STATE FLAGS AND FLOWERS II

MAINE
Pine Tree State

Pine Cone and Tassel

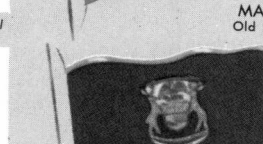

MARYLAND
Old Line State

Black-eyed Susan

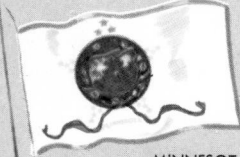

MASSACHUSETTS
Bay State

Mayflower

MICHIGAN
Wolverine State

Apple Blossom

MINNESOTA
Gopher State

Moccasin Flower

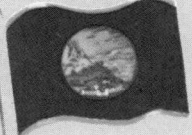

MISSISSIPPI
Bayou or Magnolia State

Magnolia

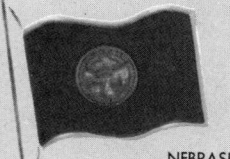

MISSOURI
Show-Me State

Hawthorn

MONTANA
Treasure State

Bitterroot

NEBRASKA
Cornhusker State

Goldenrod

NEVADA
Silver or Sagebrush State

Sagebrush

NEW HAMPSHIRE
Granite State

Purple Lilac

NEW JERSEY
Garden State

Violet

NEW MEXICO
Sunshine State

Yucca Flower

NEW YORK
Empire State

Rose

NORTH CAROLINA
Tarheel State

Dogwood

NORTH DAKOTA
Sioux or Flickertail State

Wild Prairie Rose

Webster's Encyclopedia of Dictionaries

THE SPACIOUS FIRMAMENT

The Earth upon which we live has been carefully mapped. Every continent, every ocean and every island has been measured, and charts of the whole world have been produced. When we come to map the universe, the situation is not nearly so straightforward. There is no hard and fast standard of reference, as has been known ever since men first realized that the Earth is a globe whirling through space.

Ptolemy of Alexandria, the last great scientist of ancient times, drew up maps of the world—and also charted the sky. His star catalogue remained the best for centuries after his death about A.D.180, but it was strictly limited. All that he could do was to plot the apparent positions of the stars : he could know nothing about their nature. It was only with the invention of the telescope, in the early 17th century, that men could study the celestial bodies in real detail.

The first important astronomer of the telescope era was Galileo. Within three and a half centuries after his time, immensely powerful telescopes had probed out to distant parts of the universe ; also, rocket vehicles had been sent out to our nearer neighbours in space. The direct exploration of the universe had begun.

Nature of the universe

Hundreds of years ago, men believed the Earth to be the central body of the universe, with the Sun, Moon, planets and stars moving round it once every day. This was Ptolemy's view, and at the time it was quite logical, but the modern picture is very different. The Earth is known to be a planet, moving round the Sun ; the Sun itself is an ordinary star ; and our own particular star-system, or galaxy, contains about 100,000 million stars of the same kind as ours.

The Galaxy is a flattened system, although seen at a suitable angle it would show spiral arms. It, too, is a minor part of the universe as a whole. The world's largest telescopes can show thousands of millions of galaxies, all of which contain thousands of millions of stars, and almost all of which are moving away from us—so that the universe is in a state of expansion.

Origins

How did the universe begin ? We have to confess that we do not know. On the so-called evolutionary or 'big bang' theory, all the material in the universe was created at one moment, more than 10,000 million years ago. The steady-state theory, now largely discredited, supposes that the universe has always existed, and will exist for ever ; as old stars and galaxies die, new ones are formed from matter which is being created out of nothingness. Then there is the 'cyclic' universe, assumed to be in a state of alternate expansion and contraction. If this is correct, then the galaxies will eventually draw together again, and the present systems will be destroyed, though subsequently the universe will be re-born rather in the manner of the mythological phœnix.

Of one thing we may be certain. The Sun cannot last for ever, and neither can the Earth. Life on our world must end, though not for millions of years yet. We depend entirely upon the Sun ; without its energy, we could not survive.

Scale

Our Sun is a star, and appears so much larger and hotter than the other stars simply because it is much closer to us. The distance between the Sun and Earth is 93,000,000 miles—which is very great by our normal everyday standards, but is insignificant astronomically. All the stars visible in the night sky are much more remote; their distances amount to millions of miles.

On the distance-scale of our Galaxy, the mile is too short to be a convenient unit of length. Instead, astronomers make use of the velocity of light, which amounts to 186,000 miles per second. In a year, therefore, light can cover rather less than 6 million million miles ; and it is this unit, the light-year, which is generally used to measure stellar distances. The nearest star beyond the Sun, a faint one known as Proxima Centauri, is more than four light-years or 24 million million miles away.

It follows from this that our view of the Universe is bound to be out of date. If a star is, say, 50 light-years away, we are seeing it not as it is now, but as it used to be 50 years ago; if the distance is 3,000 light-years, we are seeing it as it used to be a thousand years before the death of Christ.

On the other hand, the distances in our own particular part of the Universe —the Sun's family, or Solar System— are much less. Light from the Sun can reach us in 8·3 minutes, and the distance of the Moon is only 1¼ light-seconds.

External Systems

The Galaxy in which we live is not the only one. There are millions upon millions of others, at tremendous distances from us. One of the nearest is the Andromeda Galaxy, which is considerably larger than our own, and which can just be seen with the naked eye. Its distance from us is 2,200,000 light-years, so that we are seeing it as it used to be long before the start of civilization on Earth. Even so, the Andromeda Galaxy is one of the very closest of the external systems. The most distant galaxies known are well over 5,000 million light-years away.

Quasars

For reasons which are not yet properly understood, some of the galaxies are strong emitters of radio waves; also, there are the mysterious quasars, which seem to be relatively small (at least in comparison with normal galaxies) and incredibly luminous. Quasars were identified less than ten years ago, and their nature is by no means clear as yet.

Life?

If each galaxy consists of thousands of millions of stars, and if there are so many millions of galaxies, it is surely absurd to suggest that our own totally unimportant Sun is unique in being attended by an inhabited planet. It seems that life is likely to be widespread in the Universe—but the nearest intelligent beings are so remote that we cannot contact them directly, at least in the present state of our knowledge. The only possibility is to communicate by means of radio, but the chances of success are very slight. Sending a rocket to a planet moving round another star is out of the question at the moment, simply because any such journey would take millions of years. Whether we shall ever manage to get in touch with other intelligent races remains to be seen.

Other Planetary Systems?

The Earth and the eight other planets move round the Sun, as we shall see. Since the Sun is merely a normal star, there is no reason to doubt that many other stars have planet-families of their own. Unfortunately, direct proof is hard to obtain, because a planet is much smaller than a star (our own Sun could swallow up more than a million Earths), and shines only by reflected light. In the photograph shown here, taken with the

The Great Spiral in Andromeda
The Galaxy in which we live contains about 100,000 million stars, arranged in a flattened system about 100,000 light-years in diameter by 20,000 light-years broad at its centre.
Our Sun, with its attendant planets, lies some 25,000 light-years from the galactic nucleus or centre. When we look along the main plane of the Galaxy, we can see many stars in roughly the same line of sight; this causes the familiar aspect of the Milky Way.
Unfortunately, we cannot see the centre of the Galaxy, because there is too much gas and dust in the way, but the new science of radio astronomy has come to the rescue. A radio telescope collects long-wavelength radiations, which are not blocked out by interstellar material.
One of the closest of the outer galaxies is the Andromeda Spiral. It is 2,200,000 light-years away; it is larger than our Galaxy, and—like our Galaxy—it is spiral in form. It is dimly visible to the naked eye as a faint, hazy patch.

The Rosette Nebula (below), a mass of gas contained in our own Galaxy.

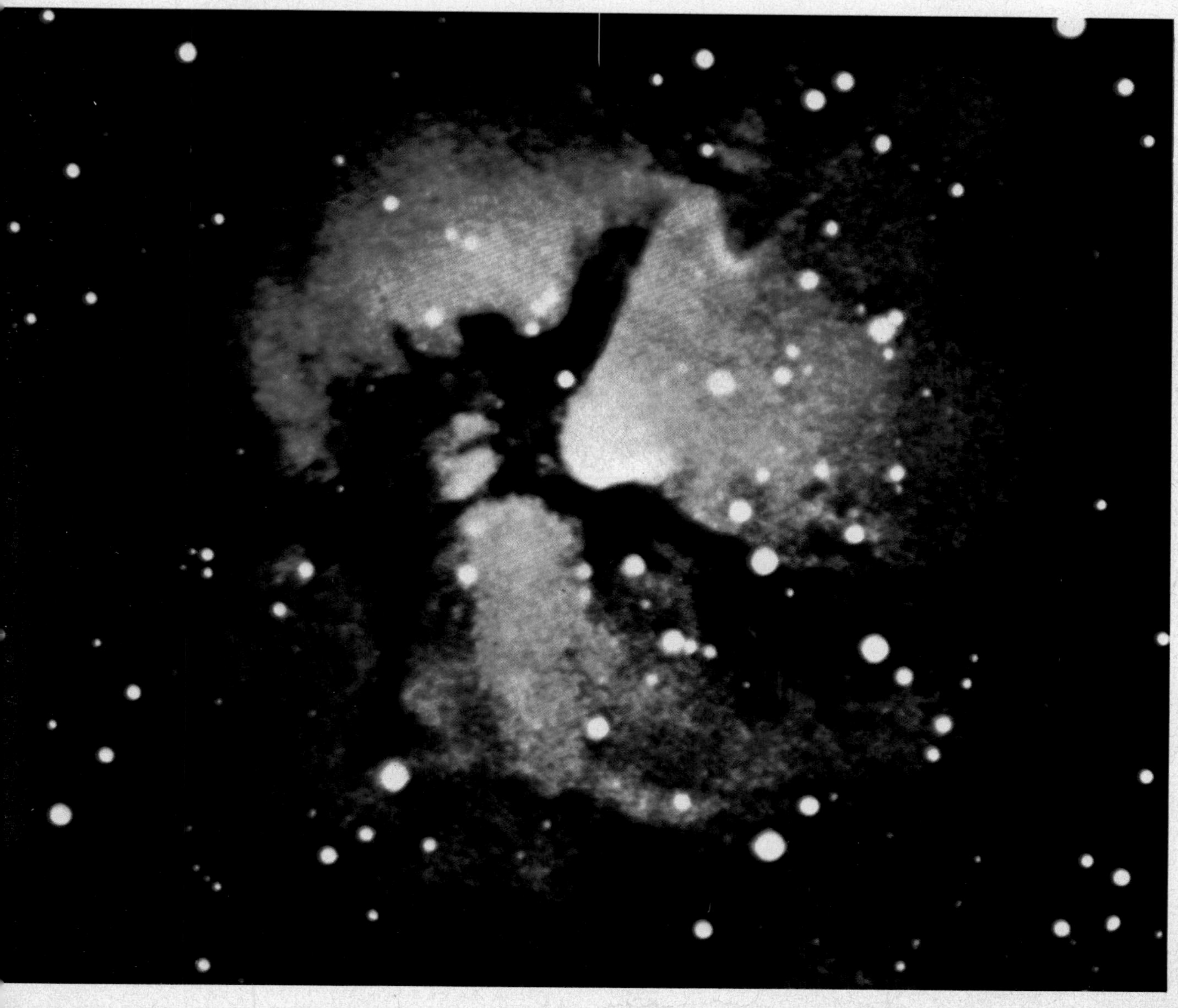

world's largest telescope, every speck of light is a star. If our Sun were seen at such a distance, so that it appeared as a tiny dot, a much smaller and non-luminous body could not be seen at all. No telescope yet planned will show planets of other stars. However, a few nearby stars seem to be moving in an irregular fashion, so they are presumably being pulled out of position by invisible companions which may well be planets.

THE SUN'S FAMILY

The planets look starlike, but they have no light of their own; they shine only by reflected sunlight, and are not so important in the universe as they appear. Five of them—Mercury, Venus, Mars, Jupiter and Saturn—are visible to the naked eye, and have been known since the dawn of recorded history; all except Mercury are brilliant objects. Because they are so much closer to us than the stars, they seem to wander slowly about against the starry back-

The most important members of the Sun's family are the planets, of which the Earth is one. Some of them are attended by secondary bodies, known as satellites; we have one natural satellite—our familiar Moon—but

Jupiter, the largest planet, has as many as 12 satellites.

Also moving round the Sun are various bodies of lesser importance, such as the comets and meteoroids. Scattered through the Solar System

there is a large amount of thinly-spread material, sometimes visible in the west after sunset or in the east before dawn as the cone-shaped glow which extends upward from the horizon and which is called the Zodiacal Light.

MERCURY

Mercury is the closest of the planets to the Sun. It has a diameter that is not a great deal larger than the Earth's Moon. It has practically no atmosphere and it is quite unsuited for any form of life. Because it is closer to the Sun than we are, it shows lunar-type phases similar to those of the Moon, but very large telescopes are needed to show the darkish patches on its disk. It may well be covered with craters. A Mercury probe is planned for 1972.

- ☐ *Mean distance from Sun:* 36 million miles
- ☐ *Year (Sidereal Period):* 88 days
- ☐ *Day (Axial Rotation):* 58·5 days
- ☐ *Diameter:* 3,000 miles
- ☐ *Escape Velocity:* 2·6 miles per second
- ☐ *Satellites:* none.

VENUS

Venus is much the brightest of the planets: it can even be seen in full daylight when at its most brilliant. This great brightness is partly because Venus is the closest planet to Earth (it can approach us to within 25,000,000 miles) and partly because its cloud-covered surface reflects over 70% of the sunlight falling on it. Because no telescope can see through Venus' atmosphere, little could be discovered about the surface conditions until the launching of the space probes, from 1962 onwards. The Russian probes of 1969 confirmed that the surface is very hot, and that conditions there are extremely hostile.

- ☐ *Mean distance from Sun:* 67 million miles
- ☐ *Year (Sidereal Period):* 224·7 days
- ☐ *Day (Axial Rotation):* 243 days
- ☐ *Diameter:* 7,700 miles
- ☐ *Escape Velocity:* 6·4 miles per second
- ☐ *Satellites:* none.

EARTH

Earth, the third planet in order of distance from the Sun, has an equatorial diameter of 7,927 miles. It has a strong magnetic field, whereas the magnetism of Venus and Mars is too weak to be measured; and, with the possible exception of Pluto, it is the densest of the planets. Its albedo, or reflecting power, is known to be 39%, much less than that of cloud-covered Venus but far greater than that of Mars.

- ☐ *Mean distance from Sun:* 93 million miles
- ☐ *Year (Sidereal Period):* 365 days
- ☐ *Day (Axial Rotation):* 23 hours 56 minutes
- ☐ *Diameter:* 7,927 miles
- ☐ *Escape Velocity:* 7 miles per second
- ☐ *Satellites:* one.

MARS

Mars is always recognizable because of its strong red colour. It is much smaller than the Earth, and its escape velocity is only 3·2 miles per second, but it retains a thin atmosphere, and it is not unlikely that the dark patches on its surface are due to living material. In any case, Mars is of particular interest to us because it is the only planet in the Solar System, apart from the Earth, which may possibly support life in some form. It has two satellites, Phobos and Deimos, both of which are less than 10 miles in diameter.

- ☐ *Mean distance from Sun:* 141·5 million miles
- ☐ *Year (Sidereal Period):* 687 days
- ☐ *Day (Axial Rotation):* 24 hours 37 minutes
- ☐ *Diameter:* 4,220 miles
- ☐ *Escape Velocity:* 3·2 miles per second
- ☐ *Satellites:* two.

Asteroids

Mercury 36 million miles

Venus 67 million miles

Earth 93 million miles

Mars 141·5 million miles

Jupiter 483 million miles

Saturn 886 million miles

Uranus 1,783 milli

THE SUN

The Sun is immensely large. Its volume is more than a million times as great as that of the Earth; it is made up of incandescent gas, and the surface temperature is of the order of 6,000 degrees Centigrade.

Telescopically, the Sun shows darkish patches known as sunspots, which are associated with strong magnetic fields.

Active spot groups often produce short-lived, violent outbreaks called flares, which emit charged particles; these particles may possibly present a hazard to astronauts, though it seems that the danger may not be so great as was once feared. Every 11 years or so the Sun is particularly active, and there are many spot-groups; the last maximum occurred

in 1968, and by 1972 the activity will be at a minimum.

It is extremely dangerous to look at the Sun through a telescope, even when a dark filter is placed over the telescope eyepiece. The only safe method is to use the telescope as a projector and show the Sun's image on a white screen. Different kinds of instruments, based on

the principle of the spectroscope, can show the prominences, huge masses of gas rising from the Solar surface. Further out comes the corona, which may be called the Sun's outer atmosphere; it is visible to the naked eye only when the Moon covers the Sun at the time of a total solar eclipse.

The Sun contains a high percentage of

Earth's nearest neighbours

Venus

In 1962, the U.S. probe Mariner II by-passed Venus at little over 20,000 miles, and sent back the first definite information that the surface is very hot. More recently, the Russians have landed three probes there: Venera-4 in 1967, Venera-5 and Venera-6 in May 1969. All these vehicles were para-chuted down through the planet's atmosphere, which is now thought to be up to 100 times as dense as the Earth's air at sea-level. The results of the Russian space-vehicles, together with Mariner II and the later Mariner V, seem to show that Venus must be a scorching hot dust-desert, with a surface temperature of at least 400 degrees Centigrade, in which case no life may be expected there. Whether manned expeditions to this planet will ever be possible remains to be seen, but certainly Venus appears to be much more hostile to man than Mars.

Crescent Venus

Through a telescope Venus shows no obvious surface detail. Generally all that can be made out is a bright disk, showing the characteristic phase: when at its brightest Venus shows up as a crescent. The markings are vague and impermanent, and represent nothing more than the top of a layer of dense atmosphere. The planet's year or revolution period is 224·7 days; recent measurements indicate that the rotation period is 243 days, and that Venus spins in the opposite direction to the Earth.
Venus showing Ashen Light, Patrick Moore 12¼" reflector. For the sake of clarity the brightness of the Ashen Light has been exaggerated.

Mars, 1969

When observed through a telescope, Mars shows considerable detail on its surface. The planet's poles are covered with whitish deposits which are usually thought to be due to a thin layer of some icy or frosty material, though solid carbon dioxide is another possibility. Much of the surface is reddish-ochre in colour, and is often termed 'desert', though there is no real comparison with an Earth desert such as the Sahara; for one thing the temperature is very much lower, because Mars is further from the Sun. On a summer day at the planet's equator the temperature may rise to 70 degrees Fahrenheit, but drops to below —100 degrees Fahrenheit during the night.

The most important result obtained from Mariner IV concerned the atmosphere of Mars, which proved to be much thinner than expected, and to be made up chiefly of carbon dioxide. The Martian atmosphere may be ineffective ground. The word 'planet' really means 'wandering star'.

There has been much discussion about the origin of the planets. It used to be thought that they were pulled off the Sun by the action of a passing star, but this attractive theory has been disproved on mathematical grounds. It is more likely that the planets were gradually built up from material collected by the Sun from space. The age of the Earth is known to be about 4,700 million years, and most authorities consider that all the planets were formed at about the same time.

The Solar System seems to be divided into two parts. The inner group of planets is made up of four relatively small worlds (Mercury, Venus, the Earth and Mars), beyond which comes a wide gap containing the small planets known as asteroids, of which the largest (Ceres) is a mere 430 miles in diameter. Jupiter and Saturn are quite unlike the Earth; they are much larger, and their outer layers, at least, are made up of gas, so that they are totally hostile to life. Moreover, they are so far from the Sun that they are intensely cold.

Beyond Saturn, outermost of the planets known in ancient times, there are three more planets. Uranus, another gas-giant, was discovered by William Herschel in the year 1781; it can just be seen with the naked eye, but it is not surprising that the old astronomers failed to notice it. Yet another gas-giant, Neptune, was tracked down in 1846 as a result of mathematical calculations by U. Le Verrier in France and J. C. Adams in England. Neptune is a large body, but it is so remote that it cannot be seen without optical aid. Finally, on the fringe of the Solar System, comes Pluto, which was discovered in 1930 by C. Tombaugh following mathematical work by Percival Lowell.

JUPITER

Jupiter is the giant of the Solar System. However, it is not a solid, rocky globe. In its outer layers, at least, it is made up of gas, chiefly hydrogen and hydrogen compounds. The most famous surface features are the cloud belts. There are also spots—in particular the Great Red Spot, which has been under observation for centuries, but whose exact nature is still uncertain. Of its twelve satellites, two—Ganymede and Callisto—are larger than our moon, and two more—Io and Europa—are about our Moon's size.

☐ *Mean distance from Sun:*
   483 million miles
☐ *Year (Sidereal Period):* 11·9 years
☐ *Day (Axial Rotation):*
   9 hours 51 minutes
☐ *Diameter:* 88,700 miles
☐ *Escape Velocity:* 37 miles per second
☐ *Satellites:* twelve.

SATURN

Saturn is a world of the same general type as Jupiter, but it is further away from the Sun (886,000,000 miles on average) and so is extremely cold. Its beautiful rings are made up of small particles spinning round the planet in a dense swarm. They may well be the remains of a former satellite which approached closely to Saturn and was torn to pieces by the gravitational pull of the planet. However, Saturn still has ten satellites; the largest, Titan, is bigger than our Moon.

☐ *Mean distance from Sun:*
   886 million miles
☐ *Year (Sidereal Period):* 29·5 years
☐ *Day (Axial Rotation):*
   10 hours 14 minutes
☐ *Diameter:* 75,100 miles
☐ *Escape Velocity:* 22 miles per second
☐ *Satellites:* ten.

URANUS

Uranus is 29,700 miles in diameter; it is therefore smaller than Jupiter or Saturn, but still much larger than the Earth. Telescopically it shows a pale greenish disk; the surface is, of course, gaseous. Uranus has a curious axial tilt so that at times its pole may be facing the Sun. The revolution period is 84 Earth years. Not much detail can be seen on its surface, but there seems to be a brightish band centred on the equator. Uranus has five satellites, none of which is as large as our Moon. Because it is so far away, it seems to be very slow-moving against the starry background.

☐ *Mean distance from Sun:*
   1,783 million miles
☐ *Year (Sidereal Period):* 84 years
☐ *Day (Axial Rotation):*
   10 hours 48 minutes
☐ *Diameter:* 29,700 miles
☐ *Escape Velocity:* 14 miles per second
☐ *Satellites:* five.

NEPTUNE

Neptune has been called the twin of Uranus. It is much further away, with a mean distance from the Sun of 2,793,000,000 miles and is too faint to be seen with the naked eye, though binoculars will show it. Like Uranus and the other giants, it has a gaseous surface; the colour is distinctly bluish. Of its two satellites, one (Triton) is relatively large, with a diameter of well over 2,000 miles. The other satellite (Nereid) is small and faint; it has a strange, high eccentric orbit around Neptune.

☐ *Mean distance from Sun:*
   2,793 million miles
☐ *Year (Sidereal Period):* 164·8 years
☐ *Day (Axial Rotation):* about 14 hours
☐ *Diameter:* 31,000 miles
☐ *Escape Velocity:* 15·5 miles per second
☐ *Satellites:* two.

PLUTO

Pluto was discovered by Clyde Tombaugh, at the Lowell Observatory, in 1930. It is not a giant and seems to be considerably smaller than the Earth. Its orbit is peculiar and at perihelion, or closest approach to the Sun, it comes within the path of Neptune, but its mean distance from the Sun is much greater, and its 'year' is 248 times as long as ours; its path is tilted at an angle of 17° so that there is no fear of a collision with Neptune. Pluto is much too faint to be seen at all except through telescopes of considerable size.

☐ *Mean distance from Sun:*
   3,666 million miles
☐ *Year (Sidereal Period):* 247·7 years
☐ *Day (Axial Rotation):* 6 days 9 hours
☐ *Diameter:* 4,000 miles?
☐ *Escape Velocity:* unknown
☐ *Satellites:* none.

Neptune 2,793 million miles

Pluto 3,666 million miles

COMETS AND METEORIC BODIES

the light element hydrogen. Deep inside the solar globe, where the temperature rises to over 14,000,000 degrees Centigrade, this hydrogen is being converted into another element, helium; energy is being released, and it is this energy which keeps the Sun radiating. Mass is being lost at the rate of 4,000,000 tons every second, but the Sun will not change perceptibly for several thousands of millions of years in the future. Eventually, however—in perhaps 8,000 million years, the supply of hydrogen 'fuel' will start to run low; the Sun will rearrange itself, and will go through a period of increased luminosity which will certainly mean the end of all life on Earth.

The comets and meteoric bodies are the most unpredictable members of the Sun's family. The orbits of bright comets are generally very eccentric, so that their periods of revolution round the Sun are very long; the only conspicuous comet with a period of less than a century is Halley's, which will be seen again in 1986. A comet is made up of small solid particles together with thin gas and fine dust; its motion against the stars is too slow to be noticed except by careful watching over a period of hours.

A meteor is a small particle, moving round the Sun in the same way as a planet. If it comes too close to the Earth and enters the upper atmosphere, it rubs against the air particles, and is destroyed in the luminous streak which we call a shooting star. The average meteor is smaller than a grain of sand. Larger bodies may reach the ground without being destroyed, and are then termed meteorites; they may be of iron or of stony material. Large meteorites are very rare, and probably do not constitute a serious risk to space-ships.

---

as a shield against various harmful radiations coming from space, and it is even possible that there is no life whatsoever on the planet. One thing is certain: because the ground pressure of the atmosphere is so low (no greater than that of the Earth's air at 95,000 feet above sea-level), it will never be possible for an astronaut to walk about there without wearing a full pressure-suit. Martian conditions seem to be unsuited to any advanced life-forms, and it is most unlikely that advanced life has ever existed there.

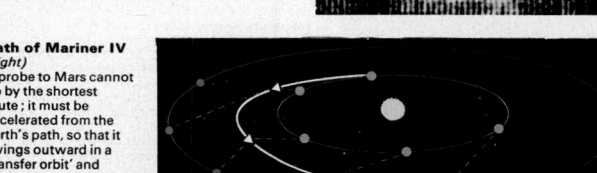

Path of Mariner IV
(right)
A probe to Mars cannot go by the shortest route; it must be accelerated from the Earth's path, so that it swings outward in a 'transfer orbit' and meets Mars at a pre-computed point.

The Craters of Mars
(left)
In 1965 the U.S. probe Mariner IV passed Mars at a minimum distance of 6,118 miles, and sent back photographs showing that the surface is covered with lunar-type craters. To the surprise of most astronomers, Mars appears to be very similar to the Moon in its surface features. This photograph *(left)* is the best of the Mariner IV series.

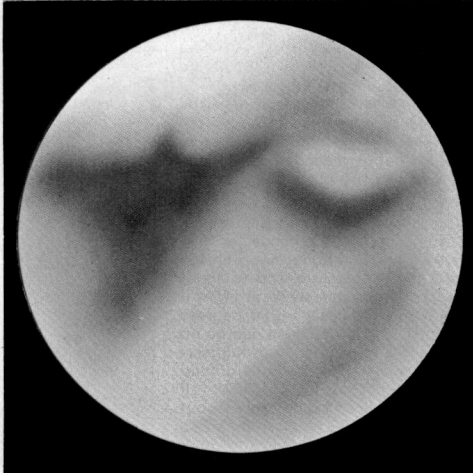

Mars, May 16th 1969
23.25 hours
12½" reflector,
magnification 360,
Patrick Moore.

EARTH'S NATURAL SATELLITE

A Satellite?

Apart from the Sun, the Moon appears much the most magnificent object in our sky, and we tend to regard it as an important body. Yet appearances are misleading. The Moon is a very junior member of the Solar System, and is officially regarded as the Earth's one natural satellite. Its mean distance from us is 238,840 miles : Venus, the closest of the planets, is always at least one hundred times as remote.

Yet it may be misleading to regard the Moon as a mere satellite. Its diameter is 2,160 miles, as against 7,927 for that of the Earth, so that the two bodies are comparable; if the Earth is represented by a tennis-ball, the Moon will be a table-tennis ball. The Moon's mass is 1/81 of that of the Earth, and its escape velocity is 1½ miles per second. It may be better to regard the system as making up a double planet.

Through a telescope, the Full Moon is dominated by the bright rays which are associated with some of the craters, notably Tycho in the southern uplands and Copernicus on the grey sea-area to the north of the equator. The rays are surface deposits, and are only well seen under high illumination. The dark seas, or maria, occupy large areas of the Earth-turned side of the Moon; there are comparatively few on the far side.

The Airless Moon

The mass-difference between the Earth and the Moon means that the surface conditions are very dissimilar. The Earth, with its escape velocity of 7 miles per second, has been able to hold on to a dense atmosphere, but this is not true for the Moon. The low lunar escape velocity of only 1½ miles per second means that any atmosphere has leaked away into space, and nowadays the Moon is to all intents and purposes airless. There may be a trace of atmosphere, but so little that it is

negligible by any standards. Shadows will be jet-black and sharp, with no air to spread the sunlight around and make the familiar blueness; there will be no clouds, no weather and no sound. On the Moon all communication has to be carried out by means of radio, once the astronauts are out of their space-craft.

This lack of atmosphere also means that the temperature range is un-pleasantly great. At lunar noon on the equator the temperature rises to about that of boiling water, while at night it goes down to at least —250 degrees Fahrenheit. Of course, there can be no liquid water on the Moon—and suggestions that there may be underground oceans do not seem to be at all convincing. Everything we know about the lunar world indicates that there is a complete lack of life and that the Moon has always been sterile.

Our Nearest Neighbour
The Moon's distance from us is only just under thirty times the diameter of the Earth *(left)*, and it is for this reason that it must be our first target in space. A lunar journey now takes less than a week; the first circum-lunar voyage, that of Apollo 8 at Christmas 1968, was completed in a mere 8 days, where a journey to Mars or Venus and back will take many months. The Moon is our faithful companion, and stays with us in our never ending journey round the Sun. The diagram below shows the Earth and Moon to scale, at the correct relative distance between them.
The Full Moon *(above)*

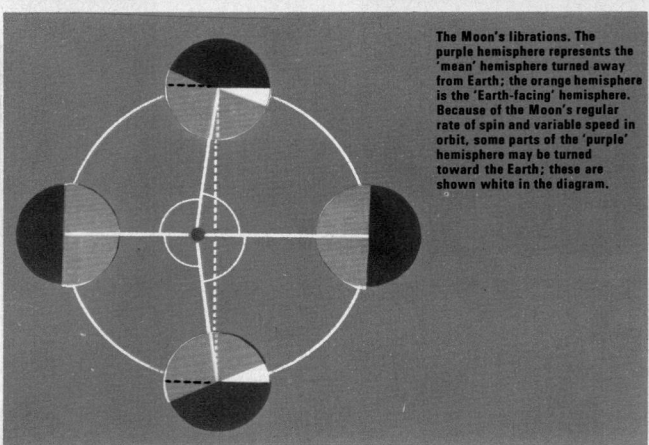

The Moon's librations. The purple hemisphere represents the 'mean' hemisphere turned away from Earth; the orange hemisphere is the 'Earth-facing' hemisphere. Because of the Moon's regular rate of spin and variable speed in orbit, some parts of the 'purple' hemisphere may be turned toward the Earth; these are shown white in the diagram.

Captured Rotation

The Moon goes round the Earth in the same time that it takes to spin once on its axis : 27·3 days. This means that it always keeps the same face turned toward the Earth, and there is a part of the Moon that we can never see. Because the Moon spins at a constant rate, but speeds up and slows down regularly in its revolution round the Earth, the amount of rotation and the position in orbit become periodically 'out of step', as it were; the Moon rocks slowly to and fro, and the result is that we can see for a short distance round alternate edges. This, together with other 'librations' of the same sort, means that from Earth we can examine a total of 59% of the Moon's surface, though of course, we can never see more than 50% at any one moment. The remaining 41% remained unknown until photographed from space-probes, the first of which was Russia's Lunik 3 of 1959. Note that the day and night conditions are the same all over the Moon. Each day and each night is equal to almost a fortnight on Earth. Near the Moon's limb as seen from Earth, the foreshortening is so great that the craters seem to be drawn out into long, narrow ellipses, and it is often difficult to tell a crater-wall from a ridge. Before the space-probes were sent Moonward, these 'libration regions' were very poorly mapped, and not much was known about them.

The surface gravity is 1/6 of that of the Earth, so that a man who weighs 180 lb at home will weigh only 30 lb under lunar conditions. The relatively feeble pull must be borne in mind when the construction of a lunar base is planned, but on the whole it may well make matters easier! Certainly there is every reason to hope that a full-scale scientific base will be set up on the Moon within the next few decades.

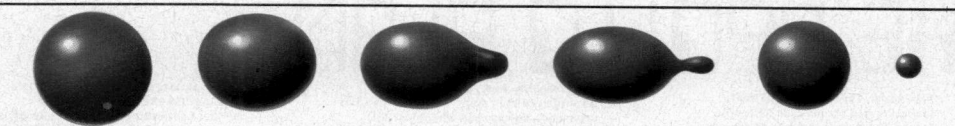

Origins of the Moon
It used to be thought that the Earth and Moon once formed a single body. According to Sir George Darwin the Earth-Moon globe spun round so quickly that it became distorted, and eventually the Moon broke away, leaving the deep scar now filled by the Pacific Ocean. This theory sounds attractive, but it has now been rejected on mathematical grounds, and we may be sure that the two bodies were never one. Either the Moon is an ex-planet which approached the Earth and became gravitationally linked with us, or else the Earth and the Moon were formed in the same manner, at about the same time and in the same region of space.

The Month
The diagram illustrates a *synodical month* or *lunation*, the 29.53 days between successive New Moons. The *sidereal month*, 27.3 days, is the time taken for the Moon to go once round the Earth: see *Captured Rotation*. Arrows align Earth and Moon with the Sun 93,000,000 miles away.

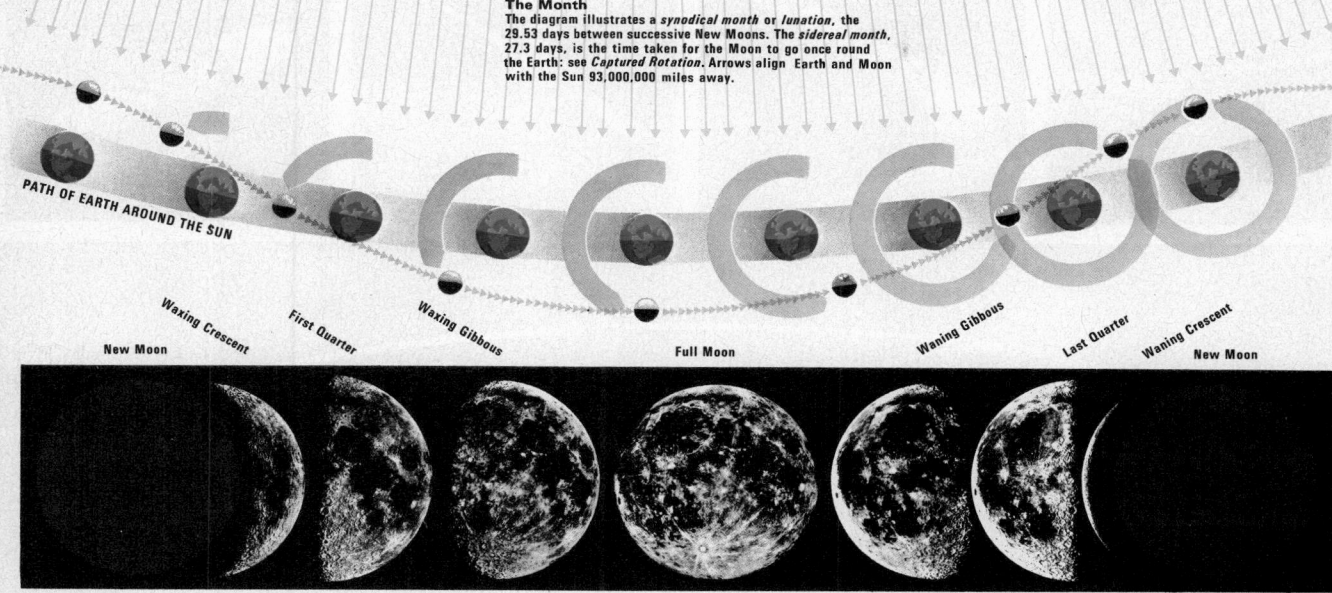

PATH OF EARTH AROUND THE SUN

New Moon   Waxing Crescent   First Quarter   Waxing Gibbous   Full Moon   Waning Gibbous   Last Quarter   Waning Crescent   New Moon

Lunar Phases

Everyone must be familiar with the Moon's phases, or apparent changes of shape from new to full. The average interval between one full moon and the next is 29½ days, so that it is approximately correct to say that there is one full moon and one new moon every month. The line between the sunlit and dark sides is called the terminator. Because the Moon's surface is so rough, the terminator is not smooth; it is irregular and broken, since the Sun's rays will obviously catch the top of a peak before illuminating an adjacent valley. When the Moon shows up as a crescent in the evening or morning sky,

the 'dark' side may often be seen shining faintly. This is due to light reflected from the Earth onto the Moon, and is known as the Earthshine. Oddly enough, the Moon reflects only 7% of the sunlight which falls upon it, so that despite appearances, its rocks are decidedly dark in hue.

As the Earth and Moon move round the Sun, it is interesting to note that the Moon's orbit is always concave to the Sun. The Earth and Moon move together round their common centre of gravity, or barycentre. This may be an extra reason for regarding the Earth-Moon system as a double planet.

Because the Moon's rotation is captured or synchronous—that is to say, it keeps the same face turned towards us apart from the minor changes due to librations—the markings on the disk always seem to keep in approximately the same positions; for instance, the conspicuous dark plain of the Mare Crisium (Sea of Crises) always appears near one edge or limb. In this and other Moon photographs in this book, north is at the top, following the American custom. (Most astronomical telescopes give an inverted picture, with south at the top and north at the bottom.)

There is almost no marked local

colour on the Moon, and the surface appears yellowish-grey, though there are many differences in intensity. During the 1950's much argument was caused by a theory that the surface was partly or completely covered with dust; it was even suggested that a landing space-craft would sink out of sight into a treacherous dust-ocean, and this idea was not finally disproved until 1966 when Russia's Luna 9 made the first successful soft landing on the Moon. The soft landing probes following Luna 9 confirmed that the Moon's surface is firm enough to support even a massive space-craft.

Eclipses of the Moon

Like all non-luminous bodies, the Earth casts a shadow in space, and this shadow extends well beyond the distance of the Moon. Therefore, when the Moon passes into the cone of shadow cast by the Earth its supply of direct sunlight is cut off; it is eclipsed, and turns a dim, often coppery colour until it passes out of the shadow again.

A lunar eclipse may be either total or partial; totality may last for an hour or so. If the Moon misses the main cone, it may still pass through the area of 'penumbra' caused by the fact that the Sun is a disk and not a point source of light. Penumbral eclipses are faint.

Even during totality, the Moon does not usually disappear completely, be-

cause some of the Sun's rays are bent on to the lunar surface by way of the atmosphere surrounding the Earth. The diagram, which is not to scale, shows the general theory of a lunar eclipse, which is quite straightforward.

Lunar eclipses are particularly interesting because as soon as the direct sunlight is cut off, a wave of

intense cold sweeps across the Moon's surface. There is no atmosphere to blanket in any warmth, and the lunar surface materials are very poor at retaining heat, so the temperature drops very sharply. Some areas, notably the great ray-crater Tycho, cool down less rapidly than their surroundings and have been called 'hot spots'.

Lunar eclipses are not really important, but they are interesting to watch; the Earth's shadow is impressive as it creeps slowly across the Moon's disk. Because the Moon's orbit is inclined by 5° to that of the Earth, eclipses do not occur every month. For obvious reasons, a lunar eclipse can take place only at Full Moon. Any place on Earth will see several lunar eclipses in each decade.

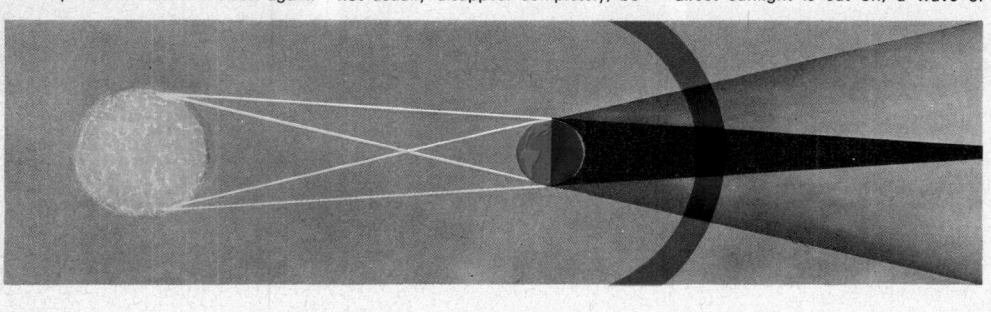

(left) A diagram showing the theory of Lunar Eclipse (not to scale).

THE APOLLO PLAN

1 Pre-launch. The Saturn rocket on its launching-pad stands over 360 feet in height. There are five clustered engines on the 138-foot first stage; these burn 470 tons of propellant in 2 minutes 10 seconds, and raise the speed to 6,000 m.p.h. The launching is suitably spectacular!

2 The launching must, of course, be according to the "step" principle. The first separation comes soon after blast-off; the lower stage, its work done, falls back to the ground. This part of the manœuvre too is spectacular—and probably looks more alarming to watchers from Earth than it seems to the astronauts themselves!

3 The second stage separates. The single engine of the third stage fires for 2 minutes; the vehicle is now at a height of 115 miles. Then the engine of the third stage fires again, and raises the velocity to over 24,000 m.p.h. This sends the vehicle into an orbit which will take it to the Moon.

4 The next manœuvre is the separation of the L.E.M., or Lunar Excursion Module. It must be remembered that on its own, the L.E.M. could not return to Earth; it is designed entirely for the lunar landing. Here the Command Module separates from the launching position with the L.E.M. to re-dock for the flight position.

   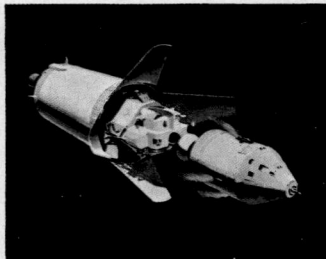

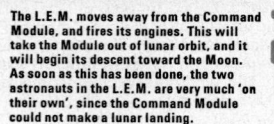

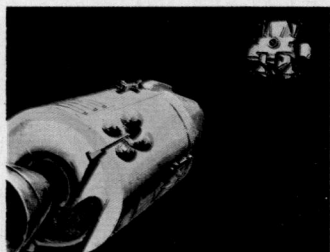

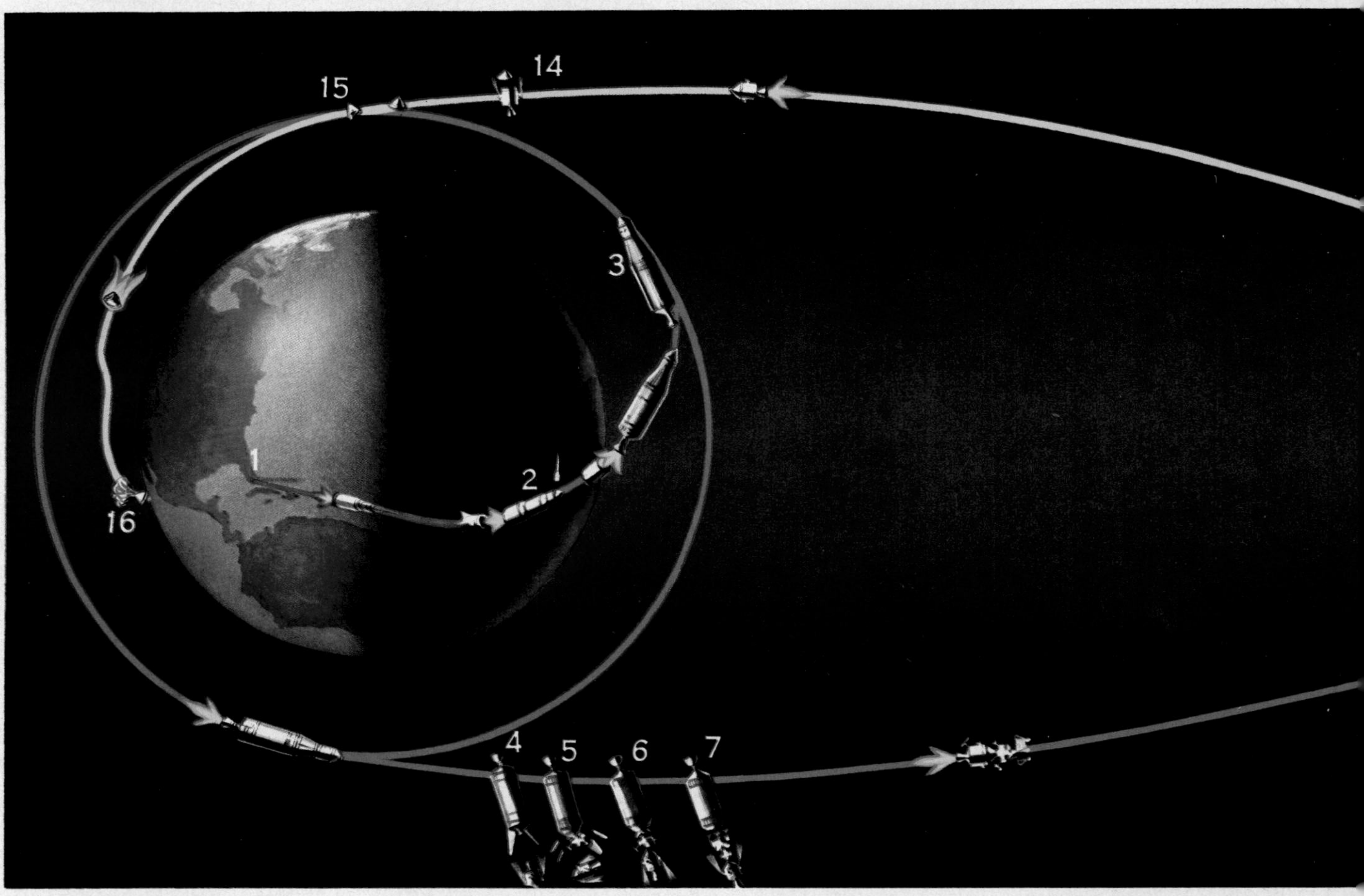

9 The L.E.M. moves away from the Command Module, and fires its engines. This will take the Module out of lunar orbit, and it will begin its descent toward the Moon. As soon as this has been done, the two astronauts in the L.E.M. are very much 'on their own', since the Command Module could not make a lunar landing.

10 Landing on the Moon. The engines of the L.E.M. slow it down until it is immediately above the surface, and the final touch-down is gentle. A certain amount of manœuvrability is possible, but only within rather restricted limits, so that this is one of the most hazardous moments of the entire expedition.

11 After the service investigations are over, the engines of the L.E.M. are again fired, so that the module can return to rendezvous with the waiting Command Module. The bottom part of the L.E.M. acts as a launching pad, and is left behind on the Moon.

12 Rendezvous with the Command Module, which has been circling the Moon while the astronauts in the L.E.M. have been on the surface. Radio contact has been maintained. Docking is carried out, and the two astronauts of the L.E.M. re-enter the Command Module ready for the return to Earth.

5 The Command Module now turns on its axis to dock with the L.E.M. to make the complete lunar craft for the flight to the Moon. The Command Module will remain in orbit round the Moon while the L.E.M. descends to the surface.

6 The lunar craft is separated from the third stage; the vehicle is now correctly assembled for the final journey to the Moon. Launching could not have been carried out in this way, as the astronauts had then to be in the top of the vehicle.

7 The separation is completed. The third stage of the launcher is jettisoned, as its work too is done, and the astronauts are left in the actual Moon vehicle. Relatively little now remains of the immense structure which was originally assembled on the launching pad at Cape Kennedy.

8 After the 239,000 mile flight from Earth the Command Module fires its rockets to brake the lunar craft 80 miles above the Moon's surface. This sends the craft into a pre-calculated orbit round the Moon. Now the lunar-landing crew crawl through the docking hatch from the Command Module to the L.E.M.

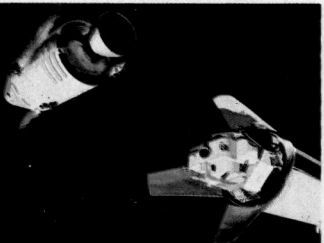  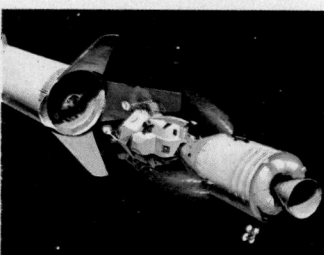 

 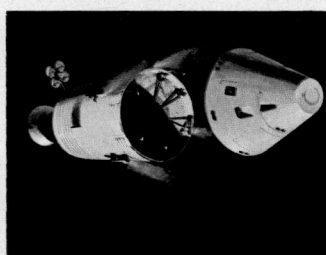  

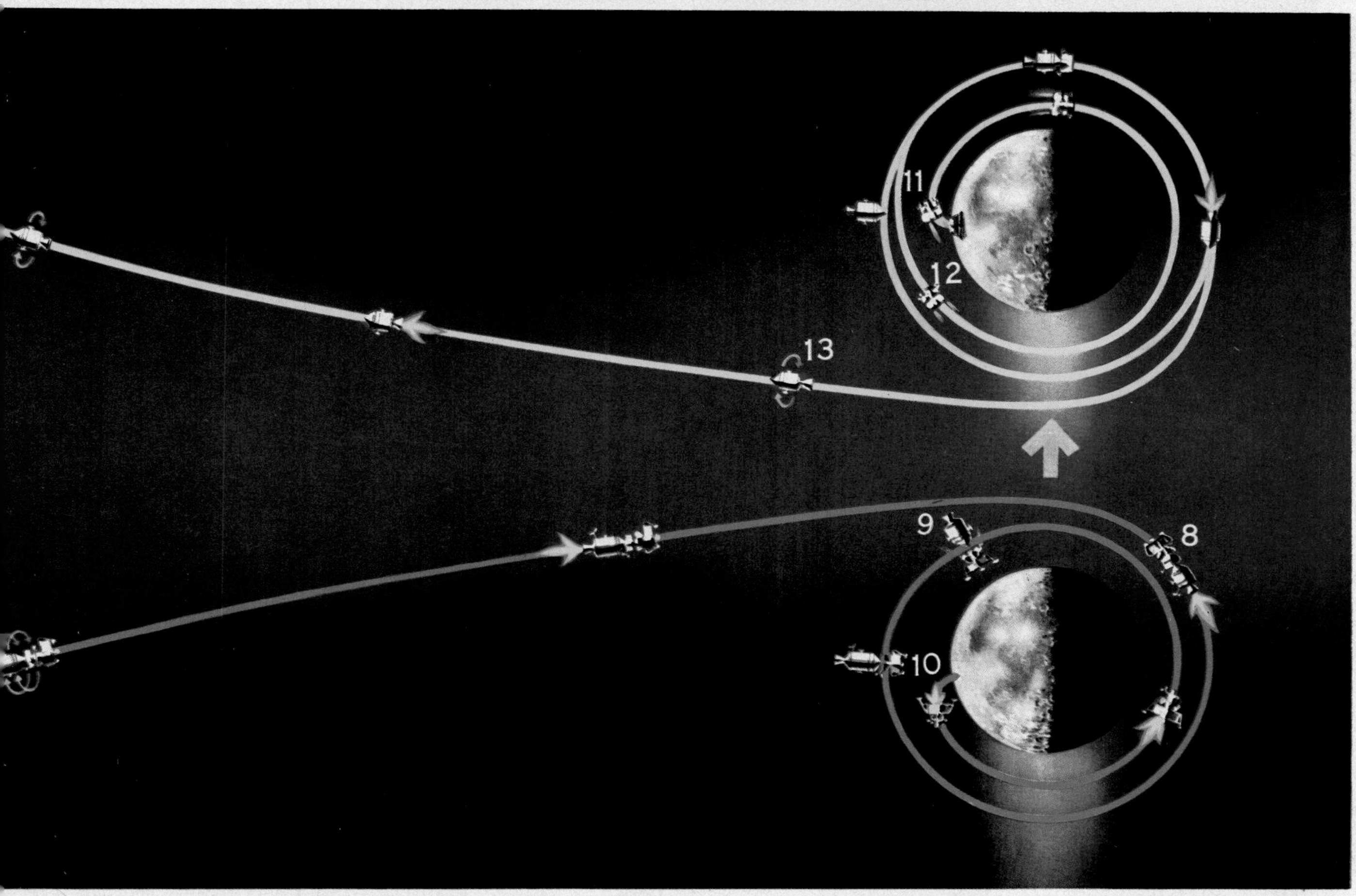

13 Before firing the engines of the Command Module for the homeward journey, the top stage of the L.E.M. is jettisoned, and is fired off into space; its work is done, and it cannot be recovered. It must be separated so that there is no danger of subsequent collision with it.

14 Just before the vehicle enters the Earth's atmosphere, the Service Module section is jettisoned, leaving only the Command Module—a small cone 13 feet in diameter at the blunt end. The Service Module does not return to the ground, but is put into orbit.

15 Reaction control jets are fired, turning the Command Module so that its heat-shield points toward the Earth. The temperature on the heat-shield will inevitably rise to at least 5000 degrees Centigrade, and it is essential for the re-entry angle to be correct.

16 Drogue parachutes are used, followed by the main parachutes which bring the Command Module down gently into the sea. The final landing is made at a speed of less than 25 m.p.h. Rescue ships are waiting for the returned astronauts; the long journey to the Moon and back is over.

MEN IN SPACE

(left) **The Apollo 7 Launch**

The Astronauts

It is one thing to develop a vehicle which can send men to the Moon; it is quite another to select and train the men who are to make the journey. An astronaut has to have both ability and stability. He must be physically fit, so that he can cope with the immense stress of a space-voyage; he must be familiar with every detail of his vehicle; he must be able to make scientific observations of all kinds, and he must be ready for any emergency. Moreover, he must be able to work in perfect harmony with his companions.

Few people could meet all these requirements, and it is no coincidence that all the early astronauts (and Russian cosmonauts) were also test pilots. The training, too, is remarkably rigorous. There are physical and psychological tests; the astronaut must be so well prepared that nothing is left to chance. It takes several years to make an astronaut ready for his first voyage beyond the Earth.

The initial blast-off means that the astronauts are subjected to considerable pressure. Also, it is notable that it takes a very large vehicle to send a very small module to the Moon. Fully assembled, the Saturn rocket on its launching pad stands over 360 feet in height, but the L.E.M. or Lunar Excursion Module, is a mere 22 feet 11 inches high and 31 feet wide. The L.E.M. itself, of course, never returns to the Earth, and would be incapable of doing so. All that comes back is the cone-shaped capsule containing the three astronauts. The rest of the huge structure on the launching-pad is expendable—and this is one reason why lunar voyages are so expensive; the vehicle can be used only once. In the future, atomic motors will no doubt be developed, and this will mean that there will be no need to use the cumbersome 'step-method' which is so wasteful; but adequate atomic motors are not in sight as yet.

The Space-Suit

Another essential piece of equipment is the space-suit. The design actually in use today is very different from the rigid suit described in so many science-fiction novels. It is comparatively flexible, and is not so uncomfortable as might be expected, but it has to have many special features, and it must be foolproof. The Moon has to all intents and purposes no atmosphere, so that a lunar suit and a 'deep-space' suit are identical—and any astronaut who is standing on the Moon's surface will have to be on his guard; he depends entirely upon his suit. To describe one of many features, there is the question

of the disposal of body waste. Urine is collected in a container attached to the inside of the suit; more solid waste is dealt with by absorbent material. Needless to say, the oxygen supply is of

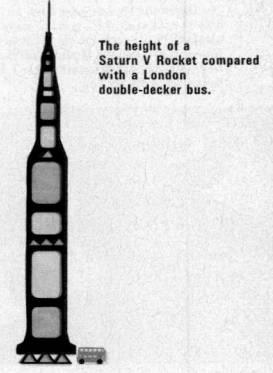

The height of a Saturn V Rocket compared with a London double-decker bus.

prime importance, and there are special cooling devices in the under-suit—without which the astronaut would become dangerously overheated when carrying out any tasks involving physical exertion.

One of the most important tasks of the Apollo mission is to find out more about the Moon itself. Samples of the lunar crust are collected, and brought back for analysis. Though the Moon is almost certainly sterile, and has never known life, stringent precautions must be taken; there is always the chance, however remote, that harmful contamination will be brought back to the Earth, in which case it might spread with alarming rapidity. (The danger is very real in the case of Mars, which has an appreciable atmosphere, and may well support some form of primitive life.) The lunar samples are 'quarantined' until the scientific teams are satisfied that no risk of contamination remains. Only then are the samples brought out and distributed to research workers.

Sampling Equipment

The samples are collected by means of special tools, which are really in the

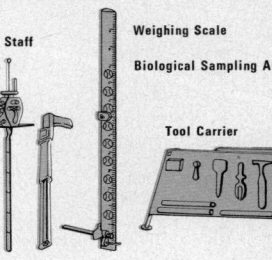
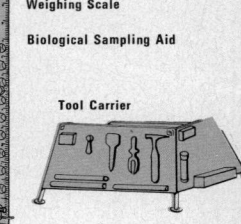

Staff

Weighing Scale

Biological Sampling Aid

Tool Carrier

Rocket Development

1902
Tsiolkovskii—In 1902 Konstantin Eduardovich Tsiolkovskii, a shy, deaf Russian school-teacher, published the first of his papers dealing with rocketry and space-flight. His work attracted no attention at the time, but a surprising number of his theories proved to be correct, and he is justly regarded as 'the father of space-flight'.

(below) Tsiolkovskii and one of his designs.

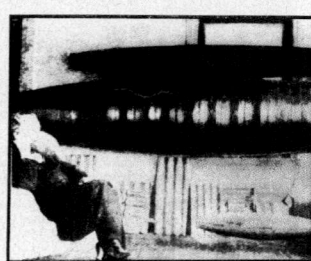

1926
Goddard—Tsiolkovskii was purely a theorist, and the greatest of the early practical rocket experimenters was Robert Goddard, who began his research in the first decade of the 20th century—quite independently of Tsiolkovskii. In 1926 he fired the first liquid-fuel rocket. It was primitive and feeble, but it was successful. *(right)* Goddard's Rocket Launcher.

1949
The First Step-Rocket—During the war, high-altitude rockets were developed by the German team led by Wernher von Braun. After 1945, captured rockets were taken to America. In 1949 a WAC Corporal rocket was mounted on top of a German vehicle, and sent up to 244 miles—a record at that time. This was the first time that the step-rocket principle had been used.

1957
Sputnik 1—In 1955 the Americans announced that they meant to launch an artificial satellite during the International Geophysical Year of 1957-8. However, the first orbital vehicle was Russian, Sputnik 1, launched on October 4, 1957. It remained aloft until January 1958, and sent back radio signals. Tiny by modern standards, it marked the beginning of the Space Age. *(below)* Sputnik 1.

1961
First Man in Space—The first man in space was also a Russian. On April 12, Major (later Colonel) Yuri Gagarin was launched in Vostok 1, and made a complete circuit of the Earth, landing safely near the pre-arranged position. It 1s tragic that Gagarin did not live to see the full results of his pioneer flight, he was killed in an aircraft crash in 1967. *(below)* Vostok 1.

nature of 'core-samplers of the type used by geologists. Storage cases are, of course, included in the astronauts' equipment. Another interesting experiment is to leave seismological instruments on the lunar surface. We do not yet know whether there are any minor ground tremors which may be called 'moonquakes'; if there are, the seismological equipment will detect them and send back information. As the Apollo programme goes on, more and more equipment will have to be left on the Moon.

All this is a preliminary to the setting-up of full-scale lunar bases. As yet the design of these bases is very much a matter of opinion. The attractive, dome-like structures, made of plastic and kept inflated by the pressure of air inside them, may or may not prove to be practicable, and it is quite likely that lunar stations will have to be constructed underground, either by making caves or by utilizing natural ones. Clearly, it is desirable to establish a proper base as soon as possible, so that an adequately-equipped scientific laboratory can be brought into operation.

The Return to Earth

There remains the question of the return to Earth, and the final landing. With the Apollo programme, the astronauts splash down in the ocean, following their re-entry into the air and the release of parachutes. This means that ships must be ready in the splashdown area, so that the astronauts can be picked up—and incidentally, to make sure that the capsule floats. (On one occasion, in the Mercury programme, a capsule actually sank, and the astronaut narrowly escaped drowning.) By now, the landing procedure has become so accurate that the capsule is brought down within sight of the waiting rescue ships.

The Russian procedure has been somewhat different, inasmuch as the landings have been made on land instead of in the sea. No doubt this will also be adopted by the Americans eventually, but at the moment the ocean splashdown is regarded as safer, and has proved to be quite satisfactory.

Sample Return Containers

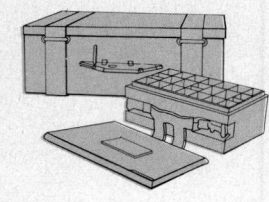

Extra-vehicular suit The outer layer is of Teflon-coated yarn and Beta glass-fibre fabric, which is completely non-inflammable in an oxygen atmosphere. Beneath this are another seven layers of synthetic materials which serve as insulators and liners.

VHF antenna linked to space craft

Extravehicular visor A polycarbonate shell placed over the helmet. It is thermally controlled, coated with gold to reduce light and heat from the sun, and is of high impact strength.

Oxygen purge system Provides an emergency 30-minute supply of oxygen in two 2-lb bottles.

Backpack control

Backpack Supplies oxygen and cooling water to the liquid cooling garment; return oxygen is cleansed. The pack also includes communications equipment, controls and a main power supply.

Penlight pocket

Oxygen purge system umbilical

Lunar Module restraint ring

Gloves Made of Chromel-R fabric and with thermal insulation for protection against extremes of heat and cold.

Utility pocket

Urine transfer connector

Lunar overshoes

Liquid cooling garment A knitted nylon-spandex garment worn next to the skin, with a network of plastic tubing through which cooling water from the portable life support system is circulated.

Connector
Zipper
Manifold
Tygon tubing

Diagram of the Tygon tubing carrying the liquid cooling system.

1961
First American Sub-Orbital Flight— When Gagarin made his ascent in Vostok 1, the Americans were still not ready to begin their manned space programme, but on May 5, 1961, Commander Alan Shepard made a sub-orbital flight to a height of 116 miles. It was more or less of an 'up and down' trip, and was of short duration, but it was entirely successful, and Shepard has the honour of being the first American to enter space.

1962
Project Mercury — The Mercury project involved space-orbits by single astronauts. Following Shepard's sub-orbital flight, and a second similar trip by the late Virgil Grissom, Colonel John Glenn achieved a complete orbit, like Gagarin. This was the first of several similar trips, though Glenn himself did not make another space-flight. *(right)* Mercury Capsule.

1964
The Ranger Programme— Project Mercury was followed by the Gemini launchings, involving two astronauts in one capsule, and complicated manoeuvres such as 'space-walks'. Meanwhile, probes were being sent to the Moon. The Ranger vehicles were crash-landed on the Moon; during the last few minutes of their flights, they sent back close-range pictures of the lunar surface. The first six failed, but the last three were successful. *(below)* Ranger vehicle.

1966
The Orbiters—The Russians were the first to put a vehicle into orbit round the Moon, but particularly good results were obtained from the U.S. Orbiters, which were placed in lunar orbit and which sent back many thousands of detailed photographs of almost the entire surface—including the side of the Moon which is always turned away from the Earth. The information obtained from the Orbiters was an essential preliminary to the Apollo programme. *(below)* An Orbiter.

1966-8
Soft Landings on The Moon—Once again the Russians took the lead in bringing a vehicle down gently on the Moon, so that pictures could be sent back from the lunar surface; this was first done with Luna 9 in 1966. Subsequently, more soft landings were made both by Russian Luna probes and by the U.S. Surveyors. The photographs obtained were invaluable. *(below)* A detail of the lunar surface showing a landing pad from a Surveyor.

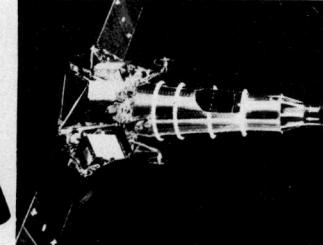

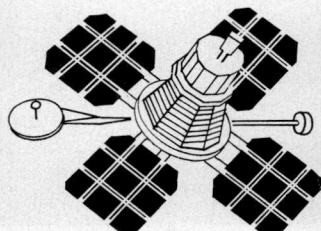

APOLLO 11: THE LANDING

The Giant Leap

"That's one small step for a man; a giant leap for mankind." Those words, never to be forgotten, were spoken by Neil Armstrong at 2.56 GMT on July 21st 1969, as he stepped out on to the surface of the Moon. Apollo 11 was a triumphant success; the dreams of twenty centuries had come true at last.

Apollo 11 had blasted away from Cape Kennedy on July 16th. The crew consisted of Astronaut Armstrong, destined to be the first man on the Moon; Colonel Edwin Aldrin, who would accompany him on the lunar surface; and Lieutenant-Colonel Michael Collins, who would remain in the Command Module, orbiting at a height of approximately 60 miles above the Moon during the final stages of the expedition. There were no complications during the launching or during the trans-lunar flight: all the instruments functioned perfectly, communications were good, and all three astronauts were in excellent shape. Neither was there any trouble with the insertion into lunar orbit. Exactly on schedule, Apollo 11 was given the 'go' signal for the landing manœuvre. This time there were no comic strip cartoon nicknames. The call sign for the Lunar Module was Eagle, and for the Command Module Columbia.

The Descent

The preparations followed the pattern set by Apollo 10. The Lunar Module had been inspected; Armstrong and Aldrin went into it, and prepared to blast away from the mother craft. The descent engine was fired at 10 per cent of its power for 15 seconds, and the throttle was then opened to 40 per cent of its full power. During this vital manœuvre, Apollo 11 was on the far side of the Moon, and so out of touch with Mission Control; but when contact was re-established it was clear that all was well with Columbia and Eagle. (Diagram 1).

The descent engine burn for Descent Orbit Injection (DOI for short) was made under the guidance of the Lunar Module's, "electronic brain", PGNS (Primary Guidance and Navigation System), but Armstrong was able to keep track of events by means of his instruments. In particular, both he and Aldrin could consult the attitude indicator, which summarized all information about the Module's position in space. Any movement in pitch, roll or yaw was indicated at once, so it was always possible for the astronauts to take over control manually if need be. In case of sudden emergency, the ABORT button would have been pressed, and Eagle would have blasted back into orbit to rendezvous with Collins in the Command Module.

The DOI manœuvre lowered the Module toward the Moon, until the height above the lunar surface was a mere 50,000 feet; at that moment the ground distance from the intended landing site was approximately 260 nautical miles (Diagram 2). Next, there began the powered descent initiation (PDI), using the descent engine to brake Eagle out of the descent transfer orbit. What had to be done, in fact, was to fire the engine against the direction of motion, slowing the Module down and reducing the velocity almost to zero for the start of the vertical descent. The braking manœuvre ended at about 7,000 feet above the surface, and the Module was rotated to an upright windows-forward attitude. The start of the final approach phase was called the "high-gate" (Diagram 3), and the start of the landing phase, at only 500 feet, was called the "low-gate" (Diagram 4).

Still all went well, but everybody—the astronauts, Mission Control at Houston, and the millions of people watching their television screens at home — knew that the most dangerous moments of the entire mission were approaching.

Leaving the Earth *(above)*
The Earth, seen from over 100,000 miles during Apollo 11's outward journey to the Moon. Africa can be seen clearly, together with parts of Europe and Asia.

Approaching the Moon *(below)*
The approach to the landing-site in the Sea of Tranquillity is seen in this photograph. taken from the Lunar Module when it was still orbiting the Moon and was docked to the Command Module. The large crater is Maskelyne; the Hypatia Cleft (U.S.1) upper left centre, with Möltke to the right. The landing site is in the centre, close to the edge of the sunlit area.

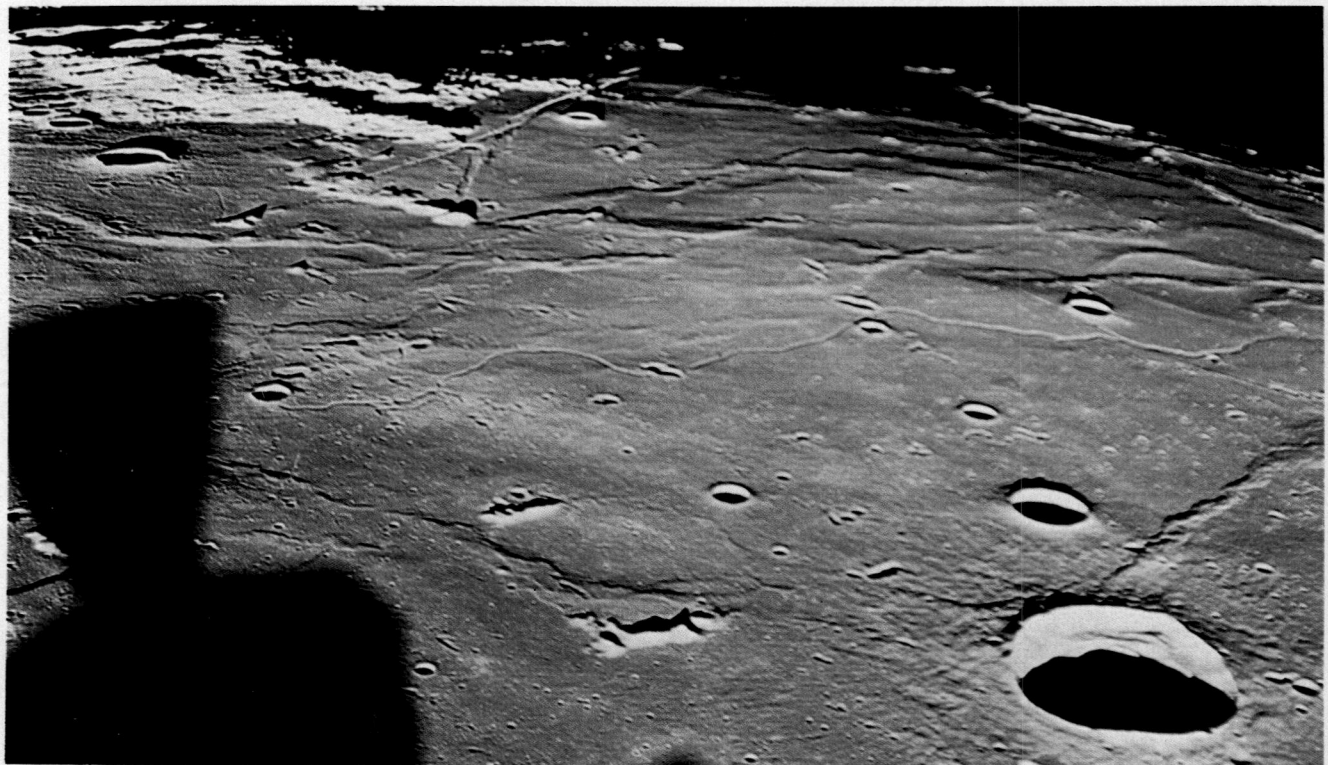

At low-gate, Armstrong took over manual control; the computers had done their work, and it was time for human intelligence and skill. Eagle was hovering at 500 feet above the Sea of Tranquillity, and it could continue there for only two minutes. Within that time, Armstrong had to make up his mind whether to go on down, or to fire the engine and blast back into orbit. There could be no second chance. If he and Aldrin were to land on the Moon, it must be now.

First, he had to check that the ground below was smooth, and free from boulders and pits. Armstrong had orders to "abort" if the tilt exceeded 6½ degrees. Since he could not see straight down through the space-craft, he had to tilt it as it hovered while he and Aldrin looked out of the windows. The manual control was delicate; on the instrument panel there were handles which allowed him to turn the module, or to shift it by using the thrust controller. In fact, the landing site below *(0 deg. 41 m. 15s. North 23 deg. 26m. East)* was 22,257 ft. West and 4,290 ft. North of the planned

Diagram 1 *(below)*
The diagram shows the procedure for the undocking of the Lunar Module from the Command Module, and the start of its moonward descent by the use of its own power. The LEM's descent orbit was calculated so that it would land in the Sea of Tranquillity close to the terminator (i.e. the boundary between the sunlit and night hemispheres of the Moon).

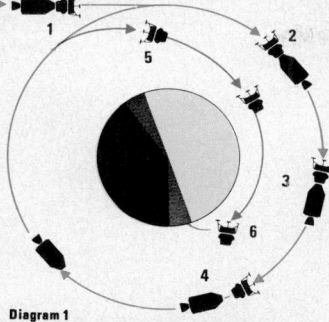

Diagram 1
1. Path from Earth. 2. Turns to tail-first position and fires into lunar orbit. 3. Correction to circular orbit. 4. LEM undocks. 5. Descent transfer orbit before final descent. 6. Descent begins.

landing ellipse centre since they had to avoid a boulder-strewn crater "about the size of a football pitch". Armstrong used the thrust control and Eagle moved slowly to one side above a smoother surface. The decision was made. All forward velocity was cancelled out, and Armstrong began the final descent at a rate of three feet per second. The engines were still working; had they faltered at that moment, disaster would have been complete.

At the last moments of descent, five-foot wires (lunar surface sensing probes) projecting from the Module's landing pads touched the surface. Lunar contact lights on the instrument panel flashed on. Exactly one second later, Armstrong shut off the descent engine by operating the thrust controller — and Eagle fell the last few feet, landing on the Sea of Tranquillity and coming to rest. The long journey was over, and after scarcely a pause Neil Armstrong reported : "Houston. Tranquillity Base here. The Eagle has landed."

Though the whole manœuvre had been planned down to the last detail, it

had never been rehearsed under realistic conditions, simply because no re-hearsal was possible. The Moon has no atmosphere, so that nothing in the way of a parachute could be used. Yet the touch down was faultless, a tribute not only to the efficiency of the computers and the motors, but also to the supreme courage and skill of Armstrong and Aldrin.

Their calm, level voices told the world that the first men on the Moon had arrived.

Diagram 2 *(below)*
Approaching the Moon. The orbit of the Command Module is shown, with its approximately constant height of more than 60 miles above the Moon ; the path of the Lunar Module is also shown during the descent stage PDI (Powered Descent Initiation) began at 260 miles, surface range, from the landing-site. At 235 miles the throttle was put to FTP (Fixed Throttle Position), and the Module then passed more or less over the conspicuous crater Maskelyne. Still descending, it reached the High-Gate position, ready for the final approach phase.

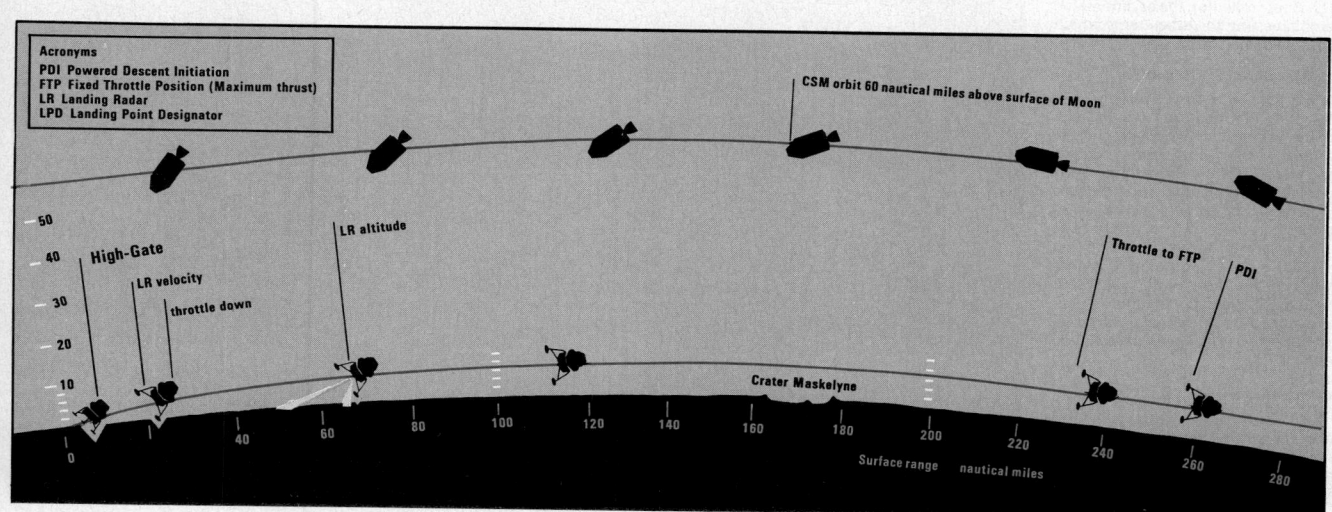

Acronyms
PDI Powered Descent Initiation
FTP Fixed Throttle Position (Maximum thrust)
LR Landing Radar
LPD Landing Point Designator

CSM orbit 60 nautical miles above surface of Moon

High-Gate
LR velocity
throttle down
LR altitude
Throttle to FTP
PDI
Crater Maskelyne
Surface range   nautical miles

Diagram 3 *(right)*
At High-Gate, the Module was positioned so that the astronauts could see the landing site. Needless to say, the radar readings were all-important ; it was only during the very last moments that Armstrong took over manual control. The forward velocity had now been reduced to almost zero, so that the Module was descending slowly and "balancing" itself against gravity by means of its engine. When the height over the surface of the Moon was only 500 feet, at Low-Gate, there came the start of the most critical manœuvre of all : the touch-down.

Forward Window View at High-Gate

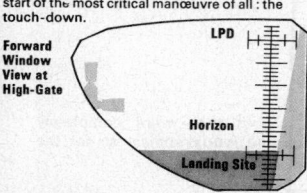

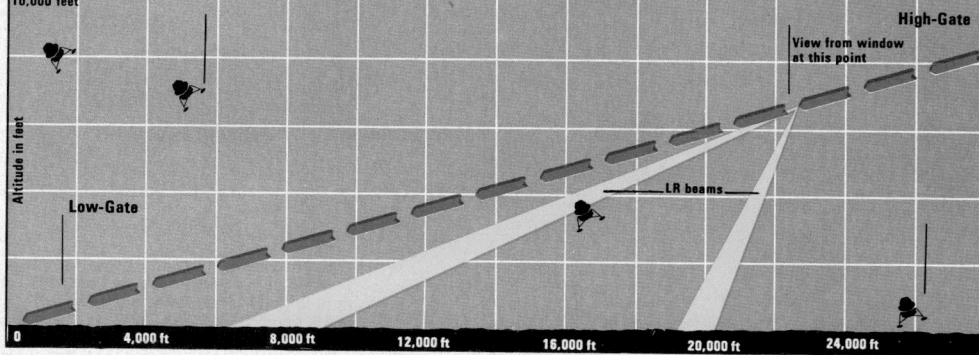

10,000 feet
High-Gate
View from window at this point
Low-Gate
LR beams
Altitude in feet
0   4,000 ft   8,000 ft   12,000 ft   16,000 ft   20,000 ft   24,000 ft

Diagram 4 *(right)*
With still very slight forward velocity, Eagle continued its descent, now under manual control. Armstrong could tilt the Module so as to see the Moon's surface through the window, and he manœuvred so as to avoid a crater which seemed to have too rocky an interior to be welcoming. At 150 feet he was satisfied that the surface below would be suitable as a landing-site, and he began the final descent, at a rate of 3 feet per second and nil forward velocity. At last the projecting foot-wires touched the Moon ; the engines were cut, and Eagle touched down safely.

Forward Window View at Low-Gate

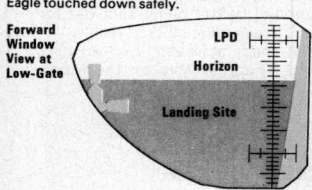

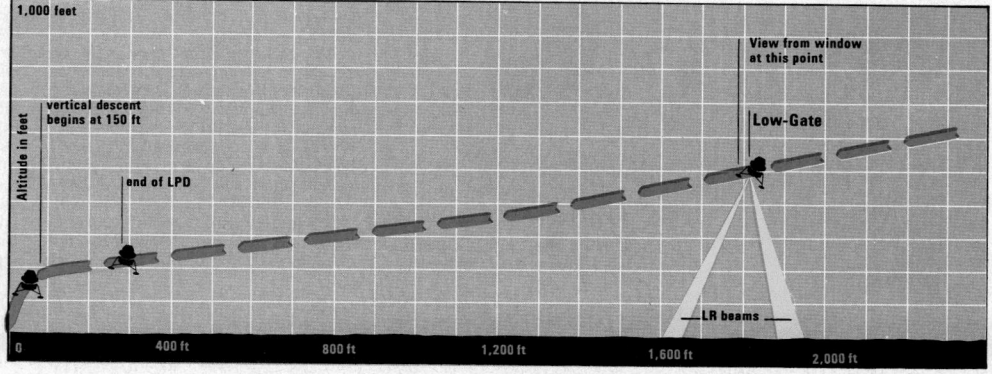

1,000 feet
vertical descent begins at 150 ft
end of LPD
View from window at this point
Low-Gate
Altitude in feet
LR beams
0   400 ft   800 ft   1,200 ft   1,600 ft   2,000 ft

APOLLO 11: RETURN JOURNEY

Lift Off

Landing on the Moon had been hazardous, because there were so many unknown factors. The subsequent lift off back to orbit was expected to be straightforward, but it was just as tense, because everything depended on the correct functioning of the single engine of the ascent stage of the Lunar Module. If it failed, there could be no rescue operation: Collins, in the circling Command Module, was unable to attempt a landing on the lunar surface.

Following a rest period, Armstrong and Aldrin prepared to blast off. Exactly on schedule, they fired the engine – and it worked perfectly. It burned for 7 minutes 14 seconds, and sent the upper part of the Eagle back to rendezvous with the waiting Columbia (see diagram). The lower part of the Lunar Module was left on the Moon, together with the laser reflector, the seismometer, the emblems, and the other items which the astronauts had discarded.

Rendezvous with Columbia

The next step was to rendezvous and dock with Columbia, and it was here that the astronauts experienced their first and only unexpected crisis. During docking there were uncontrollable movements of Eagle which led to a temporary loss of contact with Mission Control. Fortunately, the crisis was brief; after a few minutes the docking manœuvre was carried out, and before long Aldrin and Armstrong were back inside the Command Module with their precious cargo of lunar samples. Eagle, its work done, was despatched into space.

The Journey Home

On July 22nd there came the last 'lunar manœuvre' – the engine burn behind the Moon that put Apollo back into a homeward path. The return journey was comparatively uneventful, and some-

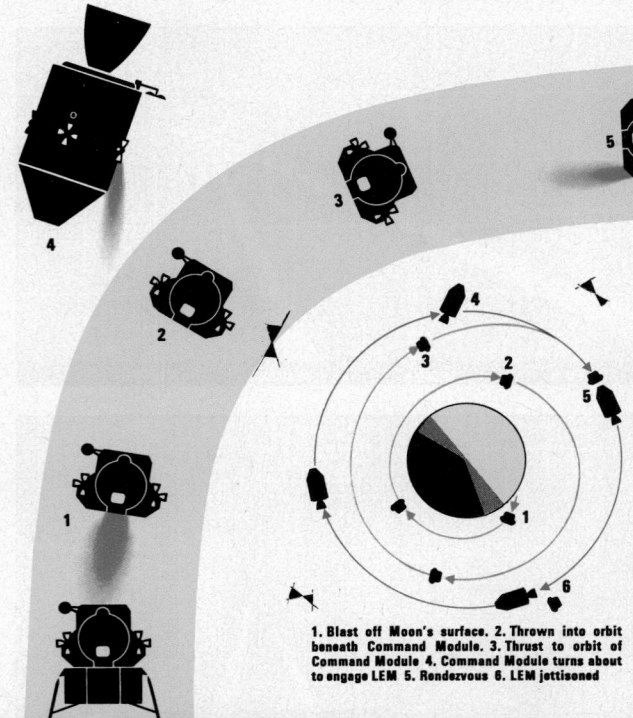

1. Blast off Moon's surface. 2. Thrown into orbit beneath Command Module. 3. Thrust to orbit of Command Module 4. Command Module turns about to engage LEM 5. Rendezvous 6. LEM jettisoned

thing in the nature of an anti-climax right up until splashdown in the Pacific at 16 hours 50 minutes GMT on July 24th, thirteen miles away from the waiting recovery ship, the U.S.S. *Hornet*, when the Command Module hit the sea upside down and had to be righted.

On this occasion there were no red-carpet ceremonies for the astronauts, because of the need for immediate and strict quarantining. They left the capsule in their contamination suits, boarded a raft, and were taken up into a helicopter. As soon as they reached the *Hornet* they went into a quarantine caravan, and it was while they were inside that Richard Nixon, President of the United States, addressed them. The astronauts could be seen behind their

window, but they were completely isolated and would remain so for the next eighteen days.

Quarantine

Many people felt that the quarantine restrictions were too strict, but the NASA authorities were entirely justified. Even though the Moon is almost certainly a sterile world, there is always a million-to-one chance that contact with lunar material may involve as yet unknown hazards for Man – and a single mistake would be one too many. The rocks brought back were also strictly quarantined before being sent out for analysis in scientific laboratories.

Man had achieved his greatest triumph. The First Men on the Moon were home.

Crater *(below)*
This striking photograph of the lunar terrain near the landed LEM shows a small crater with central mound in foreground. Note the shadow on the crater wall.

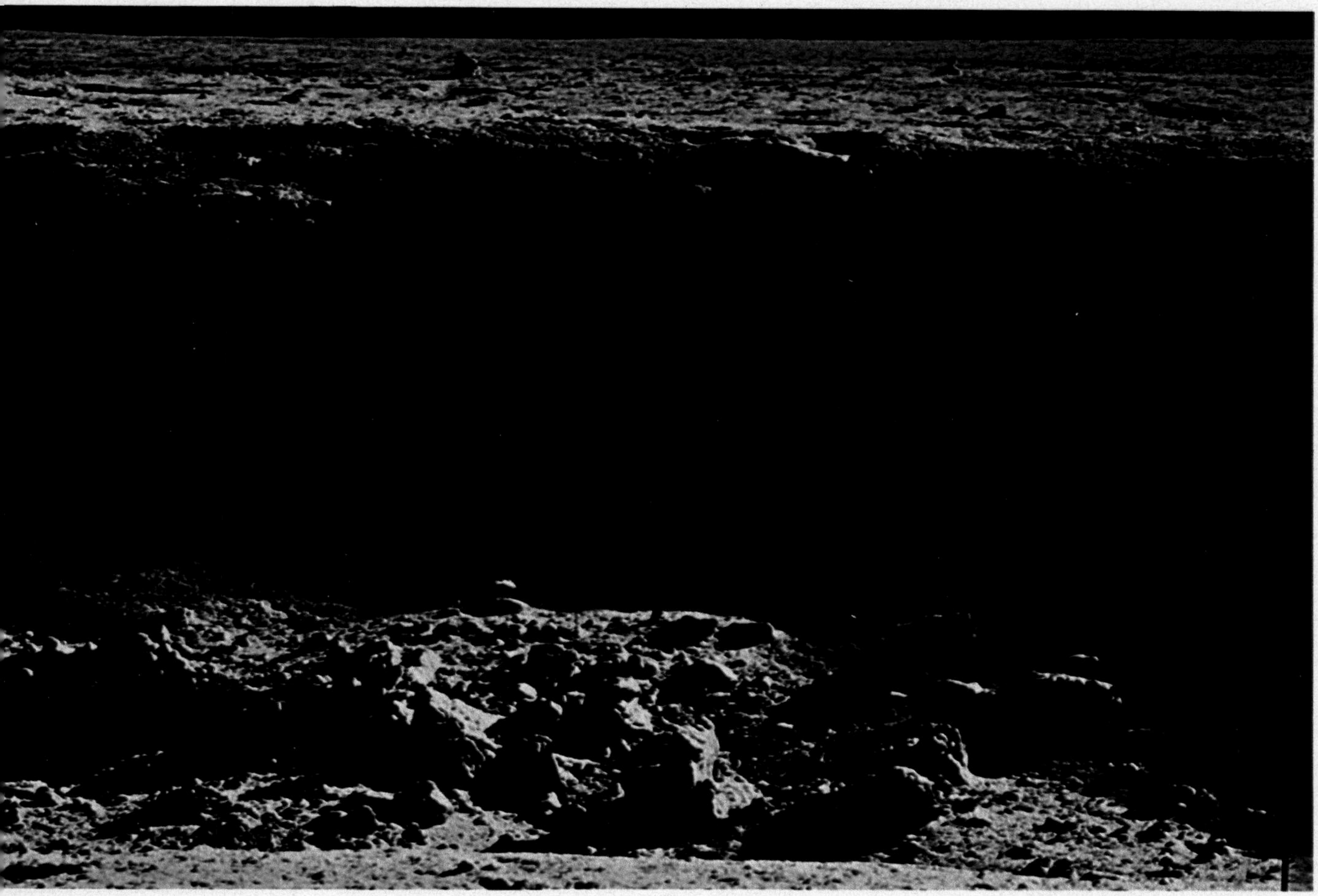

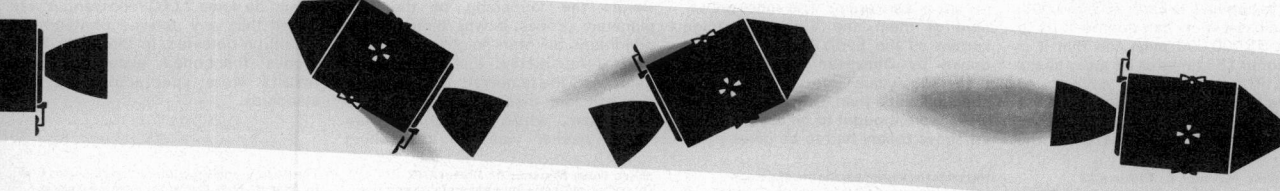

The First Men on the Moon

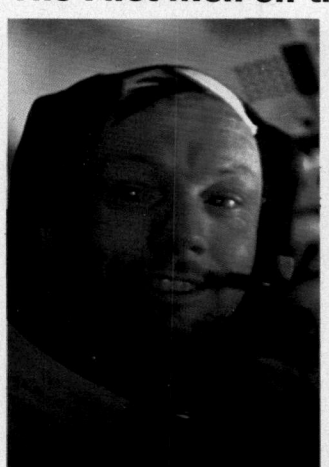

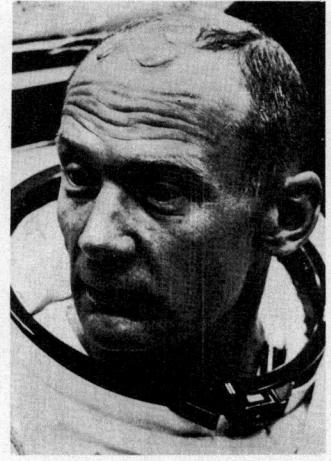

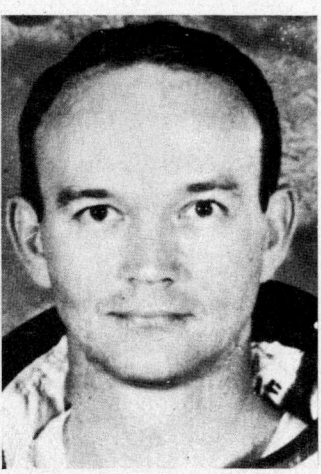

Neil Armstrong, commander of Apollo 11, was born in Wapakoneta, Ohio, on August 5, 1930. In 1955, joined NASA as an aeronautical research pilot. He was selected as an astronaut in 1962, and commanded the Gemini 8 mission, carrying out the first orbital docking manœuvre. He is married, with two sons.

Edwin Aldrin, known by his nickname of "Buzz", was born in Montclair, N.J., on January 30, 1930. He carried out his first space mission with Gemini 12; he had been selected as an astronaut in 1963. Colonel Aldrin has the reputation of being the best scientist of all the astronauts, and has a doctorate from the Massachusetts Institute of Technology. He is married, with two sons and a daughter.

Michael Collins, a Lieutenant-Colonel in the U.S. Air Force, was born in Rome in 1930 (October 31), but is of course purely American. He was selected as an astronaut in 1963, and flew in Gemini 10, launched on July 18, 1966; during that mission he undertook two 'space-walks". It was typical of him that he was very ready to concede the honour of an actual Moon-landing to his colleagues, while he carried out the equally essential rôle of Command Module pilot. He, too, is married, and has one son and two daughters.

WHERE NEXT? MARS

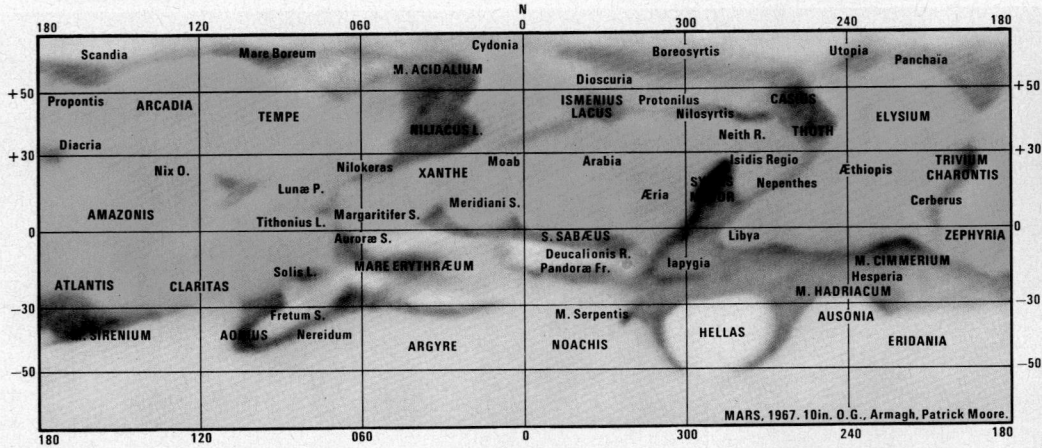

MARS, 1967. 10in. O.G., Armagh, Patrick Moore.

Map of Mars
This map, on Mercator's projection, shows the main features of Mars visible with a telescope of moderate size. It was compiled by Patrick

Moore from his observations made in 1967 with the 10 in. refractor at Armagh Observatory. North is at the top – following the American custom, as opposed to astronomical practice.

The most prominent features are the Syrtis Major in the equatorial region, and the Mare Acidalium in the northern hemisphere.

Mars from Mariner 6
This photograph was sent back from Mariner 6 on July 29, 1969, when the probe was 503,050 miles from Mars. The Syrtis Major, to the upper right, is clearly seen, and may be identified on the map ; the feature slightly to the left of centre is the 'Martian Greenwich'', Sinus Meridiani (longtitude 0 degrees). The southern polar cap is excellently shown, and there are indications of whiteness also in the far north.

Venus or Mars?

Now that the Moon has been reached, it is time to look further afield. Two planets are within range : Venus, closer to the Sun than we are, and Mars, which is further away.

The surface conditions on Venus, discovered by the American and Russian space probes and described on page 6, effectively preclude any manned landings there in the forseeable future. Not so with Mars, which, though forbidding in many respects, is a practicable and fascinating proposition. Mars must therefore be our next target.

Mars Data

Mars has a diameter of 4200 miles, so that in size it is intermediate between the Moon and the Earth. It has an appreciable atmosphere, and has always been regarded as a likely abode of life. Its climate is much cooler than that of the Earth, because it is further from the Sun ; its mean distance is 141,500,000 miles, as opposed to Earth's 93,000,000. At its closest Mars can approach us to within 35,000,000 miles, so that it is then about 150 times as far away as the Moon. The Martian year amounts to 687 days, while the rotation period is 24 hours 37 minutes – roughly half an hour longer than ours. The tilt of the

axis is much the same as that of the Earth, so that the seasons are of the same basic type, though they are, of course, much longer. The surface gravity is relatively low ; a man who weighs 150 lbs on Earth would weigh a mere 50 lbs on Mars.

Through a telescope, Mars shows definite markings, which are permanent surface features and which have been carefully mapped. First, there are the white caps which cover the poles ; it is tempting to regard them as ice-caps, but there can be no true analogy with the deep snowy caps which cover the poles of Earth. From the rate at which the Martian caps shrink in the spring and early summer, and the tiny amount of moisture which they release into the atmosphere, it is clear that they must be very thin. Their depth cannot be so much as one foot, and is more probably less than one inch.

The dark areas are characteristic, and seem to be to all intents and purposes permanent. The most prominent of them, the V-shaped region known as the Syrtis Major, was first drawn by Christiaan Huygens more than 300 years ago, and has not changed since then. Originally the dark areas were thought to be seas, but this attractive theory had to be given up as

soon as it became obvious that Mars is desperately short of water. Alternatively, it was suggested that they might be due to organic matter – or, using the term in a broad sense, "vegetation" It is true that there are seasonal changes on Mars, affecting the dark areas and linked with the shrinking of the polar caps, which might well be due to the growth of Martian organisms with the arrival of moisture wafted from the poles.

Much of the surface is reddish-ochre in hue. The Martian "deserts", to give them their common name, are not in the least like the deserts of Earth ; for one thing, they are extremely cold, and at night their temperature, even at the equator, must fall to below —100 degrees Fahrenheit. Neither are they likely to be made up of sand, and are more probably coated with some reddish mineral.

Rockets to Mars

Before the launching of the first planetary probes, it was thought that conditions on Mars might not be too severe. Admittedly, the climate was chilly, and the temperature could never rise to more than about 80 degrees Fahrenheit, while the nights were bitter ; neither was the atmosphere

breathable. However, Mars appeared much more friendly than the Moon, and the chances of underground water supplies could not be ruled out.

Then, in 1965, the American probe Mariner 4 by-passed Mars and sent back the first detailed photographs. The results came as something of a surprise. Instead of being flat, Mars proved to be crater-scarred ; its surface was not unlike that of the Moon. though there was considerable evidence of erosion. To make matters worse, the atmosphere proved to be much thinner than had been expected, and to be composed chiefly of carbon dioxide.

Though Mariner 4 was a success, it sent back only a few good pictures, and astronomers eagerly awaited the results from Mariners 6 and 7, launched in 1969. Neither was scheduled to land on Mars. Mariner 6 was destined to 'fly-by' over the planet's equator, while Mariner 7 was to pass over the pole ; in each case the closest approach would be some 2,000 miles, and it was hoped that very detailed photographs would be obtained. In the event, both probes functioned excellently, and results were spectacular by any standards.

Mars from Mariner 6 : Picture 22
This narrow-angle view of Mars spans 52 miles E-W by 45 miles N-S. The large crater to the south (at the bottom of the picture) is 15 miles in diameter ; the irregular terrain to the N.W. of

this crater is débris near the rim of a much larger crater over 150 miles across, shown in Picture 21. The local time was one hour before sunset. The photograph was taken on July 30, 1969, with Mariner at 2,150 miles from Mars.

Mars from Mariner 6 : Picture 18
One of the most striking photographs ever obtained from a space-probe. It was taken on July 30, 1969 during a twenty-minute period at Mariner's closest approach to the planet.

The narrow-angle picture extends 63 miles E-W by 48 miles N-S. The large crater, 24 miles in diameter, shows several slump terraces and radial gullies on the south wall ; the younger crater on the wall shows a central peak.

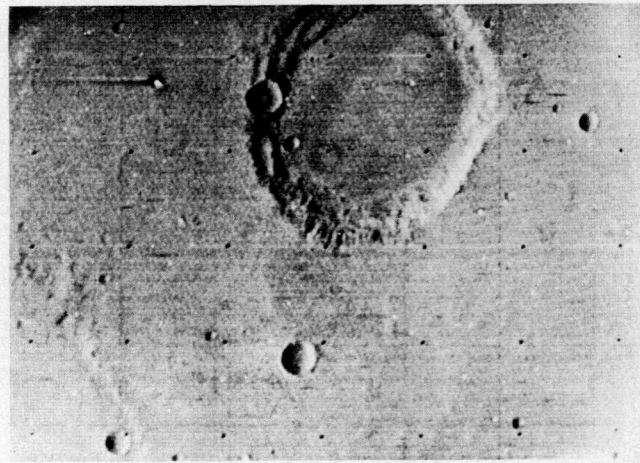

For latest space information see "U.S. History" page 1157.

Webster's Encyclopedia of Dictionaries

12 complete dictionaries in one

Nearly 150,000 entries for school, home, office

- **WEBSTER'S DICTIONARY**
  Over 50,000 entries: a standard guide for spelling, pronunciation and definition.

- **CROSSWORD PUZZLE DICTIONARY**
  Over 50,000 answers for nearly 20,000 crossword puzzle "sticklers."

- **BIBLE DICTIONARY**
  Biblical names, places and things clearly defined with book and chapter reference for each entry.

- **BOOK of FAMILIAR QUOTATIONS**
  Best known, most widely recognized quotations readily found under topic headings.

- **SCIENTIFIC TERMS**
  Definitions of terms used in Astronomy, Chemistry, Physics, etc.

- **SYNONYMS, ANTONYMS & HOMONYMS**
  Unexcelled for finding the right word with ease and rapidity.

- **MUSIC DICTIONARY**
  An authoritative guide for a complete understanding of musical terms.

- **RHYMING DICTIONARY**
  Thousands of rhyming words—indispensable for writing poetry or jingles.

- **LEGAL DICTIONARY**
  Simple, clear language insures understanding of legal phrases and terminology.

- **MEDICAL DICTIONARY**
  In efficient dictionary format, medical definitions, simplified for easy understanding.

- **OUTLINE OF U.S. HISTORY**
  From colonial days through the present, highlighting major events.

- **ATLAS & GAZETTEER**
  World, each continent, U.S., detail maps of U.S. geographical divisions—all in full color. The effectiveness of the Atlas is increased by the current geographical information to be found in the Gazetteer.

5	WEBSTER A–B
57	WEBSTER C–D
121	WEBSTER E–G
171	WEBSTER H–L
227	WEBSTER M–P
301	WEBSTER Q–S
379	WEBSTER T–Z
451	Synonym Ant/Hom
517	X–WORD DICT
591	MEDICAL DICT
629	BIBLE DICT
729	RHYMING DICT
801	MUSIC DICT
835	FAM QUOTES
931	LEGAL DICT
1027	Science Terms
1091	U.S. HISTORY
1165	GAZETTE ATLAS

WEBSTER'S DICTIONARY

Edited by

John Gage Allee, Ph.D.

**Professor of English Philology,
The George Washington University**

KEY TO THIS DICTIONARY

The entries in this Dictionary are arranged in groups, derived and related words being placed under the main entry.

A. Each main entry, in bold-faced type, is syllabized with the phonetic spelling and accented syllable shown in parentheses. The part of speech, in italics, follows; then the definition.

Ex.: **cross** (kraws) *a.* intersecting; interchanged. . . .

B. Sub-entries are shown in bold-faced type following the definition of the main entry.

1. If a hyphen precedes the sub-entry, the ending is added to the main entry.

Ex.: **-ing** (crossing)

2. If a dash precedes the sub-entry, a hyphenated word is indicated.

Ex.: **—examination** (cross-examination)

3. If a dash and a space precede the sub-entry, this indicates words that are commonly found together.

Ex.: **— reference** (cross reference)

4. If the sub-entry is spelled out and/or pronunciation shown, this may indicate differences from the main entry. (In some instances, sub-entries are spelled out where confusion may otherwise develop).

C. The etymology of the main-entry is found in brackets following the entry paragraph; lack of etymology indicates uncertain or unknown word origin.

Note: Irregularities of verb forms, plurals and comparisons are included as sub-entries to facilitate word usage.

ABBREVIATIONS USED IN THIS DICTIONARY

a. adjective
abbrev. abbreviation
ablat. ablative; ablatival
Aborig. Aboriginal
acc. accusative
A.D. Anno Domini
  (in the year of Our Lord)
adv. adverb
Aero. Aeronautics
Afr. Africa; African
Agric. Agriculture
Alg. Algebra
alt. alternative
Amer. America; American
Anat. Anatomy
Anglo-Ind. Anglo-Indian
Anthropol. Anthropology
Ar. Arabic
Arch. Archaic
Archaeol. Archaeology
Archit. Architecture
Arith. Arithmetic
Astrol. Astrology
Astron. Astronomy
aux. auxiliary
Aviat. Aviation

Bacter. Bacteriology
B.C. before Christ
Bib. Biblical
Biol. Biology
Bot. Botany
Br., Brit. British
Braz. Brazilian
Bret. Breton
Build. Building

c. about (L. = *Circa*)
C. Centigrade; Central
Can. Canada; Canadian
Cap. capital letter
Carib. Caribbean
Carp. Carpentry
Celt. Celtic
cent. century
Cent. Central
cf. compare (L. = *confer*)
ch. Chapter
Chem. Chemistry
Chin. Chinese
Class. Myth. Classical
  Mythology
Colloq. Colloquial;
  Colloquialism
Comm. Commerce;
  Commercial
comp. comparative
conj. conjunction
conn. connected
contr. contraction
corrupt. corruption

Dan. Danish
dat. dative
def. art. definite article
demons. demonstrative
der. derivation; derived
Dial. Dialect; Dialectal
Dict. Dictionary
dim. diminutive
Dut. Dutch
Dyn. Dynamics

E. East; English
Eccl. Ecclesiastical
e.g. for example (L. =
  exempla gratia)
E.Ind. East Indian
Elect. Electricity
Embryol. Embryology
Engin. Engineering
Entom. Entomology
esp. especially
Ethnol. Ethnology
etym. etymology

F., Fahr. Fahrenheit
fem. feminine
fig. figuratively
Finn. Finnish
Flem. Flemish
Fort. Fortification
fr. from
Fr. French
freq. frequentative

Gael. Gaelic
gen. genitive
Geog. Geography
Geol. Geology
Geom. Geometry
Ger. German
Gk. Greek
Gk. Myth. Greek Mythology
Gram. Grammar

Heb. Hebrew
Her. Heraldry
Hind. Hindustani
Hist. History
Hort. Horticulture
Hung. Hungarian

i. intransitive
Ice. Icelandic
i.e. that is (L. = *id est*)
imit. imitation; imitative
imper. imperative
impers. impersonal
Ind. Indian
indef. art. indefinite article
indic. indicative
infin. infinitive
interj. interjection
interrog. interrogative
Ir. Irish
It. Italian

Jap. Japanese

L. Latin
l.c. lower case letter
L.Ger. Low German
lit. literally
Lit. Literature
L.L. Low (Late) Latin

masc. masculine
Math. Mathematics
M.E. Middle English
Mech. Mechanics
Med. Medicine
Metal. Metallurgy
Meteor. Meteorology
Mex. Mexican

M.H.Ger. Middle High
  German
Mil. Military
Min. Mineralogy
Mod. Modern
Mus. Music
Myth. Mythology

n. noun
N. North; Norse
Nat.Hist. Natural History
Naut. Nautical
neg. negative
neut. neuter
nom. nominative
Norw. Norwegian
n.pl. noun plural
n.sing. noun singular
N.T. New Testament

obj. object; objective
obs. obsolete
O.E. Old English
O.Fr. Old French
O.H.Ger. Old High German
O.L.Ger. Old Low German
O.N. Old Norse
Onomat. Onomatopoeic
opp. opposite; opposed
Opt. Optics
orig. originally
Ornith. Ornithology
O.T. Old Testament

Paint. Painting
pa.p. past participle
pass. passive
pa.t. past tense
Path. Pathology
perh. perhaps
pers. person
Pers. Persian
pert. pertaining
Peruv. Peruvian
Pharm. Pharmacy
Philol. Philology
Philos. Philosophy
Phon. Phonetics
Photog. Photography
Phys. Physics
Physiol. Physiology
pl. plural
Poet. Poetry; poetical
Pol. Polish
Port. Portuguese
poss. possessive
pref. prefix
prep. preposition
pres. present
Print. Printing
prob. probably
pron. pronoun
Pros. Prosody
Prov. Provincial
pr.p. present participle
Psych. psychology

q.v. which see (L. =
  quod vide)

R. River
R.C. Roman Catholic

recip. reciprocal
redup. reduplication
ref. reference; referring
refl. reflexive
rel related; relative
Rhet. Rhetoric
Rom. Roman
Rom.Myth. Roman
  Mythology
Russ. Russian

S. South
S.Afr. South African
S.Amer. South American
Sans. Sanskrit
Scand. Scandinavian
Scot. Scots; Scottish
Sculp. Sculpture
sing. singular
Singh. Singhalese
Slav. Slavonic
Sp. Spanish
St. Saint
superl. superlative
Surg. Surgery
Sw. Swedish
Syn. Synonym

t. transitive
Teleg. Telegraphy
Teut. Teutonic
Theat. Theatre
Theol. Theology
Trig. Trigonometry
Turk. Turkish

U.S.(A.) United States (of
  America)
usu. usually

v. verb
var. variant; variation
v.i. verb intransitive
v.t. verb transitive
vulg. vulgar

W. Welsh; West

Yid. Yiddish

Zool. Zoology

These pronunciation symbols are used for the sounds indicated by the bold face letter or letters in the key words.

Vowels and diphthongs:

a—bat
ȧ—botany
a̱—about, soda
  (unstressed)
ā—bait
aw—bought
e—bet
ē—beet
i—bit
i·—city (final syllable)

ī—bite
ō—boat
oo—book
o̅o̅—boot
oi—boil
ou—bout
u—but
ū—butte
ur—Bert (stressed)
er—blubber (unstressed)

Consonants:

b—bill
ch—church
d—dill
f—fill
g—get
h—hill
hw—wheel
j—judge
k—kill
l—lily
m—mill
n—nil
ng—sing

ngg—finger
p—pill
r—rill
s—sill
sh—shall, sure
t—till
th—thin
TH—then
v—villa
w—will
y—yet
z—zillion
zh—pleasure

WEBSTER'S DICTIONARY

A

A (ā, ạ) *a*, the indefinite *article*, meaning *one*. A contraction of *an* (fr. O.E. an, *one*), used before vowels.

A-1 (ā wun) first-rate; excellent; physically fit.

aard·vark (ård′·vårk) *n.* animal resembling the ant-eater, found in parts of Africa. [Dut. *aarde*, earth; *vark*, a pig].

A.B. (ā bē) Bachelor of Arts [L. *Artium Baccalaureus*]

ab- (ab) *prefix* meaning from, away, off [L.].

a·ba·cá (åb′·ạ·ká) *n.* Manila hemp, or the plant producing it [Malay].

a·back (ạ·bak′) *adv.* backwards; on the back; (*Naut.*) against the masts, of sails pressed back by the wind. **taken aback**, taken by surprise; disconcerted [O.E. *on bacc*].

a·ba·cus (åb′·ạ·kạs) *n.* an instrument with parallel wires on which arithmetical calculations are made with sliding balls or beads; a counting-frame; (*Archit.*) a tablet crowning a column and its capital [L., from Gk. *abax*, a reckoning-board].

a·baft (ạ·baft′) *adv.* and *prep.* (*Naut.*) at or towards the stern; behind [O.E. *aeftan*, behind].

ab·a·lo·ne (ab·ạ·lō′·nē) *n.* the name of several species of limpet-like molluscs or "earshells," yielding mother-of-pearl [Sp.].

a·ban·don (ạ·ban′·dạn) *v.t.* to give up wholly and finally; to relinquish; to surrender; *n.* careless freedom; a yielding to unrestrained impulse; dash. **-ed** *a.* deserted; forsaken; unrestrained; given up entirely to, esp. wickedness. **-edly** *adv.* **-ment** *n.* the act of abandoning, or state of being abandoned; (*Law*) the relinquishing of an interest or claim [Fr. *abandonner*, to give up].

a·base (ạ·bās′) *v.t.* to bring low; to cast down; to humble. **-ment** *n.* humiliation [L. *ad*, to; L.L. *bassare*, to lower].

a·bash (ạ·bash′) *v.t.* to strike with shame or fear; to excite a consciousness of guilt, inferiority, etc. **-ment** *n.* confusion from shame, etc. [Fr. *ébahir*, to astound].

a·bate (ạ·bāt′) *v.t.* to beat down, lessen; (*Law*) to put an end to, as a nuisance; to annul, as a writ; *v.i.* to decrease, subside, decline. **-able** *a.* **-ment** *n.* **-r** *n.* [L. *ad*, and *batere*, for *batuere*, to strike].

a·bat·toir (a·bạ·twår′) *n.* a slaughter-house [Fr. *abattre*, to fell].

ab·ba·cy (ab′·ạ·si·) *n.* the office or dignity of an abbot; the building under the control of an abbot; an abbey. **abbatial** (ạ·bā′·shạl) *a.* pert. to an abbot, or an abbey. **abbé** (ab′·i·) *n.* designation of and mode of address for an R.C. priest in France; an abbot. **abbey** *n.* a church establishment forming the dwelling-place of a community of monks or nuns. **abbot** (*fem.* **abbess**) *n.* the head of an abbey or monastery. **abbotship** *n.* [Syriac *abba*, father; Heb. *ab*, father].

ab·bre·vi·ate (ạ·brē′·vi·āt) *v.t.* to shorten, reduce by contraction or omission. **abbreviation** *n.* the act of abbreviating; a shortened form. **abbreviator** *n.* **abbreviatory** *a.* [L. *abbreviare*, fr. *brevis*, short].

A·b·c (ā·bē·sē′) *n.* the first three letters of the alphabet; the alphabet; the rudiments of any subject; a primer.

ab·di·cate (ab′·di·kāt) *v.t.* and *i.* formally to give up power or office. **abdication** *n.* [L. *ab*, from; *dicare*, to proclaim].

ab·do·men (ab·dō′·mạn, ab′·dạ·mạn) *n.* the lower part of the trunk of the body; the belly.

abdominal *a.* **abdominous** *a.* having a big belly; paunchy [L.].

ab·duct (ab·dukt′) *v.t.* to take away by fraud or force; to kidnap; (*Anat.*) to draw, e.g. a limb away from its natural position. **abducent** (ab·dū′·sent) *a.* (*Anat.*) abducting. **abduction** *n.* [L. *ab*, from; *ducere*, *ductum*, to lead].

a·beam (ạ·bēm′) *adv.* (*Naut.*) at right angles to a ship's length; hence, straight across a ship; abreast [E. *beam*].

a·bed (ạ·bed′) *adv.* in bed [E. *on bed*].

a·bele (ạ·bēl′) *n.* the white poplar-tree [L. *albus*, white].

ab·er·rate (ab′·ẹr·āt) *v.i.* to deviate from the right path or normal course. **aberrant** (ab·e′·rạnt) *a.* deviating from the normal. **aberration** (ab·ạ·rā′·shun) *n.* a wandering, esp. mental disorder, forgetfulness; mental instability or peculiarity; moral lapse [L. *ab*, from; *errare*, to wander].

a·bet (ạ·bet′) *v.t.* to encourage or aid, esp. in doing wrong. *pr.p.* **-ting.** *pa.p.* and *pa.t.* **-ted.** **-ment** *n.* **-ter**, **-tor** *n.* [O.Fr. *abeter*, to incite].

a·bey·ance (ạ·bā′·ans) *n.* a state of suspension or temporary inactivity; the condition of not being in use or action. Also **abeyancy** [O.Fr. *abeer*, to gape at].

ab·hor (ab·hawr′) *v.t.* to hate extremely. *pr.p.* **-ring.** *pa.p.* and *pa.t.* **-red.** **-rence** *n.* detestation; loathing. **-rent** *a.* detestable; abominable; repugnant. **-rer** *n.* [L. *ab*, from; *horrere*, to shiver].

a·bide (ạ·bīd′) *v.i.* to stay; reside; continue firm or stable; *v.t.* to tolerate; bear; wait for; *pa.p.* and *pa.t.* **abode or abided.** **abidance** *n.* **abiding** *a.* lasting; enduring [O.E. *abidan*].

a·bil·i·ty (ạ·bil′·i·ti·) *n.* quality, state, or condition of being able; power to act; skill; capacity; competence. [L. *habilitas*, cleverness].

ab·i·o·gen·e·sis (ab·i·ō·jen′·ạ·sis) *n.* (*Biol.*) the theory of spontaneous generation from non-living matter [Gk. *a-*; neg.; *bios*, life; *genesis*, birth].

ab·ject (ab′·jekt) *a.* base; degraded; mean and worthless; contemptible; miserable. **-ly** *adv.* **-tion**, **-ness** *n.* degradation; abasement; servility [L. *ab*, away; *jacere*, *jactum*, to throw].

ab·jure (ab·joor′) *v.t.* to renounce upon oath; to abandon allegiance to a cause, doctrine, or principle; repudiate; forswear. **abjuration** *n.* [L. *abjurare*, to deny on oath].

ab·la·tive (ab′·lạ·tiv) *a.* (used as *n.*) the sixth case of Latin nouns and pronouns expressing *time when;* originally implied *separation from.* **ablatival** *a.* [L. *ab*, from; *ferre*, *latum*, to carry].

ab·laut (ab′·lout) *n.* (*Philol.*) variation of root vowel in certain related words, as *sink*, *sank*, *sunk* [Ger. *ab*, from; *laut*, sound].

a·blaze (ạ·blāz′) *a.* on fire; aglow; gleaming.

a·ble (ā′·bl) *a.* having skill, strength to perform a task; competent; talented; vigorous. **—bodied** *a.* of sound body; robust; (of a seaman, *abbrev.* **A.B.**) having all-round knowledge of seamanship. **ability** *n.* being able. **-ness** *n.* **ably** *adv.* competently [L. *habilis*, manageable].

a·bloom (ạ·bloom′) *adv.* or *a.* in bloom.

ab·lu·tion (ab·loo′·shạn) *n.* cleansing or washing; (usually plural) the purification of the body or of sacred vessels before certain religious ceremonies, e.g., Eucharist; the wine and water used. **-ary** *a.* pert. to cleansing [L. *ab*, from; *luere*, *lutum*, to wash].

ab·ne·gate (ab′·ne·gāt) *v.t.* to deny; surrender; relinquish. **abnegation** *n.* denying; renunciation [L. *ab*, away; *negare*, to deny].

ab·nor·mal (ab·nawr′·mạl) *a.* contrary to rule, or system; deviating from a recognized standard; exceptional; psychologically maladjusted. Also **-ity, -ism** *n.* the state of being abnormal; deformity; idiosyncrasy. **-ly** *adv.* **abnormity** *n.* abnormality; monstrosity [L. *ab*, from; *norma*, rule].

a·board (ạ·bōrd′) *adv.* and *prep.* (*Naut.*) on board; within a vessel; on a train.

a·bode (ạ·bōd′) *n.* residence, permanent or temporary; a dwelling place [from *abide*].

a·bol·ish (ạ·bȧl′·ish) *v.t.* to do away with; to repeal; to obliterate. **-ment** *n.* [L. *abolescere*, to destroy].

ab·o·li·tion (ab·ạ·lish′·an) *n.* the act of abolishing, as of laws, taxes, etc. **-al** *a.* **-ist** *n.* **-ism** *n.* the policy of an abolitionist [L. *abolescere*, to destroy].

A-bomb (ā′·bȧm) *n.* atomic bomb.

a·bom·i·nate (ạ·bȧm′·i·nāt) *v.t.* to loathe; detest extremely; abhor. **abominable** *a.* loathsome; morally detestable; odious. **abominableness** *n.* **abominably** *adv.* **abomination** *n.* the act or object of loathing; a despicable practice [L. *abominari*, to detest].

ab·o·rig·i·nes (ab·ạ·rij′·i·nēz) *n.pl.* the original inhabitants of a country. **aboriginal** *a.* [L. *ab origine*, from the beginning].

a·bort (ab·awrt′) *v.i.* to miscarry in giving birth; (*Fig.*) to fail to come to fruition. **abortifacient** (ạ·bawr′·ti·fā·shạnt) *n.* a drug causing abortion; *a.* capable of producing abortion. **-ion** *n.* miscarriage; one born permaturely. **-ionist** *n.* **-ive** *a.* prematurely produced; undeveloped; imperfect; rudimentary. **-ively** *adv.* [L. *aboriri*, *abortus*, to miscarry].

a·bound (ạ·bound′) *v.i.* to be in great plenty (used with preps. *with* and *in*). **-ing** *a.* plentiful [L. *abundare*, to overflow].

a·bout (ạ·bout′) *adv.* and *prep.* on every side; concerning; approximately; (before an infin.) on the point of. **to bring about**, to effect. **about face**, *n.* and *v.* turn in opposite direction [O.E. *būtan*, outside].

a·bove (ạ·buv′) *adv.* and *prep.* and *a.* higher than; more in number, quantity or degree. **above board**, open or openly; honorably. [O.E. *abufan*, upwards].

ab·ra·ca·dab·ra (ab′·rạ·kạ·dab′·rạ) *n.* corruption of sacred Gnostic term, derived from ancient Egyptian magical formula; a catchword; gibberish.

a·brade (ạ·brād′) *v.t.* to rub or wear off; to scrape or grate off; to graze (of skin). **abradant** *n.* a substance, e.g. emery powder, for polishing. **abrading** *n.* soil-erosion. **abrasion** *n.* a rubbing or scraping off; a grazing of the skin. **abrasive** *a.* tending to abrade; scouring; *n.* something used for scouring. [L. *ab*, from; *radere*, *rasum*, to scrape].

ab·re·ac·tion (ab·rē·ak′·shạn) *n.* in psychoanalysis, elimination of a morbid complex by expression through conscious association with the original cause. **abreact** *v.t.* [L. *ab*, from; and *reaction*].

a·breast (ạ·brest′) *adv.* side by side; on a line with [E.].

a·bridge (ạ·brij′) *v.t.* to shorten; curtail; reduce; diminish; epitomize. **-ment** *n.* a cutting-off; a summary; a précis; an abstract of evidence. **-r** *n.* [Fr. *abréger*; L. *abbreviare*, to shorten].

a·broad (ạ·brawd′) *adv.* and *a.* at large, over a wide space; beyond or out of a house, camp, or other enclosure; in foreign countries; overseas [E.].

ab·ro·gate (ab′·rạ·gāt) *v.t.* to annul; repeal (a law); do away with; put an end to; cancel. **abrogation** *n.* [L. *ab*, away; *rogare*, to ask].

ab·rupt (ạ·brupt′) *a.* broken off; steep; precipitous; describing a sudden change of subject, etc. in speech or writing; curt; unceremonious; brusque; (*Bot.*) without a terminal leaf. **-ly** *adv.* **-ness** *n.* [L. *ab*, away; *rumpere*, *ruptum*, to break].

ab·scess (ab′·ses) *n.* gathering of pus in any infected organ or tissue of the body [L. *abscessus*, a going away].

ab·scind (ab·sind′) *v.t.* to cut off; pare away; separate; rend apart. **absciss, abscissa** *n.* (*Geom.*) the distance of a point from a fixed line measured horizontally; one of the elements of reference by which a point, as of a curve, is referred to a system of fixed rectilineal coordinate axes; *pl.* **abscissas, abscissae. abscission** *n.* act or process of cutting off [L. *ab*, away; *scindere*, *scissum*, to cut].

ab·scond (ab·skȧnd′) *v.i.* to take oneself off; to flee from justice. **-ence** *n.* **-er** *n.* [L. *abs*, away; *condere*, to hide].

ab·sence (ab′·sạns) *n.* being absent; failure to appear when cited to a court of law; inattention to prevailing conditions. **absent** *a.* not present; inattentive. **absent** (ab·sent′) *v.t.* to withdraw (oneself); deliberately to fail to appear. **absentee** *n.* one who is not present. **absently** *adv.* casually; forgetfully. **absent-minded** *a.* abstracted; absorbed; pre-occupied [L. *ab*, away; *esse*, to be].

ab·sinthe, ab·sinth (ab′·sinth) *n.* a green-colored liqueur flavored with wormwood and other aromatics [L. *absinthium*, wormwood].

ab·so·lute (ab′·sa·lŏŏt) *a.* unconditional; without restraint; (*Gram.*) not dependent; pure. **-ly** *adv.* positively; very; entirely. **-ness** *n.* **absolution** *n.* a remission of sin after confession, pronounced by the R. C. Church; formal acquittal by a judge. **absolutism** *n.* unrestricted and unlimited rule; arbitrary government. **absolutist** *n.* **absolutory, absolvatory** *a.* **absolute alcohol**, alcohol free from water. **absolute pressure** (*Phys.*) pressure of gas, steam, or liquid measured as excess over zero pressure, i.e. over atmospheric pressure. **absolute zero** (*Phys.*) the lowest possible temperature —273.1° C. **nominative (ablative) absolute**, a grammatical construction consisting of a substantive and a participle independent of the main sentence [L. *absolutus*, freed].

ab·solve (ab·sȧlv′) *v.t.* to set free from an obligation, guilt, debt, penalty; to pardon; acquit. **-r** *n.* [L. *ab*, away; *solvere*, to loosen].

ab·sorb (ab·sawrb′) *v.t.* to swallow up; drink in; soak up; to engage one's whole attention. **-ability** *n.* **-able** *a.* **-ing** *a.* **-ent** *a.* absorbing; *n.* anything which absorbs. **-ency** *n.* [L. *ab*, away; *sorbere*, *sorptum*, to suck].

ab·sorp·tion (ab·sawrp′·shạn) *n.* the act of absorbing. **absorptive** *a.* able to absorb [fr. *absorb*].

ab·stain (ab·stān′) *v.i.* to forbear; to refrain. **-er** *n.* one who abstains, esp. from alcohol [L. *abs*, from; *tenere*, to hold].

ab·ste·mi·ous (ab·stē′·mi·ạs) *a.* showing moderation in the use of food and drink. **-ly** *adv.* **-ness** *n.* [L. *abs*, from; *temetum*, strong drink].

ab·sten·tion (ab·sten′·shạn) *n.* the act of abstaining or refraining from. **-ist** *n.* [L. *abs*, from; *tenere*, to hold].

ab·sti·nence (ab′·sti·nạns) *n.* voluntary forbearance from using or doing something. Also **abstinency. abstinent** *a.* temperate; refraining from. **abstinently** *adv.* [L. *abs*, from; *tenere*, to hold].

ab·stract (ab·strakt′) *v.t.* to separate from; remove, summarize; reduce. **-ed** *a.* **-edly** *adv.* *a.* not concrete, theoretical. (ab′·strakt) *n.* that which comprises in itself the essential qualities of a larger thing, or of several things; a summary. **-ion** *n.* abstracting or separating; a theoretical idea. **in the abstract**, without reference to particular cases [L. *abs*, from; *trahere*, *tractum*, to draw].

ab·struse (ab·stroòs′) *a.* hidden; difficult or hard to be understood. **-ly** *adv.* **-ness** *n.* [L. *abs,* from; *trudere, trusum,* to thrust].

ab·surd (ab·surd′) *a.* contrary to reason; ridiculous; silly. **-ly** *adv.* **-ity** *n.* that which is absurd. Also **-ness** [L. *absurdus,* out of tune].

a·bun·dance (a·bun′·dans) *n.* ample sufficiency; great plenty. **abundant** *a.* fully sufficient; plentiful. **abundantly** *adv.* [L. *abundare,* to overflow].

a·buse (a·būz′) *v.t.* to make a wrong use of; to ill-treat; to violate; revile; malign. **abuse** (a·būs′) *n.* ill-usage; improper treatment; a corrupt practice; rude language. **abusive** *a.* practicing abuse; rude; insulting. **abusiveness** *n.* [Fr. *abuser*].

a·but (a·but′) *v.i.* to end; to touch with one end; to border on; to adjoin. *pr.p.* **-ting.** *pa.p.* **-ted. -ment** *n.* (*Archit.*) the support at end of an arch or bridge [O.Fr. *abouter,* to join at the end].

a·byss (a·bis′) *n.* any deep chasm; a gulf. formerly, **abysm** (a·bizm′) *n.* **abysmal** *a.* bottomless; vast; profound. **abysmally** *adv.* **abyssal** *a.* inhabiting, or characteristic of, the depths of the ocean; abysmal [Gk. *abussos,* bottomless].

a·ca·cia (a·kā′·sha) *n.* thorny, leguminous tree or shrub, yielding gum arabic [Gk. *akakia,* from *akē,* a sharp point].

a·cad·e·my (a·kad′·a·mi·) *n.* a place of education or specialized training; popularly a school; a society of men united for the promotion of the arts and sciences. **academic, academical** *a.* belonging to an academy or other institution of learning. **academician** (a·kad··a·mish′·an) *n.* a member of an academy or society for promoting the arts and sciences [Gk. *akademeia*].

a·can·thus (a·kan′·thas) *n.* a prickly plant, also called 'bear's breech' or 'brank-ursine'; (*Archit.*) an ornament like this leaf, esp. on the capitals of Corinthian pillars [Gk. *ake,* a point; *anthos,* a flower].

a cap·pel·la (à ka·pel′·a) *mus.* singing without instrumental accompaniment [It.].

a·cat·a·lec·tic (a·kat·a·lek′·tik) *a.* not stopping short; complete in syllables; *n.* a verse that has the complete number of syllables.

a·cat·a·lep·sy (a·kat·a·lep′·si·) *n.* incomprehensibility; **acatalepsia** *n.* (*Med.*) uncertainty in the diagnosis of a disease. **acataleptic** *a.* [Gk. *a-,* neg.; *kata,* down; *lepsis,* a seizing].

a·cat·a·pha·si·a (a·kat·a·fā′·zi·a) *n.* difficulty or inability in expressing ideas logically.

ac·cede (ak·sēd′) *v.i.* to agree; assent; consent; to arrive at a certain state or condition; to succeed as heir. **-r** *n.* [L. *ad,* to; *cedere,* to go].

ac·cel·er·an·do (ak·sel·a·ran′·dō) *a.* and *n.* (*Mus.*) a direction to quicken the time [It. fr. L. *celer,* swift].

ac·cel·er·ate (ak·sel′·a·rāt) *v.t.* and *i.* to cause to move faster; to become swifter. **acceleration** *n.* an increase in speed, action, etc.; the rate of increase in the velocity of a moving body. **accelerative** *a.* quickening. **accelerator** *n.* a mechanism for increasing speed. **acceleratory** *a.* [L. *celer,* swift].

ac·cent (ak′·sent) *n.* stress on a syllable or syllables of a word; a mark to show this; inflection of the voice; manner of speech; pronunciation and inflection of the voice peculiar to a country, town, or individual. **accent** (ak·sent′) *v.t.* to utter, pronounce, or mark with accent; to emphasize; to stress. **-ual** *a.* **-uate** *v.t.* to accent; to stress; to make more prominent. **-uation** *n.* [Fr. fr. L. *accentus,* a tone].

ac·cept (ak·sept′) *v.t.* to take; receive; admit; believe; to agree to; (*Comm.*) to agree to pay a bill. **-able** *a.* welcome; pleasing; agreeable. **-ably** *adv.* **-ability** *n.* **-ance** *n.* the act of accepting. **-ation** *n.* the usual meaning of a word, statement, etc. **-ed** *a.* **-er, -or** *n.* [L. *acceptare*].

ac·cess (ak′·ses) *n.* a coming to the means or way of approach; admission; entrance; attack; fit. **-ary** *a.* (*Law.* See accessory). **-ible** *a.* easy of access or approach; approachable. **-ibility** *n.* **-ion** *n.* increase; a coming to, esp. to a throne, office, or dignity. **-ory** (ak·ses′·a·ri·), **-ary** *a.* aiding; contributing; additional; *n.* an additional, secondary piece of equipment; an accompaniment; (*Law*) one implicated in a felony (though not as a principal); a confederate [L. *accedere, accessum,* to go to].

ac·ci·dence (ak′·si·dans) *n.* the part of grammar dealing with changes in the form of words, e.g. plurals, etc. [fr. *accidents*].

ac·ci·dent (ak′·si·dent) *n.* chance; a mishap; a casualty; contingency; a quality not essential. **-al** *a.* **-ally** *adv.* [L. *ad,* to; *cadere,* to fall].

ac·claim (a·klām′) *v.t.* and *i.* to receive with applause, etc.; cheer; to hail as; **acclamation** (ak·la·mā′·shan) *n.* general applause. **acclamatory** (a·klam′·a·tōr·i·) *a.* [L. *acclamare,* to shout to].

ac·cli·ma·tize (a·klī′·ma·tīz) *v.t.* to accustom to a new climate. Also **acclimate** (a·klī′·mit). **acclimatization** *n.* Also **acclimatation, acclimation** (ak·li·mā′·shun) *n.* [fr. *climate*].

ac·cliv·i·ty (a·kliv′·i·ti·) *n.* an upward slope [L. *ad,* to; *clivus,* a slope].

ac·co·lade (ak′·a·lād) *n.* a ceremony used in conferring knighthood, consisting now of a tap given on the shoulder; award, praise [L. *ad,* to; *collum,* the neck].

ac·com·mo·date (a·kàm·a·dāt) *v.t.* to render fit or suitable; adapt; adjust; reconcile; provide room for. **accommodating** *a.* obliging. **accommodation** *n.* (usually pl.) a loan of money; convenience; room or space for; lodgings. **accommodative** *a.* obliging; supplying accommodation; adaptive [L. *accommodare,* to fit].

ac·com·pa·ny (a·kum′·pa·ni·) *v.t.* to go with; (*Mus.*) to play the accompaniment. **accompaniment** *n.* that which goes with; (*Mus.*) the instrumental parts played with a vocal or other instrumental part. **accompanist** *n.* [Fr. *accompagner*].

ac·com·plice (a·kàm′·plis) *n.* a companion in evil deeds; an associate in crime [Earlier *complice,* fr. L. *complex,* woven together].

ac·com·plish (a·kàm′·plish) *v.t.* to carry out; to finish; to complete; to perform. **-ed** *a.* complete; perfect; having accomplishments; hence, talented. **-ment** *n.* completion; finish; that which makes for culture, elegant manners, etc. [L. *ad,* to; *complere,* to complete].

ac·cord (a·kawrd′) *n.* agreement; harmony; *v.t.* to grant; settle; compose; *v.i.* to agree; to agree in pitch and tone. **-ance** *n.* **-ant** *a.* corresponding. **-ing** *a.* in accordance; agreeing; suitable. **-ingly** *adv.* **of one's own accord,** of one's own free will; voluntarily [L. *ad,* to; *cor, cordis,* the heart].

ac·cor·di·on (a·kawr′·di·an) *n.* wind instrument fitted with bellows and button keyboards; in the **piano-accordion** the right hand keyboard is like that of a piano. **accordion-pleated** *a.* having narrow folds like those of the bellows of an accordion.

ac·cost (a·kawst′) *v.t.* to speak first to; to address; to approach [L. *ad,* to; *costa,* a rib].

ac·count (a·kount′) *n.* a reckoning; a record; a report; a description; a statement of debts and credits in money transactions; value; advantage; profit; *v.t.* to reckon, judge; *v.i.* to give a reason; to give a financial reckoning. **-able** *a.* liable to be held responsible; able to be explained. **-ably** *adv.* **-ability** *n.* **-ancy** *n.* the profession of an accountant. **-ant** *n.* one skilled in recording financial transactions, esp. as a profession. **-ing** *n.* or *a.* [O.Fr. *aconter,* to reckon].

ac·cou·ter (a·koò′·ter) *v.t.* to furnish with dress or equipment, esp. military; to equip.

-ments *n.pl.* dress; military dress and equipment [Fr. *accoutrer*, to dress].

ac·cred·it (a·kred'·it) *v.t.* to give trust or confidence to; to vouch for; to recommend; to furnish with credentials, as an envoy or ambassador. -ed *a.* -ation *n.* [Fr. *accréditer*].

ac·crete (a·krēt') *v.i.* to grow together; *v.t.* to add by growth. **accretion** *n.* an increase in growth, esp. by an addition of parts externally. **accretive** *a.* [L. *ad*, to; *crescere*, to grow].

ac·crue (a·krōō') to increase; to result naturally; to come as an addition, e.g. interest, profit, etc. **accrual** *n.* [Fr. *accrue*, an extension, from L. *ad*, to; *crescere*, to grow].

ac·cu·mu·late (a·kū'·mū·lāt) *v.t.* to heap up; to collect; *v.i.* to grow into a mass; to increase. **accumulation** *n.* a collection; a mass; a pile. **accumulative** *a.* **accumulatively** *adv.* **accumulator** *n.* one who, or that which, collects; an apparatus for the storage of electricity [L. *ad*, to; *cumulus*, a heap].

ac·cu·rate (ak'·ū·rit) *a.* correct. -ly *adv.* -ness *n.* **accuracy** *n.* correctness; exactness; precision [L. *ad*, to; *cura*, care].

ac·curse (a·kurs') *v.t.* to doom to destruction; to curse. -ed *a.* under a curse. -dness *n.*

ac·cuse (a·kūz') *v.t.* to charge with a crime or fault; to blame. -d *a.* charged with a crime; *n.* one so charged. -r *n.* **accusation** (ak·ū·zā'·shun) *n.* a charge. **accusative** *a.* producing or containing accusations; (*Gram.*) of the case which forms the direct object of a transitive verb (the objective case); *n.* the accusative case. **accusatory** *a.* [L. *accusare*].

ac·cus·tom (a·kus'·tam) *v.t.* to make familiar by use; to familiarize; to habituate. -ed *a.* often practiced; usual; ordinary [O.Fr. *acostumer*].

ace (ās) *n.* a card with only one spot; a single point; the best, highest; an outstanding fighter pilot; an expert player; an unreturnable service in tennis [L. *as*, a unit].

ac·er·bate (as'·er·bāt) *v.t.* to make bitter; to exasperate; *a.* embittered; severe; exasperated. **acerbity** *n.* sourness of taste, with bitterness and astringency; hence bitterness, or severity in persons [L. *acerbus*, bitter].

a·ce·tic (a·set'·ik, a·sē'·tik) *a.* pert. to acetic acid, the acid in vinegar. **acetate** *n.* (*Chem.*) a salt formed by acetic acid; also a rayon material made from the acetic ester of cellulose. **acetify** *v.t.* and *v.i.* to turn into vinegar. **acetification** *n.* **acetous** (a·sē'·tas) *a.* sour. [L. *acetum*, vinegar].

a·cet·y·lene (a·set'·i·lēn) *n.* a highly inflammable gas used as an illuminant [L. *acetum*, vinegar].

ache (āk) *n.* a continuous dull, heavy pain; often found compounded in such words as *earache*, *headache*; *v.i.* to be in pain. **aching** *a.* and *n.* [O.E. *acan*].

a·chieve (a·chēv') *v.t.* to bring to a successful end; to accomplish. **achievable** *a.* -ment *n.* performing; a performance; an exploit; a feat. -r, *n.* [O.Fr. *à chef*, to a head].

ach·ro·ma·si·a (ak·rō·mā'·zi·a) *n.* (*Med.*) absence of color. **achromate** *a.* without color; showing color-blindness [Gk. *a-*, neg.; *chroma*, color].

ach·ro·ma·tic (ak·ra·mat'·ik) *a.* (*Opt.*) free from color; transmitting light without decomposing it; of a lens, giving an image free from color around the edges. -ity (ak·rō·ma·ti'·si·ti·) **achromatism** (a·krō'·ma·tizm) *n.* **achromatize** *v.t.* to deprive of color. **achromatous** *a.* [Gr. *a-*, neg.; *chroma*, color].

ac·id (as'·id) *a.* sour; sharp to the taste; having the taste of vinegar; *n.* a sour substance; (*Chem.*) a substance which contains hydrogen replaceable by a metal, is generally sour and reacts with a base to form salt and water. -ify *v.t.* and *i.* to make or become sour; to turn into an acid. -ity *n.* the state or quality of being acid; sourness; sharpness. -osis (as·i·-

dō'·sis) *n.* (*Med.*) fatty-acid poisoning in the blood, due to over-production of acids in it. -ulate *v.t.* to make slightly acid or sour; (*Fig.*) to embitter. -ulated, -ulous *a.* slightly sour; sourish; severe. **acid test** (*Fig.*) a conclusive proof of genuineness (referring to the test of gold by acid) [L. *acidus*, sour].

ack-ack (ak'·ak) *a.* (*Mil. slang*) anti-aircraft; *n.* anti-aircraft fire.

ac·know·ledge (ak·nal'·ij) *v.t.* to admit as true; to give a receipt for; to give thanks for; to reward. -ment *n.* [M.E. *knowlechen*, to perceive].

ac·me (ak'·mē) *n.* the highest point, the top; perfection [Gk. *akmē*, the top].

ac·ne (ak'·nē) *n.* a skin disease characterized by hard, reddish pimples often appearing as blackheads [fr. Gk. *akmē*, a point].

ac·o·lyte (ak'·a·līt) *n.* a candidate for priesthood in the R. C. Church; a lesser church officer; an assistant; a novice [Gk. *akolouthos*, a follower].

ac·o·nite (ak'·a·nīt) *n.* (*Bot.*) wolf's-bane or monk's-hood; a poisonous drug extracted from it [Gk. *akoniton*].

a·corn (ā'·kawrn) *n.* the seed or fruit of the oak. [O.E. *aecern*, fruit of the open country].

a·cous·tic (a·kōō'·stik, a·kou'·stik) *a.* pert. to the sense of hearing. **acoustics** *n.pl.* the science of sounds; the estimation of audibility in a theater, etc. [Gk. *akouein*, to hear].

ac·quaint (a·kwānt') *v.t.* to make fully known or familiar; to inform. -ance *n.* familiar knowledge; a person known slightly. -anceship *n.* -ed *a.* [O.Fr. *acointier*; L. *cognoscere*, *cognitum*, to know].

ac·qui·esce (ak·wi·es') *v.i.* to agree in silence; to assent without objection. -nce *n.* -ent *a.* submissive; consenting [L. *ad*, to; *quiescere*, to keep quiet].

ac·quire (a·kwīr') *v.t.* to gain; to obtain; to get. **acquirable** *a.* -ment *n.* **acquisition** (ak·wi·zi'·shan) *n.* the act of acquiring; the thing acquired. **acquisitive** *a.* grasping; greedy for gain. **acquisitiveness** *n.* [L. *ad*, to; *quaerere*, to seek].

ac·quit (a·kwit') *v.t.* to set free; release; declare innocent; to conduct oneself; to discharge a debt. *pr.p.* -ting. *pa.p.* and *pa.t.* -ted. -tal *n.* judicial release; declaration of 'not guilty.' -tance *n.* [Fr. *aquitter*, fr. L. *quies*, rest].

a·cre (ā'·ker) *n.* a measure of land containing 4840 square yards. -age (ā'·crē·ij) *n.* extent of a piece of land in acres [O.E. *aecer*, a field].

ac·rid (ak'·rid) *a.* bitter; sharp; pungent; harsh; ill-tempered. -ly *adv.* -ness, -ity *n.* [L. *acer*, sharp].

ac·ri·mo·ny (ak'·ri·mōn·i·) *n.* bitterness of temper or of language. **acrimonious** (ak·ri·mō'·ni·us) *a.* sharp; bitter; stinging; sarcastic. **acrimoniously** *adv.* [L. *acer*, sharp].

ac·ro·bat (ak'·ra·bat) *n.* one skilled in gymnastic feats; a rope-dancer; a tumbler. -ic *a.* -ics *n.pl.* skill of an acrobat. [Gk. *akrobatein*, to walk on tiptoe].

ac·ro·nym (ak'·ra·nim) *n.* a word formed from initials, e.g., *radar*.

ac·ro·pho·bi·a (ak·ra·fō'·bi·a) *n.* a morbid fear of heights. [Gk. *akros*, extreme; *phobia*, fear].

a·crop·o·lis (a·krap'·a·lis) *n.* the fortified summit of a Greek city; a citadel, esp. the citadel of Athens, on which stands the Parthenon [Gk. *akros*, topmost; *polis*, city].

a·cross (a·kraws') *adv.* and *prep.* from side to side; transversely; athwart; at an angle with [*a*, and *cross*].

a·cros·tic (a·kraws'·tik) *n.* a composition in verse, in which the first, and sometimes last, letters of the lines read in order form a name, a sentence, or title [Gk. *akros*, extreme; *stichos*, a line].

act (akt) *v.t.* to perform, esp. upon stage; to behave as; *v.i.* to exert energy; to fulfil a function; to operate. *n.* deed; performance; actuality; action; a decree, law, edict, or judgment; principal division of a play. **-ing** *a.* performing a duty; performing on the stage; serving for, as *Acting Captain*. **-or** *n.* one who performs. **-ress** *n.* a female actor [L. *agere, actum,* to do].

ACTH Adreno-corticotropic-hormone used in the treatment of rheumatic diseases.

ac·tin·i·a (ak·tin′·i·a) *n.* the sea anemone. *pl.* **actiniae** [Gk. *aktis,* a ray].

ac·tin·ism (ak′·ti·nizm) *n.* the radiation of light or heat; the property possessed by the sun's ray, of producing chemical changes, as in photography. **actinic** *a.* pert. to actinism. **actiniform** *a.* having a ray-like structure [Gk. *aktis,* a ray].

ac·tin·i·um (ak·tin′·i·um) *n.* a radio-active element; symbol **Ac** [Gk. *aktis,* a ray].

ac·ti·nol·o·gy (ak·ti·nàl′·a·ji·) *n.* that branch of science concerned with chemical action of light [Gk. *aktis,* a ray; *logos,* word].

ac·ti·no·ther·a·py (ak·tin·a·ther′·a·pi·) *n.* the treatment of disease by natural or artificial light rays; often known as 'sunlight treatment' [Gk. *aktis,* a ray; *therapeia,* service].

ac·tion (ak′·shan) *n.* a thing done; behavior; physical movement; function; a battle; the development of events in a play, etc.; legal proceedings; (*Chem.*) effect. **-able** *a.* affording grounds for legal proceedings. **-ably** *adv.* **reflex action,** an involuntary motor reaction to a sensory impulse [L. *agere, actum,* to do].

ac·ti·vate (ak′·ti·vāt) *v.t.* to make active. **activation** *n.*

ac·tive (ak′·tiv) *a.* having the power to act; agile; busy; alert; (*Gram.*) implying action by the subject. **-ly** *adv.* vigorously. **activism** *n.* policy of those who, by energetic action, seek to fulfil the promises of a political program. **activist** *n.* one who advocates or practices activism. **activity, -ness** *n.* [L. *agere, actum,* to do].

ac·tu·al (ak′·choo·al) *a.* existing now or as a fact; real; effectual. **-ize** *v.t.* to make real in fact or by vivid description. **-ist** *n.* a realist. **-ity** (ak·choo·al′·a·ti·) *n.* reality, existence. **-ly** *adv.* [L. *actualis,* active].

ac·tu·a·ry (ak′·choo·ar·i·) *n.* registrar or clerk; an official who calculates for insurance companies. **actuarial** *a.* **actuarially** *adv.* [L. *actuarius,* a clerk].

ac·tu·ate (ak′·choo·āt) *v.t.* to put into action; incite; motivate; influence. **actuation** *n.* **actuator** *n.* [L. *actus,* action].

a·cu·men (a·kū′·man) *n.* quickness of perception or discernment; sharpness; penetration. **acuminous** *a.* [L. *acumen,* a point].

a·cute (a·kūt′) *a.* sharp; pointed; sagacious; subtle; penetrating; (*Med.*) of disease with severe symptoms and sharp crisis; (*Geom.*) less than a right angle. **-ly** *adv.* **-ness** *n.* **acute accent,** a mark (′) over a letter, as in French, to indicate pronunciation [L. *acutus,* sharp].

ad (ad) *n.* (*Colloq.*) advertisement.

A.D. (ā dē) in the year of our Lord [L. *anno Domini*].

ad·age (ad′·ij) *n.* saying or maxim that has obtained credit by long use; a proverb; a byword. **adagial** *a.* [L. *adagium,* proverb].

a·da·gio (a·dà′·jō) *adv.* (*Mus.*) slowly and expressively; *n.* a slow movement, in a symphony or sonata. **adagio cantabile,** slowly and in a singing manner [It.].

ad·a·mant (ad′·a·mant) *n.* a stone of impenetrable hardness; the diamond; *a.* very hard; unyielding. **adamantine** (a·da·man′·tin) *a.* [Gk. *a-,* neg.; *damaein,* subdue].

Ad·am's ap·ple (ad′·amz a′·pl) *m.* projection of cartilage at the front of one's throat.

a·dapt (a·dapt′) *v.t.* to make fit or suitable; to make to correspond. **-ability, -ableness** *n.* the quality of being adaptable. **-able** *a.* may be adapted; versatile; **-ation** (a·dap·tā′·shan)

n. the gradual process of adjustment to new physical conditions exhibited by living organisms. **-er** *n.* any appliance which makes possible a union of two different parts of an apparatus. **-ive** *a.* **-ively** *adv.* **-iveness** *n.* **-or** *n.* a device to make possible the use of a machine, tool, etc. with modification [L. *ad,* to; *aptare,* to fit].

add (ad) *v.t.* to join, unite to form one sum or whole; to annex; to increase; to say further. **-able, -ible** *a.* **-er** *n.* a machine which adds; a comptometer. **-ibility** *n.* **-ition** *n.* the act of adding; anything added; the branch of arithmetic which deals with adding. **-itional** *a.* supplementary; extra. **-itionally** *adv.* **-itive** *a.* to be added; of the nature of an addition [L. *ad,* to; *dare,* to give].

·ad·dend (ad′·end) *n.* number to be added.

ad·den·dum (a·den′·dam) *n.* a thing to be added; an appendix; *pl.* **addenda** [L.].

ad·der (ad′·er) *n.* a venomous serpent [M.E. an *addere* for a *naddere,* fr. O.E. *naeddre,* snake].

ad·dict (a·dikt′) *v.t.* to apply habitually; habituate. **addict** (ad′·ikt) *n.* one addicted to evil habit, e.g. drug-taking. **-ed** *a.* devoted, wholly given over to. **-ion, -ness,** *n.* [L. *addicere,* to assign].

ad·dle (ad′·l) *v.t.* to corrupt; putrify; confuse; to make addled. **addle, addled,** *a.* diseased, e.g. an egg; putrid; unfruitful. **-brained, -headed, -pated** *a.* confused [O.E. *adela,* filth].

ad·dress (a·dres′) *v.t.* to direct in writing, as a letter; to apply (oneself); to make a speech; to present a congratulatory message or petition; accost; *n.* a formal speech; manner of speaking; direction of a letter; skill. **-es** *n.pl.* attentions in courtship. **-ee** *n.* person to whom a communication is sent. **-er** *n.* **-ograph** *n.* a machine for addressing envelopes, etc. [Fr. *adresser*].

ad·duce (a·dūs′) *v.t.* to bring forward as proof; to cite; to quote. **-nt** *a.* **-r** *n.* **adducible** *a.* **adduction** (a·duk′·shan) *n.* drawing together or bringing forward. **adductive** *a.* tending to bring together. **adductor** *n.* adducent muscle [L. *ad,* to; *ducere,* to lead].

ad·en (o) - (ad′·n-(o)) a combining form. **-itis** *n.* inflammation of the lymphatic glands. **-oid, -oidal** *a.* glandular; gland-shaped. **-oids** *n.pl.* a swelling of tissue between nose and throat [fr. Gk. *aden,* a gland].

a·dept (a·dept′) *n.* one skilled in any art; an expert; *a.* well skilled; expert [L. *adeptus,* having attained].

ad·e·quate (ad′·a·kwit) *a.* equal to; sufficient. **adequacy. -ness** *n.* **-ly** *adv.* [L. *adaequatus,* made equal to].

ad·here (ad·hēr′) *v.i.* to stick fast; to be devoted to; to hold to (an opinion). **-nce** *n.* state of adhering; steady attachment. **-nt** *a.* united with or to; *n.* supporter of person or cause. **adhesion** *n.* act of adhering. **adhesive** *a.* sticky; tenacious; *n.* an agent which sticks things together. **adhesively** *adv.* **adhesiveness** *n.* [L. *ad,* to; *haerere,* to stick].

ad·hib·it (ad·hib′·it) *v.t.* to use or apply; to attach [L. *adhibitus,* added to].

a·dieu (a·dū′) *interj.* good-bye; farewell; *n.* a farewell; a leave-taking. *pl.* **adieus, adieux** (a·dūz′) [Fr. meaning, "*to God*"].

ad in·fi·ni·tum (ad in·fa·nī′·tam) to infinity, without limit [L.].

ad in·ter·im (ad in′·ter·im) in the meantime [L.].

a·di·os (à·dōs′) good-bye [Sp.].

ad·i·pose (ad′·i·pōs) *a.* pert. to animal fat; fatty. **adiposity** (ad·i·pàs′·i·ti·) *n.* fatness. **adipic** *a.* pert. to, or derived from, fatty substances [L. *adeps,* soft fat].

ad·it (ad′·it) *n.* horizontal or inclined entrance into a mine [L. *aditus,* an entrance].

ad·ja·cent (a·jā′·sant) *a.* lying close to; adjoining, bordering on. **-ly** *adv.* **adjacency** *n.* [L. *ad*, to; *jacere*, to lie].

ad·jec·tive (ad'·jik·tiv) *n.* a word used with a noun to qualify, limit, or define it; *a.* pert. to an adjective. **adjectival** (ad·jik·tī'·v'l) *a.* **adjectivally** *adv.* [L. *adjicere*, to add].

ad·join (a·join') *v.t.* to join or unite to; to be next or contiguous to; *v.i.* to be next to. **-ing** *a.* [L. *adjungere*, to join to].

ad·journ (a·jurn') *v.t.* to put off to another day; to postpone. **-ment** *n.* [L. *diurnus*, daily].

ad·judge (a·juj') *v.t.* to settle judicially; to pronounce judgment; to award; to regard or deem. **adjudgment** *n.* **adjudicate** (a·jōō'·di·kāt) *v.t.* to settle judicially; *v.i.* to pronounce judgment. **adjudication** *n.* **adjudicator** *n.* a judge [L. *adjudicare*, to award as a judge].

ad·junct (ad'·jungkt) *n.* something joined to another thing, but not essential to it; (*Gram.*) a word or phrase added to modify meaning; *a.* added to; united with. **-ive, -ively** *adv.* [L. *adjunctus*, united to].

ad·jure (ad·jōōr') *v.t.* to charge or bind, under oath; to entreat earnestly. **adjuration** *n.* a solemn command on oath; an earnest appeal. **adjuratory** *a.* [L. *adjurare*, to confirm by oath].

ad·just (a·just') *v.t.* to adapt; to put in working order; to accommodate. **-able** *a.* **-ment** *n.* **-er, -or** *n.* arrangement; settlement; adaptation [L. *ad*, to; *justus*, just].

ad·ju·tant (aj'·a·tant) *n.* an assistant; staff officer who helps the commanding officer issue orders. **adjutancy** *n.* the office of an adjutant. **adjutant bird** a species of Indian stork [L. *ad*, to; *juvare*, to help].

ad lib (ad lib') *v.i.* and *v.t.* (*Colloq.*) to improvise something not in the script [L. *abbrev.* for *ad libitum*, at pleasure].

ad·min·is·ter (ad·min'·is·ter) *v.t.* to manage public affairs or an estate; to dispense, as justice or relief; to give, as medicine; to apply, as punishment or reproof; (*Law*) to settle the estate of one who has died intestate; *v.i.* to give aid (to). **administrable** *a.* **administrant** *a.* executive; *n.* one who administers. **administration** *n.* the executive part of a government: dispensation; direction. **administrative** *a.* **administrator** *n.* (*fem.* **administratrix**) one who directs; executes affairs of any kind [L. *ad*, to; *ministrare*, to give service].

ad·mi·ral (ad'·mi·ral) *n.* a naval officer of the highest rank (graded as—admiral, vice-admiral, or rear-admiral). **-ty** *n.* rank or authority of an admiral; maritime law [Fr. *amiral*, fr. Ar. *amir-al-bahr*, prince of the sea].

ad·mi·ral (ad'·mi·ral) *n.* a species of butterfly, esp. the red admiral.

ad·mire (ad·mīr') *v.t.* to regard with wonder and approval, esteem, or affection; to prize highly; *v.i.* to wonder; to marvel. **-r** *n.* **admiring** *a.* **admiringly** *adv.* **admirable** (ad'·mi·ra·bl) *a.* excellent; praiseworthy. **admirably** *adv.* **admiration** *n.* wonder mingled with esteem, love, or veneration [L. *ad*, to; *mirari*, to wonder].

ad·mis·si·ble (ad·mis'·i·bl) *a.* allowable. **admissibly** *adv.* **admissibility** *n.* **admission** *n.* permission to enter; the price paid for this [L. (*part.*) *admissus*, allowed to go].

ad·mit (ad·mit') *v.t.* to grant entrance; to concede as true; to acknowledge. *pr.p.* **-ting.** *pa.p.* and *pa.t.* **-ted. -tance** *n.* permission to enter [L. *ad*, to; *mittere*, to send].

ad·mix (ad·miks') *v.t.* to mingle with something else. **-ture** *n.* [L. *admiscere*, to mix].

ad·mon·ish (ad·màn'·ish) *v.t.* to reprove gently; to instruct or direct. **-er** *n.* **admonition** (ad·ma·ni'·shan) *n.* rebuke. **admonitory** *a.* [L. *ad*, to; *monere, monitum*, to warn].

ad nau·se·am (ad naw'·shi·am, also ·nawz·) to a sickening degree [L.].

a·do (a·dōō') *n.* fuss; bustle; trouble.

a·do·be (a·dō'·bi·) *n.* sun-dried brick [Sp.].

ad·o·les·cence (ad·a·les'·ens) *n.* stage between childhood and manhood; youth. **adolescent** *a.* growing up; *n.* a young man or woman [L. *adolescere*, to grow up].

a·dopt (a·dàpt') *v.t.* to receive the child of another and treat it as one's own; to select and accept as one's own, e.g. a view. **-er** *n.* **-able** *a.* **-ion** *n.* **-ive** *a.* that adopts or is adopted [L. *ad*, to; *optare*, to choose].

a·dore (a·dōr') *v.t.* to worship; to love deeply; **-r** *n.* a lover. **adorable** *a.* **adorably** *adv.* **adorableness** *n.* **adoration** (ad·a·rā'·shan) *n.* profound veneration; ardent devotion [L. *ad*, to; *orare*, to pray].

a·dorn (a·dawrn') *v.t.* to decorate; to deck or ornament; to set off to advantage. **-ing** *a.* beautifying; ornamental. **-ment** *n.* ornament; embellishment [L. *ad*, to; *ornare*, to deck].

ad·re·nal (ad·rē'·nal) *n.* a small, ductless gland situated close to upper end of each kidney (same as *supra-renal*). **adrenalin** (ad·ren'·al·in) *n.* the hormone of the adrenal glands; the most effective hemostatic agent known [L. *ad*, to; *renes*, kidneys].

a·drift (a·drift') *adv.* and *a.* floating at random; at mercy of the wind and tide; (*Fig.*) at a loss.

a·droit (a·droit') *a.* dexterous; skillful; ingenious; adept. **-ly** *adv.* **-ness** *n.* [Fr.].

ad·sorb (ad·sawrb') *v.t.* said of solids, to condense and hold a gas on the surface. **adsorption** *n.* [L. *ad*, to; *sorbere*, to drink in].

ad·u·late (aj'·ū·lāt) *v.t.* to praise or flatter in a servile manner; to fawn; to cringe. **adulation** *n.* **adulator** *n.* **adulatory** (aj·a·la·tawr'·i·) *a.* excessively [L. *adulari*, to flatter].

a·dult (a·dult', ad'·ult) *a.* grown to maturity, or to full size and strength; appropriate for a grown-up; *n.* a grown-up person. **-ness** *n.* **-hood** *n.* [L. *adultus*, grown up].

a·dul·ter·ate (a·dul'·ta·rāt) *v.t.* to debase by addition of inferior materials; to vitiate; to corrupt. *a.* debased; guilty of adultery. **adulteration** *n.* the act of debasing a substance [L. *adulterare*, to defile].

a·dul·ter·y (a·dul'·ter·i·) *n.* violation of the marriage vows. **adulterer** *n.* (*fem.* **adulteress**). **adulterous** *a.* pert. to or guilty of adultery. **adulterously** *adv.* [L. *adulterare*, to defile].

ad·um·brate (ad·um'·brāt) *v.t.* to shadow forth; to give faint outline of; to forecast; to typify. **adumbral** *a.* shady. **adumbrant** *a.* showing a slight resemblance. **adumbrative** *a.* **adumbration** *n.* [L. *ad*, to; *umbra*, a shade].

ad·vance (ad·vans') *v.t.* to bring or push forward; to raise in status, price, or value; to propose as a claim; to supply beforehand, as money; *v.i.* to go forward; to improve; to rise in rank, etc. *a.* before the time, as in *advance-booking*. *n.* a forward movement; gradual approach; a paying out of money before due; an increase in price; expansion of knowledge. **-d** *a.* in the front rank; progressive; well on in years; beyond the elementary stage (in education). **-ment** *n.* promotion; improvement; success; the state of being progressive in opinion; a loan of money. **-r** *n.* a promoter [Fr. *avancer*, to go forward].

ad·van·tage (ad·van'·tij) *n.* any state or means favorable to some desired end; upperhand; profit; in tennis, a point gained after deuce; *v.t.* to benefit, to promote the interests of; to profit. **-able** *a.* able to be turned to advantage. **-ous** (ad·van·tā'·jus) *a.* beneficial; opportune; convenient. **-ously** (ad·van·tā'·jus·li·) *adv.* [Fr. *avantage*].

ad·vent (ad'·vent) *n.* arrival; approach; the anticipated coming of Christ; the four weeks from the Sunday nearest to St. Andrew's Day (30th Nov.) to Christmas. **-ual** *adv.* pertaining to the season of Advent [L. *ad*, to; *venire*, to come].

ad·ven·ti·tious (ad·ven·tish′·ạs) *a.* accidental; out of the proper place; extraneous. **-ly** *adv.* [L. *ad*, to; *venire*, to come].

ad·ven·ture (ạd·ven′·chẹr) *n.* risk; bold undertaking; chance; trading enterprise of a speculative nature; *v.t.* to risk. *v.i.* to venture; to dare. **-r** *n.* (*fem.* **adventuress**). **-some** *a.* bold; daring; enterprising; facing risk. **-someness** *n.* **adventurous** *a.* inclined to take risks; perilous; hazardous. **adventurously** *adv.* [L. *adventurus*, about to arrive].

ad·verb (ad′·vurb) *n.* a word used to modify a verb, adjective, or other adverb. **-ial** *a.* **-ially** *adv.* [L. *ad*, to; *verbum*, a word].

ad·ver·sa·ry (ad′·vẹr·ser·i·) *n.* an opponent; one who strives against us; an enemy [L. *adversus*, opposite to].

ad·ver·sa·tive (ạd·vẹrs′·ạ·tiv) *a.* expressing opposition; not favorable [L. *adversus*].

ad·verse (ad·vurs′) *a.* contrary; opposite in position; unfortunate; opposed. **-ly** *adv.* **-ness** *n.* **adversity** *n.* adverse circumstances; misfortune [L. *adversus*, opposite to].

ad·vert (ạd·vurt′) *v.i.* to turn the mind or attention to; to remark upon; allude; refer. **-ence, -ency** *n.* [L. *ad*, to; *vertere*, to turn].

ad·ver·tise (ad′·vẹr·tīz) *v.t.* and *v.i.* to give public notice of; to inform; to make known through agency of the press. **-ment** *n.* a public intimation in the press; legal notification. **-r** *n.* one who advertises; **advertising** *n.* and *a.* [Fr. *avertir*, from L. *ad*, to; *vertere*, to turn].

ad·vice (ạd·vīs′) *n.* opinion offered as to what one should do; counsel; information [Fr. *avis*].

ad·vise (ạd·vīz′) *v.t.* to give advice to; to counsel; to give information to; to consult (with). *v.i.* to deliberate. **advisability, advisableness** *n.* expediency. **advisable** *a.* prudent; expedient. **advisably** *adv.* **advised** *a.* acting with due deliberation; cautious; prudent; judicious. **advisedly** *adv.* purposely. **advisedness, -ment** *n.* deliberate consideration. **-r** or **advisor** *n.* **advisory** *a.* having power to advise; containing advice [Fr. *avis*].

ad·vo·cate (ad′·vạ·kit) *n.* a vocal supporter of any cause; one who pleads or speaks for another. (ad′·vạ·kāt) *v.t.* to recommend; to maintain by argument. **advocacy** *n.* a pleading for; judicial pleading. **advocator** *n.* an intercessor; a pleader [L. *ad*, to; *vocare*, to call].

adz, adze (adz) *n.* a carpenter's tool for chipping, having a thin arching blade set at right angles to the handle [O.E. *adesa*].

ae·gis (ē′·jis) *n.* originally the shield of Jupiter; (*Fig.*) protection [Gk. *aigis*].

ae·on, eon (ē′·ạn) *n.* an infinitely long period of time; an age [Gk. *aion*, an age].

aer·ate (ā′·ẹr·āt) *v.t.* to charge with carbon dioxide or other gas; to supply with air. **aeration** *n.* the act of exposing to the action of the air; saturation with a gas. **aerator** *n.* **aerated waters,** beverages charged with carbon dioxide [Gk. *aer*, air].

aer·i·al (ār′·i·al) *a.* pert. to, consisting of, air; *n.* and *a.* (*Radio and Television*) an insulated wire or wires, generally elevated above the ground and connected to a transmitting or receiving set. **-ly** *adv.* [Gk. *aēr*, air].

aer·i·al·ist (ār′·i·ạl·ist) *n.* high wire acrobat.

a·er·ie, a·er·y (ā′·ri·, e′·ri·) *n.* the nest of a bird of prey, esp. of the eagle [O.Fr. *aire*].

a·er·o (ā′·er·ō) a combining form from Gk. *aēr*, air, used in many derivatives.

a·er·o·dy·nam·ics (er·ạ·dī·nam′·iks) *n.pl.* the science that treats of gases in motion [Gk. *aēr*, air; *dunamis*, power].

aer·o·lite (er′·ạ·līt) *n.* a meteorite; a meteoric stone. Also **aerolith, aerolithic** *a.* **aerology** *n.* the science which treats of the air and its phenomena [Gk. *aēr*, air; *lithos*, stone; *logos*, discourse].

a·er·o·me·ter (er·ȧm′·ạ·tẹr) *n.* an instrument for measuring the weight or density of air and other gases. **aerometry** *n.* this science [Gk. *aer*, air; *metron*, a measure].

aer·o·naut (ār′·ạ·nawt) *n.* a balloonist. **-ic** *a.* pert. to aeronautics. **-ics** *n.* the science of flight. [Gk. *aēr*, air; *nautes*, a sailor].

aer·o·sol (ār′·ạ·sȧl) *n.* a smoke, suspension of insoluble particles in a gas.

aer·o·stat (ār′·ạ·stat) *n.* a generic term for all lighter than air flying machines. **-ics** *n.* the science that treats of the equilibrium of gases, or of the buoyancy of bodies sustained in them; the science of air-navigation [Gk. *aēr*, air; *statos*, standing].

aes·thet·ics (es·thet′·iks) *n.* the laws and principles determining the beautiful in nature, art, taste, etc. **aesthetic, aesthetical** *a.* **aesthetically** *adv.* **aesthete** (es′·thēt) *n.* a disciple of aestheticism; a lover of the beautiful. **aestheticism** *n.* [Gk. *aisthanesthai*, to perceive].

a·far (ạ·fàr′) *adv.* from, at, or to a distance; far away [E. *far*].

af·fa·ble (af′·ạ·bl) *a.* ready to converse; easy to speak to; courteous; friendly. **affably** *adv.* **affability** *n.* [L. *ad*, to; *fari*, to speak].

af·fair (ạ·fār′) *n.* what is to be done; a business or matter; a concern; a thing; (*Mil.*) a minor engagement. **affairs** *n.pl.* public or private business; finances. **affair of honor,** a duel [L. *ad*, to; *facere*, to do].

af·fect (ạ·fekt′) *v.t.* to act upon; to produce a change in; to put on a pretense of; to influence. **-ed** *a.* inclined or disposed; not natural. **-edly** *adv.* **-edness** *n.* **-ing** *a.* moving; pathetic. **-ingly** *adv.* **-ation** *n.* a striving after artificial appearance or manners. **affective** *a.* **affectively** *adv.* [L. *affectare*, to apply onself to].

af·fec·tion (ạ·fek′·shạn) *n.* disposition of mind; good-will; tender attachment; disease. **-ate** *a.* loving. **-ately** *adv.* [L. *affectare*, to apply oneself to].

af·fer·ent (af′·ẹr·ạnt) *a.* conveying to, esp. of nerves carrying sensations to the centers [L. *ad*, to; *ferre*, to carry].

af·fi·ance (ạ·fī′·ạns) *n.* plighted faith; betrothal; the marriage contract; reliance; confidence; *v.t.* to betroth [O.Fr. *afiance*, trust].

af·fi·da·vit (af·i·dā′·vit) *n.* (*Law*) a written statement of evidence on oath [L.L. = he pledged his faith, from L. *ad*, to; *fides*, faith].

af·fil·i·ate (ạ·fil′·i·āt) *v.t.* to adopt as a son; to receive into fellowship; to unite a society, firm, or political party with another, but without loss of identity. **affiliation** *n.* act of being affiliated; relationship. (ạ·fil′·i·ạt) *n.* one who affiliates [L. *ad*, to; *filius*, a son].

af·fin·i·ty (ạ·fin′·i·ti·) *n.* relationship by marriage; close agreement; resemblance; attraction; similarity. **affined** (ạ·fīnd′) *a.* **affinitive** *a.* closely related [L. *affinis*, related].

af·firm (ạ·furm′) *v.t.* to assert positively; to confirm; to aver; to strengthen; to ratify a judgment; *v.i.* (*Law*) to make a solemn promise to tell the truth without oath; to ratify a law. **-able** *a.* **-ably** *adv.* **-ance** *n.* **-ant, -er** *n.* **-ative** *a.* ratifying; *n.* positive; speaking in favor of a motion or subject of debate. **in the affirmative,** yes. **-atively** *adv.* [L. *affirmare*, to assert].

af·fix (ạ·fiks′) *v.t.* to fasten to; to attach; to append to. **affix** (a′·fiks) *n.* addition to either end of word to modify meaning or use (includes *prefix* and *suffix*) [L. *affigere*].

af·la·tus (ạ·flā′·tạs) *n.* inspiration; impelling inner force [L. a blast].

af·flict (ạ·flikt′) *v.t.* to give continued pain to; to cause distress or grief to. **-ed** *a.* distressed in mind; diseased. **-ing** *a.* distressing. **-ingly** *adv.* **-ion** *n.* a cause of continued pain of body or mind. **-ive** *a.* causing distress. **-ively** *adv.* [L. *affligere*].

af·flu·ence (af′·lŏŏ·ạns) *n.* abundance, esp. riches. **affluent** *a.* wealthy; flowing to; *n.*

tributary of river. **affluently** *adv.* **afflux, af-fluxion** *n.* flowing to; that which flows to [L. *ad*, towards; *fluere*, to flow].

af·ford (ạ·fōrd') *v.t.* to yield, supply, or produce; to be able to bear expense [O.E. *geforthian*, to further].

af·for·est (ạ·fär'·est) *v.t.* to plant trees on a big scale. **-ation** *n.* [from *forest*].

af·fran·chise (ạ·fran'·chīz) *v.t.* to enfranchise; to free from slavery; to liberate. **-ment** *n.* [Fr. *affranchir*, make free].

af·fray (ạ·frā') *n.* a noisy quarrel or fight in public; *v.t.* to frighten; to startle [Fr. *effrayer*, to frighten].

af·fright, af·fright·en (ạ·frīt', -ạn) *v.t.* to impress with sudden and lively fear [O.E. *afyrhtan*, to terrify].

af·front (ạ·frunt') *v.t.* to confront; to meet face to face; to insult one to the face; to abash. **-ed** *a.* [L. *ad*, to; *frons, frontis*, forehead].

a·field (ạ·fēld') *adv.* to or in the field; abroad; off the beaten track; astray [E.].

a·fire (a·fīr') *adv.* and *a.* on fire.

a·flame (ạ·flām') *adv.* and *a.* flaming; on fire; glowing; ablaze [E.].

a·float (ạ·flōt') *adv.* and *a.* borne on the water; not aground or anchored.

a·flut·ter (ạ·flut'·ẹr) *a.* fluttering

a·foot (ạ·foot') *adv.* on foot; astir [E.].

a·fore (ạ·fōr') *adv.* and *prep.* before. **-hand** *adv* beforehand; before; *a.* provided; prepared. **-mentioned** *a.* spoken of, or named before. **-said** *a.* said or mentioned before. **-thought** *a.* thought of beforehand; premeditated. **-time** *adv.* in times past; at a former time; previously [O.E. *on foran*, in front].

a·foul (ạ·foul') *adv.* in collision, in a tangle.

a·fraid (ạ·frād') *a.* filled with fear; frightened [orig. *affrayed*].

a·fresh (ạ·fresh') *adv.* anew; over again.

aft (aft) *adv.* or *a.* (*Naut.*) toward, or at, the stern. **fore and aft,** lengthwise [O.E. *afta*, behind].

af·ter (af'·tẹr) *prep.* behind; later; in pursuit of; in imitation of; according to; *adv.* behind; *a.* in the rear; succeeding. **-birth** *n.* (*Med.*) the placenta, etc. expelled from uterus after childbirth. **-crop** *n.* a later crop in same year from same soil. **-damp** *n.* a gas formed in a mine after an explosion of fire-damp; chokedamp. **-deck** *n.* weather deck aft of midship house. **-effect** *n.* a secondary result, an effect coming after. **-glow** *n.* a glow in the sky after sunset. **-math** *n.* result; consequence. **-most** *a.* hindmost; nearest to stern. **-noon** *n.* time from noon to evening. **-pains** *n.pl.* pains succeeding childbirth. **-thought** *n.* reflection after an act; an idea occurring later. **-ward(s)** *adv.* later; subsequently [O.E. *aefter*, farther away].

a·gain (ạ·gen') *adv.* another time; once more; in return; moreover [O.E. *ongean*].

a·gainst (ạ·genst') *prep.* in contact with; opposite to; in opposition to; in preparation for; in exchange for [fr. *again*].

a·gape (ạ·gāp') *a.* or *adv.* open-mouthed, as in wonder, expectation, etc.; gaping.

ag·ate (ag'·it) *n.* a precious stone, composed of layers of quartz of different colors [Gk. *Achatēs*, so called because found near the river *Achates*, in Sicily].

age (āj) *n.* the length of time a person or thing has existed; a period of time; periods of history; maturity; (*Colloq.*) a long time; *v.t.* to cause to grow old; *v.i.* to grow old; *pr.p.* **aging.** **-d** *a.* of the age of. **aged** (āj'·ed) *a.* **agedness** *n.* **-less** *a.* **-long** *a.* **to come of age,** to attain one's 21st birthday [Fr. *âge*, from L. *aetas*, age].

a·gen·cy (ā'·jen·si·) *n.* instrumentality; a mode of exerting power; office or duties of an agent [L. *agere*, to do.]

a·gen·da (ạ·jen'·dạ) *n.* literally, things to be done; the items of business to be discussed at a meeting [L. *pl.* of *agendum*].

a·gent (ā'·jent) *n.* a person or thing that exerts power or has the power to act; one entrusted with the business of another; a deputy or substitute [L. *agere*, to do].

ag·glom·er·ate (ạ·glám'·ạ·rāt) *v.t.* and *i.* to collect into a mass; *a.* heaped up; *n.* (*Geol.*) a mass of compacted volcanic debris. **agglomeration** *n.* **agglomerative** *a.* [L. *ad*, to; *glomus*, mass or ball].

ag·glu·ti·nate (ạ·glŏŏ'·ti·nāt) *v.t.* to unite with glue; *a.* united, as with glue. **agglutination** *n.* **agglutinative** *a.* having a tendency to cause adhesion; (*Phil.*) applied to languages which are non-inflectional [L. *ad*, to; *gluten*, glue].

ag·gran·dize (ạ·gran'·dīz) *v.t.* to make greater in size, power, rank, wealth, etc.; to promote; to increase; to exalt. **aggrandizement** *n.* [L. *ad*, to; *grandis*, great].

ag·gra·vate (ag'·rạ·vāt) *v.t.* to make more grave, worse; (*Colloq.*) to irritate. **aggravating** *a.* making worse; provoking. **aggravatingly** *adv.* **aggravation** *n.* [L. *aggravare*, to make heavier].

ag·gre·gate (ag'·rạ·gāt) *v.t.* to collect into a total; to accumulate into a heap; (ag'·rạ·git) *n.* a sum or assemblage of particulars; the sum total; *a.* collected together. **aggregation** *n.* the act of aggregating; a combined whole. **aggregative** *a.* collective; accumulative [L. *aggregare*, to form into a flock, fr. *grex, gregis*, a flock].

ag·gress (ạ·gres') *v.i.* to attack; to start a quarrel. **-ion** *n.* a first act of hostility; an unprovoked attack. **-ive** *a.* **-ively** *adv.* **-iveness** *n.* **-or** *n.* the one who first attacks [L. *aggredi*, to attack].

ag·grieve (ạ·grēv') *v.t.* to give pain or sorrow to; to bear heavily upon; to vex; to afflict. **-d** *a.* [L. *aggravare*, to make heavier].

a·ghast (ạ·gast') *a.* struck with amazement, horror, terror; transfixed with fright [earlier *agast*, fr. O.E. *gaestan*, to terrify].

ag·ile (aj'·il) *a.* having the power of quick motion; nimble. **-ly** *adv.* **-ness, agility** *n.* [L. *agilis*, fr. *agere*, to do].

ag·i·tate (aj'·i·tāt) *v.t.* to throw into violent motion; to stir up; to disturb, excite, upset; to debate earnestly; *v.i.* to cause a disturbance. **agitatedly** *adv.* **agitation** *n.* violent and irregular motion; perturbation; inciting to public disturbance. **agitator** *n.* [L. *agitare*, to keep in motion].

a·gleam (ạ·glēm') *adv.*, *a.* gleaming.

a·glow (ạ·glō') *adv.*, *a.* glowing.

ag·nate (ag'·nāt) *n.* any male relation on the father's side. *a.* related on the father's side; akin; allied. **agnatic** *a.* **agnation** *n.* [L. *ad*, to; *natus*, born].

ag·no·men (ag·nō'·mạn) *n.* an additional name given by the Romans, generally because of some famous exploit, as Alexander the Great [L. *ad*, to; *nomen*, name].

ag·nos·tic (ag·nás'·tik) *n.* one who believes that God, life hereafter, etc., can neither be proved nor disproved, and who accepts material phenomena only; *a.* pert. to agnosticism. **-ism** *n.* [Gk. *a-*, neg.; *gnostikos*, knowing].

a·go, a·gone (ạ·gō', ạ·gawn') *adv.*, *a.* past; gone; in time past [O.E. *agan*, to pass away].

a·gog (ạ·gág') *a.* and *adv.* eagerly excited; expectantly [Fr. *en gogues*, in a merry mood].

a·gon·ic (a·gán'·ik) *a.* not forming an angle [Gk. *a-*, neg.; *gonia*, an angle].

ag·o·ny (ag'·ạ·ni·) *n.* extreme physical or mental pain; the death struggle; throes; pang. **agonize** *v.t.* to distress with great pain; to torture. *v.i.* to writhe in torment. **agonizing** *a.* **agonizingly** *adv.* **agony column,** section of newspaper containing advertisements for lost relatives, personal messages, etc. [Gk. *agon*, a contest].

ag·o·ra (ag'·ạ·rạ) *n.* forum, public square, or market of ancient Greek towns. **-phobia** *n.*

fear of open spaces [Gk. *agora*, a market place; *phobia*, fear].

a·gou·ti (a·gŏŏ′·ti·) *n.* a genus of rodents or gnawing animals, natives of S. America, allied to the guinea-pig [Native].

a·grar·i·an (a·grar′·i·an) *a.* relating to lands, their management and distribution; (*Bot.*) growing in a field. *n.* one who favors an equal division of property. **-ize** *v.t.* **-ism** *n.* an equal division of land or property [L. *ager*, a field].

a·gree (a·grē′) *v.i.* to be of one mind; to acquiesce; to resemble; (*Gram.*) to correspond in gender, case, or number. *pr.p.* **-ing.** *pa.p.* **-d. -able** *a.* consenting; favorable; suitable; pleasant; congenial. **-ably** *adv.* **-ableness** *n.* **-ment** *n.* agreeing; bargain; a written statement accepting certain conditions [L. *ad*, to; *gratus*, pleasing].

ag·ri·cul·ture (ag′·ri·kul·cher) *n.* the science and practice of the cultivation of the soil. **agricultural** *a.* **agriculturist** or **agriculturalist** *n.* one skilled in agriculture; a farmer [L. *ager*, a field; *colere*, *cultum*, to till].

a·gron·o·my (a·grán′·a·mi·) *n.* rural economy; husbandry. **agronomial, agronomic, agronomical** *a.* **agronomics** *n.pl.* the science of management of farms. **agronomist** *n.* [Gk. *agros*, field; *nemein*, to deal out].

a·ground (a·ground′) *adv.* and *a.* on the ground; stranded; run ashore; beached.

a·gue (ā′·gū) *n.* (*Med.*) intermittent malarial fever, marked by fits of shivering, burning, sweating. **agued, aguish** *a.* [L. *acuta febris*, acute fever].

a·head (a·hed′) *adv.* farther forward; in advance; in front; head foremost [E.].

a·hoy (a·hoi′) *interj.* used in hailing, as in *ship ahoy* [form of *interj.* hoy].

ai (ā′·ē) *n.* the three-toed sloth of S. America, named from its cry [Braz.].

aid (ād) *v.t.* and *v.i.* to help; to relieve. *n.* help; assistance; the person or thing which aids; auxiliary; assistant. **aide** *n.* [Fr. *aider*].

aide-de-camp (ād·de·kamp′) *n.* an officer attached to the personal staff of a general to assist him in his military routine. *pl.* **aides-de-camp** [Fr.].

ai·grette (ā′·gret) *n.* a tuft or spray, as of feathers, diamonds, etc.; the small white heron; an egret [Fr.].

ai·guille (ā·gwēl′) *n.* (*Geol.*) a sharp, slender rock; a drill for boring rock. **aiguillette, aiguillet** (ā·gwē·let′) *n.* the tag of a shoe-lace; *pl.* ornamental spangles of a dancer's dress [Fr. = a needle].

ail (āl) *v.t.* to trouble; disturb; to pain; afflict. *v.i.* to feel pain; to be ill. **-ing** *a.* **-ment** *n.* illness. [O.E. *eglan*, to pain].

ai·le·ron (ā′·la·rán) *n.* adjustable flaps near the tips of the wings of an airplane for balance and lateral control [Fr.].

aim (ām) *v.t.* to point at; to direct; to endeavor after; to intend; *n.* direction; end; purpose; intention. **-less** *a.* without aim or purpose. **-lessly** *adv.* **-lessness** *n.* [O.Fr. *esmer*, esteem].

ain't (ānt) (*Colloq.*) contracted form of *am not*, extended to *is not*, or *are not*.

air (ār) *n.* the atmosphere; a gas; a light breeze; a tune; manner, bearing of a person; carriage; appearance; mien. *v.t.* to expose to air or heat, for drying or warming; to parade before the public. **airs** *n.pl.* an affected manner. **-ing** *n.* a ride or walk in the open air. **-y** *a.* of air; exposed to the air; light-hearted. **-ily** *adv.* gaily; merrily; lightly. **-iness** *n.* openness to the air; gaiety. **air base** *n.* a place for housing, or directing operations of, aircraft. **airborne** *a.* carried by aircraft; supported by the air (of aircraft). **air brake** *n.* brake worked by compressed air. **air condenser** *n.* an electrical condenser insulated between the plates by air. **air-condition** *v.t.* to provide a building, etc. with air through a filtering apparatus.

air conditioning *n.* **air cool** *v.t.* to cool by air, to air condition. **aircraft** *n.* all kinds of machines for flying. **aircraft carrier**, an armed vessel built to carry aircraft. **airdrome** *n.* an airport. **airfield** *n.* tract of land, used for accommodation and maintenance of aircraft. **airfoil** *n.* any surface wing, etc. to help in lifting or controlling an aircraft. **air force**, the whole of a nation's aircraft. **air gun** *n.* a gun discharged by elastic force of air. **air lift** *n.* large-scale transport operation by aircraft. **air line** *n.* a service of aircraft plying regularly; a telephone line above ground level. **air liner** *n.* a large passenger airplane flying on a definite route. **air load** *n.* cargo carried by aircraft. **air lock** *n.* the stoppage of the flow of liquid in a pipe caused by the presence of air; a small chamber to allow the passage of men or materials at the top of a caisson. **air mail** *n.* the transport of letters, parcels, etc., by airplane. **airman** *n.* an aviator. **air-minded** *adj.* interested in aviation; **airplane** *n.* a heavier than air aircraft. **airport** *n.* a terminal station for passenger airplanes. **air pressure** *n.* pressure of atmosphere. **air pump** *n.* a machine for exhausting the air from a closed vessel. **air raid** *n.* an attack by hostile aircraft. **air rifle** *n.* a rifled air gun. **air sacs** *n. pl.* air-cells in the bodies of birds. **air ship** *n.* lighter-than-air machine, developed from balloon. **airsick** *adj.* ill from air travel. **airstrip** *n.* concrete runway on an airfield. **airtight** *a.* admitting no air. **airway** *n.* a prepared route for travel by airplane; a ventilating passage [Gk. *aēr*, air].

aire·dale (ār′·dāl) *n.* a kind of large terrier, with a close, wiry coat of tan and black [originally fr. *Airedale*, Yorkshire].

aisle (īl) *n.* the wing of a building; any lateral division of a church; the passage-ways between rows [L. *ala*, a wing].

aitch·bone (āch′·bōn) *n.* the rump bone of an ox; the cut of beef surrounding it [L. *natis*, the rump; *E.* bone].

a·jar (a·jár′) *adv.* partly open, as a door [M.E. *on char*, on the turn].

a·kim·bo (a·kim′·bō) *adv.* with a crook; bent. **with arms akimbo**, with hands on hips and elbows turned outward [M.E. *in kenebow*, into a crooked bend].

a·kin (a·kin′) *a.* related by blood; allied by nature; having the same properties.

-al (al) a *suffix* to *n.* to form *a.*; or to form *n.* from *v.*

à la (a·là), according to [Fr.].

al·a·bas·ter (al′·a·bas·ter) *n.* gypsum; a semitransparent kind of soft marble-like mineral; *a.* made of, or white as, alabaster. **alabastrian, alabastrine** *a.* [Gk. *alabastros*].

a·lack (a·lak′) *interj.* (*Arch.*) an exclamation expressive of sorrow. **alack-a-day** (a·lak′·-a·dā) *interj.* an exclamation of regret [E.].

a·lac·ri·ty (a·lak′·ri·ti·) *n.* cheerful readiness; eagerness; briskness [L. *alacer*, brisk].

a·lar (ā′·ler) *a.* wing-like; pert. to wings; having wings [L. *ala*, a wing].

a·larm (a·lárm′) *n.* sound giving notice of danger; a mechanical contrivance to rouse from sleep; a summons to arms; sudden fear or apprehension; dismay; trepidation. *v.t.* to fill with apprehension; to call to arms. **-ingly** *adv.* **-ist** *n.* one given to exciting alarm, esp. needlessly. **alarum** *n.* an old spelling of 'alarm' [O.Fr. *a l'arme*, to arms].

a·las (a·las′) *interj.* an exclamation of sorrow, pity, etc. [O.Fr. *a las*, ah weary].

a·late (āl′·āt) *a.* having wings; winged. Also **-d** *a.* [L. *ala*, a wing].

alb (alb) *n.* a vestment of white linen, reaching to the feet, worn by R.C. clergy officiating at the Eucharist [L. *albus*, white].

al·ba·core (al′·ba·kōr) *n.* tunny fish [Ar. *al*, the; *bukr*, a young camel].

al·ba·tross (al′·ba·traws) *n.* a large web-footed sea-bird commonest in the South Seas [fr. obsolete *alcatras*, a frigate-bird].

al·be·it (awl·bē′·it) *conj.* although; even though; notwithstanding that [E. *al* = although, *be*, and *it*].

al·bi·no (al·bī′·nō) *n.* a person, or animal, with an abnormal whiteness of the skin and hair, and a pink color in the eyes. **albinism** *n.* [L. *albus*, white].

al·bum (al′·bam) *n.* a book for autographs, photographs, stamps, etc.; a book of selections [L. *album*, a white tablet].

al·bu·men (al·bū′·man) *n.* white of egg; a similar substance found in the tissues of animals and plants. **albumin** *n.* any of a class of proteins, necessary for growth in the body. **albuminoid** *n.* a substance resembling albumen. **albuminous** *a.* [L. *albumen*, white of egg].

al·bur·num (al·bur′·nam) *n.* sapwood, part of tree under bark and outside heart up which sap rises [L. *albus*, white].

al·che·my (al′·ka·mi·) *n.* the forerunner of modern chemistry. Its chief aims were (*a*) transmuting the baser metals into gold, and (*b*) discovery of an elixir of life. **alchemic** *a.* **alchemist** *n.* [Ar. *al*, the; *kimia* fr. Gk. *chumeia*, alloying of metals].

al·co·hol (al′·ka·hál) *n.* pure spirit; a liquid of strong pungent taste, the intoxicating element in fermented or distilled liquor. **-ism** *n.* a morbid condition caused by over-indulgence in alcoholic liquor. **-ic** *a.* pert. to alcohol; *n.* one addicted to the immoderate use of alcohol; a habitual drunkard. **absolute alcohol**, alcohol entirely free from water [Ar. *al-koh′l*, powder of antimony to stain the eyelids].

al·cove (al′·kōv) *n.* a recess in a room; a covered seat in a garden [Sp. *alcoba*].

al·de·hyde (al′·da·hīd) *n.* a liquid produced by the oxidation of alcohol [fr. letters of *alcohol dehy*drogenatum, i.e. alcohol without hydrogen].

al·der (awl′·der) *n.* a tree of birch family, growing in marshy soil [O.F. *alor*].

al·der·man (awl′·der·man) *n.* a civic dignitary. *pl.* **aldermen** [O.E. *ealdorman*].

ale (āl) *n.* liquor made from malt by fermentation; a festivity (from the amount of ale drunk at it. **alehouse** *n.* a place where ale is sold [O.E. *ealu*].

a·lem·bic (a·lem′·bik) *n.* a vessel of glass or metal formerly used in distillation; (*Fig.*) a refining medium, as in the *alembic of the mind* [Ar. *al-ambig*, a cup].

a·lert (a·lurt′) *a.* watchful; vigilant; brisk; nimble; active; *n.* a signal by sirens of air attack; period of air-raid. **-ly** *adv.* **-ness** *n.* [It. *all′ erta*, on the look-out].

al·ex·an·drine (al·eg·zan′·drin) *n.* a verse of six iambic feet, probably from O.Fr. poems dealing with Alexander the Great; found as ninth line of Spenserian Stanza.

a,lex·i·a (a·lek′·si·a) *n.* inability to understand written language.

al·fal·fa (al·fal′·fa) *n.* plant of the pea family, valued as fodder [Sp. *alfalfa*, three-leaved grass].

al·fres·co (al·fres′·kō) *a.* and *adv.* in the fresh air, as an *alfresco meal* [It.].

al·ga (al·ga) *n.* (Bot.) one of the **algae** (al′·jē) *pl.* plants found in sea-water, and in slow-moving fresh or stagnant water. **algal, algoid, algous** *a.* **algology** *n.* scientific study of marine plants [L. *alga*, seaweed].

al·ge·bra (al′·je·bra) *n.* a branch of mathematics in which calculations are made by using letters to represent numbers or quantities and symbols to denote arithmetical operations of these numbers; a kind of abstract arithmetic used in almost all branches of science. **-ic(al)** (al·je·brā′·ik(al)) *a.* **-ically** *adv.* **-ist** *n.* [Ar. *al′jebr*, joining together of fragment].

al·gid (al′·jid) *a.* cold. **algid cholera** Asiatic cholera. **-ity, -ness** *n.* coldness. **algific** *a.* causing cold [L. *algere*, to be cold].

a·li·as (ā′·li·as) *adv.* otherwise; *n.* an assumed name [L. *alias*, at another time].

al·i·bi (al′·i·bī) *n.* (*Law*) a plea that the prisoner was elsewhere when the crime was committed; excuse [L. *alibi*, elsewhere].

al·ien (āl′·yan) *a.* of another country; foreign; different in nature; estranged; *n.* a non-naturalized foreigner. **-able** *a.* (of property) capable of being sold or handed over. **-ability** *n.* **-ate** *v.t.* to transfer to another; estrange; **-ation** *n.* (*Med.*) insanity. **-ator** *n.* **-ism** *n.* study of mental diseases. **-ist** *n.* specialist in treatment of mental diseases; a psychiatrist [L. *alienus*, belonging to another].

a·lif·er·ous (al·if′·er·as) *a.* having wings.

a·light (a·līt′) *adv.* or *a.* on fire; illuminated; kindled [O.E. *on;* *lēoht*, light].

a·light (a·līt′) *v.i.* to dismount; to finish one's journey; to fall; to descend. **-ing** *n.* [O.E. *alihtan*, to descend].

a·lign (a·līn′) *v.t.* to adjust by a line; to line up; to range; *v.i.* to form in a line; to fall in, as troops. Also **aline, -ment** *n.* [Fr. *aligner*, to put in line].

a·like (a·līk′) *a.* having likeness; similar; *adv.* similarly; equally [O.E. *gelic*, like].

al·i·ment (al′·i·mant) *n.* nourishment; nutriment; (*Law*) provision for maintenance. *v.t.* to maintain. **-al** *adv.* **-ary** *a.* pert. to food; nutritive. **-ation** *n.* the process of introducing nutriment into the body. **-ary canal**, the large intestine [L. *alimentum*, nourishment].

al·i·mo·ny (al′·i·mō·ni·) *n.* means of living, esp. an allowance made to a wife out of her husband's income, after legal separation [L. *alimonia*, sustenance].

al·i·quant (a′·li·kwant) *a.* (of a number) not dividing without remainder [L. *aliquantus*, considerable].

al·i·quot (al′·i·kwat) *a.* dividing exactly, or without remainder [L. *aliquot*, some].

a·live (a·līv′) *a.* having life; existent; active; alert; thronged with [O.E. *on life*, living].

al·ka·li (al′·ka·li) *n.* one of a class of chemical compounds which combine with acids to form salts—used with fats to form soap. **alkalify** (al′·ka·li·fī), **alkalize** *v.t.* to render alkaline; *v.i.* to become alkaline; *pa.p.* **-fied. -fiable** *a.* capable of being converted into an alkali. **-metry** (al·ka·lim′·a·tri·) *n.* the quantitative estimation of the strength of alkalis. **-ne** *a.* pert. to alkali; with qualities of alkali. **-nity** (al·ka·lin′·i·ti·) *n.* **alkaloid** *n.* nitrogenous organic compound which acts chemically like an alkali; *a.* resembling an alkali in properties [Ar. *al*, the; *qaliy*, calcined ashes].

all (awl) *a.* the whole of; every one of; *n.* whole amount; whole duration of; *adv.* wholly; entirely. **all-American** *adj.* chosen best in U.S.; *n.* player so chosen. **all-around** *adj.* versatile, having many abilities. **all-fours** *n.* hands and feet. **all-hail!** *interj.* welcome! good health! **all-in** *a.* exhausted. **all out** *adj.* total. **all-powerful** *a.* omnipotent. **all but**, nearly; almost. **all in all**, in all respects [O.E. *all. eall*].

al·lay (a·lā′) *v.t.* to lighten; to make quiet; to lessen grief or pain. **-er** *n.* **-ment** *n.* [O.E. *alecgan*, to put down].

al·le·ga·tion (al·a·gā′·shan) *n.* affirmation; that which is positively asserted; the act of alleging [L. *allegare*, to allege]. **allege** (a·lej′) *v.t.* to bring forward with positiveness; to plea, or excuse; to declare; affirm; cite. **allegeable** *a.* **allegedly** *adv.* [L. *allegare*, to allege].

al·le·giance (a·lē′·jans) *n.* the duty of a subject to his government or superior; loyalty; an oath of homage. **allegiant** *a.* loyal; *n.* one who owes allegiance [fr. O.Fr. *ligeance*].

al·le·go·ry (al′·a·gō·ri·) *n.* a narrative in which abstract ideas are personified; a description to convey a different meaning from that which is expressed; a continued metaphor. **allegoric, (-al)** *a.* **allegorically** *adv.* **allegorize** *v.t.* to write in allegorical form; *v.i.* to use figurative language. **allegorist** *n.* [Gk. *allos*, other; *agoreuein*, to speak].

al·le·gret·to (al·lạ·gret′·tō) *a.* (*Mus.*) livelier than *andante* but not so quick as *allegro* [It. dim. of *allegro*, gay].

al·le·gro (ạ·lā′·grō) *a.* (*Mus.*) brisk, gay, sprightly (movement). **allegro vivace** (vē·-vàtch′·e), allegro in an even more spirited manner [It. *allegro*, gay].

al·le·lu·iah (al·ạ·lōō′·yạ) *interj.* hallelujah; *n.* song of praise to the Almighty [Heb.].

al·ler·gy (al′·ẹr·ji·) *n.* hyper-sensitivity to particular substances; susceptibility to ill-effects from eating some foods. **allergen** *n.* a substance which induces allergy. **allergic** *a.* [Gk. *allos*, other; *ergon*, work].

al·le·vi·ate (ạ·lē′·vi·āt) *v.t.* to make light; to lighten; to ease; to afford relief; to mitigate. **alleviation** *n.* **alleviative** *a.* **alleviator** *n.* [L. *alleviare* fr. *levis*, light].

al·ley (al′·i·) *n.* a narrow passage between buildings; a garden path; a long, narrow passage for bowling. **alley-way** *n.* an alley [Fr. *aller*, to go].

al·li·ance (ạ·lī′·ạns) *n.* persons, parties, or states allied together for a common purpose; union by marriage [Fr. *allier*].

al·li·ga·tor (al′·i·gā·tẹr) *n.* a reptile distinguished from crocodile by a broad flat head, depressed muzzle and unequal teeth [Sp. *el lagarto*, the lizard].

al·lit·er·ate (ạ·lit′·ẹr·āt) *v.i.* to begin each word with the same letter or sound. **alliteration** *n.* recurrence of a letter or letters at the beginning of words in close succession; head rhyme. **alliterative** *adj.* [L. *ad*, to; *littera*, letter].

al·lo·cate (al′·ō·kāt) *v.t.* to distribute; to assign to each his share; to place. **allocation** *n.* **allocatur** *n.* (*Law*) a certificate that costs have been allowed [L. *ad*, to; *locus*, a place].

al·lo·cu·tion (al·ō·kū′·shạn) *n.* a formal address, esp. of the Pope to his clergy [L. *ad*, to; *locutio*, a speech].

al·lot (ạ·lát′) *v.t.* to divide by lot; to distribute as shares. *pr.p* **-ting.** *pa.p.* and *pa.t.* **-ted.** **-ment** *n.* what is alloted; distribution; a share; a portion [L. *ad*, to; O.E. *hlot*, a share].

al·lot·ro·py (ạ·làt′·rạ·pi·) *n.* property of some chemical substances of being found in two or more different forms, e.g. coal, graphite, and diamond are all carbon. **allotropic** *a.* **allotropism** *n.* [Gk. *allos*, other; *tropos*, manner].

al·low (ạ·lou′) *v.t.* to acknowledge; to permit; to give; to set apart; *v.i.* to provide. **-able** *a.* permissible; lawful; acceptable. **-ance** *n.* what is allowed; permission; a stated quantity to be added or deducted; a rebate; a grant. **-edly** *adv.* **to make allowance for,** to take into consideration [O.Fr. *allouer*].

al·loy (ạ·loi′) *v.t.* to melt together two or more metals; to reduce the purity of a metal by mixing with a less valuable one; to debase. **alloy** (al′·oi, ạ·loi′) *n.* any mixture of metals e.g. copper and zinc to form brass; a combination; an amalgam; (*Fig.*) evil mixed with good [L. *ad*, to; *ligare*, to join].

all right (awl rīt) satisfactory, yes, certainly.

all·spice (awl′·spīs) *n.* a spice [E. *all*, and *spice*].

al·lude (ạ·lōōd′) *v.i.* to refer indirectly to; to hint at; to suggest; to mention lightly [L. *ad*, at; *ludere*, to play].

al·lure (ạ·loor′) *v.t.* to tempt by a lure, offer, or promise. **-ment** *n.* that which allures. **alluring** *a.* enticing; attractive; fascinating. **alluringly** *adv.* [L. *ad*, to; Fr. *leurre*, bait].

al·lu·sion (ạ·lōō′·zhun) *n.* a passing or indirect reference; a hint; a suggestion. **allusive**

a. referring to indirectly; marked by allusions; symbolical. **allusively** *adv.* [fr. *allude*].

al·lu·vi·on (ạ·lōō′·vi·ạn) *n.* land formed by washed-up earth and sand. **alluvium** *n.* water-borne matter deposited on low-lying lands. [L. *alluvio*, an overflowing].

al·ly (a·lī′) *v.t.* to join by treaty, marriage, or friendship; *pr.p.* **-ing;** *pa.p.* and *pa.t.* **allied.** **ally** (ạ·lī′, or a′·lī) *n.* a person, family, country, etc., bound to another, esp. of nations in war-time; a partner. *pl.* **allies** (ạ·līz′, or a′·līz) [L. *ad*, to; *ligare*, to bind].

al·ma ma·ter (al′·mạ mä′·tẹr) *n.* college or school one attended [L. fostering mother].

al·ma·nac (awl′·mạ·nak) *n.* a calendar of days, weeks and months, to which astronomical and other information is added [etym. uncertain].

al·might·y (awl·mīt′·i·) *a.* all-powerful; omnipotent. **The Almighty,** the Supreme Being; God; **almightiness** *n.* [O.E. *ealmihtig*].

al·mond (á′·mạnd) *n.* the kernel of the nut of the almond-tree [Gk. *amugdalē*, an almond].

al·mon·er (á′·, ál′·mạn·ẹr) *n.* one who distributes alms or bounty. **almonry** *n.* a place for distributing alms [O.Fr. *almosnier*].

al·most (awl′·mōst) *adv.* very nearly; all but [O.E. *eallmoest*].

alms (ámz) *n.* gift offered to relieve the poor; a charitable donation. **alms-house** *n.* a building, usually erected and endowed by private charity, for housing the aged poor [Gk. *eleēmosunē*, pity].

al·oe (al′·ō) *n.* a bitter plant used in medicine; a purgative drug, made from the juice of several species of aloe. — **wood** [Gk. *aloe*, a bitter herb].

a·loft (ạ·lawft′) *adv.* on high; (*Naut.*) on the yards or rigging [O.N. *a lopt*, in the air].

a·lo·ha (ạ·lō′·a, ȧ·lō′·hȧ) *n., interj.* greetings, farewell [Hawaiian].

a·lone (ạ·lōn′) *a.* solitary; single; *adv.* by oneself; singly [E. *all* and *one*].

a·long (ạ·lawng′) *adv.* in a line with; throughout the length of; lengthwise; onward; in the company of (followed by *with*); *prep.* by the side of. **-side** *adv.* by the side of, esp. of a ship [O.E. *andlang*].

a·loof (ạ·lōōf′) *a.* reserved in manner, almost unsociable; *adv.* at a distance; apart. **-ness** *n.* [fr. Dut. *to loef*, to windward].

al·o·pe·ci·a (al·ạ·pē′·shi·ạ) *n.* disease causing loss of hair [Gk. *alopekia*, fox-mange].

a·loud (ạ·loud′) *adv.* with a loud voice or noise; loudly; audibly [fr. E. *loud*].

alp (alp) *n.* a high mountain; mountain pastureland. **Alps** *n.pl.* the mountains of Switzerland. **alpine** *a.* pert. to the Alps; *n.* a plant that grows on high ground. **alpinist** (al′·pin·ist) *n.* [L. *Alpes*].

al·pac·a (al·pak′·ạ) *n.* a sheeplike animal of Peru; a species of llama; a thin kind of cloth made of the wool of the alpaca [Sp.].

al·pen·horn, alp·horn (al′·pen·hawrn, alp′·hawrn) *n.* a long wooden horn curving towards a wide mouth-piece, used by Swiss herds. **alpenstock** *n.* a long, stout staff, shod with iron, used by mountaineers [Ger.=horn (stick) of the Alps].

al·pha (al′·fạ) *n.* the first letter of Greek alphabet. **alpha and omega,** the first and the last. **alpha particle,** a helium nucleus travelling at high speed, given out when atoms of Uranium, Radium, etc., undergo radioactive breakdown. **alpha rays,** streams of alpha particles [Gk.].

al·pha·bet (al′·fạ·bet) *n.* letters of a language arranged in order; first principles. **-ic, -al** *a.* **-ically** *adv.* **-ize** *v.* [Gk. *alpha, beta*, the first two Greek letters].

al·read·y (awl·red′·i·) *adv.* before this; even now; even then; previously to the time specified [E. *all ready*, prepared].

al·so (awl′·sō) *adv.* and *conj.* in like manner; likewise; further.

al·tar (awl′·ter) *n.* a table or raised structure in a place of worship, on which gifts and sacrifices are offered to a deity; the communion table [L. *altare*].

al·ter (awl′·ter) *v.t.* to change; *v.i.* to become different. **-ably** *adv.* **-ability** *n.* **-ation** *n.* the act of altering; change; modification [L. *alter*, other].

al·ter·cate (awl′·ter·kāt) *v.i.* to contend in words; to wrangle. **altercation** *n.* a dispute; a controversy [L. *altercari*, to wrangle].

al·ter·nate (awl·ter′·nit) *a.* occuring by turns; one following the other in succession. **-ly** *adv.* by turns. **alternate** (awl·ter·nāt) *v.t.* to cause to follow by turns; *v.i.* to happen by turns. **alternation** *n.* **alternative** *a.* offering a choice of two things; *n.* a choice of two things. **alternatively** *adv.* **alternator** *n.* (*Elect.*) a dynamo for producing alternating current. **alternating current** (*Elect.*) a current which reverses its direction of flow at fixed periods. *Abbrev.* **A.C.** [L. *alternare*, fr. *alter*, other].

al·though (awl·THō′) *conj.* admitting that; notwithstanding that [E. *all* and *though*].

al·tim·e·ter (al·tim′·a·ter) *n.* an instrument for taking altitudes; in aviation, barometer to show height [L. *altus*, high; Gk. *metron*, a measure].

al·ti·tude (al′·ti·tūd) *n.* height; perpendicular elevation above a given level [L. *altitudo*].

al·to (al′·tō) *n.* (*Mus.*) part once sung by highest male voice or counter-tenor, now sung by lowest female voice; singer with voice higher than tenor, lower than soprano; contralto [L. *altus*, high].

al·to·geth·er (awl·ta·geTH′·er) *adv.* wholly, entirely, quite; on the whole [E.].

al·tru·ism (al′·troo·izm) *n.* the principle of living for the good of others (opp. to *egoism*). **altruist** *n.* **altruistic** *a.* unselfish. **altruistically** *adv.* [L. *alter*, another].

al·um (al′·am) *n.* a double sulphate of alumina and potash; a mineral salt used as a styptic, astringent, etc., as a mordant in dyeing, and in tanning [L. *alumen*].

a·lu·mi·num (a·lòò′·mi·nam) *n.* a whitish metal produced largely from bauxite; it is strong, light, malleable. **alumina, alumine** *n.* an oxide of aluminum; the clay, loam, etc., from which alum is obtained. **aluminate** *v.t.* to impregnate with alum. **aluminic** *a.* **aluminiferous** *a.* containing alum or alumina. **aluminite** *n.* a sulphate of alumina [L. *alumen*, alum].

a·lum·nus (a·lum′·nus) *n.* (*fem.* **alumna**, *pl.* **alumnae**) a graduate or former student of a school, college, or university. *pl.* **alumni** [L. *alumnus*, foster-child].

al·ve·o·lar (al·vē′·ō·ler) *a.* pert. to or resembling the sockets of the teeth. **alveolate** *a.* pitted; honeycombed. **alveolus** *n.* (*pl.* **alveoli**) a tooth socket; a cell in a honeycomb [L. *alveolus*, a small cavity].

al·ways (awl′·wāz) *adv.* at all times; perpetually; invariably; regularly [O.E. *ealne weg*, the whole way].

a·lys·sum (a′·li·sam) *n.* a species of rock plant with white or yellow flowers; madwort [Gk. *alussos*, curing madness].

am (am) the *first person sing. pres. indic.* of the verb **to be**.

a. m. (ā em) before noon [L. *ante meridiem*].

a·mah (á′·ma) *n.* a nurse, in the Orient [Port. *ama*].

a·main (a·mān′) *adv.* (*Arch.*) with all strength or force [E. *on; main*, strength].

a·mal·gam (a·mal′·gam) *n.* a compound of mercury with another metal; a mixture of different substances. **-ate** *v.t.* to mix a metal with quicksilver; to compound; to consolidate; to combine (esp. of business firms); *v.i.* to coalesce; to blend; to fuse. **-ation** *n.* the act or results of amalgamating. **-ative** *a.* **-ator** *n.*

[Gk. *malagma*, an emollient].

a·man·u·en·sis (a·man·ū·en′·sis) *n.* one who writes what another dictates, or copies what another has written; a secretary. *pl.* **amanuenses** [L. *ab*, from; *manus*, hand].

am·a·ranth (am′·a·ranth) *n.* an imaginary purple flower which never fades; 'love-lies-bleeding'; a purplish color; also a real flower. **amaranthine** *a.* never-fading; purplish [Gk. *amaranthos*, never-fading].

am·a·ryl·lis (a′·ma·ril·as) *n.* a plant, the belladonna lily [Gk.].

a·mass (a·mas′) *v.t.* to heap up; to collect; accumulate [L. *ad*, to; *massa*, a lump].

am·a·teur (am′·a·ter) *n.* one who cultivates any study, art, or sport for the love of it, and not for money; *a.* like an amateur. **amateurish** *a.* unskilled; clumsy. **amateurism, amateurishness** *n.* [L. *amare*, to love].

am·a·tive (am′·a·tiv) *a.* pert. to love; amorous [L. *amare*, to love].

am·a·tol (am′·a·tal) *n.* explosive of ammonium nitrate of trinitrotoluene (**T.N.T.**) [name from parts of names of ingredients].

am·a·to·ry (am′·a·tōr·i·) *a.* pert. to or causing love. **amatorial** *a.* amorous; affectionate. **amatorially** *adv.* [L. *amare*, to love].

a·maze (a·māz′) *v.t.* to fill with astonishment or wonder; to confound; to perplex. **-dly** (a·māz·ad·li′) *adv.* **-ment** *n.* astonishment, surprise. **amazing** *a.* causing amazement, wonder, or surprise. **amazingly** *adv.* [O.E. *amasian*, to confound].

Am·a·zon (am′·az·an) *n.* one of a mythical race of female warriors of Scythia; a masculine woman. **Amazonian** *a* [Gk. *a*-, neg. and *mazos*, breast].

am·bages (am′·bājz) *n.pl.* circumlocution; subterfuge; evasion; used in *pl.* [L. *ambages*, a winding].

am·bas·sa·dor (am·bas′·a·der) *n.* an envoy of highest rank sent to a foreign country; (*Fig.*) an intermediary; a messenger. **ambassadress** *n. fem.* **ambassadorial** *a.* **-ship** *n.* [L. *ambactus*, vassal].

am·ber (am′·ber) *n.* a yellowish, brittle fossil resin of vegetable origin, used in making jewelry, etc.; *a.* of or like, amber [Ar. *anbar*, ambergris].

am·ber·gris (am′·ber·grēs) *n.* a fragrant, ash-colored. waxy substance, derived from a biliary secretion of the spermaceti whale [Fr. *ambre gris*, grey amber].

am·bi·dex·ter (am·bi·leks′·ter) *n.* one able to use either hand with equal dexterity; a double-dealer. **ambidexterity** *n.* **ambidextrous** *a.* able to use either hand equally skilfully. **ambidextrously** *adv.* [L. *ambo*, both; *dexter*, right hand].

am·bi·ent (am′·bi·ant) *a.* encompassing on all sides [L. *ambire*, to go round].

am·bi·gu·i·ty (am·bi·gū′·i·ti·) *n.* any statement that may be interpreted in more than one way. **ambiguous** *a.* doubtful or uncertain; equivocal; susceptible of two or more meanings. **ambiguously** *adv.* **ambiguousness** *n.* [L. *ambigere*, to waver].

am·bit (am′·bit) *n.* circuit or compass; sphere of action; scope [L. *ambire*, to go round].

am·bi·tion (am·bish′·an) *n.* an eager desire for the attainment of honor, fame, or power; aim; aspiration. **ambitious** *a.* ardently desirous of acquiring power, rank, office, etc. **ambitiously** *adv.* [L. *ambitio*, going about for votes].

am·biv·a·lence, am·biv·a·len·cy (am·biv′·a·lans, -i·) *n.* in psychoanalysis, the simultaneous operation in the mind of two conflicting wishes. **ambivalent** *a.* [L. *ambo*, both; *valere*, to be strong].

am·ble (am′·bl) *v.i.* to move along easily and gently; *n.* a peculiar gait of a horse; a stroll. **ambler** *n.* **ambling** *a.* **amblingly** *adv.* [L. *ambulare*, to walk].

am·bro·sia (am·brō′·si·ạ) n. (Myth.) the food of the Ancient Greek gods which conferred immortality; an exquisite dish. **ambrosial** a. [Gk. a-, neg.; brotos, mortal].

am·bu·lance (am′·bū·lạns) n. a covered vehicle for the transport of the injured or sick; a hospital unit in the field [Fr. ambulance].

am·bu·lant (am′·bū·lạnt) a. walking. **ambulate** v.i. to walk backwards and forwards. **ambulation** n. walking. **ambulatory** a. having power of walking; used for walking; moving from place to place; n. a cloister for walking exercise [L. ambulare, to walk].

am·bush (am′·boosh) same as **ambuscade** (am·bạs·kād) n. a surprise attack; the place of ambush; the force concealed; v.i. to lie in wait; v.t. to attack from a concealed position [L. in; Late L. boscus, a wood].

a·me·ba. See **amoeba**.

a·mel·io·rate (ạ·mēl′·yẹr·āt) v.t. and v.t. to make better; to improve. **amelioration** n. **ameliorative** a. [L. ad, to; melior, better].

A·men (ā·men′, ä′·men) adv. or interj. so be it; truly; verily (uttered at the end of a prayer) [Heb. = certainly].

a·me·na·ble (ạ·mē′·nạ·bl, ạ·men′·ạ·bl) a. liable to be brought to account; easily led; willing to yield or obey. **amenability, -ness** n. the state of being amenable. **amenably** adv. [Fr. amener, to lead near].

a·mend (ạ·mend′) v.t. to change for the better; to improve; to alter in detail as a law, etc.; v.i. to grow better. **-able** a. **-atory** a. **-ment** n. the act of amending; a change for the better. **amends** n.pl. reparation for loss or injury; compensation [L. emendare, to remove a fault].

a·men·i·ty (ạ·men′·i·ti·) n. pleasantness in situation, climate, manners, or disposition. **amenities** n.pl. pleasant ways or manners; agreeable surroundings [L. amoenus, agreeable].

a·merce (ạ·murs′) v.t. to punish by a fine. **-able** a. liable to a fine. **-ment** n. a pecuniary penalty [L. merces, a fine].

A·mer·i·can (ạ·mer′·i·kạn) n. in, of, or characteristic of the United States or America. n. a native, citizen or resident of America or the United States. **-a** n.pl. collection of facts, books, data pert. to America. **-ism** n. **-ize** v.t. and v.i. **-ization** n. [fr. Amerigo Vespucci, Italian navigator].

am·e·thyst (am′·ạ·thist) n. a kind of quartz; violet, purple, or blue color. **amethystine** a. pert. to amethyst; bluish-violet [Gk. a-, neg.; methein, to be drunken].

a·mi·a·ble (ā′·mi·ạ·bl) a. worthy of love or affection; sweet-tempered. **amiably** adv. **amiability** n. Also **-ness** [L. amicabilis, friendly].

am·i·ca·ble (am′·i·kạ·bl) a. friendly; peaceable. **amicably** adv. **amicability** n. Also **-ness** [L. amicabilis, friendly].

a·mid, a·midst (ạ·mid′, ạ·midst′) prep. in the middle of; among [O.E. on middan].

am·i·no ac·ids (ạ·mē′·nō as′·idz) a group of nitrogenous organic compounds, basic constituents of proteins.

a·miss (ạ·mis′) a. wrong; faulty; improper; adv. in a faulty manner [E. miss, a failure].

am·i·ty (am′·i·ti·) n. friendship [Fr. ami, a friend, fr. L. amicus].

am·me·ter (am′·mē·tẹr) n. an instrument used to measure the strength of an electric current in amperes [fr. ampere, and Gk. metron, a measure].

am·mo (am′·ō) n. (Army Slang) ammunition.

am·mo·ni·a (ạ·mō′·ni·ạ) n. a pungent, alkaline gas, very soluble in water; a solution of this gas in water, for household use. **ammoniac, ammoniacal** a. **ammoniated** a. combined with, containing, ammonia. **ammonium** n. hypothetical base of ammonia [fr. sal ammoniac].

am·mu·ni·tion (am·ū·nish′·an) n. military projectiles and missiles of all kinds; originally, military stores. a. [O.Fr. l'amunition, for la munition].

am·ne·sia (am·nē′·zhi·ạ) n. memory loss [Gk.]

am·nes·ty (am′·nes·ti·) n. an act of oblivion; a general pardon of political offenders [Gk. amnesia, a forgetting].

a·moe·ba (ạ·mē′·bạ) n. a minute animalcule of the simplest structure constantly changing in shape. pl. **amoebae, amoebas. amoeboid, amoebic** a. [Gk. amoibē, change].

a·mok (ạ·mȧk′) See **amuck**.

a·mong, a·mongst (ạ·mung′, ạ·mungst′) prep. mixed with; making part of; amidst [M.E. amonge].

a·mor·al (ā·mȧr′·ạl) a. non-moral; heedless of morals [Gk. a-, neg.; and E. moral].

am·o·rous (am′·ẹr·as) a. having a propensity for love and sexual enjoyment; in love; pert. to love. **-ly** adv. **-ness** n. [L. amor, love].

a·mor·phous (ạ·mawr′·fạs) a. without regular shape; shapeless; irregular; uncrystallized [Gk. a-, neg.; morphe, form].

a·mor·tize (am′·ẹr·tīz) v.t. to pay off a debt usually by periodic payments. **amortization** n.

a·mount (ạ·mount′) v.i. to rise to; to result in; to come to (in value or meaning); to be equal to; n. the sum total; the whole, or aggregate [O.Fr. amonter, to mount up].

am·pere (am′·pir) n. the unit of electric current; (Abbrev. amp.). **amperage** n. strength of electric current in amperes [named after André Ampère, a French physicist, 1775-1836].

am·per·sand (am′·pẹr·sand) n. the name given to the sign & [fr. and per se and, i.e. 'and' by itself = 'and.'].

Am·phib·i·a (am·fib′·i·ạ) n.pl. animals that can live either on land or in water, as frogs, toads, newts, etc. **amphibian** a. pert. to or having the qualities of Amphibia. n. an animal of the class Amphibia. **amphibious** a. [Gk. amphi, on both sides; bios, life].

am·phi·brach (am′·fi·brak) n. in prosody, a foot of three syllables, the middle one long, the first and last short. (   ). In English the term is applied to a foot of three syllables of which only the middle one is stressed. a. \[Gk. fr. amphi, on both sides; brachus, short].

am·phi·the·a·ter (am′·fi·thē·a·tẹr) n. an edifice, having tiers of seats, encircling an arena, used for sports or spectacles; a rising gallery in a theater, concert-hall, etc. [Gk. amphi, on both sides: theatron, a theater].

am·pho·ra (am′·fạ·rạ) n. a two-handled earthenware vessel or jar, used by the ancient Greeks and Romans; 6 gallons [Gk. amphi, on both sides; pherein, to bear].

am·ple (am′·pl) a. of full dimensions; of adequate size; of sufficient quantity; abundant; copious. **amply** adv. **-ness** n. [L. amplus].

am·pli·fy (am′·pli·fī) v.t. to make larger; to extend; to enlarge; v.i. to dilate; to expatiate upon. **amplification** n. **amplifier** n. an apparatus which increases the volume of sound [L. amplus, large; facere, to make].

am·pli·tude (am′·pli·tūd) n. largeness; extent; abundance; (Radio) (of a wave) vertical distance between its highest and lowest levels; **amplitude modulation (AM)** radio transmission by changing the amplitude of waves (contrasted with frequency modulation, FM); (Elect.) maximum value of an alternating current [L. amplus, large].

am·poule (am′·pōōl) n. also **ampule** (am′·pūle), a small sealed glass container holding hypodermic dose [Fr.].

am·pul·la (am·pūl′·ạ) n.; pl. **-e;** a sacred vessel for holding oil; cruet holding wine and water for Mass [L. ampulla].

am·pu·tate (am′·pū·tāt) v.t. to cut off, as a limb of the body, or bough of a tree. **amputation** n. **amputee** n. one who has lost a limb through amputation [L. amputare, to cut off].

a·muck, a·mok (ạ·muk′, ạ·mȧk′) adv. to rush about frantically or murderously [Malay amuq, rushing in frenzy].

am·u·let (am′·yạ·lit) *n.* a talisman; a charm; *a.* [Fr. *amulette*, fr. L. *amuletum*].

a·muse (ạ·mūz′) *v.t.* to entertain agreeably; to occupy pleasantly; to divert. **-ment** *n.* anything which entertains or pleases; a pastime. **amusing** *a.* [Fr. *amuser*, to entertain].

an (an) *a.* the form of the indefinite article used before a vowel sound. See **a.** Also *Arch. conj.* if = a form of *and* [O.E. *an*, one].

an·a·bap·tist (an·ạ·bap′·tist) *n.* one who denies the validity of infant baptism and advocates re-baptism of adults (by immersion) [Gk. *ana*, again; *baptizein*, to dip].

a·nab·a·sis (ạ·nab′·ạ·sis) *n.* a military expedition. *pl.* **anabases** [Gk.].

a·nab·o·lism (an·ab′·ạl·izm) *n.* (*Physiol.*) the constructive form of metabolism; the building-up of tissues by plant or animal which process alternates with the breaking down (katabolism) in the chemical routine [Gk. *ana*, up; *bole*, a throwing].

a·nach·ro·nism (an·ak′·rạn·izm) *n.* a chronological error; post- or ante-dating of an event or thing. **anachronistic** *a.* **anachronous** *a.* [Gk. *ana*, back; *chronos*, time].

an·a·con·da (an·ạ·kán′·dạ) *n.* a gigantic, non-venomous snake of tropical S. America.

a·nae·mia See **anemia.**

an·aes·the·sia, anesthesia See **anesthesia.**

an·a·glyph (an′·a·glif) *n.* a figure or ornament cut in low relief; a cameo. **anaglyphic** *a.* [Gk. *ana*, up; *gluphein*, to engrave].

an·a·gram (an′·ạ·gram) *n.* a transposition of the letters of a word or phrase to form a new word or phrase. **anagrammatic, -al** *a.* **anagrammatically** *adv.* **anagrammatize** *v.t.* to form anagrams. **anagrammatism** *n.* [Gk. *ana-*, again; *gramma*, letter].

a·nal (ā′·nạl) *a.* pert. to or near the anus.

an·a·lects, an·a·lec·ta (an′·ạ·lekts, an·ạ·lek′·tạ) *n.pl.* an anthology of short literary fragments. **analectic** *a.* [Gk. *analektos*, choice].

an·a·lep·sis (an·ạ·lep′·sis) *n.* (*Med.*) restoration of strength after disease. Also **analepsy. analeptic** *a.* [Gk. *ana*, up; *lepsis*, a taking].

an·al·ge·sia (an·ạl·jē′·zi·ạ) *n.* (*Med.*) absence of pain while retaining tactile sense; painlessness. **analgesic** *a.* insensible to or alleviating pain; *n.* a drug which relieves pain [Gk. *an-*, neg.; *algesis*, pain].

a·nal·o·gy (ạ·nal′·ạ·ji·) *n.* resemblance in essentials between things or statements otherwise different; relationship; likeness; parallelism; correspondence. **analogic, -al** *a.* **analogically** *adv.* **analogize** *v.t.* to explain by analogy. **analogism** *n.* an argument proceeding from cause to effect; investigation by, or reasoning from, analogy. **analogist** *n.* **analogous** (a·nal′·ạ·gus) *a.* having analogy. **analogously** *adv.* **analogue** *n.* a word or thing resembling another [Gk. *analogia*, proportion].

a·nal·y·sis (ạ·nal′·i·sis) *n.* the resolution, separating, or breaking up of anything into its constituent elements; a synopsis; (*Chem.*) determination of elements comprising a compound or mixture; (*Gram.*) logical arrangement of a sentence into its component parts; (*Math.*) theory of real and complex numbers. *pl.* **analyses. analyzable** *a.* **analyzation** *n.* **analyze** *v.t.* to take to pieces; to examine critically part by part. **analyst** *n.* one skilled in analysis; an analytical chemist. **analytic, -al** *a.* **analytically** *adv.* **analytics** *n.pl.* the technique of logical analysis [Gk. *ana*, up; *lusis*, a loosening].

an·a·pest, an·a·paest (an′·ạ·pest) *n.* in prosody, a foot of three syllables, two short or unaccented followed by one long or accented syllable (⌣⌣—). **anapestic** *a.* [Gk. *anapaistos* reversed].

an·ar·chy (an′·ẹr·ki·) *n.* want of government in society; lawless disorder in a country; a political theory, which would dispense with all laws, founding authority on the individual conscience. **anarchic, anarchically** *adv.* **anarchize** *v.t.* **anarchism** *n.* confusion, chaos. **anarchist** *n.* [Gk. *an-*, neg.; *archein*, to rule].

a·nath·e·ma (ạ·nath′·ạ·mạ) *n.* the word used in the R.C. church as part of the formula in excommunication; something highly distasteful to one; accursed thing. **-tic** *a.* **-tization** *n.* **-ize** *v.t.* to pronounce a curse against; to excommunicate [Gk.].

a·nat·o·my (ạ·nat′·ạ·mi·) *n.*, *pl.* **-mies,** art of dissecting an animal or a plant; study of form or structure of an animal; the body; a skeleton. **anatomic, -al** *a.* **anatomically** *adv.* **anatomize** *v.t.* to dissect; to lay open the interior structure for examining each part. **anatomist** *n.* [Gk. *ana*, up; *tome*, cutting].

an·ces·tor (an′·ses·ter) *n.* (*fem.***ancestress**) forefather; progenitor; forebear. **ancestral** *a.* **ancestry** *n.* lineage [L. *ante*, before; *cedere*, *cessum*, to go].

an·chor (ang′·ker) *n.* a heavy iron instrument by which a ship is held fast to the sea-bottom; a molder's chaplet; *v.t.* to place at anchor; to weight down; *v.i.* to cast anchor; to stop; **anchorage** *n.* a sheltered place where a ship may anchor; dues chargeable on ships which wish to anchor in harbor. **anchored** *a.* at anchor; firmly fixed. **to cast anchor,** to let down anchor. **to weigh anchor,** to raise anchor preparatory to sailing [L. *ancora*].

an·chor·ite, an·chor·et (ang′·ke·rīt, -ret) *n.* one who lives apart, renouncing the world for religious reasons; a hermit. **anchoress, anchoritess** *n.* a female hermit. **anchorage** *n.* home of anchorite [Gk. *anachoretes*, one who retires].

an·cho·vy (an′·chō·vi·; an·chō′·vi·) *n.* small fish of the herring family [Sp. *anchova*].

an·cient (ān′·shạnt) *a.* very old; antique; venerable; former; *n.* an aged or venerable person; one who lived in olden times. **-ly** *adv.* **-ness** *n.* **-ry** *n.* ancestry; seniority [L. *ante*, before].

an·cil·lar·y (an′·sạl·er·i·) *a.* giving help to; attending upon; auxiliary; subordinate [L. *ancilla*, a maid-servant].

and (and) *conj.* added to; together with; a word that joins words, clauses, or sentences [O.E.].

an·dan·te (an·dan′·ti·, ȧn·dàn′·ti·) *a.* or *adv.* (*Mus.*) moving rather slowly, but in a steady, flowing manner, faster than *larghetto*, but slower than *allegretto*; *n.* a moderately slow, flowing movement [It. *andare*, to go].

and·i·ron (and′·ī·ẹrn) *n.* a utensil for supporting logs in a fireplace; a firedoy [O.Fr. *andier*].

an·dro·gen (an′·drạ·jạn) *n.* male sex hormone [Gk. *andros* man, and *gen*].

an·drog·y·nous (an·dráj′·i·nus) *a.* having the characteristics of both sexes; hermaphrodite. Also **androgynal. androgyny** *n.* [Gk. *aner, andros*, a man; *kephale*, the head; *gune*, a woman].

an·ec·dote (an′·ik·dōt) *n.* a biographical incident; a brief account of any fact or happening (often amusing); **anecdotage** *n.* anecdotes collectively. **anecdotal** *a.* **anecdotist** *n.* a writer or teller of anecdotes [Gk. *anekdotos*, not published].

an·e·lec·tric (an·i·lek′·trik) *a.* non-electric; *n.* a body that does not become electric; a conductor of electricity [Gk. *an-*, neg., and *electric*].

a·ne·mi·a (a·nē′·mi·ạ) *n.* Also **anaemia** (a·nē′·mi·a) *n.* disease characterized by a deficiency of blood or of hemoglobin. **anemic** *a.* [Gk. *an-*, neg.; *haima*, blood].

a·nem·o·ne (ạ·nem′·ạ·nē) *n.* plant of crowfoot family; wind-flower. **sea-anemone** *n.* name given to certain plant-like marine animals [Gk. *anemos*, wind].

a·nent (ạ·nent′) *prep.* concerning; about; in respect of; as to [O.E. *on; efen*, even].

an·e·roid (an′·e·roid) *a.* denoting a barometer

depending for its action on the pressure of the atmosphere on a metallic box almost exhausted of air, without the use of mercury or other fluid [Gk. *a-*, neg.; *neres*, wet; *eidos*, form].

an·es·the·sia, an·aes·the·sia (an·ạs·thē'·-zh·ạ) *n.* absence of sensibility to external impressions, particularly touch. Also **anesthesis. anesthetic** *n.* a drug which induces insensibility to pain; *a.* producing loss of feeling and sensation. **anesthetically** *adv.* **anesthetize** *v.t.* **anesthetist** *n.* [Gk. *an-*, not; *aisthesis*, feeling].

an·eu·rism (an'·yạ·rizm) *n.* (*Med.*) a local widening or dilatation in the course of an artery [Gk. *ana*, up; *eurus*, wide].

a·new (ạ·nū') *adv.* in a new form or manner; newly; over again; afresh [M.E. *of newe*].

an·gel (ān'·jel) *n.* a heavenly messenger; a spirit who conveys God's will to man; a guardian spirit; (*Colloq.*) a lovable person; a dear. **angel fish** *n.* a bright-colored tropical fish. **angel food cake** *n.* a spongy, light, white cake. **angelic(al)** (an·jel'·ic) *a.* like an angel. **angelically** *adv.* [Gk. *angelos*, a messenger].

an·ge·lus (an'·jạ·las) *n.* a short devotional service in the R.C. Church held morning, noon, and sunset; the bell rung to remind the faithful to recite the prayer [L.].

an·ger (ang'·gẹr) *n.* a strong passion or emotion excited by injury; rage; *v.t.* to excite to wrath; to enrage. **angry** (ang'·gri·) *a.* roused to anger; displeased; enraged; inflamed. **angrily** *adv.* **angriness** *n.* [O.N. *angr*, trouble].

an·gi·na (an·jī'·nạ, an'·ji·nạ) *n.* (*Med.*) inflammation of the throat, e.g., quinsy. **angina pectoris,** a heart disease characterized by attacks of agonizing pain [L.].

an·gi·o·sperm (an'·ji·ō·spurm) *n.* (*Bot.*) a plant whose seeds are enclosed in a seed-vessel [Gk. *nageion*, a vessel; *sperma*, a seed].

an·gle (ang'·gl) *n.* a fish-hook; a rod and line for fishing; *v.i.* to fish with rod, line, and hook; (*Fig.*) to use artifice. **angler** *n.* one who angles. **angling** *n.* [O.E. *angul*].

an·gle (ang'·gl) *n.* a corner; the point at which two lines meet; (*Geom.*) the amount of turning made by revolving a straight line in a plane, round a point in itself, from one direction to another. **acute angle,** one less than 90°. **obtuse angle,** greater than 90° but less than 180°. **right angle,** a quarter of a complete revolution, i.e. 90°. (*Fig.*) a point of view. [L. *angulus*, a corner].

An·gli·can (ang'·gli·cạn) *a.* English; of, or belonging to, Church of England; *n.* a member of Church of England. **Anglicanism** *n.* [L. *Angli*, the Angles].

an·gli·cize (ang'·glạ·sīz) *v.t.* to make or express in English idiom. **anglicism** *n.* an English idiom; an English custom or characteristic. **anglify** *v.t.* to make English [L. *Angli*, the Angles].

An·glo- (ang'·glō) *prefix* fr. L. *Anglus*, an Angle, combining to form many compound words. **Anglo-American** *a.* involving English and Americans. **Anglo-Saxon** *a.* pert. to Anglo-Saxons or their language; *n.* one of the nations formed by the union of the Angles, Saxons. **Anglophile** (ang'·glō·fīl) *a.* favoring anything English; *n.* a supporter of English customs, manners, or policy.

An·go·ra (ang·gō'·rạ) *n.* a Turkish province in Asia minor, famous for a breed of goats; cloth made from hair of these goats.

an·guish (ang'·gwish) *n.* acute pain of body or of mind; grief; anxiety; moral torment. **-ment** *n.* [L. *angustia*, straitness].

an·gu·lar (ang'·gū·lạr) *a.* having angles; sharp-cornered; (of people) not plump; gawky; irascible. **angularity** *n.* **-ly** *adv.* **angulate** *a.* having angles [L. *angulus*, a corner].

an·hy·dride (an·hī'·drīd) *n.* (*Chem.*) a com-

pound formed from an acid by evaporation of water. **anhydrous** *a.* entirely without water [Gk. *an-*, neg.; *hudor*, water].

an·il (an'·il) *n.* a West Indian shrub from the leaves and stalks of which indigo is made. **aniline** (an'·il·in, or -in) *n.* a product orig. obtained from indigo, now mainly from coaltar, and used in the manufacture of brilliant dyes, colored inks, soaps, explosives, etc.; *a.* pert. to anil or aniline [Fr. fr. Sans. *nila*, dark blue].

an·ile (an'·īl) *a.* like an old woman; imbecile. **anility** *n.* senility [L. *anus*, an old woman].

an·i·mad·vert (an·i·mad·vurt') *v.t.* to turn the mind to; to consider disparagingly; to comment on censoriously; to reprove. **animadversion** *n.* [L. *animus*, the mind; *vertere*, to turn].

an·i·mal (an'·i·mạl) *n.* a living creature having sensation and power of voluntary motion; a living organism, distinct from plants; *a.* pert. to or got from animals. **-cule** *n.* a very minute animal (*pl.* **-cules** or **-cula**). **-culine** *a.* pert. to animalcula. **-ism** *n.* sensuality. — **magnetism,** mesmerism, hypnotism. — **spirits,** natural buoyance [L. *anima*, breath].

an·i·mate (an'·i·māt) *v.t.* to give natural life to; to endow with spirit or vigor; to energize; to inspire; to make alive; *a.* living or organic. **-d** *a.* **-dly** *adv.* **animating** *a.* inspiring. **animation** *n.* the state of possessing life or spirit; vivacity. **animator** *n.* one who or that which animates; a movie cartoonist [L. *animatus*, filled with life].

an·i·mism (an'·i·mizm) *n.* the belief that all forms of organic life have their origin in the soul; that all natural objects have a soul. **animist** *n.* **animistic** *a.* [L. *anima*, life or soul].

an·i·mos·i·ty (an·i·màs'·i·ti·) *n.* violent hatred; active enmity; acrimony; orig. meant courage [L. *animosus*, full of spirit].

an·i·mus (an'·i·mạs) *n.* animosity; temper; grudge; (*Law*) intention, purpose [L. *animus*, spirit, temper].

an·ise (an'·is) *n.* an herb with pungent smell and bearing aromatic seeds. **aniseed** *n.* seed of anise used for flavoring and in manufacture of liqueurs [Gk. *anis*].

an·kle (ang'·kl) *n.* the joint connecting the foot with the leg. **anklet** *n.* a sock which reaches just above the ankle; an ornament for the ankle [M.E. *ancle*].

an·nals (an'·alz) *n.pl.* history of events recorded each year; a yearly chronicle. **annalize** *v.t.* to write annals; to record chronologically. **annalist** *n.* [L. *annus*, a year].

an·neal (ạ·nēl') *v.t.* to heat, and then cool slowly, for the purpose of rendering less brittle; to heat in order to fix colors. **-ing** *n.* [O.E. *an; aclan*, to kindle].

an·nex (an'·eks) *v.t.* to unite at the end; to subjoin; to bind to; to take additional territory under control; *n.* something joined on; building attached to, or sufficiently near, main building to be considered part of it. **annexation** *n.* the act of annexing; what is annexed. **annexion, annexment** *n.* [L. *ad*, to; *nectere*, to bind].

an·ni·hi·late (ạ·nī'·hil·āt) *v.t.* to reduce to nothing; to destroy; to make null and void. **annihilable** *a.* **annihilation** *n.* **annihilator** *n.* [L. *ad*, to; *nihil*, nothing].

an·ni·ver·sa·ry (an·i·vur'·sạ·ri·) *a.* yearly; annual; *n.* day on which event is yearly celebrated [L. *annus*, year; *vertere*, to turn].

an·no·tate (an'·ō·tāt) *v.t.* to mark in writing; to write explanatory notes, esp. upon literary text. **annotation** *n.* a written commentary. **annotator** *n.* **annotatory** *a.* [L. *annatotus*, marked with notes].

an·nounce (ạ·nouns') *v.t.* to give first public notice of; to proclaim; to promulgate; to publish. **-ment** *n.* giving public notice; proclamation; declaration. **-r** *n.* a broadcasting official who gives the news, etc. [L. *ad*, to; *nuntiare*, to announce].

an·noy (ạ·noi′) v.t. to injure, disturb continually; to torment; tease; vex; pester; molest; trouble. **-ance** n. [fr. L. *in odio*, in hatred].

an·nu·al (an′·ū·ạl) a. yearly; performed in the course of a year; n. a periodical published once a year; a plant which completes its life-cycle within a year. **-ly** adv. [L. *annus*, a year].

an·nu·i·ty (ạ·nū′·i·ti·) n. a fixed sum of money payable each year for a number of years, or for life. **annuitant** n. one in receipt of an annuity [L. *annus*, a year].

an·nul (ạ·nul′) v.t. to make void; to nullify; repeal; cancel; pr.p. **-ling**; pa.t. and pa.p. **-led**. **-ment** n. [L. *ad*, to; *nullus*, none].

an·nu·lar (an′·ū·lạr) a. ring-shaped; like a ring. **annulated** a. having rings or belts. **annulet** n. a little ring. **annularly** adv. **annulose** a. ringed. **annulation** n. ring-like formation [L. *annulus*, a ring].

an·num (a′·nạm) n. year [L.].

an·nun·ci·ate (ạ·nun′·sī·āt) v.t. to announce; to make known; to proclaim. **annunciation** n. an announcing; (cap.) a holy day (March 25) in R.C. Church. **annunciator** n. **annunciatory** a. [L. *ad*, to; *nuntiare*, to announce].

an·ode (an′·ōd) n. positive electrode of a voltaic current; (Radio) plate of an electron tube [Gk. *anodos*, way up].

an·o·dyne (an′·ō·dīn) n. a drug or measures which relieve pain [Gk. *an-*, neg.; *odunē*, pain].

a·noint (ạ·noint′) v.t. to pour oil upon; to rub over with an ointment or oil; to consecrate by unction. **-ed** a. consecrated; n. a consecrated person. **-ment** n. consecration; a salve. **the Lord's anointed,** Christ [L. *in*, on; *ungere*, to anoint].

a·nom·a·ly (ạ·nàm′·ạ·li·) n. deviation from the common rule or type; irregularity. **anomalism** n. **anomalistic** a. **anomalous** a. irregular; incongruous [Gk. *anomalos*, not even].

a·non (ạ·nàn′) adv. quickly; at once; forthwith; soon. **ever and anon,** every now and then [O.E. *on*, in; *an*, one].

a·non·y·mous (ạ·nàn′·i·mạs) a. applied to a writing or work of which the author is not named. **anonym** n. one who remains anonymous. **-ly** adv. **anonymity** n. [Gk. *an-*, neg.; *onoma*, name].

a·noph·e·les (ạn·àf′·ạl·ēz) n. the mosquito carrying the parasite which causes malaria [Gk. *an-*, neg.; *ophelein*, benefit].

an·oth·er (ạ·nuTH′·ẹr) a. not the same; different; one more; pron. any one else [E.].

an·swer (an′·sẹr) v.t. to speak or write in return; to vindicate; to witness for; v.i. to reply; to suit; to suffer the consequence of; n. something said or written in return to a question, etc.; the solution of a problem; response. **-able** a. capable of being answered; responsible. **-er** n. **to answer for,** to be responsible for [O.E. *andswarian*, to swear back].

ant (ant) n. a small mebranous-winged insect living in colonies in wood or the ground; an emmet. **ant-bear** n. the great ant-eater of South America. **ant-eater** n. one of several quadrupeds, e.g. ant-bear, aardvark, that feed chiefly on ants. **ant-hill** n. a mound raised by a colony of ants or termites [O.E. *aemette*].

ant- (ant) a combining form fr. Gk. *anti*, against, used to form compounds. **-acid** (ant·-as′·id) a. counteracting acidity; n. a remedy for acidity of the stomach.

an·tag·o·nize (an·tag′·ạ·nīz) v.t. to contend violently against; to act in opposition; to oppose; to make hostile. **antagonism** n. opposition; hostility; hatred; dislike. **antagonist** n. **antagonistic** a. **antagonistically** adv. [Gk. *anti*, against; *agon*, a contest].

ant·arc·tic (ant·àrk′·tik) a. opposite to arctic pole; relating to southern pole or region near it [Gk. *anti*, against; E. *arctic*].

an·te (an′·te) n. in poker, a player's stake [L. *ante*, before].

an·te- (an′·te) prefix fr. L. *ante*, meaning *before* (place, time, or order), combining to form derivatives. **antebellum** a. [L.] before the war (esp. U.S. Civil War). **antecedent** (an·tạ·sēd′·ạnt) a. going before in time, place, rank, etc.; preceding; prior; n. that which goes before; (Gram.) the noun or pronoun to which a relative refers. **antichamber** n. a chamber leading to the chief apartment. **antecursor** n. a forerunner [L. *cedere*, to go; *camera*, a room; *currere*, to run].

an·te-date (an′·tạ·dāt) v.t. to date before the true time; to precede in time [L. *ante*, before, E. *date*].

an·te·di·lu·vi·an. (an·tạ·di·lóo′·vi·ạn) a. pert. to before the Flood; ancient; antiquated [L. *ante*, before; *diluvium*, a flood].

an·te·lope (an′·tạ·lōp) n. (pl. **-lope, lopes**) a hoofed ruminant, notable for its graceful and agile movement [Gk. *antholops*].

an·te·me·rid·i·an (an·te·mẹ·rid′·i·ạn) a. before noon (abbrev. **a.m.**) [L. *ante meridiem* = before midday, the period of time between midnight and noon].

an·ten·na (an·ten′·ạ) n. feeler of an insect, crustacean, etc. pl. **antennae** (an·ten′·ē). **antenna** n. (Radio) a wire for sending or receiving electric waves; an aerial. pl. **antennas. -ry** a. [L. *antenna*, a sailyard].

an·te·pe·nult (an·te·pē′·nạlt) n. last syllable but two of word. **antepenultimate** a. [L. *ante*, before; *paene*, almost; *ultimus*, last].

an·te·ri·or (an·tē′·ri·ẹr) a. before; occurring earlier. **anteriority** n. [L. *ante*, before].

an·te·room (an′·te·ròòm) n. a room giving entry to another [L. *ante*, before; E. *room*].

an·them (an′·thạm) n. a hymn sung in alternate part; Church music adapted to passages from the Scriptures; song of praise [Gk. *antiphonon*, a response sung].

an·ther (an′·thẹr) n. the little sac in a flower, containing the pollen or fertilizing dust. **-al** a. [Gk. *antheros*, flowery].

an·thol·o·gy (an·thàl′·ạ·ji·) n. orig. a collection of flowers; a collection of literary passages or poetry. **anthologist** n. [Gk. *anthos*, a flower; *legein*, to gather].

an·thra·cene (an′·thrạ·sēn) n. product from distillation of coal-tar, used in manufacture of dyes. **anthracite** n. coal, nearly pure carbon, burning without smoke or flame [Gk. *anthrax*, coal].

an·thrax (an′·thrax) n. a carbuncle; a malignant disease in cattle and sheep; a malignant pustule [Gk. *anthrax*, coal].

an·thro·po- (an′·thrạ·pō) prefix fr. Gr. *anthropos*, meaning man, combining to form derivatives. **anthropogency** (·poj′·en·i·) n. science of development of man. **anthropoid** a. man-like [Gk. *genesthai*, to be born; *graphein*, to write; *eidos*, form; *lithos*, a stone].

an·thro·pol·o·gy (an·thrạ·pàl′·ạ·ji·) n. study of man, including all aspects of his evolution, physical and social. **anthropological** a. **anthropologically** adv. **anthropologist** n. [Gk. *anthropos*, man; *logos*, discourse].

an·thro·pom·e·try (an·thrạ·pàm′·e·tri·) n. the scientific measurement of the human body [Gk. *anthropos*, man; *metron*, a measure].

an·thro·po·mor·phism (an·thrạ·pạ·mawr′·-fizm) n. the conception of God as a human being with human attributes. **anthropomorphist** n. **anthropomorphize** v.t. to invest with human qualities. **anthropomorphic** a. [Gk. *anthropos*, man; *morphe*, form].

an·thro·po·mor·pho·sis (an·thrạ·pạ·mawr′·-fō·sis) n. transformation into human shape [Gk. *anthropos*, man; *morphe*, form].

an·ti- (an′·ti) prefix fr. Gk. *anti*, meaning *against, opposite, instead of*, combining to form derivations; contracted to **ant-** before a vowel. **anti-aircraft** a. used against aircraft.

an·ti·bi·ot·ic (an·ti·bī·àt′·ik) n. substance which acts as an antibacterial agent [Gk. *anti*, against; *bios*, life].

an·ti·bod·y (an'·ti·bàd·i·) *n.* a substance in blood which counteracts growth and harmful action of bacteria; anti-toxin.

an·tic (an'·tik) *a.* odd; fanciful; fantastic; grotesque; *n.* a buffoon; a comical trick or action [L. *antiquus*, old].

An·ti·christ (an'·ti·krīst) *n.* a name given in the New Testament to various incarnations of opposition to Christ.

an·tic·i·pate (an·tis'·ạ·pāt) *v.t.* to be before another; to be beforehand in thought or action; to enjoy prematurely; to forestall. **anticipant** *a.* anticipating; (*Med.*) occurring before the regular time. **anticipation** *n.* the act of anticipating. **anticipative** *a.* full of expectation. **anticipatively, anticipatorily** *adv.* **anticipatory** *a.* happening in advance [L. *ante*, before; *capere*, to take].

an·ti·cli·max (an·ti·klī'·maks) *n.* a sentence or figure of speech in which ideas are arranged in descending order of importance; opp. of *climax*; a sudden drop from the dignified to the trivial.

an·ti·cy·clone (an'·ti·sī'·klōn) *n.* an outward flow of air in a spiral movement (clockwise in N. Hemisphere, anti-clockwise in S. Hemisphere) from an atmospheric area of high pressure, tending to produce steady weather, frosty in winter, hot in summer.

an·ti·dote (an'·ti·dōt) *n.* a remedy which counteracts the effects of a poison; (*Fig.*) anything which counteracts evil. **antidotal** *a.* [Gk. *anti*, against; *doton*, given].

an·ti·freeze (an·ti·frēz') *n.* a substance added to water in automobile radiators to prevent freezing in very cold weather.

an·ti·gen (an'·ti·jạn) *n.* a substance, such as an anti-toxin, which can produce the formation of antibodies in the blood-stream [Gk. *anti*, against; *genesthai*, to be born].

an·ti·his·ta·mine (an·ti·his'·tạ·mēn) *n.* any of several drugs used to treat allergies.

an·ti·knock (an·ti·nạk') *n.* a substance added to fuel to eliminate or decrease the knocking noise in an internal-combustion engine.

an·ti·log·a·rithm (an·ti·làg'·ạ·rithm) *n.* the complement of a logarithm or of a sine, tangent, or secant; the number corresponding to a logarithm. (*Abbrev.*) **antilog.**

an·til·o·gy (an·til'·ạ·ji·) *n.* a contradiction in terms, or in two separate passages of a book. **antilogous** *a.* [Gk. *logos*, a discourse].

an·ti·ma·cas·sar (an·ti·ma·kas'·ẹr) *n.* an ornamental covering for chair backs, etc. [Gk. *Macassar oil* from Celebes].

an·ti·mo·ny (an'·ti·mōn·i·) *n.* a whitish, brittle chemical element; a bad conductor of heat, it is used as an alloy in medicine and the arts. **antimonial** *a.* **antimoniate** *n.* a salt of antimonic acid. **antimonic, antimonious** *a.* of or containing antimony. **antimonite** *n.* stibnite [L. *antimonium*, antimony].

an·ti·pas·to (àn·ti·pàs'·tō) *n.* an appetizer course; hors d'oeuvres [It.].

an·tip·a·thy (an·tip'·ạ·thi·) *n.* opposition; aversion; dislike; enmity; hatred. **antipathetical** *a.* **antipathic** *a.* hostile to; having an opposite nature. **antipathist** *n.* [Gk. *anti*, against; *pathos*, feeling].

an·ti·phon, an·tiph·o·ny (an'·ti·fàn) (an·tif'·ạ·ni·) *n.* the chant, or alternate singing, in choirs; an anthem; a response. **-al** *a.; n.* a book of antiphons. **-ally** *adv.* **-ic, -ical** *a.* [doublet of *anthem*].

an·ti·phra·sis (an·tif'·rạ·sis) *n.* (*Rhet.*) use of words in a sense opposite to their proper meaning. **antiphrastic, antiphrastical** *a.* pert. to antiphrasis. **antiphrastically** *adv.* [Gk. *anti*, against; *phrazein*, speak].

an·tip·o·des (an·tip'·ạ·dēz) *n.pl.* those living on opposite side of globe; regions directly opposite any given point on globe; (*Fig.*) anything diametrically opposed to anything else [Gk. *anti*, against; *pous*, a foot].

an·ti·pope (an'·ti·pōp) *n.* one who usurps the papal office; rival to Pope properly elected by Cardinals. **antipapal** *a.*

an·ti·py·ret·ic (an·ti·pī·ret'·ik) *n.* any agent which lowers temperature in fevers; *a.* counteracting fever [Gk. *anti*, against; *puretos*, fever].

an·tique (an·tēk') *a.* ancient; old-fashioned; obsolete; aged; *n.* relic of bygone times; ancient work of art; the style of ancient art. **antiquarian** *n.* student of antiquity or antiquities; a collector of relics of former times; *a.* pert. to old times or objects; out-of-date; obsolete. **antiquarianism** *n.* study of antiquities. **antiquary** *n.* an antiquarian. **antiquate** *v.t.* to render obsolete. **antiquated** *a.* very old; out of date. **antiquity** *n.* ancient times; former ages; great age; the people of ancient times. **antiquities** *n.pl.* the remains and relics of ancient times; manners and customs of ancient times [Fr. fr. L. *antiquus*, ancient].

an·ti·sem·i·tism (an·ti·sem'·i·tizm) *n.* widespread outburst of hatred against members of the Hebrew race leading to persecution. **antisemite** *n.* one animated with hatred against the Jews. **anti-semitic** *a.*

an·ti·sep·sis (an·ti·sep'·sis) *n.* prevention of sepsis; destruction or arresting of growth of living micro-organisms which cause putrefaction. **antiseptic** *n.* a disinfectant; a substance which destroys bacteria; *a.* [Gk. *anti*, against; *sepsis*, putrefaction].

an·ti·so·cial (an·ti·sō'·shạl) *a.* averse to social intercourse; opposed to social order.

an·ti·the·ism (an·ti·thē'·izm) *n.* opposition to the belief in the existence of God. **antitheist** *n.* **antitheistic** *a.*

an·tith·e·sis (an·tith'·ạ·sis) *n.* a direct opposition of words or ideas; a figure in rhetoric in which words or thoughts are set in contrast. *pl.* **antitheses. antithetic, antithetical** *a.* [Gk. *anti*, opposite; *thesis*, placing].

an·ti·tox·in (an·ti·tạk'·sin) *n.* a toxin which neutralizes another toxin in the blood serum. **antitoxic** *a.* [Gk. *anti*, against; *toxikon*, arrow-poison].

an·ti·trust (an·ti·trust') *a.* opposed to trusts or monopolies.

ant·ler (ant'·lẹr) *n.* a horn of an animal of the deer family. **-ed** *a.* [L. *ante*, before; *oculus*, the eye].

an·to·nym (an'·tạ·nim) *n.* a word of contrary meaning; the opposite of *synonym* [Gk. *anti*, against; *onoma*, a name].

an·trum (an'·trum) *n.* a cavity, esp. sinus of the upper jaw. *pl.* **antra** [Gk. *ántron*].

a·nus (ā'·nus) *n.* the lower orifice of the alimentary canal [L.].

an·vil (an'·vil) *n.* an iron block, usually steel-faced, upon which blacksmith's forgings are hammered and shaped. **-led** *a.* [O.E. *anfilte*].

anx·i·e·ty (ang·zi'·e·ti·) *n.* distress of mind; disquietude; uneasiness; eagerness (to serve, etc.). **anxious** (angk'·shạs) *a.* uneasy; eager. **anxiously** *adv.* [L. *anxius*, anxious].

an·y (en'·i·) *a.* one out of many; some; *adv.* to any extent; at all. **-body** *n.* any person; an ordinary person. **-how** *adv.* at any rate; in a careless manner; in any case. **-one** *pron.* any person. **-thing** *n.* any one thing, no matter what. **-way,** *adv.* in any way or manner; anyhow; carelessly. **-where** *adv.* in any place. **-wise** in any way or respect [O.E. *an*, one].

A-one (ā'·wun') *a.* (*Colloq.*) first class, excellent.

a·or·ta (ā·awr'·tạ) *n.* the great artery leading from the left ventricle of the heart. **aortal, aortic** *a.* [Gk. *aorte*].

a·pace (ạ·pās') *adv.* at a quick pace; hastily; swiftly; fast [*a-* and *pace*, at a walk].

A·pach·e (ạ·pa'·chi·) *n.* one of a tribe of American Indians. **apache** (ạ·pàsh') *n.* a bandit of the Paris underworld, a street hooligan [Amer. Ind. *e patch*, an enemy].

ap·a·nage See **appanage**.

a·part (a·pàrt') *adv.* separately; aside, asunder; at a distance [Fr. *à part*, aside].

a·part·heid (a·pàrt'·hād) *n.* racial segregation [S. Afr.].

a·part·ment (a·pàrt'·ment) *n.* a room in a house; a suite of rooms; lodgings [Fr. *appartement*, a suite of rooms].

ap·a·thy (ap'·ath·i·) *n.* want of feeling; indifference. **apathetic** *a.* void of feeling; indifferent; insensible [Gr. *c-*, neg.; *pathos*, feeling].

ape (āp) *n.* a monkey, esp. one without a tail; one of the larger species, e.g. chimpanzee, gorilla, etc.; a mimic; *v.t.* to imitate; to mimic. **-r** *n.* one who apes; a servile imitator. **apery** *n.* mimicry. **apish** *a.* ape-like; inclined to imitate in a foolish manner [O.E. *apa*].

a·pe·ri·tif (a·pā'·rē·tif) *n.* alcoholic drink taken before meals [L. *aperire*, to open].

ap·er·ture (a'·per·cher) *n.* an opening; a hole [L. *aperire*, to open].

a·pex (ā'·peks) *n.* the top, peak, or summit of anything. *pl.* **apexes** or **apices**.

a·pha·sia (a·fā'·zi·a) *n.* loss of power of expressing ideas in words, often due to brain disease; loss of power of remembering words. **aphasic** *a.* [Gk. *a-*, neg.; *phasis*, speech].

ap·er·ture (a'·per·cher) *n.* an opening; a hole

a·phe·li·on (a·fē'·li·an) *n.* point of planet's orbit most distant from sun [Gk. *apo*, away; *helios*, the sun].

aph·o·rism (af'·er·izm) *n.* a pithy saying; a maxim. **aphoristic** *a.* **aphoristically** *adv.* **aphorize** *v.t.* and *i.* to make or use aphorisms. **aphorist** *n.* [Gk. *aphorismos*, a definition].

a·phra·sia (a·frā'·zi·a) *n.* inability to use connected language; speechlessness [Gk. *a-*, neg.; *phrasis*, speech].

Aph·ro·di·te (af·ra·dī'·tē) *n.* (*Myth.*) the Greek goddess of love and beauty. **aphrodisiac** (af·rō·diz'·i·ak) *a.* exciting sexual desire; *n* anything which so excites.

a·pi·ar·y (ā'·pi·er·i·) *n.* place where bees are kept. **apiarian** (ā·pi·e'·ri·an) *a.* pert. to bees or to bee-keeping. **apiarist** *n.* one who keeps or studies bees. **apiculture** *n.* [L. *apis*, a bee].

a·piece (a·pēs') *adv.* for each one; to each one [orig. two words].

a·plomb (a·plàm') *n.* perpendicularity; uprightness; (*Fig.*) self-assurance; coolness [L. *ad*, to; *plumbum*, lead].

a·poc·a·lypse (a·pàk'·a·lips) *n.* an unveiling of hidden things; revelation; disclosure **Apocalypse** *n.* (*Bib.*) the last book of the New Testament, called the Revelation of St. John. **apocalyptic, -al** pert. to revelation; of style, allegorical; obscure. **apocalyptically** *adv.* [Gk. *apokalupsis*, unveiling].

a·poc·ry·pha (a·pàk'·ri·fa) *n.pl.* originally hidden or secret things not suitable to be seen by the uninitiated. **Apocrypha** *n.pl.* (*Bib.*) the collective name for the fourteen books not included in the Old Testament, but incorporated in the Vulgate of the R.C. Church. **apocryphal** *a.* spurious; unauthentic; pert. to the Apocrypha [Gk. *apo*, away; *kruptein*, to hide].

a·pod·o·sis (a·pàd'·a·sis) *n.* (*Gram.*) the clause, in a conditional sentence, which expresses result as distinct from the *protasis*. *pl.* **apodoses** [Gk. *apo*, back; *didonai*, to give].

ap·o·gee (ap'·a·jē) *n.* that point in the orbit of a heavenly body at the greatest distance from the earth (opposed to *perigee*); the culmination; highest point; zenith. **apogeal** (ap·a·jē'·al), **apogean** *a.* [Gk. *apo*, from; *ge*, the earth].

ap·o·logue (ap'·a·lawg) *n.* a parable; a fable [Gk. *apo*, from; *logos*, speech].

a·pol·o·gy (a·pàl'·a·ji·) *n.* something spoken in defense; expression of regret at offense; an excuse; a poor substitute (with for). **apologize** *v.i.* to make an apology, or excuse; to express regret. **apologist** *n.* one who makes an apology; a defender of a cause. **apologetic**

(a·pàl·a·jet'·ik), **apologetical** *a.* **apologetically** *adv.* **apologetics** *n.* the branch of theology charged with the defense of Christianity. **apologia** (ap·a·lō·ji·a) *n.* a defense in writing of the author's principles, etc. [Gk. *apologia*, a speaking away].

ap·o·thegm (a'·pa·thèm) *n.* a short, pithy saying; a maxim; a proverb. **apothegmatic** (a·pa·theg·mat'·ik), **apothegmatical** *a.* [Gk. *apo*, from; *phthengesthai*, to utter].

ap·o·plex·y (ap'·a·plek·si·) *n.* a sudden loss of consciousness, sensation, and voluntary motion, due generally to rupture of a blood-vessel in the brain. **apoplectic** *a.* [Gk. *apoplexia*].

a·pos·ta·sy, a·pos·ta·cy (a·pàs'·ta·si·) *n.* the act of renouncing one's faith, principles, or party; desertion of a cause. **apostate** *n.* renegade; traitor; deserter; *a.* false; traitorous. **apostatic, -al** *a.* **apostatize** *v.i.* to abandon one's faith [Gk. *apo*, apart; *stasis*, a standing].

a·pos·te·ri·o·ri (à·pàs·tir'·i·ōr·i) from effect to cause [L. from the subsequent].

a·pos·tle (a·pàs'·l) *n.* one sent out to preach or advocate a cause; one of the twelve disciples of Christ sent to preach the Gospel. **apostolate** (a·pàs'·ta·lat) *n.* the office or dignity or mission of an apostle. **apostolic, apostolical** *a.* **apostolically** *adv.* **apostolicism** *n.* **Apostles' Creed,** creed supposedly used by apostles, summarizing Christian faith. **Apostolic Church,** church derived from, and incorporating the spirit of, the apostles. **Apostolic see,** the jurisdiction of the Pope. **Apostolic succession,** the derivation of spiritual authority in an unbroken line from the Apostles, through bishops [Gk. *apo*, away; *stellein*, to send].

a·pos·tro·phe (a·pas'·tra·fi) *n.* an address delivered to the absent or the dead, or to an inanimate thing, as if present; a mark (') indicating possessive case, or omission of one or more letters of a word. **apostrophic** *a.* **apostrophize** *v.t.* and *i.* to address by, or to use, apostrophe [Gk. *apostrophē*, a turning away].

a·poth·e·car·y (a·pàth'·a·ker·i·) *n.* one who prepares or sells drugs for medicines [Gk. *apothēkē*, a store house].

a·poth·e·o·sis (a·pà·thi·ō'·sis or a·pà·thē'·a·sis) *n.* the act of raising a mortal to the rank of the gods; deification. **apotheosize** *v.t.* to exalt to the dignity of a god [Gk. *apo*, apart; *theos*, a god].

ap·pall (a·pawl') *v.t.* to overwhelm with sudden fear; to confound; to scare; to terrify; **-ing** *a.* shocking. [O.Fr. *apalir*, to make pale].

ap·pa·ra·tus (ap·a·rā'·tas or ·rat'·as) *n.* things provided as a means to an end; collection of implements or utensils for effecting an experiment, or given work. *s.* and *pl.* [L. *ad*, to; *parare*, to prepare].

ap·par·el (a·par'·el) *n.* clothing; dress; garments; (*Naut.*) rigging, etc.; *v.t.* to dress; *pr.p.* [O.Fr. *apareiller*, to dress].

ap·par·ent (a·par'·ant) *a.* visible; evident; obvious. **-ly** *adv.* [L. *apparere*, to appear].

ap·pa·ri·tion (ap·a·rish'·an) *n.* appearance (esp. inexplicable); ghost. **-al** *a.* [Fr. fr. L. *apparitio*, appearance].

ap·peal (a·pēl') *v.i.* to invoke; to call to witness; to solicit aid; (*Law*) to reopen a case before a higher court; to be pleasing to mind or senses. *n.* an urgent call for sympathy or aid; personal attraction. **-able, -ing** *a.* **-ingly** *adv.* **-ingness** *n.* [O.Fr. *apeler*, to call].

ap·pear (a·pēr') *v.i.* to come in sight; to become visible; to seem; to be obvious or manifest. **-ance** *n.* a coming in sight; semblance; outward look or show; likeness; personal presence. **-er** *n.* [L. *apparere*, to appear].

ap·pease (a·pēz') *v.t.* to quiet; to calm; to pacify; to satisfy (hunger, etc.); to dispel anger or hatred. **appeasable** *a.* **-ment** *n.* pacifying; policy of making substantial concessions in order to preserve peace. **-r** *n.* [Fr. *apaiser*; O.Fr. *a pais*, at peace].

ap·pel·lant (ạ·pel′·ạnt) n. (Law) one who appeals to a higher court against the verdict of a lower tribunal; one who makes any appeal. **appellancy** n. an appeal. **appellate** a. (Law) pert. to appeals; having power to hear and give decision on appeals. **appellation** n. name; title; designation. **appellational** a. **appellative** a. naming; common to many; pert. to the common noun; n. common noun as distinct from proper noun. **appellatively** adv. **appellee** n. (Law) the defendant in an appeal [L. appellare, to call].

ap·pend (ạ·pend′) v.t. to hang or attach to; to add. -**age** n. something added. -**ant** n. an adjunct or unessential thing; a. hanging to; annexed [L. appendere, to hang on].

ap·pen·di·ci·tis (ạ·pen·di·sī′·tis) n. (Path.) inflammation of the appendix vermiformis. **appendectomy** (a·pen·dek′·tạ·mi·) n. surgical removal of appendix [fr. appendix].

ap·pen·di·cle (ạ·pen′·di·kl) n. a small appendage. **appendicular** a. [L. appendicula].

ap·pen·dix (ạ·pen′·diks) n. thing added; an adjunct; supplement at end of book; (Med.) the blind tube extending from caecum into pelvis. pl. -**es, appendices** [L. ad, to; pendere, to hang].

ap·per·cep·tion (ap·ẹr·sep′·shạn) n. (Philos.) an act of voluntary consciousness; a mental perception of self as a conscious agent; spontaneous thought [L. ad, to; percipere, perceptum, to perceive].

ap·per·tain (ap·ẹr·tān′) v.i. to belong by nature; to relate. -**ing** a. -**ment** n. **appertinent** (ạ·pur′·tạ·nạnt) a. belonging to [L. ad, to; pertinere, to belong].

ap·pe·tite (ap′·ạ·tīt) n. desire as for food, drink, rest, etc. **appetitive** a. **appetize** v.t. to create an appetite. **appetizer** n. something taken before a meal to create appetite. **appetizing** a. [L. ad, to; petere, to seek].

ap·plaud (ạ·plawd′) v.t. and v. i. to praise by clapping; to acclaim; commend; extol. -**er** n. **applause** n. approval publicly expressed [L. ad, to; plaudere, to clap].

ap·ple (ap′·l) n. fruit of the apple-tree; the apple-tree. —**faced,** —**cheeked** a. of rosy hue. chubby. — **jack** n. brandy distilled from hard cider. — **pie order,** perfect order. — **polisher** n. (slang) flatterer, one who seeks favors by gifts, etc. [O.E. aeppel].

ap·pli·ance See under **apply.**

ap·pli·cant (ap′·li·kạnt) n. one who applies; a candidate; a petitioner. **applicability** n. the quality of being suitable. **applicable** a. suitable; adapted. **applicableness** n. **applicably** adv. **applicate** a. applied or put to some use. **application** n. the act of applying; the thing applied; close attention. **applicatory** a. [L. applicare, to attach to].

ap·plied (a·plīd′) pa.p. and pa.t. of **apply.**

ap·pli·qué (ap·li·kā′) n. any ornamentation, sewn or fixed on a material or metal [Fr.].

ap·ply (ạ·plī′) v.t. to place one thing upon another; to employ for a particular purpose; to fix the attention upon; to administer a remedy; v.i. to agree with; to be relevant; to have recourse to; to become a candidate. **appliance** n. act of applying; thing applied; an instrument or tool [L. ad, to; plicare, to fold].

ap·point (ạ·point′) v.t. to set apart; to assign; to ordain; to decree; to designate for an office; to fix (a date); to equip. -**ed** a. established, furnished. -**ee** n. the person appointed. -**ment** n. the act of appointing; a new situation; date. -**ments** n.pl. equipment; furnishings; fittings [Fr. à point, fitly].

ap·por·tion (ạ·pôr′·shạn) v.t. to divide and share in just proportion. -**ment** n. [L. ad, to; portio, a share].

ap·po·site (ap′·ạ·zit) a. appropriate; well adapted. -**ly** adv. -**ness** n. **apposition** (ap·ạ··zish′·ạn) n. the act of placing beside; (Gram.) the relation to a noun (or pronoun) of a noun,

adjective, or clause, added by way of explanation. **appositional** a. [L. appositus, put near].

ap·praise (ạ·prāz′) v.t. to put a price upon; to fix the value of. **appraisal** n. the act of appraising; a valuation. -**ment** n. -**r** n. **appraising** a. [L. ad, to; pretium, price].

ap·pre·ci·ate (ạ·prē′·shi·āt) v.t. to value justly; v.i. to rise in value. **appreciation** (ạ·prē·-shi·ā′·shạn) n. the setting of a value on; a just estimate; rise in value. **appreciative, appreciatory** a. **appreciatively** adv. **appreciable** a. that may be estimated. **appreciably** adv. [L. ad, to; pretium, price].

ap·pre·hend (ap·ri·hend′) v.t. to seize; to arrest; to understand; to fear. **apprehensible** a. **apprehension** n. **apprehensive** a. filled with dread; suspicious. **apprehensively** adv. [L. ad, to; prehendere, to grasp].

ap·pren·tice (ạ·pren′·tis) n. one bound to another to learn a trade or art; beginner; v.t. to bind as apprentice. -**ship** n. [L. ad, to; prehendere, to grasp].

ap·prise (ạ·prīz′) v.t. to inform; to tell; to give notice [Fr. apprendre, to inform].

ap·proach (ạ·prōch′) v.i. to come near; v.t. to come near to; to enter into negotiations with; to resemble; (Golf) to play a shot intended to reach the green; n. the act of drawing near; access; a road; approximation; negotiation. -**es** n.pl. the works thrown up by besiegers in their advances towards a fortress. -**able** a. accessible. -**ability** n. [L. ad, to; prope, near].

ap·pro·ba·tion (ap·rạ·bā′·shạn) n. approval; sanction. **approbate** v.t. to approve of. **approbative, approbatory** a. approving [L. ad, to; probare, to test].

ap·pro·pri·ate (ạ·prō′·pri·āt) v.t. to take as one's own; to set apart for a particular purpose; to claim; a. suitable; fitting. -**ly** adv. -**ness** n. **appropriation** n. the act of setting apart. **appropriative** a. **appropriator** n. [L. ad, to; proprius, one's own].

ap·prove (ạ·prò͞ov′) v.t. to be pleased with; to commend; to accept; to sanction officially. **approval** n. **approving** a. [L. ad, to; probare, to test].

ap·prox·i·mate (ạ·pråk′·si′·māt) v.t. to come near to; to bring near; a. near to; nearly correct; not quite exact. -**ly** adv. **approximation** n. a coming near; a close estimate [L. ad, to; proximus, near].

ap·pur·te·nance (ạ·pur′·tạ·nạns) n. that which appertains or is annexed to another thing; adjunct; accessory. **appurtenant** a. [O.Fr. apartenance, a belonging].

a·pri·cot (ā′·pri·kåt) n. an oval, orange-yellow fruit [L. praecox, early ripe].

A·pril (ā′·pril) n. the fourth month of the year [L. Aprilis, fr. aperire, to open].

à pri·o·ri (ā·pri·ō′·ri·) from cause to effect [L. from something prior].

a·pron (ā′·prạn) n. a covering or protection worn in front to protect the clothes; concrete-surfaced area in front of aircraft hangar [O.Fr. naperon, a cloth].

a·pro·pos (a·prạ·pō′) adv. at the right time; adj. apt, relevant [Fr.].

apse (aps) n. semi-circular recess at east end of church. **apsidal** a. [Gk. hapsis, loop].

ap·sis (ap′·sis) n. the point at which a planet is nearest to, or farthest from, the sun; pl. **apsides** (ap′·si·dēz). **apsidal** a. [Gk. hapsis, a loop, a vault].

apt (apt) a. fit; suitable; prompt; quick-witted. -**ly** adv. **aptitude** n. natural capacity for; suitableness; faculty for learning; talent. -**ness** n. fitness; appropriateness [L. aptus, fit].

aq·ua (ak′·wạ, ā′·kwa) n. L. = water. **aqua fortis** n. nitric acid. **aqua pura,** pure water. **aqua vitae,** any distilled alcoholic liquor.

aq·ua·ma·rine (ak·wa·ma·rēn′) n. a semi-precious stone; a. of a sea-green color [L. aqua, water; mare, the sea].

aq·ua·plane (ak'·wạ·plān) n. a plank or boat towed by a fast motor-boat [L. *aqua*, water; *planus*, flat].

a·quar·i·um (ạ·kwā'·ri·ạm) n. a glass tank in which is kept living specimens of water animals and plants; pl. **-s**, or **aquaria** [L. *aqua*, water].

A·quar·i·us (ạ·kwā'·ri·us) n. (*Astron.*) the Waterbearer, the 11th sign of the Zodiac.

a·quat·ic (ạ·kwat'·ik) a. growing or living in water; practiced on, or in, water [L. *aqua*, water].

aq·ua·tint (ak'·wạ·tint) n. an etching process; v.i. [L. *aqua*, water, and *tint*].

aq·ue·duct (ak'·we·dukt) n. a course, channel, or bridge for conveying water either under or above ground [L. *aqua*, water; *ducere*, to lead].

a·que·ous (ā'·kwi·ạs) a. watery; made of, or from, water. **-ly** adv. [L. *aqua*, water; *ferre*, to bear].

aq·ui·line (ak'·wi·līn, ·lin) a. belonging to the eagle; curving; hooked like the beak of an eagle [L. *aquila*, an eagle].

Ar·ab (ar'·ạb) n. native of Arabia; an Arab horse. **street arab**, a homeless urchin of the streets. **Arabian** (ạ·rā'·bi·ạn) n. the native of Arabia; a. relating to Arabia. **Arabic** (ar'·a·bik) n. the language of the Arabians.

ar·a·besque (ar·ạ·besk') n. an ornament after the Arabian manner, with intricate interlacing of foliage, fruits, etc. **arabesqued** a. [It. *Arabesco*, Arabian-like]. [L. *arare*, to plough].

ar·a·ble (ar'·ạ·bl) a. fit for ploughing or tillage

a·rach·nid (a·rak'·nid) n. one of the *Arachnida*, the spiders, scorpions, mites, etc. **arachnoid** a. resembling *Arachnida*; cobweb-like. **arachnoidal** a. [Gk. *arachne*, a spider].

ar·bi·ter (ár'·bi·tẹr) n. (*fem.* **arbitress**) an umpire; a judge in a dispute; one who has supreme control. **arbitrable** a. capable of settlement by discussion. **arbitrage** n. **arbitral** a. pertaining to an arbiter or arbitration. **arbitrament** n. decision; authoritative judgment; award of arbitration. **arbitrary** a. guided by will only; high-handed; despotic; absolute. **arbitrarily** adv. **arbitrariness** n. **arbitrate** v.t. and v.i. to hear and give an authoritative decision in a dispute. **arbitration** n. a method of settling disputes between persons, parties and nations by an agreement on both sides to accept the findings of a third party. **arbitrator** n. (*fem.* **arbitratrix**) a referee; an umpire [L. *arbiter*, a judge].

ar·bor (ár'·bẹr) n. the Latin word for a *tree*. **arboraceous** a. tree-like; wooded; **arboreal** a. living in trees. **arboreous** a. wooded. **arborescent** a. growing like a tree. **arboretum** n. botanical garden for special planting and growing of trees; (pl. **arboreta**). **arborous** a. formed by trees [L. *arbor*, a tree].

ar·bor (ár'·bẹr) n. a garden seat sheltered or enclosed by trees; a bower; a shady retreat. [L. *arbor*, a tree].

ar·bu·tus (ár·bū'·tạs) n. evergreen shrub with scarlet berries. [L. *arbutus*, the wild strawberry tree].

arc (árk) n. a curved line or any part of a curve forming segment of a circle; the arc-shaped band of light formed by passage of an electric current between two carbon points. **— lamp**, n. an electric lamp making use of electric arc, used in spotlights, searchlights, etc. **— welding**, n. a method of joining metals by use of electric arc [L. *arcus*, bow].

ar·cade (ár·kād') n. a series of arches, generally supported by pillars; a walk, arched above; a covered street, usually with shops on both sides [L. *arcus*, bow].

Ar·ca·di·a (ár·kā'·di·ạ) n. region in the Peloponnesus conceived by poets to be a land of shepherds and shepherdesses. **Arcadian** a. **Arcady** n. an ideal rustic place.

ar·ca·num (ár·kā'·num) n. a secret; mystery.

pl. **arcana** [L. *arcanum*, secret].

arch (árch) a. cunning; sly; mischievous; roguish. **-ness** n. [Gk. *archein*, to rule].

arch (árch) prefix used as a. chief; first of a class, as in *arch-bishop*, etc. **-angel** n. an angel of supreme order. **-deacon** n. a Church dignitary next below bishop. **-duke** n. a grand duke. **-duchess** n. **-duchy** n. the territory of an archduke. **-ducal** a. **-enemy** n. chief enemy [Gk. *archein*, to rule].

arch (árch) n. an arc of a circle; a structure for support; v.t. or v.i. to form an arch; to bend into an arch. **-ed** a. **-way** n. arched passage or entrance [L. *arca*, a chest, and *arcus*, a bow].

ar·chae·ol·o·gy, archeology (ár·kē·ál'·ạ-·ji·) n. the study of human antiquities. **archaeologist** n. **archaeological** a. [Gk. *archaios*, ancient; *logos*, a discourse].

ar·cha·ic (ár·kā'·ik) a. antiquated; ancient; antique; obsolete; primitive. **archaically** adv. **archaism** n. a word, expression or idiom out of date. **archaist** n. an antiquary; one who revives the use of archaisms in his writings. **archaistic** a. [Gk. *archaios*, ancient].

ar·che·an (ár·kē'·an) a. pert. to the oldest period of geological time [Gk. *archaios*, ancient].

arch·er (árch'·ẹr) n. one who shoots with a bow; a bowman. **-y** n. art and practice of shooting with bow and arrow [L. *arcus*, a bow].

ar·che·type (ár'·kẹ·tīp) n. the original pattern or model from which a thing is made or copied; prototype. **archetypal** a. [Gk. *archi-*, chief; *tupos*, a model].

ar·chi·pel·a·go (ár·ki·pel'·ạ·gō) n. name originally of Aegean Sea; a group of islands; a stretch of water scattered with isles; pl. **archipelagoes. archipelagic** (·aj'·ik) a. [Gk. *archi-*, chief; *pelagos*, the sea].

ar·chi·tect (ár'·ka·tekt) n. one skilled in the art of building; designer or contriver. **architectonics** n.pl. the science or art of architecture. **architectural** a. **architecturally** adv. **architecture** n. the art of building; a distinct style of designing buildings [Gk. *archi-*, chief; *tekton*, worker].

ar·chives (ár'·kīvz) n.pl. place in which public or historical records, charters and documents are stored and preserved; public records. **archival** a. **archivist** n. a keeper of archives [Gk. *archeion*, a town-hall].

arc·tic (árk'·tik) a. pert. to the regions near the N. Pole; northern; extremely cold; frigid [Gk. *arktos*, a bear].

ar·dent (ár'·dạnt) a. burning; passionate; eager. **-ly** adv. **ardency** n. warmth of passion; zeal. **ardor** (ár'·dẹr) n. heat; warmth of affection; eagerness; zeal [L. *ardere*, to burn].

ar·du·ous (ár'·dū·ạs) a. high and lofty; steep; difficult to overcome; laborious; strenuous. **-ly** adv. [L. *arduus*, steep].

are (ár) present indicative plural of the verb **to be** [O.E. *aron*].

are (ár) n. metric unit of land measure containing 100 square meters, about 119.6 square yards [Fr. fr. L. *area*].

a·re·a (ā'·ri·ạ) n. an open space; a tract of land; a region; scope; total outside surface of a thing; superficial extent [L. *area*, open space].

a·re·na (ạ·rē'·nạ) n. oval space of a Roman amphitheater, any place of public contest; a battlefield. **arenaceous** (ar·ạ·nā'·shạs), a. like sand; sandy [L. *arena*, sand].

ar·e·om·e·ter (a·re·ám'·e·tẹr) n. an instrument for measuring the specific gravity of fluids [Gk. *araios*, rare; *metron*, a measure].

a·rete (ạ·rāt') n. a sharp mountain ridge; a rocky spur [Fr. = a fish-bone].

ar·gent (ár'·jent) a. made of, or like, silver; silvery; n. white or silver color in heraldry. **-iferous** a. bearing silver. **-ine** a. pert. to, or like, silver; sounding like silver; n. a variety of carbonate of lime [L. *argentum*, silver].

ar·gil (år′·jil) *n.* pure clay; potter's earth. [L. *argilla*, white clay].

ar·gon (är′·gån) *n.* an inert gas used for filling electric light bulbs [Gk. *argos*, inactive].

ar·go·sy (är′·ga·si·) *n.* a large, richly-laden merchant ship [earlier *ragusye*, a ship of *Ragusa*, a Dalmatian port].

ar·got (är′·gō, är′·gat) *n.* slang; cant [Fr.]. tious. [L. *arguere*, to chide].

ar·gue (är′·gū) *v.t.* to prove by reasoning; to discuss; to persuade by debate; *v.i.* to prove; to offer reasons; to dispute. **arguable** *a.* capable of being argued. **-r** *n.* one who argues. **argument** *n.* a reason offered in proof for or against a thing; the subject of a speech, etc. **argumentation** *n.* arguing, reasoning. **argumentative** *a.* given to arguing; contentious. **argumentatively** *adv.* **argumentativeness** *n.* [L. *arguere*, to chide].

a·ri·a (ȧ′·ri·a̧, a′·ri·a̧) *n.* (*Mus.*) a melody as distinct from harmony; a solo part in a cantata, opera, oratorio, etc., with musical accompaniment [It. *aria*, an air].

ar·id (ar′·id) *a.* dry; parched; barren; (*Fig.*) uninteresting. **aridity** *n.* absence of moisture; dryness; barrenness [L. *aridus*].

a·right (a̧·rīt′) *adv.* rightly [E. *on right*].

a·rise (a̧·rīz′) *v.t.* to come up; to stand up; to get up; to come into view; to spring up; to occur; *pr.p.* **arising.** *pa.p.* **arisen** (a̧·rizn′). *pa.t.* **arose** [O.E. *arisan*].

ar·is·toc·ra·cy (ar·is·tåk′·ra̧·si·) *n.* originally the rule of the best; later, the rule of an hereditary upper class; privileged class in a state; the nobility; upper classes. **aristocrat** (a·ris′·ta̧·krat) *n.* a member of the aristocracy. **aristocratic** *a.* **aristocratically** *adv.* [Gk. *aristos*, best; *kratos*, power].

Ar·is·tot·le (ar·is·tåt′·l) *n.* (384-322 B.C.), a great Greek philosopher, pupil and disciple of Plato. **Aristotelian** (ar·is·ta̧·tē′·li·a̧n) *n.* a follower of Aristotle.

a·rith·me·tic (a̧·rith′·ma̧·tik) *n.* the science of numbers; the art of reckoning by figures; a work on this subject. **arithmetical** *a.* **arithmetically** *adv.* **arithmetician** (a̧·rith·ma̧·-tish′·a̧n) *n.* one skilled in arithmetic. **arithmetical progression,** a series of numbers which increase or decrease by a common difference, e.g. 2, 4, 6, 8, or 21, 18, 15, 12 [Gk. *arithmos*, number].

ark (årk) *n.* the large floating vessel in which Noah lived during the Flood (Genesis 6-8); vessel of bulrushes in which the infant Moses was placed (Exodus 2). **ark of the Covenant,** the chest containing the two Tables of the Law, a pot of manna, and Aaron's rod (Exodus 25); a chest; a coffer [O.E. *arc*, a box].

arm (årm) *n.* the limb extending from shoulders to hand; anything projecting from main body, as a branch; *v.t.* to give an arm to for support. **-less** *a.* without arms. **-ful** *a.* as much as the arms can hold. **—chair** *n.* a chair with arms. **—pit** *n.* the cavity under the shoulder. **at arm's length,** at a safe distance. **with open arms,** cordially [O.E. *earm*].

arm (årm) *n.* a weapon; a branch of the army, e.g. infantry, artillery, etc.; *pl.* all weapons; exploits; military profession; armor; heraldic bearings; *v.t.* to equip with weapons; *v.i.* to take up arms. **-ed** (årmd, or årm′·ed) *a.* equipped with, or supported by, arms; fortified; strengthened. **armed neutrality,** the condition of holding aloof from a contest, while ready to repel attack. **small arms,** weapons that can be carried by hand, e.g. pistols, revolvers, shotguns, rifles, etc. **under arms,** enlisted for military service; fully equipped for battle. **up in arms,** eager to give battle; roused to anger. **to lay down arms,** to surrender [L. *arma*, weapons].

ar·ma·da (år·mȧ′·da̧, år·mā′·da̧) *n.* a fleet of armed ships [Sp. *armar*, to arm].

ar·ma·dil·lo (år·ma̧·dil′·ō) *n.* an animal, having the body encased in armor-like covering of small, bony shell plates [Sp. dimin. of *armado*, a man-in-armor].

Ar·ma·ged·don (år·ma̧·ged′·a̧n) *n.* the scene of the last battle between the powers of good and evil, before Day of Judgment; final decisive battle between great nations. [Or. *Megiddo*, in Palestine].

ar·ma·ment (är′·ma̧·ma̧nt) *n.* land, naval, or air forces equipped for war; munitions; the process of equipping forces in time of war [L. pl. *armamenta*, equipment].

ar·ma·ture (är′·ma̧·cher) *n.* armor; protective covering (of plants); part of magnet or dynamo which rotates in electrical generator; coil of wire in electric motor which breaks magnetic field [L. *armare*, to arm].

ar·mi·stice (är′·mis·tis) *n.* a temporary or lasting cessation of hostilities; a truce [L. *arma*, weapons; *sistere*, to cause to stop].

arm·let (årm′·lit) *n.* a small arm, as of sea; band worn round arm. [O.E. *earm*].

ar·mor (är′·mer) *n.* defensive covering for the body in battle; orig. chain-mail, etc.; steel plates used to protect ships of war, tanks, cars, etc. **-bearer** *n.* one who carried arms of a superior. **—clad** *a.* **-ed car,** a metal-plated car with machine-gun in revolving turret. **-ed division,** a mobile unit with tanks, armored cars, etc. [L. *armare*, to arm].

ar·mor·y (är′·mer·i·) *n.* place where arms are stored; building for headquarters and drill area of National Guard unit; arsenal; (*Arch.*) science of heraldry. [L. *arma*, weapons or arms].

ar·my (är′·mi·) *n.* a body of men trained and equipped for war; a military force commanded by a general; an organized body for some special purpose, e.g. *Salvation Army*; large number of people. **army corps,** a large unit comprising various branches of the service. **standing army,** the regular army in peacetime [L. *arma*, weapons].

a·ro·ma (a̧·rō′·ma̧) *n.* fragrance in plants; perfume or flavor; charm; atmosphere. **aromatic** *a.* fragrant; spicy; *n.* a plant, drug with fragrant smell [Gk. *aroma*, spice].

a·round (a̧·round′) *adv.* in a circle; near; *prep.* on all sides of; about [E. *a*, on; *round*].

a·rouse (a̧·rouz′) *v.t.* to excite to action; to awaken; *v.i.* to wake; to become active. **arousal** *n.* [E. *a*, on, and *rouse*].

ar·peg·gi·o (år·pe′·ji·ō) *n.* (*Mus.*) the sounding of notes of a chord in quick succession [It. *arpeggiare*, to play the harp].

ar·que·bus (år′·kwi·bas) *n.* an ancient form of handgun. Also **harqueous. arquebusier** *n.* [O.H.Ger. *Haken*, hook; *Büchse*, a gun].

ar·raign (a̧·rān′) *v.t.* to call or set a prisoner at the bar; to call to account; to accuse publicly. **-ment** *n.* [L. *ad*, to; *ratio*, account].

ar·range (a̧·rānj′) *v.t.* to put into order; to settle terms; to prepare; to adapt; to adjust; *v.i.* to make agreement; to take steps. **-ment** *n.* act of arranging; the way or manner in which things are placed; needful preparation; (*Mus.*) transcription or adaptation of a piece of music to an instrument other than that for which it was originally composed. **-r** *n.* [Fr. *rang*, rank]. [utter. **-ly** *adv.* (doublet of errant).

ar·rant (ar′·ant) *a.* notorious; unmitigated;

ar·ras (ar′·as) *n.* tapestry; large tapestries, used as wall hangings [fr. the city of *Arras*, France, where first woven].

ar·ray (ar·rā′) *v.t.* to set in order; to draw up, as troops for battle; to dress; to equip; *n.* order; equipment; fine apparel [O.Fr. *aréer*].

ar·rear (a̧·rēr′) *n.* the state of being behind. **-s** *n.pl.* moneys still owing; work still to be overtaken. **-age** *n.* [Fr. *arrière*, behind].

ar·rest (a̧·rest′) *v.t.* to stop; to check; to hinder; to seize by authority of law; to engage the attention; *n.* the apprehending of a person by the authority of law; any seizure, physical or moral; stoppage. **arrestation** *n.* act of arresting. **-er**, **-or** *n*. one who, or that which, arrests. **-ing**. *a*. impressive; striking. **-ive** *a*. calculated to draw attention. **-ment** *n*. an arrest of a criminal; the seizure of a person's wages, etc. in debt claims [O.Fr. *arester*].

ar·rive (ạ·rīv′) *v.i.* to reach a point; to come to; to attain to any aim or object. **arrival** *n*. act of arriving [Fr. *arriver*, to arrive].

ar·ro·gance (ar′·ạ·gạns) *n*. insolent pride; intolerable presumption; overbearing manner. **arrogant** *a*. presuming on one's rank or power; haughty; proud. **arrogantly** *adv*. **arrogate** *v.t.* to claim unduly; to take upon one's self without authority; to demand overbearingly; to presume [L. *ad*, for; *rogare*, to ask].

ar·row (ar′·ō) *n*. a barbed missile shot from a bow; a sign ▶→ to show direction. **-y** *a*. of, like an arrow. **—grass** *n*. small, erect, grasslike plants [O. E. *arwe*].

ar·row·root (ar′·ō·ròot) *n*. a nutritious starch used in puddings, cookies, etc. [So-called because used to counteract the poison of arrows].

ar·roy·o (ạ·roi′·ō) *n*. gulch, small watercourse having steep sides and usually dry [Sp.].

ar·se·nal (ár′·sạn·ạl) *n*. factory for military and naval arms and stores; an armory [It. *arsenale*, fr. Ar. *al-sina'ah*, workshop].

ar·se·nic (ár′·sạ·nik) *n*. a semi-metallic element; the poisonous, whitish, or steel-grey powder of white oxide of arsenic. **arsenic**, **arsenical** *a*. pert. to arsenic. [Gk. *arsēn*, male. The alchemists classed metals as male and female]. **arsenous** *a*. [Gk. *arsēn*, male. The alchemists classed metals as male and female].

ar·son (ár′·sạn) *n*. the crime of intentionally setting on fire houses, buildings, ships, or other property [L. *ardere*, *arsum*, to burn].

art (árt) *n*. skill; human skill as opposed to nature; skill applied to music, painting, poetry, etc.; any of the subjects of this skill; a system of rules; a profession or craft; cunning; trick. **arts** *n.pl.* certain branches of learning, languages, history, etc. as distinct from natural science. **-ful** *a*. exhibiting art or skill; crafty; cunning. **-fully** *adv*. **-fulness** *n*. **-less** *a*. free from art; guileless. **-lessly** *adv*. **-lessness** *n*. **-y** *a*. (*Colloq.*) affectedly artistic. **black art**, magic. **fine arts**, painting, sculpture, architecture, music. **useful arts**, those in which the hands, rather than the mind, are used [L. *ars*, *artis*].

ar·ter·y (ár′·te·ri·) *n*. a vessel carrying blood from the heart; (*Fig.*) any essential channel of communication. **arterial** (ár·tē′·ri·ạl) *a*. pert. to an artery; pert. to a first-class road. **arterialize** *v.t.* to change venous blood into arterial blood by oxygenization. **arterialization** *n*. **arteriole** *n*. a small artery. **arteriosclerosis** *n*. (*Med.*) a hardening of the arteries [Gk. *arteria*, the windpipe, an artery; *logos*, discourse; *skleros*, hard].

ar·te·sian well (ár·tē′·zhạn wel) *n*. a well bored deep enough so that water rises to the surface of the ground by internal pressure (the first such well was sunk at *Artois* in the 12th cent.) [Fr. *Artésien*].

ar·thri·tis (ár·thrī′·tis) *n*. inflammation of a joint; gout. **arthritic(al)** (ár·thrit′·ik) *a*.

ar·thro·pod (ár′·thrạ·pád) *n*. an animal with segmented body and jointed limbs, e.g. a spider, crustacean, etc. **arthropodal** *a*. [Gk. *arthron*, a joint; *pous*, *podos*, a foot].

ar·ti·choke (ár′·ti·chōk) *n*. a plant with thistlelike head, which can be cooked and the fleshy base eaten. **Jerusalem artichoke** *n*. an entirely different plant, bearing edible tubers which resemble the potato in appearance [It. *articiocco*, fr. Ar., Jerusalem is corrupt. of It. *girasole*, sun-flower].

ar·ti·cle (ár′·ti·kl) *n*. a clause or term in a contract, treaty, etc.; a literary composition in a journal, etc.; a paragraph or section; a

point of faith; a rule or condition; an item; a commodity or object; (*Gram.*) one of the words *a*, *an* (the indefinite article) and *the* (the definite article); *v.t.* to apprentice; to accuse specifically [L. *articulus*, a little joint].

ar·tic·u·lar (ár·tik′·yoo·lạr) *a*. pert. to the joints [L. *articulus*, a little joint].

ar·tic·u·late (ár·tik′·yoo·lāt) *v.t.* to connect by a joint; to utter clearly-defined sounds; *v.i.* to be connected by joints; to speak in distinct syllables or words; *a*. jointed; of speech, clear, distinct. **-ly** *adv*. **-ness** *n*. **articulation** *n*. the act of articulating; a consonant; a joint between two or more bones [L. *articulus*, a little joint, fr. *artus*, a limb].

ar·ti·fact (ár′·ti·fakt) *n*. object made by man [L. *ars*, *artis*, art; *facere*, to make].

ar·ti·fice (ár′·ti·fis) *n*. an artful or skilful contrivance; a ruse; a trick; cunning. **artificer** *n*. a skilled workman; an inventor. **artificial** (ár·ti·fish′·ạl) *a*. made by art; manufactured; affected in manners. **artificially** *adv*. **artificiality** *n*. [L. *artificium*, a trade, fr. *ars*, art; *facere*, to make].

ar·til·ery (ár·til′·ạ·ri·) *n*. cannon; troops trained in the use of guns; a branch of the armed forces. **artilleryman** *n*. a soldier serving in the artillery [Fr. *artillerie*, fr. O.Fr. *artillier*, to equip].

ar·ti·san (ár′·ti·zạn) *n*. a craftsman; a mechanic [Fr. fr. L. *ars*, *artis*, art].

art·ist (ár′·tist) *n*. one who practices one of the fine arts, e.g. painting, sculpture, etc.; applicable to any craftsman whose work is of high standard. **-ic(al)**, *a*. **-ically** *adv*. **artistry** (ár′·tis·tri·) *n*. artistic ability or effect; beauty of work [L. *ars*, *artis*, art].

ar·tiste (ár·tēst′) *n*. an expert in some art, not one of the fine arts; often applied to a member of the theatrical profession [L. *ars*, *artis*, art].

Ar·y·an (ā′·ri·ạn) *n*. the progenitors of the Indo-European group, i.e. Celtic, Teutonic, etc. [Sans. *Arya*, noble].

as (az) *adv*. like; in like manner; similar to; for example; *conj*. since; because; when; while; *pron*. that [form of *also*].

as·bes·tos (as·bes′·tạs) *n*. a fibrous noninflammable mineral, used in manufacture of fire-proof materials [Gk. *a-*, neg.; *sbestos*, to be quenched].

as·cend (ạ·send′) *v.t.* to climb, to mount; to walk up; *v.i.* to rise; to arise; to soar; to climb; to mount; to go back in time. **-able**, **-ible** *a*. **-ancy**, **-ency** *n*. superior or controlling influence; authority; domination [L. *ad*, to; *scendere*, to climb].

as·cent (ạ·sent′) *n*. the act of rising; the way by which one rises; a slope; a way up [L. *ad*, to; *scandere*, to climb].

as·cer·tain (as·ẹr·tān′) *v.t.* to get to know; to find out for a certainty. **-able** *a*. **-ment** *n*. [L. *ad*, to; *certus*, sure].

as·cet·ic (ạ·set′·ik) *a*. sternly self-denying; austere; strict; *n*. one who practices rigorous self-denial; a hermit; an anchorite. **asceticism** *n*. **-ally** *adv*. [Gk. *askein*, to exercise].

as·cot (as′·kạt) *n*. a kind of scarf or broad tie.

as·cribe (as·krīb′) *v.t.* to attribute; to impute; to assign. **ascribable** *a*. **ascription** *n*. [L. *ascribere*, to add in writing].

a·sep·sis (ạ·sep′·sis) *n*. freedom from putrefaction; freeing from bacteria by use of antiseptics. **aseptic** *a*. not liable to putrefaction; sterilized [Gk. *a-*, neg.; *sepsis*, decay].

a·sex·u·al (ā·sek′·shoo·ạl) *a*. without sex; lacking sexual instinct or reproductive organs. **asexuality** *n*. [L. *a*, away; *sexus*, sex].

ash (ash) *n*. a genus of trees of the olive family having a tough, hard, elastic wood. **-en** *a*. [O.E. *aesce*, the ash-tree].

ash (ash) *n*. the dry white or greyish dust left after a substance has been burned. **-es** *n.pl.* the remains of a human body after cremation;

(*Fig.*) a dead body; (*Chem.*) potash. (*Naval Slang*) a depth-charge; a multiple arc lamp used in theaters. **-en** *a.* of the color of ashes; pale. **— tray** *n.* receptacle for cigarette ash. **-y** *a.* **Ash Wednesday,** the first day of Lent [M.E. *asche,* ash].

a·shamed (ạ·shămd′) *a.* affected by shame; covered with confusion, caused by awareness of guilt [O.E. *ascamian,* to be ashamed].

a·shore (ạ·shōr′) *adv.* on or to shore; on land, opp. to *aboard* [E. *a,* on; M. E. *shore* fr. O.E. *sciran,* to cut].

A·sian, A·si·at·ic (ā′·zhạn, ā·zhi·at′·ik) *a.* pert. to Asia or to the people of Asia [Gk. *Asia,* a part of Lydia].

a·side (ạ·sīd′) *n.* something said in an undertone, esp. on stage by an actor and supposed not to be heard by the other actors; *adv.* on or to one side; apart; dismissed from use [O.E. *a,* on; *sid,* broad].

as·i·nine (as′·in·īn) *a.* pert. to an ass; stupid. **asininity** *n.* [L. *asinus,* an ass].

ask (ask) *v.t.* to seek information; to interrogate; *v.i.* (*for, about*) to request; to inquire. **-er** *n.* [O.E. *ascian,* to seek].

a·skance, a·skant (ạ·skans′, ạ·skant′) *adv.* towards one corner of the eye; awry; with disdain or suspicioun; not straightforward.

a·skew (ạ·skū′) *adv.* askant; aside; awry; obliquely; off the straight [See **skew**].

a·slant (ạ·slant′) *adv.* in a slanting direction.

a·sleep (ạ·slēp′) *adv.* and *a.* in a state of sleep; at rest; benumbed; dormant; dead.

a·slope (ạ·slōp′) *a.* sloping; tilted; oblique. *adv.* with a slope [O.E. *slūpan,* to slip].

a·so·cial (ā·sō′·shạl) *a.* not social, selfish [Gk. *a-,* neg.; social]. [poisonous serpent [Gk. *aspis*].

asp, as·pic (asp, asp′·ik) *n.* a small, hooded,

as·par·a·gus (as·par′·ạ·gạs) *n.* a succulent vegetable with tender shoots [Gk.].

as·pect (as′·pekt) *n.* look; appearance; position or situation; view [L. *aspicere,* look at].

as·pen (as′·pin) *n.* a tree known also as the trembling poplar; *a.* trembling [O.E. *aespe*].

as·per·ate (as·per′·āt) *v.t.* to make harsh or uneven; to roughen [L.].

as·per·i·ty (as·per′·i·ti·) *n.* roughness of surface, manner, or speech; harshness; crabbedness; sharpness; acrimony [L. *asper,* rough].

as·perse (as·purs′) *v.t.* to slander; to defame; to vilify; to calumniate; to bespatter (with). **-er** *n.* **aspersion** *n.* slander. **aspersive, aspersory** *a.* [L. *ad,* to; *spargere,* to sprinkle].

as·phalt (as′·fawlt), *n.* a black, hard, tar-like substance, used for paving, roofing, etc. **asphalt** *v.t.* to cover with asphalt. **asphaltic** *a.* bituminous [Gk. *asphaltos*].

as·phyx·i·a, as·phyx·y (as·fik′·si·ạ, -si·) *n.* suspended animation due to lack of oxygen in the blood; it is caused by obstructed breathing, as in drowning, inhalation of gases, etc. **-te** *v.t.* to suffocate. **-tion** *n.* [Gk. *asphuxia,* pulse stoppage].

as·pic (as′·pik) *n.* the asp; (*Bot.*) the great lavender [L. *spica,* a spike].

as·pic (as′·pik) *n.* savory jelly containing pieces of fish, fowl, egg, etc. [Fr.].

as·pi·rate (as′·pi·rāt) *v.t.* to pronounce with a full breathing sound; to prefix the sound *h* to a word or letter; *n.* a letter marked with a note of breathing; a breathed sound; *a.* pronounced with a rough breathing. **aspiration** *n.* act of breathing; (*Med.*) the removal of fluids from a cavity in the body by suction [L. *aspiratus,* breathed upon].

as·pire (as·pīr′) *v.i.* to desire with eagerness; to strive towards something higher (usually followed by *to* or *after*). **aspirant** *a.* ambitious; *n.* one who aspires; a candidate. **aspiration** *n.* **-r** *n.* [L. *ad,* to; *spirare,* breathe].

as·pi·rin (as′·pi·rin) *n.* a drug used for relief of headache, fever, etc.

ass (as) *n.* a quadruped of the horse family; a donkey; (*Fig.*) a stupid person [L. *asinus*].

as·sail (ạ·sāl′) *v.t.* to leap or fall on; to attack; to assault; to ply with arguments, reproaches, etc. **-able** *a.* **-ant** *a.* and *n.* [L. *ad,* to; *salire,* to leap].

as·sas·sin (ạ·sas′·in) *n.* one who murders by secret or treacherous assault, esp. a hired murdered. **-ate** *v.t.* to murder by guile or by sudden violence. **-ation** *n.* **-ator** *n.* [Moslem *hashish,* an intoxicating drug].

as·sault (ạ·sawlt′) *n.* a violent onset or attack; *v.t.* to attack violently, both physically and with words or arguments; to storm. **-able** *a.* **-er** *n.* **assault and battery** (*Law*) violent attacking and beating a person [L. *ad,* to; *salire,* to leap].

as·say (ạ·sā′) *n.* trial; test; examination; analysis of the amount of metal in ores or coins, or of ingredients in drugs; *v.t.* to test. **-er** *n.* [Fr. *essayer,* to try].

as·sem·ble (ạ·sem′·bl) *v.t.* to bring or call together; to collect; to fit together the parts, e.g. of a machine; *v.i.* to meet together. **assemblage** *n.* a group, gathering. **assembly** *n.* a meeting; a company gathered; the putting together of all the different parts to make a complete machine [L. *ad,* to; *simul,* together].

as·sent (ạ·sent′) *v.i.* to agree; to admit; to concur; *n.* acquiescence; approval. **assentation** *n.* servile assent; obsequiousness. **-er, -or** *n.* one who assents. **assentient** (ạ·sen′·shạnt) *a.* giving assent; *n.* one who assents [L. *ad,* to; *sentire,* to think].

as·sert (ạ·surt′) *v.t.* to declare strongly; to maintain or defend by argument. **-er, -or** *n.* **assertion** *n.* the act of asserting; affirmation; declaration. **-ive** *a.* positive; self-confident. **-ively** *adv.* **-iveness** *n.* **-ory** *a.* affirmative [L. *asserere,* to claim].

as·sess (ạ·ses′) *v.t.* to fix the amount of a tax or fine; to tax or fine; to estimate for damage, taxation, etc.; to rate; to appraise. **-able** *a.* **-ment** *n.* assessing; valuation for taxation; a tax; evaluation of merits. **-or** *n.* [L. *assidere, assessum,* to sit by a judge].

as·sets (as′·ets) *n.pl.* funds or property available for payment of debts, etc.; the estate of an insolvent or deceased person; the entire property of a business company, association, society, etc.; *n.sing.* an item of such property; a thing of value [Fr. *assez,* enough].

as·sev·er·ate (ạ·sev′·ẹr·āt) *v.t.* and *i.* to assert positively or solemnly; to aver. **asseveration** *n.* [L. *asseverare,* fr. *severus,* serious].

as·sid·u·ous (ạ·sid′·joo·us) *a.* constant in application or attention; diligent; hard-working. **-ly** *adv.* **-ness, assiduity** (as·i·dū′·i·ti·) *n.* close application; unremitting attention; devotion [L. *assiduus,* constantly near].

as·sign (ạ·sīn′) *v.t.* to allot; to apportion; to give out; to fix; to transfer; to ascribe. **-able** *a.* **assignation** (a·sig·nā′·shạn) *n.* the act of assigning; an appointment, esp. if made by lovers; a tryst; (*Law*) an assignment, or the deed by which it is made. **assignee** (a·sī·nē′) *n.* one to whom something is assigned; a person appointed to act for another. **-ment** *n.* an allotting to a particular person or use; a transfer of legal title or interest; a task assigned. [L. *assignare,* to allot by sign (*signuum*)].

as·sim·i·late (ạ·sim′·i·lāt) *v.t.* to make similar; to change into a like substance; to absorb into the system; to digest; *v.i.* to become similar; to be absorbed. **assimilation** *n.* the act of assimilating; (*Fig.*) full comprehension of anything. **assimilative** *a.* capable of assimilating [L. *assimilare,* to make like].

as·sist (ạ·sist′) *v.t.* to help; to aid; to give support to; *v.i.* to lend aid; to be present. **-ance** *n.* help; aid. **-ant** *a.* helping; acting under the direction of a superior; *n.* one who assists; a helper [L. *assistere,* to stand by].

as·size (ạ·sīz′) *v.t.* to fix the rate of; to assess; *n.* orig. the regulation of a court fixing selling price of bread, ale, etc.; edict; a sitting of a court of justice. **-ment** *n.* inspection of weights and measures. **-r** *n.* [O.Fr. *assise*, an assembly of judges].

as·so·ci·ate (ą·sō′·shi·āt) *v.t.* to join with as a friend, colleague, confederate or partner; to class together; (*reflex.*) to express agreement with; *v.i.* (foll. by *with*) to keep company; to combine; *n.* (ą·sō′·shi·it) a companion; a co-adjutor; a member of a group; a junior member; *a.* affiliated. **associable** *a.* companionable. **associableness, associability,** *n.* friendly, companionable quality; sympathy; **-ship** *n.* **associative** *a.* [L. *associare*, fr. *socius*, an ally].

as·so·nance (as′·ą·nąns) *n.* a resemblance of sounds; imperfect rhyme in which vowel sounds are same, but consonants following are different, e.g *blunder, slumber.* **assonant(al)** *a.* **assonate** *v.t.* to correspond in sound [L. *ad,* to; *sonare,* to sound].

as·sort (a·sawrt′) *v.t.* to classify; to arrange; *v.i.* to suit or agree or match (foll. by *with*). **-ed** *a.* classified; varied. **-edness, -ment** *n.* act of arranging in groups; a miscellaneous collection [Fr. *assortir,* to match].

as·suage (ą·swāj′) *v.t.* to soften; to allay; to mitigate. **-ment** *n.* **-r** *n.* **assuasive** *a.* [L. *ad,* to; *suavis,* sweet].

as·sume (a·sóóm′) *v.t.* to take upon oneself; to take for granted; to appropriate; to usurp; *v.i.* to claim unduly; to be pretentious or arrogant. **assumable** *a.* **assumed** *a.* supposed; feigned; hypothetical. **assumedly** *adv.* **assuming** *a.* arrogant. **assumingly** *adv.* **assumption** *n.* the act of taking to or upon oneself by force or right; the act of taking for granted; the thing supposed to be true, or to have happened. **assumptive** *a.* [L. *ad,* to; *sumere,* to take].

as·sure (a·shoor′) *v.t.* to make sure or certain; to affirm; to ensure; to convince. **assurable** *a.* **assurance** *n.* the act of assuring; promise; self-confidence; presumption; *Br.* insurance. **-d** *a.* certain, safe; confident. **assuredly** *adv.* **assuredness** *n.* certainty. **-r** *n.* **assuringly** *adv.* confidently [L. *ad,* to; *securus,* safe].

as·ter (as′·tęr) *n.* a genus of plants so called because the expanded flowers of various hues are like stars [Gk. *aster,* star].

as·ter·isk (as′·tą·risk) *n.* the mark (*) used in printing to indicate words for reference or words omitted. **asterism** *n.* small cluster of stars; three asterisks (***), indicating point or passage of special interest [Gk. *asterikos,* a little star]. [hinder part of ship; behind.

a·stern (ą·sturn′) *adv.* in, at, or toward the

as·ter·oid (as′·tęr·oid) *a.* star-shaped; *n.* one of the smaller planets; (*Zool.*) star-fish. **asteroidal** *a.* [Gk. *aster,* a star; *eidos,* a form].

asth·ma (az′·mą, as′·mą) *n.* a chronic disorder of the respiratory organs, marked by cough, labored breathing and feeling of suffocation. **asthmatic(al)** *a.* **asthmatically** *adv.* [Gk. *asthma,* panting].

a·stig·ma·tism (ą·stig′·mą·tizm) *n.* a defect of eye, attended with dimness of vision, due to malformation of lens of eye. **astigmatic** *a.* [Gk. *a-,* neg.; *stigma,* point]. [in motion [E.].

a·stir (ą·stur′) *adv.* or *a.* on the move; alert;

as·ton·ish (as·tán′·ish) *v.t.* to impress with sudden surprise, wonder or admiration; to strike with sudden terror; to amaze; to astound. **-ed** *a.* **-ing** *a.* **-ingly** *adv.* **-ment** *n.* [Formerly, also *astony,* fr. O.Fr. *astoner*].

as·tound (ą·stound′) *v.t.* to strike dumb with terror or amazement; to astonish greatly; to stun. **-ing** *a.* [By-form of *astony, astonish*].

as·tra·khan (as′·trą·kan) *n.* the skin of the young Persian lamb with soft, curling ringlets of wool; a cheap fabric, made in imitation [*Astrakhan,* city on the Caspian Sea].

as·tral (as′·tral) *a.* pert. to the stars; star-shaped [Gk. *astron,* star].

a·stray (ą·strā′) *adv.* out of the right way; in

the wrong direction.

a·strict (ą·strikt′) *v.t.* to bind fast; to confine; to restrict; to contract. **astriction** *n.* restriction; (*Med.*) constipation. **astrictive** *a.* astringent [L. *astrictus,* drawn close].

a·stride (ą·strīd′) *adv.* straddling; with the legs apart; *prep.* with one foot on each side of an object.

as·tringe (ą·strinj′) *v.t.* to bind together; to draw together; to astrict; to constipate. **astringency** *n.* the condition of being astringent. **astringent** *a.* binding; strengthening; constricting; contracting; *n.* a drug which causes contraction of the muscular fiber-tissues. **-ntly** *adv.* [L. *ad,* to; *stringere,* to bind].

as·tro- (as′·trō) *prefix* used in the construction of compound words having some reference to stars [Gk. *astron,* star].

as·tro·labe (as′·trą·lāb) *n.* instrument for finding altitude of stars, etc. [Gk. *astron,* star, *lambnein,* to take].

as·trol·o·gy (ą·strál′·a·ji·) *n.* science which professes to interpret the influence of heavenly bodies on human affairs **astrologer** *n.* **astrologic, -al** *a.* [Gk. *astron,* a star; *logos,* a discourse].

as·trom·e·try (ą·strám′·a·tri·) *n.* the determination of the magnitudes of the fixed stars [Gk. *astron,* a star; *metron,* measure].

as·tro·naut (as′·trą·nawt) *n.* a space traveler; **-ical** *a.* **-ics** *n.* science of traveling outside the earth's atmosphere [Gk. *astron,* a star, *naut(ilos),* a sailor].

as·tron·o·my (ą·strán′·a·mi·) *n.* the science which studies the heavenly bodies. **astronomer** *n.* one versed in astronomy. **astronomic, -al,** *a.* pert. to astronomy; boundless, countless, prodigious. **astronomize** *v.i.* [Gk. *astron,* a star; *nomos,* law].

as·tro·phys·ics (ąs·trō·fiz′·iks) *n.* (*Astron.*) the study of the physical components of the stars by means of the spectroscope and other instruments [Gk. *astron,* a star; *phusis,* nature].

as·tute (ą·stóót′) *a.* cunning; shrewd; sagacious; crafty; wily; sly; subtle; keen. **-ly** *adv.* **-ness** *n.* [L. *astutus*].

a·sun·der (ą·sun′·dęr) *adv.* apart; into different pieces; in a divided state.

a·sy·lum (ą·sī′·ląm) *n.* a sanctuary; refuge for criminals, debtors and others liable to be pursued; any place of refuge; an institution for the deaf and dumb, the blind, or the insane; the protection afforded by such places [Gk. *asulon,* inviolate].

a·sym·me·try (ā·sim′·ą·tri·) *n.* want of symmetry. **asymmetric, -al** *a.*

as·symp·tote (as′·im·tōt) *n.* (*Math.*) a straight line that continually approaches a curve, but never meets it within a finite distance [Gk. *a-,* neg.; *sun,* with; *ptosis,* a falling].

a·syn·chro·nism (ā·sin′·krą·nizm) *n.* lack of synchronism; want of correspondence in time. **asynchronous** *a.* not simultaneous.

a·syn·de·ton (ą·sin′·dą·tąn) *n.* (*Rhet.*) the omission of conjunctions. **asyndetic** *a.* [Gk. *asyndetos,* unjoined].

at (at) *prep.* denoting rest in a place, presence, or nearness; near to, by, in; engaged on; in the direction of [O.E. *aet*]. [drug.

at·a·brine (at′·ą·brin) *n.* an anti-malarial

at·a·vism (at′·ą·vizm) *n.* the recurrence in living organisms of hereditary characteristics, diseases, etc. which have skipped one or more generations; reversion to type. **atavistic** [L. *atavus,* a great-grandfather's grandfather].

a·tax·i·a (ą·tak′·si·ą) *n.* (*Med.*) irregularity of bodily functions; irregularity of movement, due to defective muscular control. **ataxic** *a.* [Gk. *a-,* neg.; *taxis,* order].

ate (āt) past tense of the verb **eat.**

at·el·ier (at·ąl·yā′) *n.* a workshop, esp. of an artist; hence, a studio [Fr. a workshop].

a·the·ism (ā′·thē·izm) *n.* disbelief in the existence of God. **atheist** *n.* one who denies the existence of God. **atheistic, -al** a. **athiesti-cally** adv. [Gk. a-, neg.; theos, a god] .

A·the·na, A·the·ne (a·thē′·na, -nē) n. (Myth.) Greek goddess of wisdom, art, industries, and prudent warfare. **Athenian** a. pert. to Athens. n. native of Athens.

a·thirst (a·thurst′) a. thirsty; eager [fr. thirst].

ath·lete (ath′·lēt) n. one trained to physical exercises, feats or contests of strength, etc.; a man strong and active by training. **athletic** (ath·let′·ik) a. pert. to physical exercises, contests, etc.; strong; vigorous; muscular. **athletics** n.pl. athletic sports [Gk. athlētēs, a contestant for a prize].

a·thwart (a·thwawrt′) prep. across; from side to side; adv. crosswise in opposition [O.N. a and thvert, across].

a·tilt (a·tilt′) a., adv. tilted.

a·tin·gle (a·ting′·gal) a. tingling.

At·lan·tic (at·lan′·tik) a. pert. to the ocean (named after Mt. Atlas) separating Europe and Africa from America; n. the ocean itself.

At·las (at′·las) n. (Myth.) a Titan, condemned by Zeus to carry the world on his shoulders. **atlas** n. a book of maps.

at·mos·phere (at′·mas·fēr) n. the mass of air, clouds, gases, and vapor, surrounding the earth or other heavenly body; any similar mass; atmospheric pressure; the air in any place, esp. if enclosed, e.g. in a theater; (Fig.) any surrounding influence. **atmospheric, atmospherical** a. pert. to, or depending on, the atmosphere. **atmospherically** adv. [Gk. atmos, vapor; sphaira, a ball].

at·oll (at′·al, a·tál′) n. a ring-shaped coral reef surrounding a lagoon [Native].

at·om (at′·am) n. the smallest unit. **-ary** constituent of a chemical element; (Fig.) anything very small; a tiny bit. **atomic, atomical** a. pert. to the atom. **atomicity** n. the number of atoms in the molecule of any element; **atomization** n. the changing of any liquid into the form of fine spray. **atomize** v.t. to reduce to atoms. **atomizer** n. an instrument for reducing a liquid to the form of spray. **atomy** n. an atom; a tiny being; (Anat.) a skeleton. **atom (atomic) bomb,** a bomb of unimaginable destructive power, whose energy is derived from the nuclear disintegration of atoms of elements of high atomic mass, e.g. uranium 235. **atomic energy,** energy derived from the disintegration of the nucleus of an atom. **atomic fission,** the action of disintegrating; the disintegration of the atom. **atomic pile,** apparatus for producing energy by the disintegration of atoms. **atomic weight,** the weight of an atom of an element, [Gk. a-, neg.; tome, a cuttnig].

a·ton·al (ā·tōn′·al) a. (Mus.) without tone; unreferred to any scale or tonic. **atonality** n. **atonic** (ā·tán′·ik) a. without tone; unaccented; (Med.) lacking tone or energy. **atony** (at′·a·ni·) n. lack of tone or accent [Gk. a-, neg; tonos, tone].

a·tone (a·tōn′) v.t. to appease; to expiate (rare); v.i. to make amends or reparation for an offense; to satisfy by giving an equivalent (with for). **-ment** n. amends; reconciliation, esp. the reconciliation of God and man [E. (to set) at one].

a·top (a·táp′) a., adv. on or at the top; prep. [on top of.

a·tri·um (ā′·tri·um) n. the principal room of an ancient Roman house; (Anat.) an auricle of the heart [L. = a hall].

a·tro·cious (a·trō′·shas) a. savagely brutal; extremely cruel; very wicked; grievous; (Colloq.) of work, etc., of very poor quality. **-ly** adv. **-ness** n. **atrocity** (a·trås′i·ti·) n. extreme wickedness; a brutal act [L. atrox, fierce].

a·tro·phy (at′·ra·fi·) n. a wasting away through lack of nutrition or use; emaciation. Also v.t. and i. to waste away; to cause to waste away. **atrophic, atrophied** a. [Gk. a-, neg.; trophē, nourishment].

at·ro·pin, at·ro·pine (at′·ra·pēn, ·pin) n. a

poisonous alkaloid obtained from the deadly nightshade, used as a drug to dilate the pupil of the eye [Gk. Atropos, one of the Fates].

at·tach (a·tach′) v.t. to bind, fasten, or tie; to take by legal authority; to bind by affection; to assign, e.g. an officer to a regiment; v.i. to adhere; to be ascribed to. **-able** a. **-ed** a. fixed; fond of. **-ment** n. [Fr. attacher].

at·ta·ché (at·a·shā′) n. one attached to the staff of an ambassador. **— case,** n. small hand-case [Fr. attacher].

at·tack (a·tak′) v.t. to fall on with force; to assail with hostile criticism in words or writing; to set to work on; to begin to affect (of illness); n. a violent onset or assault [Fr. attaquer].

at·tain (a·tān′) v.t. to reach by exertion; to obtain by effort; to accomplish; to achieve; v.i. to arrive at (generally foll. by to). **-able** a. **-ability, -ableness** n. **-ment** n. [L. attingere, to reach].

at·taint (a·tānt′) v.t. to stain or disgrace; to accuse of; to find guilty; to deprive of civil rights for treason; n. a taint or disgrace. **attainder** n. loss of civil rights after sentence of death or outlawry for treason or felony. **-ment** n. [O.Fr. ataint, convicted].

at·tar (at′·er) n. a fragrant oil obtained from flower-petals [Pers. atar, fragrance].

at·tempt (a·tempt′) v.t. to try; to endeavor to do; to attack; n. trial; an effort, esp. unsuccessful; an assault. a. [L. ad, to; temptare, to try].

at·tend (a·tend′) v.t. to accompany; to be present with or at; to give medical care to; v.i. to be present; to pay attention; to take care of; to wait on. **-ance** n. the act of attending; persons present. **-ant** a. being present; consequent; n. one who accompanies as friend or servant; a caretaker. **attention** n. careful observation; watching; act of civility; command issued, as in a military sense, to ensure readiness to act. **attentions** n.pl. courtship. **attentive** a. full of attention. **attentively** adv. [L. ad, to; tendere, to stretch].

at·ten·u·ate (a·ten′·ū·āt) v.t. to make thin or fine, to make slender; to weaken the potency of; a. slender; thin; (Bot.) tapering. **attenuant** a. tending to make thin, esp. of liquids; diluting. **-d** a. **attenuation** n. **attenuator** n. [L. ad, to; tenuis, thin].

at·test (a·test′) v.t. and v.i. to bear witness to; to vouch for; to certify; (Law) to witness officially (a signature). **-able, -ative** a. **-ation** n. [L. attestari, to bear witness].

At·tic (a′·tik) a. pert. to Attica or Athens; resembling the refined and elegant style of the Athenian writers. **attic** n. a room under the roof of a house where ceiling follows line of the roof (common in Greek archit.); a garret [Gk. Attikos, pert. to Attica].

at·tire (a·tīr′) v.i. to dress; to array in splendid garments; n. apparel; dress. **-ment, attiring** n. [O.Fr. atirier, to put in order].

at·ti·tude (at′·a·tòòd) n. posture of a person; pose (in portrait); (Fig.) mental or moral disposition [L. aptus, fit].

at·tor·ney (a·tur′·ni·) n. one put in the turn or place of another; one legally authorized by another to transact business; lawyer; solicitor. **attorn** v.t. to transfer; v.i. to transfer homage; to acknowledge a new landlord. **-ship** n. **-dom** n. **— general** n. chief law officer of a state or nation. **power, letter** or **warrant of attorney,** a legal authorization by which one person may act for another [O.Fr. atorner, to direct].

at·tract (a·trakt′) v.t. and v.i. to draw toward; to cause to approach; (Fig.) to allure; to provoke notice. **-able** a. **-ile** a. attractive. **attraction** n. the act of drawing to; the force which draws together bodies or particles; the affinity existing between one chemical body and another; (Fig.) that which allures, or fascinates. **-ive** a. **-ively** adv. **-iveness** n. [L. ad, to;

trahere, tractum, to draw].

at·tri·bute (ạ·trib′·yoot) *v.t.* to consider as belonging to; to ascribe to. **attribute** (at′·rạ·būt) *n.* something inherent in a person or thing; an inseparable property; (*Gram.*) a qualifying word used, not as part of predicate, but adjectivally, as in *red* hair. **attributable** *a.* that may be ascribed to. **attribution** *n.* the act of ascribing to; the quality attributed. **attributive** *a.* [L. *ad,* to; *tribuere,* to bestow].

at·tri·tion (ạ·trish′·ạn) *n.* the act of wearing away by friction; state of being worn; (*Mil.*) deliberate exhaustion of enemy's men and resources before making an attack. **attrite** *a.* worn away by rubbing or friction; (*Theol.*) penitent through fear [L. *attritus,* rubbed away].

at·tune (ạ·tòòn′) *v.t.* to put in tune; to make musical; to make one instrument accord with another; (*Fig.*) to bring into spiritual harmony; to fit for a purpose. *a.* in harmony. **-ment** *n.* [L. *ad,* to; *tune*].

a·typ·i·cal (ā·tip′·ạ·kạl) *a.* not typical; abnormal. **-ly** *adv.* [Gk. *a-,* neg.; *typical*].

au·burn (aw′·burn) *a.* reddish brown; *n.* rich chestnut color [L.L. *alburnus,* blond].

auc·tion (awk′·shạn) *n.* a method of public sale whereby the object for sale is secured by highest bidder; *v.t.* to sell by auction. **-eer** *n.* one licensed to sell by auction; *v.i.* to sell by auction [L. *augere, auctum,* to increase].

auc·tion bridge (awk′·shạn brij′) *n.* a card game in which the players bid.

au·da·cious (aw·dā′·shạs) *a.* bold, fearless; impudent; insolent. **-ly** *adv.* **-ness** *n.* **audacity** (aw·da′·si·ti·) *n.* boldness, effrontery, impudence. [L. *audix,* bold].

au·di·ble (aw′·dạ·bl) *a.* capable of being heard. **audibly** *adv.* **audibility** *n.* [L. *audire,* to hear].

au·di·ence (aw′·di·ạns) *n.* the act of hearing; an assembly of hearers or spectators; a ceremonial reception or interview; a judicial hearing. **audient** *a.* listening [L. *audire,* to hear].

au·di·o (aw′·di·ō) *a.* electronic apparatus using audible frequencies (between 15-20,000 cycles) [L. *audire,* hear].

au·dit (aw′·dit) *n.* an examination, by qualified persons, of accounts of a business, public office, or undertaking; *v.t.* to test and vouch for the accuracy of accounts; listen. **audition** *n.* the act, or sense, of hearing; hearing given to a performer as test. **-or** *n.* a hearer; one authorized to investigate the financial condition of a company or society. **auditorium** *n.* the body of a concert hall or theater where the audience are seated; the nave of a church. **-ory** *a.* pert. to the sense of hearing; *n.* a lecture room; an audience [L. *audire,* to hear].

au·ger (aw′·gẹr) *n.* a boring tool for woodwork, like a large gimlet. [*An auger* for *a nauger,* fr. O.E. *nafu,* nave; *gār,* dart].

aught (awt) *n.* anything; any part; zero; *adv.* to any extent [O.E. *awiht,* fr. *a,* ever, and *wiht,* thing].

aug·ment (awg·ment′) *v.t.* to increase; to add to; to make larger; to enlarge; *v.i.* to grow larger. **augment** *n.* an increase; a prefix added to the past tense of verbs to distinguish them from other tenses. **-able** *a.* **-ation** *n.* act of enlarging; an increase. **-ative** *a.* increasing; *n.* a word which expresses with increased force the idea conveyed by the simpler word. **-er** *n.* [L. *augumentum,* an increase].

au·gur (aw′·gẹr) *n.* a soothsayer; a diviner; a member of a college of priests in Rome who claimed to be able to foretell events by observing the flight or other actions of birds; *v.t.* to foretell; to presage; to prognosticate. **-al** *a.* **-ship** *n.* **-y** *n.* divination; omen [L.].

au·gust (aw·gust′) *a.* majestic; imposing; sublime; grand; magnificent; sacred. **-ly** *adv.* **-ness** *n.* [a title first bestowed on the Emperor Octavianus by the Roman Senate, fr. L.

augere, to increase].

Au·gust (aw′·gạst) *n.* the eighth month of the year [named in honor of the Emperor *Augustus*].

Au·gus·tan (aw·gus′·tạn) *a.* classic; refined; pertaining to the Emperor *Augustus,* 31 B.C.-A.D. 14; *n.* a writer of the Augustan age.

Au·gus·tine (aw·gạs·tēn′) *n.* a member of a monastic order which follows rules framed by St. Augustine (354-430) or deduced from his writings; a Black Friar.

auk (awk) *n.* a marine bird, of the Arctic regions [Icel. *alka*].

aunt (ȧnt, ȧnt) *n.* a father's or a mother's sister; also applied to an uncle's wife. [L. *amita,* a father's sister].

au·ra (aw′·rạ) *n.* a subtle invisible essence or fluid said to emanate from human and animal bodies, and even from things; (*Fig.*) the atmosphere surrounding a person; character; personality; (*Path.*) a premonitory symptom of epilepsy and hysteria, as of cold air rising to the head. **-l** *a.* pert. to the air, or to an aura [L. *aura,* a breeze].

au·ral (aw′·rạl) *a.* pert. to the ear, or sense of hearing. **-ly** *adv.* [L. *auris,* the ear].

au·re·ole, au·re·ola (aw′·ri·ōl, aw·rē′·ạ·lạ) *n.* a radiance around a sacred figure, in art; a halo; a nimbus [L. *aureus,* golden].

au·re·o·my·cin (aw′·ri·ō·mī′·sin) *n.* an antibiotic [L. *aureus,* Gk. *mukes,* mushroom].

au·ric (aw′·rik) *a.* pert. to gold; (*Chem.*) applied to compounds in which gold is trivalent. **aureate** *a.* golden [L. *aurum,* gold].

au·ri·cle (aw′·ri·kl) *n.* the external ear; each of the two upper cavities of the heart. **auricula** (aw·rik′·yoo·lạ) *n.* a part like an ear. **auricular** *a.* pert. to ear, or to hearing; told in the ear (of confession). **auriculate, auriform** *a.* ear-shaped [L. *auris,* the ear].

au·rif·er·ous (aw·rif′·ạ·rạs) *a.* yielding gold [L. *aurum,* gold; *ferre,* to bear].

Au·ro·ra (aw·raw′·rạ) *n.* (*Myth.*) the Roman goddess of the dawn. **aurora** *n.* the dawn; the rosy tint in the sky before the sun rises; an orange-red color. **aurora borealis** (bō·ri·a′·lis), a luminous phenomenon, supposed to be of electrical origin, seen at night in the northern sky. Also called 'northern lights.'

aus·cul·ta·tion (aws·kul·tā′·shạn) *n.* (*Med.*) listening to the movement of heart and lungs either directly with the ear, or with a stethoscope. **ausculate** *v.t.* and *i.* to examine thus [L. *auscultare,* to listen to].

aus·pice (aw′·spis) *n.* favoring influence; an omen based on observing birds; augury; divination; *n.pl.* **auspices,** protection; patronage esp. **under the auspices of. auspicate** *v.t.* to predict; to inaugurate in favorable conditions. **auspicious** (aw·spi′·shus) *a.* giving promise of success; favorable; propitious. **auspiciously** *adv.* **auspiciousness** *n.* [L. *auspicium,* fr. *avis,* a bird; *specere,* to behold].

aus·tere (aw·stēr′) *a.* harsh; severe; strict; simple and without luxury. **-ly** *adv.* **-ness, austerity** *n.* severity; extreme simplicity; asceticism [Gk. *austeros,* harsh].   [south wind].

aus·tral (aws′·trạl) *a.* southern [L. *auster,* the

au·tar·chy (aw′·tȧr·ki·) *n.* absolute power; despotism; dictatorship. **autarchic** *a.* [Gk. *autos,* self; *archein,* to rule].

au·then·tic (aw·then′·tik) *a.* genuine; real; not of doubtful origin; trustworthy; of attested authority. Also **-al. -ally** *adv.* **-ate** *vt.* to prove to be genuine; to confirm. **-ation** *n.* **authenticity** *n.* (aw·then·tis′·ạ·ti·) the quality of genuineness [Gk. *authentikos,* warranted, fr. *authentein,* to have full power].

au·thor (aw′·thẹr) *n.* (*fem.* **-ess**) the beginner or originator of anything; the writer of a book, article, etc. **-ial** *a.* pert. to an author. **-ship** *n.* the quality or function of being an author; source; origin [L. *auctor*].

au·thor·i·ty (aw·thăr′·i·ti·) n. legal power or right; accepted source of information; a writing by an expert on a particular subject; the writer himself; justification; influence; permission; a body or group of persons in control (often *pl.*). **authoritarian** a. advocating obedience to authority as opposed to individual liberty; n. an advocate of authority. **authoritative** a. having the weight of authority; justified. **authoritatively** adv. [L. *auctoritas*].

au·thor·ize (aw′·tha·riz) v.t. to clothe with authority; to empower; to sanction; to make legal; to justify. **authorization** n. [L. *auctorari*].

au·to- (aw′·tō) a combining form fr. Gk. *autos*, self, used in many derivatives and meaning *self*, *oneself*, *by oneself*, etc.

au·to (aw′·tō) n. (*Colloq.*) abbrev. for automobile. **-ist** n. a motorist. **-mobile** (aw·tà··mà′·bĕl) n. a road vehicle driven by mechanical power. **-motive** a. pertaining to automobiles; self-propelling [Gk. *autos*, self; L. *mobilis*, mobile].

au·to·bahn (aw′·tạ·bàn) in Germany, a highway specially constructed for motor traffic [Ger. *Bahn*, a road].

au·to·bi·og·ra·phy (aw·tạ·bī·ág′·rạ·fi·) n. the story of a person's life, written by himself. **autobiographer** n. **autobiographic** a. [Gk. *autos*, self; *bios*, life; *graphein*, to write].

au·to·crat (aw′·tạ·krat) n. monarch who rules by his own absolute right; despot. **-ic** a. **-ically** adv. **autocracy** (aw·tok′·rạ·si·) n. uncontrolled power; a state ruled thusly [Gk. *autos*, self; *kratein*, to rule].

au·to·gi·ro (aw·tạ·jī··rō) n. airplane using horizontal revolving wings for vertical ascent and descent [Gk. *autos*, self; *guros*, a ring].

au·to·graph (aw′·tạ·graf) n. a person's own handwriting or signature; an original manuscript; a. written in one's own handwriting; v.t. to write with one's own hand; to write one's signature [Gk. *autos*, self; *graphein*, to write].

au·to·mat·ic (aw·tạ·mat′·ik) a. self-acting; mechanical; not voluntary; done unconsciously; n. an automatic pistol. **automat** n. a restaurant which serves food using automatic devices. **-ally** adv. mechanically. **automate** v.t. **automation** (aw·tạ·mā′·shạn) n. the automatic control of production processes by electronic apparatus. **automatism** n. involuntary action; power of self-movement without external stimulus. **automaton** (aw·tăm′·ạ·tan) n. [Gk. *automatso*, self-acting].

au·to·mo·bile. See **auto**.

au·ton·o·my (aw·tàn′·ạ·mi·) n. the right of self-government; independence; **autonomous**, **autonomic** a. [Gk. *autos*, self; *nomos*, a law].

au·top·sy (aw′·tàp·si·) n. the dissection and examination of a dead body; a post-mortem examination; personal observation. **autoptic**, **(al)** a. self-observed. **autoptically** adv. [Gk. *autos*, self; *opsis*, sight].

au·to·sug·ges·tion (aw·tō·sạg·jes′·chạn) n. a mental process similar to hypnotism but applied by the subject to himself.

au·tumn (aw′·tạm) n. the third season of the year, generally applied to September, October, and November; fall; the season of decay; the time of declining powers. **-al** a. [L. *autumnus*].

aux·il·ia·ry (awg·zil′·yạ·ri·) a. helping; assisting; subsidiary; n. a helper; (*Gram.*) a verb which helps to form moods, tenses, or voice of another verb, e.g. *be*, *have*, *shall*, *will*, *may* [L. *auxilium*, help].

a·vail (a·vāl′) v.i. to profit by; to take advantage of; v.t. to benefit; to profit; n. advantage; profit; benefit; utility. **-able** a. capable of being used to advantage; procurable. **-ability** **-ability** n. [L. *ad*, to; *valere*, to be strong].

av·a·lanche (av′·ạ·lansh) n. mass of snow and ice moving down from a height and gathering momentum in its descent; (*Fig.*) tremendous downpour [O.Fr. *a val*, into the valley].

av·a·rice (av′·ạ·ris) n. excessive love of money; greed; miserliness; cupidity. **avaricious** a. covetous; grasping. **avariciously** adv. **avariciousness** n. [L. *avarus*, greedy].

a·vast (a·vast′) interj. cease! hold! stop! enough! [Dut. *houd vast*, hold fast].

a·ve (á′ vi, à′·vā) interj. hail! farewell; n. an Ave Maria or Hail Mary; angel Gabriel's salutation (Luke 1) [L.].

a·venge (ạ·venj′) v.t. and v.i. to take satisfaction for an injury to; to punish a wrong-doer; to seek retribution. **-ful** a. desiring retribution. **-ment** n. **-r.** n. (*fem.* **-ress**) one who avenges [O.Fr. *avengier*, to seek retribution].

av·e·nue (av′·e·nòò) n. a wide street with houses and row of trees down each side; (*Fig.*) a means towards, as in *avenue to fame* [L. *ad*, to; *venire*, to come].

a·ver (ạ·vur′) v.t. to declare positively; to avouch; to assert; to allege. *pr.p.* **-ring**; *pa.p.* **-red. -ment** n. the act of averring; a positive assertion; (*Law*) proof of a plea [L. *ad*, to; *verus*, true].

av·er·age (av′·ạ·rij) a. containing a mean proportion; ordinary; normal; n. a medial estimate obtained by dividing the sum of a number of quantities by the number of quantities; v.t. to reduce to a mean [O.Fr. *average*, cattle or possessions; fr. L. *habere*, to have].

a·verse (ạ·vurs′) a. reluctant (to do) or disinclined for; unwilling; set against (foll. by *to*). **-ly** adv. with repugnance. **-ness** n. **aversion** n. a strong dislike; instinctive antipathy; object of dislike [L. *aversus*, turned away].

a·vert (ạ·vurt′) v.t. to turn away from or aside; to ward off. **-ed** a. **-edly** adv. **-ible** a. capable of being avoided [L. *a*, from; *vertere*, to turn].

a·vi·an (ā′·vi·ạn) a. pert. to birds. **aviary** n. an enclosed space for breeding, rearing and keeping of birds [L. *avis*, a bird].

a·vi·a·tion (ā·vi·ā′·shạn) n. the art of flying aircraft. **aviate** v.i. to fly. **aviator** n. (*fem.* **aviatress, axiatrix**) [L. *avis*, a bird].

av·id (av′·id) a. eager; greedy; desirous (foll. by *of* or *for*). **avidity** n. greediness; eagerness; hunger; (*Fig.*) zest [L. *avidus*, greedy].

a·vo·ca·do (av·ạ·kà′·dō) n. the alligator pear; juicy eible fruit [Mex.].

av·o·ca·tion (av·ạ·kā′·shạn) n. a distraction; a minor plausible occupation; a hobby; a side interest; **avocative** a. calling off; n. a dissuasion [L. *a*, away; *vocare*, to call].

a·void (ạ·void′) v.t. to shun; to elude; to keep clear of; to eschew; to abstain from; to escape; (*Law*) to invalidate; to annul. **-able** a. **-ance** n. the act of shunning [L. *ex*, out; and *void*].

av·oir·du·pois (av·ẹr·dạ·poiz′) n. a common system of weights; (*Colloq.*) heaviness [corrupt. of O.Fr. *avoir de pois*, goods by weight i.e. not by numbers].

a·vouch (a·vouch′) v.t. to declare positively; to guarantee [L. *ad*, to; *vocare*, to call].

a·vow (ạ·vou′) v.t. to declare openly; to own; to confess freely; to acknowledge. **-able** a. **-al** n. an open declaration or admission. **-ance**, evidence; testimony. **-edly** adv. [Fr. *avouer*].

aw (aw) interj. sound of protest; dislike.

a·wait (ạ·wāt′) v.t. to wait for; be in store for; attend; be ready for.

a·wake (ạ·wāk′) v.t. to rouse from sleep; to stir up; v.i. to cease from sleep; to bestir oneself; *pa.t.* **awoke**; *pa.p.* **awoke, awaked**; a. not asleep; alert; vigilant; alive. **awaken** v.t. and v.i. to rouse from sleep; to awake; to excite. **awak(en)ing** n. a revival of interest or conscience [O.E. *awacian*].

a·ward (ạ·wawrd′) v.t. to adjudge; to determine (a point submitted); to decide authoritatively; to assign judicially; n. judgment; the recorded decision of an arbitrator in a court of law; thing awarded; prize [fr. O. Fr. *eswarder*].

a·ware (ạ·wār′) a. watchful; mindful; conscious of; possessing knowledge of; sensible. **-ness** n.

[O.E. *gewaer*, conscious].

a·wash (a.wásh') *adv.* (*Naut.*) level with the surface of the water; washed by the waves.

a·way (a.wā') *adv.* absent; at a distance; on the way; apart; be gone! [O.E. *onweg*, on the way].

awe (aw) *n.* wonder mingled with veneration and dread; *v.t.* to inspire with awe. **-some** *a.* **-struck, -stricken** *a.* **awful** *a.* full of awe; filling with fear and admiration; impressive; venerable; majestic, dreadful; terrible; horrible; ugly; unsightly. **awfulness** *n.* **awfully,** *adv.* (*Colloq.*) very, extremely [O.E. *ege*, awe].

a·weigh (a.wā') *adv.* (*Naut.*) when a ship's anchor is just broken out of the ground by the initial strain on the cable; atrip.

aw·ful. See under **awe.**

a·while (a.whil') *adv.* for a while.

awk·ward (awk'.wērd) *a.* unskilful; ungainly; clumsy; difficult to manage; inconvenient; embarrassing. **-ly** *adv.* **-ness** *n.* **awkward age,** adolescence [M.E. *awk*, wrong; and *ward*].

awl (awl) *n.* a small pointed instrument for boring holes in leather [O.E. *awel*].

awn·ing (aw'.ning) *n.* a covering of canvas, etc. to shelter from the sun's rays.

a·woke. See **awake.**

a·wry (a.rī') *adv.* and *a.* twisted to one side; crooked [See **wry**]. [earlier, *on wry*].

ax, axe (aks) *n.* for cutting, chopping or hewing. **an axe to grind,** a private end or purpose to serve [O.E. *aex*].

ax·es (ak'.ses) plural form of **axe** and **axis.**

ax·i·om (ak'.si.am) *n.* a necessary and self-evident proposition, requiring no proof. **-atic, -atical** *a.* self-evident. **-atically** *adv.* [Gk. *axioma* fr. *axioein*, to require].

ax·is (ak'.sis) *n.* the imaginary line round which a solid body rotates or a geometrical figure is symmetrically disposed. *pl.* **axes** (ak'.sēs). **axial** *a.* forming the axis. **axially** (*adv.* [L. *axis*, an axle].

ax·le, ax·le·tree (ak'.sl.trē) *n.* a bar of wood or iron rod on which a wheel, or a system of wheels, turns [O.N. *oxul-tre*].

ay, aye (ī) *adv.* yes; yea. **ayes** (īz) *n.pl.* affirmative votes or voters [*yea*].

aye, ay (ā) *adv.* always; ever [O.N. *ei*].

a·za·le·a (a.zā'.li.a) *n.* a genus of plants allied to the rhododendron [Gk. *azaleos*, dry].

a·zo·ic (a.zō'.ik) *a.* pert. to that part of geologic time before animal life existed [Gk. *a-*, neg.; *zoe*, life].

Az·tec (az'.tek) *n.* a member of a people dominant in Mexican Empire at the time of the Sp. conquest; their language; *a.* pert to the race or its language.

az·ure (azh'.er) *n.* sky blue; the sky; *a.* sky-blue [Fr. *azur*, from Ar.].

B

Ba·al (bā'.al) *n.* a false deity. *pl.* **Baalim. Baalist** *n.* a worshipper of Baal. [Heb.].

babble (ba'.bl) *v.t.* and *i.* to chatter senselessly; to prate; to reveal secrets; *n.* prattling; idle talk; murmuring of running water. **-r** *n.* **babbling** *n.* [Onomat.].

babe (bāb) *n.* an infant; a young child [earlier *baban*, imit. of baby speech].

ba·bel (bā'.bal) *n.* a confusion of unintelligible sounds; noisy babble of many people talking at the one time; uproar, at a public meeting. **-dom** *n.* uproar. [Heb. = confusion].

ba·boon (ba.bòòn') *n.* a species of monkey with large body, big canine teeth and capacious cheek-pouches [Fr. *babouin*].

ba·by (bā'.bi.) *n.* an infant; a young child; *a.* pert. to a baby; small, as in — **grand** (piano), etc. **-hood** *n.* the period of infancy. **-ish** *a.*

infantile; behaving like a young child. [earlier *baban*, imit of baby speech].

bac·ca·lau·re·ate (bak.a.law'.ri.at) *n.* the university degree of bachelor; an address to a graduating class [fr. L. *baccalarius*].

Bac·chus (bak.'as) *n.* (*Myth.*) the god of wine. **bacchanal** *n.* a worshipper of Bacchus; a drunken reveller; an orgy in honor of Bacchus; *a.* pert. to Bacchus; riotous; drunken. **bacchanalia** *n.pl.* feasts in honor of Bacchus; drunken revels. **bacchanalian** *n.* and *a.* **bacchic** *a.* relating to Bacchus; jovial due to intoxication [L.].

bach·e·lor (bach'.a.ler) *n.* an unmarried man; a celibate; one who has taken the first degree at a university; a monk who performed menial duties. **-hood, -ism, -ship** *n.* [M.L. *baccalarius*, a small farmer].

ba·cil·lus (ba.sil'.as) *n.* microscopic, rod-like organisms capable of causing certain diseases. *pl.* **bacilli, bacillar, bacillary** *a.* **bacilliform** *a.* of a rod-like shape [L. *baculus*, a rod].

back (bak) *n.* the upper or hinder part of the trunk of an animal; the hinder part of an object; a football player whose position is behind the line of scrimmage; *a.* of the back; at the rear of; not current (as a magazine); reversed; remote; *adv.* to or toward a former place, state, condition, or time; away from the front; in return; *v.t.* to get, or ride, upon the back of; to provide with a back; to force backward; to place a bet on; to support; to endorse (a check, etc.); *v.i.* to move or go back; of the wind, to change direction counter-clockwise. **-bite** *v.t.* to speak evil of someone in his absence. **backbiter** *n.* **-bone** *n.* the spine or vertebral column; firmness; courage. **backboned** *a.* **-er** *n.* supporter; **-field** *n.* the backs as in football who play behind the line. **-fire** *n.* in internal combustion engines, premature ignition of fuel; *v.i.* to do this; to go awry; **-ground** *n.* part behind foreground of a picture or stage setting; knowledge gained by experience. —**hand** *n.* writing sloped from left to right; a stroke in tennis with the hand turned backwards. **-handed** *a.* with the back of the hand; deceitful; indirect; sarcastic; doubtful. **-ing** *n.* support; sympathy; providing anything with a support; **-lash** *n.* the jarring reaction of a machine due to the degree of play; **-log** *n.* an accumulation, a reserve amount. — **number** *n.* a copy of an out-of-date publication; one behind the times or unprogressive. **-side** *n.* back or hinder part; the rear side; the buttocks; the rump. **-sight** *n.* the rear sight of a rifle. **-slide** *v.i.* to slide backwards; to lapse from a high moral standard. **-stage** *adv.* behind the stage, in the wings, etc. **-stays** *n.pl.* ropes supporting the upper mast. — **talk** *n.* insolent reply; impertinence. **-track** *v.i.* to retreat; to return over the same route. **-ward** *adv.* with the back in advance; towards, or on, the back; to a worse state; in a reverse direction; *a.* directed to the back or rear; dull; behind in one's education; shy; unwilling; late. **-wash** *n.* backward current; (*Slang*) the dire consequences. **-water** *n.* water held back by a dam; water thrown back by a paddle-wheel; a by-way in a river or creek. **-woods** *n.pl.* outlying forest districts or remote undeveloped country. **-woodsman** *n.* [O.E. *bacc*].

back·gam·mon (bak.gam'.an) *n.* a game played by two with 15 pieces each on a special board [E. fr. *back* and M.E. *gamen*, play].

ba·con (bā'.kn) *n.* back and sides of hogs after being salted and smoked [O.Fr.].

bac·te·ri·um (bak.ti'.ri.am) *n.* group of non-spore forming bacteria. *pl.* **bacteria. bacterial** *a.* **bactericide** *n.* any agent capable of destroying bacteria. **bactericidal** *a.* **bacteriology** *n.* the study of bacteria [Gk. *bakterion*, a little stick].

bad (bad) *a.* ill or evil; wicked. **-dish** *a.* rather bad. **-ly** *adv.* **-ness** *n.* **bad blood,** ill feeling. **bad lands** *n.pl.*, badly eroded, barren land esp. in the Dakotas. **to go bad,** to rot or decay [M.E. *badde*].

bade (bad) past tense of the verb **bid.**

badge (baj) *n.* an emblem, usually symbolic, worn to distinguish members of societies, regiments, etc.; token; mark; symbol [M.E. *bage*].

badg·er (baj′·ẹr) *n.* a greyish-brown hibernating animal; *v.t.* to follow hotly as dogs do the badger; to tease, by persistent questioning; to pester or annoy [from the white stripe or *badge* on the animal's forehead].

bad·i·nage (bad·ạ·nij′) *n.* playful or sportive talk; banter [Fr. *badin*, frivolous].

bad·min·ton (bad′·min·tạn) *n.* a game similar to tennis with the substitution of shuttlecocks for tennis balls [fr. *Badminton* House in Gloucestershire where the game was invented].

baf·fle (baf′·l) *v.t.* to frustrate; to confuse; to check or turn, as wind baffles a ship. **-r** *n.* **baffling** *a.* disconcerting; confusing.

baf·fle (baf′·l) *n.* a plate for regulating the flow of a liquid or gas; a metal plate used between the cylinders of an air-cooled motor engine to break up a stream of heated gases; a baffle-plate; a rigid mounting usually of wood, holding the reproducing diaphragm of a radio receiver.

bag (bag) *n.* a sack or pouch; content of a sack; results of one's fishing or hunting; an udder; *v.t.* to put into a bag; to seize; *v.i.* to hang loosely; to bulge or swell out. *pr.p.* **-ging.** *pa.p.* **-ged. -gage,** *n.* tents and stores of an army; luggage; a dissolute woman. **bag and baggage,** with all one's belongings. **-ging** *n.* cloth or material for bags. **-giness** *n.* the state of being baggy (as trousers). **-gy** *a.* hanging loosely; puffy. **in the bag,** certain, assured. **to let the cat out of the bag,** to reveal a secret unwittingly [O.N. *baggi*].

bag·a·telle (bag·ạ·tel′) *n.* a trifle; a thing of little worth or importance; a game played with balls and a cue on a board; a short piece of music in light style [Fr.].

ba·gel (bā·′gl) *n.* a doughnut-shaped roll.

bag·pipe (bag′·pīp) *n.* musical reed instrument, common to Scotland. **-r** *n.* [M.E. *baggepipe*].

bail (bāl) *n.* (*Law*) security taken by the court that a person charged will attend at a future date to answer to the charge; one who furnishes this security; *v.t.* to obtain the release of a person from prison by giving security against his reappearance. **-able** *a.* — **bond** *n.* a bond given by a person who is being bailed and his surety. **-ee** *n.* the holder of goods in trust who must obey the direction with which the delivery to him is made. **bail out** *v.i.* to jump from an aircraft and descend by parachute [O.Fr. *bailler*].

bail (bāl) *n.* a scoop; a shallow vessel for clearing water out of a boat; *v.t.* to empty of water with some kind of water scoop. **-er** *n.* [F. *baille*, bucket].

bail·iff (bā′·lif) *n.* an under-officer of a sheriff; a minor officer of a court; (*Br.*) land-owner's agent [O.Fr. *baillir*].

bail·i·wick (bāl′·a·wik) *n.* bailiff's jurisdiction; (*Fig.*) one's special domain, or area of skill, work, etc. [O.Fr., *baillif*, a justice; O.E. *wice*, office].

bairn (bern) *n.* (*Scot.*) a child (O.E. *bearn*].

bait (bāt) *n.* food set to entice fish or an animal; a lure; snare; *v.t.* to put food on a hook or in a trap as a lure; to set dogs on an animal; to harass; to tease. **-er** *n.* **-ing** *a.* and *n.* [Icel. *beita*, to cause to bite].

baize (bāz) *n.* a woolen or cotton cloth with long nap [O.Fr.].

bake (bāk) *v.t.* to harden by heat; to cook in an oven or over a fire; *v.i.* to work at baking; to be baked. **-house** *n.* **bakery** *n.* a bakehouse. **baking** *n.* a batch of bread, etc. **a baker's dozen,** thirteen [O.E. *basan*].

Ba·ke·lite (bāk′·ạ·līt) *n.* a hard, strong synthetic resin used as a substitute for wood, bone, celluloid, etc., a trade name [L. H. *Baekeland*, the inventor].

bal·a·lai·ka (bal·a·lī′·kạ) *n.* an old Slavic stringed instrument [Russ.].

bal·ance (bal′·ans) *n.* an apparatus for determining the weight, or comparing the masses, of bodies; a poised beam with two opposite scales; any condition of equilibrium; part of a watch or clock which regulates the beats; a sense of proportion and discretion; poise; payment still due, or cash in hand; *v.t.* to weigh, as in a balance; to render equal in proportion, etc.; to adjust, as an account; *v.i.* to be of the same weight; to be in equipoise. — **sheet** *a.* statement of the assets and liabilities of a company [L. *bis*, twice; *lanx*, a plate].

bal·co·ny (bal′·kạ·ni) *n.* a platform or gallery projecting from a building; a gallery in a theater or concert hall [It. *balcone*].

bald (bawld) *a.* destitute of hair or feathers on the crown of the head; bare; unadorned; undisguised; without literary style; monotonous. **-head, -pate** *n.* one destitute of hair. **-ly** *adv.* **-ness** *n.* [M.E. *balled*].

bal·der·dash (bawl′·dẹr·dash) *n.* a jargon of meaningless words jumbled together; nonsense.

bale (bāl) *n.* that which causes sorrow or ruin; evil; misery; mischief; injury; woe. **-ful** *a.* **-fully** *adv.* [O.E. *bealu*, evil].

bale (bāl) *n.* a package, compactly compressed, and wrapped in a protecting cover; *v.t.* to pack in bales. **-r** *n.* one employed in baling goods [N.E. *balle*]. [whale].

ba·leen (bạ·lēn′) *n.* whalebone [L. *balaena*, a

balk (bawk) *n.* a crossbeam or rafter, of squared timber, stretching from wall to wall; an unploughed ridge of land; a barrier or check; a disappointment; a part of a billiard table; in *baseball*, an uncompleted pitch, entitling base runners to advance one base; *v.t.* to frustrate; to bar the way; *v.i.* to stop abruptly; refuse to move. **-y** *a.* [O.E. *balca*, a ridge].

ball (bawl) *n.* any round body; a sphere; a globe; the earth; bullet or shot; a delivery outside the strike zone by a pitcher; the heavy piece of a pendulum; *v.t.* and *i.* to form into a ball. — **bearings** *n.* hardened steel balls interposed in channels or 'races' between the rotating and stationary surfaces of a bearing to lessen friction. — **point pen** *n.* fountain pen with a tiny ball point leaving a fine trace of ink on the paper. —**race** *n.* the grooves in which the balls of a ball-bearing run. **ball and socket,** a joint formed by a ball partly enclosed in a cup and so adjusted that it can move freely in all directions. [Scand. origin].

ball (bawl) *n.* a social gathering for the purpose of dancing; an assembly. **-room** *n.* [L.L. *ballare*, to dance].

bal·lad (bal′·ạd) *n.* a story in verse, of popular origin, generally patriotic and sung orig. to the harp; a concert-room melody, usually sentimental. **-ist** *n.* a composer or singer of ballads. **-ry** *n.* collected ballads; folk songs. **-eer** *n.* [L.L. *ballare*, to dance].

bal·lade (bạ·lád′) *n.* a short poem of one to three triplet stanzas of eight lines, each with the same rhymes and refrain, and an envoy of four or five lines [Fr.].

bal·last (bal′·ạst) *n.* heavy material taken on board ship to increase the vessel's draft and steadiness; sandy material dredged from river beds used for concrete; that which renders anything steady; *v.t.* to load with ballast; to steady [obs. *last*, burden].

bal·le·ri·na (bal·ạ·rē′·nạ) *n.* a female ballet dancer [It.].

bal·let (bal′·ā) *n.* a representation, consisting of dancing and miming, aiming to express an idea or tell a story, to the accompaniment of music. **balletomane** (bal·ạt·ạ·mān′) *n.* an enthusiast for ballet [Fr.].

bal·lis·ta, balista (ba̩·lis′·ta̩) *n.* an ancient military contrivance for hurling huge stones. **ballistic** *a.* pert. to a projectile and its flight. **ballistics** *n.pl.* scientific study of motion of projectiles [Gk. *ballein*, to throw].

bal·loon (ba̩·lŏon′) *n.* bag designed to float in the air and unequipped for mechanical propulsion; anything inflated. **-ing** *n.* **ist** *n.* [Fr. *ballon*].

bal·lot (bal′·a̩t) *n.* secret voting; slip of paper used in secret voting; *v.t.* to vote on by ballot; to draw lots [Fr. *ballotte*, little ball].

bal·ly·hoo (bal′·i·hŏo)*n.* (*Slang*) advertising; bombast.

balm (bám) a fragrant plant; any fragrant or healing ointment; anything which soothes pain. **-iness** *n.* **-y** *a.* fragrant; bearing balm [Fr. *balsamum*].

ba·lo·ney, boloney (ba̩l·ō′·ni·) *n.* (*Slang*) misleading talk; nonsense; (*Colloq.*) bologna sausage [etym. unknown].

bal·sa, (bawl′·sa̩) *n.* the extremely light wood of a W. Indian tree [Sp.].

bal·sam (bawl′·sa̩m) *n.* a name applied to many aromatic resins and oils with stimulant and tonic properties; a soothing ointment; a healing agent. **-ic** *n.* soothing, oily. **-ous** *a.* soothing. **-y** *a.* [Gk. *balsamon*].

bal·us·ter (bal′·a̩s·te̩r) *n.* a stone or wooden shaft turned and molded, used to support a handrail. **-ed** *a.* provided with balusters. **balustrade** *n.* a row of balusters supporting a railing [Gk. *balaustion*, the pomegranate, whose flowers it resembles].

bam·bi·no (bam·bē′·nō) *n.* a child or baby [It.].

bam·boo (bam·bŏo′) *n.* a genus of immense grasses in the tropics [Malay].

bam·boo·zle (bam·bŏo′·zl) *v.t.* (*Slang*) to mystify; to trick; hoax; cheat; swindle. **-r** *n.*

ban (ban) *n.* proclamation; a sentence of outlawry; excommunication; a curse; a prohibition; *v.t.* to prohibit; to curse; *pr.p.* **-ning.** *pa.t.* and *pa.p.* **-ned** [O.E. *bannan*, to summon, curse].

ba·nal (bān′·a̩l, ban·ál′, ban′·a̩l) *a.* trite, trivial, petty, vulgar, commonplace. **-ity** *n.*

ba·nan·a (ba̩·na′·na̩) *n.* the edible fruit of a tropical plant [Sp.].

band (band) *n.* a cord, tie, or fillet; part of a clerical, legal, or university vestment consisting of two pieces of cambric or linen joined together and worn under the chin; an ornamental strip separating moldings on a building or dividing a wall space; an endless belt used for driving wheels or rollers. **-box** *n.* a light cardboard box for millinery. [O.E. *bindan*, to bind].

band (band) *n.* players of musical instruments in combined performance; a company united for common purpose; a number of armed men; *v.t.* to bind together; *v.i.* to associate, join together. **-master** *n.* director of a military or brass band. **bandsman** *n.* a member of a brass band. **-stand** *n.* an open-air structure suitable for musical performances. **to climb aboard the band wagon,** to participate in a movement when its success is assured. [Fr.].

band·age (band′·ij) *n.* a strip of cloth, used for binding up wounds, etc. *v.t.* to bind with a bandage [Fr. *bande*].

ban·dan·na, ban·dan·a (ban·dan′·a̩)*n.* a large patterned silk or cotton handkerchief [Hind.].

ban·deau (ban′·dō) *n.* a narrow band worn by women to bind the hair; narrow brassiere; *pl.* **bandeaux** [Fr.].

ban·dit (ban′·dit) *n.* robber; brigand; outlaw; highwayman; *pl.* **-s, -ti. -ry** *n.* [It. *bandito*, fr. *bandire*, to outlaw].

ban·do·leer, ban·do·lier (ban·da̩·lēr′) *n.* a broad belt worn over the shoulder and fitted with pockets to hold cartridges [It. *bandoliera*].

ban·dy (ban′·di·) *a.* crooked; bent; bandied; bandy-legged; *v.t.* to beat to and fro; to toss from one to another, as 'to bandy words.' **ban-**

died *a.* **—legged** *a.* having crooked legs, bending outwards [Fr. *bander*, to bend].

bane (bān) *n.* any cause of ruin; destruction; mischief; noxious substance; poison. **-ful** *a.* **-fulness** *n.* [O.E. *bana*, a murderer].

bang (bang) *v.t.* to beat, as with a club; to handle roughly; to make a loud noise; *n.* a blow with a club or a fist; a loud noise; an explosion. **-ing** *n.* [Scand. *banga*, to hammer].

bang (bang) *v.t.* to cut the front hair square across; *n.* a straight fringe over the forehead or at the end of a horse's tail [nasal variant of *bag*-(cut)].

ban·gle (bang′·gl) *n.* an ornamental ring worn round arm or ankle; bracelet [Urdu, *bangri*, a bracelet].

ban·ish (ban′·ish) *v.t.* to condemn to exile; to drive away; to expel; to cast from the mind. **-ment** *n.* exile [fr. *ban*].

ban·is·ter (ban′·is·te̩r) *n.* Same as **baluster.**

ban·jo (ban′·jō) *n.* a stringed musical instrument [Gk. *pandoura*, a musical instrument].

bank (bangk) *n.* a ridge of earth; a shoal; a sandbank; the edge of a stream or lake; the raised edge of a road, etc.; a mass of heavy clouds or fog; *v.t.* to raise a mound; to dike; to cover a fire with small coal to procure slow combustion; to tilt about the longitudinal axis when turning. **to bank on** *v.t.* to depend on [O.E. *banc*, a bench].

bank (bangk) *n.* a bench on which rowers sit; a tier of oars; a row of objects [Fr. *banc*].

bank (bangk) *n.* an establishment where money is received for custody and repaid on demand; money-box; the money at stake in games of chance; a pool; *v.t.* to deposit money in a bank. **-book** *n.* a pass-book in which a customer's dealings with a bank are recorded. **-er** *n.* one employed in banking; in games of chance the proprietor against whom the other players stake. **— note** *n.* a promissory note on bank of issue promising to pay its face value to bearer on demand. **— rate** *n.* the rate of discount, fixed by a bank or banks [Fr. *banque*].

bank·rupt (bangk′·rupt) *n.* insolvent person compelled to place his affairs in the hands of creditors; *v.t.* to cause to go bankrupt; *a.* insolvent, unable to pay debts; lacking in (ideas, etc.). **-cy** *n.* [E. *bank;* L. *ruptus*, broken].

ban·ner (ban′·e̩r) *n.* a flag or ensign. **-ed** *a.* [Fr. *bannière*].

ban·nock (ban′·a̩k) *n.* (*Scot.*) a flat, thick, cake of oatmeal or barley [Gael. *bonnach*].

banns (banz) *n.pl.* proclamation of intended marriage [fr. *ban*].

ban·quet (bang′·kwet) *n.* a feast; a rich repast; something specially delicious; *v.t.* to entertain at a banquet. **-ing** *n.* [Fr. dim. of *banc*, bench].

ban·shee (ban′·shē) *n.* in Ireland and W. Highlands of Scotland, a fairy-elf who, by shrieks and wailing, foretells the approaching death of a member of a family [Ir. *bean sidhe*, woman of the fairies].

ban·tam (ban′·ta̩m) *n.* a variety of the small common domestic fowl; *a.* of very light weight; plucky. **-weight,** a boxer weighing less than 118 lbs. [fr. *Bantam*, a village in Java].

ban·ter (ban′·te̩r) *v.i.* to make good-natured fun of someone; to joke, jest; to rally; *n.* wit at expense of another; chaff; pleasantry. **-er** *n.*

Ban·tu (ban′·tŏo) *n.* an African language.

ban·yan (ban′·ya̩n) *n.* the Indian fig; a tree whose branches, bending to the ground, take root and form new stocks, till they become a forest. Hence—**to flourish like the banyan-tree** [Port.].

bap·tize (bap′·tīz) *v.t.* to administer the sacrament of baptism to; to christen; give a name to. **baptism** *n.* sacrament by which a person is initiated into the membership of the Christian Church. **baptismal** *a.* **Baptist** *n.* one who baptizes; one who insists that the rite of initiation is duly administered only by immersion upon personal profession of faith. **bap-**

tistery, baptistry *n.* an ancient circular building in which baptisms took place [Gk. *baptizein*, to immerse].

bar (bàr) *n.* a long piece of any solid material, used as barrier; the bolt of a door; a sand-bank; part of a tavern with a counter for the sale of liquor; a public-house; the rail before the judge's seat where prisoners appear; members of the legal profession allowed to plead in court; (*Her.*) a band crossing the shield; (*Mus.*) a perpendicular line drawn across the stave immediately before the primary accent; *v.t.* to fasten or mark with a bar; to obstruct; to prevent; to exclude; *prep.* except. **-maid, -man, -tender** *n.* a bar attendant. **-ring** *prep.* excepting; *n.* exclusion of any kind. *pr.p.* **-ring**. *pa.p.* **-red**. [Fr. *barre*].

barb (bàrb) *n.* a hooked hair; the spike of an arrow, fish-hook, etc.; a horse of great speed and endurance, originally from Barbary; *v.t.* to furnish with barbs or prongs, as an arrow; to trim the beard. **-ed** *a.* bearded; furnished with a barb or barbs. **-ed wire** *n.* a wire armed with sharp points used for defensive purposes [L. *barba*, beard].

bar·bar·i·an (bàr·be'·ri·an) *n. orig.* one who could not speak Greek, now an uncivilized being without culture; a cruel, brutal man; *a.* savage; rude. **barbaric** *a.* uncivilized; rude; nobly savage. **barbarize** *v.t.* to render barbarous. **barbarism** *n.* incorrect use of idiom or word; want of civilization. **barbarity** *n.* cruelty; savagery. **barbarous** *a.* uncivilized or savage [Gk. *barbaros*, foreign].

bar·be·cue (bàr'·bi·kū) *n.* a grid-iron on which meat is roasted over an open fire; an animal so roasted; a lavish open-air feast [Haitian].

bar·ber (bàr'·ber) *n.* one who shaves or trims and dresses the hair; a hair-dresser [L. *barba*, beard].

bar·ber·ry (bàr'·ber·i·) *n.* (*Bot.*) a shrub with clusters of red berries [M.L. *berberis*].

bar·bi·tu·rates (bàr-bit'·ū·rātz) *n.* (*Med.*) derivatives of barbituric acid, non-habit forming, hypnotic and sedative drugs.

bar·ca·role, bar·ca·rolle, (bàr'·ka·rōl) *n.* a musical composition written in imitation of the gondoliers' songs of Venice. [It. *barca*, a boat].

bard (bàrd) *n.* a Celtic minstrel who celebrated in song the great deeds of heroes; a poet. **-ic** *a.* pert. to bards or their poetry [Celt.].

bare (bār) *a.* without covering; naked; empty; open to view; paltry; *v.t.* to strip off or uncover. **-ly** *adv.* openly; poorly; scarcely. **-ness** *n.* **-facedness** *n.* sheer impudence. [O.E. *baer*].

bar·gain (bàr'·gin] *n.* an agreement between parties in buying and selling; a profitable transaction; something purchased cheaply. *v.i.* to make a contract; to chaffer. **-er** *n.* one who haggles over the price. **into the bargain,** over and above what is agreed upon [O.Fr. *bargaigner*].

barge (bàrj) *n.* flat-bottomed boat; a ship's boat; *v.i.* to push forward roughly. **-man** *n.* [L. *barca*, a boat].

bar·i·tone (bàr'·a·tōn) *n.* the male human voice between tenor and bass [Gk. *barys*, heavy; *tonos*, tone].

bar·i·um (bār'·i·am) *n.* metallic element (symbol *Ba*). **baric** *a.* [fr. Gk. *barys*, heavy].

bark (bàrk) *n.* the outer covering of a tree; rind; waste tan used in manufacturing white-lead; *v.t.* to strip off bark; to graze the skin. [Scand.].

bark (bàrk) *v.t.* to utter a cry like a dog; to yelp; (*Slang*) to advertise by shouting; to speak sharply; **-er,** *n.* **to bark up the wrong tree,** to be on the wrong trail [O.E. *beorcan*].

bark, barque (bàrk) *n.* a three masted vessel; a small sailing-ship; (*Poet.*) a ship [Fr. *barque*].

bar·ley (bàr'·li·) *n.* a cereal, the grain being used for malt-making, bread, and food for cattle. **-corn** *n.* a grain of barley; the third part of an inch. **John Barleycorn** (*Fig.*) whisky. — **flour** *n.* flour made by grinding barley. — **sugar** *n.* a confection made from sugar boiled till brittle in barley water. [O.E. *bere*, barley].

barm (bàrm) *n.* the froth on fermenting malt liquors, used in making bread; yeast. **-y** *a.* pert. to barm; light-headed, flighty, or giddy [O.E. *beorma*, yeast].

barn (bàrn) *n.* a covered farm-building for storing grain, hay, etc. and for stabling live stock; *v.t.* to store in a barn. — **dance** *n.* a lively dance in 4-4 time, resembling the schottische. **-yard** *a.* pert. to domestic fowls. *n.* open enclosure attached to barn. **-stormer** *n.* an itinerant actor [O.E. *bere*, barley; *ern*, a place].

bar·na·cle (bàr'·na·kl) *n.* a shell-fish which attaches itself to the bottoms of ships and to rocks. **-d** *a.* [O.Fr. *bernac*].

ba·rom·e·ter (ba·ràm'·a·ter) *n.* an instrument for recording the weight or pressure of the atmosphere which indicates impending weather changes. **barometric, barometrical** *a.* [Gk. *baros*, weight; *metron*, measure].

bar·on (bar'·an) *n.* a title of nobility, the lowest of the British peerage to sit in the House of Lords; a commercial magnate. (*fem.* **baroness**) [L.L. *baro*, a man].

bar·o·net (bar'·a·net) *n.* hereditary title ranking below a baron and above a knight but without privilege of peerage. **baronetcy** *n.* the rank of a baronet [dim. of *baron*].

ba·roque (ba·rōk') *n. orig.* a jeweller's trade term for ill-shaped pearls; (*Art.*) a florid style of the late Renaissance; *a.* over-lavish; extravagantly ornamented [Port. *barrocco*].

bar·o·scope (bar'·a·skōp) *n.* an instrument giving rough indications of variations in the atmospheric pressure [Gk. *baros*, weight; *skopein*, to see].

bar·rack (bar'·ak) *n.* a building for the accommodation of soldiers (generally used in the plural) [Sp. *barraca*, a tent].

bar·ra·cu·da (bar·a·kōō'·da) *n.* a large edible pike-like fish, found in the Atlantic [Sp.].

bar·rage (ba·razh') *n.* an artificial bar erected across a stream to regulate its flow; a screen of continuous military fire produced to protect the advance of troops or to stop hostile attacks; heavy prolonged attack.

bar·ra·try (bar'·a·tri·) *n.* fraudulent breach of duty by the master of a ship entailing loss by the owners or insurers of ship or cargo; habitually inciting riot or stirring up suits and quarrels [O.Fr. *barat*, fraud].

bar·rel (bar'·al) *n.* a cylindrical wooden container consisting of staves bound by hoops; a measure of capacity; anything cylindrical, as a gun-barrel; *v.t.* to stow in barrels. — **organ** *n.* street-organ played by rotating a wooden barrel [Fr. *baril*].

bar·ren (bar'·an) *a.* incapable of producing offspring or fruit; empty, lacking. **-ly** *adv.* **-ness** *n.* sterility [O.Fr.].

bar·rette (ba·ret') *n.* small bar or clasp worn to hold hair in place [Fr. *barre*].

bar·ri·cade (bar'·i·kād) *n.* a make-shift fortification, built as an obstruction; an obstruction which hinders free passage; *v.t.* to build this; formerly **barricado** [Fr. *barrica*, a cask].

bar·ri·er (bar'·i·er) *n.* a chain of military posts to protect frontiers; a railing, fence, or wall; any obstruction; a line of separation [O.Fr. *barrière*].

bar·ris·ter (bar'·is·ter) *n.* (*Br.*) a member of the highest branch of the legal profession, with exclusive right of practicing in the superior courts of England [fr. *bar*].

bar·row (bar'·ō) *n.* a small kind of light frame provided with two shafts, for carrying loads [O.E. *beran*, to hear].

bar·row (bar′·ō) *n.* an artificial mound of stone, wood, or earth, piled up in prehistoric times over the remains of the dead; a hillock [O.E. *beorg*, a mound].

bar·ter (bår′·tẹr) *v.t.* to exchange or give in exchange; *v.i.* to traffic by exchange of one kind of goods for another; *n.* direct exchange of commodities [O.Fr. *barater*, to haggle].

bas·al See **base** *n.*

ba·salt (bạ·sawlt′) *n.* an igneous rock of a greenish-black color. **-ic** *a.* [L. *basaltes*, black basalt].

bas·cule (bas′·kūl) *n.* a balancing lever. **bas·cule-bridge** *n.* a counterpoise bridge [Fr. *bas*, down; *cul*, the posterior].

base (bās) *a.* of humble birth or of low degree; morally low. **-ly** *adv.* **-born** *a.* illegitimate [Fr. *bas*, low].

base (bās) *n.* bottom; part of a thing on which it rests; foundation; support; starting-place; fixed point; supply point of an army; station at baseball; main ingredient; (*Chem.*) a substance capable of combining with an acid to form a salt; *v.t.* to put on a base; to found. **basal** *a.* situated at the base. **-less** *a.* having no foundation. **-lessness** *n.* **-ly** *adv.* **-ment** *n.* the lowest story of a building. **basic** *a.* **-board** *n.* a skirting board covering the lower part of a wall [Gk. *basis*].

base (bās) (*Mus.*). See **bass**.

base·ball (bās′·bawl) *n.* ball game, played by two teams of nine players in which a player after batting must make the complete circuit of four bases to score a run; the ball used.

bash (bash) *v.t.* (*Colloq.*) to smash in; to beat in; to knock out of shape; to beat; *n.* a severe blow; a dent. **-ing** *n.* a thrashing [blend of *bat* and *mash*].

bash·ful (bash′·ful) *a.* shy; not desiring to attract notice. **-ly** *adv.* **-ness** *n.* [fr. *abashfull*].

ba·sic (bā′·sik) *a.* relating to or serving as a base; primary; containing a small amount of silica. **English**, simplification of English. **— slag** *n.* a by-product in the manufacture of steel, used as a manure [Gk. *basis*, a base].

bas·il (baz′·il) *n.* aromatic culinary plant; sweet basil [Gk. *basilikos*, royal].

ba·sil·i·ca (bạ·sil′·i·kạ) *n.* a public building or hall of the Romans, later often converted into a church by early Christians; a spacious church built on the model of the original basilicas. **basilican** *a.* [Gk. *basilikos*, royal].

bas·i·lisk (bas′·ạ·lisk) *n.* a fabulous creature; a cockatrice; (*Zool.*) a harmless tree-dwelling American lizard; [Gk. *basilikos*, royal].

ba·sin (bā′·sn) *n.* a wide, hollow, bowl-shaped container; a sink; a land-locked bay with a good anchorage; the whole tract of country drained by a river [Fr. *bassin*].

ba·sis (bā′·sis) *n.* that on which a thing rests; foundation. *pl.* **bases** [Gk.].

bask (bask) *v.i.* to sun oneself; to lie in warmth or sunshine [Scand.].

bas·ket (bas′·kit) *n.* a container made of willow, cane, rushes, or other flexible materials, interwoven. **-ball** *n.* a game where a ball has to be thrown through a basket. **-ful** *n.* **-ry**, **-work** *n.* wickerwork.

Basque (bask) *n.* a native or the language of the Basque country (Western Pyrenees); part of a lady's dress, resembling a jacket with a short skirt; *a.* relating to the Basques [Fr.].

bas-re·lief, bass-re·lief (bà *or* bás·rạ·lēf′) *n.* or *a.* low relief, sculpture in which figures or objects are raised slightly upon a flat surface, like embossed work [Fr.].

bass (bass) *n.* name applied to any perch-like fish [M.E. *barse*, *bace*].

bass (bas) *n.* the basswood or linden tree or its inner bark; fiber; matting [O.E. *baest*].

bass, base (bās) *n.* (*Mus.*) the lowest part of harmony, whether vocal or instrumental; the deepest quality of the human voice or a stringed instrument; *a.* low. **— clef** *n.* the sign

on the fourth line of the bass stave. **double-bass** *n.* the largest of the stringed instruments [It. *basso*, low].

bas·set (bas′·it) *n.* a hound formerly used in badger hunting; (*Geol.*) emergence of strata at the surface; out-crop. **— horn** *n.* a rich-toned wind instrument [Fr. *bas*, low].

bas·si·net, bas·si·nette (bas·ạ·net′) *n.* a baby's basket with a hood [Fr. dim. of *bassin*].

bas·so (bas′·ō) *n.* a bass singer; the bass part of a harmony [It. = low].

bas·soon (bạ·sôon′) *n.* a wood-wind musical instrument with a double reed mouthpiece; organ reed stop of that name. **double —**, one which sounds an octave lower. **-ist** *n.* [It. *basso*, low].

bast (bast) *n.* inner bark of a tree, used for binding purposes; raffia, matting, cordage, etc., made of the bark [O.E. *baest*].

bas·tard (bas′·tẹrd) *n.* a child born out of wedlock; an impure, coarse brown refuse product of sugar-refining, used to color beer; *a.* illegitimate; false; counterfeit; **-y** *n.* act of begetting a bastard; being a bastard. **-ize** *v.t.* to render illegitimate. [O.Fr. *bastard*, from *fils de bast*, son of a pack-saddle].

baste (bāst) *v.t.* to sew loosely with long stitches; to moisten (meat) with butter, drippings, etc. while cooking [O.Fr. *bastir*, to stitch loosely].

bas·tille (bas·tēl′) *n.* originally a tower or bastion; a state prison. **The Bastille**, the famous state prison of Paris [Fr. *bastille*, a building].

bas·ti·na·do (bas·ti·nā′·dō) *n.* an oriental form of punishment by beating the soles of the feet [Sp. *baston*, a stick]. [fense [Fr.].

bas·tion (bast′·chạn) *n.* a stronghold of defense.

bat (bat) *n.* a club or stick; a shaped club used in cricket or baseball; a piece of a brick; wad of clay; *v.i.* to strike or hit with a bat; *pr.p.* **-ting**; *pa.p.* **-ted, -ter, -man** *n.* [O.E. *batt*, club].

bat (bat) *n.* nocturnal, flying mammal. **-ity** *a.* (*Slang*) crazy. Also **bats, to have bats in the belfry**, to be crazy or eccentric [Scand. *bakke*].

bat (bat) *v.t.* (*Colloq.*) to wink. **never batted an eyelid**, showed no emotion whatever; never slept. [var. of *late*, flutter].

batch (bach) *n.* the quantity of bread baked at one time; a number of articles received or dispatched at one time; a set of similar articles [M.E. *batche*, fr. bake]. [abate].

bate (bāt) *v.t.* to lessen; to abate [form of

bath (bath) *n.* a vessel or place to bathe in; the water in which to bathe; a solution in which photographic plates are immersed; *v.t.* to wash oneself. **-s** *n.pl.* hot or mineral springs resorted to by invalids. **-house** *n.* **-room** *n.* **blood—** *n.* a massacre. **Turkish bath**, steam bath followed by massage. **sitz bath**, a shallow bath, for bathing hips and buttocks [O.E. *baeth*].

bathe (bāTH) *v.t.* to wash by immersion; *v.i.* to be immersed; to swim; *pr.p.* **bathing. -r** *n.* **bathing** *n.* **bathing-pool** *n.* [O.E. *bathian*].

ba·thet·ic See under **bathos**.

bath·i·nette (bath′·i·net) *n.* portable folding bathtub for babies.

ba·thom·e·ter (bạ·thám′·ạ·tẹr) *n.* a spring balance for determining the depth of water [Gk. *bathos*, depth; *metron*, measure].

ba·thos (bā′·thás) *n.* a term which indicates a ludicrous descent from the sublime to the ridiculous in speech or writing; anti-climax. **bathetic** *a.* [Gk. *bathos*, depth].

bath·y- (bath′·i-) *prefix* from Gk. *bathus*, deep, used in the construction of compound terms relating to sea-depths. **bathysphere** *n.* a form of deep-sea diving-bell [Gk. *bathus*, deep; *metron*, to measure; *sphaira*, a ball].

ba·tiste (bạ·tēst′) *n.* a fine kind of linen cloth from Flanders; a variety of cambric [Fr.].

ba·ton (bạ·tán′) *n.* a short staff or club; a truncheon, symbolic of authority or used as an offensive weapon; in music, wand used by conductor in beating time; a marshal's staff. *v.t.* to strike with a baton [Fr. *baton*].

batt, batt·ing (bat, bat'·ing) *n.* fiber wadded into sheets [O.E. *batt*].

bat·tal·ion (ba·tal'·yan) *n.* a military tactical and administrative unit of command consisting of three or more companies or similar units. **-s** *n.pl.* great numbers, swarms [Fr. *bataillon*, cf. **battle**].

bat·ten (bat'·n) *v.t.* to fatten; *v.i.* to grow fat in luxury [Icel. *batna*, to grow better].

bat·ten (bat'·n) *n.* a piece of wood nailed on a surface to give it strength; board used on ships to fasten down the hatch-covers in stormy weather; *v.t.* to fasten or form with battens [a form of *bâton*].

bat·ter (bat'·er) *v.t.* to strike or beat continuously; to assault; to wear by hard use; *n.* a mixture moistened to a paste and briskly beaten up. **-ing ram** *n.* a suspended beam used to breach walls [Fr. *battre*, to beat].

bat·ter·y (bat'·er·i·) *n.* act of battering; a place where cannon are mounted; a division of artillery; electric cells which store electric current; the pitcher and catcher in baseball [Fr. *battre*, to beat].

bat·tle (bat'·l) *n.* an encounter between enemies; struggle of any kind; *v.i.* to fight on a large scale. **—axe** *n.* primitive weapon; (*Slang*) cantankerous woman. **— cry** *n.* a war-shout; a slogan. **-field, -ground** *n.* scene of battle. **-r** *n.* one who take part in a battle. **— royal** *n.* a regular melée where firsts are freely used. **-ship** *n.* the largest and most heavily armed of fast warships [Fr. *bataille*].

bat·tle·ment (bat'·l·mant) *n.* a protective parapet on a wall [M.E. *batilment*].

bau·ble (baw'·bl) *n.* a trifling piece of finery; a gew-gaw; a stick with a fool's head on the end, carried by jesters of former times; *a.* trifling [O.Fr. *baubel*, a toy].

baulk (bawk) See **balk**.

baux·ite (bak'·sit, bō'·zit) *n.* a hydrated oxide of aluminum and ferric oxide; the principal source of aluminum [fr. *Baux*, near Arles, S. France].

bawd (bawd) *n.* a procurer or procuress of women for immoral purposes. **-ily** *adv.* **-iness** *n.* **-ry** *n.* **-y** *a.* obscene; filthy; unchaste. **—house**, *n.* a brothel (O.Fr. *baud*, gay].

bawl (bawl) *v.t.* to shout, to proclaim; *v.i.* to shout out with a loud voice; *n.* a loud, prolonged cry. **bawl out** (*Colloq.*) reprimand [M.L. *laulare*, to bark].

bay (bā) *a.* reddish-brown; *n.* a chestnut horse. **-ard** *n.* a bay horse; a spirited horse; one foolishly self-confident; a knight of good fame [L. *badius*, chestnut-colored].

bay (bā) *n.* an inlet of the sea [Fr. *baie*].

bay (bā) *n.* the subdivision longitudinally of a building by piers, arches, girders, etc. **— window** *n.* a window projecting beyond the wall. **sick —**, ship's hospital [Fr. *baie*].

bay (bā) *n.* the laurel tree. **-s** *n.pl.* the victor's garland or crown. **— rum** *n.* an aromatic liquid used as a perfume and cosmetic for the hair [Fr. *baie*, berry].

bay (bā) *n.* barking, esp. of hounds in pursuit of prey; *v.t.* to bark at. **at bay**, said of a hunted animal, when all escape is cut off [O.Fr. *baier*, to bark].

bay·ber·ry (bā'·ber·i·) *n.* evergreen shrub, used for making bay rum; one variety used in candle making [*bay* and *berry*].

bay·o·net (bā'·a·net) *n.* a short spear-like weapon attached to the muzzle of a rifle; *v.t.* to stab with a bayonet. [fr. *Bayonne*, the town where first made].

ba·zaar, bazar (ba·zàr') *n.* an Oriental market-place; a sale where articles are sold for charity; shop selling miscellaneous goods [Pers.].

ba·zoo·ka (ba·zoo'·ka) *n.* a portable light rocket-gun.

B.C. before Christ.

be (bē) *v.i.* and *aux.* (*pres. indic.* **am;** *past indic.* **was;** *past part.* **been**), to exist; to live; to have a state, existence, or quality; to remain; to happen; to belong [O.E. *beon*].

be- *prefix* used in the construction of compound words, as *becalm*, etc.

beach (bēch) *n.* the shore of the sea or of a lake, esp. where sandy or pebbly; the shore; *v.t.* to run or haul a boat up on to a beach. **-comber** *n.* a long, rolling wave; a lounger who frequents beaches or seaports; scrounger. **-head** *n.* a footing gained on hostile shores by an army.

bea·con (bē'·kn) *n.* a fire lit on a high eminence, usually as a warning; a warning light; a floating buoy; traffic sign indicating a pedestrian crossing; *v.t.* to mark a channel by beacons [O.E. *beacn*].

bead (bēd) *n.* a little ball pierced for stringing; any small spherical object such as a front sight on a gun; *v.t.* to furnish with beads; *v.i.* to string beads. **-s** *n.pl.* a rosary, a necklace; flange of a tire; **-ed** *a.* in bead form. **-ing** *n.* a small rounded molding imitating beads. **-y** *a.* bead-like. **to draw a bead on,** to aim a gun at. [O.E. *gebed*, a prayer].

bea·gle (bē'·gl) *n.* the smallest hound used in hunting; (*Fig.*) a spy or informer.

beak (bēk) *n.* the horny bill of a bird, turtle, etc.; anything shaped like a beak (*Slang*) a beak-shaped nose [Fr. *bec.*].

beak·er (bē'·ker) *n.* a large drinking-cup or vessel; a tumbler-shaped vessel of thin glass used by chemists [Scand. *bikarr*].

beam (bēm) *n.* a strong, horizontal piece of timber or reinforced concrete for spanning and supporting weights; the part of a balance from which the scales hang; the cross-timber of a ship; the extreme width, measured athwartships, of a ship; wooden cylinder on which the warp is wound in a loom; the pole of a carriage; the shaft of an anchor; a sharply defined ray of light; the sparkle in a person's eyes manifesting extreme pleasure or interest; *v.t.* to emit beams of light; *v.i.* to send forth rays of light; to shine; to smile benignly. **-ing** *a.* radiantly happy; shining; *n.* rays of light; manifestation of pleasure by smiling. **-less** *a.* [O.E. *beam*, a tree].

bean (bēn) *n.* the flat, kidney-shaped seed of various plants, chiefly of the genus *Phaseolus*; (*Slang*) head. **-bag** *n.* a toy, a small cloth bag partly filled with beans. **full of beans,** in good fettle; energetic. [O.E. *bean*].

bear (bār) *v.t.* to support or to carry; to endure; to suffer; to behave; to give birth to; *v.i.* to produce (as fruit); to endure; to press; *pa.t.* **bore;** *pa.p.* **borne** or **born. -able** *a.* able to be borne; tolerable. **-ably** *adv.* **-er** *n.* carrier or messenger; a person who helps to carry a coffin; a presenter of a check. **-ing** *n.* the manner in which a person acts or behaves; the direction in which one thing lies from another; relation to or connection with; **-ings** *n.pl.* machine surfaces carrying a moving part and bearing friction. **to bear out,** to corroborate. **to bear with,** to endure patiently. **to bring to bear,** to apply pressure. **to lose one's bearings,** to lose all sense of direction [O.E. *beran*].

bear (bār) *n.* a carnivorous mammal of the Ursidae order; a rough, boorish person; one who sells stocks before he has bought them, in the hope of a fall in price before settlement; (*Astron.*) one of two constellations in the northern hemisphere, called respectively the **Great Bear** and the **Lesser Bear. — baiting** *n.* a form of sport where dogs were employed to worry the animal. **-like** *a.* **skin** *n.* [O.E. *bera*].

beard (bērd) *n.* the hair that grows on the chin and cheeks; the awns or prickles of an ear of corn; the gills of oysters; the barb of an arrow; *v.t.* to pluck the beard of; to confront or defy someone. **-ed** *a.* **-less** *a.* [O.E.].

beast (bēst) *n.* any inferior animal as opposed

to man; a four-footed animal especially if wild; cattle; person of brutal nature or of dirty habits. **-ly** a. like a beast in form or nature; filthy; displeasing. **-liness** n. [L. *bestia*].

beat (bēt) v.t. to strike or hit repeatedly; to pommel; to crush;to defeat; to be too difficult for; to spread flat and thin with a tool, as gold leaf; to drive game out of cover; to mark time in music; v.i. to throb; to dash against as waves, wind, etc. pa.t. **beat**; pa.p. **-en**; n. a recurrent stroke; a pulse throb; (*Mus.*) the divisions in a bar, the movement of a conductor's baton; zig-zag sailing of a ship working up against the wind; the round or course followed repeatedly by someone, e.g. a policeman, a postman; a. (*Colloq.*) exhausted. **-en** a. hammered into shape by a tool; worn by continual use. **-er** n. **-ing** n. act of giving blows; a thrashing; throbbing; driving out game. **-nik** n. (*Colloq.*) one who rebels against the conventions of society. **to beat about the bush,** to approach a subject in a round about way. **to beat a tatoo,** to sound the drums at roll-call. **dead beat** n. (*Colloq.*) one with a reputation for not paying his bills; (*Slang*) a loafer; sponger [O.E. *beatan*].

be·at·i·fy (bē·at′·a̧·fī) v.t. to render supremely blessed or happy; to bless with celestial enjoyment (preliminary to canonization in R.C. Church). **beatific(al)** a. having power of making happy or blessed. **beatifically** adv. **beatification** n. [L. *betaus*, happy].

be·at·i·tude (bē·at′·a̧·tūd) n. highest form of heavenly happiness; supreme blessedness. **the beatitudes** (*Bib.*) blessings spoken in regard to particular virtues (Matt. 5) [L. *beatus*, happy].

beau (bō) n. a fop; dandy; sweetheart; suitor. pl. **beaux** (bōz). — **monde** n. the fashionable world and its people [Fr.].

beau·ty (bū′·ti·) n. the inherent quality in an object of pleasing the eye, ear, or mind; a particular grace or excellence; a beautiful woman; a fine specimen. **beauteous** a. full of beauty; very handsome. **beauteously** adv. **beauteousness** n. **beautician** n. expert in use of cosmetics. **beautifier** n. a cosmetic; a decorator. **beautiful** a. highly pleasing to eye, ear, or mind; handsone; lovely; fine; excellent. **beautifully** adv. **beautifulness** n. **beautify** v.t. to make beautiful. **beautiless** a. lacking beauty. — **spot** n. a place noted for its attractive surroundings; a patch placed on the face to heighten beauty [Fr. *beauté*].

bea·ver (bē′·ver) n. an amphibious, four-footed rodent valued for its fur and for castoreum, an extract from its glands used in medicine; the fur of the beaver; a beaver hat; a. made of beaver fur [O.E. *beofor*].

be·bop (bē′·bàp) n. (*Slang*) jazz music characterized by improvization.　　　　　　[**-ed** a.

be·calm (bē·kàm′) v.t. to make calm or quiet.

be·came (bi·kām′) past tense of **become**.

be·cause (bi·kawz′) adv. and conj. for the reason that; since [E. *by*, and *cause*].

beck (bek) n. sign or gesture of the head or hand; a nod; v.i. to make such a gesture; v.t. to call by a nod or a sign; to beckon. **at one's beck and call,** entirely at someone's disposal [fr. *beckon*].

beck·on (bek′·n) v.t. and v.i. to make a sign with the hand or head; to summon with hand or finger [O.E. *becnan*].

be·come (bi·kum′) v.t. to pass from one state to another; to suit or be suitable to; pa.t. **became;** pa.p. **become. becoming** a. appropriate or fit [O.E. *becuman*].

bed (bed) n. a couch on which to sleep or take rest; a plot of ground in which plants are cultivated; channel of a stream; the bearing surface of anything; a thin layer of mortar between two surfaces; a layer of rock; stratum; v.t. to place in bed; to plant out; to arrange in layers; pr.p. **-ding;** pa.p. **-ded. -bug** n.

bloodsucking insect. **-clothes** n.pl. bed coverings, clothes worn to bed. **-ding** n. materials of a bed. **-fast** a. confined to bed; bed-ridden. **-fellow** n. one who sleeps in the same bed with another. **-pan** n. a pan for warming a bed; pan used as toilet. **-plate** n. the foundation plate of an engine lathe, etc. **-post** n. one of the upright supports of a bed. **-rid, -ridden** a. permanently confined to bed by age or infirmity. **-rock** n. the solid rock beneath loose material as sand, etc.; fundamentals. **-room** n. a room for sleeping. **-sore** n. ulcer caused by constant pressure on a part of the body of a bed-ridden patient. **-spread** n. a covering of fine material for a bed. **-stead** n. the framework, of iron or wood, of a bed. **-ticking** n. the cloth case for holding the feathers, hair, etc. of a mattress. **bed and board,** food and lodging [O.E. *bedd*].

be·daub (bi·dawb′) v.t. to smear.

be·daz·zle (bi·daz′·l) v.t. to overpower by employing too strong a light or by a magnificent show.

be·deck (bē·dek′) v.t. to deck, adorn, ornament.

be·dev·il (bi·dev′·l) v.t. to beat with devilish malignity; to torment; to throw into confusion, to confound; to bewitch.

be·dew (bi·dū′) v.t. to moisten with dew.

be·dight (bi·dīt′) a. decked out with ornaments; adorned; arrayed (*Poet.*).

be·dim (bi·dim′) v.t. to make dim; to darken. pr.p. **-ming;** pa.t. **-med. bedimmed** a.

be·diz·en (bi·diz′·n, bi·dī′·zn) v.t. to dress gaudily or with false taste. **-ed** a.

bed·lam (bed′lam) n. a mad-house; a lunatic asylum; a mental institution; a scene of uproar; pandemonium. **-ite** n. a lunatic [corrupt. of *Bethlehem*, an asylum].

Bed·ou·in (bed′·oo·in) n. Arab; nomad [Ar. *bādāwin*, dwellers in the desert].

be·drag·gle (bi·drag′·l) v.t. to soil by trailing in the wet or mud. **-d** a.

bee (bē) n. highest form of insect belonging to the order Hymenoptera; the honey-bee; a social gathering for amusement or mutual help, e.g. a spelling-bee; a busy person. **-culture** n. the rearing of bees, apiculture. **-hive** n. a case or box where the bees are housed; a. shaped like a bee-hive. **-keeper** n. **-line** n. the shortest route from one place to another. **-swax** n. the wax secreted by bees; a floor-polish; v.t. to polish with beeswax [O.E. *bēo*].

beech (bēch) n. a tree of the temperate and sub-frigid zones, greatly valued for its wood. **-coal** n. charcoal made from beechwood. **-en** a. made of beech. **beechnut** n. the triangular, edible nut of the beech [O.E. *bēce*].

beef (bēf) n. the flesh of an ox, bull, or cow; flesh and muscle; muscular strength; vigor; a. consisting of beef; v.i. (*Slang*) to make complaints. **beeves** (bēvz) n.pl. oxen. **-eater** n. one of the Yeomen of the Guard; a Warder of the Tower of London. **-iness** n. tendency to put on flesh. **-steak** n. a thick slice of beef. **-y** a. stolid; fat; stout [Fr. *boeuf*, ox].

been (bin) pa.p. of the verb **be.**

beer (bēr) n. an alcoholic beverage made by brewing and fermentation of cereals. **-y** a. pert. to the taste or smell of beer; discolored with beer slops [O.E. *beor*].

beest·ings, biest·ings (bēs′·tingz) n. the first milk taken from a cow after calving, thicker than ordinary milk [O.E. *bysting*].

beet (bēt) n. a garden or field plant having a succulent tap root, the red variety being used as a vegetable, the white yielding sugar. — **sugar** n. crystallized sugar extracted from beetroot [O.E. *bēte*, fr. L. *bēta*].

bee·tle (bē′·tl) n. heavy wooden mallet for beating down paving-stones or driving in piles; wooden utensil for beating linen, mashing potatoes or stirring porridge, etc. [O.E. *betel*, a mallet].

bee·tle (bē′·tl) n. name of a large order of insects, Coleoptera [O.E. *bitula*, a biter].

bee·tle (bē'·tl) *v.i.* to be prominent; to jut out; to overhang. **beetling** *a.* overhanging. **—browed** *a.* with overhanging brows; scowling. **-head** *n.* a dull, stupid person [O.E. *bitel*].

beeves (bēvz) *n.pl.* cattle, oxen [See **beef**].

be·fall (bi·fawl') *v.t.* to happen to; *v.i.* to come to pass; to happen; *pr.p.* **-ing**; *pa.t.* **befell**; *pa.p.* **-en** [O.E. *befeallan*].

be·fit (bi·fit') *v.t.* to fit or be suitable to; to become; be right for; *pr.p.* **-ting**; *pa.t.*, *pa.p.* **-ted. -ting** *a.* **-tingly** *adv.*

be·fog (bi·fawg') *v.t.* to envelop in a fog; perplex. *pr.p.* **-ging**. *pa.t.* **-ged.**

be·fore (bi·fōr') *prep.* in front of; preceding; in the presence of; prior to; previous to; superior to; *adv.* in front of; in advance; a short time ago; already. *conj.* sooner than; rather than. **-hand** *adv.* previously. **-time** *adv.* of old; formerly [O.E. *beforan*].

be·foul (bi·foul') *v.t.* to foul, soil, dirty.

be·friend (bi·frend') *v.t.* to act as a friend to; to favor; to help a stranger.

be·fud·dle (bi·fu'·dl) *v.t.* to confuse.

beg (beg) *v.t.* to ask earnestly and humbly; to ask for alms; to practice begging; to beseech; *pr.p.* **-ging**; *pa.t.* and *pa.p.* **-ged. -gar** *n.* one who solicits alms; a mendicant; *v.t.* to reduce to beggary; to ruin financially. **-garliness** *n.* **-garly** *a.* like a beggar; poor; mean; squalid; worthless; meagre; trifling; *adv.* meanly. **-gary** *n.* extreme poverty. **-ging** *n.* soliciting alms; *a.* pert. to begging; imploring; soliciting. **to beg the question**, to assume truth of thing to be proved [M.E. *beggen*].

be·gan (bi·gan') *pa.t.* of **begin**.

be·get (bi·get') *v.t.* to generate; to procreate; to produce or to cause; to get; give rise to. *pr.p.* **-ting**; *pa.t.* **begot, begat**; *pa.p.* **begot, begotten** [O.E. *begitan*, fr. *get*].

be·gin (bi·gin') *v.t.* to enter on; to start, to commence; *v.i.* to take the first step; to set about. *pr.p.* **-ning**; *pa.t.* **began**; *pa.p.* **begun**. **-ner** *n.* one who begins; novice. **-ning** *n.* source; first part [O.E. *beginnan*].

be·gird (bi·gurd') *v.t.* to gird or bind with a girdle or band; *pa.t.* **begirt** or **-ed**.

be·gone (bi·gawn') *interj.* go away! depart! **woebegone** *a.* gloomy and miserable.

be·go·ni·a (bi·gōn'·ya) *n.* a genus of tropical plants [Michel *Bégon*, Fr. botanist].

be·got (bi·gát') **begotten** *pa.p.* of **beget**.

be·grime (bi·grīm') *v.t.* to soil with grime.

be·grudge (bi·gruj') *v.t.* to grudge; to allow reluctantly. **begrudgingly** *adv.*

be·guile (bi·gīl') *v.t.* to cheat or deceive by trickery; to ensnare; to delude; to while away (time); to amuse or divert. **-ment** *n.* **-r** *n.* **beguilingly** *adv.*

be·gum (bē'·gam) *n.* the Hindustani name given to a Moslem princess.

be·gun (bi·gun') *pa.p.* of **begin**.

be·half (bi·haf') *n.* favor; advantage; benefit; support; vindication; defense [O.E. *be healfe*, by the side].

be·have (bi·hāv') *v.t.* and *v.i.* to conduct oneself; to act. **behavior** *n.* bearing or conduct; deportment. **behaviorism** *n.* theory that man's actions are automatic responses to stimuli and not dictated by consciousness.

be·head (bi·hed') *v.t.* to sever the head from the body. **-al, -ing** *n.*

be·held (bi·held') *pa.p.* of **behold**.

be·hest (bi·hest') *n.* that which is willed or ordered [O.E. *behaes*].

be·hind (bi·hīnd') *prep.* at the back of; in the rear (of); after; late; farther back than; in an inferior position; *n.* rump; buttocks; posterior. **-hand** *adv.* and *a.* late; backward; in arrears [O.E. *behindan*].

be·hold (bi·hōld') *v.t.* to look at; to fix the eyes upon; to observe carefully; *v.i.* to look; fix the attention. *pa.t.* and *pa.p.* **beheld. -en** *a.* obliged (to); owing a debt of gratitude (to).

-er *n.* an on-looker; spectator [O.E. *behealdan*].

be·hoof (bi·hòof') *n.* advantage; benefit; profit; use. **behoove, behove** *v.t.* to be necessary, convenient for; to befit [O.E. *behōf*].

beige (bāzh) *n.* very light brown color of unbleached wool [Fr.]. [an animal [fr. *to be*].

be·ing (bē'·ing) *n.* existence; that which exists.

be·la·bor (bi·lā'·ber) *v.t.* to beat soundly; to cudgel; to exert much labor upon; to assail verbally. [tard. **-d** *a.* **-dness** *n.*]

be·late (bi·lāt') *v.t.* to cause to be late; to retard.

be·lay (bi·lā') *v.t.* to make fast a rope, by winding it round a fixed pin or cleat; *n.* in mountaineering, a rock to which a climber anchors himself by a rope. **-ing-pin** *n.* a pin or cleat, to which running rigging may be belayed [Dut. *beleggen*].

belch (belch) *v.t.* to emit wind from the stomach by way of the mouth; to cast forth; *n.* eructation [O.E. *bealcam*].

bel·dam (bel'·dam) *n.* a grandmother; an ugly, old woman; a hag; an irate woman. Also **beldame** [orig. *grandmother*, Fr. *belle dame*].

be·lea·guer (bi·lē'·ger) *v.t.* to surround with an army so as to preclude escape. **-ment** *n.* [Dut. *belegeren*, to besiege].

bel·fry (bel'·fri·) *n.* a bell-tower, or a part of a steeple, where bells are hung. Orig. a watchtower, a bell being the signal [Fr. *beffroi*].

Ba·li·al (bēl'·yal) *n.* Satan; the devil [Heb. = that which is without profit or worth].

be·lie (bi·lī') *v.t.* to give the lie to; to falsify; to speak falsely of; to misrepresent; *pr.p.* **belying** [O.E. *beleogan*, to deceive].

be·lieve (bi·lēv') *v.t.* to regard as true; to trust; *v.i.* to have faith (in); to think; to suppose. **belief** *n.* that which is believed; full acceptance of a thing as true; faith; a firm persuasion of the truth of a body of religious tenets. **believable** *a.* credible. **-r** *n.* **to make believe**, to pretend; to fancy [M.E. *beleven*].

be·lit·tle (bi·lit'·l) *v.t.* to make small; to think lightly of; to disparage. **-ment** *n.*

bell (bel) *n.* a hollow, cup-shaped metal vessel which gives forth a clear, musical note when struck; anything shaped like a bell; *v.t.* to provide with a bell. **bells** *n.pl.* (Naut.) half hours of a watch at sea, struck on a ship's bell. **-boy** *n.* page-boy in hotel. **-buoy** *n.* a buoy which by its swaying rings a bell attached.

bell (bel) *n.* the cry of an animal; the bellow of the stag in rutting time. Also **-ing**; *v.i.* to bellow; to roar [O.E. *bellan*, to roar].

bel·la·don·na (bel·a·dán'·a) *n.* deadly nightshade from which drugs, hyoscine and atropine, are obtained [It. = fair lady].

belle (bel) *n.* a particularly beautiful woman [Fr. *belle*, fair].

belles-let·tres (bel·let'·r) *n.pl.* polite literature, i.e. literature which includes poetry, the drama, criticism, aesthetics, etc. [Fr.].

bel·li·cose (bel'·a·kōs) *a.* pugnacious; contentious; war-like; quarrelsome. **-ly** *adv.* **bellicosity** *n.* [L. *bellum*, war].

bel·lig·er·ence (be·lij'·er·ans) *n.* the state of being at war; warlike attitude. **belligerency** *n.* a state of war. **belligerent** *n.* a nation, party, or person taking part in war; a contending party; *a.* waging war; pugnacious; bellicose [L. *bellum*, war; *gerere*, to carry on].

bel·low (bel'·ō) *v.i.* to roar like a bull; to shout loudly; to make an outcry; to roar, as of cannon; *n.* a loud hollow roar, as of a bull, cannon, etc.; any deep cry [O.E. *bellan*, to bellow].

bel·lows (bel'·ōz, bel'·az) *n.pl.* an instrument for producing a strong blast of air (to stimulate a fire, to work an organ, etc.) [fr. O.E. *bielg*, belly; the full O.E. name was *blaestbelg*, blast-bag].

bel·ly (bel'·i·) *n.* part of the body which contains bowels; abdomen; stomach; part of anything bulging like a paunch; *a.* ventral; abdominal; *v.i.* to swell out; to bulge. **-ache** *n.* abdominal pains. **-band** *n.* a band under the belly of a horse to secure saddle. **-ful** n. sufficiency of food, etc. [O.E. *belg*].

be·long (bi·lawng') v.i. to pertain to; be connected with; to be property or attribute of; to be resident or native of. **-ings** n.pl. what belongs to one; possessions [M.E. *belongen*].

be·loved (bi·luv'·ad, bi·luvd') a. greatly loved; n. one very dear to others.

be·low (bi·lō') prep. under; beneath; of inferior rank or status; on a lower level than; unworthy of; adv. in a lower place; beneath; on earth or hell, as opposed to heaven [by, and *low*].

belt (belt) n. a band, girdle, or zone, used for encircling; a zone given over to the raising of one plant, e.g. wheat—v.t. to encircle, as with a belt; to thrash with a belt. **-ed** a. wearing a belt, esp. as a mark of honor, as in 'a belted knight'; thrashed with a belt. **conveyor —** n. an endless belt used for conveying material from one place to another. **-ing** n. material for skirt or bodice bands; a thrashing [E.].

be·moan (bi·mōn') v.t. to express deep grief for, by moaning; to lament; to mourn for.

be·muse (bi·mūz') v.t. to put into a state of confusion; to stupefy; to daze. **-d** a.

ben (ben) n. a geographical term, a mountain peak, as Ben Lomond [Gael]; son of [Heb.].

bench (bensh) n. a long seat; a table on which woodwork is done; the seat in court of a judge or magistrate; collective name for the body of judges sitting in judgment; v.t. to furnish with benches; to place, for exhibit, on a bench [M.E. *benche* fr. O.E. *benc*].

bend (bend) v.t. to curve; to arch; to turn out of direct course; to incline; to sway; to subdue or make submissive; to tie, make fast—of ropes and sails; v.i. to be moved out of a straight line; to stoop; to lean, to incline; to bow; to yield; pa.t. **bent**, pa.p. **bent** or **-ed**; n. a curve; crook; curvature; turn. **-er** n. an instrument for bending; a hard drinker; a drinking spree. **the bends**, aenoembolism. **to be bent upon**, to be determined upon [O.E. *bendan*].

be·neath (bi·nēth') prep. under; below; lower than; unworthy of; below the level of; adv. below [O.E. *beneothan*].

ben·e·dict (ben'·a·dikt) n. a man newly married, esp. if considered a confirmed bachelor.

Ben·e·dict (ben'·a·dikt) n. the founder of Western monasticism. **Benedictine** a. pert. to St. Benedict or his monastic order; n. a Black Friar; a cordial or liqueur originally distilled by the Benedictine monks.

ben·e·dic·tion (ben·a·dik'·shan) n. a blessing of a formal character; the blessing at the end of a religious service. **benedictory** a. imparting a blessing [L. *bene*, well; *dicere*, to speak].

ben·e·fac·tion (ben·a·fak'·shan) n. act of doing good; a benefit conferred; donation. **benefactor** n. (fem. **benefactress**) one who helps others; a donor; a patron. **benefactory** a [L. *bene*, well; *facere*, *factum*, to do].

ben·e·fice (ben'·a·fis) n. an ecclesiastical living. **-d** a. in enjoyment of a benefice [L. *beneficium*].

be·nef·i·cence (ba·nef'·i·sens) n. habitual practice of doing good; charity. **beneficent** a. kindly disposed; generous; doing good. **beneficently** adv. [L. *beneficium*].

ben·e·fi·cial (ben·a·fish'·al) a. conferring benefits; advantageous; helpful. **-ly** adv. **-ness** n. **beneficiary** n. one who benefits from the act of another; a holder of an ecclesiastical benefice [L.L. *beneficialis*].

ben·e·fit (ben'·a·fit) n. an act of kindness; a favor conferred; an advantage; profit; interest; a theatrical or other exhibition, the proceeds of which go to charity or an individual; a payment or allowance such as given by an insurance company or public agency; v.t. to do good to; to be useful to; to profit; v.i. to gain advantage (from). **fringe benefits**, such things as health insurance paid in addition to regular salary [L. *bene*, well; *facere*, to do].

Ben·e·lux (ben'·a·luks) n. the economic bloc of the three countries Belgium, the Netherlands, and Luxemburg.

be·nev·o·lence (ba·nev'·a·lans) n. disposition to do good; love of mankind; an act of kindness; generosity. **benevolent** a. of a kindly nature [L. *bene*, well; *velle*, to wish].

be·night·ed (bi·nīt'·ad) a. overtaken by night; enveloped in moral or mental darkness; ignorant; unenlightened; lost.

be·nign (bi·nīn') a. of a kindly disposition; mild, not malignant (of disease); propitious (of climate). **-ancy** (bi·nig'·nan·si·) n. benignant quality. **-ant** a. kind; gracious; favorable; beneficial. **-antly** adv. **-ity** n. **-ly** adv. in benign fashion [L. *benignus*, kind].

ben·i·son (ben'·i·zn) n. benediction; blessing [L. *benedictio*. Doublet of *benediction*].

Ben·ja·min (ben'·ja·min) n. (Bib.) a youngest son; a favorite child [Heb. = son of the right hand].

ben·ja·min (ben'·ja·min) n. benzoin, a kind or resin or gum used as a medicine [corrupt. of *benzoin*].

bent (bent) pa.t. and pa.p. of **bend**.

bent (bent) n. (of mind), leaning, bias, or inclination for; a tendency [fr. *bend*].

bent (bent) n. bent grass; any stiff, wiry, coarse grass. **-y** a. overrun with bent [O.E. *beonet*].

be·numb (bi·num') v.t. to make numb, through cold or fear; to deprive of all sensation; to deaden. **-ed** a. [O.E. *beniman*, to deprive].

Ben·ze·drine (ben'·za·drēn) n. amphetamine, a synthetic drug [Trade Name].

be·queath (bi·kwēTH') v.t. to leave by will, said of personal property; to leave to those who follow on, as a problem, trouble, etc. **bequest** n. that which is left by will; legacy [O.E. *becwethan*].

be·rate (bi·rāt') v.t. to scold vigorously.

be·reave (bi·rēv') v.t. to make destitute; to deprive of; pa.p. **-d** or **bereft**. **-d** a. robbed by death, esp. of a relative. **-ment** n. loss, esp. by death [E. pref. *be*; O.E. *rēafian*, to spoil].

be·ret (ber'·ā, ber'·it) n. a soft, round tight-fitting cap without any peak [Fr. fr. L.L. *birretum*, a cap].

berg (burg) n. a large mass or mountain of ice; an iceberg [Ger. = a mountain].

ber·i·ber·i (ber'·i·ber'·i·) n. a nervous disease due to deficiency of vitamin B [Singh.].

ber·lin (bur'·lin) n. a four-wheeled closed carriage with two seats [fr. *Berlin*, Germany].

ber·ry (ber'·i·) n. a small, pulpy, juicy fruit; strictly a simple fruit with succulent pericarp. **-ing** n. **berried** a. [O.E. *berie*].

ber·serk, ber·serk·er (ber'·surk, ·ker) n. a battle-frenzied Norse warrior; a. frenzied. **to go berserk**, to go mad with fury [Scand. = poss. bare of sark or shirt of mail].

berth (burth) n. the place where a ship is anchored or moored; a sleeping-place on a ship, etc.; a situation or job. v.t. to bring to anchorage. **-age** n. dock or harbor dues. **to give a wide berth to**, to steer clear of; to shun; to avoid [Doublet of *birth*].

ber·yl (ber'·il) n. a group of green or bluish-green precious stones of exceptional hardness. **-lium** n. a rare metal of the magnesium group [Gk. *bērullos*].

be·seech (bi·sēch') v.t. to ask or entreat earnestly; to solicit; beg; implore; pa.t. and pa.p. **besought**. **-er** n. **-ing** a. [M.E. *sechen*, to seek]

be·seem (bi·sēm') v.t. to be fit for; to befit; to suit, to become. **beseeming** a.

be·set (bi·set') v.t. to place on, in, or around; to hem in on all sides; to surround; to enclose; to assail; pr.p. **-ting**. pa.t. and pa.p. **beset**, **-ment** n. **-ter** n. **-ting** a. customary; habitual, as in 'besetting sin' [O.E. *besettan*].

be·shrew (bi'·shrōō') v.t. (Arch.) to wish some slight evil to befall one; to curse; to rate.

be·side (bi·sīd') prep. and adv. at the side of;

over and above; in addition to; apart from; distinct from. **-s** *adv.* moreover; *prep.* over and above. — **oneself**, out of one's wits [O.E. *bi sidan*].

be·siege (bi·sēj′) *v.t.* to lay siege to; to surround with armed forces; to pay court to; to beleaguer. **-ment** *n.* **-r** *n.* **besieging** *a.* **besiegingly** *adv.* [M. E. *asege*, fr. Fr. *assiéger*].

be·smear (bi·smir′) *v.t.* to smear over; to soil; to bedaub [O.E. *besmerian*].

be·smirch (bi·smurch′) *v.t.* to soil; to sully; to tarnish one's reputation, etc.

be·sot (bi·sat′) *v.t.* to make sottish by drink; to make stupid. **-ted** *a.* [O.E.].   [seech.

be·sought (bi·sawt′) *pa.t.* and *pa.p.* of **be·spat·ter** (bi·spat′·er) *v.t.* to sprinkle or splash with mud, ink, etc.; to defame.

be·speak (bi·spēk′) *v.t.* to order, speak for, or engage beforehand; to foretell; to indicate; *pa.t.* **bespoke**. *pa.p.* **bespoke** and **bespoken**. **bespoke, bespoken** *a.* ordered beforehand; of goods [O.E. *besprecan*].

be·speck·le (bi·spek′·l) *v.t.* to mark with speckles or spots; to variegate. **-d** *a.*

Bes·se·mer (bes′·am·er) *a.* applied to steel prepared by the Bessemer process of forcing atmospheric air into molten cast iron [Sir H. *Bessemer*, (1813-98), the inventor].

best (best) *a. superl.* good in the highest degree; excellent beyond all others; most suitable, advantageous, advisable, or appropriate; *adv.* in the most excellent manner; *n.* utmost; highest endeavor; perfection. — **man**, chief attendant to the groom at a wedding. — **seller**, a current popular book with an enormous sale. **to make the best of**, to resign oneself to conditions, etc. [O.E. *bet(e)st*].

bes·tial (bēs′·tyal) *a.* pert. to a beast; having the instincts of a beast; like a repulsive beast. **-ity** *n.* beastly depravity [Fr. fr. L. *bestialis*].

be·stir (bi·stur′) *v.t.* to rouse into vigorous action; to exert (oneself); to stimulate. *pr.p.* **-ring**. *pa.t.* **-red** [O.E. *bestyrian*].

be·stow (bi′·stō′) *v.t.* to lay up in store; to expend, as energy; to give ceremoniously; to confer; to award; grant; present; impart. **-al** *n.* **-er** *n.* **-ment** *n.* bestowing; what is bestowed [M.E. *bestowen*, to place].

be·strew (bi·strōō′) *v.t.* to scatter over; to besprinkle. *pa.p.* **-ed, -n.**

be·stride (bi′·strīd′) *v.t.* to stride over; to stand or sit with the legs extended across. *pr.p.* **bestriding**; *pa.t.* **bestrode, bestrid**; *pa.p.* **bestrid, bestridden.** [O.E. *bestridan*].

bet (bet) *n.* a stake or wager on some problematical event; *v.t.* to stake money upon some contingency; *pr.p.* **-ting**; *pa.t.* and *pa.p.* **bet** or **-ted. -ter, -tor** *n.* [fr. *abet*].

be·ta (bā′·ta, bē′·ta) *n.* the second letter of the Greek alphabet, printed thus, *β*. — **particles**, fast electrons emitted when certain atoms undergo radioactive breakdown. — **rays**, streams of beta particles emanated by radioactive substances.

be·take (bi·tāk′) *v.t.* to have recourse to; (with reflexive) to go, to repair to; to make one's way; *pr.p.* **betaking**; *pa.t.* **betook**; *pa.p.* **-en** [M.E. *betaken*].

be·tel (bē′·tl) *n.* a species of pepper. — **nut** *n.* the nut of the areca palm [Port. *betle*].

be·think (bi·thingk′) *v.t.*) to call to mind; to remind oneself; to cogitate. *pa.t.* **bethought.**

be·tide (bi·tīd′) *v.t.* to happen to; *v.i.* to occur; happen [M.E. *betiden*, to happen].

be·times (bi·tīmz′) *adv.* in good time; seasonably; soon; early; forward [M.E.].

be·token (bi·tō′·kn) *v.t.* to show by some visible sign; to foreshow [M.E. *betacnien*].

be·took (bi·tòòk′) *pa.t.* of **betake.**

be·tray (bi·trā′) *v.t.* to give up treacherously; to be disloyal to; to disclose (a secret); to seduce; to show signs of; deceive. **-al** *n.* **-er** *n.* a traitor; a seducer [L. *tradere*, to give up].

be·troth (bi·trōTH′, ·trawTH′) *v.t.* to promise to give or take in marriage; to affiance. **-al** *n.* an agreement with a view to marriage. **-ed** *n.* a person engaged to be married; fiancé, (*fem.*) fiancée. **-ment** *n.* the state of being betrothed [M.E. *bitreuthien*].

bet·ter (bet′·er) *a.* (compar. of *good*), showing a greater degree of excellence; improved in health; *adv.* (compar. of *well*), in a more excellent or superior manner; more fully; *v.t.* and *i.* to make better; to amend; to raise one's worldly position. **-ment** *n.* improvement; enhanced value of property due to local improvements. **-s** *n.pl.* one's superiors in rank or wealth. — **half**, a jocular term for spouse. — **off**, in more prosperous circumstances. **to get the better of**, to gain an advnatage over. **to think better of**, to reconsider [O.E. *betera*].

be·tween (bi·twēn′) *prep.* in the middle of two (of space, time, etc.); in the middle or intermediate space; shared by two; *adv.* midway. **go-between** *n.* an intermediary [O.E. *betweonum*, by twain].

be·twixt (bi·twikst′) *prep.* between; midway.

bev·el (bev′·l) *n.* an angle, not being a right angle, formed by two surfaces; an adjustable instrument used in building, etc. for testing angles; *a.* having the form of a bevel; slanting; *v.t.* to cut to a bevel angle. **-led** *a.* **-ing, -ment** *n.* [Fr. *biveau*, carpenter's rule].

bev·er·age (bev′·a·rij) *n.* a refreshing liquid suitable for drinking [O.Fr. *bevrage*].

bev·y (bev′·i·) *n.* a flock of birds; an assembly; a collection or group.

be·wail (bi·wāl′) *v.t.* to express grief for; to lament; deplore; mourn over.

be·ware (bi·wār′) *v.i.* to be wary of; to be on one's guard; to be alive to impending danger; to take care (lest).

be·wil·der (bi·wil′·der) *v.t.* to lead astray or into confusion; to confound; perplex; puzzle. **-ed** *a.* **-ing** *a.* confusing. **-ment** *n.* [fr. obs. *wildern*, wilderness].

be·witch (bi·wich′) *v.t.* to gain power over, by sorcery; to charm; captivate; entrance. **-er** *n.* **-ery, -ment** *n.* power to bewitch; enchantment. **-ing** *a.* [M.E. *bewicchen*].

be·wray (bi·rā′) *v.t.* to divulge; to disclose; to reveal without intent [O.E. *wregan*, to accuse].

be·yond (bi·yánd′) *prep.* on the farther side of; out of reach of; above; past in time; later than; superior to; *adv.* farther off; at a distance; *n.* the future life [O.E. *geond*, across].

bez·el (bez′·al) *n.* the piece of metal under the setting holding the jewel of a ring; the groove in which the glass of a watch is set; the sloped cutting edge of a tool; the sloping facets of a cut gem. Also **basil** or **bezil** [O.Fr. *bisel*].

bi-, (bī) *prefix* used in the construction of compound nouns, indicating two, twice, or double [L. *bis*, twice].   [twice a year. **-ly** *adv.*

bi·an·nu·al (bī·an′·yoo·al) *a.* happening

bi·as (bī′·as) *n.* prejudice; prepossession that sways the mind; a diagonal line of direction; *v.t.* to influence; to prejudice; to prepossess (often unduly; *pa.t.* and *pa.p.* **-sed** or **-ed** [Fr. *biais*, oblique].

bib (bib) *n.* piece of cloth worn mainly by children over the breast when eating; part of a workman's overalls to protect chest; *v.t.* and *v.i.* to sip; tipple; drink frequently. *pr.p.* **-bing;** *pa.t.* and *pa.p.* **-bed. -acious** *a.* addicted to tippling. **-ber** *n.* a person given to frequent and excessive imbibing of liquor or wines; a tippler [L. *bibere*, to drink].

Bi·ble (bī′·bl) *n.* the volume which contains the Scriptures of the Old and/or New Testament; an authoritative book on a specific subject. **biblical** *a.* scriptural [Gk. *biblia*, books].

bib·li·o- (bib′·li·ō) *prefix* from Gk. *biblion*, a book, used in the formation of compound words referring to books. **-graphy** *n.* expert knowledge of history of books; a list of books on a specific subject. **-grapher** *n.* one who compiles lists of books for further study of a subject; one interested in various editions of certain books. **-graphic(al)** a. **-logy** n. knowledge of the production and distribution of books. **-mania** n. a mania for possessing rare books. **-maniac** n. **-phile** n. a lover of books. **-pole, -polist** n. a dealer in books, esp. rare books. **-poly** n. **-theca** n. a library. **-thecary** n. a librarian [Gk. biblion, a book].

bib·u·lous (bib'·ū·las) a. given to excessive or frequent drinking; absorbent; spongy. **-ly** adv. [L. bibere, to drink].

bi·cam·er·al (bī·kam'·a·ral) a. pert. to or containing two legislative or other chambers [L. bis, twice; camera, chamber].

bi·car·bon·ate (bī·kár'·ba·nāt) n. a salt or compound containing two equivalents of carbonic acid to one of a base—usually applied loosely for 'bicarbonate of soda.'

bice (bīs) n. a blue or green pigment [Fr. bis].

bi·ceps (bī'·seps) n. two-headed muscle of arm or leg; a flexor muscle. **biciptial** a. [L. bis, twice; caput, head].

bick·er (bik'·er) v.i. to bandy words; to wrangle; to move quickly and lightly. **-ing** n. **-ment** n. [M.E. biker(en)].

bi·cus·pid (bī·kus'·pid) n. a tooth with two fangs; a. having two cusps or fangs. Also **-ate** [L. bis, twice; cuspis, a point].

bi·cy·cle (bī'·si·kl) n. a vehicle with two wheels, one in front of the other, propelled by pedals; v.i. to cycle. **bicyclist** n. one who rides a bicycle. **bike** n. (Colloq.) [L. bis, twice; Gk. kuklos, a wheel].

bid (bid) v.t. to ask; to invite; to order or direct; to offer a price; to give, as good-bye; pr.p. **bidding;** pa.t. **bid** or **bade;** pa.p. **bid, -den** n. an offer of a price, esp. at auctions; an attempt. **-dable** a. compliant; docile; obedient; submissive; willing; (Cards) that may be bid without undue risk. **-der** n. **-ding** n. invitation; command; offer at an auction; series of bids at cards [confusion of O.E. beodam, offer, and biddan, request].

bid·dy (bid'·i·) n. chicken; hen [orig. uncert.].

bide (bīd) v.i. to dwell permanently; abide; remain; continue; tarry; sojourn; reside. v.t. to endure; put up with; suffer; tolerate; bear [O.E. bidan, to remain].

bi·en·ni·al (bī·en'·i·al) a. happening once in two years; lasting for only two years; n. a plant which requires two seasons to bloom. **-ly** adv. [L. bis, twice; annus, a year].

bier (bēr) n. a frame or carriage for conveying the dead to the grave; a coffin; grave; tomb [O.E. baer]. [faces or opposite surfaces.

bi·fa·cial (bī·fā'·shal) a. having two like

bi·fo·cal (bī·fō'·kal) a. having two foci; n.pl. spectacles with a small lens for reading, set into a larger lens for distant vision [L. bis, twice; E. focal].

bi·fo·li·ate (bī·fō'·li·āt) a. (Bot.) having two leaflets springing from the same point L. bis, twice; folium, leaf].

bi·fur·cate (bī'·fur·kāt) v.t. to divide into two; v.i. to fork. **bifurcate, -d** a. **bifurcation** n. **bifurcous** a. [L. bis, twice; furca, a fork].

big (big) a. bulky; massive; huge; great; pregnant; generous; magnamimous; important. **—hearted** a. **-ness** n. size; bulk; largeness; importance. **— shot** n. (Colloq.) **-wig** n. (Colloq.) a person of great importance or influence.

big·a·my (big'·a·mi·) n. the crime of having two wives or husbands at one time. **bigamist** n. **bigamous** a. **bigamously** adv. [L. bis, twice; Gk. gamos, marriage].

big·horn (big'·hawrn) n. a Rocky Mountain wild sheep.

bight (bīt) n. a curve; a loop of a rope when folded; a bend in the sea-coast; an open bay [O.E. byht].

big·ot (big'·at) n. one obstinately and unreasably wedded to a particular belief or creed; dogmatist. **-ed** a. **-ry** n. the blind zeal of a bigot [Fr. of unknown origin].

bike (bīk) n. (Colloq.) a bicycle.

bi·ki·ni (bi·kē'·ni·) n. a scanty two-piece bathing suit [Bikini, Pacific island].

bi·lat·er·al (bī·lat'·a·ral) a. having two sides; affecting two parties. **-ly** adv. [L. bis, twice; latus, lateris, side].

bil·bo (bil'·bō) n. formerly a rapier or sword. **bilboes** n.pl. shackles for the feet, formerly used for prisoners on ships [fr. Bilbao, Spain].

bile (bīl) n. a greenish, viscous, bitter fluid secreted by the liver; gall; general disorder of health due to faulty secretion of bile; bad temper. **biliary** (bil'·yer·i·) a. pert. to the bile. **bilious** a. pert. to the bile; affected by bile; choleric; peevish; crabbed; ill-humored. **biliousness** n. a disturbance of the digestive system associated with an excess of bile [L. bilis].

bilge (bilj) n. the swelling part of a cask; the broadest part of a ship's bottom nearest the keel, acting as a sump; (Colloq.) nonsense; v.i. to spring a leak. **— water** n. evil-smelling water which gathers in a ship's botton.

bi·lin·gual (bī·ling'·gwal) a. speaking, or written in, two languages. Also **bilinguar. bilinguist** n. a person who can speak fluently in two languages [L. bis, twice; lingua, tongue].

bilk (bilk) v.t. to defraud, to swindle. **-er** n.

bill (bil) n. a kind of axle with two sharp pointed spikes mounted on a long staff; a hook-shaped pruning instrument. **-hook** n. a small bill with a hooked end for lopping branches [O.E. bil].

bill (bil) n. printed notice for public display; an account of money owed; a written engagement to pay money under the hand of the granter; a declaration of certain facts in legal proceedings; the draft of a proposed law; v.t. to announce by posters; to cover with posters; to placard; to send a statement of money owed. **-board** n. a signboard for advertising. **-fold** n. a wallet. **-ing** n. advertising; invoicing [L.L. billa = bulla, a seal].

bil·let (bil'·it) n. a short note; an order requisitioning accommodation for soldiers; the quarters occupied by soldiers in private houses, etc.; v.t. to quarter or lodge troops. **billet-doux** (bil·i·dóò') n. a love letter; pl. **billets-doux** [Fr. = a note].

bil·liard (bil'·yerd) a. pert. to billiards. **billiards,** n. a table game played with three balls which are hit by a cue [Fr. bille, log].

bil·lion (bil'·yan) n. a thousand millions (10⁹). **-aire** n. a fabulously wealthy person. **-th** a. [L. bis, twice; million].

bil·low (bil'·ō) n. a great, swelling wave of the sea; a surge of flame, smoke, cloud, etc.; a breaker; v.i. to swell or roll, as waves. **-ed, -y** a. [O.N. bylgja].

bil·ly (bil'·i·) n. (Colloq.) a policeman's stick. **bil·ly·goat** (bil'·i·gōt) n. a he-goat; a tufted beard [billy = Willie].

bi·met·al·lism (bī·met'·al·izm) n. in currency, the use of both gold and silver coins at a fixed relative value.

bi·month·ly (bī·munth'·li·) a. once in two months or twice in a month; n. a periodical which appears once in two months or twice a month.

bin (bin) n. a box or enclosed place with a lid, for corn, bread, etc.; a receptacle for bottles of wine; v.t. to store in a bin. pr.p. **-ning.** pa.t. **-ned.** [O.E. binn, crib].

bi·na·ry (bī'·na·ri·) a. composed of two; two-fold; double; dual; n. a double star. **binate** a. growing in pairs [L. bini, two by two].

bind (bīnd) v.t. to tie together as with a band, cord, etc.; to constrain by moral influence; to secure together and enclose in a cover; to place under legal obligation; to be obligatory; to apprentice; to constipate; pa.t. and pa.p. **bound. -er** n. a person who binds; a machine for binding, as sheaves, books, etc.; cover in filing and loose-leaf systems. **-ery** n. a bookbinding establishment. **-ing** a. obligatory; constipating; n. act of fastening; anything which birds; partial locking of a sliding part of a machine due to faulty lubrication [O.E. *bindan*].

binge (binj) n. concerted eating and especially drinking, to celebrate an occasion; a spree [slang].

bin·na·cle (bin′·a·kl) n. the box containing the compass of a ship [earlier *bittacle*, fr. L. *habitaculum*, little dwelling].

bin·o·cle (bin′·a·kl) n. a telescope fitted with two tubes. **binocular** (bi·nok′·ya·ler) a. adapted for the use of both eyes; n. a binocular telescope. **binoculars** n.pl. field-glasses. **binoculate** a. having two eyes; adapted for the use of two eyes [L. *bini*, two by two; *oculus*, eye]

bi·no·mi·al (bi·nō′·mi·al) n. an algebraic expression involving two terms connected by the sign plus (+) or minus (—), e.g. a + b, or c — d; a. pert. to binomials. [L. *bis*, twice; *nomen*, name].

bi·nom·i·nal (bi·nám′·i·nal) a. (*Bot.*) having two names, the first indicating the genus, the second indicating the species.

bi·o- (bī′·ō) a *prefix* used in the construction of compound terms, to express having organic life [Gk. *bios*, life].

bi·o·chem·is·try (bī·ō·kem′·is·tri·) n. physiology considered from the chemical point of view; the chemistry of living things.

bi·o·dy·nam·ics (bī·ō·dī·nam′·iks) n.pl. the science which investigates the vital forces; the energy of living functions.

bi·o·gen (bī′·a·jen) n. a hypothetical protein molecule assumed to be the primary source of all living matter. **biogenesis** n. the theory that life develops only from living organisms [Gk. *bios*, life; *genesis*, beginning].

bi·o·graph, bi·o·scope (bī′·ō·graf, -skōp′) n. early motion picture projector [Gk. *bios*, life; *graphein*, to write; *skopein*, to see].

bi·og·ra·phy (bī·ág′·ra·fi·) n. the detailed story of a person's life and achievements; the section of literature devoted to the writing of the life-stories of individuals. **biographic, -al** [Gk. *bios*, life; *graphien*, to write].

bi·ol·o·gy (bī·al′·a·ji·) n. the science of life, whether animal or vegetable. **biologic, biological** a. **biologically** adv. **biologist** n. **biological warfare**, a method of fighting in which disease bacteria would be used [Gk. *bios*, life; *logos*, a discourse].

bi·o·nom·ics (bī·a·nám′·iks) n. study of influence of environment on organisms; ecology [Gk. *bios*, life; *nomos*, law].

bi·o·phys·ics (bī·ō·fiz′·iks) n. physics of living organisms. [of living tissue for diagnosis.

bi·op·sy (bī′·áp·si·) n. the excision of a piece

bi·o·scope See **biograph**.

bi·ot·ic (bī·át′·ik) a. (*Biol.*) relating to life; vital. **biotics** n. the functions, properties, and activities of living things [Gk. *bios*, life].

bi·o·tin (bī′·a·tin) n. a constituent of the vitamin B₂ complex essential to many forms of life [Gk. *bios*, life].

bi·par·ti·san (bī·pár′·ti·zan) a. pert. to, representing, or composed of, members of two parties [L. *bis*, twice; *partire*, to divide].

bi·par·tite (bī·pár′·tīt) a. consisting of two corresponding parts; shared by the two parties concerned. **bipartition** n. [L. *bis*, twice; *partire*, to divide].

bi·ped (bī′·ped) n. a two-footed animal. **biped, bipedal** a. [L. *bis*, twice; *pse*, a foot].

bi·plane (bī′·plān) n. an airplane or glider having two main wings.

bi·pod [bī′·pád] n. a two-legged stand.—cf. **tripod**.

bi·po·lar (bī·pōl′·er) a. having two poles [L.].

bi·quad·rate (bī·kwād′·rāt, ·rit) n. (*Math.*) the value of the fourth power of a number. **biquadratic** a.; n. the fourth power [L. *bis*, twice; *quadratus*, squared].

birch (burch) n. a tree with slim branches and silvery bark-scales; the hard, close-grained wood of the birch; v.t. flog with a birch-rod. **birch, -en** a. of birch. **-rod** n. a rod of birch twigs for inflicting punishment [O.E. *birce*].

bird (burd) n. a feathered animal with wings. **— cage** n. a cage made of wire and wood for keeping birds. **-call** n. the sounds made by a bird; instrument used to allure birds by imitating their notes [O.E. *brid*, a bird].

bird·ie (burd′·i) n. (*Golf*) holing a ball in one stroke under par.

bi·ret·ta (bi·ret′·a) n. a flat, square, stiff cap worn by Catholic clergy [It. *berretta*].

birr (bur) n. a whirring noise like that of a revolving wheel; an energetic push; a pronounced accent; strongly trilling the consonant r. Also **burr** [Scand. *burr*].

birth (burth) n. act of coming into life or of being born; the delivery of a newly born child alive; descent; origin. **— control** n. restriction of conception. **-day** n. the day on which one is born; the anniversary of that day. **-mark** n. peculiar mark on the body at birth. **-place** n. the place where a person is born. **— rate** n. the ration of births to the total population. **-right** n. anything to which one is entitled by birth [M.E. *birthe*, perh. fr. Scand.].

bis (bis) adv. twice; (*Mus.*) to show that the bar or passage is to be performed twice.

bis·cuit (bis′·kit) n. a quick bread in small soft cakes; stoneware, earthenware, porcelain, etc. after firing but before being glazed [L. *bis*, twice; *coctus*, cooked].

bi·sect (bī·sekt′) v.t. to divide into two equal parts. **bisection** n. one of two equal parts. **-or** n. a bisecting line. **bisegment** n. one of two segments of a bisected line [L. *bis*, twice; *secare*, to cut].

bi·sex·u·al (bī·sek′·shoo·al) a. having the organs of both sexes [L. *bis*, twice].

bish·op (bish′·ap) n. a clergyman of high rank, chess man moving diagonally. **-ric** n. diocese, jurisdiction, or office of a bishop. **-'s lawn**, a fine kind of linen [fr. Gk. *episkopos*, overseer].

bis·muth (biz′·math) n. a reddish-white metal the salts of which are used in medicine.

bi·son (bī′·san) n. the large buffalo of Western N. Am. [L.].

bisque (bisk) n. a smooth, creamy soup; a thick soup made with shellfish or game; unglazed porcelain [Fr.].

bis·tro (bis′·trō) n. a small tavern or café [Fr.]

bi·sul·phate (bī·sul′·fāt) n. a salt of sulphuric acid in which one-half of the hydrogen in the acid is replaced by a metal.

bit (bit) pa.t. of **bite**.

bit (bit) n. a mouthful; a morsel; small piece of anything; a fragment; a boring tool generally for use in brace; part of bridle which is placed in a horse's mouth; v.t. to put the bit in the mouth of a horse.

bitch (bich) n. the female of the dog, wolf, or fox; (*Colloq.*) an opprobrious term for a woman; v. (*Slang*) to complain [O.E. *bicce*].

bite (bīt) v.t. to cut, crush, seize, or wound with the teeth; to pinch with cold; to eat into, as acid; to corrode, to gnaw; to champ; to nip; to defraud; to cheat; v.i. to be given to biting; to be pungent; pr.p. **biting**; pa.t. **bit**; pa.p. **bit** or **bitten** n. act of biting; a portion bitten off; food; morsel; sharp, pungent taste; the nibble of a fish at a hook; the grip of an edged tool on metal. **-r** n. **biting** a. sharp; severe; sarcastic; caustic; pungent; chilling [O.E. *bitan*].

bitt (bit) n. a post for securing cables, etc. usually pl.; v.t. to put around a bitt [Scand.].

bit·ter (bit′·er) a. biting or acrid to the taste; causing pain or smart to the feelings; n. bitter beer. **-ly** adv. **-ness** n. the quality of being bitter to the taste; animosity. **-s** n. alcoholic liquor containing bitter flavorings. **-sweet** n. the woody nightshade whose root, when chewed, tastes first bitter then sweet [O.E. *biter*].

bit·tern (bit'·ern) *n.* a wading marsh-bird of the heron family [O.Fr. *butor*].

bi·tu·men (bi·tū'·men) *n.* an inflammable, mineral pitch, as asphalt, petroleum, etc. **bituminize** *v.t.* to prepare or treat with bitumen. **bituminous** *a.* [L.].

bi·valve (bī'·valv) *a.* having two valves; *n.* an animal with a shell of two parts opening like a hinge; a seed case of this kind. **bivalvous** *a.*

biv·ou·ac (biv'·ŏŏ·ak) *n.* an encampment in the open air, without any cover; *v.i.* to encamp without covering. *pr.p.* **bivouacking;** *pa.t.* and *pa.p.* **bivouacked** [Fr.].

bi·week·ly (bī·wĕk'·li·) *a.* occurring once in every two weeks; occurring twice in each week; *n.* a periodical issued twice a week or once in two weeks [L. *bis*, twice]. [Fr.].

bi·zarre (bi·zår') *a.* odd; eccentric; strange

blab (blab) *v.t.* to reveal imprudently secrets entrusted to one; *v.i.* to tell tales; *pr.p.* **-bing**; *pa.t.* and *pa.p.* **-bed.** *n.* a chatterer; a gossip; a tell-tale. Also **-ber** [Scand. *blabbre*, to babble].

black (blak) *a.* of the darkest color; dark; nightlike; destitute of light; funereal; ominous; *n.* the darkest color; negro; mourning; *v.t.* to make black. **-en** *v.t.* to make black; to polish with blacking; to defame; *v.i.* to grow or turn black. **-ly** *adv.* **-ness** *n.* **-amoor** *n.* a Negro or Moor. — **art** *n.* magic; necromancy. **-ball** *v.t.* to reject a candidate for admission to a club by putting a black ball in the ballot box. **-berry** *n.* a fruit-bearing shrub, the bramble. **-bird** *n.* any of a number of birds which have predominantly black plumage. **-board** *n.* a board painted black, a slate, or any dark surface to write on with chalk. **-bread** *n.* rye bread. — **diamonds** (*Colloq.*) coal. — **eye** *n.* discoloration due to a blow. — **face** *n.* (*Theat.*) entertainer made up as a Negro, usually for a minstrel show. **-flag** *n.* flag popularly associated with pirates. — **friar** *n.* a Dominican friar, from his black mantle. — **frost** *n.* severe frost. **-guard** (blag'· erd) *n.* orig. a menial of the scullery; a low scoundrel; *a.* low; vile; *v.t.* to treat as a blackguard; to revile; *v.i.* to act in a vile manner. **-guardism** *n.* **-guardly** *a.* **-head** *n.* a small black-topped mass which plugs the mouths of the follicles of the skin. **-ing** *n.* an old form of boot polish. **-jack** *n.* a short, leather-covered club with a heavy head on an elastic shaft; the flag of a pirate; a miner's name for zinc-blende. — **lead** *n.* graphite, a form of nearly pure carbon obtained from plumbago, and used in the manufacture of stove-polish and lead pencils. —**list** *n.* any list of undesirable persons; *v.t.* to place on such a list. **-mail** *n.* extortion of money by threats of exposure or denunciation; hush-money; orig. moneys paid over to robbers to obviate constant pillaging. — **mark** *n.* a mark of censure or failure. — **market** *n.* a clandestine market for the sale of goods whose distribution is regulated, and which are not on free sale. —**out** *n.* temporary loss of vision or memory; a total cutting off of all lights. — **sheep** *n.* a loose, dissolute member of a respectable family [O.E. *blaec*].

blad·der (blad'·er) *n.* a thin musculo-membranous bag, in the pelvis, serving as a reservoir for urine; the windbag of a bagpipe; any membranous sac. **-ed** *a.* swollen like a bladder. **-wort** *n.* water-plant with floating leaves. **-y** *a.* thin and inflated; blistered [O.E. *blaedre*, a blister].

blade (blād) *n.* the leaf, or flat part of the leaf, of a plant; the cutting part of a knife, or tool; the broad part of an oar; a sword; (*Colloq.*) a dashing fellow. **-bone** *n.* the upper bone in shoulder, scapula. **-d** *a.* [O.E. *blaed*].

blame (blām) *v.t.* to express disapprobation of; to censure; *n.* fault. **-less** *a.* **-lessness** *n.* [O.Fr. *blasmer*, to speak evil of].

blanch (blanch) *v.t.* to whiten; to bleach; to strip (the husk); *v. i.* to become white; to turn

pale; to gloss over. **-ing** *n.* [Fr. *blanc*, white].

blanc-mange (blạ·mȧnzh') *n.* a pudding [Fr. *blanc*, white; *manger*, to eat].

bland (bland) *a.* mild; gentle; affable. **-ly** *adv.* **-ness** *n.* [L. *blandus*, flattering].

blan·dish (blan'·dish) *v.t.* to flatter and coax; to wheedle. **-ment** *n.* [L. *blandus*].

blank (blangk) *a.* without writing or any marks; empty; confused; *n.* an empty space; a lottery ticket not drawing a prize; the white disc of a target. **-ly** *adv.* — **verse**, unrhymed heroic [Fr. *blanc*, white].

blan·ket (blang'·kit) *n.* a loosely woven woollen bedcover; a covering; a thick canopy of cloud; *v.t.* to cover with a blanket; to toss in a blanket. **-ing** *n.* thick material for blankets; tossing in a blanket. **a wet blanket,** one who depresses others; kill-joy [Fr. *blanc*, white].

blare (blār) *v.t.* and *v.i.* to sound loudly; to trumpet; *n.* a long, prolonged noise [O.E. *blaesan*, to blow].

blar·ney (blȧr'·ni·) *n.* coaxing, cajoling talk; outrageous flattery; blandishing [fr. *Blarney-stone*, near Cork, Ireland].

bla·sé (blȧ'·sā) *a.* surfeited with everything; absolutely bored; sophisticated [Fr.].

blas·pheme (blas·fēm') *v.t.* to speak irreverently of God; to desecrate by impious talk; *v.i.* to take God's name in vain; to curse and swear. **-r** *n.* **blaspheming** *n.* impious talk. **blasphemous** *a.* **blasphemously** *adv.* **blasphemy** *n.* irreverence in speaking of sacred matters; profane talk [Gk. *blasphēmein*].

blast (blast) *n.* a gust or puff of air; a forced stream of air; the blowing of a wind instrument; an explosion of gunpowder in rending rocks; a blight affecting plants or cattle. *v.t.* to injure, as by a noxious wind; to blight; to split, as by gunpowder; to abuse vehemently. **-ed** *a.* blighted; accursed; (*Colloq.*) confounded; infernal. **-er** *n.* — **furnace** *n.* a smelting-furnace in which hot air is furnished by bellows or other apparatus. **-ing** *n.* a blast; explosion [O.E. *blaest*].

bla·tant (blā'·tạnt) *a.* offensively noisy; loud-(voiced); brawling; obtrusive. **blatancy** *n.* **-ly** *adv.* [coined by Spenser].

blath·er, blether (bla'·THer) *n.* one who talks nonsense; *v.i.* to talk nonsense. **-s** nonsensical, foolish talk. **-ing** *n.* **-skite** *n.* one who talks sheer nonsense [Scand. *blathra*, to talk nonsense].

blaze (blāz) *n.* bright flame; a big conflagration; outburst of activity or zeal; display; *v.i.* to burn brightly; to glow with anger. **-r** *n.* sports jacket of bright color. **-s** *pl.* hell, as in **'Go to blazes'** [O.E. *blaese*, a flame].

blaze (blāz) *n.* white mark upon a horse's forehead; a mark on a tree made by pathfinders; *v.t.* to mark a trail [L.G. *blāse*, white mark on head of horse].

blaze (blāz) *v.t.* to proclaim; spread abroad [O.E. *blaesan*, to blow].

bla·zon (blā'·zn) *v.t.* to make known to everybody; to display armorial bearings in their proper colors; to embellish; *n.* art of drawing or explaining coats of arms. **-er** *n.* **-ment** *n.* **-ry** *n.* art of describing or explaining coats of arms in heraldic terms [Fr. *blason*, shield].

bleach (blēch) *v.t.* to whiten by exposure to sunlight and air, or by chemical action; *v.i.* to become whiter or paler; *n.* a decolorizing, chemical agent. **-er** *n.* one who, or that which, bleaches. **bleachers** *n.pl.* outdoor, uncovered seat for a spectator in a stadium [O.E. *blaecan*, fr. *blaec*, pale].

bleak (blēk) *a.* without color; pale; desolate and exposed. **-ly** *adv.* **-ness** *n.* [O.E. *blaec*, pale].

blear (blēr) *a.* dim or watery, due to inflammation of the eye or tears; *v.i.* to dim or blur. **-y** *a.* dim [M.E. *bleren*, to have sore eyes].

bleat (blēt) *v.i.* to cry as a sheep; to talk in a complaining, whining fashion; *n.* the sound made by a sheep [O.E. *blaetan*].

bleed (blēd) *v.t.* to draw blood surgically; to extort money from someone; *v.i.* to lose blood; to die in battle; *pa.t.* and *pa.p.* **bled.** **-er** *n.* a person who is afflicted by haemophilia, excessive bleeding. **-ing** *n.* [O.E. *bledan*].

blem·ish (blem'·ish) *n.* any deformity, physical or moral; flaw; disfigurement; *v.i.* to mark with a flaw; to mar or disfigure [Fr. *blémir*].

blench (blensh) *v.i.* to start back from lack of courage; to flinch [O.E. *blencan*, to deceive].

blend (blend) *v.t.* to mix allied articles together smoothly and inseparably; *v.i.* to intermix; to mingle well; *pa.p.* **-ed** or **blent;** *n.* a mixture. **-er** *n.* **-ing** *n.* [Scand. *blanda*, to mix].

blende (blend) *n.* an ore of zinc, consisting of zinc and sulphur; name given to certain lustrous minerals [Ger. *blenden*].

bless (bles) *v.t.* to consecrate; glorify; sanctify; praise; to give thanks to; invoke happiness on; magnify. *pa.p.* **-ed** or **blest. blessed** (bles'·id), **blest** *a.* happy; favored with blessings; hallowed. **-edness** *n.* happiness; heavenly joy; felicity. **-ing** *n.* a source of happiness or gratitude; benefaction; boon; benediction; prayer [O.E. *bletsian*, to consecrate (with blood)].

blew (blōō) *pa.t.* of **blow.**

blight (blīt) *n.* disease of plants caused by certain fungi or parasitic bacteria; anything which has an adverse effect, injures, or destroys; *v.t.* to affect with blight.

blimp (blimp) *n.* a small non-rigid airship.

blind (blīnd) *a.* destitute of sight; ignorant; undiscerning; reckless; unaware of; heedless; at random; invisible; concealed; closed at one end; (*Slang*) drunk; *v.t.* to deprive of sight; to dazzle; to darken or obscure; to hide; to deceive; *n.* a window-covering or screen; something intended to mislead. — **date** *n.* a date arranged with someone not previously known; the person involved. **-ed** *a.* rendered sightless; dazzled; oblivious to all other factors. **-ers** *n.pl.* a horse's blinkers. **-fold** *a.; v.t.* to cover the eyes with something; to mislead. **-ing** *a.* — **landing** *n.* grounding an aircraft by depending on radio signals. **-ly** *adv.* **-ness** *n.* lacking power of sight; ignorance; obstinacy [O.E. *blind*].

blink (blingk) *v.i.* to wink; to look with the eyes half-shut; to glimmer, as a candle; *v.t.* to shut out of sight, as a fact or question; to ignore; *n.* a glimpse; a glance. **-ard** *n.* one who blinks; a stupid person. **-ers** *n.pl.* pieces of leather preventing a horse from seeing to either side [M.E. *blenken*].

bliss (blis) *n.* the acme of happiness; perfect felicity; heavenly rapture. **-ful** *a.* supremely happy; enjoyable. **-fully** *adv.* **-fulness** *n.* **-less** *a.* [O.E. *bliths*, fr. *blithe*].

blis·ter (blis'·tẹr) *n.* a vesicle of the skin filled with a clear or blood-stained serum; a pustule; any like swelling as on plants, paint or steel; a plaster applied to skin to raise a blister; *v.t.* to raise blisters upon; to wither up with scorn and sarcasm; *v.i.* to rise in blisters. **-y** *a.* [O.Fr. *blestre*].

blithe (blīTH) *a.* gay; happy; gladsome; jolly; merry; sprightly. **-ly** *adv.* **-ness** *n.* **-some** *a.* merry; cheerful [O.E. *blithe*, joyous].

blitz (blits) *n.* a heavy, sudden attack by enemy bombers; *v.t.* to bomb from the air. **-ed** *a.* also **blitz·krieg** [Ger. *Blitz*, lightning; *krieg*, war]. [Ger. *bletz*, lightening].

bliz·zard (bliz'·ẹrd) *n.* a blinding snowstorm

bloat (blōt) *v.t.* to cause to have an unhealthy swollen appearance; to swell or puff out; to cure fish by salting and smoking. **-ed** *a.* swollen. **-edness** *n.* **bloater** *n.* a herring—salted, smoked, and dried [fr. Scand. *blautr*, soft].

blob (blåb) *n.* anything small and globular; small, round mass [var. of *bleb*, blister (?)].

bloc (blåk) *n.* a combination of two or more countries or political parties [Fr.].

block (blåk) *n.* a solid mass of matter; a roughly squared piece of wood, stone, etc.; the large piece of wood on which persons were beheaded; the wheel of a pulley with its case of wood; a number of buildings forming one compact mass; an obstruction, esp. on roads; mounted plate for printing; *v.t.* to shut in, to enclose; to obstruct; to shape (a hat); to sketch out roughly. **-buster** *n.* a heavy explosive bomb. **-ing** *n.* the process of stamping bookcovers with a decorative pattern. **-head** *n.* a dullard. **-house** *n.* an improvised fort made of logs; a fortified place. — **letters** *n.* a form of script where the letters are printed instead of in the usual cursive style. **block and tackle,** a pulley enclosed in a block used for lifting weights [Fr. *bloc*].

block·ade (blå·kād') *n.* prevention of imports into countries usually during a war; *v.t.* to shut up hostile troops in a town by surrounding it; to prevent trade with a hostile country. — **runner** *n.* a vessel employed to slip through to a blockaded country [fr. *block*].

blond (blånd) *n.* (*fem.* **blonde**) a person of fair complexion and generally, light blue eyes; *a.* fair; light golden-brown [Fr.].

blood (blud) *n.* the red, viscid fluid which circulates in the body of men and animals; relationship, consanguinity, kindred; honorable birth; descent; a rake, man about town; *v.t.* (*Med.*) to let blood, to bleed. — **bank** *n.* a store of blood for use in a transfusion. — **count** *n.* the number of red and white cells in a specific quantity of blood. **-curdling** *a.* terrifying. **-hound** *n.* a hound, with keen sense and perseverance. **-ily** *adv.* **-less** *a.* without blood; anemic; spiritless. **-lessness** *n.* **-letting** *n.* the withdrawal of blood to allay fever; phlebotomy. **-mobile** *n.* a mobile unit for collecting blood for blood banks. **-money** *n.* money paid for betraying another; wages earned at a sweated rate of labor. — **plasma,** the fluid part of blood. — **poisoning** *n.* a condition due to circulation of bacteria in blood stream. —**pressure** *n.* the pressure exerted by the blood on the walls of the arteries. —**red** *a.* crimson. — **serum** *n.* the fluid part of the blood after the fibrin and the corpuscles have been eliminated. **-shed** *n.* the shedding of blood; slaughter. **-shot** *a.* of the eyes, red or congested with blood. **-stain** *n.* the dried and darkened stain left on clothing, floors, etc. after contact with blood. **-stone** *n.* a semiprecious stone, a variety of crystalline silica, dark green in color with red spots. Also called heliotrope. **-sucker** *n.* an animal which sucks blood, esp. the leech; an extortioner. — **test** *n.* an examination of the blood often to determine to which of the four groups it belongs. **-thirsty** *a.* eager to shed blood. —**transfusion** *n.* the transference of blood from one person to another. — **vessel** *n.* an artery or vein through which blood flows. **-y** *a.* pert. to blood; stained with or containing blood; ruthless in shedding blood; (*Br.*) used vulgarly as an expletive to add an intensive force; *v.t.* to make bloody [O.E. *blod*].

bloom (blōōm) *n.* a flower; a blossom; state of freshness and vigor; flush of youth; powdery coating on freshly picked fruit; *v.i.* to blossom; to glow with youthful vigor; to flourish; *v.t.* to cause to blossom or flourish.

bloom·ers (blōō'·mẹrz) *n.pl.* women's loose trousers gathered at the knee, worn for sports; an undergarment of the same design [Mrs. *Bloomer*, of New York, 1849].

blos·som (blås'·ạm) *n.* the flower of a plant, esp. a tree; *v.i.* to put forth blossoms; to flourish. **-ed** *a.* **-y** *a.* rich in blossoms [O.E. *blostm*].

blot (blåt) *v.t.* to spot or bespatter esp. with ink; to stain with infamy; to obliterate; to dry with blotting-paper; *pr.p.* **-ting;** *pa.p.* **-ted;** *n.* a spot or stain, as of ink; blemish; disgrace. **-ter** *n.* a blotting-pad. **-ting-paper** *n.* a kind of unsized paper for drying ink [Scand.].

blotch (blåch) *n.* an irregular, colored spot; an eruption upon the skin; pimple; *v.t.* to mark with blotches; to make spotted. **-y** a. [O.Fr. *bloche*].

blot·to (blåt'·ō) a. (*Slang*) very drunk.

blouse (blous, blouz) n. a light, loose upper garment; v.i. and v.t. to drape loosely [Fr.].

blow (blō) n. a mass or bed of flowers; v.i. to blossom [O.E. *blowan*, to blossom].

blow (blō) n. a stroke; a knock; a thump; a smack; a rap; sudden calamity.

blow (blō) v.i. to produce a current of air; to move, as air; to breathe hard or quickly; to puff; to pant; (*Slang*) to brag; (*Slang*) to squander; to spout (of whales); v.t. to direct a current of air on; to sound a wind instrument; to put out of breath; pa.t. **blew**; pa.p. **-n**; n. a high wind. **-fly** n. insect, e.g., blue-bottle which blows eggs in meat. **-lamp** n. a portable lamp for applying intense local heat. **-n** a. swelled ;tired; out of breath; tainted. **-out** n. (*Slang*) a feast or big meal; a burst tire. **—pipe** n. an instrument for concentrating the heat of a flame on some point, by blowing; a blowgun. **-y** a. windy [O.E. *blawan*].

blub·ber (blub'·ẹr) n. the fat of whales and other marine animals; v.i. to weep unrestrainedly. **-ed** a. swollen by weeping. **-ing** n. [imit. formation, with first meaning of *bubble*].

bludg·eon (bluj'·ạn) n. a short cudgel with one end loaded; v.t. to knock out with a club [probably Celt., fr. *plug*].

blue (blōō) n. the color of the clear sky; one of the seven primary colors; a dye or pigment; indigo powder used in laundering; the sea; n.pl. (*Slang*) a fit of depression; a very slow jazz dance of Negro origin. **blue** a. of the color blue; azure; livid; melancholy; glum; v.t. to make or dye blue. **bluish** a. slightly blue. **-bell** n. the wild hyacinth. **-berry** n. a shrub with edible small berries. **-bird** n. a migratory bird of N. Am. belonging to the thrush family. **— blood** n. an aristocrat. **-bonnet** n. Scottish trooper, from the blue woolen cap at one time in general use. **— book** n. a directory of socially prominent people; a college examination book. **-bottle** n. the cornflower; a large fly whose larvae are often parasites of domestic animals. **Blue Cross**, a system of nonprofit health insurance. **-grass** n. meadow grass of Kentucky which forms thick turf. **-heat**, about 550° F. **-jacket** n. a sailor. **-jay** n. a crested bird of the eastern U.S. and Canada. **— laws** n. laws restricting activities on Sunday. **-pencil** v.t. to edit, to alter. **-print** n. a simple photographic reproduction of technical drawings leaving white lines of plan on a blue background; (*Fig.*) any projected plan with its details. **— ribbon**, first prize; an emblem of temperance [Fr. *bleu*].

bluff (bluf) a. steep and broad; rough and ready; frank and hearty in manner; n. a high bank or cliff presenting a steep front; a headland; a cluster of trees on the prairie. **-ness** n. steepness; a frank, blunt manner of speech.

bluff (bluf) n. an attempt to mislead in regard to one's real purpose; v.t. to mislead one by giving a wrong impression. **-er** n. **-ing** n., a.

blun·der (blun'·dẹr) v.i. to make a gross mistake; to err through thoughtlessness; to flounder about; n. a gross mistake. **-er** n. **-head** n. one continually blundering. **-ing** n. and a. continually making mistakes; bungling; clumsy; fumbling. **-ingly** adv. [M.E. *blondren*, to confuse].

blun·der·buss (blun'·dẹr·bus) n. an obsolete short gun with a bell-shaped muzzle and a wide bore [Dut. *donderbus*, thunder-box].

blunt (blunt) a. having a dull edge or point; dull; brusque in speech; v.t. to render less sharp; to weaken appetite or desire. **-ly** adv. **-ness** [origin unknown].

blur (blur) n. a spot; stain; smudge; whatever dims without effacing; v.t. to smear; to make indistinct. pr.p. **-ring**; pa.t. and pa.p. **-red**.

blurb (blurb) n. an advertisement, esp. ex-

travagant in praise [word invented by Gelett Burgess].

blurt (blurt) n. a sudden outburst. **to blurt out** v.t. to give information suddenly, indiscreetly, or tactlessly [imit.].

blush (blush) v.i. to redden in the face, from shame, modesty, or confusion; n. a rosy tint; a red color suffusing the face; first glance or view. **-ing** n. a rosy glow on the face; a. modest; coy; bashful. **-ingly** adv. [O.E. *blyscan*, to shine].

blus·ter (blus'·tẹr) v.i. to blow in boisterous gusts, of wind; to talk with violence and noise; to bully or swagger; n. fitful noise and violence. **-er** n. **-ous** a. **-y** a. stormy.

bo·a (bō'·ạ) n. a genus of constricting, non-venomous serpents; a long round coil of fur or feathers for the neck. **—constrictor** n. a serpent which crushes its victims [L.].

boar (bōr) n. the male of the swine. **—hound** n. a large dog used in hunting boars [O.E. *bar*].

board (bōrd) n. a long, narrow strip of timber; a table, hence food or diet; council-table; council itself; a thick paper made by pasting together several layers (card-board, paste-board, etc.); v.t. to cover with boards; to supply with meals and lodging for payment; to embark on a ship, airplane, etc.; v.i. to be a lodger. **-s** n.pl. the stage in a theater; the covers of a book. **-er** n. one who boards a vehicle; one reriving food and lodging. **-ing** n. a wooden fence, floor, etc.; entering a vehicle; obtaining food and lodging. **-ing-house** n. a house in which boarders are accommodated. **-ing-school** n. a school in which the students are in residence [O.E. *bord*].

boast (bōst) v.t. to speak with vanity of; to be unduly proud of; v.i. to brag; to vaunt; to praise oneself extravagantly; n. a statement, expressive of pride or vain glory; that which is boasted of. **-er** n. **-ful** a. **-fully** adv. **-fulness**, **-ing** n. indulging in boasting. **-ingly** adv. [M.E. *bost*].

boat (bōt) n. a small vessel, generally undecked, moved by oars or sails or small motor; a ship; anything resembling a boat, e.g. a sauce-boat; v.t. to carry in a boat; v.i. to row or sail about in a boat. **boatswain** (bō'·sun) n. a ship's officer [O.E. *bat*].

bob (bàb) n. a short, jerking motion; anything which swings when suspended; a jerk; a pendant; the weight of a pendulum; hair cut short and square across; a docked tail; v.t. to move with a jerk; to cut hair semi-short; v.i. to dangle; to move up and down or in and out; pr.p. **-bing**; pa.p. **-bed**.

bob·bin (bàb'·in) n. a cylinder or spool on which thread is wound [Fr. *bobine*].

bob-o-link (bàb'·ạ·lingk) n. a common North American songbird.

bob·by·sox (bàb'·i·sàks) n. (*Colloq.*) ankle socks, usually worn by girls in their teens. **-er** n. a girl in her teens.

bob·sled, bob·sleigh (bàb'·sled, ·slā) n. two small sleds coupled together; a long toboggan; v.i. to use a bobsled.

bock (bàk) n. dark beer [Ger. fr. *Eimbeck* where first brewed].

bode (bōd) v.t. and v.i. to portend; to presage; to foretell; to foreshadow; to be an omen of. **-ful** a. **-ment** n. an omen; portent; presentiment. **boding** a. ominous; n. an omen; a presentiment [O.E. *bodian*, to announce].

bod·ice (bàd'·is) n. that part of a woman's dress above the waist, with or without sleeves, and close-fitting [orig. pl. *bodies*].

bod·kin (bàd'·kin) n. (*Obs.*) a short, sharp dagger or stiletto; an instrument for piercing holes in material; a large blunt needle; a pin for dressing hair [M.E. *boidekin*].

bod·y (bàd'·i·) n. the frame of a human being or of an animal; the main part of anything; coachwork, seating and upholstery of a car; an assemblage of things or persons; a solid substance; strength or consistency of a liquid; v.t. to produce in definite shape; pa.t. and pa.p. **bodied. bodied** a. used in compounds, e.g. able-bodied. **bodiless** a. possessing no body. **bodily** a. pert. to the body; adv. physically, in the body, in the flesh; altogether; completely; in the mass. **-guard** n. life-guard of an important individual; an escort [O.E. bodig].

Boe·o·tian (bē·ō'·shan) a. pert. to Boeotia in ancient Greece; boorish, dull, stupid, as the inhabitants were so considered.

Boer (bōr) n. a S. African of Dutch descent [Dut. cf. boor].

bo·gey (bō'·gi·) n. (Golf) one over par for hole. See bogle [fr. imaginary partner, Colonel Bogey].

bog·gle (bág'·l) v.i. to stop or shrink back through fear; to hesitate; to equivocate; to bungle.

bo·gle (bō'·gl') n. a ghost or demon; a fearsome apparition, imp, or hobgoblin associated with the nursery. **bogey, bogy** n. the devil; a bugbear; a goblin. **bogeyman, boggard** n. [fr. bug].

bo·gus (bō'·gus) a. sham; counterfeit; spurious; false [etym. unknown].

Bo·he·mi·an (bō·hē'·mi·an) a. pert. to Bohemia or its inhabitants; pert. to the gypsies; unconventional; n. a native of Bohemia; a gypsy; one who leads a loose and unsettled life [Fr. bohémien, gypsy].

boil (boil) v.t. to bring to a seething condition, by heating; to cook, by boiling; v.i. to be agitated by the action of heat; to seethe; to reach boiling-point. **-er** n. one who boils; a vessel for boiling. **-ing point**, the temperature at which a liquid boils; of water 212° Fahr. [Fr. bouillir, to boil].

boil (boil) n. local inflammation of the skin round a hair follicle [O.E. bule, sore].

bois·ter·ous (bois'·ter·as) a. wild; noisy; hearty; turbulent; stormy; windy. **-ly** adv. **-ness** n. [M.E. boistous].

bo·la, bo·las (bol'·a) n. a missile used by S. American cowboys, consisting of two or three stone balls attached to the ends of a rope, to entangle the feet of cattle [Sp.].

bold (bōld) a. daring; ready to meet danger; courageous; brave; intrepid; valorous; fearless; cheeky. **—faced** a. impudent; forward; brazen; of letters, printed with heavy thick strokes. **-ly** adv. **-ness** n. [O.E. bald].

bole (bōl) n. the trunk of a tree. **bolling** n. a tree with the top and branches cut off; a pollard [Scand. bolr].

bo·le·ro (bō·le'·rō) n. a national Spanish dance, in triple time; the music for this dance; a short jacket, usually without sleeves, worn over a blouse [Sp.].

boll (bōl) n. a seed capsule of cotton, flax, etc. **-weevil, -worm**, larvae of various moths destructive of cotton crops [O.E. bolla].

bol·lard (bál'·erd) n. a strong post on a wharf, etc., for making fast hawsers [fr. bole].

bo·lo·gna (ba·lō'·ni, ·na) n. a large smoked, seasoned type of sausage.

bo·lo·ney See **baloney**.

Bol·she·vik (bál'·sha·vik, also bōl·) n. a member of the Communist Party; a violent revolutionary. **bolshevism** n. theory and practice of Russian or other communism. **bolshevist** n. and a. **bolshevistic** a. **bolshevize** v.t. [Russ. bolshe, comp. of veliki, great].

bol·ster (bōl'·ster) n. a long round bed-pillow; anything designated as a support; v.t. to sustain; to support; to prop. **-er** n. **to bolster up**, to support a weak case or person [O.E.].

bolt (bōlt) n. a bar for fastening a door, window, etc.; part of a lock which engages with the keeper; a metal pin with a head at one end and screw threads at the other to receive a nut; a roll of cloth; a thunderbolt; an arrow; a sudden rush; v.t. to fasten with a bolt; to swallow food hurriedly; to expel suddenly; v.i. to rush away; to start suddenly forward [E.].

bomb (bám) n. a cast-iron container filled with high explosives, gas, incendiary contents, or smoke-producing substances exploding by percussion or by a timing mechanism. **-er** n. an airplane for bombs. **-proof** a. secure against small bomb splinters. **-shell** n. a bomb; something devastating and quite unexpected. **atom(ic) bomb**, a bomb depending on the release of atomic energy. **bomb sight**, instrument for aiming bombs [Gk. bombos, a booming sound].

bom·bard (bám'·bárd) n. an early mortar with a wide bore, using stone-shot. **bombard** (bam.-bard') v.t. to batter with heavy artillery fire; to ply with many questions. **-ier** n. a gunner in the artillery. **-ment** n. a sustained attack with guns, bombs, etc. [O.Fr. bombarde].

bom·bast (bám'·bast) n. inflated, high-sounding language. **-ic** a. **-ically** adv. [O.Fr. bombace, cotton-wool].

bom·ba·zine, bom·ba·sine (bám·ba·zēn') n. a twilled fabric of silk and worsted or cotton [Fr. bombasin].

bombe (bōmb) n. a melon-shaped or round mold of ice cream [Fr.].

bo·nan·za (bō'·nan'·za) n. an exceptionally rich and persistent vein of ore; a profitable enterprise [Sp.].

bon bon (bán'·bán) n. a fondant candy. **-nere** (nyār) n. candy dish [Fr. bon, good].

bond (bánd) n. that which binds, a band, a link, a tie; an oath or promise; obligation; duty; the arrangement of bricks or stones in a wall so that successive courses interlock and give stability. **-s** n.pl. fetters; chains; captivity. **-age** n. a state of being bound; slavery; political subjection [O.E. bindan, to bind].

bond (bánd) n. a legal engagement in writing to fulfill certain conditions; a certificate of ownership of capital lent to a government, municipality, etc.; a mortgage on a house, etc.; v.t. to put dutiable articles on or under bond. **-ed** a. placed in bond; mortgaged. **-ed warehouse**, a warehouse for holding goods in bond [O.E. bindan, to bind].

bone (bōn) n. the hard tissue which forms the skeleton of mammals, birds, reptiles and fishes. **-r** n. (Slang) a mistake. v.t. to remove the bones; to filet (fish); to stiffen corsets with whale-bone, etc. **-s** n.pl. human remains; corpse; dice; castanets. **— ash** n. calcined bones. **-black** n. finely ground animal charcoal. **— china** n. china in which bone ash is used. **-dry** a. absolutely dry. **—head** n. (Slang) a stupid person. **— meal** n. a fertilizer for dry soils, made from ground bones. **boniness** n. **bony** a. full of bones [O.E. ban].

bon·fire (bán'·fīr) n. orig. a fire for burning bones; a large fire specially built and lit to express public joy [fr. bone and fire].

bon·ho·mie (bon'·a·mē) n. frank and simple good nature; geniality [Fr.].

bo·ni·to (ba·nē'·tō) n. a fish of the striped tunny kind [Sp.].

bon·net (bán'·et) n. a woman's head-gear, often tied under the chin. **-ed** a.

bon·ny (bán'·i·) a. pretty [Fr. bon, bonne].

bo·nus (bō'·nas) n. something over and above that which is due [L. bonus, good].

boo (bòò) interj. an exclamation of disapproval or contempt, often used to startle. **-es** n.pl. v.t. and v.i. to hoot; to show disapproval; pr.t. (he) **booes**; pa.t. **-ed** [imit.].

book (book) n. a number of sheets of paper, etc. bound together; a literary composition or treatise, written or printed; a record of betting transactions; the words of a play, the libretto; v.t. to put into a book; to obtain, or give, a business order, ticket (theater, etc.). **-s** n.pl. record of business transactions, especially financial; ledgers. **-binder** n. one who binds books. **-binding** n. **-case** n. a case with shelving for books. **— club** n. a club to distribute specially chosen books to subscribers. — **ends** n. pl. weighted props to keep books upright on a shelf. **-ie** n. (Slang) a bet taker. **-ing** n. entering in a book a business transaction; recording field observations in surveying; an engagement to perform. **-ing-clerk** n. a clerk who issues railway, etc., tickets or registers orders. **-ish** a. fond of books and study. **-ishness** n. — **jacket** n. an attractively printed outer paper wrapper of a book. **-keeper** n. **-keeping** n. the art of keeping a systematic account of financial transactions. — **learning, -lore** n. knowledge acquired by extensive reading. **-let** n. a small book; a pamphlet. **-maker** n. one who compiles a book from various sources; a professional bettingman who accepts bets. **-mark** n. something placed in a book to mark a particular page. **the Book of Books,** the Holy Bible. **-plate** n. a label, often illustrated, pasted on the front end-papers of a book to denote ownership. **-seller** n. one who sells books. **-selling** n. **-shelf** n. a shelf for displaying books. **-shop, -stall, -stand** n. a place for exhibiting books and periodicals for sale. **-worm** n. one who reads intensively; larvae of insects which bore holes through the pages and bindings [O.E. boc, a book, the beech].

boom (bŏŏm) n. light spar for stretching bottom of a sail [Dut.].

boom (bŏŏm) v.i. to make a deep hollow sound; to be extremely popular and successful; to flourish; n. a hollow roar; the cry of the bittern; a sudden advance in popular favor; a sudden demand for an article; economic prosperity. **-er** n. **-ing.** a. [M.E. bommen].

boom·er·ang (bŏŏ'·ma·rang) n. a curved wooden missile used by the natives of Australia

boon (bŏŏn) n. some good thing given or asked for; a benefit [Fr. bon, good].

boon (bŏŏn) a. gay; merry; jolly [Fr. bon].

boor (bŏŏr) n. a peasant; a rustic; a churl; lout; clown, bumpkin. **-ish** a. **-ishly** adv. **-ishness** n. [Dut. boer, peasant].

boost (bŏŏst) v.t. to raise by pushing from beneath; to give a lift to; to help forward; to advertise on a big scale; to increase the output or power of a machine; n. a push up. **-er** n.

boot (bŏŏt) n. a covering for the foot and leg; a kick; an instrument of judicial torture in which the leg was crushed; v.t. to put on boots; to kick. **-black** n. one who polishes the shoes of passers-by. **-ee** n. a knitted boot. **-leg** v.t. to sell illicitly alcoholic liquor; to smuggle. **-legger** n. **-legging** n. **-licker** n. (Colloq.) a hanger-on; a flatterer; a sycophant. **-licking** n. [Fr. botte].

booth (bŏŏth) n. a temporary structure of boards or other materials; a covered stall at a market or fair; a small restaurant compartment [O.N. buth, a dwelling].

boo·ty (bŏŏ'·ti·) n. spoils of war [Fr. butin].

booze (bŏŏz) n. (Colloq.) alcoholic liquor; v.i. to drink excessively. **-r.** n. one who drinks to excess. **-y** a. a little intoxicated [Dut.].

bo·rax (bō·raks) n. hydrated sodium borate, used in the manufacture of enamels and glazes, as a softener for hard water, an antiseptic, a soldering flx, etc. **boracic** a. **boracic acid,** white powder used as an antiseptic or for checking excessive perspiration. **borate** n. a salt of boracic acid [Ar. būraq.]

bor·deaux (bawr·dō') n. red or white wines of Bordeaux, France [Fr.].

bor·der (bawrd'·er) n. the outer part or edge of anything; the exterior limit of a place; a frontier; an ornamental design around the outside edge of anything; a flower-bed; v.t. to adorn with a border; to adjoin; v.i. to touch at the edge; to come near. **-ing** n. material for a border. **-land** n. land contiguous to a frontier; an indeterminate state, or condition. **-line** a. on the verge of [Fr. bordure].

bore (bōr) v.t. to make a hole in; to pierce; to

drill; to weary by uninteresting talk; to fatigue; n. the hole made by boring; the inside diameter measurement of a cylinder; the hollow interior part of a gun barrel; a thing or person that wearies one. **-dom** n. the state of being bored; ennui. **-r** n. tool for drilling; insect [O.E. borian, to pierce].

bore (bōr) pa.t. of **bear.**

Bo·re·as (bō'·ri·as) n. (Myth.) the god of the North wind. **boreal** a. northern [Gk.].

bo·ric (bōr'·ik) a. pert. to boron [shortened form of boracic].

born (bawrn) pa.p. of **bear,** to bring forth; a. natural; innate; perfect.

borne (bōrn) pa.p. of **bear,** to carry.

bo·ron (bō'·ran) n. a non-metallic element whose compounds are useful in the arts and medicine [fr. borax].

bor·ough (bur'·ō) n. an incorporated town [O.E. burg, burh, a fort, a manor-house].

bor·row (bår'·ō) v.t. to obtain on loan or trust; to adopt from abroad. **-ed** a. **-er** n. **-ing** n. [O.E. borgian, fr. borg, a pledge].

bor·zoi (bawr'·zoi) n. the Russian wolf-hound, remarkable for grace and swiftness [Russ.].

bosh (båsh) n. empty talk; nonsense [Turk.].

bosk (bosk) n. (Arch.) a thicket or small wood. **-y** a. bushy; covered with underbrush. **-iness** n.

bos·om (boo'·zum) n. the breast of a human being; part of the dress over the breast; the heart; embrace; enclosure; a shirtfront; v.t. to press to the bosom; a. intimate; cherished [O.E. bosm].

boss (baws) n. a prominent circular projection on any article; a knob; a round, slightly raised ornament; v.t. to emboss; to provide with bosses. **-ed** a. embossed. **-y** a. containing, or ornamented with, bosses [Fr. bosse, a hump].

boss (baws) n. master; employer; one in charge; v.t. to manage; to supervise; (Colloq.) to browbeat. **-iness** n. **-y** a. fussy and masterful. **-ism** n. [Dut. baas, master].

bo·s'un See **boatswain** (under **boat**).

bot, bott (båt) n. usually pl. **bots, botts,** larvae of species of gad-fly found in intestines of horses, etc., causing tumor-like swellings [Gael. botus, belly-worm].

bot·a·ny (båt'·a·ni·) n. that branch of biology which is concerned with the structure and growth of plants. **botanic, botanical** a. pert. to botany. **botanically** adv. **botanic garden,** a garden where plants are scientifically studied. **botanist** n.; **botanize** v.i. to study plants; to search for and collect plants for further study [Gk. botanē, herb].

botch (båch) n. a clumsy patch of a garment; bungled work; v.t. to bungle; to patch clumsily; to blunder; spoil. **-er** n. a bungler. **-ery, -work** n. **-ily** adv. **-y** a. [M.E. bocchen, to patch].

both (bōth) a. and pron. the one and the other; conj. (foll. by and) as well [O.E. bā].

both·er (båTH'·er) v.t. to annoy; worry; trouble; vex; perplex; flurry; tease; plague; v.i. to fuss; to be troublesome; n. trouble; annoyance; fuss; worry; interj. an excalmation of annoyance. **-ation** n. trouble and worry; a mild imprecation. **-some** a. troublesome.

bot·tle (båt'·l) n. a vessel with a narrow neck for holding liquids; its contents; hard drinking; a thermionic valve; v.t. to put into bottles; to restrain; to curb. **-d** a. enclosed in bottles; of a bottle shape. **-d-up** a. confined; not allowed to speak. — **green** a. of a dark-green color. **bottling** n. and a. **-neck** n. a narrow outlet which impedes the smooth flow of traffic or production of goods. **-nose** n. a whale with a beaked snout. — **party** n. one where the guests provide the liquid refreshments. **-r** n. [O.Fr. botel, fr. botte, a truss].

bot·tom (båt'·am) n. the lowest part of anything; the posterior of human body; the base; bed or channel of a river or lake; foundation or groundwork; origin; v.t. to put a bottom on an article; to lay a foundation for a road, etc.

-less *a.* **-less pit**, hell [O.E. *botm*].

bot·u·lism (bàch'·a·lizm) *n.* a rare and dangerous form of food poisoning caused by spoiled foods [L. *botulus*, a sausage].

bou·cle (bòò'·klā') *n.* a woven material with raised pile; *a.* pert. to such material [Fr.].

bou·doir (bòò'·dwàr) *n.* a lady's private room.

bouf·fant (bòò·fànt') *a.* puffed out, full, as in draperies, skirts, hair [Fr.].

bou·gain·vil·le·a (bòò'·gan·vil'·i·a) *n.* a S. American plant with great masses of red or lilac bracts [Louis *Bougainville* (1729-1814)].

bough (bou) *n.* an arm or large branch of a tree [O.E. *bog, boh*].

bought (bawt) *pa.t.* and *pa.p.* of **buy**.

bouil·lon (bòòl'·yàn) *n.* broth; stock. **bouilla-baisse** (bòò·ya·bes') *n.* a Provençal fish soup or stew [Fr. *bouillir*, to boil].

boul·der (bōl'·der) *n.* a rock torn from its bed, and rounded by water. —**clay** *n.* a stiff clay of the glacial or ice-drift age [M.E. *bulderston*].

boul·e·vard (bòòl'·a·vàrd) *n.* a street or promenade planted with trees. **-ier** *n.* one who haunts the boulevards; a man-about-town [Fr. fr. Ger. *Bollwerk*].

bounce (bouns) *v.i.* to move with a bound and rebound; to leap or spring suddenly; *v.t.* to cause to rebound, as a ball; to eject; *n.* a sudden spring or leap; rebound; **-r** *n.* (*Slang*) one who expels disorderly persons. **bouncing** *a.* vigorous; big [Dut. *bonzen*, to strike].

bound (bound) *pa.t.* and *pa.p.* of **bind**.

bound (bound) *v.i.* to leap; jump; spring; skip; frisk; *n.* a leap; jump [Fr. *bondir*, to leap].

bound (bound) *a.* tending to go or on the way, as in *homeward bound* [Scand.].

bound (bound) *n.* usually in *pl.* limit or boundary; confines; precincts; *v.t.* to restrain; to form the boundary of; to set bounds to. **-ed** *a.* restricted; bordered; cramped. **-less** *a.* without limits; wide and spacious; vast; infinite. **-lessness** *n.* [O.E. *bindan*, to bind].

bound·a·ry (bound'·ar·i·) *n.* a border or limit; a dividing line; barrier.

boun·ty (boun'·ti·) *n.* liberality; generosity; munificence; a payment formerly made to men enlisting voluntarily in the army or navy; a premium offered by a government. **bounteous, bountiful** *a.* generous; liberal; ample; plentiful. **bounteously, bountifully** *adv.;* **bounteousness, bountifulness** *n.* [Fr. *bonté*, goodness].

bou·quet (bō'·kā, bòò'·kā) *n.* a nosegay; a bunch of flowers; a perfume; the aromatic flavor and aroma of wine; (*fig.*) a compliment [Fr.].

bour·bon (bur'·ban) *n.* a whisky distilled from corn and rye [*Bourbon*, Kentucky].

bour·geois (boor·zhwà) *n.* a member of middle-class society; *a.* of commercial or non-manual classes; middle-class; conventional; humdrum; stodgy. **bourgeoisie** (boor'·zhwà·zē) *n.* [Fr.].

bourgeon See **burgeon**.

bourn (bōrn) *n.* a stream; a burn [O.E. *burna*].

bourn, bourne (bōrn, boorn) *n.* a boundary; a limit; a realm; a domain; goal. **last bourne**, the grave [Fr. *borne*, limit].

bourse (boors) *n.* the stock exchange, esp. in Paris [Fr.]. [See **purse**].

bout (bout) *n.* a turn; a conflict; contest; continuous drinking [Doublet of *bight*].

bou·ton·nier (bòò'·tan·yẽr) *n.* a flower or flowers worn in a buttonhole or on a lapel [Fr.].

bo·vine (bō'·vīn) *a.* pert. to cattle; ox-like; dull; stupid; stolid; obtuse [L. *bovinus*].

bow (bou) *v.i.* to bend body in respect, assent, etc.; to submit; *v.t.* to bend downwards; to cause to stoop; to crush; to subdue; *n.* an inclination of head or body; the rounded forward part of a ship; the stem or prow. **-line** (bō'·lin) *n.* a rope used to keep the weather edge of the sail tight forward; knot used for tying a rope to a post. **-man** *n.* the one who rows the foremost oar in a boat. **-sprit** (bō'·sprit) *n.* a large spar projecting over the stem of a vessel [O.E. *bugan*, to bend].

bow (bō) *n.* anything bent or curved; weapon from which an arrow is discharged; any curved instrument, as a fiddle-stick; a lace or ribbon tied in a slip-knot; a rainbow; *v.t.* to manipulate ithe bow of a violin, etc. **-ed** *a.* bent like a bow; crooked. **-er** *n.* **-legged** *a.* having crooked legs. **-man** *n.* an archer. — **tie** *n.* a small bow-shaped tie [O.E. *boga*].

bowd·ler·ize (boud'·ler·īz) *v.t.* to leave out indelicate words or passages in a book in the alleged interest of moral purity. **bowdlerism** *n.* [fr. T. *Bowdler's* expurgated edition of Shakespeare, 1818].

bow·el (bou'·al) *n.* an entrail; the entrails; the inside of everything; (*Fig.*) the seat of pity, tenderness, etc. **-s** *n.pl.* the intestines [O.Fr. *boel*].

bow·er (bou'·er) *n.* a shady recess; an arbor; (*Poetic*) a small country dwelling; a boudoir. **-y** *a.* shady [O.E. *bur*, dwelling].

bow·ie-knife (bō'·i·nīf) *n.* a long hunting-knife, the point double-edged, the blade straight and single-edged at the hilt [invented by Col. James *Bowie*].

bowl (bōl) *n.* a round vessel; a deep basin; a drinking-cup; the hollow part of anything, as a pipe for smoking; a stadium [O.E. *bolle*].

bowl (bōl) *n.* anything rounded by art; a ball rolled in certain games; a ball with bias; *pl.* a game played on a bowling-green with bowls; *v.t.* to roll, as a bowl; *v.i.* to play with bowls; to move rapidly and smoothly; to deliver a ball. **-er** *n.* one who bowls. **-ing** *n.* [O.Fr. *boule*].

bow·ler (bōl'·er) *n.* (*Br.*) a derby [fr. name of original maker].

bow·sprit (bō'·sprit) *n.* See **bow**.

box (bàks) *n.* a small case or chest, generally with a lid; its contents; a compartment. — **kite** *n.* a kite consisting of a square frame strength. — **office** *n.* ticket office at a theater. — **pleat** *n.* a double fold with material turned under on both sides with knife edges [O.E.].

box (bàks) *n.* a small evergreen shrub. —**berry** *n.* the wintergreen. **-en** *a.* made of or like boxwood. **-wood** *n.* a tree [L. *buxus*].

box (bàks) *n.* a blow on the head or the ears; *v.t.* to buffet; *v.i.* to fight with the fists. **-er** *n.* a pugilist. **-ing** *n.* the sport of fighting with fists.

boy (boi) *n.* a male child; a lad. **-hood** *n.* **-ish** *a.* boy-like; puerile. **-ishly** *adv.* **-ishness** *n.* the natural actions of a boy [M.E. *boi, boy*].

boy·cott (boi'·kàt) *n.* a method of coercion by refusing to deal with; *v.t.* to act as above; to ostracize. **-er** *n.* **-ing** *n.* [fr. Capt. *Boycott*].

bra (brà) See **brassiere**.

brace (brās) *n.* a rod or bar crossing a space diagonally to connect two structural parts; a pair; a support; a fastener; a carpenter's tool for boring; a printer's mark ({) used in bracketing words; *v.t.* to furnish with braces; to support; to tighten; to nerve or strengthen. **-s** *n.pl.* suspenders; an arm guard; wires for straightening teeth. **and bit**, small interchangeable boring tool fitted into the socket of a brace. **-r** *n.* a wrist-guard of leather or metal, used esp. by archers; (*Colloq.*) stimulating drink. **bracing** *a.* strengthening; invigorating; refreshing [Fr. *bras*, arm].

brace·let (brās'·let) *n.* an encircling ornament for the wrist. **-s** *n.* *pl.* (*Colloq.*) handcuffs.

bra·chi·al (brā'·ki·al, brak'·i·al) *a.* belonging to the arm; of the nature of an arm; resembling an arm [L. *brachium*, arm].

brack·en (brak'·an) *n.* a large coarse species of fern [M.E. *braken*].

brack·et (brak'·it) *n.* a projecting support fastened to a wall; one of two hooks, [ ], { }, or ( ), used to enclose explanatory words; *v.t.* to place within brackets; to couple names together as of equal merit, etc. [Fr. *braguette*, fr. L. *bracae*, breeches].

brack·ish (brak'·ish) *a.* somewhat salty; distasteful. **-ness** *n.* [Dut. *brak*, briny].

bract (brakt) *n.* a leaf in the axil of which a flower or inflorescence arises. **-eal** *a.* of the nature of a bract. **-eate** *a.* having bracts; bracteal [L. *bractea*, a thin plate].

brad (brad) *n.* a cut nail tapering in width with a small head projecting at one end. **-awl** *n.* a small hand-boring tool [Scand.].

brag (brag) *v.i.* to boast; to praise oneself or one's belongings; *pr.p.* **-ging**; *pa.t.* and *pa.p.* **ged**; *n.* boasting; bragging. **-gadocio** (brag·- a·dō'·shi·ō) *n.* a boasting fellow. **-gart** *a.* boastful; *n.* a boaster. **-ging** *a.*, *n.* **-gingly** *adv.*

Brah·ma (brä'·ma) *n.* the 1st aspect of the Trimurti, or Hindu Trinity, the Creator. **brahman** (Also **brahmin**) *n.* a person of the highest or priestly caste among the Hindus.

braid (brād) *v.t.* to plait, entwine, or interweave; to bind with braid; *n.* a narrow ribbon or tape used as a dress-trimming or in upholstery; a tress of hair. **-ed** *a.* **-ing** *n.* [O.E. *bregdan*].

braille (brāl) *n.* a system of printing books in relief to be read by the blind; also the letters used, consisting of raised dots in combination [Louis *Braille*, inventor].

brain (brān) *n.* the whitish, soft mass in the skull in which are the nerve centers; intellect; mental capacity; understanding; intelligence; *v.t.* to dash out the brains of. **-ed** *a.* having the brains beaten out; used in compound terms as *feather-brained*, etc. **-less** *a.* witless; stupid. **—storm** *n.* (*Colloq.*) a sudden idea, inspiration. **brain trust**, body of experts engaged in research or planning. **-wash** *v.t.* (*Colloq.*) to effect a radical change in beliefs by intensive indoctrination. **— wave** *n.* (*Colloq.*) a spontaneous bright idea. **-y** *a.* highly intellectual; clever [O.E. *braegen*].

braise (brāz) *v.t.* to cook meat by browning in fat and simmering in a covered dish with a small amount of liquid [Fr.].

brake (brāk) *n.* a place overgrown with ferns, etc.; a thicket; brushwood [Scand.].

brake (brāk) *n.* instrument for breaking flax or hemp; a harrow; any device for checking speed; any restraining influence or curb; *v.t.* to pound or crush flax, hemp, etc., by beating; to check by applying a brake. **braking** *n.* **— shoe** *n.* the surface of a block brake.

bram·ble (bram'·bl) *n.* a prickly hedge-plant; the wild blackberry [O.E. *brembel*].

bran (bran) *n.* the ground husk of wheat and other grain, separated in milling from the flour [O.Fr.].

branch (branch) *n.* a limb of a tree or shrub; a bough; a department of a business, etc.; a line of family descent; an off-shoot; ramification; section; part; sub-division; *a.* pert. to a subsidiary section of any business; *v.t.* to divide, as into branches; *v.i.* to spread, in branches; to diverge; **-ed** *a.* **-ing** *a.* shooting out; starting from. **-y** *a.* [Fr. *branche*].

bran·chi·ae (brang'·ki·ē) *n.pl.* the breathing organs of fishes, the gills. **branchial** *a.* pert. to gills. **branchiate** *a.* furnished with gills [Gk. *branchia*, gills].

brand (brand) *n.* a burning, or partly burnt, piece of wood; an iron used for burning marks on; a mark made by a hot iron; a trade-mark; a grade; a sword; a mark of infamy; stigma; *v.t.* to burn a mark on; to fix a stamp on; to designate a commodity by a special name or trade-mark; to stigmatize; to reproach. **-ed** *a.* **-er** *n.* **-ing-iron** *n.* [O.E.].

bran·dish (bran'·dish) *v.t.* to flourish or wave, as a weapon [Fr. *brand*, sword].

bran·dy (bran'·di·) *n.* a spirit distilled from wine [Dut. *brandewijn*, burnt wine].

brant (brant) *n.* small dark wild goose.

brash (brash) *a.* hasty; insolent; **-ness** *n.*

brass (bras) *n.* a yellow alloy of two parts of copper to one of zinc; (*Colloq.*) money; effron-

tery; impudence; obstinacy; *a.* brazen; made of brass. **-es** *n.pl.* the brass instruments of an orchestra. **— band** *n.* musicians who perform on brass instruments; (*Colloq.*) a military band. **— hat** *n.* (*Colloq.*) staff-officer (from gold braid on hat). **-iness** *n.* bold; impudent. **-y** *a.* pert. sole. **— knuckles** *n.pl.* metal pieces fitted across the knuckles, used in fighting. **to get down to brass tacks** (*Colloq.*) to return to essentials, fundamentals [O.E. *braes*].

bras·sard (bras'·ärd) *n.* a band worn around arm to signify special duty; armor for upper arm [Fr. *bras*, arm].

bras·si·ere (bra·zēr') *n.* a woman's undergarment supporting the breasts; short form **bra** [Fr.]. [offspring [O.E. *bratt*, a pinafore].

brat (brat) *n.* a child (used contemptuously);

bra·va·do (bra·vä'·dō) *n.* showy bravery [Sp.].

brave (brāv) *a.* courageous; noble; fearless; *n.* an Indian warrior; *v.t.* to encounter with courage. **-ly** *adv.* **-ry** *n.* courage; heroism [Fr.].

bra·vo (brä'·vō) *interj.* an expression of applause, well done!; *pl.* **-es** [It.].

brawl (brawl) *v.i.* to flow noisily, as water; to squabble noisily; *n.* a noisy quarrel. **-er** *n.* [Fr. fr. Scand.].

brawn (brawn) *n.* muscular strength. esp. of the arms and legs; muscles; the flesh of a boar; a preparation of meat made from pigs' head. **-er** *n.* a boar fattened for the table. **-iness** *n.* **-y** *a.* muscular; sinewy; athletic; robust; stout [O.Fr. *braon*, fleshy part].

bray (brā) *n.* the harsh noise of a donkey; any harsh, strident noise; continual complaining; *v.i.* to utter a harsh noise, like a donkey [Fr. *braire*].

bray (brā) *v.t.* to pound; to powder; to pulverize; to grind small [O.Fr. *breier*].

braze (brāz) *v.t.* to solder metals with a hard alloy; to make or ornament with brass. **brazing** *n.* [Fr. *braser*, to solder].

bra·zen (brā'·zn) *a.* pert. to, or made of, brass; impudent; shameless; sounding like a brass instrument; *v.t.* to face a situation in a bold, impudent manner. **-ly** *adv.* [M.E. *brasen*].

bra·zier (brāzh'·yer) *n.* a portable iron container to hold burning coals; a worker in brass [Fr. *brasier*].

Bra·zil·i·an (bra·zil'·yan) *n.* a native of Brazil, in S. America; *a.* pert. to Brazil.

breach (brēch) *n.* a break or opening, esp. in a wall; a hole or gap; non-fulfillment of a contract, promise, etc.; an infringement of a rule, duty, etc.; a quarrel; *v.t.* to make a breach or gap in something. **— of promise**, the non-fulfillment of a promise, esp. of marriage [Fr. *brèche*].

bread (bred) *n.* form of food prepared by baking dough made from a cereal; food in general. **— winner** *n.* one who earns a living for his dependents [O.E.].

breadth (bredth) *n.* distance from side to side; width; freedom from narrowness of mind [O.E. *braedu*].

break (brāk) *v.t.* to shatter by force; to mitigate (a blow, a fall); to tame (a horse, etc.); to wean from (a habit); to bankrupt; to weaken or impair (health); to subdue (a person's temper); to violate (promises, etc.); to interrupt (friendship, silence, monotony, etc.); *v.i.* to divide into several parts; to open (as an abscess); curl over (as waves); to burst forth (as a storm); to dawn (as an idea, day, etc.); to crack or falter (as the voice); to make the first stroke at billiards; to change (as a horse); *pa.t.* **broke**; *pa.p.* **broken** [O.E. *brecan*].

break (brāk) *n.* the act or state of being broken; a fracture; a gap; an opening; dawn; separation; interruption; a breathing space; (*Slang*) a chance, good luck; a sudden fall in price; a scoring sequence at billiards. **-able** *a.* fragile. **-age** *n.* act of breaking; an allowance for articles broken. **-down** *n.* loss of health; an accident to machinery; suspension of negotiations; *v.t.* to divide into small categories. **-er** *n.* one who breaks; a long wave or crest as it breaks into foam. **-fast** (brek·fạst) *n.* the first meal of the day. **-neck** *a.* dangerous to life and limb. **-up** *n.* disintegration; collapse; separation. **-water** *n.* a strong structure to break the force of the waves [O.E. *brecan*, to break].

breast (brest) *n.* the external part of the thorax or chest between neck and abdomen; bosom; seat of the affections and passions; *v.t.* to bear the breast against; to oppose, face, or meet boldly (a wave); to mount (a hill, etc.). **-s** *n.pl.* the milk or mammary glands of women and female animals. **-bone** *n.* the sternum, the flat narrow bone to which the first seven ribs are attached. **-plate** *n.* a metal plate or piece of armor for protecting the chest. **— stroke** *n.* a long-distance stroke in swimming [O.E. *breost*].

breath (breth) *n.* air respired by the lungs; the act of breathing freely; life; respite; a single respiration, or the time of making it; a very slight breeze; whisper; fragrance. **-less** *a.* out of breath; panting; dead; eager and excited; expectant. **-lessness** *n.* **under one's breath,** in a low voice or whisper. **with bated breath,** breath held from fear or excitement [O.E. *braeth*, exhalation].

breathe (brēTH) *v.t.* to draw in and give out air from the lungs; to infuse or inspire, as life, courage, etc.; *v.i.* to inhale and emit air—hence to live; to take breath. **breathable** *a.* **-d** (brēTHd) *a.* (*Phon.*) uttered with breath only. **-r** *n.* a short spell of rest. **breathing** *n.* respiration; a mark (') placed over a vowel in Greek grammar giving it the sound of *h*. **breathing-space, breathing-time,** *n.* a pause; relaxation; a short respirte [fr. *breath*].

bred *pa.t.* and *pa.p.* of **breed.**

breech (brēch) *n.* the buttocks; the hinder part, esp. of a gun-barrel; *v.t.* to put (a young child for the first time) into breeches; to whip; to flog. **-es** *n.pl.* trousers, esp. those which fit tightly around knees. **-es-buoy** *n.* an apparatus consisting of a canvas bag slung along a rope, used for saving persons from a wreck. **-ing** *n.* that part of the harness which passes round a horse's haunches [O.E. *brec*].

breed (brēd) *v.t.* to beget; to engender; to generate; to propagate; to hatch; to train or bring up; *v.i.* to be produced; to be with young; to increase in number; *pa.t.* and *pa.p.* **bred;** *n.* a race of animals from the same stock; kind; sort. **-er** *n.* one who breeds cattle or other live stock. **-ing** *n.* producing; the rearing of live stock; manners; deportment; courtesy [O.E. *bredan*, to nourish].

breeze (brēz) *n.* a wind of moderate strength. **breezy** *a.* windy; gusty; of a person, animated and brisk [Fr. *brise*].

br'er (brur, brer) *n.* brother; used in the animal stories of Uncle Remus [S. Dial.].

breth·ren (breTH'·rin) *n.pl.* members of the same society or profession [See **brother**].

Bre·ton (bret'·an) *n.* pert. to Brittany; *a.* one of the Celtic dialects, spoken in Brittany; a native of Brittany; a hat with turned-up brim [O.Fr.].

breve (brēv) *n.* the longest note now used in music; a mark distinguishing short vowels; a writ issued by a court [It. fr. L. *brevis*, short].

bre·vet (brev'·et) *a.* a commission, which entitles an officer to an honorary rank in the army above his actual rank. **-cy** *n.* brevet rank [Fr. fr. L. *brevis*, short].

bre·vi·ar·y (brēv'·i·e·ri·) *n.* a book containing the daily service of the R.C. Church [L. *brevis*, short].

brev·i·ty (brev'·ạ·ti·) *n.* shortness; conciseness; briefness; terseness [L. *brevis*, short].

brew (brōo) *v.t.* to prepare a fermented liquor, from malt, hops, etc.; to infuse (tea); to plot; concoct; mix; *v.i.* to perform the operations of brewing; to be impending; *n.* something

brewed; a particular brand or quality of beer. **-er** *n.* **-ery** *n.* a place where brewing is carried on [O.E. *breowan*].

bri·ar See **brier.**

bribe (brīb) *n.* anything bestowed, with a view to influence judgment and conduct; *v.t.* to influence by gifts; *v.i.* to practice bribery. **bribable** *a.* **bribery** *n.* [Fr. *bribe*, fragment].

bric-à-brac (brik'·ạ·brak) *n.* curios; ornamental articles; knickknacks [Fr.].

brick (brik) *n.* a building material made from a special clay molded into a rectangular block and hardened by drying in the sun or firing in a kiln; (*Colloq.*) a sterling friend; *v.t.* to lay, or pave, with bricks. **-bat** *n.* a fragment of a brick. **-bats** *n.pl.* uncomplimentary comments. **-kiln** *n.* a kiln in which bricks are baked or burnt. **-layer** *n.* one who is skilled in building with bricks. **-laying** *n.* **— red** *a.* of a dull scarlet color like brick [Fr. *brique*].

bride (brīd) *n.* a woman about to be, or just, married. **bridal** *n.* wedding; *a.* pert. to a bride or a wedding; nuptial; connubial; conjugal. **bridal-suite** *n.* apartments set aside for a honeymoon couple. **-groom** *n.* a man newly-married, or about to be married. **-s maid** *n.* an unmarried woman who acts as attendant on a bride [O.E. *bryd*].

bridge (brij) *n.* a structure spanning a river or a valley, etc., in order to afford passage; a support for the strings of a violin; the hurricane deck or bridge deck of a vessel; the bone of the nose, etc.; mounting for false teeth; (*Mus.*) connecting passage; *v.t.* to build a bridge or bridges over. **-head** *n.* a work protecting the end of a bridge nearest the enemy; a footing gained by an attacking force on the far bank of a river. [O.E. *brycg*].

bridge (brij) *n.* a card game for four players.

bri·dle (brī'·dl) *n.* the headgear of a beast of burden, of a horse; a curb; constraint; *v.t.* to put a bridle upon; to check; subdue; curb; control. **-path** *n.* a narrow track used by riders on horseback [O.E. *bridel*].

brief (brēf) *a.* short in duration; using few words; *n.* an abridged statement of a case; an outline of an argument; a writ, summoning one to answer in an action; *v.t.* to instruct or retain counsel by giving him a brief; to inform personnel of the details of an impending action. **— case** *n.* a small flat case for carrying papers, cash, etc. **-ly** *adv.* **-ness** *n.* **-s** *n.pl.* undershorts [Fr. *bref*, fr. L. *brevis*, short].

bri·er, bri·ar (brī'·ẹr) *n.* the heath of S. France; a pipe made from the root of this brier [Fr. *bruyère*, heather].

bri·er (brī'·ẹr) *n.* any prickly bush; a tangled mass of them; a smoking pipe [O.E.].

brig (brig) *n.* a sailing-ship with two masts, both square-rigged; (*Slang*) guardhouse [shortened *brigatine*, q.v. but not to be confused with it].

bri·gade (bri·gād')' *n.* a sub-division of an army under the command of a general officer; a group of people organized for a specific purpose, such as a *fire brigade*. **brigadier-general** *n.* [It. *brigata*, a troop].

brig·and (brig'·and) *n.* a lawless fellow who lives by plunder; bandit; highwayman. **-age** *n.* [O.Fr. *brigand*, a foot-soldier].

bright (brīt) *a.* shining; full of light or splendor; cheerful; vivacious; sparkling; luminous; radiant; clear; clever; intelligent. **-en** *v.t.* to make bright; *v.i.* to grow bright. **-ly** *adv.* **-ness** *n.* [O.E. *beorht*].

bril·liant (bril'·yạnt) *a.* glittering; sparkling; radiant; shining; illustrious; distinguished; splendid; very clever; *n.* a polished diamond cut to a definite pattern. **-ly** *adv.* **-ness** *n.* **brilliance** *n.* **brilliancy** *a.* [Fr. *brillant*].

brim (brim) *n.* rim or border; the rim of a hat; *v.i.* to be full to the brim. **-ful** *a.* **-med** *a.* **-ming** *a.* [M.E. *brimme*].

brim·stone (brim'·stōn) *n.* sulphur; hellfire; *a.*

lemon-colored [M.E. *brenston* = burning-stone].

brin·dle, brindled (brin'·dl, ·dld) *a.* streaked with dark stripes, or spots, on a gray or tan ground [Scand.].

brine (brīn) *n.* water containing an admixture of salt; sea-water; the sea. **brinish** *a.* salty, like brine. **briny** *a.* [O.E. *bryne*].

bring (bring) *v.t.* to carry; to fetch, to convey from one person or place to another; to transfer; to transport; to draw; to lead; to prevail on; *pa.t.* and *pa.p.* **brought** (brawt) [O.E. *bringan*].

brink (bringk) *n.* edge, margin of a steep slope; verge [M.E. *brenk*].

bri·o (brē'·ō) *n.* (*Mus.*) liveliness; vivacity [It.].

bri·quette (bri·ket') *n.* a brick of compressed coal dust. Also **briquet** [Fr.].

brisk (brisk) *a.* full of activity; *v.t.* and *i.* to enliven; to cheer up. **-ly** *adv.* **-ness** *n.* [Celt.].

bris·ket (bris'·kit) *a.* part of animal's breast which lies next to ribs [O.Fr.].

bris·tle (bris'·l) *n.* a very stiff, erect, coarse hair, as of swine; a quill; *v.t.* to erect the bristles of; *v.i.* to stand up erect, like bristles; to show anger; to be surrounded with. **-d** (bris'·ld) *a.* provided with bristles [O.E. *bryst*].

Bri·tan·ni·a (bri·tan'·ya) *n.* Great Britain personified; a female figure forming an emblem of Great Britain. **Britannic** *a.* pert. to Great Britain [L.].

Brit·ish (brit'·ish) *a.* of or pertaining to Britain; *n.* the inhabitants of Britain. **-er** *n.* a British subject [fr. *Briton*].

Brit·on (brit'·an) *n.* a native of Britain [L. *Brito*].

brit·tle (brit'·l) *a.* easily broken; apt to break; frail; fragile [fr. O.E. *breotan*, to break].

broach (brōch) *n.* a roasting-spit; a tapered, hardened-steel bit for enlarging holes in metal; *v.t.* to pierce; to tap, as a cask; to open; to approach a subject [Fr. *broche*, a roasting-spit].

broad (brawd) *a.* wide, ample, open; outspoken, unrestrained; coarse, indelicate, gross; tolerant, literal-minded; with a marked local dialect; plain, unmistakable (hint); full (daylight); *n.* (*Slang*) coarse for a woman. **broad, -ly** *adv.* **-brim** *n.* a wide-brimmed hat, much affected by Quakers, and so a Quaker. **-cast** *v.t.* to scatter seed; *n.* a casting of seed from the hand in sowing [See **broadcast**]. **-cloth** *n.* a finely woven woollen, cotton, or rayon cloth for clothing. **-en** *v.t.* and *v.i.* to make or grow broad. **— jump** *n.* (*Sports*) a horizontal jump from rest or from a run. **-loom** *n.* woven on a wide loom, of carpets and rugs. **—minded** *a.* tolerant. **-ness** *n.* **-side** *n.* a sheet of paper printed on one side of the paper only; the whole side of a ship above water-line; a volley from the gun on one side of a naval craft; violent abuse [O.E. *brad*].

broad·cast (brawd'·kast) *n.* a transmission by radio of lectures, music, etc.; a program; *a.*; *v.t.* to disseminate by radio-telephone transmitter, news, plays, music, etc., for reception by receiving apparatus. **-er** *n.* a person or organization broadcasting [O.E. *brad*, and Dan. *kaste*].

bro·cade (brō·kād') *n.* a fabric woven with elaborate design; *v.t.* to make brocade; to ornament a fabric with raised designs. **-d** *a.* [Sp. *brocado*].

broc·co·li (brak'·a·li·) *n.* a variety of the cauliflower [It. pl. dim. fr. *brocco*, a shoot].

bro·chette (brō·shet') *n.* skewer.

bro·chure (brō·shoor') *n.* a printed work of a few sheets of paper; a booklet; a pamphlet [Fr. *brocher*, to stitch].

brogue (brōg) *n.* a stout, comfortable, ordinary shoe. Also **brogan** [Ir. *brog*].

brogue (brōg) *n.* a mode of pronunciation peculiar to Irish speakers [Ir. *brog*, shoe].

broi·der (broi'·der) *v.t.* to adorn with figured needlework; to embroider [Fr. *broder*].

broil (broil) *n.* a noisy quarrel; contention; altercation [Fr. *brouiller*, to trouble].

broil (broil) *v.t.* to cook on a gridiron over coals, or directly under gas or electric heat in a stove; to grill; *v.i.* to suffer discomfort through heat; to be overheated [Fr. *brûler*, to burn].

broke (brōk) *pa.t.* and old *pa.p.* of **break**; *a.* (*Colloq.*) penniless; ruined; degraded. **-n** *pa.p.* of **break**; *a.* shattered; fractured; severed; separated; parted; abrupt; rough; impaired; exhausted; spent. **-n English,** imperfect English, as spoken by a non-native. **-n hearted** *a.* crushed with grief; inconsolable. **-nly** *adv.* intermittently. **-nness** *n.* [*break*].

brok·er (brōk'·er) *n.* a person employed in the negotiation of commercial transactions between other parties in the interests of one of the principals; a pawn-broker; a dealer in second-hand goods; an agent. **-age, brokage,** *n.* the business of a broker; the commission charged by a broker [M.E. *brocour*].

bro·mide (brō'·mīd) *n.* a compound of bromine with some other element; a sedative drug, employed to induce sleep [See **bromine**].

bro·mine (brō'·mēn, -min) *n.* one of the elements, related to chlorine, iodine, and fluorine. **bromic** *a.* [Gk. fr. *bromos*, stench].

bron·chi, bron·chi·a (brang'·kī, ·ki·a) *n.pl.* the two tubes forming the lower end of the trachea. **-al** *a.* pert. to the bronchi. **bronchi·tis,** *n.* inflammation of the bronchial tubes. [Gk. *bronchia*].

bron·chus (brang'·kus) *n.* one of the bifurcations of the windpipe; *pl.* see **bronchi** [Gk. *bronchos*, windpipe].

bron·co (brang'·kō) *n.* an unbroken, or partly broken horse. **— buster** *n.* [Sp. rough].

bronze (branz) *n.* an alloy of copper, tin, and zinc; a work of art cast in bronze; the color of bronze; *a.* made of or colored like bronze; *v.t.* to give the appearance of bronze to; to sunburn; to harden. **Bronze Age,** pre-historic period between the Stone and Iron Ages. **bronzy** *a.* [It. *bronzo*].

brooch (brōch, brŏŏch) *n.* an ornamental clasp with a pin for attaching it to a garment [Fr. *broche*, a spike, a brooch].

brood (brŏŏd) *v.t.* to sit upon, as a hen on eggs; to ponder; *v.i.* to sit upon to hatch; to meditate moodily; *n.* off-spring; a family of young, esp. of birds; a tribe; a race. **-er** *n.* an appliance for rearing incubator-hatched chickens by artificial heat. **— mare —** a mare kept for breeding. **-y** *a.* wishing to sit, as a hen; moody; sullen [O.E. *brod*]. [streamlet [O.E. *broc*].

brook (brook) *n.* a small stream. **-let** *n.* a

brook (brook) *v.t.* to bear; to endure; to support [O.E. *brucan*, use, enjoy].

broom (brŏŏm, broom) *n.* a wild evergreen shrub producing yellow flowers and pods; an implement for sweeping [O.E. *brom*].

broth (brawth) *n.* water in which meat has been boiled with vegetables [O.E. *brodh*].

broth·el (brath'·al) *n.* house of prostitution [O.E. *brothen*, degenerate].

broth·er (bruTH'·er) *n.* a male born of the same parents; one closely resembling another in manner or character; an associate or fellow-member of a corporate body; *pl.* **-s, brethren.** **-hood** *n.* the state of being a brother; an association of men of the same religious order, profession, or society; the mutual regard resulting from this association. **—in-law** *n.* the brother of one's husband or wife; a sister's husband. **—like, -ly** *a.* like a brother, affectionate. **-liness** *n.* [O.E. *brothor*].

brough·am (brŏŏm, brō'·am) *n.* a closed horse-carriage with two or four wheels, with an elevated seat for the driver [fr. Lord *Brougham*].

brought (brawt) *pa.t.* and *pa.p.* of **bring**.

brow (brou) *n.* the ridge over the eyes; the eye-brow; the forehead; the rounded top of a hill. **-beat** *v.t.* to bully or over-rule a person by over-bearing speech. **-beater** *n.* [O.E. *bru*].

brown (broun) *n*. a dark color inclining to red or yellow; a mixture of black, red, and-yellow; *a*. of a brown color; swarthy; sunburnt; *v.t*. to make or give a brown color to; to sunbathe; to grill or roast brown. — **betty** *n*. a spiced, bread and apple pudding. — **shirt** *n*. a member of the German Nazi party. -**stone** *n*. a reddish-brown sandstone used in building. — **study,** serious reverie. — **sugar,** unrefined or partly refined sugar [O.E. *brun*].

brown·ie (broun'·i·) *n*. a good-natured household elf; a member of the junior section of the Girl scouts; a chocolate cookie.

browse (brouz) *v.t.* and *i*. to nibble; to graze; to glance through a book shop, etc. **browsing** *n*. [O.Fr. *broust*, a shoot].

bruise (brŏoz) *v.t*. to injure by striking or crushing; to contuse; to pound or pulverize; *n*. a contusion. -**r** *n*. a prize-fighter; (*Colloq*.) a tough bully [O.E. *brysan*, to break].

bruit (brŏot) *v.t*. to report; to rumor [Fr.].

bru·mal (brŏo'·mal) *a* relating to winter [L. *bruma*, winter].   [*a*. foggy [Fr. *brume*, fog].

brume (brŏom) *n*. mist, fog, vapor. **brumous**

brunch (brunch) *n*. (*Colloq*.) breakfast and lunch combined [Portmanteau word].

bru·nette (brŏo·net') *n*. a woman with dark brown hair or brown complexion; *a*. [Fr.].

brunt (brunt) *n*. the main shock of onset; the force of a blow [E., conn. with *burn*].

brush (brush) *n*. an implement made of bristles, twigs, feathers, etc., bound together and used for removing dust, dressing the hair, applying paint, and the like; the smaller trees of a forest, brushwood; a sharp skirmish; the bushy tail of a fox or squirrel; in electricity, the stationary contact pieces which collect current from the commutator of a dynamo; *v.t*. to remove dust, etc., with a brush; to touch lightly in passing; *v.i*. to touch with light contact. -**off** *n*. (*Slang*) an abrupt refusal. -**wood** *n*. small branches broken or cut from trees; thicket of small trees and shrubs. -**y** *a*. rough, shaggy [O.Fr. *brosse*, brushwood].

brusque (brusk), *a*. blunt; abrupt in speech. -**ness** *n*. [Fr.].

brute (brŏot) *a*. irrational; ferocious; brutal; *n*. a beast; one of lower animals; a low-bred, unfeeling person. **brutal** *a*. savage; inhuman. **brutalism** *n*. brutality. **brutality** *n*. inhumanity; savagery; **brutalize** *v.t*. to make brutal, cruel, or coarse; to treat with brutality; *v.i*. to become brutal. **brutally** *adv*. **brutish** *a*. [L. *brutus*, dull; stupid].

bry·ol·o·gy (brī·ăl'·ạ·ji·) *n*. the science of mosses [Gk. *bruon*, moss; *logos*, discourse].

Bry·thon·ic (brith·ăn'·ik) *a*. a term embracing the Welsh, Cornish and Breton group of Celtic languages [W. *Brython*, a Briton].

bub·ble (bub'·l) *n*. a hollow globe of water or other liquid blown out with air or gas; a globule of air or gas in liquid or solid substances; a small bladder-like excrescence on surface of paint, metals, etc.; *v.i*. to rise in bubbles; to effervesce; to make a noise like bubbles; to gurgle; *v.t*. to cause to bubble. **bubbly** *a*. [earlier *burble*, of imit. origin].

bu·bo (bū'·bō) *n*. lymphatic swelling of the glands in the groin or armpit. **bubonic** *a.; pl*. **buboes. bubonic plague,** the Black Death of the 14th cent [Gk. *boubon*, the groin].

buc·ca·neer (buk·ạ·nir') *n*. a pirate; *v.i*. to play the buccaneer [Fr. *boucanier*, a grill].

bu·cen·taur (bū·sen'·tawr) *n*. a fabulous monster, half bull, half man [Gk. *bous*, ox; *centaur*].

buck (buk) *n*. the male of the rabbit, hare, sheep, goat, and deep; a gay, spirited young dandy; (*Colloq*.) a male Indian or Negro; *v.i*. to attempt to unseat a rider by jumping vertically with arched back and head down; to foil all attempts at improvement. -**shot** *n*. large leaden shot for killing big game. -**skin** *n*. a soft leather made of deerskin or sheepskin. -**tooth** *n*. a tooth which protrudes. **buck up!**

(*Colloq*.) hurry up! cheer up! [M.E. *bukke*, a he-goat].

buck·board (buk·bŏrd) *n*. a four-wheeled vehicle in which a long elastic board takes the place of steel springs.

buck·et (buk'·it) *n*. a vessel for carrying water; *v.t*. to handle anything in a bucket. -**ful** *n*. the quantity held by a bucket. — **seat** *n*. a small round-backed seat for one [O.E. *buc*, pitcher].

buck·le (buk'·l) *n*. a metal clasp with a rim and tongue, for fastening straps, bands, etc.; a bend, bulge, or kink; *v.t*. and *v.i*. to fasten or clasp with a buckle; to twist out of shape; to bend; to gird with a shield and sword [M.E. *bokel*].

buck·ram (buk'·ram) *n*. a coarse linen or cotton cloth stiffened with glue and sizing; *a*. made of buckram [O.Fr. *boucaran*, goat's skin].

buck·wheat (buk'·hwēt) *n*. an herb, the seeds of which are ground into flour or fed to animals [O.E. *boc*, beech tree].

bu·co·lic (bū·kăl'·ik) *a*. rustic; countrified; *n*. a pastoral poem [Gk. *boukolos*, cowherd].

bud (bud) *n*. the shoot or sprout on a plant containing an unexpanded leaf, branch, or flower; *v.i*. to put forth buds; to begin to grow; *v.t*. to graft by budding. -**ding** *n*. the act of inserting the bud of one tree under the bark of another, for propagation. -**let** *n*. a little bud. **to nip in the bud,** to destroy at the beginning. *pr.p*. -**ding**. *pa.t*. -**ded** [M.E. *budde*].

Bud·dhism (boo'·dizm) *n*. the chief religion of E. Asia. **Buddhist** *n*. a worshipper of Buddha [Sans. *buddha*, wise].

bud·dy (bud'·i·) *n*. a person; a bosom friend; a comrade [fr. *body*].   [*bouger*, to move].

budge (buj) *v.t*. and *i*. to move; to stir [Fr.

budg·et (buj'·it) *n*. a plan for systematic spending; *v.t*. to plan one's expenditures of money, time, etc. -**ary** *a*. [Fr. *bougette*].

buff (buf) *n*. a soft, yellow leather prepared from the skin of the buffalo, elk, and other animals; a revolving wooden disc covered with layers of leather or cloth used with an abrasive for polishing; a buff-wheel; a polishing pad or stick; a light yellow-tan color; (*Colloq*.) a fan or devotee; *a*. made of, or colored like, buff leather; *v.t*. to polish with a buff. -**y** *a*. of a buff color [Fr. *buffle*, buffalo].

buf·fa·lo (buf'·ạ·lō) *n*. a ruminating horned animal, resembling an ox, but larger and more powerful [Port. *bufalo*].

buf·fer (buf'·er) *n*. a resilient cushion or apparatus to deaden the concussion between a moving body and one on which it strikes; a polisher. — **state,** a country lying between two powerful and rival nations [O.Fr. *bouffe*, a slap].

buf·fet (buf'·ā) *n*. a cupboard for displaying fine china, plate, etc.; a freshment bar; *a*. (a meal) spread on tables or a counter from which guests serve themselves [Fr.].

buf·fet (buf'·it) *n*. a blow with the fist; a slap; a cuff on the ears; *v.t*. to strike with the fist; to contend against. -**s** *n.pl*. hardships [O.Fr. *buffet*, a slap].

buf·foon (bu·fŏon') *n*. a person who acts the clown by his clumsy attempts at humor; a fool. -**ery** *n*. the silly, vulgar antics or practical jokes of a buffoon. -**ish** *a*. [Fr. *bouffon*].

bug (bug) *n*. name applied to various insects; a difficulty of a defect in a mechanism; a concealed microphone; (*Slang*) an enthusiast. -**aboo** *n*. a terrifying object; an imaginary fear. -**bear** *n*. anything that frightens or annoys. -**gy** *a*. crazy; swarming with bugs [corrupt. of O.E. *budda*, bettle]. [types of carriages].

bug·gy (bug'·i·) *n*. a word applied to various

bu·gle (bū'·gl) *n*. a wind instrument used because of its penetrating note for conveying orders by certain calls; long glass bead; *v.i*. to sound a call. -**r** *n*. [for *bugle-horn* fr. L. *buculus*, dim. of *box*, ox].

build (bild) *v.t*. to erect a structure; to construct a public work, as a railway, etc.; to fabricate; to establish (a reputation, etc.); to raise (hopes); *v.i.* to exercise the art or work of building; to depend with *on, upon; pa.t.* and *pa.p.* **built;** *n.* form; construction; physique; style of construction. **-er** *n.* **-ing** *n.* [O.E. *byldan*].

bulb (bulb) *n.* a modified leaf-bud emitting roots from its base and formed of fleshy leaf scales containing a reserve supply of food; any globular form, shaped like a bulb; a dilated glass tube containing filament for electric lighting; *v.i.* to form bulbs; to bulge. **-aceous, -ar, -ed, -ose, -y** *a.* pert. to bulbs. **-iform** *a.* shaped like a bulb. **-osity** *n.* the state of being bulbous. **-ous** *a.* having the appearance of a bulb; growing from bulbs [L. *bulbus*].

bulge (bulj) *n.* anything rounded which juts out; the part of a cask which swells out; an outer protective hull, below the water-line; *v.i.* to swell out. **bulgy** *a.* [O.Fr. *boulge*].

bulk (bulk) *n.* size; the main body; the majority; the largest portion; unpackaged goods; *v.i.* to pile up; *v.i.* to be of some importance; to swell. **-age** *n.* roughage. **-iness** *n.* **-y** *a.* voluminous and clumsy in shape, so difficult to handle. **in bulk**, unpackaged, in large quantity [O.N. *bulki*, heap, cargo].

bulk·head (bulk'·hed) *n.* a partition in a ship made with boards, etc., to form separate compartments; a horizontal or sloping cover to outside step leading to the cellar of a building.

bull (bool) *n.* the male of any bovine; the male of numerous animals as elephant, whale, seal, moose, elk, deer; a sign of the zodiac, the constellation Taurus; a speculator who buys stocks or shares to make a profit by selling at a higher rate before time of settlement arrives; *v.t.* to attempt to bring about a rise in the price of stocks and shares; *a.* to denote a male animal. **-baiting** *n.* an ancient sport of setting ferocious dogs on a bull tied to a stake. **-dog** *n.* a breed of dog formerly used for bull-baiting; a person who displays obstinate courage; **-dozer** *n.* a tractor with an attached horizontal blade in front. **-fight** *n.* the national sport of certain Latin races, esp. in Spain and consisting of a combat between men and specially bred bulls. **-finch** *n.* a bird of the thrush family with a thicker head and neck. **-frog** *n.* a large, dusky-brown frog. **-headed** *n.* obstinate, headstrong. — **pen**, fenced enclosure; (*Sports*) where baseball pitchers practice. — **ring** *n.* the arena in which a bull-fight is held. **bull's-eye** *n.* the central spot of a target; a shot that hits the center of the target; a small circular window. — **session** (*Colloq.*) informal discussion. — **terrier** *n.* a cross between bulldog and terrier. **to take the bull by the horns**, to face a difficulty resolutely [M.E. *bole*].

bull (bool) *n.* the seal appended to the edicts of the pope; papal edict. **-ary** *n.* a collection of papal bulls [L. *bulla*, a bubble, a seal].

bul·let (bool'·it) *n.* a small projectile to be discharged from a gun. **—headed** *a.* roundheaded; stubborn [L. *bulla*, a bubble, a knob].

bul·le·tin (bool'·a·tin) *n.* a periodical report or publication; a brief statement of facts issued by authority. **-board** *n.* [Fr.].

bul·lion (bool'·yan) *n.* uncoined, refined gold or silver, generally in ingots; the precious metals, including coined metal, when exported or imported [etym. uncertain].

bul·ly (bool'·i·) *n.* noisy, over-bearing person who tyrannizes the weak; *v.t.* to domineer; intimidate; ill-treat; *v.i.* to bluster.

bul·ly (bool'·i·) *n.* canned or corned meat. Also **beef** [Fr. *bouilli*, boiled].

bul·rush (bool'·rush) *n.* name applied to several species of marsh plants [O.E. *bulrysche*].

bul·wark (bool'·werk) *n.* an outwork for defense; sea defense wall; *pl.* a railing round the deck of a ship; any defense of a ship; *v.t.* to fortify with a rampart [Ger. *Bollwerk*].

bum (bum) *n.* an idle, dissolute person; *a.* worthless, bad; *v.i.* to loaf; to sponge on others; cadge [Ger. *bummeln*, to loaf].

bum·ble-bee (bum'·bal·bē) *n.* a large, hairy, social bee [E. *bumble* = keep bumming].

bum·bling (bum'·bling) *a.* noisy and blundering [See **bumble-bee**].

bump (bump) *n.* a dull, heavy blow; a thump; a swelling resulting from a bump or blow; one of the protuberances on the skull, said by phrenologists to give an indication of mental qualities, character, etc.; *v.t.* to strike against; *v.i.* to collide. **-y** *a.* covered with bumps [imit.].

bump·er (bum'·per) *n.* a cup or glass filled to the brim, esp. when toasting a guest; (*Auto.*) a horizontal bar in front and rear of car; a buffer; *a.* very large; excellent [fr. *bump*].

bump·kin (bump'·kin) *n.* an awkward, stupid person; a country lout; yokel [E. = *bumkin*, a thick log, fr. Dut.].

bump·tious (bump'·shas) *a.* rudely self-assertive; self-important. **-ness** *n.* [fr. *bump*].

bun (bun) *n.* a kind of bread roll, light in texture and slightly sweetened; hair twisted into a knot at the back of a woman's head [O.Fr. *bugne*].

bunch (bunch) *n.* a cluster of similar things, tied or growing together; a tuft or knot; a bouquet of flowers; a lump or protruberance; (*Slang*) a group, gang, or party; *v.t.* to tie up or gather together; to crowd; *v.i.* to swell out like a bunch. **bunched** *a.* crowded together. **-y** *a.* growing in bunches [Dan. *bunke*, a heap].

bun·dle (bun'·dl) *n.* a number of things bound together; a package; a definite number of things; *v.t.* to make up into a bundle or roll; *v.i.* to dress warmly [O.E. *byndel*].

bung (bung) *n.* the stopper for an opening in a cask; a large cork; *v.t.* to close or stop up; (*Slang*) to bruise.

bun·ga·low (bung'·ga·lō) *n.* a house in India of a single floor; small detached one-storied house [Hind. *bangla*, fr. *Banga*, Bengalese].

bun·gle (bung'·gl) *v.t.* to make or mend clumsily; to manage clumsily; to botch; *v.i.* to act awkwardly; *n.* a blundering performance. **-r** *n.* **bungling** *a.* [etym. uncertain].

bun·ion (bun'·yan) *n.* an inflamed swelling occurring on the foot.

bunk (bungk) *n.* a box-like structure used as a seat by day and a bed at night; a sleeping-berth on board ship; in a camp, etc.; *v.i.* to sleep in a bunk [Scand.]. [fr. *bunkum*].

bunk (bungk) *n.* (*Colloq.*) humbug; nonsense.

bunk·er (bung'·ker) *n.* a large hopper or bin for holding coal, etc.; storage room on board ship for coal or oil fuel; an underground fortification; a sand-pit placed as an obstacle on a golf course [Scand.].

bun·ny (bun'·i·) *n.* a pet name for a rabbit. **-hug** *n.* a kind of jazz dance [etym. unknown].

Bun·sen burn·er (bun'·san bur'·ner) *n.* a gas burner in which a strong current of air produces a weakly luminous, but very hot, flame [fr. the inventor, Prof. *Bunsen*].

bunt (bunt) *n.* the middle or furled part of a sail. **-line** *n.* a rope fastened to the bottom of a sail used to haul it up [Scand.].

bunt (bunt) *v.t.* to butt with horns or head; (baseball) to bounce ball a short distance off the bat.

bun·ting (bun'·ting) *n.* a group of birds of the finch family, including the indigo-, reed-, and snow-buntings; coarse woolen fabric of which flags are made; flags in general.

buoy (boi) *n.* any floating body of wood or iron employed to point out the particular situation of a ship's anchor, a shoal, a navigable channel, etc.; a life-buoy; *v.t.* to fix buoys. **to buoy up**, to keep afloat; to sustain (hopes, etc.). **-age** *n.* a series of buoys in position; the providing of buoys. **-ancy** *n.* capacity for floating in water or air; cheerfulness. **-ant** *a.* floating lightly; lighthearted; hopeful; of stocks and shares, tending to increase in price [Dut. *boci*].

bur (bur) *n.* the rough, sticky seed-case of certain plants with hooked spines to help in its distribution; a burr. See **burr**.

bur·ble (bur'·bl) *v.i.* to bubble up; to gurgle, as of running water; (*Colloq.*) to talk idly.

bur·den (bur'·dn) *n.* that which is borne or carried; anything difficult to bear, as care, sorrow, etc.; *v.t.* to load; to oppress; to encumber. Also (*Arch.*) **burthen. -ous, -some** *a.* heavy, onerous; felt as a burden [O.E. *burthen*].

bur·den (bur'·dn) *n.* the refrain of a song; a chorus [Fr. *bourdon*, deep murmur].

bur·dock (bur'·dàk) *n.* a coarse reed with wide leaves and prickly burs [Dan. *borre*, a bur].

bu·reau (bū'·rō) *n.* a small chest of drawers; an office, esp. for public business; a government department [Fr.].

bu·reau·c·ra·cy (bū·rà'·krạ·si·) *n.* administration by bureaus, often excessively numerous and powerful; the officials engaged in such an administration; identified with officialdom and 'red tape.' **bureaucrat** *n.* one who advocates or takes part in such a system of government. **bureaucratic** *a.* [Fr. *bureau*; Gk. *kratein*, to govern].

bu·rette (bū·ret') *n.* a graduated glass tube provided with a stop-cock at the lower end, used for delivering accurately measured quantities of liquid [Fr.].

burg (burg) *n.* (*Colloq.*) a town or village; a common ending of the names of cities in Holland or Germany [O.E. *burh*].

bur·geon (bur'·jạn) *v.i.* to sprout; to bud; to put forth branches [Fr.].

bur·glar (burg'·lẹr) *n.* one who is guilty of house-breaking. **-y** *n.* breaking and entering into a dwelling-house originally between 9 p.m. and 6 a.m. with intent to commit a felony but extended by statute to include daytime.

Bur·gun·dy (bur'·gạn·di·) *n.* name given to various wines, red or white [*Burgundy*, Fr.].

bur·i·al (ber'·i·ạl) *n.* the act of burying; interment; entombment. — **ground,** a cemetery [O.E. *byrgels*, tomb]. [See **bury**].

burke (burk) *v.t.* to murder, esp. by smothering; to put an end to quietly [fr. *Burke*].

burl (burl) *n.* a knot in wood, thread or yarn. **-ed** *a.* [L. *burra*, coarse].

bur·lap (bur'·lap) *n.* gunny sacking; a coarsely woven canvas of flax, hemp, or jute, used for packing and as a wall covering, etc.

bur·lesque (bur·lesk') *n.* distorting, exaggerating, and ridiculing a work of art; travesty; parody; theatrical performance featuring vulgar comedy and dancing; *a.* comical; ludicrous; risqué; *v.t.* to turn into burlesque [It. *burlesco*].

bur·ly (bur'·li·) *a.* of stout build; big and sturdy. **burliness** *n.* [M.E. *borlich*, massive].

burn (burn) *v.t.* to consume with fire; to subject to the action of fire; to char; to scorch; *v.i.* to be on fire; to flame; flare; blaze; glow; be excited or inflamed with passion; *pa.t.* and *pa.p.* **-ed** or **-t;** *n.* injury or damage caused by burning. **-er** *n.* part of a lamp or gas jet from which the flame issues. **-ing** *n.* act of consuming by fire; inflammation; *a.* flaming; scorching; parching; ardent; excessive. **-ing-glass** *n.* a convex lens which causes intense heat by bending the rays of the sun and concentrating them upon a single point. **burning question,** a topic of universal discussion. **burnt-offering** *n.* a sacrifice of a living person or animal by burning. **burnt sienna,** a fine, reddish-brown pigment from calcined Sienna earth. **burnt umber,** a brown pigment obtained from calcined umber [O.E. *baernan*].

bur·nish (bur'·nish) *v.t.* to polish by continual rubbing; *n.* polish; gloss; luster [O.Fr. *burnisant*, polishing].

burnoose (bur·nòos') *n.* a hooded cloak worn by Arabs. Also **burnous** [Ar.].

burnt *pa.t.* and *pa.p.* of **burn.**

burr (bur) *n.* a tool for cutting or drilling; a

rough edge left on metal by a cutting tool. Also **bur** [Dan. *borre*].

burr (bur) *n.* the trilled guttural sound of *r,* as heard in Northumberland and Scotland; *v.t.* and *i.* to roll the 'r' sound [imit.].

bur·ro (bur'·ō) *n.* a donkey [Sp.].

bur·row (bur'·ō) *n.* a hole dug in the ground by certain small animals to serve as an abode or for concealment; *v.i.* to tunnel through earth; to search assiduously; to live in a burrow [var. of *borough*].

bur·sar (bur'·sẹr) *n.* a treasurer of a college. **bursary** *n.* (in Scotland) a scholarship [L.L. *bursa,* Fr. *bourse,* a purse].

bur·sa (bur'·sạ) *n.* a sac or cavity, especially between joints; **-l** *a.;* **bursitis** *n.* [LL. = a *purse, bag*].

burst (burst) *v.t.* to fly asunder; to break into pieces; to break open violently; to break suddenly into some expression of feeling; to split; *v.i.* to shatter; to break violently; *pa.t.* and *pa.p.* **burst;** *n.* a bursting; an explosion; an outbreak; spurt [O.E. *berstan*].

bur·y (ber'·i·) *v.t.* to inter in a grave; to put underground; to hide or conceal by covering; *pa.p.* **buried. -ing** *n.* burial; interment. **to bury the hatchet,** to cease from strife; to restore friendly relations [O.E. *byrigan*].

bus, 'bus (bus) *n.* a contraction for *omnibus;* a vehicle for public conveyance of passengers; *pl.* **-es.** [L. *omnibus,* for all and sundry].

bush (boosh) *n.* a shrub; a low woody plant with numerous branches near ground-level; a thicket of small trees and shrubs; the interior of a country; the backwoods; *v.i.* to grow thick or bushy; *v.t.* to plant bushes about. — **fighting** *n.* guerilla warfare where advantage is taken of trees and bushes. **-iness** *n.* the quality of being bushy. **-man** *n.* a member of a negroid race of S. Africa; a settler in the backwoods; a woodsman. **-master** *n.* a large venemous snake. **-whacker** *n.* one skilled in travelling through brush or woods; a guerilla. **-y** *a.* full of bushes; thick and spreading [M.E. *busch*].

bush (boosh) *n.* the internal lining of a bearing, to form a plain bearing surface for a pin or shaft. **-ing** *n.* a removable lining to reduce friction [Dut. *bus,* a box].

bush·el (boosh'·ạl) *n.* a dry measure of 4 pecks, for corn, fruit, etc. [O.Fr. *boissel,* a little box].

busi·ness (biz'·nis) *n.* employment; profession; vocation; any occupation for a livelihood; trade; firm; concern; action on the stage, apart from dialogue. **-like** *a.* practical; systematic; methodical. **-man** *n.* [fr. *busy*].

bus·kin (busk'·in) *n.* a kind of half-boot worn by ancient Greeks and Roman tragic actors.

buss (bus) *n.* a hearty kiss; *v.t.* to kiss, esp. boisterously [Fr. *baiser,* to kiss].

bust (bust) *n.* sculptured representation of a person from the waist upwards; the upper part of the human body; a woman's bosom. **-ed** *a.* breasted [Fr. *buste*].

bust (bust) *v.i.* and *v.t.* (*Slang*) to burst; to break; *n.* a drinking bout.

bus·tle (bus'·l) *v.i.* to busy oneself with much stir and movement; *n.* great stir. **-r** *n.* [O.E. *bysig,* busy].

bus·tle (bus'·l) *n.* a stuffed pad worn by ladies to support and elevate the back of the skirt just below the waist [Fr. *buste*].

bus·y (biz'·i·) *a.* having plenty to do; active and earnest in work; diligent; industrious; officious; meddling; *v.t.* to make or keep busy; to occupy (oneself). **busily** *adv.* **-body** *n.* a person who meddles in other people's business. **-ness** *n.* state of being busy [O.E. *bysig*].

but (but) *conj.* yet; unless; that not; nevertheless; notwithstanding; *prep.* except; without; *adv.* only. **all but,** nearly [O.E. *butan,* outside].

bu·tane (bū'·tān) *n.* a natural gas used in refrigeration and as a fuel [L. *butyrum,* butter].

butch·er (booch'·ẹr) *n.* one who slaughters animals for food or retails the meat; one who recklessly destroys human life; *v.t.* to slaughter animals for food; to murder in cold blood; to spoil work. **-ing,** *n.* killing for food or lust of blood. **-y** *n.* wanton slaughter [O.Fr. *bochier,* one who kills goats].

but·ler (but'·ler) *n.* a male servant who has charge of the liquors, plate, etc. **-y** *n.* a butler's pantry [O.Fr. *bouteillier,* a bottler].

butt (but) *n.* the lower end of a tree-trunk providing the strongest timber; the end of anything; one continually subject to ridicule; (*Slang*) a cigarette; *v.t.* to strike by thrusting the head downwards; to abut on; to protrude. **-s** *n.pl.* a mound with targets where shooting is practiced. **-er** *n.* an animal, e.g. the goat, which butts. **to butt in** (*Colloq.*) to intervene without permission [Fr. *but,* end].

butt (but) *n.* a large cake. **-ery** *n.* [Fr. *bote*].

butte (būt) *n.* a steep hill standing alone [Fr.].

but·ter (but'·er) *n.* the fatty ingredients of milk, emulsified by churning; gross flattery; *v.t.* to spread with butter; to flatter. **-cup** *n.* plant with cup-shaped, glossy, yellow flowers. **-fingers** *n.* (*Colloq.*) one who has failed to hold a catch or who drops things easily. **-milk** *n.* the fluid residue after butter has been churned from cream. **-scotch** *n.* a kind of taffy with butter as an ingredient. **-y** *a.* [O.E. *butere*].

but·ter·fly (but'·er·flī) *n.* the common name of all diurnal, lepidopterous insects; a gay, flighty woman [O.E. *buter-flege*].

but·tock (but'·ak) *n.* the rump; rounded lower posterior part of the body; hip; haunch (usually in *pl.*) [prob. dim. of *butt,* thick end].

but·ton (but'·n) *n.* a knob or stud for fastening clothing; a bud; the safety knob at the end of a fencing foil; a small round protuberance, e.g. that of an electric bell; an emblem of membership; *v.t.* to fasten with buttons; *v.i.* to be fastened by a button. **-hole** *n.* the hole or loop in which a button is fastened; *v.t.* to detain a person in talk again his will. **-hook** *n.* a hook for pulling a button through a buttonhole [Fr. *bouton,* bud].

but·tress (but'·ris) *n.* a projecting support to a wall; any prop or support; *v.t.* to support [O.Fr. *bouter,* to thrust].

bu·tyl (bū'·til) *n.* an alcohol radical; a highly elastic synthetic rubber, made from butane, a natural gas [L. *butyrum,* butter].

bux·om (buk'·sam) *a.* full of health; lively; cheery, plump; gay [O.E. *bugan,* to bend].

buy (bī) *v.t.* to obtain by payment; to purchase; to pay a price for; to bribe; *pa.t.* and *pa.p.* **bought. -er** *n.* a purchaser [O.E. *bycgan*].

buzz (buz) *v.i.* to make a humming or hissing sound; *v.t.* to spread news abroad secretly; to tap out signals by means of a buzzer. **-er** *n.* one who buzzes; an apparatus used for telephonic signaling. **-ingly** *adv.* [imit. word].

buz·zard (bus'·erd) *n.* a genus of birds of the hawk family [O.Fr. *busard*].

by (bī) *prep.* near; beside; in the neighborhood of; past; through the agency of; according to; *adv.* near; in the neighborhood; close; out of the way; beyond. **by and by,** soon; in the near future. **-name** *n.* a nick-name. **—pass** *n.* a road for the diversion of traffic from crowded centers; *v.t.* to avoid a place by going round it. **—path** *n.* a side path. **-play** *n.* action carried on apart from the main part of a play; diversion. **—product** *n.* secondary product obtained during manufacture of principal commodity. **-road** *n.* a less frequented side road. **-stander** *n.* an onlooker. **-way** *n.* a secluded path or road. **-word** *n.* a common saying; a proverb [O.E. *bi*].

bye (bī) *n.* anything subordinate; having no opponent in a round of competition. **-bye** (*Colloq.*) good-bye [var. of *by*].

by·law, bye-law (bī'·law) *n.* a local law made by an association [M.E. *bilaw,* fr. *bi,* a borough]

Byz·an·tine (biz·an'·tin, biz'·an·tīn, -tin) re-

lating to *Byzantium,* the original name for Constantinople; pert. to Asiatic architecture with Grecian characteristics.

C

cab (kab) *n.* a taxicab; the covered part of a locomotive; driver's accomodation on a truck. **-by** *n.* a taxi driver [short for Fr. *cabriolet,* a light carriage].

ca·bal (ka·bal') *n.* a secret scheming faction in a state. **-istic** *a.* [Heb. *gabbalah*].

cab·a·la, cabbala (kab'·a·la) *n.* occultism. **cabalism** *n.* **cabalist, cabalistic(al)** *a.* mysterious; occult [Heb. *gabbalah,* mystical interpretation].

cab·a·ret (ka'·ba·rā, -ret) *n.* restaurant providing entertainment and space for dancing [Fr. *cabaret,* a tavern].

cab·bage (kab'·ij) *n.* a garden vegetable of Brassica family [L. *caput,* the head].

cab·in (kab'·in) *n.* a small house; a hut; an apartment in a ship; the space in an airplane for the pilot and passengers; *v.t.* to confine in a cabin; *v.i.* to live in a cabin; to lodge. **boy,** a boy who waits on the officers of a ship [Fr. *cabine,* a cabin; *cabane,* a hut].

cab·i·net (kab'·a·net) *n.* a private room; a council of ministers who advise the chief executive; a chest or case for holding or displaying objects; **—maker** *n.* a maker of cabinets and other furniture [Fr. *cabinet,* fr. *cabine*].

ca·ble (kā'·bl) *n.* a large, strong rope or chain; a stranded insulated conductor of electricity; a submarine telegraph line; a message sent by such line; *v.t.* to fasten with a cable; to send a message by cable. **car** *n.* a car pulled by a moving cable. **—gram** *n.* a telegram sent by cable; a cable [fr. L.L. *capulum,* a halter].

ca·boo·dle (ka·bōō'·dl) *n.* (*Slang*) collection.

ca·boose (ka·bōōs') *n.* a car attached to a freight train for the crew [Dut. *kombuis*].

cab·ri·o·let (kab·ri·a·lā') *n.* a light one-horse carriage with a hood [Fr. fr. L. *caper,* a goat].

ca·ca·o (ka·kā'·ō, ka·kā'·ō) *n.* a tropical tree from the seeds of which cocoa and chocolate are prepared [Mex.].

cache (kash) *n.* orig. a hole in the ground for storing or hiding provisions, etc.; any hiding-place; articles so hidden; *v.t.* to put in a cache; to conceal [Fr. *cacher,* to hide].

ca·chet (ka'·shā) *n.* a seal, as on a lette; distinctive mark [Fr. *cacher,* to hide].

cach·in·na·tion (kak·i·nā'·shan) *n.* loud, immoderate, or hysterical laughter. **cachinnate** *v.i.* [L. *cachinnare,* to laugh loudly].

ca·chou (ka·shōō') *n.* a tablet or pellet, used to perfume the breath [Fr.].

cack·le (kak'·l) *v.i.* to make a noise like a hen or goose; to gossip noisily; *n.* [imit.].

cac·o- (kak'·a) a combining form fr. Gk. *kakos,* bad, used in derivatives.

ca·cog·ra·phy (ka·kåg'·ra·fi·) *n.* bad writing or spelling [Gk. *kakos,* bad; *graphia,* writing].

ca·coph·o·ny (ka·kåf'·a·ni·) *n.* a harsh or disagreeable sound; a discord; a use of ill-sounding words. **cacophonous** *a.* [Gk. *kakos,* bad; *phōnē,* sound].

cac·tus (kak'·tas) *n.* an American desert plant with thick, fleshy, prickly stems, generally no leaves but frequently producing showy flowers. *pl.* **-es,** or **cacti.** [Gk. *kaktos,* a cardoon].

cad (kad) *n.* a low, mean, vulgar fellow. **-dish** *a.* ill-bred, mean [short for Fr. *cadet,* junior].

ca·dav·er (ka·da'·ver) *n.* (*Med.*) a corpse. **-ous** *a.* corpse-like; gaunt; sickly-looking [L.].

cad·die, cad·dy (kad'·i·) *n.* an attendant who carries a golfer's clubs; *v.i.* [fr. Fr. *cadet*].

cad·dis, cad·dice (kad'·is) *n.* worm-like aquatic larva of caddis-fly [etym. unknown].

cad·dy (kad'·i·) *n.* a small box for holding tea [Malay, *kati*, a weight, 1⅓ lbs. (for tea)].

ca·dence (kā'·dens) *n.* a fall of the voice in reading or speaking; a modulation; the beat of any rhythmical action; (*Mus.*) the subsiding of a melody towards a close. **-d** *a.* rhythmical. **cadency** *n.* [L. *cadere*, to fall].

ca·den·za (ka·den'·za) *n.* (*Mus.*) an ornamental passage for a voice or solo instrument in an aria or concerto [It.].

ca·det (ka·det') *n.* a youth in training for commissioned ranks in the army or air force; **-ship** *n.* [Fr. *cadet*, younger].

cadge (kaj) *v.t.* and *i.* to peddle goods; to beg. **-r** *n.* a peddlar; a beggar; a sponger.

cad·mi·um (kad'·mi·am) *n.* (*Chem.*) a soft, bluish-white metal of zinc group. **cadmia** *n.* an oxide of zinc [Gk. *kadmeia*].

ca·dre (kȧ'·dri·) *n.* the framework of a military unit [Fr. = a frame].

ca·du·ce·us (ka·dū'·si·as) *n.* the staff carried by Mercury, messenger of the gods; the emblem of the medical profession.

cae·cum (sē'·kam) *n.* (*Med.*) the first part of the large intestine, opening into the colon; *pl.* **caeca. caecal** *a.* [L. *caecus*, blind].

Cae·sar (sē'·zer) *n.* one who acts like Julius Caesar (100-44 B.C.), Roman emperor and dictator; hence, autocrat; dictator. **Caesarean, Caesarian** *a.* pert. to Julius Caesar. **Caesarian section** (*Med.*) delivery of child through an opening cut in abdominal wall (Julius Caesar is said to have been born thus).

cae·si·um See cesium.

cae·su·ra, cesura (sē·zū'·ra) *n.* a break or division in a line of poetry; in English prosody, the natural pause of the voice. **-l** *a.* [L. *caedere, caesum*, to cut].

ca·fé (ka·fā') *n.* a coffee-house; a restaurant, usually licensed for the sale of light refreshments only [Fr. *café*, coffee].

caf·e·te·ri·a (kaf·i·tir'·i·a) *n.* a restaurant where the customers help themselves [Amer.-Sp. = a coffee-shop].

caf·feine (kaf·ēn') *n.* the stimulating alkaloid in coffee and tea [Fr. *café*, coffee].

cage (kāj) *n.* a place of confinement; a box-like enclosure, with bars of iron or wire, for keeping animals or birds; *v.t.* to confine in a cage; to imprison. **-ling** *n.* a bird kept in a cage. **-work**, *n.* open frame-work. **-y** *a.* cautious, wary [L. *cavea*, hollow].

ca·hoot (ka·hŏŏt') *n.* (*Slang*) league or partnership. *usu. pl.* **in cahoots.**

cai·man See **cayman.**

cairn (kern) *n.* a rounded or conical pile of stones [Gael. *carn*, a heap].

cais·son (kā'·san) *n.* an ammunition chest or wagon; (*Engineering*) a water-tight chamber of sheet-iron or wood, used for workmen in laying the foundations of piers or bridges, quay-walls, etc.; an apparatus for raising sunken vessels [Fr. *caisse*, a case].

ca·jole (ka·jōl') *v.t.* to persuade by flattery; to coax; to wheedle. **-r** *n.* **-ry** *n.* the act of cajoling [Fr. *cajoler*].

cake (kāk) *n.* a piece of dough baked; fancy bread; a flattish mass of matter, esp. soap, tobacco, etc.; *v.t.* to make into a cake; *v.i.* to become a flat, doughy mass. **caky** *a.* **-walk** *n.* an American negro dance [O.N. *kaka*].

cal·a·bash (kal'·a·bash) *n.* the bottle-gourd tree; the fruit of this tree; a vessel made from the gourd, or the gourd itself; a species of pear [Ar.].

cal·a·boose (kal'·a·bŏŏs) *n.* (*Slang*) a prison; a jail [Sp.].

cal·a·mine (kal'·a·mīn) *n.* a silicate of zinc, used as a pigment in painting pottery and in skin ointments [Gk. *kadmeia*].

ca·lam·i·ty (ka·lam'·a·ti) *n.* any great misfortune; disaster; affliction; mischance. **calamitous** *a.* producing distress and misery. **calamitously** *adv.* [Fr. *calamité*].

cal·a·mus (kal'·a·mas) *n.* a reed used in ancient times as a pen, or made into a musical instrument [L. fr. Gk.].

ca·lash (ka·lash') *n.* a light carriage with low wheels, and a top or hood that can be raised or lowered; a silk hood [Fr. *calèche*].

cal·car·e·ous (kal·ke'·ri·as) *a.* chalky [L. *calx, calcis*, lime].

cal·cif·er·ol (kal·sif'·a·ral) *n.* crystalline vitamine D. used in fortifying margarine. **calciferous** *a.* containing carbonate of lime [L. *calx, calcis*, lime; *ferre*, to bear].

cal·ci·fy (kal'·si·fī) *v.t.* and *i.* to turn into lime; to harden or petrify, by a deposit of lime. **calcification** *n.* [L. *calx*, lime; *facere*, to make].

cal·ci·mine (kal'·si·mīn) *n.* a white or tinted wash for ceiling and walls.

cal·cine (kal'·sin, -sin) *v.t.* to reduce to powder by heat; to expel water and other volatile substances by heat; *v.i.* to be turned into powder. **calcinable** *a.* **calcination** *n.* **calcinatory** *n.* a vessel used in calcination [Fr. *calciner*].

cal·ci·um (kal·si·am) *n.* the metallic base of lime. **calcic** *a.* containing calcium. **calcite** *n.* native carbonate of lime [L. *calx, calcis*, lime].

cal·cu·late (kal'·kya·lāt) *v.t.* to count; to estimate; to compute; to plan; to expect; *v.i.* to make a calculation. **calculable** *a.* **-d** *a.* adapted to a purpose; intended to produce a certain effect. **calculating** *a.* capable of performing calculations; shrewd in matters of self-interest; scheming. **calculation** *n.* **calculative** *a.* tending to calculate. **calculator** *n.* one who computes; a machine which does automatic computations [L. *calculare*, to count].

cal·cu·lus (kal'·kya·las) *n.* a branch of higher mathematics concerned with the properties of continuously varying quantities; *n.* a hard concretion which forms, esp. in kidney, bladder, etc. usually called stone or gravel; *pl.* **calculi. calculose, calculous** *a.* hard, like stone; gritty [L. *calculus*, a pebble].

cal·dron, cauldron (kawl'·dran) *n.* a large metal kettle or boiler [L. *caldera*, warm pot].

cal·a·fac·tion (kal·a·fak'·shan) *n.* the act of heating, the state of being heated. **calefacient** (kal·a·fā'·shi·ant) *a.* making warm; *n.* a heat-giving remedy. **calefactor** *n.* that which gives heat. **calefactory** *a.* [L. *calere*, to be warm; *facere*, to make].

cal·en·dar (kal'·an·der) *n.* a table of days, months or seasons; an almanac; a list of criminal cases; a list of saints; *v.t.* to enter in a list [L. *Calendae*, the calends].

cal·en·der (kal'·an·der) *n.* a hot press with rollers, used to make cloth, etc. smooth and glossy [Fr. *calandre*, a cylinder].

cal·ends (kal'·endz) *n.pl.* the first day of each month, among the Romans. **at the Greek calends**, never (because the Greeks had no calends). Also **kalends** [L. *Calendae*].

calf (kaf) *n.* the young of the cow, and of some other mammals, such as elephant, whale, etc.; a mass of ice detached from a glacier, iceberg, or floe; *pl.* **calves** (kavz). **—love**, a youthful, transitory attachment to one of the opposite sex. **—skin** *n.* a fine, light-colored leather made from the skin of a calf. **calve** (kav) *v.i.* to bring forth a calf [O.E. *cealf*].

calf (kaf) *n.* the thick, fleshy part of the leg below the knee; *pl.* **calves** [O.N. *kalfi*].

cal·i·ber (kal'·a·ber) *n.* the diameter of the bore of a cannon, gun, etc.; the internal diameter of a tube or cylinder; (*Fig.*) capacity; quality of mind; character. **calibrate** *v.t.* to determine the caliber of a firearm tube or other cylindrical object. **calibration** *n.* [Fr. *calibre*].

cal·i·co (kal'·a·kō) *n.* white cotton cloth, first made in *Calicut* in India; printed cotton cloth; *a.* made of calico.

cal·i·pers, callipers (kal'·i·perz) *n.* a two-legged instrument for measuring diameters [Fr. *calibre*].

ca·liph, ca·lif (kal′·if, kā′·lif) *n.* a title given to the successors of Mohammed [Ar. *khalifah*, a successor].

ca·lix See **calyx**.

calk, caulk (kawk) *v. t.* to press tarred oakum into the seams between the planks of a boat to prevent leaks; to fill or close joints or crevices to make air- or water-tight. **-er** *n.* **-ing** *n.* [L.L. *calicare*, to stop up with lime, *calx*].

calk (kawk) *n.* a pointed stud on a horse-shoe to prevent slipping; *v.t.* [L. *calcar*, a spur].

call (kawl) *v.t.* to announce; to name; to summon; to name, as for office; to utter in a loud voice; *v.i.* to speak in a loud voice; to cry out; to make a brief visit; *n.* a shout; a summons or invitation; a short visit; a public claim; a requisition; authorized command; an invitation, as to be minister of a church; a note blown on a horn, bugle, etc.; the characteristic cry of a bird or animal. **-er** *n.* one who calls. **-ing** *n.* a person's usual occupation. **at call**, on demand. **on call**, of a person, ready if summoned. **-boy** *n.* a boy who calls actors to go on the stage; a bellboy. **to call down**, to rebuke. **to call up** (*Mil.*) to summon to military service; to telephone [O.E. *ceallian*].

cal·ligra·phy (ka·lig′·ra·fi·) *n.* the art of beautiful writing; penmanship. **calligrapher, calligraphist** *n.* **calligraphic** *a.* [Gk. *kallos*, beauty; *graphein*, to write].

cal·li·o·pe (ka·lī′·a·pē) *n.* musical instrument with steam whistles, played like an organ.

cal′lis·then·ics (kal·is·then′·iks) *n.pl.* light gymnastic exercises to promote beauty and grace of movement. **callisthenic** *a.* [Gk. *kallos*, beauty; *sthenos*, strength].

cal·lous (kal′·us) *a.* hardened; hardened in mind; unfeeling; having a callus; **-ly** *adv.* **-ness** *n.* **callosity** *n.* a horny hardness of the skin [L. *callus*, hard skin].

cal·low (kal′·ō) *a.* pert. to the condition of a young bird; unfledged; (*Fig.*) inexperienced; raw. **-ness** *n.* [L. *calvus*, bald].

cal·lus (kal′·as) *n.* a hardened or thickened part of the skin [L. = hard skin].

calm (kàm) *a.* still; quiet; at rest; *n.* the state of being calm; *v.t.* **to make calm. -ly** *adv.* **-ness** *n.* [Fr. *calme*].

cal·o·mel (kal′·a·mel) *n.* (*Med.*) sub-chloride of mercury, used as a purgative [Gk. *kalos*, fair; *melas*, black].

ca·lor·ic (ka·lawr′·ik) *n.* heat; *a.* pert. to heat; heat-producing. **caloricity** *n.* the power of animals to develop heat. **calorifacient** *a.* heat-producing. **calorific** *a.* pert. to heat; heat-producing. **calorification** *n.* the production of heat [L. *calor*, heat].

cal·o·rie, calory (kal′·er·i·) *n.* (*Phys.*) the unit of heat; the unit of heat or energy produced by any food substance. **calorimeter** *n.* a scientific instrument for determining the amount of heat produced by any substance [L. *calor*, heat].

cal·u·met (kal′·yoo·met) *n.* the 'pipe of peace' of the N. Amer. Indians [L. *calamus*, a reed].

ca·lum·ni·ate (ka·lum′·ni·āt) *v.t.* to accuse falsely; to slander; *v.i.* to utter slanders. **calumniation** *n.* false and slanderous representations. **calumniator** *n.* **calumniatory, calumnious** *a.* slanderous. **calumniously** *adv.* **calumny** *n.* a false accusation; malicious slander; libel [L. *calumnia*].

Cal·va·ry (kal′·va·ri·) *n.* the place of Christ's crucifixion [L. *calvaria*, a skull].

calve (kav) See **calf**.

Cal·vin·ism (kal′·vin·izm) *n.* the doctrines of John *Calvin*, which lay special stress on the sovereignty of God in the conferring of grace. **Calvinist** *n.* **Calvinistic** *a.*

calx (kalks) *n.* the crumbly substance that remains after the calcination of a metal or mineral; *pl.* **calxes, calces** (kalk′·siz, kal′·sēz) [L. = lime].

ca·lyp·so (ka·lip′·sō) *n.* an improvised song in native rhythm from the West Indies.

ca·lyx, ca·lix (kā′·liks) *n.* a cup-shaped cavity; the outer covering or leaf-like envelope of a flower [Gk. *kalux*, a husk, a cup].

cam (kam) *n.* a projecting part of a wheel used to give an alternating or variable motion to another wheel or piece. **-shaft** *n.* the shaft on which cams are formed for opening the valves [Dut. *kam*, a comb].

ca·ma·ra·de·rie (kàm·a·ràd′·a·rē) *n.* good-fellowship [Fr. *comarade*, a companion].

cam·ber (kam′·ber) *n.* a slight convexity of an upper surface, as of a ship's deck, a bridge, a road surface [Fr. *cambrer*, to arch].

Cam·bri·an (kam′·bri·an) *a.* Welsh; pert. to Cambria or Wales; *n.* a Welshman. [L. fr. *Cymru*, Wales].

cam·bric (kām′·brik) *n.* a fine white linen fabric first made at *Cambrai*, in N. France.

came (kām) *pa.t. of the verb* **come**.

cam·el (kam′·al) *n.* a large ruminant animal of Asia and Africa, with one or two humps, used as a beast of burden. **-eer** *n.* a camel driver [Gk. *kamēlos*].

ca·mel·lia (ka·mēl′·ya) *a.* a species of Asiatic shrub with showy flowers and elegant dark-green, laurel-like leaves [fr. *Kamel*, botanist].

Cam·em·bert (ka′·mam·ber) *n.* a small, soft, rich cheese [fr. a village in Normandy].

cam·e·o (kam′·i·ō) *n.* a gem stone of two layers cut in ornamental relief [etym. unknown].

cam·e·ra (kam′·a·ra) *n.* device for taking photographs. **-man** *n.* a professional motion picture or press photographer [L. *camera*, a vault].

cam·e·ra (kam′·a·ra) *n.* a judge's private room; hence (*Law*) 'to hear a case' **in camera** [L. *camera*, a room].

cam·i·sole (kam′·a·sōl) *n.* a lady's under-bodice; light dressing-jacket [Fr.].

cam·o·mile, chamomile (kam′·a·mīl) *n.* an aromatic creeping plant whose flowers are used medicinally [Gk. *chamaimēlon*, the earth-apple].

cam·ou·flage (kam′·a·flazh) *n.* (*Mil.*) a method of visual deception of the enemy by disguising; any form of disguise; *v.t.* to cover with camouflage material; to disguise [Fr.].

camp (kamp) *n.* the area of ground where soldiers or other groups of people are lodged in huts or tents; permanent barracks near a suitable exercise ground; group in agreement; *v.t.* and *i.* to pitch tents. **-er** *n.* one who lives in a camp in open country, esp. living in a tent. **-ing** *n.* the act of living in camp. — **chair** *n.* a light, portable chair with folding legs. — **follower** *n.* a non-combatant who follows the troops, *i.e.*, a prostitute, washer woman, etc. — **meeting** *n.* a religious meeting in the open air. — **out** *v.* to live without conveniences [L. *campus*, a field].

cam·paign (kam·pān′) *n.* a series of operations in a particular theater of war; hence, in politics, business, etc. an organized series of operations (meetings, canvassing, etc.); *v.i.* to serve in a war; to conduct, or assist in political, etc. operations. **-er** *n.* [L. *campus*, a plain].

cam·pa·ni·le (kam·pa·nē·li·, kam′·pa·nil) *n.* a bell-tower constructed beside a church, but not necessarily attached to it. **campanology** *n.* the art of bell-ringing, or of bell-founding; bell-lore. [It. *campana*, a bell].

cam·phor (kam′·fer) *n.* a whitish substance with an aromatic taste and smell, obtained from the camphor laurel-tree. **-aceous** (kam.-fer.·ā′·shas) *a.* resembling camphor. **-ate** *v.t.* to impregnate with camphor. **-ate, -ic** *a.* pert. to camphor [Malay, *kapur*, chalk].

cam·pus (kam′·pas) *n.* the grounds of a college or school [L. *campus*, a plain].

can (kan) *pres. indic.* of a defective, intransitive verb meaning, to be able, to have the power, to be allowed. *pa.p., pa.t.* **could** (kood) [O.E. *cunnan*, to know].

can (kan) *n.* a metal vessel or container for holding liquids, etc.; *v.t.* to put into a can for the purpose of preserving; *pr.p.* **-ning.** *pa.p.* and *pa.t.* **-ned. -nery** *n.* a factory where foods are preserved by canning [O.E. *canne*].

Ca·na·di·an (ka̤·nā′·di·a̤n) *n.* an inhabitant of Canada; *a.* pert. to Canada.

ca·naille (ka̤·nāl′) *n.* the dregs of society; the mob; rabble [Fr. fr. I. *canis*, a dog].

ca·nal (ka̤·nal′) *n.* an artificial watercourse for transport, drainage or irrigation purposes; a duct in the body; a groove. **canalize** *v.t.* to make a canal through; to convert into a canal [L. *canalis*].

can·a·pé (ka′·na̤·pi·) *n.* a small piece of toast or bread, with anchovies, etc. on it served as an appetizer [Fr. *canapé*, a sofa].

ca·nard (ka·na̤rd′) *n.* a false rumor; an absurd or extravagant piece of news [Fr.].

ca·nar·y (ka̤·nā′·ri·) *n.* a yellow singing bird, a species of finch; a pale-yellow color; a light wine made in the Canary Islands [Fr. *canari*].

ca·nas·ta (ka̤·nas′·ta̤) *n.* a card game played with two packs.

can-can (kan′·kan) *n.* a kind of dance, once popular in music-halls in France [Fr.].

can·cel (kan′·sa̤l) *v.t.* to cross out; to blot out; to annul; to suppress; (*Math.*) to strike out common factors; to balance; to offset. **-lation** *n.* the act of canceling [L. *cancellatus*, latticed].

can·cer (kan′·ser) *n.* (*Med.*) a malignant growth or tumor. **-ate** *v.i.* to grow into a cancer.**-ation** *n.* **-ous** *a.* pert. to or resembling cancer [L. *cancer*, a crab].

can·de·la·brum (kan·da̤·lȧ′·bra̤m) *n.* a branched and highly ornamented candle-stick; a chandelier. **candelabra** *n.sing.* and *pl.* [L. fr. *candela*, a candle].

can·did (kan′·did) *a.* fair; open; frank. **-ly** *adv.* **-ness** *n.* frankness; ingenuousness [L. *candidus*, white].

can·di·date (kan′·da̤·dāt) *n.* one who seeks an appointment, office, honor, etc. **candidature, candidacy** *n.* the position of being a candidate [L. *candidus*, white (one wearing a white toga)].

can·dle (kan′·dl) *n.* a stick of tallow, wax, etc. with a wick inside, used for light. **power,** the unit of luminosity. **-stick** *n.* an instrument for holding a candle [L. *candela*].

Can·dle·mas (kan′·dl·ma̤s) *n.* a religious festival to commemorate the Purification of the Virgin and the presentation of Jesus in the temple [*candle* and *mass*].

can·dor (kan′·der) *n.* candidness; sincerity; frankness [L. *candor*, whiteness].

can·dy (kan′·di·) *n.* a kind of sweetmeat made of sugar; *v.t.* to preserve in sugar; to form into crystals, as sugar; *v.i.* to become candied. **candied** (kan′·did) *a.* [Ar. *qand*, sugar].

can·dy·tuft (kan′·di·tuft) *n.* a large genus of herbs or shrubs [fr. *Candia*].

cane (kān) *n.* the stem of a small palm or long, strong reed; the bamboo, etc.; the sugar-cane; a walking-stick; *v.t.* to beat with a cane; to fix a cane bottom to, e.g. a chair. **-brake** *n.* a dense growth of canes. **— sugar** *n.* sugar from the sugar-cane [Gk. *kanna*, a reed].

ca·nine (kā′·nīn) *a.* of, or pert. to a dog. **teeth,** the two pointed teeth in each jaw, one on each side, between the incisors and the molars [L. *canis*, a dog].

can·is·ter (kan′·is·ter) *n.* a small case or box for holding tea, coffee, etc. **— shot** *n.* a number of small iron balls enclosed in a case of a size to fit the gun-barrel (an early form of shrapnel) [L. *canistrum*, a wicker basket].

can·ker (kang′·ker) *n.* ulceration of the mouth; a disease of trees; a disease affecting horses' feet; (*Fig.*) anything that eats away, corrupts, etc.; *v.i.* to consume; to gnaw at; to corrupt; *v.i.* to decay, to become cankered. **-ed** *a.* corrupted; malignant. **-ous** *a.* corrupting like a canker. **-y** *a.* cankered. **-worm** *n.* a destructive caterpillar [L. *cancer*, a crab].

can·nel-coal (kan′·el·kōl) *n.* a kind of coal,

burning with a clear, smokeless flame, used in the manufacture of gas. Also **candle-coal.**

can·ni·bal (kan′·a̤·bal) *n.* one who eats human flesh; *a.* relating to this practice. **-ism** *n.* the practice of eating human flesh. **-istic** *a.* **cannibalize** *v.t.* to dismantle in the hope of getting spare parts to be used for re-conditioning. [Sp. *canibal = Caribal*, a Carib].

can·non (kan′·a̤n) *n.* a large gun; *v.i.* to cannonade. **-ade** *n.* an attack with cannon; the firing of cannon; *v.t.* to bombard. **-eer, -ier** (kan·a̤n·ir′) *n.* one who loads or fires cannon; an artilleryman. **— ball** *n.* an iron ball to be discharged by cannon. **— shot** *n.* a cannonball; the range of a cannon [L. *canna*, a tube].

can·not (kan′·a̤t) combination of *can* and *not*, therefore, = not to be able.

can·ny (kan′·i·) *a.* (*Scot.*) cautious; thrifty.

ca·noe (ka·nōō′) *n.* a light, narrow boat propelled by a hand paddle.**-ist** *n.* [Haiti, *canoa*].

can·on (kan′·a̤n) *n.* a law or rule, esp. of the church; the books of the Scriptures accepted by the Church as of divine authority; rules of faith; a standard; the list of saints; a church dignitary, esp. one connected with a cathedral; (*Mus.*) a form of composition in which the melody is repeated at set intervals by the other parts. **-ess** *n.* a member of a religious association of women. **canonic, canonical** *a.* **canonicals** *n.pl.* official dress worn by a clergyman. **canonically** *adv.* **-ization** *n.* **-ize** *v.t.* to place in the list of saints. **-ist** *n.* one skilled in canon law. **-ry** *n.* the office of canon. [Gk. *kanōn*, a rule].

can·o·py (kan′·a̤·pi·) *n.* a covering fixed above a bed, or a dais, or carried on poles above the head; any overhanging shelter [Gk. *kōnōpion*, a couch with mosquito curtains].

cant (kant) *n.* an inclination from the level; a tilted position; *v.t.* to tilt; to jerk; to toss; *v.i.* to have, or take a leaning position [O.Fr.].

cant (kant) *n.* an insincere or conventional mode of speaking; an expression peculiar to a group [L. *cantare*, to sing].

can't (kant) *v.* contr. of **cannot.**

can·ta·bi·le (kȧn·tȧ′·bi·lā) *adv.* (*Mus.*) in a flowing, graceful, style, like singing [It.].

can·ta·loupe, can·ta·loup (kan′·ta̤·lōp) *n.* a variety of muskmelon, having a furrowed rind [*Cantalupo*, a town in Italy].

can·tan·ker·ous (kan·tang′·ker·as) *a.* perverse; ill-natured; quarrelsome. **-ly** *adv.*

can·ta·ta (kan·tȧ′·ta̤) *n.* a short musical composition in oratorio or lyric drama form. **cantatrice, cantatrici** (kan′·ta̤·trēs, kan·tȧ··trē′·chā) a professional female singer [It.].

can·teen (kan·tēn′) *n.* a small container for carrying water; a store and refreshment-room in camps and barracks for soldiers, sailors, etc.; a similar place in a social or institutional club [It. *cantina*, a cellar].

can·ter (kan′·ter) *v.i.* to move at an easy gallop; *n.* an easy gallop or gait [fr. *Canterbury gallop*, easy pace of the pilgrims].

can·ti·cle (kan′·ti·kl) *n.* a little song; a non-metrical hymn. **Canticles** (*Bib.*) the Song of Songs [L. *canticulum*, a little song].

can·ti·lev·er (kan′·ti·lēv·er) *n.* a bracket for supporting a cornice or balcony. **cantilever bridge,** a bridge built on the same principle [fr. *cant*, an angle; Fr. *lever*, to raise].

can·to (kan′·tō) *n.* a division or part of a poem. **-r** *n.* a precentor; the leader of the singing, esp. in a synagogue [It. fr. L. *canere*, to sing].

can·ton (kan′·ta̤n) *n.* a small district (in Switzerland, administered by a separate government); a section of something; *v.t.* to divide into districts, as territory. **-al** *a.* **-ment** *n.* quarters for troops [Fr.].

can·vas (kan′·va̤s) *n.* a coarse cloth made of hemp, for sails, tents, etc.; the sails of a vessel; a special prepared material for painting on; painting [O.Fr. *canevas*; L. *cannabis*, hemp].

can·vass (kan′·va̤s) *v.t.* to sift; to examine

thoroughly; to solicit support, or votes, or contributions; *v.i.* to solicit votes; *n.* a close examination (by discussion); a scrutiny; solicitation; a seeking to obtain votes. **-er** *n.* [fr. *canvas* = to sift, as through canvas].

can·yon (kan′·yạn) *n.* a ravine; a deep gorge. Also **cañon** [Sp.].

cap (kap) *n.* a brimless covering, for the head; the top or highest point; a small lid used as a cover; *v.t.* to cover the top or end of; to surpass; (*University, etc.*) to confer a degree on; *pr.p.* **-ping.** *pa.p.* and *pa.t.* **-ped** [O.E. *cappe*, a hood].

ca·pa·ble (kā′·pạ·bl) *a.* competent; gifted; skillful. **capably** *adv.* **-ness** *n.* **capability** *n.* power [L. *capere*, to hold].

ca·pa·cious (kạ·pā′·shạs) *a.* roomy; spacious; **-ly** *adv.* **-ness** *n.* [L. *capere*, to hold].

ca·pac·i·ty (kạ·pas′·i·ti·) *n.* power of holding or grasping; room; volume; power of mind; character; ability; cubic content. **capacitate** *v.t.* to render capable [L. *capacitas*].

cap·à·pie (kap·ạ·pē′) *adv.* from head to foot [O.Fr. fr. L. *caput*, the head; *pes*, the foot].

ca·par·i·son (kạ·par′·ạ·sạn) *n.* a covering laid over a horse; trappings; harness; *v.t.* to cover with a decorated cloth; to adorn with rich dress [O.Fr. *caparasson*, preparation].

cape (kāp) *n.* a covering for the shoulders [L.L. *cappa*].

cape (kāp) *n.* a point of land running out into the sea; a headland [L. *caput*, the head].

ca·per (kā′·pẹr) *v.i.* to leap about like a goat, in a sprightly manner; to skip; to dance; to frolic; *n.* a frolicsome skip [L. *caper*, a goat].

ca·per (kā′·pẹr) *n.* a herb or shrub whose flower-buds when pickled in vinegar are used in sauces [Gk. *kapparis*].

cap·il·lar·y (kap′·ạ·ler·i·) *a.* resembling a hair; as fine as a hair; descriptive of the very fine bore of a tube or similar passage; *n.* one of the microscopic blood-vessels connecting the arteries and veins. **capillarity** *n.* **capilliform** *a.* hair-shaped [L. *capillus*, hair].

cap·i·tal (kap′·ạ·tạl) *a.* pert. to the head; involving the forfeiture of life; first in importance; chief; principal; excellent; *n.* (*Archit.*) the head of a column, pillaster, etc.; the city or town which is the seat of government in a state or nation; the estimated total value of a business, property, stock, etc.; ready money; — **punishment** *n.* the death penalty; **-ize** *n.* to take advantage of. **-ization** *n.* to provide with capital letters; to supply with capital [L. *caput*, the head].

cap·i·tal·ism (kap′·ạ·tạl·izm) *n.* form of economic, industrial, and social organization of society involving ownership, control, and direction of production by privately owned business organizations. **capitalist** *n.*

cap·i·ta·tion (kap·ạ·ta′·shạn) *n.* a census; a tax or grant per head [L. *capitatio*, a poll-tax].

Cap·i·tol (kap′·ạ·tạl) *n.* the temple of Jupiter in Rome; the building used by the U.S. Congress in Washington for its sessions; a state legislature building [L. *Capitolium*].

ca·pit·u·late (kạ·pit′·ū·lāt) *v.i.* to surrender; to draw up terms of an agreement. **capitulation** *n.* **capitulator** *n.* [L.L. *capitulare*, to draw up a treaty].

ca·pon (kā′·pạn) *n.* a young castrated cock fed for the table. **caponize** *v.t.* [O.E. *capun*].

ca·price (kạ·prēs′) *n.* illogical change of feeling or opinion; a whim; a fancy. **capricious** (kạ·pri′·shạs) *a.* [L. *caper*, a goat].

cap·si·cum (kap′·sạ·kạm) *n.* a genus of tropical plants, whose fruits when dried and ground give Cayenne pepper [L. *capsa*, a box].

cap·size (kap·sīz′) *v.t.* and *i.* to overturn.

cap·stan (kap′·stạn) *n.* a heavy cable-holder revolving on an upright spindle [L. *capistrum*, a halter].

cap·stone (kap′·stōn) *n.* a finishing stone.

cap·sule (kap′·sạl) *n.* the seed-vessel of a plant; a small gelatinous case containing medicine; a metal cap placed over the mouth of a corked bottle; *a.* condensed [L. *capsa*, a box].

cap·tain (kap′·tin) *n.* in the army, an officer commanding a company of infantry; in the navy, an officer in command of a man-of-war; the master of a merchant ship or other vessel; in sport, the leader of a team; *v.t.* to command; to lead. **-cy** *n.* the rank or commission of a captain [L. *caput*, the head].

cap·tion (kap′·shạn) *n.* the heading of a newspaper, chapter, page, etc.; the title of an illustration [fr. L. *capere*, to take].

cap·tious (kap′·shạs) *a.* apt to find fault; difficult to please. **-ly** *adv.* **-ness** *n.* fault-finding [L. *captiosus*, deceiving].

cap·ti·vate (kap′·tạ·vāt) *v.t.* to capture the fancy of. **captivating** *a.* winning, charming. **captivation** *n.* [L. *captivus*, captive].

cap·tive (kap′·tiv) *n.* a prisoner; one held in captivity; *a.* made prisoner. **captivity** *n.* imprisonment; bondage; servitude. **captor** *n.* one who takes a prisoner or a prize. **capture** *n.* the act of seizing by force or stratagem; arrest; the thing seized; the prize; *v.t.* to take captive; to take possession of [L. *capere*, to take].

Cap·u·chin (kap′·yoo·chin) *n.* a Franciscan monk (from the hood he wears); a hooded cloak for women; a hooded pigeon; a long-tailed S. American monkey. **capuche** (kạ-pòòsh′) *n.* a hood; a cowl [It. *cappucino*, a cow].

car (kär) *n.* any kind of vehicle on wheels; abbrev. for motor-car; automobile; the part of a balloon in which the aeronauts sit [L. *carrus*].

car·a·cole (kar′·a·kōl) *v.i.* to wheel [Sp.].

ca·rafe (kạ·räf′) *n.* a glass water-bottle or decanter [Fr.].

car·a·mel (kar′·a·mel) *n.* burnt sugar, used for coloring and in cooking; a kind of candy [Sp. *caramelo*].

car·at (kar′·ạt) *n.* a measure of weight for gold and precious stones, the standard carat being 3.16 grains troy [Gk. *keration*, a carob-tree seed].

car·a·van (kar′·a·van, kar·a·van′) *n.* parties of merchants, pilgrims, or others traveling together for greater security, esp. across deserts. **-eer** *n.* the leader of a caravan. **-sary, -serai** *n.* a large Eastern inn, with a court in the middle; a large inn [Pers. *karwan*].

car·a·vel (kar′·a·vel) *n.* a light sailing-ship. Also **carvel** [L. *carabus*, a wicker boat].

car·a·way (kar′·a·wā) *n.* a biennial aromatic plant; its seed, used as a flavoring for bread, cakes, etc. [Gk. *karon*].

car·bide (kär′·bīd) *n.* a compound of carbon with certain elements, including calcium, manganese, iron, etc. [L. *carbo*, coal].

car·bine, carabine (kär′·(a)·bīn) *n.* a short rifle. **carbineer, carabineer** *n.* a soldier armed with a carbine [etym. uncertain].

car·bo·hy·drate (kär·bō·hī′·drāt) *n.* a substance, such as sugar, starch, cellulose, etc. composed of carbon, hydrogen, and oxygen [L. *carbo*, coal; Gk. *hudo*, water].

car·bol·ic (kär·bál′·ik) *a.* derived from carbon; *n.* carbolic acid. **carbolated** *a.* treated with or containing carbolic acid. **carbolic acid,** a poisonous acid distilled from coal tar [L. *carbo*, coal].

car·bon (kär′·bạn) *n.* a non-metallic element existing pure in nature as diamond, graphite, charcoal, etc. and as a compound of animal and vegetable substances; a thin rod of hard carbon used in an electric arc-lamp; a copy made by using carbon paper. **-aceous** (kär.bạn.ā′.shus) *a.* pert. to, or composed of, coal. **-ize** *v.t.* to make into carbon; to coat with carbon. **-ization** *n.* — **paper,** type of paper used for duplicating written work [L. *carbo*, coal]. carbon dioxide. **-d** *a.* **carbonation** *n.*

car·bo·run·dum (cär·bạ·run′·dạm) *n.* silicon

carbide, a black, crystalline substance, of exceptional hardness.

car·boy (kàr'·boi) *n.* a large, globular glass bottle, encased in basket-work [Pers. *garabah*].

car·bun·cle (kàr'·bung·kl) *n.* a variety of garnet; an inflamed bunion or boil. **carbuncular** *a.* [L. *carbunculus*, a small coal].

car·bu·ret·or (kàr'·ba·rā·tẹr) *n.* an apparatus in an internal-combustion engine to convert liquid gasoline into vaporized form. **carburation** *n.* **carburize** *v.t.*, cause to unite with carbon [L. *carbo*, coal].

car·cass, carcase (kàr'·kas) *n.* the dead body of man or animal, esp. of the latter; the framework or shell of anything [It. *carcassa*, the framework of a ship, etc.].

car·ci·no·ma (kàr·si·nō'·ma) *n.* a cancer.

card (kàrd) *n.* pasteboard; a small piece of pasteboard often with figures, pictures, etc. on it for playing games; a piece of pasteboard having on it a person's name and address; an ornamented piece of paper or cardboard with a greeting, such as a birthday card; (*Slang*) a humorous fellow. **-board** *n.* finely finished pasteboard. **-sharp** *n.* one who cheats at cards [L. *charta*, paper].

card (kàrd) *n.* a toothed instrument for combing wool, flax, etc.; *v.t.* to comb, as wool, flax, etc. **-er** *n.* one who cards [L. *carduus*, a thistle].

car·di·ac See **cardio-**

car·di·gan (kàr'·di·gan) *n.* a knitted jacket or jacketlike sweater [fr. an Earl of *Cardigan*].

car·di·nal (kàr'·di·nal) *a.* chief; main; of great importance; fundamental; (*Color*) deep scarlet. **-ly** *adv.* — **numbers**, 1, 2, 3, 4, 5, etc. [L. *cardo*, a hinge].

car·di·nal (kàr'·di·nal) *n.* the highest rank next to the Pope, in the Catholic Church. **-ate**, **-ship** *n.* the office of a cardinal [L. *cardo*, a hinge].

car·di·o- (kàr'·di·a) *prefix* from Gk. *kardia*, the heart, combining to form derivatives. **cardiac** *a.* pert. to the heart; *n.* a heart stimulant. **-gram** *n.* the graphic tracing of the movements of the heart as recorded by an instrument called the **cardiograph. cardiology** *n.* (*Med.*) the branch of medicine which deals with the functions and diseases of the heart.

care (ker, kär) *n.* concern or anxiety; an object of anxiety; pains or heed; caution; charge or oversight; trouble; grief (formerly); *v.i.* to be anxious, concerned; to be affected with solicitude; to have a fondness (with *for*). **-ful** *a.* full of care or solicitude; cautious or watchful; painstaking. **-fully** *adv.* **-fulness** *n.* **-less** *a.* heedless; thoughtless; regardless. **-lessly** *adv.* **-lessness** *n.* **-worn** *a.* showing the wearing effects of care. **-taker** *n.* one who takes over the care of anything or anyone [O.E. *caru*].

ca·reen (ka·rēn') *v.t.* to turn a ship over on one side; *v.i.* to lean over [L. *carina*, a keel].

ca·reer (ka·rēr') *n.* rapid motion; a course of action; profession; conduct in life, or progress through life; *v.i.* to speed along; to rush wildly. **-ist** *n.* one who makes his personal advancement his one aim in life [Fr. *carrière*, orig. a chariot course].

ca·ress (ka·res') *v.t.* to treat with affection; to fondle; to kiss; *n.* a loving touch; an embrace. **-ing** *a.* [L. *carus*, dear].

car·et (kar'·at, kā'·rat) *n.* a mark (ʌ) which shows where something should be inserted [L. *caret*, is wanting].

car·go (kàr'·gō) *n.* the freight of a ship; the goods or merchandise carried [Sp. fr. *cargar*, to load].

car·i·bou (kar'·i·boö) *n.* the N. American reindeer [Canadian Fr.].

car·i·ca·ture (kar'·i·ka·cher) *n.* a ludicrous exaggeration (usually in picture form) of peculiar personal characteristics; *v.t.* to exaggerate or distort, in words or in pictorial form. **caricaturist** *n.* [It. *caricare*, to load].

car·ies (kār'·ēz) *n.* decay of bone, teeth, etc.

car·i·ous *a.* [L.].

car·il·lon (kar'·i·làn, ka·ril'·yan) *n.* a set or peal of bells of different tones; a melody played on such bells [Fr.].

car·i·ole (kar'·i·ōl) *n.* a small, open, two-wheeled carriage or light cart. Also **carriole** [L. *carrus*].

Car·mel·ite (kàr'·mel·īt) *n.* a begging friar of the order of Our Lady of Mount Carmel, established in the 12th cent. [fr. Mount *Carmel*].

car·mine (kàr'·min, mīn) *n.* a brilliant crimson, prepared from cochineal. Also *a.* [Fr. or Sp. *carmin*].

car·nage (kàr'·nij) *n.* slaughter; massacre; bloodshed [L. *caro, carnis*, flesh].

car·nal (kàr'·nal) *a.* pert. to the flesh; sensual; animal; worldly; material, as opposed to spiritual. **-ize** *v.t.* to make carnal. **carnality** *n.* fleshly lust. **-ly** *adv.* — **knowledge**, sexual intercouse [L. *caro, carnis*, flesh].

car·na·tion (kàr·nā'·shan) *n.* a flesh-color; a variety of the clove-pink, noted for its beauty and sweet scent [L. *carnatio*, fleshiness].

car·nel·ian (kàr·nēl'·yan) *n.* a variety of light-red chalcedony, used for jewelry. Also **cornelian** [L. *cornu*, horn].

car·ni·val (kàr'·na·val) *n.* a traveling show with amusements such as merry-go-rounds, etc. [L. *carnem levare*, to take away flesh].

car·niv·o·ra (kàr·niv'·a·ra) *n.pl.* animals that feed on flesh. **carnivore** (kàr'·ni·vōr) *n.* a flesh-eating animal. **carnivorous** *a.* **carnivorously** *adv.* **carnivorousness** *n.* [L. *caro, carnis*, flesh; *vorare*, to devour].

car·ol (kar'·al) *n.* a song of joy, esp. a Christmas hymn; *v.i.* to sing a carol [O.Fr. *carole*].

ca·rot·id (ka·ràt'·id) *n.* each of the two main arteries in the neck conveying blood to the head; *a.* pert. to these [Gk. *karōtides*].

ca·rouse (ka·rouz') *v.i.* to revel; to drink deeply; to hold a drinking-party. **carousal** *n.* a noisy drinking-party. **-r** *n.* [O.Fr. *carous*, fr. Ger. *gar aus* (drink) right to the bottom (of the glass)].

car·ou·sel See **carrousel**.

carp (kàrp) *v.i.* to catch at small faults or errors; to find fault petulantly and without reason [O.N. *karpa*, to chatter].

carp (kàrp) *n.* a fresh-water fish [Fr. *carpe*].

car·pel (kàr'·pal) *n.* (*Bot.*) the seed-bearing part of a plant; part of a compound ovary. **-lary** *a.* [Gk. *karpos*, fruit].

car·pen·ter (kàr'·pan·tẹr) *n.* a worker in lumber as used in building of houses, ships, etc. **carpentry** *n.* [L.L. *carpentarius*, a cartwright]

car·pet (kàr'·pit) *n.* a woven or felted covering for floors; **-ing** *n.* a covering similar to a carpet. **-bag** *n.* a 19th cent. traveling bag made of carpet. **-bagger** *n.* a political adventurer. [L.L. *carpita*, patchwork].

car·ra·way See **caraway**.

car·riage (kar'·ij) *n.* the act of carrying passengers or goods; the cost of carrying; a vehicle for passengers; a wheeled or moving support or conveyor; one's posture or bearing; conduct. **-able** (kar'·ij·a·bl) *a.* carriable; passable for carriages [O.Fr. *cariage*, luggage].

car·ri·er (kar'·i·ẹr) *n.* one who carries; one who carries goods for hire, often called a 'common carrier'; a receptacle for carrying objects; a pigeon used for carrying messages; (*Med.*) one who, without showing symptoms of disease, can convey infection to others [O.Fr. *carier*, to loa].

car·ri·ole See **cariole**.

car·ri·on (kar'·i·an) *n.* dead, rotting flesh; anything putrid [L. *caro*, flesh].

car·rot (kar'·at) *n.* a plant cultivated for its edible root. **-y** *a.* reddish-yellow; red-haired [L. *carota*].

car·rou·sel, car·ou·sel (kar·a·sel') *n.* a merry-go-round; military ornament [Fr.].

car·ry (kar'·i·) *v.t.* to convey; to transport; to

impel; to transfer; to obtain possession of by
force; to behave; *v.i.* to reach, of a projectile;
n. range. [O.Fr. *carier* fr. *car*, a vehicle].

cart (kàrt) *n.* a two-wheeled vehicle used for
the transport of heavy goods; a small four-
wheeled vehicle pulled by hand; *v.t.* to convey
in a cart. **-age** *n.* carting; the price paid for
carting. **-er** *n.* **-wright** *n.* builder or maker of
carts [O.N. *kartr*, a cart].

carte blanche (kàrt·blànsh) *n.* full authority.

car·tel (kàr'·tel) *n.* an international industrial
combination for regulating volume and price
of output; a trust; an agreement between
states at war for exchange of prisoners; a
challenge [Fr. fr. L. *cartello*].

car·ti·lage (kàr'·ti·lij) *n.* (Anat.) gristle; a
strong, transparent tissue in the body, very
elastic and softer than bone. **cartilaginous**
(kàr·ti·la'·ji·nạs) *a.* [L. *cartilago*, gristle].

car·tog·ra·phy (kàr·tàg'·ra·fi·) *n.* the art of
making charts or maps. **cartographer** *n.* [L.
charta, chart; Gr. *graphein*, to draw].

car·ton (kàr'·tạn) *n.* a pasteboard box [Fr.
carton, pasteboard].

car·toon (kàr·tòòn') *n.* a design drawn on
strong paper for transference to mosaics, tapestries, frescoes, etc.; an illustration treating
current affairs in an amusing fashion; a pictorial caricature; a comic strip; movie comics.
-ist *n.* [Fr. *carton*, pasteboard].

car·tridge (kàr'·trij) *n.* a case made of metal,
cardboard, etc. to contain the charge for a gun.
[Fr. *cartouche*, fr. L. *charta*, paper].

carve (kàrv) *v.t.* and *i.* to fashion artistically
by cutting; to hew out, as a path, a career,
etc.; to cut in pieces or slices, as meat, etc.; to
divide. **-r** *n.* one who carves; a large knife for
carving. **carving** *n.* [O.E. *ceorfan*].

car·y·at·id (kar·i·at'·id) *n.* (*Archit.*) a draped,
female figure used in place of a column.
caryatides (kar·i·at'·i·dēz) [Gk. *Karuatis*,
a woman of *Caryae* in Laconia].

cas·cade (kas·kàd') *n.* a waterfall; anything
resembling this; a wavy fall of lace; *v.i.* to fall
in cascades [L. *cadere*, to fall].

cas·car·a (kas-ke'·rạ) *n.* **cascara sagrada**,
a fluid extracted from dried California buckthorn bark and used as a laxative [Sp. *cascara*, bark; *sagrada*, sacred].

case (kās) *n.* a receptacle; a covering; a sheath;
anything which encloses or contains; a box and
its contents; a set; (*Print.*) a frame for holding
type; *v.t.* to put in a case. **casing** *n.* a case or
covering. **-room** *n.* (*Print.*) the room in which
type is set. **— shot** *n.* canister shot; small projectiles put in cases or canisters, to be shot
from cannon. **-harden** *v.t.* to heat soft steel
in contact with carbonaceous material, so that
carbon is absorbed, and a surface of harder
steel produced. **lower case** (*Print.*) denoting
small letters. **upper case** (*Print.*) denoting
capital letters [O.Fr. *casse*].

case (kās) *n.* an event, occurrence, or circumstance; a state or condition of things or persons; a question of facts or principles requiring
investigation or solution; (*Med.*) a patient under treatment; (*Gram.*) an inflection or terminal change in nouns, pronouns, etc. **casal** *a.*
(*Gram.*) pert. to case [L. *cadere*, to fall].

ca·se·in (kā'·si·in) *n.* the curd or cheesy part
of milk; a protein [L. *caseus*, cheese].

case·ment (kās'·ment) *n.* a window-frame; a
window, or part of a window, opening on
hinges [fr. *encase*].

cash (kash) *n.* money, esp. ready money; coin;
also, paper-money, bank-note, etc.; *v.t.* to turn
into, or exchange for, money. **—register** *n.* an
automatic money-till which registers and indicates the amount paid for goods sold [O.Fr.
casse, a box].

cash·ew (ka'·shòò) *n.* a tropical American
tree whose fruit, the cashew-nut, is eaten raw
or roasted [Fr. *acajou*].

cash·ier (kash·ir') *n.* one who has charge of
the cash [O.Fr. *casse*, a box].

cash·ier (kash·ir') *v.t.* to dismiss from office in
disgrace; to discard [Fr. *casser*, to annul, to
dismiss].

cash·mere (kash'·mir) *n.* a shawl made from
the hair of the Kashmir (Cashmere) goat; the
material; *a.* [fr. *Cashmere*, in India].

ca·si·no (kạ·sē'·nō) *n.* a public assembly-room
or building for dancing, gambling, etc. [It.
casino, a little house].

cask (kask) *n.* a large wooden vessel for holding liquor; a barrel; *v.t.* to put in a cask [Sp.
casco, a potsherd, a cask].

cas·ket (kas'·kit) *n.* a coffin; a small cask or
case; a small box..   [*casco*, a helmet].

casque (kask) *n.* a sort of military helmet [Sp.

cas·se·role (kas'·ạ·rōl) *n.* a covered baking
dish in which food is both cooked and served;
a food mixture cooked in such a dish [Fr.].

cas·sia (kash'·ạ) *n.* a genus of plants, including senna, whose pods are used medicinally as
a laxative; a cheap kind of cinnamon [L. *casia*].

cas·si·mere (kas'·ạ·mir) *n.* a thin twilled,
wollen cloth [form of *cashmere*].

cas·sock (kas'·ạk) *n.* a long, close-fitting black
gown worn by clergymen [Fr. *casaque*].

cast (kast) *v.t.* to fling; to hurl; to direct or
bestow, as a glance; to project, as a shadow;
to shed, as a skin; to reckon or compute (with
up); to shape in a mold (as metal); to distribute
the parts of a play among the actors; to throw
a line in angling; to forecast (to cast a horoscope); to let down (an anchor); to give (a
vote); to give birth prematurely; *n.* the act of
casting; a throw; the distance a thing is thrown;
a mold or form; a change of direction; that
which is shed or ejected; a reckoning; a forecast; the actors appearing in a play; expression (of the face); squint (of the eye). **—
down** *a.* depressed. **-ing** *n.* an article cast in
a mold; the act of foundling and molding.
-ing-vote *n.* the vote of a chairman, which
decides a question when votes are equally divided. **—iron** *a.* made of cast iron; rigid; indefatigable; unshakable; (*Slang*) irrefutable
[O.N. *kasta*].

cas·ta·nets (kas'·tạ·nets) *n.pl.* two small concave shells of ivory or hard wood, fastened to
the thumb and clicked in time to dances and
music of a Spanish type [L. *castanea*, a chest-
nut-tree].

cast·a·way (kast'·ạ·wā) *n.* a shipwrecked
person; an outcast [fr. to *cast away*].

caste (kast) *n.* an exclusive social order [L.
castus, pure].

cas·tel·lat·ed (kas'·tạ·lā·tạd) *a.* adorned with
turrets and battlements like a castle [L. *cas-
tellatus*].

cast·er, castor (kas'·tẹr) *n.* a small bottle
with perforated top for sugar, pepper, etc.; a
stand for a set of such bottles; a small swivelled
wheel on the foot of a chair-leg, etc. [fr. *cast*].

cas·ti·gate (kas'·tạ·gāt) *v.t.* to correct; to rebuke severely; to chastise; to punish. **castigation** *n.* severe chastisement; discipline.
castigator *n.* [L. *castigare*, to punish].

castle (kas'·l) *n.* a fortified residence; a stronghold, esp. of nobleman; any imposing mansion;
a piece (also called rook) in chess. **-d** *a.* having
a castle; built like a castle [L. *castellum*].

cas·tor (kas'·tẹr) *n.* the beaver; a hat made
of beaver fur. See **caster** [Gk. *kastor*].

cas·tor-oil (kas'·tẹr·oil) *n.* an oil used as a
cathartic.

cas·trate (kas'·trāt) *v.t.* to deprive of the
testicles; to emasculate; to render incapable of
generation; to render imperfect. **castration**
n. [L. *castrare*].

cas·u·al (kazh'·òò·ạl) *a.* accidental; incidental;
occasional; offhand or careless; *n.* a casual or
occasional worker, etc. **-ly** *adv.* **-ness** *n.* **-ty** *n.*
an accident, mishap. **-ties** *n.pl.* (*Mil.*) losses

caused by death, wounds, capture, etc. [L. *casuc*, accident, chance].

cas·u·ist (kazh'·o͝o·ist) *n.* one versed in casuistry. **-ry** *n.* the science of dealing with problems of right or wrong conduct by applying principles drawn from the Scriptures, etc.; the use of specious reasoning and fallacious argument, esp. on matters of morals. **casuistic, casuistical** *a.* **casuistically** *adv.* [Fr. *casuiste*].

cat (kat) *n.* a small domestic quadruped, of the family of felines; the undomesticated cat, usually called wild-cat; related carnivores such as the lion, tiger, leopard, lynx, etc.; a spiteful woman; strong tackle used to hoist an anchor; *v.t.* and *i.* to hoist an anchor. **-ty, -tish** *a.* spiteful. **-bird** *n.* a gray N. Am. songbird having a cry similar to a cat's mew. — **burglary,** a burglar who makes his entry by climbing to windows, roofs, etc. **-call** *n.* a cat-like cry, used by audiences to express disapproval. **—eyed** *a.* able to see in the dark. — **nap** *n.* a very short, light sleep. **-'s-eye** *n.* a gem with reflections like those from a cat's eye. **cat's-paw** *n.* a dupe of another; (*Naut.*) a light breeze. **cat-o-nine-tails** *n.* a whip with nine thongs or lashes. **tabby cat,** a female cat; a striped cat. **tom cat,** a male cat [O.E. *catt*].

cat·a- (kat'·a) a combining form fr. Gk. *kata,* meaning down, away, against, fully, used to form derivatives.

cat·a·chre·sis (kat·a·krē'·sis) (*Rhet.*) a figure by which one word is wrongly used for another [Gk. *katachresis,* misuse].

cat·a·clysm (kat'·a·klizm) *n.* a social or political upheaval; a catastrophe; a sudden and violent alteration in earth's surface. **-al** *a.* **-ic** *a.* [Gk. *kata,* down; *kluzein,* to wash over].

cat·a·combs (kat'·a·kōmz) *n.pl.* underground passageways with niches for tombs [Gr. *kata,* down; *kumbē,* a cavity].

cat·a·falque (kat'·a·falk) *n.* a structure on which a coffin is placed for a lying-in-state [It.]

cat·a·lec·tic (kat·a·lek'·tik) *a.* lacking a syllable at the end of a verse; applied to an incomplete foot in prosody [Gk. *kata,* down; *legein,* to stop].

cat·a·lep·sy (kat'·a·lep·si·) *n.* (*Med.*) suspension of senses and bodily powers, with muscular rigidity; a trance. **cataleptic** *a.* [Gk. *kata,* down; *lēpsis,* a seizure].

cat·a·logue (kat'·a·lawg) *n.* a list, usually alphabetical, of names, books, goods, etc.; a descriptive price-list; also **catalog.** *v.t.* to make such a list. **-r** *n.* [Gk. *kata,* throughout; *legein,* to choose].

ca·tal·y·sis (ka·tal'·a·sis) *n.* (*Chem.*) the chemical change effected in one substance by the aid of another which itself undergoes no change. **catalyst** *n.* a substance producing such a change. **catalytic** *a.* [Gk. *kata,* down; *lusis,* a loosening].

cat·a·ma·ran (kat·a·ma·ran') *n.* a raft consisting of pieces of wood lashed together; a craft with twin parallel hulls; (*Colloq.*) a quarrelsome person [Tamil = a tied tree].

cat·a·pult (kat'·a·pult) *n.* a siege engine for hurling stones, arrows, etc.; a device for launching airplanes from the deck of a ship; *v.t.* [Gk. *kata,* against; *pallein,* to hurl].

cat·a·ract (kat'·a·rakt) *n.* a waterfall; the flow of a large body of water over a precipice; a torrent; (*Med.*) a disease of the eye, characterized by an opaque condition in the lens [Gk. *katarrhaktēs*].

ca·tarrh (ka·tár') *n.* (*Med.*) inflammation of the mucous membranes of the body. **-al** *a.* [Gk. *katarrhein,* to flow down].

ca·tas·ta·sis (ka·tas'·ta·sis) *n.* part of drama where action has reached its height [Gk.].

ca·tas·tro·phe (ka·tas'·tra·fe) *n.* a disaster; a calamity; a decisive event in drama; the denouement; the culmination. **catastrophic** *a.* *katastrophē,* an overturning].

catch (kach) *v.t.* to take hold of; to seize; to grasp; to arrest; to trap; to get a disease by infection or contagion; to detect; to understand; to come upon unexpectedly; *v.i.* to seize, and keep hold; to grasp at; *pa.t.* and *pa.p.* **caught** (kawt) *n.* a seizure; anything that holds, stops, etc.; that which is caught; a sudden advantage; gain; the total amount of fish taken by a fisherman; a form of musical composition (a round). **-able** *a.* able to be caught. **-er** *n.* **-ing** *a.* **-y** *a.* containing a hidden difficulty; (*Mus.*) (usually of light music) captivating; attractive. **-all** *n.* a receptacle for miscellaneous objects [L. *capere,* to take].

catch·fly (kach'·fli) *n.* the name of certain plants to whose stems insects adhere.

catch·ment (kach'·ment) *n.* drainage area [fr. *catch*].

catch·pen·ny (kach'·pen·i·) *n.* something of little value and usually showy, made to sell quickly; *a.* cheap and showy.

catch·up, catsup, ketchup (kach'ap, kat'·sap, kech'·ap) *n.* a bottled sauce made from tomatoes, vinegar, sugar and spices [E. Ind.].

catch·word (kach'·wurd) *n.* a word or short phrase that takes the popular fancy; a slogan; (*Theat.*) an actor's cue; the first word in the column of a dictionary, etc., repeated above the column as a reference.

cat·e·chize (kat'·e·kiz) *v.t.* to instruct by question and answer, esp. in Christian doctrine; to question; to examine orally. **catechism** (kat'·e·kizm) *n.* a set form of question and answer to teach the tenets of religion; a book containing this system. **catechist** *n.* one who catechizes. **catechetical** *a.* consisting of question and answer. **catechetically** *adv.* **catechesis** (kat'a·kē'·sis) *n.* oral instruction as given to catechumens [Gk. *katēchizein,* to teach by word of mouth].

cat·e·chu·men (kat·a·kū'·man) *n.* one being instructed in the fundamentals of a subject, esp. religion [See **catechize**].

cat·e·go·ry (kat'·a·gōr·i·) *n.* a class, group, or division; in logic, any fundamental conception. **categorical** *a.* pert. to a category; admitting no conditions; absolute; precise. **categorically** *adv.* **categorize** *v.t.* to place in a category [Gk. *katēgoria,* an assertion].

ca·te·na (ka·tē'·na) *n.* a chain; a series of connected things. **catenate** *v.t.* to connect in a series of links. **catenary** (ka'·ta·ne·ri·) *n.* the curve of a chain, wire, etc., hanging freely between two supports. **catenation** *n.* [L. = a chain].

ca·ter (kā'·ter) *v.i.* to buy or procure food; to provide food, entertainment, etc. **-er** *n.* [O.Fr. *acat,* a purchase].

cat·er·cor·nered (kat'·a·kàwrn'·erd) *a.* diagonal [F. *quatre,* four, cornered].

cat·er·pil·lar (kat'·er·pil·er) *n.* the grub or larva of butterflies and moths [O.Fr. *chatepelose,* lit. a hairy cat].

cat·er·waul (kat'·er·wawl) *v.i.* to cry like cats in heat [E. *cat,* and imit. sound].

ca·thar·tic (ka·thár'·tik) *a.* (*Med.*) purgative; cleansing the bowels; *n.* a purging medicine. **catharize** *v.t.* to cleanse; to purify. **catharsis** *n.* purgation, also of the emotions, through art [Gk. *katharos,* pure].

Ca·thay (ka·thā') *n.* an old name for China or Chinese Tartary.

ca·the·dral (ka·thē'·dral) *n.* the principal church in a diocese, which contains the bishop's throne; *a.* pert. to a cathedral [Gk. *kata,* down; *hedra,* a seat].

cath·ode (kath'·ōd) *n.* the negative pole of an electric cell; the conductor by which an electric current leaves an electrolyte, and passes over to the negative pole; opp. of *anode.* — **rays,** negative ions or electrons [Gk. *kathodos,* descent].

cath·o·lic (kath'·a·lik) *a.* universal; embracing

all Christians; pert. to Roman Catholics; liberal or comprehensive in understanding and sympathies; *n.* a member of the Church Universal, or of the R.C. Church. **catholicism** (kạ·thǎl'·-ạ·sizm) *n.* the faith and practice of Catholic Church, or of R.C. Church; breadth of view; liberality of opinion; catholicity. **catholicity** (·lis·ạ·ti·) *n.* [Gk. *katholikos*, general].

cat·nip (kat'·nip) *n.* an aromatic plant with blue flowers, attractive to cats [*cat* and *mint*].

cat·sup See **catchup**.

cat·tle (kat'·tl) *n.pl.* domestic livestock, esp. cows and bulls [L.L. *capitale*, stock.]

Cau·ca·sian (kaw·kā'·zhạn) *a.* belonging to *Caucasia;* Indo-European, i.e. pert. to the white race. *n.* [fr. the *Caucasus*, mountains near the Black Sea].

cau·cus (kaw'·kạs) *n.* a meeting of leaders of a political party to decide policies, etc.

cau·dal (kaw'·dal) *a.* pert. to a tail. **caudate** *a.* having a tail [L. *cauda*].

cau·dle (kaw'·dl) *n.* a warm drink for invalids [L. *calidus*, hot].

caught (kawt) *pa.p.* and *pa.t.* of **catch**.

caul (kawl) *n.* a net, etc. worn on the head; the membrane covering the head of some babies at birth [etym. unknown].

caul·dron See **caldron**.

cau·li·flow·er (kaw'·lạ·flou·ẹr) *n.* a variety of cabbage [L. *caulis*, a stalk, and *flower*].

caulk See **calk**.

cau·sal (kaw'·zạl) *a.* relating to a cause or causes. **causality** *n.* the manner in which a cause works; the relation of cause and effect. **causation** *n.* agency by which an effect is produced. **causative** *a.* [L. *causa*, cause].

cause (kawz) *n.* that which produces a result or effect; the origin or motive of an action; an action or lawsuit in court; principle supported by a person or party; *v.t.* to produce; to be the occasion of; to induce. **-r** *n.* **-less** *a.* without reason or motive [L. *causa*].

cau·se·rie (kō'·zạ·rē) *n.* a chat; an informal article or essay [Fr. = a talk].

cause·way (kawz'·wā) *n.* a raised paved road [L.L. *calciata*, trodden, fr. *calx*, a heel].

caus·tic (kaws'·tik) *a.* burning; (*Fig.*) biting, bitter, satirical; *n.* a substance that corrodes and destroys animal tissue. **-ally** *adv.* **causticity** *n.* [Gk. *kaustos*, burned].

cau·ter (kaw'·tẹr) *n.* a hot, searing iron. **-ize** *v.t.* to burn or sear animal tissue in order to destroy diseased tissue, or promote healing. **-ization** *n.* **-y** *n.* the act of cauterizing; a hot iron for searing [Gk. *kautērion*, a branding-iron].

cau·tion (kaw'·shạn) *n.* carefulness; prudence; wariness; a warning; (*Colloq.*) an odd or droll person; *v.t.* to advise to take care; to warn or admonish. **cautious** *a.* wary; prudent; discreet. **cautiously** *adv.* **-ary** *a.* containing a warning. **-er** *n.* [L. *cavere, cautum*, to beware].

cav·al·cade (kav'·al·kād') *n.* procession on horseback [L.L. *caballus*, a horse].

cav·a·lier (kav·a·lir') *n.* a horseman; a knight; a gallant; an attendant escort to a lady; *a.* gay and offhand; supercilious; haughty and discourteous. **-ly** *adv.* [L.L. *caballus*, a horse].

cav·al·ry (kav'·al·ri·) *n.* horse-soldiery [L.L. *caballus*, a horse].

cave (kāv) *n.* a small chamber hollowed out of the earth horizontally, either by nature or by man; a den. — **man** *n.* a very masculine male of primitive ways. **to cave in** (of ground) to fall in, to subside; (*Fig.*) to yield; to admit defeat [L. *cavus*, hollow].

ca·ve·at (kā'·vi·at) *n.* a warning; a legal notice to stop proceedings [L. = let him beware, fr. *cavere*, to beware].

cav·en·dish (kav'·ạn·dish) *n.* tobacco, softened and pressed into plugs [fr. *Cavendish*, the first maker].

cav·ern (kav'·ẹrn) *n.* a deep, hollow place under the earth; a large dark cave. **-ed** *a.* full of caverns. **-ous** *a.* hollow; deep-set [L. *caverna*].

cav·i·ar, caviare (kav'·i·är) *n.* a delicacy made from the roes of the sturgeon [Turk.].

cav·il (kav'·il) *v.i.* (with 'at') to raise frivolous objections; to find fault unreasonably. *n.* a frivolous objection. **-er** *n.* [L. *cavilla*, raillery].

cav·i·ty (kav'·i·ti·) *n.* a hole; a hollow place of any size [L. *cavus*, hollow].

ca·vort (kạ·vawrt') *v.i.* (*Colloq.*) to prance; to frisk about [etym. uncertain].

caw (kaw) *v.i.* to cry like a crow or raven; *n.* the sound made by the crow, rook, or raven.

cay·enne (kā·yen') *n.* a pungent red pepper [fr. *Cayenne*, in S. America].

cease (sēs) *v.t.* to put a stop to; *v.i.* to stop; to discontinue. **-less** *a.* without stopping. **-lessly** *adv.* [L. *cessare*, to cease].

ce·dar (sē'·dẹr) *n.* species of coniferous, evergreen trees yielding durable, fragrant wood. **-n, cedrine** *a.* [Gk. *kedros*].

cede (sēd) *v.t.* to yield; to surrender; to give up, esp. of territory [L. *cedere*].

ce·dil·la (sạ·dil'·ạ) *n.* a small sign (ç), used, principally in French, as a pronunciation mark. It is placed under 'c', when followed by a, o, or u, to indicate that the 's' sound is to be used [Gk. *zēta*, z].

ceil·ing (sē'·ling) *n.* the interior part of the roof of a room; the maximum height to which a particular airplane can ascend; (*Fig.*) the upper limit of production, wages, prices, etc. [Fr. *ciel*, the sky].

cel·e·brate (sel'·ạ·brāt) *v.t.* to make famous; to mark by ceremony, as an event or festival; to observe with solemn rites. **-d** *a.* renowned; famous. **celebration** *n.* the act of celebrating. **celebrant** *n.* one who celebrates. **celebrity** (sạ·leb'·rạ·ti·) *n.* renown; fame; a person of distinction [L. *celebrare*].

ce·ler·i·ty (sạ·ler'·ạ·ti·) *n.* rapidity of motion; speed; swiftness [L. *celer*, swift].

cel·er·y (sel'·ẹr·i·) *n.* an edible plant cultivated for eating with salads or as a cooked vegetable [Fr. *céléri*, fr. Gk. *selinon*, parsley].

ce·les·ta (sạ·les'·tạ) *n.* (*Mus.*) a small piano-like instrument [Fr.].

ce·les·tial (sạ·les'·chạl) *a.* heavenly; divine; blessed; *n.* an inhabitant of heaven. **-ly** *adv.* [L. *caelum*, heaven].

cel·i·ba·cy (sel'·ạ·bạ·si·) *n.* single life; the unmarried state. **celibate** *n.* one unmarried; *a.* unmarried [L. *caelebs*, unmarried].

cell (sel) *n.* a small room, as in a prison or monastery; a small cavity; the simplest unit in the structure of living matter; a small group of members of a political party; a division of a voltaic or galvanic battery. **-ed** (seld) *a.* furnished with, or containing, cells; contained in cells. **-ular** *a.* consisting of, or containing, cells, as cellular tissue. **-ulated** *a.* having a cellular structure [L. *cella*, a small room].

cel·lar (sel'·ẹr) *n.* an underground room, the lowest story under a building; a storeroom, esp. for wines, liquors. [L. *cellarium*, a pantry].

cel·lo, 'cel·lo (chel'·ō) *n.* (*Mus.*) a contraction for violoncello, a stringed musical instrument. **cellist, 'cellist** *n.* a player on the violoncello.

cel·lo·phane (sel'·ạ·fān) *n.* a tough, transparent, waterproof material used as wrapping tissue, etc. [Trade Name].

cel·lu·loid (sel'·yạ·loid) *n.* name for a hard compound used in the manufacture of imitation ivory, coral, amber, etc. [L. *cellula*, a little cell].

cel·lu·lose (sel'·yạ·lōs) *n.* a chemical substance, one of the carbohydrates, forming the chief constituent of the walls of plant cells; an essential part of wood, paper, linen, cotton, etc. [L. *cellula*, a little cell].

Celt, Kelt (selt, kelt) *n.* one of a race, including the Highlanders of Scotland, the Irish, Welsh, Bretons, Manx, and Cornish. **Celtic, Keltic** *n.* the language spoken by the Celts. *a.* pert. to the Celts [L. *Celticus*].

ce·ment (sa̤·ment′) *n.* a plastic mixture that can unite two bodies; mortar; a material used in making concrete for building or paving; a bond or union; *v.t.* to unite by using cement; to join closely. **-ation** *n.* the act of cementing; the conversion of iron into steel [L. *caementum*, stone for building].

cem·e·ter·y (sem′·a̤·ter·i·) *n.* a graveyard; a burying ground [Gk. *koimētērion*, a sleeping-room].

ce·no·bite, coenobite (sē′·na̤·bīt) *n.* member of a religious order, dwelling in community [Gk. *koinos*, common; *bios*, life].

cen·o·taph (sen′·a̤·taf) *n.* a monument erected to one buried elsewhere; an empty sepulcher [Gk. *kenos*, empty, *taphos*, a tomb].

Cen·o·zo·ic (sēn·a̤·zō′·ik) *a.* (*Geol.*) belonging to the third or Tertiary period; the present period of geologic time. Also **Cainozoic** [Gk. *kainos*, recent; *zōe*, life].

cen·ser (sen′·ser) *n.* a metal vessel in which incense is burned. **cense** *v.t.* to perfume with incense [L. *incendere*, to burn].

cen·sor (sen′·ser) *n.* a Roman official who looked after property, taxes, and the people's morals; one appointed to examine books, plays, newspaper articles, etc. before publication, and ban them if containing anything objectionable; also, in time of war or crisis, to examine letters, etc., and erase anything calculated to convey information to the enemy; one who blames or finds fault; *v.t.* to blame or reprove; to subject to examination by the censor. **-ial** *a.* pert. to correction of morals; pert. to a censor. **-ious** *a.* apt to find fault. **-iously** *adv.* **-iousness** *n.* **-ship** *n.* the office of a censor; the act of censoring [L. *censere*, to estimate].

cen·sure (sen′·sher) *n.* the act of finding fault; disapproval; *v.t.* to reprove; to express disapproval of; to criticize adversely. **censurable** *a.* [L. *censura*, opinion].

cen·sus (sen′·sa̤s) *n.* an official numbering of the inhabitants of a country. **censual** *a.* [L. *census*, register].

cent (sent) *n.* a hundredth, as 10 per *cent;* a U.S. coin worth the hundredth part of a dollar [L. *centum*].

cen·taur (sen′·tawr) *n.* (*fem.* **centauress**) (*Myth.*) a fabulous being, half man and half horse [Gk. *kentaurion*].

cen·te·nar·y (sen′·te·ner·i·, sen·ten·a̤r·i·) *n.* a period of a hundred years; a century; the commemoration of a hundredth anniversary; a centennial. **centenarian** (sen·ta̤·ne′·ri·a̤n) *n.* a person a hundred years old [L. *centum*, a hundred].

cen·ten·ni·al (sen·ten′·i·a̤l) *a.* pert. to a period of 100 years; happening once in a hundred years; *n.* a hundredth anniversary [L. *centum; annus*, a year].

cen·ter (sen′·ter) *n.* the mid-point of anything; pivot; axis; a point to which things move or are drawn; a point of concentration; *v.t.* and *i.* to place in the center; to be fixed. **-piece** *n.* an ornament or cloth covering for the center of a table. **centric(al)** *a.* placed in center or middle. **centrically** *adv.* **centricity** (sen-·tris′·i·ti·) *n.* the state of being centric. **center of gravity,** the point in a body about which it will balance [L. *centrum*].

cen·ti- (sen′·ti) *prefix fr.* L. *centum*, a hundred, combining to form derivatives. **-grade** *a.* divided into 100 degrees, as the centigrade thermometer on which freezing-point is marked 0°, and boiling-point 100°. **-meter** (sen′·ti-·mē·ter) *n.* 100th part of a meter = .394 inch.

cen·ti·pede (sen′·ti·pēd) *n.* an insect, of flat and elongated shape, with a segmented body [L. *centum*, a hundred; *pes, pedis*, a foot].

cen·tral (sen′·tra̤l) *a.* relating to, or placed in, the center; chief; important. **-ly** *adv.* **-ize** *v.t.* to draw to a central point; to concentrate; to put under one control. **-ization** *n.* **-ism** *n.* centralization, esp. of government. **centrality** *n.*

the state of being central. **— heating,** heating of a building or group of buildings from one central furnace [L. *centralis*, fr. L. *centrum*].

cen·tri·fu·gal (sen·trif′·yoo·ga̤l) *a.* tending to move away from the center of a revolving body [L. *centrum*, the center; *fugere*, to flee].

cen·trip·e·tal (sen·trip′·a̤·ta̤l) *a.* tending to move towards the center [L. *centrum*, the center; *petere*, to seek].

cen·tu·ple (sen′·too·pl) *a.* hundredfold. [L. *centum*, a hundred; *plicare*, to fold].

cen·tu·ry (sen′·cha̤·ri·) *n.* a period of a hundred years; a set of a hundred; a company of a Roman legion numbering a hundred soldiers under the command of a **centurion** [L. *centuria*].

ce·phal·ic (sa̤·fal′·ik) *a.* pert. to the head; *n.* a medicine for headaches [Gk. *kephale*, the head].

ce·ram·ic (sa̤r·am′·ik) *a.* pert. to pottery. **ceramics** *n.pl.* the art of molding, modelling, and baking clay; the study of pottery as an art [Gk. *keramos*, pottery].

cere (sir) *v.t.* (*Obs.*) to cover with wax; *n.* the wax-like membrane at base of bill in some birds. **ceraceous** (si·rā′·sha̤s) *a.* waxy. **cerate** *n.* an ointment of wax, oil, etc. **-cloth** *n.* a cloth smeared with melted wax in which dead bodies used to be wrapped. **-ment** *n.* (usually *pl.*) gravecloths [L. *cera*, wax].

ce·re·al (si′·ri·a̤l) *a.* pert. to edible grain; *n.* any edible grain (wheat, barley, oats, etc.); a breakfast food made of such grains. [L. *Ceres*, Roman goddess of corn].

ce·re·brum (ser′·a̤·bra̤m) *n.* the upper and larger division of the brain. **cerebellum** *n.* the part of the brain behind and below the cerebrum. **cerebral** *a.* pert. to the brain. **cerebral hemorrhage,** rupture of an artery of the brain with a consequent escape of blood. **cerebral palsy** *n.* paralysis from cerebral lesion, chiefly characterized by spasms. **cerebrate** *v.i.* to have the brain in action. **cerebration** *n.* **cerebrospinal** *a.* pert. to both brain and spinal cord [L. *cerebrum*, the brain].

ce·re·mo·ny (ser′·a̤·mō·ni·) *n.* a sacred rite; formal observance; formality; usage of courtesy; prescribed rule; a public or private function. **ceremonial** *a.* pert. to ceremony; formal; *n.* an outward observance; usage followed in performing rites. **ceremonially** *adv.* **ceremonious** *a.* full of ceremony; particular in observing forms. **ceremoniously** *adv.* **ceremoniousness** *n.* **master of ceremonies** *n.* at public functions, etc. one whose business it is to see that all forms, rules, and courtesies are observed [L. *caerimonia*, a rite].

ce·rise (sa̤r·ēs′) *n.* and *a.* light clear red; cherry-colored [Fr. = cherry].

cer·tain (sur′·tin) *a.* sure; settled; undoubted; inevitable; one; constant; of moderate quantity, degree, etc. **-ly** *adv.* **-ty** *n.* the quality of being certain. **certitude** *n.* freedom from doubt; certainty. **certes** (sur′·tēz) *adv.* (*Arch.*) certainly; in truth [L. *certus*].

cer·ti·fi·cate (ser·tif′·a̤·ka̤t) *n.* a written testimony to the truth of a fact; a testimonial or written statement of qualifications or of accomplishment; *v.i.* (ser·ti·fa̤·kāt) to attest by a certificate; to furnish with a certificate. **certify** (sur′·ti·fī) *v.t.* to testify to in writing; to vouch for the truth of. **certifiable** *a.* able to be vouched for. **certification** *n.* the act of certifying. **certified** *a.* [L. *certus*, certain; *facere*, to make].

ce·ru·le·an (sa̤·roŏ′·li·a̤n) *a.* sky-blue; deep blue. **ceruleous** *a.* sky-blue [L. *caeruleus*].

ce·ruse (si′·roŏs) *n.* white lead. **cerussite** *n.* a carbonate of lead [L. *cerussa*, white lead].

cer·vi·cal (ser′·vi·ka̤l) *a.* pert. to the neck or neck of the uterus [L. *cervix*, the neck].

ce·si·um, caesium (sē′·zi·a̤m) *n.* a silver-white alkaline metal belonging to the sodium and potassium family [L. *caesius*, bluish-gray].

ces·sa·tion (se·sā′·shạn) n. stoppage; discontinuance [L. *cessare*, to cease].

ces·sion (seʃ′·shạn) n. act of surrendering, as by treated; something yielded, ceded [L. *cessio*].

cess·pool (sesʃ′·pòol) n. a pit or hollow for collection of drainage water or sewage.

chafe (chāf) v.t. to warm by rubbing; to wear away by rubbing; to irritate; to vex; v.i. to be worn by rubbing or friction; to rage or fret; n. friction; injury caused by rubbing. **-r** n. one who chafes. **chafing dish** n. a dish and heating apparatus for cooking or keeping food warm on the table [Fr. *chauffer*, to warm].

chaff (chaf) n. the husk of grains; straw cut small for cattle-feeding; worthless matter; refuse. **-y** a. [O.E. *ceaf*].

chaff (chaf) n. banter; jesting talk; v.t. to tease; to make fun of (without spite) [form of *chafe*, to irritate].

cha·grin (shạ·grin′) n. ill-humor; vexation; mortification; v.t. to vex deeply [Fr.].

chain (chān) n. a series of metal rings or links connected and forming a flexible cable; a fetter; a succession of things or events; a mountain range; a measure such as used by engineers or surveyors; v.t. to fasten or connect with a chain; to fetter; to restrain. **— bridge** n. a suspension bridge. **-drive** n. the transmitting of driving-power by means of chain-gear. **— gang** n. a number of convicts chained together. **— reaction** n. in nuclear physics, a self-sustaining process in which some neutrons from one splitting atom are able to split more atoms, setting free still more neutrons which carry on the reaction indefinitely [L. *catena*, a chain.

chair (chār) n. a seat with a back, legs, and sometimes arms, usually for one person; a portable covered vehicle for carrying one person, e.g. a sedan; an official seat occupied by the president of a meeting, a university professor, a bishop, etc.; v.t. to install in a chair or office; to provide with chairs. **to take the chair**, to act as chairman of a meeting; to preside. **-man** n. the presiding officer of a meeting, board, committee, etc. **-manship** n. **-woman** n. [Fr. *chaire*, a pulpit, fr. Gk. *kathedra*].

chaise (shāz) n. a light, one-horse carriage; a posting-carriage. **— longue** (lawng) n. an elongated seat with backrest at one end and support for legs [Fr. *chaise*, a chair, a seat].

chal·ced·o·ny (kal′·se·dō·ni·) n. a whitish or bluish-white variety of quartz. **chalcedonic** a. [fr. *Chalcedon*, a town in Asia Minor].

cha·let (shạ·lā′) n. a timber-built house in the Alps; a country residence like a Swiss mountain cottage [Fr.]. [communion-cup L. *calix*].

chal·ice (chal′·is) n. a wine-cup; a goblet; a

chalk (chawk) n. a soft, white, carbonate of lime; a chalk-like material used for marking; v.t. to rub or mark with chalk. **-y** a. containing or like chalk. **-iness** n. **— up** v.t. to score; to earn. **French chalk**, tailor's chalk [L. *calx*, limestone].

chal·lenge (chal′·inj) n. an invitation to a contest, esp. to a duel; defiance; the warning call of a sentry; exception taken to a juror; v.t. to call upon a person to settle a dispute by fighting; to defy; to summon to answer; to call in question. **-able** a. **-r** n. [L. *calumnia*. Doublet of E. *calumny*]. [fabric.

chal·lis, challie (sha′·li·) n. a lightweight

cham·ber (chām′·bẹr) n. a room, esp. one used for lodging, privacy, or study; a place where an assembly, such as a legislature meets, and the assembly itself; a cavity; the cavity at the rear end of the bore of a gun; a vessel for urine; v.t. to shut up or confine, as in a chamber; v.i. to occupy as a chamber. **-ed** a. **-s** n.pl. a room or rooms where a judge hears cases not requiring action in court. **-maid** n. a woman servant who has the care of bedrooms, esp. in

hotels, etc. **— music** n. music suitable for performance in a house or small hall [L. *camera*, a room].

cham·ber·lain (chām′·bẹr·lin) n. court official. **-ship** n. [fr. *chamber*].

cham·bray (sham′·brā) n. a fine cotton material, a variety of gingham [fr. *Cambrai*, Fr.].

cha·me·le·on (kạ·mēl′·yạn) n. a small lizard, which changes color with its surroundings; (*Fig.*) an inconstant person [Gk. *chamai*, on the ground; *leōn*, a lion].

cham·fer (cham′·fẹr) v.t. to cut a groove in; to bevel; n. a groove; a bevel. **-ed** a. [O.Fr. *chanfraindre*, edge and fragile].

cham·ois (sham′·oi·) n. a goat-like species of antelope; a kind of soft leather [L.L. *camox*].

champ (champ) v.t. and i. to bite, chew, or munch noisily. **to champ at the bit** (*Fig.*) to be impatient; n. (*Slang*) champion.

cham·pagne (sham·pān′) n. a light effervescent, white wine, made in the province of *Champagne* in N.E. France, or elsewhere.

cham·pi·on (cham′·pi·ạn) n. one who fought in single combat to defend the honor of another; a defender of any cause; one capable of defeating his competitors in any form of sport; a. first-class; v.t. to defend; to maintain or support. **-ship** n. the position of a champion; defense; advocacy [L.L. *campio*, a fighter in the arena].

chance (chans) n. an unforeseen occurrence; risk; likelihood; opportunity; possibility; a. accidental; v.t. to risk; v.i. to happen. **by —,** accidentally [O.Fr. *cheance*, fall of dice].

chan·cel (chan′·sạl) n. the east part of a church, where the altar is placed, orig. shut off from the nave [L. *cancelli*, lattice-work].

chan·cel·lor (chan′·sạ·ler) n. the title of various high officials in the state, and in the law; the head of a university; the chief secretary of an embassy. **-ship** n. the office of chancellor. **chancellery** n. the premises of a chancellor. [Fr. *chancelier*, orig. keeper of a barrier].

chan·cer·y (chan′·sẹr·i·) n. the office of a chancellor; a chancellery; a court of equity [orig. *chancellory*].

chan·de·lier (chan·dạ·lir′) n. a branched framework for holding lights, esp. one hanging from the ceiling; orig. for holding candles [L. *candela*, a candle].

chand·ler (chand′·lẹr) n. orig. a candle-maker; now a grocer or dealer in small wares [L. *candela*, a candle].

change (chānj) v.t. to alter or make different; to put one thing for another; to shift; to quit one state for another; to exchange, as money; to convert; v.i. to become different; to change one's clothes; n. the act of changing; alteration; that which makes for variety; money of small denomination given in exchange for money of larger; balance of money returned after payment; fresh clothing; an exchange. **-able** a. variable; fickle; unsteady. **-ful** a. **-fully** adv. **-fulness** n. **-less** a. unchanging; constant. **-ling** n. a child left in place of another taken by the fairies [L. *cambire*, to barter].

chan·nel (chan′·ạl) n. a waterway; the deeper part of a river, harbor, etc.; a strait; a groove or furrow; means of access; a. frequency band for transmission of radio, television, etc.; v.t. to form a channel; to groove or furrow; to direct in a particular course [L. *canalis*].

chant (chant) v.t. and i. to sing; to celebrate in song; to intone; n. a song; melody; sacred words recited in a singing manner. **-er** n. (*fem.* **-euse** or **-ress**). **-y** (shan′·ti·) n. a sailor's song [L. *cantare*, to sing].

chant·i·cleer (chant′·i·klir) n. a cock, rooster [O.Fr. *chanté-cler*, sing-clear].

cha·os (kā′·ás) n. complete confusion; state of the universe before creation. **chaotic** a. [Gk.].

chap (chap) v.t. to cleave; to split; to crack; v.i. to become cracked, red, and rough (as the skin in cold weather); pr.t. **-ping**. pa.t. **-ped**.

n. a chink; a crack in the skin [related to *chip, chop*].   [dler O.E. *caep*, a bargain].

chap (chap) *n.* (*Colloq.*) a fellow; (*Br.*) a ped-

chap·el (chap′·ȧl) *n.* a private church; a subordinate place of worship; a division of a church with its own altar [L.L. *cappella*, a sanctuary for relics].

chap·e·ron (shap′·ȧ·rŏn) *n.* a kind of hood; a mature person who escorts an unmarried lady in public or is in attendance at social gatherings of young people; *v.t.* to escort, accompany. **-age** *n.* [Fr. = a hood].

chap·lain (chap′·lin) *n.* a clergyman. **-cy** *n.* [Fr. *chapelain*].

chap·let (chap′·lit) *n.* a garland or wreath for the head; a string of beads; a division of the rosary [O.Fr. *chapelet*].

chaps (shaps) *n.pl.* leather over-trousers worn by a cowboy [fr. Sp. *chaparejos*].

chap·ter (chap′·tẹr) *n.* a divison of a book or treatise; a bishop's council in a diocese; an organized branch of a society, fraternity, or military order; *v.t.* to divide into chapters [L. *caput*, the head].

char (chär) *n.* a species of trout [Celt.].

char (chär) *v.t.* to reduce to charcoal; to burn to a black cinder; *pr.p.* **-ring**. *pa.p.* and *pa.t.* **-red**. **-coal** *n.* the residue of partially burnt animal or vegetable matter, esp. wood.

char, chare (chär) *n.* a job; work done by the day; *v.i.* to work by the day; to do small jobs. **-woman** *n.* [O.E. *cerr*.]

char·ac·ter (kar′·ik·tẹr) *n.* a mark, letter, figure, sign, stamp; any distinctive mark; an essential feature; nature; the total of qualities making up an individuality; moral excellence; (*Colloq.*) a person noted for eccentricity; a personage in a play or novel; *v.t.* to characterize; to portray; to represent. **-ize** *v.t.* to depict the peculiar qualities of; to distinguish; to give character to. **-istic** *a.* serving to mark the character of; peculiar; distinctive; *n.* that which distinguishes a person or thing from another; **-istically** *adv.* **-ization** *n.* the act or characterizing literary or dramatic portrayal of character [Gk. *charactēr*, an engraved mark].

cha·rade (shạ·rād′) *n.* a game, consisting of the interpretation (usually dramatic) of a word for others to guess [Fr.].

chard (chärd) *n.* leafy vegetable.

charge (chärj) *n.* a load or burden; price or cost; care or trust; an earnest exhortation, as of a judge or bishop; accusation or allegation; a clergyman's parish or the people of that parish; the amount of powder, etc., that a gun is fitted to hold; an impetuous onset or attack, or the signal for it; custody; electrical contents of accumulator or battery; *v.t.* to lay a task, command, trust upon; to ask as payment; to accuse; to load, as a gun; *v.i.* to make an onset. **-able** *a.* **-r** *n.* a large, flat dish; a war-horse [L.L. *carricare*, to load a cart].

char·gé d'af·fairs (shȧr·zhā′·da·fer′) *n.* a minor diplomatic emissary; a deputy ambassador [Fr. = charged with business].

char·i·ot (char′·i·ạt) *n.* in ancient times, a two-wheeled cart used in warfare; a four-wheeled state carriage. **-eer** *n.* [Fr. dim. of *char*, a car, cart].

char·i·ty (char′·i·ti·) *n.* (*Bib.*) love and good-will to men; liberality to the poor; leniency in judging others; any act of kindness; alms; a charitable cause or institution. **charitable** *a.* pert. to charity; liberal to the poor; generous. **charitably** *adv.* [L. *caritas*, affection].

cha·riv·a·ri (shȧ·ri·vȧ′·ri·) *n.* a mock serenade. Also **shivaree** (shi′·vạ·ri·) [Fr.].

char·la·tan (shär′·lạ·tạn) *n.* a quack or imposter [It. *ciarlare*, to prate, chatter].

char·lotte (shȧr′·lạt) *n.* (*Cookery*) a kind of pudding made by lining a mold with bread or cake and filling it [Fr.].

charm (chärm) *n.* a magic spell; anything sup-

posed to possess magic power; a talisman; a trinket worn on a bracelet; attractiveness; *v.t.* to subjugate by magic; to attract irresistibly; *v.i.* to please greatly; to be fascinating. **-er** *n.* **-ing** *a.* attractive; alluring; delightful [Fr. *charme*, fr. L. *carmen*, a song].

char·nel (chär′·nel) *a.* containing dead bodies. **— house** *n.* a place where the bodies or bones of the dead are deposited; a sepulcher [L. *caro, carnis*, flesh].

chart (chärt) *n.* a map of part of the sea, showing currents, depths, islands, coasts, etc.; a diagram giving information in tabular form; a graph; *v.t.* to represent on a chart; to map; to delineate. **-er** *n.* [L. *charta*, a paper].

char·ter (chär′·tẹr) *n.* a formal document confirming privileges, titles, or rights; an act of incorporation; the hiring of a vessel; *v.t.* to establish by charter; to hire, as a ship. **-ed** *a.* **— member** *n.* one of the original members [L. *charta*, a paper].

char·treuse (shär·trẹz′) *n.* a liqueur; a light yellowish-green color [Fr.].

char·y (chär′·i·) *a.* careful; sparing. **charily** *adv.* [O.E. *cearig*, full of care].

chase (chās) *v.t.* to pursue; to run after; to hunt; to drive away; *v.i.* to hasten; to hurry; *n.* pursuit; hunting of enemy, game, etc.; what is pursued or hunted. **-r** *n.* one who chases; a mild beverage taken after liquor [L. *captare*, to seize].

chase (chās) *v.t.* to enchase; to engrave metal. **-r** *n.* [abbrev. of *enchase*].

chase (chās) *n.* (*Print.*) an iron frame to hold type when set up; a wide groove [L. *capsa*, a box. Doublet of *case*].

chasm (kazm) *n.* a deep opening in the earth; a cleft [Gk. *chasma*].

chassé (sha·sā′) *n.* in dancing, a rapid gliding step to the right or left [Fr.].

chas·sis (sha′·si·) *n.* the framework and undercarriage of an automobile, including the engine; the framework on which a gun is moved; landing gear of an airplane [Fr. *chassis*, a frame].

chaste (chāst) *a.* pure; virtuous; undefiled; pure and simple in taste and style. **-ly** *adv.* **-ness** *n.* **chastity** *n.* purity; virginity [L. *castus*, pure].

chas·ten (chā′·sn) *v.t.* to correct by punishment; to subdue [L. *castigare*, to punish].

chas·tise (chas′·tīz) *v.t.* to inflict pain in order to reform; to punish. **-ment** *n.* [L. *castigare*, to punish].

chas·u·ble (chaz′·yoo·bl) *n.* a sleeveless vestment worn over the alb by the priest during Mass [L.L. *casula*, a mantle].

chat (chat) *v.i.* to talk idly or familiarly; *n.* light, informal talk; *pr.p.* **-ting**; *pa.p.* and *pa.t.* **-ted**. **-ter** *v.i.* to talk idly or rapidly; to rattle together, of the teeth. **-terbox** *n.* one who chatters excessively. **-terer** *n.* one who chatters. **-tiness** *n.* **-ty** *a.* talkative; gossipy.

cha·teau (sha·tō′) *n.* a castle; a country-seat, esp. in France; a mansion; *pl.* **chateaux** (sha-tōz′). **chatelain** (sha′·tạ·len) *n.* the mistress of a castle or other fashionable household; a chain fastened around a lady's waist, with keys, seals, etc. attached [O.Fr. *chastel*. Doublet of *castle*].

chat·tel (chat′·l) *n.*, usually in *pl.* **chattels**, any kind of property, except land and buildings. **— mortgage** *n.* a mortgage on personal property [O.Fr. *chatel*, a castle].

chat·ter See **chat**.

chauf·feur (shō·fur′·, shō′·fẹr) *n.* the paid driver of private automobile; *v.t.* to drive [Fr. = a stoker].

chau·vin·ism (shō′·vin·izm) *n.* absurdly exaggerated patriotism; blind enthusiasm for a cause. **chauvinist** *n.* **chauvinistic** *a.* [fr. Nicolas *Chauvin*].

chaw (chaw) *n.* (*Dial.*) See **chew**.

cheap (chēp) *a.* low in price; of low cost, as

compared with the value, or the usual cost; contemptible, inferior, vulgar. **-ly** adv. **-ness** n. **-en** v.t. to bring down the price; to lessen the value; to belittle [O.E. ceap, a bargain].

cheat (chēt) v.t. to deceive; to defraud; to trick; v.i. to practice trickery; n. a fraud; one who cheats; an impostor. **-er** n. [short for escheat].

check (chek) n. a stop; a restraint; an interruption in progress; an obstacle, obstruction; control or supervision, or one employed to carry out such; a mark placed against items in a list; an order to a bank to pay money; a term in chess to indicate that opponent's king must be moved or guarded; a pattern of squares in cloth, etc.; v.t. to restrain; to hinder; to chide or reprove; to verify; to put a mark against, in a list; to leave articles in the custody of another; in chess, to put in check; v.i. to come to a sudden stop; to pause. **-ers** n.pl. a board game for 2. **-book** n. book of blank checks or orders on a bank. **-mate** n. the final movement in chess, when the king can be neither moved or protected; complete defeat. **-room** n. a place where articles may be left under the temporary protection of others. **-up** n. a medical examination [fr. Pers. shah, king].

check·er (chek'·ẹr) v.t. to variegate with cross lines; to diversify; v.i. to produce a checkered effect, esp. of alternate light and shade; n. a square; a pattern like a chess-board; a piece in the game of checkers. **-ed** a. [Fr. échiquier].

Ched·dar (ched'·ạr) n. a kind of hard, smooth cheese [fr. Cheddar, in Somerset].

cheek (chēk) n. the fleshy wall or side of the mouth; each side of the face below the eyes; (Colloq.) insolence or impudence. **-bone** n. the bone below the outer corner of the eye. **-y** a. [O.E. ceace, the cheek, jaw].

cheep (chēp) v.i. to chirp, as a small bird; n. a small shrill sound [imit. origin].

cheer (chēr) n. good spirits; disposition; state of mind; gaiety; expression of approval, or encouragement, by shouting; rich food; v.t. to render cheerful; to comfort; to hearten or encourage; to salute with cheers; v.i. to shout hurrah. **-er** n. **-ful** a. having good spirits. **-fully** adv. **-fulness** n. **-ily** adv. with cheerfulness. **-iness** n. **-io!** interj. an informal salutation at parting. **-less** a. gloomy; comfortless. **-lessness** n. **-y** a. in good spirits; promoting cheerfulness [O.Fr. chiere, countenance; L.L. cara, the face].

cheese (chēz) n. a curd of milk, separated from the whey, and prepared in several ways as food; a solid mass or cake of this food. **-cloth** n. a thin loosely woven cotton cloth, orig. used for wrapping cheese. **cheese it** (Slang) Look out! Run! [O.E. cese, cyse, curdled milk].

chee·tah (chē'·tạ) n. the hunting leopard of India and Africa [Hind.].

chef (shef) n. a head cook. **chef-d'oeuvre** (shā·devr') n. a masterpiece, esp. in art or literature [Fr.].

chei·ro- See chiro..

chem·i·cal (kem'·i·kạl) a. pert. to, or made by, chemistry; n. a substance used in chemistry, or produced by chemical processes. **-ly** adv. according to chemical principles [fr. Alchemy].

che·mise (shạm·ēz') n. a woman's undershirt [Fr. chemise, a shirt].

chem·ist (kem'·ist) n. a person versed in chemistry or professionally engaged in it. **-ry** n. the study of the various substances which compose the universe, their combinations, and the processes by which they act one upon another [shortened form of alchemist].

chem·o·ther·a·peu·tics (kem'·ō·ther·a·pū'·tiks) n. (Med.) the use of chemical compounds in the treatment of disease. **chemotherapy** n. [E. chemical; Gk. therapeuein, to heal].

chem·ur·gy (kem'·ẹr·ji·) n. applied chemistry directed to developing industrial uses for agricultural produce.

che·nille (shạ·nēl') n. a soft plush-like cord of silk, wool, worsted, etc. used for ornamental trimmings, fringes, etc.; a soft, velvety fabric [Fr. = a caterpillar].

cher·ish (cher'·ish) v.t. to hold dear; to treat tenderly; to foster [L. carus, dear].

che·root (shạ·rŏot') n. a kind of cigar, open at both ends [Hind.].

cher·ry (cher'·i·) n. the bright red fruit of a tree akin to the plum; a cherry tree; a. pert to a cherry; red [Gk. kerasos].

cher·ub (cher'·ạb) n. a winged creature with a human face; an angel; a celestial spirit; a beautiful child; pl. **cherubim** (cher'·ạ·bim) or **-s. cherubic** (chạ·rŏo'·bik) a. [Heb. kerub]

chess (ches) n. a game of Eastern origin played by two persons on a board containing sixty-four squares, with two differently colored sets of sixteen pieces or 'men.' **-man** n. a piece used in the game [Pers. shah, a king].

chest (chest) n. a large box; a coffer; a trunk; part of the body enclosed by ribs and breastbone; v.t. to place in a chest. **chest of drawers**, a piece of furniture fitted with drawers. **-y** a. having a large chest; conceited [O.E.].

ches·ter·field (ches'·tẹr·fēld) n. a long overcoat, a heavily padded sofa [after Earl of Chesterfield].

chest·nut (ches'·nut) n. the nut of a forest tree; the tree itself, or its timber; a reddish-brown color; (Colloq.) a stale joke or story; a. reddish-brown [L. castanea].

che·val (shạ·val') n. a support or frame. **— glass** n. a large mirror within a supporting frame. **chevalier** (shev·ạ·lir') n. orig. a horseman; a cavalier [Fr. cheval, a horse].

Chev·i·ot (chev'·i·ạt) n. a famous breed of sheep; cloth made from or like their wool [fr. Cheviot Hills, Eng. & Scot.].

chev·ron (shev'·rạn) n. a V-shaped bar worn on the sleeve to designate rank [Fr. chevron, a rafter].

chew (chŏo) v.t. to bite and crush with the teeth; to masticate; to ruminate; to champ; n. action of chewing; a quid of tobacco. **-ing gum** n. a sweet and flavored substance for chewing prepared from chicle, the gum of a Mexican rubber-tree [O.E. ceowan].

Chi·an·ti (kē·an'·ti·) n. an Italian red or white wine [fr. Chianti hills in Italy].

chi·a·ro·scu·ro (ki·ár·ạ·skyoo'·rō) n. the reproduction in art of the effects of light and shade in nature [It. = bright, dark].

chic (shēk) n. style and elegance; effectiveness; a. stylish; modish [Fr.].

chi·cane (shi·kān') n. trick or artifice; sharp practice, esp. in legal proceedings; (Cards) a bridge hand with no trumps in it; v.i. to use trickery. **-ry** n. trickery. **-r** n. [Fr.].

chick, chicken (chik, chik'·ạn) n. the young of fowls, esp. of hen. **-en-hearted** a. cowardly; timid. **-en-pox** n. a mild, contagious, eruptive disease. **-weed** n. weed with small white blossoms [O.E. cicen].

chic·le (chik'·l) n. a gum-like, milky juice obtained from several Central American trees [Sp. Amer.].

chic·o·ry (chik'·ạ·ri·) n. a plant whose taproot when roasted and ground is used to mix with coffee and whose greens are used for salad [Fr. chicorée].

chide (chīd) v.t. to scold; to rebuke; v.i. to find fault; pr.p. **chiding**. pa.p. **chided** or **chid**. pa.t. **chid** [O.E. cidan].

chief (chēf) a. foremost in importance; principal; main; at the head; most influention; n. a head or leader; a principal person or thing. **-ly** adv. principally; for the most part. **-tain** n. (fem. **-tainess**) the head of a clan or tribe; a commander [Fr. chef. fr. L. caput, the head].

chif·fon (shi·fan') n. a thin, soft, gauzy material. **chiffonier** (shif-ạn·ēr') n. a high narrow chest of drawers [Fr. chiffon, a rag].

chig·ger (chig'·ẹr) n. a flea.

chi·gnon (shēn'·yȧng) n. a rolled-up pad or

bun of hair at the back of a woman's head or on the nape of the neck [Fr.].

chil·blain (chil'·blān) *n.* an inflammatory swelling caused by cold and bad circulation [fr. *chill* and *blain*].

child (chīld) *n.* a very young person of either sex; offspring; descendant; *pl.* **children** (chil'·drin) offspring, descendants. **-birth** *n.* the act of bearing a child. **-bearing** *n.* producing children. **-bed** *n.* childbirth. **-hood** *n.* the state of being a child; the time during which one is a child. **-ish** *a.* pert. to a child; silly; trifling. **-ishly** *adv.* **-ishness** *n.* **-less** *a.* **-lessness** *n.* **-like** *a.* like a child; innocent; trustful. **with child**, pregnant [O.E. *cild*].

chil·i, chilli (chil'·i·) *n.* the red pepper, or fruit of the capsicum, called Cayenne pepper when dried and ground [Mex.].

chill (chil) *a.* cold; tending to cause shivering; cool in manner or feeling; discouraging; *n.* a feeling of coldness, attended with shivering; illness caused by cold; discouragement; *v.t.* to cool; to cause to shiver; to benumb; to dispirit; to keep cold; *v.i.* to grow cold. **-y**, cold; creating cold; depressing; ungenial. **-iness** *n.* [O.E. *cele, ciele,* coldness].

chime (chīm) *n.* the musical sound of bells; a set of bells tuned to the musical scale (generally used in the plural); *v.t.* and *i.* to sound harmoniously; to be in harmony; to agree with [M.E. *chimbe,* orig. = *cymbal*].

chi·me·ra, chimaera (ki·mi'·ra) *n.* a fabulous, fire-breathing monster; a creature of the imagination. **chimeric(al)** *a.* [Gk. *chimaira*].

chim·ney (chim'·ni·) *n.* the passage through which the smoke of a fireplace, etc., is carried off; a glass tube around the flame of a lamp. **— sweep** *n.* one who removes the soot from chimneys [Gk. *kaminos,* a furnace].

chim·pan·zee (chim·pan'·zē) *n.* a large African anthropoid ape [W. Africa].

chin (chin) *n.* the part of the face below the mouth; *v.t.* (*Colloq.*) to chat; to raise oneself on a horizontal bar so that the chin is level with the bar. *pr.t.* **-ning.** *pa.t.* **-ned** [O.E. *cin*].

Chi·na (chī'·na) *n.* a vast country in E. Asia; (*l.c.*) a translucent, vitreous ceramic ware; porcelain. **-man** *n.* a native of China. **Chinese** (chī·nēz') *n.* a native, the natives, or the language of China; *a.* **-ware** *n.* dishes of china.

chin·chil·la (chin·chil'·a) *n.* a small animal, with very fine, soft fur; the fur itself; a heavy woolen material used esp. for coats [Sp.].

chine (chīn) *n.* the backbone or spine of an animal; a piece of the backbone, with the flesh, cut for cooking [Fr. *échine,* the spine].

chink (chingk) *n.* a small cleft, rent, or fissure; a gap or crack; *v.t.* to open; *v.i.* to crack [O.E. *cinu,* a fissure].

chink (chingk) *n.* the sound of a piece of metal when struck; the ring of coin; *v.i.* to ring.

Chi·nook (chi·nook') *n.* a tribe of N.W. American Indians; (*l.c.*) a wind; a kind of Salmon.

chintz (chintz) *n.* a printed cotton cloth, glazed or unglazed [Hind. *chint*].

chip (chip) *v.t.* to chop off into small pieces; to break little pieces from; to shape by cutting off pieces; *v.i.* to break or fly off in small pieces; *pr.p.* **-ping;** *pa.p.* and *pa.t.* **-ped;** *n.* a piece of wood, etc. separated from a larger body by an axe, etc.; a fragment; a counter, instead of money, used in gambling. **-s** *n.pl.* fried slices of potato; (*Naut.*) a ship's carpenter. **-per** *a.* (*Colloq.*) cheerful; lively. **— shot** *n.* (*Golf*) a short, lofted shot onto the green. **— in,** *v.t.* to contribute [fr. E. *chop*].

chip·munk (chip'·mungk) *n.* a burrowing ground-squirrel or striped gopher [Native].

chip·pen·dale (chip'·pan·dāl) *n.* a style of furniture [fr. cabinet-maker *Chippendale*].

chi·ro- (kī'·rō) *prefix* fr. Gk. *cheir,* the hand, combining to form derivatives.

chi·ro·man·cy (kī'·rō·man·si·) *n.* divination by inspection of the hand; palmistry [Gk.

cheir, the hand; *manteia,* divination].

chi·rop·o·dist (ki·rap'·a·dist) *n.* one skilled in the treatment of diseases of the feet. **chiropody** *n.* [Gk. *cheir,* hand; *podos,* foot].

chi·ro·prac·tic (kī·ra·prak'·tik) *n.* a method of healing which relies upon the removal of nerve interference by manual adjustment of the spine. **chiropractor** *n.* [Gk. *cheir,* the hand; *prassein,* to do].

chirp, chir·rup (churp, chir'·ap) *n.* a short, sharp note, as of a bird or cricket; *v.i.* to make such a sound; to twitter; to talk gaily.

chis·el (chiz'·al) *n.* a tool sharpened to a cutting edge at the end, used in carpentry, sculpture, etc.; *v.i.* to cut or carve with this tool; (*Slang*) to cheat [O.Fr. *cisel*].

chit (chit) *n.* an informal note; a voucher; a permit or pass [Hind. *chitthi*].

chit-chat (chit'·chat) *n.* prattle; trivial talk.

chi·tin (kī'·tin) *n.* a white, horny substance, forming the outer covering of insects, crustacea, etc. *a.* [Gk. *chiton,* a tunic].

chit·ter·lings (chit'·er·lingz) *n.pl.* the smaller intestines of swine, etc., used as food.

chiv·al·ry (shiv'·al·ri·) *n.* the system of knighthood in medieval times; the qualities of a knight, viz. dignity, courtesy, bravery, generosity, gallantry. **chivalric, chivalrous** *a.* pert. to chivalry. **chivalrously** *adv.* [Fr. *chevalerie,* fr. *cheval,* a horse].

chive (chīv) *n.* a small herb of the onion kind [L. *cepa,* an onion].

chlor-, chlo·ro- (klōr) combining forms fr. Gk. *chloros,* green; also denoting chlorine.

chlo·rine (klō'·rēn) *n.* a heavy gas of yellowish-green color used in disinfecting, bleaching, and poison-gas warfare. **chloral** *n.* a sleep-producing drug. **chlorate** *n.* a salt of chloric acid. **chloric** *a.* pert. to chlorine. **chloride** *n.* a compound of chlorine with another element. **chlorinate** *v.t.* disinfect, bleach, or combine with chlorine. **chlorination** *n.* **chlorite** *n.* a mineral of a green color, soft and friable. **chloroform** *n.* a colorless, volatile liquid used as an anesthetic; *v.t.* to make insensible by using chloroform [Gk. *chloros,* pale-green].

chlo·ro·phyll (klō'·ra·fil) *n.* (*Bot.*) the green coloring matter of plants [Gk. *chloros,* palegreen; *phullon,* a leaf].

chock (chak) *n.* a wedge to steady a wheel or a cask lying on its side; *v.t.* to make fast, with a block or wedge. **-ful** *a.* packed [fr. *choke*].

choc·o·late (chak'·a·lit) *a.* a paste or hard cake made from the powdered seeds of the cacao plant, mixed with sugar, etc.; a beverage made by pouring boiling water or milk over this; candy; *a.* dark brown [Mex. Sp.].

choice (chois) *n.* the act of choosing; the power or opportunity of choosing; selection; the thing chosen; alternative; *a.* worthy of being chosen; rare; superior [Fr. *choisir,* to choose].

choir (kwīr) *n.* a company of singers, esp. belonging to a church; that part of the church set apart for them [L. *chorus*].

choke (chōk) *v.t.* to stop the breath as by compression of the windpipe; to stifle or smother; *v.i.* to have the wind-pipe stopped; to be suffocated; *n.* the act of choking; an obstructing piece in mechanism; a valve regulating the proportion of gas to air in a motor. **-r.** *n.* one who chokes; something worn closely about the neck, as beads, etc. [M.E. *choken*].

chol·er (kal'·er) *n.* bile; anger; wrath. **choleric** *a.* passionate; easily angered. **cholera** *n.* deadly, epidemic, bilious disease, marked by purgings, vomiting and gripping pains. [Fr. *colère,* anger, fr. Gk. *cholē,* bile].

cho·les·ter·ol (ka·les'·ta·rōl) *n.* a fatlike substance found in bile, gallstones, blood, and the brain, also in egg yolks, etc. [Gk. *cholē,* bile; *stereos,* solid].

cho·lic (kol'·ik) *a.* pert. to, or obtained from, bile [Gk. *cholē,* bile].

choose (chŏŏz) *v.t.* to pick out; to select; to take one thing in preference to another; *v.i.* to decide; to think fit. *pa.p.* **chosen**; *pa.t.* **chose. choosey** *a.* (*Slang*) fastidious, difficult to please [O.E. *ceosan*].

chop (chǎp) *n.* (usually *pl.*) the jaw of an animal; the jaw of a vice [etym. uncertain].

chop (chǎp) *v.t.* to cut into pieces; to mince, by striking repeatedly with a sharp instrument; to sever by blows; *v.i.* to make a quick stroke or repeated strokes with a sharp instrument, as an axe; *n.* the act of chopping; a piece chopped off; a thick slice of meat attached to a rib or other bone; a cutlet. *pr.p.* **-ping.** *pa.p.* and *pa.t.* **-ped. -per** *n.* one who chops; a large heavy knife; cleaver. **-py** *a.* full of fissures; of the sea, having short, broken waves.

chop sticks (chǎp stiks) *n.* one of two small sticks of wood, ivory, etc. used by the Chinese in taking food.

chop su·ey (chǎp sŏŏ'·i·) also **chop sooey.** A Chinese-American dish of meat, bean sprouts, etc. [fr. Chin.].

cho·ral (kō'·rạl) *a.* pert. or belonging to a choir or chorus. **-ly** *adv.* **choric** *a.* pert. to a chorus, esp. Greek dramatic chorus. [Gk. *choros*, a band of dancers and singers].

cho·rale (kō·rāl') *n.* a simple, dignified melody sung to religious words [Gk. *choros*].

chord (kawrd) *n.* the string of a musical instrument; (*Mus.*) a series of tones having a harmonic relation to each other, and sounded simultaneously; (*Geom.*) a straight line between two points in the circumference of a circle [Gk. *chordē*, a string].

chore (chōr) *n.* any odd job, or occasional piece of housework; (*pl.*) routine work [O.E. *cerr*, work].

cho·re·a (kō·rē'·ạ) *n.* (*Med.*) uncontrollable spasms of limbs, body and facial muscles; St. Vitus's dance [Gk. *choreia*, a dancing].

cho·re·og·ra·phy (kō·ri·ǎ'·grạ·fi·) *n.* ballet dancing; the art of creating dance compositions for ballet. **choreographer** *n.* **choreographic** *a.* [Gk. *choros*, dance; *graphein*, to write].

chor·is·ter (kawr'·is·tẹr) *n.* a choir member.

cho·rog·ra·phy (kō·rǎg'·rạ·fi·) *n.* the art of making a map, or writing a description, of a region or country. **chorology** *n.* the study of the geographical distribution of plants and animals [Gk. *chora*, land; *graphein*, to write].

chor·tle (chawr'·tl) *v.i.* to chuckle gleefully. **chortling** *n.* [invented by Lewis Carroll from *ch*uckle and sn*ort*].

cho·rus (kō'·rạs) *n.* orig. a band of singers and dancers; a combination of voices singing together; what is sung or spoken by the chorus; in a Greek play, certain performers who witness the action, and at intervals express their feelings regarding it; the refrain; *v.t.* to join in the refrain; to call out or sing together. **choric** *a.* pert. to a chorus [Gk. *choros*, a band of dancers and singers].

chose (chōz) *pa.t.* of **choose.**

chosen (chō'·zn) *pa.p.* of **choose.**

chow·der (chou'·dẹr) *n.* a stew made of fish, pork, onions, etc. [Fr. *chaudièr*, a pot].

Christ (krīst) *n.* The Anointed—a name given to Jesus of Nazareth. **-like, -ly** *a.* resembling Christ [Gk. = anointed].

chris·ten (kris'·n) *v.t.* to baptize in the name of Christ; to give a name to. **Christendom** *n.* all Christian countries; the whole body of Christians. **-ing** *n.* baptism [Gk.].

Chris·tian (kris'·chạn) *n.* a follower or disciple of Christ; a professed adherent of the Church of Christ; *a.* pert. to Christ or his religion. **-ize** *v.t.* to make Christian; to convert to Christianity. **Christianity** *n.* the religion of the followers of Christ. **— era,** the era counting from the birth of Christ. **— name,** the name given at baptism; individual name, as opposed to surname or family name.

— Science, a religious doctrine of faith-healing founded in America by Mrs. Mary Eddy [Gk. *Christos*, anointed].

Christ·mas (kris'·mạs) the annual celebration of the birth of Christ, observed on Dec. 25 [E. *Christ* and *Mass*].

chrom- (krōm) combing form fr. Gk. *chroma*, color; word element referring to chromium.

chro·mat·ic (krō·mat'·ik) *a.* pert. to color; (*Mus.*) proceeding by semitones. **-s** *n.* the science of colors; (*Mus.*) chromatic notes. **-ally** *adv.* [Gk. *chroma*, color].

chrome, chro·mi·um (krōm, krō'·mi·um) *n.* a metal, very resistant to corrosion, used generally for plating other metals. **chromic** *a.* pert. to, or obtained from, chrome or chromium. **chromate** *n.* a salt of chromic acid. **chromite** *n.* a mineral, the chief source of chromium [Gk. *chroma*, color].

chro·mo·some (krō'·mạ·sōm) *n.* (*Biol.*) one of the gene-carrying bodies in the tissue of a cell, regarded as the transmitter of hereditary factors from parent to child [Gk. *chroma*, color; *soma*, a body].

chron·ic (krǎn'·ik) *a.* continuing for a long time; of disease, deep-seated and lasting; confirmed; inveterate. **-ally** [Gk. *chronos*, time].

chron·i·cle (krạn'·i·kl) *n.* a register of events in order of time; a history or account; *v.t.* to record in order of time. **-r** *n.* [Gk. *chronika*, annals, fr. *chronos*, time].

chro·no- (krǎn'·ạ) a combining form fr. Gk. *chronos*, time. **-graph** *n.* an instrument for measuring and recording time very exactly. **chronology** (krạ·nǎl'·lạ·ji·) *n.* the science that treats of historical dates and arranges them in order; a table of events and dates. **chronologer, chronologist** *n.* one who records historical events, etc. **chronological** *a.* arranged in order of time. **chronologically** *alv.* **chronometer** *n.* a very accurate watch or time-keeper. **-metric, -metrical** *a.* **chronometry** *n.* the process of measuring time by instruments.

chrys·a·lis (kris'·ạ·lis) *n.* the case in which a caterpillar encloses itself before it becomes a butterfly or moth; *pl.* **chrysalides** (kris·al'·i·dēz) **chrysalid** *a.* [Gk. *chrusos*, gold].

chrys·an·the·mum (kris·an'·thạ·mạm) *n.* a mop-headed garden flower [Gk. *chrusos*, gold; *anthemon*, a flower].

chry·so- (kris'·ạ) a combining form fr. Gk. *chrusos*, gold. **chrysocracy** (kris·ǎk'·rạ·si·) *n.* the rule of wealth. **chrysolite** *n.* a yellowish-green precious stone. **chrysoprase** (kris'·ạ·prāz) used as a gem.

chub (chub) *n.* a fish of the carp family, small and fat. **-by** *a.* round and plump. **-biness** *n.* [M.E. *chubbe*].

chuck (chuk) *v.t.* (*Colloq.*) to throw; to toss; to tap under the chin; *n.* a toss; a pat under the chin.

chuck (chuk) *n.* in machinery, part of a lathe for holding an object while it is being operated on; a cut of beef from the neck to the shoulder blade [etym. uncertain].

chuck·le (chuk'·l) *v.i.* to laugh in a suppressed manner; *n.* a short, quiet laugh [imit. origin].

chuck·le·head (chuk'·l·hed) *n.* a dolt, a lout [E. *chock*, a block].

chug (chug) *n.* an explosive sound made by an engine exhaust; *v.i.* to make an explosive sound. *pa.p., pa.t.* **-ged.** *pr.p.* **-ging.**

chum (chum) *n.* an intimate friend; a pal; a roommate; *v.i.* to be friendly (with); to share a room with. *pr.p.* **-ming.** *pa.p.* and *pa.t.* **med. -my** *a.* friendly; sociable.

chump (chump) *n.* a lump of wood; the thick end of anything; (*Slang*) a blockhead.

chunk (chungk) *n.* a short, thick piece of wood, etc. **-y** *a.* [etym. uncertain].

church (church) *n.* building for Christian worship; collective body of Christians; a denomination or sect of the Christian religion; the clergy; the church service; *v.t.* to bring to church. **-goer** *n.* one who attends church regularly. **-ly** *a.* **-man** *n.* an ecclesiastic; a member of a church. **-warden** *n.* an officer entrusted with the interests of the church or parish. **-yard** *n.* the ground adjoining a church [O.E. *circe*, belonging to the Lord].

churl (churl) *n.* a countryman. **-ish** *a.* **-ishly** *adv.* **-ishness** *n.* [O.E. *ceorl*, a man].

churn (churn) *n.* a vessel in which cream is violently stirred to produce butter; *v.t.* to agitate cream so as to produce butter; to stir up violently; *v.i.* to produce butter [O.E. *cyrin*].

chute (shòòt) *n.* a rapid descent in a river; a rapid; a sloping contrivance for transferring coal, rubbish, etc. to a lower level [Fr. *chute*, a fall].

chut·ney, chutnee (chut'·ni·) *n.* an E. Indian condiment, generally made with mangoes, peppers and spices [Hind. *chatni*].

ci·ca·da, cicala (si·ká'·da, si·ká'·la) *n.* an insect, the male of which emits a shrill, chirping sound [L. *cicada*, a cricket].

cic·a·trix, cicatrice (sik'·a·triks) *n.* a scar left after a healed wound; *pl.* **cicatrices** (sik·a·trī'·sēz). **cicatrize** (sik'·a·trīz) *v.t.* to heal and induce the formation of new tissue [L.].

cic·e·ro·ne (sis·a·rō'·ni·; It. chē·chā·rō'·nā) *n.* one who shows strangers over a place, as a cathedral, etc.; a guide [It. fr. L. *Cicero*].

ci·der (sī'·dēr) *n.* a drink made from the juice of apples [Heb. *shakar*, to be intoxicated].

ci·gar (si·gár') *n.* tobacco leaf made up in a roll for smoking. **-ette** *n.* finely cut tobacco rolled in thin paper [Sp. *cigarillo*].

cil·i·a (sil'·i·a) *n.pl.* the eyelashes; (*Anat.*) hair-like, vibratile processes. **ciliary, ciliate, ciliated, ciliferous, ciliform** *a.* [L.].

cinch (sinch) *n.* a saddle-girth; (*Slang*) a certainty; *v.t.* to fasten a cinch around; to tighten (girth) [L. *cingula*, a girth].

cin·cho·na (sin·kō'·na) *n.* a genus of trees from which quinine is extracted; the bark. **-ceous** (sin·ka·nā'·shas) *a.* [Sp. fr. Countess of *Chinchon*, who was cured by it in 1638].

cinc·ture (singk'·cher) *n.* a belt; a girdle; a zone; *v.t.* to encircle. **-d** *a.* [L. *cinctura*, a girdle]

cin·der (sin'·dēr) *n.* the remains of burned coal; any partially burned combustible substance [O.E. *sinder*].

cin·e·ma (sin'·a·ma) *n.* a hall or theater where moving pictures are shown; a motion picture; **-scope** *n.* a wide, panoramic motion picture screen. **-tography** *n.* **-tographer** *n.* [Gk. *kinema*, movement].

cin·er·ar·y (sin'·a·re·ri·) *a.* pert. to ashes; made to hold ashes. **cinerarium** *n.* (*pl.* **-raria**) *n.* a place for ashes after cremation. **cineration** *n.* a reducing to ashes; incineration [L. *cinerarius*, ashy].

cin·na·bar (sin'·a·bàr) *n.* red sulphide of mercury used as a pigment; vermilion; *a.* vermilion colored [Gk. *kinnabari*, vermilion].

cin·na·mon (sin'·a·man) *n.* the inner bark of a laurel tree of Ceylon; an aromatic substance obtained from the bark, used as a spice; *n.* and *a.* a light-brown color [Heb. *qinnamon*].

ci·pher, cy·pher (sī'·fer) *n.* the arithmetical symbol 0; any figure; a person of no account; a secret writing; a code; the key to a code; *v.i.* to write in cipher; to work at arithmetic [Fr. *chiffre*, a figure].

cir·ca (sur'·ka) *prep.* about; around; approximately; (*abbrev.*) **ca.** or **c.** [L. *circa*, *circiter*].

cir·cle (sur'·kl) *n.* a plane figure bounded by a singel curved line called its circumference, every point of which is equally distant from a point within called the center; the curved line that bounds such a figure, a circumference; a round body; a sphere; an orb; a ring; the company associated with a person; a society group; club or group, esp. literary; a never-ending series; *v.t.* to move or revolve round; to encompass, as by a circle; to surround; *v.i.* to

move in a circle [L. *circulus*].

cir·cuit (sur'·kit) *n.* the act of moving round; the space enclosed within a fixed limit; area; (*Law*) the round made by judges holding court; the district thus visited; the path of an electric current. **-eer** (sur·ki·tir') one who moves in a circuit. **circuitous** (sur·kū'·i·tas) *a.* indirect [L. *circuitus*, a going round].

cir·cu·lar (sur'·kya·lar) *a.* in the form of a circle; round; moving in a circle; roundabout; addressed to a circle of people; *n.* a notice sent out in quantities. **-ly** *adv.* **circularity** *n.* **-ize** *v.t.* to send circulars to [L. *circularis*].

cir·cu·late (sur'·kya·lāt) *v.t.* to cause to pass round as in a circle; to spread abroad; *v.i.* to move around and return to the same point; to be spread abroad. **circulation** *n.* the act of moving around; the flow of blood from, and back to, the heart; the extent of sale of a newspaper, etc.; the money circulating in a country; currency. **circulative, circulatory** *a.* circulating. **circulator** *n.* [L. *circulare*].

cir·cum- (sur'·kam) *prefix* fr. Latin meaning *round, about*, combining to form many derivatives as in **-ambient** *a.* surrounding; enclosing. **-ambiency** *n.* environment. **-ambulate** *v.t.* and *i.* to walk around or about [L. *ambire*, to go round; *ambulare*, to walk].

cir·cum·cise (sur'·kam·sīz) *v.t.* to cut off the foreskin. **circumcision** *n.* [L. *circum*; *caedere*, to cut].

cir·cum·fer·ence (ser·kum'·fer·ans) *n.* the line that bounds a circle; the distance around; area. **circumferential** *a.* [L. *circum*; *ferre*, to carry].

cir·cum·flex (sur'·kam·fleks) *n.* an accent mark placed over a vowel to denote length, contraction, etc. [L. *circum*; *flectere*, to bend].

cir·cum·flu·ent (sur·kam'·flòò·ant) *a.* flowing round. **circumfluence** *n.* [L. *circum*; *fluere*, to flow].

cir·cum·ja·cent (sur·kam·jā'·sant) *a.* bordering on every side [L. *circum*; *facere*, to lie].

cir·cum·lo·cu·tion (sur·kam·lō·kū'·shan) *n.* a roundabout manner of speaking. **circumlocutory** *a.* [L. *circum*; *locutos*, to speak].

cir·cum·nav·i·gate (sur·kam·nav'·i·gāt) *v.t.* to sail around. **circumnavigable** *a.* capable of being sailed round. **circumnavigation** *n.* **circumnavigator** *n.* one who sails around, esp. the world [L. *circum*; *navigare*, to sail].

cir·cum·scribe (sur'·kam·skrīb) *v.t.* to draw a circle around; to enclose within limits; to confine; to define. **circumscription** *n.* limitation. **circumscriptive** *a.* confined or limited in space [L. *circum*; *scribere*, to write].

cir·cum·spect (sur'·kam·spekt) *a.* watchful on all sides; prudent; discreet. **-ly** *adv.* **circumspection** *n.* caution; prudence; discretion; tact. **-ive** *a.* [L. *circum*; *spicere*, to look].

cir·cum·stance (sur'·kam·stans) *n.* a particular fact, event, or case; anything attending on, relative to, or affecting, a fact or event; accident; incident; particular; *v.t.* to place in a particular situation. **-s** *n.pl.* worldly estate; condition as to pecuniary resources; situation; position; details. **circumstantial** *a.* accidental; not essential; full of details; minute. **circumstantially** *adv.* **circumstantiality** *n.* minuteness of detail. **circumstantiate** *v.t.* to detail exactly [L. *circum*; *stare*, to stand].

cir·cum·vent (sur·kam·vent') *v.t.* to get around by stratagem; to outwit; to go around. **-ion** *n.* **-ive** *a.* [L. *circum*; *venire*, to come].

cir·cus (sur'·kas) *n.* a travelling company of performers, animals, etc.; a circular enclosure for performances; the performance itself [L.].

cir·rho·sis (si·rō'·sis) *n.* (*Med.*) hardening and enlargement of the liver. **cirrhotic** *a.* [Gk. *kirrhos*, tawny].

cir·rus (sir'·as) *n.* a tendril; a curled filament; a lofty, fleecy cloud; *pl.* **cirri** (sir'·ī) (L. *cirrus*, a curl of hair].

cis·tern (sis′·tern) n. a large tank for holding water; a reservoir [L. *cisterna*].

cit·a·del (sit′·a·del) n. a fortress or castle in or near a city [It. *cittadella*].

cite (sīt) v.t. to summon; to quote; to name; to bring forward as proof. **citation** n. an official notice to appear; the act of quoting; the passage or words quoted; the mention of gallantry in military orders. **citator** n. **citatory** a. [L. *citare*].

cith·a·ra (sith′·a·ra) n. the ancient Greek lyre. **cithern, cittern** n. a kind of flat-backed guitar [Gk. *kithara*].

cit·i·zen (sit′·i·zn) n. an inhabitant of a city; a member of a state; a. having the character of a citizen. **-ry** n. citizens collectively. **-ship** n. the state of being a citizen; the rights and duties of a citizen [O.Fr. *citeain*].

cit·ron (sit′·ran) n. the fruit of the citron tree, resembling a lemon; the tree itself; the preserved rind of the fruit; a yellow color. **citrate** n. a salt of citric acid. **citric** a. extracted from the citron lemon, etc. **citrus fruits**, citrons, lemons, oranges, etc. [L. *citrus*, a citron-tree].

cit·ron·el·la (sit·ra·nel′·a) n. a sharp smelling oil to keep insects away [See **citron**].

cit·tern, cithern See **cithara**.

cit·y (sit′·i·) n. a large town; a corporate town; the business or shopping center of a town; a. pert. to a city [L. *civitas*, a city].

civ·et (siv′·it) n. a perfume, with a strong musk-like smell; the animal from which this perfume is obtained. Also, — cat. [Ar. *zabad*].

civ·ic (siv′·ik) a. pert. to a city or a citizen. **-s** n.pl. the study of civic affairs, municipal or national [L. *civis*, a citizen].

civ·il (siv′·il) a. pert. to city, state, or citizen; lay, as opposed to military, etc.; polite. **-ly** adv. **civilian** (sa·vil′·yan) n. one whose employment is non-military; a. pert. to civilian life (e.g. civilian dress). **civility** n. courtesy; politeness; pl. acts of politeness. **civil defense**, an organization to deal with civilians during air raids, etc. **civil engineer**, one who plans bridges, roads, dams, canals, etc. **civil service**, the government positions obtained by examination. **civil war**, war between citizens of the same country [L. *civis*, a citizen].

civ·i·lize (siv′·il·īz) v.t. to reclaim from a savage state; to refine; to enlighten. **-d** a. **civilization** n. the act of civilizing, or state of being civilized [L. *civilis*].

clack (klak) v.i. to make a sudden, sharp noise, as by striking; to talk rapidly and continually; to chatter; n. a sharp, repeated, rattling sound; continual talk [imit. origin].

clad (klad) pa.p. and pa.t. of **clothe;** a. clothed.

claim (klām) v.t. to demand as a right, or as due; to call for; to assert as true; n. the demand of a right or supposed right; a title; the thing claimed. **-ant** n. one who claims. **—jumper** n. one who seizes a piece of land marked out by a settler or miner [L. *clamare*, to shout].

clair·voy·ance (kler·voi′·ans) n. the power of seeing things not normally perceptible to the senses; second sight. **clairvoyant** n. one who claims the power of clairvoyance. Also a. [Fr.].

clam (klam) n. an edible bivalve shell-fish; (*Colloq.*) a reticent person [O.E. *clam*, a bond].

cla·mant (klā′·mant) a. crying out; clamorous. **clamancy** n. [L. *clamare*, to cry out].

clam·ber (klam′·ber) v.i. to climb with difficulty, holding on with the hands [cf. Ger. *klammern*, to cling to].

clam·my (kla′·mi·) a. sticky and moist; cold and damp. **clamminess** n. [O.E. *claeman*, to anoint].

clam·or (klam′·er) n. loud shouting; tumult; outcry; uproar; v.i. to shout loudly; to utter loud complaints or demands. **-ous** a. [L. *clamare*, to cry out].

clamp (klamp) n. any appliance with parts brought together by a screw for holding anything; a brace; v.t. to make firm [Dut. *klamp*].

clan (klan) n. a tribe bearing the same surname, united under a chieftain; a set or clique of persons having a common interest. **-nish** a. disposed to associate only with members of the same sect or clique. **-nishly** adv. **-nishness** n. [Gael. *clann*, children].

clan·des·tine (klan·des′·tin) a. secret, and contrary to law, morals, etc. **-ly** adv. **-ness** n. [L. *clandestinus*, fr. *clam*, secretly].

clang (klang) v.t. to strike with a ringing, metallic sound; v.i. to give forth a ringing, metallic sound; n. a sharp, ringing sound. **-ing** n. a clang [L. *clangere*].

clan·gor (klang′·er) n. a loud harsh, ringing sound. **-ous** a. **-ously** adv. [L. *clangere*].

clank (klangk) n. a brief, hard, metallic sound; v.t. and i. to produce such a sound [imit.].

clap (klap) v.t. to bring together with a sharp sound; to strike the hands together in approval; to slap; v.i. to strike the hands together in applause; n. a sudden, sharp noise caused by impact; applause; a slap or pat; pr.p. **-ping.** pa.p. and pa.t. **-ped. -per** n. one who claps; the tongue of a bell. **-board** n. thin board used to cover wooden houses. **-trap** n. in speech-making, tricks to win applause; a. cheap and showy [M.E. *clap*].

clar·et (klar′·it) n. any red Bordeaux wine; a. a purplish-red. [Fr. *clairet*, fr. *clair*, clear].

clar·i·fy (klar′·i·fī) v.t. to make clear or pure; to explain or clear up; to remove possibility of error; v.i. to become clear. **clarification** n. **clarity** n. clearness; lucidity of mind [L. *clarus*, clear; *facere*, to make].

clar·i·on (klar′·i·an) n. trumpet with shrill piercing note; its sound. **clarinet, clarionet** n. a wood wind instrument. **clarinettist** n. [Fr. *clairon*].

clash (klash) v.t. to strike noisily together; v.i. to dash noisily together; to collide; to conflict; to disagree; n. a loud noise; a conflict [imit.].

clasp (klasp) v.t. to shut or fasten together with a catch or hook; to embrace; to grasp; to surround and cling to; n. a catch or hook for fastening; a close embrace; a grasping of the hands [M.E. *clapse*, fr. *clyppan*, to embrace].

class (klas) n. an order or division or grouping of persons or things possessing the same characteristics or status; a group of pupils or students taught together; a grouping of plants or animals; rank or standing in society. v.t. to arrange in classes; to rank together; v.i. to rank. **-able, -ible** a. **-y** a. (*Colloq.*) high-class [L. *classis*].

clas·sic (klas′·ik) n. a work, writer of recognized worth; an ancient Latin or Greek writer or book; a. of model excellence in literature or art; conforming to standards of Greek and Roman art. **-s** n.pl. ancient Latin or Greek literature. **-al** a. **-ally** adv. **ality, -alness** n. the quality of being classical. **classicism** (klas′·i·sizm) n. classic principles in art and literature; classic style; a classical idiom. **classicist** n. [L. *classicus*, of the first rank].

clas·si·fy (klas′·i·fī) v.t. to arrange in classes; to put into a class. **classifiable** a. **classification** n. the act of classifying [L. *classis*, a class; *facere*, to make].

clat·ter (klat′·er) v.t. to strike and so make a rattling noise; v.i. to make rattling sounds; to prattle; to talk rapidly and idly; n. a repeated rattling noise; noisy and idle talk [fr. *clack*].

clause (klawz) n. (*Gram.*) a subordinate part of a sentence; (*Law*) an article or distinct portion of a document, contract, etc.; a paragraph; a subdivision [L. *claudere*, to shut].

claus·tral (klaws′·tral) a. pert. to a cloister; cloister-like; secluded. **claustration** n. the state of being confined in a cloister [L. *claustrum*, a bar or bolt].

claus·tro·pho·bi·a (klaws·tra·fō′·bi·a) n. (*Med.*) a morbid dread of confined spaces [L. *claustrum*, bolt; Gk. *phobia*, fear].

clav·i·chord (kla'·vi·kawrd) n. a medieval musical instrument like a spinet [L. *clavis*, a key; *chorda*, a string].

clav·i·cle (klav'·i·kl) n. the collarbone. **cla·vicular** a. [L. *clavicula*, dim. fr. *clavis*, a key].

cla·vi·er (kla'·vyẹr) n. (*Mus.*) a stringed musical instrument with a keyboard [L. *clavis*, a key].

claw (klaw) n. a sharp, hooked nail, as of a beast or bird; anything like this; v.t. to pull, tear, or scratch with claws or nails; to grasp [O.E. *clawu*].

clay (klā) n. soft earth, consisting of alumina and silica, with water used in making pottery, bricks, etc.; earth in general; the human body. **-ey** a. consisting of clay; like clay [O.E. *claeg*].

clean (klēn) a. free from dirt, stain, or any defilement; pure; guiltless; v.t. to free from dirt; to purify; adv. so as to leave no dirt; quite; entirely. **-er** n. one who, or that which, cleans. **-liness** (klen'·li·nes) n. freedom from dirt; purity. **-ly** (klen'·li) a. habitually clean in persons and habits; pure. **-ly** (klēn'·li·) adv. in a clean manner; neatly. **-ness** (klēn'·nes) n. **—cut** a. well-shaped; definite. [O.E. *claene*].

clear (klēr) a. bright; free from cloud; undimmed; pure; free from obstruction; plain; distinct; manifest; without defect or drawback; transparent; adv. clearly; wholly; v.t. to make bright or clear; to make evident; to free from accusation; to acquit; to pass over or through; to cleanse; to empty; to make as profit; to free by payment of dues; to settle a debt; to free from difficulty, obstruction, suspicion, etc.; v.i. to become clear, bright, transparent, free; (*Naut.*) to leave a port. **-age** n. clearance. **-ance** n. the act of clearing; a certificate that a ship has been cleared at the custom house; in machinery, distance by which one part is clear of another. **-ing** n. a tract of land cleared of wood. **-ing-house** n. an office maintained by several banks for balancing accounts, exchanging checks, etc. **-ly** adv. **-ness** n. **—cut** a. sharply defined. **—eyed**, **—seeing**, **—sighted** a. having acuteness of sight or intellect [L. *clarus*, clear].

clear·sto·ry See **clerestory**.

cleat (klēt) n. a wedge; (*Naut.*) a piece of wood or iron with two projecting ends, round which ropes are fastened; a piece of metal fastened to a shoe [O.E. *cleat*].

cleave (klēv) v.t. to split asunder; to cut in two; v.i. to fall apart; to split; to open; to crack asunder; pa.p. **cloven** or **cleft**. pa.t. **clove** or **cleft**. **cleavage** n. of rocks, the quality of splitting naturally; (*Fig.*) separation due to a difference of opinions, etc.; a rupture. **-r** n. one who, or that which, cleaves; a butcher's chopper [O.E. *cleofan*].

cleave (klēv) v.i. to adhere closely; to stick; to agree; to be faithful to [O.E. *clifian*].

clef (klef) n. (*Mus.*) a sign used to indicate the pitch [Fr., fr. L. *clavis*, a key].

cleft (kleft) pa.p. and pa.t. of the verb **cleave**; n. a fissure or split; a chasm; a chink [O. E. *cleofan*].

clem·a·tis (klem'·a·tis) n. a woody vine [Gk. *klēmatis*, fr. *klēma*, a twig].

clem·en·cy (klem'·en·si·) n. leniency; mildness; gentleness; mercy. **clement** a. mild; compassionate [L. *clemens*].

clench, clinch (klensh, klinsh) v.t. to grasp firmly; to close together tightly (the hands, the teeth); to confirm (a bargain); n. a firm closing; decisive proof; a firm grip. **-er** n. an unanswerable argument [O.E. *clencean*].

clere·sto·ry (klēr'·stō·ri·) n. the upper part of the central nave of churches, which rises clear of the other buildings and has its own row of windows [fr. *clear* and *story*].

cler·gy (klur'·ji·) n. the body of men ordained for religious service. **-man** n. a minister [Fr. *clergé* fr. L. *clericus*].

cler·ic (kler'·ik) n. a clerk or clergyman; a.

clerical. **clerical** a. belonging to the clergy; pert. to a clerk or copyist [L. *clericus*].

clerk (klurk) n. one who is employed to do correspondence, keep accounts, etc. in an office; salesman or saleswoman; v.i. to act as a clerk or secretary. **-ship** n. [O.E. *clerc*, a priest].

clev·er (klev'·ẹr) a. able; skillful; ingenious; intelligent. **-ly** adv. **-ness** n.

clew, clue (klōō) n. a ball of thread or cord; (*Myth.*) a ball of thread used as a guide through a maze; hence, anything that serves to guide one in an involved affair or helps to solve a mystery; (*Naut.*) the lower corner of a sail [O.E. *cliven*].

cli·ché (klē·shā') n. (*Print.*) an electrotype or stereotype plate; a stereotyped or hackneyed phrase [Fr.].

click (klik) n. a slight, short sound, as of a latch in a door; v.i. to make such a sound; (*Slang*) to be successful [imit. origin].

cli·ent (klī'·ạnt) n. one who employs another (esp. a lawyer) professionally as his agent; a customer. **clientele** (klī'·en·tel) n. clients or customers collectively [L. *cliens*, a follower].

cliff (klif) n. a high rock-face; the sheer side of a mountain [O.E. *clif*].

cli·mac·ter·ic (klī·mak'·tạ·rik) n. a period in human life in which a change takes place in the constitution; the menopause; any critical period; a. pert. to a climacteric; critical. **-al** a. [Gk. *klimaktēr*, rung of a ladder].

cli·mate (klī'·mit) n. the general atmospherical conditions (temperature, moisture, etc.) of a country or region. **climatic** a. **climatical** a. [Gk. *klima*, *klimatos*, slope].

cli·max (klī'·maks) n. an arrangement of words, phrases, etc. such that they rise in rhetorical force and impressiveness; acme; the point of greatest excitement or tension in a play, story, etc. **climactic** a. [Gk. = a ladder].

climb (klīm) v.t. and i. to go up, ascend (as a hill, tree, etc.); to grow upward as a plant by tendrils; to rise in the social scale; to slope upward; n. an ascent. **-er** n. [O.E. *climban*].

clime (klīm) n. a region or country; (*Poet.*) climate [Gk. *klima*, fr. *klinein*, to slope].

clinch (klinsh) v.t. and i. to grapple or struggle at close quarters in wrestling or boxing; to fasten with a rivet; (*Fig.*) to settle or conclude, as an agreement; n. a close holding in wrestling or boxing; a rivet. **-er** n. [fr. *clench*].

cling (kling) v.i. to adhere or stick close to; to be attached firmly to; pa.p. and pa.t. **clung** [O.E. *clingan*].

clin·ic (klin'·ik) n. the teaching of medical subjects at the bedside; an institution where non-resident patients attend for treatment. **-al** a. [Gk. *klinē*, a bed].

clink (klingk) n. a slight, sharp, tinkling sound; (*Slang*) prison [imit. origin].

clink·er (kling'·kẹr) n. a mass of slag or cinders from furnaces; a kind of brick [Dut.].

clink·er·built (kling'·kẹr·bilt) a. (*Naut.*) built with overlapping boards or plates (opp. of *carvel-built*) [fr. *clench*].

clip (klip) v.t. to grip tightly. pr.p. **-ping**. pa.t., pa.p. **-ped**. n. any device for grasping or holding a thing firmly [O.E. *clyppan*, to embrace].

clip (klip) v.t. to cut with scissors or shears; to prune or cut short; to shear sheep; to pare the edge of a coin; to shorten or slur words; v.i. to move quickly; n. act of clipping; a season's shearing of wool; a rapid pace; (*Colloq.*) a sharp blow. pr.p. **-ping**. pa.p. and pa.t. **-ped**. **-per** n. one who clips; a fast sailing-vessel, with a long sharp bow; fast, long distance airliner. **-pers** n. a two-bladed instrument for cutting hair, shearing sheep, etc. **-ping** n. an item cut from a newspaper, etc. [Scand.].

clique (klik) n. a narrow circle of persons with common interests; a coterie. **cliquish** a. **cliquishness** n. [Fr.].

cloak (klōk) n. a long, loose, outer garment;

something that conceals; a pretext; *v.t.* to cover with a cloak; to hide; to mask or dissemble. **-room** *n.* a room where coats, hats, etc. may be temporarily left [O.Fr. *cloque*].

clob·ber (klǎb'·ẹr) *v.t.* (*Slang*) to beat decisively.

cloche (klōsh) *n.* glass covering used for intensive cultivation of vegetables, etc.; a close-fitting bell-shaped hat [Fr. = a bell].

clock (klǎk) *n.* a device which measures time. **-wise** *adv.* in the direction of the hands of a clock. **counterclockwise** *adv.* circling in the opposite direction. **-work** *n.* the movements or machinery of a clock; regular movement as of clock; *a.* mechanically regular. **o'clock,** by the clock [Fr. *cloche,* a bell].

clock (klǎk) *n.* an ornament worked on a stocking on each side of the ankle.

clod (klǎd) *n.* a lump of earth clay, or turf; the earth; a dull, stupid fellow. **-hopper** *n.* a rustic; a boor; a clumsy, heavy shoe [O.E. fr. *clot*].

clog (klǎg) *n.* a strong, clumsy shoe with a thick wooden sole; an impediment; an obstruction; *v.t.* to hinder; to encumber; to choke up; *v.i.* to become choked, encumbered. *pr.p.* **-ging.** *pa.p. pa.t.* **-ged** [M.E. *clogge,* a block of wood].

clois·ter (klois'·tẹr) *n.* covered arcade running along one or more walls of the inner court of a monastery or college; a monastery or nunnery; a secluded spot; *v.t.* to confine. **-al, cloistral** *a.* **-ed** *a.* [L. *claustrum,* enclosed place].

close (klōz) *v.t.* to shut; to stop up; to finish; to conclude; to complete (a wireless circuit); *v.i.* to come together; to unite; to end. **closing** *a.* ending; *n.* the act of shutting; the end; the conclusion. **closure** (klō'·zhẹr) *n.* the act of shutting; a closing; the close of a debate. [L. *claudere,* to shut].

close (klōs) *a.* shut up; confined; tight; stifling; near at hand; secret; niggardly; familiar; intimate; compact; crowded; searching; *adv.* in a close manner or state; nearly; tightly; *n.* an enclosed place; the precinct of a cathedral; (*Mus.*) a cadence. **-ly** *adv.* **-ness** *n.* **—** by, near. **— call,** a very narrow escape. **—fisted** or **—handed** *a.* miserly, penurious. **—mouthed** *a.* uncommunicative. **— quarters** *n.pl.* a crowded space. **a close shave,** a very narrow escape. **—up** *n.* a close view of anything [L. *claudere,* to shut].

clos·et (klǎz'·it) *n.* a small room or recess for storing things; a small private room; a lavatory; a water closet; *v.t.* to take into a private room for consultation [L. *claudere,* to shut].

clot (klǎt) *n.* a mass or lump, esp. of a soft, slimy character; (*Med.*) a coagulated mass of blood; *v.t.* to form into clots; *v.i.* to coagulate. *pr. p.* **-ting.** *pa.p.* and *pa.t.* **-ted** [O.E. *clod*].

cloth (klawth) *n.* any woven fabric of wool, hair, silk, cotton, flax, or oher fibers; a cover for a table. *pl.* **cloths** (klawTHz). **the Cloth** (*Fig.*) clergymen [O.E. *clath*].

clothe (klōTH) *v.t.* to put garments on; to cover as with a garment; to furnish raiment; (*Fig.*) to surround with; to wrap up in. *pr.p.* **clothing.** *pa.p.* and *pa.t.* **-d** or **clad. -s** *n. pl.* garments; wearing apparel; short for bedclothes, i.e. sheets, blankets, etc. **clothier** (klōTH'·yẹr) *n.* one who makes, or sells, clothes; a tailor; an outfitter. **clothing** *n.* garments in general; dress; wearing-apparel; raiment. **clotheshorse** *n.* a frame for hanging clothes; one who like clothes [O.E. *clath*].

clo·ture (klō'·chẹr) *n.* closure, applied to parliamentary debate [L. *clasura,* closure].

cloud (kloud) *n.* a body of visible vapor floating in the atmosphere; a mass of smoke, flying dust, etc.; that which has a dark, threatening aspect; a state of obscurity or impending trouble; a great multitude; *v.t.* to overspread with clouds; to darken; to sadden; to defame; *v.i.* to grow cloudy; to be blurred. **-y** *a.* darkened with clouds; overcast; hazy; dim; blurred; indistinct; gloomy. **-ily** *adv.* **-iness** *n.* **-burst** *n.* a vio-

lent downpour of rain; a deluge [O.E. *clud*].

clout (klout) *n.* the center of the target at which archers shoot; (*Colloq.*) a slap or blow; a piece of old cloth used for cleaning, scouring, etc.; *v.t.* (*Colloq.*) to strike with the open hand [O.E. *clut*].

clove (klōv) *n.* the flower-bud of the clove-tree, used as a spice; also yields oil [Fr. *clou,* a nail, fr. L. *clavus*].

clove (klōv) *pa.t.* of **cleave.**

clove hitch (klōv'·hich) *n.* (*Naut.*) a hitch used to secure a rope around a spar.

clo·ven (klōv'·n) *pa.p.* of **cleave.** Also *a.* split; divided into two parts [fr. *cleave*].

clo·ver (klō·vẹr) *n.* a common field plant of the trefoil family, used for fodder. **-leaf** *n.* a highway intersection in the shape of a four-leaf clover [O.E. *clafre*].

clown (kloun) *n.* the fool or buffoon in a play or circus; a peasant or rustic; an ill-bred man; a boor; *v.i.* to play the fool; to behave like a fool. **-ishly** *adv.* **-ishness** *n.*

cloy (kloi) *v.t.* to induce a sensation of loathing by overmuch of anything, esp. of sweetness, sentimentality, or flattery; to satiate. **-ing** *a.* satiating; disgusting [Fr. *clouer,* to nail].

club (klub) *n.* a heavy stick, thickening towards one end, used as a weapon; a cudgel; a stick used in the game of golf; an association of people united in pursuance of a common interest; the premises in which such an association meets; *v.t.* to beat with a club; to gather into a club; *v.i.* to form a club; to unite for a common end; to pay shares in a common expense. *pr.p.* **-bing.** *pa.p.* and *pa.t.* **-bed. -foot** *n.* a congenitally deformed or crooked foot; talipes [O.N. *klubba*].

clump (klump) *n.* a shapeless mass of any substance; a cluster of trees or shrubs; a heavy extra sole on a shoe; a tramping sound; *v.t.* to put in a clump or group; *v.i.* to tramp heavily [Dut. *klomp*].

clum·sy (klum'·zi·) *a.* ill-made; awkward; ungainly. **clumsily** *adv.* **clumsiness** *n.* [M.E. *clumsen,* to benumb].

clung (klung) *pa.p.* and *pa.t.* of **cling.**

clus·ter (klus'·tẹr) *n.* a bunch; a number of things growing together, as grapes; a collection; *v.t.* to collect into a bunch; *v.i.* to grow, or be, in clusters [O.E. *clyster*].

clutch (kluch) *v.t.* and *i.* to seize or grip with the hand; to grasp; *n.* a grasp; a tight grip; a set of eggs hatched at one time; a brood of chicks; the coupling of two working parts, used in motor vehicles to connect or disconnect engine and transmission gear. **-es** *n.pl.* the claws; the hands; power [O.E. *clyccan*].

clut·ter (klut'·ẹr) *n.* crowded confusion; disorder; noise; *v.t.* to crowd together in disorder; to make untidy [origin uncertain].

co- (kō) *prefix* meaning together, joint, etc. [fr. L. *cum,* with].

coach (kōch) *n.* a railroad passenger car; a tutor who prepares students for examination; a trainer in athletics; *v.i.* to travel in a coach; *v.t.* to tutor or train [Fr. *coche,* a coach].

co·ac·tion (kō·ak'·shạn) *n.* compulsion [L. *co-gere, coactum,* to compel].

co·ad·ju·tant (kō·aj'·oo·tạnt) *a.* assisting; *n.* an assistant. **coadjutor** (·tạr) *n.* an assistant; an associate and destined successor [L. *co-,* together; *adjuvare,* to help].

co·ag·u·late (kō·ag'·ya·lāt) *v.t.* to cause to curdle or congeal; to solidify; *v.i.* to curdle; to clot. **coagulant** *n.* a substance that causes coagulation. **coagulation** *n.* **coagulative** *a.* [L. *co-,* together; *agere,* to drive].

coal (kōl) *n.* a black substance used for fuel, composed of mineralized vegetable matter; a piece of this substance; *v.t.* to supply with coal; *v.i.* to take in coal. **-s** *n.pl.* glowing embers. **— bin** *n.* a recess for storing coal. **— field** *n.* a district where coal abounds. **— gas** *n.* gases produced from the distillation of coal or from burning coal. — **mine**, — **pit** n. the excavation from which coal is dug. — **oil** n. kerosene. — **tar** n. a thick, sticky substance, produced during the distilling of coal [O.E. *col*].

co·a·lesce (kō·a·les′) v.t. to grow together; to unite into one body or mass; to fuse. **coalescent** a. coalescing. **coalescence** n. [L. *co-*, together; *alescere*, to grow up].

co·a·li·tion (kō·a·lish′·an) n. a union or combination of persons, parties, or states into one body; a league. **-ist** n. [L. *co-*, together; *alescere*, to grow up].

coarse (kōrs) a. rough, rude; not refined; without grace or elegance; ill-mannered; vulgar; inferior. **-ly** adv. **-n** v.t. and i. to make or become coarse. **-ness** n. [M.E. *cors*; Fr. *gros*].

coast (kōst) n. land bordering the sea; the seashore; the country near the shore; v.t. and i. to sail near or along the coast; to run shut off, or on a bicycle without pedaling; to toboggan. **-al** a. pert. to the coast. **-er** n. a vessel trading between towns along the coast; a small tray placed under glasses to protect a table. **-guard** n. a service organized orig. to prevent smuggling; since 1925, largely a life-saving service; a member of this service. **-line** n. the outline of a coast. **-wards** adv. toward the coast. **-wise** adv. along the coast [L. *costa*, a rib].

coat (kōt) n. an outer garment; a jacket; an overcoat; the fur or skin of an animal; a covering; a layer spread over another, as paint; v.t. to cover with a coat; to clothe. **-ed** a. **-ing** n. any covering; a layer; cloth for making coats [Fr. *cotte*, an overall].

coax (kōks) v.t. to win over by fond pleading or flattery. **-ingly** adv. [etym. uncertain].

co·ax·i·al (kō·ak′·si·al) a. having a common axis [fr. *axis*].

cob (kob) n. a corn-cob; a male swan.

co·balt (kō′·bawlt) n. a metallic element classified with iron and nickel, and used as an ingredient of many alloys. — **blue** n. a pigment containing an oxide of cobalt; a. a dark-blue color. **-ic** a. [Ger. *Kobalt*].

co·balt bomb n. a type of atomic bomb equal in power to the hydrogen bomb and with more lethal and lasting effects.

cob·ble (kab′·l) v.t. to mend or patch coarsely; to mend boots or shoes. **-r** n. a mender of shoes; a deep-dish fruit pie with a biscuit crust.

cob·ble (kab′·l) n. a stone rounded by the action of water; v.t. to pave with cobbles. **-stone** n. a rounded stone used in paving.

co·bra (kō′·bra) n. the venomous 'hooded' snake of Africa and India. **cobric** a. [L. *colubra*, a snake].

cob·web (kab′·web) n. a spider's web; anything flimsy, transparent, and fragile; a trap or entanglement [O.E. *coppe*, a spider].

co·ca (kō′·ka) n. a Peruvian plant or its dried leaf, which is a nerve stimulant. **cocaine** (kō·kān′) n. a drug made from coca leaves, used as a local anesthetic [Native].

coc·cyx (kak′·siks) n. the triangular bone ending spinal column. pl. **coccyges** (kak′·si·jēz). **coccygeal** a. [Gk. *kokkux*, cuckoo].

coch·i·neal (kak′·i·nēl) n. a scarlet dye-stuff, made from the dried bodies of insects [L. *coccineus*, scarlet].

coch·le·a (kak′·li·a) n. a spiral passage of the inner ear [Gk. *kochlias*, a snail from the shape of its shell].

cock (kak) n. the male of birds, esp. of the domestic fowl; a weather-cock; a tap to regulate the flow of fluids; the hammer of a firearm; the cocked position of a hammer (of a firearm); a chief or leader; v.t. to draw back the hammer of a gun; to set up, set erect, set at an angle, as a hat; v.i. (*Dial.*) to swagger. **-crow** n. early morning. **-erel** n. a young cock; a swaggering youth. **-eyed** a. squinting; (*Slang*) on a slant; foolish. **-scomb** n. the comb of a cock; a flowering plant. **-sure** a. quite sure. **-tail** n. a horse not of pure breed; a drink concocted of liquor, bitters, sugar, etc; a mixture of fruit, or of seafood, served as an appetizer. **-y** a. vain and confident; full of self-assurance. **-ily** adv. **-iness** n. [O.E. *coc*].

cock (kak) n. a pile of hay [O.E. *coc*].

cock·ade (ka·kād′) n. a knot of ribbons, a rosette or badge, often worn on the hat [Fr. *cocarde*, fr. *coq*, a cock].

cock·a·too (kak·a·tòò′) n. a kind of parrot with a crested head [Malay].

cock·a·trice (kak′·a·tris) n. a fabulous animal represented as a cock with a dragon's tail; a fabulous serpent imagined to possess the powers of the basilisk, whose glance deals death [O.Fr. *cocatrice*].

cock·er (kak′·er) n. a cocker spaniel, a small variety of spaniel, used for retrieving game.

cock·le (kak′·l) n. a weed that grows among corn; the corn rose [O.E. *coccel*].

cock·le (kak′·l) n. a bivalve shell-fish, with a thick ribbed shell; v.t. to cause to pucker; to wrinkle. **-shell** n. the shell of a cockle; a shallow boat [Fr. *coquille*].

Cock·ney (kak′·ni·) n. a native of London. **-dom** n. the home of cockneys. **-fied** a. like a cockney.

cock·pit (kak′·pit) n. in aircraft, a compartment in the fuselage for the pilot and controls; the pit or ring in which game cocks fought, hence any arena of frequent strife.

cock·roach (kak′·rōch) n. a black or brown beetle infesting houses [Sp. *cucaracha*].

cock·swain See **coxswain**.

co·co, co·coa (kō′·kō) n. a palm tree producing the coconut. **-nut** n. the fruit of the coco palm [Sp. and Pot. *coco*, a bugbear].

co·coa (kō′·kō) n. a powder made from the kernels of the cacao or chocolate plant; a beverage from this [corrupt. fr. *cacao*].

co·coon (ka·kòòn′) n. the silky envelope which the silkworm and other larvae spin for themselves before passing into the pupa stage [O.Fr. *coque*, a shell].

cod, cod·fish (kad, kad′·fish) n. a large fish from northern seas, much used as food.

co·da (kō′·da) n. (*Mus.*) a short passage added at the end of a composition to round it off [It. fr. L. *cauda*, a tail].

cod·dle (kad′·l) v.t. to boil gently; to pamper or spoil [etym. uncertain].

code (kōd) n. an orderly collection of laws; a system of words, symbols, or numbers adopted for secrecy or economy; a cipher; v.t. to put into the form of a code. **codify** (ka′·di·fī) v.t. to collect laws, etc. into a digest. **codification** n. act of collecting laws. [L. *codex*, a book].

co·dex (kō′·deks) n. an ancient manuscript of a book, esp. of the Bible; a collection of manuscripts; pl. **codices** [L. *codex*, a book].

codg·er (kaj′·er) n. (*Colloq.*) an eccentric.

cod·i·cil (kad′·a·sil) n. a supplement or appendix to a will [L. *codicillus*, dim. of *codex*, a book].

co·ed·u·ca·tion (kō·ed·ū·kā′·shan) n. the education of boys and girls together in mixed classes. **-al** a. **co-ed** n. (*Colloq.*) a female student at a coeducational college or university.

co·ef·fi·cient (kō·a·fish′·ant) a. cooperating; combining; n. that which unites with something else to produce a result; (*Math.*) a number or other factor placed before another as a multiplier; (*Phys.*) a constant number or factor measuring some specified property of a substance. **coefficiency** n.

co·e·qual (kō·ē′·kwal) a. equal; of the same rank or power as another; n. a person having equality with another.

co·erce (kō·urs′) v.t. to compel by force; to constrain; to restrain. **coercible** a. **coercive** a. having power to compel. **coercively** adv. **coercion** (kō·ur′·shan) n. coercing; state of being coerced; compulsory force; restraint [L. *coercere*].

co·e·val (kō·ē'·vạl) *a.* of same age; *n.* contemporary [L *co-*, together; *aevum*, age].

co·ex·ist (kō·ig·zist') *v.i.* to exist at the same time or together. **-ence** *n.* **-ent** *a.*

cof·fee (kawf'·i·) *n.* an evergreen shrub, valuable for its berries; the seeds of the berries, esp. when ground and roasted; a drink from this. **-bean** *n.* the seed of the berry. **-house** *n.* a restaurant where coffee and other refreshments are supplied [Ar. *qahwah*].

cof·fer (kawf'·ẹr, kåf'·ẹr) *n.* a chest for valuables; a large money-box; an ornamental panel in a ceiling or archway; *v.t.* to put in a coffer; to hoard (money, etc.). **-dam** *n.* in engineering, a watertight, box-like, iron structure, used in the construction of the underwater foundations of bridges, etc. [Fr. *coffre*, a box].

cof·fin (kawf'·in) *n.* a box or casket in which the dead are enclosed before burial; *v.t.* to place in a coffin [Gk. *kophinos*, a basket].

cog (kåg) *n.* one of a series of teeth on a wheel; *v.t.* to fit a wheel with cogs. *pr.p.* **-ging.** *pa.p.* and *pa.t.* **-ged** [M.E. *cogge*].

co·gent (kō'·jạnt) *a.* having great force; powerful; convincing. **-ly** *adv.* **cogence, cogency** *n.* force; convincing power [L. *cogere*, to force].

cog·i·tate (kåj'·i·tāt) *v.i.* to reflect deeply; to meditate. **cogitable** *a.* **cogitation** *n.* contemplation. **cogitative** *a.* [L. *cogitare*].

co·gnac (kōn'·yak) *n.* a French brandy, so called from the town of *Cognac* in S.W. France; brandy in general.

cog·nate (kåg'·nāt) *a.* allied by blood or birth; of the same stock; from the same origin, formation, etc.; *n.* a relative by birth; anything of the same origin, kind, nature, or effect [L. *cognatus*, born together].

cog·ni·zance (kåg·nạ·zans) *n.* knowledge; perception. **cognizable** *a.* capable of being perceived or known. **cognizably** *adv.* **cognizant** *a.* having cognizance or knowledge of; competent to take judicial notice [L. *cognoscere*, to know].

cog·ni·tion (kåg·ni·shạn) *n.* awareness; state of being able to perceive objects or to remember ideas. **cognitive** *a.* [L. *cogniscere*, to know].

cog·no·men (kåg·nō'·men) *n.* a surname; a nickname [L. *nomen*, a name].

co·ha·bit (kō·hab'·it) *v.i.* to live together as husband and wife (usually of unmarried persons). **-ation, -ant** *n.*

co·here (kō·hir') *v.i.* to stick together; to be connected; to follow regularly in natural order; to be consistent; to coalesce; to adhere. **-nce, -ncy** *n.* **-nt** *a.* sticking together; connected; consistent. **-ntly** *adv.* **cohesible** *a.* capable of cohesion. **cohesion** *n.* the act of sticking together. **cohesive** *a.* having the power of cohering. **cohesiveness, cohesibility** *n.* [L. *cohaerere*, to stick together].

co·hort (kō'·hawrt) *n.* a division of a Roman legion, from 300 to 600 soldiers; a company of persons; an associate [L. *cohors*].

coif (koif) *n.* a headdress in the form of a close-fitting cap, worn by nuns. **-feur** (kwå-·fur') (*fem.* **coiffeuse**) *n.* a hairdresser. **coiffure** (kwå·fyoor') *n.* a headdress; a style of dressing the hair [Fr. *coiffe*].

coign (koin) *n.* a corner; a corner-stone; a wedge [same as *coin*, fr. L. *cuneus*, a wedge].

coil (koil) *v.t.* to wind in rings, as a rope; to twist into a spiral shape; *v.i.* to take on a spiral shape; *n.* the spiral of rings into which anything is wound; one of the rings of the spiral [L. *colligere*, to gather].

coil (koil) *n.* turmoil; tumult; fuss.

coin (koin) *n.* a piece of stamped metal issued by government authority to be used as money; money; a wedge or cornerstone; *v.t.* to make into money; to mint; or invent or fabricate, as a word or phrase. **-age** *n.* the act of coining;

money coined; currency. **-er** *n.* one who makes coins; an inventor [L. *cuneus*, a wedge].

co·in·cide (kō-in-sīd') *v.i.* to correspond in detail; to happen at the same time; to agree (in opinion). **coincidence** (kō·in'·si·dẹns) *n.* correspondence in nature, circumstances, etc. **coincident, coincidental** *a.* occupying the same space; agreeing; simultaneous. **coincidently** *adv.* [L. *co-*, together; *incidere*, to happen].

coir (koir) *n.* the fiber from the husk of the coconut, used for cordage, matting, etc. [Malay, *kayar*, cord].

co·i·tion (kō'·ī·shạn) *n.* sexual intercourse; copulation. Also **coitus** (kō·i·tạs) [L. *co-*, together; *ire*, *itum*, to go].

coke (kōk) *n.* coal half burnt, and used as fuel; *v.t.* to turn into coke [origin uncertain].

col·an·der (kål'·an·dẹr) *n.* a vessel with a perforated bottom, used for draining off liquids in cookery; a sieve. Also **cullender** [L. *colare*, to strain].

cold (kōld) *a.* wanting in heat; chill; deficient in the emotions; spiritless; *n.* absence of warmth; chilliness; cold weather; a disorder of the nose, throat and chest, often caused by cold, and characterized by running at the nose, hoarseness and coughing; catarrh. **-ly** *adv.* **-ish** *a.* somewhat cold. **-ness** *n.* **—blooded** *a.* having cold blood, like fish; susceptible to cold; callous or heartless. Also **—hearted** (hårt'·ạd). **— war,** campaign carried on by means of economic pressure, press, radio, etc. [O.E. *ceald*].

cole (kōl) *n.* a name for plants of the cabbage family. **—slaw** *n.* a salad of finely sliced or chopped cabbage. **-wort** *n.* any kind of cabbage whose leaves do not form a compact head [L. *caulis*, a stalk, esp. a cabbage stalk].

Co·le·op·ter·a (kōl·i·åp'·tẹr·ạ) *n.pl.* the order of insects, such as beetles, whose outer wings form a horny sheath or covering for the true wings [Gk. *koleos*, a sheath; *pteron*, a wing].

col·ic (kål'·ik) *n.* severe paroxysmal pain in the abdomen [Gk. *kolon*, the lower intestine].

co·li·se·um (kå·lạ·sē'·ạm) *n.* a stadium, amphitheater, or large auditorium [M.L. *colosseum*].

col·lab·o·rate (kạ·lab'·ạ·rāt) *v.i.* to work or labor together; to act jointly, esp. in works of literature, art, science. **collaboration** *n.* joint labor; (*World War* 2) willing cooperation with the enemy given by an inhabitant of an occupied country. **collaborator** *n.* [L. *co-*, *laborare*, to work].

col·lapse (kạ·laps') *v.i.* to fall in; to break down; to fail suddenly; to lose strength; to give way under physical or mental strain; *v.t.* to cause to collapse (as of a lung); *n.* a falling in or down; a sudden and complete failure; a breakdown. **collapsable, collapsible** *a.* [L. *collabi*, *collapsus*, to fall to pieces].

col·lar (kål'·ẹr) *n.* something worn around the neck; the part of a garment that fits around the neck; *v.t.* to seize by the collar; to arrest; to capture; to grab; to put a collar on. **-bone** *n.* the bone from the shoulders to the breast-bone; the clavicle [L. *collum*, the neck].

col·late (kạ·lāt') *v.t.* to compare critically; to arrange in order, as the sheets of a book for binding; to appoint to a benefice. **collation** *n.* the act of collating; a lunch or repast. **collative** *a.* **collator** *n.* [L. *conferre*, *collatum*, to bring together].

col·lat·e·ral (kạl·at'·ạ·rạl) *a.* side by side; running parallel; subordinately connected; descended from the same ancestor but through a different line; additional (of a security); *n.* a collateral relative; a kinsman; additional security. **-ly** *adv.* **-ness** [L. *con*; *latus*, the side].

col·league (kål'·ēg) *n.* as associate or companion [L. *collega*, an associate].

col·lect (kạ·lekt') *v.t.* to bring together; to gather; to assemble; to receive payment of; *v.i.* to be assembled; to come together. **collect**

(kȧl′·ekt) n. a very short prayer. **-able, -ible** a. **-ed** a. not disconcerted; cool; self-possessed. **-edly** adv. **-edness** n. **collection** n. the act of collecting; a contribution or sum of money gather at a meeting for a religious, charitable, etc. object; assemblage. **-ive** a. formed by gathering; gathered into a mass, sum, or body; expressing a collection or aggregate. **-ively** adv. **-ivism** n. a term embracing all systems on the Socialistic doctrine of the state, municipal, cooperative, etc. control of the economic life of the country. **-ivist** n. **-or** n. one who colletcs; an officer appointed to receive taxes, customs, duties, tolls, etc. [L. colligere, collectum, to gather together].

col·leen (kȧl′·ēn) n. a girl [Ir. cailin].

col·lege (kȧl′·ij) n. an institution for higher education; the buildings, etc. of such an institution; an association of professional men, e.g. of physicians; an assembly, as of electors or cardinals. **collegial** a. pert. to a college. **collegian** (ka·lē′·ji·an) n. a member of a college; a student. **collegiate** a. pert. to, or instituted like, a college; corporate [L. collegium, a society].

col·let (kȧl′·it) n. a collar; a neckband; the rim in which the stone of a ring is set [Fr. fr. L. collum, the neck].

col·lide (ka·līd′) v.i. to strike or dash together; to clash; to come into conflict. **collision** n. (ka·lizh′·an) n. the act of striking together; a violent impact; a clash; conflict [L. collidere, to dash together].

col·lie (kȧl′·i·) n. a breed of sheep dog.

col·lier·y (kȧl′·ya·ri·) n. a coal mine [fr. coal]

col·lin·e·ar (ka·lin′·i·er) a. in the same straight line; aligned [L. collineare].

col·lo·cate (kȧl′·ō·kāt) v.t. to set or place together; to arrange. **collocation** n. [L. collocare, to place together].

col·lo·di·on (ka·lō′·di·an) n. a solution of guncotton in ether, used in preparing photographic plates and in surgery [Gk. kolla, glue; eidos, form].

col·loid (kȧl′·oid) a. like glue; gelatinous; n. a glue-like, non-crystalline substance unable to pass through animal membranes. **-al** a. like a colloid [Gk. kolla, glue; eidos, form].

col·lo·quy (kȧl′·a·kwi·) n. conversation; dialogue; discussion; a conference, esp. political; a debate. **colloquial** (ka·lō′·kwi·al) a. pert. to, or used in, ordinary conversation. **colloquially** adv. **colloquialism** n. an expression used in cordinary conversation, but not regarded as slang [L. colloqui, to speak together].

col·lu·sion (ka·lòò′·zhan) n. a secret agreement between two or more persons for a fraudulent purpose, usually in connection with legal proceedings. **collusive** a. [L. colludere, collusum, to play together].

co·logne (ka·lōn′) n. a perfumed toilet water.

co·lon (kō′·lan) n. a punctuation mark (:), separating parts of a sentence that are almost independent and complete in themselves; (Anat.) that part of the large intestine extending from the caecum to the rectum. **colonic** a. [Gk. kolon, a limb or member].

colo·nel (kur′·nal) n. the officer ranking between lieutenant colonel and a brigadier general, usually commanding a regiment. **-cy**, **-ship** n. the rank or quality of colonel [L. columna, a column. The pronunciation is due to a Sp. form coronel, one also used].

col·on·nade (kȧl′·a·nād′) n. a series of colums arranged symmetrically [L. columna, a column].

col·o·ny (kȧl′·an·i·) n. a body of people who settle in a new country but remain subject to the parent state; the country thus occupied; a group of people living in a community for a common purpose; a group of animals or plants living and growing together. **colonial** a. pert. to a colony; n. a colonist. **colonize** v.t. to plant or establish a colony; v.i. to settle.

colonist n. **colonization** n. [L. colonia].

col·o·phon (kȧl′·a·fȧn) n. individual device or inscription used by publishers and printers on the title pages of books, etc. [Gk. colophon, the finish].

col·or (kul′·er) n. any hue or tint as distinguished from white; paint; complexion; a flush; outward appearance; kind or general character; vividness in writing; in music, variety of timbre; v.t. to paint or tinge with color; v.i. to blush. **colors** n.pl. a flag or standard; a colored badge, device, rosette, etc. used as a distinguishing mark. **-able** a. capable of being colored; specious; plausible. **-ably** adv. **-ed** a. having color; biased; belonging to some other race than white, esp. Negro. **-ful** a. having plenty of color. **—blind** a. unable to distinguish colors. **— line**, discrimination in status between white and colored races [L. color, color].

col·or·a·tion (kul·a·rā′·shan) n. coloring; arrangement or dispostion of colors in art. Also **coloration** [L. color, color].

col·or·a·tu·ra (kȧl·ar·a·tū′·ra) n. (Mus.) ornamental runs and trills in vocal music [It.].

co·los·sus (ka·làs′·us) n. a gigantic statue, esp. that of Apollo at Rhodes; hence (Fig.) any person of great stature or enormous strength. **colossal** a. of enormous size [Gk. kolossos].

colt (kōlt) n. young horse, esp. a male. [O.E.].

Colt (kōlt) n. a repeating rifle; also a revolver invented by Samuel Colt.

col·ter (kōl′·ter) n. the sharp blade of iron placed at the front end of a plow to act as a cutter. Also **coulter** [O.E. culter].

col·um·bine (kȧl′·am·bīn) a. of, or like, a dove; dove-colored; n. a small bell-shaped flower, with five spurred petals [L. columba, a dove].

col·umn (kȧl′·am) n. a round pillar; a support; a body of troops drawn up in deep files; a division of a page; a perpendicular line of figures. **-ar** (ka·lum′·ner) a. formed in columns; having the form of columns. **-ated, -ed** a. furnished with, or supported on, columns. **-ist** n. a writer who contributes articles to a newspaper. **fifth column,** group of people residing in a country who are in sympathy with and assist its enemies [L. columna].

co·ma (kō′·ma) n. (Med.) a deep sleep or stupor generally resulting from injury to the brain, alcoholic or narcotic poisoning; (Fig.) lethargy; drowsiness. **-tose** a. lethargic; drowsy [Gk. koma].

comb (kōm) n. a toothed instrument for separating, cleansing, adjusting, or fastening hair, dressing wool, etc.; also a decoration for a lady's hair; a cock's crest; the crest of a wave; the cell structure in which bees store their honey; v.t. to separate, cleanse, dress, etc. with a comb; v.i. to roll over or break with a white foam (said of waves). **-er** n. one who, or that which, combs; a long, curling wave. **-ing** n. **-ings** n.pl. hair, wool, etc. removed by combing [O.E. camb].

com·bat (kam·bat′) v.t. to fight against; to oppose by force; to contend with; v.i. to struggle; to contend. **combat** (kȧm′·bat) n. a fight; a struggle; a contest. **-ant** a. contending; disposed to contend; n. one engaged in a fight. **-ive** a. disposed to combat; quarrelsome [Fr. combattre, to fight].

com·bine (kam·bīn′) v.t. to join together; to unite; to connect; v.i. to form a union; to cooperate; (Chem.) to unite and form a new compound. **combine** (kȧm′·bīn) n. an association formed to further political or commercial interests; a trust; a syndicate; a harvester; an agricultural machines that reaps, threshes and bags the grain in one operation. **combinable** a. capable of combining. **combinative, combinatory** a. tending to combine. **combination** (kȧm·ba·nā′·shan) n. union or connection; association of persons; alliance; chemical union; series of letters or numbers for operating a lock; an undergarment combining vest and pants. [L.L. *combinare*].

com·bus·tion (kạm·bus′·chạn) *n.* the act of fire on inflammable substances; the act of burning; chemical action accompanied by heat and light. **combustible** *a.* liable to take fire; inflammable; *n.* a substance that burns readily [L. *comburere*, to burn up].

come (kum) *v.i.* to approach; to arrive; to arrive at some state or condition; to move towards; to reach; to happen (to); to originate (from); to occur; to turn out to be; to appear. *pr.p.* **coming.** *pa.p.* **come.** *pa.t.* **came.** **-back** *n.* a return to a former activity; (*Slang*) a retort [O.E. *cuman*].

com·e·dy (kȧm′·ạ·di·) *n.* a play dealing with the lighter side of life; the humorous element in literature, life, or an incident.

co·me·di·an (kạ·mē′·di·ạn) *n.* an actor in comedy; an entertainer whose songs or stories are light and humorous; (*Colloq.*) a funny person; a comic. **comedienne** (kạm·ē·di·en′) *n. fem.* [Gk. *komoidia*, fr. *komos*, revel; *odē*, song].

come·ly (kum′·li·) *a.* good-looking; graceful. **comeliness** *n.* [O.E. *cyme*, fair].

co·mes·ti·ble (kạ·mes′·ti·bl) *a.* fit for eating. [L. *comedere*, to eat up].

com·et (kȧm′·it) *n.* a heavenly body consisting of a diffuse, nebulous head, a nucleus, and a tail [Gk. *komētēs*, long-haired].

come·up·pance (kum·up′·ạns) *n.* (*Slang*) deserved punishment.

com·fort (kum′·fẹrt) *v.t.* to allay grief or trouble; to console, cheer, gladden; *n.* solace or consolation; ease of body or mind, or whatever causes it. **-s** *n.pl.* appurtenances or circumstances which give greater ease to life. **-able** *a.* promoting or enjoying comfort. **-ably** *adv.* **-er** *n.* one who comforts; a quilted bedcover. **-less** *a.* **Job's comforter,** one who, in seeking to comfort, achieves the opposite [L. *confortare*, to strengthen].

com·ic (kȧm′·ik) *a.* pert. to comedy; mirth-provoking; funny; *n.* that which induces amusement or laughter; (*Colloq.*) a comedian; (*Colloq.*) (*pl.*) a comic magazine or newspaper strip. **-al** *a.* droll; ludicrous. **-ally** *adv.* **-ality** *n.* [Gk. *komos*, revel].

com·in·form (kȧm′·in·fawrm) *n.* Communist Information Bureau.

Com·in·tern (kȧm′·in·turn) *n.* Communist International, the international association of Communist parties.

com·i·ty (kȧm′·ạ·ti·) *n.* courtesy; civility; suavity of manners [L. *comitas*].

com·ma (kȧm′·ạ) *n.* a punctuation mark (,), used to mark the shortest pauses in the division of a sentence [Gk. fr. *komma*, short clause].

com·mand (kạ·mand′) *v.t.* to order or demand with authority; to govern or control; to have at one's disposal; to overlook or have a view over; *v i.* to be at the head; *n.* an order; the body of troops under an officer; a district or region under a commander; a word of command; mastery or facility. **-ing** *a.* fitted to control; impressive or imperious. **-ant** *n.* officer in charge of a military station or a body of troops. **-eer** (kȧ·mạn·dēr′) *v.t.* to seize for military purposes; to take forcible possession of. **-er** (kạ·man′·dẹr) *n.* a leader; a commanding officer; in the navy, an officer ranking between a lieutenant commander and a captain. **-ment** *n.* a command; precept. **-er-in-chief,** the officer in supreme command of the forces of a state [L. *commendare*, to entrust].

com·man·do (kạ·man′·dō) *n.* (*Mil.*) a selected body of men, who undergo special training for particularly dangerous enterprises against the enemy; a member of this body [Sp.].

com·mem·o·rate (kạ·mem′·ạ·rāt) *v.t.* to call to remembrance; to celebrate the memory of

someone or something by a solemn act of devotion. **commemoration** *n.* **commemorative, commemoratory** *a.* [L. *commemorare*].

com·mence (kạ·mens′) *v.t.* to begin, to start, to originate; *v.i.* to originate; to take rise; to begin. **-ment** *n.* beginning; the ceremony of conferring degrees in colleges and universities [Fr. *commencer*].

com·mend (kạ·mend′) *v.t.* to praise; to speak favorably of; to present as worthy; to entrust to. **-able** *a.* **-ably** *adv.* **-ableness** *n.* **-ation** *n.* the act of commending; praise; approval. **-atory** *a.* [L. *commendare*, to entrust].

com·men·su·rate (kạ·men′·shạ·rit) *a.* equal in extent; proportionate; adequate. **-ly** *adv.* **-ness** *n.* **commensuration** *n.* **commensurable** *a.* having a common measure; suitably proportioned. **commensurably** *adv.* **commensurability** *n.* [L. *con-; mensura*, a measure].

com·ment (kȧ′·ment) *v.t. and i.* to make remarks, notes, criticisms; *n.* a note; a collection of notes; an explanation; a critical remark; an observation. **-ary** (kȧ·mạn·te′·ri) *n.* a series of notes; an exposition of a book; an historical narrative. **running commentary,** the description of an event while in actual progress, broadcast by an eye-witness. **-ate** *v.t.* to annotate; to interpret the meaning of. **-ator** *n.* an annotator; an expositor; one who speaks a commentary, either on events for broadcasting, or with a film [L. *comminisci, commentus*, to contrive].

com·merce (kȧm′·urs) *n.* buying and selling; trade; social or personal intercourse. **commercial** (kạ·mur′·shạl) *a.* pert. to commerce; (*Radio*) broadcast program paid for by an advertiser. **commercialism** *n.* business principles, methods, or viewpoint. **commercialize** *v.t.* **commercially** *adv.* [L. *con-; merx*, merchandise]. [gle together.

com·min·gle (kạ·ming′·gl) *v.t. and i.* to min-

com·mis·er·ate (kạ·miz′·ạ·rāt) *v.t. and i.* to have compassion for; to condole with; to pity; to sympathize. **commiseration** *n.* [L. *commiserari*, to bewail with].

com·mis·sar (kȧm′·i·sȧr) *n.* one of the heads of a Soviet government department or commissariat [L. *committere*, to entrust].

com·mis·sar·i·at (kȧm·i·sa′·ri·ạt) *n.* the army department which supplies food, stores, equipment, transport; any of the governmental divisions of the U.S.S.R. [L. *committere*, to entrust].

com·mis·sa·ry (kȧm′·i·ser·i·) *n.* one to whom duty is assigned; a deputy; a commissioner; (*Mil.*) a store which supplies food and equipment. **commissarial** *a.* [L. *committere*, to entrust].

com·mis·sion (kạ·mish′·ạn) *n.* the act of committing; something entrusted to be done; payment by a percentage for doing something; a group of people authorized to deal with specified matters; a legal warrant to execute some office, trust, or duty; the power under such warrant; the document that contains it; the thing to be done as agent for another; (*Mil., Naval, etc.*) a warrant of appointment, by the head of a state, to the rank of officer in the army, navy, etc.; *v.t.* to give power to; to authorize; to give an order for; to appoint to the rank of officer. **-ed** *a.* **-er** *n.* one holding a commission to act; the head of a governmental department [L. *committere*, to entrust].

com·mit (kạ·mit′) *v.t.* to entrust; to give in charge; to perform; to be guilty of; to pledge or bind; to send for trial or confinement; *pr.p.* **-ting,** *pa.p. and pa.t.* **-ted. -tal** *a.* **-ment** *n.* [L. *committere*].

com·mit·tee (kạ·mit′·i·) *n.* a number of persons appointed to attend any particular business by a legislative body, court, society, etc. [L. *committere*, to entrust].

com·mode (kạ·mōd′) *n.* a chest of drawers; a small piece of furniture containing a chamber pot [L. *commodus*, suitable].

com·mo·di·ous (kạ·mō′·di·ạs) *a.* convenient; roomy; spacious. **-ly** *adv.* **-ness** *n.* **commodity** *n.* any useful thing; an article of trade. **commodities** *n.pl.* goods [L. *commodus*, suitable].

com·mo·dore (kàm′·ạ·dōr) *n.* (*Naval*) the rank just below rear admiral; captain of a convoy of ships [etym. uncertain].

com·mon (kàm′·ạn) *a.* shared by or belonging to all, or to several; public; general; ordinary; usual; frequent; vulgar; inferior; of little value; of low social status; *n.* a tract of land belonging to a community for public use. **commons** *n.pl.* the lower House of Parliament, called the **House of Commons;** (*l.c.*) a dining room at a university. **-alty** *n.* the general body of the people with reference to rank, position, etc. **-er** *n.* one of the common people, i.e. not a member of the nobility. **-ly** *adv.* in a common manner; usually; jointly; meanly. **-ness** *n.* **-place** *a.* ordinary; trite; hackneyed; *n.* a common topic; a trite remark. — **sense** *n.* sound and practical understanding; well-balanced judgment. — **law,** (*Eng.*) law based on usage and custom, and confirmed by judicial decision; the unwritten law as distinguished from statute law. **the common good,** the welfare of the community as a whole [L. *communis*].

com·mon·weal (kàm′·ạn·wēl) *n.* the public welfare; the common good. **commonwealth** (welth) *n.* the whole body of people; a republican or democratic state. **Commonwealth** *n.* since 1947 the comprehensive term for all territories within the British Empire, including the Dominions [*common* and *weal*].

com·mo·tion (kạ·mō′·shạn) *n.* violent motion; agitation; tumult; public disorder [L. *commorere, motum*, to move].

com·mune (kạ·mūn′) *v.i.* to converse together intimately; to have spiritual intercourse (*with*); (*Eccl.*) to receive the communion. **communion** (kạm·ūn′·yạn) *n.* the act of communing; (*Christianity*) the celebration of the Lord's Supper [L. *communish*, common].

com·mune (kàm′·ūn) *n.* a small administrative district (esp. in France) governed by a mayor. **communal** *a.* pert. to a commune or community; for common use. **communalize** *v.t.* to make over for common use. **communalism** *n.* a system by which small local governments have large powers. **communism** *n.* the theory of a social system in which everything is held in common, private property being abolished. **communist** *n.* **communistic** *a.* [L. *communis*, common].

com·mu·ni·cate (kạ·mū′·nạ·kāt) *v.t.* to impart information; to reveal; to convey; *v.i.* to have connection with; to have dealings, correspondence, with. **communicable** *a.* **communicably** *adv.* **communication** *n.* the act of making known; intercourse by speech, correspondence, messages, etc.; information; means of passing from one place to another; a connecting passage. **communicant** *n.* one who imparts information; one who receives communion. **communicative** *a.* ready to converse or to impart information; talkative. [L. *communicare*]. [announcement [Fr.].

com·mu·ni·qué (kạ·mū′·ni·kā) *n.* an official

com·mu·ni·ty (kạ·mū′·nạ·ti·) *n.* a locality where people reside; people having common interests; the public, or people in general; common possession or enjoyment [L. *communis*].

com·mute (kạ·mūt′) *v.t.* to exchange; to substitute; to mitigate a sentence; travel regularly between home and work. **commutable** *a.* exchangeable. **commutability** *n.* **commutation** *n.* **commutator** *n.* (*Elect.*) a device for reversing the direction of an electric current. **-r** *n.* [L. *con-*; *mutare*, to change].

com·pact (kạm·pakt′) *a.* firm; solid; closely packed; condensed; terse; *v.t.* to press closely together; to make firm. **compact** (kàm′·

pakt) *n.* a pocket vanity-case. **-ly** *adv.* **-ness** *n.* **-ed** *a.* firmly united [L. *con-*; *pangere, pactum*, to fix].

com·pact (kạm′·pakt) *n.* an agreement or contract; a mutual bargain; a league or covenant [L. *con-*; *pactus*, to make an agreement].

com·pan·ion (kạm·pan′·yạn) *n.* one who is in another's company, habitually or for the moment; comrade; an associate or partner; a match or mate. **-able** *a.* fitted to be a companion; sociable. **-ably** *adv.* **-ability, -ableness** *n.* **-ship** *n.* [L. *companium*, fellowship, fr. *con-, panis*, bread].

com·pan·ion (kạm·pan′·yạn) *n.* (*Naut.*) a skylight on upper deck, to let light into cabin below. **-way**, cabin staircase [O.Fr. *compagne*].

com·pa·ny (kum′·pa·ni·) *n.* a gathering of persons; an assembly; a group; an association of persons in business, etc.; visitors; a division of a regiment; a ship's crew [L. *con-*; *panis*, bread]

com·pare (kạm·pār′) *v.t.* to notice or point out the likeness and differences of two or more things; to liken or contrast; (*Gram.*) to state the comparative and superlative of an adjective or adverb; *v.i.* to be like; to compete with. **comparable** (kàm′·par·ạ·bl) *a.* capable of being compared; of equal regard or value. **comparably** *adv.* **comparative** (kạm·par′·ạ·tiv) *a.* estimated by comparison; not absolute; relative; partial; (*Gram.*) expressing 'more'. **comparatively** *adv.* **comparison** *n.* the act of comparing [L. *comparare*, to match].

com·part·ment (kạm·pàrt′·mạnt) *n.* a part divided off; a section; a division of a railway car [L. *compartiri*, to divide].

com·pass (kum′·pạs) *n.* an instrument for showing directions (north, east, etc.); (*Mus.*) the range of a voice in the musical scale; circuit; a circumference; measurement around; space; area; scope; reach; *v.t.* to go round; to surround; to contrive; to attain; to accomplish. **-es** *n.pl.* a mathematical instrument for drawing circles, measuring, etc. [L. *con-*; *passus*, a step].

com·pas·sion (kạm·pash′·ạn) *n.* sympathy with the distress or suffering of another; pity. **-ate** *a.* full of sympathy; showing pity; merciful; *v.t.* to pity. **-ately** *adv.* **-ateness** *n.* [L. *con-*; *pati, passus*, to suffer].

com·pat·i·ble (kạm·pat′·ạ·bl) *a.* consistent; agreeing with; capable of harmonious union. **compatibly** *adv.* **compatibility** *n.* [L. *con-*; *pati*, to suffer].

com·pa·tri·ot (kạm·pā′·tri·ạt) *n.* one of the same country; a fellow countryman [L. *con-*; and *patriot*].

com·peer (kạm·pir′) *n.* an equal; a companion; an associate [L. *con-*; *par*, equal].

com·pel (kạm·pel′) *v.t.* to force; to overpower; to bring about by force; *pr.p.* **-ling.** *pa.p.* and *pa.t.* **-led. -lable** *a.* [L. *compellere*, to drive together].

com·pen·di·um (kạm·pen′·di·ạm) *n.* an abridgement or summary; an abstract. Also **compend.** *pl.* **-s,** or **compendia. compendious** *a.* abridged. **compendiously** *adv.* [L.].

com·pen·sate (kàm′·pạn·sāt) *v.t.* to recompense suitably; to reward; to pay; *v.i.* to make amends; to make up for. **compensation** *n.* recompense; payment for some loss, injury, etc. **compensative, compensatory** *a.* [L. *compensare*, to weigh together].

com·pete (kạm·pēt′) *v.i.* to strive against others to win something; to vie with. **competition** (kàm·pạ·tish′·ạn) *n.* the act of competing; a contest. **competitive** *a.* **competitively** *adv.* **competitor** *n.* one who competes. **competitory** *a.* [L. *competere*, to seek with].

com·pe·tent (kàm′·pạ·tạnt) *a.* able; properly qualified; proper; suitable; skillful. **-ly** *adv.* **competence, competency** *n.* the state of being fit or capable; sufficiency, esp. of means of subsistence [L. *competere*, to seek together].

com·pile (kạm·pīl′) *v.t.* to put together literary

materials into one book or works; to collect or amass. **-r** n. **compilation** n. [L. *compilare*, to plunder].

com·pla·cent (kạm·plā′·sạnt) a. self-satisfied; pleased or gratified. **-ly** adv. **complacence, complacency** n. self-satisfaction [L. *complacere*, to please greatly].

com·plain (kạm·plān′) v.i. to express distress, grief, dissatisfaction; to lament; to grumble; to be ailing. **-ant** n. a complainer; (*Law*) a plaintiff; one who brings an action against another. **complaint** n. the expression of distress, dissatisfaction, etc.; a malady or ailment [L. *con-; plangere*, to bewail].

com·plai·sant (kạm·plā′·zạnt) a. desirous to please; affable; obliging; gracious. **-ly** adv. **complaisance** n. [L. *complacere*, to please greatly].

com·ple·ment (kåm′·plạ·mạnt) n. that which supplies a deficiency; something completing a whole; the full quantity or number; v.t. to complete; to supply a deficiency. **-al, -ary** a. completing [L. *complere*, to fill up].

com·plete (kạm·plēt′) a. entire; finished; perfect, with no part lacking; v.t. to bring to a state of entirety; to make perfect; to fulfill; to accomplish. **-ly** adv. **-ness** n. **completion** (kạm·plē′·shạn) n. the act of completing; fulfilment; conclusion [L. *complere*, to fill up].

com·plex (kåm′·pleks) a. consisting of two or more parts; not simple; involved or intricate; n. a complicated whole; (*Psych.*) a group of repressed emotional ideas responsible for abnormal mental condition; (*Colloq.*) an obsession. **-ly** adv. **-ness, -ity** n. [L. *complectere*, to interweave].

com·plex·ion (kạm·plek′·shạn) n. color of the skin, esp. of the face; aspect or appearance; quality or texture; character [L. *complexio*].

com·pli·ance (kạm·plī′·ạns) n. submission; a yielding; acquiescence. **compliant** a. yielding; obedient; civil. **compliantly** adv. **compliable** a. inclined to comply [fr. *comply*].

com·pli·cate (kåm′·plạ·kāt) v.t. to fold or twist together; to entangle; to make intricate. **-d** a. tangled; involved. **complication** n. [L. *con-; plicare*, to fold].

com·plic·i·ty (kạm·plis′·ạ·ti·) n. the state of being an accomplice, of having a share in the guilt [Fr. *complice*, an accomplice].

com·pli·ment (kåm′·plạ·mạnt) n. an expression of regard or admiration; flattering speech; a formal greeting (usually *pl.*); v.t. to express approbation; to congratulate; to express respect for. **-ary** a. expressing praise, admiration; free, a *complimentary* ticket [L. *complete*, to fill up].

com·ply (kạm·plī′·) v.i. to yield to; to agree; to consent; to conform; to adapt oneself to. **complier** n. [L. *complere*, to fill up].

com·po·nent (kạm·pō′·nạnt) a. constituting; composing; making up; helping to form a compound; n. a part helping to make a whole [L. *componere*, to put together].

com·port (kạm·pōrt′) v.t. to behave; to conduct oneself; v.i. to agree; to accord; to suit [L. *comportare*, to carry together].

com·pose (kạm·pōz′) v.t. to form by uniting parts; to arrange; to put in order; to write; to invent; to adjust; to calm; to soothe; to set up the types in proper order for printing; v.i. to practice composition. **-d** a. sedate; quiet; calm. **-dly** adv. **-dness** n. **-r** n. one who composes; an author. **composite** (kạm·pàz′·it) a. made up of distinct parts or elements. **composition** (kåm·pạ·zish′·ạn) n. the act of composing; the thing formed by composing; a pupil's essay; a literary, musical, artistic, etc. work; the organization of the parts of a work of art. **compositor** (kạm·pàz′·ạ·tẹr) n. a typesetter. **composure** (kạm·pō′·zhẹr) n. calmness [Fr. *composer*].

com·post (kåm′·pōst) n. a fertilizing mixture; a composition for plaster work, etc. [L. *componere*, to put together].

com·pote (kåm′·pōt) n. fruit stewed or preserved in syrup; a stemmed candy dish [Fr.].

com·pound (kạm·pound′) v.t. to put together, as elements or parts, to form a whole; to combine; to compromise; to make a settlement of debt by partial payment. **to compound a felony** (*Law*) to refrain, for some consideration, from prosecuting [L. *componere*, to put together].

com·pound (kåm′·pound) a. composed of elements, ingredients, or parts; not simple; composite; n. a mixture; a joining; a substance to which something has been added; a word, etc. made up of parts; (*Chem.*) a substance composed of two or more elements, which are always present in the same fixed proportions. **— fracture,** a fracture of a bone where a portion pierces the skin, making a surface wound. **— interest,** interest paid on capital plus accumulated interest [L. *componere*, to put together].

com·pound (kåm′·pound) n. in the Orient, an enclosure about a house; in S. Africa, an enclosed area in which native laborers reside [Malay, *kampong*, an enclosure].

com·pre·hend (kåm·pri·hend′) v.t. to understand; to grasp with the mind; to take in; to include; to comprise. **comprehensible** (kåm·pri·hen′·sạ·bl) a. understandable; conceivable. **comprehensibly** adv. **comprehensibility, comprehensibleness** n. **comprehension** n. the act of comprehending; the capacity of the mind to perceive and understand. **comprehensive** a. including much within narrow limits; extensive; large; capacious; inclusive [L. *comprehendere*, to grasp].

com·press (kạm·pres′) v.t. to press together; to reduce the volume by pressure; to condense. **-ed** a. **-ible** a. **-ibility** n. **-ion** (kạm·presh′·ạn) n. the act or effect of compressing. **-ive** a. tending to compress. **-or** n. [L. *compressus*, pressed together].

com·press (kåm′·pres) n. (*Med.*) a pad to make pressure on a wound; a wet pad to reduce inflammation.

com·prise (kạm·prīz′) v.t. to include; to be composed of; to consist of [Fr. *comprendre*, to include].

com·pro·mise (kåm′·prạ·mīz) n. a settling of matters by mutual adjustment, each side making some concessions; a middle course; v.t. and i. to settle by making mutual concessions; to commit oneself; to expose to the risk of scandal or disgrace [L. *con-; promittere*, to promise].

comp·tom·e·ter (kåm(p)·tàm′·ạ·tẹr) n. a calculating machine [Trade Name].

comp·trol·ler (kạn·trōl′·ẹr) n. a form of controller [L.].

com·pul·sion (kạm·pul′·shạn) n. the act or effect of compelling; force; constraint; violence; (*Psych.*) an irresistible impulse. **compulsive** a. exercising compulsion. **compulsory** a. compelling; constraining; obligatory; enforced [L. *compulsus*, driven together].

com·punc·tion (kạm·pungk′·shạn) n. remorse of conscience; scruple. **compuctious** a. conscience-stricken; regretful; remorseful [L. *con-; pungere*, to prick].

com·pute (kạm·pūt′) v.t. to count; to calculate; to estimate. **computable** a. **computation** n. calculation; reckoning [L. *con-; putare*, to reckon].

com·rade (kåm′·rad) n. a close friend or companion; a mate; an associate. **-ship** n. close friendship; fellowship; affectionate association [Sp. *camarada*, a room-mate].

con (kàn) v.t. to study; to pore over; to learn by heart. pr.p. **-ning**. pa.t. **-ned** [O.E. *cunnan*, to know].

con (kàn) (*Naut.*) v.t. and i. to superintend the steering of a vessel [L. *conducere*, to guide].

con (kàn) adv. (abbrev. of **contra**), against, e.g. in the phrase **pro and con**, for and against. **the pro and con** n. Also pl. **the pros and cons,** the advantages and disadvantages [L.].

con (kån) *a.* (*Slang*) confidence; *v.t.* to swindle. *pr.p.* **-ning.** *pa.t.* **-ned.**

con- prefix fr. L. *cum,* with, together.

con·cat·e·nate (kån·kat′·a·nāt) *v.i.* to link together; to unite in a series. **concatenation** *n.* a series of things depending on each other; a connected chain, as of circumstances [L. *con-; catena,* a chain].

con·cave (kån′·kāv) *a.* hollow and curved inwards, as the inner surface of a vault. **concavity** (kån·kav′·i·ti·) *n.* hollowness [L. *con-; cavus,* hollow].

con·ceal (kån·sēl′) *v.t.* to hide or secrete; to mask or disguise; to withhold from knowledge. **-ment** *n.* [L. *con-; celare,* to hide].

con·cede (kån·sēd′) *v.t.* to yield; to admit to be true; to grant; to surrender; *v.i.* to admit [L. *concedere,* to yield].

con·ceit (kån·sēt′) *n.* over-estimation of self-vanity; opinion; fanciful thought. **-ed** *a.* vain. **-edly** *adv.* [fr. *conceive*].

con·ceive (kån·sēv′) *v.t.* to form an idea in the mind; to think; to imagine; to understand; *v.i.* to become pregnant; to have a notion. **conceivable** *a.* that may be believed, imagined, or understood. **conceivably** *adv.* [L. *con-; capere,* to take, seize].

con·cen·trate (kån′·sen·trāt) *v.i.* to bring to a common center; to reduce to small space; to increase in strength; to condense; *v.i.* to come together; to devote all attention. **concentration** *n.* the act of concentrating; increased strength; the fixation of the mind on something. **concentration camp,** a place of detention. [L. *con-; centrum,* the center].

con·cen·tric (kan·sen′·trik) *a.* having the center. **-al** *a.* **-ally** *adv.* **concentricity** (kån·-san·tris′·a·ti·) *n.*

con·cept (kån′·sept) *n.* an abstract notion; a mental impression of an object. **conception** (kån·sep′·shan) *n.* the act of conceiving; the thing conceived; a mental picture; an idea; a notion; (*Med.*) the beginning of pregnancy. **conceptive** *a.* pert. to conception; capable of conceiving. **conceptual** *a.* pert. to conception or to a concept [L. *concipere,* to conceive].

con·cern (kån·surn′) *v.t.* to relate or belong to; to be of importance to; to be the business of; to make uneasy; *n.* that which relates or belongs to one; interest in, or care for, any person or thing; worry; a business establishment. **-ed** *a.* interested; worried; anxious; troubled; involved. **-ing** *prep.* regarding; with respect to. **-ment** *n.* [L. *con-; cernere,* to distinguish].

con·cert (kån·surt′) *v.t.* to plan together; to arrange; to design. **-ed** *a.* mutually planned; (*Mus.*) arranged in parts. **concert** (kån′·sert) *n.* agreement in a plan; harmony; a musical entertainment. **concertina** (·tē′·na) *n.* a small hexagonal accordion. **concerto** (kån·-cher′·tō) *n.* a musical composition arranged for a solo instrument with orchestral accompaniment [Fr. *concerter*].

con·ces·sion (kån·sesh′·an) *n.* the act of conceding; a special privilege; a grant; an admission. **-aire** *n.* one who holds a concession. **-ary** *a.* [L. *con-; cedere,* to yield].

conch (kånk, kånch) *n.* a seashell; the spiral shell used as a trumpet by the Tritons [L. *concha,* a shell].

con·chol·o·gy (kång·kål′·a·ji·) *n.* the scientific study of shells and shellfish. **conchologist** *n.* [Gk. *konchē,* a shell; *logos,* discourse].

con·cil·i·ate (kån·sil′·i·āt) *v.t.* to win over to goodwill; to appease; to make peace; to pacify. **conciliation** *n.* **conciliative** *a.* conciliatory. **conciliatory** *a.* tending to pacify [L. *conciliare,* to bring together].

con·cise (kån·sīs′) *a.* brief; condensed; comprehensive. **-ly** *adv.* in few words; tersely. **-ness** *n.* [L. *concisus,* fr. *caedere,* to cut].

con·clave (kån′·klāv) *n.* a private meeting of cardinals for the election of a pope; where they meet; any secret meeting [L. *conclave,* a room; fr. *clavis,* a key].

con·clude (kån·klōōd′) *v.t.* to bring to an end; to close; to finish; to complete; to make a final judgment of; to infer; *v.i.* to come to an end [L. *concludere*].

con·clu·sion (kån·klōō′·zhan) *n.* the end; the last part of anything; the final judgment; inference; result from experiment. **conclusive** *a.* final; convincing [L. *concludere,* to end].

con·coct (kån·kåkt′) *v.t.* to make a mixture; to make up, esp. a story. **concoction** *n.* [L. *concoctus,* cooked].

con·com·i·tant (kån·kåm′·a·tant) *a.* accompanying; attending; going along with; *n.* an accompanying circumstance. **concomitance, concomitancy** *n.* the state of being concomitant; coexistence [L. *concomitari,* to go with as companion].

con·cord (kån′·kawrd) *n.* agreement; union between persons, as in opinions, etc.; harmony; unison; consonance; *v.i.* to agree. **concordance** *n.* agreement; an index to the words of a book (esp. of the Bible) with references to the places of their occurrence. **concordant** *a.* harmonious [L. *con-; cor, cordis,* the heart].

con·cor·dat (kån·kawr′·dat) *n.* an agreement between the Pope and a sovereign or government on religious questions; a pact; a treaty [L. *con-; cor, cordis,* the heart].

con·course (kån′·kōrs) *n.* a gathering together; an assembly; a crowd; a promenade or roadway in a park; a large space in a railroad station [L. *concursus,* running together].

con·cres·cence (kån·kres′·ans) *n.* a growing together [L. *con-; crescere,* to grow].

con·crete (kån′·krēt) *a.* made of concrete; consisting of matter, facts, etc.; solid; not abstract; specific; *n.* a mixture of sand, cement, etc., used in building; anything real or specific; *v.t.* to form into a solid mass; *v.i.* to unite into a mass; to harden. **-ly** *adv.* **-ness** *n.* **concretion** *n.* the state of being concrete; a mass formed of parts pressed together [L. *concrescere,* to grow together].

con·cu·bine (kång′·kū·bīn) *n.* a woman who lives with a man without being his lawful wife. **concubinage** (kån·kū′·ba·nij) *n.* the living together of a man and a woman not legally married [L. *con-; cubare,* to lie].

con·cu·pis·cence (kån·kū′·pas·ans) *n.* violent sexual desire; lust. **concupiscent, concupiscible** *a.* lustful [L. *con-; cupere,* to desire].

con·cur (kån·kur′) *v.i.* to agree; to express agreement; to meet in the same point; to coincide. *pr.p.* **-ring** *pa.p.* and *pa.t.* **-red. -rence** *n.* **-rent** *a.* acting in conjunction; agreeing; taking place at the same time; accompanying; *n.* a joint or contributory cause. **-rently** *adv.* [L. *concurrere,* to run together].

con·cus·sion (kån·kush′·an) *n.* act of shaking by sudden striking; shock; (*Med.*) a violent disturbance of the brain caused by a blow or fall [L. *concussio,* a shaking together].

con·demn (kån·dem′) *v.t.* to blame; to censure; to pronounce guilty; to sentence; to reprove; to declare unfit for use. **-ation** *n.* **-atory** *a.* [L. *condemnare*].

con·dense (kån·dens′) *v.t.* to make more dense, close, or compact; to make more solid; to concentrate; to change a vapor or gas into liquid or solid; to pack into few words; *v.i.* to become more dense or compact; to pass from vapor to liquid or solid. **condensation** *n.* the act of condensing; the state of being condensed; conciseness; in psycho-analysis, the symbolization of two or more ideas by one symbol. **-d** *a.* compressed; concise; (of milk) evaporated and preserved in cans. **-r** *n.* one who, or that which, condenses; an apparatus for changing vapor or gas into liquid or solid; (*Elect.*) a device for accumulating and holding an electric charge [L. *condensare,* fr. *densus, dense*].

con·de·scend (kån·da·send′) *v.i.* to come down from one's position, rank, or dignity; to stoop;

to deign; to be gracious or affable to inferiors; to patronize. **-ing** *a.* **condescension** *n.* [L. *condescendere*, to come down].

con·dign (kạn·dīn′) *a.* deserved; adequate. **-ly** *adv.* [L. *dignus*, worthy].

con·di·ment (kȧn′·dạ·mạnt) *n.* a relish; seasoning for food [L. *condire*, to pickle].

con·di·tion (kạn·dish′·ạn) *n.* a thing on which a statement, happening, or existing depends; state or circumstances of anything; position as to worldly circumstances; rank; disposition; a prerequisite; a stipulation; *v.t.* to stipulate; to impose conditions on; to render fit and in good health; *v.i.* to make terms. **-al** *a.* depending on conditions; not absolute. **-ally** *adv.* **-ed** *a.* **conditioned reflex,** in psychology, an automatic response [L.].

con·dole (kạn·dōl′) *v.i.* to grieve with; to offer sympathy. **condolence, -ment** *n.* an expression of sympathy [L. *condolere*, to suffer with].

con·do·min·i·um (kȧn·dạ·min′·i·ạm) *n.* joint rule of a state by two or more states [L. *con-*; and *dominium*, dominion].

con·done (kạn·dōn′) *v.t.* to pardon; to forgive; to overlook [L. *condonare* to, remit].

con·duce (kạn·dūs′) *v.i.* to lead to some end or result; to help; to promote. **conducive** *a.* having a tendency to promote, help, or forward. **conduciveness** *n.* [L. *conducere*, to bring together, to lead].

con·duct (kȧn′·dukt) *n.* the act of guiding; guidance; management; behavior. **conduct** (kạn·dukt′) *v.t.* to guide; to lead; to direct; to manage; to behave. **-ance** *n.* (*Elect.*) the property of a body for conducting electricity. **conductible** *a.* **conduction** *n.* the act of conducting; the transmission or flow of heat from one body to another. **conductive** *a.* able to transmit heat, electricity, etc. **conductivity** *n.* the quality of being conductive. **conductor** *n.* a guide; the leader of a choir or orchestra; one in charge of a bus, train, etc. who collects fares; a substance capable of transmitting heat, electricity, etc. [L. *conducere*, to lead].

con·duit (kȧn′·dit, ·doo·it) *n.* a pipe or channel for conveying fluids [Fr. fr. *conduire*, to lead].

cone (kōn) *n.* a solid body tapering to a point from a circular base; anything of this shape; the fruit of the pine, fir, etc. **conic, conical** (kȧn′·i·kạl) *a.* having the form of, or pert. to, a cone. **conically** *adv.* **conics** *n.* (*Geom.*) the branch dealing with conic sections. [Gk. *kōnos*].

con·el·rad (kȧn′·l·rad) *n.* a system used by radio in time of war to prevent the enemy from locating cities by radio beams.

con·fab (kȧn′·fab) *n.* (*Colloq.*) a chat.

con·fab·u·late (kạn·fab′·yạ·lāt) *v.i.* to chat. **confabulation** *n.* [L. *confabulari*]

con·fec·tion (kạn·fek′·shạn) *n.* the act of compounding different substances into one compound; candy, ice cream, etc. **-ary** *a.* **-er** *n.* one who makes or sells confections. **-er's sugar** *n.* finely powdered sugar. **-ery** *n.* candies, etc.; a shop where these are sold [L. *conficere*, to make up].

con·fed·er·ate (kạn·fed′·ẹr·it) *a.* united in a league; bound by treaty; allied; *n.* an ally; an accomplice; *v.t.* and *i.* (kạn·fed′·ẹr·āt) to unite in a league. **confederacy** *n.* a union; an alliance. **confederation** *n.* the act of forming a confederacy; an alliance [L. *con-*; *foedus*, a league].

con·fer (kạn·fur′) *v.t.* to bestow upon; to grant; to award; *v.i.* to consult together; to take advice; to discuss. **pr.p. -ring.** *pa.p.* and *pa.t.* **-red. -ee** *n.* one who takes part in a conference; a recipient of an award. **conference** *n.* a meeting; a consultation [L. *conferre*, to bring together].

con·fess (kạn·fes′) *v.t.* to admit; to own; to acknowledge; to grant; to declare one's sins orally to a priest; (of a priest) to hear the sins of; to make confession; plead guilty. **-edly** *adv.*

admittedly. **confession** (kạn·fesh′·ạn) *n.* admission; avowal of sins; declaring one's sins to priest. **confessional** *n.* the stall where a priest sits to hear confessions; *a.* pert. to confession. **-or** *n.* a priest who hears confessions. **confession of faith,** a statement of religious beliefs [L. *confiteri, confessus,* to acknowledge].

con·fet·ti (kạn·fet′·i·) *n.pl.* small bits of colored paper, for throwing at weddings, carnivals, etc. [It.].

con·fide (kạn·fīd′) *v.t.* to hand over to the charge of; to entrust to; to tell a secret to; *v.i.* to put faith in; to rely on. **confidant** *n.* (*fem.* **confidante**) a person in whom one can confide [L. *con-*; *fidere,* to trust].

con·fi·dence (kȧn′·fạ·dạns) *n.* that in which faith is put; belief; trust; feeling of security; self-reliance; presumption; intimacy; a secret. **confident** *a.* having assurance; bold. **confidently** *adv.* **confidential** (kạn·fạ·den′·shạl) *a.* treated with confidence; private; secret. **confidentially** *adv.* [L. *con-*; *fidere,* to trust].

con·fig·u·ra·tion (kạn·fig·yạ·rā′·shạn) *n.* outward shape, form, or figure; grouping; outline; aspect [L. *con-*; *figurare,* to fashion].

con·fine (kạn·fīn′) *v.t.* to keep within bounds; to limit; to enclose; to imprison; *v.i.* to have a common boundary; **confine** (kȧn′·fīn) *n.* usually in *pl.* **confines,** boundary; limit. **-ment** *n.* imprisonment; restraint; detention; childbirth [L. *confinis,* having a common frontier].

con·firm (kạn·furm′) *v.t.* to make strong; to settle; to make valid by formal assent; to ratify; to make certain; to verify. **confirmation** *n.* the act of making strong, valid, certain, etc.; proof; a religious rite. **-ative** *a.* **-atory** *a.* **-ed** *a.* [L. *confirmare*].

con·fis·cate (kȧn′·fis·kāt) *v.t.* to seize by authority; to take possession of without compensation; *a.* forfeited. **confiscation** *n.* **confiscator** *n.* **confiscatory** *a.* [L. *confiscare*].

con·fla·gra·tion (kȧn·flạ·grā′·shạn) *n.* a destructive fire [L. *con-*; *flagrare,* to blaze].

con·flict (kạn·flikt′) *v.i.* to dash together; to clash; to be at odds with; to be inconsistent with; to differ. **conflict** (kȧn′·flikt) *n.* a prolonged struggle; a trial of strength; strong disagreement. **-ing** *a.* differing; contradictory [L. *configere, conflictum,* to strike against].

con·flu·ence (kȧn′·floo·ạns) *n.* a flowing together; the meeting of two or more rivers, streams, etc.; a large assemblage; a crowd. **confluent** *a.* Also **conflux** [L. *confluere,* to flow together].

con·form (kạn·fawrm′) *v.t.* to make like; to bring into agreement; *v.i.* to comply; to agree; *a.* in accord. **-able** *a.* corresponding in form; similar; submissive. **-ably** *adv.* **-ation** *n.* the manner in which a body is formed or shaped; structure. **-ist** *n.* one who complies with usage or custom. **-ity** *n.* [L. *conformare,* to give the same shape].

con·found (kạn·found′) *v.t.* to mix up; to bring to confusion; to bewilder. **-ed** *a.* confused; baffled; perplexed; (*Colloq.*) odious [L. *confundere,* to pour together].

con·front (kạn·frunt′) *v.t.* to face boldly; to oppose; to bring face to face; to compare. **confrontation** *n.* [Fr. *confronter,* fr. *front,* the brow].

Con·fu·cius (kạn·fū′·shạs) *n.* Chinese philosopher.

con·fuse (kạn·fūz′) *v.t.* to mix up; to jumble together; to muddle; to perplex; hence, to mistake one thing for another. **-d** *a.* mixed up; perplexed. **confusedly** *adv.* **confusion** *n.* the state of being confused; disorder; bewilderment [L. *confundere,* to pour together].

con·fute (kạn·fūt′) *v.t.* to prove to be wrong; to disprove. **confutable** *a.* **confutation** *n.* [L. *confutare*].

con·geal (kạn·jēl′) *v.t.* and *i.* to freeze, as a fluid; to stiffen; to solidify; to curdle; to coagulate; *v.i.* to become stiff or solidified, from cold.

-able *a.* **-ment** *n.* a thing congealed; a clot. **congelation** *n.* [L. *con-; gelare,* to freeze].

con·gen·ial (kạn·jēn′·yạl) *a.* allied in disposition and tastes; kindred; agreeable. **-ly** *adv.* **congeniality** *n.* [L. *con-; genius,* spirit].

con·gen·i·tal (kạn·jen′·a·tạl) *a.* existing at the time of birth [L. *con-; genitus,* born].

con·gest (kạn·jest′) *v.t.* to collect into a mass; to produce a hampering accumulation; to overcrowd. **-ed** *a.* overcrowded. **congestion** *n.* [L. *con-; gerere, gestum,* to bring, to carry].

con·glom·er·ate (kạn·glăm′·ẹr·it) *a.* gathered into a mass; clustered; *v.t.* (·rāt′) to bring together into a united mass; *n.* (*Geol.*) rock composed of fragments of rock cemented together. **conglomeration** *n.* a mixed collection; a cluster [L. *con-; glomus,* a mass].

con·grat·u·late (kạn·gra′·chạ·lāt) *v.t.* to wish joy to; to compliment; to felicitate. **congratulation** *n.* an expression of pleasure at the good fortune of someone; felicitation. **congratulatory** *a.* [L. *congratulari*].

con·gre·gate (kảng′·grạ·gāt) *v.t.* to gather into a crowd or assembly; *v.i.* to meet together, in a body; (·git) *a.* assembled; collective. **congregation** *n.* the act of assembling; an assemblage; a gathering of persons for worship; a religious body. **congregational** *a.* **Congregationalism** *n.* a system of church government that gives independence to each local church [L. *con-; grex,* a flock].

con·gress (kảng′·grạs) *n.* a meeting together of persons; a formal assembly, e.g. of envoys or representatives of governments. **Congress** *n.* the legislative body of the United States. **-man** *n.* a member of the U.S. House of Representatives. **-woman** *n.* **congressional** *a.* [L. *congredi, congressus,* to meet].

con·gru·ent (kảng′·groo·ạnt) *a.* agreeing together; corresponding. **congruence, congruency** *n.* suitableness. **congruity** *n.* **congruous** *a.* accordant; suitable [L. *congruere,* to run together].

con·ic See **cone.**

co·nif·e·rae (kŏ·nif′·a·rē) *n.pl.* an order of trees bearing a cone-shaped fruit. **coniferous** *a.* [L. *conus,* a cone; *ferre,* to bear].

con·jec·ture (kạn·jek′·cher) *n.* a guess; an opinion founded on insufficient proof; surmise; inference; *v.t.* to guess; to surmise; to infer on insufficient grounds. **conjecturable** *a.* **conjectural** *a.* [L. *con-; jacere,* to throw].

con·join (kạn·join′) *v.t.* to join together; *a.* united; concerted; associated [L. *conjungere,* join together].

con·ju·gal (kản′·joo·gạl) *a.* pert. to marriage; connubial; matrimonial. **-ly** *adv.* **conjugality** (kản′·jạ·gal′·i·ti·) *n.* the married state [L. *conjux, conjugis,* a spouse].

con·ju·gate (kản′·joog·āt) *v.t.* (*Gram.*) to recite or write all the different parts of a verb. **conjugation** *n.* the act of uniting; (*Gram.*) a class of verbs inflected in the same manner; (*Biol.*) the fusion of cells or individuals for reproduction [L. *con-; jugum,* a yoke].

con·junct (kạn·jungkt′) *a.* joined together; united; associated. **-ly** *adv.* **conjunction** *n.* union; concurrence of events; (*Gram.*) a word used to join clauses, etc. **conjunctive** *a.* closely connected; serving to connect [L. *con-; jungere,* to join].

con·junc·ti·vi·tis (kạn·jungk·tạ·vī′·tạs) *n.* inflammation of the mucous membrane lining the eyelid [L. *con-; jungere,* to join].

con·jure (kạn·joor′) *v.t.* to call on by a sacred name; solemnly to implore. **conjure** (kun′·jẹr) *v.i.* to practice magic; to practice the arts of a conjurer; (*Fig.*) to imagine. **conjuration** *n.* the act of calling upon or summoning by a sacred name. **conjurer, conjuror** *n.* a magician; a juggler [L. *con-; jurare,* to swear].

conk (kảnk) (*Slang*) a blow; — **out,** fail suddenly.

con·nect (kạ·nekt′) *v.t.* to fasten together; to associate; to relate; to attach; to join; *v.i.* to unite; to have a close relation. **-ed** *a.* joined; coherent. **-edly** *adv.* **connection** *n.* a link; the act of uniting, or state of being united; that which connects; a kinsman. **-ive** *a.* binding; *n.* a connecting word. **-or** *n.* **well connected,** of good family [L. *con-; nectere,* to bind].

con·nive (kạ·nīv′) *v.i.* to wink at; to pretend not to see; to co-operate secretly (with 'at'). **connivance** *n.* consent in wrong-doing. **-r** *n.* [L. *connivere,* to shut the eyes].

con·nois·seur (kản·a·sur′) *n.* an expert, esp. in fine arts [Fr. *connaître,* to know].

con·note (kạ·nōt′) *v.t.* to mean; to imply; to signify; to have a meaning in addition to the primary meaning. **connotate** *v.t.* to connote. **connotation** *n.* a secondary implied meaning. **connotative** *a.* [L. *con-; notare,* to mark].

con·nu·bi·al (kạ·nū′·bi·al) *a.* pert. to marriage. **connubiality** *n.* [L. *con-; nubere,* to marry].

co·noid (kō′·noid) *n.* any object shaped like a cone [Gk. *konos,* a cone; *eidos,* form].

con·quer (kảng′·kẹr) *v.t.* to reduce by force, as of arms; to overcome; to subjugate or subdue; to vanquish; to surmount; *v.i.* to be victorious; to prevail. **-able** *a.* **-or** *n.* **conquest** (kảng′·kwest) *n.* the act of conquering; that which is conquered [L. *con-; quaerere,* to seek].

con·quis·ta·dor (kản·kwis′·tạ·dawr) *n.* a conqueror, applied to the Spanish conquerors of Mexico and Peru in the 16th cent. [Sp.].

con·san·guin·e·ous (kản·sang·gwin′·i·ạs) *a.* of the same blood; related by birth. **consanguinity** *n.* [L. *con-; sanguis,* blood].

con·science (kản′·shạns) *n.* the faculty by which we know right from wrong. **conscientious** (kản·shi·en′·shạs) *a.* governed by dictates of conscience. **conscientiously** *adv.* **conscientiousness** *n.* **conscionable** (kản′·shạn·a·bl) *a.* governed by conscience. **—stricken** *a.* seized with scruples. **conscientious objector,** a man who refuses to serve in the armed forces, on moral or religious grounds [L. *conscire,* to be well aware].

con·scious (kản′·shạs) *a.* having inward knowledge (of); aware (of); having the use of one's faculties. **-ly** *adv.* **-ness** *n.* the state of being mentally awake to one's surroundings [L. *conscire,* to be aware].

con·script (kạn·skript′) *v.t.* to enroll compulsorily for service in the armed forces. **conscript** (kan′·skript) *n.* one compelled to serve as a soldier, sailor, or airman, etc. **conscription** *n.* [L. *con-; scribere,* to write].

con·se·crate (kản′·sạ·krāt) *v.t.* to set apart for sacred uses; to dedicate. **consecration** *n.* [L. *con-; sacrare,* to hallow].

con·sec·u·tive (kạn·sek′·yạ·tiv) *a.* following one another in unbroken order; successive; resulting; (*Gram.*) expressing consequence. **-ly** *adv.* **-ness** *n.* [L. *con-; sequi,* to follow].

con·sen·sus (kạn·sen′·sạs) *n.* a general agreement; unanimity [L.].

con·sent (kạn·sent′) *n.* agreement; assent; permission; *v.i.* to agree. **consentient** (kạn·sen′·shant) *a.* united in opinion. **consentience** *n.* [L. *con-; sentire,* to feel].

con·se·quent (kản′·sạ·kwent) *a.* following as a result; *n.* effect. **-ly** *adv.* therefore; as a result; by logical sequence. **consequence** *n.* that which naturally follows; result; importance; value. **consequential** (kản·sạ·kwen′·shạl) *a.* [L. *con-; sequi,* to follow].

con·serve (kạn·surv′) *v.t.* to keep safe; to preserve, to maintain; *n.* anything conserved; fruit, etc. prepared with sugar. **conservation** *n.* preservation; safe-guarding; protection; the official safe-guarding of forests, rivers, ports, etc.; the area so protected. **conservative** *a.* tending to conserve; disposed to maintain existing institutions; hostile to change; *n.* one opposed to hasty changes or innovations.

n. a greenhouse for plants; a school of music. **conservatory** [L. *con-; servare*, to keep].

con·sid·er (kạn·sĭd'·ẹr) *v.t.* to reflect upon carefully; to examine carefully; to be of opinion; to regard as; *v.i.* to deliberate seriously. **-able** *a.* worthy of attention; moderately large. **-ably** *adv.* **-ate** *a.* thoughtful for others; circumspect. **-ately** *adv.* **-ateness** *n.* **-ation** *n.* the act of considering; deliberation; fee or recompense; thoughtful regard for others. **-ed** *a.* carefully thought out. **-ing** *prep.* in view of; taking into account [L. *considerare*, observe].

con·sign (kạn·sīn') *v.t.* to give, transfer, or deliver in a formal manner; to entrust (goods) to a carrier for transport by rail, ship, etc.; *v.i.* to agree. **consignee** (cạn·sī·nē') *n.* the person to whom goods are consigned. **-er, -or** *n.* the person who consigns goods. **-ment** *n.* [L. *consignare*, to seal].

con·sist (kạn·sĭst') *v.i.* to be composed of; to be in a fixed or permanent state; to be compatible with. **-ence, -ency** *n.* a condition of being fixed; a degree of firmness or density; agreement or harmony. **consistent** *a.* compatible; constant in adhering to principles, etc. [L. *con-; sistere*, to stand].

con·sis·to·ry (kạn·sĭs'·tạr·i·) *a.* pert. to an ecclesiastical court; *n.* any solemn assembly or council [L. *consistorium*, a council].

con·sole (kạn·sōl') *v.t.* to comfort in distress; to solace; to encourage. **consolable** *a.* able to be consoled. **consolation** *n.* the act of comforting; that which comforts; solace; encouragement. **consolatory** *a.* [L. *consolari*].

con·sol·i·date (kạn·sǎl'·ạ·dāt) *v.t.* and *i.* to make solid; to make firm; to combine into a connected whole; to strengthen. **consolidation** *n.* the act of making or becoming compact and firm [L. *con-; solidus*, solid].

con·som·mé (kạn·sạ·mā') *n.* a clear meat soup [Fr.].

con·so·nant (kạn'·sạ·nạnt) *a.* agreeing with; in accord; *n.* a sound (or letter) making a syllable only with a vowel; a non-vowel. **-ly** *adv.* **consonance, consonancy** *n.* agreement; harmony [L. *consonare*, to sound with].

con·sort (kạn'·sawrt) *n.* a companion or partner; a wife or husband. **consort** (kạn·sawrt') *v.t.* to join; *v.i.* to keep company; to associate; to agree [L. *consors*, fr. *sors*, fate].

con·sor·ti·um (kạn·sawr'·shi·ạm) *n.* an association for a common end; an agreement between countries for mutual assistance and joint action [L.].

con·spec·tus (kạn·spek'·tạs) *n.* a general sketch or outline of a subject; a synopsis [L. fr. *conspicere*, to look at].

con·spic·u·ous (kạn·spĭk'·yoo·ạs) *a.* easy to be seen; very noticeable. **-ly** *adv.* **-ness, conspicuity** *n.* [L. *conspicere*, to catch sight of].

con·spire (kạn·spīr') *v.i..* to unite for an evil purpose; to plot together. **conspiracy** (kạn·spir'·ạ·si·) *n.* a combination of persons for an evil purpose; a plot. **conspirator** *n.* (*fem.* **conspiratress**). **conspiratorial** *a.* [L. *conspirare*, lit. to breathe together].

con·sta·ble (kạn'·stạ·bl, kun·stạ'·bl) *n.* a peace officer; a high officer in the Middle Ages. **constabulary** (kạn·stab'·yạ·ler·i·) *a.* pert. to constables; *n.* [L.L. *comes stabuli*, count of the stable, marshal].

con·stant (kạn'·stạnt) *a.* fixed; steadfast; invariable, permanent; *n.* that which is not subject to change. **-ly** *adv.* **constancy** *n.* steadfastness; resolution; fidelity [L. *constare*, to stand firm].

con·stel·la·tion (kạn·stạ·lā'·shạn) *n.* a group of fixed stars; an assemblage of notable persons or things [L. *con-; stella*, a star].

con·ster·na·tion (kạn·stẹr'·nā'·shạn) *n.* amazement or terror that throws the mind into confusion. **consternate** *v.t.* to fill with alarm or dismay [L. *con-; sternere*, to strew].

con·sti·pate (kạn'·stạ·pāt) *v.t.* to clog or make sluggish. **constipation** *n.* insufficient; irregular evacuation of the bowels [L. *con-; stipare*, to pack].

con·sti·tute (kạn'·sti·tōōt) *v.t.* to appoint to an office or function; to establish; to set up; to form; to compose. **constitution** *n.* the act of constituting; the natural state of body or mind; composition; the system or body of laws under which a state exists. **constitutional** *a.* pert. to the constitution; due to a person's physical or mental composition; *n.* a walk for the benefit of health. **constitutionally** *adv.* **constitutionalist** *n.* one who upholds constitutional government. **constitutionality** *n.* **constitutive** (kạn'·sti·tū·tiv) *a.* having powers to enact or establish. **constituent** (kạn·stich'·ȯȯ·ạnt) *a.* serving to compose or make up; an element [L. *constituere*, to place together].

con·strain (kạn·strān') *v.t.* to force or compel; to confine; to restrain; to limit. **-t** *n.* compelling force; restraining force; unnaturalness or embarrassment of manner [L. *con-; stingere*, to press].

con·strict (kạn·strikt') *v.t.* to draw together; to cramp; to cause to shrink or contract; to squeeze. **constriction** *n.* **-ive** *a.* that which constricts; the boa-constrictor [L. *con-; stringere*, to bind].

con·struct (kạn·strukt') *v.t.* to build; to fabricate; to devise or invent; to compile. **construction** *n.* the act of building; erection; structure; interpretation or meaning. **-ive** *a.* **-iveness** *n.* **-or** *n.* [L. *construere*, to build].

con·strue (kạn·strōō') *v.t.* to interpret; to put a construction upon; to deduce; to explain the structure of a sentence and the connection of the words in it; to translate. **construable** *a.* **-r** *n.* [L. *construere*, to build].

con·sub·stan·ti·ate (kạn·sạb·stan'·shi·āt) *v.t.* and *i.* to unite in one substance or nature. **consubstantial** *a.* **consubstantiation** *n.* (*Theol.*) the doctrine of the substantial union of Christ's body and blood with the elements of the sacrament [L. *consubstantialis*, of like nature].

con·sul (kạn'·sạl) *n.* an officer appointed by a government to represent it in a foreign country. **-ar** *a.* **-ate** *n.* the offices of a consul. **-ship** *n.* [L.].

con·sult (kạn·sult') *v.t.* to ask advice of; to seek the opinion of; to look to for information; to refer to; *v.i.* to confer. **-ant** *n.* one who consults; one who gives expert advice. **-ing** *a.* **-ation** *n.* the act of consulting; a council or conference. **-ative** *a.* advisory [L. *consulere*].

con·sume (kạn·sōōm') *v.t.* to waste; to destroy; to use up; to eat or drink up; *v.i.* to waste away. **consumable** *a.* **-r** *n.* [L. *consumere*, to use up].

con·sum·mate (kạn'·sạm·āt) *v.t.* to complete; to finish; to perfect; (*Law*) to complete marriage by sexual intercourse. **consummate** (kạn·sum'·it) *a.* complete; perfect. **-ly** *adv.* **consummation** *n.* [L. *consummare*].

con·sump·tion (kạn·sump'·shạn) *n.* the act of consuming: the amount consumed; (*Med.*) a wasting disease of the lungs; pulmonary tuberculosis. **consumptive** *a.* destructive; wasteful; wasting; affected with, or inclined to, pulmonary tuberculosis; *n.* (*Med.*) a person suffering from consumption [L. *consumere, consumptum*, to use up].

con·tact (kạn'·takt) *n.* a touching; (*Colloq.*) a meeting; *v.t.* to get in touch with a person. **-ual** (kạn·tak'·choo·al) *a.* implying contact. **— lens,** an invisible eye-glass fitting over the eyeball [L. *tangere, tactum*, to touch].

con·ta·gion (kạn·tā'·jạn) *n.* the transmission of a disease from one person to another; physical or moral pestilence. **contagious** *a.* communicable [L. *contagio*, fr. *tangere*, to touch].

con·tain (kạn·tān') *v.t.* to hold; to have room for; to comprise; to include; to restrain. **-able**

**WEBSTER
C–D**

a. **-er** *n.* [L. *con-; tenere*, to hold].

con·tam·i·nate (kạn·tam′·ạ·nāt) *v.t.* to soil; to taint; to corrupt; to infect. **contaminable** *a.* **contamination** *n.* pollution; taint; (*War*) the result of coming into contact with liquid gases or radioactive particles [L. *contamen, contagion*].

con·temn (kạn·tem′) *v.t.* to despise; to scorn. **-er** *n.* [L. *contemnere*].

con·tem·plate (kȧn′·tem·plāt) *v.t.* to look at with attention; to meditate on; to have in view; to intend; *v.i.* to think studiously; to reflect. **contemplation** *n.* **contemplative** *a.* **contemplatively** *adv.* [L. *contemplari*, to observe].

con·tem·po·ra·ne·ous (kạn·tem·pạ·rā′·ni··ạs) *a.* having or happening at the same time. **-ly** *adv.* **-ness** *n.* **contemporary** *a.* living or happening at the same time; contemporaneous; present-day; *n.* one who lives at the same time as another; a person approximately of one's own age [L. *con-; tempus, temporis*, time].

con·tempt (kạn·temt′) *n.* scorn; disgrace; disregard; open disrespect to court orders or rule. **-ible** *a.* worthy of contempt; despicable. **-ibleness** *n.* **-ibly** *adv.* **-uous** *a.* expressing contempt or disdain; scornful. **-uously** *adv.* **-uousness** *n.* [L. *contemnere, contemptum*, to despise].

con·tend (kạn·tend′) *v.i.* to fight or struggle with; to strive for; to dispute; to assert strongly; **-er** *n.* [L. *con-; tendere*, to stretch].

con·tent (kạn·tent′) *a.* satisfied; pleased; willing; *v.t.* to satisfy the mind of; to please; to appease; *n.* satisfaction; freedom from anxiety. **-edly** *adv.* **-edness** *n.* **-ment** *n.* satisfaction; pleasure; ease of mind [L. *contentus*].

con·tent (kȧn′·tent) *n.* that which is contained; extent or area; volume. **-s** *n.pl.* an index of the topics treated in a book [L. *continere, contentum*, to contain].

con·ten·tion (kạn·ten′·shạn) *n.* strife; debate; subject matter of argument or discussion. **contentious** *a.* quarrelsome [L. *con-; tendere, tentum*, to stretch].

con·ter·mi·nous (kạn·tur′·mạn·ạs) *a.* having the same boundary; bordering; touching. Also **conterminable, conterminal.**

con·test (kạn·test′) *v.t.* to strive for; to question or resist, as a claim; to dispute; to oppose; *v.i.* to contend or vie (with). **contest** (kȧn′··test) *n.* struggle; conflict; competition; dispute; strike. **-able** *a.* **-ant** *n.* a disputant; a competitor [L. *contestari*, to call to witness].

con·text (kȧn′·tekst) *n.* that which comes immediately before or after a passage or word quoted, and therefore helps to explain it; the setting of a text. **-ual** *a.* pert. to the context. **contexture** *n.* the weaving of parts into one body; structure; style of composition in writing [L. *con-; texere*, to weave].

con·ti·gu·i·ty (kạn·ti·gū′·ạ·ti·) *n.* the state of being contiguous. **contiguous** *a.* touching; near; adjacent [L. *contiguous*, touching].

con·ti·nent (kạn′·tin·ạnt) *n.* one of the large divisions of unbroken land. **-al** *a.* pert. to a continent [L. *con-; tenere*, to hold].

con·ti·nent (kȧn′·tin·ạnt) *a.* chaste; temperate; moderate. **continence, continency** *n.* [L. *con-; tenere*, hold].

con·tin·gent (kạn·tin′·jạnt) *a.* liable to happen, but not sure to do so; possible; dependent; *n.* contingency; a quota, esp. of troops. **-ly** *adv.* **contingence, contingency** *n.* [L. *contingere*, to happen].

con·tin·ue (kạn·tin′·ū) *v.t.* to prolong or extend in duration; to go on with; to persist in; to resume; *v.i.* to remain in a state or place; to persevere; to last. **continual** *a.* lasting; without interruption; often repeated; unceasing. **continually** *adv.* **continuance** *n.* a remaining in existence; duration; uninterrupted

succession. **continuant** *a.* **continuate** *a.* uninterrupted. **continuation** *n.* the act of continuing. **continuity** (kȧn·ti·nòò′·i·ti·) *n.* the state of being continuous; uninterrupted succession; close union. **continuous** *a.* united without break; uninterrupted; constant. **continuously** *adv.* [L. *continuare*].

con·tort (kạn·tawrt′) *v.t.* to twist violently; to writhe; to bend out of shape. **contortion** *n.* a twisting; writhing. **contortionist** *n.* one who practices contortion. **contortive** *a.* [L. *con-; torquere, tortum*, to twist].

con·tour (kȧn′·toor) *n.* a bounding line; outline; *v.t.* to draw the contour of [L. *con-; tornare*, to round off].

con·tra- Latin *prefix* meaning against, contrary, in opposition to, used to form many compounds.

con·tra·band (kȧn′·trạ·band) *a.* prohibited by law or treaty; *n.* goods, the exportation or importation of which is forbidden; smuggled goods. **contraband of war**, goods not to be supplied by a neutral to a belligerent [L. *contra;* L.L. *bandum*, a ban].

con·tra·bass (kȧn′·trạ·bās) *n.* (*Mus.*) the double-bass. Also **contrabasso.**

con·tra·cep·tion (kȧn·trạ·sep′·shạn) *n.* the prevention of conception; by artificial means; birth control. **contraceptive** *a.* and *n.* a drug or appliance for preventing conception [L. *contra;* and *conception*].

con·tract (kạn·trakt′) *v.t.* to draw together; to shorten; to reduce to a less volume; to incur or bring on; *v.i.* to become smaller; to become shorter; to agree upon; to become involved in. **contract** (kȧn′·trakt) *n.* a bargain; an agreement. **-ed** *a.* drawn together; narrow; mean. **-ible** *a.* **-ile** *a.* tending to contract; producing contraction. **-ility** *n.* **-ion** *n.* the act of contracting; the shortening of a word by the omission of a letter or syllable. **-or** *n.* one who undertakes to execute work for a fixed sum. **-ual** *a.* implying, or connected with, a contract [L. *contractus*, drawn together].

con·tra·dict (kȧn·trạ·dikt′) *v.t.* to assert the contrary of; to deny. **contradiction** *n.* denial; direct opposition; discrepancy of statements. **contradictious** *a.* inclined to contradict. **-ive** *a.* containing contradiction. **-ory** *a.* implying a denial; diametrically opposed; inconsistent [L. *contradicere*, to speak against].

con·tra·dis·tinc·tion (kȧn·trạ·dis·tingk′··shạn) *n.* direct contrast. **contradistinctive** *a.* **contradistinguish** *v.t.* to note the difference between two things by contrasting their different qualities.

con·tral·to (kạn·tral′·tō) *n.* the lowest of the three female voices; a singer of that voice [It. *contra; alto*].

con·trap·tion (kạn·trap′·shạn) *n.* (*Colloq.*) a device; a gadget [perh. fr. *contrivance*].

con·tra·pun·tal (kȧn·trạ·pun′·tạl) *a.* pert. to counterpoint [See **counterpoint**].

con·tra·ry (kȧn′·tre·ri·) *a.* opposed; opposing; different; adverse; self-willed; *n.* something the exact opposite of. **contrariety** (kȧn·trạ··rī′·ạ·ti·) *n.* something contrary. **contrarily** *adv.* **contrariness** *n.* **contrariwise** *adv.* on the contrary [L. *contrarius*, fr. *contra*, against].

con·trast (kạn·trast′) *v.t.* to bring out differences; to set in opposition for the purpose of comparing; *v.i.* to be or stand in opposition. **contrast** (kȧn′·trast) *n.* a striking difference; a comparison to show their relative excellence [L. *contra; stare*, to stand].

con·tra·vene (kȧn·trạ·vēn′) *v.t.* to oppose; to break or infringe, as a law. **contravention** *n.* [L. *contravenire*, to come against].

con·tri·bute (kạn·trib′·yoot) *v.t.* to give or pay to a common fund; to help to a common result; to write for a newspaper, magazine, etc.; *v.i.* to lend assistance. **contributable** *a.*

contribution (kȧn·tri·bū′·shạn) *n.* that which is contributed. **contributive** *a.* **contributory** *a.* [L. *contribuere*].

con·trite (kȧn′·trīt) *a.* penitent; remorseful. **-ly** *adv.* **-ness** *n.* **contrition** (kạn·trish′·ạn) *n.* remorse [L. *con-; terere*, to grind].

con·trive (kạn·triv′) *v.t.* and *i.* to plan; to effect or bring about; to invent. **contrivance** *n.* the act of planning; the thing contrived; artifice or device; mechanical invention. **-r** *n.* [L. *con-;* O.Fr. *trover*, to find].

con·trol (kạn·trōl) *v.t.* to have under command; to regulate; to check; to restrain; to direct; *n.* authority or power; government; restraint; in spiritualism, the spirit supposed to control the medium; the control system of levers, switches, etc. in aircraft, motor vehicles, etc. *pr.p* **-ling.** *pa.p.* and *pa.t.* **-led.** **-lable** *a.* **-ler** *n.* one who controls. **-lership** *n.* **-ment** *n.* [L. *contra*, against; *rotulus*, a roll].

con·tro·vert (kȧn′·trạ·vurt) *v.t.* to oppose or dispute by argument; to deny or refute. **-ible** *adv.* **controversy** *n.* disputation; argument, esp. by published writings; debate. **contro·versial** *a.* consisting of controversy; leading to controversy; likely to provoke argument. **controversially** *adv.* **controversialist** *n.* [L. *contra; vertere*, to turn].

con·tu·ma·cy (kȧn′·tyoo·mạ·si·) *n.* contempt of orders or authority; stubborn disobedience. **contumacious** *a.* rebellious. **-ly** *adv.* **-ness** *n.* [L. *contumacia*].

con·tu·me·ly (kȧn′·tyoo·mạ·li·) *n.* insult; affront; indignity; disdainful insolence. **con·tumelious** (kȧn·tū·mē′·li·us) *a.* insolent; haughtily disdainful [L. *contumelia*].

con·tuse (kạn·tūz′) *v.t.* to bruise or injure without breaking the skin. **contusion** *n.* a bruise [L. *con-; tundere, tusum*, to beat].

co·nun·drum (kạ·nun′·drạm) *n.* a riddle; anything that puzzles [etym. unknown].

con·va·lesce (kȧn·vạ·les′) *v.i.* to recover from illness. **convalescent** *a.* **convalescence** *n.* [L. *convalescere*].

con·vec·tion (kạn·vek′·shạn) *n.* the act or process of transmission, esp. of heat by means of currents in liquids or gases [L. *con-; vehere, vectum*, to carry].

con·vene (kạn·vēn′) *v.t.* to call together; *v.i.* to come together or assemble. **-r** *n.* **conven·able** *a.* [L. *con-; venire*, to come].

con·ven·ient (kạn·vēn′·yạnt) *a.* fit; suitable; affording saving of trouble; handy or easy of access. **-ly** *adv.* **convenience** *n.* that which is convenient; any appliance which makes for comfort [L. *con-; venire*, to come].

con·vent (kȧn′·vent) *n.* a community, esp. of nuns, devoted to a religious life; a nunnery. **conventual** *a.* [L. *con-; venire*, to come].

con·ven·ti·cle (kạn·ven′·tạ·kl) *n.* secret gathering, esp. for worship [L. *con-; venire*, to come].

con·ven·tion (kạn·ven′·shạn) *n.* the act of coming together; a formal assembly of representatives; a provisional treaty; accepted usage, custom, or rule. **-al** *a.* formed by agreement or compact; sanctioned by usage; customary. **-ally** *adv.* **-alism** *n.* that which is established by usage. **-ality** *n.* [L. *con-; venire*, to come].

con·verge (kạn·vurj′) *v.i.* to tend to one point; to tend to meet; to approach. **convergent** *a.* **convergence, convergency** *n.* coming together [L. *con-; vergere*, to incline].

con·verse (kạn·vurs′) *v.i.* to talk with. **con·versable** *a.* disposed to talk; affable. **con·versably** *adv.* **conversance, conversancy** *n.* the state of being acquainted with. **con·versant** *a.* familiar or acquainted with by use or study. **conversation** *n.* talk. **conversa·tional** *a.* **conversation(al)ist** *n.* one who excels in conversation [L. *conversari*, to dwell with].

con·verse (kạn·vurs′) *a.* opposite; turned around; reversed in order or relation; *n.* (kȧn′·vurs) the opposite; the contrary **-ly** *adv.* [L. *conversus*, turned about].

con·vert (kạn·vurt′) *v.t.* to apply to another purpose; to change; to cause to adopt a religion, an opinion, etc.; *v.i.* to be turned or changed. **convert** (kȧn′·vurt) *n.* a converted person; one who has turned from sin to holiness. **conversion** *n.* a change from one state to another. **-er** *n.* one who, or that which, converts; (*Elect.*) a machine for changing alternating current into direct current, or altering the pressure of direct current; an iron retort. **-ible** *a.* capable of change; transformable; transmutable; *n.* (*Colloq.*) an automobile with a folding top [L. *convertere*, to turn about].

con·vex (kȧn·veks′) *a.* curving outwards; the opposite of *concave*; bulging. **-ity, -ness** *n.* [L. *convexus*, arched].

con·vey (kạn·vā′) *v.t.* to carry; to transport; to transfer; to make over by deed; to impart; to communicate. **-able** *a.* **-ance** *n.* the act of conveying; a means of transit; a vehicle; the transference of property; the legal document by which property, titles, etc., are transferred. **-ancing** *n.* **-er, -or** *n.* [L. *con-; via*, a way].

con·vict (kạn·vikt′) *v.t.* to prove guilty; to pronounce guilty. **convict** (kȧn′·vict) *n.* a person serving a sentence. **-ion** *n.* the act of convicting; a verdict of guilty; the state of being convinced; a firm belief [L. *convincere, convictum*, to prove guilty].

con·vince (kạn·vins′) *v.t.* to bring to a belief; to persuade by argument; to satisfy by proof. **convincible** *a.* **convincing** *a.* **convincingly** *adv.* [L. *convincere*, to prove].

con·viv·i·al (kạn·viv′·i·ạl) *a.* festive; jovial; social; merry. **-ly** *adv.* **conviviality** *n.* [L. *convivium*, a feast].

con·voke (kạn·vōk′) *v.t.* to call together; to convene; to assemble. **convocation** *n.* the act of calling together; an assembly [L. *convocare*, to call together].

con·volve (kạn·vȧlv′) *v.t.* and *i.* to roll or wind together; to twist; to coil. **convolute** (kȧn′·vạ·lòòt), **convoluted** *a.* rolled together; involved; spiral. **convolution** *n.* the act of rolling together; the state of being coiled; a turn of a coil; a fold of the brain [L. *convolvere*, to roll together].

con·voy (kạn·voi′) *v.t.* to accompany or escort for protection, by land, sea, or air. **convoy** (kȧn′·voi) *n.* the act of convoying; escort; escorting protection [L. *con-; via*, a way].

con·vulse (kạn·vuls′) *v.t.* to shake violently; to affect with violent and irregular spasms; to cause violent disturbance. **convulsion** *n.* any violent agitation; *pl.* (*Med.*) violent and involuntary contractions of the muscles; spasms; fits of laughter. **convulsive** *a.* characterized by convulsion; spasmodic; jerky [L. *con-; vellere, velsum,* to pluck].

coo (kóò) *v.i.* to make a low, melodius sound like the note of a dove; to act in a loving manner [imit.].

cook (kook) *v.t.* to prepare food by boiling, roasting, baking, etc.; (*Colloq.*) to concoct; to falsify; *v.i.* to prepare food by the action of heat; to undergo cooking; *n.* one whose occupation is to cook food. **-ery** *n.* the art or process of cooking. **-er** *n.* **-out** *n.* meal cooked and eaten outdoors [O.E. *coc*].

cook·y, cook·ie (kook′·i·) *n.* a small sweet cake made of stiff dough which is rolled, dropped, or sliced, and baked [Dut. *koek*, cake].

cool (kóòl) *a.* slightly cold; self-possessed; dispassionate; chilly or frigid in manner; impudent; *n.* a moderate state of cold; *v.t.* to cause to cool; to moderate or calm; *v.i.* to become cool; to lose one's ardor or affection. **-er** *n.* a container for cooling; (*Slang*) jail. **-ish** *a.*

fairly cool. **-ly** *adv.* **-ness** *n.* **—headed** *a.* calm; self-possessed. **— one's heels,** to wait a long time [O.E. *col*].

coo·lie (kòó'·li·) *n.* an Asiatic laborer. Also **cooly** [prob. *Kuli,* name of tribe].

coon (kòòn) *n.* a raccoon [abbrev. of *raccoon*].

coop (kòòp) *n.* pen for poultry; (*Slang*) jail; *v.t.* to put up in a coop; confine [M.E. *cupe,* a basket].

coop·er (kòòp'·ẽr) *n.* a maker of casks or barrels [L. *cupa,* a cask].
shop [L. *cupa,* a cask].

co·op·er·ate (kō·áp'·a·rāt) *v.i.* to act jointly with other; to unite for a common effort. **co-operation** *n.* **co-operative** *a.* **co-operator** *n.* **co-operative store,** the shop of a co-operative society, where members make their purchases and share the profits. Also **co-op** *n.* short form [L. *co-*; *operari,* to work].

co·opt (kō·ápt') *v.t.* to choose or elect into a body or committee by the votes of its own members. **-ion, -ation** *n.* [L. *co-*; *optare,* to choose].

co·or·di·nate (kō·awr'·di·nāt) *a.* equal in degree, rank, importance, etc.; *v.t.* to make equal in degree, etc.; to bring into order as parts of a whole; to adjust; *n.* a person or thing of the same rank, importance, etc. as another. **-ly** *adv.* in the same order. **-ness** *n.* **coordination** *n.* **coordinative** *a.* [L. *co-*; *ordo,* rank, order].

coot (kòòt) *n.* a small water-fowl of the rail family [M.E. *cote*].

cop (káp) *v.t.* (*Slang*) to catch or arrest. *pr.p.* **-ping.** *pa.t.* **-ped.** *n.* (*Slang*) a policeman..

co·part·ner (kō·párt'·nẽr) *n.* a partner; an associate. **-ship** *n.*

cope (kōp) *n.* cloak or mantle; a long, sleeveless vestment worn by ecclesiastics during divine service; *v.t.* to dress with a cope. **coping** *n.* the highest course of masonry in a wall [form of *cape*].

cope (kōp) *v.i.* to contend, esp. on equal terms or with success; to deal successfully (with) [L. *colaphus,* a blow with the fist].

Co·per·ni·can (kō·pur'·ni·kạn) *a.* pert. to *Copernicus* the founder of modern astronomy.

cop·i·er (káp'·i·ẽr) *n.* See **copy.**

co·pi·ous (kō'·pi·ạs) *a.* abundant; plentiful; of style, not concise. **-ly** *adv.* **-ness** *n.* [L. *copia,* plenty].

cop·per (káp'·ẽr) *n.* a red-colored metal; a copper coin; *a.* copper-colored; made of copper; *v.t.* to cover with copper. **-y** *a.* made of copper; like copper. **-head** *n.* a poisonous N. American snake [L. *Cyprium aes,* bronze from the island of Cyprus].

cop·pice, copse (káp'·is) *n.* a wood of small trees. Also **copsewood** *n.* [O.Fr. *coper,* to cut].

cop·ra (káp'·rạ) *n.* the dried kernel of the coconut palm [Malay.].

cop·u·la (káp'·ya·lạ) *n.* a connecting link; a bond; (*Gram.*) the word uniting the subject and predicate. **copulate** *v.i.* to unite sexually. **copulation** *n.* **-tive** *a.* pert. to copulation; serving to unite [L. = a bond].

cop·y (káp'·i·) *n.* an imitation of an original; a writing like another writing; an exact reproduction; a transcript; a single specimen; anything to be imitated; the manuscript, etc. placed in the compositor's hands; the basic matter for a journalistic article; *v.t.* to write, print, etc. in imitation of an original; to imitate. **-ist** *n.* **copier** *n.* one who copies; an imitator. **-book** *n.* a book in which copies are written for learners to imitate. **-writer** *n.* a writer of advertisements. **-right** *n.* the legal exclusive right which an author, musician, or artist has to print, publish, and sell his own works, during a certain period of time; *a.* protected by the law of copyright [L. *copia,* abundance].

co·quet (kō·ket') *v.i.* to attempt to attract the notice, admiration, or love of; to flirt with.

pr.p. **-ting.** *pa.p.* and *pa.t.* **-ted. coquetry** (kō'·ket·ri·) *n.* affectation of amorous advances; trifling in love; airy graces to attract admirers. **coquette** *n.* a flirt. **-tish** *a.* [Fr. *coquet,* dim. of *coq,* a cock].

cor·al (kár'·, kawr'·al) *n.* a hard reddish yellow, white, etc. substance growing on the bottom of tropical seas, and composed of the skeletons of zoophytes; *a.* coral-colored; made of coral [Gk. *korallion*].

cord (kawrd) *n.* a thick string or a thin rope of several strands; anything like a cord (e.g. spinal cord, vocal cord); a cubic measure esp. for fuel wood; *v.t.* to bind with a cord or rope. **-age** *n.* an assemblage of ropes and cords, esp. the rigging of a ship. **-ed** *a.* **-ing** *n.* ribbed surface [Gk. *chordē*].

cor·dial (kawr'·jal) *a.* expressing warmth of heart; sincere; stimulating; *n.* anything that invigorates or strengthens; a refreshing drink or medicine. **-ly** *adv.* **-ity** *n.* [L. *cor, cordis,* the heart].

cord·ite (kawrd'·īt) *n.* a smokeless explosive [fr. *cord*].

cor·don (kawr'·dạn) *n.* a line of military posts enclosing an area to prevent passage; hence, a circle of persons round any place or thing to prevent access; a tasseled cord or ribbon worn as a badge of honor. **— bleu,** a person of great distinction in his field [Fr.].

cor·do·van (kawr'·dạ·vạn) *n.* Spanish leather; goatskin tanned and dressed [fr. *Cordoba,* in Spain].

cor·du·roy (kawr'·dạ·roi·) *n.* a thick cotton fabric, corded or ribbed on the surface. *n.pl.* trousers made of this fabric [Fr. *corde du roi,* king's cord].

core (kōr) *n.* the heart or inner part, esp. of fruit; *v.t.* to take out the core [L. *cor,* the heart].

co·res·pon·dent (kō·ri·spán'·dạnt) *n.* in a divorce suit the man or woman charged along with the respondent as guilty of adultery.

cork (kawrk) *n.* the outer bark of the cork-tree; a stopper for a bottle, cask, etc.; *a.* made of cork; *v.t.* to stop up with a cork; to stop up generally; to give wine, beer, etc. a corky taste. **-er** *n.* (*Slang*) anything first-class. **-ing** *a.* (*Slang*) excellent. **-screw** *n.* a tool for drawing corks from bottles; *a.* shaped like a corkscrew; with a spiral twist. [L. *cortex,* bark].

cor·mo·rant (kawr'·mạ·rạnt) *n.* a voracious seabird; gluttonous person [Fr. *cormoran*].

corn (kawrn) *n.* a single seed of oats, wheat, rye, barley, maize, etc.; an inclusive term for grain of all kinds; *v.t.* to preserve meat by salting. **-cob** *n.* the head or seed-pod in which are encased the grains of the maize plant; a tobacco pipe with the bowl made from a corn-cob. **-flour** *n.* a foodstuff consisting of the finely ground starch granules of Indian corn (maize). **-flower** *n.* an annual weed growing in corn-fields and bearing blue flowers. **-husk** *n.* the outer leaves enclosing an ear of corn. **-starch** *n.* a starch used for thickening puddings, sauces, etc. **-y** *a.* (*Slang*) trite, old-fashioned, unsophisticated [O.E. *corn*].

corn (kawrn) *n.* a horny growth of the skin, usually on toes and feet. **-y** *a.* pert. to a corn [L. *cornu,* a horn].

cor·ne·a (kawr'·ni·ạ) *n.* the transparent membrane which forms part of the outer coat of the eyeball [L. *corneus,* horny].

cor·ner (kawr'·nẽr) *n.* the point where two lines meet; the part of a room where two sides meet; an angle; a nook; an embarrassing position; *v.t.* to drive into a corner; to put into a position of difficulty, leaving no escape; to establish a monopoly. **-stone** *n.* the stone which lies at the corner of two walls, and unites them; in an important edifice a corner foundation stone laid with ceremony; something of fundamental importance; **-wise** *adv.* diagonally; with the corner in front. **to corner the market,** to obtain a monopoly [L. *cornu,* a horn].

cor·net (kawr·net′) *n.* a kind of trumpet with valves; a cone of paper [L. *cornu,* a horn].

cor·nice (kawr′·nis) *n.* an ornamental molding around the top of the walls of a room [Fr. *corniche,* a ledge].

cor·nu·co·pi·a (kawr·na̧·kō′·pi·a̧) *n.* the horn of plenty, an emblem of abundance [L. *cornu,* a horn; *copia,* plenty].

cor·ol·lar·y (kár′·, kawr′·a̧·ler·i·) *n.* an inference from a preceding statement; a deduction; a consequence [L. *corolla,* a garland].

co·ro·na (ka̧·rō′·na̧) *n.* the flat projecting part of a cornice; a top or crown; a halo around a heavenly body; a make of cigar (Trade Name). **-l** (kawr′·a̧·na̧l) *a.* pert. to a corona; *n.* a crown; a wreath. **coronary** *a.* resembling a crown or circlet; (*Anat.*) encircling, as of a vessel or nerve; pertaining to the arteries which supply the heart tissues. **coronary thrombosis** (*Med.*) a heart condition caused by a blood clot in a coronary artery. **coronate** *v.t.* to crown. **coronation** *n.* the crowning of a sovereign. **coronet** *n.* a small crown worn by the nobility [L. *corona,* a crown].

cor·o·ner (kár′·, kawr′·a̧·ner) *n.* a legal officer appointed to hold an inquest in cases of death [L. *corona,* a crown].

cor·po·ral (kawr′·pa̧·ral) *n.* non-commissioned officer of a company or troop, next below a sergeant [L. *caput,* the head].

cor·po·ral (kawr′·pa̧·ral) *a.* belonging or relating to the body; bodily; *n.* a communion ti·) *n.* the state of having a body; bodily sub-cloth. **-ly** *adv.* **corporality** (kawr·pa̧·ral′·a̧·stance. **corporate** (kawr′·pa̧·rit) *a.* united legally in a body; pertaining to a corporation. **corporately** *adv.* **corporateness** *n.* **corporation** (kawr·pa̧·rā′·shan) *n.* united body; a legal, municipal, mercantile, or professional association. **corporative** *a.* **corporeal** (kawr·paw′·ri·al) *a.* pert. to the body; having a body; bodily; physical. **corporeally** *adv.* **corporal punishment,** punishment inflicted on the body [L. *corpus,* body].

corps (kawr) *n.* a division of an army forming a unit; any organized body of persons. *pl.* **corps** (kawrz) [Fr. fr. L. *corpus,* a body].

corpse (kawrps) *n.* a dead body, esp. of a human being [L. *corpus,* the body].

cor·pu·lence (kawr′·pya̧·lans) *n.* excessive fatness; fleshiness; stoutness. Also **corpulency** *n.* **corpulent** *a.* [L. *corpus,* the body].

cor·pus (kawr′·pa̧s) *n.* a body; the main substance of anything. *pl.* **corpora** [L. = a body].

cor·pus·cle (kawr′·pus·l) *n.* a little body; a minute particle; (*Anat.*) an organic cell, either moving freely, as in the blood, or intimately connected with others, as bone-corpuscles [L. *corpusculum,* dim. of *corpus,* a body].

cor·ral (ka̧·ral′) *n.* an enclosure for cattle, or for defense; *v.t.* to drive into a corral [Sp. fr. *corro,* a circle].

cor·rect (ka̧·rekt′) *a.* right; free from faults; accurate; *v.t.* to make right; to indicate the errors in; to bring to the standard of truth; to punish; to counteract. **-ly** *adv.* **-tion** *n.* amendment; a change to remedy a fault; punishment. **itude** *n.* **-ional** *a.* **-ive** *a.* having power to correct; *n.* that which corrects or counteracts. **-ness** *n.* **-or** *n.* [L. *corrigere,* to make right].

cor·re·late (kár′·, kawr′·a̧·lāt) *v.i.* to be mutually related, as father and son; *v.t.* to place in reciprocal relations; *n.* a correlative; either of two things or words necessarily implying the other. **correlation** *n.* reciprocal relation. **correlative** *a.* reciprocally related; *n.* one who, or that which, is correspondingly related to another person of thing. **correlativity** *n.*

cor·re·spond (kár′·, kawr·a̧·spánd′) *v.i.* to

exchange letters; to answer or agree with in some respect; to be congruous. **-ence** *n.* exchange of letters; the letters themselves; mutual adaptation of one thing to another; suitability. **-ent** *a.* suitable; conformable; congruous; *n.* one with whom intercouse is maintained by exchange of letters. **-ing** *a.* **-ingly** *adv.* [L. *correspondere,* answer with].

cor·ri·dor (kár′·, kawr′·a̧·der) *n.* a gallery or passage in a building [L. *currere,* to run].

cor·ri·gen·dum (kawr·a̧·jen′·dam) *n.* something to be corrected, esp. a misprint in a book; *pl.* **corrigenda** [L. = to be corrected].

cor·ri·gi·ble (kár′·, kawr·′a̧·ja̧bl) *a.* capable of being corrected [L. *corrigere,* to correct].

cor·rob·o·rate (ka̧·ráb′·a̧·rāt) *v.t.* to add strength to; to confirm; to support a statement, etc. **corroborant** *a.* giving strength. **corroboration** *n.* **corroborative** *a.* confirming; strengthening [L. *con-; robur, roboris,* strength]

cor·rode (ka̧·rōd′) *v.t.* to eat away by degrees (by chemical action, disease, etc.); to rust. **corrodent** *a.* corrosive; *n.* a substance which eats away. **corrodible, corrosible** *a.* capable of being corroded. **corrosion** *n.* **corrosive** *a.* having the power of corroding; fretting or vexing; *n.* any corrosive substance [L. *con-; rodere,* to gnaw].

cor·ru·gate (kár′·, kawr′·a̧·gāt) *v.t.* to form into folds or alternate furrows and ridges. **corrugation** *n.* **— iron,** sheet-iron, corrugated to increase its rigidity [L. *con-; ruga,* a wrinkle].

cor·rupt (ka̧·rupt′) *v.t.* and *i.* to make rotten; to rot; to defile; to contaminate; to make evil; to bribe; *a.* putrid; depraved; tainted with vice or sin; influenced by bribery; spoiled, by mistakes, or altered for the worse (of words, literary passages, etc.). **-er** *n.* **-ible** *a.* capable of being corrupted .**corruption** *n.* **-ive** *a.* **-ly** *adv.* **-ness** *n.* [L. *corrumpere, corruptum*].

cor·sage (kawr′·sáj) *n.* a small bouquet worn by a lady; the bodice of a lady's dress [L. *corpus,* the body].

cor·sair (kawr′·sār) *n.* a pirate; a pirate's vessel [Fr. *corraire*].

cor·set (kawr′·sit) *n.* undergarment; girdle. **corselet** (kawr′·sa̧·let), **corselette** (kawrs′·lit) *n.* a corset. **corslet, corselet** *n.* a piece of armor to cover the trunk of the body [Fr. *corselet,* double dim. of O.Fr. *cors,* the body, fr. L. *corpus,* the body] .

cor·tège (kawr·tezh′) *n.* a train of attendants or procession; a funeral procession [Fr.].

cor·tex (kawr′·teks) *n.* bark; sheath or skin of a plant. (*Anat.*) the outer covering of an organ, esp. the outer layer of gray matter of the brain; *pl.* **cortices** (kawr′·ti·sēz). **cortical** *a.* **corticate, corticated** *a.* [L. = the bark of tree].

cor·ti·sone (kawr′·ti·zōn) *n.* a substance produced in the adrenal glands [fr. *cortex*].

co·run·dum (ka̧·run′·dam) *n.* common mineral noted for hardness [Hind. *kurand*].

cor·us·cate (kár′· kawr′·as·kāt) *v.i.* to flash; to sparkle, to glitter; to gleam. **coruscation** *n.* [L. *coruscare,* to glitter, vibrate].

cor·y·bant·ic (kawr′·a̧·bant·ik) *a.* rural estate; *a.* frenzied and delirious [*Myth.* goddess Cybele].

co·se·cant (kō·sē′·kant) *n.* (*Trig.*) the secant of the complement of an angle. (*Abbrev.*) **cosec** [L. *co-; secare,* to cut].

co·sig·na·to·ry (kō·sig′·na̧·tōr·i·) *a.* signing jointly; *n.* a joint signer of a document.

co·sine (kō′·sin) *n.* (*Trig.*) the sine of the complement of an angle. (*Abbrev.*) **cos.**

cos·met·ic (káz·met′·ik) *a.* making for beauty, esp. of the skin; *n.* any substance helping to improve or enhance the appearance [Gk. *kosmein,* to arrange, adorn].

cos·mic (káz′·mik) *a.* See **cosmos.**

cos·mo- (koz′·mō) a combining form from Gk. *kosmos,* the universe.

cos·mog·o·ny (kås·måg′·ạ·ni·) *n.* a theory of the creation of the universe and its inhabitants. [Gk. *kosmos*, the universe; *gignesthai*, to be born].

cos·mol·o·gy (kås·mål′·ạ·ji·) *n.* the science of the laws which control the universe. **cosmological** *a.* **cosmologist** *n.* [Gk. *kosmos*, the universe; *logos*, discourse].

cos·mo·naut (kåz′·mạ·nåt) *n.* a space traveler.

cos·mo·pol·i·tan (kås·mạ·pål′·i·tạn) *a.* relating to all parts of the world; free from national prejudice; *n.* a cosmopolitan person; a citizen of the world. Also **cosmopolite** *n.* [Gk. *kosmos*, the universe; *politēs*, a citizen].

cos·mos (kåz′·mạs) *n.* the ordered universe; order (as opposed to 'chaos'); a genus of flowering plant. **cosmic, cosmical** *a.* pert. to the universe, or to the earth as a part of the universe; orderly. **cosmically** *adv.* **cosmic rays**, radiations of great penetrating power, coming to the earth from outer space [Gk. *kosmos*, order].

Cos·sack (kås′·k) *n.* member of S. Russ. tribe [Turk. *quazzaq*, an adventurer].

cost (kawst) *v.i.* to entail the payment, loss, or sacrifice of; to cause to bear or suffer; *n.* price; the amount paid, or to be paid, for anything; expenditure of time, labor, etc.; suffering undergone for any end. **-liness** *n.* great cost or expense; expensiveness. **-ly** *a.* very expensive. **— price**, the wholesale, as opposed to the retail, price [L. *constare*, fr. *stare*, to stand].

cos·tal (kås′·tạl) *a.* pert. to the ribs or to the side of the body [L. *costa*, a rib].

cos·tive (kås′·tiv) *a.* having sluggish motion; constipated. **-ness** *n.* [L. *con-; stipare*, to press together].

cos·tume (kås′·tūm) *n.* dress peculiar or appropriate, as to country, period, office, or character; a person's dress or attire. **-r** *n.* one who makes or deals in costumes. Also **costumier** (kås·tūm′·i·ẹr) *n.* [It. *costume*, custom, fashion].

co·sy See **cozy**.

cot (kåt) *n.* a cottage [O.E. *cot*].

cot (kåt) *n.* a light, portable bed; (*Naut.*) a swinging bed on board ship [Hind. *khat*].

co·tan·gent (kō·tan′·jạnt) *n.* (*Trig.*) the tangent of the complement of an angle; (*Abbrev.*) **cot.**

cote (kōt) *n.* a shelter or enclosure for animals or birds; a sheep-fold [O.E. *cote*].

co·te·rie (kō′·ti·ri·) *n.* a set or circle of persons usually with common interests [Fr.].

co·til·lion, cotillon (kō·til′·yạn) *n.* a lively dance, of French origin; a complex dance of elaborate figures; music for the dance [Fr. *cotillon*, a petticoat].

cot·tage (kåt′·ij) *n.* a small dwelling house, esp. in the country or at a resort. **-r** *n.* one who inhabits a cottage. **— cheese** *n.* a soft, white cheese [O.E. *cot*].

cot·ter (kåt′·ẹr) *n.* a pin or wedge used for tightening or fastening; a split pin.

cot·ton (kåt′·n) *n.* a soft, downy, substance, resembling wool; cloth or thread made of cotton; *a.* made of cotton; *v.i.* (*Colloq.*) to become friendly; to take to. **— gin** *n.* a machine for separating the seeds from cotton. **-mouth** *n.* the water moccasin. **-tail** *n.* American rabbit. **-wood** *n.* a type of American poplar tree. **-y** *a.* [Ar. *qutum*].

cot·y·le·don (kåt·ạ·lē′·dạn) *n.* (*Bot.*) seed-lobe or primary leaf of the embryo plant [Gk. *kotulēdon*, a cup-shaped cavity].

couch (kouch) *v.t.* to cause to lie down, esp. on a bed; to phrase; to express; to lower a lance, spear, etc. for action; *v.i.* to lie down; to crouch; *n.* a sofa; davenport. **couchant** (kouch′·ạnt) *a.* lying down [Fr. *coucher*, fr. L. *collocare*, to place together].

cou·gar (kōō′·gẹr) *n.* the puma or American panther [Native S. Amer.)].

cough (kawf) *n.* noisy, violent, explosive effort to expel irritating matter from the lungs; *v.i.* to make such an effort; *v.t.* to expel from the lungs by a cough. **— up** (*Slang*) hand over [M.E. *coughen*].

could (kood) *p.at.* of the verb **can**.

cou·lomb (kōō·låm′) *n.* the quantity transferred by a current of one ampere in one second [Charles de *Coulomb*, a French physicist].

coul·ter See **colter**.

coun·cil (koun′·sạl) *n.* an assembly summoned for consultation or advice; a municipal body; the deliberation carried on in such an assembly. **-man** *n.* **-lor** *n.* [L. *concilium*].

coun·sel (koun′·sạl) *n.* advice; opinion; deliberation together; one who gives advice, esp. legal; a lawyer; an advocate; *v.t.* to advise; admonish; recommend. **-or** *n.* an adviser; a trial lawyer. **-orship** *n.* [L. *consulere*, to consult].

count (kount) *n.* (*fem.* **countess**) a title of nobility [L. *comes, comitis*, companion].

count (kount) *v.t.* to number; to reckon; to sum up; to consider or esteem; to include; to recite the numerals in regular succession; *v.i.* to depend or rely (with 'on'); *n.* the act of reckoning; the number ascertained by counting; (*Law*) a charge in an indictment. **-able** *a.* **— down** *n.* the last check before a missile is launched. **-less** *a.* not capable of being counted; innumerable. **-er** *n.* one who counts; a token or disc of metal, wood, etc. is used in reckoning; a table on which money is counted, goods displayed, or business transacted [L. *computare*].

coun·te·nance (koun′·tạ·nạns) *n.* the face; the features; aspect; look; appearance; encouragement; support; *v.i.* to favor; to support; to encourage; to approve. **to keep one's countenance**, to preserve one's composure [L. *continentia*, manner of holding oneself].

count·er (koun′·tẹr) *a.* contrary; opposite; opposed; adverse; reciprocal; *adv.* in opposition; the opposite way; *n.* that which is opposite; a return blow or parry; *v.t.* and *i.* to parry; to oppose; to hinder; to do any act which opposes another; to make a counter-move. **-attack** *n.* an attack launched to recapture a position or to stop and drive back an enemy attack. **-attraction** *n.* rival attraction. **-claim** *n.* (*Law*) a claim set up by the defendant in a suit to counter that of the plaintiff. **-clockwise** *adv.* revolving in a direction opposite to the movement of the hands of a clock. **-espionage** *n.* spying directed against the enemy's system of espionage. **-irritant** *n.* a substance, the application of which, by inducing superficial irritation, relieves a more deep-seated irritation. **-tenor** *n.* a high tenor; a man's voice singing alto [L. *contra*, against].

coun·ter·act (koun·tẹr·akt′) *v.t.* to act in opposition to; to hinder; to defeat.

coun·ter·bal·ance (koun′·tẹr·bal·ạns) *v.t.* to act against with equal power or effect; to neutralize; *n.* equal opposing weight, power, or agency; a weight balancing another.

coun·ter·charge (koun′·tẹr·chárj) *n.* a charge brought in opposition to another.

coun·ter·check (koun·tẹr·chek′) *v.t.* to check by an opposing check; to reprimand.

coun·ter·feit (koun′·tẹr·fit) *v.t.* to copy without authority; to imitate with intent to deceive; to forge; to feign; *a.* sham; forged; false; *n.* an imitation; a forgery; an impostor. **-er** *n.*

coun·ter·mand (koun·tẹr·mand′) *v.t.* to cancel an order; *n.* a contrary order [L. *contra; mandare*, to command].

coun·ter·march (koun′·tẹr·márch) *v.i.* to march back; *n.* a marching back.

coun·ter·mine (koun′·tẹr·mīn) *n.* (*Mil.*) to destroy enemy mines; any scheme to frustrate the designs of an opponent.

coun·ter·pane (koun′·tẹr·pān) *n.* a coverlet; a quilt [L. *culcita puncta*, a stitched quilt].

coun·ter·part (koun'·tẹr·pȧrt) *n.* a duplicate; something complementary or correlative.

coun·ter·point (koun'·tẹr·point) *n.* (*Mus.*) the art of combining melodies; the addition of a subsidiary melody to another so as to form a perfect melody.

coun·ter·poise (koun'·tẹr·poiz) *v.t.* to act against with equal weight or power; *n.* a weight sufficient to balance another.

coun·ter·sign (koun'·tẹr·sīn) *v.t.* to sign a document already signed by another; to ratify; to attest authenticity; *n.* a password.

coun·try (kun'·tri·) *n.* a region; a district; a tract of land; the territory of a nation; the nation itself; land of birth, residence, etc.; rural districts as opposed to town; *a.* rural; rustic; pert. to territory distant from a city. **countrified** *a.* **countrify** *v.t.* to make rural. — **club** *n.* a club with grounds, a house, and facilities for outdoor sports. **-man** *n.* one who lives in the country; a rustic; one born in the same country; a compatriot. **-side** *n.* any rural district [L.L. *contrata*].

coun·ty (koun'·ti·) *n.* a division of a country or state for administrative purposes; the inhabitants of a county. — **seat**, the chief town or capital of a county [Fr. *comté,* fr. *comte,* a count].

coup (kȯȯ) *n.* lit. a stroke or blow; then, a successful stroke or move *pl.* (kȯȯz) [Fr.].

coup de grâce (kȯȯ·dȧ·grȧs) *n.* blow, shot, etc. that brings death to a sufferer [Fr.].

coup d'é·tat (kȯȯ·dā·tä') *n.* lit. a stroke of state; a sudden and revolutionary change of government achieved by force [Fr.].

coupe (kȯȯp) *n.* a two-seat automobile with enclosed body [Fr. *couper,* to cut].

cou·ple (kup'·l) *n.* two things of the same kind taken together; two; a pair; a brace; husband and wife; a leash for two hounds; that which joins two things together; *v.t.* to join together; (*Colloq.*) to marry; *v.i.* to connect. **couplet** *n.* a pair of lines of verse. **coupling** *n.* a connection; that which couples, esp. the device joining railroad cars [L. *copula,* a bond].

cou·pon (kȯȯ'·pȧn) *n.* an interest certificate attached to a bond; a dividend warrant; a negotiable ticket or voucher; a pass [Fr. *couper,* to cut off].

cour·age (kur'·ȧj) *n.* bravery; fearlessness; daring. **courageous** (kȧ·rā'·jȧs) *a.* full of courage. **courageously** *adv.* **courageousness** *n.* [O.Fr. *corage,* fr. L. *cor,* the heart].

cour·i·er (kȯȯ'·ri·ẹr) *n.* a runner or messenger; a state messenger; a tourist guide who accompanies travelers [L. *currere,* to run].

course (kōrs) *n.* the act of passing from one point to another; progress or movement, both in space and in time; the ground traversed; way or direction; line of conduct; the track or ground on which a race is run; career; a series (of lessons, lectures, etc.); each of the successive divisions of a meal; a continuous line of masonry at one level in a building; *v.t.* to hunt; to pursue; to chase; *v.i.* to run swiftly; to gallop. **-r** *n.* one who courses or hunts; a swift horse [L. *cursus,* running].

court (kōrt) *n.* an uncovered area enclosed by buildings, or by buildings and railings; a yard; the residence of a sovereign; the retinue of a sovereign; the homage or attention paid to a sovereign; a legal tribunal; the judge or judges, as distinguished from the counsel; the hall where justice is administered; (*Sport*) a space, usually rectangular, laid out for certain sports, as tennis, etc. **courteous** (kurt'·i·ȧs) *a.* polite; well-bred; of courtlike manners. **courteously** *adv.* **courteousness** *n.* **courtier** (kōrt'·yẹr) one who frequents the courts of princes; one with the manners of a frequenter of courts. **-ly** *a.* elegant; flattering; with the manners of a courtier. **-liness** *n.* — **martial** *n.* a court of military or naval officers for the trial of persons in the army or navy; *pl.* **-s-martial.** [L.

cohors, an enclosure].

court (kōrt) *v.t.* to seek the favor of; to try to gain the affections of; to seek in marriage; *v.i.* to woo; to play the lover. **-ship** *n.* [L. *cohors,* an enclosure].

cour·te·san (kōr'·tȧ·zạn) *n.* a prostitute [It. *cortigiana*].

cour·te·sy (kur'·tȧ·si·) *n.* politeness of manners; urbanity [O.Fr. *cortoisie*].

cou·sin (kuz'·n) *n.* formerly any kinsman; now, the son or daughter of an uncle or aunt [Fr. fr. L. *consobrinus*].

cou·tu·rier (kȯȯ·tu·rya') *n.* a man dressmaker. **-rieré** (·ryār') *n. fem.*

cove (kōv) *n.* a small bay [O.E. *cofa,* a chamber].

cov·e·nant (kuv'·ȧ·nạnt) *n.* a mutual and solemn agreement; a contract; a compact; a written agreement; *v.t.* to agree to by covenant; *v.i.* to enter into an agreement. **-er** *n.* one who makes a covenant or agreement. **Covenanters** later [L. *cno-; venire,* to come].

cov·er (kuv'·ẹr) *v.t.* to be over the whole top of; to overspread; to enclose; to include; to protect; to put hat on; to point a revolver, gun, etc. at; to wager an equal sum of money; *n.* anything that covers; a lid; a wrapper; an envelope; a binding; a cloak; disguise; concealment; shelter; defense. **-ing** *n.* **-let** *n.* a bedcover. **covert** *a.* covered over; concealed; sheltered; secret; veiled; *n.* a thicket; a place sheltering game. **covertly** *adv.* secretly; in private. **coverture** (kuv'·ẹr·chẹr) *n.* covering; shelter; defense. [Fr. *couvrir,* to cover].

cov·et (kuv'·it) *v.t.* to long to possess, esp. what belongs to another; to desire unreasonably or unlawfully; *v.i.* to have strong desire. **-able** *a.* that may be coveted. **-ous** *a.* very desirous; excessively eager; avaricious for gain. **-ously** *adv.* **-ousness** *n.* [L. *cupiditas,* desire].

cov·ey (kuv'·i·) *n.* a brood of partridges or quail; (*Fig.*) a company; a set [Fr. *couveé,* fr. *couver,* to brood].

cow (kou) *n.* the female of a bovine animal; the female elephant, whale, etc. **-ish** *a.* **-boy** *n.* a boy who herds cows; on the western plains, a herdsman employed on a ranch to look after cattle. **-catcher** *n.* a frame in front of a locomotive to remove obstructions. **-herd** *n.* one who herds cows. **-hide** *n.* the hide of a cow; leather made from the hide of a cow. **-lick** *n.* a tuft of hair not easily flattened [O.E. *cu*].

cow (kou) *v.t.* to frighten into submission; to overawe [O.N. *kuga,* to oppress].

cow·ard (kou'·ẹrd) *n.* one given to fear; one who lacks courage. **-ly** *a.* lacking in courage; afraid. **-ice** (·dis) *n.* want of courage; fear. [Fr. *couard,* fr. L. *cauda,* a tail].

cow·er (kou'·ẹr) *v.i.* to crouch down through fear, shame, cold [etym. uncertain].

cowl (koul) *n.* a monk's hooded cloak; the hood itself; a hooded top for a chimney. **-ed** *a.* [L. *cucullus,* the hood of a cloak].

cow·slip (kou'·slip) *n.* the marsh marigold [OE. *cu-slyppe,* cow dung].

cox·comb (kȧks'·kōm) *n.* one given to showing off; a fool; a fop. **-ry** *n.*

cox·swain (kȧk'·sn), **cox** (kȧks) *n.* the steersman of a boat. **to cox** *vt.* and *i.* to act as coxswain [fr. *cock*-boat and *swain*].

coy (koi) *a.* shy; modest; pretending to be shy. **-ly** *adv.* **-ness** *n.* [Fr. *coi,* fr. L. *quietus*].

coy·o·te (kī'·ōt) *n.* the Amer. prairie wolf [Mex.].

coz·en (kuz'·n) *v.t.* to flatter in order to cheat; to defraud [Fr. *cousiner,* to play the part of *cousin,* in order to sponge on people].

co·zy (kō'·zi·) *a.* snug; comfortable; *n.* a covering to keep a teapot hot (*tea cozy*). Also **cosy. cozily** *adv.* **coziness** *n.*

crab (krab) *n.* an edible crustacean; a disagreeable person; *v.t.* to fish for crabs; (*Slang*) to complain. *pr.p.* **-bing.** *pa.t.* **-bed. -biness** *n.* **-by** *a.* — **grass** *n.* rapid growing coarse grass

[O.E. *crabbd*, snatcher].

crab·bed (krab'·ad) *a.* harsh; austere; fault-finding; perverse; bad-tempered; of writing, hard to read. **-ly** *adv.* **-ness** *n.*

crack (krak) *v.t.* to break with a sharp noise, either wholly or partially; to split or break; to produce a sudden sharp sound; to snap; *v.i.* to break partially; to burst open in chinks; to give forth a sudden, sharp sound; *n.* a partial break; fissure; a sharp noise; a flaw; a break in the voice; a mental flaw; (*Colloq.*) *a.* superior; special; expert. **-ed** *a.* **-er** *n.* one who cracks, that which cracks; a fire-cracker; a thin crisp biscuit.**-er-jack** (*Slang*) *n.* a person or thing of exceptional quality. — **up** *n.* a collision; a defeat; a breakdown [O.E. *cracian*].

crack·le (krak'·l) *v.i.* to produce slight but repeated cracking sounds; *n.* a noise composed of frequent, slight cracking sounds; over-all fine cracks in porcelain glaze. **crackling** *n.* a succession of small sharp reports; rind of roasted pork [O.E. *cracian*, to crack].

cra·dle (krā'·dl) *n.* a bed for infants that can be rocked; infancy; the place of origin of anyone or anything; a framework used as a support; *v.t.* to place or rock in a cradle; to tend or train in infancy; to support on a cradle (as a vessel) [O.E. *cradol*].

craft (kraft) *n.* skill or dexterity; a skilled trade; cunning, artifice, or guile; a vessel; vessels collectively. **-y** *a.* cunning; artful. **-ily** *adv.* **-iness** *n.* **-sman** *n.* one engaged in a craft or trade. **-smanship** *n.* [O.E. *craeft*].

crag (krag) *n.* a steep, rugged rock or peak. **-ged** (krag'·ad) *a.* **-gy** *a.* full of crags; rough; rugged. **-giness** *n.* [W. *craig*, a rock].

cram (kram) *v.t.* and *i.* to stuff; to pack tightly; (*Colloq.*) to prepare hastily for an examination. *pr.p.* **-ming.** *pa.t.* **-med.** *n.* (*Colloq.*) a crush or crowd of people [O.E. *crammian*].

cramp (kramp) *n.* a painful contraction of muscles of the body; that which restrains; a clamp for holding masonry, timbers, etc. together; *v.t.* to affect with cramp; to restrict or hamper; to hold with a cramp; *a.* narrow; cramped; restricted [O.Fr. *crampe*].

cran·ber·ry (kran'·ber·i·) *n.* a red, sour, berry [prob. orig. *crane-berry*].

crane (krān) *n.* a tall wading-bird with long legs, neck, and bill; a machine for lifting and lowering heavy weights; *v.t.* to stretch out the neck to look at something [O.E. *cran*].

cra·ni·um (krā'·ni·am) *n.* the skull. *pl.* **crania. cranial** *a.* pert. to the skull. **craniology** *n.* the study of skulls. **craniological** *a.* [Gk. *kranion*, the skull].

crank (krangk) *n.* a handle attached to a shaft for turning it; the bent portion of an axis, used to change horizontal or vertical into rotatory motion, etc.; a fanciful twist or whimsy in speech; (*Colloq.*) a faddist; an eccentric or crotchety person; *v.t.* to provide with a crank; to shape like a crank; to operate by a crank; *v.i.* to turn the crank as in starting an automobile engine (usually with 'up'). **-case** *n.* the housing for a crankshaft. **-shaft** *n.* (*Mach.*) a shaft driven by or driving a crank. **-y** *a.* shaky or in bad condition, of machinery; (*Fig.*) irritable or crotchety; bad-tempered. **-iness** *n.* [O.E. *cranc*].

cran·ny (kran'·i·) *n.* an open crack; a small opening; a crevice; a chink [Fr. *cran*, a notch].

crap, craps (krap, -s) *n.* gambling game played with dice.

crash (krash) *n.* a violent fall or impact accompanied by loud noise; a burst of mixed, loud sound, e.g. of thunder, breaking crockery, etc.; bankruptcy; a sudden collapse or downfall; *v.i.* to make a crash; to fall, come with, strike with, a crash; to collapse; *v.t.* to break into pieces. **—helmet** *n.* a padded helmet worn by aviators and racing motorists [imit. of the sound].

crash (krash) *n.* a coarse linen cloth.

cra·sis (krā'·sis) *n.* (*Gram.*) union of two vowels into one long vowel or diphthong [Gk.].

crass (kras) *a.* thick; gross; dense; stupid. **-ly** *adv.* **-ness** *n.* [L. *crassus*, coarse].

crate (krāt) *n.* a wicker hamper, or open-work packing-case [L. *cratis*, a hurdle].

cra·ter (krā'·ter) *n.* the cup-shaped mouth of a volcano; the cavity resulting from the explosion of a large shell, bomb, mine, etc. [Gk. *kratēr*, a mixing-bowl].

cra·vat (kra·vat') *n.* a man's necktie or scarf [Fr. *cravate*, Croation (scarf)].

crave (krāv) *v.t.* and *i.* to have a very strong desire for; to long for; to ask with earnestness, submission, or humility; to beg. **-r.** *n.* **craving** *n.* an inordinate desire [O.E. *crafian*, to crave].

cra·ven (krāv'·n) *a.* cowardly; spiritless; chicken-hearted; *n.* a spiritless fellow; a coward [O.Fr. *cravanter*, to overthrow].

craw (kraw) *n.* crop or first stomach of fowls; stomach of any animal [M.E. *crawe*].

craw·fish, crayfish (kraw'·, krā'·fish) *n.* a fresh-water crustacean, resembling the lobster but smaller [Fr. *écrevisse*].

crawl (krawl) *v.i.* to move along the ground on the belly or on the hands and knees; to move very slowly; to move abjectly; to swim with an overarm stroke; *n.* a crawling motion; swimming stroke [O.N. *krafla*, to claw].

cray·on (krā'·an) *n.* a coloring pencil; a drawing made with crayons; *v.t.* to draw with crayons [Fr. *crayon*, a pencil; *craie*, chalk].

craze (krāz) *n.* a strong, habitual desire or passion; a general or individual mania; a very common fashion; *v.t.* to make crazy; (*Pottery*) to crackle. **-d** *a.* weak in mind. **craziness** *n.* **crazy** *a.* insane; extremely foolish; madly eager (for); falling to pieces. **crazily** *adv.* [Fr. *écraser*, to break].

creak (krēk) *n.* a harsh, grating sound; *v.i.* to make a sharp, harsh, grating sound. **-y** *a.* [imit. sound].

cream (krēm) *n.* the fatty substance that rises to the surface of milk; the best part of anything; anything resembling cream; *v.t.* to take off the cream; to add cream to; *v.i.* to become covered with cream; to froth. **-y** *a.* full of cream; resembling cream. **-ery** *n.* a butter and cheese factory; a center to which milk is sent for distribution. **-iness** *n.* **— cheese** *n.* a soft, smooth, white cheese. **— of tartar,** acid potassium tartrate, a component of baking powder [Gk. *chrisma*, unguent].

crease (krēs) *n.* a line or mark made by folding anything; *v.t.* to make a crease or mark on; *v.i.* to become creased [etym. uncertain].

cre·ate (krē·āt') *v.t.* to bring into existence out of nothing; to originate; to make. **creation** (krē·ā'·shan) *n.* the act of creating, esp. of bringing the world into being; the world; anything created; any original production of the human mind. **creative** *a.* capable of creation; original. **creator** *n.* one who creates; a maker. **Creator** *n.* God. **creature** (krē'·cher) *n.* anything created; any living being [L. *craere*].

cre·dence (krē'·dans) *n.* trust; belief; (*Eccles.*) a small altar table. **credentials** (kri·den'·shalz) *n.pl.* testimonials showing that a person is entitled to belief or credit. **credible** (kred'·a·bl) *a.* worthy of belief. **credibility** *n.* [L. *credere*, to believe].

cre·den·za (kra·den'·za) *n.* a sideboard [fr. *credence*].

cred·it (kred'·it) *n.* belief; trust; trustworthiness; honor or reputation; anything that procures esteem or honor; the amount at a person's disposal in a bank; in commerce, the general system of buying, borrowing and lending based on good faith and confidence; *v.t.* to believe; to put trust in. **-able** *a.* reliable; meriting credit. **-ably** *adv.* **-ableness** *n.* **-or** *n.* one to whom money is due [L. *credere*, to believe].

cred·u·lous (kre'·ja·las) *a.* too prone to believe. **-ly** *adv.* **-ness** *n.* **credulity** (kra·dū'·-

la·ti·) n. gullibility [L. *credulus*, believing].

creed (krēd) n. a statement of religious belief; any statement of principles. **credo** (krē'·dō) n. a creed [L. *credere*, to believe].

creek (krēk) n. a small inlet; a branch or small tributary of a river [O.N. *kriki*].

creel (krēl) n. an angler's basket [Celt.].

creep (krēp) v.i. to move along with the body close to the ground, like a worm or reptile; to spread, like certain plants, by clinging. pa.t., pa.p. **crept. -er** n. esp. a creeping plant; a genus of small birds. **-y** a. causing a creeping sensation on the skin [O.E. *creopan*].

cre·mate (krē'·māt) v.t. to consume by burning, esp. the dead; to reduce to ashes. **cremation** (krē·mā'·shan) n. the act of cremating the dead. **cremator** n. **crematorium** n. an establishment for the cremation of bodies. **crematory** a. or n. [L. *cremare*, to burn].

cre·nate (krē'·nāt) a. with the edge notched. **-d** a. [L. *crena*, a notch].

Cre·ole (krē'·ōl) n. a native of Spanish America or the W. Indies, of European parentage; a white person descended from the French or Spanish settlers of Louisiana; a native of mixed parentage [Fr. fr. Sp. *criollo*].

cre·o·sote (krē'·a·sōt) n. an oily liquid obtained from the distillation of coal tar, extensively used to preserve wood from decay [Gk. *sōtēr*, preserver].

crepe (krāp) n. a thin crinkled fabric or paper; mourning cloth; a kind of rough-surfaced rubber used for the soles of shoes, etc. [Fr.].

crept (krept) pa.p. and pa.t. of **creep**.

cre·pus·cu·lar (kri·pus'·kya·ler) a. pert. to twilight; dim. [L. *crepusculum*, twilight].

cre·scen·do (kra·shen'·dō) n. (*Mus.*) a gradual increase in loudness; adv. with increase in loudness. (*Abbrev.*) **cresc.** [It.].

cres·cent (kres'·ant) a. like the young moon in shape; increasing; n. the moon in first quarter; a crescent-shaped object [L. *crescere*, to grow].

cress (kres) n. various salad greens[O.E. *cerse, cresse*, creeper].

cres·set (kres'·it) n. an iron basket or cage-like container, filled with inflammable material used as a torch [O.Fr. *craisse*, grease].

crest (krest) n. the comb or tuft on a bird's head; the plume or top of a helmet; the top of a mountain, ridge, etc.; the highest part of a wave; a badge above the shield of a coat of arms; v.t. to reach the top of. **-fallen** a. dispirited; dejected [L. *crista*].

cre·tin·ism (krēt'·in·izm) n. condition caused by thyroid deficiency; a form of idiocy. **cretin** n. one suffering from cretinism. **cretinous** a. [Swiss *crestin*, a Christian].

cre·tonne (kri·tán) n. a strong, unglazed printed cotton cloth [*Creton*, in France].

cre·vasse (kra·vas') n. a deep open chasm in a glacier; a fissure; a cleft [Fr.].

crev·ice (krev'·is) n. a cleft; a narrow fissure; a crack [Fr. *crever*, to burst].

crew (kr̄oo) n. a group of workmen; a ship's or boat's company [earlier *crue, accrue*, a reinforcement].

crew·el (kr̄oo'·al) n. embroidery yarn. **-work** n.

crib (krib) n. a manger; a stall for cattle; a child's bed with barred sides; a hut or small dwelling; a key or translation (used by students); an enclosure for storing grain [O.E. *cribb*, an oxstall].

crib·bage (krib'·ij) n. (*Cards*) a game played by two or four players.

crick (krik) n. neck or back spasm or cramp.

crick·et (krik'·it) n. a small, brown, chirping insect [Fr. *criquer*, to creak].

crick·et (krik'·it) n. a game played with bats, ball, and wickets; (*Colloq.*) fair play.

cri·er (krī'·er) n. See **cry**.

crime (krīm) n. a violation of the law (usually of a serious nature); an offense. **criminal** (krim'·a·nal) a. guilty of, or pert. to, crime;

wicked; n. one guilty of a crime. **criminality** n. guiltiness. **criminally** adv. **criminate** v.t. to charge with a crime. **crimination** n. **criminative, criminatory** a. accusing. **criminologist** n. **criminology** n. science dealing with the cause and treatment of crime and criminals [L. *crimen*, a charge].

crimp (krimp) v.t. to form into curls or pleats; to wrinkle; to decoy or press into military or naval service; n. an agent who procures men for service as soldiers or sailors; a small waves, as in hair [O.E. *crimpan*, to curl].

crim·son (krim'·zn) a. of a rich deep red color; n. the color itself [O.Sp. *cremesin*, fr. Arab. *qirmiz*, the cochineal insect].

cringe (krinj) v.t. to shrink; to cower; to behave obsequiously [M.E. *crengen*].

crin·kle (kring'·kl) v.t. to wrinkle; to make a series of bends or twists in a line or surface; to rustle. **crinkly** adv. [O.E. *crincan*].

crin·o·line (krin'·a·lin) n. a hoop skirt; a stiff, coarse fabric petticoat [L. *crinis*, hair; *linum*, flax].

crip·ple (krip'·l) n. a person without the use of a limb or limbs; a lame person; a. lame; v.t. to lame [O.E. *crypel*].

cri·sis (krī'·sis) n. the decisive moment; the turning point, esp. in an illness; emergency; a time of difficulty or danger; pl. **crises** (krī'·sēz) [Gk. *krisis*, decision].

crisp (krisp) a. brittle; breaking with a short snap; of hair, curly; sharp; v.t. to make crisp; **-ly** adv. **-ness** n. [L. *crispus*, curled].

criss·cross (kris'·kraws) a. crossing; arranged in crossing lines; adv. crossing one another in different directions; v.t. and i. to mark or be marked with cross lines [corrupt. of *Christ's-cross*].

cri·te·ri·on (krī·tir'·i·an) n. a standard of judging; a rule or test by which opinions may be judged. pl. **criteria** [Gk.].

crit·ic (krit'·ik) n. one who expressed a reasoned judgment on any matter, esp. on art or literature; one whose profession it is to write reviews; one given to expressing adverse judgment or finding fault. **-al** a. pert. to criticism or critics; captious or fault-finding; pert. to a crisis; crucial; decisive. **-ally** adv. **criticism** n. the art of making a reasoned judgment, a critical appreciation. **criticize** v.t. and i. to pass judgment; to censure. **critique** (kri·tēk') n. criticism; review [Gk. *krinein*, to judge].

croak (krōk) v.t. and i. to make a low, hoarse noise in the throat; (*Slang*) to die; n. the hoarse, harsh sound made by a frog or a crow. **-y** a. [imit.].

cro·chet (krō·shā') n. a kind of needlework consisting of loops; v.t. and i. to work in crochet [Fr. *crochet*, a small hook].

crock (krák) n. an earthenware pot or pitcher; a piece of broken earthenware. **-ery** n. vessels and dishes of all kinds, generally made of earthenware [Gael. *crog*, a pitcher].

croc·o·dile (krák'·a·dīl) n. a large, amphibious reptile of the lizard kind. **— tears**, hypocritical tears; sham grief [Gk. *krokodilos*, a lizard].

cro·cus (krō'·kas) n. a bulbous plant; saffron [Gk. *krokos*, crocus, saffron].

crone (krōn) n. a wizened old woman.

cro·ny (krō'·ni·) n. an intimate friend; a chum [earlier *chrony*, a contemporary, fr. Gk.].

crook (krook) n. any hook, bend, or sharp turn; a shepherd's or a bishop's staff; a thief; a swindler; v.t. to bend into a crook; to curve; to pervert; v.i. to be bent or curved. **-ed** a. bent; twisted; (*Fig.*) not straightforward. **-edly** adv. **-edness** n. **by hook or by crook**, by some means or other; by fair or foul [O.N. *krokr*].

croon (kroon) v.t. and i. to sing or hum softly; to sing in a sentimental manner. **-er** n. **-ing** n. [imit.].

crop (kráp) n. the cultivated produce of any plant or plants, in a farm, field, country, etc.; a harvest; the best ore; a pouch in a bird's gullet; the craw; a hunting-whip; a closely-cut head of hair; *v.t.* to reap the produce of a field. *pr.p.* **-ping.** *pa.p.* and *pa.t.* **-ped** *a.* with clipped ears; with hair cut close to head. **-per** *n.* one who, or that which, crops; (*Colloq.*) a heavy fall. **to crop up**, to appear unexpectedly [O.E. *cropp*, the head of a plant, ear of corn, etc.].

cro·quet (krō'·kā) *n.* an outdoor game played with balls, mallets and hoops.

cro·quette (krō·ket') *n.* (*Cookery*) a ball of finely minced meat, fish, etc. seasoned and fried [Fr. *croquer*, to mince].

cro·sier, cro·zier (krō'·zhẹr) *n.* the pastoral staff of a bishop [O.Fr. *crosse*, a crook].

cross (kraws) *n.* a stake used for crucifixion, consisting of two pieces of timber placed upon one another in the shape † or ✕; in particular, **the Cross,** the one on which Christ was crucified; a model or picture of this; anything in the shape of a cross; (*Fig.*) (the Cross being the symbol of suffering) affliction; tribulation; a misfortune; *v.t.* to mark with a cross; to make the sign of the cross. **-let** *n.* a small cross. **-wise** *adv.* in the form of a cross [L. *crux*, a cross].

cross (kraws) *a.* transverse; intersecting; interchanged; contrary, adverse; out of temper; dishonest; *n.* an intermixture of breeds or stocks, esp. in cattle-breeding; *v.t.* to place so as to intersect; to pass from one side to the other of; to pass over; to thwart; to oppose; to clash; to modify the breed of animals, plants, etc. by intermixture; *v.i.* to intersect; to move or pass from one side to the other; *adv.* across. **-ing** *n.* the act of passing across; an intersection; a place of crossing; the intermixture of breeds. **-ly** *adv.* **—action** *n.* (*Law*) an action brought by a defendant against a plaintiff on points pert. to the same case. **-bones** *n. pl.* two thigh bones crossed and surmounted by a skull, used as symbol of death, a sign of deadly danger, or the flag of a pirate ship. **-breed** *n.* parents of different breeds; a hybrid. **—examination** *n.* the examination of a witness by counsel on the other side. **—eyed** *a.* with eyes turned in toward the nose. **—grained** *a.* of wood, having the grain running across, or irregularly; of a person, ill-natured. **-hatching** *n.* in drawing, etching, etc. the art of shading by parallel intersecting lines. **— reference** *n.* in a book, e.g. a dictionary, the directing of the reader to another part for related information [L. *crux*, a cross].

cross·bill (kraws'·bil) *n.* a bird of the Finch family, whose mandibles cross.

cross·bow (kraws'·bō) *n.* a medieval weapon. **-man** *n.*

crotch (krach) *n.* a fork or bifurcation; the angle where the legs branch off from the human body. **-ed** *a.* [etym. uncertain].

crotch·et (krach'·ẹt) *n.* a small hook. **-y** *a.* full of whims, or fads [Fr. *crochet*, dim. of *croc.* a hook].

crouch (krouch) *v.i.* to huddle down close to the ground; to stoop low; to cringe or fawn servilely [prob. Fr. *croc*, a hook, crook].

croup (krōop) *n.* the rump or hindquarters of a horse [Fr. *croupe*].

croup (krōop) *n.* (*Med.*) acute inflammation of the windpipe, accompanied by a hoarse cough. **-y** *a.* [O.E. *kropan*, to cry].

crou·pi·er (krōo'·pi·ẹr) *n.* one who assists the chairman at a public banquet; an official in charge of a gaming table [Fr.].

crou·ton (krōo'·tän) *n.* a small cube of toasted bread used in soups, etc. [Fr. *croûte*].

crow (krō) *n.* a large bird, usually wholly black, of the genus Corvus; the cry of the cock; the name of a tribe of American Indians; a crowbar; *v.i.* to give the shrill cry of the cock; to utter a sound of pleasure. **crow's-foot** *n.* a wrinkle about the outer corners of the eyes in adults. **crow's-nest** *n.* a box or perch for the lookout man near the top of the mast [O.E. *crawan*].

crowd (kroud) *v.t.* to press or drive together; to fill or occupy by crushing together; *v.i.* to be numerous; to gather in numbers; *n.* a number of things or persons collected into a close body; a dense multitude or throng; (*Colloq.*) a set or clique [O.E. *crudan*].

crown (kroun) *n.* the diadem or state headdress worn by a sovereign; the sovereign; royalty; anything resembling a crown; something achieved or consummated; the topmost part of the head; the upper part of a hat; the summit; (*Br.*) a five-shilling piece (stamped with a crown); *v.t.* to invest with a crown or with royal dignity; to bestow upon as a mark of honor; to top or surmount; to complete. **— prince** *n.* the heir apparent to the throne. **— wheel** *n.* a wheel with cogs at right angles to its plane [L. *corona*, a crown].

cro·zier See **crosier.**

cru·cial (krōo'·shal) *a.* decisive; critical; crossshaped [L. *crux*, a cross].

cru·ci·ble (krōo'·si·bl) *n.* vessel capable of withstanding great heat, used for melting metals, etc.; (*Fig.*) a severe test [L.L. *crucibulum*].

cru·ci·fy (krōo'·sa·fī) *v.t.* to put to death by nailing to a cross; to torture; to mortify. **crucifier** *n.* **crucifix** *n.* an image of Christ on the Cross. **crucifixion** (krōo·sa·fik'·shan) *n.* **cruciform** *a.* cross-shaped [L. *crux*, a cross; *figere*, to fix].

crude (krōod) *a.* in the natural or raw state; unripe; rough; unfinished. **-ly** *adv.* **-ness** *n.* **crudity** *n.* [L. *crudis*, raw].

cru·el (krōo'·el) *a.* hard-hearted. **-ly** *adv.* **-ty** *n.* the quality of being cruel [See **crude**].

cru·et (krōo'·it) *n.* a small stoppered bottle for holding vinegar, oil, etc.; a stand for holding such bottles [O.Fr. *cruie*, a jar].

cruise (krōoz) *v.i.* to sail about without precise destination; in motoring and aviation, to go at a normal operating speed; *n.* an organized pleasure-sail. **-r** *n.* [L. *crux*, a cross].

crumb (krum) *n.* a small particle; a bit, esp. of bread; *v.t.* to reduce to crumbs; to cover with crumbs. **-y** *a.* **crummy** *a.* (*Slang*) inferior [O.E. *cruma*].

crum·ble (krum'·bl) *v.t.* to break into crumbs or fragments; *v.i.* to fall into crumbs. **crumbly** *a.* [O.E. *cruma*].

crum·pet (krum'·pit) *n.* (*Br.*) a flat, soft pancake [origin uncertain].

crum·ple (krum'·pl) *v.t.* to wrinkle; to crease; to rumple; *v.i.* to become wrinkled or creased; to shrink irregularly; to collapse.

crunch (krunch) *n.* the sound made by chewing crisp food, treading on gravel, hard snow, etc.; *v.t.* and *i.* to chew, tread, etc. with this sound [imit. origin].

cru·sade (krōo·sād') *n.* a medieval Christian war to recover the Holy Land from the Saracens; a campaign against any evil or vice; *v.i.* to join in a crusade. **-r** *n.* [Fr. *croisade*, fr. L. *crux*, a cross].

cruse (krōoz) *n.* a small earthen pot for holding water, oil, etc. [O.N. *krus*].

crush (krush) *v.t.* to press between two hard bodies so as to break, bruise, or crumple; to break into fragments; to squeeze out by pressure; to defeat utterly; *v.i.* to be broken or compressed by weight or force; *n.* violent pressure; a closely packed crowd of people [O.Fr. *crussir*].

crust (krust) *n.* the hard outer coat or covering of anything; the outer part of baked bread; pastry, etc. forming the covering of a pie; a deposit from wine collected on the interior of bottles; *v.t.* to cover with a crust; *v.i.* to gather into a crust; to form a crust. **-ated** *a.* covered with a crust; incrusted. **-ation** *n.* **-ily** *adv.* in a crusty manner; peevishly; morosely. **-iness** *n.* **-y** *a.* having a crust; like a crust; hard; peevish; surly [L. *crusta*].

Crus·ta·ce·a (krus·tā'·shi·a) *n.pl.* (*Zool.*) a

class of mainly aquatic animals including lobsters, crabs, shrimps, prawns, etc. **-n** *a.* and *n.* pert. to, or one of, the crustacea. **crustaceous** *a.* having a hard shell [L. *crusta*, a rind].

crutch (kruch) *n.* a staff with a cross-piece to go under the armpit for the use of cripples; a support; *v.t.* to support; to aid [O.E. *cryce*].

crux (kruks) *n.* a perplexing problem; a knotty point; the real issue [L. *crux*, a cross].

cry (krī) *v.t.* to call out; to shout; to proclaim; *v.i.* to call loudly; to exclaim vehemently; to weep; *n.* a loud utterance; the shedding of tears; the sound of a pack of hounds on the scent. **crier** *n.* one who cries; a public announcer. **-ing** *a.* **a far cry**, a great distance. **to cry wolf**, to give a false alarm [L. *quiritare*, to wail].

cry·o·lite (krī'·a·līt) *n.* a mineral used in making aluminum [Gk. *kruos*, frost; *lithos*, stone].

crypt (kript) *n.* a cell or chapel under a church, or underground, used for burial. **crytic(al)** *a.* hidden; secret; mysterious. **cryptically** *adv.* [Gk. *kruptein*, to conceal].

cryp·to- a *prefix* fr. Gk. *kruptos*, hidden, secret, combining to form many compounds.

cryp·to·gram (krip'·ta·gram) *n.* a writing in secret characters. Also **cryptograph** *n.* **cryptology** *n.* a secret language. **cryptonym** (krip'·ta·nim) *n.* a secret name [Gk. *kruptos*, hidden; *graphein*, to write].

crys·tal (kris'·tal) *n.* a transparent, colorless quartz; an ornament made from it; a ball cut from it for crystal gazing; a superior sort of glass; a table article made from such glass with ornamental cutting; (*Chem.*) a mineral body which has assumed a regular geometrical form; *a.* consisting of, or like, crystal; clear; transparent. **-line** *a.* **-lize** *v.t.* to cause to form crystals; (*Fig.*) to cause to assume a definite shape; *v.i.* to be formed into crystals; (*Fig.*) to become definite in shape. **-lizable** *a.* **-lization** *n.* [Gk. *krustallos*, fr. *kruos*, frost].

cub (kub) *n.* the young of the bear, fox, wolf, etc.; a junior Boy Scout; *v.i.* to bring forth young (of animals) [etym. unknown].

cub·by hole (kub'·i·hōl) *n.* a small place for storing things, or for hiding in [dial. E. *cub*, a pen or shed].

cube (kūb) *n.* (*Geom.*) a solid body with six equal square sides; (*Math.*) the product of a number multiplied twice by itself, as $4 \times 4 \times 4 = 64$, the cube of 4, or 4, to the third power; *v.t.* to raise to the third power. **cubic(al)** *a.* having the form of a cube; of three dimensions, e.g. **cubic foot. cuboid** *a.* resembling a cube in shape. — **root** *n.* the number which gives the stated number if raised to the third power, or cubed, e.g. 4 is the cube root of 64 [Gk. *kubos*].

cu·bi·cle (kū'·bi·kl) *n.* a small partitioned compartment [L. *cubiculum*, a bedroom].

cub·ism (kū'·bizm) *n.* (*Art*) a phase of modern art based on geometrical forms. **cubist** *n.*

cu·bit (kū'·bit) *n.* a measure of length, about 18 inches. **-al** *a.* [L. *cubitum*, the elbow].

cuck·old (kuk'·ald) *n.* a man whose wife is unfaithful to him; *v.t.* to be unfaithful to a husband [O.Fr. *cucu*, a cuckoo].

cuck·oo (koo'·kŏŏ) *n.* a migratory bird named from its call; the call of the bird; a fool; *a.* (*Slang*) crazy; foolish [imit. origin].

cu·cum·ber (kū'·kum·ber) *n.* plant of the gourd family and its fruit [L. *cucumis*].

cud (kud) *n.* food brought up by ruminating animals, from their first stomach, and chewed a second time. **to chew the cud** (*Fig.*) to meditate [O.E. *cudu*].

cud·dle (kud'·l) *v.t.* to caress; to hug; to fondle; *v.i.* to lie close or snug; to nestle; *n.* a close embrace. **-some** *a.* [etym. uncertain].

cudg·el (kuj'·al) *n.* a short thick stick; *v.t.* to beat with a cudgel [O.E. *cycgel*, club].

cue (kū) *n.* the last words of an actor's speech as a signal to the next actor to speak; a hint

[earlier 'q,' standing for L. *quando*, when (i.e. to come on)].

cue (kū) *n.* a long tapering rod used in pool, billiards, etc. [Fr. *queue*, pigtail].

cuff (kuf) *n.* a blow with the open hand; *v.t.* to strike with the open hand [etym. uncertain].

cuff (kuf) *n.* the ending of a sleeve; the turned-up end of a trouser leg; the wrist-band of a sleeve [M.E. *cuffe*].

cui·rass (kwi·ras') *n.* metal or leather armor, consisting of a breastplate and backplate [Fr. *cuir*, leather].

cui·sine (kwi·zēn') *n.* literally a kitchen; style of cooking [Fr. fr. *cuire*, to cook].

cul-de-sac (kool'·da·sak') *n.* a blind alley [Fr. *cul*, bottom; *sac*, a bag].

cu·li·nar·y (kū'·li·ner·i·) *a.* pert. to the kitchen or cookery [L. *culina*, a kitchen].

cull (kul) *v.t.* to select, or pick out; to gather [Fr. *cueillir*, to gather].

cul·mi·nate (kul'·ma·nāt) *v.i.* to reach the highest point (with 'in'); to reach a climax. **culmination** *n.* the attainment of the highest point; climax [L. *culmen*, summit].

cu·lottes (koo·lots') *n.pl.* knee length trousers resembling a skirt [Fr.].

cul·pa·ble (kul'·pa·bl) *a.* deserving blame or censure. **culpably** *adv.* **culpability, -ness** *n.* [L. *culpa*, fault].

cul·prit (kul'·prit) *n.* one accused of a crime; a criminal; an offender [L. *culpa*, a fault].

cult (kult) *n.* a system of religious worship, or rites and ceremonies [L. *cultus*, worship].

cul·ti·vate (kul'·ta·vāt) *v.t.* to prepare for the raising of crops; to till; to produce by tillage, labor, or care; to train; to foster. **-d** *a.* [L. *colere, cultum,* to till].

cul·ture (kul'·cher) *n.* tillage or cultivation; mental training and development; refinement; civilization; the propagation of bacteria and other micro-organisms in artificial media; *v.t.* to cultivate. **cultural** *a.* pert. to culture. **-d** *a.* educated and refined [L. *colere*, to cultivate].

cul·vert (kul'·vert) *n.* an arched drain or conduit for the passage of water under a road, railway, or canal [Fr. *couler*, to flow].

cum·ber (kum'·ber) *v.t.* to burden or hinder with a useless load. **-some** *a.* burdensome; clumsy and unmanageable. **cumbrous** *a.* [O.Fr. *combrer*, to hinder].

cum·mer·bund (kum'·er·bund) *n.* a broad sash worn as a belt [Pers. *kamarband*, a loin band].

cu·mu·late (kū'·mya·lāt) *v.t.* to heap together; *a.* heaped up. **cumulation** *n.* **cumulative** *a.* becoming greater by successive additions; gaining force or effect by additions. **cumulatively** *adv.* [L. *cumulus*, a heap].

cu·mu·lus (kū'·mya·las) *n.* a heap; a piled-up cloud mass with rounded outlines. *pl.* **cumuli** [L. *cumulus*, a heap].

cu·ne·i·form, cuniform (kū'·ni·a·fawrm) *a.* wedge-shaped [L. *cuneus*, a wedge].

cun·ning (kun'·ing) *a.* wily; sly; artful; *n.* craft or skill; guile; deceit. **-ly** *adv.* [O.E. *cunnan*, to know].

cup (kup) *n.* a drinking vessel; the contents of a cup; anything resembling a teacup in shape; an ornamental vessel given as a prize for sport, etc.; *v.t.* to let blood; to hold, as in a cup; to form into a cup shape. *pr.p.* **-ping.** *pa.t.* **-ped.** **-ful** *n.* the quantity that a cup holds, 8 fluid oz. **cupboard** (kub'·erd) *n.* a small closet with shelves for cups, plates, etc. **loving cup** *n.* a large cup; trophy, given as a prize [L. *cupa*, a tub].

cu·pid·i·ty (kū·pid'·a·ti·) *n.* an eager desire for possession; greed [L. *cupidus*, desirous].

cu·po·la (kū'·pa·la) *n.* a spherical vault or small domed tower on the top of a building [It. *cupola*, fr. L. *cupa*, a tub].

cu·pre·ous (kū'·pri·as) *a.* of, pert. to, or containing copper [L. *cuprum*, copper].

cur (kur) *n.* a dog of mixed breed; a mongrel;

[O.N. *kurra*, to grumble].

cu·rate (kjoo'·rit) *n.* (*chiefly Br.*) an assistant to a vicar or rector. **curacy** *n.* [L. *cura*, care].

cu·ra·tor (kyoo·rā'·ter) *n.* a superintendent, as of a museum, library, etc.; a guardian. **-ship** *n.* [L. *fr. curare*, to care].

curb (kurb) *n.* a chain or strap attached to the bit of a bridle to give control with the reins; any check or means of restraint; an edging to a pavement or sidewalk; *v.t.* to apply a curb to (a horse); to restrain; to confine. **-ing** *n.* [Fr. *courber*, fr. L. *curvare*, to bend].

curd (kurd) *n.* the cheesy part of milk; coagulated milk; the coagulated part of any liquid. **-le** *v.t.* and *i.* to turn into curd; to coagulate [O.E. *crudan*, to press].

cure (kūr) *v.t.* to heal; to restore to health; to remedy; to preserve fish, skins, etc. by salting, drying, etc.; *n.* the act of healing; that which heals; a remedy. **curable** *a.* **curative** *a.* **cure-all** *n.* a remedy for all ills; a panacea [L. *cura*, care].

cu·rette (kū·ret') *n.* instrument for scraping body tissue. **-ment** *n.* [Fr. *curer*, to cleanse].

cur·few (kur'·fū) *n.* the time after which persons may not be out of doors [Fr. *couvre-feu* = cover fire].

cur·ie (kyoo'·ri) *n.* (*Chem.*) the standard unit of emanation from one gram of radium. **curium** (kyoo'·ri·am) *n.* a radioactive, inert, gaseous element [fr. M. and Mme. *Curie*, discoverers of radium].

cu·ri·o (kyoo'·ri·ō) *n.* a rare or curious object; a curiosity [abbrev. of *curiosity*].

cu·ri·ous (kyoo'·ri·as) *a.* eager to know; inquisitive; (*Colloq.*) puzzling; strange. **-ly** *adv.* **curiosity** *n.* eagerness to know; inquisitiveness; a strange or rare object; a novelty [L. *curiosus*, inquisitive].

curl (kurl) *v.t.* to twist into ringlets; to coil; to bend into spiral or curved shape; *v.i.* to take a spiral or curved shape or path; to turn into ringlets; to ripple; to play at the game of curling; *n.* a ringlet of hair; anything of a similar shape. **-y** *a.* having curls; tending to curl; full of ripples. **-icue** *n.* a lock of hair; a fancy curve in writing. **-iness** *n.* **-ing** *n.* a game like bowls played on ice with large, rounded stones. **-er** *n.* a pin used as a fastener to retain a curl or wave in position [M.E. *crul*, curly].

cur·lew (kur'·lòò) *n.* a long-billed wading bird [Fr. *courlieu*, imit. of its cry].

cur·mudg·eon (ker·muj'·an) *n.* a grasping ill-natured fellow; a churl [origin unknown].

cur·rant (kur'·ant) *n.* the fruit of various plants allied to the gooseberry.

cur·rent (kur'·ant) *a.* belonging to the present time; in circulation or general use; *n.* a flowing body of water or air in motion; the flow of a river, etc.; tendency; drift; transmission of electricity through a conductor. **-ly** *adv.* in a current manner; commonly. **currency** *n.* money in use or circulation [L. *currere*, to run].

cur·ric·u·lum (ku·rik'·ya·lam) *n.* a specified course of study at a school, college, university, etc.; *pl.* **curricula** [L. *curriculum*, a running, a race-course].

cur·ry (kur'·i·) *n.* (*Cookery*) a highly-flavored and pungent condiment much used in the East. **— powder** *n.* [Tamil].

cur·ry (kur'·i·) *v.t.* to dress leather; to comb, rub down, and clean a horse; to beat or thrash. **currier** *n.* one who dresses tanned leather. **to curry favor**, to try to win favor by flattery. [O.Fr. *correer*, to prepare].

curse (kurs) *v.t.* to utter a wish of evil against; to invoke evil upon; to swear at; to torment; *v.i.* to utter blasphemous words; to swear; *n.* the invocation of evil or injury upon a person; profane words or oaths. **cursed** (kurs'·ad, kurst) *a.* hateful. **cursedly** *adv.* [O.E. *cursian*].

cur·sive (kur'·siv) *a.* written with a running hand, i.e. with all the letters joined; flowing.

-ly *adv.* **cursory** *a.* characterized by haste; careless; superficial [L. *currere*, to run].

curt (kurt) *a.* short; concise to the point of rudeness; abrupt; terse. *n.* [L. *curtus*, shortened].

cur·tail (kur·tāl') *v.t.* to cut short; to abridge; to diminish. **-ment** *n.* [L. *curtus*, shortened].

cur·tain (kur'·tin) *n.* a drapery; a screen in front of stage of a theater; anything that shuts off or conceals; *v.t.* to enclose or furnish with curtains. **— raiser** *n.* a short play preceding the main piece in a theater. **iron curtain** (*Fig.*) any hindrance to obtaining information about conditions in a country [L.L. *cortina*].

curt·sy, curtsey (kurt'·si·) *n.* a gesture of civility or respect made by women or girls; *v.i.* to make a curtsy [form of *courtesy*].

curve (kurv) *n.* a bending without angles; that which is bent; an arch; *a.* bent; *v.t.* and *i.* to bend. **curvate** *a.* curved. **curvature** *n.* [L. *curvus*, crooked].

cush·ion (koosh'·an) *n.* any stuffed or padded surface used as a rest or protector; *v.t.* to seat on a cushion; to provide or protect with a cushion [Fr. *coussin*, a cushion, fr. L. *coxa*, the hip].

cusp (kusp) *n.* a point or horn of a crescent, as of the moon; a prominence on a molar tooth; the point at which the two branches of a curve have a common tangent. **-id** *n.* a canine tooth. **-idal** *a.* ending in a point [L. *cuspis*, a point].

cus·pi·dor (kus'·pa·dawr) *n.* a spittoon [Port.].

cuss (kus) *n.* (*Slang*) a fellow; a curse. **-ed** *a.* corrupt. of cursed [fr. *curse*].

cus·tard (kus'·terd) *n.* a sweet dish made with milk and eggs [M.E. *crustade*, a pie with a crust].

cus·to·dy (kus'·ta·di·) *n.* a keeping or guarding; care; guardianship; imprisonment. **custodial** (kus·tō'·di·al) *a.* **custodian, custodier** *n.* a keeper; a caretaker [L. *custodia*, fr. *custos*, a keeper].

cus·tom (kus'·tam) *n.* fashion; usage; habit; business patronage; toll, tax, or tribute; **-s** *n.pl.* duties levied on imports. **-able** *a.* liable to duty. **-ary** *a.* according to custom; established by common usage; usual; habitual. **-arily** *adv.* **-er** *n.* one who enters a shop to buy. **-house** *n.* office where customs are paid. [O.Fr. *coustume* fr. L. *consuetudo*].

cut (kut) *v.t.* to severe, penetrate, or wound with an edged instrument; to divide; to separate; to intersect; to cross; to mow; to hew; to carve; to trim; to shape; to reduce; to abridge; intentionally to ignore a person; (*Sports*) to hit the ball obliquely in order to impart spin to it. *pr.p.* **-ting**. *pa.p.* and *pa.t.* **cut** *n.* an act of cutting; opening made with an edged instrument; a gash; a wound; a piece cut off, as e.g. a joint of meat; a notch; a reduction, esp. in salary or wages. **-ter** *n.* he who, or that which, cuts; a warship's rowing and sailing boat. **-ting** *n.* an incision; a small branch, slip, etc. cut from a plant, bush, etc. *a.* sarcastic. **— glass** *n.* glass ornamented with cut designs. **-off** *n.* a road that is a short cut; a device to shut off. **—rate** *a.* below usual price. **-throat** *n.* a murderer; *a.* merciless. **to cut a caper**, to frisk about; to gambol.

cu·ta·ne·ous (kū·tā'·ni·as) *a.* belonging to, or affecting, the skin [L. *cutis*, the skin].

cute (kūt) *a.* (*Colloq.*) attractive [short for *acute*].

cu·ti·cle (kū'·ti·kl) *n.* the epidermis, esp. around the fingernails and toenails [L. *cutis*, skin].

cut·las (kut'·las) *n.* a short, broad-bladed, curving sword [O.Fr. *coutel*, a knife fr. L. *culter*, a ploughshare].

cut·ler (kut'·ler) *n.* one who makes, repairs, or deals in knives and cutting implements. **-y** *n.* business of a cutler; cutting instruments; esp. tableware [Fr. *coutelier*; *couteau*, a knife].

cut·let (kut'·lit) *n.* a piece of meat or chop from the rib bones [Fr. *cotelette*, fr. *côte*, a rib].

cy·a·nide (sī'·a·nīd) *n.* a poisonous compound.

cy·an·o·gen (si·an'·a·jen) *n.* (*Chem.*) a colorless, poisonous gas. **cyanic** *a.* blue [Gk. *kuanos*, blue, and root *gen*].

cy·ber·net·ics (si·ber·net'·iks) *n.* the study of the self-organizing machine or mechanical brain [Gk. *kubornasis*, a pilot].

cyc·la·men (sik'·la·man) *n.* a tuberous plant of the Primrose family [Gk. *kuklaminos*].

cy·cle (si'·kl) *n.* a regularly recurring succession of events or phenomena, or the period of time occupied by such a succession; a body of myths or legends, relating to some period, person, or event; a series of songs dealing with various phases of the same subject, and meant to be sung one after the other; a bicycle or tricycle; *v.i.* to pass through a cycle of changes; to ride a bicycle or tricycle. **cyclist** *n.* one who rides a bicycle or tricycle. **cycloid** *n.* (*Geom.*) a curve traced by a point in a circle when the circle revolves along a straight line [Gk. *kuklos*, a circle].

cy·clone (si'·klōn) *n.* a violent storm characterized by strong winds. **cyclonic** [Gk. *kuklos*, a circle].

cy·clo·pe·di·a See **encyclopedia.**

cy·clo·ram·a (si·kla·rā'·ma) *n.* circular panorama [Gk. *kuklos*, a circle; *orama*, a view].

cy·clo·tron (si'·kla·tran) *n.* a radio oscillator developed to disintegrate atoms, in order to study their internal structure [Gk. *kuklos*, a circle].

cyg·net (sig'·nit) *n.* a young swan [Fr. *cygne*, a swan].

cyl·in·der (sil'·in·der) *n.* a roller-like body with straight sides, the ends being equal, parallel circles; any object of similar shape. **cylindric, cylindrical** *a.* **cylindriform** *a.* [Gk. *kulindros*, a roller].

cym·bal (sim'·bal) *n.* musical percussion instrument [Gk. *kumbalon*].

cyn·ic (sin'·ik) *n.* one of a set of Greek philosophers who regarded virtue as the supreme good and despised all comfort or refinement; one who believes man's conduct is based on self-interest. **cynic(al)** *a.* sneering; distrustful of people's motives. **cynically** *adv.* **cynicalness** *n.* **cynicism** (sin'·i·sizm) *n.* principles of a cynic; disbelief in goodness; misanthropy [Gk. *kunikos*, doglike, fr. *kuon*, a dog].

cy·no·sure (si'·nō·, sin'·ō·shoor) *n.* (*Astron.*) the constellation of the Lesser Bear, containing the Pole-star; hence, something to which all eyes are turned; a guiding star [Gk. *kuon*, a dog; *oura*, a tail].

cy·press (si'·pras) *n.* a slender coniferous tree with evergreen foliage [L. *cypressus*].

cyst (sist) *n.* (*Med.*) a bladder or membranous sac containing liquid secretion or morbid matter; **-ic** *a.* pert. to cysts [Gk. *kustis*, a bladder].

Czar (zar) *n.* a title used by various Slavonic rulers, esp. by the Emperors of Russia. **Czarina** (za·rē'·na) *n.* the wife of a Czar. (Other forms are **Tsar, Tzar, Tsarina, Tzarina,** etc.) [fr. L. *Caesar*].

Czech (chek) *n.* a member of the Slavonic race of people inhabiting the western region of Czechoslovakia; the language spoken by them; *a.* pert. to the people or their language. **Czechoslovak** (chek·a·slō'·vak, chek·a··slō·vak'), **Czechoslovakian** *a.* pert. to the country, the people, or the language of Czechoslovakia; *n.* a native of the country; the language.

D

dab (dab) *n.* Eur. flatfish.

dab (dab) *v.t.* to pat gently and intermittently, **-bing.** *pa.p.* and *pa.t.* **-bed.** *n.* a gentle blow with a soft substance; a small lump of any-

thing soft, as butter [M.E. *dabban*, to strike].

dab·ble (dab'·l) *v.t.* to wet by little dips; to moisten; *v.i.* to play in water; to pursue a subject superficially [M.E. *dabban*, to strike].

dace (dās) *n.* a small fresh-water river fish. Also **dart, dare** [O.Fr. *dars*, dart].

dach·shund (daks'·hoont) *n.* dog with long body, short legs, and drooping ears [Ger. *Dachs*, a badger; *Hund*, a dog].

dac·tyl (dak'·til) *n.* a metrical foot in poetry, consisting of one accented syllable followed by two unaccented syllables (— u u). **-ic** *a.* pert. to or consisting of a dactyl. **-iography** *n.* the history of gem engraving. **-ogram** *n.* a finger print. **-ography** *n.* the science of finger prints. **-ology** *n.* the finger language of the deaf and dumb [Gk. *daktulos*, a finger].

dad, dada, daddy (dad, da'·da, dad'·i·) *n.* father, a word used by little children [W. *tad*, a father].

da·da·ism (da'·da·izm) *n.* a school of art and literature which aims at suppressing all relation between thought and expression.

dad·dy-long-legs (dad'·i·lawng'·legz) *n.* a flying insect; a harvestman [fr. *dad*].

da·do (dā'·dō) *n.* (*Archit.*) the part of a pedestal between the base and cornice; the lower part or wide skirting of the walls of a room [It. *dado*, a pedestal].

dae·mon (dē'·man) *n.* an inspiring influence; a divinity; genius. **-ic** *a.* more than human; supernatural [Gk. *daimon*, spirit].

daf·fo·dil (daf'·a·dil) *n.* a spring plant of the genus Narcissus; the yellow color of the daffodil [Gk. *asphodelos*, a lily flower].

daft (daft) *a.* insane; foolish. **-ness** *n.* [M.E. *daft*, mild].

dag·ger (dag'·er) *n.* a short, two-edged sword used in close combat; a mark of reference in typography (†) or (‡) [M.F. *daggen*, to slit].

dag·gle (dag'·l) *v.t.* to trail through mud; to bedraggle [Scand. *dagg*, dew].

da·guerre·o·type (da·ger'·a·tip) *n.* in photography, an early method of taking pictures on plates of silver or silvered copper [fr. Louis *Daguerre* of Paris, the 19th cent. inventor].

dahl·ia (dal'·ya) *n.* a genus of plants with large, brightly colored flowers [fr. *Dahl*, a Swedish botanist].

dai·ly (dā'·li·) *a.* or *adv.* happening each day; *n.* a newspaper published each day or each weekday [O.E. *daeg*, day].

dain·ty (dān'·ti·) *a.* pleasing to the taste; refined; pretty and delicate; scrupulous; *n.* a delicacy. **daintily** *adv.* [L. *dignus*, worthy].

dair·y (dā'·ri·) *n.* the place where milk and cream are kept cool, butter is churned, and cheese is made; the shop where milk and its products are sold; a dairy farm. **-ing** *n.* the business of conducting a dairy. **-maid, -man** *n.* [Icel. *deigja*, a dairymaid].

da·is (dā'·is) *n.* the raised platform at the end of a room, esp. of dining hall [O.Fr. *deis*, fr. L.L. *discus*, a table].

dai·sy (dā'·zi·) *n.* a common wild flower; (*Slang*) a person or thing unusually pleasing. **daisied** *a.* [O.E. *daeg*, a day; *eage*, an eye].

dale (dāl) *n.* a low place between hills; a valley or vale; a glen [O.E. *dael*, a valley].

dal·ly (dal'·i·) *v.i.* to waste time; to trifle; to fondle or interchange caresses. **dalliance** *n.* the act of trifling and wasting time; flirtation [M.E. *dalien*, to play].

Dal·ma·tian (dal·mā'·shan) *n.* a breed of large white dogs with black or liver-colored spots [fr. *Dalmatia*].

dam (dam) *n.* a female parent—used of animals [form of *dame*].

dam (dam) *n.* a barrier of earth, stones, etc. to obstruct the flow of water; the water confined by a dam; *v.t.* to confine water by a dam; to block up [M.E. *dam*, an obstruction].

dam·age (dam'·ij) *n.* any injury or harm to person, property, or reputation; *v.t.* to harm;

to hurt. **-s** *n.pl.* legal compensation paid to injured party. **-able** *a.* [L. *damnum*, loss].

dam·ask (dam'·ask) *n.* a figured silk or linen fabric, orig. made at Damascus; steel ornamented with wavy pattern; a rose-pink color, like that of damask rose; *a.* woven with figured pattern like damask [fr. *Damascus*, in Syria].

dame (dām) *n.* (*Arch.*) a noble lady; (*Slang*) a woman. **Dame** *n.* (*Br.*) title of the wife of a knight or baronet [Fr. *dame*, a lady].

damn (dam) *v.t.* to consign to everlasting punishment; (*Colloq.*) to condemn irritably (used as interjection); to destroy the reputation of; *n.* an oath; a curse; (*Colloq.*) a trifle. **-able** *a.* **-ably** *adv.* **-ation** *n.* **-ed** *a.* odious [L. *damnare*, to condemn].

dam·o·sel, damozel (dam'·ō·zel) *n.* archaic and poetic var. of *damsel* [O.Fr. *damoisele*, a maiden].

damp (damp) *n.* moist air; humidity; fog; vapor; noxious gases in coal mines, wells, etc. (as fire-damp, choke-damp); *a.* slightly moist; *v.t.* to moisten slightly; to retard combustion (to *damp* down a fire). **-en** *v.t.* to moisten; (*Fig.*) to depress. **-er** *n.* one who or that which damps; a contrivance in a flue to regulate the draft; a device to minimize vibration. **-ish** *a.* [Ger. *Dampf*, steam].

dam·sel (dam'·sal) *n.* a young unmarried woman [M.E. *damizel*, Fr. *demoiselle*, a maiden].

dam·son (dam'·zan) *n.* a small dark plum [O.Fr. *damascene*, of Damascus].

dance (dans) *v.t.* and *v.i.* to move with measured steps; to move rhythmically; to caper; *n.* a lively and rhythmical movement with certain steps and gestures; a social gathering for the purpose of dancing. **-r** *n.* one who dances. **danseuse** *n.* a female dancer, esp. in ballet. **to lead someone a dance**, to lead someone in vain pursuit. **St. Vitus's dance** (*Med.*) nervous disorder accompanied by twitching of muscles [Fr. *danser*, to dance].

dan·de·li·on (dan·da·lī'·an) *n.* a plant with large yellow flowers, and tooth-edged leaves [Fr. *dent de lion*, lion-toothed].

dan·der (dan'·der) *n.* (*Colloq.*) anger; passion; temper [fr. *dandriff*].

dan·dle (dan'·dl) *v.t.* to move up and down in affectionate play, as an infant; to pet; to caress [It. *dondolare*, to swing].

dan·druff, dandriff (dan'·draf, ·drif) *n.* a disease affecting the scalp and producing scurf or small scales of skin under the hair.

dan·dy (dan'·di·) *n.* one who affects special finery in dress; a fop; *a.* (*Colloq.*) fine; first-rate. **dandify** *v.t.* to make like a dandy. **dandified** *a.* foppish [etym. poss. Scots corrupt. of St. Andrew].

Dane (dān) *n.* a native of Denmark; a breed of dog, large and smooth coated, usually *great Dane.* **Danish** *a.* pert. to Denmark or the Danes; *n.* the language of the Danes [O.E. *Dene*, a Dane].

dan·ger (dān'·jer) *n.* exposure to injury or evil; peril; hazard; jeopardy. **-ous** *a.* **-ously** *adv.* **dangerousness** *n.* [M.E. *danger*, power].

dan·gle (dang'·l) *v.t.* to swing loosely or carelessly; (*Fig.*) to use as a bait; *v.i.* to hang loosely [Scand. *dangle*, to swing].

dank (dangk) *a.* unpleasantly damp or moist. **-ness** *n.* [Scand. *danka*, moist].

dap·per (dap'·er) *a.* neat; trim; smart; little and active [Dut. *dapper*, brave].

dap·ple (dap'·l) *n.* a spot; *a.* spotted, applied to horses and deer. **-d** *a.* spotted, esp. of pattern made by sunlight through trees.

dare (dār) *v.i.* to have courage for; to venture (to); to be audacious enough; *v.i.* to defy; to challenge. **daring** *n.* audacity; a bold action; *a.* bold; courageous; audacious. **daringly** *adv.* **—devil** *n.* a foolhardy, reckless fellow. **I dare say**, I presume [M.E. *durran*, to dare].

dark (dark) *a.* lacking light; black; somber; evil; unenlightened; *n.* absence of light; gloom;

obscurity; evil. **-en** *v.t.* to obstruct light; to render dim; to cloud; (*Fig.*) to sully; *v.i.* to grow dark. **-ish** *a.* rather dark. **-le** *v.i.* to grow dark; to lie hid. **-ling** *adv.* in the dark. **darkly** *adv.* **-ness** *n.* **-y, -ey** *n.* a Negro. **— horse** *n.* (*Fig.*) one unexpectedly nominated for an office. **to darken a door**, to enter a door [O.E. *deorc*, dark.

dar·ling (dar'·ling) *n.* a beloved or lovable one; *a.* cherished [dim. of O.E. *deore*, dear].

darn (darn) *v.t.* to mend; to repair a hole by weaving threads at right angles to one another; *n.* the place darned. **-ing-needle** *n.* [prob. O.E. *dernan*, to hide].

dart (dart) *n.* a pointed arrow-like weapon; anything similar which pierces or wounds; a small seam or intake in garment to make it fit more closely; a sharp, forward movement; *v.t.* to send forward quickly; to throw suddenly; *v.i.* to run forward swiftly; to move like a dart. **-s** *n.pl.* a popular game using darts and dartboard [M.E. *dart*, a javelin].

Dar·win·i·an (dar·win'·i·an) *a.* pert. to Charles *Darwin* or to his Theory of Evolution; *n.* one who accepts the theories of Darwin.

dash (dash) *v.t.* to throw violently; to cast down; to shatter; *v.i.* to rush forward or move violently; to strike violently against; *n.* a violent clashing of two bodies; a rapid movement; a mark of punctuation (—) to denote parenthesis; a small amount, as a *dash of soda.* **-ing** *a.* daring; spirited; showy. **-y** *a.* showy [M.E. *daschen*, to strike down].

das·tard (das'·terd) *n.* mean or cowardly fellow; *a.* cowardly. **-ly** *a.* **-liness** *n.* [M.E. *dastard*, a stupid or mean person].

da·ta (dā'·ta) *n.pl.* (sing. **datum**) things known and from which inferences may be deduced [L. *data*, things given].

date (dāt) *n.* period of time of an event; epoch; duration; (*Slang*) appointment or engagement; *v.t.* to note or fix the time of; to refer to as a starting point; *v.i.* to reckon back to a given time (foll. by *from* or *back* to). **—line** *n.* approximately the 180° parallel of longitude on each side of which the date of the day differs [L. *datum*, a thing given].

date (dāt) *n.* the stone fruit of the Eastern date palm. **— palm** *n.* tree bearing date fruit [Gk. *dakulos*].

da·tive (dā'·tiv) *n.* the case of a noun which is the indirect object of a verb, or which is preceded by certain prepositions [L. *dare*, to give].

da·tum (dā'·tum) *n.* a fact given; *pl.* **data** [L. *dare*, to give].

daub (dawb) *v.t.* to smear with mud or plaster; to soil; to paint crudely; *n.* a crude painting; a smudge. **-er** *n.* one who daubs; *n.* a daub; rough cast for exterior of houses [O.Fr. *dauber*, to plaster].

daugh·ter (daw'·ter) *n.* a female child; *a.* like a daughter. **—in-law** *n.* the wife of one's son [O.E. *dohtor*].

daunt (dawnt, dant) *v.t.* to subdue the courage of; to dismay; to dishearten; to disconcert. **-less** *a.* fearless; intrepid [O.Fr. fr. L. *domare*, to tame].

dau·phin (daw'·fin) *n.* (*fem.* **dauphiness**) the French Crown prince [O.Fr. *daulphin*].

dav·en·port (dav'·an·port) *n.* a sofa [fr. the name of the maker].

dav·its (da'·vits) *n.* uprights fitted with tackle for lowering life-boats over side of ship [Fr. *davire*, forceps].

Da·vy Jones (dā'·vi·jōnz') *n.* a sailor's name for the Devil.

daw (daw) *n.* a bird of the crow family; a jack-daw [imit.].

daw·dle (daw'·dl) *v.i.* to loiter; to move very slowly [prob. conn. with *dandle*].

dawn (dawn) *v.i.* to grow towards daylight; to begin to be visible; (*Fig.*) to come to the mind; *n.* daybreak; morning half-light; beginning [O.E. *daeg*, a day].

day (dā) *n.* the period from sunrise to sunset; the period of the sun's revolution on its axis; 24 hrs.; time of life; epoch. — **bed** *n.* a divan. **-book** *n.* a book kept to record daily transactions. **-break** *n.* dawn. **-dream** *n.* a reverie; *v.i.* to indulge in reveries [O.E. *daeg*, a day].

daze (dāz) *v.t.* to confuse; to stupefy; to bewilder; to stun; *n.* the state of being bewildered; stupefaction. **dazzle** *v.t.* to daze with sudden light; to make temporarily blind; to confuse mentally; *n.* brilliancy. **dazzling** *a.* [M.E. *dāsen*, to stupefy].

dea·con (dē′·kạn) *n.* an assistant to a priest or minister; a layman elected to certain duties in the church. **-ess** *n.* **-hood** *n.* the office of deacon. **-ry** *n.* the body of deacons. **-ship** *n.* office of deacon [Gk. *diakonos*, a servant].

dead (ded) *a.* without life; *adv.* wholly; *n.* the most death-like time. **-en** *v.t.* to benumb. **-ness** *n.* —**beat** *a.* without oscillation, applied to measuring instruments in which the pointer comes to rest. —**end** *n.* a street with only one entrance. **-fall** *n.* a trap, esp. for large animals. — **heat** *n.* a race where two or more competitors reach the winning post at exactly the same time. — **language**, a language no longer spoken. — **letter** *n.* an undelivered or persons must not pass; last available date. **-liness** *n.* **-lock** *n.* a state of affairs which renders further progress impossible; an impasse. **-ly** *a.* causing death; virulent; lethal; *adv.* completely. — **pan** (*Slang*) *n.* an immobile face. — **reckoning** *n.* (*Naut.*) the steering of a vessel by compass and not by the stars. — **weight** *n.* the unrelieved weight of inert objects [O.E. *dead*, dead].

deaf (def) *a.* lacking partially or wholly the sense of hearing; heedless; unwilling to listen. **-en** *v.t.* to make deaf; to stun with sound. **-ening** *a.* very loud; thunderous, as applause. **-ly** *adv.* —**mute** *n.* one who is deaf and dumb. —**mutism** *n.* **-ness** *n.* [O.E. *deaf*, deaf].

deal (dēl) *v.t.* to divide; to dole out; to distribute, as in card games; *v.i.* to traffic; to act; to give one's business to; to behave towards; *n.* a part or portion; distribution of playing cards; a business transaction; a bargain. *pa.p.* **dealt** (delt). **-er** *n.* **-ing** *n.* buying and selling; traffic; treatment; *pl.* intercourse or relations with others. **a raw deal**, iniquitously unfair treatment. **a square deal**, fair treatment [O.E. *daelen*, to divide].

dean (dēn) *n.* a dignitary in cathedral or collegiate churches; (in universities) the head of a faculty; an official of a college with disciplinary authority [O.Fr. *deien*, fr. L. *decanus*, an official].

dear (dēr) *a.* precious; much loved; highly esteemed or valued; costly; expensive; scarce; *interj.* expressing sorrow, pity or wonder, as in 'Oh, dear!' **-ly** *adv.* [O.E. *deore*, precious].

dearth (durth) *n.* scarcity; lack [M.E. *derthe*].

death (deth) *n.* extinction of life; manner of dying; state of being dead; decease; dissolution; (*Fig.*) termination. — **blow** *n.* a fatal stroke. **-less** *a.* immortal. **-lessness** *n.* **-like** *a.* **-ly** *adv.*; *a.* like death. — **mask** *n.* a plaster cast of a person's face taken immediately after death. — **rate** *n.* the mortality rate per thousand of the population at a given time. —**throes** *n.pl.* last struggle before death. — **warrant** *n.* an official document authorizing execution of a criminal. **-watch** *n.* a vigil [O.E. *death*, death].

de·ba·cle (dā·bàk′·ạl) *n.* a sudden collapse; a rout; the breaking up of ice in a river [Fr.].

de·bar (di·bàr)′ *v.t.* to cut off from entrance; to hinder; to prohibit; to exclude; *pr.p.* **-ring.** *pa.t., pa.p.* **-red. -ment** *n.* [L. *de*; and *bar*].

de·bark (di·bàrk′) *v.t.* and *v.i.* to disembark, oppos. of *embark*. **-ation, -ment** *n.* [Fr. *débarquer*, to disembark].

de·base (di·bās′) *v.t.* to reduce to a lower state; to disagree; to degrade; to adulterate. **-ment** *n.* **debasing** *a.* corrupting, esp. in moral sense.

de·bate (di·bāt′) *n.* controversy; wrangle; argument; dispute; *v.t.* to discuss; to dispute; to contend; to argue in detail; *v.i.* to take part in a discussion; to reflect. **debatable** *a.* **-r** *n.* [L. *de*, from; *batuere*, to strike or beat].

de·bauch (di·bawch′) *v.t.* to corrupt; to make depraved; to seduce; to pervert; *n.* excess in eating and drinking. **-ed** *a.* **-ee** *n.* a dissipated person. **-ery** *n.* moral corruption. **-ment** *n.* [O.Fr. *debaucher*, to corrupt].

de·ben·ture (di·ben′·chạr) *n.* a certificate acknowledging a debt and guaranteeing repayment of loan with interest [L. *debentur mihi*, first words of certificate meaning 'these sums are owing to me.'].

de·bil·i·tate (di·bil′·ạ·tāt) *v.t.* to weaken; to make infirm; to enervate. **debilitation, debility** *n.* [L. *debilitare*, to weaken].

deb·it (deb′·it) *n.* an item entered on debtor side of an account (oppos. of *credit*); *v.t.* to charge with debt [L. *debere, debitum*, to owe].

deb·o·nair (deb′·ạ·nãr) *a.* bearing oneself cheerfully and well; sprightly; spruce [Fr. *de bon air*, of amiable disposition].

de·bris, dé·bris (dạ·brē′, dā′·brē) *n.* fragments (taken collectively); rubble; ruins [Fr. *briser*, to break].

debt (det) *n.* something owed to another; a liability; an obligation. **-or** *n.* one who owes a debt [L. *debere, debitum*, to owe].

de·bunk (dạ·bungk′) *v.t.* (*Slang*) to remove false sentiment from.

de·but, dé·but (di·bū′, dā·bū′) *n.* a first appearance in public, socially or as an artist. **debutante** *n.* one, esp. a girl, making her first appearance in society; abbrev. **deb.** [Fr. *début*, a first stroke, aim, or goal].

dec·a- *prefix* fr. Gk. *deka*, ten.

dec·ade (dek′·ād) *n.* a group of ten things; a period of ten years [Gk. *deka*, ten].

de·ca·dence (dek′·ạ·dạns, di·kā′·dạns) **decadency** *n.* deterioration; degeneration; decay; a falling off in moral or aesthetic standards.

dec·a·dent (dek′·ạ·dạnt) *a.* deteriorating [L. *decadentia*, a falling away].

dec·a·gon (dek′·ạ·gàn) *n.* a plane figure of ten sides and ten angles [Gk. *gonia*, an angle].

dec·a·gram(me) (dek′·ạ·gram) *n.* in the metric system, a weight of 10 grams, i.e. 0.353 oz. [Gk. *deka*, ten; *gramma*, a weight].

dec·a·he·dron (dek·ạ·hē′·drạn) *n.* a solid figure of a body having ten sides. **decahedral** *a.* [Gk. *deka*, ten; *hedra*, face of a solid].

de·cal·ci·fy (dē·cal′·si·fī) *v.t.* to deprive bones (esp. teeth) of lime.

de·cal·i·ter (dek′·ạ·lē·tẹr) *n.* a measure of capacity equal to 10 liters—about 2.64 imperial gallons [Gk. *dega*, ten; Fr. *litre*].

Dec·a·logue (dek′·ạ·lawg) *n.* the Ten Commandments [Gk. *deka*, ten; *logos*, a word of discourse].

dec·a·me·ter (dek′·ạ·mē·tẹr) *n.* in the metric system a measure of ten meters, or 32.8 ft. [Gk. *deka*, ten; *metron*, measure].

de·camp (dē·kamp′) *v.i.* to move away from a camping ground; to move off suddenly or secretly [Fr. *décamper*, to break camp].

de·cant (di·kant′) *v.t.* to pour off liquid without disturbing sediment, esp. used of wines. **-er** *n.* a slender necked glass bottle into which wine is decanted [L. *de*, from; *canthus*, rim of a cup].

de·cap·i·tate (di·kap′·i·tāt) *v.t.* to cut off the head; to behead. **decapitation** *n.* [L. *de*, from; *caput*, head].

dec·a·pod (dek′·ạ·pàd) *n.* a shellfish of the crab family having five pairs of legs; a ten-footed crustacean; *a.* having ten legs. **-al, -ous** *a.* [Gk. *deka*, ten; *pous*, a foot].

de·car·bon·ize (dē·kàr′·bạ·nīz) *v.t.* to deprive of carbon; to remove a deposit of carbon, as from a motor cylinder. Also **decarbonate, decarburize. decarbonization, decarburi-**

zation n.

dec·a·syl·lab·ic (dek·a·si·lab′·ik) a. having ten syllables. **decasyllable** n. [Gk. deka, ten; syllable].

de·cath·lon (di·kath′·lån) n. a group of ten different contests at Olympic games [Gk. deka, ten; athlon, a contest].

de·cay (di·kā′) v.i. to rot away; to become decomposed; to waste away; to deteriorate; v.t. to impair; n. gradual decline or corruption; deterioration. **-ed** a. rotting. [L. de, down; cadere, to fall].

de·cease (di·sēs′) n. death; v.i. to die. **-d** a. dead; n. a dead person [L. decessus, a departure].

de·ceit (di·sēt′) n. fraud; duplicity; wile. **-ful** a. crafty; fraudulent. **-fulness** n. **deceive** v.t. to delude; to cheat. **deceivable** a. **deceivably** adv. **deceiver** n. [L. decipere, deceptum, to beguile].

de·cel·er·ate (dē·sel′·ẹr·āt) v.t. and v.i. to reduce speed [L. de, from; celer, swift].

De·cem·ber (di·sem′·bẽr) n. orig. the tenth month of the Roman calendar; the twelfth month of the year [L. decem, ten].

de·cen·nial (di·sen′·i·ạl) a. lasting for ten years or happening every ten years. **decennary** n. [L. decem, ten; annus, a year].

de·cent (dē′·sent) a. fitting or becoming; modest; suitable; comely; sufficient. **decency** n. the state or quality of being decent. **-ly** adv. [L. decere, to be fitting].

de·cen·tral·ize (dē·sen′·tral·īz) v.t. to remove from the center or point of concentration and distribute among small areas; esp. to enlarge powers of local government at expense of central authority. **decentralization** n.

de·cep·tion (di·sep′·shạn) n. the act of deceiving; fraud; illusion. **deceptible** a. **deceptibility** n. **deceptive** a. causing a false impression. **deceptively** adv. [L. deceptus, deceived].

dec·i·bel (des′·ạ·bel) n. one transmission unit; one tenth of a bel; the smallest variation in sound that the human ear can detect [L. decem, ten; bel, a coined word].

de·cide (di·sīd′) v.t. to determine the result of; to make up one's mind about; to settle an issue; v.t. to give a decision; to come to a conclusion. **-d** a. clear; not ambiguous; determined. **decidedly** adv. **decision** (di·sizh′·ạn) n. the act of settling; determination; settlement; judgment. **decisive** a. conclusive; resolute. **decisively** adv. **decisiveness** n. [L. decidere, to cut off].

de·cid·u·ous (di·sid′·yoo·ạs) a. (of trees) shedding leaves in autumn, oppos. of coniferous or evergreen; not lasting; liable to fall; (used also of a deer's horns) [L. decidere, to fall down].

dec·i·mal (des′·ạ·mạl) a. pert. to tens; numbered or proceeding by tens; n. some power of 10. **-ization** n. **-ize** v.t. to reduce to the decimal system. **— fraction**, a fraction the (unexpressed) denominator of which is 10 or a power of 10 [L. decimus, tenth].

dec·i·mate (des′·ạ·māt) v.t. to kill (as in Ancient Rome) every tenth man, chosen by lot, as punishment; to reduce the numbers of, very considerably. **decimation** n. [L. decimus, tenth].

de·ci·pher (di·sī′·fẹr) v.t. to read a cipher; to make out what is illegible, unintelligible or written in strange symbols.

de·ci·sion See decide.

deck (dek) v.t. to adorn; to cover; to dress up; to cover with a deck (of a ship); n. a covering; the horizontal platform extending from one side of ship to the other; a pack of cards, or part of pack remaining after dealing. **—chair** n. a light-weight, collapsible chair, made partly of canvas. **— hand** n. a person employed on deck of ship. **-ing** n. adornment. **hurricane-deck** n. a half-deck. **main-deck** n. deck below the upper deck. **quarter-deck** n. part of the deck abaft the main mast. **double-decker** n. a vehicle, as bus, or ferry, with upper and lower passenger-decks [Dut. dekken, to cover].

deck·le (dek′·l) n. the gauge on a paper-making machine. **—edge** n. untrimmed edge of paper. **—edged** a. [Ger. deckel, cover].

de·claim (di·klām′) v.t. to recite in a rhetorical manner; v.i. to make a formal speech. **declamation** n. a set speech; a rhetorical and dramatic address. **declamatory** (di·klam′·ạ·tōr·i·) a. pert. to a declamation; ostentatiously rhetorical [L. declamare, to shout out].

de·clare (di·kler′) v.t. to proclaim; to make clear; to state publicly; to state in the presence of a witness; v.i. to make a declaration; (at Customs) to admit possession of dutiable goods. **declarable** a. **declaration** n. the act of declaring; a solemn statement. **declaratory** a. making clear or manifest; explanatory [L. declarare, to make clear].

de·clen·sion (di·klen′·shạn) n. the act of falling away; (Fig.) deterioration; (Gram.) the inflection of nouns, pronouns, adjectives; a class of nouns, etc. so inflected. **-al** a. [L. declinare, to fall away].

de·cline (di·klīn′) v.t. to bend downward; to refuse; to avoid; (Gram.) to give inflections of a word in oblique cases; v.i. to slope; to hang down; to fall in value or quantity; to pine away; to languish; n. a downward slope; a falling off. **declinable** a. able to be inflected. **declination** (de·kli·nā′·shạn) n. a sloping away [L. declinare, to fall away].

de·cliv·i·ty (di·kliv′·ạ·ti·) n. a downward slope; a gradual descent. **declivitous, declivous** a. [L. declivis, sloping down].

de·code (dē·kōd′) v.t. to translate a message in code into ordinary language.

de·col·le·tage (dā·kạl·tazh′) n. the line of a woman's low cut evening dress; the neck and shoulders of a person wearing such a dress. **décolleté** a. low-necked [Fr.].

de·com·pose (dē·kạm·pōz′) v.t. to break up into elements; to separate the constituent parts of; v.i. to decay; to rot. **decomposition** n. act of decomposing; decay; putrefaction.

de·con·tam·i·nate (dē·kạn·tam′·ạ·nāt) v.t. to cleanse from effects of poison gas, etc. **decontamination** n.

de·con·trol (dē·kạn·trōl′) v.t. to release from government or state control.

de·cor (dā·kawr′) n. the decoration, or setting of a theater, stage, or room [Fr.].

dec·o·rate (dek′·ạ·rāt) v.t. to beautify; to embellish; to honor a person by giving a medal or badge of honor. **-d** a. **decoration** n. an ornament; a badge of honor; insignia. **decorative** a. **decorativeness** n. **decorator** n. [L. decus, an ornament].

dec·o·rous (dek′·ạ·ras) a. seemly; decent; staid. **-ly** adv. **-ness** n. **decorum** (di·kōr′·ạm) n. behavior, etc. in keeping with social conventions [L. decus, an ornament].

de·coy (di·koi′) v.t. to lead into a snare; (Fig.) to allure; to entice by specially tempting means; (dē′·koi) n. a device for leading wild birds into a snare; an enticement [Dut. kooi, a cage].

de·crease (di·krēs′) v.t. to lessen; to make smaller; to reduce gradually; v.i. to become less; to wane; to abate; (dē·krēs′) n. gradual diminution; a lessening [L. de, from; crescere, to grow].

de·cree (di·krē′) n. an order made by a competent authority; an edict; decision in a law court; an established law; (Theol.) divine purpose; v.t. to determine judicially; to order; v.i. to decide authoritatively. **decretal** a. pert. to a decree; n. an order given by a high authority, esp. the Pope. **decretive** a. [L. decretum, decreed].

dec·re·ment (dek′·ra·mạnt) n. the act or state of decreasing; the quantity lost by decrease [L. decrementum, a decrease].

de·crep·it (di·krep′·it) a. worn out or enfeebled by old age; infirm; broken down; (of things) ramshackle. **-ude, -ness** *n.* [L. *decrepitus*, very old].

de·cres·cent (di·kres'·ant) *a.* becoming gradually less; waning.

de·cre·tal See **decree.**

de·cry (di·krī') *v.t.* to bring into disrepute; to abuse. **decrial** *n.* act of decrying [L. *de*, from; Fr. *crier*, to cry].

ded·i·cate (ded'·i·kāt) *v.t.* to set apart and consecrate to a holy purpose; to give oneself wholly to a worthy purpose; to inscribe a book or other object to someone as mark of appreciation or admiration. **-d** *a.* devoted. **dedication** *n.* **dedicatory** *a.* containing a dedication; complimentary [L. *dedicare*, to announce].

de·duce (di·dūs') *v.t.* to draw from; to reach a conclusion by deductive reasoning; to infer; to trace down. **deducible** *a.* inferred. **deduct** *v.t.* to remove; to subtract. **deductible** *a.* **deduction** *n.* the act or process of deducting; the amount subtracted; the inference or conclusion arrived at. **deductive** *a.* capable of being deduced. **deductively** *adv.* [L. *deducere*, to lead down].

deed (dēd) *n.* that which is done; an act; exploit; achievement; a legal document or contract; *v.t.* to convey by deed [O.E. *daed; don,* to do].

deem (dēm) *v.t.* to believe on consideration; to judge [O.E. *dēman*, to judge].

deep (dēp) *a.* extending far below the surface; low in situation; dark; intense; abstruse; low in pitch; sagacious; *adv.* to a great depth; *n.* that which is deep; the sea. **-en** *v.t.* to make deep; *v.i.* to become deeper. **-most** *a.* deepest. **-ness** *n.* depth. **—rooted** *a.* firmly established. **—seated** *a.* not superficial. **depth** *n.* the quality of being deep [O.E. *deop*, deep].

deer (dir) *n.* any of the ruminant quadrupeds, such as stag, roebuck, fallow deer, etc. [O.E. *dēor*, an animal].

de·face (di·fās') *v.t.* to destroy or mar the external appearance of; to disfigure. **-able** *a.* **-ment** *n.* [Fr. *défacer*, to mar].

de·fal·cate (di·fal'·kāt) *v.t.* to misappropriate money; to embezzle. **defalcation** *n.* **defalcator** *n.* [L. *de*, from; *falx,* a sickle].

de·fame (di·fām') *v.t.* to harm or destroy the good name or reputation of; to slander. **defamation** *n.* **defamatory** *a.* [L. *diffamare,* to spread an evil report].

de·fault (di·fawlt') *n.* fault; neglect; defect; failure to appear in a law court when summoned; failure to account for money held in trust; *v.i.* to fail to meet an obligation. **-er** *n.* [O.Fr. *defaillir,* to fail].

de·fea·sance (di·fē'·zans) *n.* defeat; a rendering null and void. **defeasible** *a.* capable of being annulled [O.Fr. *desfaire,* to undo].

de·feat (di·fēt') *v.t.* to overcome; to subdue; to conquer; *n.* act of defeating; overthrow; conquest. **-ism** *n.* the attitude of mind of those who accept defeat as inevitable. **-ist** *n.; a.* pert. to defeatism [O.Fr. *desfait,* undone].

def·e·cate (def'·a·kāt) *v.t.* to clear or strain impurities from, as lees, dregs, etc.; *v.i.* to void excrement from the bowels. **defecation** *n.* [L. *de*, from; *faex,* dregs].

de·fect (dē·fekt', di·fekt') *n.* a want; an imperfection; absence of something necessary for completeness. **defection** *n.* a failure in duty; the act of abandoning allegiance to a cause. **-ive** *a.* incomplete; imperfect; faulty; (*Gram.*) not having all the parts to make the complete conjugation of a verb. **-ively** *adv.* **-iveness** *n.*

de·fend (dē·fend') *v.t.* to protect; to ward off attack; to maintain; to justify; to vindicate; (*Law*) to state the case of an accused person (by counsel). **-able** *a.* **-ant** *n.* one who defends; the accused in a criminal case; the one prosecuted in a civil case. **-er** *n.* [L. *defendere,* to protect].

de·fense (di·fens') *n.* the act of defending; that which shields or protects; vindication; justification; (*Law*) a plea or reply to a charge. **-less** *a.* open to attack. **-lessly** *adv.* **-lessness** *n.* **Civil Defense,** an organization in World War 2 and since, for protection of civilians. **defensible** *a.* **defensibility** *n.* **defensive** *a.* serving to defend; resisting attack; *n.* the position of defending against attack. **defensively** *adv.* [L. *defendere,* to protect].

de·fer (di·fur') *v.i.* to submit; to yield or bow to the opinion of another. **deference** (def'·er·ans) *n.* the act of deferring. **deferential** *a.* showing deference [L. *deferre,* to bring before].

de·fer (di·fur') *v.t.* to put off; to postpone; *v.i.* to delay. *pr.p.* **-ring;** *pa.p.* **-red. -able, -rable** *a.* **-ment** *n.* delay; postponement [L. *deferre,* to postpone].

de·fi·ance (di·fī'·ans) *n.* the act of defying; a challenge to combat; contempt; opposition. **defiant** *a.* aggressively hostile; insolent. **defiantly** *adv.* [Fr. *défier,* to challenge].

de·fi·cient (di·fish'·ant) *a.* wanting; failing; lacking a full supply; incomplete. **deficiency, deficience** *n.* shortcoming, shortage; defect. **-ly** *adv.* **deficit** (def'·a·sit) *n.* shortage or deficiency of revenue; excess of expenditure over income [L. *deficere,* to be wanting].

de·file (di·fīl') *n.* a narrow pass; *v.i.* to march by files [Fr. *défiler,* to thread].

de·file (di·fīl') *v.t.* to make unclean; soil; to dirty; to desecrate. **-ment** *n.* the act of defiling [L. *de.*; O.E. *fylan,* to pollute].

de·fine (di·fīn') *v.t.* to determine the boundaries of; to state the exact meaning of; to circumscribe; to designate; to specify. **definable** *a.* **definite** (def'·a·nit) *a.* fixed or defined; exact; precise; specific; restricted. **definitely** *adv.* **definiteness** *n.* **definition** *n.* description of a thing by its properties; explanation of the exact meaning of a word or term; distinctness. **definitive** *a.* limiting; determining; final; positive [L. *de*, down; *finis,* end].

de·flate (di·flāt') *v.t.* to empty of air or gas; to reduce inflated currency. **deflation** *n.* [L. *de*, down, *flare,* to blow].

de·flect (di·flekt') *v.t.* to turn aside; to divert from the right direction; *v.i.* to swerve; to deviate. **-ed** *a.* **deflection** *n.* **-or** *n.* [L. *de*, from; *flectere,* to bend].

de·flow·er (di·flour') *v.t.* to deprive of flowers; to ravish. [O.Fr. *defleurer,* to strip of flowers].

de·fo·li·a·tion (di·fō·li·ā'·shan) *n.* the shedding of leaves. **defoliate** *v.t.* to deprive of leaves. **defoliate, defoliated** *a.* [L. *de, folium,* leaf].

de·for·est (dē·fawr'·ast) *v.t.* to deprive of forests. **-ation** *n.*

de·form (di·fawrm') *v.t.* to mar or alter the form of; to make misshapen; to disfigure. **-ed** *a.* **-ation** *n.* **-ity** *n.* the state of being disfigured; a malformation [L. *deformare,* disfigure].

de·fraud (di·frawd') *v.t.* to deprive of, by fraud; cheat [L. *defraudare*].

de·fray (di·frā') *v.t.* to bear the cost of; to provide the money for, as in to *defray the expenses.* **-al** *n.* [O.Fr. *desfrayer,* to pay the cost].

de·frock (dē·frok') *v.t.* to unfrock, as of a priest deprived of ecclesiastical status.

deft (deft) *a.* dexterous; adroit; handy. **-ly** *adv.* **-ness** *n.* [O.E. *gedaeftan,* to make smooth].

de·funct (di·fungkt') *a.* dead; deceased; (of things) obsolete; *n.* a dead person [L. *defunctus,* finished].

de·fy (di·fī') *v.t.* to challenge; to dare; to resist authority [L. *dis,* away; *fidere,* to trust].

de·gen·er·ate (di·jen'·er·āt) *v.i.* to decline from a noble to a lower state of development; to become worse physically and morally; *n.* a person of low moral standards; *a.* having become less than one's kind. **degeneracy** *n.* **-ly** *adv.* **-ness** *n.* **degeneration** *n.* **degenerative** *a.* [L. *degenere,* unlike one's race].

de·grade (di·grād') *v.t.* to reduce in status; to

lower the moral reputation of; to disgrace. **deg·ra·da·tion** (deg.ra.dā′.shan) *n.* the act of degrading; the state or process of being degraded; abasement [L. *de*, down; *gradus*, a step].

de·gree (di.grē′) *n.* a step upward or downward; station or status; extent, as in *degree of proficiency;* rank to which one is admitted by a university; the 360th part of a revolution; a measured space on a thermometer, protractor, etc. (*Gram.*) modification of adjectives and adverbs by adding of suffix —*er* (comparative), and —*est* (superlative) to indicate intensifying of meaning. **third degree** (*U.S.*) a long, searching cross-examination by police of a suspect [L. *de*, down; *gradus*, a step].

de·gres·sion (di.gresh′.an) *n.* a going down; a lowering of rate of taxation on certain wage levels [L. *degredi*, to go down].

de·hy·drate (dē.hī′.drāt) *v.t.* to remove water from; *v.i.* to lose water; **dehydration** *n.* the process of reducing bulk and weight of food by removing water from products (e.g. dried eggs, milk, potatoes, etc.) [L. *de*, from; Gk. *hydor*, water].

de·i·cide (dē′.a.sīd) *n.* the killing of a god [L. *deus*, god; *caedere*, to kill].

de·i·fy (dē′.a.fī) *v.t.* to make a god of; to exalt to the rank of divinity; to worship. **deific, -al** *a.* making godlike. **deification** *n.* **deiform** *a.* of godlike form [L. *deus*, a god; *facere*, to make].

deign (dān) *v.i.* to condescend; to stoop; *v.t.* to condescend to do; to grant [L. *dignari*, to deem worthy].

de·ism (dē′.izm) *n.* belief, on purely rational grounds, in the existence of God without accepting the revelation implied in religious dogma. **deist** *n.* **deistic, -al** *a.* **deity** *n.* God, the Supreme Being; a pagan god or goddess [L. *deus*, god].

de·ject (di.jekt′) *v.t.* to cast down; to dishearten; to depress; to dispirit. **-ed** *a.* downcast; moody; in low spirits. **-edly** *adv.* **-edness** *n.* **-ion** *n.* lowness of spirits; (*Med.*) evacuation of the bowels [L. *de*, down; *jacere*, to throw].

de·lay (di.lā′) *v.t.* to put off; to postpone; to stop temporarily; *v.i.* to linger; to dawdle; to procrastinate; *n.* a stoppage; tardiness. **-er** *n.* [O.Fr. *delaier*, to prolong].

de·lec·ta·ble (di.lek′.ta.bl) *a.* highly pleasing; delightful; enjoyable. **-ness** *n.* **delectably** *adv.* **delectation** *n.* pleasure; delight [L. *delectare*, to delight].

del·e·gate (del′.a.gāt) *v.t.* to entrust authority to a deputy. *n.* also (del′.a.git) a deputy; a representative. **delegation** *n.* act of delegating; body of delegates. **delegacy** *n.* [L. *de*, from; *legare*, to send].

de·lete (di.lēt′) *v.t.* to erase; to strike out (word or passage). **delenda** *n.pl.* things to be blotted out. **deletion** *n.* [L. *delere*, to blot out].

del·e·te·ri·ous (del.a.tē′.ri.as) *a.* capable of harming or destroying health; pernicious. **-ly** *adv.* **-ness** *n.* [Gk. *dēleisthai*, to harm].

delft (delft) *n.* glazed earthenware, orig. made at *Delft* in Holland. Also **delf, delft-ware.**

de·lib·er·ate (di.lib′.a.rāt) *v.t.* to weigh in the mind; to discuss; *v.i.* to consider carefully; to take counsel; to hesitate. *a.* (di.lib′.a.rit) carefully considered; slow. **-ly** *adv.* **-ness** *n.* **deliberation** *n.* the act of carefully considering; slowness of action or speech. **deliberative** *a.* [L. *deliberare*, to ponder].

del·i·cate (del′.a.kat) *a.* dainty; frail; exquisitely wrought; nicely adjusted; highly sensitive or perceptive. **delicacy** *n.* fineness of shape, color, texture, or feeling; something which pleases the palate; a dainty; tact. **-ly** *adv.* **-ness** *n.* [L. *delicatus*, delightful].

del·i·ca·tes·sen (del.a.ka.tes′.an) *n.pl.* a shop selling cold cooked meats and other foods requiring little or no preparation [Ger.].

de·li·cious (di.lish′.as) *a.* extremely pleasing

to the taste or sense of smell; delightful. **-ly** *adv.* [L. *deliciae*, delight].

de·light (di.līt′) *v.t.* to give great pleasure to; to charm; *v.i.* to take delight; *n.* the source of pleasure; great satisfaction; joy. **-ed** *a.* **-edly** *adv.* **-ful** *a.* [L. *delectare*, to delight].

de·lim·it (di.lim′.it) *v.t.* to fix the limit or boundaries of. **-ation** *n.*

de·lin·e·ate (di.lin′.i.āt) *v.t.* to draw an outline; to sketch; to portray; (*Fig.*) to describe clearly in words. **delineation** *n.* the act of delineating; a portrayal in line or words; a sketch. **delineator** *n.* [L. *de*, from; *linea*, a line].

de·lin·quent (di.ling′.kwant) *n.* one who fails in duty; an offender or criminal, esp. of a young person; *a.* failing in duty. **delinquency** *n.* [L. *de*, from; *linquere*, to leave].

del·i·quesce (del.a.kwes′) *v.i.* to liquefy by absorbing moisture from the air. **deliquescence** *n.* **deliquescent** *a.* [L. *deliquescere*, to melt away].

de·lir·i·ous (di.lir′.i.as) *a.* wandering in the mind; light-headed; raving; incoherent. **deliration** *n.* madness. **-ly** *adv.* **-ness** *n.* **delirium** *n.* mental disturbance caused by grave physical illness or nervous shock; strong excitement. **delirium tremens** (*abbrev.* D.T.) violent delirium resulting from excessive alcoholism [L. *delirus*, crazy].

de·liv·er (di.liv′.er) *v.t.* to liberate from danger, captivity, restraint; to save; to distribute or hand over; to pronounce (as a speech); to execute (as an attack); to give birth to a child (used passively). **-able** *a.* **-ance** *n.* liberation; state of being delivered; the formal statement of an opinion. **-er** *n.* **-y** *n.* the act of delivering; the style of utterance of a public speech or sermon; (*Med.*) the act of giving birth [L. *de*, from; *liberare*, to set free].

dell (del) *n.* a small, deep valley; a hollow [M.E. *delle*, a dell].

Del·phic, Del·phian (del′.fik, del′.fi.an) *a.* pert. to the town of *Delphia* in Ancient Greece, to the oracle of Apollo in that town; oracular.

del·phin·i·um (del.fin′.i.am) *n.* a genus of flowering plants [Gk. *delphinion*, larkspur].

del·ta (del′.ta) *n.* the fourth letter of the Greek alphabet, Δ (small letter = δ); (*Geog.*) a triangular tract of alluvium at the mouth of a large river. **delta rays,** rays from radioactive metals much less powerful and penetrating than the *alpha* rays [Gk.].

de·lude (di.lood′) *v.t.* to lead into error; to mislead; to deceive. **deludable** *a.* **-r** *n.* **delusion** *n.* the act of deluding; that which deludes; a mistaken belief. **delusive** *a.* **delusory** *a.* [L. *de; ludere*, to play].

de·luge (del′.ūj) *n.* a great flow of water; torrential rain; a flood; *v.t.* to flood; to inundate [L. *diluvium*, a washing away]. [quality [Fr.].

de luxe (di looks′) *a.* sumptuous; of superlative

delve (delv) *v.t.* and *v.i.* to carry on intensive research [O.E. *delfan*, to dig].

dem·a·gogue (dem′.a.gàg) *n.* an unprincipled agitator. **demagogic, -al** (dem.a.gàj′(g).ik.-al) *n.* **demagogy** (dem′.a.gàj(g).i.) *n.* the beliefs and actions of a demogague. Also **demagoguery** [Gk. *dēmos*, the people; *agein*, to lead].

de·mand (di.mand′) *v.t.* to ask authoritatively or peremptorily; to question; to require; *n.* the act of demanding; urgent claim; earnest inquiry; (*Econ.*) the requirement of purchaser or consumer, oppos. of *supply*. **-ant** *n.* a plaintiff [L. *demandare*, to entrust].

de·mar·ca·tion, demarkation (dē.mar.kā′.shun) *n.* the act of marking a line or boundary; a boundary. **demarcate** *v.t.* [Fr.].

de·mean (di.mēn′) *v.t.* to conduct or comport oneself. **demeanor** *n.* behavior; conduct [O.Fr. *demener*, to conduct].

de·mean (di.mēn′) *v.t.* to make mean; to debase; to degrade (used reflexively).

de·ment·ed (di.men′.tad) *a.* insane; crazy;

suffering from dementia. **dement** v.t. to drive mad. **dementia** (di·men′·shi·ạ) n. incipient loss of reason; insanity marked by complete mental deterioration. **dementia praecox**, insanity in adolescence [L. de, from; mens, the mind].

de·mer·it (dē·mer′·it) n. a fault; a mark against one's record [L. de, from; merere, to deserve].

de·mesne (di·mān′, di·mēn′) n. a manor house and the estate adjacent to it; private ownership of land. Also **domain** [Fr.].

dem·i- prefix signifying half [L. dimidium, half; Fr. demi].

demi·i·god (dem′·i·gạd) n. a classical hero half human, half divine.

dem·i·john (dem′·ạ·jàn) n. a glass bottle with large body, slender neck, and enclosed in wicker work [prob. fr. Fr. dame-Jeanne].

dem·i·monde (dem′·i·mạnd) n. a class of women of doubtful reputation; prostitutes. [Fr. demi, half; monde, world].

de·mise (di·mīz′) n. death; transmission by will to a successor; the conveyance of property; v.t. to bequeath; to transmit to a successor [L. demittere, to send down].

dem·i·tasse (de·mạ·tås′) n. a small-sized cup, esp. for after-dinner coffee [Fr.].

de·mo·bi·lize (dē·mō′·bạ·līz) v.t. to dismiss (troops); to disband. **demobilization** n.

de·moc·ra·cy (dạ·màk′·rạ·si·) n. a form of government for the people by the will of the majority of the people (based on conception of the equality of man); a state having this form of government. **democrat** (dem′·ạ·krat) n. one who adheres to democracy; member of Democratic party (opp. of Republican party). **democratic, democratical** a. [Gk. dēmos, the people; kratein, to rule].

de·mog·ra·phy (di·màg′·rạ·fi·) n. science of vital and social statistics [Gk. dēmos, people; graphein, to write].

de·mol·ish (di·màl′·ish) v.t. to destroy; to pull down (of a building); to ruin. **-er** n. **demolition** (dem·ạ·li′·shạn) n. the act or process of pulling down; destruction [L. de, down; moles, a heap].

de·mon (dē′·mạn) n. a spirit (esp. evil); a devil; sometimes like daemon, a friendly spirit. **demoniac** a. pert. to a demon; possessed of an evil spirit; devilish—also **demoniacal**; n. a human being possessed of an evil spirit. **-olatry, -ism** n. the worship of evil spirits. **-olater** n. [Gk. daimon, a spirit].

de·mon·e·ti·za·tion (dē·màn·ạ·tī·zā′·shạn) n. the act of demonetizing. **demonetize** v.t. to diminish or deprive of monetary value [L. de, down; moneta, money].

dem·on·strate (dem′·ạn·strāt) v.t. to prove by pointing out; to exhibit; to explain by specimens or experiment. **demonstrable** a. capable of being demonstrated. **demonstrably** adv. **demonstration** n. the act of making clear, esp. by practical exposition; proof beyond doubt; a display of emotion. **demonstrative** a. proving by evidence; exhibiting with clearness; inclined to show one's feelings openly;; (Gram.) of an adjective or pronoun which points out, as this or that. **demonstrator** n. [L. demonstrare, to show].

de·mor·al·ize (di·mawr′·ạl·īz) v.t. to injure the morale of; to corrupt; to throw into confusion.

de·mos (dē′·mạs) n. the people [Gk.].

de·mur (di·mur′) v.i. to object. pr.p. **-ring**; pa.p. **-red**; n. statement of objections. **-rable** a. **-rage** n. undue detention of a ship, railroad car, etc.; compensation paid for such detention. **-rer** n. one who demurs; (Law) a plea that a case has insufficient evidence to justify its being pursued further [L. de; morari, to delay].

de·mure (di·mūr′) a. grave; staid; shy; seemingly modest. **-ly** adv. **-ness** n. [O.Fr. de murs, of good manners].

den (den) n. a cave or hollow place; lair or cage of a wild beast; disreputable haunt; a private sanctum, study or workshop [O.E. denn, a cave].

de·nar·i·us (di·nạr′·i·ạs) n. a Roman silver coin; the 'penny' of the N.T. pl. **denarii. denary** a. containing ten [L.].

de·na·ture (dē·nā′·chẹr) v.t. to make unfit for eating or drinking by adulteration. **denaturant** n. that which changes the nature of a thing. **denaturation** n.

den·dri-, dendro- prefix from Gk. dendron, a tree, as in **-form** (den′·dri·fawrm) a. having the shape or appearance of a tree. **-tic, -tical** a. tree-like; arborescent. **dendroid, dendroidal** a. having the shape of a tree.

de·ni·al (di·nī′·ạl) n. the act of denying; a flat contradiction; a refusal [L. de; negare, to deny].

den·i·gra·tion (den·ạ·grā′·shạn) n. a blackening of; defamation of a person's character. **denigrate** v.t. [L. de; nigrare, to blacken].

den·im (den′·im) n. a stout cotton twill cloth [Fr. serge de Nimes].

den·i·zen (den′·ạ·zn) n. a dweller (human or animal); anything successfully naturalized; v.t. to make a denizen of [L. de intus, from within].

de·nom·i·nate (di·nàm′·ạ·nāt) v.t. to give a name to; to designate; to style. **denominable** a. **denomination** n. the act of naming; a title; a class; a religious sect; (Arith.) unit of measure (money, length, etc.). **denominational** a. **denominative** a. conferring or having a distinctive name; (Gram.) a verb made from a noun or adjective. **denominatively** adv. **denominator** n. the one who, or that which, designates a class; the divisor; the number below the line in a fraction [L. de; nominare, to name].

de·note (di·nōt′) v.t. to signify or imply; to express by a sign; to mean; to be the symbol of; (Logic) to indicate the objects to which a term refers. **denotable** a. **denotation** n. [L. denotare, to mark].

dé·noue·ment (dā·nòò′·mạng) n. the unraveling of the complication of a dramatic plot; the issue or outcome of a situation [Fr. fr. L. de, from; nodare, to tie with knots].

de·nounce (di·nouns′) v.t. to inform against; to accuse in public; to repudiate, as a treaty. **-ment** n. **-er** n. [L. de; nuntiare, to announce].

dense (dens) a. compact; thick, crowded; (of vegetation) impenetrable, luxuriant; (Fig.) stupid. **-ly** adv. **-ness** n. **density** n. the quality of being dense; (Chem.) the mass per unit volume of a substance [L. densus, thick].

dent (dent) n. a small depression made (by a blow) in a surface; v.t. to mark by a blow or pressure [O.E. dynt, a stroke].

den·tal (den′·tạl) a. pert. to the teeth or to dentistry; n. and a. a consonant sound (e.g. d or t) made by tip of tongue behind the upper front teeth. **dentate** a. toothed; sharply notched (e.g. leaf). **dentiform** a. having the shape of a tooth. **dentifrice** n. powder, paste, or liquid used to clean and whiten teeth. **dentist** n. a medically trained specialist in the care of the teeth (also dental surgeon). **dentistry** n. **dentition** n. arrangement of teeth. **dentoid** a. tooth-like. **denture** n. set or part set of teeth, esp. artificial teeth [L. dens, a tooth].

den·ti·cle (den′·tạ·kl) n. a small tooth or projection. **denticular, denticulate, denticulated** a. having notches or sharp prejections [L. dens, tooth].

de·nude (di·nūd′) v.t. to lay bare; to strip. **denudation** n. [L. denudare, to make bare].

de·nun·ci·ate (di·nun′·si·āt) v.t. Same as **denounce. denunciation** n. **denunciator** n. [L. de; nuntiare, to announce].

de·ny (di·nī′) v.t. to declare to be untrue; to gainsay; to refuse a request; to disavow; to disown; to withhold; (reflex.) to abstain from [L. de; negare, to deny].

de·o·dor·ize (dē·ō′·dạ·rīz) v.t. to deprive of

odor. **deodorant, deodorizer** n. something which destroys an odor [L. *de*, from; *odor*, smell].

de·ox·i·dize (dē·ȧks′·ȧ·dīz) v.t. to remove oxygen from; to reduce from the state of an oxide.

de·part (di·pärt′) v.i. to go away; to leave; to die; to deviate (as from a policy); v.t. to leave (e.g. *to depart this life*). **-ed** n. (*sing.* and *pl.*) the dead. **-ment** n. a section of a business or administration; a special branch of the arts or science; an administrative district of a country, as in France. **-mental** a. pert. to a department.; affecting only a section of a business, etc. **-ure** n. the act of going away; divergence from rule [L. *de*, from; *partiri*, to part].

de·pend (di·pend′) v.i. to rely on; to be sustained by; to be contingent on; to hang; (*Law*) to be awaiting final judgment. **-able** a. trustworthy. **-ably** adv. **-ant, -ent** n. one who is supported, esp. financially by another; a retainer; a subordinate; a. hanging down; relying on for support or favor; varying according to; (spellings -ant, -ent are interchangeable in noun and adjective, but *-ant* is more common in noun, and *-ent* in adjective). **-ence** n. **-ency** n. **-ently, -antly** adv. [L. *dependere*, to hang down].

de·pict (di·pikt′) v.t. to portray; to present a visual image of; to describe in words. **-tion** n. **-ive** a. [L. *de*; *pingere*, *pictum*, to paint].

dep·i·late (dep′·ȧ·lāt) v.t. to remove hair from. **depilation** n. **depilatory** n. agent for removing superfluous hair from body; a. able to remove hair [L. *de*, from; *pilus*, a hair].

de·plete (di·plēt′) v.t. to empty; to diminish; to reduce. **depletion** n. **depletive, depletory** a. [L. *de*, from; *plere*, to fill].

de·plore (di·plōr′) v.t. to suffer remorse for; to regret; to express disapproval of. **deplorable** a. **deplorably** adv. [L. *de*; *plorare*, to weep].

de·ploy (di·ploi′) v.t. to spread out; to extend troops in line; v.i. to extend from column into line. **-ment** n. [Fr. *déployer*, to spread out].

de·po·lar·ize (dē·pō′·lȧ·rīz) v.t. to deprive of polarity [Gk. *poloz*, pivot].

de·pone (di·pōn′) v.t. to give evidence under oath, in a law court. **deponent** n. [L. *de*, down; *ponere*, to lay].

de·port (di·pōrt′) v.t. to carry away; to expel; to banish into exile (of undesirable aliens); (reflex.) to behave; to bear oneself. **-ation** n. the compulsory removal of people from one country to another. **-ment** n. conduct of a person [L. *de*, from; *portare*, to carry].

de·pose (di·pōz′) v.t. to remove from a throne; to oust from a high position; to degrade; (*Law*) to state upon oath. **deposable** a. **deposal** n. **deposition** (de·pȧ·zi′·shȧn) n. removal of someone from a high position; (*Law*) act of deponing; a written declaration by a witness [L. *de*, down; *ponere*, to place].

de·po·sit (di·pȧz′·it) v.t. to lay down; to entrust; to let fall (as a sediment); to lodge (in a bank); to store; n. that which is deposited or laid down; sediment falling to the bottom of a fluid; money placed in safe-keeping of a bank (usually with interest); a security; partial payment. **-ary** n. one with whom anything is left in trust. **-or** n. **-ory** n. [L. *de*, down; *ponere*, to place].

de·pot (dē′·pō) n. a railway station; (*Mil.*) (de′·pō) a storage center for supplies and materials; (formerly) training center for recruits [Fr. *dépôt*].

de·prave (di·prāv′) v.t. to make bad or worse; to corrupt; to pervert. **depravation** n. **-d** a. immoral; vicious. **depravity** n. [L. *de*; *pravus*, vicious].

dep·re·cate (dep′·rȧ·kāt) v.t. to express disapproval of. **deprecatingly** adv. **deprecation** n. **deprecative, deprecatory** a. **deprecator** n. [L. *de*, from; *precari*, to pray].

de·pre·ci·ate (di·prē′·shi·āt) v.t. to lower in value; (*Fig.*) to disparage; to underrate; v.i. to lose quality; to diminish in market value.

depreciation n. decline in value. **depreciative, depreciatory** a. **depreciator** n. [L. *de*, down; *pretium*, price].

dep·re·date (dep′·ri·dāt) v.t. to plunder; to lay waste. **depredation** n. the act of laying waste; pillaging [L. *de*, from; *praeda*, plunder].

de·press (di·pres′) v.t. to deject or cast a gloom over; to press down; to lower; to diminish the vigor of. **-ed** a. dejected; pressed down. **-ible** a. **depression** n. a hollow; a dip; a sinking; dejection; despondency; a slump (in trade); in meteorology, an area of low barometric pressure. **-or** n. [L. *depressus*, pressed down].

de·prive (di·prīv′) v.t. to take away; to dispossess; to debar a person from **deprivation** n. the act of depriving; the state of being deprived or dispossessed. **deprivable** a. **depriver** n. [L. *de*, from; *privare*, to deprive].

depth (depth) n. deepness; distance measured downwards from surface; distance from front to back, as of a shelf, etc.; profundity or penetration, as of mind [O.E. *deop*, deep].

de·pute (di·pūt′) v.t. to send with commission to act for another; to delegate duties to another. **deputation** n. the act of deputing; persons authorized to transact business for others; **deputize** v.i. to appoint as deputy. **deputy** n. (dep′·yoo·ti·) one who is appointed to act for another [L. *deputare*, to esteem, to allot].

de·range (di·rānj′) v.t. to put out of order or place; to upset; to make insane. **-d** a. mentally unstable; insane. **-ment** n. [Fr. *déranger*, to disturb].

der·by (dur′·bi·) n. a man's felt hat, with stiff rounded crown and narrow brim.

der·e·lict (der′·ȧ·likt) a. forsaken; abandoned and disclaimed by owner, esp. used of ships; n. a ship abandoned by captain and crew; a person abandoned by society. **dereliction** n. [L. *de*, from; *relinquere*, to leave].

de·ride (di·rīd′) v.t. to ridicule; to mock; to laugh at with scorn. **-r** n. **deridingly** adv. **derision** (di·rizh′·ȧn) n. mockery; ridicule. **derisive** a. **derisively** adv. **derisiveness** n. **derisory** a. [L. *de*, down; *ridere*, to laugh].

de·rive (dȧ·rīv′) v.t. to obtain or draw from a source; to trace the etymology (of a word); to trace the descent or origin(of a person); v.i. to have as an origin; to proceed (foll. by *from*). **derivable** a. **derivation** (der·ȧ·vā′·shȧn) n. act of deriving or process of being derived; tracing of a word back to its roots; etymology. **derivative** n. that which is derived or traceable back to something else; a word derived from another; a. obtained by derivation; secondary [L. *de*, down; *rivus*, a stream].

der·ma, der·mis (dur′·mȧ, dur′·mis) n. the true skin below epidermis. **dermal** a. **dermatic** a. consisting of skin. **-titis** n. inflammation of the skin. **-tology** n. branch of medical science concerned with the skin and skin diseases. **-tologist** n. skin specialist [Gk. *derma*, a skin].

der·o·gate (der′·ȧ·gāt) v.i. to lessen (as reputation). **derogation** n. **derogatory** a. tending to impair the value of; detracting. **derogatorily** adv. [L. *de*, from; *rogare*, to ask].

der·rick (der′·ik) n. an apparatus like a crane for hoisting heavy weights [fr. *Derrick*, a Tyburn hangman of 17th cent.].

der·rin·ger (der′·in·jer) n. a short-barrelled pistol with a large bore [U.S. inventor].

der·vish (dur′·vish) n. a member of one of the mendicant orders among the Mohammedans [Pers. *darvish*, a poor man].

des·cant (des′·kant) n. a melody harmonizing with and sung or played as accompaniment to a musical theme; a discourse on a theme; v.i. to discourse fully; to sing. **-er** n. [L. *dis*, apart; *cantus*, song].

de·scend (di·send′) v.t. to go down; to traverse downwards; to flow down; v.i. to sink; to lower oneself or stoop to something; to fall (upon an enemy); to be derived by birth. **-ant** *n.* one descended from an ancestor; offspring. **-ent** *a.* descending. **descending** *a.* **descent** *n.* act of coming down; a slope or declivity; lineage [L. *de*, down; *scandere*, to climb].

de·scribe (di·skrīb') *v.t.* to represent the features of; to portray in speech or writing. **describable** *a.* **description** (de·skrip'·shan) *n.* act of describing; a representation, in words, of the qualities of a person or thing; sort; kind. **descriptive** *a.* **descriptively** *adv.* [L. *de*, down; *scribere*, to write].

de·scry (di·skrī') *v.t.* to discover by the eye; to perceive from a distance; to make out. **descrier** *n.* [L. *de*, down; *scribere*, to write].

des·e·crate (des'·a·krāt) *v.t.* to violate the sanctity of; to profane. **-r, -or** *n.* **desecration** *n.* [L. *de*, away, *sacer*, holy].

de·sert (di·zūrt') *n.* that which is deserved; reward (for merit); punishment (for demerit) [L. *desevire*, to serve zealously].

des·ert (dez'·ert) *n.* a wide, sandy waste region; *a.* uncultivated; solitary [L. *deserere*, to abandon].

de·sert (di·zūrt') *v.t.* to abandon; to leave; *v.i.* to quit the armed forces without authorization. **-ed** *a.* abandoned. **-er** *n.* **desertion** *n.* [L. *deserere*, to abandon].

de·serve (di·surv') *v.t.* to earn by service; to merit; to be entitled to; to warrant; *v.i.* to be worthy of reward. **deservedly** *adv.* justly. **deserving** *a.* worthy; meritorious [L. *deservire*, to serve zealously].

des·ic·cate (des'·a·kāt) *v.t.* to extract all moisture from; to dry up; to dehydrate. **desiccant** *a.* drying; *n.* (*Chem.*) substance capable of absorbing moisture. **desiccation** *n.* [L. *desiccare*, to dry up].

de·sign (di·zīn') *v.t.* to draw the outline of; to plan; *v.i.* to purpose; *n.* sketch in outline (esp. in architecture); a pattern (as in wallpaper, printed cloth, etc.); scheme or plan; purpose. **-able** *a.* **designate** (dez'·ig·nāt) *v.t.* to mark out and make known; to nominate or appoint. **designation** *n.* distinctive title. **designative** *a.* **-edly** *adv.* intentionally. **-er** *n.* one who designs or makes plans or patterns; a schemer or plotter. **-ful** *a.* **-ing** *a.* artful; selfishly interested [L. *de*, down; *signare*, to mark].

de·sire (di·zīr') *v.t.* to yearn for the possession of; to request; to entreat; *n.* anything desired; a longing; object of longing; lust. **desirable** *a.* worth possessing. **desirably** *adv.* **desirableness, desirability** *n.* the state or quality of being desired. **desirous** *a.* full of desire; covetous [O.Fr. *desirer*, to want].

de·sist (di·zist') *v.t.* to cease; to discontinue. **-ance, -ence** *n.* [L. *de*, from *sistere*, to stand].

desk (desk) *n.* a table for reading or writing; a lectern [L.L. *desca*, a table].

des·o·late (des'·a·lāt) *v.t.* to devastate; to depopulate; to make lonely or forlorn; *a.* (des'·a·lit) waste; deserted; unfrequented; dismal. **-ly** *adv.* **ness** *n.* **-r** *n.* **desolation** *n.* the act of laying waste; loneliness; misery. **desola-tory** *a.* [L. *desolare*, to forsake].

de·spair (di·sper') *v.i.* to be without hope; to lose heart; *n.* despondency; hopelessness. **-ing** *a.* full of despair. **-ingly** *adv.* [L. *desparare*].

des·patch See **dispatch**.

des·pi·ca·ble (des'·pik·a·bl) *a.* contemptible; vile; deserving to be despised. **despicably** *adv.* **despicability** *n.* [L. *despicere*, to despise].

de·spise (di·spīz') *v.t.* to look down upon; to hold in contempt; to disdain; to scorn. **despisable** *a.* [L. *despicere*, to look down on].

de·spite (di·spīt') *n.* contemptuous treatment; *prep* in spite of, notwithstanding. **-ful** *a.* **-fully** *adv.* [L. *despicere*, to look down on].

de·spoil (di·spoil') *v.t.* to take away by force; to rob; to strip. **-er** *n.* a plunderer. **-ment, despoliation** *n.* [L. *de*, from; *spolium*, spoil].

de·spond (di·spánd') *v.i.* to be cast down in spirit. **-ence, -ency** *n.* dejection of mind; depression. **-ent** *a.* depressed. **-ently** *adv.* **-ingly** *adv.* [L. *de*, from; *spondere*, to promise].

des·pot (des'·pat) *n.* one who rules with absolute power; a tyrant; one who enforces his will on others. **-ic** *a.* **-ically** *adv.* **-ism** *n.* the absolute power of one man unlimited by constitution [Gk. *despotēs*, a master].

des·sert (di·zurt') *n.* a course served at end of a dinner [O.Fr. *desservir*, to clear the table].

des·tine (des'·tin) *v.t.* to predetermine (usu. passive). **destination** *n.* the purpose for which anything is destined; the place to which one is traveling. **destiny** *n.* state appointed; foreordained lot; fate [L. *destinare*, to establish].

des·ti·tute (des'·ta·tūt) *a.* in want; needy; deprived of means of sustenance. **destitution** *n.* [L. *de*, from; *statuere*, to place].

de·stroy (di·stroi') *v.t.* to pull down; to turn to rubble; to put an end to; to annihilate. *pa.p.* **-ed. -able** *a.* **-er** *n.* a type of fast warship armed with guns and torpedoes [L. *destruere*].

de·struc·tion (di·struk'·shan) *n.* the act of destroying; state of being destroyed; ruin; death. **destructible** *a.* capable of being destroyed. **destructibleness, destructibility** *n.* **destructive** *a.* [L. *destruere*, to destroy].

des·ue·tude (des'·wi·tūd) *n.* discontinuance of a custom or practice [L. *desuetudo*].

de·sul·tor·y (des'·al·tōr·i·) *a.* leaping from one thing to another; unmethodical; aimless; rambling. **desultorily** *adv.* **desultoriness** *n.* [L. *desultor*, a circus rider].

de·tach (di·tach') *v.t.* to separate; to disunite; to withdraw; to detail for special service (as troops). **-able** *a.* **-ed** *a.* standing alone (e.g. of a house); impersonal; disinterested; unprejudiced. **-edly** *adv.* **-edness, -ment** *n.* process or state of being detached; that which is detached (as troops) [Fr. *détacher*, to unfasten].

de·tail (di·tāl') *v.t.* to relate minutely; to record every item; to appoint for a special duty (e.g. troops). **detail** (dē'·tāl or di·tāl') *n.* a minute part; item; (*Mil.*) special duty. **-ed** *a.* giving every particular fact [Fr. *tailler*, to cut].

de·tain (di·tān') *v.t.* to keep back or from; to prevent someone proceeding; to maintain possession of; to keep in custody. **-er** *n.* one who detains; (*Law*) illegal detention of another's possessions; a writ to keep in custody. **-ment** *n.* **detention** *n.* [L. *detinere*, to keep back].

de·tect (di·tekt') *v.t.* to uncover; to discover; to expose; to bring to light (esp. a crime); to perceive. **-able, -ible** *a.* **-or** *n.* one who or that which detects. **-ion** *n.* **-ive** *a.* employed in detecting; *n.* a member of the police force, not in uniform, who apprehends criminals and investigates cases [L. *detergere*, to uncover].

de·ter (di·ter') *v.t.* to frighten from; to discourage; to restrain. *pr.p.* **-ring**; *pa.p.* **-red. -ment** *n.* hindrance. **-rent** *a.* having the power to deter; *n.* that which deters. **deterrence** *n.* [L. *deterrere*, to frighten off].

de·terge (di·turj') *v.t.* to cleanse (wound); to wipe off; to purge. **detergence, detergency** *n.* **detergent** *a.* cleansing *n.* cleansing substance [L. *detergere*, to wipe off].

de·te·ri·o·rate (di·tir'·i·a·rāt) *v.t.* to make worse; to cause to depreciate; *v.i.* to become worse; to degenerate. **deterioration** *n.* [L. *deterior*, worse].

de·ter·mine (di·tur'·min) *v.t.* to fix the limits of; to define; to regulate the form, scope, or character of; to decide; to ascertain with precision; *v.i.* to make a decision or resolution; (*Law*) to terminate. **determinable** *a.* **determinant** *a.* serving to determine, fix, or limit; *n.* that which determines or causes determination. **determinate** *a.* having fixed limits; decisive; established. **determinately** *adv.* **determination** *n.* the act or process of determining fixed purpose; resolution; adherence to a definite line of action. **-d** *a.* resolute; unwavering; firm; purposeful. **-dly** adv. **determinism** n. the doctrine that man is not a free agent, and that his actions and mental activity are governed by causes or motives outside his own will [L. determinare, to limit].

de·test (di·test') v.t. to dislike intensely; to hate; to abhor. **-able** a. **-ableness, -ability** n. **-ation** n. [L. detestari, to execrate].

de·throne (dē·thrōn') v.t. to remove from a throne; to depose. **-ment** n.

de·to·nate (det'·a·nāt) v.t. to cause to explode; v.i. to explode with a loud report. **detonation** n. a sudden and violent explosion. **detonator** n. a detonating substance; device to make another substance explode [L. detonare, to thunder].

de·tour (dē'·toor) n. a roundabout way, a circuitous route; a digression [Fr. détour].

de·tract (di·trakt') v.t. to take away a part from; to defame; v.i. (with from) to diminish. **-or** n. **-ingly** adv. **detraction** n. disparagement; depreciation; slander [L. detrahere, to draw away].

de·tri·ment (det'·ra·mant) n. injury; harm; loss. **-al** a. [L. detrimentum, a rubbing off].

de·trun·cate (di·trung'·kāt) v.t. to lop off from the trunk; to shorten. **detruncation** n.

deuce (dūs) n. a card or die with two spots; (Tennis) score of 40 all [L. duo, two].

deuce (dūs) n. the devil (in mild imprecations); bad luck [prob. deus, a god].

deu·te·ri·um (dū·tir'·i·am) n. a form of hydrogen twice as heavy as the normal gas [Gk. deutereion, second place].

deu·ter·on·o·my (dū·tẹr·ȧn'·a·mi·) n. the fifth book of the Pentateuch [Gk. deuteros, second; nomos, law].

de·val·u·ate, devalue (dē·val'·yoo·āt) v.t. to reduce the value of (esp. the currency). **devaluation** n. [L. de, down; valere, to be worth].

dev·as·tate (dev'·as·tāt) v.t. to lay waste. **devastation** n. act of laying waste; the state of being devastated; destruction; havoc [L. devastare, to lay waste].

de·vel·op (di·vel'·ap) v.t. to cause to grow; to unfold gradually; to increase the resources of; (Photog.) to produce image on photographic plate or film by chemical application; v.i. to evolve by natural processes; to expand; to open out; to assume definite character. **-er** n. one who or that which develops; (Photog.) a chemical for producing image on plate or film. **-ment** n. a gradual unfolding or growth; expansion; evolution; unraveling of a plot; the result of previous causes [Fr. développer, to grow gradually].

de·vi·ate (dē'·vi·āt) v.i. to diverge; to turn away from the direct line; to swerve; v.t. to cause to swerve. **deviation** n. [L. de, from; via, a way].

de·vice (di·vīs') n. that which is planned out or designed; contrivance; stratagem; (Her.) emblem on a shield [M.E. devisen, to contrive].

dev·il (dev'·l) n. the spirit of evil; in Scripture, tempter; Satan; fiend; any very wicked person; (Colloq.) a fellow; v.t. (Colloq.) to torment; (cookery) to prepare with hot or savory seasoning. **-ish** a. **-ishly** adv. **—may-care** a. reckless; happy-go-lucky. **-ment** n. mischief; prank. **-ry; -try** n. devilish conduct. **-'s advocate**, one appointed by papal court to oppose a proposed canonization; (Colloq.) one who maintains an argument with which he really disagrees. **give the devil his due**, give even the worst person credit for something [O.E. deofol, the devil; fr. Gk. diabolos, slandered].

de·vi·ous (dē'·vi·as) a. not direct; circuitous; erring. **-ly, -ness** n. [L. de, from; via, a way].

de·vise (di·vīz')v.t. to invent; to contrive; to scheme; to plan; (Law) to leave as a legacy; v.i. to consider; n. (Law) the act of bequeathing real estate by will; clause in will to this effect. **devisable** a. **devisal,** n. **-r** n. one who schemes or contrives. **devisor** n. one who be-

queaths by will [M.E. devisen, to divide].

de·vi·tal·ize (dē·vī'·ta·līz) v.t. to deprive of life or vitality. **devitalization** n.

de·void (di·void') a. empty; free from; without [L. de, from; viduus, deprived].

dev·o·lu·tion (dev·a·lōō'·shan) n. delegation of powers to subsidiary or local bodies; gradual retrogression (oppos. of evolution) [L. devolutus, rolled down]. [See **devolve**].

de·volve (di·vȯlv') v.t. to transmit; to transfer; to delegate; v.i. (foll. by upon) to fall to the lot of; (Law) to pass, by inheritance, from one to another [L. devolvere, to roll down].

de·vote (di·vōt') v.t. to give oneself wholly to; to dedicate; to consecrate. **-d** a. **-dly** adv. **devotedness** n. **devotee** (de·va·tē') n. one who is devoted to a cause; a zealous supporter. **devotion** n. **devotions** n.pl. worship and prayer. **devotional** a. pert. to devotions; religious [L. devovere, to dedicate by vow].

de·vour (di·vour') v.t. to swallow ravenously; to consume completely and wantonly; to destroy; (Fig.) to read avidly. **-ing** a. [L. devorare, to swallow up].

de·vout (di·vout') a. pious; passionately religious; sincere. **-ly** adv. [L. devovere, to vow].

dew (dū) n moisture in the atmosphere or in the soil itself, condensed on exposed surfaces, esp. at night; v.t. to moisten; to bedew. **-fall** n. the falling of dew, or the time when it falls. **-iness** n. **-y** a. [O.E. deaw, dew].

dex·ter (deks'·tẹr) a. pert. to the right hand; on the right hand side. **dexterity** n. manual skill; mental adroitness; cleverness; right-handedness. **-ous, dextrous** a. **-ously** adv. **-ousness** n. **dextral** a. right as opposed to left. **dextrality** n. right-handedness. **dextrally** adv. [L. dexter, on the right hand].

dex·trin, dextrine (deks'·trin) n. a soluble gummy substance used for stiffening fabrics, sizing paper, mucilage, etc. [L. dexter, on the right].

di·a·be·tes (dī·a·bē'·tis, ·ēz) n. a disease marked by excessive flow of sugar-urine due to failure of pancreas to produce insulin [Gk. diabetes, fr. dia, through; bainein, to go].

di·a·bol·ic, diabolical (dī·a·bȧl'·ik, ·i·kal) a. devilish; fiendish; pert. to the devil. **-ally** adv. [Gk. diabolos, the devil].

di·ac·o·nal (dī·ak'·a·nal) a. pert. to a deacon.

di·a·dem (dī'·a·dem) n. a fillet or head band worn as the symbol of royal power; a headdress or crown significant of royalty; (Fig.) sovereignty. **-ed** a. wearing a crown [Gk. diadēma, fr. diadein, to bind round].

di·a·glyph (dī'·a·glif) n. an intaglio [Gk. dia, through; gluphein, to carve].

di·ag·no·sis (dī·ag·nō'·sis) n. a scientific discrimination of any kind; (Med.) the identification of a disease from its signs and symptoms; pl. **diagnoses. diagnose** v.t. (Med.) to ascertain from signs and symptoms the nature of a disease; to identify the root-cause of any social or other problems. **diagnostic** a. distinguishing; symptomatic; n. a symptom distinguishing one disease from another; a clue. **diagnostician** n. [Gk. dia, through; gnosis, an inquiry].

di·ag·o·nal (dī·ag'·a·nal) n. (Geom.) a straight line joining two opposite angles in a rectilineal figure; a line, plane, part, etc. having an oblique direction or position; a. from corner to opposite corner; oblique. **-ly** adv. [Gk. dia, through; gonia, a corner].

di·a·gram (dī'·a·gram) n. a figure drawn to demonstrate a theorem; a drawing or plan in outline. **-matically** adv. [Gk. dia, through; graphein, to write].

di·al (dī'·al) n. an instrument for showing the time of day from the sun's shadow; the face of a sundial, clock, watch, etc.; any plate or face on which a pointer moves, as on a weighing machine; v.t. to measure on a dial; to call a number on automatic telephone; pr.p. **-ling**. pa.p. **-led**.

di·a·lect (dī′·a̱·lekt) *n.* a group variation of language; a mode of speech peculiar to a district or social group; vernacular [Gk. *dialektos,* manner of speech].

di·a·lec·tic, -al (dī·a̱·lek′·tik, ·a̱l) *a.* pert. to dialectics; *n.* (usually *pl.*) the art of discussion, disputation, or debate; the science of reasoning. **-ally** *adv.* **dialectician** *n.* one skilled in debate; one who studies dialects [Gk. *dialektikē,* the art of debate].

di·a·logue (dī′·a̱·lawg) *n.* a conversation between two (or more) persons. **dialogistic** *a.* pert. to dialogue. **dialogize** *v.i.* to speak in dialogue [Gk. *dialogos,* a conversation].

di·al·y·sis (dī·al′·a̱·sis) *n.* (*Chem.*) separation of colloid (non-crystalline) from crystalline substances in solution, by filtration through a membrane; *pl.* **dialyses. dialytic** *a.* [Gk. *dia,* through; *luein,* to loosen].

di·am·e·ter (dī·am′·a̱·ter) *n.* (*Geom.*) a line passing through the center of a circle or other curvilinear figure, and terminated by the circumference; transverse measurement; unit of magnifying power of a lens. **diametric (-al)** *a.* pert. to the diameter; directly opposite [Gk. *dia,* through; *metron,* a measure].

di·a·mond (dī′·a̱·ma̱nd) *n.* one of the crystalline forms of carbon and the hardest substance known; a popular gem stone; a four-sided figure with two acute and two obtuse angles; a rhombus; one of the four suits of playing-cards; one of the smallest types of English printing (4½ point); playing field for baseball. *a.* resembling, set with, consisting of, shaped like diamonds. — **wedding,** the sixtieth anniversary of a marriage. **black diamonds** (*Colloq.*) coal. **rough diamond,** (*Colloq.*) a worthy but uncultured person [Fr. *diamant,* diamond].

di·a·pa·son (dī·a̱·pā′·za̱n) *n.* correct pitch; harmony; the entire compass of a voice or instrument; the two foundation stops of an organ (*open* and *stopped diapason*) [Gk. *dia pason* = through all (the notes)].

di·a·per (dī′·a̱·per) *n.* a linen or cotton cloth with diamond pattern; a baby's breechcloth; *v.t.* to change a baby's diaper; to ornament with a diaper pattern [O.Fr. *diapre*].

di·aph·a·nous (dī·af′·a̱·na̱s) *a.* having the power to transmit light; transparent; translucent [Gk. *dia,* through; *phainein,* to show].

di·a·pho·ret·ic (dī·a̱·fa̱·ret′·ik) *n.* (*Med.*) a medicine which induces perspiration; *a.* promoting perspiration [Gk. *dia,* through; *phorein,* to carry].

di·a·phragm (dī′·a̱·fram) *n.* (*Anat.*) a dividing membrane; a dome-shaped muscular partition between chest and abdomen; vibrating disc in telephone or microphone; a disc with a circular hole used in telescope or camera to cut off part of a ray of light. **-atic, -al** *a.* [Gk. *diaphragma,* a barrier].

di·ar·chy (dī′·a̱r·ki·) *n.* a system of government in which power is held jointly by two authorities [Gk. *dis,* twice; *archein,* to rule].

di·ar·rhe·a, diarrhoea (dī·a̱·rē′·a̱) *n.* an excessive and frequent looseness of the bowels. **diarrhetic** *a.* [Gk. *dia,* through; *rhein,* to flow].

di·a·ry (dī′·a̱·ri·) *n.* a daily record; a book in which a personal record of thoughts, action, etc. is kept. **diarist** *n.* [L. *dies,* a day].

di·a·stase (dī′·a̱·stās) *n.* an enzyme capable of converting starch into sugar. **diastasic** *a.* [Gk. *diastasis,* separation].

di·as·to·le (dī·as′·ta̱·lē) *n.* (*Med.*) a rhythmical dilatation of the heart and arteries alternating with *systole* (contraction); the lengthening of a syllable usually short, before a pause [Gk. = a putting apart].

di·a·ther·mal (dī·a̱·thurm′·a̱l) *a.* permeable by heat. **diathermanous, diathermous, diathermic** *a.* having the property of transmitting radiant heat. **diathermy** *n.* [Gk. *dia,* through; *thermē,* heat].

di·a·tom (dī′·a̱·ta̱m) *n.* one of an order of

microscopic unicellular marine or vegetable organisms [Gk. *dia,* through; *tomē,* a cutting].

di·a·tom·ic (dī·a̱·ta̱m′·ik) *a.* (*Chem.*) consisting of two atoms.

di·a·ton·ic (dī·a̱·ta̱n′·ik) *a.* (*Mus.*) pert. to major or minor scales; proceeding by the tones, intervals, and harmonies of the natural scale [Gk. *dia,* through; *tonos,* tone].

di·a·tribe (dī′·a̱·trīb) *n.* a vituperative harangue; a wordy denunciation. **diatribist** *n.* [Gk. *diatribē,* a means of passing the time].

dib·ble (dib′·l) *n.* a pointed instrument used in gardening for making holes. Also **dibber.** *v.t.* to plant with a dibble; *v.i.* to make holes. **-r** *n.* [form of *dab*].

dice (dīs) *n.pl.* small cubes on each of the six faces of which are spots representing numbers 1-6; used from Egyptian times in games of chance; *Sing.* form **die;** *v.t.* to cut into small squares; *v.i.* to play with dice. **dicer** *n.* a gambler [O.Fr. *dez,* fr. L. *datus,* given, thrown].

di·ceph·a·lous (dī·sef′·a̱·la̱s) *a.* having two heads [Gk. *dis,* twice; *kephalē,* the head].

di·chot·o·my (dī·ka̱t′·am·i·) *n.* a cutting in two; (*Logic*) division of ideas into two classes. **dichotomize** *v.t.* and *v.i.* **dichotomous** *a.* [Gk. *dicha,* apart; *temnein,* to cut].

dick·er (dik′·er) *v.t.* and *v.i.* to barter; to haggle; to quibble; *n.* a bargain; a deal [L. *decuria,* a group of ten (esp. hides)].

dick·ey, dicky (dik′·i·) *n.* a waist front for women; detachable shirt front; seat for servants at back of old-fashioned carriage.

Dic·ta·phone (dik′·ta̱·fōn) *n.* a machine into which letters, etc. can be dictated and which re-dictates to the typist [Trade Name].

dic·tate (dik·tāt′) *v.t.* to read aloud a passage for another to transcribe; to give orders; *v.i.* to speak with authority; to prescribe; to deliver commands; *n.* an order; command; direction that must be obeyed (usually *pl.*). **dictation** *n.* art or practice of dictating; that which is read aloud for another to write down. **dictator** *n.* one who holds absolute power. **dictatorial** *a.* pert. to or like a dictator; tending to force one's opinions on another. **dictatorially** *adv.* **dictatorship** *n.* [L. *dicere,* to say].

dic·tion (dik′·sha̱n) *n.* choice of words in speaking and writing; verbal style; enunciation [L. *dicere,* to say].

dic·tion·ar·y (dik′·sha̱n·er·i·) *n.* a book containing, alphabetically arranged, the words of a language, their meanings and etymology; a lexicon [L. *dicere,* to say].

dic·to·graph (dik′·ta̱·graf) *n.* sound-recording telephonic instrument [Trade Name].

dic·tum (dik′·ta̱m) *n.* a positive assertion; an authoritative statement or opinion; a maxim; *pl.* **dicta** [L. = a thing said].

did (did) *pa.t.* of verb **do** [O.E. *dyde*].

di·dac·tic (dī·dak′·tik) *a.* designed to instruct; containing precepts or doctrines; (of people) opinionated. **-ally** *adv.* **-s** *n.* the science of teaching [Gk. *didaskein,* to teach].

did·y·mous (did′·a̱·ma̱s) *a.* twin [Gk. *didumos*].

die (dī) *n.* a small cube of wood, bone, or ivory used in games of chance; *pl.* **dice** (dīs). **the die is cast,** one's fate is irrevocably settled [O.Fr. *det,* fr. L. *datus,* given, thrown].

die (dī) *v.i.* to cease to live; to become extinct or extinguished; to wither; to decline. *pr.p.* **dying.** *pa.p.* **-d. dying** *a.* pert. to a person at the point of death; fading; languishing. **to die for** (*Colloq.*) to want desperately. **to die hard,** to resist stubbornly; to be long in dying [M.E. *deyan,* to die].

die (dī) *n.* a device for cutting in a press; an engraved metal block used for stamping a design as on a coin; the cubical part of a pedestal; a steel block used for cutting screws; *pl.* **dies.** — **casting** *n.* method of making castings in permanent molds [L. *dare,* to give].

di·e·lec·tric (dī·a·lek′·trik) *a.* non-conducting; *n.* name for a substance through or across which electric induction takes place [Gk. *dia,* through; *elektron,* amber].

di·er·e·sis, diaeresis (dī·er′·a·sis) *n.* a mark (··) placed over the second of two consecutive vowels to indicate that each is to be pronounced separately, as in coöperate. *pl.* **diereses, diaereses** (-ēz) [Gk. *diairesis,* division].

Die·sel en·gine (dē′·zl en′·jan) *n.* an internal combustion engine [fr. R. *Diesel,* the inventor].

di·e·sis (dī′·a·sis) *n.* (*Print.*) a mark of reference, the double dagger (‡); *pl.* **dieses** [Gk. *diesis,* a quarter tone].

di·et (dī′·at) *n.* a system of food; what one habitually eats and drinks; food specially prescribed by a doctor; a regulated allowance of provisions; *v.i.* to prescribe a special course of foods; *v.i.* (*Colloq.*) to slim. **-ary** *n.* special course of feeding; daily allowance of food; *a.* pert. to diet. **-etic** *a.* pert. to diet. **-etics** *n.* the science and study of food values, and their effect on health. **-ician, -itian** *n.* [L. *diaeta,* a mode of living].

di·et (dī′·at) *n.* a legislative assembly in certain countries; an international conference [L. *dies,* a day].

dif·fer (dif′·er) *v.i.* to be unlike; to have distinctive characteristics; to disagree (foll. by *from* or *with*); to be at variance. **-ence** *n.* unlikeness; dissimilarity; distinguishing characteristic; disagreement; contention; the amount by which one thing exceeds another in weight or number. **-ent** *a.* unlike; distinct; not the same (used with *from*). **-entia** *n.* (*Logic*) the essential quality or characteristic distinguishing any one species from another in a genus (e.g. rational power in *man*); *pl.* **-entiae.** **-ential** *a.* characteristic; special; discriminating; (*Math.*) pert. to infinitely small quantitative differences; proceeding by increments infinitely small. **-entially** *adv.* **-entiate** *v.t.* to make different; to distinguish; to classify as different; *v.i.* to acquire different characteristics. **-entiation** *n.* **-ently** *adv.* **-ential gear,** a mechanism by which two sets of wheels are made to rotate at different speeds, as wheels of a car [L. *dis-,* apart; *ferre,* to bear].

dif·fi·cult (dif′·a·kult) *a.* hard to do or understand; not easy; laborious; (of persons) hard to please; not amenable. **-ly** *adv.* **-y** *n.* laboriousness; a trouble; objection; demur; that which is not easy to do or understand. **-ies** *n.pl.* financial embarrassment [L. *dis-,* not; *facilis,* easy].

dif·fi·dent (dif′·a·dant) *a.* wanting confidence; timid; shy. **diffidence** *n.* lack of confidence; modesty. **-ly** *adv.* [L. *dis-,* not; *fidere,* to trust].

dif·fract (di·frakt′) *v.t.* to break or separate into parts, esp. of rays of light and sound waves. **diffraction** *n.* breaking up of wave motion (light, sound, etc); the phenomenon caused by light passing through a narrow slit [L. *dis,* apart; *frangere,* to break].

dif·fuse (dif·ūz′) *v.t.* to pour out in every direction; to spread; to scatter; to cause gases to mix by diffusion; *v.i.* to mix; to spread, as a liquid. **diffuse** (dif·ūs′) *a.* widely spread; wordy. **diffusely** (di·fūs′·li·) *adv.* **-ness** *n.* **diffusible** *a.* **diffusion** *n.* act or process of scattering abroad; (*Chem.*) term applied to the intermixture of two gases or fluids without chemical combination. **diffusive** *a.* spreading; expanding; prolix. **diffusively** *adv.* **diffusiveness** *n.* [L. *dis,* away; *fundere,* to pour].

dig (dig) *v.t.* to break and turn up earth, as with a spade; to excavate; to delve; (*Colloq.*) to poke or nudge someone; *v.i.* to till the soil; to use a spade, etc. *pr.p.* **-ging.** *pa.p., pa.t.* **dug.** *n.* a thrust; poke; jibe or taunt. **-ger** *n.* **-gings** *n.pl.* areas where mining or other digging is carried on [prob. O.Fr. *diguer,* to hallow out].

di·gest (da·jest′) *v.t.* to convert, as food in the stomach, into a substance which can be readily absorbed into the blood; to assimilate in the mind; to think over; *v.i.* to undergo digestion. **digest** (dī′·jest) *n.* a concise summary or *the Digest,* an abridged version of the Roman laws compiled by order of Emperor Justinian; a magazine containing condensed version of articles already published elsewhere. **-er** *n.* **-ible** *a.* capable of being digested; easily assimilated. **-ibility** *n.* **digestion** *n.* the act of digesting. **digestive** *a.* promoting, or pert. to digestion; *n.* any medicine that aids digestion [L. *digerere,* to arrange].

dig·it (dij′·it) *n.* a finger; a finger's breadth, or three-quarters of an inch; (*Arith.*) integer under 10, so-called from counting on the fingers. **-al** *a.* pert. to the fingers; *n.* one of the keys of piano or organ. **-alin** *n.* the drug obtained from leaves of digitalis. **-alis** *n.* a genus of hardy plants including the foxglove; a strong drug obtained from foxglove, and used medicinally as sedative, narcotic and as cardiac stimulant. **-ate, -ated** *a.* having divisions like fingers. **-igrade** *n.* an animal which walks on its toes (e.g. dog); *a.* walking on the toes [L. *digitus,* a finger or toe].

di·glot (dī′·glat) *a.* speaking two languages [Gk. *dis,* twice; *glotta,* tongue].

dig·ni·fy (dig′·na·fi) *v.t.* to invest with dignity or honor; to exalt; to ennoble. **dignified** *a.* [L. *dignus,* worthy; *facere,* to make].

dig·ni·ty (dig′·na·ti·) *n.* state of being dignified in mind, character, or bearing; loftiness; high office or rank. **dignitary** *n.* one who holds a high position [L. *dignus,* worthy].

di·graph (dī′·graf) *n.* two vowels or two consonants combined to express one sound as *ea* in head [Gk. *dis,* twice; *graphein,* to write].

di·gress (da·gres′, dī·gres′) *v.i.* to wander from the main theme, topic, or argument; to be diffuse. **digression** *n.* **digressional, -ive** *a.* [L. *dis-,* aside; *gradus,* a step].

di·he·dral (dī·hē′·dral) *a.* having two plane faces. **dihedron** *n.* a figure with two plane surfaces [Gk. *dis,* twice; *hedra,* base].

dike, dyke (dīk) *n.* an artificial embankment to prevent inundation of low lying ground, as in Holland; (*Geol.*) igneous rock, once molten, which has filled up fissures of stratified rocks [O.E. *dic,* a ditch].

di·lap·i·date (da·lap′·a·dāt) *v.t.* (*Lit.*) to pull stone from stone; to suffer to fall into ruin; to despoil; *v.i.* to be in a condition of disrepair. **-d** *a.* in ruins; decayed; tumbled down; (of persons) shabby; unkempt. **dilapidation** *n.* [L. *di-,* asunder; *lapis,* a stone].

di·late (dī·lāt′) *v.t.* to swell out; to expand in all directions; to distend; *v.i.* to widen; (*Fig.*) to expatiate; to speak at length. **dilatable** *a.* capable of dilation; elastic. **dilatancy, dilatation, dilation** *n.* expansion; a spreading or extending in all directions. **dilatant** *a.* **dilator, -r** *n.* [L. *di-,* apart; *latus,* borne].

dil·a·tory (dil′·a·tōr·i·) *a.* tardy; inclined to procrastination; loitering. **dilatorily** *adv.* **dilatoriness** *n.* [L. *dilatus,* postponed].

di·lem·ma (di·lem′·a) *n.* choice between alternatives equally undesirable; a predicament; (*Logic*) an argument which presents an antagonist with alternatives equally conclusive against him, whichever he chooses. **on the horns of a dilemma,** confronted with a perplexity [Gk. *dis,* twice; *lemma,* an assumption].

dil·et·tante (dil·a·tan′·te·) *n.* a lover of the fine arts, esp. in a superficial way; a dabbler. *pl.* **dilettantes, -ti. dilettantish** *a.* **dilettantism, dilettanteism** *n.* [It.].

dil·i·gent (dil′·a·jant) *a.* steady and constant in application; industrious; assiduous. **diligence** *n.* **-ly** *adv.* [L. *diligere,* to choose].

dill (dil) *n.* a perennial yellow-flowered herb used in medicines and flavoring [O.E. *dile*].

dil·ly-dal·ly (dil′·i-dal′·i·) *v.i.* (*Colloq.*) to

loiter; to delay [reduplication of *dally*].

di·lute (di·lōōt′) *v.t.* to make thinner or more liquid by admixture; to reduce the strength of by addition of something, esp. water; to weaken the force of; *v.i.* to become thin; *a.* reduced in strength; attenuated; thinned down; **diluent** *a.* diluting; making weaker; *n.* that which thins or weakens the strength, color, etc. **-ness** *n.* **dilution** *n.* [L. *diluere*, dissolve].

di·lu·vi·um (di·lōō′·vi·ạm) *n.* a surface deposit of sand, gravel, etc. regarded as glacial drift. **diluvial, diluvian** *a.* pert. to or produced by a flood, esp. the deluge in Noah's time [L. *diluvium*, flood].

dim (dim) *a.* not bright or distinct; faint; partially obscure; shadowy; (*Fig.*) dull of apprehension; vague; *v.t.* to cloud; to cause to grow dim; *v.i.* to become dull or indistinct. *pr.p.* **-ming.** *pa.p.*, *pa.t.* **-med. -ly** *adv.* **-mer** *n.* in motoring, a device to diminish power of headlights. **-ness** *n.* [O.E. *dim*].

dime (dīm) *n.* U.S. silver coin equal to 10 cents [L. *decima*, a tenth].

di·men·sion (di·men′·shạn) *n.* a measurement of extent in a single direction (length, breadth, height, or thickness); usually *pl.* measurement in three directions (e.g. of a room); extent; capacity; (*Fig.*) importance. **-al** *a.* capable of being measured; pert. to a dimension [L. *dimensio*, a measuring].

dim·e·ter (dim′·ạ·tẹr) *n.* a verse with two measures or accents [Gk. *dis*, twice; *metron*, a measure].

di·min·ish (di·min′·ish) *v.t.* to cause to grow less; to weaken; to reduce; (*Mus.*) to lower a note by a semi-tone; *v.i.* to become smaller. **-ed** *a.* lessened; lowered; (*Mus.*) lowered by a semi-tone [L. *diminuere*, to break in small pieces].

di·min·u·en·do (di·min·yoo·en′·dō) *n.* (*Mus.*) a gradual decrease in volume of sound and marked >, the opposite of *crescendo* [It.].

dim·i·nu·tion (dim·ạ·nū′·shạn) *n.* the act or process of diminishing; state of being reduced in size, quality, or amount. **diminutive** *a.* of small size; minute; (*Gram.*) applied to a suffix expressing smallness, e.g. *-let, -ock*; *n.* a word formed from another by addition of such a suffix, as *hamlet, hillock* [L. *diminuere*, to break in small pieces].

dim·i·ty (dim′·i·ti·) *n.* a thin cotton cloth ribbed or figured [prob. Gk. *dimitos*, of double thread].

di·morph·ic (dī·mawr′·fik) *a.* existing in two forms; (*Chem.*) capable of crystallizing in two forms under different degrees of temperature. **dimorphism** *n.* **dimorphous** *a.* [Gk. *dis*, twice; *morphē*, shape].

dim·ple (dim′·pl) *n.* a slight natural depression or hollow on cheek, chin, arm, etc.; a slight indentation in any surface; *v.t.* to mark with dimples; *v.i.* to become dimpled [prob. dimin. of *dip*].

din (din) *n.* a loud, continuous noise; racket; clamor; *v.t.* to strike, stun with noise; to harass with insistent repetition. *pr.p.* **-ning.** *pa.p.*, *pa.t.* **-ned** [O.E. *dyn*, noise].

dine (dīn) *v.t.* to entertain at dinner; to give facilities or accommodation for dining; *v.i.* to take dinner. **-r** *n.* one who dines; a compartment on a railway train for serving meals to passengers. Also **dining car. dinette** (dī-net′) *n.* a small dining room. **dinner** (din′·ẹr) *n.* the principal meal of the day. **dinner jacket,** a black coat (without tails) worn as informal evening dress [Fr. *diner*, to dine].

ding (ding) *v.t.* to ring, as a bell. **—dong** *n.* the sound of bells continuously rung; *a.* monotonous; strenuously contested as in *ding-dong* struggle [Scand.].

din·ghy, dingy, dingey (ding′·gi·) *n.* a small boat [Hind. *dengi*, a boat].

din·gy (din′·ji·) *a.* soiled; sullied; of a darkish color. **dinginess** *n.* [prob. conn. with *dung*].

di·no·saur (dī′·nạ·sawr) *n.* a gigantic extinct four-footed reptile of the Mesozoic age [Gk. *deinos*, terrible; *sauros*, a lizard].

dint (dint) *n.* a mark or depression made by a blow; force or energy exerted; *v.t.* to make a mark or dent by a blow. **by dint of,** by means of [O.E. *dynl*, a blow].

di·o·cese (dī′·ạ·sēs) *n.* the district in which a bishop exercises ecclesiastical jurisdiction. **diocesan** (dī·ás′·es·ạn or dī′·ạ·sē·zạn) *a.* pert. to a diocese; *n.* a bishop or holder of a diocese [Gk. *dioikēsis*, administration].

di·oe·cious, diecious (dī·ē′·shus) *a.* (*Bot.*) having the stamens (male) and pistils (female) borne by separate plants of the same species; (*Zool.*) having the male and female reproductive organs separate [Gk. *dis*, twice; *oikos*, a dwelling].

di·op·ter, dioptre (dī·áp′·tẹr) *n.* the unit for measuring power of a lens [Gk. *dioptron*, instrument for measuring angles].

di·o·ram·a (dī·ạ·ra′·mạ) *n.* a miniature, three-dimensional scene; a painting viewed through an opening, varied effects of reality being realized by manipulation of lights [Gk. *dia*, through; *horama*, a sight].

di·ox·ide (dī·ák′·sīd) *n.* a substance the molecules of which comprise one part metal, two parts oxygen [Gk. *dis*, twice; *oxus*, acid].

dip (dip) *v.t.* to immerse momentarily in a liquid; to dye; to lower and raise again, as a flag; to wash as a sheep; to baptize by immersion; *v.i.* to sink below at a certain level; to glance cursorily at; (*Geol.*) to incline downwards. *pr.p.* **-ping.** *pa.p.*, *pa.t.* **-ped.** *n.* a liquid into which something is dipped; immersion; (*Geol.*) inclination downward of rock strata; a candle made by dipping wick in melted tallow. **-per** *n.* something used for dipping; a semi-aquatic diving bird; (*Astron.*) the Great Bear; the Little Bear. **-py** *a.* (*Slang*) crazy [O.E. *dyppan*, to plunge].

diph·the·ri·a (dif·thẹr′·i·ạ) *n.* epidemic disease affecting mainly throat and air passages. **-l, diphtheric, diphtheritic,** *a.*

diph·thong (dif′·thawng) *n.* a union of two vowel sounds pronounced as one, as in p*oi*se, m*ou*th. **-al** *a.* **-ally** *adv.* **-ize** *v.t.* to develop a diphthong from a single vowel. **diphthongization** *n.* [Gk. *dis*, twice; *phthongos*, sound].

di·plex (dī′·pleks) *a.* (*Radio*) pert. to the reception or transmission of two messages simultaneously.

dip·lo·car·di·ac (dip′·lō·kár′·di·ak) *a.* (*Biol.*) having, as some birds, a double or divided heart [Gk. *diplous*, double; *kardia*, the heart].

di·plo·ma (di·plō′·mạ) *n.* a document or certificate conferring some honor, privilege, or degree, as that granted to graduates of a university; *v.t.* to furnish with a diploma [Gk. *diploma*, a folded letter].

di·plo·ma·cy (di·plō′·mạ·si·) *n.* the art of conducting international negotiations; political dexterity; tact in dealing with people. **diplomat, diplomatist** *n.* one skilled in the art of handling difficult international or personal relations; one engaged in administering international law. **diplomatic, -al** *a.* pert. to diplomacy. **diplomatically** *adv.* **diplomatic corps,** the body of accredited foreign diplomatists resident in any capital [Gk. *diploma*, a folded letter].

di·po·lar (dī·pō′·lẹr) *a.* having two poles, as a magnet. **dipolarize** *v.t.* to magnetize.

dip·so·ma·ni·a (dip·sạ·mā′·ni·ạ) *n.* an uncontrollable craving for alcoholic stimulants. **dipsomaniac** *n.* **dipsomaniacal** *a.* [Gk. *dipsa*, thirst; *mania*, madness].

Dip·ter·a (dip′·tẹr·ạ) *n.* an order of insects, including common housefly, gnat, mosquito, which have only two wings. **dipteral** *a.* **dipteran** *n.* a dipterous insect. **dipterous** *a.* of the order *Diptera* [Gk. *dis*, twice; *pteron*, a wing].

dip·tych (dip'·tik) *n.* an ancient writing tablet hinged in the middle and folding together like a book; a pair of carvings or pictures similarly hinged [Gk. *diptuchos*, folded double].

dire (dīr) *a.* dreadful; calamitous; disastrous. Also **-ful. -ly, -fully** *adv.* [L. *dirus*, terrible].

di·rect (di·rect', dī'·rect) *a.* straight; straightforward; immediate; in line of descent; sincere; unambiguous; *v.t.* to aim at; to guide; to point out the way; to manage (a business); to prescribe a course or line of procedure; to write the name and address on a missive, etc.; *v.i.* to give direction; to act as a guide; *adv.* in a straight line. **direction** *n.* act of directing; instruction; guidance; management; order; superscription; prescription; address (on a letter); line taken by a moving body. **directional, -ing, -ive** *a.* tending to guide or to advise. **-ive** *n.* orders from a supreme authority. **-ly** *adv.* in a straight line; straightway; immediately after. **-ness** *n.* the quality of being direct, frank, or unimpeded by extraneous details. **-or** *n.* (*fem.* **-ress**) one who directs; a member of a board of managers in a large commercial firm, hospital, etc.; that which regulates a machine; in gunnery, an optical instrument for calculating line of firing. **-orate** *n.* a board of directors. **-orial** *a.* **-ory** *a.* containing directions; guiding; *n.* a book containing the alphabetically arranged names and addresses of the residents of a town or district; a collection of rules. — **current** (*abbrev.* D.C.) (*Elect.*) a current flowing in one direction (contrasting with *alternating current* (A.C.)). **direction finder** (*Radio*) an aerial which determines direction of incoming radio signals (*abbrev.* D/F) [L. *dirigere, directum*, to make straight].

dirge (durj) *n.* a funeral chant; a lament. **-ful** *a.* funereal [fr. L. *dirige* (lead thou), the opening word of Latin burial anthem].

dir·i·gi·ble (dir'·a·ja·bl) *a.* capable of being directed or steered; *n.* a navigable balloon elongated in shape and propelled by engine-driven propellers [L. *dirigere*, to direct].

dirk (durk) *n.* a short dagger; *v.t.* to stab with a dirk.

dirn·dl (durn'·dl) *n.* a type of skirt [Ger. *Dirne*, a girl].

dirt (durt) *n.* any filthy substance, as mud, dust, excrement; loose soil; rubbish; squalor; obscenity. —**cheap** *a.* (*Colloq.*) uncommonly cheap. **-ily** *adv.* in a dirty manner; meanly. **-iness** *n.* **-y** *a.* foul; unclean; muddy; base; (of weather) stormy; rainy; *v.t.* to befoul [M.E. *drit*, excrement].

dis- *pref.* implying *separation*, as in *dismiss*; *negation*, as in *disband*; *deprivation*, as in *disanimate*; *thoroughness*, as in *disannul*.

dis·a·ble (dis·ā'·bl) *v.t.* to make incapable or physically unfit; to disqualify. **-ment** *n.* disability. **disability** *n.* the state of being disabled; incapacity.

dis·a·buse (dis·a·būz') *v.t.* to free from misapprehension or error; to undeceive.

dis·ad·van·tage (dis·ad·van'·tij) *n.* want of advantage; a drawback; a hindrance; a handicap; detriment; hurt. **disadvantageous** (dis·-ad·van·tā'·jas) *a.* **disadvantageously** *adv.*

dis·af·fect (dis·a·fekt') *v.t.* to alienate the affection of; to estrange; to fill with discontent. **-ed** *a.* discontented; disloyal (esp. to government). **-edly** *adv.* **-edness, disaffection** *n.*

dis·af·firm (dis·a·furm') *v.t.* to annul; to invalidate; to reverse a decision. **disaffirmation** *n.*

dis·a·gree (dis'·a·grē) *v.i.* to be at variance; to differ in opinion; to be incompatible; to be detrimental to health (of food, climate, etc.). **-able** *a.* **-ably** *adv.* **-ment** *n.* difference of opinion; discord; discrepancy.

dis·al·low (dis·a·lou') *v.t.* to refuse to allow; to reject as untrue or invalid. **-able** *a.* **-ance** *n.*

dis·ap·pear (dis·a·pir') *v.i.* to vanish; to become invisible; to cease to exist. **disappearance** *n.*

dis·ap·point (dis·a·point') *v.t.* to fail to realize the hopes of; to frustrate; to foil. **-ed** *a.* **-ing** *a.* causing disappointment. **-ment** *n.* state of being disappointed; the frustration of one's hopes; miscarriage which disappoints.

dis·ap·pro·ba·tion (dis·ap·ra·bā'·shan) *n.* act of disapproving; censure; mental condemnation of what is considered wrong.

dis·ap·prove (dis·a·proov') *v.t.* to form an unfavorable judgment of; to censure; to refuse to sanction; to dislike; *v.i.* (foll. by *of*). **disapproval** *n.* **disapprovingly** *adv.*

dis·arm (dis·arm') *v.t.* to deprive of arms; to render unable to attack; (*Fig.*) to conciliate; to allay; *v.i.* to lay down arms, esp. national armaments. **-ament** *n.* the act of reducing, in peacetime, the output of military and naval weapons as a prevention of war; the state of being disarmed. **-ing** *a.* ingenuous.

dis·ar·range (dis·a·rānj') *v.t.* to disturb the order or arrangement of; to throw into confusion. **-ment** *n.*

dis·ar·ray (dis·a·rā') *v.t.* to break the array of; to throw into disorder; to undress; *n.* disorder; confusion; state of undress.

dis·as·so·ci·ate (dis·a·sō'·shi·āt) *v.t.* to disunite; to dissociate.

dis·as·ter (diz·as'·ter) *n.* an adverse happening; sudden misfortune; catastrophe. **disastrous** *a.* [L. *dis*; *astrum*, a star].

dis·a·vow (dis·a·vou') *v.t.* to refuse to acknowledge; to repudiate. **-al, -ment** *n.*

dis·band (dis·band') *v.t.* to disperse (troops); to break up an organization; to dismiss; *v.i.* to break up; to disperse. **-ment** *n.*

dis·bar (dis·bar') *v.t.* (*Law*) to expel a lawyer from the bar or from the legal profession. *pr.p.* **-ring.** *pa.p., pa.t.* **-red. -ment** *n.*

dis·be·lieve (dis·ba·lēv') *v.t.* to maintain to be untrue; to refuse to believe; *v.i.* to place no reliance or belief (foll. by *on* or *in*). **disbelief** *n.* **disbeliever** *n.*

dis·burse (dis·burs') *v.t.* to pay out money; to expend. **-ment** *n.* expenditure. **-r** *n.* [L. *dis*, apart; Fr. *bourse*, purse].

disc See **disk**.

dis·card (dis·kard') *v.t.* and *v.i.* to put aside; to cast off; *n.* (dis'·kard) the act of discarding; anything thrown out as useless.

dis·car·nate (dis·kar'·nit) *a.* bereft of flesh; having no physical body.

dis·cern (di·surn') *v.t.* to distinguish clearly esp. by the sight; to perceive by the mind; to behold as separate. **-er** *n.* **-ible** *a.* **-ing** *a.* discriminating; judging with insight. **-ment** *n.* power or faculty of judging [L. *dis*, apart; *cernere*, to sift].

dis·charge (dis·charj') *v.t.* to free from a load or weight; to unload a cargo; to fire off the charge with which gun is loaded; to emit, as smoke; to perform, as a duty; to pay, as an account or a debt; to demobilize, as soldiers, etc.; to dismiss, as for failure in service or duty; *n.* act of discharging; performance; matter which exudes, as from an abscess; that which is discharged; the rate of flow of a liquid or waste matter through a pipe [Fr. *décharger*, to unload].

dis·ci·ple (di·sī'·pl) *n.* one who receives instruction from another; one who adheres to a particular school of philosophy, religious thought, or art; a follower, esp. one of the twelve apostles of Christ. **-ship** *n.* [L. *discipulus*, a pupil].

dis·ci·pline (dis'·a·plin) *n.* instruction; training of the mind, or body, or the moral faculties; subjection to authority; self-control; *v.t.* to train; to improve behavior by judicious penal methods. **disciplinarian** *n.* one who enforces rigid discipline; a martinet. **disciplinary** *a.* **-r** *n.* [L. *disciplina*, training].

dis·claim (dis·klām') *v.t.* to renounce claim to, or responsibility for; to disown; to repudiate; *v.i.* to give up all claim (foll. by *to*).

-ant *n.* **-er** *n.* denial; disavowal; repudiation.
dis·close (dis·klōz′) *v.t.* to unclose; to reveal; to divulge; to bring to light. **-r** *n.* **disclosure** *n.*
dis·col·or (dis·kul′·ẹr) *v.t.* to spoil the color of; to stain; *v..i* to become discolored or stained. **-ation, -ment** *n.* **-ed** *a.* stained.
dis·com·fit (dis·kum′·fit) *v.t.* to defeat; to disconcert; to foil; to baffle. **-ure** *n.* [O.Fr. *desconfit*, defeated].
dis·com·fort (dis·kum′·fẹrt) *n.* want of comfort; uneasiness; pain; *v.t.* to impair the comfort of; to make uneasy.
dis·com·mode (dis·kạ·mōd′) *v.t.* to put to inconvenience; to incommode; to disturb.
dis·com·pose (dis·kạm·pōz′) *v.t.* to upset the self-possession of; to disturb; to disarrange. **discomposure** *n.*
dis·con·cert (dis·kạn·surt′) *v.t.* to discompose; to embarrass. **-ment** *n.* state of disagreement.
dis·con·nect (dis·kạn·ekt′) *v.t.* to separate; to sever; to disjoint. **-ed** *a.* separated; incoherent.
dis·con·so·late (dis·kȧn′·sạ·lit) *a.* destitute of comfort or consolation; forlorn; utterly dejected. **-ly** *adv.* **-ness, disconsolation** *n.*
dis·con·tent (dis·kạn·tent′) *a.* not content; dissatisfied; *n.* want of contentment; dissatisfaction; state of being aggrieved; *v.t.* to cause to be ill-pleased; to dissatisfy. **-ed** *a.* **-edly** *adv.* **-edness, -ment** *n.*
dis·con·tin·ue (dis·kạn·tin′·ū) *v.t.* to interrupt; to break off; to stop; *v.i.* to cease. **discontinuance, discontinuation** *n.* interruption; cessation. **discontinuity** *n.* want of continuity. **discontinuous** *a.* intermittent.
dis·cord (dis′·kawrd) *n.* want of concord or agreement; lack of harmony; strife; (*Mus.*) a combination of inharmonious sounds. **discord** (dis·kawrd′) *v.i.* to disagree; to be out of tune. **discordance, discordancy** *n.* lack of spiritual (or musical) harmony. **discordant** *a.* out of harmony; jarring; dissonant. **discordantly** *adv.* [L. *discordia*, variance].
dis·count (dis·kount′) *v.t.* to pay in advance (a bill of exchange not yet due); to deduct a sum or rate per cent from; to disregard; *v.i.* to lend money with discount. **discount** (dis′·kount) *n.* a sum of money refunded on prompt payment of a bill; the allowance made on the retail price by a wholesaler to a retailer; a deduction [O.Fr. *descompter*, to count off].
dis·coun·te·nance (dis·koun′·tạn·ạns) *v.t.* to refuse to countenance or give approval to.
dis·cour·age (dis·kur′·ij) *v.t.* to deprive of courage; to dishearten; to deter. **-ment** *n.* act of discouraging; state of being discouraged; dissuasion; dejection. **discouraging** *a.*
dis·course (dis′·kōrs) *n.* a formal speech; a sermon; a dissertation; reasoning from premises; conversation. **discourse** (dis·kōrs′) *v.t.* to utter; *v.i.* to lecture; to converse; to hold forth (foll. usually by *upon*) [L. *discursus*, running to and fro].
dis·cour·te·ous (dis·kur′·ti·ạs) *a.* lacking in courtesy; rude. **-ly** *adv.* **discourtesy** *n.*
dis·cov·er (dis·kuv′·ẹr) *v.t.* to find out (esp. something hitherto unknown); to bring to light. **-able** *a.* **-er** *n.* **-y** *n.* the act of finding out; that which is discovered [Fr. *découvrir*, to reveal].
dis·cred·it (dis·kred′·it) *v.t.* to bring into disrepute; to disbelieve; *n.* loss of credit or of reputation. **-able** *a.* damaging; injurious to reputation.
dis·creet (dis·krēt′) *a.* prudent; circumspect; judicious; cautious (in action or speech). **-ly** *adv.* [L. *discretus*, separated, prudent].
dis·crep·an·cy (dis·krep′·an·si·) *n.* inconsistency; variance; difference. **discrepant** *a.* not tallying; inconsistent [L. *discrepare*, to jar].
dis·crete (dis·krēt′) *a.* separate; distinct. **-ly** *adv.* **-ness** *n.* [L. *discretus*, separated].
dis·cre·tion (dis·kresh′·ạn) *n.* the quality of being discreet; prudence; discernment; liberty to act according to one's judgment. **-al, -ary**

a. **ally** *adv.* [L. *discretus*, separated, prudent].
dis·crim·i·nate (dis·krim′·ạ·nāt) *v.t.* to detect as different; to distinguish; to select; *v.i.* to make a distinction in. **-ly** *adv.* **discriminating** *a.* able to observe subtle differences; distinctive. **discriminatingly** *adv.* **discrimination** *n.* faculty of drawing nice distinctions; perception; a difference in treatment between persons, things, etc. **discriminative** *a.* marking a difference; characteristic [L. *discriminare*, to divide].
dis·cur·sive (dis·kur′·siv) *a.* passing from one topic to another; rambling; digressive; arguing from premises to conclusion. **-ly** *adv.* **-ness** *n.* **discursory** *a.* [L. *discursus*].
dis·cus (dis′·kạs) *n.* a circular plate of stone or metal, used in athletic contests [Gk. *diskos*, quoit].
dis·cuss (dis·kus′) *v.t.* to examine critically; to exchange ideas on; (*Colloq.*) to consume, as wine. **-able (or -ible)** *a.* **discussion** *n.* debate; act of exchanging opinions [L. *discutere*, to agitate].
dis·dain (dis·dān′) *v.t.* to look down upon, as unworthy or despicable; to scorn; *n.* scorn; arrogance; contempt. **-ful** *a.* **-fully** *adv.* **-fulness** *n.* [O.Fr. *desdeigner*, to scorn].
dis·ease (di·zēz′) *n.* an unhealthy condition of mind or body; malady; **-d** *a.* [O.Fr. *desaise*, discomfort].
dis·em·bark (dis·em·bȧrk′) *v.t.* to put on shore; to land passengers, goods, etc.; *v.i.* to land. **-ation, -ment** *n.*
dis·em·bod·y (dis·im·bȧd′·i·) *v.t.* to free from the body or flesh. **disembodiment** *n.*
dis·em·bowel (dis·im·bou′·ạl) *v.t.* to take out the bowels; to gut; to eviscerate.
dis·en·chant (dis·in·chant′) *v.t.* to free from enchantment or glamor; to disillusion.
dis·en·fran·chise (dis·in·fran′·chīz) *v.t.* to deprive of the right to vote. **-ment** *n.*
dis·en·gage (dis·in·gāj′) *v.t.* to unfasten; to separate from an attachment; to release. **-d** *a.* unattached; available; at leisure. **-ment** *n.*
dis·en·tan·gle (dis·in·tang′·gl) *v.t.* to unravel; to untwist; to put in order.
dis·es·tab·lish (dis·ạs·tab′·lish) *v.t.* to deprive of established position; to deprive (a church) of state aid and recognition. **-ment** *n.*
dis·fa·vor (dis·fā′·vẹr) *n.* disapproval; dislike; state of being out of favor; *v.t.* to regard unfavorably.
dis·fig·ure (dis·fig′·yẹr) *v.t.* to mar the appearance of; to deface; to deform. **-ment** *n.* a defect; a blemish.
dis·fran·chise See **disenfranchise.**
dis·frock (dis·frȧk′) *v.t.* to unfrock; to deprive of the right to wear clerical garb.
dis·gorge (dis·gawrj′) *v.t.* to eject from the throat; to pour out (as a river into the sea); to hand over. **-ment** *n.*
dis·grace (dis·grās′) *n.* dishonor; discredit; shameful conduct; *v.t.* to bring dishonor to; to degrade. **-ful** *a.* shameful; discreditable.
dis·grun·tled (dis·grun′·tld) *a.* vexed; sulky.
dis·guise (dis·gīz′) *v.t.* to change the outward appearance of; to misrepresent; *n.* dress, manner, voice, etc. assumed to hide a person's real identity [O.Fr. *desguiser*, to change costume].
dis·gust (dis·gust′) *n.* loathing; nausea; aversion; repugnance; *v.t.* to provoke disgust in. **-edly** *adv.* **-ing** *a.* [L. *dis*; *gustus*, taste].
dish (dish) *n.* a plate or shallow concave vessel for serving food; the food in such a vessel; any concave object, like a dish; *v.t.* to put in a dish; [O.E. *disc*, a plate].
dis·ha·bille (dis·ạ·bēl′) *n.* partial undress; careless toilet for indoors. Also **deshabille** [Fr.]. [harmony; discord.
dis·har·mo·ny (dis·har′·mạ·ni·) *n.* lack of
dis·heart·en (dis·hȧr′·tn) *v.t.* to deprive of courage, confidence, or hope; to depress.
di·shev·el (di·shev′·ạl) *v.t.* to ruffle the hair;

to cause the hair or clothes to be untidy or unkempt; *v.i.* to spread in disorder. **-ment** *n.* [L. *dis*, in different directions; *capillus*, the hair].

dis·hon·est (dis·ȧn'·ist) *a.* lacking in honesty; inclined to cheat; unprincipled. **-ly** *adv.* **-ty** *n.*

dis·hon·or (dis·ȧn'·er) *n.* loss of honor; disgrace; shame; indignity; *v.t.* to disgrace; to seduce; to refuse payment of. **-able** *a.* shameful; lacking integrity. **-ableness** *n.* **-ably** *adv.*

dis·il·lu·sion (dis·i·lŏŏ'·zhan) *v.t.* to free from illusion; to make the truth apparent; *n.* state of being disillusioned. **-ment** *n.*

dis·in·cline (dis·in·klīn') *v.t.* to make unwilling; to excite dislike or aversion. **disinclination** *n.* unwillingness; reluctance; dislike.

dis·in·fect (dis·in·fekt') *v.t.* to free from infection; to destroy disease germs. **-ant** *n. a.* germicide. **disinfection** *n.* **-or** *n.*

dis·in·her·it (dis·in·her'·it) *v.t.* to deprive of rights and privileges of an heir.**-ance** *n.*

dis·in·te·grate (dis·in'·tȧ·grāt) *v.t.* to break up; *v.i.* to crumble to pieces; to be resolved into elements. **disintegration** *n.* a gradual breaking up.

dis·in·ter (dis·in·tur') *v.t.* to disentomb; to exhume; to unearth.

dis·in·ter·est·ed (dis·in'·tȧ·res·tȧd) *a.* free from self-interest; unprejudiced; (*Colloq.*) indifferent. **-ness** *n.*

dis·join (dis·join') *v.t.* to sever; to disunite. **-t** *v.t.* to separate at the joints; to make incoherent; *v.i.* to fall to pieces. **-ted** *a.* unconnected; (of speech) rambling; incoherent.

dis·junct (dis·jungkt') *a.* disjoined. **disjunction** *n.* disunion; severance; disconnection; (*Logic*) a statement of alternative possibilities. **-ive** *a.* [L. *dis; jugere, junctum*, to join].

disk, disc (disk) *n.* a at circular plate or surface; the face of sun or moon. **-al** *a.* — **jockey** *n.* (*Colloq.*) announcer of a radio program of recorded music [Gk. *diskos*, a round plate].

dis·like (dis·līk') *v.t.* to have an aversion to; *n.* distaste; antipathy.

dis·lo·cate (dis·lō·kāt') *v.t.* to put out of place or out of joint; to upset the normal working of. **dislocatedly** *adv.* **dislocation** *n.* (*Med.*) the displacement of a bone.

dis·lodge (dis·làj') *v.t.* to remove from a position of rest, hiding, or defense; *v.i.* to depart. **dislodg(e)ment** *n.*

dis·loy·al (dis·loi'·ȧl) *a.* failing in duty or allegiance; faithless; treacherous. **-ly** *adv.* **-ty** *n.*

dis·mal (diz'·mȧl) *a.* gloomy; dreary; depressing; bleak. **-ly** *adv.* **-ness, -ity** *n.* [L. *dies mali*, ill-omened days].

dis·man·tle (dis·man'·tl) *v.t.* to strip of furnishings; to take apart [O.Fr. *desmanteler*, to strip].

dis·may (dis·mā') *v.t.* to alarm; to deprive of courage; to fill with apprehension; *n.* consternation; loss of courage [L. *dis*, neg.; O.H. Ger. *magan*, to be strong].

dis·mem·ber (dis·mem'·ber) *v.t.* to tear limb from limb; to mutilate. **-ment** *n.*

dis·miss (dis·mis') *v.t.* to send away; to disperse; to allow to go; to discharge from employment; to banish (from the mind). **-al** *n.*

dis·mount (dis·mount') *v.i.* to alight from a horse, bicycle, etc.; *v.t.* to bring down from a place of elevation.

dis·o·bey (dis·ȧ·bā') *v.t.* to disregard orders or instructions; to refuse to do what is commanded. **disobedient** *a.* refusing to obey. **disobediently** *adv.* **disobedience** *n.*

dis·o·blige (dis·ȧ·blīj') *v.t.* to offend by an act of incivility; to refuse to grant a request to. **disobliging** *a.* ungracious; unwilling to accede to another's wishes.

dis·or·der (dis·awr'·der) *n.* want of order; muddle; confusion; discomposure; ailment of body or mind; *v.t.* to throw out of order; to upset. **-ed** *a.* out of order; deranged. **-ly** *a.*

dis·or·gan·ize (dis·awr'·gȧ·nīz) *v.t.* to upset the structure or regular system of; to throw into disorder. **disorganic** *a.* **disorganization**

dis·own (dis·ōn') *v.t.* to repudiate ownership; to renounce.

dis·par·age (dis·par'·ij) *v.t.* to belittle; to lower in rank or reputation; to depreciate. **-ment** *n.* unjust comparison; act of undervaluing [O.Fr. *desparagier*, to marry unequally].

dis·pa·rate (dis'·pȧ·rit) *a.* essentially different; dissimilar. **-ness** *n.* [L. *dis*, neg.; *par*, equal].

dis·par·i·ty (dis·par'·ȧ·ti·) *n.* difference in form, character, or degree; incongruity.

dis·pas·sion (dis·pash'·ȧn) *n.* lack of feeling; serenity. **-ate** *a.* free from passion; impartial.

dis·patch, despatch (des·pach') *v.t.* to send away, esp. in haste; to execute promptly (as an order); to dispose of; to kill; *n.* something which is dispatched; speed; official message or document sent by special messenger; the sending out of mails, etc. **-er** *n.* [Fr. *dépêcher*, to expedite].

dis·pel (dis·pel') *v.t.* to drive away; to scatter; to cause to disappear. *pr.p.* **-ling.** *pa.p., pa.t.* **-led** [L. *dis*, apart; *pellere*, to drive].

dis·pense (dis·pens') *v.t.* to divide out in parts; to administer, as laws; to make up and distribute medicines; *v.i.* to excuse from; **dispensable** *a.* **dispensary** *n.* a place where medicines are made up and distributed. **dispensation** *n.* the act of distributing; the mode of God's dispensing mercies (e.g. *Mosaic, Christian*); a license to do what is normally prohibited. **-r** *n.* **to dispense with,** to do without [L. *dispensare*, to distribute by weight].

dis·perse (dis·purs') *v.t.* to scatter here and there; to spread; to distribute; to place at intervals (as troops); *v.i.* to separate; to vanish; to be dispelled. **dispersal** *n.* **dispersedly** *adv.* **dispersedness** *n.* **dispersion** *n.* the act of dispersing; the state of being dispersed; (*Opt.*) the separation of light into its constituent rays by refraction through a prism. **dispersive** *a.* [L. *di-*, asunder; *spargere, sparsum*, to scatter].

dis·pir·it (dis·pir'·it) *v.t.* to deject; to depress; to discourage. **-ed** *a.*

dis·place (dis·plās') *v.t.* to put out of position; to oust from situation or office. **-able** *a.* **Displaced Persons,** homeless war victims (*abbrev.* **D.P.**). **-ment** *n.* the act of putting out of place or removing from office; the weight of water, measured in tons, displaced by a floating ship.

dis·play (dis·plā') *v.t.* to unfold; to exhibit; to set out conspicuously; *n.* exhibition; ostentation; exaggerated expression of feeling [L. *displicare*, to unfold].

dis·please (dis·plēs') *v.t. and v.i.* to offend; to cause dissatisfaction to. **displeasure** (dis·plezh'·er) *n.* slight anger or irritation; dislike.

dis·pose (dis·pōs') *v.t.* to arrange; to regulate; to adjust; to bestow for an object or purpose; to produce a tendency or inclination; *v.i.* to settle; to determine. **disposable** *a.* liable, free, to be disposed of or employed. **disposal** *n.* the the act of disposing or disposing of; control; regulation; management; transference (of property by a will). **disposed** *a.* inclined; minded; arranged. **disposedly** *adv.* **disposition** *n.* the act of disposing; arrangement; guidance; temperament. **to dispose of,** to get rid of; to refute (an argument); to finish (a task) [L. *dis*, apart; *ponere*, to place].

dis·pos·sess (dis·pȧ·zes') *v.t.* to put out of possession; to deprive of property; to eject. **-ion** *n.* **-or** *n.*

dis·proof (dis·prŏŏf') *n.* the act of disproving; refutation; a proving to be erroneous.

dis·pro·por·tion (dis·prȧ·pōr'·shan) *n.* want of proportion, symmetry, proper quantity; *v.t.* to make unsuitable; to mismatch. **-able, -al, -ate, -ed** *a.*

dis·prove (dis·prŏŏv') *v.t.* to prove to be false; to refute; to prove the opposite of.

dis·pute (dis·pūt') *v.t.* to consider for and

against; to debate; to question the validity of; to argue; to discuss; to contend; *n.* an argument; a debate; a quarrel. **disputable** *a.* **disputably** *adv.* **disputability** *n.* the quality of being disputable. **disputant** *n.* one who takes part in a dispute; a controversialist. **disputation** *n.* a controversy in words; an academic discussion or argument. **disputatious, disputative** *a.* [L. *dis*, apart; *putare*, to think].

dis·qual·ify (dis·kwál'·a·fī) *v.t.* to make unfit for some special purpose; to incapacitate, to make ineligible; to deprive of legal power or right. **disqualification** *n.*

dis·qui·et (dis·kwī'·at) *v.t.* to render uneasy in mind; to disturb; to make restless; *n.* apprehensiveness; uneasiness **-ment, -ude** *n.* uneasiness; want of tranquility.

dis·qui·si·tion (dis·kwa·zish'·an) *n.* a formal enquiry into a subject by argument or discussion; a systematic treatise. **-al, -ary** *a.* [L. *disquirere*, to investigate].

dis·re·gard (dis·ri·gàrd') *v.t.* to take no notice of; to ignore; *n.* indifference; lack of attention.

dis·re·pair (dis·ri·per') *n.* state of being out of repair; delapidation.

dis·re·pute (dis·ri·pūt') *n.* discredit; state of being unpopular. **disreputable** *a.* degraded; discreditable. **disreputableness** *n.*

dis·re·spect (dis·ri·spekt') *n.* want of respect or deference; rudeness. **-ful** *a.* **-fully** *adv.*

dis·robe (dis·rōb') *v.t.* to undress; to discard official dress.

dis·rupt (dis·rupt') *v.t.* to break or burst asunder; to create a schism. **disruption** *n.* the act or process of disrupting; rent; breach. **disruptive** *a.* **disrupture** *n.* a bursting asunder [L. *dis*, apart; *rumpere*, to break].

dis·sat·is·fy (dis·sat'·is·fī) *v.t.* to fail to satisfy; to make discontented. **dissatisfaction** *n.*

dis·sect (dis·sekt') *v.t.* to cut up; to divide a plant or a dead body of man or animal for minute examination of its parts; (*Fig.*) to criticize in detail. **dissection** *n.* the act or science of dissecting; the part dissected. **-or** *n.* [L. *dis*, apart; *secare*, cut].

dis·sem·ble (dis·sem'·bl) *v.t.* to hide under a false semblance; to disguise; to ignore; *v.i.* to give an erroneous impression; to assume a false appearance; to be hypocritical. **-r** *n.* [L. *dissimulare*, to conceal a fact].

dis·sem·i·nate (dis·sem'·a·nāt) *v.t.* to sow, as seed; to scatter abroad; (*Fig.*) to broadcast; to circulate. **dissemination** *n.* scattering; circulation. **disseminative** *a.* **disseminator** *n.* [L. *dis*, asunder; *seminare*, to sow].

dis·sent (dis·sent') *v.i.* to differ in opinion; to disagree; to hold views differing from those of the established church; *n.* disagreement; difference of opinion; nonconformity. **dissension** *n.* open disagreement; quarrelling; discord. **-er** *n.* [L. *dis*, apart; *sentire*, to feel].

dis·ser·tate (dis·er·tāt) *v.i.* to discourse. **dissertation** *n.* a formal treatise or discourse, esp. a written thesis by a candidate for the Doctor's degree [L. *disserere*, to discuss].

dis·serve (dis·surv') *v.i.* to serve badly another's interests. **disservice** *n.* injury; harm; a bad turn.

dis·sev·er (dis·sev'·er) *v.t.* to separate; to disunite. **-ance, -ation, -ment** *n.*

dis·si·dent (dis'·a·dant) *a.* differing; disagreeing; *n.* a dissenter; a non-conformist. **dissidence** *n.* dissent [L. *dissidere*, to disagree].

dis·sim·i·lar (dis·sim'·a·ler) *a.* unlike; not similar. **dissimilarity, dissimilitude** *n.* unlikeness; difference. **-ly** *adv.*

dis·sim·u·late (dis·sim'·ya·lāt) *v.t.* to dissemble; to feign; *v.i.* to conceal one's true feelings; to be hypocritical. **dissimulation** *n.* the act of pretending [L. *dissimulare*].

dis·si·pate (dis'·a·pāt) *v.t.* to scatter; to squander; to dispel; *v.i.* to disappear; to waste away; to lead a dissolute life. **-d** *a.* dissolute; debauched. **dissipation** *n.* **dissipative** *a.* [L.

dissipare, to scatter].

dis·so·ci·ate (dis·sō'·shi·āt) *v.t.* to separate; to disunite; (*reflex.*) to disclaim connection with. **dissociability** *n.* **dissociable** *a.* capable of being dissociated; incongruous. **dissocial** *a.* anti-social. **dissociation** *n.* the act of dissociating or state of being dissociated; separation; (*Psych.*) term used to describe disunion of the mind, or split personality. **dissociative** *a.* [L. *dis*, asunder; *sociare*, to unite].

dis·sol·u·ble (di·sál'·ya·bl) *a.* capable of being dissolved, liquefied, melted, or decomposed.

dis·so·lute (dis'·a·lŏŏt) *a.* lax in morals; dissipated. **-ly** *adv.* **-ness** *n.* **dissolution** *n.* act of dissolving or passing into solution; disintegration, esp. of body at death; dismissal of an assembly; termination (of marriage, partnership, etc.) [L. *dis*, asunder; *solvere*, to loosen].

dis·solve (di·zálv') *v.t.* to break up, esp. a solid by the action of a liquid; to terminate (as a parliament); to annul (as a marriage); *v.i.* to melt; to waste away; to fade out; to be dismissed. **dissolvability, dissolvableness** *n.* **dissolvable** *a.* **dissolvent** *a.* having the power of dissolving substances [L. *dis*, asunder; *solvere*, to loosen].

dis·so·nant (dis'·a·nant) *a.* discordant; harsh; unharmonious. **dissonance** *n.* Also **dissonancy** [L. *dissonare*, to fail to harmonize].

dis·suade (di·swād') *v.t.* to persuade not to; to advise against. **-r** *n.* **dissuasion** *n.* **dissuasive** *a.* [L. *dis*, apart; *suadere*, to advise].

dis·syl·la·ble. See **disyllable.**

dis·taff (dis'·taf) *n.* a cleft stick for holding the fiber (wool, flax, etc.) from which thread is made in the process of hand spinning. **the distaff side**, the female line [O.E. *distaef*, the staff holding flax for spinning].

dis·tance (dis'·tans) *n.* the space between two objects; the interval between two events; remoteness; aloofness; reserve; *v.t.* to place at a distance; to outstrip; to surpass. **distant** *a.* far off; remote in time, place, or blood-relationship; aloof; reserved; faint. **distantly** *adv.* [L. *distantia*, remoteness].

dis·taste (dis·tāst') *n.* dislike, esp. of food; aversion. **-ful** *a.* unpleasant.

dis·tem·per (dis·tem'·per) *n.* a method of painting (also called *tempera*) with pigments, in powder form, mixed with any glutinous substance soluble in water; paint of this kind; *v.t.* to paint in distemper. [O.Fr. *destremper*, to moisten with water].

dis·tem·per (dis·tem'·per) *n.* a disordered state of mind or body; disease, esp. a highly infectious inflammatory disease in young dogs [L. *dis*, apart; *temperare*, to control].

dis·tend (dis·tend') *v.t.* to stretch out; to swell; to inflate. *v.i.* to become swollen or puffed out. **distensible** *a.* **distention, distension** *n.* [L. *dis*, apart; *tendere*, to stretch].

dis·till (dis·til') *v.t.* to vaporize and recondense a liquid; to cause to fall in drops; to cause to trickle; (*Fig.*) to extract the essential quality of (as wisdom); *v.i.* to undergo distillation; to drop; to trickle; to ooze. **-ate** *n.* the essence produced by distilling. **-ation** *n.* act of distilling. **-atory** *a.* used in distilling. **-er** *n.* **-ery** *n.* a place where distilling is carried on, esp. of alcohol [L. *de*, down; *stillare*, to drip].

dis·tinct (dis·tingkt') *a.* of marked difference; separate; clear; well-defined; obvious; precise. **distinction** *n.* separation; that which indicates individuality; eminence; repute; mark of honor bestowed for merit. **-ive** *a.* marking distinction or difference. **-ively** *adv.* **-iveness** *n.* **-ness** *n.* clarity [L. *distinctus*, separate].

dis·tin·guish (dis·ting'·gwish) *v.t.* to observe the difference between; to keep apart; to give individuality to; to discern; *v.i.* to make distinctions. **-ed** *a.* eminent; dignified. **-ing** *a.* peculiar; characteristic [L. *distinguere*, to separate].

dis·tort (dis·tawrt') *v.t.* to twist out of shape; to misrepresent; to pervert. **-ed** *a.* **-edly** *adv.*

distortion n. a twisting awry; misrepresentation; (Radio) any deviation from the original wave-form of speech or sound during transmission [L. dis, asunder; tortum, to twist].

dis·tract (dis·trakt') v.t. to draw away (the mind); to divert; to bewilder; to disturb mentally. **-ed** a. **-edly** adv. **-edness** n. **distraction** n. **-ive** a. **distraught** (dis·trawt') a. perplexed; bewildered; frantic [L. distractus, drawn aside].

dis·train (dis·trān') v.t. to seize goods, esp. to enforce payment of debt. **-ment, -t** n. seizure of goods. **-or, -er** n. [L. dis, asunder; stringere, to draw tight].

dis·tress (dis·tres') n. extreme pain, mental or physical; misfortune; extreme poverty; v.t. to cause pain or anguish to; to harass; (Law) to distrain. **-ful** a. causing suffering. **-fully** adv. **distressed area**, a part of the country where unemployment is rife [L. distringere, to pull asunder].

dis·tri·bute (dis·trib'·ūt) v.t. to divide among several; to allot or hand out; to spread out; to classify. **distributable** a. **distribution** n. act of distributing; arrangement. **distributive** a. **distributor(-er)** n. [L. dis, asunder; tribuere, to allot].

dis·trict (dis'·trikt) n. a defined tract of land; an administrative division of a country; a region; a. local; regional; v.t. to divide into specified areas [L. distringere, tighten].

dis·trust (dis·trust') v.t. to have no faith in; to suspect; to doubt; n. want of trust; doubt.

dis·turb (dis·turb') v.t. to upset the normal condition of; to disquiet; to agitate; to ruffle. **-ance** n. uproar; confusion; derangement [L. dis, asunder; turbare, to agitate].

dis·un·ion (dis·ūn'·yan) n. separation; discord; dissension. **disunite** v.t. to cause separation; to cause a breach between. **disunity** n.

dis·use (dis·ūs') n. cessation of use or practice. **disuse** (dis·uz') v.t. to cease to use.

di·syl·la·ble (di·sil'·a·bl) n. a word of two syllables. Also **dissyllable** [Gk. disyllabos].

ditch (dich) n. a trench dug esp. for drainage or defense; a natural waterway; v.t. to cut a ditch in; (Colloq.) to get rid of; v.i. to make a forced 'landing' on the sea [O.E. dic, a ditch].

dith·er (diTH'·er) n. (Colloq.) a state of nervous agitation or confusion [etym. uncertain].

dit·to (dit'·ō) n. that which has been said; the same; — **symbol** ", placed below thing to be repeated; adv. as aforesaid; v.t. to copy [L. dictus, said].

dit·ty (dit'·i·) n. a song; a short poem to be sung [L. dictare, to dictate or compose].

dit·ty bag (dit'·i·bag) n. a small bag used by soldiers and sailors for holding needles, thread, etc. **ditty box** n. a box for the same purpose.

di·u·ret·ic (di·yoo·ret'·ik) a. exciting the discharge of urine; n. a medicine which tends to increase the flow of urine. **diuresis** n. excessive urinary excretion [Gk. dia, through; ourein, to make water].

di·ur·nal (di·ur'·nal) a. belonging to the day (opp. of nocturnal); daily; n. a book containing the canonical hours of the R.C. breviary. **-ly** adv. [L. dies, a day].

di·va (dē'·va) n. a popular female singer; a prima donna [L. diva, fem. of divus, divine].

di·va·lent (di·vā'·lent or div'·a·lent) a. (Chem.) capable of combining with two radicals; bivalent [Gk. dis, twice; L. valere, to be strong].

di·van (di·van') n. a long cushioned seat; a Turkish council of state; a council room; a smoking room [Pers. divan, a long seat].

dive (dīv) v.i. to plunge into water head first; to remain under water, as a diver; to penetrate deeply into; to plunge the hand into; n. a plunge head-first; (Slang) a cheap restaurant of ill-repute. **diving bell** n. an apparatus by which deep-sea divers can work under water [O.E. dufan, to plunge].

di·verge (da·vurj') v.i. to turn in different directions; to deviate from a course; to differ. **-ment, -nce, -ncy** n. deviation from a common center. **-nt** a. branching off; deviating. **-ntly** adv. [L. dis, asunder; vergere, to incline].

di·vers (dī'·verz) a. several; sundry. **diverse** a. (modern var. of divers) of different kinds. **diversely** adv. **diversity** n. state of being unlike; variety [L. diversus, different].

di·ver·si·fy (da·vur'·sa·fi) v.t. to make diverse or various; to give variety to [L. diversus, varied; facere, to make].

di·vert (da·vurt') v.t. to turn aside; to alter the direction of; to draw off; to amuse or entertain. **diversion** n. **-ing** a. **divertissement** (dē·ver·tēs'·mong) n. a diversion; a short ballet or interlude between the acts of a play [L. dis, aside; vertere, to turn].

di·vest (da·vest') v.t. to strip, as of clothes, equipment, etc.; to dispossess **-iture, -ment** n. [L. dis; vestire, to clothe].

di·vide (da·vid') v.t. to separate into parts; to share; to keep apart; to antagonize; (Math.) to find how many times one number is contained in another; v.i. to be separated; to part; n. act of dividing; a watershed. **-rs** n.pl. compasses for measuring or dividing lines. **the Great Divide**, death [L. dividere, to distribute].

div·i·dend (div'·a·dend) n. (Arith.) the sum to be divided by the divisor to obtain the quotient; interest payable on loans, invested money, etc.; the share of profits paid to holders of stocks, insurance, etc. [L. dividere, to share out].

di·vine (da·vin') a. belonging to or having the nature of God, or a god; devoted to the worship of God; holy; sacred; heavenly; superhuman; n. a priest; a clergyman; a theologian; v.t. and v.i. to forecast by supernatural means; to practice divination. **divination** n. the art or act of foretelling the future by non-rational methods; intuitive prevision; augury. **divinator, diviner** n. one who divines. **-ly** adv. **-ness** n. **divining rod**, a forked twig, usually of hazel, used to locate underground water. **divinity** n. state of being divine; God; a pagan deity; the study of theology [L. divinus, divine].

di·vi·sion (da·vizh'·an) n. the act of dividing; part of a whole; a section; a partition; difference in opinion; (Mil.) an army unit, the normal command of a major-general. **divisibility** n. **divisible** a. capable of being divided. **-al, divisionary** a. pert. to or belonging to a division; indicating a separation. **divisor** (da·vi'·zer) n. (Math.) the number by which another is divided [L. divisus, divided].

di·vorce (da·vōrs') n. the legal dissolution of a marriage contract; separation; v.t. to obtain legal dissolution of a marriage; to separate; to sever; to disunite. **divorcee** n. a divorced person. **-ment** n. [L. divortium].

div·ot (div'·at) n. (Golf) a piece of turf cut out accidentally by golfer [etym. unknown].

di·vulge (da·vulj') v.t. to disclose something secret or unknown; **divulgate** v.t. to publish. **-ment, -nce** n. [L. dis, asunder; vulgus, the common people].

Dixie (diks'·i·) n. the Southern States of the U.S.; a song [etym. unknown].

diz·zy (diz'·i·) a. giddy; light-headed; causing giddiness; (Colloq.) stupid; v.t. to make dizzy. **dizzily** adv. **dizziness** n. giddiness; vertigo [O.E. dysig, foolish].

do (dō) (Mus.) the first tone of the major diatonic scale. Also **doh**.

do (dōō) v.t. to perform; to execute; to affect; to finish; to prepare; to confer; (Colloq.) to swindle; v.i. to act; to be; as auxil. verb, used to give emphasis to principal verb as in I do think you should go; to avoid repetition of another verb, and in negative, emphatic and interrogative sentences. pr.p. **-ing**. pa.t. **did**. pa.p. **done**. n. **to do away with**, to destroy. **-er** n. an agent. **to do in**, to murder. **-ings** n.pl. things done; activities. **done-out** a. exhausted. [O.E. don, to do].

dob·bin (dob'·in) n. a name for patient, quiet

workhorse [nickname for *Robin*].

do·cent (dō'·sạnt) *n.* a teacher in a university below professorial rank [L. *docere*, to teach].

doc·ile (dás'·il) *a.* easily instructed or managed; tractable. **-ly** *adv.* [L. *docere*, to teach].

dock (dák) *v.t.* to cut short; to deduct; to clip (as an animal's tail); *n.* the part of tail left after clipping [M.E. *dok*, a tail].

dock (dák) *n.* wharf, or row of piers with buildings, etc. where ships are berthed, loaded, etc.; enclosed space in a law court where accused stands. **-age** *n.* space available in docks for ships; charge made for use of docks. **-er** *n.* one who works at the docks, esp. loading and unloading cargoes. **-yard,** *n.* an enclosed dock area where ships are built or repaired. **dry dock,** *n.* a dock from which water can be pumped out [O.Dut. *dokke*].

dock·et (dák'·it) *n.* (*Law*) a list of cases for trial; a summary of a written document; a memorandum; a bill or label affixed to goods giving instructions; *v.t.* to summarize; to mark the contents of papers on the back or outside sheet [prob. dim. of *dock*, to curtail].

doc·tor (dák'·tẹr) *n.* one who holds the highest degree granted by any faculty of a university; a medical practitioner; *v.t.* to treat medically; (*Colloq.*) to adulterate; to falsify; to repair temporarily; *v.i.* to practice medicine; to take medicine. **-ate** *n.* the degree or status of a university doctor. **-ship** *n.* **-ial** *a.* [L. = a teacher, fr. *docere*, to teach].

doc·trine (dák'·trin) *n.* principle of belief; instruction; that which is taught. **doctrinal** *a.* pert. to doctrine, esp. Christian Church. **doctrinally** *adv.* **doctrinaire** (dák·tri·ner') *n.* a theorist who tends to urge the application of a doctrine beyond all practical considerations; *a.* impracticable [Fr. fr. L. *doctrina*, teaching].

doc·u·ment (dák'·yạ·mạnt) *n.* an official paper containing information, giving instructions, or establishing facts; *v.t.* to furnish with written evidence of. **-al, documentary** *a.* pert. to, derived from, or in the form of a document. **-ation** *n.* the use of documentary evidence; the furnishing of such evidence. **-ed** *a.* [L. *documentum*, example].

dod·der (dád'·ẹr) *v.t.* or *v.i.* to totter or tremble, as with age. **-ing** *a.* [prob. dialect word].

do·dec·a·gon (dō·dek'·ạ·gàn) *n.* a plane figure with twelve sides and twelve angles. **-al** *a.* [Gk. *dodeka*, twelve; *gonia*, an angle].

dodge (dáj) *v.t.* to evade or escape by a sudden turning; to prevaricate; *v.i.* to twist aside (physically or morally); *n.* a quick, evasive movement; a trick; (*Colloq.*) **-r** *n.*

do·do (dō'·dō) *n.* an extinct flightless bird. *pl.* **-(e)s** [Port. *doudo*, silly].

doe (dō) *n.* the female of the fallow deer; also female of antelope, rabbit, hare, goat, rat, mouse, ferret. **-skin** *n.* the skin of a doe; a fine close-woven cloth [O.E. *da*, a doe].

does (duz) *3rd pers. sing. pr. ind.* of verb **do.**

doff (dáf) *v.t.* to take off, esp. the hat; to rid oneself of [contr. of *do off*].

dog (dawg) *n.* a common, carnivorous quadruped of the same genus as the wolf, mainly domesticated; a worthless fellow; (*Colloq.*) a young man-about-town; one of the two constellations of stars (*Canis Manjor, Canis Minor*); a metal bar for holding logs of wood or supporting fireirons; *a.* male, as in *dog-wolf*; *v.t.* to follow closely, as a dog does; to keep at the heels of; to pursue relentlessly. *pr.p.* **-ging.** *pa.p.* **-ged.** **—collar. — days** *n.pl.* the hottest period of the northern summer, generally considered from July 3rd-August 11th. **—eared** *a.* (of a book) having the corners of the pages turned down. **-ged** *a.* stubborn; persistent. **-gedly** *adv.* **-gedness** *n.* **-gish** *a.* like a dog; surly. **-gy** *a.* pert. to dogs; fond of dogs (*Colloq.*) fashionable. **-house** *n.* a small hut for dogs. **dog Latin,** incorrect barbarous Latin. **-like** *a.* faithful. **— star** *n.* alternative name for Sirius,

the principal star in the constellation *Canis Major*, and the brightest star in the heavens. **—tired,** *a.* dead-beat; completely exhausted. **-tooth,** *n.* a canine tooth; the eye-tooth (of a human being). **-watch** *n.* one of the two-hour watches on board ship from 4-6 or 6-8 p.m. **a dog in the manger,** a spoil-sport; one who refuses to let another enjoy what he himself has no use for. **a hot dog,** a hot sausage inside a roll. **in the doghouse,** in disfavor. **to go to the dogs,** to be ruined. **to let sleeping dogs lie,** not to stir up trouble unnecessarily [O.E. *docga*, a dog].

dog·ger·el (dog'·ẹr·ẹl) *n.* irregular, unpoetical burlesque verse; *a.* [etym. unknown].

dog·ma (dáwg'·mạ) *n.* a philosophical tenet; theological doctrine authoritatively asserted; a principle or belief. **dogmatic, -al,** *a.* pert. to a dogma; opinionated; authoritative. **dogmatically** *adv.* **dogmatics** *n.* the science of systematized Christian doctrines; doctrinal theology. **-tize** *v.i.* to formulate a dogma; to express an opinion positively or arrogantly. **-tism** *n.* positive assertion; laying down the law. **-tist** *n.* [Gk. *dogma*, an opinion].

doi·ly (doi'·li·) *n.* a small table mat placed under dishes; a small, round, linen or paper mat put on plate holding cakes, etc. [fr. *Doily*, a haberdasher].

dol·ce (dōl'·chā) *a.* (*Mus.*) sweet; soft. [It. *dolce*, sweet].

dol·drums (dál'·dramz) *n.pl.* a belt of calms at the Equator; (*Colloq.*) a state of depression.

dole (dōl) *v.t.* to distribute in small portions; *n.* something given or paid out; alms; a small portion [O.E. *dal*, a part].

dole·ful (dōl'·fạl) *a.* grievous; melancholic; dismal. **-ly** *adv.* **-ness** *n.* [O.Fr. *doel*, mourning].

doll (dál) *n.* a puppet; a toy baby as a child's plaything; (*Colloq.*) a pretty, rather brainless girl. **to doll up** (*Colloq.*) to dress up smartly [prob. fr. *Dolly*, abbrev. of Dorothy].

dol·lar (dál'·ẹr) *n.* a silver coin or paper note, the monetary unit of U.S.A. and Canada [Ger. *Taler*, short for *Joachimstaler*, the coin being first made at the silver mines of *Joachimstal*, Bohemia].

dol·lop (dál'·ạp) *n.* a lump, a shapeless mass [prob. Scand. *dolp*, a lump].

doll·y (dál'·i·) *n.* a wooden shaft attached to a disc with projecting arms, used in mining, piledriving, etc.; a mobile platform; a small locomotive used in quarries, etc. **dollied** *a.* [prob. fr. *Dolly*].

dol·man (dál'·man) *n.* a long, loose Turkish garment; Hussar's coat worn like a cape; similar garment worn by women in Victorian days [Turk. *dolaman*, a cloak].

dol·men (dál'·men) *n.* a prehistoric tomb formed by a large unhewn stone resting on two or more unhewn uprights [Breton, *tol*, table; *men*, stone].

dol·or·ous (dō'·lẹr·ạs) *a.* full of, expressing, or causing grief. **-ly** *adv.* [L. *dolere*, to grieve].

dol·phin (dál'·fin) *n.* a sea mammal; a mooring buoy [Gk. *delphis*, a dolphin].

dolt (dōlt) *n.* a dull, stupid fellow; a blockhead. **-ish** *a.* **-ishly** *adv.* [M.E. *dold*, dulled].

do·main (dō·mān') *n.* that which one has dominion over; property; (*Fig.*) the scope or sphere of any branch of human knowledge. **-al, dominial** *a.* [L. *dominus*, a lord].

dome (dōm) *n.* a hemispherical vault reared above the roof of a building; a large cupola. **-d, domical** *a.* possessing a dome [L. *domus*, a house].

Domes·day, Doomsday-book. See **doom.**

do·mes·tic (dạ·mes'·tik) *a.* pert. to a house or home; devoted to home and household affairs; tame (of animals); not foreign (of a country's policy); *n.* a household servant. **-ally** *adv.* **-ate** *v.t.* to make fond of domestic life; to tame animals. **domesticity** *n.* life in a household. **— science,** science of home management, etc.

[L. *domus*, a house].

dom·i·cile (dăm′·a̧·sĭl) *n.* an abode; a dwelling-house; (*Law*) a person's permanent residence; *v.t.* to establish in a fixed residence. **domiciliary** *a.* [L. *domicilium*, a dwelling].

dom·i·nant (dăm′·a̧·na̧nt) *a.* ruling; prevailing; (*Mus.*) having harmonic importance; *n.* (*Mus.*) the fifth note of the diatonic scale. **dominance** *n.* authority; ascendancy. **dominancy** *n.* **-ly** *adv.* **dominate** *v.t.* and *v.i.* to rule; to influence strongly; to sway; to tower over. **domination** *n.* authority. **dominative** *a.* ruling. **dominator** *n.* **domineer** *v.i.* to rule with arbitrary sway; to be overbearing. **domineering** *a.* arrogant. **dominion** *n.* lordship; sovereignty; territory under one government; a self-governing British colony [L. *dominari*, to be master].

do·min·i·cal (da̧·mĭn′·i·ka̧l) *a.* belonging to Jesus as Lord, or the Lord's Day [L. *dominicus*, belonging to a lord].

Do·min·i·can (da̧·mĭn′·i·ka̧n) *a.* belonging to St. *Dominic*, or to the order of preaching friars, founded by him (called also the *Black Friars*); *n.* a member of St. Dominic's order.

dom·i·no (dăm′·a̧n·ō) *n.* a long cloak of black silk with a hood, worn at masquerades; the person wearing such a cloak; a mask; one of the 28 oblong pieces marked each with a certain number of spots used in the game of *dominoes* [L. *dominus*, a master].

Don (dăn) *n.* (*fem.* **Doña** (dawn′·ya̧); **Donna** (Italian spelling) *n.* a Spanish title, the equivalent of the English *Sir* (formerly applied only to noblemen); a Spaniard. **don**, *n.* a fellow or tutor of Oxford or Cambridge University; a master at Winchester [Sp. fr. L. *dominus*, a master].

don (dăn) *v.t.* to put on; to assume. *pr.p.* **-ning** *pa.p.*, *pa.t.* **-ned** [short fr. *do on*].

do·na·tion (dō·nā′·sha̧n) *n.* act of giving; a gift; a contribution. **donate** *v.t.* to present a gift. **donative** *n.* **donor** *n.* one who gives a donation; a benefactor [L. *donare*, to give].

done (dun) *pa.p.* of the verb **do. done!** agreed.

don·key (dăng′·ki·) *n.* an ass; (*Colloq.*) a foolish person. — **engine** *n.* a small auxiliary steam engine.

don't (dōnt) *contr.* of **do not.**

doo·dle (doō′·dl) *v.i.* to scribble aimlessly [prob. form of *dawdle*].

doom (doōm) *n.* fate; evil destiny; judgment; legal decree; ruin; *v.t.* to destine; to pass sentence on; to condemn. **-ed** *a.* under sentence. **-ful** *a.* **-sday** *n.* the Day of Judgment. **Doomsday or Domesday Book,** the census compiled by order of William the Conqueror, for purposes of taxation [O.E. *dom*, a judgment].

door (dōr) *n.* the wooden or metal structure, hinged or sliding, giving access to house, room, passage, or cupboard; the frame by which an entrance is closed; (*Fig.*) a means of approach. **dead as a door nail** (*Colloq.*) quite dead. **-post** *n.* the jamb. **-step** *n.* the step outside a door. **-way** *n.* the entrance to a house, room, etc. **to darken one's door,** to enter one's house [O.E. *duru*, a door].

dope (dōp) *n.* any thick liquid, or semi-liquid lubricant; a varnish; a preparation for coating the fabric surfaces of aircraft; a drug (orig. given to a horse before a race); any narcotic; (*Slang*) a stupid person; inside information (esp. about racehorses); *v.t.* to apply dope or varnish to; to administer dope to; (*Fig.*) to hoodwink. **dopey** *a.* stupefied with drugs; slow-witted [Dut. *doop*, a dipping].

Do·ri·an (dōr′·i·a̧n) *a.* pert. to *Doris*, in ancient Greece, or to its inhabitants. **Doric,** *a.* pert. to Doris, the Dorians, or the simple style of architecture of the Dorians; (of dialect) unpolished; *n.* a mode of Greek music; the Doric dialect characterized by broad vowel sounds.

dor·mant (dōr′·ma̧nt) *a.* sleeping; hibernating;

quiescent; not in action; unclaimed (as a title). **dormancy** *n.* state of being quiescent. **dormer-window** *n.* a small vertical window projecting from a roof slope. **dormitory** *n.* a building primarily containing sleeping rooms; a large sleeping apartment. **dormouse** *n.* a small, hibernating rodent [L. *dormire*, to sleep].

dor·sal (dawr′·sal) *a.* pert. to, near, or belonging to, the back [L. *dorsum*, the back].

do·ry (dō′·ri·) *n.* a flat-bottomed boat.

dose (dōs) *n.* the prescribed quantity of medicine to be taken at one time; a portion; anything disagreeable that must be taken or done; *v.t.* to administer or order in doses; (*Colloq.*) to adulterate. **dosage** *n.* the practice of dosing; the amount of a dose. **dosimeter** *n.* an instrument for measuring minute doses accurately; (*Atomic Warfare*) a small instrument for recording the total dose of radioactivity accumulated up to the moment [Gk. *dosis*, a giving].

dos·si·er (dăs′·i·ā) *n.* a set of documents [Fr.].

dot (dăt) *n.* a small point or spot made with a pen, pencil, or sharp instrument; a speck; (*Mus.*) a point placed after a note or rest to lengthen the sound or pause by one-half; *v.t.* to mark with dots; to diversify as with small objects; *v.i.* to make dots. *pr.p.* **-ting.** *pa.p.* **-ted. -ty** *a.* marked with or consisting of dots. **dot and dash,** in Morse code, the short and long symbols [O.E. *dott*, a speck].

dot (dăt) *n.* a dowry. **dotal** *a.* [Fr.].

dote (dōt) *v.i.* to be in one's dotage; to be foolishly sentimental; to be over-fond of. **dotage** *n.* childishness of old people; senility; excessive fondness. **dotard** *n.* one whose intellect is impaired by old age [O.Dut. *doten*, to be silly].

dou·ble (dub′·l) *a.* denoting two things of the same kind; existing in pairs; twice as much (quantity); twice as good (quality); serving for two; acting two parts; deceitful; ambiguous; *adv.* twice; two-fold; *v.t.* to multiply by two; to make twice as great; to fold in two; *v.i.* to increase to twice as much; to return upon one's track; to run (after marching); *n.* twice as much; that which is doubled over; a fold; a duplicate; an actor's substitute or understudy; a game with two on each side; two faults in succession; a running pace, twice as quick as marching. — **bass** *n.* the largest and lowest pitched of the stringed instruments, played with a bow. **—breasted** *a.* (of a coat) able to fasten over on either side. — **cross** *v.t.* (*Slang*) to cheat a swindler. **—dealing** *n.* duplicity. **—decker** *n.* a ship or bus with two decks. **—edged** *a.* having two edges; (*Fig.*) cutting both ways; effective for and against. — **entry** *n.* in bookkeeping, a system by which every entry is made both on debit and credit side of an account. **—faced** *a.* hypocritical. **-r** *n.* **doublet** *n.* one of a pair; a close-fitting garment for the upper part of body as worn by Elizabethan men; one of two words derived orig. from the same root but varying in spelling and meaning. — **time** *n.* the fastest marching pace next to a run. [L. *duo*, two].

doubt (dout) *v.t.* to disbelieve; to hold questionable; *v.i.* to be in a state of uncertainty; to hesitate; *n.* uncertainty of mind; misgiving; distrust of others. **-able** *a.* **-er** *n.* **-ful** *a.* dubious; uncertain in opinion. **-fully** *adv.* **-fulness** *n.* **-ing** *a.* undecided; hesitant. **-ingly** *adv.* **-less** *adv.* without doubt; probably. **-lessly** *adv.* [L. *dubitare*, to be uncertain].

douche (doōsh) *n.* a jet of water directed upon or into the body; an apparatus for douching [It. *doccia*, a water-pipe].

dough (dō) *n.* a mass of flour moistened and kneaded, to be baked afterwards; (*Slang*) money. **-boy** *n.* (*Colloq.*) an infantryman. **-nuts** *n.* sweetened dough in shape of balls or rings, fried in fat and finally dipped in sugar. **-y** *a.* [O.E. *dah*].

dough·ty (dou′·ti·) *a.* (*Arch.*) brave; valiant. **doughtily** *adv.* [O.E. *dyhtig*, valiant].

dour (dour) *a.* sullen; gloomy; obstinate; forbidding in manner. **-ly** *adv.* [L. *durus*, hard].

douse, dowse (dous) *v.t.* to dip or plunge into water; (*Naut.*) to lower a sail; to put out.

dove (duv) *n.* a pigeon; a symbol of peace or of the Holy Ghost. **—colored** *a.* soft pinkish grey. **-cot(e)** *n.* nesting box of pigeons, usually on top of a pole. **-tail** *n.* a joint made by fitting one piece toothed with wedge like projections (tenons) (shaped like a dove's tail) into cavities of corresponding shape (mortises) in another piece of timber; *v.t.* to join together by this method; (*Fig.*) to link together [O.E. *dufe-doppa*, cf. Ger. *Taube*].

dow·a·ger (dou'·a·jer) *n.* (*Law*) widow with property or title left by her husband; (*Colloq.*) a dignified elderly lady [O.Fr. *douage*, a dower].

dow·dy (dou'·di·) *a.* untidy; lacking style; *n.* a dowdy woman. **dowdily** *adv.* **dowdiness** *n.*

dow·el (dou'·al) *n.* a wooden or iron pin for joining two adjacent boards or stones [cf. Ger. *dobel*, a plug].

dow·er (dou'·er) *n.* a widow's share of her husband's property; portion a worman brings in marriage; gift; talent. **-ed** *a.* **-less** *a.* **dowry** *n.* goods given to the husband by the bride or her family at marriage; a natural gift [L. *dotare*, to endow].

down (doun) *n.* the fine, soft feathers of birds. **-y** *a.* resembling or covered with down [Scand. *dunn*].

down (doun) *n.* a hillock of sand by the sea (same as *dune*); treeless land [O.E. *dun*, a hill].

down (doun) *prep.* along a descent; towards a lower place, situation, etc.; towards the mouth of a river; in the same direction as, as in *down-wind*; passing from the past to less remote times, as *down* the ages; *adv.* in a downward direction; on the ground; to the bottom; below the horizon. *v.t.* to knock down; used also as an *interjection* with verb *get, kneel,* etc. understood; *n.* a reversal of fortune (as in the *ups and downs* of life). **-cast** *a.* depressed; (of eyes) lowered; *n.* (in mining) a shaft for ventilation. **-fall** *n.* ruin; a heavy fall of rain, snow. **-fallen** *a.* **-hearted** *a.* despondent. **-hill** *a.* sloping; *adv.* on a slope. **-pour** *n.* a heavy fall of water, esp. rain. **-right** *adv.* completely; in plain terms; *a.* straightforward; unqualified. **-stairs** *adv.* in or to a lower floor of a house; *a.* pert. to the ground floor; *n.* the ground floor. **-stream** *adv.* with the current. **-trodden** *a.* trampled underfoot; oppressed. **-ward** *a.* **-wards** *adv.* **—town,** towards the center of the town [O.E. *of dune*, from the hill].

dowse (douz) *v.t.* and *v.i.* to find subterranean water supply by means of a divining rod. **-r** *n.*

dox·ol·o·gy (dáks·al'·a·ji·) *n.* a short hymn of praise to God. [Gk. *daxa*, glory; *legein*, speak].

doze (dōz) *v.i.* to sleep lightly; to be half asleep; *n* a nap [Scand. *dose*].

doz·en (duz'·n) *n.* a group of twelve things of the same kind; *a.* twelve. **baker's dozen, devil's dozen,** thirteen [Fr. *douzaine*, twelve].

drab (drab) *n.* a dingy brownish-grey color; *a.* (*Fig.*) dull; monotonous [Fr. *drap*, cloth].

drach·ma (drak'·ma) *n.* a Greek coin; an ancient Greek weight [Gk. *drachmē*, a handful].

draft (draft) *n.* a sketch or rough copy; a current of air; a selection of men for military service; an order directing payment of money by a bank; a drink; drawing of liquid from a cask. *v.t.* to draw the outline of; to compose and write; to take for military service. **-sman** *n.* one who draws plans for buildings, etc. **-smanship** *n.* **-y** *a.* **-iness** *n.* [var. of *draught*].

drag (drag) *v.t.* to draw with main force; to trail slowly; to trawl with a drag or net; to harrow (the fields); *v.i.* to move heavily or slowly; to pass tediously. *pr.p.* **-ging.** *pa.p.* **-ged.** *n.* a net or hook to bring up submerged things; a heavy harrow; (*Slang*) a puff; a device acting as a brake on a wheel; anything that slows progress. **-ger** *n.* **-net** *n.* a fishing net for dragging along the sea floor [O.E. *dragan*, to draw].

drag·gle (drag'·l) *v.t.* and *v.i.* to make or become wet and dirty by trailing on the ground.

dra·gon (drag'·an) *n.* a fabulous winged reptile represented as breathing out fire and smoke; (*Fig.*) an over-vigilant chaperon. **-et** *n.* a little dragon; a fish of the *Pegasus* genus. **-fly** *n.* an insect of brilliant coloring, with long slender body and two pairs of large, transparent wings. **-'s blood,** a carmine fruit resin used for coloring varnishes and lacquers; [Gk. *drakon*, a large serpent].

dra·goon (dra·gòòn') *n.* a cavalryman; *v.t.* to oppress; to enforce harsh disciplinary measures [Fr. *dragon*, a fire-spitting carbine].

drain (drān) *v.t.* to filter; to draw off by degrees; to make dry; to swallow down; to exhaust; to impoverish; *v.i.* to flow off or drip away gradually; *n.* a watercourse; a pipe, sewer or ditch; a gradual exhaustion of means, health, etc. **-able** *a.* **-age** *n.* act of draining; system of carrying away surplus water from an area by rivers, canals. **-er** *n.* a kitchen utensil like a rack, on which plates, etc. are placed to dry; a colander or sieve [O.E. *dragan*, to draw].

drake (drāk) *n.* the male of the duck.

dram (dram) *n.* (contr. of *drachma*) a unit of weight; (*apothecary*) $\frac{1}{8}$ of an ounce [Gk. *drachmē*, a weight; orig. a handful].

dra·ma (dra'·ma) *n.* a composition to be acted on the stage; the branch of literature dealing with plays; a series of real emotional events. **dramatic** *a.* pert. to the drama; striking; tense. **dramatically** *adv.* **dramatization** *n.* **dramatize** *v.t.* to adapt a novel, etc. for acting. **dramatist** *n.* a writer of plays. **-turge** *n.* **-turgy** *n.* the art of writing or producing plays. **dramatis personae** (dram'·a·tis per·sòn'·ā) characters of a drama [Gk. *draein*, to do].

drank (drangk) *pa.t.* of **drink.**

drape (drāp) *v.t.* to hang something loosely in folds; to adorn with drapery. **drapery** *n.* cloth; hangings [Fr. *drap*, cloth].

dras·tic (dras'·tik) *a.* very powerful; harsh; thorough [Gk. *drastikos*, active].

drat (drat) *interj.* a mild expletive expressing annoyance [corrupt. of *God rot*].

draught (draft) *n.* **-s** *n.pl.* the game of checkers; *a.* drawn from a barrel, as beer. **-(s)man** *n.* checker. See **draft** [O.E. *dragan*, to draw].

draw (draw) *v.t.* to pull along; to haul towards oneself; to entice; to extract (as a tooth); to elicit an opinion from another; to deduce; to receive (as money, salary, etc.); to inhale; to sketch; to describe; to cast lots; to bring game, such as fox, out of hiding; to take out the entrails; *v.i.* to pull; to attract; to move towards; to pull out a weapon for action; to be equal in a match; to sketch; to cast lots; to have a free passage of air (as a chimney). *pr.p.* **-ing.** *pa.t.* **drew.** *pa.p.* **-n.** *n.* the act of drawing; a game ending with same score for both sides; an attraction. **-able** *a.* **-back** *n.* a disadvantage. **-bridge** *n.* a bridge that can be raised or let down. **-er** *n.* one who or that which draws; one who draws an order, draft, etc.; a lidless, sliding box in a table, chest, etc. **-ers** *n.pl.* close fitting undergarment for lower limbs. **-ing** *n.* the art of pulling; a lottery; the art of representing objects by line or color on paper, canvas, etc. **-ing-room** *n.* orig. a withdrawing room; a room in which guests are entertained; a private compartment on a train. **to draw a blank,** to fail to find what one is seeking. **to draw the line,** to stop. **drawn and quartered** quartered and disemboweled [O.E. *dragan*, to draw].

drawl (drawl) *v.i.* to speak with slow and lengthened tone; *v.t.* to utter (words) in this way; *n.* a manner of speech, slow and drawn out [Scand. *dralla*, to loiter].

dray (drā) *n.* a low cart for heavy goods. [O.E. *dragan*, to draw].

dread (dred) *n.* overwhelming apprehension; awe; terror; *a.* dreadful; awful; *v.t.* to regard with fear; *v.i.* to have fear of the future. **-ed** *a.* feared. **-ful** *a.* terrifying; terrible. **-fully** *adv.* **-fulness** *n.* **-nought** *n.* a large-sized battleship mounting heavy guns; a thick woolen overcoat [O.E. *ondraeden*, to fear].

dream (drēm) *n.* a series of images or thoughts in the mind of a person asleep; an idle fancy; a vision; an aspiration; *v.i.* to imagine things during sleep; to have yearnings; *v.t.* to see in a dream; *pa.t.* and *p.p.* **-ed** or **-t** (drēmd or dremt). **-er** *n.* **-ily** *adv.* **-iness** *n.* **-land** *n.* an imaginary land seen in dreams. **-less** *a.* **-like** *a.* visionary; unreal. **-y** *a.* [O.E. *dream*].

drear·y (drir′·i·) *a.* dismal; gloomy; bleak. **drearily** *adv.* **dreariness** *n.* (*Poetic*) **drear** *a.* [O.E. *dreorig*, mournful].

dredge (drej) *v.t.* to sprinkle. **-r** *n.* a flour can with perforated lid [O.Fr. *dragie*, a sweetmeat].

dredge (drej) *n.* a machine like a large scoop for taking up mud from a river bed, harbor, etc.; a dragnet for oysters or zoological specimens. Also **-r.** *v.t.* to scoop up or deepen with a dredge [conn. with *drag*].

dregs (dregz) *n.pl.* sediment in a liquid that falls to the bottom; lees; grounds; (*Fig.*) the most worthless class [Scand. *dreggjar*, dregs].

drench (drench) *v.t.* to wet thoroughly; to soak [O.E. *drencan*, to give to drink].

dress (dres) *v.t.* to put clothes on; to provide with clothes; to adorn; to treat (a sore); *v.i.* to put on one's clothes; *n.* clothes; a frock; adornment. **— circle** *n.* the lowest gallery in a theater, orig. for people in evening-dress. **-er** *n.* one who dresses; a dressing table or bureau. **-ing** *n.* clothes; a sterile substance for a wound; manure; substance used to stiffen fabrics; a sauce (as salad-dressing); stuffing for a fowl. **-ing-down** *n.* (*Colloq.*) a scolding. **-ing gown** *n.* a robe worn while dressing. **-ing table** *n.* a table with mirror used while dressing. **-maker** *n.* a person who makes women's dresses, etc. **-making** *n.* **-y** *a.* fond of dress; fashionable [O.Fr. *dresser*, to prepare].

drew (drōō) *pa.t.* of **draw**.

drib·ble (drib′·l) *v.i.* to trickle down, esp. of saliva of babies and idiots; (*Basketball*) to bounce the ball repeatedly; (*Other Sports*) to kick the ball forward by short kicks. **driblet** *n.* a small drop [dim. of *drip*].

dried (drīd) *pa.t.* and *pa.p.* of verb **dry**.

drift (drift) *n.* the state or process of being driven; that which is driven; the accumulation of substance driven by the wind, as snow; a slow surface current in the sea caused usually by the prevailing wind; deviation or tendency; *v.t.* to drive into heaps; to cause to float in a certain direction; *v.i.* to be floated along; to be piled in heaps; (*Fig.*) to follow unconsciously some trend in policy, thought or behavior. **-age** *n.* that which has drifted, as snow, seaweed, etc.; deviation of a ship from its course. **— anchor** *n.* an anchor for keeping a ship's head to the wind during a storm. **-er** *n.* an aimless wanderer. **-wood** *n.* wood cast on shore by tide [O.E. *drifan*, to drive].

drill (dril) *v.t.* to pierce; to bore a hole through; to sow, as seeds, in a row; to train in military tactics; to instruct thoroughly (in mental or physical exercises); *n.* revolving tool for boring holes in metal, stone, etc.; an implement for making holes for seed; a row of seeds or root crops; physical exercise or military training; instruction. **drilling** *n.* the process of making drills [prob. Dut. *drillen*, to bore].

drink (dringk) *v.t.* to swallow, as a liquid; to empty, as a glass; to breathe in, as air; *v.i.* to swallow a liquid; to consume intoxicating liquor. *pa.t.*, *pa.p.* **drunk.** *n.* liquid for drinking; intoxicating liquor. **-able** *a.* **-er** *n.* a tippler. **to drink in,** to absorb through the senses [O.E. *drincan*, to drink].

drip (drip) *v.t.* to let fall, drop by drop; *v.i.* to ooze; to trickle. *pr.p.* **-ping.** *pa.t.*, *pa.p.* **-ped.** *n.* a drop; the sound made by water dripping; the projecting edge of a roof; (*Slang*) an insipid person. **-ping** *a.* thoroughly wet; *n.* that which falls in drops; *pl.* fat, from meat while roasting. **-stone** *n.* a projecting molding over doors to deflect rain water [O.E. *dryppan*, to fall in drops].

drive (drīv) *v.t.* to urge on; to keep in motion; to guide the course of; to cause (a machine) to work; to strike in, as a nail; to compel; to hurry; to conclude, as a bargain; to hit a ball with force, as in golf, tennis; to chase game towards sportsmen; *v.i.* to be forced along; to ride in a vehicle. *pr.p.* **driving.** *pa.t.* **drove.** *pa.p.* **driven.** *n.* an excursion in a vehicle; a private roadway; driving game towards sportsmen; the capacity for getting things done. **-r** *n.* one who or that which drives; a golf club for hitting ball from the tee; a drover. **to drive at,** to hint at [O.E. *drifan*, to drive].

driv·el (driv′·l) *v.i.* to dribble like a child; to talk nonsense; to be weak or foolish; *n.* nonsense. **-er** *n.* [O.E. *dreflian*, to slobber; conn. with *dribble*].

driz·zle (driz′·l) *v.t.* and *v.i.* to rain gently; *n.* fine rain [O.E. *dreosan*, to fall].

droit (drwa, droit) *n.* legal right [Fr. *droit*].

droll (drōl) *a.* laughable; funny; queer; *n.* a buffoon; a jester; an odd character. **-ery** *n.* [Fr. *drôle*, an amusing rascal].

drom·e·dar·y (dram′·e·der·i·) *n.* a one-humped Arabian camel [Gk. *dromas*, running].

drone (drōn) *n.* the male of the honey-bee; an idler who lives on the work of others; a deep, humming sound; the largest pipe of the bagpipes; its sound; *v.t.* and *v.i.* to hum; to speak or sing in a monotone [O.E. *dran*, a drone].

drool (drōōl) *v.i.* to slaver; to drivel; to speak foolishly [See **drivel**].

droop (drōōp) *v.i.* to hang down; to grow weak; to pine; to sag; to wilt (as flowers); *v.t.* to lower [Scand. *drupa*, to sink].

drop (drap) *n.* a globular particle of fluid that falls or is allowed to fall; a minute quantity of fluid in medical dose; anything hanging like a drop, or resembling a drop in size (as a jewel in a pendant, ear-ring, etc.); a fall; the trap door of a gallows; *v.t.* to let fall drop by drop; to let fall; to dismiss or break off (as an acquaintance); to set down from a vehicle; to write a letter or pass a remark, in a casual manner; (of animals) to give birth to prematurely; *v.i.* to fall in drops; to fall down suddenly; to sink to a lower level (as prices); to come to an end. *pr.p.* **-ping.** *pa.t.* and *pa.p.* **-ped. — curtain** *n.* a painted curtain lowered in front of theater stage between scenes in a play. **—kick** *n.* (*Football*) a kick effected by letting the ball fall from the hands to the ground to be kicked immediately on the rebound. **-let** *n.* a tiny drop of liquid. **-per** *n.* a small glass tube from which liquid is measured out in drops. **-pings** *n.pl.* dung. **to drop in,** to make an informal visit. **a drop in the bucket,** a small amount [O.E. *dropa*, a drop].

drop·sy (drap′·si·) *n.* a morbid collection of fluid in any part of body. **dropsical** *a.* [Gk. *hudrops*, fr. *hudor*, water].

dross (dras) *n.* the scum of metals thrown off in smelting; refuse [O.E. *dros*, dregs].

drought, drouth (drout, drouth) *n.* dryness; absence of rain over a prolonged period. **-iness** *n.* **-y** *a.* [O.E. *drugath*, dryness].

drove (drōv) *n.* a herd or flock, esp. on the move. **-r** *n.* one who drives cattle or sheep, esp. to market [O.E. *drifan*, to drive].

drown (droun) *v.t.* to suffocate by submerging in water; to deluge; to render inaudible; to overpower; *v.i.* to be suffocated in water [O.E. *druncnian*, to be drunk, to get drowned].

drowse (drouz) *v.t.* to make sleepy; *v.i.* to doze; be heavy with sleep; *n.* a half-sleep; a doze.

drowsy *a.* **drowsily** *adv.* **drowsiness** *n.* [O.E. *drusian,* to be sluggish].

drub (drub) *v.t.* to beat; to cudgel; *v.i.* to defeat. *pr.p.* **-bing.** *pa.p.,* *pa.t.* **-bed. -bing** *n.* a thrashing [prob. Scand. *drabba,* to hit].

drudge (druj) *v.i.* to toil hard; to labor at menial tasks; *n.* one who must do menial work. **drudgery** *n.* hard, monotonous, toil. **drudgingly** *adv.* [O.E. *dreogan,* to perform].

drug (drug) *n.* any substance used in the composition of a medicine; a narcotic; (*Fig.*) a commodity unsaleable because of over-production; *v.t.* to mix with drugs; to administer a drug to someone; *v.i.* to take drugs habitually and in excess. *pr.p.* **-ging.** *pr.p.* **-ged. -gist** *n.* dealer in drugs; a pharmaceutical chemist.

Dru·id (drŏō′·id) *n.* a priest of the ancient Celtic peoples of Britain, Gaul, etc. who worshipped the oak tree. **-ism** *n.* [Celt.].

drum (drum) *n.* (*Mus.*) a percussion instrument comprising a hollow, parchment-covered cylinder beaten with a drumstick; anything drum-shaped; (*Anat.*) the middle portion of ear; *v.t.* to play on a drum; to teach by constant repetition; *v.i.* to beat on drum; to beat rhythmically. *pr.p.* **-ming.** *pa.p.,* *pa.t.* **-med.** **— major** *n.* the leader of a marching drum corps or band. **-mer** *n.* one who plays a drum; a commercial traveler. **-stick** *n.* a padded stick for beating a drum; lower part of leg of cooked fowl [prob. imit. word].

drunk (drungk) *pa.p.* of **drink;** *a.* overcome by strong drink; intoxicated; *n.* a drunk person. **-ard** *n.* one who habitually drinks to excess. **-en** *a.* given to excessive drinking. **-enness** *n.* [O.E. *drincan,* to drink].

drupe (drŏōp) *n.* a fleshy fruit, such as plum, cherry, or peach, with a stone or kernel containing the seed [L. *drupa,* an over-ripe olive].

dry (drī) *a.* free from moisture, rain, or mist; sear; not giving milk, as a cow; thirsty; unsweetened, as wines; uninteresting; sarcastic; plain, as facts; pert. to a district subject to prohibition laws; *v.t.* to free from moisture or wetness; to drain; *v.i.* to grow dry; to evaporate; (*Fig.*) to become void of ideas. **drier** *n.* **— battery** *n.* a battery composed of *dry cells* sealed in a container to prevent leakage. **to dry clean,** to clean garments with chemicals. **—fly** *n.* an artificial fly (in dry-fly fishing) played over surface of water. **— goods** *n.pl.* textile fabrics. **-ly, drily** *adv.* **— measure,** a measure of bulk, used for grain, etc. **-ness** *n.* **— rot** *n.* a decay caused by fungous disease. **—shod** *a.* with dry feet; without wetting one's feet [O.E. *dryge,* dry].

dry·ad (drī′·ad) *n.* in Greek mythology a spirit of the trees; a wood-nymph [Gk. *drus,* an oak tree].

du·al (dū′·al) *a.* consisting of two; twofold; (*Gram.*) of noun, etc. denoting two persons or things; *n.* (*Gram.*) the dual number. **duad** *n.* pair of things regarded as one. **-ism** *n.* a twofold division; the belief that two separate elements co-exist in the universe, namely spirit and matter; the belief in the existence of good and evil as separate entities. **-ist** *n.* **-ity** *n.* state of being double [L. *duo,* two].

dub (dub) *v.t.* to knight; to give a nickname to; to make smooth; to dress a fly for fishing; (*Film*) to provide a film with a sound track not in the original language. *pr.p.* **-bing.** *pa.p.* and *pa.t.* **-bed** [M.E. *dubben,* to adorn].

du·bi·ous (dū′·bi·as) *a.* doubtful; liable to turn out well or ill; (of a character) shady. **-ly** *adv.* **-ness** *n.* **dubiety** (dū·bī′·a·ti·) *n.* hesitancy; uncertainty. **dubitable** *a.* doubtful. **dubitancy, dubitation** *n.* [L. *dubius,* doubtful].

du·cal (dū′·kal) *a.* pert. to a duke. **-ly** *adv.* in a ducal manner. **ducat** (duk′·at) *n.* a coin. **duce** (dŏō′·chā) *n.* leader, esp. 'Il Duce,'. **duchess** (duch′·is) *n.* the wife or widow of a duke; a woman who holds a duchy in her own right. **duchy** *n.* dominions of dukes [L. *dux*].

duch·ess (duch′·es) *n.* See **ducal.**

duck (duk) *n.* a coarse cloth or light canvas used for small sails and clothing. **-s** *n.pl.* trousers made of this [Dut. *doeck,* linen cloth].

duck (duk) *n.* any broad-beaked, web-footed, short-legged water bird; female duck as distinct from male *drake;* (*Colloq.*) a darling; a sudden dip; a sudden lowering of head; (*World War* 2) an amphibious truck; *v.i.* to dip suddenly in water; to bend (head) suddenly; to cringe; *v.i.* to plunge into water; to dodge. **-bill** *n.* an Australian burrowing, egg-laying mammal. Also called **-billed platypus. -board** *n.* planking to cross swampy areas. **duckling** *n.* a young duck. **-pins,** small bowling pins. **-weed** *n.* minute, floating, green plants growing on all standing waters. [O.E. *ducan,* to dive].

duct (dukt) *n.* a canal or tube for conveying fluids, esp. in animal bodies, plants, etc. **-less glands** (*Anat.*) endocrine glands which discharge their secretions directly into the blood (e.g. thyroid, pituitary) [L. *ducere,* to lead].

duc·tile (duk′·tal) *a.* (of metals) capable of being drawn out in fine threads or hammered thin; (*Fig.*) tractable; easily influenced. **ductility** *n.* [L. *ducere,* to lead].

dud (dud) *n.* anything defective or worthless; *n.pl.* clothes, esp. old and sloppy.

dude (dūd, dŏōd) *n.* (*Slang*) a fop; a brainless dandy; an Easterner (a tenderfoot) who vacations on a ranch.

dudg·eon (duj′·an) *n.* anger; resentment, as in phrase *in high dudgeon* [etym. doubtful].

due (dū) *a.* owing; fitting to be paid or done to another; adequate; appointed to arrive (as a train); attributable; *adv.* exactly; duly; directly; *n.* that which is owed; right; (*pl.*) fee; tax. **duly** *adv.* properly; at the right time [O.Fr. *deu,* fr. L. *debere,* to owe].

du·el (dū′·al) *n.* a combat between two persons, generally an affair of honor; any two-sided contest; *v.i.* to fight a duel. **-ist** *n.* [It. from L. *duellum,* a fight between two].

du·en·na (dū·en′·a) *n.* a chaperon [Sp.].

du·et (dū·et′) *n.* a musical composition for two performers, vocal or instrumental. **-ist** *n.* [It. *duetto,* fr. L. *duo,* two].

duff (duf) *v.t.* to make old things look like new; to fake; (*Golf*) to make a bad stroke. **-er** *n.* (*Slang*) a poor player, an incompetent person [etym. doubtful, prob. Scand. *dowf,* stupid].

duf·fel, duffle (duf′·l) *n.* a coarse woolen cloth with a thick nap; camping kit. **— bag** *n.* a canvas bag used for carrying clothes, etc. [fr. *Duffel* in Belgium].

dug (dug) *n.* a teat, esp. of an animal [Scand. *daegge,* to suckle].

dug (dug) *pa.t.* and *pa.p.* of **dig. -out** *n.* a canoe hollowed out of a tree trunk; a hole in the ground roughly roofed over to protect in trench warfare; (*Baseball*) covered shelter for players not on field [fr. *dig*].

duke (dūk) *n.* (*fem.* **duchess**) the highest order of nobility in the British peerage. **-dom** *n.* the status or possessions of a duke. See **ducal.**

dul·cet (dul′·sit) *a.* sweet to the ear; melodious [L. *dulcis,* sweet].

dul·ci·mer (dul′·sa·mer) *n.* an old musical instrument probably like a small harp; a modern instrument related to the guitar [L. *dulcis,* sweet; Gk. *melos,* a song].

dull (dul) *a.* stupid; slow of hearing or seeing; tedious; uninspired; sleepy; dim or cloudy; obtuse; blunt; heavy; *v.t.* to stupefy; to blunt; to mitigate; *v.i.* to become dull. **-ard** *n.* a slow-witted person. **-ness** *n.* [O.E. *dol,* dull-witted].

dulse (duls) *n.* an edible reddish-brown seaweed [Gael. *duileasg*].

duly See **due.**

dumb (dum) *a.* lacking permanently the power of speech; mute; temporarily silent; inarticulate; (*Slang*) stupid; unresponsive; *v.t.* to silence. **-bell** *n.* two heavy iron balls connected by a bar for a handle, used in gymnastic exercises; (*Slang*) a nitwit, moron. **-ly** *adv.* mutely; in silence. **-ness** *n.* — **show**, pantomime. —**waiter** *n.* a hand-operated elevator. **dum(b)found** *v.t.* to strike dumb; to nonplus; to amaze; **-ed** *a.* **dummy** *a.* dumb; sham; *n.* a dumb person; a tailor's mannequin; a sham package in a shop window; (*Cards*) the exposed hand in bridge or whist [O.E. *dumb*, mute].

dum-dum (dum'·dum) *n.* a soft nosed bullet [Bengal].

dump (dump) *v.t.* to throw down heavily; to deposit; to unload; to sell off surplus goods at a low price; *n.* refuse or scrap heap; a temporary store for munitions, etc.; (*Slang*) a poorly kept up place. **-ling** *n.* a ball of dough boiled in water, stock, etc.; a pudding, boiled or baked containing fruit. **-y** *a.* short; thick; squat. **-iness** *n.* — **truck** *n.* a truck whose body tilts and end opens for unloading.

dun (dun) *a.* greyish-brown color; dark; *n.* this color [O.E. *dunn*, dark brown].

dun (dun) *v.t.* to importune for payment of a debt. *pr.p.* **-ning.** *pa.p.* **-ned** [allied to *din*].

dunce (duns) *n.* one who is slow at learning; a dullard [fr. *Duns Scotus*, 13th cent.].

dun·der·head (dun'·der·hed) *n.* a stupid person; a dunce. **-ed** *a.*

dune (dūn) *n.* a low hill of sand in desert areas or on the seacoast [O.Dut. *duna*, a hill].

dung (dung) *n.* the excrement of animals; manure; *v.t.* to treat with manure; *v.i.* to drop excrement. **-hill** *n.* a mound of dung; (*Fig.*) any mean condition [O.E. *dung*, muck].

dun·ga·ree (dung'·ga·rē) *n.* a coarse hard-wearing cotton cloth. **-s** *n.pl.* trousers or overalls of this material [Hind.].

dun·geon (dun'·jan) *n.* orig. the principal tower or 'keep' of a castle; a damp subterranean prison cell; *v.t.* to confine in a dungeon [Fr. *donjon*, fr. L. *dominus*, a master].

dunk (dungk) *v.t.* to dip (bread) into tea, coffee, soup, etc. [Ger. *Tunker*, a dipper].

du·o (dū'·ō) *n.* a duet; a pair of stage artistes.

du·o·de·cen·ni·al (dū·a·da·sen'·i·al) *a.* occurring every twelve years. **duodenary** *a.* pert. to 12 [L. *duodecim*, twelve; *annus*, a year].

du·o·dec·i·mo (dū·a·des'·a·mō) *n.* formed of sheets folded into twelve leaves (*abbrev.* 12 mo.); a 12 mo. book. **duodecimal** *a.* proceeding by twelves; *n.* a twelfth part. **duodecimals** *n.pl.* a method of computation by denominations of 12 instead of 10. **duodecimally** *adv.* [L. *duodecim*, twelve].

du·o·de·num (dū·a·dē'·nam) *n.* upper part of intestines so called as it is about 12 fingerbreadths long; *pl.* **duodena. duodenal** *a.* pert. to duodenum [L. *duodeni*, twelve each].

dupe (dūp) *n.* one who is easily cheated; *v.t.* to cheat; to mislead. **-ry** *n.* the art of cheating.

du·plex (dū'·pleks) *a.* twofold; double; *n.* a house consisting of two family units. **duple** *a.* double [L. *duplex*, double].

du·pli·cate (dū'·pli·kit) *a.* double; exactly resembling another; *n.* an exact copy; a replica, facsimile; a method of playing tournament bridge; *v.t.* (dū'·pli·kāte) to double; to make a copy. **duplication** *n.* **duplicator** *n.* a machine for making copies of written matter. **duplicity** *n.* double-dealing; deception [L. *duplicatus*, to double].

du·ra·ble (dyoor'·a·bl) *a.* lasting; able to resist wear and tear; not perishable; abiding. **-ness, durability** *n.* **durably** *adv.* **durance** *n.* confinement. **duration** *n.* continuance in time; period anything lasts [L. *durare*, to last].

du·ress (dyoo·res') *n.* compulsion; imprisonment; coercion [O.Fr. *duresce*, hardship].

dur·ing (dyoor'·ing) *prep.* in the time of; in course of [*pr.p.* of obsolete *dure*].

dusk (dusk) *a.* tending to darkness; darkish; *n.* twilight; gloaming. **-y** *a.* partially dark;

dim; dark-skinned [O.E. *dosc*, dark-colored].

dust (dust) *n.* very fine particles of matter deposited on the ground or suspended in the air; minute particles of gold in a river bed; powder; the ashes of the dead; *v.t.* to remove dust from; to sprinkle with powder. — **jacket** *n.* a book cover. **-er** *n.* one who dusts; a cloth for dusting; a tin with perforated lid for sprinkling flour, sugar, etc.; a light garment used as a robe. **-ily** *adv.* **-iness** *n.* **-ing** *n.* the act or process of removing dust from furniture, etc.; a sprinkling [O.E. *dust*, dust].

Dutch (duch) *a.* pert. to Holland, to its inhabitants, or to their language; *n.* the language, the people of Holland. **-man** *n.* — **treat,** an entertainment for which each person pays his own share. **like a Dutch uncle,** with frankness [M.Dut. *dutsch*, pert. to the Netherlands].

du·ty (dū'·ti·) *n.* that which is due; that which is demanded by law, morality, social conscience, etc.; military service; one's proper employment; a period of work set down for each person on a roster; customs or excise dues. **duteous** *a.* dutiful; obedient. **duteously** *adv.* **dutiable** *a.* subject to customs duties. Also **dutied. dutiful** *a.* attentive to duty; submissive; proceeding from a sense of duty. **dutifully** *adv.* **dutifulness** *n.* —**free** *a.* exempt from customs duty [O.Fr. *dueté*, what is owed].

dwarf (dwawrf) *n.* an animal, plant, or man abnormally small in size; *v.t.* to hinder the growth of; to make diminutive by comparison. **dwarf, -ish** *a.* undersized [O.E. *dweorg*].

dwell (dwel) *v.i.* to abide; to be domiciled; to deal with in detail, as in a speech. **-er** *n.* **-ing** *n.* habitation; abode [O.E. *dwellan*, to tarry].

dwin·dle (dwin'·dl) *v.i.* to grow less; to shrink; *v.t.* to lessen [O.E. *dwinan*, to fade].

dye (dī) *v.t.* to give a new color to; to stain; *v.i.* to undergo change of color. *pr.p.* **-ing.** *pa.p.* **-d** *n.* a coloring matter. **-r** *n.* one who is employed in dyeing. **-stuff** *n.* substance used for dyeing [O.E. *deagian*, to dye].

dying (dī'·ing) *pr.p.* of **die.**

dyke (dīk) *n.* See **dike.**

dy·nam·ic (dī·nam'·ik) *a.* pert. to force in motion; pert. to dynamics; (*Med.*) functional; (*Fig.*) possessing energy and forcefulness (of character). Also **-al. -s** *n.* branch of mechanics which deals with *force in motion.* **dynamism** *n.* a school of scientific thought which explains phenomena of universe as resulting from action of natural forces. **dynamist** *n.* **dynamite** *n.* a powerful high explosive, with great disruptive force; *v.t.* to blow up with dynamite. **dynamiter** *n.* one who uses dynamite, esp. for criminal purposes. **dynamo** *n.* a generator for transforming mechanical energy into electrical energy (short for *dynamo-electric machine*); *pl.* **dynamos. dynamograph** *n.* the recording registered on a dynamometer. **dynamometer** *n.* an instrument for measuring force [Gk. *dunamis*, power].

dy·nas·ty (dī'·nas·ti·) *n.* a line of kings of the same family: the period of a family's rule. **dynast** *n.* a ruler. **dynastic** *a.* [Gk. *dunastēs*, a lord].

dyne (dīn') *n.* a centimeter-gram-second unit of force, or system [Gk. *dunamis*, force].

dys- (dis) *prefix* fr. Gk. meaning bad, ill, difficult.

dys·en·ter·y (dis'·an·ter·i·) *n.* inflammation of the mucous membrane of the large intestine, accompanied by excessive discharge of the bowels, pain and fever. **dysenteric, -al** *a.* [*dus-*, ill; *entera*, the entrails].

dys·pep·sia (dis·pep'·si·a) *n.* indigestion. **dyspeptic** *a.* suffering from indigestion; morbid; *n.* one who suffers from dyspepsia [Gk. *dys-*, bad; *peptein*, to digest].

dys·pro·si·um (dis·prō'·zi·um) *n.* one of the rare earths, and the most magnetic metal known [Gk. *dusprositos*, hard to get at].

E

each (ēch) a. and pron. denoting every one of a number, separately considered. Abbrev. **ea.** [O.E. aelc].

ea·ger (ē′·gẹr) a. inflamed by desire; ardent; yearning; earnest. **-ly** adv. **-ness** n. [Fr. aigre, sour, keen].

ea·gle (ē′·gl) n. large bird of prey; a gold 10 dollar piece of the U.S.; a military standard; (Golf) a hole played in two under par. —**eyed** a. sharp-sighted. **eaglet** n. a young eagle.

ear (ēr) n. the fruiting spike of a cereal plant; v.i. to form ears [O.E. ear].

ear (ēr) n. the organ of hearing, esp. external part of it; sensitiveness to musical sounds; attention; ear-shaped projection. **-ache** n. acute pain in ear. **-drum** n. the middle ear or tympanum. **-ed** a. **-lobe** n. **-mark** v.t. to mark the ears for identification; to reserve for a particular purpose. **-shot** n. distance at which sounds can be heard. **-splitting** a. exceedingly loud and piercing. **-wax** n. cerumen, a waxy secretion of glands of ear. **-wig** n. an insect with a body terminating in a pair of horny forceps [O.E. eare].

earl (url) n. a nobleman ranking between a marquis and a viscount. **-dom** n. territory or dignity of an earl [O.E. eorl].

ear·ly (ur′·li·) a. and adv. in the beginning of a period of time; belonging far back in time; in the near future. **earliness** n. [O.E. aerlice].

earn (urn) v.t. to gain money by labor; to merit by service; to get. **-ings** n.pl. wages; savings [O.E. earnian].

ear·nest (ur′·nist) a. serious in intention; sincere; zealous; n. seriousness. **-ly** adv. **-ness** n. [O.E. eornest, zeal].

ear·nest (ur′·nist) n. a pledge; sum paid as binding [M.E. ernes].

earth (urth) n. the planet on which we live; the soil, dry land, on the surface of the earth; world matters, as opposed to spiritual. **-s** n.pl. term in chemistry for certain metallic oxides. —**bound** a. fixed firmly in the earth; worldly; **-en** a. made of earth. **-enware** n. crockery made of earth. **-iness** n. **-ling** n. a dweller on the earth. **-ly** a. belonging to the earth; terrestial; worldly. **-nut** n. a name of certain plants whose tubers are edible. **-quake** n. disturbance of the earth's surface due to contraction of a section of the crust of the earth. **-work** n. embankments. **-worm** n. the common worm. **-y** a. like or pertaining to earth; gross [O.E. erothe].

ease (ēz) n. leisure; quiet; freedom from anxiety, bodily effort, or pain; facility; natural grace of manner; v.t. to free from pain, disquiet, or oppression. **-ful** a. **-ment** n. something that comforts; (Law) a right in another's land, e.g. right of way. **easily** adv. **easiness** n. **easing** n. the act of alleviating or slackening. **easy** a. at ease; free from pain, care, anxiety; moderate; comfortable. **stand at ease!** military term to relax. **easy-chair** n. an armchair. **easy-going** a. taking matters in an easy way [Fr. aise].

ea·sel (ē′·zl) n. a wooden frame to support pictures, etc. [Ger. Esel, an ass].

east (ēst) n. one of the four cardinal points; the part of the horizon where the sun rises; regions towards that; a. on, in, or near the east; adv. from or to the east. **-ern** a. toward, in, or from the east; oriental. **-ing** n. distance eastward from a given meridian. **-ward** adv. or a. toward the east. **-wards** adv. **Far East,** China, Japan, etc. **Middle East,** Iran, Iraq, etc. **Near East,** Turkey, Syria, Palestine, etc. [O.E. east].

East·er (ēs′·tẹr) n. a festival commemorating Christ's resurrection, falling on the Sunday after Good Friday [O.E. Eastre, spring festi-

val of goddess of dawn].

eas·y See under **ease.**

eat (ēt) v.t. to chew and swallow, as food; to consume gradually; to destroy; gnaw; corrode; wear away; v.i. to take food. pa.t. **ate** (āt). pa.p. **-en.** **-able** a. or n. anything that may be eaten. **-s** n.pl. (Slang) food ready for consumption [O.E. etan].

eau (ō) n. French for water; pl. **eaux.** **eau de Cologne,** a perfume obtained by distillation.

eaves (ēvz) n.pl. the lower edges of a sloping roof overhanging the walls of a building. **-drop** v.i. to listen furtively to a conversation. **-dropper** n. [O.E. efes, an edge].

ebb (eb) n. the reflux of tide-water to the sea; a decline; growing less; diminution; v.i. to flow back; to sink; to decline. — **tide** n. the ebbing or retiring tide [O.E. ebba].

eb·on (eb′·ạn) a. black as ebony. **-y,** a cabinet wood which is jet black. **-ite** n. hard rubber or form of a vulcanite [L. ebenus].

e·bul·lient (i·bul′·yạnt) a. boiling over; overflowing; exuberant; enthusiastic. **ebullience** n. **ebullition** n. act of boiling; outburst of feeling; agitation [L. bullire, to boil].

ec·cen·tric (ik·sen′·trik) a. departing from the center; not placed, or not having the axis placed, centrally; not circular (in orbit); irregular; odd; of a whimsical temperament; n. a disc mounted off center upon a shaft to change the rotary movement of a shaft into an up and down motion; a whimsical person; one who defies the social conventions. **-ally** adv. **eccentricity** n. the distance of a focus from the center of an ellipse; the deviation of two or more circles from a common center; departure from normal way of conducting oneself [Gk. ek, from; kentron, center].

ec·cle·si·a (i·klē′·zi·a) n. the general assembly of the freemen of Athens in classical times; a church; a religious assembly. **ecclesiastic** n. a clergyman; a priest; a. **ecclesiastical** a. **ecclesiasticism** n. adherence to ecclesiastical principles. **ecclesiology** n. the science and study of church architecture and decoration. **ecclesiologist** n. [Gk. ekklēsia, church].

ech·e·lon (esh′·a·lán) n. a level of command; an arrangement of troops in parallel lines, each a little to left or right of another; (Flying) formation of airplanes in which each plane flies slightly above and to the right or left of the one in front [Fr. échelle, a ladder].

e·chi·nus (e·kī′·nạs) n. a sea-urchin; a rounded molding as that below the abacus of a Doric capital [Gk. echinos, a hedgehog].

ech·o (ek′·ō) n. repetition of sound produced by sound waves reflected from an obstructing object; close imitation of another's remarks or ideas; reverberation; repetition; answer. pl. **-es.** v.t. to send back the sound of; to repeat with approval; to imitate closely; v.i. **-ism** n. forming words to imitate natural sounds. [Gk.].

é·clair (ā·klār′) n. a pastry filled with cream and frosted chocolate [Fr.].

é·clat (ā·klà′) n. splendor; approbation of success; renown; acclamation [Fr.].

ec·lec·tic (ik·lek′·tik) a. selecting at will; n. a thinker who selects and reconciles principles, opinions, belonging to different schools of thought. **-ally** adv. [Gk. eklegein, to pick out].

e·clipse (i·klips′) n. an interception of the light of one heavenly body by another; temporary effacement; v.t. to obscure or hide; to surpass [Gk. ek, out; leipein, to leave].

e·clip·tic (i·klip′·tik) n. the great circle on the celestial sphere which lies in the plane of the sun's apparent orbit round the Earth; a. Also **-al** a. [Gk. ek, out; leipein, to leave].

ec·logue (ek′·lawg) n. a short poem of a pastoral nature [Gk. eklogē, a selection].

e·col·o·gy (e·kál′·a·ji·) n. a study of relations between animals, plants, people and their environment [Gk. aikos, a house; logos, discourse].

e·con·o·my (e·kán′·a·mi·) n. wise expenditure of money; careful use of materials; management of the resources of a community; a saving harmonious organization. **economic, (al)** *a.* **economically** *adv.* **economics** *n.pl.* **political economy,** the science which deals with the production, distribution, and consumption of the world's resources and the management of state income and expenditure in terms of money. **economize** *v.i.* to expend with care and prudence; *v.t.* **economist** *n.* a student of economics; an economizer [Gk. *oikos*, a house; *nomos*, law].

é·cru (ek'·rŏŏ) *n.* beige [Fr. *écru*, unbleached].

ec·sta·sy (ek'·sta·si·) *n.* abnormal emotional excitement when the mind is ruled by one idea, object, or emotion; a sense of uplift and joyfulness and increased well-being; excessive joy. **ecstatic** *a.* to be in a state of rapture; overjoyed. **ecstatically** *adv.* [Gk. *ekstasis*]

ec·to-, ect-, a prefix implying *outside, without* [Gk. *ektos*].

ec·to·plasm (ek'·ta·plasm) *n.* (*Zool.*) exterior protoplasm of a cell; in spiritualism, an ethereal substance in which psychic phenomena may manifest themselves. **ectoplasmic** *a.* [Gk. *ektos*, outside; *plasma*, anything formed].

ec·u·men·ic, ecumenical (ek·yoo·men'·ik, ·i·kal) *a.* universal; representative of the Church, universal or catholic. Also **oecumenic, -al** [Gk. *oikoumenē*, the inhabited world].

ec·ze·ma (ek'·sa·ma, eg·zē'·ma) *n.* disease of the skin, characterized by itchiness and inflammatory eruption [Gk. *ekzema*].

ed·dy (ed'·i·) *n.* a current of air, smoke, or water, swirling back contrary to the main current; a vortex; *v.i.* to move in a circle [O.E. *ed* = black].

e·del·weiss (ā'·dl·vīs) *n.* a small white flowering plant found in the Swiss Alps [Ger. *edel*, noble; *weiss*, white].

E·den (ē'·dan) *n.* the garden where Adam and Eve lived; a place of delight; a paradise.

e·den·tate (ē·din'·tāt) *a.* without front teeth; lacking teeth; *n.* an edentate animal [L. *e*, out of; *dens*, tooth].

edge (ej) *n.* the thin cutting side of the blade of an instrument; the part adjacent to the line of division; rim; keenness; *v.t.* to put an edge on; to sharpen; to fringe; to move almost imperceptibly; *v.i.* to move sideways. **-d** *a.* sharp; bordered. **-less** *a.* **-ways, -wise** *adv.* in the direction of the edge; sideways. **edging** *n.* border or fringe; narrow lace. **edgy** *a.* having an edge; irritable. **to be on edge,** to be irritable [O.E. *ecg*].

ed·i·ble (ed'·a·bl) *a.* fit for eating; *n.* an eatable. **edibility** *n.* [L. *edere*, to eat].

e·dict (ē'·dikt) *n.* a law or decree; order proclaimed by a government or king [L. *e*; *dicere*, to say].

ed·i·fy (ed'·a·fī) *v.t.* to build up, esp. in character or faith; to instruct in moral and religious knowledge. *pa.t.* and *pa.p.* **edified. edification** *n.* improvement of the mind or morals. **edifice** *n.* a fine building. **edifier** *n.* **edifying** *a.* [L. *aedificare*, to build].

ed·it (ed'·it) *v.t.* to prepare for publication; to compile; to direct a newspaper or periodical; to revise and alter or omit. **edition** *n.* the form in which a book is published; the number of copies of a book, newspaper, etc. printed at one time; an issue; copy or prototype. **-or** *n.* one who edits; **editorial** *n.* an article in a newspaper presenting the newspaper's point of view; *a.* pert. to or written by an editor [L. *edere*, to give out].

ed·u·cate (ej'·oo·kāt) *v.t.* to cultivate and discipline the mind and other faculties by teaching; send to school. **educable** *a.* able to absorb education. **educability** *n.* **education** *n.* process of training; knowledge. **educational** *a.* **educationally** *adv.* **educative** *a.* tending to educate. **educator** *n.* one who educates [L. *e*, out; *ducere*, to lead].

e·duce (i·dŏŏs') *v.t.* to draw or bring out that which is latent; to elicit; to extract; to develop. **educible** *a.* **educt** *n.* that which is educed. **eduction** *n.* [L. *educere*, to lead out].

eel (ēl) *n.* a group of fishes with elongated bodies [O.E. *ael*].

e'en, e'er (ēn, er) *contr.* for *even, ever*.

ee·rie, eery (ē'·ri·) *a.* weird, superstitiously timid; frightening. **eerily** *adv.* **eeriness** *n.* [O.E. *earg*, timid].

ef·face (i·fās') *v.t.* to erase or scratch out. **-ment** *n.* the act of effacing [Fr. *effacer*].

ef·fect (a·fekt') *n.* that which is produced by an agent or cause; result; consequence; *v.t.* to bring about. **-s** *n.pl.* property. **-ive** *a.* in a condition to produce desired result; efficient; powerful. **-ively** *adv.* **-iveness** *n.* **-ual** *a.* producing the intended result; efficacious; successful. **-uality** *n.* **-ually** *adv.* **-uate** *v.t.* to bring to pass; to achieve; to effect. **in effect,** really; for practical purposes. **to take effect,** to become operative [L. *efficere*, to bring about].

ef·fem·i·nate (i·fem'·a·nit) *a.* unmanly; womanish [L. *effeminatus*, made womanish].

ef·fer·ent (ef'·er·ant) *a.* conveying outward, or away from the center [L. *ex*, out; *ferre*, to carry].

ef·fer·vesce (ef·er·ves') *v.i.* to bubble, to seethe, as a liquid giving off gas; to be in a state of excitement; to froth up. **-nce** *n.* **-ent** *a.* bubbling; lively; sparkling [L. *effervescere*].

ef·fete (e·fēt') *a.* no longer capable of bearing young; sterile; unfruitful; worn-out; spent [L. *effetus*, exhausted by breeding].

ef·fi·ca·cious (ef·a·kā'·shas) *a.* productive of effects; producing the desired effect. **-ly** *adv.* **-ness, efficacity, efficacy** *n.* power to produce effects [L. *efficere*, to effect].

ef·fi·cient (a·fish'·ant) *a.* causing effects; producing results; capable; able; effective. **efficiency** *n.* power to produce the result required; competency. **-ly** *adv.* [L. *efficere*, to effect].

ef·fi·gy (ef'·a·ji·) *n.* an image or representation of a person. **hang in effigy,** to hang an image of a person as a public expression of hatred [L. *effigies*, fr. *fingere*, to form].

ef·flo·resce (ef·lō·res') *v.i.* to burst into bloom; to blossom; (*Chem.*) to lose water of crystallization on exposure to air, so that crystals fall into powder. **-nce, -ncy** *n.* blooming; the time of flowering. **-ent** *a.* [L. *efflorescere*].

ef·flu·ent (ef'·loo·ant) *a.* flowing out; *n.* a stream which flows out from another river or lake. **effluence** *n.* a flowing out; issue; emanation [L. *efflorescens*].

ef·flu·vi·um (e·flŏŏ'·vi·am) *n.* an exhalation with a disagreeable smell. *pl.* **effluvia. effluvial** *a.* [L. fr. *effluere*].

ef·flux (ef'·luks) *n.* the act of flowing out; that which flows out [L. *effluere*, flow out].

ef·fort (ef'·ert) *n.* putting forth an exertion of strength or power, bodily or mental; attempt; achievement. **-less** *a.* [L. *ex*, out; *fortis*, strong]

ef·fron·ter·y (i·frun'·ter·i·) *n.* brazen impudence; audacity [Fr. *effronté* = without brow (for blushing)].

ef·fulge (e·fulj') *v.i.* to shine brightly. **-nce** *n.* **-nt** *a.* diffusing a flood of light; radiant [L. *ex*, out; *fulgere*, to shine].

ef·fuse (e·fūz') *v.t.* to pour out or forth; *a.* (*Bot.*) spread out; (of shells) slightly separated. **effusion** *n.* act of pouring out; that which is poured out. **effusive** *a.* gushing; demonstrative [L. *ex*, out; *fundere, fusum*, to pour].

e·gad (i·gad') *interj.* a mild imprecation = by God.

egg (eg) *v.t.* to urge on; to encourage one to take action [O.N. *eggja*, fr. *egg*, edge].

egg (eg) *n.* an oval body laid by birds and a few animals in which the embryo continues development apart from parent body; matured female germ cell or ovum; anything egg-shaped. **— cell** *n.* the ovum, as distinct from any other cells associated with it. **-nog** *n.* a drink made of egg, milk, sugar, and wine. **-shell** *n.* **-plant** *n.* an edible plant with somewhat egg-shaped purple fruit [O.N. *egg*].

e·gis See **aegis.**

eg·lan·tine (eg'·lan·tīn) *n.* the sweet brier; the honeysuckle [Fr. *églantine*].

e·go (ē'·gō, eg'·ō) *n.* I; the whole person; self; the personal identity. **-centric** *a.* self-centered. **-centricism, -centricity** *n.* systematic selfishness; theory that bases morality on self-interest. **-ist** *n.* **-istic, -istical** *a.* **-mania,** *n.* abnormal self-esteem. **-tism** *n.* the habit of talking or writing incessantly of oneself; selfishness. **-tist** *n.* **-tistic, -tistical** *a.* **-tistically** *adv.* [L. *ego*, I].

e·gre·gious (i·grē'·jas) *a.* remarkably flagrant. **-ly** *adv.* [L. *e*, out; *grex*, a flock].

e·gress (ē'·gres) *n.* act of leaving an enclosed place; exit; the right of departure. **egression** *n.* [L. *egressus*].

e·gret (ē'·grit) *n.* several species of heron [Fr. *aigrette*].

E·gy·ptian (ē·jip'·shan) *a.* pert. to Egypt; *n.* a native of Egypt. **Egyptology** *n.* study of Egyptian history, antiques, and inscriptions. **Egyptologist** *n.*

ei·der (ī'·der) *n.* **the eider duck,** a species of sea ducks. — **down** *n.* the breast down of the *eider duck*; a quilt stuffed with this down [O.N. *aethr*].

eight (āt) *n.* and *a.* one more than seven, written as 8 or VIII. **-een** *n.* and *a.* eight more than ten, written 18 or XVIII. **-eenth** *n.* and *a.* the eighth after the tenth, written 18th. **-fold** *a.* eight times any quantity. **eighth** *n.* and *a.* the first after the seventh; *n.* one of eight equal parts; 8th; (*Mus.*) the interval of an octave; the eighth note of the diatonic scale. **-ieth** *a.* ordinal corresponding to eighty, coming after the seventy-ninth; written 80th; *n.* one of eighty equal parts of a whole, written 1/80. **-y** *n.* and *a.* eight times ten; four-score [O.E. *eahla*].

ei·ther (ē'·, ī'·THer) *a.* or *pron.* one or the other; one of two; each; *adv.* or *conj.* bringing in the first of alternatives or strengthening an added negation [O.E. *aegther*].

e·jac·u·late (i·jak'·ya·lāt) *v.t.* to utter suddenly and briefly; to eject; *v.i.* to utter ejaculations. **ejaculation** *n.* a short, sudden exclamation; a sudden emission. **ejaculatory** *a.* [L. *e*, out; *jacere*, to throw].

e·ject (i·jekt') *v.t.* to throw out; to cast forth; to turn out; to dispossess of a house or estate. **-a** *n.* waste matter. **ejection** *n.* the act of casting out. **-ment** *n.* expulsion; dispossession; (*Law*) the forcible removal of a defaulting tenant by legal process from land or house. **-or** *n.* [L. *e*, out; *jacere*, to throw].

eke (ēk) *v.t.* to add or augment. — **out,** to supplement; to use makeshifts [O.E. *ecan*].

e·lab·o·rate (i·lab'·a·rāt) *v.t.* to put much work and skill on; to work out in detail; to take pains with; *v.i.* to give fuller treatment; *a.* (i·lab'·a·rit) worked out in details; highly finished; complicated. **-ly** *adv.* **-ness, elaboration** *n.* act of elaborating; progressive improvement [L. *e*, out; *labor*, labor].

é·lan (ā·làng') *n.* dash; impetuosity [Fr.].

e·land (ē'·land) *n.* the largest of the antelopes, found in Africa [Dut.].

e·lapse (i·laps') *v.i.* of time, to pass by; to slip away [L. *e*; *labi, lapsus*, slide].

e·las·tic (i·las'·tik) *a.* possessing the property of recovering the original form when a distorting or constraining force has been removed; flexible; resilient; springy; *n.* a fabric whose threads are interwoven with strands of rubber; a rubber band. **elasticity** *n.* [Gk. *elaunein*, to drive].

e·late (i·lāt') *v.t.* to raise or exalt the spirit of; make proud. **-d** *a.* **elation** *n.* exultation [L. *elatus*, lifted up].

el·bow (el'·bō) *n.* the joint between the arm and forearm; right angle bend for joining two pipes; any sharp bend or turn; *v.t.* and *v.i.* to push with the elbows; to jostle. — **grease** *n.* (*Colloq.*) hard work, as in rubbing vigorously. — **room** *n.* ample room for free movement [O.E. *elnboga*].

el·der (el'·der) *a.* older; senior; prior; *n.* one who is older; a senior; an office bearer in certain Protestant churches. **-liness** *n.* **-ly** *a.* somewhat old; up in years. **eldest** *a.* the oldest of a family [O.E. *eldo*].

el·der (el'·der) *n.* a flowering shrub which yields berries [O.E. *ellern*].

El Do·ra·do, Eldorado (el·da·rá'·dō) *n.* a fabulous city abounding in gold and precious stones; any similar place [Sp.=the gilded one].

e·lect (i·lekt') *v.t.* to choose; to choose by vote; to appoint to office; to select; *v.i.* to determine on a course of action; *a.* chosen; selected from a number; (after a noun), appointed but not yet in office; *n.* those predestined to eternal life. **election** *n.* the act of electing or choosing; public voting for office. **electioneer** *v.i.* to work for the election of a candidate. **-ive** *a.* appointed by; dependent on choice. **-ively** *adv.* **-or** *n.* one with right to vote at election. **-oral** *a.* pertaining to electors or to elections. **-oral college** *n.* a body of electors chosen by voters in the states to elect the president and vice-president of the U.S. **-orate** *n.* the whole body of electors [L. *eligere*].

e·lec·tric (i·lek'·trik) *a.* pertaining to, charged with, worked by, producing electricity; thrilling. — **chair,** used for electrocuting criminals. — **eel,** a fresh water fish of S. America which is capable of inflicting powerful shocks. **-al** *a.,* **-ally** *adv.* **-ity** (tris'·a·ti·) *n.* a form of energy generated by friction, induction, or chemical change, and having magnetic and radiant effects; state of strong tension. — **unit,** of pressure = *volt*; of current = *ampere*; of power = *watt*; of resistance = *ohm* [Gk. *ēlektron*, amber].

e·lec·tri·cian (i·lek·trish'·an) *n.* a mechanic who makes or repairs electrical apparatus.

e·lec·tri·fy (i·lek'·tra·fī) *v.t.* to charge with electricity; to thrill, startle, excite by an unexpected statement or action.

e·lec·tro- (i·lek'·trō) *prefix*, used in the construction of compound words referring to some phase of electricity. **-analysis** *n.* chemical analysis by electrolysis. **-cardiogram** *n.* a tracing of electrical changes of contractions of heart. **-cardiograph** *n.* machine which makes the tracing.

e·lec·tro·cute (i·lek'·tra·kūt) *v.t.* to cause death by electric shock. **electrocution** *n.*

e·lec·trode (i·lek'·trōd) *n.* a metallic conductor of an open electric circuit in contact with some other kind of conductor [Gk. *ēlektron*, amber; *hodos*, way].

e·lec·tro·dy·nam·ics (i·lek·trō·dī·nam'·iks) *n.* a branch of the science of electricity which treats of the laws of electricity in motion or of electric currents and their effects.

e·lec·tro·ki·net·ics (i·lek'·trō·ki·net·iks) *n.* Same as **electrodynamics.**

e·lec·trol·y·sis (i·lek·tral'·a·sis) *n.* the resolution of dissolved or fused chemical compounds into elements by passing a current of electricity through them; (*Surg.*) destruction of hair roots, tumors, by an electric current. **electrolyze** *v.t.* to subject to electrolysis. **electrolyte** *n.* the liquid which carries the electric current between two electrodes [Gk. *ēlektron*, amber; *luein*, to loosen].

e·lec·tro·mag·net (i·lek·trō·mag'·a·nit) *n.* a mass of soft iron temporarily magnetized by being placed within a coil of insulated copper wire through which a current of electricity is passing. **-ic** *a.* **-ism** *n.* branch of electrical science which deals with the relation of magnetism and electricity.

e·lec·trom·e·ter (i·lek·tråm'·e·tẹr) *n.* an instrument for measuring electricity.

e·lec·tro·mo·tion (i·lek·trå·mō'·shạn) *n.* the flow of an electric current in a voltaic circuit. **electromotive** *a.* producing motion by means of electricity.

e·lec·tron (i·lek'·tràn) *n.* the lightest known particle, a constituent of all atoms around whose nuclei they revolve in orbits. **electronics** *n.* the branch of physics which deals with the behavior of free electrons. — **microscope**, an instrument of immense magnifying power in which controlled rays of electrons are used instead of light rays.

e·lec·tro·neg·a·tive (i·lek·trạ·neg'·ạ·tiv) *a.* carrying a negative charge of electricity.

e·lec·trop·a·thy (i·lek·tråp'·ạ·thi·) *n.* treatment of disease by means of electricity. Also **electrotherapy. electrotherapeutics** *n.*

e·lec·tro·plate (i·lek'·trạ·plåt) *v.t.* to cover with a coating of metal by means of electrolysis; *n.* an article so covered.

e·lec·tro·pos·i·tive (i·lek·trạ·pås'·ạ·tiv) *a.* carrying a positive charge of electricity.

e·lec·tro·stat·ics (i·lek·trạ·stat'·iks) *n.* the branch of electrical science which treats of the behavior of electricity in equilibrium or at rest.

e·lec·tro·type (i·lek'·trạ·tīp) *n.* a facsimile printing plate of type or illustrations.

e·lec·trum (i·lek'·trạm) *n.* an alloy of gold and silver [Gk. *ēlektron*].

el·ee·mos·y·nar·y (el·ạ·mos'·ạ·nẹr·i·) *a.* by way of charity; given in charity [Gk. *eleēmosunē*, alms].

el·e·gant (el'·ạ·gạnt) *a.* graceful; tasteful; refined; luxurious. **-ly** *adv.* **elegance** *n.* grace; beauty; propriety; gentility; delicate taste [L. *elegans*].

el·e·gy (el'·ạ·ji·) *n.* a poem of mourning; a funeral song. **elegiac** *a.* pertaining to elegy; written in elegiacs. **elegiacs** *n.pl.* elegiac verse or couplets, each made up of a hexameter and a pentameter. **elegiacal** *a.* **elegiast, elegist** *n.* a writer of elegies [Gk. *elegos*, a lament].

e·lek·tron (i·lek'·tràn) *n.* a magnesium alloy of unusual lightness. See **elektrum** [Gk. = amber].

el·e·ment (el'·ạ·mạnt) *n.* the first principle or rule; a component part; ingredient; constituent; essential point; the habitation most suited to a person or animal; (*Chem.*) a substance which cannot be separated into two or more substances. **-s** *n.pl.* the bread and wine used in the Lord's Supper; fire, air, water and earth, supposed to be foundation of all things; the physical forces of nature which determine the state of the weather. **-al** *a.* of the powers of nature; not compounded; basic; fundamental. **-ary** *a.* pertaining to the elements or first principles of anything; rudimentary; simple [L. *elementum*].

el·e·phant (el'·ạ·fạnt) *n.* the largest four-footed animal, having a long flexible trunk, two ivory tusks, and exceedingly thick skin. **-ine** *a.* huge; unwieldy; ungainly. **-oid** *a.* like an elephant [Gk. *elephas*].

el·e·phan·ti·a·sis (el·ạ·fạn·tī'·ạ·sis) *n.* disease in which there is gross enlargement of the affected parts [Gk. *elephas*, an elephant].

el·e·vate (el'·ạ·våt) *v.t.* to lift up; to raise to a higher rank or station; to elate. **elevated** *a.* raised; dignified; exhilarated; *n.* a railroad on elevated tracks. **elevation** *n.* the act of elevating or the state of being raised; elevated place, a hill, a height; (*Archit.*) geometrical projection, drawn to scale, of the vertical face of any part of a building or object. **elevator** *n.* the person or thing which lifts up; a lift or hoist; a silo where grain is stored; the rudder-like airfoil hinged to the tail of an aircraft. **elevatory** *a.* tending or having power to elevate [L. *levis*, light].

e·lev·en (i·lev'·n) *n.* and *a.* one more than ten,

written as 11 or XI; a full team at football or hockey. **-th** *a.* the ordinal number corresponding to eleven, the next after tenth; *n.* one of 11 equal parts of a whole [O.E. *endlufan*].

elf (elf) *n.* a supernatural, diminutive being of folk-lore with mischievous traits; a hobgoblin; a dwarf; *pl.* **elves** (elvz). **-in** *n.* a little elf; **elfish** *a.* elf-like; roughish [O.E. *aelf*].

e·lic·it (i·lis'·it) *v.t.* to draw out; to extract; to bring to light facts by questioning or reasoning [L. *elicere*].

e·lide (i·līd') *v.t.* to cut off or suppress a vowel or syllable. **elision** *n.* the suppression of a vowel or syllable [L. *elidere*, to strike out].

el·i·gi·ble (el'·i·jạ·bl) *a.* legally qualified; fit and worthy to be chosen; desirable. **eligibility** *n.* [L. *eligere*, to choose].

e·lim·i·nate (i·lim'·ạ·nåt) *v.t.* to remove; get rid of; set aside; separate; leave out of consideration; excrete; expel; obliterate. **elimination** *n.* **eliminator** *n.* [L. *eliminare*, to put out of doors].

e·li·sion See **elide.**

e·lite (i·lēt') *n.* a choice or select body; the best part of society [Fr.].

e·lix·ir (i·lik'·sẹr) *n.* a cure-all; a medicine; the essence, vainly sought by the alchemists, which would have the power to transmute base metals into gold [Ar. *al-iksir*].

E·liz·a·be·than (i·liz·ạ·bē'·thạn) *a.* pert. to Queen Elizabeth I or her times; *n.* a writer or distinguished person of her reign.

elk (elk) *n.* the largest member of the deer family in the N. of Europe; in America, the wapiti; a leather used for shoes, etc. [O.E. *eolh*].

ell (el) *n.* an addition to a building, usually at right angles [from letter L].

el·lipse (i·lips') *n.* a regular oval, formed by the line traced out by a point moving so that the sum of its distance from two fixed points always remains the same; the plane section across a cone not taken at right angles to the axis. **ellipsoid** *n.* a closed solid figure of which every plane section is an ellipse. **elliptic(al)** *a.* oval; pertaining to an ellipse [See **ellipsis**]. [Gk. *elleipsis*, a defect].

el·lip·sis (i·lip'·sis) *n.* in English syntax a term denoting the omission of a word or words from a sentence whereby the complete meaning is obtained by inference. **elliptic(al)** *a.* [Gk.].

elm (elm) a genus of trees [O.E.].

el·o·cu·tion (el·ạ·kū'·shạn) *n.* art of effective public speaking from the point of view of enunciation, voice-production, delivery. **-ary** *a.* **-ist** *n.* [L. *e*, out; *loqui*, to speak].

e·lon·gate (i'·lawng·gåt) *v.t.* to make longer; to lengthen; to extend; to draw out; *a.* (*Bot.*) tapering. **elongation** *n.* the act of stretching out; the part extended [L. *e*; *longus*, long].

e·lope (i·lōp') *v.i.* to run away with a lover; to marry secretly; to bolt unexpectedly. **-ment** *n.* [O.Fr. *alouper*].

el·o·quence (el'·ạ·kwạns) *n.* the art or power of expressing thought in fluent, impressive and graceful language; oratory; rhetoric; fluency. **eloquent** *a.* **eloquently** *adv.* [L. *e*, out; *loqui*, to speak].

else (els) *adv.* besides; other; otherwise; instead. **-where** *adv.* in or to some other place [O.E. *elles*].

e·lu·ci·date (i·lòò'·sạ·dåt) *v.t.* to make clear or manifest; to throw light upon; to explain; illustrate. **elucidation** *n.* act of throwing light upon or explaining. **elucidative, elucidatory** *a.* **elucidator** *n.* [L. *e*; *lux*, light; *dare*, to give].

e·lude (i·lòòd') *v.t.* to keep out of sight; to escape by stratagem, artifice, or dexterity; to evade; to baffle. **elusion** *n.* act of eluding; evasion. **elusive** *a.* **elusory** *a.* [L. *e*, out; *ludere*, to play].

el·van, elves, elvish See **elf.**

E·ly·si·um (e·lizh'·i·ạm) *n.* (*Myth.*) according

to the Greeks, the abode of the virtuous dead where the inhabitants lived a life of passive blessedness; any place of perfect happiness. **Elysian** *a.* like a paradise; blissful.

em- *prefix* in or with; or adding a transitive or casual force in the composition of verbs.

em (em) *n.* (*Print.*) Typographical unit of width, known as a pica or 12 pt. em (approx. ⅙th of an in.) used for measuring the length of a line of type.

e·ma·ci·ate (i·mā′·shi·āt) *v.t.* to make lean; to reduce one to flesh and bones; *v.i.* to waste away; to become extremely thin. **-d.** *a.* **emaciation** *n.* [L. *emaciare*, fr. *macies*, leanness].

em·a·nate (em′·a·nāt) *v.i.* to issue from; to originate; to proceed from; to arise (of intangible things). **emanant** *a.* flowing from. **emanation** *n.* a flowing out from; that which issues from a source; radioactive, chemically inert gas given off by radium, thorium and actinium. **emanative, emanatory** *a.* [L. *emanare*, to flow out].

e·man·ci·pate (i·man′·sa·pāt) *v.t.* to set free from slavery or servitude; to set free from any restraint or restriction. **emancipation** *n.* **emancipator** *n.* [L. *emancipare*].

e·mas·cu·late (i·mas′·ka·lāt) *v.t.* to castrate; to deprive of masculine qualities; to render effeminate. **emasculation** *n.* **emasculatory** *a.* [L. *e*; *masculus*, masculine].

em·balm (im·bám′) *v.t.* to preserve a corpse from decay by means of antiseptic agents, balm, aromatic oils and spices; to perfume; to cherish tenderly some memory of. **-er** *n.* **-ing**, **-ment** *n.* [Fr. *embaumer*].

em·bank (im·bangk′) *v.t.* to enclose or defend with a bank, mound, or earthwork. **-ment** *n.* the act of embarking; an earthwork built to prevent flooding or hold up a road, etc.

em·bar·go (im·bár′·gō) *n.* in international law, an order by which a government prevents a foreign ship from entering or leaving port; an order forbidding the despatch of a certain class of goods, usually munitions, to another country; a general prohibition. *pl.* **embargoes.** *v.t.* to lay an embargo upon [Sp. *embargar*, to impede].

em·bark (im·bárk′) *v.t.* to put on board a ship; to enter on some business or enterprise; *v.i.* to go on board a ship. **-ation** *n.* [Fr. *embarquer*].

em·bar·rass (im·bar′·as) *v.t.* to disconcert; to perplex; to abash; to impede; to involve one in difficulties, esp. regarding money matters. **-ed** *a.* **-ing** *a.* disconcerting. **-ment** *n.* [Fr. *embarrasser*].

em·bas·sy (em′·ba·si·) *n.* the person sent abroad as an ambassador along with his staff; the residence of an ambassador [O.Fr. *ambasée*].

em·bat·tle (em·bat′·l) *v.t.* to furnish with battlements. **-ment** *n.*

em·bat·tle (em·bat′·l) *v.t.* to draw up in order of battle. **-d** *a.* [O.F. *embatailler*].

em·bed (im·bed′) *v.t.* to lay as in a bed; to bed in soil. Also **imbed.**

em·bel·lish (im·bel′·ish) *v.t.* to make beautiful or elegant with ornaments; to add fanciful details to a report or story. **-er** *n.* **-ingly** *adv.* **-ment** *n.* [Fr. *embellir*, to beautify].

em·ber (em′·ber) *n.* a live piece of coal or wood; *pl.* red-hot ashes [O.E. *aemerge*].

em·bez·zle (im·bez′·l) *v.t.* to misappropriate fraudulently. **-ment** *n.* **-r** *n.* [O.Fr. *enbesiler*, to damage, steal].

em·bit·ter (im·bit′·er) *v.t.* to make bitter. **-ed** *a.*

em·bla·zon (em·blā′·zan) *v.t.* to adorn with heraldic figures; to deck in blazing colors; to proclaim. **-ment** *n.* **-ry** *n.* emblazoning.

em·blem (em′·blam) *n.* an object, or a representation of an object, symbolizing and suggesting to the mind something different from itself; sign; badge; symbol; device. **-atic, -al** *a.* **-atically** *adv.* **-atize** *v.t.* to represent by

an emblem; to be an emblem of [Gk. *emblema*, a thing put in].

em·bod·y, imbody (im·bod′·i.) *v.t.* to form into a body; to incorporate; to give concrete expression to; to represent. **embodiment** *n.* an act of embodying; bodily representation.

em·bold·en (im·bōl′·d'n) *v.t.* to give boldness or courage to; to encourage.

em·bo·lism (em′·ba·lizm) *n.* the insertion of days between other days to adjust the reckoning of time; (*Med.*) the result of the presence in the blood stream of a solid foreign substance, as a clot. **embolismal** *a.* [Gr. *embole*, an insertion].

em·bos·om, imbosom (em·, im·booz′·am) *v.t.* to clasp or receive into the bosom; to enclose; to shelter; to foster.

em·boss (im·baws′) *v.t.* to raise or form a design above the surrounding surface. **-ed** *a.* **-ment** *n.* a boss or protuberance [O.Fr. *bosc*].

em·bow·el (em·bou′·al) *v.t.* to disembowel.

em·bow·er (em·bou′·er) *v.t.* to lodge, or set in a bower; to surround (with flowers).

em·brace (em·brās′) *v.t.* to clasp in the arms; to press to the bosom; to avail oneself of; to accept; to encircle; *n.* a clasping in the arms; a hug [Fr. *embrasser*, fr. *bras*, arm].

em·bra·sure (em·brā′·zher) *n.* the splay or bevel of a door or window where the sides slant on the inside; opening in a parapet of a fort to allow cannon-fire [Fr.].

em·bro·cate (em′·brō·kāt) *v.t.* to moisten and rub with lotion, etc. **embrocation** *n.* [Gk. *embroche*, lotion].

em·broi·der (im·broi′·der) *v.t.* to ornament fabrics with threads of silk, linen, etc. to form a design; to embellish, exaggerate a story. **-er** *n.* **-y** *n.* ornamental needlework [O.Fr. *broder*].

em·broil (em·broil′) *v.t.* to involve in a quarrel or strife; to entangle; to confound. **-ment** *n.* [Fr. *embrouiller*, to entangle].

em·bry·o (em′·bri·ō), **embryon** (em′·bri·an) *n.* foetus during first months of gestation before quickening; a plant in rudimentary stage of development within seed; initial or rudimentary stage of anything; *a.* rudimentary; in the early stage. **-logic, -logical** *a.* pert. to embryology. **-logist** *n.* **-logy** *n.* science which deals with the growth and structure of the embryo. **-nic** *a.* rudimentary; at an early stage of development [Gk. *embruon*].

e·mend (i·mend′) *v.t.* to remove faults or blemishes from; to amend, esp. of correcting a literary text; to alter for the better. **emendate** *v.t.* **emendation** *n.* correction of errors or blemishes. **emendator** *n.* **-atory** *a.*

em·er·ald (em′·er·ald) *n.* precious stone of beryl species, transparent and bright green in color. **Emerald Isle,** Ireland [Fr. *émeraude*].

e·merge (i·merj′) *v.i.* to rise out of a fluid; to come forth; to come into view; to come to notice. **-nce** *n.* coming into view; an outgrowth from a plant. **-ncy** *n.* state of pressing necessity; difficult situation; urgent need. **-nt** *a.* emerging; rising into view [L. *e*, out; *mergere*, to plunge].

e·mer·i·tus (i·mer′·a·tas) *n.* and *a.* one who has honorably resigned or retired from a position of trust or responsibility but is retained on the rolls [L. = a veteran, fr. *e*, out; *merere*, to earn].

e·mer·sion (ē·mur′·shan) *n.* an emerging.

em·er·y (em′·er·i.) *n.* a naturally occurring mixture of corundum and iron oxide, used as an abrasive for polishing; *v.t.* to rub with emery [Gk. *smuris*].

e·met·ic (i·met′·ik) *a.* inducing vomiting; *n.* any agent which causes vomiting [Gk. *emetikos*, provoking sickness].

em·i·grate (em′·a·grāt) *v.i.* to leave one's country to settle in another. **emigrant** *a.* pert. to emigration; *n.* one who emigrates. **emigra-**

tion n. [L. e, out; migrare, to remove].

em·i·nent (em'·a·nant) a. exalted in rank, office, or public estimation; prominent. **eminence** n. elevation; rising ground; height; rank; official dignity; fame [L. eminere, to stand out].

e·mir (a·mēr') n. a title bestowed on Moslem chiefs [Ar. amir].

em·is·sar·y (em'·a·ser·i·) n. agent charged with a secret mission; one sent on a mission [L. e, out; mittere, missum, to send].

e·mit (i·mit') v.t. to send forth; to utter (a declaration). pr.p. **-ting.** pa.p., pat. **-ted.** **emission** n. **emissive** a. [L. e, out; mittere, to send].

e·mol·lient (i·mál'·i·ant) a. softening; relaxing; assuaging; a soothing agent or medicine [L. mollis, soft].

e·mol·u·ment (i·mál'·yoo·mant) n. profit arising from office or employment; gain; pay; salary; fee [L. moliri, to toil].

e·mo·tion (i·mō'·shan) n. strong, generalized feeling; excitement or agitation. **-al** a. easily excited or upset. **-alism** n. tendency to emotional excitement. **-ally** adv. **-less** a. **emotive** a. causing emotion [L. emotio, fr. emovere, to stir].

em·pa·thy (em'·pa·thi·) n. intellectual identification of oneself with another [Gk. en, in; pathos, feeling].

em·per·or (em'·per·er) n. the title assumed by the ruler of an empire [L. imperare].

em·pha·sis (em'·fa·sis) n. stress on anything such as force of voice given to words or syllables. pl. **emphases, emphasize** v.t. to stress. **emphatic, emphatical** a. [Gk.].

em·pire (em'·pīr) n. imperial power; dominion; a country with its satellite states under the rule of an emperor or some other supreme control [L. imperium, command].

em·pir·ic, em·pir·i·cal (em·pir'·ik, -al) a. based on the results of experiment, observation, or experience, and not from mathematical or scientific reasoning; having reference to actual facts. **empiric** n. a quack; one who depends for his knowledge entirely on experience. **-ally** adv. **empiricism** n. the philosophical doctrine that sensory experience is the only source of knowledge; the formulation of scientific laws by the process of observation and experiment. **empiricist** n. [Gk. en, in; peira, trial].

em·place·ment (em·plás'·mant) n. the place or site of a building; a fortified position for a gun; placing in position.

em·ploy (em·ploi') v.t. to give occupation to; to make use of; to hire or engage; to busy; to engross; to exercise; to occupy; (em'·ploi) n. paid service. **-able** a. **-ee** n. one who is employed at a wage or salary. **-er** n. **-ment** n. [Fr. employer].

em·po·ri·um (em·pō'·ri·am) n. a place of extensive commerce or trade; a mart; a big shop. pls. **emporia** [Gk. emporos, trader].

em·pow·er (im·pou'·er) v.t. to give legal or moral power or authority to; to authorize.

em·press (em'·pris) n. the wife of an emperor; a female who exercises similar supreme power to that of an emperor.

emp·ty (emp'·ti·) a. containing nothing; wanting force or meaning; void; vacant; unoccupied; destitute; hollow; unreal; senseless; (Colloq.) hungry; v.t. to make empty; to pour out; to drain; v.i. to become empty; to discharge; **emptiness** n. [O.E. aemtig].

em·py·e·ma (em·pī·ē'·ma) n. (Med.) a collection of pus in body cavity, esp. in pleura [Gk. en; puon, pus].

em·pyr·e·al (em·pir'·i·al) a. of pure fire or light; pert. to highest and purest regions of heaven. **empyrean** a. empyreal; n. highest heaven, or region of pure elemental fire; the firmament [Gk. en, in; pur, fire].

e·mu, emeu (ē'·mū) n. a large flightless bird, native of Australia [Port.].

em·u·late (em'·yoo·lāt) v.t. to strive to equal or surpass; to rival; to imitate. **emulation** n. act of attempting to equal or excel. **emulative** a. **emulator** n. **emulous** a. anxious to emulate or outdo another [L. aemulari, to rival].

e·mul·sion (i·mul'·shan) n. a liquid mixture in which a fatty or oily substance is suspended in water and by aid of a mucilaginous medium forms a smooth milky white fluid; the coating of silver salts on a photographic film or plate. **emulsic** a. **emulsification** n. **emulsify** v.t. **emulsive** a. yielding a milk-like substance [L. e, out; mulgere, to milk].

en (en) n. a printer's unit of measurement equal to half an em [See **em**].

en- prefix in; with; or adding transitive or causal force in verb composition.

en·a·ble (in·ā'·bl) v.t. to make able; to authorize to empower; to fit; to qualify.

en·act (in·akt') v.t. to make into a law; to act the part of. **-ing** a. **-ive** a. **-ment** n. the passing of a bill into law; a decree; a law.

en·am·el (i·nam'·l) n. a vitreous compound fused into surface of metal, pottery, or glass for utility and ornament; the hard, glossy surface of teeth; paint with glossy finish; v.t. to enamel [Fr. émail, enamel].

en·am·or (in·am'·er) v.t. to inflame with love; to captivate; to charm; to fascinate.

en·camp (in·kamp') v.t. to form into a camp; v.i. to settle in or pitch a camp; to settle down temporarily. **-ment** n. an encamping; camp site.

en·case See **incase**.

en·caus·tic (en·kaws'·tik) a. pertaining to the fixing of colors by burning; n. an ancient style of decorative art, consisting in painting on heated wax [Gk. en, in; kaustikos, burnt].

en·ceinte (en·sānt') a. pregnant; with child; n. the precincts within the walls of a fort [Fr.]

en·ceph·a·lon (en·sef'·a·lán) n. the brain. **encephalic** a. cerebral; relating to the brain. **encephalitis** n. inflammation of the brain. [Gk. en, in; kephalē, the head].

en·chain (en·chān') v.t. to fasten with a chain; to hold fast. **-ment** n.

en·chant (in·chant') v.t. to charm by sorcery; to hold, as by a spell. **-ed** a. delighted; held by a spell. **-er** n. (fem. **-ress**) one who enchants; a sorcerer. **-ingly** adv. **-ment** n. act of enchanting; incantation; magic; delight; fascination [Fr. enchanter].

en·chase (en·chās') v.t. to adorn with chased work; to set with jewels. **-d** a.

en·cir·cle (in·sur'·kl) v.t. to enclose in a circle; to surround. **-ment** n.

en·clave (en'·klāv) n. a country, e.g. Switzerland, or an outlying province of a country, entirely surrounded by territories of another power; anything entirely enclosed into something else [L. in; clavis, a key].

en·clit·ic (en·klit'·ik) n. a word or particle united, for pronunciation, to another word so as to seem a part of it, e.g. thee in prithee [Gk. en, in; klinein, to lean].

en·close, inclose (in·klōz') v.t. to shut in; to surround; to envelope; to contain. **enclosure** n.

en·co·mi·um (en·kō'·mi·am) n. high commendation; formal praise. pl. **-s, encomia.** **encomiast** n. eulogist. **encomiastic(al)** a. **encomiastically** adv. [Gk.].

en·com·pass (in·kum'·pas) v.t. to include; to contain; to encircle. **-ment** n.

en·core (ang'·kōr) interj. again! once more! n. a recall awarded by an audience to a performer, artiste, etc.; the item repeated; v.t. to applaud with encore [Fr. = again].

en·coun·ter (in·koun'·ter) v.t. to meet face to face; to meet unexpectedly; to meet in a hostile manner; to contend against; to confront; n. an unexpected meeting; a fight or combat [Fr. encontrer].

en·cour·age (in·kur'·ij) v.t. to give courage to; to inspire with hope; to embolden. **-ment** n. that which gives courage; act of encouraging.

encouraging a. [Fr. encourager].

en·croach (in·krōch') v.i. to invade the rights or possessions of another; to intrude on other's property. **-er** n. **-ingly** adv. **-ment** n. [Fr. accrocher, to hook on].

en·crust, encrustation See **incrust**.

en·cum·ber (in·kum'·ber) v.t. to load; to impede; to burden; to saddle with debts. **encumbrance** n. a burden; a dependent person; a legal claim on an estate [Fr. encombrer].

en·cyc·li·cal (en·sik'·li·kl) a. intended to circulate among many people and in many places; n. an encyclical letter, a letter addressed by the Pope to the bishops of the R.C. Church. Also **encyclic** [Gk. en, in; kuklos, a circle].

en·cy·clo·pe·di·a, encyclopaedia (en·sī··kla·pē'·di·a) n. works which give detailed account, in alphabetical order, of whole field of human knowledge, or of some particular section in it. **encyclopedian** a. embracing all forms of knowledge. **encyclopedic** a. having universal knowledge; full of information. **encyclopedist** n. a compiler of an encyclopedia [Gk. enkuklios paideia, all around education].

en·cyst (en·sist') v.t. or v.i. to enclose or become enclosed in a sac or cyst.

end (end) n. the extreme point of a line; the last part in general; termination; conclusion; limit; extremity; final condition; issue; consequence; result; object; aim; death; a fragment; v.t. to bring to an end or conclusion; to destroy; to put to death; v.i. to come to the ultimate point; to finish; to be finished; to cease. **-ed** a. **-ing** n. termination; conclusion; the terminating syllable or letter of a word; suffix. **-less** a. **-lessly** adv. **-lessness** n. **at loose ends**, bored. **at one's wits' end**, perplexed; unable to proceed. **to make both ends meet**, to keep out of debt; to balance income and expenditure [O.E. ende].

en·dan·ger (in·dān'·jer) v.t. to place in jeopardy; to expose to loss or injury.

en·dear (in·dēr') v.t. to render dear or more beloved. **-ed** a. **-ing** a. **-ingly** adv. **-ment** n. the state of being, or act of, endearing; tender affection; loving word; a caress.

en·deav·or (in·dev'·er) v.i. to exert all strength for accomplishment of object; to attempt; to strive; n. attempt; effort; struggle [Fr. devoir, duty].

en·dem·ic, endemical (en·dem'·ik, -al) a. terms applied to recurring diseases confined to certain people or localities and which arise from local causes. **endemic** n. an endemic disease [Gk. en, in demos, a people].

en·dive (en'·dīv, án·dēv') n. an annual plant of the family Compositae, used for salads [Fr.].

en·do- (en'·dō) prefix indicating within [Gk. endon].

en·do·car·di·tis (en·dō·kàr·dī'·tis) n. (Med.) inflammation of the lining membrane of the heart [Gk. endon, within; kardia, heart].

en·do·car·di·um (en·da·kàr'·di·am) n. the lining membrane of the heart. **endocardiac** a. **endocardial** a.

en·do·crine (en'·da·krin) a. (Zool.) describing the tissues and organs giving rise to an internal secretion; n. any such secretion. **endocrinology** n. study of internal secretions of ductless glands [Gk. endon, within; krinein, to separate].

en·dog·a·my (en·dág'·a·mi·) n. the custom of compulsory marriage within the limits of a tribe or clan or between members of the same race. **endogamous** a. [Gk. endon, within; gamos, marriage].

en·do·plasm (en'·da·plazm) n. inner portion of cytoplasm of a cell [Gk. endon, within; plasma, a formation].

en·dorse, indorse (in·dors') v.t. to write (esp. to sign one's name) on back of, as a check; to back (a bill, etc.); to sanction; to confirm; to vouch for; to ratify; **endorsable** a. **en-**

dorsee n. the person to whom a bill of exchange, etc. is assigned by endorsement. **-ment** n. act of endorsing. **-r** n. [Fr. endosser, fr. dos, back; L. dorsum].

en·do·scope (en'·da·skōp) n. (Med.) an instrument for inspecting the cavities of internal parts of the body [Gk. endon, within; skopein, to see].

en·do·sperm (en'·dō·spurm) n. (Bot.) the nutritive starchy tissue which surrounds the embryo in many seeds. **-ic** a. [Gk. endon, within; sperma, seed].

en·dow (in·dou') v.t. to settle, by deed or will, a permanent income on; to enrich or furnish. **-er** n. **-ment** n. the act of settling a fund or permanent provision for an institution or individual; grant; bequest; natural capacity [O Fr. endouer].

en·dure (in·door') v.t. to remain firm under; to bear with patience; to put up with; to sustain; to suffer; to tolerate; v.i. to continue; to last. **endurable** a. can be endured, borne, or suffered. **endurableness** n. **endurably** adv. **endurance** n. power of enduring; act of bearing pain or distress; continuance; patience; fortitude; stamina. **-r** n. **enduring** a. and n. **enduringly** adv. [L. indurare; fr. durus, hard].

en·e·ma (en'·a·ma) n. a liquid solution injected into intestine through rectum; device for this [Gk. fr. en, in; hienai, to send].

en·e·my (en'·a·mi·) n. one actuated by hostile feelings; an armed foe; opposing state; something harmful; a. of an enemy; due to an enemy [Fr. ennemi, fr. L. inimicus].

en·er·gy (en'·er·ji·) n. vigor; force; activity; (Mech.) the power of doing mechanical work; **energetic(al)** a. exerting force; vigorous; active; forcible. **energetically** adv. **energize** v.t. to give energy to; v.i. to act energetically [Gk. energeia, activity].

en·er·vate (en'·er·vāt) v.t. to deprive of nerve, strength, or courage; a. spiritless. **enervating, enervative** a. **enervation** n. [L. enervare, to deprive of sinew].

en·fee·ble (in·fē'·bl) v.t. to render feeble.

en·fi·lade (en·fa·lād') n. a line or straight passage; narrow line, as of troops in marching; fire from either flank along a line; v.t. to direct enfilading fire [Fr. enfiler, to string on a thread].

en·fold See **infold**.

en·force (in·fōrs') v.t. to give strength to; to put in force; to impress on mind; to compel; to impose (action) upon; to urge on; to execute. **-able** a. **enforcedly** adv. under threat or compulsion. **-ment** n. [O.Fr. enforcer].

en·fran·chise (en·fran'·chīz) v.t. to set free from slavery; to extend political rights to; to grant the privilege of voting. **-ment** n.

en·gage (in·gāj') v.t. to bind by contract, pledge, or promise; to hire; to order; to employ; to undertake; to occupy; to busy; to attract; to bring into conflict; to interlock; v.i. to begin to fight; to employ oneself (in); to promise. **-d** a. **-ment** n. act of engaging; state of being engaged; obligation by contract or agreement; pledge; betrothal; occupation; affair of business or pleasure; battle; encounter. **engaging** a. attractive; pleasing [Fr. engager].

en·gen·der (in·jen'·der) v.t. to beget; to cause to exist; to sow the seeds of; to breed; to occasion or cause (strife) [Fr. engendrer].

en·gine (en'·jan) n. any mechanical contrivance for producing and conveying motive power; a machine; a. **engineer** n. one who constructs, designs, or is in charge of engines, military works, or works of public utility (roads, docks, etc.); v.t. to direct or design work as a skilled engineer; to contrive; to bring about; to arrange. **engineering** n. the art of constructing and using machines or engines; the profession of an engineer. [Fr. engin, fr. L. ingenium, skill].

Eng·lish (ing'·glish) a. belonging to England

or its inhabitants; *n.* the people or the language of England; *v.t.* to anglicize. **-man** *n.* **Old English,** language to about 1150 A.D. **Middle English,** 1150-1500. **Modern English,** from 1500. **Basic English,** a skeleton form of the English language of less than a thousand words [O.E. *Englisc,* fr. *Engle,* Angle].

en·gorge (en·gawrj′) *v.t.* to swallow greedily and in large quantities; *v.i.* to feed with voracity; to devour. **-ment** *n.* [Fr. *engorger,* fr. *gorge,* the throat].

en·graft, ingraft (en·graft′) *v.t.* to graft on; to incorporate; to add to. **-ation** *n.* **-ment** *n.*

en·grain See **ingrain.**

en·grave (in·grāv′) *v.t.* to draw on a metal plate a design or picture by means of an incised line or on wood by leaving a raised surface; to imprint; to make a deep impression; *v.i.* to practice the art of engraving. **-r** *n.* **engraving** *n.* the art of cutting designs, etc. on wood, metal, or stone; an impression on art paper taken from an engraved block or plate; a print [See **grave**].

en·gross (in·grōs′) *v.t.* to occupy wholly; to absorb; to copy in a large fair hand or in legal form; to buy wholesale with a view to cornering the market; to monopolize. **-er** *n.* **-ing** *n.* **-ment** *n.* [Fr. *en gros,* in a large hand].

en·gulf, ingulf (in·gulf′) *v.t.* to swallow up or absorb as in a gulf; to encompass wholly.

en·hance (in·hans′) *v.t.* to intensify; to increase in value or worth; to add to the effect. **-ment** *n.* [Fr. *hausser,* to raise].

en·har·mon·ic, enharmonical (en·här··mán′·ik, -al) *a.* (*Mus.*) having the same pitch but written in different notation, as G♯ and A♭; pert. to one of the three ancient Greek scales, the others being diatonic and chromatic [Gk. *en,* in; *harmonia,* harmony].

e·nig·ma (i·nig′·ma) *n.* an obscure question or saying difficult of explanation; anything or anybody puzzling; a riddle. **-tic(al)** *a.* **-tically** *adv.* [Gk. *ainigma*].

en·jamb·ment (in·jam′·mant) *n.* in verse, continuation of a sentence from one line into the next [Fr. *en,* in; *jambe,* leg].

en·join (in·join′) *v.t.* to direct with authority; to order; to impose; to prescribe; (*Law*) to prohibit by judicial order; to put an injunction on. **-ment** *n.* [Fr. *enjoindre*].

en·joy (in·joi′) *v.t.* to delight in; to take pleasure in; to have the use or benefit of. **-able** *a.* pleasurable. **-ably** *adv.* **-ment** *n.* [Fr. *joie*].

en·large (in·lárj′) *v.t.* and *v.i.* to make or become larger; to broaden. **-d** *a.* **-ment** *n.* act of enlarging; expansion; an enlarged reproduction.

en·light·en (in·lit′·n) *v.t.* to give information to; to instruct; to make clear; to free from superstition, etc. **-ment** *n.* act of enlightening; state of being enlightened; intellectual revival in Europe during 18th cent.

en·list (in·list′) *v.t.* to enter on a list; to enroll; to secure support of; *v.i.* to engage in public service, as soldiers; to enter heartily into a cause. **-ment** *n.*

en·liv·en (in·liv′·an) *v.t.* to give life, action, or motion to; to quicken; to make gay. **-er** *n.*

en masse (en mas′, án más′) in a group [Fr.].

en·mesh, immesh, inmesh (en·mesh′) *v.t.* to catch in a mesh or net; to entangle; to trap.

en·mi·ty (en′·ma·ti·) *n.* the quality of being an enemy; hostile or unfriendly disposition; hatred; rancour; hostility [Fr. *inimitié*].

en·no·ble (en·nō′·bl) *v.t.* to make noble; to raise to the peerage; to exalt; to dignify **-ment** *n.*

en·nui (án′·wē) *n.* boredom; listlessness due to satiety or lack of interest.

e·nor·mous (i·nawr′·mas) *a.* huge; vast; prodigious; immense; atrocious. **enormity** *n.* quality of being enormous; great wickedness; atrocity. **-ly** *adv.* **-ness** *n.* [L. *enormis,* abnormal].

e·nough (i·nuf′) *a.* as much or as many as need be; sufficient; adequate. *n.* a sufficiency; as

much as satisfies conditions; *adv.* sufficiently; fully [O.E. *genog*].

e·nounce (ē·nouns′) *v.t.* to state; to declare; to pronounce; to proclaim. **-ment** *n.* [L. *enuntiare,* to declare].

en·quire, enquiry See **inquire, inquiry.**

en·rage (in·rāj′) *v.t.* to fill with rage; to provoke to frenzy or madness; to anger immoderately. **-d** *a.*

en·rapture (in·rap′·cher) *v.t.* to transport with pleasure, to delight excessively; to charm. **-d,** **enrapt** *a.*

en·rich (in·rich′) *v.t.* to make rich; to add to; to enhance; to embellish. **-ment** *n.*

en·robe (en·rōb′) *v.t.* to dress; to clothe.

en·roll (in·rōl′) *v.t.* to enter a name in a roll or register; to enlist; to record. *pa.t.* **-ment** *n.* the act of enrolling; number of persons enrolled [Fr. *enrôler*].

en·sconce (en·skáns′) *v.t.* to shelter; to hide securely; to settle snugly [L. *in;* *condere,* to hide].

en·sem·ble (án·sám′bl) *n.* all the parts taken together; general effect; an entire costume; (*Mus.*) concerted playing by a number of musicians; the group of players [Fr. = together].

en·shrine (in·shrīn′) *v.t.* to enclose in a shrine; to treasure with affection. **-ment** *n.*

en·shroud (en·shroud′) *v.t.* to shroud; to hide from view.

en·sign (en′·sīn) *n.* a badge of rank or insignia of office; a flag or banner; an emblem; (*U.S. Navy*) the lowest commissioned officer. **-cy, -ship** *n.* rank of an ensign [Fr. *enseigne.*]

en·sil·age (en′·sil·ij) *n.* a process of storing crops such as hay, etc. while green, to serve as winter food for cattle; fodder so stored [Fr.].

en·slave (in·slāv′) *v.t.* to reduce to slavery or bondage. **-ed** *a.* **-ment** *n.*

en·snare, insnare (en·snār′) *v.t.* to catch in a snare; to entrap; to entangle.

en·sue (en·sōó′) *v.i.* to follow; to happen after; to be the consequence of. **ensuing** *a.* [Fr. *ensuivre,* fr. L. *insequi,* to follow up].

en·sure (in·shoor′) *v.t.* to make sure, safe, or certain; to bring about.

en·tail (in·tāl′) *n.* law restricting inheritance of land to a particular heir or line of heirs; a predetermined order of succession; an estate; *v.t.* to settle land on persons in succession, none of whom can then dispose of it; to involve as a result; to bring about or cause. **-ment** *n.* [Fr. *entailler,* to cut into].

en·tan·gle (in·tang′·gl) *v.t.* to twist or interweave so as not to be easily separated; to perplex; to ensnare. **-ment** *n.*

en·tente (án·tánt′) *n.* cordial agreement or understanding; the nations or parties involved [Fr.].

en·ter (en′·ter) *v.t.* to go or come into; to pass within; to pierce; to penetrate; to invade; to join (a society, etc.); to put down one's name; *v.i.* to go or come in; to make a beginning; to take a part or interest in. **to enter on, upon,** to begin [Fr. *entrer*].

en·ter- (en′·ter) Gk. *prefix* used in the construction of compound words relating to the intestine. **-a** *n.pl.* **-ic** *a.* of or pertaining to the intestine; **-itis** *n.* inflammation of the intestines [Gk. *enteron,* intestine].

en·ter·prise (en′·ter·prīz) *n.* that which is undertaken or attempted; force of character in launching out; daring spirit; a bold attempt; **enterprising** *a.* adventurous; energetic. **enterprisingly** *adv.* [Fr.].

en·ter·tain (en·ter·tān′) *v.t.* to receive a guest; to show hospitality to; to lodge; to amuse; to divert; to consider favorably; to cherish; to hold in the mind. **-er** *n.* **-ing** *a.* **-ment** *n.* [Fr. *entretenir*].

en·thrall (en·thrawl′) *v.t.* to thrill; to captivate; to hold spellbound; to reduce to slavery.

en·throne (in·thrōn′) *v.t.* to place on a throne; to raise to sovereignty; to exalt. **-ment** *n.*

en·thu·si·asm (in·thū'·zi·azm) *n.* passionate zeal for a person, object or pursuit; keen interest. **enthusiast** *n.* one who is carried away by enthusiasm. **enthusiastic(al)** *a.* **enthusiastically** *adv.* [Gk. *enthousiasmos*, inspiration].

en·tice (in·tīs') *v.t.* to draw on by exciting hope or desire; to lead astray. **-able** *a.* **-ment** *n.* act of enticing; that which incites to evil; allurement. **enticing** *a.* **enticingly** *adv.* [O.Fr. *enticier*, to provoke].

en·tire (in·tīr') *a.* complete in all parts; whole; unimpaired; not castrated. **-ly** *adv.* **-ness**, **-ty** *n.* completeness [Fr. *entier*, fr. L. *integer*].

en·ti·tle (in·tī'·tl) *v.t.* to give a title to; to name; to qualify; to fit for; to give claim to; O.Fr. *entiteler*].

en·ti·ty (en'·tạ·ti·) *n.* a real being; reality; existence; a material substance [L.L. *entitas*, fr. *esse*, to be].

en·tomb (in·tòòm') *v.t.* to deposit in a tomb; to inter; to bury. **-ment** *n.*

en·to·mol·o·gy (en·tạ·mål'·ạ·ji·) *n.* scientific study, classification, and collection of insects. **entomological** *a.* **entomologically** *adv.* **entomologize** *v.t.* to pursue the study of insects. **entomologist** *n.* [Gk. *entomon*, insect; *logos*, a discourse].

en·tou·rage (àn·tòò·razh') *n.* surroundings; one's habitual associates; retinue [Fr.].

en·tr'acte (àn·trakt') *n.* the interval or musical interlude between two acts of a play [Fr.].

en·trails (en'·trạlz) *n.pl.* the bowels; the intestines; the internal parts of anything [Fr.].

en·train (in·trān') *v.t.* to enter or put into a railway train.

en·trance (en'·trans) *n.* the act of entering; right of access; a door, gateway, or passage to enter by; the beginning. **entrant** *n.* one who enters; a competitor.

en·trance (in·trans') *v.t.* to put into a trance; to ravish with delight and wonder. **-ment** *n.* **entrancing** *a.*

en·trap (in·trap') *v.t.* to catch, as in a trap; to ensnare. **-ment** *n.*

en·treat (in·trēt') *v.t.* to ask earnestly; to implore; *v.i.* to make an earnest request. **-y** *n.* act of entreating; supplication [O.Fr. *entraiter*].

en·tree (àn'·trā) *n.* right of access; a dish served before the main course, as a main course, or between main courses (used mostly now as a term for the main course); right of access [Fr.].

en·trench, intrench (in·trench') *v.t.* to dig a trench; to surround, fortify as with a trench; *v.i.* to encroach. **-ment** *n.* a ditch or trench; any fortification or defense.

en·tre·pre·neur (àn·trạ·prạ·nur') *n.* a contractor; an organizer of business, trade, or entertainment [Fr. *entreprendre*, to undertake].

en·trust, intrust (in·trust') *v.t.* to charge with a responsibility; to confide to the care of.

en·try (en'·tri·) *n.* the act of entering; a place to enter by; an item noted down in a ledger, catalogue, or notebook; one entered in a contest [Fr. *entrer*].

en·twine, intwine (in·twīn') *v.t.* to twist together; to plait; to encircle.

e·nu·mer·ate (i·nòò'·mạ·rāt) *v.t.* to count, one by one; to give in detail; to count. **enumeration** *n.* **enumerator** *n.* [L. *enumerare*, to number off].

e·nun·ci·ate (i·nun'·si·āt) *v.t.* to state clearly; to proclaim; to announce; to pronounce each syllable distinctly. **enunciable** *a.* **enunciation** *n.* the act of enunciating; articulation or pronunciation; a declaration or announcement. **enunciator** *n.* [L. *e*, out; *nuntiare*, to announce].

en·ure See **inure**.

en·vel·op (in·vel'·ạp) *v.t.* to cover by folding or wrapping; to surround. **envelope** (en'·vạ·lōp) *n.* a cover or wrapper, esp. the cover of a letter. **-ment** *n.* [Fr. *envelopper*].

en·ven·om (en·ven'·ạm) *v.t.* to impregnate with venom; to poison; to embitter.

en·vi·a·ble, envious See **envy**.

en·vi·ron (in·vī'·rạn) *v.t.* to surround; to encompass; to encircle; to envelop. **-ment** *n.* that which environs; external conditions which determine modifications in the development of organic life. **-s** *n.pl.* adjacent districts; neighborhood; suburbs [Fr. = about].

en·vis·age (en·viz'·ij) *v.t.* to look in the face of; to face; to imagine; to visualize [Fr. *envisager*].

en·voy (en'·voi) *n.* a diplomatic agent of a country below the rank of ambassador; messenger [Fr. *envoyer*, to send].

en·voy, envoi (en'·voi) *n.* an author's postscript, esp. in an additional stanza of a poem.

en·vy (en'·vi·) *v.t.* to grudge another person's good fortune; to feel jealous of; *pr.p.* **-ing**; *pa.p.* **envied**. *n.* pain or vexation excited by the sight of another's superiority or success; jealousy. **enviable** *a.* **envious** *a.* full of envy. **enviously** *adv.* [Fr. *envie*].

en·wrap, inwrap (en·rap') *v.t.* to wrap up; to envelop; to engross.

en·wreathe, inwreathe (en·rēTH') *v.t.* to encircle, as with a wreath.

en·zyme, enzym (en'·zīm) *n.* a complex organic substance which in solution produces fermentation and chemical change in other substances apparently without undergoing any change itself; a form of catalyst; digestive ferment. **enzymetic** *a.* [Gk. *en*, in; *zumē*, leaven].

E·o·li·an, Eolic See **Aeolian, Aeolic**.

e·o·lith (ē'·ạ·lith) *n.* the oldest known stone implement used by pre-historic men **-ic** *a.* pertaining to the earliest stage of human culture [Gk. *eos*, dawn; *lithos*, stone].

eon See **aeon**.

e·pact (ē'·pakt) *n.* the excess of a solar over a lunar month or year in number of days [Gk. *epagein*, to intercalate].

ep·au·let, epaulette (ep'·ạ·let) *n.* an ornamental shoulder-piece or badge of rank [Fr. *épaule*, shoulder].

é·pée (ā·pā') *n.* a dueling sword with a sharp point but no cutting edge, used in fencing [Fr.].

e·pergne (i·purn') *n.* an ornamental piece for center of table [Fr.].

ep·ex·a·ge·sis (ep·eks·ạ·jē'·sis) *n.* a further explanation of a previous statement. **epexegetic, epexegetical** *a.* [Gk. *epi*, further; and *exegesis*].

e·phed·rine (ef'·ạ·drēn) *n.* an alkaloid drug, derived from plants of the genus *Ephedra* [Gk. *ephedra*].

e·phem·er·a (i·fem'·ẹr·ạ) *n.* anything of temporary interest and value; a genus of insects, better known as May flies, which as adults, live only for one day; *pl.* **ephemerae**. **-l** *a.* lasting only a very short period of time; transitory. [Gk. *epi*, for; *hēmera*, a day].

e·phem·er·is (i·fem'·ẹr·is) *n.* (*Astron.*) a table or calendar giving for successive days the positions of heavenly bodies; *pl.* **ephemerides** [Gk. *epi*, for; *hēmera*, a day].

epi- Gk. *prefix* meaning upon, at, in addition to, etc., used in the construction of compound terms.

ep·ic (ep'·ik) *n.* a long narrative poem in the grand style, usually dealing with the adventures of great soldiers or heroes whose deeds are part of the history of a nation; a worthy subject for such a poem; *a.* in the grand style; lofty in conception; memorable; heroic [Gk. *epos*, a word].

ep·i·car·di·um (ep·i·kar'·di·ạm) *n.* (*Med.*) the serous membrane of the pericardium, the sac which envelops the heart. **epicardial** *a.* [Gk. *epi*, upon; *kardia*, the heart].

ep·i·cene (ep'·ạ·sēn) *a.* common to both sexes; (*Gram.*) of common gender, of nouns with but one form for both genders, e.g. sheep; *n.* a person having characteristics of both sexes; a hermaphrodite.

ep·i·cen·ter (ep'·a·sen·ter) *n.* the point on the upper crust of the earth below which an earthquake has originated.

ep·i·crit·ic (ep·a·krit'·ik) *a.* pert. to fine sensitivity, e.g. to the slightest sensation of heat or touch.

Ep·i·cu·rus (ep'·i·kyoor·as) *n.* a Greek philosopher (342-270 B.C.), the founder of the Epicurean school. **epicure** *n.* one with a refined taste in food and dring; one who applies himself to gross sensualism, esp. the delights of the table. **epicurean** *a. n.* a follower of Epicurus; a sensualist. **epicureanism** *n.* the doctrine that the chief end of man was physical and mental happiness.

ep·i·cy·cle (ep'·a·sī·kl) *n.* a circle whose center moves round in the circumference of a greater circle [Gk. *epi,* upon; *kuklos,* a wheel].

ep·i·dem·ic, epidemical (ep·a·dem'·ik, ·al) *a.* common to, or affecting a whole people or community; prevalent; general; prevailing for a time. **epidemic** *n.* the temporary appearance of infectious disease attacking whole communities [Gk. *epi,* among; *dēmos,* the people].

ep·i·der·mis (ep·a·dur'·mis) *n.* (*Anat.*) the outer protective layer of skin, otherwise the scarf skin, which covers the dermis or true skin underneath; (*Bot.*) a sheath, usually one cell in thickness, which forms a layer over surface of leaves. **epidermatoid, epidermic, epidermal, epidermidal** *a.* [Gk. *epi,* upon; *derma,* the skin].

ep·i·glot·tis (ep·a·glat'·is) *n.* a covering of elastic, cartilaginous tissue, which closes the opening leading into the larynx during the act of swallowing. **epiglottic** *a.* [Gk. *epi,* upon; *glotta,* the tongue].

ep·i·gram (ep'·a·gram) *n.* a neat, witty, pointed saying; originally an epitaph couched in verse form, and developed by the Latin epigrammatists into a short poem designed to display their wit. **-matic, -matical** *a.* **matically** *adv.* **-matize** *v.t.* **-matist** *n.* [Gk. *epi,* on; *gramma,* a writing].

ep·i·graph (ep'·a·graf) *n.* an inscription, esp. on a building, statue, etc.; an appropriate motto or saying at the beginning of a book or chapter [Gk. *epi,* upon; *graphein,* to write].

ep·i·lep·sy (ep'·a·lep·si·) *n.* a nervous disease characterized by sudden convulsions and unconsciousness, followed by temporary stoppage of breath and rigidity of the body. **epileptic** *n.* one subject to epilepsy [Gk. *epilēpsis,* seizure].

ep·i·logue (ep'·a·lawg) *n.* a short speech or poem recited at the end of a play; conclusion of a literary work [Gk. *epi,* upon; *logos,* speech].

E·piph·an·y (i·pif'·an·i·) *n.* a Church festival held on the twelfth day after Christmas; the manifestation of a god [Gk. *epi,* to; *phainein,* to show].

ep·i·phyte (ep'·i·fīt) *n.* a plant which grows on but does not draw nourishment from another plant [Gk. *epi,* upon; *phuton,* a plant].

e·pis·co·pa·cy (i·pis'·ka·pas·i·) *n.* the government of the church by bishops; the office of a bishop; prelacy; the body of bishops. **episcopal** *a.* belonging to or vested in bishops; governed by bishops. **episcopalian** *a.* of an episcopal system or church; *n.* a member or adherent of an episcopal church. **episcopalianism** *n.* the system of church government by bishops. **episcopally** *adv.* **episcopate** *n.* a bishopric; the office or order of bishop [Gk. *episkopos,* overseer].

ep·i·sode (ep'·a·sōd) *n.* an incident; an incidental narrative or series of events; a digression, only remotely relevant to the plot of a play or novel; (*Mus.*) an intermediate passage between various parts of a fugue. **episodal, episodic, episodical** *a.* **episodically** *adv.* [Gk. *epeisodion,* the part of a play between choral songs].

e·pis·tle (i·pis'·l) *n.* a letter, usually of the less

spontaneous type, written for effect or for instruction, as the epistles of the New Testament. **epistolary** *a.* [Gk. *epistolē*].

ep·i·taph (ep'·a·taf) *n.* an inscription placed on a tombstone or cenotaph in commemoration of the dead [Gk. *epi,* upon; *taphos,* tomb].

ep·i·tha·la·mi·um (ep·i·tha·lā'·mi·am) *n.* a nuptial song.

ep·i·the·li·um (ep·i·thē'·li·am) *n.* cellular tissue covering cutaneous, mucous, and serous surfaces [Gk. *epi,* upon; *thēlē,* a nipple].

ep·i·thet (ep'·a·thet) *n.* phrase or word used adjectivally to express some quality or attribute of its object; a designation; title; appellation. **epithetic, -al** *a.* [Gk. *epithetos,* added].

e·pit·o·me (i·pit'·a·mē) *n.* a brief summary; an abridgement of a book; abstract; synopsis; digest. **epitomize** *v.t.* to make or be a short abstract of [Gk. fr. *epitemnein,* to cut into].

e·poch (ep'·ak) *n.* a fixed point or duration of time from which succeeding years are reckoned, as being specially marked by notable events; era; date; period; age. **-al** *a.* [Gk. *epochē,* a stop].

eq·ua·ble (ek'·wa·bl) *a.* uniform in action or intensity; not variable; of unruffled temperament. **equability, -ness** *n.* **equably** *adv.* [L. *aequabilis*].

e·qual (ē'·kwal) *a.* having the same magnitude, dimensions, value, degree, or the like; identical; equable; tantamount (to); not lop-sided; *n.* a person of the same rank, age, etc.; *v.t.* to be or make equal. **-ization** *n.* **-ize** *v.t.* to make or become equal. **-itarian** *n.* one who holds that all men are equal in status. **-ity** *n.* the state of being equal. **-ly** *adv.* [L. *aequus,* equal].

e·qua·nim·i·ty (ē·kwa·nim'·a·ti·) *n.* evenness of mind or temper; composure; calmness [L. *aequus,* even; *animus,* mind].

e·quate (i·kwāt') *v.t.* to make or treat as equal; to state or assume the equality of. **equation** *n.* the act of making equal; allowance for any inaccuracies; (*Math.*) an expression of the equality of two like algebraic magnitudes or functions by using the sign of equality (=) **equational** *a.* **equationally** *adv.* [L. *aequus,* equal].

e·qua·tor (i·kwā'·ter) *n.* a great circle supposed to be drawn round the earth 90° from each pole and dividing the globe into the N. & S. hemispheres; (*Astron.*) the celestial equator, another name for the equinoctial. **equatorial** *a.* of or pertaining to the equator; *n.* an astronomical telescope, so mounted that it automatically follows the diurnal course taken by the heavenly body under observation. **equatorially** *adv.* [L. *aequus,* equal].

eq·uer·ry (ek'·wer·i·) *n.* one charged with the care of horses; an officer whose duty it is to accompany the sovereign or royal prince when riding in state [Fr. *écurie,* stable].

e·ques·tri·an (i·kwes'·tri·an) *a.* pertaining to horses or horsemanship; mounted on a horse; *n.* (*fem.* **equestrienne**) a rider or circus-performer on a horse. **-ism** *n.* [L. *equus,* a horse].

e·qui- *prefix* fr. L. *aequus,* equal, used in the construction of compound words.

e·qui·an·gu·lar (ē·kwi·ang'·gya·ler) *a.* having equal angles.

e·qui·dis·tance (ē·kwa·dis'·tans) *n.* an equal distance from some point. **equidistant** *a.*

e·qui·lat·er·al (ē·kwa·lat'·er·al) *a.* having all the sides equal.

e·qui·li·brate (ē·kwa·lī'·brāt) *v.t.* to balance exactly; to equipoise. **equilibrant** *n.* (*Phys.*) the single force which will balance any system of forces or produce equilibrium when used in conjunction with these forces. **equilibration** *n.* **equilibrator** *n.* in aviation the stabilizing fin which controls the balance of an airplane [L. *aequus,* equal; *libra,* a balance].

e·qui·lib·ri·um (ē·kwa·lib'·ri·am) *n.* (*Mech.*) the state of rest of a body produced by action and reaction of a system of forces; equipoise;

a state of balance [L. *aequus*, equal; *libra*, a balance].

e·quine, equinal (e′·kwīn, ·al) *a.* pert. to a horse; *n.* a horse [L. *equis*, a horse].

e·qui·noc·tial (ē·kwạ·nåk′·shạl) *a.* pert. to the equinoxes; *n.* (*Astron.*) a great circle in the heavens corresponding to the plane of the equator when extended (cf. **equinox**).

e·qui·nox (e′·kwạ·noks) *n.* the time at which the sun crosses the plane of the equator, approx. March 21 and Sept. 22, and day and night are equal; *pl.* [L. *aequus*, equal; *nox*, night].

e·quip (i·kwip′) *v.t.* to fit out; to supply with all requisites for service; to furnish; to array; to dress; *pr.p.* -**ping** *pa.p.*, *pa.t.* -**ped. equipage** (ek′·wi·pij) *n.* furniture, especially the furniture and supplies of a vessel or army; a carriage, horses and attendants; accoutrements. -**ment** *n.* act of equipping; the state of being equipped; outfit, especially a soldier's; apparatus [Fr. *équiper*].

e·qui·poise (e′·kwạ·poiz) *n.* the state of equality of weight or force; even balance.

eq·ui·ta·ble (ek′·wit·ạ·bl) *a.* giving, or disposed to give, each his due; just. -**ness** *n.* **equitably** *adv.* fairly; justly [L. *aequus*, equal].

eq·ui·ta·tion (ek·wi·tā′·shạn) *n.* skill in horsemanship; a ride on horseback [Fr. fr. L. *equus*, a horse].

eq·ui·ty (ek′·wạ·ti·) *n.* fairness; equal adjustment or distribution; giving to each his due according to the sense of natural right [L. *aequitas*].

e·quiv·a·lent (i·kwiv′·ạ·lạnt) *a.* and *n.* equal in value, power, import, etc.; (*Chem.*) of equal valency. **equivalence** *n.* identical value; state or condition of being equivalent. **equivalency** *n.* [L. *aequus*, equal; *valere*, to be worth].

e·quiv·o·cal (i·kwiv′·ạ·kạl) *a.* of double or doubtful meaning; questionable; ambiguous; doubtful; dubious. -**ly** *adv.* -**ness** *n.* **equivocate** *v.i.* to use words of doubtful signification to mislead; to prevaricate. **equivocation** *n.* **equivocator** *n.* [L. *aequus*, equal; *vox, vocis*, a voice].

e·ra (ēr′·ạ) *n.* a fixed point of time from which a series of years is reckoned; epoch; time; age; a memorable date or period [L. *aera*, counters, used in computation].

e·rad·i·cate (i·rad′·i·kāt) *v.t.* to pull up by the roots; to extirpate; to destroy. **eradicable** *a.* **eradication** *n.* [L. *e*, out; *radix*, a root].

e·rase (i·rās′) *v.t.* to rub or scrape out; to efface. **erasable** *a.* -**d** *a.* -**r** *n.* one who or that which erases. -**ment** *n.* **erasure** *n.* [L. *e*, out; *radere*, rasum, to scrape].

ere (ār) *adv.* before; sooner; *prep.* before; *conj.* sooner than [O.E. *aer*].

e·rect (i·rekt′) *v.t.* to set upright; to raise, as a building, etc.; to elevate; to construct; *a.* upright; pointing upwards. -**ion** *n.* -**or** *n.* [L. *erectus*, set upright].

erg (urg) *n.* the absolute unit of measurement of work and energy in the metric system; the work done by a force which produces a velocity of a centimeter per second in a mass of one gram [Gk. *ergon*, work].

er·go (ur′·gō) *adv.* therefore; consequently [L.].

er·got (ur′·gạt) *n.* a dried fungus used as a drug to stop bleeding and contract muscles [Fr. = bird's spur].

Er·in (ār′·in) *n.* Ireland.

er·mine (ur′·min) *n.* a member of weasel family the white winter coat of which is highly prized as a fur; the robe of a judge in England and so used as a synonym for *judge* [O.Fr.].

e·rode (i·rōd′) *v.t.* to eat into; to wear away; to corrode. **erodent** *n.* a caustic drug. **erose** *a.* appearing as if gnawed or worn irregularly. **erosion** *n.* act or operation of eating away; corrosion; denudation. **erosive** *a.* [L. *erodere*].

E·ros (ēr′·os, er′·os) *n.* (*Myth.*) the Greek god of love. **erotic** (i·råt·ik) *a.* pertaining to love; amatory; *n.* a love poem; **erotics** *n.pl.* science and art of love. **erotica** *n.* literature dealing with sexual love. **eroticism, erotism** *n.* in psycho-analysis, love in all its manifestations [Gk. *eros*, love].

err (ur) *v.i.* to commit a mistake; to be mistaken; to deviate; to go astray; to sin. -**atic(al)** (i·rat′·ik) *a.* roving; wandering; eccentric; changeable; capricious; not dependable. -**atic** *n.* a wanderer; a boulder transported by a glacier or other natural force. -**atically** *adv.* -**atum** *n.* an error in writing or printing. *pl.* -**ata** [L. *errare*, to wander].

er·rand (er′·ạnd) *n.* commission; message [O.E. *aerende*, a message].

er·rant (er′·ạnt) *a.* wandering; roving; wild; abandoned; *n.* a knight-errant. -**ly** *adv.* -**ry** *n.* a state of wandering about, esp. of a knight-errant in search of adventures [L. *errare*, to wander].

erratic, erratum etc. See **err.**

er·ror (er′·ẹr) *n.* a deviation from right or truth; a mistake; blunder; sin. **erroneous** *a.* wrong; incorrect; inaccurate; false. **erroneously** *adv.* **erroneousness** *n.* [L. *errare*, to wander].

er·satz (er′·zåts′) *a.* substituted for articles in everyday use; artificial; makeshift [Ger.].

erst (urst) *adv.* (*Arch.*) formerly; of old; hitherto. -**while** *adv.* former [O.E. *aerest*].

e·ruct, e·ruc·tate (i·rukt′, ·tāt) *v.t.* to belch. **eructation** *n.* belching [L. *e*, out; *ructare*, to belch].

er·u·dite (er′·yoo·dīt) *a.* learned; deeply read; scholarly. -**ly** *adv.* **erudition** *n.* learning; scholarship [L. *eruditus*].

e·rupt (i·rupt′) *v.i.* to throw out; to break through; to break out in eruptions. **eruption** *n.* act of bursting forth; outburst of lava, ashes, gas, etc. from the crater of a volcano; a rash on the skin. **eruptive** *a.* breaking forth or out [L. *e*, out; *rumpere*, to burst].

er·y·sip·e·las (er·ạ·sip′·ạ·lạs) *n.* contagious disease causing acute inflammation of the skin [Gk. fr. *eruthos*, red; *pella*, skin].

es·ca·lade (es·kạ·lād′) *n.* mounting the walls of a fortress by means of ladders; *v.t.* to scale [Fr. fr. L. *scala*, a ladder].

es·ca·la·tor (es′·kạ·lā·tẹr) *n.* continuous, moving stairway [L. *scala*, a ladder].

es·cape (e·skāp′) *v.t.* to gain freedom; to evade; to elude; to pass unnoticed; *v.i.* to hasten away; to avoid capture; to become free from danger; *n.* flight from danger; evasion; leakage (of gas, etc.); an outlet for purposes of safety; a garden-plant growing wild and thriving; a conscious effort to forget mental troubles by taking up some other powerful interest. **escapable** *a.* **escapade** *n.* a wild prank or exploit. -**ment** *n.* the act or means of escaping; the contrivance in a time-piece which connects the wheel-work with the pendulum, allowing a tooth to escape at each vibration. **escapism** *n.* morbid desire to escape from the realities of life by concentrating on some other interest. **escapist** *n.* [Fr. *échapper*].

es·carp (es·kårp′) *v.t.* to make into a steep slope; *n.* -**ment** *n.* a steep, sloping bank [Fr. *escarper*].

es·cha·tol·o·gy (es·kạ·tál′·ạ·ji·) *n.* the department of theology which treats of the last things, such as death, the return of Christ, the resurrection, the end of the world, etc. [Gk. *eschatos*, last; *logos*, discourse].

es·cheat (es·chēt′) *n.* the legal process of property reverting to the crown or government on the tenant's death without heirs; an estate so lapsing; *v.t.* to forfeit; to confiscate; *v.i.* to revert to the crown or lord of the manor [O.Fr. *escheoir*, to fall due].

es·chew (es·chŏŏ′) *v.t.* to shun; to avoid; to abstain from [O.Fr. *eschuer*].

es·cort (es'·kawrt) *n.* an armed guard for a traveller, etc.; a person or persons accompanying another on a journey for protection or as an act of courtesy. **escort** (i·skawrt') *v.t.* to accompany; to convoy [Fr. *escorte*].

es·cri·toire (es·kri·twȧr') *n.* a writing-desk provided with drawers [O.Fr. *escriptoire*].

Es·cu·la·pi·an (es·kū·lā'·pi·ạn) *a.* pertaining to the art of healing [*Aesculapius*, in classic mythology, the god of medicine].

es·cu·lent (es'·kyạ·lạnt) *a.* suitable as a food for man; edible; *n.* something which is eatable [L. *esculentus*].

es·cutch·eon (is·kuch'·ạn) *n.* in heraldry, a shield bearing armorial bearings; that part of a vessel's stern on which her name is inscribed; an ornamental plate or shield placed round a keyhole opening. **-ed** *a.* [L. *scutum*, a shield].

Es·ki·mo, Esquimau (es'·kạ·mō) *n.* and *a.* one of an aboriginal people thinly scattered along the northern seaboard of America and Asia and in many of the Arctic islands; *pl.* **Eskimos, Esquimaux** [etym. doubtful].

e·soph·a·gus (ē·sȧf'·ạ·gạs) *n.* the gullet [L. *oesophagus*].

es·o·ter·ic (es·ạ·ter'·ik) *a.* term applied to doctrines intended only for the inner circle of initiates; secret; profound [Gk. *esoterikos*, fr. *eso*, within].

es·pe·cial (ạs·pesh'·ạl) *a.* distinguished; pre-eminent; more than ordinary; particular. **-ly** *adv.* [O.Fr. *especiel*, fr. L. *species*].

Es·pe·ran·to (es·pạ·rȧn'·tō) *n.* a universal auxiliary language [coined word].

es·pi·o·nage (es'·pi·ȧ·nij or ·nȧzh) *n.* the practice of employing secret agents; spying [Fr. *espion*, a spy].

es·pla·nade (es·plạ·nād) *n.* a level space, esp. for a promenade as along the seafront of a town [Fr.].

es·pouse (ȧs·pouz') *v.t.* to marry; to support, attach oneself to (a cause, etc.). **espousal** *n.* act of espousing. **espousals** *n.pl.* nuptials. **-r** *n.* [O.Fr. *espouser*].

es·prit (es·prē') *n.* spirit; wit; liveliness. **esprit de corps** (es·prē·da·kŏr') loyalty and attachment to the group of which one is a member [Fr.].

es·py (ạs·pī') *v.t.* to catch sight of [Fr. *espier*, to spy out].

-esque (esk) *suffix* in the manner or style of.

es·quire (es'·kwīr) *n.* originally, a squire or shield-bearer, one of two attendants on a knight; now a courtesy title [O.Fr. *escuyer*, fr. L. *scutarius*, a shield-bearer].

es·say (es'·ā) *n.* a literary composition, shorter than a treatise; a trial; an attempt. **essay** *v.t.* to try; to make experiment or trial of; to attempt. **-ist** *n.* a writer of essays [Fr. *essayer*, to try].

es·sence (es'·ạns) *n.* the very being or power of a thing; the formal cause of being; peculiar nature or quality; a being; essential part; a concentration of the active ingredients of a substance in a smaller mass; (*Med.*) a solution of essential oils in rectified alcohol; a perfume. **essential** *a.* belonging to the essence; necessary to the existence of a thing; inherent; *n.* something indispensable; a chief point; a leading principle. **essentiality** *n.* **essentially** *adv.* **essentialness** *n.* [Fr. from L. *esse*, to be].

es·tab·lish (ạs·tab'·lish) *v.t.* to make stable or firm; to set up; to found; to enact or decree by authority; to confirm; to prove; to verify; to substantiate; to set up and endow, as a state church by law. **-ed** *a.* fixed; settled; on the permanent staff; supported by the State. **-er** *n.* **-ment** *n.* act of establishing; that which is established; an institution; settlement; place of business, residence, etc.; the church established by the state. **-mentarian** *a.* and *n.* supporting church establishment [L. *stabilire*, fr. *stare*, to stand].

es·tate (ạs·tāt') *n.* a piece of landed property;

condition of life; rank; position; quality; property, real or personal; the total assets and liabilities of a bankrupt or of a deceased person. **the Three Estates**, in France, nobles, clergy, and middle class. **the Fourth Estate**, a satirical term for the press. **real estate**, property in land [O.Fr. *estat*].

es·teem (ạs·tēm') *v.t.* to regard with respect or affection; to set a value on; to rate highly; *n.* high regard; favorable opinion [L. *aestimare*, to estimate].

es·thet·ic See **aesthetic**.

es·ti·ma·ble (es'·tạ·mạ·bl) *a.* able to be estimated or esteemed; worthy of regard. **estimably** *adv.* [L. *aestimare*].

es·ti·mate (es'·tạ·māt) *v.t.* to judge and form an opinion of the value, size, weight, etc. of; to compute; to calculate; *v.i.* to offer to complete certain work at a stated cost; *n.* appraisement; conjecture. **estimator** *n.* one who appraises. [L. *aestimare*].

es·ti·va·tion, aestivation (es·tạ·vā'·shạn) *n.* a state of torpor, affecting some insects, during the dry summer months. **estival** *a.* pertaining to or continuing throughout the summer aestival. **estivate** *v.i.* (cf. *hibernate*) [L. *aestus*, summer].

Es·to·ni·an, Esthonian (es·t(h)ō'·ni·ạn) *a.* pert. to *Est(h)onia*, a country on the Baltic; the Finnish-Ugrian language.

es·top (es·tȧp') *v.t.* (*Law*) to impede; to bar by one's own act [Fr. *étouper*, to stop up].

es·trange (ạs·trānj') *v.t.* to alienate, as the affections; to divert from its original use, purpose, or possessor. **-d** *a.* **-ment** *n.* [O.Fr. *estrangier*, to make strange].

es·tu·ar·y (es'·choo·er·i·) *n.* a narrow arm of the sea at the mouth of a river, up which the tides penetrate twice daily. **estuarine** *a.* pert. to an estuary [L. *aestus*, tide].

e·su·ri·ent (i·soor'·i·ạnt) *a.* hungry; voracious; gluttonous [L. *esuriens*, being hungry].

et cet·er·a (et set'·ẹr·ạ) phrase meaning "and the others"; and so on; (*abbrev.*) **etc.** [L.].

etch (ech) *v.t.* to make an engraving by eating away the surface of a metal plate with acid; *v.i.* to practice this art. **-er** *n.* one who etches. **-ing** *n.* the act or art of etching; the printed impression taken from an etched plate [Ger. *ätzen*, to eat into].

e·ter·nal (i·tur'·nạl) *a.* without beginning or end in relation to time; everlasting; timeless; ceaseless; immortal; imperishable. **eternalize, eternize** *v.t.* to make eternal or immortal; to perpetuate. **-ly** *adv.* **eternity** *n.* the infinity of time; the future state after death [L. *aeternus*].

eth·ane (eth'·ān) *n.* a colorless, odorless, inflammable gas [fr. *ether*].

e·ther (ē'·thẹr) *n.* the hypothetical non-material, imponderable medium supposed by physicists to permeate the whole of space and to transmit the waves of light, radiant heat, and electromagnetic radiation; the higher regions beyond the earth. **ethereal** *a.* pertaining to the ether; celestial; airy; delicate. **etherealization** *n.* **etheralize** *v.t.* to render ethereal or spiritual. **ethereality** *n.* the quality or state of being ethereal. **ethereally** *adv.* [Gk. *aithēr*, the upper air].

e·ther (ē'·thẹr) *n.* a volatile liquid, prepared by the action of sulfuric acid on alcohol, used as a solvent and as an anesthetic.

eth·ic, eth·i·cal (eth'·ik, ·ạl) *a.* relating to morals or moral principles. **-ally** *adv.* **-s** *n.pl.* philosophy which treats of human character and conduct, of distinction between right and wrong, and moral duty and obligations to the community [Gk. *tehos*, character].

E·thi·o·pi·a (ē·thi·ō'·pi·ạ) *n.* a kingdom in E. Africa; Abyssinia. **-n** *n.* a native of Ethiopia; a Negro; *a.* pertaining to Ethiopia [Gk. *aithein*, to burn; *ops*, the countenance].

eth·nic, eth·ni·cal (eth'·nik, ·ạl) *a.* pert. to

races or peoples, esp. speech groups; ethnological; heathen; pagan. **ethnography** n. detailed study of the physical characteristics and social customs of racial groups. **ethnographer** n. **ethnographic** a. **ethnology** n. the science which traces the origin and distribution of races, their peculiarities and differences. **ethnological** a. **ethnologist** n. [Gk. ethnos, a people].

e·thos (ē′·thås) n. the character, customs, and habits which distinguish a people or community from another; in art, the inherent quality which conveys nobility, universality, etc. [Gk. ethos, custom].

eth·yl (eth′·ạl) n. (Chem.) the univalent radical C₂H₅; an antiknock fluid. — **alcohol** common alcohol [fr. ether, and Gk. hulē, material].

e·ti·o·late (ē′·ti·ạ·lāt) v.t. to render pale or unhealthy by denying light and fresh air; v.i. to become pale by being deprived of light, etc. **etiolation** n. [Fr. étioler, to become pale].

e·ti·ol·o·gy (ē·ti·ȧl′·ạ·ji·) n. the study of the causes of diseases. Also **aetiology** [Gk. aitia, cause; logos, discourse].

et·i·quette (et′·i·ket) n. the conventional code of good manners which governs behavior in society and in professional and business life decorum [Fr.].

E·ton·i·an (ē·tōn′·i·ạn) n. one educated at Eton College. **Eton collar,** white starched collar worn outside the jacket. **Eton jacket,** a boy's very short and tailless jacket.

E·tru·ri·an (i·troor′·i·ạn) a. of Etruria, the ancient Roman name of part of N.W. Italy. **Etruscan** n. a native of ancient Etruria; a. pert. to Etruria, its language, people and especially art and architecture.

e·tude (ā·tȯȯd′) n. (Mus.) a study; a short musical composition [Fr.].

et·y·mol·o·gy (et·ạ·mȧl·′ạ·ji·) n. the investigation of the origins and meanings of words and word-forms. **etymological** a. **etymologically** adv. **etymologist** n. one versed in etymology [Gk. etumon, true meaning; logos, a discourse].

eu·caine (ū·kān′) n. a synthetic drug, resembling cocaine, used as a local anesthetic [Gk. eu, well; (co)caine].

eu·ca·lypt (ū′·kạ·lipt) n. any member of the genus Eucalyptus. **eucalyptus** n. the gum tree of Australia with tough and durable wood. **eucalyptol** n. eucalyptus oil, a colorless, aromatic, oily liquid distilled from the leaves of the eucalyptus [Gk. eu, well; kaluptos, covered].

Eu·cha·rist (ū·kạ·rist) n. Holy Communion; the consecrated elements at the sacrament of the Lord's Supper. **-ic, -ical** a. [Gk. eucharistia, thanksgiving].

eu·chre (ū′·kẹr) v.t. (Colloq.) to outwit; to get the best of [game of euchre].

Eu·clid·e·an (ū·klid′·ȧ·ạn) a. pert. to Euclid of Alexandria who founded a school of mathematics about 300 B.C.; geometric; three dimensional.

eu·de·mon·ism, eudaemonism (ū·dē′·mạn· izm) n. the doctrine that the attainment of personal happiness, power and honor is the chief end and good of man. **eudemonist** n. [Gk. eu, well; daimon, a spirit].

eu·gen·ic (ū·jen′·ik) a. pertaining to eugenics; relating to, or tending towards, the production of fine offspring. **-s** n.pl. the scientific application of the findings of the study of heredity to human beings with the object of perpetuating those inherent and hereditary qualities which aid in the development of the human race. **eugenist** n. [Gk. eu, well; genes, producing].

eu·gen·nol (ū′·jạ·nȯl) n. an aromatic acid, obtained from the oil of cloves [Prince Eugène of Savoy, a patron of botany].

eu·lo·gy, eu·lo·gi·um (ū′·lạ·ji·, ū·lō′·ji·ạm) n. a speech or writing in praise, especially a speech praising a dead person. **eulogic, -al**

a. commendatory; laudatory. **eulogize** v.t. to speak in flattering terms. **eulogist** n. **eulogistic** a. commendatory; laudatory. **eulogistically** adv. [Gk. eulogia, praise].

eu·nuch (ū′·nạk) n. a castrated male, especially in the Near East, in charge of the women of the harem [Gk. eunē, a bed; echein, to keep].

eu·pep·sia (ū·pep′·shạ) n. healthy normal digestion—opposed to dyspepsia. **eupeptic** a. [Gk. eu, well; peptein, to digest].

eu·phe·mism (ū·fạ·mizm) n. a figure of speech where a less disagreeable word or phrase is substituted for a more accurate but more offensive one. **euphemize** v.t. or v.i. to soften down an expression. **euphemistic** a. [Gk. euphēmizein, to use words of good omen].

eu·pho·ny (ū′·fạ·ni·) n. pleasantness or smoothness of sound; assonance; assimilation of the sounds of syllables to facilitate pronunciation and to please the ear. **euphonic, euphonious** a. **euphoniously** adv. [Gk. eu, well; phonē, sound].

eu·pho·ri·a (yoo·fōr′·i·ạ) n. a sense of health and well-being which may, however, be misleading; state of irrational happiness. **euphoric** a. [Gk.].

eu·phu·ism (ū′·fyoo·izm) n. an affected, elaborate, bombastic prose style of language, so called from Euphues, a work by John Lyly (1553-1606), in that style; a stilted expression. **euphuist** n. **euphuistic** a.

Eu·ra·sian (yoor·ā′·zhạn) n. offspring of mixed European and Asiatic parentage; a. pert. to Europe and Asia considered as one landmass or continent [fr. Europe and Asia].

eu·rhyth·mics (yoo·riTH′·miks) n.pl. an art of rhythmical free movement to music [Gk. eu, well; rhuthmos, rhythm].

Eu·rope (yoor′·ạp) n. the continent which extends from the Atlantic Ocean to Asia. **European** a. belonging to Europe; n. a native or inhabitant of Europe.

Eu·sta·chi·an (yoo·stā′·ki·ạn, ·shạn) a. derived from Bartolommeo Eustachio (c. 1500-1574), an Italian anatoimst. **Eustachian tube,** open duct extending from throat near tonsils to middle ear.

eu·tec·tic (yoo·tek′·tik) a. easily melted or fused; n. in metallurgy, a particular mixture or alloy of metals whose melting point is lower than other mixtures of the same ingredients [Gk. eu, well; tēktos, molten].

eu·tha·na·sia (ū·thạ·nā′·zhạ) n. an easy, painless death; the putting of a person to death painlessly, esp. one in a hopeless condition. Also **euthanasy** [Gk. eu, well; thanatos, death].

e·vac·u·ate (i·vak′·yoo·āt) v.t. to make empty; to withdraw from; to excrete; v.i. to quit. **evacuant** n. a purgative. **evacuation** n. the act of evacuating, emptying out, withdrawing from; system by which noncombatants, in time of war, are sent to safe areas; (Med.) the discharge of fecal matter from the rectum. **evacuative** a. **evacuator** n. **evacuee** n. a person temporarily removed from dangerous area [L. e, out; vacuus, empty].

e·vade (i·vād′) v.t. to avoid by dexterity, artifice, or stratagem; to elude; to escape; to avoid; to shun; to frustrate; to baffle. **evadable** a. [L. e, out; vadere, to go].

e·val·u·ate (i·val′·yoo·āt) v.t. to appraise or determine the value of. **evaluation** n. estimation of worth [Fr. évaluer].

ev·a·nesce (ev·ạ·nes′) v.i. to vanish; to fade or melt away. **-nce** n. **-nt** a. vanishing; fleeting; transitory; scarcely perceptible. **-ntly** adv. [L. evanescere, to vanish].

e·van·gel (i·van′·jạl) n. good tidings; the Gospel; one of the first four books of the New Testament. **evangelic, evangelical** a. consonant with the Gospel; applied to those forms of Christianity which regard the atonement of Christ as the ground and central principle of the Christian faith; orthodox. **evangelical** n.

one who holds the views of the evangelical school. **evangelically** *adv.* **evangelicalness, evangelicism, evangelicalism, evangelism** *n.* a religious movement to spread actively the tenets of the Gospel. **-ization** *n.* the preaching of the Gospel; conversion. **-ize** *v.t.* and *v.i.* to convert, by preaching the Gospel. **-ist** *n.* **-istic** *a.* [Gk. *eu*, well; *angelia*, tidings].

e·vap·o·rate (i·vap′·ạ·rāt) *v.t.* and *v.i.* to pass off in vapor, as a fluid; to disperse; to disappear; to vaporize. **evaporable, evaporative** *a.* **evaporation** *n.* [L. *e*, out; *vapor*].

e·va·sion (i·vā′·zhạn) *n.* the act of evading or eluding; subterfuge to escape the force of an accusation, interrogation, or argument; excuse; dodge. **evasible** *a.* may be evaded. **evasive** *a.* tending to evade; marked by evasion; not straightforward. **evasively** *adv.*

eve (ēv) *n.* evening; the evening before some particular day; the period immediately preceding an event or important occasion. **even** *n.* evening (poetical). **even-song** *n.* evening prayer. **even-tide** *n.* evening [O.E. *aefen*].

e·ven (ēv′·n) *a.* level; equal in surface; uniform in rate of motion or mode of action; flat; smooth; uniform in quality; equal in amount; balanced; horizontal; equable; calm; unruffled; impartial; exactly divisible by two; *v.t.* to make even; to smooth; to equalize; *adv.* evenly; just; still; fully. **-handed** *a.* fair, impartial (of justice); just. **-ly** *adv.* **-ness** *n.* **—tempered** *a.* not irascible [O.E. *efen*].

eve·ning (ēv′·ning) *n.* the close of day; the decline or end of life. **evening dress,** formal dress worn at evening functions [O.E. *aefnung*].

e·vent (i·vent′) *n.* that which happens; a notable occurrence; affair; result; effect; item at a sports meeting. **-ful** *a.* full of exciting events; momentous. **-ual** *a.* happening as a consequence; resulting in the end; ultimate. **-uality** *n.* contingency; force of circumstances. **-ually** *adv.* **-uate** *v.i.* to happen [L. *evenire*, to come out].

ev·er (ev′·ẹr) *adv.* at any time; at all times; perpetually; constantly; unceasingly. **-glade** *n.* a swampy, grassy tract. **-green** *a.* always green; *n.* nondeciduous tree or shrub which remains green throughout the year. **-more** *adv.* unceasingly; eternally. **ever so** (*Colloq.*) extremely. **for ever and a day,** always.

ev·er·last·ing (ev·ẹr·last′·ing) *a.* enduring for ever; eternal; *n.* eternity; a flower which does not lose shape or color when dried.

e·vert (ē·vurt′) *v.t.* to turn inside out. **eversible** *a.* capable of being turned inside out. **eversion** *n.* [L. *e*, out; *vertere*, to turn].

ev·er·y (ev′·ri·) *a.* each of all; all possible. **-body** *n.* every person. **-day** *a.* ordinary. **-where** *adv.* in every place; universally. **—other**, every second; alternately [O.E. *aefre, yle,* ever each].

e·vict (i·vikt′) *v.t.* to dispossess by a judicial process; to expel; to eject; to turn out. **eviction** *n.* ejectment. **-or** *n.* [L. *evincere*, to conquer, to recover property by law].

ev·i·dent (ev′·ạ·dant) *a.* visible; clear to the vision; obvious. **evidence** *n.* that which makes evident; information in a law case; a witness; sign; indication; ground for belief; testimony; proof; attestation; corroboration; *v.t.* to render evident; to manifest. **evidential, evidentiary** *a.* furnishing evidence; proving conclusively. **-ly** *adv.* apparently; plainly. **to turn State's evidence,** to give evidence, on the part of one accused, against an accomplice [L. *e*, out; *videre*, to see].

e·vil (ē′·vl) *a.* having bad natural qualities; bad; harmful; disagreeable; vicious; corrupt; wicked; calamitous; unfortunate; *n.* harm; misfortune; wickedness; depravity; sinfulness; wrong; *adv.* in an evil manner. **— eye** *n.* the power of bewitching others by the glance of the eyes. **-ly** *adv.* **-ness** *n.* [O.E. *yfel*].

e·vince (i·vins′) *v.t.* to prove beyond any reasonable doubt; to show clearly; to make evident. **evincible** *a.* **evincibly** *adv.* **evincive** *a.* tending to prove [L. *evincere*, to prove].

e·vis·cer·ate (i·vis′·ẹr·āt) *v.t.* to disembowel; to take out the entrails or viscera. **evisceration** *n.* [L. *e*, out; *vicsera*, bowels].

e·voke (i·vōk′) *v.t.* to call up; to summon forth; to draw out; to bring to pass. **evocation** *n.* [L. *evocare*, to call out].

ev·o·lu·tion (ev·al·ōō′·shạn) *n.* gradual unfolding or growth; development; evolving; the scientific theory according to which the higher forms of life have gradually developed from simple and rudimentary forms; a movement to change position, order, and direction carried out by a body of troops. **-al, -ary** *a.* **-ism** *n.* **-ist** *n.* a biologist who accepts the scientific theory of evolution [L. *evolvere, evolutum,* to roll out].

e·volve (i·vȧlv′) *v.t.* to develop gradually; to give off, as odors; to unfold; *v.i.* to develop, esp. by natural process; to open out [L. *evolvere,* to roll out].

ewe (ū) *n.* a female sheep [O.E. *eowy*].

ew·er (yoo′·ẹr) *n.* a large water jug with a wide spout [O.Fr. *euwier*, fr. *eau*, water].

ex- *prefix* fr. L. *ex*, out of, used in the construction of compound terms, signifying *out of, from, former* (as ex-M. P.)

ex·ac·er·bate (igz-., iks·as′·ẹr·bāt) *v.t.* to render more bitter; to increase the violence of; to exasperate; to irritate; to aggravate. **exacerbation** *n.* [L. *ex*, out of; *acerbus*, bitter].

ex·act (ig·zakt′) *a.* accurate; correct; precise; strict; *v.t.* to demand; to extort; to enforce; to insist upon. **-ing** *a.* making severe demands on; demanding extreme care or accuracy. **exaction** *n.* **-itude** *n.* extreme accuracy; correctness. **-ly** *adv.* precisely [L. *ex*, out; *agere, actum,* to drive].

ex·ag·ger·ate (ig·zaj′·ạ·rāt) *v.t.* to represent as greater than truth or justice will warrant; to magnify in the telling, describing, etc. **exaggeratedly** *adv.* **exaggeration** *n.* a statement going beyond the facts. **exaggerative** *a.* **exaggerator** *n.* **exaggeratory** *a.* [L. *exaggerare*, to heap up].

ex·alt (ig·zawlt′) *v.t.* to elevate as in rank; to praise; to elate with joy. **-ation . -ed** *a.* [L. *ex*, out; *altus*, high].

ex·am·ine (ig·zam′·in) *v.t.* to inquire into and determine; to try and assay by the appropriate tests; to inspect; to scrutinize; to explore; to investigate; to interrogate. **exam** *n.* (*Colloq.*) examination. **examinee** *n.* one who undergoes an examination test. **examination** *n.* the act of examining; interrogation; a scholastic test of knowledge, written or oral; judicial inquiry. **-r** *n.* [L. *examinare*, to weigh accurately].

ex·am·ple (ig·zam′·pl) *n.* a pattern; a thing illustrating a general rule; a specimen; sample [L. *exemplum*, a sample].

ex·as·per·ate (ig·zas′·pẹr·āt) *v.t.* to irritate in a high degree; to rouse angry feelings; to provoke beyond endurance. **exasperating** *a.* extremely trying; provoking. **exasperation** *n.* **-r** *n.* [L. *ex*, out; *asper*, rough].

ex·ca·vate (eks′·kạ·vāt) *v.t.* to hollow out; to form a cavity or hole in; to dig out. **excavation** *n.* **excavator** *n.* [L.].

ex·ceed (ik·sēd′) *v.t.* to pass or go beyond the limit of; *v.i.* to be greater; to surpass; to excel. **-ing** *a.* surpassing; excessive. **-ingly** *adv.* very; to a very high degree [L. *ex*, out; *cedere*, to go].

ex·cel (ik·sel′) *v.t.* to surpass, especially in good qualities; to be better than; to exceed; to outstrip; to outdo; *v.i.* to be very good; to be pre-eminent. *pr.p.* **-ling.** *pa.t.* and *pa.p.* **-led.** **-lence** *n.* **-lency** *n.* complimentary title borne by ambassadors, etc. **-lent** *a.* worthy; choice; remarkably good. **-lently** *adv.* [L. *excellere*, to rise above].

ex·cept (ik·sept′) v.t. to leave out; to exclude; v.i. to take exception to; to object; prep. with exclusion of; leaving out; excepting; all but; save; conj. with the exception (that). **-ing** prep. excluding. **exception** n. an excepting; that which is not included in a rule; objection. **exceptionable** a. objectionable. **exceptionably** adv. **exceptional** a. outstanding; superior. **exceptionally** adv. [L. exceptus, taken out].

ex·cerpt (ik·surpt′) v.t. to extract, to quote (a passage from a book, etc.). **excerpt** (ek′·surpt) n. a passage, quoted or culled from a book, speech, etc. [L. excerpere, to pluck out].

ex·cess (ik·ses′) n. that which surpasses or goes beyond a definite limit; extravagance; intemperance. **-ive** a. more than enough.

ex·cheq·uer (iks·chek′·ẹr) n. the public treasury [O.Fr. eschequier].

ex·change (iks·chānj′) v.t. to give or take in return for; to barter; n. the act of giving or taking one thing in return for another; the transfer of goods between countries; a place for buying and selling stocks, securities, etc., or where other business of a special nature is carried on; the conversion of the currency of one country to that of another; the settling of debts by the transfer of credits or the interchange of drafts, etc. **-able** a.

ex·cheq·uer (iks·chek′·ẹr) n. the public treasury; (Brit.) the department in charge of public revenues; (Colloq.) funds [O.Fr. eschequier].

ex·cise (ek·sīz′) n. a tax or duty upon certain articles of home production and consumption; also includes licenses on certain employments, sports, etc.; v.t. to impose an excise duty on. **excisable** a. liable to excise duty [Dut. accijns, excise].

ex·cise (ik·sīz′) v.t. to cut out; to cut off; to expunge. **excision** (ik·sizh′·ạn) n. act of cutting; surgical operation [L. ex, out; caedere, to cut].

ex·cite (ik·sīt′) v.t. to rouse; to call into action; to stir up; to set in motion; to move to strong emotion; to stimulate. **excitability** n. **excitable** a. capable of being easily excited. **excitant** (ik′·si·tạnt) a stimulant. **excitation** n. the act of exciting; the excitement produced; the action of a stimulant on an organ of the body or of a plant. **excitative** a. **excitatory** a. tending to excite. **excited** a. **excitedly** adv. **-ment** n. abnormal activity; agitation; perturbation; commotion. **exciting** a. rousing to action; thrilling. **excitingly** adv. [L. excitare].

ex·claim (iks·klām′) v.i. and v.t. to utter loudly and vehemently; to declare suddenly. **exclamation** (eks·klạ·mā′·shạn) n. loud remark or cry, expressing joy, surprise, etc.; vehement utterance. **exclamation mark**, the mark (!) used to suggest sudden emotion. **exclamatory** a. [L. ex, out; clamare, to call].

ex·clude (eks·klōōd′) v.t. to thrust out; to shut out; to debar from; to eject. **exclusion** n. the act of excluding or debarring. **exclusive** a. excluding; debarring; limited to a special favored few. **exclusively** adv. **exclusiveness** n. [L. ex, out; claudere, to shut].

ex·cog·i·tate (eks·kǎj′·ạ·tāt) v.t. to find out by thinking; to think out. **excogitation** n. [L. ex, out; cogitare, to think].

ex·com·mu·ni·cate (eks·kạm·mūn′·ạ·kāt) v.t. to expel from the communion and membership of the church by an ecclesiastical sentence; to deprive of spiritual privileges. **excommunication** n. [L. excommunicare, to expel from a community].

ex·co·ri·ate (iks·kō′·ri·āt) v.t. to strip, wear, or rub the skin off; to flay. **excoriation** n. [L. ex, out; corium, the skin].

ex·cre·ment (eks′·kạ·mạnt) n. matter excreted; feces. **-al** a. **-itious** a. resembling feces [L. excrementum].

ex·cres·cence (iks·kres′·ạns) n. an abnormal protuberance which grows out of anything, as a wart or tumor; a normal outgrow, such as hair. **excrescent** a. growing out unnaturally; superfluous [L. ex, out; crescere, to grow].

ex·crete (iks·krēt′) v.t. to eject waste matter from the body; to expel. **excreta** n.pl. the normal discharges from the animal body as urine, feces, and sweat. **excretion** n. **excretive** a. **excretory** a. [L. excernere, to sift out].

ex·cru·ci·ate (iks·krōō′·shi·āt) v.t. to inflict the severest pain on; to torture, in body or mind. **excruciating** a. [L. ex, out; cruciare, to torture].

ex·cul·pate (iks·pạl′·pāt) v.t. to clear from a charge or imputation of fault or guilt. **exculpation** n. vindication. **exculpatory** a. [L. ex, out; culpa, fault].

ex·cur·sion (iks·kur′·zhạn) n. a short trip for a special purpose; deviation; digression. **-ist** n. one who makes a journey for pleasure. **excursive** a. prone to wander; rambling; digressive; diffusive. **excursus** n. a dissertation appended to a book and containing a fuller exposition of some relevant point [L. ex, out; currere, to run].

ex·cuse (iks·kūz′) v.t. to free from fault or blame; to free from obligation or duty; to pardon; to justify; to apologize; to exempt; to let off. **excuse** (iks·kūs′) n. a plea offered in extenuation of a fault, etc.; a pretext; an apology. **excusable** a. [L. ex, out; causa, a cause, accusation].

ex·e·crate (eks′·i·krāt) v.t. to feel or express hatred for; to curse; to abominate; to loathe; to detest utterly. **execrable** a. **execrably** adv. **execration** n. act of execrating; the object execrated; a curse; imprecation [L. exsecrari, to curse].

ex·e·cute (eks′·i·kūt) v.t. to carry out a task to the end, to accomplish; to give effect to; to perform; to complete; to enforce a judgment of a court of law; to sign a deed; to put to death by sentence of a court. **executable** a. **executant** n. a performer, esp. of music. **execution** n. the act of executing or performing; death penalty inflicted by law; performance; accomplishment; mode of performance; workmanship. **executioner** n. one who executes; a hangman. **executive** a. capable of executing or performing; administrative; n. a body appointed to administer the affairs of a corporation, a company, etc.; a high official of such a body; the administrative branch of a government. **executively** adv. **executor** n. (fem. **executrix**, **executress**) one who executes or performs; a person appointed under a will to fulfill its terms and administer the estate. **executorial** a. [L. exsequi, to follow out].

ex·e·ge·sis (eks·ạ·jē′·sis) n. literary commentary; interpretation and elucidation of Scripture. **exegete**, **exegetist** n. one versed in interpreting the text of the Scriptures. **exegetic**, **exegetical** a. [Gk. fr. ex, out; hēgeesthai, to lead].

ex·em·plar (ig·zem′·plẹr) n. a person or thing to be imitated; an original or pattern; model. **-ily** adv. in a manner to be imitated; by way of warning or example. **-iness** n. **-y** a. serving as a pattern or model; commendable [L. exemplum, sample].

ex·em·pli·fy (ig·zem′·pli·fī) v.t. to show by example; to illustrate; to make an attested copy of. pr.p. **-ing**. pa.t., pa.p. **exemplified**. **exemplification** n. [L. exemplum, an example; facere, to make].

ex·empt (ig·zempt′) v.t. to free from; to grant immunity from; a. not included; not liable for some duty; freed from; not affected by. **-ible** a. **exemption** n. act of exempting; state of being exempt; immunity [L. exemptum, taken out].

ex·er·cise (eks′·ẹr·sīz) n. the act of exercising; use (of limbs, faculty, etc.); use of limbs for health; practice for the sake of training; pl. military drill; a ceremony; v.t. to put in motion;

to use or employ; to exert; to apply; to engage; to practice; v.i. to take exercise [L. *exercere*, to keep at work].

ex·ert (ig·zurt') v.t. to put forth, as strength, force, or ability; to exercise; to strive; to labor. **exertion** n. **-ive** a. [L. *exserere*, to put forth].

ex·hale (eks·hāl') v.t. to breathe out; to give off as vapor or odor; to discharge; v.i. to rise or be given off as vapor. **exhalable** a. **exhalant** a. having the property of exhalation. **exhalation** n. [L. *ex*, out; *halare*, to breathe].

ex·haust (ig·zawst') v.t. to draw out or drain off completely; to empty; to weaken; to tire; to use up; to squander; to discuss thoroughly; n. conduit through which steam, waste gases and the like, after performing work, pass from the cylinders to the outer air; the steam or gases themselves. **-ed** a. tired out; fatigued; emptied; drawn out; consumed. **-ible** a. **exhaustion** n. act of exhausting or consuming; state of being completely deprived of strength or vitality. **-ive** a. tending to exhaust; comprehensive; thorough. **-ively** adv. [L. *ex*, out; *haurire*, *haustum*, to draw].

ex·hib·it (ig·zi'·bit) v.t. to hold forth or to expose to view; to present; to show; to display; to manifest; to express; n. anything displayed at an exhibition. **-er, -or** n. one who sends articles to an exhibition for display. **exhibition** (ek·sa·bi'·shan) n. the act of exhibiting; show; display; a public show (of works of art, etc.). **exhibitionism** n. a tendency to show off before people. **exhibitionist** n. **exhibitory** a. [L. *exhibere*, to hold forth].

ex·hil·a·rate (ig·zil'·a·rāt) v.t. to make cheerful; to animate. **exhilarant** a. exhilarating; exciting joy, mirth, or pleasure; n. anything which exhilarates. **exhilarating** a. **exhilaration** n. [L. *exhilarare*, fr. *hilaris*, happy].

ex·hort (ig·zawrt') v.t. to incite by words of advice; to advise strongly; to admonish earnestly. **-ation** n. **-ative, -atory** a. tending to exhort [L. *ex*; *hortari*, to encourage].

ex·hume (iks·hūm') v.t. to dig up, as from a grave; to unearth; to disinter. **exhumation** n. **-r** n. [L. *ex*, out; *humus*, the ground].

ex·i·gent (ek'·sa·jant) a. calling for immediate action or aid; pressing; urgent. **exigence, exigency** n. urgent want; emergency. **exigible** a.

ex·i·gu·i·ty (ek·sa·gū'·i·ti·) n. smallness; slenderness. **exiguous** a. [L. *exiguus*].

ex·ile (eg'·zīl, ek'·sīl) n. separation or enforced banishment; a banished person; one living away from his native country; v.t. to banish or expel [L. *exsilium*, banishment].

ex·ist (eg·zist') v.t. to be; to have a being, whether material or spiritual; to continue in being; to live; to subsist; to occur. **-ence** n. the condition of objectivity; being; state of being actual; entity; life; **-ential** a. consisting in existence; ontological. **-entialism** n. (*Philos.*) a school which describes, analyzes and classifies the experiences of an individual mind considered as *existences*. **-ibility** n. [L. *existere*, to come forth].

ex·it (eg'·zit, ek'·sit) n. a departure; a way out of a place; stage direction to indicate when an actor is to leave the stage. **exeunt**, stage direction [L. = he goes out].

ex·o- *prefix* fr. Gk. *exo*, outside, without.

ex·o·dus (ek'·sa·das) n. a departure, esp. of a a crowd. **Exodus** n. (*Bib.*) the second book of the Old Testament [Gk. *exodos*, way out].

ex·og·a·my (eks·ȧg'·ȧ·mi·) n. a custom compelling a man to marry outside his tribe or clan. **exogamous** a. [Gk. *exo*, outside; *gamos*, marriage].

ex·on·er·ate (eg·zȧn'·ẹr·āt) v.i. to declare free from blame or responsibility; to relieve of a charge or obligation. **exoneration** n. **exonerator** n. [L. *exonerare*, to unburden].

ex·o·ra·ble (ek'·sẹr·ȧ·bl) a. capable of being moved by entreaty [L. *exorare*, to persuade by entreaty].

ex·or·bi·tant (ig·zawr'·bȧ·tȧnt) a. very excessive; extravagant. **exorbitance, exorbitancy** n. **-ly** adv. [L. *ex*, out; *orbis*, a circle].

ex·or·cise (ek'·sawr·sīz) v.t. to cast out (evil spirits) by invocation; to free a person of evil spirits. **exorcism** n. [Gk. *exorkizein*].

ex·or·di·um (ig·zawr'·di·am) n. a beginning; the introduction part of a discourse or treatise. **exordial** a. [L. fr. *ex*, out; *ordiri*, to begin].

ex·o·skel·e·ton (ek·sō·skel'·ȧ·tan) n. (*Zool.*) external hard supporting structure such as scales, nails, feathers. **exoskeletal** a. [Gk. *exo*, outside].

ex·o·ter·ic, extrical (ek·sȧ·tẹr'·ik, ·al) a. capable of being understood by, or suited for, the many; not secret; the opposite to *esoteric* [Gk. *exoterikos*, external].

ex·ot·ic (eg·zȧt'·ik) a. introduced from a foreign country; not indigenous; unusual or colorful. **-ism** (ig·zȧt'·i·cizm) n. [Gk. *exotikos*].

ex·pand (ik·spand') v.t. to spread out; to enlarge; to increase in volume or bulk; to extend; to stretch; to develop. **expanse** n. a wide extent of surface. **-able, expansible** a. **expansibly** adv. **expansion** n. act of expanding; condition of being expanded; increase in one or more of the dimension of a body; spreading; distension; enlargement. **expansive** a. widely extended; effusive; communicative; diffusive. **expansively** adv. **expansiveness** n. [L. *ex*, out; *pandere*, to stretch].

ex·pa·ti·ate (ik·spā'·shi·āt) v.i. to speak or write at great length (on); **expatiation** n. **expatiative** a. [L. *exspatiari*, to wander].

ex·pa·tri·ate (eks·pā'·tri·āt) v.t. to banish from one's native land; to exile; (·it) n. **expatriation** n. [L. *ex*, out; *patria*, fatherland].

ex·pect (ek·spekt') v.t. to look forward to; to look on as likely to happen; to look for as one's due; to anticipate; (*Colloq.*) to suppose. **-ance, -ancy** n. the act or state of expecting; that which is expected. **-ant** a. waiting; hopeful. **-antly** adv. **-ation** n. act or state of looking forward to an event. **-ations** n.pl. prospects in life; probable gain [L. *exspectare*, to look out for].

ex·pec·to·rate (ek·spek'·tȧ·rāt) v.t. or v.i. to spit; to cough up. **expectorant** a. aiding expectoration; n. a drug or agent which promotes expectoration. **expectoration** n. the act of expectorating; sputum; spittle [L. *ex*, out; *pectus*, breast].

ex·pe·di·ent (ek·spē'·di·ant) a. suitable; fitting; advisable; politic; desirable; convenient; useful; n. suitable means to accomplish an end; means devised or employed in an exigency; shift; contrivance. **expediency** n. **-ly** adv. [L. *expedire*, to be fitting].

ex·pe·dite (ek'·spi·dīt) v.t. to free from hindrance or obstacle; to hurry forward; a. quick; ready; unencumbered. **-ly** adv. **expedition** n. a journey for a specific purpose; the persons and equipment involved; efficient promptness; speed; **expeditionary** a. **expeditious** a. prompt; speedy [L. *ex*, out; *pes, pedis*, a foot].

ex·pel (ek·spel') v.t. to drive or force out; to cast out; to eject; to exclude; pr.p. **-ling**. pa.t. and pa.p. **-led** [L. *ex*, out; *pellere*, to drive].

ex·pend (ek·spend') v.t. to consume by use; to spend; to use up; to exhaust. **-able** a. **-iture** n. act of expending; that which is expended; expense; cost. **expense** n. big outlay; cost; expenditure. **expensive** a. costly; dear [L. *expendere*, to weigh out].

ex·pe·ri·ence (ek·spir'·i·ans) n. practical knowledge gained by trial or practice; personal proof or trial; continuous practice; evidence; an event in one's life; v.t. to undergo; to feel; to endure; to encounter. **-d** a. skilled; expert; wise; capable; thoroughly conversant with. **experiential** a. relating to or having experience; empirical [L. *experiri*, to test].

ex·per·i·ment (ek·sper'·ȧ·mant) n. the action of trying anything; putting to the proof or test; practical test; a trial to find out what happens; *v.i.* to make an experiment. **-al** *a.* founded on or known by experiment; pertaining to experiment. **-alist** *n.* **-ally** *adv.* **-ation** *n.* **-tative** *a.* **-er**, **-ist** *n.* [L. *experiri*, to try].

ex·pert (ek·spurt') *a.* taught by use, practice, or experience; adroit; dexterous; skillful. (ex'·-purt) *n.* an authority; a specialist. **-ly** *adv.* **-ness** *n.* [L. *expertus*, having tried].

ex·pi·ate (eks'·pi·āt) *v.t.* to make satisfaction or reparation for; to atone for; to make amends for. **expiable** *a.* **expiation** *n.* [L. *expiare*, to make amends for].

ex·pire (ek·spīr') *v.t.* to breathe out; to emit; to exhale; *v.i.* to die; to die away; to come to an end. **expirant** *n.* one who is dying. **expiration** *n.* the exhalation of air from the lungs; end of a period of time; close; termination. **expiratory** *a.* **expiring** *a.* **expiry** *n.* conclusion [L. *ex*, out; *spirare*, to breathe].

ex·plain (eks·plān') *v.t.* to make plain, manifest, or inteligible; to account for; to elucidate; to define. **-able** *a.* **explanation** *n.* act or method of explaining, expounding, or interpreting; the meaning of or reason given for anything. **explanative, explanatory** *a.* serving to explain [L. *explanare*, to make smooth].

ex·ple·tive (eks'·pli·tiv) *a.* serving only to fill out a sentence, etc.; added for ornamentation only; *n.* a word inserted to fill up or to add force to a phrase; an exclamation; an oath [L. *expletivus*, filling out].

ex·pli·cate (eks'·pli·kāt) *v.t.* to unfold the meaning of; to explain; to interpret; to elucidate. **explicable** *a.* **explication** *n.* **explicative, explicatory** *a.* [L. *explicare*, to unfold].

ex·plic·it (iks·plis'·it) *a.* stated in detail; stated, not merely implied; unambiguous; clear; unequivocal. **-ly** *adv.* **-ness** *n.* [L. *explicitus*].

ex·plode (ik·splōd') *v.t.* to cause to blow up; to discredit; to expose (a theory, etc.); *v.i.* to burst with a loud report; to become furious with rage; to burst into unrestrained laughter. **-d** *a.* rejected; debunked. **explosion** *n.* the act of exploding; sudden release of gases, accompanied by noise and violence; a manifestation of rage. **explosive** *a.* liable to explode; *n.* a chemical intended to explode [L. *ex*, out; *plaudere*, to clap with the hands].

ex·ploit (eks·ploit') *n.* a brilliant feat; a heroic deed; remarkable action, often in a bad sense; *v.t.* to make the most of; to utilize for personal gain. **-able** *a.* **-age**, **-ation** *n.* **-er** *n.* [Fr.].

ex·plore (ik·splōr') *v.t.* to search through with the view of making discovery; to leave the beaten tracks; to investigate; to examine. **exploration** *n.* **exploratory** *a.* **-r** *n.* [L. *explorare*, to search out].

ex·plo·sive See **explode**.

ex·po·nent (ek·spō'·nạnt) *n.* one who expounds, demonstrates, or explains; a symbol; in algebra, index number or quantity, written to the right of and above another to show how often the latter is to be multiplied by itself, e.g. $a^3 = a \times a \times a$. [L. *ex*, out; *ponere*, to place].

ex·port (eks·pōrt') *v.t.* to send goods or produce out of a country. (ex'·port) *n.* act of exporting; that which is exported. **-able** *a.* **-ation** *n.* **-er** *n.* [L. *ex*, out; *portare*, to carry].

ex·pose (ik·spōz') *v.t.* to lay open; to leave unprotected; to exhibit; to disclose; to submit a photographic plate or film to the light. **exposé** (eks·pō·zā') *n.* an exposure or disclosure of discreditable facts. **exposition** *n.* act of exhibiting or expounding; exhibition; display; explanation. **expositor** *n.* **expository** *a.* **exposure** *n.* the act of exposing, laying bare, or disclosing shady or doubtful transactions; the state of being laid bare; aspect of a building relative to the cardinal points of the compass [L. *ex*, out, *ponere*, to place].

ex·pos·tu·late (ik·spás'·chạ·lāt) *v.i.* to remonstrate with; to reason earnestly. **expostu-**

lation *n.* **expostulative, expostulatory** *a.* [L. *expostulare*, to demand urgently].

ex·pound (ek·spound') *v.t.* to explain; to set forth; to interpret; [L. *exponere*].

ex·press (ik·spres') *v.t.* to make known one's opinions or feelings; to put into words; to represent by pictorial art; to designate; to press or squeeze out; to send by express; *a.* definitely stated; closely resembling; specially designed; explicit; clear; plain; speedy; *adv.* post-haste; by express messenger or train; specially; on purpose; *n.* a messenger sent on a special errand; a fast train making few stops en route; a message. **-ible** *a.* **-ion** *n.* act of expressing; lively or vivid representation of meaning, sentiment, or feeling; the reflection of character or mood in the countenance; utterance; declaration; phrase; term; remark; aspect; look; (*Math.*) a quantity denoted by algebraic symbols. **-ionism** *n.* an antirealistic art theory that all art depends on the expression of the artist's creative self. **-ionist** *n.* **-ionless** *a.* **-ive** *a.* full of expression. **-ively** *adv.* **-iveness** *n.* **-ly** *adv.* plainly; explicitly; specially [L. *expressus*, squeezed out, clearly stated].

ex·pro·pri·ate (eks·prō'·pri·āt) *v.t.* to dispossess; to take out of the owner's hand. **expropriation** *n.* [L. *ex*, out; *proprius*, one's own].

ex·pul·sion (ik·spul'·shạn) *n.* the act of expelling or casting out; ejection; banishment. **expulsive** *a.* [L. *expulsus*, driven out].

ex·punge (ik·spunj') *v.t.* to strike out; to erase; to obliterate; to cancel [L. *expungere*, to strike out].

ex·pur·gate (ek'·spẹr·gāt) *v.t.* to remove objectionable parts (from a book, etc.); to cleanse; to purify; to purge. **expurgation** *n.* **expurgator** *n.* [L. *expurgare*, to purge].

ex·qui·site (eks'·kwi·zit) *a.* of extreme beauty or delicacy; of surpassing excellence; extreme, as pleasure or pain. **-ly** [L. *exquisitus*, sought out].

ex·ser·vice (eks'·sur·vis) *a.* of or pertaining to one who has served in the armed forces.

ex·sic·cate (ek'·si·kāt) *v.t.* to dry up; to evaporate. **exsiccation** *n.* [L. *ex*, out; *siccus*, dry].

ex·tant (ik·stant', ek'·stạnt) *a.* still existing [L. *ex*, out; *stare*, to stand].

ex·tem·po·re (ik·stem'·pạ·ri·) *a.* or *adv.* without previous study or meditation; offhand; on the spur of the moment. **extemporal, extemporaneous, extemporary** *a.* impromptu. **extemporization** *n.* act of speaking extempore. **extemporize** *v.i.* to speak extempore; to create music on the inspiration of the moment [L. *ex*, out of; *tempus, temporis*, time].

ex·tend (ik·stend') *v.t.* to prolong in a single direction, as a line; to stretch out; to prolong in duration; to offer; to expand; to enlarge; *v.i.* to be continued in length or breadth; to stretch. **-ible, extensible, extensile** *a.* capable of being stretched, expanded, or enlarged. **extensibility** *n.* **extension** *n.* **extensional** *a.* **extensive** *a.* having wide extent; large; comprehensive; spacious. **extensively** *adv.* **extensiveness** *n.* **extensor** *n.* a muscle which straightens or extends a limb. **extent** *n.* space or degree to which a thing is extended; size; scope; a space; area; degree; volume; length; expanse [L. *extendere*, to stretch out].

ex·ten·u·ate (ek·sten'·yoo·āt) *v.t.* to palliate, as a crime; to mitigate; to make less blameworthy. **extenuating** *a.* **extenuation** *n.* [L. *ex*, out; *tenuare*, to make thin].

ex·te·ri·or (ek·stir'·i·ẹr) *a.* outer; outward; external; coming from without; *n.* the outside; outer surface; outward appearance.

ex·ter·mi·nate (ek·stur'·mạ·nāt) *v.t.* to root out; to destroy utterly. **extermination** *n.* **exterminator** *n.* [L. *ex*, out; *terminus*, boundary].

ex·ter·nal (ik·stur'·nạl) *a.* not inherent or essential; outward; exterior; superficial; extrinsic; apparent; **-s** *n.pl.* outward appearances; **-ly** *adv.* [L. *externus*, outside].

ex·tinct (eks·tingkt′) *a.* extinguished; put out; no longer existing; dead. **-ion** *n.* [L. *extinctus*].

ex·tin·guish (ek·sting′·gwish) *v.t.* to put out; to put an end to; to quench; to destroy; to obscure by superior splendor. **-able** *a.* **-er** *n.* [L. *extinguere*, to quench].

ex·tir·pate (ek′·ster·pāt) *v.t.* to pull or pluck up by the roots; to destroy utterly. **extirpable** *a.* **extirpation** *n.* **extirpator** *n.* [L. *exstirpare* fr. *stirps*, stem].

ex·tol (ek·stōl′) *v.t.* to praise highly. *pr.p.* **-ling.** *pa.t.* and *pa.p.* **-led** [L. *extollere*, to lift up].

ex·tort (ek·stawrt′) *v.t.* to obtain by force or threats; to extract. **extorsive** *a.* serving or tending to extort. **-ion** *n.* act of extorting; illegal compulsion; unjust exaction. **-ionary, -ionate** *a.* **-ioner, -ionist** *n.* [L. *ex*, out; *torquere*, to wrench].

ex·tra- *prefix* fr. L. meaning *beyond, on the other side of, on the outside of*; used in many compound words denoting *beyond, without, more than, further than*, or generally, *excess.* (eks′·tra) *a.* extraordinary; additional; *adv.* unusually; especially; *n.* something extra; over and above the usual charges; additional item; special edition of a news paper; a person employed casually by film producers to play a minor role in a production. **-curricular** *a.* pert. to the studies or activities which are not included in the curriculum. **-judicial** *a.* out of the proper court or the ordinary legal procedure. **-mural** *a.* beyond the walls, as outside a university. **-sensory** (eks·tra·sen′·ser·i·) *a.* beyond the senses. **-sensory perception,** (*abbrev. E.S.P.*) an awareness of events not presented to the physical senses. **-territorial** *a.* outside the limits of a country or its jurisdiction [L.].

ex·tract (ik·strakt′) *v.t.* to take out, esp. by force; to obtain against a person's will; to get by pressure, distillation, etc.; to copy out; to quote; to elicit; (*Math.*) to calculate. **extract** (eks′·trakt) *n.* matter obtained by distillation; concentrated drug, solution, syrup, etc.; a passage from a book, speech, etc. **-able, -ible** *a.* **extraction** *n.* act of extracting; that which is extracted; chemical operation of removing one or more substances from others by means of a solvent; parentage; ancestry; lineage; descent; arithmetical process of finding the root of a number. **-ive** *a.* **-or** *n.* [L. *ex*, out; *trahere, tractum*, to draw].

ex·tra·dite (eks′·tra·dīt) *v.t.* to deliver up a fugitive to another nation or authority. **extradition** *n.* [L. *ex*, out of; *tradere*, to deliver].

ex·tra·ne·ous (ek·strā′·ni·as) *a.* not naturally belonging to or dependent on a thing; not essential; foreign. **-ly** *adv.* [L. *extraneus*].

ex·tra·or·di·nar·y (eks·trawr′·da·ner·i·) *a.* beyond or out of the common order or method; exceeding the common degree or measure; employed on a special errand or duty. **extraordinarily** *adv.* **extraordinariness** *n.* [L. *extra*, beyond; *ordo, ordinis*, order].

ex·trav·a·gant (eks·trav′·a·gant) *a.* profuse in expense; excessive; prodigal; wasteful; unrestrained. **extravagance** *n.* **extravagate** *v.i.* to wander beyond proper limits [L. *extra*, beyond, *vagari*, to wander].

ex·trav·a·gan·za (eks·trav′·a·gan′·za) *n.* an extravagant, farcical, or fantastic composition, literary or musical [It.].

ex·tra·va·sate (eks·trav′·a·sāt) *v.t.* to let out of the proper vessels, as blood; *a.* let out of its proper vessel [L. *extra*, beyond; *vas*, a vessel].

ex·tra·vert See **extrovert.**

ex·treme (ek·strēm′) *a.* at the utmost point, edge, or border; outermost; of a high or highest degree; severe; excessive; last; most urgent; *n.* the utmost point or degree; a thing at one end or the other; the first and last of a series; great necessity. **-ly** *adv.* **extremism** *n.* holding extreme views or doctrines. **extremist** *n.*

extremity *n.* the most distant point or side. **extremities** *n.pl.* hands and feet; arms and legs; extreme measures [L. *extremus*].

ex·tri·cate (eks′·tra·kāt) *v.t.* to free from difficulties or perplexities. **extricable** *a.* **extrication** *n.* [L. *extricare*].

ex·trin·sic, extrinsical (eks·trin′·sik, ·al) *a.* developing or having its origin from outside the body; not essential; not inherent [L. *extrinsecus*, on the outside].

ex·tro·vert (eks′·trō·vert) *n.* in psychology, a person whose emotions express themselves readily in external actions and events, as opposed to an *introvert.* **extroversion** *n.* [L. *extra*, outside of; *vertere*, to turn].

ex·trude (eks·trōōd′) *v.t.* to thrust out; to press out; to expel. **extrusion** *n.* [L. *ex*, out; *trudere*, to thrust].

ex·u·ber·ant (ek·zōō′·ber·ant) *a.* effusive; vivacious; over abundant; prolific; **exuberance, exuberancy** *n.* state of being exuberant. **-ly** *adv.* [L. *ex:uber*, fertile].

ex·ude (eg·zōōd′) *v.t.* to discharge through the pores, as sweat; to discharge sap by incision, as a tree; *v.i.* to ooze out; to escape slowly, as a liquid [L. *ex*, out; *sudare*, to sweat].

ex·ult (eg·zult′) *v.i.* to rejoice exceedingly; to triumph; **-ance, -ancy** *n.* **-ant** *a.* **-tation** *n.* [L. *exultare*, to leap for joy].

ex·u·vi·ae (eg·zōō′·vi·ē) *n.pl.* (*Zool.*) cast off skin, teeth, shells, etc. of animals. **exuvial** *a.* **exuviate** *v.i.* [L. *exuere*, to strip off].

eye (ī) *n.* the organ of sight or vision; the power of seeing; sight; perforation; eyelet; bud; shoot; view; observation; judgment; keen sense of value; vigilance; anything resembling an eye; a small staple or ring to receive a door hook; an aperture for observing; *v.t.* to observe closely or fixedly; to look at; to view; *pr.p.* **eying** or **-ing.** *pa.t.* and *pa.p.* **-d** (īd). **-ball** *n.* the globe of the eye. **-brow** *n.* the arch of hairs. **-d** *a.* having eyes; spotted as if with eyes. **-glass** *n.* a glass to assist the sight; a monocle; the eyepiece of an optical instrument. *pl.* spectacles. **-lash** *n.* one of the hairs which edge the eyelid. **-let** *n.* a small eye or hole for a lace or cord, as in garments, sails, etc.; *v.i.* to make eyelets. **-lid** *n.* folds of skin which may be drawn at will over the eye. — **opener** *n.* surprising news; revealing statement. **-piece** *n.* lens in an optical instrument by means of which the observer views the image of the object formed in the focus of the other lenses. **-sight** *n.* power of vision; view; observation. **-sore** *n.* an object offensive to the eye. **-tooth** *n.* either of the two canine teeth of the upper jaw. **-wash** *n.* eye lotion. **-witness** *n.* one who gives testimony as to what he actually saw. **the green eye,** jealousy. **to see eye to eye,** to agree; to think alike [O.E. *eage*].

ey·rie (ār′·i·) *n.* the nest of a bird of prey.

F

fa·ble (fā′bl) *n.* a short tale or prolonged personification, often with animal characters, intended to convey a moral truth; a myth; a fiction; a falsehood; *v.t.* and *v.i.* to tell fables; to lie. *a.* mythical; legendary. **fabular fabulize** *v.i.* to compose fables. **fabulist** *n.* **fabulous** *a.* feigned or fabled; amazing; exaggerated [L. *fabula*, a story].

fab·ric (fab′·rik) *n.* structure; framework; woven, knitted or felted cloth; texture. **fabricate** *v.t.* to frame; to construct mechanically; to build according to standard specifications; to assemble from standardized components; to fake; to concoct. **-ation** *n.* **-ator** *n.* [L. *fabrica*, a workshop].

fa·cade (fa·sad′) n. the front view or elevation of a building [Fr. fr. It. *facciata*, the front of a building].

face (fās) n. the front of the head including forehead, eyes, nose, mouth, cheeks and chin; the outer appearance; cast of countenance; the outer or upper surface of any thing; the dial of a clock, etc.; the front; prestige; v.t. to confront; to stand opposite to; to admit the existence of (as facts); to oppose with courage; to put a layer of different material on to, or to trim an outer surface; v.i. to turn; — **card** n. a playing card, as king, queen and jack; — **cloth** n. a square of Turkish towelling for washing the face. — **lifting** n. an operation performed to remove wrinkles from the face. — **piece** n. the front part of a respirator. — **value** n. apparent worth. **facial** a. pert. to the face; n. (*Colloq.*) a beauty treatment for the face. **facies** (fā′·shi·ēz) n. the general appearance of anything. **facing** n. a covering in front for ornament or defense; material applied to the edge of a garment. [L. *facies*, a face].

facet (fas′·it) n. a small surface, as of a crystal or precious stone; aspect; a. having facets [Fr. *facette*, dim. of *face*].

fa·ce·tious (fa·sē′·shas) a. witty; jocular. **facetiae** (fa·sē′·shi·ē) n.pl. witty or humorous writings or sayings. adv. **-ness** n. [L. *facetus*, elegant].

fac·ile (fas′·l) a. easy; fluent; easily done; courteous; glib. **-ly** adv. **-ness** n. **facilitate** v.t. to make easy; to expedite. **facilitation** n. **facility** n. ease; deftness; aptitude; easiness of access [L. *facilis*, easy].

fac·sim·i·le (fak·sim′·a·li·) n. an exact copy; a. identical; v.t. to make a facsimile **facsimilist** n. **in facsimile**, accurately [L. *fac*, make (imper.); *simile*, like].

fact (fakt) n. anything done; anything actually true; that which has happened. **-ual** a. pert. to facts; actual. **matter-of-fact** a. prosaic; unimaginative [L. *factum*, thing done].

fac·tion (fak′·shạn) n. a group of people working together, esp. for subversive purposes; dissension; party clique. **factious** a. **factiously** adv. [Fr. fr. L. *factio*, a doing].

fac·ti·tious (fak·tish′·as) a. made or imitated by art, oppos. of *natural*; artificial; manufactured [L. *factitare*, to do frequently].

fac·tor (fak′·ter) n. (*Math.*) one of numbers which, multiplied together, give a given number; a contributory element or determining cause; v.t. (*Math.*) to express as a product of two or more quantities. **-ial** a. pert. to a factor. v.t. (*Math.*) to find the factors of a given number. **-ship** n. **-y** n. a building where things are manufactured [L. *facere*, to do].

fac·to·tum (fak·tō′·tạm) n. one who manages all kinds of work for an employer [L. *fac*, do (imper.); *totum*, all].

fac·ul·ty (fa′·kal·ti·) n. ability or power to act; mental aptitude; talent; natural physical function; a university department; the teaching body; the members of a profession, esp. medical; authorization. **facultative** a. optional [L. *facultas*, power].

fad (fad) n. a pet whim; a fancy or notion. **-dish** a. **-dy** a. **-dist** n. [etym. unknown].

fade (fād) v.i. to lose freshness, brightness, or strength gradually; to disappear slowly. **-less** a. not liable to fade; fast (of dye) [O.Fr. *fade*, dull].

fa·er·ie, faery (fē′·ri·) n. fairyland; a. pert. to fairyland; fairy-like [var. of *fairy*].

fag (fag) n. toil; a tedious task; (Br. *Slang*) a cigarette; v.t. to exhaust; **-end** n. the tail

end of anything; a remnant [etym. doubtful].

fag·ot, fag·got (fag′·ạt) n. a bundle of sticks for fuel; a bundle of steel rods cut for welding; v.t. to tie together; to embroider with a fagot stitch. **-ing, faggoting,** n. a kind of embroidery [Fr. *fagot*, a bundle of sticks].

Fahr·en·heit (far′·an·hīt) n. the term applied to a type of thermometer graduated so that freezing point of water is fixed at 32°, and boiling point at 212°. [German physicist, *Fahrenheit* (1686-1736)].

fail (fāl) v.i. to be lacking; to diminish; to deteriorate; to miss; to be unsuccessful in; to go bankrupt; v.t. to disappoint or desert; to omit; (*Colloq.*) to refuse to pass a candidate under examination. pr.p. **-ing.** pa.p. **-ed. -ing** n. a fault; a weakness; a shortcoming; prep. in default of. **-ure** n. bankru͟ptcy; lack of success [O.Fr. *faillir*, to deceive].

fain (fān) adv. (*Poetic*) gladly. [O.E. *faegen*, joyful].

faint (fānt) a. lacking strength; indistinct; giddy; timorous; v.i. to become weak; to grow discouraged; to swoon; n. a swoon. **—heart** n. and a. **—hearted** a. cowardly; timorous. adv. indistinctly [O.Fr. *feint*, pa.p. of *feindre*, to feign].

fair (fer) a. clear; free from fault or stain; light-colored; blond; beautiful; not cloudy; hopeful; just; plausible; middling; adv. in a fair or courteous manner; according to what is just. **— copy** n. a rewritten, corrected copy. **— game,** open to banter. **-ish** a. rather fair. **-ly** adv. justly; tolerably; wholly. **-ness** n. **— play** n. straightforward justice. **— spoken** n. polite; plausible. **-way** n. a navigable channel on a river; (*Golf*) the stretch of ground between the tee and the green, which is freed from rough grass. **fair and square,** honest; honestly [O.E. *faeger*, pleasant].

fair (fer) n. periodic competitive exhibition for showing produce of a district; a sale of fancy articles to raise money for charitable purposes [O.Fr. *feire*, L. *feria*, a holiday].

fair·y (fer′·i·) n. an imaginary creature in the form of a diminutive human being, supposed to meddle, for good or for ill, with the affairs of men; a. fairy-like; dainty. **-land** n. land of the fairies; wonderland. **— tale** n. a story about fairies and magic; (*Colloq.*) improbable tale [O.Fr. *faerie*, enchantment].

faith (fāth) n. belief, esp. in a revealed religion; trust or reliance; a system of religious doctrines believed in; loyalty; pledged word. **-ful** a. loyal; reliable; honorable; exact. **-fully** adv. **-fulness** n. [O.Fr. *fei*, faith].

fake (fāk) v.t. to conceal the defects of, by artifice; to copy, as an antique, and pass it off as genuine; v.i. to pretend; n. a fraud; a deception; a forgery; a faker. **-r** n. [prob. Dut. *feague*, to touch up].

fa·kir (fạ·kir′, fā′·ker) n. a member of a sect of religious mendicants in India [Ar. *faqir*, a poor man].

Fa·lan·gists (fạ·lanj′·ists) n.pl. Spanish military Fascists, who co-operated with Franco during Spanish Civil War (1936-39).

fal·cate (fal′·kāt) a. (*Bot.* and *Zool.*) sickle shaped; crescent [L. *falx*, a sickle].

fal·con (faw′·kn, fȧl′·kạn) n. a sub-family of birds of prey, allied to the hawk, with strong curved beak and long sickle-shaped claws; one of these birds, trained to hunt game; **-er** n. one who breeds and trains falcons or hawks for hunting wild-fowl. **-ry** n. the sport of flying hawks in pursuit of game [O.Fr. *faucon*, a falcon].

fal·de·ral (fal·der·al′) n. the refrain to a song; anything trifling; a gew-gaw. Also

fald·stool (fawld′·stòòl) n. a portable, folding stool; stool before which kings kneel at their coronation; a litany-desk [O.H. Ger. *faldstuol*, a folding stool].

fall (fawl) v.i. to descend from a higher to a lower position; to drop; to collapse; to abate; to decline in value; to become degraded; to happen; to be captured. *pr.p.* **-ing.** *pa.t.* **fell.** *pa.p.* **-en.** n. the act of falling; a drop; capitulation; the amount (of rain, snow, etc.) deposited in a specified time; a cascade; a wrestling bout; a moral lapse, esp. that of Adam and Eve; diminution in value, amount, or volume; the autumn. **-en** a. prostrate; degraded; of loose morals. **-ing-star** n. a meteor. **—out** n. radioactive particles which descend to earth after a nuclear explosion. [O.E. *feallan*, to fall].

fal·la·cy (fal′·a·si.) n. deceptive appearance; a delusion; an apparently forcible argument which is really illogical; sophistry. **fallacious** a. misleading; illogical. **fallaciously** adv. [L. *fallax*, deceitful].

fal·li·ble (fal′·a·bl) a. liable to error; not reliable. **fallibility** n. the quality of being fallible. **fallibly** adv. [L. *fallere*, to fail].

fal·low (fal′·ō) a. left untilled for a season; (*Fig.*) untrained (of the mind); n. land which has lain untilled and unsown for a year or more; v.t. to plough without sowing [etym. doubtful, prob. O.E. *fealh*, a harrow].

fallow (fal′·ō) a. a pale yellow or light brown color. [O.E. *fealwes*, of a brown color.]

false (fawls) a. untrue; inaccurate; dishonest; deceptive; artificial. **— face** n. a mask. **-hood** n. an untruth; a lie. **-ly** adv. **-ness** n. **falsifiable** a. capable of being falsified. **falsification** n. **falsifier** n. one who falsifies. **falsify** v.t. to distort the truth; to forge; to tamper with; to prove to be untrue. **falsity** n. an untrue statement; deception [L. *falsus*, mistaken].

fal·set·to (fawl·set′·ō) n. forced high notes esp. of a male voice [It. dim. of *falso*, false].

fal·ter (fawl′·ter) v.i to stumble; to hesitate; to lack resolution; to stammer.

fame (fām) n. public report or rumor, esp. good repute. **-d** a. celebrated. **famous** a. celebrated; noted; (*colloq.*) excellent. **famously** adv. [L. *fama*, a report].

fa·mil·iar (fa·mil′·yer) a. intimate; informal; free; unconstrained; well-known; current; conversant with; n. a close acquaintance. **-ize** v.t. to make familiar; (*Reflex.*) to get to know thoroughly (foll. by *with*). **familiarity** n. intimacy; forwardness. **-ly** adv. [L. *familiaris*, pert. to a household].

fam·i·ly (fam′·a·li.) n. parents and their children; the children of the same parents; descendants of one common ancestor; (*Biol.*) group of individuals within an order or subdivision of an order; a group of languages derived from a common parent tongue. **— tree**, a diagram representing the genealogy of a family. **— way**, pregnancy [L. *familia*].

fam·ine (fam′·in) n. large-scale scarcity of food; extreme shortage; starvation. **famish** v.t. to starve; v.i. to feel acute hunger, famished a. [L. *fames*, hunger].

fan (fan) n. an instrument to produce currents of air or assist ventilation; a decorative folding object, made of paper, silk, etc. used to cool face; a winnowing-implement; a small sail on a windmill to keep large sails to the wind; v.t. to cool with a fan; to ventilate; to winnow; to cause to flame (as a fire); to excite; to spread out like a fan. *pr.p.* **-ning.** *pa.p.* **-ned. -light** n. a window, usually semicircular, over a doorway. **-ner** n. [O.E. *fann*, a winnowing-fan].

fan (fan) n. (*Slang*) a devoted admirer [*abbrev. of fanatic*].

fa·nat·ic (fa·nat′·ik) n. a person inspired with excessive and bigoted enthusiasm, esp. a religious zealot; devotee; a. over-enthusiastic; immoderately zealous. **-al** a. **-ally** adv. **fanaticism** n. violent enthusiasm [L. *fanum*, a temple].

fan·cy (fan′·si.) n. the faculty of creating within the mind images of outward things; an image thus conceived; a whim; a notion; partiality; a. pleasing to the taste; guided by whim; elaborate; v.t. to imagine; to have a liking for; to desire; to breed (as dogs); **fancier** n. one who has a specialized knowledge, esp. of the breeding of animals. **fanciful** a. capricious; unreal; fantastic; **fancifully** adv. **fancifulness** n. **— ball** n. a ball at which the dancers wear costumes. **-free** a. heart-free [contr. fr. *fantasy*].

fan·fare (fan′·fār) n. a flourish of trumpets; a showy display. [Fr. *fanfarer*, to blow trumpets].

fang (fang) n. the canine tooth of a carnivorous animal; the long perforated tooth of a poisonous serpent [O.E. = a seizing].

fan·gled (fang′·gld) a. orig. meant fashionable, now exists only in the epithet *newfangled*, new fashioned, hence unfamiliar.

fan·tan (fan′·tan) n. a Chinese gambling game [Chin.].

fan·ta·sy (fan′·ta·si) n. fancy; mental image; caprice; hallucination. Also **phantasy. fantasia** (fan·tā′·zha) n. (*Mus.*) a composition not conforming to the usual rules of music. **fantasied** a. fanciful. **fantasm** n. same as **phantasm. fantastic, -al** a. fanciful; wild; irregular; capricious. **fantastically** adv. [Gk. *phantasia*, appearance].

far (fár) a. distant; remote; more distant of two; adv. to a great extent or distance; to a great height; considerably; very much; n. a distant place. **-ther** a. (*comp.*). **-thest** a. (*superl.*) adv. **— East**, that part of Asia including India, China, Japan. **-fetched** a. (*Fig.*) incredible; strained. **-seeing,** or **-sighted** a. seeing to a great distance; (*Fig.*) taking a long view; prudent [O.E. *feor*, far].

far·ad (far′·ad) n. the unit of electrostatic capacity—the capacity of a condenser which requires one coulomb to raise its potential by one volt. **faraday,** n. the quantity of electricity required to liberate 1 gram-equivalent of an ion. **faradaic, faradic** a. pert. to induced electrical currents [fr. M. *Faraday*, scientist].

farce (fárs) n. orig. a dramatic interlude; a style of comedy marked by boisterous humor and extravagant gesture; absurd or empty show; a pretense. **farceur** (far·sur′) n. a joker; a wag. **farcical** a. pert. to a farce; absurdly ludicrous; sham. **farcically** adv. [O.Fr. *farce*, stuffing].

fare (fer) v.i. to be in any state, bad or good; to get on; to happen; to be entertained at table; n. the sum paid by a passenger on a vehicle; a passenger; food and drink at table. **-well** interj. (*Lit.*) may it go well with you; good-bye; n. a parting wish for someone's welfare; the act of taking leave; a. parting; last [O.E. *faran*, to go].

fa·ri·na (fa·rē′·na, fa·rī′·na) n. flour or meal of cereal grains, used for cereal and puddings; starch [L. *farina*, ground corn].

farm (fárm) n. a tract of land set apart for cultivation or for other industries, as dairy farm, etc.; the buildings on this land; v.t. cultivate land for agricultural purposes; to collect (taxes, etc.) on condition of receiving a percentage of what is yielded; v.i. and t. to cultivate; to operate a farm. **-er** n. **-ing**

n. the occupation of cultivating the soil. **-stead** *n.* a farm with all the outbuildings attached to it. **-yard** *n.* enclosure surrounded by farm buildings [M.E. *ferme*, payment].

far·o (fer'·ō) *n.* a gambling game of cards [fr. *Pharaoh*, one of the cards].

far·ra·go (far·ā'·gō, far·ä'·gō) *n.* a medley; a miscellaneous collection. **farraginous** *a.* confusedly mixed [L. *farrago*, mixed fodder].

far·ri·er (far'·i·ẹr) *n.* Br. a veterinarian. **-y** *n.* [L. *ferrum*, iron].

far·row (far'·ō) *n.* a litter of pigs; *v.t.* to give birth to (pigs); *v.i.* to bring forth pigs [O.E. *fearh*, a pig].

far·ther (fär'·THẹr) *a.* more far; more remote; *adv.* to a greater distance. **-most** *a.*

far·thing (fär'·THing) *n.* (*Brit.*) the fourth of a penny [O.E. *feorthing*, a fourth part].

fas·ci·a (fash'·i·a) *n.* a band, fillet, or bandage; (*Archit.*) a strip of flat stone between two moldings; [L. *fascia*, a band].

fas·ci·cle (fas'·i·kl) *n.* (*Bot.*) a close cluster of leaves or flowers as in the sweet william; a small bundle of nerve fibers; a serial division of a book. **fasicular, fasiculate** *a.* [L. *fasciculus*, a small bundle].

fas·ci·nate (fas'·a·nāt) *v.t.* to enchant; to deprive of the power of movement, by a look. **fascinating** *a.* **fascination** *n.* the act of fascinating; enchantment; irresistible attraction. **fascinator** *n.* [L. *fascinare*].

fas·cism (fash'·ism) *n.* a centralized autocratic national regime with extremely nationalistic policies with an economic system based on state-controlled capitalism. **Fascist** *n.* [It. *fascio*, a bundle].

fash·ion (fash'·an) *n.* the style in which a thing is made or done; pattern; the mode or cut, esp. of a dress; custom; appearance; *v.t.* to form; to shape. **-able** *a.* **-ably** *adv.* [O.Fr. *facon*, a manner].

fast (fast) *v.i.* to abstain from food; to deny oneself certain foods as a form of religious discipline; *n.* abstinence from food; a day of fasting [O.E. *faestan*, to fast].

fast (fast) *a.* rapid; securely fixed; firm; tight shut; profound; immovable; permanent, as a dye; stable; in advance of the correct time, as a clock; loyal, as friends; dissipated, as *a fast life; adv.* firmly; soundly; securely; dissipatedly; rapidly. **-ness** *n.* security; a stronghold [O.E. *faest*, firm].

fas·ten (fas'·n) *v.t.* to fix firmly; to hold together; *v.i.* to fix itself; to catch (of a lock). **-er** *n.* a contrivance for fixing things firmly together. **-ing** *n.* that by which anything fastens, as a lock, bolt, nut, screw [O.E. *faest*, firm].

fas·tid·i·ous (fas·tid'·i·as) *a.* difficult to please; discriminating. **-ly** *adv.* **-ness** *n.* [L. *fastidium*, loathing].

fat (fat) *a.* (*comp.*) **-ter.** (*superl.*) **-test.** fleshy; plump; oily; yielding a rich supply; productive; profitable; *n.* an oily substance found in animal bodies; solid animal or vegetable oil; the best or richest part of anything; *v.t.* to make fat; *v.i.* to grow fat. *pr.p.* **-ting.** *pa.p.* **-ted. -head** *n.* (*Slang*) a stupid person. **-headed** *a.* **-ling** *n.* a young fattened animal. **-ness** *n.* the quality or state of being fat; corpulence; fertility. **-ted** *a.* fattened. **-ten** *v.t.* to make fat; to make fertile; *v.i.* to grow fat. **-tener** *n.* **-tiness** *n.* **-ty** *a.* resembling or containing fat; greasy [O.E. *faet*, fat].

fate (fāt) *n.* an inevitable and irresistible power supposedly controlling human destiny; appointed lot; death; doom. **the Fates,** the three goddesses supposed to preside over the course of human life. **fatal** *a.* causing death; appointed by fate; calamitous. **fatalism** *n.* the doctrine that all events are predetermined and unavoidable. **fatalist** *n.* **fatalistic** *a.* **fatality** *n.* accident causing death; the state

of being fatal; inevitable necessity. **-d** *a.* destined; pre-ordained; doomed. **-ful** *a.* momentous; irrevocable. **-fully** *adv.* **-fulness** *n.* [L. *fatum*].

fa·ther (fä'·THẹr) *n.* a male parent; a male ancestor more remote than a parent; a title of respect paid to one of seniority or rank, esp. to church dignitaries, priests, etc.; the first person of the Trinity; oldest member of a community; a producer, author or contriver; *v.t.* to make oneself the father of; to adopt; to assume or admit responsibility for. **-hood** *n.* the state of being a father; paternity. **—in-law** *n.* (*pl.* **-s-in-law**) the father of one's wife or husband. **-land** *n.* the land of one's fathers. **-less** *a.* without a father living. **-liness** *n.* **-ly** *a.* and *adv.* like a father in affection and care; paternal; benevolent. **-ship** *n.* [O.E. *faeder*, a father].

fath·om (faTH'·am) *n.* a nautical measure of depth, 6 ft. *v.t.* to ascertain the depth of; to sound; (*Fig.*) to get to the bottom of; to understand. **-able** *n.* **-less** *a.* incapable of being fathomed; unplumbed. **-lessly** *adv.* [O.E. *faethm*, the outstretched arms].

fa·tigue (fa·tēg') *n.* weariness from bodily or mental exertion; toil; non-military routine work of soldiers; *v.t.* to weary by toil; to exhaust the strength of; to tire out. *pr.p.* **-ing.** *pa.p.* **-d** [Fr. *fatiguer*, to weary].

fat·u·ous (fa'·choo·as) *a.* silly. **fatuity** *n.* unconsciously foolish; inanity; foolishness. **-ness** *n.* [L. *fatuus*, silly].

fau·cet (faw'·sit) *n.* a fixture for controlling the flow of liquid from a pipe, etc.; a tap [O.Fr. *fausset*].

faugh (faw) *interj.* an exclamation of contempt or disgust [imit.].

fault (fawlt) *n.* a failing; blunder; mistake; defect; flaw; responsibility for error; (*Geol.*) a dislocation of rock strata; in hunting, the loss of the scent trail; (*Elect.*) a defect in electrical apparatus. **-ed** *a.* (*Geol.*) broken by one or more faults. **-ily** *adv.* **-iness** *n.* **-less** *a.* without flaws; perfect. **-lessly** *adv.* **-lessness** *n.* perfection. **-y** *a.* imperfect. [O. Fr. *faute*, error].

fau·na (fawn'·a) *n.* a collective term for the animals of any given geographical region or geological epoch [L. *Fauna*, sister of *Faunus*, a god of agriculture].

fa·ve·o·late (fav·ē'·ō·lāt) *a.* pitted; cellular; resembling a honeycomb. [L. *faveolus*, a little honeycomb].

fa·vor (fā'·ver) *n.* a gracious act; kind regard; goodwill; partiality; token of generosity or esteem; a gift; *v.t.* to regard with kindness; to show bias towards; to tend to promote; (*Colloq.*) to resemble in feature. **-able** *a.* friendly; propitious; advantageous; suitable; satisfactory. **-ableness** *n.* **-ably** *adv.* **-ed** *a.* fortunate; lucky featured, as in *ill-favored.* **-ite** *n. a* person or thing regarded with special favor; the likely winner; *a.* regarded with particular affection; most esteemed. **-itism** *n.* undue partiality [L. *favor*, partiality].

fawn (fawn) *n.* a young deer; its color; *a.* delicate yellowish-brown; *v.i.* to give birth to a fawn [O.Fr. *faon*, fr. L. *fetus*, offspring].

fawn (fawn) *v.i.* to flatter unctuously; to curry favor. **-er** *n.* **-ing** *n.* servile flattery; *a.* over-demonstrative. **-ingly** *adv.* **-ingness** *n.* [M.E. *faunen*, to rejoice].

fay (fā) *n.* a fairy; an elf [O.Fr. *fae*].

fe·al·ty (fē'·al·ti·) *n.* fidelity; obligations binding a vassal to his lord [O.Fr. *fealte*, fidelity].

fear (fir) *n.* alarm; dread; solicitude; anxiety; reverence towards God; *v.t.* to regard with dread or apprehension; to anticipate (as a disaster); to hold in awe; *v.i.* to be afraid;

to be anxious. **-ful** adv. **-fulness** n. **-less** a. without fear; intrepid; dauntless. **-lessly** adv. **lessness** n. courage; intrepidity. **-some** a. causing fear; terrifying [O.E. *faer*, danger].

fea·si·ble (fē'·zạ·bl) a. capable of being done; suitable. **-ness, feasibility** n. **feasibly** adv. [Fr. *faisible*, that can be done].

feast (fēst) n. a day of joyful or solemn commemoration; a banquet; something very enjoyable; v.t. to feed sumptuously; to regale; v.i. to eat sumptuously; to be highly gratified or delighted. **-er** n. [L. *festum*, a holiday].

feat (fēt) n. an exploit or action of extraordinary strength, courage, skill, or endurance [Fr. *fait*, fr. L. *factum*, a deed].

feath·er (feTH'·ẹr) n. one of the epidermal growths forming the body-covering of a bird; a plume; the feathered end or an arrow; feathers, as a cap or arrow. **-bed** n. a mattress stuffed with feathers; v.t. (*Colloq.*) to pamper; to keep supernumeraries on a job. **-brained, -headed, -pated** a. weak-minded; inane. **-stitch** n. an embroidery stitch resembling a feather. **-weight,** the lightest weight that may be carried by a race-horse; a boxer weighing not more than 126 lbs.; any very light or insignificant person or thing. **-y** a. pert. to, covered with, or resembling feathers [O.E. *fether*, feather].

fea·ture (fē'·cher) n. any part of the face; distinctive characteristic; main attraction; pl. the face; v.t. to portray; to outline; to present as the leading attraction. **-less** a. void of striking features. [O.Fr. *faiture*, something made].

feb·ri·fuge (feb'·rạ·fūj) n. a drug taken to allay fever. **febrifugal** a. **febrile** (fē'·bril, feb'·ril) a. feverish; accompanied by fever. **febrility** n. [L. *febris*, fever].

Feb·ru·ar·y (feb'·rȯȯ·e·ri·) n. the second month of the year [L. *Februaris*, fr. *Februa*, the Roman festival of purification].

fe·ces, faeces (fē'·sēz) n.pl. dregs; the solid waste matter from the bowels. **fecal** (·kạl) a. [L. *faeces*, grounds].

fe·cund (fe'·kạnd) a. prolific; fruitful; fertile. **-ate** (fē'·kun'·dāt, fek'·un·dāt) v.t. to make fruitful; to impregnate. **-ation** n. **-ity** n. the quality or power of reproduction; fertility; productiveness [L. *fecundus*, fruitful].

fed (fed) pa.t. and pa.p. of the verb **feed.**

fed·er·al (fed'·er·al) a. pert. to a league or treaty, esp. between states; of an association of states which, autonomous in home affairs, combine for matters of wider national and international policy; pert. to such a central government; pert. to the Union in the Civil War. **federacy** n. **-ize** v.t. to form a union under a federal government. **-ism** n. **-ist** n. a supporter of such a union. **federate** v.t. to unite states into a federation. a. united; allied. **federation** n. a federal union. **federative** a. [L. *foedus*, a compact].

fee (fē) n. orig. land held from a lord on condition of certain feudal services; remuneration for professional services; payment for special privilege; v.t. to pay a fee to. **fee-simple,** unrestricted ownership or inheritance [O.E. *feoh*, cattle or property].

fee·ble (fē'·bl) a. weak; deficient in strength; frail; faint. **—minded** a. mentally subnormal. **-ness** n. **feebly** adv. [Fr. *faible*, weak].

feed (fēd) v.t. to give food to; to supply with nourishment; to supply with material (as a machine); v.i. to eat; to subsist. pa.p. and pa.t. **fed.** n. that which is consumed, esp. by animals; the material supplied to a machine or the channel by which it is fed. **-er** n. one who feeds; a device for supplying a machine with material; a channel

taking water to a reservoir; a branch railway-line. **-ing** n. act of eating; that which is consumed; grazing. [O.E. *fedan*, to feed].

feel (fēl) v.t. to perceive by the touch; to handle; to be sensitive to; to experience emotionally; to have an intuitive awareness of; v.i. to know by the touch; to be conscious of being; to give rise to a definite sensation; to be moved emotionally. pa.p. pa.t. **felt** n. the sensation of touch; the quality of anything touched. **-er** n. (*Zool.*) one of the tactile organs (antennae, tentacles, etc.) of certain insects and animals; a tentative remark, proposal, etc. to sound the opinions or attitude of others. **-ing** n. sense of touch; awareness by touch; intuition; sensibility; sympathy. **-ings** n.pl. emotions; a. kindly; responsive; possessing great sensibility. **-ingly** adv. [O.E. *felan*, to feel].

feet (fēt) n.pl. of **foot.**

feign (fān) v.t. to invent; to pretend; to counterfeit. **-ed** a. pretended; disguised. **-edly** adv. **-edness** n. **-ing** n. pretense; invention. **feint** n. an assumed appearance; a misleading move in boxing, military operations, etc. v.i. to make a deceptive move [Fr. *feindre*, to feign].

feld·spar (feld'·spàr) n. a constituent of granite and other igneous rocks; a crystalline mineral comprising silicates of aluminium with varying proportions of potassium, calcium and sodium. a. [Ger. *Feld*, field; *Spath*, a spar].

fe·lic·i·ty (fi·lis'·ạ·ti·) n. happiness; bliss; skill. **felicitate** v.t. to express joy or pleasure to; to congratulate. **felicitation** n. congratulation; the act of expressing good wishes. **felicitous** a. happy; appropriate; aptly expressed [L. *felix*, happy].

fe·line (fē'·līn) a. pert. to cats; cat-like; (*Fig.*) treacherous [L. *feles*, a cat].

fell (fel) a. cruel; ruthless; deadly [O.Fr. *fel.* cruel].

fell (fel) n. an animal's skin or hide [O.E. *fel*, a skin].

fell (fel) pa.t. of the verb **fall.**

fell (fel) v.t. to cause to fall; to cut down; to sew an overlapping flax seam. **-er** n. [O.E. *fellan*, to cause to fall].

fell (fel) n. a tract of high moorland, as in the English Lake District [Scand. *fiall*, rock].

fel·low (fel'·ō) n. a man; boy; (*Colloq.*) suitor; an associate; an equal; a person; a worthless person; a graduate student on a grant for special study; member of a literary or scientific society. **— traveller** n. sympathizer with the Communist Party, but not a member of it. **-ship** n. the state of being a fellow; companionship; community of feeling, interest, etc.; a foundation for the maintenance of a resident university graduate; the grant made by such a foundation [M.E. *felawe*, a partner].

fel·on (fel'·ạn) n. one who has committed felony; (*Med.*) inflammation of top joint of the finger; a whitlow; a. fierce; traitorous. **-ious** a. **-iously** adv. **-iousness** n. **-y** n. (*Law*) a crime more serious than a *misdemeanor* (as murder, manslaughter, etc.) [O.Fr. *felon*, a traitor].

felt (felt) pa.t. and pa.p. of **feel.**

felt (felt) n. a closely matted fabric of wool, hair, etc.; v.t. to make into felt; to cover with felt; v.i. to become matted like felt. **-ing** n. the art or process of making felt; the felt itself [O.E. *felt*, something compact]

fe·male (fē'·māl) n. one of the sex that bears young; (*Bot.*) a plant which produces fruit; a. pert. to the child-bearing sex; feminine. **femineity** (fe·mạ·nē'·ạ·ti·) n. the quality of being a woman. **feminine** a. pert. to or associated with women; womanly;

tender; (of males) effeminate. **femininely** *adv.* **feminineness, femininity** *n.* the nature of the female sex; womanliness. **feminism** *n.* the doctrine that maintains the equality of the sexes; advocacy of women's rights. **feminist** *n.* [L. *femina*].

fe·mur (fē'·mẹr) *n.* the thigh-bone. **femoral** *a.* [L. *femur*, the thigh].

fen (fen) *n.* (*Brit.*) low-lying marshy land [O.E. *fenn*, a bog].

fence (fens) *n.* a wall or hedge for enclosing; the art of fencing; a receiver of stolen goods; *v.t.* to enclose with a fence; to guard; *v.i.* to practise the art of sword-play; to evade a direct answer to an opponent's challenge; to equivocate. **-r** *n.* one who is skilled in fencing. **fencing** *n.* the art or practice of self-defense with the sword, foil, etc.; the act of enclosing by a fence; the materials of which a fence is made [abbrev. of *defence*].

fend (fend) *v.t.* to ward off; *v.i.* to resist; to parry; (*Colloq.*) to provide. **-er** *n.* that which acts as a protection; the metal part over wheels of an automobile; a metal guard to prevent coals falling beyond hearth; a device, usually a bundle of rope, to break the impact of a ship drawing alongside a wharf or other vessel [abbrev. of *defend*].

fenestra (fi·nes'·trạ) *n.* a hole; an opening. Also **fenester. fenestral** *a.* **fenestrate, fenestrated** *a.* (*Bot.*) having transpartent spots; (*Archit.*) having windows. **fenestration** *n.* the state of being perforated; arrangement of windows in a building [L. *fenestra*, a window].

fen·nel (fen'·el) *n.* a perennial umbelliferous plant with yellow flowers [O.E. *finul*, fr. L. *faenum*, hay].

fe·ral (fi'·rạl) *a.* wild; not domesticated; run wild (of plants). **ferine** *a.* [L. *ferus*, wild].

fer·ment (fur'·ment) *n.* a substance which causes fermentation, as yeast; fermentation; (*Fig.*) tumult; agitation. (fẹr·ment') *v.t.* to induce fermentation in; to arouse a commotion; *v.i.* to undergo fermentation; to work (of wine); to become excited; to be in a state of agitation. **-ability** *n.* **-able** *a.* **-ation** *n.* the decomposition of organic substances produced by the action of a living organism, or of certain chemical agents. **-ative** *a.* [L. *fermentum*, leaven].

fern (furn) *n.* plant characterized by fibrous roots, and leaves called fronds. **-y** *a.* [O.E.].

fe·roc·ity (fạ·ràs'·ạ·ti·) *n.* cruelty; savage fierceness of disposition. **ferocious** *a.* fierce; violent; wild. **ferociously** *adv.* **ferociousness** *n.* [L. *ferox*, wild].

fer·ret (fer'·it) *n.* a small, partially domesticated variety of polecat; *v.t.* to hunt out to search out [O.Fr. *furet*, a ferret].

fer·ric (fer'·ik) *a.* pert. to or extracted from iron; applied to compounds of trivalent iron, **— acid**, an acid containing iron and oxygen. [L. *ferrum*, iron].

fer·ro- (fer'·ō) *prefix* fr. L. *ferrum*, containing or made of iron, occurring in compound words **-concerte** *n.* reinforced concrete; concrete with inner skeleton of iron or steel. **-magnetic** *a.* reacting like iron in a magnetic field. **ferrous** *a.* pert. to iron.

fer·rule (fer'·ạl, fer'·ŏŏl) *n.* a metal tip or ring on a cane, etc. to prevent splitting. Also **ferule** [O.Fr. *virelle*, a bracelet].

fer·ry (fer'·i·) *v.t.* to transport over stretch of water by boat. *n.* a place where one is conveyed across a river, etc. by boat; the ferryboat; the right of transporting passengers and goods by this means. **ferriage** *n.* transport by ferry; the fare paid for such transport [O.E. *faran*, to go].

fer·tile (fur'·til) *a.* producing or bearing

abundantly; prolific; fruitful; (*Fig.*) inventive. **-ly** *adv.* **-ness, fertilization** *n.* the act of fertilizing; enrichment of soil, by natural or artificial means; (*Biol.*) union of the female and male cells. **fertilize** *v.t.* to make fruitful; (*Biol.*) to fecundate; (*Bot.*) to pollinate. **fertilizer** *n.* one who, or that which, fertilizes; material (e.g. manure, nitrates) to enrich soil. **fertility** *n.* [L. *fertilis*, fruitful].

fer·ule (fer·ạl, fer'·ŏŏl) *n.* a rod or ruler for punishing children [L. *ferula*, rod].

fer·vent (fur'·vạnt) *a.* glowing; ardent; zealous; enthusiastic. **fervency** *n.* ardor; intensity of devotion. **-ly** *adv.* **fervid** *a.* burning; vehement; intense. **fervidity** *n.* **fervidly** *adv.* **fervidness** *n.* zeal; enthusiasm. **fervor** *n.* heat; ardor; passion [L. *fervere*, to boil].

fes·cue (fes'·kū) *n.* a kind of tough grass; a teacher's small pointer [M.E. *festu*, a bit of straw].

fes·tal (fes'·tạl) *a.* pert. to feast or festival; joyous; gay. **-ly** *adv.* [O.Fr. *feste*, a feast].

fes·ter (fes'·tẹr) *v.t.* to cause to putrefy; *v.i.* to become inflamed; to suppurate; to rot; to become embittered; *n.* an ulcer; a sore [O.Fr. *festre*, an ulcer].

fes·tive (fes'·tiv) *a.* festal; joyous; convivial. **festival** *n.* a feast or celebration; an annual competition or periodic gathering of musical or dramatic societies. **-ly** *adv.* **festivity** *n.* merriment; merrymaking; festival [L. *festivus*, festive].

fes·toon (fes·tóon') *n.* garland hanging in a curve; *v.t.* [Fr. fr. L.L. *festo*, a garland].

fetch (fech) *v.t.* to go for and bring; to summon; to bring or yield (a price); *v.i.* to go and bring things; *n.* the act of bringing; a trick or artifice; an apparition; a person's double. **-ing** *a.* attractive; alluring [O.E. *feccan*, to bring].

fete (fāt) *n.* a festival; a holiday; *v.t.* to honor with celebrations. **feted** *a.* honored [L. *festum*, a feast].

fet·id (fet'·id) *a* having a strong, offensive smell. Also **foetid** [L. *fetidus*, stinking].

fe·tish, fetich, fetiche (fet'·ish) *n.* an object or image superstitiously invested with divine or demoniac power, and, as such, reverenced devoutly; anything regarded with exaggerated reverence. **-ism,** *n.* fetish worship. **-istic,** *a.* [Port. *feitico*, magic].

fet·lock (fet'·làk) *n.* the tuft of hair on a horse's leg.

fet·ter (fet'·ẹr) *n.* a chain or shackle for the feet (usually pl.); an impediment or restriction; *v.t.* to shackle; to restrain [O.E. *fetor*, fr. *fet*, the feet]. [girdle].

fet·tle (fet'·l) *n.* condition [O.E. *fetel*, a

fe·tus, foetus (fē'·tạs) *n.* the young of vertebrate animals between the embryonic and independent states. **fetal, foetal** *a.* **fetation, foetation** *n.* pregnancy. **feticide, foeticide** *n.* destroying of the fetus; abortion [L. *fetus*, a bringing forth].

feud (fūd) *n.* a lasting, hereditary strife between families or clans; deadly hatred [M.E. *fede*, enmity].

feud (fūd) *n.* an estate or land held on condition of service; a fief. **-al** *a.* pert. to feuds or to feudalism. **-alism** *n.* a system which prevailed in Europe in the Middle Ages, by which vassals held land from the King and the tenants-in-chief in return for military service. Also **feudal system. -ary, -atory** *a.* holding land by feudal tenure; *n.* a vassal holding land in fee [L. L. *feudum*, a fief].

fe·ver (fē'·vẹr) *n.* bodily disease marked by unusual rise of temperature and usually a quickening of pulse; violent mental or emotional excitement; *v.t.* to put into a fever. *v.i.* to become fevered. **-ed** *a.* affected with fever; frenzied. **ish** *a.* slightly fevered;

agitated. **-ishly** *adv.* [O.E. *fefor*, forever].

few (fū) *a.* not many; *n.* and *pron.* a small number. **-ness** *n.* [O.E. *feawe*, few].

fez (fez) *n.* a red, brimless felt hat with tassel worn in Egypt, Turkey, etc. [prob. fr. *Fez* in Morocco].

fi·a·cre (fi·à′·kr) *n.* a hackney coach [fr. *Hotel St. Fiacre* [Paris].

fi·an·ce (fē·an·sā′) *n.* (*fem.* **fiancee**) a betrothed man [Fr. *fiancer*, to betroth].

fi·as·co (fē·as′·kō) *n.* any spectacular failure [It. *fiasco*, a bottle].

fi·at (fī′·at) *n.* a formal command; an authoritative order [L. *fiat*, let it be done].

fib (fib) *n.* a falsehood; a mild lie; *v.i.* to tell a petty lie *pr.p.* **-bing.** *pa.p.; pa.t.* **-bed.**

fi·ber (fī′·ber) *n.* one of the bundles of thread-like tissue constituting muscles, etc.; any thread-like substance used for weaving fabric; character, as in *moral fiber.* **-ed** *a.* **-less** *a.* **fibriform** *a.* **fibril** *n.* a very small fiber. **fibrillose** *a.* (*Bot.*) covered with fibers. **fibrillous** *a.* composed of small fibers. **fibrin** *n.* a proteid formed in coagulation of blood. **fibroid** *a.* of a fibrous nature; *n.* a fibrous tumor. **fibrous** *a.* composed of fibers. **fibrousness** *n.* [L. *fibra*, a fiber].

fib·u·la (fib′·yạ·la) *n.* (*Archeal.*); (*Med.*) the slender outer bone of the leg between knee and ankle. **-r** *a.* [L.*fibula*, a clasp].

fich·u (fī′·shò) *n.* a triangular cape worn over the shoulders and tying in front; a ruffle of lace, etc. worn at the neck [Fr.].

fick·le (fik′·l) *a.* inconstant; capricious; unreliable. **-ness** *n.* [O.E. *ficol*, cunning].

fic·tile (fik′·til) *a.* capable of being molded; plastic; used of all objects shaped in clay by a potter [L. *fictilis*].

fic·tion (fik′·shạn) *n.* literature dealing with imaginary characters and situations; something invented, or imagined. **-al** *a.* **fictitious** *a.* imaginary; feigned; false; **fictitiously** *adv.* [L. *fictus*, invented].

fid·dle (fid′·l) *n.* a stringed musical instrument; a violin; wooden framework around dining-tables on board a ship; *v.t.* and *v.i.* to play on a fiddle; to trifle. **—bow** *n.* the bow used in playing a violin. **—de-dee** *n.* nonsense. **—faddle** *v.i.* to trifle; to dawdle; *n.* triviality; *interj.* rubbish′ **-sticks** (*interj.*) nonsense. **fiddling** *a.* trifling [O.E. *fithele*].

fi·del·i·ty (fī·del′·ạ·ti·) *n.* faithfulness; loyalty; devotion to duty; adherence to marriage vows; accuracy [L. *fidelis*, faithful].

fidg·et (fij′·it) *v.i.* to move restlessly; to be uneasy; *n.* uneasiness. **-s** *n.pl.* nervous restlessness. **-y** *a.* [fr. Scand. *fikja*].

fi·du·ci·ar·y (fī·dòō′·shi·er·i·) *a.* holding or held in trust; (of paper currency) depending for its value on public confidence; *n.* a trustee. **fiducial** *a.* having faith or confidence [L. *fiducia*, confidence].

field (fēld) *n.* cleared land; a division of farm land; scene of a battle; the battle itself; any wide expanse; areas of observation; locality of operations, as in surveying; sphere of influence within which magnetic, electrostatic, or gravitational forces are perceptible; the surface of an escutcheon; the background of a flag, coin, etc. on which a design is drawn; the people following a hunt; (sports) area of ground used for sports; (*Cricket*) the side which is not batting; a collective term for all the competitors in an athletic contest or all the horses in a race; an area rich in some natural product (e.g. coal-field, oil-field); *v.t.* (*Baseball*) to catch the ball; *v.i.* to act as fielder. **— artillery** *n.* light guns for active operations. **— battery** *n.* battery of field guns. **— book** *n.* book used for notes by land surveyor or naturalist. **— day** *n.* a day for athletic con-

tests; a gala day. **-er** *n.* one who fields at cricket, baseball, etc. **— glass** *n.* a binocular telescope. **— gun** *n.* a small cannon on a carriage. **— marshal** *n.* the highest rank in the British and several other armies. **— officer** *n.* a commissioned officer in rank between a captain and a general. **-piece** *n.* a field-gun. **—sports** *n.pl.* out-of-door sports as hunting, racing, etc. [O.E. *feld*, a field].

fiend (fēnd) *n.* a demon; the devil; a malicious foe; (*Colloq.*) one who is crazy about something, as, *a fresh-air fiend.* **-ish** *a.* [O.E. *feond*, an enemy].

fierce (fērs) *a.* ferocious; violent; savage; intense. **-ly** *adv.* **-ness** *n.* ferocity; rage [O.Fr. *fers*, bold].

fi·er·y (fī′·er·i·) *a.* flaming; hot; (*Fig.*) ardent; fierce; vehement; irritable. **fierily** *adv.* **fieriness** *n.* [fr. *fire*].

fife (fīf) *n.* a high-pitched flute. **-r** *n.* one who plays the fife [O.Fr. *fifre*, a fife].

fif·teen (fif′·tēn) *a.* and *n.* five and ten; the symbol, 15 or XV. *a.* the fifth after the tenth; making one of fifteen equal parts. [O.E. *fif*, five; *tene*, ten].

fifth (fifth) *a.* next after the fourth; *n.* one of five equal parts of a whole. **— column,** any organization within a country deliberately assisting the enemy by acts of sabotage, etc. **— columnist** *n.* **-ly** *adv.*

fif·ty (fif′·ti·) *a.* and *n.* five times ten; the symbol 50 or L. **fiftieth** *a.* next in a series of forty-nine others; making one of fifty equal parts of a whole; *n.* a fiftieth part. **to go fifty-fifty** (*Colloq.*) share and share alike [O.E. *fiftig*, fifty].

fig (fig) *n.* a Mediterranean tree or its fruit (*Colloq.*) something insignificant [Fr. *figue*].

fight (fit) *v.t.* to wage war against; to contend against; to oppose; *v.i.* to take part in single combat or battle; to resist. *pa.p.* **fought** (fawt). *n.* a combat; a battle; a struggle; pugnacity. **-er** *n.* one who fights; an aircraft designed for fighting. **-ing** *a.* able to, or inclined to, fight; pert. to a fight [O.E. *feohtan*].

fig·ment (fig′·mạnt) *n.* an invention, fiction, or fabrication [L. *figmentum*, an image].

fig·ure (fig′·yer) *n.* outward form of anything; the form of a person; a diagram, drawing, etc.; a design; an appearance; steps in a dance; the sign of a numeral, as 1, 2, 3; *v.t.* to cover with patterns; to note by numeral characters; to calculate; to symbolize; to image in the mind; *v.i.* to make a figure. **-d** *a.* esp. adorned with patterns, as *figured muslin.* **figurative** *a.* representing by a figure; not literal; abounding in figures of speech. **figuratively** *adv.* **figurativeness** *n.* **-head** *n.* the norminal head of an organization, without real authority; ornamental figure under the bowsprit of a ship. **figurine** *n.* a statuette. **figure of speech,** an unusual use of words to produce a desired effect, such as metaphor, simile, etc. [L. *figura*, fr. *fingere*, to form].

fil·a·ment (fil′·a·ment) *n.* a slender thread; a fiber, (*Bot.*) the stalk of a stamen; (*Elect.*) a fine wire, usually of tungsten, which glows to incandescence by the passage of an electric current. *a.* like a filament. **-ous** *a.* thread-like [L. *filum, thread*].

filbert (fil′·bert) *n.* the nut of the hazel-tree.

filch (filch) *v.t.* to steal; to pilfer. **-er** *n.*

file (fīl) *n.* an orderly line; a cabinet, wire, or portfolio for keeping papers in order; the papers or cards thus kept; *v.t.* to set in order in a public record office; *v.i.* to march in a file; to make application. **Indian** or **single file,** a single line of men marching one behind the other. **rank and file,** non-commissioned soldiers; the general mass of people as distinct from well-known figures [L. *filum*, a thread].

file (fīl) *n.* a steel instrument for smoothing rough surfaces or cutting through metal. *v.t.* to cut or abrade with a file. *pr.p.* **filing**. *pa.p.* **-d. filing** *n.* a particle of metal rubbed off by a file; the action of abrading stone or cutting metal [O.E. *feol*, a file].

fil·i·al (fil'·i·ạl) *a.* pert. to or befitting a son or daughter. **-ly** *adv.* **filiation** *n.* being a child of a certain parent; derivation [L. *filius*, a son].

fil·i·bus·ter (fil'·ạ·bus·tẹr) *n.* one who deliberately obstructs legislation, esp. by making long speeches; a lawless adventurer; a buccaneer. *v.i.* to act as a filibuster [Fr. *filibustier*, a freebooter].

fil·i·form (fil'·ạ·form) *a.* thread-like [L. *filum*, a thread].

fil·i·gree (fil'·i·grē) *n.* ornamental open-work of gold or silver wire; anything highly ornamental but fragile. **-d** *a.* [L. *filum*, thread; *granum*, grain].

Fil·i·pi·no (fil·ạ·pēn'·ō) *n.* a native of the Philippine Islands.

fill (fil) *v.t.* to make full; to replenish; to occupy as a position; to supply as a vacant office; to pervade; to stop up (a tooth); *v.i.* to become full; *n.* a full supply. **-er** *n.* one who, or that which, fills; a funnel-shaped vessel for filling bottles; **-ing** *n.* that which fills up a space, as gold, etc. used by dentists; a mixture put into sandwiches, cakes, etc.; *a.* satisfying; ample. **filling station,** a roadside depot for supplying gasoline, oil etc., to motorists [O.E. *fyllan*, to make full].

fil·let (fil'·it) *n.* a narrow band, esp. round the head; (fi·lā') piece of meat cut from the thigh; a piece of meat boned and rolled; fish after bones are removed; *v.t.* to bind with a fillet; to bone (meat or fish, etc.); [Fr. *filet*, a thread].

fil·lip (fil'·ap) *v.t.* to strike with the nail of the finger, first placed against the ball of the thumb then released with a sudden jerk; to incite; to spur on; a jerk of the finger; an incentive; a stimulus [form of *flip*].

fil·ly (fil'·i·) *n.* a young mare; a lively or wanton young woman [dim. of *foal*].

film (film) *n.* a thin coating or membrane; a delicate filament; dimness over the eyes; (*Photog.*) a roll of flexible, sensitized material used for photography; pictures taken on this roll; *pl.* (*Colloq.*) a movie show; *v.t.* to cover with a film; to take a moving picture of; to reproduce on a film. **-iness** *n.* **-y** *a.* composed of or covered with film; membranous; sheer [O.E. *filmen*, membrance].

fi·lose (fī'·lōs) *a.* having a thread-like ending [L. *filum*, thread].

fil·ter (fil'·tẹr) *n.* a device for separating liquids from solids, or for straining impurities from liquids; any porous material such as filter paper, charcoal, etc.; a device for removing dust from the air; (*Photog.*) a piece of colored glass placed in front of the lens, passing certain rays only; *v.t.* to purify by passing through a filter; to filtrate; *v.i.* to pass through a filter; **filtrate** *v.t.* to filter; *n.* the liquid which has been strained through a filter. **filtration** *n.* — **bed** *n.* a layer of sand or gravel at bottom of a reservoir for purifying the water. [O.Fr. *filtre*, a strainer].

filth (filth) *n.* foul matter; dirt; pollution; (*Fig.*) immorality; obscenity. **-ily** *adv.* **-iness** *n.* **-y** *a.* [O.E. *fylth*, foulness].

fim·bri·a (fim'·bri·ạ) *n.* (*Zool.*) a fringe or fringe-like structure. **fimbriate, fimbriated** *a.* fringed [L. *fimbria*, thread].

fin (fin) *n.* a paddle-like organ of fishes and other aquatic forms serving to balance and

propel; (*Aero.*) a vertical surface, fixed usually on the tail of an aircraft to aid lateral and directional stability. [O.E. *finn*, a fin].

fi·nal (fī'·nal) *a.* pert. to the end; last; decisive; conclusive; ultimate; *n.* the last stage of anything; *pl.* the last examination or contest in a series. **-ist** *n.* a competitor who reaches the finals of a contest. **-ity** *n.* the state of being final; conclusiveness. **-ize** *v.t.* to give a final form to. **-ly** *adv.* [L. *finis*, the end].

fi·na·le (fi·nä'·li·) *n.* the end; (*Mus.*) the last movement of a musical composition; final scene; a conclusion [It. *finale*, the end].

fi·nance (fạ·nans' or fī'·nans) *n.* the science of controlling public revenue and expenditure; the management of money affairs; *pl.* the income of a state or person; resources; funds; *v.t.* to provide funds for; to supply capital. **financial** *a.* pert. to finance; fiscal. **financially** *adv.* **financier** (fin·an·sēr') *n.* one who deals in large-scale money transactions [Fr. fr. L.L. *finare*, to pay a fine].

finch (finch) *n.* the name applied to various species of small, seed-eating birds including the *chaffinch, bullfinch* [O.E. *finc*, finch].

find (fīnd) *v.t.* to come to by searching; to meet with; to discover; to perceive; to experience; (*Law*) to give a verdict; *pa.t.*, *pa.p.* **found.** *n.* a discovery, esp. of unexpected value. **-er** *n.* **-ing** *n.* the act of one who finds; a legal decision arrived at by a jury after deliberation; a discovery [O.E. *findan*, to find].

fine (fīn) *a.* excellent; thin; slender; minute; delicate; noble; polished; showy; striking; refined (as *fine gold*); keen; appealing aesthetically (as the *Fine Arts*); perceptive; *v.t.* to make fine; to refine or purify; *v.i.* to become fine, pure, or slender; *adv.* **—drawn** *a.* invisibly mended (of cloth); delicately thin (of wire); subtly conceived (of an argument); **-ly** *adv.* **-ness** *n.* the state of being fine; the amount of gold in an alloy. **-r** *n.* refiner. **-ry** *n.* ornament; gay clothes; a furnace for making wrought iron. **—spun,** *a.* drawn out to a gossamer thread; (*Fig.*) subtle; ingenious. **finessé** (fạ·nes') *n.* subtlety of contrivance to gain a point; stratagem; (*Whist, Bridge, etc.*) the attempt to take a trick with a low card while holding a higher card; *v.i.* and *v.t.* to use artifice; to try to take a trick by finesse [Fr. *fin*, exact].

fine (fīn) *n.* a sum of money imposed as a penalty for an offense; conclusion, as in phrase *in fine*; *v.t.* to impose a fine on [L.L. *finis*, a payment].

fi·nesse See **fine.**

fin·ger (fing'·gẹr) *n.* a digit; any one of the extremities of the hand, excluding thumb; the width or length of a finger; something like a finger; *v.t.* to touch with fingers; to handle; to perform with fingers; to purloin; to meddle with; *v.i.* to use the fingers. **— alphabet** *n.* the finger-language of the deaf and dumb. **— board** *n.* that part of a violin, etc. on which fingers are placed; the keyboard of a piano. **— bowl** *n.* a small bowl of water to cleanse fingers at dinner. **-ing** *n.* the act of touching or handling lightly with fingers; the manner of manipulating the fingers in playing an instrument. [O.E. *finger*, a finger].

fin·i·al (fin'·i·al) *a.* ornamental topping of lamp, gable, etc. [L. *finire*, to finish].

fin·i·cal (fin'·i·kạl) *a.* affected fine; over-fastidious. **-ly** *adv.* **finicking, finicky,** *a.* over-particular [prob. fr. *fine*].

fi·nis (fī'·nis) *n.* an end; conclusion [L.].

fin·ish (fin'·ish) *v.t.* to bring to an end; to terminate; to destroy; to complete; *v.i.* to conclude; *n.* that which finishes, or perfects; last stage; the final coat of paint, etc. **-ed** *a.* terminated; perfect; polished; talented; **-er** *n.* one who or that which finishes or gives the final touches. **-ing school,** a school for completing the education of young women [Fr. *finir,* to finish].

fi·nite (fī'·nīt) *a.* limited in quantity, degree, or capacity; bounded; countable; measurable (*Gram.*) used of a *predicating* verb (limited by number and person), oppos. of *infinitive* of verb. **-ly** *adv.* **-ness, finitude** *n.* [L. *finire,* to finish].

Finn (fin) *n.* a native of Finland. **Finnic, Finnish** *a.* **Finlander** *n.* a Finn.

fin·nan-had·dock (fin'·an-ha'·dak) *n.* smoked haddock, esp. that cured at Findon, Scotland. Also **finnan haddie.**

fir (fur) *n.* cone-bearing, evergreen tree, yielding valuable timber. **—cone** *n.* fruit of the fir. [O.E. *furh- (wudu),* fir-(wood)].

fire (fīr) *n.* heat and light caused by combustion; burning; conflagration; ignited fuel; flame; discharge of firearms; ardor; spiritual or mental energy; impassioned eloquence; *v.t.* to set on fire; to kindle; to supply with fuel; to discharge (firearms, etc.); to inflame; to incite; (*Colloq.*) to dismiss; *v.i.* to be ignited; to be stimulated; to discharge firearms. **— alarm** *n.* an alarm giving warning of an discharges by fire exploding gunpowder. outbreak of fire. **-arm** *n.* a weapon which discharges by fire exploding gunpowder. **-ball** *n.* a meteor; (*Mil.*) a ball filled with combustibles. **—bomb** an incendiary bomb. **-box** *n.* the fire chamber of a locomotive. **-brand** *n.* a piece of flaming wood; a torch; (*Fig.*) one who incites others to strife. **— brigade** *n.* men specially trained to deal with fire. **-bug** *n.* an incendiary; (*Colloq.*) one quilty of arson. **-damp** *n.* gas generated in coal mines, which mixed with air, explodes violently in contact with a naked light. **-dog** *n.* (Same as andirons). **— escape** *n.* iron stair used as emergency exist from burning building. **-fly** *n.* a type of beetle which has light-producing organs. **-man** *n.* a member of a fire-fighting unit; a man who tends a furnace; a stoker. **-place** *n.* hearth or grate. **-plug** *n.* a hydrant for drawing water by hose to extinguish a fire. **-proof** *a.* **-r** *n.* **— screen** *n.* a movable protective screen in front of a fire. **-side** *n.* the hearth; (*Fig.*) home. **-water** *n.* term used by Am. Indians for whisky, brandy, etc. **-wood** *n.* wood for fuel; kindling. **-work** *n.* a preparation containing gunpowder, sulfur, etc. for making spectacular explosions. **firing line** *n.* the area of a battle zone within firing range of the enemy. **firing party** or **squad,** soldiers detailed to fire the final salute at a military funeral, or to shoot a condemned person [O.E. *fyr,* a fire].

fir·kin (fur'·kin) *n.* a small cask [O.Dut. *vierde,* four; and dim. suffix kin].

firm (furm) *a.* fixed; solid; compact; rigid; steady; unwavering; stern; inflexible. **-ly** *adv.* **-ness** *n.* [L. *firmus,* steadfast].

firm (furm) *n.* the name, title, or style under which a company transacts business [It. *firma,* a signature].

fir·ma·ment (fur'·ma·mant) *n.* the expanse of the sky; the heavens [L. *firmamentum,* a support, the sky].

first (furst) *a.* preceding all others in a series or in kind; foremost (in place); earliest (in time); most eminent; most excellent; highest; chief; *adv.* before anything else in time, place, degree, or preference; *n.* beginning; a first-class honors degree at a university. **— aid** *n.* preliminary treatment given to injured person before the arrival of a doctor. **—born** *n.* eldest child. **—class** *a.* first-rate; of highest worth; of superior accommodation; *adv.* in the first-class (of a train, boat, etc.). **—fruits** *n.pl.* earliest gathered fruits, orig. dedicated to God; (*Fig.*) earliest results or profits. **—hand** *a.* obtained direct from the source. **-ly** *adv.* **—rate** *a.* of highest excellence [O.E. *fyrst,* first].

firth (furth) *n.* (*Scot.*) a long narrow inlet of the sea or estuary of a river [O.N. *fird*].

fisc (fisk) *n.* the State treasury; public revenue. **fiscal** *a.* pert. to the public treasury or revenue; pert. to financial matters generally.

fish (fish) *n.* a cold-blooded, aquatic vertebrate animal, with limbs represented by fins, and breathing through its gills; the flesh of fish; *pl.* **fish, fishes.** *v.t.* to catch by fishing; *v.i.* to follow the occupation of a fisherman, for business or pleasure; to extract information, etc. by indirect, subtle questions (foll. by *for*). **-er** *n.* one who fishes; a marten. **-erman** *n.* one whose employment is to catch fish; one who fishes for pleasure; an angler. **-ery** *n.* the business of fishing; a fishing-ground; the legal right to fish in a certain area. **-hook** *n.* a barbed hook for catching fish by line. **-ily** *adv.* **-iness** *n.* **-ing** *n.* the act of fishing. **-ing rod** *n.* a long supple rod with line attached, used by anglers. **-ing tackle** *n.* an angler's gear comprising, rod, lines, hooks, etc. **— meal** *n.* dried fish ground into meal. **— story** (*Colloq.*) *n.* an unbelievable story. **-tail** *a.* shaped like the tail of a fish. **-wife** *n.* a woman selling fish in the streets; a shrill, nagging woman. **-y** *a.* abounding in fish; pert. to fish (of smell); expressionless; glazed (of eye); dubious (of a story). [O.E. *fisc,* fish].

fish (fish) *n.* a strip of wood fixed longitudinally to strengthen a mast, or clamp two pieces together; *v.t.* to splice; to join together. **-plate, — joint** *n.* a metal clamp used to join lengths of train rails together [Fr. *fiche,* a pin or peg].

fis·sile (fis'·il) *a.* capable of being split or cleft in the direction of the grain [L. *findere, fissum,* to cleave].

fis·sion (fish'·an) *n.* the process of splitting or breaking up into parts; (*Biol.*) cell-cleavage; in nuclear physics, the splitting of an atomic nucleus into two approx. equal fragments and a number of neutrons, with the liberation of a large amount of energy; *v.t.* and *i.* to split into two parts. **-able** *a.* [L. *findere, fissum,* to cleave].

fis·sure (fish'·ar) *n.* a cleft, crack, or slit [L. *findere, fissum,* to cleave].

fist (fist) *n.* the hand clenched with fingers doubled into the palm; (*Colloq.*) handwriting. **-ic** *a.* pugilistic. **-icuff** *n.* a blow with the fist; **-icuffs** *n.pl.* boxing; a brawl. **-y** *a.* [O.E. *fust,* the fist].

fis·tu·la (fis'·choo·la) *n.* (*Med.*) a narrow duct; an infected channel in the body leading from an internal abscess to the surface. **-r, fistulous** *a.* (*Bot.*) hollowed like a pipe [L. *fistula,* a pipe].

fit (fit) *a.* (*comp.*) **-ter.** (*superl.*) **-test.** adapted to an end or purpose; becoming; suitable; qualified; proper; vigorous (of bodily health); *v.t.* to make suitable; to qualify; to adapt; to adjust; to fashion to the appropriate size; *v.i.* to be proper or becoming. *pr.p.* **-ting.** *pa.p., p.t.* **-ted. -ly** *adv.* **-ness** *n.* the state of being fit; appropriateness; sound bodily health. **-ter** *n.* one who or that which makes fit; a tailor or dressmaker who fits clothes on a person; a mechanic who assembles separate parts of a machine. **-ting** *a.* appropriate; suitable; *n.* anything used in fitting up; a trial of a garment to see that it fits. **-tings** *n.pl.* fixtures; equipment. **-tingly** *adv.*

fit (fit) *n.* a sudden and violent attack of a disorder; a paroxysm; a seizure; a spasmodic attack (as of sneezing); a momentary impulse. **-ful** *a.* spasmodic; intermittent. **-fully** *adv.* [O.E. *fitt*, a struggle].

fit (fit) *n.* a song, or division of a poem; a canto [M.E. *fitte*, a stanza].

five (fīv) *n.* four and one; the symbol 5, or V; *a.* one more than four. **-fold** *a.* five times repeated; quintuple. **-r** *n.* (*Colloq.*) a five-dollar bill [O.E. *fíf*].

fix (fiks) *v.t.* to make firm; to establish; to secure; to make permanent, as a photograph; to make fast, as a dye; to immobilize; to determine; to gaze at; to repair; to put in order; *v.i.* to settle permanently; to become hard; *n.* (*Colloq.*) dilemma; predicament; determination of the position of a ship or airplane by observations or radio signals. **-ation** *n.* the act of fixing; steadiness; (*Med.*) in psycho-analysis, an emotional arrest of part of the psycho-sexual development. **-ative** *n.* a fixing agent; a chemical which preserves specimens in a life-like condition; *a.* capable of fixing colors or structure of specimens. **-ed** *a.* settled, permanent, not apt to change; steady. **-edly** *adv.* **-edness** *n.* **-er** *n.* one who, or that which, fixes. **-ity** *n.* fixedness; immobility. **-ings** *n.pl.* (*Colloq.*) apparatus; trimmings. **-ture** *n.* that which is fixed or attached; (house) anything of an accessory nature considered a part of the real property [L. *fixus*, fixed].

fizz (fiz) *v.i.* to make a hissing sound; to splutter; to effervesce; *n.* a hissing sound; any effervescent liquid. **fizzle** *v.i.* to fizz or splutter; *n.* (*Colloq.*) a fiasco. **-y** *a.* [imit.].

fjord See **fiord**.

flab·ber·gast (flab'·er·gast) *v.t.* (*Colloq.*) to overcome with amazement; to confound [prob. conn. with *flabby*].

flab·by (flab'·i·) *a.* soft; yielding to the touch; drooping; weak; lacking in moral fiber. **flabbily** *adv.* **flabbiness** *n.* [fr.*flap*].

flac·cid (flak'·sid) *a.* soft; flabby; limp. **-ly** *adv.* **-ness**, **-ity** *n.* [L. *flaccidus*, flabby].

flag (flag) *v.i.* to hang loosely; to grow spiritless or dejected; to become languid; to lose vigor, *pr.p.* **-ging**. *pa.p.* **-ged**.

flag (flag) *n.* a flat paving stone; a type of sandstone which splits easily into large slabs. Also **-stone** [Ice. *flaga*, a slab].

flag (flag) *n.* (*Bot.*) a popular name of certain species of plants belonging to the genus *Iris*, with long sword-shaped leaves.

flag (flag) *n.* an ensign or colors; a standard; a banner as a mark of distinction, rank, or nationality; the bushy tail of a setter dog; *v.t.* to decorate with flags or bunting; to convey a message by flag signals. **— officer** *n.* an admiral, entitled to display a flag indicating his rank; the commander of a fleet or squadron. **-ship** *n.* the ship flying the admiral's flag. **white flag**, the symbol of truce or surrender. **yellow flag**, a flag indicating that a ship is in quarantine. **to dip the flag**, to lower, then hoist, flag as a mark of respect. **to fly a flag half-mast**, to hoist flag half-way as token of mourning [etym. doubtful, prob. Scand.].

flag·el·late (flaj'·a·lāt) *v.t.* to whip; to scourge; to flog; *a.* (*Biol.*) having a long thread-like appendage, like a lash. **flagellantism**, **flagellation** *n.* **flagellant** *n.* an ascetic who voluntarily scourges himself as punishment for sin [L. *flagellare*, to scourge].

flag·eo·let (flaj·a·let') *n.* a small non-reed wind instrument [dim. of O.Fr. *flageol*, a pipe].

fla·gi·tious (fla·jish'·as) *a.* shamefully criminal [L. *flagitiosus* disgraceful].

flag·on (flag'·an) *n.* a vessel for holding liquids, usually with handle, spout and lid [Fr. *flacon*, a flask].

fla·grant (flā'·grant) *a.* glaring; notorious; scandalous. **flagrance, flagrancy** *n.* **-ly** *adv.* [L. *flagrare*, to burn].

flail (flāl) *n.* an implement for threshing grain by hand, consisting of a stout stick attached to a handle [L. *flagellum*, a whip].

flair (fler) *n.* instinctive discernment; a keen scent [Fr. *flairer*, to scent out].

flak (flak) *n.* anti-aircraft fire (*World War 2*) [Ger. (*abbrev.*) *Flugabwehrkanone*, anti-aircraft gun].

flake (flāk) *n.* a scale-like particle; a piece of a thin layer; *v.t.* to form into flakes; to cover with flakes; *v.i.* to scale; to fall in flakes. **flaky** *a.* consisting of flakes [Scand. *flaki*, flake].

flam·beau (flam'·bō) *n.* a flaming torch; an ornamental candlestick; *pl.* **flambeaux** [Fr. fr. L. *flamma*, a flame].

flam·boy·ant (flam·boi'·ant) *a.* (*Archit.*) characterized by flame-like tracery and florid ornamentation of windows, panels, etc.; florid; showy; ornate. **flamboyance, flamboyancy** *n.* [Fr. *flamboyer*, to flame].

flame (flām) *n.* a mass of burning vapor or gas; a blaze of light; fire in general; ardor; vehemence of mind or imagination; (*Slang*) a sweetheart; *v.i.* to blaze; to blush; to become violently excited, fervent, or angry. **—colored** *a.* of the color of a flame; bright red or yellow. **— thrower** *n.* a short range trench weapon throwing ignited fuel into the enemy's lines. **flaming** *a.* blazing; gaudy; fervent. **flamingly** *adv.* **flammability** *n.* **flammable** *a.* [L. *flamma*, a flame].

fla·min·go (fla·ming'·gō) *n.* tropical wading bird [L. *flamma*, a flame].

flan (flan) *n.* a pastry shell or cake filled with fruit filling [O.Fr. *flaon*, a flat cake].

flange (flanj) *n.* a projecting edge, as of a railway-car wheel to keep it on the rails, or of castings to fasten them together; *v.t.* [O.Fr. *flanche*, fr. *flanc*, a side].

flank (flangk) *n.* the fleshy part of side of animal between ribs and hip; the right or left side of an army; part of a bastion; the side of a building; *v.t.* to stand at the side of; to protect the flank of an army, etc.; to border *v.i.* [O.Fr. *flanc*, the side].

flan·nel (flan'·al) *n.* a soft-textured, loosely woven woolen cloth. **-s** *n.pl.* clothes made of this, esp. sports garments; woolen undergarments; *a.* made of flannel; *v.t.* to cover or rub with flannel. **-ette** *n.* a cotton material like flannel [W. *gwlanen*, fr. *gwlan*, wool].

flap (flap) *n.* the motion or noise of anything broad and hanging loose; a piece of flexible material attached on one side only and usually covering an opening, as of envelope; anything hinged and hanging loose; *v.t.* to cause to sway or flutter; to strike with something broad and flexible, such as a duster; to move rapidly up and down; *v.i.* to flutter; to fall like a flap; to move, as wings. *pr.p.* **-ping**. *pa.p.* **-ped. -jack** *n.* a broad, flat pancake. **-per** *n.* one who or that which flaps; (*Slang*) the hand; (*Colloq.*) an adolescent girl; a flighty, young woman [imit.].

flare (fler) *v.i.* to burn with a glaring, unsteady or fitful flame; to burst out with flame, anger, etc.; to curve out; *n.* an unsteady, blazing light; a brilliant, often colored, light used as a signal; a spreading or curving out, as the hull of a ship; a sudden burst of flame, passion, etc. **flared** *a.* (of a skirt) spreading gradually out toward the bottom. **flaring** *a.* [Scand. *flara*, to blaze].

flash (flash) *n.* a sudden brief burst of light; an instant or moment; a fleeting emotional outburst; (*Colloq.*) thieves' language; rush of water; a news story; *a.* showy; tawdry; pert. to thieves; *v.i.* to blaze suddenly and die out; to give out a bright but fitful gleam; to shine out, as a stroke of wit or sudden idea; to pass swiftly; *v.t.* to cause to flash; to transmit instantaneously, as news by radio, telephone, etc. **— back** *n.* momentary turning back to an episode in a story. **— bulb** *n.* (*Photog.*) an electric bulb giving brilliant flash for night picture. **-ily** *adv.* **-iness** *n.* **-light** *n.* a portable light powered by batteries or a small generator. **-y** *a.* showy; tawdry; cheap. [M.E. *flarihe(n)*, rise and dash].

flask (flask) *n.* a narrow-necked, usually flat bottle easily carried in the pocket; a wicker-covered bottle; a powder-horn. **-et** *n.* a small flask; a long, shallow basket [It. *fiasco*].

flat (flat) *a.* (*comp.*) **-ter.** (*superl.*) **-test.** level; even; tasteless; monotonous; dull; unqualified; without point or spirit; uniform; spread out; downright; (*Mus.*) below the true pitch (opp. of *sharp*); *n.* a level surface; low-lying sometimes flooded, tract of land; a shoal; (*Mus.*) a note, a semitone below the natural; the symbol for this; a piece of canvas or board mounted on a frame used as stage scenery. *adv.* prone; exactly. (*Mus.*) in a manner below true pitch. **—finish** *n.* a flat surface in paint work. **—footed** *a.* having fallen arches in the feet. **-iron** *n.* an iron for smoothing linen, etc. **-ly** *adv.* peremptorily. **-ness** *n.* **— rate,** uniform rate. **-ten** *v.t.* to make flat; to lower the true musical pitch of; **-top** *n.* an aircraft carrier. **-ware** *n.* silver knives, forks, etc. [Scand. *flatr*, flat].

flat·ter (flat'·er) *v.t.* to praise unduly and insincerely; to pay fulsome compliments to; to depict as being an improvement on the original. **-er** *n.* **-ing** *a.* **-ingly** *adv.* **-y** *n.* the act of flattering; undue praise [O.Fr. *flater*, to smooth].

flat·u·lent (fla'·cha·lənt) *a.* pert. to or affected with wind or gas in stomach and intestines; (*Fig.*) empty; vapid. **flatulence, flatulency** *n.* distension of stomach or intestines by excessive accumulation of wind or gas. **-ly** *adv.* **flatus** *n.* air or gas in stomach, etc. [L. *flare*, to blow].

flaunt (flawnt) *v.t.* to display ostentatiously or impudently; *v.i.* to wave or move in the wind; to parade showily; *n.* a vulgar display.

fla·vor (flā'·ver) *n.* savor; quality affecting taste or smell; distinctive quality of a thing. *v.t.* to season; (*Fig.*) to give zest to. **-ous** *a.* **-ing** *n.* substance to add flavor to a dish, e.g. spice, essence [O.Fr. *flaur*, smell].

flaw (flaw) *n.* a crack; a defect; a weak point as in an argument; *v.t.* to break; to crack; **-less** *a.* perfect [Scand. *flaga*, a slab].

flaw (flaw) *n.* a sudden gust of wind; a squall [Dut. *vlaag*, a gust of wind].

flax (flaks) *n.* the fibers of an annual blue-flowered plant, *Linum*, used for making linen; the plant itself. **-en** *a.* pert. to or resembling flax; loose or flowing; of the color of unbleached flax, hence yellowish or golden (esp. of hair) [O.E. *flaex*, flax].

flay (flā) *v.t.* to skin; (*Fig.*) to criticize bitterly [O.E. *flean*, to strike].

flea (flē) *n.* a small, wingless, very agile insect with irritating bite. **—bitten** *a.* bitten by a flea; (*Fig.*) mean; worthless [O.E. *fleah*, a flea].

fleck (flek) *n.* a spot; a streak; *v.t.* to spot; to dapple [Scand. *flekka*, to spot].

fled (fled) *pa.t.* and *pa.p.* of **flee.**

fledge (flej) *v.t.* to supply with feathers for flight, as an arrow; to rear a young bird; *v.i.* to acquire feathers; to become able to fly (of birds). **-ling** *n.* a young bird just fledged; (*Fig.*) a young untried person [O.E. *flycge*, feathered].

flee (flē) *v.i.* to fly or retreat from danger; *v.t.* to hasten from; *pr.p.* **-ing.** *pa.p., p.t.* **fled** [O.E. *fleon*, to fly].

fleece (flēs) *n.* the coat of wool covering a sheep or shorn from it; anything resembling wool; *v.t.* to shear wool (from sheep); (*Fig.*) to rob; to swindle. **fleecy** *a.* woolly; resembling wool [O.E. *fleos*, fleece].

fleet (flēt) *n.* a group of ships; a force of naval vessels under one command; (*Fig.*) a number of motor vehicles, etc. organized as a unit [O.E. *fleot*, a ship].

fleet (flēt) *n.* a creek, inlet, or small stream [O.E. *fleot*, an inlet].

fleet (flēt) *a.* swift; nimble. *v.i.* to pass swiftly; *v.t.* to make to pass quickly. **-ing** *a.* transient; ephemeral; passing. **-ingly** *adv.* **-ness** *n.* swiftness. **—footed** *a.* swift of foot [O.E. *fleotan*, to swim].

Flem·ing (flem'·ing) *n.* a native of Flanders, **Flemish** *a.* pert. to Flanders [Dut. *Vlaamsch*].

flense (flens) *v.t.* to cut up the blubber of, as a whale [Dan. *flense*].

flesh (flesh) *n.* the body tissue; the muscles, fat, etc. covering the bones of an animal; the body as distinct from the soul; mankind; kindred; sensuality; the pulpy part of fruit; *v.t.* to incite to hunt, as a hound, by feeding it on flesh; to glut; to thrust into flesh, as a sword; to remove flesh from the under side of hides preparatory to tanning process. **-color** *n.* the pale pink color of the human skin (of white races). **-iness** *n.* state of being fleshy; plumpness. **-ings** *n.pl.* flesh-colored tights worn by dancers, acrobats, etc. **-less** *a.* **-liness** *n.* **-ly** *a.* corporeal; worldly; sensual. **-pot** *n.* a vessel in which meat is cooked; (*Fig.*) luxurious living. **— wound** *n.* **-y** *a.* pert. to flesh; corpulent; gross; (*Bot.*) thick and soft. **proud flesh** (*Med.*) a growth of granular tissue over a wound [O.E. *flaesc*, flesh].

fletch (flech) *v.t.* to feather (as an arrow). *n.pl.* feathers on an arrow [Fr. *flèche*, an arrow].

fleur-de-lis (flur·da·lē') *n.* a design based on the shape of an iris; the royal insignia of France [Fr. *fleur-de-lis*, flower of the lily].

flew (floo) *pa.t.* of verb **fly.**

flex (fleks) *v.t.* and *v.i.* to bend (as the joints of the body). **-ibility** *n.* quality of being pliable; (*Fig.*) adaptability; versatility. **-ible** *a.* **-ibly** *adv.* **-ile** *a.* bendable. **-ion, flection** *n.* a bend; a fold; an inflection. **-or** *n.* a muscle. **-uose, -uous** *a.* bending; tortuous. **-ure** *n.* act of bending; a bend [L. *flexus*, bent].

flick (flik) *v.t.* to strike lightly, as with whip; *n.* light, smart stroke.

flick·er (flik'·er) *v.i.* to flutter; to waver; to quiver; to burn unsteadily. *n.* act of wavering; quivering [O.E. *flicorian*, to flutter].

flight (flīt) *n.* the act or power of flying; the distance covered in flying; a journey by airplane; a formation of planes forming a unit; a flock of birds; a soaring, as of the imagination; a discharge of arrows; a volley; a series of steps between successive landings. **— deck,** *n.* the deck of an aircraft carrier for planes to land or take off. **-y** *a.* capricious; giddy; volatile [O.E. *flyht*, flight].

flight (flīt) *n.* the act of fleeing; retreat. **to put to flight,** to rout [O.E. *fleon*, to flee].

flim·sy (flim'·zi·) *a.* thin; fragile; unsubstantial; *n.* thin, transfer-paper; (*Slang*) a banknote. **flimsily** *adv.* **flimsiness.**

flinch (flinch) *v.i.* to shrink from pain or difficulty; to wince. **-ing** *n.* the act of flinching [O.Fr. *flenchir*, to turn aside].

fling (fling) *v.t.* to throw from the hand; to hurl; to send out; to plunge; *v.i.* to flounce; to throw oneself violently. *pa.t., pa.p.* **flung.**

n. a cast or throw; a gibe; abandonment to pleasure; lively dance. **-er** *n.* [Scand. *flanga*, to move violently].

flint (flint) *n.* quartz, which readily produces fire when struck with steel; anything hard; a prehistoric stone weapon; *a.* made of flint. **-lock** *n.* a gunlock with a flint fixed on the hammer for firing the priming. **-y** *a.* made of, or resembling, flint; (*Fig.*) hard-hearted; cruel [O.E. *flint*].

flip (flip) *n.* a drink composed of eggs, sugar and liquor [prob. fr. verb *flip*].

flip (flip) *v.t.* to flick; to jerk. *pr.p.* **-ping**. *pa.t.*, *pa.p.* **-ped**, *n.* a flick; a snap. **-per** *n.* the limb of an animal which facilitates swimming; (*Slang*) the human hand [var. of *flap*].

flip·pant (flip′·ant) *a.* pert. to shallow; smart or pert in speech. **flippancy** *n.* **-ly** *adv.*

flirt (flurt) *v.t.* to jerk, as a bird's tail; to move playfully to and fro, as a fan; *v.i.* to move about briskly; to play the coquette; to dally; *n.* a jerk; a philanderer; a flighty girl. **-ation** *n.* **-atious** *a.* [etym. doubtful].

flit (flit) *v.i.* to fly away; to dart along; to flutter. *pr.p.* **-ting**. *pa.t.*, *pa.p.* **-ted** [Scand. *flytja*, to cause to float].

flit·ter (flit′·er) *v.i.* to flutter.

float (flōt) *v.i.* to rest or drift on the surface of a liquid; to be buoyed up; to be suspended in air; to wander aimlessly; *v.t.* to cause to stay on the surface of a liquid; to cover a surface with water; to set going, as a business company; to put into circulation; *n.* anything which is buoyant; a raft; cork or quill on a fishing line, or net; a hollow floating ball of metal indicating depth of liquid in tank or cistern; a plasterer's trowel; (*Aero.*) a streamlined attachment to a seaplane enabling it to float; theater footlights. **-able** *a.* **-age** *n.* See **flotage**. **-ation** *n.* See **flotation**. **-er** *n.* **-ing** *a.* buoyant on surface of the water or in air; movable; fluctuating; in circulation. **-ing dock**, a floating dry dock. **-ingly** *adv.* **-ing population**, shifting population. **-ing ribs**, lower ribs not connected to breastbone [O.E. *flotian*, to float].

flo·cus (flāk′·as) *n.* a long tuft of wool or hair; *pl.* **flocci** (flok′·sī). **floccose** (flāk′·ōs) **flocculent**, *a.* woolly; having tufts; flaky [L. *floccus*, flock of wool].

flock (flāk) *n.* a small tuft of wool; refuse of wool in cloth making, used for stuffing cushions, etc.; small wool fibers used in making wall paper [L. *floccus*, flock of wool].

flock (flāk) *n.* a collection of animals; a crowd of people; a Christian congregation; *v.i.* to come together in crowds [O.E. *flocc*, a band].

floe (flō) *n.* an extensive field of ice floating in the sea [Scand. *flo*, a layer].

flog (flāg) *v.t.* to beat or strike, as with a rod or whip; to thrash; *pr.p.* **-ging**. *pa.t.*, *pa.p.* **-ged** [L. *flagellare*, to whip].

flood (flud) *n.* an overflow of water; an inundation; a deluge; the flowing in of the tide; (*Lit.* and *Fig.*) a torrent. *v.t.* to overflow; to drench; (*Fig.*) to overwhelm; *v.i.* to spill over; to rise (as the tide). **-lighting** *n.* artificial lighting by lamps fitted with special reflectors. **— tide** *n.* the rising tide; (*Fig.*) peak of prosperity [O.E. *flod*, a stream].

floor (flōr) *n.* the horizontal surface of a room upon which one walks; a story; any level area; inside bottom surface of anything (room, sea, etc.); minimum level, esp. of prices. *v.t.* to cover with a floor; to strike down; (*Colloq.*) to perplex; to stump (in argument). **-age** *n.* floor space. **-cloth** *n.* a heavy material used for covering floors. **-er** *n.* a knock-out blow; (*Colloq.*) a baffling examination question or situation. **-ing** *n.* materials for floors. **— show** *n.* a show at a nightclub. **— walker** *n.* a person employed by a store to supervise one floor [O.E. *flor*].

flop (flop) *v.t.* to flap; to set down heavily. *v.i.* to drop down suddenly or clumsily. *pr.p.* **-ping**, *pa.t.* *pa.p.* **-ped**. *n.* a fall, as of a soft, outspread body; (*Slang*) a fiasco. **-py** *a.* slack; (of a hat brim) wide and soft [var. of *flap*].

flo·ra (flō′·ra) *n.* the plants native to a certain geographical region or geological period; a classified list of such plants. **floral** *a.* **florally** *adv.* adorned with flowers. **floriated**, *a.* **floret** *n.* a single flower in a cluster of flowers; a small compact flower head. **florist** *n.* a grower or seller of flowers [L. *Flora*, the goddess of flowers].

flo·res·cence (flō·res′·ans) *n.* a bursting into flower. **florescent** *a.* [L. *florescere*, to burst into flower].

flor·id (flawr′·id) *a.* bright in color; overelaborate; ornate; (of complexion) highly colored; (*Archit.*) overly decorative. **-ly** *adv.* **-ity** *n.* [L. *floridus*, flowery].

floss (flàs) *n.* untwisted threads of very fine silk; the outer fibers of a silkworm's cocoon. **-silk** *n.* very soft silk thread. **-y** *a.* [It. *floscio*, soft].

flo·tage (flō′·tij) *n.* state or act of floating; the floating capacity of anything; (*Colloq.*) flotsam [O.E. *flotian*, to float].

flo·ta·tion (flō·tā′·shan) *n.* the act of floating; science of floating bodies; act of launching, esp. a business venture, loan, etc. Also **floatation** [O.E. *fltian*, to float].

flo·til·la (flō·til′·a) *n.* a fleet of small vessels [Sp. *flotilla*, a little fleet].

flot·sam (flàt′·sam) *n.* goods lost by shipwreck and found floating on the sea [O.Fr. *flotaison*, a floating].

flounce (flouns) *v.i.* to turn abruptly; to flounder about; *n.* a sudden, jerky movement [Scand. *flunsa*, to plunge].

flounce (flouns) *n.* a plaited border or frill on hem of a dress; *v.t.* to trim with a flounce. **flouncing** *n.* material used for flounces [M.E. *frounce*, a plait].

floun·der (floun′·der) *n.* a small, edible flatfish [Scand. *flundra*, a flounder].

floun·der (floun′·der) *v.i.* to struggle helplessly, as in marshy ground; to tumble about; (*Fig.*) to stumble hesitatingly, as in a speech.

flour (flour) *n.* the finely ground meal of wheat, etc.; any finely powdered substance; *v.t.* to turn into flour; to sprinkle with flour. **-y** *a.* [Fr. *fleur de farine*, the flower (i.e. the best) of meal].

flour·ish (flur′·ish) *v.t.* to decorate with flowery ornament or with florid diction; to brandish; *v.i.* to grow luxuriantly; to prosper; to execute ostentatiously a passage of music; *n.* ornament; a fanciful stroke of the pen; rhetorical display; (*Mus.*) florid improvisation either as prelude or addition to a composition; a fanfare; brandishing (of a weapon); **-ing** *a.* thriving; vigorous [M.E. *florisshen*, to blossom].

flout (flout) *v.t.* to mock; to disregard with contempt; *v.i.* to jeer; *n.* an expression of contempt; a gibe; an insult [prob. fr. M.E. *flouten*, to play the flute].

flow (flō) *v.i.* to run, as a liquid; to rise, as the tide; to circulate, as the blood; to issue forth; to glide along; to proceed from; to fall in waves, as the hair; *v.t.* to overflow; *n.* a stream; a current; the rise of the tide; any easy expression of thought, diction, etc.; copiousness; output. **-ing** *a.* moving; running; fluent; curving gracefully, as lines; falling in folds, as drapery. **-ingly** *adv.* [O.E. *flowan*, to flow].

flow·er (flou′·er) *n.* (*Bot.*) the reproductive

organ in plants; a blossom; the choicest part of anything; the finest type; a figure of speech; an ornament in shape of a flower. **-s** *n.pl.* a substance in the form of a powder, as *flowers of sulphur*; *v.t.* to adorn with flowers or flower-like shapes; *v.i.* to produce flowers; to bloom; to come to prime condition. **-ed** *a.* decorated with a flower pattern, as fabric. **-et** *n.* a small flower; a floret. **-ing** *a.* having flowers. **-y** *a.* abounding in, or decorated with flowers; (of style) highly ornate; euphuistic [L. *flos*, a flower].

flown (flōn) *pa.p. of* **fly.**

flu (floo) *n.* (*Colloq.*) influenza.

fluc·tu·ate (fluk'·chŏo·āt) *v.i.* to move up and down, as a wave; to be unstable; to be irresolute. **fluctuant** *a.* **fluctuation** *n.* a vacillation [L. *fluctus*, a wave].

flue (floo) *n.* a shaft or duct in a chimney; a pipe for conveying air through a boiler; the opening in the pipe of an organ.

flu·ent (floo·ant) *a.* flowing; ready in the use of words; (of lines) gracefully curved. **fluency** *n.* *adv.* [L. *fluere*, to flow].

fluff (fluf) *n.* light, floating down; downy growth of hair on skin; *v.t.* to give a fluffy surface to; *v.i.* to become downy; (*Slang*) to make errors in the speaking of a stage part. **-y** *a.* [prob. var. of *flue*].

fluid (floo'·id) *n.* a substance which flows (liquid, gas, etc.); a non-solid; *a.* capable of flowing; liquid; gaseous; shifting. **-ify** *v.t.* to make fluid. **-ity, -ness** *n.* the state or quality of being a non-solid; (*Fig.*) the state of being alterable. **-ly** *adv.* [L. *fluidus*, flowing].

fluke (flook) *n.* the flounder; a parasitic worm [O.E. *floc*, a flat-fish].

fluke (flook) *n.* the flattened barb at the extremity of either arm of an anchor [O.E. *floc*, a flat-fish].

fluke (flook) *n.* (*Colloq.*) any lucky chance.

flung (flung) *pa.t. and pa.p. of* **fling.**

flunk (flungk) (*Colloq.*) *v.i.* to fail as in an examination or course; *v.t.* to fail in; to disqualify a student for low achievement; to give a student a failing grade; *n.* a failure.

flun·ky (flung'·ki·) *n.* a liveried manservant; a toady; an obsequious person. **-ism** *n.* [Fr. *flanquer*, to run at the side of].

flu·or (floo'·er) *n.* a mineral, fluoride of source of fluorine. **-esce** *v.i.* to exhibit calcium, usually called *fluorite*; principle fluorescence. **-escence** *n.* the property of some substances which emit surface reflections of light different in color from the mass of the material upon exposure to external radiation. **-escent** *a.* **-ide** *n.* a compound of fluorine with another element. **-ine** *n.* a pale yellow very active gaseous element. **-escent lighting,** *a* form of artificial diffused lighting, giving the effect of permanent daylight [L. *fluere*, to flow].

flur·ry (flur'·i·) *n.* a sudden, brief gust of wind; bustle; commotion; *v.t.* to agitate; to fluster [prob. imit. flutter and hurry].

flush (flush) *v.i.* to turn red in the face; to blush; to flow with a rush *v.t.* to cause to blush or turn red; to animate with high spirits; to cleanse with a rush of water; *n.* a flow of water; a rush of blood to the face; elation; freshness [origin uncertain].

flush (flush) *v.t.* to cause to start, as a hunter, a bird; *v.i.* to fly up quickly and suddenly from concealment; *n.* the act of starting up; a flock of birds flying up suddenly [M.E. *fluschen*, to fly up].

flush (flush) *n.* a run of cards of the same suit [L. *fluxus*, a flowing].

flush (flush) *v.t.* to level up; *a.* being in the same plane; well-supplied, as with money; full; (*Print.*) even with margins.

flus·ter (flus'·ter) *v.t.* to make agitated; to

flurry; *v.i.* to be confused and flurried; *n.* confusion; nervous agitation. **-ed** *a.* [Scand. *flaustr*, hurry].

flute (floot) *n.* a musical tubular wind-instrument; a stop in the pipe-organ; (*Archit.*) a vertical groove in the shaft of a column; a similar groove as in a lady's ruffle; *v.i.* to play the flute; to sing or recite in flute-like tones; *v.t.* to play (tune) on the flute; to make flutes or grooves in. **fluted** *a.* ornamented with grooves, channels, etc. **fluting** *n.* action of playing a flute; the ornamental vertical grooving on a pillar, on glass, or in a lady's ruffle. **flutist** *n.* one who plays a flute. Also **flautist. fluty** *a.* [L.L.*flauta*].

flut·ter (flut'·er) *v.t.* to cause to flap; to throw into confusion; to move quickly; *v.i.* to flap the wings; to move with quick vibrations; (of heart) to palpitate; *n.* quick and irregular motion; nervous hurry; confusion [O.E. *flotorian*, to float about].

flu·vi·al (floo'·vi·al) *a.* pert. to, or produced by, a river. [L. *fluvius*, a river].

flux (fluks) *n.* the act of flowing; fluidity; (*Phys.*) the rate of flow; (*Med.*) morbid discharge of body-fluid, esp. blood; dysentery; (*Chem.*) a substance added to another to promote fusibility; continuous process of change; *v.t.* to fuse; to melt; *v.i.* to flow. **-ion** *n.* a flow or flux [L. *fluere*, to flow].

fly (flī) *v.t.* to cause to fly; to direct the flight of; to flee from; *v.i.* to move through the air, as a bird or an aircraft; to become airborne; to travel by airplane; to move rapidly; to flee; *pr.p.* **-ing** *pa.t.* **flew** (floo). *pa.p.* **flown.** *n.* a winged insect, esp. of the order *Diptera*; a housefly; a fishhook in imitation of a fly; a flap on a garment covering a row of buttons or other fastener; (*Sports*) a ball sent high in the air (*pa.t., pa.p.* in baseball, **flied**). **flies** *n.pl.* the space above a theater stage where scenery is moved. **-ing** *n.* moving through the air; air navigation; *a.* capable of flight; streaming; swift. **-ing-boat** *n.* a seaplane. **-ing-buttress** (*Archit.*) an arched prop attached only at one point to the mass of masonry whose outward thrust it is designed to counteract. **-ing-saucer** *n.* name given to a saucer-like object reputedly seen flying at tremendous speeds and high altitudes. **-ing squirrel,** squirrel-like rodent with expanding fold of skin between front and hind legs. **-ing visit,** a hasty, unexpected visit. **-leaf** *n.* the blank page at the beginning or end of a book. **-man** *n.* a scene-shifter in the theater. **-paper** *n.* a paper smeared with sticky substance to trap flies. **-wheel** *n.* a heavy-rimmed wheel attached to the crankshaft of an engine to regulate its speed or accumulate power [O.E. *fleogan*, to fly].

foal (fōl) *n.* the young of a mare or she-ass; a colt or a filly; *v.t. and v.i.* to bring forth a foal [O.E. *fola*, a young animal].

foam (fōm) *n.* froth; spume; the bubbles of air on surface of effervescent liquid; *v.i.* to froth; to bubble; to gather foam; **-ing** *a.* **-ingly** *adv.* **— rubber** *n.* latex made into a soft, elastic, and porous substance, resembling a spong. **-y** *a.* frothy [O.E. *fam*, foam].

fob (fàb) *n.* a small pocket in the waistband for holding a watch; a chain with seals, etc. dangling from the pocket [Dial H. Ger. *fuppe*, a pocket].

fo'c's'le See **forecastle.**

fo·cus (fō'·kus) *n.* the point at which rays of light meet after reflection or refraction; (*Geom.*) one of two points connected linearly to any point on a curve; any point of concentration; *pl.* **-es, foci** (fō'·sī); *v.t.* to bring to a focus; to adjust; to concentrate; *v.i.* to converge. *pr.p.* **-ing.** *pa.p.* **-ed. focal**

a. pert. to a focus. **focalize** *v.t.* to bring into focus; to cause to converge; to concentrate. **focalization** *n.* **in focus,** clearly outlined; well defined. **out of focus,** distorted [L. *focus,* a fireplace].

foe (fō) *n.* an enemy; an adversary; a hostile army [O.E. *fah,* hostile].

foe·tus See **fetus.**

fog (fág) *n.* thick mist; watery vapor in the lower atmosphere; a cloud of dust or smoke obscuring visibility; (*Fig.*) mental confusion; *v.t.* to shroud in fog; to perplex the mind. *v.i.* to become cloudy or obscured. — **bank** *n.* a mass of fog. **-bound** *a.* hindered by fog from reaching destination, as a ship, train, etc. **-gily** *adv.* **-giness** *n.* **-gy** *a.* **-horn** *n.* a loud siren used during fog for warnings.

fo·gy, fogey (fō'·gi·) *n.* dull, old fellow; an elderly person whose ideas are behind the times.

foi·ble (foi'·bl) *n.* weakness of character; a failing [O.Fr. *foible,* weak].

foil (foil) *v.t.* to frustrate; to baffle; to put off the scent *n.* a blunt sword, with button on point, for fencing practice [O.Fr. *fuler,* to trample on].

foil (foil) *n.* a thin leaf of metal, as *tinfoil;* a thin leaf of metal placed under gems to increase their brilliancy or color; a thin coating of quicksilver amalgam on the back of a mirror; (*Archit.*) a leaf-like ornament in windows, niches, etc. (*trefoil, quatrefoil, cinquefoil,* etc.); (*Fig.*) anything serving to set off something else [L. *folium,* a leaf].

foist (foist) *v.t.* to palm off; to insert surreptitiously or unwarrantably. **-er** *n.* [prob. Dut. *vuisten,* to take in the hand].

fold (fōld) *n.* a doubling over of a flexible material; a pleat; a coil (or rope); a crease or a line made by folding; (*Geol.*) a dip in rock strata caused originally by pressure; *v.t.* to double over; to enclose within folds or layers; to embrace; *v.i.* to be pleated or doubled. **-er** *n.* the one who or that which folds; a folded, printed paper; a file for holding papers, etc. [O.E. *fealdan,* to fold].

fold (fōld) *n.* an enclosure for sheep; a flock of sheep; the church; a congregation; *v.t.* to confine in a fold [O.E. *fald,* a stall].

fol·der·al See **falderal.**

fo·li·age (fō'·li·ij) *n.* leaves of a plant in general; leafage. **-d** *a.* having leaves. **foliate** *v.t.* to hammer (metal) into laminae or foil; (*Archit.*) to ornament with leaf design; to number the leaves (not pages) of a book; *a.* resembling a leaf; having leaves. **foliated** *a.* **foliation** *n.* **foliolate** *a.* pert. to leaflets or the separate parts of a compound leaf [L. *folium,* a leaf].

fo·li·o (fō'·li·ō) *n.* a sheet of paper once folded; a book of such folded sheets; the two opposite pages of a ledger used for one account and numbered the same; (*Print*) page number in a book; *a.* pert. to or formed of sheets folded so as to make two leaves; *v.t.* to number the pages of a book on one side only [L. *folium,* a leaf].

folk (fōk) *n.* people in general, or as a specified class. **-s** *n.pl.* (*Colloq.*) one's own family and near relations; *a.* originating among the common people. — **dance** *n.* a traditional country dance. **-lore** *n.* popular superstitions or legends; the study of traditional beliefs [O.E. *folc,* the people].

fol·li·cle (fál'·i·kl) *n.* (*Bot.*) a one-celled seed vessel; (*Zool.*) a small sac; (*Anat.*) a gland, as in *hair-follicle.* **follicular** *a.* pert. to a follicle [L. *folliculus,* a little bag].

fol·low (fál'·ō) *v.t.* to go after; to move behind; to succeed (in a post); to adhere to (a belief); to practice (as a trade or profession); to comprehend; to watch carefully; to keep in touch with; *v.i.* to come after; to pursue; to occur as a consequence; *n.* the act of following. **-er** *n.* one who comes after; adherents; vocation; *a.* coming next after [O.E. *folgian,* to accompany].

fol·ly (fál'·i·) *n.* want of sense; weakness of mind; a foolish action; (*pl.*) a theatrical revue [O.Fr. *fol,* a fool].

fo·ment (fō·ment') *v.t.* to encourage or instigate; to bathe with warm water to relieve pain. **-ation** *n.* instigation, of discord, etc.; the action of applying warm lotions; the lotion applied. **-er** *n.* [L. *fomentum,* a poultice].

fond (fánd) *a.* loving; doting; very affectionate. **fond of,** much attached to; **-le** *v.t.* to caress; to stroke tenderly. **-ly** *adv.* **-ness** *n.* [M.E. *fonned,* infatuated].

fon·dant (fán'·dant) *n.* a thick, creamy sugar candy [Fr. *fondre,* to melt].

font (fánt) *n.* a stone basin for holding baptismal water; a receptable for holy water [L. *fons,* a fountain].

food (fóod) *n.* matter which one feeds on; solid nourishment as contrasted with liquids; that which, absorbed by any organism, promotes growth; (*Fig.*) mental or spiritual nourishment. **-stuff** *n.* edible commodity with nutritional value [O.E. *foda,* food].

fool (fóol) *n.* one who behaves stupidly; one devoid of common sense; a simpleton, a clown; a dupe; *v.t.* to make a fool of, to impose on; to trick *v.i.* to behave like a fool; to trifle. **-ery** *n.* silly behavior; foolish act. **-hardily** *adv.* **-hardiness** *n.* **-hardy** *a.* recklessly daring; venturesome. **-ish** *a.* weak in intellect; ill-considered; stupid. **-ishly** *adv.* **-ishness** *n.* **-ing** *n.* foolery. **-proof** *a.* (of machines) so devised that mishandling cannot cause damage to machine or personnel; **-scap** *n.* any of various sizes of writing paper. [L. *folis,* a windbag].

foot (foot) *n.* the extreme end of the lower limbs, below the ankle; a base or support, like a foot; the end of a bed, couch, etc. where the feet would normally lie; footsoldiers; a measure of length = 12 inches; (*Prosody*) a combination of syllables measured according to quantity or stress-accent; the bottom of a page, ladder, etc.; the total of an account; *pl.* **feet.** *v.t.* to traverse by walking; (*Colloq.*) to add (an account); (*Colloq.*) to pay (a bill); to put a new foot on; *v.i.* to dance; to walk. **-age** *n.* the length expressed in feet. **-ball** *n.* a game played by two teams of eleven each trying to carry or pass the ball over the opponents' goal line; the elongated inflated leather ball used in the game; the round ball used in soccer. **-ed** *a.* having feet or a foot (usually in compounds as *two-footed, sure-footed*). **-fall** *n.* a step; sound of a step. **-gear** *n.* boots and shoes; stockings, socks. **-hold** *n.* a support for the foot; space to stand on. **-ing** *n.* ground to stand on; the part of a construction contacting the ground; status (in society) **-lights** *n.pl.* a row of screened lights along the front of the stage; (*Fig.*) the theater; the profession of acting. **-loose** *a.* free to do as one likes. **-man** *n.* liveried man-servant; a trivet. **-note** *n.* a note of reference or explanation at foot of a page. **foot and mouth disease,** a highly contagious disease of sheep, swine, and esp. horned cattle. [O.E. *fot,* foot].

fop (fáp) *n.* a conceited, effeminate man; a dandy. **-pery** *n.* affection in dress and manners. **-pish** *a.* vain. **-pishly** *adv.* **-pishness** *n.* [M.E. *foppe,* a fool].

for (fawr) *prep.* in place of; instead of; because of; during; as being; considering; in return for; on behalf of; in spite of; in respect to; intended to belong to; suited to; with the purpose of. *conj.* because. **as for,**

regarding [O.E. *for, for*].

for- *prefix.* survives in a few words of O.E. origin, with various meanings; utterly, as in *forlorn*; prohibition, as in *forbid*; neglect, as in *forsake*; away, as in *forget*.

for·age (fawr'·ij) *n.* food for horses and cattle; the search for this or any provisions; *v.t.* to supply with provender; to plunder; *v.i.* to rove in search of food; (*Fig.*) to rummage. [O.Fr. *fourage*, forage].

fo·ra·men (fō·rā'·man) *n.* a small aperture, esp. in a bone; *pl.* **foramina** [L. a hole].

for·as·much (fawr·az·much') *conj.* seeing that; because; since.

for·ay (fawr'·ā) *n.* a raid to get plunder; *v.t.* to pillage.

for·bade (fer·bad') *pa.t.* of **forbid.**

for·bear (fawr·bār') *v.t.* to abstain from; to avoid; to bear with; *v.i.* to refrain from; to control one's feelings. *pa.t.* **forbore.** *pa.p.* **forborne. -ing.** *a.* long-suffering [O.E. *forberan*, to suffer, endure].

for·bid (fer·bid') *v.t.* to prohibit; to order to desist; to exclude. *pa.t.* **forbade** (fer·bad') or **forbad.** *pa.p.* **-den. -den** *a.* prohibited. **-ding** *a.* repellent; menacing; sinister. **-dingly** *adv.* [O.E. *forbeodan*, to prohibit].

force (fōrs) *n.* strength; energy; efficacy; coercion; power; operation; body of soldiers, police, etc.; (*Mech.*) that which produces a change in a body's state of rest or motion; (*Law*) unlawful violence to person or property. **Forces** *n.pl.* Army, Navy and Air Force; *v.t.* to compel (physically or morally); to strain; to ravish; to overpower (*Hort.*) to cause plants to bloom, or ripen before normal time. **-d** *a.* achieved by great effort, or under compulsion; lacking spontaneity, as *forced laugh.* **-ful** *a.* full of energy; vigorous. **-fully** *adv.* **-less** *a.* weak; inert. **-r** *n.* **forcible** *a.* having force; compelling; cogent; effective. **forcibly** *adv.* **forcing** *n.* the action of using force or applying pressure; the art of ripening plants, fruits, etc. before their season. [O.E. *force*, strength].

for·ceps (fawr'·seps) *n.* a surgical instrument like tongs. [L.].

ford (fōrd) *n.* a shallow part of a stream, etc. where a crossing can be made on foot; *v.t.* to cross by a ford. **-able** *a.* [O.E. *faran*, to go].

fore (fōr) *a.* in front; forward; prior; adv. in front, as opp. to *aft; n.* the front. *interj.* (*Golf*) a warning cry to person in the way [O.E. *fore*, before].

fore- *prefix* meaning in front or beforehand.

fore·arm (fōr'·arm) *n.* the part of the arm between the elbow and the wrist.

fore·arm (fōr·arm') *v.t.* to take defensive precautions.

fore·bear, forbear (fōr'·bār) *n.* an ancestor.

fore·bode (fōr·bod') *v.t.* to predict (esp. something unpleasant); to prognosticate; to presage. **-ment** *n.* **foreboding** *n.* an intuitive sense of impending evil or danger.

fore·cast (fōr'·kast) *n.* a prediction; (*Meteor.*) a general inference as to the probable weather to come; *v.t.* and *v.i.* to conjecture beforehand; to predict.

fore·cas·tle, fo'c'sle (fōk'·sl) *n.* (*Naut.*) the upper deck forward of the foremast; forepart under deck, forming crew's quarters.

fore·close (fōr·klōz') *v.t.* (*Law*) to prevent; to exclude; to deprive of the right to redeem a mortgage or property. **foreclosure** *n.*

fore·date (fōr·dāt') *v.t.* to antedate.

fore·doom (fōr·dóóm') *v.t.* to judge in advance; to predestine to failure, etc.

fore·fa·ther (fōr'·fà·THer) *n.* an ancestor.

fore·fin·ger (fōr'·fing·ger) *n.* the finger next to the thumb; the index finger.

fore·foot (fōr'·foot) *n.* one of the front feet of a quadruped.   [the center of interest.

fore·front (fōr'·frunt) *n.* the foremost place;

fore·go (fōr·gō') *v.t.* to precede. **-ing** *a.* preceding; just mentioned. **-ne** *a.* predetermined or inevitable, as in a *foregone conclusion.*

fore·ground (fōr'·ground) *n.* the part of the ground nearest the spectator; the part of a picture which seems nearest the observer.

fore·hand (fōr'·hand) *n.* the part of a horse in front of the rider; *a.* done beforehand; (*Tennis*) used of a stroke played *forward* on the right or natural side, as opp. to *backhand.* **-ed** *a.*

fore·head (fawr'·id, fawr'·hed) *n.* the upper part of the face above the eyes; the brow.

for·eign (fawr'·in) *a.* situated outside a place or country; alien; irrelevant; introduced from outside. **-er** *n.* a native of another country; an alien. **-ism** *n.* [O.Fr. *forain*, fr. L. *foris*, outside].

fore·know (fōr·nō') *v.t.* to know or sense beforehand. **foreknowledge** *n.*

fore·land (fōr'·land) *n.* a promontory; a cape; shore area round a port.

fore·lock (fōr'·lák) *n.* a lock of hair on the forehead.

fore·man (fōr'·man) *n.* the principal member and spokesman of a jury; the overseer of a group of workmen.

fore·mast (fōr'·mast) *n.* the mast in the forepart of a vessel, nearest the bow.

fore·most (fōr'·mōst) *a.* first in place or time; first in dignity or rank.   [tioned.

fore·named (fōr'·nāmd) *a.* already men-

fore·noon (fōr'·nóón) *n.* the part of the day before noon; morning.

fo·ren·sic (fa·ren'·sik) *a.* pert. to the law courts, public discussion, or debate. **-ally** *adv.* [L. *forensis*, pert. to the forum].

fore·or·dain (fōr·awr·dān') *v.t.* to predetermine; to decree beforehand.

fore·part (fōr'·part) *n.* the part before the rest; the beginning.

fore·run (fōr·run') *v.t.* to run before; to precede; to outrun. **-ner** *n.* a messenger sent in advance; a harbinger; a precursor.

fore·said (fōr'·sed) *a.* mentioned before.

fore·sail (fōr'·sāl or fō'sl) *n.* the lowest square sail on the foremast.

fore·see (fōr·sē') *v.t.* to see beforehand; to foreknow *pa.t.* **foresaw,** *pa.p.* **foreseen.**

fore·sight *n.* wise forethought; prudence; (*Mil.*) front sight on gun [O.E. *foreseon*].

fore·sha·dow (fōr·shad'·ō) *v.t.* to shadow or indicate beforehand; to suggest in advance.

fore·shore (fōr'·shōr) *n.* the part of the shore between the level of high tide and low tide.

fore·short·en (fōr·shōr'·ten) *v.t.* to represent (in art) according to perspective; to depict to the eye, as seen obliquely.

fore·show (fōr·shō') *v.t.* to prognosticate.

fore·skin (fōr'·skin) *n.* the skin covering the glans penis; prepuce.

for·est (fawr'·ist) *n.* a tract of wooded, uncultivated land; the trees alone; *a.* sylvan; *v.t.* to cover with trees. **-er** *n.* one who practices forestry; one who has forest land, game, etc. under supervision. **-ry** *n.* the science of growing timber [L. *foris*, outside].

fore·stall (fōr·stawl') *v.t.* to thwart by advance action; to buy up goods before they reach the market, so as to resell at maximum price; to get in ahead of someone else. **-er** *n.* **-ment** *n.* [O.E. *foresteall* intervention].

fore·taste (fōr'·tāst) *n.* a taste beforehand; anticipation; *v.t.* to taste before full possession.

fore·tell (fōr·tel') *v.t.* to predict; to prophesy. *pr.p.* **-ing** *pa.t., pa.p.* **foretold.**

fore·thought (fōr'·thawt) *n.* anticipation; provident care; a thinking beforehand.

fore·to·ken (fōr'·tō·kan) *n.* a token or sign received beforehand; a prophetic sign; *v.t.* to indicate beforehand [O.E. *foretacn*].

fore·top (fōr'·tap) *n.* (*Naut.*) platform at the

head of the foremast; an animal's forelock.

for·ev·er (fer·ev'·er) *adv.* always; eternally; *n.* eternity. **-more** *adv.* [tion in advance.

fore·warn (fōr·wawrn') *v.t.* to warn or cau-

fore·word (fōr'·wurd) *n.* a preface; an introductory note to a book.

for·feit (fōr'·fit) *v.t.* to be deprived of, as a punishment; *n.* that which is forfeited; a fine or penalty. **-able** *a.* **-ure** *n.* the act of forfeiting; the state of being deprived of something as a punishment; the thing confiscated [O.Fr. *forfaire*, to transgress].

for·gather, foregather (fōr·gaTH'·er) *v.i.* to meet with friends; to come together socially.

for·gave (fer·gāv') *pa.t.* of verb **forgive**.

forge (fōrj) *v.t.* a furnace for heating iron red hot so that it can be hammered into shape; to fabricate; to counterfeit; *v.i.* to work with metals; to commit forgery. **-r** *n.* **forgery** *n.* the making of an imitation of money, work of art, etc., and representing it as genuine; the act of falsifying a document, or illegally using another's signature; that which is forged [L. *fabrica*, a workshop].

forge (fōrj) *v.i.* to move forward steadily.

for·get (fer·get') *v.t.* to lose remembrance of; to neglect inadvertently; to disregard. *pr.p.* **-ting**. *pa.t.* **forgot**. *pa.p.* **forgot** or **forgotten**. **-table** *a.* **-ful** *a.* apt to forget; heedless; oblivious. **-fully** *adv.* **-fulness** *n.* [O.E. *forgietan*, to forget].

for·give (for·giv') *v.t.* to pardon; to cease to bear resentment against; to cancel (as a debt); *v.t.* to exercise clemency; to grant pardon. *pa.t.* **forgave**. *pa.p.* **forgiven**. **forgivable** *a.* **-ness** *n.* **forgiving** *a.* ready to pardon [O.E. *forgiefan*, to give up].

for·go (fōr·gō') *v.t.* *pa.t.* **forwent**, *pa.p.* **foregone**. To renounce; to abstain from possession or enjoyment.

fork (fōrk) *n.* an implement with two or more prongs at the end; a table utensil of silver, etc. usually with four prongs; anything shaped like a fork; a pronged instrument which when struck gives forth a fixed musical note (tuning-fork); the bifurcation of a road, etc.; each part into which anything divides, as a road, river, etc.; *v.i.* to divide into branches; *v.t.* to pitch with a fork, as hay; to lift with a fork (as food); to form a fork. **-ed**, **-y** *a.* shaped like a fork; cleft. [O.E. *forca*, a fork].

for·lorn (faur·lōrn') *a.* deserted; forsaken; *adv.* **-ness** *n.* [O.E. *forleosan*, to lose].

form (fōrm) *n.* shape or appearance; configuration; the human body; a mold; state of health; model; style; method of arrangement of details; etiquette; an official document or questionnaire with details to be filled in by applicant; *v.t.* to give shape to; to construct; to devise; to be an element of; to arrange to conceive; to build up (as a sentence); *v.i.* to assume position; to develop. **-al** *a.* according to form; regular; methodical; conventional; ceremonious. **-alization** *n.* **-alize** *v.t.* and *v.i.* to give form to; to make formal. **-alism** *n.* the quality of being formal; undue insistence on conventional forms, esp. in religion or the arts. **-alist** *n.* **-ality** *n.* quality of being conventional or pedantically precise; propriety. **-ally** *adv.* **-ation** *n.* the act of forming; structure; an arrangement, of troops, aircraft, etc. **-ative** *a.* giving form; conducive to growth. **-less** *a.* [L. *forma*, shape].

-form *suff.* in the shape of, as *cruciform* in the shape of a cross.

form·al·de·hyde (fōr·mal'·da·hīd) *n.* a colorless, pungent gas, soluble in water, used as a disinfectant and preservative.

for·mat (fōr'·mat) *n.* the general make-up of a book, its size, shape, style of binding, quality of paper, etc. [L. *forma*, a shape].

for·mer (fōr'·mer) *a.* preceding in time;

long past; first mentioned. **-ly** *adv.*

for·mic (fōr'·mik) *a.* pertaining to ants [L. *formica*, an ant].

for·mi·da·ble (fōr'·mi·da·bl) *a.* exciting fear or apprehension; overwhelming. **formidability**, **-ness** *n.* **formidably** *adv.* [L. *formidare*, to fear].

for·mu·la (fōr'·mya·la) *n.* a prescribed form; a conventional phrase; a confession of faith; (*Math.*) a general rule or principle expressed in algebraic symbols; (*Chem.*) the series of symbols denoting the component parts of a substance; (*Med.*) *a.* prescription; *pl.* **-s**, **formulae** (·lē). **formularization, formulation** *n.* **formulary** *n.* a book containing formulas, or prescribed ritual; *a.* prescribed. **formulate, formulize** *v.t.* to reduce to a formula; to express in definite form [L. dim. of *forma*, a shape].

for·ni·cate (fōr'·ni·kāt) *v.i.* to indulge in unlawful sexual intercourse. **fornication** *n.* sexual intercourse between unmarried persons. **fornicator** *n.* [L. *fornix*, a brothel].

for·sake (fer·sāk') *v.t.* to abandon; to leave or give up entirely. *pr.p.* **forsaking**. *pa.t.* **forsook** *pa.p.* **forsaken**. **forsaken** *a.* deserted [O.E. *forsacan*, to relinquish].

for·sooth (fer·sòòth') *adv.* in truth; indeed.

for·swear (fōr·swār) *v.t.* to renounce on oath; to deny; *v.i.* to swear falsely; to commit perjury. *pa.t.* **forswore**. *pa.p.* **forsworn** [O.E. *forswerian*, to renounce].

for·syth·i·a (fer·sith'·i·a) *n.* a spring-flowering shrub with bright yellow blossoms [Eng. 18th cent. botanist William *Forsyth*].

fort (fōrt) *n.* a stronghold; a small fortress; outpost [L. *fortis*, strong].

forte (fōrt) *n.* a strong point; that in which one excels [Fr. *fort*, strong].

forte (fōr'·te) *a.* and *adv.* (*Mus.*) loud; loudly; *n.* a loud passage. **fortissimo** *adv.* very loudly [It. fr. L. *fortis*, *strong*].

forth (fōrth) *adv.* forwards, in place or time; out from concealment; into view; away. **-coming** *a.* ready to come forth or appear; available. **-right** *a.* straightforward; frank. **-with** *adv.* immediately [O.E. *fore*, before].

for·ti·fy (fōr'·ta·fī) *v.t.* to strengthen, as by forts, batteries, etc.; to invigorate; to corroborate. *pr.p.* **-ing**. *pa.t.*, *pa.p.* **fortified**, **fortification** *n.* the art or act of strengthening; a defensive wall; a fortress [L. *forotis*, strong; *facere*, to make].

for·ti·tude (fōr'·ta·tūd) *n.* power to endure pain or confront danger; resolute endurance; **fortitudinous** *a.* courageous [L. *fortitudo*].

fort·night (fōrt'·nīt) *n.* the space of fourteen days; two weeks. **-ly** *a.* and *adv.* at intervals of a fortnight [contr. of O.E. *feowertyne niht*, fourteen nights].

for·tress (fōr'·tris) *n.* a fortified place; a stronghold [O.Fr. *forteresse*, a stronghold].

for·tu·i·tous (fōr·tū'·a·tas) *a.* happening by chance; accidental. **-ness, fortuity** *n.* [L. *fortuitus*, casual].

for·tune (fōr'·chan) *n.* chance; that which befalls one; good luck or ill luck; possessions, esp. money or property. **fortunate** *a.* lucky; propitious. **fortunately** *adv.* **fortunateness** *n.* **-teller** *n.* one who reveals the future by palmistry, crystal-gazing, etc. [L. *fortuna*].

for·ty (fōr'·ti·) *a.* and *n.* four times ten; a symbol expressing this, as 40, XL. **fortieth** *a.* fortieth part. [O.E. *feowertig*, forty].

fo·rum (fō'·ram) *n.* the market place of ancient Rome where legal as well as commercial business was conducted; a public discussion of questions of common interest; tribunal [L. *forum*, the market-place].

for·ward (fōr'·werd) *adv.* towards a place in front; onwards in time; in a progressive or conspicuous way; *a.* toward or at the forepart, as in a ship; eager; progressive; bold; *n.* (*Sports*) a player in the front line; *v.t.* to promote; to redirect (letter, parcel) to new address; to send out or dispatch. **-ness** *n.* the state of being advanced; precocity; presumption [O.E. *fore*, before; *weard*, in the direction of].

fos·sil (fàs′·il) *n.* any portion of an animal or vegetable organism or imprint of such, which has undergone a process of petrifaction and lies embedded in the rock strata; (*Colloq.*) an antiquated person or thing; *a.* pert. to or resembling a fossil. **-iferous** *a.* bearing or containing fossils. **-ize** *v.t.* to turn into a fossil; to petrify; *v.t.* to become a fossil [L. *fodere, fossum*, to dig].

fos·ter (faws′·ter) *v.t.* to rear; to promote; to cherish. — **brother** *n.* a boy fostered with another child of different parents. — **child** *n.* a child reared by one who is not the parent. — **daughter**, — **son** *n.* a child brought up as a daughter or son, but not so by birth. — **father**, — **mother**, — **parent** *n.* [O.E. *fostrian*, to nourish].

fought (fawt) *pa.t.* and *pa.p.* of verb **fight.**

foul (foul) *a.* filthy; containing offensive or putrescent matter; obscene; wicked; stormy of weather; contrary (of wind); full of weeds; entangled (of ropes); unfair; *n.* the breaking of a rule (in sports); *v.t.* to make foul; to obstruct deliberately; to clog or jam; *v.i.* to become foul, clogged, or jammed; to come into collision. **-ly** *adv.* **-mouthed** *a.* using language scurrilous, obscene, or profane. — **play**, cheating; (*Law*) criminal violence; murder [O.E. *ful*, filthy].

found (found) *pa.t.* and *pa.p.* of verb **find. -ling** *n.* a small child who has been found abandoned.

found (found) *v.t.* to lay the basis or foundation of; to establish; to endow; *v.i.* to rely; to depend. **-ation** *n.* the act of founding; the base or substructure of a building; groundwork; underlying principle; an endowment; an endowed institution. **-er** *n.* [Fr. *fonder*, to establish].

found (found) *v.t.* to melt (metal, or materials for glassmaking) and pour into a mold; to cast. **-er** *n.* **-ing** *n.* metal casting. **-ry** *n.* works for casting metals; the process of metal casting [Fr. *fondre*, to melt].

foun·der (foun′·der) *v.t* to cause inflammation in the feet (of a horse) so as to lame; to cause to sink (as a ship); *v.i.* to collapse; to fill with water and sink; to fail; to stumble and become lame [O.Fr. *fondrer*, to fall in].

foun·tain (foun′·tan) *n.* a natural spring; an artificial jet of water. **fount** *n.* a spring of water; a source. **-head** *n.* source of a stream; (*Fig.*) the origin. [L. *fons*, a spring].

four (fōr) *a.* one more than three; two; *n.* the sum of four units; the symbol representing this sum—4, IV. **-flusher** *n.* (*Slang*) one who bluffs. **-fold** *a.* quadruple; folded or multiplied four times. **—in-hand** *n.* a necktie; a team of four horses drawing a carriage; the carriage itself. **—poster** *n.* a bed with four posts. **-some** *n.* a group of four persons. **—square** *a.* having four equal sides and angles. **-teen** *n.* the sum of four and ten; the symbol representing this—14, XIV; *a.* four and ten. **-teenth** *a.* making one of fourteen equal parts. **-th** *a.* next after third; *n.* one of four equal parts. **-thly** *adv.* [O.E. *feower*, four].

fowl (foul) *n.* barnyard cock or hen; the flesh of a fowl; a similar game bird; *pl.* **-s, fowl.** *v.i.* to catch or kill wild fowl. **-er** *n.* one who traps wild fowl. **-ing-piece** *n.* a light shotgun for shooting wild fowl [O.E. *fugol*, a bird].

fox (fàks) *n.* (*fem.* **vixen**) an animal of the canine family, genus *Vulpes*, reddish-brown or gray in color, with large, bushy tail and erect ears; a wily person; *v.t.* to trick; to make sour, in fermenting; to mislead. — **brush** *n.* the bushy tail of a fox. **-glove** *n.* a tall plant with white or purple-pink bell-shaped flowers and leaves which yield digitalis used medicinally as heart stimulant. **-hole** *n.* (*Mil.*) a small trench; a dugout for one or more men. — **hunt** *n.* the pursuit of a fox by huntsmen and hounds. **-iness** *n.* the quality of being foxy; discoloration (in paper); the state of being sour (of beer). — **terrier** *n.* a popular breed of dog sometimes trained for unearthing foxes. — **trot** *n.* a social dance. **-y** *a.* pert. to foxes; cunning; reddish-brown in color. **-ily** *adv.* slyly [O.E. *fox*, a fox].

foy·er (foi′·er) *n.* a theater or hotel lobby; an entrance hall [Fr.].

fra·cas (frā′·kas) *n.* a noisy quarrel; a disturbance; a brawl [Fr.].

frac·tion (frak′·shan) *n.* a small portion; a fragment; (*Arith.*) a division of a unit. **decimal fraction**, a fraction expressed with numerator above, and denominator below the line. **-al** *a.* **fractious** *a.* quarrelsome; peevish. **fractiously** *adv.* **fracture** *n.* the act of breaking; a breach or rupture; the breaking of a bone; *v.t.* to break; to crack; *v.i.* to become broken. **compound fracture**, a fracture of a bone, the jagged edge of which protrudes through the skin. **simple fracture**, a fracture where the bone is broken, but surrounding tissues and skin are undamaged [L. *frangere, fractum*, to break].

frag·ile (fraj′·al) *a.* easily broken; frail; brittle. **fragility** *n.* [L. *fragilis*, breakable].

frag·ment (frag′·mant) *n.* a portion broken off; a part; an unfinished portion, as of a literary composition. **-al** *a.* (*Geol.*) composed of fragments of different rocks. **-ary** *a.* broken [L. *frangere*, to break].

fra·grant (frā′·grant) *a.* sweet smelling. **fragrance, fragrancy** *n.* sweet scent; perfume; pleasant odor. **-ly** *adv.* [L. *fragrare*].

frail (frāl) *a.* fragile; easily destroyed; infirm; morally weak. **-ly** *adv.* **-ness, -ty** *n.* quality of being weak [O.Fr. *fraile*, weak].

frame (frām) *v.t.* to construct; to contrive; to provide with a frame; to put together, as a sentence; (*Colloq.*) to bring a false charge against; *v.i.* to take shape; *n.* anything made of parts fitted together; the skeleton of anything; a structure; the case or border around a picture; a mood of the mind; a glazed structure in which plants are protected from frost; a structure upon which anything is stretched. **-work** *n.* the fabric which supports anything. **framing** *n.* [O.E. *framian*, to be helpful].

franc (frangk) *n.* a coin (100 centimes) and monetary unit of France, Belgium and Switzerland [O.Fr. *franc*].

fran·chise (fran′·chīz) *n.* the right to vote; a privilege conferred by a government; permission by a manufacturer to sell his products [O.Fr. *franc*, free].

Fran·cis·can (fran·sis′·kan) *n.* one of the order of friars founded by Francis of Assisi.

Fran·co- (frangk′·ō) *prefix*, French, in combinations. **Francophile** *n.* one who admires France and all things French. **Francophobe** *n.* one who hates things French.

fran·gi·ble (fran′·ji·bl) *a.* breakable; fragile. **frangibility** *n.* [L. *frangere*, to break].

frank (frangk) *a.* open; candid; unreserved; *v.t.* to exempt from charge, esp. postage; *n.* a signature on outside of a letter authorizing its free delivery. **-ly** *adv.* candidly. **-ness** *n.* openness; honesty; candor [Fr. *franc*, free].

Frank (frangk) *n.* a member of one of the

Germanic tribes which settled in Gaul giving France its name.

Frank·en·stein (frangk'·an·stīn) *n.* any creation which brings disaster or torment to its author [from Mary Shelley's novel].

frank·furter (frangk'·fer·ter) *n.* a smoked sausage [G. City of Frankfurt].

frank·in·cense (frangk'·in·sens) *n.* a dry, perfumed resin, burned as incense [Fr. *franc*, pure; *encens*, incense].

Frank·lin (frangk'·lin) *n.* a type of open iron stove [fr. Benj. *Franklin*].

fran·tic (fran'·tik) *a.* frenzied; wild. **-ally** *adv.* [O.Fr. *frenetique*, mad].

fra·ter·nal (fra·tur'·nal) *a.* pert. to a brother or brethren; brotherly. *adv.* **fraternization** *n.* **fraternize** *v.i.* to associate with others in a friendly way. **fraternizer** *n.* **fraternity** *n.* a student society, designated by letters of the Greek alphabet; brotherhood; a group of men associated for a common purpose [L. *frater*, a brother].

frat·ri·cide (frat'·ri·sīd) *n.* the crime of killing a brother; one who commits this crime. **fratricidal** *a.* [L. *frater*, a brother; *caedere*, to kill].

fraud (frawd) *n.* deception deliberately practiced; trickery; (*Colloq.*) a cheat; imposter. **-ulence, -ulency** *n.* trickery, deceitfulness. **-ulent** *a.* pert. to or practicing fraud; dishonest. **-ulently** *adv.* [L. *fraus*, a fraud].

fraught (frawt) *a.* loaded; charged [Dut. *vracht*, a load].

fray (frā) *n.* an affray; a brawl; a contest [contr. of *affray*].

fray (frā) *v.t.* to wear through by friction; to ravel the edge of cloth; (*Fig.*) to irritate, as the nerves, or temper; *v.i.* to become frayed [Fr. *frayer*, to rub].

fraz·zle (fraz'·l) *v.t.* to fray; to exhaust; *n.* exhaustion [etym. unknown].

freak (frēk) *n.* a sudden whim; a prank; capricious conduct; something or someone abnormal; *a.* odd; unusual. **-ish** *a.* **-ishly** *adv.* **-ishness** *n.* [prob. O.E. *frec*, bold].

freak (frēk) *v.t.* to spot or streak or dapple; *n.* a streak [prob. from *freckle*].

freck·le (frek'·l) *n.* a small brownish spot on the skin; any small spot; *v.t.* to color with freckles; *v.i.* to become covered with freckles. **freckly**, *a.* [M.E. *frakin*, a freckle].

free (frē) *a.* having political liberty; unrestricted; loose; independent; open; liberal; spontaneous; irregular; licentious; exempt from impositions, duties, or fees (as trade, education); *adv.* without hindrance; gratis; *v.t.* to set at liberty; to emancipate; to clear; to disentangle. *pr.p.* **-ing**. *pa.p.* **-d.** **-booter** *n.* one who wanders about for plunder; a pillager. **-man** *n.* one who has been freed from slavery. **-dom** *n.* liberty; immunity; indecorous familiarity; **-hand**, unrestricted authority; drawn by hand without instruments, etc. **-handed** *a.* generous; liberal. **-hold** *n.* the tenure of property in fee simple, or fee tail, or for life; *a.* held by freehold. **freeholder** *n.* **—lance** *n.* orig. a mercenary soldier who sold his services to any country, esp. said of a journalist, not attached to a particular staff. **— love** *n.* doctrine that sexual relations should be unhampered by marriage, etc. **-ly** *adv.* **-man** *n.* a man who is not a slave; one who enjoys the full privileges of a corporate body. **-mason** *n.* orig. a member of an organization of skilled masons; now, a member of a fraternal association for mutual assistance and social enjoyment. **-masonic** *a.* **-masonry** *n.* **-ness** *n.* **—spoken** *a.* accustomed to speak without reserve. **-stone** *n.* a building-stone easily quarried, cut, and carved; peach, plum, etc. in which the pit does not cling. **-thinker** *n.* one who professes to be independent of all religious authority;

a rationalist. **-thinking, — thought** *n.* **— trade,** the policy of unrestricted, international trade. **-trader** *n.* **— verse** *n.* a form of verse unrestricted in length of line, meter, stanza form, and generally without rhyme. **— will** *n.* the power of the human will to choose without restraint; *a.* voluntary [G.E. *freo*, free].

freeze (frēz) *v.t.* to harden into ice; to congeal; to preserve by refrigeration; to paralyze with cold or terror; to render credits unrealizable; become congealed or stiff with cold. *pr.p.* **freezing.** *pa.t.* **froze.** *pa.p.* **frozen** *n.* frost. **freezing point** *n.* the temperature at which a liquid turns solid, esp. that at which water freezes, marked 32° F. or 0° C. [O.E. *freosan*, to freeze].

freight (frāt) *n.* the cargo of a ship, etc.; a load; charge for conveyance of goods; *v.t.* to load a ship, etc. **-age** *n.* charge for transport of goods; freight. **-er** *n.* one who receives and forwards freight; a cargo boat [late form of *fraught*].

French (french) *a.* pert. to France or its inhabitants; *n.* the inhabitants or the language of France. **French chalk,** a variety of talc. **— horn** *n.* a musical wind instrument with mellow note like a hunting horn. **-man** (*fem.* **Frenchwoman**) *n.* a native of France. **— window,** one functioning as door and window.

fren·zy (fren'·zi·) *n.* violent agitation of the mind; madness; *v.t.* to render frantic. **frenzied** *a.* **frenetic** (also **phrenetic**) *a.* mad; frenzied [Gk. *phrenitis*, inflammation of the brain].

fre·on (frē'·an) *n.* gas used in refrigeration and for air-conditioning [fr. *freeze*].

fre·quent (frē'·kwant) *a.* happening at short intervals; constantly recurring; repeated.

frequent (fri·kwent') *v.t.* to visit often. **frequency** *n.* the state of occurring repeatedly; periodicity; (*Phys.*) number of vibrations per second of a recurring phenomenon. **-ation** *n.* the practice of visiting repeatedly. **-ative** *a.* (*Gram.*) denoting the repetition of an action; *n.* (*Gram.*) a word, usually a verb, expressing frequency of an action. **-er** *n.* **-ly** *adv.* **-ness** *n.* [L. *frequens*].

fres·co (fres'·kō) *n.* a method of mural decoration on walls of fresh, still damp, plaster. *v.t.* to paint in fresco [It. *fresco*, fresh].

fresh (fresh) *a.* vigorous; unimpaired; new; not stale; brisk; original; unsalted; (*Slang*) impudent; *n.* a stream of fresh water; a freshet. **-en** *v.t.* to make fresh; *v.i.* to grow fresh; to become vigorous. **-ener** *n.* **-et** *n.* an inundation caused by rains or melting snows; a fresh-water stream. **-man** *n.* a first-year University or high school student. **-ness** *n.* **—water** *a.* pert. to or living in water which is not salt [M.E. *fresch*, fresh].

fret (fret) *v.t.* to wear away by friction; to eat away; to ruffle; to irritate; *v.i.* to wear away; to be corroded; to be vexed or peevish; *pr.p.* **-ting.** *pa.t., pa.p.* **-ted.** *n.* irritation; erosion. **-ful** *a.* querulous. **-fully** *adv.* **-fulness** *n.* [O.E. *fretan*, to devour].

fret (fret) *n.* ornamental work, consisting usually of strips, interlaced at right angles. **-ted, -ty** *a.* ornamented with frets. **-work** *n.* decorative, perforated work on wood or metal [O.Fr. *frete*, interlaced work].

fret (fret) *n.* a small piece of wood or wire fixed on the fingerboard, as of a guitar, under the strings [prob. O.Fr. *frete*, ferrule].

Freud·i·an (froi'·di·an) *a.* pert. to *Sigmund Freud*, (1856-1939) the Austrian psychoanalyst, or to his theories.

fri·a·ble (frī·a·bl) *a.* easily crumbled or reduced to powder. **-ness, friability** *n.* [L. *friabilis*, crumbling].

fri·ar (frī'·er) *n.* a member of one of the orders (*R.C.*) of mendicant monks. **-y** *n.* a monastery [L. *frater*, a brother].

frib·ble (frib′·l) *n.* a frivolous person or thing; *v.i.* to fritter away time.

fri·cas·see (frik·ạ·sē′) *n.* a dish of fowl, rabbit, etc. stewed with rich gravy sauce; *v.t.* to make a fricassee [Fr.].

fric·tion (frik′·shạn) *n.* the act of rubbing one thing against another; (*Phys.*) the resistance which a body encounters in moving across the surface of another with which it is in contact; unpleasantness. **fricative** *a.* produced by friction. **-al** *a.* caused by friction. **-ally** *adv.* [L. *fricare*, to rub].

Fri·day (frī′·di·) *n.* the sixth day of the week [O.E. *Frig*, wife of Odin; *daeg*, a day].

fried (frīd) *pa.t.* and *pa.p.* of verb **fry**.

friend (frend) *n.* one attached to another by esteem and affection; an intimate associate; a supporter. **Friend** *n.* a member of the Quakers. **-less** *a.* without friends. **-liness** *n.* **-ly** *a.* having the disposition of a friend; kind; propitious. **-ship** *n.* attachment; comradeship. **Society of Friends,** the Quaker sect [O.E. *freond*, a friend].

frieze (frēz) *n.* a heavy woolen cloth with nap on one side [Fr. *frise*, a curl].

frieze (frēz) *n.* decoration on the upper part of the wall, around a mantel, etc. [Fr. *frise*, a fringe].

fri·gate (frig′·it) *n.* a fast 2-decked sailing ship of war of the 18th and 19th centuries. [It. *fregata*, a frigate].

fright (frīt) *n.* sudden and violent fear; extreme terror; alarm; (*Colloq.*) an ugly or grotesque person or object; *v.t.* to make afraid. **-en** *v.t.* to terrify; to scare. **-ened** *a.* **-ful** *a.* terrible; calamitous; shocking. **-fully** *adv.* terribly; (*Colloq.*) very. **-fulness** *n.* **-some** *a.* frightful [O.E. *fyrhto*, fear].

frig·id (frij′·id) *a.* very cold (esp. of climate); unfeeling; passionless; stiff. **-ity** *n.* coldness. **-ly** *adv.* **-ness** *n.* **-aire** *n.* a refrigerator [L. *frigidus*, cold].

frill (fril) *n.* a gathered cloth or paper edging; a ruffle; (*Fig.*) excessive ornament (as in style); *v.t.* to ornament with a frill; *v.i.* to become crinkled like a frill [etym. doubtful].

fringe (frinj) *n.* loose threads as ornamental edging of cloth; anything suggesting this, as a fringe of hair; the outside edge of anything; *v.t.* to adorn with fringe; to border [O.Fr. *fringe*, a border].

frip·per·y (frip′·ẹr·i·) *n.* tawdry finery; ostentation [Fr. *fripperie*, old clothes].

frisk (frisk) *v.i.* to leap; to gambol; to skip; *v.t.* (*slang*) to feel a person's clothing for concealed weapons; (*Slang*) to steal in this way; *n.* a frolic. **-ily** *adv.* playfully. **-iness** *n.* **-y** *a.* lively [O.Fr. *frisque*, lively].

frit·ter (frit′·ẹr) *n.* a slice of fruit or meat dipped in batter and fried to form a cake [O.Fr. *friture*, something fried].

frit·ter (frit′·ẹr) *v.t.* to waste (time, energy, etc.) in a futile way. **-er** *n.* [prob. conn. with L. *frangere*, to break].

friv·ol (friv′·ạl) *v.t.* and *v.i.* to squander, esp. time or energy; to fritter away. **frivolity** *n.* the act or habit of idly wasting time; lack of seriousness. **-ous** *a.* **-ously** *adv.* **-ousness** *n.* [L. *frivolus*, paltry].

frizz (friz) *v.t.* to curl; to crisp; *n.* a row of small curls. **-zle** *v.t.* to curl; in cooking, to crisp by frying; *n.* curled hair [O.Fr. *friser*].

fro (frō) *adv.* from; back, as in *to and fro.*

frock (frȧk) *n.* a woman's dress; a monk's long, wide sleeved garment. **— coat** *n.* a double-breasted, full skirted coat worn by men [O.Fr. *froc*, a monk's frock].

frog (frȧg) *n.* an amphibious, tailless animal, (developed from a tadpole); hoarseness caused by mucus in the throat; a V-shaped horny pad on the sole of a horse's foot; a V-shaped section of track where two sets of rails cross; ornamental braiding on uniform,

or ornamental fastening of loop and button; *v.t.* to ornament with frogs. **-men** *n.* the nickname given to underwater swimming men [O.E. *frogga*, a frog].

frol·ic (frȧl′·ik) *n.* a merry-making; gaiety; *a.* full of pranks; merry; *v.i.* to play merry pranks; to have fun. *pr.p.* **-king.** *pa.t., pa.p.* **-ked. -some** *a.* [Dut. *vroolijk*, merry].

from (frum) *prep.* away; forth; out of; on account of; at a distance [O.E. *fram*, from].

frond (frȧnd) *n.* (*Bot.*) an organ of certain flowerless plants, such as ferns, in which leaf and stem are combined and bear reproductive cells [L. *frons*, a leaf].

front (frunt) *n.* the forepart, the forehead; the human countenance; (*Mil.*) firing line; battle zone; (*Colloq.*) outward appearance *a.* pert. to, or at the front of, anything; *adv.* to the front; *v.t.* and *v.i.* to have the face or front towards any point. **-age** *n.* the front part of general exposure of a building; land abutting on street, river, or sea. **-al** *a.* pert. to the forehead or foremost part; (*Mil.*) direct, as an attack, without flanking movement; *n.* a bone of the forehead; an ornamental cloth for altar front [L. *frons*, the forehead].

fron·tier (frun′·tir) *n.* border of a country; the undeveloped areas of a country, knowledge, etc.; *a.* bordering; pioneering. **-sman** *n.* one who settles on a frontier [Fr.].

fron·tis·piece (frun′·tis·pēs) *n.* (*Archit.*) the main face of a building; an engraving or decorated page fronting the title page of a book [L. *frons*, the front; *specere*, to see].

frost (frawst) *n.* condition when water turns to ice, i.e. when temperature falls below 32° F.; severe cold; frozen dew; (*Slang*) a failure; a disappointment; *v.t.* to cover with hoar-frost; to nip (as plants); to ice a cake **-bite** *n.* freezing of the skin and tissues due to exposure to extreme cold. **-bitten** *a.* **-ed** *a.* covered with frost or anything resembling it. **-ily** *adv.* **-iness** *n.* **-y** *a.* accompanied with frost; chilly; white; grey-haired; frigid (in manner or feeling) [O.E. *forst*, fr. *freosan*, to freeze].

froth (frawth) *n.* spume; foam; trivial things or ideas; *v.t.* to cause to froth; *v.i.* to bubble. **-iness** *n.* **-y** *a.* [Scand. *frotha*, froth].

frounce (frouns) *v.t.* to curl the hair [O.Fr. *fronce*, a plait].

fro·ward (frō′·ẹrd) *a.* perverse; refractory. **-ly** *adv.* **-ness** *n.* [O.E. *fra*, away, and *ward*].

frown (froun) *v.i.* to wrinkle the brow; to scowl; *v.t.* to rebuke by a stern look; *n.* a wrinkling of the brow to express disapproval [O.Fr. *froignier*, to look sullen].

frow·zy (frou′·zi·) *a.* musty; unkempt.

fro·zen (frō′·zạn) *pa.p.* of the verb **freeze**.

fruc·ti·fy (fruk′·ti·fī) *v.t.* to make fruitful; to fertilize; *v.i.* to bear fruit. **fructiferous** *a.* fruitbearing. **fructose** *n.* fruit sugar; levulose [L. *fructus*, fruit].

fru·gal (frŏŏ′·gạl) *a.* sparing; thrifty; economical. **-ly** *adv.* **-ity** *n.* [L. *frugalis*, thrifty].

fruit (frŏŏt) *n.* the produce of the earth used for man's needs; the edible produce or seed of a plant; offspring; the consequence or outcome; *v.i.* to produce fruit. **-age** *n.* fruit collectively. **fruitarian** *n.* one who lives almost wholly on fruit. **-er** *n.* fruit grower; fruit-carrying ship. **-ful** *a.* producing fruit; abundant; profitable. **-fully** *adv.* **-fulness** *n.* **-ing** *n.* the process of bearing fruit. **-less** *a.* having no fruit; (*Fig.*) profitless; vain; empty. **-lessly** *adv.* **-lessness** *n.* **— sugar** *n.* glucose; levulose. **-y** *a.* resembling fruit; mellow [O.Fr. *fruit*, fruit].

fru·i·tion (frŏŏ·ish′·ạn) *n.* fulfillment of hopes and desires [L. *fruitio*, enjoyment].

frump (frump) *n.* a dowdy, cross woman.

frus·trate (frus′·trāt) *v.t.* to bring to nothing; to balk; to thwart; to circumvent. **frus-**

tration n. disappointment; defeat. **frustrative** a. [L. frustrari, to deceive].

frus·tum (frus'·tam) n. (Geom.) the remaining part of a solid figure when the top has been cut off by a plane parallel to the base. pl. **-s, frusta** [L. frustrum, a piece].

fry (frī) v.t. to cook with fat in a pan over the fire; v.i. to be cooked in a frying pan; to sizzle. pr.p. **-ing** pa.t., pa.p. **fried. -er, frier** n. [O.Fr. frire, to roast].

fry (frī) n. young fish just spawned; young children [M.E. fri, offspring].

fuch·sia (fū'·sha) n. a genus of flowering plants, with drooping bright purplish red flowers [fr. Fuchs, German botanist].

fud·dle (fud'·l) v.t. to make confused.

fudge (fuj) interj. stuff; nonsense; n. a soft chocolate candy; space reserved in a newspaper for last minute news.

fu·el (fū'·al) n. anything combustible to feed a fire, as wood, coal; v.t. to provide with fuel [O.Fr. fouaille, fr. L. focus, a health].

fu·gi·tive (fū'·ja·tiv) a. escaping; fleeing; fleeting; wandering; n. a refugee; one who flees from justice. [L. fugere, to flee].

fugue (fūg) n. (Mus.) a musical composition for voices and or instruments based on chief and subsidiary themes [L. fuga, flight].

ful·crum (ful'·kram) n. (Mech.) the pivot of a lever; (Fig.) means used to achieve a purpose. pl. **-s, fulcra** [L. fulcrum, a bedpost].

ful·fill (fool·fil') v.t. to carry into effect; to execute; to discharge; to satisfy (as hopes). **-er** n. **-ment** n. accomplishment; completion [O.E. full, full; fyllan, to fill].

ful·gent (ful'·jant) a. shining; dazzling. **fulgency** n. **-ly** adv. [L. fulgere, to shine].

fu·lig·i·nous (fū·lij'·an·as) a. sooty; dusky [L. fuligo, soot].

full (fool) a. filled to capacity; replete; crowded; complete; plump; abundant; showing the whole surface (as the moon); ample (of garments, etc.); clear and resonant (of sounds); n. the utmost extent; highest degree. adv. quite; completely; exactly. **—blooded** a. of pure race; vigorous. **—blown** a. fully developed, as a flower. **— dress** n. dress worn on ceremonial occasions; a. formal. **-y** adv. completely [O.E. full, full].

full (fool) v.t. to cleanse, shrink and thicken cloth in a mill; v.i. to become thick or felted. **-er** n. one who fulls cloth [O.E. fullian, to whiten cloth].

ful·mi·nate (ful'·mi·nāt) v.t. to flash; to explode; to thunder forth official censure; n. a compound of fulminic acid exploding by percussion, friction, or heat, as fulminate of mercury. **fulminant** a. fulminating. **fulmination** n. the act of fulminating; an explosion; a biting denunciation. **fulminatory, fulmineous, fulminous** a. pert. to or like thunder and lightening [L. fulmen, lightning].

ful·some (fool'·sam) a. excessive; insincere, **-ly** adv. **-ness** n. [O.E. full].

ful·vous (ful'·vas) a. tawny; dull yellow. [L. fulvus, tawny].

fu·ma·role (fū'·ma·rōl) n. a small fissure in volcano [Fr. fumerole, a smoke-hole].

fum·ble (fum'·bl) v.i. to grope blindly or awkwardly; v.t. to handle clumsily [Scand. fumla, to grope].

fume (fūm) n. pungent vapor from combustion or exhalation; (Fig.) excitement; rage; v.i. to smoke; to be in a rage; v.t. to send forth as fumes [L. fumus, smoke].

fu·mi·gate (fū'·mi·gāt) v.t. to expose to poisonous gas or smoke, esp. for the purpose of destroying germs; to perfume or deodorize. **fumigator** n. apparatus or substance used in fumigation [L. fumigare, to smoke].

fun (fun) n. merriment; hilarity; sport. **-nies** n.pl. (Colloq.) comic strips. **-nily** adv. **-niness** n. **-ny** a. full of fun [M.E. fonnen].

fu·nam·bu·late (fū·nam'·bya·lāt) v.i. to balance and walk on a tight-rope. **funambulist** n. [L. funis, a rope; ambulare, to walk].

func·tion (fungk'·shan) n. performance; the special work done by an organ or structure; office; ceremony; (Math.) a quantity the value of which varies with that of another quantity; a social entertainment; v.i. to operate; to fulfil a set task. **-al** a. having a special purpose; pert. to a duty or office. **-ally** adv. **-ary** n. an official [L. functus, to perform].

fund (fund) n. permanent stock or capital; an invested sum, the income of which is used for a set purpose; a store; ample supply; pl. money in hand; v.t. to establish a fund for the payment of interest or principal. **-ed** a. [L. fundus, the bottom].

fun·da·men·tal (fun·da·men'·tal) a. pert. to the foundations; basic; essential; original; n. a primary principle; (Mus.) the bottom note of a chord. **-ism** n. belief in literal truth of the Bible. **-ist** n. **-ly** adv. [L. fundamentum, the foundation].

fu·ne·ral (fū'·na·ral) n. the ceremony of burying the dead; obsequies; a. pert. to or used at burial. **funerary, funereal** a. gloomy [L. funus, burial rites].

fun·gus (fung'·gas) n. any of a group of thallophytes (molds, mushrooms, mildews, puffballs, etc.) (Path.) a spongy, morbid growth; proud flesh. pl. **fungi** (fun'·jī), **-es, fungiform** a. fungus or mushroom-shaped. **fungicide** n. any preparation which destroys molds or fungoid growths. **fungoid, fungous** a. pert. to or caused by fungus [L. fungus, a mushroom].

fu·ni·cle (fū'·ni·kl) n. (Bot.) the stalk of a seed. **funicular** a. pert. to, or worked by rope. **funicular railway**, a cable railway [L. funiculus, dim. of funis, a cord].

funk (fungk) n. (Colloq.) abject terror; panic; v.i. and v.t. to be terrified of or by.

fun·nel (fun'·al) n. an inverted hollow metal cone with tube, used for filling vessels with narrow inlet; the smokestack of a steamship [L. fundere, to pour].

fur (fur) n. the short, fine, soft hair of certain animals; animal pelts used for coats, etc.; coating on the tongue; deposit on inside of kettles, etc. v.t. to line, face, or cover with fur; to coat with morbid matter. pr.p. **-ring.** pa.p. **-red. -rier** n. a dealer in furs. **-ry** a. [M.E. forre, fur].

fur·be·low (fur'·ba·lō) n. an ornament; a ruffle [Sp. falbala, a flounce].

fur·bish (fur'·bish) v.t. to polish; to burnish; to renovate [O.Fr. fourbir, to polish].

fur·cate (fur'·kāt) a. forked; branched like a fork; v.i. to branch out [L. furca, a fork].

fu·ri·ous (fyoo'·ri·as) a. raging; violent; savage. **-ly** adv. [L. furiosus, raging].

furl (furl) v.t. to roll, as a sail [contr. of O.Fr. fardel, a bundle].

fur·long (fur'·lawng) n. eighth of mile; 220 yards [O.E. furh, a furrow; lang, long].

fur·lough (fur'·lō) n. leave of absence; v.t. to grant leave [Dut. verlof, permission].

fur·nace (fur'·nas) n. an enclosed structure for the generating of heat required for smelting ores, warming houses, etc.; a place of severe trial [L. fornus, an oven].

fur·nish (fur'·nish) v.t. to supply; to equip; to fit out. **-er** n. **-ings** n.pl. fittings, of a house, esp. furniture, curtains, carpets, etc.

fur·ni·ture (fur'·ni·cher) n. equipment; that which is put into a house, office, etc. for use or ornament [Fr. fournir, to provide].

fu·ror (fū'·rawr) n. wild excitement; enthusiasm [L. furor, rage].

fur·row (fur'·ō) n. a trench made by a plough; channel; groove; deep wrinkle; v.t. to plough; to mark with wrinkles. **-y** a. [O.E. furh, a furrow].

fur·ther (fur'·THer) a. more remote; additional; *adv.* to a greater distance; more-over. **-more** *adv.* moreover; besides. **-most** *a.* most remote. **furthest** *adv.* and *a.* most remote. (**farther, farthest** are preferred as *comp.* and *superl.* of **far**) [O.E. *furthor*, comp. of *forth*, forwards].

fur·ther (fur'·THẹr) *v.t.* to help forward; to promote. **-ance** *n.* the act of furthering [O.E. *fyrthia*, to promote].

fur·tive (fur'·tiv) *a.* done stealthily; covert; sly. **-ly** *adv.* [L. *fur*, a thief].

fu·ry (fyoo'·ri·) *n.* rage; passion; frenzy [L. *furia*, rage].

fus·cous (fus'·kạs) *a.* of a dark greyish-brown color [L. *fuscus*, dark].

fuse (fūz) *v.t.* to melt (as metal) by heat; to amalgamate; *v.i.* to become liquid; *n.* a tube filled with combustible matter, used in blasting or discharge of bombs, etc.; a device used as a safety measure in electric lighting and heating systems. **fusibility** *n.* **fusible** *a.* **fusion** *n.* the act or process of melting; the state of being melted or blended; coalition [L. *fundere, fusum, to* melt].

fu·see (fū-zē') *n.* the spindle-shaped wheel in a clock or watch, round which the chain is wound; a match; a red signal flare. Also **fuzee** [Fr. *fuseé*, a spindleful].

fu·se·lage (fū'·sa·lij or fū·zạ·lazh') *n.* the body of an airplane [O.Fr. *fusel*, a spindel].

fu·sil (fū'·sil) *n.* a light flintlock musket. **-lade** *n.* the simultaneous discharge of firearms [O.Fr. *fuisil*, a flintmusket].

fuss (fus) *n.* bustle; unnecessary ado; needless activity; *v.i.* to become nervously agitated; *v.t.* to bother another with excessive attentions. **—budget** *n.* (*Colloq.*) a fussy person. **-ily** *adv.* **-iness** *n.* **-y** *a.*

fus·tian (fust'·chạn) *n.* a coarse cotton twilled fabric, corduroy, velveteen; (*Fig.*) bombast [M.E. *fustyane*, fr. *Fustat* (*Egypt*)].

fus·ti·ga·tion (fus·tạ·gā'·shạn) *n.* a thrashing with a stick. **fustigate** *v.t.* to cudgel [L. *fustigare*, to cudgel].

fu·tile (fū'·til) *a.* ineffectual, unavailing, useless. **-ly** *adv.* **futility** *n.* uselessness; fruitlessness [L. *futilis*, worthless].

fu·ture (fūt'·cher) *a.* about to happen; that is to come hereafter; *n.* time to come. **futurism** *n.* a modern aesthetic movement marked by complete departure from tradition. **futurist** *n.* **futuristic** *a.* **futurity** *n.* time to come [L. *futurus*, about to be].

fuzz (fuz) *n.* fine, light particles; fluff; **-iness** *n.* **-y** *a.*

G

gab (gab) *n.* (*Colloq.*) trifling talk; chatter; *v.i.* to chatter. *pr.p.* **-bing.** *pa.t.* **-bed. -by** *a.* **-ble** *n., v.i.* **the gift of gab,** a talent for talking.

gab·ar·dine (gab'·ẹr·dēn) *n.* a firm, woven twilled fabric of cotton, rayon or wool. Also **gaberdine** [Sp. *gabardina*].

ga·ble (gā'·bl) *n.* the end of a house, esp. the vertical triangular ends of a building from the eaves to the top; a similar construction projecting from a roof [O.N. *gafl*].

gad (gad) *v.i.* to go about idly; to ramble. *pr.p.* **-ding.** *pa.p.* and *pa.t.* **-ded. -about** *v.i.* to wander idly; *n.* a pleasure seeker [O.E. *gaedeling*, a comrade].

gad·fly (gad'·flī) *n.* a cattle biting fly; (*Fig.*) a tormentor [fr. *gad*, a goad].

gadg·et (gaj'·it) *n.* (*Colloq.*) a general term for any small mechanical contrivance or device.

Gael (gāl) *n.* a Scottish Highlander of Celtic origin. **-ic** *a. n.* the language of the Gaels.

gaff (gaf) *n.* a barbed fishing spear; a stick with an iron hook for landing fish; *v.t.* to seize (a fish) with a gaff [Fr. *gaffe*].

gaf·fer (gaf'·ẹr) *n.* (*Brit.*) an old man, esp. a country man [contr. of *grandfather*].

gag (gag) *n.* something thrust into or over the mouth to prevent speech; *v.t.* to apply a gag to; to silence by force; *v.i.* to heave with nausea. *pr.p.* **-ging.** *pa.t., pa.p.* **-ged.** [imit.].

gag (gag) *n.* (*Colloq.*) words inserted by an actor which are not in his part; a joke.

gage (gāj) *n.* a pledge or pawn; a glove, gauntlet, cast down as challenge; a challenge; [O.Fr. *guage*]. [Sir William *Gage*].

gage (gāj) *n.* a kind of plum; a greengage [fr. gage (gāj) *v.t.* See **gauge.**

gag·gle (gag'·l) *v.i.* to cackle like geese; *n.* a flock of geese [imit.].

gai·e·ty (gā'·ạ·ti·) *n.* mirth; merriment; glee; jollity. **gaily** *adv.* merrily [Fr. *gai*].

gain (gān) *v.t.* to attain to, or reach; to get by effort; to get profit; to earn; to win; *v.i.* to have advantage or profit; to increase; to improve; to make an advance; *n.* profit; advantage; increase. **-ful** *a.* profitable; lucrative. **-fully** *adv.* **-fulness** *n.* [Fr. *gagner*, to earn].

gain·say (gān·sā') *v.t.* to contradict; to deny. *pa.p.* and *pa.t.* **-said** [O.E. *gean*, against, and *say*].

gait (gāt) *n.* manner of walking or running; pace [var. of *gate*].

gai·ter (gā'·tẹr) *n.* covering for instep and ankle fitting over the shoe; a spat [Fr. *guétre*].

gal (gal) *n.* (*Slang*) a girl.

ga·la (gā'·lạ) *n.* a show or festivity; *a.* festive [It. *gala*, finery].

gal·ax·y (gal'·ạk·si·) *n.* a band of stars encircling the heavens; a brilliant assembly of persons. (G) the Milky Way. **galactic** *a.* [Gk. *gala, galaktos*, milk].

gale (gāl) *n.* a wind between a stiff breeze and a hurricane; (*Colloq.*) an outburst of noise.

gale (gāl) *n.* a shrub found in marshes, giving off a pleasant fragrance [O.E. *gagel*].

ga·le·na (gạ·lē'·nạ) *n.* sulfide of lead, the principal ore from which lead is extracted [L. *galena*, lead ore].

gall (gawl) *n.* bile secreted in the liver; anything bitter; bitterness; rancor; (*Slang*) effrontery; impudence. **— bladder** *n.* a small sac on the under side of the liver, in which the bile is stored. **-stone** *n.* a concretion formed in the gall bladder [O.E. *gealla*].

gall (gawl) *v.t.* to fret and wear away by rubbing; to vex, irritate, or harass; *n.* a skin wound caused by rubbing. **-ing** *a.* irritating [O.E. *gealla*].

gal·lant (gal'·ạnt) *a.* splendid or magnificent; noble in bearing or spirit; brave; chivalrous; courteous to women; amorous. (ga·lant') *n.* a brave, high-spirited man; a courtly or fashionable man; a lover or paramour. **-ly** *adv.* **-ry** *n.* bravery; chivalry [Fr. *galant*].

gal·leon (gal'·i·ạn) *n.* a large, clumsy sailing ship built up high at bow and stern [Sp.].

gal·ler·y (gal'·ẹr·i·) *n.* a long corridor, hall, or room; a room or series of rooms in which works of art are exhibited; a balcony; the uppermost tier of seats, esp. in theater; audience or spectators; a passage in a mine; a tunnel [Fr. *galerie*].

gal·ley (gal'·i·) *n.* a low, one-decked vessel, navigated both with oars and sails; a large rowboat; the kitchen of a ship; (*Print.*) an oblong tray on which type is placed when set up. **— proof** *n.* (*Print.*) a proof taken from the galley on a long strip of paper, before it is made up in pages. **— slave** *n.* one who was condemned for some criminal offence to row in the galleys [L.L. *galea*].

gal·liard (gal'·yẹrd) *n.* a lively dance [Fr.].

Gal·lic (gal'·ik) *a.* pert. to ancient Gaul, or France; French. **gallicize** *v.t.* to make French in opinions, manners [L. *Gallia*, Gaul].

gal·li·mau·fry (gal·a·maw'·fri·) *n.* a hash of various meats; a hodgepodge [O.Fr. *galimafree*].

gal·li·na·ceous (gal·a·nā'·shas) *a.* belonging to the order of birds which includes domestic fowls, pheasants, etc. [L. *galling*, a hen].

gal·li·pot (gal'·i·pát) *n.* a small earthenware pot, for medicines [*galley*, and *pot*].

gal·li·um (gal'·i·am) *n.* a soft grey metal of extreme fusibility [L. *gallus*, a cock. *Lecoq* the discoverer].

gal·li·vant (gal·a·vant') *v.i.* to gad about.

gal·lon (gal'·an) *n.* a measure of capacity both for liquid and dry commodities, containing four quarts [O.Fr. *jalon*].

gal·lop (gal'·ap) *n.* fastest gait of horse, when it lifts forefeet together, and hind feet together; a ride at a gallop; *v.i.* to ride at a gallop; to go at full speed; *v.t.* to cause to gallop. **-ing** *a.* speedy; swift [Fr. *galoper*].

gal·lows (gal'·ōz) *n.* a frame from which criminals are hanged [O.E. *galga*].

gal·lus·es (gal'·as·iz) *n.pl.* suspenders [fr. *gallows*].

ga·loot (ga·lōōt') *n.* (*Colloq.*) an uncouth or awkward fellow.

gal·op (gal'·ap) *n.* a lively dance [Fr.].

ga·lore (ga·lōr') *adv.* abundantly; in plenty [Gael. *gu leor*, enough].

ga·losh, golosh (ga·lásh') *n.* (usually pl.) a rubber overshoe [Fr. *galoche*].

gal·va·nism (gal'·va·nizm) *n.* the branch of science which treats of the production of electricity by chemical action. **galvanic** *a.* **galvanize** *v.t.* to apply galvanic action to; to stimulate by an electric current; (*Fig.*) to stimulate by words or deeds; to coat metal with zinc. **galvanization** *n.* **galvanizing** *n.* coating with zinc (by galvanic action). **galvanometer** *n.* an instrument for detecting and measuring the strength and direction of electric currents. **galvanoscope** *n.* an instrument for detecting the existence and direction of an electric current. **galvanic battery**, an apparatus for generating electricity by chemical action on a series of zinc or copper plates. **galvanized iron**, iron coated with zinc to prevent rust [fr. Luigi *Galvani*, inventor].

gamb (gam) *n.* an animal's leg. **gam** *n.* (Slang) a woman's leg [L. *gamba*, leg].

gam·bit (gam'·bit) *n.* in chess, opening move involving sacrifice of pawn [It. *gambetto*, wrestler's trip, fr. *gamba*, leg].

gam·ble (gam'·bl) *v.i.* to play for money; to risk esp. by financial speculation; *v.t.* to lose or squander in speculative ventures; *n.* a risky undertaking; a reckless speculation. **-r** *n.* [O.E. *gamen*, a game].

gam·bol (gam'·bal) *v.i.* to leap about playfully; to skip and dance about. *n.* a dancing or skipping about; a frolic [Fr. *gambade*].

game (gām) *n.* any sport; a pastime; a contest for amusement; a trial of strength, skill, or chance; an exercise or play for stakes; victory in a game; frolic; mockery; hence, an object of ridicule; animals and birds protected by law and hunted by sportsmen; *a.* pert. to animals hunted as game; brave; plucky; *v.i.* to gamble. *n.pl.* athletic contests. **-ly** *adv.* **-ness** *n.* **-ster** *n.* a gambler. **gaming** *a.* playing cards, dice, etc. for money; gambling. **gamy** *a.* having the flavor of dead game which has been kept uncooked for a long time. — **cock** *n.* breed of cock trained for cockfighting. — **preserve**, land stocked with game for hunting or shooting. — **warden** *n.* an official who enforces game laws. **big game**, all large animals hunted for sport. **fair game** (*Fig.*) a person considered easy subject for jest. **to play the game**, to act in a sportsmanlike way [O.E. *gamen*].

game (gām) *a.* (*Colloq.*) of an arm or leg, lame; injured [O.Fr. *gambi*, bent].

gam·ete (gam·ēt') *n.* a protoplasmic body, ovum, or sperm, which unites with one of opposite sex for conception [Gk. *gamos*, marriage].

gam·in (gam'·in) *n.* a street-urchin [Fr.].

gam·ma (gam'·a) *n.* the third letter of the Greek alphabet. — **rays**, electro-magnetic radiations, of great penetrative powers, given off by radioactive substances, e.g. radium.

gam·mon (gam'·an) *n.* the thigh of a pig, smoked or cured [Fr. *jambon*, ham].

gam·ut (gam'·at) *n.* the whole series of musical notes; a scale; the compass of a voice; the entire range [L. *gamma*, and *ut*, names of notes]

gan·der (gan'·der) *n.* a male goose; (*Slang*) a look [O.E. *gandra*].

gang (gang) *n.* people banded together for some purpose, usually bad; body of laborers working together. *v.i.* (*Colloq.*) to act as a gang (followed by *up*) **-ster** *n.* one of a gang of criminals [O.E. *gangan*, to go].

gan·gling (gang'·gling) *a.* lanky and loosely knit in build [O.E. *gangan*, to go].

gan·gli·on (gang'·gli·an) *n.* a globular, hard tumor, situated on a tendon. *pl.* **-s**, **ganglia**. **gangliate** *a.* furnished with ganglia. **-ic** *a.* [Gk. *ganglion*, an encysted tumor].

gang plank (gang' plangk') *n.* a moveable plank bridge between a ship and the shore.

gan·grene (gang'·grēn) *n.* the first stage of mortification or death of tissue in the body; *v.t.* and *v.i.* to affect with, or be affected with, gangrene. **gangrenous** *a.* mortified; putrefying [Gk. *gangraina*].

gang·way (gang'·wā) *n.* a passageway; a platform and ladder slung over the side of a ship; *interj.* make way, please! [O.E. *gangweg*].

gan·net (gan'·it) *n.* the solan goose, a seafowl of the pelican tribe [O.E. *ganot*].

gant·let (gant'·lit) *n.* a former military or naval punishment in which the offender was made to run between files of men who struck him as he passed. **to run the gantlet** (erroneously, **gauntlet**), to undergo this ordeal; to face any unpleasant ordeal [Scand.].

gan·try (gan'·tri·) *n.* a structure to support a crane, railway-signal, etc.

gaol (jāl) *n.* (*Brit.*) a jail. **-er** *n.* [form of *jail*].

gap (gap) *n.* an opening; a breach; a mountain pass [O.N. = chasm].

gape (gāp) *v.i.* to open wide, esp. the mouth; to stare with open mouth; to yawn. *n.* a wide opening; the act of gaping. **the gapes**, a fit of yawning; a disease of poultry and other birds, characterized by gaping [O.N. *gapa*].

gar (går) *n.* a fish of the pike family. Also **garfish** [O.E. *gar*, a dart, spear].

ga·rage (ga·ràzh', ga·raj') *n.* a covered enclosure for motor vehicles; a fuel and repair station for motor vehicles; *v.t.* to place in a garage [Fr. *gare*, a station].

garb (gàrb) *n.* clothing; mode or style of dress; *v.t.* to dress [O.Fr. *garbe*, dress].

gar·bage (gàr'·bij) *n.* kitchen refuse; anything worthless.

gar·ble (gàr'·bl) *v.t.* to pervert or mutilate, as a story, a quotation, an account, etc. by picking out only certain parts [Ar. *ghirbal*, a sieve].

gar·den (gàr'·dn) *n.* ground for cultivation of flowers, vegetables, etc. generally attached to a house; pleasure grounds; *v.i.* to cultivate, or work in, a garden. **-er** *n.* **-ing** *n.* the act of tending a garden [Fr. *jardin*].

gar·de·nia (gàr·dē'·ni·a) *n.* a genus of tropical trees and shrubs with sweet-scented, beautiful white flowers [fr. A. *Garden*, Amer. botanist].

gar·gan·tu·an (gàr·gan'·choo·an) *a.* immense, enormous, esp. of appetite [fr. *Gargantua*, hero of Rabelais' book].

gar·gle (gàr'·gl) *v.t.* to rinse (mouth or throat),

preventing water from going down throat by expulsion of air from lungs; *v.i.* to make a sound of gargling; to use a gargle; *n.* a throat wash [O.Fr. *gargouille*, throat].

gar·goyle (går'·goil) *n.* a projecting spout, often in the form of a grotesque carving, found on old buildings and intended to carry off the water [O.Fr. *gargouille*, the throat].

gar·ish (gar'·ish) *a.* gaudy; showy; glaring; dazzling. **-ly** *adv.* [M.E. *gauren*, to stare].

gar·land (går'·land) *n.* a wreath of flowers, branches, feathers, etc.; an anthology; *v.t.* to ornament with a garland [O.Gr. *garlande*].

gar·lic (går'·lik) *n.* a plant having a bulbous root, a strong smell like onion, and a pungent taste. **-ky** *a.* [O.E. *garleac*].

gar·ment (går'·mant) *n.* any article of clothing [*Fr. garnement*, equipment].

gar·ner (går'·ner) *n.* a granary; *v.t.* to store in a granary; to gather up [L. *granarium*].

gar·net (går'·nit) *n.* a semi-precious stone, usually of a dark-red color and resembling a ruby; a dark-red color [Fr. *grenat*].

gar·nish (går'·nish) *v.t.* to adorn; to embellish; to ornament; (*Cookery*) to make food attractive or appetizing; *n.* ornament; decoration; **-ment** *n.* **garniture** *n.* that which garnishes [Fr. *garnir*, to furnish].

ga·rotte See **garrote**.

gar·ret (gar'·it) *n.* upper floor of a house immediately under roof; an attic [O.Fr. *garite*, a place of safety].

gar·ri·son (gar'·a·sn) *n.* a body of troops stationed in a fort, town, etc.; the fort or town itself; *v.t.* to occupy with a garrison [O.Fr. *garison*, fr. *garir*, to protect].

gar·rote (ga·råt', ·röt') *n.* a Spanish mode of execution by strangling, with an iron collar affixed to a post and tightened by a screw; apparatus for this punishment; *v.t.* to execute by strangulation; to seize by the throat, in order to throttle and rob. [Sp. *garrote*, a cudgel].

gar·ru·lous (gar'·a·las) *a.* talkative; loquacious. **-ly** *adv.* **-ness** *n.* **garrulity** *n.* [L. *garrire*, to chatter].

gar·ter (går'·ter) *n.* a string or band worn near the knee to keep a stocking up; the badge of the highest order of knighthood in Great Britain; *v.t.* to support with a garter [O.Fr. *gartier*, fr. *garet*, the bend of the knee].

gas (gas) *n.* an elastic fluid such as air, esp. one not liquid or solid at ordinary temperatures; mixture of gases, used for heating or lighting; an anesthetic; (*Warfare*) a chemical substance used to poison or incapacitate the enemy; (*Slang*) empty talk; (*Colloq.*) gasoline; *v.t.* to poison with gas; *v.i.* (*Slang*) to talk emptily; to talk unceasingly. *pr.p.* **-sing.** *pa.p.* and *pa.t.* **-sed.** **-eous** *a.* like, or in the form of gas. **-ification** *n.* **-ify** *v.t.* to convert into gas, as by the action of heat, or by chemical processes. **-sy** *a.* full of gas. **-bag** *n.* (*Slang*) a very talkative person. — **burner** *n.* a gas jet or stove. — **jet** *n.* a nozzle or burner of a gas burner; the burner itself. — **mask** *n.* a respirator worn to protect against poisonous gases. — **meter** *n.* a metal box used to measure the amount of gas consumed. **-ometer** *n.* an apparatus for measuring or storing gas. — **range** *n.* a gas cooking stove[coined by D. chemist, Van Helmont fr. Gr. *chaos*, chaos].

Gas·con (gas'·kan) *n.* a native of *Gascony*, in S.W. France; (*l.c.*) a boaster.

gash (gash) *v.t.* to make a long, deep cut in; *n.* a deep cut [O.Fr. *garser*, to slash].

gas·ket (gas'·kit) *n.* (*Naut.*) a flat, plaited cord, used to furl the sail or tie it to the yard; a washer between parts such as the cylinder head and cylinder block [Fr. *garcette*].

gas·o·line, gasolene, (gas'·a·lēn) *n.* a volatile, inflammable, liquid mixture produced by the distillation of petroleum, used as a fuel,

solvent, etc. [*gas; L. oleum,* oil; *-ine*].

gasp (gasp) *v.i.* to struggle for breath with open mouth; to pant; *v.t.* to utter with gasps; *n.* the act of gasping; a painful catching of the breath [O.N. *geispa*, to yawn].

gas·tric (gas'·trik) *a.* pert. to the stomach. **gastritis** (gas·trī'·tis) *n.* inflammation of the stomach. **gastro-enteritis** *n.* inflammation of the stomach and intestines. **gastrology** *n.* [Gk. *gaster*].

gas·tron·o·my (gas·tràn'·a·mi·) *n.* the art of good eating; epicurism. **gastronome, gastronomer** *n.* one fond of good living. Also **gastronomist, gastronomic, gastronomical** *a.* [Gk. *gaster*, the stomach; *nemein*, regulate].

gas·tro·pod (gas'·tra·pàd) *n.* a class of molluscs, e.g. snails and whelks, having a fleshy, ventral disk, which takes the place of feet. [Gk. *gaster*, the stomach; *pous, podos*, the foot].

gat (gat) *n.* (*Slang*) a pistol. Abbrev. of **gatling-gun**.

gate (gāt) *n.* an opening into an enclosure, through a fence, wall, etc.; a mountain pass or defile; an entrance; a device for stopping passage of water through a dam or lock; the number of people paying to watch a game; also the money taken; —**crasher** *n.* one attending a social function uninvited. **-way** *n.* an entrance [O.E. *geat,* a way].

gath·er (gaTH'·er) *v.t.* to bring together; to collect; to pick; in sewing, to draw into puckers; to infer or deduce; to harvest; *v.i.* to come together; to congregate; to increase; to wrinkle, as the brow; to swell up and become full of pus (of a sore or boil); *n.* a pucker or fold in cloth. **-ing** *n.* an assemblage; a crowd; an abscess [O.E. *gaderian*, fr. *gador*, together].

Gat·ling-gun (gat'·ling-gun) *n.* machine gun invented by R. J. *Gatling*.

gauche (gōsh) *a.* awkward; clumsy; tactless. **gaucherie** (gō'·sha·rē) *n.* [Fr.].

gau·cho (gou'·chō) *n.* a cowboy of the S. American pampas [Sp.].

gaud (gawd) *n.* a piece of worthless finery; a trinket. **-ily** *adv.* **-y** *a.* [L. *gaudium*, joy].

gauge (gāj) *v.t.* to ascertain the capacity of; to measure the ability of; to estimate; *n.* an instrument for determining dimensions or capacity; a standard of measure; test; criterion; the distance between the rails of a railway. **-r** *n.* one who gauges, esp. an exciseman who measures the contents of casks [O.Fr. *gauge*].

Gaul (gawl) *n.* an old name for France; a Frenchman [L. *Gallia*].

gaunt (gawnt) *a.* lean and haggard; pinched and grim; desolate. **-ly** *adv.* **-ness** *n.*

gaunt·let (gawnt'·lit) *n.* a glove with metal plates on the back, worn formerly as armor; a glove with a long cuff. **to run the gauntlet,** see **gantlet. to throw down, to take up, the gauntlet,** to give, accept, a challenge [Fr. *gant*, a glove].

gauss (gous) *n.* (*Elect.*) the unit of density of a magnetic field [fr. Karl F. *Gauss*, a German scientist, 1777-1855].

gauze (gawz) *n.* a thin, transparent fabric. **gauziness** *n.* **gauzy** *a.* [Fr. *gaze*].

gave (gāv) *p.at.* of **give**.

gav·el (gav'·al) *n.* a mallet; a small wooden hammer used by a chairman or auctioneer.

ga·votte (ga·vàt') *n.* an old dance after the style of the minuet but not so stately; the music for it [Fr. *gavotte*].

gawk (gawk) *n.* an awkward person; a simpleton; a booby; *v.i.* to stare stupidly. **-y** *a.*

gay (gā) *a.* lively; merry; light-hearted; showy; dissipated. **-ly, gaily** *adv.* **-ety, gaiety** *n.* [Fr. *gai*].

gaze (gāz) *v.i.* to look fixedly; to stare; *n.* a fixed, earnest look; a long, intent look. **-r** *n.* one who gazes.

ga·ze·bo (ga·zē'·bō) *n.* a summerhouse commanding a wide view; a belvedere.

ga·zelle (gạ·zel´) *n.* a small, swift, graceful antelope [Ar. *ghazal*].

ga·zette (gạ·zet´) *n.* a newspaper (now used in newspaper titles). **gazetteer** (gaz·ạ·tẽr´) *n.* formerly a writer for a gazette; now, a geographical dictionary [It. *gazetta*].

gear (gir) *n.* apparatus; equipment; tackle; a set of tools; harness; rigging; clothing; goods; utensils; a set of toothed wheels working together, esp. by engaging cogs, to transmit power or to change timing; *v.t.* to provide with gear; to put in gear; *v.i.* to be in gear. **-ing** *n.* the series of toothed wheels for transmitting power, changing speed, etc. **—wheel** *n.* a wheel having teeth or cogs [M.E. *gere*].

gee (jē) *interj.* a command to a horse to turn to the right; exclamation of surprise.

geese (gēs) *n.* plural of **goose.**

gee·zer (gē´·zẹr) *n.* (*Slang*) an old fellow; a queer old chap [corrupt. of *guiser*].

Gei·ger counter (gī´·gẹr) *n.* a hypersensitive instrument for detecting radio-activity, cosmic radiation, etc. [H. *Geiger*, Ger. physicist].

gei·sha (gā´·sha) *n.* a Japanese dancing girl.

gel (jel) *n.* (*Chem.*) a colloidal solution which has set into a jelly; *v.i.* to become a gel. **-ling.** *pa.t.*, *pa.p.* **-led.** **-ation** *n.* a solidifying by means of cold [L. *gelare*, to freeze].

gel·a·tin, gelatine (jel´·ạ·tin) *n.* a glutinous substance gotten by boiling parts of animals (bones, hoofs, etc.) which is soluble in hot water and sets into a tremulous jelly. **-ous** (jạ·lat´·i·nạs) *a.* of the nature or consistency of gelatin; like jelly. **-ate, -ize** *v.t.* to convert into gelatine. **-ation** *n.* [It. *gelata*, jelly].

geld (geld) *v.t.* to castrate. **-ing** *n.* a castrated animal, esp. a horse [O.N. *geldr*, barren].

gel·id (jel´·id) *a.* cold as ice. **-ly** *adv.* **-ness, gelidity** *n.* [L. *gelidus*, fr. *gelu*, frost].

gem (jem) *n.* a precious stone of any kind; a jewel; anything of great value; *v.t.* to adorn with gems. *pr.p.* **-ming.** *pa.p.*, *pa.t.* **-med** [L. *gemma*].

gem·i·nate (jem´·ạ·nāt) *a.* doubled; existing in pairs; *v.i.* and *t.* to make or become paired or doubled. **gemination** *n.* [L. *geminare*, to double].

Gem·i·ni (jem´·ạ·nī) *n.pl.* the third sign of the Zodiac; a constellation containing the two bright stars Castor and Pollux, twin heroes of Greek legend [L. *geminus*, twin-born].

gem·ma (jem´·ạ) *n.* (*Bot.*) a bud; (*Zool.*) a bud-like outgrowth which becomes a separate individual. *pl.* **gemmae. gemmate** *a.* having buds; *v.i.* to propagate by buds, as coral. **gemmation** *n.* budding; (*Zool.*) reproduction by gemmae. **gemmiparous** *a.* producing buds; (*Zool.*) propagating by buds [L. *gemma*, a bud].

gen·darme (zhàn·dàrm´) *n.* an armed military policeman in France. **gendarmeria** (zhàn·-dàrm´·rē) *n.* the corps of armed police [Fr. fr. *gens d'armes*, men-at-arms].

gen·der (jen´·dẹr) *n.* (*Colloq.*) sex, male or female; (*Gram.*) the classification of nouns according to sex (actual or attributed) or animateness [L. *genus, generis*, a kind].

gene (jēn) *n.* the hereditary factor which is transmitted by each parent to offspring and which determines hereditary characteristics [Gk. *genos*, origin].

ge·ne·al·o·gy (jēn·i·àl´·ạ·ji·) *n.* a record of the descent of a person or family from an ancestor; the pedigree of a person or family; lineage. **genealogist** *n.* one who traces the descent of persons or families. **genealogical** *a.* [Gk. *genea*, birth; *logos*, discourse].

gen·er·a (jen´·ạ·rạ) *n.* See **genus.**

gen·er·al (jen´·ạ·rạl) *a.* relating to a genus or kind; pert. to a whole class or order; not precise, particular, or detailed; usual, ordinary, or prevalent; embracing the whole, not local or partial; *n.* (*U.S. Army*) brigadier general, lieutenant general, major general, general, general of the Army, or general of the Armies. **-ly** *adv.* as a whole; for the most part; commonly; extensively. **generality** *n.* indefiniteness; vagueness; a vague statement; the main body. **-ship** *n.* military skill in a commander; leadership. **-issimo** *n.* the chief commander of all the country's forces in China and the U.S.S.R. **in general,** in most respects. **general practitioner,** a doctor whose work embraces all types of cases [L. *generalis*].

gen·er·al·ize (jen´·ẹr·ạl·īz) *v.t.* to reduce to general laws; to make universal in application; *v.i.* to draw general conclusions from particular instances; to speak vaguely. **generalization** *n.* a general conclusion from particular instances [fr. *general*].

gen·er·ate (jen´·ẹ·rāt) *v.t.* to bring into being; to produce; (*Math.*) to trace out. **generation** *n.* a bringing into being; the act of begetting; the act of producing; that which is generated; a step in a pedigree; all persons born about the same time; the average time in which children are ready to replace their parents (about 30 years); family. **generative** (jen´·ẹ·rā·tiv) *a.* having the power of generating or producing; prolific. **generator** *n.* one who, or that which, generates; a begetter; an apparatus for producing steam, etc.; a machine for converting mechanical into electrical energy [L. *generare*, to procreate].

ge·ner·ic (jạ·ner´·ik) *a.* pert. to a genus; of a general nature in regard to all members of a genus. **-ally** *adv.* [L. *generus*, kind].

gen·er·ous (jen´·ẹr·as) *a.* liberal, free in giving; abundant; copious; of wine, rich. **-ly** *adv.* **generosity** *n.* magnanimity; liberality in giving [L. *generosus*, of noble birth].

gen·e·sis (jen´·ạ·sis) *n.* origin; creation; production; birth. *pl.* **geneses** (jen´·e·sēs). **Genesis** *n.* (*Bib.*) the first book of the Old Testament [Gk.].

gen·et (jen´·it) *n.* See **jennet.**

ge·net·ic (jạ·net´·ik) *a.* pert. to origin, creation, or reproduction. **-s** *n.* the scientific study of the heredity of individuals, esp. of inherited characteristics. **geneticist** *n.* [Gk. *gignesthai*, to be born].

Ge·ne·van (jạ·nē´·vạn) *a.* pert. to *Geneva*, in Switzerland. **Geneva Conventions,** international agreements, signed at Geneva in 1864, 1868, 1906 and 1949, to lessen sufferings of the wounded in war by providing for the neutrality of hospitals, ambulances, etc.

gen·ial (jen´·yạl) *a.* kindly; sympathetic; cordial; sociable; of a climate, mild and conducive to growth. **geniality** (jē·ni·al´·ạ·ti·) *n.* the quality of being genial; friendliness; sympathetic cheerfulness. **-ly** *adv.* [L. *genialis*].

ge·ni·e (jē´·ni·) *n.* a jinni. *pl.* **genii** (jē´·ni·ī) [corrupt. of Arab. *jinnee*].

gen·i·tal (jen´·ạ·tạl) *a.* pert. to generation, or to the organs of generation. **-s** *n.pl.* the external sexual organs. Also **genitalia** (jen·ạ·tā´·-li·ạ) [L. *genitalis*, fr. *gignere*, to beget].

gen·i·tive (jen´·ạ·tiv) *a.* pert. to, or indicating, source, origin, possession, etc.; *n.* (*Gram.*) the case used to indicate source, origin, possesion and the like [L. *genitivus*].

gen·ius (jēn´·yạs) *n.* one's mental endowment or individual talent; the animating spirit of a people, generation or locality; uncommon intellectual powers; a person endowed with the highest mental gifts [L.].

gen·o·cide (jen´·ạ·sīd) *n.* race murder. **genocidal** *a.* [Gk. *genos*, race; L. *caedere*, to kill].

gen·re (zhàn´·rạ) *n.* a kind; sort; style. **— painting,** painting which portrays scenes in everyday life [Fr. = style, kind].

gent (jent) *n.* (*Colloq.*) a gentleman; a would-be gentleman [abbrev. fr. *gentleman*].

gen·teel (jen·tēl′) *a.* possessing the qaulities belonging to high birth and breeding; well-bred; stylish; refined. **-y** *adv.* **-ness** *n.* **gentility** (jen·til′·i·ti) *n.* [Fr. *gentil*].

gen·tian (jen′·shạn) *n.* the common name of Gentiana, plants whose root is used medicinally as a tonic and stomachic; its flower is usually of a deep, bright blue [L. *gentiana*].

gen·tile (jen′·tīl) *n.* one who is not a Jew; *a.* formerly (among Christians), heathen [L. *gens*, a nation].

gen·tle (jen′·tl) *a.* kind and amiable; mild and refined in manner; quiet and sensitive of disposition; meek; moderate; gradual; of good family; *v.t.* (*Colloq.*) to tame; to make docile. **gently** *adv.* **-folk** *n.pl.* persons of good breeding and family. **-ness** *n.* **gentry** (jen′·tri·) *n.* people of birth and good breeding; the class of people between the nobility and the middle class [L. *gentilis*].

gen·tle·man (jen′·tl·mạn) *n.* a man of good breeding and refined manners; a man of good family; a polite term for a man. *pl.* **gentlemen. -ly** *a.* **-like** *a.* **gentlewoman** *n.* a woman of good family or of good breeding; a woman who waits upon a person of high rank. **-'s gentleman**, a valet. **-'s agreement**, one binding in honor but not legally [L. *gentilis*].

gen·u·flect (jen′·yoo·flekt) *v.i.* to bend the knee, esp. in worship. **genuflection, genuflexion** *n.* **-or** *n.* **-ory** *a.* [L. *genu*, the knee; *flectere*, to bend].

gen·u·ine (jen′·yoo·in) *a.* real; true; pure; authentic; sincere. **-ly** *adv.* [L. *genuinus*].

ge·nus (jē′·nạs) *n.* a class; an order; a kind; (*Nat. Hist.*) a subdivision ranking next above species, and containing a number of species having like characteristics. *pl.* **genera** (jen′·ạ·rạ) [L. *genus, generis*, a kind].

ge·o-, ge- combining forms fr. Gk. *gē*, meaning earth, ground, soil. **geocentric** *a.* (*Astron.*) having reference to the earth as center [Gk. *kentron*, the center].

ge·ode (jē′·ōd) *n.* in mineralogy, a rounded nodule of stone, containing a cavity, usually lined with crystals [Gk. *geōdēs*, earth-like].

ge·od·e·sy (jē·ȧd′·ạ·si·) *n.* the mathematical survey and measurement of the earth's surface, involving allowance for curvature. **geodetic, geodetical** *a.* [Gk. *gē; daiein*, to divide].

ge·og·ra·phy (jē·ȧg′·rạ·fi·) *n.* the science of the earth's form, its physical divisions into seas, rivers, mountains, plains, etc.; a book on this. **geographer** *n.* one versed in geography. **geographic, geographical** *a.* pert. to geography. **geographically** *adv.* [Gk. *gē*, the earth; *graphein*, to write].

ge·ol·o·gy (jē·ȧl′·ạ·ji·) *n.* the science of the earth's crust, the rocks, their strata, etc. **geological** *a.* **geologically** *adv.* **geologist** *n.* [Gk. *gē*, the earth; *logos*, discourse].

ge·om·e·try (jē·ȧm′·ạ·tri·) *n.* the mathematical study of the properties of lines, angles, surfaces, and solids. **geometric(al)** *a.* pert. to geometry. **geometrically** *adv.* **geometrician** *n.* one skilled in geometry. **geometric progression** (*Math.*) a series of quantities in which each quantity is obtained by multiplying the preceding term by a constant factor, e.g. 2, 6, 18, 54, etc. (3 being the constant factor) [Gk. *gē*, the earth; *metron*, a measure].

ge·oph·a·gy (jē·ȧf′·a·ji·) *n.* the practice of eating earth, dirt, clay, etc. Also **geophagism** *n.* [Gk. *gē*, earth; *phagein*, to eat].

ge·o·pol·i·tics (jē·ō·pȧl′·ạ·tiks) *n.pl.* the study of the influence of geographical situation upon the politics of a nation. **geopolitical** *a.* [Gk. *gē*, the earth; *politēs*, a citizen].

geor·gette (jawr·jet′) *n.* a fine semi-transparent silk fabric [fr. *Georgette*, Fr. modiste].

geor·gic (jawr′·jik) *n.* a pastoral poem [Gk. *gē*, the earth; *ergon*, a work].

ge·ot·ro·pism (jē·ȧt′·rạ·pizm) *n.* (*Bot.*) the tendency of a growing plant to direct its roots downwards. **geotropic** *a.* [Gk. *gē*, the earth; *tropos*, a turning].

ge·ra·ni·um (jạ·rā′·ni·ạm) *n.* plant having showy flowers [Gk. *geranos*, a crane].

ger·i·at·rics (jer·i·at′·riks) *n.* science of the diseases and care of the old [Gk. *geras*, old age].

germ (jurm) *n.* the rudimentary form of a living thing, whether animal or plant; a microscopic organism; a microbe; a bud; that from which anything springs. **-icide** *n.* a substance for destroying disease-germs. **germicidal** *a.* **— warfare** waged with bacteria for weapons [L. *germen*, a bud].

ger·man (jur′·mạn) *a.* closely related. **germane** (jer·mān′) *a.* appropriate; relevant; allied; akin [L. *germanus*, fully akin].

Ger·man (jur′·mạn) *a.* belonging to *Germany*; *n.* a native of Germany; the German language. **Germanic** *a.* pert. to Germany; Teutonic. **Germanize** *v.t.* to make German. **German measles**, a disease like measles, but less severe [L. *Germanus*].

ger·man·der (jẹr·man′·dẹr) *a.* genus of herb-like plants having medicinal properties [Gk. *chamai*, on the ground; *drus*, a tree].

ger·ma·ni·um (jur·mā′·ni·ạm) *n.* a rare metallic element [L. *Germanus*, German].

ger·mi·nal (jur′·mạ·nal) *a.* pert. to a germ or seed-bud [L. *germen*, bud].

ger·mi·nate (jur′·mạ·nāt) *v.i.* to sprout; to bud; to shoot; to begin to grow; *v.t.* to cause to grow. **germinative** *a.* pert. to germination. **germination** *n.* [L. *germen*, a bud].

ger·on·tol·o·gy (jẹr·ạn·tȧl′·ạ·ji·) *n.* the science that studies the decline of life, esp. of man [Gk. *geron*, an old man].

ger·ry·man·der (ger-, jer·i·man′·dẹr) *v.t.* to arrange or redistribute electoral districts to private advantage [fr. Gov. *Gerry* of Mass.].

ger·und (jer′·ạnd) *n.* part of the Latin verb used as a verbal noun; the dative of the O.E. or modern English infinitive, used to express purpose. **gerundial** *a.* of the nature of a gerund. **gerundive** *n.* the future passive participle of a Latin verb expressing the action of having to be done [L. *gerere*, to do].

ge·stalt (ge·shtawlt′) *n.* pattern; a whole which is more than the sum of its parts [Ger.].

Ge·sta·po (gạ·stȧp′·ō) *n.* the secret police of the German Nazi party [contr. of *Geheime Staatspolizei* = secret state-police].

ges·ta·tion (jes·tā′·shạn) *n.* carrying young in womb; pregnancy [L. *gestare*, to bear].

ges·tic·u·late (jes·tik′·yạ·lāt) *v.i.* to make violent gestures or motions, esp. with hands and arms, when speaking. **gesticulation** *n.* a gesture [L. *gestus*, gesture].

ges·ture (jes′·chẹr) *n.* a motion of the head, hands, etc. as a mode of expression; an act indicating attitude of mind; *v.i.* to make gestures [L. *gerere*, to do].

get (get) *v.t.* to procure; to obtain; to gain possession of; to come by; to win, by almost any means; to receive; to earn; to induce or persuade; (*Colloq.*) to understand; (*Arch.*) to beget; *v.i.* to become; to reach or attain; to bring one's self into a condition. *pr.p.* **-ting**. *pa.t.* **got**. *pa.p.* **got, gotten. -away** (get′·a·wā) *n.* (*Colloq.*) escape. **get-up** *n.* (*Colloq.*) equipment; dress; energy [O.E. *gitan*].

gew·gaw (gū′·gaw) *n.* a showy trifle; a bauble [O.E. *gifu*, a gift].

gey·ser (gī′·zer) *n.* a hot spring which spouts water intermittently [O.N. *geysa*, to gush].

ghast·ly (gast′·li·) *a.* horrible; shocking. Also *adv.* **ghastliness** *n.* [O.E. *gaestlic*, terrible].

gher·kin (gur′·kin) *n.* a small species of cucumber used for pickling [Dut. *agurkje*].

ghet·to (get′·ō) *n.* a section to which Jews were restricted; a section of a city in which members of a national or racial group live or are restricted [It.].

ghost (gōst) *n.* the apparition of a dead person; a specter; a disembodied spirit; semblance or shadow; (*Colloq.*) a person who does literary or artistic work for another, who takes the credit for it. **-ly** *a.* **-liness** *n.* **-like** *a.* **Holy Ghost,** the Holy Spirit; the third element in the Trinity [O.E. *gast*].

ghoul (gōōl) *n.* imaginary evil being. **-ish** *a.* [Ar. *ghul*].

gi·ant (jī'·ant) *n.* (*fem.* **giantess**) a man of extraordinary bulk and stature; a person of unusual powers, bodily or intellectual; *a.* like a giant. **-ism** *n.* (*Med.*) abnormal development [Fr. *géant*].

gib·ber (jib'·er) *v.i.* and *t.* to speak rapidly and inarticulately; to chatter. **-ish** *n.* meaningless speech; nonsense [imit. origin].

gib·bet (jib'·it) *n.* a gallows; *v.t.* to hang on a gallows [O.Fr. *gibet*, a stick].

gib·bon (gib'·an) *n.* a tailless, long-armed ape of S.E. Asia [Fr.].

gib·bous (gib'·as) *a.* rounded and bulging [L. *gibbus*, a hump].

gibe, jibe (jīb) *v.i.* to taunt; to sneer at; to scoff at; *n.* an expression of contempt; a taunt.

gib·lets (jib'·lits) *n. pl.* the internal edible parts of poultry, e.g. heart, liver, gizzard, etc. [O.Fr. *gibelet*].

gid·dy (gid'·i·) *a.* dizzy; feeling a swimming sensation in the head; liable to cause this sensation; whirling; flighty; frivolous. **giddily** *adv.* **giddiness** *n.* [O.E. *gydig*, insane].

gift (gift) *n.* a present; a thing given; a donation; natural talent; faculty; power; *v.t.* to endow; to present with; to bestow. **-ed** *a.* possessing natural talent. **-edness** *n.* [fr. *give*].

gig (gig) *n.* a light carriage with one pair of wheels, drawn by a horse; a ship's boat.

gi·gan·tic (jī·gan'·tik) *a.* like a giant; of extraordinary size; huge. **-ally** *adv.* [Gk. *gigas*].

gig·gle (gig'·l) *v.i.* to laugh in a silly way, with half-suppressed catches of the breath; *n.* such a laugh. **-r** *n.* **giggling** *n.* [imit. origin].

gig·o·lo (jig'·a·lō) *n.* a professional male dancing-partner [Sp.].

gild (gild) *v.t.* to overlay with gold-leaf or gold-dust; to make gold in color; to brighten; to give a fair appearance to; to embellish [O.E. *gyldan*].

gill (jil) *n.* a measure of capacity containing one fourth of a pint [O.Fr. *gelle*].

gill (gil) *n.* the organ of respiration in fishes and other water animals (usually *pl.*) [Scand.].

gill (gil) *n.* a ravine or narrow valley, with a stream running through it. Also **ghyll** [O.N. *gil*, a fissure].

gilt (gilt) *n.* a thin layer of gold, or something resembling gold; *a.* yellow like gold; gilded. **-edged** *a.* having the edges gilded; of the best quality [O.E. *fyldan*].

gim·bals (jim'·balz, gim'·balz) *n.pl.* a contrivance of rings and pivots for keeping a ship's compass, etc. always in a horizontal position [L. *gemelli*, twins].

gim·crack (jim'·krak) *n.* a showy or fanciful trifle; *a.* showy but worthless [E. *jim*, neat; *crack*, a lad, a boaster].

gim·let (gim'·lit) *n.* a small implement with a screw point and a cross handle, for boring holes in woods; *v.t.* [O.Fr. *guimbelet*].

gim·mick (gim'·ik) *n.* (*Slang*) any device by which a magician works a trick; a gadget.

gimp (gimp) *n.* a narrow fabric or braid used as an edging or trimming [Fr. *guimpe*].

gin (jin) *n.* a distilled alcoholic beverage, flavored with juniper berries, orange peel, etc. [Fr. *genièvre* fr. L. *juniperus*, juniper].

gin (jin) *n.* a snare or trap; a machine for separating the seeds from cotton; *v.t.* to clear cotton of seeds by a gin; to catch in a snare. *pr.p.* **-ning.** *pa.p.* and *pa.t.* **-ned** [fr. *engine*].

gin·ger (jin'·jer) *n.* a plant of the Indies with a hot-tasting spicy root; (*Slang*) spirit; a light reddish-yellow color; *v.t.* to flavor with ginger. **— ale** *n.* an effervescent beverage. **-bread** *n.* a cake, flavored with ginger and molasses; showy ornamentation. **-y** *a.* hot and spicy [L. *zingiber*].

gin·ger·ly (jin'·jer·li·) *adv.* cautiously; carefully.

ging·ham (ging'·am) *n.* a kind of cotton cloth, usually checked or striped [Jav. *ginggang*, striped].

gin·gi·vi·tis (jin·ji·vī'·tis) *n.* inflammation of the gums [L. *gingiva*, the gum; *-itis*, inflammation].

gin rum·my (jin·rum'·i·) *n.* a card game for two or more players.

gin·seng (jin'·seng) *n.* a plant, the root valued as medicine [Chin. *jin-tsan*].

gip·sy See **Gypsy**.

gi·raffe (ja·raf') *n.* an African animal with spotted coat and very long neck and legs [Fr. fr. Ar. *zaraf*].

gird (gurd) *v.t.* to encircle with any flexible band; to put a belt around; to equip with, or belt on, a sword. *pa.p.* and *pa.t.* **-ed** or **girt.** **-er** *n.* an iron or steel beam used as a support in constructional engineering [O.E. *gyrdan*].

gir·dle (gur'·dl) *n.* that which girds or encircles, esp. the waist; a tight-fitting undergarment worn for support of the lower part of the body; *v.t.* [O.E. *gyrdel*.]

girl (gurl) *n.* a female child; a young unmarried woman. **-hood** *n.* the state, or time, of being a girl. **-ish** *a.* like a girl. **-ishly** *adv.* **-ishness** *n.* [M.E. *gurle*].

girt (gurt) alternate *pa.p.* and *pa.t.* of **gird.**

girth (gurth) *n.* band to hold a saddle, blanket, etc. in place on a horse; a girdle; the measurement around a thing [fr. *gird*].

gist (jist) *n.* the main point of a question; the substance or essential point of any matter [O.Fr. *gist*, it lies].

give (giv) *v.t.* to bestow; to make a present of; to grant; to deliver; to impart; to assign; to yield; to supply; to make over; to cause to have; to pronounce, as an opinion, etc.; to pledge, as one's word; *v.i.* to yield; to give away; to move; *n.* elasticity; a yielding to pressure. *pr.p.* **giving.** *pa.p.* **given.** *pa.t.* **gave.** **-n** *a.* granted; admitted; supposed; certain; particular; addicted to; inclined to. **-r** *n.* **to give away,** to bestow; (*Colloq.*) to betray [O.E. *giefan*].

giz·zard (giz'·erd) *n.* a bird's strong muscular second stomach [O.Fr. *gezier*].

gla·cé (gla·sā') *a.* of a cake, iced; of a kind of leather, polished or glossy; of fruits, candied [Fr. *glace*, ice].

gla·cier (glā'·sher) *n.* a mass of ice, formed by accumulated snow in high cold regions, which moves very slowly down a mountain. **glacial** (glā'·shal) pert. to ice or its action; pert. to glaciers; icy; frozen; crystallized. **glaciate** *v.t.* to cover with ice; to turn to ice. **glaciology** *n.* the scientific study of the formation and action of glaciers [Fr. *glace*, ice].

glad (glad) *a.* pleased; happy; joyous; giving joy. **-den** *v.t.* to make glad; to cheer; to please. **-ly** *adv.* with pleasure; joyfully; cheerfully. **-ness** *n.* **-some** *a.* giving joy; cheerful; gay. **glad rags** (*Slang*) dressy clothes [O.E. *glaed*].

glade (glād) *n.* a grassy open space in a wood.

glad·i·a·tor (glad'·i·ā·ter) *n.* literally, a swordsman; a combatant who fought in the arena; one involved in a fight [L. *gladius*, a sword].

glad·i·o·lus (glad·i·ō'·las) *n.* a plant of the iris family, with long sword-shaped leaves [L. *gladius*, a sword].

Glad·stone (glad'·stōn) *n.* a leather traveling-bag hinged along the bottom to open out flat [fr. Brit. statesman, W. E. *Gladstone*].

glair (gler) *n.* white of egg; size or gloss made

from it; any substance resembling it; *v.t.* to smear with glair. **-eous, -y** *a.* [Fr. *glaire*].

glam·our (glam′·ẽr) *n.* deceptive or alluring charm; witchery. **-ous** *a.* Also **glamor** [corrupt. of *gramarye*, magic].

glance (glans) *n.* a quick look; a glimpse; a flash or sudden gleam of light; an allusion or hint; an oblique hit; *v.t.* to cast a glance; *v.i.* to give a swift, cursory look; to allude; to fly off in an oblique direction; to flash or gleam. **glancing** *a.* [Ger. *Glanz*, luster].

gland (gland) *n.* an organ or collection of cells secreting and abstracting certain substances from the blood and transforming them into new compounds. **-ers** *n.* a disease of horses. **-ular, -ulous** *a.* consisting of or pert. to glands [L. *glans*, an acorn].

glare (glār) *n.* a strong, dazzling light; an overwhelming glitter; showiness; a fierce, hostile look or stare; *v.i.* to shine with a strong dazzling light; to be too showy; to stare in a fierce and hostile manner. **glaring, glary** *a.* brilliant; open and bold [O.E. *glaer*, amber].

glass (glas) *n.* a hard, brittle, generally transparent substance formed by fusing silica with fixed alkalis; articles made of glass, e.g. a drinking-glass or tumbler, a looking-glass or mirror, a telescope, a weather glass or barometer; the quantity contained in a drinking glass; *a.* made of glass; *v.t.* to cover with glass; to glaze. **-es** *n.pl.* spectacles. **-y** *a.* made of glass; vitreous; like glass; dull or lifeless. **-ily** *adv.* **-iness** *n.* **-ful** *n.* the contents of a glass. **— blowing** *n.* the art of shaping and fashioning glass by inflating it through a tube, after heating. **— blower** *n.* **-ware** *n.* articles made of glass [O.E. *glaes*].

glau·co·ma (glaw·kō′·ma) *n.* (*Med.*) a serious eye disease causing tension and hardening of the eyeball with progressive loss of vision [Gk.].

glau·cous (glaw′·kas) *a.* sea-green; covered with a fine bloom, as a plum [Gk. *glaukos*, blue-gray].

glaze (glāz) *n.* the vitreous, transparent coating of pottery or porcelain; any glossy coating; *v.t.* to furnish with glass, as a window; to overlay with a thin, transparent surface, as earthenware; to make glossy. **-r** *n.* a workman who glazes pottery, cloth, etc. **glazier** (glā′·zhẽr) *n.* one who sets glass in windows, etc. [O.E. *glaes*, glass].

gleam (glēm) *n.* a faint or transient ray of light; brightness; glow; *v.i.* to shoot or dart, as rays of light; to flash; to shine faintly [O.E.].

glean (glēn) *v.t.* to gather after a reaper, as grain; to collect with patient labor; to cull the fairest portion of; to pick up (information); *v.i.* to gather. **-er** *n.* **-ings** *n.pl.* what is collected by gleaning [O.Fr. *glener*].

glebe (glēb) *n.* soil; ground; land belonging to a parish church [L. *gleba*, a clod].

glede (glēd) *n.* a bird of prey [O.E. *glida*].

glee (glē) *n.* mirth; merriment; joy; a part song for three or more voices. **-ful** *a.* **-fully** *adv.* **-fulness** *n.* **— club** *n.* a group of singers [O.E. *gleo*, mirth].

gleet (glēt) *n.* thin watery discharge from a sore [O.Fr. *glete*, a flux].

glen (glen) *n.* a valley, usually wooded and with a stream [Gael. *gleann*].

glen·gar·ry (glen·gar′·i·) *n.* a Highlander's cap, boat-shaped, with two ribbons hanging down behind [fr. *Glengarry*, Scotland].

glib (glib) *a.* smooth; fluent. **-ly** *adv.* **-ness** *n.*

glide (glīd) *v.i.* to move gently or smoothly; to go stealthily or gradually; of an airplane, to move, or descend, usually with engines shut off; *n.* a sliding movement. **-r** *n.* one who or that which, glides; a plane capable of flight without motive power, by utilizing air currents [O.E. *glidan*].

glim·mer (glim′·ẽr) *v.i.* to shine faintly and unsteadily; to flicker; *n.* a faint, unsteady light; a faint glimpse; an inkling. Also **-ing** *n.* and *a.* [M.E. *glimeren*].

glimpse (glimps) *n.* a momentary view; a passing appearance; a faint notion; *v.t.* to catch a glimpse of; *v.i.* to look briefly [M.E. *glimsen*, to shine faintly].

glint (glint) *n.* glitter; a faint gleam; a flash; *v.i.* to glitter [M.E. *glent*].

glis·sade (gli·sād′, ·sàd′) *n.* the act of sliding down a slope of ice or snow; in dancing, a gliding step sideways; *v.i.* to perform a glissade [Fr. *glisser*, to slide].

glis·ten (glis′·n) *v.i.* to glitter; to sparkle; to shine; *n.* [O.E. *glisnian*].

glit·ter (glit′·ẽr) *v.i.* to shine with a bright, quivering light; to sparkle; to be showy and attractive; *n.* a bright, sparkling light; brilliance [O.N. *glitra*].

gloam·ing (glō·ming) *n.* twilight; dusk [O.E.].

gloat (glōt) *v.i.* to gaze with adulation; to think about with evil satisfaction. **-ing** *a.*

globe (glōb) *n.* a round body; a sphere; a heavenly sphere, esp. the earth; a sphere with a map of the earth or the stars; anything approximately of this shape, e.g. a fish bowl, a lamp shade, etc. **global** *a.* taking in the whole world. **globate, globated** *a.* spherical. **globoid** *a.* globe-shaped. **globose, globous** *a.* round, spherical (or nearly so). **globosity** *n.* **globular** *a.* globe-shaped (or nearly so). **globularity** *n.* **globularly** *adv.* **globule** (glàb′·yool) *n.* a small particle of matter of a spherical form; a tiny pill. **globulous** *a.* **-trotter** *n.* traveler; tourist [L. *globus*, a round mass].

glob·u·lin (glàb′·ya·lin) *n.* one of the proteins of the blood [fr. *globule*].

glock·en·spiel (glàk′·an·spēl) *n.* a musical instrument consisting of a row of bells suspended from a rod, or of a series of flat bars, which when struck with a mallet give forth a bell-like sound; a carillon [Ger. *Glocke*, a bell; *Spiel*, play].

glom·er·ate (glàm′·a·rit) *a.* gathered into a cluster. **glomeration** *n.* [L. *glomus*, a ball].

gloom (glŏŏm) *n.* thick shade; partial or almost total darkness; melancholy; *v.i.* to become dark or threatening; to be dejected. **-y** *a.* dark and dreary; melancholy. **-ily** *adv.* **-iness** *n.* [O.E. *glom*].

glo·ry (glō′·ri·) *n.* renown; whatever brings honor; praise and adoration; divine happiness; height of excellence or prosperity; splendor or brilliance; a halo; *v.i.* to be proud; boast; to exult triumphantly. **gloriole** (glō′·ri·ōl) *n.* a halo. **glorious** *a.* illustrious; conferring renown; splendid; noble. **gloriously** *adv.* **gloriousness** *n.* **glorify** *v.t.* to exalt; to praise esp. in worship; to make eternally blessed; to shed radiance on; to magnify. **glorifier** *n.* **glorification** *n.* [L. *gloria*].

gloss (glaws) *n.* luster from a smooth surface; polish; a deceptively fine exterior; *v.t.* to make smooth and shining; to render plausible; (with *over*) to mitigate or excuse something harsh or unpleasant. **-y** *a.* smooth and shining [O.N. *glossi*, a blaze].

gloss (glaws) *n.* an explanatory note upon some word or passage in a text, written in the margin or between the lines; *v.t.* and *i.* to annotate [Gk. *glōssa*, the tongue].

glos·sal (glàs·al) *a.* (*Anat.*) pert. to the tongue [Gk. *glōssa*, the tongue].

glos·sa·ry (glàs′·a·ri·) *n.* a vocabulary of obscure or technical words; vocabulary to a book. **glossarial** *a.* **glossarist** *n.* a compiler of a glossary [Gk. *glōssa*, the tongue].

glot·tis (glàt′·is) *n.* (*Anat.*) the narrow opening at the top of the larynx or windpipe, between the vocal chords. **glottal** *a.* [Gk. fr. *glōssa, glotta*, the tongue].

glove (gluv) *n.* a cover for the hand and wrist

with a sheath for each finger; *v.t.* to cover with a glove. **-r** *n.* one who makes or sells gloves [O.E. *glof*].

glow (glō) *v.i.* to shine with an intense heat; to be bright or red; to feel hot, as the skin; to burn; to rage; *n.* incandescence; warmth or redness; sensation of warmth; ardor. **-ing** *a.* bright; warm; excited; enthusiastic. **-ingly** *adv.* [O.E. *glowan*].

glow·er (glou'·ẹr) *v.i.* to stare sullenly or with anger; a scowl.

gloze (glōz) *v.t.* to smooth over; to explain away; to flatter [M.E. *glosen*].

glu·cose (glŏŏ'·kōs) *n.* a white crystalline sugar obtained from fruits and honey [Gk. *glukus*, sweet].

glue (glŏŏ) *n.* an adhesive, gelatinous substance made by boiling skins, hoofs, etc. of animals; *v.t.* to join with glue; to cause to stick as with glue. **-y** *a.* [O.Fr. *glu*].

glum (glum) *a.* sullen; moody; morose. **-ness** *n.* **-ly** *adv.* [M.E. *glommen*, to frown].

glut (glut) *v.t.* overindulge; to fill to excess. *pr.p.* **-ting.** *pa.p.*, *pa.t.* **-ted** *n.* an oversupply [L. *gluttire*, to swallow].

glu·ten (glŏŏ'·tẹn) *n.* the protein of wheat and other cereals. **-ous** *a.* [L.].

glut·ton (glut'·n) *n.* one who eats too much; (*Fig.*) one eager for anything in excess, e.g. work, books, etc.; carnivore of weasel family, wolverine. **-ize** *v.i.* to eat to excess. **-ous** *a.* **-ously** *adv.* **-y** *n.* [Fr. *glouton*].

glyc·er·ine (glis'·ẹr·in) *n.* a sweet, colorless, odorless, syrupy liquid. Also **glycerol** [Gk. *glukeros*, sweet].

gly·co·gen (glī'·kạ·jin) *n.* the form in which the body stores carbohydrates (starch); animal starch [Gk. *glukus*, sweet].

gly·col (glī'·kōl) *n.* an artificial compound linking glycerine and alcohol used as an antifreeze.

glyph (glif) *n.* a shallow vertical channel or carved fluting [Gk. *gluphein*, to carve].

glyp·tic (glip'·tik) *a.* pert. to carving, esp. on gems. **-s** *n.pl.* the art of engraving on precious stones. **glyptograph** *n.* the engraving. **glyptography** *n.* [Gk. *glyptos*, carved].

gnar (nạr) *v.i.* to growl; to snarl.

gnarl (nạrl) *n.* a knot in wood or on the trunk of a tree. **-ed** (nạrld), **-y** *a.* knotty; knobby [M.E. *knurre*].

gnash (nash) *v.t.* to grind the teeth together, as in anger or pain; *n.* a grinding of the teeth. **-ing** *n.* [imit. origin].

gnat (nat) *n.* a kind of small biting insect [O.E.].

gnaw (naw) *v.t.* to wear away by scraping with the teeth; to bite steadily, as a dog a bone; to fret; to corrode; *v.i.* to use the teeth in biting; to cause steady pain. **-er** *n.* **-ing** *a.*, *n.* [O.E. *gnagan*].

gneiss (nīs) *n.* a metamorphic rock similar to granite [Ger.].

gnome (nōm) *n.* a fabled being resembling a misshapen dwarf, the guardian of precious metals hidden in the earth; a goblin [Gk. *gnōmē*, intelligence].

gnome (nōm) *n.* a wise saying; a maxim. **gnomic, gnomical** *a.* [Gk. *gnōmē*, thought].

gno·mon (nō'·mạn) *n.* the pin, rod, or plate which casts the shadow on a sundial; an indicator; (*Geom.*) the part of a rectangular figure which remains when a similar rectangle is taken from one corner of it. **-ic, -ical** *a.* [Gk. *gnōmōn*, pin of a sundial.]

gno·sis (nō'·sis) *n.* mystical knowledge. **gnostic** (nás'·tik) *a.* pert. to knowledge; having special knowledge [Gk. *gignoskein*, to know].

gnu (noō) *n.* antelope, resembling an ox; the wildebeest [Kaffir, *ngu*].

go (gō) *v.i.* to pass from one place or condition to another; to move along; to be in motion; to proceed; to depart; to elapse; to be kept; to put; to be able to be put; to result; to contribute to

a result; to tend to; to pass away; to become; to fare. *pr.p.* **-ing** *pa.p.* **gone** (gawn). *pa.t.* **went.** *n.* a going; (*Colloq.*) vigor; (*Colloq.*) an attempt; (*Colloq.*) a success. **-er** *n.* **-ing** *n.* the state of the ground or roads; working conditions. *a.* moving; successful. **-ings on** (*Colloq.*) usually in a bad sense, behavior; conduct. **gone** *a.* lost; beyond recovery; weak and faint. **-between** *n.* an intermediary. **-cart** *n.* wooden framework on casters, for teaching infants to walk. **to go in for,** to indulge in. **to go off,** to depart; to explode; to disappear; to become less efficient, popular, fashionable, etc. [O.E. *gan*].

goad (gōd) *n.* a sharp, pointed stick for driving cattle; anything that urges to action; *v.t.* to drive with a goad; to urge on; to irritate. [O.E. *gad*].

goal (gōl) *n.* an object of effort; an end or aim; in a race, the winning post; in football, hockey, etc., the space marked by two upright posts and a cross-bar; the act of kicking or driving the ball between these posts [Fr. *gaule*, a pole].

goat (gōt) *n.* a long-haired, ruminant quadruped with cloven hoofs and curving horns; the 10th sign of the Zodiac, Capricorn; (*Slang*) one who must take the blame for another. **-ee** (gō·tē') *n.* a small tuft of beard on the chin. **—herd** *n.* one who tends goats. **-ish** *a.* like a goat; lecherous. **to get one's goat** (*Colloq.*) to annoy or irritate one [[O.E. *gat*].

gob (gáb) *n.* a lump or mass. **gobbet** *n.* a small mass; a mouthful [O.Fr. *gobe*, a mouthful].

gob (gáb) *n.* (*Slang*) a nickname for U.S. sailor.

gob·ble (gáb'·l) *v.t.* to eat hurriedly or greedily. **-r** *n.* a greedy eater O.Fr. *gober*, to devour].

gob·ble (gáb'·l) *n.* the throaty, gurgling cry of the turkey cock; *v.i.* to make such a noise. **-r** *n.* a turkey [imit.].

gob·ble·dy·gook (gáb'·l·di·gook) *n.* (*Slang*) pompous, wordy talk or writing [fr. **gobble**].

Gob·e·lin (gáb'·ạ·lin) *n.* rich French tapestry [fr. *Gobelin*, tapestry makers in Paris].

gob·let (gáb'·lit) *n.* a drinking glass with a stem and foot [O.Fr. *gobelèt*].

gob·lin (gáb'·lin) *n.* an evil or mischievous sprite or elf; a gnome [Gk. *kobalos*, a mischievous spirit].

god (gád) *n.* a being of more than human powers; a divinity; an idol; any person honored unduly; any object esteemed as the chief good; *n.pl.* false deities; (G) the Supreme Being; Jehovah. **-dess** *n.* a female god or idol. **godly** *a.* reverencing God; pious; devout. **godliness** *n.* holiness; righteousness. **-less** *a.* wicked; impious; acknowledging no God. **godsend** *n.* an unexpected piece of good fortune. **-speed** *n.* a prosperous journey; a wish for success given at parting. **-forsaken** *a.* dreary; dismal [O.E. *god*, cf. Ger. *Gott*].

god·child (gád'·chīld) *n.* one for whom a person becomes sponsor, guaranteeing his religious education. Also. **-daughter, -son, -parent, -mother, -father,** the sponsor.

god·wit (gád'·wit) *n.* a long-billed wading bird [O.E. *god*, good; *wiht*, a creature].

gog·gle (gág'·l) *v.i.* to roll the eyes; to stare; *n.* a rolling of the eyes; *a.* rolling; bulging; protruding (of the eyes). **-s** *n.pl.* spectacles to protect the eyes [Gael. *gog*, a nod].

goi·ter (goi'·tẹr) *n.* a swelling on the front of the neck, the enlargement of the thyroid gland. **goitrous** *a.* [L. *guttur*, the throat].

gold (gōld) *n.* a precious metal of a bright yellow color; money; riches; a bright yellow color; *a.* made of gold; of color of gold. **-en** *a.* made of gold; having the color of gold; precious. **-finch** *n.* a beautiful bird, so named from its color. **-fish** *n.* a small fish of the carp family named from its color. **-smith** *n.* one who manufactures vessels and ornaments of gold. **-beater** *n.* one who beats gold into gold leaf. **-digger** *n.* one who digs or mines gold; (*Slang*) an unscrupulous flirt, expert at obtaining money from male friends. **-dust** *n.* gold in very fine particles. **-leaf** *n.* gold beaten into an extremely thin leaf or foil, used for gilding. **-mine** *n.* a mine from which gold is due; a source of wealth. **-plate** *n.* vessels or utensils made of gold (collectively). **-rush** *n.* the mad scramble to reach a new goldfield. — **standard**, a currency system under which banknotes are exchanged for gold at any time. **-en age**, the most flourishing period in the history of a nation. **-enrod**, a plant with branching clusters of small yellow flowers. **-en rule**, the rule of doing as you would be done by. **-en wedding**, the fiftieth wedding anniversary [O.E.].

golf (gàlf) *n.* out door game played with set of clubs and a ball, in which the ball is driven with the fewest possible strokes, into a succession of holes. *v.i.* to play this game. **-er** *n.* — **course**, — **links** tract of land for playing golf [Dut. *kolf*, a club].

gol·ly (gàl'·i·) *interj.* to express joy, sorrow, surprise, etc. [fr. *God*].

go·losh See **galosh**.

gon·ad (gōn'·ad) *n.* (*Biol.*) a gland that produces reproductive cells; ovary or testis. **-al** *a.* [Gk. *gonos*, seed].

gon·do·la (gàn'·dạ·lạ) *n.* a long, narrow, flat-bottomed boat, used in the canals of Venice. **gondolier** (gon·dạ·lēr') *n.* the boatman [It.].

gone (gawn) *pa.p.* of the verb **go**. **-r** *n.* (*Slang*) one who is in a hopeless state; *a.* beyond recovery [O.E. *gan*].

gong (gàng) *n.* a circular metal plate which gives out a deep note when struck with a soft mallet; anything used in this way; as a call to meals [Malay].

gon·o·coc·cus (gàn·ạ·kàk'·ạs) *n.* (*Med.*) microbe of gonorrhea. **gonorrhea** (gàn·ạ·rē'·ạ) *n.* [Gk. *gonos*, seed; *kokkos*, a berry; *rhoia*, a flowing].

good (good) *a.* commendable; right; proper; suitable; excellent; virtuous; honest; just; kind; affectionate; safe; sound; valid; solvent; adequate; full, as weight, measure, etc.; skillful. *comp.* **better**. *superl.* **best**. *n.* that which is good; welfare; well-being; profit; advantage; *n.pl.* property; wares; commodities; merchandise; (*Colloq.*) evidence of guilt; textiles; *interj.* well! right! so be it! **-ish** *a.* (of quality) pretty good; (of quantity) fairly plentiful. **-ly** *a.* handsome; pleasant; of considerable size. **-liness** *n.* **-ness** *n.* the quality of being good; *interj.* used for emphasis; *pl.* **-ies** candy; sweets. —**by** *interj.* contraction of God be with you!; farewell! *n.* a farewell. — **day** *interj.* greeting at meeting or parting. —**for-nothing** *a.* worthless; shiftless; *n.* a shiftless person; a loafer. — **humor** *n.* a happy or cheerful state of mind. —**humored** *a.* — **nature** *n.* natural kindness of disposition; **-natured** *a.* —**naturedly** *adv.* — **turn**, a kindly action. — **will** *n.* benevolence; kindly disposition; (*Commerce*) the right, on transfer or sale of a business, to the reputation, trade, and custom of that business. **to be to the good**, to show a profit [O.E. *god*].

goof (goof) *n.* (*Slang*) a silly person; a mistake. *v.*

goose (goos) *n.* a web-footed bird like a duck but larger; the flesh of the bird; a simpleton; a tailor's smoothing iron; *pl.* **geese** (gēs). **gosling** (gàz'·ling) *n.* a young goose. — **flesh** *n.* a bristling state of the skin due to cold or fright. — **step** *n.* (*Mil.*) a marching step with legs kept stiff and lifted high at each step; *v.i.* to use the goose step [O.E. *gos*].

goose·ber·ry (goos'·ber·i·) *n.* a thorny shrub cultivated for its fruit; fruit of the shrub.

go·pher (gō'·fer) *n.* in N. America, the ground-squirrel; a kind of rat with pouched cheeks [Fr. *gaufre*, a honeycomb].

gore (gōr) *n.* thick or clotted blood; blood. **gory** *a.* bloody [O.E. *gor*, dirt].

gore (gōr) *v.t.* to pierce with a spear, horns, or tusks [O.E. *gar*, a spear].

gore (gōr) *n.* a tapering piece of material inserted in a garment or a sail, to widen it; *v.t.* to cut into a wedge shape; to supply with a gore [O.E. *gara*, a pointed piece of land].

gorge (gawrj) *n.* a narrow pass between mountains; a full meal; *v.t.* to swallow with greediness; *v.i.* to feed greedily and to excess [L. *gurges*, a whirlpool].

gor·geous (gawr'·jis) *a.* splendid; showy; magnificent; richly colored. **-ly** *adv.* [O.Fr. *gorgias*].

Gor·gon (gawr'·gạn) *n.* (*Myth.*) one of three sisters of terrifying aspect; (*l.c.*) any one, esp. a woman, who is terrifying or repulsive looking. **-esque** *a.* repulsive [Gk. *gorgos*].

Gor·gon·zo·la (gawr·gạn·zō'·lạ) *n.* a milk cheese made in Italy [fr. *Gorgonzola*, Italy].

go·ril·la (gạ·ril'·ạ) *n.* an ape inhabiting W. Africa, of great size and strength [Afr.].

gor·mand See **gourmand**.

gorse (gawrs) *n.* (*Brit.*) a prickly shrub, bearing yellow flowers [O.E. *gorst*].

gosh (gàsh) *interj.* (*Colloq.*) a minced and very mild oath [corrupt. of *God*].

gor·y See **gore**.

gosh (gàsh) *interj.* (*Colloq.*) a minced and very mild oath [corrupt. of *God*].

gos·hawk (gàs'·hawk) *n.* a large powerful hawk [O.E. *gos*, a goose; *hafoc*, a hawk].

gos·ling See **goose**.

gos·pel (gàs'·pạl) *n.* glad tidings; the revelation of the Christian faith; story of Christ's life as found in first four books of New Testament; doctrine; belief accepted as infallibly true; *a.* pert. to, or in accordance with, the gospel [O.E. *god*, good; *spell*, a story].

gos·sa·mer (gàs'·ạ·mer) *n.* a filmy substance, like cobwebs; thin, gauzy material; *a.* light, thin and filmy [M.E. *gossomer*].

gos·sip (gàs'·ạp) *n.* idle talk about others, regardless of fact; idle talk or writing; one who talks thus; *v.i.* to talk gossip; to chat [M.E *god*, God; *sib*, related].

got (gàt) *pa.p.* and *pa.t.* of **get**.

Goth (gàth) *n.* a member of ancient Teutonic tribe; a barbarian. **-ic** *a.* pert. to Goths; barbarous; pert. to pointed-arch style of architecture; *n.* the language of Goths; (*l.c.*) a printing type Gothic [L. *Gothicus*].

got·ten *pa.p.* of **get**.

gouache (gwàsh) *n.* water-color painting with opaque colors mixed with water and gum; a picture painted thus [It. *guazzo*, a wash].

Gou·da (gou'·dạ) *n.* a well-known Dutch cheese [fr. *Gouda*, Holland].

gouge (gouj) *n.* a chisel with a curved cutting edge, for cutting grooves or holes; *v.t.* to cut or scoop out with a gouge; to hollow out; to force out, as the eye of a person, with the thumb or finger [Fr.].

gou·lash (goo'·làsh) *n.* a Hungarian stew.

gourd (gawrd) *n.* trailing or climbing plant: pumpkin, squash, etc.; large, fleshy fruit of this plant; its dried rind used as bottle, drinking vessel, etc.; a small-necked bottle or flask [L. *cucurbita*, a gourd].

gour·mand (goor'·mạnd) *n.* one fond of eating; a judge of fine foods. Also **gormand**, **gourmet** (goor'·mā) [Fr.].

gout (gout) *n.* a disease characterized by acute inflammation and swelling of the smaller joints. **-iness** *n.* **-y** *a.* [Fr. *goutte*, a drop].

gov·ern (guv'·ẹrn) *v.t.* to rule; to direct; to guide; to control; to regulate by authority; to keep in subjection; (*Gram.*) to be followed by a case, etc.; *v.i.* to exercise authority; to administer the laws. **-able** *a.* **-ance** *n.* directions; control; management. **-ess** *n.* woman with authority to control and direct; a lady, usually resident in a family, in charge of children's education. **-ment** n. act of governing; exercise of authority; the system of governing in a state or community; the ruling power in a state; territory over which rule is exercised; the administrative council or body; the executive power; control; rule. **-mental** a. **-or** n. the executive head of a state; a ruler; regulating mechanical device for velocity, pressure, etc. [L. *gubernare*, to steer].

gown (goun) n. a loose, flowing garment; outer dress of a woman; official robe of professional men and scholars, as in a university; v.t. to dress in a gown; v.i. to put on a gown [O.Fr. *gonne*, loose robe].

grab (grab) v.t. to grasp suddenly; to snatch; to clutch; to seize. pr.p. **-bing**. pa.p. and pa.t. **-bed**. n. a sudden clutch; unscrupulous seizure.

grace (grās) n. charm; attractiveness; easy and refined motion, manners, etc.; favor; divine favor; a short prayer of thanksgiving before or after a meal; a period of delay granted as a favor; the ceremonious title used when addressing a duke, or archbishop; v.t. to adorn; to honor; to add grace to. **-ful** a. displaying grace or charm in form or action; elegant; easy. **-fully** adv. **-fulness** n. **-less** a. lacking grace. **gracious** (grā'·shas) a. favorable; kind; friendly; merciful; pleasing; proceeding from divine grace; **graciously** adv. **graciousness** n. — **note** n. (*Mus.*) a note that is an embellishment, not essential to the melody [L. *gratia*, favor].

grac·ile (gras'·il) a. slender; gracefully slight. **gracility** n. [L. *gracilis*, slender].

gra·da·tion (gra·dā'·shan) n. successive stage in progress; degree; a step, or series of steps; the state of being graded or arranged in ranks. **gradate** (grā'·dāt) v.t. to cause to change by imperceptable degrees, as from one color to another [L. *gradatio*].

grade (grād) n. a step or degree in rank, merit, quality, etc.; a class or category; a mark or rating of a student's work; degree of rise of a slope; a gradient; v.t. to arrange in order, degree, or class; to gradate [L. *gradus*, a step].

gra·di·ent (grā'·di·ant) a. moving by steps; rising or descending by regular degrees; n. the degree of slope of a road or railway; an incline [L. *gradiens*, going, stepping].

grad·u·al (gra'·joo·al) a. proceeding by steps or degrees; progressive; changing imperceptibly; n. (*Eccl.*) book of music sung by the choir. **-ly** adv. [L. *gradus*, a step].

grad·u·ate (graj'·oo·āt) v.t. to grant a diploma or university degree; to mark with degrees; to divide into regular steps; v.i. to receive a diploma or university degree; (graj'·oo·it) n. one who has received a diploma or degree upon completing a course of study. **graduator** n. an instrument for dividing a line into regular intervals. **graduation** n. [L. *gradus*, a step].

graft, graff (graft, graf) v.t. to insert a bud or small branch of a tree into another; to transplant living tissue, e.g. skin, bone, etc. from one part of the body to another; n. a bud, etc. so inserted, or a piece of tissue so transplanted [Fr. fr. Gk. *grapheion*, a pencil].

graft (graft) v.i. to exercise political privilige; to use influence unfairly for self-advancement or profit; n. self-advancement or profit by unfair means. **-er** n.

gra·ham (grā'·am) a. made of whole-wheat flour [S. *Graham*, Amer. physician].

grail (grāl) n. a cup. **The Holy Grail**, in medieval legend, the cup or vessel used by Jesus at the Last Supper [O.Fr. *graal*, a flat dish].

grain (grān) n. a kernel, esp. of corn, wheat, etc.; fruit of certain kindred plants, viz. corn, wheat, rye, barley, oats, etc. (used collectively); any small, hard particle; slightest amount; the smallest unit of weight; that arrangement of

the particles of any body which determines its roughness, markings or texture; (*Fig.*) natural temperament or disposition; v.t. to paint in imitation of the grain of wood; to form into grains, as sugar, powder, etc. **-ed** (grānd) a. **against the grain**, i.e. against the fiber of the wood; hence (*Fig.*) against a natural inclination [L. *granum*, seed].

gram (gram) n. unit of weight in metric system = 15.432 grains. Also **gramme** [Fr. fr. Gk. *gramma*, small weight].

gram·mar (gram'·er) n. the science of language; a system of general principles for speaking and writing according to the forms and usage of a language; a textbook for teaching the elements of language. **-ian** (gra·me'·ri·an) n. a philologist; **grammatical** (gra·mat'·i·kal) a. pert to grammar; according to the rules of grammar [Gk. *gramma*, a letter].

gramme See **gram**.

gram·o·phone (gram'·a·fōn) n. a phonograph [Gk. *gramma*, a letter; *phonē*, sound].

gram·pus (gram'·pas) n. a blowing and spouting sea creature of the dolphin family [L. *crassus piscis*, a fat fish].

gran·a·ry (gran'·a·ri·) n. a storehouse for threshed grain; a barn [L. *granum*, grain].

grand (grand) a. great; high in power and dignity; illustrious; eminent; distinguished; imposing; superior; splendid; lofty; noble; sublime; dignified; majestic; chief; final; indicating family relationship of the second degree; n. (*Mus.*) a grand piano; (*Slang*) a thousand dollars. **-child** n. a son's or daughter's child. **-daughter, -son** n. a son's or daughter's daughter. **-ee** (gran·dē') n. a Spanish or Portuguese nobleman; a great personage. **-eur** (gran'·jer) n. nobility of action; majesty; splendor; magnificence. **-father (-mother)** n. a father's or mother's father (mother). **-father('s)-clock**, n. a tall, old-fashioned clock, standing on the floor. **-iloquence** (gran·dil'·a·kwens) n. lofty words or phrases; pomposity of speech. **-iloquent** a. **-iose** (gran'·di·os) a. imposing; striking; bombastic. **-iosely** adv. **-iosity** n. **-ly** adv. in a grand manner, splendidly. **-ma** n. grandmother. **-mother-clock** n. similar to a grandfather-clock but smaller. **-ness** n. greatness; magnificence. **-pa** n. a grandfather. **-parent** n. grandfather or grandmother. **—— piano**, a large harp-shaped piano, with a horizontal frame. **—— slam** (*Cards*) the winning of all the tricks at Bridge. **-stand** n. main seating structure for spectators at a sporting event [L. *grandis*, great].

grange (grānj) n. a farm; (*Cap.*) an association of farmers [L. *granum*, grain].

gran·ite (gran'·it) n. a hard igneous rock, consisting of quartz, feldspar, and mica; gray or pink in color [It. *granito*, grained].

gran·ny (gran'·i·) n. (*Colloq.*) grandmother; an old woman [abbrev. of *grandmother*].

grant (grant) v.t. to allow; to yield; to concede; to bestow; to confer; to admit as true; n. a bestowing; a gift; an allowance. **-er, -or** n. (*Law*) the person who transfers property [O.Fr. *garanter*, to promise].

gran·ule (gran'·yool) n. a little grain; a small particle. **granular** a. consisting of grains or granules. **granulate** v.t. to form into grains; to make rough on the surface; v.i. to be formed into grains. **granulated** a. **granulation** n. the process of forming into grains; (*Med.*) the development of new tissue in a wound, characterized by the formation of grain-like cells [L. *granulum*, dim. of *granum*, a grain].

grape (grāp) n. the fruit of the vine. **-ry** n. a place for the cultivation of grapes. **—— fruit** n. a large round citrus fruit with yellow rind. **—— sugar** n. a simple sugar, found abundantly in grapes; dextrose. **-vine** n. the grape-bearing vine plant; (*Colloq.*) a person-to-person means of secret communication. **sour grapes** (*Fig.*) things falsely despised merely because unattainable [Fr. *grappe*, a bunch of grapes].

graph (graf) *n.* a diagram or curve representing the variation in value of some phenomenon or relationship of two or more things, according to stated conditions; *v.t.* to show variation by means of a diagram. **-ic(al)** *a.* pert. to writing or delineating; truly descriptive; vivid. **-ically** *adv.* **-ic arts**, drawing, engraving, and painting. **-ics** *n.* the art of drawing, esp. mechanical drawing. **-ite** *n.* a natural form of carbon used in the making of the 'lead' of pencils; plumbago; blacklead. **-ology** *n.* the study of handwriting as an index of character [Gk. *graphein*, to write].

grap·nel (grap'·nal) *n.* an iron instrument with hooks or claws for clutching an object; a small anchor with several claws [O.Fr. *grape*, a hook].

grap·ple (grap'·l) *v.t.* to seize firmly; to seize with a grapnel; *v.i.* to come to grips; to contend; *n.* a grapnel; a grip; a contest at close quarters. **grappling-iron** *n.* a large grapnel [O.Fr. *grape*, a hook].

grasp (grasp) *v.t.* to seize firmly; to clutch; to take possession of; to understand. *v.i.* to endeavor to seize; to catch at; *n.* a firm grip of the hand; the power of seizing and holding; reach of the arms; mental power or capacity. **-ing** *a.* seizing; greedy of gain [O.E. *graspen*].

grass (gras) *n.* herbage; pasture for cattle; ground covered with grass; *v.t.* to cover with grass; to feed with grass. **-y** *a.* **-hopper** *n.* a jumping, chirping insect, allied to the locust family. **-land** *n.* permanent pasture-land. **—roots** (*Colloq.*) *a.* close to, or from, the people. **— widow** *n.* a woman separated or divorced from her husband [O.E. *gaers*].

grate (grāt) *n.* a frame of bars for holding fuel while burning; a framework of crossed bars. **grating** *n.* a partition of parallel or cross bars [L. *cratis*, a hurdle].

grate (grāt) *v.t.* to rub or scrape into small bits; to rub together with a harsh sound; *v.i.* sound harshly; to irritate. **-r** *n.* an instrument with a rough surface for rubbing off small particles [Fr. *gratter*, to scratch].

grate·ful (grāt'·fal) *a.* thankful; pleasant; [L. *gratus*, pleasing].

gra·ti·fy (grat'·a·fī) *v.t.* to give pleasure to; to satisfy. **-ing** *a.* **gratifier** *n.* one who gratifies. **gratification** *n.* the act of pleasing; satisfaction [L. *gratus*, pleasing].

grat·in (grå'·tan) *n.* (*Cookery*) a dish prepared with a covering of bread crumbs or cheese. **au gratin** (ō grå'·tan) *a.* food so cooked [Fr. *gratin*, fr. *gratter*, to grate].

gra·tis (grā'·tis) *adv.* free [L. *gratia*, a favor].

grat·i·tude (grat'·a·tūd) *n.* thankfulness [L. *gratus*, pleasing, thankful].

gra·tu·i·ty (gra·tū'·a·ti·) *n.* a gift of money for services rendered; a tip; something given freely. **gratuitous** *a.* free; voluntary; granted without obligation; asserted without cause or proof. **gratuitously** *adv.* [L. *gratuitus*, done without profit].

gra·va·men (gra·vā'·man) *n.* stress laid on a part; substantial ground or reason for a charge; a grievance [L. *gravis*, heavy].

grave (grāv) *n.* a hole dug for a dead body; a place of burial; (*Fig.*) death. **-stone** *n.* a memorial stone set at a grave. **-yard** *n.* a burial ground [O.E. *braef*].

grave (grāv) *a.* solemn; serious; weighty; important. **grave** (gràv) *n.* the 'grave' accent in French or its sign ('). **-ly** *adv.* [L. *gravis*, heavy].

grave (grāv) *v.t.* to engrave; to impress deeply. **-n image**, an idol [O.E. *grafan*, to dig].

grave (grāv) *v.t.* to clean a ship's bottom [Fr. *grève*, a beach].

grav·el (grav'·al) *n.* small stones; coarse sand; small pebbles; (*Med.*) an aggregation of minute crystals in the urine; *v.t.* to cover with gravel; to puzzle. (*Colloq.*) to irritate. **-ly** *a.* [O.Fr. *grave*, the beach].

grav·id (grav'·id) *a.* pregnant [L. *gravis*, heavy].

grav·i·tate (grav'·a·tāt) *v.i.* to obey the law of gravitation; to tend towards a center of attraction; to be naturally attracted to. **gravitation** *n.* the act of gravitating; the tendency of all bodies to attract each other. **gravitational, gravitative** *a.* [L. *gravis*, heavy].

grav·i·ty (grav'·a·ti·) *n.* weight; heaviness; seriousness; the force of attraction of one body for another, esp. of objects to the earth. **specific gravity**, the relative weight of any substance as compared with the weight of an equal volume of water [L. *gravitas*, fr. *gravis*, heavy].

gra·vy (grā'·vi·) *n.* the juices from meat in cooking; sauce made with this. (*Slang*) easy profit. **— boat** *n.* a dish for holding gravy.

gray, grey (grā) *a.* between black and white in color, as ashes or lead; clouded; dismal; turning white; hoary; aged; *n.* a gray color; a gray horse; *v.t.* to cause to become gray; *v.i.* to become gray. **-ish** *a.* somewhat gray. **— matter** the gray nerve tissue of the brain and spinal cord; (*Colloq.*) brains, intellect. **-ness** *n.* **-lag** *n.* wild goose [O.E. *graeg*].

graze (grāz) *v.t.* to touch lightly in passing; to abrade the skin thus; *n.* a light touch in passing; a grazing.

graze (grāz) *v.t.* to feed, as cattle, with grass; *v.i.* to eat grass or herbage [O.E. *grasian*].

grease (grēs) *n.* soft melted fat of animals; thick oil as a lubricant; (grēz, grēs) *v.t.* to apply grease to; (*Slang*) to bribe. **greasy** *a.* like grease; oily; fat; (*Fig.*) slippery. **— monkey** (*Slang*) a mechanic. **— paint** actors' make-up. **-r** *n.* **greasiness** *n.* [Fr. *graisse*, fr. *gras*, fat].

great (grāt) *a.* large in size or number; long in time or duration; admirable; eminent; uncommonly gifted; of high rank; mighty; pregnant; denoting relationship, either in the ascending or descending line; (*Slang*) splendid. **-ly** *adv.* **-ness** *n.* **-coat** *n.* an overcoat. **great-grandchild** *n.* the child of a grandchild. **Great Britain** England, Wales and Scotland. **Great Dane**, a large dog with short, smooth hair [O.E.].

greaves (grēvz) *n.pl.* the dregs of melted tallow [O.N.].

Gre·cian (grē'·shan) *a.* Greek; pert. to Greece; *n.* a native of Greece; a Greek scholar [L. *Graecus*].

greed (grēd) *n.* an eager and selfish desire; covetousness; avarice. **-y** *a.* having a keen desire for food, drink, wealth, etc.; ravenous. **-ily** *adv.* **-iness** *n.* [O.E. *graedig*, hungry].

Greek (grēk) *a.* pert. to Greece; Grecian; *n.* a native of Greece; the language of Greece [L. *Graecus*].

green (grēn) *a.* of color between blue and yellow; grass-colored; emerald-colored; containing its natural sap; unripe; inexperienced; easily deceived; sickly; wan. *n.* the color; a communal piece of grass-covered land; (*Golf*) the putting-green. *n.pl.* fresh leaves or branches; wreaths; green leafy vegetables. **-ery** *n.* a place where plants are cultivated; vegetation. **-ish** a somewhat green. **-ness** *n.* the quality of being green; freshness. **—eyed** *a.* having green eyes; (*Fig.*) jealous. **—eyed monster**, jealousy. **-gage** *n.* a small, green plum. **-heart** *n.* a very hard wood. **-horn** *n.* an inexperienced person. **-house** *n.* a glass building for keeping or growing plants. **— light** traffic signal to go; (*Colloq.*) authorization. **— thumb** apparent skill in growing plants. **-sward** *n.* turf [O.E.].

Greenwich time, (grin'·ij, gren·ich) the basis

for calculating standard time everywhere.

greet (grēt) *v.t.* to salute; to welcome; to accost; to receive. **-ing** *n.* a salutation; expression of good wishes [O.E. *gretan*].

gre·ga·ri·ous (gri·gar'·i·ạs) *a.* living in flocks or herds; fond of company. **-ly** *adv.* **-ness** *n.* [L. *gregarius,* fr. *grex,* a flock].

Gre·go·ri·an (gre·gō'·ri·ạn) *a.* pert. to the Popes Gregory I through XIII. — **calendar,** the present day calendar, introduced in 1582. — **chants,** unaccompanied music used in R.C. worship.

grem·lin (grem'·lin) *n.* (*World War* 2) a mischievous pixy haunting aircraft and causing engine trouble [Fr. dial. *grimelin,* brat].

gre·nade (gri·nād') *n.* an explosive shell or bomb, thrown by hand or shot from a rifle; a glass projectile containing chemicals. **grena·dier** (gren·a·dir') *n.* formerly, a soldier trained to throw grenades; a soldier in the Grenadier Guards of Brit. Army [Fr. *grenade,* a pomegranate].

gren·a·dine (gren'·a·dēn) *n.* a syrup for flavoring drinks [Fr. fr. *grenade*].

grew *pa.t.* of **grow.**

grey See **gray.**

grey·hound (grā'·hound) *n.* a swift, slender dog, used in racing [O.E. *grighund*].

grid (grid) *n.* a frame of bars; a grating; a grid-iron; (*Elect.*) a lead or zinc plate in a storage battery; (*Electronics*) an electrode of wire mesh in an electron tube [O.Fr. *gredil*].

grid·dle (grid'·l) *n.* flat utensil for cooking over direct heat; *v.t.* to cook on a griddle. [O.Fr. *gredil,* fr. L. *cratis,* hurdle].

grid·i·ron (grid'·ī·ẹrn) *n.* a framework of metal bars, for broiling meats, fish, etc.; a football field [O.Fr. *gredire, gredil,* a griddle].

grief (grēf) *n.* deep sorrow; pain; the cause of sorrow or distress [Fr. fr. L. *gravis,* heavy].

grieve (grēv) *v.t.* to cause grief; to afflict; to vex; to offend; *v.i.* to feel grief; to be distressed; to lament. **grievance** *n.* a real or imaginary complaint; a cause of grief or uneasiness. **-r** *n.* **grievous** *a.* causing sadness; atrocious. **grievously** *adv.* [O.Fr. *grever,* to afflict].

grill (gril) *v.t.* to broil on a gridiron; to question relentlessly; *n.* a cooking utensil for broiling meat, fish, etc.; the food cooked on one [Fr. *gril,* a gridiron].

grille (gril) *n.* a metal grating screening a window, doorway, etc. **grillwork** *n.* [O.Fr. *gredil,* a griddle].

grim (grim) *a.* stern; severe; of forbidding aspect; fierce; surly. **-ly** *adv.* **-ness** *n.* [O.E. *grimm,* fierce].

gri·mace (gri·mās') *n.* a distortion of the face to express contempt, dislike, etc.; a wry face; *v.i.* to make a grimace [Fr.].

gri·mal·kin (gri·mawl'·kin) *n.* an old cat, esp. a she-cat; a spiteful old woman.

grime (grīm) *n.* ingrained dirt; soot; *v.t.* to soil deeply; to dirty. **grimy** *a.* dirty.

grin (grin) *v.i.* to show the teeth as in laughter derision, or pain. *pr.p.* **-ning.** *pa.t., pa.p.* **-ned.** *n.* a wide smile [O.E. *grennian*].

grind (grīnd) *v.t.* to crush to powder between hard surfaces; to sharpen by friction; to rub harshly; to turn a crank to operate; to grate; *v.i.* to grind; (*Colloq.*) to work hard. *pa.p.* and *pa.t.* **ground.** *n.* the action of grinding; (*Colloq.*) a laborious task; (*Colloq.*) a hard-working student. **-ers** *n.pl.* (*Colloq.*) the teeth [O.E. *grindan*].

grin·go (gring'·gō) *n.* in Spanish-speaking America, a contemptuous name for a foreigner.

grip (grip) *n.* a firm hold; a grasp or pressure of the hand; a clutch; mastery of a subject, etc.· a handle; a suitcase; *v.t.* to grasp or hold tightly; (*Fig.*) to hold the attention of. *pr.p.* **-ping.** *pa.p., pa.t.* **-ped. -per** *n.* [O.E. *gripa*].

gripe (grīp) *v.t.* to grip; to oppress; to afflict

with sharp pains; *v.i.* to grasp at gain; to suffer griping pains; (*Colloq.*) to complain constantly; *n.* grasp; clutch; severe intestinal pain. **griping** *a.* [O.E. *gripan*].

grippe (grip) *n.* influenza [Fr.].

gris·ly (griz'·li·) *a.* grim; horrible. **grisliness** *n.* [O.E. *grislic,* terrible].

grist (grist) *n.* a supply of grain to be ground; the meal ground; (*Fig.*) profit; gain [O.E.].

gris·tle (gris'·l) *n.* a smooth, solid, elastic substance in animal bodies; cartilage [O.E.].

grit (grit) *n.* the coarse part of meal; particles of sand; coarse sandstone; (*Fig.*) courage; spirit; resolution; *pl.* grain coarsely ground; *v.t.* to grind (the teeth); to grate; *v.i.* to cover with grit. *pr.p.* **-ting.** *pa.t., pa.p.* **-ted. -ty** *a.* [O.E. *greot,* sand].

griz·zle (griz'·l) *n.* gray hair. **-d** *a.* gray; gray-haired. **grizzly** *a.* gray; *n.* a grizzly bear, a large ferocious bear of N. Amer. [Fr. *gris,* gray].

groan (grōn) *v.i.* to make a low deep sound of grief or pain; to be overburdened; *n.* the sound. **-er** *n.* **-ing** *n.* [O.E. *granian,* to weep].

groats (grōts) *n.pl.* hulled grain, esp. oats [O.E. *greot,* a particle].

gro·cer (grō'·sẹr) *n.* storekeeper. **-y** *n.* a store. **groceries** *n.pl.* goods sold by a grocer [O.Fr. *grossier,* wholesale].

grog (grȧg) *n.* a mixture of spirits, esp. rum and cold water. **-gy** *a.* drunk; unsteady; shaky [fr. Admiral Vernon (*Brit.*) who wore *grogram* breeches].

grog·ram (grȧg'·rạm) *n.* a coarse material of silk and mohair [O.Fr. *grosgrain*].

groin (groin) *n.* the depression where the abdomen joins the thigh.

grom·met (grȧm'·it) *n.* a metal eyelet used for fastening [Fr. *gourmette,* a curb-chain].

groom (grṏom) *n.* a servant in charge of horses; a bridegroom; an officer in the English royal household; *v.t.* to dress with neatness and care; to tend a horse.

groove (grṏov) *n.* a channel or hollow, esp. one cut by a tool; a rut; a routine; *v.t.* to cut a groove in [Dut. *groefe,* a trench].

grope (grōp) *v.t.* to feel about; to search blindly as if in the dark [O.E. *grapian*].

gros·beak (grōs'·bēk) *n.* a bird of the Finch family [Fr. *gros,* big; *bec,* a beak].

gros·grain (grō'·grān) *n.* corded ribbon or cloth [Fr. *gros grain,* large grain].

gross (grōs) *a.* coarse; indecent; crude; thick; rank; glaring; total, not net; *n.* twelve dozen; mass; bulk; *v.t.* to earn a total of. **-ly** *adv.* **-ness** *n.* [Fr. *gos,* big].

gro·tesque (grō·tesk') *a.* wildly formed; irregular in design or form; *n.* a whimsical figure; a caricature. **-ness** [Fr. fr. It. *grotta,* a grotto].

grot·to (grȧt'·ō) *n.* a natural cave; an artificial structure in gardens, etc. in imitation of such a cave. [It. *grotta*].

grouch (grouch) *n.* (*Colloq.*) a complaint; a a grumbler; *v.i.* to grumble. **-y** *a.* **-iness** *n.* [fr. *grudge*].

ground (ground) *pa.p.* and *pa.t.* of **grind.**

ground (ground) *n.* the surface of the earth; dry land; territory; a special area of land; soil; the sea bottom; reason; motive; basis; (*Elect.*) a conducting line between electrical equipment and the ground; (*Art*) the surface or coating to work on; *v.t.* to establish; to instruct in elementary principles; to place on the ground; (*Naut.*) to run ashore; *v.i.* to come to the ground. **-s** *n.pl.* dregs; sediment; lands around a house. **-less** *a.* without reason. **-ed** *a.* (*Aviat.*) of aircraft, unable to fly because of weather conditions. **-ing** *n.* the background; thorough knowledge of the essentials of a subject. **-work** *n.* foundation; basis; the essential part; first principles. — **rent** *n.* rent paid to a landlord for the privilege of building on his ground.

— **swell** *n.* a broad, deep swell of the ocean felt some distance from a storm [O.E. *grund*].

group (gròòp) *n.* a number of persons or things near, placed, or classified together; a class; a cluster, crowd, or throng; a military unit; (*Art*) two or more figures forming one artistic design; *v.t.* to arrange in groups; *v.i.* to fall into groups. **-ing** *n.* [Fr. *groupe*].

grouse (grous) *n.* a round, plump game-bird.

grouse (grous) *v.i.* (*Colloq.*) to grumble; to complain; *n.* a complaint.

grout (grout) *n.* coarse meal; thin mortar to fill cracks; plaster; *v.t.* to fill with grout [O.E. *gaut*, coarse meal].

grove (grōv) *n.* a group of trees [O.E. *graf*].

grov·el (gràv'·l, gruv'·l) *v.i.* to lie face downward, from fear or humility; to crawl thus; to abase oneself. **-er** *n.* **-ing** *a.* servile [O.N. *a grufa*, face downwards].

grow (grō) *v.t.* to produce by cultivation; to raise; *v.i.* to develop naturally; to increase in size, height, etc.; to become by degrees. *pa.p.* **-n.** *pa.t.* **grew** (gròò). **-er** *n.* **-th** (grōth) *n.* the process of growing; something already grown; (*Med.*) a morbid formation; a tumor. **grown-up** *n.* an adult [O.E. *growan*].

growl (groul) *v.i.* to make a low guttural sound, of anger or menacing like an animal; to grumble; *n.* such a sound. **-er** *n.* [imit. origin].

grub (grub) *v.t.* to dig superficially; to root up; *v.i.* to dig; to rummage; (*Fig.*) to plod; *n.* the larva of a beetle; that which is dug up for food; (*Slang*) food. *pr.p.* **-bing.** *pa.p.*, *pa.t.* **-bed.** **-ber** *n.* **-biness** *n.* the state of being grubby. **-by** *a.* unclean; dirty, grimy [M.E. *grobben*, to dig].

grudge (gruj) *v.t.* to be reluctant to give or allow; to envy; *n.* a feeling of ill will; resentment. **grudging** *a.* [O.Fr. *groucer*].

gru·el (gròò'·al) *n.* a food made by boiling oatmeal in water; a thin porridge; *v.t.* to subject to great strain. **-ing** *a.* exhausting [O.E. = crushed meal].

grue·some (gròò'·sam) *a.* causing horror, fear or loathing [M.E. *grue*, to shudder].

grum·ble (grum'·bl) *v.i.* to murmur with discontent; to complain; to make growling sounds; *n.* grumbling; a complaint [imit. origin].

grump·y (grum'·pi·) *a.* surly; irritable; gruff. **grumpily** *adv.* **grumpiness** *n.* [imit. origin].

grunt (grunt) *v.i.* of a pig, to make its characteristic sound; to utter a sound like this; *n.* a deep, guttural sound; a pig's sound. **-er** *n.* **-ing** *a.* [O.E. *grunnettan*].

Gru·yère (gròò·yer') *n.* a whole-milk cheese [fr. *Gruyère*, Switzerland].

guar·an·tee (gar·an·tē') *n.* formal assurance given by way of security; an assurance of the truth, genuineness, permanence, etc. of something, the one who receives such promise or assurance; guaranty; security; an assurance; *v.t.* to promise; to answer for. **guaranty** (gar'·an·ti·) *n.* a pledge of commitment; security; basis of security. **guarantor** *n.* [Fr. *garantir*, to protect].

guard (gàrd) *v.t.* to protect from danger; to accompany for protection; to watch by way of caution or defense; *v.i.* to keep watch; to take precautions; *n.* he who, or that which, guards; a sentry; a watch, as over prisoners; a protective device. **-ed** *a.* cautious; wary. **-edly** *adv.* **-house** *n.* a place for the detention of military prisoners. **-ian** *n.* a keeper; a protector; (*Law*) one who has custody of a minor. **-ianship** *n.* [Fr. *garde*].

gua·va (gwà'·va) *n.* a genus of tropical American trees and shrubs, bearing pear-shaped fruit used for jelly [Sp. *guayaba*].

gu·ber·na·to·ri·al (gòò·ber·na·tōr'·i·al) *a.* pert. to a governor [L. *gubernare*, to govern].

gudg·eon (guj'·un) *n.* a metal pin at the end of an axle on which the wheel turns; the socket of a hinge into which the pin fits [O.Fr. *gou-*

---

jon, pivot].

guer·don (gur'·dan) *n.* (*Poetic*) a reward [O.Fr. *gueredon*].

Guern·sey (gurn'·zi) *n.* breed of dairy cattle. **guernsey** *n.* knitted woolen shirt.

guer·ril·la guerilla (ga·ril'·a) *n.* a member of a band of irregular troops taking part in a war independently of the principal combatants; *a.* pert. to this kind of warfare [Sp. *guerrilla*, dim. of *guerra*, war].

guess (ges) *v.t.* and *i.* to estimate without calculation or measurement; to judge at random; to conjecture; to suppose; *n.* a rough estimate; a random judgment [M.E. *gessen*].

guest (gest) *n.* a visitor received or entertained; one living in a hotel, boarding-house, etc. [O.E. *gest*].

guf·faw (guf·aw') *n.* a burst of boisterous laughter; *v.i.* to laugh boisterously [imit.].

guide (gīd) *n.* one who shows the way; an adviser; an official accompanying tourists; a sign, mark, or device to indicate direction; a book of instruction or information; *v.t.* to lead; to direct; to influence; to act as a guide to. **guidance** *n.* direction. **-book** *n.* a descriptive handbook for tourists, travelers, etc. **guided missile**, powered rocket or other projectile which can be directed by remote control. **-post** *n.* a sign-post [Fr. *guider*, to guide].

guild (gild) *n.* a society for mutual help, or with a common object [O.E. *gild*, money].

guile (gīl) *n.* craft; cunning. **-ful** *a.* **-less** *a.* honest; innocent; sincere [O.Fr. *guile*, deceit].

guil·lo·tine (gil'·a·tēn) *n.* a machine for beheading by the descending stroke of a heavy blade; a paper cutting machine; *v.t.* to use a guillotine upon [fr. Joseph *Guillotin*].

guilt (gilt) *n.* the fact or state of having offended; criminality and consequent liability to punishment. **-y** *a.* judged to have committed a crime. **-ily** *adv.* **-iness** *n.* **-less** *a.* innocent [O.E. *gylt*, crime, fr. *gildan*, to pay].

guimpe (gimp) *n.* a short-sleeved blouse [Fr.].

guin·ea (gin'·i·) *n.* a former Brit. gold coin. — **fowl** *n.* a fowl allied to the pheasant. — **pig** *n.* (corrupt. of *Guiana* pig) a small rodent, used frequently in scientific experiments; (*Fig.*) a person used as a subject for experimentation [fr. *Guinea*, in W. Africa].

guise (gīz) *n.* external appearance, semblance; pretense [Fr. *guise*, manner].

gui·tar (gi·tàr') *n.* a six-stringed musical instrument resembling the lute. **-ist** *n.* a player of the guitar [Fr. *guitare*].

gulch (gulch) *n.* a ravine; a deep-walled valley.

gulf (gulf) *n.* a large bay; a sea extending into the land; a deep chasm; any wide separation; *v.t.* to swallow up [Gk. *kolpos*, a bay].

gull (gul) *n.* a long-winged, web-footed sea-bird [Bret. *gwelan*, to weep].

gull (gul) *n.* a dupe; a food; *v.t.* to deceive; to trick; to defraud. **-ible** *a.* easily imposed on; credulous. **-ibility** *n* [fr. *gull*, the sea-bird considered to be stupid].

gul·let (gul'·it) *n.* the tube from mouth to stomach; the throat [L. *gula*, the throat].

gul·ly (gul'·i·) *n.* a channel or ravine worn by water; a ravine; a ditch [fr. *gullet*].

gulp (gulp) *v.t.* to swallow eagerly; to swallow in large amounts; *v.t.* to gasp; to choke; *n.* an act of gulping; an effort to swallow; a large mouthful [imit.].

gum (gum) *n.* the firm flesh in which the teeth are set [O.E. *goma*, the jaws].

gum (gum) *n.* a sticky substance issuing from certain trees; this substance used for stiffening or adhesive purposes; resin; an adhesive; chewing gum; *v.t.* to coat with gum; *v.i.* to exude gum; to become clogged. *pr.p.* **-ming.** *pa.p.*, *pa.t.* **-med.** **-miness** *n.* **-my** *a.* consisting of gum; sticky. — **elastic** *n.* rubber. **-drop** *n.* small jelly-like candy. — **tree** *n.* any species of gum yielding tree: the eucalyptus, sour gum, sweet gum, etc. **chewing gum** *n.* a sticky preparation for chewing [Fr. *gomme*].

gum·bo (gum'·bō) *n.* okra; soup thickened with this.

gump·tion (gump'·shan) *n.* (*Colloq.*) resourcefulness; courage; common sense; courage.

gun (gun) *n.* a weapon consisting of a metal tube from which missiles are thrown by explosion; a firearm, cannon, rifle, pistol, etc.; a gun-like device; *v.i.* to shoot with a gun. *pr.p.* **-ning.** *pa.p.*, *pa.t.* **-ned. -ner** *n.* one who works a gun. **-nery** *n.* the firing of guns; the science of artillery. **-ning** *n.* the shooting of game. **-boat** *n.* a small armed patrol ship. **— metal** *n.* dark gray. **-powder** *n.* an explosive. **-runner** *n.* a gun smuggler. **-shot** *n.* the range of a gun; a shot fired from a gun. **-smith** *n.* one who makes, repairs, deals in guns. **a son of a gun** (*Colloq.*) a rascal [M.E. *gunne*].

gun·ny (gun'·i·) *n.* strong, coarse sacking made from jute [Hind.].

gun·nel See **gunwale**.

gun·wale (gun'·l) *n.* upper edge of the side of a boat or ship. Also **gunnel** [fr. *Gunhilda*, a medieval war engine].

gup·py (gup'·i·) *n.* tiny fresh-water fish [fr. R. T. L. *Guppy* of Trinidad].

gur·gi·ta·tion (gur·ja·tā'·shan) *n.* a surging rise and fall [L. *gurgitare*, to flood].

gur·gle (gur'·gl) *n.* a bubbling noise; *v.i.* to make a gurgle [imit.].

gush (gush) *v.i.* to flow out suddenly and copiously; (*Colloq.*) to display exaggerated and effusive affection; *n.* a sudden copious flow; (*Colloq.*) effusive talk. **-er** *n.* a gushing person; an oil-well with a natural flow. **-iness** *n.* **-ing, -y** *a.* effusive.

gus·set (gus'·it) *n.* a triangular piece of material inserted in a garment to strengthen or enlarge it [Fr. *gousset*, the arm-pit].

gust (gust) *n.* a sudden blast of wind; a burst of rain, etc.; an outburst of passion. **-y** *a.* [O.N. *gustr*].

gus·to (gus'·tō) *n.* keen enjoyment; zest; artistic style [L. *gustus*, taste].

gut (gut) *n.* a material made from animal intestines, as violin strings, etc.; tennis rackets; a narrow passage; a strait; *n.pl.* entrails; intestines; (*Colloq.*) courage; pluck; determination; *v.t.* to remove the entrails from; to destroy the interior as by fire. *pr.p.* **-ting.** *pa.p.* and *pa.t.* **-ted** [O.E. *guttas*, (pl.)].

gut·ter (gut'·er) *n.* a passage for water; a trough or pipe for conveying rain from the eaves of a building; a channel at the side of a road for carrying water; *v.t.* to make channels in; *v.i.* to flow in streams; of a candle to melt away so that wax runs off in channels. **-snipe** *n.* the common snipe; a child homeless or living in the streets [L. *gutta*, a drop].

gut·tur·al (gut'·er·al) *a.* pert. to or produced in the throat; *n.* a guttural sound [L. *guttur*, throat].

guy (gī) *n.* a rope or chain to steady a thing; boat, tent, etc.; *v.t.* to guide with a guy. Also **-rope** [O.Fr. *guier*, to guide].

guy (gī) *n.* (*Slang*) a fellow; *v.t.* (*Slang*) to ridicule; to make fun of [fr. *Guy* Fawkes].

guz·zle (guz'·l) *v.t.* and *i.* to drink greedily. **-r** *n.* [Fr. *gosier*, the gullet].

gybe See **jib, jibe**.

gym·kha·na (jim·ka'·na) *n.* a place for athletic games; a sports meet [Urdu *gend-khana*, a racket court, *lit.* a ball house].

gym·na·sium (jim·nā'·zi·am) *n.* a building or room equipped for physical training or sports; (gim·na'·zi·am) in Germany, a High School. *pl.* **gymnasia** or **-s. gymnast** (jim'·nast) *n.* an expert in gymnastics. **gymnastic** *a.* **gymnastics** *n.pl.* muscular and bodily exercises.

gym *n.* a gymnasium; a school athletic course

[Gk. *gymnasion* fr. *gumnos*, naked].

gy·ne·col·o·gy (ji· (or gī)·na·kál'·a·ji·) *n.* (*Med.*) the science which deals with the diseases and disorders of women, esp. the organs of generation. **gynecologist** *n.* Also **gynaecology**, etc. [Gk. *gunē*, a woman; *logos*, discourse].

gyp (jip) (*Slang*) *v.t.* to swindle, to steal; *n.* a cheat; a swindle.

gyp·sum (jip'·sam) *n.* a mineral, consisting mostly of sulfate of lime, used for making plaster of Paris [Gk. *gupsos*, chalk].

Gyp·sy (jip'·si·) *n.* one of a nomadic tribe of Indian origin· (*l.c.*) a person who resembles or lives like a Gypsy; *a.* of or like a Gypsy [corrupt. fr. *Egyptian*].

gy·rate (jī'·rāt) *v.i.* to revolve around a central point; to move in a circle; to move spirally. **gyratory** *a.* **gyration** *n.* a circular or spiral motion [L. *gyrare*, to turn, whirl].

gy·ro·man·cy (ji'·rō·man·si·) *n.* divination performed by drawing a circle, and walking in it till dizziness causes a fall [Gk. *guros*, a circle; *manteia*, divination].

gy·ro·scope (jī'·ra·skōp) *n.* a wheel so mounted that its axis can turn freely in any direction when set rotating and left undisturbed, it will maintain the same direction in space, independently of its relation to the earth Gk. *guros*, a circle; *skopein*, to view].

H

ha (há) *interj.* denoting surprise, joy, or grief [imit. origin].

ha·be·as cor·pus (hā'·bi·as kawr'·pas) *n.* writ requiring that a prisoner be brought to court to determine legality of confinement [L. = that you have the body].

ha·ber·dash·er (hab'·er·dash·er) *n.* a dealer in men's furnishings. **-y** *n.* [etym. uncertain].

ha·bil·i·ment (ha·bil'·a·mant) *n.* (usually in *pl.*) dress [Fr. *habiller*, to clothe].

hab·it (hab'·it) *n.* custom; usage; tendency to repeat an action in the same way; mental condition acquired by practice; dress, esp. a *riding-habit*; *v.t.* to dress; to clothe. **-ual** *a.* formed by habit. **-ually** *adv.* **habituate** *v.t.* to accustom to a practice or usage; to familiarize; (*Colloq.*) to frequent. **-uation** *n.* **-ude** *n.* customary manner of action; repetition of an act, thought, or feeling; confirmed practice. **-ué** (ha·bich'·a·wā) *n.* a frequenter (of a place) [L. *habitus*, attire, state, fr. *habere*, to have].

hab·it·a·ble (hab'·it·a·bl) *n.* fit to live in. **-ness, habitability** *n.* **habitably** *adv.* **habitant** *n.* an inhabitant. **habitat** *n.* the natural home of an animal or plant; place of residence. **habitation** *n.* the act of inhabiting; a place of abode [L. *habitare*, to dwell].

ha·chure (hash'·oor) *n.* shading on a map to show mountains; *v.t.* to mark with this [Fr.].

ha·cien·da (há·si·en'·da) *n.* a ranch; an estate in S. America [Sp.].

hack (hak) *v.t.* to cut irregularly; to notch; *v.i.* to make cuts or notches; to give harsh dry coughs; *n.* a cut; a notch; an ax, a pick; a short cough [O.E. *haccian*].

hack (hak) *n.* a horse for ordinary riding; a horse worn out by over work; a drudge, esp. literary; *a.* hackneyed; hired; a hired carriage; (*Colloq.*) a taxi; *v.t.* to let out for hire; to hackney; *v.i.* (*Colloq.*) to drive a taxi [short for *hackney*].

hack·ney (hak'·ni·) *n.* a horse for riding or driving; a horse (and carriage) kept for hire; *a.* to let out for hire; *v.i.* to use often; to make trite or commonplace. **-ed** *a.* commonplace [Fr. *haquenée*, a pacing horse].

had (had) *pa.p.* and *pa.t.* of **have**.

had·dock (had′·ạk) *n.* a fish of the cod family.

Ha·des (hā′·dēz) (*Myth.*) the underworld; (*l.c.*) (*Colloq.*) hell [Gk. = the unseen].

haft (haft) *n.* a handle, esp. of a knife; a hilt; *v.t.* to set in a handle [O.E. *haeft*].

hag (hag) *n.* an ugly old woman; a witch. **-gish** *a.* like a hag. **-gishly** *adv.* **-ridden** *a.* troubled with nightmares [O.E. *haegtesse*, a witch].

hag·gard (hag′·ẹrd) *a.* wild-looking; lean and gaunt; *n.* untrained hawk. **-ly** *adv.* [O.Fr. *hagard*].

hag·gle (hag′·l) *v.t.* to hack; to mangle; *v.i.* to dispute terms; to be difficult in bargaining; *n.* act of haggling. **-r** *n.* [O.N. *hoggva*, to chop].

Hag·i·og·ra·pha (hag·i·, hā·ji·ag′·rạ·fạ) *n.pl.* the last of the three divisions of the Old Testament [Gk. *haigios*, holy; *graphein*, to write].

hag·i·ol·o·gy (hag·i·, hā·ji·al′·ạ·ji·) *n.* a history of the lives of saints. **hagiologist** *n.* **hagiography** *n.* the branch of literature which treats of the lives of saints [Gk. *hagios*, holy; *logos*, discourse; *graphein*, to write].

ha-ha (hà·hà′) *n.* a sunken fence [Fr.].

hail (hāl) *n.* frozen rain falling in pellets; *v.i.* to rain hail; *v.t.* to pour down like hail. **-stone** *n.* frozen raindrops [O.E. *hagol*].

hail (hāl) *v.t.* to greet, salute or call; *n.* an exclamation of respectful salutation. **— fellow** *n.* (often **hail-fellow well met**) an intimate companion; *a.* on intimate terms. **to hail from**, to come from [O.N. *heill*, healthy].

hair (hār) *n.* a filament growing from the skin of an animal; such filaments collectively, esp. covering the head; bristles; anything small or fine. **-ed** *a.* having hair. **-iness** *n.* **-y** *a.* covered with, made of, resembling hair. **-breadth** (hār′·bredth). **-s-breadth** *n.* the breadth of a hair; a very small distance; *a.* very narrow. **-brush** *n.* a brush for the hair. **-cloth** *n.* cloth made wholly or partly of hair. **-dresser** *n.* one who dresses or cuts hair; (*Brit.*) a barber. **-pin** *n.* a special two-legged pin for controlling hair. **-pin bend,** a bend of the road in the form of a U. **—raising** *a.* terrifying; alarming. **— shirt** *n.* a shirt made of haircloth, worn by penitents, ascetics, etc. **-splitting** *n.* and *n.* minute distinctions in reasoning. **-spring** *n.* a fine spring in a watch. **— trigger** *n.* a secondary trigger releasing the main one by very slight pressure [O.E. *haer*].

hal·cy·on (hal′·si·ạn) *n.* the kingfisher; *a.* calm. **— days,** peaceful, tranquil days; calm weather just before and after the winter solstice [Gk. *halkuon*, kingfisher, associated with calm sea].

hale (hāl) *a.* robust; sound; healthy, esp. in old age. **-ness** *n.* [O.E. *hal*, whole].

hale (hāl) *v.t.* to haul [O.Fr. *haler*, to pull].

half (haf) *n.* either of two equal parts of a thing. *pl.* **halves** (havz); (*Golf*) a hole neither won nor lost; *a.* forming a half; *adv.* to the extent of half. **—and-half** *n.* a mixture of two things in equal proportions; *adv.* in two equal portions. **-back** *n.* (*Football*) a player, or position, behind the forward line. **—baked** *a.* underdone; immature; silly. **—breed** *n.* one whose parents are of different races. **— brother** *n.* a brother by one parent only. **—caste** *n.* a half-breed. **— dozen** *n.* six. **— hearted** *a.* lukewarm. **— mast** *n.* the position of a flag lowered halfway down the staff, as a signal of distress, or as a sign of mourning. **— measure** *n.* inadequate means to achieve an end. **— moon** *n.* the moon when half its disk appears illuminated; a semicircle. **— nelson** *n.* a hold in wrestling. **— title** *n.* the name of a book, or subdivision of a book, occupying a full page. **—tone** *n.* an illustration printed from a

relief plate, showing light and shade by minute dots, made by photographing the subject through a closely ruled screen. **—wit** *n.* an imbecile; a blockhead. **—witted** *a.*

halve (hav) *v.t.* to divide into two equal portions; to reduce to half the previous amount [O.E. *haelf*].

hal·i·but (hal′·ạ·bạt) *n.* a large, flat sea fish [M.E. *haly*, holy; *butt*, a flatfish].

hal·i·to·sis (hal·ạ·tō′·sis) *n.* foul or offensive breath [L. *halitus*, breath].

hall (hawl) *n.* a corridor in a building; a place of public assembly; a room at the entrance of a house; a building belonging to a collegiate institution, guild, etc. **-mark** *n.* the mark used to indicate the standard of tested gold and silver; any mark of quality [O.E. *heal*].

Hal·le·lu·jah, Halleluiah (hal·ạ·lōō′·ya) *n.* and *interj.* used in songs of praise to God [Heb. *hallelu*, praise ye; *Jah*, Jehovah].

hal·liard See **halyard**.

hal·loo (hạ·lōō′) *n.* a hunting cry; a shout or call to draw attention; *v.t.* to encourage with shouts, esp. dogs in hunting [imit.].

hal·low (hal′·ō) *v.t.* to make holy; to consecrate; to treat as sacred; to reverence. **-ed** *a.* **Hallowe'en** *n.* the evening before All Hallows' or All Saints' day (Oct. 31st).

hal·lu·ci·nate (hạ·lōō′·sạ·nāt) *v.t.* to produce illusion in the mind of. **hallucination** *n.* illusion; seeing something that is not present; delusion. **hallucinative, hallucinatory** *a.* [L. *hallucinari*, to wander in mind].

ha·lo (hā′·lō) *n.* a circle of light around the moon, sun, etc.; a ring of light around a saint's head in a picture. *pl.* **-s, -es** [Gk. *halos*, a threshing-floor; a disk].

hal·o·gen (hal′·ạ·jạn) *n.* (*Chem.*) one of the elements chlorine, bromine, iodine, and fluorine [Gk. *hals*, salt; root *gen-*, producing].

halt (hawlt) *n.* a stoppage on a march or journey; *v.t.* to cause to stop; *v.i.* to make a stop [Ger. *Halt*, stoppage].

halt (hawlt) *v.i.* to falter in speech or walk; to hesitate; *n.* cripple. **-ing** *a.* [O.E. *healt*].

hal·ter (hawl′·tẹr) *n.* a rope or strap with headstall to fasten or lead horses or cattle; a noose for hanging a person; *v.t.* to fasten with a rope or strap [O.E. *haelftre*].

halve (hav) *v.t.* to divide into two equal parts.

hal·yard, halliard (hal′·yẹrd) *n.* (*Naut.*) a rope for hoisting or lowering yards or sails [corrupt. of *halier*, fr. *hale* = to haul].

ham (ham) *n.* the thigh of any animal, esp. a hog's thigh cured by salting and smoking; the region behind the knee; (*Slang*) an actor who overacts; an amateur transmitter and receiver of radio messages. **-string** *n.* a tendon at the back of the knee; *v.t.* to cripple by cutting this [O.E. *hamm*].

ham·burg·er (ham′·bur·gẹr) *n.* ground beef, seasoned and formed into cakes, frequently served in a bun [Ger. *Hamburg*].

ham·let (ham′·lit) *n.* a small village [O.E. *ham*, a dwelling].

ham·mer (ham′·ẹr) *n.* a tool, usually with a heavy head at the end of a handle, for beating metal, driving nails, etc.; a contrivance for exploding the charge of a gun; *v.t.* and *i.* to beat with, or as with, a hammer; to work hard at. **-head** *n.* a rapacious kind of shark. **-headed** *a.* having a head shaped like a hammer. **to hammer out** (*Fig.*) to find a solution by full investigation of all difficulties. **to come under the hammer,** to be sold by auction. [O.E. *hamor*].

ham·mock (ham′·ạk) *n.* a kind of hanging bed, consisting of a piece of canvas, and suspended by cords from hooks [Sp. *hamaca*].

ham·per (ham′·pẹr) *n.* a large covered basket for conveying goods [O.Fr. *hanapier*, a case for *hanaps*, goblets].

ham·per (ham′·pẹr) *n.* (*Naut.*) cumbrous

equipment; *v.t.* to impede; to obstruct the movements of [etym. uncertain].

ham·shack·le (ham'·shak·l) *v.t.* to fasten the head of an animal to one of the forelegs [fr. *hamper* and *shackle*].

ham·ster (ham'·ster) *n.* a species of rodent, remarkable for having cheek pouches [Gk.].

ham·string See **ham.**

hand (hand) *n.* the extremity of the arm beyond the wrist; a pointer on a dial, e.g. on a watch; a measure of the hand's breadth, four inches; a style of handwriting; cards dealt to a player; a manual worker; a sailor; side; direction; agency; service; aid; skill; *a.* belonging to, worn on, carried in, the hand; made or operated by hand; *v.t.* to give with the hand; to deliver; to pass; to hold out. **-y** *a.* convenient; close at hand; clever with the hands. **-y man** *n.* one hired for odd jobs. **-ily** *adv.* **-iness** *n.* **-bag** *n.* a bag for carrying in the hand. **-bill** *n.* printed sheet for circulation by hand. **-book** *n.* a short treatise; a manual. **-breath** *n.* the breadth of a hand (about four inches). **-cart** *n.* a small cart drawn or pushed by hand. **-cuff** *n.* shackle around wrist connected by a chain with one on other wrist; a manacle; *v.t.* to manacle. **-ful** *n.* as much as the hand will grasp or contain. **-maid(en)** *n.* a female servant. — **out** (*Slang*) food or money given to a beggar. **-rail** *n.* the rail of a staircase. — **to hand** *a.* in personal encounter; at close quarters. — **to mouth** *a.* precarious; without thought of the future. **-writing** *n.* the way a person writes. **at first hand,** direct from the original source. **in hand,** under control. **off-hand** *adv.* without attentive consideration; immediately. **on hand,** ready for distribution; available for disposal. **with a heavy hand,** sternly; severely. **with a high hand,** arrogantly. **an old hand,** a person with experience; a veteran. **second hand,** not new; having already been used. **to change hands,** to become the property of another. **to show one's hand,** to reveal one's intentions. [O.E. *hand*].

hand·i·cap (han'·di·kap) *n.* a race or contest in which competitors' chances are equalized by starts given, weights carried, etc.; a condition so imposed; (*Fig.*) a disability; *v.t.* to hinder or impede [fr. *hand in cap*; orig. a lottery game].

hand·i·craft (han'·di·kraft) *n.* manual occupation or skill; work performed by the hand [O.E. *handcraeft*].

hand·ker·chief (hang'·ker·chif) *n.* a small square of fabric carried in the pocket for wiping the nose, etc.; a kerchief for head or neck.

han·dle (hand'·d'l) *v.t.* to touch or feel with the hand; to manage; to wield; to deal with; to deal in; *n.* the part of a thing by which it is held; (*Fig.*) a fact that may be taken advantage of [O.E. *handlian*].

hand·some (han'·sam) *a.* of fine appearance; generous. **-ly** *adv.* **-ness** *n.* [orig. = pleasant to handle].

hang (hang) *v.t.* to suspend; to put to death by suspending from gallows; to cover with, as wallpaper, curtains, pictures, etc.; to fix on hinges, as a door; to display; *v.i.* to be suspended; to incline; to be in suspense; to linger; to cling to. *pa.p.* and *p.t.* **-ed** or **hung.** *n.* the way in which a thing hangs; (*Colloq.*) meaning; manner of doing. **-dog** *n.* a degraded fellow; *a.* having a sneaking look. **-er** *n.* that by which a thing is suspended, e.g. a *coat-hanger*. **-ing** *n.* death by suspension; that which is hung, as curtains, etc. for a room (used chiefly in *pl.*); *a.* punishable by death; suspended. **-man** *n.* one who hangs another; a public executioner. **-nail** *n.* piece of skin hanging from root of fingernail. **-over** *n.* depressing after-effects of drinking. **to hang**

in the balance, to be in doubt or suspense. **hang! hang it! hang it all!** mild oaths [O.E. *hangian*].

han·gar (hang'·er) *n.* a shed for aircraft [Fr. = *a shed*].

hank (hangk) *n.* a coil, esp. as a measure of yarn (of cotton = 840 yards; of worsted = 560 yards); (*Naut.*) a ring at the corner of a sail [O.N. *hanki*].

han·ker (hang'·ker) *v.i.* to long for; to crave. **-ering** *n.* an uneasy longing for; a craving

han·som (han'·sam) *n.* a light two-wheeled cab with the driver's seat at the back [fr. the inventor, Joseph A. *Hansom,* 1803-1882].

hap·haz·ard (hap·haz'·erd) *n.* chance; accident; *a.* random; without design. **-ly** *adv.* **-ness** *n.* [O.N. *happ,* luck]. [*happ,* luck].

hap·less (hap'·lis) *a.* unlucky. **-ly** *adv.* [O.N.

hap·pen (hap'·in) *v.i.* to come by chance; to occur; to take place. **-ing** *n.* occurrence; event [O.N. *happ,* luck].

hap·py (hap'·i·) *a.* glad; content; lucky; fortunate; apt; fitting. **happily** *adv.* **happiness** *n.* [O.N. *happ,* luck].

ha·ra·ki·ri (há·ra·ker'·i·) *n.* a method of suicide by disembowelment, practiced by the Japanese. Also **hari-kari** [Jap. *hara,* the belly; *kiri,* to cut].

ha·rangue (ha·rang') *n.* a loud, passionate speech; *v.i.* to deliver a harangue; *v.t.* to speak vehemently to. **-r** *n.* [O.H. Ger. = a ring of hearers].

har·ass (har'·as, ha·ras') *v.t.* to attack repeatedly; to worry; to trouble. **-ed** *a.* **-er** *n.* **-ing** *a.* **-ment** *n.* [Fr. *harasser*].

har·bin·ger (har'·bin·jer) *n.* one who announces another's approach; a forerunner [M.E. *herbergeour,* one sent on to provide lodgings].

har·bor (har'·ber) *n.* shelter for ships; a port; any shelter; *v.t.* to give shelter to; to protect *v.i.* to take shelter [M.E. *herberwe*].

hard (hard) *a.* firm; solid; resisting pressure; difficult; harsh; unfeeling; difficult to bear; strenuous; bitter, as winter; keen, as frost; of water, not making lather well with soap; strong; said of alcoholic liquors; *adv.* vigorously; intently; solidly. **-en** *v.t.* to make hard or more hard; to strengthen; to confirm in wickedness or obstinacy; to make less sympathetic; *v.i.* to become hard. **-ly** *adv.* with difficulty; not quite; scarcely; severely. **-ness** *n.* **-ship** *n.* severe toil or suffering; ill-luck; privation; suffering. **hard and fast,** strict; rigid. **—bitten** *a.* tough; stubborn. **—boiled** *a.* boiled till hard, e.g. of an egg; (*Slang*) tough; unfeeling. **— by,** near; close at hand. **—cash,** gold and silver coins, as opposed to paper money. **-headed** *a.* shrewd; intelligent; practical. **-hearted** *a.* cruel; merciless; unsympathetic. **-tack,** a large coarse unsalted biscuit. (*Colloq.*) **— up,** very short of money; poor. **-ware** *n.* articles made of metal, e.g. tools, locks, fixtures, etc. **to die hard,** to die after a fierce struggle. **a die-hard** (*Fig.*) one who clings desperately to long-held opinions [O.E. *heard*].

har·dy (har'·di·) *a.* robust; vigorous; bold; brave; daring; able to bear exposure. **-ily** *adv.* **-ihood** *n.* extreme boldness. **-iness** *n.* vigor; robustness [Fr. *hardi,* bold].

hare (har) *n.* a rodent with long hind legs, long ears, short tail, and divided upper lip, noted for its speed. **-brained** *a.* wild; heedless. **-lip** *n.* (*Med.*) a congenital fissure in the upper lip. **-lipped** *a.* [O.E. *hara*].

har·em (har'·am) *n.* apartment for females in a Mohammedan household; the occupants [Ar. *haram,* forbidden].

ha·ri·ka·ri, form of **hara-kari.**

hark (hark) *v.i.* to listen; *interj.* listen! hear! **to hark back** (*Fig.*) to return to some previous point in an argument [M.E. *herkien*; cf. E. *hearken*].

har·lot (hàr'·lạt) *n.* a prostitute. **-ry** *n.* prostitution [O.Fr. = a vagabond].

harm (hàrm) *n.* injury; hurt; damage; misfortune; *v.t.* to hurt; to injure. **-ful** *a.* hurtful; injurious. **-fully** *adv.* **-fulness** *n.* **-less** *a.* **-lessly** *adv.* **-lessness** *n.* [O.E. *hearm*].

har·mo·ny (hàr·mạ·ni·) *n.* agreement; concord; friendliness; peace; a melodious sound; a combination of musical notes to make chords; the science that treats of musical sounds in their combination and progression. **harmonic** (hàr·màn'·ik), **harmonical** *a.* **harmonically** *adv.* **harmonica** *n.* a mouth organ. **harmonicon** *n.* a mouth organ; an orchestration. **harmonics** *n.* the science of harmony, of musical sounds. **harmonious** (hàr·mō'·ni·ạs) *a.* vocally or musically concordant; symmetrical; living in peace and friendship. **harmoniously** *adv.* **harmoniousness** *n.* **harmonize** *v.t.* to bring into harmony; to cause to agree; to reconcile; (*Mus.*) to arrange into parts for the voice, or with instrumental accompaniments; *v.i.* to be in harmony; to agree; (*Colloq.*) to sing in harmony. **harmonizer** *n.* **harmonist** *n.* a harmonizer; a musical composer. **harmonium** *n.* a small reed organ. **harmonic progression**, a series of numbers whose reciprocals are in arithmetical progression, e.g. ½, ⅓, ¼, etc. or 10, 12, 15 [Gk. *harmonia*, fr. *harmozein*, to fit together].

har·ness (hàr'·nis) *n.* the working gear, straps, bands, etc. of a draft animal, esp. a horse; *v.t.* to put harness on [Fr. *harneis*].

harp (hàrp) *n.* a stringed musical instrument played by hand; *v.i.* to play on the harp; to dwell persistently upon a particular subject. **-ist** *n.* a player on the harp. **-sichord** (hàrp'·-si·kawrd) *n.* an old-fashioned musical instrument, a forerunner of the piano [O.E. *hearpe*].

har·poon (hàr·pòòn') *n.* a barbed spear with a rope attached for catching whales, etc.; *v.t.* to strike with a harpoon. **-er** *n.* [Fr. *harpon*].

Har·py (hàr'·pi·) *n.* (*Myth.*) ravenous monster, with head and breast of woman and wings and claws of vulture; (*l.c.*) a rapacious woman [Gk. *harpazein*, to seize].

har·ri·dan (har'·i·dạn) *n.* a haggard old woman; a shrew [corrupt. of Fr. *haridelle*, a worn-out horse].

har·row (har'·ō) *n.* a toothed agricultural implement to level, break clods, or cover seed when sown; *v.t.* to draw harrow over; (*Fig.*) to distress greatly. **-er** *n.* **-ing** *a.* [M.E. *harwe*].

har·ry (har'·i·) *v.t.* to ravage; to pillage; to torment [O.E. *hergian*, to make war].

harsh (hàrsh) *a.* rough; unpleasing to the touch or taste; severe; unfeeling. **-ly** *adv.* **-ness** *n.* [M.E. *harsk*].

hart (hàrt) *n.* a male deer or stag, esp. over five years old [O.E. *heort*].

harte·beest (hàrt'·bēst) *n.* a large S. African antelope [Dut.].

har·um-scar·um (hār'·ạm-skār'·ạm) *a.* reckless; wild; *n.* a rash person [perh. *hare*, and *scare*].

har·vest (hàr'·vist) *n.* (season for) gathering crops; the crop itself; *v.t.* to gather in. **-er** *n.* one who harvests; a reaping-machine. **— moon** *n.* the full moon nearest the autumn equinox [O.E. *haerfest*, autumn].

has (haz) 3rd sing. pres. indic. of the verb **have. —been** *n.* (*Colloq.*) a person long past his best.

hash (hash) *v.t.* to chop into small pieces; to mince; *n.* that which is hashed; a dish of hashed meat and potatoes; (*Slang*) a mess [Fr. *hacher*, to chop].

hasp (hasp) *n.* a clasp passing over a staple for fastening a door, etc.; *v.t.* to fasten with a hasp [O.E. *haepse*].

has·sock (has'·ạk) *n.* a padded cushion for kneeling or for a footstool; a tuft of grass [O.E. *hassuc*, coarse grass].

haste (hāst) *n.* speed; quickness; hurry; *v.i.* (*Poetic*) to hasten. **hasten** (hās'·n) *v.t.* to urge forward; to accelerate; *v.i.* to hurry. **hastener** *n.* **hasty** *a.* speedy; quick; over-eager; rash; passionate. **hastily** *adv.* [O.Fr. *haste*].

hat (hat) *n.* covering for head, usually with brim; red hat of cardinal, hence, dignity of a cardinal. **-ter** *n.* one who makes, or sells hats. **top hat**, a silk hat with a high crown. **to pass (round) the hat**, to make a collection, esp. to pay expenses [O.E. *haett*].

hatch (hach) *v.t.* to bring forth young birds from the shell; to incubate; to plot; *v.i.* to come forth from the shelf; *n.* the act of hatching; the brood hatched. **-er** *n.* **-ery** *n.* a place for hatching eggs, esp. of fish [M.E. *hacchen*].

hatch (hach) *n.* the lower half of a divided door; an opening in a floor or roof; the boards, etc. covering a hatchway; the hatchway itself. **-way** *n.* a square opening in a ship's deck through which cargo, etc. is lowered [O.E. *haec*, a gate]. [*hacher*, to chop].

hatch (hach) *v.t.* to shade with lines [Fr.

hatch·et (hach'·at) *n.* a small ax with a short handle. **— faced** *a.* having a face with sharp features. **to bury the hatchet**, to make peace [Fr. *hache*, an axe].

hate (hāt) *v.t.* to dislike strongly; to bear malice to; to detest; *n.* strong dislike; aversion; hatred. **-ful** *a.* detestable. **-fully** *adv.* **-fulness** *n.* **-r** *n.* **hatred** *n.* aversion; active ill-will; enmity [O.E. *hatian*, to hate; *hete*, hatred].

haugh·ty (haw'·ti·) *a.* proud. **haughtily** *adv.* **haughtiness** *n.* [Fr. *haut*, high, fr. L. *altus*].

haul (hawl) *v.t.* to pull with force; to drag; to steer a ship closer to the wind; *v.i.* to pull; of wind, to shift, to veer; *n.* a hauling; a catch; good profit, gain, or acquisition. **-age** *n.* the act of pulling; the charge for hauling; the carrying of goods, material, etc. by road. **-er** *n.* one who hauls. **close-hauled** *a.* (*Naut.*) of a ship, with the sails trimmed to keep her close to the wind [Fr. *haler*].

haunch (hawnch) *n.* the part of the body between the ribs and thighs; the hip; a leg and loin of venison, etc. [Fr. *hanche*].

haunt (hawnt) *v.t.* to frequent; of ghosts, to visit regularly; *v.i.* to loiter about a place; *n.* a place of frequent resort. **-ed** *a.* frequently visited by ghosts [Fr. *hanter*, to frequent].

haut·boy (hō'·boi) *n.* an older form of the oboe [Fr. *haut*, high; *bois*, wood].

hau·teur (hō·tur') *n.* haughtiness; haughty manner or spirit; arrogance [Fr.].

Ha·van·a (hạ·van'·ạ) *n.* a fine brand of cigar [named from *Havana*, the capital of Cuba].

have (hav) *v.t.* to hold or possess; to be possessed or affected with; to seize; to bring forth; to enjoy; to be obliged (to do); (as an auxiliary verb, forms the perfect and other tenses); *pr.p.* **having.** *pa.p.* and *pa.t.* **had** [O.E. *habban*].

ha·ven (hā'·vn) *n.* a bay or inlet giving shelter for ships; any place of shelter [O.E. *haefen*].

hav·er·sack (hav'·ẹr·sak) *n.* a soldier's canvas ration-bag; a similar bag for travelers [Ger. *Habersack*, an oat sack].

hav·oc (hav'·ạk) *n.* pillage; devastation; ruin [orig. to 'cry havoc,' to give the signal for pillage; O.Fr. *havot*, plunder].

haw (haw) *n.* a hesitation in speech; *v.i.* to speak hesitatingly [imit.].

haw (haw) *interj.* a command to horses, usually to turn left; *v.t.* and *v.i.* to turn left [O.E. *hawian*].

hawk (hawk) *n.* a bird of prey of the falcon family; *v.t.* and *i.* to hunt with hawks, as in falconry. **hawker** *n.* a falconer. **-ing** *n.* falconry [O.E. *hafoc*].

hawk (hawk) *v.i.* to clear the throat noisily;

n. an audible clearing of the throat.

hawk (hawk) *v.i.* to carry about wares for sale; to peddle. **-er** *n.* an itinerant dealer; a peddler [Dut. *heuker*, a huckster]. [plaster.

hawk (hawk) *n.* a plasterer's tool for holding

hawse (hawz) *n.* the part of a ship's bows with holes for cables [O.E. *heals*, the prow].

haw·ser (haw'·zer) *n.* a large rope or small cable [O.Fr. *haucier*, to raise].

hay (hā) *n.* grass mown and dried for fodder. **— fever** *n.* irritation of the mucous membrane of the nose (generally by pollen from grasses). **-maker** *n.* one who cuts and dries grass for hay. **-rick** *n.* **-stack** *n.* a large pile of hay with ridged or pointed top. **-seed** *n.* grass seed; (*Colloq.*) a rustic; a country bumpkin [O.E. *hieg*].

haz·ard (haz'·erd) *n.* chance; a chance; risk; danger; (*Golf*) an inclusive term for all obstacles on the golf course; a game played with dice; *v.t.* to expose to risk; to run the risk of. **-ous** *a.* dangerous; risky [Fr. *hasard*].

haze (hāz) *n.* a misty appearance in the air; mental obscurity. **hazy** *a.* **hazily** *adv.*

haze (hāz) *v.t.* to torment or punish by the imposition of disagreeable task; to play tricks on [O.Fr. *haser*, to annoy].

ha·zel (hā'·zl) *n.* a nut-bearing bush or small tree; the reddish-brown color of the nuts; *a.* of this color. **-nut** *n.* the nut of the hazel tree [O.E. *haesel*].

he (hē) *pron.* the 3rd pers. sing. masc. pronoun. **—man** *n.* (*Colloq.*) a very virile man [O.E.].

head (hed) *n.* the upper part of a man's or animal's body; the brain; intellectual capacity; upper part of anything; the top; the chief part, a chief; something the shape of a head; progress; a section of a chapter; the source of a stream; a cape or headland; a crisis; freedom to go on; *a.* chief; principal; of wind, contrary; *v.t.* to lead; to be at the head of; to direct; to go in front, so as to hinder; *v.i.* to originate; to form a head; to make for. **-y** *a.* impetuous; apt to intoxicate. **-ily** *adv.* **-iness** *n.* **-ache** (hed'·āk) *n.* a nerve-pain in the head. **-achy** *a.* **-er** *n.* (*Colloq.*) a plunge, head foremost into water; in building, a brick laid so that its end forms part of the surface of the wall. **-gear** *n.* a hat; the harness about an animal's head. **—hunting** *n.* raiding to procure human heads as trophies. **-ing** *n.* the act of providing with a head; a title. **-land** *n.* a cape; a promontory. **-light** *n.* a strong light carried on the front of a locomotive, motor vehicle, etc. **—line** *n.* a summary of news in large print in a newspaper; a caption. **-long** *adv.* with the head foremost; rashly; *a.* steep; rash; reckless. **-man** *n.* the chief, esp. of a tribe. **-master, -mistress** *n.* the person in charge of a school; the principal. **-most** *a.* most advanced; foremost. **—on** *a.* meeting head to head; head first. **-phone** *n.* a telephone-receiver to clip on head (usually in *pl.*). **-piece** *n.* a helmet; the head; brain-power; ornamental engraving at beginning of book or chapter. **-quarters** *n.pl.* (*Mil.*) a center of operations. **-sail**, any sail forward of the mast. **-sman** *n.* an executioner. **-stall** *n.* the part of the bridle that fits round the head. **-stone** *n.* a memorial stone placed at the head of a grave. **-strong** *a.* obstinate; stubborn; self-willed. **-way** *n.* progress. **head over heels,** completely; deeply. **to keep one's head,** to keep calm [O.E. *heafod*].

heal (hēl) *v.t.* to make whole; to restore to health; to make well; *v.i.* to become sound. **-er** *n.* **-ing** *a.* tending to cure [O.E. *haelan*, fr. *hal*, whole].

health (helth) *n.* soundness of body; general condition of the body; a toast drunk in a person's honor. **-y** *a.* having, or tending to give, health; sound; vigorous; wholesome. **-ily** *adv.* **-iness** *n.* **-ful** *a.* [O.E. *haelth*, fr. *hal*, whole].

heap (hēp) *n.* a number of things lying one on

another; a pile; a mass; (*Colloq.*) a great quantity; *v.t.* to throw or lay in a heap; to amass [O.E. *heap*].

hear (hēr) *v.t.* to perceive with the ear; to listen to; to heed; (*Law*) to try (a case); *v.i.* to perceive sound; to learn by report. *pr.p.* **-ing.** *pa.p.* and *pa.t.* **heard** (hurd). **-er** *n.* **-ing** *n.* the act of perceiving sound; the sense by which sound is perceived; audience; earshot. **-say** *n.* rumor; common talk. **hear! hear!** *interj.* indicating approval of a speaker's words or opinions [O.E. *hieran*].

hearse (hurs) *n.* a vehicle to carry a coffin to the place of burial [Fr. *herce*, a harrow].

heart (hårt) *n.* the hollow, muscular organ which makes the blood circulate; the seat or source of life; the seat of emotions and affections; the inner part of anything; courage; warmth or affection; a playing-card marked with a figure of a heart. **-y** *a.* cordial; friendly; vigorous; in good health; of a meal, satisfying the appetite. **-ily** *adv.* **-iness** *n.* **-less** *a.* without heart; unfeeling. **-en** *v.t.* to encourage; to stimulate. **-ache** *n.* sorrow; anguish. **-blood** *n.* life; essence. **-break** *n.* overpowering sorrow. **-broken** *a.* overwhelmed with grief. **-burn** *n.* a form of dyspepsia. **-strings** *n.pl.* (*Fig.*) affections; emotions. **at heart**, at bottom, inwardly. **by heart**, by rote; by memory. **to wear one's heart on one's sleeve**, to show one's feelings openly [O.E. *heorte*].

hearth (hårth) *n.* the fireside; the house itself; home [O.E *heorth*].

heat (hēt) *n.* hotness; a sensation of this; hot weather or climate; warmth of feeling; anger; excitement; sexual excitement in animals, esp. female; (*Sport*) a race to decide the persons to compete in a deciding one; *v.t.* to make hot; to excite; *v.i.* to become hot. **-ed** *a.* (*Fig.*) of argument, etc. passionate; intense. **-edly** *adv.* **-er** *n.* **— wave** *n.* a spell of abnormally hot weather [O.E. *haetu*].

heath (hēth) *n.* waste land; moor; shrub of genus Erica. **-y** *a.* [O.E. *haeth*].

hea·then (hē'·THạn) *n.* one who is not an adherent of a religious system; an infidel; a pagan; an irreligious person; *a.* **-ish** *a.* **-ism** *n.* pagan worship; the condition of being heathen [O.E. *haethen*].

heath·er (heTH'·er) *n.* a small plant of the genus Erica, bearing purple, and sometimes white, bell-shaped flowers; heath [fr. *heath*].

heave (hēv) *v.t.* to lift with effort; to throw (something heavy); to utter (a sigh); to pull on a rope, etc.; to haul; (*Geol.*) to displace; *v.i.* to rise and fall in alternate motions, e.g. of heavy breathing, of waves, etc.; to try to vomit; *n.* a heaving; an effort to lift something; a rise and fall; an attempt to vomit; *pr.p.* **heaving.** *pa.p.* and *pa.t.* **heaved** or **hove. to heave to,** to bring a ship to a standstill [O.E. *hebban*].

heav·en (hev'·n) *n.* the sky; the upper air; the abode of God; God Himself; a place of bliss; supreme happiness. **-ly** *a.* pert. to, or like, heaven; pure; divine; *adv.* in a heavenly manner. **-liness** *n.* **-ward, -wards** *adv.* toward heaven. **in seventh heaven,** in a state of supreme bliss [O.E. *heofon*].

Heav·i·side lay·er (hev'·i·sīd lā'·er) *n.* the upper part of the atmosphere, which reflects radio waves [fr. Oliver *Heaviside*, English physicist, 1850-1925].

heav·y (hev'·i·) *a.* weighty; striking or falling with force; large in amount, as a debt; rough, as the sea; abundant, as rain; clayey, as soil; sad; hard to bear; difficult; dull; sluggish; serious; over compact; indigestible. **heav·ily** *adv.* **heaviness** *n.* **—handed** *a.* awkward; severe; oppressive. **— headed** *a.* drowsy. **—hearted** *a.* sad. **—weight** *n.* (*Boxing*) a boxer exceeding 175 lbs. in weight [O.E. *hefig*, fr. *hebban*, to heave].

heb·do·mad (heb·da̩·mad′) *n.* a group of seven things; a week [Gk. *hebdomas*, seventh].

He·brew (hē′·bròó) *n.* one of the ancient inhabitants of Palestine; an Israelite; a Jew; the language. **Hebraic** (hē·brā′·ik) *a.* pert. to the Hebrews, or to their language [Heb. 'ibhri,' one from across the river Euphrates].

hec·a·tomb (hek′·a̩·tōm) *n.* any large number of victims [Gk. *hekaton*, a hundred; *bous*, an ox].

heck·le (hek′·l) *n.* a comb for cleaning flax; *v.t.* to comb flax; to ask awkward questions of a speaker at a public meeting.

hec·to- *prefix* combining to form derivatives used in the metric system. **-gram, -gramme** hek′·ta̩·gram) *n.* a weight of 100 grammes = 3.527 ounces. **-liter** (hek′·ta̩·lēt·e̩r) *n.* a unit of capacity, containing 100 liters = 26.418 U.S. gallons. **-meter** (hek·ta̩·mē·te̩r) *n.* a unit of length = 100 meets = 109.363 yards [fr. Gk. *hekaton*, one hundred].

hec·tic (hek′·tik) *a.* exciting; wild; consumptive affected with hectic fever [Gk. *hektikos*, habitual].

hec·to·graph (hek′·ta̩·graf) *n.* an apparatus for multiplying copies of writings [Gk. *hekaton*, a hundred; *graphein*, to write].

Hec·tor (hek′·te̩r) *n.* the chief hero of Troy in war with Greeks. (*l.c.*) *n.* a bully; a brawler; a blusterer; *v.t.* and *i.* to bully; to bluster.

hedge (hej) *n.* a fence of bushes; a protecting barrier; *v.t.* to enclose with a hedge; to fence, as fields; to obstruct; to hem in; *v.i.* to bet on both sides so as to guard against loss; to shift; to shuffle; to skulk. **hedging** *n.* **hedgy** *a.* **-hog** *n.* a small quadruped, covered on the upper part of its body with prickles or spines. **-hopping** *n.* in aviation, flying very low. **-row** *n.* a row of bushes forming a hedge [O.E. *hecg*].

he·don·ism (hē′·d′n·izm) *n.* the doctrine that pleasure is the chief good. **hedonist** *n.* [Gk. *hēdonē*, pleasure].

heed (hēd) *v.t.* to take notice of; to care for; to mind; to observe; *n.* attention; notice; care; caution. **-ful** *a.* watchful; attentive. **-fully** *adv.* **-fulness** *n.* **-less** *a.* [O.E. *hedan*].

hee·haw (hē′·haw) *v.i.* to bray, of an ass [imit. origin].

heel (hēl) *n.* back part of foot, shoe, boot, or stocking; back part of anything; (*Slang*) an undesirable person; *v.t.* to add a heel to, as in knitting; to touch ground, or a ball, with the heel. **— of Achilles** (*Fig.*) a vulnerable part. **down at the heels**, slovenly; seedy; ill-shod [O.E. *hela*].

heel (hēl) *v.i.* of a ship; to lean to one side; to incline; *v.t.* to cause to do this [O.E. *hieldan*, to incline].

heft (heft) *v.t.* to try the weight by lifting; (*Colloq.*) to heave up or lift; *n.* weight. **-y** *a.* heavy; vigorous [fr. *heave*].

he·gem·o·ny (hi·jem′·a̩·nē, hej′·a̩·mōn·i·) *n.* leadership; predominance. **hegemonic** *a.* Gk. *hēgemōn*, a leader].

He·gi·ra, hejira (hi·jī′·ra̩) *n.* Mohammed's flight from Mecca to Medina, A.D. 622 [Ar. *hijrah*, flight].

heif·er (hef′·e̩r) *n.* a young cow that has not had a calf [O.E. *heahfore*].

height (hīt) *n.* measurement from base to top; quality of being high; a high position; a hill; eminence. **-en** *v.t.* to make high or higher; to intensify [O.E. *hiehthu*].

hei·nous (hā′·nas) *a.* extremely wicked; atrocious; odious [Fr. *haineux*, hateful].

heir (ār) *n.* (*fem.* **-ess**) a person legally entitled to succeed to property or rank. **— apparent** *n.* the person who is first in the line of succession to an estate, crown, etc. **-loom** *n.* article of personal property which descends to heir along

with inheritance; a thing that has been in a family for generations [L. *heres*].

he·ji·ra See **hegira.**

held (held) *pa.p.* and *pa.t.* of **hold.**

hel·i·cal (hel′·i·ka̩l) *a.* pert. to a helix; spiral.

helicopter *n.* an airplane which can rise or descend vertically; an autogiro [Gk. *helix*, spiral; *pteron*, a wing].

he·li·o·gram (hē′·li·a̩·gram) *n.* a message transmitted by heliograph [Gk. *hēlios*, the sun; *gramma*, a writing].

he·li·o·graph (hē′·li·a̩·graf) *n.* signaling apparatus employing a mirror to reflect the sun's rays; an instrument for photographing the sun; *v.t.* to signal by means of a heliograph. **-ic** *a.* **heliography** *n.* [Gk. *hēlios*, the sun; *graphein*, to write].

he·li·o·trope (hē′·li·a̩·trōp) *n.* a plant with fragrant purple flowers; the color of the flowers, or their scent; a bloodstone. **heliotropism** *n.* (*Bot.*) the tendency of plants to direct their growth towards light [Gk. *hēlios*, the sun; *tropos*, a turn].

he·li·um (hē′·li·a̩m) *n.* (*Chem.*) an inert non-inflammable, light gas [Gk. *hēlios*, the sun].

he·lix (hē′·liks) *n.* a spiral, e.g. wire in a coil, or a corkscrew; (*Zool.*) a genus including the snail; (*Anat.*) the outer rim of the ear. **helical** *a.* spiral [Gk. *helix*, a spiral].

hell (hel) *n.* the abode of the damned; the lower regions; a place or state of vice, misery, or torture. **-ish** *a.* infernal. **-ishly** *adv.* **-ishness** *n.* **-ion** *n.* troublemaker [O.E. *hel*].

Hel·lene (hel′·ēn) *n.* an ancient Greek; a subject of modern Greece. **Hellenic** *a.* **Hellen-ism** *n.* Grecian culture; a Greek idiom. **Hellenist** *n.* a Greek scholar. **Hellenistic** *a.* [Gk. *Hellen*].

hel·lo (ha̩·lō′, he·lō′) *interj.* a greeting or call to attract attention.

helm (helm) *n.* (*Naut.*) a tiller or wheel for turning the rudder of a ship; (*Fig.*) control; guidance; *v.t.* to steer; to control [O.E. *helma*].

helm (helm) *n.* (*Arch.*) a helmet. **helmet** *n.* a defensive covering for the head; anything similar in shape or position [O.E. *helm*].

hel·minth (hel′·minth) *n.* an intestinal worm. [Gk. *helmins*, a worm].

hel·ot (hēl′·a̩t, hē′·la̩t) *n.* a serf in ancient Sparta; a slave; serfdom [Gk. *Heilōtēs*].

help (help) *v.t.* to aid; to assist; to support; to succor; to relieve; to prevent; *v.i.* to lend aid; to be useful; *n.* the act of helping; one who, or that which, helps; aid; assistance; support; a domestic servant. **-er** *n.* **-ful** *a.* **-fulness** *n.* **-ing** *n.* a portion of food. **-less** *a.* not able to take care of oneself; weak; dependent. **-lessly** *adv.* **-lessness** *n.* **-mate** *n.* an assistant; a partner; a wife or husband. Also **-meet** [O.E. *helpna*].   [order; in hurry and confusion.

hel·ter-skel·ter (hel·te̩r-skel′·te̩r) *adv.* in dis-

Hel·ve·tia (hel·vē′·sha̩) *n.* the Latin, and political, name for Switzerland.

hem (hem) *n.* border, esp. one made by sewing; *v.t.* to fold over and sew down; to edge; to enclose (followed by *in*). *pr.p.* **-ming.** *pa.p.* and *pa.t.* **-med** [O.E.].

hem (hem) *interj.* and *n.* a kind of suppressed cough, calling attention or expressing doubt; *v.i.* to make the sound.

he·ma-, hemo- (hē′·ma̩) a word element meaning "blood" [Gk. *haima*].

he·mal, haemal (hē′·ma̩l) *a.* of the blood; on same side of body as the heart and great blood-vessels [Gk. *haima*, blood].

hem·a·tin, haematin (hem′·a̩·tin, hē′·ma̩·-tin) *n.* the constituent of hemoglobin containing iron [Gk. *haima*, blood].

hem·i-, *prefix* from Greek *hēmi*, half, combining to form derivatives.

hem·i·sphere (hem′·a̩·sfe̩r) *n.* a half sphere; half of the celestial sphere; half of the earth. **hemispheric, hemispherical** *a.*

hem·i·stich (hem'·ạ·stik) *n.* half a line of verse.

hem·lock (hem'·lȯk) *n.* a poisonous umbelliferous plant; a coniferous spruce [O.E. *hemlic*].

he·mo·glo·bin, haemoglobin (hē·mạ·glō'·bin) *n.* the coloring matter of the red blood corpuscles [Gk. *haima*, blood; L. *globus*, a ball].

he·mo·phil·i·a, haemophilia (hē·mạ·fil'·i·ạ) *n.* (*Med.*) tendency to excessive bleeding due to a deficiency in clotting power of blood; *n.* a bleeder [Gk. *haima*, blood; *philein*, to love].

hem·or·rhage, haemorrhage (hem'·ạr·ij) *n.* (*Med.*) a flow of blood; a discharge of blood from the blood vessels; bleeding. **hemorrhagic** *a.* [Gk. *haima*, blood; *rhēgnunai*, to burst].

hem·or·rhoids, haemorrhoids (hem'·ạ·roidz) *n.pl.* dilated veins around anus; piles. [Gk. *haima*, blood; *rhein*, to flood].

he·mo·stat·ic, haemostatic (hē·mạ·stat'·ik) *n.* an agent which stops bleeding; a styptic. Also *a.* [Gk. *haima*, blood; *stasis*, a standing].

hemp (hemp) *n.* a plant whose fiber is used in the manufacture of coarse cloth, ropes, cables, etc. **-en** *a.* [O.E. *henep*].

hen (hen) *n.* the female of any bird, esp. the domestic fowl; (*Colloq.*) the female of certain crustaceans, e.g. the lobster, crab, etc. **-coop** *n.* a large cage for poultry. — **party** *n.* (*Slang*) a social gathering of women only. **-peck** *v.t.* to domineer over a husband [O.E. *henn*].

hence (hens) *adv.* from this point; for this reason; *interj.* go away! begone! **-forth, -forward** *adv.* from now [M.E. *hennes*].

hench·man (hench'·mạn) *n.* a servant; a loyal supporter [M.E. *henxi-man*, a groom].

hen·dec·a·gon (hen·dek'·ạ·gȧn) *n.* a plane figure having eleven sides [Gk. *hendeka*, eleven; *gōnīā*, an angle; *sullabē*, a syllable].

hen·na (hen'·ạ) *n.* a shrub or small tree of the Near East; a dye made from it [Ar. *hinna*].

hep (hep) *a.* (*Slang*) informed; smart.

he·pat·ic (hi·pat'·ik) *a.* pert. to the liver. **hepatitis** *n.* [Gk. *hēpar*, the liver].

hep·ta- (hep'·tạ) *prefix* from Greek, *hepta*, seven, combining to form derivatives. **-1** *n.* a group of seven. **-gon** *n.* a plane figure with seven sides. **-gonal** *a.* **-meter** *n.* a line of verse of seven feet.

hep·tar·chy (hep'·tȧr·ki·) *n.* government by seven persons; the country governed by them; a group of seven kingdoms [Gk. *hepta*, seven; *archein*, to rule].

her (hur) *pron.* the objective case of the pronoun **she;** also, the possessive case used adjectivally. **hers** *pron.* the absolute possessive case. **herself** *pron.* emphatic and reflexive form [O.E. fr. *hire*, gen. and dat. of *heo*, she].

her·ald (her'·ȧld) *n.* an officer who makes royal proclamations, arranges ceremonies, keeps records of those entitled to armorial bearings, etc.; a messenger; an envoy; a forerunner. **heraldic** (he·ral'·dik) *a.* **-ry** *n.* the art or office of a herald; the science of recording genealogies and blazoning armorial bearings [O.Fr. *herault*].

herb (urb, hurb) *n.* a plant with a soft stem which dies down after flowering; a plant of which parts are used for medicine, food, or scent. **-aceous** (hur·bā'·shạs) *a.* pert. to herbs. **-age** *n.* herbs; nonwoody vegetation; (*Brit.*) green food for cattle. **-al** *a.* pert. to herbs; *n.* a book on herbs. **-alist** *n.* dealer in herbs [L. *herba*, grass].

Her·cu·les (hur'·kyạ·lēz) *n.* (*Myth.*) Latin name of Greek hero Heracles distinguished for his prodigious strength; hence any person of extraordinary strength and size. **Herculean** *a.*

herd (hurd) *n.* a number of animals feeding or traveling together; a drove of cattle; a large number of people; *v.i.* to go in a herd; *v.t.* to tend (a herd); to drive together. **-er** *n.* **-sman** *n.* one who tends cattle [O.E. *hirde*].

here (hēr) *adv.* in this place; at or to this point (opposed to *there*). **-about, -abouts** *adv.* about this place. **-after** *adv.* after this; *n.* a future existence. **-by** *adv.* by means of this; by this. **-in** *adv.* in this. **-on** *adv.* hereupon. **-to** *adv.* to this. **-tofore** *adv.* up to the present; formerly. **-with** *adv.* with this [O.E. *her*].

he·red·i·ty (hạ·red'·ạ·ti·) *n.* the transmission of characteristic traits and qualities from parents to offspring. **hereditable** *a.* heritable **hereditament** *n.* (*Law*) property that may be inherited. **hereditary** *a.* descending by inheritance [L. *heres*, an heir].

her·e·sy (her'·ạ·si·) *n.* opinion contrary to orthodox opinion, teaching, or belief. **heresiarch** (hạ·rē'·zi·ȧrk) *n.* the originator or leader of a heresy. **heretic** *n.* one holding opinions contrary to orthodox faith. **heretical** *a.* [Gk. *hairesis*, a choice, a school of thought].

her·it·a·ble (her'·ạ·tạ·bl) *a.* that can be inherited; attached to the property or house, as opposed to movable. **heritage** *n.* that which may be or is inherited. **heritor** *n.* one who inherits [L. *heres*, an heir].

her·maph·ro·dite (hur·maf'·rạ·dīt) *n.* and *a.* animal or flower with the characteristics of both sexes; having normally both sexual organs. **hermaphroditic, hermaphroditical** *a.* **hermaphrodism, hermaphroditism** *n.* [Gk. *Hermaphroditos*, the son of *Hermes* and *Aphrodite* who became joined in one body with a nymph called Salmacis].

her·met·ic (hur·met'·ik) *a.* pert. to alchemy; magical; sealed. — **sealing**, the airtight closing of a vessel by fusion [Gk. *Hermes*].

her·mit (hur'·mit) *n.* a person living in seclusion, esp. from religious motives; a recluse. **-age** *n.* the abode of a hermit [Gk. *erēmitēs*, fr. *erēmos*, solitary].

her·ni·a (hur'·ni·ạ) *n.* (*Med.*) the external protrusion of any internal part through the enclosing membrane; rupture [L.].

he·ro (hē'·rō) *n.* (*fem.* **heroine** (her'·ō·in)) one greatly regarded for his achievements or qualities; the chief man in a poem, play, or story; an illustrious warrior. *pl.* **-es. heroic** *a.* pert. to a hero; bold; courageous; illustrious; narrating the exploits of heroes, as a poem; denoting the verse or measure in such poems. **heroical** *a.* **heroically** *adv.* **heroics** *n.pl.* high-flown language; bombastic talk. **heroism** (her'·ō·izm) *n.* courage; valor; bravery [Gk. *herōs*, a demigod, a hero].

her·o·in (her'·ō·in) *n.* (*Med.*) habit-forming drug used as a sedative [Ger. trade name].

her·on (her'·ạn) *n.* a long-legged wading bird. [O.Fr. *hairon*; Fr. *héron*].

her·pes (hur'·pēz) *n.* a skin disease. **herpetic** *a.* [Gk. fr. *herpein*, to creep].

her·pe·tol·o·gy (hẹr·pạ·tȧl'·ạ·ji·) *n.* the study of reptiles [Gk. *herpein*, to creep].

Herr (her) *n.* the German equivalent of Mr. *pl.* **Herren** [Ger. *Herrenvolk*, master race].

her·ring (her'·ing) *n.* a familiar sea-fish, moving in shoals, much used as a food. **-bone** *n.* a zig-zag pattern. **red herring**, herring cured and dried by a special process; (*Fig.*) subject deliberately introduced into a discussion to divert criticism from main issue [O.E. *haering*].

hers See **her.**

hes·i·tate (hez'·ạ·tāt) *v.i.* to feel or show indecision; to hold back; to stammer. **hesitant** *a.* pausing; slow to decide. **hesitance, hesitancy** *n.* **hesitation** *n.* doubt; indecision. **hesitantly, hesitatingly** *adv.* [L. *haesitare*, fr. *haerere*, to stick fast].

Hes·per·us (hes'·pẹr·as) *n.* the planet Venus as the evening star. **Hesperian** (hes·pē'·ri·an) *a.* western [Gk. *hesperos*, evening].

Hes·sian (he'·shạn) *a.* pert. to *Hesse*, in Germany; *n.* a native of Hesse. — **boots**, high, tasseled boots first worn by Hessian troops.

het·er·o·dox (het'·ạ·rạ·dȧks) *a.* contrary to

accepted opinion, esp. in theology; not ortho-dox; heretical. **-y** n. [Gk. *heteros*, different; *doxa*, an opinion].

het·er·o·ge·ne·ous (het·ẹr·ạ·jē′·ni·ạs) a. composed of diverse elements; differing in kind; dissimilar. **heterogeneity, -ness** n. [Gk. *heteros*, different; *genos*, kind].

het·er·o·gen·e·sis (het·ẹr·ō·jen′·ạ·sis) n. (*Biol.*) spontaneous generation. **heterogenetic** a. [Gk. *heteros*, different; *genesis*, generation].

het·er·o·sex·u·al (het·ẹr·ō·sek′·shoo·ạl) a. directed towards the opposite sex [Gk. *heteros*, different; L. *sexus*].

hew (hū) v.t. to chop or cut with an ax or sword; to cut in pieces; to shape or form. *pa.p.* **-ed** *or* **-n. -er** n. [O.E. *heawan*].

hex (hex) n. a witch; (*Colloq.*) a jinx.

hex·a- *prefix* from Gk. *hex*, six, combining to form derivatixes, e.g. **-gon** n. a plane figure having six sides and six angles. **-gonal** a. **-hedron** n. solid figures having six faces, e.g. a cube. [Gk. *gōnia*, an angle; *hedra*, a base; L. *angulus*, a corner].

hex·ad (hek′·sad) n. a group of six [Gk. *hex*, six].

hex·am·e·ter (hek·sam′·ạ·tẹr) n. a verse of six feet [Gk. *hex*, six; *metron*, a measure].

hex·a·pod (hek′·sạ·pàd) n. a six-footed insect [Gk. *hex*, six; *pous*, a foot].

hey (hā) *interj.* used to call attention, or to express joy, wonder, or interrogation. **-day** n. the time of fullest strength and greatest vigor.

hi·a·tus (hī·ā′·tạs) n. a gap in a series; an opening; a lacuna; the pronunciation without elision of two adjacent vowels in successive syllables [L. fr. *hiare*, to gape].

hi·ber·nate (hī′·bẹr·nāt) v.i. to winter; to pass the winter, esp. in a torpid state. **hiberna-tion** n. [L. *hibernare*, fr. *hiems*, winter].

Hi·ber·ni·a (hī·bur′·ni·ạ) the Latin name for Ireland. **Hibernian** a., n.

Hi·bis·cus (hī·bis′·kạs) n. (*Bot.*) a genus of shrubs or tree with large flowers [Gk. *hibis-kos*].

hic·cup (hik′·up) n. a spasm of the breathing organs with an abrupt cough-like sound; the sound itself; v.i. to have this. *pr.p.* **-ping.** *pa.p.* and *pa.t.* **-ped** [of imit. origin].

hick (hik) n. (*Slang*) a farmer.

hick·o·ry (hik′·ạr·i·) n. a nut-bearing tree; its tough wood [*pohickery*, native name].

hi·dal·go (hi·dal′·gō) n. a Spanish nobleman [Sp. *hijo de algo* = son of something].

hide (hīd) v.t. to put or keep out of sight; to keep secret; v.i. to lie concealed. *pa.p.* **hidden, hid.** *pa.t.* **hid. hidden** a. concealed; secret; unknown. **hiddenly** adv. **hiding** n. conceal-ment; a place of concealment [O.E. *hydan*].

hide (hīd) n. skin of an animal; the dressed skin of an animal; (*Slang*) human skin; v.t. (*Colloq.*) to flog. **-bound** a. of animals, hav-ing the skin too close to the flesh; bigoted; narrow-minded. **hiding** n. (*Colloq.*) a flogging [O.E. *hyd*].

hid·e·ous (hid′·ē·ạs) a. repulsive; revolting; horrible; frightful. **-ly** adv. [Fr. *hideux*].

hie (hī) v.i. and *refl.* to go quickly; to hurry on; to urge on [O.E. *higian*, to strive].

hi·er·arch (hī′·ẹr·àrk) n. one who has author-ity in sacred things; a chief priest. **-al, -ical** a. **-ically** adv. **-y** n. a graded system of people or things; government by priests; the organi-zation of the priesthood according to different grades; each of the three orders of angels. [Gk. *hieros*, holy; *archein*, to rule].

hi·er·at·ic (hī·ẹr·at′·ĭk) a. priestly; pert. to a cursive style of ancient Egyptian writing, used by the priests [Gk. *hieratikos*, priestly].

hi·er·o- *prefix* from Gk. *hieros*, holy, combining to form derivatives, e.g. **hierograph** n. a sacred inscription. **hierology** n. the science or study of sacred things, esp. of the writings of the ancient Egyptians.

hi·er·o·glyph·ic (hī·ẹr·ạ·glif′·ik) (usually *pl.*) n. ancient Egyptian characters or symbols used in place of letters; picture-writing. Also **hieroglyph. hieroglyphic, hieroglyphical** a. [Gk. *hieros*, holy; *gluphein*, to carve].

hig·gle (hig′·l) v.i. to dispute about terms, esp. in bargaining [fr. E. *haggle*].

high (hī) a. elevated; tall; towering; far up; elevated in rank, etc.; chief; eminent; proud; loud; angry, as words; strongly marked, as color; dear; costly; extreme; sharp, as tone or voice; tainted, as meat; remote from equator, as latitude; (*Colloq.*) drunk; adv. far up; strongly; to a great extent. **-ly** adv. **-ball** n. mixed whisky and soda. **—born** a. of noble birth. **-bred** a. of superior breeding, thorough-bred. **-brow** a. and n. (*Colloq.*) intellectual, esp. in a snobbish manner. **—falutin', —fa-luting** a. pretentious. **—frequency** n. (*Ra-dio*) any frequency above the audible range. **—flown** a. elevated; extravagant. **-flyer, -flier** n. (*Fig.*) an ambitious person. **-lands** n.pl. a mountainous region. **Highlander** n. an inhabitant of a mountainous region, esp. highlands of Scotland. **-lights** n.pl (*Art.*) the brightest parts of a painting; (*Fig.*) mo-ments of crisis; persons of importance. **-ness** n. the quality of being high; a title of honor to princes and princesses. **-pitched** a. of a shrill sound. **-road** n. a main road. **— school,** a school (grades 9 through 12), following gram-mar school; a school (grades 10 through 12), following junior high school (grades 7 through 9); **— seas,** the sea or ocean beyond the three-mile belt of coastal waters. **-spirited** a. bold; daring. **—strung** a. in a state of tension. **—treason,** any breach of allegiance due from a citizen to the government. **— water** n. a high tide at which the tide reaches its highest ele-vation. **-way** n. a main road; a public road; an ordinary route. **-wayman** n. a robber on a public road, esp. a mounted one [O.E. *heah*].

hi·jack·er (hī′·jak·ẹr) n. (*Slang*) one who robs; a smuggler or a bootlegger.

hike (hīk) v.i. to walk; to tramp; v.t. to hoist or carry on one's back; n. a journey on foot. **-r** n.

hi·lar·i·ous (hi·la′·ri·ạs) a. mirthful; joyous. **-ly** adv. **hilarity** n. merriment; boisterous joy [Gk. *hilaros*, cheerful].

hill (hil) n. a natural elevation of land; a small mountain; a mound; v.t. to heap up. **-y** a. full of hills. **-iness** n. **-ock** n. a small hill [O.E. *hyll*].

hilt (hilt) n. the handle of a sword, dagger, etc. [O.E. *hilt*].

him (him) *pron.* the objective case of the pro-noun he. **-self** *pron.* emphatic and reflexive form of **he** and **him** [O.E.].

hind (hind) n. the female of the deer.

hind, hind·er (hīnd, hīnd′·ẹr) a. at the back; placed at the back; a combining form in such words as **-leg. -most** a. the furtherest behind; the last [O.E. *hinder*].

hin·der (hin′·dẹr) v.t. to prevent from pro-gressing; to stop. **-er** n. **hindrance** n. the act of impeding progress; obstruction; obstacle [O.E. *hindrian*, to keep back].

Hin·du·stan (hind′·doo·stan) n. (*Geog.*) the name applied to the country of the upper val-ley of the R. Ganges, India. **Hindi, Hindes** (hin′·dē) n. an Indo-Germanic language spoken in N. India. **Hindu, Hindoo** (hin′·dòò) n. a native of Hindustan. **Hindustani, Hindoo-stanee** n. chief language of Hindu India; also known as 'Urdu' [Urdu, *Hind*, India].

hinge (hinj) n. a movable joint, as that on which a door, lid, etc. hangs; point on which thing depends; v.t. to attach with, or as with a hinge; v.i. to turn on; to depend on [M.E. *heng*].

hint (hint) n. a slight allusion; an indirect suggestion; an indication; v.t. and i. to allude to indirectly [O.E. *hentan*, to seize].

hin·ter·land (hint′·ẹr·land) *n.* the district inland from the coast or a river [Ger.].

hip (hip) *n.* the upper part of the thigh; the haunch; the angle of 2 sloping sides of a roof; *interj.* a cheer [O.E. *hype*].

hip (hip) *n.* the fruit of the rose, esp. of the wild-rose [O.E. *heope*].

hip·ped (hipt) *a.* (*Slang*) obsessed (with *on*) [corrupt. of *hypochondria*].

Hip·poc·ra·tes (hi·pàk′·ra̧·tēz) *n.* a Greek physician, the 'Father of Medicine,' born about 460 B.C. **Hippocratic** *a.* pert. to him.

hip·po·drome (hip′·ạ·drōm) *n.* in ancient Greece and Rome, a stadium for horse and chariot races; an arena [Gk. *hippos*, a horse; *dromos*, a course].

hip·po·pot·a·mus (hip·ạ·pàt′·ạ·mạs) *n.* a very large pachydermatous African quadruped frequenting rivers. *pl.* **-es** or **hippopotami** (hip·ạ·pàt′·ạ·mī) [Gk. *hippos*, a horse; *potamos*, a river].

hir·cine (hur′·sīn) *a.* pert. to a goat; strong-smelling (like a goat) [L. *hircus*, a goat].

hire (hīr) *n.* payment for the use of a thing; wages; a hiring or being hired; *v.t.* to pay for the use of a thing; to contract with for wages; to take care or give on hire. **-r** *n.* **-ling** *n.* one who serves for wages (generally used in contempt) [O.E. *hur*, wages].

hir·sute (hur′·sòòt) *a.* hairy; (*Bot.*) set with bristles [L. *hirsutus*, hairy].

his (hiz) *pron.* and *a.* the possessive case of the pronoun **he,** belonging to him [O.E.].

his·pid (his′·pid) *a.* (*Bot.*) bristly; having rough hairs [L. *hispidus*, rough].

hiss (his) *v.i.* to make a sound like that of *ss* as in 'ass,' esp. to express strong dislike or disapproval; *n.* the sound. **-ing** *n.* [imit.].

hist (hist) *interj.* a word used to command attention or silence.

his·ta·mine (his′·ta·mēn) *n.* substance released by the tissues in allergic reactions [*histidine* + *amine*].

his·to- *prefix* from Gk. *histos*, a web or tissue, combining to form derivatives, e.g.—**histology** (his·tàl′·ạ·ji·) *n.* the science that treats of the minute structure of the tissues of animals, plants, etc. [Gk. *histos*, tissue; *logos*, a discourse].

his·to·ry (his′·ta̧·ri·) *n.* the study of past events; a record of events in the life of a nation, state, institution, epoch, etc.; a description of animals, plants, minerals, etc. existing on the earth, called **natural history. historian** (his·tō′·ri·ạn) *n.* a writer of history. **historic** *a.* pert. to, or noted in, history. **historical** *a.* of, or based on, history: belonging to the past. **historically** *adv.* **historicity** *n.* the historical character of an event; the genuineness of it [Gk. *historia*, an inquiry].

his·tri·on·ic (his·trē·àn′·ik) *a.* theatrical; affected. **-al** *a.* **-ally** *adv.* **-s** *n.pl.* theatrical representation [L. *histrio*, an actor].

hit (hit) *v.t.* to strike with a blow or missile; to affect severely; to find; *v.i.* to strike; to light (upon). *pr.p.* **-ting.** *pa.p.* and *pa.t.* **hit.** *n.* a blow; a stroke; a success [O.E. *hyttan*].

hitch (hich) *v.t.* to raise or move with a jerk; to fasten with a loop; etc.; to harness; *v.i.* to be caught or fastened; *n.* a jerk; a fastening, loop, or knot; a difficulty; (*Slang*) to marry. **-er** *n.* **to -hike,** to travel by begging rides from motorists, etc. [etym. uncertain].

hith·er (hiTH′·ẹr) *adv.* to or toward this place; *a.* situated on this side. **-most** *a.* nearest in this direction. **-to** *adv.* up to now [O.E. *hider*].

hive (hīv) *n.* a place where bees live; place of great activity; *v.t.* to gather or place bees in a hive; *v.i.* to enter a hive; to take shelter together; to live in company [O.E. *hyf*].

hives (hīvz) *n.* an eruptive skin disease.

hoar (hōr) *a.* gray with age; grayish-white.

-y *a.* white or gray with age; venerable; of great antiquity. **-frost** *n.* white frost; frozen dew [O.E. *har*].

hoard (hōrd) *n.* a stock or store, esp. if hidden away; a treasure; *v.t.* to store secretly; *v.i.* to lay up a store. **-er** *n.* [O.E. *hord*, treasure].

hoarse (hōrs) *a.* rough and harsh sounding; husky; having a hoarse voice. **-ly** *adv.* **-ness** *n.* [O.E. *has*].

hoax (hōks) *v.t.* to deceive by an amusing or mischievous story; to play a trick upon for sport; *n.* a practical joke. **-er** *n.* [contr. fr. *hocus*].

hob (hàb) *n.* the flat-topped casing of a fireplace where things are placed to be kept warm. **-nail** *n.* a large-headed nail for boot soles.

hob (hàb) *n.* an elf; (*Colloq.*) mischief. **-goblin** *n.* a mischievous elf; a bogy [corrupt. of *Robin* or *Robert*].

hob·ble (hàb′·l) *v.i.* to walk lamely; to limp; *v.t.* to tie the legs together of a horse, etc.; to impede; *n.* a limping gait; a fetter; a rope for hobbling [etym. uncertain].

hob·ble·de·hoy (hàb′·l·di·hoi) *n.* a clumsy youth [etym. uncertain; perh. fr. *hobble*].

hob·by (hàb′·i·) *n.* formerly a small horse; a favorite pursuit or pastime. **-horse** *n.* a stick with a horse's head, or a rocking horse used as a child's toy; at fairs, etc. a wooden horse on a merry-go-round [*Hob*, for *Robert*].

hob·nail See **hob.**

hob·nob (hàb′·nàb) *v.i.* to drink together; to be very friendly with [etym. uncertain].

ho·bo (hō′·bō) *n.* a vagrant; a tramp.

hock (hàk) *n.* the joint of a quadruped's hind leg between the knee and the fetlock [O.E. *hoh*, the heel].

hock (hàk) *v.t.*, *n.* pawn [D. *hok*, debt].

hock·ey (hàk′·i·) *n.* a game played with a ball or disk and curved sticks [perh. fr. O.Fr. *hoquet*, a crook].

ho·cus (hō′·kạs) *v.i.* to hoax; to stupefy with drugs. **hocus-pocus** *n.* an incantation; a juggler's trick; trickery [a sham L. formula used by jugglers].

hod (hàd) *n.* a small trough on a staff used by builders for carrying mortar, bricks, etc. [Fr. *hotte*, a basket].

hodge-podge (hàj′·pàj) *n.* a medley or mixture. Also **hotchpotch** [fr. *hocher*, to shake; *pot*, a pot].

hoe (hō) *n.* a tool for breaking ground, scraping out weeds, etc.; *v.t.* to break up or weed with a hoe. **-r** *n.* [O.Fr. *houe*].

hoe-down (hō′·doun) *n.* lively square dance.

hog (hawg, hàg) *n.* a swine; a pig, esp. if reared for fattening; (*Colloq.*) a greedy or dirty fellow; *v.t.* (*Slang*) to take more than one's share of; to cut (horse's mane short); *v.i.* to arch the back. **-gish** *a.* like a hog. **-back, -s-back** *n.* a crested hill-ridge. **-tie** *v.* (*Colloq.*) to make incapable as if by tying up. **-wash** *n.* kitchen swill etc. used for feeding pigs; anything worthless [O.E. *hogg*].

hogs-head (hawgz′·, hàgz′·hed; hawgz′·ạd) *n.* a large cask; a liquid measure [etym uncertain].

hoi pol·loi (hoi′·pạ·loi′) *n.pl.* the masses [Obs.].

hoist (hoist) *v.t.* to raise aloft, esp. of flags; to raise with tackle, etc.; *n.* a hoisting; an elevator; a lift [Dut. *hijschen*, to hoist].

hold (hōld) *v.t.* to keep fast; to grasp; to support in or with the hands, etc.; to own; to occupy; to detain; to celebrate; to believe; to contain; *v.i.* to cling; not to give way; to abide (by); to keep (to); to proceed; to be in force. *pa.p.* and *pa.t.* **held.** *n.* a grasp; grip; handle; binding power and influence; a prison. **-er** *n.* **-ing** *n.* land, farm, etc. rented from another; stocks held. **to hold up,** to support; to cause delay; to obstruct; to commit robbery with threats of violence [O.E. *healdan*].

hold (hōld) *n.* the space below the deck of a ship, for cargo [earlier *hole*].

hole (hōl) *n.* a hollow; cavity; pit; den; lair; burrow; opening; a perforation; mean habitation; (*Colloq.*) awkward situation; *v.t.* to make a hole in; to perforate; to put into a hole; *v.i.* to go into a hole [O.E. *hol,* a hollow].

hol·i·day (hål'·a·dā) *n.* a day of rest from work esp. in memory of an event or a person [fr. *holy day*].

Hol·land·er (hål'·an·der) *n.* a native of Holland, the Netherlands.

hol·ler (hål'·er) *v.* (*Dial.*) shout; yell.

hol·low (hål'·ō) *n.* a cavity; a hole; a depression; a valley; *a.* having a cavity; not solid; empty; *v.t.* to make a hollow in. **—eyed** *a.* with sunken eyes. **—toned** *a.* deep toned. **-ware** *n.* silver serving dishes [O.E. *holh*].

hol·ly (hål'·i·) *n.* an evergreen shrub with prickly leaves and red berries [O.E. *holegn*].

hol·ly·hock (hål'·ē·håk) *n.* a tall garden plant [A.S. = *holy hock,* O.E. *hoc,* mallow].

hol·o- a combining form, fr. Gk. *holos,* whole, used in many derivatives. **-caust** (hål'·a·-kawst) *n.* a burnt offering; destruction, or slaughter. **-graph** *n.* and *a.* any writing, as a letter, deed, will, etc. wholly in the handwriting of the signer of it. **-graphic** *a.* [Gk. *kaustos,* burnt; *graphein,* to write]. [tol. **-ed** *a.* [Dut.]

hol·ster (hōl'·ster) *n.* a leather case for a pistol.

ho·ly (hō'·li·) *a.* belonging to, or devoted to, God; morally perfect; divine; sacred; pious; religious. **holily** *adv.* **holiness** *n.* the quality of being holy. **— day** *n.* a religious festival. **Holy Ghost, Holy Spirit,** the third person of the Godhead or Trinity. **Holy Land,** Palestine. **— orders** *n.* the office of a clergyman; the Christian ministry [O.E. *halig*].

hom·age (håm'·ij, åm'·ij) *n.* in feudal times, service due by a vassal to his over-lord; tribute; respect paid; reverence; deference [Fr. *hommage,* fr. *homme,* a man].

hom·burg (håm'·burg) *n.* a type of men's soft, felt hat [fr. *Homburg,* in Germany].

home (hōm) *n.* one's fixed residence; a dwelling-place; a native place or country; an institution for the infirm, sick, poor, etc.; *a.* pert. to, or connected with, home; not foreign; domestic; *adv.* to or at one's home; to the point aimed at; close. **— economics** *n.pl.,* theory and practice of homemaking. **-lessness** *n.* the state of being without a home. **-ly** *a.* belonging to home; plain; ugly. **-liness** *n.* **—grown** *a.* grown in one's own garden, locality, etc. **-land** *n.* one's native land. **—made** *a.* made at home. **— rule** *n.* self-government. **— run** *n.* (*Baseball*) a safe hit that allows a batter to touch all bases to score a run. **-sick** *a.* depressed in spirits through absence from home. **-sickness** *n.* **-spun** *a.* spun or made at home; anything plain or homely. **-stead** *n.* a house with land and buildings. **— stretch** *n.* on a racecourse, the part between the last curve and the finish line; the final stage. **-work** *n.* schoolwork to be done outside of class. [O.E. *ham*].

home (hōm) *v.i.* of a pigeon, to fly home; *v.t.* in naval warfare, to guide (another ship or aircraft) by radio to the attack of a target.

ho·me·op·a·thy (hō·mē·åp'·a·thi·) *n.* the treatment of disease by the administration of very small doses of drugs which would produce in a healthy person effects similar to the symptoms of the disease. Also **homeotherapy. homeopath, homeopathist** *n.* **homeopathic** *a.* [Gk. *homoios,* like; *pathos,* feeling].

hom·i·cide (håm'·a·sīd) *n.* manslaughter; the one who kills. **homicidal** *a.* [L. *homo,* a man; *caedere,* to kill].

hom·i·ly (håm'·a·li·) *n.* a discourse on a religious or moral subject; a sermon. **homilist** *n.* [Gk. *homilia,* converse].

hom·i·ny (håm'·a·ni·) *n.* maize porridge [Amer.-Ind.].

ho·mo- a combining form fr. Gk. *homos,* the same, used in derivatives. **-centric** *a.* having the same center.

ho·moe·o·path. See **homeopathy.**

ho·mog·e·ne·ous (hō·ma·jē'·ni·as) *a.* of the same kind or nature; similar; uniform. **-ness, homogeneity** (hō·ma·ja·nē'·a·ti·) *n.* sameness; uniformity. **homogenize** *v.* to make uniform [Gk. *homo,* the same; *genos,* a kind].

hom·o·graph (håm'·a·graf) *n.* a word having the same spelling as another, but different meaning and origin [Gk. *homos,* the same; *graphein,* to write].

ho·mol·o·gate (hō·mål'·a·gāt) *v.t.* to approve; to confirm. **homologous** *a.* having the same relative value, position, etc. **homologation** *n.* [Gk. *homos,* the same; *legein,* to say].

hom·o·nym (håm'·a·nim) *n.* a word having the same pronunciation as another but a different meaning, e.g. *air* and *heir.* Also **homophone** [Gk. *homos,* the same; *onoma,* a name].

ho·mo sa·pi·ens (hō'·mō·sā'·pi·ans) scientific term for human being, man.

ho·mo·sex·u·al·ity (hō·ma·sek·shoo·al'·a·-ti·) *n.* attraction between individuals of the same sex. **homosexual** *n.* a person thus perverted [Gk. *homos,* the same; and *sex*].

hone (hōn) *n.* a stone for sharpening knives, etc. *v.t.* to sharpen on one [O.E. *han,* a stone].

hon·est (ån'·ist) *a.* upright; dealing fairly; just; faithful; free from fraud; unadulterated. **-ly** *adv.* **-y** *n.* upright conduct or disposition; (*Bot.*) a small flowering plant with semi-transparent, silvery pods [L. *homestus,* honorable].

hon·ey (hun'·i·) *n.* the sweet, thick fluid collected by bees from flowers; anything very sweet; sweetness; (*Colloq.*) sweetheart; darling; *a.* sweet; luscious; *v.t.* to sweeten. *pa.p.* and *a.* **-ed** (hun'·id). Also **honied** *a.* sweet; (*Fig.*) flattering. **-bee** *n.* the common hive-bee. **-comb** *n.* the structure of wax in hexagonal cells in which bees place honey, eggs, etc.; anything resembling this; *v.t.* to fill with cells or perforations. **-combed** *a.* **-dew** (hun'·i·dū) *n.* a sweet sticky substance found on plants; a melon. **-moon** *n.* the holiday taken by a newly-wed couple. Also, *v.i.* **-suckle** *n.* a climbing plant with yellow flowers [O.E. *hunig*].

honk (hawngk) *n.* the cry of the wild goose; any sound resembling this [imit.].

honk·y-tonk (hång'·ki·tångk) *n.* (*Slang*) a cheap saloon [echoic].

hon·or (ån'·er) *n.* high respect; renown; glory; reputation; sense of what is right or due; a source or cause of honor; high rank or position; a title of respect given to a judge, etc.; chastity; *v.t.* to respect highly; to confer a mark of distinction on; to accept or pay (a bill, etc.) when due. **-s** *n.pl.* public marks of respect or distinction; distinction given a student for outstanding work. **-able** *a.* worthy of honor; upright; a title of distinction or respect. **-ably** *adv.* **-ableness** *n.* **an affair of honor,** a duel. **maid of honor,** a lady in the service of a queen or princess; chief attendant of a bride. [Fr. *honneur,* fr. L. *honor*].

hon·or·ary (ån'·a·rer·i·) *a.* conferred for the sake of honor only; holding a position without pay or usual requirements. **honorarium** (ån·a·re'·ri·am) *n.* a sum of money granted voluntarily to a person for services rendered. **honorific** *a.* conferring honor; *n.* term of respect [L. *honorarius*].

hooch (hooch) *n.* (*Slang*) alcoholic liquor [fr. Amer.-Ind. *hoochinoo,* spirit].

hood (hood) *n.* a covering for the head and neck, often part of a cloak or gown; an appendage to a graduate's gown designating his university and degree; the cover of an automobile engine; *v.t.* to cover with a hood. **-wink** *v.t.* to blindfold; to deceive [O.E. *hod*].

hood·lum (hood'·lam) *n.* a hooligan.

hoo·doo (hoo'·doo) (*Colloq.*) *n.* uncanny, bad luck; a cause of such luck [same as voodoo].

hoo·ey (hoo'·i·) *interj., n.* (*Slang*) nonsense.

hoof (hoof, hoof) *n.* the horny casing of the foot of a horse, ox, sheep, etc.; *pl.* **-s, hooves** [O.E.]

hook (hook) *n.* a bent piece of metal, etc. for catching hold, hanging up, etc.; a bent piece of barbed steel for catching fish; anything curved or bent like a hook; *v.t.* and *i.* to fasten, draw, catch, etc. with a hook; to catch a fish with a hook; (*Golf*) to drive a ball in a curve to the left; (*Boxing*) to deliver a blow with bent elbow. **hooks and eyes**, bent metallic clips and catches used for fastening. **-up** *n.* the interconnection of broadcasting stations for relaying program; a connection [O.E. *hoc*].

hook·ah, hoo·ka (hoo'·ka) *n.* a tobacco pipe in which the smoke is drawn through water and a long tube [Ar. *huggah*, a vessel].

hook·worm (hook'·wurm) *n.* (*Med.*) a parasitic worm, infesting the intestines.

hoo·li·gan (hool'·i·gan) *n.* one of a gang of street roughs; a rowdy [name of a person].

hoop (hoop, hoop) *n.* a band for holding together the staves of casks, etc.; a circle of wood or metal for rolling as a toy; a stiff circular band to hold out a woman's skirt; *v.t.* to bind with a hoop. [O.E. *hop*].

hoot (hoot) *n.* the cry of an owl; a cry of disapproval; *v.t.* to assail with hoots; *v.i.* to cry as an owl; to cry out in disapproval. **-er** *n.* [imit.].

hooves (hoovz, hoovz) *pl.* of **hoof.**

hop (hap) *v.i.* of persons, to spring on one foot; of animals or birds, to leap or skip on all feet at once. *pr.p.* **-ping.** *pa.p.* and *pa.t.* **-ped.** *n.* an act or the action of hopping; (*Slang*) a dance; (*Aviation*) one stage in a flight. **-per** *n.* one who hops; a device for feeding material into a mill or machine; a railroad car with dumping device for coal, sand, etc. **hop-o-my-thumb** *n.* a dwarf [O.E. *hoppian*].

hop (hap) *n.* a climbing plant with bitter cones used to flavor beer, etc.; *v.t.* to flavor with hops. **-s** *n.pl.* the cones of the hop plant [Dut.].

hope (hop) *n.* a desire combined with expectation gives grounds for hoping; thing desired; *v.t.* to desire, with belief in possibility of obtaining; *v.i.* to feel hope. **-ful** *a.* **-fully** *adv.* **-fulness** *n.* **-less** *a.* **-lessly** *adv.* [O.E. *hopian*].

hop·scotch (hap'·skach) *n.* a child's game, played on an arrangement of squares [E. *hop; scotch*, a slight cut or score].

ho·ral (hō'·ral) *a.* of or pert. to an hour; hourly [L. *hora*, an hour].

horde (hord) *n.* a great multitude; a troop of nomads or tent-dwellers [Turk. *ordu*, a camp].

hore·hound (hor'·hound) *n.* a plant with bitter juice, used for coughs or as a tonic; a candy flavored with the herb. Also **hoarhound** [O.E. *harehune*].

ho·ri·zon (ha·rī'·zan) *n.* the boundary of the part of the earth seen from any given point; the line where earth (or sea) and sky seem to meet. **horizontal** (har·a·zan'·tal) *a.* parallel to the horizon; level. **horizontally** *adv.* [Gk. *horizein*, to bound].

hor·mone (hawr'·mōn) *n.* a substance secreted by certain glands which passes into the blood and stimulates the action of various organs [Gk. *hormaein*, to set moving].

horn (hawrn) *n.* a hard projecting organ growing from heads of cows, deer, etc.; substance forming this organ; tentacle of a snail, etc.; a wind instrument of music; a drinking cup; a utensil for holding gunpowder; a sounding contrivance on motors as warning; either of the extremities of the crescent moon; *v.t.* to furnish with horns; to gore. **-y** *a.* of, or made of, horn; hard or callous. **-beam** *n.* a small tree or shrub. **-book** *n.* a primer for children, formerly covered with horn to protect it. **-pipe** *n.* an old musical instrument; a vigorous dance;

the lively tune for such a dance. **horn of plenty**, or cornucopia; a representation of a horn, filled with flowers, fruit and grain [O.E.].

hor·net (hawr'·nat) *n.* a large insect of the wasp family [O.E. *hyrnet*, dim. of *horn*].

ho·ro- from Gk. *hōra*, time; used as a combining form, e.g.—**horologe** (hawr'·a·lōj) *n.* an instrument of any kind for telling the time. **horologer, horologist** *n.* **horology** *n.* the science of measuring time; the art of making timepieces [Gk. *hōra*, time; *legein*, to tell; *metron*, a measure].

hor·o·scope (har', hawr'·a·skōp) *n.* a chart of of the heavens which predicts the character and potential abilities of the individual as well as future events. **horoscopic** *a.* [Gk. *hōra*, time; *skopein*, to observe].

hor·rent (hawr'·ant) *a.* (*Poet.*) standing erect, as bristles; bristling [L. *horrere*, to bristle].

hor·ri·ble (har', hawr'·a·bl) *a.* tending to excite horror, fear, dread. **horribly** *adv.* **-ness** *n.* **horrid** *a.* frightful; shocking; abominable. **horrify** *v.t.* to strike with horror, dread, repulsion; to shock. **horrific** (ha, haw·rif'·ik) *a.* causing horror [L. *horrere*, to bristle].

hor·ror (ha', haw'·rer) *n.* a painful emotion of fear, dread and repulsion; that which excites dread and abhorrence [L. from *horrere*, to bristle].

horse (hawrs) *n.* a large hoofed quadruped used for riding, drawing vehicles, etc.; the male of the horse species, as distinct from the female (the mare); mounted soldiers; in gymnastics, a vaulting-block; a frame for drying clothes; *v.t.* to provide with a horse, or horses; to carry or support on the back; *v.i.* to mount on a horse. **horsy** *a.* pert. to horses; fond of, or interested in, horses. **horsiness** *n.* **-back** *n.* the back of a horse. **-fly** *n.* a stinging fly troublesome to horses. **-hair** *n.* hair from the tail or mane of a horse; haircloth. **-laugh** *n.* a loud boisterous laugh. **-leech** *n.* a large kind of leech. **-man** *n.* a man on horseback; a skilled rider. **-manship** *n.* the art of riding or of training horses. — **opera** (*Film Slang*) a thriller film with a Wild West setting. **-pistol** *n.* an old kind of large pistol. **-play** *n.* rough and boisterous play. **-power** *n.* (abbrev. **h.p.**), the power a horse is capable of exerting; estimated (in *Mechanics*) to be the power of lifting 33,000 lb. one foot high in one minute. **-radish** *n.* a cultivated plant used for sauces, salads, etc. **-sense** *n.* (*Colloq.*) common sense. **-shoe** *n.* a curved, narrow band of iron for nailing to the underpart of the hoof [O.E. *hors*].

hor·ta·tive, hor·ta·tory (hawr'·ta·tiv, hawr'·ta·tō·ri·) *a.* tending or serving to exhort; advisory [L. *hortari*, to exhort].

hor·ti·cul·ture (hawr'·ti·kul·cher) *n.* gardening; the art of cultivating a garden [L. *hortus*, garden; *colere*, to cultivate].

ho·san·na (hō·zan'·a) *n.* a cry of praise to God; an exclamation of adoration [Gk.].

hose (hōz) *n.* stockings; socks; a covering for the legs and feet; tight-fitting breeches or pants; a flexible tube or pipe for conveying water; *v.t.* to water with a hose. **hosier** (hō'·zher) *n.* dealer in hosiery. **hosiery** *n.* a collective word for stockings and similar garments [O.E. *hosa*].

hos·pice (has'·pis) *n.* a traveler's house of rest kept by a religious order [L. *hospitium*, fr. *hospes*, a guest].

hos·pi·ta·ble (has'·pi·ta·bl) *a.* receiving and entertaining guests in a friendly and liberal fashion. **hospitality** *n.* generous reception of strangers and guests [L. *hospes*, a guest].

hos·pi·tal (has'·pi·tal) *n.* an institution for the care of the sick. **-ization** *n.* being in the hospital. **-ize** *v.t.* [L. *hospes*, a guest].

host (hōst) *n.* one who lodges or entertains another; an innkeeper; an animal or plant which has parasites living on it. **-ess** *n.* a woman who entertains guests. **hostel** (hás′.- tǎl) *n.* a lodging place for young people who are hiking or traveling by bicycle; (*Arch.*) an inn. **hostelry** *n.* (*Arch.*) an inn [L. *hospes*, a host or guest].

host (hōst) *n.* a large number; a multitude; a crowd; (*Arch.*) an army. **the heavenly host**, the angels and archangels; the stars and planets [L. *hostis*, an enemy].

Host (hōst) *n.* the bread consecrated in the Eucharist [L. *hostia*, a sacrificial victim].

hos·tage (hás′.tij) *n.* one handed over to the enemy as security [O.Fr. *hostage*, fr. L. *hospes*, a guest].

hos·tel See **host.**

hos·tile (hás′.tǎl) *a.* of, or pert. to, an enemy; unfriendly; opposed. **-ly** *adv.* **hostility** *n.* opposition; *pl.* state or acts of warfare [L. *hostis*, an enemy].

hos·tler, ostler (hás′.lẹr, ás′.lẹr) *n.* (*Arch.*) a groom at an inn [O.Fr. *hostel*].

hot (hát) *a.* of high temperature; very warm; of quick temper; ardent or passionate; (of dance music) florid and intricate. **-ly** *adv.* **-ness** *n.* **-bed** *n.* in gardening, a glass-covered bed for bringing on plants quickly; hence (*Fig.*) any place conducive to quick growth (e.g. of scandal, vice, etc.). **—blooded** *a.* high-spirited; quick to anger. **— dog** *n.* (*Colloq.*) a sandwich roll with hot sausage inside. **-foot** *adv.* swiftly; in great haste. **-head** *n.* an impetuous person. **-house** *n.* heated house, usually of glass for rearing of plants [O.E. *hat*].

ho·tel (hō·tel′) *n.* a large and superior kind of inn. **-keeper** *n.* [Fr. *hotel*].

Hot·ten·tot (hát′.n.tát) *n.* a member of a native race of S. Africa [Dut. imit.].

hound (hound) *n.* a dog used in hunting, esp. in hunting by scent; (*Slang*) despicable man; (*Slang*) an addict or fan; *v.t.* to chase with, or as with, hounds; (with 'on') to urge or incite; to pursue, to nag [O.E. *hund*].

hour (our) *n.* the twenty-fourth part of a day, or 60 minutes; the time of day; an appointed time or occasion; *pl.* the fixed times of work, prayers, etc. **-glass** *n.* a sand-glass running for an hour. **— hand** *n.* the index which shows the hour on the face of a watch, clock, or chronometer. **-ly** *adv.* happening every hour; frequently [L. *hora*].

hou·ri (hŏŏ′.ri; hou′.ri·) *n.* a nymph of the Mohammedan paradise [Pers. *huri*].

house (hous) *n.* a dwelling-place; a legislative or other assembly; a family; a business firm; audience at theater, etc.; dynasty; a school residence hall. *pl.* **houses** (houz′.as). **house** (houz) *v.t.* to shelter; to receive; to store; *v..i* to dwell. **housing** (hou′.zing) *n.* shelter; the providing of houses; a support for part of a machine, etc. **-ful** *n.* **-less** *a.* **-hold** *n.* the inmates of a house; *a.* domestic. **-keeper** *n.* the woman who attends to the care of the household. **-wife** *n.* the mistress of a family; a little case or bag for materials used in sewing. **-wifery** (hous′.wif·ri·) *n.* housekeeping. **-boat** *n.* a flat-bottomed barge, with a houselike superstructure. **—fly** *n.* the common fly or *musca domestica.* **— physician, — surgeon** *n.* the resident medical officer of a hospital, etc. **-warming** *n.* a merrymaking to celebrate entry into a new house. **the House**, the House of Representatives [O.E. *hus*].

hous·ing (hou′.zing) *n.* a saddle-cloth; *pl.* the trappings of a horse [Fr. *housse*].

hove (hōv) *pa.p.* and *pa.t.* of **heave.**

hov·el (huv′.ạl, háv′.ạl) *n.* a small, mean house; *v.t.* to put in a hovel [dim. of O.E. *hof*, a dwelling].

hov·er (huv′.ẹr, háv′.ẹr) *v.i.* to hang fluttering in the air, or on the wing; to loiter; to waver.

how (hou) *adv.* in what manner; by what means;

to what degree or extent; in what condition. **-beit** (hou·bē′.it) *adv.* nevertheless. **-ever** (hou·ev′.ẹr) *adv.* in whatever manner or degree; *conj.* in spite of how. **-soever** *adv.* however [O.E. *hu*].

how·itz·er (hou′.it·sẹr) *n.* a form of gun, with a high trajectory [Bohemian *houfnice*, an engine for hurling stones].

howl (houl) *v.i.* to utter a prolonged, wailing cry such as that of a wolf or dog; to cry; (*Colloq.*) to laugh heartily; *v.i.* to utter with howling; *n.* a wail or cry. **-er** *n.* one who howls; (*Colloq.*) a ridiculous blunder [imit. origin].

hoy·den, hoiden (hoi′.dn) *n.* a rude, bold girl; a tomboy. **-ish** *a.* romping; bold; boisterous.

hub (hub) *n.* the central part, or nave, of a wheel; center of activity [var. of *hob*].

hub·bub (hub′.ub) *n.* a commotion [imit.].

hub·by (hub′.i·) *n.* (*Colloq.*) husband.

huck·a·back (huk′.ạ.bak) *n.* a kind of coarse linen with an uneven surface, much used for towels. Also **huck** [L. Ger. *hukkebak*].

huck·le·ber·ry (huk′.l.ber·i·) *n.* an American shrub which bears small black or dark blue berries [O.E. *heorot-berge*].

huck·le·bone (huk′.l.bōn) *n.* the hipbone; the anklebone [dim. of *huck*, hook].

huck·ster (huk′.stẹr) *n.* retailer of small articles; a street peddler; a mean, mercenary fellow; (*Colloq.*) an advertising man; *v.i.* to peddle [O.Dut. *hoekster*].

hud·dle (hud′.l) *v.t.* to crowd together; to heap together confusedly; *v.i.* to press together. **to go into a huddle with** (*Slang*) to meet in conference with [etym. uncertain].

hue (hū) *n.* color; tint. **-d** *a.* having a color (generally in compounds) [O.Fr. *hiw*].

hue (hū) *n.* an outcry; now only used in **hue and cry**, a loud outcry [Fr. *huer*, to hoot].

huff (huf) *n.* a fit of petulance or anger; *v.t.* to bully; *v.i.* to take offense. **-y** *a.*

hug (hug) *v.t.* to clasp tightly in the arms; to embrace; to cling to. *pr.p.* **-ging.** *pa.t.*, *pa.p.* **-ged.** *n.* a close embrace [etym. uncertain].

huge (hūj) *a.* very large; immense; enormous. **-ly** *adv.* **-ness** *n.* [O.Fr. *ahuge*].

Hu·gue·not (hū′.gạ.nát) *n.* a 16th cent. French Protestant [etym. uncertain].

huh (hu) *interj.* expressing contempt, surprise or to ask a question.

hu·la (hoo′.lạ) *n.* native Hawaiian dance.

hulk (hulk) *n.* the body of a ship, esp. dismantled ship; anything big and unwieldy; *v.i.* to be bulky; (*Dial.*) to slouch. **-ing, -y** *a.* unwieldy; clumsy [O.E. *hulc*, ship].

hull (hul) *n.* husk of any fruit, seed, or grain; frame or body of a vessel; *v.t.* to remove shell or husk; to pierce hull of, as of a ship [O.E. *hulu*, husk].

hul·la·ba·loo (hul′.ạ.bạ.lŏŏ) *n.* uproar; outcry [imit. origin].

hul·lo, hul·loa (hạ.lō′) *niterj.* hello.

hum (hum) *v.t.* to sing with the lips closed; *v.i.* to make droning sound, as bee. *n.* the noise of bees or the like; a low droning; (*Colloq.*) to be very busy. *pr.p.* **-ming.** *pa.p.* and *pa.t.* **-med** [imit. origin].

hu·man (hū′.mạn) *a.* belonging to, or having the qualities of, man or mankind. **-ly** *adv.* **-ness** *n.* **humane** (hū·mān′) *a.* having the moral qualities of man; kind; benevolent. **-ness** *n.* **-ism** *n.* a philosophic mode of thought devoted to human interests; literary culture. **-ist** *n.* one who pursues the study of human nature or the humanities. **-istic** *a.* pert. to humanity; pert. to humanism or humanists. **-ize** *v.t.* to render human or humane. **humanity** *n.* the quality of being human; human nature; the human race; kindness or benevolence. **humanities** *n.pl.* language, literature, art, philosophy, etc. **humanitarian** *n.* one who denies the divinity of Jesus; a philanthropist. **-kind** n. the whole race of man [L. humanus].

hum·ble (hum'·bl) a. lowly; meek; not proud, arrogant, or assuming; modest; v.t. to bring low; to make meek. **humbly** adv. **-ness** n. [L. humilis, fr. humus, the ground].

hum·bug (hum'·bug) n. a hoax; sham; nonsense; an impostor; v.t. to hoax; to deceive.

hum·drum (hum'·drum) a. commonplace; dull [redupl. of hum, imit. of monotony].

hu·mer·al (hū'·mer·al) a. belonging to the shoulder. **humerus** n. the long bone of the upper arm [L. humerus, the shoulder].

hu·mid (hū'·mid) a. damp; moist. **-ly** adv. **humidify** v.t. to make humid. **humidity, -ness** n. dampness; moisture. **humidor** n. a device for keeping the air moist in a jar, case, etc., such a case. [L. humidus, moist].

hu·mil·i·ate (hū·mil'·i·āt) v.t. to humble; to lower the dignity of. **humiliating** a. painfully humbling. **humiliation** n. **humility** n. the state of being humble and free from pride [L. humiliare, fr. humilis, low].

hum·mock (hum'·ak) n. a hillock; a ridge on an ice field [dim. of hump].

hu·mor (hū'·, ū'·mer) n. quality of imagination quick to perceive the ludicrous or to express itself in an amusing way; fun; caprice; disposition; mood; state of mind; the fluids of animal bodies; v.t. to indulge; to comply with mood or whim of. **-esque** (hū·mer·esk') n. musical composition of fanciful character. **-ist** n. one who shows humor in speaking or writing. **-ous** a. full of humor. **-ously** adv. [L. humor, moisture].

hump (hump) n. the protuberance or hunch formed by a crooked back; a hillock; v.t. to bend into a hump shape. **-back** n. a person with a crooked back. **—backed** a. [etym. uncertain].

hu·mus (hū'·mas) n. a brown or black constituent of the soil, composed of decayed vegetable or animal matter [L. humus, the ground].

Hun (hun) n. a barbarian.

hunch (hunch) n. a hump; (Slang) an intuition or presentiment; v.t. to bend or arch into a hump; v.i. to move forward in jerks.

hun·dred (hun'·drad) n. a cardinal number, the product of ten times ten; the symbol 100 or C; a. ten times ten. **-fold** a. a hundred times as much. **-th** a. last, or one, of a hundred; n. one of a hundred equal parts. **-weight** n. an avoirdupois weight of 100 lb. written cwt. [O.E. hund, hundred, with raed, reckoning].

hung (hung) pa.p. and pa.t. of **hang**.

hun·ger (hung'·ger) n. discomfort or exhaustion caused by lack of food; a craving for food; any strong desire; v.i. to feel hunger; to long for; v.t. to starve. **hungry** a. feeling hunger. **hungrily** adv. **— strike** n. refusal of all food as a protest [O.E. hungor].

hunk (hungk) n. a lump [Prov. E.].

hunt (hunt) v.t. to pursue and prey on (as animals on other animals); to pursue animals or game for food or sport; to search diligently after; to drive away; to use in hunting (as a pack of hounds); v.i. to go out in pursuit of game; to search; n. the act of hunting; chase; search; an association of huntsmen. **-er** n. one who hunts; a horse or dog used in hunting [O.E. huntian].

hur·dle (hur'·dl) n. a barrier in a race course; an obstacle; v.t. to enclose with hurdles; to jump over; to master a problem, etc. [O.E. hyrdle].

hur·dy-gur·dy (hur'·di·gur'·di·) n. an old-fashioned musical instrument played by turning a handle; a street-organ [imit. origin].

hurl (hurl) v.t. to send whirling; to throw with violence; n. a violent throw [etym. uncertain].

hur·ly-bur·ly (hur'·li·bur'·li·) n. tumult; bustle; confusion [etym. uncertain].

hur·rah, hurra (ha·rà') interj. used as a shout of joy. Also **hurray** [Ger.].

hur·ri·cane (hur'·i·kān) n. a wind of 60 m.p.h. or over; a violent cyclonic storm of wind and rain. **— deck** n. the upper deck of steamboats. **— lamp** n. a candlestick or lamp with a chimney [Sp. huracán].

hur·ry (hur'·i·) v.t. to hasten; to impel to greater speed; to urge on; v.i. to move or act with haste; n. the act of pressing forward in haste; quick motion. **hurried** a. done in haste; working at speed. **hurriedly** adv.

hurt (hurt) v.i. to cause pain; to wound or bruise; to impair or damage; to wound feelings; v.i. to give pain; n. wound, injury, or harm. **-ful** a. [Fr. heurter, to run against].

hur·tle (hur'·tl) v.t. to fling, to dash against; v.i. to move rapidly; to rush violently; to dash (against) [See hurt].

hus·band (huz'·band) n. a married man; v.t. to manage with economy; (Obs.) to till the soil. **-man** n. a farmer. **-ry** n. farming; thrift [O.E. husbonda, the master of the house].

hush (hush) interj. or imper. be quiet! silence! n. silence or stillness; v.t. to make quiet; (with up) to keep secret; v.i. to be silent [imit.].

husk (husk) n. the dry, external covering of certain seeds and fruits; the chaff of grain; pl. waste matter; refuse; v.t. to remove the outer covering. **-y** a. full of husks; dry, esp. of the throat, hence, rough in tone; hoarse; (Colloq.) big and strong. **-ily** adv. **-iness** n.

husk·y (hus'·ki·) n. an Eskimo sled-dog.

hus·sar (hu·zàr') n. one of the light cavalry of European armies [Hung. huszar, a freebooter].

hus·sy (hus'·, huz'·i·) n. an ill-behaved woman; a saucy girl [contr. fr. housewife].

hus·tings (hus'·tingz) n. any platform from which political campaign speeches are made; election proceedings [O.E. hus, a house; thing, an assembly].

hus·tle (hus'·l) v.t. to push about; to jostle; v.i. to hurry; to bustle; n. speed; jostling. **-r** n. [Dut. hutselen, to shake up].

hut (hut) n. a small house or cabin [Fr. hutte].

hutch (huch) n. a chest or box; a grain-bin; a pen for rabbits, etc. [Fr. huche, a coffer].

huz·za, huzzah (hu·zà') n. a shout of joy or approval [Ger.].

hy·a·cinth (hī'·a·sinth) n. a bulbous plant; a purplish-blue color; a red variety of zircon. [Gk. huakinthos, doublet of jacinth].

hy·a·line (hī'·a·lin) a. glassy; transparent; crystalline [Gk. hualos, glass].

hy·brid (hī'·brid) n. the offspring of two animals or plants of different species; a mongrel; a word compounded from different languages; a. cross-bred [L. hibrida].

hy·dra (hī'·dra) n. (Myth.) a monstrous water-serpent with many heads, slain by Hercules; (Zool.) a small fresh-water polyp [Gk. hudra, a water-snake].

hy·dran·gea (hī·drān'·ja) n. a genus of shrubs producing large flower clusters [Gk. hudor, water; angeion, a vessel].

hy·drant (hī'·drant) n. a water-pipe with a nozzle to which a hose can be attached; a fireplug [Gk. hudor, water].

hy·drate (hī'·drāt) n. (Chem.) a compound of water with another compound or an element; v.t. to combine with water. **hydrated** a. **hydration** n. [Gk. hudor, water].

hy·drau·lic (hī·draw'·lik) a. pert. to hydraulics; relating to the conveyance of water; worked by water power [Gk. hudor, water; aulos, a pipe].

hy·dro- prefix fr. Gk. hudor, water, combining to form derivatives; in many compounds used to indicate hydrogen. **-carbon** n. a compound of hydrogen and carbon. **-cephalus** (hī·drō·sef'·a·las) n. (Med.) an excess of cerebro-spinal fluid in the brain; water on the brain. **-cephalic, -cephalous** a. **-chloric** a. containing hydrogen and chlorine. **-chloric acid,** a strong acid [Gk. kele, a tumor; kephale, the head; chloros, green].

hy·dro·dy·nam·ics (hī·drō·dī·nam′·iks) *n.pl.* the branch of physics which deals with the flow of fluids, whether liquid or gases [Gk. *hudor*, water; *dunamis*, power; *kinein*, to move].

hy·dro·e·lec·tric (hī·drō·i·lek′·trik) *a.* pert. to the generation of electricity by utilizing water power [Gk. *hudor*, water].

hy·dro·gen (hī′·dra·jan) *n.* an inflammable, colorless, and odorless gas, the lightest of all known substances. **hydrogenous** (hī·drå′·je·nas) *a.* — **bomb** *n.* atom bomb of enormous power [Gk. *hudor*, water; *gennaein*, to produce].

hy·drol·o·gy (hī·dràl′·a·ji·) *n.* the science of the properties, laws, etc. of water. **hydrolysis** (hī·dràl′·a·sis) *n.* a chemical process by which the oxygen or hydrogen in water combines with an element, or some element of a compound, to form a new compound. **hydrolytic** *a.* [Gk. *hudor*, water; *logos*, a discourse; *luein*, to loosen].

hy·drom·e·ter (hī·dràm′·a·ter) *n.* a graduated instrument for finding the specific gravity, and thence the strength of liquids [Gk. *hudor*, water; *merton*, a measure].

hy·drop·a·thy (hī·dråp′·a·thi·) *n.* the treatment of diseases with water, including the use of cold or warm baths. Also **hydrotherapy.** [Gk. *hudor*, water; *pathos*, suffering].

hy·dro·pho·bi·a (hī·dra·fō′·bi·a) *n.* an acute infectious disease in man caused by the bite of a mad dog; rabies; an extreme dread of water, esp. as a supposed symptom of the disease [Gk. *hudor*, water; *phobos*, fear].

hy·dro·plane (hī′·dra·plān) *n.* an airplane designed to land on and take off from water; a kind of flat-bottomed boat designed to skim over the surface of the water [Gk. *hudor*, water; *sphaira*, a sphere].

hy·drous (hī′·dras) *a.* containing water; containing hydrogen [Gk. *hudor*, water].

hy·e·na (hī·ē′·na) *n.* a carnivorous mammal of Asia and Africa, allied to the dog. **laughing hyena,** the striped hyena [Gk. *huaina*, sow-like].

hy·giene (hī·jēn) *n.* medical science which deals with the preservation of health. **hygienic** (hī·gē·en′·ik, hī·jen′·ik) *a.* pert. to hygiene; sanitary. **hygienist** *n.* [Gk. *hugiēs*, healthy].

hy·gro- *prefix* fr. Gk. *hugros*, moist, combining to form derivatives.

hy·gro·scope (hī′·gra·skōp) *n.* an instrument which indicates variations of humidity in the atmosphere, without showing its exact amount [Gk. *hugros*, moist; *skopein*, to view].

Hy·men (hī′·man) *n.* (*Myth.*) the god of marriage; (*l.c.*) membrane fold at entrance to female sex organs. **hymeneal** (hī·ma·nē′·al) *a.* pert. to marriage [Gk. *humēn*].

hy·me·nop·ter·ous (hī·ma·nåp′·ter·as) *a.* belonging or pert. to an order of insects (Hymenoptera) as the bee, the wasp, etc. [Gk. *humēn*, membrane; *pteron*, a wing].

hymn (him) *n.* an ode or song of praise, esp. a religious one; a sacred lyric; *v.t.* to praise in song; *v.i.* to sing in worship. **-al** (him′·nal) *n.* a hymn book [Gk. *humnos*, a festive song].

hy·per·bo·la (hī·pur′·ba·la) *n.* (*Geom.*) a curve formed by a section of a cone when the cutting plane makes a greater angle with the base than the side of the cone makes. **hyperbolic** *a.* [Gk. *huyer*, over; *bolē*, a throw].

hy·per·bo·le (hī·pur′·ba·lē) *n.* (*Gram.*) a figure of speech which expresses much more or much less than the truth, for the sake of effect; exaggeration. **hyperbolic, hyperbolical** *a.* **hyperbolically** *adv.* **hyperbolize** *v.t.* and *i.* to state with hyperbole [Gk. *huper*, beyond; *bolē*, a throw].

hy·per·crit·ic (hī·per·krit′·ik) *n.* one who is critical beyond measure or reason. **-al** *a.* **-ally** *adv.* [Gk. *huper*, over; *kritikos*, critical].

hy·per·phys·i·cal (hī·per·fiz′·i·kal) *a.* super-

natural [Gk. *huper*, beyond; *phusis*, nature].

hy·per·sen·si·tive (hī·per·sen′·sa·tiv) *a.* abnormally sensitive. **-ness, hypersensitivity** *n.* [Gk. *huper*, beyond; L. *sentire*, to feel].

hy·per·tro·phy (hī·pur′·tra·fi·) *n.* (*Med.*) abnormal enlargement of organ or part of body [Gk. *huper*, over; *trophē*, nourishment].

hy·phen (hī′·fan) *n.* a mark (-) used to connect syllables or compound words; *v.t.* to connect with a hyphen. **-ated** *a.* [Gk. *hupo*, under; *hen*, one].

hyp·no·sis (hip·nō′·sas) *n.* the state of being hypnotized; abnormal sleep. **hypnotic** *a.* tending to produce sleep; pert. to hypnotism; *n.* a drug that induces sleep; a hypnotized person. **hypnotize** *v.t.* to produce a mental state resembling sleep. **hypnotism** *n.* an abnormal mental state resembling sleep. **hypnotist** *n.* [Gk. *hupnos*, sleep]. [beneath, below.

hy·po- (hī′·pō) *prefix* fr. Gk. meaning under,

hy·po·chon·dri·a (hīp·a·kàn′·dri·a) *n.* a mental disorder, in which one is tormented by melancholy and gloomy views, especially about one's own health. **hypochondriac** *a.* affected by hypochondria; *n.* a person so affected [Gk. *hupo*, under; *chondros*, a cartilage].

hy·poc·ri·sy (hi·pàk′·ra·si·) *n.* stimulation or pretense of goodness; feigning to be what one is not; insincerity. **hypocrite** (hip′·a·krit) *n.* one who dissembles his real nature; a pretender to virtue or piety; a deceiver. **hypocritical** *a.* [Gk. *hupowritēs*, an actor].

hy·po·der·mic (hī·pa·dur′·mik) *a.* pert. to parts underlying the skin; *n.* the injection of a drug beneath the skin by means of a needle and small syringe. **-ally** *adv.* [Gk. *hupo*, under; *derma*, the skin].

hy·pos·ta·sis (hī·pàs′·ta·sas) *n.* essential nature of anything; the substance of each of the three divisions of the Godhead; (*Med.*) a deposit of blood in an organ; *pl.* **hypostases** [Gk. *hupo*, under; *stasis*, state].

hy·pot·e·nuse (hī·pàt′·e·nòòs) *n.* (*Geom.*) the side of a right-angled triangle which is opposite the right angle [Gk. *hupoteinousa*, extending under].

hy·poth·e·cate (hī·pà′·tha·kāt) *v.t.* to give in security; to mortgage [Gk. *hupothēkē*, a pledge].

hy·poth·e·sis (hī·pàth′·a·sis) *n.* *pl.* **hypotheses,** a supposition used as a basis from which to draw conclusions; a theory. **hypothesize** *v.i.* and *v.t.* to form and to assume by a hypothesis. **hypothetic, hypothetical** *a.* [Gk. *hupothesis*, a proposal].

hys·te·ri·a, hysterics (his·ti′·ri·a, his·ter′·iks) *n.* an affection of the nervous system, characterized by excitability and lack of emotional control. **hysteric, hysterical.** *a.* **hysterically** *adv.* [Gk. *hustera*, womb].

I

I (ī) *pron.* the pronoun of the first person singular, the word by which a speaker or writer denotes himself [O.E. *ic*; cf. Ger. *ich*; L. *ego*; Gk. *egō*].

i·am·bus (ī·am′·bas) *n.* a metrical foot of two syllables, the first short or unaccented, and the second long or accented. **iamb** *n.* shorter form of *iambus*. **iambic** *a.* [Gk.].

i·at·ric, iatrical (ī·at′·rik, ·al) *a.* pert. to physicians, medicine [Gk. *iatros*, physician].

I·ber·ri·an (ī·bi′·ri·an) *a.* pert. to Iberia, viz. Spain and Portugal; *n.* early inhabitant of ancient Iberia [L. *Iberia*, Spain].

i·bex (ī′·beks) *n.* variety of wild goat [L.].

i·bis, *n.* a stork-like wading bird, allied to the

WEBSTER
H–L

spoonbills [Gk.].

I·car·i·an (ī·ker′·i·an) *a.* adventurous in flight; rash [fr. *Icarus*].

ice (īs) *n.* frozen water; a frozen dessert made with fruit juices and water; *(Slang)* diamonds; *v.t.* to cover with ice; to freeze; to chill with ice; to frost a cake; *pr.p.* **icing.** — **age** *(Geol.)* Pleistocene period, the series of glacial epochs. —**belt** *n.* the belt of ice fringing land in Arctic and Antarctic regions. **-berg** *n.* a detached portion of a glacier floating in the sea. **-blink** *n.* a whitish light due to reflection from a field of ice. **-boat** *n.* a boat adapted for being pulled over ice. **-bound** *a.* surrounded by or jammed in ice. **-breaker** *n.* a vessel designed to open passage through ice-bound waters; social start. **-cap** *n.* a glacier formed by the accumulation of snow and ice on a plateau and moving out from the center in every direction. — **cream** *n.* a frozen food made esp. of cream or milk sweetened and flavored. —**fall** *n.* a glacier as it flows over a precipice. — **field** *n.* a vast expanse of sea either frozen or covered with floating masses of ice. — **floe** *n.* a large mass of floating ice. — **hockey** *n.* game played by skaters on ice with a hard rubber disk (the puck). — **pack** *n.* drifting field of ice, closely packed together. — **pick** *n.* an implement for cutting ice. — **skate** *n.* a shoe fitted with a metal runner for skating on ice. — **sheet** *n.* an enormous glacier covering a huge area, valleys and hills alike. **icily** *adv.* coldly. **iciness** *n.* **icing** *n.* a covering of sugar on cakes, etc.; formation of ice on part of an airplane. **icy** *a.* pert. to ice; ice-like; frigid [O.E. *is;* Ger. *Eis*].

Ice·land·er (is′·lan·der) *n.* a native of Iceland. **Icelandic** *a.*

ich·nol·o·gy (ik·nàl′·a·ji·) *n.* the classification of fossil footprints [Gk. *ichnos*, track; *logos*, a discourse].

i·chor (ī′·kawr, ·ker) *n.* *(Gk. Myth)* the fluid which flowed in the veins of the Gods; the colorless, watery discharge from ulcers. **-ous** *a.* [Gk. *ichor*].

ich·thy·ol·o·gy (ĭk·thi·àl′·a·ji·) *n.* the branch of zoology which treats of fishes. **ichthyological** *a.* **ichthyologist** *n.* **ich·thyic** *a.* pert. to fish. **ichthyoid** *a.* fish-like [Gk. *ichthus*, fish; *logos*, discourse].

i·ci·cle (ī′·si·kl) *n.* a pendent conical mass of ice, slowly built up by freezing of drops of water [O.E. *isgicel*].

i·con (ī′·kàn) *n.* any sign which resembles the thing it represents; a venerated representation of Christ, an angel, or a saint, found in Greek and Orthodox Eastern Churches. **-ic, -ical** *a.* pert. to icons. **-oclasm** *n.* act of breaking images; an attack on the cherished beliefs or enthusiasms of others. **-oclast** *n.* a breaker of images; one who exposes or destroys shams of any kind. **-ography** *n.* the making of an icon; the subject matter, or the analysis of an icon. **-olater** *n.* an image worshipper. **-olatry** *n.* image worship [Gk. *eikōn*, an image].

ic·ter·us (ik′·ta·ras) *n.* jaundice. **icteric, icterical** *a.* [Gk. *ikteros*, jaundice].

id (id) *n.* in psycho-analysis, the primary source in individuals of instinctive energy and impulses [L. = it).

i·de·a (ī·dē′·a) *n.* a product of intellectual action; way of thinking; a thought; belief; plan; aim; principle at the back of one's mind. **ideal** *a.* existing in fancy only; perfect; satisfying desires; *n.* an imaginary type or norm of perfection to be aimed at. **idealization** *n.* **idealize** *v.t.* to represent or look upon as ideal; to make or render ideal; to refine. **idealizer** *n.* an idealist.

idealism *n.* tendency to seek the highest spiritual perfection; imaginative treatment in comparative disregard of the real; the doctrine that appearances are purely the perceptions, the ideas, of subjects, that the world is to be regarded as consisting of mind; **-list** *n.* **-listic** *a.* pert. to idealism or idealists; perfect; consummate. **-lity** *n.* ideal state or quality; capacity to form ideals of beauty and perfection; condition of being mental. **-lly** *adv.* **-tion** *n.* the process of forming an idea. **-tional** *a.* [Gk. *idea*, fr. *idein*, to see].

i·den·ti·cal (ī·den′·ti·kal) *a.* the very same; not different. **-ly** *adv.* **-ness** *n.* exact sameness [L. *idem*, the same].

i·den·ti·fy (ī·den′·ta·fī) *v.t.* to establish the identity of; to ascertain or prove to be the same; to recognize; to associate (oneself) in interest, purpose, use, etc. **identifiable** *a.* **identification** *n.*

i·den·ti·ty (ī·den′·ta·ti·) *n.* state of having the same nature or character with; absolute sameness, as opposed to mere similarity; individuality [L. *idem*, the same].

id·e·o·graph (īd′·ē·a·graf) *n.* a picture, symbol, diagram, etc., suggesting an idea or object without specifically naming it; a character in Chinese and kindred languages. **ideogram** *n.* an ideograph. **-ic, -ical** *a.* **ideography** *n.* [Gk. *idea*, an idea; *graphein*, to write].

i·de·ol·o·gy (ī·dē·àl′·a·ji·) *n.* the body of beliefs of any group; *(Philos.)* science of origin of ideas; visionary theorizing. **ideologic, ideological** *a.* **ideologist** *n.* a theorist. [Gk. *idea; logos*, discourse].

ides (īdz) *n.pl.* in the Roman calendar, the 15th day of March, May, July, and October, and the 13th day of the other months [Fr. fr. L. *Idus*].

id·i·o·cy *n.* See **idiot.**

id·i·om (id′·i·am) *n.* a peculiar mode of expression; the genius or peculiar cast of a language; colloquial speech; dialect. **-atic, -atical** *a.* **-atically** *adv.* [Gk. *idios*, one's own].

id·i·o·syn·cra·sy (id·i·a·sin′·kra·si·) *n.* a peculiarity in a person; fad; peculiar view. **idiosyncratic, idiosyncratical** *a.* [Gk. *idios*, peculiar; *sunkrasis*, mixing together].

id·i·ot (id′·i·at) *n.* one mentally deficient; a born fool. **idiocy** *n.* state of being an idiot; extreme and permanent mental deficiency. **-ic, -ical** *a.* utterly senseless or stupid. **-ically** *adv.* **-ism** *n.* natural imbecility [Gk. *idiōtes*, a private person].

i·dle (ī′·dl) *a.* doing nothing; inactive; lazy; unused; frivolous; *v.t.* to spend in idleness; *v.i.* to be idle or unoccupied. **-ness** *n.* **-r** *n.* **idly** *adv.* [O.E. *idel*].

i·dol (ī′·dal) *n.* an image of a diety as an object of worship; a false god; object of excessive devotion. **-ater** *n.* *(fem.* **idolatress)** a worshipper of idols. **-atrize** *v.t.* to worship as an idol. **-atrous** *a.* **-atrously** *adv.* **-atry** *n.* worship of idols or false gods; excessive and devoted admiration. **-ization** *n.* **-ize** *v.t.* to make an idol of; to love or venerate to excess. **-izer** *n.* [Gk. *eidōlon*, image].

i·dyl, idyll (ī′·dal) *n.* a short pastoral poem; a picture of simple perfection and loveliness. **-lic** *a.* pert. to idyls; of a perfect setting; blissful [Gk. *eidullion*, dim. of *eidos*, a picture].

if (if) *conj.* on the condition or supposition that; whether; in case that [O.E. *gif*].

ig·loo (ig′·lòò) *n.* a dome-shaped house built of blocks of hard snow by Eskimos [Eskimo].

ig·ne·ous (ig′·ni·as) *a.* resembling fire; *(Geol.)* resulting from the action of intense heat [L. *ignis*, fire].

ig·nite (ig·nīt′) *v.t.* to set on fire; to kindle;

v.i. to catch fire; to begin to burn. **ignitible** *a.* **ignition** *n.* act of kindling or setting on fire; (internal-combustion engine) the process or device which ignites the fuel [L. *ignis*, fire].

ig·no·ble (ig·nō′·bl) *a.* of humble birth or family; mean; base; inferior. **ignobility, -ness** *n.* **ignobly** *adv.* [L. *in*, not; *nobilis*, noble].

ig·no·min·y (ig′·na·min·i·) *n.* public disgrace or dishonor; infamous conduct. **ignominious** *a.* humiliating; dishonorable. **ignominiously** *adv.* **ignominiousness** *n.* [L. *ignominia*].

ig·no·ra·mus (ig·na·ra′·mas) *n.* an ignorant person [L. = we are ignorant].

ig·no·rant (ig′·na·rant) *a.* uninstructed; uninformed; unlearned. **ignorance** *n.* **-ly** *adv.* [L. *ignorare*, not to know].

ig·nore (ig·nōr′) *v.t.* to refuse to take notice of; not to recognize [L. *ignorare*, not to know].

i·gua·na (i·gwa′·na) *n.* a family of lizards, found in tropical America [Sp.].

i·lex (ī′·leks) *n.* the common holly of Europe; a genus of evergreen trees and shrubs, including the holm oak [L.].

ilk (ilk) *a.* the same. **of that ilk,** family or kind [O.E. *ilc*].

ill (il) *a.* bad or evil in any respect; sick; unwell; wicked; faulty; ugly; disastrous; unfavorable; *n.* evil of any kind; misfortune; misery; pain; *adv.* not well; faultily; unfavorably; not rightly (*compar.* **worse;** *superl.* **worst**). **-ness** *n.* sickness [O.N. *illr*].

ill- (il) *prefix*, used in the construction of compound words, implying badness in some form or other. **—advised** *a.* badly advised. **—disposed** *a.* not friendly; hostile; maliciously inclined. **—fated** *a.* destined to bring misfortune. **—favored** *a.* ugly. **—gotten** *a.* not honestly obtained. **—humor** *n.* bad temper. **—natured** *a.* surly; cross; peevish. **—omened** *a.* inauspicious; attended by evil omens. **—starred** *a.* born under the influence of an unlucky star; unlucky. **—tempered** *a.* quarrelsome. **—will** *n.* malevolence; bad feeling; enmity [O.N. *illr*].

il·le·gal (i·lē′·gal) *a.* contrary to law; unlawful. **-ize** *v.t.* to render unlawful. **-ity** *n.* unlawful act. **-ly** *adv.* [L.*il* + *legalis*, law].

il·leg·i·ble (i·lej′·a·bl) *a.* incapable of being read or deciphered; unreadable; indistinct. **-ness, illegibility** *n.* **illegibly** *adv.*

il·le·git·i·mate (i·li·jit′·a·mit) *a.* unlawful; not authorized by good usage; born out of wedlock. **illegitimacy** *n.* bastardly; illegality. **-ly** *adv.* [L. *in-*, not; *legitimate*].

il·lib·er·al (i·lib′·er·al) *a.* not liberal; not free or generous; niggardly; narrow-minded; intolerant. **illiberality** *n.*

il·lic·it (i·lis′·it) *a.* not permitted; unlawful; unlicensed. **-ly** *adv.* **-ness** *n.*

il·lim·it·a·ble (i·lim′·it·a·bl) *a.* incapable of being limited or bounded; immeasurable; infinite.

il·lit·er·ate (i·lit′·er·it) *a.* unable to read or write; unlettered; *n.* a person unable to read or write. *adv.* **-ness, illiteracy** *n.*

il·log·i·cal (i·làj′·i·kal) *a.* not according to the rules of logic; unsound; fallacious. **-ly** *adv.* **-ness, illogicality** *n.*

il·lu·mi·nate (i·lŏŏ′·ma·nāt) *v.t.* to enlighten, literally and figuratively; to light up; to throw light upon; to embellish, as a book or manuscript with gold and colors. **illuminable** *a.* **illuminant** *a.* and *n.* a source of light. **illumination** *n.* act of giving light; that which supplies light; instruction; enlightenment; decoration on manuscripts and books. **illuminative** *a.* giving light; instructive; explanatory. **illuminator** *n.* **illumine** *v.t.* and *v.i.* [L. *illuminare*, to light].

il·lu·sion (i·lŏŏ′·zhan) *n.* an erroneous interpretation or unreal image presented to the bodily or mental vision; a false perception; deceptive appearance, esp. as a conjuring trick; fallacy. **illusionist** *n.* a professional entertainer who produces illusions. **illusive, illusory** *a.* deceiving by false appearances. **illusively** *adv.* **illusiveness** *n.* [L. *illusio*, mocking].

il·lus·trate (il′·as·trāt, il·us′·trāt) *v.t.* to make clear or bright; to exemplify, esp. by means of figures, diagrams, etc.; to adorn with pictures. **illustration** *n.* act of making clear or bright; explanation; a pictorial representation accompanying a printed description. **illustrative, illustratory** *a.* serving to illustrate. **illustratively** *adv.* **illustrator,** *n.* [L. *illustrare*, to light up].

il·lus·tri·ous (i·lus′·tri·as) *a.* conferring honor; possessing honor or dignity. **-ness** *n.* [L. *illustris*, clear].

im·age (im′·ij) *n.* a mental picture of any object; a representation of a person or object; a copy; a symbol; idol; figure of speech; (*Optics*) the representation of an object formed at the focus of a lens or mirror by rays of light refracted or reflected to it from all parts of the object; *v.t.* to form an image of; to reflect; to imagine. *n.* images regarded collectively; figures of speech; imagination. **imagism** *n.* clear-cut presentation of a subject. **imagist** *n.* one of a modern poetical group who concentrates on extreme clarity by the use of precise images. [L. *imago*, an image].

im·ag·ine (i·maj′·in) *v.t.* to form in the mind an idea or image; to conjecture; to picture; to believe; to suppose; *v.i.* to form an image of; to picture in the mind. **imaginable** *a.* **imaginableness** *n.* **imaginably** *adv.* **imaginary** *a.* existing only in imagination or fancy; fanciful; unreal. **imaginative** *a.* proceeding from the imagination; gifted with the creative faculty; fanciful. **imagination** *n.* the mental faculty which apprehends and forms ideas of external objects; the poetical faculty. **imaginatively** *adv.* **imaginativeness** *n.* [L. *imago*, an image].

i·mam, imaum (i·màm′, i·mawm′) *n.* a Moslem priest [Ar. *imam*, a chief].

im·be·cile (im′·ba·sil) *a.* mentally feeble; silly; idiotic; *n.* one of feeble mentality. **imbecility** *n.* [L. *imbecillus*, weak in mind or body].

im·bed (im·bed′) *v.t.* See **embed.**

im·bibe (im·bīb′) *v.t.* to drink in; to absorb; to receive into the mind; *v.t.* to drink. **imbiber** *n.* [L. *in*; *bibere*, to drink].

im·brue (im·brŏŏ′) *v.t.* to wet; to drench as in blood [O.Fr. *embuer*, to drink in].

im·bro·glio (im·brōl′·yō) *n.* an intricate, complicated plot; confusion [It.].

im·bue (im·bū′) *v.t.* to inspire; to tinge deeply; to saturate [L. *imbuere*, to wet].

im·i·tate (im′·a·tāt) *v.t.* to follow, as a pattern, model, or example; to copy. **imitable** *a.* capable or worthy of being copied. **imitation** *n.* a servile reproduction of an original; a copy; mimicry. **imitative** *a.* inclined to imitate; not original. **imitatively** *adv.* **imitativeness** *n.* **imitator** *n.* [L. *imitari*].

im·mac·u·late (i·mak′·yoo·lat) *a.* without blemish; spotless; unsullied; pure; undefiled. **-ly** *adv.* **-ness** *n.* **Immaculate Conception,** the dogma that the Blessed Virgin Mary was conceived and born without taint of sin.

im·ma·nent (im′·a·nant) *a.* abiding in; inherent; intrinsic; innate. **immanence, immanency** *n.* [L. *in*; *manere*, to dwell].

im·ma·te·ri·al (im·a·ti′·ri·al) *a.* not consisting of matter; incorporeal; of no essential consequence; unimportant. **-ize** *v.t.* to separate from matter. **-ism** *n.* doctrine that matter only exists as a process of the mind; pure idealism. **-ist** *n.*

im·ma·ture (im·a·toor′) *a.* not mature or ripe; raw; unformed; undeveloped; untimely. **-ness, immaturity** *n.*

im·meas·ur·a·ble (i·mezh′·ẹr·a·bl) *a.* incapable of being measured; illimitable; infinite; boundless. **immeasurably** *adv.*

im·me·di·ate (i·mē′·di·at) *a.* occurring at once; without delay; present; not separated by others. **immediacy** *n.* immediateness. **-ly** *adv.* **-ness** *n.* [L.L. *immediatus*].

im·me·mo·ri·al (i·ma·mōr′·i·al) *a.* beyond the range of memory; of great antiquity. **immemorable** *a.* **-ly** *adv.*

im·mense (i·mens′) *a.* unlimited; immeasureable; very great; vast; huge; prodigious; enormous. **-ly** *adv.* **-ness, immensity** *n.* vastness; boundlessness [L. *immensus*, unmeasured].

im·merge (i·murj′) *v.t.* to plunge into [L. *in; mergere*, to plunge].

im·merse (i·murs′) *v.t.* to plunge into anything, esp. a fluid; to dip; to baptize by dipping the whole body; to absorb. **immersable, immersible** *a.* **-d** *a.* doused; submerged; engrossed. **immersion** *n.* [L. *in; mergere, mersum*, to plunge].

im·mi·grate (im′·a·grāt) *v.i.* to migrate into a country. **immigrant** *n.* **immigration** *n.* [L. *in: migrare*, to remove].

im·mi·nent (im′·a·nant) *a.* threatening immediately to fall or occur. **imminence** *n.* **-ly** *adv.* [L. *imminere*, to overhang].

im·mis·ci·ble (i·mis′·i·bl) *a.* not capable of being mixed. **immiscibility** *n.*

im·mit·i·ga·ble (i·mit′·i·ga·bl) *a.* incapable of being mitigated or appeased; relentless.

im·mo·bile (i·mō′·bal) *a.* incapable of being moved; fixed; immovable. **immobilize** *v.t.* to render immobile.

im·mod·er·ate (i·mȧd′·ẹr·at) *a.* exceeding just bounds; excessive. **-ness** *n.* extravagance. **-ly** *adv.* **immoderation** *n.*

im·mod·est (i·mȧd′·ist) *a.* wanting in modesty or delicacy; indecent; shameless; impudent. **-ly** *adv.* **-y** *n.* shamelessness.

im·mo·late (im′·a·lāt) *v.t.* to sacrifice; to offer as a sacrifice; to kill as a religious rite. **immolation** *n.* **immolator** *n.* [L. *immolare*, to sprinkle with sacrificial meal].

im·mor·al (i·màr′·, i·mawr′·al) *a.* uninfluenced by moral principle; wicked. **-ity** *n.* vice; profligacy; injustice. **-ly** *adv.*

im·mor·tal (i·mawr′·tal) *a.* not mortal; having an eternal existence; undying; deathless; *n.* one exempt from death or decay; a divine being. **immortalize** *v.t.* to make famous for all time; to save from oblivion. **immortality** *n.* perpetual life. flower [Fr.].

im·mov·a·ble (i·mȯȯv′·a·bl) *a.* incapable of being moved; firmly fixed; fast; resolute. **-ness, immovability** *n.* **immovably** *adv.*

im·mune (i·mūn′) *a.* exempt; free from infection; protected against any particular infection; *n.* one who is so protected. **immunization** *n.* the process of rendering a person or animal immune. **immunize** *v.t.* **immunity** *n.* [L. *in-*, not; *munis*, serving].

im·mure (i·myoor′) *v.t.* to enclose within walls; to imprison [L. *in; murus*, a wall].

im·mu·ta·ble (i·mū′·ta·bl) *a.* not susceptible to any alteration; invariable; unalterable. **immutability, immutableness** *n.*

imp (imp) *n.* a little demon; a mischievous child. **-ish** *a.* like an imp; mischievous [O.E. *impa*, fr. Gk. *emphytos*, grafted on].

im·pact (im·pakt′) *v.t.* to press or drive forcibly together. **impact** (im′·pact) *n.* impulse communicated by one object striking another; collision [L. *in*, into; *pingere*, to strike].

im·pair (im·per′) *v.t.* to diminish in quantity, value, excellence, or strength; to injure;

to weaken [Fr. *empirer*, to grow worse].

im·pale (im·pāl′) *v.t.* to fix on a sharpened stake; inclose with stakes; to put to death by fixing on an upright, sharp stake. **-ment** *n.* [L. *in.* into; *palus*, a stake].

im·pal·pa·ble (im·pal′·pa·bl) *a.* not capable of being felt or perceived by the senses, esp. by touch; exceedingly fine in texture; not readily understood or grasped. **impalpability** *n.* **impalpably** *adv.*

im·pan·el (im·pan′·al) *v.t.* to place a name on a panel or list; to enter the names of a jury on a panel; to form a jury by roll-call. **-ment** *n.*

im·part (im·pȧrt′) *v.t.* to bestow a share or portion of; to grant; to divulge; to disclose.

im·par·tial (im·pȧr′·shal) *a.* not partial; without prejudice; not taking sides; unbiased. **impartiality, impartialness** *n.*

im·part·i·ble (im·pȧrt′·i·bl) *a.* not divisible (of landed property).

im·pas·sa·ble (im·pas′·a·bl) *a.* incapable of being passed; impervious; impenetrable; pathless. **impassability, impassableness** *n.*

im·passe (im·pas′, im′·pas) *n.* deadlock; dilemma; fix [Fr.].

im·pas·sion (im·pash′·an) *v.t.* to move or affect strongly with passion. **-ed** *a.*

im·pas·sive (im·pas′·iv) *a.* not susceptible of pain or suffering; insensible; showing no emotion; calm. **-ly** *adv.* **-ness, impassivity** *n.*

im·pa·tient (im·pā′·shant) *a.* uneasy or fretful under trial or suffering; averse to waiting; restless. **impatience** *n.* **-ly** *adv.*

im·pav·id (im·pav′·id) *a.* fearless [L. *in +pavidus*, fearing].

im·peach (im·pēch′) *v.t.* to charge with a crime or misdemeanor; to call to account; to denounce; to challenge. **-able** *a.* **-er** *n.* **-ment** *n.* the trial of a public official, by the upper house of the legislature, the lower house having made the charge [orig. to hinder, Fr. *empêcher*, to prevent].

im·pec·ca·ble (im·pek′·a·bl) *a.* not liable to sin or error; perfect. **impeccability, impeccancy** *n.* [L. *in-*, not; *peccare*, to sin].

im·pe·cu·ni·ous (im·pi·kū′·ni·as) *a.* having no money; poor; hard up. **impecuniosity** *n.* dire poverty [L. *in-*, not; *pecunia*, money].

im·pede (im·pēd′) *v.t.* to stop the progress of; to hinder; to obstruct. **impedance** *n.* hindrance; (*Elect.*) opposition offered to an alternating current by resistance, inductance, or capacity, or by combined effect of all three. **impedible** *a.* **impediment** *n.* that which hinders; stammer. **impedimenta** *n.pl.* baggage, esp. military; encumbrances. **impedimental** *a.* [L. *impedire*, to shackle].

im·pel (im·pel′) *v.t.* to drive or urge forward; to induce; to incite. *pr.p.* **-ling.** *pa.t.* and *pa.p.* **-led. -lent** *a.* impelling; *n.* a force which impels. **-ler** *n.* [L. *in*, into; *pellere*, to drive].

im·pend (im·pend′) *v.i.* to hang over; to threaten; to be imminent. **-ence, -ency** *n.* **-ent** *a.* impending; threatening [L. *impendere*, to hang over].

im·pen·e·tra·ble (im·pen′·a·tra·bl) *a.* incapable of being penetrated or pierced; obscure. **impenetrability** *n.* quality of being impenetrable; that property of matter by which it excludes all other matter from the space it occupies.

im·pen·i·tent (im·pen′·a·tant) *a.* not repenting of sin; not contrite; obdurate.

im·per·a·tive (im·per′·a·tiv) *a.* expressive of command; authoritative; obligatory; absolutely necessary; peremptory. **-ly** *adv.* [L. *imperare*, to command].

im·per·cep·ti·ble (im·per·sep′·ta·bl) *a.* not discernible by the senses; minute. **-ness, imperceptibility** *n.* **imperceptibly** *adv.* **imperceptive** *a.* not having power to perceive.

im·per·fect (im·pur'·fikt) *a.* wanting some part or parts; defective; faulty; *n.* (*Gram.*) tense denoting an action in the past but incomplete, or continuous action in the past. **-ly** *adv.* **imperfection** *n.*

im·per·fo·rate, imperforated (im·pur'·fa·rat) *a.* not perforated or pierced.

im·pe·ri·al (im·pi'·ri·al) *a.* pertaining to an empire or to an emperor; royal; sovereign; majestic. **-ism** *n.* the system of government in an empire; policy of national territorial expansion. **-ist** *n.* **-istic** *a.* [L. *imperium*].

im·per·il (im·per'·il) *v.t.* to bring into peril; to endanger; to hazard; to risk.

im·pe·ri·ous (im·pi'·ri·as) *a.* commanding; domineering; dictatorial. **-ly** *adv.* **-ness** *n.* [L. *imperiosus*, full of command].

im·per·ish·a·ble (im·per'·ish·a·bl) *a.* not liable to decay or oblivion; indestructible. **-ness** *n.* **imperishability** *n.*

im·per·ma·nence (im·pur'·ma·nans) *n.* want of permanence or stability.

im·per·me·a·ble (im·pur'·mē·a·bl) *a.* not permitting passage, as of fluid or gas, through its substance; impervious. **impermeability** *n.* **-ness** *n.* **impermeably** *adv.*

im·per·son·al (im·pur'·san·al) *a.* having no personal reference; objective; (*Gram.*) form of verb used only in 3rd person singular with nominative *it.* e.g. *it hails.* **-ly** *adv.*

im·per·son·ate (im·pur'·san·āt) *v.t.* to invest with a real form, body or character; to represent in character or form; to act a part on the stage; to imitate. **impersonation** *n.* **impersonator** *n.*

im·per·ti·nent (im·pur'·ta·nant) *a.* having no bearing on the subject; irrelevant; impudent; saucy. **impertinence** *n.*

im·per·turb·a·ble (im·per·tur'·ba·bl) *a.* incapable of being disturbed or agitated; unmoved; composed. **imperturbability** *n.* **imperturbably** *adv.* **imperturbation** *n.*

im·per·vi·a·ble, im·per·vi·ous (im·pur'·vi·abl, ·vi·us) *a.* not admitting of entrance or passage through; impenetrable; impassable; not to be moved by argument or importunity. **-ness, imperviability** *n.* **imperviously** *adv.*

im·pe·ti·go (im·pa·tī'·gō) *n.* (*Med.*) a pustulous skin disease [L. *impetere*, to rush upon].

im·pet·u·ous (im·pech'·choo·as) *a.* rushing with force and violence; vehement; hasty. **-ly** *adv.* **-ness, impetuosity** *n.* precipitancy; fury [L. *impetus*, attack].

im·pe·tus (im'·pa·tas) *n.* the force with which a body moves; momentum; boost [L.].

im·pi·e·ty (im·pī'·a·ti·) *n.* lack of reverence.

im·pinge (im·pinj') *v.i.* (foll. by *on, upon, against*) to fall or dash against; to touch on; to infringe [L. *impingere*, to strike].

im·pi·ous (im'·pi·as) *a.* not pious; proceeding from or manifesting a want of reverence. **-ly** *adv.* **-ness, impiety** *n.*

im·pla·ca·ble (im·plak'·, im·plāk'·a·bl) *a.* inexorable; not to be appeased; unrelenting. **-ness, implacability** *n.*

im·plant (im·plant') *v.t.* to set in; to insert; to sow (seed); to plant (shoots); to instill, or settle in the mind or heart.

im·plead (im·plēd') *v.t.* to sue at law.

im·ple·ment (im'·pla·mant) *n.* a weapon, tool, or instrument; a utensil; *v.t.* (im'·pla·ment) to fulfill an obligation or contract which has been entered into; to give effect to; to carry out; to supplement. **-al** *a.* **-ation** *n.* [L *implere*, to fill up].

im·pli·cate (im'·pli·kāt) *v.t.* to involve; to include; to entangle; to imply. **implication** *n.* the implied meaning; a logical deduction; entanglement. **implicative** *a.* tending to implicate. **implicatively** *adv.* **implicit** *a.* implied; without questioning. **implicitly** *adv.*

[L. *implicare* to entangle].

im·plore (im·plōr') *v.t.* to entreat earnestly; to beseech. **imploration** *n.* **-r** *n.* **imploringly** *adv.* [L. *in*, in; *plorare*, to weep].

im·ply (im·plī') *v.t.* to contain by implication; to involve as necessary; to signify; to insinuate; to suggest [L. *implicare*, to entangle].

im·po·lite (im·pa·līt') *a.* uncivil; rude; discourteous. **-ly** *adv.* **-ness** *n.*

im·pol·i·tic (im·pál'·a·tik) *a.* ill-advised; not in the best interests of; inexpedient. **impolicy** *n.* injudicious action. **-ly** *adv.*

im·pon·der·a·ble (im·pan'·der·a·bl) *a.* without perceptible weight; not able to be weighed; *n.pl.* natural phenomena such as heat, electricity, etc., which do not alter the weight of substances; the unknown factors which may influence human activities. **-ness, imponderability** *n.*

im·port (im·pōrt') *v.t.* to bring in from abroad; to convey a meaning; to be of consequence. **-ance** *n.* consequence; moment. *a.* **-antly** *adv.* **-ation** *n.* act of bringing from another country [L. *in*, into; *portare*, to carry].

im·por·tune (im·per·tūn') *v.t.* to request with urgency; to pester with requests; to entreat; to solicit. **importunacy, importunateness** *n.* **importunate** *a.* earnestly solicitous; persistent in urging a claim; troublesome. **importunately** *adv.* [L. *importunus*, troublesome].

im·pose (im·pōz') *v.t.* to lay on; to levy; to lay, as a charge or tax; to force oneself upon others; to lay on hands in ordination; *v.i.* (with *upon*) to deceive; to take undue advantage of a person's good-nature; to impress. **imposable** *a.* **imposing** *a.* adapted to impress considerably; commanding; grand. **imposition** *n.* act of imposing, laying on, enjoining, indicting, etc.; that which is imposed; a tax; a burden [Fr. *imposer*].

im·pos·si·ble (im·pás'·a·bl) *a.* that which cannot be done; incapable of existing in conception or in fact; unfeasible; unattainable. *interj.* absurd! **impossibility** *n.*

im·post (im'·pōst) *n.* tax duty [Fr. *impôt*].

im·pos·tor (im·pás'·ter) *n.* one who assumes a false character; one who deceives others; a cheat. **imposture** *n.* deception [L. *imponere*, to place upon].

im·po·tent (im'·pa·tant) *a.* powerless; wanting natural strength; without sexual power (of a male). **impotence, impotency** *n.*

im·pound (im·pound') *v.t.* to confine cattle in a pound or pen; to restrain within limits; (*Law*) to retain documents in a civil case with a view to criminal proceedings.

im·pov·er·ish (im·páy'·er·ish) *v.t.* to reduce to poverty; to exhaust the strength, richness, or fertility of land. **-ed** *a.* **-ment** *n.* [O. Fr. *empovrir*].

im·prac·ti·ca·ble (im·prak'·ti·ka·bl) *a.* not able to be accomplished; unfeasible. **impracticability, impracticableness** *n.* **impractical** *a.* not practical.

im·pre·cate (im'·pri·kāt) *v.t.* to invoke by prayer (evil) upon; to curse. **imprecation** *n.* **imprecatory** *a.* [L. *imprecari*, to invoke by prayer].

im·preg·na·ble (im·preg'·na·bl) *a.* not to be stormed or taken by assault; not to be moved, impressed, or shaken. **impregnability** *n.* **impregnably** *adv.* [Fr. *imprenable*, fr. L. *in-*, not; *prehendere*, to take].

im·preg·nate (im·preg'·nāt) *v.t.* to make pregnant; to render fertile; to saturate; to imbue. **impregnable** *a.* **impregnation** *n.* [L. *impregnare*].

im·pre·sa·ri·o (im·pra·sà'·ri·ō) *n.* an organizer of public entertainments, a teacher or manager of concert artists [It].

im·press (im·pres') *v.t.* to take forcibly, persons or goods, for public service; to commandeer. **-ment** *n.* [L. *in*, in, into; *praestare*, to furnish].

im·press (im·pres') *v.t.* to press in or upon; to make a mark or figure upon; to fix deeply in the mind; to stamp. (im'·pres) *n.* a mark made by pressure; stamp; impression wrought on the mind. **-ibility** *n.* susceptibility. **-ible** *a.* capable of being impressed. **-ibly** *adv.* **impression** *n.* act of impressing; a mark or stamp made by pressure; psychological effect or influence on the mind; opinion; idea. **impressionable** *a.* susceptible to external influences. **-ive** *a.* making or fitted to make a deep impression on the mind. **-ively** *adv.* **-iveness** *n.* [L. *imprimere*, fr. *premere*, to press].

im·pres·sion·ism (im·presh'·an·izm) *n.* a revolutionary modern movement, originating in France, in art, literature and music, aiming at reproducing the *impression* which eye and mind gather, rather than representing actual fact. **impressionist** *n.*

im·pri·ma·tur (im·prạ·mā'·ter) *n.* a license to print a book; official approval [L. = 'let it be printed'].

im·print (im·print') *v.t.* to mark by pressure; to fix indelibly, as on the mind; to print. (im'·print) *n.* an impression; name of printer or publisher on title page or at the end of a book.

im·prob·a·ble (im·prȧb'·a·bl) *a.* unlikely. **improbability** *n.* **improbably** *adv.*

im·pro·bi·ty (im·prō'·bi·ti·) *n.* want of integrity or rectitude; dishonesty.

im·promp·tu (im·prȧmp'·tóȯ) *adv.* or *a.* offhand [Fr. fr. L. *promptus*, ready].

im·prop·er (im·prȧp'·er) *a.* unsuitable to the end or design; unfit; indecent; inaccurate. **-ly** *adv.* **impropriety** *n.* offense against rules of conduct; the use of a word in its wrong sense.

im·prove (im·próȯv') *v.t.* to make better; to employ to good purpose; to make progress; *v.i.* to grow better; to become more prosperous. **improvability, improvableness** *n.* **improvable** *a.* **improvably** *adv.* **-ment** *n.* the act of improving; state of being improved; progress. **improvingly** *adv.*

im·prov·i·dent (im·prȧv'·a·dant) *a.* not prudent or foreseeing; neglecting to provide for the future. **improvidence** *n.*

im·pro·vise (im·prẹ·viz') *v.t.* to extemporize; to make the best of materials at hand; to compose, speak or perform without preparation. **improvisation** (im·prȧv·i·zā'·shan) *n.* **-r** *n.* [L. *in-*, not; *provisus*, foreseen].

im·pru·dent (im·próȯ'·dant), *a.* lacking in discretion. **imprudence** *n.* **-ly** *adv.*

im·pu·dent (im'·pyạ·dant) *a.* brazen; boldfaced; rude. **impudence** *n.* **-ly** *adv.* [L. *impudens*, shameless].

im·pugn (im·pūn') *v.t.* to call in question; to contradict; to challenge the accuracy of a statement. **-able** *a.* **-er** *n.* **-ment** *n.* [L. *impugnare*, to assail].

im·pulse (im'·puls) *n.* the motion or effect produced by a sudden action or applied force; push; thrust; momentum; sudden thought. **impulsion** *n.* impelling force; incitement. **impulsive** *a.* having the power of impelling; acting momentarily without due thought. **impulsively** *adv.* **impulsiveness** *n.* [L. *impellere, impulsion*, to urge on. Cf. *impel*].

im·pu·ni·ty (im·pūn'·a·ti·) *n.* exemption from punishment, injury, or loss [L. *impunitas*, without punishment].

im·pure (im·pyoor') *a.* not pure; mixed; adulterated; foul; unchaste. **-ly** *adv.* **impurity, impureness** *n.*

im·pute (im·pūt') *v.t.* to ascribe to (in a bad sense); to attribute to. **imputable** *a.* **imputableness, imputability** *n.* **imputation**

n. act of imputing; suggestion of evil. **imputative** *a.* **imputatively** *adv.* [L. *in; putare*, to reckon, to think].

in (in) *prep.* within; inside of; indicating a present relation to time, space, or condition; *adv.* inside; closely; with privilege or possession; immediately. **in so far as,** to the extent that. **inasmuch as,** considering that [O.E.].

in·a·bil·i·ty (in·a·bil'·a·ti·) *n.* want of strength, means, or power; impotence.

in·ac·cu·rate (in·ak'·yar·at) *a.* not correct; not according to truth or reality; erroneous. **inaccuracy** *n.* **-ly** *adv.*

in·ac·tive (in·ak'·tiv) *a.* not disposed to action or effort; idle; inert; lazy; (*Chem.*) showing no tendency to combine with other elements. **inaction** *n.* **inactivate** *v.t.* to make inactive. **inactivation** *n.* **-ly** *adv.* **inactivity** *n.* want of action or energy.

in·ad·e·quate (in·ad'·a·kwat) *a.* insufficient; too cramped; incapable. **inadequacy** *n.* **-ly** *adv.* **-ness** *n.*

in·ad·mis·si·ble (in·ad·mis'·a·bl) *a.* not allowable; improper. **inadmissibly** *adv.*

in·ad·vert·ent (in·ad·vur'·tant) *a.* not turning the mind to a matter; inattentive; thoughtless; careless. **inadvertence, inadvertency** *n.* **-ly** *adv.*

in·ad·vis·a·ble (in·ad·vī'·zạ·bal) *a.* not recommended; inexpedient. **inadvisability** *n.* **inadvisably** *adv.*

in·al·ien·a·ble (in·āl'·yan·a·bl) *a.* incapable of being separated or transferred.

in·ane (in·ān') *a.* empty; void; foolish; silly. **inanition** *n.* state of being empty; exhaustion; starvation. **inanity** *n.* vacuity; silly remark [L. *inanis*].

in·an·i·mate (in·an'·a·mat) *a.* destitute of life or spirit. **inanimation** *n.* **-ness** *n.*

in·ap·pli·ca·ble (in·ap'·lik·a·bl) *a.* not applicable; unsuitable; irrelevant; inappropriate.

in·ap·pre·ci·a·ble (in·a·prē'·shi·a·bl) *a.* not worth reckoning; not able to be valued.

in·ap·pro·pri·ate (in·a·prō'·pri·at) *a.* unsuitable; at the wrong time. **-ly** *adv.* **-ness** *n.*

in·apt (in·apt') *a.* inappropriate; unsuitable; awkward; clumsy. **-itude** *n.* unfitness; awkwardness. **-ly** *adv.*

in·ar·tic·u·late (in·ȧr·tik'·ya·lat) *a.* unable to put one's ideas in words; not uttered distinctly; not jointed. **-ly** *adv.* **-ness** *n.* **inarticulation** *n.*

in·as·much *adv.* See **in.**

in·au·di·ble (in·aw'·di·bl) *a.* not able to be heard; noiseless; silent. **inaudibility, inaudibleness** *n.* **inaudibly** *adv.*

in·au·gu·rate (in·aw'·gya·rāt) *v.t.* to induct into an office in a formal manner; to install; to set in motion or action; to begin. **inaugural, inauguratory** *a.* **inauguration** *n.* opening ceremony. **inaugurator** *n.* [L. *inaugurare*, to take auguries before action].

in·aus·pi·cious (in·aw·spish'·as) *a.* not auspicious; ill-omened. **-ly** *adv.* **-ness** *n.*

in·born (in'·bawrn) *a.* born in or with; innate; natural; inherent.

in·bred (in'·bred) *a.* bred within; innate; inherent. **inbreed** *v.t.* to mate animals of the same blood stock; to marry within the family or tribe. **inbreeding** *n.*

in·cal·cu·la·ble (in·kal'·kya·la·bl) *a.* countless; beyond calculation; uncertain. **incalculability, -ness** *n.*

in·can·des·cent (in·kan·des'·ant) *a.* glowing with white heat and providing light. **incandescense** *n.* white heat [L. *in*, in; *candescere*, to begin to glow].

in·can·ta·tion (in·kan·tā'·shan) *n.* a formula or charm-words used to produce magical or supernatural effect. **incantatory** *a.* [L. *incantare*, to sing spells. Cf. *enchant*].

in·ca·pa·ble (in·kā′·pạ·bl) *a.* wanting ability or capacity; not admitting of; not susceptible of. **incapability** *n.*

in·ca·pa·ci·tate (in·kạ·pas′·ạ·tāt) *v.t.* to render incapable. **incapacitation** *n.* act of disqualifying. **incapacity** *n.* want of capacity; lack of normal intellectual power; inability; incapability; legal disqualification.

in·car·cer·ate (in·kàr′·sẹr·āt) *v.t.* to confine; to imprison. **incarcerator, incarceration,** *n.* [L. *in; carcer,* prison].

in·car·na·dine (in·kàr′·nạ·dīn) *a.* flesh-colored; of a carnation color; crimson; *v.t.* to dye crimson [Fr. fr. L. *caro,* flesh].

in·car·nate (in·kàr′·nāt) *v.t.* to put into concrete form; to embody in flesh, esp. in human form; *a.* (in·kàr′·nạt) embodied in flesh; typified. **incarnation** *n.* embodiment; that which embodies and typifies an abstraction [L. *in; caro, carnis,* flesh].

in·cen·di·ar·y (in·sen′·di·er·i·) *n.* one who maliciously sets fire to property; an agitator who inflames passions; a fire bomb; *a.* pert. to malicious burning of property; tending to inflame dissension. **incendiarism** *n.* arson [L. *incendere,* to set on fire].

in·cense (in·sens′) *v.t.* to inflame to violent anger [L. *incendere,* to set on fire].

in·cense (in′·sens) *n.* a mixture of aromatic gums and spices which, when burned, produces a sweet-smelling smoke, used for religious purposes; flattery; adulation; *v.t.* to perfume with incense [L. *incendere,* to burn].

in·cen·tive (in·sen′·tiv) *a.* inciting; provoking; *n.* motive; spur; stimulus; encouragement [L. *incentivus,* setting the tune].

in·cep·tion (in·sep′·shạn) *n.* beginning; start; origin. **inceptive** *a.* **inceptively** *adv.* [L. *incipere, inceptum,* to begin].

in·ces·sant (in·ses′·ạnt) *a.* continuing or following without interruption. **incessancy** *n.* **-ly** *adv.* [L. *in-,* not; *cessare,* to cease].

in·cest (in′·sest) *n.* sexual intercourse of kindred within the forbidden degrees.**-uous** *a.* [L. *in-,* not; *castus,* chaste].

inch (inch) *n.* twelfth part of a linear foot; a small degree or quantity; *v.i.* to push forward by slow degrees; to edge forward [L. *uncia,* twelfth part of anything].

in·cho·ate (in′·kō·at) *a.* just begun; rudimentary; incipient. **-ly** *adv.* **inchoation** *n.* early stage or state. **inchoative** *a.* [L. *in, choare,* to begin].

in·ci·dent (in′·sạ·dạnt) *a.* liable to happen; subordinate to; falling upon, as a ray of light upon a reflecting surface; naturally attaching to; *n.* that which takes place; event; occurrence; episode; subordinate action. **incidence** *n.* range of influence; the manner of falling upon. **-al** *a.* and *n.* **-ally** *adv.* **-alness** *n.* [L. *incidere,* to fall in].

in·cin·er·ate (in·sin′·ẹr·āt) *v.t.* to consume by fire; to burn to ashes. **incineration** *n.* **incinerator** *n.* furnace for consuming refuse [L. *incinerare,* to reduce to ashes].

in·cip·i·ent (in·sip′·i·ạnt) *a.* beginning; originating. **incipience, incipiency** *n.* [L. *incipere,* to begin].

in·cise (in·sīz′) *v.t.* to cut into; to carve; to engrave. **incision** (in·sizh′·ạn) *n.* the act of cutting with a sharp instrument; a cut; gash. **incisive** *a.* having the quality of cutting or penetrating; sharp; biting; trenchant; **incisively** *adv.* **incisiveness** *n.* **incisor** *n.* one of the eight front cutting teeth[L. *incidere,* to cut into].

in·cite (in·sīt′) *v.t.* to move the mind to action; to spur on. **incitant** *n.* a stimulant; *a.* exciting. **incitation** (in·sī·tā′·shun) *n.* **-ment** *n.* act of inciting; motive; incentive. *n.* [L. *incitare,* to rouse].

in·clem·ent (in·klem′·ạnt) *a.* not clement; severe; harsh; stormy. **inclemency** *n.*

in·cline (in·klīn′) *v.t.* to cause to deviate from a line or direction; to give a tendency to, as to the will or affections; to bend; to turn from the vertical. *v.i.* to deviate from the vertical; to be disposed. (in′·klīn) *n.* an ascent or descent; a slope. **inclination** *n.* act of inclining; bent of the mind or will; leaning; tendency towards; favor for one thing more than another. **-d** *a.* [L. *in; clinare,* to lean].

in·clude (in·klood′) *v.t.* to confine within; to comprise. **inclusion** *n.* act of including; state of being included or confined. **inclusive** *a.* taking in the stated limit, number, or extremes; enclosing; embracing. **inclusively** *adv.* [L. *includere,* to shut in].

in·cog·ni·to (in·kàg′·ni·tō) *a.* and *adv.* in a disguise; in an assumed character and under an assumed name; *n.* (*fem.* **incognita**) the state of being unknown; a person who conceals his identity under a false name [L. *incognitus,* unknown].

in·co·her·ent (in·kō·hir′·ạnt) *a.* not connected or clear; confused. **incoherence** *n.* **-ly** *adv.* **incoherency** *n.*

in·com·bus·ti·ble (in·kạm·bust′·ạ·bl) *a.* not capable of being burned. **incombustibility, incombustibleness** *n.* **incombustibly** *adv.*

in·come (in′·kum) *n.* the gain or reward from one's labors or investments; annual receipts; rent; profit; interest. **-r** *n.* a newcomer. **incoming** *n.* a coming in; revenue; *a.* coming in; entering; — **tax,** tax levied on income.

in·com·men·su·ra·ble (in·kạ·men′·sạ·ra·bl) *a.* having no common measure or standard of comparison. **-ness** *n.* **incommensurably** *adv.* **incommensurate** *a.* not admitting of a common measure; unequal; out of proportion. **incommensurately** *adv.*

in·com·mode (in·kạ·mōd′) *v.t.* to put to inconvenience or discomfort; to hinder. **incommodious** *a.* inconvenient; too small. **incommodiously** *adv.* **incommodity** *n.* [L. *in-,* not; *commodus,* convenient].

in·com·mu·ni·ca·ble (in·kạ·mū′·ni·kạ·bl) *a.* incapable of being communicated or shared. **incommunicability** *n.* **-ness** *n.* **incommunicably** *adv.* **incommunicative** *a.* reserved; not ready to impart information.

in·com·mu·ni·ca·do (in·kạ·mū·ni·kà′·dō) *a.* of a prisoner, deprived of communication with other people [Sp.].

in·com·pa·ra·ble (in′·kàm′·per·ạ·bl) *a.* not admitting any degree of comparison; unequaled; unrivaled. **incomparability** *n.* **-ness** *n.* **incomparably** *adv.*

in·com·pat·i·ble (in·kạm·pat′·ạ·bl) *a.* incapable of existing side by side; unable to live together in harmony. **incompatibility, incompatibleness** *n.* **incompatibly** *adv.*

in·com·pe·tent (in·kàm′·pạ·tạnt) *a.* not efficient in the performance of function; inadequate; incapable. **incompetence** *n.* **incompetency** *n.*

in·com·plete (in·kam·plēt′) *a.* defective; unfinished; imperfect. **-ly** *adv.*

in·com·pre·hen·si·ble (in·kàm·pri·hen′·sa·bl) *a.* incapable of being comprehended or understood. **-ness, incomprehensibility, incomprehension** *n.* difficulty of understanding; quality or state of being incomprehensible. **incomprehensibly** *adv.* **incomprehensive** *a.* limited; not extensive.

in·com·pres·si·ble (in·kạm·pres′·ạ·bl) *a.* cannot be compressed or reduced in bulk.

in·con·ceiv·a·ble (in·kạn·sēv′·ạ·bl) *a.* not capable of being conceived in the mind; unthinkable. **inconceivability, inconceivableness** *n.* **inconceivably** *adv.*

in·con·clu·sive (in·kạn·klŏŏ′·siv) *a.* not decisive or conclusive; not settling a point in debate or a doubtful question. **-ly** *adv.*

in·con·gru·ous (in·kàng′·groo.ạs) *a.* inappropriate; not reciprocally agreeing;

WEBSTER
H–L

(*Math.*) not coinciding. **incongruent** *a.* **incongruity, incongruousness** *n.*

in·con·se·quent (in·kán'·sạ·kwent) *a.* not following from the premises; illogical; irrelevant. **inconsequence** *n.* **inconsequential** *a.* not to the point; illogical; of no import; trivial. **inconsequentially** *adv.*

in·con·sid·er·a·ble (in·kạn·sid'·ẹr·ạ·bl) *a.* unworthy of consideration; unimportant.

in·con·sid·er·ate (in·kạn·sid'·ẹr·ạt) *a.* thoughtless; careless of others' feelings.

in·con·sis·tent (in·kạn·sis'·tạnt) *a.* liable to sudden and unexpected change; changeable; not agreeing. **inconsistency** *n.* **-ly** *adv.*

in·con·spic·u·ous (in·kạn spik'·yoo·ạs) *a.* scarcely noticeable; hardly discernible.

in·con·stant (in·kán'·stạnt) *a.* not constant or consistent; subject to change. **inconstancy** *n.* **-ly** *adv.*

in·con·ti·nent (in·kán'·tạ·nạnt) *a.* morally incapable of restraint. **incontinence, incontinency** *n.* **-ly** *adv.*

in·con·tro·vert·i·ble (in·kán·trạ·vur'·tạ·bl) *a.* too clear or certain to admit of dispute; unquestionable. **incontrovertibly** *adv.*

in·con·ven·ient (in·kạn·vēn'·yạnt) *a.* awkward; unsuitable. **inconvenience** *v.t.* to put to trouble or annoyance. **inconvenience, inconveniency** *n.* **-ly** *adv.*

in·con·vert·i·ble (in·kạn·vur'·tạ·bl) *a.* cannot be changed or exchanged; of paper money, notes which cannot be converted into gold on demand. **inconvertibility** *n.*

in·co·or·di·nate (in·kō·awr'·dạ·nạt) *a.* not in orderly relation with one another.

in·cor·po·rate (in·kawr'·pạ·rāt) *v.t.* and *v.i.* to combine, as different ingredients, into one body or mass; to give a material form to; to constitute into a corporation; *a.* formed into an incorporation. **incorporation** *n.* act of incorporating; state of being incorporated; the formation or embodying of an association or society. **incorporative** *a.* **incorporeal** *a.* not possessed of a body; immaterial; unsubstantial; spiritual. **incorporeality** *n.*

in·cor·rect (in·kạ·rekt') *a.* not in accordance with the truth; improper. **-ly** *adv.* **-ness** *n.*

in·cor·ri·gi·ble (in·kawr'·i·jạ·bl) *a.* beyond any hope of reform or improvement in conduct; *n.* such a person.

in·cor·rupt (in·kạr·upt') *a.* morally pure; not open to bribery; free from decay. **-ible** *a.* **-ibility** *n.* **-ly** *adv.* **-ness** *n.*

in·crease (in·krēs') *v.t.* to make greater; to extend; to lengthen; *v.t.* to become greater; to multiply by the production of young. (in'· krēs) *n.* growth; produce; profit; interest; progeny; offspring; enlargement; addition. **increasable** *a.* **increasingly** *adv.* [L. *increscere*, fr. *crescere*, to grow].

in·cred·i·ble (in·kred'·ạ·bl) *a.* impossible to be believed; surpassing belief; amazing. **incredibility, -ness** *n.* **incredibly** *adv.*

in·cred·u·lous (in·krej'·ạ·lạs) *a.* not disposed to believe; showing unbelief. **incredulity** *n.* disbelief. **-ness** *n.* **-ly** *adv.*

in·cre·ment (in'·krạ·mạnt) *n.* increase; matter added; growth; annual augmentation of a fixed amount to a salary. **-al** *a.* [L. *incrementum*, fr. *increscere*, to increase].

in·crim·i·nate (in·krim'·ạ·nāt) *v.t.* to charge with a crime; to involve one in a criminal action. **incriminatory** *a.* [L. *in; crimen*, a charge].

in·crust, encrust (in·, en·krust') *v.t.* to cover with a crust; *v.i.* to form a hard covering or crust on the surface. **-ation** *n.*

in·cu·bate (ing·, in'·kyạ·bāt) *v.i.* to sit, as on eggs, for hatching; to brood; of disease germs, to pass through the stage between infection and appearance of symptoms; *v.t.* to hatch; to ponder over. **incubation** *n.* **incubative, incubatory** *a.* **incubator** *n.* a cabinet, in which the heat is automatically regulated,

used to hatch eggs; similar devices for premature infants or bacterial cultures. [L. *in; cubare*, to lie].

in·cu·bus (ing'·, in'·kyạ·bạs) *n.* a nightmare; any burdensome or depressing influence [L. *in*, upon; *cubare*, to lie].

in·cul·cate (in·kul'·kāt) *v.t.* (foll. by *in* or *on*) to urge forcibly and repeatedly; to impress by admonition. **inculcation** *n.* **inculcator** *n.* [L. *inculcare*, to stamp in].

in·cum·bent (in·kum'·bạnt) *a.* lying or resting upon; resting on, as duty; *n.* holder of an office. **incumbency** *n.* [L. *incumbere*, to lie upon].

in·cur (in·kur') *v.t.* to become liable to; to bring upon oneself. *pr.p.* **-ring.** *pa.t.* and *pa.p.* **-red** [L. *in*, into; *currere*, to run].

in·cur·a·ble (in·kyoor'·ạ·bl) *a.* not able to be cured; *n.* one beyond cure. **incurability** *n.*

in·cu·ri·ous (in·kyoo'·ri·ạs) *a.* not inquisitive or curious; indifferent. **-ly** *adv.*

in·cur·sion (in·kur'·zhạn) *n.* a raid into a territory with hostile intention. **incursive** *a.* [L. *in*, into; *currere*, to run].

in·curve (in·kurv') *v.t.* to bend into a curve; *v.i.* to bend inward. **incurvate** *v.t.* to bend inward or upward; *a.* curved in.

in·debt·ed (in·det'·ạd) *a.* placed under an obligation; owing; beholden. **-ness** *n.*

in·de·cent (in·dē'·sạnt) *a.* unbecoming; immodest; obscene. **indecency** *n.* lack of decency. **-ly** *adv.*

in·de·ci·pher·a·ble (in·di·sī'·fer·a·bl) *a.* incapable of being deciphered; illegible.

in·de·ci·sion (in·di·sizh'·ạn) *n.* want of decision; irresoluteness; shilly-shallying. **indecisive** *a.* inconclusive; doubtful; wavering. **indecisively** *adv.* **indecisiveness** *n.*

in·de·clin·a·ble (in·di·klīn'·ạ·bl) *a.* (*Gram.*) having no inflections or cases.

in·dec·o·rous (in·dek'·ạ·rạs, in·di·kōr'·ạs) *a.* contrary to good manners. **-ly** *adv.* **-ness, indecorum** *n.* impropriety.

in·deed (in·dēd') *adv.* in reality; in truth; in fact; certainly. *interj.* denotes surprise.

in·de·fat·i·ga·ble (in·di·fat'·i·gạ·bl) *a.* incapable of being fatigued; unwearied; untiring. **-ness, indefatigability** *n.* **indefatigably** *adv.* [L. *in-; defatigare*, to tire].

in·de·fea·si·ble (in·di·fēz'·ạ·bl) *a.* not to be defeated; incapable of being made void; irrevocable. **indefeasibility** *n.* **indefeasibly** *adv.* [O.Fr. *defaire*, to undo].

in·de·fen·si·ble (in·di·fen'·sạ·bl) *a.* incapable of being maintained, vindicated, or justified; untenable; unjustifiable; unexcusable.

in·de·fin·a·ble (in·di·fin'·ạ·bl) *a.* not able to be defined. **indefinably** *adv.*

in·def·i·nite (in·def'·ạ·nit) *a.* having no known limits; (*Gram.*) not pointing out with precision the person, thing, or time to which a part of speech refers. **-ly** *adv.* **-ness, indefinitude** *n.* want of precision. **— article,** a, an.

in·del·i·ble (in·del'·ạ·bl) *a.* not to be blotted out or erased; ineffaceable; ingrained. **indelibility, -ness** *n.* **indelibly** *adv.* [L. *in-*, not; *delere*, to destroy, blot out].

in·del·i·cate (in·del'·ạ·kạt) *a.* offensive to good manners or to purity of mind; indecorous. **indelicacy** *n.* **-ly** *adv.*

in·dem·ni·fy (in·dem'·nạ·fī) *v.t.* to reimburse; to give security against; to free one from the consequences of a technically illegal act. **indemnification** *n.* **indemnitor** *n.* **indemnity** *n.* an agreement to render a person immune from a contingent liability; compensation [L. *indemnis*, unharmed].

in·de·mon·stra·ble (in·de·mán'·strạ·bl) *a.* cannot be demonstrated or proved.

in·dent (in·dent') *v.t.* to cut into points or inequalities; to make notches or holes in; to make an order (*upon* some one *for*); to indenture; (*Print.*) to begin the first line of a paragraph farther away from the margin than the remaining lines; *v.i.* to wind back and forth; to make an agreement; to make out an order in duplicate. (in'·dent) *n.* a cut or notch; a dent; a mark, as of a tooth; an order for goods. **-ation** *n.* a notch; a depression. **-ure** *n.* a contract of apprenticeship; [L. *in,* in; *dens,* a tooth].

in·de·pen·dent (in·di·pen'·dant) *a.* not dependent; not subject to the control of others; unrelated; free; self-supporting. **independence, independency** *n.* **-ly** *adv.*

in·de·scrib·a·ble (in·di·skrīb'·a·bl) *a.* incapable of being described.

in·de·struct·i·ble (in·di·struk'·ta·bl) *a.* not able to be destroyed; imperishable. **indestructibility** *n.* **indestructibly** *adv.*

in·de·ter·mi·na·ble (in·di·tur'·min·a·bl) *a.* cannot be determined, classified, or fixed. **-ness** *n.* **indeterminably** *adv.* **indeterminate** *a.* not settled or fixed in detail; indefinite. **indeterminately** *adv.* **indeterminateness, indetermination** *n.* an unsettled or wavering state of the mind.

in·dex (in'·deks) *n.* any table for facilitating reference in a book; a directing sign; that which points out, shows, indicates, or manifests; a pointer or hand which directs to anything; the forefinger or pointing finger; the ratio between the measurement of a given substance and that of a fixed standard; (*Math.*) the figure or letter showing the power of a quantity; the exponent of a power. *pl.* **-es, indices.** *v.t.* to provide with an index or table references; to place in alphabetical order in an index. **-er** *n.* one who compiles an index [L. = an indicator].

In·di·a (in'·di·a) *n.* a country in Asia, named from river *Indus.* — **ink,** ink composed of lamp-black mixed into a paste with gum. — **paper,** a very thin tough and opaque paper made from fibers. — **rubber** *n.* natural rubber obtained from latex [Sans. *sindhu,* a river].

In·di·an (in'·di·an) *a.* pert. to India in Asia, to the East Indies, or to the aborigines of America; *n.* a native of India in Asia, of the East Indies, or one of the aboriginal inhabitants of America. — **club,** bottle-shaped wooden club, used in physical exercise. — **corn,** maize. — **file,** single file. — **giver** *n.* (*Colloq.*) one who takes back a gift. — **red** an earthy pigment with a purple-russet color, due to the presence of peroxide of iron. — **summer** mild, warm, hazy weather of autumn [Cans. *sindhu,* a river].

in·di·cate (in'·da·kāt) *v.t.* to point out; to be a sign of; to denote; to show; to signify. **indication** *n.* act of indicating; mark; token; sign. **indicative** *a.* pointing out; denoting; (*Gram.*) applied to that mood of the verb which affirms or denies; *n.* the direct mood of a verb. **indicatively** *adv.* **indicator** *n.* one who indicates; a pointer; an instrument used to gauge and record varying conditions. **indicatory** *a.* [L. *indicare,* to show].

in·dict (in·dīt') *v.t.* to charge with a crime; to accuse; to arraign. **-able** *a.* **-ment** *n.* the act of indicting; a formal charge of crime. [L. *in; dicere,* to declare].

in·dif·fer·ent (in·dif'·er·ant) *a.* uninterested; without concern; not making a difference; having no influence or weight; of no account; neither good nor bad. **indifference** *n.* **-ly** adv.

in·di·gene (in'·da·jēn) *n.* an aborigine; a native animal or plant. Also **indigen.** **indigenous** *a.* born or originating in a country; native. **indigenously** *adv.* [L. *indigena,* a native].

in·di·gent (in'·da·jent) *a.* destitute of property or means of subsistence; needy; poor. **indigence** *n.* [L. *indigere,* to lack].

in·di·gest·ed (in·da·jest'·ad) *a.* not digested;

lacking order or system. **indigestibility** *n.* **indigestible** *a.* incapable of being digested. **indigestibly** *adv.* **indigestion** *n.* inability to digest food or difficulty and discomfort in doing so; dyspepsia. **indigestive** *a.*

in·dig·nant (in·dig'·nant) *a.* moved by a feeling of wrath, mingled with scorn or contempt; roused. **-ly** *adv.* **indignation** *n.* righteous wrath. **indignity** *n.* affront; contemptuous treatment [L. *in-,* not; *dignari,* to deem worthy].

in·di·go (in'·di·gō) *n.* a blue dye-stuff derived from many leguminous plants; *a.* of a deep-blue color [L. *indicum,* fr. *Indicus,* of India].

in·di·rect (in·da·rekt') *a.* not direct or straight; crooked; dishonest. **-ion** *n.* roundabout way; deliberate attempt to mislead; trickery. **-ly** *adv.* **-ness** *n.*

in·dis·creet (in·dis·krēt') *a.* not discreet; imprudent; injudicious; reckless. **-ly** *adv.* **indiscretion** (in·dis·kresh'·an) *n.* an indiscreet act; the quality of being indiscreet.

in·dis·crim·i·nate (in·dis·krim'·a·nat) *a.* wanting discrimination; not making any distinction. **-ly** *adv.* **indiscriminating, indiscriminative** *a.* **indiscrimination** *n.*

in·dis·pen·sa·ble (in·dis·pen'·sa·bl) *a.* absolutely necessary; not to be set aside. **indispensability, -ness** *n.* **indispensably** *adv.*

in·dis·pose (in·di·spōz') *v.t.* to render unfit or unsuited; to make somewhat ill; to render averse or disinclined (toward). **-d** *a.* averse; ill. **indisposition** *n.*

in·dis·put·a·ble (in·dis·pū'·ta·bl, in·dis'·-pyoo·ta·bl) *a.* too obvious to be disputed.

in·dis·sol·u·ble (in·dis·al'·ya·bl) *a.* not capable of being dissolved; perpetually binding or obligatory; inviolable. **-ness, indissolubility** *n.* **indissolubly** *adv.*

in·dis·tinct (in·dis·tingkt') *a.* not distinct or distinguishable; not clearly defined or uttered; obscure; dim. **-ive** *a.* not capable of making distinctions; not distinctive. **-ly** *adv.*

in·dis·tin·guish·a·ble (in·dis·ting'·gwish·a·bl) *a.* may not be distinguished. **-ness** *n.* **indistinguishably** *adv.*

in·dite (in·dīt') *v.t.* to compose; to write. **-ment** *n.* [O. Fr. *enditer*].

in·di·vid·u·al (in·da·vij'·ȯȯ·al) *a.* not divided; single; peculiar to single person or thing; distinctive; *n.* a single being, or thing. **-ization** *n.* **-ize, individuate** *v.t.* to distinguish individually; to particularize. **-ism** *n.* quality of being individual; a political or economic theory which asserts the rights of the individual as against those of the community. **-ist** *n.* **-istic** *a.* **-ity** *n.* separate or distinct existence; personality. **-ly** *adv.* [L. *individuus,* undivided].

in·di·vis·i·ble (in·da·viz'·a·bl) *a.* not divisible; not separate. **indivisibility, -ness** *n.* **indivisibly** *adv.*

in·doc·tri·nate (in·dak'·tri·nāt) *v.t.* to instruct; to imbue with political or religious principles and dogmas. **indoctrination** *n.*

in·do·lent (in'·da·lant) *a.* habitually idle or lazy; indisposed to exertion. **indolence, indolency** *n.* **-ly** *adv.* [L. *in-,* not; *dolere,* to feel pain].

in·dom·i·ta·ble (in·dam'·at·a·bl) *a.* not to be subdued; that cannot be overcome. **indomitably** *adv.* [L. *in-,* not; *domitare,* to tame].

In·do·ne·sia (in·da·nē'·zha) *n.* Republic of S.E. Asia (since 1945). **-n** *a.* [*Indo,* and Gk. *nēsos,* an island].

in·door (in'·dōr) *a.* being within doors; under cover. **indoors** *adv.*

in·dorse, in·dorse·ment See **en·dorse.**

in·du·bi·ta·ble (in·dū'·bit·a·bl) *a.* too obvious to admit of doubt; unquestionable; quite certain. **indubitably** *adv.*

in·duce (in·dūs') *v.t.* to overcome by persuasion or argument; to persuade; to produce or cause (as electricity) **-ment** *n.* that which induces or persuades to action. **-r** *n.* **inducible** *a.* [L. *inducere*, to lead in].

in·duct (in·dukt') *v.t.* to bring in or introduce; to install or put formally into office; to bring into military service. **-ile** *a.* of a metal not capable of being drawn out into wires or threads. **-ility** *n.* **-ion** *n.* installation of a person in an office; an introduction to a poem or play; (*Elect.*) the transfer of a magnetic or electric state from an electrified to a non-electrified body, by proximity; (*Logic*) a process of finding explanations. **-ional** *a.* **-ive** *a.* **-ively** *adv.* **-or** *n.* [L. *in*, into; *ducere*, to lead].

in·dulge (in·dulj') *v.t.* to give freedom or scope to; to allow one his own way; to gratify; *v.i.* (usu. followed by *in*) to give oneself to the habit or practice of. **-nce** *n.* **-nt** *a.* yielding; compliant; very forbearing. **-ntly** *adv.* [L. *indulgere*, to be indulgent].

in·du·rate (in'·dyą·rāt) *v.t.* to make hard; to deprive of sensibility; *v.i.* grow hard; to harden. [L. *in*, in; *durus*, hard].

in·dus·try (in'·dąs·tri·) *n.* habitual diligence in any employment, bodily or mental; steady application to work; a particular branch of trade or manufacture. **industrial** *a.* pert. to industry or manufacture. **industrialism** *n.* system of industry or manufacture on a large scale. **industrially** *adv.* **industrious** *a.* diligent in business or study. **industriously** *adv.* **industriousness** *n.* [L. *industria*].

in·e·bri·ate (in·ē'·bri·āt) *v.t.* to make drunk; to intoxicate; to exhilarate; *a.* intoxicated; *n.* a habitual drunkard. **inebriation, inebriety** *n.* drunkenness. **inebrious** *a.* stupidly drunk [L. *in*; *ebrius*, drunk].

in·ed·i·ble (in·ed'·ą·bl) *a.* not eatable; unfit for food. **inedibility** *n.*

in·ef·fa·ble (in·ef'·ą·bl) *a.* incapable of being expressed in words; indescribable; unutterable. **-ness, ineffability** *n.* **ineffably** *adv.* [L. *in-*, not; *effabilis*, speakable].

in·ef·face·a·ble (in·ą·fās'·ą·bl) *a.* incapable of being rubbed out. **ineffaceably** *adv.*

in·ef·fec·tive (in·ą·fek'·tiv) *a.* incapable of producing any effect or the effect intended; useless; inefficient. **-ly** *adv.* **ineffectual** *a.* not producing the proper effect; vain; fruitless; futile. **ineffectuality, ineffectualness** *n.* **ineffectually** *adv.*

in·ef·fi·ca·cy (in·ef'·ą·ką·si·) *n.* want of power to produce the proper effect. **inefficacious** *a.* **inefficaciously** *adv.*

in·ef·fi·ci·ent (in·ą·fish'·ąnt) *a.* not fitted to perform the work in a capable, economical way. **inefficiency** *n.* **-ly** *adv.*

in·e·las·tic (in·i·las'·tik) *a.* not elastic; rigid; unyielding. **inelasticity** *n.*

in·el·e·gant (in·el'·ą·gant) *a.* lacking in form or beauty; wanting grace or ornament. **inelegance, inelegancy** *n.* **-ly** *adv.*

in·el·i·gi·ble (in·el'·i·ją·bl) *a.* unsuitable; legally disqualified. **ineligibility** *n.*

in·e·luc·ta·ble (in·i·luk'·tą·bl) *a.* inevitable. **ineluctability** *n.* [L. *in-*; *eluctari*, to struggle out].

in·ept (in·ept') *a.* not apt or fit; inexpert; unsuitable; foolish. **-itude, -ness** *n.* **-ly** *adv.* [L. *in*, not; *aptus*, fit].

in·e·qual·i·ty (in·i·kwal'·ą·ti·) *n.* want of equality; disparity; inadequacy; unevenness.

in·eq·ui·ta·ble (in·ek'·wi·tą·bl) *a.* not fair or just; not according to equity.

in·e·rad·i·ca·ble (in·i·rad'·i·ką·bl) *a.* incapable of being rooted out; deep-seated.

in·ert (in·urt') *a.* without the power of action or resistance; sluggish; without active chemical properties. **inertia** (in·ur'·shą) *n.* inactivity; that property of matter by which it tends when at rest to remain so, and when in motion to continue moving in a straight line. **-ly** *adv.* **-ness** *n.* [L. *iners*, sluggish].

in·es·cap·a·ble (in·ą·skăp'·ą·bl) *a.* inevitable; incapable of escape or of being evaded.

in·es·sen·tial (in·ą·sen'·shąl) *a.* not necessary; immaterial; of little consequence.

in·es·ti·ma·ble (in·es'·ti·mą·bl) *a.* not possible to be estimated; of untold value; incalculable; **inestimably** *adv.*

in·ev·i·ta·ble (in·ev'·i·tą·bl) *a.* unavoidable; certain to take place or appear. **-ness, inevitability** *n.* **inevitably** *adv.* [L. *in-*; *evitare*, to avoid].

in·ex·act (in·ig·zakt') *a.* not exact; not strictly true. **-itude, -ness** *n.*

in·ex·cus·a·ble (in·ik·skūz'·ą·bl) *a.* not admitting excuse or justification; unpardonable.

in·ex·haust·i·ble (in·ig·zaws'·tą·bl) *a.* incapable of being exhausted, emptied, or spent; unfailing. **inexhaustibility** *n.* **inexhaustibly** *adv.* **inexhaustive** *a.*

in·ex·o·ra·ble (in·ek'·sęr·ą·bl, in·egz'·er·ą·bl) *a.* not to be persuaded or moved by entreaty; unyielding. **-ness, inexorability** *n.* **inexorably** *adv.* [L. *in-*; *exorare*, to entreat].

in·ex·pe·di·ent (in·ik·spē'·di·ąnt) *a.* not advisable; impolitic; undesirable at the moment. **inexpedience, inexpediency** *n.*

in·ex·pen·sive (in·ik·spen'·siv) *a.* cheap.

in·ex·pe·ri·ence (in·ik·spēr'·i·ąns) *n.* absence or want of experience. **-d** *a.*

in·ex·pert (in·ek'·spurt) *a.* unskilled; clumsy; awkward. **-ness** *n.*

in·ex·pi·a·ble (in·ek'·spi·ę·bl) *a.* admitting of no atonement; implacable; inexorable.

in·ex·pli·ca·ble (in·eks'·pli·ką·bl) *a.* incapable of being explained. **inexplicability,** *n.* **inexplicably** *adv.*

in·ex·plic·it (in·iks·plis'·it) *a.* not explicit; not clearly stated; ambiguous; equivocal.

in·ex·press·i·ble (in·iks·pres'·ą·bl) *a.* cannot be expressed; indescribable. **inexpressibly** *adv.*

in·ex·pres·sive (in·iks·pres'·iv) *a.* not expressive; lacking emphasis; insignificant.

in·ex·ten·si·ble (in·ik·sten'·są·bl) *a.* not capable of extension. **inextensibility** *n.*

in·ex·tin·guish·a·ble (in·ik·sting'·gwish·ą·bl) *a.* cannot be extinguished; unquenchable.

in·ex·tri·ca·ble (in·eks'·tri·ką·bl, in·iks·tri'·ką·bl) *a.* not to be extricated or disentangled, as a knot or coil; incapable of being cleared up or explained. **inextricably** *adv.*

in·fal·li·ble (in·fal'·ą·bl) *a.* incapable of error; certain; unerring; sure. **infallibilism, infallibility** *n.* **infallibly** *adv.*

in·fa·my (in'·fą·mi·) *n.* total loss of reputation; public disgrace; ill-fame. **infamous** *a.* (in'·fą·mąs) of evil fame or reputation. **infamously** *adv.* [L. *in-*; *fama*, report].

in·fant (in'·fąnt) *n.* a young baby; (*Law*) a person under 21; *a.* pert. to infants or infancy. **infancy** *n.* the early stage of life preceding childhood; (*Law*) life to the age of twenty-one; the first stage of anything. **infanticide** (in·fan'·tą·sīd) *n.* the killing of a newly-born child. **-ile** *a.* pert. to infants; extremely childish. **infantilism** *n.* arrested development, carrying childish characteristics into adult life. **infantile paralysis,** an infectious disease, poliomyelitis, which leads to paralysis [L. *infans*, unable to speak].

in·fan·try (in'·fąn·tri·) *n.* foot-soldiers [It. *infanteria*].

in·fat·u·ate (in·fach'·ŏŏ·wāt) *v.t.* to render foolish; to inspire with a foolish passion. **-d** *a.* greatly enamored. **infatuation** *n.* excessive and foolish love [L. *in*; *fatuus*, foolish].

in·fea·si·ble (in·fē'·zą·bl) *a.* not capable of being done or accomplished; impracticable.

in·fect (in·fekt') *v.t.* to affect (with disease); to make noxious; to corrupt; to influence the mood or emotions of people. **-ion** *n.* **-ious.**

-ive a. causing infection; catching. **-iously** adv. [L. *inficere*, to dip into].

in·fe·lic·i·ty (in·fa·lis'·a·ti·) n. unhappiness; anything not appropriate. **infelicitous** a.

in·fer (in·fur') v.t. to draw as a conclusion; to deduce; to conclude; to imply. pr.p. **-ring.** pa.t. and pa.p. **-red. -able** a. **-ence** n. deduction. **-ential** a. deduced or deducible by inference. **-entially** adv. [L. *inferre*, to bring in].

in·fe·ri·or (in·fi'·ri·er) a. lower in rank, order, place, or excellence; of less value; poorer in quality; n. a person of a lower rank or station. **-ity** n. a lower state of condition. **-ly** adv. **-ity complex**, subconscious sense of inferiority [L. comp. of *inferus*, low].

in·fer·nal (in·fur'·nal) a. pert. to the lower regions; hellish. **-ity** n. **-ly** adv. **inferno** n. hell; any place resembling hell; furnace. [L. *infernus*, fr. *inferus*, low].

in·fest (in·fest') v.t. to inhabit; to swarm in such numbers as to be a source of annoyance. **-ed** a. covered with body parasites as lice, etc.; plagued **-ation** n. [L. *infestare*, fr. *infestus*, unsafe].

in·fi·del (in'·fa·dal) a. unbelieving; skeptical; n. one who is without religious faith; unbeliever; **-ity** n. unfaithfulness to the marriage contract; treachery; lack of religious faith [L. *infidelis*, unfaithful].

in·field (in'·fēld) n. (*Baseball*) the three basemen and the short stop, or the diamond; a field in close proximity to a farmhouse. **-er** n.

in·fil·trate (in·fil'·trāt) v.t. to filter into; to enter gradually; to pass through enemy's lines, one by one; v.i. to pass in or through by filtering, or as by filtering. n. that which infiltrates. **infiltration** n.

in·fi·nite (in'·fa·nit) a. unlimited in time or space; without end, limits, or bounds; (*Math.*) greater than any assignable quantity; numberless; immeasurable; n. the boundlessness and immeasurableness of the universe; the Almighty, the Infinite Being. **-ly** adv. exceedingly. **-ness** n. **infinitesimal** a. infinitely small. **infinitesimality** n. **infinitesimally** adv. **infinitude** n. boundlessness (of space and time). **infinity** n. unlimited and endless extent. [L. *infinitus*, unbounded].

in·fin·i·tive (in·fin'·a·tiv) n. the simple form of the verb which can be preceded by *to* (*to be*); a. not defined or limited. [L. *infinitus*, unbounded].

in·firm (in·furm') a. not strong; feeble; weak; sickly; irresolute. **-ary** n. a hospital for the weak and infirm. **-ity** n. disease; failing. **-ly** adv. [L. *in-; firmus*, strong].

in·flame (in·flām') v.t. to set on fire; to arouse, as desire; to provoke; to be affected with inflammation. **inflammable** a. combustible; easily aroused. **inflammability, inflammableness** n. **inflammably** adv. **inflammation** n. inflaming; diseased condition of a part of the body characterized by heat, redness and pain. **inflammatory** a. tending to arouse passions; pert. to inflammation [L. *inflammare*, to set on fire].

in·flate (in·flāt') v.t. to swell with air or gas; to raise (price) artificially; to increase (currency) abnormally. **-d** a. swollen; bloated; bombastic; pumped up. **inflatable** a. **inflation** n. swelling; increase in the amount of fiduciary (paper or token) money issued, beyond what is justified by the country's tangible resources; a rise in prices. **inflationary** a. [L. *in; flare*, to bowl].

in·flect (in·flekt') v.t. to bend; to modulate the voice; to modify (words) to show grammatical relationships. **-ion,** n. a bending inwards or deviation; a variation in the tone of the voice; variation in the terminations of words to express grammatical relations. **-ional** a. **-ive** a. subject to inflection. **inflex-**

ibility n. **inflexible** a. incapable of being bent; unyielding to influence or entreaty; unbending. **inflexibly** adv. [L. *in*, in; *flectere*, to bend].

in·flict (in·flikt') v.t. to lay on; to impose (a penalty, etc.); to afflict with something painful. **-ion** n. pain; burden. **-ive** a. [L. *in*, in; *fligere*, to strike].

in·flu·ence (in'·flóó·ans) n. power over men or things; effect on the mind; (*Electrostatics*) induction of a charge by a charged conductor; v.t. to act on the mind; to sway; to bias; to induce. **influential** a. exerting influence or power; possessing great authority. **influentially** adv. [L. *in*, in; *fluere*, to flow].

in·flu·en·za (in·flóó·en'·za) n. (*Med.*) an acute, infectious epidemic catarrhal fever [It. = influence].

in·flux (in'·fluks) n. act of flowing in; the mouth of a stream; the place where one stream flows into another.

in·fold, enfold (in-, en·fōld') v.t. to wrap up; to enclose; to encircle.

in·form (in·fawrm') v.t. to tell; to accumulate knowledge; to inspire; v.i. to give information.

in·form (in·fawrm') a. without form. **-al** a. without formality, unceremonious. **-ality** n. **-ant** n. one who imparts news. **-ation** n. knowledge; intelligence; news. **-ative, -atory** a. educational. **-ed** a. educated. **-er** n. one who gives information about a violation of the law [L. *informare*, to give form to].

in·frac·tion (in·frak'·shan) n. breach; violation.

in·fran·gi·ble (in·fran'·ja·bl) a. not capable of being broken; not to be violated. **infrangibility** n. [L. *in-*, not; *frangere*, to break].

in·fra·red (in·fra·red') a. of the longer invisible heat rays below the red end of the visible spectrum.

in·fre·quent (in·frē'·kwant) a. seldom happening; rare; uncommon. **infrequence, infrequency** n. **-ly** adv.

in·fringe (in·frinj') v.t. to violate; to transgress. **-ment** n. breach; breaking (of a law) [L. *in; frangere*, to break].

in·fu·ri·ate (in·fyoor'·i·āt) v.t. to make furious; to enrage; to madden. **infueriation** n. [L. *in; furia*, rage].

in·fuse (in·fūz') v.t. to pour into; to instill; to inspire; to steep in order to extract soluble properties. **infusible** a. capable of being infused; not capable of fusion. **infusibility** n. **infusion** n. act of infusing, instilling, or inspiring; aqueous solution containing the soluble parts of a substance, made by pouring boiling water over it, cooling and straining [L. *in*, in; *fundere, fusum*, to pour].

in·gen·ious (in·jēn'·yas) a. skilled in inventing or thinking out new ideas; curious or clever in design; skillfully contrived. **-ly** adv. **-ness, ingenuity** (in·ja·nóó'·i·ti·) n. [L. *ingenium*, natural ability].

in·ge·nue (an·zha·nóó') n. an artless, naive, girl; an actress who plays such a part [Fr.].

in·gen·u·ous (in·jen'·yoo·as) a. frank; artless; innocent. **-ly** adv. **-ness** n. [L. *ingenuus* free-born, frank].

in·got (ing'·gat) n. a metal casting, esp. of unwrought silver or gold [O.E. *in; geotan*, to pour].

in·grain, engrain (in-, en·grān') v.t. to fix firmly in the mind. (in'·grain) a. firmly fixed; dyed, before manufacture into articles. **-ed** a.

in·grate (in'·grāt) n. an ungrateful person. **ingratitude** n. want of gratitude; unthankfulness.

in·gra·ti·ate (in·grā'·shi·āt) v.t. to work oneself into favor with another **ingratiation** n. [L. *in; gratia*, favor].

in·gre·di·ent (in·grē'·di·ant) n. a component part of any mixture; one part or element of a compound [L. *ingredi*, to go in].

in·gress (in′·gres) *n.* entrance; power, right, or means of entrance [L. *ingredi, ingressum,* to go in].

in·grow·ing (in′·grō·ing) *a.* growing inwards, esp. of a toenail. **ingrowth** *n.* **ingrown** *a.*

in·gur·gi·tate (in·gur′·ja·tāt) *v.t.* to swallow up greedily or hastily; to engulf. **ingurgitation** *n.* [L. *in,* in; *gurges,* a whirlpool].

in·hab·it (in·hab′·it) *v.t.* to live or dwell in; to occupy. **-able** *a.* possible to be dwelt in. **-ant** *n.* one who inhabits; a resident. **-ation** *n.* [L. *in,* in; *habitare,* to dwell].

in·hale (in·hāl′) *v.t.* to breathe in, as air, tobacco smoke, etc.; to draw in the breath. **inhalant** *n.* a volatile medicinal remedy to be inhaled. *a.* **inhalation** *n.* act of drawing air into the lungs. **inhalator** *n.* apparatus to help one inhale [L. *in,* in; *halare,* to breathe].

in·here (in·hir′) *v.i.* (usu. followed by *in*) to exist in; to belong naturally to; to be a quality of; to be vested in, as legal rights. **-nce, -ncy** *n.* **-nt** *a.* existing in something so as to be inseparable. **-ntly** *adv.* [L. *in,* in; *haerere,* to stick].

in·her·it (in·her′·at) *v.t.* to receive by descent, or by will; to fall heir to; to derive (traits, etc.) from parents; *v.i.* to succeed as heir. **-able** *a.* **-ance** *n.* what is inherited. **-or** *n.* (*fem.* **-ress, -rix**) [L. *in,* in; *heres,* an heir].

in·hib·it (in·hib′·it) *v.t.* to hold back; to forbid; to restrain. **inhibition** (in·i·bi′·shan) *n.* a subconscious repressed emotion which controls or colors a person's attitude or behavior. **-ory** *a.* prohibiting; forbidding; restraining [L. *inhibere,* to hold in].

in·hos·pi·ta·ble (in·hås′·pi·ta·bl) *a.* averse to showing kindness to strangers or guests; discourteous. **-ness, inhospitality** *n.* **inhospitably** *adv.* [L. *hospes,* a guest].

in·hu·man (in·hū′·man) *a.* not human or humane; without feeling or pity. **inhumane** (in·hū·mān′) *a.* cruel. **-ity** *n.*

in·hume (in·hūm′) *v.t.* to put into the ground; to bury. **inhumation** *n.* [L. *humus,* ground].

in·im·i·cal (in·im′·i·kal) *a.* like an enemy; unfriendly. **-ly** *adv.* [L. *inimicus,* an enemy].

in·im·i·ta·ble (in·im′·i·ta·bl) *a.* defying imitation; incomparable. **inimitably** *adv.*

in·iq·ui·ty (in·ik′·wa·ti·) *n.* gross injustice; want of moral principle; wickedness; a crime. **iniquitous** *a.* **iniquitously** *adv.* [L. *iniquitas* fr. *in-,* not; *aequus,* fair, even].

in·i·tial (in·ish′·al) *a.* occurring at the beginning; commencing; early; *v.t.* to put one's initials to, in the way of acknowledgment. *n.* the first letter of a word, esp. a name. **initiate,** *v.t.* to begin; to start (a movement, etc.); to instruct in the rudiments of; to admit into a society, etc., with formal rites; *n.* one who is initiated. **initiation** *n.* **initiative** *a.* serving to initiate; *n.* the first step; the quality of being able to set things going for the first time. **initiator** *n.* **initiatory** *a.* introductory [L. *initialis,* fr. *initium,* a beginning].

in·ject (in·jekt′) *v.t.* to throw in; to force in; to introduce (a fluid) under the skin by means of a hollow needle. **-ion** *n.* the act of injecting or throwing into; fluid so injected. **-or** *n.* [L. *injicere,* fr. *jacere,* to throw].

in·ju·di·cious (in·jòò·dish′·as) *a.* ill-advised; imprudent; lacking in judgment **injudicial** *a.* not according to the form of law. **-ly** *adv.*

in·junc·tion (in·jungk′·shan) *n.* an order or command; an exhortation; a precept [L. *in,* in; *jungere, junctum,* to join].

in·jure (in′·jer) *v.t.* to do wrong, injury, damage, or injustice to. **injurious** *a.* causing injury or damage. **injuriously** *adv.* **injury** *n.* wrong; damage; harm [L. *injuria,* fr. *jus,* law].

in·jus·tice (in·jus′·tis) *n.* an unjust act; want of justice; wrong.

ink (ingk) *n.* a fluid, black or colored, used for writing, printing and sketching; *v.t.* to cover or smear with ink. **-well** *n.* container for ink. **-iness** *n.* **-y** *a.* resembling ink [O.Fr. *enque* = Fr. *encre*].

ink·ling (ingk′·ling) *n.* a hint or whisper; slight knowledge [etym. doubtful].

in·land (in′·land) *a.* remote from the sea; interior; carried on within a country; *n.* (in land′) the interior part of a country. **-er** *n.*

in·laws (in′·lawz) *n.pl.* (*Colloq.*) one's relations by marriage.

in·lay (in·lā′) *v.t.* to ornament, by cutting out part of a surface and inserting pieces of pearl, ivory, wood, etc., to form a pattern. *pa.p.* **inlaid.** *n.* inlaid pattern.

in·let (in′·let) *n.* an entrance; a small bay or creek; an insertion.

in·mate (in′·māt) *n.* a dweller in a house or institution; a fellow-lodger.

inn (in) *n.* a house which provides lodging accommodation for travelers; a hotel; restaurant or tavern. **-keeper** *n.* one who keeps an inn. [O.E.].

in·nate (i·nāt′) *a.* inborn; native; natural; inherent; congenital. **-ly** *adv.* [L. *innatus*].

in·ner (in′·er) *a.* farther in; interior; private; not obvious; **-most, inmost.** *a.* farthest in. [O.E. *innera,* comp. fr. *inne,* within].

in·ner·vate (in′·er·vāt). Also **innerve,** *v.t.* to give nervous strength to; to stimulate. **innervation** *n.* [L. *in; nervus,* sinew].

in·ning (in′·ing) *n.* in games, a side's turn of batting; the ingathering of grain; reclaiming of land [O.E. *inn,* in, within].

in·no·cent (in′·a·sant) *a.* free from guilt; blameless; harmless, sinless; simple; *n.* an innocent person, esp. a child; a guileless, unsuspecting person. **innocence, innocency** *n.* **-ly** *adv.* [L. *in-,* not; *nocere,* to harm].

in·noc·u·ous (in·ák′·yoo·as) *a.* producing no ill effects; harmless. **-ly** *adv.* **-ness** [L. *in-,* not; *nocere,* to harm].

in·no·vate (in′·a·vāt) *v.t.* to make changes by introducing something new. **innovation** *n.* a new idea [L. *innovare,* fr. *novus,* new].

in·nox·ious (in·ák′·shas) *a.* innocuous; harmless in effects [L. *innoxius*].

in·nu·en·do (in·ū·en′·dō) *n.* an allusive remark (usually deprecatory); an indirect hint [L. = by nodding to, fr. *nuere,* to nod].

in·nu·mer·a·ble (i·nū′·mer·a·bl) *a.* not able to be numbered; countless; very numerous. **innumerability** *n.* **innumerably** *adv.*

in·nu·tri·tion (in·nóò·trish′·an) *n.* want of nutrition. **innutritious** *a.*

in·ob·serv·ant (in·ab·zer′·vant) *a.* not observant; heedless. **inobservance** *n.* failure to observe (the law, church-going, etc.).

in·oc·u·late (in·ák′·ya·lāt) *v.t.* (*Med.*) to introduce into the body pathogenic bacteria (e.g. typhoid inoculation) or living virus (e.g. smallpox vaccination) to secure immunity; to imbue strongly with opinions. **inoculation** *n.* [L. *inoculare,* fr. *oculus,* eye, bud].

in·op·er·a·ble (in·áp′·er·a·bl) *a.* (*Surgery*) not in a condition for operating on. **inoperative** *a.* not operating; without effect.

in·op·por·tune (in·áp·er·tūn′) *a.* unseasonable in time; not convenient; untimely. **-ly** *adv.* **inopportunity** *n.*

in·or·di·nate (in·awr′·da·nat) *a.* not limited; disordered. **-ness** *n.* **-ly** *adv.* excessively.

in·or·gan·ic (in·awr·gan′·ik) *a.* devoid of an organized structure; not derived from animal or vegetable life. **-ally** *adv.*

in·os·cu·late (in·as′·kya·lāt) *v.t.* and *v.i.* to join by openings (arteries, etc.).

in·pa·tient (in′·pā·shant) *n.* a patient who is lodged and fed while receiving medical attention in a hospital.

in·put (in′·poot) *n.* (*Elect.*) the power supplied to battery, condenser, etc.

in·quest (in′·kwest) *n.* a judicial inquiry, esp. one presided over by a coroner, with or without a jury, into the cause of a person's death.

in·qui·e·tude (in·kwī′·a·tūd) *n.* uneasiness either of body or of mind; restlessness.

in·quire, enquire (in-, en·kwīr′) *v.i.* to ask questions; to make investigation; to seek information; *v.t.* to ask about. **-r** *n.* **inquiring** *a.* given to inquiring; prying. **inquiringly** *adv.* **inquiry** *n.* investigation; a question [L. *inquirere,* fr. *quaerere,* to seek].

in·qui·si·tion (in·kwa·zish′·an) *n.* a strict investigation; official inquiry; an ecclesiastical tribunal, 'the Holy Office,' established by the R.C. Church in the Middle Ages for the trial and punishment of heretics. **-al** *a.* **inquisitive** *a.* apt to ask questions; prying; curious to know. **inquisitively** *adv.* **inquisitiveness** *n.* **inquisitor** *n.* one whose official duty it is to make inquiries; a member of the Court of Inquisition. **inquisitorial** *a.* **inquisitorially** *adv.* [L. *inquisitio,* fr. *inquirere,* to search out].

in·re (in·rē′, ·rā′) *prep.* in the matter of; concerning (often abbreviated to **re**) [L.]

in·road (in′·rōd) *n.* a sudden incursion into enemy territory; a sudden invasion; raid.

in·sane (in·sān′) *a.* unsound in mind; mentally diseased; lunatic. **-ly** *adv.* **-ness, insanity** *n.* lunacy; madness.

in·sa·tia·ble (in·sā′·sha·bl) *a.* incapable of being satisfied; voracious; rapacious. **-ness, insatiability** *n.* **insatiably** *adv.*

in·sa·ti·ate (in·sā′·shi·at) *a.* not to be satisfied. **-ly** *adv.* **-ness** *n.*

in·scribe (in·skrīb′) *v.t.* to write upon; to engrave; to address or dedicate; to draw a geometrical figure inside another so as to touch but not intersect. **inscribable** *a.* **-r** *n.* **inscription** *n.* act of inscribing; words inscribed on a monument, coin, etc.; dedication of a book, etc.; **inscriptional, inscriptive** *a.* [L. *in; scribere,* to write].

in·scru·ta·ble (in·skróó′·ta·bl) *a.* incapable of being searched into and understood by inquiry or study; mysterious. **inscrutability, -ness** *n.* **inscrutably** *adv.* [L. *in-,* not; *scrutari,* to search].

in·sect (in′·sekt) *n.* one of a class of invertebrate animals called the *Insecta. a.* pert. to insects; small; insignificant. **insecta** *n.* the insect or hexapod (six-legged) class of arthropods. **insecticide** *n.* killing insect pests; chemical preparation for the destruction of noxious insects. **-ivorous** *a.* living on insects [L. *in,* in; *secare,* to cut].

in·se·cure (in·si·kyoor′) *a.* not securely fixed; dangerous to life or limb; unsafe; unguarded; having doubts and fears. **insecurity** *n.*

in·sem·i·nate (in·sem′·a·nāt) *v.t.* to sow; to impregnate. **insemination** *n.* conception [L. *in,* into; *semen,* seed].

in·sen·sate (in·sen′·sāt) *a.* destitute of sense; without power of feeling. **-ly** *adv.*

in·sen·si·ble (in·sen′·sa·bl) *a.* without bodily sensation; not perceived by the senses; unconscious; callous; imperceptible **-ness** *n.* **insensibility, insensibly** *adv.*

in·sen·si·tive (in·sen′·sa·tiv) *a.* not sensitive; callous. **-ness, insensitivity** *n.*

in·sen·ti·ent (in·sen′·shi·ant) *a.* not having perception; inanimate.

in·sep·a·ra·ble (in·sep′·a·ra·bl) *a.* not divisible or separable; always in close association; *n.pl.* persons or things that are seldom seen apart. **inseparably** *adv.*

in·sert (in·surt′) *vt.* to put in; to place among; to introduce. (in′·surt) *n.* anything inserted. **-ion** *n.* the act of inserting; that which is inserted [L. *in,* in; *serere,* to join].

in·side (in′·sīd) *prep.* or *adv.* within the sides of; in the interior; *a.* internal; interior; *n.*

the part within; *pl.* (*Colloq.*) inward parts; guts. **-r** *n.* (*Colloq.*) one who is within a certain group or has special advantages.

in·sid·i·ous (in·sid′·i·as) *a.* lying in wait; treacherous; advancing imperceptibly. **-ly** *adv.* **-ness** *n.* [L. *insidiosus,* fr. *insidere,* to lie in wait.].

in·sight (in′·sīt) *n.* view of the interior of anything; mental penetration; clear understanding; power of discernment.

in·sig·ni·a (in·sig′·ni·a) *n.pl.* symbols of authority, dignity, or office; badges; emblems [L. fr. *signum,* sign].

in·sig·ni·fi·cant (in·sig·nif′·a·kant) *a.* signifying very little; having little importance, use, or value; trifling. **insignificance, insignificancy** *n.* **-ly** *adv.*

in·sin·cere (in·sin·sir′) *a.* not sincere; dissembling; hypocritical; not to be trusted. **-ly** *adv.* **insincerity** *n.* hypocrisy.

in·sin·u·ate (in·sin′·ya·wāt) *v.t.* to introduce gently and adroitly; to suggest by remote allusion; to work oneself into favor; *v.i.* to ingratiate oneself. **insinuating** *a.* **insinuatingly** *adv.* **insinuation** *n.* act of gaining favor by artful means; hint; suggestion. **insinuative** *a.* **insinuator** *n.* **insinuatory** *a.* [L. *insinuare,* to introduce tortuously].

in·sip·id (in·sip′·id) *a.* destitute of taste; deficient in spirit, life, or animation. **-ly** *adv.* **-ness, -ity** *n.* [L. *insipidus,* tasty].

in·sip·i·ent (in·sip′·i·ant) *a.* not wise; foolish. **insipience** *n.* [L. *insipiens*].

in·sist (in·sist′) *v.i.* to dwell upon as a matter of special moment; to be urgent or pressing; (foll. by *on* or *upon*) to hold firmly to. **-ence** *n.* persistent demand or refusal to give way. **-ency** *n.* pertinacity. **-ent** *a.* [L. *insistere,* fr. *sistere,* to stand].

in·so·bri·e·ty (in·sa·brī·at·i·) *n.* drunkeness.

in·so·lent (in′·sa·lant) *a.* proud and haughty; overbearing. **insolence** *n.* contemptuous rudeness or arrogance. **-ly** *adv.* [L. *in-,* not; *solere,* to be accustomed].

in·sol·u·ble (in·sál′·ya·bl) *a.* incapable of being dissolved; inexplicable; not to be explained. **insolubility, -ness** *n.* **insolvable** *a.*

in·sol·vent (in·sál′·vant) *a.* not able to pay one's debts; bankrupt; *n.* one who is bankrupt. **insolvency** *n.*

in·som·ni·a (in·sám′·ni·a) *n.* chronic sleeplessness from any cause [L.].

in·so·much (in·sa·much′) *adv.* so that; to such a degree; in such wise that.

in·sou·ci·ance (in·sóó′·si·ans) *n.* carelessness of feeling or manner; an air of indifference. **insouciant** *a.* carefree; indifferent [Fr.].

in·spect (in·spekt′) *v.t.* to view narrowly and critically; to examine officially as troops, arms, or goods offered for sale, etc. **-ingly** *adv.* **inspection** *n.* careful survey; official examination. **inspectional, -ive** *a.* **-or** *n.* official examiner; a police officer ranking below a superintendent; anyone who inspects. **-orate** *n.* a district under an inspector; a body of inspectors generally. **-orial** *a.* [L. *inspicere,* to look into].

in·spire (in·spīr′) *v.t.* to breathe in; to infuse thought or feeling into; to affect as with a supernatural influence; to arouse; *v.i.* to give inspiration; to inhale. **inspirable** *a.* **inspiration** *n.* act of drawing in the breath; communication of ideas from a supernatural source; a bright idea. **inspirational** *a.* **inspiratory** *a.* tending to inspire; encouraging. **inspired** *a.* inhaled; actuated by Divine influence [L. *in; spirare,* to breathe].

in·sta·bil·i·ty (in·sta·bil′·a·ti·) *n.* want of stability or firmness.

in·stall (in·stawl′) *v.t.* to place in position; to have something put in; to induct, with ceremony, a person into an office. **installation** *n.* complete equipment of a building for heating, lighting, etc.; generally, placing in position for use. **-ment** n. act of installing; a periodical payment of the part cost of something; a portion.

in·stance (in'·stạns) n. case in point; example; v.t. to mention as an example; to cite.

instant a. urgent; pressing; immediate; current (usu. abbreviated to inst.); n. a particular point of time; moment. **instantaneity** n. **instantaneous** a. done in an instant; happening in a moment. **instantaneously** adv. **instantaneousness** n. **instantly** adv. at once [L. in; stare, to stand].

in·stead (in·sted') adv. in the stead, place, or room; in one's stead [stead].

in·step (in'·step) n. the arched upper part of the human foot, near the ankle, which gives spring to the step; that part of a shoe, etc., which covers the instep; the hind-leg of a horse from the hock to the pastern joint.

in·sti·gate (in'·stạ·gāt) v.t. to goad or urge forward; to incite, esp. to evil; to bring about. **instigation** n. **instigator** n. [L. instigare, to incite].

in·still (in·stil') v.t. to put in by drops; to infuse slowly; to introduce by degrees (into the mind). **-ed. -ation, -ment** n. [L. in; stillare, to drip].

in·stinct (in'·stingkt) n. intuition (in neurology) compound reflex action; (in psychology) an innate train of reflexes; inborn impulse or propensity; unconscious skill; intuition. (in·stingkt') a. charged; full; urged from within; animated. **instinctively, instinctly** adv. **instinctivity** n. [L. instinctus, fr. instinguere, to urge].

in·sti·tute (in'·stạ·tūt) v.t. to establish; to found; to appoint; to set going; to originate; to lay down as a law; n. a society or organization established for promoting some particular work, scientific, educational, etc. **institutes** n.pl. a book of precepts, principles or rules; a text-book on legal principles. **institution** n. the act of instituting or establishing; an established law, custom, or public occasion; an institute; (sociol.) an organized pattern of group behavior established and generally accepted as a fundamental part of a culture, such as slavery. **institutional** a. **institutionally** adv. **institutive** a. tending or intended to instigate or establish; endowed with the power to ordain. **institutively** adv. **institutor, -r** n. [L. instituere, to set up].

in·struct (in·strukt') v.t. to teach; to inform; to prepare someone for (e.g., an examination); to order or command; to give directions to. **-ible** a. **-ion** n. the act of instructing or teaching; education; order. **-ional** a. **-ive** a. fitted to instruct; containing edifying matter; conveying knowledge or information. **-ively** adv. **-iveness** n. **-or** n. [L. instructus].

in·stru·ment (in'·strạ·mạnt) n. a tool or implement; a person or thing made use of; a means of producing musical sounds; (Law) a formal or written document. **-al** (in·strạ·ment'·al) a. serving as an instrument or means; helpful; pert. to musical, surgical, or other instruments; performed with or composed for a musical instrument or instruments; (Gram.) in some inflected languages, denoting a case, having as chief function the indication of means or agency. **-alist** n. one skilled in playing upon a musical instrument. **-ality** n. the quality of being instrumental, of serving some purpose; agency or means; good offices. **-ally** adv. **-ation** n. the art of writing and arranging musical compositions for the individual instruments of a band or orchestra; orchestration. [L. instruere, to build].

in·sub·or·di·nate (in·sạ·bawr'·dạ·nit) a. disobedient; unruly. **insubordination** n.

in·suf·fer·a·ble (in·suf'·ẹr·ạ·bl) a. not able to be endured; intolerable. **insufferably** adv.

in·suf·fi·cient (in·sạ·fish'·ạnt) a. not enough; deficient. **insufficiency** n. **-ly** adv.

in·su·lar (in'·syoo·lẹr) a. pert. to or like an island; isolated; narrow-minded or prejudiced. **-ism, -ity** n. **-ly** adv. [L. insula, an island].

in·su·late (in'·sạ·lāt) v.t. to keep rigidly apart from contact with other people; to bar the passage of electricity, heat, sound, light, dampness, or vibration by the use of nonconducting materials. **insulation** n. [L. insula, an island].

in·su·lin (in'·sạ·lin) n. a hormone secreted in the pancreas; organic drug for the treatment of diabetes [L. insula, island].

in·sult (in·sult') v.t. to treat with insolence or contempt by words or action; to abuse; to affront. (in'·sult) n. gross abuse offered to another [L. insultare, to leap upon].

in·su·per·a·ble (in·sōō'·pẹr·a·bl) a. not able to be overcome or surmounted; invincible. **insuperability, n. insuperably** adv.

in·sup·port·a·ble (in·sạ·pōr'·tạ·bl) a. incapable of being borne or endured. **-ness** n. **insupportably** adv.

in·sure (in·shoor') v.t. to make sure or certain; to make safe (against); to ensure; to secure the payment of a sum in event of loss, death, etc., by a contract and payment of sums called premiums. **insurable** a. **insurance** n. contract between two parties whereby the insurer agrees to indemnify the insured upon the occurrence of a stipulated contingency [L. in; securus, secure].

in·sur·gent (in·sur'·jạnt) a. rising in opposition to lawful authority; rebellious; n. one in revolt; a rebel. **insurgency** n. incipient stage of revolt. Also **insurgence**.

in·sur·mount·a·ble (in·sẹr·moun'·tạ·bl) a. not able to be surmounted or overcome. **insurmountability** n. **insurmountably** adv.

in·sur·rec·tion (in·sạ·rek'·shạn) n. a rising against civil or political authority. **-al, -ary** a. **-ist** n. [L. insurgere, to rise upon].

in·sus·cep·ti·ble (in·sạ·sep'·tạ·bl) a. not susceptible; not to be moved, affected, or impressed. **insusceptibility** n.

in·take (in'·tāk) n. that which is taken in; quantity taken in; inlet of a tube or cylinder; a point of narrowing or contraction.

in·tan·gi·ble (in·tan'·jạ·bl) a. not perceptible to the touch; not clear to the mind. **-ness, intangibility** n. **intangibly** adv.

in·te·ger (in'·tạ·jẹr) n. the whole of anything; whole number (as opposed to a fraction or a mixed number). **integral** (in'·tạ·grạl) a. denoting a whole number or quantity; constituting an essential part of a whole; n. a whole number; (Math.) a sum of differentials. **integrally** adv. **integrate** v.t. to make entire; to give the sum or total. **integration** n. act of making a whole out of parts. **integrator** n. **integrity** n. the state of being entire; wholeness; probity; honesty; uprightness [L. integer, entire].

in·teg·u·ment (in·teg'·yạ·mạnt) n. the outer protective layer of tissue which covers a plant or animal; the skin. **integumentary** a. [L. integumentum, fr. integere, to cover].

in·tel·lect (in'·tạ·lekt) n. the faculty of reasoning and thinking; mental power; mind; understanding; pl. the senses. **-ive** a. pert. to intellect as distinguished from the senses.

in·tel·lec·tu·al (in·tạ·lek'·choo·ạl) a. of high mental capacity; having the power of understanding; n. one well endowed with intellect. **-ism** n. the doctrine that knowledge is derived from pure reason; emphasis on the value of the rational faculties. **-ity** n. intellectual powers. **-ly** adv. [L. intelligere, to understand].

in·tel·li·gent (in·tel'·ạ·jạnt) a. having or showing good intellect; quick at understanding. **intelligence** n. inborn quickness of understanding an dadaptability to relatively new situations; information. **-ly** *adv.* **-sia** *n.* the intellectual or cultured classes. **intelligible** *a.* that can be readily understood; rational. **intelligibleness, intelligibility** *n.* **intelligibly** *adv.* **intelligence quotient** (abbrev. I.Q.) the numerical rating of general intelligence by use of psychological tests [L. *intelligere*, to understand].

in·tem·per·ate (in·tem′·pẹr·ạt) *a.* immoderate; indulging to excess any appetite or passion; addicted to an excessive use of liquor; extreme in climate. **intemperance** *n.* excess of any kind. **-ly** *adv.* [L. *intemperatus*].

in·tend (in·tend′) *v.t.* and *v.i.* to design; to purpose; to mean; to have in mind. **-ant** *n.* one who has the charge of some public business. **-ancy** *n.* the office of an intendant. **-ed** *a.* and *n.* (*Colloq.*) betrothed [L. *intendere*, to bend the mind on].

in·tense (in·tens′) *a.* to an extreme degree; very strong or acute; emotional. **-ly** *adv.* **-ness, intensity** *n.* severity; ardor; earnestness; the strength of an electric current. **intensification** *n.* **intensify** *v.t.* to render more intense; to increase or augment; *v.i.* to become more intense. *pa.t.* and *pa.p.* **intensified. intensive** *a.* giving emphasis; unrelaxed; increasing in force. **intensively** *adv.* [L. *intendere, intensum*, to stretch].

in·tent (in·tent′) *a.* having the mind bent on an object; eager in pursuit of; firmly resolved; preoccupied; absorbed; *n.* intention; aim; purpose; view; object. **-ion** *n.* design; aim; purpose. **-ional, -ioned** *a.* done purposely. **-ionally** *adv.* **-ly** *adv.* **-ness** *n.* [L. *intendere*, to turn the mind to].

in·ter- (in′·tẹr) *prefix* fr. L. *inter*, between, among, with, amid.

in·ter (in·tur′) *v.t.* to bury. *pr.p.* **-ring.** *pa.t.* and *pa.p.* **-red. -ment** *n.* burial [Fr. *enterrer*, fr. L. *in; terra*, earth].

in·ter·act (in·tẹr·akt′) *v.i.* to act mutually on each other. **-ion** *n.*

in·ter·cede (in·tẹr·sēd′) *v.i.* to act as peacemaker; to plead in favor of one; to mediate. **-r** *n.* **intercession** *n.* the act of interceding. **intercessor** *n.* a mediator; a pleader. **intercessorial, intercessory** *a.* [L. *inter*, between; *cedere*, to go].

in·ter·cept (in·tẹr·sept′) *v.t.* to stop or obstruct passage; to seize in transit; (*Math.*) to cut off a part of a line at two points; *n.* the part of a line between any two points. **-er, -or** *n.* **-ion** *n.* **-ive** *a.* [L. *inter*, between; *capere, captum*, to seize].

in·ter·ces·sion, intercessor See **intercede.**

in·ter·change (in·tẹr·chānj′) *v.t.* to exchange; to reciprocate; *v.i.* to succeed alternately; to exchange places; *n.* (in′·tẹr·chānj) access to a freeway; a mutual exchange. **-able** *a.* **-ability, -ableness** *n.*

in·ter·com (in′·tẹr·kàm) (*Slang*) *n.* internal telephonic system. **municate** (in·tẹr·kạ·mū′·ni·kāt) *v.t.* to exchange conversations or messages. **-munication** *a.,n.* **-municative** *a.*

in·ter·con·nect (in·tẹr·kạ·nekt′) *v.t.* and *v.i.* to connect mutually and intimately.

in·ter·cos·tal (in·tẹr·kàs′·tạl) *a.*(*Anat.*) between the rigs [L. *inter*, between; *costa*, a rib].

in·ter·course (in′·tẹr·kōrs) *n.* communication between individuals; exchange of goods; correspondence by letter; coition [O.Fr. *entrecours*, fr. L. *inter*, between; *currere*, to run].

in·ter·cur·rent (in·tẹr·kur′·ạnt) *a.* running between or among; occurring during the course of another (disease); intervening.

in·ter·de·pend (in·tẹr·di·pend′) *v.i.* to depend mutually. **-ence** *n.* **-ent** *a.* **-ently** *adv.*

in·ter·dict (in·tẹr·dikt′) *v.t.* to forbid; to prohibit; to restrain; to debar from communion with a church; to lay under an interdict. (in′·tẹr·dikt) *n.* prohibition; (*Law*) a prohibitory act or decree; a papal ordinance by which certain persons are debarred from participating in the sacraments, church offices or ecclesiastical burial. **-ion** *n.* **-ive, -ory** *a.* [L. *interdicere*, to prohibit].

in·ter·est (in′·tẹr·ạst, in′·trist) *v.t.* to engage and keep the attention of; to arouse the curiosity of; to cause to feel interest; *n.* special attention; concern; regard to personal profit or advantage; curiosity; the profit per cent derived from money lent. **-ed** *a.* having a share in; feeling an interest in. **-edly** *adv.* **-edness** *n.* **-ing** *a.* appealing to or exciting one's interest or curiosity. **-ingly** *adv.* **compound —,** interest on the principal and also on the added interest as it falls due. **simple interest,** interest only on the principal during the time of loan. [L. *interesse*, to be of concern to].

in·ter·fere (in·tẹr·fir′) *v.i.* to be in or come into, opposition; to enter into or take part in the concerns of others; to intervene. **-nce** *n.* meddling with other people's business; uncalled-for intervention; (*Radio*) anything generally which prevents the proper reception of radio waves. **-r** *n.* **interferingly** *adv.* [L. *inter*, between; *ferire*, to strike].

in·ter·im (in′·tẹr·im) *n.* the time between; the meantime; *a.* for the time being; temporary; provisional [L.].

in·te·ri·or (in·tī′·ri·ẹr) *a.* inner; internal; inland, away from coast or frontiers; *n.* the inside part or portion; the inland part of a country. **-ly** *adv.* [L. compar. of *interus*, fr L. *intra*, within].

in·ter·ject (in·tẹr·jekt′) *v.t.* to throw between; to insert; to exclaim abruptly. **-ion** *n.* act of throwing between; a word which expresses strong emotion or passion when suddenly uttered. **-ional, -ionary, .-ory** *a.* **-ionally** *adv.* [L. *inter*, between; *jacere, jactum*, to throw].

in·ter·lace (in·tẹr·lās′) *v.t.* to lace together; to entwine; to unite; to interweave.

in·ter·lard (in·tẹr·làrd′) *v.t.* to diversify by mixture (of words, etc.).

in·ter·line (in·tẹr·līn′) *v.t.* to write or mark between the lines of a book, document, etc.; to put an inner lining in a garment between the outer material and the regular lining. **-al, -ar** *a.* between lines. **-ate** *v.t.* to mark between the lines. **interlining** *n.* inner lining of a garment; interlineation [L. *interlineare*].

in·ter·lock (in·tẹr·lak′) *v.t.* to unite by locking together; to fasten together so that one part cannot move without the other; *v.i.* to be locked or jammed together.

in·ter·lo·cu·tion (in·tẹr·lō·kū′·shạn) *n.* dialogue; a conference; speaking in turn. (in·tẹr·làk′·yạ·ter) *n.* one who speaks in his turn; one who questions another [L. *interloqui*, to speak between].

in·ter·lope (in·tẹr·lōp′) *v.i.* to traffic without a proper license; to intrude into other people's affairs. **-r** *n.* [L. *inter*, between; Dut. *loopen*, to run].

in·ter·lude (in′·tẹr·löòd) *n.* a dramatic or musical performance given between parts of an independent play; an interval; an incident during a pause in the proceedings [L. *inter*, between; *ludus*, play].

in·ter·mar·ry (in·tẹr·mar′·i·) *v.i.* to connect families or races by a marriage between two of their members; to marry within close relationship. **intermarriage** *n.*

in·ter·me·di·ate (in·tẹr·mē′·di·ạt) *a.* lying or being between two extremes; in a middle position; intervening; *n.* anything between; *v.i.* to mediate; to intervene. **intermediacy** *n.* state of being intermediate; mediation. **intermediary** *a.* acting between; interposed; intermediate; *n.* one who acts as a go-between or mediator. **intermedium** *n.* intervening person or instrument. **intermedi-**

ation n. [L. *inter*, between; *medius*, middle].
in·ter·ment See **inter.**
in·ter·mez·zo (in·tẹr·met'·sō, med'·zō) n. a light dramatic entertainment between the acts of a tragedy, grand opera, etc.; an interlude; (*Mus.*) a short movement connecting more important ones in a symphony, sonata, opera, etc. [It. = in between].
in·ter·mi·na·ble (in·tur'·mi·nạ·bl) a. endless; unlimited. **-ness** n. **interminably** adv.
in·ter·min·gle (in·tẹr·ming'·gl) v.t. to mingle or mix together.
in·ter·mit (in·tẹr·mit') v.t. to give up or forbear for a time; to interrupt; v.i. to cease for a time. pr.p. **-ting.** pa.t., pa.p. **-ted. intermission** n. intervening period of time; suspension; interval. **intermissive.** a. coming after temporary cessations. **-tence, -tency** n. **-tent** a. occurring at intervals; ceasing at intervals; coming and going. **-tently** adv. [L. *inter*, between; *mittere*, *missum*, to send].
in·ter·mix (in·tẹr·miks') v.t. and v.i. to mix together. **-ture** n.
in·tern (in·turn') v.t. to confine (in a place), esp. aliens or suspects in time of war; (in'·turn) n. a resident doctor in a hospital. Also **interne. internee** n. one who is confined to a certain place. **-ment** n. **-ship** n. [L. *internus*, internal].
in·ter·nal (in·tur'·nạl) a. interior; inner; inward; domestic, as opposed to foreign. **-ly** adv. — **combustion**, the process occurring by exploding in one or more piston-fitted cylinders a mixture of air and fuel [L. *internus*, inward].
in·ter·na·tion·al (in·tẹr·nash'·ạn·al) a. pert. to the relations between nations; n. a game or match between teams representing their respective countries; a player who participates in such. **-ism** n. a political theory which aims at breaking down the artificial barriers which separate nations. **-ist** n. **-ly** adv.
in·ter·ne·cine (in·tẹr·nē'·sin) a. mutually destructive; deadly [L. *inter*; *necare*, to kill].
in·ter·nee See **intern.**
in·ter·nist n. (in·tur'·nist) a specialist in internal medicine.
in·ter·nun·ci·o (in·tẹr·nun'·shi·ō) n. the pope's representative; an envoy. **internuncial** a. [L. *internuntius*, a messenger].
in·ter·pel·late (in·tẹr·pel'·āt) v.t. to interrupt a speaker in a legislative assembly by demanding an explanation. **interpellation** n. **interpellator** n. [L. *inter*; *pellere*, to drive].
in·ter·pen·e·trate (in·tẹr·pen'·ạ·trāt) v.t. to grow through one another; to penetrate thoroughly. **interpenetration** n.
in·ter·plan·e·tar·y (in·tẹr·plan'·ạ·ter·i·) a. situated between the planets.
in·ter·play (in'·tẹr·plā) n. reciprocal action of two things; interchange of action and reaction; give and take.
in·ter·po·late (in·tur'·pạ·lāt) v.t. to insert new (esp. misleading) matter into a text; to interpose with some remark; (*Math.*) to infer the missing terms in a known series of numbers. **interpolation** n. **interpolator** n. [L. *interpolare*, to furbish up].
in·ter·pose (in·tẹr·pōz') v.t. and i. to place or come between; to thrust in the way; to offer, as aid or service; to interrupt. **interposal** n. **-r** n. **interposition** n. [L. *inter*; *ponere*, to place].
in·ter·pret (in·tur'·prẹt) v.t. to explain the meaning of; to put a construction on; to translate orally for the benefit of others. **-able** a. **-ation** n. act of interpreting; translation; meaning; artist's version of a dramatic part or musical composition. **-ative** a. explanatory. **-er** n. [L. *interpres*, an interpreter].
in·ter·reg·num (in·tẹr·reg'·nạm) a. the time a throne is vacant between the death or abdi-

cation of a king and the accession of his successor; any interruption in continuity. [L. *inter*; *regnum*, rule].
in·ter·re·la·tion (in·tẹr·ri·lā'·shạn) n. reciprocal or mutual relation.**-ship** n.
in·ter·ro·gate (in·tẹr'·ạ·gāt) v.t. to question; to examine by questioning, esp. officially. **interrogation** n. close questioning; a question. **interrogation mark**, the mark (?) placed after a question. **interrogative** a. **interrogatory** a. [L. *inter*; *rogare*, to ask].
in·ter·rupt (in·tạ·rupt') v.t. to break in upon; to stop course of; to break continuity of. **-edly** adv. **-er** n. **-ion** n. intervention; suspension; hindrance. **-ive** a. [L. *interruptus*, broken apart].
in·ter·sect (in·tẹr·sekt') v.t. to cut into or between; to divide into parts; to cross one another. **-ion** n. an intersecting; the point where lines, roads, etc., cut or cross one another. **-ional** a. [L. *intersectus*, cut off].
in·ter·sperse (in·tẹr·spurs') v.t. to scatter or place here and there, in no fixed order; to mingle. **interspersion** n. [L. *inter*, among; *spargere*, *sparsum*, to scatter].
in·ter·stel·lar (in·tẹr·stel'·ẹr) a. passing between, or situated among, the stars. Also**-y.**
in·ter·stice (in·tur'·stis) n. a small gap or chink in the body of an object or between two things; a crevice. **interstitial** (in·tẹr·stish'·ạl) a. [L. *interstitium*].
in·ter·twine (in·tẹr·twīn') v.t. to twine or twist together.
in·ter·val (in'·tẹr·val) n. time or distance between; a pause; a break; (*Mus.*) difference in pitch between any two tones [L. *intervallum*, fr. *inter*; *vallum*, a wall].
in·ter·vene (in·tẹr·vēn') v.i. to come or be between; to happen in the meantime; to interfere; to interrupt; to interpose.**-r** n. **intervention** n. **interventionist** n. or a. [L. *inter*; *venire*, to come].
in·ter·view (in'·tẹr·vū) n. a meeting or conference; a meeting of a journalist and a person whose views he wishes to publish; v.t. to have an interview with. **-er** n. [Fr. *entrevue*].
in·tes·tate (in·tes'·tāt) a. not having made a valid will; not disposed of by will; n. a person who dies intestate. **intestacy** n. [L. *in-*, not; *testari*, to make a will].
in·tes·tine (in·tes'·tin) a. internal; domestic; civil (of war, etc.); n.pl. the bowels; the entrails. **intestinal** a. [L. *intestinus*].
in·ti·mate (in'·tạ·mạt) a. innermost; familiar; closely-related; close; n. an intimate friend; v.t. **intimate** (in'·tạ·māt) to hint; to imply. **intimacy** n. the state of being intimate; sexual relations. **-ly** adv. **intimation** n. a notice; a hint [L. *intimus*, inmost].
in·tim·i·date (in·tim'·a·dāt) v.t. to force or deter by threats; to inspire with fear; to frighten into action; to cow. **intimidation** n. **intimidator** n. [L. *in*; *timidus*, fearful].
in·to (in'·too) prep. expresses motion to a point within, or a change from one state to another.
in·tol·er·a·ble (in·tȧl'·ạ·rạ·bl) a. insufferable; unbearable.**-ness** n. **intolerably** adv. **intolerance** n. **intolerant** a. **intolerantly** adv.
in·tone (in·tōn') v.t. to utter or recite with a long drawn out musical note or tone; to chant; v.i. to modulate the voice; to give forth a deep protracted sound. **intonate** v.t. to intone. **intonation** n.
in·tox·i·cate (in·tȧk'·sạ·kāt) v.t. to make drunk; to excite beyond self-control. **intoxicating** a. producing intoxication; heady. **intoxicant** n. an intoxicating liquor. **intoxication** n. [Gk. *toxikon*, poison].
in·tra- (in'·tra) prefix fr. L. *intra*, within, inside of, used in the construction of many compound terms. **-cellular** a. within a cell.

-muscular *a.* inside a muscle. **-venous** *a.* within a vein.

in·trac·ta·ble (in·trak′·ta̯·bl) *a.* not to be managed or governed; unmanageable; stubborn. **intractability, intractably** *adv.*

in·tra·mu·ral (in·tra̯·myoo′·ral) *a.* pert. to a single college or its students; within the walls or limits.

in·tran·si·gent (in·tran′·sa̯·ja̯nt) *a.* refusing in any way to compromise or to make a settlement (esp. in political matters); irreconcilable; *n.* one who adopts this attitude. **intransigence,** *n.* **-ly** *adv.* [Fr. *intransigeant*].

in·tran·si·tive (in·tran′·sa̯·tiv) *a.* (*Gram.*) denoting such verbs as express an action or state which is limited to the agent, or which does not pass over to, or operate upon, an object.

in·trep·id (in·trep′·id) *a.* free from fear or trepidation. **-ity** *n.* undaunted courage. **-ly** *adv.* [L. *in-*, not; *trepidus*, alarmed].

in·tri·cate (in′·tri·ka̯t) *a.* involved; entangled; complicated; difficult. **intricacy, -ness** *n.* **-ly** *adv.* [L. *intricare*, to entangle].

in·trigue (in′·trig) *n.* a plot to effect some purpose by secret artifices; illicit love; (in·trēg′) *v.i.* to scheme secretly; to plot; to carry on illicit love; *v.t.* to fascinate; to arouse interest in; to puzzle. *pr.p.* **intriguing. intrigant, -r** *n.* **intriguing** *a.* **intriguingly** *adv.* [Fr. fr. L. *intricare*, to entangle].

in·trin·sic (in·trin′·sik) *a.* from within; having internal value; inherent. **-ality** *n.* **-ally** *adv.* [L. *intrinsecus*, inwardly].

in·tro- (in′·trō) *prefix*, a variation of intra, *inwards*, used in compound terms.

in·tro·duce (in·tra̯·dūs′) *v.t.* to lead or bring in; to bring forward; to insert; to make known formally (one person to another); to import; to begin. **introduction** (in·tra̯·duk′·shan) *n.* act of introducing or bringing into notice; the act of making persons formally acquainted with one another; the preliminary section of a speech or discourse; prologue; the preface to a book; an elementary treatise on some branch of knowledge. **introductory, introductive** *a.* **introductively, inductorily** *adv.* [L. *introducere*, to lead in].

in·tro·spect (in·tra̯·spekt′) *v.t.* to look within; to inspect; *v.i.* to pre-occupy oneself with one's own thoughts, emotions and feelings. **-ion** *n.* close (often morbid) examination of one's thoughts and feelings. **-ive** *a.* **-ively** *adv.* [L. *intro*, within; *specere*, to look].

in·tro·vert (in·tra̯·vurt′) *v.t.* to turn inward; (in′·tra̯·vurt) *n.* a self-centered, introspective individual. Cf. *extrovert.* **introversion** *n.* **introversive, -ive** *a.* [L. *intro*, within; *vertere*, to turn].

in·trude (in·trōōd′) *v.i.* to thrust oneself in; to enter unwelcome or uninvited into company; to trespass; *v.t.* to force in. **-r** *n.* **intrusion** *n.* **intrusive** *a.* **intrusively** *adv.* **intrusiveness** *n.* [L. *in*; *trudere*, to thrust].

in·trust See **entrust.**

in·tu·i·tion (in·tōō·ish′·a̯n) *n.* immediate and instinctive perception of a truth; direct understanding without reasoning. **intuit** *v.t.* and *v.i.* to know intuitively. **-al** *a.* **-alism, -ism** *n.* the doctrine that the perception of good and evil is by intuition. **-alist** *n.* **intuitive** *a.* having instinctively immediate knowledge or perception of something. **intuitively** *adv.* [L. *intueri*, to look upon].

in·tu·mesce (in·tōō·mes′) *v.i.* to swell; to enlarge or expand, owing to heat. **-nce** *n.*

in·twine See **entwine.**

in·un·date (in′·a̯n·dāt, in·un′·dāt) *v.t.* to overflow; to flood; to overwhelm. **inundation** *n.* [L. *inundare*, to flood, fr. *unda*, a wave].

in·ure (in·yoor′) *v.t.* to accustom (to); to habituate by use; to harden (the body) by toil, etc. **-ment** *n.* [*in*, into + obs. *ure*, to work,

fr. Fr. *œuvre*, work].

in·vade (in·vād′) *v.t.* to attack; to enter with hostile intentions; to violate; to encroach upon. **-r** *n.* **invasion** *n.* **invasive** *a.* [L. *invadere*, to go in].

in·val·id (in·val′·id) *a.* not valid; void; of no legal force; weak. *v.t.* to render invalid. **-ate** *v.* **-ation** *n.* **-ity, -ness** *n.*

in·va·lid (in′·va·lid) *n.* a person enfeebled by sickness or injury; *a.* ill; sickly; weak; *v.t.* and *v.i.* to make invalid; to send away as an invalid. [L. *invalidus*, infirm].

in·val·u·a·ble (in·val′·ya̯·bl) *a.* incapable of being valued; priceless; of very great value.

in·var·i·a·ble (in·ve′·ri·a̯·bl) *a.* not displaying change; always uniform; (*Math.*) constant. **-ness, invariability** *n.* **invariably** *adv.* **invariant** *n.* a constant quantity.

in·va·sion (in·vā′·zhan) *n.* See **invade.**

in·vec·tive (in·vek′·tiv) *n.* violent outburst of censure; abuse; vituperation. *a.* abusive [L. *invectio,* fr. *invehere,* to bring against].

in·veigh (in·vā′) *v.i.* to exclaim or rail against. **-er** *n.* [L. *invehere,* to bring against].

in·vei·gle (in·vā′·gl) *v.t.* to entice by deception or flattery; to allure; to mislead into something evil; to seduce. **-ment** *n.* **-r** *n.* [Fr. *aveugler,* to blind].

in·vent (in·vent′) *v.t.* to devise something new or an improvement; to contrive; to originate; to think out something untrue. **-ion** *n.* act of producing something new; an original contrivance; a deceit, fiction, or forgery. **-ive** *a.* able to invent; of an ingenious turn of mind; resourceful. **-ively** *adv.* **-or** *n.* [L. *invenire,* to come upon, to discover].

in·ven·to·ry (in′·va̯n·tōr·i·) *n.* a detailed list of articles comprising the effects of a house, etc.; a catalog of moveables; *v.t.* to make a list or enter on a list [L. *inventarium,* a list of things found].

in·verse (in′·vurs) *a.* inverted; opposite in order or relation. **-ly** *adv.* **inversion** *n.* the act of inverting; the state of being inverted; change of order or time; (*Gram.*) a change of the natural arrangement of words. **inversive** *a.* [L. *in, vertere, versum,* to turn].

in·vert (in·vurt′) *v.t.* to turn over; to put upside down; to place in a contrary order. **-edly** *adv.* [L. *in; vertere,* to turn].

in·ver·te·brate (in·vur′·ta̯·brat, -brāt) *a.* not having a vertebral column or backbone; spineless, weak-willed; *n.* animal, such as an insect, snail, etc., with no spinal column.

in·vest (in·vest′) *v.t.* to lay out capital with a view to profit; to clothe, as with office or authority; to dress; to lay siege to; *v.t.* to make a purchase or an investment. **-iture** *n.* ceremony of installing anyone in office. **-ment** *n.* the act of investing; the capital invested to produce interest or profit; blockade. **-or** *n.* [L. *investire,* to clothe].

in·ves·ti·gate (in·ves′·ta̯·gāt) *v.t.* to inquire into; to examine thoroughly. **investigable** *a.* **investigation** *n.* **investigator** *n.* **investigatory** *a.* [L. *vestigare,* to track].

in·vet·er·ate (in·vet′·er·it) *a.* firmly established by long continuance; obstinate; deep-rooted. **-ly** *adv.* **-ness, inveteracy,** *n.* [L. *inveterare,* to grow old].

in·vid·i·ous (in·vid′·i·a̯s) *a.* likely to provoke envy, ill-will or hatred; offensive. **-ly** *adv.* **-ness** *n.* [L. *invidia,* envy].

in·vig·or·ate (in·vig′·er·āt) *v.t.* to give vigor to; to animate with life and energy; to strengthen. **invigoration** *n.* **-d** *a.* [L. *in; vigor,* force].

in·vin·ci·ble (in·vin′·sa̯·bl) *a.* unconquerable; insuperable. **-ness, invincibility** *n.* **invincibly** [L. *in-,* not; *vincere,* to conquer].

in·vi·o·la·ble (in·vī′·a̯l·a̯·bl) *n.* not to be violated; sacred. **inviolably** *adv.* **inviolate** *a.* unprofaned; uninjured. **inviolately** *adv.* **in-**

violateness n. [L. in; violare, to violate].

in·vis·i·ble (in·viz'·a·bl) a. incapable of being seen; unseen; indiscernible, **invisibility, -ness** n. **invisibly** adv.

in·vite (in·vīt') v.t. to ask by invitation; to attract. **invitation** (in·vi·tā'·shan) n. act of inviting; the spoken or written form with which a request for a person's company is extended. **-r** n. **inviting** a. alluring, attractive. **invitingly** adv. [L. invitare].

in·vo·ca·tion (in·va·kā'·shan) n. act of addressing in prayer; a petition for divine help and guidance. **invocatory** a. [See **invoke.**]

in·voice (in'·vois) n. a detailed list of goods, with prices, sold or consigned to a purchaser; v.t. to make such a list. [pl. of obs. invoy, fr. Fr. envoi, a sending].

in·voke (in·vōk') v.t. to address (esp. God) earnestly or solemnly in prayer; to beg for protection or assistance; to implore; to summon [L. in; vocare, to call].

in·vol·un·ta·ry (in·val'·an·te·ri·) a. outside the control of the will; not proceeding from choice; unintentional; instinctive. **involuntarily** adv. **involuntariness** n.

in·vo·lute (in'·va·lòòt) a. (Bot.) rolled inwardly or spirally; n. the locus of the far end of a perfectly flexible thread unwound from a circle and kept constantly taut. **involution** n. that in which anything is involved; the process of raising a quantity to any power; entanglement; complication. [See **involve**].

in·volve (in·valv') v.t. to envelop; to wrap up; to include; to comprise; to embrace; to implicate (a person); to complicate (a thing); to entail; to include; to twine; to interlace; to overwhelm; to multiply a number any number of times by itself. **-ment** n. [L. in; volvere, volutum, to roll].

in·vul·ner·a·ble (in·vul'·ner·a·bl) a. incapable of being wounded or injured. **invulnerability,** n. **invulnerably** adv.

in·ward (in'·werd) a. placed within; towards the inside; interior; internal; seated in the mind or soul; n. that which is within. esp. in pl., the viscera; adv. toward the inside; into the mind. Also **inwards; -ly** adv. in the parts within, secretly; in the mind or soul [O.E. inneward].

i·o·dine (ī'·a·dīn, dēn) n. a non-metallic chemical element belonging to the halogen group. **iodiferous** a. yielding iodine. **iodize,** to treat with compounds of iodine, e.g. common salt. **iodoform** n. a powdered crystalline compound of iodine [Gk. ioeidēs, violet-like, from the color of its fumes].

i·on (ī'·an, ·ån) n. electrically charged atom or radical which has gained, or lost, one or more electrons and which facilitates the transport of electricity through an electrolyte or the gas in a gas-discharge tube. **ionic** a. pert. to ions. **-ization** n. splitting up of a liquid during electrolysis or of a gas during a glow discharge, into ions. **-ize** v.t. **ionosphere** n. the layer of ionized molecules in the upper atmosphere beyond the stratosphere [Gr. ion].

I·on·ic (ī·àn'·ik) a. pert. to section of Greece; (Archit.) denoting type of column with fluted molding and ram's horn design.

i·on·o·sphere (ī·àn'·a·sfir) n. See **ion.**

i·o·ta (ī·ō'·ta) n. a very small quantity or degree; a jot [Gk. the name of the smallest letter of the Greek alphabet = I. i.].

ir- (ir) prefix for in; not, before 'r.'

i·ras·ci·ble (i·ras'·a·bl) a. easily provoked; hot-tempered, **irascibility** n. **irascibly** adv. [L. irasci, to be angry].

i·rate (ī·rāt') a. angry; incensed; enraged [L. iratus, fr. irasci, to be angry].

ire (īr) n. anger; wrath. **-ful** a. **-fully** adv. **-fully** adv. **-fulness** n. [L. ira, anger].

irid-, irido-, prefix fr. Gk. iris, rainbow, used in the construction of compound terms, per-

taining to the iris of the eye or to the genus of plants, as **iridescence** (i·ra·des'·ans) n. rainbow-like display of colors. **iridescent** a.

iris (ī·ris) n. (Anat.) the thin contractile, colored membrane between the cornea and the lens of the eye, perforated in the center by an opening called the pupil; (Bot.) a genus of flowering plants of the natural order Iridaceae, the rainbow; an appearance resembling the rainbow [Gk. iris, rainbow].

I·rish (ī'·rish) a. pert. to Ireland; n. the early language spoken in Ireland—now known as Erse. **-ism** n. a mode of speaking, phrase, or idiom of Ireland. **-man, -woman** n. — **moss,** carageen, a form of edible seaweed.

irk (urk) v.t. to weary; to trouble; to distress (used impersonally as, **it irks me**). **-some** a. wearisome; annoying. **-somely** adv. [M.E.]

i·ron (ī'·ern) n. the most common and useful of the metallic elements; something hard and unyielding; an instrument or utensil made of iron; an instrument used, when heated, to press and smooth cloth; in golf, an iron-headed club. **-s** n.pl. fetters; manacles; a. made of iron; resembling some aspect of iron; robust; inflexible; unyielding; v.t. to smooth with a heated flat iron; v.i. to furnish or arm with iron; to fetter. **-clad** a. covered or protected with sheets of iron; n. a vessel prepared for naval warfare by having the parts above water plated with iron. **-er** n. — **gray** a. of a dark color. — **horse** n. a locomotive. — **lung** n. an apparatus which maintains artificial respiration continuously. — **ore** n. a rock containing iron-rich compounds from which commercial iron is obtained. **-smith** n. a worker in iron. **-stone** n. any ore of iron mixed with clay, etc. **-y** a. made of or resembling iron. **cast iron, pig iron** n. the iron obtained by smelting iron ore with charcoal, coke, or raw coal in a blast furnace. **corrugated iron,** plate of galvanized iron, corrugated to give it stiffness, used for temporary roofing, fencing, etc. **galvanized iron,** sheet iron coated with zinc to minimize the effects of rusting. — **age,** period following Bronze age, when iron was substituted for bronze in the making of tools, weapons, and ornaments. — **Curtain,** the ban placed by the U.S.S.R. on free exchange of information, news, etc., between Eastern and Western Europe. **to have too many irons in the fire,** to attempt to do too many things at the same time [O.E. iren].

i·ro·ny (ī'·ra·ni·) n. a mode of speech in which the meaning is the opposite of that actually expressed; sarcasm; satire. **ironic, ironical** (i·ràn'·ik, ·al) a. **ironically** adv. [Gk. eirōneia, dissimulation in speech].

ir·ra·di·ate (i·rā'·di·āt) v.t. to shine upon, throw light upon; to illuminate; v.i. to emit rays; to give forth light; a. illumined with beams of light. **irradiance, irradiancy** n. effulgence; emission of rays of light; splendor. **irradiant** a. **irradiation** n. exposure to X-rays, ultra-violet rays, solar rays, etc.; illumination; brightness; enlightenment. **irradiative** a. **irradiator** n.

ir·ra·tion·al (i·rash'·an·al) a. incompatible with or contrary to reason. **-ity** n. **-ly** adv.

ir·re·claim·a·ble (ir·i·klā·ma·bl) a. incapable of being reclaimed. **irreclaimably** adv.

ir·rec·on·cil·a·ble (i·rek·an·sīl'·a·bl) a. incapable of being reconciled; inconsistent. **-ness, irreconcilability** n. **irreconcilably** adv.

ir·re·cov·er·a·ble (ir·i·kuv'·er·a·bl) a. cannot be recovered; irreparable; irretrievable. **-ness** n. **irrecoverably** adv.

ir·re·deem·a·ble (ir·i·dēm'·a·bl) a. not redeemable; incorrigible; hopelessly lost; not convertible (as paper money into specie). **-ness, irredeemability** n. **irredeemably** adv.

ir·re·duc·i·ble (ir·i·dūs′·ạ·bl) *a.* that which cannot be reduced or lessened. **-ness, irreducibility** *n.* **irreducibly** *adv.*

ir·ref·u·ta·ble (i·ri·fū′·tạ·bl, ir·ref′·yạ·tạ·bl) *a.* that cannot be refuted. **irrefutability** *n.* **irrefutably** *adv.*

ir·reg·u·lar (i·reg′·yạ·ler) *a.* not regular; not according to rule; deviating from the moral standard; (*Gram.*) not inflected according to normal rules; *n.* a member of an armed force outside government control. **-ity** *n.* **-ly** *adv.*

ir·rel·a·tive (i·rel′·ạ·tiv) *a.* not relative; unconnected. **-ly** *adv.*

ir·rel·e·vant (i·rel′·ạ·vạnt) *a.* not logically pertinent. **irrelevancy** *n.* **-ly** *adv.*

ir·re·li·gion (ir·i·lij′·ạn) *n.* state of indifference or opposition to religious beliefs. **irreligious** *a.* **irreligiously** *adv.* profanely; impiously. **irreligiousness** *n.* ungodliness.

ir·re·me·di·a·ble (ir·i·mē′·di·a·bl) *a.* not to be remedied or redressed. **-ness** *n.* **irremediably** *adv.*

ir·re·place·able (ir·i·plā′·sạ·bl) *a.* that cannot be passed by or forgiven; unpardonable.

ir·rep·a·ra·ble (i·rep′·ạr·ạ·bl) *a.* that cannot be repaired or rectified. **-ness** *n.* **irreparability** *n.* **irreparably** *adv.*

ir·re·place·able (ir·i·plā′·sạ·bl) *a.* that cannot be replaced; indispensable; unique.

ir·re·press·i·ble (ir·i·pres′·ạ·bl) *a.* not able to be kept under control. **irrepressibility** *n.* **-ness** *n.* **irrepressibly** *adv.*

ir·re·proach·a·ble (ir·i·prō′·chạ·bl) *a.* free from blame; faultless. **irreproachably** *adv.*

ir·re·sist·i·ble (ir·i·zis′·tạ·bl) *a.* incapable of being resisted; too strong, fascinating, charming, etc., to be resisted. **-ness, irresistibility** *n.* **irresistibly** *adv.*

ir·res·o·lute (i·rez′·a·lŏŏt) *a.* infirm or inconstant in purpose; vacillating. **-ly** *adv.* **-ness, irresolution** *n.*

ir·re·spec·tive (ir·i·spek′·tiv) *a.* and *adv.* without regard to; apart from. **-ly** *adv.*

ir·re·spon·si·ble (ir·i·spạn′·sạ·bl) *a.* not liable to answer (for consequences); carefree; without a due sense of responsibility. **irresponsibility** *n.* **irresponsibly** *adv.*

ir·re·spon·sive (ir·i·spạn′·siv) *a.* not responsive (to); unanswering; taciturn. **-ness** *n.*

ir·re·triev·a·ble (ir·i·trē′·vạ·bl) *a.* incapable of recovery or repair. **-ness** *n.* **irretrievability** *n.* **irretrievably** *adv.*

ir·rev·er·ent (i·rev′·ạ·rạnt) *a.* not reverent; disrespectful. **irreverence** *n.* **-ly** *adv.*

ir·re·vers·i·ble (ir·i·vur′·sạ·bl) *a.* that cannot be reversed, turned back, recalled, or annulled. **irreversibly** *adv.*

ir·rev·o·ca·ble (i·rev′·ạ·kạ·bl) *a.* incapable of being recalled or revoked. **-ness, irrevocability** *n.* **irrevocably** *adv.*

ir·ri·gate (ir′·ạ·gāt) *v.t.* to water (by artificial channels). **irrigable, irrigative** *a.* **irrigation** *n.* the artificial application of water to the land for the purpose of increasing its fertility; (*Med.*) the washing out of a wound, etc. to keep it moist. **irrigator** *n.* [L. *irrigare*, fr. *rigare*, to moisten].

ir·ri·tate (ir′·ạ·tāt) *v.t.* to excite to anger; to annoy; to excite heat and redness in the skin by friction. **irritability** *n.* **irritable** *a.* easily provoked or annoyed; fretful; able to be acted upon by stimuli. **irritableness** *n.* **irritably** *adv.* **irritant** *a.* irritating; *n.* that which irritates or causes irritation. **irritation** *n.* exasperation; anger; the act of exciting heat, redness, or action in the skin or flesh by external stimulus. **irritative** *a.* tending to irritate [L. *irritare*].

ir·rup·tion (i·rup′·shạn) *n.* a sudden invasion; a violent incursion into a place; a breaking or bursting in. **irruptive** *a.* **irruptively** *adv.* [L. *irruptio*].

is (iz) *v.* the *third pers. sing. pres. indic.* of the verb **to be** [O.E.].

is·land (ī′·lạnd) *n.* a piece of land surrounded by water; anything resembling this, e.g. a street-refuge. **-er** *n.* an inhabitant of an island [earlier *iland*, O.E. *iegland*].

isle (īl) *n.* an island. **islet** (ī′·let) *n.* a tiny island [O.Fr. *isle*. L. *insula*].

-ism (izm) *n.* a jocular reference to any distinctive doctrine, theory, or practice [English suffix, *-ism*].

i·so- (ī′·so) *prefix fr.* Gk. *isos*, equal, used in the construction of compound terms.

i·so·bar (ī′·sạ·bàr) *n.* a line on a map joining up all those points where the mean height of the barometer is the same; *pl.* species of atoms having the same atomic weight but different atomic numbers. **-ic** *a.* consisting of isobars. **-ometric** *a.* showing equal barometric pressure (Gk. *isos*, equal; *baros*, weight].

i·so·dy·nam·ic (ī·sạ·dī·nam′·ik) *a.* having equal force or power.

i·so·gon (ī′·sạ·gàn) *n.* a plane figure having equal angles. **isogonal** (ī·sàg′·ạ·nạl) *a.* **-ic** *a.* [Gk. *isos*, equal; *gonia*, angle].

i·so·late (ī′·sạ·lāt) *v.t.* to place in a detached position; to place apart or alone; to insulate; (*Chem.*) to obtain a substance in a pure state. **isolation** *n.* state of being isolated. **isolation hospital**, a hospital for infectious diseases. **isolationist** *n.* one who advocates non-participation in world-politics [It. *isolato*, detached, fr. L. *insula*, an island].

i·so·met·ric (ī·sạ·met′·rik) *a.* of equal measurement.

i·so·mor·phism (ī·sạ·mawr′·fizm) *n.* similarity of structure, esp. between the crystals of different chemical substances. **isomorphic** *a.* **isomorphous** *a.* [Gk. *isos*, equal; *morphē*, shape].

i·sos·ce·les (ī·sàs′·ạ·lēz) *a.* having two sides which are equal (said of a triangle) [Gk. *isos*, equal; *skelos*, a leg].

i·so·topes (ī′·sạ·tōps) *n.pl.* (*physics*) of most of the elements, atoms with nuclei of slightly different weights [Gk. *isos*, equal; *topos*, place].

Is·ra·el (iz′·ri·ạl) *n.* since 1948, the name of the Jewish State in Palestine; (*Bib.*) the Jewish people **Israeli** (iz·rāl′·i·) *n.* an inhabitant of Israel. **-ite** *n.* (*Bib.*) a descendant of Israel or Jacob; a Jew. **-itic, -itish**, *a.* [Heb. *Israel*, he who striveth with God].

is·sue (ish′·ŏŏ) *n.* act of passing or flowing out; the act of sending out; that which is issued; a topic of discussion or controversy; a morbid discharge from the body; outlet; edition; consequence; result; progeny; offspring; (*Law*) the specific point in a suit between two parties requiring to be determined; *v.t.* to send out (a book, etc.); to put into circulation; to proclaim or set forth with authority; to supply with equipment, etc.; *v.i.* to pass or flow out; to come out; to proceed; to be born or spring from. **-less** *a.* **-er** *n.* **at issue** (point) to be debated or settled. **to join issue**, to take opposite views on a point in debate [O.Fr. *issir*, to go out].

isth·mus (is′·mạs) *n.* a narrow neck of land connecting two larger portions. **isthmian** *a.* [Gk. *isthmos*].

it (it) *pron.* the neuter pronoun of the third person; *n.* (*Colloq.*) sexual attractiveness; sex appeal; perfection [O.E. *hit*].

I·tal·ian (i·tal′·yạn) *a.* pert. to Italy, its inhabitants or their language.

i·tal·ics (i·tal′·iks) *n.pl.* a printing type having the type sloping from the right downwards. *as these letters.* **italicization** *n.* **italicize** *v.t.* to print thus.

itch (ich) *n.* an irritation in the skin; scabies; an irrepressible desire; *v.i.* to feel uneasiness or irritation in the skin; to be inordinately anxious or desirous to; to be hankering after. **-iness** n. **-y** a. **an itching palm,** a grasping disposition; greed [O.E. *giccan,* to itch].

i·tem (ī'·tạm) n. a piece of news, as in a newspaper; an entry in an account or list; a detail. **itemize** v.t. to list by items; to give particulars [L.].

it·er·ate (it'·ạ·rāt) v.t. to repeat; to do again. **iteration** n. **iterative, iterant** a. repeating [L. *iterare,* fr. *iterum,* again].

i·tin·er·ant (ī·tin'·ạ·rạnt) a. traveling from place to place; traveling on circuit; of no settled abode. n. one who goes from place to place, esp. on business. **itineracy, itinerancy** n. **-ly** adv. **itinerary** n. a record of travel; a route, line of travel; a guide-book for travelers. **itinerate** v.i. to travel up and down a country, esp. in a regular circuit. **itineration** n. [L. *iter, itineris,* a journey].

its (its) the *possessive case of pron. it.* **itself** pron. the neuter reciprocal pronoun applied to things; the reflexive form of it.

i·vo·ry (ī'·vạ·ri.) n. the hard, white, opaque, dentine constituting tusks of elephant, walrus, etc.; as carving of ivory; creamy white color. n.pl. (*Colloq.*) keys of a piano; the teeth. a. made of or like ivory [Fr. *ivoire,* fr. L. *ebur,* ivory].

i·vy (ī'·vi.) n. a climbing evergreen plant. **ivied** a. covered with ivy [O.E. *ifig*].

J

jab (jab) v.t. to poke sharply; to stab; pr.p. **-bing.** pa.t., pa.p. **-bed.** n. a sharp poke, stab, or thrust [prob. imit.].

jab·ber (jab'·ẹr) v.i. to chatter; to speak quickly and indistinctly; v.t. to utter indistinctly; n. rapid, incoherent talk. **-er** n. **-ingly** adv. [prob. imit.].

ja·bot (zha·bō') n. a frill or fall of lace on a woman's dress; orig. a ruffle on a man's shirt.

ja·cinth (jā'·sinth) n. the hyacinth [contr. of L. *hyacinthus,* a precious stone].

Jack (jak) n. a popular nickname and diminutive of *John;* (*l.c.*) a fellow; a laborer, as *steeple-jack;* a sailor; the knave in a pack of cards; a device to facilitate removal of boots, as a *boot-jack;* a mechanical device for turning a roasting-spit; a portable apparatus for raising heavy weights, esp. for raising a motor vehicle to change a tire; a flag or ensign; the male of certain animals, as *jackass; v.t.* to raise with a jack. Also **jack up. -boot** n. a long boot reaching above the knee formerly worn by cavalry. **—in-the-box** n. a child's toy comprising a small figure which springs out of a box when the lid is lifted. **-knife** n. a strong clasp knife. **— o' lantern,** a lantern made from hollowed-out pumpkin, with holes cut to make a face. **—of-all-trades** n. one who can turn his hand to anything. **-pot** n. a pool, in poker, which cannot be opened except by player holding two jacks or better; (*Slang*) the pay-off. **-rabbit** n. a hare with very long ears. **-tar,** a sailor. **Union Jack,** the national flag of Gt. Britain. **yellowjack** n. yellow fever [fr. *John,* infl. by Fr. *Jacques*].

jack·al (jack'·ạl, ·awl) n. a bashy-tailed carnivorous animal of Asia and Africa; wild dog; (*Fig.*) a servile creature [Pers. *shaghal*].

jack·ass (jack'·as) n. a male ass; a stupid fellow; a blockhead [*Jack,* the male; and *ass*].

jack·daw (jak'·daw) n. a glossy, black bird of the crow family [fr. *Jack; daw*].

jack·et (jak'·it) n. a short, sleeved coat; outer covering or skin (as of potatoes); an outer casing, as for a boiler to keep in heat; a loose dust-cover for a book; v.t. to cover with a jacket [O.Fr. *jaquet,* dim. of *jaque,* a coat of mail].

Jac·o·be·an (jak·ạ·bē'·ạn) a. pert. to reign of James I; used mainly of architecture, indoor decoration, and furniture (dark oak) of Stuart period; n. person of this period [L. *Jacobus,* James].

Jac·o·bin (jak'·ạ·bin) n. a French Dominican friar, so called from monastery of *St. Jacques,* Paris; a member of society of French Revolutionists [Fr. fr. L. *Jacobus,* James].

Ja·cob's lad·der (jā'·kạbz·lad'·ẹr) n. (*Naut.*) a rope ladder with wooden rungs [Heb. *ya'aqob,* Jacob].

jac·quard (ja·kárd') n., a. pattern woven into fabrics [fr. Fr. inventor of loom, *Jacquard*].

jade (jād) n. an over-worked, worn-out horse; a mean woman; a saucy wench; v.t. to tire; to wear out. pr.p. **jading.** pa.p. **jaded. jaded** a. tired; weary; sated [Scand. *jalda,* a mare].

jade (jād) n. a very hard, compact silicate of lime and magnesia, of various colors, carved for ornaments [Span. (*piedra de*) *ijada,* a stone for curing a pain in the side].

jag (jag) n. a notch; a ragged protuberance; (*Bot.*) cleft or division; v.t. to notch; to slash. pr.p. **-ging.** pa.p. **-ged. -ged, -gy** a. notched; rough-edged; sharp. **-gedness** n. (*Slang*) a spree, as **a talking jag** [etym. doubtful].

jag·uar (jag'·wàr) n. a large spotted yellowish beast of prey [Braz.].

jail (jāl) n. a prison; v.t. to take into custody. (*Br.*) **goal. — bird** n. a prisoner; a criminal. **-er, -or** n. one who has charge of prisoners in the cells [O.Fr. *gaole,* a prison].

jal·ap (jal'·ạp) n. a drug used as a purgative esp. in dropsy [fr. *Xalapa,* in Mexico]. [car.

ja·lop·y (ja·lập'·i·) n. (*Slang*) an old, decrepit

jal·ou·sie (jal'·ạ·sē) n. a blind or shutter with slats at an angle. **-d** a. [Fr. *jalousie,* suspicion].

jam (jam) n. preserve made from fruit, boiled with sugar. **-my** a. [etym. doubtful].

jam (jam) v.t. to squeeze tight; to wedge in; to block up; to stall (a machine); v.i. to cease to function because of obstruction. pr.p. **-ming.** pa.p. **-med.** n. a crush; a hold-up (as of traffic); (*Colloq.*) a tight corner. **-ming** n. (*Radio*) to interfere with signals by sending out others of like frequency [prob. var. of *champ*].

jamb (jam) n. the side piece of a door, fireplace, etc. [Fr. *jambe,* a leg].

jam·bo·ree (jam·bạ·rē') n. a large, usually international, rally of Boy Scouts; (*Slang*) a noisy gathering [etym. unknown].

jan·gle (jang'·gl) v.t. to ring with a discordant sound; v.i. to sound out of tune; to wrangle; n. a discordant sound; a dispute. **jangling** n. [imit. O.Fr. *jangler*].

jan·i·tor (jan'·i·tẹr) n. (*fem.* **janitress**) a caretaker of a building; a doorkeeper; a porter [L. *janitor*].

Jan·i·zar·y (jan'·ạ·zạr·i·) n. a soldier of the Turkish Sultan [Turk. *yenitsheri,* the new soldiers].

Jan·u·ar·y (jan'·yạ·wer·i·) n. the first month, dedicated by Romans to *Janus,* the god with two faces. **janus-faced** a. untrustworthy [L. *Janus,* a Roman deity].

Ja·pan (jạ·pan') n. a N.E. Asiatic insular country. **-ese** (jạ·pạ·nēz') n. a native of Japan; a. pert. to Japan, the people or language. **japan** v.t. to make black and glossy; to lacquer with black varnish. pr.p. **-ning.** pa.p. **-ned.** n. the black laquer japanned [Jap.].

jape (jāp) n. a jest [O.Fr. *japer,* to jest].

jar (jàr) n. vessel narrower at top than at base, with or without handles [Fr. *jarre*].

jar (jár) v.i. to give forth a discordant sound; to vibrate discordantly; to affect the nerves, feelings, etc. unpleasantly; to conflict; v.t. to cause to vibrate by sudden impact; to shake physically or mentally. pr.p. -**ring**. pa.p. -**red**. n. a harsh, grating sound; a jolting movement; conflict. -**ringly** adv. [prob. imit.].

jar·gon (jar'·gạn) n. confused speech; gibberish; slang; technical phraseology.

jas·mine (jas'·min) n. a shrub with fragrant white, yellow or pink flowers. Also **jessamine** [Pers. yasmin, jasmine].

jas·per (jas'·pẹr) n. an opaque form of quartz, often highly colored [Gk. iaspis, chalcedony].

ja·to (jā'·tō) n. kind of rocket to assist the take-off of heavily loaded aircraft [Jet Assisted Take Off].

jaun·dice (jawn'·dis, jȧn'·dis) n. a disease, characterized by yellowness of skin and eyes; v.t. to affect with jaundice. -**d** a. affected with jaundice; (Fig.) jealous; prejudiced [Fr. jaune, yellow].

jaunt (jawnt, jȧnt) v.i. to make an excursion; n. an outing; a ramble. -**ing** a. rambling.

jaun·ty (jawn'·ti·, jȧn'·ti·) a. sprightly; airy; trim. **jauntily** adv. [Fr. gentil, genteel].

jave·lin (jav'·lin) n. a light hand-thrown spear [Fr.].

jaw (jaw) n. one of the two bones forming framework of mouth and containing the teeth; the mouth; part of any device which grips or crushes object held by it, as a vice; (Slang) loquacity; pl. narrow entrance to a gorge; v.t. (Slang) to scold; (Slang) to gossip. -**bone** n. bone of the mouth in which teeth are set. -**breaker** (Colloq.) a word hard to pronounce; (Colloq.) a large piece of hard candy.

jay (jā) n. a chattering, perching bird with gay plumage; (Fig.) a foolish person. -**walker** n. (Colloq.) a careless or absent-minded pedestrian who disregards traffic rules [etym. doubtful].

jazz (jaz) n. syncopated, noisy music played as accompaniment to dancing; a. like or pert. to jazz; v.t. and v.i. to dance to or play jazz music; (Slang) to put vigor and liveliness into. -**y** a. [Negro word].

jeal·ous (jel'·as) a. envious; suspicious; apprehensively watchful; solicitous; zealously careful. -**y** n. [O.Fr. fr. Gk. zelos, emulation].

jean (jēn) n. a strong, twilled cotton cloth; n.pl. overalls; trousers [prob. fr. L. Genua, Genoa].

jeep (jēp) n. light motor utility truck designed in World War 2 [G.P., of general purposes].

jeer (jir) v.i. to mock; to deride; v.t. to treat scoffingly; n. a gibe; a railing remark. -**er** n.

Je·ho·vah (ji·hō'·vạ) n. (Bib.) Hebrew name of the supreme God [Heb. Yahweh].

je·june (ji·jōōn') a. empty; barren; uninteresting; dry. -**ly** adv. [L. jejunus, hungry].

jel·ly (jel'·i·) n. any gelatinous substance; the juice of fruit boiled with sugar. **jell** v.i. to stiffen. **jellied** a. of the consistency of jelly. **jellify** v.t. to make into jelly; v.i. to become set like a jelly. -**fish** n. popular name given certain marine animals of soft gelatinous structure [Fr. gelée, frost].

jen·ny (jen'·i·) n. a spinning machine; a female ass; a female bird, the wren (usually jenny-wren) [dim. of Jane].

jeo·par·dy (jep'·ẹr·di·) n. danger; risk. **jeopardize** v.t. to endanger; to imperil [Fr. jeu parti, a divided game].

Jer·e·mi·ah (jer·ạ·mī'·ạ) n. (Bib.) a Hebrew prophet and author of the Book of Lamentations; any doleful prophet. **jeremiad** n. a tale of grief or complaint.

jerk (jurk) v.t. to throw with a quick motion; to twitch; to give a sudden pull, twist, or push; n. a short, sudden thrust, pull, start, etc.; a spasmodic twitching. -**er** n. -**ily** adv. -**iness** n. -**water** a. (Colloq.) insignificant. -**y** a. fitful;

spasmodic; lacking rhythm [imit. word].

jerk (jurk) v.t. to cure (meat) by cutting in long slices and drying in the sun. -**ed** a. [Peruv. charqui, dried beef].

jer·kin (jur'·kin) n. a close-fitting jacket or waistcoat [prob Dut. jurk, a frock].

jer·o·bo·am (jer·a·bō'·am) n. a large bowl; a huge bottle, in capacity eight times the ordinary size [1 Kings, 11].

Jer·ry (jer'·i·) n. (Slang) a German soldier [shortening of German].

Jer·sey (jur'·zi·) n. the largest of the Channel Islands; a cow of Jersey breed; a. pert. to State of New Jersey. **jersey** n. a close-fitting, knitted, woolen jacket, vest, or pullover; a knitted cloth [fr. Jersey].

jess (jes) n. a strap of leather or silk tied round the legs of a hawk; v.t. to put jesses on [O.Fr. ges, a throw].

jest (jest) n. a joke; a quip; banter; an object of ridicule; v.i. to joke; to scoff. -**er** n. one who jests; a professional fool, originally attached to the court or lord's manor. -**ful** a. -**ingly** adv. [M.E. jeste, an exploit].

Jes·u·it (jezh'·ū·it) n. one of a religious order founded by Ignatius Loyola in 1534 under the title of The Society of Jesus; (commonly) a crafty person; a prevaricator [fr. Jesus].

jet (jet) n. a variety of very hard, black lignite, capable of a brilliant polish and much used for ornaments; a. made of, or having the glossy blackness of jet. — **black** a. black like jet. -**tiness** n. -**ty** a. [O.Fr. jet].

jet (jet) n. a sudden rush, as of water or flame, from a pipe; the spout or nozzle emitting water, gas, etc.; a jet airplane; v.t. to spout; v.i. to shoot forth. **jet propulsion**, propulsion of a machine by the force of a jet of fluid or of heated gases, expelled backwards from the machine. pr.p. -**ting**. pa.t. -**ted** [Fr. jeter, to throw].

jet·sam (jet'·sam) n. goods thrown overboard to lighten a ship in distress; goods washed ashore from a wrecked ship. **jettison** n. act of throwing overboard; jetsam; v.t. to throw overboard, as cargo; (Fig.) to abandon, as a scheme [O.Fr. jetée, thrown out].

jet·ty (jet'·i·) n. a structure of piles, stones, etc. built to protect a harbor; a landing pier [O.Fr. jetée, thrown out].

Jew (jōō) n. (fem. -**ess**) a Hebrew or an Israelite. —**baiting**, persecution of the Jews. -**ish** a. of or belonging to Jews. -**ishness** n. -**ry** n. the Jewish people; a ghetto. **jew's harp**, a small, lyre-shaped musical instrument [Heb. Yehudah, Judah].

jew·el (jōō'·al) n. a precious stone; an ornament set with gem(s); a highly valued person or thing; v.t. to adorn with jewels; to fit (as a watch) with a jewel for pivot-bearings. -**er** n. one who makes or deals in jewels. -**ery** n. jewels collectively [O.Fr. joel, jewel].

Jez·e·bel (jez'·ạ·bel) n. a wicked, wanton woman [Jezebel, wife of Ahab].

jib (jib) n. (Naut.) a triangular stay-sail in front of forward mast; the projecting beam of a crane or derrick; v.t., v.i. jibe [var. of gybe]. (Colloq.) to agree; n. a jeer [var. of gibe].

jibe (jīb) v.t. to swing (the sail) from one side of the ship to the other; v.i. to swing round (of the sail) when running before the wind; to alter the course so that the sail shifts; (Colloq.) to agree; n. a jeer (var. of **gibe**).

jif·fy (jif'·i·) n. (Colloq.) a moment; an instant.

jig (jig) n. a lively dance; music for this; (Slang) a trick; a tool or fixture used to guide cutting tools in the making of duplicate parts; v.t. to jerk up and down; v.i. to dance; to bob up and down. pr.p. -**ging**. pa.p. -**ged**. -**saw** n. a narrow saw in a frame for cutting curves, etc. -**saw puzzle**, a picture cut into irregular pieces for putting together again.

jig·ger (jig'·ẹr) *n.* one who or that which jigs; any mechanical device which operates with jerky movement esp. an apparatus for washing and separating ores by shaking in sieves under water; an iron-headed golf club for approach shots; a bridge for a billiard cue; (*Naut.*) light tackle; (*Naut.*) a sail nearest the stern; (*Colloq.*) any gadget; a 1½ oz. measure for liquor.

jig·ger (jig'·ẹr) *n.* Also **chigger.** a flea, the female of which burrows under the human flesh to lay its eggs [var. of *chigoe*].

jig·gle (jig'·l) *v.i.* and *v.t.* to move with repeated short, quick jerks; *n.* a short, quick movement [etym. uncertain].

ji·had (ji·hàd') *n.* a holy war to the death proclaimed by Mohammedans against the foes of Islam; (*Fig.*) a campaign launched against any doctrine. Also **jehad** [Ar.].

jilt (jilt) *n.* one, esp. a woman, who capriciously disappoints a lover; *v.t.* to deceive or disappoint in love; to break an engagement to marry [prob. fr. *jillet*, dim. of *Jill*].

Jim Crow (jim-krō) *a.* discriminating against or segregating Negroes [*Jim* and *crow*].

jim·my (jim·i·) *n.* a small crowbar, as used by burglars; *v.t.* to force open [var. of *James*].

jin·gle (jing'·gl) *v.t.* to cause to give a sharp, tinkling sound; *v.i.* to tinkle; to give this effect in poetry; *n.* a tinkling sound, as of bells; correspondence of sounds, rhymes, etc., in verse to catch the ear [imit.].

jin·go (jing'·gō) *n.* a mild oath, as in *By Jingo;* one who expresses vehement patriotism (from the popular songs of the late 1870's, 'We don't want to fight, but *by Jingo* if we do...'). **jingo, -ish** *a.* **-ism** *n.*

jinks (jingks) *n.pl.* lively pranks [Scot.]. spirits of Mohammedan mythology [Ar. *jinni*].

jinn (jin) *n.pl.* (*sing.* **jinnee, jinni, genie**) spirits of Mohammedan mythology, supposedly able to assume the forms of men and animals [Ar. *jinni*].

jin·rik·i·sha (jin·rik'·shạ) *n.* a small, two-wheeled hooded carriage pulled by one or more men, commonly used in Japan (*abbrev.* **rickshaw**) [Jap. *jin*, a man; *riki*, power; *sha*, a carriage].

jinx (jingks) *n.* a person or thing of ill-omen.

jit·ney (jit'·ni·) *n.* public bus or car traveling a regular route.

jit·ters (jit'·ẹrs) *n.pl.* (*Slang*) a state of nervous agitation. **jitterbug** *n.* a jazzdancer. **jittery** *a.* [prob. imit.].

jiu·jit·su See **jujutsu.**

jive (jīv) *n.* and *v.i.* (*Slang*) exuberant variation on modern swing-time dance steps.

job (jàb) *n.* a piece of work; labor undertaken at a stated price or paid for by the hour; position; habitual employment or profession; *a.* lumped together (of miscellaneous articles); *v.i.* to do odd jobs; to act as a jobber; to use influence unscrupulously; *v.t.* to buy and sell as a jobber; to let out work in portions. *pr.p.* **-bing.** *pa.p.* **-bed. -ber** *n.* a wholesale dealer who sells to retailers; one who transacts public business to his own advantage; one who does odd jobs. **-bery** *n.* underhand means to gain private profit at the expense of public money; fraudulent dealings. **-bing** *a.* — **lot,** a large amount of goods as handled by a jobber; a lot of inferior quality. — **printing,** — **work,** the printing of handbills, circulars, etc.

Job (jōb) *n.* (*Bib.*) a Hebrew patriarch of the Old Testament regarded as a monument of patience; any person accepting continued disaster with infinite patience. **a Job's comforter,** one who aggravates the distress of another while pretending to console him.

jock·ey (jàk'·i·) *n.* a professional rider in horse-races; *v.t.* to ride as a jockey; to maneuver for one's own advantage; to trick; *v..i* to

cheat. **-ism, -ship** *n.* [dim. of *Jock*].

jo·cose (jō·kōs') *a.* given to jesting; waggish. **-ly** *adv.* **-ness, jocosity** (jō·kás'·ạ·ti·) *n.* the quality or state of being jocose. **jocular** (jàk'·yạ·lẹr) *a.* given to jesting; facetious. [L. *jocus*, a jest].

joc·und (jàk'·ạnd) *a.* merry; gay; genial. **-ity, -ness** *n.* **-ly** *adv.* [L. *jucundus*, gay].

jodh·purs (jàd'·poorz) *n.pl.* long riding breeches, close-fitting from knee to ankle [fr. *Jodhpur*, a native Indian State].

jog (jàg) *v.t.* to push with the elbow or hand; to nudge; to stimulate (as the memory); *v.i.* to move on at a slow jolting pace; to plod on. *pr.p.* **-ging.** *pa.p.* **-ged;** *n.* a nudge; a reminder; a slow walk, trot, etc.

jog (jàg) *n.* a projecting part [var. of **jag**].

jog·gle (jàg'·l) *v.t.* to shake slightly; to join by notches to prevent sliding apart; *v.i.* to shake; to totter; *n.* a jolt; a joint of two bodies so constructed by means of notches, that sliding apart is prevented; a metal pin joining two pieces of stone [dim. of **jog**].

John (jàn) *n.* a proper name; a familiar appellation. — **Barleycorn,** whisky. — **Bull,** the typical Englishman. — **Doe,** fictitious plaintiff in a law-case. — **Hancock** (*Colloq.*) one's signature. **johnny cake** corn bread; *l.c.* (*Slang*) a toilet [L. *Johannes*, John].

John·so·ni·an (jàn·sō'·ni·ạn) *a.* pert. to *Dr. Samuel Johnson* (1709-84), or to his literary style.

join (join) *v.t.* to bring together; to fasten; to unite; to act in concert with; to become a member of; to return to (as one's ship); to unite in marriage; *v.i.* to meet; to become united in marriage, partnership, league, etc.; to be in contact; *n.* a junction; a fastening. **joinder** *n.* (*Law*) a union. **-er** *n.* one who or that which joins; a carpenter. **-ery** *n.* the trade of a joiner. **to join battle,** to begin fighting. **to join issue,** to take different sides on a point in debate [Fr. *joindre*, to join].

joint (joint) *n.* the place where two things are joined; the articulation of two or more bones in the body; a hinge; (*Bot.*) the point where a leaf joins the stem; a cut of meat with bone prepared by butcher for the table; (*Slang*) a low-class public house; *v.t.* to unite; to provide with joints; to cut at a joint, as meat; *v.i.* to fit like joints; *a.* jointed; held in common. **-ed** *a.* having joints. **-ly** *adv.* together; co-operatively. — **stock company,** a mercantile, banking, or co-operative association with capital made up of transferable shares. **-ure** *n.* property settled on a woman at marriage to be hers on the decease of her husband. **out of joint,** dislocated; (*Fig.*) disordered [Fr. *joindre*, to join].

joist (joist) *n.* a beam to which the boards of a floor or the laths of a ceiling are nailed [O.Fr. *giste*, fr. *gésir*, to lie].

joke (jōk) *n.* something said or done to provoke laughter; a witticism; a prank; *v.t.* to make merry with; to banter; *v.i.* to make sport; to be merry. **-r** *n.* one who makes jokes or plays pranks; (*Slang*) a fellow; (*Cards*) an extra card in the pack, used in some games, such as poker; a hidden clause which changes the original intent of a bill, document, etc. **jokingly** *adv.* [L. *jocus*, a joke].

jol·ly (jàl'·i·) *a.* jovial; gay; enjoyable; *v.t.* (*Colloq.*) to humor a person with pleasant talk; (*Colloq.*) to tease. **jollification** *n.* a celebration; a noisy party. **jolliness, jollity** *n.* mirth; boisterous fun [O.Fr. *joli*, gay].

jol·ly·boat (jàl'·i·bōt) *n.* a ship's small boat [prob. Dut. *jolle*, a boat].

jolt (jōlt) *v.t.* to shake with a sudden jerk; *v.i.* to shake, as a vehicle on rough ground; *n.* a sudden jerk [etym. unknown].

Jo·nah (jō'·nạ) *n.* (*Bib.*) a Hebrew prophet; (*Colloq.*) a person who brings bad luck.

Jon·a·than (jăn′·a·than) *n.* a variety of eating apple.   [Fr. fr. L. *juncus*, a rush].

jon·quil (jŏn′·kwil) *n.* a variety of narcissus.

jo·rum (jō′·ram) *n.* a large drinking vessel; a large quantity of liquid.   [to banter.

josh (jăsh) *v.t.* and *v.i.* to make fun of, to tease,

joss (jăs) *n.* a Chinese idol [corrupt of Port. *deos*, a god].

jos·tle (jăs′·l) *v.t.* to push against, esp. with the elbow; *v.i.* to push; to strive for position; *n.* a pushing against [fr. *joust*].

jot (jăt) *n.* an iota; something negligible; *v.t.* to scribble down; to make a memorandum of. *pr.p.* **-ting.** *pa.p.* **-ted.** **-ter** *n.* **not to care a jot,** not to care at all [Gk. *iota*, the letter i].

joule (jōōl, joul) *n.* (*Elect.*) a unit of work; the energy expended in 1 sec. by 1 ampere flowing through a resistance of 1 ohm [fr. *J. P. Joule*, English physicist, 1818-89].

jour·nal (jur′·nal) *n.* a diary; a book recording daily transactions of a business firm; a daily newspaper; a periodical. **-ese** *n.* a term of contempt for the second-rate literary style of journalists. **-ize** *v.i.* to write for a journal; to keep a daily record of events. **-ism** *n.* **-ist** *n.* one who writes professionally for a newspaper or periodical. **-istic** *a.* [Fr. fr. L. *diurnalis*, daily].

jour·ney (jur′·ni·) *n.* travel from one place to another; distance covered in a specified time; *v.i.* to travel. *pr.p.* **-ing.** *pa.p.* **-ed.** **-man** *n.* orig. one hired to work by the day; a skilled mechanic or artisan who has completed his apprenticeship [O.Fr. *journée*, a day].

joust (joust, just) *n.* a mock encounter on horseback; a tournament; *v.i.* to tilt [O.Fr. *juster*, to approach].

Jove (jōv) *n.* Jupiter. **jovial** *a.* orig. born under the influence of the planet Jupiter; gay; convivial. **joviality, jovialness** *n.* **jovially** *adv.* [L. *jovialis*, of Jupiter].

jowl (joul) *n.* the jaw; the cheek; the dewlap, of cattle [O.E. *ceafl*, a jaw].

joy (joi) *n.* gladness; exhilaration of spirits; *v.i.* to rejoice; to exult. *pr.p.* **-ing.** *pa.p.* **-ed.** **-ful** *a.* **-fully** *adv.* **-fulness** *n.* **-less** *a.* dismal. **-lessly** *adv.* **-lessness** *n.* **-ous** *a.* full of joy. **-ously** *adv.* **-ousness** *n.* **-ride** *n.* (*Slang*) a pleasure ride or stolen ride. **-stick** *n.* (*Colloq.*) the control stick of an aircraft [O.Fr. *joie*, joy].

ju·bi·lant (jōō′·ba·lant) *a.* exulting; rejoicing. **-ly** *adv.* **jubilate** *v.i.* to rejoice; to exult. **jubilate** (jōō·ba·lá′·tē) *n.* the hundredth psalm as a canticle in the Anglican church service. **jubilation** *n.* rejoicing; exultation [L. *jubilare*, to shout for joy].

ju·bi·lee (jōō′·bi·lē) *n.* the fiftieth anniversary of any outstanding event; a festival or time of rejoicing. **silver jubilee,** the twenty-fifth anniversary. **diamond jubilee,** the sixtieth anniversary [Heb. *yobel*, a ram, or ram's horn trumpet].

Ju·da·ism (jōō′·dē·izm) *n.* the religious doctrines and rites of the Jewish people. **Judaic, -al** *a.* pert. to the Jews. **Judaically** *adv.* [L. *Judacus*, a Jew].

Ju·das (jōō′·das) *n.* (*Bib.*) the disciple of Christ who betrayed him; a traitor. **—kiss** *n.* a treacherous act disguised as kindness.

judge (juj) *n.* one who judges; an officer authorized to hear and determine civil or criminal cases, and to administer justice; an arbitrator; *pl.* a book of the Old Testament; *v.t.* to decide; to hear and try a case in a court of law; to give a final opinion or decision (as in a performance); to criticize; *v.i.* to act as a judge; to form an opinion; to come to a conclusion. **-ship** *n.* the office of a judge. **judgment** *n.* the act of judging; a legal decision arrived at by a judge in a court of law; discernment; an opinion. **Judgment Day,**

doomsday [L. *judex*, a judge].

ju·di·ca·ture (jōō′·i·ka·cher) *n.* the power of of justice; a judge's period of office. **judicable** dispensing justice; judges collectively; a court *a.* capable of being tried or judged. **judicative** *a.* having the power to judge. **judicatory** *a.* dispensing justice. **judicial** *a.* pert to a court of justice or to a judge; impartial. **judicially** *adv.* **judiciary** *n.* judicial branch of government; the judicial system; judges collectively; *a.* pert. to the courts of law; passing judgment or sentence. **judicious** *a.* wise; prudent; showing discrimination [L. *judicare*, to judge].

ju·do (jōō′·dō) *n.* a form of jujitsu [Jap.].

jug (jug) *n.* a vessel of earthenware, glass, etc., with handle and narrow neck; other vessels for holding liquids; (*Slang*) jail; *v.t.* to put in a jug; (*Slang*) to put in jail. *pr.p.* **-ging.** *pa.p.* **-ged** [etym. uncertain].

jug·ger·naut (jug′·er·nawt) *n.* any fanatical idea for which people are prepared to sacrifice their lives; any irresistible, tyrannical force which crushes all that obstructs its path [Hind. *Jagannath*, the lord of the universe].

jug·gle (jug′·l) *v.t.* to toss up and keep in motion a number of balls, plates, etc.; to defraud; *v.i.* to perform tricks with the hands; to use trickery; *n.* a trick by sleight of hand; verbal trickery. **juggler** *n.* one who juggles; a twister; a cheat. **jugglery** *n.* [O.Fr. *jogler*, to jest].

jug·u·lar (jug′·ya·ler) *a.* pert. to the neck or throat; *n.* one of the large veins of the neck [L. *jugulum*, the throat].

juice (jōōs) *n.* sap; the liquid constituent of fruits or vegetables; (*Slang*) gasoline or electricity. **juiciness** *n.* **juicy** *a.* [L. *jus*, broth].

ju·jit·su (jōō·jit′·sōō) *n.* a form of wrestling, originating in Japan. Also **jujutsu** [Jap.].

juke box (jōōk′·băks) *n.* (*Colloq.*) a coin operated phonograph.

ju·lep (jōō′·lap) *n.* a sweet drink, esp. one in which medicine is taken. **mint julep** [Pers. *gul*, rose; *ab*, water].

Jul·ian (jōōl′·yan) *a.* pert. to Julius Caesar. **Julian Calendar,** the calendar as adjusted by Julius Caesar in 46 B.C. in which the year was made to consist of 365 days, 6 hours.

ju·li·enne (jōō·li·en′) *n.* a clear soup containing vegetables finely shredded; *a.* of vegetables in thin strips [Fr.].

Ju·ly (joo·lī′) *n.* the seventh month of the year [fr. *mensis Julius*, month of Julius Caesar].

jum·ble (jum′·bl) *v.t.* to mix in a confused mass; *v.i.* to be in a muddle; *n.* a miscellaneous collection; a chaotic muddle [prob. from *jump* and *tumble*].

jum·ble (jum′·bl) *n.* a thin, sweet, sticky cake.

jum·bo (jum′·bō) *n.* a huge person, animal, or thing, esp. the famous elephant in the 1880's.

jump (jump) *v.t.* to spring over; to spring off; to skip (as page of a book); *v.i.* to lift feet from ground and alight again; to spring; *n.* a leap; a bound; a sudden, nervous start; *pl.* (*Colloq.*) nervousness. **-er** *n.* **-iness** *n.* nervous twitching. **-y** *a.* **-ing-bean** *n.* the seed of a Mexican plant containing larva which make it appear to jump [prob. imit.].

jum·per (jum′·er) *n.* a one-piece sleeveless dress [prob. fr. Fr. *jupe*, a petticoat].

junc·tion (jungk′·shan) *n.* the act of joining; the place or point of joining; a connection. **juncture** *n.* a joint; an exigency; a particular moment in the trend of affairs [L. *jungere*, to join].

June (jōōn) *n.* the sixth month of the year [L. *Junius*, the month of Juno].

jun·gle (jung′·gl) *n.* land covered with forest trees, tangled undergrowth, esp. the dense forests of equatorial latitudes. **— fever** *n.* a severe form of malaria [Hind. *jungal*, forest].

jun·ior (jōōn′·yer) *a.* younger, esp. of a son with the same name as his father; of lower status; *n.* a young person; the younger of two; a minor; one in a subordinate position; a student in the next to last year of study [L. compar. of *juvneis*, young].

ju·ni·per (jōō′·nạ·pẹr) *n.* a genus of evergreen coniferous shrub [L. *juniperus*].

junk (jungk) *n.* a flat-bottomed Chinese vessel [Port. *junco*, a boat].

junk (jungk) *n.* useless, discarded articles; pieces of old cordage used for oakum; (*Naut.*) hard, dry salted meat; *v.t.* to turn into junk. **—dealer, -man** *n.* one who buys and sells junk [L. *juncus*, a rush].

Jun·ker (yoong′·kẹr) *n.* a young German noble; a member of that reactionary political party in Prussia which stood for the landed interests of the aristocracy. **-ism** *n.* [Ger. *Junker*, a young noble].

jun·ket (jung′·kit) *n.* a dessert of milk curded with flavored rennet; a pleasure excursion; *v.i.* to feast; to picnic; to go on a pleasure trip; *v.t.* to entertain [L. *juncus*, a rush].

jun·ta (hoon′·tạ, jun′·tạ) *n.* a meeting; a council of state in Spain or Italy [Sp. *junta*, a committee].   [cabal [Sp. *junta*, a committee].

jun·to (jun′·tō) *n.* a group of conspirators; a

Ju·pi·ter (jōō′·pạ·tẹr) *n.* in Roman mythology, the supreme god and ruler of heaven. Also **Jove;** the largest and brightest of the outer planets [L. fr. *Jovis*, *pater*, father Jove].

ju·rid·i·cal (joo·rid′·ik·ạl) *a.* pert. to law, or the administration of justice. **-ly** *adv.* [L. *juridicus*, judicial].

ju·ris·dic·tion (joor·is·dik′·shạn) *n.* the administration of justice; legal authority; the limit or extent within which this authority may be exercised. **-al, jurisdictive** *a.* [L. *jus*, law; *dicere*, to say].

ju·ris·pru·dence (joor·is·prōō′·dạns) *n.* the science of law; the study of the fundamental principles underlying any legal system; a body of laws. **medical jurisprudence,** forensic medicine, study of medicine as it concerns criminal law [L. *jus*, law; *prudentia*, knowledge].   [*jus*, law].

ju·rist (joor′·ist) *n.* one versed in the law [L.

ju·ry (joor′·i·) *n.* a body of citizens selected and sworn to give a verdict from the evidence produced in court; a committee chosen to decide the winners in a competition. **juror** *n.* one who serves on a jury. **-man, -woman** [O.Fr. *jurée*, an oath].

jus·sive (jus′·iv) *a.* (*Gram.*) expressing a command; *n.* a grammatical form expressing a command [L. *jubere*, to command].

just (just) *a.* equitable; true; founded on fact; proper; fair; well-deserved; *adv.* exactly; closely; scarcely. **-ly** *adv.* in a just manner; deservedly; uprightly. **-ness** *n.* equity; fairness [L. *justus*, upright].

jus·tice (jus′·tis) *n.* the quality of being just; equity; merited reward or punishment; the administration of the law; a judge; a magistrate. **-ship** *n.* the office of a judge. **justiciary** *a.* pert. to the administration of the law. **Justice of the Peace** (J.P.), a local officer authorized to try minor cases, administer oaths, perform marriages, etc. [L. *justitia*, justice].

jus·ti·fy (jus′·tạ·fī) *v.t.* to prove the justice of; to vindicate; to excuse; to adjust. *pr.p.* **justifying.** *pa.p.* **justified. justifiable** *a.* defensible; excusable. **justifiableness** *n.* **justifiably** *adv.* **justification** *n.* vindication; (*Theol.*) absolution [L. *justificare*, to justify].

jut (jut) *v.i.* to project. *pr.p.* **-ting.** *pa.t.*, *pa.p.* **-ted** [a form of *jet*].

jute (jōōt) *n.* fiber of an Indian plant [Bengali fr. Sans. *juta*, a tress of hair].

Jutes (jōōts) *n.pl.* a Teutonic tribe [O.E. *Jote*].

ju·ve·nes·cent (jōō·vạn·es′·ạnt) *a.* becoming young. **juvenescence** *n.* [L. *juvenis*, young].

ju·ve·nile (jōō′·vạ·nīl, -nạl) *a.* young; youthful; puerile; *n.* a young person; a book written for children. **-ness, juvenility** *n.* **juvenilia** *n.pl.* works of author produced in childhood and early youth [L. *juvenilis*, youthful].

jux·ta·pose (juks·tạ·pōs′) *v.t.* to place side by side. **juxtaposition** *n.* the act of placing side by side; contiguity [L. *juxta*, near; *ponere*, to place].

K

ka·i·nite (kā′·nīt) *n.* hydrated compound of the chlorides and sulphates of magnesium and potassium [Gk. *kainos*, new].

Kai·ser (kī′·zẹr) *n.* the name derived from the Latin *Caesar*, given to the emperors of the Old Holy Roman Empire, and of the rulers of the German Empire. **-ship** *n.* [Ger.].

kale (kāl) *n.* colewort; a hardy member of the mustard family with curled leaves; [O.E. *cawel*, fr. L. *caulis*, a stalk].

ka·lei·do·scope (kạ·lī′·dạ·skōp) *n.* an optical instrument, varying symmetrical, colorful patterns being displayed on rotation. **kaleidoscopic** *a.* ever-changing in beauty and form; variegated [Gk. *kalos*, beautiful; *eidos*, form; *skopein*, to view].

kame (kāme) *n.* a high narrow ridge of gravel and sand left by a glacier.

ka·mi·ka·ze (kạ·ma·ká′·zi·) *n.* a suicide attack by Jap. pilot [Jap.].

kam·pong (kam·pawng′) *n.* a native Hawaiian; a native of any South Sea island [Hawaiian = a man].

kan·ga·roo (kang·gạ·rōō′) *n.* a ruminating marsupial found in Australia.

Kant·i·an (kan′·ti·ạn) *a.* pert. to the German philosopher, Immanuel Kant, or his school of philosophy.

ka·o·lin (kā′·ạ·lin) *n.* China clay; fine porcelain clay chiefly produced from feldspar in China, U.S.A. and Cornwall by weathering [Chin. *kaoling*, high hill].

ka·pok (kā·pák′) *n.* a silky white vegetable fiber used for stuffing and for sound insulation; W. Indian evergreen tree [Malay].

ka·put (kạ·poot′) *n.* (*Slang*) finished; no good; all over; done for [Ger.].

kar·at (kar′·ạt) *n.* in fineness of gold, a twenty-fourth part (pure gold being 24 karats fine) (Gk. *Keras*, horn].

kath·ode See **cathode.**

kat·i·on, cation (kat′·i·ạn) *n.* an electro-positive ion which, in electrolysis, travels towards the cathode; a neutral atom which in consequence of losing an electron, has a positive charge [Gk. *kata*, down; *ienai*, to go].

ka·ty·did (kā′·ti·did) *n.* a green insect of the grasshopper family [Imit.]

ka·va (ká′·vạ) *n.* an intoxicating Polynesian beverage [Hawaiian].

kay·ak (kī′·ak) *n.* the Eskimo seal-skin canoe, long, narrow and covered over.

keck (kek) *v.i.* to retch, as if about to vomit; to show disgust [imit. of the sound].

keck·le (kek′·l) *v.t.* to protect a cable or hawser from damage by fraying, by wrapping old rope, etc., round the length likely to be affected [etym. doubtful].

kedge (kej) *n.* a small anchor *v.t.* to warp, as a ship; to move a ship by means of small anchors and hawsers [Fr.].

keel (kēl) *n.* the length-wise beam of a ship on which the frames of the ship rest; hence, a ship; a similar part on some other structure; *v.i.* to turn up the keel; to provide with a keel **-haul** *v.t.* to haul under the keel of a ship by ropes attached to the yard-arms

to keel over, (*Collog.*) to fall over; to capsize [O.E. *ceol*, a ship].

keen (kēn) *a.* having a fine cutting edge; sharp; penetrating; piercing (of wind); eager; intense; acrimonious; caustic (tongue); shrewd; discerning. **-ly** *adv.* [O.E. *cene*].

keen (kēn) *n.* Irish dirge; *v.i.* to wail over the dead before burial [Ir. *caoine*].

keep (kēp) *v.t.* to retain possession of; to detain; to observe; to carry out; to have the care of; to maintain; to cause to continue; to reserve; to manage; to commemorate; *v.i.* to remain (in good condition); to continue; *pa.p., pa.t.* **kept** *n.* guardianship; maintenance; the chief tower or dungeon (donjon) of a castle; a stronghold. **-er** *n.* one who keeps or guards; an attendant; a gamekeeper; a finger-ring to prevent another from slipping off. **-ing** *n.* care; custody; support; harmony. **-sake** *n.* anything given to recall the memory of the giver [O.E. *cepan*].

keg (keg) *n.* a small barrel [O.N. *kaggi*, cask].

kelp [kelp] *n.* the calcined ash of certain seaweeds, used as a source of iodine; a general name for large sea-weeds [etym. unknown].

Kelt, Keltic Same as **Celt, Celtic.**

kelt (kelt) *n.* a salmon which has just spawned.

kemps (kemps) *n.pl.* coarse rough hairs in wool.

ken (ken) *n.* view; range of sight or knowledge [O.E. *cennan*, to know].

ken·nel (ken'·al) *n.* a house or shelter for dogs; an establishment where dogs are bred or lodged; the hole of a fox or other animal; a small hovel of a house; *v.t.* to confine in a kennel; *v.i.* to live in a kennel. *pr.p.* **-ling.** *pa.p.* **-led** [Fr. *chenil*, fr. L. *canis*, a dog].

ken·ning (ken'·ing) *n.* a descriptive, poetical name used in place of the usual name of a thing or person [Ice.].

kent·ledge (kent'·lij) *n.* pig iron placed in a ship's hold for permanent ballast.

kep·i (kep'·i·) *n.* a light military cap, flat-topped with a straight peak [Fr.].

kept (kept) *pa.t.* and *pa.p.* of **keep.**

ker·a·sine (ker'·a·sin) *a.* horny; [Gk. *keros*, a horn].

ker·at'(o)-, ker·at(a)) *prefix,* fr. Gk. *keras,* a horn, used in the formation of compound terms. **keratin** (ker'·a·tin) *n.* an essential constituent of horny tissue. **keratoid** *a.* horny. **keratosis** *n.* (*Med.*) a skin disease characterized by abnormal thickening.

ker·chief (kur'·chif) *n.* any cloth used in dress, esp. on the head or round the neck. **-ed** *a.* [Fr. *couvre-chef*, cover-head].

ker·mis, kermess (kur'·mis) *n.* a festival or fair in the Low Countries; (*U.S.*) a similar affair, usually for charitable purposes; originally a dedication service at the opening of a new church [Dut. *kerk*, church; *mis*, mass].

kern (kurn) *n.* (*Print.*) a part of the face of a type projecting beyond the body, as an italic *f* [L. *cardo*, hinge].

ker·nel (kur'·nal) *n.* the inner portion, the seed, of the stony endocarp of a drupe; the edible part of a nut; the body of a seed; central or essential part; the nucleus [O.E. *cyrnel*, dim. of *corn*].

ker·o·sene (ker'·a·sēn) *n.* an illuminating or burning oil [Gk. *kēros*, wax].

ker·sey (kur'·zi·) *n.* coarse woolen cloth, usually ribbed [*Kersey*, England].

ketch (ketch) *n.* a small two-masted vessel.

ketch·up, catch·up, cat·sup (kech'·ap) *n.* a sauce made from mushrooms, tomatoes or walnuts [Malay *kechap*].

ket·tle (ket'·l) *n.* a metal vessel, with spout and handle, used for heating and boiling water or other liquids; a cooking pot. **-drum** *n.* a musical percussion instrument made of a hemispherical copper shell covered with vellum. **-drummer** *n.* **a pretty kettle**

of fish, an awkward affair [O.N. *ketilla*].

key (kē) *n.* a low-lying island or reef near the coast, used esp. of Spain's former possessions off the coast of Florida [Sp. *cayo*, a reef].

key (kē) *n.* an instrument which shuts or opens a lock; an instrument by which anything is turned or opened; a spanner; the highest central stone of an arch; a lever in a musical instrument, depressed by the fingers in playing; a lever on a typewriter for actuating the mechanism; in engineering, a hand tool for valve control; a switch adapted for making and breaking contact in an electric circuit; in carpentry, a small piece of hardwood inserted in joints to prevent sliding; (*Mus.*) the keynote of a scale, or tonality; the pitch of a voice; solution or explanation; a translation of a book, esp. the classics, or solutions to questions set. *a.* critical; of vital importance; controlling. **-board** *n.* the whole range of keys on a keyed instrument. **-hole** *n.* a hole in a door or lock for receiving a key. **— industry,** an industry on which vital interests of the country or other industries depend. **— man** *n.* an indispensable employee. **-note** *n.* (*Mus.*) the first tone of the scale in which a passage is written; the essential spirit of speech, thought, etc.; the policy to be followed by a political party, etc., as set forth in an initial address. **— ring** *n.* a ring for keeping a number of keys together. **— signature** *n.* (*Mus.*) the essential sharps and flats placed at the beginning of a piece after the clef to indicate the tonality. **-stone** *n.* the wedge-shaped central stone at the crown of an arch; something on which other things depend. **all keyed up,** agog with excitement and expectation [O.E. *caeg*].

khak·i (ka'·ki·) *a.* dust-colored or buff; *n.* a cloth of this color, used for the uniforms of soldiers [Urdu = *dusty*].

khan (kán) *n.* a title of respect in various Mohammedan countries among Mongol races, a king, prince, or chief. **-ate** *n.* the dominion of a Khan [Pers. = a lord or prince].

khe·dive (ka·dēv') *n.* the title of the Turkish ruler of Egypt [Fr. fr. Pers. = prince].

kib·itz (kib'·its) *v.i.* (*Colloq.*) to act as a kibitzer. **-er** *n.* (*Colloq.*) a spectator of a game, esp. cards, who looks at a player's hand over his shoulder; someone who gives unwanted advice [G. *kiebitz*].

kib·lah, keb·lah (kib'·la, keb'·la) *n.* the point towards which Mohammedans turn their faces in prayer [Ar. *qiblah*].

ki·bosh (kī'·bàsh, ki·bàsh') *n.* (*Colloq.*) nonsense; rubbish. **to put the kibosh on,** to silence; to defeat; to make impossible.

kick (kik) *v.t.* to strike or hit with the foot; *v.i.* to strike out with the foot; (*Colloq.*) to resist; to recoil violently (of a rifle, etc.); *n.* a blow with the foot; the recoil of a gun; (*slang*) stimulation; (*Colloq.*) thrill (*Colloq.*) complaint. **-er** *n.* **-back** *n.* (*Colloq.*) a vigorous response; a portion of a worker's wages taken out by his supervisor. **-off** *n.* the commencement of a game of football. **to kick over the traces,** to throw off all restraint; to rebel openly. **to kick the bucket** (*Slang*) to die. **drop kick** *n.* (*football*) a kick made as the ball, just dropped from the hand, rebounds from the ground. **place kick** *n.* kicking a football placed or held on the ground [M.E. *kiken*, of unknown origin].

kid (kid) *n.* a young goat; leather made from the skin of a goat; (*Slang*) a child; *pl.* gloves of smooth kid leather; *a.* made of kid leather [O.N. *kith*].

kid (kid) *vt.* and *i.* (*Slang*) to tease; to fool. *pr.p.* **-ding.** *pa.p., pa.t.* **-ded.** *n.* teasing. **-der** *n.*

kid·nap (kid'·nap) *v.t.* to carry off, abduct, or forcibly secrete a person (esp. a child). **-er** *n.*

-ing *n.* [E.*kid*, a child; *nap*, to nab].

kid·ney (kid'·ni·) *n.* one of two glandular organs in the lumbar region of the abdominal cavity which excrete urine; animal kidney used as food; kind; temperament. — **bean,** the kidney-shaped seed of a bean plant.

kill (kil) *v.t.* to deprive of life; to slay; to put to death; to destroy; to neutralize; to weaken or dilute; to render inactive; to pass (time); *n.* the act or time of killing; the animal killed. **-er** *n.* **-er whale** *n.* the grampus, a whale capable of swallowing seals, porpoises, etc., whole. **-ing** *a.* depriving of life; very exhausting; fascinating; (*Colloq.*) exceedingly funny. *n.* the act of destroying life; game killed on a hunt; (*Colloq.*) a profitable business deal. **-ingly** *adv.*

kiln (kil, kiln) *n.* furnace or oven for burning, baking or drying something. —**dry** *v.t.* to dry in a kiln [L. *culina*, an oven].

ki·lo- *prefix* fr. Gk. *chilioi*, one thousand, in the metric system denoting a thousand. **-cycle** *n.* the unit for measuring vibrations, esp. the frequency of electromagnetic waves, 1000 cycles or oscillations per second. **-gram** *n.* 1000 grams, equal to 2.2046 lbs. avoirdupois. **-liter** *n.* 1000 liters. **-meter** *n.* 1000 meters, 3280.899 feet or nearly ⅝ of a mile. **-watt** *n.* an electric unit of power equal to 1000 watts. **-watt-hour,** *n.* one kilowatt expended for one hour, approximately 1.34 hp.

kilt (kilt) *n.* a short skirt usually of tartan cloth, deeply pleated, reaching from waist to knees [Dan. *kille*, to tuck up].

kim·bo (kim'·bō) *a.* crooked; bent; **akimbo.**

ki·mo·no (ka·mō'·na) *n.* a striped or flowered overgarment with short wide sleeves, worn in Japan by both men and women; a dressing-gown in imitation of this style [Jap.].

kin (kin) *n.* family relations; relationship; affinity; *a.* of the same nature or kind; kindred; akin. **next of kin,** the person or persons closest in relationship to a deceased person [O.E. *cynn*].

-kin (kin) *noun suffix,* used as a diminutive, e.g. *lambkin,* a little lamb.

kind (kīnd) *n.* genus; sort; variety; class; particular nature; *a.* having a sympathetic nature; considerate; good; benevolent; obliging. **-hearted** *a.* **-heartedness** *n.* **-liness** *n.* benevolence. **-ly** *a.* and *adv.* **-ness** *n.* kind feeling or action. [O.E. *gecynde,* nature].

kin·der·gar·ten (kin'·der·gar'·tn) *n.* a school for young children where they are taught by the organizing of their natural tendency to play [Ger. = children's garden].

kin·dle (kin'·dl) *v.t.* to set on fire; to light; to excite (the passions); to inflame; *v.i.* to catch fire; to become bright or glowing; to grow warm or animated. **kindling** *n.* the act of starting a fire; the material for starting a fire [O.N. *kynda*].

kin·dred (kin'·drad) *n.* relation by birth; affinity; relatives by blood or marriage; *a.* related; cognate; of like nature; congenial; similar [M.E. *kinrede*].

kine (kīn) *n.pl.* a plural form of **cows.**

kin·e·mat·ic, kin·e·mat·i·cal (kin·a·mat'·ik, ·i·kal) *a.* relating to pure motion. **-s** *n.pl.* the branch of mechanics dealing with problems of motion [Gk. *kinēma,* movement].

kin·es·the·si·a (kin·as·thē'·zha) *n.* muscle sense; the perception of muscular effort. **kinesthetic** *a.* Also **kinaesthesia, kinesthesis** [Gk. *kinein,* to move; *aisthēsia,* perception].

ki·net·ic, kinetical (ka·net'·ik, ·i·kal) *a.* relating to motion; imparting or growing out of motion. **-s** *n.* the science which treats of changes in movements of matter produced by forces [Gk. *kinein,* to move].

king (king) *n.* (*fem.* **queen**) supreme ruler of a country; a sovereign; a monarch; one who

is distinguished above all others of his compeers; a playing card in each suit with a picture of a king; the chief piece in the game of chess; in checkers, a man which is crowned. **-craft. -dom** *n.* realm; sphere; domain; one of the great divisions (animal, vegetable, and mineral) of Natural History. **-fisher** *n.* a stout-billed bird, with brilliant plumage. **-hood** *n.* kingship. **-let** *n.* a petty king; small bird **-like, -ly** *a.* **-pin** *n.* (*Fig.*) in bowling, the pin at the front apex when the pins are set up (*Fig.*) the most important person in a group. **-'s English,** correct English usage. [O.E. *cyning*].

kink (kingk) *n.* a short twist, accidentally formed, in a rope, wire, chain, etc.; in the neck, a cramp or crick; a mental twist; a whim; *v.i.* and *v.t.* to twist spontaneously; to form a kink (in).

kins·folk (kinz'·fōk) *n.* blood relations; kin; members of the same family; also **kinfolk. kinship** *n.* state or condition of being related by birth. **kinsman, kinswoman** *n.* [*kin*].

ki·osk (kē·ask') *n.* an open pavilion or summerhouse, supported by pillars; an erection, resembling a sentry box, for the sale of periodicals, candy, tobacco, etc.; a bandstand [Turk. *kioshk*].

kip (kip) *n.* the untanned hide of young cattle; a bundle of a definite number of hides.

kip·per (kip'·er) *n.* herring, salmon, etc. split, then smoked; *v.t.* to cure fish by splitting, salting, smoking, or drying.

kirk (kurk) *n.* (*Scot.*) a church building; the (Established) Church of Scotland [Scand.].

kis·met (kis'·met) *n.* fate or destiny [Ar.].

kiss (kis) *v.t.* and *v.i.* to touch with the lips, in affection or reverence; to touch gently; *n.* a salute by touching with lips. **-able** *a.* **-er** *n.* one who kisses; (*Slang*) the mouth. [O.E. *cyssan*].

kit (kit) *n.* a soldier's outfit, excluding his uniform; a set of tools or implements; personal effects; a wooden tub.

kitch·en (kich'·an) *n.* a room in which food is prepared and cooked. **-ette** *n.* a small kitchen. — **garden** *n.* a garden for raising vegetables for the table. — **police** (abbrev. (**K.P.**) soldiers on kitchen duty. **-ware** *n.* cooking utensils [L. *coquina,* a kitchen].

kite (kīt) *n.* bird of prey of Falcon family; a sheet of paper, silk, etc., stretched over a light frame and flown by means of a cord attached and held from ground [O.E. *cyta*].

kith (kith) *n.* in phrase **kith and kin,** friends and acquaintances [O.E. *cuththu*].

kit·ten (kit'·n) *n.* a young cat; *v.i.* to bring forth young cats. **-ish** *a.* like a kitten; playful. **kitty** *n.* a pet name for a cat [dim. of *cat*].

kit·ty (kit'·i·) *n.* the pool in card games; cards left over after a deal to be used as part of the game.

ki·wi (kē'·wē) *n.* a New Zealand flightless bird; the apteryx [imit. fr. its cry].

klang (klang) *n.* the sound of metal striking metal; a complex musical tone, consisting of a fundamental with its harmonics [Ger.].

klax·on (klak'·san) *n.* electric horn on motor cars. [Trade Name].

klep·to·ma·ni·a (klep·ta·mā'·ni·a) *n.* an uncontrollable impulse to steal or secrete things. **-c** *n.* [Gk. *kleptein,* to steal; *mania,* madness].

klick See **click.**

klieg eyes (klēg īz) *n.pl.* eye strain due to the excessive brilliancy of incandescent floodlighting lamps. **klieg light** *n.* a powerful incandescent lamp used in film studios for floodlighting [proper name].

knack (nak) *n.* inborn dexterity; adroitness; mannerism; habit [etym. uncertain].

knag (nag) *n.* a knot in wood; *a.* knotty;

rough [M.E. *knagge*, a knot in wood].

knap·sack (nap'·sak) *n.* a bag for food and clothing, borne on the back; a rucksack [Dut. *knapzak*].

knar (nar) *n.* a knot in a tree or in timber. [Dut. *knorf.* knot].

knave (nāv) *n.* a dishonest person; a rascal; (*Cards*) a jack. **-ry** *n.* roguery; trickery; sharp practice. **knavish** *a.* fraudulent; mischievous; roguish. **knavishly** *adv.* [O.E. *cnafa*, a boy. Cf. Ger. *Knabe*, a boy].

knead (nēd) *v.t.* to work dough by pressing with the heel of the hands, and folding over; to work or shape anything by pressure; to massage. **-er** *n.* [O.E. *cnedan*].

knee (nē) *n.* the joint formed by the articulation of the femur and the tibia, the two principal bones of the leg; a similar joint or region in other vertebrates; part of a garment covering the knee; *v.t.* to touch with the knees. — **breeches** *n.pl.* breeches reaching and fastened just below the knee. **-cap** *n.* the patella, a flattened bone in front of knee joint; a covering to protect the knees, esp. of horses. [O.E. *cneow*].

kneel (nēl) *v.i.* to bend a knee to the floor; to fall on the knees; to rest on the knees as in prayer. *pa.t.* and *pa.p.* **-ed** or **knelt. -ing** *n.* [fr. *knee*].

knell (nel) *n.* the stroke of a bell rung at a funeral or death; a death signal; a portent of doom; *v.i.* to toll; *v.t.* to summon by tolling bell [E. *cnyll*].

knew (nū) *pa.t.* of **know.**

knick·er·bock·ers (nik'·er·bak'·erz) *n.pl.* loose breeches gathered in at the knees. Also **knickers** [fr. the pseudonym of Washington Irving].

knick-knack (nik'·nak) *n.* a trifle, toy, or trinket. **-ery** *n.* knick-knacks collectively [reduplication of *knack*].

knife (nīf) *n.pl.* **knives** (nīvz) a cutting instrument; *v.t.* to stab with a knife. — **edge** *n.* the sharp edge of a knife; anything with a thin, sharp edge [O.E. *cnif*].

knight (nīt) *n.* orig. in feudal times, a young man admitted to the privilege of bearing arms; a minor piece in chess bearing a horse's head; *v.t.* to dub or create a knight. —**errant** *n.* a knight who wandered about in search of adventures. —**errantry** *n.* **-hood** *n.* the dignity or order of knights. **-liness** *n.* **-ly** *a.* and *adv.* [O.E. *cniht*, youth].

knit (nit) *v.t.* to form fabric by the interlooping of yarn or thread by means of needles or a machine; to cause to grow together, as a fractured bone; to contract (the brows); to unite closely; *v.i.* to be united closely. *pr.p.* **-ting** *pa.t.* and *pa.p.* **-ted. -ter** *n.* **-ting** *n.* **-wear** *n.* knitted garments [O.E. *cynttan*].

knives (nīvz) pl. of **knife.**

knob (nab) *n.* a rounded lump; a hard protuberance or swelling; a boss or stud; small round handle of a door, etc.; a rounded hill. **-bed** *a.* set with or containing knobs. **-biness** *n.* **-by** *a.* full of knobs; lumpy. [M.E. *knop*].

knock (nak) *v.t.* and *v.i.* to strike or beat with something hard or heavy; to strike against; to rap; to make a periodic noise, due to a faulty bearing in a reciprocating engine or to pinking in a gasoline engine; (*Colloq.*) to disparage, to criticize adversely; *n.* a stroke with something heavy; a rap on a door; a blow; the noise of a faulty engine. **-er** *n.* one who knocks; an ornamental metal attachment on a door. —**kneed** *a.* having the knees bent inward. **-out** *n.* (*Slang*) something or someone overwhelmingly attractive; a blow in a boxing match which knocks out an adversary [O.E. *cnocian*].

knoll (nōl) *n.* a small rounded hill; the top of a hill; a hillock; a mound [O.E. *cnoll*].

knoll Same as **knell.**

knot (nat) *n.* a complication of threads, cords, or ropes, formed by tying or entangling; in cordage, a method of fastening a rope to an object or to another rope; an epaulet; ribbon folded in different ways; a bond of union; a small group (of people or things); a difficulty; a hard lump, esp. of wood where a branch has sprung from the stem; (*Bot.*) a node in a grass stem; (*Naut.*) a measure of speed of ships, equal to one nautical mile (6,080 ft.) per hour; *v.t.* to form a knot in; *v.i.* to form knots. *pr.p.* **-ting.** *pa.t. pa.p.* **-ted. -hole** *n* a hole in a board where a piece of a knob has fallen out. **-tiness** *n.* **-ty** *a.* full of knots; difficult; puzzling [O.E. *cnotta*].

knout (nout) *n.* a whip consisting of leather, thongs, [Russ. *knut*, a whip].

know (nō) *v.t.* to be aware of; to have information about; to have fixed in the mind; to be acquainted with; to recognize; to have experience; to understand; to have sexual intercourse with; *v.i.* to have information or understanding. *pa.t.* **knew** (nū). *pa.p.* **-n.** **-ing** *a.* professing to know; shrewd; deliberate; clever. **-ingly** *adv.* **to know the ropes,** to know from experience what to do [O.F. *cnawan*].

know·ledge (nal'·ij) *n.* direct perception; understanding; acquaintance with; practical skill; information; learning. **-able** *a.* well informed [E. *know*].

knuck·le (nuk'·l) *n.* the joint of a finger; the knee-joint of a calf or pig; *v.t.* to strike with the knuckles; *v.i.* to hold the knuckles close to the ground in the game of marbles. **brass knuckle** *n.pl.* iron or brass rings fitting across the knuckles, used to deliver murderous blows. **to knuckle down,** to tackle a job vigorously. **to knuckle down** or **under,** to yield or submit [M.E. *knokel*].

knurl (nurl) *n.* a series of ridges or rough indentations on the edge of a thumbscrew, coin, etc.; *v.t.* to roughen edges of a circular object; to mill; to indent. **-ed.** *a.*

ko·a·la (kō·à'·la) *n.* a small marsupial of arboreal habit, native to Australia [Aborig].

Ko·dak (ko·dak) *n.* (an arbitrarily coined word) a trademark for photographic film, apparatus and supplies (orig. a small hand camera).

kohl (kōl) *n.* powdered antimony or lead sulfide used in the East for darkening eyebrows and eyelashes [Ar.]

kohl·ra·bi (kōl'·rà·bi·) *n.* a variety of cabbage with an edible turnip-shaped stem [Ger.].

ko·la (kō'·la) *n.* an African tree whose seeds or nuts contain a large quantity of caffeine and are used as a stimulant [Native].

ko·lin·sky (ka·lin'·ski·) *n.* Siberian polecat or mink; its fur [*Kola Peninsula*].

kood·doo (kóó'·dòò) *n.* the striped antelope of Africa. Also **kudu** [S. Afr.].

kook·a·bur·ra (kook'·a·ber'·a) *n.* the great kingfisher with a laugh-like cry [Austral.].

Koran (ka·ràn', kō'·ran) *n.* sacred book of Islam, containing revelations received by Mohammed. [Ar. *quaran*, reading].

ko·sher (kō'·sher) *a.* (of food) pure, clean, esp. meat, made ceremonially clean according to Jewish ordinances [Heb. *kasher*, proper].

kow·tow, kotow (kou'·tou) *v.i.* to perform the Chinese ceremony of prostration; to abase oneself; to fawn on someone [Chin.].

kraal (kral) *n.* a Hottentot or Kaffir village consisting of a group of huts encircled by a stockade [Dut. fr. Port. *curral*, a cattlepen].

kra·sis (krā'·sis) *n.* mixture of wine and water used for the Eucharist [Gk.].

krem·lin (krem'·lin) *n.* the citadel of a Russian town or city; (*cap.*) the citadel of Moscow, the seat of Soviet government [Russ.].

kreut·zer (kroit'·zer) *n.* an old German coin: a modern Austrian monetary unit.

Krish·na (krish′·na̞) *n.* in Hinduism the last incarnation of Vishnu [Sans.].

kro·ne (krōn′·e) *n.* a silver coin of Denmark and Norway; *pl.* **kroner.** Also an old coin of Austria and Germany. *pl.* **kronen.**

kryp·ton (krip′·tàn) *n.* a non-metallic chemical element belonging to the group of rare-gases, present in the proportion of about one part in twenty mililons in the atmosphere [Gk. *kruptein,* to conceal].

ku·dos (kū′·dàs) *n.* fame; glory; credit [Gk.].

ku·du Same as **koodoo.**

Ku Klux Klan (kū′·kluks-klan) *n.* a lawless secret society, founded c. 1865, to oppose granting of privileges to the freed Negroes [Gk. *kuklos,* a circle].

ku·lak (kòò′·làk) *n.* a prosperous land holder in Russia who resisted the efforts of the Soviet to nationalize agriculture [Russ. = a fist, a forestaller].

kum·mel (kim′·al) *n.* a liqueur flavored with cumin and caraway seeds [Ger. = caraway].

kum·quat (kum′·kwàt) *n.* a shrub, native to China and Japan, producing a small orange-like fruit [Chinese = a golden orange].

Kuo·min·tang (kwŏ′·min·tàng) *n.* political party in China, founded by Sun Yat Sen.

ky·pho·sis (kì·fŏ′·sis) *n.* humpback, angular deformity of the spine [Gk.].

kyr·i·e (kir′·i·ē) *n.* the words and music of part of the service in the R.C. Church; the response in the Anglican communion service after each of the Ten Commandments [Gk.].

L

la (là) *n.* (*Mus.*) syllable for sixth tone of scale in tonic sol-fa notation.

lab·da·num (lab·da̞·nam) *n.* a fragrant resin used in perfumes, etc. [Also **ladanum** [Gk. *ladanon*].

la·bel (lā′·bal) *n.* paper, card, etc., affixed to anything, denoting its contents, nature, ownership, destination, etc.; (*Fig.*) a classifying phrase or word applied to persons, etc.; (*Archit.*) a dripstone; *v.t.* to affix a label to; to identify by a label [O.Fr. *label,* a strip].

la·bel·lum (la̞·bel′·am) *n.* the posterior petal of a flower of the orchid type [L. *labellum,* a small lip].

la·bi·al (lā′·bi·al) *a.* pert. to the lips; formed by the lips, as certain speech sounds such as *p, b, w, o; n.* a sound formed by the lips. **-ize** *v.t.* to give a labial character to a sound. **labiate, -d** *n.* (*Bot.*) with calyx or corolla formed in two parts, resembling lips [L. *labium,* lip].

la·bi·o·den·tal (lā′·bi·ō·den′·tal) *a.* pert. to the lips and teeth; *n.* a sound made with the lips and teeth, as *f* and *v.* **labium** *n.* a lip or lip-like structure. *pl.* **labia** [L. *labium,* a lip].

la·bor (lā′·ber) *n.* exertion of body or mind; toil; work demanding patience and endurance; manual workers collectively or politically; (*Med.*) the pains of childbirth; *v.i.* to work strenuously; to take pains; to move with difficulty; (*Med.*) to suffer the pains of childbirth; (*Naut.*) to pitch and roll. **-ious** *a.* toilsome; industrious. **-iously** *adv.* **-iousness** *n.* **-ed** *a.* **-er** *n.* — **union** *n.* an organization of workers for mutual aid and protection and for collective bargaining [L. *labor,* work].

lab·o·ra·to·ry (lab′·ra̞·tŏr·i·) *n.* a placed used for experiments or research in science, pharmacy, etc., or for manufacture of chemicals in industry (*Colloq.* abbrev. **lab.**) [L. *laborare,* to work].

la·bret (lā′·bret) *n.* an ornament inserted into a hole pierced in the lip, worn by some primitive tribes. **labral** *a.* **labrose** *a.* having thick lips. **labrum** *n.* a liplike structure. *pl.* **labra** [L. *labrum,* a lip].

la·bur·num (la̞·bur′·nam) *n.* a small, hardy deciduous tree [L.].

lab·y·rinth (lab′·a̞·rinth) *n.* a system of intricate winding passages; a maze; (*Med.*) the intricate passages of the internal ear. **-ian, -ine** *a.*: [Gk. *laburinthos,* a maze].

lac, lakh (lak) *n.* one hundred thousand, as a *lac of rupees* [Hind. *lakh,* 100,000].

lac (lak) *n.* a deep-red resinous substance, the excretion of an insect, found specially on trees in southern Asia, and used as a dye, in varnishes, sealing wax, etc. **seed-lac** *n.* the resinous substance cleared from twigs, etc. **shell-lac, shellac** *n.* the resin melted and cleared of impurities [Hind. *lakh,* 100,000].

lace (lās) *n.* a string or cord used for fastening dress, shoes, etc.; a net-like fabric of linen, cotton or silk with ornamental design interwoven by hand or machine; a tissue of silver or gold threads used as trimming; *v.t.* to fasten with a lace; to ornament with lace; to mix, as coffee, with a dash of brandy; *v.i* to be fastened with a lace. **lacing** *n.* a fastening formed by a lace threaded through eyeholes; a trimming of lace; (*Colloq.*) a thrashing. **lacy** *a.* [O.Fr. *las,* a noose].

lac·er·ate (las′·e̞·rāt) *v.t.* to tear; to rend; to injure; to afflict sorely. **-d** *a.* torn; mangled. **laceration** *n.* [L. *lacerare,* to tear].

lach·ry·mal (lak′·ra̞·mal) *a.* pert. to or producing tears, as *lachrymal duct,* the tear duct; *n.* one of the tear glands; a small vessel, in ancient graves, supposed to contain tears of the bereaved [L. *lacrima,* a tear].

lack (lak) *v.t.* and *v.i.* to be destitute of; to want; *n.* deficiency; shortage; need; want. **-luster** *a.* dim; wanting in brightness; *n.* dimness [M.Dut. *lak,* deficiency].

lack·a·dai·si·cal *a.* affectedly pensive or languid [abbrev. of *Alack-a-day*].

lack·ey (lak′·i·) *n.* a liveried manservant; a footman; a follower; *v.t.* or *v.i.* to attend or serve as a lackey. Also **lacquey** [O.Fr. *laquais*].

la·con·ic (la̞·kàn′·ik) *a.* brief; concise; expressing maximum meaning in the minimum of words. Also **-al, -ally** *adv.* **laconism** *n.* a brief, pithy style of speech; terse, sententious saying [Gk. *lakōn,* Spartan].

lac·quer, lacker (lak′·e̞r) *n.* a varnish consisting of a solution of shellac in alcohol; *v.t.* to cover with a film of lacquer; to varnish [Fr. *lacre,* a kind of sealing-wax].

la·crosse (la̞·kraws′) *n.* an outdoor ball game played with a *crosse* or stick which has a net at the end [Fr. *la crosse,* the crook].

lac·te·al (lak·ti·al) *a.* pert. to milk; milky; resembling chyle; *n.* an absorbent vessel conveying chyle from the intestines to the thoracic duct. **lactate** *n.* (*Chem.*) a salt of lactic acid; *v.i.* to produce milk. **lactation** *n.* the act of giving or secreting milk; the period during which a mother suckles her child. **lacteous** *a.* resembling milk. **lactic** *a.* pert. to milk; procured from milk or whey, as *lactic acid.* **lactose** *n.* milk-sugar [L. *lacteus,* milky].

la·cu·na (la·kū′·na̞) *n.* a hollow; a hiatus; an omission. *pl.* **lacunae** [L. *lacuna,* a pit].

lad (lad) *n.* (*fem.* **lass**) a young man; a boy [M.E. *ladde,* a serving-man].

lad·der (lad′·e̞r) *n.* a frame of wood, steel, ropes, etc., consisting of two sides connected by rungs for climbing; anything resembling a ladder; a means of ascent [O.E. *hlaeder*].

lade (lād) *v.t.* to load; to burden; to draw (fluid) by means of a ladle. *pa.t.* **-d.** *pa.p.* **-n. lading** *n.* the act of loading; freight [O.E. *hladan,* to load].

la·dle (lā'·dl) n. a long-handled spoon; v.t. to draw off with a ladle [O.E. *hladan*, to lade].

la·dy (lā'·di·) n. a well-bred woman; orig. a woman having authority over a household or estate; a woman of social distinction, position; a polite term for any woman. pl. **ladies. Lady** n. (*Brit.*) the title given to the wife of any nobleman ranking below a duke; the title of the daughter of a duke, marquis, or earl; the courtesy title of the wife of a knight or baronet. **-bird** n. a small spotted beetle. **-finger** n. a finger-shaped cake. — **in waiting** n. a lady appointed to attend a queen or princess. **-ish** a. affecting the airs of a lady. **—killer** n. (*Slang*) a man who imagines he has a fascination to women. **-like** a. **-love** n. a sweetheart. **-ship** n. the title of a lady [O.E. *hlaefdige*, a kneader of bread].

lag (lag) v.t. to bind round, as pipes, boiler, etc., with non-conducting material to prevent loss of heat; n. piece of lagging material [Scand. *lög*, a barrel stave].

lag (lag) n. time lapse; retardation; v.i. to move slowly; to fall behind. pr.p. **-ging.** pa.p. **-ged. -gard** n. a listless person. **-ger** n. **-ging** a. loitering. **-gingly** adv. [Celt.].

lag (lag) n. (*Colloq.*) a convict [etym. unknown]

la·ger-beer (là'·ger-bēr) n. a light German beer [Ger. *lager*, a store; *Bier*, beer].

la·goon (la·gōon') n. a shallow pond or lake; a lake in a coral atoll [It. *laguna*].

la·ic (lā'·ik) a. lay; secular; n. a layman. **-ally** adv. **-ize** (lā·a·sīz) v.t. to secularize; to render lay or laic [Gk. *laos*, the people].

laid (lād) pa.t. and pa.p. of the verb **lay;** a. put down; (of paper) having a slightly ribbed surface showing the marks of the close parallel wires on which pulp was laid. — **up,** indisposed; (*Naut.*) dismantled; temporarily out of service, for repairs [Fr. verb *lay*].

lain (lān) pa.p. of verb **lie.**

lair (lār) n. a den or bed of a wild animal; a place to rest. v.t. and v.i. to place or lie in a lair [O.E. *leger*, a bed].

lais·sez-faire (les'·ā·fār') n. a policy of non-interference. Also **laisser-faire** [Fr. *laissez-faire*, 'let do.'].   [from the clergy [See **lay**].

la·i·ty (lā'·a·ti·) n. the people, as distinct

lake (lāk) n. a large sheet of water within land. [O.E. *lac*, a lake].

lake (lāk) n. a deep-red coloring matter [Fr. *laque*]. [See **lac**].

lakh Same as **lac**. [100,000].

lam (lam) v.t. (*Slang*) to beat; to flog [Scand. *lamu*, to beat].

lam (lam) n. (*Slang*) hasty escape; v.i. to run off quickly.

la·ma (là'·ma) n. a Buddhist priest in Tibet. **Lamaism** n. form of Buddhist religion practiced in Tibet. **Dalai-Lama** n. or **Grand Lama,** the chief of the lamas [Tib. *blama*, a spiritual teacher].

lamb (lam) n. the young of a sheep; the flesh of lamb as food; a young and innocent person; v.i. to bring forth lambs. **-kin** n. a little lamb. **-like** a. gentle. **-skin** n. [O.E. *lamb*, a lamb].

lam·baste (lam·bāst') v.t. (*Slang*) to beat or scold severely.

lam·bent (lam'·bant) a. playing on the surface; gleaming; flickering; playing lightly and gracefully over a subject; said of wit. **lambency** n. [L. *lambere*, to lick].

lame (lām) a. crippled in a limb; hobbling; (*Fig.*) unsatisfactory, as an excuse; imperfect; v.t. to cripple. — **duck** n. (*Colloq.*) formerly, a Congressman serving at the last session of his term; temporarily disabled. **-ly** adv. **-ness** n. **-ish** a. rather lame [O.E. *lama*].

lamé (la·mā') n. a textile containing metal threads giving a gold or silver effect [Fr.].

la·mel·la (la·mel'·a) n. a thin plate-like structure or scale. pl. **lamellae. lamellar, lamel-**

late a. composed of thin plates or scales. [L. *lamella*, a thin plate].

la·ment (la·ment') v.i. to utter cries of sorrow; to bemoan; to mourn for; v.t. to deplore; n. a heartfelt expression of sorrow; an elegy or dirge. **lamentable** (lam'·an·ta·bl) a. grievous; sad. **lamentably** adv. **-ation** n. the act of lamenting; audible expression of grief. **Book of Lamentations** (*Bib.*) one of the poetical books of the Old Testament. **-ed** a. mourned. **-ing** a. grieving. **-ingly** adv. [L. *lamentari*, to wail].

lam·i·na (lam'·a·na) n. a thin plate or scale lying over another; (*Bot.*) the blade of a leaf. pl. **laminae. laminable, laminar, laminary** a. consisting of, or resembling, thin plates. **laminate** v.t. to cause to split into thin plates; to make into thin layers (as metal); to cover with one layer or build up with many layers; v.i. to split into layers. **laminate, -d** a. formed of thin plates; stratified. **lamination** n. [L. *lamina*, a thin plate].

lamp (lamp) n. a vessel containing combustible oil to be burned by a wick, or inflammable gas from a jet; any light-giving contrivance. **-black** n. a fine soot formed by the smoke of burning gas, oil, etc.; the pigment from this soot [Gk. *lampas*, a torch].

lam·poon (lam·pōon') n. a bitter personal satire, usually in verse; abusive or scurrilous publication; v.t. to abuse in written satire. **-er** n. **-ery** n. [O.Fr. *lampon*, a drinking song].

la·nate (lā'·nāt) a. wooly; (*Bot.*) covered with fine hairs resembling wool [L. *lama*, wool].

lance (lans) n. a former war weapon consisting of a spearhead on a long wooden shaft; the soldier armed with a lance; a lancet; v.t. to pierce with a lance; to open with a lancet. **-r** n. a cavalry soldier armed with a lance; pl. a square dance, like quadrilles. **lancet** n. a small two-edged surgical knife. **lancet arch** n. narrow, pointed arch. **a free lance,** one who acts on his own initiative; a journalist not attached to the staff of any particular newspaper [O.Fr. *lance*, a light spear].

lan·ci·nate (lan'·sa·nāt) v.t. to tear; to lacerate [L. *lancinare*, to tear].

land (land) n. earth; the solid matter of surface of globe; any area of the earth; ground; soil; the inhabitants of a country; real estate; v.t. to set on shore; to bring to land; (*Colloq.*) to gain; to catch; v.i. to go on shore; to disembark; (*Aero.*) to bring an aircraft to rest on land or water. — **breeze** n. an off-shore current or air. **-ed** a. pert. to, or possessing, real estate. **-fall** n. sighting of land by a ship at sea. — **grant** n. a grant of land from the government esp. for colleges, railroads, etc. **—grant college** n. a college supported with the aid of such grants according to the Morrill Acts (1862, 1890). **-holder** n. a proprietor of land. **-ing** n. the act of coming to land; disembarkation; the level part of a staircase between two flights of steps; the place where passengers land. **-ing gear** n. the wheeled under-carriage of an airplane on which it rests when landing or taking off. **-ing net** n. a net used by anglers for landing a fish already caught by rod. **-lady** n. the owner of property who leases land, buildings, etc. to tenants; one who lets rooms in a house; the proprietress of an inn. **-locked** a. enclosed by land. **-lord** n. the owner of houses rented to tenants; the proprietor of an inn, etc. **-lubber** n. a landsman (term used by sailors); one who knows little or nothing about boats. **-mark** n. a mark to indicate a boundary; any outstanding or elevated object indicating general direction or distinguishing a particular locality. — **mine** n. military high-explosive bomb. — **office** n. a government office for business concerning public lands. **-scape** n. that portion of land which the eye can comprehend in a single view; a pictorial representation of an actual or imagined inland scene. **-scape architecture** n. art of aesthetically arranging or changing features of the landscape. **-scape gardener,** one who is employed professionally to lay out gardens, etc. **-scapist** n. a painter of landscape. **-slide** n. a fall of rock from a hillside or cliff; (*Fig.*) a sudden overwhelming victory [O.E. *land,* land].

lan·dau (lan'·daw) n. a carriage, the top of which may be opened and thrown back. **landaulet, landaulette** n. an automobile with folding hood [fr. *Landau* (in Germany)].

land·grave (land'·grāv) n. a German nobleman [Ger. *Land,* land; *Graf,* a count].

lane (lān) n. a narrow track between hedges or across fields; a narrow street or road; a specified route followed by ships or airplanes; part of a street or highway for one line of traffic [O.E. *lane,* an alley].

lan·guage (lang'·gwij) n. speech; expression of ideas by words or written symbols; mode of speech peculiar to a nation, a class, profession, etc.; communication of animals, etc. or by any means. **dead language,** a language not spoken now, as opposed to *living language* [Fr. *langue,* language].

lan·guid (lang'·gwid) a. indifferent; listless; flagging from exhaustion. **-ly** adv. **-ness** n. **languish** v.i. to become languid; to droop with weariness; to pine or suffer; to become wistful. **-ing** a. drooping; sentimental. **-ingly** adv. **-ment** n. **languor** n. lassitude; sentimental softness [L. *languere,* to be weary].

lan·gur (lung'·gòòr) n. a long-tailed Indian monkey [Hind.].

lank (langk) a. drooping; gaunt and thin; long and straight, as hair. **-y** a. tall and slender. **-ly** adv. **-ness, -iness** n. [O.E. *hlanc,* lean].

lon·o·lin, lanoline (lan'·a·lin) n. an oily substance obtained from wool [L. *lana,* wool; *oleum,* oil].

lan·tern (lan'·tern) n. something portable or fixed, enclosing a light and protecting it from wind, rain, etc.; a little dome over a roof to give light; a square turret placed over the junction of the cross in a cathedral, with windows in each side of it; the light chamber of a lighthouse. **— jaws** n. hollow cheeks. **Chinese lantern,** a colored, collapsible paper lantern. **magic lantern,** an instrument by means of which magnified images of small objects or pictures are thrown on a screen in a dark room [Fr. *lanterne,* a lamp].

lan·yard, laniard (lan'·yerd) n. a short rope or line for fastening; a cord, with knife attached, worn round the neck [Fr. *lanière,* a rope].

La·od·i·ce·an (lā·a·da·sē'·an) a. like the Christians of *Laodicea;* lukewarm in religion; lacking strong feeling on any subject; (Rev. 3) ([fr. *Laodicea*].

lap (lap) n. that part of the clothing between waist and knees of a person who is sitting; the part of the body thus covered; an overlying part of any substance or fixture; a course or circuit, as in bicycle-racing, etc.; that in which anything rests or is fostered as the *lap of luxury;* v.t. to lay over or on; v.i. to be spread or laid on or partly over; to be turned over or on; to lie upon and extend beyond. **-el** n. that part of a coat or dress which laps over the facing. **-ped** a. **-ful** n. that which fills a lap. **-pet** n. a part of a garment which hangs loose; a fold of flesh. **-peted** a. [O.E. *laeppa,* loosely].

lap (lap) v.i. to take up food or drink by licking; to make a sound like an animal lapping its food; v.t. to lick up; to wash or flow against. pr.p. **-ping.** pa.p. **-ped.** n. the act or sound of lapping; something lapped up [O.E. *lapian,* to drink].

la·pel See **lap.**

lap·i·dar·y (lap'·a·der·i·) a. pert. to stones or to the art of cutting stones; pert. to inscriptions and monuments; n. one who is skilled in the cutting, polishing and engraving of precious stones. **lapidate** v.t. to stone (to death). **lapillus** n. a small rounded fragment of lava. pl. **lapilli, lapis lazuli** n. an opaque mineral, sapphire-blue in color, much used in jewelry, ornaments, mosaics, etc. [L. *lapis,* a stone].

Lapp (lap) n. a native of Lapland. Also **Laplander. Laplandish, Lappish** a.

lapse (laps) v.i. to slip or fall; to fail to maintain a standard of conduct; to pass from one proprietor to another because of negligence; to pass slowly or by degrees; n. a slip or fall; a gliding; a passing of time; an error of omission; failure to do one's duty; (*Law*) termination of legal possession through negligence. **lapsable** a. **-d** a. no longer valid or operative; [L. *lapsus,* a fall].

lar·ce·ny (lár'·san·i·) n. theft. **larcenist** n. a thief. **larcenous** a. thieving; pilfering [O.Fr. *larrecin,* theft].

larch (lárch) n. a genus of cone-bearing deciduous tree [L. *larix*].

lard (lárd) n. the clarified fat of swine; v.t. to smear with fat; to stuff, as meat or fowl, with bacon or pork; (*Fig.*) to embellish, as to *lard one's speech with metaphors.* **-aceous** a. fatty. **-y** a. [L. *lardum,* the fat of bacon].

lard·er (lár'·der) n. a pantry where meat and food stuffs are kept; supply of provisions [O.Fr. *lardier,* a bacon tub].

large (lárj) a. of great size; spacious; extensive; liberal; numerous; extravagant; adv. in a large way. **-hearted** a. generous; liberal. **-ly** adv. **-ness** n. bigness [L. *largus,* abundant].

lar·gess (lár'·jes) n. a generous gift; a donation. Also **largesse** [L. *largiri,* to give freely].

lar·ghet·to (lár·get'·ō) a. (*Mus.*) rather slow; less slow than *largo.* **largo** (*Mus.*) a. and adv. slow and stately [It. *largo,* slow].

lar·i·at (lar'·i·at) n. a lasso; a rope or thong of leather, with a noose for catching wild horses, etc. [Sp. *la reata,* the rope].

lark (lárk) n. a frolic; a prank; v.i. to play practical jokes [O.E. *lac,* play].

lark (lárk) n. a small songbird. **-spur** n. the delphinium [M.E. *laverock,* a lark].

lar·rup (lar'·ap) v.t. (*Colloq.*) to thrash. **-er** n. [Dut. *larpen,* to beat].

lar·va (lár·va) n. an insect in the caterpillar, grub, or maggot stage. pl. **larvae. -l** a. [L. *larva,* a ghost].

lar·ynx (lar'·ingks) n. the upper part of the trachea or windpipe; a cartilaginous cavity containing the vocal cords. pl. **-es, larynges** (·in·jēz). **laryngeal, laryngal** a. pert. to the larynx. **laryngitis** n. inflammation of the larynx. **laryngoscope** n. a special mirror for examining the larynx [Gk. *larunx,* the throat].

las·civ·i·ous (la·siv'·i·as) a. loose; lustful; wanton. **-ly** adv. **-ness** n. [L. *lascivus,* wanton].

lash (lash) n. the thong of a whip; a cord; a stroke with a whip; a satirical or sarcastic reproof; an eyelash; v.t. to strike with a lash; to dash against, as waves; to bind with a rope; to scourge with bitter criticism; v.i. to ply the whip. **-ing** n. the act of whipping; the ropes fastening anything securely [etym. doubtful].

lass (las) n. a young woman; a girl; a sweetheart. **lassie** n. a little girl [prob. Scand.].

las·si·tude (las'·a·tūd) n. exhaustion of body or mind; languor [L. *lassus,* faint].

las·so (las'·ō) n. a long rope with a noose, used for catching wild horses; a lariat. pl. **-s, es** v.t. to catch with the lasso [Sp. fr. L. *laqueus,* a noose].

last (last) a. following all the rest; most recent; most unlikely; final; supreme; adv. finally; immediately before in time; in conclusion; n. the end. **-ly** *adv.* **the Last Supper,** the memorial supper celebrated by Jesus on the eve of his betrayal. **at last,** finally [contr. of *latest*.]

last (last) *n.* a model of the human foot in wood on which shoes are made or repaired; *v.t.* to fit with a last [O.E. *last*, a trace or track].

last (last) *v.i.* to continue in time; to endure; to remain unimpaired in strength or quality; to suffice. **-ing** *a.* durable; permanent [O.E. *laestan*, to continue on a track].

las·tex (las'·teks) *n.* a fine rubber thread wound with cotton, rayon, or silk and woven into cloth or knitted into fabrics [coined word].

lat·a·ki·a (lat·a·kē'·a) *n.* a superior quality of Turkish tobacco from *Latakia* in Syria.

latch (lach) *n.* a small piece of iron or wood used to fasten a door; a catch; *v.t.* to fasten with a latch. **-key** *n.* a key used for raising the latch of a door; a pass-key [O.E. *laeccan*, to catch].

late (lāt) *a.* behindhand; coming after; delayed; earlier than the present time; occurring at the close of a period of time; no longer in office; deceased; *adv.* after the usual time; not long ago; far into the night, day, week, etc. **-ly** *adv.* **-ness** *n.* tardiness. **-r** *a.* (comp. of *late*) subsequent; posterior. **-st** *a.* (superl. of *late*) longest after the usual time; most recent or up-to-date, as news. **latter** (lat'·ẹr) *a.* (var. of *later*) later or more recent; the second of two just mentioned; modern. **latterly** *adv.* **of late,** recently [O.E. *laet*, slow].

la·tent (lā'·tạnt) *a.* not visible or apparent; dormant; hid; concealed. **latency** *n.* **-ly** *adv.* **— heat,** heat which is absorbed in changing a body from solid to liquid, or liquid to gas, without increasing its temperature [L. *latere*, to lie hid].

lat·er·al (lat'·ẹr·ạl) *a.* relating to the side. **-ly** *adv.* **— pass** (*Football*) a short pass parallel to the goal line [L. *latus, lateris*, side].

Lat·er·an (lat'·ẹr·ạn) *n.* the Pope's cathedral Church in Rome; *a.* pert. to church councils [fr. *Lateranus*, orig. owner of land].

la·tex (lā'·teks) *n.* the milky sap of trees, plants, the milky juice of the rubber tree. *pl.* **latices** [L. *Latex*, a liquid].

lath (lath) *n.* a thin, narrow slip of wood to support plaster, slates, etc. *pl.* **laths** (laTHz); *v.t.* to line with laths. **-er** *n.* **-ing** *n.* the process of constructing with laths; the work done [O E. *laettu*, a thin strip].

lathe (lāTH) *n.* a machine-tool for turning articles of wood, metal, etc.; *v.t.* to shape on a lathe [Scand.].

lath·er (laTH'·ẹr) *n.* foam or froth made with soap and water; froth from sweat; *v.t.* to spread over with lather; *v.i.* to form a lather [O.E. *leathor*, lather].

Lat·in (lat'·in) *a.* pert. to *Latium*, a part of ancient Italy with Rome as its chief center, or its inhabitants; written or spoken in Latin; pert. to the Roman Catholic Church (as distinct from the Greek Church); *n.* language or person descended linguistically from the ancient Latins. **-ize** *v.t.* to give a Latin form to; to translate into Latin; *v.i.* to use Latin words. **-ism** *n.* a Latin idiom. **-ist** *n.* a Latin scholar or expert. **-ity** *n.* the Latin language and its idiom. **— America,** parts of Central and South America where Romance languages are spoken. **— Church,** the Roman Catholic Church using Latin as its official language. **— languages,** those languages derived mainly from Latin as French, Italian, Spanish, Rumanian.

lat·i·tude (lat ·a·tūd) *n.* distance, measured in degrees, north or south of the equator; any region defined according to latitude; the angular distance of a heavenly body from the ecliptic; (*Fig.*) breadth of signification; deviation from a standard, esp. religious or ethical; scope; range. **latitudinal** *a.* pert. to latitude.

latitudinarian *a.* broad; liberal, esp. in religious principles; *n.* one who departs from, or is indifferent to, strictly orthodox religious principles. **latitudinal** *a.* [L. *latitudo*, breadth].

la·trine (la·trēn') *n.* a toilet, esp. in barracks, hospitals, etc. [L. *latrina*, bath].

lat·ten (lat'·ạn) *n.* a metallic alloy of copper and zinc, with appearance of brass; metal in thin sheets [Ger. *Latte*, a thin plate].

lat·ter See **late.**

lat·tice (lat'·is) *n.* framework of wood, metal, etc., formed by strips, laths, or bars crossing each other; a gate, trellis, or window thus formed; *v.t.* to furnish with a lattice. **-work** *n.* a trellis, etc. [Fr. *latte*, a lath].

Lat·vi·an (lat'·vi·ạn) *a.* pert. to the Baltic state of Latvia; Lettish.

laud (lawd) *v.t.* to praise in words or singing; to extol; *n.* a eulogy; praise; *pl.* in R.C. services, the prayers immediately after matins. **-ability** *n.* praiseworthiness. **-able** *a.* commendable. **-ableness** *n.* **-ably** *adv.* **-ation** *n.* praise; eulogy; the act of praising highly. **-atory** *a.* expressing praise [L. *laudare*, to praise].

laugh (laf) *v.i.* to express mirth spontaneously; to make an involuntary explosive sound of amusement; to be merry or gay; *n.* mirth peculiar to human species; laughter. **-able** *a.* droll; ludicrous; comical. **-ableness** *n.* **-ably** *adv.* **-er** *n.* **-ing** *a.* happy; merry. **-ing gas** *n.* nitrous oxide gas used as anesthetic in dental operations. **-ing hyena** *n.* the spotted hyena with a peculiar cry like a human laugh. **-ing jackass** *n.* the great kingfisher of Australia. **-ingly** *adv.* **-ing stock** *n.* object of ridicule. **-ter** *n.* merriment; audible expression of amusement. **to laugh up one's sleeve,** to laugh inwardly [O.E. *hlihan*, to laugh].

launch, lanch (lawnch, lạnch) *v.t.* to throw as a lance; to let fly; to cause to slide into the water for the first time, as a ship; to initiate, as an attack; to start a new activity; *v.i.* to go into the water; to push out to sea; to go forth; to expatiate, as in talk; to embark upon; *n.* the sliding of a ship into the water for the first time. **— vehicle** *n.* a rocket used to place a satellite or space vehicle in orbit. **-ing pad** *n.* platform from which a missile is fired by remote control [M.E. *lanchen*, to drop].

launch (lawnch, lạnch) *n.* the largest boat carried on a warship; an open boat driven by steam, gasoline, or electricity [Sp. *lancha*, a pinnace].

laun·dry (lawn'·dri·, lạn'·dri·) *n.* a place where clothes are washed, dried, and ironed; the process of washing clothes, etc.; clothes thus washed, etc. **launder** *v.t.* to wash clothes; *n.* (*Mining*) a long hollow trough for conveying powdered ore from the box where it is bruised. **launderer** *n.* **laundress** *n.* a woman who washes and irons clothes. **-man** *n.* a man who collects and delivers laundry or who works in a laundry [L. *lavandus*, to be washed].

lau·rel (law'·rạl) *n.* evergreen shrub, much used formerly to make wreaths symbolic of honor; *pl.* (*Fig.*) honors; *a.* consisting of laurel. **laureate** *a.* crowned with laurel; *n.* esp. in *Poet Laureate*. **laureateship** *n.* **-ed** *a.* [L. *laurus*, a bay-tree].

la·va (lä'·va) *n.* the molten rock, ejected by a volcano, hardening as it cools [It. fr. L. *lavare*, to wash].

la·va·bo (la·vä'·bō) *n.* ceremonial washing of a celebrant's hands after the offertory and before the eucharist, esp. in R.C. service; the towel or basin used in this ceremony [L.].

lave (lāv) *v.t.* (*Poetic*) to wash; to bathe; *v.i.* to bathe; to wash oneself. **lavatory** *n.* a place for washing [L. *lavare*, to wash].

lav·en·der (lac'·ạn·dẹr) *n.* an aromatic plant of mint family, yielding an essential oil; pale-lilac color of lavender flowers; dried flowers used as a sachet; *v.t.* to sprinkle or perfume with lavender [Fr. *lavande*, fr. L. *lavare*, to wash].

lav·ish (lav′·ish) *a.* over-generous; extravagant; ample; *v.t* to expend or bestow extravagantly. **-ly** *adv.*, *n.* [O. E. *lafian*, to pour out].

law (law) *n.* a rule established by authority; a body of rules the practice of which is authorized by a community or state; legal science; established usage; a rule, principle, or maxim of science, art, etc.; the legal profession; legal procedure; (*Theol.*) the Jewish or Mosaic code, as distinct from the Gospel. **—abiding** *a.* well-behaved; conforming to the law. **— court** *n.* a court in which lawcases are heard and judged. **-ful** *a.* allowed by law; legitimate. **-fully** *adv.* **-fulness** *n.* **-giver** *n.* a legislator. **-less** *a.* not conforming to the law; violent. **-lessly** *adv.* **-lessness** *n.* **— officer** *n.* a policeman. **-suit** *n.* a process in law for recovery of a supposed right. **-yer** *n.* a practitioner of law. **common law**, body of laws established more by custom than by definite legislation. **written law**, statute law, codified and written down, as distinct from *Common law* [O.E. *lagu*, a thing laid down].

lawn (lawn) *n.* a stretch of closely-cut, carefully-tended grass. **— mower** *n.* a machine for cutting grass [O.Fr. *launde*, a plain].

lawn (lawn) *n.* a fine linen or cambric; *a.* made of lawn [fr. *Laon*, a town in France].

lax (laks) *a.* slack; flabby; loose, esp. in moral sense; careless; not constipated. **-ative** *a.* having purgative effect; *n.* an aperient. **-ity**, **-ness** *n.* slackness; looseness of moral standards; want of exactness [L. *laxus*, loose].

lay (lā) *v.t.* to place or put down; to apply; to beat down, as corn; to cause to subside; to exorcise, as an evil spirit; to spread on a surface; to wager; to produce, to prepare; to station, as an ambush; to form, as a plot; to set out dishes, etc. (on a table); to charge, as with a responsibility; *v.i.* to produce eggs. *pr.p.* **-ing**. *pa.t.*, *pa.p.* **laid**. *n.* a situation; disposition. **-er** *n.* a person who or that which lays, as a bricklayer, hen, etc.; a thickness or coating laid down; a stratum of rock or vegetation; the shoot of a plant partly covered with earth, thus laid to encourage propagation. **-erage** *n.* the artificial propagation of plants by layers. **— off** *n.* a slack time in industry. **— out** *n.* that which is laid out; the design or plans, as of a garden. **— over** *n.* stop, or break, in a trip. [O.E. *lecgan*, to lay].

lay (lā) past tense of **lie** (to recline).

lay (lā) *n.* a song; a narrative poem such as was recited by minstrels [O.Fr. *lai*, a song].

lay (lā) *a.* pert. to the laity, as distinct from the clergy; unprofessional. **laicize** *v.t.* to deprive of clerical character. **laity** *n.* **— brother** *n.* a servant in a monastery. **-figure** *n.* a jointed figure used by artists in imitation of the human form; a person of rather negative character. **-man** *n.* one of the laity, or people; one who is not an expert in a branch of knowledge. **— sister** *n.* a woman who serves the nuns in a convent [Gk. *laos*, the people].

lay·ette (lā·et′) *n.* a complete outfit for a new-born baby [Fr.].

laz·ar (laz′·ẹr) *n.* a person afflicted with a loathsome disease, like *Lazarus*, the beggar [fr. *Lazarus*, the beggar, Luke 16].

laze (lāz) *v.i.* (*Colloq.*) to be lazy; to lounge [fr. *lazy*].

la·zy (lā′·zi·) *a.* disinclined to exertion; slothful; *v.i.* to be lazy. **lazily** *adv.* **laziness** *n.* **-bones** *n.* (*Colloq.*) a lazy fellow; an idler [O.Fr. *lasche*, weak].

lea (lē) *n.* (*Poetic*) a meadow; land left untilled; pasturage [O.E. *leah*, a field].

leach (lēch) *v.t.* to wash by causing water to pass through; (*Bot.*) to remove salts from soil by percolation; *v.i.* to pass through by perco-

lation; *n.* act of leaching; material leached; a vessel used for leaching. Also **letch.** **-y** *a.* porous [O.E. *leccan*, to moisten].

lead (led) *n.* a well-known malleable bluish-grey metal, ductile and heavy, used for roofing, pipes, etc.; a plummet for sounding ocean depths; a thin strip of type metal to separate lines of print; graphite for pencils; bullets; *pl.* sheets of lead for roof coverings; *a.* made of, or containing lead. **-ed** *a.* fitted with lead; set in lead, as panes of glass. **-en** *a.* made of lead; heavy; dull. **-ing** *n.* frame or cover of lead. **— pencil** *n.* a pencil containing graphite. **— poisoning** *n.* a form of poisoning called plumbism caused by lead being absorbed into the blood and tissues. **-y** *a.* [O.E. *lead*, lead].

lead (lēd) *v.t.* to show the way; to guide; to direct; to persuade; to precede; (*Cards*) to play the first card of a round; *v.i.* to go in front and show the way; to outstrip; to conduct; to tend to; *n.* front position; precedence; guidance; direction; priority; principal part in a play or film; an electric wire or cable; the first card played in a card-game; a dog's chain or leash. **-er** *n.* a guide; a conductor; a commander; (chiefly *Brit.*) the leading editorial in a newspaper; the foremost horse in a team; (*Mus.*) a performer who leads an orchestra or choir; (*Print.*) a series of dots (...) to guide the eye across the page. **-ership** *n.* the state or function of a leader. **-ing** *n.* direction; the act of guiding. **-ing-article** *n.* a leader or editorial in a newspaper. **-ing-lady, -man** *n.* the actress (or actor) playing the principal role. **-ing-question** *n.* (*Law*) a question so phrased as to suggest the answer expected. **to lead astray**, to tempt from virtue [O.E. *laedan*, to lead].

leaf (lēf) *n.* thin deciduous shoot from the stem or branch of a plant; anything resembling a leaf in shape or thinness; a sheet of paper, esp. as part of a book, with a page on each side; side of a double door or a shutter; one of the sections of a dropleaf or extension table; a hinged flap; a very thinly beaten plate, as of gold. *pl.* **leaves**. *v.i.* to shoot out leaves. **-age** *n.* leaves collectively; foliage. **-iness** *n.* **-less** *a.* devoid of leaves. **-let** *n.* a tiny leaf; a printed sheet advertisement, notice of meeting, etc. **— mold** *n.* leaves decayed and reduced to mold, used as manure. **-y** *a.* full of leaves. **to turn over a new leaf**, to reform [O.E. *leaf*, leaf].

league (lēg) *n.* an old nautical measure equal to three geographical miles [O.Fr. *legue*, fr. (L.L.) *leuca*, a Gallic mile of 1500 paces].

league (lēg) *n.* a compact made between nations or individuals for mutual aid and the promoting of common interests; an association, as of football clubs, for match games to be played during a season; *v.i.* to combine in an association [Fr. *ligue*, a conspiracy].

lea·guer (lē′·gẹr) *n.* a military camp, esp. a siege camp [Dut. *leger*, a camp].

leak (lēk) *n.* a crack, crevice, fissure, or hole in a vessel; the oozing of liquid from such; (*Elect.*) an escape of electrical current from a faulty conductor; *v.i.* to let fluid into, or out of, a defective vessel. **-age** *n.* an oozing or quantity of liquid which passes through a defect in a vessel; (*Fig.*) the giving away of secrets, news, etc., through unauthorized channels. **-iness** *n.* **-y** *a.* having leaks. **spring a leak**, to develop a crack or flaw [Scand. *leka*, a drip].

lean (lēn) *v.t.* to incline; to cause to rest against; *v.i.* to deviate from the perpendicular; to incline. *pa.t.* and *pa.p.* **leaned** or **leant** (lent). *n.* a slope; a rest against. **-ing** *n.* inclination (of body or mind). **—to** *n.* a shed built against a wall or side of a house or supported at one end by posts or trees [O.E. *hlaenan*, to cause to incline].

lean (lēn) *a.* thin; wanting in flesh or fat; (*Fig.*) empty; impoverished; *n.* that part of meat consisting of flesh without fat. **-ly** *adv.* **-ness** *n.* [O.E. *hlaene*, thin].

leap (lēp) *v.i.* to spring; to jump up or forward; to vault; *v.t.* to pass over by leaping. *pr.p.* **-ing** *pa.t.* and *pa.p.* **-ed** or **leapt** (lept). *n.* jumping up or forward; a sudden rise (as of book-sales). **-frog** *n.* a game, in which one stoops down, and another vaults over his head. **— year** *n.* a year of 366 days [O.E. *hleapan*, to leap].

learn (lurn) *v.t.* to acquire knowledge; to get to know; to gain skill by practice; *v.i.* to gain knowledge; to take example from. *pa.t.* and *pa.p.* **-ed** (lurnd) or **-t. -ed** (lurn'.ad) *a.* having knowledge; erudite. **-edly** *adv.* **-edness** *n.* **-er** *n.* **-ing** *n.* that which is learned; letters; science; literature, erudition [O.E. *leornian*].

lease (lēs) *n.* a contract renting lands, houses, farms, etc., for a specified time; time covered by lease; any tenure; *v.t.* to grant possession of lands, etc., to another for rent; to hold a lease. **— hold** *a.* held on lease [O.Fr. *laissier*, to transmit].

leash (lēsh) *n.* a line by which a hawk, dog, or other animal is held; a set of three hounds, or hares or foxes held in leash; *v.t.* to hold by a leash; to bind [O.Fr. *lesse*, a thong].

least (lēst) *a.* (superl. of **little**) smallest; faintest; most minute; *adv.* in the smallest degree; *n.* the smallest amount. **-ways, -wise** (*Colloq.*) *adv.* at least; however. **at least**, at any rate [O.E. *laest*, smallest].

leath·er (leTH'.er) *n.* the skin of an animal dressed and prepared for use; anything made of leather; *v.t.* to apply leather to; (*Colloq.*) to thrash with a strap. **-back** *n.* a large sea turtle. **— bound** *a.* (of a book) bound in calf, morocco, or other leather. **-ing** *n.* (*Colloq.*) a thrashing. **-n** *a.* made of leather. **-neck** *n.* (*Slang*) a U.S. marine. **-y** *a.* like leather; tough. **patent leather**, leather with shiny, varnished surface [O.E. *lether*, leather].

leave (lēv) *n.* liberty granted; formal good-bye; furlough; permission to be temporarily absent from duty. **French leave**, absence without permission [O.E. *leaf*, permission].

leave (lēv) *v.t.* to quit; to forsake; to omit; to remove; to allow to remain unaltered; to bequeath; to permit; to entrust; to refer; *v.i.* to depart from; to withdraw. *pr.p.* **leaving.** *pa.p.* **left. leavings** *n.pl.* things left; relics; refuse [O.E. *laefan*, to bequeath].

leav·en (lev'.n) *n.* a substance due to fermentation which causes bread dough to rise; (*Fig.*) anything which causes a general change in the mass; *v.t.* to raise with leaven; to create a spiritual change [L. *levare*, to raise].

lech·er (lech'.er) *n.* a man given to lewdness; a fornicator. **-ous** *a.* lascivious; lustful. **-ously** *adv.* **-ousness, -y** *n.* [O.Fr. *lechier*, to lick].

lec·tern (lek'.tern) *n.* a reading desk in a church [L.L. *lectrum*, a reading-desk].

lec·tion (lek'.shan) *n.* a variation in copies of a manuscript; a portion of scripture read during a church service. **-ary** *n.* a book containing portions of the Scripture to be read on particular days. **lector** *n.* a reader; a minor ecclesiastic in the early church; a lecturer in a college or university [L. *legere*, to read].

lec·ture (lek'.cher) *n.* a discourse on any subject; a formal reproof; *v.t.* to instruct by discourses; to reprove; *v.i.* to deliver a formal discourse. **-r** *n.* one who lectures; an assistant to a professor in a university department. **-ship** *n.* [L. *legere, lectum*, to read].

led (led) *pa.t.* and *pa.p.* of verb **lead**.

ledge (lej) *n.* a projection, as from a wall or cliff; a shelf; a ridge of rock near the surface of the sea [M.E. *legge*, a bar].

ledg·er (lej'.er) *n.* a book in which a business firm enters all debit and credit items in sum-

mary form; a cash book; a flat stone lying horizontally as on a grave; one of the pieces of timber used in a scaffolding; *a.* stationary (only in compound words). **— line** *n.* a line with hook and sinker to keep it stationary; (*Mus.*) an additional line above or below the staff for notes outside the normal range. Also **leger** [prob. M.E. *leggan*, to lie].

lee (lē) *n.* a place protected from the wind; shelter; *a.* pert. to the part or side farthest from the wind. **-board** *n.* a plank lowered on the side of a boat to diminish its drifting to leeward. **-gage** *n.* the sheltered side. **— shore** *n.* the shore on the lee-side of a vessel. **—side** *n.* the side of a vessel opposite to the direction from which the wind is blowing. **— tide** *n.* a current running in the direction the wind is blowing. **-ward** (lē'.werd, lōō'.werd) *a.* pert. to, or in, the direction towards which the wind is blowing. **-way** *n.* the side movement of a vessel to the leeward of her course; loss of progress; (*Colloq.*) extra time, space, etc. [O.E. *hleo*, a shelter].

leech (lēch) *n.* a blood-sucking worm used for bloodletting; (*Archaic*) physician; *v.t.* to bleed by application of leeches [O.E. *laece*, one who heals].

leek (lēk) *n.* a biennial bulbous plant allied to the onion; also, the national emblem of Wales [O.E. *leac*, leek].

leer (lēr) *n.* a sly or furtive look expressive of malignity, lasciviousness, or triumph; *v.i.* to look with a leer [O.E. *hleor*, cheek].

leer·y (lēr'.i.) *a.* wary; suspicious.

lees (lēz) *n.pl.* the sediment which settles at the bottom of a wine-cask; dregs [Fr. *lie*].

left (left) *a.* on the side of the body which is westward when one is facing north. Also **left-hand.** *n.* the side opposite to the right; in some legislative assemblies, the left side of the speaker's chair where the opposition members sit, hence an extreme or radical party; *adv.* to or on the left. **—hand** *n.* the left side; *a.* situated on the left side; executed with the left hand. **—handed** *a.* using the left hand more easily than the right; awkward. **—handedness** *n.* **— wing** *n.* a political group with extremist views [M.E. *lift*, weak].

left (left) *pa.t.* and *pa.p.* of the verb **leave.**

leg (leg) *n.* the limb of an animal used in supporting the body and in walking, esp. that part of the limb between the knee and the foot; any support, as leg of a table; one of the two divisions of a forked object, as compasses; part of a garment covering the leg; (*Naut.*) a ship's course covered on one tack; *v.i.* (*Colloq.*) to walk briskly; to run. *pr.p.* **-ging.** *pa.t.* and *pa.p.* **-ged. -ged** *a.* having legs, as *three-legged stool.* **-ging** *n.* a garment to cover the legs. **-gy** *a.* having disproportionately long legs, as a very young animal. **-less** *a.* without legs. **—of-mutton** *a.* shaped like a leg of mutton, as of a sleeve; triangular, as a sail [Scand. *legar*, a leg].

leg·a·cy (leg'.a.si.) *n.* a bequest; a gift of personal property by will. **legatee** *n.* one who receives a legacy [L. *legare*, to bequeath].

le·gal (lē'.gal) *a.* pert. to, or according to, the law; defined by law; statutory; binding; constitutional. **-ization** *n.* **-ize** *v.t.* to make lawful; to sanction. **-ity** *n.* conformity to law. **-ly** *adv.* **— tender**, the form of money, coin, or notes, which may be lawfully used in paying a debt [L. *lex, legis*, a law].

leg·ate (leg'.at) *n.* Pope's highest diplomatic envoy; a diplomatic minister below ambassadorial rank. **-ship** *n.* **legatine** *a.* of a legate. **legation** (li.gā'.shan) *n.* a minister and his staff; the official residence or offices of a diplomatic minister [L. *legatus*, an envoy].

le·ga·to (li.gà'.tō) *adv.* (*Mus.*) in a smooth, gliding manner [L. *ligare*, to tie].

leg·end (lej'.and) *n.* orig. a chronicle of the

lives of the saints; any traditional story of ancient times; an inscription on a coin, medal, etc. **-ary** *n.* book of, relater of, legends; *a.* comprising legends; fabulous; strange. **-ry** *n.* legends collectively [L. *legendus*, to be read].

le·ger·de·main (lej·ẹr·dạ·mān′) *n.* a sleight of hand; trickery [Fr. *léger de main*, light of hand].

leg·er·line (lej′·ẹr·līn) *n.* See **ledger**.

Leg·horn (leg′·hawrn) *n.* a plaited straw, from Leghorn in Italy; (*l.c.*) a hat made of this straw; a breed of domestic fowl.

leg·i·ble (lej′·ạ·bl) *a.* capable of being read. **legibly** *adv.* **-ness, legibility** *n.* [L. *legere*, to read].

le·gion (lē′·jạn) *n.* in ancient Rome, a body of infantry of from three to six thousand; a military force; a great number. **-ary** *a.* relating to, or consisting of, a legion or legions; containing a great number; *n.* a soldier of a legion. **-naire** *n.* a legionary; (*Cap.*) member of the American Legion [L. *legio, legionis*].

leg·is·late (lej′·is·lāt) *v.i.* to make or enact laws. **legislation** *n.* act of legislating; laws made. **legislative** *a.* having power to make laws; constitutional. **legislatively** *adv.* **legislator** *n.* one who enacts laws; a member of the legislature. **legislature** *n.* the body empowered to make and repeal laws [L. *lex*, a law; *ferre, latum*, to carry].

le·git·i·mate (li·jit′·ạ·mit) *a.* lawful; in accordance with the law; born in lawful wedlock; justifiable; reasonable; genuine; *v.t.* (li·jit′·ạ·māt) to make lawful; to render legitimate; to pronounce lawful or proper. **legitimacy** *n.* the state of being legitimate. **-ly** *adv.* **-ness** *n.* **legitimation** *n.* the act of investing with the rights and privileges of lawful birth. **legitimize** *v.t.* to legitimate. **legitimism** *n.* **legitimist** *n.* one who upholds legitimate authority, esp. hereditary monarchical government [L. *legitimus*, lawful].

leg·ume (leg′·ūm) *n.* a seed pod with two valves and having the seeds attached at one suture, as the pea; a plant bearing seed-pods. Also **legumen**. *pl.* **legumens, legumina. leguminous** *a.* [Fr. *légume*, a vegetable].

lei (lā) *n.* a garland of flowers worn around the neck [Haw.].

lei·sure (lē′·zhẹr) *n.* freedom from occupation; spare time; *a.* unoccupied. **leisurable** *a.* **-d.** *a.* free from business duties. **-ly** *a.* unhurried; slow; *adv.* slowly [O.Fr. *leisir*, to be lawful].

leit·mo·tif (līt′·mō·tēf) *n.* (*Mus.*) a theme associated with a person or idea, constantly recurring in a composition [Ger. *leit*, leading; Fr. *motif*, motive].

lem·ma (lem′·ạ) *n.* (*Math.*) a subsidiary proposition; (*Logic*) a premise taken for granted; a theme; a heading of an entry [Gk. *lemma*, something taken for granted].

lem·on (lem′·ạn) *n.* an oval-shaped fruit with rind pale yellow in color and containing very acid pulp and juice; the tree which provides this fruit; (*Colloq.*) an inferior product; *a.* of the color of lemon rind. **-ade** *n.* a cooling drink made of lemon juice, sugar, and water [Fr. *limon*, the lemon fruit].

le·mur (lē′·mẹr) *n.* one of a family of nocturnal monkey-like mammals found in Madagascar [L. *lemur*, a ghost].

lend (lend) *v.t.* to grant the temporary use of, to give in general; to let out money at interest; to serve for; *v.i.* to make a loan. *pr.p.* **-ing**. *pa.p.* **lent. -er** *n.* [O.E. *laen*, a loan].

lend-lease, the pooling of material resources of Allied nations in the struggle against Germany and Japan (W.W. II); *v.t.* to grant (material aid) to a foreign country in accordance with the Lend-Lease Act of March 11, 1941.

length (length) *n.* the measurement of anything from end to end; extension; duration of

time; extent; intervening distance, as in a race; the quantity of a syllable or vowel in prosody. **-en** *v.t.* to extend in length; to protract; *v.i.* to grow longer. **-ily** *adv.* **-iness** *n.* **-wise** *a.* in the direction of the length. **-y** *a.* [O.E. *lang*, long].

le·ni·ent (lē′·ni·ẹnt) *a.* clement; acting without severity. **lenience, leniency** *n.* the quality of being lenient; clemency. **-ly** *adv.* **lenitive** *n.* a medicine with eases pain; *a.* soothing; emollient. **lenity** *n.* [L. *lenis*, soft].

lens (lenz) *n.* (*Optics*) a piece of glass or other transparent substance ground with one or both sides curved so as to refract rays of light, and thereby modify vision; the crystalline biconvex tissue between the cornea and retina of the eye. *pl.* **lenses** [L. *lens*, a lentil].

Lent (lent) *n.* the season of 40 days from Ash Wednesday until Easter Day. **-en** *a.* pert. to Lent [O.E. *lencten*, spring].

len·tic·u·lar (len·tik′·yoo·lẹr) *a.* shaped like a lens or lentil; resembling a double-convex lens. Also **lentiform. lentoid** *a.* lens-shaped [L. *lenticula*, a small lentil].

len·til (len′·til) *n.* a Mediterranean plant allied to the bean [L. *lens*, a lentil].

len·to (len′·tō) *adv.* (*Mus.*) slowly [It.].

l'en·voi (len·voi′ or lawng′·vwà) *n.* a kind of postscript to a poem; a short, final stanza [O.Fr. *l'envoi*, the sending].

Le·o (lē′·ō) *n.* the lion, the fifth sign of the Zodiac which the sun enters about July 22nd. **leonine** *a.* of or like a lion [L. *leo*, a lion].

leo·pard (lep′·ẹrd) *n.* a large carnivorous member of the cat family, of a yellow or fawn color with black spots [Gk. *leōn*, lion; *pardos*, pard].

le·o·tard (lē′·ạ·tárd) *n.* a one-piece tight-fitting garment worn by dancers [after *Léotard*, 19th cent. Fr. aerial performer].

lep·er (lep′·ẹr) *n.* a person afflicted with leprosy; (*Fig.*) an outcast. **leprosy** *n.* a chronic contagious disease affecting skin, tissues and nerves. **leprous** *a.* [Gk. *lepros*, scaly].

Lep·i·dop·ter·a (lep·ạ·dáp′·tẹr·ạ) *n.pl.* an order of insects having four wings covered with gossamer scales, as moths, butterflies, etc. **-l, lepidopterous** *a.* [Gk. *lepis*, a scale; *pteron*, a wing].

lep·re·chaun (lep′·rạ·kawn) *n.* a sprite; a brownie commonly referred to in Irish folk-stories [Ir.].

lep·ro·sy (lep′·rạ·si·) *n.* See **leper**.

Les·bi·an (lez′·bi·ạn) *a.* pert. to the island of *Lesbos* (Mytilene) in the Aegean Sea, or to the ancient school of lyric poets there; amatory; *n.* a woman who is sexually attracted to another woman; a homosexual woman [Gk. *lesbrōs*].

lese maj·es·ty (lēz′·maj·is·ti·) *n.* (*Law*) a crime committed against the sovereign, or sovereign power of a state; high treason [Fr. fr. L. *laesa majesta*, injured majesty].

le·sion (lē′·zhạn) *n.*(*Med.*) any morbid change in the structure or functioning of the living tissues of the body; injury; (*Law*) loss or injury [L. *laedere, laesum*, to hurt].

less (les) *a.* smaller in size; not equal to in number; lower; inferior; *adv.* in a smaller or lower degree; *n.* a smaller portion; the inferior. **-en** *v.t.* to make less; to diminish; *v.i.* to contract; to decrease. **-er** *a.* smaller; inferior [O.E. *laes*, less].

les·see (les·ē′) *n.* one to whom a lease is granted [fr. *lease*].

les·son (les′·n) *n.* a reading; a piece of instruction; something to be learned by pupils; a Scripture passage read aloud as part of church service; instruction gained by experience; reproof; *v.t.* to teach [Fr. fr. L. *legere*, to read].

lest (lest) *conj.* for fear that [O.E.].

let (let) *v.t.* to allow; to give permission; to cause to do (foll. by *infin.* without *to*); to grant the temporary use of, for hire; *v.i.* to be rented; (*Colloq.*) to be dismissed (foll. by *out*). *pr.p.* **-ting**. *pa.t.* and *pa.p.* **let.** [O.E. *laeten*, to permit].

le·thal (lē′·thal) *a.* deadly; mortal. **lethifer-ous** *a.* deadly [L. *letum*, death].

leth·ar·gy (leth′·er·ji·) *n.* unnaturally heavy drowsiness; overpowering lassitude; inertia. **lethargic, lethargical** *a.* drowsy; apathetic. **lethargically** *adv.* [Gk. *lēthargos*, forgetful].

le·the (lē′·thē) *n.* oblivion. **-an** [Gk. *lēthē*, a forgetting].

let·ter (let′·er) *n.* a mark or symbol used to represent an articulate, elementary sound; a written or printed communication; an epistle; the literal statement; printing-type; *pl.* learning; erudition; *v.t.* to impress or form letters on. — **box** *n.* a box for receiving letters, as on inside of house door. — **carrier** *n.* a postman. **-ed** *a.* literate; educated; versed in literature, science, etc.; inscribed with lettering. **-er** *n.* — **file** *n.* a device for holding letters for reference. **-head** *n.* printed heading on business stationery. **-ing** *n.* the act of impressing letters; the letters impressed. **-press** *n.* printed matter as distinct from illustrations, diagrams, etc.; print. **letter of credit**, a letter authorizing money to be paid by a bank to the bearer. **letters patent**, a document under seal of the state, granting some property privileges or authority, or conferring the exclusive right to use an invention or design [L. *littera*, a letter].

Let·tic (let′·ik) *a.* pert. to the Letts or to their language; *n.* the language of the Letts. Also **Lettish. Letts** *n.pl.* the inhabitants of Lithuania and Latvia.

let·tuce (let′·is) *n.* a common garden plant, used in salads [L. *lactuca*, lettuce].

leu·co·cyte (lōō′·ka·sīt) *n.* one of the white corpuscles of the blood, destroying bacteria [Gk. *leukos*, white; *kutos*, a cell].

leu·ke·mi·a, leukaemia (lōō·kē′·mē·a̞) *n.* a disease characterized by an excessive number of white corpuscles in the blood [Gk. *leukos*, white].

Le·vant (la̞·vant′) *n.* Eastern Mediterranean countries; (*l.c.*) a superior grade of morocco leather. **-er** *n.* wind blowing from E. Spain towards Levant. **-ine** *a.* pert. to Levant; *n.* native of the Levant [L. *levare*, to raise].

le·va·tor (la̞·vā′·ter) *n.* a muscle in the body which raises any part, as the eyelid, lips, etc. [L. *levare*, to raise].

lev·ee (lev′·ē, la̞·vē′) *n.* a reception; orig. a reception held by royal personage on rising from bed [Fr. *lever*, to rise].

lev·ee (lev′·ē) *n.* a river embankment to prevent flooding; a quay [Fr. *levée*, raised].

lev·el (lev′·al) *n.* a line or plane which is everywhere parallel to the horizon; the horizontal plane on which a thing rests; a state of equality; an instrument for finding or drawing a true horizontal line; *a.* not having one part higher than another; even; horizontal; equal in rank or degree; *v.t.* to make horizontal; to reduce to the same height with something else; to raze; to make equal in rank, etc.; to point a gun or arrow at the mark. **—headed** *a.* balanced; prudent. **-er** *n.* **-ing** *n.* the act of making a surface even with another; the process of ascertaining the difference of elevation between two points, by the use of a *leveling* instrument. **-ing rod** *n.* a graduated rod used in surveying [L. *libella*, a water-level].

lev·er (lev′·er, lē′·ver) *n.* a bar used to exert pressure or sustain a weight at one point of its length by receiving a force or power at a second, and turning at a third on a fixed point called a fulcrum; a crowbar for forcing open; *v.t.* to raise up; to force open. **-age** *n.* the action of a lever; mechanical advantage gained by use of the lever [L. *levare*, to raise].

le·vi·a·than (la̞·vī′·a̞·than) *n.* a huge aquatic animal; a whale; a sea-monster; anything of colossal size [Heb. *livyathan*, a sea-monster].

lev·i·ta·tion (lev·a̞·tā′·shan) *n.* the act of making buoyant or light; the phenomenon of heavy bodies being made to float in air by spiritual agencies. **levitate** *v.t.* [L. *levis*, light].

Le·vite (lē′·vīt) *n.* one of the tribe of Levi; lesser priest in ancient Jewish synagogue. **Levitic, -al** (le·vit′·ik, ·al) *a.* **Leviticus** *n.* (*Bib.*) third book of Old Testament [fr. *Levi*].

lev·i·ty (lev′·a̞·ti·) *n.* lightness; buoyancy; lack of seriousness [L. *levis*, light].

le·vo·ro·ta·tion (lē·va̞·rō·tā′·shan) *n.* counterclockwise or left-hand rotation. **levorotatory** *a.* [L. *laevus*, left].

lev·u·lose (lev′·yoo·lōs) *n.* fruit sugar found in honey and certain fruits [L. *laevus*, left].

lev·y (lev′·i·) *v.t.* to raise by assessment, as taxes; to enlist or collect, as troops; to impose, as a fine; *v.i.* to make a levy; *n.* collection of assessment by authority or compulsion, for public services; the money or troops thus collected [L. *levare*, to raise].

lewd (lōōd) *a.* obscene; indecent; given to unlawful indulgence. **-ly** *adv.* **-ness** *n.* [O.E. *laewede*, lay].

lew·is (lōō′·is) *n.* an iron clamp dove-tailed into a stone block to raise it [etym. unknown].

lex·i·con (lek′·si·kán) *n.* a dictionary, esp. of Greek, Latin, or Hebrew; a vocabulary list relating to a particular subject, class, etc. **lexical** *a.* pert. to a lexicon. **lexicographer** *n.* one who compiles a dictionary. **lexicographic, -al** *a.* **lexicologist** *n.* an expert in lexicology. **lexicography** *n.* the art or process of compiling a dictionary. **lexicology** *n.* the science which deals with the exact significance and use of vocabulary [Gk. *lexis*, speech; *graphein*, to write; *logos*, a discourse].

li·a·ble (lī′·a̞·bl) *a.* obliged in law or equity; subject; answerable; responsible. **liability** *n.* the state of being liable; responsibility; obligation; *pl.* debts [Fr. *lier*, to bind].

li·ai·son (lē·ā·zán′) *n.* a union; connection; illicit intimacy between a man and a woman; (*Mil.*) contact maintained between one unit or command and another; the sounding, as in French, of the final consonant of a word before the initial vowel or mute *h* of the next word [Fr. fr. L. *ligare*, to bind].

li·a·na (li·án′·a̞) *n.* a climbing tropical plant [Fr. *liane*].

li·ar (lī′·er) *n.* one who tells lies [fr. *lie*].

li·ba·tion (lī·bā′·shan) *n.* the ceremonial pouring of wine in honor of some deity; the liquid itself; (*Colloq.*) a drink [L. *libare*, to pour].

li·bel (lī′·bal) *n.* a defamatory writing or printed picture; (*Law*) a written statement by the plaintiff of his allegations in a law case; (*Colloq.*) a statement injurious to a person's character; *v.t.* to defame by a writing, picture, etc.; to proceed against, by filing a libel. **-er** *n.* **-ous, -lous** *a.* defamatory; containing a libel. **-ously** *adv.* [L. *libellus*, a little book].

lib·er·al (lib′·er·al) *a.* open-minded; generous; catholic; unbiased; (in politics) favoring democratic or progressive ideals, and freedom of religion; *n.* one who favors greater political and religious freedom from tradition; supporter of a liberal political party. **-iaztion** *n.* the process of gaining greater freedom. **-ize** *v.t.* to cause to be freer or more enlightened. **-ism** *n.* liberal principles. **-ist** *n.* **liberality** *n.* generosity; munificence; catholicity of mind. **-ly** *adv.* **liberate** *v.t.* to set free. **liberation** *n.* the act of setting free; the state of being free from bondage. **liberator** *n.* one who sets others free, esp. from tyranny [L. *liberalis*, befitting a freeman].

lib·er·ty (lib′·er·ti·) *n.* freedom from bondage or restraint; power to act according to one's natural rights as an individual; privilege; undue freedom of act or speech; *pl.* rights, privileges, etc., conferred by grant or prescription. **libertarian** n. one who upholds the doctrine of freewill. **libertarianism** n. **libertine** (lib′·er·tēn) n. one who leads a dissolute life; a. dissolute [L. libertas, liberty].

li·bi·do (li·bē′·dō, li·bi′·dō) n. in psychology, the emotional craving behind all human impulse; esp. used by Freud to denote the sexurge. **libidinous** (li·bid′·a·nas) a. lewd; obscene; lustful. **libidinously** adv. [L. libido, desire].

Li·bra (lī′·bra) n. the balance, the 7th sign of the Zodiac [L. libra, a balance].

li·brar·y (lī′·bre·ri·) n. a collection of books; the room or building which contains it. **librarian** n. the person in charge of a library; one trained and engaged in library work. **librarianship** n. — **science** n. the knowledge and skills required for library service [L. liber, a book].

li·brate (lī′·brāt) v.i to be poised; to oscillate. **libration** n. balancing; a quivering motion. **libratory** a. [L. libra, a balance].

li·bret·to (li·bret′·ō) n. the words of an opera or oratorio. **librettist** n. the writer of librettos [It. = a little book].

Lib·y·an (lib′·i·an) a. pert. to Libya in N. Africa or to the language of the district.

lice (līs) pl. of **louse.**

li·cense (lī′·sans) n. authority granted to do any act; a legal permit; excess of liberty; v.t. to permit by grant of authority. **licensable** a. **-d** a. privileged; holding a license. **licensee** n. one who is given a license. **-r** n. one legally entitled to grant a license. **licentiate** n. one who has a license to practice a profession. **licentious** a. using excessive license; dissolute. **licentiously** adv. **licentiousness** n. [L. licentia, freedom].

li·chen (lī′·kan) n. one of an order of cellular flowerless plants; (Med.) a skin eruption [L. fr. Gk. leichēn, moss].

lic·it (lis′·it) a. lawful; allowable. **-ly** adv. [L. licitus, lawful].

lick (lik) v.t. to pass or draw the tongue over; to lap; to take in by the tongue; to touch lightly (as flames); (Colloq.) to thrash; to be superior over; n. a lap with the tongue; a small portion; (Colloq.) a brief attempt; pl. a beating. **-er** n. **-ing** n. a lapping with tongue; a flogging; a beating (in a competition) [O.E. liccian].

lic·o·rice, liquorice (lik′·a·ris) n. a Mediterranean plant, the root of which contains a sweet juice; the brittle, black substance extracted from the roots of this plant, and used medicinally and in candy [Gk. glukus, sweet; rhiza, a root].

lic·tor (lik′·ter) n. an officer who attended a Roman magistrate, bearing the fasces [L. fr. ligare, to bind].

lid (lid) n. a cover of a vessel or box; the covering of the eye [O.E. hlid, a cover].

lie (lī) v.i. to utter untruth; to misrepresent; to deceive; to make false statement. pr.p. **lying.** pa.t. and pa.p. **-d.** n. a deliberate falsehood. **liar** n. one who utters a falsehood. **lying** a. spares one embarrassment, difficulty, etc. **-size** addicted to telling lies [O.E. leogan, to lie].

lie (lī) v.i. to be recumbent; to be in a horizontal position or nearly so; to be situated; to lean; to be at rest; to press upon; (Law) to be admissible. pr.p. **lying.** pa.t. **lay.** pa.p. **lain.** n. manner of lying [O.E. licgan, to lie].

lie·der (lē′·der) n.pl. German lyrics set to music; sing. **lied** [Ger. Lied, a song].

lief (lēf) adv. gladly; willingly [O.E. leof, loved].

liege (lēj) a. bound by feudal tenure; (of a lord) entitled to receive homage; n. a vassal; a feudal lord to whom allegiance is owed [O.Fr. liege, an overlord].

li·en (lēn, lē′·an) n. (Law) a legal claim upon real or personal property for the satisfaction of some debt or duty [Fr. fr. L. ligare, to bind].

lieu (loō) n. place; stead, as in phrase 'in lieu of' [Fr.].

lieu·ten·ant (loō·ten′·ant) n. a deputy; an officer who takes the place of a superior in his absence; rank below a captain (Army) or below a lieutenant commander (Navy). — **colonel** n. the rank below a colonel. — **commander** n. (Navy) the rank intermediate between that of lieutenant and commander corresponding to that of major (Army). — **general** n. military rank intermediate between that of major general and general. — **governor** n. state official ranking below a governor [Fr. lieu, place; tenant, holding].

life (līf) n. existence; vitality; condition of plants, animals, etc. in which they exercise functional powers; the span between birth and death; mode of living; narrative of a person's history; animation; pl. **lives.** — **and death** a. desperate. — **assurance** or **insurance** n. insurance of a person's life. — **belt** n. a belt either inflated, or made buoyant with cork, for keeping person afloat in case of shipwreck. **-boat** n. a special type of boat, designed for stability in stormy seas, for saving of human lives — **expectancy** n. probable life span. **-guard** n. someone employed at a swimming pool, etc. to prevent accidents. — **history** n. the cycle of life of a person, organism, etc. — **interest** n. interest in an estate or business which continues during one's life, but which cannot be bequeathed by will. —**jacket** n. a life belt. **-less** a. inanimate; dead; inert. **-lessly** adv. **-lessness** n. **-like** a. like a living creature; resembling closely. **-line** n. a line attached to a lifebuoy or lifeboat; a line fired by rocket from the shore to a ship in distress; the line which lowers and raises a deep-sea diver; (Fig.) that which keeps a nation alive. **-long** a. lasting a lifetime. — **preserver** n. any apparatus (as life belt, -buoy, -line) for preserving or rescuing life. **-r** n. (Colloq.) a criminal who has received a life sentence.**-saver** n. someone who rescues a person, esp. from drowning; (Slang) a person or thing which spares one embarrassment, difficulty, etc. **-size** a. resembling in proportions the living model. **-time** n. the duration of person's life. **-work** n. any task, usually creative, demanding a lifetime's work [O.E. lif, life].

lift (lift) v.t. to raise; to take up and remove; to elevate socially; to exalt spiritually; (Colloq.) to steal; to take passengers on a bus, etc.; v.i. to rise; to be dispersed; n. the act of lifting; assistance; the helping of a person on his way by offering conveyance in one's car; (chiefly Brit.) an elevator; a rise in the ground; (Aero.) an air force acting at right angles on aircraft's wing, thereby lifting it [Scand. lypta, to raise].

lig·a·ment (lig′·a·mant) n. anything which binds one thing to another; (Anat.) strong fibrous tissue bands connecting the bones of the body; a bond. **-al, -ary, -ous** a. **ligate** (lī·gāt) v.t. to bind; to bandage. **ligation** n. the act of binding; the state of being bound with a ligature. **ligature** n. anything which binds; a bandage; (Mus.) a line connecting two notes; (Print.) type consisting of two or more letters joined [L. ligare, to bind].

light (līt) v.i. to come to by chance; to alight; to settle. pr.p. **-ing.** pa.p. **-ed** or **lit** [O.E. lihtan, to dismount].

light (līt) a. having little weight; not heavy; easy; active; nimble; loose or sandy, as soil; moderate; as wind; spongy, as cake; not heavily armed, as a cruiser; unsettled; volatile; trivial; wanton; easily disturbed, as sleep. **-en** v.t. to make less heavy; to jettison; to enliven; v.i. to become less heavy or gloomy. **light, -ly** adv. **-er** n. a barge used in loading and unloading ships anchored out from the dock. **-erage** n.

the price paid for loading and unloading ships.
-erman n. **—fingered** a. dexterous, esp. in picking pockets. **—footed** a. agile. **—handed** a. delicate of touch; empty-handed. **—headed** a. delirious; frivolous. **—hearted** a. carefree; gay. **—minded** a. frivolous. **—s** n.pl. the lungs of a slaughtered animal. **-some** a. lively; cheerful. **-weight** a. (of a boxer) weighing less than 135 lbs.; n. (Colloq.) a person of little importance; **-ness** n. quality of being light [O.E. leoht, light].

light (līt) n. that form of radiant energy which stimulates visual perception; anything which has luminosity; day; illumination; a source of illumination; the illuminated part of a scene or picture; point of view; aspect; spiritual or mental enlightenment; any opening admitting light into a building; a. bright; not dark; whitish; pale (of color); v.t. to give light or fire to; v.i. to begin to burn; to become bright; to express joy (as in the face). pr.p. -ing. pa.t. and pa.p. -ed or lit. -en v.t. to illuminate. **-er** n. a mechanical device for producing a flame, as a cigarette-lighter; one who lights street lamps, etc. **-house** n. a tower-like structure built at danger points on seacoast and provided with very powerful light to serve as warning to ships. **-ing** n. illumination; the arrangement of lights in a building; the effect of light, esp. in a picture. **-ish** a. rather light or pale in color. **-ness** n. **-ship** n. a floating lighthouse. **— year** n. (Astron.) the distance in a year (calculated at 5,878,000,000,000 miles) light travels. **to see the light,** to be born; to comprehend. **footlights** n.pl. the row of electric lights along the edge of the stage in a theater. **Northern Lights,** aurora borealis. **lit** (Slang) drunk [O.E. leoht, light].

light·ning (līt'·ning) n. a flash produced by an electrical discharge between two clouds, or between cloud and ground. **— bug** n. a firefly. **— rod** n. a rod serving, by a connected wire called a **lightning-conductor,** to carry electric current into the earth or water, thereby preventing building from being struck by lightning [M.E. lihtnen, to flash].

lig·ne·ous (lig'·ni·as) a. woody; resembling wood. **lignify** v.t. to convert into wood. **lignin** n. an organic substance formed in the woody tissues of plants. **lignite** n. coal of recent origin still showing ligneous texture; brown coal [L. lignum, wood].

lig·ure (lig'·yoor) n. a precious stone [fr. Liguria, a district of Italy].

like (līk) a. equal; similar; n. an equal; a person or thing resembling another; an exact resemblance; prep. similarly to; conj. (Colloq.) as; as if. **-lihood** n. probability. **-ly** a. probable; credible; of excellent qualities; adv. probably. **liken** v.t. to represent as similar; to compare. **-ness** n. resemblance; an image, picture, or statue. **-wise** adv. in like manner; also; moreover [O.E. gelic, similar].

like (līk) v.t. to be pleased with or attracted by; to enjoy; to approve; v.i. to be pleased; n. a liking, as in phrase, 'likes and dislikes.' **lik(e)-able** a. pleasing; congenial; attractive. **lik(e)-ableness** n. **-ly** a. pleasing. **liking** n. [O.E. lician, to please].

li·lac (lī'·lak) n. a shrub, with delicately perfumed flower clusters, purple, pale mauve, or white in color; a pale mauve color; a. of lilac color [Pers. lilak, the indigo flower].

li·li·pu·tian (lil·i·pū'·shan) n. an inhabitant of Lilliput described by Jonathan Swift in his Gulliver's Travels; a person of diminutive size; a. diminutive; dwarfed. [v.i. to sing.

lilt (lilt) n. a light or rhythmic tune; v.t. and **li·ly** (lil'·i·) n. a bulbous plant, with fragrant and showy bell-shaped flowers; a. resembling a lily; pure; pale; delicate. **liliaceous** a. pert. to lilies. **—livered** a. cowardly. **—white** a. pure white; unsullied [O.E. lilie, a lily].

limb (lim) n. an extremity of the human body, as an arm or leg; a branch of a tree [O.E.].

limb (lim) n. an edge or border; (Astron.) the rim of a heavenly body; (Bot.) the expanded part of a petal [L. limbus, a hem].

lim·ber (lim'·ber) n. the detachable front part of a gun-carriage; v.t. to attach to a gun-carriage [Fr. limonière, a cart with shafts].

lim·ber (lim'·ber) a. easily bent; pliant; supple.

lim·bo (lim'·bō) n. a region intermediate between heaven and hell in which the souls of unbaptized children etc., are confined after death; a region of forgotten things; neglect; oblivion; jail [L. limbus, the edge].

lime (līm) n. the linden tree; a. pert to the linden tree [corrupt. of O.E. lind, the linden tree].

lime (līm) n. a tree which produces a small sour kind of lemon; the fruit of this tree [Fr. fr. Span. lima].

lime (līm) n. birdlime; oxide of calcium; white, caustic substance obtained from limestone, shells, marble, etc.; a calcium compound to enrich soil; v.t. to smear with lime; to ensnare; to cement; to manure with lime. **-kiln** n. a furnace in which limestone is heated to produce lime. **-light** n. a powerful light, as on a stage; the public view. **-stone** n. a rock consisting chiefly of carbonate of lime. **limy** a. covered with or impregnated with lime; sticky; resembling lime [O.E. lim, cement].

li·men (lī'·man) n. the threshold of consciousness. **liminal** a. [L. limen, threshold].

lim·er·ick (lim'·er·ik) n. a five-lined nonsense verse [said to be from a song introducing the place name Limerick]. [esp. a sailor.

lim·ey (lī'·mi·) n. (Slang) a British person,

lim·it (lim'·it) n. boundary; edge; utmost extent; (Slang) an outrageous or intolerable person or thing; v.t. to confine within certain bounds; to curb; to restrict the signification of. **-able** a. that may be bounded or restricted. **-ary** a. of, pert. to, or serving as a limit; restricted. **limitation** n. **-ative, -ed** a. circumscribed; narrow. **-edly** adv. **-edness** n. **-less** a. boundless; immeasurable; infinite. **limited liability,** said of a joint stock company in which liability of the shareholder is in proportion to the amount of his stock [L. limes, a boundary].

limn (lim) v.t. to draw or paint; to illuminate a manuscript. **limner** n. painter; one who decorates books with pictures [M.E. limnen, to decorate].

lim·ou·sine (lim'·a·zēn) a. pert. to a type of closed automobile with roof over the driver's head; n. a closed car [fr. Limousin, a French province]. [O.E. lemp-healt, lame].

limp (limp) v.i. to walk lamely; n. lameness

limp (limp) a. wanting in stiffness, as covers of a book; flaccid; flexible; (Fig.) lethargic; exhausted [Scand. limpa, weakness].

lim·pet (lim'·pat) n. a small, univalve conical shaped shellfish which clings firmly to rocks. **—mine** n. (World War 2) a small suction mine attached by hand to the hull of a ship [O.E. lempedu, a lamprey].

lim·pid (lim'·pad) a. clear; translucent; crystal. **-ness, -ity** n. **-ly** adv. [L. limpidus, clear].

linch·pin (linch'·pin) n. a pin used to prevent a wheel from sliding off the axle tree [O.E. lynis, axletree; and pin].

lin·den (lin'·dan) n. a tree with yellowish flowers and heart-shaped leaves [O.E. lind, the lime-tree].

line (līn) n. a rope, wire or string; a slender cord; a thread-like mark; an extended stroke; (Math.) that which has one dimension, length, but no breadth or thickness; a curve connecting points which have a common significance (as the Equator, isotherms, isobars, contours, etc.); a boundary; a row or continued series; progeny; a verse; a short letter or note; a course of conduct, thought, or policy; a trend;

a department; a trade, business or profession; a system of buses, trains, or passenger aircraft under one management; a railway track; a formation of naval vessels; the regular infantry of an army; harmony; graceful cut (as of a costume, dress); a path; a thin crease; parts of a play memorized by an actor or actress; military fieldworks; *v.t.* to mark out with lines; to form in a line; to border. **linage** *n.* number of lines on a page; payment according to the number of lines. **lineage** *n.* descendants in a line from common progenitor; pedigree. **lineal** *a.* composed of lines; pert. to, or in the direction of, a line; directly descended from a common ancestor. **lineality** *n.* **lineally** *adv.* **lineament** *n.* feature; form; characteristic; outline of a body or figure. **linear** *a.* pert. to, or consisting of, a line; drawn in lines. **linearly** *adv.* **lineate(d)** *a.* marked by lines. **lineation** *n.* the act of marking with lines; the lines marked or engraved. **-d** *a.* marked with lines; ruled. — **engraving** *n.* a process of engraving lines on a copper plate. **-r** *n.* a steamship or passenger aircraft belonging to a regular transport line. **linesman** *n.* one who installs and repairs telephone and electric lines, etc.; an official (at football or tennis match) who determines whether ball has crossed the outside line or not. —**up** *n.* a marshaling of forces, or resources. **the line**, the Equator [L. *linea*, a string of flax].

line (līn) *v.t.* to cover on the inside, as a garment, pan, etc. **lining** *n.* the material used; contents [M.E. *linen*, to cover].

lin·en (lin'·ạn) *n.* thread or cloth made from flax; underclothing; napery; *a.* made of flax or linen [O.E. *lin*, flax].

lin·ger (ling'·gẹr) *v.i.* to delay; to dally; to loiter. **-er** *n.* **-ing** *a.* protracted [O.E. *lengan*, to protract].

lin·ge·rie (làn'·jạ·rā, làn'·zhạ·rē) *n.* orig. linen goods; women's underclothing [Fr. *linge*, linen].

lin·go (ling'·gō) *n.* language; a dialect; jargon corrupt. of L. *lingua*, language].

lin·gual (ling'·gwạl) *a.* pert. to the tongue; *n.* a sound or letter made by the tongue, as *d*, *l*, *n.* **-ly** *adv.* **linguiform** *a.* shaped like a tongue. **linguist** *n.* fluent speaker of several languages; an expert in linguistics. **linguistic** *a.* **linguistically** *adv.* **linguistics** *n.* study of human speech including its sounds, history, nature, structure, etc.; comparative philology. **lingulate, lingular** *a.* (*Bot.*) shaped like a tongue [L. *lingua*, a tongue].

lin·i·ment (lin'·ạ·mạnt) *n.* a lotion or soft ointment [L. *linere*, to besmear].

link (lingk) *n.* a single ring of a chain; anything doubled and closed like a link; a connection; the 1/100 part of a chain (7.92 inches). *v.t.* to connect by a link; to combine for a common purpose; *v.i.* to be coupled. **-age** *n.* a system of connections. **missing link**, a connection without which a chain of argument is incomplete; (*Zool.*) that form of animal life the scientific knowledge of which is required to complete the chain of evolution of man from the ape [O.E. *hlence*, a ring]. [ridge].

links (lingks) *n.pl.* a golf course [O.E. *hlinc*, a

lin·net (lin'·at) *n.* a small song bird of the finch family [O.Fr. *linette*, fr. L. *linum*, flax].

li·no·le·um (li·nō'·li·ạm) *n.* a hard floor covering of burlap impregnated with a cement of linseed oil, cork, etc. [L. *linum*, flax; *oleum*, oil].

lin·o·type (lin'·a·tīp) *n.* a type-setting machine in which the matter is cast in solid lines of type [L. *linea*, line, and *type*].

lin·seed (lin'·sēd) *n.* flaxseed. — **cake**, compressed mass of husks of linseed, after oil has been pressed out, much used for cattle feeding. — **oil**, the oil pressed out of linseed [O.E. *linsaed*, flaxseed].

lin·sey-wool·sey (lin'·zi--wool'·zi·) *a.* made of wool and linen mixed; (*Fig.*) shoddy; *n.* inferior stuff [O.Fr. *linsel*, and *wool*].

lint (lint) *n.* a linen material, one side with a soft, wooly surface formerly used for dressing wounds; scraps of thread; fluff from cloth [L. *linteum*, a linen cloth].

lin·tel (lin'·tạl) *n.* a horizontal beam or stone over a doorway or window [L.L. *lintellus*].

li·on (lī'·ạn) *n.* (*fem.* **-ess**) the largest of the cat tribe, tawny-colored, with powerful, tufted tail, the male having a shaggy mane; (*Fig.*) a person of fierce courage; a celebrity; (*Astron.*) a sign of the Zodiac (Leo). —**hearted** *a.* courageous. **-ize** *v.t.* to treat as a celebrity [L. *leo*, a lion].

lip (lip) *n.* one of the two fleshy, outer edges of the mouth; a liplike part; the edge of anything; brim; (*Slang*) impertinent talk; *pl.* the organs of speech as represented by the lips; *v.t.* to touch with the lips; to speak; *a.* pert. to or made by the lips. **-ped** *a.* having a lip or lips. — **reading** *n.* the art of 'hearing' by reading the motions of a speaker's lips; this system as taught to the deaf. — **service** *n.* superficial devotion to a person or cause. **-stick**, a salve, in the form of a small stick, used by women to redden the lips [O.E. *lippa*].

li·quate (li'·kwāt) *v.t.* to melt; to separate or purify solids or gases by liquefying. **liquation** *n.* [L. *liquare*, to be fluid].

liq·ue·fy (lik'·wạ·fī) *v.t.* to transform a liquid; to melt; *v.i.* to become liquid. **liquefaction** *n.* the act of liquefying; the state of being liquefied. **liquefiable** *a.* [L. *liquefacere*, to melt].

li·queur (li·kur') *n.* a preparation of distilled liquors flavored with fruits or aromatic substances [Fr.].

liq·uid (lik'·wid) *a.* fluid; in a state intermediate between a solid and a gas; flowing smoothly; (of sounds) pleasing to the ear; *n.* a substance intermediate between a solid and a gas which assumes the shape of the vessel which contains it; the name popularly applied to a consonant which has a smooth flowing sound (*l*, *r*). **-ate** *v.t.* to settle a debt; to wind up the affairs of business, etc.; to convert into cash; to destroy; *v.i.* (of business) to be wound up. **-ation** *n.* **-ator** *n.* **-ity** *n.* [L. *liquidus*, fluid].

liq·uor (lik'·ẹr) *n.* any liquid or fluid, esp. alcoholic [Fr. fr. L. *liquere*, to be fluid].

li·ra (li'·rạ, lē'·rạ) *n.* the monetary unit and a silver coin of Italy; a monetary unit and gold coin of Turkey [It.].

lisle (līl) *n.* a fine hard-twisted cotton or linen thread [formerly made at *Lille*, France].

lisp (lisp) *v.i.* to speak imperfectly, esp. to substitute the sound *th* for *s*; *v.t.* to pronounce with a lisp; *n.* the habit of lisping. **-ing** *n.* [O.E. *wlisp*, stammering].

lis·some (lis'·um) *a.* supple; flexible; lithe. **-ness** *n.* [fr. *lithesome*].

list (list) *n.* the outer edge or selvage of woven cloth; a row or stripe; a roll; a catalogue; a register; a boundary line enclosing a field of combat at a tournament, esp. in *pl.* **lists**; the field thus enclosed; *v.t.* to sew together strips of cloth; to enter in a catalogue or inventory; *v.i.* to enlist [O.E. *liste*, a border].

list (list) *v.i.* (*Naut.*) to lean or incline (of a ship); *v.t.* to cause to lean; *n.* an inclination to one side [O.E. *lystan*, to desire].

lis·ten (lis'·n) *v.i.* to attend closely; to yield to advice. **list** *v.t.* and *v.i.* to listen (*Poet*). **-er** *n.* **to listen in**, to listen without taking part; to eavesdrop [O.E. *hlyst*, hearing].

list·less (list'·lạs) *a.* indifferent; languid; apathetic. **-ly** *adv.* **-ness** *n.* [O.E. *lust*, pleasure].

lit (lit) *pa.t.* and *pa.p.* of verb **light**.

lit·a·ny (lit'·ạ·ni·) *n.* an earnest prayer of supplication [Gk. *litaneia*, supplication].

li·ter (lē'·tẹr) *n.* a unit of volume in the

metric system, equal to 1.0567 quarts. Also **litre** [Gr. *litra*, pound].

li·te·ral (lit'·a·ral) *a.* according to the letter; real; not figurative; word for word, as a translation. **-ism** *n.* keeping to the literal sense; exact representation in art or literature. **-ist** *n.* **-istic** *a.* **-ize** *v.t.* **-ly** *adv.* [L. *litera*, a letter].

lit·er·ar·y (lit'·er·er·i·) *a.* pert. to letters or literature; versed in literature. **literacy** *n.* state of being literate, opp. of *illiteracy*. **literate** *a.* versed in learning and science; educated; *n.* one who is able to read and write. **literati** *n.pl.* men of letters; educated people. [L. *litera*, a letter].

lit·er·a·ture (lit'·a·ra·choor, ·cher) *n.* the body of writings of a language, period, subject, etc.; (*Colloq.*) any printed matter, as advertisements, brochures [L. *litteratura*, learning].

lithe (lith) *a.* capable of being easily bent; supple; pliant. **-ly** *adv.* **-ness** *n.* **-some** *a.* [O.E. *lithe*, gentle].

li·thog·e·nous (li·thȧj'·a·nas) *a.* rock-producing, as certain corals [Gk. *lithos*, a stone; *genesthai*, to be born].

lith·o·glyph (lith'·ō·glif) *n.* an engraving on a precious stone [Gk. *lithos*; *gluphein*, to carve].

lith·o·graph (lith'·a·graf) *v.t.* to trace on stone, zinc, or aluminium, and transfer to paper by special printing process; *n.* a print from stone, etc. **lithographer** (li·thȧg'·ra·fer) *n.* **lithographic, -al** *a.* **lithographically** *adv.* **lithography** *n.* the art of tracing designs on stone or other media, and taking impressions of these designs [Gk. *lithos*, a stone; *graphein*, to write].

lith·oid, -al (lith'·oid, ·al) *a.* resembling a stone [Gk. *lithos*, a stone].

li·thol·o·gy (li·thȧl'·a·ji·) *n.* the science which treats of the characteristics of rocks; (*Med.*) the study of calculi in the body [Gk. *lithos*, a stone; *logos*, a discourse].

lith·o·tint (lith'·a·tint) *n.* the lithographic production of a tinted picture; the picture itself [Gk. *lithos*, a stone; and *tint*].

lith·o·tome (lith'·a·tōm) *n.* a stone resembling an artificially cut gem; (*Surg.*) an instrument for performing a lithotomy. **lithotomic** *a.* **lithotomist** *n.* **lithotomy** (li·thȧt'·a·mi·) *n.* (*Surg.*) the operation by which stones are removed from the bladder [Gk. *lithos*, a stone; *tomē*, a cutting].

lith·o·type (lith'·a·tīp) *n.* a stereotype plate; print from this plate. **lithotypy** *n.* [Gk. *lithos*, a stone; *tupos*, type].

Lith·u·a·ni·an (lith·oo·ā'·ni·an) *n.* a native of Lithuania; the language. Also **Lett**.

lit·i·gate (lit'·a·gāt) *v.t.* to contest in law; *v.i.* to carry on a lawsuit. **litigable** *a.* **litigant** *n.* a person engaged in a lawsuit; *a.* engaged in a lawsuit. **litigation** *n.* judicial proceedings. **litigator** *n.* one who litigates. **litigiosity** (la·tij·i·ȧs'·a·ti·) *n.* **litigious** *a.* given to engaging in lawsuits [L. *litigare*, to dispute].

lit·mus (lit'·mas) *n.* a bluish purple vegetable dye (obtained from lichens) which turns red with an acid, and blue with an alkali. — **pa-per**, used to test solutions.

li·to·tes (lī'·ta·tēz) *n.* a figure of speech which expresses a strong affirmative, by using the negative of its contrary, as in phrase, *not a few* [Gk. *litos*, simple].

lit·ter (lit'·er) *n.* a heap of straw as bedding for animals; a vehicle containing bed carried on men's shoulders; a stretcher; odds and ands left lying about; state of disorder; a family of young pigs, puppies, etc., brought forth at one birth; *v.t.* to bring forth young; to scatter indiscriminately about; to make untidy with odds and ends [Fr. *litière*, a bed].

lit·tle (lit'·l) *a.* small in size, extent, or quantity; brief; slight; mean; *n.* a small quantity or space; *adv.* in a small quantity or degree (*comp.*

less; *superl.* **least**). **-ness** *n.* [O.E. *lytel*].

lit·to·ral (lit'·er·al) *a.* pert. to a lake or sea-shore [L. *litoralis*, pert. to the seashore].

lit·ur·gy (lit'·er·ji·) *n.* the established ritual for public worship in a church, esp. the Mass. **liturge** *n.* a leader in public worship. **liturgic, -al** *a.* **liturgically** *adv.* **liturgics** *n.* the study of church worship and its ritual. **liturgist** *n.* [Gk. *leitourgia*, a public service].

live (liv) *v.i.* to have life; to subsist; to be conscious; to dwell; to enjoy life; to keep oneself (as on one's income); *v.t.* to spend; to pass. **livable** *a.* habitable [O.E. *lifian*, to live].

live (līv) *a.* having life; quick; active; vital; unexploded, as a mine; burning, as coal; full of zest; dynamite. **lived** (līvd) *a.* used in compounds as *long-lived*, *short-lived*. —**circuit** *n.* a circuit through which an electric current is passing. **liven** *v.t.* to enliven. **-stock** *n.* the general term for horses, cattle, pigs, etc., on a farm. — **wire** *n.* a wire carrying an electric current; an energetic person [O.E. *lif*, life].

live·li·hood (līv'·li·hood) *n.* a means of living; sustenance [O.E. *lif*, life; *lad*, a way].

live·long (liv'·lawng) *a.* the entire [O.E. *leof*, dear].

live·ly (līv'·li·) *a.* animated; active; gay; exciting; light; *adv.* briskly. **livelily** *adv.* **liveliness** *n.* [O.E. *liflic*, life-like].

liv·er (liv'·er) *n.* (*Anat.*) glandular organ in body secreting bile; the flesh of this organ in animals or fowls used as food. **-ish** *n.* off-color because of a disordered liver. **-wort** *n.* a moss-like plant with liver-shaped leaves. **-wurst** *n.* a sausage with a large amount of liver. **lily-livered** *a.* cowardly [O.E. *lifer*, liver].

liv·er·y (liv'·er·i·) *n.* orig. the special dress or food *delivered* by a lord to his household retinue; a dress peculiar to a certain group, as members of a medieval guild or trade; any characteristic uniform of an employee, as of a chauffeur; a livery stable; the body of liverymen. **liveried** *a.* clothed in a livery. **-man** *n.* one who works in a livery stable. — **stable** *n.* a stable where horses and vehicles are kept for hire [O.Fr. *livrée*, an allowance].

liv·id (liv'·id) *a.* black and blue; discolored, as flesh, by bruising. **-ness, lividity** *n.* [L. *lividus*, bluish].

liv·ing (liv'·ing) *a.* having life; active; flowing (of water); resembling closely; contemporary; *n.* livelihood; maintenance; mode of life. — **language**, a language still in use. — **room** *n.* *n.* a sitting-room [O.E. *lif*, life].

liz·ard (liz'·erd) *n.* an order of four-footed scale-clad reptiles [L. *lacerta*].

lla·ma (lȧ'·ma) *n.* a S. America two-toed ruminant, used as a beast of burden [Peruv.].

lo (lō) *interj.* look! behold! [O.E. *lā*, (imit.)].

loach (lōch) a small river fish [Fr. *loche*].

load (lōd) *n.* a burden; the amount normally carried at one time; any heavy weight; a cargo; (*Elect.*) amount of electrical energy drawn from a source; (*Fig.*) burden of anxiety; *pl.* (*Colloq.*) plenty; heaps; *v.t.* to burden; to put on, for conveyance; to freight; to overweight; to overwhelm (with gifts, adulation, etc); to charge (a gun); to weight (as dice); to insert a spool into (as a camera); *v.i.* to take on a load or cargo; to charge a firearm; to become loaded. **-ed** *a.* weighted; (*Slang*) drunk. **-ing** *n.* the act of loading; freight. — **line** *n.* a line painted on the side of a vessel to indicate maximum immersion when loaded. **-stone** *n.* a metal which attracts other metals [O.E. *lad*].

loaf (lōf) *n.* shaped portion of dough baked in the oven; a lump of sugar. *pl.* **loaves. meat-loaf** *n.* meat cooked in a loaf tin or shaped in a mass [O.E. *hlaf*, a loaf].

loaf (lōf) *v.i.* to spend (time) idly; to lounge. **-er** *n.* one who loafs; a moccasin style of shoe.

loam (lōm) *n.* a rich, fertile soil of clay, sand,

oxide of iron, and carbonate of lime; a mixture of clay, sand, and chopped straw used in making molds for founding [O.E. *lam*, clay].

loan (lōn) *n.* the act of lending; that which is lent, esp. money for interest; *v.t.* to lend; to lend at interest. **-ee, -er** *n.* — **office** *n.* a pawnbroker's shop [O.N. *lan*, loan].

loath, loth (lōth) *a.* unwilling; reluctant; disinclined [O.E. *lath*, hateful].

loathe (lōTH) *v.t.* to detest; to abominate; to be nauseated by. **loathing** *n.* disgust; repulsion. **loathly** *a.* **loathsome** *a.* detestable; repugnant. **loathsomely** *adv.* **loathsomeness** *n.* [O.E. *lath*, hateful].

lob (lȧb) *n.* (*Tennis*) a ball rising high in air over opponent's head; *v.t.* to bowl underhand; to hit (tennis ball, shuttle-cock) high into air; *v.i.* to deliver a lob. *pr.p.* **-bing.** *pa.p.* **-bed.** [Scand. *lobbe*, a lump of fat].

lob·by (lȧb'·i·) *n.* a passage, or hall, forming the entrance to a public building or private dwelling; a waiting-room; a pressure group seeking to influence members of a legislature; *v.i.* to solicit votes of members of a legislature; *v.t.* to secure the passage of a bill, to influence a legislator by lobbying. **-ing** *n.* **-ism** *n.* **-ist** *n.* [L.L. *lobia*, a portico].

lobe (lōb) *n.* a rounded division of an organ; the lower, fleshy, rounded part of human ear; a division of the lung; (*Bot.*) rounded division of a leaf. **lobar** *a.* **lobate, lobed, lobose** *a.* having a lobe or lobes [Gk. *lobos*].

lo·bel·ia (lō·bē'·li·a̧) *n.* a genus of herbaceous plants (including the blue dwarf variety) [fr. *Lobel*, botanist to James I].

lob·lol·ly (lȧb'·lȧl·i·) *n.* a pine tree of the southern U.S.

lob·ster (lȧb'·stẹr) *n.* an edible, marine, long-tailed crustacean, with pincer-claws. — **pot,** a trap in which lobsters are caught [corrupt. of L. *locusta*, a lobster].

lo·cal (lō'·ka̧l) *a.* pert. to a particular place; confined to a definite spot, district, or part; circumscribed; *n.* some person or thing belonging to a district; a suburban train. **locale** *n.* the scene of an occurrence; the scene of a film-shot. **localization** *n.* the act of localizing. **localize** *v.t.* to assign to a definite place; to decentralize. **locality** *n.* position of a thing; site; neighborhood. **-ly** *adv.* **locate** *v.t.* to set in a particular place; to find the exact position of. **location** *n.* act of locating; situation; geographical position; the out-of-doors site of a film production. **locative** (lȧk'·a̧·tiv) *n.* (*Gram.*) the case form denoting the 'place where.' [L. *locus*, a place].

loch (lȧk) *n.* a lake, esp. in Scotland; an arm of the sea (as Loch Fyne) [Gael.].

lock (lȧk) *n.* a strand or tress of hair; *pl.* hair of the head [O.E. *locc*, a tress].

lock (lȧk) *n.* a device for fastening a door, box, case, etc.; a mechanism on a gun to keep it from firing; an appliance to check the revolution of a wheel; an accidental stoppage of any mechanism; an enclosure in a canal with gate at each end for allowing vessels to pass from one level to another; the grappling hold, in wrestling; *v.t.* to fasten with a lock and key; to furnish with locks, as a canal; to hold tightly; *v.i.* to become fastened; to jam. **-er** *n.* a drawer, small chest, etc. where valuables may be locked. **-et** *n.* a small case containing portrait, lock of hair, worn on a chain. **-jaw** *n.* a contraction of the muscles of the jaw; tetanus. **-nut** *n.* a second nut screwed on top of the first nut to prevent loosening. **-out** *n.* a refusal by an employer to admit employees until a dispute has been amicably settled. **-smith** *n.* one who makes and repairs locks. **-up** *n.* a prison [O.E. *loc*, a fastening].

lo·co·mo·tion (lō·ka̧·mō'·sha̧n) *n.* the act or process of moving from place to place. **loco-**

motive *a.* capable of moving from one place to another; *n.* an engine which moves by its own power, as a railway engine. **locomotivity** *n.* **locomotor** *n.* person or thing with power to move; *a.* pert. to locomotion [L. *locus*, a place; *movere, motum*, to move].

lo·cus (lō'·ka̧s) *n.* the exact position of anything; (*Math.*) the path traced out by a point moving in accordance with some mathematical law; *pl.* **loci** (lō'·sī) [L. *locus*, a place].

lo·cust (lō'·ka̧st) *n.* a winged insect, allied to the grasshopper and found in N. Africa, Asia, and the U.S.; a thorny-branched N. American tree with very durable wood [L. *locusta*].

lo·cu·tion (lō·kū'·sha̧n) *n.* speech; mode or style of speaking [L. *loqui*, to speak].

lode (lōd) *n.* a metallic vein; a body of ore. **-star, loadstar** *n.* a star by which one steers, esp. the Pole-star. **lodestone** see **loadstone** [O.E. *lad*, a course].

lodge (lȧj) *n.* a small country-house; a cottage at the entrance to an estate; a branch of a society, as of Freemasons, or the building where such a society meets; *v.i.* to dwell in temporarily; to reside; to become embedded in; *v.t.* to deposit for preservation; to infix; to rent out rooms; to lay flat; to harbor; to put (as money) in a bank; to allege, as an accusation. **lodg(e)ment** *n.* lodgings; accumulation of something deposited; (*Mil.*) occupation of a position by a besieging party. **-r** *n.* one who occupies rooms for rent. **lodging(s)** *n.* room(s) let temporarily [O.Fr. *loge*, an apartment].

loft (lawft) *n.* an upper room; an attic in space between top story and roof; the gallery in a church, as the *organ-loft; v.t.* (*Golf*) to strike a ball high. **-ily** *adv.* **-iness** *n.* **-y** *a.* elevated; towering; haughty [Scand. *lopt*, air].

log (lawg, lȧg) *n.* an unhewn piece of timber; an apparatus to measure the speed of a ship and distance covered; the tabulated record of a ship's voyage; a logbook; *a.* made of logs; *v.t.* to fell and trim trees; to clear woodland; to keep records of. *pr.p.* **-ging.** *pa.t., pa.p.* **-ged.** **-book** *n.* a daily record of events on a ship's voyage. — **cabin** *n.* a hut made of lopped tree trunks. **-ger** *n.* a lumberjack. **-ging** *n.* the process of cutting trees and getting the logs to a sawmill to be cut for lumber. **-rolling** *n.* act of clearing logs, esp. from a neighbor's land, hence mutual help esp. in politics [M.E. *logge*].

lo·gan·ber·ry (lō'·ga̧n·ber·i·) *n.* a shrub, a cross between raspberry and blackberry [hybridized by *Logan*, 1881].

log·a·rithm (lawg'·, lȧg'·a̧·riTHm) *n.* the index of the power to which a fixed number or base must be raised to produce the number; a method of reducing arithmetical calculations to a minimum by substituting addition and subtraction for multiplication and division. [Gk. *logos*, ratio; *arithmos*, a number].

log·ger·head (lawg'·, lȧg'·ẹr·hed) *n.* a blockhead; a dunce; a kind of turtle. **at loggerheads,** quarrelling; at cross-purposes [fr. *log* and *head*].

log·gia (lȧj'·i·a̧, law'·jȧ) *n.* a kind of open elevated gallery with pillars, common in Italian buildings [Cf. **lodge**].

log·ic (lȧj'·ik) *n.* the science of reasoning; the science of pure and formal thought; (*Colloq.*) commonsense. **-al** *a.* pert. to formal thought; skilled in logic; reasonable. **logicality, -alness** *n.* **-ally** *adv.* **logician** *n.* one skilled in logic [Gk. *logos*, speech].

lo·gis·tic, -al (lȧj·is'·tik, -a̧l) *a.* pert. to calculating. **-s** *n.pl.* (used as *sing.*); (*Mil.*) branch of military science which deals with the moving of and providing for troops [Gk. *logizesthai*, to compute].

log·o·gram (lawg'·, lȧg'·a̧·gram) *n.* a symbol representing a whole word or phrase [Gk. *logos*, a word; *gramma*, a letter].

lo·go·gra·pher (lō·găg′·rạ·fẹr) *n.* a speech-writer in ancient Greek times. **logography** *n.* a method of printing in which words cast in a single type are used instead of single letters [Gk. *logos*, a word; *graphein*, to write].

loin (loin) *n.* part of animal or man above hips and on either side of spinal column; a cut of meat from this part of an animal. **-cloth** *n.* [L. *lumbus*, loin].

loi·ter (loi′·tẹr) *v.i.* to linger; to be slow in moving; to spend time idly. **-er** *n.* **-ingly** *adv.* [Dut. *leuteren*, to delay].

loll (lȧl) *v.i.* to lounge about lazily; to hang out, as the tongue; *v.t.* to permit to hang out [Scand. *lolla*, to be lazy].

lol·li·pop lollipop (lȧl′·i·pȧp) *n.* a piece of flavored toffee or hard candy on a stick [etym. doubtful].

lone (lōn) *a.* solitary; standing by itself. **-liness, -ness** *n.* **-ly** *a.* alone; unfrequented. **-some** *a.* solitary. **-somely** *adv.* **-someness** *n.* [abbrev. fr. *alone*].

long (lawng) *a.* extended in distance or time; drawn out in a line; protracted; slow in coming; continued at great length; *adv.* to a great extent; at a point of duration far distant; *v.i.* to be filled with a yearning to desire. **— ago** *adv.* in the remote past. **-boat** *n.* the largest boat carried by a sailing ship. **-bow** *n.* a bow drawn by hand, and usually 5½-6 feet long—so called to distinguish it from the *Cross*-bow. **—drawn** *a.* protracted. **longeron** (lȧn′·jẹr·ȧn) *n.* (*Aero.*) a main longitudinal strength member of a fuselage. **longevity** (lawng·-jev′·ạ·ti·) *n.* length of life; uncommonly prolonged duration of life. **longevous** *a.* long-lived. **-hand** *n.* ordinary handwriting (opp. *shorthand*). **—headed** *a.* far-seeing; prudent. **-horn** *n.* a kind of cattle of Mexico and U.S. **— house** *n.* a long communal dwelling of the Iroquois Indians. **— hundred** *n.* Br. hundredweight, 120 pounds. **-ing** a yearning; a craving. **-ingly** *adv.* **-ish** *a.* rather long. **longitude** (lȧn′·jạ·tūd) *n.* angular distance east or west of a given meridian, measured in degrees; (*Astron.*) angular distance from vernal equinox on the ecliptic. **longitudinal** *a.* pert. to length or longitude; lengthwise; *n.* a girder running lengthwise in a ship or airship. **longitudinally** *adv.* **— measure** *n.* linear measure. **—range** *a.* having the power to fire a great distance, as a gun; able to fly or sail great distances without refueling, as aircraft, submarine, etc. **-shore** *a.* existing or employed on the shore. **-shoreman** *n.* a dock laborer. **-sightedness** *n.* (*Med.*) hypermetropia, an abnormal eye condition whereby the rays of light are focused *beyond* and not on the retina. **—standing** *a.* having existed for some time. **—suffering** *a.* patiently enduring. **—winded** *a.* able to run a great distance without becoming short of breath; tedious; loquacious. **-wise, -ways** *a.* lengthwise. **before long,** soon [O.E. *lang*, long].

loo (lŏŏ) *n.* a card-game; *v.t.* to win in a game of loo [abbrev. fr. *lanterloo*].

look (look) *v.i.* to turn one's eyes upon; to seem to be; to consider; to seem; to face, as a dwelling; *v.i* to express by a look; *n.* the act of directing one's gaze upon; facial expression generally; aspect; view. **-er** *n.* one who looks. **-er-on** *n.* a spectator. **-ing** *n.* a search. **-ing glass** *n.* a mirror. **-out** *n.* a watch; a place from which a careful watch is kept; person stationed to keep watch [O.E. *lōcian*, to look].

loom (lŏŏm) *n.* a machine for weaving cloth from thread by interlacing threads called the *woof* through threads called the *warp*; part of the shaft of an oar inside the rowlock [O.E. *geloma*, a tool].

loom (lŏŏm) *v.i.* to emerge indistinctly and larger than the real dimensions; to appear over the horizon; (*Fig.*) to assume great importance.

loom (lŏŏm) *n.* a kind of guillemot; a puffin; a loon [Scand. *lomr*, a sea bird].

loon (lŏŏn) *n.* a large fish-eating diving bird of the northern regions [same as *loom*].

loon·y (lŏŏn′·i·) *n.* (*Colloq.*) a crazy person; *a.* (*Slang*) very foolish [fr. *lunatic*].

loop (lŏŏp) *n.* a doubling of string or rope, through which another string may run; anything with a similar shape; (*Aero.*) an aerial maneuver in which plane describes a complete circle; *v.t.* to fasten by a loop; to form into a loop. **-ed** *a.* [prob. Ir. *lub*, a bend].

loop·hole (lŏŏp′·hōl) *n.* a narrow slit or opening as in the walls of a fortification; (*Fig.*) a way out of a difficult situation.

loose (lŏŏs) *v.t.* to free from constraint; to untie; to disconnect; to relax; to discharge; *v.i.* to set sail; to let go; *a.* free; slack; unsewed; unbound; flowing; diffuse; incoherent; careless; inaccurate; lax; inclined to diarrhea. **—jointed** *a.* loosely built. **—leaf** *a.* having sheets of paper which can be removed and rearranged. **-ly** *adv.* **loosen** *v.t.* to make loose; to unfasten; *v.i.* to become loose; to become relaxed. **loosener** *n.* **-ness** *n.* **—tongued** *a.* prating; indiscreet [O.E. *leas*, loose].

loot (lŏŏt) *n.* plunder; the act of plundering; *v.t.* and *v.i.* to plunder; to appropriate illegally [Sans. *lut*, booty].

lop (lȧp) *v.t.* to cut off, esp. top of anything; to cut away superfluous parts. *pr.p.* **-ping.** *pa.t.*, *pa.p.* **-ped.** *n.* twig from tree; act of lopping. **-per** *n.* **-ping** *n.* [Dut. *lubben*, to cut].

lop (lȧp) *v.i.* to hang down loosely. *pr.p.* **-ping.** *pa.t.*, *pa.p.* **-ped.** **—eared** *a.* having drooping ears. **—sided** *a.* heavier on one side than the other; askew [prob. imit.].

lope (lōp) *v.i.* to run with a long, leisurely gait; *n.* an easy gait [O.N. *hlaupa*, to leap].

lo·qua·cious (lō·kwā′·shạs) *a.* talkative; babbling; garrulous. **-ly** *adv.* **-ness, loquacity** *n.* talkativeness [L. *loquax*, talkative].

lo·quat (lō′·kwȧt) *n.* a low-growing Japanese plum tree; the fruit itself [Chinese].

lo·ran (lō′·rạn) *n.* (*Flying*) a navigational device which locates the position of an airplane [From *long* + *range* + *navigation*].

lord (lawrd) *n.* a master; a ruler; a king; (*Brit.*) a proprietor of a manor; any peer of the realm; courtesy title; the holder of certain high government offices; (*Cap.*) the Supreme Being; Jehovah; God; Christ; *v.i.* to play the lord; to domineer. **-liness** *n.* **-ling** *n.* a petty or unimportant lord. **-ly** *a.* pert. to, or like, a lord; imperious; proud; magnificent. **-ship** *n.* the state of being a lord; authority; estate owned by a lord; (*Brit.*) (with *his, your*) a formal mode of address in speaking to a lord, bishop [O.E. *hlaford*, the keeper of the bread].

lore (lōr) *n.* learning; erudition; traditional knowledge [O.E. *lar*, lore].

lor·gnette (lawr·nyet′) *n.* a pair of eyeglasses attached to a long handle; an opera glass [Fr. *lorgner*, to stare at].

lo·ri·ca (lạ·rī′·kạ) *n.* a cuirass; (*Zool.*) a protective covering of bony plates, scales, etc., like a cuirass. **loricate** *v.t.* to clothe in mail; to cover with a coating; *a.* (*Zool.*) having protective covering of bony plates, as crocodiles [L. *lorica*, a breastplate].

lorn (lawrn) *a.* (*Arch.*) lost; forsaken; desolate [O.E. *loren*, *pa.p.* of *leosan*, to lose].

lor·ry (lawr′·i·) *n.* (*esp. Brit.*) a wagon for transporting heavy loads; a car on rails, used in factories, mines, etc.; (*Brit.*) a truck.

lose (lŏŏz) *v.t.* to be deprived of; to mislay; to forfeit; to fail to win; to miss; to waste, as time; to destroy; *v.i.* to fail; to suffer loss; to become bewildered. *pr.p.* **losing.** *pa.t.* and *pa.p.* **lost. losable** *a.* **-r** *n.* **losing** *a.* producing loss. **loss** *n.* the act of losing; that which is lost; defeat; diminution; bereavement; harm; waste by escape or leakage; number of casualties suffered in war. **lost** *a.* mislaid; bewildered; bereft [O.E. *leosan*, to lose].

lot (lŏt) *n.* what happens by chance; destiny; object used to determine something by chance; the choice thus determined; a separate part; a large number of articles such as at an auction sale; (*Motion Pictures*) the area covered by film studio and its subsidiary buildings; (*Colloq.*) a great many; *v.t.* to allot; to separate into lots. **-tery** *n.* a scheme by which prizes are given to people, not on merit, but by drawing lots. **a job-lot,** a miscellaneous collection of articles, sold as one item [O.E. *hlot*, a share].

loth (lōth) *a.* Same as **loath.**

Lo·thar·i·o (lō·thar'·i·ō) *n.* libertine, rake [fr. *Lothario*, in Rowe's *The Fair Penitent*].

lo·tion (lō'·shan) *n.* a fluid with healing, antiseptic properties esp. for the skin [L. *lavare*, *lotum*, to wash].

lot·to (lăt'·ō) *n.* a game of chance [fr. *lot*].

lo·tus (lō'·tas) *n.* the Egyptian water lily; a decorative representation, as in Egyptian and Hindu art; a genus of plants including the British bird's-foot trefoil; a N. African shrub, the fruit of which was reputed, in Greek legend, to induce in those who consumed it an overpowering lethargy. Also **lotos.** **—eater** *n.* (*Fig.*) one who gives up an active life for one of slothful ease [Gk. *lōtus*].

loud (loud) *a.* making a great sound; noisy; flashy; obtrusive; vulgar. **loud, -ly** *adv.* **-ness** *n.* **-speaker** *n.* a device which makes speech, music, etc. audible at a distance [O.E. *hlud*].

lou·is (lōō'·i·) *n.* an obsolete French gold coin worth 20 francs. Also **— d'or.** **— quatorze,** **— quinze,** **— seize,** applied to architecture, furniture, style of interior decoration characteristic of the reigns of the French Kings Louis XIV, VX, XVI [Fr.].

lounge (lounj) *v.i.* to recline at ease; to loll; to spend time idly; *n.* the act of lounging; a room in which people may relax; a kind of sofa.

louse (lous) *n.* a small wingless parasitic insect infesting hair and skin of human beings; a sucking parasite found on mammals or plants. *pl.* **lice. lousily** (louz'·a·li·) *adv.* **lousiness** *n.* **lousy** *a.* infested with lice; (*Slang*) mean; despicable [O.E. *lus*, a louse].

lout (lout) *n.* a clumsy fellow; a bumpkin; *v.i.* to bend. **-ish** *a.* **-ishly** *adv.* [etym. uncertain].

lou·ver (lōō'·ver) *n.* an opening in the roof of ancient buildings for the escape of smoke or for ventilation; a slot for ventilation [O.Fr. *louvert* for *l'ouvert*, the open space].

love (luv) *n.* affection; strong liking; goodwill; benevolence; charity; devoted attachment to one of the opposite sex; passion; the object of affection; the personification of love: Cupid; (*Tennis*) no score; *v.t.* to show affection for; to be delighted with; to admire passionately; *v.i.* to be in love; to delight. **lovable** *a.* worthy of affection; engaging. **lovableness** *n.* **— affair** *n.* a passionate attachment between two members of the opposite sex. **— apple** *n.* the tomato. **—bird** *n.* a small parrot with bright-colored plumage. **—charm** *n.* a philter. **—child** *n.* an illegitimate child. **— feast** *n.* a religious festival among the early Christians during which collections were made for the poor. **—in-a-mist** *n.* fennel. **—in-idleness** *n.* the pansy. **—knot** *n.* a bow of ribbon tied in a special way, as a token of love. **-less** *a.* lacking love; not founded on love. **— letter** *n.* a letter written to a sweetheart. **—lies-bleeding** *n.* a garden flower with reddish-purple spike flowers. **-liness** *n.* **—lock** *n.* a curl worn on the forehead or over the temple. **-lorn** *a.* forsaken. **-ly** *a.* very beautiful; **-making** *n.* courtship. **— match** *n.* a marriage founded on true love. **— philter** *or* **— potion** *n.* a drink

supposed to induce the emotion of love towards a chosen person. **-r** *n.* one who loves, esp. one of the opposite sex; an admirer, as of the arts. **loverlike** *a.* **loverly** *adv.* **— seat** *n.* a seat for two. **-sick** *a.* pining because of love. **—song** *n.* lyric inspired by love. **—token** *n.* an object, as a ring, given as a symbol of love. **loving** *a.* affectionate; loyal. **loving-cup** *n.* large drinking-vessel with two handles, given as a prize or trophy. **lovingly** *adv.* **lovingness** *n.* [O.E. *lufu*, love].

low (lō) *a.* not high; lying near the ground; depressed below the adjacent surface; near the horizon; shallow; not loud, as a voice; moderate, as prices; dejected; lewd; weak; cold, as a temperature; humble; (of dress) décolleté; *adv.* not high; in a low voice; cheaply. **-born** *a.* of humble birth. **-boy** *n.* a chest about three feet high usu. with two tiers of drawers and on slender legs. **-brow** *n.* a non-intellectual. **Low Countries,** the Netherlands, Belgium, and Luxemburg. **-down** *a.* mean; underhand; *n.* (*Slang*) full information. **-er** *v.t.* to cause to descend; to take down; to humble; to diminish resistance; to make cheap; to reduce pitch; *a.* (*compar.* of *low*) less exalted. **-er case** *n.* abbrev. *l.c.*) small letters as opposed to capitals. **-land** *n.* country which is relatively flat in comparison with surrounding hilly district. **-lander** *n.* an inhabitant of flat land, esp. in Scotland. **-liness** *n.* **-ly** *a.* humble; meek; **—pressure,** having only a small expansive force (less than 50 lbs. to the square inch) said of steam and steam engines [O.N. *lagr*].

low (lō) *v.i.* to bellow as an ox or cow; *n.* the noise made [O.E. *hlowan*, to low].

low·er (lou'·er) *v.i.* to frown; to look gloomy or threatening, as the sky; *n.* a scowl; sullenness. **-ing** *a.* **-ingly** *adv.* Also **lour** [M.E. *louren*, to frown].

lox (lǎks) *n.* liquid oxygen [from liquid *oxygen*]. *n.* salty smoked salmon [Yid. *lachs*, salmon].

loy·al (loi'·al) *a.* faithful to the lawful government, the sovereign, a cause, or a friend. **-ist** *n.* a faithful follower of a cause. **-ly** *adv.* **-ty** *n.* fidelity [Fr. fr. L. *lex*, a law].

loz·enge (lăz'·inj) *n.* a figure with two acute and two obtuse angles; small (often medicated) confection orig. lozenge-shaped.

lub·ber (lub'·er) *n.* a heavy, clumsy fellow.

lu·bri·cate (lōō'·bri·kāt) *v.t.* to make smooth or slippery; to smear with oil, grease, etc., to reduce friction. **lubricant** *n.* any oily substance used to reduce friction; *a.* having the property of reducing friction. **lubrication** *n.* **lubricative** *a.* **lubricator** *n.* **lubricity** *n.* slipperiness [L. *lubricare*, to make slippery].

luce (lōōs) *n.* a fresh-water fish, the pike when full grown [O.Fr. *lus*, a pike].

lu·cent (lōō'·sant) *a.* shining; bright. **lucency** *n.* **lucernal** *a.* pert. to a lamp [L. *lucere*].

lu·cid (lōō'·sid) *a.* shining; clear; easily understood, as of style; normally sane. **-ness, -ity** *n.* **-ly** *adv.* [L. *lux*, light].

Lu·ci·fer (lōō'·sa·fer) *n.* the planet Venus, when appearing as the morning star; Satan. [L. *lucifer*, light-bearing].

lu·cite (lōō'·sīt) *n.* a very clear plastic compound [Trade Name].

luck (luk) *n.* accidental fortune, good or bad; fate; chance. **-ily** *adv.* **-iness** *n.* **-less** *n.* unfortunate. **-lessly** *adv.* **-lessness** *n.* **-y** *a.* fortunate; fortuitous [Dut. *luk*, fate].

lu·cre (lōō'·ker) *n.* material gain; profit, esp. ill-gotten. **lucrative** *a.* profitable. **lucratively** *adv.* **filthy lucre** (*Slang*) money [L. *lucrum*].

lu·cu·brate (lōō'·kya·brāt) *v.i.* to study by lamp or candlelight, or at night. **lucubration** *n.* nocturnal study; the product of such study. **lucubrator** *n.* **lucubratory** *a.* [L. *lucubrare*, to work by candlelight].

lu·cu·lent (lōō'·kya·lant) *a.* clear; self-evident.

-ly *adv*. [L. *lux*, light].

lu·di·crous (lōō'·di·krạs) *a*. provoking laughter; ridiculous; droll. **-ly** *adv*. **-ness** *n*. [L. *ludus*, sport].

luff (luf) *v.ı.* to turn the head of a ship towards the wind; to sail nearer the wind; *n*. the windward side of a ship [M.E. *lof*, a paddle].

Luft·waf·fe (looft'·vả·fạ) *n*. the German Air Force [Ger. *Luft*, the air; *Waffe*, a weapon].

lug (lug) *v.t.* to pull with force; to tug; to haul; to drag. *pr.p.* **-ging**. *pa.t.* and *pa.p.* **-ged**. **-gage** *n*. a traveler's trunks, baggage, etc. [Scand. *lugga*, to pull the hair].

lug (lug) *n*. a projecting piece by which an object may be grasped, supported, etc. [Scand. *lugga*, a forelock].

lu·gu·bri·ous (lōō·gū'·bri·ạs) *a*. mournful; woeful; dismal. **-ly** *adv*. [L. *lugere*, to mourn].

lug·worm (lug'·wurm) a large earthworm.

luke·warm (look'·wawrm) *a*. moderately warm; tepid; indifferent. **-ly** *adv*. **-ness** *n*. [M.E. *leuk*, tepid; *warm*].

lull (lul) *v.t.* to soothe to sleep; to quiet; *v.i.* to become quiet gradually; *n*. a period of quiet in storm or noise. **-aby** (·a·bī) *n*. a song sung to a child to soothe it to sleep [Scand. *lulla*].

lum·ba·go (lum·bā'·gō) *n*. a painful rheumatic affection of the lumbar muscles. **lumbaginous, lumbar, lumbral** *a*. pert. to the lower part of the back [L. *lumbus*, the loin].

lum·ber (lum'·bẹr) *n*. anything useless and cumbersome; odds and ends hoarded; timber cut and split for market; *v.i.* to prepare timber for market; *v.t.* to heap in disorder. **-er, -jack, -man**, *n*. **-ing** *n*. **-yard** *n*. [fr. *Lombard*, a pawnbroker's shop].

lum·ber (lum'·bẹr) *v.i.* to move heavily. **-er** *n*. **-ing** *a*. [Scand. *lomra*, to resound].

lu·mi·nar·y (lōō'·mạ·ner·i·) *n*. any body which gives light, esp. one of the heavenly bodies; (*Fig.*) a person of outstanding qualities. **luminant** *a*. giving out light. **lumination** *n*. **luminescence** *n*. the quality of being luminescent; phosphorescence. **luminescent** *a*. **lumeniferous** *a*. yielding light. **luminous** *a*. shining; brilliant; glowing; brilliant in mind; lucid; comprehensible. **luminously** *adv*. [L. *lumen*, a light].

lump (lump) *n*. a small mass of matter of indefinite shape; a swelling; the gross; (*Colloq.*) a stupid, clumsy person; *a*. in a mass; *v.t.* to throw into a mass; to take in the gross. **lumpy** *a*. full of lumps; uneven. **in the lump**, taken as an aggregate [Scand. *lump*, a block].

lu·nar (lōō'·nẹr) *a*. pert. to the moon; measured by revolutions of the moon. Also **lunary**. **lunacy** *n*. madness, formerly supposed to be influenced by changes of moon. **lunatic** *a*. insane; *n*. a mad person. **lunation** *n*. the period from one new moon to the next. **lunar month**, period of the moon's revolution, about 29½ days. **lunar year**, period of twelve synodic lunar months (354⅓ days). **lunate** *a*. crescent-shaped [L. *luna*, the moon].

lunch (lunch) *n*. a light meal taken between breakfast and dinner. Also **-eon**. *v.i.* to take lunch. **-eonette** *n*. [dial. *lunsh*, a lump].

lune (lōōn) *n*. anything in the shape of a half-moon. **lunette** *n*. a crescent-shaped opening in a vault to let in light [L. *luna*, the moon].

lung (lung) *n*. one of the two main organs of respiration in a breathing animal. **-ed** *a*. [O.E. *lungen*, lungs].

lunge (lunj) *n*. in fencing, a sudden thrust; *v.i.* to thrust [Fr. *allonger*, to stretch].

lu·pine (lōō'·pin) *a*. wolflike [L. *lupus*, a wolf].

lu·pine (lōō'·pạn) *n*. a genus of leguminous plants, some cultivated for their flowers, others for cattle fodder [L. *lupinus*, pert. to a wolf].

lu·pus (lōō'·pạs) *n*. a spreading tubercular condition affecting the skin [L. *lupus*, a wolf].

lurch (lurch) *n*. a sudden roll of a ship to one side; a staggering movement; *v.i.* to stagger.

lurch (lurch) *n*. a critical move in the game of cribbage. **to leave in the lurch**, to desert in a moment of need [Fr. *lourche*, a game].

lure (loor) *n*. a decoy used by the falconer to recall the hawk; an artificial bait; *v.t.* to entice; to decoy [Fr. *leurre*, a bait].

lu·rid (lōō'·rid) *a*. extravagantly colored; (*Fig.*) startling; ghastly pale. **-ly** *adv*. [L. *luridus*, pale yellow].

lurk (lurk) *v.i.* to lie hidden; to lie in wait. **-er** *n*. [Scand. *lurka*, to go slowly].

lus·cious (lush'·ạs) *a*. excessively sweet; cloying. **-ly** *adv*. **-ness** *n*. [etym. doubtful].

lush (lush) *a*. luxuriant; juicy [*luscious*].

lush (lush) *n*. (*Slang*) a habitually drunken person.

lust (lust) *n*. longing desire; sexual appetite; craving; *v.i.* to desire passionately; to have sexual appetites. **-ful** *a*. having inordinate carnal desires; sensual. **-fully** *adv*. **-fulness** *n*. **-iness** *n*. **-ily** *adv*. **lusty** *a*. vigorous; robust [O.E. *lust*, pleasure].

lus·ter (lus'·tẹr) *n*. clearness; glitter; gloss; renown; radiance; chandelier with drops or pendants of cut glass; a cotton dress fabric with glossy, silky surface; a pottery glaze. **lustrous** *a*. gleaming; bright. **lustrously** *adv*. [L. *lustrare*, to make bright].   [Fr.].

lus·trine (lus'·trin) *n*. a glossy silk fabric.

lus·trum (lus'·trạm) *n*. a period of five years; purification, (Rom. times) every five years. **lustral** *a*. pert. to, or used in, purification. **lustration** *n*. the act of purifying; the sacrifice or ceremony by which cities, fields, armies, or people were purified [L. *lustrare*, to purify].

lute (lōōt) *n*. a stringed instrument with a pear-shaped body. **lutanist, luter, lutist** *n*. a lute-player. **—string** *n*. [O.Fr. *lut*].

Lu·ther·an (lōō'·thẹr·ạn) *a*. pert. to *Luther* the German reformer, or to his doctrines; *n*. a follower of Martin Luther; a member of the Lutheran Church. **-ism, Lutherism**.

lu·thern (lōō'·thẹrn) *n*. a dormer-window.

lux·ate (luk'·sāt) *v.t.* to put out of joint; to dislocate. **luxation** *n*. [L. *luxare*, to dislocate].

luxe See **de luxe**.

lux·u·ry (luk'·shạ·ri·) *n*. indulgence in the pleasures which wealth can procure; that which is not a necessity of life. **luxuriance, luxuriancy, luxuriety** *n*. **luxuriant** *a*. in great abundance; dense or prolific, as vegetation. **luxuriantly** *adv*. **luxuriate** *v.i.* to grow luxuriantly; to live luxuriously. **luxurious** *a*. self-indulgent in appetite, etc.; sumptuous. **luxuriously** *adv*. **luxuriousness** *n*. [L. *luxus*, excess].

Ly·ce·um (lī·sē'·ạm) *n*. orig. a place in Athens where Aristotle taught his pupils; (*l.c.*) a lecture hall [Gk. *Lukeion*].

lydd·ite (lid'·īt) *n*. picric acid; a powerful explosive used in shells [fr. *Ludd* in Kent].

lye (lī) *n*. alkaline solution of wood ashes and water; used in soap making [O.E. *leah*].

ly·ing (lī'·ing) *a*. recumbent. **lying-in** *n*. the confinement of a pregnant woman [fr. *lie*].

ly·ing (lī'·ing) *a*. untruthful; *n*. habit of being untruthful. **-ly** *adv*. [fr. *lie*].

lymph (limf) *n*. an alkaline fluid, watery in appearance, contained in the tissues and organs of the body. **-atic** *a*. pert. to lymph; sluggish. **-atics** *n.pl.* small vessels in the body containing lymph. **-oid** *a*. like, composed of, lymph [L. *lympha*, water].

lynch (linch) *v.t.* to inflict capital punishment (on an accused) illegally [fr. *Charles Lynch*, Virginia planter (18th cent.)].

lynx (lingks) *n*. an animal of the cat tribe with abnormally keen sight [Gk. *lunx*].

ly·on·naise (lī'·ạ·nāz) *a*. prepared with onions [Fr.].

lyre (līr) *n*. a stringed, musical instrument in

use among ancient Greeks, esp. to accompany minstrels. **lyrate** *a.* shaped like a lyre. **-bird** *n.* an Australian bird with tail feathers which curve upward in the shape of a lyre. **lyric.** *n.* orig. a poem sung to music; a short, subjective poem expressing emotions of poet. **lyric, -al** *a.* pert. to the lyre; suitable to be sung to a musical accompaniment; used of poetry expressing emotion. **lyricism** *n.* lyrical quality of a poem; emotional expression. **lyrist** *n.* **lyricist** *n.* [Gk. *lura*, a lyre].

M

ma'am (mam) *n.* contr. of **madam**.

ma·ca·bre (mạ·kả′·bẹr) *a.* gruesome; ghastly; grim. **macaberesque** *a.* [O.Fr. *macabre*].

mac·a·dam (mạ·kad′·ạm) *n.* a road-surface material of crushed stones. **-ize** *v.t.* [fr. J. L. *MacAdam*, the inventor (d. 1836)].

ma·caque (mạ·kȧk′) *n.* a genus of Asian monkeys. **macaco** *n.* Braz. monkey [Port. *macaco*, a monkey].

mac·a·ro·ni (mak·ạ·rō′·ni·) *n.* a paste of wheat flour made in long slender tubes; a dandy of the 18th cent. **macaronic** *a.* affected; burlesque verse in modern words with Latinized endings [It.].

mac·a·roon (mak′·ạ·rȯȯn) *n.* a small cooky made of white of egg, ground almonds and sugar [Fr. *macaroon*].

ma·caw (mạ·kaw′) *n.* a long-tailed S. Amer. parrot [Brazil. *macao*].

mace (mās) *n.* a heavy club of metal; a staff carried as an emblem of authority; a billiard cue [O. Fr. *mace*, a mallet].

mace (mās) *n.* a spice made from nutmeg.

mac·er·ate (mas′·ạ·rāt) *v.t.* to soften by soaking; to cause to grow thin; *v.i.* to become soft; to waste away. **maceration** *n.* [L. *macerare*, to steep].

ma·che·te (mạ·che′·ti·) *n.* a heavy knife or cleaver used to cut down sugar canes, and as a weapon [Sp.].

Mach·i·a·vel·lian (mak·i·ạ·vel′·i·ạn) *a.* pert. to Machiavelli; unscrupulous; crafty; *n.* an unprincipled ruthless ruler. **-ism** *n.* [fr. *Machiavelli*, Florentine statesman].

mach·i·nate (mak′·ạ·nāt) *v.t.* to contrive, usually with evil or ulterior motive; *v.i.* to conspire. **machination** *n.* the act of contriving or plotting, with evil intent; an intrigue. **machinator** *n.* one who plots [L. *machinari*, to plot].

ma·chine (mạ·shēn′) *n.* (*Mech.*) any contrivance for the conversion and direction of motion; an apparatus for doing some kind of work; an engine; a vehicle; a person who acts like an automaton; a politically controlled organization; a contrivance in the ancient Greek theater to indicate a change of scene; *v.t.* to use a machine. — **gun** *n.* an automatic small-arms weapon capable of continuous firing. **machinery** *n.* machines collectively; the parts of a machine; any combination of means to an end. — **tool** *n.* a tool for cutting, shaping and turning operated by machinery. **machinist** *n.* one who makes machinery; one who works at a machine [L. *machina*, a machine].

mack·er·el (mak′·ẹr·ạl) *n.* an edible sea fish with blue and black stripes above and silver color below [O.Fr. *mackerel*].

mack·i·naw (mak′·ạ·naw) *n.* a short woolen coat, usually plaid [Ojibwa Indian, turtle].

mack·in·tosh (mak′·in·tȧsh) *n.* a waterproof coat [fr. *Charles MacIntosh*, the inventor].

mac·ra·mé (mak′·rạ·mā) *n.* a coarse fringe.

mac·ro·bi·ot·ic (mak·rō·bī·ȧt′·ik) *a.* long

lived. **macrobiosis** *n.* long life. **macrobiotics** *n.* study of longevity [Gk. *makros*, long; *bios* life].

mac·ro·cosm (mak′·rȧ·kȧzm) *n.* the great universe. **-ic** *a.* [Gk. *makros*, long; *cosmos*, the world].

ma·cron (mā′·krȧn) *n.* short line put over vowel to show it is long in quantity or quality, as *fāte* [Gk. *makros*, long].

mac·ro·scop·ic (mak·rạ·skȧp′·ik) *a.* visible to the naked eye; opp. of *microscopic*. **-ally** *adv.* [Gk. *makros*, long; *skopein*, to see].

mac·u·la (mak′·yạ·lạ) *n.* a spot. *pl.* **maculae**. **maculate** *v.t.* to spot. **maculation** *n.* the act of spotting; a spot. **maculose** *a.* spotted [L.].

mad (mad) *a.* (*comp.* **-der**; *superl.* **-dest**) deranged in mind; insane; crazy; frenzied; angry; infatuated; irrational, as a scheme. **-cap** *n.* a rash person; *a.* uncontrolled. **-den** *v.t.* to enrage; to drive mad; to annoy; *v.i.* to behave as a madman. **-dening** *a.* **-ly** *adv.* **-house** *n.* an asylum for patients with mental disorders; a place of confusion. **-man** *n.* a lunatic. **-ness** *n.* insanity; anger [O.E. *gemaed*, foolish].

mad·am (mad′·ạm) *n.* a formal mode of address in speaking to a married or elderly woman. **madame** (mạ·dam′) *n.* French form. *pl.* **mesdames** (mā·dȧm′) [O.Fr. *ma dame*, my lady].

Ma·dei·ra (mạ·dir′·ạ) *n.* a rich amber-colored wine from *Madeira*, Port.

ma·de·moi·selle (mad·ạ·mạ·zel′) *n.* French mode of addressing unmarried lady [Fr.].

Ma·don·na (mạ·dȧn′·ạ) *n.* the Virgin Mary; a statue of the Virgin [It. *mia*, my; *donna*, a lady].

mad·ras (mad′·rạs) *n.* a fine cotton cloth, usu. striped or plaid [fr. *Madras*, India].

mad·re·pore (mad′·rạ·pōr) *n.* white perforate coral [It. *madre*, a mother; L. *porus*, a pore].

mad·ri·gal (mad·ri·gạl) *n.* a short love poem; an unaccompanied part-song, usually syncopated in rhythm, popular in 16th and 17th cents.

mael·strom (māl′·strạm) *n.* a whirlpool; (*Fig.*) menacing state of affairs [Dut. = a whirlpool].

ma·es·to·so (mī·stō′·sō) *a.* and *adv.* (*Mus.*) with dignity [It.].

maes·tro (mīs′·trō) *n.* master, esp. an eminent composer, conductor, or teacher of music [It.].

Mae West (mā·west) *n.* an inflatable life-jacket [fr. *Mae West*, film star].

ma·fi·a (má′·fi·a) *n.* a criminal Sicilian secret society; hostility to the law. Also **maffia** [It.].

mag·a·zine (mag′·ạ·zēn) *n.* a military store-house; part of a ship where ammunition is stored; compartment in a rifle holding the cartridges; a periodical containing miscellaneous articles [Fr. *magasin*, a warehouse].

ma·gen·ta (mạ·jen′·tạ) *n.* a purplish dye from coal tar [discovery in *Magenta*, It.].

mag·got (mag′·at) *n.* a grub; larva of a house-fly; (*Fig.*) a whim [M.E. *maddok*, a flesh worm].

Ma·gi (mā′·jī) *n.pl.* a class of priests among the ancient Persians; in the N.T. the Wise Men who came to visit the infant Jesus [Gk. *magos*, a magician].

mag·ic (maj′·ik) *n.* the feigned art of influencing nature or future events by occult means; sorcery; charm. **-al** *a.* **-ally** *adv.* **-ian** (mạ·jish′·ạn) *n.* one skilled in magic; a conjurer. — **lantern**, early form of projector using slides. **black magic**, magic by aid of evil spirits [Gk. *magikos*].

mag·is·te·ri·al (maj·ạs·tir′·i·ạl) *a.* pert. to or conducted by a magistrate; authoritative; judicial; overbearing. **-ly** *adv.* [L. *magister*].

mag·is·trate (maj′·ạs·trāt) *n.* a person vested with public judicial authority; a justice of the peace. **magistracy** *n.* the position of a magistrate; the body of magistrates [L. *magistratus*].

mag·ma (mag′·mạ) *n.* a paste of mineral or organic matter; (*Geol.*) the molten rock beneath the earth's crust; (*Pharm.*) a salve [Gk. to knead].

Mag·na Car·ta (Charta) (mag'·nạ kàr'·tạ) *n.* Great Charter of English public and private liberties signed by King John, 1215 (L.)].

mag·na·nim·i·ty (mag·nạ·nim'·ạ·ti·) *n.* greatness of mind; generosity of heart esp. in forgiveness. **magnanimous** *a.* **magnanimously** *adv.* [L. *magnus*, great; *animus*, the mind].

mag·nate (mag'·nāt, -net) *n.* an eminent person, esp. a wealthy business man [L. *magnus*, great].

mag·ne·si·um (mag·nē'·zē·ạm, -zhạm) *n.* the silvery-white metallic base of magnesia, burning with an intensely brilliant white light and used for fireworks, flash bulbs, etc. [Gk. *Magnesia* (lithos), magnesian stone].

mag·net (mag'·nạt) *n.* the loadstone; a bar of iron having property of attracting iron or steel and, when suspended, of pointing N. and S.; a person or thing with powers of attraction. **-ic, (al)** *a.* pert. to a magnet; attractive. **-ically** *adv.* **-ist** *n.* an expert in magnetism. **-izable** *a.* **-ization** *n.* **-ize** *v.t.* to give magnetic properties to; to attract; *v.i.* to become magnetic. **-ism** *n.* the natural cause of magnetic force; the science of the phenomena of magnetic force; attraction. **magneto** *n.* a magnetoelectric machine, esp. used to generate ignition spark in internal-combustion engine. **magnetic field**, the sphere of influence of magnetic forces. **magnetic needle**, a small magnetized pivoted steel bar of a compass which always points approximately north. **magnetic north**, the north as indicated by the pivoted bar of the mariner's compass. **magnetic poles**, two nearly opposite points on the earth's surface [Gk. *magnētis* (lithos), a magnet].

mag·ni·fy (mag'·nạ·fī) *v.t.* to make greater; to cause to appear greater. **Magnificat** *n.* the song of the Virgin Mary. **magnification** *n.* the act of magnifying. **magnificent** *a.* splendid; brilliant;. **magnificence** *n.* **magnificently** *adv.* **magnifico** *n.* a Venetian nobleman; person of importance. **magnified** *n.* one who or the instrument which magnifies [L. *magnus*, great; *facere*, to make].

mag·nil·o·quent (mag·nil'·ạ·kwạnt) *a.* speaking pompously; boastful. **magniloquence** *n.* [L. *magnus*, great; *loqui*, to speak].

mag·ni·tude (mag'·nạ·tūd) *n.* greatness; size; importance [L. *magnitudo*, greatness].

mag·no·li·a (mag·nō'·li·ạ) *n.* a species of tree bearing large perfumed flowers [fr. *Magnol*, French botanist].

mag·num (mag'·nạm) *n.* a wine-bottle holding two quarts. **— opus** *n.* one's best artistic or literary work [L. *magnus*, great].

mag·pie (mág'·pī) *n.* a bird of the crow family, with a harsh chattering cry; an idle chatterer [contr. of *Margaret* and *pie*].

Mag·yar (mag'·yàr) *n.* dominant people of Hungary; the language of Hungary.

ma·ha·ra·jah (mà·hạ·rà'·jạ) *n.* (*fem.* **maharani** or **maharanee**) the title of an Indian prince [Sans. *maha*, great; *raja*, a prince].

ma·hat·ma (mạ·hàt'·mạ) *n.* a man of saintly life with supernatural powers derived from purity of soul [Sans. *mahatma*, high-souled].

mah·jong (mà·jàng') *n.* old Chinese game for four played with small tiles [Chin.].

ma·hog·a·ny (mạ·hág'·a·ni·) *n.* a tree of hard, reddish wood used for furniture; the red-brown color of mahogany [W. Ind.].

maid (mād) *n.* a girl or unmarried woman; a female domestic servant. **old maid**, a spinster; a game of cards. **-en**, *n.* a maid; *a.* pert. to a maid; unmarried; unused; first. **-enhair** *n.* a kind of fern with delicate fronds. **-enhood**, *n.* virginity; purity. **-enliness** *n.* **-enly** *a.* gentle;

modest. **-en name**, surname of a woman before marriage [O.E. *maegden*, a maid].

mail (māl) *n.* defensive armor composed of steel rings or plates; *v.t.* to clothe in armor [O.Fr. *maille*, mail].

mail (māl) *n.* letters, packages, etc., carried by post; the person or means of conveyance for transit of letters, parcels, etc.; *v.t.* to post; to send by mail. **-bag** *n.* the sack in which letters are put for transit. **-boat, -car, -plane, -train, -man** *n.* means of conveyance of letters [O.Fr. *male*, a trunk or mail].

maim (mām) *v.t.* to deprive of the use of a limb; to disable; to disfigure. **-er** *n.* [O.Fr. *mahaing*, a bruise].

main (mān) *a.* principal; first in size, importance, etc.; sheer; *n.* the chief part; strength, as in *might and main*; (*Poet.*) the open sea or ocean or the mainland; the principal pipe or line in water, gas, or electricity system. **-land** *n.* a continent as distinct from islands. **-ly** *adv.* **-spring** *n.* the principal spring in a watch or other mechanism; motive power. **-stay** *n.* the chief support [O.E. *maegen*, main].

main·tain (mān·tān') *v.t.* and *v.i.* to hold or keep in any state; to sustain; to preserve; to defend, as an argument; to support. **-able** *a.* **-er** *n.* **maintenance** *n.* the act of maintaining; means of support [Fr. *maintenir*, to hold].

maize (māz) *n.* Indian corn, a cereal; yellow [Sp. *maiz*].

maj·es·ty (maj'·ạs·ti·) *n.* grandeur; exalted dignity; royal state; the title of a sovereign. **majestic, -al** *a.* [L. *majestas*, dignity].

ma·jol·i·ca (mạ'·jạl'·i·kạ) *n.* a decorative, enameled pottery [fr. *Majorca*].

ma·jor (mā'·jẹr) *a.* greater in number, quality, quantity, or extent; (*Mus.*) greater by a semitone; pert. to a field of study; *n.* a person who has reached the age of 21; an officer in the army ranking below a lieutenant-colonel; a principal field of study. *v.i.* to specialize. **—domo** *n.* a steward; (*Colloq.*) an organizer. **— general** *n.* an army officer in rank below a lieutenant-general. **majority** *n.* the greater part; more than half; full legal age (21) [L. *major*, greater].

make (māk) *v.t.* to cause to be or do; to create; to constitute; to compel; to appoint; to secure; to arrive at; to reckon; to perform; *v.i.* to go; to start; *pa.t.* and *pa.p.* **made.** *n.* structure; texture; form; style; brand. **—believe** *n.* pretense; *v.i.* to pretend. **-r** *n.* **Maker** *n.* God. **-shift** *n.* a temporary expedient. **-up** *n.* arrangement or layout of a printed page, magazine, etc.; cosmetics; nature; a making up for [O.E. *macian*, to make].

mal·a·chite (mal'·ạ·kīt) *n.* a green carbonate of copper, used for inlaid work [Gk. *malachē*, mallow].

mal·ad·just·ment (mal·ạ·just'·mạnt) *n.* faulty adjustment; inability to adjust to one's environment.

mal·ad·min·is·tra·tion (mal·ạd·min·ạ·strā'shạn) *n.* faulty administration, esp. of public affairs. [ward. **-ness** *n.*

mal·a·droit (mal·ạ·droit') *a.* clumsy; awk

mal·a·dy (mal'·ạ·di·) *n.* a disease; ailment. **mal de mer**, seasickness [Fr. *malade*, sick].

Mal·a·gas·y (mal·ạ·gas'·i·) *n.* a native of, or the language of, Madagascar; *a.* [[Fr.].

ma·laise (ma·lāz') *n.* a physical discomfort

mal·a·prop(ism) (mal'·ạ·pràp·(izm) *n.* the ludicrous misuse of a word [Fr. *mal à propos*, ill-suited].

ma·lar·i·a (mạ·lar'·i·ạ) *n.* a febrile disease transmitted by the bite of mosquito; **malarious** *a.* [It. *malaria*, bad air].

Ma·lay (mā'·lā) *n.* a native of the Malay Peninsula; *a.* Also **Malayan.**

mal·con·tent (mal'·kạn·tent) *a.* discontented; rebellious. **-ed** *a.* **-edly** *adv.* **-edness** *n.*

WEBSTER M–P

male (māl) *a.* pert. to the sex which begets young; masculine; (*Bot.*) having stamens; *n.* a male animal [L. *masculus*, male].

mal·e·dic·tion (mal·a·dik'·shan) *n.* evil-speaking; a curse. **maledictory** *a.* slander [L. *male*, badly; *dicere*, to speak].

mal·e·fac·tor (mal'·a·fakter) *n.* an evil-doer; a criminal. **malefaction** *n.* a crime [L. *male*, badly; *facere*, to do].

ma·lev·o·lent (ma·lev'·a·lant) *a.* evilly disposed; malicious. **malevolence** *n.* ill will; malice. **-ly** *adv.* [L. *male*, badly; *velle*, to wish].

mal·fea·sance (mal·fē'·zans) *n.* misconduct, esp. in public affairs [Fr.].

mal·for·ma·tion (mal·fawr·mā'·shan) *n.* irregular formation. **malformed** *a.* deformed.

mal·func·tion (mal·fungk'·shan) *v.i.* to fail to operate correctly or normally [L. *male*, badly; L. *functio*]. [apple].

mal·ic (mā'·lik) *a.* from the apple [L. *malum*, **mal·ice** (mal'·is) *n.* ill will; spite; desire to injure others; (*Law*) criminal intention. **malicious** *a.* spiteful; showing malice. **maliciously** *adv.* **maliciousness** *n.* **with malice aforethought** (*Law*) with deliberate criminal intention [L. *malitia*, ill-will].

ma·lign (ma·līn') *a.* malicious; evil; spiteful; *v.t.* to slander; to vilify. **malignance, malignancy** *n.* **malignant** *a.* being evilly disposed; harmful; (of disease) virulent; likely to prove fatal. **malignantly** *adv.* **-er** *n.* **malignity** *n.* [L. *malignus*, ill-disposed].

ma·lin·ger (ma·ling'·ger) *v.i.* to feign illness in order to avoid duty. **-er** *n.* a shirker [Fr. *malingre*, ailing].

mall (mawl) *n.* a level, shaded walk; a heavy mallet used in game of pall-mall (var. of *maul*) L. *malleus*, a hammer].

mal·lard (mal'·erd) *n.* a wild drake or duck.

mal·le·a·ble (mal'·i·a·bl) *a.* capable of being hammered or extended by beating; amenable; tractable. **malleability** *n.* **malleate** *v.t.* to hammer; to draw into a plate or leaf by beating. **malleation** *n.* [L. *malleus*, a hammer].

mal·let (mal'·at) *n.* any of various types of wooden hammer [Fr. *maillet*, a small hammer].

mal·low (mal'·ō) *n.* plant with downy leaves, and having emollient properties [L. *malva*].

mal·nu·tri·tion (mal·nū·tri'·shan) *n.* the state of being undernourished.

mal·o·dor·ous (mal·ō'·der·as) *a.* having an offensive odor. **malodor** *n.*

mal·prac·tice (mal·prak'·tis) *n.* professional impropriety or negligence.

malt (mawlt) *n.* barley or other grain steeped in water till it germinates, then dried in a kiln for use in brewing; *v.t.* to make into malt; *v.i.* to become malt. **-ed milk** *n.* a powder of malted grains and dried milk; a drink made by mixing this with milk and ice cream. **— extract** *n.* a medicinal body-building food. **— liquor**, a liquor made from malt by fermentation and not by distillation, as beer, stout, ale. **-ose** *n.* a sugar produced by the action of malt on starch [O.E.]. [dialect and people.

Mal·tese (mawl'·tēz) *n.* a native of *Malta*; its **mal·treat** (mal·trēt') *v.t.* to ill-treat; to abuse; to handle roughly. **-ment** *n.*

mal·ver·sa·tion (mal·ver·sā'·shan) *n.* corruption in office; fraudulent handling of public funds [L. *male*, ill; *versari*, to be engaged in].

mam·bo (mám'·bō) *n.* rhythmic music and dance of Sp. Amer. origin. [Africa [Kaffir].

mam·ba (mám'·ba) *n.* a poisonous snake of **mam·ma** (mam'·a) *n.* child's name for mother [imit.].

mam·ma (mam'·a·) *n.* milk-secreting gland in females. *pl.* **mammae. mammary** *a.* [L. the breast].

Mam·ma·li·a (ma·mā'·li·a) *n.pl.* (*Zool.*) the class of mammals or animals which suckle their young. **mammal** *n.* one of the *Mammalia*. **-n**

a. [L. *mamma*, the breast].

mam·mon (mam'·an) *n.* wealth personified and worshipped [Syrian *mamon*, wealth].

mam·moth (mam'·ath) *n.* a huge extinct elephant; *a.* colossal [Russ. *mammant*].

mam·my (mam'·i·) *n.* a Negro woman who took care of white children in the South; Mother: a child's word [Dial.].

man (man) *n.* a human being; an adult male; a manly person; a male servant; a husband; the human race; a piece used in such games as chess, checkers, etc. *pl.* **men.** *v.t.* to furnish with men; to fortify; *pr.p.* **-ning.** *pa.t.* and *pa.p.* **-ned. —eater**, a cannibal; a tiger, etc.; a shark. **-ful** *a.* vigorous; sturdy. **-fully** *adv.* **-fulness** *n.* **-hole** *n.* an opening large enough to admit a man leading to a drain, sewer, etc. **-hood** *n.* the state of being a man; courage. **—hour** *n.* work performed by one man in one hour. **-kind** *n.* human beings. **-liness** *n.* **-ly** *a.* bold; resolute; dignified; not effeminate; masculine. **-nish** *a.* like a man. **-nishly** *adv.* **-nishness** *n.* **—of-war**, a warship. **—power** *n.* a unit of power equal to one-eighth of a horse-power; the total number of people in industry, the armed forces, etc. **-servant** *n.* a male servant. **-slaughter** *n.* culpable homicide without malice aforethought. **man in the street,** average man [O.E. *mann*].

man·a·cle (man'·a·kl) *n.* a handcuff; *v.t.* to fetter with handcuffs [O.Fr. *manicle*].

man·age (man'·ij) *v.t.* to direct; to control; to carry on; to cope with; *v.i.* to direct affairs; to succeed. **-ability** *n.* **-able** *a.* capable of being managed. **-ment** *n.* the act of managing; administration; body of directors controlling a business. **-r** *n.* one who manages: one in charge. **managerial** *a.* [L. *manus*, the hand].

Man·chu (man'·chōō) *n.* one of the original inhabitants of Manchuria; *a.* of Manchuria [Chin.].

man·ci·ple (man'·si·pl) *n.* a steward; a caterer [L. *manceps*, a purchaser].

man·da·mus (man·dā'·mus) *n.* a written order [L., we command].

man·da·rin (man'·da·rin) *n.* a European name for a Chinese provincial governor; the language used in Chinese official circles; a small orange; a long brocade coat with loose sleeves [Port. *mandarin*].

man·date (man'·dāt) *n.* an official order; a precept; a prescript of the Pope; a commission to act as representative of a body of people. **mandatary** *n.* one to whom a mandate is given by a **mandator. -d** *a.* committed to a mandate, as *mandated territories.* **mandatory** *a.* containing a mandate; obligatory [L. *mandatum*, an order].

man·di·ble (man'·di·bl) *n.* a jaw; in vertebrates, the lower jaw; in birds, the upper or lower beak. **mandibular** *a.* [L. *mandibula*].

man·do·lin (man'·da·lin) *n.* a musical instrument with a rounded pear-shaped body [It. *mandola*, a lute].

man·drake (man'·drāk) *n.* a narcotic plant, the root thought to resemble human form [M.E. *mandragge*].

man·drel (man'·drel) *n.* a shaft on which objects may be fixed for turning, milling, etc.; the spindle of a lathe. Also **mandril.**

man·drill (man'·dril) *n.* a large African baboon [Fr.].

mane (mān) *n.* long hair on the neck of an animal [O.E. *manu*, neck].

ma·nège (ma·nezh') *n.* the art of horsemanship; a riding-school [Fr.].

ma·neu·ver (ma·nōō'·ver) *n.* a controlled strategic movement; scheme; artiface. *pl.* peacetime exercises of troops; *v.t.* to direct skillfully; **-able** *a.* **-ability** *n.* **-er** *n.* [Fr. fr. L. to work by hand].

man·ga·nese (mang'·ga·nēz) *n.* a greyish, hard, brittle metal which oxidizes rapidly in humid atmosphere [O.Fr. *manganese*].

mange (mānj) *n.* a parasitic disease affecting the skin of animals causing hair to fall out. **manginess** *n.* **mangy** *a.* [O.Fr. *manjue*, itch].

man·ger (mān'·jer) *n.* a trough for holding fodder for cattle [Fr. *manger*, to eat].

man·gle (mang'·gl) *n.* a machine for pressing linen between rollers; *v.t.* to smooth with a mangle. **-r** *n.* [Dut. *mangel*].

man·gle (mang'·gl) *v.t.* to hack; to mutilate; to spoil the beauty of [prob. O.Fr. *mahaigner*, to maim].

man·go (mang'·gō) *n.* a tropical tree, the unripe fruit used in making chutney [Malay, *mangga*].

man·grove (man'·grōv) *n.* a tropical tree the bark of which is used in tanning [Malay, *man-gri + grove*].

man·han·dle (man'·han·dl) *v.* to handle roughly.

man·hat·tan (man·hat'·n) *n.* a cocktail containing whisky, vermouth, bitters [Amer.].

ma·ni·a (mā'·ni·a) *n.* madness; a violent excitement; extravagant enthusiasm; an obsession. **maniac** *n.* a madman; *a.* raving; frenzied. **maniacal** *a.* [Gk.].

man·i·cure (man'·a·kyoor) *n.* the care of the hands and nails. **manicurist** *n.* one who gives this treatment; *v.t.* to file, and polish the nails [L. *manus*, the hand; *cura*, care].

man·i·fest (man'·a·fest) *a.* clearly visible; apparent to the mind or senses; *v.t.* to make clear; to reveal; *n.* a detailed list of goods transported. **-able**, **-ible** *a.* capable of being clearly revealed. **-ation** *n.* the act of revealing; the state of being revealed; display; disclosure. **-ly** *adv.* obviously. **manifesto** *n.* a public declaration of the principles or policy of a leader or party; *pl.* **manifestoes** [L. *manifestus*, clear].

man·i·fold (man'·a·fōld) *a.* many and varied; numerous; *v.t.* to make many copies of, as letters, by a machine, such as a duplicator; *n.* something with many parts; (*Mech.*) a pipe fitted with several lateral outlets [fr. *many* and *fold*].

man·i·kin (man'·a·kin) *n.* a little man; a dwarf; a model of the human body used in medical schools; a mannequin. Also **manakin** [Dut. *mannekin*, a double dim. of **man**].

ma·nil·a (ma·nil'·a) *n.* a cigar made in *Manila*, capital of the Philippine Islands. — **hemp**, a fiber used for making ropes, twine, sails, etc. — **paper**, a stout buff-coolred paper

man·i·ple (man'·a·pl) *n.* part of a Roman legion; a scarf worn by celebrant at mass. **manipular** *a.* [L. *manipulus*, a handful].

ma·nip·u·late (ma·nip'·yoo·lāt) *v.t.* to operate with the hands; to manage (a person) in a skillful, esp. unscrupulous way; to falsify; *v.i.* to use the hands. **manipulation** *n.* **manipular, manipulative, manipulatory** *a.* **manipulator** *n.* [L. *manipulus*, a handful].

man·na (man'·a) *n.* the food supplied miraculously to the Israelites in the wilderness; sweetish juice of the ash; spiritual nourishment; [Heb. *man*, a gift].

man·ne·quin (man'·a·kin) *n.* one employed to model new fashions; figure for a similar purpose. Also **manequin, manikin** [Fr. *manne-quin*, a puppet].

man·ner (man'·er) *n.* way of doing anything; custom; style; a person's habitual bearing; *pl.* social behavior; customs. **-ed** *a.* having manners (in compound *well-mannered*). **-ism** *n.* a personal peculiarity of bearing, speech, or style of expression; affection. **-liness** *n.* politeness; decorum. **-ly** *a.* having good manners; courteous; civil; respectful; *adv.* civilly; respectfully. **to the manner born**, having natural talent for special work or position [Fr. *manière*, manner].

man·or (man'·er) *n.* (*Brit.*) the land belonging to a lord; a unit of land in feudal times over which the owner had full jurisdiction [O.Fr. *manoir*, a dwelling].

man·sard roof (man'·sard ròòf) *n.* roof in which lower slope is nearly vertical and upper much inclined (fr. F. *Mansard*, Fr. arcritect].

manse (mans) *n.* a minister's residence [L.L. *mansa*, a dwelling].

man·sion (man'·shan) *n.* a large, imposing house; a manor house [L. *manere*, to remain].

man·sue·tude (man'·swa·tòòd) *n.* gentleness; tameness [L. *manus*, a hand; *suescere*, to accustom].

man·tel (man'·tl) *n.* the shelf above a fireplace; the framework around a fireplace. **-piece** *n.* the shelf [form of *mantle*].

man·til·la (man·til'·a) *n.* a veil covering head and shoulders, worn by Spanish women; a short cape [dim. of Sp. *mante*, a cloak].

man·tis (man'·tis) *n.* a genus of insects holding the forelegs folded as if praying [Gk. *man-tis*, a prophet].

man·tis·sa (man·tis'·a) *n.* the decimal part of a logarithm [L. *mantissa*, a makeweight].

man·tle (man'·tl) *n.* a loose outer garment; a cloak; a covering; *v.t.* to cover; to hide; *v.i.* to form a covering; to suffuse; to flush. **mantlet** *n.* (*Mil.*) a bullet-proof shelter [L. *mantellum*, a cloak].

man·tu·a (man'·choo·a) *n.* a woman's loose gown [Fr. *manteau*].

man·u·al (man'·yoo·al) *a.* pert. to, made by or done with the hand; *n.* a handbook or small textbook; a keyboard of a pipe-organ. **-ly** *adv.* [L. *manus*, the hand].

man·u·fac·ture (man·ya·fak'·cher) *n.* making goods either by hand or by machine (esp. mass-production; anything produced from raw materials; *v.t.* to make from raw materials; to fabricate; *v.i.* to be engaged in manufacture. **manufactory** *n.* a factory. **-r** *n.* [L. *manus*, the hand; *facere*, to make].

man·u·mit (man·ya·mit') *v.t.* to give freedom to a slave; to emancipate. *pr.p.* **-ting.** *pa.p.*, *pa.t.* **-ted. manumission** *n.* [L. *manumit-tere*, to send from one's hand].

ma·nure (ma·noor') *v.t.* to enrich soil with fertilizer; *n.* animal excrement used as fertilizer [contr. of Fr. *manoeuvrer*, to work with the hands].

man·u·script (man'·ya·skript) *a.* written, or typed, by hand; *n.* a book written by hand; an author's script or typewritten copy for perusal by publisher [L. *manus*, hand; *scribere*, *scrip-tum*, to write].

man·y (men'·i·) *a.* comprising a great number (*comp.* **more**; *superl.* **most**); *n. pro.* a number of people or things. **-sided** *a.* talented [O.E. *manig*, many].

map (map) *n.* a representation, esp. on a plane surface, of the features of the earth, or of part of it; a chart of the heavens; a plan or delineation; *v.t.* to draw a map of; to fill in details in a blank map; to plan; *pr.p.* **-ping.** *pa.t.* and *pa.p.* **-ped** [L. *mappa*, a napkin].

ma·ple (mā'·pl) *n.* a deciduous tree, valuable for its timber and the sap from which sugar is extracted [O.E. *mapultreow*, the maple tree].

mar (mår) *v.t.* to injure; to impair; to disfigure. *pr.p.* **-ring.** *pa.p.* **-red** [O.E. *merran*, to hinder].

mar·a·bou (mar'·a·bòò) *n.* a kind of stork; the feathers of this bird used as trimming.

ma·ra·ca (ma·rá'·ka) *n.* gourd shaped rattle [Braz.].

mar·a·schi·no (mar·a·skē'·nō) *n.* a sweet liqueur distilled from cherries [It. *amarasca*, a sour cherry].

mar·a·thon (mar'·a·than) *n.* a foot race (approx. 26 miles); endurance contest [Gk. Myth. runner, *Marathon to Athens*)].

ma·raud (ma·rawd') *v.i.* to rove in quest of plunder; to loot. **-er** *n.* **-ing** *n.* and *a.* [O.Fr. *marauder*, to play the rogue].

mar·ble (mår'·bl) *n.* hard limestone which takes on a brilliant polish and is used for ornaments, statuary, etc.; a little ball of marble, glass, etc., used in games; *a.* made of marble; cold; insensible; *v.t.* to color like streaked marble. **-ed** *a.* veined like marble. **marbly** *a.* **-ize**, *v.t.* make like marble [Gk. *marmairein*, to sparkle].

mar·ca·site (mår'·ka·sīt) *n.* white iron pyrite used in jewelry because of its brilliance [Fr.].

mar·cel (mår·sel') *n.* an artificial hair wave. **-led** *a.* [fr. *Marcel*, the inventor].

March (mårch) *n.* third month of year, named after *Mars*, Roman god of war.

march (mårch) *n.* a border; a frontier; *pl.* [O.E. *mearc*, mark].

march (mårch) *v.i.* to move in order, as soldiers; to proceed at a steady pace; *v.t.* to cause to move in military array; *n.* distance marched; a musical composition to accompany a march; steady advance, as the *march of time.* **-er** *n.* [Fr. *marcher*, to walk].

mar·chion·ess (mår'·shan·is) *n.* the wife of a marquis; lady, holding in her own right, the rank of marquis [L.L. *marchionissa*, fem. of *marchio*, ruler of the march].

march·pane See **marzipan.**

mare (mer) *n.* the female of the horse, mule, donkey, etc. [O.E. *merc*, fem. of *mearh*, a horse].

mar·ga·rine (mår'·ja·ran) *n.* pearly wax-like substance obtained from animal fat; a fatty extract of certain vegetable oils; a butter substitute made from vegetable oils or animal fats [Gk. *margaron*, a pearl].

mar·gin (mar'·jan) *n.* a border; a blank space at top, bottom and sides, of a written or printed page; allowance made for contingencies; *v.t.* to provide with margin; to enter in the margin. **-al** *a.* pert. to a margin; entered in the margin. **-alia** *n.pl.* notes jotted in the margin. **-al** *a.* **-ally** *adv.* **-ate**, **-d** *a.* [L. *margo*, the edge].

mar·gue·rite (mår'·ga·rēt) *n.* a large ox-eye daisy [L. *margarita*, a pearl].

mar·i·gold (mar'·a·gōld) *n.* name applied to a plant bearing yellow or orange flowers [prob. fr. Virgin *Mary* and *gold*].

ma·ri·jua·na (mar·a·hwå'·na) *n.* a type of hemp dried and used as tobacco, having a narcotic effect [Sp.].

ma·rim·ba (ma·rim'·ba) *n.* a jazz-band instrument resembling the xylophone [Afr.].

ma·ri·na (ma·rē'·na) *n.* a small harbor or boat basin [L. *marinus*, the sea].

mar·i·nade (mar·a·nåd') *n.* a seasoned vinegar or wine used for steeping meat, fish, vegetables. *v.t.* to marinate. **marinate** *v.t.* to let food stand in a marinade [Fr. *mariner*, pickle in brine].

ma·rine (ma·rēn') *a.* pert. to the sea; found in, or near, the sea; pert. to shipping or overseas trade. **-r** (mar'·i·ner) *n.* a sailor or seaman [L. *mare*, the sea].

mar·i·o·nette (mar·i·a·net') *n.* a puppet worked by strings [Fr. dim. of *Marion*].

mar·i·tal (mar'·a·tal) *a.* pert. to a husband or to marriage [L. *maritus*, married].

mar·i·time (mar'·a·tīm) *a.* pert. to the sea; bordering on the sea; living near the sea; pert. to overseas trade or navigation [L. *maritimus*, fr. *mare*, the sea].

mar·jo·ram (mår'·ja·ram) *n.* an aromatic plant of the mint family used in cookery.

mark (mårk) *n.* a visible sign; a cross; a character made by one who cannot write; a stamp; a proof; a target; a point; an attainable standard; a numerical assessment of proficiency, as in an examination; a flaw or disfigurement; a peculiarity or distinguishing feature; (*Running*) starting post; indication of position,

depth, etc. *v.t.* to make a sign upon; to stamp or engrave; to notice; to assess, as an examination paper; *v.i.* to observe particularly. **-ed** *a.* outstanding; notorious. **-edly** *adv.* noticeably. **-er** *n.* **-ing** *n.* design of marks. **-sman** *n.* one who is expert at hitting a target. **-smanship** *n.* shooting skill. **-up** *n.* the amount added to the cost of an article in determining the selling price. **trade mark**, a special symbol marked on commodities to indicate the maker [O.E. *mearc*, a boundary].

mark (mårk) *n.* unit of exchange of various countries [O.E. *marc*].

mar·ket (mår'·kit) *n.* a public meeting place for the purchase and sale of commodities; a trading-center; demand; country or geographical area regarded as a buyer of goods; price or value at a stated time; *v.i.* to buy or sell; *v.t.* to produce for sale in a market. **-able** *a.* suitable for selling. **-ably** *adv.* — **place** *n.* — **price** *n.* the current price of a commodity [L. *mercatus*, trade].

marl (mårl) *n.* a crumbly soil used for fertilizer and in brick making; *v.t.* to manure with marl. **-y** *a.* [O.Fr. *marle*, marl].

mar·lin (mår'·lin) *n.* a large slender deep-sea fish [fr. *marlin*, spike (snout)].

mar·line (mår'·lin) *n.* a small rope used to secure a splicing. **-spike** *n.* a pointed tool used to separate strands of a rope in splicing [Dut. *marren*, to bind; *lijn*, a line].

mar·ma·lade (mår'·ma·lād) *n.* a preserve made of the pulp and peel of fruit [Port. *marmelo*, a quince].

mar·mo·set (mår'·ma·set, ·zet) *n.* a small monkey of S. America [Fr. *marmouset*, a small grotesque figure (on fountains)].

mar·mot (mår'·mat) *n.* a bushy-tailed rodent; the prairie dog [Fr. *marmot*, a mountain rat].

ma·roon (ma·rōōn') *n.* orig. a fugitive slave of the W. Indies; a marooned person; *v.t.* to put ashore on a desolate island; to isolate, cut off; *v.i.* to live as if marooned [Sp. (*ci*)*marron*, a runaway slave].

ma·roon (ma·rōōn') *a.* brownish-crimson; *n.* [Fr. *marron*, a chestnut].

marque (mårk) *n.* seizure by way of retaliation. usually **letter of marque** [Fr. fr. Prov. *marcar*, to seize as a pledge].

mar·quee (mår·kē') *n.* a roof-like structure or awning outside a public building [orig. *marquees*, fr. Fr. *marquise*, the tent of a marquis].

mar·que·try (mår'·ka·tri) *n.* decorative, inlaid wood; the process of inlaying wood with designs. Also **marqueterie** [Fr. *marqueter*, to variegate].

mar·quis (mår'·kwis, ·kē) *n.* noble ranking next below a duke. Also **marquess** (*fem.* **marchioness**). **marquise** (mår·kēz') *n.* in France, the wife of a marquis; pointed oval diamond [O.Fr. *marchis*, ruler of the marches].

mar·que·sette (mår·kwi·zet', ·ki·zet') *n.* thin, lightweight fabric.

mar·riage See **marry.**

mar·row (mar'·ō) *n.* the soft substance in the cavities of bones; the essence of anything. **-bone** *n.* a bone containing marrow; *pl.* the knees [O.E. *meary*, marrow].

mar·ry (mar'·i·) *v.t.* to unite, take, or give in wedlock; *v.i.* to enter into matrimony. **marriage** (mar'·ij) *n.* the legal union of husband and wife; the ceremony, civil or religious, by which two people of opposite sex become husband and wife. **-able** *a.* [L. *maritare*, to marry].

Mars (mårz) *n.* the Roman god of war; the planet nearest to the earth. **Martian** *n.* an imaginary inhabitant of Mars [L.].

Mar·seil·laise (mår·sa·yez' or mår·sa·lāz') *n.* the French national anthem.

marsh (mårsh) *n.* a tract of low, swampy land; *a.* pert. to swampy areas. **-fever** *n.* malaria. **-gas** *n.* a gaseous product of decomposing organic matter. **-mallow** n. a red flowered plant growing in marshes; a confection made from the root of this, or from gelatin. **-y** a. boggy; swampy [O.E. *merisc*, full of meres].

mar·shal (mår'·shạl) n. a civil officer of a district with powers of a sheriff; a person in charge of arrangements for ceremonies, etc.; military rank in Fr. and Brit. armed forces. v.t. to dispose in order, as troops; (*Fig.*) to arrange, as ideas [O.Fr. *mareschal*, a horse servant].

mar·su·pi·al (mår·sòó'·pi·ạl) a. having an external pouch, to carry the young; n. a marsupial or pouched animal (opossum, kangaroo) [L. *marsupium*, a pouch].

mart (mårt) n. a market [contr. of *market*].

mar·ten (mår'·tạn) n. a kind of weasel, valued for its fur [O.Fr. *martre*].

mar·tial (mår'·shạl) a. pert. to war or to the armed services; warlike; military. (*Cap.*) a. pertaining to Mars. **-ly** adv. **— law**, law enforced by military authorities and superseding civil law [L. *Mars*, the god of war].

mar·tin (mår'·tin) n. a bird of the swallow family [fr. *Martin*].

mar·ti·net (mår'·tạ·net) n. a strict disciplinarian [fr. Fr. officer, *Martinet*].

mar·tin·gale (mår'·tạn·gāl) n. a strap fastened to a horse's girth to keep its head down; (*Naut.*) a stay for a jib boom. Also **martingal.**

mar·ti·ni (mår·tē'·ni·) n. a cocktail of vermouth, gin and bitters.

mar·tyr (mår'·tẹr) n. one who suffers punishment or the sacrifice of his life for adherence to principles or beliefs; a constant sufferer; v.t. to put to death for refusal to abandon principles. **-dom** n. the suffering and sacrifice of a martyr. **-ology** n. a history of martyrs [L. Gk. *martus*, a witness].

mar·vel (mår'·vạl) n. anything wonderful; v.i. to wonder exceedingly. **-ous** a. wonderful; astonishing. **-ously** adv. **-ousness** n. [O.Fr. *merveille*, a wonder].

Marx·ism (mårk'·sizm) n. the doctrines of *Karl Marx*, which profoundly influenced Socialists and communists of Europe in later part of 19th cent. **Marxian, Marxist** a. **Marxist** n.

mar·zi·pan (mår'·zạ·pan) n. a paste of ground almonds, sugar and egg white made into confections. Also **marchpane.**

mas·car·a (mas·ka'·rạ) n. a cosmetic preparation for eyelashes.

mas·cot (mas'·kåt) n. a person or thing reputed to bring good luck.

mas·cu·line (mas'·kyạ·lin) a. male; strong; virile; (of a woman) mannish; (*Gram.*) of male gender. **-ness, masculinity** n. [L. *masculus*, male].

mash (mash) v.t. to beat to a pulp or soft mass; to mix malt with hot water; n. a thick mixture of malt and hot water for brewing; a mixture of bran meal, etc. given to horses and cattle; a pulpy mass [O.E. *masc*, mash].

mash (mash) v.t. (*Slang*) to pay court to; to flirt. **-er** n. a lady-killer.

mash·ie (mash'·i·) n. a golf club with short iron head [prob. corrupt. of Fr. *massue*, a club].

mask (mask) n. a covering for the face; an impression of a human face, as a *deathmask;* a respirator to be worn as protection against poison gas; a false face, as worn by children at Hallowe'en; a disguise; a masquerade; (*Fig.*) a pretext; v.t. to hide, as with a mask; v.i. to assume a disguise [Fr. *masque*].

mas·och·ism (mas'·ạ·kizm) n. a form of sex gratification by endurance of physical or mental pain. **masochist** n. [fr. *von Sascher-Masoch*, Austrian novelist].

ma·son (mā'·sn) n. a builder in stone, brick, etc.; a Freemason. **-ic** a. pert. to freemasonry. **-ry** n. the work of a mason; stonework; freemasonry [Fr. *maçon*, a mason].

ma·son·ite (mā'·sạn·īt) n. a fiberboard made from pressed wood fibers used in building [fr. W. H. *Mason*, Amer. engineer].

mas·quer·ade (mas·kạ·rād') n. an assembly of masked persons; disguise; v.i. to take part in a masquerade; to disguise [Fr. *mascarade*].

mass (mas) n. the quantity of matter in a body; a shapeless lump; magnitude; crowd; chief portion; v.t. to collect in a mass; v.i. to assemble in large numbers. **-ive** a. forming a mass; bulky; weighty. **-ively** adv. **-iveness** n. **— meeting** n. a large public meeting or demonstration. **— production** n. cheap production in great quantities. **the masses,** the common people [L. *massa*, a lump].

Mass (mas) n. the communion service in the R.C. Church; the music to accompany High Mass. **High Mass**, Mass celebrated with music. **Low Mass**, a simple celebration of Mass without music. Also **mass** [O.E. *maesse*, fr. L. *missa*, mass].

mas·sa·cre (mas'·ạ·kẹr) n. general, ruthless slaughter; carnage; v.t. to slaughter indiscriminately [O.Fr. *maçacre*, slaughter].

mas·sage (mạ·sàzh') n. a treatment of physical disorders by kneading, rubbing, carried out by specialists; v.t. to treat by massage. **massagist, masseur** n. (*fem.* **masseuse**) a specialist in massage [Fr. fr. Gk. *massein*, to knead].

mas·sive See **mass**.

mast (mast) n. upright pole supporting rigging and sails of a ship; v.t. to furnish with mast or masts. **-ed** a. **-head** n. top portion of a ship's mast; newspaper or magazine trademark or business information [O.E. *maest*, the stem of a tree].

mast (mast) n. fruit of oak, beech, esp. as food for swine [O.E. *maest*, fodder].

mas·ter (mas'·tẹr) n. one who directs and controls; an employer of labor; male head of a household; a ship captain; a graduate degree in arts, or science (*abbrevs.* M.A., M.Sc.); courtesy title given the sons of a family, esp. by servants; an expert; a famous artist, esp. an *old master;* one who organizes and leads a fox hunt, as *master of foxhounds; a.* chief; dominant; skilled; v.t. to become the master of; to become expert at; to overcome. **-ful** a. compelling; domineering. **-fully** adv. **-fulness** n. **— key** n. a key which opens several locks. **-ly** a. highly competent; supremely proficient; adv. with the skill of an expert. **-mind** n. a first-class mind; chief controlling power behind a scheme. **— of ceremonies** n. one who presides over entertainment. **-piece** n. a brilliantly executed work. **-stroke** n. a masterly action. **— switch** n. an electric switch which must be turned on before other switches will function. **-y** n. supremacy; action of mastering; consumate skill; victory [L. *magister*, a master].

mas·ti·cate (mas'·tạ·kāt) v.t. to chew; to reduce to a pulp. **masticable** a. capable of being chewed. **mastication** n. the process of chewing. **masticator** n. crushing machine [L. *masticare*, to chew].

mas·tiff (mas'·tif) n. a powerful breed of dog [O.Fr. *mastin* confused with *mestif*, mongrel].

mas·ti·tis (mas·tī'·tis) n. (*Med.*) inflammation of the breast [Gk. *mastos*, the breast].

mas·to·don (mas'·tạ·dàn) n. an extinct mammal resembling an elephant. **mastodontic** a. [Gk. *mastos*, the breast; *odous*, the tooth].

mas·toid (mas'·toid) a. nipple-shaped; n. the prominence on the temporal bone behind the human ear. **-itis** n. inflammation of the mastoid area [Gk. *mastos*, the breast].

mas·tur·bate (mas'·tẹr·bāt) v.i. to practice self-excitation; auto-eroticism. **masturbation** n. **masturbator** n. [L. *masturbari*].

mat (mat) n. a coarse fabric of twin, rope, or rushes for wiping the shoes on; a rug; a heat-resisting covering of cork, plastic, etc., for protecting surface of a table; a border or frame

WEBSTER M-P

for a picture; a tangled mass of hair; *v.t.* to lay or cover with mats; *v.i.* to become a tangled mass. *pr.p.* **-ting**. *pa.t.* and *pa.p.* **-ted** [L. *matta*, a mat].

mat, matte (mat) *a.* having a dull finish; not shiny [Fr. *mate*].

mat·a·dor, matadore (mat′·a·dawr) *n.* the man who kills the bull in a Sp. bullfight [Sp. fr. L. *mactare*, to kill].

match (mach) *n.* splint of wood or taper tipped with a substance capable of ignition by friction with a rough surface; a piece of rope for firing a gun; a fuse [Fr. *mèche*, a wick].

match (mach) *n.* a person or thing equal to or resembling another; a sporting contest; a marriage; a mate; *v.i.* to correspond in quality, quantity, color, etc.; *v.t.* to compete with; to unite in marriage; to be the same as. **-less** *a.* having no match; peerless; unique. **-maker** *n.* one who schemes to bring about a marriage [O.E. *gemaecca*, a mate].

mate (māt) *n.* a companion; a spouse; one of a pair; an assistant; *v.t.* to match; to mar; *v.i.* to pair [O.Dut. *maet*, a companion].

mate (māt) *v.t.* to checkmate (chess); *n.* checkmate [abbrev. of *checkmate*].

ma·té, mate (má′·tā) *n.* an evergreen tree of Brazil and Paraguay, the leaves of which are dried and used as tea [Native *mati*, the vessel for infusing tea].

ma·te·ri·al (ma·ti′·ri·al) *a.* consisting of matter corporeal; (of persons) not spiritually minded; essential; appreciable; worthy of consideration; *n.* the substance out of which something is fashioned; fabric; the accumulated data out of which a writer creates a work of literary, historical, or scientific value; materials collective. **-ization** *n.* **ize** *v.t.* to render material; to give bodily form to; *v.i.* to become fact. **-ism** *n.* the theory that matter, and matter only, exists in the universe; an attitude which ignores spiritual values. **-istic, -al** *a.* **-ly** *adv.* appreciably [L. *materia*, matter].

ma·té·ri·el (ma·tir·i·el′) *n.* weapons, equipment, tools, supplies necessary [Fr. = material].

ma·te·ri·a med·i·ca (mat·tir′·i·a med′·i·ka) *n.* (*Med.*) the substances used in the making of medicines, drugs, etc.; the science relating to medicines and their curative properties [L.].

ma·ter·nal (ma·tur′·nal) *a.* pert. to a mother; motherly; related on the mother's side. **-ly** *adv.* **maternity** *n.* motherhood; childbirth [L. *mater*, a mother].

math·e·mat·ics (math·a·mat′·iks) *n.* the science of quantity and space, including arithmetic, algebra, trigonometry, geometry. **mathematical** *a.* pert. to mathematics; accurate. **mathematician** *n.* [Gk. *mathēma*, learning].

mat·in (mat′·in) *n.* a morning song; a morning service [Fr. *matin*, morning].

ma·tri·arch (mā′·tri·ärk) *n.* a woman in a position analagous to that of a patriarch. **-al** *a.* **-alism** *n.* government exercised by a mother [L. *mater*, a mother; Gk. *archein*, to rule].

ma·tri·cide (mat′·ra·sīd) *n.* the murder of a mother; one who kill his own mother [L. *mater*, a mother; *caedere*, to kill].

ma·tric·u·late (ma·trik′·ya·lāt) *v.t.* and *i.* to enroll as a student, esp. of a college; to enter, by matriculation. **matriculation** *n.* [L. *matricula*, a register].

mat·ri·mo·ny (mat′·ra·mō·ni·) *n.* marriage; wedlock. **matrimonial** *a.* [L. *matrimonium*].

ma·trix (mā′·triks or mat′·riks) *n.* the womb; the cavity where anything is formed; a mold, esp. for casting printer's type; rock where minerals are embedded. *pl.* **matrices, -es** [L. *matrix*, the womb].

ma·tron (mā′·tran) *n.* a married woman; a woman in charge of domestic affairs of an institution. **-like, -ly** *adv.* like a matron; mature; staid [L. *matrona*, a married lady].

matte See **mat.**

mat·ter (mat′·er) *n.* that which occupies space and is the object of the senses; substance; cause of a difficulty; subject of a book, speech, sermon; occasion; (*Med.*) pus; *v.i.* to be of importance; to signify; (*Med.*) to discharge pus. **-of-fact** *a.* prosaic; unimaginative [L. *materia*, matter].

mat·ting (mat′·ing) *n.* mat work; coarse material used as floor covering [fr. *mat*].

mat·tock (mat′·ak) *n.* a kind of pickaxe with only one end pointed, used for loosening soil [O.E. *mattuc*].

mat·tress (mat′·ras) *n.* a casing of strong fabric filled with hair, foam rubber, cotton, etc. used on or as a bed [O.E. fr. Ar. *natrah*, a place where anything is thrown].

mat·u·rate (mach′·a·rāt) *v.i.* to mature. **maturation** *n.* [L. *maturus*, ripe].

ma·ture (ma·toor′) *a.* ripe; fully developed; (*Med.*) come to suppuration; resulting from adult experience; due for payment, as a bill; *v.t.* to ripen; to perfect; *v.i.* to become ripe; to become due, as a bill. **maturable** *a.* **-ly** *adv.* **-ness, maturity** *n.* ripeness; the state or quality of being fully developed [L. *maturus*, ripe].

ma·tu·ti·nal (ma·tōō′·te·nal) *a.* morning; early. **-ly** *adv.* [L. *matutinus*, of the morning].

maud·lin (mawd′·lin) *a.* over-sentimental; tearful [contr. of O.Fr. *Maudeleine*, Mary Magdalen, painted as weeping].

maul (mawl) *n.* a heavy wooden hammer; *v.t.* to maltreat; to handle roughly. **-er** *n.* [L. *malleus*, a hammer].

Mau Mau (mou′·mou′) *n.* a secret, terrorist society in Kenya.

maun·der (mawn′·der) *v.i.* to mutter; to talk or to wander aimlessly.

mau·so·le·um (maw·sa·lē′·am) *n.* a large imposing tomb. **mausolean** *a.* [orig. the tomb of *Mausolus*, King of Caria, 350 B.C.].

mauve (mōv, mawv) *n.* a delicate purple color; *a.* of this color [Fr. fr. L. *malva*, the mallow].

mav·er·ick (mav′·er·ik) *n.* an unbranded calf; an independent [fr. S. *Maverick*, Texas rancher].

maw (maw) *n.* the stomach of an animal; in birds, the craw [O.E. *maga*, maw].

mawk·ish (mawk′·ish) *a.* loathsome; sickly sweet; maudlin. **-ly** *adv.* [M.E. *mathek*, a maggot].

max·il·lar·y (mak′·sa·ler·i·) *a.* pert. to the upper jawbone or jaw; *n.* a jawbone. **maxilla** *n.* the upper jaw; *pl.* **maxillae** [L. *maxilla*, a jawbone].

max·im (mak′·sim) *n.* an accepted principle; an axiom; a proverb or precept [L. *maximus*].

max·i·mum (mak′·sa·mam) *a.* greatest; *n.* the greatest number, quantity or degree; the highest point; peak; opp. *minimum*. **maximal** *a.* of the greatest value [L. superl. of *magnus*, great].

may (mā) *v.i.* expressing possibility, permission, contingency; uncertainty; hope. *pa.t.* **might** (mīt). **maybe, (mayhap,** *Arch.*) *adv.* perhaps; possibly [O.E. *maeg*, may].

May (mā) *n.* the fifth month of the year; (*Fig.*) youthful prime. **-day** *n.* the first day of May. (*l.c.*)**-flower** *n.* trailing arbutus; any flower blooming in May. **-flower** *n.* the ship in which the Pilgrims sailed to Plymouth, Mass. in 1620. **-fly** *n.* an ephemeral insect; an artificial fly for fishing. **-pole** *n.* a pole with streamers, around which people danced on May Day [L. *Maius*, the month of May].

may·hem (mā′·hem) *n.* (*Law*) the offense of maiming by violence [O.Fr. *mahaigne*, injury].

may·on·naise (mā·a·nāz′) *n.* a sauce or dressing for salads [Fr.].

may·or (mā′·er) *n.* the chief official of a city or town. **-al** *a.* **-alty, -ship** *n.* the office of mayor [Fr. *maire*, mayor].

maze (māz) *n.* a network of intricate paths; a labyrinth; confused condition; mental perplexity [M.E. *masen*, to confuse].

ma·zur·ka, ma·zour·ka (ma·zur′·ka) *n.* a Polish dance; the music for this [Pol.].

me (mē) *pron.* the objective case of first pers. pronoun, '*I*'.

mead (mēd) *n.* a fermented drink made of honey, yeast and water [O.E. *meodu*].

mead·ow (med′·ō) *n.* a low, level tract of grassland; pasture. — **lark** *n.* a yellow-breasted Amer. songbird. **-y** *a.* [O.E. *mæwan*, to mow].

mea·ger (mē′·gẹr) *a.* scanty; having little flesh; gaunt. **-ly** *adv.* **-ness** *n.* [Fr. *maigre*, thin].

meal (mēl) *n.* the food served at one time; a repast [O.E. *mæl*, time].

meal (mēl) *n.* edible grain coarsely ground. **-iness** *n.* — **worm** *n.* an insect found in meal. **-y** *a.* like meal; powdery; spotty. **-y-mouthed** *a.* apt to mince words; not blunt [O.E. *melo*, meal].

mean (mēn) *a.* humble in rank or birth; sordid; lacking dignity; stingy; malicious; (*Colloq.*) disagreeable; selfish; (*Slang*) skillful. **-ly** *adv.* **-ness** *n.* [O.E. *gemæne*, common].

mean (mēn) *a.* in a middle position; average; *n.* the middlepoint of quantity, rate, position, or degree; *pl.* resourcees; wealth; agency. **-time,** the interval between two given times. **-time, -while** *adv.* in the intervening time [L. *medius*, the middle].

mean (mēn) *v.t.* to have in view; to intend; to signify; *v.i.* to form in the mind; to be disposed. *pa.t.* and *pa.p.* **meant** (ment). **-ing** *n.* that which is meant; sense; signification; *a.* expressive. **-ingful** *a.* **-ingless** *a.* [O.E. *mænan*, to signify].

me·an·der (mē·an′·dẹr) *v.i.* to flow with a winding course; to saunter aimlessly; *n.* a circuitous stroll; the winding course of a river (usu. *pl.*). **-ing** *a.* winding. **meandrous** *a.* [Gk. *Maiandros*, a winding river of Asia Minor].

mea·sles (mē′·zạlz) *n.* (*Med.*) a highly contagious disease, charatcerized by rash of bright red spots; a disease affecting cattle and pigs caused by tapeworms. **measly** *a.* having measles; (*Fig.*) worthless; skimpy. **German measles,** a disease resembling measles but less severe [Dut. *mazelen*, measles].

meas·ure (mezh′·ẹr) *n.* dimension reckoned by some standard; an instrument for measuring; a vessel of predetermined capacity; a course of action; an act of the legislature; means to an end; (*Mus.*) tempo; the notes between two bars in staff notation; *pl.* (*Geol.*) layers of rock; strata; *v.t.* to ascertain the quantity or dimensions of; to assess; to distribute by measure; *v.i.* to have an ascertained value or extent; to compare favorably with. **measurable** *a.* capable of being measured. **measurably** *adv.* **-d** *a.* of specified measure; uniform; calculated. **-less** *a.* boundless; infinite. **-ment** *n.* dimension, quantity, etc., ascertained by measuring with fixed unit. **-r** *n.* [L. *mensura*, a measure].

meat (mēt) *n.* flesh used as food; food of any kind. **-iness** *n.* **-y** *a.* full of meat; (*Fig.*) pithy; compact with ideas [O.E. *mete*, food].

Mec·ca (mek′·a) *n.* the reputed birthplace of Mohammed; a holy city; (*l.c.*) the focal point for people drawn by common interest.

me·chan·i·cal (ma·kan′·i·kạl) *a.* pert. to machines, mechanism, or mechanics; produced or operated by machinery; automatic. **mechanic** *n.* one who works with or repairs machines or instruments. **-ly** *adv.* **mechanician** *n.* a machine-maker or repairer. **mechanics** *n.* that branch of applied mathematics which deals with force and motion; the science of machines. **mechanization** *n.* the change to mechanical power. **mechanize** *v.t.* to make mechanical; to equip with machines. **mech-**

anized *a.* **mechanism** *n.* the structure of a machine; machinery; a piece of machinery; (*Fig.*) technique; the philosophical doctrine that all phenomena of life admit of physio-chemical proof. **mechanist** *n.* **mechanistic** *a.* [Gk. *mēchanē*, a contrivance].

Mech·lin (mek′·lin) *n.* and *a.* a kind of lace, made in *Mechlin* (Malines) in Belgium.

med·al (med′·l) *n.* a piece of metal, struck like a coin, as a memento or reward; *v.t.* to decorate with a medal. **-ic** (ma·dal′·ik) *a.* pert. to medals. **medallion** *n.* a large medal; a metal disk, usually round, with portrait in bas-relief. **-ist** *n.* a maker of medals; one who has been awarded a medal [Fr. *médaille*, a metal disc].

med·dle (med′·l) *v.i.* to interfere officiously; to tamper with. **-r** *n.* **-some** *a.* interfering [L. *miscere*, to mix].

me·di·a See **medium.**

me·di·al (mē′·di·ạl) *a.* in, or through, the middle; pert. to a mean or average. **median** *a.* situated in the middle; *n.* (*Geom.*) a line drawn from vertex of a triangle to the middle point of the opposite side [L. *medius*, the middle].

me·di·ate (mē′·di·ạt) *a.* being between two extremes; intervening; depending on an intermediary; not direct; (mē′·di·āte) *v.i.* to interpose between contending parties to effect a reconciliation; *v.t.* to settle by mediation. **mediacy** *n.* **-ly** *adv.* **mediation** *n.* the act of mediating; the steps taken to effect a reconciliation. **mediatize** *v.t.* to annex a small state, still leaving the ruler his title. **mediator** *n.* [L. *medius*, the middle].

med·ic (med′·ik) *n.* a leguminous plant with leaves like clover, used as fodder; (*Colloq.*) a doctor [Gk. *mēdikē* (*poa*), 'Median' grass].

med·i·cal (med′·i·kạl) *a.* pert. to medicine or the art of healing; medicinal. **medicable** *a.* capable of being cured. **-ly** *adv.* **medicament** *n.* any healing remedy. **medicate** *v.t.* to treat with medicine. **medicated** *a.* **medication** *n.* **medicative** *a.* [L. *medicus*, a physician].

med·i·cine (med′·a·sin) *n.* any substance used in the treatment of disease; the science of healing and prevention of disease; magic (as practiced in primitive tribes); (*Fig.*) salutary lesson; *v.t.* to administer medicine to. **medicinal** *a.* pert. to medicine; remedial. **medicinally** *adv.* — **man,** a magician with supposed powers of healing; a witch doctor. **medico** *n.* (*Colloq.*) a doctor or medical student [L. *medicus*, a physician].

me·di·e·val, mediaeval (med·i·ē′·vạl) *a.* pert. to or characteristic of the Middle Ages. **medi(a)evalist** *n.* one who makes a special study of the Middle Ages [L. *medius*, middle; *aevum*, an age].

me·di·o·cre (mē′·di·ō·kẹr) *a.* middling; neither good nor bad; second-rate. **mediocrity** *n.* [L. *mediocris*].

med·i·tate (med′·a·tāt) *v.t.* to consider thoughtfully; to intend; *v.i.* to ponder, esp. on religious matters. **-d** *a.* planned. **meditation** *n.* the act of meditating; deep thought. **meditative** *a.* given to reflection. **meditatively** *adv.* [L. *meditari*, to consider].

med·i·ter·ran·e·an (med·a·tẹr·rā′·ni·ạn) *a.* (of water) encircled by land. **Mediterranean** *a.* pert. to the almost landlocked water between S. Europe and N. Africa, so called because it was regarded as being in the *middle* of the Old World. **Mediterranean climate,** a climate of warm wet winters, hot dry summers [L. *medius*, the middle; *terra*, the earth].

me·di·um (mē′·di·ạm) *n.* that which is in the middle; a means; an agency; in spiritualism, an intermediary professing to give messages from the dead; in bacteriology, a substance used for cultivation of bacteria. *pl.* **-s** or **media.** *a.* middle; average; middling [L. *medius*, the middle].

med·ley (med'·li·) *n.* a miscellaneous collection of things; a miscellany [O.Fr. *medler*, to mix].

me·dul·la (mạ·dul'·ạ) *n.* marrow in a bone; inner tissue of a gland; pith of hair or plants. *pl.* **-e.** *a.* comprising or resembling marrow, covered with medullary substance, etc. **med·ullate(d)** *a.* **medullose** *a.* like pith [L. *medulla*, marrow].

me·du·sa (mẹ·dŏŏ'·sạ) *n.* a kind of jellyfish, with tentacles [Gk. *Medousa*].

meed (mēd) *n.* reward; recompense [O.E. *med*].

meek (mēk) *a.* submissive; humble; mild. **-ly** *adv.* **-ness** *n.* [O.E. *meoc*, meek].

meer·schaum (mir'·shạm, ·shawm) *n.* a fine, white clay used for the bowl of tobacco pipes; a pipe of this [Ger. *Meer*, the sea; *Schaum*, foam].

meet (mēt) *a.* fit; suitable. **-ly** *adv.* **-ness** *n.* [O.E. (*ge*)*maele*, suitable].

meet (mēt) *v.t.* to encounter; to join; to find; to satisfy; to pay, as a debt; to await arrival, as of a train; *v.i.* to converge at a specified point; to combine; to assemble in company. *pa.t.* and *pa.p.* **met.** *n.* an assembly of people, as at a fox-hunt. **-ing** *n.* a coming together, as of roads, rivers; encounter; people gathered together for worship, entertainment, discussion, sport, etc. [O.E. *metan*, to meet].

me·ga- Gr. *prefix* meaning great, mighty.

meg·a·cycle (meg'·ạ·sī·kl) *n.* (*Elect.*) one million cycles [Gk. *megas*, great; *kuklos*, a circle].

meg·a·lith (meg'·ạ·lith) *n.* a huge stone. **-ic** *a.* pert. to huge ancient stone monuments or circles [Gk. *megas*, great; *lithos*, a stone].

meg·a·lo·ma·ni·a (meg·ạ·lạ·mā'·ni·ạ) *n.* a form of insanity in which the patient has grandiose ideas of his own importance; lust for power. **-c** *n.* [Gk. *megas*, great; *mania*, madness].

meg·a·phone (meg'·ạ·fōn) *n.* a large funnel-shaped device to increase the volume of sounds [Gk. *megas*, great; *phōnē*, a sound].

meg·a·ton (meg'·ạ·tạn) *n.* a unit for measuring the power of thermonuclear weapons.

meg·ohm (meg'·ōm) *n.* one million ohms [Gk. *megas*, great; and *ohm*].

me·grim (mē'·grim) *n.* a severe headache usu. on one side; *pl.* depression [Gk. *hemi-*, half; *kranion*, the skull].

mei·o·sis (mī·ō'·sis) *n.* (*Rhet.*) a figure of speech which makes a deliberate understatement to achieve emphasis; a form of litotes [Gk. *meiosis*, lessening].

mel·an·chol·y (mel'·ạn·kạl·i·) *n.* depression of spirits; morbidity; *a.* gloomy; depressed; pensive. **melancholia** *n.* morbid state of depression; abnormal introspectiveness bordering on insanity [Gk. *melas*, black; *cholē*, bile].

Mel·a·ne·sian (mel·ạ·nē'·shạn) *a.* pert. to *Melanesia*, a S. Pacific dark-skinned island group; *n.* a native; the language of Melanesia [Gk. *melas*, black; *nēsos*, island].

mé·lange (mā·lȧnzh') *n.* a mixture; a medley [Fr. *méler*, to mix].

mel·a·nin (mel'·ạ·nin) *n.* a black pigment found in the eye, hair and skin. **melanic** *a.* black. **melanism** *n.* an excess of coloring matter in the skin [Gk. *melas*, black].

Mel·ba toast (mel'·bạ tōst') *n.* thin slice of toast.

meld (meld) *v.t.* and *i.* to blend; merge; a combination of cards melded [fr. *melt, weld*].

mê·lée (mā'·lā) *n.* a confused, hand-to-hand fight [Fr. *méler*, to mix].

mel·io·rate (mēl'·yạ·rāt) *v.t.* to improve; *v.i.* to become better. **melioration** *n.* **meliorator** *n.* **meliorism** *n.* the doctrine that the world is capable of improvement [L. *melior*, better].

mel·lif·er·ous (mạ·lif'·ẹr·ạs) *a.* producing honey. **mellifluence** *n.* a flowing sweetly or smoothly. **mellifluent, mellifluous** *a.* **mellifluently, mellifluously** *adv.* [L. *mel*, honey; *ferre*, to bear].

mel·low (mel'·ō) *a.* soft and ripe; well-matured; genial; jovial; resonant, as a voice; (*Slang*) somewhat intoxicated; *v.t.* to soften; to ripen; *v.i.* to become soft or ripe; to become maturely wise. **-ly** *adv.* **-ness** *n.* [O.E. *meary*, soft].

me·lo·de·on (mạ'·lō·di·ạn) *n.* a small hand keyboard organ; a kind of accordion [Gk.].

me·lod·ic See **melody**.

mel·o·dra·ma (mel·ạ·drám'·ạ) *n.* a dramatic entertainment, sensational and emotional; a play of romantic sentiment and situation. **-tic** *a.* [Gk. *melos*, a song; *drama*, a play].

mel·o·dy (mel'·ạ·di·) *n.* a rhythmical succession of single sounds forming an agreeable musical air; a tune. **melodic** *a.* pert. to melody; melodious. **melodious** *a.* tuneful; pleasing to the ear. **melodiously** *adv.* **melodiousness** *n.* **melodist** *n.* a musical composer or singer [Gk. *melōidia*, a song].

mel·on (mel'·ạn) *n.* a kind of gourd with a sweet, juicy pulp, and a center full of seeds [Gk. *mēlon*, an apple].

melt (melt) *v.t.* to reduce to a liquid state; to dissolve; to soften; to make tender; *v.i.* to become liquid or molten; to blend; to vanish; to become tender. **-ing** *n.* making liquid; *a.* softening; languishing, as looks; tender. **-ingly** *adv.* [O.E. *meltan*, to melt].

mem·ber (mem'·bẹr) *n.* a limb, esp. of an animal body; a constituent part of a complex whole; one of a society, group, etc. **-ed** *a.* having limbs. **-ship** *n.* the state of being a member, or one of a group; members collectively [L. *membrum*, a limb].

mem·brane (mem'·brān) *n.* (*Anat.*) a thin, flexible tissue forming or lining an organ of the body; a sheet of parchment. **membranous** *a.* [L. *membrana*, parchment].

me·men·to (mi·men'·tō) *n.* anything which serves as a reminder of a person or event; a souvenir [L. *meminisse*, to remember].

mem·o (mem'·ō) *n.* (*Colloq.*) memorandum.

mem·oir (mem'·wȧr) *n.* a short, biographical sketch; a scientific record of personal investigations on a subject; *pl.* reminiscences. **-ist** *n.* [L. *memoria*, memory].

mem·o·ry (mem'·ạ·ri·) *n.* the faculty of retaining and recalling knowledge; recollection; remembrance. **memorabilia** *n.pl.* things worthy of note. **memorable** *a.* noteworthy; remarkable. **memorably** *adv.* **memorandum** *n.* a note or reminder; (*Law*) a summary of a transaction; in diplomacy, an outline of the state of a question. *pl.* **-s** or **memoranda.** **memorial** *a.* serving as a reminder; contained in the memory; *n.* anything intended to commemorate a person or an event; a written statement of facts in the form of a petition presented to a governing body. **memorialize** *v.t.* to commemorate; to present a memorial. **memorize** *v.t.* to commit to memory. **memorization** *n.* [L. *memoria*, memory].

men (men) *n.pl.* of **man.**

men·ace (men'·ạs) *n.* a threat or threatening; potential danger; *v.t.* to threaten. **menacing** *a.* **menacingly** *adv.* [L. *minari*, to threaten].

mé·nage (mạ·nȧzh') *n.* a household; housekeeping [Fr. fr. L. *mansio*, a dwelling].

me·nag·er·ie (mạ·naj'·ẹr·i·) *n.* a collection of caged wild animals for exhibition [Fr. *ménage*, a household].

mend (mend) *v.t.* to repair; to set right; to improve; *v.i.* to improve; *n.* a mended place; improvement. **-er** *n.* **-ing** *n.* the act of repairing [fr. *amend*].

men·da·cious (men·dā'·shạs) *a.* given to telling lies; untruthful. **-ly** *adv.* **mendacity** *n.* prevarication; a tendency to lying [L. *mendax*].

men·di·cant (men'·di·kạnt) *a.* begging; living as a beggar; *n.* a beggar. **mendicancy, mendicity** *n.* the practice of living by alms [L. *mendicare*, to beg].

me·ni·al (mē'·ni·ạl) *a.* pert. to domestic service; servile; *n.* a servant; a servile person. **-ly** *adv.* [O.Fr. *mesnee*, a household].

me·nin·ges (mạ·nin'·jēz) *n.pl.* the three membranes enveloping the brain and spinal cord. *sing.* **meninx, meningitis** (·jī'·tis) *n.* (*Med.*) inflammation of these membranes [Gk. *mēninx*, a membrane].

me·nis·cus (mạ·nis'·kạs) *n.* a lens convex on one side and concave on the other; the curved surface of a liquid in a vessel; (*Math.*) a crescent. **meniscal, meniscate** *a.* **menisciform** *a.* crescent-shaped [Gk. *mēniskos*, a crescent].

Men·non·ite (men'·ạn·īt) *n.* a member of or pert. to a Prot. sect favoring plain dress and plain living [fr. *Menno* Simons, leader].

men·o·pause (men'·ạ·pawz) *n.* female change of life [Gk. *mēn*, a month; *pausis*, cessation].

men·sal (men'·sạl) *a.* monthly [L. *mensis*].

men·ses (men'·sēz) *n.pl.* the monthly discharge from the uterus of the female. **menstrual** *a.* monthly; pert. to the menses. **menstruate** *v.i.* to discharge the menses. **menstruation** *n.* **menstruous** *a.* [*pl.* of L. *mensis*, a month].

men·stru·um (men'·stroo·ạm) *n.* a solvent [L. *menstrua*, the menses].

men·sur·a·ble (men'·sher·a·bl) *a.* capable of being measured. **mensurability** *n.* **mensural** *a.* pert. to measure. **mensuration** *n.* the act, process, or art of measuring; (*Math.*) the determination of length, area, and volume. **mensurative** [L. *mensura*, measure].

men·tal (men'·tạl) *a.* pert. to, or of, the mind; performed in the mind; (*Colloq.*) mentally ill. **-ity** (men·tal'·ạ·ti·) *n.* intellectual power; mental attitude. **-ly** *adv.* — **deficiency** subnormal intelligence [L. *mens*, the mind].

men·thol (men'·thawl) *n.* a camphor obtained from oil of peppermint. **-ated** *a.* treated or flavored with menthol [L. *mentha*, mint].

men·tion (men'·shạn) *n.* a brief notice; a casual comment; *v.t.* to notice; to name. **-able** *a.* fit to be remarked on [L. *mentio*].

men·tor (men'·tẹr) *n.* an experienced and prudent adviser. **-ial** *a.* [Gk. *Mentōr*, the adviser of Telemachus].

men·u (men'·ū) *n.* a bill of fare; the food served [Fr. *menu*, a list].

Meph·i·stoph·e·les (mef·is·tåf'·ạ·lēz) *n.* (*Myth.*) the devil. **Mephistophelean** *a.* sinister.

me·phi·tis (me·fī'·tis) *n.* noxious exhalation, esp. from the ground or from decaying matter. **mephitic** *a.* [L.].

mer·can·tile (mur'·kạn·til, ·tīl) *a.* pert. to commerce. **mercantilism** *n.* the mercantile system. **mercantilist** *n.* — **system**, the economic theory that money alone is wealth and that a nation's exports should far exceed its imports [L. *mercari*, to traffic].

mer·ce·nar·y (mur'·se·ner·i·) *a.* working merely for money or gain; hired; greedy. *n.* a hired soldier. **mercenarily** *adv.* **mercenariness** *n.* [L. *merces*, wages].

mer·cer·ize (mur'·sạ·rīz) *v.t.* to treat cotton fabrics with caustic lye to impart a silky finish. **-d** *a.* [fr. J. *Mercer*, inventor of the process].

mer·chant (mur'·chant) *n.* one who engages in trade; a storekeeper. *a.* pert. to trade or merchandise. **merchandise** *n.* commodities bought and sold. **-man** *n.* a ship carrying goods. — **marine**, the ships and men engaged in commerce [L. *mercari*, to traffic].

Mer·cu·ry (mur'·kyạ·ri·) *n.* the planet of the solar system nearest to the sun. (**m**) *n.* a metallic chemical element, silvery white in color, with very low melting point (also called *quicksilver*), used in barometers, thermometers, etc. **mercurial** *a.* pert to, or consisting of, mercury; sprightly; agile; erratic. **mercurialize** *v.t.* to make mercurial; to treat with mercury. **mercurous, mercuric** *a.* (*Chem.*) pert. to compounds of mercury [L. *Mercurius*, prob. fr.

merx, goods; also Gk. *Myth*].

mer·cy (mur'·si·) *n.* forbearance; clemency; leniency shown to a guilty person; compassion. **merciful** *a.* full of mercy; compassionate. **mercifully** *adv.* **mercifulness** *n.* **merciless** *a.* void of pity; callous; cruel. **mercilessly** *adv.* **mercilessness** *n.* [L. *merces*, reward].

mere (mēr) *n.* (*Poetic*) a pool or lake [O.E. *mere*, a stretch of water].

mere (mēr) *a.* nothing but; simple. **-ly** *adv.* simply; solely [L. *merus*, undiluted].

mer·e·tri·cious (mer·ạ·trish'·ạs) *a.* tawdry; cheap (as of style). **-ly** *adv.* **-ness** *n.* [L. *meretrix*, a harlot].

mer·gan·ser (mẹr·gan'·sẹr) *n.* a diving fish-eating bird [L. *mergus*, a diving bird; *anser*, a goose].

merge (murj) *v.t.* to cause to be swallowed up; to plunge or sink; *v.i.* to lose identity by being absorbed in something else; to be swallowed up or lost. **-r** *n.* a combine of commercial or industrial firms [L. *mergere*, to dip].

me·rid·i·an (mạ·rid'·i·ạn) *n.* an imaginary line passing through the poles at right angles to the equator; (*Astron.*) a circle passing through the poles of the heavens and the zenith of the observer; the highest attitude of sun or star; midday; *a.* pert. to midday; supreme. **meridional** *a.* pert. to the meridian; southerly. **meridionally** *n.* [L. *meridianus*, pert. to noon].

me·ringue (mạ·rang') *n.* a mixture of sugar and white of egg whipped till stiff, and baked in a cool oven; a small cake or pie topping of this [Fr.].

me·ri·no (mạ·rē'·nō) *n.* a breed of sheep with very fine, thick fleece, orig. from Spain; a dress fabric of this wool; *a.* pert. to the merino [Sp. *merino*, an inspector of sheepwalks].

mer·it (mer'·it) *n.* quality of deserving reward; excellence; worth; *pl.* the rights and wrongs, as of a law case; *v.t.* to earn; to deserve. **-orious** *a.* deserving reward. **-oriously** *adv.* [L. *meritum*, desert].

mer·lin (mur'·lin) *n.* a species of falcon [O.Fr. *esmerillon*, a falcon].

mer·lon (mur'·lạn) *n.* solid part of a parapet between two openings [Fr. fr. L. *murus*, a wall].

mer·maid (mur'·mād) *n.* an imaginary sea-creature with the upper body and head of a woman, and the tail of a fish. **merman** *n.* the male equivalent [O.E. *mere*, a lake; and *maid*].

mer·ry (mer'·i·) *a.* gay; hilarious; lively. **merrily** *adv.* **merriment, merriness** *n.* gaiety with noise and laughter; hilarity. **—go-round** *n.* a revolving platform with horses, cars, etc. **—making** *n.* festivity [O.E. *myrge*, pleasant].

mer·thi·o·late (mẹr·thī'·ạ·lāt) *n.* an antiseptic and germicide [fr. *mercuri-thiosalicylate*].

me·sa (mā'·sạ) *n.* a high plateau [Sp. = table].

mes·dames (mā·dạm') *n.pl.* of madam, Mrs. [Fr.].

mes·en·te·ry (mes'·ạn·ter·i·) *n.* a fold of abdominal tissue keeping the intestines in place. **mesenteric** *a.* [Gk. *mesos*, middle; *enteron*, intestine].

mesh (mesh) *n.* the space between the threads of a net; network; *v.t.* to net; to ensnare; *v.i.* to become interlocked, as gears of a machine [O.E. *max*, net].

mes·mer·ism (mez'·mẹr·izm) *n.* exercising an influence over will and actions of another; hypnotism. **mesmeric, -al** *a.* of or pert. to mesmerism. **mesmerization** *n.* **mesmerize** *v.t.* to hypnotize. **mesmerizer, mesmerist** *n.* [fr. F. A. *Mesmer*, a Ger. physician].

mesne (mēn) *a.* middle; (*Law*) intermediate [O.Fr. *mesne*, middle].

mes·o·lith·ic (mez·ạ·lith'·ic) *a.* of period between paleolithic and neolithic ages [Gk.

mesos, middle; *lithos*, a stone].

me·son (mez′·ån) *n.* a particle equal in charge to, but having greater mass than, an electron or positron, and less mass than a neutron or proton [Gk. *meson*, neut. of *mesos*, middle].

Mes·o·po·ta·mi·a (mes·a·pa·tā′·mi·a) *n.* the land between Euphrates and Tigris; now Iraq [Gk. *mesos*, middle; *potamos*, a river].

Mes·o·zo·ic (mes·a·zō′·ik) *a.* pert. to the second geological period [Gk. *mesos*, middle; *zōe*, life].

mess (mes) *n.* unpleasant mixture; disorder; a muddle; *v.t.* to dirty; to muddle. **-y** *a.* dirty; untidy; chaotic [form of *mash*].

mess (mes) *n.* a dish of food served at one time; the meal; a number of people who eat together, esp. in army, navy, etc.; *v.t.* to supply meals to; *v.i.* to eat in company. **-kit** *n.* a soldier's portable eating equipment [O.Fr. *mes*, a dish].

mes·sage (mes′·ij) *n.* a communication, verbal or written, sent by one person to another; an inspired utterance. **messenger** *n.* one who delivers a communication; one employed to deliver goods [L. *mittere*, to send].

mes·si·ah (ma·sī′·a) *n.* an expected savior or liberator. **messianic** *a.* [Heb. *mashiah*, anointed].

mes·suage (mes′·wij) *n.* (*Law*) a dwelling-house with lands and outbuildings [O.Fr. *mesuage*, a holding of land].

mes·ti·zo (mes·tē′·zō) *n.* a half-caste, esp. the offspring of a Spaniard and an Amer. Indian [Sp. fr. L. *miscere*, to mix].

met (met) *pa.t.* and *pa.p.* of the verb **meet**.

me·ta·bo·lism (ma·tab′·al·izm) *n.* the name given to the chemical changes continually going on in the cells of living matter. **metabolic** *a.* **metabolize** *v.t.* [Gk. *metabole*, change].

me·ta·car·pus (met·a·kår′·pas) *n.* the hand between the wrist and fingers; the bones of this part. **metacarpal** *a.* [Gk. *meta*, after; *karpos*, the wrist].

met·age (mēt′·ij) *n.* official weighing, as of coal; the price paid for this [fr. *mete*].

met·al (met′·al) *n.* a mineral substance, opaque, fusible and malleable, capable of conducting heat and electricity; molten glass; (*Fig.*) courage; mettle; *v.t.* to furnish or cover with metal. **-lic** (ma·tal′·ik) *a.* pert. to, like, or consisting of, metal. **-lically** *adv.* **-ize** *v.t.* to make metallic. **-loid** *n.* an element with both metallic and non-metallic properties, as arsenic; *a.* pert. to a metal. **base metals,** copper, lead, zinc, tin as distinct from precious metals, gold and silver [Gk. *metallon*, a mine].

met·al·lur·gy (met′·al·ur·ji·) *n.* the art of working metals or of obtaining metals from ores. **metallurgic** *a.* **metallurgist** *n.* [Gk. *metallon*, a metal; *ergon*, a work].

met·a·mor·pho·sis (met·a·mawr′·fa·sis) *n.* a change of form or structure; evolution; *pl.* **metamorphoses. metamorphic** *a.* subject to change of form. **metamorphism** *n.* the state of being metamorphic. **metamorphose** *v.t.* to transform in form or nature [Gk. *meta*, over; *morphe*, shape].

met·a·phor (met′·a·fawr, fer) *n.* a figure of speech which makes an *implied* comparison between things which are not *literally* alike. **-ically** *adv.* **-ist** *n.* **mixed metaphor,** a combination of metaphors drawn from different sources [Gk. *metapherein*, to transfer].

met·a·phrase (met′·a·frāz) *n.* literal, word for word translation from foreign language (opp. of *paraphrase*); *v.t.* to translate literally. **metaphrast** *n.* one who makes a literal translation. **metaphrastic** *a.* literal [Gk. *meta*, over; *phrasis*, a saying].

met·a·phys·ics (met·a·fiz′·iks) *n.* the science which investigates first causes of all existence and knowledge; speculative philosophy. **metaphysical** *a.* **metaphysically** *adv.* **metaphy-**

sician *n.* [Gk. *meta*, after; *phusis*, nature].

me·tas·ta·sis (ma·tas′·ta·sis) *n.* change of position, state, or form; shift of malignant cells from one part of the body to another. *pl.* **metastases. metasticize** *v.i.* [Gk. removal].

met·a·tar·sus (met·a·tår′·sas) *n.* the front part of the foot excluding the toes. **metatarsal** *a.* [Gk. *meta*, beyond; *tarsos*, the flat of the foot].

me·tath·e·sis (ma·tath′·a·sis) *n.* the transposition of a letter or letters in a word, as in *curl*, orig. *crul.* **metathetic** *a.* [Gk. *meta*, over; *thesis*, a placing].

met·a·zo·a (met·a·zō′·a) *n.pl.* multi-cellular organisms. **metazoan** *n. sing.* and *a.* **metazoic** *a.* [Gk. *meta*, after; *zoon*, an animal].

mete (mēt) *v.t.* to distribute by measure; to allot, as punishment [O.E. *metan*, to measure].

me·te·or (mē′·ti·er) *n.* any rapidly passing, luminous body seen in the atmosphere; a shooting star. **-ic** *a.* pert. to a meteor; influenced by atmospheric conditions; swift; dazzling. **-ite** *n.* a mass of stone or metal from outer space which lands on earth. **-ograph** *n.* an intsrument for automatically recording weather conditions. **-ography** *n.* **-oid** *n.* a body in space which becomes a meteor on passing through the atmosphere of the earth. **-ological** *a.* **-ologist** *n.* **-ology** *n.* the science which treats of atmospheric phenomena, esp. in relation to weather forecasts [Gk. *meteoros*, lofty].

me·ter (mē′·ter) *n.* a unit of length in the metric system, 39.37 U.S. inches. **metric** *a.* **metric system,** a decimal system based on the French meter. **metrology** *n.* the science of weights and measures [Gk. *metron*, a measure].

me·ter (mē′·ter) *n.* an instrument for recording the consumption of gas, electricity, water, etc. [Gk. *metron*, a measure].

me·ter (mē′·tr) *n.* in poetry, the rhythmical arrangement of syllables, these groups being termed *feet*; verse; stanza-form; (*Music*) rhythmical structure indicated by measures; time or beat. **metrical** *a.* pert. to meter or measurement. **metrically** *adv.* **metronome** *n.* (*Mus.*) an instrument like an inverted pendulum for beating out time in music [Gk. *metron*].

meth·ane (meth′·ān) *n.* an inflammable, hydrocarbon gas. **methanol** *n.* methyl or wood alcohol [fr. *methyl*].

meth·od (meth′·ad) *n.* manner of proceeding esp. in scientific research; orderliness; system; technique. **-ic, -ical** *a.* arranged systematically; orderly. **-ically** *adv.* **-ology** *n.* [Gk. *meta*, after; *hodos*, a way].

Meth·o·dist (meth′·a·dist) *n.* a member of Protestant sect founded in 18th cent. by Charles and John Wesley [fr. *method*].

meth·yl (meth′·al) *n.* the chemical basis of wood [Gk. *methu*, wine; *hule*, wood].

me·tic·u·lous (ma·tik′·ya·las) *a.* orig. afraid to make a mistake; over-scrupulous as to detail; over-exact. **-ly** *adv.* **-ness** *n.* [L. *metus*, fear].

mé·tier (māt′·yā) *n.* one's profession or vocation; the occupation for which one is best suited [Fr.].

me·ton·y·my (me·tàn′·a·mi) *n.* (*Rhet.*) a figure of speech in which the name of one thing is put for another associated with it. **metonym** *n.* **metonymic, -al** *a.* **metonymically** *adv.* [Gk. *meta*, expressing change; *onoma*, a name].

me·tro·nym·ic (mē·tra·nim′·ik) *a.* a name derived from a female ancestor.

me·trop·o·lis (ma·tråp′·a·lis) *n.* the chief city of an area; a large city; a diocese. **metropolitan** *a.* pert to a metropolis; pert. to the see of a metropolitan bishop; *n.* one who lives in a metropolis or has the manners, etc. of one who does [Gk. *meter*, a mother; *polis*, a city].

met·tle (met′·l) *n.* spirit; courage. **-some** *a.* **to be on one's mettle,** to be roused to do one's best [fr. *metal*].

mew (mū) *n.* a seagull [O.E. *maew*, a gull].

mew (mū) *v.t.* to shed or cast; to confine, as in a cage; *v.i.* to molt; *n.* a cage for hawks; a den. *n.pl.* stables around a court or alley [O.Fr. *muer*, to change; *mew*, a cage].

mewl (mūl) *v.i.* to whimper or whine [fr. *mew*].

Mex·i·can (mek′·sạ·kạn) *n.* a native or inhabitant of Mexico; *a.*

mez·za·nine (mez′·ạ·nēn) *n.* (*Archit.*) a low story between two main ones; in a theater usu. the first few rows in the balcony [It. *mezzo*, middle].

mez·zo (met′·sō) *a.* middle; moderately. —**soprano** *n.* voice between soprano and contralto. **-tint** *n.* a method of copperplate engraving in which a roughened surface is scraped according to degrees of light and shade required. [It. *mezzo*, half].

mi·as·ma (mī·az′·mạ) *n.* noxious exhalations from decomposing matter. **-l, -tic, miasmic** *a.* [Gk. *miasma*, a stain].

mi·ca (mī′·kạ) *n.* a group of mineral silicates capable of cleavage into very thin, flexible, and often transparent laminae. *a.* [L. *mica*, a crumb].

mice (mīs) *pl.* of **mouse.**

Mich·ael·mas (mik′·l·mạs) *n.* the feast of the archangel Michael, Sept. 29.

mi·crobe (mī′·krōb) *n.* a minute organism; a bacterium or disease germ. **microbial, microbian, microbic** *a.* **microbiology** *n.* the science of microbes. **microbiological** *a.* [Gk. *mikros*, small; *bios*, life].

mi·cro·ceph·a·lous (mī·krō·sef′·ạ·lạs) *a.* (*Med.*) having a very small head [Gk. *mikros*, small; *kēphalā*, the head].

mi·cro·coc·cus (mī·krō·kàk′·ạs) *n.* a spherical or oval organism or bacterium [Gk. *mikros*, small; *kokkos*, a berry].

mi·cro·cosm (mī′·krạ·kàzm) *n.* miniature universe; man, regarded as the epitome of the universe; a community symbolical of humanity as a whole. **microcosmic**, *a.* [Gk. *mikros*, small; *kosmos*, the universe].

mi·cro·film (mī′·krạ·film) *n.* film used to make reduced photographic copies of books, etc. [Gk. *mikros*, small; and *film*].

mi·cro·graph (mī′·krạ·graf) *n.* an instrument for producing microscopic engraving; a microphotograph. **micrographer** *n.* **micrography** *n.* the study of microscopic objects; the art of writing or engraving on a minute scale [Gk. *mikros*, small; *graphein*, to write].

mi·crol·o·gy (mī·kràl′·ạ·ji·) *n.* the science which deals with microscopic objects; (*Fig.*) overscrupulous attention to small details [Gk. *mikros*, small; *logos*, a discourse].

mi·crom·e·ter (mī·kràm′·ạ·ter) *n.* an instrument for measuring very small distances or angles. **micrometric, -al** *a.* [Gk. *mikros*, small; *metron*, a measure].

mi·cron (mī′·kràn) *n.* the millionth part of a meter [Gk. *mikros*, small].

mi·cro-or·gan·ism (mī·krō·awr′·gạn·izm) *n.* a microscopic organism [Gk. *mikros*, small; *organon*, an instrument].

mi·cro·phone (mī′·krạ·fōn) *n.* an instrument for turning sound waves into electrical waves so enabling them to be transmitted; mouthpiece for broadcasting (*Colloq.* abbrev. **mike**); an instrument for making faint sounds louder. [Gk. *mikros*, small; *phōne*, a sound].

mi·cro·pho·tog·ra·phy (mī·krạ·fạ·tàg′·rạ·fi·) *n.* the art of producing minute photographs. **microphotograph** *n.* [Gk. *mikros*, small; *phos*, light; *graphein*, to write].

mi·cro·scope (mī′·krạ·skōp) *n.* an optical instrument for magnifying minute objects. **microscopic, -al** *a.* visible only with a microscope; very minute. **microscopically** *adv.* **microscopy** *n.* [Gk. *mikros*, small; *skopein*, to see].

mi·cro·zo·a (mī·krạ·zō′·ạ) *n.pl.* microscopic animals. **-n** *a.* and *n. sing.* [Gk. *mikros*, small; *zōon*, an animal; *zumē*, leaven].

mic·tu·ri·tion (mik·chạ·rish′·ạn) *n.* (*Med.*) the passing of urine. **micturate** *v.i.* [L. *micturire*, to pass urine].

mid (mid) *a.* situated between extremes; middle, as in *mid-air, mid-Atlantic.* **-day** *n.* and *a.* noon; pert. to noon. **-night** *n.* twelve o'clock at night. **-shipman** *n.* rank in U.S. Navy and Coast Guard held by young men attending service academies; **-ships** *adv.* amidships. **-summer** *n.* the middle of summer. **-way** *adv.* halfway. **-winter** *n.* middle of the winter [O.E.].

mid (mid) *prep.* amidst (in poetry).

mid·dle (mid′·l) *a.* equidistant from the extremes; intermediate; *n.* middle point. **-aged** *a.* pert. to the period of life between 40 and 60. **-man** *n.* an agent acting between producer and consumer; a go-between. **-weight** *n.* (*Boxing*) a boxer of a weight not more than 160 lbs. **middling** *a.* of medium size, quality; *adv.* moderately. **Middle Ages,** the period of European history from the Fall of the Roman Empire (about A.D. 476) to the Fall of Constantinople (1453). — **class,** that section of the community between the very wealthy higher social classes and the laboring classes; the bourgeoisie. **Middle East,** that part of the world between the *Near East* and the *Far East*; Egypt, Syria, Palestine, Arabia, Iraq and Iran. **Middle English,** the English language as written and spoken between 1150-1500 (approx.) [O.E. *middel*].

mid·dy (mid′·i·) *n.* (*Colloq.*) a midshipman; a loose blouse with a sailor collar.

midge (mij) *n.* a gnat; a very small person. **midget** *n.* a dwarf; *a.* miniature [O.E. *mycge*, a gnat].

mid·riff (mid′·rif) *n.* the diaphragm; body part between chest and abdomen [O.E. *mid*, middle; *hrif*, the belly].

midst (midst) *n.* the middle; *prep.* amidst [M.E.].

mid·wife (mid′·wīf) *n.* a woman who assists another at childbirth. *pl.* **midwives** [O.E. *mid*, with; *wif*, a woman]. [pearance.

mien (mēn) *n.* manner; bearing; general appearance.

miff (mif) *v.t.* and *i.* to offend or take offense [Ger. *muffen*, to sulk].

might (mīt) *pa.t.* of verb **may.**

might (mīt) *n.* power; strength; energy. **-iness** *n.* the state of being powerful; greatness. **-y** *a.* having great strength or power; exalted [O.E. *meaht*, might].

mi·gnon·ette (min′·yạ·net) *n.* a sweet-scented, greenish-gray flowered plant [dim. Fr. *mignon*, a darling].

mi·graine (mī′·grān) *n.* severe headache often accompanied by nausea. cf. **megrim.**

mi·grate (mī′·grāt) *v.i.* to remove one's residence from one place to another; (of birds) to fly to another place in search of warmer climate. **migrant** *n.* a person or creature who migrates. **migration** *n.* the act of migrating; a mass removal. **migratory** *a.* [L. *migrare*, to go].

Mi·ka·do (mạ·kà′·dō) *n.* the Emperor of Japan [Jap. *mi*, august; *kado*, the door].

mike (mīk) *n.* (*Colloq.* abbrev.) a microphone.

mil (mil) *n.* .001 in., a unit of measurement in calculating the diameter of wire [L. *mille*, a thousand].

milch (milch) *a.* giving milk [M.E. *milch*, milk].

mild (mīld) *a.* gentle; kind; placid; calm, or temperate, as weather. **-ly** *adv.* **-ness** [O.E. *milde*, gentle].

mil·dew (mil′·dòò) *n.* whitish coating of minute fungi on plants; a mold on paper, cloth, leather caused by dampness; *v.t.* and *v.i.* to taint or be tainted with mildew. **-y** *a.* [O.E. *mele*, honey; *deaw*, dew].

mile (mīl) n. a measure of length equal to 5280 ft. **geographical** or **nautical mile,** 1/60 of 1 degree of the earth's equator, 6,080.2 ft. **-age** n. distance in miles; rate of travel calculated in miles; traveling expenses calculated on the number of miles traveled. **-r** n. a man or horse trained to run a mile. **-stone** n. roadside marker; a stage or crisis in one's life [O.E. *mil,* fr. L. *mille passus,* 1000 paces].

mil·i·ar·y (mil'·i·er·i·) a. like millet seeds. **miliaria,** n. (*Med.*) a fever, accompanied by a rash resembling millet seeds (heat rash) [L. *milium,* millet]. [dle].

mi·lieu (mēl·yoo') n. environment [Fr. = mid-

mil·i·tant (mil'·i·tạnt) a. aggressive; serving as a soldier. **militancy** n. war-like, fighting spirit. **-ly** adv. **militarism** n. military spirit; excessive emphasis on military power; opp. of *pacifism.* **militarist** n. one who upholds the doctrine of militarism; a student of military science. **military** a. pert. to soldiers, arms, or war; warlike; n. the army. **military police,** soldiers performing duties of police in the army. **militate** v.i. to be combative; to work against (or for); to have an adverse effect on [L. *miles,* a soldier].

mi·li·tia (mạ·lish'·ạ) n. a citizen army, liable to be called out in an emergency [L. *miles,* a soldier].

milk (milk) n. a white fluid secreted by female mammals for nourishment of their young and in some cases used for humans; the juice of certain plants; v.t. to draw milk from; (*Colloq.*) to fleece or exploit a person; v.i. to give milk. **— and water** a. insipid. **—bar** n. a counter where milk drinks, etc. are sold. **-er** n. a milking-machine; a cow which yields milk. **— fever,** a fever sometimes contracted after childbirth. **-iness** n. **-ing** n. the quantity of milk yielded at one time; the drawing of milk. **-like** a. **-maid** n. a dairymaid or woman who milks cows. **-man** n. a man who milks cows; a man who delivers milk. **-sop** n. a weak, effeminate man. **-tooth** n. one of the temporary baby teeth. **-weed** n. wild plant with milky sap. **-wood** n. kind of tropical trees yielding latex. **-y** a. like, full of, or yielding milk. **Milky Way,** the Galaxy, an irregular, luminous belt in the heavens, from the light of innumerable stars. **condensed milk,** milk with sugar added and evaporated to the consistency of syrup. **evaporated milk,** unsweetened condensed milk [O.E. *meolc,* milk].

mill (mil) n. a building equipped with machinery to grind grain into flour; an apparatus for grinding, as *coffee-mill;* a factory or machinery used in manufacture, as *cotton-mill, paper-mill;* (*Slang*) a boxing match. v.t. to grind; to cut fine grooves on the edges of (coins); to full (cloth); to dress or puify (ore); (*Slang*) to box; v.i. to go round in circles, as cattle, or crowds of people. **-board** n. stout pasteboard used in bookbinding. **-dam** n. a dam built to provide water for turning a mill wheel. **-ed** a. having the edges raised and grooved, as coins; rolled into sheets, as metal. **-er** n. **-ing** n. grinding in a mill; fulling cloth, or grooving raised edges of a coin, or pressing crude rubber under rollers; a. (*Slang*) confused; without direction, as *milling crowds.* **-pond** n. milldam. **-race** n. the current of water which turns millwheel. **-stone** n. one of the flat stones used in grinding grain; a burden. **— wheel** n. a water wheel for driving mill machinery. **-wright** n. one who sets up machinery in a mill [O.E. *myln,* to grind].

mill (mil) n. one thousandth of a dollar; one tenth of a cent [L. *mille,* thousand].

mil·len·ni·um (mil·en'·i·ạm) n. a thousand years; a future time or perfect peace on earth. **millennarian** n. one who believes in the millennium. **millennary** a. comprising a thou-

sand; n. a period of a thousand years. **millennial** a. [L. *mille,* a thousand; *annus,* a year].

mil·li·pede (mil'·i·pēd) n. an insect with many legs [L. *mille,* thousand; *pes,* a foot].

mil·li- *prefix* one thousandth of. **-gram** n. one thousandth of a gram. **-meter** n. one thousandth of a meter [L. *mille,* a thousand].

mil·liard (mil'·yẹrd) n. a thousand millions; a billion [Fr.].

mil·li·ner (mil'·ạn·ẹr) n. one who makes or sells ladies' hats. **-y** n. [fr. *Milan*].

mil·lion (mil'·yạn) n. a thousand thousands (1,000,000); **-aire** n. one whose wealth amounts to a million (or more) dollars. **-fold** a. **-th** n. a. one of a million parts; **the millions,** the masses [Fr.].

milque·toast (milk·tōst) n. a timid shrinking person [fr. H. T. Webster's comic strip character].

milt (milt) n. the spleen; the reproductive glands or secretion of the male fish; v.t. to impregnate the female roe. **-er** n. [O.E. *milte*].

mime (mīm) n. a farce in which scenes of real life are expressed by gesture only; an actor in such a farce; v.i. to act in a mime; to express by gesture. **mimetic(al)** a. imitative. **mimic** (mi'·mik) v.t. to imitate; to burlesque; to ridicule by imitating another. pr.p. **-king** pa.p., pa.t. **-ked.** n. one who mimics or caricatures; a. mock, as in *mimic battle;* feigned. **mimicry** n. the art or act of mimicking [Gk. *mimos,* an actor].

mim·e·o·graph (mim'·i·ạ·graf) n. a form of duplicating-machine [Gk. *mimeisthai,* to imitate; *graphein,* to write].

Mi·mo·sa (mi·mō'·sạ) n. a genus of leguminous plants, shrubs, or trees, with small, fluffy flowers [Gk. *mimos,* an imitator].

min·a·ret (min·ạ·ret') n. a turret on a Mohammedan mosque [Ar. *manarat,* a lighthouse].

min·a·to·ry (min'·ạ·tōr·i·) a. threatening; menacing. **minacious** a. **minacity** n. [L. *minari,* to threaten].

mince (mins) v.t. to cut or chop into very small pieces; (*Fig.*) to tone down; v.i. to speak or walk with affected elegance. **-meat** n. currants, raisins, spices, apple, suet and sugar, chopped and mixed together, used as pie filling (*Fig.*) anything chopped up. **mincing** a. speaking or walking with affected elegance. **mincingly** adv. [O.E. *minsian,* to make small].

mind (mīnd) n. the intellectual faculty; the understanding; memory; opinion; inclination; purpose; a person regarded as an intellect; v.t. to obey; to attend to; to heed; to object to; to take care of; v.i. to be careful; to care. **-ed** a. disposed; inclined. **-edness** n. **-ful** a. attentive; observant; aware. **-fully** adv. **-fulness** n. **-less** a. stupid; careless. **— reader** n. one who can sense another's thoughts. **absent minded,** forgetful [O.E. *gemynd,* the mind].

mine (mīn) n. a pit in the earth from which minerals are excavated; a hidden explosive to blow up a wall, vessel, etc.; a profitable source; pl. the mining industry; v.i. and v.t. to place mines; to dig a mine or in a mine; to burrow; to undermine; to sap. **— field** n. an area of land or stretch of the sea where mines have been placed. **— layer** n. a vessel which places submarine or floating mines. **— sweeper** n. a vessel with nets for clearing a mine field [Fr. *miner,* to mine].

mine (mīn) poss. pron. belonging to me; [O.E. *min*].

min·er·al (min'·ẹr·ạl) n. any substance, generally inorganic, taken from the earth by mining; a chemical element or compound occurring in nature; a. pert. to or containing minerals; inorganic. **-ization** n. **-ize** v.t. to convert into or impregnate with minerals. **-ogy** (min·ẹr·-ạl'·ạ·ji·) n. the science of minerals and their classification. **mineralogist** n. **— water,**

water, impregnated with mineral substance, used medicinally [Fr. *miner*, to mine].

mi·ne·stro·ne (min·a·strō'·ni·) *n.* thick vegetable soup [It.].

min·gle (ming'·gl) *v.t.* to mix; to blend; to join in; *v.i.* to become mixed. **-r** *n.* **mingling** *n.* blend [O.E. *mengan*, to mix].

min·i·a·ture (min'·i·a·cher) *n.* a small-sized painting done on ivory, vellum, etc.; anything on a small scale; *a.* minute. **miniaturize** *v.t.* to make on a small scale [L. *miniare*, to paint red].

min·i·fy (min'·i·fī) *v.t.* to lessen; to minimize [L. *minor*, less; *facere*, to make].

min·im (min'·im) *n.* anything very minute; (*Med.*) 1/60 of a fluid dram; a drop; (*Mus.*) a half note. **minimal** *a.* smallest possible. **minimize** *v.t.* to reduce; to depreciate. **minimization** *n.* **minimum** *n.* the least to which anything may be reduced [L. *minimus*, least].

min·ion (min'·yan) *n.* a favorite; a servile flatterer; (*Print.*) a small type [Fr. *mignon*, a darling].

min·is·ter (min'·is·ter) *n.* an agent or instrument; a clergyman; (*Brit.*) one entrusted with a govt. department; to serve; *v.i.* to supply things needed. **-ial** *a.* executive; pert. to the work of a minister. **-ially** *adv.* **-ing** *a.* serving. **ministrant** *n.* one who ministers; a helper. **ministration** *n.* the act of performing a service. **ministrative** *a.* **ministry** *n.* the act of ministering; the office or functions of a minister; the clergy [L. *minister*, a servant].

min·i·ver (min'·a·ver) *n.* fine white fur [O.Fr. *menu*, small; *vair*, fur].

mink (mingk) *n.* a semiaquatic animal of the weasel tribe; its fur [Scand.].

min·now (min'·ō) *n.* a small freshwater fish [O.E. *myne*, a small fish].

mi·nor (mī'·ner) *a.* lesser; inferior in bulk, degree, importance, etc.; subordinate; (*Mus.*) lower by a semi-tone; *n.* a person under 21. **-ity** (mī·när'·i·ti·) *n.* the state of being under age; the lesser number, oppos. of *majority*. — **key** (*Mus.*) a key characterized by a minor third, sixth, or seventh [L. *minor*, less].

Mi·nor·ca (min·awr'·ka) *n.* a breed of fowl [Sp. fr. *Minorca* island].

min·ster (min'·ster) *n.* church cathedral [O.E. *mynster*, a monastery].

min·strel (min'·stral) *n.* a medieval poet or wandering singer; an entertainer in a minstrel show (a comic variety show with performers in blackface) [O.Fr. *menestrel*, a jester].

mint (mint) *n.* the place where money is coined; a great amount of money; *a.* as issued (before use); *v.t.* to make by stamping, as coins; to invent. **-age** *n.* process of minting money [O.E. *mynet*, money].

mint (mint) *n.* an aromatic plant used for medicinal and culinary purposes; a candy flavored with it. — **julep**, an iced drink of whiskey and sugar flavored with mint [O.E. *minte*].

min·u·end (min'·ū·end) *n.* the number from which another is to be subtracted [L. *minuendus*, to be made less].

min·u·et (min·ū·et') *n.* a slow, stately dance; music, to which the minuet is danced [Fr. *menuet*, fr. *menu*, small].

mi·nus (mī'·nas) *prep.* less by; *a.* showing subtraction; negative *n.* the sign (—) of subtraction; an amount less than nothing. **-cule** (mi·nus'·kūl) *a.* small; *n.* a lower-case letter, oppos. of *majuscule* [L. *minor*, less].

mi·nute (mī·nóòt') *a.* very small; slight; particular; exact. **-ly** *adv.* **-ness** *n.* **minutiae** (min·ū'·shi·ē) *n.pl.* minute details [L. *minuere*, *minutum*, to lessen].

min·ute (min'·it) *n.* the 60th part of an hour or degree; a moment. *pl.* the official record of a meeting; *v.t.* to make a note of. — **hand** *n.* longer of two hands on clock or watch indicat-

ing minutes. **-ly** *adv.* occurring every minute [L. *minuere minutum*, to lessen].

minx (mingks) *n.* a pert, saucy girl [Ger. *mensch*].

mir·a·cle (mir'·a·kl) *n.* a wonder; a supernatural happening; a prodigy. — **play**, a popular medieval form of drama based on the lives of the saints, or on Biblical history. **miraculous** *a.* supernatural; extraordinary. **miraculously** *adv.* [L. *miraculum*, wonder].

mi·rage (mi·ràzh') *n.* an optical illusion; a delusion [L. *mirare*, to wonder at].

mire (mīr) *n.* slimy soil; mud; defilement; *v.t.* to plunge into or cover with mud; *v.i.* to sink in mud. **miriness** *n.* **miry** *a.* [O.N. *myrr*, marsh].

mir·ror (mir'·er) *n.* a looking glass; a brilliantly polished reflecting surface; a pattern or model; a reflection, as a *mirror of the times*. *v.t.* to reflect [L. *mirare*, to look at].

mirth (murth) *n.* gaiety; merriment; joyousness; laughter. **-ful** *a.* **-fulness** *n.* **-less** *a.* grim. **-lessly** *adv.* [O.E. *myrgth*, merry].

mis- (mis) *prefix.* wrong; ill. prefixed to words of O.E. or O.Fr. origin.

mis·ad·ven·ture (mis·ad·ven'·cher) *n.* an unlucky adventure; a mishap.

mis·ad·vise (mis·ad·vīz') *v.t.* to advise wrongly. **-d** *a.* ill-advised.

mis·al·li·ance (mis·a·lī'·ans) *n.* an unfortunate alliance, esp. in marriage.

mis·an·thrope (mis'·an·thrōp) *n.* a hater of mankind; one who has no faith in his fellow men. **misanthropically** *adv.* **misanthropy** *n.* hatred of mankind [Gk. *miseein*, to hate; *anthrōpos*, a man].

mis·ap·ply (mis·a·plī') *v.t.* to apply wrongly or dishonestly. **misapplication** *n.*

mis·ap·pre·hend (mis·ap·ri·hend') *v.t.* to apprehend wrongly; to misconceive. **misapprehension** *n.* **misapprehensive** *a.*

mis·ap·pro·pri·ate (mis·a·prō'·pri·āt) *v.t.* to use wrongly, esp. to embezzle money. **misappropriation** *n.*

mis·be·got·ten (mis·bi·gàt'·n) *a.* unlawfully conceived; illegitimate.

mis·be·have (mis·bi·hāv') *v.i.* to behave badly, improperly or dishonestly. **misbehavior** *n.*

mis·be·lieve (mis·bi·lēv') *v.t.* to believe wrongly. **misbelief** *n.* belief in false ideas.

mis·cal·cu·late (mis·kal'·kya·lāt) *v.t.* to calculate wrongly. **miscalculation** *n.*

mis·car·riage (mis·kar'·ij) *n.* failure; premature birth. **miscarry** *v.i.* to fail to fulfill the intended effect; to give birth prematurely.

mis·ce·ge·na·tion (mis·i·ja·nā'·shan) *n.* a mixture of races by interbreeding [L. *miscere*, to mix; *genus*, a race].

mis·cel·la·ne·ous (mis·al·ā'·ni·as) *a.* mixed; heterogeneous. **-ly** *adv.* **miscellanist** *n.* a writer of miscellanies. **miscellany** *n.* a medley, esp. a collection. **miscellanea** *n.pl.* odds and ends [L. *miscellaneus*, fr. *miscere*, to mix].

mis·chance (mis·chans') *n.* a mishap; ill-luck.

mis·chief (mis'·chif) *n.* harm; damage; conduct intended to annoy; the cause of such trouble. — **maker** *n.* one who stirs up trouble. **mischievous** *a.* tending to stir up trouble; playfully annoying. **mischievously** *adv.* **mischievousness** *n.* [O.Fr. *meschever*, to come to grief].

mis·ci·ble (mis'·i·bl) *a.* capable of being mixed. **miscibility** *n.* [L. *miscere*, to mix].

mis·con·ceive (mis·kan·sēv') *v.t.* to misunderstand. **misconception** *n.*

mis·con·duct (mis·kàn'·dukt) *n.* bad management; dishonest conduct. **misconduct** (mis·kan·dukt') *v.t.* to mismanage.

mis·con·strue (mis·kan·strōò') *v.i.* to interpret wrongly; misunderstand. **misconstruction** *n.*

mis·count (mis·kount') *v.t.* to count wrongly; to miscalculate; (mis'·kount) *n.* a wrong count.

mis·cre·ant (mis′·krē·ạnt) *n.* unprincipled person [O.Fr. *mescreant*, unbeliever].

mis·cue (mis·kū′) *n.* (*Billiards*) a stroke spoiled by the cue slipping; a mistake; *v.t.*

mis·date (mis·dāt′) *v.t.* to put a wrong date on; *n.* a wrong date.

mis·deal (mis·dēl′) *v.t.* and *i.* to deal cards wrong. *pa.t.* **misdealt** *n.* wrong deal.

mis·deed (mis·dēd′) *n.* an evil deed, a crime.

mis·de·mean·or (mis·dạ·mēn′·ẹr) *n.* dishonest conduct; (*Law*) a crime less than felony. **misdemean** *v.i.* to misbehave.

mis·di·rect (mis·dạ·rekt′) *v.t.* to direct or advise wrongly. **-tion** *n.*

mi·ser (mī′·zẹr) *n.* one who hoards money and lives in wretched surroundings. **-ly** *a.* greedy; stingy. **-liness** *n.* [L. = wretched].

mis·er·a·ble (miz′·ẹr·ạ·bl) *a.* unhappy; causing misery; worthless; deplorable. **miserably** *adv.* [L. *miser*, wretched].

mis·e·re·re (miz·ạ·re′·ri·) *n.* Psalm 51, a cry for mercy [L. = take pity].

mis·er·y (miz′·ẹ·ri·) *n.* great unhappiness; extreme pain of body or mind [L. *miser*].

mis·fea·sance (mis·fē′·zạns) *n.* (*Law*) wrongdoing; a misuse of lawful authority [O.Fr. *mesfaire*, to do wrong].

mis·fire (mis·fīr′) *n.* (of internal combustion engine, gun, etc.) failure to start or go off; *v.i.* to fail to start or fire.

mis·fit (mis′·fit) *n.* a bad fit; *v.t.* and *i.*

mis·for·tune (mis·fawr′·chạn) *n.* ill luck; a calamity.

mis·give (mis·giv′) *v.t.* to fill with doubt; to cause to hesitate; *v.i.* to fail *pa.t.* **misgave**. *pa.p.* **misgiven**. **misgiving** *n.* distrust; suspicion. [ly. **-ment** *n.*

mis·gov·ern (mis·guv′·ẹrn) *v.t.* to govern bad-

mis·guide (mis·gīd′) *v.t.* to lead astray; to advise wrongly. **misguidance** *n.*

mis·han·dle (mis·hand′·dl) *v.t.* to maltreat; to bungle.

mis·hap (mis′·hap) *n.* accident.

mish·mash (mish′·mȧsh) *n.* a jumble [fr. *mash*].

mis·in·form (mis·in·fawrm′) *v.t.* to give wrong information to. **-ant, -ation** *n.*

mis·in·ter·pret (mis·in·tur′·prit) *v.t.* to interpret or explain wrongly. **-ation** *n.* **-er** *n.*

mis·join·der (mis·join′·dẹr) *n.* (*Law*) introduction into court of parties or causes not belonging.

mis·judge (mis·juj′) *v.t.* to judge wrongly; to miscalculate. **-ment** *n.*

mis·lay (mis·lā′) to lay down something in a place which cannot later be recollected. *pa.t.*, *pa.p.* **mislaid**.

mis·lead (mis·lēd′) *v.t.* to lead astray; to delude. *pa.p.* **misled**. **-ing** *a.*

mis·man·age (mis·man′·ij) *v.t.* to manage incompentently. **-ment** *n.*

mis·name (mis·nām′) *v.t.* to call by the wrong name.

mis·no·mer (mis·nō′·mẹr) *n.* a wrong name; incorrect designation [O.Fr. *mesnommer*, to name wrongly].

mi·sog·a·my (mi·sȧg′·ạ·mi·) *n.* hatred of marriage. **misogamist** *n.* [Gk. *miseein*, to hate; *gamos*, marriage].

mi·sog·y·ny (mi·sȧj′·ạ·ni·) *n.* hatred of women. **misogynist** *n.* **misogynous** *a.* [Gk. *miseein*, to hate; *gunē*, a woman].

mis·place (mis·plās′) *v.t.* to place wrongly; to mislay.

mis·print (mis·print′) *v.t.* to make an error in printing; (mis′·print) *a.* a printing error.

mis·pro·nounce (mis·prạ·nouns′) *v.t.* to pronounce incorrectly. **mispronunciation** *n.*

mis·quote (mis·kwōt′) *v.t.* to quote incorrectly.

mis·reck·on (mis·rek′·n) *v.t.* to estimate or reckon incorrectly. **-ing** *n.*

mis·rep·re·sent (mis·rep·ri·zent′) *v.i.* to represent falsely; to report inaccurately. **-ation** *n.*

mis·rule (mis·rōōl′) *n.* disorder; misgovernment.

Miss (mis) *n.* title of unmarried women; girl [contr. of *mistress*]..

miss (mis) *v.t.* to fail to hit, reach, find, catch, notice; to be without; to feel the want of; to avoid; to omit; *v.i.* to fail to hit; to fall short of one's objective; *n.* failure to hit, reach, find, etc.; escape, as in *a lucky miss*. **-ing** *a.* lost; failing [O.E. *missan*, to fail].

mis·sal (mis′·ạl) *n.* a book containing the R.C. service of the mass for a year [L. *missa*, mass].

mis·sel (mis′·l) *n.* the large European thrush, supposed to eat *mistletoe berries* [O.E. *mistel*, mistletoe].

mis·shape (mis·shāp′) *v.t.* to shape badly; to deform. **-en** *a.*

mis·sile (mis′·l) *n.* that which is thrown or shot. **guided missile** *n.* a projected unmanned object which travels above the earth and performs some specific function, such as communication; *a.* capable of being thrown or shot [L. *mittere, missum*, to send].

mis·sion (mish′·ạn) *n.* the act of sending; the duty on which one is sent; a group of people sent to a foreign country for religious work; a delegation sent to a foreign country; vocation. **-ary** *a.* pert. to missions or missionaries; *n.* one sent to preach religion, esp. in a foreign country; one who does social service among the poor. [L. *mittere, missum*, to send].

mis·sive (mis′·iv) *n.* a letter or message [L. *missum*, to send].

mis·spell (mis·spel′) *v.t.* to spell incorrectly. **-ing** *n.* an error in spelling.

mis·spend (mis·spend′) *v.t.* to spend foolishly; to squander. *pa.t.* and *pa.p.* **misspent**.

mist (mist) *n.* visible vapor in the lower atmosphere; droplets of rain; a cloudiness or film; *v.t.* or *v.i.* to dim or be dimmed, as by a mist. **-y** *a.* dim; obscured. **-ily** *adv.* **-iness** *n.* [O.E. *mist*, darkness].

mis·take (mis·tāk′) *v.t.* to misunderstand; to take one person for another; *v.i.* to err; *n.* an error. *pa.t.* **mistook**. *pa.p.* **mistaken**. **mistakable** *a.* **mistaken** *a.* wrong; misunderstood. **mistakenly** *adv.* [M.E. *mistaken*, to take wrongly].

mis·ter (mis′·tẹr) *n.* sir; title of courtesy to a man (*abbrev.* **Mr.**) [form of *master*].

mis·time (mis·tīm′) *v.t.* to time wrongly. **-d** *a.*

mis·tle·toe (mis′·l·tō) *n.* a parasitic, evergreen plant with white berries [O.E. *mistel*, mistletoe; *tan*, a twig].

mis·tral (mis′·trạl) *n.* a cold, often violent, N.W. wind which blows over S. France [Fr. *mistral*, a master (wind)].

mis·tress (mis′·tris) *n.* (*fem.* of **master**) a woman in authority (as over a household, animal, institution); a kept woman; formerly, a title of address [O.Fr. *maistresse*, fem.]

mis·tri·al (mis·trī′·al) *n.* a trial made invalid by an error in proceedings.

mis·trust (mis·trust′) *n.* lack of confidence; *v.t.* to suspect; to lack faith in. **-ful** *a.*

mis·un·der·stand (mis·un·dẹr·stand′) *v.t.* to interpret incorrectly; to form a wrong judgment. **-ing** *n.* a misconception; a slight quarrel.

mis·use (mis·ūz′) *v.t.* to use improperly; to maltreat. (mis·ūs′) *n.* improper use. **misusage** *n.* abuse.

mite (mīt) *n.* any very small thing or person; a kind of arachnid, as *cheese-mite*; a very small coin [O.Dut. *mijt*, a small coin].

mi·ter (mī′·tẹr) *n.* a bishop's headdress, a tall cap; in carpentry, a joint made by two pieces of wood fitting into each other at an angle of 45°; *v.t.* to confer a miter on; to join at an angle. **mitral, mitriform** *a.* shaped like a miter; (*Bot.*) conical. **— block, — board,** or **— box** *n.* a piece of wood acting as a guide in sawing a *miter-joint*. **-d** *a.* wearing a miter; cut like a miter [Gk. *mitra*, a headboard].

mit·i·gate (mit′·ạ·gāt) *v.t.* to relieve; to alleviate; to temper. **mitigable** *a.* capable of being lessened. **mitigation** *n.* alleviation. **mitigative, mitigatory** *a.* **mitigator** *n.* [L. *mitigare*, to lessen].

mi·to·sis (mī·tō'·sis) *n.* (*Biol.*) method of cell division in which chromatin divides into chromosomes [Gk. *mitos*, thread; *osis*, action].

mitt (mit) *n.* a covering for wrist and hand leaving fingers exposed; a baseball glove, with palm heavily padded; (usu. *pl.*) padded mitten worn by boxers. **-ten** *n.* a glove with thumb, but palm and fingers all in one [L. *medius*, middle].

mix (miks) *v.t.* to unite into a mass; to blend; to combine a mixture; to associate; *v.i.* to become mingled; to associate; *n.* a muddle; a mixture. **-able** *a.* **-ed** *a.* mingled; blended; **-er** *n.* one who or that which mixes; one who is sociable, as a *good mixer.* (*Slang*) a social gathering. **-ture** *n.* the act of mixing; that which is mixed; (*Chem.*) a combination of substances which retain their individual properties, as contrasted with a *compound.* **-up** *n.* (*Colloq.*) confusion. **-ed marriage**, a marriage between two people of different religions [L. *miscere*].

miz·zen, mizen (miz'·n) *n.* fore-and-aft sail of a vessel. **-mast** *n.* the mast bearing the mizzen [Fr. *misaine*, a fore-sail].

mne·mon·ic, -al (ni·màn'·ik, ·al) *a.* assisting the memory. **-s** *n.pl.* the art of assisting the memory; artificial aids to memory [Gk. *mnēnōn*, mindful].

mo·a (mō'·à) *n.* an extinct N. Z. flightless bird of very large size [Maori].

moan (mōn) *n.* a low cry of grief or pain; *v.i.* to utter a low, wailing cry; *v.t.* to lament [O.E. *maenan*, to lament].

moat (mōt) *n.* a deep trench around a castle, usu. filled with water [O.Fr. *mote*, a trench].

mob (màb) *n.* a disorderly crowd of people; a rabble; the populace; *v.t.* to attack in a disorderly crowd; to jostle. *pr.p.* **-bing.** *pa.p.*, *pa.t.* **-bed. -ocracy** *n.* the rule of the mob. **-ocrat** mob leader. **-ster** *n.* (*Slang*) gangster [L. *mobile vulgus*, the fickle masses].

mob·cap (màb'·kap) *n.* a frilled cap, tied under the chin, worn by women in the 18th cent. [Dut. *mop*, a coif].

mo·bile (mō'·bl) *a.* easily moved; changing; facile; (of troops) mechanized; capable of moving rapidly from place to place; *n.* (mō'·bēl) an artistic arrangement of wires, etc., easily set in motion. **mobilization** *n.* the wartime act of calling up men and women for active service. **mobilize** *v.t.* to gather together available resources. **mobility** *n.* the state of being mobile [L. *mobilis*, movable].

moc·ca·sin (màk'·à·sin) *a.* shoe of soft leather worn by N. American Indians, trappers, etc.; a bedroom slipper of similar shape; a poisonous water snake [N. Amer. Ind.].

mo·cha (mō'·kà) *n.* a coffee orig. from *Mocha* in Yemen; *a.* flavored with coffee.

mock (màk) *v.t.* to laugh at; to ridicule; to make a fool of; to defy; to mimic; substitute. **-er** *n.* **-ery, -ing** *n.* the act of mocking; derision; travesty; false show. **-heroic** *a.* burlesquing the serious or heroic style. **-ing.** *a.* scornful; derisive. **-ing bird**, a N. American bird which imitates other birds. — **orange**, shrub with fragrant white flowers. — **turtle**, a soup made of calf's head and spices to imitate turtle soup [Fr. *moquer*].

mode (mōd) *n.* manner, form, or method; custom; fashion; (*Mus.*) one of the two classes of keys (major or minor); (*Gram.*) the *mood* of the verb. **modal** *a.* relating to mode or form. **modality** *n.* **modish** *a.* fashionable. **modishly** *adv.* **modishness** *n.* **modiste** (mōd·ēst') *n.* a dealer in the latest fashions [L. *modus*, manner].

mod·el (màd'·l) *n.* an exact, three-dimensional representation of an object, in miniature; a pattern or standard to copy; one who poses for an artist; a mannequin; *a.* serving as a model or criterion; *v.t.* to make in model; to copy from a pattern or standard to shape, as clay, wax, etc.; *v.i.* to practice modeling. **-er** *n.* **-ing** *n.* the art of working in plastic materials or of making models; shaping [O.Fr. *modelle*, a pattern].

mod·er·ate (màd'·er·it) *a.* restrained; temperate; average; not extreme; (màd'·er·āt) *v.t.* to restrain; to control; to decrease the intensity or pressure of; *v.i.* to become less violent or intense; to act as moderator; *n.* a person of moderate opinions in politics, etc. **-ly** *adv.* **-ness** *n.* **moderation** *n.* moderating; freedom from excess. **moderatism** *n.* non-extremist views. **moderator** *n.* arbitrator [L. *moderare*, to limit].

mod·ern (màd'·ern) *a.* pert. to present or recent time; up-to-date; *n.* a person living in modern times; one up-to-date in outlook and ideas. **-ization** *n.* **-ize** *v.t.* to bring up-to-date. **-ism** *n.* sympathy with modern ideas. **-ist** *n.* one who upholds modern ideas. **modernity** *n.* the state or quality of being modern [L. *modernus*, fr. *modo*, just now].

mod·est (màd'·ist) *a.* unassuming; restrained; decent; retiring in manner; not excessive, as *modest* means. **-ly** *adv.* **-ty** *n.* the quality of being modest [L. *modestus*, moderate].

mod·i·cum (màd'·i·kam) *n.* a small amount [L. *modicus*, moderate].

mod·i·fy (màd'·à·fī) *v.t.* to moderate; to alter the form or intensity of; (*Philol.*) to change the sound of a vowel by the influence of a following vowel; (*Gram.*) to qualify the meaning of, as of a verb by an adverb. **modifiable** *a.* **modification** *n.* the act of modifying; the state of being modified; a change of form, manner, or intensity. **modifier** *n.* [L. *modificare*].

mod·u·late (màj'·oo·lāt) *v.t.* to regulate, esp. the pitch of the voice; to adapt; (*Mus.*) to change the key of; *v.i.* (*Mus.*) to pass from one key to another. **modular** *a.* of a mode, modulation, or module. **modulation** *n.* the act of modulating; the changing of the pitch or key; (*Elect.*) the variation of the amplitude or frequency of continuous waves, usu. by a lower frequency. **modulator** *n.* one who, or that which modulates. **module** *n.* a unit of measurement; (*Archit*.) the radius of a shaft at its base. **modulus** *n.* (*Math.*) a constant number, coefficient, or quantity which measures a force, function, or effect. (*pl.* **moduli**) [L. *modulari*, to measure].

mo·gul (mō'·gul) *n.* a powerful or important person [Pers. *Mughul*, Mongolian conqueror].

mo·hair (mō'·hār) *n.* the silky hair of the Angora goat; fabric from this or similar hair. *a.* [Ar. *mukhayyar*, hair-cloth].

Moslem religion

Mo·ham·me·dan (mo·ham'·à·dàn) *a.* of Mohammed or the Moslem religion; *n.* a Moslem. **-ism** *n.* Moslem religion; Islam [fr. *Mohammed*, Ar. prophet, 570?-632].

Mo·ha·ve (mō·hà'·vi·) *n.* a tribe of Amer. Indians. Also **Mojave** [Native].

Mo·hawk (mō'·hawk) *n.* the name of a N. Amer. Indian tribe [Native].

Mo·hi·can (mō·hē'·kàn) *n.* a N. Amer. Indian tribe of Algonquin stock. Also **Mahican, Mohegan** [Native].

moi·e·ty (moi'·à·ti·) *n.* half [Fr. *moitié*, half].

moire (mwà·rā') *n.* watered fabric; *a.* having a wavy pattern [var. of *mohair*].

moist (moist) *a.* damp; humid; rather wet. **-en** (mois'·n) *v.t.* to make moist; to dampen. **moistness, moisture** (mois'·cher) *n.* that which causes dampness; condensed vapor. **-ureless** [O.Fr. *moiste*, fresh].

mo·lar (mō'·ler) *a.* grinding or able to grind,

as back teeth; *n.* a back double-tooth [L. *molere*, to grind].

mo·las·ses (ma·las'·az) *n. sing.* a dark-colored syrup obtained from sugar; treacle [L. *mellaceus*, honey-like].

mold (mōld) *n.* a pattern, form or matrix for giving shape to something in a plastic or molten state; a shape to form a model; character; *v.t.* to shape; to influence. **-er** *n.* one who molds or makes molds. **-ing** *n.* anything molded, esp. anything molded, esp. ornamentation of wood. Also **mould** [L. *modulus*, a small measure].

mold (mōld) *n.* fine, soft soil; the upper layer of the earth. **-er** *v.i.* to decay; to crumble away; to turn to dust. Also **mould** [O.E. *molde*].

mold (mōld) *n.* a downy fungus which grows on leather, cheese, bread, etc. if exposed to dampness; mildew. **-iness** *n.* **-y** *a.* affected by mold; musty; (*Fig.*) antiquated. Also **mould**.

mole (mōl) *n.* a slightly raised, dark spot on the skin [O.E. *mal*, a spot].

mole (mōl) *n.* a small burrowing animal; *v.t.* to burrow. **-hill** *n.* a small mound of earth. **-skin** *n.* the fur of a mole; a fabric with soft surface [M.E. *molle*, a mole].

mole (mōl) *n.* a breakwater [L. *moles*, a mass].

mol·e·cule (mál'·a·kūl) *n.* the smallest portion of a substance which can retain the characteristics of that substance. **molecular** *a.* **molecular weight**, the weight of a molecule of a substance in relation to the weight of a hydrogen atom [dim. fr. L. *moles*, a mass].

mo·lest (ma·lest') *v.t.* to trouble; to accost with sinister intention. **-ation** *n.* [L. *molestus*, troublesome].

mol·li·fy (mál'·a·fī) *v.t.* to appease; to placate; to soften. **mollifiable** *a.* **mollification** *n.* **mollifier** *n.* [L. *mollificare*, to make soft].

mol·lusk, mol·lusc (mál'·ask) *n.* an invertebrate animal with soft, pulpy body and a hard outer shell (oyster, snail, etc.) **molluscan** *a.* **molluscoid, -cous** *a.* like a mollusk [L. *mollusca*, a soft nut].

mol·ly·cod·dle (mál'·i·kád·l) *n.* a milksop; *v.t.* or *v.i.* to coddle or be coddled or pampered [dim. of *Mary; coddle*].

molt (mōlt) *v.t.* and *i.* to shed feathers, as of birds, or skins, as of snakes; *n.* the act of shedding. Also **moult** [L. *mutare*, to change].

mol·ten (mōl'·tan) *a.* melted; of metals, liquified [*Arch. pa.p.* of *melt*].

mo·lyb·de·num (mal·ib'·da·nam) *n.* a rare metal, used in alloys [Gk. *molubdos*, lead].

mom (mám) *n.* (*Colloq.*) mother. Also **mommy**.

mo·ment (mō'·mant) *n.* a short space of time; interval; importance; the measure of a force by its effect in causing rotation. **-arily** *adv.* **-ariness** *n.* **-ary** *a.* very brief. **-ous** (mō·men'·tas) very important. **-tum** (mō·men'·tam) *n.* the impetus in a body; increasing force [L. *momentum*, movement].

mon·a·chism (mán'·a·kizm) *n.* monasticism. **monachal** *a.* of monks [L. *monachus*, a monk].

mon·ad (mán'·ad) *n.* (*Biol.*) a single-celled organism; (*Chem.*) an atom with the valence of one; (*Philos.*) an individual thought of as a microcosm. **-ism, -ology** *n.* the theory of monads [Gk. *monos*, alone].

mon·arch (mán'·erk) *n.* a hereditary sovereign; the supreme ruler of a state; *a.* supreme. **-ial, -ic, -al** *a.* pert. to a monarch or a monarchy. **-ically** *adv.* **-ism** *n.* the principles of monarchy; devotion to a royalist acuse. **-ist** *n.* advocate of monarchy; a royalist. **-y** *n.* government by a single ruler; a kingdom or empire [Gk. *monos*, alone; *archein*, to rule].

mon·as·ter·y (mán'·as·ter·i·) *n.* a settlement of monks. **monasterial, monastic** *a.* pert. to monasteries, monks or nuns. **monastic** *n.* a monk. **monasticism** (man·as'·ti·sizm) *n.* the monastic way of life [Gk. *monasterion*].

mon·au·ral (mán·aw'·ral) *a.* of sound reproduction from one source only.

Mon·day (mun'·di·) *n.* the second day of the week [O.E. *mona*, the moon].

mon·e·tary (mán'·a·ter·i) *a.* concerning money or coinage [L. *moneta*, a mint].

mon·ey (mun'·i·) *n.* any form of token, as coin, banknote, used as medium of exchange, and stamped by state authority; currency; wealth. *pl.* **monies.** **— bags** *n.pl.* a wealthy person. **-ed** *a.* wealthy. **— lender** *n.* one who lends money and charges interest. **—making** *a.* profitable. **— order,** an order for money, issued at one post office and payable at another [L. *moneta*, a mint].

mon·ger (mung'·ger) *n.* (*Brit.*) a dealer, usu. in compound words, as *fishmonger, ironmonger, rumormonger* [O.E. *mangere*, a merchant].

Mon·gol (máng'·gal) *n.* a native of Mongolia (Asia); *a.* Also **Mongolian. -ism** *n.* arrest of physical and mental development with Asiatic features. **-oid** *a.* resembling the Mongols.

mon·goose (máng'·gòòs) *n.* a small weasel-like animal, a snake-killer. *pl.* **mongooses** [Tamil]

mon·grel (máng'·gral) *a. n.* impure; hybrid of mixed breed [O.E. *mang*, a mixture].

mon·ism (mōn'·izm) *n.* the philosophical doctrine which seeks to explain varied phenomena by a single principle. **monist** *n.* **monistic** *a.* [Gk. *manos*, single].

mo·ni·tion (mō·nish'·an) *n.* cautionary advice; admonition; notice; (*Law*) a summons. **monitive** *a.* expressing warning [L. *monitio*, warning].

mon·i·tor (mán'·i·ter) *n.* one who cautions; one appointed to help keep order; a large lizard; (*Arch.*) armed warship for coastal service; *v.t.* to watch or check on a person or thing, radio or TV. **-ial** (mán·i·tōr'·i·al) *a.* **-ially** *adv.* **-y** *a.* warning [L. *monere, monitum*, to warn].

monk (mungk) *n.* a hermit; a member of a religious community living in a monastery. **-hood** *n.* **-ish** *a.* monastic. **-hood** *n.* a herbaceous poisonous plant [Gk. *monachos*].

mon·key (mung'·ki·) *n.* a long-tailed mammal of the order of Primates resembling man in organization; mischievous child; the weighted head of a pile driver; a hammer for driving home bolts; *v.i.* to imitate as a monkey; (*Colloq.*) to meddle with, as to *monkey with*. **-shine** (*Slang*) *n.* a prank. **— wrench** *n.* wrench with movable jaw.

mo·no- *prefix* meaning sole, single [Gk. *monos*, alone, single].

mon·o·bloc (mán'·a·blák) *n.* the cylinders of the internal-combustion engine in one casting [Gk. *monos*, single; and *block*].

mon·o·car·pous (mán·a·kárp'·as) *a.* bearing fruit only once. **monocarp** *n.* [Gk. *monos*, single; *karpos*, fruit].

mon·o·chord (mán'·a·kawrd) *n.* a one-stringed instrument; a one-stringed device for measuring musical intervals.

mon·o·chrome (mán'·a·krōm) *n.* a painting in different tones of the same color. **monochromatic, monochromic** *a.* **monochromatism** *n.* color-blindness [Gk. *monos*, single; *chrōma*, color].

mon·o·cle (mán'·a·kl) *n.* a single eyeglass [Gk. *monos*, single; L. *oculus*, the eye].

mon·o·cot·y·le·don (mán·a·kát·a·lē'·dan) *n.* a plant with only one seed lobe. **-ous** *a.* [Gk. *monos*, single; *kotule*, a cup].

mo·noc·ra·cy (ma·nák'·ra·si·) *n.* government by a single person. **monocrat** *n.* [Gk. *monos*, single; *kratein*, to rule].

mon·o·dy (mán'·a·di·) *n.* an elegy expressive of mourning; a monotonous tone. **monodic, -al** *a.* **monodist** *n.* [Gk. *monos*, single; *ōdē*, song].

mo·nog·a·my (ma·nág'·a·mi·) *n.* the state of being married to one person at a time. **monogamist** *n.* **monogamous** *a.* [Gk. *monos*, single; *gamos*, marriage].

mon·o·gen·e·sis (mån·a·jen'·a·sis) *n.* the descent of an organism or all living things, from a single cell. **monogenetic** *a.* **monogenism** *n.* the theory of the descent of all human beings from an original single pair. Also **monogeny** [Gk. *mnoos*, single; *gignesthai*, to be born].

mon·o·gram (mån'·a·gram) *n.* two or more letters, as initials of a person's name, interwoven. **monogrammatic** *a.* [Gk. *manos*, alone; *gramma*, a letter].

mon·o·graph (mån'·a·graf) *n.* a specialized treatise on a single subject or branch of a subject. **-er** (ma·någ'·ra·fer) **-ist** *n.* **monographic, -al** *a.* [Gk. *monos*, single; *graphein*, to write] .

mo·nog·y·nous (ma·nåj'·a·nus) *a.* (*Bot.*) having single pistil; (*Zool.*) mating with a single female. **monogyny** *n.* the custom of having only one female mate [Gk. *monos*, single; *gunē*, a female].

mon·o·lith (mån'·a·lith) *n.* a monument or column fashioned from a single block of stone. **-al, -ic** *a.* [Gk. *monos*, alone; *lithos*, a stone].

mon·o·logue (mån'·a·lawg) *n.* a dramatic scene in which an actor soliloquizes; a dramatic entertainment by a solo performer. **-ist** *n.* Also **monolog. monologist** *n.* [Gk. *monos*, single; *logos*, a speech].

mon·o·ma·ni·a (mån·a·mā'·ni·a) *n.* a form of mental derangement in which sufferer is irrational on one subject only, or is obsessed by one idea. **monomaniac** *n.* **monomaniacal** *a.* [Gk. *monos*, single; *mania*, madness].

mo·no·mi·al (mån·ō'·mi·al) *a.* (*Math.*) comprising a single term or expression; *n.* an algebraic expression containing a single term [Gk. *monos*, single; *onoma*, a name].

mon·o·nym (mån'·a·nim) *n.* a name comprising a single term. **mononymic** *a.* [Gk. *monos*, single; *onoma*, a name].

mon·o·pho·bia (mån·a·fō'·bi·a) *n.* (*Path.*) a morbid fear of being alone [Gk. *monos*, single; *phobos*, fear].

mon·o·plane (mån'·a·plān) *n.* an aircraft with only one set of wings.

mo·nop·o·ly (ma·nåp'·a·li·) *n.* the sole right to trade in certain commodities; exclusive possession or control; a commodity so controlled; a controlling company. **monopolize** *v.t.* to have a monopoly; to take possession to exclusion of others. **monopolizer, monopolist** *n.* **monopolistic** *a.* [Gk. *manos*, single; *pōlein*, to sell].

mon·o·syl·la·ble (mån·a·sil'·a·bl) *n.* a word of one syllable. **monosyllabic** *a.* having one syllable; speaking in words of one syllable. **monosyllabism** *n.*

mon·o·the·ism (mån'·a·thē·izm) *n.* the doctrine which admits of one God only. **monotheist** *n.* **monotheistic** *a.*

mon·o·tint (mån'·a·tint) *n.* a sketch or painting in one tint.

mon·o·tone (mån'·a·tōn) *n.* a single, unvaried tone or sound; a series of sounds of uniform pitch; sameness of any kind. **monotonic, monotonous** (ma·nåt'·a·nas) uttered or recited in one tone; dull; unvaried. **monotony** (ma·nåt'·a·ni·) *n.* tedious uniformity of tone; lack of variety or variation; sameness [Gk. *monos*, single; *tonos*, a tone].

mon·o·type (mån'·a·tīp) *n.* (*Biol.*) a genus with one species; (*Print.*) a two-part machine for setting and casting type in individual letters, as distinct from *linotype*. **monotypic** *a.* [Gk. *monos*, single; and *type*].

mon·o·va·lent (mån·a·vā'·lant) *a.* (*Chem.*) having a valency of one; univalent. **monovalence, monovalency** *n.*

mon·ox·ide (ma·nak'·sīd) *n.* oxide containing one oxygen atom in a molecule.

Mon·sei·gneur (mawn·se'·nyer) *n.* my lord; a title (*abbrev.* **Mgr.**) given in France to princes, bishops, etc. *pl.* **Messeigneurs** (me·sen·yurz') **Monsignor** (mån·sēn'·yer) (*abbrev.* **Mgr.** or **Monsig.**), an Italian title given to prelates. Also **monsignore.** *pl.* **monsignori** [L. *meus*, my; *senior*, older].

mon·soon (mån·sòòn') *n.* a seasonal wind of S. Asia which blows *on-shore* from the S.W. in summer, and *off-shore* from the N.E. in winter; the very heavy rainfall season in summer, esp. in India. **-al** *a.* [Ar. *mausin*, a season].

mon·ster (mån'·ster) *n.* a creature of unnatural shape; a person of abnormal callousness, cruelty, or wickedness. **monstrosity** *n.* an unnatural production; an abnormal creature; a freak. **monstrous** *n.* abnormal; enormous; horrible; shocking. **monstrously** *adv.* [L. *monstrum*, a marvel] .

mon·strance (mån'·strans) *n.* a shrine for the consecrated host in R.C. services [L. *monstrare*, to show].

mon·tage (mån·tazh') *n.* (*Motion pictures*) assembling various shots of a film into one well-arranged series: a picture made by superimposing various elements from several sources [Fr. *monter*, to mount].

Mon·tes·so·ri Sys·tem (mån·ta·sō'·ri sis'·-tam) *n.* educational system to give free scope to child's individuality and creative powers [fr. Maria *Montessori*].

month (munth) *n.* one of the twelve divisions of the year—a **calendar month**, 31, 30 or 28 (29) days; the period of the complete revolution of the moon—a **lunar month**, about 29 days; a period of 28 days, or four complete weeks. **-ly** *a.* lasting, performed in, a month; *n.* a publication produced once each month; *pl.* the menses; *adv.* once a month [O.E. *monath*, a month].

mon·u·ment (mån'·ya·mant) *n.* any structure, as a tombstone, building tablet, erected to the memory of person, or event; an ancient record; an achievement of lasting value. **-al** *a.* like, or worthy of a monument; massive; colossal. **-ally** *adv.* [L. *monumentum*, fr. *monere*, to remind].

moo (mòò) *v.i.* to make the noise of a cow; to low; the lowing of a cow [imit.].

mooch (mòòch) *v.t.* and *v.i.* (*Colloq.*) to loiter; to sponge from another [O.Fr. *muchier*, to hang about].

mood (mòòd) *n.* (*Gram.*) the inflection of a verb expressing its function, as *indicative, imperative, subjunctive, infinitive;* (*Logic*) a form of syllogism; (*Mus.*) mode; the arrangement of intervals in the scale, as *major, minor* [var. of *mode*].

mood (mòòd) *n.* disposition; frame of mind; temper. **-ily** *adv.* **-iness** *n.* temporary depression of spirits; captiousness. **-y** *a.* peevish; sulky; depressed; angry [O.E. *mod*, mind].

moon (mòòn) *n.* the satellite which revolves around the earth in the period of a lunar month; any secondary planet; a month; anything crescent-shaped or shining like the moon; *v.i.* to gave or wander about aimlessly. **-beam** *n.* a ray of moonlight. **-calf** *n.* a fool. **-faced** *a.* having a round, expressionless face. **-shine** *n.* light of the moon; nonsense; (*Colloq.*) smuggled liquor. **-stone** *n.* an almost pellucid form of feldspar. **-struck** *a.* dazed [O.E. *mona*].

Moor (moor) *n.* a native of the Barbary States; one of the conquerors of Spain in the 8th cent. **-ish** *a.* [L. *Maurus, Mauretania*].

moor (moor) *n.* (*Brit.*) marshy wasteland. **-ish, -y** *a.* **-land** *n.* a heath [O.E. *mor*, marshland].

moor (moor) *v.t.* to secure by cables and anchors, as a vessel. **-age** *n.* place where vessel or airship is moored; charge for mooring. **-ing** *n.* the act of securing a ship; the place where a ship is moored [prob. Dut. *marren*, to tie].

moose (mòòs) *n.* largest species of deer; elk [Amer. Ind.].

moot (mòòt) *v.t.* to debate; to discuss; *a.* debat-

able; *n.* a discussion; in olden times, a council.
— **court** *n.* a mock court [O.E. *gemot*, an assembly].

mop (mȧp) *n.* a bunch of soft cotton yarn or rags attached to handle for washing or polishing; a bushy head of hair; *v.t.* to wipe or polish. *pr.p.* **-ping**. *pa.p.* **-ped** [L. *mappa*, a napkin].

mope (mōp) *v.i.* to be dull or depressed; to sulk. **moping** *a.* listless; gloomy. **mopishly** *adv.* dispiritedly [Dut. *moppen*, to sulk].

mop·pet (mȧp'·ȧt) *n.* (*Colloq.*) a doll; a child [fr. *mop*].

mo·raine (mȧ·rān') *n.* rock debris which accumulates along the sides or at the end of a glacier [Fr.].

mor·al (mȧr'·ȧl, mawr'·ȧl) *a.* pert. to right conduct or duties of man; ethical; virtuous; chaste; discriminating between right and wrong; didactic; verified by reason or probability; *n.* the underlying meaning implied in a fable, allegory, etc. *pl.* ethics; conduct, esp. concerning sex-relations; habits. **-ization** *n.* **-ize** *v.t.* to explain in a moral sense; to draw a moral from; *v.i.* to reflect on ethical values of. **-izer** *n.* **-ist** *n.* one who moralizes; one who studies or teaches ethics; one who accepts ethics instead of religion as an adequate guide to good living. **-istic** *a.* **-ity** (mȧ·ral'·i·ti·) *n.* the practice of moral duties; virtue; ethics; an early form of drama, in which the characters were the virtues and vices of men personified. **-ly** *adv.* — **victory**, a defeat, which in a deeper sense, is a victory [L. *moralis*, of manners or customs].

mo·rale (mȧ·ral') *n.* the disposition or mental state which causes a man or body of people to face an emergency with spirit, fortitude and unflagging zeal [Fr.].

mo·rass (mȧ·ras') *n.* marshy ground; difficult state of affairs [Dut. *moeras*, a marsh].

mor·a·to·ri·um (mawr·ȧ·tō'·ri·ȧm) *n.* a law to delay payment of debts for a given period of time; the period of suspension of payments; **moratory** *a.* delaying [L. *mora*, delay].

mo·ray (maw'·rā) *n.* a sharp-toothed marine eel [Gk. *muraina*].

mor·bid (mawr'·bid) *a.* diseased; unhealthy; (of the mind) excessively gloomy. **-ity** *n.* **-ly** *adv.* **-ness** *n.* **morbific** *a.* causing unhealthiness of body or mind [L. *morbus*, disease].

mor·dant (mawr'·dȧnt) *n.* any substance, metallic or vegetable, which fixes dyes; a corrosive acid used in etching; *a.* biting; corrosive; sarcastic. **mordacious** *a.* acrid; sarcastic. **mordaciously** *adv.* **mordacity** *n.* **-ly** *adv.* [L. *mordere*, to bite].

mor·dent (mōr'·dȧnt) *n.* (*Mus.*) a trill [L. *mordere*, to bite].

more (mōr) *a.* greater in amount, degree, quality, etc.; in greater number; additional; *adv.* in a greater quantity, extent, etc.; besides; *n.* something additional. (*comp. of* **much, many;** *superl.* **most**) [O.E. *mara*].

mor·el (mȧ·rel') *n.* an edible mushroom [Fr. *morille*].

mo·rel (mȧ·rel') *n.* the common and deadly nightshade [O.Fr. *morel*, black].

mo·rel·lo (mȧ·rel'·ō) *n.* a variety of dark red cherry used in manufacture of brandy. Also **morel** [It. *morello*, dark-skinned].

more·o·ver (mōr·ō'·ver) *adv.* besides; also; further [fr. *more*].

mor·ga·nat·ic (mawr·gȧ·nat'·ik) *a.* applied to a marriage between a man of high, esp. royal rank, and a woman of lower station, the issue having no claim to his rank or property. **-ally** *adv.* [Ger. *Morgengabe*, a morning gift].

mo·res (maw'·rāz) *n.pl.* customs [L.].

morgue (mawrg) *n.* a place where bodies of people killed in accidents, etc., are taken to await identification; a library of clippings, etc. kept by a newspaper or publication [Fr.].

mor·i·bund (mawr'·i·bund) *a.* at the point of death [L. *moribundus*, dying].

Mor·mon (mawr'·mȧn) *n.* a member of 'The Church of Jesus Christ of Latter-day Saints' founded by Joseph Smith in 1830 in Utah and professing theocracy and, formerly, polygamy. **-ism** *n.* [fr. the Book of *Mormon*].

morn (mawrn) *n.* (*Poetic*) the early part of the day [O.E. *morgen*, morning].

morn·ing (mawr'·ning) *n.* the first part of the day between dawn and midday; (*Fig.*) the first part of anything; *a.* pert. to or happening at this time. **—glory** *n.* a twining vine with flowers. **—coat** *n.* a tail-coat with cutaway front. **— star** *n.* a planet visible before sunrise [M.E. *morwening*, the coming of the day].

mo·ron (mōr'·ȧn) *n.* an adult with the mental development of an 8-12 yr. old child. **moronic** *a.* [Gk. *moros*, stupid].

mo·rose (mȧ·rōs') *a.* sullen; gloomy; soured in nature. **-ly** *adv.* **-ness** *n.* [L. *morosus*, fretful].

mor·pheme (mawr'·fēm) *n.* (*Gram.*) the smallest meaningful linguistic unit; *free form* as **boy**, or *bound form* as **ish** in **boyish**.

mor·phine (mawr'·fēn) *n.* an alkaloid of opium; a drug used to induce sleep and to deaden pain. [fr. *Morpheus*, Gk. god of sleep].

mor·ph-, morphic, morphous word elements meaning form or shape [Gk.].

mor·row (mȧr'·ō) *n.* next day; (*Poet.*) morning [O.E. *morgen*, the morning].

Morse (mawrs) *n.* a system of telegraphic signals in which the alphabet is represented by combinations of dots and dashes [fr. Amer. inventor S. F. B. *Morse*].

mor·sel (mawr'·sȧl) *n.* a mouthful; a small piece [O.Fr. dim fr. L. *morsus*, a bite].

mor·tal (mawr'·tȧl) *a.* subject to death; fatal; meriting damnation, as sin; implacable, as a foe; *n.* a human being. **-ity** (mawr·tal'·i·ti·) *n.* death; death-rate; the human race. **-ly** *adv.* [L. *mortalis*, fr. *mors*, death].

mor·tar (mawr·ter) *n.* a thick bowl of porcelain, glass, etc., in which substances are pounded with a pestle; a mill for pulverizing ores; (*Mil.*) a short-barreled cannon for short-distance firing of heavy shells; a cement made of lime, sand and water, used in building; *v.t.* to pound in a mortar; to cement, with mortar. **-board** *n.* a square board used when mixing mortar; an academic cap [L. *mortarium*].

mort·gage (mawr'·gij) *n.* (*Law*) a conveyance of property in security of a loan; the deed effecting this; *v.t.* to pledge as security. **mortgagee** *n.* one to whom a mortgage is given. **mortgagor** *n.* one who gives a mortgage to a mortgage [O.Fr. *mort*, dead; *gage*, a pledge].

mor·ti·cian (mawr·tish'·ȧn) *n.* an undertaker [L. *mors*, death].

mor·ti·fy (mawr'·tȧ·fī) *v.t.* to discipline the flesh; to humiliate; to vex; *v.i.* (*Med.*) to become gangrenous. **mortification** *n.* the act of mortifying or the state of being mortified; humiliation; (*Med.*) gangrene; the death of one part of a living body L. *mors*, death; *facere*, to make].

mor·tise (mawr'·tis) *n.* a hole in a piece of wood to receive the projection or tenon of another piece, made to fit it. Also **mortice.** *v.t.* to cut or make a mortise in; to join with a mortise.

mort·main (mawrt'·mān) *n.* an inalienable bequest; the holding of land by a corporation, which cannot be transferred [O.Fr. *mortmain*, dead hand].

mor·tu·ar·y (mawr'·choo·er·i·) *n.* a place for the temporary reception of dead bodies; *a.* pert. to burial [L. *mortus*, dead].

mo·sa·ic (mō·zā'·ik) *a.* pert. to or made of mosaic; *n.* inlaid work of colored glass or marble [Gk. *mousa*, a muse].

Mo·sa·ic (mō·zā'·ik) *a.* (*Bib.*) pert. to *Moses*, or to the laws and writing attributed to him.

Mo·selle (mō·zel′) *n.* a light wine (fr. *Moselle*, Fr.).

Mos·lem (màz′·lạm) *n.* a Mohammedan; *a.* pert. to the Mohammedans or their religion. Also **Muslim** [Ar. *salama*, submit to God].

mosque (màsk) *n.* a Mohammedan temple [Ar. *masjid*, temple].

mos·qui·to (mạ·skē′·tō) *n.* an insect which draws blood, leaving a raised, itchy spot. **-net**, a net covering to ward off mosquitos [L. *musca*, a fly].

moss (maws) *n.* a small, thickly growing plant which thrives on moist surfaces; lichen. — **agate** *n.* an agate with moss-like markings. **-back** *n.* (*Colloq.*) an extreme conservative. **-iness** *n.* **-y** *a.* covered with moss [O.E. *mos*, bog-land].

most (mōst) *a.* (*superl.* of **much, many;** *comp.* is **more**) the greatest number or quantity; greatest; *adv.* in the greatest degree; *n.* the greatest quantity, number, etc. **-ly** *adv.* for the most part [O.E. *maest*, most].

mot (mō) *n.* pithy, witty saying [Fr. = word].

mote (mōt) *n.* a small particle; a speck of dust [O.E. *mot*, a particle].   [+ hotel].

mo·tel (mō′·tel) *n.* lodging for travelers [motor

mo·tet (mō·tet′) *n.* a musical composition for (unaccompanied) voices, to words from Scripture [Fr. dim. of *mot*, a word].

moth (mawth) *n.* a nocturnal winged insect; larva of this insect which feeds on cloth, esp. woolens. — **balls** *n.pl.* balls of moth repellent. **—eaten** *a.* eaten into holes by moth larva; decrepit [O.E. *moththe*].

moth·er (muTH′·ẹr) *n.* a female parent; the head of a convent; the origin of anything; *a.* characteristic of a mother; native; original; *v.t.* to be the mother or author of; to adopt as one's own; to cherish, as a mother her child. **-hood** *n.* the state of being a mother. **—in-law** *n.* the mother of one's wife or husband. **-liness** *n.* **-ly** *a.* having attributes of a mother. — **of pearl** *n.* the iridescent lining of several kinds of shells. **Mother Superior,** the head of a convent. — **tongue** *n.* one's native language [O.E. *modor*, a mother].

mo·tif (mō·tēf′) *n.* the dominant theme in a literary or musical composition [Fr.].

mo·tion (mō′·shạn) *n.* the act of moving; movement; a gesture; a proposal made in an assembly; *v.t.* to guide by gesture; *v.i.* to gesture. **-less** *a.* still; immobile. — **picture** *n.* a series of photographs projected on a screen rapidly, as to approximate lifelike movement [L. *movere*, *motum*, to move].

mo·tive (mō′·tiv) *n.* that which incites to action; inner impulse; motif; *a.* causing movement or motion; *v.t.* to impel; to motivate. **motivate** *v.t.* to incite. **motivation** *n.* **-less** *a.* without purpose or direction. **motivity** *n.* capacity to produce motion [L. *movere, motum*, to move].

mot·ley (màt′·li·) *a.* vari-colored; diversified; *n.* a jester's dress; a diversified mixture.

mo·tor (mō′·tẹr) *n.* that which imparts motion; a machine which imparts motive power, esp. the internal-combustion engine; *a.* causing motion; (*Anat.*) producing muscular activity, as *motor nerves; v.t.* and *v.i.* to travel by, or convey in, a motor driven vehicle. **-cade** *n.* procession of automobiles. **-ize** *v.t.* to mechanize (the transport of the army). **-ist** *n.* one who drives or travels in an automobile. **-man** *n.* one who drives a streetcar [L. *motor*, a mover].

mot·tle (màt′·l) *v.t.* to mark with spots of different colors; to dapple. **-d** *a.* variegated [prob. fr. *motley*].

mot·to (màt′·ō) *n.* a maxim or principle of behavior [L. *muttum*, a murmur].

moue (mòò) *n.* a pout [Fr.].

mou·lage (mòò′·làzh) *n.* the making of molds [Fr.].

mound (mound) *n.* an artificial elevation of earth; a knoll; an earthwork for defensive purposes; a heap; (*Baseball*) point from which pitcher delivers the ball; *v.t.* to fortify with a mound; to heap [O.E. *mund*, a defense].

mount (mount) *n.* (*poet.*, except in proper names) a mountain or hill; that on which anything is mounted for exhibition; a horse for riding; *v.t.* to raise up; to ascend; to get on a horse or bicycle; to frame (a picture); to set (gem-stones); to put on a slide for miscroscope examination; to stage a play with costumes, scenery, etc.; to raise guns into position; *v.i.* to rise up; to get up; to increase. **-ed** *a.* **-ing** *n.* **to mount guard,** to be on sentry duty; to keep watch over [L. *mons*, a mountain].

moun·tain (mount′·n) *n.* a high hill; *a.* pert. to a mountain; growing or living on a mountain. — **ash** *n.* any of a variety of small trees. — **dew** *n.* (*Slang*) whisky. **-eer** *n.* one who lives on or climbs high mountains. — **goat** *n.* the Rocky Mountain goat. — **laurel** *n.* American laurel. **-ous** *a.* very steep; full of mountains; colossal. — **range** *n.* a series or system of mountains [L. *mons*, a mountain].

moun·te·bank (moun′·tạ·bangk) *n.* a quack doctor; a charlatan [It. *montambanco*, mount on bench or platform].

Mount·ie (moun′·ti·) *n.* a member of the Canadian N.W. Mounted Police.

mourn (mōrn, mawrn) *v.t.* to grieve over; to lament; *v.i.* to express grief; to wear mourning. **-er** *n.* **-ful** *a.* sad; dismal. **-fully** *adv.* **-fulness** *n.* **-ing** *n.* the act of grieving; lamentation; wearing of black as a sign of grief; the period during which such clothes are worn [O.E. *murnan*, to grieve].

mouse (mous) *n.* a small rodent found in fields, or houses; a timid person. *pl.* **mice. mouse** (mouz) *v.t.* and *v.i.* to catch mice; to search for patiently or slyly; to prowl. **—color** *a.* dark greyish brown. **-r** *n.* an animal which catches mice. **—trap** *n.* **mousy** *a.* resembling a mouse in color; timid; quiet drab [O.E. *mus*, a mouse].

mousse (mòòs) *n.* a light-frozen dessert [Fr. *mousse*, froth].

mouth (mouth) *n.* an opening between lips of men and animals through which food is taken; lips, as a feature; the cavity behind the lips containing teeth, tongue, palate, and vocal organs; an opening as of a bottle, cave, etc.; the estuary of a river; a wry face. *pl.* **mouths** (mouTHz); *v.t.* (mouTH) to speak, with noticeable use of the mouth; to put or take into the mouth; to mumble; *v.i.* to make grimaces. **-ful** as much as the mouth conveniently holds; a small amount. — **organ** *n.* harmonica. **-piece** *n.* the part of a musical instrument, pipe, etc., held in mouth; (*Fig.*) a spokesman; a newspaper (as expressing public opinion) [O.E. *muth*, the mouth].

move (mòòv) *v.t.* to set in motion; to stir emotions of; to prevail on; to incite; to propose for consideration; *v.i.* to change one's position, posture, residence, etc.; to march; to make a proposal or recommendation; *n.* the act of moving; a change of residence; a movement, as in game of checkers. **movable, moveable** *a.; n.pl.* (*Law*) the furnishings of a house which are not permanent fixtures; **-ment** *n.* the act of moving; the part of a machine which moves; organized activity of a society; a division of a musical composition; evacuation of the bowels. **-r** *n.* **movies** *n.pl.* (*Colloq.*) motion pictures. **moving** *a.* causing motion; affecting the emotions: pathetic. **moving picture** *n.* motion picture. **moving staircase,** an escalator [L. *movere*, to move].

mow (mō) *v.t.* to cut down with a scythe or machine; to cut down in great numbers, as enemy. **-er** *n.* one who or that which mows [O.E. *mawan*, to mow].

mow (mou) *n.* a heap of hay, or corn, in a barn;

v.t. to put in a mow as a *haymow* [O.E. *muga*, a heap].

much (much) *a.* (*comp.* **more**; *superl.* **most**) great in quantity or amount; abundant; *n.* a great quantity; *adv.* to a great degree or extent; almost. **-ness** *n.* greatness. **-ly** *adv.* (*Colloq.*) much. **to make much of**, to treat as of great importance [M.E. *muchel*].

mu·cid (mū'·sid) *a.* moldy, musty. Also **-ous**. **-ness** *n.* [L. *mucidus*, moldy].

mu·ci·lage (mū'·sa·lig) *n.* a gummy substance extracted from plants and animals; an adhesive. **mucilaginous** *a.* slimy; sticky [L. *mucus*, mucus].

muck (muk) *n.* moist manure; anything vile or filthy; *v.t.* to manure; to make filthy. **-iness** *n.* **-y** *a.* filthy [O.N. *myki*, dung].

muck·rake (muk'·rāk) *n.* one esp. a reporter, who searches for corruption, scandal [fr. a *muck raker*, coined by T. Roosevelt].

mu·cus (mū'·kas) *n.* a viscid fluid secreted by the mucous membranes; slimy. **mucoid** *a.* like mucus. **mucous** *a.* of mucus; slimy [L.].

mud (mud) *n.* soft, wet dirt; aspersions, as in *to throw mud at a person* **-dily** *adv.* **-diness** *n.* **-dy** *a.* consisting of mire or mud; dull; cloudy, as liquid; *v.t.* to soil with mud; to confuse. *pr.p.* **-ding**. *pa.p., pa.t.* **-ded. -flat** *n.* a stretch of mud below high-water. **-guard** *n.* a shield to protect from mud splashes [O.L. Ger. *mudde*, mud].

mud·dle (mud'·l) *v.t.* to make muddy; to confuse; to bewilder; to mix up; *v.i.* to be confused; *n.* confusion; jumble [fr.*mud*].

muff (muf) *n.* a warm covering for both hands, usu. of fur, shaped like a cylinder and open at both ends; (*Baseball*) failure to hold a ball one has caught; *v.t.* to bungle [fr. Dut. *mof*, mitten]

muf·fin (muf'·in) *n.* a small cup-shaped bread, usu. eaten hot.

muf·fle (muf'·l) *v.t.* to wrap up for warmth or to hide something; to deaden (sound of); *n.* something used to deaden sound or provide warmth. **-d** *a.* **-r** *n.* a scarf; a silencer [O.Fr. *moufle*, a thick glove].

muf·ti (muf'·ti·) *n.* a Mohammedan advisor in regard to religious law; civilian dress worn by soldiers when off duty [Ar.].

mug (mug) *n.* a straight-sided earthenware or metal cup with or without a handle; the contents of this; (*Slang*) the face or mouth, a grimace, a rough person; *v.t.* (*Slang*) to attack from behind, by strangling, with intent to rob. *v.i.* (*Slang*) to grimace or overact. *pr.p.* **-ging**. *pa.p., pa.t.* **-ged. -ger** *n.*

mug·gins (mug'·inz) *n.* (*Brit.*) a simpleton; a game of dominoes.

mug·gy (mug'·i·) *a.* warm and humid, as weather; close; enervating. **mugginess** *n.* [O.N. *mugga*, a mist].

mug·wump (mug'·wump) *n.* one who holds independent political views [N. Amer. Ind. *mugquomp*, big chief].

mu·lat·to (ma·lat'·ō) *n.* offspring of white person and Negro. *pl.* **-es** [Port. *mulato*, of mixed breed].

mul·ber·ry (mul'·ber·i·) *n.* a deciduous tree on the leaves of which the silkworm feeds; the fruit of this tree; a purplish-brown color [L. *morum*; A.S. *herie*].

mulch (mulch) *n.* a protective covering of straw, manure, etc., for plants; *v.t.* to treat with mulch [M.E. *molsh*, soft].

mulct (mulkt) *n.* a fine imposed as a penalty; *v.t.* to punish with a fine; to deprive of [L. *mulcia*, a fine].

mule (mūl) *n.* the hybrid offspring of a donkey or horse; a small tractor for hauling, in mines, along canals, etc.; a heelless bedroom slipper; an obstinate person. **-teer** *n.* a mule driver. **mulish** *a.* obstinate; pig-headed. **mulishly** *adv.* **mulishness** *n.* [O.E. *mul*, a he-ass].

mull (mul) *v.t.* to heat, sweeten and spice (wine, ale, etc.). **-ed** *a.*

mull (mul) *v.i.* to muse upon; to cogitate.

mul·let (mul'·at) *n.* an edible fish [L. *mullus*].

mul·li·gan (mul'·i·gan) *n.* a stew made from left-over meat and vegetables.

mul·li·ga·taw·ny (mul·i·ga·taw'·ni·) *n.* a rich soup flavored with curry, thickened with rice [Tamil].

mul·lion (mul'·yan) *n.* a dividing upright between the lights of windows, panels, etc. *v.t.* to divide by millions. **-ed** *a.* [L. *mancus*, maimed].

mul·ti- *prefix*, fr. L. *multus*, many.

mul·ti·col·or (mul'·ti·kul·er) *a.* having many colors. **-ed** *a.*

mul·ti·far·i·ous (mul·ta·far'·i·as) *a.* manifold; made up of many parts [L. manifold].

mul·ti·form (mul'·ti·fawrm) *a.* having many forms. **-ity** *n.*

mul·ti·lat·e·ral (mul·ti·lat'·er·al) *a.* having many sides. **-ly** *adv.* [L. *multus*, many; *latus*, a side].

mul·ti·mil·lion·aire (mul'·ti·mil'·yan·er) *n.* a person who is worth several million dollars.

mul·ti·par·tite (mul·ti·par'·tīt) *a.* having many parts; (*Govt.*) pert. to an agreement among three or more states; multilateral.

mul·ti·ped (mul'·ti·ped) *n.* and *a.* (animal) with many feet. Also **multipede.**

mul·ti·ple (mul'·ta·pl) *a.* manifold; of many parts; repeated many times; *n.* (*Math.*) a quantity containing another an exact number of times. **— fission** *n.* repeated division [L. *multiplex*, manifold].

mul·ti·ply (mul'·ta·plī) *v.t.* to increase in number; to add a number to itself a given number of times; *v.i.* to increase; to grow in number. **multiplex** *a.* multiple; (of telegraph) capable of transmitting numerous messages over the same wire. **multipliable, multiplicable** *a.* **multiplicand** *n.* the number to be multiplied. **multiplication** *n.* the act of multiplying; a rule or operation by which any given number may be added to itself any specified number of times (the symbol ✕). **multiplicative** *a.* **multiplicator** *n.* a multiplier. **multiplicity** *n.* the state of being multiplied; great number. **multiplier** *n.* a number by which another, the **multiplicand**, is multiplied [L. *multus*, many; *plicare*, to fold].

mul·ti·tude (mul'·ta·tūd) *n.* a great number; numerousness; a crowd; an assemblage. **multitudinous** *a.* made up of a great number [L. *multitudo*].

mul·ti·va·lent (mul·ta·vā'·lant) *a.* (*Chem.*) having a valency of more than two. **multivalence, multivalency** *n.*

mul·ti·valve (mul'·ti·valv) *a.* having many valves; *n.* a mollusk with a shell of many valves.

mum (mum) *a.* silent; *n.* silence. **mum's the word**, keep it a secret [imit.].

mum (mum) *v.t.* to perform in dumb show; to act in a mask. **-mer** *n.* one who performs. **-mery** *n.* exaggerated ceremony. *pr.p.* **-ming**. *pa.p., pa.t.* **-med** [Dut. *mommen*, to mask].

mum·ble (mum'·bl) *v.t., i.* to utter, speak indistinctly; *n.* an indistinct utterance [fr. *mum*].

mum·bo jum·bo (mum'·bō jum'·bō) *n.* meaningless ritual [fr. Afr. idol worship].

mum·my (mum'·i·) *n.* a dead body preserved by embalming. **mummified** *a.* **mummification** *n.* **mummify** *v.t.* to embalm and dry as a mummy; *v.i.* to become dried up like a mummy [Pers. *mum*, wax].

mumps (mumps) *n.* a highly infectious disease causing painful swelling of face and neck glands (form of *mum*).

munch (munch) *v.t.* and *v.i.* to chew noisily and steadily [M.E. imit.].

mun·dane (mun'·dān) *a.* pert. to this world; worldly [L. *mundus*, the world].

mu·nic·i·pal (mū·nis'·a·pal) *a.* pert. to local

government or to internal affairs (not international). **-ity** (mū·nis·a·pal′·i·ti·) *a* town or district with its own local self-government. **-ly** *adv.* [L. *municipium*, a free town].

mu·nif·i·cence (mū·nif′·a·sans) *n.* liberality; generosity. **munificent** *a.* very generous. **munificently** *adv.* [L. *munus*, a gift; *facere*, to make].

mu·ni·ment (mū′·na·mant) *n.* means of protection. *pl.* title deeds; charter [L. *munire*, to fortify].

mu·ni·tion (mū·nish′·an) *v.t.* to equip with the weapons of war; *n.* (usually *pl.*) military stores or weapons [L. *munifus*, fortified].

mu·ral (mūr′·al) *a.* pert. to a wall; on a wall; *n.* a wall painting [L. *muralis*].

mur·der (mur′·der) *n.* homicide with premeditated and malicious intent; *v.t.* to commit a murder; to kill; to mar by incompetence. **-er** *n.* (*fem.* **-ess**) **-ous** *a.* bloody; homicidal. **-ously** *adv.* [O.E. *morthor*, murder].

mu·ri·ate (myoo′·ri·āt) *n.* a chloride. **muriated** briny. **muriatic acid**, hydrochloric acid [L. *muria*, brine].

murk (murk) *a.* dark; *n.* darkness; gloom. **-y** *a.* dark; misty. **-ily** *adv.* **-iness** *n.* [O.E. *mirce*, dark].

mur·mur (mur′·mer) *n.* a low, unbroken sound, as of wind, water, etc.; a complaint expressed in subdued tones; softly uttered speech; *v.i.* to make a low sound; to speak in subdued tones; to complain. **-er** *n.* [L. *murmur*, a low sound].

mur·rain (mur′·in) *n.* a disease affecting cattle, foot-and-mouth disease [O.Fr. *morine*, a plague].

mus·cat (mus′·kat) *n.* a sweet grape; **-el** (mus·ka·tel′) *n.* a wine made from this grape [It. *moscato*, musk-flavored].

mus·cle (mus′·l) *n.* a band of contractile fibrous tissue which produces movement in an animal body; strength. **—bound** *a.* with muscles enlarged and stiffened from too much exercise. **-d** *a.* having muscle; muscular. **muscular** *a.* pert. to muscle; brawny; strong. **muscularity** *n.* **muscularly** *adv.* **to muscle in** (*Slang*) to break in by force [L. *musculus*, a muscle].

mus·coid (mus′·koid) *a.* (*Bot.*) like moss. **muscology** *n.* the study of mosses [L. *muscus*, moss].

Mus·co·vite (mus′·ka·vīt) *n.* a native or inhabitant of Moscow or of Russia. **muscovite** *n.* white mica; *a.* pert. to Moscow or to Russia.

Muse (mūz) *n.* (*Gk. myth.*) one of the nine daughters of Zeus and Mnemosyne, who each presided over one of the liberal arts. *n.* inspiration. **the muse**, poetry [Gk. *Mousa*].

muse (mūs) *v.i.* to think over dreamily; to ponder; to consider meditatively; *n.* reverie; contemplation. **musingly** *adv.* reflectively [O.Fr. *muser*, to loiter].

mu·settte (mū·zet′) *n.* a small bagpipe; a melody for this instrument; a reed stop on an organ; a country dance [O.Fr. a small bagpipe].

mu·se·um (mū·zē′·am) *n.* a building or room housing a collection of works of art, antiques, objects of natural history, the sciences, etc. [Gk. *Mouseion*, a temple of the Muses].

mush (mush) *n.* a pulp; (*U.S.*) porridge of corn meal; a soft mass; (*Slang*) sentimentality. **-y** *a.* **-iness** *n.* [form of *mash*].

mush (mush) *v.t.* to journey on foot with dogs over snowy wastes; *interj.* command to dogs to start or speed up.

mush·room (mush′·room) *n.* an edible fungus of very quick growth; (*Fig.*) an upstart; *a.* of rapid growth; shaped like a mushroom; *v.i.* to gather mushrooms; to grow quickly [prob. fr. Fr. *mousse*, moss].

mu·sic (mū′·zik) *n.* the art of combining sounds or sequences of notes into harmonious patterns pleasing to the ear and satisfying to the emotions; melody; musical composition or score. **-al** *a.* pert. to music; set to music; ap-

preciative of music; trained or skilled in the art of music. **-ally** *adv.* — **box** *n.* a box which when wound up plays a tune. **-al comedy**, a form of light entertainment in which songs, dialogue, dancing, humor are combined with a not too serious plot. **-ale** (mū·zi·kal′) *n.* a private party with music. — **hall** *n.* a hall for musical programs. **-ian** (mū·zi′·shan) *n.* a composer or skilled performer of musical compositions. **-ology** *n.* the scientific study of music [Gk. *mousikos*, pert. to the Muses].

musk (musk) *n.* a fragrant substance obtained from a gland of the musk deer; the perfume of this; any plant with a musky perfume. **-cat** *n.* civet. — **deer** *n.* a small, hornless deer. Also **Muscovy-duck.** **-melon** *n.* common melon. — **ox** *n.* a sheep-like ox with brown, long-haired shaggy coat. **-rat** *n.* a large N. Amer. water rat with musk-gland, valued for its fur. — **rose** *n.* a climbing rose with white blossoms faintly perfumed with musk. **-y** *a.* having the smell of musk [L. *muscus*, musk].

mus·ket (mus′·kit) *n.* (formerly) a hand gun or matchlock. **-eer** *n.* a soldier armed with a musket [O.Fr. *mousquet*, a sparrow hawk].

Mus·lim (muz′·lam) *n.* See **Moslem.**

mus·lin (muz′·lin) *n.* a thin cotton cloth of open weave; *a.* made of muslin [fr. *Mosul*, in Iraq].

mus·quash (mus′·kwàsh) *n.* the muskrat, or its fur [Amer. Ind.].

muss (mus) *v.t.* (*Colloq.*) to disorganize; to make messy. **-y** *a.*

mus·sel (mus′·l) *n.* a class of marine bivalve shellfish [L. *musculus*, mussel].

must (must) *v.i.* to be obliged, by physical or moral necessity; *v.aux.* to express compulsion, obligation, probability, certainty, dependent on verb used with it; *n.* a necessity [O.E. *moste*, pret. of verb, *not*, may].

must (must) *n.* wine newly pressed from grapes but not fermented [L. *mustus*, new].

mus·tache (mas·tash′) *n.* the hair on the upper lip [Fr. *moustache*].

mus·tang (mus′·tang) *n.* a wild horse of the Amer. prairies; a bronco [Sp. *mestengo*, belonging to graziers].

mus·tard (mus′·terd) *n.* a plant with yellow flowers and pungent seeds; a powder or paste made from the seeds, used as a condiment. — **gas**, dichlorodiethyl sulphide, an oily liquid, irritant war-gas [O.Fr. *moustarde*].

mus·ter (mus′·ter) *v.t.* to assemble, as troops for a parade; to gather together, as one's resources; *v.i.* to be assembled together; *n.* an assembling of troops, etc. **to pass muster**, to be up to standard [O.Fr. *mostre*, show].

mus·ty (mus′·ti·) *a.* moldy; stale. **mustily** *adv.* **-iness** *n.* [L. *mustum*, new wine].

mu·ta·ble (mū′·ta·bl) *a.* subject to change; inconstant. **-ness, mutability,** *n.* **mutably** *adv.* **mutate** *v.t.* to change, as a vowel by the influence of another in a subsequent syllable. **mutation** *n.* change; the process of vowel change; (*Biol.*) a complete divergence from racial type which may ultimately give rise to a new species. **mutative, mutatory** *a.* [L. *mutare*, to change].

mute (mūt) *a.* dumb; silent; unexpressed in words; not sounded, as *e* of *cave*; *n.* a person who cannot speak; (*Mus.*) a device to soften or muffle tone; *v.t.* to muffle the sound of. **-ly** *adv.* **-ness** *n.* [L. *mutus*, dumb].

mu·ti·late (mū′·ta·lāt) *v.t.* to maim; to cut off; to impair by removing an essential part. **mutilation** *n.* **mutilator** *n.* [L. *mutilus*, maimed].

mu·ti·ny (mū′·ti·ni·) *n.* insurrection against lawful authority, esp. military or naval; *v.i.* to rise in mutiny. **mutineer** *n.* **mutinous** *a.* rebellious; seditious [Fr. *mutin*, mutinous].

mutt (mut) *n.* (*Slang*) a fool; a dog, a mongrel.

mut·ter (mut'·ẽr) *v.t.* to speak indistinctly or in a low voice; to grumble. **-er** *n.* **-ing** *n.*

mut·ton (mut'·n) *n.* the flesh of sheep, esp. mature sheep, as food. **—chop whiskers,** side whiskers [Fr. *mouton,* a sheep].

mu·tu·al (mū'·choo·ạl) *a.* reciprocally acting or related; interchanged; done by each to the other; common to several; as a *mutual friend.* **-ity** *n.* the quality of being reciprocal. **-ly** *adv.* [L. *mutuus,* borrowed].

mu·zhik (mŏŏ·zhĕk') *n.* a Russian peasant.

muz·zle (muz'·l) *v.t.* the snout; the mouth and nose of an animal; a cage-like fastening for the mouth to prevent biting; the open end of a gun; *v.t.* to put a muzzle on; to gag; to enforce silence [L. *musus,* a snout].

muz·zy (muz'·i·) *a.* (*Colloq.*) dazed; bewildered.

my (mī) *poss. a.* belonging to **me** [contr. of *mine;* O.E. *min,* of me].

my·col·o·gy (mī·kạl'·ạ·ji·) *n.* the science of fungi. **mycologist** *n.* **mycophagy** *n.* the eating of fungi [Gk. *mukēs,* a mushroom].

my·e·lin (mī'·ạ·lạn) *n.* (*Zool.*) the fatty substance forming the sheath of nerve fibers. **myelitis** *n.* inflammation of the spinal cord or bone marrow [Gk. *muelos,* marrow].

my·na(h) (mī'·nạ) *n.* a tropical starling, one variety mimics human speech [Hind.].

my·o- *prefix* from Gk. **mys, myos** meaning muscle.

my·o·car·di·tis (mī·ạ·kár·dīt'·ạs) *n.* (*Med.*) inflammation of the heart muscle.

my·o·ma (mī·ō'·mạ) *n.* tumor of muscle tissue.

my·o·pi·a (mī·ō'·pi·ạ) *n.* near-sightedness. **myopic** *a.* [Gk. *muein,* to close; *ōps,* the eye].

my·o·sis (mī·ō'·sis) *n.* prolonged contraction of the pupil of the eye [Gk. *myein,* to close; *-osis*].

my·o·so·tis (mī·ạ·sō'·tis) *n.* a genus of herbs including the forget-me-not [Gk. = mouse-ear].

myr·i·ad (mir'·i·ạd) *n.* an indefinitely large number; *a.* countless [Gk. *murias,* ten thousand].

myr·i·a·pod (mir'·i·ạ·pàd) *n.* (*Zool.*) an animal with great number of legs, as centipede [Gk. *murias,* ten thousand; *pous,* a foot].

myr·me·col·o·gy (mur·mạ·kál'·ạ·ji·) *n.* the scientific study of ants and ant life [Gk. *murmēx,* an ant].

myrrh (mur) *n.* a transparent yellow-brown aromatic gum resin formerly used as incense, now used in antiseptics [Gk. *murrha,* myrrh].

myr·tle (mur'·tl) *n.* an evergreen plant with fragrant flowers and glossy leaves; (*U.S.*) the periwinkle [O.Fr. *myrtille,* the myrtle-berry].

my·self (mī·self') *pron.* I or me, used emphatically, or reflexively.

mys·ter·y (mis'·tẽr·i·) *n.* anything strange and inexplicable; a puzzle; a religious truth beyond human understanding; secrecy; a medieval drama based on Scripture; *pl.* rites known to and practiced by initiated only. **mysterious** *a.* strange; occult; incomprehensible. **mysteriously** *adv.* [Gk. *mystēria,* secret religious rites].

mys·tic (mis'·tik) *a.* pert. to a mystery, to secret religious rites, or to mysticism; symbolical of spiritual truth; strange; *n.* one who believes in mysticism; one who seeks to have direct contact with the Divine by way of spiritual ecstasy and contemplation. **-al** *a.* **-ally** *adv.* **-ism** (mis'·ti·sizm) *n.* the doctrine of the mystics; study of spiritual experience; obscurity of doctrine. **mystification** *n.* **mystify** *v.t.* to perplex; to puzzle [Gk. *mustikos,* pert. to one initiated in the mysteries].

myth (mith) *n.* a fable; a legend embodying primitive faith in the supernatural; an invented story; an imaginary person or thing. **-ic, -ical** *a.* pert. to myths; fabulous; non-existent. **-ically** *adv.* **-ologic, (-al)** *a.* pert. to mythology; legendary. **-ologically** *adv.* **-ologist** *n.* one who has studied myths of various countries; a writer of fables. **-ology** *n.* a collection of myths; the science of myths; a treatise on myths [Gk. *muthos,* a story].

myx·e·de·ma (mik·sạ·dē'·mạ) *n.* (*Med.*) a disease caused by deficiency of secretion from thyroid gland [Gk. *muxa,* mucus; *oidēma,* swelling].

N

nab (nab) *v.t.* to catch hold of; to seize suddenly. *pr.p.* **-bing.** *pa.t., pa.p.* **-bed** [Dan. *nappe,* to catch].

na·bob (nā'·báb) *n.* a Mohammedan chief in India; any man of great wealth [Hind. *nawwab*].

na·celle (nạ·sel') *n.* the part fixed to the wing of any aircraft serving to enclose engine, crew, passengers, and goods [Fr. fr. L. *navicella,* a little ship].

na·cre (nā'·kẽr) *n.* mother-of-pearl. **nacreous** *a.* [Fr. fr. Sp. *nacar*].

na·dir (nā'·dẽr) *n.* point of the heavens directly opposite the zenith; the lowest or most depressed stage [Ar. *nazir,* opposite].

nag (nag) *n.* a small horse; an old horse; (*Colloq.*) any horse [etym. uncertain].

nag (nag) *v.t.* and *v.i.* to worry by constant faultfinding; to scold. *pr.p.* **-ging.** *pa.t.* and *pa.p.* **-ged. -ger** *n.* [Sw. *nagga,* to peck].

nai·ad (nā'·ad, or nī'·ad) *n.* (*Class. Myth.*) a nymph of the streams. [Gk. *naias*].

nail (nāl) *n.* the horny shield covering the ends of the fingers or toes; a claw; a strip of pointed metal provided with a head, for fastening wood, etc.; *v.t.* to fasten with a nail; to fix or secure; to confirm or pin down; (*Colloq.*) to seize hold of. **— brush** *n.* a small brush for cleaning the fingernails. **-er** *n.* **-ery** *n.* a factory where nails are made. [O.E. *naegel*].

na·ïve (nȧ·ēv') *a.* having native or unaffected simplicity; childishly frank; artless. **-ly** *adv.* **naïveté** (nȧ·ēv·tā') *n.* childlike ingenuousness. Also **naivety** [Fr.].

na·ked (nā'·kid) *a.* having no clothes; exposed; bare; nude; uncovered; unarmed; manifest; evident; undisguised; simple; sheer. **-ly** *adv.* **-ness** *n.* [O.E. *nacod*].

nam·by-pam·by (nam'·bi·pam'·bi·) *a.* insipid, lacking strength of character; weakly sentimental [a nickname for *Ambrose Philips,* a poet who wrote childishly affected verse].

name (nām) *n.* the term by which any person or thing is known; appellation; designation; title; fame; reputation; family; *v.t.* to give a name to; to call or mention by name; to nominate; to specify; to christen; **-less** *a.* without a name; dishonored; obscure; unspeakable. **-lessly** *adv.* **-ly** *adv.* by name; that is to say. **-sake** *n.* a person who bears the same name as another [O.E. *nama*].

nan·keen (nan·kēn') *n.* a cotton fabric dyed buff [*Nanking,* China, where first woven].

nan·ny (nan'·i·) *n.* (*Brit.*) a child's nurse. **— goat** *n.* a she-goat.

nap (nap) *n.* a short sleep; a doze; *v.i.* to indulge in a short sleep; to be unprepared. *pr.p.* **-ping** *pa.t., pa.p.* **-ped** [O.E. *knappian*].

nap (nap) *n.* fine hairy surface of cloth; the pile of velvet [Dut. *nop*].

na·palm (nā'·pám) *n.* jellied gasoline used in flame throwers.

nape (nāp) *n.* the back part of the neck [O.E. *hnaepp,* bowl].

na·per·y (nā'·per·i·) *n.* household linen, esp. for the table [O.Fr. *naperie*].

naph·tha (nap'·tha, naf'·thạ) *n.* a clear,

volatile, inflammable liquid distilled from petroleum, wood, etc. **-lene** *n.* a white, solid crystalline hydrocarbon distilled from coal tar and familiar in the form of moth balls [Gk.].

nap·kin (nap'·kin) *n.* a cloth used for wiping the hands or lips at table [Fr. *nappe*, cloth].

na·po·le·on (na·pōl'·yan) *n.* a pastry of several cream-filled layers; a French gold coin; a card game. **-ic** *a.* pert. to Napoleon I or III.

Nar·cis·sus (nár·sis'·as) *n.* bulbous plant genus including the daffodil, jonquil, narcissus; **narcissim** *n.* in psychoanalysis, an abnormal love and admiration for oneself. **narcissist** *n.* [fr. *Gk. Myth.*].

nar·cot·ic (nár·kàt'·ik) *a.* producing stupor or inducing sleep; *n.* a substance which relieves pain and induces sleep, and in large doses, insensibility and stupor; one addicted to the habitual use of narcotics. **narcosis** *n.* a state of unconsciousness or stupor with deadening of sensibility to pain, produced by narcotics [Gk. *narkōtikos*, benumbed].

nard (nàrd) *n.* the spikenard, a plant which yields an odorous unguent. **-ine** *a.* [Pers.].

nar·rate (na·rāt', nar'·āt) *v.t.* to relate; to tell (story) in detail; to give an account of; to describe. **narration** *n.* an account. **narrative** *n.* a tale; a detailed account of events; *a.* pert. to, containing, narration, **narratively** *adv.* **narrator** *n.* [L. *narrare*].

nar·row (nár'·ō) *a.* of little breadth; not wide or broad; limited; bigoted; illiberal; *v.t.* to make narrow; *v.i.* to become narrow; *n.pl.* straits. **-ly** *adv.* **—minded** *a.* bigoted; illiberal; prejudiced [O.E. *nearu*].

nar·whal (nar'·whàl) *n.* a cetaceous mammal, closely related to the white whale, with one large protruding tusk. [Dan. *narhval*].

na·sal (nā'·zal) *a.* pert. to the nose; *n.* a nasal sound or letter, such as *m* or *n.* **-ize** *v.i.* to render (a sound) nasally. **-ity** *n.* the quality of being nasal. **-ly** *adv.* [L. *nasus*, the nose].

nas·cent (nas'·, nās'·ant) *a.* at the moment of being born; just beginning to exist **nascence, nascency** *n.* [L. *nasci*, to be born].

na·stur·tium (na·stur'·sham) *n.* (*Bot.*) a common trailing garden plant of the genus Tropaeolum [L. = twisting the nose].

nas·ty (nas'·ti·) *a.* very dirty; filthy; disgusting; offensive; repulsive; unpropitious (of the weather, etc.); ill-natured; indecent. **nastily** *adv.* **nastiness** *n.* [etym. uncertain].

na·tal (nā'·tal) *a.* pert. to one's place of birth or date of birth; **-ity** *n.* birth rate. **— day,** birthday [L. *natus*, born].

na·tant (nā'·tant) *a.* (*Bot.*) floating on the surface. **natation** *n.* swimming. **natatorial** *a.* natatory. **natatorium** *n.* a swimming pool. **natatory** *a.* used or adapted for swimming [L. *nature*, to swim].

na·tion (nā'·shan) *n.* a people inhabiting a country under the same government; an aggregation of persons of the same origin and language [L. *natio*, a tribe].

na·tion·al (nash'·an·al) *a.* belonging to or pertaining to a nation; public; general; *n.* member of a nation. **-ization** *n.* **-ize** *v.t.* to make national; to acquire and manage by the state; to make a nation of. **-ism** *n.* devotion to the interests of one's nation, often to the detriment of common interests of all nations. **-ist** *n.* one who advocates a policy of national independence. **-ity** *n.* the quality of being a nation or belonging to a nation; one's nation; patriotism. **-ly** *adv.* **— anthem,** a hymn or song expressive of patriotism, praise, or thanksgiving, commonly sung by people of a nation at public gatherings. **— debt,** the debt due from a nation to individual creditors. **National Guard,** State military force which can be called to active duty [L. *natio*].

na·tive (nā'·tiv) *a.* pert. to one's birth; belonging by birth; innate; indigenous; natural; of metals, occurring in a natural state; pert. to natives; *n.* a person born in a place; **-ly** *adv.* **nativity** *n.* the time or circumstances of birth; in astrology, the position of the stars at a person's birth [L. *nativus*, inborn].

nat·ty (nat'·i·) *a.* neat; trim; tidy; spruce. **nattily** *adv.* [etym. unknown].

nat·u·ral (nach'·a·ral) *a.* in accordance with, belonging to, or derived from, nature; inborn; unconstrained; normal; in a state of nature; unaffected; unassuming; true to life; illegitimate; (*Mus.*) not modified by a flat or sharp; *n.* an idiot; (*Colloq.*) a person or thing naturally suitable; (*Mus.*) a character used to remove the effect of an accidental sharp or flat which has preceded it. **-ization** *n.* **-ize** *v.t.* to give to an alien the rights of a native subject; to adopt a foreign word etc., as native; to accustom, as to a climate. **-ism,** *n.* natural condition or quality; the system of those who deny miracles, prophecies, etc.; theory of art, etc. which holds that any artistic creation must be a reproduction of nature or reality. **-ist** *n.* one versed or interested in natural history. **-istic** *a.* in accordance with nature. **-istically** *adv.* **-ly** *adv.* **-ness** *n.* **— gas,** an inflammable product, usually methane, occurring in association with mineral oil deposits. **— history,** the science which deals with the earth's crust and its productions, but applies more especially to biology or zoology. **— philosophy,** the science of nature and of the physical properties of bodies; physics. **— religion,** religion which is derived from nature and reason without resource to revelation. **— science,** the science of nature as distinguished from mental and moral science and mathematics. [fr. *nature*].

na·ture (nā'·cher) *n.* the world, the universe, known and unknown; the power underlying all phenomena in the material world; the innate or essential qualities of a thing; the environment of man; the sum total of inheritance; natural disposition; innate character; of a material, the average excellence of its qualities when unaffected by deteriorating influences; sort; kind; vital functions of organs of the body; state of nakedness. **-d** *a.* in compounds, **good-, bad-natured** *a.* showing one's innate disposition. [L. *natura*].

naught (nawt) *n.* (*Arch.*) nothing; figure 0; zero; Also **nought. -y** *a.* wayward; not behaving well; mischievous; bad. **-ily** *adv.* **naughtiness** *n.* [O.E. *nawiht*, no whit].

nau·se·a (naw'·zē·a, naw'·s(h)ē·a, naw'·zha) *n.* any sickness of the stomach accompanied with a propensity to vomit; a feeling of disgust; sea-sickness. **-te** *v.i.* to feel nausea; *v.t.* to loathe; to fill with disgust; to affect with nausea. **nauseous** *a.* loathsome; disgusting; producing nausea. **nauseously** *adv.* [Gk. = seasickness, fr. *naus*, a ship].

nau·ti·cal (naw'·ti·kal) *a.* pert. to ships, seamen, or to navigation. **-ly** *adv.* **— mile,** 6,080.2 ft. [Gk. *nautēs*, a sailor].

nau·ti·lus (naw'·ta·las) *n.* a genus of cephalopod mollusc with many-chambered spiral shells. **nautiloid** *a.* [Gk. *nautilos*, a sailor].

na·val (nā'·val) *a.* pert. to ships, esp. warships; belonging to or serving with the navy [L. *navis*, a ship].

nave (nāv) *n.* the middle or body, of a church [L. *narvis*, a ship].

na·vel (nā'·vl) *n.* the umbilicus, place of attachment of the umbilical cord to the body of the embryo, marked by a rounded depression in the center of the lower part of the abdomen; the central part [O.E. *nafela*].

na·vic·u·lar (na·vik'·ya·ler) *a.* shaped like a boat; relating to small ships or boats; *n.* one of the bones of the wrist and ankle [L. *navic-*

ularis; fr. *navis,* a ship].

nav·i·gate (nav′·i·gāt) *v.t.* and *v.i.* to steer or manage a ship or aircraft; to sail upon or through; **navigable** *a.* may be sailed over or upon; seaworthy; steerable (of balloons). **navigability, navigableness** *n.* **navigably** *adv.* **navigation** *n.* the science of directing course of seagoing vessel and of ascertaining its position at any given time; the control and direction of aircraft in flight; **navigator** *n.* [L. *navigare,* to sail].

na·vy (nā′·vi·) *n.* a fleet; the warships of a country with their crews and organization. — **blue** *n.* and *a.* dark blue [L. *navis,* a ship].

nay (nā) *adv.* no; not only this, but; *n.* denial; refusal [O.N. *nei,* never].

Naz·a·rene (naz′·a·rēn) *n.* a native of *Nazareth;* name given to Jesus; *pl.* an early Christian sect.

Na·zi (nàt′·zi·) *n.* and *a.* a member of the National Socialist Party of Germany (1922-1945). **-sm, -ism** *n.* [Ger. *nazional,* national].

Ne·an·der·thal (nē·an′·der·tàl) *a.* denoting a man of the earliest long-headed race in Europe which became extinct at least 20,000 years ago [fr. a cave in *Neanderthal,* Ger.].

neap (nēp) *a.* low; *n.* neap tide. — **tide** *n.* the tide whose rise and fall is least marked [O.E. *nep.*].

Ne·a·pol·i·tan (nē·a·pàl′·a·tan) *a.* and *n.* pert. to Naples or its inhabitants [Gk. *Neapolis,* fr. *neos,* news; *polis,* a city].

near (nir) *adv.* at or to a short distance; *prep.* close to; *a.* close; closely related; stingy; *v.t.* and *v.i.* to approach. **-by** *a.* in close proximity; adjacent. — **East,** part of Asia nearest Europe, from Asia Minor to Persia. **-ly** *adv.* closely; intimately; almost. **-ness** *n.* **-side** *n.* of horses, vehicles, etc., the left side. **-sighted** *a.* myopic; short-sighted. **-sighted-ness** *n.* [O.E. *near,* nigher].

neat (nēt) *a.* orderly; clean; trim; well-fitting; undiluted; clever; in good taste; dexterous; precise; net. **-ly** *adv.* **-ness** *n.* [Fr. *net,* clean, pure].

neb (neb) *n.* the bill or beak of a bird; the nose [O.E. *nebb* the face].

neb·u·la (neb′·ya·la) *n.* a slight greyish speck on the cornea of the eye; a cloudlike celestial phenomenon consisting of vastly diffused gas or of tenuous material throughout which fine dust in an incandescent state is distributed. *pl.* **-e. -r** *a.* **nebulosity** *n.* cloudiness; vagueness. **nebulous** *a.* cloudy, hazy, indistinct; vague; formless; pert. to nebula. **nebulousness** *n.* [L. = mist].

nec·es·sar·y (nes′·a·ser·i·) *a.* needful; requisite indispensable; that must be done; *n.* a needful thing; essential need. **necessarily** *adv.* [L. *necessarius*].

ne·ces·si·ty (na·ses′·a·ti·) *n.* pressing need; indispensability; compulsion; needfulness; urgency; poverty; a requisite; an essential. **necessitate** *v.t.* to make necessary or indispensable; to force; to oblige. **necessitous** *a.* needy; destitute [L. *necessitas*].

neck (nek) *n.* the part of the body joining the head to the trunk; the narrower part of a bottle, etc.; a narrow piece of anything between wider parts; *v.t.* (*Slang*) to hug; to cuddle. **-erchief** *n.* a band of cloth or kerchief worn round the neck. **-lace** *n.* a string of beads or precious stones worn round neck. **-piece** *n.* a scarf, usually of fur, **-tie** *n.* a tie for the neck. **neck and neck,** just even [O.E. *hnecca,* nape of neck].

ne·cro- *prefix,* fr. Gk. *nekros,* a dead body, used in the construction of compound terms, signifying death in some form. **-logy** *n.* a register of deaths; a collection of obituary notices. **-mancy** *n.* the art of predicting future events by conjuring up the spirits of the dead; black magic; enchantment. **-mancer** *n.* a sorcerer; a magician. **-mantic** *a.* pert. to magic. **-polis** *n.* a cemetery. **-scopy** *n.* a postmortem; autopsy. **-sis** *n.* gangrene, mortification. **-tic** *a.*

nec·tar (nek′·ter) *n.* the fabled drink of the gods; any delicious beverage; honey-like secretion of the nectary gland of flowers. **-eal, -ean,- -eous, -ous** *a.* sweet as nectar; resembling nectar; delicious. **-ed** *a.* flavored with nectar; very sweet. **-ine** *a.* sweet as nectar; *n.* a smooth-skinned variety of peach. [Gk. *nektar*].

need (nēd) *n.* a constitutional or acquired craving or want, appeased by recurrent satisfactions; want; necessity; requirement; poverty; destitution; extremity; urgency; *v.t.* to be in want of; to require; *v.i.* to be under a necessity. **-ful** *a.* necessary; requisite **-fully** *adv.* **-fulness** *n.* **-ily** *adv.* **-iness** *n.* condition of need. **-less** *a.* unnecessary; not needed. **-lessly** *adv.* **-lessness** *n.* **-y** *a.* in need; indigent [O.E. *nied*].

nee·dle (nēd′·l) *n.* a slender pointed instrument with an eye, for passing thread through cloth, etc.; a slender rod for knitting; anything like a needle, as the magnet of a compass, a hypodermic syringe, an etcher's burin, an obelisk, a sharp-pointed rock, leaf of the pine, etc.; the reproducing needle of a phonograph. **-point** *n.* a hand-made lace; canvas with a design worked in yarn. **-work** *n.* **-ly** *a.* thorny [O.E. *naedl*].

ne'er (ner) *adv.* poetical form of never. **—do-well** *a.* and *n.* good-for-nothing; worthless.

ne·far·i·ous (ni·fa′·ri·as) *a.* wicked in the extreme; iniquitous. **-ly** *adv.* **-ness** *n.* [L.].

ne·gate (ni·gāt′) *v.t.* to deny; to prove the contrary. **negation** *n.* the act of denying; negative statement; disavowal; contradiction [L. *negare,* to deny].

neg·a·tive (neg′·a·tiv) *a.* expressing denial, prohibition, or refusal; lacking positive qualities; not positive; stopping or withholding; (*Elect.*) at a lower electric potential; (*Algebra*) minus; *n.* a proposition in which something is denied; a negative word; a photographic plate in which lights and shades are reversed; *v.t.* to refuse to sanction; to reject. **-ly** *adv.* **-ness** *n.* [L. *negare,* to deny].

neg·lect (ni·glekt′) *v.t.* to disregard; to take no care of; to fail to do; to omit through carelessness; to slight; *n.* omission; disregard; careless treatment; slight. **-edness** *n.* **-er** *n.* **-ful** *a.* careless; inclined to be heedless. **-fully** *adv.* [L. *negligere,* to neglect].

neg·li·gee (neg·la·zhā′) *n.* a woman's loose dressing gown [Fr.].

neg·li·gence (neg′·la·jans) *n.* want of due care; carelessness; habitual neglect. **negligent** *a.* careless; inattentive; untidy. **negligently** *adv.* **negligible** *a.* hardly worth noticing [L. *neglegere,* to neglect].

ne·go·ti·ate (ni·gō′·shi·āt) *v.t.* to settle by bargaining; to arrange; to transfer (a bill, etc.); (*Colloq.*) to surmount; *v.i.* to discuss with a view to finding terms of agreement; to bargain. **negotiable** *a.* capable of being negotiated; transferable. **negotiability** *n.* **negotiation** *n.* **negotiant, negotiator** *n.* [L. *negotiari,* fr. *negotium,* business].

Ne·gro (nē′·grō) *n.* member of one main ethnological group of human race, with dark skin. *a.* pert. to black African race. **Negress** *n.* Negro woman. **-id** *a.* resembling or related to the Negroes [Sp. fr. L. *nger,* black].

neigh (nā) *v.i.* to whinny, like horse; *n.* cry of horse [O.E. *hnaegan*].

neigh·bor (nā′·ber) *n.* a person who lives, works, near another; *a.* neighboring; *v.t.* to adjoin; to be near. **-hood** *n.* adjoining district and its people; proximity; vicinity. **-ing** *a.*

close by. **-ly** *a.* friendly; sociable; helpful. **-liness** *n.* [O.E. *neahgebur*].

nei·ther (nē'·THẹr, nī'·THẹr) *a.* and *pron.* not the one or the other; *adv.* not on the one hand; not either; *conj.* nor yet; not either [O.E. *nahwaether*, not whether].

nem·a·tode, nematoid (nem'·ạ·tōd, ·toid) *a.* thread-like. **nematoidea** *n.pl.* roundworms, threadworms [Gk. *nēma*, thread; *eidos*, form].

nem·e·sis (nem'·ạ·sis) *n.* inevitable retributive justice [Gk. *nemein*, to distribute, deal out].

ne·o- (nē'·ō) *prefix* used in the construction of compound terms, signifying *new, recent* [Gk.].

ne·o·dym·i·um (nē·ō·dim'·i·ạm) *n.* a metallic element belonging to the group of rare earth metals [Gk. *neos*, new; and *didymium* (a once supposed element)].

ne·o·lith·ic (nē·ō·lith'·ik) *a.* (*Geol.*) pert. to the late Stone Age.

ne·ol·o·gy (nē·ál'·ạ·ji·) *n.* the introduction of new words into a language; new doctrines, esp. rationalistic, in theology. **neologian, neologist** *n.* one who coins new words or holds novel doctrines in religion. **neologic, neological** *a.* **neologize** *v.i.* to coin new words. **neologism** *n.* a newly-coined word or phrase; a new doctrine [Gk. *neos*, new; *logos*, word].

ne·on (nē'·ạn) *n.* a non-metallic chemical element belonging to the group of the rare gases. **— light, — sign,** or **— tube,** one containing neon gas and glowing with a characteristic reddish-orange light [Gk. *neos*, new].

ne·o·pho·bi·a (nē·ō·fō'·bi·ạ) *n.* a dread of the unknown [Gk. *neos*, new; *phobos*, fear].

ne·o·phyte (nē'·ạ·fit) *n.* a novice; a convert [Gk. *neos*, new; *phutos*, grown].

ne·pen·the, nepenthes (ni·pen'·thē, ·thēz) *n.* in Greek mythology, a drug with power of banishing grief; any narcotic drug to relieve pain; genus of Asiatic plants [Gk. *nē-*, not; *phenthos*, grief].

neph·ew (nef'·ū) *n.* a brother's or sister's son; son of one's husband's or wife's brother or sister [Fr. *neveu*, fr. L. *nepos*, a nephew].

nephr- (or nephro-) *prefix* used in the construction of compound terms, from Greek *nephros*, a kidney. **-algia, -algy** *n.* pain in the kidney. **-ic** *a.* pert. to the kidneys. **-itic(al)** *a.* pert. to (diseases of) the kidneys. **-itis** *n.* Bright's disease, non-infective inflammation of the kidney.

nep·o·tism (nep'·ạ·tizm) *n.* undue favoritism in awarding public appointments to one's relations [L. *nepos*, a nephew].

Nep·tune (nep'·tòòn) *n.* (*Myth.*) the Roman god of the sea; second most remote planet of solar system [L.].

nerve (nurv) *n.* one of the bundles of fibers which convey impulses either *from* brain (motor nerves) to muscles, etc., producing motion, or *to* brain (sensory nerves) from skin eyes, nose, etc., producing sensation; mid-rib or vein of a leaf; sinew; tendon; fortitude; courage; cool assurance; (*Slang*) impudence. *pl.* irritability; unusual sensitivity to fear, annoyance, etc.; *v.t.* to give courage or strength to. **-d** *a.* **-less** *a.* lacking in strength or will; incapable of effort. **-lessness** *n.* **nervine** *a.* acting on the nerves; *n.* a nervetonic. **nervy** *a.* (*Slang*) bold; showing courage [L. *nervus*, sinew].

nerv·ous (nurv'·ạs) *a.* pert. to, containing, or affecting nerves; uneasy; apprehensive. **-ly** *adv.* **-ness** *n.* **— breakdown** *n.* a condition of mental depression [L. *nervus*, a sinew].

nes·cience (nesh'·ạns) *n.* the condition of complete ignorance; lack of knowledge; agnosticism. **nescient** *a.* ignorant; agnostic [L. *nescier*, not to know].

nest (nest) *n.* the place in which a bird or other animal lays and hatches its eggs; any snug retreat; a set of boxes, tables, etc., which fit into one another; *v.t.* to form to place in a nest; *v.i.* to occupy or build a nest. **-ling** *n.* a bird too young to leave the nest. **— egg** *n.* an egg left in a nest to induce a bird to lay; a small sum of money put aside for some later purpose [O.E.].

nes·tle (nes'·l) *v.i.* to settle comfortably and close to one another; to lie snugly, as in a nest; (of a house) to be situated in a sheltered spot [O.E. *nestlian*].

net (net) *n.* an open-work fabric of meshes of cord, etc.; sections of this used to catch fish, protect fruit, etc.; lace formed by netting; a snare. *a.* made of netting; reticulate; caught in a net; *v.t.* to cover with, or catch in, a net; to veil; *v.t.* to make net or network. *pr.p.* **-ting.** *pa.t.* and *pa.p.* **-ted. -ted** *a.* **-ting** *n.* the act or process of forming network; netlike fabric; snaring by means of a net. **-work** *n.* anything made like, or resembling, a net; (*Radio*) a group of transmitting stations producing programs carried by long-distance telephone wires to affiliated stations for broadcasting [O.E. *nett*.].

net (net) *a.* left after all deductions; free from deduction; *v.t.* to gain or produce as clear profit; *pr.p.* **-ting.** *pa.p.* **-ted. — price,** net price without discount [Fr. = clean].

neth·er (neTH'·ẹr) *a.* lower; low-lying; lying below; belonging to the lower regions.**-most** *a.* lowest. **-ward(s)** *adv.* in a downward direction [O.E. *neothera*].

net·tle (net'·l) *n.* a common weed covered with fine stinging hairs; *v.t.* to irritate; to provoke; to make angry; to rouse to action. **— rash** *n.* an irritating eruption in the skin [O.E. *netele*].

neur-, neuro- *prefix* from Gk. *neuron*, a nerve.

neu·ral (nyoo'·rạl) *a.* pert. to the nerves or nervous system [Gk. *neuron*, a nerve].

neu·ral·gia (nyoo·ral'·jạ) *n.* a spasmodic or continuous pain occurring along the course of one or more distinct nerves. **neuralgic** *a.* [Gk. *neuron*, a nerve; *algos*, pain].

neu·ras·the·ni·a (nyoor·ạs·thē'·ni·ạ) *n.* a condition of nervous debility characterized by lack of energy, restlessness, headache and insomnia. **neurasthenic** *a.* [Gk. *neuron*, a nerve; *astheneia*, weakness].

neu·rax·is (nyoo·rak'·sis) *n.* the cerebrospinal axis, or central nervous system, including the brain and spinal cord.

neu·ri·tis (nyoo·rī'·tis) *n.* an inflammatory condition of a nerve [Gk. *nueron*, a nerve].

neu·rol·o·gy (nyoo·rál'·ạ·ji·) *n.* the study of the structure, function and diseases of the nervous system. **neurological** *a.* **neurologist** *n.* [Gk. *neuron*; *logos*, discourse].

neu·ron (nyoor'·ạn) *n.* a nerve cell and all its processes [Gk. = nerve].

neu·ro·path (nyoo'·rạ·path) *n.* a person subject to a nervous disorder. **-ic, -ical** *a.* pert. to nervous diseases. **-ist** (nyoo·rạp'·ạ·thist) *n.* an abnormal or diseased condition of the nervous system [Gk. *neuron*, nerve; *pathos*, suffering].

neu·ro·sis (nyoo·rō'·sis) *n.* a psychic or mental disorder resulting in partial personality disorganization. *pl.* **neuroses. neurotic** (nyoo·rát'·ik) *a.* pert. to the nerves; *n.* a highly strung person [Gk. *neuron*, a nerve].

neu·ter (nū'·tẹr) *a.* neither masculine nor feminine; (*Bot.*) possessing neither stamens nor carpels; *n.* the neuter gender; an imperfectly developed female, as the worker-bee [L. = neither].

neu·tral (nū'·trạl) *a.* taking neither side in

a war, dispute, etc.; indifferent; without bias; grey; intermediate (shade of color); neither acid nor alkaline; asexual; *n.* nation, person, not taking sides in a dispute; the position in a gear-mechanism when no power is transmitted. **-ize** *v.t.* to render neutral; to make ineffective; to counterbalance. **-izer** *n.* nonintervention by a state or third-party in a dispute; the state of being neutral. **-ly** *adv.* **-ity** *n.* [L. *neuter*, neither].

neu·tron (nū′·trån) *n.* one of the minute particles composing the nucleus of an atom [L. *neuter*, neither].

nev·er (nev′·er) *adv.* at no time; not ever; in no degree; (*Colloq.*) surely not. **-more** *adv.* **-theless** *conj.* none the less; in spite of that; notwithstanding [O.E. *naefre*].

new (nū) *a.* not existing before; lately discovered or invented; not ancient; *adv.* (usually **new-**), recently; freshly; **-ly** *adv.* **-ish** *a.* somewhat new. **-ness** *n.* **-born** *a.* recently born; born anew. **-comer** *n.* one who has just settled down in a strange place or taken up a new post. **-fangled** *a.* lately devised; novel (in a depreciatory sense). **—fashioned** *a.* just come into fashion; the latest in style. **New Style** *n.* a term to denote dates reckoned by the Gregorian calendar. **New Deal**, a campaign initiated in 1933 by President Franklin Roosevelt involving social reforms. **New Englander**, a native or resident of any of the six N. E. states of the U.S.A. **New Learning**, the Renaissance. **— moon**, the period when the first faint crescent of the moon becomes visible. **New Testament**, later of the two main divisions of Bible. **New World**, N. and S. America [O.E. *niwe*].

new·el (nū′·al) *n.* the post supporting the balustrade to a flight of stairs [L. *nodus*, a knot].

news (nōōz) *n.sing.* report of recent happenings; fresh information; tidings; intelligence. **-boy** *n.* a boy who sells or distributes newspapers. **— bulletin** *n.* the latest news, esp. as disseminated by radio or television. **-monger** *n.* busy-body; *gossip.* **-paper** *n.* a regular publication giving latest news. **-print** *n.* cheap paper for newspapers. **-reel** *n.* a short film depicting items of news and topical features. **-stand** *n.* a stand where newspapers, and sometimes magazines, are sold. **-y** *a.* gossipy; full of news.

newt (nūt) *n.* a salamander; an eft [*a newt* for *an ewt*, fr. O.E. *efeta*, an *eft*].

next (nekst) *a.* nearest; immediately following in place or time; *adv.* nearest or immediately after; on the first future occasion; *prep.* nearest to. **-ly** *adv.* in the next place. **— of kin**, *n.* nearest blood relative **-door** *a.* [O.E. *niehst*, superl. of *neah*, nigh].

nex·us (nek′·sås) *n.* a tie, connection, or bond [L. *nectere*, to bind].

nib (nib) *n.* something small and pointed; beak of a bird; point of a pen; **-bed** *a.* having a nib [form of *neb*].

nib·ble (nib′·l) *v.t.* to bite a little at a time; *v.i.* to catch at (as a fish); to bite gently; to dally with; *n.* a tiny bite [L.G. *nubbelen*].

nib·lick (nib′·lik) *n.* a golf-club with an iron-head, well laid back, designed for lofting.

nice (nīs) agreeable; attractive; kind; exact; discriminating; delicate; dainty. **-ly** *adv.* **-ness** *n.* **-ty** (nī′·så·ti·) *n.* precision; delicacy; exactness; refinement [O.Fr. *nice*, foolish].

niche (nich) *n.* a recess in a wall for a statue, bust, etc.; one's ordained position in life or public estimation; *v.t.* to place in a niche. **-d** *a.* [Fr. fr. It. *nicchia*].

nick (nik) *v.t.* to make a notch in; to indent; to catch exactly; *n.* a notch; a slit; the opportune moment as *in the nick of time*.

nick·el (nik′·al) *n.* a silver white metallic element, malleable and ductile, and much used in alloys and plating; a five-cent piece; *v.t.* to plate with nickel. **— plating** *n.* plating of metals with nickel to provide a bright surface and to keep down rust. **— silver** *n.* an alloy of copper, nickel and zinc; German silver [Sw. abbrev. fr. Ger. *Kupfernickel*, copper nickel (ore)].

nick·el·o·de·an (nik·al·ō′·di·ån) *n.* a player phonograph operated by the insertion of a nickel [Fr.].

nick·nack See **knickknack**.

nick·name (nik′·nām) *n.* a name given in contempt, derision, or familiarity to some person, nation, or object [orig. *an eke name*, an added name, fr. *eke*, to increase].

nic·o·tine (nik′·a·tēn) *n.* a colorless, highly poisonous alkaloid present in the tobacco plant; [Jean *Nicot*, who introduced the plant into Fr.].

nid·i·fi·ca·tion (nid·a·fa·kā′·shn) *n.* the act of building a nest. **nidify** *v.i.* to build a nest. **nidus** (ī) *n.* a nest; (*Med.*) a nucleus of infection [L. *nidus*, a nest; *facere*, to make].

nidus See **nidification**.

niece (nēs) *n.* the daughter of a brother or sister or of one's husband's or wife's brother or sister [Fr. *nièce*, fr. L. *neptis*].

nif·ty (nif′·ti·) *a.* (*Colloq.*) fine; smart.

nig·gard (nig′·erd) *n.* a very miserly person; *a.* stingy. Also **-ly. -liness** *n.* meanness.

nig·ger (nig′·er) *n.* (*offensive*) a Negro [Fr. *nègre*].

nig·gle (nig′·l) *v.i.* to trifle; to be too particular about details. **-r** *n.* **niggling, niggly** *a.* and *n.* [etym. uncertain].

nigh (nī) *a.* near; direct. *adv.* near [O.E. *neah*].

night (nīt) *n.* the time of darkness from sunset to sunrise; end of daylight; intellectual or spiritual darkness; ignorance; death. **-ly** *a.* happening or done every night; of the night; *adv.* every night; by night. **-cap** *n.* a cap worn in bed; (*Colloq.*) an alcoholic drink at bedtime. **— club** *n.* establishment for dancing and entertainment remaining open until early morning. **-dress, -gown** *n.* a loose gown worn in bed. **-fall** *n.* the close of day. **-hawk** *n.* a nocturnal bird; (*Colloq.*) one who is up late habitually. **-light** *n.* bulb of low wattage kept burning all night. **-long** *a.* persisting all night. **-mare** *n.* a terrifying feeling of oppression or suffocation arising during sleep; a frightening dream. **— owl** *n.* (*Colloq.*) one who habitually keeps late hours. **— school** *n.* a school for the continuation of studies after working hours. **— shift** *n.* employees who work regularly during night; duration of this work. **-shirt** *n.* a loose shirt used for sleeping in. **-time** *n.* period of night; **-ward** *a.* towards night. **— watchman** *n.* [O.E. *niht*].

night·in·gale (nīt′·an·gāl) *n.* a bird of the thrush family, the male being renowned for its beautiful song at night [O.E. *niht*, night; *galan*, to sing].

ni·hil, nil (nī′·hil, nil) *n.* nothing; zero. **nihilism** *n.* the rejection of all religious and moral principles as the only means of obtaining social progress; the denial of all reality in phenomena; in 19th cent. the opposition in Russia to all constituted authority or government. **nihilist** *n.* **nihilistic** *a.* [L.].

Ni·ke (nī′·kē) *n.* a U.S. Army supersonic guided missile [fr. *Gk. Myth* goddess of victory].

nim·ble (nim′·bl) *a.* light and quick in motion. **-ness** *n.* **—witted** *a.* quick-witted. **nimbly** *adv.* [O.E. *niman*, to take].

nim·bus (nim′·bås) *n.* a cloud or atmosphere

around a person or thing; in representation of saints, angels, etc., the circle of light surrounding the head; a halo; an aureole. *pl.* **-es** *or* **nimbi** [L. = cloud].

nin·com·poop (nin'·kạm·pòóp) *n.* a foolish person; a simpleton [origin uncertain].

nine (nīn) *a.* and *n.* one more than eight; the symbol 9 or IX; a baseball team; **-fold** *a.* nine times repeated. **-teen** *a.* and *n.* nine and ten. **-teenth** *a.* and *n.* **ninetieth** *a.* the tenth after the eightieth. **-ty** *a.* and *n.* **ninth** *a.* the first after the eighth; *n.* **ninthly** *adv.* **-pins** *n.* a game in which nine erect wooden pegs are to be knocked down by a ball. **the Nine,** the Muses [O.E. *nigon*].

nin·ny (nin'·i·) *n.* a fool; a dolt [It. *ninno*, a child].

ni·non (nē'·nàn) *n.* a glossy lightweight dress fabric of silk [Fr. proper name].

nip (nip) *v.t.* to pinch sharply; to detach by pinching; to check growth (as by frost); to smart. *pr.p.* **-ping.** *pa.t.* and *pa.p.* **-ped.** *n.* a pinch; sharp touch of frost; a sip. **-per** *n.* one who or that which nips; the great claw (as of a crab); *pl.* small pincers. **-piness** *n.* **-pingly** *adv.* **-py** *a.* sharp in taste; curt; smarting [etym. uncertain, cf. Dut. *nijpen*].

nip·ple (nip'·l) *n.* the protuberance in the center of a breast by which milk is obtained from the female during breast-feeding; a teat; the mouthpiece of a nursing bottle; a small metal projection pierced so that oil or grease may be forced into a bearing surface by means of a grease gun [etym. uncertain, cf. *nib*].

Nip·pon (nip'·àn) *n.* Japan. **-ese** *n., a.* [Jap. = rising of the sun].

Nir·va·na (nir·và'·nạ) *n.* in Buddhism, that state of blissful repose or absolute existence reached by one in whom all craving is extinguished [Sans].

ni·sei (nē'·sā') *n.* Am. citizen born of immigrant.

ni·si (nī'·sī) *conj.* unless. **decree nisi** (*Law*) a decree to take effect after a certain period of time has elapsed unless some valid objection arises [L.].

nit (nit) *n.* the egg of an insect parasite, esp. of a louse [O.E. *hnitu*].

ni·ter (nī'·tẹr) *n.* potassium nitrate; saltpeter, a white crystalline solid used in the manufacture of gunpowder, acids, etc. **nitrate** *n.* a salt of nitric acid; a fertilizer. **nitrated** *a.* combined with nitric acid. **nitration** *n.* the conversion of nitrites into nitrates by the action of bacteria; the introduction of a nitro-group (NO$_2$) into an organic substance. **nitric** *a.* containing nitrogen. **nitric acid,** a powerful, corrosive acid. **nitride** *n.* a compound of a metal with nitrogen. **nitrify** *v.t.* to treat a metal with nitric acid; to oxidize to nitrates or nitrites, esp. by action of bacteria. **nitrite** *n.* a salt of nitrous acid. **nitrous oxide,** laughing gas, used as an anaesthetic in dentistry [Gk. *nitron*].

ni·tro- (nī·trạ) *prefix* used in the formation of compound terms, signifying, formed by, or containing, *niter*. **-glycerine** *n.* a powerful oily liquid explosive [Gk. *nitron*, native soda].

ni·tro·gen (nī'·trạ·jạn) *n.* a non-metallic gaseous chemical element, colorless, odorless and tasteless, forming nearly four-fifths of the atmosphere. **nitrogenous** *a.*

nit·wit (nit'·wit) *n.* (*Colloq.*) a fool. **-ted** *a.* [Dut. *niets*, nothing; O.E. *witan*, to know].

nix (niks) *n.* (*Slang*) nothing [Dut. *niets*].

no (nō) *a.* not any; *adv.* expresses a negative reply to a question or request; not at all; *n.* a refusal; a denial; a negative vote. **-es** *n.pl.* term used in parliamentary proceedings, *the noes have it*. **no man's land,** the terrain between the front lines of opposing forces [O.E. *na*].

nob (nàb) *n.* (*Slang*) the head [fr. *knob*].

No·bel Prize (nō·bel' prīz) *n.* one of a series of five prizes awarded annually to persons who have distinguished themselves in physics, chemistry, medicine, literature, or the promotion of peace [Alfred *Nobel*, Swedish inventor (1833-96)].

no·bil·i·ty (nō·bil'·ạ·ti·) *n.* the class holding special rank, usually hereditary, in a state; the quality of being noble; grandeur; loftiness and sincerity of mind or character [L. *nobilis*, noble].

no·ble (nō'·bl) *a.* distinguished by deeds, character, rank, or birth; of lofty character; titled; *n.* a nobleman; a peer; an old English gold coin. **-man** *n.* (*fem.* **-woman**). **-ness** *n.* **nobly** *adv.* **the noble art,** boxing [L. *nobilis*].

no·bod·y (nō'·bàd·i·) *n.* no one; a person of no importance.

nock (nàk) *n.* notch, esp. of bow or arrow; upper end of fore-and-aft sail [*notch*].

noc·turn (nàk'·turn) *n.* a service held during the night. **nocturne** *n.* a painting of a night scene; a musical composition of a gentle and simple character. **-al** *a.* pertaining to night; happening or active by night; *n.* a primitive instrument for determining latitude at night. **-ally** *adv.* [L.*nocturnus*, of the night].

noc·u·ous (nàk'·yoo·ạs) *a.* hurtful; noxious. **-ly** *adv.* [L. *nocere*, to hurt].

nod (nàd) *v.t.* and *v.i.* to incline the head forward by a quick motion, signifying assent or drowsiness; to droop the head; to be sleepy; to sway; to bow by way of recognition. *pr.p.* **-ding.** *pa.t.* and *pa.p.* **-ded.** *n.* an act of nodding. **-der** *n.* [etym. uncertain].

nod·al See **node.**

nod·dle (nàd'·l) *n.* (*Colloq.*) the head; *v.i.* to nod repeatedly.

nod·dy (nàd'·i·) *n.* a simpleton; a fool; a sea-bird [fr. *nod*].

node (nōd) *n.* a knot or knob; (*Geom.*) a point at which a curve crosses itself to form a loop; (*Elect.*) a point in a circuit carrying alternating currents at which the amplitude of current or voltage is a minimum; (*Astron.*) one of two points at which the orbit of a planet intersects the plane of the ecliptic; (*Phys.*) a point of permanent rest in a vibrating body; (*Med.*) á small protuberance or hard swelling; (*Bot.*) the part of a stem to which a leaf is attached; an articulation. **nodal, nodical** *a.* pert. to nodes. **nodated** *a.* knotted. **nodation** *n.* the knots. **nodular** *a.* like a nodule. **nodulated** *a.* having nodules. **nodule** *n.* a small node or act of making knots. **nodiferous** *a.* (*Bot.*) having nodes. **nodose, nodous** *a.* full of swelling [L. *nodus*, a knot].

No·ël (nō'·el) *n.* Christmas; a carol. Also **Nowel** [Fr. fr. L. *natalis*, birthday].

nog (nàg) *n.* a wooden peg or block [Scand.].

nog (nàg) *n.* a beverage made with eggs and usually liquor; eggnog; a kind of strong ale. **-gin** *n.* a small mug; a very small drink; (*Slang*) the head [Ir. *noigin*].

no·how (nō'·hou) *adv.* (*substandard*) in no way; not at all; (*Colloq.*) ability.

noise (noiz) *n.* sound; din; loud outcry; *v.t.* to spread by rumor; *v.i.* to sound loud. **-less** *a.* making no noise; silent. **-lessly** *adv.* **-lessness** *n.* **noisy** *a.* making much noise; clamorous. **noisily** *adv.* **noisiness** *n.* [Fr.].

noi·some (noi'·sạm) *a.* injurious to health; noxious; offensive; disgusting; evil smelling. **-ly** *adv.* **-ness** *n.* [obs. *noy*, for *annoy*].

no·mad (nō'·mad) *a.* roaming from pasture to pasture; *n.* a wanderer; a member of a wandering tribe. **nomadic** *a.* pert. to nomads; having no fixed dwelling place. **nomadically** *adv.* **-ism** *n.* [Gk. *nomas*, pasturing].

nom·de·plume (nàm'·dạ·plòóm) a pen name [Fr.].

no·men·cla·tor (nō'·mạn·klā·tẹr) *n.* one who gives names to things. **nomenclatural** *a.* **nomenclature** (nō'·mạn·klā·chẹr) *n.* a system of naming; the vocabulary of a science, etc. [L. *nomen*, a name; *calare*, to call].

nom·i·nal (nạm'·ạ·nạl) *a.* pert. to a name; existing only in name, ostensible; titular; (*Gram.*) pert. to a noun. **-ism** *n.* the doctrine that the universal, or general, has no objective existence or validity, being merely a name expressing the qualities of various objects resembling one another in certain respects. **-ist** *n.* one who holds these views, the opposite of a *realist*. **-istic** *a.* **-ly** *adv.* in name only; not really [L. *nominalis*, fr. *nomen*, a name].

nom·i·nate (nạm'·ạ·nāt) *v.t.* to put forward the name of, as a candidate; to propose; to designate. **nomination** *n.* act of nominating; power or privilege of nominating. **nominative** *a.* (*Gram.*) denoting the subject; *n.* a noun or pronoun which is the subject of a verb. **nominator** *n.* one who nominates. **nominee** *n.* one who is nominated [L. *nominare*, to name].

non- *prefix* from L. *non* = not, used in the formation of compound terms signifying absence or omission. **-combatant** *n.* a member of the armed forces whose duties do not entail an active part in military operations, e.g., chaplain, surgeon, etc.; an unarmed civilian. **-commissioned** *a.* of ranks between a private and warrant officer; (*abbrev.* **noncom**) **-commital** *a.* deliberately avoiding any direct statement as to one's opinions or course of future action. **-conductor** *n.* a substance which will not conduct electricity, heat, or sound; insulator. **-ferrous** *a.* of an alloy or metal containing no, or only the merest trace of, iron. **-intervention** *n.* not intervening or interfering in the affairs or policies of another, esp. in international affairs, **-stop** *a.* not stopping.

non·age (nạn'·ij) *n.* minority (under 21 years of age); a period of immaturity [L. *non*, not; and *age*].

non·a·ge·nar·i·an (nạn·ạ·jạ·ner'·i·ạn) *n.* one who is ninety years old or upwards; *a.* relating to ninety [L. *nonaginta*, ninety].

nonce (nạns) *n.* **for the nonce**, for the occasion only; for the present [earlier *the*(*n*) *-anes*, the once].

non·cha·lance (nạn'·shạ·lạns) *n.* unconcern; coolness; indifference; **nonchalant** *a.* **nonchalantly** *adv.* [Fr. *non*, not; *chaleur*, heat].

non·con·form·ist (nạn·kạn·fawr'·mist) *n.* one who refuses to comply with the usages and rites of an established church, etc. **nonconforming** *a.* **nonconformity** *n.*

non·de·script (nạn'·dạ·skript) *a.* lacking in distinction; hard to classify; *n.* [*nom*, not; *descriptus*, described].

none (nun) *a.* and *pron.* no one; not anything. **-such, nonsuch** *n.* a person or thing without a rival or equal. **nonetheless**, nevertheless; all the same [O.E. *nan*].

nones (nōnz) *n. pl.* one of the canonical hours of the R.C. Breviary, the *ninth* hour after sunrise at the equinox, viz. 3 p.m., or the appropriate mass celebrated at this time [L. *nonus*, ninth].

non·en·ti·ty (nạn·ẹn'·tạ·ti·) *n.* a thing not existing; nonexistence; a person of no importance; a mere nobody [L. *non*, not; *ens, entis*, a being].

non·ju·ror (nạn·joor'·ẹr) *n.* one who refuses to swear allegiance or take an oath. **nonjuring** *a.*

non·pa·reil (nạn·pạ·rel') *n.* a person or thing without an equal; a printing type, between ruby and emerald, counting 6 points; *a.* unrivalled; peerless; matchless [Fr. *non*, not; *pareil*, equal].

non·plus (nạn'·plus) *n.* perplexity; puzzle; inability to say or do more; quandary; *v.t.* to confound or bewilder completely [L. *non*, not; *plus*, more].

non·sense (nạn'·sens) *n.* lack of sense; language without meaning; absurdity; silly conduct. **nonsensical** *a.* **nonsensically** *adv.* [L. *non*, not].

non·such See **none**.

noo·dle (nóo'·dl) *n.* a simpleton; (*Slang*) the head [conn. with *noddy*].

noo·dle (nóo'·dl) *n.* a strip of dough, made of flour and eggs, baked and served in soups [Ger. *nudel*].

nook (nook) *n.* a corner; a recess; a secluded retreat [ME. *nok*].

noon (nóon) *n.* midday; twelve o'clock by day; the exact instant when, at any given place, the sun crosses the meridian. **-day, -tide** *n.* and *a.* midday [L. *nona* (*hora*), ninth hour; See **nones**.

noose (nóos) *n.* a running loop with a slip knot which binds closer the more it is drawn; snare; tight knot; *v.t.* to tie, catch in noose [L. *nodus*, knot].

nor (nawr) a particle introducing the second clause of a negative proposition; and not [M.E. *nother*].

Nor·dic (nawr'·dik) *a.* of or pert. to peoples of Germanic, esp. Scandinavian, stock.

norm (nawrm) *n.* a rule or authoritative standard; a unit for comparison; a standard type or pattern; a model; a class-average test score. **-a** *n.* a rule, pattern, or standard; a pattern or templet; a mason's square for testing. **-al** *a.* conforming to type or natural law; (*Math.*) perpendicular; *n.* (*Math.*) a perpendicular to a line, surface, or tangent at point of contact; the standard; the average. **-alcy** (nawr'·mal·si·) *n.* normality. **normality** *n.* normal state or quality. **-ly** *adv.* **-ative** *a.* setting up a norm; regulative. **-al school**, a training college for teachers [L. *norma*, a rule].

Nor·man (nawr'·mạn) *n.* a native of Normandy; *a.* pert. to Normandy or the Normans. **— architecture**, a style of medieval architecture characterized by rounded arch and massive simplicity. [O.Fr. *Normant*, fr. Scand. = Northmen].

Norse (nawrs) *a.* pert. to ancient Scandinavia, esp. Norway, its language, or its people; *n.* Norwegians or ancient Scandinavians; the old Scandinavian language [Scand. *norsk*, north].

north (nawrth) *n.* the region or cardinal point in the plane of the meridian to the left of a person facing the rising sun; the part of the world, of a country, etc., towards this point; *adv.* towards or in the north; *a.* to, from, or in the north. **northerly** (nawr'·THẹr·li·) *a.* towards the north; of winds, coming from the north. **northern** *a.* pert. to the north; in or of the north. **northerner** *n.* an inhabitant of the northern parts of a country. **northernly** *adv.* in a northern direction. **northernmost** *a.* situated at the most northerly point. **-ward, -wardly** *a.* situated towards the north; *adv.* in a northerly direction. **-wards** *adv.* **-east (-west)** *n.* the point between the north and the east (west); *a.* pert. to, or from, the northeast (-west) **-easter (-wester)** *n.* a wind from the northeast (-west). **-easterly (-westerly)** *a.* towards or coming from the northeast (-west). **-eastern (-western)** *a.* belonging to the northeast (-west). **-eastward (-westward)** *a.* towards the northeast (-west). **northern lights**, aurora borealis. **North Pole**, northern extremity of earth's axis. **North Star** *n.* polar star, the only star which does not change its apparent position [O.E.].

Nor·we·gian (nawr·wē'·jạn) *a.* pert. to Norway; *n.* a native or language of Norway.

nose (nōz) *n.* the organ for breathing and smelling; power of smelling or detecting; any projection resembling a nose, as prow of a ship; *v.t.* to detect by smell; to nuzzle; to sniff; to move forward; *v.i.* to smell; to pry; to push forward. — **bag** *n.* a bag containing provender fastened to a horse's head. — **dive** *n.* in aviation, a sudden steep plunge directly towards an objective, usually from a great height; *v.i.* to perform this evolution. **-gay** *n.* a bunch of sweet-smelling flowers; a bouquet. **nosing** *n.* the molded projecting edge of the tread of a step. **nosy** *a.* (*Colloq.*) inquisitive [O.E. *nosu*].

nose- *prefix* fr. Greek, *nosos*, disease, used in formation of compound words. **nosology** (nō·sòl'·a·ji·) *n.* branch of medicine treating generally of diseases; systematic classification of phases of disease. **nosological** *a.* **nosologist** *n.*

nos·tal·gia (nàs·tal'·ja) *n.* homesickness; a phase of melancholia due to the unsatisfied desire to return home. **nostalgic** *a.* [Gk. *nostos*, return; *algos*, pain].

nos·tril (nàs'·tril) *n.* one of the external openings of the nose [O.E. *nosy*, nose; *thyrel*, opening].

nos·trum (nàs'·tram) *n.* a quack remedy; a patent medicine of doubtful efficacy; a pet scheme, pushed by some visionary [L. = our].

not (nàt) *adv.* a word expressing denial, negation, or refusal [*nought*].

no·ta·ble (nō'·ta·bl) *a.* worthy of notice; remarkable; *n.* a person of distinction. **nota-bilia** *n.pl.* things worth noting; famous remarks. **notability** *n.* an eminent person. **-ness** *n.* **notably** *adv.* [L. *nota*, note].

no·ta·ry (nō'·ta·ri·) *n.* a *notary-public*, a person authorized to record statements, to certify deeds, to take affidavits, etc., on oath [L. *notarius*, a secretary].

no·ta·tion (nō·tā'·shan) *n.* any system of figures, signs and symbols which conveys information; the act or process of noting; a note [L. *nota*, a mark].

notch (nàch) *n.* a V-shaped cut or indentation; nick; a groove formed in a piece of timber to receive another piece; (*U.S.*) a pass between mountains; *v.t.* to make notches in; to indent; to secure by a notch; to score (a run) [O.F. *osche*, a notch].

note (nōt) *n.* a mark; a brief comment; *pl.* a record of a lecture, speech, etc.; a memorandum; a short letter; a diplomatic paper; a written or printed promise of payment; a musical tone; a character to indicate a musical tone; notice; distinction; fame; *v.t.* to observe; to set down in writing; to attend to; to heed. **-book** *n.* a book for jotting down notes, memoranda, etc. **-d** *a.* well-known by reputation or report; celebrated; **-dly** *adv.* **-dness** *n.* — **paper** *n.* a small size of writing paper. **-worthy** *a.* worthy of notice; remarkable. — **of hand**, a promissory note [L. *notare*, to mark].

noth·ing (nuth'·ing) *n.* not anything of account, value, note, or the like; non-existence; nonentity; nought; zero; trifle; *adv.* in no degree; not at all. **-ness** *n.* [fr. no thing].

no·tice (nō'·tis) *n.* act of noting; remarking, or observing; cognizance; regard; note; heed; consideration; news; a review; a notification; *v.t.* to observe; to remark upon; to treat with regard. **-able** *a.* **-ably** *adv.* **to give notice**, to warn beforehand. **to receive one's notice**, to be informed that one's services are about to be terminated [L. *notus*, known].

no·ti·fy (nō'·ta·fī) *v.t.* to report; to give notice of or to; to announce; to inform.

notifiable *n.* **notification** *n.* act of making known or giving notice; official notice or announcement [L. *notus*, known; *facere*, to make].

no·tion (nō'·shan) *n.* apprehension; idea; conception; opinion; belief; sentiment; fancy; inclination; *pl.* small articles such as sewing supplies, etc. [L. *notio*].

no·to·ri·e·ty (nō·ta·rī'·at·i·) *n.* the state of being generally known, esp. in a disreputable way; discreditable publicity. **notorious** *a.* generally known (usually in a bad sense); infamous. **notoriously** *adv.* **notoriousness** *n.* [L. *notus*, known].

not·with·stand·ing (not·with·stand'·ing) *adv.* nevertheless; however; yet; *prep.* in spite of; despite; *conj.* although.

nou·gat (noo'·gat) *n.* a confection of almonds, pistachio-nuts, or other nuts, in a sugar and honey paste [Fr.].

nought See **naught**.

noun (noun) *n.* (*Gram.*) a word used as a name of a person, quality, or thing; a substantive [L. *nomen*, a name].

nour·ish (nur'·ish) *v.t.* to supply with food; to feed and cause to grow; to nurture; to encourage. **-ing** *a.* nutritious. **-ment** *n.* food; nutriment; the act or state of nourishing [Fr. *nourrir*, fr. L. *nutrire*, to feed].

no·va (nō'·va) *n.* a new star. *pl.* **novae** [L. = new].

nov·el (nàv'·al) *a.* of recent origin or introduction; new; unusual; *n.* a fictitious prose tale dealing with the adventures or feelings of imaginary persons so as to portray, by the description of action and thought, the varieties of human life and character. **-ette** *n.* a shorter form of novel. **-ist** *n.* a writer of novels. **-ty** *n.* newness; something new or unusual [L. *novus*, new].

No·vem·ber (nō·vem·ber) *n.* the eleventh month of the year [L. *novem*, nine].

no·vena (nō·vē'·na) *n.* (*R.C.*) devotions on nine consecutive days; lasting nine days [L. *novem*, nine].

nov·ice (nàv'·is) *n.* a candidate for admission to a religious order; one new to anything; an inexperienced person; a beginner. **novicate, novitiate** *n.* the state or time or being a novice; a novice [L. *novus*, new].

no·vo·caine (nō'·va·kān) *n.* a nonirritant drug which has replaced cocaine as a local anesthetic [L. *novus*, new; and *cocaine*].

now (nou) *adv.* at the present time; *conj.* this being the case; *n.* the present time. **-adays** *adv.* in these days. **now! now!** a form of admonition. **now and then**, occasionally [O.E. *nu*].

no·where (nō'·hwer) *adv.* not in any place. **nowise** *adv.* not in any manner or degree.

nox·a (nàk'·sa) *n.* (*Med.*) anything harmful to the body; *pl.* **-e**. **noxal** *a.* **noxious** *a.* hurtful; pernicious; unwholesome. **noxiously** *adv.* **noxiousness** *n.* [L. *noxa*, injury].

noz·zle (nàz'·l) *n.* a projecting spout or vent; the outlet end of a pipe, hose, etc.; (*Colloq.*) the nose [dim. of *nose*].

nu·ance (noo·àns') *n.* a shade or subtle variation in color, tone of voice, etc.; (*Mus.*) a delicate gradation of tone and expression in performance on an instrument [Fr. = a shade].

nub (nub) *n.* a knob; lump; protuberance; (*Colloq.*) point; gist.

nu·cle·us (nū'·kli·as) *n.* a central part of anything; the starting point of some project or idea; (*Astron.*) the dark center of a sunspot; the denser core or head of a comet; (*Biol.*) the inner essential part of a living cell; (*Physics*) the core of the atom, com-

WEBSTER M–P

posed of protons and neutrons. *pl.* **nuclei** (nū'·kli·ī). **nuclear** *a.* **nuclear energy,** a more exact term for atomic energy; energy freed or absorbed during reactions taking place in atomic nuclei. **nuclear fission,** a process of disintegration which breaks up into chemically different atoms. **nucleate** *v.t.* to gather into or round a nucleus. **nucleolus** *n.* a minute body of condensed chromatin inside a nucleus [L. = kernel].

nude (nūd) *a.* bare; naked; undraped; uncovered; *n.* a picture or piece of sculpture in the nude. **-ly** *adv.* **-ness, nudity,** *n.* nakedness. **nudism** *n.* cult emphasizing practice of nudity for health. **nudist** *n.* [L. *nudus,* naked].

nudge (nuj) *v.t.* to touch slightly with the elbow; *n.* a gentle push [etym. uncertain].

nug·get (nug'·it) *n.* rough lump or mass, esp. of native gold [etym. uncertain].

nui·sance (nū'·sans) *n.* something harmful, offensive, or annoying; a troublesome person; a pest; an inconvenience [Fr. *nuisant,* harming; fr. L. *nocere,* to harm].

null (nul) *a.* of no legal validity; void; nonexistent; of no importance; *v.t.* to annul; to render void. **-ify** *v.t.* to make null; to render useless; to invalidate; **-fication** *n.* **ifier** *n.* **-ity** *n.* state of being null and void [L. *nullus,* none].

numb (num) *a.* insensible; insensitive; chilled; *v.t.* to benumb; to paralyze. **-ness** *n.* [O.E. *numen,* taken].

num·ber (num'·ber) *n.* a word used to indicate how great any quantity is when compared with the unit quantity, one; a sum or aggregate of quantities; a collection of things; an assembly; a single issue of a publication; a piece of music; (*Gram.*) classification of words as to singular or plural; *pl.* metrical feet or verse; rhythm; *v.t.* to give a number to; to count; to reckon; to estimate; *v.i.* to amount to. **-s** *n.pl.* (*Bib.*) fourth book of Pentateuch. **-er** *n.* **-less** *a.* innumerable. **numerability, numerableness** *n.* **numerable** *a.* may be numbered or counted [Fr. *nombre,* fr. L. *numerus*].

nu·mer·al (nū'·mer·al) *a.* designating a number; *n.* a sign or word denoting a number. **numerable** *a.* able to be counted. **numerably** *adv.* **-ly** *adv.* according to number. **numerary** *a.* belonging to, or an integral part of, a certain number, as opposed to *supernumerary.* **numerate** *v.t.* to count; to read figures according to their notation. **numeration** *n.* **numerator** *n.* top part of a fraction, figure showing how many of the fractional units are taken. **numeric(al)** *a.* of, or in respect of, numbers. **numerically** *adv.* **numerous** *a.* many. **numerously** *adv.* **numerousness** *n.* [L. *numerus,* a number].

nu·mis·mat·ic (nū·mis·mat'·ik) *a.* pert. to coins and medals, esp. as an aid to study of archaeology. **numismatist** *n.* **numismatography, numismatology** *n.* science of coins and medals in relation to archaeology and history. **numismatologist** *n.* [L. *numisma,* current coin].

num·skull (num'·skul) *n.* (*Colloq.*) dolt; dunce; a stupid person [*numb, skull*].

nun (nun) *n.* a female member of a religious order, vowed to celibacy, and dedicated to active or contemplative life. **-nery** *n.* convent of nuns [L.L. *nonna*].

nun·ci·o (nun'·shi·ō) *n.* a diplomatic representative of the Pope abroad. **nunciature** *n.* [It. fr. L. *nuntius,* a messenger].

nun·cu·pate (nung'·kyoo·pāt) *v.t.* and *v.i.* to vow publicly; to dedicate; to declare orally, as a will. **nuncupation** *n.* **nuncupative** *a.* oral; not written. **nuncupator** *n.* **nuncupatory** *a.*

oral; verbal [L. *nuncupare,* to name].

nup·tial (nup'·shal, ·chal) *a.* pert. to or constituting ceremony of marriage; *pl.* wedding ceremony; marriage [L. *nuptiae,* wedding].

nurse (nurs) *n.* a person trained for the care of the sick or injured; a woman tending another's child; *v.t.* to tend, as a nurse; to suckle; to foster; to husband; to harbor (a grievance); to manage skillfully (the early stages of some project). **-maid, nurserymaid** *n.* a girl in charge of young children. **-r** *n.* **nursery** *n.* a room set aside for children; a place for the rearing of plants. **nurseryman** *n.* one who raises plants for sale. **nursery rhymes,** jingling rhymes written to amuse young children. **nursery school,** a school for children of 2-5 years of age. **nursling** *n.* an infant; anything which is carefully tended at inception. **wet-nurse** *n.* woman who suckles infant of another [Fr. *nourrice,* fr. L. *nutrix,* a nurse].

nur·ture (nur'·cher) *n.* nurturing; education; rearing; breeding; nourishment; (*Biol.*) the various environmental forces, which combined, act on an organism and further its existence; *v.t.* to nourish; to cherish; to tend; to train; to rear; to bring up. **-r** *n.* [Fr. *nourriture,* nourishment].

nut (nut) *n.* a fruit consisting of a hard shell enclosing a kernel; a hollow metal collar, the internal surface of which carries a groove or thread into which the thread of a screw fits; (*Slang*) the head; blockhead; *v.i.* to gather nuts; *pr.p.* **-ting.** *pa.t.* and *pa.p.* **-ted.** **-brown** *a.* of the color of a nut. — **butter,** a butter substitute made from nut oil. **-cracker** *n.* an instrument for cracking nuts; bird of crow family. **-hatch** *n.* a climbing bird, allied to titmice. **-shell** *n.* the hard shell enclosing the kernel of a nut. **-ter** *n.* one who gathers nuts. **-tiness** *n.* taste of nuts. **-ting** *n.* **-ty** *a.* abounding in nuts; having a nut-flavor; (*Slang*) silly; imbecile. **a hard nut to crack,** a difficult problem to solve; a person difficult to deal with [O.E. *hnutu*].

nu·tant (nū'·tant) *a.* (*Bot.*) hanging with the apex of the flower downwards; nodding. **nutation** *n.* nodding; (*Astron.*) slight periodic wobbling of direction of Earth's axis [L. *nutare,* to nod].

nut·meg (nut'·meg) *n.* an aromatic flavoring spice [E. *nut*; O.Fr. *mugue,* musk].

nu·tri·ent (nū'·tri·ant) *a.* nourishing; *n.* something nutritious. **nutriment** *n.* that which nourishes; food; sustenance. **nutrition** *n.* the act of nourishing. **nutritional, nutritious, nutritive, nutritory** *a.* nourishing; promoting growth [L. *nutrire,* to nourish].

nuz·zle (nuz'·l) *v.t.* and *v.i.* to rub with the nose; to nestle; to burrow or press with the nose [*nose*].

nyc·ta·lo·pi·a (nik·ta·lō'·pi·a) *n.* night blindness [Gk. *nux,* night; *alaos,* blind; *ēps,* eye].

ny·lon (nī'·lan) *n.* an artificial fabric the yarn of which is produced synthetically; *n.pl.* stockings made of nylon yarn [fr. *N* (ew) *Y* (ork), *Lon*(don)].

nymph (nimf) *n.* a lesser goddess inhabiting a mountain, grove, fountain, river, etc.; a girl distinguished by her grace and charm. **-al, -ean, -ic, -ical** *a.* **-like** *a.* **-omania** *n.* a morbid and uncontrollable sexual desire in women. **-omaniac** *n.* [Gk. *nymphē,* a bride].

nymph (nimf) *n.* the pupa or chrysalis of an insect [Gk. *nymphē,* a nymph].

nys·tag·mus (nis·tag'·mas) *n.* eye disease with involuntary twitching oscillation of eyes [Gk. *nustazein,* to nod].

O

O, oh (ō) *interj.* an exclamation of address, surprise, sorrow, wonder, entreaty [O.E. *ea*].

oaf (ōf) *n.* a changeling; dolt; lout; simpleton. *pl.* **oafs** or **oaves. -ish** *a.* loutish; awkward [O.N. *alfr*, an elf].

oak (ōk) *n.* a familiar forest tree yielding a hard, durable timber and acorns as fruit. **-en** *a.* made of oak. — **apple** *n.* a gall or swelling on oak leaves caused by the gallfly [O.E. *ac*].

oar (ōr) *n.* a wooden lever with a broad blade worked by the hands to propel a boat; an oarsman; *v.t.* and *v.i.* to row. **-ed** *a.* having oars. **-man** *n.* a rower. **-manship** *n.* art of rowing. **to put in one's oar** (*Slang*) to meddle; to interfere [O.E. *ar*].

o·a·sis (ō·ā'·sis) *n.* a fertile spot in the desert. *pl.* **oases** (ō·ā'·sēz) [Gk.].

oat (ōt) *n.* but usually in *pl.* **oats**, the grain of a common cereal plant, used as food; the plant; (*Poet.*) a shepherd's musical pipe; a pastoral song. **-en** *a.* made of oat-straw or oatmeal. **-cake** *n.* a thin cake of oatmeal. **-meal** *n.* meal made from oats. **to sow wild oats**, to indulge in youthful follies before settling down [O.E. *ate*].

oath (ōth) *n.* confirmation of the truth by naming something sacred, esp. God; a statement or promise confirmed by an appeal to God; a blasphemous use of the name of God; any imprecation. *pl.* **oaths** (ōTHz) [O.E. *ath*].

ob·bli·ga·to (ab·li·ga'·tō) *n.* (*Mus.*) a part in a musical composition for a particular instrument, of such importance that it is indispensable to the proper rendering of the piece; —also *a.* Also **obligato** [It.].

ob·du·rate (ab'·dyoo·rat) *a.* hard-hearted; stubborn; unyielding. **-ly** *adv.* **obduracy** *n.* [L. *obduratus*, hardened].

o·be·di·ent (ō·bē'·di·ant) *a.* subject to authority; willing to obey. **-ly** *adv.* **obedience** *n.* submission to authority; doing what one is told [L. *obedire*].

o·bei·sance (ō·bā'·sans) *n.* a bow, curtsy or gesture of deference [Fr. *obéissance*, obedience].

ob·e·lisk (ab'·a·lisk) *n.* a tall, four-sided, tapering pillar, ending in a small pyramid; in printing, a reference mark (†) also called 'dagger'; an **obelus** (*pl.* **obeli**), the marks — or ÷ [Gk. *obeliskos*].

o·bese (ō·bēs') *a.* fat; fleshy. **obesity** *n.* excessive fatness [L. *obesus*].

o·bey (ō·bā') *v.i.* to be obedient; *v.t.* to comply with the orders of; to yield submission to; to be ruled by [L. *obedire*].

ob·fus·cate (ab·fus'·kāt) *v.t.* to darken; to confuse or bewilder. **obfuscation** *n.* obscurity; confusion [L. *obfuscare*, to darken].

o·bit (ō'·bit) *n.* (*Slang*) abbrev. of **obituary. obituary** *a.* pert. to death of person; *n.* a notice, often with a biographical sketch, of the death of a person [L. *obitus*, approach, fr. *obire*, to go to meet].

ob·ject (ab'·jekt) *n.* anything presented to the mind or senses; a material thing; an end or aim; (*Gram.*) a noun, pronoun, or clause governed by, and dependent on, a transitive verb or a preposition. **-less** *a.* having no aim or purpose [L. *objetus*, thrown in the way].

ob·ject (ab·jekt') *v.t.* to offer in opposition; to put forward as reason against; *v.i.* to make verbal opposition; to protest against; to feel dislike or reluctance. **objection** (ab·jek'·shan) *n.* act of objecting; adverse reason; difficulty or drawback; argument against. **objectionable** *a.* **objectionably** *adv.* **-or** *n.* [L. *ob*, in the way of; *jacere*, to throw].

ob·jec·tive (ab·jek'·tiv) *a.* pert. to the object; relating to that which is external to the mind; unbiased; (*Gram.*) denoting the case of the object. **-ly** *adv.* **objectivity** *n.* the quality of being objective [Fr. *objectif*].

ob·jur·gate (ab'·jer·gāt) *v.t.* to reprove; to blame; to berate. **objurgation** *n.* **objurgatory** *a.* [L. *objurgare*, to blame].

ob·late (ab·lāt') *a.* (*Geom.*) flattened at the poles (said of a spheroid, like the earth). **-ness** *n.* [L. *oblatus*, brought forward].

ob·late (ab'·lāt) *n.* a person dedicated to religious work, esp. the monastic service. **oblation** *n.* something offered to God, or a god; a gift to the church [L. *oblatus*, brought forward, offered].

ob·li·gate (ab'·li·gāt) *v.t.* to bind, esp. by legal contract; to put under obligation. **obligation** *n.* the binding power of a promise or contract; indebtedness for a favor of kindness; a duty; a legal bond. **obligatory** (a·blig'·a·tōr·i·) *a.* binding legally or morally; compulsory. **obligatorily** *adv.* [L. *obligare*, fr. *ligare*, to bind].

o·blige (a·blīj') *v.t.* to constrain by physical, moral, or legal force; to lay under an obligation; to do a favor to; to compel. **-d** *a.* grateful; indebted. **-ment** *n.* a favor. **obliging** *a.* helpful; courteous. **obligingly** *adv.* **obligingness** *n.* [L. *obligare*, fr. *ligare*, to bind].

ob·lique (ō·blēk') *a.* slanting; inclined; indirect; obscure; not straightforward; underhand. **-ly** *adv.* **-ness, obliquity** (a·blik'·wi·ti·) *n.* slant or inclination; deviation from moral uprightness; dishonesty [L. *obliquus*.].

ob·lit·er·ate (a·blit'·a·rāt) *v.t.* to blot out; to efface or destroy. **obliteration** *n.* the act of blotting out; destruction; extinction. **obliterative** *a.* [L. *obliterare*, fr. *litera*, a letter].

ob·liv·i·on (a·bliv'·i·an) *n.* a forgetting, or being forgotten; forgetfulness; heedlessness. **oblivious** *a.* forgetful; causing to forget; heedless. **obliviously** *adv.* **obliviousness** *n.* [L. *oblivisci*, to forget].

ob·long (ab'·lawng) *a.* longer than broad; *n.* (*Geom.*) a rectangular figure with adjacent sides unequal [L. *oblongus*].

ob·lo·quy (ab'·la·kwi·) *n.* abusive speech; disgrace [L. *obloquium*, a speaking against].

ob·nox·ious (ab·nak'·shas) *a.* offensive; objectionable. **-ly** *adv.* **-ness** *n.* [L. *obnoxius*, exposed to harm].

o·boe (ō'·bō) *n.* (*Mus.*) a woodwind instrument, long and slender, with tone produced by a double reed; an organ reed stop. **oboist** *n.* [Fr. *hautbois*, high, wood].

ob·scene (ab·sēn) *a.* offensive to modesty; indecent; filthy. **-ly** *adv.* **-ness** *n.* **obscenity** (ob·sen'·i·ti·) *n.* lewdness; indecency [L.].

ob·scure (ab·skūr') *a.* dark; hidden; dim; uncertain; humble; *v.t.* to dim; to conceal; to make less intelligible; to make doubtful. **-ly** *adv.* **-ness** *n.* **obscurity** *n.* absence of light; a state of retirement; lack of clear expression or meaning [L. *obscurus*, covered over].

ob·se·quy (ab'·sa·kwi·) *n.* funeral rite; a funeral. **obsequial** *a.* [L.L. *obsequiae*].

ob·se·qui·ous (ab·sē'·kwi·as) *a.* servile; fawning. **-ly** *adv.* **-ness** *n.* [L. *obsequi*, to comply with].

ob·serve (ab·zurv') *v.t.* to watch; to note systematically; to perform or keep religiously; to remark; *v.i.* to take notice; to make a remark; to comment. **observable** *a.* **observance** *n.* the act of observing; a paying attention; the keeping of a law, custom, religious rite; a religious rite; a rule or practice. **observant** *a.* quick to notice; alert; carefully attentive; obedient to. **observantly** *adv.* **observation** *n.* the action or habit of observing; the result of watching, examining, and noting; attentive watchfulness; a comment; a remark. **observatory** *n.* a building for the observation and study of astronomical, meteorological, etc., phenomena. **-r** *n.* [L. *observare*, to watch].

ob·sess (ạb·ses') *v.t.* to haunt; to fill the mind completely; to preoccupy. **-ion** *n.* complete domination of the mind by one idea; a fixed idea [L. *obsidere, obsessum*, to besiege].

ob·sid·i·an (ạb·sid'·i·an) *n.* vitreous lava or glassy volcanic rock [fr. *Obsius*, the discoverer].

ob·so·lete (ạb·sạ·lēt) *a.* no longer in use; out of date. **-ly** *adv.* **-ness** *n.* **obsolescent** *a.* becoming obsolete; going out of use. **obsolescence** *n.* [L. *obsolescere*, to grow out of use].

ob·sta·cle (ạb'·stạ·kl) *n.* anything that stands in the way; an obstruction; a hindrance [L. *ob*, in the way of; *stare*, to stand].

ob·stet·rics (ạb·stet'·riks) *n.* (*Med.*) the science dealing with the care of pregnant women; midwifery. **obstetric, obstetrical** *a.* **obstetrician** *n.* [L. *obstetrix*, a midwife].

ob·sti·nate (ạb'·stạ·nạt) *a.* stubborn; not easily moved by argument; unyielding. **-ly** *adv.* **-ness** *n.* **obstinacy** *n.* unreasonable firmness; stubbornness [L. *obstinatus*].

ob·strep·er·ous (ạb·strep'·ạ·rạs) *a.* noisy; clamorous; vociferous; unruly; *adv.* **-ness** *n.* [L. *ob*, against; *strepere*, to make a noise].

ob·struct (ạb·strukt') *v.t.* to block up; to impede; to hinder the passage of; to retard; to oppose; to block out. **-er, -or** *n.* **-ion** *n.* the act of obstructing; that which obstructs or hinders. **-ive** *a.* **-ively** *adv.* [L. *ob*, against; *struere*, to build up].

ob·tain (ạb·tān') *v.t.* to gain; to acquire; to procure; *v.i.* to be customary or prevalent; to hold good. **-able** *a.* procurable. **-ment** *n.* Also **obtention** [L. *obtinere*].

ob·trude (ạb·trōōd') *v.t.* to thrust forward unsolicited; to push out; *v.i.* to intrude. **-r** *n.* **obtrusion** *n.* the act of obtruding. **obtrusive** *a.* **obtrusively** *adv.* [L. *ob; trudere*, to thrust].

ob·tuse (ạb·tōōs') *a.* blunt; dull of perception; stupid; (*Geom.*) greater than a right angle, but less than 180°. **-ly** *adv.* **-ness** *n.* [L. *obtundere, obtusum*, to blunt].

ob·verse (ạb'·vurs, ạb·vurs') *a.* having the base narrower than the apex; being a counterpart; facing the observer; of a coin, bearing the head; *n.* face of a coin, medal, etc. (opp. of 'reverse'); the front or principal aspect. **-ly** *adv.* [L. *ob*, toward; *versum*, to turn].

ob·vi·ate (ạb'·vi·āt) *v.t.* to intercept and remove (as difficulties); to make unnecessary [L. *ob; viare*, to go].

ob·vi·ous (ạb'·vi·ạs) *a.* easily seen or understood; evident; apparent. **-ly** *adv.* **-ness** *n.* [L. *obvius*, in the way].

oc·a·ri·na (ạk·ạ·rē'·nạ) *n.* a small musical wind-instrument with finger holes [It. *oca*, a goose, from its shape].

oc·ca·sion (ạ·kā'·zhạn) *n.* opportunity; a juncture favorable for something; reason or justification; a time of important occurrence; *v.t.* to cause; to bring about. **-al** *a.* occurring now and then; incidental; meant for a special occasion. **-ally** *adv.* from time to time [L. *occasio*, fr. *cadere*, to fall].

oc·ci·dent (ạk'·sạ·dạnt) *n.* part of the horizon where the sun sets, the west. **occidental** *a.* western; *n.* (*Cap.*) native of Europe or America [L. *occidere*, to go down].

oc·ci·put (ạk'·si·put) *n.* the back part of the head. **occipital** (ạk·sip'·i·tạl) *a.* [L. *ob*, over against; *caput*, the head].

oc·clude (ạ·klōōd') *v.t.* to shut in or out; (*Chem.*) to absorb gas. **occlusion** *n.* **occlusive** *a.* [L. *ob; claudere, clausum*, to shut].

oc·cult (ạ·kult') *a.* secret; mysterious; magical; supernatural; *v.t.* to conceal; to hide from view; to eclipse. **-ly** *adv.* **occultation** *n.* the eclipse of a heavenly body by another. **-ism** *n.* the doctrine or study of the supernatural, magical, etc. [L. *occulere*, to hide].

oc·cu·py (ạk'·yạ·pī) *v.t.* to take possession of; to inhabit; to fill; to employ. **occupancy** *n.* the act of having or holding possession; tenure. **occupant** *n.* one who occupies or is in possession. **occupation** *n.* occupancy; possession; temporary possession of enemy country by the victor; employment; trade; calling; business, profession. **occupational** *a.* **occupier** *n.* [L. *occupare*, to take possession of].

oc·cur (ạ·kur') *v.i.* to come to the mind; to happen; to be met with. *pr.p.* **-ring.** *pa.p.* and *pa.t.* **-red. -rence** *n.* a happening; an event. [L. *occurrere*, to run against].

o·cean (ō'·shạn) *n.* great body of salt water surrounding land of globe; one of the large divisions of this; the sea; *a.* pert. to the great sea. **oceanic** (ō·shi·an'·ik) *a.* pert. to, found, or formed in the ocean. **-ography** *n.* the scientific description of ocean phenomena. **-ographer** *n.* **-ographic, -ographical** *a.* **-ology** *n.* science which relates to the ocean [Gk. *ōkeanos*, a stream encircling the world].

o·ce·lot (ō'·sạ·lạt) *n.* a S. Amer. quadruped of the leopard family [Mex. *ocelotl*].

o·cher (ō'·kẹr) *n.* various natural earths used as yellow, brown, or red pigments. **-ous, -y** *a.* [Gk. *ōchra*, yellow ocher].

o'clock (ạ·klạk') *adv.* by the clock.

oct-, octa-, octo- prefix fr. Gk. *oktō*, eight, combining to form derivatives. **-agon** (ạk'·tạ·gạn) *n.* a plane figure with 8 sides and 8 angles. **-agonal** *a.* **-ahedron** *n.* a solid figure with 8 plane faces. **-ahedral** *a.* **-ane** *n.* (*Chem.*) a hydrocarbon of the paraffin series, obtained from petroleum and used as a fuel, esp. for airplanes. **-angular** *a.* having 8 angles. **-ant** *n.* the eighth part of a circle; an instrument for measuring angles, having an arc of 45°.

oc·tave (ạk'·tāv) *n.* the week following the celebration of a principal Church festival; the day falling a week after a festival; a stanza of 8 lines; (*Mus.*) an interval of 8 diatonic notes comprising a complete scale; a note 8 tones above or below another note; a group of 8 [L. *octavus*, eighth].

oc·ten·ni·al (ạk·ten'·i·ạl) *a.* happening every eighth year; lasting for 8 years [L. *octo*, eight; *annus*, a year].

oc·tet (ạk·tet') *n.* (*Mus.*) a group of 8 musicians or singers; a composition for such a group; a group of 8 lines, esp. the first 8 lines of a sonnect. Also **octette** [L. *octo*, eight].

Oc·to·ber (ạk·tō'·bẹr) *n.* tenth month [eighth month of ancient Roman year].

oc·to·ge·nar·i·an (ạk·tạ·jạ·ne'·ri·ạn) *a.* and *n.* (one) between 80 and 90 years of age [L. *octogenarius*, of eighty].

oc·to·pus (ạk'·tạ·pạs) *n.* a mollusk with 8 arms or tentacles covered with suckers [Gk. *okto*, eight; *pous*, a foot].

oc·u·lar (ạk'·yạ·ler) *a.* pert. to the eye, or to sight; visual; *n.* the eyepiece of an optical instrument. **oculist** *n.* a specialist in the defects and diseases of the eye [L. *oculus*, the eye].

o·da·lisque (ō'·dạ·lisk) *n.* a female slave or concubine in a Turkish harem. Also **odalisk** [Fr. fr. Turk.].

odd (ạd) *a.* not even; not divisible by two; left over after a round number has been taken; extra; surplus; casual or outside the reckoning; occasional; out-of-the-way; queer or eccentric; strange. **-ity** *n.* quality of being odd; peculiarity; queer person or thing. **-ly** *adv.* **-ness** *n.* **odds** *n.pl.* the difference in favor of one as against another; advantage or superiority; the ratio by which one person's bet exceeds another's; likelihood or probability. [O.N. *odda-* (*tala*), odd- (number)].

ode (ōd) *n.* a lyric poem of exalted tone [Gk. *ōdē*, a song].

o·di·um (ō'·di·ạm) *n.* hatred; the state of being hated; general abhorrence incurred by a person or action; stigma. **odious** *a.* **odiously** *adv.* **odiousness** *n.* [L. = hatred].

o·dont- (ō·dạnt′) *prefix* from the Gk. *odous, odontos,* a tooth. **odontalgia** (ō·dạn·tạl′·ji·ạ) *n.* toothache. **odontology** *n.* the science of the teeth [Gk. *algos,* pain; *logos,* discourse].

o·dor (ō′·dẹr) *n.* smell; fragrance; perfume; repute or estimation. **-iferous** (ō·dạ·rif′·ạ·rạs) *a.* sweet-scented; having a strong smell. **-iferously** *adv.* **-iferousness** *n.* **-less** *a.* **-ous** *a.* fragrant; scented. [L. *odor*].

O·dys·seus (ō·dis′·ūs, ō·dis′·ē·ạs) *n.* (*Myth.*) (L. Ulysses) hero of Homer's **Odyssey** (od′·i·si·) *n.* a Greek epic poem glorifying the adventures and wanderings of Odysseus; hence, any long, adventurous journey.

Oed·i·pus (ē·dạ·pạs) *n.* (*Myth.*) a king of Thebes who unwittingly slew his father and married Jocasta, his mother. **Oedipus complex,** in psychoanalysis, a complex involving an abnormal love by a person for the parent of opposite sex.

o'er (ōr) *prep.* (*Poet.*) a contr. for **over.**

oe·soph·a·gus See **esophagus.**

of (ạv, uv) *prep.* belonging to; from; proceeding from; relating to; concerning [O.E.].

off (awf) *adv.* away; in general, denotes removal or separation, also completion, as in *to finish off; prep.* not on; away from; *a.* distant; on the farther side; less than satisfactory; discontinued; free; *interj.* begone! depart! **-ing** *n.* the more distant part of the sea visible to an observer; **-ish,** *a.* inclined to stand aloof; **-ishly** *adv.* **-ishness** *n.* in the offing, not very distant. **—chance** *n.* a slight chance. **—color** *a.* poor in color; of doubtful propriety. **-hand** *a.* without preparation; free and easy; curt; *adv.* without hesitation; impromptu. **-set** *n.* a shoot or side-branch; a sum set off against another as an equivalent; compensation; (*Print.*) the smudging of a clean sheet; a process in lithography; *v.t.* to counterbalance or compensate. **-shoot** *n.* that which shoots off or separates from a main branch or channel; a descendant. **— side** *a.* (*Football, etc.*) of a player, being illegally ahead of the ball, etc. **-spring** *n.* children; progeny; issue. **off and on,** intermittently [form of *of*].

of·fal (awf′·ạl) *n.* waste meat; entrails of animals; refuse [fr. *off* and *fall*].

of·fend (ạ·fend′) *v.t.* to displease; to make angry; to wound the feelings of; *v.i.* to cause displeasure; to do wrong; to sin. **-er** *n.* [L. *offendere,* to strike against].

of·fense (ạ·fens′) *n.* transgression; sin; insult; wrong; resentment; displeasure; a cause of displeasure. **offensive** *a.* causing or giving offense; used in attack; insulting; unpleasant; *n.* attack; onset; aggressive action. **offensively** *adv.* **offensiveness** *n.* [L. *offendere,* to strike against].

of·fer (awf′·ẹr) *v.t.* to present for acceptance or refusal; to tender; to bid, as a price; to propose; to attempt; to express readiness to do; *v.i.* to present itself or to occur; *n.* an act of offering; a presentation; a price bid; a proposal, esp. of marriage. **-ing** *n.* that which is offered, as a contribution through the church; a sacrifice; a gift. **-er** *n.* [L. *offerre*].

of·fer·to·ry (awf′·ẹr·tor·i·) *n.* (*R.C.*) a part of the mass during which the elements are offered up; the collection of money during the church service; the part of the service, or the music, when offerings are made [L. *offertorium*].

of·fice (awf′·is) *n.* a place for doing business; a duty; a service; a function; an official position; a form of worship; a religious service; **-s** *n.pl.* acts of kindness; help. **-r** *n.* a person who holds an official position; one who holds

commissioned rank in the navy, army, air force, etc. [L. *officium,* duty].

of·fi·cial (ạf·ish′·ạl) *a.* pert. to an office; vouched for by one holding office; authorized; *n.* one holding an office, esp. in a public body. **-ly** *adv.* **-dom** *n.* officials collectively; their work, usually in contemptuous sense [L. *officium,* a duty].

of·fi·ci·ate (ạ·fish′·i·āt) *v.i.* to perform the duties of an officer; to perform a divine service [L. *officium,* duty].

of·fi·cious (ạ·fish′·ạs) *a.* given to exaggerate the duties of an office; importunate in offering service; meddlesome. **-ly** *adv.* **-ness** *n.* [L. *officium,* a duty].

of·ten (awf′·n) *adv.* frequently; many times. **oft, -times, ofttimes,** *adv.* archaic forms of 'often' [O.E. *oft.*].

o·gle (ō′·gl, à′·gl) *v.i.* to make eyes: *v.t.* to make eyes at; to cast amorous glances at; *n.* an amorous glance. **-r** *n.* [L.Ger. *oegeln,* fr. *oegen,* to eye].

o·gre (ō·gẹr) *n.* (*fem.* **ogress**) a fabulous man-eating giant. **-ish, ogrish** *a.* [Fr.]

oh (ō) *interj.* an exclamation of surprise, sorrow, pain, etc. Also **oho!**

ohm (ōm) *n.* the standard unit of electrical resistance. **-meter** *n.* an instrument for measuring electrical current and resistance [fr. George S. *Ohm* (1787-1854)].

oil (oil) *n.* one of several kinds of light viscous liquids, obtained from various plants, animal substances, and minerals, used as lubricants, illuminants, fuel, medicines, etc.; *v.t.* to apply oil to; *v.i.* to take oil aboard as fuel. **-er** *n.* one who, or that which, oils; an oilcan. **-y** *a.* consisting of, or resembling, oil; greasy; fawning; subservient. **-ily** *adv.* **-iness** *n.* **-s** *n.pl.* (*Paint.*) short for 'oil-colors' **-cloth** *n.* coarse canvas cloth coated with oil and pigment to make waterproof, used for table coverings, etc. **— colors** *n.pl.* (*Paint.*) colors made by grinding pigments in oil. **— field** *n.* a region rich in mineral oil. **— painting** *n.* one done in oil colors. **-skin** *n.* cloth made waterproof with oil; *pl.* rain clothes of this material. **— well** *n.* boring made in district yielding petroleum [L. *oleum*].

oint·ment (oint′·mạnt) *n.* an unguent; [O.Fr. *oignement*].

o·kay (ō·kā′) *a.* and *adv.* abbrev. to **O.K.,** an expression signifying approval.

old (ōld) *a.* advanced in age; having lived or existed long; belonging to an earlier period; not new or fresh; stale; out of date. **-en** *a.* old; ancient; pert. to the past. **-ish** *a.* somewhat old. **-ness** *n.* **-fashioned** *a.* out of date; not modern. **Old Harry,** the devil; Satan. **— maid,** a spinster; (*Cards*) a round game. **— master,** a painting by a famous artist, esp. of 15th and 16th cents. **Old Nick,** the devil. **— school.** *a.* old-fashioned. **Old Testament,** the first division of Bible. **Old World,** the Eastern hemisphere [O.E. *eald*].

o·le·ag·i·nous (ō·lē·aj′·ạ·nạs) *a.* oily; greasy; (*Fig.*) fawning; unctuous [L. *oleum,* oil].

o·le·an·der (ō·lē·an′·dẹr) *n.* a beautiful, evergreen shrub with red and white flowers [Fr.].

o·le·as·ter (ō·lē·as′·tẹr) *n.* the wild olive [L. fr. *olea,* an olive].

o·le·o (ō′·lē·ō) *prefix* fr. L. *oleum,* oil. **-graph** *n.* a lithograph in oil colors [Gk. *graphein,* to write].

o·le·o·mar·ga·rine (ō·lē·ō·màrj′·ạ·rạn) *n.* a butter substitute. *Abbrev.* oleo.

ol·fac·tion (ạl·fak′·shạn) *n.* smelling; sense of smell. **olfactory** *a.* pert. to smelling [L. *olere,* to smell; *facere,* to make].

ol·i·gar·chy (ạl′·i·gàr·ki·) *n.* government in which supreme power rests with a few; those who constitute the ruling few. **oligarch** *n.* a member of an oligarchy. **oligarchal** a. Also **oligarchic(al)** [Gk. *oligos*, few; *archein*, to rule].

ol·i·go·cene (ăl'·i·gō·sēn) a. (*Geol.*) pert. to a geological period between the eocene and miocene [Gk. *oligos*, little; *kainos*, recent].

o·li·o (ō'·li·ō) n. a highly-spiced stew of meat and vegetables; a medley [Sp. *olla*, fr. L. *olla*, a pot].

ol·ive (ăl'·iv) n. an evergreen tree, long cultivated in the Mediterranean countries for its fruit; its oval, oil-yielding fruit; a color, of a greyish, ashy green; a. of the color of an unripe olive, or of the foliage. —**branch** n. an emblem or offer of peace. — **oil** n. oil expressed from olives [L. *oliva*].

O·lym·pi·a (ō·lim'·pi·a) (*Class. Hist.*) a plain in ancient Greece, the scene of the Olympic Games. **Olympiad** n. the name given to period of four years between each celebration of Olympic Games. **Olympic** a. pert. to Olympia, or to the games. **Olympics** n.pl. the OlympicGames. -**n** pert. to Mount *Olympus*.

o·me·ga (ō·meg'·a) n. the last letter of the Greek alphabet; hence, the end. **the alpha and omega**, the beginning and the end [Gk.].

om·e·let, omelette (ăm'·let) n. (*Cookery*) a dish of eggs beaten with milk and seasonings and cooked in a frying pan [Fr.].

o·men (ō'·man) n. a sign of future events; a foreboding; v.t. to foreshadow by means of signs; to augur [L.].

om·i·nous (ăm'·a·nas) a. foreboding evil; threatening; inauspicious. -**ly** adv. -**ness** n. [L. *ominosus*, fr. *omen*].

o·mit (ō·mit') v.t. to leave out; to neglect; to fail to perform. *pr.p.* -**ting** *pa.p.*, *pa.t.* -**ted**. **omission** n. the act of omitting; neglect; failure to do; that which is omitted or left undone. **omissible** a. that may be omitted. **omissive** a. [L. *omittere*].

om·ni- (ăm'·ni·) *prefix* fr. L. *omnis*, all.

om·ni·bus (ăm'·na·bus) n. a bus; a. used in the sense of 'several in one,' e.g. — **volume**, a book containing reprints of several works originally published separately; an anthology [L. *omnibus* = for all].

om·ni·far·i·ous (ăm'·ni·făr'·i·as) a. consisting of all varieties [L.].

om·ni·po·tent (ăm·nip'·a·tant) a. all-powerful, esp. of God; almighty. -**ly** adv. **omnipotence** n. unlimited power.

om·ni·pres·ent (ăm·ni·prez'·ant) a. present in all places at the same time. **omnipresence** n. [L. *omnis*, all; and *present*].

om·nis·cience (ăm·nish'·ans) n. infinite knowledge. **omniscient** a. all-knowing.

om·niv·o·rous (ăm·niv'·a·ras) a. all-devouring; eating every kind of food. -**ly** adv. [L. *omnis*, all; *vorare*, to devour].

on (awn, ăn) *prep.* above and touching; in addition to; following from; referring to; at; near; towards, etc.; adv. so as to be on; forwards; continuously [O.E.].

once (wuns) adv. at one time; on one occasion; formerly; ever; n. one time. **at once,** immediately [fr. *one*].

on·com·ing (awn'·, ăn'·kum·ing) a. approaching; n. approach [fr. *on* and *coming*].

one (wun) a. single; undivided; only; without others; identical; n. the number or figure 1, I; the lowest cardinal number; unity; a single specimen; *pron.* a particular but not stated person; any person. -**ness** n. unity; uniformity; singleness. -**self** *pron.* one's own self or person. —**horse** a. drawn by one horse; (*Colloq.*) of no importance; insignificant; paltry. —**sided** a. esp. of a contest, game, etc., limited to one side; considering one side only; partial; unfair. —**way** a. denoting a system of traffic circulation in one direction only [O.E. *an*].

on·er·ous (ăn'·er·as) a. burdensome; oppres-

sive. -**ly** adv. -**ness** n. [L. *oneris*, a load].

on·go·ing (awn'-, ăn'·go·ing) n. a going on; advance; procedure; a. continuing.

on·ion (un'·yan) n. an edible, bulbous plant with pungent odor. — **skin** n. thin, glazed paper [L. *unio*.].

on·look·er (awn'·, ăn'·look·er) n. a spectator; an observer [fr. *on* and *look*].

on·ly (ōn'·li·) a. being the one specimen; single; sole; adv. solely; singly; merely; exclusively; *conj.* but then; except that; with this reservation [O.E. *anlic*, one like].

on·o·mat·o·poe·ia (ăn·a·mat·a·pē'·ya) n. the formation of a word by using sounds that resemble or suggest the object to be named; e.g. *hiss, ping-pong.* **onomatopoeic, onomatopoetic** a. [Gk. *onoma*, a name; *poiein*, to make].

on·set (awn'·, ăn·set) n. a violent attack; an assault [fr. *on* and *set*].

on·shore (awn'·, ăn'·shōr) a. towards the land, esp. of a wind [fr. *on* and *shore*].

on·slaught (awn'·, ăn'·slawt) n. attack; an onset; an assault [Dut. *aanslag*].

on·to (awn'·, ăn'·tòó) *prep.* upon; on the top; to.

on·tol·o·gy (ăn·tăl'·a·ji·) n. the science that treats of reality of being; metaphysics. **ontological** a. **ontologist** n. [Gk. *ōn, ontos*, being; *logos*, discourse].

o·nus (ō'·nas) n. burden; responsibility [L.].

on·ward (awn'·, ăn·werd) a. and adv. advancing; going on; forward. -**s** adv. in a forward direction; ahead [E. *on*; O.E. *weard*, in the direction of].

on·yx (ăn'·iks) n. a variety of quartz [Gk. *onux*, a fingernail].

oo·dles (òó'·dlz) n.pl. (*Slang*) superabundance.

ooze (òóz) n. soft mud or slime; a gentle flow; a kind of deposit on the bottom of the sea; v.i. to flow gently as if through pores; to leak or percolate; v.t. to exude or give out slowly. **oozy** a. [M.E. *wose*, fr. O.E. *wase*, mud].

o·pad·i·ty See **opaque**.

o·pal (ō'·pal) n. a mineral much used as a gem owing to its beautiful and varying hues of green, yellow and red. -**escent** (ō·pal·es'·ant) a. of changing iridiscent color, like an opal. -**escence** n. -**ine** (ō'·pal·in) a. like opal [L. *opalus*].

o·paque (ō·pāk') a. not transparent; impenetrable to light; not lucid; dull-witted. -**ly** adv. -**ness** n. **opacity** n. [L. *opacus*].

ope (ōp) v.t. and i. (*Poet.*) to open.

o·pen (ō'·pn) a. not shut or blocked up; allowing passage in or out; not covered (with trees); not fenced; without restrictions; available; exposed; frank and sincere; n. clear, unobstructed space; v.t. to set open; to uncover; to give access to; to begin; to cut or break into; v.i. to become open; to begin; (*Theater*) to have a first performance. -**er** n. one who or that which opens. -**ing** a. first in order; initial; n. a hole or gap; an open or cleared space; an opportunity; a beginning. -**ly** adv. publicly; frankly. -**ness** n. -**cast** a. (*Mining*) excavated from the surface, instead of from underground. —**handed** a. generous; liberal. —**hearted** a. frank. —**minded** a. free from prejudices [O.E.].

op·er·a (ăp'·a·ra) n. a musical drama; (*Colloq.*) the theater where opera is performed. **operatic** a. pert. to opera. **operetta** n. a short light opera. **grand opera**, opera in which no spoken dialogue is permitted. — **bouffe** (bòóf) n. a farcical play set to music. — **glass** (or **glasses**) n. a small binocular used in theaters. — **hat** n. a man's collapsible tall hat [It. fr. L. *opera*, work].

op·er·ate (ăp'·a·rāt) v.t. to cause to function; to effect; v.i. to work; to produce an effect; to exert power; to perform an act of surgery;

to deal in stocks and shares, esp. speculatively.
operation *n.* the act of operating; a method
or mode of action; treatment involving surgical skill; movement of an army or fleet (usu.
in *pl.*). **operational** *a.* **operative** *a.* having
the power of acting; exerting force; producing the desired effect; efficacious; *n.* artisan or
workman; factory hand. **operator** *n.* [L.
operari, to work].

op·er·cu·lum (ō·pur′·kya·lam) *n.* a lid or
cover, in plants; a lid-like structure in mollusks [L. fr. *operire*, to cover].

op·er·ose (ȧp′·a·rōs) *a.* laborious; industrious.
-ly *adv.* **-ness** *n.* [L. *opus*, work].

oph·i·(o)- *prefix* fr. Gk. *ophis*, a snake.
ophidian (ō·fid′·i·an) *n.* a snake; *a.* snakelike.

oph·thal·mi·a (ȧf·thal′·mi·a) *n.* (*Med.*) inflammation of the eye. **ophthalmic** *a.* of the
eye. **ophthalmologist** *n.* a physician skilled
in the study and treatment of the eye. **ophthalmology** *n.* the science dealing with the
structure, functions, and diseases of the eye.
ophthalmoscope *n.* an instrument for view-
ing the interior of the eye [Gk. *ophthalmos*,
the eye; *logos*, discourse; *skopein*, to view].

o·pi·ate (ō′·pi·at) *n.* any preparation of
opium; a narcotic; anything that dulls or
stupefies; *a.* containing opium; inducing
sleep. **opiatic** *a.* [fr. *opium*].

o·pine (ō·pīn′) *v.t.* and *i.* to think or suppose;
to hold or express an opinion [L. *opinari*].

o·pin·ion (a·pin′·yan) *n.* judgment or belief;
estimation; formal statement by an expert.
-ated *a.* dogmatic [L. *opinio*].

o·pi·um (ō′·pi·am) *n.* narcotic used to induce
sleep or allay pain [Gk. *opion*, poppy-juice].

o·pos·sum (a·pȧs′·am) *n.* a small marsupial
animal. Also **possum** [N. Amer. Ind.].

op·po·nent (a·pō′·nant) *a.* opposite; opposing; antagonistic; *n.* one who opposes [L.
opponere, to place against].

op·por·tune (ȧp·er·tūn′) *a.* well-timed; convenient. **-ly** *adv.* **-ness** *n.* **opportunism** *n.*
the policy of doing what is expedient at the
time regardless of principle. **opportunist** *n.*
opportunity *n.* a fit or convenient time; a
good chance [L. *opportunus*].

op·pose (a·pōz′) *v.t.* to set against; to resist;
to compete with. **opposable** *a.* **-r** *n.* [L.
opponere, to place against].

op·po·site (ȧp′·a·zit) *a.* contrary facing;
contrary; diametrically different; *n.* the contrary; *prep.* and *adv.* in front of; on the
other side; across from; **-ly** *adv.* facing each
other. **-ness** *n.* **opposition** (ȧp·a·zish′·an)
n. the state of being opposite; resistance;
contradiction; an obstacle; a party opposed to
that in power [L. *opponere, oppositum*, to
place against].

op·press (a·pres′) *v.t.* to govern with tyranny; to treat severely; to lie heavily on. **-ion**
(a·presh′·an) *n.* harshness; tyranny; dejection. **-ive** *a.* unreasonably burdensome; hard
to bear. **-ively** *adv.* **-iveness** *n.* **-or** *n.* [L.
opprimere, oppressum, to press down].

op·pro·bri·um (a·prō′·bri·am) *n.* reproach;
disgrace; infamy. **opprobrious** *a.* reproachful and contemptuous; shameful. [L.].

op·pugn (a·pūn′) *v.t.* to dispute; to oppose.
-er *n.* **oppugnant** (a·pug′·nant) *a.* opposing. **-ancy** *n.* opposition [L. *oppugnare*, to
fight against].

opt (ȧpt) *v.i.* to make a choice; to choose.
-ative (ȧp′·ta·tiv) *a.* expressing wish or
desire; *n.* (*Gram.*) a mood of the verb expressing wish. [L. *optare*, to wish].

op·tic (ȧp′·tic) *a.* pert. to the eye or to sight;
pert. to optics; *n.* the eye. **-s** *n.* the science
which deals with light and its relation to
sight. **-al** *a.* pert. to vision; visual. **-ally** *adv.*
optician (ȧp·tish′·an) *n.* a maker of, or

dealer in, optical instruments, esp. spectacles
[Gk. *optikos*].

op·ti·mism (ȧp′·ta·mizm) *n.* belief that everything is ordered for the best; disposition to
look on bright side. **optimist** *n.* believer in
optimism; one who takes hopeful view. **opti-
mistical** *a.* [L. *optimus*, best].

op·tion (ȧp′·shan) *n.* the power or right of
choosing; choice. *a.* left to one's free choice.
-ally *adv.* [L. *optare*, to choose].

op·u·lent (ȧp′·ya·lant) *a.* wealthy; abundantly rich. **-ly** *adv.* **opulence, opulency** *n.*
wealth; riches [L. *opulentus*].

o·pus (ō′·pas) *n.* a work; a musical composition; *pl.* **opera** (ȧp′·a·ra). **magnum opus**,
a writer's most important work [L. *opuscu-
lum* dim. of *opus*, work].

or (awr) *conj.* introducing an alternative;
if not; (*Arch.*) before [M.E. *other*].

or·a·cle (awr′·a·kl) *n.* shrine where ancient
Greeks consulted deity; response given, often
obscure; a person of outstanding wisdom.
o·rac·u·lar (aw·rak′·ya·ler) *a.* **oracularly**
adv. [L. *oraculum*].

o·ral (ō′·ral) *a.* spoken; pert. to the mouth.
-ly *adv.* [L. *os, oris*, the mouth].

or·ange (awr′·inj) *n.* a juicy, gold-colored
citrus fruit; tree bearing it; reddish yellow
color like an orange; *a.* reddish yellow in
color. **-ade** (or·anj·ād′) *n.* drink of orange
juice, sugar, and water [Arab. *naranj*].

o·rang-u·tan, o·rang-ou·tang (ō·rang′·oo·
tang) *n.* a large long-armed ape [Malayan =
man of the woods].

o·rate (ō·rāt′) *v.i.* to talk loftily; to harangue.
oration (ō·rā′·shan) *n.* a formal and dignified public speech. **orator** *n.* one who delivers
an oration; one distinguished for gift of public speaking. **oratorical** *a.* pert. to orator(y);
rhetorical. **oratorically** *adv.* **oratorio** (or·
a·tō′·ri·ō) *n.* a religious musical composition
for voices and orchestra. **oratory** *n.* the art
or exercise of speaking in public; eloquence;
a chapel or small room for private devotions
[L. *orare*, to speak].

orb (awrb) *n.* a sphere or globe; (*Poet.*) a
heavenly body; the globe surmounted by a
cross, which forms part of the regalia in
England; (*Poet.*) the eye. **-it** *n.* (*Astron.*)
path traced by one heavenly body in its revolution round another; range of influence or
action; the eye socket. **-ital** *a.* [L. *orbis*, a
circle].

or·chard (awr′·cherd) *n.* a garden or enclosure containing fruit trees [O.E. *ortgeard*].

or·ches·tra (awr′·kis·tra) *n.* the space in a
theater occupied by musicians; the main floor
of a theater; a group of performers on various musical instruments. **orchestral** *a.* **orchestrate** *v.t.* to arrange music for performance by an orchestra. **-tion** *n.* [Gk.
orcheisthai, to dance].

or·chid, orchis (awr′·kid, awr′·kis) *n.* a
genus of plants with fantastically-shaped
flowers of varied and brilliant colors. **-aceous**
a. pert. to the orchid [Gk. *orchis*, a testicle].

or·dain (awr·dān′) *v.t.* to decree; to destine;
to appoint; to admit to the Christian ministry; to confer holy orders upon. **-ment** *n.*
(rare). **ordination** *n.* the act of ordaining
admission to the ministry [L. *ordo*, order].

or·deal (awr′·dēl, awr′·dē·al) *n.* an ancient
method of trial by requiring the accused to
undergo a dangerous physical test; a trying
experience; a test of endurance [O.E. *ordal*,
a judicial test].

or·der (awr′·der) *n.* rank; class; group; regular arrangement; sequence; succession; method; regulation; a command or direction;
mode of procedure; an instruction; a monastic
society; one of the five styles of architecture
(Doric, Ionic, Corinthian, Tuscan, and Com-

posite); a subdivision of a class of plants or animals, made up of genera; an honor conferred for distinguished civil or military services; in trade, detailed instructions, by a customer, of goods to be supplied. *v.t.* to arrange; to command; to require; to regulate; to systematize; to give an order for. **-ly** *a.* methodical; tidy; well regulated; peaceable; *n.* a soldier following an officer to carry orders; in a hospital, an attendant; *adv.* in right order. **-liness** *n.* **holy orders,** generally, ordination to the Christian ministry. **to take orders,** to accept instructions; (*Church*) to be ordained. **by order,** by command. **in order to,** for the purpose of [L. *ordo,* order].

or·di·nal (awr'·dạ·nạl) *a.* and *n.* showing order or position in a series, e.g. *first, second,* etc.; pert. to an order, of plants, animals, etc. a church service book for use at ordinations [L. *ordo,* order].

or·di·nance (awr'·dạ·nạns) *n.* an established rule, religious rite, or ceremony; a decree [O. Fr. *ordenance*].

or·di·nar·y (awr'·dạ·nẹr·i·) *a.* usual; regular; habitual; normal, commonplace; plain; *n.* something customary; a church service book. **ordinarily** *adv.* [L. *ordo,* order].

or·di·na·tion See **ordain.**

ord·nance (awrd'·nạns) *n.* collective term for heavy mounted guns; military weapons of all kinds, ammunition, etc. [var. of *ordinance*].

or·dure (awr'·jẹr) *n.* dung; filth [O.Fr. *ord.* vile].

ore (ōr) *n.* a native mineral from which metal is extracted [O.E. *ora*].

or·gan (awr'·gạn) *n.* a musical instrument of pipes worked by bellows and played by keys; a member of an animal or plant exercising a special function; a medium of information. **organic** *a.* pert. to or affecting bodily organs; having either animal or vegetable life; derived from living organisms; systematic; organized. **organically** *adv.* **-ism** *n.* an organized body or system; a living body. **-ist** *n.* a player on the organ. — **grinder** *n.* a player of a barrel organ. — **loft** *n.* gallery for an organ. — **stop** *n.* a series of pipes of uniform tone or quality; one of a series of knobs for manipulating and controlling them. **organic chemistry,** the branch of chemistry dealing with the compounds of carbon [Gk. *organon,* an instrument].

or·gan·dy (awr'·gạn·di·) *n.* a muslin of great transparency and lightness. Also **organdie** [Fr. *organdi*].

or·gan·ize (awr·'gạ·nīz) *v.t.* to give a definite structure; to prepare for transaction of business; to get up, arrange, or put into working order; to unite in a society. **organizable** *a.* **organization** *n.* act of organizing; the manner in which the branches of a service, etc., are arranged; individuals systematically united for some work; a society. **-r** *n.* [Gk. *organon,* an instrument].

or·gasm (awr'·gazm) *n.* immoderate action or excitement, esp. sexual. **orgastic** *a.* [Gk. *orgaein,* to be lustful].

or·gy (awr'·ji·) *n.* a drunken or licentious revel; a debauch. **orgiastic** *a.* [Gk. *orgia* (*pl.*) Bacchic rites].

o·ri·el (ō'·ri·ạl) *n.* a projecting window; the recess in a room formed by such a window [O.Fr. *oriol,* a porch].

o·ri·ent (ō'·ri·ạnt) *a.* rising, as the sun; lustrous (applied to pearls); *n.* the east; Eastern countries; *v.t.* to place so as to face the east; to determine the position of, with respect to the east; to take one's bearings. **oriental** *a.* eastern; pert. to, coming from, of, the east; *n.* (*Cap.*) an Asiatic. **orientate** *v.t.* and *i.* to orient; to bring into clearly understood relations. **orientation** *n.* the act of turning to, or determining, the east; sense of

direction; determining one's position [L. *oriens,* rising, fr. *oriri,* to rise].

or·i·fice (awr'·ạ·fis) *n.* a mouth or opening; perforation; vent [L. *orificium,* fr. *os,* the mouth; *facere,* to make].

or·i·gin (awr'·ạ·jin) *n.* beginning; starting point; a source; parentage; birth; nationality. **original** (ạ·rij'·ạ·nạl) *a.* earliest; first; new, not copied or derived; thinking or acting for oneself; *n.* origin; model; a pattern. **originally** *adv.* **originality** *n.* the quality of being original; initiative. **originate** *v.t.* to bring into being; to initiate; *v.i.* to begin; to arise. **originative** *a.* **origination** *n.* **originator** *n.* [L. *origo,* fr. *oriri,* to rise].

o·ri·ole (ō'·ri·ōl) *n.* bird of the thrush family [O.Fr. *oriol,* fr. L. *aurum,* gold.]

or·i·son (awr'·i·zạn) *n.* a prayer [L. *orare,* to pray].

or·mo·lu (awr·mạ·lóó) *n.* an alloy of copper, zinc and tin [Fr. *or,* gold; *moulu* ground, fr. *moudre,* to grind].

or·na·ment (awr'·nạ·mạnt) *n.* decoration; any object to adorn or decorate; *v.t.* to adorn; to beautify; to embellish. **ornamental** *a.* serving to decorate. **ornamentally** *adv.* **ornamentation** *n.* decoration. **ornate** *a.* richly decorated. **ornately** *adv.* **ornateness** *n.* [L. *ornamentum*].

or·ni·tho- *prefix* fr. Gk. *ornis, ornithos,* a bird, used in derivatives. **ornothology** (awr·nạ·thạl'·ạ·ji·) the scientific study of birds. **ornithological** *a.* **ornithologist** *n.* [Gk. *logos,* discourse; *rhunchos,* the beak].

o·ro·tund (ō'·rạ·tund) *a.* of voice or speech, full, clear, and musical; of style, pompous [L. *os, oris,* the mouth; *rotundus,* round].

or·phan (awr'·fan) *n.* and *a.* a child bereft of one or both parents; *v.t.* to make an orphan. **-age** *n.* a home or institution for ophans. **-hood, -ism** *n.* [Gk. *orphanos,* bereaved].

or·pi·ment (awr'·pi·mạnt) *n.* a yellow mineral of the arensic group, used as a dye [L. *aurum,* gold; *pigmentum,* a pigment].

or·rer·y (awr'·ạ·ri·) *n.* a mechanical model of the solar system, showing the revolutions of the planets, etc. [fr. the Earl of *Orrery,* for whom one was made in 1715].

or·ris (awr'·is) *n.* a kind of iris. **-root** *n.* the dried root, used as a powder in perfumery and medicine [form of *iris*].

or·tho·dox (awr'·thạ·dàks) *a.* having the correct faith; sound in opinions or doctrine; conventional. **-ly** *adv.* **-y** *n.* soundness of faith, esp. in religion. **-ness** *n.* [Gk. *orthos,* right; *doxa,* opinion].

or·thog·ra·phy (awr·thàg'·rạ·fi·) *n.* correct spelling. **orthographer** *n.* **orthographic, orthographical** *a.* **orthographically** *adv.* [Gk. *orthos,* correct; *graphein,* to write].

or·tho·pe·dics, orthopaedics (awr·thạ·pēd'·iks) *n.* treatment and cure of bodily deformities, esp. in children. Also **orthop(a)edia, orthop(a)edy. orthopedic** *a.* **orthopedist** *n.* [Gk. *orthos,* straight; *pais, paidos,* a child].

os·cil·late (às'·ạ·lāt) *v.i.* to swing to and fro; to vibrate; to vary between extremes; (*Radio*) to set up wave motion in a receiving set. **oscillation** *n.* a pendulum-like motion; variation between extremes. **oscillator** *n.* **oscillatory** *n.* [L. *oscillare,* to swing].

os·cu·late (às'·kyạ·lāt) *v.t.* and *i.* to kiss; (*Math.*) to touch, as curves; *a.* of species sharing characteristics. **osculant, osculation** *n.* kissing; contact. **osculatory** *a.* [L. *osculum,* a kiss].

os·mi·um (àz'·mi·ạm) *n.* (*Chem.*) a hard, bluish-white metal [fr. Gk. *osmē,* smell].

os·mo·sis (às·mō'·sis) *n.* (*Chem.*) the tendency of fluid substances, if separated by a porous membrane, to filter through it and become equally diffused. **osmotic** (às·màt'·ik) *a.* [Gk. *ōsmos,* fr. *ōthein,* to push].

os·prey (ás'·prē, ·prā) *n.* the fish hawk or sea eagle; erroneously applied to an egret plume used in millinery [corrupt. of *ossifrage,* the sea eagle].

oss- (ás-) *prefix fr.* L. *os, ossis,* bone, used in many derivatives. **-eous** (ás'·ē·ás) *a.* pert. to or resembling bone; bony. **-icle** *n.* a small bone, esp. of the middle ear. **-iferous** *a.* containing, or yielding, bones. **-ification** *n.* hardening into bone. **-ify** *v.t.* to harden into bone; *v.i.* to become bone, of cartilage, etc. **-uary** (ás'·ū·er·i·) *n.* a memorial place for holding the bones of the dead.

os·si·frage (ás'·ạ·frij) *n.* the osprey [L. *ossifraga,* the bonebreaker].

os·te·al (ás'·ti·ạl) *a.* (*Med.*) pert. to, or like, bone. **osteitis** *n.* inflammation of the bone [Gk. *osteon,* bone].

os·ten·si·ble (ás·ten'·sạ·bl) *a.* professed; used as a blind; apparent. **ostensibly** *adv.* **ostensibility** *n.* [L.*ostendere,* to show].

os·ten·ta·tion (ás·tạn·tā'·shạn) *n.* vainglorious display; showing off. **ostentatious** *a.* fond of display; characterized by display **ostentatiously** *adv.* **ostentatiousness** *n.* [L. *ostendere,* to show].

os·te·o- (ás'·ti·ō) *prefix fr.* Gk. *osteon,* bone, used in derivatives mainly medical. **-arthritis** (ár·thrī'·tis) *n.* chronic inflammation of a joint. **osteoid** *a.* resembling bone. **osteology** *n.* that branch of anatomy dealing with bones, their structure, etc. **osteologist** *n.*

os·te·op·a·thy (ás·ti·á'·path·i·) *n.* a system of healing, based on the belief that the human body can effect its own cure with the aid of manipulative treatment of the spinal column, joints, etc.; manipulative surgery. **osteopath** *n.* a practitioner of this system. **osteopathic** *a.* [Gk. *osteon,* bone; *pathos,* feeling].

os·tra·cise (ás'·trạ·sīz) *v.t.* to exclude from society; to exile; to boycott. **ostracism** *n.* exclusion from society; social boycotting [Gk. *ostrakon,* a shell].

os·trich (ás'·trich) *n.* a large flightless bird, native of Africa [Gk. *strouthos*].

oth·er (uTH'·ẹr) *a.* and *pron.* not this; not the same; different; opposite; additional; *adv.* otherwise. **-wise** *adv.* differently; in another way; *conj.* else; if not. **every other,** every second (one); each alternate. **-worldly** *a.* spiritual [O.E. *other*].

o·ti·ose (ō'·shi·ōs, ō'·ti·ōs) *a.* at ease; at leisure; superfluous; futile [L. *otium,* easel].

o·ti·tis (ō·tī'·tis) *n.* (*Med.*) inflammation of the ear. **otology** *n.* [Gk. *ous, ōtos,* the ear].

ot·ta·va ri·ma (a·tà·vạ·rē'·mạ) *n.* a stanza of eight lines [It. *ottava,* octave + *rhyme*].

ot·ter (át'·ẹr) *n.* an aquatic, fish-eating animal of the weasel family [O.E.*otor*].

Ot·to·man (át'·ạ·mạn) *a.* pert. to the Turks; *n.* a cushioned seat without back or arms [fr. Turkish Sultan *Othman,* or *Osman*].

ought (awt) *auxil. v.* to be bound by moral obligation or duty [O.E. *ahte,* owed].

ought (awt) *n.* a form of 'nought'; nothing.

oui·ja (wē'·jạ, ·jē) *n.* board with letters, used at seances to answer questions [Trademark, coined fr. Fr. *oui,* yes; Ger. *ja,* yes].

ounce (ouns) *n.* a unit of weight, abbrev. oz.; in avoirdupois weight = 1/16 of a pound; in troy weight 1/12 of a pound; a fluid measurement [L. *uncia,* a twelfth part].

ounce (ouns) *n.* snow leopard [O.Fr. *once*].

our (our) *n.* belonging to us. **-s** *poss. pron.* used with a noun. **-self** *pron.* myself (in regal or formal style). **-selves** *pron. pl.* we, i.e. not others [O.E. *ure*].

oust (oust) *v.t.* to put out; to expel; to dispossess, esp. by unfair means [O.Fr. *oster;* Fr. *ôter,* to remove].

out (out) *adv.* on, at, or to, the outside; from within; from among; away; not in the usual or right place; not at home; in bloom; disclosed; exhausted; destitute; in error; at a loss; on strike; unemployed; *a.* outlying; remote; *prep.* outside; out of; *interj.* away! begone! *v.t.* to put out; to knock out; **-er** *a.* being on the outside; away from the inside. **-ermost, -most** *a.* [O.E. *ut*].

out·bal·ance (out·bal'·ans) *v.t.* to exceed in weight; to be heavier than.

out·bid (out·bid') *v.t.* to bid more than; to offer a higher price.

out·board (out'·bōrd) *a.* projecting beyond and outside the hull of a ship, e.g. of a ladder; also, of a detachable motor.

out·break (out'·brāk) *n.* a sudden breaking out; a burst, esp. of anger; the beginning, esp. of an epidemic of disease, of war, etc.

out·build·ing (out'·bild·ing) *n.* an outhouse; a building detached from the main building.

out·burst (out'·burst) *n.* a bursting out, esp. of anger, laughter, cheering, etc.

out·cast (out'·kast) *a.* cast out as useless; *n.* one rejected by society.

out·class (out·klas') *v.t.* to exceed in skill or quality; to surpass.

out·come (out'·kum) *n.* issue; result.

out·crop (out'·krảp) *n.* the coming out of a stratum of rock, coal, etc.

out·cry (out'·krī) *n.* a loud cry; a cry of distress, complaint, disapproval, etc.

out·dis·tance (out·dis'·tạns) *v.t.* to surpass in speed; to get ahead of.

out·do (out·dóó') *v.t.* to excel; surpass.

out·door (out'·dōr) *a.* out of doors; in the open air. **-s** *adv.* outside.

out·field (out'·fēld) *n.* the field or fields farthest from the farm buildings; (*Baseball*) the part of the field beyond the diamond or infield; the players there.

out·fit (out'·fit) *n.* a supply of things, esp. clothes, tools, etc., required for any purpose; equipment; kit; (*Slang*) a company of people; a crowd; *v.t.* to supply with equipment, etc. **-ter** *n.* one who supplies equipment.

out·flank (out·flangk') *v.t.* (*Mil.*) to succeed in getting beyond the flank of the enemy.

out·go (out·gō') *v.t.* to go beyond; *n.* (out'·gō) expenditure; outlay. **-ing** *a.* sociable; departing; going out.

out·grow (out·grō') *v.t.* to surpass in growth; to become too large or old for; to grow out of. **-th** *n.* what growth out of anything.

out·house (out'·hous) *n.* a building, separate from main building; a privy.

out·ing (out'·ing) *n.* a going out; an excursion; a trip; an airing.

out·land·ish (out·lan'·dish) *a.* remote; barbarous; not according to custom; queer.

out·law (out'·law) *n.* one placed beyond the protection of the law; a bandit; *v.t.* to declare to be an outlaw. **-ry** *n.* defiance of the law.

out·lay (out'·lā) *n.* expenditure; expenses.

out·let (out'·let) *n.* a passage or way out; an exit; a vent; an opening.

out·line (out'·līn) *n.* the lines that bound a figure; a boundary; a sketch without details; a rough draft; a general plan; *v.t.* to draw in outline; to give a general plan of.

out·live (out·liv') *v.t.* to live longer than.

out·look (out'·look) *n.* a looking out; a prospect; a person's point of view; prospects.

out·ly·ing (out'·lī·ing) *a.* lying at a distance; remote; isolated; detached.

out·mod·ed (out·mō'·dạd) *a.* out of fashion.

out·num·ber (out·num'·bẹr) *v.t.* to exceed in number.

out·pa·tient (out'·pā'·shạnt) *n.* a patient who comes to a hospital, infirmary, etc., for treatment but is non-resident.

out·post (out'·pōst) *n.* (*Mil.*) a small detachment posted some distance from the main body.

out·pour (out·pōr') *v.t.* to pour out; to flow

WEBSTER
M–P

over. **-pour, -ing** n. an overflow.

out·put (out'·poot)n. production; the amount of goods produced in a given time.

out·rage (out'·rāj) n. excessive violence; violation of others' rights; gross insult or indignity; v.t. to do grievous wrong or violence to; to insult grossly. **outrageous** (out·rā'·jas) a. violent; atrocious. **outrageously** adv.

out·ride (out·rīd') v.t. to ride faster than; to ride farther than; (Naut.) of a ship, to live through a storm. **-r** n. a servant on horseback who rides beside a carriage.

out·rig·ger (out'·rig·er) n. (Naut.) a projecting spar for extending sails, ropes, etc.; a frame on the side of a rowing-boat with a rowlock at the outer edge; projecting framework, with a float attached to it, to prevent a canoe from upsetting [earlier outligger; Dut. uitlegger, outlyer].

out·run (out·run') v.t. to exceed in speed; to run farther or faster than; to leave behind.

out·set (out'·set) n. a setting out; commencement; beginning; start.

out·side (out·sīd') n. the outer surface; the exterior; the farthest limit; a. pert. to the outer part; exterior; external; outdoor; adv. not inside; out of doors; in the open air; prep. on the outer part of.**-r** n. one not belonging to a particular party, set, circle, etc.

out·size (out'·sīz) a. and n. larger than the normal size, esp. of garments.

out·skirt (out'·skurt) n. generally in pl. the border; the suburbs of a town.

out·spo·ken (out·spō'·kn) a. not afraid to speak aloud one's opinions; bold of speech.

out·stand·ing (out·stand'·ing) a. standing out; prominent; conspicuous; of debts, unpaid; of work, etc., still to be done.

out·strip (out·strip') v.t. to surpass; to outrun; to leave behind.

out·vote (out·vōt') v.t. to defeat by a greater number of votes.

out·ward (out'·werd) a. pert. to the ouside; external; exterior; adv. towards the outside. **-s** adv. outward; toward the outside. **-ly** adv.

out·weigh (out·wā') v.t. to exceed in weight, value, influence, etc.

out·wit (out·wit') v.t. to defeat by cunning, stratagem, etc.; to get the better of.

o·va (ō'·va) n.pl. eggs; the female germ cells; sing. **ovum** (ō'·vum) **ovary** n. one of two reproductive organs in female animal in which the ova are formed and developed; (Bot.) the part of the pistil containing the seed. **ovarial, ovarian** (ō·ver'·i·al, -an) a. pert. to the ovary [L. ovum, an egg].

o·val (ō'·val) a. egg-shaped; elliptical; n. an oval figure. **-ly** adv. [L. ovum, and egg].

o·va·tion (ō·vā'·shan) n. an enthusiastic burst of applause; a triumphant reception [L. ovatio, to celebrate a triumph].

ov·en (uv'·n) n. an enclosed chamber in a stove, for baking or heating [O.E. ofēn].

o·ver (ō'·ver) prep. above; on; upon; more than; in excess of; across; from side to side of; throughout; etc.; adv. above; above and beyond; going beyond; in excess; too much; past; finished; across; a. upper; outer; covering; n. **-all** a. inclusive [O.E. afer].

o·ver·act (ō·ver·akt') v.t. and i. to play a part (in a play) in an exaggerated manner.

o·ver·all (ō'·ver·awl) n. loose trousers worn over the ordinary clothing as a protection against dirt, etc. Also n.pl.

o·ver·arm (ō'·ver·arm) a. and adv. in swimming, ball, etc., with the hand and arm raised.

o·ver·awe (ō·ver·aw') v.t. to restain by awe.

o·ver·bal·ance (ō·ver·bal'·ans) v.t. to exceed in weight, value, etc.; v.i. to lose balance.

o·ver·bear (ō·ver·ber') v.t. to bear down; to repress; to overpower. **-ing** a. domineering.

o·ver·board (ō'·ver·bōrd) adv. over the side of a ship; out of a ship into the water.

o·ver·cast (ō·ver·kast') v.t. to cast over; to

cloud; to darken; to stitch over roughly. **overcast** a. cloudy; dull.

o·ver·charge (ō·ver·charj') v.t. and i, to load too heavily; to charge too high a price.

o·ver·coat (ō'·ver·kōt) n. an outdoor garment for men worn over ordinary clothing.

o·ver·come (ō·ver·kum') v.t. and i. to conquer; to overpower; to get the better of.

o·ver·do (ō·ver·dóò') v.t. to do to much; to fatigue; to exaggerate. pa.t. **overdid.** pa.p. **overdone** a. exaggerated; over-acted; overcooked.

o·ver·dose (ō·ver·dōs') v.t. to give an excessive dose; n. to take too great a dose.

o·ver·draw (ō·ver·draw') v.t. and i. to exaggerate; to draw money in excess of one's credit. **overdraft** n. act of overdrawing; amount drawn from bank in excess of credit.

o·ver·dress (ō·ver·dres') v.t. and i. to dress too showily for good taste.

o·ver·due (ō·ver·dū') a. unpaid at right time; not having arrived at right time.

o·ver·es·ti·mate (ō·ver·es'·ta·māt) v.t. to estimate too highly.

o·ver·flow (ō·ver·flō) v.t. to flow over; to flood; to fill too full; v.i. to flow over the edge, bank, etc.; to abound. n. what flows over; flood; excess; superabundance; surplus.

o·ver·grow (ō·ver·grō') v.t. to grow beyond; to cover with growth; v.i. to grow beyond normal size. **overgrown** a. covered with grass, weeds, etc. **overgrowth** n.

o·ver·hand (ō'·ver·hand) a. and adv. (Ball, Swimming, etc.) with the hand raised.

o·ver·hang (ō·ver·hang') v.t. and i. to hang over; to jut over; to threaten.

o·ver·haul (ō·ver·hawl') v.t. to examine thoroughly and set in order; to overtake in pursuit. **overhaul** n. a thorough examination, esp. for repairs; repair.

o·ver·head (ō'·ver·hed) a. and adv. over the head; above; aloft; in the sky; the permanent expenses of running a business.

o·ver·hear (ō·ver·hir') v.t. to hear by accident. pa.p. and pa.t. **overheard.**

o·ver·joy (ō·ver·joi') v.t. to fill with great joy.

o·ver·land (ō'·ver·land) a. and adv. wholly by land, esp. of a journey.

o·ver·lap (ō·ver·lap') v.t. and i. to lap over; to rest upon and extend beyond.

o·ver·lay (ō·ver·lā') v.t. to spread over, to cover completely; to span. n. a covering, as a transparent sheet, superimposed on another.

o·ver·lie (ō·ver·lī') v.t. to lie on the top of; to smother a baby by lying on it in bed.

o·ver·load (ō·ver·lōd') v.t. to place too heavy a load on. n. an excessive load.

o·ver·look (ō·ver·look') v.t. to look over; to inspect; to superintend; to fail to notice by carelessness; to excuse; to pardon.

o·ver·lord (ō'·ver·lawrd) n. one who is lord over another; a feudal superior.

o·ver·much (ō·ver·much') a. and adv. too much.

o·ver·night (ō·ver·nīt') adv. through and during the night; on the previous evening.

o·ver·pow·er (ō·ver·pou'·er) v.t. to conquer by superior strength; to subdue; to crush.

o·ver·rate (ō·ver·rāt') v.t. to put too high a value on; to assess too highly.

o·ver·reach (ō·ver·rēch') v.t. to reach beyond; to cheat.

o·ver·ride (ō·ver·rīd') v.t. to ride over; to ride too much; to set aside; to cancel. n. a gear; larger than usual payment.

o·ver·rule (ō·ver·róòl') v.t. to rule against or over; to set aside by superior authority.

o·ver·run (ō·ver·run') v.t. to run over; to grow over, e.g. as weeds; to take possession by spreading over, e.g. as an invading army.

o·ver·seas (ō'·ver·sēz) a. and adv. from or to a country of place over the sea; foreign.

o·ver·see (ō·ver·sē') v.t. to superintend; to

supervise. **overseer** n. a supervisor.

o·ver·shad·ow (ō·ver·shad′·ō) v.t. to cast a shadow over; to outshine (a person).

o·ver·shoe (ō′·ver·shōō) n. a shoe made of rubber, felt, etc., worn over the ordinary shoe.

o·ver·shoot (ō·ver·shōōt′) v.t. to shoot beyond or over; to send too far; to go too far.

o·ver·sight (ō·ver·sīt) n. failure to notice; unintentional neglect; management.

o·ver·state (ō·ver·stāt′) v.t. to exaggerate, **-ment** n. exaggeration.

o·ver·strain (ō·ver·strān′) v.t. and i. to strain too much; (Fig.) to work too hard; n. overwork. **-ed** a.

o·ver·strung (ō·ver·strung′) a. too highly strung; in a state of nervous tension.

o·vert (ō′·vurt) a. open to view. **-ly** adv. [Fr. ouvert, open].

o·ver·take (ō·ver·tāk′) v.t. to come up with; to catch; to take by surprise.

o·ver·throw (ō·ver·thrō′) v.t. to throw over or down; to upset; to defeat. pa.t. **over-threw;** pa.p. **overthrown. overthrow** n. the act of throwing over; defeat; ruin; fall.

o·ver·time (ō′·ver·tīm) n. time at work beyond the regular hours; the extra wages paid for such work.

o·ver·ture (ō·ver·cher) n. an opening of negotiations; a proposal; an offer; (Mus.) an orchestral introduction [Fr. ouvrir, to open].

o·ver·turn (ō·ver·turn′) v.t. and i. to throw down or over; to upset; to turn over.

o·ver·ween·ing (ō·ver·wē′·ning) a. conceited; arrogant [O.E. oferwenian, to become insolent].

o·ver·weight (ō·ver·wāt′) n. excess weight; extra weight beyond the just weight.

o·ver·whelm (ō·ver·hwelm′) v.t. to crush; to submerge; to overpower. **-ing** a. decisive; irresistible. **-ingly** adv. [M.E. whelmen, to overturn].

o·ver·work (ō·ver·wurk′) v.t. and i. to work too hard. **overwork** n. **overwrought** (ō·ver-rawt′) a. tired out; highly excited.

o·vi- (ō′·vi) prefix fr. L. ovum, an egg, used in derivatives. **oviduct** n. a passage for the egg, from the ovary. **oviferous** a. egg-bearing. **oviform** a. egg-shaped. **oviparous** a. producing eggs.

o·vine (ō′·vīn) a. pert. to sheep; like a sheep [L. ovis, a sheep].

o·vo- prefix fr. L. ovum, an egg, used in derivatives. **ovoid** (ō′·void) a. egg-shaped; oval.

o·vum See **ova.**

owe (ō) v.t. to be bound to repay; to be indebted for. **owing** (ō′·ing) a. requiring to be paid [O.E. agan].

owl (oul) n. a night bird of prey; a solemn person. **-et** n. a young owl; a small owl. **-ish** a. owllike in appearance [O.E. ule].

own (ōn) a. is used to emphasize possession, e.g. my own money; v.t. to possess; to acknowledge; to admit; v.i. to confess. **-er** n. the rightful possessor. **-ership** n. right of possession [O.E. agen (a.), agnian (v.)].

ox (åks) n. a large cloven-footed and usually horned farm animal; a male cow. pl. **-en**. **-eye** n. daisylike plant. **-bow** n. U-shaped part of ox yoke [O.E. oxa].

ox·al·ic ac·id (åk·sal′·ik as′·ad) n. a poisonous acid found as an acid salt in wood sorrel. [Gk. oxus, sharp bitter].

ox·blood (åks′·blud) n. deep red color.

ox·ford (åks′·ferd) n. a low shoe laced over the instep [Oxford (England)].

ox·ide (åk′·sīd) n. a compound of oxygen and one other element. **oxidize, oxidate** v.t. and i. to combine with oxygen to form an oxide; of metals, to rust, to become rusty. **oxidiza-tion** n. [Gk. oxus, acid].

ox·y- prefix fr. Gk. oxus sharp, used in derivatives. **-acetylene** (åk′·si·a·set′·a·lēn) a.

denoting a very hot blowpipe flame, produced by a mixture of oxygen and acetylene, and used in cutting steel plates, etc.

ox·y·gen (åk′·si·jan) n. a colorless, odorless, and tasteless gas, forming about ½ by volume of the atmosphere, and essential to life, combustion, etc. **-ate, -ize** v.t. to combine or treat with oxygen. **-ation** n. **-ous** (åk·sij′·a·nas) a. pert. to or obtained from, oxygen [Gk. oxas, acid; gignesthai, to be born].

ox·y·mo·ron (åk·si·mō′·ràn) n. a figure of speech in which two words or phrases of opposite meaning are set together for emphasis or effect, e.g. 'falsely true' [Gk. oxus, sharp; mōros, dull, stupid].

oys·ter (ois′·ter) n. an edible, bivalve shellfish; something from which one may get an advantage [Gk. ostreon].

o·zone (ō′·zōn) n. a condensed and very active form of oxygen with a peculiar, pungent odor; (Colloq.) invigorating air. **ozonic** a. [Gk. ozein, to smell.]

P

pab·u·lum (pab′·ya·lam) n. food; nourishment (for body and mind). **pabular** a. [L.].

pace (pās) n. a step; the length of a step in walking (about 30 inches); gait; rate of movement; v.t. to measure by steps; to set the speed for; v.t. to walk with measured fashion. **-d** a. having a certain gait. **-r** n. one who sets the pace for another [L. passus, a step].

pach·y (pak′·i·) prefix from Gk. pachus, thick, **-derm** (pak′·i·durm) n. a thick-skinned, nonruminant quadruped, e.g. the elephant. **-dermatous** a. thick-skinned; insensitive.

pac·i·fy (pas′·a·fī) v.t. to appease; to tranquilize. **pacifism** n. a doctrine which advocates abolition of war; antimilitarism. **pacifist** n. **pacific** a. peaceful; calm or tranquil; peaceable; not warlike. **pacification**. n. **pacificatory** a. tending to make peace; conciliatory. **pacifier** n. [L. pacificus, peacemaking, fr. pax, peace].

pack (pak) n. bundle for carrying, esp. on back; a lot or set; a band (of animals); a set of playing cards; mass of floating ice; treatment of a fevered patient by enveloping in moist wrapping; army rucksack; v.t. to arrange closely in a bundle, box or bag; to stow away within; to fill, press together; to carry; to load; (with off) to dismiss summarily; v.i. to collect in packs, bales, or bundles. **-age** n. a bundle or parcel. **-er** n. **-et** n. a small package; a packet boat or mail boat. **-et boat** n. a ship that sails regularly for the conveyance of mail and passengers. **— horse** n. a horse for carrying burdens, in panniers or in packs. **-ing** n. any material used to pack, fill up, or make close. **-ing case** n. a box in which to pack goods. **-man** n. a pedlar. **-saddle** n. a saddle for supporting loads on animal's back [Fr. paquet].

pact (pakt) n. an agreement; a compact [L. pactum, a thing covenanted].

pad (pad) n. anything stuffed with soft material, to fill out or protect; a cushion; sheets of paper fastened together in a block; the foot or sole of certain animals; v.t. to furnish with a pad; to stuff; to expand; pr.p. **-ding.** pa.p. and pa.t. **-ded. -ding** n. the material used in stuffing; unnecessary matter inserted in a book, speech, etc., to expand it [etym. uncertain].

pad (pad) n. an easy-paced horse; a highway

robber; *v.i.* to trudge along; to travel on foot [Dut. *pad*, a path].

pad·dle (pad'·l) *n.* a short oar with a broad blade at one or each end; a balance or float of a paddle wheel, a flipper; *v.t.* and *i.* to propel by paddles [etym. uncertain].

pad·dle (pad'·l) *v.i.* to walk with bare feet in shallow water; to dabble [etym. uncertain].

pad·dock (pad'·ak) *n.* a small grass field or enclosure where horses are saddled before race [earlier *parrock*, fr. O.E. *pearroc*, a park].

pad·dy (pad'·i·) *n.* rice in the husk; rice in general [Malay *padi*].

pad·lock (pad'·lak) *n.* a detachable lock with a hinged hoop to go through a staple or ring; *v.t.* to fasten with a padlock [etym. uncertain].

pa·dre (pa'·dra, drē) *n.* priest; chaplain [It. and Sp. = father, fr. L. *pater*].

pae·an (pē'·an) *n.* orig. a joyful song in honor of Apollo; hence, any shout, song, or hymn of triumph or praise [Gk. *Paian*, the physician of the Gods, epithet of Apollo].

pa·gan (pā'·gan) *n.* a heathen; *a.* heathenish; idolatrous, **-ish** *a.* **-ize** *v.t.* to render pagan. **-ism** *n.* [L. *paganus*, a peasant].

page (pāj) *n.* one side of a leaf of a book or manuscript; *v.t.* to number the pages of. [Fr. *page*, fr. L. *pagina*, a leaf].

page (pāj) *n.* formerly a boy in service of a person of rank; a uniformed boy attendant esp. in a hotel; *v.t.* to summon by sending a page to call [Fr. *page*].

pag·eant (paj'·ant) *n.* a show of persons in costume in procession, dramatic scenes, etc. a spectacle. **-ry** *n.* a brilliant display; pomp [L. *pagina*, a stage].

pa·go·da (pa·gō'·da) *n.* a temple or sacred tower in India, Burma, etc. [Port. *pagode*].

paid (pād) *pa.p.* and *pa.t.* of the verb **pay**.

pail (pāl) *n.* a round, open vessel of wood, tin, etc., for carrying liquids; a bucket.

pain (pān) *n.* bodily or mental suffering; distress; *pl.* trouble; exertion; *v.t.* to inflict bodily or mental suffering upon. **-ful** *a.* full of pain; causing pain; difficult; **-fully** *adv.* **-fulnes** *n.* **-less** *a.* **-lessly** *adv.* **-lessness** *n.* **-staking** *a.* carefully laborious [L.*poema*, punishment].

paint (pānt) *n.* coloring matter for putting on surface with brush, etc.; *v.t.* to cover or besmear with paint; to make a picture with paint; to adorn with, or as with, paint; *v.i.* to practice the art of painting. **-er** *n.* **-ing** *n.* laying on colors; the art of representing natural objects in colors; a picture in paint [L. *pingere*, to paint].

paint·er (pān'·ter) *n.* a rope at the bow of a boat used to fasten it to any other object [Gk. *panthera*, hunting net].

pair (par) *n.* two things of a kind; a single article composed of two similar pieces, e.g. a pair of scissors; a courting, engaged, or married couple; a mated couple of animals or birds; *v.t.* to unite in couples; *v.i.* to be joined in couples; to mate [L. *par*, equal].

pa·ja·mas (pa·ja'·maz) *n.pl.* loose trousers, worn by Mohammedans; a sleeping suit. Also **pyjamas** [Pers. *pāejāmas*, a leg garment].

pal (pal) *n.* (*Colloq.*) a close friend [Gipsy].

pal·ace (pal'·is, as) *n.* the house in which a great personage, resides; any magnificent house. **palatial** (pa·lā'·shal) *a.* [L. *palatium*].

pal·a·din (pal'·a·din) *n.* a knight-errant; one of the twelve peers of Charlemagne [L. *palatinus*, an officer of the palace].

pal·an·quin, palankeen (pal·an·kēn') *n.* a light, covered litter suspended from poles and borne on the shoulders of men—used in India and the East. [Hind. = a bed].

pal·ate (pal'·at) *n.* the roof of the mouth; sense of taste; relish; liking. **palatable** *a.*

agreeable to the taste or mind; savory. **palatably** *adv.* **palatal** *a.* pert. to palate; of a sound, produced by placing tongue against palate [L. *palatum*].

pa·la·tial See **palace.**

pal·a·tine (pal'·a·tīn) *a.* pert. to a palace; having royal privileges; *n.* one who possesses royal privileges; a count palatine. **palatinate** *n.* the office or dignity of a palatine; the territory under his jurisdiction [L. *Mons Palatinus*, the Palatine hill].

pa·lav·er (pa·la'·ver) *n.* idle talk; empty conversation [Port. *palavra*, a word].

pale-, palae-, paleo-, palaeo- *prefix* from Gk. *palaios*, ancient. **-ography** (pāl·ē·ag'·ra·fi·) *n.* ancient writings; act of deciphering ancient writings. **-ographic** *a.* **-ographer** *n.* **-olith** (pāl'·ē·a·lith) *n.* an unpolished stone implement of the earlier stone age. **-olithic** *a.* **-ology** (pāl·ē·al'·a·ji·) *n.* study of antiquities; archaeology. **-ologist** *n.* **-ontology** (pāl·ē·an·tal'·a·ji) *n.* study of fossils. **-ontologist** *n.* **-ontological** *a.* **-ozoic** (pāl·ē·a·zō'·ik) *a.* denoting the lowest fossiliferous strata and the earliest forms of life.

pale (pāl) *a.* faint in color; not ruddy or fresh; whitish; dim; wan; *v.t.* to make pale; *v.i.* to become pale. **-ly** *adv.* **-ness** *n.* **palish** *a.* somewhat pale. **-face** *n.* name given to a white person by Red Indians [Fr. *pâle*, fr. L. *pallidus*, pale].

pale (pāl) *n.* a pointed wooden stake; a narrow board used for making a fence; a boundary; *v.t.* to enclose with stakes; to encompass. [fr. L. *palus*, a stake].

pal·ette (pal'·it) *n.* a thin oval board on which a painter mixes his colors [L. *pala*, a spade].

pal·frey (pawl'·fri·) *n.* a small saddle horse, esp. for a lady [O. Fr. *palefrei*, fr. L. *paraveredus*, an extra post horse].

Pa·li (pa'·lē) *n.* the sacred language of the Buddhists [Sans. *pāli*, canon].

pal·in·drome (pal'·in·drōm) *n.* a word or sentence that is the same when read backward or forward, e.g. *level* [Gk. *palin*, back; *dromos*, running].

pal·i·sade (pal·a·sād') *n.* fence of pales or stakes; (*pl.*) an expanse of high cliffs; *v.t.* to enclose with palisades [L. *palus*, stake].

pall (pawl) *n.* a large, usually black cloth laid over the coffin at a funeral; an ecclesiastical mantle; something that spreads gloom [L. *pallium*, a cloak].

pall (pawl) *v.t.* to make tedious or insipid; *v.i.* to become tedious or insipid [prob. shortened fr. *appal*].

Pal·la·di·an (pa·lā'·di·an) *a.* denoting a classical style of architecture [fr. Andria *Palladio*, a 16th cent. Italian architect].

pal·la·di·um (pa·lā'·di·am) *n.* a rare metal of the platinum group [fr. Gk. *Pallas*].

pal·la·di·um (pa·lā'·di·am) *n.* a safeguard; *pl.* **paladia**. [Gk. *Palladion*].

pal·let (pal'·it) *n.* a palette; a tool with a flat blade used by potters, etc. [form of *palette*].

pal·li·ate (pal'·i·āt) *v.t.* to lessen or abate without curing; to excuse or extenuate. **palliation** *n.* **palliative** (pal'·i·ā·tiv) *a.* serving to extenuate, to mitigate. *n.* that which mitigates, alleviates [L. *palliatus*, dressed in a cloak].

pal·lid (pal'·id) *a.* deficient in color; pale; wan, **-ly** *adv.* **-ness** *n.* **pallor** *n.* paleness [L. *pallidus*, pale].

palm (pam) *n.* the inner, slightly concave surface of hand, between wrist and fingers; lineal measure, reckoned as 3 or 4 inches; flat, expanding end of any arm-like projection, esp. blade of oar; that part of glove that covers palm; *v.t.* to conceal in the palm; to impose by fraud (with 'off'). **palmar** (pal'·

mer) *a.* pert. to the palm. **palmate** *a.* having shape of hand; (*Zool.*) web-footed. **-ist** *n.* one who claims to tell fortunes by the lines on the palm of the hand. **-istry** *n.* [L. *palma,* the palm].

palm (pám) *n.* a branchless, tropical tree; a branch or leaf of this tree used as a symbol of victory; prize or honor. **-er** (pá'·mer) *n.* in the Middle Ages, one who visited the Holy Land, and bore a branch of palm in token thereof; an itinerant monk. **-etto** *n.* a species of palm tree. **-y** *a.* bearing palms; (*Fig.*) prosperous; flourishing. (*Cap.*) — **Sunday,** Sunday before Easter [L. *palma,* a palm].

pal·my·ra (pal·mĭ'·ra) *n.* a tall E. Indian palm [Port. *palmeira*].

pal·pa·ble (pal'·pa·bl) *a.* capable of being touched or felt; certain; obvious. **palpably** *adv.* **-ness** *n.* **palpate** *v.t.* (*Med.*) to examine with the hand. **palpation** *n.* [L. *palpare,* to feel].

pal·pi·tate (pal'·pa·tāt) *v.i.* to beat rapidly, as heart; to throb; to pulsate. **palpitation** *n.* [L. *palpitare,* fr. *palpare,* to feel].

pal·sy (pawl'·zi·) *n.* paralysis; *v.t.* to paralyze. **palsied** *a.* [fr. *paralysis*].

pal·ter (pawl'·ter) *v.i.* to trifle with; to deal evasively; to use trickery; to dodge. **-er** *n.* **paltry** *a.* mean; worthless. **paltriness** *n.*

pam·pas (pam'·paz) *n.pl.* vast grassy, treeless plains in S. America [Sp. *pampas,* fr. Peruv. *bamba,* a plain].

pam·per (pam'·per) *v.t.* to gratify unduly; to over-indulge; to coddle. **-er** *n.* [perh. L. Ger. *pampen,* to cram].

pam·phlet (pam'·flit) *n.* a thin, paper-covered, unbound book; a short treatise or essay on a current topic. **-eer** *n.* a writer of pamphlets [O.Fr. *Pamphilus,* the title of a medieval poem].

pan (pan) *n.* a broad, shallow metal vessel for house hold use; anything resembling this; of an old type of gun, part of the flintlock that held the priming; abbrev. of brainpan, the upper part of the skull; *v.t.* and *i.* to wash gold-bearing soil in a pan in order to separate earth and gold; (*Colloq.*) to criticize; to turn out (fr. *panorama*) [O.E. *panne*].

pan- (pan) *prefix* fr. Gk. *pas, pantos,* all, used in such words as **Pan-American** *a.* pert. to movement of the American republics to foster collaboration between N. and S. America.

pan·a·ce·a (pan·a·sē'·a) *n.* a cure for all diseases; a universal remedy [Gk. *panakeia,* a universal remedy].

pa·nache (pa·nash') *n.* plume of feathers used as an ornament on a cap, etc. [Fr.].

Pan·a·ma (pan·a·má') *n.* a hat made of fine, pliant strawlike material [made in S. America, but not in *Panama*].

pan·cake (pan'·kāk) *n.* a thin cake of batter fried in a pan; *v.i.* to land an airplane almost vertically and in a level position.

pan·chro·mat·ic (pan·krō·mat'·ik) *a.* (*Phot.*) pert. to plates or films which, although reproduced in monochrome, give to all colors their proper values [Gk. *pan,* all; *chrōma,* color].

pan·cre·as (pan'·krē·as) *n.* (*Anat.*) digestive gland behind stomach; in animals, the sweetbread. **pancreatic** *a.* [Gk. *pan,* all; *kreas,* flesh].

pan·da (pan'·da) *n.* a raccoon-like animal; the bearcat [Native word].

pan·dect (pan'·dekt) *n.* usually a treatise that contains the whole of any science; *pl.* any code of laws [Gk. *pandektēs,* all receiving, comprehensive].

pan·dem·ic (pan·dem'·ik) *a.* of a disease, universal; widely distributed; affecting a nation [Gk. *pan,* all; *dēmos,* people].

pan·de·mo·ni·um (pan·da·mō'·ni·am) *n.* the abode of evil spirits; any disorderly, noisy place or gathering; a riotous uproar [Gk. *pan,* all; *daimōn,* a demon].

pan·der (pan'·der) *n.* a go-between in base love intrigues; *v.i.* to act as a pander; to help to satisfy any unworthy desires [fr. *Pandarus,* in Chaucer's *Troilus and Cressida*].

pane (pān) *n.* a sheet of glass in a window; a square in a pattern. **-d** (pānd) *a.* [Fr. *pan,* a flat section].

pan·e·gyr·ic (pan·a·jir'·ik) *n.* a speech or writing of praise; a eulogy. **-al** *a.* **panegyrist** *n.* one who writes or pronounces a eulogy. **panegyrize** *v.t.* to praise highly [Gk. *pan,* all; *agora,* an assembly].

pan·el (pan'·al) *n.* a rectangular piece of cloth, parchment, or wood; a sunken portion of a door, etc.; a list of jurors; a jury; a group of speakers, etc. *v.t.* to divide into, or decorate with panels. **-ing** *n.* paneled work. **-ist** *n.* member of a panel [O.Fr. = a small panel].

pang (pang) *n.* a sudden pain, physical or mental [etym. doubtful].

pan·ic (pan'·ik) *n.* sudden terror, often unreasoning; infectious fear; *a.* extreme and illogical (of fear); *v.i.* to be seized with sudden, uncontrollable fright. *pr.p.* **panicking.** *pa.p. and pa.t.* **panicked. panicky** *a.* affected by panic. — **stricken,** — **struck** *a.* seized with paralyzing fear [Gk. = fear excited by *Pan*].

pan·ier (pan'·yer) *n.* one of a pair of baskets carried on each side of a pack animal; a puffing-out round hips of a lady's skirt; framework to achieve this [L. *panarium,* a breadbasket].

pan·o·ply (pan'·a·pli·) *n.* a complete suit of armor; anything that covers or envelops completely. **panoplied** *a.* fully armed [Gk. *pan,* all; *hopla,* arms].

pan·o·ram·a (pan·a·rá'·ma) *n.* a complete view in every direction; a picture exhibited by being unrolled and made to pass continuously before the spectator. **panoramic** *a.* [Gk. *pan.* all; *horama,* a view].

pan·sy (pan'·zi·) *n.* a cultivated species of violet with richly colored flowers; (*Slang*) an effeminate man [Fr. *pensée,* thought].

pant (pant) *v.i.* to breathe quickly and in a labored manner; to gasp for breath; to yearn (with 'for' or 'after'); *v.t.* to utter gaspingly; *n.* a gasp [O.Fr.].

pan·ta·loon (pan·ta·lóon') *n.(pl.)* tight trousers [It. *pantalone,* buffoon].

pan·the·ism (pan'·thē·izm) *n.* the doctrine that identifies God with the universe, everything being considered as part of or a manifestation of Him. **pantheist** *n.* **pantheistic (al)** *a.* **pantheology** *n.* a system which embraces all religions and all gods [Gk. *pan,* all; *theos,* god].

pan·ther (pan'·ther) *n.* (*fem.* **-ess**) a variety of leopard [Gk. *panthēr*].

pan·to- (pan'·ta) *prefix* fr. Gk. *pas, pantos,* all, used in derivatives. **-graph** (pant'·a·graf) *n.* an instrument for copying drawings, maps, etc., on an enlarged, a reduced, or the same scale [Gk. *graphein,* to write].

pan·to·mime (pant'·a·mīm) *n.* a dramatic entertainment in dumb show; a gesture without speech; *v.t.* and *i.* to act or express by gestures only. **pantomimic** *a.* **pantomimist** *n.* [Gk. *pas, pantos,* all; *mimos,* mimic].

pan·try (pan'·tri·) *n.* a small room for storing food or kitchen utensils [L. *panis,* bread].

pants (pants) *n.pl.* (*Colloq.*) trousers [abbrev. of *pantaloons*].

pap (pap) *n.* soft food for infants, etc. [fr. baby language].

pap (pap) *n.* a nipple; a teat; something resembling a nipple [M.E. *pappe*].

pa·pa·cy (pā'·pa·si·) *n.* the office and dignity of the Pope; Popes collectively. **papal** (pā'·pál) *a.* [It. *papa,* father].

pa·pav·er·ous (pa·pav'·er·as) *a.* pert. to or resembling the poppy. Also **papaveraceous** *a.* [L. *papaver,* the poppy].

pa·paw, pawpaw (pạ·paw′) *n.* a N. American tree with purple flowers and edible yellow fruit [Sp. *papayo*].

pa·per (pā′·pẹr) *n.* a material made by pressing pulp of rags, straw, wood, etc., into thin flat sheets; a sheet of paper written or printed on; a newspaper; an article or essay; a document; wall covering; a set of examination questions; *n.pl.* document(s) establishing one's identity; ship's official documents; *a.* consisting of paper; *v.t.* to cover with paper. **-y** *a.* resembling paper. — **clip** *n.* a device for holding together sheets of paper. — **hanger** *n.* one who hangs paper on walls. — **knife** *n.* a knife with a blunt blade for opening envelopes, etc. — **money** *n.* official pieces of paper issued by a government or bank for circulation. **-weight** *n.* small, heavy object to prevent loose sheets of paper from being displaced [O.F. *papier*, fr. L. *papyrus*, paper].

pa·pier-mâ·ché (pā·pẹr·mạ·shā′) *n.* paper pulp, mixed with glue, etc., shaped or molded into articles [Fr. *papier*, paper; *mâché*, chewed].

pa·pil·la (pạ·pil′·ạ) *n.* a small nipple-shaped protuberance in a part of the body, e.g. on surface of tongue [L. *papilla*, the nipple].

pa·pist (pā′·pist) *n.* a supporter of the papal system; a Roman Catholic. **papistic(al)** *a.* **-ry** *n.* [Fr. *papiste*, fr. *pape*, the Pope].

pa·poose (pa·pòós′) *n.* a N. Amer. Indian baby.

pap·pus (pap′·ạs) *n.* down, as on the seeds of the thistle, dandelion, etc. **pappose** (pap·ōs′) *a.* downy [Gk. *pappos*, down].

pap·ule (pap′·ūl) *n.* a pimple [L.].

pa·py·rus (pạ·pī′·rạs) *n.* a species of reed, the pith of which was used by the ancients for making paper; a manuscript on papyrus. *pl.* **papyri** [Gk. *papyros*, an Egyptian rush].

par (pạr) *n.* equality of value or circumstances; face value (of stocks and shares); (*Golf*) the number of strokes for hole or course in perfect play [L. *par*, equal].

par·a·ble (par′·ạ·bl) *n.* story or allegory with a moral. **parabolical** *a.* **parabolically** *adv.* [Gk. *parabolē*, a comparison].

pa·rab·o·la (pạ·rab′·ạ·la) *n.* (*Geom.*) a conic section made by a plane parallel to side of cone. **parabolic** *a.* **paraboloid** *n.* solid formed when parabola is revolved round its axis [Gk. *para*, beside; *bolē*, a throw].

par·a·chute (par′·ạ·shòòt) *n.* a collapsible umbrellalike device used to retard the descent of a falling body. **parachutist** *n.* — **troops** *n.pl.* See **paratroops** [Fr. *parer*, to make ready; *chute*, a fall].

par·a·clete (par′·ạ·klēt) *n.* (*Bib.*) the name given to the Holy Spirit; one called to aid or support; an advocate [Gk. *paraklētos*, called to help].

pa·rade (pạ·rād′) *n.* a public procession; a muster of troops for drill or inspection; the ground on which such a muster takes place; display; show; *v.t.* to make a display or spectacle of; to marshal in military order; *v.i.* to march in military array; to march in procession with display [L. *parare*, to prepare].

par·a·digm (par′·ạ·dim) *n.* an example; a model; (*Gram.*) a word, esp. a noun, verb, etc., given as an example of grammatical inflexions. **-atic** (par·ạ·dig·mat′·ik) *a.* **-atically** *adv.* [Gk. *paradeigma*, a model].

par·a·dise (par′·ạ·dīs) *n.* the garden of Eden; Heaven; a state of bliss. **paradisaic** (par·ạ·di·sā′·ik), **paradisaical** *a.* pert. to or like paradise [Gk. *paradeisos*, a pleasure-ground].

par·a·dox (par′·ạ·dáks) *n.* a statement seemingly absurd or self-contradictory, but really founded on truth. **-ical** *a.* **-ically** *adv.* [Gk. *para*, against; *doxa*, an opinion].

par·af·fin (par′·ạ·fin) *n.* a white wax-like substance obtained from crude petroleum, shale, coal tar, wood, etc. [L. *parum*, little; *affinis*, related].

par·a·gon (par′·ạ·gạn) *n.* a pattern of excellence [It. *paragone*].

par·a·graph (par′·ạ·graf) *n.* a distinct part of a writing; a section or subdivision of a passage, indicated by the sign ¶, or begun on a new line; *v.t.* to arrange in paragraphs. **-ic** *a.* [Gk. *paragraphos*, a marginal stroke].

par·a·keet (par′·ạ·kēt) *n.* a small long-tailed parrot. Also **parrakeet, paroquet** [Fr. *perroquet*, a parrot].

par·al·de·hyde (pạ·ral′·dạ·hīd) *n.* a powerful hypnotic [Gk. *para* and *aldehyde*].

par·al·lel (par′·ạ·lel) *a.* continuously at equal distance apart; precisely corresponding; similar; *n.* a line equidistant from another at all points; a thing exactly like another; a comparison; a line of latitude; *v.t.* to make parallel; to represent as similar; to compare. **-ism** *n.* the state of being parallel; comparison, resemblance. — **bars**, horizontal bars for gymnastic exercises [Gk. *parallēlos*, beside one another].

par·al·lel·o·gram (par·ạ·lel′·ạ·gram) *n.* a four-sided plane figure with both pairs of opposite sides parallel [Gk. *parallēlos*, beside one another; *gramma*, a line].

pa·ral·y·sis (pạ·ral′·ạ·sis) *n.* (*Med.*) loss of power of movement or sensation. **paralyze** (par′·ạ·liz) *v.t.* to affect with paralysis; to make useless; to cripple. **paralytic** *a.* pert. to, affected with, paralysis; *n.* one affected with paralysis. **infantile paralysis**, inflammation of grey matter in spinal cord, usually in children; poliomyelitis [L., fr. Gr. *paralysis*, to loosen at the side].

par·a·mount (par′·ạ·mount) *a.* superior; of highest importance; chief. **-cy** *n.* **-ly** *adv.* [Fr. *par amont*, upwards].

par·a·mour (par′·ạ·moor) *n.* a partner in an illicit love intrigue [Fr. *par amour*, through love].

par·a·noi·a, paranoea (par·ạ·noi′·ạ, ·nē′·ạ) *n.* (*Med.*) a form of chronic insanity, often characterized by delusions of grandeur, persecution, etc. **paranoiac** *a.* and *n.* [Gk. *para*, beside; *noein*, to think].

par·a·pet (par′·ạ·pet) *n.* a low wall or railing at the edge of a bridge, quay, balcony, etc.; a breastwork to protect soldiers [It. *parare*, to ward off; *petto*, the breast].

par·a·pher·na·li·a (par·ạ·fẹ(r)·nā′·li·ạ, ·nāl′·yạ) *n.pl.* personal belongings; furnishings or accessories; (*Law*) goods of wife beyond dowry [Gk. *para*, beyond; *phernē*, a dower].

par·a·phrase (par′·ạ·frāz) *n.* a restatement of a passage; a free translation into the same or another language; an interpretation; *v.t.* to express in other words; to interpret freely. [Gk. *para*; *phrazein*, to speak].

par·a·site (par′·a·sīt) *n.* formerly, one who habitually ate at the table of another, repaying with flattery; a hanger-on; a plant or animal that lives on another. **parasitic** *a.* **parasitically** *adv.* **parasitology** *n.* the study of parasites, esp. as causes of disease. **parasitological** *a.* **parasitologist** *n.* [Gk. *parasitos*; fr. *para*, beside; *sitos*, food].

par·a·sol (par′·ạ·sawl) *n.* a small, light sun umbrella [It. *parare*, to ward off; *sole*, the sun].

par·a·troops (par′·ạ·tròóps) *n.pl.* (*World War* 2) troops organized to descend by parachute with their equipment from airplanes and gliders. **paratrooper** *n.*

par·boil (pàr′·boil) *v.t.* to boil partially; to precook [L. *per*, thoroughly, confused with 'part'; *boil*].

par·cel (pàr′·sạl) *n.* (*Arch.*) a part or portion, a bundle or package (wrapped in paper);

a number of things forming a group or lot; a piece of land; *v.t.* to divide into portions; to distribute; to wrap up. [Fr. *parcelle*, a little part].

parch (pàrch) *v.t.* to scorch; to shrivel with heat; to dry to an extreme degree; *v.i.* to be dry from heat [M.E. *parchen*].

parch·ment (pàrch′·mạnt) *n.* the skin of a sheep or goat, etc., prepared for writing on; a document written on this [fr. *Pergamum* in Asia Minor, here first used].

par·don (pàr′·dạn) *v.t.* to forgive; to free from punishment; to excuse; *n.* forgiveness; remission of a penalty. **-able** *a.* excusable. [Fr. *pardonner*].

pare (par) *v.t.* to cut or shave off; to remove the outer skin; to peel. **-er** *n.* **paring** *n.* the action of peeling; that which is pared off [Fr. *parer*, to make ready].

par·e·gor·ic (par·ạ·gawr′·ik) *a.* soothing; assuaging pain; *n.* a soothing medicine [Gk. *parēgorikos*, comforting].

par·ent (par·ạnt) *n.* a father or mother; one who, or that which, brings forth or produces. **-age** *n.* descent from parents; birth; extraction. **parental** (pạ·ren′·tạl) *a.* pert. to, or becoming, parents; tender; affectionate. **parentally** *adv.* [L. *parere*, to bring forth].

pa·ren·the·sis (pạ·ren′·thạ·sis) *n.* a word or sentence inserted in a passage independently of the grammatical sequence and usually marked off by brackets, dashes, or commas; **parentheses** (-sēz) *n.pl.* round brackets ( ), used for this. **parenthetic, parenthetical** *a.* expressed as a parenthesis; interposed. [Gk. *para*, beside; *en*, in; *thesis*, a placing].

pa·ri·ah (pạ·rī′·ạ) *n.* in S. India, one deprived of all religious or social rights; a member of the lowest or no caste; an outcast from society [Tamil, *paraiyar*, a drummer].

pa·ri·e·tal (pạ·rī′·ạ·tạl) *a.* pert. to a wall; pert. to the wall of the body or its cavities [L. *paries* a wall].

par·ish (par′·ish) *n.* an ecclesiastical district under a priest or clergyman; a local church and its area of activity; *a.* pert. to a parish. **parishioner** (pạ·rish′·an·er) *n.* an inhabitant of a parish; a member of a parish church [Gk. *para*, beside; *oikos*, a dwelling].

par·i·ty (par′·ạ·ti·) *n.* equality; analogy; close correspondence [L. *par, paris*, equal].

park (pàrk) *n.* a large piece of ground, usually with grass and trees for public use and recreation; a sports' ground; grounds around a country house; *v.t.* to enclose in a park; to leave an automobile in a certain place [O.E. *pearroc*; Fr. *parc*].

par·ka (pàr′·kạ) *n.* an Eskimo garment of undressed skin; a hooded outer garment [Aleutian].

par·lance (pàr′·lạns) *n.* a way of speaking; **parley** (pàr′·li·) *n.* a meeting between leaders of opposing forces to discuss terms; *v.i.* to hold a discussion about terms [Fr. *parler*, to speak].

par·lia·ment (pàr′·lạ·mạnt) *n.* (*usually cap.*) the supreme legislature of the United Kingdom, composed of the House of Lords and House of Commons; any similar assembly. **-ary** *a.* pert. to, enacted by, or according to, the established rules of parliament; of language, admissible in parliamentary debate, hence, decorous and non-abusive. **-arian** *n.* a skilled debater in parliament [Fr. *parlement*, fr. *parler*, to speak].

par·lor, parlour (pàr′·lẹr) *n.* living room; a semi-private room in an inn [Fr. *parloir*, fr. *parler*, to speak].

par·lous (pàr′·lạs) *a.* (*Arch.*) perilous; critical [fr. *perilous*].

Par·nas·sus (pàr·nas′·ạs) *n.* a mountain in ancient Greece, sacred to Apollo and the

Muses; (*Fig.*) poetry; an anthology of poetry.

pa·ro·chi·al (pạ·rō′·ki·ạl) *a.* pert. to a parish; provincial; narrow-minded **-ly** *adv.* **-ism** *n.* [L. *parochia*, a parish, fr. Gk. *paroikein* to dwell near].

par·o·dy (par′·ạ·di·) *n.* an imitation of a poem, song, etc., where the style is the same but the theme ludicrously different; a feeble imitation; *v.t.* to write a parody of; to burlesque in verse. **parodist** *n.* [Gk. *para*, beside (i.e. imitating); *ōdē*, a song].

pa·role (pạ·rōl′) *n.* release of a prisoner on condition of good behavior; word of honor, esp. a promise given by a prisoner of war not to attempt to escape [Fr. *parole*, a word].

par·o·no·ma·si·a (par·ạ·nō·mā′·zhi·ạ, ·zi·ạ) *n.* a play on words; a pun. **paronym** *n.* a word similar to another in having the same derivation or root. **paronymous** *a.* [Gk. *para*, beside; *anoma*, a name].

pa·rot·id (pạ·ràt′·id) *a.* near the ear; *n.* a large salivary gland, in front of and below the ear [Gk. *para*, beside; *ous, ōtos*, the ear].

par·ox·ysm (par′·ák·sizm) *n.* sudden, violent attack of pain, rage, laughter; fit; convulsion [Gk. *para*, beyond; *oxus*, sharp].

par·quet (pàr′·kā, -ket) *n.* flooring of wooden blocks; *v.t.* to lay such a floor. **-ry** *n.* [Fr. flooring].

parr (pàr) *n.* a young salmon.

par·ri·cide (par′·ạ·sīd) *n.* one who murders his parent, a near relative, or a person who is venerated; the crime itself [L. *pater*, a father; *caedere*, to kill].

par·rot (par′·ạt) *n.* tropical bird; one who repeats words, actions, ideas, etc. of another [Fr. *perroquet*, a parrot].

par·ry (par′·i·) *v.t.* to ward off; to turn aside; to avoid [L. *parare*, to prepare].

parse (pàrs) *v.t.* to classify a word or analyze a sentence in terms of grammar. **parsing** *n.* [L. *pars*, part, *pars orationis*, part of speech].

Par·see, parsi (pàr′·sē) *n.* a follower of the disciples of Zoroaster; a fire worshipper. **-ism** *n.* [Pers. *Parsi*, a Persian].

par·si·mo·ny (pàr′·sạ·mō·ni·) *n.* stinginess; undue economy. **parsimonious** *a.* **parsimoniously** *adv.* **parsimoniousness** *n.* [L. *parcere*, to spare].

pars·ley (pàrs′·li·) *n.* a garden herb, used as a flavoring or garnish in cookery [Gk. *petroselinon*, rock parsley].

pars·nip (pars′·nip) *n.* a root vegetable, carrot-like in shape [L. fr. *pastinare*, to dig up].

par·son (pàr′·sn) *n.* a clergyman; the incumbent of a parish. **-age** *n.* the residence of a parson. (*Colloq.*) **-'s nose,** the rump of a fowl [*person*].

part (pàrt) *n.* a portion, fragment, or section of a whole; a share or lot; a division; an actor's role; duty; interest; a melody in a harmonic piece; *pl.* accomplishments or talents; region; *v.t.* to divide; to separate; to share; *v.i.* to separate; to take leave; to part with or give up. **-ing** *n.* the act of separating; leave-taking; division; dividing line; *a.* given on taking leave. **-ly** *adv.* in part; in some measure or degree. **-ible** *a.* divisible. **-ibility** *n.* [L. *pars*, a part].

par·take (pàr·tāk′) *v.t.* and *i.* to have or take a share in; to take food or drink. *pr.p.* **partaking.** *pa.p.* **-n.** *pa.t.* **partook.** **-r** *n.* [fr. *part* and *take*].

par·terre (pàr·ter′) *n.* an ornamental arrangement of flower beds; the rear section of the main floor of a theater [Fr. *par terre*, on the earth].

par·the·no·gen·e·sis (pàr·thạ·nō·jen′·ạ·sis) *n.* reproduction without sexual union [Gk. *parthenos*, virgin; *genesis*, birth].

Par·the·non (par′·thạ·nàn) *n.* famous Doric temple of Athena [Gr. *parthenos*, virgin].

par·tial (pár'·shạl) *a.* affecting only a part; not total; inclined to favor unreasonably. **-ly** *adv.* **partiality** *n.* quality of being partial; favoritism; fondness for [L. *pars*, part].

par·tic·i·pate (pár·tis'·ạ·pāt) *v.t.* and *i.* to share in; to partake (foll. by 'in'). **participant** *n.* a partaker; *a.* sharing. **participator** *n.* **participation** (pár·tis·ạ·pā'·shạn) *n.* [L. *pars*, part; *capere*, to take].

par·ti·ci·ple (pár'·tạ·si·pl) *n.* (*Gram.*) an adjective formed by inflection from a verb. **participial** *a.* [L. *particeps*, sharing].

par·ti·cle (pár·'tạ·kl) *n.* a minute portion of matter; (*Gram.*) a part of speech which is uninflected and of subordinate importance [L. *particula*, a little part].

par·ti·col·ored, party-colored (pár'·ti·kul·ẹrd) *a.* having different colors; variegated.

par·tic·u·lar (pár·tik'·yạ·lẹr) *a.* relating to a single person or thing, not general; considered apart from others; minute in details; fastidious in taste; *n.* a single point or circumstance; a detail or item. **-ly** *adv.* especially; in a high degree; with great attention. **particularity** *n.* quality or state of being particular; individual characteristic. **-ize** *v.t.* and *i.* to mention one by one; to give in detail; to specify. **-ization** *n.* [L. *particularis*].

par·ti·san, partizan (pár'·tạ·zạn) *n.* adherent, often prejudiced, of a party or cause; a member of irregular troops engaged in risky enterprises; *a.* adhering to a faction. **-ship** *n.* [Fr.].

par·ti·san (pạr'·tạ·zạn) *n.* a long-handled pike [O.Fr. *pertuisane*].

par·ti·tion (pár·tish'·ạn) *n.* division or separation; any of the parts into which a thing is divided; that which divides or separates, as a wall, etc.; *v.t.* to divide into shares; to divide by walls. **partitive** *n.* a word expressing partition; a distributive; *a.* denoting a part. **partitively** *adv.* [L. *partitio*].

part·ner (párt'·nẹr) *n.* a partaker; a sharer; an associate, esp. in business; a husband or wife; one who dances with another; in golf, tennis, etc., one who plays with another; *v.t.* in games, to play with another against opponents. **-ship** *n.* the state of being a partner; the association of two or more persons for business [L. *pars*, a part].

par·tridge (pár'·trij) *n.* a small game bird of the grouse family [Gk. *perdix*].

par·tu·ri·ent (pár·tyoo'·ri·ạnt) *a.* bringing forth or about to bring forth young. **parturition** *n.* the act of bringing forth young [L. *parturire*, to be in labor].

par·ty (pár'·ti·) *n.* a number of persons united in opinion; a political group; a social assembly; a participator; an accessory; a litigant; *a.* pert. to a party or faction. **—colored** *a.* parti-colored [O.Fr. *partir*, to divide].

par·ve·nu (pár'·vạ·nū) *n.* an upstart; one who has risen socially, esp. by the influence of money [Fr. fr. *parvenir*, to arrive at].

Pasch (pask) *n.* Passover; Easter. **-al** *a.* **— lamb**, lamb eaten at Passover; (P-L. in *Christ.*) Christ [Heb. *pesach*, to pass over].

pas·quin (pas'·kwin) *n.* a writer of lampoons or satires; a lampoon or satire; *v.t.* and *i.* to lampoon. **-ade** *n.* a lampoon [fr. It. *Pasquino*, Roman statue on which political lampoons were posted].

pass (pas) *v.t.* to go by, beyond, through etc.; to spend; to exceed; to approve; to disregard; to circulate; to send through; to move; *v.i.* to go; to elapse; to undergo examination successfully; to happen; to die; to circulate. *pa.p.* **-ed, past.** *pa.t.* **-ed.** *n.* a passage or narrow way, esp. a narrow and difficult one; a passport; a permit; success in an examination, test, etc.; in football, hockey, etc., the passing of the ball from one player to another.

-able *a.* that may be passed or crossed; fairly good; admissible; current. **-ably** *adv.* **-book** *n.* a bankbook. **-key** *n.* a latchkey; a masterkey. **-port** *n.* an official document, issued by a State Department, granting permission to travel abroad. **-word** *n.* (*Mil.*) a selected word given to sentries, soldiers, etc. used to distinguish friend from enemy. **to pass the buck** (*Slang*) to shift responsibility to another [L. *passus*, a step].

pas·sage (pas'·ij) *n.* the act, time, or right of passing; movement from one place to another; a voyage across the sea; fare for a voyage; an entrance or exit; part of a book, etc.; the passing of a law. **passage of arms,** a feat of arms. **bird of passage,** a migratory bird [Fr. fr. L. *passus*, a step, a pace].

pas·sé (pa·sā') *a.* past one's best; faded; rather out of date; antiquated [Fr.].

pas·sen·ger (pas'·ạn·jẹr) *n.* a traveller, esp. by some conveyance; *a.* adapted for carrying passengers [O.Fr. *passager*].

Pas·ser·i·for·mes (pas'·ẹr·i·fawr·mēz) *n.* the largest order of birds [L. *passer*, a sparrow].

pas·sim (pas'·im) *a.* here and there [L.].

pas·sion (pash'·ạn) *n.* intense emotion, as of grief, rage, love; eager desire; (*Cap.*) the story of Christ's suffering and last agony. **-ate** *a.* easily moved to anger; moved by strong emotions; vehement. **-ately** *adv.* **-ateness** *n.* **-less** *a.* **— play** *n.* a theatrical representation of Christ's passion. **— week** *n.* the week immediately preceding Easter [L. *passio*, fr. *pati*, to suffer].

pas·sive (pas'·iv) *a.* inactive; submissive; acted upon, not acting; *n.* (*Gram.*) (or passive voice) the form of the verb which expresses that the subject is acted upon. **-ly** *adv.* **-ness** *n.* [L. *pati, passus*, to suffer].

Pass·o·ver (pas'·ō·vẹr) *n.* a feast of the Jews to commemorate the time when God, smiting the first-born of the Egyptians, passed over the houses of Israelites [*pass* and *over*].

past *pa.p.* of **pass.**

past (past) *a.* pert. to former time; gone by; elapsed; ended; *n.* former state; bygone times; one's earlier life; *prep.* beyond; after; exceeding; beyond the scope of; *adv.* by; beyond. **— master,** a former master of a guild, freemasons, etc.; one adept or proficient [fr. *pass*].

paste (pāst) *n.* a soft composition, as of flour and water; dough prepared for pies, etc.; any soft plastic mixture or adhesive; a fine glass for making artificial gems; *v.t.* to fasten with paste; (*Slang*) to strike. **pasty** *a.* (pās'·ti·) like paste. **pastry** (pās'·tri·) *n.* the crust of pies and tarts; articles of food made of paste or dough. **pastry-cook** *n.* who makes and sells pastry. **-board** (pāst'·bōrd) *n.* a stiff, thick paper; *a.* made of pasteboard; flimsy or unsubstantial [O.Fr.].

pas·tel (pas'·tel) *n.* a colored chalky crayon; a drawing made with such crayons. **— shades,** delicate and subdued colors [F., fr. It. *pastello*, dim. fr. L. *pasta*, paste].

pas·tern (pas'·tern) *n.* part of horse's leg between fetlock and hoof [O.Fr. *pasturon*, shackle of horse at pasture].

Pas·teur (pas·tur') *n.* a French chemist and biologist. **pasteurization** *n.* the sterilization of milk, etc. by heating to 140° F. or over and then cooling. **pasteurize** *v.t.*

pas·tic·cio, pastiche (pas·tēch'·ō, pas·tēsh') *n.* a medley made up from various sources; a picture or literary composition in the style of a recognized author or artist [It.].

pas·tille, pastil (pas·tēl', pas'·til) *n.* an aromatic substance burned for cleansing or scenting a room; a small lozenge, aromatic or medicated [Fr. fr. L. *pastillus*, a little loaf].

pas·time (pas'·tīm) *n.* that which amuses and

makes time pass agreeably; recreation; diversion [fr. *pass* and *time*].

pas·tor (pas'·tẹr) *n.* a minister of the gospel. **-al** *a.* pert. to shepherds or rural life; relating to a pastor and his duties. *n.* a poem describing rural life; an idyll. **-ally** *adv.* **-ate** *n.* the office or jurisdiction of a spiritual pastor. **-ship** *n.* [L. *pastor*, a herdsman].

pas·ture (pas'·chẹr) *n.* grass for food of cattle; ground on which cattle graze; *v.t.* to feed on grass; *v.i.* to graze. **pasturable** *a.* **pasturage** *n.* pasture land; the business of grazing cattle [L. *pascere*, to feed].

past·y See **paste.**

pat (pat) *n.* a light, quick blow, esp. with hand or fingers; a small lump, esp. of butter; *v.t.* to strike gently. *pr.p.* **-ting.** *pa.p.* and *pa.t.* **-ted** [imit. origin].

pat (pat)*a.* ready; apt; at right moment; *adv.* opportunely; exactly. **-ness** *n.* [fr. *pat*].

patch (pach) *n.* a piece of material used to mend a hole, rent, etc.; a covering for a wound; small spot of black silk formerly worn on cheek by ladies; *v.t.* to mend with a patch; to repair clumsily. **-y** *a.* full of patches; unequal. **-work** *n.* work made by sewing together pieces of cloth of different material and color [O.Fr. *pieche*, a piece].

pate (pāt) *n.* the top of the head; the head.

pâ·té de foie gras (pát·ā' dạ fwạ·grạ) a paste of goose liver [Fr.].

pa·tel·la (pạ·tel'·ạ) *n.* the kneecap [L. = small pan].

pat·en (pat'·ạn) *n.* the plate on which the bread of the Eucharist is placed [L. *patina*, a plate].

pat·ent (pā'·tạnt, pat'·ạnt) *a.* open; evident; protected by a patent; *n.* short for *letters patent*, an official document granting a right or privilege, or securing the exclusive right to invention; the invention itself. *v.t.* to secure or protect by a patent. **-ly** *adv.* openly; evidently. **-ee** (pat·ạn·tē') *n.* one who has secured a patent. **— leather,** leather with a varnished or lacquered surface [L. *patens*, open].

pa·ter·nal (pạ·tur'·nạl) *a.* pert. to a father; fatherly; hereditary. **-ly** *adv.* **paternity** *n.* the relation of a father to his offspring; authorship [L. *pater*, a father].

pa·ter·nos·ter (pat·ẹr·nás'·tẹr) *n.* the Lord's Prayer [L. *pater*, father; *noster*, our].

path (path) *n.* a way, course, or track of action, conduct, or procedure. **-finder** *n.* a pioneer. **-way** *n.* a narrow footway [O.E. *paeth*].

pa·thet·ic (pạ·thet'·ik) *a.* affecting or moving the tender emotions; causing pity; touching. Also **-al. -ally** *adv.*

path·o- *prefix* fr. Gk. *pathos*, suffering, feeling, used in derivatives. **-genesis, pathogeny** (path·ạ·jen'·a·sis, pạ·tháj'·a·ni·) *n.* the origin and development of disease. **-genetic, -genic** *a.* causing disease. **-logy** *n.* the science and study of diseases, their causes, nature, cures, etc.**-logic, -logical** *a.* **-logically** *adv.* **-logist** *n.* [Gk. *genesis*, birth; *logos*, discourse].

pa·thos (pā'·thǎs) *n.* the power of exciting tender emotions; deep feeling [Gk. *pathos* fr. *paschein*, to suffer].

pa·tient (pā'·shạnt) *a.* bearing trials without murmuring; not easily made angry; calm; not hasty; *n.* a person under medical treatment. **-ly** *adv.* **patience** *n.* the quality of enduring with calmness; quiet perseverance [L. *pati*, to suffer].

pa·ti·o (pa'·ti·ō) *n.* the inner court of a Spanish house [Sp.].

pat·ois (pat'·wạ) *n.* a dialect; illiterate or provincial form of speech; jargon [Fr.].

pa·tri·arch (pā'·tri·ark) *n.* the father and ruler of a family, esp. in Biblical history; the highest dignitary in the Eastern church; a venerable old man. **-al** *a.* **-ate** *n.* dignity or jurisdiction of a patriarch. **-y** *n.* government by the head or father of a tribe [Gk. *pater*, father; *archein*, to rule].

pa·tri·cian (pạ·trish'·ạn) *a.* pert, to the senators of ancient Rome and their descendants; of high birth; noble or aristocratic; *n.* [L. *patricius*, fr. *pater*, father, senator].

pat·ri·cide (pat'·rạ·sīd) *n.* murder of one's father [L. *pater*, father; *caedere*, to kill].

pat·ri·mo·ny (pat'·rạ·mō·ni·) *n.* a right or estate inherited from one's father or ancestors; heritage; a church estate or revenue. **patrimonial** *a.* **patrimonially** *adv.* [L. *patrimonium* fr. *pater*, father].

pa·tri·ot (pā'·tri·ạt) *n.* one who loves his country and upholds its interests. **-ic** *a.* filled with patriotism. **-ically** *adv.* **-ism** *n.* love for, and loyalty to, one's country [L. *patria*, fatherland].

pa·trol (pạ·trōl') *v.t.* and *i.* to go or walk around a camp, garrison, etc. in order to protect it. *pr.p.* **-ling.** *pa.p.* and *pa.t.* **-led.** *n.* a going of the rounds by a guard; the man or men who go to the rounds [O.Fr. *patrouiller*].

pa·tron (pā'·trạn) *n.* (*fem.* **-ness**) a man who protects or supports a person, cause, entertainment, artistic production, etc.; a guardian saint; (*Eccles.*) one who has the right of appointment to a benefice; a regular customer. **-age** *n.* countenance, support, or encouragement given to a person or cause; condescending manner; in trade, regular customer. **-ize** *v.t.* to act as a patron to; to assume the air of a superior towards; to frequent, as a customer. **patronizing** *a.* **patronizingly** *adv.* **— saint,** a saint who is regarded as the special protector of a person, city, trade, etc. [L. *patronus*, fr. *pater*, father].

pat·ro·nym·ic (pat·rạ·nim'·ik) *n.* a name derived from parent or ancestor; a surname [Gk.*patōr*, father; *onoma*, a name].

pat·ten (pat'·ạn) *n.* a wooden sandal worn in wet weather [Fr. *patin*].

pat·ter (pat'·ẹr) *v.i.* to make a quick succession of small taps or sounds, like those of rain falling [frequentative of *pat*].

pat·ter (pat'·ẹr) *v.t.* to speak rapidly and indistinctly; to mutter; *v.i.* to talk glibly or mechanically; to say prayers; *n.* chatter; prattle; lingo of a professoin or class; jargon [fr. *paternoster*].

pat·tern (pat'·ẹrn) *n.* a model, example, or guide; a decorative design; *v.t.* to design from a pattern; to imitate [M.E. *patron*, a model].

pat·ty (pat'·i·) *n.* a little pie [Fr. *pâté*].

pau·ci·ty (paw'·sa·ti·) *n.* fewness; scarcity; smallness of quantity [L. *paucus*, few].

paunch (pawnch, pánch) *n.* the belly **-iness** *n.* **-y** *a.* [L. *pantex*].

pau·per (paw'·pẹr) *n.* (*fem.* **-ess**) a very poor person, esp. one supported by the public. **-ize** *v.t.* to reduce to pauperism [L., poor].

pause (pawsz) *n.* a temporary stop or rest; cessation; hesitation; a break in speaking, reading, or writing; in music, a sign · or · placed under or over a note to indicate the prolongation of a note or rest; *v.i.* to make a short stop; to cease for a time [Gk. *pausis*].

pave (pāv) *v.t.* to form a level surface with stone, brick, etc.; to make smooth and even; (*Fig.*) to prepare. **-ment** *n.* a paved floor, road, or sidewalk; material used [L. *pavire*, to ram down].

pav·id (pav'·id) *a.* timid; shy [L. *pavidus*].

pa·vil·ion (pạ·vil'·yạn) *n.* orig. a tent; hence, anything like a tent, e.g. a garden summerhouse [Fr. fr. L. *papilio*, a butterfly, a tent].

paw (paw) *n.* the foot of an animal having claws; (*Slang*) the hand; *v.t.* and *i.* to scrape with the paws; (*Colloq.*) to stroke or fondle with hands clumsily, rudely [O.Fr. *poe*].

pawn (pawn) *n.* something deposited as security for money borrowed; a pledge; the state of being pledged; *v.t.* to deposit as security for a loan; to pledge. **-broker** *n.* one who lends money on something deposited with him. [L. *pannus*, cloth].

pawn (pawn) *n.* a piece of the lowest rank in the game of chess; (*Fig.*) a person who is a mere tool in the hands of another [L.L. *pedo*, a foot soldier].

pay (pā) *v.t.* to discharge one's obligations to; to give money, etc., for goods received or services rendered; *v.i.* to recompense; to be remunerative; to be worth the trouble. *pa.p.* and *pa.t.* **paid** (pād). *n.* reward; compensation; wages; salary. **-able** *a.* justly due; profitable. **-ee** (pā·ē´) *n.* one to whom money is paid. **-er** *n.* one who pays. **-ment** *n.* the act of paying; discharge of a debt; recompense [L. *pacare*, to appease].

pay (pā) *v.t.* (*Naut.*) to cover with pitch; to make waterproof [L. *picare*, to pitch].

pea (pē) *n.* the fruit, growing in pods, of a leguminous plant; the plant itself. **-nut** *n.* the earth nut. — **soup** *n.* soup made of dried peas. **sweet pea**, a climbing garden annual, bearing sweet-scented flowers [Gk. *piscos*].

peace (pēs) *n.* calm; repose; freedom from disturbance, war, or hostilities. **-able** *a.* in a state of peace; disposed to peace; not quarrelsome. **-ably** *adv.* **-ableness** *n.* **-ful** *a.* free from war, tumult, or commotion; mild; undisturbed. **-fully** *adv.* **-fulness** *n.* **-maker** *n.* one who makes peace [L. *pax, pacis*].

peach (pēch) *n.* a juicy fruit with light orange flesh, and a velvety skin; the tree which bears this fruit; a pale orange-pink color. **-y** *a.* peach-like; (*Slang*) excellent [Fr. *pêche*].

peach (pēch) *v.i.* (*Slang*) to inform against; to tell tales [abbrev. fr. *impeach*].

pea·cock (pē´·kȧk) *n.* (*fem.* **peahen**) *a.* bird remarkable for the beauty of its plumage, and for its large tail; a person vain of his appearance. **peafowl** *n.* the peacock or peahen. — **blue**, lustrous greenish blue [L. *pavo*, a peacock; and *cock*].

peak (pēk) *v.i.* to waste or pine away. **-y** *a.* thin, sickly. **-ed** *a.* [etym. unknown].

peak (pēk) *n.* the sharp top of a hill; the pointed top of anything; the projecting part of a cap brim; the maximum point of a curve or record. [Fr. *pic*; conn. with *pike*].

peal (pēl) *n.* a loud sound, or succession of loud sounds, as of thunder, bells, laughter, etc.; a set of bells attuned to each other; *v.t.* and *i.* to sound loudly [abbrev. fr. *appeal*].

pear (pâr, per) *n.* a sweet, juicy fruit of oval shape; tree on which it grows [L. *pirum*].

pearl (purl) *n.* a hard, smooth, lustrous substance, found in several mollusks, particularly pearl oyster, and used as a gem; something very precious; a small size of printing type, a creamy grey; *a.* made of pearls; pert. to pearls; *v.t.* to adorn with pearls; to take a round form like pearls. **-y** *a.* of the color of pearls; like pearls; abounding in pearls; clear; pure. **-iness** *n.* [Fr. *perle*].

peas·ant (pez´·ȧnt) *n.* a rural laborer; a rustic; *a.* rural. **-ry** *n.* peasants collectively [Fr. *paysan*].

peat (pēt) *n.* a brown, fibrous turf, formed of decayed vegetable matter, which is used as fuel. **-y** *a.* like peat, in texture or color. **-bog**, **-moss** *n.* marshland of which the foundation is peat [etym. uncertain].

peb·ble (peb´·l) *n.* a small, roundish stone; transparent and colorless rock crystal used for spectacle lenses. **-d, pebbly** *a.* full of pebbles [O.E. *papol*].

pe·can (pi·kȧn´, ·kan´) *n.* a smooth-shelled

oval nut with edible kernel; the tree on which it grows [Amer. Indian].

pec·ca·ble (pek´·ȧ·bl) *a.* liable to sin. **peccability** *n.* liability to sin. **peccant** *a.* sinful; offensive; causing trouble; (*Med.*) morbid. **peccancy** *n.* [L. *peccare*, to sin].

pec·ca·dil·lo (pek·ȧ·dil´·ō) *n.* a trifling offense; an indiscreet action. [Sp. *pecadillo*, fr. *pecado*, a sin; L. *peccare*, to sin].

peck (pek) *n.* a measure of capacity for dry goods = 2 gallons, or the fourth part of a bushel; a great deal [O.Fr. *pek*].

peck (pek) *v.t.* and *i.* to strike with the beak; to pick up with the beak; to dab; to eat little quantities at a time; *n.* (*Colloq.*) a kiss. **-er** *n.* [form of *pick*].

pec·tin (pek´·tin) *n.* a carbohydrate from fruits which yields a gel [Gr. *pektos*, congealed].

pec·to·ral (pek´·tȧr·ȧl) *a.* pert. to the breast or chest [L. *pectus*, the breast].

pec·u·late (pek´·yȧ·lāt) *v.t.* and *i.* to embezzle. **peculation** *n.* **peculator** *n.* [L. *peculari*].

pe·cul·iar (pi·kūl´·yer) *a.* belonging solely to; appropriate; particular; singular; strange. **-ly** *adv.* **peculiarity** (pi·kū·li·ar´·a·ti·) *n.* something that belongs to only one person, thing, class, people; a distinguishing feature; characteristic [L. *peculium*, property].

pe·cu·ni·ar·y (pe·kū´·ni·e·ri·) *a.* pert. to, or consisting of, money. **pecunniarily** *adv.* [L. *pecunia*, money, fr. *pecus*, cattle].

ped·a·gogue (ped´·ȧ·gog) *n.* a schoolteacher; a pedantic person. **pedagogic** (ped·a·gȧj´·ik), **pedagogical** *a.* **pedagogy** (ped´·ȧ·gō·ji·), **pedagogics** *n.* science of teaching [Gk. *pais*, a boy; *agogos*, leading].

pe·dal (ped´·ȧl) *a.* pert. to the foot; *n.* a mechanical contrivance to transmit power by using foot as a lever, e.g. on bicycle, sewing-machine. *v.t.* and *i.* to use the pedals of an organ, piano, etc.; to propel a bicycle by pedaling. [L. *pes, pedis*, the foot].

ped·ant (ped´·ȧnt) *n.* one who insists unnecessarily on petty details of book learning, grammatical rules, etc.; one who shows off his learning. **-ic, -ical** *a.* **pedantically** *adv.* **-ry** *n.* [perh. conn. with *pedagogue*].

ped·dle (ped´·l) *v.t.* to travel from place to place selling small articles; *v.t.* to sell or hawk goods thus. **-r; pedlar** *n.* one who peddles goods; [O.E. *ped*, a basket].

ped·es·tal (ped´·is·tȧl) *n.* anything that serves as a support or foundation; the base of a column, statue, etc. [Fr. *piédestal*].

pe·des·tri·an (pȧ·des´·tri·ȧn) *a.* going on, performed on, foot; of walking; commonplace; *n.* a walker; one who journeys on foot [L. *pedester*, fr. *pes*, a foot].

pe·di·at·rics (pēd·i·at´·riks) *n.* (*Med.*) the branch dealing with the diseases and disorders of children. **pediatric** *a.* **pediatrician** *n.* [Gk. *paidos*, a child; *iatrikos*, healing].

pe·dic·u·lar (pi·dik´·yȧ·ler) *pert.* to lice [L. *pediculus*, a louse].

ped·i·cure (ped´·i·kūr) *n.* treatment of the feet [L. *pes, pedis*, the foot; *cura*, care].

ped·i·gree (ped´·ȧ·grē) *n.* a line of ancestors; genealogy; *a.* having a line of ancestors [M.E. *pedegru* fr. Fr. *pied de grue*, crane's foot].

ped·i·ment (ped´·ȧ·mȧnt) *n.* (*Archit.*) the triangular ornamental facing of a portico door, or window, etc. **pedimental** *a.* [earlier *periment*, perh. fr. *pyramid*].

pe·dom·e·ter (pi·dȧm´·ȧ·ter) *n.* an instrument which measures the distance walked by recording the number of steps [L. *pes, pedis*, the foot; Gk. *metrom*, a measure].

pe·dun·cle (pi·dung´·kl) *n.* a flower stalk; (*Zool.*) a stalk or stalklike process in an animal body. **peduncular** *a.* [dim. of L. *pes, pedis*, a foot].

peek (pēk) *v.i.* to peep; to peer; *n.* a glance [etym. uncertain].

peel (pēl) *v.t.* to strip off the skin, bark, or rind; to free from a covering; *v.i.* to come off, as the skin or rind; *n.* the outside skin of a fruit; rind or bark [L. *pilare*, to deprive of hair].

peel (pēl) *n.* wooden shovel used by bakers [L. *pala*, a spade].

peep (pēp) *v.i.* to look through a crevice; to look furtively or slyly; to emerge slowly; *n.* a furtive or sly glance. — **show** *n.* a small exhibit, viewed through an aperture containing a magnifying glass [etym. uncertain].

peep (pēp) *v.i.* to cry, as a chick [imit.].

peer (pir) *n.* (*fem.* **-ess**) an equal in any respect; a nobleman; a member of the House of Lords; an associate. **-age** *n.* the rank of a peer; the body of peers. **-less** *a.* having no equal. **-lessly** *adv.* **-lessness** *n.* [L. *par*, equal].

peer (pir) *v.i.* to look closely and intently; to peer; to appear [etym. doubtful].

pee·vish (pē′·vish) *a.* fretful; irritable; hard to please; childish. **-ly** *adv.* **-ness** *n.* **peeve** *v.t.* to annoy.

peg (peg) *n.* a nail or pin of wood or other material; (*Colloq.*) a step or degree; *v.t.* to fix or mark with a peg; *v.i.* to persevere. *pr.p.* **-ging** *pa.t.*, *pa.p.* **-ged** [etym. uncertain].

Pe·king·ese′ (Pē·kan·ēz′) *n.* a breed of Chinese lap-dog. *abbrev.* **peke**.

pe·koe (pē′·kō) *n.* a black tea of superior quality [Chin. *pek*, white; *ho*, down (i.e. with 'down' on the leaves)].

pel·i·can (pel′·i·kan) *n.* a large water fowl [Gk. *pelekan*].

pe·lisse (pa·lēs′) *n.* formerly, a robe of silk or other material, worn by ladies; a fur-lined coat [L. *pellis*, skin].

pel·let (pel′·it) *n.* a little ball; a pill; small shot [Fr. *pelote*, a ball].

pell-mell (pel-mel′) *adv.* in utter confusion; helter-skelter [Fr. *mêler*, to mix; *pêle*, being a rhyme with *mêle*].

pel·lu·cid (pa·lōō′·sid) *a.* perfectly clear; translucent. **-ly** *adv.* **-ness** *n.* [L. *per*, very; *lucidus*, clear].

pelt (pelt) *n.* raw hide; undressed skin of fur-bearing animal [L. *pellis*, skin].

pelt (pelt) *v.t.* to strike with missiles; *v.i.* of rain, etc. to fall heavily; to throw missiles; to run fast [etym. uncertain].

pel·vis (pel′·vis) *n.* (*Anat.*) the bony basin-shaped cavity at the base of the human trunk. **pelvic** *a.* [L. = a basin].

pen (pen) *n.* an instrument for writing with ink; a large wing feather (a quill) used for writing; *v.t.* to write; to compose and set down. *pr.p.* **-ning**. *pa.p.* and *pa.t.* **-ned**. **-knife** *n.* a pocketknife. **-man** *n.* one who writes a good hand; an author. **-manship** *n.* — **name** *n.* an assumed name of author. [L. *penna*, a feather].

pen (pen) *n.* a small enclosure, as for sheep; a coop. *v.t.* to confine in a pen: to shut in. *pr.p.* **-ning** *pa.p.*, *pa.t.* **-ned** [O.E. *penn*].

pe·nal (pē′·nal) *a.* pert. to, prescribing, incurring, inflicting, punishment. **-ize** *v.t.* to make penal; to impose a penalty upon; to handicap. **-ly** *adv.* **penalty** (pen′·al·ti·) *n.* punishment for a crime or offense; in games, a handicap imposed for infringement of rule, etc.; **penology** *n.* study and arrangement of prisons and prisoners [L. *poena*, punishment].

pen·ance (pen′·ans) *n.* suffering submitted to in penitence; act of atonement [L. *penitentia*].

pence (pens) *n.pl.* See **penny**.

pen·chant (pen′·chant) *n.* a strong mental inclination [Fr. *pencher*, to lean].

pen·cil (pen′·sil) *n.* a stick of graphite encased in wood, used for writing or drawing; (*Math.*) a system of rays which converge to, or diverge from, a point; *v.t.* to draw, write with pencil. **-ed** *a.* marked, as with pencil; having pencils or rays. **-ing** *n.* the work of a pencil [L. *penicillum*, a little tail].

pend·ant (pen′·dant) *n.* a hanging ornament, esp. a locket or earring; a lamp or chandelier hanging from the ceiling; a complement or parallel. **pendent** *a.* suspended; hanging; projecting. **pendently** *adv.* **pending** *a.* awaiting settlement; in suspense; undebted; *prep.* during; until [L. *pendere*, to hang].

pen·du·lous (pen′·ja·las) *a.* hanging loosely; swinging. **-ly** *adv.* **-ness** *n.* **pendulum** *n.* a body suspended from a fixed point, and swinging freely; the swinging rod with weighted end which regulates movements of a clock, etc. [L. *pendulus*, hanging].

pen·e·trate (pen′·a·trāt) *v.t.* to enter into; to pierce; to pervade or spread through; to touch with feeling; to arrive at the meaning of; *v.i.* to make a way to, or through. **penetrating** *a.* **penetrable** *a.* capable of being entered or pierced; susceptible. **penetrably** *adv.* **penetrability** *n.* **penetration** *n.* [L. *penetrare*].

pen·guin (pen′·gwin) *n.* a flightless sea bird inhabiting the S. temperate and Antarctic regions [W. *pen*, head; *gwyn*, white].

pen·i·cil·lin (pen·i·sil′·in) *n.* an antibacterial agent produced from the fungus *penicillium*.

pen·in·su·la (pa·nin′·sa·la) *n.* a portion of land nearly surrounded by water, and connected with the mainland by an isthmus **-r** *a.* [L. *paene*, almost; *insula*, an island].

pe·nis (pē′·nis) *n.* the male organ of generation. **penial** *a.* [L.].

pen·i·tent (pen′·a·tant) *a.* deeply affected by sense of guilt; contrite; repentant; *n.* one who repents of sin. **-ly** *adv.* **penitence** *n.* sorrow for having sinned; repentance. **penitential** (pen·a·ten′·shal) *a.* pert. to or expressing penitence; *n.* among R.C.s, a book containing rules of penance. **penitentially** *adv.* **penitentiary** (pen·a·ten′·sha·ri·) *a.* pert. to punishment by confinement; *n.* a prison; (*R.C.*) an officer who prescribes penance; [L. *paenitere*, to repent].

pen·nant (pen′·ant) *n.* a very long, narrow flag tapering to a point. Also **pennon** [Fr. *pennon*, fr. L. *penna*, a feather].

pen·nate (pen′·āt) *a.* winged; feathered. Also **pennated**. **penniform** *a.* feather-shaped [L. *penna*, a feather].

pen·ny (pen′·i·) *n.* the U.S. and Canadian cent; an English coin (about 2 U.S. cents); a small sum. *pl.* **pennies**. **penniless** *a.* without money; poor. **-weight** (pen′·i·wāt) *n.* a troy weight of 24 grains (*abbrev.* **pwt.**).

pen·sile (pen′·sl) *a.* hanging; suspended; pendulous [L. *pensilis*].

pen·sion (pen′·shan) *n.* an annual grant of money for past services; an annuity paid to retired officers, soldiers, etc.; *v.t.* to grant a pension to. **-er** *n.* one who receives a pension [L. *pensio*, payment].

pen·sive (pen′·siv) *a.* thoughtful; deep in thought; somewhat melancholy **-ly** *adv.* **-ness** *n.* [Fr. *pensif*, fr. *penser*, to think].

pent (pent) *a.* closely confined; shut up [fr. *pen* = an enclosure].

pen·ta- (pen′·ta) *prefix* fr. Gk. *pente*, five, used in derivatives. **-gon**, **-gram** *n.* (*Geom.*) a plane figure having five angles and five sides. **-gonal** *a.* **-cle** *n.* a five-pointed star, formerly a magic symbol. **-meter** *n.* verse of five feet.

pen·tane (pen′·tān) *n.* a paraffin hydrocarbon, a very inflammable liquid [Gk. *pente*, five].

Pen·ta·teuch (pen′·ta·tūk) *n.* the first five books of the Old Testament [Gk. *pente*, five; *teuchos*, a book].

Pen·te·cost (pen′·tạ·kawst) *n.* a Jewish festival, celebrated on the 50th day after the Passover; a Christian festival (Whitsunday) commemorating the descent of the Holy Ghost on the Apostles.**Pentecostal** *a.* [Gk. *pentō-kostos*, fiftieth].

pent·house (pent′·hous) *n.* an apartment, or structure, on the roof of a building; a shed attached to a main building, its roof sloping down from the wall [Fr. *appentis*, fr. L. *pendere*, to hang].

pen·to·thal (pen′·tạ·thawl) *n.* sometimes called the 'truth' drug; an anesthetic [Trade Name].

pe·nult (pē·nult′) *n.* the next to last syllable of a word. **penultimate** (pi·nul′·ti·mạt) *a.* next to last [L. *paene*, almost; *ultimus*, last].

pe·num·bra (pin·um′·brạ) *n.* in an eclipse, the partially shadowed region which surrounds the full shadow [L. *paene*, almost; *umbra*, shade].

pen·u·ry (pen′·yạ·ri·) *n.* extreme poverty; want or indigence; scarcity. **penurious** (pạ·noo′·ri·ạs) *a.* miserly. **penuriously** *adv.* **penuriousness** *n.* [L. *penuria*].

pe·on (pē′·ạn, ·an) *n.* in Mexico, a day laborer or serf; in India, a foot soldier, or messenger. **-age** *n.* [Sp., L. *pes*, a foot].

pe·o·ny (pē′·ạ·ni·) *n.* plant having beautiful, showy flowers [Gk. *paiōnia*, healing, fr. *Paiōn*, the physican of the gods].

peo·ple (pē′·pl) *n.* the body of persons that compose a community, tribe, nation, or race; the populace as distinct from rulers; *v.t.* to populate [L. *populus*].

pep (pep) *n.* (*Slang*) vigor; energy. **-py** *a.* **-piness** *n.* [short for *pepper*].

pep·per (pep′·ẹr) *n.* a pungent, spicy condiment obtained from an E. Indian plant; *v.t.* to sprinkle with pepper; to pelt with missiles. **-y** *a.* having the qualities of pepper; pungent; irritable. **-iness** *n.* **—corn** *n.* the berry or fruit of the pepper-plant; something of insignificant value. **-mint** *n.* a pungent plant which yields a volatile oil; essence gotten from this oil; a lozenge flavored with this essence [Gk.*peperi*].

pep·sin, pepsine (pep′·sin) *n.* a ferment formed in gastric juice of man and animals, and serving as an aid to digestion. **peptic** *a.* pert. to pepsin and to digestion; *n.pl.* medicines that promote digestion. **peptone** (pep′·tōn) *n.* one of the soluble compounds due to the action of pepsin, etc. on proteins. **peptonize** *v.t.* to convert food into peptones [Gk. *pepsis*, digestion].

per·ad·ven·ture (pur·ad·ven′·chẹr) *adv.* by chance; perhaps; possibly; *n.* doubt; question [O.Fr. *par aventure*].

per·am·bu·late (pẹr·am′·byạ·lāt) *v.t.* to walk through or over; formerly to survey the boundaries of; *v.i.* to walk about; to stroll. **perambulation** *n.* **perambulator** *n.* one who perambulates; a small carriage for a child. **perambulatory** *a.* [L. *per*; *ambulare*, to walk].

per·an·num (pẹr·an′·nạm) L. by the year; annually.

per·cale (pẹr·kal′) *n.* closely woven cotton cloth [Per. *pargal*].

per cap·i·ta (pẹr·kap′·ạ·tạ) L. for each person.

per·ceive (pẹr·sēv′) *v.t.* to obtain knowledge of through the senses; to see, hear, or feel; to understand. **perceivable** *a.* **perceivably** *adv.* **-r** *n.* **perceptible** (pẹr·sep′·ti·bl) *a.* capable of being perceived; discernible. **perceptibly** *adv.* **perceptibility** *n.* **perception** (pẹr·sep′·shan) *n.* the faculty of perceiving; intuitive judgment. **perceptive** *a.* having perception; used in perception.**perceptual** *a.* involving perception [L. *percipere*].

per·cent·age (pẹr·sen′·tij) *n.* proportion or

rate per hundred. **per centum** (*abbrev.* **per cent**) by, in, or for, each hundred; portion [L. *per*, through; *centum*, a hundred].

perch (purch) *n.* an edible fresh-water fish [Gk. *perkē*].

perch (purch) *n.* roosting bar for birds; high place; lineal measure (also 'pole' or 'rod') = 5½ yards; a measure of area = 30¼ square yards; *v.t.* to place on a perch; *v.i.* to alight or settle on a perch [L. *pertica*, a pole].

per·chance (pẹr·chans′) *adv.* perhaps; by chance [L. *per*, through; and *chance*].

per·cip·i·ent (pẹr·sip′·i·ạnt) *a.* having the faculty of perception; perceiving; *n.* one who has the power of perceiving. **percipience, percipiency** *n.* [L. *percipere*, to perceive].

per·co·late (pẹr′·kạ·lāt) *v.t.* and *i.* to pass slowly through small openings, as a liquid; to filter. **percolation** *n.* **percolator** *n.* a coffee pot fitted with a filter [L. *per*, through; *colare*, to strain].

per·cuss (pẹr·kus′) *v.t.* to strike sharply. **percussion** (pẹr·kush′·ạn) *n.* a collision; an impact; (*Med.*) tapping the body to determine condition of internal organ. **-ive** *a.* [L. *percutere*, to strike].

per·di·em (pẹr·dī′·am) L. daily.

per·di·tion (pẹr·dish′·ạn) *n.* utter loss; ruin; damnation [L. *perdere*, to lose].

per·e·gri·nate (pẹr′·ạ·gri·nāt) *v.i.* to travel from place to place; to journey. **peregrination** *n.* a wandering about. **peregrinator** *n.* [L. *peregrinus*, foreign].

per·emp·to·ry (pạ·remp′·tạ·ri·) *a.* authoritative; dictatorial; non-debatable; decsive; absolute. **peremptorily** *adv.* **peremptoriness** *n.* [L. *perimere*, *peremptum*, to destroy].

per·en·ni·al (pạ·ren′·i·ạl) *a.* lasting through the year; lasting; everlasting; lasting more than two years; *n.* a plant lasting for such a time.**-ly** *adv.* [L. *per*, through; *annus*, a year].

per·fect (pur′·fikt) *a.* complete; faultless; correct; excellent; of the highest quality; (*Gram.*) a tense denoting completed action; **perfect** (pur′·fekt or pẹr·fekt′) *v.t.* to finish or complete; to make perfect; to improve; to make skillful. **-ly** *adv.* **perfectible** *a.* capable of becoming perfect. **perfectibility** *n.* **perfection** *n.* state of being perfect. **perfectionist** *n.* one who believes that moral perfection is attainable, or that he has attained it [L. *perfectus*, done thoroughly].

per·fer·vid (pẹr·fur′·vid) *a.* very eager [L.].

per·fi·dy (pur′·fạ·di·) *n.* treachery; breach of faith; violation of trust. **perfidious** *a.* treacherous. **perfidiously** *adv.* **perfidiousness** *n.* [L. *perfidia*, faithlessness].

per·fo·rate (pur′·fạ·rāt) *v.t.* to pierce; to make a hole or holes in. **perforation** *n.* act of perforating; a hole, or series of holes [L. *per*. through; *forare*, to bore].

per·force (pẹr·fōrs′) *adv.* by force; of necessity [L. *per*; and *force*].

per·form (pẹr·fawrm′) *v.t.* to do; to accomplish; to fulfill; to represent on the stage; *v.i.* to do; to play, as on a musical instrument. **-ing** *a.* trained to act a part or do tricks. **-er** *n.* **-ance** *n.* act of performing; execution or carrying out; the thing done [L. *per*, thoroughly; Fr. *fournir*; to furnish or complete].

per·fume (pur′·fūm) *n.* a sweet scent or fragrance; a substance which emits an agreeable scent. (pẹr·fūm′) *v.t.* to fill or imbue with an agreeable odor; to scent. **-r** *n.* a maker or seller of perfumes. **perfumery** *n.* perfumes in general; the art of making perfumes [L. *per*, through; *fumare*, to smoke].

per·func·to·ry (pẹr·fungk′·tạ·ri·) *a.* done as a duty, carelessly and without interest; indifferent; superficial. **perfunctorily** *adv.* [L. *perfungi*, to perform].

per·go·la (pur′·gạ·lạ) *n.* an arbor or covered

walk formed of growing plants trained over trelliswork. [It.].

per·haps (per·haps') *adv.* it may be; possibly; perchance [L. *per*, through; E. *hap*, chance].

per·i·car·di·um (per·i·kár'·di·am) *n.* (Anat.) the double membranous sac which encloses the heart. **pericardiac, pericardial** *a.* [Gk. *peri*, round; *kardia*, the heart].

per·i·gee (per'·a·jē) *n.* that point in the moon's orbit nearest to the earth. opp. to *apogee* [Gk. *peri*, round; *gē*, the earth].

per·il (per'·al) *n.* danger; hazard; exposure to injury or loss; *v.t.* to expose to dangers, etc. **-ous** *a.* full of peril. **-ously** *adv.* **-ousness** *n.* [L. *periculum*, danger].

per·im·e·ter (pa·rim'·a·ter) *n.* (Geom.) the outer boundary of a plane figure; the sum of all its sides; circumference. **perimetrical** *a.* [Gk. *peri*, around; *metron*, a measure].

pe·ri·od (pi'·ri·ad) *n.* a particular portion of time; the time in which a heavenly body makes a revolution; a series of years; a cycle; conclusion; a punctuation mark (.), at the end of a sentence; menstruation; *a.* of furniture, dress, a play, etc., belonging to a particular period in history. **periodic** *a.* recurring at regular intervals. **periodical** *a.* periodic; pert. to a periodical; *n.* a publication, esp. a magazine issued at regular intervals. [Gk. *peri*, around; *hodos*, a way].

per·i·pa·tet·ic (per·a·pa·tet'·ik) *a.* walking about; pert. to the philosophy of Aristotle. **-ism** *n.* [Gk. *peri*, around, about; *patein*, to walk].

pe·riph·er·y (pa·rif'·a·ri·) *n.* circumference; perimeter; the outside. **peripheral** *a.* [Gk. *peri*, around; *pherein*, to bear].

pe·riph·ra·sis (pa·rif'·ra·sis) *n.* a roundaway of speaking or writing; circumlocution. *pl.* **periphrases. periphrastic** *a.* circumlocutory. **periphrastically** *adv.* [Gk. *peri*, around; *phrasis*, speaking].

per·i·scope (per'·a·skōp) *n.* an optical instrument which enables an observer to view surrounding objects from a lower level [Gk. *peri*, around; *skopein*, to see].

per·ish (per'·ish *v.t.* and *i.* to die; to waste away; to decay; to be destroyed. **-able** *a.* liable to perish, decay, etc., e.g. fish, fruit, etc. [L. *perire; per*, completely; *ire*, to go].

per·i·to·ne·um (per·a·ta·nē'·am) *n.* membrane which lines abdominal cavity, and surrounds intestines, etc. **peritonitis** *n.* inflammation of peritoneum [Gk. *peritonaion*, stretch over].

per·i·wig (per'·i·wig) *n.* a wig; a peruke. **-ged** *a.* [Fr. *perrugue*, a wig].

per·i·win·kle (per'·i·wing·kl) *n.* an edible shellfish [O.E. *pinewincle*, a whelk].

per·i·win·kle (per'·i·wing·kl) *n.* a trailing shrub with blue flowers; myrtle [L. *pervinca*].

per·jure (pur'·jer) *v.t.* to violate one's oath (used reflex.). **-d** *a.* guilty of perjury. **perjury** *n.* false testimony; the crime of violating one's oath. **-r** *n.* [L. *per; jurare* to swear].

perk (purk) *v.t.* to make spruce or trim; *v.i.* to become brisk and lively again (with 'up'). **-y** *a.* jaunty; pert; trim [Celt.].

per·ma·nent (pur'·ma·nant) *a.* remaining unaltered; lasting. *n.* a wave put into the hair to last several months. **-ly** *adv.* **permanence** *n.* [L. *per*, through; *manere*, to remain].

per·man·ga·nate (pur·mang'·ga·nāt) *n.* a salt of an acid of manganese, which, dissolved in water, forms a disinfectant and antiseptic.

per·me·ate (pur'·mi·āt) *v.t.* to penetrate and pass through; to diffuse itself through; to saturate. **permeable** *a.* admitting of passage of fluids. **permeably** *adv.* **permeability** (pur·mē·a·bil'·a·ti·) *a.* capable of permeating [L. *per*, through; *meare*, to pass].

per·mit (per·mit') *v.t.* to allow; to give leave or liberty to; *v.t.* to give leave. **permit** (pur'·mit) *n.* written permission. *pr.p.* **-ting.** *pa.p.* and *pa.t.* **-ted. permission** *n.* authorization; leave or license granted. **permissible** *a.* allowable. **permissibly** *adv.* **permissive** *a.* allowing. **permissively** *adv.* [L. *permittere*].

per·mute (per·mūt') *v.t.* to change the order of **permutable** *a.* **permutably** *adv.* **permutableness, permutability** *n.* **permutation** *n.* (Math.) the arrangement of a number of quantities in every possible order [L. *per*, thoroughly; *mutare*, to change].

per·ni·cious (per·nish'·as) *a.* having the quality of destroying or injuring; wicked. **-ly** *adv.* **-ness** *n.* [L. *per* thoroughly; *nex*, death by violence].

per·nick·et·y (per·nik'·a·ti·) *a.* (Colloq.) unduly fastidious about trifles [Scot.].

per·o·ra·tion (per·a·rā'·shan) *n.* the concluding part of an oration. **perorate** *v.i.* to deliver a speech [L. *perorare*, to speak to the end].

per·ox·ide (pa·rak'·sīd) *n.* (Chem.) oxide containing more oxygen than the normal oxide of an element; *v.t.* (Colloq.) to bleach the hair with peroxide of hydrogen.

per·pen·dic·u·lar (pur·pan·dik'·ya·ler) *a.* exactly upright or vertical; at right angles to the plane of the horizon; at right angles to a given line or surface; *n.* a line at right angles to the plane of the horizon or to any line or plane; the latest of the styles of English Gothic architecture, marked by stiff, straight lines; upright position. **-ly** *adv.* [L. *perpendiculum*, a plumb-line].

per·pe·trate (pur'·pa·trāt) *v.t.* to commit (something bad, esp. a crime). **perpetration** *n.* **perpetrator** *n.* [L. *perpetrare*, to accomplish].

per·pet·u·al (per·petch'·oo·wal) *a.* continuing indefinitely; everlasting. **-ly** *adv.* **perpetuate** *v.t.* to make perpetual; not to allow to be forgotten. **perpetuation** *n.* **perpetuity** (pur·pa·tū'·a·ti·) *n.* the state or quality of being perpetual [L. *perpetualis*].

per·plex (per·pleks') *v.t.* to make intricate, or difficult; to puzzle; to bewilder. **-ed** *a.* puzzled; bewildered. **-ing** *a.* **-ity** *n.* bewilderment; a confused state of mind [L. *per*, thoroughly; *plectere*, to weave].

per·qui·site (pur'·kwa·zit) *n.* a casual payment in addition to salary, etc.; a tip [L. *perquisitum*, a thing eagerly sought].

per·se·cute (pur'·si·kūt) *v.t.* to oppress unjustly for the holding of an opinion; to subject to persistent ill-treatment; to harass. **persecution** *n.* **persecutor** *n.* [L. *persequi*, to pursue].

per·se·vere (pur·sa·vēr) *v.i.* to persist; to maintain an effort; not to give in. **persevering** *a.* **perseveringly** *adv.* **perseverance** *n.* [L. *per*, thoroughly; *severus*, strict].

per·sian (pur'·zhan) *a.* pert. to Persia (now Iran) its people, or the language. **— cat**, a breed of cat with long, silky fur.

per·si·flage (pur'·si·flázh) *n.* idle banter [Fr. fr. L. *per*, through; *sifilare, sibilare*, to hiss].

per·sim·mon (per·sim'·an) *n.* an American tree with plumlike fruit [Amer.-Ind.].

per·sist (per·sist') *v.i.* to continue firmly in a state or action in spite of obstacles or objections. **-ent** *a.* persisting; steady; persevering; lasting. **-ently** *adv.* **-ence, -ency** *a.* [L. *persistere*, fr. *sistere*, to stand].

per·son (pur'·san) *n.* a human being; an individual; the body of a human being; a character in a play; (Gram.) one of the three classes of personal pronouns (first, second, or third) showing the relation of the subject to a verb, as speaking, spoken to, or spoken of. **-able** *a.* attractive in appearance. **-age** *n.* a person, esp. of rank or social position. **-al** *a.*

pert. to, peculiar to, or done by, a person; pert. to bodily appearance; directed against a person; (*Gram.*) denoting the pronouns, I, you, he, she, it, we, you, and they. **-ally** *adv.* in person; individually. **-ality** *n.* individuality; distinctive personal qualities. **personalty** (pur'·san·al·ti·) *n.* (*Law*) personal effects; movable possessions. **-ate** *v.t.* to assume character of; to pretend to be. **-ator** *n.* **-ation** *n.* [L. *persona*].

per·son·i·fy (per·sán'·a·fī) *v.t.* to endow inanimate objects or abstract ideas with human attributes; to be an outstanding example of. **personification** *n.* [L. *persona*, a person; *facere*, to make].

per·son·nel (pur·san·el') *n.* the persons employed in a public service, business, office, etc.; staff [Fr. fr. L. *persona*, person].

per·spec·tive (per·spek'·tiv) *n.* the art of drawing objects on a plane surface to give impression of the relative distance of objects, indicated by the convergence of their receding lines; relation of parts of a problem, etc. in the mind [L. *per*, through; *specere*, to look].

per·spi·ca·cious (pur·spi·kā'·shas) *a.* of acute discernment; of keen understanding. **-ly** *adv.* **perspicacity** (pur·spi·kas'·a·ti·) *n.* quick mental insight or discernment. **perspicuous** (per·spik'·ū·as) *a.* clear to the understanding; lucid. **perspicuously** *adv.* **perspicuousness** *n.* **perspicuity** (pur·spi·kū'·a·ti·) *n.* clearness [L. *perspicax*, keen of sight].

per·spire (per·spīr') *v.t.* to emit through the pores of the skin; *v.i.* to evacuate the moisture of the body through the pores of the skin; to sweat. **perspiration** *n.* the process of perspiring; the moisture emitted [L. *per*, through; *spirare*, to breathe].

per·suade (per·swād') *v.t.* to influence by argument, entreaty, etc.; to win over. **persuasive** (per·swā'·siv) *a.* having the power of persuading. **persuasively** *adv.* **persuasiveness** *n.* **persuasion** (per·swā'·zhan) *n.* the act of persuading; the quality of persuading; conviction; belief; sect. **persuasible** *a.* [L. *per*, thoroughly; *suadere*, to advise].

pert (purt) *a.* bold; forward; saucy. **-ly** *adv.* **-ness** *n.* [O.Fr. *apert*].

per·tain (per·tān') *v.i.* to belong; to concern [L. *pertinere*, to belong].

per·ti·na·cious (pur·ta·nā'·shas) *a.* adhering to an opinion, etc. with obstinacy; persevering; resolute. **-ly** *adv.* **-ness** *n.* **pertinacity** (per·ti·nas'·i·ti·) *n.* [L. *pertinax*, tenacious].

per·ti·nent (pur'·ta·nant) *a.* related to the subject or matter in hand. **-ly** *adv.* **pertinence, pertinency** *n.* [L. *pertinere*, to belong].

per·turb (per·turb') *v.t.* to disturb; to trouble greatly. **-ation** (pur·ter·bā'·shan) *n.* mental uneasiness or disquiet; disorder [L. *per*, thoroughly; *turbare*, to disturb].

Pe·ru (pa·róo') *n.* a republic on the west coast of S. America. **-vian** *n.* a native of Peru; *a.* pert. to Peru.

pe·ruse (pa·róoz') *v.t.* to read through, esp. with care. **perusal** *n.* the act of perusing [*per*, thoroughly; and *use*].

per·vade (per·vād') *v.t.* to spread through the whole of; to be diffused through all parts of. **pervasion** (per·vā'·zhun) *n.* **pervasive** *a.* [L. *per*, through; *vadere*, to go].

per·verse (per·vurs') *a.* obstinately or unreasonably wrong; refusing to do the right, or to admit error; self-willed. **-ness**, **perversity** *n.* [L. *per*, thoroughly; *vertere*, to turn].

per·ver·sion (per·vur'·zhan) *n.* a turning from the true purpose, use, or meaning; corruption; unnatural manifestation of sexual desire. **perversive** *a.* tending to pervert [L. *per*, thoroughly; *vertere*, to turn].

per·vert (per·vurt') *v.t.* to turn from its

proper purpose; to misinterpret; to lead astray; to corrupt. **pervert** (pur'·vert) *n.* one who has deviated from the normal, esp. from right to wrong [L. *per*, thoroughly; *vertere*, to turn].

per·vi·ous (pur'·vi·as) *a.* giving passage to; penetrable. **-ness** *n.* [L. *per*, through, *via*, way].

pes·si·mism (pes'·a·mizm) *n.* the doctrine that the world is fundamentally evil; the tendency to look on the dark side of things (opp. of *optimism*); melancholy. **pessimist** *n.* **pessimistic** *a.* **pessimistically** *adv.* [L. *pessimus*, worst].

pest (pest) *n.* a plague or pestilence; a troublesome or harmful thing or person; nuisance. **-iferous** *a.* pestilential; carrying disease; (*Colloq.*) annoying [L. *pestis*, a plague].

pes·ter (pes'·ter) *v.t.* to trouble or vex persistently; to annoy [O.Fr. *empestrer*, fr. L.L. *pastorium*, a foot shackle].

pest·i·cide (pes'·ta·sīd) *n.* a pest killer.

pes·ti·lence (pes'·ti·lens) *n.* any infectious or contagious, deadly disease. **pestilent** *a.* producing disease; noxious; harmful to morals. **pestilential** (pes·ta·len'·shal) *a.* pert. to, or producing, pestilence; destructive; wicked [L. *pestis*, plague].

pes·tle (pes'·l, pes'·tl) *n.* an instrument for pounding substances in a mortar [L. *pistillum*, fr. *pinsere*, to pound].

pet (pet) *n.* an animal or person kept or regarded with affection; a favorite; *a.* favorite; *v.t.* to make a pet of; to indulge. *pr.p.* **-ting.** *pa.p.* and *pa.t.* **-ted** [etym. uncertain].

pet (pet) *n.* a sudden fit of peevishness [etym. uncertain].

pet·al (pet'·al) *n.* a colored flower-leaf. **-ed,** **-led** *a.* having petals. **-ine** *a.* pert. to, resembling, a petal [Gk. *petalon*, a thin plate].

pe·ter (pē'·ter) *v.i.* (*Colloq.*) to become exhausted, gradually smaller, weaker, etc. (with *out*) [fr. name *Peter*].

pet·it (pet'·i·, pe·tē') (*Law*) small; minor. *fem.* **petite** (pa·tēt') small, dainty, trim of figure. — **point** *a.* slanting stitch used in embroidery and tapestry [Fr.].

pe·ti·tion (pa·tish'·an) *n.* a formal request or earnest prayer; *v.t.* and *i.* to present a petition to; to entreat. **-ary** *a.* **-er** *n.* [L. *petere*, to ask].

pet·ri·fy (pet'·ra·fī) *v.t.* to turn into stone; to make hard like stone; to make motionless with fear; *v.i.* to become like stone. *pr.p.* **petrified, pertifactive** *a.* [L. and Gk. *petra*, rock, stone; *facere*, to make].

pe·tro *prefix* fr. L. and Gk. *petra*, rock, stone, used in derivatives. **petrography** (pa·trág'·ra·fi·) *n.* the science of describing and classifying rocks. **petrographic(al)** *a.* **petrology** *n.* a branch of geology dealing with the composition, structure, and classification of rocks, their origin and sequence of formation. **petrologic(al)** *a.* **petrous** (pe'·tras) *a.* pert. to, or like, rock; rocky; hard [Gk. *graphein*, to write; *logos*, discourse].

pe·tro·le·um (pa·trō'·li·am) *n.* a mineral oil drawn from the earth by means of wells. **petrol** *n.* (*Brit.*) gasoline. **petrolic** *a.* [L. *petra*, rock; *oleum*, oil].

pet·ti·coat (pet'·i·kōt) *n.* a woman's underskirt; (*Colloq.*) a woman; *a.* feminine [orig. *petty coat*, a small coat].

pet·ti·fog·ger (pet'·i·fág·er) *n.* a low class person given to mean dealing in small matters. **pettifog** *v.i.* **-y** *n.* low trickery. **pettifogging** *a.* [etym. uncertain].

pet·tish (pet'·ish) *a.* petulant; easily annoyed. **-ly** *adv.* **-ness** *n.* [fr. *pet*, a fit of temper].

pet·ty (pet'·i·) *a.* small; unimportant; trivial; small-minded; of lower rank. **pettily** *adv.* **pettiness** *n.* — **cash,** small items of expenditure, esp. in an office. — **officer,** a non-commissioned officer in the Navy [Fr. *petit*, small].

pet·u·lant (pech′·a·lant) *a.* given to small fits of temper; irritable. **-ly** *adv.* **petulance, petulancy** *n.* peevishness; crossness; fretfulness [L. *petulans*, wanton].

pe·tu·ni·a (pa·tū′·ni·a) *n.* a common garden plant with showy flowers [Braz. *petun*, tobacco].

pew (pū) *n.* a long, fixed bench in a church [O.Fr. *puie*, a platform].

pe·wee (pē′·wē) *n.* a small bird, the phoebe. Also **pewit** [imit. of its note].

pew·ter (pū′·ter) *n.* an alloy of tin and lead or some other metal, esp. copper; ware made of this; *a.* made of pewter [O.Fr. *peutre*].

phae·ton (fā′·tan) *n.* a light, four-wheeled, open carriage.

phal·ange See **phalanx.**

pha·lan·ger (fa·lan′·jer) *n.* genus of furry marsupial, some winged; flying squirrel [Gk. *phalangion*, a spider's web].

pha·lanx (fā′·langks) *n.* in ancient Greece, a company of soldiers in close array; hence, any compact body of people; (*Anat.*) a small bone of a toe or finger. *pl.* **-es, phalanges** [Gk.].

phal·lus (fal′·as) *n.* sexual organs. *pl.* **phalli. phallic** *a.* [Gk. *phallos*].

phan·tasm (fan′·tazm) *n.* an imaginary vision; a phantom; a specter. **-al, -ic** *a.* **phantasmagoria** (fan·taz·ma·gō′·ri·a) *n.* an exhibition of optical illusions; a shifting scene of dim or unreal figures. **phantasmagoric** *a.* **phantasy** *n.* See **fantasy. phantom** (fan′·tam) *n.* an apparition; a specter; a ghost; *a.* spectral [Gk. *phainein*, to show].

Phar·aoh (fā′·rō) *n.* 'The Great House' a title of the kings of ancient Egypt.

Phar·i·see (far′·i·sē) *n.* (*Bib.*) one of a Jewish sect noted for their strict observance of the forms of the Law. **Pharisaic** (far·a·sā′·ik), **Pharisaical** *a.* **Pharisaically** *adv.* **-ism, Pharisaism,** *n.* [Heb. *parash*, to separate].

phar·ma·ceu·ti·cal (far·ma·sū′·tik·al) *a.* pert. to pharmacy. **pharmaceutics** *n.pl.* the science of pharmacy. **pharmaceutist** *n.* [Gk. *pharmakon*, a drug].

phar·ma·cy (far′·ma·si·) *n.* the science of preparing, compounding, and dispensing drugs and medicines; a drugstore. **pharmacist** *n.* one skilled in pharmacy. **pharmacology** *n.* the study of drugs and their action. **pharmacologist** *n.* one skilled in pharmacy. **pharmacopoeia** (far·ma·ka·pē′·ya) *n.* an authoritative book containing information on medicinal drugs [Gk. *pharmakon*, a drug].

phar·ynx (far′·ingks) *n.* the cavity at back of mouth, opening into the gullet. *pl.* **pharynges. pharyngeal** (fa·rin′·jal) *a.* Also **pharyngal. pharyngitis** (far·in·jī′·tis) *n.* (*Med.*) inflammation of pharynx. **pharyngoscope** *n.* instrument for examining throat [Gk. *pharunx*, the pharynx].

phase (fāz) *n.* (*Astron.*) an aspect of moon or a planet; a stage in development; an aspect of a subject or question. **phasic** *a.* [Gk. *phasis*, an appearance].

pheas·ant (fez′·ant) *n.* a gamebird with brilliant plumage [Gk. *Phasis*, a river in Colchis, whence the bird first came].

phe·nom·e·non (fa·nàm′·a·nàn) *n.* anything appearing or observed, esp. if having scientific interest; a remarkable person or thing; (*Philos.*) sense appearance as opposed to real existence. *pl.* **phenomena. phenomenal** *a.* pert. to a phenomenon; remarkable; extraordinary. **phenomenally** *adv.* [Gk. *phainomenon*, a thing appearing].

phew (fū) *interj.* expressing disgust, impatience, relief, etc.

phi·al (fī′·al) *n.* a small glass bottle; a vial [Gk. *phialē*, a flat vessel].

phi·lan·der (fa·lan′·der) *v.i.* to flirt. **-er** *n.* [Gk. *philos*, loving; *anēr*, a man].

phi·lan·thro·py (fi·lan′·thra·pi·) *n.* love of mankind, esp. as shown in acts of charity; an act of charity. **philanthropic** (fil·an·throp′·ik), **philanthropical** *a.* **philanthropically** *adv.* **philanthropist** *n.* one who loves and seeks to do good to his fellowmen. Also **philanthrope** [Gk. *philos*, loving; *anthrōpos*, man].

phi·lat·e·ly (fa·lat′·a·li·) *n.* stamp collecting. **philatelic** *a.* **philatelist** *n.* [Gk. *philos*, loving; *atelēs*, franked].

phil·har·mon·ic (fil·er·màn′·ik, fil·har·màn′·ik) *a.* loving harmony or music; musical [Gk. *philos*, loving; *harmonia*, harmony].

Phi·lis·tine (fil′·as·tīn, ·tin) *n.* one with no love of music, painting, etc.; an uncultured person [*Bib.* Phillistine].

phi·lol·o·gy (fi·làl′·a·ji·) *n.* scientific study of origin, development, etc. of languages. **philological** *a.* **philologian** (fi·la·lō′·ji·an) **philologist** *n.* one versed in philology [Gk. *philos*, loving; *logos*, word, speech].

phi·los·o·phy (fa·làs′·a·fi·) *n.* originally, any branch of investigation of natural phenomena; now, the study of beliefs regarding God, existence, conduct, etc. and of man's relation with the universe; a calmness of mind; composure. **philosopher** *n.* a student of philosophy. **philosophic** (fil·a·saf′·ik) **philosophical** *a.* pert. to philosophy; wise; calm. **philosophically** *adv.* **philosophize** *v.i.* to reason like a philosopher; to theorize; to moralize. **philosophism** *n.* a pretended system of philosophy; sophism [Gk. *philos*, loving; *sophia*, wisdom].

phil·ter (fil′·ter) *n.* a drink supposed to excite love; any magic potion. Also **philtre** [Gk. *philtron*, fr. *philos*, loving].

phle·bi·tis (fla·bī′·tis) *n.* (*Med.*) inflammation of a vein. **phlebitic** *a.* **phlebotomy** *n.* (*Surg.*) blood-letting [Gk. *phleps*, a vein].

phlegm (flem) *n.* a secretion of thick mucous substance discharged from throat by expectoration; calmness; apathy; sluggishness. **phlegmatic** (fleg·mat′·ik) *a.* cool and collected; unemotional. [Gk. *phlegma*].

phlox (fláks) *n.* a genus of garden plants [Gk. = a flame].

phoe·be (fē·bi·) *n.* a small American flycatcher [imit.]

pho·bi·a (fō′·bi·a) *n.* a morbid dread of anything; used esp. as a suffix, e.g. claustrophobia, hydrophobia, etc. [Gk. *phobos*, fear].

Phoe·nix, Phenix (fē′·niks) *n.* (*Myth.*) a fabulous Arabian bird, symbol of immortality; a paragon [Gk. *phoinix*].

phone (fōn) *n., v.t.* and *i.* (*Colloq.*) abbrev. of **telephone** [Gk. *phōnē*, sound].

phone (fōn) *n.* a sound made in speaking. **phonic** *a.* pert. to sound, esp. to speech sounds. **phonics** *n.* method of teaching reading, etc. on basis of speech sounds [Gk. *phone*].

pho·neme (fō′·nēm) *n.* a member of the set of smallest units of speech sounds that serve to distinguish utterances. **phonemic** *a.* **phonemically** *adv.* **phonemics** *n.* branch of linguistics which deals with phonemes. [F.]

pho·net·ic (fō·net′·ik) *a.* pert. to the voice; pert. to, or representing, vocal sounds. Also **-al** *a.* **-ally** *adv.* **-s** *n.* the branch of the study of language which deals with speech sounds, and their production. **-ize** *v.t.* to represent phonetically. — **spelling,** a simplified system of spelling in which same letter or symbol is always used for same sound, e.g. cat = kat [Gk. *phōnē*, sound].

pho·no- (fō′·nō) *prefix* fr. Gk. *phōnē*, sound, used in many derivatives. **-gram** *n.* a character or symbol, esp. in shorthand, used to represent a speech sound. **-graph** *n.* an instrument for reproducing sounds from records. **phonography** *n.* a system of shorthand. **phonology** (fō·nàl'·ạ·ji·) *n.* study of speech sounds; phonetics. **-logic(al)** *a.*

pho·ny, phoney (fō'·ni·) *a.* (*Slang*) sham; counterfeit.

phos·phate (fàs'·fāt) *n.* a salt of phosphoric acid. **phosphatic** *a.* — **of lime,** commercially, bone-ash. **phosphide** *n.* a compound of phosphorus with another element, e.g. copper [fr. *phosphorus*].

phos·pho·rus (fàs'·fẹr·ạs) *n.* a non-metallic element, a yellowish waxlike substance giving out a pale light in the dark. **phosphorous** *a.* pert. to phosphorus. **phosphorescence** (fàs·fẹr·es'·ạns) *n.* the giving out of light without heat, as phosphorus, the glow-worm, decaying fish, etc. **phosphorescent** *a.* **phosphoric** *a.* pert. to, or obtained from, phosphorus; phosphorous. **phosphureted** *a.* combined with phosphorus [Gk. *phōs*, light; *phoros*, bearing].

pho·to (fō'·tō) *n.* (*Colloq.*) *abbrev.* of photograph; *v.t.* to photograph.

pho·to (fō'·tō) *prefix* fr. Gk. *phōs*, *phōtos*, light, used in derivatives. **-chemistry** (fō·tō·kem'·is·tri·) *n.* the branch of chemistry which treats of the chemical action of light. **-electron** *n.* an electron liberated from a metallic surface by the action of a beam of ultraviolet light. — **finish,** in racing, a photo taken at the finish to show correct placing of contestants. **-genic** *a.* producing light; of a person, having features, etc. that photograph well.

pho·tog·ra·phy (fạ·tàg'·rạ·fi·) *n.* the art of producing pictures by the chemical action of light on a sensitive plate or film. **photograph** *n.* a picture so made; *v.t.* to take a photograph of. **photographer** *n.* **photographic(al)** *a.* pert. to, resembling, or produced by, photography. **photographically** *adv.* [Gk. *phōs*, light; *graphein*, to write; Fr. *gravure*, an engraving; Gk. *lithos*, a stone].

pho·tol·o·gy (fō·tàl'·ạ·ji·) *n.* the science of light. **photometer** *n.* an instrument for measuring the intensity of light [Gk. *phōs*, light; *logos*, discourse; *metron*, a measure].

pho·ton (fō'·tàn) *n.* the unit of measurement of light intensity [Gk. *phōs*, *phōtos*, light].

pho·to·stat (fō'·tō·stat) *n.* a photographic apparatus for making copies of documents, etc. directly on paper; *v.t.* to copy thus. **photostatic** *a.* [Trade Name].

pho·to·syn·the·sis (fō·tō·sin'·thạ·sis) *n.* the process by which a plant, under the influence of sunlight, can build up, in its chlorophyll-containing cells, carbohydrates from the carbon dioxide of the atmosphere and from the hydrogen of the water in the soil [Gk. *phōs*, *phōtos*, light; *sun*, together; *thesis*, a placing].

phrase (frāz) *n.* a small group of words forming part of a sentence; a short pithy expression; a characteristic mode of expression; (*Mus.*) a short, distinct part of a longer passage; *v.t.* to express suitably in words. **phraseogram** (frā'·zi·ạ·gram) *n.* in shorthand, a symbol used to represent a phrase. **-ology** *n.* a mode of expression; the choice of words used in speaking or writing [Gk. *phrazein*, to speak].

phre·net·ic (fri·net'·ik) *a.* having the mind disordered; frenzied; frantic [Gk. *phrēn*, the diaphragm, the mind].

phre·nol·o·gy (fri·nàl'·ạ·ji·) *n.* character reading from the shape of the head. **phrenologic(al)** *a.* **phrenologically** *adv.* **phrenologist** *n.* [Gk. *phrēn*, mind; *logos*, discourse].

phthi·sis (thī'·sis) *n.* (*Med.*) a wasting away of the lungs; consumption. **phthisic** (tiz'·ik), **phthisical** (tiz'·ik·ạl) *a.* [Gk. fr. *phthiein*, to waste away].

phy·lac·ter·y (fạ·lak'·tạ·ri·) *n.* a charm or amulet; a small leather case containing strips of vellum, inscribed with certain verses of the Law and worn on the forehead or left arm by male Jews during morning prayer [Gk. *phylassein*, to guard].

phy·log·e·ny (fi·làj'·ạ·ni·) *n.* (*Bot.*) the evolution of an animal or plant type. **phylum** (fī'·lạm) *n.* one of the primary divisions of the animal or plant kingdoms. *pl.* **phyla** [Gk. *phylon*, a race; *genesis*, origin].

phys·ic (fiz'·ik) *n.* (*Arch.*) a cathartic; medicine; *v.t.* to give a dose of physic to. *pr.p.* **physicking.** *pa.p.* and *pa.t.* **physicked. physician** (fạ·zish'·ạn) *n.* one skilled in the art of healing; a medical doctor [Gk. *physis*, nature].

phys·i·cal (fiz'·ik·ạl) *a.* pert. to physics; pert. to nature; bodily, as opposed to mental or moral; material. **-ly** *adv.* [Gk. *physis*, nature].

phys·ics (fiz'·iks) *n.* sciences (excluding chemistry and biology) which deal with natural phenomena, e.g. motion, force, light, sound, electricity, etc. **physicist** (fiz'·i·sist) *n.* [Gk. *physis*, nature].

phys·i·og·no·my (fiz·i·àg'·nạ·mi·, fiz·i·àn'·ạ·mi·) *n.* art of judging character from contours of face; face itself; expression of the face. **physiognomic, physiognomical** *a.* **physiognomist** *n.* [Gk. *physis*, nature; *gnōmōn*, a judge].

phys·i·og·ra·phy (fiz·i·àg'·rạ·fi·) *n.* the study and description of natural phenomena; physical geography. **physiographer** *n.* [Gk. *physis*, nature; *graphein*, to write].

phys·i·ol·o·gy (fiz·i·àl'·ạ·ji·) *n.* science which deals with functions and life processes of plants, animals, and human beings. **physiological** *a.* **physiologist** *n.* [Gk. *physis*, nature; *logos*, discourse].

phys·i·o·ther·a·py (fiz·i·ō·ther'·ạ·pi·) *n.* the application of massage, manipulation, light, heat, electricity, etc., for treatment of certain disabilities [Gk. *physis*, nature; *therapeuein*, to cure].

phy·sique (fi·zēk') *n.* bodily structure and development [Fr. fr. Gk. *physis*, nature].

phy·to (fī'·to) *prefix* fr. Gk. *phyton*, a plant. **phytogenesis** (fī·tō·jen'·ạ·sis), **phytogeny** (fī·tàj'·ạ·ni·) *n.* the evolution of plants.

pi (pī) *n.* the Greek letter π, esp. as a mathematical symbol for the ratio of the circumference of a circle to its diameter, approx. 3⅐, or 3.14159.

pi·a·no (pē·à'·nō) *adv.* (*Mus.*) softly. **pianissimo** *adv.* very softly [It.].

pi·a·no (pē·a'·nō) *n.* *abbrev.* of **pianoforte** (pē·à·nō·fōr'·te) *n.* a musical instrument having wires of graduated tension, struck by hammers moved by notes on a keyboard. **pianist** (pē'·ạ·nist, pē·an'·ist) *n.* one who plays the piano [It. *piano e forte* = soft and strong].

pi·as·ter (pi·as'·tẹr) *n.* a monetary unit of several Eastern countries [It. *piastra*].

pi·az·za (pē·az'·ạ, pē·at'·sạ) *n.* a porch of a house; a public square [It.].

pi·ca (pī'·kạ) *n.* (*Print.*) a size of type, having 6 lines to the inch [L. *pica*, a magpie].

pic·a·dor (pik·ạ·dawr') *n.* a mounted bullfighter armed with a lance to prod the bull [Sp. *pica*, a pike].

pic·a·roon (pik'·ạ·ròòn) *n.* an adventurer; a pirate. **picaresque** (pik·ạ·resk') *a.* of a novel, dealing with the lives and adventures of rogues [Sp. *picaro*, a rogue].

pic·ca·lil·li (pik·ạ·lil'·i·) *n.* a pickle of vegetables [etym. uncertain].

pic·co·lo (pik´·a·lō) n. (Mus.) a small flute, sounding an octave higher than the ordinary flute [It.].

pick (pik) v.t. to peck at, like birds with their bills; to pierce with a pointed instrument; to open with a pointed instrument, as a lock; to pluck, or cull, as flowers, etc.; to raise or lift (with 'up'); to choose or select; to rob; to pluck the strings of a musical instrument; (Colloq.) to eat; v.i. to eat daintily or without appetite; n. a sharp-pointed tool; the the choicest or best of anything. **-ax** n. an instrument for digging. **-ing** n. the act of one who picks; stealing; pl. gleanings; perquisites, often obtained by slightly underhand methods. **— on** (Colloq.) to nag; to find fault. **— pocket** n. one who steals from pockets. **—me-up** n. a drink that acts as a stimulant or restorative [M.E.].

pick·a·nin·ny (pik´·a·nin·i·) a small child; a Negro baby [Sp. pequeño, small].

pick·er·el (pik´·a·ral) n. a young pike; a kind of pike [dim. fr. pike].

pick·et (pik´·it) n. a sharpened stake (used in fortifications, etc.); a peg or pale; a guard posted in front of an army; a party sent out by trade unions to dissuade men from working during a strike; v.t. to fence with pickets [Fr. piquet, fr. pic, a pike].

pick·le (pik´·l) n. brine or vinegar in which fish, meat, or vegetables are preserved; any food preserved in brine or vinegar; (Colloq.) a difficult situation; v.t. to preserve with salt or vinegar. **-d** a. (Slang) drunk. **-s** n.pl. vegetables in vinegar and spices [M.E. pykyl, pikille].

pic·nic (pik´·nik) n. pleasure excursion with meal out of doors; agreeable situation; v.i. to go on a picnic. pr.p. **-king**. pa.p. and pa.t. **-ked** [Fr. pique-nique, etym. uncertain].

pi·cot (pē´·kō) n. a small projecting loop of thread forming part of an ornamental edging to ribbon, lace, etc. [Fr.].

pic·ric (pik´·rik) a. pert. to **— acid**, a poisonous, crystalline substance used in solution as a dressing for burns, for dyes, explosives, etc. [Gk. pikros, bitter].

pic·to·graph (pik´·ta·graf) n. a picture representing an idea [L. pingere, pictum, to paint; Gk. graphein, to write].

pic·to·ri·al (pik·tō´·ri·al) a. pert. to pictures; expressed by pictures; illustrated. **-ly** adv. [L. pictor, a painter, fr. pingere, to paint].

pic·ture (pik´·cher) n. a representation of objects or scenes on paper, canvas, etc., by drawing, painting, photography, etc.; a mental image; a likeness or copy; an illustration; picturesque object; a graphic or vivid description in words; v.t. to draw or paint an image or representation of; to describe graphically; to recall vividly. **picturesque** (pik·cher·esk´) a. making effective picture; vivid in description. **-squely** adv. **-squeness** n. **— gallery** n. a hall containing a collection of pictures for exhibition. [L. pingere, pictum, to paint].

pid·dle (pid´·l) v.i. to trifle. **piddling** a. trifling [etym. uncertain].

pidg·in (pij´·in) n. Chinese corruption of English word business. **pidgin** or **pigeon English**, a jargon used in China between foreigners and natives.

pie (pī) n. (Cookery) a dish of meat or fruit covered with upper or lower pastry crust or both; (Print.) a confused mass of type [etym. uncertain].

pie (pī) n. a magpie. **-bald** (pī´·bawld) a. irregularly marked; streaked with any two colors. **-d** a. piebald; variegated [L. pica, a magpie; bald = balled, streaked].

piece (pēs) n. a part of anything; a bit; a portion; a single object; a separate example; a coin; a counter in chess, checkers, etc.; a literary work; a musical composition; a gun; a plot of land; v.t. to mend; to put together. **— goods** n.pl. textile fabrics sold by measured lengths of the material. **— meal** adv. little by little; gradually. **— work** n. work paid for by the amount done, and not by the hour, day, etc. **— of eight**, an old Spanish dollar = eight reals [Fr. pièce].

pier (pir) n. a piece of solid, upright masonry, as a support or pillar for an arch, bridge, or beam; a structure built out over the water as a landing. **— glass** n. a tall mirror, esp. a wall mirror between two windows [Fr. pierre, stone, fr. L. Petra].

pierce (pirs) v.t. to thrust into, esp. with a pointed instrument; to make a hole in; to penetrate; v.i. to enter; to penetrate. **piercing** a. penetrating; sharp; keen. **piercingly** adv. [Fr. percer].

pi·e·ty (pī´·a·ti·) n. the quality of being pious; devotion to religion; affectionate respect for one's parents. **pietist** n. an ultrapious person; a sanctimonious person. **pietistic** a. **pietism** n. [L. pietas, fr. pius, pious].

pig (pig) n. a hoofed domestic animal, reared for its flesh; oblong mass of smelted metal, as pig iron; v.i. to bring forth pigs. **-gish** a. pert. to, or like, pigs; dirty; greedy; stubborn. **-tail** n. the tail of a pig; a braid of hair hanging from the back of the head; a roll of twisted tobacco. **—eyed** a. having small, sly eyes. **-headed** a. obstinate; stupidly perverse. **— iron, — lead**, iron, lead, cast in rough oblong bars. **-nut** n. the nut of the brown hickory. **-skin** n. strong leather made from the pig's skin, and used for saddles, etc. (Colloq.) a football. **-sticking** n. hunting wild boar with a spear, popular in India. **-sty** n. a covered enclosure for keeping pigs; a dirty house or room [M.E. pigge].

pi·geon (pij´·an) n. any bird of the dove family, both wild and domesticated; a simpleton or dupe. **— English** n. See **pidgin English**. **—hearted** a. timid. **-hole** n. a little division in a desk or case, for holding papers, etc.; v.t. to place in the pigeonhole of a desk, etc.; to shelve for future reference; to classify. **—toed** a. having turned-in toes [Fr. fr. L. pipio, pipionis, a young piping bird].

pig·ment (pig´·mant) n. paint; coloring matter; coloring matter in animal tissues and cells. **-ation** n. (Biol.) coloring matter [L. pigmentum].

pigmy. See **pygmy**.

pike (pīk) n. a sharp point; an old weapon consisting of a long, wooden shaft with a flat-pointed steel head; a voracious freshwater fish; a turnpike or tollgate. **-staff** n. a staff with a sharp metal spike [O.E. pic, a point].

pi·las·ter (pi´·las·ter, pi·las´·ter) n. a square column, usually set in a wall [It. pilastro, fr. L. pila, a pillar].

pil·chard (pil´·cherd) n. a sea fish resembling the herring, but smaller [etym. uncertain].

pile (pīl) n. a mass or collection of things; a heap; a large building or mass of buildings; in atomic energy research, the nuclear energy furnace, made by accumulation of uranium and graphite. (Colloq.) a large fortune; v.t. to throw into a pile or heap; to accumulate [L. pila, a pillar].

pile (pīl) n. a beam driven vertically into the ground to support a building, a bridge etc.; v.t. to drive piles into; to support with piles. **-driver** n. a machine for driving in piles [O.E. pil, a dart].

pile (pīl) n. fur or hair; nap of a fabric, esp.

if thick and close-set, as in velvet [L. *pilus*, a hair].

piles (pīlz) *n.pl.* a disease of the rectum; hemorrhoids [L. *pila*, a ball].

pil·fer (pil′·fẹr) *v.t.* and *i.* to steal in small quantities [O.Fr. *pelfrer*].

pil·grim (pil′·grim) *n.* a traveler, esp. one who journeys to visit a holy place. **-age** *n.* journey to a holy place; any long journey [O.Fr. *pelegrin*, fr. L. *peregrinus*, a stranger].

pill (pil) *n.* a small ball of medicine, to be swallowed whole; anything disagreeable that has to be endured; (*Slang*) an unpopular person. **-box** *n.* (*Mil.*) a small concrete fort [L. *pilula*, dim. fr. *pila*, a ball].

pil·lage (pil′·ij) *n.* the act of plundering; plunder or spoil; *v.t.* to plunder [Fr. *piller*, fr. L. *pilare*, to plunder].

pil·lar (pil′·ẹr) *n.* a slender upright structure of stone, iron, etc.; a column; a support. **-ed** *a.* [L. *pila*, a column].

pil·lion (pil′·yạn) *n.* a cushioned pad put behind the saddle on a horse as a seat for a second person [Gael. *pillean*, a pack-saddle].

pil·lo·ry (pil′·ạ·ri·) *n.* an old instrument used to punish offenders, consisting of a frame with holes for head and hands in which the person was confined and exposed to pelting and ridicule; *v.t.* to punish by putting into a pillory; to expose to ridicule and abuse. [Fr. *pilori*]

pil·low (pil′·ō) *n.* a cushion, esp. for the head of a person in bed; *v.t.* to place on a pillow. **-case**, **-slip** *n.* a removable covering for a pillow [O.E. *pyle*].

pi·lose (pī′·lōs) *a.* hairy; covered with hair. Also **pilous pilosity** *n.* [L. *pilosus*, hair].

pi·lot (pī′·lạt) *n.* a person qualified to take charge of a ship entering or leaving a harbor, or where knowledge of local waters is needed; one qualified to operate an aircraft; a steersman; a guide; a small jet of gas kept burning in order to light a stove, etc.; *v.t.* to direct the course of; to guide through dangers or difficulties. **— engine** *n.* a locomotive sent on ahead to clear the way for a train [Fr. *pilote*].

pi·men·to (pi·men′·tō) *n.* allspice; pimiento, a reddish pepper [Sp. fr. L. *pigmentum*, spice].

pimp (pimp) *n.* a procurer; a pander; *v.i.* to pander [Fr. *pimper*, to dress up].

pim·per·nel (pim′·pẹr·nel) *n.* an annual plant of the primrose family [Fr. *pimprenelle*].

pim·ple (pim·′pl) *n.* a small, red, pustular spot on the skin. **-d, pimply** *a.*

pin (pin) *n.* a short, thin piece of stiff wire with a point and head for fastening soft materials together; a wooden or metal peg or rivet; an ornament that fastens on cloth; (*Golf*) a thin metal or wooden stick (with a flag) to mark the position of the hole; a rolling pin; a clothespin; a trifle; *pl.* (*Slang*) the legs; *v.t.* to fasten with pins; to seize and hold fast. *pr.p.* **-ning.** *pa.p.* and *pa.t.* **-ned. -cushion** *n.* a small pad in which pins are stuck. **— money** *n.* an allowance for incidental or personal expenses. **-point** *v.t.* to locate (a target) with great accuracy. **-up girl** (*Colloq.*) one whose photograph is pinned up on the wall; hence, any good-looking girl [O.E. *pinn*, a peg].

pin·a·fore (pin′·ạ·fōr) *n.* an apron for a child or young girl [E. *pin* and *afore*].

pince·nez (pans′·nā) *n.* a pair of eyeglasses fixed to the nose by a spring clip [Fr. *pincer*, to pinch; *nez*, the nose].

pin·cers (pin′·sẹrz) *n.pl.* a tool for gripping, composed of two limbs crossed and pivoted; nippers; pliers; the claw of a lobster, crab, etc. [Fr. *pincer*, to pinch)].

pinch (pinch) *v.t.* to nip or squeeze, e.g. between the thumb and finger; to stint; to make thin, e.g. by hunger; (*Slang*) to steal; to arrest; *v.i.* to press hard; to be miserly; *n.*

as much as can be taken up between the thumb and finger; a nip; an emergency. **-ed** *a.* (*Fig.*) thin and hungry looking [Fr. *pincer*].

Pin·dar (pin′·dẹr) *n.* great lyric poet of ancient Greece (522-443 B.C.). **Pindaric** (pin·dar′·ik) *a.* pert. to the poet or his poetry; *n.* an imitation of one of his odes.

pine (pīn) *n.* a coniferous tree with evergreen, needlelike leaves; wood of this tree; (*Colloq.*) a pineapple. **-y, piny** *a.* **-apple** *n.* tropical plant and its fruit resembling a pine cone; the ananas; (*Mil. Slang*) a hand grenade. **— cone** *n.* fruit of the pine [L. *pinus*].

pine (pīn) *v.i.* to waste away from grief, anxiety, want, etc.; to languish; to wither; to desire eagerly [O.E. *pinian*, fr. *pin*, pain].

pin·fold (pin′·fōld) *n.* a pound; enclosure for stray cattle [for *pindfold* = pound-fold].

ping (ping) *n.* the sound that a bullet makes **—pong** *n.* table tennis [imit.].

pin·ion (pin′·yạn) *n.* the outermost joint of a bird's wing; wing; feather; a small wheel with teeth working into the teeth of a larger wheel; *v.t.* to cut off the pinion; to restrain by binding arms to body; to shackle [O.Fr. *pignon*].

pink (pingk) *n.* a carnation, a garden flower of various colors; a light crimson color; that which is supremely excellent; *a.* of a pale crimson color [etym. uncertain].

pink (pingk) *v.t.* to pierce with small holes; to pierce with a sword, etc.; to ornament the edge with notches, etc. [M.E. *pinken*, to prick].

pink (pingk) *v.t.* of a motor engine, to make a metallic, knocking sound [imit.].

pin·na (pin′·ạ) *n.* a feather; the fin of a fish. **-te, -ted** *a.* feather-shaped; having wings or fins [L.*pinna*, for *penna*, a feather].

pin·na·cle (pin′·ạ·kl) *n.* a slender turret elevated above the main building; a rocky mountain peak; a summit; (*Fig.*) the climax [L. *pinna*, a feather, a battlement].

pint (pīnt) *n.* a liquid and a dry measure equal to ½ quart [Fr. *pinte*].

pin·to (pin′·tō) *n.* a piebald horse [Sp.].

pi·o·neer (pī·ạ·nēr′) *n.* one who originates anything or prepares the way for others; *v.i.* to open a way or originate; an explorer; (*Mil.*) one of an advance body clearing or repairing a road for troops [Fr. *pionnier*, fr. *pion*, a foot-soldier].

pi·ous (pī′·ạs) *a.* having reverence and love for God; marked by pretended or mistaken devotion;**-ly** *adv.* [L. pius].

pip (pip)*n.* the seed of an apple, orange, etc. **-less** *a.* [abbrev. fr. *pippin*].

pip (pip) *n.* a disease in the mouth of fowls [L.L. *pipita*, fr. *pituita*, phlegm].

pip (pip) *n.* a rootstock of a plant; (*Radio*) each of the six shrill notes broadcast as a time signal.

pipe (pīp) *n.* a tubular instrument of music; any long tube; a tube of clay, wood, etc. with a bowl for smoking; a bird's note; a pipeful of tobacco; a pipe-like vein of ore; *pl.* bagpipes; *v.t.* to perform on a pipe; to utter in a shrill tone; to convey by means of pipes; to ornament with a piping or fancy edging; *v.i.* to play on a pipe, esp. the bagpipes; to whistle. **piped** (pīpt) *a.* furnished with a pipe; tubular; conveyed by pipes. **piping** *a.* giving forth a shrill sound; *n.* the act of playing on a pipe; a system of pipes (for gas, water, etc.); a kind of cord trimming for ladies' dresses; ornamentation made on cakes **— clay** *n.* a fine, whitish clay used in the manufacture of tobacco pipes; *v.t.* to whiten with pipe clay. **— line** *n.* a long line of piping for conveying water, oil, etc. [O.E. *pipe*, fr. L. *pipa*].

pi·pette (pi·pet′) *n.* a thin, glass tube used for withdrawing small quantities of a liquid from a vessel [Fr. dim. of *pipe*].

pip·it (pīp'·it) *n.* small bird resembling the lark [imit.].

pip·pin (pip'·in) *a.* one of several kinds of apple [O.Fr. *pepin*, a seed].

pi·quant (pē'·kạnt) *a.* agreeably pungent to the taste; arousing interest. **-ly** *adv.* **piquancy** (pē'·kạn·si·) *n.* [Fr. *piquer*, to prick].

pique (pēk) *v.t.* to irritate; to hurt the pride of; to displease; to stimulate; to pride oneself. *pr.p.* **piquing.** *pa.p.* and *pa.t.* **piqued** (pēkt); *n.* annoyance from a slight; vexation [Fr. *piquer*, to prick].

pi·qué (pi·kā') *n.* a ribbed cotton fabric [Fr.].

pi·rate (pī'·rạt) *n.* a sea robber; a vessel manned by sea robbers; a publisher, etc. who infringes copyright; *v.t.* and *v.i.* to act as a pirate; to plunder; to publish or reproduce regardless of copyright. **piratical** *a.* **piratically** *adv.* **piracy** *n.* [Gk. *peirates*, fr. *peirein*, to attempt].

pir·ou·ette (pir·óò·et') *n.* a spinning round on the toes of one foot; *v.i.* to do this [Fr.].

pis·ca·tol·o·gy (pis·kạ·tál'·ạ·ji·) *n.* the study of fishing. **piscator** (pis·kā'·tor) *n.* an angler; a fisherman. **piscatorial, piscatory** *a.* pert. to fishermen or fishing. [L. *piscis*, a fish].

Pis·ces (pis'·ēz) *n.pl.* (*Astron.*) the Fishes, the twelfth sign of the zodiac [L. *piscis*, a fish].

pis·ci·na (pis·ī·na) *n.* a stone basin near the altar. **-l** *a.* [L. *piscis*, a fish].

pis·cine (pis'·īn) *a.* pert. to fishes [L.].

pis·ta·chi·o (pis·ta'(tā')·shi·ō) *n.* the nut of an Asiatic tree, whose kernel is used for flavoring [Sp. fr. Gk. *pistakion*].

pis·til (pis'·tl) *n.* the seed-bearing organ of a flower, consisting of the stigma, style, and ovary. **-late** *a.* having a pistil but sometimes no stamen [L. *pistillum*, a pestle].

pis·tol (pis'·tl) *n.* a small handgun; *v.t.* to shoot with a pistol [Fr. *pistole*].

pis·ton (pis'·tạn) *n.* a closely fitting metal disk moving to and fro in a hollow cylinder, e.g. as in a steam engine, automobile, etc. — **rod** *n.* a rod which connects the piston with another part of the machinery [It. *pistone*, fr. L. *pinsere*, *pistum*, to pound].

pit (pit) *n.* a deep hole in the ground, esp. one from which coal etc. is dug or quarried; the abyss of hell; a hollow or depression; an area for cock-fighting, etc.; in the theater, the section for musicians in front of stage; in motor racing, the base where cars are refilled, etc.; *v.t.* to mark with little hollows, as by pustules; to place in a pit; to put forward as an antagonist in a contest. *pr.p.* **-ting.** *pa.p.* and *pa.t.* **-ted;** *a.* marked with small hollows. **-fall** *n.* a pit lightly covered, intended to entrap animals; any hidden danger [O.E. *pytt*, fr. L. *puteus*, a well].

pit·a·pat (pit'·ạ·pat) *adv.* in a flutter; with palpitation; *n.* a light, quick step; *v.i.* to go pitapat. *pr.p.* **-ting.** *pa.p.*, *pa.t.* **-ted** [reduplication of *pat*].

pitch (pich) *n.* a thick, black, sticky substance obtained by boiling down tar; *v.t.* to cover over, smear with pitch. **-iness** *n.* **—black, —dark** *a.* very dark [L. *pix*].

pitch (pich) *v.t.* to throw, toss, fling; to set up (a tent, camp, wickets, etc.); (*Music*) to set the keynote of; *v.i.* to alight; to fix one's choice on (with 'on'); to plunge or fall forward; to slope down; of a ship, to plunge. *n.* the act of tossing or throwing; a throw or toss; steepness of a roof; downward slope; the highest point; the plunging motion of a vessel lengthwise; degree of acuteness of musical note; the distance between consecutive threads of a screw, or between successive teeth of a gear. **-ed** (picht) *a.* **-er** *n.* **-fork** *n.* a fork for tossing hay, etc.; *v.t.* to lift with a pitchfork [form of *pick*].

pitch·er (pich'·er) *n.* a jug; a vessel for pouring liquids, usually with a handle and a lip or spout [L.L. *picarium*, a goblet].

pith (pith) *n.* the soft, spongy substance in the center of plant stems; the essential substance; force or vigor. **-y** *a.* consisting of pith; terse and forceful; energetic. **-ily** *adv.* **-iness** *n.* **-less** *a.* [O.E. *pitha*].

pit·tance (pit'·ạns) *n.* an allowance for living expenses; a very small income [Fr. *pitance*, allowance of food in a monastery].

pi·tu·i·tar·y (pi·tū'·a·ter·i·) *a.* pert. to the pituitary gland. — **gland,** a ductless gland at base of the brain, secreting an endocrine influencing growth [L. *pituita*, mucus].

pit·y (pit'·i·) *n.* sympathy or sorrow for others' suffering; a cause of grief or regret; *v.t.* to feel grief or sympathy for. **-ing** *a.* expressing pity. **-ingly** *adv.* **pitiable** *a.* deserving pity. **pitiably** *adv.* **pitiful** *a.* full of pity; tender; woeful; exciting pity. **pitifully** *adv.* **pitifulness** *n.* **pitiless** *a.* feeling no pity; hardhearted. **pitilessly** *adv.* **pitilessness** *n.* **piteous** (pit'·i·as) *a.* fitted to excite pity; sad or sorrowful [L. *pietas*, piety].

piv·ot (piv'·ạt) *n.* a pin or shaft on which a wheel or other body turns; that on which important results depend; *v.t.* to turn as on a pivot. **-al** *a.* **-ally** *adv.* [Fr.].

pix·y, pixie (pik'·si·) *n.* a fairy or elf. **pixilated** *a.* amusingly accentric [etym uncert.].

piz·zi·ca·to (pit·si·kā'·to) *a.* (*Mus.*) a direction for stringed instruments denoting that the strings be plucked with the fingers [It.].

pla·ca·ble (plak'·à·b], plā'·kạ·bl) *a.* readily appeased or pacified; willing to forgive. **-ness, placability** *n.* **placate** (plàk'·āt) *v.t.* to appease, conciliate. **placatory** *a.* [L. *placare*, to appease].

plac·ard (plak'·erd) *n.* a written or printed paper posted in a public place. **placard** (plạ·kard') *v.t.* to post placards [Fr.].

place (plās) *n.* a particular part of space; a spot; a locality; a building; rank; position; priority of position; stead; duty; office or employment; (*Sport*) a position among the first three competitors to finish; *v.t.* to put in a particular spot; to find a position for; to appoint; to fix; to put; to identify. **-d** *a.* in a race, etc., to be first, second, or third at the finish. — **kick** *n.* (*Football*) one made by kicking the ball after it has been placed on the ground for the purpose. **to give place,** to make room for [L. *platea*, a broad street; fr. Gk. *platus*, broad].

pla·cen·ta (plạ·sen'·tạ) *n.* (*Med.*) the soft, spongy substance (expelled from the womb after birth) through which the mother's blood nourishes the fetus; (*Bot.*) the part of the plant to which the seeds are attached. **-l** *a.* [L. = a flat cake].

plac·id (plas'·id) *a.* calm; peaceful. **-ly** *adv.* **-ity** *n.* mildness; sweetness; serenity [L. *placidus*, fr. *placere*, to please].

plack·et (plak'·it) *n.* a slit at the top of a woman's skirt [Fr. *plaquet*].

pla·gi·a·rize (plā'·ji·ạ·rīz) *v.t.* to steal the words, ideas, etc. of another and use them as one's own. **plagiarism** *n.* the act of plagiarizing; literary theft. **plagiarist** *n.* **plagiary** *n.* [L. *plagiarius*, a kidnapper].

plague (plāg) *n.* a deadly, epidemic, and infectious disease; a pestilence; a nuisance; *v.t.* to vex; to trouble or annoy. *pr.p.* **plaguing.** *pa.p.* and *pa.t.* **-d. plaguy** (plā'·gi·) *a.* [L. *plaga*, a blow].

plaid (plad) *n.* a long, woolen garment, usually with a tartan pattern, worn as a wrap by Scottish Highlanders; *a.* marked with stripes. **-ed** *a.* [Gael. *plaide*].

plain (plān) *a.* evident; clear; unobstructed; not intricate; simple; ordinary; without decoration; not beautiful; level; flat; even; *adv.* clearly; *n.* a tract of level country.**-ly** *adv.* **-ness** *n.* — **sailing** *n.* an unobstructed course of action. — **song** *n.* the traditional chants of the Christian church, sung in unison [L. *planus*, smooth].

plaint (plānt) *n.* (*Poet.*) a lamentation; (*Law*) a statement in writing of the complaint, accusation, etc. **-iff** *n.* the one who sues in a court of law. **-ive** *a.* expressing grief; sad; mournful. **-ively** *adv.* [L. *plungere*, *planctum*, to lament].

plait (plāt, plat) *n.* a fold; a braid of hair, straw, etc., *v.t.* to interweave strands of hair, straw, etc. Also **pleat** [L. *plicatus*, folded].

plan (plan) *n.* a drawing representing a thing's horizontal section; a diagram; a map; a project; a design; a scheme; *v.t.* to make a plan of; to arrange beforehand. *pr.p.* **-ning** *pa.p.* and *pat.* **-ned** [L. *planus*, flat].

plane (plān) *n.* a flat, level surface; (*Geom.*) a surface such that, if any two points on it be joined by a straight line, that line will lie wholly on the surface; *a.* perfectly level; pert. to, or lying in, a plane. — **geometry,** branch of geometry which deals with plane, not solid, figures [L. *planus*, level].

plane (plān) *n.* abbrev. of 'airplane'; the wing of an airplane or glider; *v.i.* to glide [Fr. *planer*, to hover].

plan·et (plan'·ạt) *n.* a celestial body revolving round the sun (e.g. Venus, Mars, etc.) as distinct from the fixed stars. **-arium** (plan·ạ·tē'·ri·ạm) *n.* a working model of the planetary system; a projected representation of the heavens on a dome. **-ary** *a.* pert. to planets; of the nature of a planet; erratic; wandering; (*Astrol.*) under the influence of a planet. **-oid** *n.* a minor planet [Gk. *planētēs*, wanderer].

plan·gent (plan'·jạnt) *a.* of sound, vibrating; resounding. **plangency** *n.* [L. *plangere*, to beat].

plan·ish (plan'·ish) *v.t.* to make smooth or flat by light hammering; to flatten between rollers. **-er** *n.* [L. *planus*, level].

plank (plangk) *n.* a thick, heavy board; an article of policy in a political program; *v.t.* to lay with planks. **-ing** *n.* planks collectively [L. *planca*].

plank·ton (plangk'·tạn) *n.* (*Biol.*) the minute animal and vegetable organisms floating in the ocean [Gk. *planktos*, wandering].

plant (plant) *n.* a living organism belonging to the vegetable kingdom, generally excluding trees and shrubs; a slip or cutting; machinery, tools, etc., used in an industrial undertaking; (*Slang*) a swindle, hoax, trick; *v.t.* to set in ground for growth; to implant (ideas, etc.). **-ation** (plan·tā'·shạn) *n.* large estate for growing a certain crop. **-er** *n.* one who plants; the owner of a plantation [O.E.].

plaque (plak) *n.* a thin, flat, ornamental tablet hung on a wall or inserted into a wall or furniture [Fr.].

plash (plash) *n.* a puddle; a splashing sound; *v.i.* to dabble in water. **-y** *a.* [Dut. *plassen*, to splash].

plas·ma (plaz'·mạ) *n.* (*Biol.*) protoplasm; the fluid part of the blood, as opposed to the corpuscles. Also **plasm. -tic, plasmic** *a.* [Gk. *plasma*, fr. *plassein*, to form or mold].

plas·ter (pas'·tẹr) *n.* a composition of lime, water, and sand, for coating walls; gypsum, for making ornaments, molds, etc.; (*Med.*) an adhesive, curative application; (*Surg.*) a composition used to hold a limb, etc. rigid; *v.t.* to cover with plaster; to smooth over or conceal. **-er** *n.* [Gk. *plassein*, to mold].

plas·tic (plas'·tik) *a.* capable of molding or of being molded; pliable; capable of change; *n.*

a substance capable of being molded; a group of synthetic products derived from casein, cellulose, etc. which may be molded into any form. **plasticity** (plas·tis'·ạ·ti·) *n.* quality of being plastic. — **art,** the art of representing figures in sculpture or by modeling in clay. — **surgery,** the art of restoring lost or damaged parts of the body by grafting on sound tissue [Gk. *plassein*, to mold].

Plas·ti·cine (plas'·ti·sẽn) *n.* modeling material easily manipulated [Trade Name].

plat (plat) *n.* map [fr. *plot*].

plate (plāt) *n.* a shallow, round dish from which food is eaten; a plateful; a flat, thin sheet of metal, glass, etc.; (*Dentistry*) a thin sheet of vulcanic, or metal, to hold artificial teeth; (*Photog.*) short for 'photographic plate'; a separate page of illustrations in a book; *v.t.* to cover with a thin coating of gold, silver, or other metal; to protect with steel plates, *e.g.* as a ship. **-r** *n.* — **armor** *n.* very heavy, protective armor for warships. — **glass** *n.* thick glass, rolled in sheets and used for windows, mirrors, etc. [Gk. *platus*, broad].

pla·teau (pla·tō') *n.* a tract of level, high ground. *pl.* **plateaus, plateaux** (pla·tōz') [Fr. fr. Gk. *platus*, flat].

plat·en (plat'·ạn) *n.* (*Print.*) the plate which presses the paper against the type; the roller of a typewriter [O.Fr. *platine*, a flat piece].

plat·form (plat'·fawrm) *n.* a wooden structure raised above the level of the floor, as a stand for speakers; a landing area at a railway-station; (*Mil.*) a stage on which a gun is mounted; policy of a political party [Fr. *plate-forme* = flat form].

plat·i·num (plat'·ạ·nạm) *n.* a hard, silvery-white, malleable metal. **platinic, platinous** *a.* **platinoid** *n.* a metal found associated with platinum, e.g. iridium; an alloy of copper, zinc, nickel, and tungsten [Sp. *platina*, fr. *plata*, silver].

plat·i·tude (plat'·ạ·tūd) *n.* a commonplace remark; dullness of writing or speaking. **platitudinous** *a.* [Fr. fr. Gk. *platus*, flat].

Pla·to (plā'·tō) *n.* a famous Greek philosopher (427-347 B.C.). **Platonic** (plạ·tàn'·ik), **-nical** *a.* pert. to Plato or to his philosophy. **-nism** *n.* the doctrines of Plato. **-nist** *n.* **Platonic love,** spiritual affection between man and woman without sexual desire.

pla·toon (plạ·tòòn') *n.* (*Mil.*) a small body of soldiers employed as a unit [Fr. *peloton*, a knot, a ball].

plat·ter (plat'·ẹr) *n.* a large, shallow plate or dish [Fr. *plat*, a dish].

plat·y·pus (plat'·ạ·pạs) *n.* a small, acquatic, furred animal of Australia; the duckbill [Gk. *platus*, flat; *pous*, a foot].

plau·dit (plaw'·dit) *n.* enthusiastic applause. **-ory** *a.* expressing approval [L. *plaudere*, to clap the hands].

plau·si·ble (plaw'·zạ·bl) *a.* having the appearance of being true; apparently right; fair-spoken. **plausibly** *adv.* **plausibility** *n.* [L. *plaudere*, to praise].

play (plā) *v.t.* and *i.* to move with light or irregular motion; to frolic; to flutter; to amuse oneself; to take part in a game; to gamble; to act a part on the stage; to perform on a musical instrument; to operate; to trifle with; *n.* a brisk or free movement; activity; action; amusement; fun; frolic; sport gambling; a dramatic piece or performance. **-er** *n.* **-ful** *a.* fond of play or fun; lively. **-fully** *adv.* **-bill** *n.* a bill or poster to advertise a play. **-boy** *n.* a habitual pleasure-seeker. **-fellow** *n.* a playmate. **-ground** *n.* an open space or courtyard for recreation. **-house** *n.* a theater. **-mate** *n.* a companion in play.**-pen** *n.* a portable enclosure for small children to play in. **-thing**

n. a toy. **playwright** (plā′·rīt) *n.* a writer of plays; a dramatist. **-ing card** *n.* one of a set of cards, usually 52 in number, used in card games [O.E. *plegan,* to play].

plea (plē) *n.* (*Law*) the defendant's answer to the plaintiff's declaration; an excuse; entreaty [Fr. *plaider,* to plead].

plead (plēd) *v.t.* to allege in proof or vindication; (*Law*) to argue at the bar; *v.i.* to carry on a lawsuit; to present an answer to the declaration of a plaintiff; to urge reasons in support of or against; to beg or implore. *pa.p.* and *pa.t.* **-ed.** Also (*Colloq.*) **pled. -er** *n.* **-ing** *a.* entreating; *n.* the art of conducting a cause as an advocate; entreaty; supplication [Fr. *plaider*].

pleas·ance (plez′·ạns) *n.* a pleasure garden [L. *placere,* to please].

please (plēz) *v.t.* to excite agreeable sensations or emotions in; to gratify; to delight; to satisfy; *v.i.* to give pleasure; used as *abbrev.* of 'if you please,' in a polite request. **pleasant** (plez′·ạnt) *a.* fitted to please; cheerful; lively; merry; agreeable. **pleasantly** *adv.* **pleasantness** *n.* **pleasantry** (plez′·ạnt·ri·) *n.* playfulness in conversation; a joke; a humorous act; *pl.* **pleasantries. pleasing** (plē′·zing) *a.* agreeable; gratifying. **pleasingly** *adv.* **pleasingness** *n.* **pleasure** (plezh′·ẹr) *n.* agreeable sensation or emotion; gratification of the senses or mind; amusement, diversion, or self-indulgence; choice; a source of gratification. **pleasurable** *a.* **pleasurably** *adv.* [L. *placere,* to please].

pleat (plēt) *n.* a flattened fold fastened in position; *v.t.* to make pleats [var. of *plait*].

ple·be·ian (pli·bē′·an) *a.* pert. or belonging to the common people; vulgar; uncultured; *n.* a common person [L. *plebs,* common people].

pleb·i·scite (pleb′·i·sīt, pleb′·i·sit) *n.* a vote of the whole community or nation [L. *plebis citum,* a decree of the plebs].

plec·trum (plek′·trạm) *n.* a small device used for plucking the strings of a mandalin, etc. Gk. *plēktron,* fr. *plēssein,* to strike].

pledge (plej) *n.* something deposited as a security; a sign or token of anything; a drinking to the health of; a solemn promise; *v.t.* to deposit in pawn; to leave as security; to engage for, by promise or declaration; to drink the health of [O.Fr. *plege*].

ple·na·ry (plē′·nạ·ri·, ple′·nạ·ri·) *a.* full, entire, complete; unqualified; (for an assembly) fully attended. **plenarily** *adv.* **plenariness** *n.* **plenipotentiary** (plen·ạ·pạ·ten′·shạ·ri·) *n.* an ambassador with full powers; *a.* possessing full powers. **plenitude** (plen′·ạ·tūd) *n.* fullness; abundance [L. *plenus,* full; *potens,* potent].

plen·ty (plen′·ti·) *n.* a full supply; abundance; quite enough; sufficiency. **plenteous** (plen′·ti·ạs) *a.* copious; abundant; rich. **plenteously** *adv.* **plentiful** *a.* abundant; ample. **plentifully** *adv.* [L. *plenus,* full].

ple·num (plē′·nạm) *n.* space as considered to be full of matter (opposed to *vacuum*); a condition of fullness [L. *plenus,* full].

pleth·o·ra (pleth′·ạ·ra) *n.* an excess of red corpuscles in the blood; superabundance. **plethoric** *a.* [Gk. *plethōra,* fullness].

pleu·ra (ploo′·ra) *n.* (*Med.*) the membrane lining the chest and covering the lungs. *pl.* **-e. -l** *a.* **pleurisy** *n.* (*Med.*) inflammation of the pleura [Gk. *pleura,* the side].

plex·us (pleks′·ạs) *n.* a network, esp. of nerves, blood vessels, fibers, etc. **plexal** *a.* [L. = a twining].

pli·a·ble (plī′·ạ·bl) *a.* easily bent; easily influenced. Also **pliant** (plī′·ant). **pliably, pliantly** *adv.* **pliability, pliancy** *n.* [L. *plicare,* to fold].

pli·ca (plī′·kạ) *n.* a fold. **-te, -ted** *a.* (*Bot.*) folded; pleated [L. *plicare,* to fold].

pli·ers (plī′·ẹrz) *n.pl.* small pincers with a flat grip [fr. *ply,* to bend].

plight (plīt) *n.* a state or condition of a distressing kind; predicament [L. *plicare,* to fold; O.E. *plit,* a fold or plait].

plight (plīt) *v.t.* to pledge, as one's word of honor; to betroth [O.E. *pliht,* risk].

plinth (plinth) *n.* a square slab, forming the base of a column; the projecting band running along the foot of a wall [Gk. *plinthos,* a brick].

plod (plåd) *v.t.* to tread with a heavy step; *v.i.* to walk or work laboriously; to toil or drudge *pr.p.* **-ding** *pa.t., pa.p.* **-ded** [imit.].

plot (plåt) *n.* a small patch of ground; a plan of a field, farm, etc. drawn to scale; the plan of a play, novel, etc.; a secret scheme; a conspiracy. *v.t.* to draw a graph or plan of; to plan or scheme. *v.i.* to conspire. *pr.p.* **-ting** *pa.t., pa.p.* **-ted** [O.Fr. *pelote* clod; Fr. *complot*].

plov·er (pluv′·ẹr) *n.* one of various kinds of wading birds [L. *pluvia,* rain].

plow (plou) *n.* an implement with a heavy cutting blade for turning up the soil; *v.t.* to turn up with the plow; to furrow; to advance laboriously; *v.i.* to till the soil with a plow. **-share** *n.* the heavy iron blade of a plow [O.E. *ploh*].

pluck (pluk) *v.t.* to pull off; to pick, as flowers; to strip off feathers, as a fowl; to snatch, or pull with sudden force; *n.* a pull or jerk; the act of plucking; courage or spirit. **-y** *a.* brave; spirited. **-iness** *n.* [O.E. *pluccian*].

plug (plug) *n.* anything used to stop a hole; a cake of compressed tobacco; (*Elect.*) a device for connecting and disconnecting of a circuit; *abbrev.* for spark plug; *v.t.* to stop with a plug; to insert a plug in; (*Slang*) to shoot; (*Slang*) to advertise a song or tune by having it played constantly; *v.i.* (*Colloq.*) to keep doggedly at work (with 'at'). *pr.p.* **-ging.** *pa.p.* and *pa.t.* **-ged** [Dut.].

plum (plum) *n.* a round or oval fruit; the tree that bears it; a particularly good appointment or position; a dark purplish color [O.E. *plume*].

plum·age (plòò′·mij) *n.* a bird's feathers, collectively [Fr. fr. L. *pluma,* a feather].

plumb (plum) *n.* a weight of lead attached to a line, and used to determine perpendicularity; the perpendicular position; *a.* perpendicular; *adv.* perpendicularly; (*Colloq.*) utterly, absolutely; *v.t.* to adjust by a plumb line; to sound or take the depth of water with a plummet. **-er** (plum′·ẹr) *n.* one who installs or repairs water and sewage systems. **-ic** *a.* (*Chem.*) containing lead. **-ing** (plum′·ing) *n.* the trade of a plumber; the system of water and sewage pipes in a building. **— line** *n.* a weighted string for testing the perpendicular. **— bob** *n.* the weight at the end of this line [L. *plumbum,* lead].

plum·ba·go (plum·bā′·gō) *n.* black lead; graphite [L. *plumbum,* lead].

plume (plòòm) *n.* a feather or tuft of feathers; a crest on a helmet; a token of honor; *v.t.* to furnish with plumes; (*Fig.*) to boast of [L. *pluma,* a feather].

plum·met (plum′·it) *n.* a plumb bob; a weight; *v.i.* to fall like a dead weight [L. *plumbum,* lead].

plump (plump) *a.* of rounded form; moderately fat. **-ness** *n.* [Dut. *plomp,* blunt].

plump (plump) *v.i.* to fall or sit down heavily and suddenly; to vote for one candidate; *v.t.* to drop or throw abruptly; *a.* direct; abrupt; downright; *adv.* heavily; abruptly; bluntly; *n.* a sudden fall [perh. imit. origin].

plu·mule (plòò′·mūl) *n.* a small, downy feather; [L. *pluma,* a feather]

plun·der (plun′·dẹr) *v.t.* to rob systematically;

to take by force; *n.* the act of robbing by force; property so obtained. [Ger. *plündern*].

plunge (plunj) *v.t.* to thrust forcibly into; to immerse suddenly in a liquid; *v.i.* to throw oneself headlong into; (*Colloq.*) to gamble recklessly; *n.* the act of plunging; a dive; a sudden rush. **-r** *n.* one who plunges; a solid, cylindrical rod used as a piston in pumps [Fr. *plonger*, fr. L. *plumbum*, lead].

plu·per·fect (plōó'·pur·fikt) *a.* (*Gram.*) of a tense, expressing action completed before another action in the past [L. *plus quam perfectum*, more than perfect].

plu·ral (ploo'·ral) *a.* more than one; (*Gram.*) denoting more than one person or thing; *n.* (*Gram.*) a word in its plural form. **-ly** *adv.* **-ism** *n.* (*Philos.*) doctrine that existence has more than one ultimate principle. **-ist** *n.* **-istic** *a.* **-ity** *n.* large number; a majority of votes; state of being plural [L. *plus*, more].

plus (plus) *n.* symbol of addition (+); positive quantity; extra quantity; *a.* to be added; (*Math., Elect.*, etc.) positive; *prep.* with the addition of. — **fours** *n.pl.* wide knickers worn by golfers [L. *plus*, more].

plush (plush) *n.* a fabric with a long, velvet-like nap [Fr. *peluche*, fr. L. *pilus*, hair].

Plu·to (plōó'·tō) *n.* (*Myth.*) god of the lower world; the planet farthest from the sun. **-nic rocks** (*Geol.*) name given to igneous rocks formed by action of intense subterranean heat. **-nium** *n.* a metal of high atomic weight made by bombarding atoms of uranium with neutrons.

plu·toc·ra·cy (plōó·tàk'·ra·si·) *n.* government by the wealthy class. **plutocrat** *n.* a wealthy person. **plutocratic** *a.* [Gk. *ploutos*; wealth; *kratein*, to rule].

plu·vi·al (plōó'·vi·al) *a.* pert. to rain; rainy. Also **pluvious** [L. *pluvia*, rain].

ply (plī) *v.t.* to wield; to work at steadily; to use or practice with diligence; to urge; *v.i.* to work steadily; of a boat, etc. to run regularly between fixed places [fr. *apply*].

ply (plī) *n.* a fold; a strand of yarn; thickness. *pl.* **plies. -wood** *n.* board made of two or more thin layers of wood cemented together [Fr. *plier*, to fold, fr. L. *plicare*].

pneu·mat·ic (nū·mat'·ik) *a.* pert. to air or gas; inflated with wind or air; operated by compressed air. **-s** *n.pl.* the branch of physics dealing with the mechanical properties of gases [Gk. *pneuma*, breath].

pneu·ma·tol·o·gy (nū·ma·tàl'·a·ji·) *n.* the doctrine of spiritual existences [Gk. *pneuma*, spirit; *logos*, a discourse].

pneu·mo·nia (nū·mō'·ni·a) *n.* acute inflammation of a lung [Gk. *pneuma*, breath].

poach (pōch) *v.t.* to cook eggs, by breaking them into a pan of boiling water [Fr. *pocher*].

poach (pōch) *v.t. and i.* (*chiefly Brit.*) to take game or fish from another's property without permission. **-er** *n.* [Fr. *poche*, a pocket].

pock (pàk) *n.* pustule on skin, as in smallpox. — **mark** *n.* pit left in skin by pock [O.E. *poc*, a pustule].

pock·et (pàk'·it) *n.* a small pouch or bag inserted into a garment; a cavity or hollow; (*Mil.*) isolated area held by the enemy; *v.t.* to put in the pocket; to take surreptitiously, esp. money; to accept without resentment, as an insult. — **battleship** *n.* a heavily armored, high-powered, German battleship, of not more than 10,000 tons. **-book** *n.* a small bag or case for holding money or papers. — **money** *n.* money for small, personal expenses, e.g. allowance to child. **in pocket**, having funds [Fr. *pochette*, dim. of *poche*, pouch].

pod (pàd) *n.* a seed vessel of a plant, esp. a legume, as peas, beans, etc.

po·em (pō'·am) *n.* a composition in verse; any composition written in elevated and imaginative language; opp. to 'prose.' **poesy** *n.*

poetry. **poetically** *adv.* **poetics** *n.* principles of art of poetry; criticism of poetry.

poetry (pō'·it·ri·) *n.* language of imagination expressed in verse; metrical composition.

poetaster (pō'·it·as·ter) *n.* a would-be poet; a petty rhymster. **poeticize, poetize** *v.t. and i.* to treat poetically; to write poetry. **poetic justice**, ideal justice, in which crime is punished and virtue rewarded. **poetic license**, latitude in grammar or facts, allowed to poets. **poet laureate**, official poet [Gk. *poiēma*, fr. *poiein*, to make].

poign·ant (poin'·ant, poin'·yant) *a.* acutely painful; strongly appealing; pungent. **-ly** *adv.* **poignancy** *n.* [L. *pungere*, to prick].

point (point) *n.* sharp or tapering end of anything; dot or mark; dot in decimal system; punctuation mark; full stop; (*Geom.*) that which has position but no magnitude; item or detail; gist of argument; striking or effective part of a speech, story, etc.; moment of time; purpose; physical quality in animals, esp. for judging purposes; (*Geog.*) headland; one of the 32 direction marks of a compass; unit of scoring in certain games; (*Print.*) unit of measurement of size of type (72 points = 1 inch); a fine lace made with a needle; *v.t.* to sharpen; to give value, force, etc. to words, etc.; to aim or direct; to fill up joints with mortar; to punctuate; *v.i.* to show direction or position by extending a finger, stick, etc.; of a dog, to indicate the position of game by standing facing it. **-ed** *a.* having a sharp point; direct; telling; aimed; (*Archit.*) pert. to the style having pointed arches, i.e. Gothic. **-edly** *adv.* **-edness** *n.* **-less** *a.* having no point; blunt; irrelevant; insipid. **-er** *n.* **-ing** *n.* punctuation; filling the crevices of walls with mortar. — **blank** *a.* aimed horizontally; straightforward; *adv.* at short range [L. *punctum*, fr. *pungere*, to prick].

poise (poiz) *v.t.* to place or hold in a balanced or steady position; *v.i.* to be so held; to hover; to balance; *n.* equilibrium; carriage of the head, body, etc.; self-possession [L. *pendere*, to weigh].

poi·son (poi'·zn) *n.* any substance which kills or injures when introduced into a living organism; that which has an evil influence on health or moral purity; *v.t.* to give poison to; to infect; to corrupt. **-er** *n.* **-ous** *a.* having a deadly or injurious quality; corrupting. **-ously** *adv.* — **ivy** *n.* a vine which, if touched, causes a skin rash. — **pen** *n.* writer of malicious, anonymous letters [L. *potio, potion*].

poke (pōk) *v.t.* to push or thrust against with a pointed object, e.g. with a finger, stick, etc.; to thrust in; to tease; *v.i.* to make thrusts; to pry; to dawdle; a thrust or push; a woman's bonnet with a projecting brim. **-r** *n.* a metal rod for stirring the fire. **poky** *a.* small; slow [M.E. *poken*].

poke (pōk) *n.* (*Dial.*) a sack; a small bag [Fr. *poche*, a pocket].

pok·er (pō'·ker) *n.* a card game in which the players bet on the value of their hands. — **faced** *a.* having an expressionless face.

po·lar (pō'·ler) *a.* pert. to, or situated near, the North or South Poles; pert. to the magnetic poles (points on the earth's surface where a magnetic needle dips vertically); pert. to either pole of a magnet; directly opposed; having polarity. **-ity** (pō·lar'·a·ti·) *n.* the state of being polar; the condition of having opposite poles; the power of being attracted to one pole, and repelled from the other. — **bear**, a large, white bear, found in the Arctic regions [Gk. *polos*, a pivot].

po·lar·ize (pō'·la·rīz) *v.t.* to give polarity to; (*Elect.*) to reduce the electromotive force (E.M.F.) of a primary cell by the accumulation of certain electrolytic products on the plates; (*Chem.*) to separate the positive and negative charges on a molecule; (*Light*) to confine the vibrations of light waves to certain directions, e.g. to a plane. **polarization** *n.* **polaroid** *n.* [fr. *polar*].

pole (pōl) *n.* a long, rounded piece of wood or metal; a measure of length = 5½ yards; a measure of area = 30¼ square yards; *v.t.* to propel with a pole. — **jump** *n.* in athletics, a jump over a high bar with the help of a long pole [L. *palus*, a stake].

pole (pōl) *n.* either of the ends of the axis of a sphere, esp. of the earth (in the latter case called the North Pole and South Pole); either of the opposite ends or terminals of a magnet, electric battery, etc. **-star** *n.* the North Star; a guide; an indicator [Gk. *polos*, a pivot].

Pole (pōl) *n.* a native of Poland. **Polish** *a.* pert. to Poland or the Poles.

pole·axe (pōl'·aks) *n.* a battle axe with a long handle. [E. *poll*, the head, and *axe*].

pole·cat (pōl'·kat) *n.* a small, carnivorous animal, resembling the weasel; a skunk [O.Fr. *pole*, a hen (fr. its preying on poultry)].

po·lem·ic (pō·lem'·ik) *a.* controversial; disputatious; *n.* controversy; controversialist. **-s** *n.pl.* art of controversy; controversial writings or discussions, esp. religious. Also **polemical** *a.* **polemically** *adv.* [Gk. *polemos*, war].

po·lice (pạ·lēs') *n.* the civil force which maintains public order; the members of the force; *v.t.* to control with police; to keep in order. **-man**, — **officer** *n.* (*fem.* **-woman**) member of a police force. — **court** *n.* a court for the trial of minor offenses. — **station** *n.* the headquarters of the police [Gk. *polis*, a city].

pol·i·cy (pál'·ạ·si·) *n.* a course of action adopted, esp. in state affairs; prudent procedure [Gk. *polis*, a city].

pol·i·cy (pál'·ạ·si·) *n.* a document containing a contract of insurance [Gk. *apodeixis*, proof].

pol·i·o·my·e·li·tis (pōl·i·ō·mī·ạ·li'·tis) *n.* (*Med.*) inflammation of the grey matter of the spinal cord; infantile paralysis. *abbrev.* **polio** [Gk. *polios*, grey; *muelos*, marrow].

pol·ish (pál'·ish) *v.t.* to make smooth and glossy; to make polite and cultured; *v.i.* to become polished; *n.* the act of polishing; a smooth, glassy surface; a substance used in polishing; refinement; elegance of manners. **-er** *n.* [Fr. *polir*, fr. L. *polire*].

Pol·ish See **Pole.**

po·lite (pạ·līt') *a.* elegant in manners; well-bred; courteous; refined. **-ly** *adv.* **-ness** *n.* [L. *politus*, polished].

pol·i·tic (pál'·ạ·tik) *a.* prudent; wise; shrewd; cunning; advisable. **-s** *n.pl.* the art of government; political affairs, life, or principles. **-ly** *adv.* **-al** *a.* pert. to the state or its affairs; pert. to politics. **-ally** *adv.* **politician** (pál·ạ·tish'·ạn) *n.* a holder of a political position; a statesman; a member of a political party. **polity** *n.* civil government; the form or constitution of government. **political economy,** the science dealing with the nature, production, distribution, and consumption of wealth [Fr. *politique*, fr. Gk. *polis*, a city].

pol·ka (pōl'·kạ) *n.* a lively dance of Bohemian origin; music for it [fr. *Polish*].

poll (pōl) *n.* (top of) the head; a register of persons; a list of persons entitled to vote; (the place) of voting; number of votes recorded; *v.t.* to cut off the top of, e.g. tree; to cut short horns of cattle; to canvass; to receive (votes); to cast a vote; *v.i.* to vote. — **tax** *n.* a tax on each person who votes. [Low Ger. *polle*, the head].

pol·lack (pál'·ạk) *n.* fresh water fish.

pol·lard (pál'·ẹrd) *n.* a tree on which a close head of young branches has been made by polling; a hornless animal of a normally horned variety. See **poll.**

pol·len (pál'·ạn) *n.* the fertilizing dust of a flower. **pollinate** *v.t.* to fertilize a flower by conveying pollen to the pistil [L. = fine flour].

pol·lute (pạ·lōōt') *v.t.* to make foul or unclean; to defile; to desecrate. **pollution** *n.* [L. *polluere*].

po·lo (pō'·lō) *n.* a game like hockey played on horseback; also **water polo.**

po·lo·naise (pōl·ạ·nāz) *n.* a slow stately dance, of Polish origin; the music for it [Fr. = Polish].

po·lo·ni·um (pạ·lō'·ni·ạm) *n.* a metallic, radio active chemical [fr. *Poland*].

pol·ter·geist (pōl'·tẹr·gīst) *n.* a mysterious spirit believed to create noise and disturbance [Ger. *Polter*, uproar; *Geist*, a ghost].

pol·troon (pál·trōōn') *n.* a coward. **-ery** *n.* [Fr. *poltron*, fr. It. *poltro*, lazy].

pol·y- *prefix* fr. Gk. *polus*, many words used in derivatives. **polyandry** (pál'·i·an·dri·) *n.* a custom by which a wife is shared by several husbands. **-androus** *a.* (*Bot.*) having more than 20 stamps. **-chrome** *n.* a picture, statue, etc. in several colors. **-chromatic, -chromic, -chromous** *a.* many-colored.

po·lyg·a·my (pạl·ig'·ạ·mi·) *n.* the practice of having more than one wife at the same time. **polygamous** *a.* **polygamist** *n.* [Gk. *polus*, many; *gamos*, marriage].

pol·y·glot (pál'·i·glát) *a.* pert. to, or speaking, several languages; *n.* a person who speaks several languages; a book, esp. the Bible, in which the text is printed side by side in different languages [Gk. *polus*, many; *glōtta*, the tongue].

pol·y·gon (pál'·i·gán) *n.* a plane figure with more than four sides or angles. **polygonal** *a.* [Gk. *polus*, many; *gōnia*, an angle].

po·lyg·y·ny (pạ·lij'·a·ny) *n.* practice of polygamy by a man [See *polygamy*].

pol·y·he·dron (pál·i·hē'·drạn) *n.* (*Geom.*) a solid figure with many faces, usually more than six [Gk. *polus*, many; *hedra*, a base].

pol·y·mor·phous (pál·i·mawr'·fạs) *a.* assuming many forms. Also **polymorphic. polymorphism** *n.* [Gk. *polus*, many; *morphē*, form].

Pol·y·ne·sia (pál·ạ·nē'·zhạ) *n.* (*Geog.*) a group of islands in the S. Pacific, east of Australia. **-n** *a.* [Gk. *polus*, many; *nēsos*, an island].

pol·y·no·mi·al (pál·i·nō'·mi·ạl) *n.* (*Alg.*) a quantity having many terms [Gk. *polus*, many; L. *nomen*, a name].

pol·y·phon·ic (pál·i·fán'·ik) *a.* pert. to polyphony. **polyphony** (pạl·if'·ạn·i·) *n.* (*Mus.*) a kind of composition in which melodic strains are simultaneously developed without being subordinate to each other [Gk. *polus*, many; *phonē*, a voice].

pol·y·syl·a·ble (pál·i·sil'·ạ·bl) *n.* a word of three or more syllables. **polysyllabic** *a.* [Gk. *polus*, many, and *syllable*].

pol·y·tech·nic (pál·i·tek'·nik) *a.* pert. to many arts and sciences; *n.* a school or college of applied arts and sciences [Gk. *polus*, many; *technē*, art]

pol·y·the·ism (pál'·i·thē·izm) *n.* belief in the existence of many gods, or in more than one. **polytheist** *n.* **polytheistic** *a.* [Gk. *polus*, many; *theos*, a god].

po·made (pō·mad') *n.* scented ointment for the hair. Also **pomatum. pomander** *n.* ball of or case for mixture of perfumes [L. Fr. *pommade*].

pome (pōm) *n.* any fruit having a fleshy body, core, etc. like the apple, pear, pomegranate, etc. [L. *pomum*, an apple].

pome·gran·ate (pám'·gra·nit) *n.* a large fruit containing many seeds in a red pulp [L. *pomum*, an apple, *granatum*, having seeds].

pom·er·a·ni·an (pám·ạ·rā'·ni·ạn) *n.* a small

breed of dog with bushy tail, sharp pointed muzzle, pointed ears and long silky hair [fr. *Pomerania*, in Germany].

pom·mel (pum'·al) *n.* the knob of a sword hilt; the front part of a saddle; *v.t.* to strike repeatedly, as with the fists [O. Fr. *pomel*, a little apple].

pomp (pamp) *n.* splendid display or ceremony; magnificence. **-ous** *n.* showy with grandeur; of a person, self-important; of language, inflated. **-ously** *adv.* **-ousness** *n.* **-osity** *n.* [Gk. *pompē*, a solemn procession].

pom·pa·dour (pam'·pa·dōr) *n.* woman's high swept hairstyle; man's hair style with hair brushed up from forehead [Fr. Marquese de *Pompadour*].

pom·pa·no (pam'·pa·nō) *n.* food fish [Sp.].

pom·pon (pam'·pan) *n.* the ball of colored wool worn in front of the shako, etc.; small, compact chrysanthemum [Fr.].

pond (pand) *n.* a pool of water, either naturally or artificially enclosed [same as *pound*].

pon·der (pan'·der) *v.t.* to weigh in the mind; to consider attentively; *v.i.* to mediate. **-er** *n.* **-ing** *a.* [L. *pondus*, weight].

pon·der·ous (pan'·der·as) *a.* very heavy; weighty; massive; unwieldy; dull or lacking in spirit. **-ly** *adv.* **-ness** *n.* **ponderosity** *n.*

pon·iard (pan'·yerd) *n.* a slender dagger [Fr. *poignard*, fr. *poing*, the fist].

pon·tiff (pan'·tif) *n.* the Pope; a bishop; a high priest. **pontifical** *a.* belonging to a high priest; popish; pompous and dogmatic; *n.pl.* the garb of a priest, bishop, or pope. **pontifically** *adv.* **pontificate** *n.* the state, dignity, or term of office of a priest, bishop, or pope. [L. *pontifex*, a high priest].

pon·toon (pan·tōōn') *n.* a low, flat-bottomed boat; a support in building a temporary bridge [Fr. fr. L. *pons*, a bridge].

po·ny (pō'·ni·) *n.* a small breed of horse; [O.Fr. *poulenet*, fr. *poulain*, a colt].

poo·dle (pōō'·dl) *n.* one of a breed of dogs with thick, curly hair, often clipped into ornamental tufts [Ger. *Pudel*].

pooh (pōō) *interj.* an exclamation of scorn or contempt. **pooh-pooh** *v.t.* to express contempt.

pool (pōōl) *n.* a small body of still water; a deep place in a river [O.E. *pol*].

pool (pōōl) *n.* the collective stakes in various games; the place where the stakes are put; a variety of billiards; a combination of capitalists to fix prices and divide into a common fund; *v.i.* to form a pool [Fr. *poule*, a hen].

poop (pōōp) *n.* the stern of a ship; raised deck at the stern [L. *puppis*, the stern].

poor (poor) *a.* having little or no money; without means; needy; miserable; wretched; unfortunate; feeble; deserving of pity; unproductive; of inferior quality. **-ly** *adv.* inadequately; with little or no success; without spirit; *a.* (*Colloq.*) somewhat ill; out of sorts. **-ness** *n.* **-spirited** *a.* cowardly; mean. **-house** *n.* an institution for lodging the poor at public expense [L. *pauper*, poor].

pop (pap) *n.* an abrupt, small explosive sound; a shot; an effervescing drink; *v.i.* to make a sharp, quick sound; to go or come unexpectedly or suddenly; to dart; *v.t.* to put or place suddenly; *adv.* suddenly. *pr.p.* **-ping** *pa.p.* and *pa.t.* **-ped. -corn** *n.* Indian corn exposed to heat causing it to burst open. **-gun** *n.* a child's toy gun for shooting pellets, etc. by the expansion of compressed air [imit. origin].

Pope (pōp) *n.* the Bishop of Rome and head of the R.C. Church. **popish** (pō'·pish) *a.* pert. to the Pope or the papacy. **-dom** *n.* the office, dignity, or jurisdiction of the Pope. [L. *papa*, father].

pop·in·jay (pap'·in·jā) *n.* a vain, conceited fellow [O.Fr. *papegai*, a parrot].

pop·lar (pap'·ler) *n.* a tree noted for its slender tallness [L. *populus*].

pop·lin (pap'·lin) *n.* a corded fabric of silk, cotton, or worsted [etym. uncertain].

pop·py (pap'·i·) *n.* a bright flowered plant, one species of which yields opium [L. *papaver*, a poppy].

pop·py·cock (pap'·i·kak) *n.* nonsense.

pop·u·lace (pap'·ya·lis) *n.* the common people; the masses. **populate** *v.t.* to people. **population** *n.* the total number of people in a country, town, etc. **populous** *a.* thickly inhabited [L. *populus*, the people].

pop·u·lar (pap'·ya·ler) *a.* pert. to the common people; liked by the people; finding general favor; easily understood. **-ly** *adv.* **-ize** *v.t.* to make popular; to make familiar, plain, easy, etc. to all. **-ization** *n.* **-ity** *n.* public favor [L. *populus*, the people].

por·ce·lain (pōrs'·lin, pōr'·sa·lin) *n.* the finest kind of earthenware—white, glazed and semi-transparent; china; *a.* made of porcelain [It. *porcellana*, a delicate shellfish].

porch (pōrch) *n.* a covered entrance to a doorway; a veranda [L. *porticus*, a colonnade].

por·cine (pawr'·sīn) *a.* pert. to, or like, swine; swinish [L. *porcus*, a pig].

por·cu·pine (pawr'·kya·pīn) *n.* a large quadruped of the rodent family, covered with spines [L. *porcus*, a pig; *spina*, a spine].

pore (pōr) *n.* a minute opening in the skin for the passage of perspiration. **porous** *a.* full of pores [Gk. *poros*, a passage].

pore (pōr) *v.i.* to look at with steady attention, esp. in reading or studying (with 'over').

pork (pōrk) *n.* the flesh of swine used for food. **-y** *a.* like pork; fat; greasy. **-er** *n.* a hog, fattened for eating. [L. *porcus*, a pig].

por·nog·ra·phy (pawr·nag'·ra·fi·) *n.* obscene literature or pictures. **pornographer** *n.* **pornographic** *a.* [Gk. *pornē*, a harlot; *graphein*, to write].

por·poise (par'·pas) *n.* a blunt-nosed cetacean mammal 5 to 8 feet long, frequenting the northern seas; a dolphin [L. *porcus*, a hog; *piscis*, a fish].

por·ridge (pawr'·ij) *n.* (*Brit.*) a soft breakfast food [form of *pottage*].

por·rin·ger (pawr'·in·jer) *n.* a small bowl for porridge [Fr. *potager*, a soup-basin].

port (pōrt) *n.* a harbor; a town with a harbor; a haven; a refuge [L. *portus*].

port (pōrt) *n.* the way in which a person carries himself; *v.t.* (*Mil.*) to carry (a rifle) slanting upwards in front of the body. **-ly** *a.* dignified in appearance; corpulent [L. *portare*, to carry].

port (pōrt) *n.* a strong, sweet, dark-red wine [fr. *Oporto*, Portugal].

port (pōrt) *n.* the left side of a ship, looking towards the bow.

port-a-ble (pōr'·ta·bl) *a.* capable of being easily carried. **portability** *n.* [L. *portare*, to carry].

por·tage (pōr'·tij) *n.* the act of carrying or transporting goods; the charge for transport; [L. *portare*, to carry].

por·tal (pōrt'·al) *n.* a gate or entrance. [Fr. *portail*, fr. L. *porta*, a gate].

por·tend (pōr·tend') *v.t.* to foretell; to give warning in advance; to be an omen of. **portent** *n.* an omen, esp. of evil. **portentous** *a.* serving to portend; omnious [L. *portendere*, to foretell].

por·ter (pōr'·ter) *n.* a door- or gatekeeper; railway sleeping-car attendant [L. *porta*, gate].

por·ter (pōr'·ter) *n.* one employed to carry baggage, esp. at stations or hotels. **-age** *n.* fee for hire of a porter.

por·ter·house (pōr'·ter·house) *n.* place where beer (porter) was served. — **steak** choice cut of beef next to the sirloin [L. *portare*, to carry].

port·fo·li·o (pōrt·fō′·li·ō) *n.* case for holding loose documents, drawings, etc.; office of a minister of state [L. *portare*, to carry; *folium*, a leaf].

port·hole (pōrt′·hōl) *n.* window in side of ship [L. *porta*, gate].

por·ti·co (pōr′·ti·kō) *n.* (*Archit.*) a row of columns in front of the entrance to a building; a covered walk [L. *porticus*].

por·tion (pōr′·shan) *n.* a piece; a part; a share; a helping of food; destiny; lot; a dowry; *v.t.* to divide into shares; to give a dowry to. **-less** *a.* [L. *portio*].

por·tray (pōr·trā′) *v.t.* to represent by drawing, painting, acting, or imitating; to describe vividly in words. **-al** *n.* the act of portraying; the representation. **-er** *n.* **portrait** (pōr′·trāt) *n.* picture of a person, esp. of the face; a graphic description of a person in words. **portraiture** *n.* the art of portrait painting [L. *protrahere*, to draw forth].

Por·tu·guese (pōr′·cha·gēz′) *a.* pert. to Portugal, its inhabitants, or language.

pose (pōz) *n.* attitude or posture of a person, natural or assumed; a mental attitude or affection; *v.t.* to place in a position for the sake of effect; to lay down or assert; *v.i.* to assume an attitude; to affect or pretend to be of a certain character [Fr. *poser*, to place].

pose (pōz) *v.t.* to puzzle; to embarrass by a difficult question. **-r** *n.* [short fr. *oppose*].

pos·it (pàz′·it) *v.t.* to place or set in position; to lay down as a fact or principle [L. *ponere*, *positum*, to place].

po·si·tion (pa·zish′·an) *n.* place; situation; the manner in which anything is arranged; posture; social rank or standing; employment [L. *ponere positum*, to place].

pos·i·tive (pàz′·a·tiv) *a.* formally laid down; clearly stated; absolute; dogmatic; of real value; confident; not negative; plus; (*Math.*) pert. to a quantity greater than zero; (*Gram.*) denoting the simplest value of an adjective or adverb; (*Colloq.*) utter; downright; *n.* the positive degree of an adjective or adverb, i.e. without comparison; in photography, a print in which the lights and shadows are not reversed (as in the negative). **-ly** *adv.* **-ness** *n.* **positivism** *n.* the philosophical system which recognizes only matters of fact and experience. **positivist** *n.* a believer in this doctrine. **— pole,** of a magnet, the north-seeking-pole. **— sign,** the sign (+ read *plus*) of addition [L. *ponere, positum,* to place].

pos·i·tron (pàz′·a·trān) *n.* particle differing from an electron in that it has positive electrical charge; a **pos**itive **el**ectron.

pos·se (pás′·i·) *n.* a company or force, usually with legal authority; men under orders of the sheriff, maintaining law and order [L. *posse*, to be able].

pos·sess (pa·zes′) *v.t.* to own or hold as property; to have as an attribute; to enter into and influence, as an evil spirit or passions. **-ed** *a.* influenced, as by an evil spirit; demented. **-ion** *n.* the act of possessing; ownership; actual occupancy; the state of being possessed; the thing possessed. **-ive** *a.* denoting possession; *n.* (*Gram.*) the possessive case or pronoun. **-ively** *adv.* **-or** *n.* [L. *possidere, possessum,* to possess].

pos·si·ble (pás′·a·bl) *a.* capable of being or of coming into, being; feasible. **possibly** *adv.* **possibility** *n.* [L. *possibilis*].

pos·sum (pás′·sam) *n.* (*Colloq.*) an opossum. **to play possum,** to feign; to pretend; to deceive [fr. *opossum*].

post (pōst) *n.* a piece of timber or metal, set upright as a support; a prop or pillar; *v.t.* to attach to a post or wall, as a notice or advertisement. **-er** *n.* one who posts bills; a large placard for posting [L. *postis*].

post (pōst) *n.* a fixed place; a military station or the soldiers occupying it; an office or position of trust, service, or emolument; a trading settlement; formerly, a stage on the road for riders carrying mail; *v.t.* to station or place; *v.i.* to inform; to travel with speed. **-age** *n.* the cost of conveyance by mail. **-al** *a.* pert. to the post office or mail service. **-man** *n.* one who delivers mail. **-mark** *n.* a post office mark which cancels the postage stamp and gives place and time of mailing. **-master** *n.* the manager of a post office. **-master general** *n.* the chief of the post office department of a government. **— card** *n.* a stamped card on which a message may be sent through the mail. **-haste** *adv.* with great speed. **— office** *n.* an office where letters and parcels are received for distribution; the government postal department. **-age stamp** *n.* an adhesive stamp, affixed to mail to indicate payment [L. *ponere*, to place].

post- (pōst) *adv.* and *prefix* fr. L. *post*, after, behind, used in many compound words. **-date** *v.t.* to put on a document, letter, etc., a date later than the actual one. **-diluvian** *a.* living or happening after the Flood. **-graduate** *a.* of academic study, research, etc., undertaken after taking a university degree. **-impressionism** *n.* a movement in painting, sculpture, etc. which aims at artistic self-expression, or subjective as opposed to objective representation of things. **—mortem** *a.* after death; *n.* the dissection of a body after death; an autopsy. **-natal** *a.* after birth. **-primary** *a.* of education, beyond the elementary school.

pos·te·ri·or (pàs·ti′·ri·er) *a.* coming after; situated behind; later; hinder; *n.* the rump. **-ly** *adv.* **-ity** *n.* the state of being later or subsequent. **posterity** (pàs·ter′·at·i·) *n.* future generations [L. *posterus*, behind].

pos·tern (pōs′·tern) *n.* a back door or gate; *a.* rear; private [L. *posterus*, behind].

post·hu·mous (pàs′·cha·mas) *a.* born after the death of the father; published after the death of the author; occurring after death. **-ly** *adv.* [L. *postumus*, last, but confused with L. *humus*, the ground].

pos·til·ion, postillion (pōs·til′·yan) *n.* the rider mounted on the near horse of a team drawing a carriage [Fr. *postillon*].

post·pone (pōst·pōn′) *v.t.* to put off till a future time; to defer; to delay. **-ment** *n.* **-r** *n.* [L. *post*, after; *ponere*, to place].

post·pran·di·al (pōst·pran′·di·al) *a.* after-dinner [L. *post*, after; *prandium*, repast].

post·script (pōst′·skript) *n.* something added to a letter after the signature; *abbrev.* **P.S.** [L. *post*, after; *scribere, scriptum*, to write].

pos·tu·late (pàs′·cha·lāt) *v.t.* to assume without proof; to lay down as self-evident; to stipulate; *n.* a prerequisite; a proposition assumed without proof. **postulant** *n.* one who makes a request or petition; a candidate, esp. for admission to a religious order. **postulation** *n.* [L. *postulare*, to demand].

pos·ture (pàs′·cher) *n.* the position of a body, figure, etc. or of its several members; attitude; *v.i.* to assume an artificial or affected attitude. **postural** *a.* [L. *ponere, positum,* to place].

po·sy (pō′·zi·) *n.* a bouquet; a flower [*poesy*].

pot (pàt) *n.* a rounded vessel of metal, earthenware, etc., used for cooking, holding fluids, plants, etc.; the contents of a pot; (*Slang*) a large sum of money; *v.t.* to plant in pots; to preserve (as jam, chutney, etc.). *pr.p.* **-ting.** *pa.p.* and *pa.t.* **-ted. -bellied** *a.* corpulent. **-hole** *n.* cavity formed in rock by action of stones in the eddy of a stream; a hole in the roadway. **-luck** *n.* whatever may happen to have been provided for a meal. **-shot** *n.* a shot at random [O.E. *pott*].

po·ta·ble (pō′·ta·bl) *a.* drinkable. **potation**

n. a drinking; a draft [L.*potare*, to drink].

pot·ash (pàt'·ash) *n.* a powerful alkali obtained from wood ashes. **potassium** *n.* metallic base of potash [*pot* and *ash*].

po·ta·to (pạ·tā'·tō) *n.* an edible tuber widely grown for food. *pl.* **-es** [Sp. *patata*].

po·tent (pō'·tnt) *a.* having great authority or influence; powerful; mighty; procreative. **-ly** *adv.* **potency** *n.* moral or physical power; influence; energy; efficacy. **-ate** *n.* one who possesses power; a monarch. **-ial** (pạ·ten'·shạl) *a.* latent; existing in possibility but not in actuality; *n.* inherent capability of doing anything; (*Elect.*) the level of electric pressure. **-ially** *adv.* **-iality** (pạ·ten·shi·al'·ạ·ti·) *n.* possibility as distinct from actuality. **-ial difference** (*Elect.*) the difference of pressure between two points; voltage [L. *potens*, powerful, fr. *posse*, to be able].

poth·er (pàTH'·ẹr) *n.* disturbance; fuss; *v.i.* and *v.t.* to harass; to worry [etym. uncertain].

po·tion (pō'·shạn) *n.* a dose, esp. of liquid, medicine, or poison [fr. L. *potare*, to drink].

pot·pour·ri (pō·poo·rē') *n.* a mixture of dried rose petals, spices, etc.; a musical or literary medley [Fr. *pot*, a pot; *pourri*, rotten].

pot·tage (pàt'·ij) *n.* soup or stew; (*Bib.*) a dish of lentils [Fr. *potage*, soup].

pot·ter (pàt'·ẹr) *n.* a maker of earthenware vessels. **-y** *n.* pots, vessels, etc. made of earthenware; the place where it is made; the art of making it [fr. *pot*].

pouch (pouch) *n.* a small bag or sack; a baglike receptacle in which certain animals, e.g. the kangaroo, carry their young; *v.t.* to pocket; to cause to hang like a pouch [Fr. *poche*, a pocket].

poult (pōlt) *n.* a young fowl. **poultry** (pōl'·tri·) *n.* domestic fowls. **-erer** *n.* a dealer in poultry [Fr. *opulet*, a chicken].

poul·tice (pōl'·tis) *n.* a hot, moist mixture applied to a sore, etc.; *v.t.* to apply a poultice to [L. *puls*, porridge].

pounce (pouns) *v.i.* to spring upon suddenly; to swoop; *n.* a swoop or sudden descent.

pounce (pouns) *n.* a fine powder used to prevent ink from spreading on unsized paper; a powder used for dusting over perforations in order to trace a pattern; *v.t.* to sprinkle with pounce [L. *pumex*, pumice].

pound (pound) *n.* a measure of weight (*abbrev.* **lb.**), 16 ounces avoirdupois, or 12 ounces troy; a unit of British money (*abbrev.* £), **-age** *n.* charge of so much per pound. **-al** *n.* a unit of force [L. *pondus*, weight].

pound (pound) *v.t.* and *i.* to beat or strike; to crush to pieces or to powder; to walk, run, etc., heavily [O.E. *punian*].

pound (pound) *n.* an enclosure for animals; *v.t.* to shut up in one [O.E. *pund*].

pour (pōr) *v.i.* to come out in a stream, crowd, etc.; to flow freely; to rain heavily; *v.t.* to cause to flow, as a liquid from a vessel; to shed; to utter [etym. unknown].

pout (pout) *v.i.* to thrust out the lips, as in displeasure, etc.; to look sullen or sulky; *n.* the act of pouting; a protrusion of the lips. **-er** *n.* one who pouts; a pigeon with the power of inflating its crop [etym. uncertain].

pov·er·ty (pàv'·ẹr·ti·) *n.* the state of being poor; poorness; lack of means [L. *pauperlas*, fr. *pauper*, poor].

pow·der (pou'·dẹr) *n.* dust; a solid matter in fine dry particles; a medicine in this form; short for gunpowder, face powder, etc.; *v.t.* to reduce to powder; to pulverize; to sprinkle with powder; *v.i.* to fall into powder; to crumble. **-y** *a.* like powder. — **magazine** *n.* a place where ammunition is stored. [Fr. *poudre*, fr. L. *pulvis*, dust].

pow·er (pou'·ẹr) *n.* a capacity for action, physical, mental, or moral; energy; might; agency or motive force; authority; one in authority; influence or ascendancy; a nation; mechanical energy; (*Math.*) the product arising from the continued multiplication of a number by itself. **-ful** *a.* having great power; capable of producing great effect. **-fully** *adv.* **-fulness** *n.* **-less** *a.* **-lessly** *adv.* **-lessness** *n.* **-house, — station** *n.* a building where electric power is generated [O.Fr. *poer*].

pow·wow (pou'·wou) *n.* orig. a feast, dance, or conference among N. American Indians; hence, any conference [N. Amer. Ind.].

pox (pàks) *n.* a disease attended with pustules on the skin, as smallpox, chickenpox, etc.; syphilis [orig. pl. of *pock*].

prac·tice (prak'·tis) *n.* performance or execution, as opposed to theory; custom or habit; systematic exercise for instruction; training; exercise of a profession. **practice** or **practise** *v.t.* to put into action; to do frequently or habitually; to exercise a profession; to exercise in; to train; *v.i.* to perform certain acts customerily; to exercise a profession. **practicable** (prak'·ti·kạ·bl) *a.* capable of being accomplished or put into practice; capable of being used, e.g. a weapon, a road, etc. **practicably** *adv.* **practicableness** *n.* **practicability** *n.* **practical** *a.* pert. to practice or action; capable of being turned to account; useful; virtual. **practically** *adv.* **practicalness** *n.* **practicality** *n.* **practitioner** (prak·tish'·ạn·ẹr) *n.* one engaged in a profession, esp. law or medicine [Gk. *praktikos*, concerned with action].

prag·mat·ic, pragmatical (prag·mat'·ik, ·i·kạl) *a.* pert. to state affairs; concerned with practical consequences; matter-of-fact; officious or meddlesome. **-ally** *adv.* **-alness** *n.* **pragmatize** *v.t.* to represent an imaginary thing as real. **pragmatism** *n.* a philosophy based on the conception that the truth of a doctrine is to be judged by its practical consequences. **pragmatist** *n.* [Gk. *pragmatikos*, pert. to business].

prai·rie (prē'·ri·) *n.* a large tract of grassland, destitute of trees. — **chicken** *n.* grouse. — **dog** *n.* a small burrowing rodent. — **schooner** *n.* a covered wagon. — **wolf** *n.* the coyote [Fr. fr. L. *pratum*, a meadow].

praise (prās) *v.t.* to express approval or admiration; to glorify; *n.* approval of merit; commendation; worship. —**worthy** *a.* deserving of praise [O.Fr. *preiser*].

pra·line (prà'·lēn) *n.* a candy made by roasting almonds in boiling sugar [Fr. fr. *Duplessis-Praslin*, who first made it].

prance (prans) *v.i.* to spring or bound like a high-spirited horse; to swagger; to caper, esp. of children; *n.* a prancing movement. *n.*

pran·di·al (pran'·di·ạl) *a.* pert. to dinner [L. *prandium*, lunch].

prank (prangk) *n.* a mischievous trick; a practical joke.

prate (prāt) *v.t.* and *i.* to talk idly; to utter foolishly; *n.* chatter. **prattle** *n.* [M.E. *praten*].

prawn (prawn) *n.* an edible crustacean of the shrimp family [etym. unknown].

prax·is (prak'·sis) *n.* practice; a set of examples for practice [Gk. fr. *prassein*, to do].

pray (prā) *v.i.* to ask earnestly; to entreat; to petition; *v.i.* to make a request or confession, esp. to God; to commune with God. **-er** *n.* one who prays; the act of praying; an earnest entreaty; the words used; the thing asked for; a petition **-erful** *a.* devout [L. *precari*].

pre- *prefix* fr. L. *prae*, before, beforehand, used with many nouns and verbs.

preach (prēch) *v.i.* and *t.* to deliver a sermon; to speak publicly on a religious subject, esp. as a clergyman; to advocate. **-er** *n.* **-ment** *n.* a sermon, esp. one of exaggerated solemnity [L. *praedicare*, to proclaim].

pre·am·ble (prē'·am·bl) *n.* the introductory

part of a discourse, story, document, etc.; a preface [L. *praeambulus*, walking before].

pre·ar·range (prē·a·rānj′) *v.t.* to arrange beforehand. **-ment** *n.*

pre·car·i·ous (pri·ka′·ri·as) *a.* depending on the will or pleasure of another; depending on circumstances; uncertain; dangerous; perilous. **-ly** *adv.* **-ness** *n.* [L. *precarius*, obtained by entreaty].

pre·cau·tion (pri·kaw′·shan) *n.* care taken beforehand; *v.t.* to forewarn. **-ary** *a.* characterized by precaution.

pre·cede (prē·sed′) *v.t.* to go before in place, time, rank, or importance. **-nt** *a.* preceding; **-nt** (pre′·sa·dant) *n.* something done, or said, that may serve as an example in similar cases. **-ntly** *adv.* **-nce** (prē·se′·dans) *n.* the act of preceding; priority in position, rank, or time. **preceding** *a.* [L. *prae*, before; *cedere*, to go].

pre·cen·tor (prē·sen′·ter) *n.* one who leads a church choir [L. *prae*, before; *cantor*, a singer].

pre·cept (prē′·sept) *n.* an instruction intended as a rule of conduct, esp. moral conduct; a maxim; a commandment or exhortation; (*Law*) a written warrant or mandate given to an administrative officer. **-ive** *a.* [L. *praecipere*, *praeceptum*, to order].

pre·ces·sion (prē·sesh′·an) *n.* a going before. **-al** *a.* [L. *praecedere*, to go before].

pre·cinct (prē′·singt) *n.* a division of a city for police protection, voting, etc.; a boundary or limit; a minor territorial division. [L. *prae*, before; *cigere*, to gird].

pre·cious (presh′·as) *a.* of great value or price; costly; highly esteemed; over-refined; fastidious; *adv.* (*Colloq.*) extremely. **-ly** *adv.* [Fr. *précieux*, fr. L. *pretium*, price].

prec·i·pice (pres′·a·pis) *n.* a very steep or perpendicular place, as a cliff-face. **precipitous** *a.* very steep. **precipitously** *adv.* **precipitousness** *n.* [L. *praeceps*, headlong].

pre·cip·i·tate (pri·sip′·a·tāt) *v.i.* to throw headlong; to urge on eagerly; to hasten the occurrence of; (*Chem.*) to cause to separate and fall to the bottom, as a substance in solution; of vapor, to condense; *v.i.* (*Chem.*) to fall to the bottom of a vessel, as a sediment; *n.* (*Chem.*) that which is precipitated in a liquid; sediment; *a.* headlong; rash or over-hasty. **-ly** *adv.* **precipitable** *a.* **precipitance, precipitancy** *n.* headlong hurry; rash haste. **precipitant** *a.* falling headlong; too hasty; unexpectedly hastened; *n.* (*Chem.*) a substance which, added to a liquid, decomposes it and precipitates a sediment. **precipitantly** *adv.* **precipitation** (pre·sip·i·tā′·shun) *n.* the act of precipitating; rash haste; a falling headlong; condensation of vapor, rain, snow, etc. [L. *praeceps*, headlong].

pré·cis (prā·sē′) *n.* a concise statement; an abstract or summary [Fr.].

pre·cise (pri·sīs′) *a.* exact; definite; distinct; prim. **-ly** *adv.* **-ness** *n.* **precision** (pre·sizh′·un) *n.* accuracy; definiteness; *a.* done with great accuracy [Fr. *précis*, exact].

pre·clude (pri·klood′) *v.t.* to shut out; to hinder; to prevent from happening **preclusion** *n.* **preclusive** *a.* [L. *prae*, before; *claudere*, to shut].

pre·co·cious (pri·kō′·shas) *a.* (*Bot.*) ripe or developed too soon; having the mental powers or bodily growth developed at an early age; premature; forward. **-ly** *adv.* **-ness, precocity** *n.* [L. *praecox*; early ripe].

pre·con·ceive (prē·kan·sēv′) *v.t.* to form an opinion or idea of beforehand. **preconception** *n.* a prejudice.

pre·con·cert (prē·kan·surt′) *v.t.* to settle beforehand.

pre·cur·sor (prē·kur′·ser) *n.* a person or thing going before; a forerunner; a harbinger.

-y, precursive *a.* [L. *prae*, before; *currere*, to run].

pre·da·cious (pri·dā′·shus) *a.* living on prey; predatory. **predatory** (pred′·a·tōr·i·) *a.* living by preying on others; plundering; pillaging. Also **predaceous** [L. *praeda*, booty].

pre·date (prē·dāt′) *v.t.* to date earlier than the true date; to antedate [*pre* and *date*].

pred·e·ces·sor (pre·da·ses′·er) *n.* one who has preceded another in an office, position, etc. [L. *prae*, before; *decedere*, to withdraw].

pre·des·tine (prē·des′·tin) *v.t.* to destine beforehand; to foreordain. **predestinate** *v.t.* to determine beforehand; to foreordain. **predestination** *n.* (*Theol.*) the doctrine that the salvation or damnation of individuals has been foreordained by God; the determination beforehand of future events; destiny; fate. **predestinarian** *n.* a believer in this doctrine.

pre·de·ter·mine (prē·di·tur′·min) *v.t.* to determine beforehand. **predeterminate** *a.* determined beforehand. **predetermination** *n.*

pred·i·ca·ble (pred′·i·ka·bl) *a.* able to be predicated or affirmed; *n.* anything that can be affirmed of something. **predicability** *n.* [L. *praedicare*, to proclaim].

pre·dic·a·ment (pri·dik′·a·mant) *n.* an awkward plight; a trying situation [L. *praedicare*, to proclaim].

pred·i·cate (pred′·i·kāt) *v.t.* to affirm; to assert; to declare; (pred′·i·kat) *n.* that which is predicated; (*Gram.*) a statement made about the subject of the sentence. **predication** *n.* **predicative** *a.* **predicatively** *adv.* [L. *praedicare*, to proclaim].

pre·dict (prē·dikt′) *v.t.* to tell beforehand; to foretell; to prophesy. **-able** *a.* **-ion** *n.* the act of foretelling; prophecy. **-ive** *a.* **-or** *n.* [L. *praedicere*, to say before].

pre·di·gest (prē·di·jest′) *v.t.* to subject food to artificial digestion before eating.

pre·di·lec·tion (prē·di·lek′·shan) *n.* a prepossession of mind in favor of something; partiality [L. *prae*, before; *dilectus*, chosen].

pre·dis·pose (prē·dis·pōz′) *v.t.* to incline beforehand; to give a tendency or bias to; to render susceptible to. **predisposition** *n.*

pre·dom·i·nate (pri·dàm′·a·nāt) *v.i.* to surpass in strength, influence, or authority; to rule; to have ascendancy; to prevail. **predominance, predominancy** *n.* ascendancy; superiority. **predominant** *a.* superior in influence, authority, etc.; having ascendancy. **predominantly** *adv.* [*pre* and *dominate*].

pre·em·i·nent (prē·em′·a·nant) *a.* distinguished above others; outstanding. **-ly** *adv.* **preeminence** *n.*

pre·emp·tion (prē·em(p)′·shan) *n.* the act or right of purchasing before others. **pre·empt** (prē·em(p)t′) *v.t.* to appropriate beforehand. [L. *prae*, before; *emptio*, a buying].

preen (prēn) *v.t.* to trim or dress with the beak, as birds do their feathers; to primp [form of *prune*].

pre·ex·ist (prē·ig·zist′) *v.i.* to exist beforehand, or before something else. **-ence** *n.* **-ent** *a.*

pre·fab (prē·fab′) *n.* a prefabricated house.

pre·fab·ri·cate (prē·fab′·ra·kāt) *v.t.* to build houses and ships in standardized units in factories for rapid assembly. **prefabrication** *n.*

pref·ace (pref′·as) *n.* introductory remarks at beginning of book, or spoken before a discourse; foreword; *v.t.* to furnish with a preface. **prefatory** (pref′·a·tō·ri·) *a.* introductory [L. *prae*, before; *fari*, to speak].

pre·fect (prē′·fekt) *n.* an ancient Roman magistrate; head of a department. **-orial** *a.* **-ship** *n.* [L. *praetectus*, set before].

pre·fer (pri·fur′) *v.t.* to like better; to choose rather; to promote to an office or dignity. **-able** (pref′·er·a·bl) *a.* worthy of preference; more desirable. **-ably** *adv.* **-ence** *n.*

what is preferred; choice. **-ential** (pref·a·ren'·shal) a. giving or receiving a preference. **-ment** n. advancement or promotion; a position of honor [L. *prae*, before; *ferre*, to bear].

pre·fix (prē'·fiks) n. a letter, syllable, or word put at the beginning of another word to modify its meaning, e.g. *predigest*, *underground*. **prefix** (prē·fiks') v.t.

preg·na·ble (preg'·na·bl) a. able to be taken by assault or force [L. *prehendere*, to take].

preg·nant (preg'·nant) a. being with child; fruitful; full of meaning. **-ly** adv. **pregnancy** n. [L. *praegnans*].

pre·hen·sile (prē·hen'·sil) a. (*Zool.*) capable of grasping [L. *prehendere*, to seize].

pre·his·to·ry (prē·hist'·er·i·) n. the period before written records were kept; the study of this period. **prehistoric** a.

prej·u·dice (prej'·oo·dis) n. an opinion, favorable or unfavorable (more often the latter), formed without fair examination of facts; bias; v.t. to bias; to influence; to injure. **prejudicial** (prej·oo·dish'·al) a. injurious. [L. *prae*, before; *judicium*, judgment].

prel·ate (prel'·at) n. a bishop, or other church dignitary of equal or higher rank. **prelatic, prelatical** a. **prelacy** n. the office or dignity of a prelate; government by prelates; episcopacy; bishops collectively. [L. *praelatus*, put before].

pre·lect (prē·lekt'·) v.i. to deliver a lecture or discourse in public. **prelection** n. a lecture. [L. *prae*, before; *legere, lectum*, to read].

pre·lim·i·nary (pri·lim'·a·ner·i·) a. introductory; preparatory; n. an introduction; a preparatory measure; (often used in *pl.*) [L. *prae*, before; *limen*, a threshold].

prel·ude (prel'·ūd) n. an introductory performance or event; a musical introduction; a preliminary; v.t. to serve as a prelude or forerunner to. **prelusive, prelusory** a. introductory [L. *prae*, before; *ludere*, to play].

pre·ma·ture (prē'·ma·tūr) a. ripe before the natural or proper time; untimely; overhasty. **-ly** adv. **-ness, prematurity** n.

pre·med·i·tate (prē·med'·a·tāt) v.t. to consider, or revolve in the mind beforehand.

pre·mier (prē'·myer) a. first; chief or principal; most ancient; n. (*Great Britain, France*) the prime minister. **-ship** n. [Fr. fr. *primarius*, of the first rank].

pre·miere (pri·myir') n. a first public performance of a play, etc. [Fr. = first].

prem·ise (pri·mīz') v.t. to set forth beforehand, or as introductory to the main subject; to lay down general propositions on which the subsequent reasonings rest. **premise** (prem'·is) n. Also **premiss,** a proposition previously supposed or proved; a proposition from which an inference or conclusion is drawn. *n.pl.* a building with its adjuncts [L. *prae*, before; *mittere, missum*, to send].

pre·mi·um (prē'·mi·am) n. a prize; a fee paid to learn a trade or profession; money paid for insurance; the amount exceeding the par value of shares of stock. **at a premium,** in great demand [L. *praemium*, reward].

pre·mo·ni·tion (prē·ma·nish'·an) n. previous warning; an instinctive foreboding; presentment. **premonitory. premonitorily** adv. [L. *prae*, before; *monere*, to warn].

pre·na·tal (prē·nā'·tal) a. previous to birth.

pre·oc·cu·py (prē·ak'·ya·pī)v.t. to take possession of before another; to engage the attention of. **preoccupied** a. occupied previously; engrossed in thought; absorbed in mediation. **preoccupancy** n. **preoccupation** n.

pre·or·dain (prē·awr·dān') v.t. to ordain beforehand; to foreordain. **preordination** n.

prep (prep) n. (*Colloq.*) preparatory school.

pre·paid (prē·pād') a. paid in advance.

pre·pare (pri·par') v.t. to make ready for

use; to fit for a particular purpose; to provide; to fit out; v.i. to make things ready; to make oneself ready. **preparation** (prep·a·rā'·shan) n. the act of making ready for use; readiness; a substance, esp. medicine or food, made up for use. **preparative** a. tending to prepare for; n. anything which serves to prepare. **preparatively** adv. **preparatory** a. preparing the way; preliminary; introductory. **preparedness** (pra·par'·ad·nas) n. [L. *prae*, before; *parare*, to make ready].

pre·pay (prē·pā') v.t. to pay beforehand [*pre* and *pay*].

pre·pon·der·ate (pri·pan'·der·āt) v.i. to exceed in power, influence, numbers, etc.; to outweigh. **preponderance** n. superiority of power, numbers, etc. **preponderant** a. **preponderantly** adv. [L. *prae*, before; *pondus, ponderis*, a weight].

prep·o·si·tion (prep·a·zish'·an) n. (*Gram.*) a word, e.g. *with, by, for*, etc., used before a noun or pronoun to show the relation to some other word in the sentence. **-al** a. [L. *prae*, before; *ponere, positum*, to place].

pre·pos·sess (prē·pa·zes') v.t. to possess beforehand; to influence a person's mind, heart, etc. beforehand; to prejudice favorably. **-ing** a. tending to win a favorable opinion; attractive. **-ingly** adv. **prepossession** n.

pre·pos·ter·ous (pri·pas'·ter·as) a. contrary to nature, truth, reason, or common sense; utterly absurd. **-ly** adv. **-ness** n. [L. = before, behind, fr. *prae*, before; *posterus*, after].

pre·rog·a·tive (pri·rag'·a·tiv) n. an exclusive right or privilege by reason of rank, position, etc. [L. *prae*, before; *rogare*, to ask].

pres·age (pres'·ij) n. an indication of what is going to happen; an omen. **presage** (pri·sāj') v.t. to foretell; to forebode; to have a presentiment of. **-ful** a. warning [L. *prae*, before; *sagire*, to perceive acutely].

pres·by·o·pi·a (prez·bi·ō'·pi·a) n. farsightedness (occurring in advancing age) [Gk. *presbutēs*, an old man; *ops*, an eye].

pres·by·ter (prez'·bi·ter) n. a priest or elder in the early Christian Church; in Episcopal churches, one ordained to the second order in the ministry; a member of a presbytery. **Pres·by·te·ri·an** (prez·bi·tir'·i·an) n. one belonging to Presbyterian Church. **-ism** n. **presbytery** n. a body of elders; court of pastors [Gk. *presbuteros*, elder, fr. *presbuteros*, elder, fr. *presbus*, old].

pre·sci·ence (prē'·shi·ans) n. knowledge of events before they take place. **prescient** a. [O.Fr. fr. L. *praescientia*, foreknowledge].

pre·scribe (pri·skrīb') v.t. to lay down authoritatively for direction; to set out rules for; (*Med.*) to order or advise the use of. **-r** n. **prescript** n. direction; ordinance. **prescription** (pri·skrip'·shan) n. the act of prescribing or directing; a doctor's direction for use of medicine. **prescriptive** a. [L. *praescribere*, to write before].

pres·ent (prez'·ant) a. being in a certain place; here or at hand; now existing; (*Gram.*) pert. to time that now is; n. present time; (*Gram.*) the present tense. **presence** n. the state of being present; nearness or proximity; the person of a superior; mien or appearance; apparition. **-ly** adv. at once; soon; by and by [L. *praesens*, being present].

pre·sent (pri·zent') v.t. to introduce into the presence of; to exhibit or offer to the notice; to offer as a gift; to bestow; to aim, as a weapon; n. (prez'·ant) a gift. **-able** a. fit to be presented. **-ation** (prez·an·tā'·shan) n. the act of presenting; the state of being presented; that which is presented. **-ment** n. the act or state of presenting; representation; the laying of a formal statement [L. *praesentare*, to place before].

pre·sen·ti·ment (pri·zen'·ta·mant) n. a

previous notion or opinion; anticipation of evil; foreboding.

pre·serve (pri·zurv´) v.t. to keep from injury or destruction; to keep in a sound state; n. that which is preserved, as fruit, etc.; any medium used in preserving; a place for the preservation of game, fish, etc. **-r** n. **preservable** a. **preservation** (prez·er·va´·shan) n. the act of preserving or keeping safe; the state of being preserved; safety. **preservative** n. that which preserves; a. having the power of preserving. **preservatory** a. [L. prae, before; servare, to protect].

pre·side (pri·zīd´) v.i. to be chairman of a meeting; to direct; to control; to superintend. **president** (prez´·a·dant) n. the head of a society, company, association, etc.; the elected head of a republic. **presidency** n. the office, or term of office, of a president. **presidential** a. pert. to a president, his office, dignity, etc. [L. prae, before; sedere, to sit].

press (pres) v.t. to push or squeeze; to crush; to hug; to embrace closely; to drive with violence; to hurry; to urge steadily; to force; to solicit with importunity; to constrain; to smooth by pressure; v.i. to exert pressure; to strive eagerly; to crowd; to throng; to hasten; n. an instrument or machine for squeezing, compressing, etc.; a printing machine; printing and publishing; newspapers collectively; a crowd; a throng; urgent demands; stress; a cupboard for clothes, etc. **-ing** a. urgent; persistent. **— agent** n. one employed to advertise and secure publicity for any person or organization. **to go to press**, of a newspaper, to start printing [L. pressare, fr. premere, to squeeze].

press (pres) v.t. to force to serve in the navy or army [L. praestare, to furnish].

pres·sure (presh´·er) n. the act of pressing; state of being pressed; influence; urgency.

pres·su·ri·za·tion (presh·er·a·zā´·shan) n. maintenance of pressure inside aircraft at great altitudes. **pressurize** (presh´·er·īz) v.t.

pres·ti·dig·i·ta·tion (pres·ta·dij·a·tā·shan) n. conjuring; sleight of hand. **prestidigitator** n. a conjurer (conjuror); a magician [L. praesto, ready; digitus. a finger].

pres·tige (pres·tēzh´, pres´·tēj) n. influence resulting from past achievement, character, reputation, etc. [Fr. = marvel].

pres·to (pres´·tō) adv. (Mus.) quickly [It. fr. L. praesto, ready].

pre·sume (pri·zóom´) v.t. to take for granted; to suppose to be true without proof; to venture; v.i. to act in a forward manner; to take liberties. **presumable** a. probable. **presumably** adv. **presumption** (pri·zum(p)´·shan) n. the act of, or grounds for, presuming; strong probability; that which is taken for granted; arrogance of opinion or conduct; boldness. **presumptive** (pri·zum(p)´·tiv) a. presuming; based on probability; that may be assumed as true or valid until the contrary is proved. **presumptively** adv. **presumptuous** a. forward; taking liberties. n. [L. prae, before; sumere, to take].

pre·sup·pose (prē·sa·pōz´) v.t. to assume or take for granted beforehand.

pre·tend (pri·tend´) v.t. to assert falsely; to counterfeit; to make believe; v.i. to lay claim (to); to make pretense; to aspire (to) **-er** n. one who simulates or feigns; a claimant, esp. to the throne. **pretense** n. simulation; the act of laying claim; assumption; pretext. **pretentious** (pri·ten´·shas) a. given to outward show; presumptuous and arrogant. **pretentiously** adv. **pretentiousness** n. [L. prae, before; tendere, to stretch].

pre·ter- prefix fr. L. praeter, meaning beyond, above, more than, etc., used in combining forms. **-natural** (pre·ter·nach´·er·al) a. beyond or different from what is natural.

pret·er·it, preterite (pret´·er·it) a. (Gram.) past (applied to the tense that expresses past action or state); n. (Gram.) the preterit or past definite tense [L. praeter, beyond; ire, itum, to go].

pre·text (prē´·tekst) n. ostensible reason or motive which cloaks the real reason; pretense [L. prae, before; texere, to weave].

pret·ty (prit´·i·) a. of a beauty that is charming and attractive; but not striking or imposing; neat and tasteful; pleasing; fine or excellent in an ironical sense; adv. in some degree; moderately; fairly; rather. **prettily** adv. **prettiness** n. [O.E. praettig, crafty].

pre·vail (pri·vāl´) v.i. to gain the upper hand or mastery; to succeed; to be current; to be in force; to persuade or induce (with 'on' or 'upon'). **-ing** a. **prevalent** (prev´·a·lant) a. most generally; extensively existing; rife. **prevalently** adv. **prevalence** n. [L. prae, before; valere, to be strong].

pre·var·i·cate (pri·var´·a·kāt) v.i. to evade the truth. **prevarication** n. **prevaricator** n. [L. prae, before; varus, crooked].

pre·vent (pri·vent´) v.t. to keep from happening; to stop. **-able** a. **-ion** n. obstruction; hinderance; preventive. **-ive** a. tending to prevent or ward off; n. that which prevents; antidote to keep off disease [L. prae, before; venire, ventum, to come].

pre·view (prē´·vū) n. a private showing of works of art, films, etc. before being exhibited in public [pre and view].

pre·vi·ous (prē´·vi·as) a. preceding; happening before; (Slang) hasty. **-ly** adv. **-ness** n. [L. prae, before; via, a way].

pre·vise (pri·vīz´) v.t. to foresee; to forewarn. **prevision** n. foresight; foreknowledge [L. prae, before; videre, visum, to see].

prey (prā) n. any animal hunted and killed for food by another animal; a victim; v.i. (with 'on' or 'upon') to seize and devour; to weigh heavily; to pillage [Fr. proie, fr. L. praeda].

price (prīs) n. the amount at which a thing is valued, bought, or sold; value; cost; v.t. to fix the price of; to ask the cost of. **-less** a. beyond any price. [L. pretium, price].

prick (prik) n. a sharp-pointed instrument; a puncture made by a sharp point; the act of pricking; a sharp, stinging pain; hence, (Fig.) remorse; a spur; v.t. to pierce slightly with a sharp point; to incite; to affect with sharp pain; to sting; to erect (the ears). **-er** n. [O.E. prica, a point].

prick·le (prik´.l) n. a small sharp point; a thorn; a spike; a bristle; (Colloq.) a pricking feeling; v.t. to prick slightly; v.i. to feel a tingling sensation. **prickly** a. full of prickles; stinging; tingling [O.E. prica, a point].

pride (prīd) n. the state or quality of being proud; too high an opinion of oneself; worthy self-esteem. **-ful** a. **to pride oneself on** (upon), to be proud of; to take credit for [O.E. pryte, fr. prut, proud].

priest (prēst) n. (fem. **-ess**) a clergyman; in R.C. and Episcopal churches; in pagan times, one who officiated at the altar, or performed the rites of sacrifice. **-like, -ly** a. **-liness** n. **-hood** n. [O.E. preost, fr. Gk. presbuteros, elder].

prig (prig) n. a conceited person who professes superiority. **-gish** a.

prim (prim) a. formal and precise; affectedly nice; prudish. **-ly** adv. **-ness** n. [O.Fr. fr. L. primus, first].

pri·ma (prē´·ma) a first. **— donna**, the principal female singer in an opera. **— facie** (fā´·shi·) at first view. **— facie case**, a case based on sufficient evidence to go to a jury [It. prima, first; donna, a woman; L. facies, appearance].

pri·ma·cy See primate.

pri·mal (prī´·mal) a. first, original; chief.

primary *a.* first in order of time, development, importance; preparatory; elementary; *n.* that which stands highest in rank or importance; a preliminary election (often *pl.*); **primarily** *adv.* in the first place. **primary colors,** red, yellow and blue from which other colors may be made [L. *primus*, first].

pri·mate (prī'·māt) *n.* (*Brit.*) the chief dignitary in a church; an archbishop. **primacy** (prī'·ma·si·) *n.* the chief dignity in a national church; the office or dignity of an archbishop [L.L. *primas*, a chief, fr. *primus*, first].

prime (prīm) *a.* first in time; original; first in degree or importance; foremost; of highest quality; (*Math.*) that cannot be separated into factors; *n.* the earliest stage or beginning; spring; youth; full health or strength; the best portion; *v.t.* to prepare a firearm by charging with powder; to prepare wood with a protective coating before painting it; to fill with water, etc., as a pump, to make it start working; to instruct beforehand. **-r** *n.* one who, or that which, primes, esp. a percussion cap, etc. used to ignite the powder of cartridges, etc.; (prim'·er) a small elementary book used in teaching. **-ly** *adv.* **-ness** *n.* **priming** *n.* the powder, etc. used to fire the charge in firearms. — **minister,** the first minister of state in some countries. — **number,** a number divisible without remainder only by itself or one [L. *primus*, first].

pri·me·val (prī·mē'·val) *a.* original; primitive;**-ly** *adv.* [L. *primus*, first; *aevum*, age].

prim·i·tive (prim'·a·tiv) *a.* pert. to the beginning or origin; being the earliest of its kind; old-fashioned; plain and rude; (*Biol.*) rudimentary; undeveloped; **-ly** *adv.* **-ness** *n.* [L. *primitivus*, fr. *primus*, first].

pri·mo·gen·i·ture (prī·ma·jen'·a·cher) *n.* the state of being the first-born child; the right of the eldest son to inherit his parents' property. **primogenital, primogenitary** *a.* **primogenitor** *n.* the earliest ancestor [L. *primus*, first; *genitor*, a father, fr. *gignere*, to beget].

pri·mor·di·al (prī·mawr'·di·al) *a.* existing from the beginning; first in order; primeval [L. *primus*, first; *ordiri*, to begin].

prim·rose (prim'·rōz) *n.* a plant bearing pale-yellow and other colored flowers in spring [M.E. *primerole*, fr. L. *primus*, first].

prince (prins) *n.* (*fem.* **princess**) a ruler or chief; the son of a king or emperor; a title of nobility. **-dom** *n.* the jurisdiction, rank, or estate of a prince. **-ly** *a.* stately; august; dignified. **-liness** *n.* **Prince Consort,** the husband of a reigning queen [L. *princeps*, a prince].

prin·ci·pal (prin'·sa·pal) *a.* chief in importance; first in rank, character, etc.; *n.* the chief person in authority; a leader; the head of certain institutions, esp. a school; the chief actor in a crime; a chief debtor; a person for whom another is agent; a sum of money lent and yielding interest. **-ly** *adv.* **-ship** *n.* the office or dignity of a principal. **principality** *n.* the territory or dignity of a prince; sovereignty [L. *principalis*].

prin·cip·i·a (prin·sip'·i·a, pring·kip'·i·a) *n.pl.* first principles; beginnings [L. *principium*, a beginning].

prin·ci·ple (prin'·sa·pl) *n.* a fundamental truth or law; a moral rule or settled reason of action; uprightness; honesty; an element.**-d** *a.* guided by certain rules of conduct [L. *principium*, a beginning].

print (print) *v.t.* to impress; to reproduce words, pictures, etc. by pressing inked types on paper, etc.; to produce in this way; to write in imitation of this; to publish; *n.* an impression or mark left on a surface by something pressed against it; printed fabric; printed lettering; an engraving; a photograph. **-er** *n.* one engaged in the setting of type for, and the printing of books, newspapers, etc. **-ing press** *n.* a machine for reproducing on paper, etc. impressions made by inked type [L. *premere*, to press].

pri·or (prī'·er) *a.* previous; former; earlier; preceding in time; *n.* (*fem.* **-ess**) the superior of a priory; one next in dignity to an abbot. **-ity** (prī·awr'·a·ti·) *n.* the state of being antecedent in time; precedence; preference in regard to privilege. **-y** *n.* a religious house, [L. *prior*, former].

prism (prizm) *n.* (*Geom.*) a solid whose bases or ends are any similar, equal, and parallel plane figures, and whose sides are parallelograms; (*Optics*) a transparent figure of this nature, usually with triangular ends. **-atic(al)** *a.* **-atically** *adv.* **prismatic colors,** the seven colors, red, orange, yellow, green, blue indigo, violet, into which a ray of light is separated by a prism [Gk. *prisma*; *eidos*, form].

pris·on (priz'·n) *n.* building for confinement of criminals; jail; any place of confinement or restraint. **-er** (priz'·ner) *n.* one confined in prison; one captured in war [L. *prensio*, fr. *praehendere*, to seize].

pris·tine (pris'·tēn) *a.* belonging to the earliest time; original; pure [L. *pristinus*, fr. *priscus*, of old].

private (prī'·vat) *a.* not public; belonging to or concerning an individual; peculiar to oneself; personal; secluded; secret; of a soldier, not holding any rank; *n.* a common soldier. **-ly** *adv.* **-ness** *n.* **privacy** (prī'·va·si·) *n.* the state of being in retirement from company; solitude; seclusion; secrecy [L. *privatus*, fr. *privus*, single].

pri·va·teer (prī·va·tir') *n.* an armed private vessel commissioned by a government to attack enemy ships.

pri·va·tion (prī·vā'·shan) *n.* the state of being deprived, esp. of something required; destitution; want. **privative** (priv'·a·tiv) *a.* causing privation; consisting in the absence of something; denoting negation.

priv·et (priv'·it) *n.* an evergreen shrub.

priv·i·lege (priv'·i·lij) *n.* a special right or advantage; *v.t.* to grant some special favor to. **-d** *a.* enjoying a special right or immunity [L. *privilegium*, private law, fr. *lex*, a law].

priv·y (priv'·i·) *a.* private; admitted to knowledge of a secret; *n.* a person having an interest in a law suit; a latrine. **privily** *adv.* **privity** *n.* private knowledge; connivance. — **to,** secretly informed of. **Privy Council,** (*Brit.*) the council which advises the sovereign on matters of government [Fr. *privé*, fr. L. *privatus*, private].

prize (prīz) *n.* a reward given for success in competition; a reward given for merit; a thing striven for; a thing won by chance, e.g. in a lottery. *v.t.* to value highly; to esteem. — **fight** *n.* a professional boxing match. — **fighter** *n.* [O.Fr. *pris*].

prize (prīz) *n.* an enemy ship or property captured in naval warfare. — **court** *n.* court to adjudicate on prizes captured in naval warfare [Fr. *prise*, a seizing].

pro- (prō) *prefix* fr. L. or Gk. meaning for; instead of; on behalf of; in front of; before; forward; according to.

prob·a·ble (prab'·a·bl) *a.* likely; to be expected; having more evidence for than against. **probably** *adv.* **probability** *n.* likelihood; anything that has appearance of truth [L. *probare*, to prove].

pro·bate (prō'·bāt) *n.* the process by which a last will and testament is legally authenticated after the testator's death; an official copy of a will; *v.t.* to establish the validity of a will [L. *probare*, to prove].

pro·ba·tion (prō·bā'·shan) *n.* a trial or test of a person's character, conduct, ability, etc.; the testing of a candidate before admission to full membership of a body, esp. a religious sect or order; a system of releasing offenders, esp. juveniles, and placing them under supervision of.**-al** *a.* **-ary** *a.* **-er** *n.* a person undergoing probation. **probative** (prō'·ba̧·tiv) *a.* pert. to, serving for, or offering, trial or proof [L. *probare*, to prove].

probe (prōb) *n.* (*Med.*) instrument for examining a wound, ulcer, cavity, etc.; an investigation; *v.t.* to explore a wound, etc. with a probe; to examine thoroughly [L. *probare*, to prove].

pro·bi·ty (prō'·ba̧·ti·) *n.* integrity; rectitude; honesty [L. *probus*, good].

prob·lem (prāb'·lem) *n.* a matter proposed for solution; a question difficult of solution; a puzzle. **-atical** *a.* questionable; uncertain; disputable; doubtful. **-atically** *adv.* [Gk. *problēma*, a thing thrown before].

pro·bos·cis (prō·bás'·is) *n.* an elephant's trunk; the snout of other animals [Gk. fr. *pro*, before; *boskein*, to feed].

pro·ceed (prō·sēd') *v.i.* to move onward; to advance; to renew progress; to pass from one point or topic to another; to come forth; to carry on a series of acts; to take legal proceedings. **-ing** *n.* going forward; movement or process; *pl.* (*Law*) the several steps of prosecuting a charge, claim, etc.; a record of business done by a society. **proceeds** (prō'·sēdz) *n.pl.* yield; sum realized by a sale. **procedure** (pra̧·sē'·jȩr) *n.* act, method of proceeding [L. *procedere*, to go forward].

pro·cess (prá'·ses) *n.* continued forward movement; lapse of time; a series of actions or measures; a method of operation; (*Anat.*) a projecting part or growth; (*Law*) procedure; *v.t.* to subject to some process, as food or material. **procession** (pra̧·, prō·sesh'·an) *n.* a moving line of people, cars, animals, etc.; regular progress. **-ional** *a.* pert. to a procession; *n.* a hymn sung during a church procession — **server** *n.* one who serves notices to appear in court [L. *processus*].

pro·claim (prō·klām') *v.t.* to make known by public announcement; to declare.**-ant, -er** *n.* one who proclaims. **proclamation** (prak·la̧·mā'·shan) *n.* the act of announcing publicly; an official public announcement [L. *pro*, before; *clamare*, to cry out].

pro·cliv·i·ty (prō·kliv'·a̧·ti·) *n.* inclination; propensity; proneness; aptitude [L. *pro*, forward; *clivus*, a slope].

pro·cras·ti·nate (prō·kras'·ta̧·nāt) *v.i.* to put off till some future time. **procrastination** *n.* **procrastinator** *n.* [L. *procrastinare*, fr. *cras*, tomorrow].

pro·cre·ate (prō'·krē·āt) *v.t.* to bring into being; to beget; to generate. **procreation** *n.* **procreative** *a.* having the power to beget; productive. **procreativeness** *n.* **procreator** *n.* [L. *pro*, forth; *creare*, to produce].

proc·tor (prāk'·tȩr) *n.* (*Law*) one who manages the affairs of another in a court; one who supervises students in an examination; *v.t.* to supervise in an examination. **-ial** *a.* **-ship** *n.* [abbrev. of *procurator*].

pro·cum·bent (prō·kum'·bant) *a.* lying face down; (*Bot.*) growing along the ground [L. *pro*, forward; *cumbere*, to lie down].

proc·u·ra·tion (prāk·ya̧·rā'·shan) *n.* management of another's affairs; power of attorney. [L. *pro*, for; *curare*, to see to].

pro·cure (prō·kyoor')*v.t.* to acquire; to obtain; to get; to bring about; *v.i.* to act as a procurer. **procurable** *a.* obtainable. **-ment** *n.* **-r** *n.* (*fem.* **procuress**) one who procures; one who supplies women for immoral purposes [L. *pro*, for; *curare*, to see to].

prod (prād) *v.t.* to poke with something pointed; to goad; *n.* a pointed instrument; a poke, *pr.p.* **-ding.** *pa.p.* and *pa.t.* **-ded.**

prod·i·gal (prād'·i·ga̧l) *a.* wasteful; spending

recklessly; *n.* one who spends recklessly; a spendthrift. **-ly** *adv.* **-ity** *n.* reckless extravagance [L. *prodigere*, to squander].

prod·i·gy (prād'·i·ji·) *n.* a person or thing causing wonder; a marvel; a very gifted person; a monster; a portent. **prodigious** (pra̧·dij'·as) *a.* like a prodigy; marvelous; enormous; extraordinary. **prodigiously** *adv.* [L. *prodigium*, a portent or sign].

pro·duce (pra̧·dóós') *v.t.* to bring forth; to exhibit; to give birth to; to yield; to make; to cause; of a play, to present it on the stage. **produce** (prād'·óós) *n.* that which is produced; product; agricultural products; crops. **-r** *n.* [L. *pro*, forward; *ducere*, to lead].

prod·uct (prād'·a̧kt) *n.* that which is produced; (*Arith.*) a number resulting from the multiplying of two or more numbers. **production** (pra̧·duk'·shan) *n.* the act of producing; the things produced. **-ive** *a.* having the power to produce; creative; fertile; efficient. **-ively** *adv.* **-iveness, -ivity** *n.* [L. *pro*, forward; *ducere*, to lead].

pro·em (prō'·em) *n.* a preface; an introduction. **-ial** *a.* [Gk. *pro*, before; *oimos*, a path].

pro·fane (prō·fān') *a.* not sacred; irreverent; blasphemous; vulgar; *v.t.* to treat with irreverence; to put to a wrong or unworthy use; to desecrate. **-ly** *adv.* **-ness** *n.* **-r** *n.* **profanation** (prāf·a̧·nā'·shan) *n.* the act of violating sacred things. **profanity** (pro·fan'·i·ti·) *n.* profaneness; irreverence; the use of bad language [L. *pro*, before; *fanum*, a temple].

pro·fess (pra̧·fes') *v.t.* to make open declaration of; to confess publicly; to affirm belief in; to pretend to knowledge or skill in. **-ed** *a.* openly acknowledged. **-ion** (pra̧·fesh'·an) *n.* the act of professing; that which one professes; occupation or calling, esp. one requiring learning. **-ional** *a.* pert. to a profession or calling; engaged in for money, as opposed to *amateur*; *n.* one who makes a livelihood in sport or games (*abbrev.* **pro**). **-ionally** *adv.* [L. *profiteri, professus*, to acknowledge].

pro·fes·sor (pra̧·fes'·ȩr) *n.* one who makes profession; a teacher of the highest rank in a university. **professorial** (prō·fa̧·sō'·ri·a̧l) *a.* **-ially** *adv.* **professoriate** (prō·fa̧·sō'·ri·it) *n.* the office of a professor; his period of office; body of professors. **-ship** *n.* [L. *profiteri, professus*, to acknowledge].

prof·fer (prāf'·ȩr) *v.t.* to offer for acceptance; **-er** *n.* [L. *proferre*, to bring forward].

pro·fi·cient (pra̧·fish'·a̧nt) *a.* thoroughly versed or qualified in any art or occupation; skilled; *n.* an expert. **-ly** *adv.* **proficience, proficiency** *n.* [L. *proficere*, to be useful].

pro·file (prō'·fīl) *n.* an outline or contour; a portrait in a side view; the side face; short biographical sketch; *v.t.* to draw the outline of [L. *pro*, before; *filum*, thread].

prof·it (prāf'·it) *n.* advantage or benefit; the excess of returns over expenditure; pecuniary gain in any transaction or occupation; *v.t.* to be of service to; *v.i.* to gain advantage; to grow richer. **-able** *a.* yielding profit or gain; advantageous; helpful. **-ably** *adv.* **-ableness** *n.* **profiteer** (prāf·a̧·tēr')*n.* one who makes excessive profits; *v.i.* to make such profits [L. *profectus*, fr. *proficere*, to make progress].

prof·li·gate (prāf'·la̧·gat, ·gāt) *a.* abandoned to vice; dissolute; extravagant; *n.* a depraved person. **-ly** *adv.* **-ness** *n.* **profligacy** (prāf'·li·ga̧·si·) *n.* a vicious and dissolute manner of living [L. *profligatus*, ruined].

pro·found (pra̧·found') *a.* deep; intellectually deep; learned; deeply felt. **-ly** *adv.* **profundity** *n.* depth of place, knowledge, skill, feeling [L. *profundus*, deep].

pro·fuse (pra̧·fūs') *a.* giving or given generously; lavish; extravagant. **-ly** *adv.* **-ness, profusion** (pra̧·fū'·shan) *n.* great abundance [L. *pro*, forth; *fusum*, to pour].

prog·e·ny (prăj'·ạ·ni·) n. descendants; offspring; children. **progenitive** a. pert. to the production of offspring. **progenitor** (prō·jen'·i·ter) n. ancestor; forefather [L. pro. before; gignere, to beget].

prog·no·sis (prăg·nō'·sis) n. a forecast; (Med.) foretelling the course of a disease. pl. **prognoses. prognostic** (prăg·năs'·tik) a. foretelling; forecasting; predicting; n. a forecast; a prediction. **prognosticate** v.t. to foretell; to predict; to prophesy. **prognostication** n. **prognosticator** n. [Gk. pro, before; gnōsis, knowledge].

pro·gram, programme (prō'·gram) n. a plan or detailed notes of intended proceedings at a public entertainment, ceremony, etc.; a party policy at election time [Gk. pro, before; gramma, a writing].

prog·ress (prăg'·res) n. a moving forward; advancement; development. **progress** (prạ·gres') v.i. to move forward; to advance; to develop; to improve. **-ion** (prạ·gresh'·ạn) n. the act of moving forward; onward movement; progress. **-ional** a. **-ive** a. moving forward gradually; advancing; improving; favoring progress or reform. **-ively** adv. **-iveness** n. **arithmetical progression**, a series of numbers increasing or decreasing by the same amount, e.g. 3, 6, 9, 12, 15, etc. **geometrical progression**, a series of numbers increasing or decreasing by a common ratio, e.g. 3, 9, 27, 81, etc. [L. progredi, progressus, to go forward].

pro·hib·it (prō·hib'·it) v.t. to forbid; to prevent; to hinder. **-er, -or -ion** (prō·(h)ạ·bish'·ạn) n. the act of forbidding; interdict; the forbidding by law of manufacture, importation, sale, or purchase of alcoholic liquors. **-ionist** n. one in favor of prohibition. **-ive, -ory** a. tending to forbid, prevent, or exclude; exclusive. **-ively** adv. [L. prohibere].

pro·ject (prạ·jekt') v.t. to throw or cast forward; to plan; to contrive; to throw a photographic image on a screen; v.i. to jut out; to protrude. **project** (prăj'·ekt) n. a plan; a scheme; a task. **-ile** (prạ·jek'·til) a. capable of being thrown; n. a heavy missile, esp. a shell or cannon ball. **-ion** n. the act of projecting; something that juts out; a plan; delineation; the representation on a plane of a curved surface or sphere; in psychology, mistaking for reality something which is only an image in the mind. **-ive** a. **-or** n. an apparatus for throwing photographic images, esp. films, on a screen [L. projicere, propectum, to throw forward].

pro·lapse (prō'·laps) n. (Med.) the falling down of a part of the body from its normal position, esp. womb or rectum [L. prolapsus, fr. prolabi, to fall or slide forward].

pro·lep·sis (prō·lep'·sis) n. a figure of speech by which objections are anticipated and answered; an error in chronology, consisting in antedating an event; pl. **prolepses. proleptical** a. [Gk. pro, before; lēpsis, a taking].

pro·le·tar·i·an (prō·lạ·te'·ri·ạn) a. pert. to the proletariat; belonging to the working class; n. one of the proletariat. **proletariat** (prō·lạ·te'·ri·ạt) n. propertyless wage-earners who live by sale of their labor [L. proles, offspring].

pro·lif·er·ous (prō·lif'·ẹr·ạs) a. (Biol.) reproducing freely by cell division; developing anthers. **-ly** adv. **proliferate** v.t. to bear; v.i. to reproduce by repeated cell division. **proliferation** n. increase [L. proles, offspring; ferre, to bear].

pro·lif·ic (prạ·lif'·ik) a. bringing forth offspring; fruitful, abundantly productive; bringing about results. **-ally** adv. [L. proles, offspring; facere, to make].

pro·lix (prō'·liks) a. long drawn out; diffuse; wordy. **-ly** adv. **-ity** n. [L. prolixus].

pro·loc·u·tor (prō·lăk'·yạ·ter) n. a chairman of an assembly [L. pro; locutus, to speak].

pro·logue (prō'·lawg) n. the preface or introduction to a discourse, poem, book, or performance, esp. the address spoken before a dramatic performance; v.t. to preface [Gk. pro, before; logos, discourse].

pro·long (prō·lawng') v.t. to lengthen out; to extend the duration of. **-ation** n. the act of lengthening out; a part prolonged; extension [L. pro; longus, long].

prom (prám) n. (Colloq.) a formal ball [Abbrev. of promenade].

prom·e·nade (prám·ạ·nād', nád) n. a leisurely walk, generally in a public place; a place adapted for such a walk; a march of dancers, as at the opening of a ball or in a square dance; v.i. to walk for pleasure, display, or exercise. **-r** n. [Fr.].

prom·i·nent (prám'·ạ·nạnt) a. sticking out; projecting; conspicuous; distinguished. **-ly** adv. **prominence, prominency** n. [L. prominere, to jut out].

pro·mis·cu·ous (prạ·mis'·kyoo·ạs) a. mixed without order or distinction; indiscriminate. **-ly** adv. **-ness, promiscuity** (prám·is·kū'·ạ·ti·) n. [L. promiscuus, fr. miscere, to mix].

prom·ise (prám'·is) n. an undertaking to do or not to do something; cause or grounds for hope; v.t. to give one's word to do or not to do something; to give cause for expectation; to agree to give; v.i. to assure by a promise; to give grounds for hope. **-r** n. **promisor** n. (Law) the person by whom a promise is made. **promising** a. likely to turn out well or to succeed; hopeful [L. promittere, promissum, to promise].

prom·is·so·ry (prám'·ạ·sōr·i·) a. containing a promise. **— note**, written agreement to pay sum to named person at specified date [L. promittere, to promise].

prom·on·to·ry (prám'·ạn·tōr·i·) n. a point of high land jutting out into the sea [L. promontorium, fr. mons, a mountain].

pro·mote (prạ·mōt') v.t. to move forward; to move up to a higher rank or position; to encourage the growth or development of; to help organize a new business venture or company. **-r** n. a supporter; an initiator, esp. of a new business venture, etc. **promotion** n. advancement; preferment; a higher rank, station, or position. **promotive** a. [L. promovere, promotum, to move forward].

prompt (prámpt) a. ready and quick to act; done at once; punctual; v.t. to excite to action; to suggest; to help out (actor or speaker) by reading, suggesting next words. **-ly** adv. **-er** n. one who reminds or helps out an actor, speaker, etc. **-itude, -ness** n. readiness; quickness of decision and action. [L. promptus, fr. promere, to put forth].

pro·mul·gate (prám'·ạl·gāt) v.t. to proclaim; to publish; to make known officially. **promulgation** n. [L. promulgare].

prone (prōn) a. lying face downward; sloping; inclined; naturally disposed. **-ly** adv. **-ness** n. inclination; tendency [L. pronus].

prong (prăng) n. one of the pointed ends of a fork; a spike [etym. uncertain].

pro·noun (prō'·noun) n. (Gram.) a word used instead of a noun [pro and noun].

pro·nounce (prạ·nouns') v.t. to speak with the correct sound and accent; to speak distinctly; to utter formally or officially; to declare or affirm. **-d** a. strongly marked; very definite or decided. **-able** a. **-ment** n. a formal declaration. **-r** n. **pronouncing** a. teaching or indicating pronunciation. **pronunciation** (prạ·nun·si·ā'·shạn) n. the act of uttering with the proper sound and accent; [L. pronuntiare, to proclaim].

pron·to (prán'·tō) adv. (Colloq.) promptly; quickly [Sp.].

proof (próóf) *n.* something which proves; a test or trial; any process to ascertain correctness, truth, or facts; demonstration; evidence that convinces the mind and produces belief; argument; standard strength of alcoholic spirits; (*Print.*) a trial impression from type, on which corrections may be made; *a.* firm in resisting; impenetrable; serving as proof or designating a certain standard or quality; *v.t.* to render proof against. **-reader** *n.* one who corrects printer's proofs [L. *probare*, to prove].

prop (práp) *v.t.* to support by placing something under or against; to sustain. *pr.p.* **-ping.** *pa.t.*, *pa.p.* **-ped.** *n.* that which supports; a stay [M.E. *proppe*].

prop·a·gan·da (práp·a·gan'·da) *n.* the propagating of doctrines or principles; the opinions or beliefs thus spread; (*R.C.*) a society in Rome charged with the management of missions. **propagandize** *v.t.* and *i.* to spread propaganda. **propagandist** *n.* [fr. L. *de propaganda fide*, concerning the spreading of the faith].

prop·a·gate (práp'·a·gāt) *v.t.* to cause to multiply or reproduce by generation; to breed; to spread the knowledge of; to transmit or carry forward; *v.i.* to have young; to breed. **propagator** *n.* **propagation** *n.* [L. *propagare*, to propagate plants by slips].

pro·pel (pra·pel') *v.t.* to drive forward; to press onward by force; to push. *pr.p.* **-ling.** *pa.p.* **-led. -ler** *n.* one who, or that which, propels; a revolving shaft with blades for driving a ship or airplane [L. *pro*, forward; *pellere*, to drive].

pro·pen·si·ty (pra·pen'·sa·ti·) *n.* bent of mind; leaning or inclination [L. *pro*, forward; *pendere*, *pensum*, to hang].

prop·er (práp'·ẹr) *a.* fit; suitable; correct or according to usage.**-ly** *adv.* — **fraction** (*Arith.*) one in which the numerator is less than the denominator [L. *proprius*, own].

prop·er·ty (práp'·ẹr·ti·) *n.* an inherent or essential quality or peculiarity; ownership; the thing owned; possessions; land; *pl.* theatrical requisites, as scenery, costumes, etc. [L. *proprietas*, fr. *proprius*, own].

proph·e·cy (práf'·a·si·) *n.* the foretelling of future events; prediction; revelation of God's will. **prophesy** (práf'·a·sī) *v.t.* to foretell; to predict; to utter by divine inspiration; *v.i.* to utter predictions. **prophet** (práf'·it) *n.* (*fem.* **prophetess**) one who foretells future events; an inspired teacher or revealer of the Divine Will. **prophetic(al)** *a.* [Gk. *prophētēs*, aforespeaker].

pro·phy·lac·tic (prō·fa·lak'·tik) *a.* (*Med.*) tending to prevent disease, preventive; *n.* medicine or treatment tending to prevent disease. **prophylaxis** *n.* preventive treatment of disease [Gk. *phulassein*, to guard].

pro·pin·qui·ty (prō·ping'·kwa·ti·) *n.* nearness in time or place; nearness in blood relationship [L. *propinquitas*, fr. *prope*, near].

pro·pi·ti·ate (pra·pish'·i·āt) *v.t.* to appease; to conciliate; to gain the favor of. **propitiation** *n.* appeasement; conciliation; atonement. **propitiator** *n.* **propitiatory** *a.* serving, or intended, to propitiate. **propitious** (pra·pish'·as) *a.* favorable; favorably inclined. **propitiously** *adv.* [L. *propitiare*].

pro·po·nent (pra·pō'·nant) *n.* one who supports or makes a proposal [see **propound**].

pro·por·tion (pra·pōr'·shan) *n.* relative size, number, or degree; comparison; relation; relation between connected things or parts; symmetrical arrangement, distribution, or adjustment; (*Arith.*) equality of ratios; the rule of three; *n.pl.* dimensions; *v.t.* to arrange the proportions of. **-al** *a.* *n.* a number of quantity in arithmetical or mathematical

proportion. **-ally** *adv.* **-ality** *n.* **-ate** *a.* **-ed** *a.* **-ment** *n.* [L. *proportio*, fr. *portio*, a share].

pro·pose (pra·pōz') *v.t.* to offer for consideration; to suggest; to nominate; *v.i.* to form a plan; to intend; to offer oneself in marriage. **proposal** *n.* the act of proposing; what is offered for consideration; an offer, esp. of marriage. **-r** *n.* **proposition** (práp·a·zish'·an) *n.* a proposal; a statement or assertion. **propositional** *a.* [L. *proponere*, to put forward].

pro·pound (pra·pound') *v.i.* to offer for consideration; to propose; to set (a problem) [L. *pro*, forth; *ponere*, to place].

pro·pri·e·tor (pra·prī'·a·tẹr) *n.* (*fem.* **proprietress, proprietrix**) one who is the owner of property, a business, restaurant, etc. **proprietary** *a.* pert. to an owner; made and sold by an individual or firm having the exclusive rights of manufacture and sale. **-ship** *n.* [L. *proprius*, one's own].

pro·pri·e·ty (pra·prī'·a·ti·) *n.* properness; correct conduct [L. *proprius*, one's own].

pro·pul·sion (pra·pul'·shan) *n.* the act of driving forward. **propulsive, propulsory** *a.* tending, or having power, to propel [L. *pro*, forward; *pellere, pulsum*, to drive].

pro·rate (prō'·rāt) *v.t.* and *i.* to divide or distribute proportionally. **proratable** *a.* **pro rata** in proportion [fr. L].

pro·sa·ic (prō·zā'·ik) *a.* dull and unimaginative; commonplace. Also **-al, -ally** *adv.* [L. *prosus*, straight-forward].

pro·sce·ni·um (prō·sē'·ni·am) *n.* the part of the stage in front of the curtain [Gk. *pro*, before; *skēnē*, the stage].

pro·scribe (prō·skrīb') *v.t.* to put outside the protection of the law; to outlaw; to prohibit. **-r** *n.* **proscription** *n.* **proscriptive** *a.* [L. *proscribere*, to publish].

prose (prōz) *n.* ordinary language in speech and writing; language not in verse; *a.* pert. to prose; not poetical; *v.i.* to write prose; to speak or write in a dull, tedious manner. **prosy** *a.* dull and tedious. **prosily** *adv.* [L. *prosa (oratio)*, direct (speech)].

pros·e·cute (prás'·i·kūt) *v.t.* to follow or pursue with a view to reaching or accomplishing something; (*Law*) to proceed against judicially; *v.i.* to carry on a legal suit. **prosecution** *n.* (*Law*) the institution and carrying on of a suit in a court of law; the party by which legal proceedings are instituted, as opposed to the *defense*. **prosecutor** *n.* (*fem.* **prosecutrix**) [L. *prosequi*, to follow].

pros·e·lyte (prás'·a·līt) *n.* a convert to some party or religion; *v.t.* to convert. **proselytize** *v.t.* to make converts. **proselytism** *n.* [Gk. *prosēlutos*, a newcomer].

pros·o·dy (prás'·a·di·) *n.* the science of versification. **prosodic** (pra·sád'·ik) *a.* **prosodist** *n.* one skilled in prosody [Gk. *pros*, to, *ōdē*, a song].

pros·pect (prás'·pekt) *n.* a wide view; anticipation; reasonable hope; promise of future good. *v.t.* and *i.* to search or explore (a region), esp. for precious metals, oil, etc. **-ive** *a.* looking forward; relating to the future. **-ively** *adv.* **-or** *n.* **-us** *n.* a preliminary statement of an enterprise [L. *prospicere*, to look forward].

pros·per (prás'·pẹr) *v.t.* to cause to succeed; *v.i.* to succeed; to do well. **-ity** *n.* **-ous** *a.* **-ously** *adv.* [L. *prosper*, fortunate].

pros·tate (prás'·tāt) *n.* a small gland at the neck of the bladder in males. Also — **gland** [Gk. *pro*, before; *statos*, placed].

pros·ti·tute (prás'·ta·tūt) *n.* a harlot; *v.t.* to make a prostitue of; to put to base, infamous, or unworthy use. **prostitution** *n.* [L. *prostituere*, to offer for sale].

pros·trate (prás'·trāt) *a.* lying on the

ground, esp. face downwards; mentally or physically exhausted; *v.t.* to lay flat, as on the ground; to bow down in adoration; to overcome. **prostration** *n.* [L. *pro*, forward; *sternere*, *stratum*, to lay flat].

pro·tag·o·nist (prō·tag′·an·ist) *n.* the principal actor in a drama; a leading character [Gk. *prōtos*, first; *agōnistēs*, an actor].

pro·tect (pra·tekt′) *v.t.* to defend; to guard; to put a tariff on imports to encourage home industry. **-ion** *n.* defending from injury or harm; state of being defended; that which defends. **-ionism** *n.* the doctrine of protecting industries by taxing competing imports. **-ive** *a.* affording protection; sheltering. **-ively** *adv.* **-or** *n.* one who or that which, defends. **-orate** *n.* (period of) office of a protector of a state; political administration of a state or territory by another country [L. *pro*. in front of; *tegere*, to cover].

pro·té·gé (prō′·ta·zhā) *n.* (*fem.* **protégée**) one under the care, protection, or patronage of another (Fr. *protéger*, to protect].

pro·te·in (prō′·tēn) *n.* a nitrogenous compound required for all animal life processes. Also **proteid** [Gk. *prōtos*, first].

pro·test (pra·test′) *v.i.* to assert formally; to make a declaration against; *v.t.* to affirm solemnly; to object to. **protest** (prō′·test) *n.* a declaration of objection. **-ant** (pra·tes′·tant) *n.* one who holds an opposite opinion. **Protestant** (prát′·as·tant) *a.* pert. or belonging to any branch of the Western Church outside the Roman communion; *n.* a member of such a church. **Protestantism** *n.* **protestation** *n.* a solemn declaration, esp. of dissent [L. *pro*, before; *testari*, to witness].

pro·tha·la·mi·on (prō·tha·lā′·mi·an) *n.* a song written in honor of a marriage. Also **prothalamium** [Gk. *pro*, before; *thalamos*, the bridal chamber].

pro·to- (prō′·tō) *prefix* fr. Gk. *prōtos*, first; hence, original; primitive. **-plasm** *n.* a semifluid substance forming the basis of the primitive tissue of animal and vegetable life; living matter. **-plasmatic**, **-plasmic** *a.* **-type** (prō′·ta·tīp) *n.* original or model from which anything is copied; a pattern. **-typal**, **-typic(al)** *a.* **Protozoa** (prō·ta·zō′·a) *n.pl.* first or lowest division of animal kingdom, consisting of microscopic, unicellular organisms. **-zoon** (prō·ta·zō′·an) *n.* a member of this division. **-zoal**, **-zoan**, **-zoic** *a.*

pro·to·col (prō′·ta·kál) *n.* an original copy; a rough draft, esp. a draft of terms signed by negotiating parties as the basis of a formal treaty or agreement; rules of diplomatic etiquette [Gk. *prōtokollon*, a flyleaf glued on to a book].

pro·ton (prō′·tán) *n.* in physics, the unit of positive electricity, found in the nuclei of all atoms [Gk. *prōtos*, first].

pro·tract (prō·trakt′) *v.t.* to lengthen; to draw out; to prolong; to draw to scale. **-ed** *a.* prolonged; long drawn out; tedious. **-ion** *n.* **-ive** *a.* **-or** *n.* a mathematical instrument for measuring angles; (*Anat.*) a muscle which draws forward or extends a limb [L. *pro*, forward; *trahere*, *tractum*, to draw].

pro·trude (prō·trōōd′) *v.t.* and *i.* to stick out; to project; to thrust forward. **protrusion** *n.* the act of thrusting forward; the state of being protruded or thrust forward; that which protrudes. **protrusive** *a.* [L. *pro*, forward; *trudere*, *trusum*, to thrust].

pro·tu·ber·ant (prō·tū′·ber·ant) *a.* bulging; swelling out; prominent. **-ly** *adv.* **protuberance** *n.* [L. *protuberare*, to swell].

proud (proud) *a.* haughty; self-respecting. **-ly** *adv.* **— flesh**, excessive granulation in tissue of healing wound [O.E. *prut*, proud].

prove (prōov) *v.t.* to try by experiment; to ascertain as fact, by evidence; to demonstrate;

to show; to establish the validity of (a will, etc.) *v.i.* to turn out (to be, etc.); to be found by trial. *pr.p.* **proving**. *pa.p.* **-d** or **-n**. *pa.t.* **provable** *a.* able to be proved. [L. *probare*, to test].

prov·e·nance (práv′·a·nans) *n.* source or place of origin. Also **provenience** (prō·vē′·ni·ans [L. *pro*, forth; *venire*, to come].

prov·en·der (práv′·an·der) *n.* a dry food for beasts; fodder; hence provisions; food [O.Fr. *provendre*].

proverb (práv′·erb) *n.* a short pithy saying to express a truth or point a moral; an adage. **Proverbs** *n.pl.* (*Bib.*) book of Old Testament. **-ial** *a.* pert. to or resembling a proverb; well-known. **-ially** *adv.* [L. *proverbium*, fr. *verbum*, a word].

pro·vide (pra·vīd′) *v.t.* to supply; to furnish; to get or make ready for future use; *v.i.* to make preparation; to furnish support (for). **providence** (prov′·i·dens) *n.* prudence; wise economy; God's care; an event regarded as an act of God. **Providence** *n.* God Himself. **provident** *a.* prudent; thrifty. **providently** *adv.* **providential** (práv·a·den′·shal) *a.* effected by divine foresight; fortunate; lucky. **-r** *n.* [L. *pro*, before; *videre*, to see].

prov·ince (práv′·ins) *n.* a division of a country or empire; an administrative district; a district under the jurisdiction of an archbishop; a sphere of action; a department of knowledge; one's special duty. **provincial** pra·vin′·shal) *a.* pert. to a province or the provinces; countrified; narrow; *n.* an inhabitant of a province. **provincially** *adv.* [L. *provincia*].

pro·vi·sion (pra·vizh′·an) *n.* the act of providing; measures taken beforehand; store esp. of food (generally in *pl.*); a condition or proviso; *v.t.* to supply with provisions. **-al** *a.* temporary; adopted for the time being. **-ally** *adv.* [L. *pro*, before; *videre*, *visum*, to see].

pro·vi·so (pra·vī′·zō) *n.* a condition or stipulation in a deed or contract. *pl.* **-s** or **-es**. **-ry** *a.* containing a proviso or condition; temporary [L. *proviso quod*, it being provided that].

pro·voke (pra·vōk′) *v.t.* to excite or stimulate to action, esp. to arouse to anger or passion; to bring about or call forth. **provoking** *a.* **provocation** (práv·a·kā′·shan) *n.* the act of provoking; that which provokes. **provocative** (pra·vák′·a·tiv) *a.* serving or tending to provoke. **provocatively** *adv.* **provocativeness** *n.* [L. *provocare*, to call forth].

prov·ost (práv′·ast) *n.* in certain colleges on administrative assistant to the president. **— marshal** (prō′·vō·már′·shal) *n.* an officer in charge of the military police (army), or of prisoners (navy) [L. *praepositus*, placed before].

prow (prou) *n.* the forepart or bow of a ship; (*Poetic*) a ship [L. *prora*].

prow·ess (prou′·is) *n.* bravery, esp. in war; valor; achievement [Fr. *prouesse*].

prowl (proul) *v.i.* to roam about stealthily; *n.* the act of prowling [M.E. *prollen*].

prox·i·mate (prák′·si·mit) *a.* next or nearest; closest; immediately following or preceding. **-ly** *adv.* **proximity** *n.* being next in time, place, etc.; immediate nearness. **proximo** *adv.* in or of the coming month [L. *proximus*, nearest].

prox·y (prák′·si·) *n.* an authorized agent or substitute; one deputed to act for another; a writing empowering one person to vote for another [short fr. *procuracy*].

prude (prōōd) *n.* a woman of affected or over-sensitive modesty or reserve. **prudish** *a.* **-ry** *n.* affected modesty; primness; stiffness [O.Fr. *prode*, discreet].

pru·dent (prōō·dant) *a.* cautious and judi-

cious; careful; not extravagant. **-ly** *adv.*
prudence *n.* **prudential** (proŏ·den′·shạl) *a.*
ially *adv.* [L. *prudens*, foreseeing].
prune (proŏn) *n.* a dried plum [Fr. fr. L.
prunum, a plum].
prune (proŏn) *v.t.* to cut off dead parts, excessive branches, etc.; to remove anything
superfluous. [O.Fr. *proignier*].
pru·ri·ent (proŏr·i·ạnt) *a.* given to, or
springing from, unclean or lewd thoughts.
-ly *adv.* **prurience, pruriency** *n.* [L.
prurire, to itch].
Prus·sia (prush′·ạ) *n.* (*Geog.*) formerly the
leading state of Germany, and the recognized
home of German militarism. **-n** *n./a.* **-n blue**,
a deep blue salt of potassium and iron, used as
a pigment. **prussic acid**, hydrocyanic acid.
pry (prī) *v.i.* to look curiously; to peer; to
nose about. *pr.p.* **-ing.** *pa.p.* and *pa.t.* **pried**
(prīd). **prier, -er** *n.* [M.E. *prien*, to peer].
psalm (sám) *n.* a sacred song or hymn. **the
Psalms** (*Bib.*) a book of the Old Testament.
psalmist (sám′·ist, sal′·mist) *n.* a writer of
psalms. **psalmody** (sa′·mạ·di·, sal′·mạ·
di·) *n.* the art or practice of singing sacred
music; psalms collectively. **-odist** *n.* a singer
of psalms. **Psalter** (sawl′·tẹr) *n.* the Book of
Psalms. **psaltery** *n.* an obsolete stringed instrument like the zither [Gk. *psalmos*, a
twanging of strings].
pseu·d(o)- (sū′·dō) *prefix* fr. Gk. *pseudes*,
false, used in many derivatives to signify,
false; pretended; sham; not real; wrongly
held to be, etc. **-nym** (sū′·dạ·nim) *n.* a fictitious name; a pen name. **pseudonymous** *a.*
pshaw (shaw) *interj.* expressing contempt,
impatience, etc. [imit.].
psit·ta·co·sis (sit·ạ·kō′·sis) *n.* (*Med.*) a
fatal disease found in parrots and communi-
cable· to man [L. *psittacus*, a parrot].
pso·ri·a·sis (sạ·rī·ạ·sis) *n.* (*Med.*) chronic
skin disease.
psy·che (sī·kē) *n.* the soul personified; the
principle of life [Gk. *psyche*, soul, mind].
psy·chi·a·try (sī·kī′·ạ·tri·) *n.* study and
treatment of mental disorders. **psychiater,
psychiatrist** *n.* a specialist in mental disorders. **psychiatric(al)** *a.* [Gk. *psuche*,
mind; *iatros*, a physician].
psy·chic(al) (sī′·kik, ·ki′·kạl) *a.* pert. to
soul, spirit, or mind; spiritualistic. **-ally** *adv.*
psychic *n.* one sensitive to spiritualistic
forces; medium. **-ist** *n.* [Gk. *psuche*, soul,
mind].
psy·cho·a·nal·y·sis (sī′·kō·ạn·al′·ạ·sis) *n.*
process of studying the unconscious mind;
psychoanalyze *v.t.* **psychoanalyst** *n.* **psy-
choanalytic(al).**
psy·chol·o·gy (sī·kàl′·ạ·ji·) *n.* the scientific
study of the mind, its activities, and human
and animal behavior. **psychological** *a.* **psychologically** *adv.* **psychologist** *n.* [Gk.
psyche, the mind; *logos*, a discourse].
psy·cho·pa·thol·o·gy (sī·kō·pạ·thàl′·ạ·ji·)
n. the science or study of mental diseases.
psychopathy (sī·kàp′·ạ·thi·) *n.* mental
affliction. **psychopath** *n.* one so afflicted.
psychopathic *a.*
psy·cho·sis (sī·kō′·sis) *n.* a general term for
any disorder of the mind. *pl.* **psychoses** [Gk.
psyche, the mind].
psy·cho·so·mat·ic (sī·kō·sạ·mat′·ik) *a.* of
mind and body as a unit; treatment of physical diseases as having a mental origin [Gk.
soma, body].
psy·cho·ther·a·py (sī·kō·ther′·a·pi·) *n.* the
treatment of disease through the mind, e.g.
by hypnotism, auto-suggestion, etc. **psycho-
therapeutic (-al)** *a.*
ptar·mi·gan (tår′·mạ·gạn) *n.* a bird of the
grouse family [Gael. *tårmachan*].

pter·o- (ter′·ō) *prefix* fr. Gk. *pteron*, a wing.
-dactyl (ter·ạ·dak′·til) *n.* extinct flying reptile with bat-like wings [Gk. *dactylos*, a fin-
ger].
pto·maine (tō′·mān, tō·mān′) *n.* substance,
usually poisonous, found in putrefying organic
matter [Gk. *ptōma*, a corpse].
pu·ber·ty (pū′·bẹr·ti·) *n.* the earliest age at
which an individual is capable of reproduction.
pubescence (pū·bes′·ạns) *n.* the period of
sexual development; puberty. **pubescent** *a.*
[L. *pubertas*, fr. *pubes*, adult].
pub·lic (pub′·lik) *a.* of, or pert. to, the people;
not private or secret; open to general use;
accessible to all; serving the people; *n.* community or its members; a section of community. **-ly** *adv.* **-ation** *n.* making known to the
public; proclamation; printing a book, etc.
for sale or distribution; a book, periodical,
magazine, etc. **publicize** *v.t.* to make widely
known; to advertize. **publicist** *n.* one versed
in, or who writes on, international law, or
matters of political or economic interest. **publicity** (pub·lis′·ạ·ti·) *n.* the state of being
generally known; notoriety; advertisement.
— prosecutor, the legal officer appointed to
prosecute criminals in serious cases on behalf
of the state. **— school,** one of a system of
schools maintained at public expense [L. *publicus*, fr. *populus*, the people].
pub·lish (pub′·lish) *v.t.* to make generally
known; to proclaim; to print and issue for
sale (books, music, etc.); to put into circulation. **-er** *n.* [L. *publicus*].
puce (pūs) *a.* brownish purple; *n.* the color
[Fr. = a flea].
puck (puk) *n.* a rubber disk used in ice
hockey; a mischievous sprite.
puck·er (puk·ẹr) *v.t.* and *i.* to gather into
small folds or wrinkles; to wrinkle; *n.* a wrinkle; a fold; **-y** *a.* [fr. *poke*, a bag].
pud·ding (pood′·ing) *n.* name of various
forms of cooked foods, usually in a soft mass,
served as a dessert.
pud·dle (pud′·l) *n.* a small pool of dirty
water; a mixture of clay and water used as
rough cement; *v.t.* to make muddy; to line
embankments, etc. with puddle; to stir molten
pig iron; *v.i.* to make muddy. **puddling** *n.*
-r *n.* [O.E. *pudd*, a ditch].
pu·er·ile (pū′·ẹr·il) *a.* childish; foolish;
trivial. **-ly** *adv.* **puerility** *n.* childishness;
triviality [L. *puer*, a boy].
pu·er·per·al (pū·ur′·pẹr·ạl) *a.* pert. to, or
caused by childbirth. **— fever** (*Med.*) a fever
developing after childbirth [L. *puer*, a child;
parere, to bear].
puff (puf) *n.* a short blast of breath or wind;
its sound; a small quantity of smoke, etc.; a
swelling; a light pastry; a soft pad for applying powder; exaggerated praise, esp. in a
newspaper; a quilt; *v.i.* to send out smoke,
etc. in puffs; to breathe hard; to pant; to
swell up; *v.t.* to send out in a puff; to blow
out; to smoke hard; to cause to swell; to
praise unduly. **-er** *n.* **-ing** *n.* **-ingly** *adv.* **-y**
a. inflated; swollen; breathing hard. **-iness**
n. **— paste** *n.* a short, flaky paste for making
light pastry [imit. origin].
puf·fin (puf′·in) *n.* a sea bird of the auk
family with a parrot-like beak [M.E. *pofin*].
pug (pug) *n.* a small, snub-nosed dog; *a.*
— nose *n.* a turned-up nose.
pug (pug) *v.t.* to make clay plastic by grinding with water; to fill in spaces with mortar
in order to deaden sound [etym. uncertain].
pu·gil·ism (pū′·jạ·lizm) *n.* the art of fighting with the fists; boxing. **pugilist** *n.* a boxer. **pugilistic** *a.* [L. *pugil*, a boxer, fr.
pugnus, the fist].
pug·na·cious (pug·nā′·shạs) *a.* given to
fighting; quarrelsome. **-ly** *adv.* **pugnacity**
(pug·nas′·ạ·ti·) *n.* [L. *pugnare*, to fight].

pu·is·sant (pū'·i·sant, pwis'·ant) a. powerful; mighty. **-ly** adv. **puissance** n. power [Fr. fr. L. potens, powerful].

puke (pūk) v.t. and i. to vomit.

pul·chri·tude (pul'·kri·tūd) n. beauty; comeliness [L. pulcher, beautiful].

pule (pūl) v.i. to chirp; to cry weakly; to whimper; to whine [imit. origin].

pull (pool) v.t. to draw towards one; to drag; to haul; to tug at; to pluck; to row a boat: v.i. to draw with force; to tug; n. act of pulling; force exerted by it; a tug; a means of pulling; effort; (Slang) influence, unfair advantage; (Print.) a rough proof; (Golf) a curving shot to the left. **-er** n. **—over** n. sweater put on by pulling over head [O.E. pullian].

pul·let (pool'·it) n. a young hen [Fr. poulet].

pul·ley (pool'·i·) n. a small wheel with a grooved rim on which runs a rope, used for hauling or lifting weights [Fr. poulie].

Pull·man·car (pool'·man·kar) n. a railway car. Also **Pullman** [fr. G. M. Pullman (1831-97), the inventor].

pul·mo- (pul'·ma) prefix from L. pulmo, the lung. **-nary** (pul'·ma·ner·i·) a. pert. to or affecting the lungs. **-nic** a. pert. to, or affecting, the lungs.

pulp (pulp) n. a soft, moist, cohering mass of animal or vegetable matter; the soft, succulent part of fruit; the material of which paper is made; v.t. to reduce to pulp; to remove the pulp from. **-y** a. like pulp. **-iness** n. [L. pulpa, flesh, pith].

pul·pit (pool'·pit) n. elevated place in a church for preacher [L. pulpitum, a stage].

pul·sate (pul'·sāt) v.t. to beat or throb, as the heart; to vibrate; to quiver. **pulsation** n. **pulsatile** a. pulsating; producing sounds by being struck, as a drum. **pulsative, pulsatory** a. capable of pulsating; throbbing [L. pulsare, to throb].

pulse (puls) n. the beating or throbbing of the heart or blood vessels, esp. of the arteries; the place, esp. on the wrist, where this rhythmical beat is felt; any measured or regular beat. v.i. to throb or pulsate [L. pulsus, beating].

pulse (puls) n. leguminous plants or their seeds, as beans, peas, etc. [L. puls, porridge].

pul·ver·i·ze (pul'·ver·īz) v.t. to reduce to a fine powder; to smash or demolish; v.i. to fall down into dust. **pulverization** n. **-r** n. [L. pulvis, dust].

pu·ma (pū'·ma) n. a large American carnivorous animal of the cat family; cougar [Peruv.].

pum·ice (pum'·is) n. Also **— stone**, a light, porous variety of lava, used for cleaning, polishing, etc. [L. pumex].

pum·mel See **pommel**.

pump (pump) n. an appliance used for raising water, putting in or taking out air or liquid, etc.; v.t. to raise with a pump, as water; to free from water by means of a pump; to extract information by artful questioning; v.i. to work a pump; to raise water with a pump [Fr. pompe].

pump (pump) n. a low, thin-soled shoe [Dut.].

pump·kin (pump'·kin) n. a plant of the gourd family; its fruit, used as food [O.Fr. pompon, fr. Gk. pepon, ripe].

pun (pun) n. a play on words similar in sound but different in sense; v.i. to use puns. pr..p. **-ning**. pa.p. and pa.t. **-ned. -ster** n. one who makes puns.

punch (punch) n. a drink made of fruit juices, sugar, and water, sometimes carbonated or with liquor [Hind. panch, five (ingredients)].

punch (punch) n. a tool used for making holes or dents; a machine for perforating or stamping; v.t. to perforate, dent, or stamp with a punch [Fr. poinçon, an awl, fr. L. pungere, to pierce].

punch (punch) v.t. to strike with the fist; to beat; to bruise; of cattle, to drive; n. a blow with the fist; (Slang) energy [fr. punish].

punc·tate (pungk'·tāt) a. having many points; having dots scattered over the surface. Also **punctated** [L. pungere, to pierce].

punc·til·i·o (pungk·til·i·ō) n. a fine point of etiquette; formality. a. attentive to punctilio; strict in the observance of rules of conduct, etc.; scrupulously correct. **-usly** adv. **-usness** n. [L. punctum, a point].

punc·tu·al (pungk'·choo·al) a. arriving at the proper or fixed time; prompt; not late; (Geom.) pert. to a point. **-ly** adv. **-ity** n. [L. punctum, a point].

punc·tu·ate (pungk'·choo·āt) v.t. to separate into sentences, clauses, etc. by periods, commas, colons, etc.; to emphasize in some significant manner; to interrupt at intervals. **punctuation** n. the act or system separating by the use of **punctuation marks** (the period, comma, colon, semi-colon, etc.) [L. punctum, a point].

punc·ture (pungk'·cher) n. an act of pricking; a small hole made by a sharp point; a perforation; v.t. to make a hole with a sharp point [L. pungere, to prick].

pun·dit (pun'·dit) n. a title given to a Hindu scholar; any learned person [Hind. pandit].

pun·gent (pun'·jant) a. sharply affecting the taste or smell; stinging; sarcastic; caustic. **-ly** adv. **pungency** n. [L. pungere, to prick].

pun·ish (pun'·ish) v.t. to inflict a penalty for an offense; to chastise. **-able** a. **-ment** n. **punitive** (pū'·ni·tiv) a. pert. to or inflicting punishment [L. punire, to punish].

punk (pungk) n. crumbly, decayed wood; a. (Slang) worthless [etym. uncertain].

punt (punt) v.t. and i. to kick a football, when dropped from the hands, before it touches the ground; n. such a kick

pu·ny (pū'·ni·) a. small and feeble; petty. **puniness** n. [O.Fr. puisne].

pup (pup) n. a puppy or young dog; a young seal; v.i. to bring forth puppies or whelps. pr.p. **-ping**. pa.p., pa.t. **-ped** [short fr. puppy, fr. Fr. poupée, a doll or puppet].

pu·pa (pū'·pa) n. the third stage in the metamorphosis of an insect, when it is in a cocoon; a chrysalis. pl. **pupae** (pū'·pē). **-l** a. **-te** v.i. to become a pupa [L. pupa, a girl].

pu·pil (pū'·pil) n. a student; a boy or girl under the care of a guardian; the small circular opening in the center of the iris of the eye. **-age** n. the state of being a pupil; the period of time during which one is a pupil. **-lary** a. pert. to a pupil or ward; pert to the pupil of the eye [L. pupillus, an orphan boy].

pup·pet (pup'·it) n. a marionette; a person whose actions are completely controlled by another. **-ry** n. a puppet show [Fr. popuée, a doll; L. puppa].

pup·py See **pup**.

pur·blind (pur'·blīnd) a. almost blind; dull in understanding. **-ly** adv. **-ness** n. [fr. pure and blind].

pur·chase (pur'·chas) v.t. to buy; to obtain by any outlay of labor, time, sacrifice, etc.; (Law) to obtain by any means other than inheritance; n. acquisition of anything for a price or equivalent; a thing bought; **purchasable** a. **-r** n. [Fr. pourchasser, to obtain by pursuit].

pure (pyoor) a. free from all extraneous matter; untainted; spotless; blameless; unsullied; chaste; innocent; absolute; theoretical, not applied. **-ly** adv. entirely; solely. **-ness** n. **purity** n. freedom from all extraneous matter; freedom from sin or evil [L. purus].

pu·rée (pyoo·rā') n. a thick soup [Fr.].

purge (purj) v.t. to purify; to cleanse; to clear out; to clear from guilt, accusation, or the charge of a crime, etc.; to remove from an organization, political party, army, etc. undesirable or suspect members; to cleanse the bowels by taking a cathartic medicine; *n.* a cleansing, esp. of the bowels; a purgative. **purgation** (pur·gā′·shạn) *n.* act of cleansing or purifying; act of freeing from imputatiaon of guilt; purging. **purgative** (pur′·gạ·tiv) *a.* having the power of purging; *n.* any medicine which will cause evacuation of bowels. **purgatory** (pur′·gạ·tōr·i·) *a.* tending to cleanse; purifying; expiatory; *n.* in R.C. faith, place where souls of dead are purified by suffering; (*Fig.*) a place or state of torment. **purgatorial** *a.* [L. *purgare*, fr. *purus*, pure].

pu·ri·fy (pyoor′·ạ·fī) *v.t.* to make pure, clear, or clean; to free from impurities; to free from guilt or defilement; *v.i.* to become pure. **purification** (pyoor·ạ·fạ·kā′·shạn) *n.* **purificative** *a.* **purifier** *n.* [L. *purus*, pure; *facere*, to make].

pur·ist (pyoor′·ist) *n.* an advocate of extreme care or precision in choice of words, etc.; a stickler for correctness [L. *purus*, pure].

Pu·ri·tan (pyoor′·ạ·tạn) *n.* a member of the extreme Protestant party, who desired further *purification* of the Church after the Elizabethan reformation; (*l.c.*) a person of extreme strictness in morals or religion; *a.* pert. to Puritans or to puritan. **-ic(al)** *a.* pert. to Puritans, their doctrine and practice; over-scrupulous. **-ically** *adv.* **-ism** *n.* doctrine and practice of Puritans; narrow-mindedness [L. *puritas*, purity, fr. *purus*].

purl (purl) *n.* an embroidered border; a knitting stitch that is reverse of plain stitch; *v.t.* to ornament with purls; *v.i.* to knit in purl. Also **pearl** [fr. *purfle*].

purl (purl) *v.i.* to flow with a burbling sound or gentle murmur [imit. origin].

pur·lieu (pur′·lōō) *n.* ground bordering on something; *pl.* outlying districts; outskirts [O. Fr. *puraliee*, a survey].

pur·loin (pur·loin′) *v.i.* to steal; to pilfer [O.Fr. *purloigner*, to put far away].

pur·ple (pur′·pl) *n.* a color between crimson and violet; robe of this color, formerly reserved for royalty; royal dignity; *a.* purple-colored; dark red; *v.i.* to make or dye a purple color; *v.i.* to become purple. **born to the purple**, of princely rank [Gk. *porphura*, shellfish that gave Tyrian purple].

pur·port (pur′·pōrt) *n.* meaning; apparent meaning; import; aim. **purport** (per·pōrt′) *v.t.* to mean; to be intended to seem [O. Fr. *porporter*, to embody].

pur·pose (pur′·pạs) *n.* object in view; aim; end; plan; intention; effect; purport; *v.t.* to intend; to mean to. **-ly** *adv.* intentionally; expressly. **-ful** *a.* determined resolute. **-fully** *adv.* **-less** *a.* aimless. **-lessly** *adv.* **purposive** *a.* done with a purpose [O.Fr. *porpos*, fr. *porposer*, to propose].

pur·pu·ra (pur′·pyạ·rạ) *n.* (*Med.*) the appearance of purple patches under the skin, caused by hemorrhage; shellfish, yielding purplish fluid. **purpureal** (per·pū′·rē·ạl) *a.* purple. **purpuric** *a.* pert. to purpura [Gk. *porphura*]. See **purple**.

purr (pur) *n.* a low, murmuring sound made by a cat; *v.i.* to utter such a sound.

purse (purs) *n.* a small bag or pouch to carry money in; money offered as a prize, or collected as a present; money; *v.t.* to wrinkle up; to pucker. **-r** *n.* (*Naut.*) officer in charge of accounts, etc. on board a ship. **-ful** *a.* enough to fill a purse. **— strings** *n.pl.* power to control expenditure [Fr. *bourse*, a purse, fr. Gk. *bursa*, a hide].

pur·sue (per·sū′) *v.t.* to follow with the aim of overtaking; to run after; to chase; to aim

at; to seek; to continue; *v.i.* to go on; to proceed; **-r** *n.* **pursuance** *n.* the act of pursuing. **pursuant** *a.* done in consequence, or performance, of anything. **pursuit** (per·sūt′) *n.* the act of pursuing; a running after; chase; profession; occupation. **pursuivant** (pur′·swi·vạnt) *n.* an attendant [Fr. *poursuivre*, fr. L. *prosequi*, to follow].

pu·ru·lent (pyoor′·ạ·lạnt) *a.* pert. to, containing, or discharging pus, or matter; septic; suppurating. **purulence, purulency** *n.* [L. *pus, puris*, matter].

pur·vey (per·vā′) *v.t.* (*Brit.*) to furnish or provide; to supply, esp. provisions. **-ance** *n.* act of purveying; supplies; former royal prerogative of requisitioning supplies, or enforcing personal service. **-or** *n.* [L. *providere*, to provide].

pur·view (pur′·vū) *n.* the enacting clauses of a statute; scope; range. [Fr. *pourvu*, provided].

pus (pus) *n.* the yellowish-white matter produced by suppuration [L. *pus*, matter].

push (poosh) *v.t.* to move or try to move away by pressure; to drive or impel; to press hard; to press or urge forward; to shove; *v.i.* to make a thrust; to press hard in order to move; *n.* a thrust; any pressure or force applied; emergency; enterprise; (*Mil.*) an advance or attack on a large scale. **-er** *n.* **-ing** *a.* given to pushing oneself or one's claims; self-assertive. **-ingly** *adv.* [Fr. *pousser*, fr. L. *pellere*, to drive].

pu·sil·lan·i·mous (pū·sạ·lan′·ạ·mạs) *a.* cowardly; faint-hearted; mean-spirited. **-ly** *adv.* **pusillanimity** *n.* [L. *pusillus*, very small; *animus*, spirit].

a young girl. **-y** *n.* dim. of puss; a cat.

pus·tule (pus′·chool) *n.* a small swelling or pimple containing pus. **pustular, pustulous** *a.* [L. *pustula*, a blister].

put (poot) *v.t.* to place; to set; to lay; to apply; to state; to propose; to throw; *v.i.* to go. *pr.p.* **-ting.** *pa.p.* and *pa.t.* **put.** *n.* a throw, esp. of a heavy weight. **to put about** (*Naut.*) to alter a ship's course [Late O.E. *putian*].

pu·ta·tive (pū′·tạ·tiv) *a.* commonly thought; supposed; reputed. **-ly** *adv.* **putation** *n.* [L. *putare*, to think].

pu·tre·fy (pū′·trạ·fī) *v.t.* and *i.* to make or become rotten; to decompose; to rot. **putrefaction** *n.* the rotting of animal or vegetable matter; rottenness; decomposition. **putrefactive** *a.* **putrescence** *n.* tendency to decay; rottenness. **putrescent** *a.* **putrid** (pū′·trid) *a.* in a state of decay; (*Colloq.*) very bad. **putridity, putridness** *n.* [L. *putere*, to rot; *facere*, to make].

putt (put) *v.t.* and *i.* (*Golf*) to hit a ball in the direction of the hole; (*Scot.*) to throw (a weight or iron ball) from the shoulder; *n.* the stroke so made in golf; the throw of the weight. **-er** *n.* one who putts; a short golf club [var. of *put*].

put·ter (put′·er) *v.i.* to work or act in a feeble, unsystematic way; to dawdle. Also **potter**. [var. of *potter*, O.E. *potian*, to poke].

put·ty (put′·i·) *n.* a kind of paste or cement, used by plasterers; *v.t.* to fix, fill up, etc. with putty. **puttier** *n.* [Fr. *potée*, the contents of a pot].

puz·zle (puz′·l) *n.* a bewildering or perplexing question; a problem, etc. requiring clever thinking to solve it; a conundrum; *v.t.* to perplex; to bewilder; (with 'out') to solve after hard thinking; (with 'over') to think hard over; *v.i.* to be bewildered. **-r** *n.* **puzzling** *a.* bewildering, perplexing [fr. M.E. *opposal*, a question, interrogation].

py·e·mi·a, pyaemia (pī·ē′·mi·ạ) *n.* (*Med.*) blood-poisoning [Gk. *pyon*, pus; *haima*, blood].

Pyg·my, Pigmy (pig′·mi·) *n.* one of a race

of dwarf Negroes of C. Africa. (*l.c.*) a very small person or thing; a dwarf; *a.* diminutive [Gk. *pygmē*, a measure of length from elbow to knuckles].

py·lon (pī'·lạn) *n.* a post or tower marking an entrance, a course for air races, etc.; the gateway of an ancient support; power-transmission cables [Gk. *pylōn*, a gateway].

py·or·rhe·a (pī·ạ·rē'·ạ) *n.* (*Med.*) a dental discharge of pus from the gums. Also **pyor-rhoea** [Gk. *pyon*, pus; *rhoia*, a flowing].

pyr·a·mid (pir'·ạ·mid) *n.* a solid figure on a triangular, square, or polygonal base, and with sloping sides meeting at an apex; a structure of this shape. **-al** *a.* pert. to, or having the form of a pyramid. **-ally** *adv.* [Gk. *pyramis*].

pyre (pīr) *n.* a pile of wood for burning a dead body; funeral pile [Gk. *pyra*, fire].

py·ret·ic (pī·ret'·ik) *a.* (*Med.*) pert. to, producing, or relieving, fever; feverish. **pyrexia** *n.* fever [Gk. *pyretos*, fever, fr. *pur*, fire].

py·rite (pī'·rīt) *n.* a yellow mineral formed of sulphur and iron; iron pyrites. **pyrites** (pī·rī'·tēz, pī'·rīt) *n.pl.* a name for many compounds of metals with sulphur, esp. iron pyrites, or copper pyrites. **pyritic, pyritif-erous, pyritous** *a.* pert. to, or yielding, pyrites [Gk. *pyra*, fire].

py·ro- (pī'·rạ) *prefix* fr. Gk. *pur*, fire, used in many derivatives. **— electricity** *n.* the property possessed by some crystals, of becoming electrically polar when they are heated.

py·ro·ma·ni·a (pī·rạ·mā'·ni·ạ) *n.* a mania for setting things on fire. **pyromaniac** *n.* [Gk. *pyr*, fire; and *mania*].

py·ro·tech·nics (pī·rạ·tek'·niks) *n.pl.* the art of making fireworks; the art of displaying them. Also **pyrotechny. pyrotechnic, pyro-technical** *a.* [Gk. *pyr*, fire; *technē*, art].

Py·thag·o·ras (pi·thag'·ạ·ras) *n.* a Greek philosopher and mathematician (582-507 B.C.).

py·thon (pī'·thạn) *n.* a large, non-poisonous snake that kills its prey by crushing it; a spirit; [Gk. *Pythōn*, the serpent slain by Apollo near Delphi].

pyx (piks) *n.* the vessel in which the conse-crated bread or Host is kept; a box at a Brit. mint in which specimen coins are kept for trial and assay; *v.t.* to test by assay. **-is** *n.* a small pyx; a casket [Gk. *pyxis*, fr. *pyxos*, a box tree].

Q

quack (kwak) *v.i.* to cry like a duck; to act as a quack; *n.* cry of duck or like sound; one who pretends to skill in an art, esp. in medicine; a charlatan; *a.* pert. to quackery. **-ery** *n.* **-salver** *n.* a quack doctor [imit.].

Quad·ra·ges·i·ma (kwod·ra·jes'·i·mạ) *n.* (*Church*) the first Sunday of Lent. **-l** *a.* pert. to Lent [L. *quadragesimus*, fortieth].

quad·ran·gle (kwåd'·rang·gl) *n.* in geome-try, a plane figure having four sides and angles; a square or court surrounded by build-ings (*abbrev.* **quad**) **quadrangular** *a.* [L. *quattuor*, four and *angle*].

quad·rant (kwåd'·rant) *n.* the fourth part of the area of a circle; an arc of 90°; an in-strument for taking altitude of heavenly bodies; in gunnery, an instrument to mark the degrees of a gun's elevation [L. *quadrans*, a fourth part].

quad·rate (kwåd'·rāt) *a.* having four sides and four right angles; square; divisible by four (used chiefly in anatomical names); *n.* ‌ square; **quadrate** *v.i.* to agree; to suit.

quadratic (kwåd·rat'·ik) *a.* pert. to, or re-sembling, a square; square; (*Alg.*) involving the second but no higher power of the un-known quantity, esp. in **quadratic equation.**

quadrature (kwåd'·rạ·cher) *n.* the act of squaring or reducing to a square; the posi-tion of one heavenly body with respect to another 90° away [L. *quadratus*, squared].

quad·ri- (kwod'·ri·) *comb. form,* four [L. *quattuor*, four].

quad·ri·cen·ten·ni·al (kwåd·rạ·sen·ten'·i·al) *a.* pert. to a period of four hundred years; *n.* the four hundredth anniversary [L. *quat-tuor*, four; *centum*, hundred; *annus*, a year].

quad·ri·lat·er·al .. (kwåd·rẹ·lat'·er·ạl) *a.* having four sides; *n.* (*Geom.*) a plane figure having four sides [L. *quattuor*, four; *latus*, side].

qua·drille (kwạ·dril', kạ·dril') *n.* an 18th cent. card game; a square dance; also, the music played to such a dance [L. *quadrus*, square].

quad·ril·lion (kwåd·ril'·yon) *n.* a number represented in the Fr. and U.S. notation by one with 15 ciphers annexed; in Great Britain and Ger. by one followed by 24 ciphers [L. *quattuor*, four and *million*].

quad·ri·no·mi·al (kwåd·rạ·nō'·mi·ạl) *a.* (*Alg.*) consisting of four terms.

quad·ri·par·tite (kwåd·rạ·pár'·tīt) *a.* divided into four parts.

quad·roon (kwåd·róon·) *n.* offspring of mu-latto and white; one who is one-fourth Negro [Sp. *cuarteró*, fr. L. *quartus*, fourth].

quad·ru·mane (kwåd'·roo·mān) *n.* an animal which has all four feet formed like hands. **quadrumanous** *a.* four-handed [L.*quatiuor*, four; *manus*, the hand].

quad·ru·ped (kwåd'·roo·ped) *n.* an animal having four feet; *a.* having four feet [L. *quattuor*, four; *pes, pedis*, a foot].

quad·ru·ple (kwåd'·róo·pl) *a.* fourfold; *n.* a four fold amount; a sum four times as great as another; *v.t.* to multiply by four; *v.i.* to be multiplied by four. **-t** *n.* one of four chil-dren born at a birth. **quadruplicate** *v.t.* to multiply by four; *n.* one of four things corre-sponding exactly; *a.* fourfold. **quadruplica-tion** *n.* [L. *quadru-plus*, fourfold].

quaff (kwåf) *v.t.* and *i.* to swallow in large drafts; *n.* a drink.

quag·mire (kwag'·mīr) *n.* soft, wet land, yielding under the feet; a bog; (*Fig.*) a difficult position. **quaggy** *a.* spongy; boggy; like quagmire. [fr. *quake*].

quail (kwāl) *v.i.* to lose spirit; to shrink or cower; to flinch [Fr. *cailler*, to curdle].

quail (kwāl) *n.* a game bird [Fr. *caille*].

quaint (kwānt) *a.* interestingly old-fashioned or odd; curious and fanciful; whimsical. **-ly** *adv.* **-ness** *n.* [O.Fr. *cointe*, prudent].

quake (kwāk) *v.i.* to tremble or shake with fear, cold, or emotion; to quiver or vibrate; *n.* a shaking or trembling; *abbrev.* of 'earth-quake' [O.E. *cwacian*].

Quak·er (kwāk'·ẹr) *n.* (*fem.* **-ess**) a member of the Society of Friends, a religious sect founded in the 17th cent. by George Fox. **-ism** *n.*

qual·i·fy (kwål'·ạ·fī) *v.t.* to ascribe a quality to; to describe (as); to fit for active service or office; to prepare by requisite training for special duty; to furnish with the legal title to; to limit; to diminish; *v.i.* to make oneself competent; to show oneself fit for. **qualifier** *n.* **qualifiable** *a.* **qualification** *n.* the act of qualifying or condition of being qualified; any endowment or acquirement that fits a person for an office or employment; modifica-tion; restriction [L. *qualis*, of what kind; *facere*, to make].

qual·i·ty (kwål'·ạ·ti·) *n.* a particular property inherent in a body or substance; an essential attribute, distinguishing feature, or characteristic; character or nature; degree of excellence; excellence or superiority of sound, tonal color. **qualitative** *a.* relating to quality; concerned with quality. [L. *qualitas*, of what kind.]

qualm (kwám) *n.* a sudden attack of illness, faintness, nausea, distress; a scruple of conscience [Ger. *qualm*, vapor].

quan·da·ry (kwan′.dri, dạ.ri.) *n.* a state of perplexity; a predicament; a dilemma.

quan·ti·fy (kwản′.tạ.fī) *v.t.* to fix or express the quantity of; to measure. **quantification** *n.* [L. *quantus*, how much; *facere*, to make].

quan·ti·ty (kwản.tạ.ti.) *n.* property of things ascertained by measuring; amount; bulk; a certain part; a considerable amount; number; (*Pros.*) the length or shortness of vowels, sounds, or syllables; *pl.* abundance; profusion. **quantitative** (kwản′.tạ.tā.tiv) *a.* relating to quantity [L. *quantus*, how much].

quan·tum (kwản′.tạm) *n.* quantity or amount; a specified, desired, or required amount. *pl.* **quanta**. [L. *quantus*, how much].

quar·an·tine (kwawr′.ạn.tēn) *n.* isolation of infected persons to prevent spread of serious disease; the period during which a ship, with infectious disease aboard, is isolated; *v.t.* to put under quarantine [Fr. *quarantaine*, forty days].

quar·rel (kwawr′.ạl) *n.* rupture of friendly relations; an angry altercation; a dispute; *v.i.* to dispute; to wrangle; to disagree; *pr.p.* **-er** *n.* **-some** *a.* apt to quarrel; irascible; contentious [L. *queri*, to complain].

quar·ry (kwawr′.i.) *n.* an excavation whence stone is dug for building; any source from which material may be extracted; *v.t.* to dig from a quarry. *pa.p.* and *pa.t.* **quarried** [L. *quadrare*, to square, hew (stones)].

quar·ry (kwawr′.i.) *n.* prey; victim [O.Fr. *cuiree*, fr. L. *corium*, skin].

quart (kwawrt) *n.* the fourth part of a gallon; one eighth of a peck [L. *quartus*, fourth].

quart·er (kwawr′.tẹr) *n.* fourth part; (*U.S. and Canada*) one fourth of a dollar, or the coin valued at this amount; one of the four cardinal points of the compass; one limb of a quadruped with the adjacent parts; a term in a school, etc.; part of a ship's side aft of mainmast; a region; a territory; a division of a town, or county; clemency; *pl.* assigned position; lodgings, esp. for soldiers; shelter; *v.t.* to divide into four equal parts; to divide up a traitor's body; to furnish with shelter; *v.i.* to have temporary residence. **-ing** *n.* an assignment of quarters for soldiers. **-ly** *a.* consisting of a fourth part; occurring every quarter of a year; *n.* a review or magazine published four times a year; *adv.* by quarters; once in a quarter of a year. **—deck** *n.* a part of deck of a ship which extends from stern to mainmast. **-master** *n.* (*Mil.*) an officer in charge of quarters, clothing, stores, etc.; (*Naut.*) a petty officer who attends to steering, signals, stowage, etc. **-master-sergeant** *n.* the N.C.O. assistant to the quartermaster. [L. *quartarius*, fr. *quartus*, fourth].

quar·tet, quartette (kwawr.tet′) *n.* (*Mus.*) a composition of four parts, each performed by a single voice or instrument; set of four who perform this; a group of four [Fr.].

quar·to (kwawr′.tō) *a.* denoting the size of a book in which the paper is folded to give four leaves to the sheet (*abbrev.* **4to**); *n.* a book of the size of the fourth of a sheet [L. *in quarto*, in a fourth part].

quartz (kwawrts) *n.* kinds of mineral, consisting of pure silica or silicon dioxide [Ger. *quarz*].

quash (kwȧsh) *v.t.* to crush; to quell; (*Law*) to annul, overthrow, or make void [L.

quassare, to shake].

qua·si (kwā′.sī, kwȧ′.sē) as if; as it were; in a certain sense or degree; seeming; apparently; it is used as adj. or adv. and as prefix to noun, adj., or adv. [L.].

quat·rain (kwȧt′.rān) *n.* (*Pros.*) a stanza of four lines [L. *quattaor*, four].

qua·ver (kwā′.vẹr) *v.i.* to shake, tremble, or vibrate; to sing or play with tremulous modulations; *v.t.* to utter or sing with quavers or trills; *n.* a trembling, esp. of the voice.

quay (kē, kwā) *n.* a landing place used for the loading and unloading of ships; a wharf. **-age** *n.* payment for use of a quay; space occupied by quays [Fr. *quai*].

quea·sy (kwē′.zi.) *a.* affected with nausea; squeamish; fastidious. **queasily** *adv.* **queasiness** *n.* [etym. uncertain].

queen (kwēn) *n.* the consort of a king; a woman who is the sovereign of a kingdom; the sovereign of a swarm of bees, ants, etc.; any woman who is pre-eminent; one of the chief pieces in a game of chess. *v.i.* to act the part of a queen (usu. 'to queen it'). **-ly** *a.* like, appropriate to a queen; majestic. **-liness** *n.* **-hood** *n.* state or position of a queen. **— consort** *n.* the wife of a king. **— dowager** *n.* the widow of a king. **— mother** *n.* a queen dowager who is also mother of reigning monarch. **— regent** *n.* a queen reigning in her own right. [O.E. *cwen*, a woman].

queer (kwir) *a.* odd; singular; quaint; (*Colloq.*) of a questionable character; faint or out of sorts; *v.t.* (*Slang*) to spoil. **-ly** *adv.* **-ish** *a.* somewhat queer. **-ness** *n.* [Ger. *quer*, oblique, crosswise].

quell (kwel) *v.t.* to subdue; to put down; to suppress forcibly. **-er** *n.* [O.E. *cwellan*, to kill].

quench (kwench) *v.t.* to extinguish; to put out, as fire or light; to cool or allay; to stifle; to slake (thirst). **-able** *a.* **-less** *a.* **-er** *n.* [O.E. *cwencan*].

quer·u·lous (kwer′.ạ.lạs) *a.* peevish; fretful. **-ly** *adv.* **-ness** *n.* [L. *queri*, to complain].

que·ry (kwir′.i.) *n.* a question; an inquiry; a mark of interrogation; *v.t.* to inquire into; to call in question; to mark as of doubtful accuracy [L. *quaerere* to seek or inquire].

quest (kwest) *n.* search; the act of seeking; the thing sought; *v.i.* to search; to seek [L. *quaerere, quaestum*, to seek].

ques·tion (kwes′.chạn) *n.* interrogation; inquiry; that which is asked; subject of inquiry or debate; (subject of) dispute; a matter of doubt or difficulty; a problem; *v.t.* to inquire of by asking questions; to be uncertain of; to challenge; to take objection to; to interrogate; **-able** *a.* doubtful; suspicious. **-ably** *adv.* **-ableness** *n.* **-er** *n.* **— mark** *n.* a mark of interrogation (?). **out of the question**, not to be thought of. **to beg the question**, to assume as fact something which is to be proved [L. *quaestio*, fr. *quaerere*, to seek, ask].

ques·tion·naire (kwes.chạ.ner′) *n.* a list of questions. [Fr.].

queue (kū) *n.* a pigtail [Fr. fr. L. *cauda*, a tail].

quib·ble (kwib′.l) *n.* an evasion of the point in question by a play upon words, or by stressing unimportant aspect of it; equivocation; *v.i.* to use quibbles. **-r** *n.* [dim. of obs. *quib*].

quick (kwik) *a.* animated; sprightly; ready or prompt; sensitive; rapid; hasty; impatient; fresh and invigorating; pregnant; *n.* living persons; sensitive flesh under nails; (*Fig.*) one's tenderest susceptibilities; *adv.* also **-ly**, rapidly; promptly. **-ness** *n.* **-en** *v.t.* to make alive; to make active or sprightly; to hasten; to sharpen or stimulate; *v.i.* to become alive; to move with greater rapidity. **-ener** *n.* **-ening** *n.* a making or becoming quick; first movement of fetus in womb. **-sand** *n.* sand, readily yielding to pressure, esp. if loose and mixed with water. **-silver** *n.* mercury. **-step** *n.* a march; a lively dance step [O.E. *cwic, alive*].

quid (kwid) *n.* a portion suitable for chewing, esp. of tobacco; a cud [form of *cud*].

quid (kwid) *n.* (*Brit. Slang*) a pound sterling.

quid·di·ty (kwid'·a·ti·) *n.* a trifling nicety; a quibble; the essence of anything [L. *quidditas* fr. *quid*, what?].

qui·es·cent (kwī·es'·ant) *a.* still; inert; motionless; at rest. **-ly** *adv.* **quiescence, quiescency** *n.* [L. *quiescere*, to rest].

qui·et (kwī'·at) *a.* still; peaceful; not agitated; placid; of gentle disposition; not showy; *n.* calm; peace; tranquillity; *v.t.* to reduce to a state of rest; to calm; to allay or appease; to silence; *v.i.* to become quiet. **-en** (*Dial.*) *v.t.* and *i* to quiet. **-ly** *adv.* **-ness** *n.* **-ude** *n.* freedom from noise, disturbance, alarm; tranquillity; repose. **quietus** (kwi·ē'·tas) *n.* final acquittance, of debt, etc.; (*Fig.*) extinction [L. *quietus*].

quill (kwil) *n.* a large, strong, hollow feather used as a pen; a spine or prickle, as of a porcupine; a piece of small reed on which weavers wind thread; an implement for striking the strings of certain instruments; *v.t.* to plait or form into small ridges [M.E. *quil*].

quilt (kwilt) *n.* any thick, warm coverlet; *v.t.* to stitch together, like a quilt, with a soft filling; to pad. **-ed** *a.* [L. *culcita*, a cushion].

qui·na·ry (kwī'·na·ri·) *a.* consisting of, or arranged in, fives [L. *quinque*, five].

quince (kwins) *n.* a hard, yellow, acid fruit, somewhat like an apple [Fr. *coing*; L. *cydonium*; fr. *Cydonia*, a city in Crete].

qui·nine (kwī·nīn) *n.* a bitter alkaloid obtained from various species of cinchona bark; it is used as a tonic and febrifuge. **quinic** *a.* [Peruv. *kina*, bark].

quin·qu(e)- (kwin'·kw(a)), *prefix* fr. L. *quinque*, five.

Quin·qua·ges·i·ma (kwing·kwa·jes'·a·ma) *n.* the Sunday before Ash Wednesday, so called because fifty days before Easter [L. *quinquagesimus*, fiftieth].

quin·sy (kwin'·zi·) *n.* a severe inflammation of the throat and tonsils [Gk. *kunanchē*, fr. *kuōn*, a dog; *anchein*, to choke].

quin·tes·sence (kwin·tes'·ans) *n.* the pure essence of anything; the perfect embodiment of a thing. **quintessential** *a.* [L. *quinta essentia*, fifth essence].

quin·tet, quintette (kwin·tet') *n.* (*Mus.*) a composition for five voices or instruments; a company of five singers or players; a set of five [L. *quintus*, fifth].

quin·til·lion (kwin·til'·yan) *n.* (*U.S. and France*) a number represented by one with 18 ciphers following; (*Great Britain and Germany*) one with 30 ciphers following [fr. L. *quintus*, fifth, and million].

quin·tu·ple (kwin'·tōō·pl) *a.* multiplied by five; fivefold; *v.t.* to make fivefold; to multiply by five. **-ts** *n.pl.* five children at a birth (*Colloq.* **quints**) [fr. L. *quintus*, fifth, by imit. of quadruple].

quip (kwip) *n.* a smart, sarcastic turn of phrase; a gibe; a witty saying. **-ster** *n.* [L. *quippe*, indeed (ironical)].

quire (kwīr) *n.* 24 sheets of paper of the same size, the twentieth part of a ream [O.Fr. *quaier*, fr. L. *quattuor*, four].

quirk (kwurk) *n.* sudden turn or twist; a quibble; a peculiarity. **-y** *a.* [etym. uncertain].

quit (kwit) *v.t.* to depart from; to leave; to cease from; to give up; to let go; *v.i.* to depart; to stop doing a thing; *a.* released from obligation; free. *pr.p.* **-ting** *pa.p., pa.t.,* **quit** or **-ted. -tance** *n.* discharge from a debt of obligation; receipt. **-ter** *n.* (*Colloq.*) a person easily discouraged. **to be quits,** to be equal

with another person by repayment (of money, of good, or evil) [O.Fr. *quiter*, fr. L. *quietare*, to calm].

quite (kwīt) *adv.* completely; wholly; entirely; positively [M.E. *quite*, free].

quiv·er (kwiv'·er) *n.* a case or sheath for holding arrows [O.Fr. *cuivre*, fr. Ger.].

quiv·er (kwiv'·er) *v.i.* to shake with a tremulous motion; to tremble; to shiver; *n.* the act of quivering; a tremor [O.E. *cwifer*, to risk].

Qui·xo·te (kē·hōt'·i·, kwik'·sat) *n.* the hero of the great romance of Miguel Cervantes. **quixotic** (kwik·sat'·ik) *a.* like Don Quixote; ideally and extravagantly romantic. **quixotically** *adv.* **quixotism. quixotry** *n.*

quiz (kwiz) *n.* a test or examination; a hoax or jest. *v.t.* to question. *pr.p.* **-zing.** *pa.p. pa.t.* **zed, -zer** *n.* **-zical** *a.* odd; amusing; teasing [etym. unknown].

quoin (koin) *n.* (*Archit.*) the external angle, esp. of a building; a cornerstone; (*Gun.*) a metalic wedge inserted under the breech of a gun to raise it; (*Print.*) a small wooden wedge used to lock the types in the galley etc. [Fr. *coin*, a corner].

quoit (kwoit) *n.* a flat, iron ring to be pitched at a fixed object in play; *pl.* game of throwing these on to a peg; *v.i.* to play at quoits.

quon·dam (kwän'·dam) *a.* former; that was once; sometime [L. = formerly].

quo·rum (kwō'·ram) *n.* the number of members that must be present at a meeting to make its transactions valid [L.]

quo·ta (kwō'·ta) *n.* a proportional part or share [L. *quot*, how many?].

quote (kwōt) *v.t.* to copy or repeat a passage from; to cite; to state a price for; *n.* a quotation; *pl.* quotation marks. **quotation** (kwō·tā'·shan) *n.* — **marks** *n.pl.* marks ("—") used to indicate beginning and end of a quotation [Late L. *quotare*, to distinguish by numbers, fr. L. *quot*, how many?].

quoth (kwōth) *v.t.* (*Arch.*) said; spoke (used only in the 1st and 3rd persons) [O.E. *cwethan*, to say].

quo·tid·i·an (kwō·tid'·i·an) *a.* daily; *n.* thing returning daily, esp. fever [L. *quotidie*, daily].

quo·tient (kwō'·shant) *n.* number resulting from division of one number by another [L. *quotients*, how many times?].

R

rab·bet (rab'·it) *n.* a groove made so as to form, with a corresponding edge, a close joint; *v.t.* to cut such an edge [O.Fr. *raboter*, to plane].

rab·bi (rab'·ī), **rab·bin** (rab'·in) *n.* a Jewish teacher of the Law. **-nic(al)** [Heb. = my master].

rab·bit (rab'·it) *n.* a small, burrowing rodent mammal, like the hare, but smaller. — **hutch** *n.* an enclosure for rearing tame rabbits. **-ry,** — **warren** *n.* the breeding place of wild rabbits [etym. uncertain].

rab·ble (rab'·l) *n.* a noisy, disorderly crowd; the common herd; *v.t.* to mob.

rab·id (rab'·id) *a.* furious; fanatical; affected with rabies. **-ly** *adv.* **-ness, -ity** *n.* [L. *rabidus*].

ra·bies (rā'·bēz) *n.* canine madness; hydrophobia [L. fr. *rabere*, to be mad].

rac·coon, racoon (ra·kōōn') *n.* one of a genus of plantigrade carnivorous mammals of N. America [Algonquin].

race (rās) *n.* the descendants of a common ancestor; distinct variety of human species; a peculiar breed, as of horses, etc.; lineage;

descent. **racial** *a.* pert. to race or lineage. **racially** *adv.* **racialism, racism** *n.* animosity shown to peoples of different race [It. *razza*].

race (rās) *n.* swift progress; rapid motion; a contest involving speed; a strong current of water; the steel rings of an antifriction ball bearing; *v.t.* to cause to run rapidly; *v.i.* to run swiftly; of an engine, pedal, etc., to move rapidly without control. **-r** *n.* one who races; a racehorse, yacht, car, etc., used for racing. **— horse** *n.* a horse bred to run for a stake or prize. **— track** *n.* a track used for horse racing, etc. **racing** *n.* [O.E. *ras*, a swift course].

ra·chis (rā′·kis) *n.* an axial structure, such as vertebral column in animals, the stem of a plant, a quill, etc. *pl.* **rachides. rachitic** *a.* having rickets. **rachitis** (ra·kī′·tis) *n.* rickets [Gk. *rhachis*, the spine].

rack (rak) *n.* an instrument for stretching; an instrument of torture by which the limbs were racked to point of dislocating; hence, torture; an open framework for displaying books, bottles, hats, baggage, etc.; a framework in which hay is placed; a straight cogged bar to gear with a toothed wheel to produce linear motion from rotary motion, or vice-versa; *v.t.* to stretch almost to breaking point; to overstrain; to torture; to place in a rack. **-ed** *a.* **-ing** *a.* agonizing (pain). **— and ruin** destruction [Dut. *rak*, fr. *rekken*, to stretch].

rack·et racquet (rak′·it) *n.* bat used in tennis, etc.; *pl.* a ball game played in a paved court with walls; a snowshoe [Fr. *raquette*].

rack·et (rak′·it) *n.* a confused, clattering noise′ din; (*Slang*) an occupation by which much money is made illegally; *v.i.* to make noise or clatter. **-eer** *n.* a gangster.

rac·on·teur (rak·ản·tur′) *n.* one skilled in telling anecdotes [Fr. *raconter*, to recount].

rac·y (rā′·si·) *a.* lively; having a strong flavor; spicy; pungent. **racily** *adv.* **raciness** *n.*

ra·dar (rā′·dảr) *n.* radiolocation or apparatus used in it (fr. initial letters of *radio, detection,* and *ranging*).

ra·di·al (rā′·di·al) *a.* pert. to a ray, radius, or radium; branching out like spokes of a wheel [L. *radius*, a ray].

ra·di·an (rā′·di·an) *n.* (*Math.*) the angle subtended by an arc of a circle equal in length to the radius of a circle.

ra·di·ant (rā′·di·ant) *a.* emitting rays; beaming; radiating; *n.* (*Astron.*) point in sky from which a shower of meteors appears to come; (*Opt.*) luminous point from which rays of light emanate. **radiance, radiancy** *n.* radiant intensity; brilliancy; splendor. **-ly** *adv.* [L. *radius*, a ray].

ra·di·ate (rā′·di·āt) *v.i.* to branch out like the spokes of a wheel; to emit rays; to shine; *v.t.* to emit rays, as heat, etc. *a.* with rays diverging from a center. **radiation** *n.* emission and diffusion of rays from central point. **radiator** *n.* any device which radiates or emits rays of heat or light; apparatus for heating rooms; in motoring, apparatus to split up and cool circulating water in water-cooling system [L. *radius*, a ray].

rad·i·cal (rad′·i·kal) *a.* pert. to the root; original; basic; complete; thorough; of extreme or advanced liberal views; *n.* (*Gram.*) a root; a primitive word; a politician who advocates thorough reforms; (*Chem.*) a basal atomic group of elements which passes unchanged through a series of reactions of the compound of which it is a part; (*Bot.*) a radicle; a rootlet; (*Math.*) a quantity expressed as the root of another. **-ism** *n.* root and branch political reform. **-ly** *adv.* **-ness** *n.* [L. *radix*, a root].

rad·i·cle (rad′·i·kal) *n.* (*Med.*) the initial fibril of a nerve; (*Bot.*) the primary root of an embryo plant; any rootlet [L. *radix*, a root].

ra·di·o- (rā′·di·ō) *prefix* used in forming compound terms with the meaning 'of rays,' 'of radiation,' 'of radium,' as in **— active** (rād·ē·ō·ak′·tiv) *a.* emitting from an atomic nucleus invisible rays which penetrate matter. **-activity** *n.* **-element** *n.* metallic chemical element having radioactive properties. **-graph** *n.* an instrument for measuring and recording the intensity of the heat given off by the sun; a photograph taken by means of X-ray or other rays. **-grapher** *n.* **-graphy** *n.* **-logy** *n.* the science of radioactivity in medicine. **-logist** *n.* **-scopy** *n.* examination by X-rays. **-therapy, -therapeutics** *n.* treatment of disease by radium or X-rays [L. *radius*, a ray].

ra·di·o (rā′·di·ō) *n.* wireless telephony or telegraphy; apparatus for reception of broadcast; a radio telegram. **-gram** *n.* a telegram transmitted by radio. [L. *radius*, a ray].

rad·ish (rad′·ish) *n.* an annual herb with pungent edible root [L. *radix*, a root].

ra·di·um (rā′·di·am) *n.* a metallic, radioactive element [L. *radius*, a ray].

ra·di·us (rā′·di·as) *n.* a straight line from center of circle to circumference; the spoke of a wheel; distance from any one place; the bone on the thumb side of forearm; movable arm of a sextant. *pl.* **-es, radii** [L. = a ray].

ra·dix (rā′·diks) *n.* a root; source; origin; a radical; (*Anat.*) the point of origin of a structure, as the root of a tooth; (*Math.*) fundamental base of system of logarithms or numbers. *pl.* **-es, radices** [L. = root].

ra·don (rā′·dån) *n.* a gaseous, radioactive element; radium emanation.

raff (raf) *n.* the mob; a worthless fellow. **-ish** *a. cf.* **riff-raff** [O. Fr. *raffer*, to snatch].

raf·fi·a (raf′·i·a) *n.* the fiber from a cultivated palm used for mats, baskets, etc. [Native].

raf·fle (raf′·l) *n.* a lottery; *v.t.* to sell by raffle. **-r** *n.* [orig. a dicing game, Fr. *rafle*].

raft (raft) *n.* an improvised float of planks fastened together; a mass of logs chained together for easy transportation down a river; *v.i.* to proceed by raft [O.N. *raptr*].

raft (raft) *n.* (*Colloq.*) a great quantity.

raft·er (raf′·ter) *n.* a sloping beam, from the ridge to the eaves, to which the roof covering is attached; *v.t.* to provide with rafters [O.E. *raefter*].

rag (rag) *n.* a fragment of cloth; a remnant; a scrap; (*Slang*) a newspaper; *pl.* mean or tattered attire; *a.* made of rags. **-amuffin** *n.* a ragged, dirty and disreputable person. **-man, -picker** *n.* one who collects rags. **-tag** *n.* the rabble; riffraff. **-time** *n.* popular dance music, of Negro origin, marked by strong syncopation. **-weed** *n.* a widespread weed, common cause of hay fever. [O.E. *ragg*].

rag (rag) *v.t.* to tease; to nag; *pr.p.* **-ging** *pa.t.* and *pa.p.* **-ged** [etym. uncertain].

rage (rāj) *n.* violent excitement; extreme anger; craze; fashion; *v.i.* to be furious with anger; to rave; to proceed violently and without check (as a storm; battle, etc.]. **raging** *a.* **ragingly** *adv.* [Fr. fr. L *rabies*, madness].

rag·ged (rag′·ad) *a.* worn to tatters; dressed in rags; jagged; slip-shod; imperfectly performed; not rhythmical. **-ly** *adv.* **-ness** *n.*

rag·lan (rag′·lan) *n.* an overcoat with wide sleeves running up to the neck, not to the shoulders [fr. Lord *Raglan*, 1788-1855].

ra·gout (ra·gòò′) *n.* fragments of meat, stewed and highly seasoned; a hash [Fr.].

raid (rād) *n.* a hostile incursion depending on surprise and rapidity; surprise visit by police to suspected premises; an attack on a town by hostile aircraft; *v.t.* to make a sudden attack upon. **-er** *n.* [var. of *road*].

rail (rāl) *n.* a piece of timber or metal extending from one post to another, as of a fence or balustrade; bars of steel on which the flanged wheels of vehicles run; a track for locomotives; a railway; a horizontal bar for support; top of ship's bulwarks; *v.t.* to enclose with rails; to send by railway. **-ing** *n.* material for rails; a construction of rails. **-road** n. a road on which steel rails are laid for wheels to run on; a system of such rails and all equipment; the company that runs it. **-way** n. a line of tracks, for wheeled vehicles [O.Fr. *reille*, fr. L. *regula*, a rule].

rail (rāl) n. wading birds [Fr. *râle*].

rail (rāl) v.i. to use insolent and reproachful language; to utter abuse. **-er** n. **-lery** n. good-humored banter; ridicule [Fr. *railler*].

rai·ment (rā'·mənt) n. (*Poetic*) clothing dress; apparel [for *arraiment*, fr. *array*].

rain (rān) n. condensed moisture, falling in drops from clouds; a shower; v.t. and v.i. to fall as rain; to pour down like rain. **-bow** n. arch showing seven prismatic colors and formed by refraction and reflection of sun's rays in falling rain. — **check** n. a ticket for a future performance, game, etc. when one is stopped by rain. **-coat** n. a light, rainproof overcoat. **-fall** n. a fall of rain; the amount of rain, in inches, which falls in a particular place in a given time. **-iness** n. **-less** a. **-proof** a. impervious to rain. **-y** a. [O.E. *regn*].

raise (rāz) v.t. to cause to rise; to elevate; to promote; to build up; to collect; to produce by cultivation; to rear; to increase; to enliven; to give up (seige); to heighten (voice); a. **-d** a. elevated. **raising** n. [O.N. *reisa*].

rai·sin (rā'·zn) n. a dried grape [O.Fr. *raizin* fr. L. *racemus*, a bunch of grapes].

raj (ràj) n. sovereignty; rule; dominion. **raja, rajah** n. king, prince, or noble of the Hindus [Hind. *raja*].

rake (rāk) n. a long-handled garden implement; an agricultural machine used in hay-making; v.t. and v.i. to scrape with a toothed implement; to draw together, as mown hay; to sweep or search over; to ransack; to scour; to fire shot lengthwise into a ship, etc. **a rake-off** (*Slang*) a monetary commission esp. if illegal [O.E. *raca*].

rake (rāk) n. a dissolute man of fashion; a libertine **rakish** a. **rakishly** adv. [M.E. *rakel*; corrupt, of *rake-hell*].

rake (rāk) n. an angle of inclination; the inclination of masts from the perpendicular; the projection of the upper parts of the stem and stern beyond the keel of a ship; v.i. to incline from perpendicular. **rakish** a. having a backward inclination of the masts; speedy-looking. **rakishly** adv. [Scand. *raka*, to reach].

ral·ly (ral'·i·) v.t. and v.i. to reassemble; to collect and restore order, as troops in confusion; to recover (strength; health); to return a ball (in tennis). n. act of rallying; assembly; outdoor demonstration; lively exchange of strokes in tennis [Fr. *rallier*].

ram (ram) n. male sheep; a swinging beam with a metal head for battering; a hydraulic engine; a beak projecting from bow of warship; (*Astron.*) Aries, one of the signs of zodiac; v.t. to consolidate loose material with a rammer; to drive against with violence; to butt; to cram; pr.p. **-ming**. pa.t. and pa.p. **-med**, **-er** n. [O.E. *ram*].

ram·ble (ram'·bl) v.i. to walk without definite route; to talk or write incoherently; n. a short stroll or walk. **-r** n. one who rambles; a climbing rose. **rambling** a. wandering.

ram·bunc·tious (ram·bung(k)'·shəs) a. boisterous; noisy (*Slang*).

ram·e·kin (ram'·ə·kin) n. a cheese preparation or other food mixture baked in a small dish; the dish itself [F. *ramequin*].

ram·i·fy (ram'·ə·fī) v.t. and v.i. to branch out in various directions. **ramification** n. a branch; any subdivision proceeding from a main structure [L. *ramus*, a branch; *facere*, to make].

ramp (ramp) v.i. to rear up on hind legs; n.

a gradual slope; [Fr. *ramper*, to climb].

ram·page (ram'·pāj) n. a state of excitement or passion, as **on the rampage**; v.i. (ram·pāj') to rush about, in a rage; to act violently. **-ous** a. [fr. *ramp*].

ram·pant (ramp'·ənt) a. rearing; violent; in full sway; rank. **rampancy** n. [Fr. *ramper*, to climb].

ram·part (ram'·part) n. mound of earth around fortified place; that which provides security; v.t. to strengthen with ramparts [Fr. *rempart*].

ram·rod (ram'·rod) n. rod used in ramming down charge of a gun; a rod for cleaning barrel of a rifle, etc. [fr. *ram*.].

ram·shack·le (ram'·shak·l) a. tumble-down; rickety; beyond repair [fr. *shake*].

ran (ran) pa.t. of run.

ranch (ranch) n. prairie land for sheep and cattle rearing; v.i. to keep a ranch. **-er** n. man who owns or works on a ranch [Sp. Amer. *rancho*, a grazing farm].

ran·cid (ran'·sid) a. having a rank smell; smelling or tasting like stale fat. **-ly** adv. **-ness**, **-ity** n. [L. *rancidus*].

ran·cor (rang'·ker) n. bitter and inveterate ill-feeling. **-ous** a. evincing intense and bitter hatred; malignant. **-ously** adv. [L. *rancor*].

rand (rand) n. thin inner sole of shoe; high land above river valley [O.E. *rand*, a border].

ran·dom (ran'·dəm) a. done haphazardly; aimless; fortuitous; n. in phrase, **at random**, haphazard [O.Fr. *random*, headlong rush].

ra·nee, rani (rän'·ē) n. in India, a queen or wife of a prince.

rang (rang) pa.t. of ring.

range (rānj) v.t. to set in a row; to rank; to rove over; v.i. to extend; to roam; to be in line with; to pass from one point to another; to fluctuate between, as prices, etc.; n. limits, or distance within which something is possible; a row; a large kitchen stove; line of mountains; compass or register of voice or instrument; distance to a target; place for practice shooting; pasture land. **-er** n. keeper of park or forest. **rangy** a. roaming; long-limbed; slender [Fr. *ranger*, fr. *rang*, a rank].

rank (rangk) n. row or line; soldiers standing side by side; grade in armed services; status; a class; social position; eminence; relative position; pl. enlisted soldiers; v.t. to arrange in class, order, or division; to place in line or abreast; to take rank over; v.i. to be placed in a rank or class; to possess social or official distinction. **-er** n. **-ing** n. arrangement; disposition [Fr. *rang*].

rank (rangk) a. growing too thickly; exuberant; offensively strong of smell; rancid; gross; vile; excessive. **-le** v.i. to be inflamed; to become more violent; to remain a sore point with. **-ly** adv. **-ness** n. [O.E. *ranc*, strong, proud].

ran·sack (ran'·sak) v.t. to search thoroughly; to plunder [O.N. *rannsaka*].

ran·som (ran'·səm) n. a price paid for release of prisoner; immense sum of money; v.t. to redeem from captivity [O.Fr. fr. L. *redemptio*, buying back].

rant (rant) v.i. to rave; to talk wildly and noisily; n. noisy and meaningless declamation; boisterous talk. **-er** n. [O.Dut. *ranten*, to rave].

rap (rap) n. a smart, light blow; a knock on door, etc.; a tap; v.t. and v.i. to deliver a smart blow; to knock; pr.p. **-ping**. pa.t. and pa.p. **-ped** [prob. imit.].

ra·pa·cious (ra·pā'·shəs) a. subsisting on prey; greedy; grasping. **-ly** adv. **-ness**, **rapacity** n. [L. *rapere*, to seize].

rape (rāp) n. carnal knowledge of a female against her will; the act of snatching or carrying off by force; v.t. to ravish or violate [L. *rapere*, to seize].

rape (rāp) *n.* an annual of the cabbage family, the seeds of which yield vegetable oils [L. *rapum*, turnip].

rap·id (rap'·id) *a.* very quick; fast; speedy; hurried; descending steeply. **-s** *n.pl.* part of a river where current rushes over rocks. **-ity** *n.* **-ly** *adv.* **-ness** *n.* [L. *rapidus*].

ra·pi·er (rā'·pi·ẹr) *n.* a light, slender, pointed sword, for thrusting only [Fr. *rapière*].

rap·ine (rap'·in) *n.* act of plundering; pillage; plunder [L. *rapina*, fr. *rapere*, to snatch].

rap·port (ra·pōr') *n.* harmony; agreement. **en rapport**, in relation to; in harmony with [Fr.].

rap·proche·ment (ra·prōsh·mȧng') *n.* reconciliation; restoration of friendly relations [Fr.].

rap·scal·lion (rap·skal'·yạn) *n.* a scamp; a rascal. See **rascal**.

rapt (rapt) *a.* intent; transported; in a state of rapture. **-ure** *n.* extreme joy; ecstasy; bliss; exultation. **-urous** *a.* ecstatic; exulting. **-urously** *adv.* [L. *rapere*, *raptum*, to snatch away].

rare (rer) *a.* underdone (of meat) [O.E. *hrere*, boiled gently].

rare (rer) *a.* uncommon, few and far between; thin, not dense, as air; extremely valuable; of the highest excellence. **-faction** *n.* act of rarefying; decrease of quantity of a gas in fixed volume. **rarefy** (rer'·a·fī) *v.t.* to make rare or less dense; *v.i.* to become less dense. **-ly** *adv.* **-ness** *n.* **rarity** *n.* state of being rare; thinness; something rare or seldom seen [L. *rarus*].

rare·bit (rer'·bit) *n.* (*Cookery*) Welsh rabbit; cheese sauce on toast, etc. [corrupt. of *rabbit*].

ras·cal (ras'·kạl) *n.* a rogue; a scoundrel; a scamp; *a.* dishonest; low. **-ity** *n.* knavery; base villainy. **-ly** *a.* [O.Fr. *rascaille*, the rabble].

rash (rash) *a.* without reflection; precipitate. **-ly** *adv.* **-ness** *n.* [Dut. *rasch*, quick].

rash (rash) *n.* a temporary, superficial eruption of the skin [O.Fr. *rasche*, itch].

rash·er (rash'·ẹr) *n.* a thin slice of bacon [Fr. *arracher*, to tear up].

rasp (rasp) *v.t.* to rub or file; to scrape (skin) roughly; to speak in grating manner; to irritate; *n.* a form of file with one side flat and the other rounded; a rough, grating sound. **-ing** *a.* emitting a harsh, grating sound; irritating. **-ingly** *adv.* [O.Fr. *rasper*].

rasp·ber·ry (raz'·ber·i·) *n.* a plant, cultivated for its fruit; a small drupe, the fruit of the plant; (*Slang*) derisory applause [E. *rasp*, rough, like a file].

rat (rat) *n.* large rodent; (*Slang*) one who deserts his party; (*Colloq.*) padding to puff out women's hair; *v.i.* to hunt rats; to abandon party or associates in times of difficulty. *pr.p.* **-ting** *pa.t.* and *pa.p.* **-ted. -ter** *n.* a rat-catcher; a terrier which kills rats. **-ting** *n.* [O.E. *raet*].

rat·a·fi·a (rat·a·fē'·a) *n.* a liquer, such as curaçoa; a cordial [Fr.].

ratch·et (rach'·it) *n.* a bar or piece of mechanism turning at one end upon a pivot, while the other end falls into teeth of wheel, allowing the latter to move in one direction only [Fr. *rochet*, ratchet of a clock].

rate (rāt) *n.* established measure; degree; standard; proportion; ratio; value; price; movement, as fast or slow; *v.t.* to estimate value; to settle relative scale, rank, price or position of; *v.i.* to be set in a class; to have rank. **-able, ratable** *a.* **ratability** *n.* **rating** *n.* assessment; (*Naut.*) classification of a ship; amount set as a rate [O.Fr. fr. L. *rata* (*pars*), fixed portion].

rate (rāt) *v.i.* to take to task; to chide.

rather (raTH'·ẹr) *adv.* preferably; on the other hand; somewhat [O.E. *hrathe*, quickly].

rat·i·fy (rat'·a·fī) *v.t.* to confirm or sanction officially; to make valid. **ratification** *n.* [L. *ratus*, fixed; *facere*, to make].

rat·ing See **rate**.

ra·tio (rā'·shō) *n.* relation one quantity has to another, as expressed by number of times one can be divided by the other; proportion [L.].

ra·ti·oc·i·nate (rash·i·ás'·a·nāt) *v.i.* to reason logically. **ratiocination** *n.* deductive reasoning. **ratiocinative** *a.* [L. *ratiocinari*, to reckon].

ra·tion (ra'·shạn, rā'·shạn) *n.* fixed allotted portion; daily allowance of food, drink, etc., to armed forces; *pl.* provisions; *v.t.* to limit to fixed amount [Fr. fr. L. *ratio*].

ra·tion·al (rash'·an·ạl) *a.* sane; sensible; reasonable; (*Math.*) a quantity expressed in finite terms or whose root is a whole number. **-e** (rash·a·nal') *n.* logical basis; exposition of principles. **-ization** *n.* in psychology, the attempt to square one's conscience by inventing reasons for one's own conduct; **-ize** *v.t.* **-ism** *n.* philosophy which makes reason the sole guide; system opposed to supernatural or divine revelation. **-ist** *a.* **istic(al)** *a.* **-istically** *adv.* **-ity** *n.* the power or faculty of reasoning; soundness of mind. **-ly** *adv.* [L. *rationalis*, fr. *ratio*, reason].

rats·bane (ratz'·bān) *n.* rat poison.

rat·tan, ratan (ra·tan') *n.* a species of palm found in India and the Malay Peninsula; the stems used for wickerwork, etc.; a walking-stick made from a rattan cane [Malay, *rotan*].

rat·tle (rat'·l) *v.i.* to clatter; to speak (on) eagerly and noisily; to move along, quickly and noisily; *v.t.* to shake briskly, causing sharp noises; (*Colloq.*) to disconcert, or ruffle; *n.* a rapid succession of clattering sounds; a toy for making a noise; rings at the end of a rattlesnake's tail. **-brained, -headed, -pated** *a.* empty-headed; giddy; lacking stability. **-snake** *n.* an American poisonous snake. **rattling** *n.* clattering; *a.* brisk; lively; first-rate; *adv.* extremely; very [M.E. *ratelen*].

rat·ty (rat'·i·) *a.* full of rats; (*Slang*) shabby.

rau·cous (raw'·kạs) *a.* hoarse; harsh; rough. **-ly** *adv.* [L. *racus*].

rav·age (rav'·ij) *v.t.* to lay waste; to despoil; to plunder; *n.* ruin; destruction [Fr.].

rave (rāv) *v.i.* to talk in delirium or with great enthusiasm. **-r** *n.* **raving** *n.* delirium; incoherent or wild talk; *a.* delirious; (*Colloq.*) exceptional. **ravingly** *adv.* [O.Fr. *raver*].

rav·el (rav'·ạl) *v.t.* to entangle; to make intricate; to fray out; *v.i.* to become twisted and involved; to fall into confusion. *n.* complication; unraveled thread [Dut. *ravelen*].

ra·ven (rā'·vạn) *n.* crow with glossy black plumage, predatory in habit; *a.* glossy black, esp. of hair [O.F. *hraefn*].

rav·en, ravin (rav'·n) *v.t.* and *v.i.* to devour; to prowl for prey; to be ravenous; *n.* rapine; plunder; spoil. **-er** *n.* a plunderer. **-ous** *a.* famished; voracious; eager for prey. **-ously** *adv.* [Fr. *ravir*, fr. L. *rapere*, to seize].

ra·vine (ra·vēn') *n.* a deep, narrow gorge; a gully [O.Fr. fr. L. *rapere*, to carry off].

rav·ish (rav'·ish) *v.t.* to seize and carry away by violence; to rape; to enrapture; to charm eye or ear. **-er** *n.* **-ing** *a.* entrancing; captivating. **-ingly** *adv.* **-ment** *n.* [Fr. *ravir*, fr. L. *rapere*, to carry off].

raw (raw) *a.* not cooked; not covered with skin; chilly and damp; untrained; not manufactured. *n.* a sore; naked state. **-boned** *a.* having little flesh; gaunt. **-hide** *n.* compressed untanned leather; a riding whip of untanned leather. **-ly** *adv.* **-ness** *n.* — **deal,** unfair and undeserved treatment [O.E. *hreaw*].

ray (rā) *n.* a narrow beam of light; the path along which light and electro-magnetic waves travel in space; a heat radiation; one of a number of lines diverging from a common point or center; a gleam or suggestion (of hope, truth, etc.); *v.t.* and *v.i.* to radiate; to send forth rays. **-ed** *a.* having rays [O.Fr. *raye*, fr. L. *radus*, a beam].

ray (rā) *n.* a flat fish allied to skate, shark, and dogfish [O.Fr. *raye*].

ray·on (rā′·àn) *n.* a synthetic fibrous material in imitation of silk [Fr.].

raze, rase (rāz) *v.t.* to level to the ground; to destroy completely; to demolish [Fr. *raser*, fr. L. *radere, rasum*, to scrape].

ra·zor (rā′·zẹr) *n.* a keen-edged cutting appliance for shaving. **-back** *n.* kind of hog; rorqual or finbacked whale [Fr. *rasoir*, fr. L. *radere, rasum*, to scrape].

razz (raz) *v.t.* to ridicule [fr. *raspberry*].

re-, *prefix* used in the formation of compound words,usually to signify *back* or *again* [L.]

re (rē) *prep.* in reference to; concerning. **in re**, in the case (of) [L. *res*, thing].

reach (rēch) *v.t.* to extend; to stretch; to touch by extending hand; to attain to or arrive at; to come to; to obtain; to gain; *v.i.* to stretch out the hand; to strain after; to be extended; to arrive; *n.* reaching; easy distance; mental range; scope; grasp; straight stretch of water, etc. **-able** *a.* [O.E. *raecan*, to stretch out].

re·act (rē·akt′) *v.i.* to respond to stimulus; to exercise a reciprocal effect on each other; to resist the action of another body by an opposite effect; (*Chem.*) to cause or undergo a chemical or physical change when brought in contact with another substance or exposed to light, heat, etc. **-ance** *n.* (*Elect.*) resistance in a coil to an alternating current due to capacity or inductance in the circuit. **-ion** *n.* action in opposite direction to another; the response to stimulus, influence, events, etc. **-ionary** *a.* tendency to reaction. *n.* one opposed to progressive ideas in politics, religion, thought, etc. **-ionist** *n.* **-ivation** *n.* restoration to an activated state. **-ive** *a.*

re·act (rē′·akt) *v.t.* to act again; to repeat.

re·ac·tor (rē·act′·ẹr) *n.* apparatus for generating heat by nuclear fission.

read (rēd) *v.t.* to peruse and understand written or printed matter; to interpret mentally; to read and utter; to understand any indicating instrument (as a gas meter); *v.i.* to perform the act of reading; to find mentioned in writing or print; to surmise. *pa.t.* and *pa.p.* **read** (red). **read** (red). *a.* versed in books; learned. **-able** (rēd) *a.* well written; informative; interesting; legible. **-ably** (rēd) *adv.* **-er** (rēd) *n.* one who reads; one whose office is to read prayers; one who determines suitability for publication of manuscripts offered to publisher; corrector of printer's proofs; a reading book. **-ing** (rēd) *a.* pert. to reading; *n.* act of reading; a public recital of passages from books; interpretation of a passage from a book [O.E. *raedan*, to make out].

read·i·ly, readiness See **ready.**

re·ad·just (rē·a·just′) *v.t.* to adjust or put in order again. **-ment** *n.*

read·y (red′·i·) *a.* prepared; fitted for use; handy; prompt; quick; willing; apt; *v.t.* to prepare. *n.* position of a fighting unit or their weapons, as *at the ready.* **readily** *adv.* **readiness** *n.* **—made** *a.* not made to measure. **— money,** cash in hand [O.E. *raede*].

re·a·gent (rē·ā·′jạnt) *n.* any substance employed to bring about a characteristic reaction in chemical analysis. **reagency** *n.*

re·al (rē′·al) *a.* actual; not sham; not fictitious or imaginary; not assumed; unaffected; (*Law*) heritable; denoting property not movable or personal, as lands and tenements. **reality** (ri·al′·a·ti·) *n.* actuality; fact; truth. **-ly** *adv.* actually; indeed; *interj.* is that so? **-ty** *n.* real estate. **— estate, — property,** immovable property [L.L. *realis*, fr. L. *res*, a thing].

re·al (rē′·ạl) *n.* an obsolete Spanish coin [Sp. fr. L. *regalis*, royal].

re·al·ize (rē′·ạl·īz) *v.t.* to make real; to yield (profit); to convert into money; to apprehend or grasp the significance of. **realization** *n.* **realism** *n.* interest in things as they are; practical outlook on life; representation in art or letters of real life, even if sordid and repellent; (*Philos.*) doctrine that matter has a separate existence apart from conceptions of it in the mind; doctrine that general terms and ideas have objective existence and are not mere names. **realist** *n.* **realistic** *a.* pert. to realism; factual; practical; true to life. **realistically** *adv.* [Fr. *réaliser*].

reality, realtor, realty See **real** (1).

realm (relm) *n.* kingdom; province; region [O.Fr. *realme*, fr. L. *regalis*, royal].

ream (rēm) *n.* a paper measure containing from 472 to 516 sheets, usually 500 sheets (20 quires) [Ar. *rizmah*, bundle].

ream (rēm) *v.t.* to enlarge or make a tapered or conical hole with a reamer. **-er** *n.* a machine tool for enlarging a hole [O.E. *rum*, room].

reap (rēp) *v.t.* to cut down ripe grain for harvesting; to harvest; to receive as fruits of one's labor. **-er** *n.* a harvester; a reaping machine [O.E. *ripan*].

rear (rir) *n.* back of hindmost part; part of army or fleet behind the others. **-most** *a.* last of all; at the very back [L. *retro*, behind].

rear (rir) *v.t.* to raise; to bring to maturity, as young; to erect or build; *v.i.* to rise up on the hindlegs, as a horse [O.E. *raeran*].

re·arm (rē·arm′) *v.t.* to equip the fighting services with new weapons. **-ament** *n.*

re·ar·range (rē·a·rānj′) *v.t.* to arrange anew; to set in a different order. **-ment** *n.*

rea·son (rē′·zn) *n.* a faculty of thinking; power of understanding; intelligence; the logical premise of an argument; cause; motive; purpose; excuse; *v.i.* to exercise rational faculty; to deduce from facts or premises; to argue with; *v.t.* to discuss by arguments. **-able** *a.* rational; just; fair. **-ableness** *n.* **-ably** *adv.* **-er** *n.* **-ing** *n.* [Fr. *raison*, fr. L. *ratio*, reason].

re·as·sure (rē·a·shoor′) *v.t.* to free from fear; to allay anxiety; to restore confidence, or spirit to **reassurance** *n.* **reassuring** *a.*

re·bate (rē′·bāt) *v.t.* to allow as discount; *n.* deduction [Fr. *rabattre*, to beat down].

re·bate. See **rabbet.**

reb·el (reb′·ạl) *n.* one who resists the lawful authority of a government; revolter; revolutionist; one who is defiant; *a.* rebellious. **rebel** (ri·bel′) *v.i.* to take up arms against state or government; to revolt. *pr.p.* **-ling.** *pa.t.* and *pa.p.* **-led. -lion** *n.* organized resistance to authority; insurrection; mutiny. **-lious** *a.* [L. *rebellare*, fr. *bellum*, war].

re·birth (rē·burth′) *n.* state of being born again, spiritually; renaissance, as in the Rebirth of Learning.

re·bound (rē·bound′) *v.i.* to leap back; to recoil; to bound repeatedly; *v.t.* to cause to fly back; (rē′·bound) *n.* rebounding; recoil.

re·buff (ri·buf′) *n.* a blunt, contemptuous refusal; a snub; a repulse; *v.t.* to beat back; to check; to snub [It. *rebuffo*, reproof].

re·buke (ri·būk′) v.t. to censure; to reprove; to reprimand; n. reprimand; reproof [O.Fr. *revuchier*, repulse].

re·bus (rē′·bąs) n. an enigmatical representation of a name, word, or phrase by pictures suggesting syllables [L. = by things].

re·but (ri·but′) v.t. to refute, to disprove; pr.p. **-ting**. pa.t. and pa.p. **-ted**. **-table** a. **-tal** n. refutation of an argument [Fr. *revoutier*, to repulse].

re·cal·ci·trate (ri·kal′·si·trāt) v.i. to kick back; to be refractory. **recalcitrant** n. one who defies authority; a. refractory; willfully disobedient. **recalcitrance, recalcitration** n. [L. *recalcitrare*, to kick back].

re·call (ri·kawl′) v.t. to call back; to take back (a gift, etc.); to annul or revoke; to call to mind; to remember; n. (rē′·kawl) act of recalling; a summons to return.

re·cant (ri·kant′) v.t. to take back, words or opinions; to retract; v.i. to unsay. **-ation** n. [L. *recantare*, fr. re-, back; *contare*, to sing].

re·ca·pit·u·late (rē·ka·pich′·a·lāt) v.t. to relate in brief the matter or substance of a previous discourse; v.i. to sum up what has been previously said. **recapitulation** n. [L. *capitulum*, a small head].

re·cap·ture (rē·kap′·cher) v.t. to capture back; to regain; n. act of retaking.

re·cast (rē·kast′) v.t. to cast or mold again; to remodel; to throw back; to add up figures in a column a second time.

re·cede (ri·sēd′) v.i. to move or fall back; to retreat; to withdraw; to ebb. **receding** a.

re·ceipt (ri·sēt′) n. the act of receiving; a written acknowledgment of money received; a recipe in cookery; pl. money received; v.t. to give a receipt for [L. *recipere, receptum*, to receive].

re·ceive (ri·sēv′) v.t. to take; to accept; to get (an offer, etc.); to acquire; to welcome or entertain; to hold; to take or buy stolen goods. **receivable** a. **-r** n. one who receives; receptacle, place of storage, etc.; one who receives goods knowing them to have been stolen; appointed by court to receive profits of business being wound up by that court; (*Chem.*) a vessel into which spirits are emitted in distillation; a radio receiving set; earpiece of a telephone. **receiving** n. [O.Fr. fr. L. *recipere*, to take back].

re·cent (rē′·sąnt) a. that has lately happened; new; **-ly** adv. **-ness** n. [L. *recens*].

re·cep·ta·cle (ri·sep′·ta·kal) n. a vessel— that which receives, or into which anything is received and held [L. *recipere, receptum*, to receive].

re·cep·tion (ri·sep′·shan) n. receiving; welcome; ceremonial occasion when guests are personally announced; the quality of signals received in broadcasting. **receptible** a. receivable. **-ist** n. person in hotel, office, etc., who receives guests or clients. **receptive** a. able to grasp ideas or impressions quickly. **receptiveness, receptivity** n. [L. *recipere, receptum*, to receive].

re·cess (rē′·ses) n. a withdrawing from usual activity; suspension of business; vacation, as of legislative body or school; a secluded place; a niche or cavity in a wall; (*Zool.*) a small cleft or indentation in an organ; v.t. to make, or place in, a recess; v.i. to go on a recess. **-ed** a. fitted with recess. **-ion** n. act of receding or withdrawing; a period of reduced trade or business; a procession at the close of a service. **-ional** a. pert. to recession; n. hymn sung as clergyman leaves chancel. **-ive** a. **-iveness** n. [L. *recessus*, fr. *recedere* to recede].

re·cher·che (re·shur′·shā) a. of studied elegance; choice; exquisite; exclusion [Fr.]

rec·i·pe (res′·a·pē) n. a prescription; a cookery receipt [L. imper. *recipere*, take].

re·cip·i·ent (ri·sip′·i·ant) a. receptive; n. one who receives [L. *recipere*, to receive].

re·cip·ro·cal (ri·sip′·ra·kal) a. moving backwards and forwards; alternating; mutual; complementary; (*Gram.*) reflexive; n. idea or term alternating with, or corresponding to, another by contrast or opposition; quantity arising from dividing unity by any quantity; pl. two numbers which multiplied give unity, e.g. $\frac{2}{3} \times \frac{3}{2} = 1$. **-ly** adv. **-ness** n. **reciprocate** v.t. to make return for; to interchange; v.i. to move backwards and forwards; to act interchangeably; to alternate. **reciprocating, reciprocatory** a. **reciprocation** n. mutual giving and receiving. **reciprocative** a. **reciprocity** (res·a·pràs′·a·ti·) n. action and reaction; the discharge of mutual duties or obligations; in international trade, equal facilities or advantages gained by abolition of prohibitory or protective duties, or by equalizing rates [L. *reciprocus*, turning back].

re·ci·sion (ri·sizh′·an) n. the act of cutting, annulling [L. *rescindere, rescissus*, to cut off].

re·cite (ri·sīt′) v.t. and v.i. to repeat aloud esp. before an audience. **recital** n. act of reciting; what is recited; detailed narration; a musical or dramatic performance by one person or by one composer or author. **recitation** n. reciting; repetition of something from memory. **recitative** (res·a·ta·tēv′) n. declamation to musical accompaniment, as in opera; a. in the style of recitative. **-r** n. [L. *recitare*, to read aloud].

reck (rek) v.t. and v.i. (*Arch.*) to heed. **-less** a. rashly negligent. **-lessly** adv. **-lessness** n. [O.E. *reccan*, to care for].

reck·on (rek′·n) v.t. and v.i. to count; to calculate; to estimate; to value; (*Colloq.*) to think; to be of opinion. **-er** n. one who reckons; table of calculations. **-ing** n. computing; calculation; a bill [Ger. *rechnen*, to count].

re·claim (ri·klām′) v.t. to bring into a state of productiveness, as waste land, etc.; to win back from error or sin. **-able** a. able to be reclaimed or reformed. **reclamation** (rek·la·mā′·shan) n.

re·claim (rē·klām′) v.t. to demand the return of.

re·cline (ri·klīn′) v.t. to lean back; v.i. to assume a recumbent position; to rest. **-r** n. [L. *reclinare*].

re·cluse (rek′·lòòs) a. secluded from the world; solitary; n. a hermit. [L. *reclusus*, shut away.]

rec·og·nize (rek′·ag·nīz) v.t. to know again; to identify; to acknowledge; to treat as valid; to realize; to salute. **recognizable** a. **recognizably** adv. **recognizance** n. acknowledgment of a person or thing; an obligation, under penalty, entered into before some court or magistrate to do, or to refrain from doing, some particular act; sum pledged as surety. **recognition** n. recognizing; acknowledgment. **recognitive, recognitory** a. [L. *recognoscere*].

re·coil (ri·koil′) v.i. to start, roll, bound, fall back; to draw back; to rebound; n. return motion; a starting or falling back [Fr. *reculer*, to spring back].

re·col·lect (rek·a·lekt′) v.t. to recall; to remember. **recollection** n. power of recalling ideas to the mind; remembrance; things remembered. [L. *recolligere*, to collect again].

rec·om·mend (rek·a·mend′) v.t. to speak well of; to commend; to advise. **-able** a. worthy of recommendation. **-ation** n. recommending; a statement that one is worthy of favor or trial.

rec·om·pense (rek′·am·pens) v.t. to repay; to reward, to make an equivalent return for service, loss, etc.; to make up for; n. repayment; requital [Fr. *récompenser*].

rec·on·cile (rek'·an·sīl) *v.t.* to conciliate; to restore to friendship; to make agree; to become resigned (to); to adjust or compose. **reconcilable** *a.* **-ment, reconciliation** *n.* renewal of friendship; harmonizing of apparently opposed ideas, etc.; (*Bib.*) expiation; **reconciliatory** *a.* [L. *reconciliare*].

rec·on·dite (rek'·an·dīt) *a.* hidden from view or mental perception; obscure; little known. **-ness** *n.* [L. *reconditus*, hidden away].

re·con·di·tion (rē·kan·dish'·an) *v.t.* to restore to sound condition, either person or thing; to renovate; to repair.

re·con·nais·sance (ri·kan'·a·sans) *n.* an examination or survey, by land or air, for engineering or military operations [Fr.].

re·con·noi·ter (rē·ka·noi'·ter) *v.t.* to make a preliminary survey of, esp. with a view to military operations; *v.i.* to make reconnaissance; to scout; *n.* a preliminary survey [Fr. *reconnoître, reconnaître*, to recognize].

re·con·sid·er (rē·kan·sid'·er) *v.t.* to consider again; to take up for renewed discussion.

re·con·sti·tute (rē·kan'·sta·tōōt) *v.t.* to constitute anew; to reconstruct; to restore a dehydrated substance to original form.

re·con·struct (rē·kan·strukt') *v.t.* to rebuild; to enact (*crime*) on actual spot, in course of judicial proceedings. **reconstruction** *n.*

re·cord (ri·kawrd') *v.t.* to commit to writing; to make a note of; to register (a vote); to inscribe; to make a sound record; *v.i.* to speak, sing, etc. for reproduction on a record. **record** (rek'·erd) *n.* register; authentic copy of any writing; personal history; list; finest performance or highest amount ever known; a disk, cylinder, roll, etc. for mechanical reproduction of sound; *pl.* public documents. **-er** *n.* one who registers writings or transactions; apparatus for registering data, by some form of symbol or line; instrument which transforms sounds into disk impressions; an instrument which registers sounds on wire tape; an ancient, flute-like musical instrument. **-ing** *n.* the making, or reproduction of, sound by mechanical means. **off the record**, unofficial [L. *recordari*, to remember].

re·count (rē·kount', ri·kount') *v.t.* to count again; to relate; to recite; to enumerate; *n.* a second enumeration [O.Fr. *reconter*].

re·coup (ri·kōōp') *v.t.* to recover equivalent for what has been lost or damaged; to compensate [Fr. *recouper*, to cut again].

re·course (rē'·kōrs) *n.* application made to another in difficulty or distress; person or thing resorted to [L. *recurrere*, to run back].

re·cov·er (ri·kuv'·er) *v.t.* to get back; to revive; to reclaim; to rescue; (*Law*) to obtain (damages) as compensation for loss, etc.; *v.i.* to regain health or a former state; **-able** *a.* **-y** *n.* regaining, retaking, or obtaining possession; restoration to health; amends for a bad start in business, sport, etc. [O.Fr. *recuvrer*, fr. L. *recuperare*].

re·cov·er (rē·kuv'·er) *v.t.* to put a fresh cover on; to cover again.

rec·re·ant (rek'·ri·ant) *a.* cowardly; craven; false; *n.* a craven; an apostate. **recreancy** *n.* [O.Fr. *recroire*, to take back one's pledge].

re·cre·ate (rek'·ri·āt) *v.t.* to give fresh life to; to restore; to reanimate; to refresh from weariness. **recreation** *n.* recreating; any pleasurable interest; amusement. **recreational** *a.* [L. *recreare*, to make again].

re·crim·i·nate (ri·krim'·a·nāt) *v.t.* and *v.i.* to charge an accuser with a similar crime. **recrimination** *n.* a counter-charge brought by the accused against the accuser; mutual abuse and blame. **recriminative, recriminatory** *a.* [L. *re-*, back; *crimen*, charge].

re·cru·desce (rē·krōō·des') *v.i.* to break out again; to revive; **-nce, -ncy** *n.* **-nt** *a.* [L. *recrudescere*, to become raw again].

re·cruit (ri·krōōt') *v.t.* to enlist persons for army, navy, etc.; to repair by fresh supplies; to renew in strength; *v.i.* to obtain new adherents; to gain health, spirits, etc.; *n.* a newly enlisted soldier; a fresh adherent. **-al, -ing, -ment** *n.* [O.Fr. *recruter*, fr. L. *recrescere*, to grow again].

rec·tan·gle (rek'·tang·gl) *n.* a four-sided figure with four right angles. **rectangular** *a.* [L. *rectus*, right, straight; *angulus*, an angle].

rec·ti·fy (rek'·ta·fī) *v.t.* to set right; to correct; to purify; to convert an alternating current of electricity into a direct current; **rectifiable** *a.* **rectification** *n.* **rectifier** *n.* one who corrects; a device which rectifies; a transformer; one who refines spirits by repeated distillations [L. *rectus*, straight; *facere*, to make].

rec·ti·lin·e·al, rectilinear (rek·ta·lin'·i·al, -ar) *a.* consisting of, or bounded by straight lines [L. *rectus*, straight; *linea*, a line].

rec·ti·tude (rek'·ta·tūd) *n.* moral uprightness; honesty of purpose [L. fr. *rectus*, right].

rec·to (rek'·tō) *n.* the right-hand page of an open book—opp. to *verso* [L. = on the right].

rec·tor (rek'·ter) *n.* clergyman of Episcopal Church who has charge of a parish; (*R.C.*) head of a religious house, college. **-y** *n.* house of a rector [L. fr. *regere, rectum*, to rule].

rec·tum (rek'·tam) *n.* lower end of the large intestine. *pl.* **recta. rectal** *a.* [L. *rectus*, straight].

re·cum·bent (ri·kum'·bant) *a.* reclining; lying on back [L. *recumbere*, to lie down].

re·cu·per·ate (ri·kū'·per·āt) *v.i.* to win back health and strength; to recover from financial loss. **recuperation** *n.* convalescence. **recuperative** *a.* [L. *recuperare*, to recover].

re·cur (ri·kur') *v.i.* to happen again; to return periodically; *pr.p.* **-ring** *pa.t.* and *pa.p.* **-red. -rence, -rency** *n.* **-rent** *a.* returning periodically [L. *re-*, again; *currere*, to run].

re·curve (ri·kurv') *v.t.* to bend backwards.

rec·u·sant (rek'·ū·zant) *a.* obstinate in refusal; *n.* dissenter or nonconformist who refuses to conform to authority, esp. in religious matters. [L. *recusare*, to refuse].

red (red) *a.* (*comp.* **-der**; *superl.* **-dest**) of the color of aterial blood, rubies, glowing fire, etc.; of color, including shades, as scarlet, crimson, vermilion, orange-red and the like; of or connected with bloodshed, revolution, left-wing politics, etc.; *n.* color of blood; a socialist; communist, bolshevist; a Russian soldier; a danger signal. **-den** *v.t.* to make red; *v.i.* to become red; to blush; **-ness** *n.* state or quality of being red. **—blooded** *a.* vigorous; manly. **-breast** *n.* the robin. **-cap** *n.* a porter at a transportation terminal. **-coat** *n.* a British soldier, because of the bright scarlet tunic. **— corpuscle,** a colored blood corpuscle, containing hemoglobin and carrying oxygen. **Red Cross,** international emblem of organization for relief of sick and wounded in war time and for helping distressed persons in emergencies, as floods. **—handed** *a.* having red hands—hence, in the very act, orig. of a murderer. **— hat,** a cardinal's hat. **— heat** *n.* temperature of a body emitting red rays, about 700°-800° C. **— herring,** the common herring, cured by drying, smoking and salting; (*Colloq.*) any topic introduced to divert attention from main issue. **—hot** *a.* heated to redness; eager; enthusiastic. **Red Indian** *n.* a copper-colored aboriginal native of N. America. **—letter** *a.* applied to principal holy days, —hence, any memorable (day). **— pepper,** seasoning, such as cayenne. **-skin** *n.* a N. American Indian. **— tape,** slavish adherence to official regulations, fr. red tape used for tying up government documents. **-wing** *n.* a blackbird with a red patch on wings. **-wood** *n.* any wood yielding a red dye; the sequoia tree of California, a gigantic evergreen coniferous tree. **to paint the town red,** to have a noisy good time. **to see red,** to become infuriated [O.E. *read*].

re·dact (ri·dakt') *v.t.* to digest or reduce to order, literary, or scientific materials. **-ion** *n.* **-or** *n.* an editor [L. *redactum*, to drive back].

re·deem (ri·dēm') *v.t.* to purchase back; to regain, as mortaged property, by paying principal, interest and costs of mortgage; to take out of pawn; to ransom; to deliver from sin; to make good; to recover. **-able** *a.* **-ableness** *n.* **-er** *n.* [L. *redimere*, to buy back].

re·demp·tion (ri·demp'·shạn) *n.* redeeming or buying back; deliverance from sin; salvation. **-er** *n.* one who has redeemed himself. **redemptive** *a.* **redemptory** *a.* [L. *redimmere, redemptum*, to buy back].

red·in·te·grate (ri·din'·tạ·grāt) *v.t.* to make whole again; to renew. **redintegration** *n.* [L. *redintegrare*, to make whole again].

re·di·rect (rē·di·rekt') *v.t.* to direct again; to readdress a communication. **-ion** *n.*

re·dis·trib·ute (rē·dis·trib'·ūt) *v.t.* to deal out or apportion again. **redistribution** *n.*

red·o·lent (red'·ạ·lạnt) *a.* diffusing a strong or fragrant odor; scented; reminiscent (of). **redolence** *n.* [L. *redolere*, to smell strongly].

re·doubt (ri·dout') *n.* a central part within fortifications for a final stand by the defenders [Fr. *reduote*, fr. L. *re-*, back; *ducere*, to lead].

re·doubt·able (ri·dou'·tạ·bl) *a.* dreaded; formidable; valiant. [O.Fr. *redouter*, to fear].

re·dound (ri·dound') *v.i.* to contribute or turn to; to conduce (to); to recoil; to react (upon) [L. *re-*, back; *undare*, to surge].

re·draft (rē·draft') *v.t.* to draft or draw up a second time; *n.* a second copy; a new bill of exchange.

re·dress (ri·dres') *v.t.* to make amends for; to set right; to compensate; to adjust; (rē·dress) *n.* reparation; amendment; relief; remedy. **-er** *n.* **-ible** *a.* [Fr. *redresser*].

re·duce (ri·dūs') *v.t.* to diminish in number, length, quantity, value, price, etc.; to lower; to degrade; (*Chem.*) to remove oxygen or add hydrogen; to decrease valency number; to separate metal from its ore by heat and chemical affinities; to add electrons to an ion; (*Arith.*) to change, as numbers, from one denomination into another without altering value; to slim; to impoverish; to subdue; to capture (as a fort). **-d** *a.* **reducible** *a.* **reduction** *n.* reducing; subjugation; diminution; curtailment; amount by which something is reduced. **reductive** *a.* having the power of reducing. **reductively** *adv.* **reducing agent,** a reagent for abstracting oxygen or adding hydrogen [L. *re-*; *ducere*, to lead].

re·dun·dant (ri·dun'·dạnt) *a.* superfluous; serving no useful purpose; using more words than necessary for complete meaning **redundance, redundancy** *n.* **-ly** *adv.* [L. *redundare*, to overflow].

re·ech·o (rē·ek'·ō) *v.t.* to echo back.

reed (rēd) *n.* a tall hollow-stemmed grass growing in water or marshes; in certain wind-instruments, a thin strip of cane or metal which vibrates and produces a musical sound; a musical instrument made of the hollow joint of some plant; a pastoral pipe; thatching straw; an arrow; *pl.* a molding *v.t.* to thatch; to fit with a reed. **-ed** *a.* covered with reeds; molded like reeds. **-er** *n.* a thatcher. **-iness** *n.* **—instrument** *n.* (*Mus.*) a wind-instrument played by means of a reed, as the oboe, English horn, bassoon, clarinet, saxophone, etc. **— pipe** *n.* organ pipe whose tone is produced by vibra-

tion of metal tongue. **— stop** *n.* organ stop owing its tone to vibration of little metal tongues. **-y** *a.* [O.E. *hreod*].

reef (rēf) *n.* a portion of a square sail which can be rolled up and made fast to the yard or boom; *v.t.* to reduce the area of sail by taking in a reef. **-er** *n.* one who reefs; a sailor's close-fitting jacket. **— knot** *n.* (*Naut.*) a square knot [O.N. *rif*, reef, rib].

reef (rēf) *n.* a ridge of rock near the surface of the sea; a lode of auriferous rock [O.N. *rif*].

reek (rēk) *n.* smoke; vapor; fume; *v.i.* to emit smoke; to steam; to smell strongly unpleasant. **-ing** *a.* **-y** *a.* [O.E. *rec*].

reel (rēl) *n.* frame or bobbin on which yarn or cloth is wound; cylinder turning on an axis on which seamen wind the log lines, and anglers their fishing line; in motion pictures, a flanged spool on which film is wound; a portion of film, usually 1000 feet; *v.t.* to wind upon a reel; to draw (in) by means of a reel. **to reel off,** to recite rapidly [O.E. *hreol*].

reel (rēl) *v.i.* to stagger; to sway from side to side; to whirl; to be dizzy [O.E. *hreol*].

reel (rēl) *n.* a sprightly dance tune; a Scottish dance for two or more couples [Gael. *righil*].

reeve (rēv) *v.t.* to pass line through any hole in a block, cleat, ring, etc., for pulling a larger rope after it [Dut. *reef*, a reef].

reeve (rēv) *n.* official in early English times as shire reeve (sheriff) [O.E. *gerefa*].

re·fec·tion (ri·fek'·shạn) *n.* refreshment; a simple repast; a lunch. **refectory** *n.* a hall in a monastery, convent, school, or college where meals are served [L. *reficere, refectum*, to remake].

re·fer (ri·fur') *v.t.* to direct to; to assign to; *v.i.* to have reference or relation to; to offer, as testimony in evidence of character, qualification, etc.; to allude (to). *pr.p.* **-ring.** *pa.t.* and *pa.p.* **-red. referable, referrable** *a.* may be referred to or assigned to. **referee** *n.* an arbitrator; an umpire; a neutral judge in various sports. **reference** *n.* appeal to the judgment of another; relation; one of whom inquiries can be made; one named by a candidate for a post as willing to give testimony of character, etc.; a passage in a book to which reader is referred; a quotation; a testimonial. **referendum** *n.* a popular vote for ascertaining the public will on a single definite issue. **referential** *a.* containing a reference; used for reference [L. *re-*, back; *ferre*, to carry].

re·fine (ri·fīn') *v.t.* to purify; to reduce crude metals to a finer state; to clarify; to polish or improve; to free from coarseness, vulgarity, etc.; *v.i.* to become pure; to improve in accuracy, excellence, or good taste. **-d** *a.* purified or clarified; polished; well-bred. **-dly** *adv.* **-ment** *n.* **-ry** *n.* place where process of refining sugar, oil, metals, etc. is effected [Fr. *raffiner*].

re·flect (ri·flekt') *v.t.* to throw back, esp. rays of light, heat, or sound, from surfaces; to mirror; *v.i.* to throw back light, heat, etc.; to meditate; to consider attentively; to cast discredit on; to disparage. **-ed** *a.* **-ing** *a.* thoughtful; throwing back rays of light, etc. **ingly** *adv.* **-ion** *n.* reflecting; return of rays of heat or light, or waves of sound, from a surface; image given back from mirror or other reflecting surface; meditation; contemplation. **-ive** *a.* reflecting; meditative; (*Gram.*). reflective; reciprocal. **-ively** *adv.* **-iveness** *n.* **-or** *n.* a reflecting surface [L. *reflectere*, to bend back].

re·flex (rē'·fleks) *a.* turned, bent, or directed backwards; reflected; (*Mech.*) produced by reaction; (*Anat.*) denoting the involuntary action of the motor nerves under a stimulus from the sensory nerves; involuntary; automatic; *n.* reflection; a reflected image; a reflex action; *v.t.* (ri·fleks') to bend back; to reflect. **-ible** *a.* **-ibility** *n.* **-ive** *a.* bending or turned backwards; reflective; of certain verbs, whose subject and object are the same person or thing; of pronouns which serve as objects to reflexive verbs; as *myself*, etc. **-ively** *adv.* **-ly** *adv.* **conditioned reflex,** reflex action due to power of association and suggestion [L. *re-*, back; *flectere*, to bend].

re·flux (rē'·fluks) *n.* a flowing back; ebbing.

re·form (ri·fawrm') *v.t.* to restore; to reclaim; to amend; to improve; to eliminate (abuse, malpractice); *v.i.* to amend one's ways; to improve; *n.* amendment; improvement; rectification; correction. **-able** *a.* **reformation** (ref'·er·mā·shan) *n.* reforming; change for the better; religious movement of 16th cent. in which a large section of the church broke away from Rome. **-ative** *a.* aiming at reform. **-atory** *a.* tending to reform; *n.* institution for reforming young law-breakers. **-ed** *a.* amended; reclaimed **-er** *n.* one who reforms; an advocate of reform.

re·fract (ri·frakt') *v.t.* to bend sharply; to cause to deviate from a direct course, as rays of light on passing from one medium to another. **-able** *a.* **-ed** *a.* **-ing** *a.* serving to refract; refractive. **-ion** *n.* **-tive** *a.* **-or** *n.* [L. *re-*, back; *frangere, fractum*, to break].

re·frac·to·ry (ri·frak'·ta·ri·) *a.* sullen or perverse in opposition or disobedience; suitable for lining furnaces because of resistance to fusion at very high temperatures; (*Med.*) resistent to treatment. **refractorily** *adv.* [L. *re-*, back; *frangere*, to break].

re·frain (ri·frān') *v.i.* to abstain. **-ment** *n.* [L. *refrenare*, to bridle].

re·frain (ri·frān') *n.* chorus recurring at end of each verse of song; constant theme [Fr. fr. L. *refringere*, to break off].

re·fran·gi·ble (ri·fran'·ja·bl) *a.* able to be refracted [L. *re-*, back; *frangere*, to break].

re·fresh (ri·fresh') *v.t.* to make fresh again; to revive; to renew; to enliven; to provide with refreshment; to freshen up. **-er** *n.* one who, or that which, refreshes; (*Slang*) a refreshing drink. **-ing** *a.* invigorating; reviving. **-ment** *n.* restoration of strength; that which adds fresh vigor, as rest, drink, or food—hence, *pl.* food and drink [O.Fr. *refrescher*].

re·frig·e·rate (ri·frij'·er·āt) *v.t.* to make cold or frozen; to preserve food, etc., by cooling; *v.i.* to become cold. **refrigerant** *a.* **refrigeration,** *n.* **refrigerative, refrigeratory** *a.* cooling. **refrigerator** *n.* apparatus and plant for the manufacture of ice; chamber for preserving food by mechanical production of low temperatures [L. *re-*, again; *frigus*, cold].

ref·uge (ref'·ūj) *n.* shelter; asylum; retreat; harbor. **refugee** *n.* one who flees to a place of safety [L. *re*, back; *fugere*, to flee].

re·ful·gent (ri·ful'·jant) *a.* shining; splendid. **refulgence** *n.* splendor. Also **refulgency** [L. *re-*, again; *fulgere*, to shine].

re·fund (ri·fund') *v.t.* to return in payment or compensation for; to repay. **refund** (rē'·fund) *n.* repayment [L. *re-*, back; *fundere*, to pour].

re·fur·bish (rē·fur'·bish) *v.t.* to furbish up again; to retouch; to renovate; to polish up.

re·fuse (rē·fūz') *v.t.* to deny or reject; to decline; *v.i.* to decline something offered; not to comply. **refusal** *n.* act of refusing; the first chance of accepting or declining an offer; an option [Fr. *refuser*, fr. L. recusare, to refuse].

ref·use (ref'·ūs) *a.* rejected; worthless; *n.* waste matter; trash [Fr. *refuser*, to refuse].

re·fuse (rē·fūz') *v.t.* of metals, to fuse or melt again. **refusion** *n.*

re·fute (ri·fūt') *v.t.* to overthrow by argument; to prove to be false. **refutable** *a.* capable of being refuted. **refutably** *adv.* **refutation** *n.* [L. *refutare*, to repel].

re·gain (ri·gān') *v.t.* to recover; to retrieve; to get back; to reach again.

re·gal (rē'·gal) *a.* pert. to a king; kingly; royal. **regalia** (re·gā'·li·a) *n.pl.* insignia of royalty, as crown, scepters, orbs, etc. **regality** *n.* royalty; sovereignty; an ensign of royalty. **-ly** *adv.* [L. *regalis*, royal].

re·gale (ri·gāl') *v.t.* to entertain in sumptuous manner; *v.i.* to feast [Fr. *régaler*].

re·gard (ri·gàrd') *v.t.* to observe; to gaze; to consider; to pay respect to; *n.* aspect; esteem; account; gaze; heed; concern; *pl.* compliments; good wishes. **-able** *a.* **-ful** *a.* heedful. **-fully** *adv.* **-ing** *prep.* concerning—also **in, with, regard to, as regards. -less** *a.* without regard; careless; neglectful. **-lessly** *adv.* [Fr. *regarder*].

re·gat·ta (ri·gat'·a) *n.* boat races [*It.* orig. a gondola race in Venice].

re·gen·cy See **regent.**

re·gen·er·ate (ri·jen'·er·āt) *v.t.* and *v.i.* to give fresh life or vigor to; to reorganize; to recreate the moral nature; to cause to be born again; *a.* born anew; changed from a natural to a spiritual state; regenerated. **regeneracy, regeneration** *n.* **regenerative** *a.*

re·gent (rē'·jant) *a.* holding the office of regent; exercising vicarious authority; *n.* one who governs a kingdom during the minority, absence, or disability of sovereign. **regency** *n.* office and jurisdiction of a regent [L. *regere*, to rule].

reg·i·cide (rej'·a·sīd) *n.* one who kills, or the killing of, a king. **regicidal** *a.* [L. *rex, regis*, a king; *caedere*, to slay].

re·gime (rā·zhēm') *n.* style or tenure of rule or management; administration; an ordered mode of dieting [Fr.].

reg·i·men (rej'·a·man) *n.* orderly government; systematic method of dieting, exercising, etc. [L. = rule, government].

reg·i·ment (rej'·a·mant) *n.* a body of soldiers commanded by a senior officer and consisting of companies, batteries, battalions, or squadrons, according to branch of service; *v.t.* to form into a regiment: to systematize. **-al** *a.* **-ation** *n.* thorough systemization and control [L. *regimentum*, government].

re·gion (rē'·jan) *n.* territory of indefinite extent; district; part of body; sphere or realm. **-al** *a.* **-ally** *adv.* [L. *regio*, a district].

reg·is·ter (rej'·is·ter) *n.* a written account; an official record; a list; the book in which a record is kept; an alphabetical index; an archive; a catalog; a registration; a metal damper to close a heating duct; any mechanical contrivance which registers or records; (*Mus.*) row of organ pipes with same tone color; organ stop; compass of a voice or instrument; *v.t.* to record; to enroll; to indicate, by cash register, scales, etc., by facial expression. **registrable** *a.* **-ed** *a.* **registrant** *n.* one who registers. **registrar** *n.* an official who keeps a register or record. **registration** *n.* entry or record; total entries registered. **registry** *n.* office for registering births, deaths and marriages. **-ed mail,** a method of postal delivery by which mail is insured against loss or damage in transit [O.Fr. *registre*].

reg·nal (reg'·nal) *a.* pert. to reign of monarch. **regnancy** *n.* rule; reign [L. *regnare*, to reign].

re·gress (rē'·gres) *n.* passage back; the power of passing back; re-entry; *v.i.* (ri·gres') to go or fall back; to return to a former state; (*Astron.*) to move from east to west. **-ion** *n.* returning; retrogression; (*Psych.*) diversion of psychic energy, owing to obstacles encountered, into channels of fantasy instead of reality. **-ive** *a.* [L. *regressus*, fr. *regredi*, to go back].

re·gret (ri·gret') *v.t.* to grieve over; to lament; to deplore; *pr.p.* **-ting.** *pa.t.* and *pa.p.*

-ted. *n.* grief; sorrow; remorse. **-ful** *a.* **-fully** *adv.* **-table** *a.* deserving regret; lamentable. **-tably** *adv.* **-ter** *n.* [Fr. *regretter*].

reg·u·lar (reg'·yạ·lẹr) *a.* conforming to, governed by rule; periodical; symmetrical; orderly; strict; habitual; straight; level; natural; standing (army); (*Colloq.*) out and out; belonging to a monastic order (opp. to *secular*); *n.* a member of any religious order who professes to follow a certain rule (*regula*) of life; a soldier belonging to a permanent, standing army. **-ization** *n.* **-ity** *n.* conformity to rule; uniformity. **-ly** *adv.* [L. *regula*, a rule].

reg·u·late (reg'·yạ·lāt) *v.t.* to adjust by rule, method, etc.; to arrange; to control. **regulation** *n.* regulating or controlling; state of being reduced to order; a law; an order. **regulator** *n.* [L. *regula*, a rule].

re·gur·gi·tate (rē·gur'·jạ·tāt) *v.t.* to throw, flow, or pour back in great quantity; *v.i.* to be thrown or poured back. **regurgitation** *n.* [L. *re-*, back; *gurges*, a gulf].

re·ha·bil·i·tate (rē·(h)ạ·bil'·ạ·tāt) *v.t.* to restore to reputation or former position; to recondition. **rehabilitation** *n.* [L. *re-*, again; *habitare*, to make *fit*].

re·hash (rē·hash') *v.t.* to mix together and use or serve up a second time.

re·hearse (ri·hẹrs') *v.t.* and *v.i.* to repeat aloud; to practice (play, etc.); to recite; to recapitulate; to narrate. **rehearsal** *n.* trial performance of a play, opera, etc. [O.Fr. *rehercer*, to repeat (lit. rake over again)].

Reich (rīk) *n.* German Confederation of States. **-stag** *n.* the German parliament. [Ger.].

re·i·fy (rē'·i·fī) *v.t.* to make concrete or real. **reification** *n.* [L. *res*, a thing; *facere*, to make].

reign (rān) *n.* royal authority; the period during which a sovereign occupies throne; influence; *v.i.* to possess sovereign power [O.Fr. *regne*, fr. L. *regnare*, to rule].

re·im·burse (rē·im·bẹrs') *v.t.* to refund; to pay back; to give the equivalent of. **-ment** *n.* **-r** *n.* [Fr. *rembourser*, fr. *bourse*, a purse].

rein (rān) *n.* strap of bridle to govern a horse, etc.; means of controlling, curbing; restraint; *pl.* power, or means of exercising power [O.Fr. *reine*, fr. L. *retinere*, to hold back].

re·in·car·nate (rē·in·kár'·nāt) *v.t.* to embody again in the flesh. **reincarnation** *n.*

rein·deer (rān'·dir) *n.* large deer of colder regions. — **moss** *n.* lichen, the winter food of reindeer [O.N. *hreinndyri*].

re·in·force (rē·in·fōrs') *v.t.* to strengthen with new force, esp. of troops or ships; to increase. **-ment** *n.* **reinforced concrete** *n.* concrete strengthened by the inclusion in it of steel nets, rods, girders, etc. [Fr. *renforcer*].

re·in·state (rē·in·stāt') *v.t.* to restore to former position. **-ment** *n.*

re·is·sue (rē·ish'·ōō) *v.t.* to issue again; to republish; *n.* a new issue; a reprint.

re·it·er·ate (rē·it'·ẹr·āt) *v.t.* to repeat again and again. **reiterant** *a.* **reiteration** *n.*

re·ject (ri·jekt') *v.t.* to cast from one; to throw away; to refuse; to put aside; (rē'jekt) *n.* a person or thing rejected as not up to standard. **-ion** *n.* [L. *re-*, back; *jacere*, to throw].

re·joice (ri·jois') *v.t.* to give joy to; to cheer; to gladden; *v.i.* to exult; to triumph. **rejoicing** *n.* act of expressing joy; *pl.* public expression of joy; festivities. [Fr. *réjouir*].

re·join (rē·join') *v.t.* to unite again; to meet again; to enter again, as society, etc.; *v.i.* to become united again; to reply. **-der** *n.* an answer to a reply [Fr. *rejoindre*].

re·ju·ve·nate (ri·jōò'·vạ·nāt) *v.t.* to make young again. **rejuvenation** *n.* **rejuvenator** *n.* **rejuvenesce** *v.i.* to grow young again. **rejuvenescence** *n.* **rejuvenescent** *a.* [L.

re-, again; *juvenis*, young].

re·lapse (ri·laps') *v.i.* to slide back, esp. into state of ill health, error, evil ways; *n.* a falling back [L. *relapsus*, to slip back].

re·late (ri·lāt') *v.t.* to tell; to establish relation between; *v.i.* to have relation (to); to refer (to). **-d** *a.* connected by blood or marriage; allied; akin. **relation** *n.* telling; *pl.* dealings between persons or nations; connection between things; kindred; connection by consanguinity or affinity; a relative. **relational** *a.* indicating some relation. **relationship** *n.* [L. *referre*, *relatum*, to bring back].

rel·a·tive (rel'·ạ·tiv) *a.* dependent on relation to something else, not absolute; comparative; respecting; connected; related; (*Gram.*) noting a relation or reference to antecedent word or sentence; *n.* a person connected by blood or affinity; a word relating to an antecedent word, clause, or sentence. **-ly** *adv.* comparatively. **-ness** *n.* **relativity** *n.* being relative; doctrine that measurement is conditioned by the choice of co-ordinate axes e.g., all observable motion, and time, are relative [fr. *relate*].

re·lax (ri·laks') *v.t.* to make less severe or stern; to loosen; *v.i.* to become loosened or feeble; to unbend; to become less severe; to ease up. **-ation** *n.* act of relaxing; recreation; mitigation. **-ing** *a.* [L. *re-*, again; *laxus*, loose].

re·lay (rē·lā', ri·lā') *n.* supplies conveniently stored at successive stages of a route; a gang of men, a fresh set of horses, etc., ready to relieve others; a device for making or breaking a local electrical circuit; an electro-magnetic device for allowing a weak signal from a distance to control a more powerful local electrical circuit; a low-powered broadcasting station which broadcasts programs originating in another station; *v.t.* to pass on, as a message, broadcast, etc. — **race**, a race between teams of which each runner does a part of the distance [Fr. *relais*, a rest].

re·lease (ri·lēs') *v.t.* to set free; to allow to quit; to exempt from obligation; (*Law*) to remit a claim; *n.* liberation; exemption; discharge; acquittance; a catch for controlling mechanical parts of a machine; (*Law*) a surrender of a right or claim. **releasable** *a.* [O.Fr. *relaissier*].

rel·e·gate (rel'·ạ·gāt) *v.t.* to send away; to banish; to consign; to demote. **relegation** *n.* [L. *re-* back; *legare*, to send].

re·lent (ri·lent') *v.i.* to give up harsh intention; to yield. **-less** *a.* showing no pity or sympathy. **-lessly** *adv.* **-lessness** *n.* [Fr. *ralentir*, to slacken].

rel·e·vant (rel'·ạ·vạnt) *a.* bearing upon the case in hand; pertinent. **relevance**, **relevancy** *n.* **-ly** *adv.* [L. *relevare*, to raise up].

re·li·a·ble (ri·lī·ạ·bl) *a.* trustworthy; honest; creditable. **-ness, reliability** *n.* **reliably** *adv.* **reliance** *n.* trust; confidence; dependence. **reliant** *a.* [fr. *rely*].

rel·ic (rel'·ik) *n.* something surviving from the past [L. *reliquus*, remaining].

re·lief (ri·lēf') *n.* removal or alleviation of pain, distress, or other evil; help; remedy; one who relieves another at his post; prominence; a sculptured figure standing out from a plane surface. — **map** *n.* a map showing the elevations and depressions of a country in relief [L. *re-*, again; *levare*, to raise].

re·lieve (ri·lēv') *v.t.* to alleviate; to free from trial, evil, or distress; to release from a post by substitution of another; to remedy; to lighten (gloom, etc.). **relieving** *a.* serving to relieve. [L. *re-*, again; *levare*, to raise].

re·li·gion (ri·lij'·ạn) *n.* belief in supernatural power which governs universe; recognition of God as object of worship; practical piety; any system of faith and worship. **-ist -ary, -er** *n.* one who makes inordinate professions of religion.**religiosity** *n.* sense of, or tendency towards, religiousness. **religious** *a.* pert. to religion; pious; teaching religion; conscientious. **religiously** *adv.* [L. *religio*].

re·lin·quish (ri·ling'·kwish) *v.t.* to give up; to yield.**-er** *n.* **-ment** *n.* [L. *relinquere*].

rel·i·quar·y (rel'·a·kwer·i·) *n.* a depository or casket in which relics of saints or martyrs are preserved; a shrine [Fr. *reliquaire*].

rel·ish (rel'·ish) *v.t.* to taste with pleasure; to like immensely; *v.t.* to have a pleasing taste; to savor; *n.* savor; flavor; what is used to make food more palatable, as sauce, seasoning, etc.; liking [O.Fr. *reles*, aftertaste].

re·luc·tant (ri·luk'·tant) *a.* unwilling; disinclined. **reluctance** *n.* **reluctancy** *n.* **-ly** *adv.* [L. *reluctari*, to struggle against].

re·ly (ri·lī') *v.i.* to trust; to depend; **relier** *n.* [L. *religare*, to bind fast].

re·main (ri·mān') *v.i.* to stay; to continue or endure; to be left; *n.pl.* a corpse; unpublished literary works of deceased. **-der** *n.* what remains; remnant; in real property law, an interest in an estate which only operates after the termination of a prior interest [L. *re-*, back; *manere*, to stay].

re·mand (ri·mand') *v.t.* to send back, as an accused person sent back to prison while further inquiries are made; *n.* such a recommittal [*re-*, back; *mandare*, to commit].

re·mark (ri·márk') *v.t.* to take notice of; to express in words or writing; to comment; notice; heed; regard. **-able** *a.* extraordinary. **-ableness** *n.* **-ably** *adv.* [Fr. *remarquer*].

rem·e·dy (rem'·a·di·)*n.* a means of curing or relieving a disease, trouble, fault, etc.; legal means to recover a right, or to obtain redress; cure; antidote; *v.t.* to restore to health; to heal; to cure; to put right. *a.* curable. **remedial** *a.* affording a remedy [L. *remedium*].

re·mem·ber (ri·mem'·ber) *v.t.* to retain in the memory; to recollect; to reward for services rendered; *v.i.* to have in mind. **-able** *a.* **remembrance** *n.* act or power of remembering; state of being remembered; recollection; memory; token; memento; keepsake [L. *re-*; *memor*, mindful].

re·mind (ri·mīnd') *v.t.* to cause to remember. **-er** *n.* one who, or that which reminds.

rem·i·nis·cence (rem·a·nis'·ans) *n.* state of calling to mind; a recollection of past events; a remembrance; *pl.* memoirs. **reminiscent** *a.* [L. *reminisci*, to remember].

re·mise (ri·mīz') *v.t.* to send back or remit, esp. in law; to resign or surrender (property, etc.) by deed; *n.* (*Law*) a surrender [O.Fr.].

re·miss (ri·mis') *a.* not prompt or exact in duty; careless. **-ful** *a.* **-ible** *a.* able to be pardoned or remitted. **-ion** *n.* act of remitting; abatement; diminution; period of moderation of intensity of a fever or other disease; pardon; forgiveness of sin. **-ive** *a.* **-ly** *adv.* **-ness** *n.* [L. *remissus*, sent back].

re·mit (ri·mit') *v.t.* to send back; to transfer; to send accused for trial back to a lower court; to transmit to a distance, as money bills; to return; to restore; to slacken (efforts); to forgive; to refrain from exacting debt, etc.); *v.i.* to abate in force; to slacken off. *pa.p.* **-ting.** *pa.t.* and *pa.p.* **-ted.** *n.* **remittal** *n.* act of remitting to another court. **remittance** *n.* transmitting money bills, or the like to a distant place; the money sent. **remittent** *a.* increasing and decreasing at periodic intervals [L. *remittere*, to send back].

rem·nant (rem'·nant) *n.* fragment of cloth; scrap; residue; remainder [O.Fr. *remanant*].

re·mon·strate (ri·mán'·strāt) *v.t.* to make evident by strong protestations *v.i.* to present strong reasons against; to speak strongly against. **remonstrance** *n.* expostulation; protest. **remonstrant** *n.* one who remon-

strates; *a.* expostulatory. **remonstration** *n.* **remonstrative, remonstratory** *a.* [L. *re-*, again; *monstrare*, to point out].

re·morse (ri·mawrs') *n.* self-reproach excited by sense of guilt; repentance. **-ful** *a.* penitent; repentant. **-fully** *adv.* **-less** *a.* relentless; pitiless [L. *remordere*, to bite back].

re·mote (ri·mōt') *a.* far back in time or space; not near; slight; **-ly** *adv.* **-ness** *n.* **— control,** control of apparatus from a distance [L. *re-*, back; *movere*, *motum*, to move].

re·move (ri·mòòv') *v.t.* to take or put away; to dislodge; to transfer; to withdraw; to extract; to banish; to dismiss from a post; *v.i.* to change place or residence; *n.* removal; change of place; a step in any scale of gradation. **removable** *a.* not permanently fixed. **removal** *n.* removing; transferring to another house; dismissal from a post. **-d** *a.* denoting distance of relationship. **-r** *n.* [L. *re-*, back; *movere*, to move].

re·mu·ner·ate (ri·mū'·na·rāt) *v.t.* to reward for services; to recompense; to conpensate. **remunerable** *a.* that may, or should be, remunerated. **remuneration** *n.* reward; recompense; salary **remunerative** *a.* [L. *re-*, again; *munerare*, to give].

ren·ais·sance (ren·a·sán(t)s', ·zàn(t)'s) (*Cap.*) *n.* a rebirth; a period of intellectual revival, esp. of learning in fourteenth to sixteenth, cents.; *a.* pert. to renaissance. Also **renascence** [Fr.].

re·nal (rē'·nal) *a.* pert. to kidneys [L. *renes*].

re·nas·cent (ri·nas'·ant) *a.* springing into being again; regaining lost vigor. **renascence** *n.* See **renaissance** [L. *re-*, again; *nasci*, to be born].

rend (rend) *v.t.* to tear asunder; to pull to pieces; to split; to lacerate. *pa.t.* and *pa.p.* **rent** [O.E. *rendan*, to cut].

ren·der (ren'·der) *v.t.* to give in return; to deliver up; to supply; to present; to make or cause to be; to translate from one language into another; to interpret music; to portray; to extract animal fats by heating. **-able** *a.* **-er** *n.* **-ing** *n.* **rendition** *n.* rendering [Fr. *rendre*].

ren·dez·vous (rán'·da·vòò) *n.* an appointed place for meeting; *v.i.* to assemble at a prearranged place [Fr. = betake yourselves].

ren·di·tion See **render.**

ren·e·gade (ren'·a·gād) *n.* one faithless to principle or party; a deserter; *a.* apostate; false. **renege** (ri·nig') *v.t.* and *v.i.* to deny; to desert; to break a promise; to revoke at cards [L. *re-*, again; *negare*, to deny].

re·new (ri·nū') *v.t.* and *v.i.* to restore; to renovate; to revive; to begin again; to recommence.**-able** *a.* **-al** *n.* revival; restoration; regeneration.

ren·net (ren'·it) *n.* any preparation used for curdling milk and in preparation of cheese; junket, etc. [M.E. *rennen*, to run, congeal].

re·nounce (ri·nouns') *v.t.* to disavow; to give up; to reject; *v.i.* to fail in following suit when a card of the suit is in the player's hand. **-ment, renunciation** *n.* [L. *renuntiare*, to protest against].

ren·o·vate (ren'·a·vāt) *v.t.* to make as good as new; to overhaul and repair. **renovation** *n.* [L. *renovare*, fr. *novus*, new].

re·nown (ri·noun') *n.* great reputation; fame. **-ed** *a.* famous; noted; eminent [O.Fr. *renoun*, fr. *renomer*, to make famous].

rent (rent) *pa.t.* and *pa.p.* of **rend**; *n.* an opening made by rending; a tear; a fissure; a split; a breach; a rupture; a rift.

rent (rent) *n.* a periodical payment at an agreed rate for use and enjoyment of something, esp. land, houses; rental; hiring charge; *v.t.* to lease; to hold by lease; to hire; *v.i.* to be leased or let for rent. **-able** *a.* **-al** *n.* the amount of rent; a rent roll; *a.* pert.

to rent.**-er** *n.* one who rents [Fr. *rente*, income].

re·nun·ci·a·tion (ri·nun·si·ā′·shạn) *n.* a surrender of claim or interest; rejection; repudiation. Also **renunciance. renunciative, renunciatory** ·*a.* See **renounce**.

re·or·gan·ize (rē·awr′·ga·nīz) *v.t.* to organize anew. [cotton, or silk fabric.

rep, repp (rep) *n.* a thick corded worsted,

re·pair (ri·per′) *v.t.* to restore to a sound or good state after injury; to mend; to redress; *n.* restoration; mending. **-able** *a.* **-er** *n.* [O. Fr. *reparer*].

re·pair (ri·pār′) *v.i.* to go; to betake oneself [L. *repatriare*, to return to one's country].

rep·a·ra·ble (rep′·a·ra·bl) *a.* that can be made good. **reparably** *adv.* **reparation** *n.* repairing or making amends; redress; compensation. **reparative** *a.* [O.Fr. *reparer*].

rep·ar·tee (rep·ẹr·tē′) *n.* apt, witty reply; gift of making such replies [Fr. *repartie*, orig. answering thrust in fencing].

re·past (ri·past′) *n.* a meal [Fr. *repas*, a meal].

re·pa·tri·ate (rē·pā′·tri·āt) *v.t.* to restore to one's country; to bring back prisoners of war and refugees from abroad. **repatriation** *n.* [L.L. *repatriare*].

re·pay (rē·pā′) *v.t.* to pay back; to make return or requital for; to require. *pa.t.* and *pa.p.* **repaid. -able** *a.* **-ment** *n.*

re·peal (ri·pēl′) *v.t.* to revoke, rescind, annul, as a deed, will, law, or statute; to abrogate; to cancel; *n.* revocation; abrogation.**-able** *a.* [O.Fr. *rapeler*, fr. *appeler*, to appeal].

re·peat (ri·pēt′) *v.t.* to say or do again; to reiterate; to echo; to tell; *n.* repetition; encore; (*Mus.*) sign that a movement is to be performed twice, indicated by inclusion within dots of part to be repeated. **-able** *a.* **-ed** *a.* frequent; recurring **-edly** *adv.* **-er** *n.* one who, or that which, repeats; firealarm which may be discharged many times in quick succession; a person who repeats a course of study.**-ing** *n.* **-ing decimal** (*Arith.*) a decimal in which same figure(s) repeat ad infinitum. [L. *repetere*, to try or seek again].

re·pel (ri·pel′) *v.t.* to drive back; to repulse; to oppose; to excite revulsion in; *v.i.* to have power to drive away; to cause repugnance. *pr.p.* **-ling.** *pa.t.* and *pa.p.* **-led. -lence, -lency** *n.* **-lent** *a.* driving back; tending to repel; *n.* that which repels. **-ler** *n.* [L. *re-*, back; *pellere*, to drive].

re·pent (ri·pent′) *v.t.* and *v.i.* to feel regret for a deed or omission; to desire to change one's life as a result of sorrow for one's sins. **-ance** *n.* sorrow for a deed or regret; contrition; penitence **-ant** *a.* [Fr. *se repentir*].

re·per·cus·sion (rē·pẹr·kush′·ạn) *n.* act of driving back; reverberation; rebound; recoil; echo; indirect effect. [fr. *percussion*].

rep·er·toire (rep·ẹr·twár′) *n.* list of plays, operas, musical works, dramatic rôles, within sphere of operations of a company or of an individual.**repertory** *n.* a repertoire; a place in which things are disposed in an orderly manner; *a.* pert. to the stock plays of a resident company [Fr. fr. L. *repertorium*].

rep·e·ti·tion (rep·a·tish′·ạn) *n.* act of repeating; the thing repeated; a copy. **repetitious** *a.* full of repetitions. **repetitive** *a.* involving much repetition [fr. *repeat*].

re·pine (ri·pīn′) *v.i.* to fret. **repining** *n.*

re·place (ri·plās′) *v.t.* to put back into place; to supply an equivalent for; to substitute for. **-able** *a.* **-ment** *n.* restoration; substitution.

re·plen·ish (ri·plen′·ish) *v.t.* to fill up again; to restock; to refill; to furnish; to supply. **-ment** *n.* [L. *re-*, again; *plenus*, full].

re·plete (ri·plēt′) *a.* full; completely filled; surfeited. **-ness, repletion** *n.* satiety; sur-

feit; (*Med.*) fullness of blood; plethora [L. *re-*, again; *plere, pletum*, to fill].

rep·li·ca (rep′·li·ka) *n.* exact copy of work of art by the artist of the original; facsimile. **-te** *v.t.* to fold or bend back; to duplicate. **-tion** *n.* an answer; reply; (*Law*) reply of a plaintiff to defendant's plea; a copy [L. *replicare*, to fold back].

re·ply (ri·plī′) *v.t.* and *v.i.* to return an answer; to respond; to rejoin. *n.* answer; response [O.Fr. *replier*, fr. L. *replicare*, to fold back].

re·port (ri·pōrt′) *v.t.* to relate; to take down in writing; to give an account of; to name as an offender; to narrate; *v.i.* to make official statement; to furnish in writing an account of a speech, or the proceedings of a public assembly; to present oneself as to superior officer; *n.* an official statement of facts; rumor; reverberation, as of gun; account of proceedings, debates, etc. of public bodies; repute; reputation. **-er** *n.* one who reports, esp. for newspapers. [L. *reportare*, to bring back].

re·pose (ri·pōz′) *v.t.* to rely on; to put trust (in). **reposit** *v.t.* to lay up, to lodge, in a place of safety. **repository** *n.* place where valuables are deposited for safety; a burial vault; a storehouse [Fr. *reposer*, fr. L. *reponere*, to place back].

re·pose (ri·pōz′) *v.i.* to rest; to sleep; to recline; to depend on; *v.t.* to lay at rest; *n.* sleep; relaxation. **-al** *n.* **-ful** *a.* **-fully** *adv.* [L. *repausare*, to pause again].

re·pous·sé (ra·pòò·sā′) *a.* embossed; hammered into relief from reverse side; *n.* a style of raised ornamentation in metal [Fr.].

rep·re·hend (rep·ri·hend′) *v.t.* to find fault with; to blame; to rebuke. **reprehensible** *a.* blameworthy. **reprehensibly** *adv.* **reprehension** *n.* act of reprehending; reproof. [L. *reprehendere*, lit. to take hold again].

rep·re·sent (rep·ri·zent′) *v.t.* to be or express the counterpart or image of; to recall by description or portrait; to pretend to be; to be the agent for; to act or play the part of; to personate; to be the member (of the House of Representatives, etc.) for. **-able** *a.* **-ation** *n.* describing, or showing; that which represents, as a picture; description; account; a dramatic performance; the act of representing (in parliament, etc.). **-ational** *a.* **-ative** *a.* typical; representing; exhibiting a likeness; *n.* an agent, deputy, delegate, or substitute; local member of a legislative body. [Fr. *représenter*].

re·press (ri·pres′) *v.t.* to keep under control; to put down; to reduce to subjection; to quell; to check. **-er, -or** *n.* **-ible** *a.* **-ibly** *adv.* **-ion** *n.* check; restraint; in psychoanalysis, the rejection from consciousness of anything unpleasant. **-ive** *a.* [L.*reprimere, repressum*, to repress].

re·prieve (ri·prēv′) *v.t.* to remit or commute a sentence; to grant temporary relief; *n.* temporary suspension of execution of sentence; rest or relief [fr. Fr. *reprendre*, to take back].

rep·ri·mand (rep′·ra·mand) *v.t.* to reprove severely; to chide. *n.* a sharp rebuke; a severe admonition [Fr. *réprimande*].

re·print (rē·print′) *v.t.* to print again. (rē′·print) *n.* a second or a new impression or edition of any printed work.

re·pris·al (ri·prī′·zạl) *n.* an act of retaliation or retribution [Fr. *représaille*].

re·proach (ri·prōch′) *v.t.* to censure; to upbraid; to rebuke; *n.* reproof; rebuke; discredit; an object of scorn. **-ful** *a.* expressing censure. **-fully** *adv.* **-fulness** *n.* [Fr. *reprocher*].

rep·ro·bate (rep′·ra·bāt) *v.t.* to disapprove with signs of extreme dislike; to exclude from hopes of salvation; *a.* depraved; cast off by

God; *n.* profligate; hardened sinner; scoundrel. **reprobation** *n.* condemnation; censure; rejection [L. *reprobare*, to reprove].

re·pro·duce (rē·prạ·dūs′) *v.t.* to produce over again; to produce likeness or copy of; to imitate; *v.i.* to propagate; to generate. **reproducible** *a.* **reproduction** *n.* a repeat; a facsimile, as of a painting, photograph, etc.; process of multiplication of living individuals or units whereby the species is perpetuated, either sexual or asexual. **reproductive** *a.* pert. to reproduction; yielding a return or profits.

re·proof (ri·pròòf′) *n.* reprimand; rebuke; censure; admonition. **reprove** *v.t.* to charge with a fault; to rebuke. **reprovable** *a.* deserving or calling for censure. **reproval** *n.* [O.Fr. *reprover*, fr. L. *reprobare*, to reprove].

rep·tile (rep′·tīl) *n.* animal of class **Reptilia**, cold-blooded, air-breathing vertebrates which move on their bellies or by means of small, short legs; a groveling or contemptible person [L. *reptilis*, creeping].

re·pub·lic (ri·pub′·lik) *n.* a state, without a hereditary head, in which supremacy of the people or its elected representatives is formally acknowledged; commonwealth. **-an** *a.* pert. to republic; (*Cap.*) one of the two traditional political parties of the U.S.A. **-anism** *n.* [L. *res publica*, common weal].

re·pu·di·ate (ri·pū′·di·āt) *v.t.* to cast off; to reject; to disclaim; to disown. **repudiation** *n.* [L. *re-*, away; *pudere*, to be ashamed].

re·pug·nance (ri·pug′·nạns) *n.* state or condition of being repugnant. **repugnancy** *n.* a settled or habitual feeling of aversion. **repugnant** *a.* contrary; distasteful in a high degree; offensive; adverse [L. *repugnare*, to fight back].

re·pulse (ri·puls′) *v.t.* to beat or drive back; to repel decisively; to reject; *n.* state of being repulsed; act of driving off; rebuff; rejection. *n.* **repulsion** *n.* act of driving back; state of being repelled; feeling of aversion; repugnance. **repulsive** *a.* loathsome. **repulsively** *adv.* [L. *repulsum*, to drive back].

re·pute (ri·pūt′) *v.t.* to account or consider; to reckon; *n.* good character; reputation; credit; esteem. **reputation** (rep·yạ·tā′·shạn) *n.* estimation in which a person is held; repute; known or reported character; general credit; good name; fame; renown. **reputable** *a.* held in esteem; respectable; creditable. **reputably** *adv.* **reputedly** *adv.* generally understood or believed [L. *reputare*, to reckon].

re·quest (ri·kwest′) *v.t.* to ask for earnestly; to petition; to beg; *n.* expression of desire for; petition; suit; demand **-er** *n.* [O.Fr. *requeste*].

Re·qui·em (rek′·wi·ạm) *n.* (*R.C.*) celebration of the mass for soul of a dead person; dirge; music for such a mass [L.].

re·quire (ri·kwīr′) *v.t.* to claim as by right; to make necessary; to demand; to need. **-ment** *n.* act of requiring; what is required; need; an essential condition [L. *requirere*, to seek].

req·ui·site (rek′·wạ·zit) *a.* necessary; needful; indispensable; essential; *n.* something necessary or indispensable. **requisition** *n.* a demand made on a community by a military force; formal demand made by one state to another; a written order for materials or supplies; a formal demand; *v.t.* to demand certain supplies or materials, esp. for troops; to request formally; to seize. **requisitionist** *n.* one who makes a requisition [L. *requirere*, *requisitum*, to seek].

re·quite (ri·kwīt′) *v.t.* to return an equivalent in good or evil; to repay; to make retaliation. **requital** *n.* that which requires or repays; compensation [*re-*, and *quit*].

re·scind (ri·sind′) *v.t.* to annul; to cancel; to revoke; to repeal; to reverse; to abrogate. **-able** *a.* **recission** *n.* act of rescinding. **rescissory** *a.* [L. *rescindere*, to cut off].

re·script (rē′·skript) an edict or decree [L. *rescriptum*, written back].

res·cue (res′·kū) *v.t.* to free from danger, evil, or restraint; to set at liberty; to deliver. *n.* rescuing; deliverance. **-r** *n.* [O.Fr. *rescourre*].

re·search (ri·surch′, rē′·surch) *n.* diligent search or inquiry; scientific investigation and study to discover facts; *a.* pert. to research; *v.i* to make research; to examine with care. **-er** *n.*

re·seat (rē·sēt′) *v.t.* to provide with a new seat or set of seats; to patch (trousers, etc.).

re·sem·ble (ri·zem′·bl) *v.t.* to be like or similar to; **resemblance** *n.* likeness; similarity. **resembling** *a.* [Fr. *ressembler*].

re·sent (ri·zent′) *v.t.* to consider as an injury or affront; to take ill; to be angry at. **-er** *n.* **-ful** *a.* full of, or readily given to, resentment. **-fully** *adv.* **-ment** *n.* deep sense of affront; indignation; [L. *re-*, again; *sentire*, to feel].

re·serve (ri·zurv′) *v.t.* to hold back; to set apart; to keep for future use; to retain; to keep for some person; *a.* acting as a reserve; *n.* keeping back; what is reserved; supply of stores for future use; troops, etc., held back from line of battle to assist when necessary; body of men discharged from armed forces but liable to be recalled in an emergency; funds set aside for possible contingencies; reticence; an area of land for a particular purpose. **reservation** *n.* reserving or keeping back; what is kept back; booking of a hotel room, etc.; a proviso or condition; a tract of land reserved for some public use. **-d** *a.* kept back; retained or booked; self-restrained; uncommunicative. **-dly** *adv.* **-dness** *n.* **reservist,** a member of the armed forces belonging to reserves. [L. *reservare*, to keep back].

res·er·voir (rez′·ẹr·vwȧr) *n.* area for storage and filtering of water; a large supply [Fr.].

re·set (rē·set′) *v.t.* to set again. *pr.p.* **-ting.** *pa.p.* and *pa.t.* **reset.**

re·side (ri·zīd′) *v.i.* to dwell permanently; to abide; to live; to be vested in; to be inherent in. **-nce** *n.* act, or time, of dwelling in a place; place where one resides; house. **-ncy** *n.* a residence. **-nt** *a.* dwelling; residing; *n.* one who resides in a place. **-ntial** *a.* pert. to a residence; pert. to a part of a town consisting mainly of dwelling houses. **-ntiary** *a.* having residence; *n.* a resident, esp. clergyman required to reside for a certain time within precincts of cathedral [L. *residere*, fr. *sedere*, to sit].

res·i·due (rez′·ạ·dū) *n.* balance or remainder. **residual** *a.* remaining after a part is taken away. **residuary** *a.* pert. to residue or part remaining. **residuum** *n.* what is left after any process of separation or purification; balance or remainder [L. *residuum*].

re·sign (ri·zīn′)*v.t.* and *v.i.* to relinquish formally (office, etc.); to yield to; to give up; to submit to. **resignation** (rez·ig·nā′·shạn) *n.* giving up, as a claim, possession, office, or place; relinquishment; patience and endurance. **-ed** *a.* relinquished; surrendered; acquiescent; submissive; patient. **-edly** *adv.* [L. *resignare*, to unseal].

re·sile (ri·zīl′) *v.i.* to draw back from a previous offer, decision, etc.; to retreat; to recoil; to rebound. **resilience** (ri·zil′·yạns), **resiliency** *n.* springing back or rebounding; elasticity, esp. of mind. **resilient** *a.* springing back; rebounding; elastic; buoyant; possessing power of quick recovery [L. *resilire*, to jump back].

res·in (rez′·in) *n.* general term for brittle, glassy, thickened juices exuded by certain plants; a resinous substance left after distillation of crude turpentine; fossilized remains, as amber, copal, kauri gum, etc.; *v.t.* to dress or coat with resin. **-ous** a. [L. *resina*].

re·sist (ri·zist') v.t. and v.i. to oppose; to withstand; to strive against. **-ance** n. opposition; hindrance; (*Elect.*) opposition offered by a circuit to passage of a current through it; power possessed by an individual to resist disease; in physics, forces tending to arrest movements. **-ant** n. one who, or that which, resists. a. offering or making resistance. **-er** n. **-ibility, -ibleness** n. the quality or state of being resistible; **-ible** a. **-ibly, -ingly** adv. **-less** a. irresistible; unable to resist. **-lessly** adv. **-lessness** n. **-or** n. a resistance coil or similar apparatus possessing resistance to electrical current. **-ance coil,** a coil of insulated wire whose resistance has been adjusted to a stated value. **-ance movement,** the organized, underground movement [L. *resistere*, to oppose].

res·o·lute (rez'·a·lūt) a. having a decided purpose; determined; n. a determined person; **-ly** adv. **-ness** n. determination. **resolution** n. act, purpose, or process of resolving; intention; firmness; solution; decision of court or vote of assembly; motion or declaration [L. *resolvere, resolutum*, to unite].

re·solve (ri·zȧlv') v.t. to separate the component parts of; to solve and reduce to a different form; to make clear; to unravel; (*Math.*) to solve; (*Med.*) to clear of inflammation; v.i. to determine; to decide; to purpose; to melt; to dissolve; to determine unanimously or by vote; n. act of resolving; that which is resolved on; firm determination. **resolvable** a. **-d** a. determined; resolute. **-dly** adv. **-dness** n. [L. *resolvere*, to untie].

res·o·nant (rez'·a·nant) a. resounding; echoing; sonorous; ringing. **resonance** n. [L. *re-*, again; *sonare*, to sound].

re·sort (ri·zawrt') v.i. to go; to have recourse; to frequent; n. a frequented place; vacation spot; recourse; aid. **last resort,** the last resource [Fr. *ressortir*, to rebound, to go back].

re·sound (ri·zound') v.i. to sound back; to send back sound; v.i. to echo; to reverberate.

re·source (ri·sōrs', rē·sōrs') n. that to which one resorts, or on which one depends, for supply or support; skill in improvising; means; contrivance; pl. pecuniary means; funds; wealth. **-ful** a. clever in devising fresh expedients. **-fully** adv. **-fulness** n. [Fr. *ressource*].

re·spect (ri·spekt') v.t. to esteem; to honor; to refer to; to relate to; n. consideration; deference; pl. expression of esteem; good wishes. **-able** a. worthy of respect; reputable; decent; moderate. **-ability, -ableness** n. **-ably** adv. **-ful** a. deferential; polite. **-fully** adv. **-fulness** n. **-ing** prep. regarding; concerning. **-ive** a. relative; not absolute. **-ively** adv. each [L. *respicere*, to look back].

re·spire (ri·spīr') v.t. and v.i. to breathe. **respirable** a. fit to be breathed. **respiration** n. process of breathing. **respirational** a. respiratory. **respirator** n. a device to produce artificial respiration. **respiratory** (res'. or res·pi') a. serving for, pert. to, respiration [L. *respirare*].

res·pite (res'·pit) n. a temporary intermission; suspension of execution of a capital sentence; v.t. to grant a respite to; to reprieve; to relieve by interval of rest [O.Fr. *respit*].

re·splend·ent (ri·splen'·dant) a. shining with brilliant luster; very bright; dazzling. **resplendence, resplendency** n. **-ly** adv. [L. *resplendere*, to shine].

re·spond (ri·spȧnd') v.i. to answer; to reply; to correspond to; to react **-ent** a. answering; giving response; n. (*Law*); defendant; one who refutes in a debate [L. *respondere*, to reply].

re·sponse (ri·spȧns') n. answer or reply; part of liturgy said or sung by choir and congregation in answer to versicles of priest; in R.C. church, anthem after morning lessons, etc. **responsibility** n. state of being responsible; that for which any one is responsible; a duty; a charge; an obligation **responsible** a. accountable; trustworthy; rational. **responsibly** adv. **responsive** a. able, ready, or inclined, to respond. **responsively** adv. **responsiveness** n. [L. *respondere, responsum*, to reply].

rest (rest) n. repose; a cessation from motion or labor; that on which anything rests or leans; a place where one may rest; a pause; v.t. to lay at rest; v.i. to cease from action; to repose; to stand or be fixed (on); to sleep; to be dead; to remain (with), for decision, etc.; to be undisturbed. **-ful** a. soothing; peaceful; quiet. **-fully** adv. **-fulness** n. **-less** a. continually on the move; unsettled in mind; uneasy. **-lessly** adv. **-lessness** n. **to lay to rest,** to bury [O.E.].

rest (rest) v.i. to remain; to continue to be; n. that which is left over or remainder [L. *restare*, to remain].

res·tau·rant (res'·ta·rȧnt) n. a place where customers are provided with meals on payment. **restaurateur** (res·to'·rạ·ter) n. proprietor of a restaurant [Fr.].

res·ti·tu·tion (res·ta·tōō'·shạn) n. the act of restoring, esp. to the rightful owner; reparation; indemnification; compensation. **restitutive** a. **restitutor** n. [L. *restituere, restitutum*, to replace].

res·tive (res'·tiv) a. impatient; fidgety; uneasy; obstinate; stubborn. **-ly** adv. **-ness** n. [O.Fr. *restif*, stubborn].

re·store (ri·stōr') v.t. to give back or return; to recover from ruin or decay; to repair; to renew; to replace; to reinstate; to heal; to revive; to cure. **restorable** a. **restoration** n. replacement; recovery; reconstruction; re-establishment; (*Cap.*) establishment of monarchy by return of Charles II in 1660. **restorative** a. having power to renew strength, vigor, etc.; n. a remedy for restoring health and vigor [L. *restaurare*, to repair].

re·strain (ri·strān') v.t. to hold back; to hinder; to check. **-able** a. **-edly** adv. with restraint. **-ment** n. **-t** n. curb; repression; hinderance; imprisonment [O.Fr. *restraindre*, fr. L. *re-*, back; *stringere*, to bind].

re·strict (ri·strikt') v.t. to restrain within bounds; to limit **-ed** a. limited. **-edly** adv. **-ion** n. act of restricting; state of being restricted; limitation, confinement; restraint. **-ive** a. **-ively** adv. [L. *restringere*, to bind fast].

re·sult (ri·zult') v.i. to follow, as a consequence; to issue (in); to terminate; n. issue; effect; outcome; answer to a calculation. a. following as a result [L. *resultare*, to leap back].

re·sume (ri·zūm)' v.t. to renew; to recommence; to take again. **résumé** (rā·zū·mā') n. a summing up; an abstract. **resumable** a. **resumption** n. act of taking back or taking again; a fresh start. **resumptive** a. resuming [L. *re-*, again; *sumere*, to take].

re·surge (ri·surj') v.i. to rise again. **-nce** n. **-nt** a. rising again (from the dead) [L. *re-*, again; *surgere*, to rise].

res·ur·rect (rez'·a·rekt) v.t. to restore to life; to use again. **-ion** n. rising of the body after death; (*Cap.*) Christ's arising from the grave after Crucifixion; a revival. **-ion, -ionary** a. **-ionist** n. one who resurrects, revives, etc.; a believer in resurrection; one who stealthily exhumed bodies from the grave to sell for anatomical purposes [L. *re-*, again; *surgere*, to rise].

re·sus·ci·tate (ri·sus'·a·tāt) v.t. to restore to

life one apparently dead; to revive; *v.i.* to come to life again. **resuscitable** *a.* **resuscitation** *n.* **resuscitative** *a.* tending to revive or reanimate. **resuscitator** *n.* [L. *resuscitare*, to raise up again].

re·tail (rē·tāl′) *v.t.* to sell to consumer, esp. in small quantities; to tell. **retail** *a.* denoting sale to consumer, as opposed to wholesale; *n.* sale in small quantities. **-er** *n.* **-ment** *n.* [O.F. *retailler*, to cut up].

re·tain (ri·tān′) *v.t.* to continue to keep in possession; to hold; to reserve; to engage services of. **-able** *a.* **-er** *n.* one who retains; adherent or follower; a fee paid to secure services of, esp. lawyer. **-ment** *n.* [L. *retinere*, to hold back].

re·tal·i·ate (ri·tal′·i·āt) *v.t.* and *v.i.* to repay in kind; to return like for like; to requite. **retaliation** *n.* **retaliative, retaliatory** *a.* **retaliator** *n.* [L. *retaliare*, fr. *talis*, like].

re·tard (ri·tȧrd′) *v.t.* to hinder progress; to make slow or late; to impede. **-ation** *n.* delaying; hindrance; diminishing velocity of a moving body; rate of loss of velocity; delayed mental development in children. **-ment** *n.* [L. *retardare*, fr. *tardus*, slow].

retch (rech) *v.i.* to strain at vomiting. **-ing** *n.* [O.E. *hraecan*].

re·ten·tion (ri·ten′·shan) *n.* act or power of retaining; memory. **retentive** *a.* **retentively** *adv.* **retentiveness** *n.* [fr. *retain*].

ret·i·cent (ret′·a·sant) *a.* reserved; uncommunicative. **reticence** *n.* also **reticency.** **-ly** *adv.* [L. *reticere*, fr. *tacere*, to be silent].

ret·i·cle (ret′·a·kl) *n.* a group of lines or wires in the focus of an optical instrument. **reticule** *n.* a little bag; a reticle. **reticular, reticulary** *a.* having the form of a net; intricate. **reticulate** *v.t.* to cover with netlike lines; to make like a net; *a.* Also **reticulated.** **reticulation** *n.* [Fr. *reticule*, fr. L. *rete*, a net].

re·ti·form (rē′·ta·fawrm) *a.* having form of a net; reticulated [L. *rete*, a net; *forma*, form].

ret·i·na (ret′·i·na) *n.* innermost, semi-transparent, sensory layer of the eye from which sense impressions are passed to the brain. **-l** *a.* [L. *rete*, a net].

ret·i·nue (ret′·i·nū) *n.* a body of hired servants or followers; a train of attendants; suite [Fr. *retenir*, to retain].

re·tire (ri·tīr′) *v.t.* to compel one to retire from office; to withdraw from circulation notes or bills; *v.i.* to go back; to withdraw; to retreat; to give up formally one's work or office; to go to bed. **retiral** *n.* act of retiring; occasion when one retires from office, etc. **-d** *a.* secluded; private; sequestered; withdrawn permanently from one's daily work. **-dly** *adv.* **-ment, -dness** *n.* act of retiring; state of being retired. **retiring** *a.* reserved; modest [Fr. *retirer*, to pull back].

re·tort (ri·tawrt′) *v.t.* to repay in kind; to hurl back (chare, etc.); *v.i.* to make a smart reply; *n.* vigorous reply or repartee; a vessel in which substances are distilled [L. *retorquere, retortum,* to twist back].

re·trace (rē·trās′) *v.t.* to trace back or over again; to go back the same way. **-able** *a.*

re·tract (ri·trakt′) *v.t.* and *v.i.* to draw back; to take back, as a statement; to go back on one's word. **-able** *a.* **-ation** *n.* recalling of a statement or opinion; recantation. **-ile** *a.* (*Zool.*) capable of being drawn back or inwards, as claws, etc. **-ion** *n.* the act of drawing back; disavowal; recantation; retractile power. **-ive** *a.* **-ively** *adv.* [L. *re-,* back; *trahere, tractum,* to draw].

re·tread (rē·tred′) *v.t.* to tread again; to replace a worn tread on the outer cover of a rubber tire with a new tread.

re·treat (ri·trēt′) *n.* retiring or withdrawing; a military signal for retiring; a military call at sunset, on a bugle; place of seclusion; period of retirement for prayer and meditation; *v.i.* to move back; to betake oneself to a place of security; to retire before an enemy. **-ing** *a.* sloping backward, as forehead or chin [Fr. *retraite,* fr. *retraire,* to draw back].

re·trench (ri·trench′) *v.t.* to cut down (expense, etc.); to curtail; to remove; *v.i.* to economize. **-ment** *n.* diminution of expenditure; economy; (*Fort.*) extra parapet and ditch within a rampart to prolong defense [Fr. *retrancher,* to cut off].

ret·ri·bu·tion (ret·ra·bū′·shan) *n.* just or suitable return; esp. for evil deeds; requital; repayment. **retributive, retributory** *a.* [L. *retributio*].

re·trieve (ri·trēv′) *v.t.* to gain back; to recover; to reestablish (former position, fortune, etc.); to repair; (of a dog) to find and bring back shot game. **retrievable** *a.* **retrievably** *adv.* **-ment, retrieval** *n.* **-r** *n.* dog trained to find and bring back game [Fr. *retrouver,* to find again].

ret·ro- (ret′·rō) *prefix* fr. L. *retro,* back, backward, used in the formation of compound words.

ret·ro·act (ret·rō·akt′) *v.i.* to act backwards; to react **-ion** *n.* **-ive** *a.* acting in regard to past events; retrospective. **-ively** *adv.* [L. *retro,* backward; *agere, actum,* to act].

ret·ro·cede (ret·rō·sēd′) *v.t.* to go or move back. **retrocession** *n.* going back [L. *retro,* backward; *cedere,* to go].

ret·ro·grade (ret′·rō·grād) *v.i.* to move backward; to deteriorate; to decline; *a.* tending to a backward direction; deteriorating; reactionary; retrogressive. **retrogradation** *n.* *n.* **retrogress** *v.i.* to move backwards; to deteriorate. **retrogression** *n.* act of going backward; a decline into an inferior state of development. **retrogressive** *a.* moving backward; reactionary; degenerating; assuming baser characteristics. **retrogressively** *adv.* [L. *retro,* backward; *gradi,* to go].

re·trorse (rē·trawrs′) *a.* bending or pointing backwards, as feathers of birds. Also **retroverse. -ly** *adv.* [L. *retro,* backwards; *vertere, versum,* to turn].

ret·ro·spect (ret′·rō·spekt) *n.* a looking back; survey of past events; a review. **-ion** *n.* **-ive** *a.* tending to look back; applicable to past events; of laws, rules, etc., having force as if enacted or authorized at earlier date. **-ively** *adv.* [L. *retro,* backward; *specere,* to look].

ret·ro·verse (ret′·rō·vers) *a.* bent backwards; retrorse. **retroversion** *n.* **retrovert** (rē′·, ret·′) *v.t.* to turn back [L. *retro,* backward; *vertere, versum,* to turn].

re·turn (ri·turn′) *v.t.* to bring, give, or send back; to restore; to report officially; to elect; to yield (a profit); to reciprocate; *v.i.* to go or come back; to recur; to reply; *n.* coming back to the same place; what is returned, as a payment; profit; an official report, esp. as to numbers; repayment; restitution. **-able** *a.* **— match** *n.* second game played by same opponents. **— ticket** *n.* ticket for journey, there and back [Fr. *retourner*].

re·un·ion (rē·ūn′·yan) *n.* union formed anew after separation; a social gathering. **reunite** *v.t.* and *v.i.* to unite again; to join after separation.

rev (rev) *n.* (*Colloq.*) revolution of an engine; *v.t.* and *v.i.* to run (an engine). *pr.p.* **-ving.** *pa.t.* and *pa.p.* **-ved.**

re·veal (ri·vēl′) *v.t.* to disclose; to show. **-able** *a.* **-er** *n.* **-ment** *n.* disclosure; revelation. **-ed law,** divine law. **-ed religion,** founded on revelation. Opposite of *natural religion* [L.

revelare, to draw back the veil].

rev·eil·le (rev′·a̱·li·) *n.* the bugle call or roll of drums sounded in military establishments at daybreak to rouse inmates [Fr. *réveillez* (*-vous*) wake up!].

rev·el (rev′·al) *v.i.* to make merry; to carouse; to delight in. *pr.p.*, *pa.t.*, *pa.p. and n.* festivity; noisy celebration; *pl.* entertainment, with music and dancing. **-er** *n.* **-ment, -ry** *n.* [O.Fr. *reveler*, to make tumult].

rev·e·la·tion (rev·a̱·lā′·shan) *n.* act of revealing; God's disclosure of himself to man; (*Cap.*) last book of New Testament. **-al, revelatory** *a.* [L. *revelare*, to draw back the veil].

rev·e·nant (rev′·a̱·nant) *n.* one returned from long absence or apparently from the dead; a specter; a ghostly visitant [Fr.].

re·venge (ri·venj′) *v.t.* to make retaliation for; to return injury for injury; to avenge; *n.* revenging; infliction of injury in return for injury; passion for vengeance. **-ful** *a.* **-fully** *adv.* **-fulness** *n.* [O.Fr. *revenger*, fr. L. *re-*, again; *vindicare*, to claim].

rev·e·nue (rev′·a̱·nū) *n.* income derived from any source, esp. annual income of a state or institution; proceeds; receipts; profits. [Fr. *revenue*, return, fr. L. *revenire*, to come back].

re·ver·ber·ate (ri·vur′·beṟ·āt) *v.t. and v.i.* to send back, as sound; to reflect, as light or heat; to re-echo; to resound. **reverberant** *a.* resounding; beating back. **reverberation** *n.* **reverberative** *a.* tending to reverberate. **reverberator** *n.* **reverberatory** *a.* producing reverberation [L. *reverberare*, to beat back].

re·vere (ri·vir′) *v.t.* to regard with mingled fear, respect and affection; to reverence. **-nce** *n.* awe mingled with respect and esteem; veneration; a bow, curtsy, or genuflection; (*Cap.*) a title applied to a clergyman; *v.t.* to revere; to venerate. **-nd** *a.* worthy of reverence; venerable; a title of respect given to clergy (*abbrev.* **Rev.**) **-nt** *a.* feeling, showing, behaving with, reverence. **-ntial** *a.* respectful. **-ntially, -ntly** *adv.* [O.Fr. *reverer*, fr. L. *vereri*, to feel awe].

rev·er·ie, revery (rev′·eṟ·i·) *n.* state of mind, akin to dreaming; rhapsody; musing [Fr. *rêverie*, fr. *rêver*, to dream].

re·vers (ra̱·vir′) *n.* part of garment turned for ornamentation, as lapel [O.Fr. = *reverse*].

re·verse (ri·vurs′) *v.t.* to change completely; to turn in an opposite direction; to give a contrary decision; to annul; to overturn; to transpose; to invert; *v.i.* to change direction; *n.* side which appears when object is turned round; opposite or contrary; crest side of coin or medal, as distinguished from *obverse*; check; defeat; misfortune; gear to drive a car backward; *a.* turned backward; opposite. **reversal** *n.* reversing, changing, overthrowing, annulling. **-d** *a.* turned in opposite direction; inverted; annulled. **-ly** *adv.* **reversibility** *n.* property of being reversible. **reversible** *a.* capable of being used on both sides or in either direction. **reversibly** *adv.* **reversion** *n.* returning or reverting; a deferred annuity; right or hope of future possession; (*Law*) return of estate to grantor or his next-of-kin, after death of grantee or legatee; interest which reverts to a landlord after expiry of lease; (*Biol.*) a tendency to revert to long-concealed characters of previous generations; atavism. **reversional, reversionary** *a.* involving a reversion. **reversive** *a.* [L. *re-*, back; *versum, versus*, to turn].

re·vert (ri·vurt′) *v.i.* to return to former state or rank; to come back to subject; to turn backwards; (*Law*) to return by reversion to donor; *v.t.* to turn back or reverse. **-ible** *a.* [L. *re-*, again; *vertere*, to turn].

re·view (ri·vū′) *v.t.* to re-examine; to consid-

er critically (book); to inspect troops, etc. *n.* revision; survey; inspection, esp. of massed military forces; a critical notice of a book, etc.; periodical devoted to critical articles, current events, etc. **-er** *n.* one who writes critical reviews; examiner; inspector [Fr. *revoir*, to see again].

re·vile (ri·vīl′) *v.t.* to abuse with opprobrious language; to vilify; to defame. **-ment** *n.* **-r** *n.* [O.Fr. *reviler*].

re·vise (ri·vīz′) *v.t.* to look over and correct; to review, alter and amend; *n.* a revised form; a further printer's proof to ensure all corrections have been made. **revisal** *n.* review; reexamination. **revision** *n.* revisal; revised copy of book or document. **-r** *n.* **revisional, revisionary** *a.* pert. to revision. **revisory** *a.* having power to revise (*Cap.*). **-d Version,** new translation of Bible in 1881 (New Testament) and 1884 (Old Testament) [L. *revisere*].

re·vive (ri·vīv′) *v.i.* to come back to life, vigor, etc.; to awaken; *v.t.* to resuscitate; to re-animate; to renew; to recover from neglect; to refresh (memory). **revivability** *n.* **revivable** *a.* capable of being revived. **revivably** *adv.* **revival** *n.* reviving or being revived; renewed activity, of trade, etc.; a wave of religious enthusiasm worked up by powerful preachers; awakening; reappearance of old, neglected play, etc. **revivalism** *n.* religious fervor of a revival. **revivalist** *n.* one who promotes religious revivals. **-r** *n.* one who, or that which, revives; a stimulant. **revivification** *n.* renewal of life and energy. **revivify** *v.t.* to reanimate; to reinvigorate [L. *re-*, again; *vivere*, to live].

re·voke (ri·vōk′) *v.t.* to annul; to repeal; to reverse (a decision); *v.i.* at cards, to fail to follow suit. *n.* neglect to follow suit at cards. **-r** *n.* **revocable** *a.* able to be revoked. **revocableness, revocability** *n.* **revocably** *adv.* **revocation** *n.* repeal; reversal. **revocatory** *a.* [L. *revocare*, to recall].

re·volt (ri·vōlt′) *v.i.* to renounce allegiance; to rise in rebellion; to feel disgust; *v.t.* to shock; to repel; *n.* act of revolting; rebellion; mutiny; disgust; loathing. **-er** *n.* **-ing** *a.* disgusting. **-ingly** *adv.* [Fr. *révolter*].

rev·o·lu·tion (rev·a̱·lū′·shan) *n.* motion of body round its orbit or focus; turning round on axis, time marked by a regular recurrence (as seasons); a radical change in constitution of a country after revolt. **-ary** *a.* pert. to revolution; marked by great and violent changes; *n.* one who participates in a revolution. **-ize** *v.t.* to change completely [L. *revolvere, revolutum*, to turn round].

re·volve (ri·valv′) *v.i.* to turn round on an axis; to rotate; to meditate; *v.t.* to cause to turn; to rotate; to reflect upon. **revolvable** *a.* **-r** *n.* pistol [L. *revolvere*, to turn round].

re·vue (ri·vū′) *n.* theatrical entertainment, partly musical comedy, with little continuity of structure or connected plot [Fr.].

re·vul·sion (ri·vul′·shan) *n.* sudden, violent change of feeling; repugnance or abhorrence; ·reaction; (*Med.*) counterirritation. **revulsive** *a.* [L. *revellere, revulsum*, to tear away].

re·ward (ri·wawrd′) *v.t.* to give in return for; to recompense; to remunerate; *n.* what is given in return; return for voluntary act; assistance in any form. **-er** *n.* **-ing** *a.* [O.Fr. *rewarder* = Fr. *regarder*, to look upon].

rhab·do- (rab·da̱) *prefix* used in formation of scientific compound terms, signifying *a rod* or *rod-like*. **rhaboid** *a.* rod-shaped. **-mancy** *n.* divination by rod or wand, to trace presence of ores or water underground [Gk. *rhabdos*, a rod].

rhap·so·dy (rap′·sa̱·di·) *n.* collection of verses; an intense, rambling composition or discourse; (*Mus.*) an irregular composition in a free style. **rhapsodic(al)** *a.* in extravagant, irregular style. **rhapsodically** *adv.* **rhapsodize** *v.t.* and *v.i.* to sing or recite, as a rhapsody; to be ecstatic over. **rhapsodist** *n.* one who recites or composes a rhapsody [Gk. *rhapsōdia*].

Rhen·ish (ren′·ish) *a.* of or pert. to River Rhine; *n.* wine from grapes grown in Rhineland [L. *Rhenus*].

rhe·o- *prefix* used in the formation of scientific compound terms, signifying *flowing* from Gk. *rhein*, to flow. **rheometer** (rē·am′·a·ter) *n.* instrument for measuring force of flow of fluids. **-stat** *n.* instrument for controlling and varying within limits value of resistance in electrical circuit. **rheostatic** *a.*

rhe·sus (rē′·sas) *n.* small Indian monkey. **rhesian** *a.* **rhesus factor** (*Med.*) Rh factor; a peculiarity of red cells of blood of most individuals, the so-called **rhesus positive**, rendering transfusion of their blood unsuitable for rhesus negative minority of patients. [L.]

rhet·o·ric (ret′·a·rik) *n.* art of persuasive or effective speech or writing; declamation; artificial eloquence or sophistry; exaggerated oratory. **rhetorical** *a.* concerning style or effect; of the nature of rhetoric. **rhetorical question**, statement in the form of question to which no answer is expected. **rhetorically** *adv.* **rhetorician** *n.* a teacher of or one versed in principles of rhetoric [Gk. *rhētorikos*, fr. *rhētōr*, a public speaker].

rheum (rŏŏm) *n.* thin, serous fluid secreted by mucous glands and discharged from nostrils or eyes during catarrh or a common cold. **-atic, -atical** *a.* pert. to or suffering from rheumatism. **-atism** *n.* a disease with symptoms of sharp pains and swelling in muscles and larger joints. **-atoid** *a.* resembling rheumatism. **-y** *a.* (*Literary*) full of rheum (esp. eyes); damp. **rheumatoid arthritis**, severe chronic inflammation of joints, esp. knees and fingers [Gk. *rheuma*, flow].

rhi·nal (rī′·nal) *a* pert. to the nose [Gk. *rhis, rhinos*, nose].

rhine·stone (rīn′·stōn) *n.* paste imitation of diamonds [fr. the *Rhine*].

rhi·noc·er·os (rī·nas′·a·ras) *n.* thick-skinned mammal allied to elephant, hippopotamus, etc. with strong horn (sometimes two) on nose [Gk. *rhis, rhinos*, the nose; *keras*, a horn].

rhi·zo- (rī·zō) *prefix* used in construction of compound terms, from Greek, *rhiza*, a root. **rhizome** (rī′·zōm) *n.* subterranean shoot, often bearing scales which are membranous, and usually giving off adventurous roots. **-matous** *a.* of the nature of a rhizome.

rhod-, rhodo- *prefix* used in the formation of compound terms, signifying rose-colored from Greek, *rhodon*, a rose. **-ocyte** *n.* red blood corpuscle. **rhododendron** *n.* evergreen flowering shrub with magnificent red or white blossoms.

rhom·bus (ram′·bas) *n.* (*Geom.*) parallelogram whose sides are all equal but whose angles are not right angles. **rhomb** *n.* a lozenge or diamond-shaped figure; rhombus. **rhombic, rhombiform, rhomboid, rhomboidal** *a.* **rhomboid** *n.* parallelogram like rhombus, but having only opposite sides and angles equal [Gk. *rhombos*].

rhu·barb (rŏŏ′·barb) *n.* two species of cultivated plants, familiar rhubarb of kitchen garden, and an eastern variety whose roots are used as a purgative. (*Slang*) heated discussion [Gk. *rha*, rhubarb; *barbaron*, foreign].

rhumb, rumb (rum, rumb) *n.* any of 32 cardinal points on compass [Gk. *rhombos*, a rhomb].

rhyme (rīm) *n.* identity of sound in word endings of verses; verses in rhyme with each other; word answering in sound to another word; *v.t.* to put into rhyme; *v.i.* to make verses. **-r, rhymster** *n.* one who makes rhymes; a minor poet; a poetaster. **— scheme**, pattern or arrangement of rhymes in stanza [O.E. *rim*, number].

rhythm (rithm) *n.* regular or measured flow of sound, as in music and poetry, or of action, as in dancing; measured, periodic movement, as in heart pulsations; regular recurrence; symmetry. **-ic(al)** *a.* **-ically** *adv.* **-ics** *n.* science of rhythm [Gk. *rhuthmos*, fr. *rhein*, to flow].

ri·ant (rī′·ant) *a.* laughing; merry; genial. **-ly** *adv.* [Fr. *rire*, to laugh].

rib (rib) *n.* one of arched and very elastic bones springing from vertebral column; anything resembling a rib, as a bar of a firegrate, wire support of umbrella. *v.t.* to furnish with ribs. *pr.p.* **-bing.** *pa.t.* and *pa.p.* **-bed. -bing** *n.* an arrangement of ribs [O.E. *ribb*].

rib·ald (rib·ald) *a.* low; vulgar; indecent. **-ry** *n.* vulgar language or conduct; obscenity. **-ish** *a.* [Fr. *ribaud*].

rib·bon (rib′·an) *n.* woven strip of material such as silk or satin, as trimming or fastening for a dress; colored piece of silk as war medal; part of insignia of order of knighthood; anything in strips resembling ribbon; inked tape in a typewriter. **Blue Ribbon**, first prize award [O.Fr. *riban*].

ri·bo·fla·vin (rī·ba·flā′·vin) *n.* chemical substance present in vitamin B2 complex, with marked growth promoting properties [L.L. *ribus*, currant; *flavus*, yellow].

rice (rīs) *n.* annual grass plant, cultivated in Asia, the principal food of one-third of world. **— paper** *n.* very thin and delicate paper used in China and Japan for drawing and painting [Gk. *oruza*].

rich (rich) *a.* wealthy; abounding in possessions; well supplied; fertile; abounding in nutritive qualities; of food, highly seasoned or flavored; mellow and harmonious (voice); *n.* the wealthy classes. **-es** *n.pl.* wealth. **-ly** *adv.* **-ness** *n.* [O.E. *rice*, rich].

rick·ets (rik′·its) *n.* rachitis, infantile disease marked by defective development of bones. **rickety** *a.* affected with rickets; shaky; unstable; insecure [etym. uncertain].

rick-shaw. See **jinrickisha.**

ric·o·chet (rik′·a·shā) *n.* glancing rebound of object after striking flat surface at oblique angle; *v.t.* and *v.i.* to rebound [Fr.].

rid (rid) *vt.* to free of; to relieve of; to remove by violence; to disencumber. *pr.p.* **-ding.** *pa.t.* and *pa.p.* **rid** or **-ded. -dance** *n.* deliverance; removal. **a good riddance**, a welcome relief [O.E. *hreddan*, to snatch away].

rid·den (rid′·n) *pa.p.* of **ride.**

rid·dle (rid′·l) *n.* large sieve for sifting or screening gravel, etc.; *v.t.* to separate, as grain from chaff, with a riddle; to pierce with holes as in a sieve; to pull (theory, etc.) to pieces. **riddlings** *n.pl.* coarse material left in sieve [O.E. *hridder*].

rid·dle (rid′·l) *n.* enigma; puzzling fact, thing, person; *v.i.* to speak in, make, riddles [O.E. *raedelse.* fr. *raedan*, to read, to guess]

ride (rīd) *v.t.* to be mounted on horse, bicycle, etc.; to traverse or cover distance; *v.i.* to be carried on back of an animal; to be borne along in a vehicle; to lie securely at anchor; to float lightly. *pr.p.* **riding.** *pa.t.* **rode;** *pa.p.* **ridden.** *n.* act of riding; journey on horseback, in a vehicle, etc.; roadway, etc. **-r** one who rides; addition to a document; supplement to original motion or verdict. **riding** *a.* used for riding on; used by a rider; *n.* act of riding. **riding habit** *n.* outfit worn by ladies on horseback. **to ride over**, to tyrannize. **to ride rough-shod**, to show no consideration for others [O.E. *ridan*].

ridge (rij) *n.* line of meeting of two sloping surfaces; long narrow hill; strip of upturned soil between furrows; highest part of roof; horizontal beam to which tops of rafters are fixed; tongue of high pressure on meteorological map; *v.t.* to form into ridges; *v.i.* to rise in ridges; to wrinkle. **-d** *a.* having ridges on its surface. — **pole** *n.* horizontal beam at peak of roof, tent, etc. [O.E. *hrycg*, the back].

rid·i·cule (rid'·a·kūl) *n.* mockery; raillery; derision; *v.t.* to deride; to mock; to make fun of. **-r** *n.* **ridiculous** *a.* exciting ridicule; ludicrous, laughable. [L. *ridere*, to laugh].

rife (rīf) *a.* prevailing; prevalent; abundant; plentiful. **-ly** *adv.* **-ness** *n.* [O.E.].

riff·raff (rif'·raf) *n.* the rabble (*Dial*) trash [M.E. *rif* and *raf*].

ri·fle (rī·fl) *v.t.* to search and rob; to strip; to plunder. **-r** *n.* **rifling** *n.* pillaging [O.Fr. *rifler*, fr. Ice. *hrifa*, to seize].

ri·fle (rī'·fl) *v.t.* to make spiral grooves in (gun barrel, etc.), *n.* a shoulder weapon or artillery piece whose barrel is grooved. **rifling** *n.* the arrangement of grooves in a gun barrel or rifle tube. **-man.** *n.* a man armed with rifle [Dan. *rifle*, to groove].

rift (rift) *n.* cleft; fissure; *v.t.* and *v.i.* to crack [fr. *rive*, to rend].

rig (rig) *v.t.* to provide (ship) with spars, ropes, etc.; to equip; (*Colloq.*) to arrange fraudulently; to clothe. *pr.p.* **-ging.** *pa.t.* and *pa.p.* **-ged** *n.* manner in which masts and sails of vessel are rigged; equipment used in erecting or installing machinery, etc.; (*Colloq.*) dress; a horse and trap. **-ger** *n.* **ging** *n.* system of ropes and tackle, esp. for supporting mast or controlling sails; adjustment of different components of an aircraft [Scand.].

right (rīt) *a.* straight; proper; upright; in accordance with truth and duty; being on same side of person toward the east when facing north; in politics, implying preservation of existing, established order or of restoring former institutions; (*Geom.*) applied to regular figures rising perpendicularly; correct; true; *adv.* in a right manner; according to standard of truth and justice; very; correctly; properly; exactly; to the right hand; *n.* that which is correct; uprightness; a just claim; legal title; that which is on right side, or opposite to left; political party inclined towards conservatism and preservation of status quo; *v.t.* to set upright; to do justice to; to make right; *v.i.* to recover proper or natural position; to become upright. **-ful** *a.* legitimate; lawful; true; honest; reasonable; fair. **-fully** *adv.* **-fulness** *n.* **-ly** *adv.* in accordance with justice; correctly. **-ness** *n.* correctness; justice. **-about** *adv.* in to the opposite direction. **—angled** *a.* having a **right angle**, one of ninety degrees. **—hand** *a.* belonging to the right hand; pert. to most reliable assistant. **— of way** *n.* right of passage [O.E. *riht*].

right·eous (rī'·chas) *a.* doing what is right; just; upright; godly. **-ly** *adv.* **-ness** *n.* [O.E. *riht*, right; *wis*, wise].

rig·id (rij'·id) *a.* stiff; not easily bent; strict; rigorous. **-ness**, **-ity** *n.* **-ly** *adv.* [L. *rigidus*].

rig·ma·role (rig'·ma·rōl) *n.* a succession of meaningless, rambling statements; foolish talk [corrupt. of *ragman roll*, a list of names].

rig·or (rig'·er) *n.* strictness, severity, stiffness, (*Med.*) a chill with fever; insensitive state of plants or animals. **-ism** *n.* strictness; austerity. **-ist** *n.* a person of strict principles. **-ous** *a.* **-ously** *adv.* **-ousness** *n.* **— mortis**, stiffening of body after death [L.].

rile (rīl) *v.t.* (*Colloq.* or *Dial.*) to anger; to exasperate; to irritate [a form of *roil*].

rill (ril) *n.* a small brook; rivulet; a streamlet. **-et** *n.* a tiny stream [Ger. *Rille*, a furrow].

rim (rim) *n.* margin; brim; border; metal ring forming outer part of a car wheel and carrying the tire; *v.t.* to furnish with a rim; *pr.p.* **-ming.** *pa.t.* and *pa.p.* **-med.** **-less** *a.* [O.E. *rima*].

rime Same as **rhyme**.

rime (rīm) *n.* white or hoarfrost; frozen dew or vapor. **rimy** *a.* [O.E. *hrim*].

ri·mose (rī'·mōs) *a.* having surface covered with fissures or cracks. Also **rimous** [L. *rimosus*].

rind (rīnd) *n.* the external covering or coating of trees, fruits, cheese, bacon, etc.; skin; peel; etc. *v.t.* to strip off rind [O.E. *rindle*].

ring (ring) *n.* small circle of gold, etc. esp. on finger; band, coil, rim; circle formed for dance or sports; round enclosure, as in circus, auction mart, etc.; area within roped square for boxing, etc.; a combination of persons to control prices within a trade; *v.t.* to encircle; to put ring through an animal's nose; to cut a ring around trunk of a tree. **-ed** *a.* wearing, marked with, formed of, or surrounded by, a ring or rings. **-ing** *n.* **-leader** *n.* the leader of people associated together for a common object, usually in defiance of law and order. **-less** *a.* **-let** *n.* small ring; long curl of hair. **-mail** *n.* chain armor. **-master** *n.* one who directs performance in circus ring. **-worm** *n.* contagious disease of skin, esp. of scalp, leaving circular bare patches [O.E. *hring*].

ring (ring) *v.t.* to cause to sound, esp. by striking; to produce, by ringing; *v.i.* to give out a clear resonant sound, as a bell; to chime; to resound; to be filled, as with praise, tidings, etc.; to continue sounding, as ears. *pa.t.* **rang**, rarely **rung**. *pa.p.* **rung.** *n.* a resonant note; chime (of church bells); act of ringing; a telephone call. **to ring down**, to cause theater curtain to be lowered. **to ring false**, to sound insincere [O.E. *hringan*].

rink (ringk) *n.* place for skating or curling; members of a side at bowling or curling; floor for roller skating, etc.; broad strip of a bowling-green [etym. doubtful].

rinse (rins) *v.t.* to wash out, by filling with water, etc., and emptying; to wash without the use of soap; **rinsing** *n.* [Fr. *rincer*].

ri·ot (rī'·at) *n.* tumultuous disturbance of peace; wanton behavior; noisy festivity; tumult; uproar; profusion, as of color. *v.i.* to make, or engage in, riot; to revel; to disturb peace. **-er** *n.* **-ing** *n.* **-ous** *a.* engaging in riot; unruly; boisterous. **-ously** *adv.* **-ousness** *n.* **-ry** *n.* riotous conduct. **to read the riot act** (*Colloq.*) to scold and threaten punishment. **to run riot,** to behave wildly, without restraint [O.Fr. *riotte*].

rip (rip) *v.t.* to rend; to slash; to tear off or out; to slit; to saw wood along direction of grain; *v.i.* to tear; to move quickly and freely. *pr.p.* **-ping.** *pa.t.* and *pa.p.* **-ped.** *n.* rent; tear. **-per** *n.* **-ping** *a.* **-cord** *n.* cord to withdraw parachute from pack so that ascending air forces it open. **— roaring** (*Slang*) *a.* hilarious. **-saw** *n.* saw with large teeth for cutting timber in direction of grain [O.N. *rippa*, to scratch].

rip (rip) *n.* a stretch of broken water in sea or river. **— current, — tide** [etym. doubtful].

ri·par·i·an (ra·, rī·pār·i·an) *a.* pert. to, or situated on, banks of a river [L. *ripa*, a river bank].

ripe (rīp) *a.* ready for reaping; mature; fully developed; sound (judgment, etc.); ready (for) **-ly** *adv.* **-n** *v.t.* to hasten process of riping; to mature; *v.i.* to grow ripe; to come to perfection. **-ness** *n.* [O.E.].

ri·poste (ri·pōst') *n.* quick return thrust in fencing; smart reply; repartee [Fr.].

rip·ple (rip'·l) *n.* fretting or dimpling of surface of water; a little wave; subdued murmur or sound; *v.t.* to cause ripple in; *v.i.* to flow or form into little waves. [var. of *rimple*, for O.E. *hrimpan*, to wrinkle].

rise (rīz) *v.i.* to ascend; to get up; to get out of bed; to appear above horizon; to originate; to swell; to increase in value, price, power; to revolt; to reach a higher rank; to revive. *pr.p.* **rising.** *pa.t.* **rose.** *pa.p.* **-n.** *n.* act of rising; that which rises or seems to rise; increase, as of price, wages, etc.; source; elevation. **-r** *n.* one who, or that which, rises; vertical part of a step. **rising** *n.* getting up; revolt; insurrection; *a.* mounting; advancing. **to get a rise out of,** to tease someone to the point of anger [O.E. *risan*].

ris·i·ble (riz′·a·bl) *a.* very prone to laugh; capable of exciting laughter; mirth provoking. **-ness, risibility** *n.* **risibly** *adv.* [L. *risibilis*, fr. *ridere*, to laugh].

risk (risk) *n.* danger; peril; hazard; amount covered by insurance; person or object insured; *v.t.* to expose to danger or possible loss. **-er** *n.* **-y** *a.* [Fr. *risque*].

ris·qué (ris·kā) *a.* daringly close to impropriety [F. *risquer*].

ri·sot·to (ri·zawt′·tō) *n.* Italian dish of shredded onions, meat, and rice [It.].

ris·sole (ris′·ōl) *n.* fish or meat minced and fried with bread crumbs and eggs [Fr.].

rite (rīt) *n.* formal practice or custom, esp. religious; form; ceremonial. **ritual** *a.* pert. to rites; ceremonial; *n.* manner of performing divine service; prescribed book of rites. **ritualism** *n.* adherence to and fondness for decorous ceremonial customs in public worship. **ritualist** *n.* **ritualistic** *a.* **ritually** *adv.* [L. *ritus*].

ri·val (rī′·val) *n.* competitor; opponent; *a.* having same pretensions or claims; competing; *v.t.* to vie with; to strive to equal or excel. **-ry** *n.* keen competition; emulation [L. *rivalis*].

rive (rīv) *v.t.* to rend asunder; to split; to cleave; *v.i.* to be split or rent asunder. **-d.** *pa.p.* **-d, -n** [O.N. *rifa*].

riv·er (riv′·er) *n.* natural stream of water flowing in a channel; a copious flow; abundance. **-ine** *a.* situated near or on river. **— basin** *n.* area drained by a river and its tributaries. **-bed** *n.* channel of a river. **— horse** *n.* the hippopotamus. **-side** *n.* the bank of a river [Fr. *rivière*].

riv·et (riv′·it) *n.* cylindrical iron or steel pin with strong flat head at one end, used for uniting two overlapping plates, etc. by hammering down the stub end; *v.t.* to fasten with rivets; to clinch; to fasten firmly [Fr.].

riv·u·let (riv′·ya·lit) *n.* a little river.

roach (rōch) *n.* fresh-water fish [O. Fr. *roche*].

roach. See **cockroach.**

road (rōd) *n.* a track or way prepared for passengers, vehicles, etc., direction; way; route; a place where vessels may ride at anchor. **-block** *n.* an obstruction placed across a road to stop someone. **-house** *n.* a restaurant, hotel, etc., at the roadside. **— show,** traveling company of actors. **-side** *n.* strip of ground along edge of road. **-way** *n.* a road. **to take to the road,** to adopt life of a tramp [O.E. *rad*, riding].

roam (rōm) *v.t.* and *v.i.* to wander; to ramble; to rove; *n.* a ramble; a walk. **-er** *n.*

roan (rōn) *a.* having coat in which the main color is thickly interspersed with another, esp. bay or sorrel or chestnut mixed with white or grey; *n.* a roan horse; smooth-grained sheepskin, dyed and finished [Fr. *rouan*].

roar (rōr) *v.t.* and *v.i.* to shout; to bawl; to make loud, confused sound, as winds, waves,

traffic, etc.; to laugh loudly; *n.* sound of roaring, deep cry. **-ing** *n.* act or sound of roaring. **-ingly** *adv.* **-ing trade,** brisk, profitable business [O.E. *rarian*].

roast (rōst) *v.t.* to cook by exposure to open fire or in oven; to expose to heat (as coffee, etc.); (*Slang*) to reprimand; *v.i.* to become over-heated; *n.* what is roasted, as joint of meat; *a.* roasted. **-ing** *n.* **-er** *n.* [O.Fr. *rostir*].

rob (rab) *v.t.* to take by force or stealth; to plunder; to steal. *pr.p.* **-bing.** *pa.t.* and *pa.p.* **-bed. -ber** *n.* **-bery** *n.* forcibly depriving a person of money or of goods [O.Fr. *rober*].

robe (rōb) *n.* a long outer garment, esp. of flowing style; ceremonial dress denoting state, rank, or office; gown; large covering, as lap robe; *v.t.* to invest with a robe; to array; to dress. **robing** *n.* [Fr.].

rob·in (rab′·in) *n.* brown red-breasted bird of thrush family; Also **— redbreast** [O.Fr. *Robin*, for *Robert*].

ro·bot (rō′·bat) *n.* automaton; mechanical man; person of machine-like efficiency [fr. play, R.U.R. (Rossum's Universal Robots, by Karel Capek). Pol. *robotnik*, workman].

ro·bust (rō·bust′) *a.* strong; muscular, sound; vigorous. **-ly** *adv.* **-ness** *n.* [L. *Robustus*, fr. *robur*, an oak, strength].

Ro·chelle salt (rō·shel′·sawlt) *n.* tartrate of sodium and potassium, used as aperient [*La Rochelle*, a town in France.]

roch·et (rach′·it) *n.* garment like a surplice, of white lawn, usually with tight sleeves, worn by bishops [O.Fr.].

rock (rak) *n.* large mass of stone; (*Geol.*) any natural deposit of sand, earth, or clay when in natural beds; firm foundation. **-ery** *n.* small artificial mound of stones planted with flowers, ferns, etc. **-iness** *n.* **-y** *a.* full of rocks; resembling rocks; unfeeling. **— bottom** *a.* lowest possible; *n.* lowest level. **— crystal** *n.* transparent quartz used in making certain lenses. **— garden** *n.* a garden laid out with rocks and plants. **— salt** *n.* unrefined sodium chloride found in great natural deposits. **the Rock,** Gibraltar. **on the rocks** (*Colloq.*) having no money or resources [Fr. *roche*].

rock (rak) *v.t.* to sway to and fro; to put to sleep by rocking; to lull; to sway, with anger, etc.; *v.i.* to be moved, backward and forward; to reel; to totter. **-er** *n.* curving piece of wood on which cradle or chair rocks; rocking horse or chair; pivoted lever having a rocking motion. **-y** *a.* disposed to rock; shaky. **-ing** *n.* **-ing chair** *n.* chair mounted on rockers. **-ing horse** *n.* wooden horse mounted on rockers; a hobbyhorse. **off one's rocker** (*Slang*) eccentric [O.E. *roccian*].

rock·et (rak′·it) *n.* cylindrical tube filled with a mixture of sulfur, niter, and charcoal, which, on ignition, hurls the tube forward by action of liberated gases; a similar tube which draws a life-line towards ship in distress; firework; *v.i.* to soar up; to increase rapidly in price, etc. [It. *rochetta*, dim. of *rocca*, a distaff].

ro·co·co (rō·kō′·kō) *n.* style of architecture, overlaid with profusion of delicate ornamentation [Fr.].

rod (rad) *n.* slender, straight, round bar, wand, stick, or switch; birch rod for punishment; cane; emblem of authority; fishing-rod; lightning conductor; linear measure equal to $5\frac{1}{2}$ yards or $16\frac{1}{2}$ feet [O.E. *rodd*].

rode (rōd) *pa.t.* of **ride.**

ro·dent (rō′·dant) *a.* gnawing; *n.* gnawing animal, as rabbit, rat [L. *rodere*, to gnaw].

ro·de·o (rō′·di·ō) *n.* roundup of cattle to be branded or marked; exhibition and contest in steer wrestling and bronco busting by cowboys [Sp.].

rod·o·mont (rad′·a·mant) *n.* a braggart; *a.*

boasting; bragging. **rodomontade** *n.* vain boasting; bluster; rant; *v.i.* to boast; to brag; to bluster [*Rodomonte*, the blustering opponent of Charlemagne, depicted in Ariosto's *Orlando Furioso*].

roe (rō) *n.* small deer; female hart. **-buck** *n.* male of roe [O.E. *rah*].

roe (rō) *n.* the eggs or spawn of fish [Scand.].

roent·gen (rent'·gen) *n.* (*Nuclear Physics*) measuring unit of radiation dose. — **rays** *n.pl.* X-rays. **-ize** *v.t.* to submit to action of X-rays. Also **Röntgen** [Wilhelm von Roentgen (1845-1923), German physicist].

ro·ga·tion (rō·gā'·shan) *n.* in ancient Rome demand, by consuls or tribunes, of a law to be passed by people; supplication. **Rogation Days**, three days preceding Ascension Day, on which special litanies are sung or recited by R.C. clergy and people in public procession, invoking a blessing on crops. **rogatory** *a.* commissioned to gather information [L. *rogare*, to ask].

rogue (rōg) *n.* vagrant; rascal; knave; mischievous person. **roguery** *n.* knavish tricks; cheating; waggery. **roguishly** *adv.* **roguishness** *n.* **rogues' gallery**, a collection of photographs of convicted criminals [O.Fr. *rogue*, proud].

rogue (rōg) *v.t.* and *v.i.* to remove plant from crop (potatoes, cereals, etc.) when that plant falls short of standard or is of another variety from the crop, in order to keep strain pure; *n.* plant so removed; plant that falls short of a standard or has reverted to original type.

rois·ter (rois·ter) *v.i.* to bluster; to bully; to swagger. **-er** *n.* **-ous** *a.* [O.Fr. *ruster*, a rough, rude fellow, fr. L. *rusticus*, rustic].

role (rōl) *n.* a part played by an actor in a drama—hence, any conspicuous part or task in public life [Fr.].

roll (rōl) *v.t.* to turn over and over; to move by turning on an axis; to form into a spherical body; to drive forward with a swift and easy motion; to level with a roller; to beat with rapid strokes, as a drum; to utter vowels, letter *r* with a full, long-drawn sound; *v.i.* to move forward by turning; to revolve upon an axis; to keep falling over and over; to sway; to reel; to rock from side to side, as ship; of aircraft, to turn about the axis, *i.e.* a line from nose to tail, in flight; *n.* rolling; a piece of paper, etc. rolled up; any object thus shaped; bread baked into small oval or rounded shapes; official list of members; register; catalog; continuous sound, as thunder; a full corkscrew revolution of an airplane about its longitudinal fore and aft axis during flight. **-able** *a.* — **call** *n.* calling over list of names to check absentees. **-er** *n.* cylinder of wood, stone, metal, etc. used in husbandry and the arts; a cylinder which distributes ink over type in printing; long, swelling wave; long, broad bandage; small, insectivorous bird which tumbles about in the air. **-er skate** *n.* skate with wheels or rollers instead of steel runner. **-ing** *a.* moving on wheels; turning over and over; undulating, as a plain; *n.* (*Naut.*) reeling of a ship from side to side. **-ing pin** *n.* cylindrical device for rolling out dough. **-ing stone**, person incapable of settling down in any one place [Fr. *rouler*, fr. L. *rotula*, a little wheel].

rol·lick (ràl'·ik) *v.i.* to move about in a boisterous, careless manner; *n.* frolicsome gaiety. **-ing** *a.* jovial; high-spirited [etym. unknown].

ro·ly-po·ly (rō'·li-pō'·li·) *a.* plump and rounded. [redupl. of *roll*].

Ro·ma·ic (rō·mā'·ik) *n.* modern Greek [Fr. *romaïque*, fr. Mod. Gk. *Rhōmaikos* fr. *Rhōmē*, Rome].

Ro·man (rō'·man) *a.* pert. to Rome or Roman people; pert. to R.C. religion; in printing, up-right letters as distinguished from *Italic* characters; expressed in letters, not in figures, as I., IV., i., iv., etc. (as distinguished from Arabic numerals, 1, 4, etc.). **-ic** *a.* **-ize** *v.t.* to introduce many words and idioms derived from Latin; to convert to Roman Catholicism; *v.i.* to use Latin expressions; to conform to R.C. opinions or practices. **-ism** *n.* tenets of Church of Rome. **-ist** *n.* **Romish** *a.* relating to Rome or to R.C. church. **Romist** *n.* Roman Catholic. — **candle**, a firework which throws out differently colored stars. — **Catholic**, a member or adherent of section of Christian Church which acknowledges supremacy of Pope; *a.* pert. to Church of Rome. — **Catholicism** [L. *Romanus*, fr. *Roma*, Rome].

Ro·mance (rō·mans') *n.* languages; *a.* pert. to these languages. **romance** *n.* narrative of knight-errantry in Middle Ages; ballad of adventures in love and war; any fictitious narrative treating of olden times; historical novel; story depending mainly on love interest; romantic spirit or quality; (*Mus.*) composition sentimental and expressive in character; *v.i.* to write or tell romances; embroider one's account or description with extravagances. **-r**, *n.* **romansque**, *a.* pert. to the portrayal of fabulous or fanciful subjects in literature (*Cap.*) pert. to any form of architecture derived from Roman, as Lombard, Saxon, etc., devleoped in the 10th to 13th centuries in southern western Europe. **romantic** *a.* pert. to romance; fictitious; fanciful; sentimental; imaginative. **romantically** *adv.* **romanticism** *n.* the reactionary movement in literature and art against formalism and classicism; state of being romantic. **romanticist** *n.* [O.Fr. *romans*, It. *romanza*.]

Rom·a·ny, Rommany (ràm'·a·ni·) *n.* a Gypsy; the language of the Gypsies [Gypsy *rom*, a man].

romp (ràmp) *v.i.* to leap and frisk about in play; to frolic; *n.* a tomboy; a boisterous form of play. **-ers** *n.pl.* a child's overall, with leg openings. **-ish** *a.* [earlier, *ramp*].

ron·deau (ron'·dō) *n.* poem, usually of thirteen lines with only two rhymes, the opening words recurring additionally, after eighth and thirteenth lines;. (*Mus.*) rondo. **rondel** *n.* poem of thirteen or fourteen iambic lines, first two lines of which are repeated in middle and at close. **rondo** *n.* musical setting of a rondeau; sanota movement in music in which a principal theme is repeated two or three times [Fr.].

Rönt·gen. See **roentgen.**

rood (róod) *n.* a length of 5½ to 8 yards; fourth part of acre, equal to 40 square rods or 1,210 square yards; a cross or crucifix, esp. one placed in a church over entrance to choir. — **loft** *n.* a small gallery over rood screen of church. [O.E. *rōd*, a rod, a cross].

roof (róof, roof) *n.* outside structure covering building; framework suppporting this covering; stratum immediately above seam in mine; upper part of any hollow structure or object, as roof of cave, mouth, etc.; ceiling; *v.t.* to cover with a roof; to shelter. — **garden** *n.* miniature garden on flat roof. **-tree** *n.* the ridgepole or roof itself. [O.E. *hrof*].

rook (rook) *n.* in chess, one of the four pieces placed on corner squares of the board; also known as a castle [Pers. *rukh*].

rook (rook) *n.* blueblack, hoarse-voiced bird of crow family; swindler; a card-sharp; *v.t.* to cheat; to swindle. **-ery** *n.* colony of rooks and their nests **-ie** *n.* Army slang for a recruit [O.E. *hroc*].

room (ròòm, room) *n.* (enough) space; apartment or chamber; scope; opportunity; occasion; *pl.* lodgings; *v.i.* to lodge. **-ful** *a.* **-ily** *adv.* **-iness** *n.* spaciousness. **-y** *a.*

spacious; wide [O.E. *rum*].

roost (ròòst) *n.* pole on which birds rest at night; perch; collection of fowls roosting together; *v.i.* to settle down to sleep, as birds on a perch; to perch. **-er** *n.* a cock [O.E. *hrost*].

root (ròòt, root) *n.* part of plant which grows down into soil seeking nourishment for whole plant; plant whose root is edible, as beetroot; part of anything which grows like root, as of tooth, cancer, etc.; source; origin; vital part; basis; bottom; primitive word from which other words are derived; (*Math.*) factor of quantity which, when multiplied by itself the number of times indicated by the index number, will produce that quantity, e.g. 4 is third (or cube) root of 64 (symbol $\sqrt{}$), for $4 \times 4 \times 4 = 64$; *v.t.* to plant and fix in earth; to impress deeply in mind; to establish firmly; to pull out by roots (followed by *out*) *v.i.* to enter earth, as roots; to be firmly fixed or established. **-ed** *a.* firmly established. **-stock** *n.* a rhizome. **root and branch,** entirely; completely [O.E. *wyrt*].

root (ròòt) *v.t.* and *v.i.* to turn up with the snout, as swine; to rummage; to uncover (with *up*) [O.E. *wrot*, a snout].

root (ròòt) *v.i.* to cheer [*Slang*].

rope (rōp) *v.t.* stout cord of several twisted strands of fiber or metal wire; row of objects strung together, as onions, pearls, etc.; *v.t.* to fasten with a rope; to mark off a race track, etc., with ropes; to lasso. **-ladder, -bridge,** etc. *n.* one made of ropes [O.E. *rap*].

Roque·fort (rōk'·fert) *n.* a cheese of ewe's milk [*Roquefort*, in France].

ror·qual (rawr'·kwal) *n.* a genus of whale [Scand. *röd*, red; *hval*, whale].

Ro·sa·ceae (rō·zā'·sē·ī) *n.pl.* order of plants including rose, strawberry, blackberry, spiraea. **rosaceous** *a.* roselike; belonging to rose family. **rosarium** *n.* rose garden [L. *rosa*, rose].

ro·sa·ry (rō'·za·ri·) *n.* rose garden; string of prayer beads [L. *rosa*, a rose].

rose (rōz) *pa.t.* of **rise.**

rose (rōz) *n.* typical genus (*Rosa*) of plant family of Rosaceae; shade of pink; rosette; perforated nozzle of tube or pipe, as on watering can. **-ate** *a.* rosy; full of roses; blooming; optimistic. **-bud** *n.* the bud of the rose; **—colored** *a.* having color of a rose; unwarrantably optimistic. **— water** *n.* water tinctured with roses by distillation **— window** *n.* circular window with a series of mullions diverging from center. **-wood** *n.* rich, dark red hardwood from S. America, used for furniture making. **rosily** *adv.* **rosiness** *n.* **rosy** *a.* like a rose; blooming; red; blushing; bright; favorable [L. *rosa*, a rose].

rose·mar·y (rōz'·me·ri·) *n.* a small fragrant evergreen shrub, emblem of fidelity [L. *ros*, dew; *marinus*, marine].

ro·sette (rō·zet') *n.* something fashioned to resemble a rose, as ribbon; a rose-shaped architectural ornament. [Fr. dim. of *rose*].

ros·in (ràz'·in) *n.* resin in solid state; *v.t.* to rub or cover with rosin. **-y** *a.* [Fr. *résine*].

ros·ter (ràs'·ter) *n.* a list or plan showing turns of duty; register of names [Dut. *rooster*, a corrupt. of L. *register*].

ros·trum (ràs'·tram) *n.* snout or pointed organ; beak of a ship; raised platform; pulpit. **rostral** *a.* pert. to a rostrum. **rostrate, rostrated** *a.* beaked [L. = a beak].

ros·y, See **rose.**

rot (ràt) *v.t.* and *v.i.* to decompose naturally; to become morally corrupt; to putrefy; to molder away. *pr.p.* **-ting.** *pa.t.* and *pa.p.* **-ted** *n.* rotting; decomposition; decay; disease of sheep, as **foot-rot; dry rot** (*Slang*) nonsense [O.E. *rotian*].

ro·ta (rō'·ta) *n.* roster, list, or roll; an ecclesiastical tribunal in the R.C. church which

acts as court of appeal [L. = wheel].

ro·ta·ry (rō'·ter·i·) *a.* turning, as a wheel; rotatory; *n.* (*Cap.*) international association of business men's clubs. **Rotarian** *n.* member of Rotary Club. **— engine** (*Aero.*) engine in which cylinder and crankcase rotate with propeller [L. *rota*, a wheel].

ro·tate (rō'·tāt) *v.t.* to cause to revolve; *v.i.* to move around pivot; to go in rotation; to revolve; *a.* (*Bot.*) wheel-shaped, as a calyx. **rotation** *n.* turning, as a wheel or solid body on its axis; (*Astron.*) period of rotation of planet about its imaginary axis; serial change, as **rotation of crops. rotational** *a.* **rotator** *n.* **rotatory** *a.* turning on an axis, as a wheel; going in a circle; following in succession [L. *rota*, a wheel].

rote (rōt) *n.* mechanical repetition [O.Fr. *rote*, track].

ro·tis·ser·ie (rō·tis'·er·i·) *n.* grill with a turning spit [Fr. *rotir*, to roast].

ro·tor (rō'·ter) *n.* revolving portion of dynamo, motor, or turbine [short for *rotator*].

rot·ten (ràt'·n) *a.* putrefied; decayed; unsound; corrupt; (*Slang*) bad; worthless. **-ly** *adv.* **-ness** *n.* **rotter** *n.* (*Slang*) a worthless, unprincipled person [fr. *rot*].

ro·tund (rō·tund') *a.* round; globular; plump. **-a** *n.* circular building or hall, covered by dome. **-ity, -ness** *n.* globular form; roundness [L. *rotundus*, fr. *rota*, a wheel].

rou·é (ròò'·ā) *n.* a libertine; a profligate; a rake [Fr. = one broken on the wheel].

rouge (ròòzh) *n.* fine red powder used by jewelers; cosmetic for tinting cheeks; *v.t.* and *v.i.* to tint (face) with rouge [Fr. = red].

rough (ruf) *a.* not smooth; rugged; uneven; unhewn; shapeless; uncut; unpolished; rude; harsh; boisterous; stormy; approximate; having aspirated sound of *h*; *adv.* in rough manner; *n.* crude, unfashioned state; parts of golf course adjoining fairway and greens; *v.t.* to make rough; to roughen; to rough-hew; to shape out in rough and ready way. **-age** *n.* fibrous, unassimilated portions of food which promote intestinal movement. **— diamond,** uncut diamond; a person of ability and worth, but uncouth. **-en** *v.t.* to make rough; *v.i.* to become rough. **—hew** *v.t.* to hew coarsely; to give first form to a thing. **-house** *n.* rowdy, boisterous play. **-ly** *adv.* **-neck** *n.* (*Slang*) ill-mannered fellow; a tough. **-ness** *n.* **to rough it,** to put up with hardship and discomfort [O.E. *ruh*].

rou·lade (ròò·làd') *n.* (*Mus.*) embellishment; trill [Fr. *rouler*, to roll].

rou·leau (ròò·lō') *n.* little roll; roll of coins in paper; little roll or chain of red corpuscles; *pl.* **-x, -s** [Fr. dim. of O.Fr. *role*, a roll].

rou·lette (ròò·let') *n.* game of chance, played with a revolving disk and a ball [Fr. dim. of O.Fr. *roule*, wheel].

round (round) *a.* circular; spherical; curved; whole; total; not fractional, as a number; plump; smooth; flowing, as style or diction; plain; (of vowel) pronounced with rounded lips; *n.* circle; ring; globe; circuit; cycle; series; a course of action performed by persons in turn; toasts; a certain amount (of applause); walk by guard to visit posts, sentries, etc.; beat of policeman, milkman, etc.; a game (of golf); one of successive stages in competition; 3-minute period in boxing match; step of a ladder; ammunition unit; circular dance; short, vocal piece, in which singers start at regular intervals after each other; *adv.* on all sides; circularly; back to the starting point; about; *v.t.* to make circular, spherical, or cylindrical; to go around; to smooth; to finish; *v.i.* to grow or become round or full in form. **-about** *a.* indirect; circuitous. **-el** *n.* round window or panel; kind of dance; rondel; small circular shield. **-elay** *n.* round or country dance; an air or tune in three parts, in which the first strain is repeated in the others. **-er** n. a tool for rounding off objects; one who makes rounds; habitual drunkard or criminal. **Roundhead** n. a Puritan (so called from practice of cropping hair close); republican in time of Commonwealth. **-house** n. (Naut.) a cabin built on after part of quarterdeck; circular building for locomotives. **-ly** adv. vigorously; fully; open. **-ness** n. — **robin** n. petition, etc. having signatures arranged in a circular form so as to give no clue to order of signing. **-table conference,** one where all participants are on equal footing. **-up,** n. collecting cattle into herds; throwing cordon around area by police or military for interrogating all found within; v.t. to collect and bring into confined space. **to round off,** to [Fr. rond].

roup (roop) n. a contagious disease of domestic poultry [O.E. hropan, to cry].

rouse (rouz) v.t. to wake from sleep; to excite to action; to startle or surprise; v.i. to awake from sleep or repose. **-r** n. **rousing** a.

rout (rout) n. tumultuous crowd; rabble; defeat of army or confusion of troops in flight; v.t. to defeat and throw into confusion [L. ruptus, broken].

rout (rout) v.i. to roar; to snore [O.E. hrutan].

rout (rout) v.t. to turn up with the snout; to cut grooves by scooping or gouging; to turn out of bed; v.i. to poke about [fr. root, dig.].

route (root) n. course or way which is traveled or to be followed. **en route,** on the way [Fr.].

rou·tine (roo·tēn′) n. regular course of action adhered to by order or habit; a. in ordinary way of business; according to rule [Fr.].

rove (rōv) v.t. to wander or ramble over; to plough into ridges; v.i. to wander about; to ramble. **-r** n. wanderer; pirate ship; roving machine. **roving** n. and a. [Dut. roofer, a robber].

row (rō) n. persons or things in straight line; a rank; a file; a line [O.E. raw].

row (rō) v.t. to impel (a boat) with oars; to transport, by rowing; v.t. to labor with oars; n. spell of rowing; a trip in a rowboat. **-boat** n. boat impelled solely by oars [O.E. rowan].

row (rou) n. riotous, noisy disturbance; a dispute. **-dy** a. noisy and rough; n. hooligan. **-dyism, -diness** n. [etym. uncertain].

row·an (rō′·an) n. mountain ash producing clusters of red berries. [Scand.].

row·el (rou′·al) n. wheel of a spur, furnished with sharp points [Fr. roue, a wheel].

roy·al (roi′·al) a. pert. to the crown; worthy of, befitting, patronized by, a king or queen; kingly; n. a size of paper; small sail above topgallant-sail; third shoot of stag's horn. **-ism** n. principles of government by king. **-ist** n. adherent to sovereign, or one attached to kingly government. **-ly** adv. **-ty** n. kingship; kingly office; person of king or sovereign; members of royal family; royal prerogative; royal domain; payment to owner of land for right to work minerals, or to inventor for use of his invention, or to author depending on sales of his book [Fr. fr. L. regalis, fr. rex, a king].

rub (rub) v.t. to subject to friction; to abrade; to chafe; to remove by friction; to wipe; to scour; to touch slightly; v.i. to come into contact accompanied by friction; to become frayed or worn with friction. pr.p. **-bing.** pa.t. and pa.p. **-bed.** n. rubbing; difficulty, impediment; a sore spot from rubbing; **-ber** n. **-bing** n. impression of coin, lettering on book, etc. obtained by rubbing thin paper placed on object with pencil or similar article; applying friction to a surface. **to rub in,** to emphasize by constant reiteration [etym. obscure].

rub·ber (rub′·er) n. coagulated sap of certain tropical trees; caoutchouc; gum elastic; India rubber for erasing pencil marks, etc. a series of an odd number, usually three, of games; the winning game in the series; pl. overshoes; galoshes: a. made of rubber. **-ized** a. impregnated or mixed with rubber, as rubberized fabrics. **-neck** n. (Slang) a tourist eager to see every important building, sight, or spectacle [fr. rub].

rub·bish (rub′·ish) n. waste or rejected matter; anything worthless: refuse; nonsense [etym. uncertain].

rub·ble (rub′·l) n. upper fragmentary decomposed mass of stone overlying a solid stratum of rock; masonry built of rough stone, of all sizes and shapes; rough stones used to fill up spaces between walls, etc. **-rubbly** a. [O.Fr. robel, dim. of robe, robbe, trash].

rube (roob) n. (Slang) a farmer; a rustic [abbrev. fr. Reuben].

Ru·bi·con (roo′·bi·kan) n. stream in Italy, between Roman Italy and Cisalpine Gaul. **to cross the Rubicon,** to take a decisive, irrevocable step.

ru·bi·cund (roo′·ba·kund) a. ruddy; florid; reddish. **-ity** n. [L. rubicundus, fr. ruber, red].

ru·bid·i·um (roo·bid′·i·am) n. rare silvery metallic element, one of the alkali metals [L. rubidus, red].

ru·ble (roo′·ble) n. Russian monetary unit. Also **rouble** [Russ. rubl].

ru·bric (roo′·brik) n. medieval manuscript or printed book in which initial letter was illumined in red; heading or portion of such a work, printed in red—hence, the title of a chapter, statute, etc. originally in red; an ecclesiastical injunction or rule; v.t. to illumine with or print in red. **-al** a. colored in red; to formulate as a rubric. **-ian** n. one versed in the rubrics. **rubricist** n. a strict adherent to rubrics; a formalist [L. rubrica, red earth, fr. ruber, red].

ru·by (roo′·bi·) n. a red variety of corundum valued as a gem; purple-tinged red color; a. having the dark-red color of a ruby [L. ruber, red].

ruche (roosh) n. pleated trimming for dresses, sewn down the middle and not at top, as in box pleatings. **ruching** n. material for ruches; ruches collectively [Fr.].

ruck (ruk) v.t. to wrinkle; to crease; v.i. to be drawn into folds; n. fold; crease; wrinkle [O.N. hrukka].

ruck (ruk) n. rank and file; common herd [etym. doubtful].

ruck·sack (ruk′·sak) n. pack carried on back by climbers, etc. [Ger. = 'back-pack'].

ruc·tion (ruk′·shan) n. (Colloq.) disturbance; row; rumpus [perh. fr. eruption].

rudd (rud) n. British fresh-water fish allied to the roach [O.E. rudu, redness].

rud·der (rud′·er) n. flat frame fastened vertically to stern of ship, which controls direction; in plane, flat plane surface hinged to tail unit and used to provide directional control and stability; anything which guides, as a bird's tail-feathers [O.E. rothor].

rud·dle (rud′·l) red ocher, used for marking sheep; v.t. to mark (sheep) with ruddle [O.E. rudu, redness].

rud·dock (rud′·ok) n. European robin [O.E. rudig, reddish].

rud·dy (rud′·i·) a. of a red color; of healthy flesh color; rosy; **ruddiness** n. [O.E. rudig, reddish].

rude (rood) a. uncivil; primitive; roughly made. **-ly** adv. **-ness** n. [L. rudis, rough].

ru·di·ment (roo′·da·mant) n. beginning; germ; vestige; (Biol.) imperfectly developed or formed organ; pl. elements, first principles, beginning (of knowledge, etc.) **-al, -ary** a. **-arily** adv. [L. rudimentum, fr. rudis, rude].

rue (roo) v.t. and v.i. to grieve for; to regret;

to repent of. *pr.p.* **-ing. -ful** *a.* woeful; mournful; sorrowful. **-fully** *adv.* [O.E. *hreowan*, to be sorry for].

rue (ròò) *n.* aromatic, bushy, evergreen shrub; any bitter infusion [L. *ruta*].

ruff (ruf) *n.* broad, circular collar, plaited, crimped, or fluted; something similar; light-brown mottled bird, the male being ringed with ruff or frill of long, black, red-barred feathers during breeding season; (*fem.*) **reeve**; neck fringe of long hair or feathers on animal or bird. **-ed** *a.* [etym. uncertain].

ruff (ruf) *n.* trumping at cards when one cannot follow suit; *v.t.* to trump instead of following suit [O.Fr. *roffle*].

ruf·fi·an (ruf'·i·ạn) *n.* a rough, lawless fellow; desperado; *a.* brutal. **-ism** *n.* conduct of a ruffian. **-ly** [O.Fr. fr. It. *ruffiano*].

ruf·fle (ruf'·l) *v.t.* to make into a ruff; to draw into wrinkles, open plaits, or folds; to furnish with ruffles; to roughen surface of; to annoy; to put out (of temper); *v.i.* to flutter; to jar; to be at variance; to grow rough; *n.* a strip of gathered cloth, attached to a garment, a frill; agitation; commotion [Dut. *ruifelen*, to rumple].

ru·fous (ròò'·fạs) *a.* (*Bot.*) brownish red [L. *rufus*, red].

rug (rug) *n.* piece of carpeting [*Scand.*].

rug·by (rug'·bi·) *n.* English form of football, played with teams of 15 players each [fr. *Rugby*, public school].

rug·ged (rug'·id) *a.* rough; uneven; jagged; wrinkled; harsh; inharmonious; homely; unpolished; sturdy, vigorous. **-ly** *adv.* **-ness** *n.* [rug].

ru·gose (ròò'·gōs) *a.* wrinkled; ridged. **-ly** *adv.* **rugosity** *n.* [L. *ruga*, a wrinkle].

ru·in (ròò'·in) *n.* downfall; remains of demolished or decayed city, fortress, castle, work of art, etc.; state of being decayed; *v.t.* to bring to ruin; to injure; to spoil; to mar; to cause loss of fortune or livelihood to. **-s** *n.pl.* ruined buildings, etc. **-ation** *n.* state of being ruined; act or cause of ruining. **-er** *n.* **-ous** *a.* fallen to ruin; dilapidated; injurious; destructive. **-ously** *adv.* [L. *ruina*, fr. *ruere*, to rush down].

rule (ròòl) *n.* act, power, or mode of directing; government; sway; control; authority; precept; prescribed law; established principle or mode of action; regulation; habitual practice; standard; an instrument to draw straight lines; (*Print.*) thin strip of brass or type metal, type high, to print a line or lines; *v.t.* to govern; to control; to determine; to decide authoritatively; to mark with straight lines, using ruler; *v.i.* to have command; to order by rule; to prevail. **-r** *n.* one who rules; sovereign; instrument with straight edges for drawing lines. **ruling** *a.* governing; managing; predominant; *n.* an authoritative decision; a point of law settled by a court of law [L. *regula*, fr. *regere*, to govern].

rum (rum) *n.* spirit distilled from sugar-cane skimmings or molasses. **-runner** *n.* smuggler. **-my** *n.* (*Slang*) a drunkard [etym. uncertain].

rum·ba (rum'·bạ) *n.* Cuban dance [Sp.].

rum·ble (rum'·bl) *v.i.* to make a low, vibrant, continuous sound; to reverberate; *v.t.* to cause to roll along or utter with a low heavy sound; to polish in a tumbling box *n.* dull, vibrant, confused noise, as of thunder; seat for footmen at back of carriage; a tumbling box; (*Slang*) fight. **-r** *n.* [imit.].

ru·mi·nant (ròò'·mạ·nạnt) *n.* animal which chews cud, as sheep, cow; *a.* chewing cud. **ruminate** *v.t.* to chew over again; to ponder over; to muse on; *v.i.* to chew cud; to meditate. **ruminatingly** *adv.* **rumination** *n.* **ruminative** *a.* **ruminator** *n.* [L. *ruminare*, to chew cud].

rum·mage (rum'·ij) *v.t.* to search thoroughly into or through; to ransack; *v.i.* to make a search; *n.* careful search; odds and ends. **-r** *n.* [orig. stowage of casks, O.Fr. *arrumage*].

rum·my (rum'·i·) *n.* a simple card game for any number of players.

ru·mor (ròò'·mẹr) *n.* current but unproved report; common talk; *v.t.* to spread as a rumor [L. *rumor*, noise].

rump (rump) *n.* end of backbone of animal with the parts adjacent; buttocks; hinder part; remnant of anything [Scand.].

rum·ple (rum'·pl) *v.t.* to muss; to crease; to crumple; *n.* an irregular fold [O.E. *hrimpan*, to wrinkle].

rum·pus (rum'·pạs) *n.* (*Colloq.*) an uproar; a noisy disturbance [etym. doubtful].

run (run) *v.i.* to move rapidly on legs; to hurry; to contend in a race; to stand as candidate for; to travel or sail regularly; to extend; to retreat; to flee; to flow; to continue in operation; to continue without falling due, as a promissory note or bill; to have legal force; to fuse; to melt; to average; to turn or rotate; to be worded; *v.t.* to cause to run; to drive, push, or thrust; to manage; to maintain regularly, as bus service; to operate; to evade (a blockade); to smuggle; to incur (risk). *pr.p.* **-ning.** *pa.t.* **ran.** *pa.p.* **run.** *n.* flow; channel; act of running; course run; regular, scheduled journey; pleasure trip by car, cycle, etc.; unconstrained liberty; range of ground for grazing cattle, feeding poultry, etc.; trend; kind or variety; vogue; point gained in cricket or baseball; a great demand; period play holds the stage; (*Mus.*) rapid scale passage, roulade. **-about** *n.* motorboat or a small open car; a gadabout. **-away** *n.* fugitive; horse which has bolted. **-ner** *n.* one taking part in a race; messenger; a long, slender prostrate stem which runs along the ground; one of curved pieces on which sleigh, skate, etc slides; device for facilitating movement of sliding doors, etc.; narrow strip of carpet; smuggler. **-ner-up** *n.* one who gains second place. **-ning** *a.* flowing; entered for a race, as a horse; successive (numbers); continuous (as an order, account); discharging (pus); cursive; easy in style; effortless; *n.* moving or flowing quickly; chance of winning; operation of machine, business, etc. **-ning board** *n.* narrow, horizontal platform running along locomotive, carriage, car, etc., to provide step for entering or leaving. **-ning commentary,** broadcast description of event by eye-witness. **-ning knot,** knot made so as to tighten when rope is pulled. **-way** *n.* prepared track on airfields for landing and taking off. **also ran,** an unsuccessful competitor. **in the long run,** in the end; ultimately. **to run amok,** to go mad. **to run riot,** to give way to excess. **to run to earth,** to capture after a long pursuit [O.E. *rinnan*].

run·dle (run'·dl) *n.* a rung or step of a ladder; something which rotates like a wheel [fr. *round*].

rune (ròòn) *n.* letter or character of old Teutonic and Scandinavian alphabets; magic; mystery. **runic** *a.* [O.N. *run*, a mystery].

rung (rung) *pa.p.* of **ring.**

rung (rung) *n.* rounded step of a ladder; crossbar or spoke [O.E. *hrung*, a beam].

run·nel (run'·ạl) *n.* small brook or rivulet; a gutter [O.E. *rinnelle*, a brook].

runt (runt) *n.* small, weak specimen of any animal, person or thing [etym. doubtful].

ru·pee (ròò·pē') *n.* standard Indian monetary unit, silver coin [Urdu, *rupiyah*].

rup·ture (rup'·chẹr) *n.* breaking or bursting; state of being violently parted; breach of concord between individuals or nations; hernia; forcible bursting, breaking, or tearing of a bodily organ or structure; *v.t.* to part by violence; to burst (a blood-vessel, etc.) [L.

ruptura, fr. *rumpere*, to break].

ru·ral (roo′·rạl) *a.* pert. to the country; pert. to farming or agriculture; rustic; pastoral. **-ize** *v.t.* to make rural; *v.i.* to live in the country; to become rural. **-ism** *n.* **-ly** *adv.* [L. *ruralis*, fr. *rus*, the country].

ruse (rόoz) *n.* artifice; trick; strategem [Fr.].

rush (rush) *v.t.* to carry along violently and rapidly; to take by sudden assault; to hasten forward; *v.i.* to move violently or rapidly; to speed; *n.* heavy current of water, air, etc.; haste; eager demand (for an article); **-er** *n.* [M.E. *ruschen*].

rush (rush) *n.* name of plants of genus Juncus, found in marshy places; stem as a material for baskets, etc.; thing of little worth; taper; straw. **—bottomed** *a.* of chair with seat made of rushes. **-y** *a.* [O.E. *rysc*].

rusk (rusk) *n.* biscuit or light, hard bread [Sp. *rosca*, roll of bread].

rus·set (rus′·it) *a.* of reddish-brown color; *n.* homespun cloth dyed this color; apple of russet color [Fr. *roux*, red].

Rus·sian (rush′·ạn) *a.* pert. to Russia; *n.* general name for Slav races in Russia; native or inhabitant of Russia; Russian language. **Russo-** *prefix* Russian. **— dressing** *n.* mayonnaise mixed with catchup or chili sauce.

rust (rust) *n.* coating formed on iron or various other metals by corrosion; reddish fungus disease on plants; *v.t.* to corrode with rust; to impair by inactivity; *v.i.* to become rusty; to dissipate one's potential powers by inaction. **-ily** *adv.* **-iness** *n.* **— proof** *a.* not liable to rust. **-y** *a.* [O.E.].

rus·tic (rus′·tik) *a.* pert. to the country; rural; awkward; *n.* a simple country person. **-ally** *adv.* **-ate** *v.t.* to compel to reside in country; to make rustic; *v.i.* to live in the country. **-ation** *n.* **-ity** *n.* [L. *rusticus*, fr. *rus*, the country].

rus·tle (rus′·l) *v.i.* to make soft, swishing sounds, like rubbing of silk cloth or dry leaves; (*Slang*) to be active and on the move; *v.t.* (*U.S.*) to steal, esp. cattle; *n.* a soft whispering sound. **-r** *n.* one who, or that which, rustles; (*Slang*) hustler; cattle thief. **rustling** *n.* [imit. origin].

rut (rut) *n.* furrow made by wheel; settled habit or way of living; groove; *v.t.* to form ruts in; *pr.p.* **-ting.** *pa.t.* and *pa.p.* **-ted** [Fr. *route*, a way, track, etc.].

rut (rut) *n.* time of sexual excitement and urge among animals, esp. of deer; *v.i.* to be in heat [O.Fr. fr. L. *rugire*, to roar].

ruth·less (rόoth′·lạs) *a.* pitiless; cruel. **-ly** *adv.* **-ness** *n.* [*rue*].

rye (rī) *n.* a kind of grass allied to wheat, whiskey made from rye [O.E. *ryge*].

S

Sab·bath (sab′·ạth) *n.* seventh day of week; Sunday; Lord's Day. **Sabbatarian** *n.* member of certain Christian sects, e.g. Seventh-day Adventists, who observe seventh day Saturday, as the Sabbath; strict observer of Sabbath. **Sabbatarianism** *n.* **Sabbatic, -al** *a.* pert. to Sabbath; (*l.c.*) rest-bringing. *n.* (*l.c.*) a period of leave from a job. **Sabbatical year,** in the Jewish ritual, every seventh, in which the lands were left untilled, etc.; (*l.c.*) a year periodically interrupting one's normal course of work, wholly devoted to further intensive study or one's special subject [Heb. *shabbath*].

saber (sā′·ber) *n.* sword with broad and heavy blade, slightly curved toward the point; cavalry sword; *v.t.* to wound or cut down with saber. Also **sabre** [Fr.]

Sa·bine (sā′·bīn) *n.* one of an ancient tribe of Italy who became merged with the Romans; *a.* pert. to the Sabines.

sa·ble (sā′·bl) *n.* small carnivorous mammal of weasel tribe; sable fur; (*Her.*) tincture or color black; *pl.* mourning garments; *a.* black; made of sable [O.Fr.].

sab·ot (sab′·ō) *n.* a wooden shoe worn by the peasantry of France and Belgium [Fr.].

sab·o·tage (sa·bạ·tázh′) *n.* willful damage or destruction of property perpetrated for political or economic reasons. **saboteur** *n.* one who commits sabotage [Fr. *sabot*].

sac (sak) *n.* pouch-like structure or receptacle in animal or plant; cyst-like cavity [Fr. = sack].

saccharin, saccharine (sak′·ạ·rin) *n.* a white crystalline solid substance, with an intensely sweet taste. **saccharine** *a.* pert. to sugar; over-sweet; cloying; sickly sentimental. **saccharify** *v.t.* to convert into sugar. **saccharinity** *n.* **saccharize** *v.t.* to convert into sugar. **saccharoid, -al** *a.* having granular texture resembling that of loaf sugar. **saccharose** *n.* cane sugar [Gk. *sakchari*, sugar].

sac·cule (sak′·ūl) *n.* a small sac. **saccular** *a.* like a sac [dim. of L. *saccus*, a bag].

sac·er·do·tal (sas·er·dō′·tạl) *a.* pert. to priests, or to the order of priests. **-ism** *n.* the system, spirit, or character of priesthood; **-ist** *n.* **-ly** *adv.* [L. *sacerdos*, a priest].

sa·chem (sā′·chạm) *n.* a Red Indian chief; a political boss, esp. a Tammany leader [Amer.-Ind.].

sa·chet (sa·shā′) *n.* a small scent-bag or perfume cushion [Fr.].

sack (sak) *n.* a large bag, usually of coarse material; contents of sack; also **sacque,** loose garment or cloak; any bag; *v.t.* to put into sacks. **-cloth** *n.* coarse fabric of great strength used for making sacks; in Scripture, garment worn in mourning or as penance. **-ful** *n.* quantity which fills sack. **-ing** *n.* coarse cloth or canvas. **— race** *n.* race in which legs of contestants are encased in sacks [Heb. *saq.* a coarse cloth].

sack (sak) *n.* old name for various kinds of dry wines, esp. Spanish sherry [Fr. *sec*, dry].

sack (sak) *v.t.* to plunder or pillage; to lay waste; *n.* pillage of town. **-ing** *n.* [Fr. *sac*, plunder].

sac·ra·ment (sak′·rạ·mạnt) *n.* one of the ceremonial observances in Christian Church. Lord's Supper; solemn oath; materials used in a sacrament. **-al** *n.* any observance, ceremony, or act of the nature of a sacrament instituted by R.C. Church; *a.* belonging to, or of nature of, sacrament; sacred. **-ally** *adv.* **-arian** *n.* one who believes in efficacy of sacraments. **-arianism** *n.* [L. *sacer*, sacred].

sac·ri·fice (sak′·rạ·fīs, ·fīz) *v.t.* to consecrate ceremonially offering of victim by way of expiation or propitiation to deity; to surrender for sake of obtaining some other advantage; to offer up; to immolate; *v.i.* to make offerings to God of things consumed on the altar; *n.* anything consecrated and offered to divinity; anything given up for sake of others. **-r** *n.* **sacrificial** *a.* relating to, performing, sacrifice. **sacrificially** *adv.* [L. *sacrificium*].

sac·ri·lege (sak′·rạ·lij) *n.* profanation of sacred place or thing; church robbery. **sacrilegious** *a.* violating sacred things; profane; desecrating. **sacrilegiously** *adv.* **sacrilegiousness** *n.* [L. *sacer*, sacred; *legere*, to gather].

sac·ris·tan (sak′·ris·tạn) *n.* officer in church

entrusted with care of sacristy or vestry. sexton. **sacristy** *n.* vestry [L. *sacer*, sacred].

sac·ro·sanct (sak′·rō·sangkt) *a.* inviolable and sacred in the highest degree. **-ity** *n.* [L. *sacrosanctus*, consecrated].

sa·crum (sā′·kram) *n.* a composite bone, triangular in shape, at the base of the spinal column. *pl.* **sacra** [L. = the sacred (bone)].

sad (sad) *a.* sorrowful; affected with grief; deplorably bad; somber-colored. **-den** *v.t.* to make sad or sorrowful; *v.i.* to become sorrowful and downcast. **-ly** *adv.* **-ness** *n.* [O.E. *saed*, sated].

sad·dle (sad′·l) *n.* rider's seat to fasten on horse, or form part of a cycle, etc.; part of a shaft; joint of mutton or venison containing part of backbone with ribs on each side; ridge of hill between higher hills; *v.t.* to put a saddle upon; to burden with; to encumber. **-bag** *n.* one of two bags united by strap and hanging on either side of horse. **-bow** *n.* bow or arch in front of saddle. **-cloth** *n.* housing or cloth placed upon saddle. **-girth** *n.* band passing under belly of horse to hold saddle in place. **— horse** *n.* horse for riding, as distinguished from one for driving. **-r** *n.* one who makes saddles and harness for horses. **saddlery** *n.* materials for making saddles and harness; occupation of saddler; room for storing saddles. **—shaped** *a.* **-tree** *n.* frame of saddle [O.E. *sadol*].

sad·ism (sā′·dizm, sad′·izm) *n.* insatiate love of inflicting pain for its own sake. **sadist** *n.* one who practices this; a consistently inhumane person. **sadistic** *a.* [Marquis de *Sade* (1740-1814) whose writings exemplify it].

sa·fa·ri (sa·fà′·ri·) *n.* hunting expedition [Swahili, *safar*, a journey].

safe (sāf) *a.* free from harm; unharmed; unhurt; sound; protected; sure; *n.* a fireproof chest for protection of money and valuables; case with wire gauze panels to keep meat, etc. fresh. **—conduct** *n.* passport to pass through a dangerous zone. **— deposit** *a.* pert. to box or vault where valuables are stored and protected. **-guard** *n.* protection; precaution; convoy; escort; passport; *v.t.* to make safe; to protect. **-ly** *adv.* **-ness** *n.* **-ty** *n.* **-ty belt** *n.* belt to keep person afloat in water, to prevent injury in automobile, aircraft, etc. **-ty-catch** *n.* contrivance to prevent accidental discharge of gun. **-ty razor** *n.* one in which blade fits into holder with guard to ensure safety for rapid shaving. **-ty valve** *n.* automatic valve fitted to boiler, to permit escape of steam when pressure reaches danger point; outlet for pent-up emotion [Fr. *sauf*, fr. L. *salvus*].

saf·fron (saf′·ran) *n.* plant of iris family, used in medicine and as a flavoring and coloring in cookery; *a.* deep yellow [Fr. *safran*].

sag (sag) *v.i.* to sink in middle; to hang sideways or curve downwards under pressure; to give way; to tire. *pr.p.* **-ging**. *pa.p.* **-ged**. *n.* a droop [M.E. *saggen*].

sa·ga (sà′·ga) *n.* a prose narrative, written in Iceland in the 12th and 13th centuries, concerning legendary and historic people and actions of Iceland and Norway; novels describing life of a family [O.N. = a tale].

sa·ga·cious (sa·gā′·shas) *a.* quick of thought; acute; shrewd. **-ly** *adv.* **-ness**, **sagacity** *n.* shrewdness; discernment; wisdom [L. *sagax*].

sage (sāj) *n.* dwarf shrub of mint family, used for flavoring [Fr. *sauge*, fr. L. *salvia*].

sage (sāj) *a.* wise; discerning; solemn; *n.* wise man. **-ly** *adv.* **-ness** *n.* [Fr. fr. L. *sapere*, to be wise].

sage-brush (sāj′·brush) *n.* a shrub smelling like sage and found chiefly on western plains of U.S.

Sa·git·ta (saj′·it·a) *n.* a constellation north

of Aquila—the Arrow. **sagittal, sagittate** *a.* shaped like an arrow or arrowhead. **sagittally** *adv.* **Saggitarius** *n.* the Archer, 9th sign of zodiac; constellation in Milky Way [L. = arrow].

sa·go (sā′·gō) *n.* dry, granulated starch [Malay, *sagu*].

sa·hib (sà′·ib) *n.* (fem. **sahiba** or **mem sahib**) courtesy title in India for European or high-born Indian [Ar. = lord, master].

said (sed) *pa.t.* and *pa.p.* of **say**; the before-mentioned; already specified; aforesaid.

sail (sāl) *n.* sheet of canvas to catch wind for propelling ship; sailing vessel; a journey upon the water; arm of windmill; *v.t.* to navigate; to pass in a ship; to fly through; *v.i.* to travel by water; to begin a voyage; to glide in stately fashion. **-able** *a.* navigable. **-boat** *n.* a boat propelled by sails. **-cloth** *n.* canvas used in making sails. **-ing** *n.* art of navigating. **-less** *a.* **-or** *n.* mariner; seaman; tar. **-or-hat** *n.* straw hat. **full sail**, with all sails set. **under sail**, to have sails spread. **to sail close to the wind**, to sail with sails of ship barely full; to run great risks. **to sail under false colors**, to act under false pretenses [O.E. *segel*].

saint (sānt) *n.* outstandingly devout and virtuous person; one of the blessed in heaven; one formally canonized by R.C. Church; *v.t.* to canonize. **-ed** *a.* pious; hallowed; sacred; dead. **-hood** *n.* **—like, -ly** *a.* devout; godly; pious. **-liness** *n.* **-'s day**, day on which falls celebration of particular saint. **All-Saints' Day**, 1st November. **St. Bernard**, dog famous for guiding and rescuing travelers lost in snow. **St. Patrick's Day**, 17th March. **St. Valentine's Day**, 14th February. **St. Vitus's dance**, chorea. **Latter-day Saints**, the Mormons. **patron saint**, saint held to be a protector [Fr. fr. L. *sanctus*, consecrated].

sake (sāk) *n.* cause; behalf; purpose; account; regard. **for the sake of**, on behalf of [O.E. *sacu*, dispute at law].

sa·ke (sà′·ki) *n.* national beverage of Japan, fermented from rice [Jap.].

sal (sal) *n.* salt (much used in compound words pert. esp. to pharmacy).**— ammoniac** *n.* ammonium chloride, used in composition of electric batteries and in medicine as expectorant and stomachic. **— volatile** *n.* mixture of ammonium carbonate with oil of nutmeg, oil of lemon and alcohol, used as a stimulant, antacid, or expectorant [L.].

sa·laam (sa·làm′) *n.* salutation, a low bow, of ceremony or respect in the East; *v.t.* to salute; to greet [Ar. = peace].

sa·la·cious (sa·lā′·shas) *a.* lustful; lewd; lecherous. **-ly** *adv.* **-ness**, **salacity** *n.* [L. *salax*, fr. *salire*, to leap].

sal·ad (sal′·ad) *n.* green vegetables raw or cooked, meat, fish, fruit, dressed with various seasonings or dressings. **—dressing** *n.* a sauce for salads. **— days**, early years of youthful inexperience [Fr. *salade*, fr. L. *sal*, salt].

sal·a·man·der (sal′·a·man·der) *n.* small, tailed amphibian, allied to newt. **salamandriform, salamandrine** *a.* pert. to or shaped like a salamander; fire-resisting [Gk. *salamandra*].

sa·la·mi (sa·là′·mi·) *n.* Italian salted sausage.

sal·a·ry (sal′·a·ri·) *n.* fixed remuneration, usually monthly, for services rendered; stipend. **salaried** *a.* [L. *salarilum*, saltmoney, soldier's pay].

sale (sāl) *n.* exchange of anything for money; demand (for article); public exposition of goods; a special disposal of stock at reduced prices. **-able, salable** *a.* capable of being sold. **-ableness** *n.* **-ably** *adv.* **— price** *n.*

special, low price. **-sman** *n.* man who sells. **-smanship** *n.* art of selling goods. **-swoman** *n.* [O.E. *sala*].

sal·i·cin (sal'·a·sin) *n.* a bitter white crystalline glucocide obtained from bark of aspen and used as drug. **salicylate** *n.* any salt of salicylic acid. **salicylic** *a.* derived from salicin. **salicylic acid,** white crystalline solid obtained from aspen bark or synthetically from phenol [L. *salix*, a willow].

sa·li·ent (sā'·li·ant) *a.* moving by leaps; pro-angle formed by intersection of adjacent surfaces; projecting angle in line of fortifications, etc. **-ly** *adv.* [L. *salire*, to leap].

sa·lif·er·ous (sa·lif'·er·as) *a.* bearing or producing salt [L. *sal*, salt; *ferre*, to bear].

sal·i·fy (sal'·a·fī) *v.t.* to form a salt by combining an acid with a base; to combine with a salt. **salifiable** *a.*

sa·line (sā'·līn) *a.* of or containing salt; salty; *n.* a saline medicine. **salina** *n.* salt marsh; saltworks. **saliniferous** *a.* producing salt. **salinity** *n.* [L. *salinus*].

sa·li·va (sa·lī'·va) *n.* digestive fluid or spittle, secreted in mouth by salivary glands. **-ry** *a.* pert. to, producing saliva. **-te** *v.t.* to produce abnormal secretion of saliva [L.].

sal·low (sal'·ō) *a.* of sickly yellow color; of pale, unhealthy complexion. **-ish** *a.* **-ness** *n.* [O.E. *salo*].

sal·ly (sal'·i·) *n.* sudden eruption; issuing of troops from besieged place to attack enemy; sortie; witticism; *v.i.* to issue suddenly. [L. *satire*, to leap].

salm·on (sam'·an) *n.* silver-scaled fish with orange-pink flesh. **—pink** *n.* orange pink. **— trout** *n.* sea or white-trout, fish resembling salmon in color but smaller [L. *salmo*].

sa·lon (sa·lȧn') *n.* spacious apartment for reception of company; half for exhibition of art [Fr.]

sa·loon (sa·lòòn') *n.* public dining room; principal cabin in steamer; a place where liquor is sold and drunk. [Fr. *salon*].

sal·si·fy, salsafy (sal'·sa·fi·) *n.* hardy, biennial, composite herb with edible root; oyster plant [Fr. fr. It. *sassefrica*, goat's beard].

salt (sawlt) *n.* sodium chloride or common salt, substance used for seasoning food and for preservation of meat, etc; compound resulting from reaction between acid and a base; savor; piquancy; wit; (*Colloq.*) an old sailor; *pl.* (*Chem.*) combinations of acids with alkaline or salifiable bases; (*Med.*) saline cathartics, as Epsom, Rochelle, etc.; *a.* containing or tasting of salt; preserved with salt; pungent; *v.t.* to season or treat with salt. **-er** *n.* **-ern** *n.* saltworks. **-ing** *n.* land covered regularly by tide. **-less** *a.* **— lick** *n.* salt for animals to lick. **— marsh** *n.* land with low growth liable to be overflowed by sea. **-ness** *n.* salt taste; state of being salt. **—water** *n.* water impregnated with salt; sea water. **-y** *a.* **salt of the earth,** persons of the highest reputation or worth. **to take with a grain of salt,** to be sceptical of [O.E. *sealt*].

sal·tant (sal'·tant) *a.* leaping; jumping; dancing. **saltation** *n.* [L. *salire*, to leap].

sal·tire, saltier (sal'·tir) *n.* cross in the shape of an X, or St. Andrew's cross [O.Fr. *saulloir*].

salt·pe·ter (sawlt'·pē'·ter) *n.* common name for niter or potassium nitrate, used in manufacture of glass, nitric acid, etc. [L. *sal petrae*, salt of the rock].

sa·lu·bri·ous (sa·lū'·bri·as) *a.* wholesome; healthy. **-ly** *adv.* **-ness, salubrity** *n.* [L. *salus*, health].

sal·u·tar·y (sal'·ya·ter·i·) *a.* wholesome; resulting in good; healthful; beneficial. **salutar-**

ily *adv.* **salutariness** *n.* [L. *salus*, health].

sa·lute (sa·lūt') *v.t.* to address with expressions of kind wishes; to recognize one of superior rank by a sign; to honor by a discharge of cannon or small arms, by striking colors, etc.; to greet; *n.* greeting showing respect. **salutation** *n.* saluting; words uttered in welcome; opening words of a letter. **salutatory** *a.* welcoming; *n.* opening address of welcome at commencement exercises of school or college. **salutatorian** *n.* student of graduating class who delivers such an address [L. *salutare*, to wish health to].

salvage See **salve.**

sal·va·tion (sal·vā'·shan) *n.* preservation from destruction; redemption; deliverance. **Salvation Army,** international religious organization for revival of religion among the masses. **Salvationist** *n.* active member of Salvation Army [L. *salvare*, to save].

salve (salv) *v.t.* to save or retrieve property from danger or destruction. **salvability** *n.* **salvable** *a.* capable of being used or reconstructed in spite of damage. **salvage** *n.* compensation allowed to persons who assist in saving ship or cargo, or property in general, from destruction; property, so saved; *v.t.* to save from ruins, shipwreck, etc. **-r, salvor** *n.* [L. *salvare*, to save].

salve (sav) *n.* healing ointment applied to wounds or sores; *v.t.* to anoint with such; to heal; to soothe (conscience) [O.E. *sealf*].

sal·ver (sal'·ver) *n.* a tray for visiting cards [Sp. *salva*, a foretasting, fr. L. *salvare*, to save].

sal·vo (sal'·vō) *n.* guns fired simultaneously, or in succession as salute; sustained applause or welcome from large crowd. *pl.* **salvo(e)s** [It. *salva*, a volley].

sal volatile See **sal.**

Sa·mar·i·tan (sa·mar'·a·tan) *a.* pert. to Samaria in Palestine; *n.* native or inhabitant of Samaria; kind-hearted, charitable person (fr. parable of good Samaritan, Luke 10).

sam·ba (sam'·ba) *n.* a dance of S. American origin; the music for such a dance [Sp.].

sam·bo (sam'·bō) *n.* offspring of black person and mulatto [Sp. *zambo*].

Sam Browne (sam broun) *n.* military belt.

same (sām) *a.* identical; not different; of like kind; unchanged; uniform; aforesaid. **-ly** *adv.* **-ness** *n.* near resemblance; uniformity [O.N. *samr*].

sam·ite (sam'·īt) *n.* rich silk material; any lustrous silk stuff [Fr. *samit*, fr. Gk. *hexamitos*, woven with six threads].

sam·o·var (sam'·a·vȧr) *n.* Russian tea urn.

Sam·o·yed (sam'·a·yed) *n.* Mongolian race inhabiting N. shores of Russia and Siberia; breed of dog, orig. a sledge dog.

sam·pan (sam'·pan) *n.* a Chinese light river vessel. Also **sanpan** [Malay fr. Chin. *san*, three; *pan*, a board].

sam·phire (sam'·fīr) *n.* European herb found on rocks and cliffs, St. Peter's wort [corrupt. fr. Fr. *Saint Pierre*].

sam·ple (sam'·pl) *n.* specimen; example; *v.t.* to take or give a sample of; to try; to test; to taste. **-r** *n.* one who samples; beginner's exercise in embroidery [M.E. *essample*; fr. L. *exemplum*, example].

sam·u·rai (sam'·oo·rī) *n.* (*s.* and *pl.*) member of hereditary military caste in Japan from 12th to mid 19th cent. [Jap.].

san·a·tive (san'·a·tiv) *a.* having power to cure or heal. **-ness** *n.* **sanatorium** *n.* (*pl.* **sanatoria**) institution for open-air treatment of tuberculosis; institution for convalescent patients. Also **sanitarium.** See **sanitary.** **sanatory** *a.* healing [L. *sanare*, to heal].

sanc·ti·fy (sangk'·ta·fī) *v.t.* to set apart as sacred or holy; to hallow; to consecrate; to purify. **sanctification** n. purification and freedom from sin. **sanctified** a. hallowed; sanctimonious. **sanctifiedly** adv. **sanctimonious** a. hypocritically pious. **sanctimoniously** adv. **sanctimoniousness, sanctimony** n. affected piety. **sanctitude** n. saintliness; holiness. **sanctity** n. quality of being sacred; state of being pure and devout; state of being solemnly binding on one; inviolability [L. sanctus, holy].

sanc·tion (sangk'·shan) n. solemn ratification; express permission; authorization; approval; legal use of force to secure obedience to law; anything which serves to secure obedience to law; anything which serves to move a person to observe or refrain from given mode of conduct; v.t. and v.i. to confirm; to authorize; to countenance. **sanctions** n.pl. measures to enforce fulfillment of international treaty obligations [L. sanctus, holy].

sanc·tu·ar·y (sangk'·choo·er·i·) n. holy place; shrine; the chancel; a church or other place of protection for fugitives. **sanctum** n. sacred place; private room or study. **sanctum sanctorum,** holy of holies in Jewish temple; exclusive private place [L. sanctus, holy].

sand (sand) n. fine, loose grains of quartz or other mineral matter formed by disintegration of rocks; n.pl. sandy beach; desert region; moments of time; v.t. to sprinkle or cover with sand; to smooth with sandpaper. **-bag** n. bag filled with sand or earth, for repairing breaches in fortification, etc. **-bank** n. shoal of sand thrown up by sea. — **bar** n. barrier of sand facing entrance of river estuary. **-blast** n. jet of sand driven by a blast of air or steam, for roughening, cleaning, cutting. — **dune** n. ridge of loose sand. **-ed** a. sprinkled with sand. — **glass** n. hourglass, instrument for measuring time by running of sand. **-iness** n. state of being sandy; a sandy color. **-ing** n. cleaning up wood by rubbing with sandpaper. **-paper** n. stout paper or cloth coated with glue and then sprinkled over with sand, used as an abrading agent for smoothing wood, etc. v.t. to smooth with sandpaper. **-piper** n. small wading bird of plover family. **-stone** n. rock employed for building and making grindstones. **-storm** n. a storm of wind carrying dust. **-y** a. like or covered with sand; not firm or stable; yellowish brown [O.E.].

san·dal (san'·dal) n. a shoe consisting of flat sole, bound to foot by straps or thongs. **-led** a. [Gk. sandalon].

san·dal·wood (san'·dal·wood) n. fragrant heartwood of santalum [Ar. sandal].

sand·er·ling (san'·der·ling) n. a wading bird of the plover family.

sand·wich (sand'·wich) n. two thin pieces of bread with slice of meat, etc., between them (said to have been a favorite dish of Earl of Sandwich); v.t. to make into sandwich; to form of alternating layers of different nature; to insert or squeeze in between, making a tight fit. — **man** n. man carrying two advertising boards, one slung before and one behind him.

sane (sān) a. of sound mind; not deranged; rational; reasonable; lucid. **-ly** adv. **-ness** n. [L. sanus, healthy].

sang (sang) pa.t. of **sing.**

sang-froid (sản·frwả') n. composure of mind; imperturbability [Fr. sang, blood; froid, cold].

san·guine (sang'·gwin) a. hopeful; confident; cheerful; deep red; florid; n. a crayon; blood-red color. **sanguinarily** adv. **sanguinariness** n. **sanguinary** a. bloody; bloodthirsty; murderous. **-ly** adv. **-ness** n. **-ous** a. bloody; blood-red; blood-stained; containing blood. [L. sanguis, blood].

San·he·drin (san'·hē·drin) n. supreme court

of Ancient Jerusalem; any similar Jewish assembly. Also **Sanhedrim.** [Heb. fr. Gk. sun, together; hedra, seat].

san·i·tar·y (san'·a·te·ri·) a. pert. to health; hygienic; clean; free from dirt, germs, etc. **sanitarian** n. one interested in the promotion of hygienic reforms. **sanitarily** adv. **sanitation** n. the measures taken to promote health and to prevent disease; hygiene. **sanitarium,** n. private hospital for treatment of special or chronic diseases; health retreat; sanitorium. **sanitary napkin,** pad or absorbent material for use during menstruation [L. sanitas, health].

san·i·ty (san'·a·ti·) n. state of being sane; soundness of mind [L. sanus, sane].

sank (sangk) pa.t. of the verb **sink.**

sans·cu·lotte (sanz·kū·lat') n. ragged fellow; a name given in the first French Revolution to extreme republican party [Fr. = without knee breeches].

San·skrit, Sanscrit (san'·skrit) n. classic literary language of ancient India, member of Indo-European family of languages [Sans. samskrita, perfected, finished].

San·ta Claus (san'·ta klawz) n. traditional 'Father Christmas' of children [corrupt. of St. Nicholas, patron saint of children].

sap (sap) n. watery juice of plants, containing mineral salts, proteins and carbohydrates; (Slang) a stupid person. **-head** n. (Slang) dolt. **-less** a. **-ling** n. young tree; youth. doltishness. **-py** a. juicy; (Slang) silly. **-wood** n. alburnum, exterior part of wood of tree next to bark [O.E. saep].

sap (sap) n. tunnel driven under enemy positions for purpose of attack; v.t. and v.i. to undermine; to impair insidiously; to exhaust gradually. pr.p. **-ping.** pa.t. and pa.p. **-ped** [It. zappa, a spade].

sap·id (sap'·id) a. savory; palatable; tasty. **-ity** n. [L. sapere, to taste].

sa·pi·ent (sā'·pi·ant) a. discerning; wise; sage. **sapience** n. **-ly** adv. [L. sapiens, wise].

sap·o·na·ceous (sap·a·nā'·shas) a. resembling soap; slippery, as if soaped. **saponify** v.t. to convert into soap. **saponin** n. glucoside obtained from many plants used for foam baths, fire extinguishers, detergents, etc. due to frothy qualities [L. sapo, soap].

sa·por (sā'·per) n. taste; savor; flavor. **-oific** a. producing taste or flavor. **-osity** n. [L. = taste].

Sap·phic (saf'·ik) a. pert. to Sappho, lyric poetess of Greece of 7th cent. B.C.; denoting verse in which three lines of five feet each are followed by line of two feet; n. Sapphic verse. **sapphism** n. unnatural sexual relations between women.

sap·phire (saf'·īr) n. translucent precious stone of various shades of blue; a. deep, pure blue [Gk. sapheiros].

sar·a·band (sar'·a·band) n. slow, stately dance, introduced by Moors into Spain in 16th cent.; in England, country dance [Pers. sarband, a fillet].

Sar·a·cen (sar'·a·san) n. Arab or Mohammedan who invaded Europe and Africa; an infidel. **-ic, -ical** a. [L. Saracenus].

Sar·a·to·ga trunk (sar·a·tō'·ga·trungk) n. a large trunk for ladies' dresses.

sar·casm (sár·kazm) n. taunt; scoffing gibe; veiled sneer; irony; use of such expressions. **sarcastic, -al** a. bitterly satirical and cutting; taunting. **sarcastically** adv. [Gk. sarkasmos].

sar·coph·a·gus (sár·káf'·a·gas) n. kind of limestone used by Greeks for coffins and believed to consume flesh of bodies deposited in it; stone coffin; monumental chest or case of stone, erected over graves. pl. **sarcophagi** [Gk. sarx, flesh; phagein, to eat].

sar·dine (sár·dēn') *n.* small fish of herring family in young stage salted and preserved in oil [It. *sardina*, fr. the island of Sardinia].

sar·don·ic (sár·dän'·ik) *a.* (of laugh, smile) bitter, scornful, derisive, mocking. **-ally** adv. [L. *sardonicus*].

sar·do·nyx (sár'·dá·niks) *n.* semi-precious stone [Gk. = Sardinian onyx].

sar·gas·sum (sár·gas'·ạm) *n.* genus of sea-weeds. **sargasso** *n.* gulfweed. **Sargasso Sea,** part of Atlantic covered with seaweed [Sp. *sargazo*].

sa·ri (sá'·rē) *n.* long outer garment of Hindu women. Also **saree** [Hind.].

sa·rong (sạ·rawng') *n.* garment draped round waist by Malayans [Malay].

sar·sa·pa·ril·la (sárs·(a)·pạ·ril'·ạ) *n.* sev-eral plants of genus Smilax, with roots yield-ing medicinal sarsaparilla, a mild diuretic; a soft drink flavored with the extract [Sp. *zarza-parilla*].

sar·to·ri·al (sár·tō·'·ri·ạl) *a.* pert. to tailor, tailoring [L. *sartor*, a tailor].

sash (sash) *n.* silken band; belt or band, usu-ally decorative, worn round body [Arab. *shash*].

sash (sash) *n.* frame of window which carries panes of glass [Fr. *chassis*].

sas·sa·fras (sas'·ạ·fras) *n.* a tree of the laurel family; the dried bark of the root, used for flavoring beverages, etc.

sat (sat) *pa.t.* and *pa.p.* of **sit.**

Sa·tan (sā'·tạn) *n.* the devil. **-ic, -al** *a.* devilish; infernal; diabolical. **-ically** adv. [Heb. = enemy].

satch·el (sach'·ạl) *n.* small bag for books, etc. [L. *saccellus*, small sack].

sate (sāt) *v.t.* to satisfy appetite of; to glut [earlier *sade*, to make sad].

sa·teen (sạ·tēn') *n.* glossy cloth for linings, made of cotton in imitation of satin [fr. satin].

sat·el·lite (sat'·a·līt) *n.* one constantly in attendance upon important personage; an obsequious follower; (*Astron.*) a secondary body which revolves round planets of solar system; a moon. **satellite** (earth) *n.* an object launched into space by man to orbit the earth for scientific purposes. **satellitic** *a.* [L. *satelles*].

sa·ti·ate (sā'·shi·āt) *v.t.* to satisfy appetite of; to surfeit; to sate. **satiability** *n.* **satia-ble** *a.* capable of being satisfied. **satiation** *n.* state of being satiated. **satiety** (sạ·tī'·a·ti·) *n.* state of being satiated; feeling of having had too much [L. *satiare*, fr. *satis*, enough].

sat·in (sat'·n) *n.* soft, rich, usually silk fabric with smooth, lustrous surface; *a.* made of satin; smooth; glossy. **-et** *n.* thin kind of satin; glossy cloth of cotton warp and woolen weft, to imitate satin. **-wood** *n.* beautiful hard yellow wood, valued in cabinet work for veneers. **-y** *a.* [Fr. fr. It. *seta*, silk].

sat·ire (sat·īre) *n.* literary composition hold-ing up to ridicule vice or folly of the times; use of irony, sarcasm, invective, or wit. **satiric, -al** *a.* **satirically** adv. **satirical-ness** *n.* **satirize** *v.t.* to make object of satire. **satirist** *n.* [L. *satira*, a literary medley].

sat·is·fy (sat'·is·fī) *v.t.* to gratify fully; to pay, fulfill, supply, recompense, adequately; to convince; to content; to answer; to free from doubt; *v.i.* to give content; to supply to the full; to make payment. **satisfaction** *n.* **sat-isfactorily** adv. **satisfactoriness** *n.* **satis-factory** *a.* **-ing** *a.* affording satisfaction, esp. of food. **-ingly** adv. [L. *satisfacere*].

sa·trap (sā'·trap) *n.* governor of province un-der ancient Persian monarchy; petty, despotic governor. **-al** *a.* **-y** *n.* government, jurisdiction of satrap [Gk. *satrapēs*].

sat·u·rate (sach'·ạ·rāt) *v.t.* to soak thor-oughly; to steep; to drench. **-d** *a.* **saturation** *n.* act of saturating; complete penetration; condition of being saturated; solution of a body in a solvent, until solvent can absorb no more; in magnetism, state when increase of magnetizing force produces no further in-crease of flux-density in magnet; purity of color, free from white **saturator** *n.* contriv-ance for saturating air of factory, etc. with water-vapor [L. *saturare*].

Sat·ur·day (sat'·ẹr·di) *n.* seventh day of week [O.E. *Saeterdaeg*, day of Saturn].

Sat·urn (sat'·ẹrn) *n.* old deity, father of Jupiter; sixth of major planets in order of distance from sun. **Saturnalia** *n.pl.* festival in ancient Rome in honor of Saturn; time of carnival and unrestrained license; orgy. **sat-urnalian** *a.* **Saturnian** *a.* pert. to epoch of Saturn; golden; distinguished for prosperity and peacefulness. **saturnine** *a.* gloomy, slug-gish in temperament [L. *Saturnus*, god of agriculture].

sat·yr (sā'·tẹr, sat'·ẹr) *n.* woodland deity in Greek mythology, part human and part goat, fond of sensual enjoyment; lecherous person. **satyriasis** *n.* excessive and morbid desire for sexual intercourse exhibited by men. **-oma-niac** *n.* **-ical** *a.* pert. to satyrs [Gk. *saturos*].

sauce (saws) *n.* liquid or soft seasoning for food to render it more palatable or to whet appetite; condiment; relish; (*Colloq.*) impu-dence; cheek; *v.t.* to season with sauce; to give flavor or interest to; (*Colloq.*) to be rude in speech or manner. **-pan** *n.* meal pot with lid and long handle used for cooking. **saucy** *a.* bold; pert; cheeky. **saucily** adv. **sauci-ness** *n.* [Fr. fr. L. *sal.* salt].

sau·cer (saw'·sẹr) *n.* orig. vessel for sauce; small plate put under cup [Fr. *saucière*].

sauer·kraut (sour'·krout) *n.* cabbage cut fine and allowed to ferment in brine [Ger.].

saun·ter (sawn'·tẹr) *v.i.* to stroll. *n.* leisurely walk or stroll. **-er** *n.* **-ing** *n.*

sau·ri·an (saw'·ri·an) *n.* lizard-like reptile [Gk. *sauros*, a lizard].

sau·sage (saw'·sij) *n.* meat minced and seasoned and enclosed in thin membranous casing obtained from small entrails of pig or sheep [Fr. *saucisse*].

sau·té (sō·tā) *a.* cooked in little fat [Fr.].

sau·terne (sō·turn') *n.* a well-known white wine, from *Sauternes*, S. W. France.

sav·age (sav'·ij) *a.* remote from human ha-bitation; wild; uncivilized; primitive; cruel; *n.* man in native state of primitiveness; a barbarian. **-ly** adv. **-ry** *n.* ferocity; barbar-ism [L. *silvaticus*, fr. *silva*, a wood].

sa·vant (sạ·vánt', sav'·ạnt) *n.* a man of learning [Fr. fr. *savoir*, to know].

save (sāv) *v.t.* to rescue, preserve from dan-ger, evil, etc.; to redeem; to protect; to secure; to maintain (face, etc.); to keep for future; to lay by; to hoard; to obviate need of; to spare; to except; *v.i.* to lay by money; to economize; *prep.* except; *conj.* but. **savable** *a.* capable of being saved; re-trievable. **-r** *n.* **saving** *a.* frugal; thrifty; delivering from sin; implying reservation, as *saving clause*; *prep.* excepting; with apol-ogy to; *n.* economy; *pl.* earnings or gains put by for future. **savingly** adv. **savings bank** *n.* bank for receipt and accumulation of savings [Fr. *sauver*, fr. L. *salvare*, to save].

sav·ior (sāv'·yẹr) *n.* one who saves or delivers from destruction or danger; (*Cap.*) the Re-deemer, Jesus Christ. Also **saviour** [L. *sal-vare*, to save].

sa·voir-faire (sav·wár·fer') *n.* the knack of knowing the right thing to do at the right time; tact [Fr.].

sa·vor (sā'·ver) *n.* taste; flavor; relish; odor; smack; distinctive quality; *v.t.* to like; to taste or smell with pleasure; to relish; *v.i.* to have a particular smell or taste; to resemble; to indicate the presence of. **-ily** *adv.* **-less** *a.* **-y** *a.* having savor; tasty. Also *savour* [L. *sapor*, taste].

sa·vor·y (sā'·ver·i·) *n.* genus of aromatic plants, often grown as pot-herbs, the leaves being used in cooking as flavoring [fr. *savour*].

sav·vy (sav'·i·) *v.t.* (Slang) to understand; *n.* intelligence [Sp. *saber*; Fr. *savoir*, to know].

saw (saw) *pa.t.* of the verb **see.**

saw (saw) *n.* old saying; maxim; proverb; aphorism; adage [O.E. *sagu*].

saw (saw) *n.* hand or mechanical tool with thin blade, band, or circular disk with serrated edge, used for cutting; *v.t.* and *v.i.* to cut with a saw; *pa.t.* **sawed.** *pa.p.* **sawed** or **sawn. -bones** *n.* (Slang) surgeon. **-dust** *n.* small particles of wood, etc. made by action of a saw. **-er** *n.* **-mill** *n.* place where logs are sawn by mechanical power. **—toothed** *a.* having serrations like a saw. **-yer** *n.* one who saws timber; wood-boring larva of longicorn beetle [O.E. *saga*].

sax·horn (saks'·hawrn) *n.* brass wind instrument [Adolphe *Sax*, inventor, c. 1842].

sax·i·frage (sak'·sa·frij) *n.* popular name of various plants, most of them true rock plants [L. *saxum*, a stone; *frangere*, to break].

Sax·on (sak'·san) *n.* one of the people who formerly dwelt in N. Germany and who invaded England in the 5th and 6th cents.; a person of English race; native of Saxony; language of Saxons; *a.* pert. to Saxons, their country, their language; Anglo-Saxon [O.E. *Seaxa*, *Seaxan*, fr. *seax*, a knife].

Sax·o·ny (sak'·sa·ni·) *n.* very fine quality of wool; flannel [*Saxony*, where first produced].

sax·o·phone (sak'·sa·fōn) *n.* brass wind-instrument, with a reed and clarinet mouthpiece, fingered like an oboe [A. J. *Sax*, the inventor; Gk. *phōnē*, a sound].

say (sā) *v.t.* to utter with speaking voice; to state; to express; to allege; to repeat (lesson, etc.); to recite; to take as near enough. *pa.t.* and *pa.p.* **said** (sed). *n.* something said; what one has to say; share in a decision. **-er** *n.* **-ing** *n.* a verbal utterance; spoken or written expression of thought; proverbial expression; adage [O.E. *secgan*].

scab (skab) *n.* crust forming over open wound or sore; contagious skin disease, resembling mange, which attacks horses, cattle and sheep; disease of apple and pear; non-union worker; (Slang) despicable person; *v.i.* to heal over; to form a scab. *pa.t.* and *pa.p.* **-bed.** *pr.p.* **-bing. -bed** *a.* covered with scabs. **-bedness** *n.* **-by** *a.* [O.N. *skabbi*].

scab·bard (skab'·erd) *n.* sheath for sword or dagger; *v.t.* [O.Fr. *escalberc*].

sca·bies (skā'·bēz) *n.* skin disease caused by parasite; the itch; the scab [L.].

sca·bi·ous (skā'·bi·as) *a.* consisting of scabs; scabby; itchy [L. *scabies*, the itch].

sca·brous (skā'·bras) *a.* rough; scaly; harsh; full of difficulties; indelicate. **-ly** *adv.* **-ness** *n.* [L. *scaber* rough].

scad (skad) *n.* a species of mackerel; *pl.* (Slang) a great quantity [form of *shad*].

scaf·fold (skaf'·ald) *n.* temporary structure for support of workmen, used in erecting, altering, or repairing buildings; framework; stage; platform, esp. for execution of criminal; *v.t.* to furnish with a scaffold; to prop up. **-ing** *n.* scaffold [O.Fr. *eschafault*].

scal·a·wag, scallawag (skal'·a·wag) *n.* (Colloq.) scamp; worthless fellow.

scald (skawld) *v.t.* to burn with moist heat or hot liquid; to cleanse by rinsing with boiling water; to heat to point approaching boiling point; *n.* injury by scalding [L. *ex*, out of; *calidus*, hot].

scald See **skald.**

scale (skāl) *n.* dish of a balance; balance itself; machine for weighing, chiefly in *pl.*; Libra, one of signs of zodiac; *v.t.* to weigh, as in scales [O.N. *skal*, bowl].

scale (skāl) *n.* horny or bony plate-like outgrowth from skin of certain mammals, reptiles, and fishes; any thin layer or flake on surface; *v.t.* to deprive of scales; *v.i.* to come off or peel in thin layers. **-d** *a.* having scales. **-less** *a.* **scaliness** *n.* being scaly. **scaling** *n.* removing of scales. **scaly** *a.* covered with scales; resembling scales [O.Fr. *escale*, husk].

scale (skāl) *n.* series of steps or gradations; comparative rank in society; ratio between dimensions as shown on map, etc. to actual distance, or length; scope; basis for a numerical system, as *binary scale*; instrument for measuring, weighing, etc. (Mus.) succession of notes arranged in order of pitch between given note and its octave; gamut; *v.t.* to climb as by a ladder; to clamber up; to measure; *v.i.* to mount [L. *scala*, a ladder].

sca·lene (skā·lēn) *a.* uneven; (Geom.) having all three sides unequal; *n.* a scalene triangle [Gk. *skalēnos*, uneven].

scal·lion (skal'·yan) *n.* a variety of shallot [L. (*cepa*) *Ascalonia*, onion of Ascalon].

scal·lop, scollop (skal'·ap) *n.* bivalve mollusk with ribbed, fan-shaped shell and beautiful coloring; ornamental edge of rounded projections; dish resembling scallop shell to serve oysters, etc.; *v.t.* to cut edge of material into scallops [O.Fr. *escalope*, a shell].

scalp (skalp) *n.* covering dome of cranium consisting of skin and hair; skin and hair torn off by Indian warriors as token of victory; *v.t.* to deprive of integument of head; to make quick profits in buying and prompt reselling [contr. of *scallop*].

scal·pel (skal'·pel) *n.* small, straight surgical knife with convex edge [L. *scalpere*, to cut].

scamp (skamp) *n.* scoundrel; rascal; rogue; *v.t.* to execute work carelessly [O.Fr. *escamper*, to decamp].

scam·per (skam'·per) *v.i.* to run about; to run away in haste and trepidation; *n.* a hasty, impulsive flight [fr. *scamp*].

scan (skan) *v.t.* to examine closely; to scrutinize; to measure or read (verse) by its metrical feet (Radar) to traverse an area with electronic beams. *v.i.* to be metrically correct. *pr.p.* **-ning.** *pa.t.* and *pa.p.* **-ned. -ning** *n.* (Television) process of dissecting a picture to be transmitted. **-sion** *n.* act or mode of scanning poetry [L. *scandere*, to climb].

scan·dal (skan'·dal) *n.* malicious gossip; disgraceful action; disgrace; injury to a person's character; **-bearer, -monger** *n.* one who delights in spreading malicious scandal and gossip. **-ize** *v.t.* to shock by disgraceful actions **-ous** *a.* bringing shame; disgraceful. **-ously** *adv.* **-ousness** *n.* [Gk. *skandalon*, a cause of stumbling].

Scan·di·na·vi·a (skan·da·nā'·vi·a) *n.* peninsula of Norway, Sweden, and Finland, but historically and linguistically includes Denmark and Iceland. **-n** *a.* pert. to Scandinavia [L. *Scandinavia* or *Scandia*].

scansion. See **scan.**

scant (skant) *a.* barely sufficient; inadequate; *v.t.* to put on short allowance; to fail to give full measure; **-ily** *adv.* **-iness** *n.* **-ly** *adv.* sparingly; scarcely; barely. **-ness** *n.* scantiness; insufficiency. **-y** *a.* [O.N. *skamt*, short].

scant·ling (skant'·ling) *n.* a small amount; a small piece of timber; a stud [Fr. *échantillon*, a sample].

scape·goat (skāp'·gōt) *n.* in Mosaic ritual, goat upon whose head were symbolically placed sins of people; one who has to shoulder blame due to another. **scapegrace** *n.* graceless, good-for-nothing fellow [fr. *escape*].

scaph·oid (skaf′.oid) *a.* boat-shaped [Gk. *skaphē*, a boat; *eidos*, form].

scap·u·la (skap′.yạ.lạ) *n.* shoulder blade. *pl.* **scapulae. -r** *a.* pert. to scapula; *n.* bandage for shoulder blade; part of habit of certain religious orders in R.C. church; sleeveless monastic garment. Also **-ry** [L. *scapulae*, the shoulder blades].

scar (skär) *n.* permanent mark left on skin after healing of a wound, burn; a cicatrix; any blemish; *v.t.* to mark with scar; *v.i.* to heal with a scar [O.Fr. *escare*].

scar·ab (skar′.ạb) *n.* bettle regarded by ancient Egyptians as emblematic of solar power; gem cut in shape of this bettle, as amulet [L. *scarabaeus*].

scarce (skers) *a.* not plentiful; deficient; wanting; rare; infrequent; uncommon; scanty; **-ly** *adv.* hardly; not quite. **-ness**, **scarcity** *n.* being scarce; lack; deficiency [O.Fr. *escars*].

scare (sker) *v.t.* to terrify suddenly; to alarm; to drive away by frightening; *n.* sudden alarm (esp. causeless); panic; fright. **-crow** *n.* figure set up to frighten away birds from crops; a miserable-looking person in rags. **-monger** *n.* alarmist [O.N. *skirra*].

scarf (skärf) *n.* long, narrow, light article of dress worn loosely over shoulders or about neck; a muffler. *pl.* **-s, scarves** [O.Fr. *escrepe*, a purse hanging from the neck].

scarf (skärf) *v.t.* to unite lengthways to pieces of timber by letting notched end of one into a similar end of the other, then securing them with bolt or strap. *n.* joint for connecting timbers lengthways, the two pieces overlapping [Scand. = *skarf*, a joint].

scar·i·fy (skar′.ạ.fī) *v.t.* to scratch or slightly cut the skin; to stir the surface soil of; to lacerate; to criticize unmercifully. **scarification** *n.* **scarifier** *n.* [L. *scarificare*].

scar·la·ti·na (skar.lạ.tē′.nạ) *n.* scarlet fever [It.].

scar·let (skär′.lit) *n.* bright red color of many shades; cloth of scarlet color; *a.* of this color — **fever** *n.* childhood disease characterized by a scarlet rash. **-hat** *n.* a cardinal's hat. — **pimpernel**, small annual herb with red flowers. — **runner** *n.* bean plant with twining stem and scarlet flowers [O.Fr. *escarlate*].

scarp (skärp) *n.* steep inside slope of ditch in fortifications; *v.t.* to make steep. **-ed** *a.* steeply sloping [It. *scarpa*].

scar·y (sker′·i·) *a.* (*Colloq.*) producing fright or alarm; exceedingly timid [fr. *scare*].

scat (skat) *v.i.* to hurry off; *v.t.* to order off with "scat!"

scathe (skāth) *v.t.* to criticize harshly. **scathing** *a.* damaging; cutting; biting. **scathingly** *adv.* [O.N. *skatha*].

sca·tol·o·gy (skạ.tàl′.ạ.ji.) *n.* scientific study of fossilized excrement of animals; interest in obscene literature. **scatological** *a.* [Gk. *skor, skatos*, dung].

scat·ter (skat′.ẹr) *v.t.* to strew about; to sprinkle around; to put to rout; to disperse; *v.i.* to take to flight; to disperse. **-brain** *n.* a giddy, thoughtless person. **-brained** *a.* **-ed** *a.* widely separated or distributed; distracted. **-er** *n.* **-ing** *n.* act of dispersing; effect of irregularly reflected light; (*Radio*) general re-radiation of wave-energy when a ray meets an obstacle in its path; *a.* dispersing; sporadic; diversified. **-ingly** *adv.*

scav·en·ger (skav′.in.jẹr) *n.* one employed in cleaning streets, removing refuse, etc.; animal which feeds on carrion; *v.i.* to scavenge. **scavenge** *v.t.* to cleanse streets, etc. [orig. *scavager*, inspector of goods for sale, later, of street cleansing, fr. O.E. *sceawian*, to inspect].

sce·nar·i·o (sạ.ner′.i.ō) *n.* script or written version of play to be produced by motion picture; plot of a play. **scenarist** *n.* [It.].

scene (sēn) *n.* place, time of action of novel, play, etc.; a division of a play; spectacle, show, or view; episode; unseemly display of temper; minor disturbance. **-ry** *n.* stage settings; natural features of landscape which please eye. — **shifter** *n.* one who manages the scenery in theatrical representation. **scenic** *a.* pert. to scenery; theatrical; picturesque. **scenographic, -al** *a.* drawn in perspective. **scenographically** *adv.* **scenography** *n.* [L. *scena*].

scent (sent) *v.t.* to discern or track by sense of smell; to give a perfume to; to detect; to become suspicious of; *v.i.* to smell; *n.* odor or perfume; fragrance; aroma; trail left by odor. **-ed** *a.* perfumed. **to put off the scent**, to mislead wilfully [Fr. *sentir*, to smell].

sceptic. See **skeptic**.

scepter (sep′.tẹr) *n.* ornamental staff or baton, as symbol of royal power; royal or imperial dignity. **-ed** *a.* invested with a scepter, regal. Also **sceptre** [Gk. *skēptron*, a staff].

sched·ule (skej′.ool) *n.* document containing list of details forming part of principal document, deed, etc.; tabulated list; order of events; timetable; *v.t.* to note and enter in a schedule [L. a small scroll].

sche·ma (skē′.mạ) *n.* plan or diagram; outline; scheme; *pl.* **-ta. -tic** *a.* **-tically** *adv.* **-tize** *v.t.* to form a scheme [Gk.].

scheme (skēm) *n.* plan; design; system; plot; draft; outline; a syllabus; tabulated statement; diagram; *v.t.* to plan; to contrive; to frame; *v.i.* to intrigue; to plot. *pr.p.* **scheming. -r** *n.* **scheming** *n.* and *a.* planning; plotting. **schemist** *n.* schemer [Gk. *schēma*, form].

scher·zo (sker′.tsō) *n.* (*Mus.*) composition of a lively, playful character [It. = a jest].

schil·ling (shil′.ing) *n.* orig. a German coin, re-introduced into Austrian monetary system in 1925 [Ger.].

schism (sizm) *n.* split of a community into factions; division of a church or religious denomination; crime of promoting this. **schismatic** *a.—n.* one who separates from a church. **-atical** *a.* schismatic. **-atically** *adv.* [Gk. *schisma*, a cleft].

schiz·o- (skiz′.ō) *prefix* fr. Greek, *schizein*, to cleave, used in the construction of compound terms. **schizoid** *a.* exhibiting slight symptoms of schizophrenia. **-phrenia** (skiz.ạ.frē′.ni.ạ) *n.* mental disorder known as 'split personality,' characterized by a social behavior, introversion, and loss of touch with one's environment. **-phrenic** *a.*

schnapps, schnaps (shnaps) *n.* kind of Holland gin [Ger.].

schol·ar (skàl′.ẹr) *n.* learned person; holder of scholarship. **-ly** *a.* learned. **-ship** *n.* learning; erudition; a grant to aid a student. **scholastic** *a.* pert. to schools, scholars, or education; pert. to schools or scholars of philosophy of Middle Ages; pedantic; *n.* schoolman who expounded medieval philosophy; Jesuit student who has not yet taken Holy Orders. **scholastically** *adv.* **Scholasticism** *n.* system of philosophy during Middle Ages [Gk. *scholē*, a school].

scho·li·ast (skō′.li·ast) *n.* ancient commentator or annotator of classical texts. **scholiastic** *a.* **scholium** *n.—pl.* **scholia**, marginal note or comments [Gk. *scholiastēs*, commentator].

school (skóol) *n.* a shoal (of fish, whales, etc.) [Dut. *school*, crowd]

school (skóol) *n.* institution for teaching or giving instruction in any subject; pupils of a school; sessions of instruction; group of writers, artists, thinkers, etc. with principles

WEBSTER Q–S

or methods in common; branch of study, in a university; *v.t.* to educate; to discipline; to instruct; to train. **-boy** *n.* boy attending school or of school age. **-mate** *n.* contemporary at school. **-man** *n.* learned doctor of Middle Ages, versed in scholasticism. **-master** *n.* master in charge of school; male teacher in school. **-room** *n.* **-teacher** *n.* **boarding school,** residential school for boys or girls. **preparatory school,** private school which prepares young people for college. **public school,** see **public** [Gk. *scholē,* leisure; place for discussion].

schoon·er (skoŏ'·ner) *n.* small sharp-built vessel, having two masts, fore-and-aft rigged; (*Colloq.*) extra large glass for holding beer; [orig. *scooner,* fr. Prov. E. *scoon,* to make flat stone skip along surface of water. O.E. *scunian*].

schot·tische, shottish (shåt'·ish) *n.* round dance resembling polka; music in ²⁄₄ time for this dance. **Highland schottische,** lively dance to strathspey tunes, Highland fling [Ger. = Scottish].

sci·at·i·ca (sī·at'·i·ka) *n.* neuralgia of sciatic nerve, with pains in region of hip. **sciatic, -al** *a.* situated in, or pert. to, hip region. **-lly** *adv.* [Late L. fr. Gk. *ischion,* hip-joint].

sci·ence (sī'·ans) *n.* systematic knowledge of natural or physical phenomena; truth ascertained by observation, experiment, and induction; ordered arrangement of facts known under classes or heads; theoretical knowledge as distinguished from practical; knowledge of principles and rules of invention, construction, mechanism, etc. as distinguished from art. **scientific, -al** *a.* **scientifically** *adv.* **scientism** *n.* outlook and practice of scientist. **scientist** *n.* a person versed in science, esp. natural science. **Christian Science,** religious doctrine of faith healing, bodily diseases being due to errors of mortal mind and therefore curable by faith and prayer. **domestic science,** study of good housekeeping. **natural science, physical science,** science which investigates nature and properties of material bodies and natural phenomena. **pure science,** science based on self-evident truths, as mathematics, logic, etc. [L. *scientia,* knowledge].

scim·i·tar (sim'·a·ter) *n.* short saber with curved, sharp-edged blade broadening from handle [Pers. *shimshir*].

scin·til·la (sin·til'·a) *n.* spark; least particle. **-nt** *a.* emitting sparks; sparkling. **-te** *v.i.* to emit sparks; to sparkle; to glisten. **-tion** *n.* [L. = a park].

sci·o·lism (sī'·a·lizm) *n.* superficial knowledge used to impress other. **sciolist** *n.* one possessed of superficial knowledge; charlatan. **sciolistic** *a.* [L. *scire,* to know].

sci·on (sī'·an) *n.* slip for grafting; offshoot; a descendant; heir [Fr.].

scis·sile (sis'·al) *a.* (*Bot.*) capable of being cut, split, or divided. **scission** *n.* act of cutting; division [L. *scindere, scissum,* to cut].

scis·sors (siz'·erz) *n.pl.* instrument of two sharp-edged blades pivoted together for cutting; small shears. **scissor** *v.t.* to cut with scissors [Fr. *ciseaux*].

scle·ro- (sklēr'·a) *prefix* fr. Gk. *sklēros,* hard, used in the construction of compound terms, implying hardness or dryness. **sclera** (sklir'·a) *n.* strong, opaque fibrous membrane forming outer coat of eyeball, the white of the eye. **scleral** *a.* hard, bony. **scleritis** *n.* inflammation of sclera of eye. **scleroderma, sclerodermia** *n.* chronic skin disease characterized by hardness and rigidity. **sclerodermatous** *a.* (*Zool.*) possessing a hard, bony, external structure for protection. **sclerodermatous, sclerodermic, sclerodermous** *a.* pert. to scleroderma; having a hard outer skin. **scleroid** *a.* of hard texture. **scleroma** *n.* hard-

ening of tissues. **sclerosal** *a.* pert. to sclerosis. **sclerosis** *n.* hardening of organ as a result of excessive growth of connective tissue; induration.

scoff (skåf, skawf) *v.i.* to treat with derision; to mock; to jeer; *n.* expression of scorn; an object of derision. **-er** *n.* **-ingly** *adv.* [Scand.].

scold (skōld) *v.t.* and *v.i.* to find fault (with); to chide; to reprove angrily; to rebuke; *n.* one who scolds; a nagging, brawling woman. **-er** *n.* **-ing** *n.* rebuke. **-ingly** *adv.* [Ger. *schelten,* to brawl].

sconce (skåns) *n.* ornamental bracket fixed to wall, for carrying a light; small fort or breastwork; [O.Fr. *esconce,* fr. L. *abscondere,* to bide].

scone (skōn) *n.* a thin, flat cake.

scoop (skoŏp) *n.* article for ladling; kind of shovel; hollow place; (*Colloq.*) lucrative speculation; (*Slang*) publication of exclusive news in newspaper; *v.t.* to ladle out, shovel, lift, dig or hollow out with scoop; (*Slang*) to publish exclusive news; [prob. fr. Sw. *skopa,* a scoop].

scoot (skoŏt) *v.i.* to move off quickly; to dart away suddenly; to scamper off. **-er** *n.* a toy consisting of flat board mounted on two wheels, on which one foot rests, propelled by other foot and guided by handle attached to front wheel [fr. *shoot*].

scope (skōp) *n.* range of activity or application; space for action; room; play; outlet; opportunity [It. *scopo,* a target].

scor·bu·tic (skawr·bū'·tik) *a.* affected with, or relating to, scurvy.

scorch (skawrch) *v.t.* to burn the surface of; to parch; to shrivel; to char; to singe; to wither; to blast; *v.i.* to be burnt on surface; to dry up; to parch; (*Colloq.*) to drive at excessive speed. **scorched-earth policy,** destroying everything of value in path of hostile army. **-er** *n.* anything which scorches; a biting,, sarcastic remark; (*Colloq.*) one who drives furiously; hot, sultry day. **-ing** *a.* burning superficially; oppressively hot.

score (skōr) *n.* a cut, notch, line, stroke; tally-mark, reckoning, bill, account; number twenty; reason; sake; number of points, runs, goals, etc. made in a game; arrangement of different parts of a musical composition on the page so that each bar may be read in all parts simultaneously; *v.t.* to mark with lines, scratches, furrows; to cut; to write down in proper order; to orchestrate; to enter in account book, to record; to make (points, etc.) in game; *v.i.* to add a point, run, goal, etc. in a game; to make a telling remark; to achieve a success. **-r** *n.* one who keeps official record of points, runs, etc. made in the course of a game; one who makes the point, run, etc. in a game. **scoring** *n.* **-book, -card, -sheet,** *n.* [O.N. *skor,* notch].

sco·ri·a (skō'·ri·a) *n.* dross or slag resulting from smelting of metal ores; rough, angular material sent out by volcano. *pl.* **scoriae. scorify** *v.t.* to reduce to dross or slag [Gk. *skoria,* dross].

scorn (skawrn) *n.* extreme disdain or contempt; object of derision; *v.t.* to contemn; to despise; to spurn. **-ful** *a.* **-fully** *adv.* [O.Fr. *escarnir*].

Scor·pi·o (skawr'·pi·ō) *n.* Scorpion, 8th sign of zodiac; scorpion. **-n** *n.* insect allied to spiders having slender tail which ends in very acute sting; whip armed with points like scorpion's tail; vindicative person with virulent tongue [L.].

scot (skåt) *n.* formerly, tax, contribution, fine. **—free** *a.* unhurt; exempt from payment [O.N. *skot,* a tax].

Scot (skåt) *n.* native of Scotland [O.E. *Scottas* (*pl.*) Irishmen].

Scotch (skåch) *a.* pert. to Scotland or its inhabitants; Scots (adj. form usually preferred in Scotland); Scottish; *n.* Scots; Scots dialect; Scotch whiskey. — **broth,** broth made of pearl barley, various vegetables and beef for seasoning. — **pine,** Northern pine and Baltic fir or pine. **-man** *n.* a Scotsman. — **terrier,** small short-legged, rough-coated dog.

scotch (skȧch) *v.t.* to support, as a wheel, by placing some object to prevent its rolling; to prevent progress being made; to kill project in its initial stages; *n.* prop., wedge, strut.

scotch (skȧch) *v.* to wound slightly; to cut; *n.* scratch; mark or score.

Scots (skȧts) *n.* dialect of English spoken in lowland Scotland; *a.* pert. to Scotland; Scottish. **-man, -woman** *n.* [O.E. *Scottas*].

Scot·tish (skȧt′·ish) *a.* pert. to Scotland or its people; Scots; Scotch [O.E. *Scottas*].

scoun·drel (skoun′drel) *n.* rascal; villain. **-ly** *a.* [etym. uncertain].

scour (skour) *v.t.* to clean or polish the surface of, by hard rubbing; to purge violently; to flush out; *v.i.* to clean by rubbing; *n.* act or material used in scouring. **-er** *n.* [O.Fr. *escurer*].

scour (skour) *v.t.* to pass rapidly along or over in search of something; to range; *v.i.* to scamper; to rove over; to scurry along. **-er** *n.* [etym. uncertain].

scourge (skurj) *n.* whip made of leather thongs; lash; punishment; a grievous afflu-tion; one who or that which inflicts pain or devastates country; *v.t.* to flog; to lash; to chastise; to torment [L. *excoriare*].

scout (skout) *n.* one sent out to reconnoiter; lookout; a Boy Scout or Girl Scout; reconnaissance airplane; *v.t.* to reconnoiter; to spy out. **-master** *n.* adult instructor and organizer in the Boy Scouts [O.Fr. *escoute*, fr. *escouter*, to listen].

scout (skout) *v.t.* to reject with contempt; to sneer at [O.N. *skuta*, a taunt].

scow (skou) *n.* large flat-bottomed barge, with square ends; lighter [Dut. *schouw*].

scowl (skoul) *v.i.* to wrinkle brows in displeasure; to frown gloomily or sullenly; to look sullen, or annoyed; *n.* an angry frown [Scand.].

scrab·ble (skrab′·l) *v.t.* to scribble; to scrawl; *v.i.* to scratch with hands; [var. of *scrapple*, frequentative of *scrape*].

scrag (skrag) *n.* anything thin, lean, gaunt, or shrivelled; (*Slang*) long, thin neck; lean end of neck of mutton; *v.t.* (*Slang*) to wring neck of; to hang; to execute. **-ged** *a.* lean; thin. **-gedness, -giness** *n.* **-gily** *adv.* **-gly** *a.* rough and unkempt. **-gy** *a.* lean; jagged [earlier *crag*].

scram (skram) *interj.* (*Slang*) clear out′

scramble (skram′·bl) *v.t.* to move by crawling, climbing, etc. on all fours; to clamber; to struggle with others for; *v.t.* to collect together hurriedly and confusedly; to cook eggs by stirring when broken, in frying pan; *n.* scrambling; disorderly proceeding. **scrambling** *a.*

scrap (skrap) *n.* small detached piece or fragment; material left over which can be used as raw material again; *pl.* odds and ends; *v.t.* to make into scraps; to discard; *pa.t.* and *pa.p.* **-ped,** *pr.p.* **-ping. -book** *n.* a blank book in which to put clippings, pictures, etc. **-heap** *n.* a rubbish heap; pile of old iron, etc. **-py** *a.* consisting of scraps; fragmentary [O.N. *skrap*].

scrap (skrap) *n.* and *v.i.* (*Slang*) fight; quarrel. **-pily** *adv.* **-piness** *n.* [var. of *scrape*].

scrape (skrāp) *v.t.* to abrade; to grate; to scratch; to remove by rubbing; to clean or smooth thus; *v.i.* to produce grating noise; to live parsimoniously; to bow awkwardly with drawing back of foot; to scratch in earth, as fowls; *n.* act or sound of scraping;

scratch; predicament; embarrassing situation. **-r** *n.* one who, or that which, scrapes; tool with thin blade for scraping [O.E. *scrapian*].

scratch (skrach) *v.t.* to score or mark a narrow surface wound with claws, nails, or anything pointed; to abrade skin; to erase; to scrape; to withdraw name of entrant for race or competition; to write in a hasty, careless manner; to rub an itchy spot; *v.i.* to use claws or nails in tearing, abrading, or shallow digging; to strike out one's name from list of competitors; *n.* slight wound, mark, or sound made by sharp instrument; mark indicating the starting point in a handicap race; one who concedes a start in distance, time, etc. to other competitors; *a.* taken at random, brought together in a hurry, as a *scratch team;* denoting competitor without handicap. **-er** *n.* **-y** *a.* [mixture of earlier *scrat* and *cratch*, both of Teut. origin].

scrawl (skrawl) *v.t.* to write or draw untidily; to scribble; *v.i.* to write unskillfully; *n.* hasty, careless writing; **-er** *n.* [perh. fr. *scrabble*].

scraw·ny (skraw′·ni·) *a.* lean; scraggy; rawboned. **scrawniness** *n.* [var. of *scranny*].

scream (skrēm) *v.t.* and *v.i.* to utter a piercing cry; to shriek; to laugh immoderately; *n.* a shrill, piercing cry; a person who excites much laughter; laughter-provoking incident. **-ing** *a.* [imit. origin].

scree (skrē) *n.* pile of débris at base of cliff or hill; a talus [etym. uncertain].

screech (skrēch) *v.i.* to utter a harsh, shrill cry; *n.* a shrill and sudden, harsh cry. — **owl** *n.* owl with persistent harsh call [earlier *scritch*, of imit. origin].

screed (skrēd) *n.* long letter or passage; long boring speech [O.E. *screade*, a shred].

screen (skrēn) *n.* covered frame to shelter from heat, light, draft, or observation; partition of stone, metal, or wood, cutting off one part of ecclesiastical building from the rest; coarse, rectangular sieve for grading coal, pulverized material, etc.; white surface on which image is projected by optical means; troops thrown out towards enemy to protect main body; *v.t.* to provide with shelter or concealment; to protect from blame or censure; to sift; to film; to project film, latern slide, etc. on a screen; to subject a person to political scrutiny. **-ing** *n.* employing a metal sheath to screen a magnetic field from the outside surroundings; (*Nuclear Physics*) reduction in intensity of radiations on passing through matter. **the screen,** the movies. **smoke screen** *n.* dense smoke artificially disseminated to conceal movements [O. Fr. *escran*].

screw (skroŏ) *n.* in mechanics, a machine consisting of an inclined plane wound round a cylinder; cylinder with a spiral ridge running round it, used as holding agent or as mechanical power; turn of screw; twist to one side; a screw propeller; *v.t.* to fasten with screw; to press or stretch with screw; to work by turning; to twist round; to obtain by pressure; to extort; *v.i.* to assume a spiral motion; to move like a screw. **-driver** *n.* tool for turning screws. **-ed** *a.* **-er** *n.* **-ing** *a.* — **propeller** *n.* revolving shaft carrying two or more symmetrically arranged fan-like blades or flanges to create forward thrust of a ship. — **thread** *n.* spiral ridge, triangular or rectangular in section, on a screw cylinder. **-y** *a.* tortuous, like the thread or motion of a screw; (*Slang*) crazy; daft [O.Fr. *escroue*].

scrib·ble (skrib′·l) *v.t.* and *v.i.* to write carelessly; to draw meaningless lines; to scrawl; *n.* something scribbled. **-r** *n.* bad or careless writer; a writer of unimportant trifles; **scribbling** *a.* used for scribbling; *n.* careless writing [L. *scribere*, to write].

scribe (skrīb) *n.* a writer; official or public

writer; clerk; copyist; official copyist and expounder of Mosaic and traditional Jewish law; *v.t.* to incise wood, metal, etc. with a sharp point as a guide to cutting; **scribal** *a.* pert. to a scribe. **-r** *n.* sharp-pointed instrument used to mark off work [L. *scribere*, to write].

scrim·mage (skrim'·ij) *n.* a confused struggle; a tussle for the ball in football [Cf. *skirmish*].

scrimp (skrimp) *v.t.* to make too short or small; to stint. **-ed** *a.* **-ily** *adv.* **-iness** *n.* **-y** *a.* [O.E. *scrimman*, to shrink].

scrim·shaw (skrim'·shaw) (*Naut.*) *v.t.* and *v.i.* to make decorative article out of bone, whale's tooth, shell, etc.; *n.* such work.

scrip (skrip) *n.* a writing; interim certificate of holding bonds, stock, or shares [var. of *script*].

script (skript) *n.* kind of type, used in printing and typewriting, to imitate handwriting; handwriting; text of words of play, or of scenes and word of film; text of spoken part in broadcast; (*Law*) original or principal document [L. *scribere*, *scriptum*, to write].

scrip·ture (skrip'·cher) *n.* anything written; sacred writing; passage from Bible. **the Scriptures,** Old and New Testaments. **scriptural, scripture** *a.* according to Scriptures; biblical [L. *scribere*, *scriptum*, to write].

scrive·ner (skriv'·an·er) *n.* rotary [L. *scribere*, to write].

scrof·u·la (skrof'·ya·la) *n.* a tuberculous condition most common in childhood. **scrofulitic, scrofulous** *a.* [L. = a little sow]

scroll (skrōl) *n.* roll of paper or parchment; a list; flourish at end of signature; ornament consisting of spiral volutes; (*Her.*) motto-bearing ribbon or inscription. **-ed** *a.* formed like, or contained in, a scroll [O.Fr. *escrou*].

scro·tum (skrō'·tam) *n.* external muscular sac which lodges testicles of the male.

scrounge (skrounj) *v.t.* and *v.i.* (*Slang*) to pilfer. **-r** *n.* **scrounging** *n.*

scrub (skrub) *v.t.* to clean with a hard brush, etc. and water; to scour; to rub; *v.i.* to clean by rubbing; to work hard for a living; *pa.t.* and *pa.p.* **-bed.** *pr.p.* **-bing.** *n.* act of scrubbing [D. *schrubben*].

scrub (skrub) *n.* stunted growth of trees and shrubs; an animal of unknown or inferior breeding; *a.* stunted; inferior; (*Sports*) pert. to a substitute team without training. **-by** *a.* mean and small; stunted; covered with scrub; unshaved [var. of *shrub*].

scruff (skruf) *n.* the back of the neck; nape. Also **skruff** (etym. uncertain].

scrump·tious (skrump'·shas) *a.* (*Slang*) delicious; delightful; nice.

scrunch (skrunch) *v.t.* to crush with the teeth; to crunch; to crush [fr. *crunch*].

scru·ple (skrōō'·pl) *n.* very small quantity; feeling of doubt; conscientious objection; qualm; *v.i.* to hesitate from doubt; to have compunction. **scrupulous** *a.* extremely conscientious; attentive to small points. **scrupulously** *adv.* **scrupulousness, scrupulosity** *n.* [L. *scrupulus*].

scru·ti·ny (skrōō'·ta·ni·) *n.* close search; critical examination; searching look or gaze. **scrutator** *n.* one who examines closely. **scrutinate, scrutinize** *v.t.* to examine into critically [L. *scrutari*, to examine closely].

scud (skud) *v.i.* to move quickly; to run before a gale; *pr.p.* **-ding.** *pa.t.* and *pa.p.* **-ded.** *n.* act of moving quickly; ragged cloud drifting rapidly in strong wind [Scand.].

scuff (skuf) *v.t.* to graze against; *v.i.* to shuffle along without raising the feet. *n.* a mark left by scuffing; a flat slipper with covering only over toes [Sw. *skuffa*, to push].

scuf·fle (skuf'·l) *v.i.* to struggle at close quarters; to fight confusedly; to shuffle along;

n. confused fight, or struggle; a shuffling. **-r** *n.* [Sw. *skuffa*, to push].

scull (skul) *n.* short light oar pulled with the one hand; light racing boat of a long, narrow build; *v.t.* to propel boat by two sculls; to propel boat by means of oar placed over stern and worked alternately, first one way and then the other [O.Fr. *escuelerie*, fr. *escuele*, a dish].

scul·lion (skul'·yan) *n.* (*Arch.*) male underservant who performed menial work; low, mean, dirty fellow [O.Fr. *escouillon*, a dish-cloth].

sculp·ture (skulp'·cher) *n.* art of reproducing objects in relief or in the round out of hard material by means of chisel; carved work; art of modeling in clay or other plastic material, figures or objects to be later cast in bronze or other metals; *v.t.* to represent by sculpture. **sculptor** *n.* (*fem.* **sculptress**) one who carves or molds figures. **sculptural** *a.* [L. *sculpere*, *sculptum*, to carve].

scum (skum) *n.* impurities which rise to surface of liquids; foam or froth of dirty appearance; vile person or thing, riffraff; *v.t.* to take scum off; *v.i.* to form scum. *pr.p.* **-ming.** *pa.t.* and *pa.p.* **-med, -my** *a.* covered with scum; low-bred [Dan. *skum*, froth].

scup·per (skup'·er) *n.* channel alongside bulwarks of ship to drain away water from deck; [O.Fr. *escopir*, to spit out].

scurf (skurf) *n.* dry scales or flakes formed on skin; anything scaly adhering to surface. **-y** *a.* covered with scurf [O.E. *sceorf*].

scur·ril·ous (skur'·i·las) *a.* indecent; abusive; vile. **-ness, scurrility** *n.* vulgar language; vile abuse. **-ly** *adv.* [L. *scurrilis*].

scur·ry (skur'·i·) *v.i.* to hurry along; to run hastily. **-ing** *n.* [fr. *scour*].

scur·vy (skur'·vi·) *n.* deficiency disease due to lack of vitamin C; (*Med.*) scorbutus; *a.* afflicted with the disease; mean; low; vile. **scurvily** *adv.* in a scurvy manner. **scurviness** *n.* [fr. *scurf*].

scut (skut) *n.* a short tail, as that of a hare [O.N. *skjota*, to jut out].

scu·tate (skū'·tāt) *a.* (*Bot.*) shield-shaped; (*Zool.*) protected by scales or shieldlike processes [L. *scutum*, a shield].

scutch·eon. See escutcheon.

scu·tel·lum (skū·tel'·am) *n.* horny plate or scale. **scutellate, -d** *a.* (*Bot.*) rounded and nearly flat, like a saucer. **scutelliform** *a.* scutellate. **scutiform** *a.* (*Bot.*) shield-shaped [L. = a salver].

scut·tle (skut'·l) *n.* wide-mouthed vessel for holding coal [O.E. *scutel*].

scut·tle (skut'·l) *n.* hole with a cover, for light and air, cut in ship's deck or hatchway; hinged cover of glass to close a port-hole; *v.t.* to make holes in ship, esp. to sink it. **-butt** *n.* (*Naut.*) a water cask; (*Slang*) rumor [O.Fr. *escoutille*, a hatchway].

scut·tle (skut'·l) *v.i.* to rush away; to run hurriedly [freq. of *scud*].

scythe (sïTH) *n.* mowing implement; *v.t.* to cut with scythe; to mow [O.E. *sithe*].

sea (sē) *n.* mass of salt water covering greater part of earth's surface; named broad tract of this; certain large expanses of inland water, when salt; billow, or surge; swell of ocean; vast expanse; flood; large quantity. **— anemone** *n.* beautifully colored radiate marine animal, found on rocks on seacoast. **-board** *n.* coastline and its neighborhood; seashore. **—borne** *a.* carried on the sea or on a seagoing vessel. **— breeze** *n.* one which blows from sea toward land. **-coast** *n.* shore or border of land adjacent to sea. **— dog** *n.* dogfish; seal; pirate; old, experienced sailor. **-faring** *a.* **-girt** *a.* encircled by the sea. **-going**

a. pert. to vessels which make long voyages by sea. — **green** *a.* having color of sea water; being of faint green color, with a slightly bluish tinge. — **gull** *n.* any gull. — **horse** *n.* a small fish, allied to pipedish, with horselike head; the walrus; fabulous animal, part horse, part fish. — **legs** *n.pl.* ability to walk on ship's deck in spite of rough seas. — **level** *n.* level of the sea taken at mean tide. — **lion** *n.* lion-headed, eared type of seal, eared seal. **-man** *n.* a sailor. **-manlike, -manly** *a.* **-manship** *n.* art of managing and navigating properly ship at sea. **-plane** *n.* airplane which can take off from and alight on sea. **-port** *n.* town with harbor. — **power,** command of the seas; nation with powerful fleet. **-scape** *n.* a picture representing maritime scene or view. — **serpent** *n.* enormous marine animal of serpenting form said to inhabit ocean. — **shell** *n.* a marine shell. **-shore** *n.* land adjacent to sea; (*Law*) ground between ordinary high-water mark and low-water mark. **-sick** *a.* suffering from seasickness. **-sickness** *n.* a disturbance of the nervous system with nausea and vomiting, produced by rolling and pitching of vessel at sea. **-side** *n.* and *a.* land adjacent to the sea. — **wall** *n.* embankment to prevent erosion or flooding. **-ward** *a.* and *adv.* towards the sea. **-weed** *n.* collective name for large group of marine plants (Algae). **-worthy** *n.* fit for proceeding to sea; able to stand up to buffetings of waves. **-worthiness** *n.* **at sea,** on the ocean; away from land; bewildered. **high seas,** the open sea [O.E. sae].

seal (sēl) *n.* an aquatic carnivorous animal with flippers as limbs, of which the eared variety furnishes rich fur pelt as well as oil; *v.i.* to hunt for seals. **-er** *n.* ship, or person, engaged in seal fishing. **-ery** *n.* seal-fishing station. **-skin** *n.* dressed skin or fur of eared seal; *a.* made of sealskin [O.E. seolh].

seal (sēl) *n.* piece of metal or stone engraved with a device, cipher, or motto for impression on wax, lead, etc.; impression made by this (on letters, documents, etc.); that which closes or secures; symbol, token, or indication; arrangement for making drainpipe joints airtight; *v.t.* to affix a seal to; to confirm; to ratify; to settle, as doom; to shut up; to close up joints, cracks, etc. **-ed** *a.* having a seal affixed; enclosed; ratified. **-ing wax** *n.* wax composed of shellac or other resinous substances and turpentine tinted with coloring matter. — **ring** *n.* a signet ring. [O.Fr. seel, fr. L. sigillum, a seal].

seam (sēm) *n.* line of junction of two edges, e.g. of two pieces of cloth, or of two planks; thin layer or stratum, esp. of coal; *v.t.* to join by sewing together; to mark with furrows or wrinkles; to scar. **-less** *a.* having no seams; woven in the piece. **-ster** *n.* (*fem.* **-stress, sempstress**) one who sews by profession. **-y** *a.* showing seams; sordid [O.E. fr. siwian, to sew].

sé·ance (sā'·ans) *n.* essembly; meeting of spiritualists for consulting spirits and communicating with 'the other world' [Fr.].

sear (sir) *v.t.* to scorch or brand with a hot iron; to dry up; to wither; to render callous; to brown meat quickly *a.* (*Poetic.*) dry; withered [O.E. searian].

search (surch) *v.t.* to look over or through in order to find; to probe into; *v.i.* to look for; to seek; to explore; *n.* searching; quest; inquiry; investigation. **-ing** *a.* thorough; penetrating; keen; minute. **-ingly** *adv.* **-ingness** *n.* **-light** *n.* electric arc-light which sends concentrated beam in any desired direction. — **warrant** *n.* warrant to enable police to search premises of suspected person [Fr. chercher, to look for].

sea·son (sē'·zn) *n.* one of four divisions of

year—spring, summer, autumn, winter; in tropical regions, the wet or dry period of year; busy holiday period; time of the year for certain activities, foods, etc.; convenient time; period; time; *v.t.* to render suitable; to habituate; to give relish to; to spice; to mature; *v.i.* to grow fit for use; to become adapted. **-able** *a.* suitable or appropriate for the season; opportune; timely; fit. **-ableness** *n.* **-ably** *adv.* **-al** *a.* depending on, or varying with, seasons. **-ally** *adv.* **-ing** *n.* flavoring. — **ticket** *n.* one valid for definite period. **open season,** time when something is permitted [L. satio, sowing].

seat (sēt) *n.* thing made or used for sitting; manner of sitting (of riding, etc.); right to sit (e.g. in council, etc.); sitting part of body; part of trousers which covers buttocks; locality of disease, trouble, etc.; country house; place from which a country is governed; *v.t.* to place on a seat; to cause to sit down; assign a seat to; to fit up with seats; to establish. **-ed** *a.* fixed; confirmed; settled. [O.N. saeti].

se·ba·ceous (si·bā'·shas) *a.* made of, or pert. to tallow or fat; secreting oily matter [L. sebum, tallow].

se·cant (sē'·kant, kant) *a.* cutting; dividing into two parts; *n.* any straight line which cuts another line, curve, or figure; a straight line drawn from center of circle through one end of an arc, and terminated by a tangent drawn through other end; in trigonometry, ratio of hypotenuse to another side of a right-angled triangle is secant of angle between these two sides. [L. secare, to cut].

se·cede (si·sēd') *v.i.* to withdraw formally from federation, alliance, etc. **-er** *n.* **secession** *n.* seceding from fellowship, alliance, etc.; withdrawal; departure [L. secedere, to go apart].

se·clude (si·klood') *v.t.* to shut up apart; to guard from or to remove from sight or resort. **-d** *a.* shut off; remote; sequestered. **-dly** *adv.* **seclusion** *n.* **seclusive** *a.* tending to seclude; retiring [L. secludere, to shut away].

sec·ond (sek'·and) *a.* next to first; other; another; inferior; subordinate; *n.* one who, or that which, follows the first; one next and inferior; one assisting, esp. principal in duel or boxing-match; sixtieth part of a minute; (*Mus.*) interval contained between two notes on adjacent degrees of the staff; moment; *n.pl.* inferior quality of commodity or article; *v.t.* to support, esp. a motion before a meeting or council; to back; to encourage. **Second Advent,** belief that Christ will return to earth in visible form. — **best** *n.* and *a.* best except one. — **childhood,** dotage, senility. — **class** *a.* of an inferior order; mediocre. — **hand** *a.* not new; having been used or worn; indirect. — **lieutenant** *n.* lowest commissioned rank in Army. **-ly** *adv.* in the second place. — **nature,** acquired habit. — **rate** *a.* of inferior quality, value, etc. — **sight** *n.* prophetic vision. **to play second fiddle,** to play or act subordinate part [L. secundus].

sec·ond·ar·y (sek'·an·der·i·) *a.* succeeding next in order to the first; of second place, origin, rank; second-rate; inferior; unimportant; pert. to education and schools intermediate between elementary schools and university; (*Geol.*) relating to Mesozoic period; *n.* one who occupies a subordinate place. — **color,** color obtained by combination of primary colors, blue, red, and yellow. **secondarily** *adv.* in a secondary or subordinate manner; not primarily. [fr. second].

se·cret (sē'·krit) *a.* kept or meant to be kept from general knowledge; concealed; unseen; private; *n.* something kept secret or concealed; a mystery; governing principle known only to initiated. **secrecy** n. keeping or being kept secret; fidelity in keeping a secret; retirement; privacy; concealment. **-ly** adv. **-ness** n. secrecy. **secretive** (or ·krē′·) a. uncommunicative; reticent; underhand. **-ively** adv. **-iveness** n. [L. secretus, separated].

sec·re·tar·y (sek′·ra·ter·i·) n. one employed to deal with papers and correspondence, keep records, prepare business, etc.; confidential clerk; official in charge of a particular department of government; a desk with bookshelves on top. **secretarial** a. pert. to duties of a secretary. **secretariat** n. administrative office or officials controlled by secretary; the secretarial force of an office. **-ship** n. office or post of a secretary [L. secretum (something) secret].

se·crete (si·krēt) to hide or conceal; of gland, etc. to collect and supply particular substance in body; a. separate; distinct. **secreta** n.pl. products of secretion. **secretion** n. substance elaborated by gland out of blood or body fluids; process of so secreting or elaborating. **secretional** a. **secretive** a. promoting or causing secretion. **secretor** n. a secreting organ or gland. **secretory** a. [L. secernere, secretum, to set apart].

sect (sekt) n. religious denomination; followers of philosopher or religious leader; faction. **-arian** a. pert. to a sect; n. one of a sect; a bigot; a partisan. **-arianism** n. devotion to the interests of a sect. **-ary** n. one of a sect; a dissenter [L. secta, fr. sequi, to follow].

sec·tion (sek′·shan) n. cutting or separating by cutting; part separated from the rest; division; portion; a piece; a subdivision of subject matter of book, chapter, statute; printer's reference mark (§) used for footnotes; representation of portion of building or object exposed when cut by imaginary vertical plane so as to show its construction and interior; surveyor's scaled drawing showing variations in surface level of ground along base-line; (Geom.) plane figure formed by cutting a solid by another plane; line formed by intersection of two surfaces; distinct part of a city, country, people, etc.; small military unit; (Bot. and Zool.) thin, translucent slice of organic or inorganic matter mounted on slide for detailed microscopic examination. **-al** a. pert. to, made up of sections; partial; local; (of paper) ruled in small squares. **-alism** n. partial regard for limited interests of one particular class at expense of others. **-ally** adv. **-ize** v.t. to divide out in sections [L. secare, sectum, to cut].

sec·tor (sek′·ter) n. portion of circle enclosed by two radii and the arc which they intercept; mathematical instrument; (Mil.) a subdivision of the combat area. **-al** a. [L. secare, sectum, to cut].

sec·u·lar (sek′·ya·ler) a. worldly; temporal, as opposed to spiritual; lay; pert. to anything not religious; lasting for, occurring once in, a century or age; n. layman; clergyman, not bound by vow of poverty and not belonging to religious order. **-ization** n. **secularize** v.t. to convert from spiritual to secular use; to make worldly. **secularism** n. ethical doctrine which advocates a moral code independent of all religious considerations or practices. **-ist** n. **-ity** n. worldliness; secularism. **-ly** adv. [L. saecularis, fr. saeculum, an age, a century].

se·cure (si·kūr′) a. free from care, anxiety, fear; safe; fixed; stable; in close custody; certain; confident; v.t. to make safe, certain, fast; to close, or confine, effectually; to gain possession of; to obtain; to assure. **securable** a. **securance** n. assurance; act of securing. **-ly** adv. **-ness** n. free from anxiety; feeling

of security. **-r** n. **security** n. being secure; what secures; protection; assurance; anything given as bond, caution, or pledge. **Security Council** n. branch of United Nations Organization, set up in 1945, to settle international disputes and to prevent aggression. **securities** n.pl. general term for shares, bonds, stocks, debentures, etc.; documents giving to holder right to possess certain property [L. securus, fr. se-, without; cura, care].

se·dan (si·dan′) n. old-time closed conveyance with a chair inside for one, carried on two poles; a sedan chair; a closed automobile with two full seats [orig. made at Sedan, France].

se·date (si·dāt′) a. staid; not excitable, composed; calm. **-ly** adv. **-ness** n. **sedative** a. tending to calm; soothing; n. agent, external or internal, which soothes [L. sedare, to calm].

sed·en·tar·y (sed′·an·ter·i·) a. sitting much; requiring sitting posture, as certain forms of employment; inactive. **sedentariness** n. [L. sedere, to sit].

sedge (sej) n. any marshgrass. **sedgy** a. [O.E. secg].

sed·i·ment (sed′·a·mant) n. matter which settles to bottom of liquid; lees; dregs. **-ary** a. composed of sediment, esp. of rock laid down as deposits by water action. **-ation** n. [L. sedere, to settle].

se·di·tion (si·dish′·an) n. any act aimed at disturbing peace of realm or producing insurrection. **-ary** n. one who incites sedition. **seditious** a. pert. to, tending to excite sedition. **seditiously** adv. **seditiousness** n. [L. seditio, a going apart].

se·duce (si·dūs′) v.t. to lead astray; to draw aside from path of rectitude and duty; to induce woman to surrender chastity; to allure. **-ment** n. seduction. **-r** n. **seducible** a. liable to be led astray; corruptible. **seduction** n. act of seducing. **seductive** a. **seductively** adv. **seductiveness** n. [L. seducere, to lead aside].

sed·u·lous (sej′·a·las) a. diligent; steady; industrious; persevering. **sedulity** n. **-ness** n. **-ly** adv. [L. sedulus].

see (sē) n. diocese or jurisdiction of bishop; province of archbishop. **the Holy See,** the papal court [O.Fr. siet, fr. L. sedere, to sit].

see (sē) v.t. to perceive by eye; to behold; to observe; to form an idea; to understand; to have interview with; to visit; to meet with; v.i. to have the power of sight; to pay regard; to consider; to give heed; to understand; to apprehend. pa.t. **saw.** pa.p. **seen. -r** n. one who sees; one who foresees events, has second-sight; a prophet. **-ing** conj. considering; since; n. act of perceiving; sight [O.E. seon].

seed (sēd) n. ovule, which gives origin to new plant; one grain of this; such grains saved or used for sowing; that from which anything springs; origin; source; progeny; offspring; sperm; first principle; v.t. to sow with seed; to remove seeds from; to arrange draw for sports tournament, so that best players, etc. should not be drawn against each other in earlier rounds; v.i. to produce seed; to shed seed. **-ed** a. sown. **-ily** adv. in seedy manner. **-iness** n. being seedy; shabbiness. **-less** a. **-ling** n. young plant or tree, grown from seed. **-y** a. abounding with seeds; run to seed; shabby; worn out; miserable looking. **to run to seed,** to produce flowers and seed at expense of leaves or roots; to go to waste or ruin [O.E. saed].

seek (sēk) v.t. to make search or enquiry for; to look for; to ask for; to strive after; v.i. to make search. pa.t. and pa.p. **sought. -er** n. [O.E. secan].

seem (sēm) v.i. to appear (to be or to do); to look; to appear to one's judgment. **-ing** a. appearing like; apparent; n. appearance; apparent likeness; **-ingly** adv. **-liness** n. **-ly**

a. fit; becoming; *adv.* in a decent or proper manner [O.N. *sōma*].

seen (sēn) *pa.p.* of **see.**

seep (sēp) *v.i.* to ooze; to trickle; to leak away. **-age** *n.* [O.E. *sipian*, to soak].

se·er (sē′·ẹr) *n.* a prophet [fr. *see*].

seer·suck·er (sir′·suk·ẹr) *n.* a cotton fabric of alternating plain and crinkled stripes [fr. Pers. *shir o shakkar* = milk and sugar].

see·saw (sē′·saw) *n.* game in which two children sit at opposite ends of plank supported in middle and swing up and down; plank for this; up-and-down motion; *a.* moving up and down or to and fro; reciprocal; *v.i.* to move up and down [imit.].

seethe (sēTH) *v.t.* to soak; *v.i.* to be in a state of ebullition; to be violently agitated; [O.E. *seothan*, to boil].

seg·ment (seg′·mạnt) *n.* part cut off from a figure by a line; part of circle contained between chord and arc of that circle; section; portion; part; *v.t.* and *v.i.* to separate into segments. **-al** *a.* relating to a segment. **-ary, -ate** *a.* **-ation** *n.* **-ed** *a.* [L. *segmentum*].

seg·re·gate (seg′·rạ·gāt) *v.t.* and *v.i.* to set or go apart from the rest; to isolate; to separate; *a.* set apart; separate from the others. **segregation** *n.* [L. *segregare*, to remove from the flock (*grex*)].

se·gui·dil·la (se·gē·dē′·lyạ) *n.* graceful, lively Spanish dance; music for it [Sp.].

seign·ior (sēn′·yawr), **sei·gneur** (sēn·yur′) *n.* a feudal lord of a manor; title of honor or respectful address. **-age, seignorage** *n.* anything claimed by sovereign or feudal superior as prerogative. **-ality** *n.* authority or domains of a seignior. **-ial, -ial, signorial** *a.* manorial. **grand seignor,** Sultan of Turkey [Fr. fr. L. *senior*, elder].

seine (sān) *n.* open net for sea fishing. *v.t.* to catch fish by dragging a seine through water [Fr. fr. L. *sagena*, a fishing net].

seism (sīzm) *n.* earthquake. **-al, -ic** *a.* pert. to or produced by earthquake. **-ogram** *n.* record of earthquake made by seismograph. **-ograph** *n.* instrument which records distance and intensity of slightest earth tremors. **-ologic, -al -ologist** *n.* one versed in seismology. **-ology** *n.* the study of earthquakes and their causes and effects [Gk. *seismos*, an earthquake].

seize (sēz) *v.t.* to grasp; to take hold of; to take possession of by force or legal authority; to arrest; to capture; to comprehend; *v.i.* to take hold. **seizable** *a.* **seizure** *n.* act of seizing; thing or property seized; sudden attack, as apoplectic stroke [Fr. *saisir*].

sel·dom (sel′·dạm) *adv.* rarely [O.E. *seldum*].

se·lect (sạ·lekt′) *v.t.* to choose; to cull; to prefer; *a.* of choice quality; of special excellence; chosen; picked; exclusive; *n.* the best people. **-ed** *a.* **-edly** *adv.* **-ion** *n.* selecting; things selected; variety of articles from which to select; (*Mus.*) medley; (*Biol.*) process, according to the evolutionary theory, by which certain members of species survive and others, unfit, are gradually eliminated. **-ive** *a.* having power of selection; discriminating. **-ively** *adv.* **-ivity** *n.* **-or** *n.* [L. *seligere, selectum*].

sel·e·nite (sel′ạn·īt) *n.* a colorless and translucent crystalline form of gypsum (calcium sulphate) [Gk. *selēnē*, the moon].

self (self) *n.* one's individual person; one's personal interest; ego; subject of individual consciousness; selfishness. *pl.* **selves** (selvz). *pron.* affix used to express emphasis or a reflexive usage; *a.* of color, uniform, same throughout; of same material, etc.; *prefix* used in innumerable compounds. **—abandonment** *n.* disregard of self. **—abnegation** *n.* self-denial. **—abuse** *n.* masturbation; abuse of one's own powers. **—assurance** *n.* self-

confidence. **—centered** *a.* egoistic. **—confidence** *n.* whole-hearted reliance on one's own powers and resources. **—confident** *a.* **—consciousness** *n.* an embarrassed state of mind leading to confusion due to belief that one is object of critical judgment by others present. **—conscious** *a.* **—contained** *a.* of a reserved nature; complete in itself; (of a house) having a separate entrance, detached. **—control** *n.* control over oneself, temper, emotions, and desires. **—defense** *n.* the act of defending one's person or justifying one's actions. **—denial** *n.* refraining from gratifying one's desires or appetites; unselffishness, to the point of deprivation. **—determination** *n.* free will; right of a people or nation to work out its own problems and destiny, free from intereference from without. **—governing** *a.* autonomous; having a legislature elected by, and responsible to, those governed. **—government** *n.* **—indulgence** *n.* undue gratification of one's appetites or desires. **—interest** *n.* selfishness. **-ish** *a.* concerned unduly over personal profit or pleasure; lacking consideration for others; mercenary; greedy. **-less** *a.* unselfish. **—pity** *n.* morbid pleasure in nursing one's own woes. **—possessed** *a.* calm and collected; able to control one's feelings and emotions; composed; undisturbed. **—preservation** *n.* instinctive impulse to avoid injury or death. **—respect** *n.* a proper regard for one's own person, character, or reputation. **—respecting** *a.* **—respectful** *a.* **—righteous** *a.* thinking oneself faultless; esteeming oneself as better than others; pharisaical; sanctimonious. **—sacrifice** *n.* foregoing personal advantage or comfort for the sake of others. **-same** *a.* the very same; identical. **—satisfaction** *n.* personal reassurance; (in a bad sense) smug conceit. **—satisfied** *a.* **—seeker** *n.* one who seeks only his own own profit or pleasure. **—seeking** *a.* seeking one's own interest or happiness. **—starter** *n.* an automatic contrivance used for starting internal-combustion engine of automobile. **—styled** *a.* so-called, without any real warrant or authority; self-assumed. **—sufficient** *a.* sufficient in itself; relying on one's own powers. **—supporting** *a.* not dependent on others for a living [O.E.].

sell (sel) *v.i.* to dispose of for an equivalent, usually money; to deal in; to betray for money or a consideration; to delude; (*Slang*) to trick; to have for sale; to promote sale of; *v.t.* to fetch a price; to be in demand; *pa.t.* and *pa.p.* **sold.** *n.* deception; hoax. **-er** *n.* one who sells; vendor [O.E. *sellan*].

Selt·zer (selt′·sẹr) *n.* a carbonated mineral water; artificial mineral water; aerated with carbon dioxide [corrupt. of *Selters*].

sel·vage, selvedge (sel′·vij) *n.* edge of cloth finished to prevent raveling; strong edging of web [for *self-edge*].

selves (selvz) *n.pl.* of **self.**

se·man·tic (sạ·man′·tik) *a.* pert. to meaning of words. **-s** *n.pl.* branch of linguistic research concerned with studying meaning and changes in meaning of words [Gk. *sēmainein*, to mean].

sem·a·phore (sem′·ạ·fōr) *n.* a post with movable arm or arms used for signaling; a system of signaling by human or mechanical arms [Gk. *sēma*, sign; *pherein*, to bear].

se·ma·si·ol·o·gy (sạ·mā·si·ål′·ạ·ji) *n.* the science of the development of the meanings of words, semantics. **semasiological** *a.* [Gk. *sēmasia*, meaning; *logos* a discourse].

sem·blance (sem′·blạn(t)s) *n.* real or seeming likeness; appearance; image; form; figure [Fr. *sembler*, to seem].

se·men (sē′·mạn) *n.* male secretion containing sperm [L. = seed].

se·mes·ter (sạ·mes'·tẹr) *n.* one of two or three divisions of the school year [Fr. *semestre*, fr. L. *sex*, six; *mensis*, a month].

sem·i- (sem'·i) *prefix* with the meaning of half, partly, imperfectly, etc., used in the construction of compound terms, the meaning being usually obvious. **-annual** *a.* half-yearly. **-breve** *n.* (*Mus.*) a whole note. **-circle** *n.* plane figure bounded by diameter and portion of circumference of a circle which it cuts off. **-circled, -circular** *a.* **-colon** *n.* punctuation mark (;) used to separate clauses of a sentence requiring a more marked separation than is indicated by a comma. **-final** *n.* a match, round, etc. qualifying winner to contest the final. **-tone** *n.* (*Mus.*) half a tone; smallest interval used in music [L. = half].

sem·i·nal (sem'·ạ·nạl) *a.* pert. to seed of plants or semen of animals; reproductive. **semination** *n.* act of sowing or disseminating; seeding. **seminiferous, seminific** *a.* seedbearing [L. *semen*, seed].

sem·i·nar (sem'·ạ·nȧr) *n.* group of advanced students pursuing research in a specific subject under supervision [L. *semen*, seed].

sem·i·nar·y (sem'·ạ·ner·i·) *n.* academy; secondary school for girls; a training college for priesthood or ministry; *a.* trained in seminary. **seminarist** *n.* [L. *seminarium*, nursery].

Sem·i·nole (sem'·ạ·nōl) one of a nomadic tribe of American Indians, formerly living S.E. of the Mississippi (Florida, etc.).

se·mi·ol·o·gy (sē·mi·al·a·ji·) *n.* (*Med.*) study of signs and symptoms of disease; symptomatology. **semiotics** *n.* science or language of signs. [Gk. *sémeion*, a mark].

Sem·ite (sem'·it) *n.* member of a speech family comprising Hebrews, Arabs, Assyrians, etc.; descendant of Shem (Genesis x). **Semitic** *a.*

sem·o·li·na (sem·ạ·lē'·nạ) *n.* hard grains of wheat used in production of spaghetti, macaroni, etc. Also **semola** [L. *simila*, wheatmeal].

sen (sen) *n.* Japanese copper coin.

sen·ate (sen'·it) *n.* supreme legislative and administrative assembly in ancient Rome; upper house of legislature, e.g. U.S., France, Canada, and others; governing or advisory body in many universities. **senator** *n.* a member of a senate. **senatorial** *a.* [L. *senatus*, council of old men, fr. *senex*, old man].

send (send) *v.t.* to cause to go; to transmit; to forward; to despatch; to throw; *v.i.* to despatch messenger; to transmit message. *pa.t.* and *pa.p.* **sent** [O.E. *sendan*].

se·nes·cence (sạ·nes'·ạns) *n.* the state of growing old; decay; old age. **senescent** *a.* growing old [L. *senescere*, to grow old].

sen·es·chal (sen'·ạ·shạl) *n.* functionary who superintended household affairs of feudal lord in Middle Ages; steward [O.Fr.].

se·nile (sē'·nīl) *a.* pert. to old age; aged; doting. **senility** *n.* degenerative physical or mental conditions accompanying old age; old age [L. *senex*, old man].

sen·ior (sēn'·yẹr) *a.* older; superior in rank or standing; pert. to highest class of school or college; *n.* a person older, or of higher rank, or of longer service, than another; an aged person; a member of a senior class. **-ity** *n.* state of being older; precedence in rank, or longer in service; priority [L. = older].

sen·na (sen'·ạ) *n.* a valuable purgative drug [Ar. *sana*].

se·ñor (sān·yawr') *n.* Spanish form of address; sir; gentleman; equivalent to Mr.;**-a** *n.* lady; madam; Mrs. **-ita** *n.* young lady; Miss.

sen·sa·tion (sen·sā'·shạn) *n.* what we learn through senses; state of physical consciousness; effect produced on a sense organ by external stimulus; excited feeling or state of excitement; exciting event; strong impression. **sensate** *a.* perceived by the senses. **-al** *a.* pert. to perception by senses; producing great excitement and surprise; melodramatic. **-alist** *n.* **-ally** *adv.* [L. *sensus*, feeling].

sen·sa·tion·al·ism (sen·sā'·shạn·ạ·liz·ạm) *n.* matter, language or style designed to excite and please vulgar taste; sensualism. (*philos.*) doctrine that all knowledge originates in sense perception [L. *sensus*, feeling].

sense (sens) *n.* any of the bodily faculties of perception or feeling; sensitiveness of any or all of these faculties; ability to perceive; mental alertness; consciousness; significance; meaning; coherence; wisdom; good judgment; prudence. *pl.* wits; faculties; *v.t.* to perceive; to suspect; (*Colloq.*) to understand. **-less** *a.* destitute of sense; insensible; unfeeling; silly; foolish; stupid; absurd. **-lessly** *adv.* **-lessness** *n.* [L. *sentire, sensum*, to feel].

sen·si·ble (sen'·sạ·bl) *a.* capable of being perceived by the senses; characterized by good sense; perceptible; aware; conscious; appreciable; reasonable. **sensibility** *n.* power of experiencing sensation; faculty by which mind receives intuitions; capacity of feeling. **sensibly** *adv.* [fr. *sense*].

sen·si·tive (sen'·sạ·tiv) *a.* open to, or acutely affected by, external stimuli or impressions; easily affected or altered; responsive to slight changes; easily upset by criticism. **-ly** *adv.* **-ness** *n.* quality or state of being sensitive. **sensitivity** *n.* sensitiveness; keen sensibility; capacity to receive and respond to external stimuli [Fr. *sensitif*, fr. L. *sentire*, to feel].

sen·si·tize (sen'·sạ·tīz) *v.t.* to render sensitive; in photography, to render film, paper, etc. sensitive to the chemical action of light. **sensitizer** *n.* [L. *sensus*, feeling].

sen·so·ry (sen'·sạ·ri·) *a.* pert. to, or serving, senses; conveying sensations, as the nerve-fibers [L. *sensus*, feeling].

sen·su·al (sen'·shoo'·al) *a.* pert. to the senses; given to pursuit of pleasures of sense; self-indulgent; voluptuous; lewd. **-ization** *n.* **-ize** *v.t.* to make or render sensual. **-ism** *n.* fleshly indulgence. **-ist** *n.* one given to lewd or loose mode of life; **-istic** *a.* **-ity** *n.* **-ly** *adv.* **sensuous** *a.* stimulating, or apprehended by, senses. **sensuously** *adv.* **sensuousness** *n.* [L. *sensus*, feeling].

sent (sent) *pa.t.* and *pa.p.* of **send.**

sen·tence (sen'·tạns) *n.* combination of words, which is complete as expressing a thought; opinion; judgment passed on criminal by court or judge; decision; *v.t.* to pass sentence upon; to condemn. **sententious** (sen·ten'·chạs) *a.* abounding with axioms and maxims; short and energetic; pithy; moralizing [L. *sententia*, an opinion].

sen·tient (sen'·shi·ant) *a.* feeling or capable of feeling; perceiving by senses; sensitive. **sentience, sentiency** *n.* consciousness at a sensory level. **-ly** *adv.* [L. *sentire*, to feel].

sen·ti·ment (sen'·tạ·mant) *n.* abstract emotion; tendency to be moved by feeling rather than idea; opinion. **sentimental** (sen·tạ·men'·tal) *a.* abounding with sentiment; romantic; emotional; foolishly tender. **-alism, -ality** *n.* affected and distorted expression of sentiment revealing a superficiality of feeling. **-alist** *n.* one given to sentimental talk; one swayed by emotions rather than by reason. [O.Fr. *sentement*, fr. L. *sentire*, to feel].

sen·ti·nel (sen'·tạ·nạl) *n.* guard; sentry; *a.* acting as sentinel; watching [Fr. *sentinelle*].

sen·try (sen'·tri·) *n.* soldier on guard; sentinel; duty of sentry. **— box** *n.* small shelter used by sentry [fr. *sanctuary*, a place of safety].

se·pal (sē'·pạl) *n.* (*Bot.*) leaf-like member of outer covering, or calyx, of flower. **-ous** *a.*

having sepals [Fr. *sépale*].

sep·a·rate (sep'·a·rāt) *v.t.* to part in any manner; to divide; to disconnect; to detach; to withdraw; to become disunited; *a.* divided; disconnected; apart; distinct; individual. **separability** *n.* **separable** *a.* **-ly** *adv.* **-ness** *n.* **separation** *n.* act of separating; state of being separate. **separationist** *n.* one who supports policy of breaking away from a union of states or countries; a separatist. **separatism** *n.* act or policy of separating or withdrawing from any union, esp. religious or political. **separatist** *n.* [L. *separare*].

se·pi·a (sē'·pi·a) *n.* brown pigment obtained from ink bags of cuttlefish, uased as water-color [Gk. = cuttlefish].

sep·sis (sep'·sis) *n.* (*Med.*) state of having bodily tissue infected by bacteria. **septic** *a.* [Gk. = putrefaction].

sept (sept) *n.* clan, race, or family, proceeding from common progenitor.

Sep·tem·ber (sep·tem'·ber) *n.* ninth month of year (L. *septem*, seven, as being 7th month of Roman year].

sep·te·nar·y (sep'·ta'·ner·i·) *a.* crossing of seven; lasting seven years; occurring once in seven years. [L. *septem*, seven].

sep·tet, septette (sep·tet') *n.* (*Mus.*) composition for seven voices or instruments [L. *septem*, seven].

sep·tic (sep'·tik) *a.* pert. to sepsis; infected. **-emia, -aemia** (sep·ta·sē·mi·a) *n.* blood poisoning. **-ally** *adv.* [Gk.].

sep·tu·a·ge·nar·i·an (sep·t(y)oo·a·ja·ner'·i·an) *n.* person between seventy and eighty years of age. **septuagenary** *a.* consisting of seventy; seventy years old; *n.* a septuagenarian [L. *septuaginta*, seventy].

Sep·tu·a·ges·i·ma (sep·t(y)oo·a·jes'·a·ma) *n.* third Sunday before Lent, seventy days before Easter. [L. *septuagesimus*, seventieth].

Sep·tu·a·gint (sep'·too·a·jint) *n.* the first and only complete version in Greek of the Old Testament. **-al** *a.* [L. *septuaginta*, seventy (compilers)].

sep·tu·ple (sep'·too·pl) *a.* sevenfold; *v.t.* to multiply by seven [L. *septem*, seven].

sep·ul·cher (sep'·al·ker) *n.* tomb; grave; burial vault; *v.t.* to place in a sepulcher. **sepulchral** (sa·pul'·kral) *a.* pert. to burial, the grave, or monuments erected to dead; funereal; mournful. **sepulture** *n.* act of burying dead [L. *Sepulcrum*].

se·qua·cious (sa·kwā'·shas) *a.* following; attendant; easily led. **-ness, sequacity** *n.* [L. *sequi*, to follow].

se·quel (sē'·kwal) *n.* that which follows; consequence; issue; end; continuation, complete in itself, of a novel or narrative previously published [L. *sequi*, to follow].

se·quence (sē'·kwans) *n.* connected series; succession; run of three or more cards of same suit in numerical order; part of scenario of film; (*Mus.*) repetition of musical figure, either melodic or harmonic, on different degrees of sale. **sequent** *a.* following; succeeding; *n.* sequence. **sequential** *a.* in succession. **sequentially** *adv.* [L. *sequi*, to follow].

se·ques·ter (si·kwes'·ter) *v.t.* to put aside; to separate; to seclude; to cause to retire into

se·quin (sē'·kwin) *n.* small, ornamental metal disk on dresses, etc. [It. *zecchino*, fr. *zecca*, mint].

Se·quoi·a (si·kwoi'·a) *n.* genus of gigantic coniferous evergreen trees native to California [fr. *Sequoiah*, a Cherokee Indian chief].

se·rag·lio (si·ral'·yō) *n.* harem or women's quarters in royal household [It. *serraglio*, an enclosure, fr. L. *sera*, a bolt].

ser·aph (ser'·af) *n.* member of the highest order of angels. **-s, -im** *n.pl.* **-ic, -ical** *a.* [Heb.].

Serb, Serbian (surb, sur'·bi·an) *a.* pert. to Serbia; *n.* native or inhabitant of Serbia, the chief constituent state of Yugoslavia.

sere (sir) *a.* dry; withered [fr. *sear*].

ser·e·nade (ser·a·nād') *n.* music of quiet, simple, melodious character sung or played at night below person's window, esp. by lover; *v.t.* to entertain with serenade. **-r** *n.* **serenata** *n.* instrumental work, between suite and symphony [It. *serenata*, fr. *sereno*, the open air].

ser·en·dip·i·ty (ser·an·dip'·a·ti·) *n.* knack of stumbling upon interesting discoveries in a casual manner ['The Three Princes of Serendip' by Horace Walpole].

se·rene (sa·rēn') *a.* clear and calm; unclouded; fair; unruffled; quiet; placid; composed. **-ly** *adv.* **-ness, serenity** *n.* condition or quality of being serene [L. *serenus*, clear].

serf (surf) *n.* under feudalism; a bondman; vassal. **-age, -dom, -hood** *n.* [L. *servus*, a slave].

serge (surj) *n.* hard-wearing worsted fabric [L. *serica*, silk].

ser·geant, sergeant (sàr'·jant) *n.* noncommissioned officer in army, ranking above corporal; police officer ranking above constable; officer of a law court. **-ship, sergeancy** *n.* **— at arms** *n.* officer attendant on legislative body, charged with preservation of order. **— major** *n.* highest noncommissioned officer [Fr. *sergent*, fr. L. *serviens*, serving].

se·ri·al (sir'·i·al) *a.* consisting of a series; appearing in successive parts or installments; *n.* a periodical publication; a tale or writing published or broadcast, etc., in successive numbers or programs. **-ize** *v.t.* to publish as a serial. **-ly, seriately** *adv.* in a regular series or order. **seriatim** (sir·ē·āt'·am) *adv.* point by point; one after another [fr. *series*].

se·ries (sir'·ēz) *n. s.* and *pl.* succession of related objects or matters; sequence; order; related objects or matters; sequence; set; books, bound and printed in same style, usually on kindred subjects; (*Elect.*) end-to-end arrangement of batteries or circuits which are traversed by the same current [L.].

ser·if (ser'·if) *n.* (*Printing*) a fine line at the end of the stems and arms of unconnected Roman type letters, as M, y, etc.

se·ri·ous (sir'·i·as) *a.* grave in manner or disposition; earnest; important; attended with danger; in earnest. **-ly** *adv.* **-ness** *n.* [L. *serius*].

ser·jeant. See **sergeant.**

ser·mon (sur'·man) *n.* discourse for purpose of religious instruction usually based on Scripture; serious and admonitory address. **-ic, -al** *a.* of the nature of a sermon. **-ize** *v.t.* to preach earnestly; to compose a sermon. **-izer** *n.* [L. *sermo*, a discourse].

se·rous (sir'·as) *a.* pert. to, containing, or producing serum; watery; thin. **serosity** *n.* state of being serous [L. *serum*].

ser·pent (sur'·pant) *n.* snake; reptile without feet; treacherous or malicious person; kind of firework; (*Cap.*) constellation in northern hemisphere (*Mus.*) bass wooden wind instrument bent in a serpentine form; *a.* deceitful treacherous. **-ine** *a.* relating to, or like, serpent; winding; spiral; meandering; crafty; treacherous; *n.* skin; *v.i.* to wind in and out like a serpent. **-inely** *adv.* [L. *serpere*, to creep].

ser·rate, serrated (ser'·āt, ·ed) *a.* notched or cut like saw, as a leaf edge. **serration** *n.* formation in shape of saw. **serrature** *n.* series of notches, like that of saw. **serriform** *a.* toothed like a saw. [L. *serra*, a saw].

ser·ried (ser'·id) *a.* in close order; pressed shoulder to shoulder [Fr. *serrer*, to lock].

se·rum (sir'·am) *n.* watery secretion; whey; thin straw-colored fluid, residue of plasma or liquid part of the blood; such fluid used for inoculation or vaccination [L. = whey].

serv·ant (sur′·vant) *n.* personal or domestic attendant; one who serves another. **civil servant,** member of the civil service; government employee [L. *servire,* to serve].

serve (surv) *v.t.* to work for; to be a servant to; to minister to; to wait on; to attend; to help; to distribute, as rations, stores, etc.; to promote; to advance; to forward; to satisfy; to deliver formally; *v.i.* to work under another; to carry out duties; to be a member of a military, naval, etc. unit; to be useful, or suitable, or enough; in tennis, to resume play by striking the ball diagonally across court; *n.* in tennis, act of serving a ball. **servable** *a.* capable of being served. **-r** *n.* one who serves; a salver or small tray [L. *servire,* to serve].

serv·ice (sur′·vis) *n.* state of being a servant; work done for and benefit conferred on another; act of kindness; department of public employment; employment of persons engaged in this; military, naval, or air-force duty; advantage; use; form of divine worship; regular supply, as water, bus, electricity, etc.; (*Law*) serving of a process or summons; turn for serving ball at tennis, etc.; a set of dishes, etc.; *v.t.* to perform service for, e.g., automobiles, etc. **-able** *a.* useful; helpful; convenient; in fair working order. **— station** *n.* a place for buying gasoline, oil, etc. and making minor repairs on automobiles. **active service,** military, naval, or air force service against an enemy. **dinner-service, table-service, tea-service,** complete set of the appropriate dishes. **the Services,** the armed forces [L. *servire,* to serve].

serv·ice (sur′·vis) *n.* a small fruit tree; the shadbush [corrupt. of L. *sorbus*].

ser·vi·ette (sur·vi·et′) *n.* a table napkin [Fr.].

ser·vile (sur′·val) *a.* pert. to or befitting a servant or slave; submissive; dependent; menial. **-ly** *adv.* **servility** *n.* [L. *servilis,* slavish].

ser·vi·tor (sur′·va·ter) *n.* attendant; follower or adherent. **servitude** *n.* slavery; bondage [L. *servire,* to serve].

ses·a·me (ses′·a·mē) *n.* annual herbaceous plant cultivated in India and Asia Minor for seeds from which oil is extracted. [Gk.].

ses·qui- (ses′·kwi) *prefix* denoting a proportion of 3:2. **-alteral, -alterate, -alterous** *a.* one and a half more. **-centennial** *a.* pert. to a century and a half; *n.* the 150th anniversary. **-pedalian** *a.* measuring a foot and a half long; applied humorously to any long cumbersome technical word or to one given to using unnecessarily long words. **-pedalianism** *n.* [L. *sesqui,* one half more].

ses·sile (ses′·al) *a.* attached by the base, as a leaf; fixed and stationary [L. *sessilis,* low, fr. *sedere, sessum,* to sit].

ses·sion (sesh′·an) *n.* actual sitting of a court, council, etc. for transaction of business; term during which a court, council, and the like, meet for business; a period of time at school or college when a definite course of instruction is given. **-al** *a.* [L. *sessio,* fr. *sedere,* to sit].

ses·tet, seste (ses′·tet) *n.* (*Mus.*) composition for six instruments or voices; last six lines of a sonnet [L. *sextus,* sixth].

set (set) *v.t.* to put; to cause to sit; to seat; to place; to plant; to make ready; to adjust; to arrange (of hair) while wet; to fix, as precious stone in metal; to convert into curd; to extend (sail); to reduce from dislocated or fractured state, as limb; to adapt, as words to music; to compose type; to place a brooding fowl on nest of eggs; to crouch or point,

as dog, to game; to clench (teeth); to stake; *v.i.* to pass below horizon; to go down; to strike root; to become fixed or rigid; to congeal or solidify; to put forth an effort; to begin. *pr.p.* **-ting.** *pa.t.* and *pa.p.* **set.** [O.E. *settan*].

set (set) *n.* a number of things or persons associated as being similar or complementary or used together, etc.; the manner in which a thing is set, hangs, or fits, as a dress; permanent change of shape or figure in consequence of pressure or cooling; an attitude or posture; young plant, cutting, or slip for planting out; direction, tendency, drift; figure of square dance; group or clique; setting of sun; equipment to form the ensemble of a scene for stage or film representation; (*Radio*) complete apparatus for reception (or transmission) of radio signals and broadcasts; (*Tennis*) series of games forming unit for match-scoring purposes; (*print.*) width of type character; a wooden or granite block or set; *a.* fixed; firm; prescribed; regular; established; arranged; appointed; obstinate; determined. **-back** *n.* check to progress [O.Fr. *sette,* sect or O.E. *settan*].

se·ta (sē′·ta) *n.* bristle or bristlelike structure. **setaceous, setose** *a.* bristly [L. = a bristle].

set·tee (se·tē′) *n.* couch or sofa [Cf. *settle*].

set·ter (set′·er) *n.* hunting, formerly dog trained to crouch or set when game was perceived [fr. *set*].

set·ting (set′·ing) *n.* fixing, adjusting, or putting in place; descending below horizon, as of sun; bezel which holds a precious stone, etc. in position; mounting of scene in play or film; background or surroundings [fr. *set*].

set·tle (set′·l) *v.t.* to put in place, order, arrangement, etc.; to fix; to establish; to make secure or quiet; to decide upon; to bring (dispute) to an end; to reconcile; to calm; to pay; to liquidate; to secure by legal deed, as a pension, annuity, etc.; to take up residence in; to colonize; *v.i.* to become fixed or stationary; to arrange; to come to rest; to (cause to) sink to bottom; to subside; to take up residence in; to dwell; to become calm; to become clear (of liquid). **-d** *a.* fixed; permanent; deep-rooted; decided; quiet; methodical; adjusted by agreement. **-ment** *n.* act of settling; state of being settled; colonization; a colony; (*Law*) transfer of real or personal property to a person; sum secured to a person. **-r** *n.* one who makes his home in a new country; colonist. **settling** *n.* the act of making a settlement; act of subsiding; adjusting of matters in dispute; *pl.* sediment [O.E. *setl,* a seat].

set·tle (set′·l) *n.* long high-backed bench; settee [O.E. *setl,* a seat].

sev·en (sev′·an) *a.* one more than six; *n.* number greater by one than six, symbol 7 or VII; **-fold** *a.* repeated seven times; increased to seven times the size; *adv.* seven times as much or as often. [O.E. *seofon*].

sev·en·teen (sev′·an·tēn) *a.* one more than sixteen; *n.* sum of ten and seven; symbol 17, or XVII *a.* and *n.* the seventh after the tenth [O.E. *seofontiene*].

sev·enth (sev′·anth) *a.* constituting one of seven equal parts; *n.* one of seven equal parts. **Seventh-day Adventists,** Christian sect observing seventh day as Sabbath. **Seventh heaven,** supreme ecstasy or beatitude. [fr. *seven*].

sev·en·ty (sev′·an·ti·) *a.* seven times ten; *n.* sum of seven times ten; the symbol 70 or LXX. **seventieth** *a.* constituting one of seventy equal parts [O.E. *seofontig*].

sev·er (sev′·er) *v.t.* to part or divide by violence; to sunder; to cut or break off; *v.i.* to divide; to make a separation. **-able**

a. **-ance** *n.* separation; partition [Fr. fr. L. *separare*].

sev·er·al (sev′·ẹr·ạl) *a.* more than two; some; separate; distinct; various; diff`ierent`; *pron.* several persons or things. **-ly** *adv.* apart from others [O.Fr. fr. L. *separare*].

se·vere (sạ·vir′) *a.* serious; rigidly methodical; harsh; not flowery, as style. **-ly** *adv.* **-ness, severity** *n.* sternness; harshness; rigor; austerity; intensity [L. *severus*].

Sè·vres (se′·vr) *n.* and *a.* name of a fine porcelain made at *Sèvres*, France.

sew (sō) *v.t.* to fasten together with needle and thread; to join with stitches; *v.i.* to practice sewing. **-er** *n.* one who sews. **-ing** *n.* and *a.* **-ing-machine** *n.* automatic machine adapted for all kinds of sewing operations [O.E. *seowian*].

sew·age (sòò′·ij) *n.* drainage; organic refuse carried off by a regular system of underground pipes [fr. *sewer*].

sew·er (sòò′·ẹr) *n.* underground drain or conduit to remove waste water and organic refuse. **-age** *n.* underground system of pipes and conduits to carry off surface water and organic refuse [O.Fr. *esseveur*].

sex (seks) *n.* state of being male or female; sum total of characteristics which distinguish male and female organisms; function by which most animal and plant species are perpetuated; males or females collectively. **— appeal,** what makes person sexually desirable or attractive. **-ual** *a.* pert. to sex or sexes; pert. to genital organs. **-ual intercourse,** coition. **-uality** *n.* **-ually** *adv.* [L. *sexus*].

sex-, comb. form, six.

sex·ag·e·nar·y (seks·aj·ạ·ner·i·) *a.* pert. to the number sixty; proceeding by sixties. **sexagenarian** *n.* person of age of sixty [L. *sexaginta*, sixty].

Sex·a·ges·i·ma (seks·ạ·jas′·ạ·mạ) *n.* second Sunday before Lent, sixty days before Easter **sexagesimal** *a. sexagesimus*, sixtieth].

sex·en·ni·al (seks·en′·i·ạl) *a.* continuing for six years; happening once every six years. Also **sextennial. -ly , sextennially** *adv.* [L. *sex*, six; *annus*, a year].

sex·tant (seks′·tant) *n.* an astronomical instrument used in measuring angular distances [L. *sextus*, sixth].

sex·ten·nial. See **sexennial.**

sex·tet, sex·tette (seks·tet′) *n.* musical composition for six voices or instruments; company of six singers or instrumentalists [L. *sex*, six].

sex·ton (seks′·tạn) *n.* church lay officer acting as caretaker and may also be grave digger [corrupt, of *sacristan*].

sex·tu·ple (seks′·yoo·pl) *a.* sixfold; six times as many; *v.t.* to multiply by six [L. *sex*, six; *plicare*, to fold].

sfor·zan·do (sfawr·tsàn′·dō) *a.* (*Mus.*) forced or pressed; strongly accented. Usually *abbrev.* to **sf., sfz.,** or denoted by symbols ∧, >. [It.].

shab·by (shab′·i·) *a.* torn or worn to rags; poorly dressed; faded; worn; mean. **shabbily** *adv.* **shabbiness** *n.* [O.E. *sceabb*, scab].

shack (shak) *n.* roughly built wooden hut; shanty [fr. *ramshackle*].

shack·le (shak′·l) *n.* metal loop or staple; U-shaped steel link with a pin closing the free ends; *pl.* fetters; manacles; anything which hampers; restraints; *v.t.* to fetter; to hamper [O.E. *sceacul*, a bond].

shad (shad) *n.* name of several species of herring family [O.E. *sceadd*].

shade (shād) *n.* partial darkness, due to interception of light; place sheltered from light, heat, etc.; screen; darker part of anything; depth of color; tint; hue; a very minute difference; *pl.* invisible world or region of the dead; Hades; *v.t.* to shelter or screen, from light or

a source of heat; to darken; to dim; to represent shades in a drawing; to pass almost imperceptibly from one form or color to another. **-d** *a.* **shadily** *adv.* in shady manner. **shadiness** *n.* quality of being shady. **shading** *n.* interception of light; slight variation; light and color values in a painting or drawing. **shady** *a.* providing shade; in shade; (*Colloq.*) disreputable; not respectable; doubtful; suspicious [O.E. *sceadu*].

shad·ow (shad′·ō) *n.* patch of shade; dark figure projected by anything which intercepts rays of light; darker or less illuminated part of picture; inseparable companion; ghost; phantom; gloom; slight trace; *v.t.* to cast a shadow over; to follow and watch closely. **— boxing** *n.* boxing practice, without opponent. **-er** *n.* one who dogs the footsteps of another. **-iness** *n.* **-ing** *n.* gradation of light and color; shading. **-y** *a.* full of shadow; serving to shade; faint; unsubstantial; obscure; unreal [O.E. *sceadu*].

shaft (shaft) *n.* straight rod, stem, or handle; shank; stem of arrow; arrow; anything long and slender, as a tall chimney, the well of an elevator, vertical passage leading down to mine or excavation, etc.; part of column between base and capital; revolving rod for transmitting power; stem of feather; pole of carriage. **-ing** *n.* system of long rods and pulleys used to transmit power to machinery [O.E. *sceaft*].

shag (shag) *n.* coarse, matted wool or hair; long and coarse nap on some types of woolen fabrics; strong mixture of tobacco leaves cut and shredded for smoking; *a.* rough; shaggy. **-gedness, -giness** *n.* **-gy** *a.* covered with rough hair or wool; rough; unkempt [O.E. *sceacga*, a head of hair].

shah (shạ) *n. abbrev.* of Shah-in-Shah (King of Kings), the title given to the monarchs of Iran, Persia [Pers.].

shake (shāk) *v.t.* to cause to move with quick vibrations; to weaken stability of; to impair resolution of; to trill, as note in music; to agitate; *v.i.* to tremble; to shiver; to totter. *pa.t.* **shook.** *pa.p.* **-n.** *n.* shaking; vibration; jolt; severe shock to system; friendly grasping of hands by two individuals; (*Mus.*) trill; (*Colloq.*) moment. **-down** *n.* (*Colloq.*) extortion of money. **-n** *a.* weakened; agitated; cracked. **shakily** *adv.* **shakiness** *n.* **shaky** *a.* easily moved; unsteady; weak; tottering; unreliable. **to shake off,** to get rid of [O.E. *sceacan*].

shak·o (shak′·ō) *n.* military peaked headdress, shaped like truncated cone and usually plumed in front [Hung. *csako*].

shale (shāl) *n.* (*Geol.*) clay or mud become hardened and which splits into thin plates, parallel to stratification [O.E. *scealu*, scale].

shall (shall) *v.i.* and *aux.* used to make compound tenses or moods to express futurity, obligation, command, condition or intention [O.E. *sceal*].

shal·low (shal′·ō) *a.* having little depth of water; having little knowledge; superficial; *n.* place where water is of little depth; shoal, flat, or sandbank. **-ly** *adv.* **-ness** *n.*

sham (sham) *n.* any trick, fraud, or device which deludes; pretense; counterfeit; imitation; *a.* counterfeit; false; pretended; *v.t.* to counterfeit; to feign, to pretend; *v.i.* to make false pretenses. *pr.p.* **-ming.** *pa.t.* and *pa.p.* **-med** [etym. uncertain].

sham·ble (sham′·bl) *v.i.* to walk unsteadily with shuffling gait [etym. uncertain].

shame (shām) *n.* emotion caused by consciousness of something wrong or dishonoring in one's conduct or state; cause of disgrace; dishonor; ignominy; *v.t.* to cause to feel shame; to disgrace; to degrade; to force by shame (into). **-faced** *a.* bashful; modest. **-facedly** *adv.* **-facedness** *n.* **-ful** *a.* disgraceful. **-fully**

adv. **-fulness** n. **-less** a. destitute of shame; brazen-faced; immodest. **-lessly** adv. **-lessness** n. [O.E. *sceamu*].

sham·my. See **chamois.**

sham·poo (sham·póó′) v.t. to wash (scalp); to massage; n. act of shampooing; preparation used. **-er** n. [Hind. *champna*, to knead].

sham·rock (sham′·ràk) n. small trefoil plant; national emblem of Ireland [Ir. *seamrog*, trefoil].

shang·hai (shang·hī′) v.t. to drug or render a man unconscious by violence so that he may be shipped as member of a crew; to bring by deceit and force; pa.t. and pa.p. **shanghaied** [*Shanghai*, China].

Shan·gri·la (shang′·gri·là) n. a peaceful, untroubled place to which one may escape [From the name of the hidden retreat in James Hilton's *Lost Horizon*].

shank (shangk) n. lower part of leg, from knee to ankle; shin-bone; stem of anchor, pipe, etc.; shaft of a column; long connecting part of an appliance. **-'s mare**, one's own legs [O.E. *sceanca*, leg].

shan·tung (shan·tung′) n. silk cloth with rough, knotted surface made from the wild silkworm [Chinese province].

shan·ty (shant′·i·) n. shabby dwelling; crude wooden building [Fr. *chantier*, a workshop].

shan·ty (shant′·i·) n. sailor's song. Also **chanty, chantey** [Fr. *chanter*, to sing].

shape (shāp) v.t. to mold or make into a particular form; to give shape to; to figure; to devise; v.i. to assume a form or definite pattern; n. form; figure; appearance; outline; pattern; mold; condition; **-able, shapable** a. capable of being shaped; shapely. **-less** a. without regular shape or form; deformed; ugly. **-lessness** n. **-liness** n. beauty of shape or outline. **-ly** a. [O.E. *scieppan*].

shard (shàrd) n. broken fragment, esp. of earthenware; hard wing-case of bettle. Also **sherd** [O.E. *sceard*, a fragment].

share (sher) n. pointed, wedge-shaped, cutting blade of plough [O.E. *scear*].

share (sher) n. part allotted; portion; unit of ownership in public company entitling one to share in profits; v.t. to give or allot a share; to enjoy with others; to apportion; v.i. to take a share; to partake; to participate. **-cropper** n. a tenant farmer, esp. in the South. **-r** n. [O.E. *scearu*, a cutting or division].

shark (shàrk) n. general name applied to certain voracious marine fishes; swindler; rapacious fellow; (*Slang*) an expert. **-skin** n. stiff, smooth-finished rayon fabric [etym. unknown].

sharp (shàrp) a. having keen, cutting edge or fine point; abrupt; having ready perception; quick; shrewd; acid; acrid; pungent; sarcastic; harsh; painful intense dealing cleverly but unfairly artful; strongly marked, esp. in outline; shrill; (*Mus.*) raised a semi-tone in pitch; n. acute sound, esp. note raised semitone above its proper pitch; (*Mus.*) sign indicating this; (*Colloq.*) an expert; v.t. and v.i. to raise or sound a half tone above a given tone; adv. punctually. **-en** v.t. to give a keen edge or fine point to; to make more eager or intelligent; to make more tart or acid; (*Mus.*) to raise a semi-tone. **-ener** n. one who, or that which, sharpens; instrument for putting fine point on lead-pencil, etc. **-er** n. swindler; cheat; **—eyed** a. very observant. **-ly** adv. **-ness** n. **-shooter** n. skilled, long-range marksman. **-shooting** n. **-sighted** a. **-witted** a. having acute mind [O.E. *scearp*].

shat·ter (shat′·er) v.t. to break into many pieces; to smash; to disorder; v.i. to fly in pieces [doublet of *scatter*].

shave (shāv) v.t. to pare away; to cut close, esp. hair of face or head with razor; to cut

off thin slices; to miss narrowly; to graze; v.i. to shave oneself; pa.p. **-d** or **-n**. n. act of shaving; thin slice or shaving; tool for shaving; narrow escape; close miss. **-r** n. one who shaves; (*Colloq.*) a young lad. **shaving** n. act of shaving; what is shaved off. **close** or **near shave**, very narrow escape from danger [O.E. *sceafan*, to scrape].

Sha·vi·an (shā′·vi·an) n. of or pertaining to George Bernard Shaw.

shawl (shawl) n. cloth used by women as loose covering for neck and shoulders; v.t. to wrap in a shawl [Pers. *shal*].

shay (shā) n. an obsolete one-horse carriage [var. of *chaise*].

she (shē) pron. this or that female; feminine pronoun of the third person; a female (used humorously as a noun); also, in compound words, as *she-bear* [O.E. *seo*].

sheaf (shēf) n. bundle of stalks of wheat, rye, oats, or other grain; any similar bundle; a sheave; pl. **sheaves**. v.t. to make sheaves; v.i. to collect and bind corn, etc. into sheaves [O.E. *sceaf*].

shear (shir) v.t. to clip or cut through with shears or scissors; to clip wool (from sheep); to fleece; to deprive. v.i. to divide by action of shears; to reap with a sickle. pa.t. **-ed** pa.p. **-ed, shorn** n. (*Engineering*) stress in a body in a state of tension due to a force acting parallel with its section; shearing; curve; pl. a cutting instrument, consisting of two blades movable on a pin; large pair of scissors. **-er** n. **-ing** n. operation of clipping or cutting with shears; wool, etc. cut off with shears [O.E. *sceran*].

sheath (shēth) n. close-fitting cover, esp. for knife or sword; scabbard; thin protective covering. **-e** v.t. to put into a sheath; to envelop; to encase. **-ing** n. that which sheathes; metal covering for underwater structures as a protection against sea organisms, etc. [O.E. *scaeth*].

sheave (shēv) n. grooved wheel in block, etc. on which a rope works [doublet of *shive*].

sheave (shēv) v.t. to bind into sheaves; to sheaf [fr. *sheaf*].

shed (shed) n. shelter used for storage or workshop; [doublet of *shade*].

shed (shed) v.t. to cause to emanate, proceed, or flow out; to spill; to let fall; to cast off, as hair, feathers, shell; to spread; to radiate; v.i. to come off. pr.p. **-ding**. pa.t. and pa.p. **shed**. [O.E. *sceadan*, to divide].

sheen (shēn) n. gloss; glitter; brightness; light reflected by a bright surface. **-y** a. [O.E. *sciene*, beautiful].

sheep (shēp) n. sing. and pl. ruminant mammal, valued for its flesh and its solf fleecy wool; simple, bashful person; pl. pastor's church congregation. **-cote** n. enclosure affording shelter for sheep. **-dip** n. tank containing insecticide through which sheep are passed to free them from ticks; anti-parasitic solution or sheep-wash so used. **-dog** n. any breed of dog trained to tend and round up sheep. **-fold** n. sheepcote. **-ish** a. like a sheep; bashful; shy and embarrassed; awkwardly timid and diffident. **-ishly** adv. **-ishness** n. **-'s eyes**, fond, languishing glances. **-shank** n. knot or hitch for temporarily shortening rope, halyard, etc. **-shearer** n. one who clips wool from sheep. **-shearing** n. **-skin** n. skin of sheep; leather, parchment, or rug made from this; (*Colloq.*) diploma; **black sheep**, disreputable member of family; rogue [O.E. *sceap*].

sheer (shir) a. pure; unmixed; absolute; downright; perpendicular; of linen or silk, very thin; adv. quite; completely [O.E. *scir*, pure, bright].

sheer (shir) v.i. to deviate from the right course; to swerve; n. longitudinal, upward curvature of ship's deck towards bow or stern; a swerve [Dut. *scheren*].

sheet (shēt) *n.* any broad expanse; a broad piece of cloth spread on bed; broad piece of paper; newspaper; broad expanse of water, or the like; broad, thinly expanded portion of metal or other substance; *v.t.* to cover, as with a sheet. — **metal,** etc. *n.* metal in broad, thin sheets. **-ing** *a.* process of forming into sheets; cloths used for bed coverings; — **lightning** *n.* sudden glow appearing on horizon due to reflection of forked lightning. —**music** *n.* music printed on unbound sheets of paper [O.E. *scete*].

sheik, sheikh (shēk, shāk) *n.* Arab chief; a title of respect to Moslem ecclesiasts [Ar.].

shek·el (shek'·l) *n.* among ancient Hebrews, orig. weight, and later name of a gold or silver coin. *pl.* (*Colloq.*) money; coins; cash [Heb. *sheqel*].

shel·drake (shel'·drāk) *n.* (*fem.* **shelduck**) genus of wild duck [O.E. *sheld, variegated;* and *drake*].

shelf (shelf) *n.* board fixed horizontally on frame, or to wall, for holding things; ledge of rocks; sandbank in sea, rendering water shallow. *pl.* **shelves** (shelvz). *a.* [O.E. *scelf*].

shell (shel) *n.* hard, rigid, outer, protective covering of many animals, particularly mollusks; outer covering of eggs of birds; protective covering of certain seeds; hollow steel container, filled with high explosive, for discharging from mortar or gun; outer part of structure left when interior is removed; frail racing boat or skiff; group of electrons in atom all having same energy. **-back** *n.* old sailor. **-ed** *a.* having shell; stripped of shell; damaged by shellfire. **-fish** *n.* aquatic animal with external covering of shell, as oysters, lobster, crustacean, mollusk. **-proof** *a.* capable of withstanding bombs or high-explosives. **-shock** *n.* war neurosis, disturbance of mind and nervous system due to war conditions [O.E. *sciell*].

shel·lac (shạ·lak') *n.* refined, melted form of seed lac, obtained from resinous deposit secreted by insects on certain Eastern trees, used as varnish. *v.t.* to cover with shellac [*shel(l)* and *lac*].

shel·ter (shel'·tẹr) *n.* place or structure giving protection; that which covers or defends; a place of refuge; asylum; *v.t.* to give protection to; to screen from wind or rain; *v.i.* to take shelter. **-er** *n.* [etym. uncertain].

shelve (shelv) *v.t.* to furnish with shelves; to place on a shelf; to put aside, as unfit for use; to defer consideration of; *v.i.* to slope gradually; to incline. **shelving** *n.* [fr. *shelf*].

she·nan·i·gan (shạ·nan'·ạ·gạn) *n.* (*Slang*) nonsense. *usu. pl.* foolishness.

shep·herd (shep'·ẹrd) *n.* (*fem.* **shepherdess**) one who tends sheep; pastor of church; *v.t.* to tend sheep; to watch over and guide. **-'s-crook** *n.* long staff, with end curved to form large hook. [O.E. *sceaphirde*].

Sher·a·ton (sher'·ạ·tạn) *n.* style of furniture design distinguished for grace and beauty [Thomas *Sheraton* (1751-1806), the designer].

sher·bet (sher'·bạt) *n.* a frozen dessert made with fruit juices, milk, egg white or gelatin [Ar. *sharbat*, a drink].

sherd. *See* **shard.**

she·rif, shereef (shạ·rēf') *n.* a descendant of Mohammed [Ar. *sharif*, noble].

sher·iff (sher'·if) *n.* orig. governor of a shire, a 'shire-reeve' in England; chief law enforcement officer [O.E. *scirgerefa*, a shire-reeve].

Sher·pa (sher'·pạ) *n.* one of Nepal tribe, employed as porter or guide on Himalayan mountaineering expeditions.

sher·ry (sher'·i·) *n.* Spanish wine of deep amber color [fr. *Jerez*, near Cadiz].

Shet·land (shet'·lạnd) (*Geog.*) group of islands off N. coast of Scotland. **-er** *n.* — **pony** small breed of pony.

shib·bo·leth (shib'·bạ·leth) *n.* testword or password; a distinctive custom [Heb.].

shield (shēld) *n.* broad piece of armor carried on arm; buckler; anything which protects or defends; escutcheon or field on which are placed bearings in coats of arms; *v.t.* to protect; to defend; to screen; to ward off; to forfend [O.E. *scield*].

shift (shift) *v.t.* to change position (of); to transfer from one place to another; to move; to change gears in an automobile; *v.i.* to move; to change place, course; to change in opinion; *n.* change; evasion; expedient; squad or relay of workmen; time of their working. **-er** *n.* **-iness** *n.* trickiness of character or behavior. **-ing** *a.* changing place or position; displacing; fickle; unreliable. **-less** *a.* lacking in resource or character; aimless; not to be depended upon. **-lessness** *n.* **-y** *a.* not to be trusted; unreliable. **make-shift,** to manage or contrive somehow [O.E. *sciftan,* to arrange].

shil·le·lagh, shillelah (shạ·lā'·li·) *n.* a club or cudgel. [*Shillelagh,* Co. Wicklow].

shil·ling (shil'·ing) *n.* British silver coin of the value of twelve pence [O.E. *scilling*].

shil·ly-shal·ly (shil'·i·shal'·i·) *n.* vacillation; indecision; *v.i.* to hesitate or trifle; to waver. **shilly-shallier** *n.* [redupl. of *shall I*].

shim·mer (shim'·ẹr) *v.i.* to shine with faint, tremulous light; to glisten; *n.* faint, quivering light or gleam. **-ing** *n.* **-y** *a.* [O.E. *scimian*].

shim·my (shim'·i·) *n.* dance characterized by exaggerated wriggling; wobbling, as in wheel of a car; *v.i.* to wobble [fr. *chemise*].

shin (shin) *n.* forepart of leg, between ankle and knee; shank; *v.i.* to climb (up) with aid of one's arms and legs. Also **-ny. -bone** *n.* tibia, larger of two bones of leg [O.E. *scinu*].

shin·dig (shin'·dig) *n.* (*Colloq.*) social affair [var. of *shindy*].

shin·dy (shin'·di·) *n.* (*Slang*) excessive noise and tumult; uproar [Romany, *chindi*, quarrel].

shine ((shīn) *v.i.* to give out or reflect light; to radiate; to sparkle; to perform in brilliant fashion. *pa.t.* and *pa.p.* **shone.** *v.t.* to cause to shine; to polish, shoes, etc. *pa.t.* and *pa.p.* **shined.** *n.* brightness; gloss; (*Colloq.*) liking. **-r** (*Slang*) a black eye. **shining** *a.* glistening; splendid. **shininess** *n.* **shiny** *a.* bright; glossy; unclouded [O.E. *scinan*].

shin·gle (shing'·gl) *n.* rounded water-worn pebbles. **shingly** *a.* [Norw. *singel*].

shin·gle (shing'·gl) *n.* thin, rectangular slat for roofing and house siding; a short haircut; small signboard (esp. of physician, lawyer); *v.t.* to cover with shingles; to crop women's hair close [L. *scindula*].

shin·gles (shing'·glz) *n.pl.* (*Med.*) *herpes zoster,* viral infection of nerve ganglia, accompanied by severe pain and a vesicular eruption along the nerve course [L. *cingulum*, a belt].

Shin·to (shin'·tō) *n.* native religion of Japan, **-ism** *n.* [Chin. *shin*, god; *tao*, the way].

ship (ship) *n.* a vessel for carriage of passengers and goods by sea; *v.t.* to engage for service on board a ship; to place object in position, as oar; to take in water (over the side); *v.i.* to transport. *pr.p.* **-ping.** *pa.t.* and *pa.p.* **-ped. -board** *n.* deck or side of ship. **-builder** *n.* one who constructs ships; naval architect. **-building** *n.* **-master** *n.* captain **-mate** *n.* fellow sailor. **-ment** *n.* process of shipping; cargo. **-owner** *n.* **-per** *n.* one who forwards commodities. **-ping** *n.* collective body of ships in one place; mercantile vessels generally; tonnage; the business of transporting goods. **-shape** *a.* orderly, trim; *adv.* properly. **-wreck** *n.* loss of ship by accident; total destruction; ruin. **-wright** *n.* one engaged in building or repairing ships. **-yard** *n.* place where ships are built or repaired [O.E. *scip*].

shire (shīr) *n.* territorial division in Great Britain; county [O.E. *scir*. district].

shirk (shurk) *v.t.* to evade; to try to avoid (duty, etc.) **-er** *n.* one who seeks to avoid duty.

shirr (shur) *n.* in needlework, row of puckering or gathering; *v.t.* to gather with parallel threads; to bake eggs.

shirt (shurt) *n.* garment for upper part of body. **-sleeve** *a.* simple; plain. **-waist** *n.* woman's blouse. **to keep one's shirt on** (*Slang*) to be patient [O.E. *scyrfe*].

shiv·er (shiv'·er) *v.t.* to quiver or shake from cold or fear; to tremble; to shudder; *v.t.* to cause to shake; *n.* shaking or shuddering; a vibration. **-y** *a.* inclined to shiver; tremulous.

shiv·er (shiv'·er) *n.* small piece or splinter; *v.t.* and *v.i.* to break into many small pieces or splinters; to shatter [M.E. *scifre*].

shoal (shōl) *n.* large number of fish swimming together; a crowd; *v.i.* to crowd together [O.E. *scolu*, company, fr. L. *schola*, a school].

shoal (shōl) *n.* a sandbank or bar; shallow water; *a.* shallow; *v.i.* to become shallow. **-y** *a.* full of shoals [O.E. *sceald*, shallow].

shoat (shōt) *n.* a young pig [M.E. *schote*].

shock (shåk) *n.* violent impact or concussion when bodies collide; clash; percussion; conflict; emotional disturbance produced by anything unexpected, offensive, or displeasing; sudden depression of the system due to violent injury or strong mental emotion; paralytic stroke; effect of electric discharge through body; *v.t.* to strike against suddenly; to strike with surprise, horror, or disgust. **—absorber** *n.* anything to lighten a blow, shock, or ordeal. **-er** *n.* **-ing** *a.* appalling; terrifying; frightful; repulsive; offensive. **-ingly** *adv.* **—proof** *a.* able to withstand shocks [Fr. *choquer*].

shock (shåk) *n.* disordered mass of hair; *a.* shaggy; bushy. [O.E. *scucca*, a demon].

shock (shåk) *n.* group of sheaves of grain; *v.t.* to make into shocks [Dut. *schocke*].

shod (shåd) *pa.t.* and *pa.p.* of verb **shoe.**

shod·dy (shåd'·i·) *n.* inferior textile material; *a.* inferior; of poor quality.

shoe (shoo) *n.* covering for foot, but not enclosing ankle; metal rim or curved bar nailed to horse's hoof; various protective plates or under-coverings; apparatus which bears on the live rail in an electric railways in order to collect current to actuate the motor; *v.t.* to furnish with shoes; to put shoes on. *pr.p.* **-ing.** *pa.t.*, *pa.p.* **-horn** *n.* curved piece of horn, metal, etc. used to help foot into shoe. **lace** *n.* for fastening shoe on foot. **-less** *a.* **-maker** *n.* **-r** *n.* one who makes or repairs shoes. **-string** *n.* a shoelace; (*Colloq.*) small amount of money [O.E. *scoh*].

shone (shōn) *pa.t.* and *pa.p.* of **shine.**

shoo (shoo) *interj.* begone (used esp. in scaring away fowls and other animals); *v.t.* to scare or drive away [imit.].

shook (shook) *pa.t.* of **shake.**

shoot (shoot) *v.t.* to discharge missile from gun, etc.; to kill or wound with such a missile; to propel quickly; to thrust out; to pass swiftly over (rapids) or through (arch of bridge); to photograph episode or sequence of motion picture; *v.i.* to move swiftly and suddenly; to let off a gun, etc.; to go after game with gun; to just out; to sprout; to bud; to dart through (as severe pain); to advance; to kick towards goal. *pa.t.* and *pa.p.* **shot.** *n.* shooting; young branch or stem. **-er** *n.* **-ing** *n.* act of discharging firearms, etc.; the act of killing game. **-ing-gallery** *n.* long room for practice with rifles. **-ing-star** *n.* incandescent meteor. [O.E. *sceotan*].

shop (shåp) *n.* building where goods are made, or sold; workshop; store *v.i.* to visit shops to purchase articles. *pr.p.* **-ping** *pa.t.* and *pa.p.* **-ped.** **-keeper** *n.* one who keeps retail shop. **-keeping** *n.* **-lifter** *n.* one who makes petty thefts from shop counters. **-ping** *n.* visiting shops with view to purchasing. **-ping-bag,** or **-basket** *n.* receptacle for holding articles purchased. **-worn** *a.* soiled or tarnished by long exposure in shop. [Fr. *échoppe*, a booth].

shore (shōr, shawr) *n.* land adjoining sea or large lake; *v.t.* to put ashore [Dut. *schor*].

shore (shōr, shawr) *n.* strong beam set obliquely against wall of building or ship to prevent movement during alterations; *v.t.* to support by post or buttress; to prop. **shoring** *n.* props for support [etym. uncertain].

shorn (shawrn) *pa.p.* of **shear;** *a.* cut off; having the hair or wool cut off [fr. *shear*].

short (shawrt) *a.* having little length; not long in space; low; not extended in time; limited or lacking in quantity; hasty of temper; crumbling in the mouth; pronounced with less prolonged accent; brief; near; concise; pithy; abrupt; destitute; crisp; *adv.* suddenly; abruptly; without reaching the end; *n.* short film to support feature film; short circuit; *pl.* short trousers reaching down to above knees. **-age** *n.* insufficient supply; deficiency. **-bread** *n.* rich cake or butter cooky. **-cake** *n.* sweetened biscuit or cake filled and topped with fruit and whipped cream. **— circuit** *n.* passage of electric current by a shorter route than that designed for it; *v.t.* to cause short circuit; to by-pass. **-coming** *n.* failing; fault; defect. **-cut** *n.* quicker but unorthodox way of reaching a place or of accomplishing a task, etc. **-en** *v.t.* to make shorter; to render friable, as shortbread, with butter or lard; to abridge; to lessen; *v.t.* to contract; to lessen. **-ening** *n.* lard, butter, or other fat used when baking pastry, etc. **-hand** *n.* system of rapid reporting by means of signs or symbols. **—handed** *a.* not having the full complement or sta ffon duty. **-horn** *n.* a breed of English cattle with short horns. **-ly** *adv.* in a brief time; soon; in a few words; curtly. **-ness** *n.* **— shrift,** summary treatment. **-sighted** *a.* not able to see distinctly objects some distance away; lacking in foresight. **—sightedly** *adv.* **-sightedness** *n.* **—tempered** *a.* easily roused to anger. **— waves** (*Radio*) electromagnetic waves whose wave length is, by international definition, between 10 and 50 meters. **—winded** *a.* affected with shortness of breath; easily made out of breath. **in short,** briefly. [O.E. *schort*].

shot (shåt) *pa.t.* and *pa.p.* of **shoot.**

shot (shåt) *a.* pert. to fabrics woven with warp and weft of contrasting tints or colors, so that shade changes according to angle of light [fr. *shoot*].

shot (shåt) *n.* act of shooting; skilled marksman; one of small pellets, contained in cartridge fired from sporting rifle; heavy, solid, round missile, formerly fired from cannon; range of such missiles; charge of blasting powder; stroke in billiards, tennis, etc.; a photograph; a try to attempt; (*Slang*) injection of a drug; *v.t.* to load or weight with shot. *pr.p.* **-ting.** *pa.t.* and *pa.p.* **-ted.** **-gun** *n.* smoothbore gun for shooting small game or birds. [O.E. *sceot*].

should (shood) *v.* and *aux.* used in Future-in-the-Past tenses of verbs with pronouns I or we; auxiliary used after words expressing opinion, intention, desire, probability, obligation, etc. (Cf. *shall*).

shoul·der (shōl'·der) *n.* ball and socket joint formed by humerus (bone of the upper arm) with scapula (shoulder-blade); upper joint of foreleg of animal; anything resembling human shoulder, as prominent part of hill; graded strip along edge of road; v.t. to push forward with shoulders; to bear (burden, etc.); to accept (responsibility); v.i. to push forward through crowd. — **blade** n. flat bone of shoulder; scapula. [O.E. sculdor].

shout (shout) n. loud, piercing cry; call for help; v.t. and v.i. to utter loud sudden cry.

shove (shuv) v.t. to push; to press against; to jostle; v.i. to push forward; to push off from shore in a boat, using oar; n. act of pushing; push [O.E. scufan].

shov·el (shuv'·l) n. spade wtih broad blade slightly hollowed; scoop; machine for scooping and lifting; v.t. to lift or move with a shovel; v.i. to use shovel. **-ler** n. [O.E. scofl].

show (shō) v.t. to present to view; to point out; to display; to exhibit; to disclose; to explain; to demonstrate; to prove; to conduct; to guide; v.i. to appear; to be visible; to come into sight. pa.p. **-n** or **-ed.** n. act of showing; that which is shown; spectacle; exhibition; display; (Colloq.) theatrical performance or movie. **-bill** n. broad sheet containing advertisement. **-bread** n. Same as **shewbread.** **-case** n. glass case for display of goods, museum exhibits, etc. **-down** n. laying down of cards, face upwards, at poker or other card games; open disclosure of truth, clarification. **-er** (shō'·ẹr) n. one who shows or exhibits. **-ily** n. **-man** n. one who presents a show; one who is skilled at presenting things. **-manship** n. — **place** n. place of local interest made especially attractive to draw tourists. **-room** n. room where goods are laid out for inspection. **-y** a. gaudy; attracting attention; ostentatious. **to show off,** to make an ostentatious display. **to show up,** to stand out prominently; to hold up to ridicule; to appear [O.E. sceawian, to look at].

show·er (shou'·ẹr) n. a brief fall of rain or hail; anything coming down like rain; great number; v.t. to wet with rain; to give abundantly; v.i. to rain; to pour down. — **bath** n. bath equipped with fine-spraying apparatus. — **proof** a. impervious to rain. **-y** a. raining intermittently [O.E. scur].

shrank (shrangk) pa.t. of **shrink.**

shrap·nel (shrap'·nạl) n. shell timed to explode over, and shower bullets and splinters on, personnel; shell splinters [Gen. Shrapnel].

shred (shred) n. long, narrow piece cut or torn off; strip; fragment; scrap; v.t. to cut or tear to shreds; to tear into strips. pr.p. **-ding.** pa.t. and pa.p. **-ded** [O.E. screade].

shrew (shröò) n. noisy, quarrelsome woman; a termagant; diminutive mammal, resembling, but unrelated to, mouse. **-ish** a. having manners of a shrew. **-ishly** adv. **-ishness** n. [O.E. screawa, shrew mouse].

shrewd (shröòd) a. intelligent; discerning; sagacious; knowing; cunning. **-ly** adv. **-ness** n. [fr. shrew].

shriek (shrēk) v.t. and v.i. to scream, from fright, anguish, or bad temper; to screech; n. a loud, shrill cry [imit. origin].

shrift (shrift) n. confession made to a priest; absolution. **short shrift,** summary treatment [O.E. scrifan, to prescribe (penance)].

shrike (shrīk) n. bird which preys on birds, frogs, and insects, and impales victims on thorns; butcherbird [imit. of cry O.E. scric].

shrill (shril) a. uttering an acute sound; piercing; high-pitched; v.i. to sound in a shrill tone. **-y** adv. piercingly [M.E. shrille].

shrimp (shrimp) n. small edible crustacean allied to prawns; small person; v.i. to catch shrimps with net. **-er** n. [M.E. shrimpe].

shrine (shrīn) n. case in which sacred relics are deposited; tomb of saint; place of worship; any sacred place [L. scrinium, chest, box].

shrink (shringk) v.i. to contract; to dwindle; to recoil; to draw back; v.t. to cause to contract. pa.t. **shrank, shrunk.** pa.p. **shrunk.** **-age** n. act or amount of shrinking. **shrunken** a. narrowed in size [O.E. scrincan].

shrive (shrīv) v.t. to give absolution to; to confess (used reflexively); v.i. to receive or make confession pa.t. **-d** or **shrove.** pa.p. **shriven** [O.E. scrifan, to prescribe].

shriv·el (shriv'·l) v.t. and v.i. to cause to contract and wrinkle; to wither.

shroud (shroud) n. that which clothes or covers; sheet for a corpse; winding sheet; pl. strongest of the wire-rope stays which support mast athwartships; v.t. to enclose in winding sheet; to cover wtih shroud; to screen; to wrap up; to conceal [O.E. scrud, a garment].

shrove (shrōv) pa.t. of the verb **shrive.** **Shrovetide** n. period immediately before Lent, ending on Shrove Tuesday [fr. shrive].

shrub (shrub) n. any hard-wooded plant of smaller and thicker growth than tree; bush; low, dwarf tree. **-bery** a. collection of shrubs. **-by** a. of nature of shrub; full of shrubs [O.E. scrybb].

shrug (shrug) v.i. to raise and narrow shoulders in disdain, etc. v.t. to move (shoulders) thus. pr.p. **-ging.** pa.t. and pa.p. **-ged.** n. drawing up of shoulders [ME schruggen].

shrunk, shrunken See **shrink.**

shuck (shuk) n. husk or pod; shell of nut; v.t. to remove husk, pod, or shell from [Cf. chuck, to throw].

shud·der (shud'·ẹr) v.i. to tremble violently, esp. with horror or fear; to shiver; to quake; n. trembling or shaking. **-ing** n. and a. trembling; shivering [M.E. Cf. Ger. schaudern].

shuf·fle (shuf'·l) v.t. to shove one way and the other; to throw into disorder; to mix (cards); to scrape (feet) along ground; v.i. to change position of cards in pack; to prevaricate; to move in a slovenly manner; to scrape floor with foot in dancing or walking; n. act of throwing into confusion by change of places; artifice or pretext; scraping movement of foot in dancing. —**board** n. a game in which disks are shoved into numbered divisions at the end of a long playing area.

shun (shun) v.t. to keep clear of; to avoid. pr.p. **-ning.** pa.t. and pa.p. **-ned** [O.E. scunian].

shunt (shunt) v.t. to move or turn off to one side; to move (train) from one line to another; to divert (electric current); v.i. to go aside; to turn off. n. act of shunting. **-er** n. railway employee who shunts rolling-stock.

shut (shut) v.t. to close to hinder ingress or egress; to forbid entrance to; v.i. to close itself; to become closed. pr.p. **-ting.** pa.t. and pa.p. **shut.** a. closed; made fast. **-down** n. stoppage of work or activity. **-ter** n. one who, or that which, shuts; movable protective screen for window; automatic device in camera which allows light from lens to act on film or plate for a predetermined period. **to shut down,** to stop working; to close (business, etc.). **to shut up,** to close; to fasten securely; (Colloq.) to stop talking [O.E. scyttan].

shut·tle (shut'·l) n. instrument used in weaving for shooting thread of woof between threads of warp; similar appliance in sewing machine to form a lock stitch; v.t. and v.i. to move backwards and forwards. **-cock** n. cork with fan of feathers for use with battledore or in badminton; game itself. [O.E. scytel, a missile].

shy (shī) a. sensitively timid; reserved; easily frightened; bashful; cautious; falling short; v.i. to start suddenly aside. pa.t. and pa.p. **shied.** **-ly** adv. **-ness** n. **-ster** n. un-

WEBSTER Q–S

scrupulous lawyer or person. [*eschif*].

shy (shī) *v.t.* to throw; to fling. *pa.t.* and *pa.p.* **shied.** *n.* throw; cast.

Si·a·mese (sī·a·mēz′) *a.* pert. to Siam, the people, or language; *n.* native of Siam; the language. — **twins,** joined twins.

sib (sib) *a.* having kinship; related by blood; akin; *n.* a blood relation [O.E. Cf. Ger. *sippe*].

Si·be·ri·an (sī·bi′·ri·an) *a.* pert. to Siberia, part of the Soviet Union.

sib·i·lance (sib′·a·lans) *n.* hissing sound; quality of being sibilant. Also **sibilancy. sibilant** *a. n.* letter uttered with hissing of voice, as *s, x,* etc. **sibilate** *v.t.* to pronounce with hissing sound [L. *sibilare,* to whistle].

sib·yl (sib′·il) *n.* a name applied to certain votaresses of Apollo, endowed with visionary, prophetic power; prophetess; witch. **-lic, -line** *a.* [Gk. *Sibulla*].

sic (sik) *adv.* abbreviated form of *sic in originail* (Lat. = so it stands in the original) printed in brackets as guarantee that passage has been quoted correctly; so; thus[L.].

sic·ca·tion (si·kā′·shan) *n.* act or process of drying. **siccative** *a.* drying; causing or tending to dry; *n.* a drier [L. *siccus,* dry].

Si·cil·i·an (si·sil′·yan) *a.* pert. to island of Sicily; *n.* native of Sicily.

sick (sik) *a.* affected with physical or mental disorder; diseased; ill; ailing; tired of. — **bay** *n.* place set aside on ship for treating the sick. — **benefit** *n.* allowance made to insured person while ill and off duty. **-en** *v.t.* to make sick; to disgust; *v.i.* to become sick; to be filled with abhorrence. **-ening** *a.* causing sickness or disgust; nauseating. **-eningly** *adv.* — **headache** *n.* migraine. **-ly** *a.* somewhat sick; ailing; weak; pale; arising from ill health. **-ness** *n.* state of being sick; illness; disordered state of stomach [O.E. *seoc*].

sick·le (sik′·l) *n.* reaping hook with semi-circular blade and a short handle [L. *secula,* fr. *secare,* to cut].

side (sīd) *n.* one of surfaces of object, esp. upright inner or outer surface; one of the edges of plane figure; margin; border; any part viewed as opposite to another; part of body from hip to shoulder; slope, as of a hill; one of two parties, teams, or sets of opponents; body of partisans; sect or faction; line of descent traced through one parent; *a.* being on the side; lateral; indirect; incidental; *v.i.* (with) to hold or embrace the opinions of another; to give support to one of two or more contending parties. — **arms** *pl.* weapons carried on side of body. **-board** *n.* piece of furniture designed to hold dining utensils, etc. in dining room. **-car** *n.* small box-shaped body attached to motorcycle. **—issue** *n.* subsidiary to main argument or business. — **light** *n.* any source of light situated at side of room, door, etc.; lantern, showing red or green, on side of a vessel; incidental information or illustration. — **line** *n.* any form of profitable work which is ancillary to one's main business or profession; (*Sports*) line marking the side boundaries of playing field. **—long** *a.* lateral; oblique; not directly forward; *adv.* obliquely; on the side. **-r** *n.* **-saddle,** saddle for woman on horseback, not astride, but with both feet on one side of horse. **-show** *n.* minor entertainment or attraction; subordinate affair. **-slip** *n.* involuntary skid or slide sideways; *v.i.* to skid. **-splitting** *a.* exceedingly ludicrous and laughter-provoking. **—step** *n.* to step to one side; *v.i.* to step to one side. **-stroke** *n.* style of swimming where body is turned on one side. **-swipe** (*U.S.*) *n.* a blow with or on the side; *v.t.* to strike such a blow. **-track** *v.t.* to shunt into siding; to postpone

indefinitely; to shelve; *n.* a railway siding.

siding *n.* short line of rails on which trains are shunted from main line. **sidle** *v.i.* to move sideways; to edge

si·de·re·al (sī·di′·rē·al) *a.* relating to constellations and fixed stars; measured or determined by apparent motion of stars [L. *sidus, sideris,* a star].

sid·er·ite (sid′·er·īt) *n.* brown ironstone [Gk. *sidēritis,* the lodestone].

siege (sēj) *n.* the surrounding of a town or fortified place by hostile troops in order to induce it to surrender either by starvation or by attack at suitable juncture; continuous effort to gain (affection, influence, etc.); *v.t.* to besiege [Fr. *siège,* seat, siege].

si·en·na (sē·en′·a) *n.* natural yellow earth which provides pigment. **burnt sienna,** pigment giving reddish-brown tint. **raw sienna,** pigment giving a yellowish-brown tint [fr. *Sienna,* Italy].

si·er·ra (sē·er′·a) *n.* chain of mountains with saw-like ridge [Sp. fr. L. *serra,* a saw].

si·es·ta (sē·es′·ta) *n.* rest or sleep in afternoon esp. in hot countries; afternoon nap [Sp. = the sixth (hour) i.e. moon].

sieve (siv) *n.* utensil with wire netting or small holes for separating fine part of any pulverized substance from the coarse; *v.t.* to sift [O.E. *sife*].

sift (sift) *v.t.* to separate coarser portion from finer; to sieve; to bolt; to scrutinize; to examine closely [O.E. *sife,* a sieve].

sigh (sī) *v.i.* to make a deep, single respiration, as expression of exhaustion or sorrow; *v.t.* to utter sighs over; *n.* long, deep breath, expression of sorrow, fatigue, regret, or relief [O.E. *sican*].

sight (sīt) *n.* one of the five senses; act of seeing; faculty of seeing; that which is seen; view; glimpse; anything novel or remarkable; exhibition; spectacle; (*Colloq.*) pitiful object; a piece of metal near breech of firearm to assist the eye in correct aiming; any guide for eye to assist direction; *v.t.* to catch sight of; to see; to give proper elevation and direction to instrument by means of a sight; *v.i.* to take aim by means of a sight. **-less** *a.* blind; invisible. **-lessly** *adv.* **-lessness** *n.* **-liness** *n.* comeliness. **-ly** *a.* pleasing to the eye; graceful; handsome. **second-sight** *n.* gift of prophetic vision [O.E. *sihth,* fr. *seon,* to see].

sig·il (sij′·il) *n.* seal; signet; occult sign. **sigillary** *a.* [L. *sigillum,* a seal].

sig·ma (sig′·ma) *n.* the Greek letter (Σ, σ, ϛ) corresponding to letter *s;* symbol indicating, in mathematics, etc., summation; 200; millesecond or $\frac{1}{1000}$ second. **sigmate, sigmoid** *a.* curved like letter S. [Gk.].

sign (sīn) *n.* movement, mark, or indication to convey some meaning; token; symbol; omen; signboard; password; (*Math.*) character indicating relation of quantities, or operation to be performed, as $+$, $\times$, $\div$, $=$ etc.; (*Mus.*) any character, as flat, sharp, dot, etc.; (*Astron.*) the twelfth part of the ecliptic or zodiac; *v.t.* to represent by sign; to affix signature to; to ratify; *v.i.* to make a signal, sign, or gesture; to append one's signature. **-board** *n.* board displaying, advertising, name of business firm, etc. **-manual** *n.* an autograph signature appended [L. *signum*].

sig·nal (sig′·nal) *n.* sign to give notice of some occurrence, command, or danger to persons at a distance; that which in the first place impels any action; sign; token; semaphore, esp. on railway; (*Radio*) any communication made by emission of radio waves from a transmitter; *v.t.* to communicate by signals; *v.i.* to make signals. *pr.p.* **-ing.** *pa.t.* and *pa.p.* **-ed.** *a.* pert. to a signal; remarkable; conspicuous. **-ize** *v.t.* to make notable, distinguished, or remarkable; to point out. **-er** *n.* **-ly** *adv.* eminently; remarkably [L. *signum*, a sign].

sig·na·to·ry (sig′·nạ·tō·i·) *a.* and *n.* (one) bound by signature to terms of agreement. [L. *signare*, to sign].

sig·na·ture (sig·′nạ·cher) *n.* a sign, stamp, or mark impressed; a person's name written by himself; act of writing it; letter or number printed at bottom of first page of section of book to facilitate arrangement when binding; (*Mus.*) the flats or sharps after clef which indicate key (**key signature**), followed by appropriate signs giving value of the measures contained in each bar (**time signature**). [L. *signare*, to sign].

sig·net (sig′·nit) *n.* seal used for authenticating documents. — **ring** *n.* finger ring on which is engraved monogram or seal of owner [L. *signum*, a mark].

sig·ni·fy (sig′·nạ·fī) *v.t.* to make known by a sign; to convey notion of; to denote; to indicate; to mean; *v.i.* to express meaning; to be of consequence. *pa.t.* and *pa.p.* **signified. significance** *n.* importance; weight; meaning; import. **significant** *a.* fitted or designed to signify or make known something; important. **significantly** *adv.* **signification** *n.* act of signifying that which is expressed by signs or words; meaning; sense. **significative** *a.* **significatory** *a.* having meaning [L. *significare*, fr. *signum*, a sign; *facere*, to make].

si·gnor (sē′·nyōr) *n.* Italian lord or gentleman; ttile of respect or address equivalent to *Mr.* **signora** (sē·nyō′·rạ) *n. fem.* [It.].

si·lage (sī′·lij) *n.* compressed, acid-fermented fodder, orig. packed green in a silo for preservation [fr. *ensilage*].

si·lence (sī′·lans) *n.* stillness; quietness; calm; refraining from speed; muteness; secrecy; oblivion; *interj.* be quiet!; *v.t.* to cause to be still; to forbid to speak; to hush; to calm; to refute; to gag; to kill. **-r** *n.* **silent** *a.* **silently** *adv.* **silentness** *n.* [L. *silentium*].

si·lex (sī′·leks) *n.* silica; trade name for coffee maker made of heat-resistant glass [L. = flint].

sil·hou·ette (sil·o͡o·et′) *n.* portrait or picture cut from black paper or done in solid black upon a light ground; outline of object seen against the light; *v.t.* to represent in outline; to cause to stand out in dark shadow against a light background [Fr.].

sil·i·ca (sil′·i·kạ) *n.* silicon dioxide, main component of most rocks, occurring in nature as sand, flint, quartz, etc. **silicate** *n.* salt of silicic acid. **silicated** *a.* combined or coated with silica. **silicate of soda**, waterglass. **siliceous** (sạl·ish′·ạs) *a.* pert. to silica in a finely divided state. Also **silicious. silicic** (sạl·is′·ik) *a.* derived from or containing silica [L. *silex*].

sil·i·cones (sil′·ạ·kōnz) *n.pl.* new family of materials—petroleum, brine, ordinary sand [L. *silex*, flint].

silk (silk) *n.* fine, soft, lustrous thread obtained from cocoons made by larvae of certain moths, esp. silkworm; thread or fabric made from this; *a.* made of silk. **-en** *a.* made of, or resembling, silk; soft; smooth; silky. **-iness** *n.* **-screen** *a.* and *n.* (pert. to) the reproduction of a design by means of a pattern made on a screen of nylon or silk. **-worm** *n.* caterpillar of any moth which produces silk, esp. Bombyx mori. **-y** *a.* [O.E. *seoloc*].

sill (sil) *n.* base or foundation; horizontal member of stone, brick, or wood at the bottom of window frame, door, or opening [O.E. *syll*].

sil·ly (sil′·i·) *a.* weak in intellect; foolish;

senseless; stupid; (*Arch.*) simple; *n.* silly person. **sillily** *adv.* **silliness** *n.* foolishness [O.E. *saelig*, happy, fortunate].

si·lo (sī′·lō) *n.* large, airtight tower, elevator, or pit in which green crops are preserved for future use as fodder; *v.t.* to preserve in a silo. Cf. [Sp.].

silt (silt) *n.* fine, alluvial, soil, particles; mud; sediment; *v.t.* to choke or obstruct with silt (generally with up); *v.i.* to become filled up with silt [etym. uncertain].

sil·ver (sil′·ver) *n.* soft, white, metallic element, very malleable and ductile; silverware; silver coins; anything resembling silver; *a.* made of, or resembling, silver; white or gray, as hair; having a pale luster, as moon; soft and melodious, as voice or sound; bright, silvery; *v.t.* to coat or plate with silver; to apply amalgam of tinfoil and quicksilver to back of a mirror; to tinge with white or gray; to render smooth and bright; *v.i.* to become gradually white, as hair. **-ize** *v.t.* to coat or cover thinly with a film of silver. *n.* — **lining**, prospect of better times to come. **-plate** *n.* metallic articles coated with silver. **-plated** *a.* **-plating** *n.* deposition of silver on another metal by electrolysis. **-ware** *n.* articles made of silver. — **wedding**, 25th anniversary of marriage. **-ry** *a.* like silver; lustrous; (of sound) soft and clear [O.E. *siolfor*].

sim·i·an (sim′·i·ạn) *a.* pert. to or like an ape generally; *n.* a monkey or ape [L. = ape].

sim·i·lar (sim′·ạ·ler) *a.* like; resembling; exactly corresponding; (*Geom.*) of plane figures, differing in size but having all corresponding angles and side ratios uniform. **-ity** *n.* quality or state of being similar. **-ly** *adv.* [L. *similis*, like].

sim·i·le (sim′·ạ·lē) *n.* figure of speech using some point of resemblance observed to exist between two things which differ in other respects [L. *similis*, like].

si·mil·i·tude (sạ·mil′·ạ·tūd) *n.* state of being similar or like; resemblance; likeness; parable [L. *similis*, like].

sim·mer (sim′·er) *v.t.* to cause to boil gently; *v.i.* to be just bubbling or just below boiling-point; to be in a state of suppressed anger or laughter; *n.* gentle, gradual heating [imit.].

si·mo·ni·ac (sạ·mō′·ni·ak) *n.* one guilty of simony. **-al** *a.* **-ally** *adv.* **simonist** *n.* one who practices simony [Cf. *simony*].

si·mo·ny (sī′·mạ·ni·, sim′·a·ni·) *n.* the offense of offering or accepting money or other reward for nomination or appointment to an ecclesiastical office or other benefit [See *Acts* 8].

sim·per (sim′·per) *v.i.* to smile in a silly, affected manner; *n.* smile with air of silliness or affectation. **-er** *n.* [etym. uncertain].

sim·ple (sim′·pl) *a.* single; not complex; entire; mere; plain, sincere; clear; intelligible; simple-minded; (*Chem.*) composed of a single element; *n.* something not compounded. — **interest**, money paid on principal borrowed but not on accrued interest as in compound interest. —**minded** *a.* ingenuous; open; frank; mentally weak. **-ness** *n.* **-ton** *n.* foolish person; person of weak intellect. **simplicity** *n.* artlessness; sincerity; clearness; simpleness. **simplification** *n.* act of making simple or clear; thing simplified. **simplificative** *a.* tending to simplify. **simplify** *v.t.* to make or render simple, plain, or easy. *pa.t.* and *pa.p.* **simplified. simply** *adv.* in a simple manner; plainly; unostentatiously; without affectation [L. *simplus*].

sim·u·la·crum (sim·yạ·lā′·kram) *n.* image; representation. *pl.* **simulacra** [L.].

sim·u·lant (sim′·yạ·lant) *a.* simulating; having the appearance of; *n.* one simulating something. **simular** *a.* simulated; counterfeit; feigned; *n.* one who pretends to be what he is not; a simulator.

sim·u·late (sim'·yạ·lāt) *v.t.* to assume the mere appearance of, without the reality; to feign. **simulation** *n.* **simulator** *n.* [L. *simulare*, to make like].

si·mul·ta·ne·ous (sim·ạl·tā'·nē·ạs) *a.* existing or occurring at same time. **-ness, simultaneity** *n.* **-ly** *adv.* [L. *simul*].

sin (sin) *n.* transgression against divine or moral law, esp. when committed consciously; conduct or state of mind of a habitual or unrepentant sinner; iniquity; evil; *v.i.* to depart from path of duty prescribed by God; to violate any rule of duty; to do wrong. *pr.p.* **-ning.** *pa.t.* and *pa.p.* **-ned.** **-ful** *a.* iniquitous; wicked; unholy. **-fully** *adv.* **-fulness** *n.* **-ner** *n.* [O.E. *synn*].

since (sins) *adv.* from then till now; subsequently; ago; *prep.* at some time subsequent to; after; *conj.* from the time that; seeing that; because; inasmuch as [earlier *sithens*, O.E. *siththan*].

sin·cere (sin·sir') *a.* not assumed or merely professed; straightforward. **-ly** *adv.* **-ness, sincerity** (sin·ser'·ạ·ti·) *n.* state or quality of being sincere; honesty of mind or intention; truthfulness [L. *sincerus*, pure].

sine (sīn) *n.* (*abbrev.* **sin**) (*Math*) perpendicular from one extremity of an arc to diameter drawn through other extremtiy; function of one of the two acute angles in a right-angle triangle, ratio of line subtending this angle to hypotenuse [L. *sinus*, a curve].

si·ne·cure (sī'·ni·kŭr, sin'·ạ·kŭr) *n.* office, position, etc. with salary but with few duties. **sinecurist** *n.* one who holds, or seeks sinecure [L. *sine cura*, without care].

sin·ew (sin'·ū) *n.* ligament or tendon which joins muscle to bone; strength; source of strength or vigor. **-ed** *a.* having sinews; strong; firm. **-y** *a.* well braced; muscular; strong [O.E. *sinu*].

sing (sing) *v.t.* to utter with musical modulations of voice; to celebrate in song; to praise in verse; *v.i.* to utter sounds with melodious modulations of voice; to pipe, twitter, chirp, as birds; to hum; to reverberate. *pa.t.* **sang** or **sung.** *pa.p.* **sung.** **-er** *n.* one who sings; vocalist. **-ing** *n.* art of singing; vocal music; a humming noise (in the ear, on a telephone circuit, etc.) [O.E. *singan*].

singe (sinj) *v.t.* to burn the surface slightly; to burn loose fluff from yarns, etc. *pr.p.* **-ing.** *n.* superficial burn [O.E. *sencgan*, to make hiss].

Sin·gha·lese (sing·gạ·lēz') *a.* pert. to Ceylon, its people, or language. *n.* a native of Ceylon [Sans. *Sinhala*].

sin·gle (sing'·gl) *a.* sole; alone; separate; individual; not double; unmarried; sincere; whole-hearted; straightforward; upright; *n.* unit; (*Cricket*) one run; (*Tennis*) game confined to two opponents; *v.t.* (with *out*) to select from a number; to pick; to choose. **—breasted** *a.* of a garment, buttoning on one side only. **— entry** *n.* in bookkeeping, entry of each transaction on one side only of an account. **—handed** *a.* and *adv.* without help; unassisted. **—hearted** *a.* sincere. **—minded** *a.* having but one purpose or aim; sincere. **-ness** *n.* state of being single; honesty of purpose; freedom from deceit or guile; sincerity. **singly** *adv.* one by one; by oneself [L. *singuli*, one at a time].

sin·gle·ton (sing'·gl·tạn) *n.* (*Cards*) hand containing only one card of some suit, or the card itself [dim. of *single*].

sing·song (sing'·sawng) *n.* rhythmical, monotonous fashion of uttering. *a.* monotonous;

droning [redup. of *sing*].

sin·gu·lar (sing'·gyạ·lẹr) *a.* existing by itself; denoting one person or thing; individual; unique; outstanding; *n.* single instance; word in the singular number. **-ize** *v.t.* to make singular or unique. **-ity** *n.* state of being singular; anything unusual or remarkable; oddity. **-ly** *adv.* [L. *singularis*].

Sin·ic (sin'·ik) *a.* Chinese. **Sinicise** (sin'·ạ·sīz) *v.t.* to give a Chinese character to. **-ism** *n.* mode of thought or customs peculiar to the Chinese [Gk. *Sinai*, the Chinese].

sin·is·ter (sin'·is·tẹr) *a.* on left hand; evil-looking; unlucky (left being regarded as unlucky side). **sinistral** *a.* to the left; reversed; (*Bot.*) having whorls not turning normally [L. = on the left hand].

sink (singk) *v.t.* to cause to descend; to submerge; to lower out of sight; to dig; to excavate; to ruin; to suppress; to invest; *v.i.* to subside; to descend; to penetrate (into); to decline in value, health, or social status; to be dying; to droop; to decay; to become submerged. *pa.t.* **sank** or **sunk.** *pa.p.* **sunk.** *n.* a receptacle for washing up, with pipe for carrying away waste water; marsh or area in which river water percolates through surface and disappears; place notoriously associated with evildoing. **-er** *n.* weight fixed to anything to make it sink, as on net, fishing-line, etc. **-ing** *n.* operation of excavating; subsidence; settling; abatement; ebb; part sunk below surrounding surface. **-ing fund,** fund set aside at regular intervals to provide replacement of wasting asset or repayment of particular liability [O.E. *sincan*].

Si·no-, in compounds, meaning Chinese [Gk. *Sinai*, Chinese].

Si·nol·o·gy (sī·nȧl'·ạ·ji·) *n.* that branch of knowledge which deals with the Chinese language, culture, history, religion and art. [Gk. *Sinai*, the Chinese; *logos*, a discourse].

sin·u·ate (sin'·yoo·āt) *v.i.* to bend in and out; to wind; to turn; *a.* (sin'·yoo·it) (*Bot.*) wavy; tortuous; curved on the margin, as a leaf. Also **-d. sinuation** *n.* **sinuose, sinuous** *a.* bending in and out; of serpentine or undulating form; morally crooked; supple. **sinuously** *adv.* [L. *sinus*, a fold].

si·nus (sī'·nạs) *n.* (*Anat.*) opening; hollow; cavity; (*Path.*) groove or passage in tissues leading to a deep-seated abscess, usually in nose or ear. **-itis** *n.* inflammation of sinus [L. *sinus*, a curve].

Sioux (sóo) *n.* member of great Siouan division of N. American aborigines; their language. *pl.* **Sioux** (sóo, sóoz).

sip (sip) *v.t.* and *v.i.* to drink or imbibe in very small quantities; to taste. *pr.p.* **-ping.** *pa.t.* and *pa.p.* **-ped.** *n.* a small portion of liquid sipped with the lips [O.E. *sypian*, to soak].

si·phon, syphon (sī'·fạn) *n.* a bent tube or pipe by which a liquid can be transferred by atmospheric pressure from one receptacle to another; bottle provided with internal tube and lever top, for holding and delivering aerated water; projecting tube in mantle of shell of bivalve; *v.t.* to draw off by means of a siphon. *n.* action of a siphon [Gk. = tube].

sir (sur) *n.* a title of respect to any man of position; title of knight or baronet [var. of *sire*].

sire (sīr) *n.* title of respect to a king or emperor; male parent of an animal (applied esp. to horses); *pl.* (*Poetic*) ancestors; *v.t.* to beget (of animals) [Fr. fr. L. *senior*, elder].

si·ren (sī'·rạn) *n.* (*Myth.*) one of several nymphs said to sing with such sweetness that sailors were lured to death; seductive alluring woman; form of horn which emits series of loud, piercing notes used as warning signal;

steam whistle; the mud-eel; *a.* pert. to, or resembling a siren; alluring; seductive [Gk. *Seirēn*].

Sir·i·us (sir′·i·as) *n.* (*Astron.*) a star of the first magnitude known as the Dog Star [L.].

sir·loin (sur′·lion) *n.* the upper part of a loin of beef [O.Fr. *surloigne*].

si·roc·co (si·rák′·ō) *n.* a hot, southerly, dust-laden wind from Africa, chiefly experienced in Italy, Malta and Sicily [It.].

si·sal (sis′·al, sī′·sal) *n.* fiber plant, native to Florida and Yucatan providing **sisal-grass** (**sisal-hemp**) [*Sisal*, a seaport in *Yucatan*].

sis·sy (sis′·i·) *n.* (*Colloq.*) ineffective effeminate man or boy; *a.* effeminate.

sis·ter sis′·ter) *n.* female whose parents are same as those of another person; correlative of brother; woman of the same faith; female of the same society, convent, abbey; nun; *a.* standing in relation of sister; related; of a similar nature to, as institute, college, etc. **-hood** *n.* state of being a sister; society of women united in one faith or order. **—in-law** *n.* husband's or wife's sister; brother's wife. *pl.* **-s-in-law, -like, -ly** *a.* [O.N. *systir*].

Sis·tine (sis′·tēn) *a.* pert. to any Pope named Sixtus. **— Chapel,** the Pope's private chapel in the Vatican at Rome.

sit (sit) *v.i.* to rest upon haunches, a seat, etc.; to remain; to rest; to perch, as birds; (of hen) to cover and warm eggs for hatching; to be officially engaged in transacting business, as court, council, etc.; to be in session; to be representative in legislative for constituency; to pose for portrait; to press or weigh (upon); to fit (of clothes); *v.t.* to keep good seat, upon, as on horseback; to place upon seat; *pr.p.* **-ting.** *pa.t.* and *pa.p.* **sat.** *n.* position assumed by an object after being placed. **-ter** *n.* one who sits; one who poses for artist; bird sitting on its eggs; one who stays with children while parents are out. **-ting** *n.* state of resting on a seat, etc.; act of placing oneself on a seat; session; business meeting; time given up to posing for artist; clutch of eggs for incubation; *a.* resting on haunches; perched. **-ting-room** *n.* [O.E. *sittan*].

site (sīt) *n.* situation; plot of ground for, or with, building; locality; place where anything is fixed; *v.t.* to place in position; to locate [L. *situs*, a site].

si·tol·o·gy (sī·tál′·a·ji·) *n.* dietetics [Gk. *silos*, food; *logos*, a discourse].

sit·u·ate (sich′·oo·āt) *v.t.* to give a site to; to place in a particular state or set of circumstances; to locate; **-d** *a.* located; placed with reference to other affairs, etc. **situation** *n.* location; place or position; site; condition; job; post; plight [L. *situs*, a site].

six (siks) *a.* one more than five; *n.* sum of three and three; symbol 6 or VI. **-fold** *a.* six times as much or as many. **-footer** *n.* person six feet in height. **-pence** *n.* silver coin in British currency of value of six pennies. **-penny** *a.* worth sixpence; paltry; of small value. **-shooter** *n.* a six-chambered revolver. **-teen** *n.* and *a.* six and ten, symbol 16 or XVI. **-teenth** *a.* sixth after the tenth; being one of sixteen equal parts into which anything is divided; *n.* one of sixteen equal parts; a division of the inch; (*Mus.*) semiquaver. **-th** *a.* next in order after the fifth; one of six equal parts; *n.* (*Mus.*) an interval comprising six degrees of the staff, as A to F. **-ty** *a.* six times ten; three score; *n.* symbol 60 or LX. **-tieth** *a.* next in order after the fifty-ninth; one of sixty equal parts; *n.* **at sixes and sevens,** in disorder and confusion [O.E. *siex*].

size (sīz) *n.* bulk; bigness; comparative magnitude; dimensions; extent; conventional measure of dimension; *v.t.* to arrange according to size. **-able, sizable** *a.* of considerate size or bulk. **to size up,** to estimate possibili-

ties of; to take measure of [contr. of *assize*].

size (sīz) *n.* substance of a gelatinous nature, like weak glue; *v.t.* to treat or cover with size [Fr. *assise*, a layer (e.g. of paint, etc.)].

siz·zle (siz′·l) *v.i.* to make hissing or sputtering noise; (*Colloq.*) to suffer from heat. *n.* hissing, sputtering noise. **sizzling** *n.* [imit.].

skald (skáld) *n.* ancient Scandinavian poet **-ic** *a.* Also **scald** [O.N. *skald*].

skate (skāt) *n.* steel blade attached to boot, used for gliding over ice; *v.i.* to travel over ice on skates. **-r** *n.* **skating** *n.* **skating-rink** *n.* stretch of ice or flat expanse for skating; ice-rink. **roller skate** *n.* skate with wheels in place of steel blade [Dut. *schaats*].

skate (skāt) *n.* a large, edible, flat fish of the ray family [O.N. *skata*].

skean (skēn) *n.* Highland dagger or dirk; long knife [Gael. *sgian*, knife].

ske·dad·dle (ski·dad′·l) *v.i.* (*Colloq.*) to scamper off; *n.* hasty, disorderly flight.

skeet (skēt) *n.* trapshooting with clay targets thrown into the air.

skein (skān) *n.* small hank, of fixed length, of thread, silk, or yarn, doubled and secured by loose knot [O.Fr. *escaigne*].

skel·e·ton (skel′·a·tạn) *n.* body framework providing support for human or animal body; any framework, as of building, plant, etc.; general outline; *a.* pert. to skeleton; containing mere outlines. Also **skeletal. — crew, staff, etc.,** minimum number of men employed on some essential duty [Gk. *skeletos*, dried up].

skel·ter. See **helter-skelter.**

skep (skep) *n.* beehive made of straw; light basket [O.N. *skeppa*, a basket].

skep·tic (skep′·tik) *n.* one who doubts, esp. existence of God, or accepted doctrines; rationalist; agnostic; unbeliever; **-al** *a.* doubtful; doubting; disbelieving. **-ally** *adv.* **-alness** *n.* **skepticize** *v.i.* to doubt everything. **skepticism** *n.* doubt in absence of conclusive evidence; theory that positive truth is unattainable by human intellect [Gk. *skeptesthai*, to investigate].

sker·ry (sker′·i·) *n.* rocky isle; reef [O.N.].

sketch (skech) *n.* first rough draft or plan of any design; outline; drawing in pen, pencil, or similar medium; descriptive essay or account, in light vein; a short, humorous one-act play; *v.t.* to draw outline of; to make rough draft of; *v.i.* to draw; to make sketches. **-er** *n.* **-ily** *adv.* **-iness** *n.* lack of detail. **-y** *a.* containing outline or rough form; inadequate; incomplete [Dut. *schets*].

skew (skū) *a.* awry; oblique; askew; turned aside; *n.* anything set obliquely or at an angle to some other object; a deviation; *v.t.* to put askew; to skid. **—bald** *a.* of horse, bay and white in patches. [O.Fr. *escuer*].

skew·er (skū′·er) *n.* pointed rod for fastening meat to a spit, or for keeping it in form while roasting; *v.t.* to fasten with skewers.

ski (skē, in Norway, shē) *n.* long wooden runner strapped to foot, for running, sliding and jumping over snow; *v.i.* to run, slide, or jump on skis. **-er** *n.* [Norw.].

ski·a·graph (skī′·a·graf) *n.* an X-ray photograph. Also **skiagram. -er** *n.* one who takes X-ray photographs. **-ic** *a.* [Gk. *skia*, a shadow; *graphein*, to write].

skid (skid) *n.* a piece of timber to protect side of vessel from injury; drag placed under wheel to check speed of vehicle descending steep gradient; inclined plane down which logs, etc. slide; low, wooden platform for holding and moving loads; *v.i.* to slide or slip sideways; *v.t.* to slide a log down a skid; to place on skids. *pr.p.* **-ding** *pa.p.*, *pa.t.* **-ded** [O.N. *skidh*].

skiff (skif) *n.* a small rowboat or sailboat [Fr. *esquif*].

skill (skil) *n.* practical ability and dexterity; knowledge; expertness; aptitude. **-ful** *a.* expert; skilled; dexterous. **-fully** *adv.* **-fulness** *n.* **-ed** *a.* [O.N. *skil*, distinction].

skil·let (skil'.it) *n.* a frying pan [O.Fr. *escuellete*].

skim (skim) *v.t.* to remove from surface of liquid; to glide over lightly and rapidly; to glance over in superficial way; to graze; *v.i.* to pass lightly over; to glide along; to hasten over superficially. *pr.p* **-ming.** *pa.t.* and *pa.p.* **-med.** *n.* skimming; matter skimmed off. **-mer** *n.* — **milk** *n.* milk from which cream has been removed [O.Fr. *escumer*].

skimp (skimp) *v.t.* to stint; *v.i.* to be mean or parsimonious; to economize in petty fashion. **-y** *a.* scant; meager; stingy.

skin (skin) *n.* external protective covering of animal bodies; epidermis; a hide; a pelt; coat of fruits and plants; husk or bark; thick scum; *v.t.* to strip off skin or hide of; to flay; to graze; to peel; (*Slang*) to cheat; to swindle. **—deep** *a.* superficial. **—flint** *n.* miser. **— game** *n.* cheating and swindling. **— grafting** *n.* transplanting healthy skin to wound to form new skin. **-ner** *n.* dealer in hides; furrier. **-niness** *n.* leanness. **-ny** *a.* of skin; very lean or thin. **—tight** *a.* fitting close to skin. [O.N. *skinn*].

skip (skip) *v.t.* to leap over lightly; to omit without noticing; *v.i.* to leap lightly, esp. in frolic; to frisk; to pass from one thing to another; to clear repeatedly a rope swung in play under one's feet; (*Colloq.*) to run away hastily. *pr.p.* **-ping.** *pa.t.* and *pa.p.* **-ped.** *n.* light leap, spring, or bound; an omission. **-ping** *a.* characterized by skips.

skip·per (skip'.er) *n.* captain of ship or team [Dut. *schipper*].

skirl (skurl) *v.i.* to sound shrilly. *n.* shrill, high-pitched sound of bagpipe [var. of *shrill*].

skir·mish (skur'.mish) *n.* irregular, minor engagement between two parties of soldiers; *v.i.* [Fr. *escarmouche*].

skirt (skurt) *n.* lower part of coat, gown; outer garment of a woman fitted to and hanging from waist; petticoat; flap; border; margin; edge; rim; *v.t.* to be on border; to go around. **-ing** *n.* material for women's skirts; border [O.N. *skyria*].

skit (skit) *n.* satirical gibe; lampoon; short, usually humorous, play; *v.i.* to leap aside. **-tish** *a.* frisky; frivolous; fickle; apt to shy, of a horse. **-tishly** *adv.* **-tishness** *n.*

skit·tle (skit'.l) *n.* game of ninepins.

skive (skīv) *v.t.* in shoe-making, to pare away edges of leather [Ice. *skifa*, to split].

skiv·vy (skiv'.i.) *n.* (*Slang*) undershirt.

skoal (skōl) *interj.* salutation, hail! in toasting [Dan. *skaal*, bowl; a toast].

skulk (skulk) *v.i.* to sneak out of the way; to lurk or keep out of sight in a furtive manner; to act sullenly; *n.* one who skulks.

skull (skul) *n.* bony framework which encloses brain; cranium along with bones of face. **— cap** *n.* brimless cap fitting close to head. **— and crossbones,** a symbol for poison, formerly used on pirate flags [M.E. *skulle*].

skunk (skungk) *n.* small N. American burrowing animal, allied to weasel, which defends itself by emitting evil-smelling fluid; (*Colloq.*) a base, mean person [Amer.-Ind. *seganku*].

sky (skī) *n.* the apparent vault of heaven; heavens; firmament; climate. *v.t.* **—blue** *n.* and *a.* azure; cerulean. **-ey** *a.* (*Poetic*) like the sky. **—gazer** *n.* visionary.**—high** *a.* and *adv.* at a great elevation; carried away with excitement or anticipation. **-lark** *n.* bird which sings as it soars; *v.i.* (*Colloq.*) to indulge in boisterous byplay. **—larking** *n.* **-light** *n.* glazed opening in roof or ceiling.

-line *n.* horizon; silhouette of buildings, etc. on horizon. **-scraper** *n.* lofty building with numerous stories. **-writing** *n.* writing in air for advertising or propaganda purposes by smoke from an airplane [O.N. *sky*, a cloud].

Skye (skī) *n.* or **Skyeterrier,** breed of Scotch terrier, with long hair. [Isle of *Skye*].

slab (slab) *n.* thickish, flat, rectangular piece of anything; concrete paving-block; thick slice of cake, etc.

slack (slak) *a.* not taut; not closely drawn together; not holding fast; remiss about one's duties; easy-going; *n.* part of a rope which hangs loose; quiet time. **-en** *v.t.* to loosen; to moderate; to relax; to leave undone; to slake; *v.i.* to become slack; to lose cohesion; to relax; to dodge work; to languish; to flag. **-er** *n.* one who shirks work. **-ly** *adv.* **-ness** *n.* **-s** *n.pl.* loose trousers worn by men or women. [O.E. *slaec*].

slack (slak) *n.* the finer screenings of coal which pass through a half-inch mesh; coaldust; dross. **-heap** *n.* [Ger. *Schlacke*, dross].

slag (slag) *n.* silicate formed during smelting of ores; scoria of a volcano; *v.i.* to form slag [Ger. *Schlacke*, dross].

slain (*slān*) *pa.p.* of the verb **slay.**

slake (slāk) *v.t.* to quench; to extinguish; to combine quicklime with water; to slacken; *v.i.* to become mixed with water [O.E. *slacian*].

slam (slam) *v.t.* to shut violently and noisily; to bang; to hit; to dash down; to win all, or all but one, of the tricks at cards. *pr.p.* **-ming.** *pa.t.* and *pa.p.* **-med.** *n.* act of slamming; bang; **slam (grand** or small) thirteen or twelve tricks taken in one deal in cards.

slan·der (slan'.der) *n.* false or malicious statement about person; defamation of character by spoken word; calumny; *v.t.* to injure by maliciously uttering false report; to defame. **-er** *n.* **-ous** *a.* [Fr. *esclandre*].

slang (slang) *n.* word or expression in common colloquial use but not regarded as standard English; jargon peculiar to certain sections of public, trades, etc.; argot; *a.* pert. to slang; *v.t.* to vituperate; to revile; to scold.

slant (slant) *v.t.* to turn from a direct line; to give a sloping direction to; *v.i.* to lie obliquely; to slope; to incline; *n.* slanting direction or position; slope; point of view or illuminating remark (on); *a.* sloping; oblique. **-ingly** *adv.* **-ly, -wise** *adv.* [Swed. *slinta*, to slide].

slap (slap) *n.* blow with open hand or flat instrument; insulting remark; *v.t.* to strike with open hand or something flat. *pr.p.* **-ping.** *pa.t.* and *pa.p.* **-ped.** *adv.* with a sudden blow; (*Colloq.*) instantly; directly. **-stick** *n.* boisterous farce of pantomine or low comedy. [imit. origin].

slash (slash) *v.t.* to cut by striking violently and haphazardly; to make gashes in; to slit; *v.i.* to strike violently and at random with edged weapon; *n.* long cut; gash; cutting stroke; large slit in garment. **-er** *n.* [O.Fr. *esclachier*, to sever].

slat (slat) *n.* narrow strip of wood, metal, etc. a lath *pl.* (*Slang*) ribs. **-ted** *a.* covered with slats [O.Fr. *esclat*, fragment].

slate (slāt) *n.* a form of shale, composed mainly of aluminium silicate, which splits readily into thin leaves; prepared piece of such stone, esp. thin piece for roofing houses, etc.; dark blue-gray color; list of candidates for offices; *a.* made of slate; bluish-gray; *v.t.* to cover with slates; to put on a list for nomination, etc. **slating** *n.* act of covering with slates; roof-covering thus put on. **slaty** *n.* [O.Fr. *esclat*, a splinted].

slat·tern (slat'.ern) *n.* slut; slovenly woman or girl. **-liness** *n.* **-ly** *a.* like a slattern; *adv.* in slovenly manner [Scand. *slat*, to strike].

slaugh·ter (slaw'.ter) *n.* act of slaughtering; carnage; massacre; butchery; killing of animals to provide food; *v.t.* to kill; to slay in battle; to butcher, **-er** *n.* **-house** *n.* place where cattle are slaughtered. **-ous** *a.* bent on slaughter; destructive. **-ously** *adv.* [O.N. *slatr*, butcher's meat].

Slav (slàv) *n.* a member of a group of peoples in E. and S.E. Europe, comprising Russians, Ukrainians, White Russians, Poles, Czechs, Slovaks, Serbians, Croats, Slovenes and Bulgarians; *a.* relating to the Slavs; Slavic; Slavonic. **-ic** *a.* **-onic** *a.* [etym. unknown].

slave (slāv) *n.* person held legally in bondage to another; bondman; one who has lost all powers of resistance to some pernicious habit or vice; *v.i.* to work like a slave, to toil unremittingly. **-driver** *n.* an overseer in charge of slaves at work; exacting taskmaster. **-r** *n.* person or ship engaged in slave traffic. **-ry** *n.* condition of slave compelled to perform compulsory work for another; bondage; servitude. **— trade** *n.* traffic in human beings. **— trader** *n.* **slavish** *a.* pert. to slaves; menial; drudging; servile; base; mean; imitative. **slavishly** *adv.* **slavishness** *n.* **white slavery,** traffic in women and girls for immoral purposes [Fr.*esclave*, fr. *Slav*].

slav·er (slàv'·er) *n.* saliva running from mouth; sentimental nonsense; *v.t.* to smear with saliva issuing from mouth; *v.i.* to slobber; to talk in a weakly sentimental fashion. **-er** *n.* [O.N. *slafra*, to slaver].

slaw (slaw) *n.* sliced cabbage served cooked, or uncooked, as a salad [Dut. *sla*, salad].

slay (slā) *v.t.* to kill; to murder; to slaughter. *pa.t.* **slew.** *pa.p.* **slain. -er** *n* [O.E. *slean*, to smite].

sleave (slēv) *n.* knotted or entangled part of silk or thread; a fine wisp of silk made by separating a thread; *v.t.* to separate and divide as into threads [etym. uncertain].

slea·zy (slē'·zi) *a.* thin or poor in texture.

sled, sledge (sled, slej) *n.* a vehicle on runners, for conveying loads over hard snow or ice; a sleigh; a small flat sled for coasting; *v.t.* to convey on a sled; *v.i.* to ride on a sled [Dut. *slede*].

sledge (slej) *n.* large, heavy hammer. [O.E. *slecg*].

sleek (slēk) *a.* having a smooth surface; glossy; not rough; ingratiating; *v.t.* to make smooth; to calm; to soothe; *adv.* **-ly** *adv.* **-ness** *n.* [O.N. *slikr*, smooth].

sleep (slēp) *v.i.* to rest by suspension of exercise of powers of body and mind; to become numb (of limb); to slumber; to doze; to repose; to rest; to be dead. *pa.t.* and *pa.p.* **slept.** *n.* slumber; repose; rest; death. **-er** *n.* one who sleeps; railway sleeping car; **-ily** *adv.* in drowsy manner. **-iness** *n.* **-ing** *a.* resting in sleep; inducing sleep; adapted for sleeping; *n.* state of resting in sleep; state of not being raised or discussed. **-ing-bag** *n.* bag of thick material, waterproofed on outside, for sleeping in the open. **-ing-car** *n.* railway car with berths, compartments, etc. **-ing sickness** *n.* brain infection causing increased drowsiness. **-less** *a.* wakeful; restless; alert; vigilant; unremitting. **-lessly** *adv.* **-lessness** *n.* **-walker** *n.* one who walks in his sleep or in trance; somnambulist. **-walking** *n.* **-y** *a.* inclined to sleep; drowsy [O.E. *slaepan*].

sleet (slēt) *n.* rain that is partly frozen; *v.i.* to fall as fine pellets of ice. **-iness** *n.* **-y** *a.* [M.E. *slete*].

sleeve (slēv) *n.* part of garment which covers arm; casing surrounding shaft of engine; wind-sock used on airfields as wind-indicator; *v.t.* to furnish with sleeves. [O.E. *sliefe*].

sleigh (slā) *n.* a sled; an open carriage on runners, usually horse-drawn; *v.i.* to drive in a sleigh [Dut. *slee*].

sleight (slīt) *n.* artful trick; skill. **— of hand** *n.* legerdemain; juggling [O.N. *slaegth*].

slen·der (slen'·der) *a.* thin or narrow; weak; feeble; not strong. **-ly** *adv.* **-ness** *n.* [M.E. *slendre*].

slept (slept) *pa.t.* and *pa.p.* of **sleep.**

sleuth (slooth) *n.* bloodhound; a relentless tracker; (*Colloq.*) detective. **-hound** *n.* bloodhound [O.N. *sloth*, a track].

slew (slōó) *pa.t.* of **slay.**

slew, slue (slōó) *v.t.* and *v.i.* to turn about; to swing round [etym. unknown].

slice (slīs) *v.t.* and *v.i.* to cut off thin flat pieces; to strike a ball so that its line of flight diverges well to the right; to part like the cut of a knife; *n.* thin, flat piece cut off; broad, flat, thin knife for serving fish; spatula; share or portion; stroke at golf, etc. in which ball curls away to the right. **-r** *n.* [O. Fr. *esclice*].

slick (slik) *a.* smooth; sleek; smooth-tongued; smart; clever; slippery; *adv.* deftly; cleverly; *v.t.* to sleek; to make glossy. *n.* a smooth spot, as one covered with oil. See **sleek.**

slick·er (slik'·er) *n.* waterproof coat.

slid, slidden See **slide.**

slide (slīd) *v.i.* to slip smoothly along; to slip, to glide, esp. over ice; to pass imperceptibly; to deteriorate morally; *v.t.* to move something into position by pushing along the surface of another body; to thrust along; to pass imperceptibly. *pr.p.* **sliding.** *pa.t.* **slid.** *pa.p.* **slid** or **slidden.** *n.* sliding; track on ice made by sliding; sliding part of mechanism; anything which moves freely in or out; photographic film holder for projecting; smooth and easy passage; chute; a narrow piece of glass to carry small object to be examined under microscope; moving part of trombone or trumpet. **-r** *n.* **— rule** *n.* mathematical instrument for rapid calculations. **sliding-scale** *n.* schedule of wages, prices, duties, etc. showing automatic variations [O.E. *slidan*].

slight (slīt) *a.* trifling; inconsiderable; not substantial; slim; slender; *n.* contempt by ignoring another; disdain; insult; *v.t.* to ignore; to disdain; to insult. **-ing** *n.* act or instance of disrespect; *a.* disparaging. **-ingly** *adv.* **-ly** *adv.* to slight extent; not seriously. **-ness** *n.* [O.N. *slettr*].

slim (slim) *a.* of small diameter or thickness; slender; thin; slight; unsubstantial; *comp.* **-mer,** *superl.* **-mest.** *v.t.* and *v.i.* to make or become slim; *pa.t., pa.p.* **-med.** *pr.p.* **-ming. -ly** *adv.* frail [Dut. = crafty].

slime (slīm) *n.* soft, sticky, moist earth or clay; greasy, viscous mud; mire; viscous secretion of snails, etc.; **slimily** *adv.* **sliminess** *n.* **slimy** *a.* [O.E. *slim*].

sling (sling) *n.* pocket of leather, etc., with a string attached at each end for hurling a stone; catapult; swinging throw; strap attached to rifle; hanging bandage, for supporting an arm or hand; rope, chain, belt, etc. for hoisting weights; *v.t.* to throw by means of sling or swinging motion of arm; to hoist or lower by means of slings; to suspend. *pa.t.* and *pa.p.* **slung. -er** *n.* [O.N. *slyngva*].

sling (sling) *n.* American iced drink of sweetened gin (or rum) with water, fruit juice [Ger. *schlingen,* to swallow].

slink (slingk) *v.i.* to move in a stealthy, furtive manner. *pa.t.* and *pa.p.* **slunk** [O.E. *slincan,* to creep].

slip (slip) *v.t.* to move an object smoothly, secretly, or furtively into another position; to put on, or off easily; to loosen; to release (dog); to omit; to miss; to overlook; to escape (memory); to escape from; of animals, to give premature birth to; *v.i.* to lose one's foothold; to move smoothly along surface of; to withdraw quietly; to slide; to make a mistake; to lose one's chance; to pass without notice. *pr.p.* **-ping.** *pa.t.* and *pa.p.* **-ped.** *n.* act of slipping; unintentional error; false step; twig for grafting separated from main stock; leash for dog; long, narrow, piece; loose garment worn under woman's dress; covering for a pillow; skid; inclined plane from which ships are launched. — **cover** n. a removable covering for upholstered furniture. **-knot** n. running knot which slips along rope around which it is made, forming loop. **-per** n. light shoe for indoor use; dancing-shoe. **-perily** adv. **-periness** n. condition of being slippery. a. so smooth as to cause slipping or to be difficult to hold or catch; not affording a firm footing; unstable; untrustworthy; changeable; artful; wily. **-shod** a. having shoes down at heel; untidy; slovenly; inaccurate. **-up** n. (Colloq.) a mistake [O.E. slipan].

slit (slit) v.t. to cut lengthwise; to cut open; to sever; to rend; to split; v.i. to be slit. pr.p. **-ting.** pa.t. and pa.p. **slit.** n. straight, narrow cut or incision; narrow opening. **-ter** n. [O.E. slitan].

slith·er (sliTH′·er) v.i. to slide and bump (down a slope, etc.); to move in a sliding, snakelike fashion; n. act of slithering; rubble [var. of slidder].

sliv·er (sliv′·er) v.t. to divide into long, thin strips; v.i. to split; to become split off; n. thin piece cut lengthwise; splinter [O.E. slifan, to split].

slob·ber (slåb′·er) v.i. to let saliva drool from mouth; dribble; v.t. to cover with saliva. n. saliva coming from mouth; sentimental drivel. Also **slabber. -er** n. [var. of slaver].

sloe (slō) n. blackthorn; small dark fruit of blackthorn. — **gin** n. liqueur from gin and sloes [O.E. sla].

slog (slåg) v.t. to hit wildly and vigorously; v.i. to work or study with dogged determination; to trudge along; pr.p. **-ging.** pa.t. and pa.p. **-ged, -ger** n. [O.E. slean, to strike].

slo·gan (slō′·gan) n. war cry of Highland clan in Scotland; distinctive phrase used by a political party; catchword for focusing public interest, etc. [Gael. sluagh-ghairm].

sloop (slōop) n. one-masted sailing vessel [Dut. sloep].

slop (slåp) n. liquid carelessly spilled; puddle; pl. water in which anything has been washed; liquid refuse; v.t. to spill; to soil by spilling over; v.i. to overthrow or be spilled. pr.p. **-ping.** pa.t. and pa.p. **-ped.** —**basin,** —**bowl** n. basin or bowl for holding dregs from teacups. **-pily** adv. **-piness** n. **-py** a. wet; muddy; slovenly; untidy; (Colloq.) mawkishly sentimental [O.E. sloppe].

slope (slōp) n. upward or downward inclination; slant; side of hill; v.t. to form with slope; to place slanting; v.i. to assume oblique direction; to be inclined. **sloping** a. [O.E. slupan, to slip away].

slosh (slåsh) n. soft mud; v.t. to stir in liquid; v.i. to splash, stir about, in mud, water, etc. [fr. slush].

slot (slåt) n. slit cut out for reception of object or part of machine; slit where coins are inserted into automatic machines; v.t. to make a slot in. pr.p. **-ting.** pa.t. and pa.p. **-ted.** — **machine** n. automatic machine worked by insertion of coin [O.Fr. esclot].

sloth (slawth) n. lethargy; indolence. **-ful** a. inactive; sluggish; lazy. **-fully** adv. **-fulness** n. [O.E. slaewth, fr. slaw, slow].

sloth (slōth, slawth) n. group of edentate mammals of S. America which cling mostly to branches of trees [fr. slow].

slouch (slouch) n. ungraceful, stooping manner of walking or standing; shambling gait; v.i. to shamble; to sit or stand in a drooping position; v.t. to depress; to cause to hang down loosely. — **hat** n. soft hat with a broad, flexible brim. **-y** a. inclined to slouch.

slough (slou) n. bog; swamp [O.E. sloh].

slough (sluf) n. cast-off outer skin, esp. of snake; dead mass of soft tissues which separates from healthy tissues in gangrene or ulcers; v.t. to cast off, or shed, as a slough; v.i. to separate as dead matter which forms over sore; to drop off [etym. uncertain].

Slo·vak (slō·vak′) n. member of Slav people in northern Carpathians, closely related to Czechs; language spoken in Slovakia; a. pert. to Slovaks. Also **Slovakian.**

slov·en (sluv′·n) n. person careless of dress, or negligent of cleanliness. **-liness** n. **-ly** a. adv. in slipshod manner [etym. uncertain].

slow (slō) a. not swift; not quick in motion; gradual; indicating time earlier than true time; mentally sluggish; dull; wearisome; adv. slowly; v.t. to render slow; to retard; to reduce speed of; v.i. to slacken speed. **-ly** adv. — **match** n. fuse made so as to burn slowly, for firing mines, etc. — **motion** n. and a. in motion pictures, motion shown in exaggeratedly slow time. **-ness** n. **-witted** a. mentally slow, dull; apathetic. [O.E. slaw, sluggish].

sludge (sluj) n. mud which settles at bottom of waterways, of vessel containing water, or a shaft when drilling; semi-solid; slimy matter precipitated from sewage in sedimentation tank. **sludgy** a. [var. of slush].

slug (slug) n. one of land snails without a shell, a common pest in gardens. **-gard** n. person habitually lazy and idle; a. disinclined to exert oneself; habitually indolent; slothful; slow-moving. **-gishly** adv. **-gishness** n. [Scand.].

slug (slug) n. small thick disk of metal; a piece of metal fired from gun; solid line of type cast by linotype process.

slug (slug) (Colloq.) v.i. to strike heavily; to slog; n. heavy blow [O.E. slean, to strike].

sluice (slōōs) n. valve or shutter for regulating flow; a natural channel for drainage; artificial channel along which stream flows; sluicing; v.t. to drain through a sluice; to wash out, or pour over with water; v.i. to run through a sluice or other stream of water. — **box** n. trough used in goldmining [O.Fr. escluse].

slum (slum) n. squalid street, or quarter of town, characterized by gross over-crowding, dilapidation, poverty, vice and dirt; v.i. to visit slums. pr.p. **-ming** pa.t. and pa.p. **-med.**

slum·ber (slum′·ber) v.i. to sleep lightly; to be in a state of negligence, sloth, or inactivity; n. light sleep; doze. **-er** n. **-ous, slumbrous** a. inducing slumber; drowsy [O.E. sluma].

slump (slump) n. act of slumping; sudden, sharp fall in prices or volume of business done; industrial or financial depression; v.i. to drop suddenly; to droop; to decline suddenly in value, volume, or esteem; to sink suddenly when crossing snow, ice, boggy ground, etc.

slung (slung) pa.t. and pa.p. of **sling.**

slunk (slungk) pa.t. and pa.p. of **slink.**

slur (slur) v.t. to pass over lightly; to depreciate; to insult; to pronounce indistinctly; (Mus.) to sing or play in a smooth, gliding style; to run one into the other, as notes. pr.p. **-ring.** pa.t. and pa.p. **-red.** n. slight blur in print; stigma; reproach; implied insult; (Mus.) mark, thus (‿ or ⁀) connecting notes that are to be sung to same syllable, or made in one continued breath; indistinct sound [O. Dut. slooren, to trail (in mud)].

slush (slush) n. half-melted snow; soft mud; any greasy, pasty mass; overly sentimental talk or writings; v.t. to splash or cover with slush; to flush a place with water. **-y** a. [var. of sludge].

slut (slut) n. dirty, untidy woman; slattern. **-tish** a. untidy and dirty. [M.E. slutte].

sly (slī) a. artfully cunning; mischievous. **-ly** adv. **-ness** n. [O.N. slaegr].

smack (smak) v.t. to make a loud, quick noise

(with lips) as in kissing or after tasting; to slap loudly; to strike; *v.i.* to make sharp, quick noise with lips; *n.* quick, sharp noise, esp. with lips; a loud kiss; a slap [imit.].

smack (smak) *v.i.* to have a taste or flavor; to give a suggestion (of); *n.* a slight taste [O.E. *smaec*, taste].

smack (smak) *n.* small sailing vessel, usually for fishing [Dut. *smak*].

small (smawl) *a.* little in size, number, degree, etc.; not large; unimportant; short; weak; slender; mean; *n.* small or slender part, esp. of back. -**ish** *a.* rather small. -**ness** *n.* — **arms** *n.pl.* hand firearms, e.g. rifles, pistols, etc. — **change**, coins of small value, e.g. pennies, nickels, dimes, etc. — **fry** *n.* young fish; children. — **talk** *n.* gossip; light conversation [O.E. *smael*].

small·pox (smawl'·pàks) *n.* infectious disease, characterized into pustules [E. *small*; O.E. *poc.* a pustule].

smart (smàrt) *n.* sharp, stinging pain; pang of grief; hurt feelings, etc. *v.i.* to feel such a pain; to be punished (with 'for'); *a.* causing a sharp, stinging pain; clever; active; shrewd; trim; neat; well-dressed; fashionable. -**ly** *adv.* -**ness** *n.* **smarten** (smàr'·tn) *v.t.* and *v.i.* to make more spruce [O.E. *smeortan*, to feel pain].

smash (smash) *v.t.* to break into pieces to shatter; to hit hard; to ruin; *v.i.* to break into pieces; to dash violently against; of a business firm, to fail; *n.* crash; heavy blow; accident, wrecking vehicles; utter ruin; of business firm, bankruptcy. -**ing** *a.* [fr. E. *mash.* to mix up].

smat·ter (smat'·er) *v.i.* to talk superficially; -**ing** *n.* slight, superficial knowledge.

smear (smēr) *v.t.* to rub over with a greasy, oily, or sticky substance; to daub; to impute disgrace to; (*U.S. Slang*) to defeat thoroughly; *n.* mark, stain. -**iness** *n.* -**y** *a.* [O.E. *smeru*, fat].

smell (smel) *n.* sense of perceiving odors by nose; act of smelling; (unpleasant) odor; scent; perfume; *v.t.* to perceive by nose; to detect; *v.i.* to use nose; to give out odor. *pr.p.* -**ing**. *pa.p.* and *pa.t.* -**ed** or **smelt**. -**ing** *n.* -**y** *a.* having unpleasant smell. -**ing salts** *n.pl.* scented ammonium carbonate used to relieve faintness, headache, etc. [M.E. *smel*].

smelt (smelt) *n.* small, silvery fish of salmon family [O.E. *smelt*].

smelt (smelt) *v.t.* to melt or fuse ore in order to extract metal. -**ing** *n.* [Sw. *smalla*, to melt].

smi·lax (smī'·laks) *n.* genus of evergreen climbing shrubs [Gk. = bindweed].

smile (smīl) *v.i.* to express pleasure, approval, amusement, contempt, irony, etc. by curving lips; to look happy; *v.t.* to express by smile; *n.* act of smiling; pleasant facial expression. **smiling** *a.* cheerful; gay joyous. [Sw. *smila*].

smirch (smurch) *v.t.* to dirty; to soil; to stain; to bring disgrace upon; *n.* stain [M.E. *smeren*, to smear].

smirk (smurk) *v.i.* to smile in an affected or conceited manner; *n.* [O.E. *smercian*, to smile].

smite (smīt) *v.t.* to hit hard; to strike with hand, fist, weapon, etc.; to defeat; to afflict; *v.i.* to strike. *pa.p.* **smitten** (smit'·n). *pa.t.* **smote** (smōt). -**r** *n.* [O.E. *smitan*, to smear].

smith (smith) *n.* one who shapes metal, esp. with hammer and anvil; blacksmith. -**y** *n.* smith's workship; forge [O.E. *smith*].

smith·er·eens (smiTH·er·ēnz') *n.pl.* (*Colloq.*) small bits. Also **smithers** [fr. *smite*].

smit·ten (smit'·n) *pa.p.* of **smite.**

smock (smàk) *n.* a loose garment worn over other clothing as a protection while working. -**ing** *n.* embroidered gathering of dress, blouse, etc. into honeycomb pattern [O.E. *smoc*].

smog (smàg, smawg) *n.* mixture of smoke and fog in atmosphere [from *smoke* and *fog*].

smoke (smōk) *n.* cloudy mass of suspended particles that rises from fire or anything burning; spell of tobacco smoking; cigar or cigarette; *v.t.* to consume (tobacco opium, etc.) by smoking; to expose to smoke (esp. in curing fish, etc.); *v.i.* to inhale and expel smoke of burning tobacco; to give off smoke. -**r** *n.* one who smokes tobacco; railroad car or section in which smoking is permitted; social gathering for men at which smoking is allowed. **smoking** *n.* **smokiness** *n.* **smoky** *a.* emitting smoke; filled with smoke; having color, taste of smoke [O.E. *smoca*].

smol·der (smōl'·der) *v.i.* to burn slowly without flame; of feelings, esp. anger, resentment, etc., to exist inwardly [M.E. *smolder*].

smolt (smōlt) *n.* young salmon.

smooth (smòoTH) *a.* not rough; level; polished; gently flowing; calm; steady in motion; pleasant; easy; *v.t.* to make smooth; to polish; to calm; to soothe; to make easy; *adv.* in a smooth manner. -**ly** *adv.* [O.E. *smoth*].

smor·gas·bord (smōr'·gas·bōrd) *n.* meal of appetizers served buffet style [Sw.].

smote (smōt) *pa.p.* and *pa.t.* of **smite.**

smoth·er (smuTH'·er) *v.t.* to destroy by depriving of air; to suffocate; to conceal; *v.i.* to be stifled; to be without air; *n.* thick smoke or dust [O.E. *smorian*, to choke].

smudge (smuj) *n.* smear; stain; dirty mark; blot; smoky fire to drive off insects or protect fruit trees from pests; *v.t.* to smear; to make a dirty mark; *v.i.* to become dirty or blurred.

smug (smug) *a.* very neat and prim; self-satisfied; complacent. -**ly** *adv.* -**ness** *n.* [L. Ger. *smuk*, neat].

smug·gle (smug'·l) *v.t.* to import or export goods secretly to evade customs duties. -**r** *n.* **smuggling** *n.* [L. Ger. *smuggeln*].

smut (smut) *n.* black particle of dirt; spot caused by this; fungoid disease of cereals, characterized by blackening of ears of oats, barley, etc.; lewd or obscene talk or writing; *v.t.* to blacken; to smudge. *pr.p.* -**ting**. *pa.p.* and *pa.t.* -**ted**. -**ty** *a.* soiled with smut; obscene; lewd. -**tily** *adv.* -**tiness** *n.*

smutch (smuch) *v.t.* to blacken, as with soot, etc.; *n.* dirty spot; stain; smudge.

snack (snak) *n.* share; slight, hasty meal. — **bar** *n.* place for service of light, hurried meals [fr. *snatch*].

snaf·fle (snaf'·l) *n.* horse's bridle bit jointed in middle but without curb; *v.t.* to put one on a horse [Dut. *snavel*, nose of animal].

snag (snag) *n.* stump projecting from tree-trunk; stump or tree-trunk sticking up in a river, impeding passage of boats; any obstacle, drawback, or catch; *v.t.* to catch on a snag. *pr.p.* -**ging**. *pa.p.*, *pa.t.* [O.T. *snagi*, a point].

snail (snāl) *n.* slow-moving mollusk with spiral shell; slow person [O.E. *snaegel*].

snake (snāk) *n.* long, scaly, limbless reptile; serpent; treacherous person; *v.t.* (*U.S.*) to drag along, e.g. log; *v.i.* to move like a snake. **snaky** *a.* pert. to, or resembling, snake; full of snakes [O.E. *snaca*].

snap (snap) *v.t.* to break abruptly; to crack; to seize suddenly; to snatch; to bite; to shut with click; (*Photog.*) to take snapshot of; *v.i.* to break short; to try to bite; to utter sharp, cross words; to make a quick, sharp sound; to sparkle. *pr.p.* -**ping**. *pa.p.* and *pa.t.* -**ped**. *n.* act of seizing suddenly, esp. with teeth; bite; sudden breaking; quick, sharp sound; small spring catch, as of a bracelet; crisp cooky; short spell of frosty weather; (*Photog.*) short for snapshot; (*Slang*) an easy job; *a.* sudden; unprepared; without warning. -**per** *n.* one who snaps; kind of fresh-water turtle. **-py** *a.* lively; brisk; (*Colloq.*) smartly dressed; quick. **-dragon** *n.* (*Bot.*) a flowering plant. **-shot** *n.* photograph [Dut. *snappen*].

snare (snār) *n.* running noose of cord or wire, used to trap animals or birds; a trap; anything by which one is deceived; *n.pl.* (*Mus.*) catgut strings across lower head of snare drum to produce rattling sound; *v.t.* to catch with snare; to entangle. — **drum** *n.* small drum carried at the side [O.N. *snara*].

snarl (snårl) *v.i.* to growl like an angry dog; to speak in a surly manner; *n.* growling sound; surly tone of voice. **-er** *n.* [imit.].

snarl (snårl) *n.* tangle or knot of hair, wool, etc.; complication; *v.t.* and *v.i.* to entangle or become entangled [fr. *snare*].

snatch (snach) *v.t.* to seize hastily or without permission; to grasp; *v.i.* to make quick grab or bite (at); *n.* quick grab; small bit or fragment [M.E. *snacchen*].

sneak (snēk) *v.i.* to creep or steal away; to slink; *v.t.* (*Slang*) to steal; *n.* furtive, cowardly fellow. **-er** *n.* **-ers** *n.pl.* (*U.S.*) light, soft-soled shoes. **-ing** *a.* mean; contemptible; secret. **-ingly** *adv.* **-iness, -ingness** *n.* quality of being sneaky; slyness. **-y** *a.* sneaking; mean; underhand [O.E. *snican*, to creep].

sneer (snēr) *v.i.* to show contempt by facial expression, as by curling lips; to smile, speak, or write scornfully; *n.* look of contempt or ridicule; scornful utterance. **-er** *n.* **-ing** *a.*

sneeze (snēze) *v.i.* to expel air through nose and mouth with sudden convulsive spasm and noise; *n.* a sneezing [O.E. *fneosan*].

snick (snik) *n.* small cut; notch; nick; *v.t.* to cut; to notch; to clip; [Scand. *snikka*, to cut].

snicker (snik′·ẹr) *v.i.* to laugh with small, audible catches of voice; to giggle; *n.* half-suppressed laugh [imit. origin].

sniff (snif) *v.i.* to draw in breath through nose with sharp hiss; to express disapproval, etc. by sniffing; to snuff; *v.t.* to take up through nose; to smell; *n.* act of sniffing; that which is sniffed. **-le** *v.i.* to sniff noisily through nose; to snuffle. **-ler** *n.* **snifter** (*Slang*) small drink of liquor [imit. origin].

snip (snip) *v.t.* to clip off with scissors; to cut; *n.* a single, quick stroke, as with scissors; a bit cut off; small piece of anything; *pl.* strong hand shears for cutting sheet metal. *pr.p.* **-ping.** *pa.p.* and *pa.t.* **-ped. -per** *n.* **-pet** *n.* a fragment [Dut. *snippen*].

snipe (snīp) *n.* long-billed gamebird, frequenting marshy places; a shot; *v.i.* to shoot snipe; (*Mil.*) to shoot from cover; *v.t.* to hit by so shooting. **-r** *n.* [O.N. *snipa*].

sniv·el (sniv′·l) *n.* running at the nose; sham emotion; whining, as a child. *v.i.* to run at the nose; to show real or sham sorrow; to cry or whine, as children [O.E. *snyflan*].

snob (snåb) *n.* one who judges by social rank or wealth rather than merit; one who ignores those whom he considers his social inferiors. **-bery** *n.* **-bish** *a.* **-bishly** *adv.* **-bishness** *n.* [etym. uncertain].

snood (snööd) *n.* ribbon formerly worn to hold back hair; fillet; netlike covering for head or part of hat [O.E. *snod*].

snoop (snööp) *v.i.* (*Colloq.*) to investigate slyly; to pry into; *n.* one who acts thus.

snoot (snööt) *n.* snout; nose; contemptuous; **-ily** *adv.* arrogantly; **-iness** *n.*; **-y,** *a.* (*Colloq.*) snobbish [ME *snute*].

snooze (snööz) *n.* (*Colloq.*) short sleep; nap; *v.i.* to take a snooze [perh. fr. *snore*].

snore (snōr) *v.i.* to breathe heavily and noisily during sleep; *n.* such noisy breathing. **-r** *n.* [O.E. *snora*, a snore].

snor·kel (snōr′·kạl) *n.* device for submarines and divers for air intake [Gr. *Schnorkel*, spiral].

snort (snawrt) *v.i.* to force air with violence through nose, as horses; to express feeling by such a sound; *v.t.* to express by snort; *n.* snorting sound [imit. origin].

snout (snout) *n.* projecting nose and jaws of animal, esp. of pig; any projection like a snout [O.E. *snut*].

snow (snō) *n.* frozen vapor which falls in flakes; snowfall; mass of flakes on the ground; (*Slang*) narcotic drug, in powdered form; *v.t.* to let fall like snow; to cover with snow; *v.i.* to fall as or like snow.**-y** *a.* covered with, full of snow; white. **-ily** *adv.* **-iness** *n.* **-ball** *n.* round mass of snow pressed or rolled together; shrub bearing balllike clusters of white flowers; anything increasing like snowball; *i.t.* to pelt with snowballs; *v.i.* to grow rapidly; like a rolling snowball. — **blindness** *n.* temporary blindness caused by glare of sun from snow. —**bound** *a.* shut in by heavy snowfall. **-drift** *n.* mass of snow driven into a heap by wind. **-drop** *n.* bulbous plant bearing white flowers in early spring. **-fall** *n.* falling of snow; amount of snow falling in given time or place. **-flake** *n.* small, thin, feathery mass of snow. — **line** *n.* line on mountain above which snow never melts. **-plow** *n.* machine for clearing snow from roads, etc. **-shoe** *n.* light, wooden framework with interwoven leather thongs for traveling over deep snow [O.E. *snaw*].

snub (snub) *v.t.* to check or rebuke with rudeness or indifference; to repress intentionally; *pr.p.* **-bing.** *pa.p.* and *pa.t.* **-bed.** *n.* intentional slight; rebuff; check; *a.* of nose, short and slightly turned up [O.N. *snubba*, to rebuke].

snuff (snuf) *n.* charred part of wick of candle or lamp; *v.t.* to nip this off; to extinguish. **-ers** *n.pl.* instrument resembling scissors, for snuffing candles [M.E. *snoffe*].

snuff (snuf) *v.t.* to draw up or through nostrils; to sniff; to smell; to inhale; *v.i.* to draw air or snuff into nose; to take snuff; *n.* powdered tobacco for inhaling through nose; sniff. **-er** *n.* **-box** *n.* a small box for snuff [Dut. *snuffen*].

snuf·fle (snuf′·l) *v.i.* to breathe noisily through nose, esp. when obstructed; to sniff continually; to speak through nose; *n.* act of snuffling; a nasal twang. **-r** *n.* [fr. *snuff*].

snug (snug) *a.* cosy; trim; comfortable; sheltered; close fitting. **-ly** *adv.* **-ness** *n.* cosiness. **-gery** *n.* a cosy room. **-gle** *v.i.* to lie close to, for warmth or from affection; to nestle [Scand.].

so (sō) *adv.* in this manner or degree; in such manner; very; to such degree (with *as* or *that* coming after); the case being such; accordingly; *conj.* therefore; in case that; *interj.* well! — **long** (*Colloq.*) good-bye. **so-so** *a.* (*Colloq.*) fair; middling; tolerable; *adv.* fairly; tolerably [O.E. *swa*].

soak (sōk) *v.t.* to steep; to wet thoroughly; to permeate; *v.i.* to lie steeped in water or other fluid; (*Colloq.*) to drink to excess; *n.* a soaking; the act of soaking; heavy rain; (*Colloq.*) a hard drinker. **-er** *n.* **-ing** *a.* wetting thoroughly; drenched; *n.* [O.E. *socian*].

soap (sōp) *n.* compound of oil or fat with alkali, used in washing; *v.t.* and *v.i.* to apply soap to. **-y** *a.* pert. to soap; covered with soap; like soap. **-iness** *n.* — **bubble** *n.* iridescent bubble from soapsuds. — **opera** *n.* (*Colloq.*) highly dramatized radio serial. **-stone** *n.* soft, smooth stone, with soapy feel; talc. **-suds** *n.pl.* foamy mixture of soap and water [O.E. *sape*].

soar (sōr) *v.i.* to fly high; to mount into air; to glide; to rise far above normal or to a great height [L. *ex*, out of; *aura*, the air].

sob (såb) *v.i.* to catch breath, esp. in weeping;

to sigh with convulsive motion. *pr.p.* **-bing.** *pa.p.* and *pa.t.* **-bed.** *n.* convulsive catching of breath, esp. in weeping or sighing [imit.].

so·ber (sō'·bẽr) *a.* temperate; not intoxicated; exercising cool reason; subdued; *v.t.* and *v.i.* to make or become sober. **-ly** *adv.* **-ness** *n.* **sobriety** (sō·brī'·e·ti·) *n.* habit of being sober; habitual temperance; moderation; seriousness [L. *sobrius*].

so·bri·quet (sō'·bri·kā) *n.* nickname, an assumed name. Also **soubriquet** (sòò-) [Fr.].

soc·cer (sǎk'·ẽr) *n.* association football [fr. *soc* in association].

so·cia·ble (sō'·shạ·bl) *a.* inclined to be friendly; fond of company. **sociably** *adv.* **-ness** *n.* **sociability** *n.* friendliness; geniality [L. *socius*, a companion].

so·cial (sō'·shạl) *a.* pert. to society; affecting public interest; pert. to world of fashion, etc.; living in communities, as ants; sociable; companionable; convivial; *n.* social meeting. **sociably** *adv.* **-ite** (sō'·shạl·īt) *n.* member of fashionable society [L. *socius*, a companion].

so·cial·ism (sō'·shạl·izm) *n.* economic and political system, aiming at public or government ownership of means of production, etc. **socialize** *v.t.* to make social; to transfer industry, etc. from private to public or government ownership. **socialization** *n.* **socialist** *a.* pert. to socialism. **socialistic** *a.* **socialistically** *adv.* [L. *socius*, a companion].

so·ci·e·ty (sạ·sī'·ạ·ti·) *n.* people in general; community; people of culture and good breeding in any community; the wealthy classes; the world of fashion; fellowship; wealthy; a company; an association; a club [L. *socius*, a companion].

so·ci·ol·o·gy (sō·shi·ǎl'·ạ·ji·) *n.* science of origin, development, and nature of problems confronting society; social science. **sociological** *a.* **sociologist** *n.* [L. *socius*, a companion; Gk. *logos*, a discourse].

sock (sǎk) *n.* orig. a low-heeled shoe; a short stocking [L. *soccus*, a light shoe].

sock (sǎk) *v.t.* (*Slang*) to hit hard; *n.* a blow.

sock·et (sǎk'·ạt) *n.* opening or hollow into which anything is fitted; cavity of eye, tooth, etc.; *v.t.* to provide with, or place in, socket.

sock·eye (sǎk'·ī) *n.* a red salmon.

sod (sǎd) *n.* flat piece of earth with grass; turf; *v.t.* to cover with turf. *pr.p.* **-ding.** *pa.p.*, *pa.t.* **-ded.**

so·da (sō'·dạ) *n.* name applied to various compounds of sodium, e.g. *baking soda, caustic soda, washing soda.* (See **sodium**); (*Colloq.*) soda water. **— fountain** *n.* case for holding soda water; shop selling soft drinks, ices, etc. **— water** *n.* drink made by charging water with carbon dioxide [It. fr. L. *solidus*, firm].

so·dal·i·ty (sō·dǎl'·ạ·ti·) *n.* fellowship; an association [L. *sodalis*, a comrade].

sod·den (sǎd'·n) *a.* soaked; soft with moisture; dull and heavy; stupid.

so·di·um (sō'·di·ạm) *n.* silvery-white metallic alkaline element, the base of soda (symbol, **Na.** fr. L. *natrium*). **— bicarbonate,** compound of sodium and carbon, used in cooking, medicine, etc.; baking soda. **— carbonate,** washing soda. **— chloride,** common household salt [fr. *soda*].

sod·o·my (sǎd'·ạm·i·) *n.* unnatural sexual intercourse, esp. between males or with an animal [fr. *Sodom*, Bib. city].

so·fa (sō'·fà) *n.* an upholstered couch [Ar. *Suffah*, cushion].

soft (sawft) *a.* yielding easily to pressure; not hard; easily shaped or molded; smooth; gentle; melodious; quiet; susceptible; sentimental; weak; weak in intellect; not astringent; containing no alcohol; in phonetics, esp. of consonants 'c' and 'g,' pronounced with a sibilant sound; *adv.* softly; quietly. **-ish** *a.*

somewhat soft. **-ly** *adv.* **-ness** *n.* **-headed** *a.* weak in intellect. **-hearted** *a.* kind; gentle; merciful [O.E. *softe*].

soft·ball (sawft'·bawl) *n.* variant of the game of baseball [*soft* and *ball*].

soft·en (sawf'·n) *v.t.* to make soft or softer; to lighten; to mitigate; to tone down; to make less loud; *v.t.* to become soft or softer. **-ing** *n.* act, process, or result of becoming soft or softer. **-ing** *n.* act, process, or result of becoming soft or softer [O.E. *softe*].

sog·gy (sǎg'·i·) *a.* soaked with water; sodden [Icel. *soggr*, damp].

soi·gné (swàn'·yā) *a.* well finished; exquisitely groomed [Fr.].

soil (soil) *v.t.* to make dirty; to defile; to dirty marks; filth; manure; top layer of earth's surface; earth, as food for plants [O.Fr. *soile*].

soi·rée (swà·rā') *n.* a social evening, a reception [Fr. = evening].

so·journ (sō'·journ) to dwell for a time; (sō'jurn') *n.* short stay [L. *sub*, under; *diurnus*, of a day].

sol·ace (sǎl'·as) *n.* comfort in grief; consolation; *v.t.* to console [L. *solari*, to comfort].

so·lan (sō'·lan) *n.* large sea bird like a goose; a gannet. Also **— goose** [O.N. *sula*].

so·lar (sō'·lẽr) *a.* pert. to, caused by, measured by sun. **-ize** *v.t.* and *v.i.* to expose to sun's rays. **solarium** (so·lar!·i·um) *n.* a sun room or porch. *pl.* **solaria. — plexus** (*Med.*) network of nerve tissue and fibers at back of stomach; (*Colloq.*) the pit of the stomach. **— system,** sun and all the heavenly bodies revolving around it [L. *sol*, the sun].

sold (sōld) *pa.p.* and *pa.t.* of **sell.**

sol·der (sǎd'·ẽr) *n.* easily melted alloy for joining metals; *v.t.* to join or mend with solder [L. *solidare*, to make solid].

sol·dier (sōl'·jẽr) *n.* man engaged in military service; an enlisted man as distinguished from commissioned officer. **-y** *n.* soldiers collectively; troops. **— of fortune,** military adventurer [L. *solidus*, a coin].

sole (sōl) *n.* flat of the foot; under part of boot or shoe; lower part of anything, or that on which anything rests; small flatfish, used for food; *v.t.* to supply with a sole [L. *solea*].

sole (sōl) *a.* being, or acting, without another; alone; only. **-ly** *adv.* alone; only [L. *solus*].

sol·e·cism (sǎl'·ạ·sizm) *n.* breach of grammar; a breach of etiquette. **solecist** *n.* one guilty of solecism [Gk. *soloikos*, speaking incorrectly].

sol·emn (sǎl'·ạm) *a.* marked, or performed, with religious ceremony; impressive; grave; inspiring awe or dread. **-ly** *adv.* **-ness** *n.* **-ize** (sǎl'·ạm·nīz) *v.t.* to perform with ceremony or legal form. **-ity** (sol·em'·ni·ti·) *n.* sacred rite or formal celebration; gravity; seriousness [L. *sollemnis*, yearly, solemn].

so·len (sō'·lan) *n.* genus of bivalve molluscs having a long, slender shell; razor-shell. **solenoid** *n.* (*Elect.*) cylindrical coil of wire (without fixed iron core) forming electromagnet when carrying current [Gk. *sōlēn*, a channel pipe; *eidos*, form].

sol·fa (sōl·fà!) *v.i.* to sing notes of scale [It. fr. *sol, fa*].

so·lic·it (sạ·lis'·it) *v.t.* to ask with earnestness; to petition; to entreat; *v.i.* to try to obtain, as trade, etc.; to accost. **-ant** *n.* one who solicits; petitioner. **-ation** *n.* earnest request; invitation; petition. **-or** *n.* one who solicits; official in charge of legal matters of city, department of government, etc. **-ous** *a.* anxious; eager; earnest. **-ously** *adv.* **-ousness, -ude** *n.* being solicitous; uneasiness; anxiety [L. *sollicitare*, to stir up].

sol·id (sǎl'·id) *a.* not in a liquid or gaseous state; hard; compact; firm; not hollow; dependable; sound; unanimous; (*Geom.*) having length, breadth, and thickness; whole; complete; *n.* a firm, compact body; (*Geom.*) that which has length, breadth and thickness; (*Physics*) substance which is not liquid nor gaseous. **-ly** *adv.* **-arity** *n.* state of being solidly united in support of common interests, rights, etc. **-ity** *n.* state of being solid; compactness; hardness [L. *solidus*, firm].

so·lid·i·fy (sa·lid'·a·fī) *v.t.* to make solid or firm; to harden; *v.i.* to become solid [L. *solidus*, firm; *facere*, to make].

sol·i·dus (sàl'·i·das) *n.* oblique stroke (/) in fractions, dates, etc. *pl.* **solidi** [L.].

so·lil·o·quy (sa·lil'·a·kwi·) *n.* talking to oneself; monologue, esp. by actor alone on stage. **soliloquize** *v.i.* to recite a soliloquy; to talk to oneself [L. *solus*, alone; *logui*, to speak].

sol·i·taire (sàl'·a·ter) *a.* living alone; done or spent alone; lonely; secluded; single; sole; *n.* hermit; recluse; a single gem set by itself. **solitarily** *adv.* **solitariness** *n.* **solitude** *n.* being alone; seclusion; lonely place or life [L. *solus*, alone].

so·lo (sō'·lō) *n.* musical composition played or sung by one person; in aviation, flight by single person; *pl.* (sō'·lōz) or **soli** (sō'·lē); *a.* done or performed by one person; unaccompanied; alone. **soloist** (sō'·lō·ist) *n.* (*Mus.*) performer of solos [It. fr. L. *solus*, alone].

sol·tice (sàl'·stis) *n.* either of two points in sun's path at which sun is farthest N. or S. from equator, about June 21 and December 22 respectively. **solstitial** (sàl·sti'·shal) *a.* [L. *sol*, the sun; *sistere*, to cause to stand].

sol·u·ble (sàl'·ya·bl) *a.* capable of being dissolved in a liquid; able to be solved or explained. **solubility** *n.* [L. *solubilis*, fr. *solvere*, to loosen].

so·lus (sō'·las) *a.* as a stage direction, alone. *fem.* **sola**]L. = alone[.

so·lu·tion (sa·lòò'·shan) *n.* process of finding answer to problem; answer itself; dissolving gas, liquid, or solid, esp. in liquid; mixture so obtained; commonly, a mixture of a solid in a liquid; *v.t.* to coat with solution, as a puncture. **solute** *n.* substance dissolved in a solution [L. *solvere*, *solutum*, to loosen].

solve (sàlv) *v.t.* to work out; to find the answer to; to explain; to make clear. **solvable** *a.* capable of explanation; able to be worked out. **-r** *n.* **solvent** *a.* having the power to dissolve another substance; able to pay all one's debts; *n.* substance, able to dissolve another substance. **-ncy** *n.* state of being able to pay one's debts [L. *solvere*, to loosen].

so·mat·ic (sō·mat'·ik) *a.* pert. to the body; corporeal; physical. Also **-al** [Gk. *sōma*, a body].

som·ber (sàm'·ber) *a.* dark; gloomy; melancholy. **-ly** *adv.* **-ness** *n.* **sombrous** *a.* (*Poet.*) somber **sombrously** *adv.* [Fr. fr. L. *sub umbra*, under shade].

som·bre·ro (sàm·bre'·rō) *n.* broad-brimmed felt hat [Sp. *sombre*, shade].

some (sum) *a.* denoting an indefinite number, amount, or extent; amount of; one or other; a certain; particular; approximately; (*Colloq.*) remarkable; (*pron.*) portion; particular persons not named; *adv.* approximately. **-body** *n.* person not definitely known; person of importance. **-how** *adv.* in one way or another; by any means. **-one** *pron.* somebody; person not named. **-such** *a.* denoting person or thing of the kind specified. **-thing** *n.* thing not clearly defined; an indefinite quantity or degree; *adv.* in some degree. **-time** *adv.* at a time not definitely stated; at one time or other; at a future time; *a.* former. **-times** *adv.* at times; now and then;

occasionally. **-what** *n.* indefinite amount or degree; *adv.* to some extent; rather. **-where** *adv.* in an unnamed or unknown place [O.E. *sum*].

som·er·sault (sum'·er·sawlt) *n.* a movement in which one turns heels over head; *v.i.* [L. *supra*, above; *saltus*, a leap].

som·nam·bu·late (sàm·nam'·bya·lāt) *v.i.* to walk in one's sleep. **somnambulation** *n.* **somnambulism** *n.* habit of walking in one's sleep; sleepwalking. **somnambulist** *n.* a sleepwalker. **somnambulistic** *a.* [L. *somnus*, sleep; *ambulare*, to walk].

som·ni·fa·cient (sàm·ni·fā'·shant) *a.* inducing sleep; *n.* soporific. **somniferous** *a.* inducing sleep. **somnific** *a.* causing sleep [L. *somnus*, sleep; *facere*, to make; *ferre*, to bring].

som·no·lent (sàm'·na·lant) *a.* sleepy; drowsy. **-ly** *adv.* drowsily. **somnolence** *n.* sleepiness; drowsiness. Also **somnolency**. **somnolescent** *a.* half asleep [L. *somnus*].

son (sun) *n.* male child; male descendant, however distant; term of affection; native of a place; disciple. **—in-law** *n.* the husband of one's daughter [O.E. *sunu*].

so·nant (sō'·nant) *a.* pert. to sound; (*Phonetics*) of certain alphabetic sounds, voiced; *n.* a syllabic sound. **sonance** *n.* [L. *sonare*].

so·na·ta (sa·nà'·ta) *n.* a musical composition in three or four movements. **sonatina** (sà·na·tē'·na) *n.* a short sonata [It. fr. L. *sonare*, to sound].

song (sawng) *n.* singing; poem, or piece of poetry, esp. if set to music; piece of music to be sung; musical sounds made by birds; (*Colloq.*) a mere trifle. **— bird** *n.* a singing bird. **-ster** *n.* (*fem.* **songstress**) one who sings; a song bird [O.E. *sang*, fr. *singan*, to sing].

son·ic (sàn'·ik) *a.* pertaining to sound; devoting speed approximate to that of sound.

son·net (sàn'·at) *n.* poem of fourteen lines of iambic pentameter, with a definite rhyme scheme. **soneteer** *n.* a writer of sonnets [It. *sonetto*, fr. L. *sonus*, a sound].

so·no·rous (sa·nōr'·as) *a.* giving out a deep, loud sound when struck; resonant; highsounding. *adv.* **-ness**, **sonority** *n.* [L. *sonorus*, noisy].

soon (sòòn) *adv.* in a short time; shortly; without delay; willingly [O.E. *sona*, at once].

soot (soot) *n.* a black powdery substance formed by burning coal, etc.; *v.t.* to cover with soot. **-y** *a.* pert. to, or like, soot; covered with soot; black; dingy; dirty [O.E. *set*].

sooth (sòòth) *n.* (*Arch.*) truth; reality. **-sayer** *n.* one who claims to be able to foretell future. **-saying** *n.* [O.E. *soth*, true].

soothe (sòòTH) *v.t.* to please with soft words or kind actions; to calm; to comfort; to allay, as pain. **soothing** *a.* **soothingly** *adv.* [O.E. *sothian*, to show to be true].

sop (sàp) *n.* piece of bread, etc., dipped in a liquid; anything given to pacify or quieten; bribe; *v.t.* to steep in liquid. *pr.p.* **-ping**. *pa.p.* and *pa.t.* **-ped**. **-ping** *a.* soaked; wet through. **-py** *a.* soaked; rainy [O.E. *sopp*, fr. *supan*, to sip].

soph·ism (sàf'·izm) *n.* specious argument; clever but fallacious reasoning. **sophist** *n.* orig. in ancient Greece, teacher of logic, rhetoric, philosophy; one who uses fallacoius or specious arguments. **sophistry** *n.* practice of sophists. **sophistic, sophistical** *a.* **sophistically** *adv.* **sophisticate** *v.t.* to deceive by using sophisms; to make artificial; to make wise in the ways of the world. **sophisticated** *a.* **sophistication** *n.* [Gk. *sophisma*, wise].

soph·o·more (sàf'·a·mōr) *n.* second-year student of university, college, or high school [Gk. *sophos*, wise].

so·por (sō'·per) n. unnaturally deep sleep. **-ific** a. causing or inducing sleep; n. drug, which induces deep sleep. **-iferous, soporose** a. causing sleep; sleepy. [L. *sopor*, deep sleep].

so·pran·o (sạ·pra'·nō) n. highest type of female or boy's voice; soprano singer; pl. **-s, soprani** (sō·pra'·nĭ) [It. fr. *sopra*, above].

sor·cer·y (sawr'·sạ·ri·) n. witchcraft; magic; enchantment. **sorcerer** n. a magician. *fem.* **sorceress**, a witch [L. *sortiri*, to cast lots].

sor·did (sawr'·did) a. filthy; squalid; meanly avaricious. **-ly** adv. **-ness** n. [L. *sordidus*].

sore (sōr) a. painful when touched; causing pain; tender; distressed; grieved; (*Colloq.*) angry; n. diseased, injured, or bruised spot on body; **-ly** adv. **-ness** n. [O.E. *sar*].

sor·ghum (sawr'·gạm) n. cereal grasses of several varieties, used for making molasses, forage, hay, brooms, etc.; the syrup from sweet sorghums [etym. uncertain].

so·ror·i·ty (sạ·rawr'·i·ti·) n. a girls' or women's society [L. *soror*, a sister].

so·ro·sis (sạ·rō'·sis) n. compound fleshy fruit, e.g. pineapple; women's club [Gk. *sōros*, heap].

sor·rel (sawr'·al) n. meadow plant with sour taste [O.Fr. *surelle*].

sor·rel (sawr'·al) a. reddish-brown; n. (horse of) reddish-brown color [O.Fr. *sorel*].

sor·row (sár'·ō, sawr'·ō) n. pain of mind; grief; sadness; distress; cause of grief, etc.; v.i. to feel pain of mind; to grieve. **-er** n. **-ful** a. causing sorrow; sad; unhappy. **-fully** adv. **-fulness** n. [O.E. *sorh*].

sor·ry (sár'·i; sawr'·i·) a. feeling regret; pained in mind; mean; shabby; wretched; worthless. **sorriness** n. [O.E. *sarig*].

sort (sawrt) n. kind or class; persons or things having same qualities; quality; character; order or rank; v.t. to classify; to put in order. **-er** n. [L. *sors*, a share, a lot].

sor·tie (sawr'·tē) n. sally by besieged forces to attack besiegers; flight by warplane [Fr. *sortir*, to go out].

S.O.S. (es·ō·es) n. international code signal call of distress, by radio telegraph (· · · — — — · · ·); any appeal for help.

sot (sát) n. confirmed drunkard. **-tish** a. stupid through drink [Fr. *sot*, foolish].

sot·to vo·ce (sát'·tō vō'·chā) adv. under one's breath [It. *sotto*, under; *voce*, the voice].

sou (sōō) n. former French coin of various values [Fr. fr. L. *solidus*, a coin].

soubriquet See **sobriquet**.

souf·flé (sōō·flā') n. a delicate dish made of eggs and baked [Fr. *scuffler*, to blow].

sough (suf, sou) n. low murmuring, sighing sound; v.i. [O.E. *swogan*, to resound].

sought (sawt) pa.p. and pa.t. of **seek**.

soul (sōl) n. spiritual and immortal part of human being; seat of emotion, sentiment, and aspiration; the center of moral powers; spirit; the essence; the moving spirit; a human being. **-ful** a. full of soul, emotion, or sentiment. **-fully** adv. **-less** a. without a soul; not inspired; prosaic [O.E. *sawol*].

sound (sound) a. healthy; in good condition; solid; entire; profound; free from error; reliable; solvent, as a business firm; adv. soundly; completely. **-ly** adv. thoroughly. **-ness** n. [O.E. *gesund*, healthy].

sound (sound) n. long, narrow stretch of water; channel; strait [O.E. *sund*].

sound (sound) v.t. to find depth of water, by means of line and lead; (*Fig.*) to try to discover the opinions of; v.i. to find depth of water; of a whale, to dive suddenly. **-ing** n. measuring the depth of water, esp. with a weighed line; measurement obtained [Fr. *sonder*].

sound (sound) n. that which is heard; auditory effect; the distance within which a sound is heard; noise; v.t. to cause to make a sound; to utter; to play on; to signal; to examine with stethoscope; v.i. to make a noise; to be conveyed by sound; to appear; to seem. **-ing** a. making a sound; resonant. **— barrier** (*Aero.*) colloq. term for phenomena occurring when an aircraft reaches speed in excess of that of sound. **— track** n. strip on one side of motion-picture film which records sound vibrations and so produces dialogue. **—waves** n.pl. vibrations of the air producing sound. **-board, -ing box** n. board or box which reinforces sound from musical instrument; canopy over pulpit for directing voice towards the congregation [L. *sonus*].

soup (sōōp) n. liquid food made by boiling meat, vegetables, etc. [Fr. *soupe*, fr. *souper*, to sup].

soup·çon (sōōp·sán') n. suspicion; hence, very small quantity; a taste [Fr.].

sour (sour) a. acid; having a sharp taste; pungent; rancid; cross; v.t. and v.i. to make or become sour. **-ed** a. embittered; aggrieved. **-ly** adv. **-ness** n. [O.E. *sur*].

source (sōrs) n. spring; fountain; origin (of stream, information, etc. [L. *surgere*, to rise].

sour·dough (sour'·dō) n. fermented batter of flour and water used to leaven fresh dough; prospector; pioneer [*sour* and *dough*].

souse (sous) v.t. to steep in brine; to pickle; to plunge into a liquid; to soak; n. a pickle made with salt; brine; anything steeped in it; a drenching [form of *sauce*, fr. L. *sal*, salt].

sou·tane (sōō·tán') n. gown worn by R.C. priests; cassock [L. *subtus*, beneath].

south (south) n. cardinal point of compass opposite north; region lying to that side; a. pert. to, or coming from, the south; adv. toward or in the south; v.i. to move towards the south. **southerly** a. (suTH'·ẹr·li·) a. pert. to south. **-ern** a. in, from, or towards, the south. **-erner** n. native of south of a country, etc. **-ernly** adv. towards the south. **-ernmost** (also **-ermost, —most**) a. lying farthest towards the south. **—ward** a. and adv. towards south; n. southern direction. **—wardly** a. and adv. **—wards** adv. **souwester** (or **—wester**) n. a strong wind from southwest; waterproof hat [O.E. *suth*].

sou·ve·nir (sōō·vạ·nir', sōō'·vạ·nir) n. a keepsake; a memento [Fr. *souvenir*, to remind].

sov·er·eign (sáv'·rạn) n. ruler; British gold coin = one pound sterling = 20 shillings; a. supreme in power; chief; efficacious in highest degree. **-ty** n. supreme power [O.Fr. *sovrain*, fr. L. *supra*, above].

so·vi·et (sō'·vi·et) n. council. **Soviet** n. political body, consisting of representatives of workers and peasants, elected to local municipalities, regional councils, etc. and sending delegates to higher congresses. a. **Soviet Union,** short for the Union of Socialist Soviet Republics,' i.e. Russia; abbrev. **U.S.S.R.** [Russ. = a council].

sow (sou) n. female pig; in smelting, bar of cast iron [O.E. *su*].

sow (sō) v.t. to scatter or deposit (seed); to spread abroad; to disseminate; v.i. to scatter seed. pa.p. **sown** (sōn) or **sowed** (sōd). pa.t. **-ed. -er** n. [O.E. *sawan*].

soy (soi) n. sauce made from soybean **-bean** n. seed of leguminous plant of Far East [Jap. *shoyu*].

Spa (spa) n. inland watering place in Belgium. **spa** n. any place with mineral spring.

space (spās) n. expanse of universe; area; room; period of time; extent; empty place; v.t. to place at intervals. **spacious** (spā'·shas) a. roomy; capacious; extensive. **spaciously** adv. [Fr. *espace*, fr. L. *spatium*].

spade (spād) *n.* digging tool, with flat blade and long handle; *v.t.* to dig with spade. **-work** *n.* preliminary tasks [O.E. *spadu*].

spade (spād) *n.* (*Cards*) one of two black suits, marked by figure like a pointed spade [Sp. *espada*, a sword].

spa·ghet·ti (spạ·get′·ti·) *n.* footstuff resembling macaroni but thinner [It. *spago*, cord].

spake (spāk) *pa.t.* (*Arch.*) of **speak**.

span (span) *pa.t.* of **spin**.

span (span) *n.* distance between thumb and little finger, when fingers are fully extended; this distance as measure = 9 in; short distance or period of time; distance between supports of arch. roof, etc.; of airplane, distance from wing-tip to wing-tip; pair, of horses or oxen harnessed together; *v.t.* to reach from one side of to the other; to extend across. *pr.p.* **-ning**. *pa.p.* and *pa.t.* **-ned**. **-ner** *n.* one who spans; tool for tightening screw nuts [O.E. *spann*].

span·drel (span′·drẹl) *n.* (*Archit.*) the space between outer curves of arch and square head over it; ornamental design in corner of postage stamp [etym. uncertain].

span·gle (spang′·gl) *n.* a small piece of glittering metal, used to ornament dresses; *v.t.* to adorn with spangles; *v.i.* to glitter [O.E. *spang*, a buckle].

Span·iard (span′·yerd) *n.* native of Spain. **Spanish** *a.* of, or pert. to, Spain; *n.* language of Spain.

span·iel (span′·yạl) *n.* breed of dogs, with long, drooping ears; fawning person [O.Fr. *espagneul*, Sangish].

spank (spangk) *v.i.* to move with vigor or spirit. **-ing** *a.* moving with quick, lively step; dashing. **-er** *n.* fast-going horse, ship, etc.; (*Naut.*) fore-and-aft sail attached to the mast nearest the stern [Dan. *spanke*, to strut].

spank (spangk) *v.t.* to strike with flat of hand, esp. on buttocks as punishment; *n.* slap [imit. origin].

spar (spàr) *v.i.* to fight with the fists, in fun or in earnest; to fight with spurs, as in cock fighting; to dispute, bandy words. *pr.p.* **-ring**. *pa.p.* and *pa.t.* **-red** [etym. uncertain].

spar (spàr) *n.* pole or beam, esp. as part of ship's rigging [O.N. *sparri*].

spar (spàr) *n.* crystalline mineral which has luster [O.E. *spaerstan*, gypsum].

spare (sper) *v.t.* and *v.i.* to use frugally; to do without; to save; to omit; to leave unhurt; to give away; *a.* frugal; scanty; scarce; parsimonious; thin; lean; additional; in reserve; not in use; *n.* that which is held in reserve; a duplicate part. **-ly** *adv.* **-ness** *n.* thinness; leanness. **sparing** *a.* **sparingly** *adv.* [O.E. *sparian*].

spark (spàrk) *n.* small glowing or burning particle; flash of light; trace or particle of anything; in internal-combustion engines, electric flash which ignites explosive mixture in cylinder; (*Colloq.*) gay, dashing young fellow; *v.i.* to send out sparks. — **plug** *n.* in internal-combustion engines, device for igniting explosive gases; (*Colloq.*) one who animates a group [O.E. *spearca*].

spar·kle (spàrk′·l) *n.* small spark; a glitter; a gleam; vivacity; *v.i.* to emit small flashes of light; to gleam; to glitter; to effervesce. **-r** *n.* one who, or that which, sparkles; (*Slang*) a diamond. **sparkling** *a.* [O.E. *spearca*].

spar·row (spar′·ō) *n.* small brown bird of finch family. **—grass** *n.* (*Colloq.*) asparagus. [O.E. *spearwa*].

sparse (spàrs) *a.* thinly scattered; scanty; rare. **-ly** *adv.* **-ness** *n.* scantiness [L. *spargere*, *sparsum*, to scatter].

Spar·ta (spàr′·tạ) *n.* ancient Greek city-state. **Spartan** *n.* citizen of this town; one who is frugal and faces danger, etc. without flinching; *a.* pert. to Sparta; dauntless.

spasm (spaz′·ạm) *n.* sudden, involuntary contraction of muscle(s); sudden, convulsive movement, effort, emotion, etc.; fitful effort. **spasmodic(al)** *a.* pert. to spasms; convulsive; fitful. **spasmodically** *adv.* by fits and starts. **spastic** *a.* (*Med.*) pert. to spasms; in a rigid condition, due to spasm; applied to people suffering from cerebral palsy. *n.* such a person [Gk. *spasmos*, fr. *spaein*, to draw].

spat (spat) *pa.t.* of **spit**.

spat (spat) *n.* kind of cloth gaiter, reaching a little above ankle. Usually in *pl.* **spats** [*abbrev.* of *spatterdash*].

spat (spat) *n.* spawn of shellfish or oyster; *v.i.* to spawn, of oysters [fr. *spit*].

spate (spāt) *n.* flood in a river, esp. after heavy rain; inundation [Gael. *speid*].

spathe (spāTH) *n.* leaflike sheath enveloping flower cluster. **spathed, spathose** *a.* [Gk. *spathē*, a broad blade].

spa·tial (spā′·shạl) *a.* pert. to space. **-ly** *adv.* [L. *spatium*].

spat·ter (spat′·er) *v.t.* to cast drops of water, mud, etc. over; to splash; *v.i.* to fall in drops; *n.* the act of spattering; a slight splash [Dut. *spatten*, to burst].

spat·u·la (spach′·ạ·lạ) *n.* broad-bladed implement for spreading paints, turning foods in frying pan, etc. **spatular, spatulate** *a.* [Gk. *spathē*, a broad blade].

spav·in (spav′·in) *n.* swelling on horse's leg, causing lameness. **-ed** *a.* [O.Fr. *esparvain*].

spawn (spawn) *n.* eggs of fish, frogs; offspring; *v.t.* and *v.i.* of fish, frogs, to cast eggs; to produce offspring [O.Fr. *espandre*, fr. L. *expandere*, to spread out].

speak (spēk) *v.i.* to utter words; to tell; to deliver a discourse; *v.t.* to utter; to pronounce; to express in words; to express silently or by signs; *pr.p.* **-ing**. *pa.p.* **spoken**. *pa.t.* **spoke**. **-er** *n.* one who speaks; orator. **the Speaker**, presiding officer of the House of Representatives and of similar legislative bodies. **-ing** *n. a.* having power to utter words; eloquent; lifelike, e.g. of picture. **-easy** *n.* (*Slang*) illegal saloon, esp. during prohibition [O.E. *sprecan*].

spear (sper) *n.* long, pointed weapon, used in fighting, hunting, etc.; sharp-pointed instrument for catching fish; lance; pike; *v.t.* to pierce or kill with spear. **-head** *n.* iron point, barb, or prong of a spear; leader of an advance; — **side** *n.* male branch of a family [O.E. *spere*].

spe·cial (spesh′·al) *a.* pert. to a species or sort; particular; beyond the usual; distinct; intimate; designed for a particular person or purpose. **-ly** *adv.* **-ize** *v.t.* to make special or distinct; to adapt for a particular purpose; *v.i.* to devote oneself to a particular branch of study. **-ization** *n.* act of specializing. **-ist** *n.* one trained and skilled in a special branch. **-istic** *a.* **-ty** *n.* a special characteristic of a person or thing; a special product; that in which a person is highly skilled. [L. *species*, a kind].

spe·cie (spē′·shē) *n.* coined money [L. *species*, a kind].

spe·cies (spē′·shēz) *n.* kind; variety; sort; class; subdivision of a more general class or genus [L. *species*, a kind].

spe·cif·ic (spi·sif′·ik) *a.* pert. to, or characteristic of, a species; peculiar to; well defined; precise; *n.* a specific statement, etc. **-ally** *adv.* — **gravity**, weight of substance expressed in relation to weight of equal volume of water [L. *species*, a kind; *facere*, to make].

spec·i·fi·ca·tion (spes·ạ·fạ·kā′·shạn) *n.* act

of specifying; statement of details, requirements, etc. **specify** v.t. to state definitely; to give details of; to indicate precisely. **specifiable** a. [L. *species*, a kind; *facere*, to make].

spec·i·men (spes'·a·man) n. part of anything, or one of a number of things, used to show nature and quality of the whole; sample [L. *specere*, to look].

spe·cious (spē'·shas) a. having a fair appearance; superficially fair or just; apparently acceptable, esp. at first sight. **-ly** adv. **-ness speciosity** n. [L. *speciosus*, fair to see].

speck (spek) n. small spot; particle; very small thing; v.t. to mark with specks. **-le** n. a small speck or spot; v.t. to mark with small spots. **speckled** a. **-less** a. [O.E. *specca*].

spec·ta·cle (spek'·ta·kl) n. sight; show; thing exhibited; a pageant. **spectacles** n.pl. eyeglasses. **-ed** a. wearing spectacles. **spectacular** a. showy; making great display. **spectacularly** adv. [L. *spectare*, to look at].

spec·ta·tor (spek'·tā·ter) n. an onlooker; ghost; apparition. **spectral** a. pert. to a specter; ghostly; pert. to spectrum. **spectrally** adv. **spectrum** n. the colored band into which a ray of light can be separated as in the rainbow; pl. **spectra** [L. *spectrum*, an image].

spec·tro- (spek'·trō) prefix fr. L. *spectrum*, an image, used in many derivatives. **-graph** n. scientific instrument for photographing spectra. **-scope** n. instrument for production and examination of spectra. **-scopic, -scopical** a. [Gk. *graphein*, to write; *skopein*, to view].

spec·u·late (spek'·ya·lāt) v.i. to make theories or guesses; to meditate; to engage in risky commercial transactions. **speculation** n. act of speculating; theorizing; guess; practice of buying shares, etc. in the hope of selling at a high profit. **speculative** a. given to speculation. **speculatively** adv. **speculator** n. **speculatory** a. [L. *speculari*, to observe].

spec·u·lum (spek'·ya·lam) n. mirror; reflector of polished metals, esp. as used in reflecting telescopes; (*Surg.*) instrument for examining interior cavity of body. pl. **specula** [L. fr. *specere*, to observe].

sped (sped) pa.p. and pa.t. of **speed**.

speech (spēch) n. power of speaking; what is spoken; faculty of expressing thoughts in words; enunciation; remarks; conversation; language; formal address; an oration. **-less** a. without power of speech; dumb; silent. **-lessly** adv. **-lessness** n. **-ify** v.i. to make speech, esp. long and tedious one. **-ifier** n. [O.E. *spraec*].

speed (spēd) n. swiftness of motion; rate of progress; velocity; v.t. to cause to move faster; to aid; to bid farewell to; v.i. to move quickly or at speed beyond legal limit; to increase speed. pa.p. and pa.t. **sped. -y** a. quick; rapid; prompt. **-ily** adv. **-boat** n. very fast motor boat. **-ometer** n. instrument indicating speed, usually in miles per hour. **-way** n. track for racing [O.E. *sped*].

spell (spel) n word or words supposed to have magical power; magic formula; fascination. **-bind** v.t. to hold as if by spell; to enchant; to fascinate. pa.p., pa.t. **-bound** a. [O.E. *spell*, a narrative].

spell (spel) n. a turn of work or duty; a brief period of time [O.E. *spelian*, to act for].

spell (spel) v.t. to read letter by letter; to mean; v.i. to form words with proper letters. pa.p. and pa.t. **-ed** or **spelt** [O.E. *spell*, a narrative].

spe·lun·ker (spē'·lungk·er) one who explores caves.

spend (spend) v.t. and v.i. to pay out; to disburse; to pass, as time; to employ; to waste; to exhaust. pa.p., pa.t., **spent** a. exhausted; worn out; of a fish, having deposited spawn. **-er** n. **-thrift** n. one who spends money fool-

ishly or extravagantly; a. extravagant [O.E. *spenden*].

sperm (spurm) n. fertilizing fluid of male animals; the male cell. **—oil** n. oil obtained from sperm whale. **— whale.** n. cachalot, large whale, valuable for its oil and for spermaceti.

spermaceti (spur·ma·sē'·ti., spur·ma·set'·i.) n. waxlike substance obtained from head of sperm whale. **-atic** a. pert. to sperm [Gk. *sperma*, seed].

sperm·a·to- prefix fr. Gk. *sperma*, seed. **spermatoid** a. resembling sperm. **spermatozoon** (spur·ma·ta·zō'·an) n. male generative cell, found in semen. pl. **-zoa, -zoal, -zoan** a.

spew, spue (spū) v.t. and v.i. to eject from the stomach; to vomit [O.E. *spiwan*].

sphere (sfir) n. round, solid body, ball; globe; celestial body; range of knowledge, influence, etc.; field of action; social status; position; v.t. to put in a sphere; to encircle, **spheral** (sfi'·ral) a. formed like a sphere. **spheric** (sfer'·ik) a. pert. to heavenly bodies. **spherical** a. sphere-shaped. **spherically** adv. **sphericity** n. roundness. **spheroid** (sfi'·roid) n. body almost, but not quite, spherical, e.g. orange, earth, etc. **spheroidal** a. having form of spheroid. Also **spheroidic. spherule** (sfir'·ūl) n. a small sphere. **spherular, spherulate** a. [Gk. *sphaira*, a globe].

sphinc·ter (sfingk'·ter) n. (*Anat.*) circular muscle which contracts or expands orifice of an organ, e.g. round anus [Gk. *sphingein*, to bind tight].

sphinx (sfingks) n. (*Myth.*) fabulous monster, with winged body of lion and head of woman, which proposed riddles; statue of this; (*Fig.*) one whose thoughts are difficult to guess; enigmatic person. (*Cap.*) huge statue of recumbent lion with man's head in Egypt [Gk. *sphinx*, literally, the strangler].

sphyg·mus (sfig'·mas) n. (*Med.*) pulse. **sphygmic** a. [Gk. *sphugmos*, the pulse].

spice (spīs) n. aromatic substance, used for seasoning; spices collectively (*Fig.*) anything that adds flavor, zest, etc. v.t. to season with spice. **spicery** n. spices collectively. **spicy** a. **spicily** adv. [O.Fr. *espice*].

spi·der (spī'·der) n. small, eight-legged insect-like animal that spins web to catch flies, etc.; a frying pan; a trivet; an evil person. a. like a spider; full of spiders; very thin. **—monkey** n. monkey with long, thin legs and tail [O.E. *spinnan*, to spin].

spied (spīd) pa.p. and pa.t. of **spy**.

spig·ot (spig'·at) n. peg for stopping hole in cask; a faucet which controls flow [L. *spica*, an ear of corn].

spike (spīk) n. sharp-pointed piece of metal or wood; large nail; ear of corn, etc.; (*Bot.*) flower-cluster growing from central stem; v.t. furnished with spikes; pointed (*Slang*) to add liquor to a drink. **spiky** a. to supply, set, fasten, or pierce with spikes; pointed [O.N. *spik*, a nail].

spill (spil) v.t. to cause to flow out; to pour out; to shed (blood); to throw off, as from horse, etc.; to upset; v.i. to flow over; to be shed; to be lost or wasted; n. a spilling; fall or tumble, as from vehicle, horse, etc. pa.p. and pa.t. **-ed** or **spilt. -er** n. **-way** n. channel for overflow water from dam [O.E. *spillian*, to destroy].

spill (spil) n. thin strip of wood or twist of paper, for lighting a fire, pipe, etc.; a peg [Dut. *speld*, a splinter].

spin (spin) v.t. to twist into threads; to cause to revolve rapidly; to whirl; to twirl; to draw out tediously, as a story; to prolong; v.i. to make thread, as a spider, etc.; to revolve rapidly; to move swiftly; n. rapid whirling motion; short, quick run or drive. pr.p. **-ning.** pa.p. and pa.t. **spun** or (*Arch.*)

span. -ner *n.* **-ning jenny** *n.* machine for spinning several threads simultaneously. **-ning wheel** *n.* outdated device for spinning cotton, wool, flax, etc. into thread or yarn [O.E. *spinnan*].

spin·ach (spin'·ich) *n.* leafy vegetable used for food. **spinaceous** *a.* [O.Fr. *espinage*].

spin·dle (spin'·dl) *n.* long, slender rod, used in spinning, for twisting and winding the thread; measure of yarn, thread, or silk; shaft; axis; *v.i.* to grow long and slender. **spindly** *a.* long and slender. **spindling** *a.* [O.E. *spinel*, fr. *spinnan*, to spin].

spine (spīn) *n.* thorn; quill; backbone; back of book. **spinal** *a.* pert. to spine or back-bon. **-less** *a.* having no spine; weak of character. **spiny** *a.* full of spines; like a spine; thorny; prickly; perplexing. **spinule** *n.* small spine. **spinal column,** the back-bone [L. *spina*, a thorn].

spin·et (spin'·it) *n.* musical instrument like a harpsichord [O.Fr. *espinette*, fr. L. *spina*].

spin·na·ker (spin'·a·ker) *n.* a large triangu-lar sail [etym. uncertain].

spin·ster (spin'·ster) *n.* orig. one who spins; unmarried woman. **-hood** *n.* **spinstress** *n.* woman who spins [O.E. *spinnan*, to spin].

spi·ra·cle (spī'·ra·kl, spir'·a·kl) *n.* breathing-hole; blowhole of whale. **spiracular, spirac-ulate** *a.* [L. *spirare*, to breathe].

Spi·rae·a (spī·rē'·a) *n.* a genus of herbaceous plants, including meadowsweet, bearing white or pink flowers [Gk. *speira*, a coil].

spi·rant (spī'·rant) *n.* consonant pronounced with perceptible emission of breath [L. *spirare*, to breathe].

spire (spīr) *n.* winding line like threads of screw; curl; coil. **spiral** *a.* winding; coiled; *n.* spiral curve; coil; whorl; *v.i.* to follow spiral line; to coil; to curve [Gk. *speira*, coil].

spire (spīr) *n.* blade of grass; stalk; slender shoot; anything tall and tapering to point; (tapering part of) steeple; peak; *v.i.* to rise high, like spire. **spiral** *a.* like a spire. **spiry** *a.* having spires; tapering [O.E. *spir*, a stalk].

spir·it (spir'·it) *n.* vital force; immortal part of man; soul; specter; ghost; frame of mind; disposition; temper; eager desire; mental vigor; courage; essential character; (*Cap.*) Holy Spirit; liquid got by distillation, esp. alcoholic; *v.t.* to carry away mysteriously; to put energy into. **spirits** *n.pl.* a state of mind; mood; distilled alcoholic liquor. **-ed** *a.* full of spirit and vigor; lively; animated. **-edly** *adv.* **-edness** *n.* **-ism** *n.* See **spiritualism. -less** *a.* without spirit or life; lacking energy; list-less. **-essly** *adv.* **-uous** *a.* containing alcohol; distilled [L. *spiritus*, fr *spirare*, to breathe].

spir·it·u·al (spir'·it·choo·al) *a.* pert. to spirit or soul; not material; unworldly; pert. to sacred things; holy; *n.* Negro sacred song or hymn. **-ly** *adv.* **-ize** *v.t.* to make spiritual; to make pure in heart. **-ism, spiritism** *n.* be-lief that spirits of dead can communicate with living people. **-ist** *n.* [L. *spiritus*, breath].

spit (spit)) *n.* pointed rod put through meat for roasting; narrow point of land projecting into sea; *v.t.* to thrust spit through; to im-pale *pr.p.* **-ting.** *pa.p.* *pa.t.* **-ted.** [O.E. *spitu*].

spit (spit) *v.t.* to eject from mouth; to expel; *v.i.* to eject saliva from mouth; to expectorate; to hiss, esp. of cats; *pr.p.* **-ting.***pa.p.* *pa.t.* **spat.** *n.* saliva; act of spitting; like fall of fine rain; (*Colloq.*) an exact likeness. **-ter** *n.* **-tle** *n.* saliva ejected from mouth; frothy secretion of certain insects. **-toon** *n.* a vessel for spittle; cuspidor [O.E. *spittan*].

spite (spīt) *n.* malice; ill will; *v.t.* to treat maliciously; to try to injure or thwart; to annoy. **-ful** *a.* **-fully** *adv.* **-fulness** *n.* **in spite of,** in defiance of [fr. *despite*].

spit·fire (spit'·fīr) *n.* hot tempered person [*spit* and *fire*].

spitz (spitz) *n.* a kind of Pomeranian dog [Ger. = pointed].

splash (splash) *v.t.* to spatter water, mud, etc. over; to soil thus; to print in bold head-lines; *v.i.* to dash or scatter, of liquids; to dabble in water; to fall in drops; *n.* sound of object falling into liquid, water, mud, etc. dashed about; spot; daub; patch of color. **-y** *a.* full of dirty water; wet and muddy. **-board** *n.* mud guard [imit. origin].

splat·ter (splat'·er) *v.t.* and *v.i.* to splash; to spatter [fr. *spatter*].

splay (splā) *v.t.* to slope; to slant; to spread outwards; *a.* turned outwards; at and broad; *n.* slanting surface of opening, as at window. **-foot** *n.* flat foot [fr. *display*].

spleen (splēn) *n.* ductless organ lying to left of stomach; ill humor; spite; melancholy; irritability [Gk. *splēn*].

splen·did (splen'·did) *a.* magnificent; gorge-ous; (*Colloq.*) excellent. **-ly** *adv.* **splendor** (splen·der) *n.* brilliant luster; pomp. **splen-dorous** *a.* [L. *splendere*, to shine].

sple·net·ic (spli·net'·ik) *a.* pert. to spleen; morose; irritable. *n.* one suffering from disease of spleen; irritable person [Gk. *splēn*].

splice (splīs) *v.t.* to join together; to join, as wood, etc. by overlapping and binding; (*Colloq.*) to marry; *n.* union [Dut. *splissen*].

splint (splint) *n.* rigid piece of material for holding broken limb in position; bony ex-crescene on inside of horse's leg; *v.t.* to bind with splints. **-er** *n.* thin piece of wood, metal, etc. split off; *v.t.* and *v.i.* to make or break into thin pieces. **-ery** *a.* [Swed. *splint*].

split (split) *v.t.* to cut lengthwise; to cleave; to tear apart; to separate; to divide; *v.i.* to break asunder; to part lengthwise; to dash to pieces; to separate; *n.* crack; fissure; a breach; a share. *pr.p.* **-ting.** *pa.p.* *pa.t.* **split. -ing** *n.* cleaving or rending; *a.* severe; distressing. **— infinitive,** insertion of adverb or adverbial phrase between 'to' and verb of infinitive. **—level** *a.* describing a home that has several levels separated by steps. **to split hairs,** to make fine distinctions [Dut. *splitten*].

splut·ter (splut'·er) *v.t.* to utter incoherently with spitting sounds; *v.t.* to emit such sounds; to speak hastily and confusedly; *n.* such sounds or speech; a confused noise. **-er** *n.* [imit. origin].

Spode (spōd) *n.* highly decorated porcelain [Josiah *Spode*, pottery manufacturer].

spoil (spoil) *v.t.* to damage; to injure; to cause to decay; to harm character of by indul-gence; *v.i.* to go bad; to decay; *n.* booty; prey; plunder. *pa.p.* and *pa.t.* **-ed** or **-spoilt** *n.* one who takes a delight in interfering with enjoyment of others [L. *spoliare*].

spoke (spōk) *pa.t.* of the verb **speak.** *pa.p.* **spoken** (spōk'·n). **-s-man** *n.* one deputed to speak for others.

spoke (spōk) *n.* one of small bars connecting hub of wheel with rim; rung of ladder. **-shave** *n.* planning tool [O.E. *spaca*].

spo·li·ate (spō'·li·āt) *v.t.* to rob; to plunder; *v.i.* to practice plundering. **spoliative** *a.* **spoliation** *n.* the act of despoiling; robbery; destruction. **spoliator** *n.* [L. *spoliare*].

spon·dee (spán'·dē) *n.* in poetry, a foot of two long syllables, marked (— —). **spondaic** (spán·dā'·ik) *a.* [Gk. *spondē*, drink offering].

sponge (spunj) *n.* marine animal of cellular structure, outer coating of whose body is perforated to allow entrance of water; skele-ton of this animal, used to absorb water; act of cleaning with sponge; (*Colloq.*) para-site; sponger; hanger-on; (*Colloq.*) habitual drinker; *v.t.* to wipe, cleanse, with sponge; *v.i.* to live at expense of others. **-r** *n.* **spongy**

(spun'·ji·) a. sponge-like; of open texture; full of small holes; absorbent; wet and soft, esp. of ground. **sponginess** n. **-cake** n. light, sweet cake. **to throw in the sponge**, to acknowledge defeat [Gk., L. *spongia*].

spon·sor (spǎn'·ser) n. one who is responsible for another; surety; godfather or godmother; guarantor; a patron; v.t. to support; to act as guarantor or patron of; to pay for a radio or television program including advertisements of one's own goods. **-ial** a. **-ship** n. [L. *spondere, sponsum*, to promise].

spon·ta·ne·ous (spǎn·tā'·nē·as) a. of one's own free will; voluntary; natural; produced by some internal cause, said of physical effects, as combustion, growth, etc. **-ly** adv. **-ness, spontaneity** (spǎn·ta·nē'·a·ti·) n. [L. *sponte*, of one's own free will].

spoof (spoof) n. (*Slang, chiefly Brit.*) hoax; swindle; v.t. to fool; to hoax.

spook (spook) n. (*Colloq.*) ghost; apparition. **-ish, -y** a. [Dut.].

spool (spool) n. small cylinder for winding thread, wire, etc.; v.t. to wind on spool [O.Fr. *espole*].

spoon (spoon) n. implement, with bowl at end of handle, for carrying food to the mouth. etc.; golf club with wooden head; v.t. and v.i. to use, hit with spoon; (*Golf*) to scoop ball high in air; (*Colloq.*) to make love. **-ful** n. quantity spoon can hold; small quantity; (*Med.*) half an ounce. **-bill** n. long-legged wading bird with spoon-shaped bill **—feed** v.t. to feed with a spoon; (*Fig.*) to do over-much for a person, thus weakening his self-reliance pa.p., pa.t. **-fed** a. [O.E. *spon*].

spoon·er·ism (spoon'·er·ism) n. transposition of letters of spoken words, causing a humorous effect, e.g. a *half-warmed fish* for a 'half-formed wish' [fr. Dr. A. W. *Spooner*].

spoor (spoor) n. track or trail of wild animal [Dut. = a track].

spo·rad·ic (spa·rad'·ik) a. occurring singly here and there; occasional. Also **-al. -ally** adv. [Gk. *sporadikos*, fr. *speirein*, to sow].

spore (spor) n. in flowerless plants, e.g. in ferns, minute cell with reproductive powers; germ; seed. **sporangium** n. spore case. pl. **sporangia. sporangial** a. **sporoid** a. sporelike [Gk. *spora*, seed].

spor·ran (spawr'·an) n. large pouch worn in front of the kilt [Gael. *sporan*].

sport (sport) n. that which amuses; diversion; pastime; merriment; object of jest; mockery; outdoor game or recreation esp. of athletic nature; freak of nature; (*Colloq.*) a dandy; good loser; one willing to take a chance; v.t. (*Colloq.*) to display in public; to show off; v.i. to play; to take part in out-door recreation. **-s** n.pl. games; athletic meetings. **-ing** a. pert. to sport or sportsmen; (*Colloq.*) willing to take a chance. **-ive** a. pert. to sport; playful. **-s-man, -s-woman** n. **-s-manship** n. practice or skill of a sportsman; fairmindedness. **-s-manlike** a. [fr. *disport*].

spot (spǎt) n. speck; blemish, esp. on reputation; place; locality; v.t. to cover with spots; to stain; to place billiard ball on marked point; (*Colloq.*) to detect; to recognize; v.i. to become marked. pr.p. **-ting**. pa.p. and pa.t. **-ted. -less** a. without spot or stain; scrupulously clean; pure; innocent. **-lessly** adv. **-lessness** n. **-ted, -ty** a. marked with spots or stains; irregular. **-tedness, tiness** n. **-ter** n. **— cash**, immediate payment; ready money. **-light** n. apparatus used to throw concentrated beam of light on performer on stage; light thrown; the public eye. **on the spot**, immediately; (*Slang*) in a dangerous or embarrassing position [O.N. *spotti*].

spouse (spous) n. married person, husband or wife. **spousal** a. pert. to spouse, marriage [L. *sponsus*, promise].

spout (spout) v.t. to shoot out, as liquid through a pipe; (*Colloq.*) to utter in a pompous manner; to recite; v.i. to gush out in jet; (*Colloq.*) to speak volubly; n. projecting tube, pipe, etc., for pouring liquid; a pipe or tube for leading off rain from roof. **-er** n.

sprag (sprag) n. piece of wood or metal used to lock wheel of vehicle; device to prevent vehicle running backwards on hill [Dan.].

sprain (sprān) v.t. to wrench or twist muscles or ligaments of a joint; to overstrain; n. such an injury.

sprang (sprang) pa.t. of the verb **spring**.

sprat (sprat) n. small sea fish, allied to herring and pilchard [O.E. *sprot*].

sprawl (sprawl) v.i. to sit or lie with legs outstretched or in ungainly position; to move about awkwardly; to spread out irregularly; to write carelessly and irregularly; n. act of sprawling [O.E. *spreawlian*].

spray (sprā) n. twigs; small, graceful branch with leaves and blossoms; sprig.

spray (sprā) n. fine droplets of water driven by wind from tops of waves, etc.; shower of fine droplets of any liquid, e.g. medicine, perfume, etc.; spraying machine; atomizer; v.t. to sprinkle. **-er** n. [L. Ger. *Sprei*].

spread (spred) v.t. to stretch out; to extend; to cover surface with; to scatter; to unfold, as wings; to circulate, as news, etc.; to convey from one to another, as disease; to set and lay food on table; v.i. to extend in all directions; to become spread, scattered, circulated, etc.; n. extension; expanse; covering for bed, etc.; (*Colloq.*) feast. pa.p. and pa.t. **spread. -ing** n. act of extending. **—eagle** n. eagle with wings stretched out; a. with arms and legs stretched out; bombastic; v.t. to lie with outstretched limbs [O.E. *spraedan*].

spree (sprē) n. lively frolic; drinking bout [Ir. *spre*, a spark].

sprig (sprig) n. small shoot or twig; ornament in form of spray; scion; youth; small, headless nail; v.t. to mark, adorn, with figures of sprigs or sprays. pr.p. **-ging**. pa.p., pa.t. **-ged** [O.E. *spraec*, a twig].

spright·ly (sprīt'·li·) a. lively; airy; vivacious. **sprightliness** n. [old form of *sprite*].

spring (spring) v.i. to leap; to jump; to shoot up, out, or forth; to appear; to recoil; to result, as from a cause; to issue, as from parent or ancestor; to appear above ground; to grow; to thrive; v.t. to cause to spring up; to produce unexpectedly; to start, as game; to cause to explode, as a mine; to develop leak; to bend so as to weaken; to release, as catch of trap; n. a leap; a bound; a jump; recoil; a contrivance of coiled or bent metal with much resilience; resilience; flow of water from earth; fountain; any source; origin; a crack; season of year; upward curve of arch. pa.p. **sprung**. pa.t. **sprang** or **sprung**. **-er** n. one who springs; breed of spaniel. **-y** a. elastic; light in tread or gait. **-iness** n. **-board** n. springy board used in jumping and diving. **-time** n. season of spring [O.E. *springan*].

springe (sprinj) n. snare with a spring noose; v.t. to catch in a springe [fr. *spring*].

sprin·kle (spring'·kl) v.t. to scatter small drops of water, sand, etc.; to scatter on; to baptize with drops of water; v.i. to scatter (a liquid or any fine substance); n. small quantity scattered; occasional drops of rain. **-d** a. marked by small spots. **-r** n. one who sprinkles. **sprinkling** n. act of scattering; small quantity falling in drops [O.E. *sprengan*].

sprint (sprint) v.i./n. short run at full speed. **-er** n. [Cf. *spurt*].

sprit (sprit) n. (*Naut.*) small spar set diagonally across fore-and-aft sail to extend it [O.E. *spreot*, a pole].

sprite (sprīt) *n.* elf; a fairy; a goblin [older form = *spright*, fr. L. *spiritus*, spirit].

sprock·et (sprŏk'·it) *n.* toothlike projection on outer rim of wheel, e.g. of bicycle, for engaging links of chain [etym. uncertain].

sprout (sprout) *v.i.* to begin to grow; to put forth shoots; to spring up; *n.* shoot; bud. [O.E. *sprutan*].

spruce (sprŏŏs) *a.* neat in dress; smart; dapper; trim; *v.t.* and *v.i.* to dress smartly. **-ly** *adv.* **-ness** *n.* [fr. *Pruce*, Prussia].

spruce (sprŏŏs) *n.* common name of some coniferous trees [M.E. *Spruce*, Prussia].

sprung (sprung) *pa.p.* and *pa.t.* of **spring**.

spry (sprī) *a.* nimble; agile [*Scand.*].

spud (spud) *n.* small spadelike implement; (*Colloq.*) potato [etym. uncertain].

spue. See **spew.**

spume (spūm) *n. v.i.* froth; foam; scum. **spumous** *a.* **spumy** *a.* [*L.* spuma].

spun (spun) *pa.p.* and *pa.t.* of verb **spin.**

spunk (spungk) *n.* wood that readily takes fire; (*Colloq.*) spirit. **-y** *a.* (*Colloq.*) plucky [L. *spongia*, a sponge].

spur (spur) *n.* pricking instrument worn on horseman's heels, used as goad; anything that incites to action; projection on the leg of a cock; mountain projecting from range; projection; *v.t.* to apply spurs to; to urge to action; *v.i.* to ride hard; to press forward. *pr.p.* **-ring.** *pa.p.* and *pa.t.* also *a.* **-red** spurd), wearing spurs; (*Bot.*) having spur-like shoots; incited [O.E. *spora*].

spurge (spurj) *n.* plant of several species, having milky juice [L. *expurgare*, to purge].

spu·ri·ous (spyoo'·ri·as) *a.* not genuine or authentic; false. **-ly** *adv.* [L. *spurius*].

spurn (spurn) *v.t.* to reject with disdain; to scorn; *n.* disdainful rejection [O.E. *spornan*].

spurt (spurt) *v.t.* to force out suddenly in a stream; to squirt; *v.i.* to gush out with force; to make a short, sudden, and strong effort, esp. in a race; *n.* a sudden, strong flow or effort. Also **spirt** [O.E. *spryttan*].

sput·ter (sput'·er) *v.t.* to throw out in small particles with haste and noise; to utter excitedly and indistinctly; *v.i.* to scatter drops of saliva, as in excited speech; to speak rapidly; to fly off with crackling noise, as sparks from burning wood; *n.* act of sputtering; sound made. **-er** *n.* [fr. *spout*].

spu·tum (spū'·tạm) *n.* spittle; saliva. *pl.* **sputa** [L. *spuere*, *sputum*, to spit].

spy (spī) *n.* one who enters enemy territory secretly, to gain information; secret agent; one who keeps watch on others. *v.t.* to catch sight of; to notice; to discern; *v.i.* to act as a spy. **-glass** *n.* small telescope [Fr. *espion*, fr. L. *specere*, to look].

squab (skwŏb) *a.* fat and short; *n.* nestling pigeon used for food [etym. uncertain].

squab·ble (skwŏb'·l) *v.i.* to wrangle; to dispute noisily; *n.* petty, noisy quarrel [*imit.*].

squad (skwŏd) *n.* (*Mil.*) smallest unit of soldiers, etc.; small party of men at work; gang [Fr. *escouade*].

squad·ron (skwŏd'·rạn) *n.* a military tactical unit; an athletic team [It. *squadra*, a square].

squal·id (skwŏl'·id) *a.* mean and dirty, esp. through neglect; filthy; foul. *adv.* **-ity, -ness, squalor** *n.* filth; foulness [L.*squalidus*].

squall (skwawl) *v.t.* and *v.i.* to scream or cry out violently; *n.* loud scream; sudden gust of wind. **-y** *a.* [imit. origin].

squa·ma (skwā'·mạ) *n.* scale; scalelike part *pl.* **squamae** (skwā'·mē) [L. = a scale].

squan·der (skwŏn'·der) *v.t.* to waste; to dissipate. **-er** *n.* spendthrift [Scand.].

square (skwār) *n.* plane figure with four equal sides and four right angles; anything shaped like this; in town, open space of this shape; carpenter's instrument for testing or drawing right angles; body of soldiers drawn up in form of square; (*Math.*) product of a number or quantity multiplied by itself; *a.* square shaped; rectangular; at right angles; giving equal justice; fair; balanced or settled, as account or bill; *adv.* squarely; directly; *v.t.* to make like a square; to place at right angles; (*Math.*) to multiply by itself; to balance; to settle; to put right; (*Colloq.*) to win over by bribery; *v.i.* to agree exactly; **-ly** *adv.* **-ness** *n.* **squarish** *a.* nearly square. **— dance**, old-fashioned dance for four couples. **— inch, foot, yard,** etc., area equal to surface of square with sides one inch, foot, yard, etc. long. **—rigged** *a.* (*Naut.*) of a ship, fitted with square sails. **— root,** number or quantity which, when multiplied by itself, produces the number of which it is the square root. **-shooter** *a.* (*Colloq.*) person who is honest [L. *quadrare*, to square, fr. *quattuor*, four].

squash (skwŏsh) *v.t.* to beat or crush flat; to squeeze to pulp; to suppress; *v.i.* to fall into a soft, flat mass; *n.* anything soft and easily crushed; packed crowd; game played with rackets. **-iness** *n.* **-y** *a.* [L. *ex*, out; *quassus*, to shake].

squash (skwŏsh) *n.* gourdlike fruit [Amer.-Ind. *asquash*, raw, green].

squat (skwŏt) *v.i.* to sit on heels; to crouch, as animal; to settle on land without having title to it, or in order to acquire title; *a.* short and thick; sitting close to ground. *pr.p.* **-ting.** *pa.p.* and *pa.t.* **-ted. -ter** *n.* [O.Fr. *esquatir*].

squaw (skwaw) *n.* N. American Indian woman, esp. wife [N. Amer. Ind. *eskaw*].

squeak (skwēk) *n.* short, sharp, shrill sound; sharp, unpleasant, grating sound; (*Colloq.*) a narrow escape; *v.i.* to utter, or make, such sound; (*Slang*) to give away secret. **-y** *a.*

squeal (skwēl) *n.* long, shrill cry; *v.i.* to utter long, shrill cry; (*Slang*) to turn informer. **-er** *n.* [imit. origin].

squeam·ish (skwēm'·ish) *a.* easily made sick; easily shocked; over-scrupulous; fussy. **-ly** *adv.* **-ness** *n.* [O.Fr. *escoymous*].

squee·gee (skwē'·jē) *n.* implement with rubber edge on head, for clearing water from deck of ship, floor, pavement, etc. Also **squil-gee** [fr. *squeeze*].

squeeze (skwēz) *v.t.* to press or crush; to compress; to extract by pressure; to force into; (*Colloq.*) to subject to extortion; *v.i.* to force one's way; to press; *n.* pressure; compression; close hug or embrace; (*Colloq.*) difficult situation. **squeezable** *a.* [O.E. *cwisan*].

squelch (skwelch) *n.* crushing blow; suppression; sound made when withdrawing feet from sodden ground; *v.t.* to crush down; (*Colloq.*) to silence with a crushing remark; *v.i.* to make sound of a squelch [etym. uncertain].

squid (skwid) *n.* a kind of sea mollusc.

squil·gee (skwil·'·jē) *n.* Same as **squeegee.**

squill (skwil) *n.* plant of lily family whose bulb has emetic properties. **-s** *n.pl.* drug from bulb of squill [Gk. *skilla*].

squint (skwint) *a.* looking obliquely; having eyes turned in; *v.t.* to cause to squint; *v.i.* to be cross-eyed; to glance sideways; to look with eyes partly closed; *n.* act, habit of squinting; (*Med.*) strabismus; hasty glance; peep. **-eyed** *a.* squinting; cross-eyed; spiteful.

squire (skwīr) *n.* formerly, knight's attendant; (*Brit.*) rural landowner; lady's escort; *v.t.* to escort [fr. *esquire*].

squirm (skwurm) *v.i.* to move like a snake, eel, worm, etc.; to wriggle. **-iness** *n.* **-y** *a.*

squir·rel (skwur'·al) *n.* small graceful animal with bushy tail, living in trees and feeding on nuts; its fur [O.Fr. *escureul*].

squirt (skwurt) *v.t.* and *v.i.* to eject, or be ejected, in a jet; to spurt; *n.* instrument for squirting; syringe; thin jet of liquid. **-er** *n.*

stab (stab) *v.t.* to pierce or wound with pointed instrument; to hurt feelings of; *v.i.* to strike with pointed weapon; *n.* blow or wound so inflicted; sudden pain. *pr.p.* **-bing.** *pa.p.* and *pa.t.* **-bed. -ber** *n.* [fr. Gael. *stob*, stake].

sta·bi·lize (stā′·ba·līz) *v.t.* to make stable, fixed, etc.; to fix exchange value of currency of a country. **stabilization** *n.* **stabilizer** *n.* that which stabilizes; horizontal tailplane of aircraft. **stability** (sta·bil′·a·ti·) *n.* steadiness [L. *stabilis*, fr. *stare*, to stand].

sta·ble (stā′·bl) *a.* firmly fixed, established; steady; lasting; resolute; **stably** *adv.* Also **stabile.** [L. *stabilis*, fr. *stare*, to stand].

sta·ble (stā′·bl) *n.* building for horses, usually divided into stalls; racehorse trainer's establishment; *v.t.* to put into, or keep in, stable; *v.i.* to be in stable [L. *stabulum*, a stall, fr. *stare*, to stand].

stac·ca·to (sta·ka′·tō) *a.* and *adv.* (*Mus.*) short, sharp, and distinct [It. fr. L. *staccare*, to separate].

stack (stak) *n.* large heap or pile. esp. of hay, straw, or wood; number of chimneys standing together; a chimney; (*Colloq.*) a great number; *pl.* book shelves. *v.t.* to heap or pile up; to arrange cards for cheating [O.N. *stakkr*].

sta·di·um (stā·di·am) *n.* arena for sports events, entertainments, etc., with seats for spectators [L. fr. Gk. *stadion*].

staff (staf) *n. pl.* **-s** or **staves** (stāvz): pole or stick used in walking, climbing, etc. or for support or defense; prop; stick, as emblem of office or authority; flagpole; (*Mus.*) five lines and four spaces on which music is written; (*Arch.*) stanza. (with *pl.* **-s**): body of persons working in office, school, etc.; *v.t.* to provide with staff. [O.E. *staef*].

stag (stag) *n.* male of red or other large deer; man who attends party without a woman. (*Slang*) party for men only [O.E. *stagga*].

stage (stāj) *n.* raised floor or platform esp. of theater, etc.; theatrical profession; dramatic art of literature; scene of action; degree of progress; point of development; distance between two stopping places on a journey; *v.t.* to put (a play) on stage. **staging** *n.* scaffolding. **-coach** *n.* four-wheeled passenger vehicle, horse drawn. **-fright** *n.* extreme nervousness felt when facing audience.**-struck** *a* smitten with love for stage as career. **-whisper** *n.* loud whisper intended to be heard [O.Fr. *estage*, fr. L. *stare*, to stand].

stag·ger (stag′·er) *v.i.* to walk or stand unsteadily; to reel; to totter; to hestitate; *v.t.* to cause to reel; to cause to hesitate; to shock; to distribute in overlapping periods; to arrange in zigzag fashion; *n.* act of staggering; unsteady movement. **-ing** *a.* amazing; astounding [O.N. *stakra*, to push].

stag·nate (stag′·nāt) *v.i.* to cease to flow; to be motionless; to be dull. **stagnant** *a.* of water, not flowing; hence, foul; impure; not brisk; dull. **stagnantly** *adv.* **stagnation** *n.* [L. *stagnum*, pool].

staid (stād) *a.* of sober and quiet character; steady; sedate; **-ly** *adv.* **-ness** *n.* [fr. *stay*].

stain (stān) *v.t.* and *v.i.* to discolor; to spot; to blot; to dye; to color, as wood, glass, etc.; to mark with guilt; *n.* discoloration; spot; dye; taint of guilt; disgrace. **-less** *a.* without a stain; not liable to stain or rust, esp. of a kind of steel. **-ed-glass,** glass with colors fused into it [L. *tingere*, to color].

stair (stār) *n.* steps one above the other for connecting different levels. **-s** *n.pl.* flight of steps. **-case** *n.* flight of steps with railings, etc. Also **-way** [M.E. *steire*, climb].

stake (stāk) *n.* sharpened stick or post; post to which one condemned to be burned, was tied; death by burning; money laid down as wager; interest in result of enterprise; *pl.*

money in contention; *v.t.* to mark out with stakes; to wager; to risk; to pledge. **at stake,** risked; involved [O.E. *staca*].

sta·lac·tite (sta·lak′·tīt) *n.* deposit of carbonate of lime, hanging like icicle from roof of cave. **stalactic, stalactitic** *a.* **stalactical** *a.* [Gk. *stalaktos*, droppings].

sta·lag (sta′·lag) *n.* (*World War 2*) prisoner-of-war camp [Ger. *Stammlager*].

sta·lag·mite (sta·lag′·mīt) *n.* deposit of carbonate of lime from floor of cave. **stalagmitic(al)** [Gk. *stalagma*, that which drops].

stale (stāl) *a.* not fresh; kept too long, as bread; tasteless; musty; having lost originality;trite; common; *v.t.* to make tasteless; *v.i.* to lose freshness.**-ly** *adv.* **-ness** *n.* [O.Fr. *estale*, spread out].

stale (stāl) *v.i.* of horses, to make water; *n.*

stale·mate (stāl′·māt) *n.* (*Chess*) position, resulting in drawn game; deadlock; standstill; *v.t.* to bring to a standstill [*stale* and *mate*].

stalk (stawk) *n.* stem of plant, leaf, etc., [M.E.].

stalk (stawk) *v.i.*, *t.* to steal up to game cautiously; to walk in stiff and stately manner; *n.* act of stealing up to game; stiff and stately gait. **-er** *n.* **-ing-horse** *n.* horse or figure of one, behind which a sportsman takes cover when stalking game; pretense; feint; pretext [O.E. *stealcian*, to walk cautiously].

stall (stawl) *n.* compartment for animal in stable; erection for display and sale of goods; a pew or enclosed seat in cathedral or church; protective sheath for injured finger; *v.t.* and *v.i.* to place or keep in stall; to come to a standstill; of engine or automobile, to stop running unintentionally; of aircraft, to lose flying speed and controllability [O.E. *steall*, a standing place, esp. for cattle].

stall (stawl) (*Slang*) pretense, trick; *v.i.* to evade question [O.E. *stelan*, to steal].

stal·lion (stal′·yan) *n.* an uncastrated male horse kept for breeding [fr. *stall*].

stal·wart (stawl′·wert) *a.* sturdy; strong; brave; steadfast; *n.* strong, muscular person; staunch supporter. **-ly** *adv.* [O.E. *staelworthe*].

sta·men (stā′·man) *n.* (*Bot.*) male organ of flowering plant, pollen-bearing part. **staminal** *a.* pert. to stamens, or to stamina. L. = fiber, thread].

stam·i·na (stam′·a·na) *n.* power of endurance; staying power; vigor.

stam·mer (stam′·er) *v.i.* to speak with repetition of syllables or hesitatingly; to stutter; *n.* halting enunciation; stutter. **-er** *n.* **-ing** *n.* stammer; stutter [O.E. *stamerian*].

stamp (stamp) *v.i.* to put down a foot with force; *v.t.* to set down (a foot) heavily or with force; to make an official mark on; to affix postage stamp; to distinguish by a mark; to brand; to fix deeply; *n.* act of stamping; instrument for making imprinted mark; mark imprinted; die; piece of gummed paper printed with device, as evidence of postage, etc.; character; form. **-er** *n.* [O.E. *stempan*].

stam·pede (stam·pēd′) *n.* sudden, frightened rush, esp. of herd of cattle, crowd, etc.; *v.t.* to put into a state of panic; *v.i.* to take part in a stampede; to rush off in a general panic [Sp. *estampido*, a crash].

stance (stans) *n.* position of feet in certain games, e.g. golf [L. *stare*, to stand].

stanch (stanch) *v.t.* to stop or check flow (of blood). *a.* firm; loyal; trustworthy. **-ly** *adv.* **-ness** *n.* Also **staunch** [O.F. *estancher*].

stan·chion (stan′·chan) *n.* upright support; iron bar, used as prop [O.Fr. *estance*, fr. L. *stare*, to stand].

stand (stand) *v.i.* to remain at rest in upright position; to be situated; to become or remain stationary; to stop; to endure; to adhere to principles; to have a position, order, or rank; to consist; to place oneself; to adhere to; to persist; to insist; to be of certain height; (*Naut.*) to hold course or direction; to continue in force; (*Colloq.*) to treat; *v.t.* to endure; to sustain; to withstand; to set; *pa.p.* and *pa.t.* **stood**. *n.* place where one stands; place for taxicabs; structure for spectators; piece of furniture on which things may be placed; stall for display of goods; position on some question. **-by** *n.* something in reserve. **-in** *n.* (*Film*) actor or actress who stands in the place of principal player until scene is ready to be shot. **-off, -offish** *a.* haughty; reserved; aloof. **-offishness** *n.* **-point** *n.* a point of view. **to standdown** (*Law*) to leave the witness stand. **to stand out**, to be conspicuous [O.E. *standan*].

stand·ard (stan'·derd) *n.* weight, measure, model, quality, etc. to which others must conform; criterion; pole with a flag; flag esp. ensign of war; royal banner; upright support; *a.* serving as established rule, model, etc.; having fixed value; uniform; standing upright. **-ize** *v.t.* to make of, or bring to, uniform level of weight, measure, quality, etc. **-ization** *n.* [O.Fr. *estendard*, a royal banner].

stand·ing (stan'·ding) *a.* established by law, custom, etc.; settled; permanent; not flowing; erect; *n.* duration; existence; continuance; reputation. **— army**, force maintained in peacetime. **— orders**, permanent rules [O.E. *standan*].

stank (stangk) *pa.t.* of the verb **stink**.

stan·za (stan'·za) *n.* group of lines or verses of poetry having definite pattern; loosely, division of poem. **stanzaic** (stan·zā'·ik) *a.* [It. stanza, fr. L. *stare*, to stand].

sta·ple (stā'·pl) *n.* settled market; chief product of a country or district; unmanufactured material; fiber of wool, cotton, flax, etc.; *a.* established in commerce; settled; regularly produced or made for market; principal; chief; *v.t.* of textiles, to grade according to length and quality of fiber. **-r** *n.* [O.Fr. *estaple*, a general market].

sta·ple (stā'·pl) *n.* U-shaped piece of metal with pointed ends to drive into wood used with hook, as locking device for a door, etc.; piece of wire to hold sheets of paper together **-r** *n.* mechanical device for fastening papers together [O.E. *stapel*, a prop].

star (stár) *n.* shining celestial body, seen as twinkling point of light; five or six-pointed figure asterisk; leading actor or actress; *v.t.* to set or adorn with stars; to cast (in play) as leading actor; *v.i.* to shine, as star; to play principal part. *pr.p.* **-ring**; *pa.p.*, *pa.t.* **-red**. **-let** *n.* small star; beginning actress. **-light** *n.* light from stars. **-lit** *a.* **-red** *a.* **-ry** *a.* **-riness** *n.* **-fish** *n.* marine animal shaped like a star. **-gazing** *n.* practice of observing stars; astrology [O.E. *steorra*].

star·board (stár'·berd) *n.* right-hand side of a ship, looking forward; *a.* pert. to, or on this side; *v.t.* to put (the helm) to starboard [O.E. *steorbord*, the steer side].

starch (stárch) *n.* substance forming main food element in bread, potatoes, etc. and used, mixed with water, for stiffening linen, etc.; formality; primness; *v.t.* to stiffen with starch. **-y** *a.* pert. to, containing, starch; (*Colloq.*) stiff; formal. **-ily** *adv.* **-iness** *n.* [O.E. *stearc*, rigid].

stare (ster) *v.i.* to look fixedly; to gaze; *v.t.* to abash by staring at; *n.* fixed, steady look. **-r** *n.* **staring** *n.* *a.* [O.E. *starian*].

stark (stárk) *a.* stiff; rigid; desolate; naked; downright; utter; *adv.* completely. **-ly** *adv.* [O.E. *steare*, rigid].

star·ling (stár'·ling) *n.* bird, bluish-black and speckled [O.E. *staer*, starling].

start (stárt) *v.i.* to make sudden movement; to spring; to wince; to begin, esp. journey; to become loosened or displaced; *v.t.* to cause to move suddenly; to set going; to begin; to loosen; to displace; *n.* sudden involuntary movement, spring or leap; act of setting out; beginning; in sports, advantage of lead in race. **-er** *n.* [O.E. *sturtan*].

star·tle (stár'·tl) *v.t.* to cause to start; to excite by sudden alarm; to give a fright to; *v.i.* to move abruptly, esp. from fright, apprehension, etc. **startling** *a.* alarming; astonishing; surprising. **startlingly** *adv.* [fr. *start*].

starve (stárv) *v.i.* to suffer from hunger; to die of hunger; to be short of something necessary; *v.t.* to cause to suffer or die from lack of food, etc. **starvation** *n.* the suffering from lack of food, warmth, etc. [O.E. *steorfan*, to die].

state (stāt) *n.* condition of person or thing; place or situation; temporary aspect of affairs; rank; high position; formal dignity; politically organized community; civil powers of such; *a.* pert. to state; governmental; ceremonial; *v.t.* to set forth; to express in words; to specify. **-d** *a.* fixed; regular; settled. **-ly** *a.* dignified; imposing; majestic. **-liness** *n.* **-ment** *n.* act of expressing in words; what is expressed; formal account of indebtedness. **-craft** *n.* political sagacity; statesmanship. **-less** *a.* without nationality. **-room** *n.* a private cabin in a ship, train, etc. **-sman** *n.* one skilled in art of government; able politician. **-sman-like** *a.* **-smanship** *n.* [L. *status*, fr. *stare*, to stand].

stat·ic (stat'·ik) *a.* pert. to bodies at rest, or in equilibrium; motionless; *n.* (*Radio*) crackling noises during reception due to atmospheric electricity. **-al** *a.* static. **-s** *n.pl.* branch of mechanics dealing with bodies at rest [Gk. *statikos*, causing to stand].

sta·tion (stā'·shan) *n.* place where thing or person stands; position; situation; condition of life; rank; regular stopping place for trains, etc.; local or district office for police force, fire-brigade, etc.; *v.t.* to put in a position; to appoint to place of duty. **-ary** *a.* not moving; fixed; regular; stable [L. *stare*, to stand].

sta·tion·er (stā'·shan·er) *n.* one who deals in writing materials. **-ery** *n.* wares sold by stationer [L. *statiōnāries*, stationary].

sta·tis·tics (sta·tis'·tiks) *n.pl.* numerical data collected systematically, summarized, and tabulated; science of collecting and interpreting such information. **statistic(al)** *a.* **statistically** *adv.* **statistician** (stat·as·tish'·an) *n.* one skilled in statistics. **statist** (stā'·tist) *n.* statistician [Gk. *statizein*, to set up].

sta·tor (stā'·ter) *n.* (*Elect.*) the stationary part of a generator [L. *stare*, to stand].

stat·ue (stach'·ōō) *n.* image of person or animal, carved out of solid substance or cast in metal. **statuary** *n.* collection of statutes. **statuesque** (stach·ōō·esk') *a.* like a statue; imposing. **statuette** (stach·ōō·et') *n.* small statute [L. *statua*, a standing image].

stat·ure (stach'·er) *n.* the heights of a person or animal [L. *statura*, fr. *stare*, to stand].

sta·tus (stā'·tas) *n.* position; rank; position of affairs [L. fr. *stare*, to stand].

stat·ute (stach'·ōō) *n.* law passed by legislature; established rule or law. **statutory** *a.* enacted, defined, or authorized by statute [L. *statutum*, that which is set up].

staunch. See **stanch**.

stave (stāv) *n.* one of curved strips of wood forming cask; rung of ladder; staff; five lines and spaces on which musical notes are written; verse or stanza; *v.t.* to fit with staves; to break stave(s) of (cask); to knock hole in side of; to ward off; to deter. *pa.p.* and *pa.t.* **-d** or **stove** [fr. *staff*].

staves (stāvz) *n.pl.* See **staff** and **stave**.

stay (stā) *v.t.* to restrain; to check; to stop; to support; to satisfy; to last; *v.i.* to remain; to continue in a place; to dwell; to pause; *n.* remaining or continuing in a place; halt; support; postponement, esp. of a legal proceeding. **-s** *n.pl.* laced corset [O.E. *staeg*].

stay (stā) *n.* (*Naut.*) strong rope or wire to support a mast or spar; *v.t.* to support or incline to one side with stays; to put on the other track; *v.t.* to change tack; to go about [O.E. *staeg*].

stead (sted) *n.* place which another had; place; use; benefit; advantage; service; frame of bed. [O.E. *stede*, position, place].

stead·fast (sted'·fast) *a.* firmly fixed; steady; constant. **-ly** *adv.* **-ness** *n.* [O.E. *stede*, place; *faest*, firm].

stead·y (sted'·i·) *a.* firm; constant; uniform; temperate; industrious; reliable; *v.t.* to make steady; to support; *v.i.* to become steady; **steadily** *adv.* **steadiness** *n.* [O.E. *stede*, position, place].

steak (stāk) *n.* slice of meat, esp. beef; also, slice of fish [O.N. *steik*].

steal (stēl) *v.t.* to take by theft; to get by cunning or surprise; to win gradually by skill, affection, etc.; *v.i.* to take what is not one's own; to move silently, or secretly. *pa.p.* **stolen** (stōlan). *pa.t.* **stole** (stōl). **stealth** (stelth) *n.* secret means used to accomplish anything; concealed act. **stealthy** (stel'·thi·) *a.* done by stealth. **stealthiness** *n.* [O.E. *stelan*].

steam (stēm) *n.* vapor rising from boiling water; water in gaseous state; any exhalation of heated bodies; *a.* worked by steam; *v.t.* to apply steam; to; to cook or treat with steam; *v.i.* to give off steam; to rise in vapor; to move under power of steam. **-y** *a.* pert. to, or like, steam; full of steam; misty. **-iness** *n.* **-er** *n.* steamship; vessel for cooking or washing by steam; something operated by steam. **-roller** *n.* heavy roller, driven by steam, used in road making [O.E. *steam*].

ste·a·rin (stē·a·rin) *n.* solid substance occurring in natural fats; hard, waxy solid used in manufacture of candles. Also **stearine**. **stearic** *a.* [Gk. *stear*, suet].

steed (stēd) *n.* horse [O.E. *steda*, stallion].

steel (stēl) *n.* hard and malleable metal, made by mixing carbon in iron; tool or weapon of steel; *a.* made of steel; hard; inflexible; unfeeling; *v.t.* to overlay, point, or edge, with steel; to harden; to make obdurate. **-y** *a.* made of, or like, steel; hard; obdurate; relentless. **-iness** *n.* — **engraving** *n.* method of incising on steel; the print [O.E. *style*].

steel·yard (stēl'·yàrd) *n.* balance with unequal arms and movable weight [etym. uncertain].

steep (stēp) *a.* having abrupt or decided slope; precipitous; (*Colloq.*) very high or exorbitant, esp. of prices; *n.* steep place; precipice. **-ly** *adv.* **-en** *v.t.* and *v.i.* to make, or become, steep [O.E. *steap*].

steep (stēp) *v.t.* to soak in a liquid; to drench; to saturate; *v.i.* to be soaked; *n.* act or process of steeping; liquid used [O.N. *steypa*, to pour out].

stee·ple (stē'·pl) *n.* a church tower with a spire. **-chase** *n.* a cross-country horse race; horse race on a course specially set with artificial obstacles; a cross-country footrace. **-jack** *n.* a skilled workman who climbs steeples, tall chimneys, etc. [O.E. *steap*, lofty].

steer (stir) *n.* a young male ox; a bullock [O.E. *steor*, a bullock].

steer (stir) *v.t.* to guide or direct the course of (a ship, car, etc.) by means of a rudder, wheel, etc.; *v.i.* to guide a ship, automobile, etc.; to direct one's course. **-age** *n.* the part of a ship allotted to passengers paying the lowest fare. **-er, -sman** *n.* the man who steers; the helmsman of a ship. **-ing gear** *n.* the mechanism for steering a vessel, vehicle, etc. [O.E. *stieran*].

stel·lar (stel'·er) *a.* pert. to, or like, stars; starry. **stellate, stellated** *a.* arranged in the form of a star; star-shaped; radiating. **stelliform** *a.* **stellular** *a.* [L. *stella*, a star].

stem (stem) *n.* the principal stalk of a tree or plant; any slender stalk of a plant; any slender shaft resembling a stalk; branch of family; curved or upright piece of timber or metal to which two sides of ship are joined; part of word to which inflectional endings are added; *v.t.* to remove the stem of; *v.i.* to originate. *pr.p.* **-ming** *pa.p.* and *pa.t.* **-med** [O.E. *stefn*]

stem (stem) *v.t.* to check; to stop; to dam up. *pr.p.* **-ming.** *pa.p.* and *pa.t.* **-med** [O.N. *stemma*].

stench (stench) *n.* strong, offensive odor [O.E. *stenc*].

sten·cil (sten'·sil) *n.* thin sheet of metal, paper, etc. pierced with pattern or letters, so that when placed on any surface and brushed over with paint, ink, etc., the design is reproduced; design so reproduced; *v.t.* to mark or paint thus. *pr.p.* **-ing.** *pa.p.* and *pa.t.* **-ed**

ste·nog·ra·phy (ste·nag'·ra·fi·) *n.* shorthand writing. **stenograph** *n.* character used in stenography; the script; stenographic machine; *v.i.* to write in shorthand. **stenographer, stenographist** *n.* **stenotype** *n.* a machine for writing shorthand; **stenographic, stenographical** *a.* [Gk. *stenos*, narrow; *graphein*, to write].

step (step) *v.i.* to move and set down the foot; to walk, esp. short distance; to press with the foot; *v.t.* to set or place, as foot; to measure in paces; (*Naut.*) to set up (mast); *n.* act of stepping; complete movement of foot in walking, dancing, etc.; distance so covered; manner of walking; footprint; footfall; tread of stair; degree of progress; measure; grade; (*Naut.*) socket for mast; *pr.p.* **-ping.** *pa.p.* and *pa.t.* **-ped. -per** *n.* **-ping stone** *n.* stone for stepping on when crossing stream, etc.; (*Fig.*) aid to success [O.E. *staeppan*].

step- (step) *prefix*, showing relationship acquired by remarriage. **-father** *n.* second, or later, husband of one's mother. Similarly **-mother, -brother, -sister**.

steppe (step) *n.* vast, treeless plain, as in Siberia [Russ. = a heath].

ster·e·o- (ster'·i·ō, stir'·i·ō·) fr. Gk. *stereos*, solid, used in referring to hardness solidity, three-dimensionality. **-phonic** *a.*, of or denoting a system of placing microphone to impart greater realism of sound.

ster·e·o·scope (stir'·i·, ster'·i·a·skōp) *n.* optical instrument in which two pictures taken at different viewpoints are combined into one image, with effect of depth and solidity. **-scopic(al)** *a.* **-scopically** *adv.* **-scopy** *n.* [Gk. *stereos*, solid; *skopein*, to view].

ster·e·otype (stir'·i·, ster'·i·a·tīp) *n.* in printing, plate made by pouring metal into mold of plaster or papier-maché made from original type; fixed form. *a.* pert. to stereotypes; *v.t.* to make a stereotype from; to print from stereotypes; to fix unalterably; to reduce to empty formula; to make always the same. **-d** *a.* **-r, stereotypist** *n.* [Gk. *stereos*, solid; and *type*].

ster·ile (ster'·il) *a.* barren; not fertile; unable to have offspring; producing no fruit, seed, or crops; (*Med.*) entirely free from germs of all kinds. **sterilize** *v.t.* to make steril; to deprive of power of having offspring; to destroy germs, esp. by heat or antiseptics. **sterlization** *n.* **sterlizer** *n.* **sterility** *n.* barrenness [L. *sterilis*, barren].

ster·ling (stur'·ling) *a.* pert. to standard

WEBSTER Q–S

value, weight, or purity of silver 92½% pure); of solid worth; genuine; pure; denoting British money.

stern (sturn) *a.* severe; strict; rigorous.-**ly** *adv.* -**ness** *n.* [O.E. *styrne*].

stern (sturn) *n.* after part of ship; rump or tail of animal [O.N. *stjorn*, steering].

ster·num (stur'·nam) *n.* breastbone. *pl.* **sterna. sternal** *a.* [Gk. *sternon*, the chest].

ster·nu·ta·tion (ster·nya·tā'·shan) *n.* act of sneezing; sneeze [L. *sternutare*].

ster·tor (stur'·ter) *n.* heavy, sonorous breathing. -**ous** *a.* -**ously** *adv.* [L. *stertere*, to snore]

stet (stet) *v.i.* word used by proofreaders as instruction to printer to cancel previous correaction. *pr.p.* -**ting.** *pa.p.,* *pa.t.* -**ted.** [L. = let it stand]

steth·o·scope (steth'·a·skōp) *n.* instrument for listening to action of lungs or heart. [Gk. *stēthos*, chest; *skopein*, to see].

ste·ve·dore (stēv'·a·dōr) *n.* one who loads and unloads ships [Sp. *estivador*, a wool packer, fr. L. *stipare*, to press together].

stew (stū) *v.t.* to cook slowly in a closed vessel; to simmer; *v.i.* to be cooked slowly; to feel uncomfortably warm; (*Slang*) to fuss or worry; *n.* stewed meat, etc. (*Colloq.*) nervous anxiety; -**ed** *a.* [O.Fr. *estuve*, a stove].

stew·ard (stū'·erd) *n.* one who manages another's property; on ship, attendant on passengers; catering-manager of club. -**ess** *n. fem.* female steward. -**ship** *n.* office of steward; management [O.E. *stigweard*, fr. *stig*, a house; *weard*, a ward].

stib·i·um (stib'·i·am) *n.* antimony **stibial** *a.* [L.].

stich (stik) *n.* verse or line of poetry, of whatever measure or number of feet -**ic** *a.* pert. to stich. -**ometry** *n.* measurement of manuscript by number of lines it contains. -**ometric, ometrical** *a.* [Gk. *stichos*, row].

stick (stik) *n.* small branch cut off tree or shrub; staff; rod; (*Print.*) instrument in which types are arranged in words and lines; set of bombs dropped one after the other; (*Colloq.*) stiff or dull person [O.E. *sticca*].

stick (stik) *v.t.* to stab; to pierce; to jab; to puncture; to fasten; to cause to adhere; to fix; to thrust; (*Colloq.*) to endure; *v.i.* to pierce; to adhere closely; to remain fixed; to hesitate; to be unable to proceed; to be puzzled, e.g. by a problem. *pa.p.* and *pa.t.* **stuck.** -**er** *n.* -**y** *a.* adhesive; viscous; tenacious; (*Colloq.*) embarrassing. -**iness** *n.* -**ing plaster** *n.* adhesive bandage for small wounds, cuts, etc. **stuck up,** conceited [O.E. *stician*, to pierce].

stick·le (stik'·l) *v.i.* to hold out stubbornly. -**r** *n.* one who insists on trifles of procedure, etc. [O.E. *stihlan*, to control].

stick·pin (stik'·pin) *n.* necktie pin.

stiff (stif) *a.* not easily bent; not flexible or pliant; moved with difficulty; firm; hard; stubborn; formal in manner; high in price; *n.* (*Slang*) corpse. -**ly** *adv.* -**ness** *n.* -**en** *v.t.* and *v.i.* to make or become stiff or stiffer. -**ener** *n.* one who, or that which, stiffens. —**necked** *a.* stubborn; obstinate [O.E. *stif*].

sti·fle (stī'·fl) *v.t.* and *v.i.* to smother; to suppress; to repress. **stifling** *a.* airless; close.

stig·ma (stig'·ma) *n.* brand; mark of disgrace; stain on character; blemish on skin; (*Bot.*) top of pistil of a flower. *pl.* -**s** or -**ta.**

stigmata (stig'·ma·ta) *n.pl.* marks resembling five wounds of Christ, said to have been miraculously impressed on bodies of certain saints. -**tic(al)** *a.* pert. to, or marked with stigma; giving reproach or disgrace; -**tization** *n.* -**tizer** *n.* [Gk. *stigma*, a tattoo mark].

stile (stīl) *n.* arrangement of steps for climbing fence or wall; a turnstile; in paneling or framing, upright sidepiece [O.E. *stigel*].

sti·let·to (sti·let'·ō) *n.* small dagger; pointed

instrument used in needlework [It. fr. L. *stilus*, a pointed instrument].

still (stil) *a.* motionless; silent; quiet; peaceful; of wine, not sparkling; *n.* stillness; (*Photog.*) enlargement of one unit of film; *v.t.* to quiet; to silence; to calm; *adv.* to this time; yet; even; *conj.* yet; however. -**ness** *n.* -**birth** *n.* state of being dead at time of birth. -**born** *a.* — **life** (*Art*) inanimated objects as subject of painting [O.E. *stille*].

still (stil) *n.* apparatus for distilling [L. *stillare*, to drip].

stilt (stilt) *n.* pole with foot-rest, for walking raised from ground; *v.i.* to walk on stilts. -**ed** *a.* formal; stiff; pretentious [Dut. *stelt*].

stim·u·lus (stim'·ya·las) *n.* goad; incentive; stimulant; (*Bot.*) sting; prickle. *pl.* **stimuli. stimulate** *v.t.* to rouse to activity; to excite; to increase vital energy of. **stimulater** *n.* **stimulant** *a.* serving to stimulate; *n.* that which spurs on; (*Med.*) any agent or drug which temporarily increases action of any organ of body. **stimulation** *n.* **stimulative** *a., n.* [L. *stimulus*, a goad].

sting (sting) *n.* pointed organ often poisonous, of certain animals, insects, or plants; thrust, wound, or pain of one; any acute physical or mental pain; *v.t.* to thrust sting into; to cause sharp pain to; to hurt feelings; to incite to action; (*Slang*) to overcharge; *v.i.* to use a sting. *pa.p.* and *pa.t.* **stung.** -**er** *n.* -**ing** *a.* -**ingly** *adv.* [O.E. *stingan*].

stin·gy (stin'·ji) *a.* meanly avaricious; miserly. **stinginess** *n.* [fr. *sting*].

stink (stingk) *v.i.* to give out strongly offensive smell; *pa.p.* **stunk** (stungk) *pa.t.* **stank** (stangk) or **stunk.** *n.* stench. -**er** *n.* one who, or that which, stinks; (*Slang*) objectionable person or thing. -**ing** *a.* [O.E. *stincan*].

stint (stint) *v.t.* to limit; to keep on short allowance; to skimp; *v.i.* to be frugal; *n.* limitation of supply or effort; allotted task. -**ed** *a.* [O.E. *styntan*, to blunt].

sti·pend (stī'·pend) *n.* money paid for a person's services; regular payment.-**iary** *a.* receiving salary; *n.* one who performs services for fixed salary [L. *stipendium*, wages].

stip·ple (stip'·l) *v.t.* and *v.i.* to engrave, draw, or paint by using dots instead of lines; *n.* this process. -**r** *n.* **stippling** *n.* [Dut. *slip*, a point].

stip·u·late (stip'·ya·lāt) *v.i.* to arrange; to settle definitely; to insist on in making a bargain or agreement. **stipulation** *n.* specified condition. **stipulator** *n.* [L. *stipulari*].

stir (stur) *v.t.* to set or keep in motion; to move; to mix up ingredients, materials, etc. by circular motion of utensil; to rouse; to incite; *v.i.* to begin to move; to be in motion; to be emotionally moved; *pr.p.* -**ring.** *pa.p.* and *pa.t.* -**red.** *n.* act of stirring; commotion. -**rer** *n.* -**ring** *a.* active; energetic; exciting; rousing; *n.* act of stirring [O.E. *styrian*].

stir·rup (stur'·ap) *n.* metal loop hung from strap, for foot of rider on horse. [O.E. *stigrap*, mount rope].

stitch (stich) *n.* in sewing, a single pass of needle; loop or turn of thread thus made; in knitting, crocheting, etc., single turn of yarn or thread around needle or hook; bit of clothing; sharp, sudden pain in the side; *v.t.* and *v.i.* to form stitches; to sew. -**er** *n.* -**ing** *n.* work done by sewing [O.E. *stician*, to pierce].

stith·y (stith'·i·) *n.* anvil; forge [O.N. *stethi*, anvil].

stoat (stōt) *n.* ermine or weasel, esp. in its summer fur of reddish-brown color.

stock (stȧk) *n.* stump or post; stem or trunk of tree or plant; upright block of wood; piece of wood to which the barrel, lock, etc. of firearm are secured; crossbar of anchor; ancestry; family; domestic animals on farm; supply of goods merchant has on hand; government securities; capital of company or corporation; quantity; supply; juices of meat, etc. to form a liquid used as foundation of soup; close-fitting band of cloth worn round neck; garden plant bearing fragrant flowers; gillyflower; *pl.* frame of timber supporting a ship while building; old instrument of punishment in form of wooden frame with holes in it, to confine hands and feet of offenders; *v.t.* to lay in supply for future use; to provide with cattle, etc. *a.* used, or available, for constant supply; commonplace; pert. to stock. **-breeder** *n.* one who raises cattle, horses, etc. **-broker** *n.* one who buys and sells stocks or shares for others. **-broking** *n.* **— exchange,** building in which stockbrokers meet to buy and sell stocks and shares. **-in-trade** *n.* goods merchant, shopkeeper, etc. has on hand for supply to public. **-market,** stock exchange. **-still** *a.* still as stock or post; motionless. **—taking** *n.* act of preparing inventory of goods on hand; sizing up of a situation. **— yard** *n.* large yard with pens for cattle, sheep, pigs, etc., esp. for those to be slaughtered [O.E. *stocc,* a stick].

stock·ade (stà·kād′) *n.* enclosure or pen made with posts and stakes; *v.t.* to surround, enclose, or defend by erecting line of stakes [Sp. *estacada,* a stake].

stock·fish (stàk′·fish) *n.* codfish, hake, etc., split and dried in open air [fr. *stock*].

stock·ing (stàk′·ing) *n.* woven or knitted covering for foot and leg [fr. *stock*].

stock·y (stàk′·i.) *a.* short and stout; thickset. **stockily** *adv.* [fr. *stock*].

stodge (stàj) *v.i.* to stuff; to cram. **stodgy** *a.* heavy; lumpy; indigestible; (*Fig.*) dull and uninteresting. **stodginess** *n.*

sto·ic (stō′·ik) *n.* disciple of Greek philosopher Zeno; one who suffers without complaint; person of great self-control; one indifferent to pleasure or pain. **-al** *a.* suffering without complaint; being indifferent to pleasure or pain. **-ally** *adv.* **-ism** *n.* endurance of pain, hardship, etc. without complaint [Gk. *stoa,* porch (where Zeno taught his philosophy)].

stoke (stōk) *v.t.* and *v.i.* to stir up, feed, or tend (fire). **-r** *n.* [Dut. *stoken,* to kindle a fire].

stole (stōl) *pa.t.* of **steal.**

stole (stōl) *n.* long, narrow scarf worn by bishops, priests, etc. during mass; woman's long, narrow scarf [Gk. *stole,* a robe].

stol·en (stōl′·n) *pa.p.* of **steal.**

stol·id (stàl′·id) *a.* dull or stupid; not easily excited. **-ly** *adv.* **-ness, -ity** *n.* [L. *stolidus*].

stomach (stum′·ak) *n.* chief digestive organ in any animal; appetite; desire; *v.t.* to put up with; to endure. **-er** *n.* formerly part of a woman's dress. **-ic** *n.* (*Med.*) any medicine for aiding digestion [Gk. *stomachos,* the gullet, fr. *stoma,* a mouth].

stone (stōn) *n.* hard, earthy matter of which rock is made; piece of rock; (*chiefly Brit.*) a measure of weight equal to 14 lb.; hard center of certain fruits; gem; concretion in kidneys or bladder; *a.* made of stone, stoneware, earthenware; *v.t.* to pelt with stones; to remove stones from, as from fruits. **stony** *a.* like stone; full of stones; pitiless. **stonily** *adv.* **stoniness** *n.* **Stone Age,** primitive stage of human development when man used stone for tools and weapons. **-blind** *a.* entirely blind. **-crop** *n.* creeping plant found on old walls, etc. **-deaf** *a.* completely deaf. **-mason** *n.* worker or builder in stone. **-'s throw** *n.* as far as one can throw a stone; hence, not far away [O.E. *stan*].

stood (stood) *pa.p.* and *pa.t.* of **stand.**

stooge (stōoj) *n.* (*Slang*) one who bears blame for others; (*Colloq.*) actor serving as butt of another's jokes; *v.t.* to act as stooge.

stool (stōol) *n.* chair with no back; low back-less seat for resting feet on; seat for evacuating bowels; discharge from bowels. **-pigeon** *n.* pigeon used to trap other pigeons; (*Slang*) person used as decoy. [O.E. *stol*].

stoop (stōop) *v.i.* to bend body; to lean forward; to have shoulders bowed forward, as from age; to bow one's head; to condescend; to lean forward; *n.* act of stooping; stooping carriage of head and shoulders [O.E. *stupian*].

stoop (stōop) *n.* raised entrance landing or porch in front of doorway [D. *stoep*].

stop (stàp) *v.t.* to fill up opening; to keep from opening; to keep from going forward; to bring to a halt; to obstruct; to check; to impede; to hinder; to suspend; to withhold; to desist from; to bring to an end; *v.i.* to cease; to halt; *pr.p.* **-ping.** *pa.p.* and *pa.t.* **-ped;** *n.* act of stopping; state of being stopped; halt; halting place; pause; delay; hindrance; any device for checking movement, e.g. peg, pin, plug, etc.; (*Mus.*) any device for altering or regulating pitch, e.g. vent hole in wind instrument; set of organ pipes; lever for putting it in action; consonant (p, t, etc.) produced by checking escape of breath from mouth by closure of lips, teeth, etc. **-page** *n.* state of being stopped; act of stopping; obstruction; cessation. **-per** *n.* one who, or that which, stops; plug for closing mouth of bottle, etc.; *v.t.* to close with a stopper. **-cock** *n.* valve for regulating flow of liquid. **—gap** *n.* a temporary substitute. **— watch** *n.* special watch whose hands can be started or stopped instantly [O.E. *stoppian,* to plug].

store (stōr) *n.* great quantity; abundance; reserve supply; stock; shop; *pl.* supplies; *v.t.* to collect; to accumulate; to hoard; to place in a warehouse. **storage** *n.* act of placing goods in a warehouse; space occupied by them; price paid. [L. *instaurare,* to restore].

stork (stawrk) *n.* large wading bird allied to heron and ibis [O.E. *storc*].

storm (stawrm) *n.* violent wind or disturbance of atmosphere with rain, snow, etc.; tempest; gale; assault on fortified place; commotion; outburst of emotion; *v.t.* to take by storm; to assault; *v.i.* to raise tempest; to rage; to fume; to scold violently. **-y** *a.* tempestuous; boisterous; violent; passionate. **-ily** *adv.* **-iness** *n.* **—bound** *a.* delayed by storms. [O.E. *storm*].

sto·ry (stō′·ri.) *n.* history or narrative of facts or events; account; tale; legend; anecdote; plot; rumor; (*Colloq.*) falsehood; a lie. **storied** (stō′·rid) *a.* told in a story; having a history. **-teller** *n.* one who tells stories [Gk. *historia*].

story (stō′·ri.) *n.* horizontal division of building; set of rooms on one floor. **storied** *a.*

stoup (stōop) *n.* holy-water basin [O.N.].

stout (stout) *a.* strong; robust; vigorous; bold; resolute; thickset; bulky; *n.* strong, dark-colored beer; porter. **-ly** *adv.* **-ness** *n.* **-hearted** *a.* brave; courageous; intrepid [O.F. *estoul,* proud, fierce].

stove (stōv) *n.* apparatus heated by gas, electricity, etc. for cooking, warming room, etc.; oven of blast furnace; **-pipe** *n.* metal pipe for carrying off smoke from stove [O.E. *stofa,* a heated room].

stove (stōv) *pa.p.* and *pa.t.* of **stave.**

stow (stō) *v.t.* to fill by packing closely; to arrange compactly, as cargo in ship; (*Slang*) to cease; to conceal. **-age** *n.* act of packing closely; space for stowing goods; charge made for stowing goods. **-away** *n.* one who hides on ship to obtain free passage [O.E. *stow,* a place].

strad·dle (strad′·l) *v.i.* to spread legs wide; to stand or walk with legs apart; *v.t.* to bestride something; (*Colloq.*) to seem to favor both sides of an issue; *n.* act of straddling;

astraddle adv. astride [fr.stride].

Strad·i·var·i·us (strad-a-va′·ri-as) n. a violin, usually of great value, made at Cremona, Italy, by Antonio *Stradivari* (1649-1737).

strafe (strāf) v.t. (*Mil. Slang*) to bombard heavily; to attack with machine-gun fire from airplanes [Ger. *strafen*, to punish].

strag·gle (strag′·l) v.i. to wander from direct course; to stray; to get dispersed; to lag behind; to stretch beyond proper limits; as branches of plant. **-r** n. one who, or that which, straggles. **straggling** a.

straight (strāt) a. passing from one point to another by nearest course; without a bend; direct; honest; upright; frank; (*U.S.*) of whisky, etc. undiluted; n. straightness; straight part, e.g. of racing-track; adv. in a direct line or manner; directly; without ambiguity; at once. **-ly** adv. **-en** v.t. to make straight. **-ener** n. **-away** a. straight forward. **-forward** a. proceeding in a straight course; honest; frank; simple [O.E. *streht*].

strain (strān) n. race; breed; stock; inherited quality [O.E. *streon*].

strain (strān) v.t. to stretch tight; to stretch to the full or to excess; to exert to the utmost; to injure by over-exertion, as muscle; to wrench; to force; to stress; to pass through sieve; to filter; v.i. to make great effort; to filter; n. act of straining; stretching force; violent effort; injury caused by over-exertion; wrench, esp. of muscle; sound; tune; style; manner; tone of speaking or writing. **-ed** a. done with effort; forced; unnatural; **-er** n. filter; sieve [L. *stringere*, to make tight].

strait (strāt) n. narrow channel of water connecting two larger areas; difficulty; financial embarrassment. **-en** v.t. to narrow; to put into position of difficulty or distress. — **jacket** n. garment for restraint of violently insane. —**laced** a. laced tightly in stays; puritanical; austere [L. *stringere*, *strictum*, to draw tight].

strand (strand) n. (*Poetic*) edge of sea or lake; the shore; v.t. to cause to run aground; to drive ashore; to leave in helpless position; -v.i. to run aground. **-ed** a. [O.E. *strand*].

strand (strand) n. single string or wire of rope; any string, e.g. of hair, pearls, etc.; v.t. to make rope by twisting strands together [O.Fr. *estran*, a rope].

strange (strānj) a. unaccustomed; not familiar; uncommon; odd; extraordinary. **-ly** adv. **-ness** n. **-r** n. one from another country, town, place, etc.; unknown person; newcomer; one unaccustomed (to) [O.Fr. *estrange*].

stran·gle (strang′·gl) v.t. to kill by squeezing throat; to choke; to stifle; to suppress. **-r** n. **strangulate** v.t. to constrict so that circulation of blood is impeded; to compress; to strangle. **strangulation** n. [L. *strangulare*].

strap (strap) n. long, narrow strip of leather, cloth, or metal; strop; strip of any material for binding together or keeping in place; v.t. to fasten, bind, chastise with strap; to sharpen (a razor). pr.p. **-ping**. pa.p. and pa.t. **-ped. -ping** n. act of fastening with strap; material used; punishment with strap; a. (*Colloq.*) tall; robust [O.E. *strop*].

stra·ta (strā′·ta) n.pl. See **stratum**.

strat·a·gem (strat′·a·jam) n. artifice in war; scheme for deceiving enemy; ruse [Gk. *stratēgein*, to lead an army].

strat·e·gy (strat′·a·ji·) n. art of conducting military or naval operations; generalship; skillful management in getting the better of an adversary. **strategic** (stra·tē′·jik) a. pert. to, based on, strategy. **strategics** n.pl. strategy. **strategical** a. **strategically** adv. **strategist** n. [Gk. *stratēgein*, to lead army].

strat·i·fy (strat′·a·fī) v.t. to form or deposit in strata or layers. **stratification** n. [L. *stratum*, a layer].

strat·o·sphere (strat′·a·sfir) n upper part of atmosphere, six miles or more above earth [L. *stratum*, layer, and *sphere*].

stra·tum (strā′·tam, strat′·am) n. bed of earth, rock, coal, etc. in series of layers; any bed or layer; class in society. pl. **strata**. **stratus** n. cloud form, in low, horizontal layers or bands. pl. **strati** [L. *stratum*, fr. *sternere*, to spread out].

straw (straw) n. stalk of wheat, rye, etc. after grain has been thrashed out; collection of such dry stalks, used for fodder, etc.; hollow tube for sipping beverage; thing of very little value; a. made of straw [O.E. *streaw*].

straw·ber·ry (straw′·be·ri·) n. a red berry with delicious taste [O.E. *steaw*, straw; *berige*, a berry].

stray (strā) v.i. to wander from path; to digress; a. wandering; strayed; lost; occasional; n. stray animal; lost child [O.Fr. *estraier*].

streak (strēk) n. line, or long band, of different color from the background; stripe; flash of lightning; trait; strain; v.t. to mark with streaks. **-ed, -y** a. [O.E. *strica*, a stroke].

stream (strēm) n. flowing body of water, or other liquid; river, brook, etc.; current; course; trend; steady flow of air or light, or people; v.i. to issue in stream; to flow or move freely; to stretch in long line; to float or wave in air; v.t. to send out in a stream; to send forth rays of light. **-y** a. **-er** n. long, narrow flag; pennant; auroral beam of light shooting up from horizon. **-let** n. little stream. **-line** n. line of current of air; shape of a body (e.g. car, ship, etc.) calculated to offer least resistance to air or water when passing through it; v.t. to design body of this shape [O.E.].

street (strēt) n. road in town or village, usually with houses or buildings at the side. **-walker** n. one who walks the streets; prostitute [L. *strata* (*via*), a paved (way)].

strength (strength) n. quality of being strong; capacity for exertion; ability to endure; power or vigor; physical, mental, or moral force; potency of liquid, esp. of distilled or malted liquors; intensity; force of expression; vigor of style; support; security; force in numbers, e.g. of army. **-en** v.t. to make strong or stronger; to reinforce; v.i. to become or grow strong or stronger. **-ener** n. [O.E. *strengthu*].

stren·u·ous (stren′·yoo·as) a. eagerly pressing; energetic; full of, requiring effort. **-ly** adv. **-ness** n. **strenuosity** n. [L. *strenuus*].

strep·to·coc·cus (strep·ta·kak′·as) n. (*Med.*) bacterium of chain formation, the organism responsible for serious infections. pl. **streptococci** (·kak′·ī) [Gk. *streptos*, bent; *kokkos*, grain].

strep·to·my·cin (strep·tō·mī′·san) n. (*Med.*) antibiotic drug related to penicillin [Gk. *streptos*, bent; *mukēs*, fungus].

stress (stres) n. force; pressure; strain; emphasis; weight or importance; accent; (*Mech.*) force producing change in shape of body; v.t. to lay stress on [O.Fr. *estrecier*]...

stretch (strech) v.t. to pull out; to tighten; to reach out; to strain; to exaggerate; v.i. to be drawn out; to be extended; to spread; n. extension; strain; effort; extent; expanse; long line or surface; unbroken period of time. **-er** n. one who, or that which, stretches; a frame or litter for carrying sick or wounded; brick or stone laid lengthwise along line of wall [O.E. *streccan*].

strew (strōó) v.t. to scatter over surface; to spread loosely. pa.p. **-ed** or **-n**, pa.t. **-ed** [O.E. *streowian*].

stri·a (strī′·a) n. line or small groove. pl. **-e**

(strī'·ē) thread-like lines, as on surface of shells, rocks, crystals, etc. **-te, -ted** a. marked with striae. **-tion** n. [L. stria, a furrow].

strick·en (strik'·n) a. struck; smitten; afflicted; worn out [fr. strike].

strict (strikt) a. stern; severe; exacting; rigid; unswerving; without exception; accurate. **-ly** adv. **-ness** n. **-ure** n. severe criticism; (Med.) morbid contraction of any passage of body, esp. urethra [L. stringere, strictum, to tighten].

stride (strīd) n. long step, or its length; v.t. to pass over with one long step; v.i. to walk, with long steps. pa.p. **stridden** (strid'·n). pa.t. **strode** [O.E. stridan].

stri·dent (strī'·dąnt) a. harsh in tone; grating; jarring. **stridence, stridency** n. **-ly** adv. [L. stridere, to creak].

strife (strīf) n. conflict; struggle [O.Fr. estrif].

strike (strīk) v.t. to hit; to smite; to dash against; to collide; to sound; to cause to sound; to occur to; to impress; to afflict; to stamp; to cause to light, as match; to lower, as flag or sail; to take down, as tent; to ratify; to conclude; to come upon unexpectedly, as gold; to cancel; v.i. to hit; to deliver blow; to dash; to clash; to run aground; to stop work for increase of wages, etc.; to take root, of a plant; n. a stoppage of work to enforce demand; find, esp. in prospecting for gold; stroke of luck. pa.p. **struck, or -n** pa.t. **struck. striking** a. affecting with strong emotions; impressive. **strikingly** adv. [O.E. strican, to move, to wipe].

string (string) n. cord; twine; ribbon; thick thread; cord or thread on which things are arranged, e.g. string of pearls; chain; succession; series; stretched cord of gut or wire for musical instrument; vegetable fiber, as string beans; all race horses from certain stable; pl. stringed musical instruments collectively; v.t. to furnish with strings; to put on string, as beads, pearls, etc.; v.i. to stretch out into a long line; to form strings; to become fibrous. pa.p. and pa.t. **strung. -ed** a. **-y** a. fibrous; of person, long and thin. **-iness** n. [O.E. streng].

strin·gent (strin'·jąnt) a. binding strongly; strict; rigid; severe. **-ly** adv. **-ness, stringency** n. [L. stringere, to tighten].

strip (strip) v.t. to pull or tear off; to peel; to skin; to lay bare; to divest; to rob; v.i. to take off one's clothes; n. long, narrow piece of anything. pr.p. **-ping.** pa.p. and pa.t. **-ped** (stript). **-ling** n. youth [O.S. strypan, to plunder].

stripe (strīp) n. narrow line, band, or mark; strip of material of a different color from the rest; (Mil.) V-shaped strip of material worn on sleeve as badge of rank; chevron; stroke made with lash, whip, scourge, etc.; v.t. to mark with stripes; to lash. **-d** (strīpt) a. [Dut. streep].

strive (strīv) v.i. to try hard; to make an effort; to struggle; to contend. pa.p. **-n.** pa.t. **strove.** n. [O.Fr. estriver].

strode (strōd) pa.t. of **stride.**

stroke (strōk) n. blow; paralytic fit; apoplexy; any sudden seizure of illness, misfortune, etc.; sound of bell or clock; mark made by pen, pencil, brush, etc.; completed movement of club, stick, racquet, etc.; in swimming, completed movement of arm; in rowing, sweep of an oar; rower nearest stern who sets the time and pace; entire movement of piston from one end to other of cylinder; single, sudden effort, esp. if successful, in business, diplomacy, etc.; piece of luck; v.t. to set time and pace for rowers [O.E. stracian, to strike].

stroke (strōk) v.t. to pass hand gently over; to caress; to soothe; n. act of stroking [O.E. stracian, to strike].

stroll (strōl) v.i. to walk leisurely from place to place; to saunter; to ramble; n. a leisurely walk. **-er** n. [etym. uncertain].

strong (strawng) a. having physical force; powerful; muscular; able to resist attack; healthy; firm; solid; steadfast; well-established; violent; forcible; intense; determined; not easily broken; positive. **-ly** adv. [O.E. strang].

stron·ti·um (stran'·shi·ąm) n. (Chem.) a yellowish, reactive, metallic element [Strontian, Scotland].

strop (strąp) n. strip of leather for sharpening razor; v.t. to sharpen on strop. pr.p. **-ping.** pa.p. and pa.t. **-ped** (stropt) [L. struppus].

stro·phe (strō'·fē) n. in ancient Greek drama, song sung by chorus while dancing from right to left of orchestra; stanza. **strophic** a. [Gk. strophē, a turning].

strove (strōv) pa.t. of **strive.**

struck (struk) pa.p. and pa.t. of **strike.**

struc·ture (struk'·cher) n. that which is built; building; manner of building; arrangement of parts or elements; organization. **structural** a. **structurally** adv. [L. struere, structum, to build].

stru·del (stroo'·dl) n. type of Ger. pastry.

strug·gle (strug'·l) v.i. to put forth great efforts, esp. accompanied by violent twistings of body; to contend; to strive; n. violent physical effort; any kind of work in face of difficulties; strife. n. [etym. uncertain].

strum (strum) v.t. and v.i. to play badly and noisily on (stringed instrument). pr.p. **-ming.** pa.p. and pa.t. **-med** [imit. origin].

strum·pet (strum'·pit) n. prostitute; harlot.

strung (strung) pa.p. and pa.t. of **string.**

strut (strut) v.i. to walk pompously; to walk with affected dignity; n. stiff, proud and affected walk; pompous gait. pa.p. **-ting.** pa.p. and pa.t. **-ted** [O.E. strutian, to stick out stiffly].

strut (strut) n. rigid support, usually set obliquely; support for rafter; v.t. to brace.

strych·nine (strik'·nīn) n. highly poisonous alkaloid; stimulant. Also **strychnin** [Gk. nightshade].

stub (stub) n. stump of a tree; short, remaining part of pencil, cigarette, etc.; v.t. to clear (ground) by rooting up stumps of trees; to strike toe against fixed object. pr.p. **-bing.** pa.p. and pa.t. **-bed. -bed** a. short and blunt like stump; obtuse. **-by** a. abounding in stubs; short and thickset. **-biness** n. [O.E. stybb].

stub·ble (stub'·l) n. short ends of cornstalks left after reaping; short growth of beard. **-d** a. **stubbly** a. [L. stipula, fr. stipes, stalk].

stub·born (stub'·ern) a. fixed in opinion; obstinate. adv. **-ness** n. [M.E. stoburn].

stuc·co (stuk'·ō) n. plaster of lime, sand, etc. used on walls, and in decorative work; v.t. to make stucco [It.].

stuck (stuk) pa.p. and pa.t. of **stick. -up** a. (Colloq.) conceited.

stud (stud) n. a movable, double-headed flat-headed nail; boss; upright wooden support, as in wall; v.t. to furnish with studs; to set thickly in, or scatter over. pr.p. **-ding.** pa.p. and pa.t. **-ded** [O.E. studu, a post].

stud (stud) n. collection of horses, kept for breeding, or racing; place where they are kept. **-book** n. official book for recording pedigrees of thoroughbred animals [O.E. stod].

stu·dent (stū'·d(a)nt) n. one who studies; scholar at university or other institutions for higher education. [L. studere, to be zealous].

stu·di·o (stū'·di·ō) n. workroom of artist, sculptor, or professional photographer; where film plays are produced; a room equipped for broadcasting of radio and television programs [It.].

stu·di·ous (stū'·di·as) *a.* given to, or fond of, study; thoughtful; contemplative; painstaking; careful (of); deliberate. **-ly** *adv.* [L. *studium*, zeal].

stud·y (stud'·i·) *n.* application of the mind to books, etc. to gain knowledge; subject of such application; branch of learning; thoughtful attention; meditation; room for study; preliminary sketch by an artist; *v.t.* to set the mind to; to examine carefully; to scrutinize; to ponder over; *v.i.* to read books closely in order to gain knowledge. **studied** (stud'·id) also *a.* examined closely; carefully considered and planned [L. *studium*, zeal].

stuff (stuf) *n.* essential part; material; (*Brit.*) cloth not yet made into garments; goods; belongings; useless matter; worthless things, trash, esp. in *stuff and nonsense; v.t.* to fill by pressing closely; to cram; in cookery, to fill, e.g. chicken with seasoning; to fill skin, e.g. of animal, bird, etc. to preserve it as specimen; *v.i.* to eat greedily. **-ing** *n.* material used to stuff or fill anything [O.Fr. *estoffe*, fr. L. *stupa*, tow].

stuff·y (stuf'·i·) *a.* badly ventilated; airless; dull; conceited **stuffiness** *n.* [Fr. *étouffer*, to choke, stifle].

stul·ti·fy (stul'·ta·fi) *v.t.* to make to look ridiculous; to make ineffectual; to destroy the force of [L. *stultus*, foolish].

stum·ble (stum'·bl) *v.i.* to trip in walking and nearly fall; to walk in unsteady manner; to fall into error; to speak hesitatingly; *v.t.* to cause to trip; to mislead; *n.* act of stumbling; wrong step; error. **stumblingly** *adv.* **stumbling block** *n.* obstacle; hindrance [M.E. akin to *stammer*].

stump (stump) *n.* part of tree left after trunk is cut down; part of limb, tooth, etc. after main part has been removed; remnant; *pl.* (*Colloq.*) legs; *v.t.* to reduce to a stump; to cut off main part; to puzzle or perplex; (*Colloq.*) to tour (district) making political speeches; *v.i.* to walk noisily or heavily. **-y** *a.* full of stumps; short and thick [ME *stumpe*].

stun (stun) *v.t.* to knock senseless; to daze; to stupefy; to amaze. *pr.p.* **-ning.** *pa.p.* and *pa.t.* **-ned** (stund). **-ner** *n.* **-ning** *a.* rendering senseless (*Slang*) striking; excellent [O.Fr. *estoner*].

stung (stung) *pa.p.* and *pa.t.* of **sting.**

stunk (stungk) *pa.p.* and *pa.t.* of **stink.**

stunt (stunt) *v.t.* to check the growth of; to dwarf. **-ed** *a.* [O.E. *stunt*, dull].

stunt (stunt) *n.* (*Colloq.*) any spectacular feat of skill or daring, esp. if for display, or to gain publicity [etym. uncertain].

stu·pe·fy (stū'·pa·fi) *v.t.* to deprive of full consciousness; to dull the senses; to stun; to amaze. **stupefier** *n.* **stupefaction** *n.* act of making stupid; dazed condition; utter amazement. **stupefactive** *a.* **stupefacient** *a.* and *n.* [L. *stupere*, to be amazed; *facere*, to make].

stu·pen·dous (stū·pen'·das) *a.* astonishing, esp. because of size, power, etc.; amazing. **-ly** *adv.* **-ness** *n.* [L. *stupere*, to be amazed].

stu·pid (stū'·pid) *a.* slow-witted; unintelligent; foolish; dull. **-ly** *adv.* **-ness**, **-ity** *n.* [L.].

stu·por (stū'·per) *n.* complete or partial loss of consciousness; dazed state; lethargy. **-ous** *a.* [L. *stupere*, to be struck senseless].

stur·dy (stur'·di·) *a.* hard; robust; vigorous; strongly built; firm. **sturdily** *adv.* **sturdiness** *n.* [O.Fr. *estourdi*, stunned, amazed].

stur·geon (stur'·jan) *n.* large fish, whose roe is made into caviar [Fr. *esturgeon*].

stut·ter (stut'·er) *v.i.* and *v.t.* to speak with difficulty; to stammer; *n.* the act or habit of stuttering, **-er** *n.* **-ing** *a.* [M.E. *stoten*].

sty (stī) *n.* place to keep pigs; hence, any filthy place [O.E. *stig*].

sty, stye (stī) *n.* small abscess on edge of eyelid [O.E. *stigend*].

styg·i·an (stij'·i·an) *a.* pert. to river *Styx* in Hades; infernal; gloomy; dismal [L. *Stygius*].

style (stīl) *n.* pointed instrument used by the ancients for writing on waxed tablets; engraving-tool; etching-needle; manner of expressing thought in writing, speaking, acting, painting, etc.; in the arts, mode of acting, painting, etc.; in the arts, mode of expression or performance peculiar to individual, group, or period; in games, manner of play and bodily action; mode of dress; fashion; fine appearance; mode of address; title; mode of reckoning time; sort, kind, make, shape, etc. of anything; (*Bot.*) stem-like part of pistil of flower, supporting stigma; pin of a sundial; *v.t.* to give title, official or particular, in addressing or speaking of (person); to term; to name; to call. **-t** *n.* stiletto; probe.**stylize** *v.t.* to make conform to convention. **stylish** *a.* fashionable; elegant. **stylishly** *adv.* **stylishness** *n.* **stylist** *n.* writer, who is attentive to form and style; one who is master of style. **stylistic** *a.* **stylistically** *adv.* **stylus** *n.* style [L. *stilus*].

sty·mie (stī'·mi·) *n.* (*Golf*) position on putting-green resulting from one player's ball coming to rest between hole and opponent's ball; (*Fig.*) to thwart [etym. unknown].

styp·tic (stip'·tik) *a.* contracting; astringent; *n.* (*Med.*) any substance used to arrest bleeding [Gk. *stuphein*, to contract].

sua·sion (swā'·zhan) *n.* persuasion; advisory influence [L. *suadere*, to advise].

suave (swāv, swāv) *a.* pleasant; agreeable; smoothly polite; bland. **-ly** *adv.* **suavity** *n.* [L. *suavis*, sweet].

sub (sub) *n.* (*Colloq.*) shortened form of subaltern, sub-lieutenant, subscription, substitute, submarine, etc.

sub- (sub) *prefix*, meaning under, below, from below, lower, inferior, nearly, about, somewhat, slightly, moderately, used in many words, e.g. **-acute** *a.* moderately acute or severe [L.].

sub·al·tern (sa·bawl'·ten) (*Mil.*) *a.* of lower rank [L. *sub*, under; *alternus*, in turn].

sub·a·que·ous (sub·ā'·kwi·as) *a.* living, lying, or formed under water. **subaquatic** *a.*

sub·arc·tic (sub·ark'·tik) *a.* pert. to region or climate immediately next to the Arctic.

sub·con·scious (sub·kan'·shas) *a.* pert. to unconscious activities which go on in mind; partially conscious; *n.* subconscious mind.**-ly** *adv.*

sub·cu·ta·ne·ous (sub·kū·tā'·ni·as) *a.* under the skin. **-ly** *adv.*

sub·di·vide (sub·da·vīd') *v.t.* to divide a part, or parts of, into other parts; to divide again; *v.i.* to be subdivided. **subdivision** *n.* act of subdividing; result of subdividing.

sub·duc·tion (sub·duk'·shan) *n.* withdrawal; deduction [L. *subducere*, to withdraw].

sub·due (sub·dū') *v.t.* to bring under one's power; to conquer; to bring under control; to reduce force or strength of; to soften. **-d** *a.* **-r** *n.* **subdual** *n.* act of subduing; state of being subdued [L. *subducere*, to withdraw]. to withdraw].

sub·ed·it (sub·ed'·it) *v.t.* to act under an editor; to be assistant editor. **-or** *n.*

sub·head·ing (sub·hed'·ing) *n.* division of main heading.

sub·hu·man (sub·hū'·man) *a.* less than human.

sub·ject (sub'·jikt) *a.* under power or control of another; owing allegiance; subordinate; dependent; liable to; prone; exposed; *n.* one under the power or control of another; one owing allegiance to a sovereign, state, government, etc.; a person, animal, etc. as an object of experiment, treatment, operation, etc.; matter under consideration or discussion, written or spoken; topic; theme; (*Mus.*) principal theme or melody of movement; (*Gram.*) a word or words in sentence of which something is affirmed; (*Philos.*) conscious self; thinking mind. **subject** (sub·jekt′) *v.t.* to bring under power or control of; to subdue; to cause to undergo; to submit. **-ion** *n.* act of bringing under power or control; state of being under control. **-ive** *a.* pert. to subject; existing in the mind; arising from senses; relating to, or reflecting, thoughts and feelings of person; (*Gram.*) pert. to subject of sentence. **-ively** *adv.* **-iveness** *n.* **-ivity** *n.* [L. *sub*, under; *jacere*, to throw].

sub·join (sub·join′) *v.t.* to append; to annex. **-der** *n.* something added at end.

sub·ju·gate (sub′·jŏŏ·gāt) *v.t.* literally, to bring under the yoke; to force to submit; to conquer. **subjugation** *n.* **subjugator** *n.* [L. *sub*, and *jugum*, yoke].

sub·junc·tive (sąb·jungk′·tiv) *a.* denoting subjunctive mood; mood of verb implying condition, doubt, or wish [L. *sub; jungere*, to join].

sub·lease (sub′·lēs) *n.* lease granted to another tenant by one who is himself a tenant; (sub·lēs′) *v.t.* to grant or hold a sublease.

sub·let (sub·let′) *v.t.* to let to another tenant property of which one is a tenant; *pr.p.* **-ting.** *pa.t. pa.p.* **sublet.**

sub·li·mate (sub′·li·māt) *v.t.* (Chem.) to convert solid directly into vapor and then allow it to solidify again; to purify thus; to direct repressed impulses, esp. sexual, towards new aims and activities. *n.* (*Chem.*) substance that has been sublimated. **sublimation** *n.* [L. *sublimare*, to lift up].

sub·lime (są·blīm′) *a.* exalted; eminent; inspiring awe, adoration, etc.; majestic; grandiose; *n.* that which is sublime; *v.t.* to sublimate; to purify; to exalt; to ennoble. **-ly** *adv.* **-ness, sublimity** (są·blim′·ą·ti·) *n.* [L. *sublimis*, high].

sub·lim·i·nal (sub·lim′·ąn·ąl) *a.* in psychology, below level of consciousness.

sub·ma·chine gun (sub·mą·shēn′·gun) *n.* (*Mil.*) light, portable machine gun.

sub·ma·rine (sub·mą·rēn′) *a.* situated, living, or able to travel under surface of sea; *n.* submersible boat, esp. one armed with torpedoes.

sub·merge (sąb·murj′) *v.t.* to put under water; to cover with water; to flood; (*Fig.*) to overwhelm; *v.i.* to go under water. **-nce** *n.* [L. *sub; mergere*, to dip].

sub·merse (sąb·murs′) *v.t.* to submerge; to put under water. **submersible** *a.* **submersion** *n.* [L. *submergere*].

submit (sąb·mit′) *v.t.* to put forward for consideration; to surrender; *v.i.* to yield oneself to another; to surrender. *pr.p.* **-ting.** *pa.p.* and *pa.t.* **-ted. submission** *n.* act of submitting; humility; meekness. **submissive** *a.* ready to submit; obedient; docile; humble. **submissively** *adv.* **submissiveness** *n.* resignation [L. *sub; mittere*, to put].

sub·mul·ti·ple (sub·mul′·tą·pl) *n.* number or quantity that divides into another exactly.

sub·nor·mal (sub·nawr′·mąl) *a.* below normal.

sub·or·di·nate (są·bawr′·dą·nit) *a.* lower in rank, importance, power, etc.; *n.* one of lower rank, importance, etc. than another; one under the orders of another; *v.t.* (są·bawr′·dą·nāt) to make or treat as subordinate; to make subject. **-ly** *adv.* **-ness, subordinacy** *n.* **subordination** *n.* [L. *sub*, under; *ordinare*, to set in order].

sub·orn (są·bawrn′) *v.t.* to induce (person) to commit perjury; to bribe to do evil. **-ation** *n.* **-er** *n.* [L. *sub*, under; *ornare*, to furnish].

sub·poe·na (su(b)·pē′·ną) *n.* (*Law*) writ summoning person to appear in court (under penalty for non-appearance); *v.t.* to issue such an order [L. under penalty].

sub·rep·tion (sub·rep′·shąn) *n.* concealment or misrepresentation of truth. **subreptitious** *a.* [L. *sub*, under; *rapere*, to seize].

sub·scribe (sąb·skrīb′) *v.t.* to write underneath; to sign at end of paper or document; to give, or promise to give, (money) on behalf of cause; to contribute; *v.i.* to promise in writing to give a sum of money to a cause; (with *to*) to pay in advance for regular supply of issues of newspaper, magazine, etc.; to agree with or support. **-r** *n.* **subscript** *a.* written underneath. **subscription** *n.* act of subscribing; name or signature of subscriber; money subscribed or gifted; receipt of periodical for fee paid.

sub·se·quent (sub′·si·kwąnt) *a.* following or coming after in time; happening later. **-ly** *adv.* [L. *sub; sequi*, to follow].

sub·serve (sąb·surv′) *v.t.* to serve in small way; to help forward; to promote. **subservient** *a.* serving to promote some purpose; submissive; servile. **subserviently** *adv.* **subservience, subserviency** *n.* state of being subservient.

sub·side (sąb·sīd′) *v.i.* to sink or fall to the bottom; to settle; to sink to lower level; to abate. **subsidence, subsidency** *n.* act of subsiding [L. *sub*, under; *sidere*, to settle].

sub·sid·i·ar·y (sąb·sid′·e·ri·) *a.* pert. to subsidy; aiding, helping, supplementary, secondary; auxiliary; *n.* one who, or that which, helps; auxiliary [L. *subsidium*, a reserve].

sub·si·dy (sub′·si·di·) *n.* financial aid; government grant for varoius purposes, e.g. to encourage certain industries, to keep cost of living steady, etc.; also in return for help in time of war. **subsidize** *v.t.* to pay subsidy to [L. *subsidium*].

sub·sist (sąb·sist′) *v.i.* to continue to be; to exist; to live (on); *v.t.* to support with food; to feed. **-ent** *a.* having real being; existing. **-ence** *n.* act of subsisting; things or means by which one supports life; livelihood [L. *subsistere, fr. sistere*, to stand].

sub·soil (sub′·soil) *n.* the layer of earth lying just below the top layer.

sub·son·ic (sub·sán′·ik) *a.* pert. to speeds less than that of sound; below 700-750 m.p.h.

sub·stance (sub′·stans) *n.* essence; material, etc. of which anything is made; matter; essential matter of book, speech, discussion, etc.; real point; property. **substantial** (sąb·stan′·shi·āt) *v.t.* to make substantial; to give substance to; to bring evidence for; to establish truth of. **substantiation** *n.* **substantive** *a.* having independent existence; real; fixed; (*Gram.*) expressing existence; pert. to noun, or used as noun; *n.* (*Gram.*) noun. **substantively** *adv.* [L. *substart*, to be present].

sub·sti·tute (sub′·sti·tūt) *v.t.* to put in place of another; to exchange. *v.i.* to take place of another; *n.* one who, or that which, is put in place of another. **substitution** *n.* **substitutional, substitutionary** *a.* **subsitutionally** *adv.* [L. *sub*, under; *statuere*, to appoint].

sub·sra·tum (sub·strā′·tąm) *n.* underlying stratum or layer of soil, rock, etc.; a basic element. *pl.* **substrata. substrative** *a.*

sub·sume (sąb·sóóm′) *v.t.* to include under a class as belonging to it, e.g. 'all sparrows are birds.' **subsumption** *n.* **subsumptive** *a.*

sub·ten·ant (sub·ten′·ant) *n.* tenant who rents house, farm, etc. from one who is himself a tenant. **subtenancy** *n.*

sub·tend (sąb·tend′) *v.t.* (*Geom.*) of line, to

extend under or be opposite to, e.g. angle.

sub·ter·fuge (sub'·ter·fūj) *n.* that to which a person resorts in order to escape from a difficult situation, to conceal real motives, to avoid censure, etc.; an underhand trick; evasion [L. *subter*, under; *fugere*, to flee].

sub·ter·ra·ne·an (sub·ta·rā'·nē·an) *a.* being or lying under surface of earth. Also **subterraneous, subterrene** (sub·ta·rēn'), **subterrestrial** [L. *sub*, under; *terra*, the earth].

sub·ti·tle (sub'·tī·tl) *n.* additional title of book; half-title; film caption.

sub·tle (sut'·l) *a.* delicate; acute; discerning; clever; ingenious; intricate; making fine distinctions. **subtly** *adv.* **-ness, -ty** (sutl'·ti·) *n.* quality of being subtle; artfulness; a fine distinction [L. *subtilis*, fine woven].

sub·tract (sub·trakt') *v.t.* to take away (part) from rest; to deduct one number from another to find difference. **-ion** *n.* act or operation of subtracting. **-ive** *a.* **subtrahend** *n.* quantity or number to be subtracted from another [L. *sub*; *trahere*, to draw].

sub·trop·i·cal (sub·trap'·i·kal) *a.* designating zone just outside region of the tropics.

sub·urb (sub'·urb) *n.* residential district on outskirts of town; *pl.* outskirts. **suburban** *a.* and *n.* **-ia** *n.* suburbs and their inhabitants [L. *sub*, under; *urbs*, city].

sub·ven·tion (sub·ven'·shan) *n.* act of coming to the help of; government grant; subsidy [L. *sub*, under; *venire*, to come].

sub·vert (sab·vurt') *v.t.* to overthrow, esp. government; to destroy; to ruin utterly; **-er** *n.* **subversion** *n.* the act of subverting; overthrow; ruin. **subversive** *a.* [L. *sub*, under; *vertere*, to turn].

sub·way (sub'·wā) *n.* underground passage; underground railway.

suc·ceed (sak·sēd') *v.t.* to come immediately after; to follow in order; to take place of, esp. of one who has left or died; *v.i.* to come next in order; to become heir (to); to achieve one's aim to prosper. **-er** *n.* **success** *n.* favorable accomplishment; prosperity; one who has achieved success. **successful** *a.* **successfully** *adv.* **successfulness** *n.* **succession** (sak·sesh'·an) *n.* act of following in order; sequence; series of persons or things according to some established rule; line of descendants; act or right of entering into possession of property, place, office, title, etc., of another, esp. of one near of kin. **successional** *a.* **successionally** *adv.* **successive** *a.* following in order; consecutive. **successively** *adv.* **successor** *n.* one who succeeds or takes place of another [L. *succedere*].

suc·cinct (sak·singkt') *a.* closely compressed; expressed in few words; terse; concise. **-ly** *adv.* **-ness** *n.* [L. *succingere*, to gird up].

suc·cor (suk'·er) *v.t.* to help esp. in great difficulty or distress; to relieve; to comfort; *n.* aid; support. **-er** *n.* [L. *succurrere*].

suc·cu·lent (suk'·ya·lant) *a.* full of juice; juicy. **-ly** *adv.* **succulence** *n.* juiciness [L. *succus*, juice].

suc·cumb (sa·kum') *v.i.* to yield; to submit; to die [L. *sub*, under; *cumbere*, to lie down].

such (such) *a.* of like kind; of that kind; of same kind; similar; of degree, quality, etc. mentioned; certain or particular; *pron.* used to denote a certain person or thing; these or those. **-like** *a.* similar; *pron.* similar things (but not defined); this or that [O.E. *swylc*].

suck (suk) *v.t.* to draw into mouth (by using lips and tongue); to draw liquid from (by using mouth; to roll (candy) in mouth; to absorb; *v.i.* to draw in with mouth; to drink from mother's breast; *n.* act of drawing with the mouth; milk drawn from mother's breast. **-er** *n.* one who, or that which, sucks; organ by which animal adheres by suction to any

object; fresh water fish; shoot of plant from roots or lower part of stem; (*Slang*) person easily deceived. **-ing** *a.* **-le** *v.t.* to give suck to; to feed at mother's breast. **-ling** *n.* young child or animal not yet weaned [O.E. *sucan*].

su·crose (sóó'·krōs) *n.* white, sweet, crystalline substance; cane sugar, beet sugar, etc. [Fr. *sucre*, sugar].

suc·tion (suk'·shan) *n.* act of sucking or drawing in; act of drawing liquids, gases, dust, etc. into vessel by exhausting air in it; 'force' that causes one object to adhere to another when air between them is exhausted. **— pump** *n.* pump in which water or other liquid is raised by atmospheric pressure [L. *sugere*, to suck].

sud·den (sud'·n) *a.* happening without notice or warning; coming unexpectedly; done with haste; abrupt. **-ly** *adv.* **-ness** *n.* [Fr. *soudain*, fr. L. *subitus*, unexpected].

suds (sudz) *n.pl.* water in which soap has been dissolved; froth and bubbles on it [O.E. *seothan*, to seethe].

sue (sóó) *v.t.* (*Law*) to seek justice by taking legal proceedings; to prosecute; *v.i.* to begin legal proceedings; to petition [L. *sequi*, follow].

suède (swād) *n.* soft, undressed kid leather; *a.* made of undressed kid [Fr. *Suède*, Sweden].

su·et (sū'·it) *n.* hard animal fat around kidneys and loins, used in cooking. **-y** *a.* [L. *sebum*, fat].

suf·fer (suf'·er) *v.t.* to endure; to undergo; to allow; to tolerate; *v.i.* to undergo pain, punishment, etc.; to sustain a loss. **-able** *a.* **-ableness** *n.* **-ably** *adv.* **-ance** *n.* the state of suffering; toleration [L. *sub*, under; *ferre*, to bear].

suf·fice (sa·fīs'·) *v.t.* to satisfy; *v.i.* to be enough; to meet the needs of. **sufficient** (sa·fish'·ant) *a.* enough; satisfying the needs of. **sufficiently** *adv.* **sufficiency** *n.* [L. *sufficere*, to satisfy].

suf·fix (suf'·iks) *n.* letter or syllable added to end of word; affix. *v.t.* to add to end of. **-al** *a.* **-ion** *n.* [L. *sub*; *figere*, to fix].

suf·fo·cate (suf'·a·kāt) *v.t.* to kill by choking; to smother; to stifle; *v.i.* to be choked, stifled, or smothered. **suffocating** *a.* **suffocatingly** *adv.* **suffocation** *n.* [L. *suffocare*].

suf·frage (suf'·rij) *n.* vote; right to vote. **-tte** *n.* woman who agitated for women's right to vote [L. *suffragium*, a vote].

suf·fuse (sa·fūz') *v.t.* to spread over, as fluid; to well up; to cover. **suffusion** *n.* **suffusive** *a.* [L. *sub*, under; *fundere*, to pour].

sug·ar (shoog'·er) *n.* sweet, crystalline substance; any substance like sugar; (*Fig.*) sweet words; flattery; *v.t.* to sweeten with sugar; *v.i.* to turn into sugar. *a.* made of, tasting of, or containing sugar; sweet; flattering. **-iness** *n.* **— cane**, tall grass whose sap yields sugar. **— loaf** *n.* a cone-shaped mass of hard, refined sugar. **— plum** *n.* sweetmeat; bonbon [Fr. *sucre*].

sug·gest (sag·jest') *v.t.* to bring forward; to propose; to hint; to insinuate. **-er** *n.* **-ion** *n.* proposal; hint; in psychiatry, influence exercised over subconscious mind of a person, resulting in a passive acceptance by him of impulses, beliefs, etc. **-ive** *a.* tending to call up an idea to the mind; hinting at; tending to bring to the mind indecent thoughts; improper. **-ively** *adv.* **-iveness** *n.* [L. *suggerere*, to carry up].

su·i·cide (sóó'·a·sīd) *n.* one who kills himself intentionally; act of doing this. **suicidal** (sóó·a·sī'·dal) *a.* pert. to, tending to suicide; (*Fig.*) disastrous; ruinous. **suicidally** *adv.* [L. *sui*, of oneself; *caedere*, to kill].

suit (sóót) *n.* act of suing; petition; request;

action in court of law; courtship; series or set of things of same kind or material; set of clothes; any of four sets in pack of cards; *v.t.* to fit; to go with; to appropriate; to be adapted to; to meet desires of; *v.i.* to agree; to be convenient. **-able** *a.* proper; appropriate; becoming. **-ably** *adv.* **-ability, -ableness** *n.* **-ing** *n.* material for making suits. **-or** *n.* one who sues; a wooer; a lover. [Fr. *suivre*, to follow, fr. L. *sequi*].

suite (swēt) *n.* train of followers or attendants; retinue; a number of things used together, e.g. set of apartments, furniture; (*Mus.*) series of dances or other pieces [Fr. fr. *suivre*, to follow].

su·ki·ya·ki (sōó·kē·ya′·kē) *n.* Jap. dish of fried meat, vegetables, etc.

sul·cus (sul′·kąs) *n.* groove; a furrow. **sulcate, sulcated** *a.* **sulcation** *n.* [L.].

sul·fa (sul′·fą) *n.* abbrev. for *sulfa drugs*, a group of antibacterial compounds used in the treatment of disease, injury, etc.

sul·fate (sul′·fāt) *n.* salt of sulfuric acid. **sulfide** *n.* compound of sulfur with metal or other element. **sulfite** *n.* salt of sulfurous acid [L. *sulphur*].

sul·fur (sul′·fer) *n.* yellow, nonmetallic element, burning with blue flame and giving off suffocating odor. **-ous** *a.* **-y** *a.* **-ic acid,** colorless acid, having strong corrosive action [L. *sulphur*].

sulk (sulk) *v.i.* to be silent owing to ill humor, etc.; to be sullen; *n.* sullen fit or mood. **-y** *a.* silent and sullen; morose; *n.* light two-wheeled carriage for one person. **-ily** *adv.* **-iness** *n.*

sul·len (sul′·ąn) *a.* gloomily ill-humored; silently morose. **-ly** *adv.* **-ness** *n.* the state of being sullen [L. *solus*, alone].

sul·ly (sul′·i·) *v.t.* to soil; to stain; to disgrace; *v.i.* to be sullied [Fr. *souiller*, to soil].

sul·tan (sul′·tąn) *n.* Mohammedan prince or ruler. **-a** *n.* wife, mother, or daughter of sultan; kind of raisin [Fr. fr. Ar. *sultan*, victorious].

sul·try (sul′·tri·) *a.* hot, close, and oppressive; sweltering. **sultrily** *adv.* **sultriness** *n.* [form of *sweltry*, fr. *swelter*].

sum (sum) *n.* result obtained by adding together two or more things, quantities, etc.; total; aggregate; summary; quantity of money; *v.t.* (generally with *up*) to add up; to find total amount; to make summary of main parts. *pr.p.* **-ming.** *pa.p.* and *pa.t.* **-med. -mation** *n.* act of summing up; total reckoning [L. *summa*, total amount].

sum·ma·ry (sum′·ą·ri·) *a.* expressed in few words; concise; done quickly and without formality; *n.* abridgment or statement of chief points of longer document, speech; etc.; epitome. **summarily** *adv.* **summarize** *v.t.* **summarist** *n.* **summarization** *n.* **summarizer** *n.* [Fr. *sommaire*].

sum·mer (sum′·er) *n.* warmest of four seasons of year, season between spring and autumn; commonly, months of June, July, and August; *a.* pert. to period of summer; *v.i.* to pass the summer. *a.* like summer. **-y** *a.* [O.E. *sumor*].

sum·mer·sault *n.* See **somersault**.

sum·mit (sum′·it) *n.* highest point; top, esp. of mountain [L. *summus*, highest].

sum·mon (sum′·ąn) *v.t.* to demand appearance of, esp. in court of law; to send for; to gather up (energy, etc.). **-er** *n.* **-s** *n.* (*Law*) document ordering person to appear in court; any authoritative demand; *v.t.* to serve with summons [L. *summonere*, to hint].

sump (sump) *n.* lowest part of excavation, esp. of mine, in which water collects; well in crankcase of motor vehicle for oil [Dut. *somp*].

sump·tu·ar·y (sump′·chŏó·er·i·) *a.* pert. to, or regulating, expenditure. **sumptuous** *a.*

costly; lavish; magnificent. **sumptuously** *adv.* **sumptuousness** *n.* [L. *sumptus*, cost].

sun (sun) *n.* luminous body round which earth and other planets revolve; its rays; any other heavenly body forming the center of system of planets; anything resembling sun, esp. in brightness; *v.t.* to expose to sun's rays; to warm (oneself) in sunshine; to bask. *pr.p.* **-ning.** *pa.p.* and *pa.t.* **-ned. -ny** *a.* pert. to, like, sun; exposed to sun; warmed by sun; cheerful. **-niness** *n.* **-bathe** *v.i.* to expose body to sun. **-beam** *n.* ray of sunlight. **-burn** *n.* darkening of skin, accompanied often by burning sensation due to exposure to sun; *v.t.* and *v.i.* to darken by exposure to sun. **-burned, burnt** *a.* — **dial** *n.* device for showing time by shadow which a raised pin casts on plate marked with hours. **-down** *n.* sunset; **-flower** *n.* tall plant with large, round, yellowrayed flowers. **-light** *n.* light of sun. **-lit** *a.* lighted by sun. **-rise** *n.* first appearance of sun above horizon in morning; time of its appearance; dawn; east. **-set** *n.* descent of sun below horizon; time of its disappearance; west. **-shade** *n.* parasol. **-shine** *n.* light of sun; cheerfulness. **-shiny** *a.* **-spot** *n.* dark, irregular patche seen periodically on surface of sun. **-stroke** *n.* feverish and sudden prostration caused by undue exposure to very strong sunlight [O.E. *sunne*].

sun·dae (sun′·di) *n.* ice-cream served with topping [perh. fr. *Sunday*].

Sun·day (sun′·di) *n.* first day of week; [O.E. *sunnan*, sun; *daeg*, day].

sun·der (sun′·der) *v.t.* to separate; to divide; to sever; *v.i.* to come apart. **sundry** *a.* separate; several; various. **sundries** *n.pl.* sundry things; odd items [O.E. *syndrian*, separate].

sung (sung) *pa.p.* of **sing**.

sunk (sungk) *pa.p.* and alt. *pa.t.* of **sink**.

sunk·en (sungk′·ąn) alt. *pa.p.* of **sink**.

sup (sup) *v.t.* to take in sips; to sip; to eat with spoon, as soup; *v.i.* to have supper; to sip; *n.* small mouthful; *pr.p.* **-ping.** *pa.p.* and *pa.t.* **-ped** [O.E. *supan*]

su·per (sōó′·per) *n.* supernumerary (actor); (*Colloq. abbrev.*) superintendent; (*Colloq.*) short for superfine, super-excellent, etc.; hence; first-rate [L. *super*, above].

su·per- (sōó′·per) *prefix* fr. L. *super*, above, over, higher, superior, to extra, etc.

su·per·a·ble (sōó′·per·ą·bl) *a.* capable of being overcome [L. *superare*, to overcome].

su·per·a·bound (sōó′·per·ą·bound′) *v.i.* to be exceedingly abundant. **superabundant** *a.* much more than enough; excessive. **superabundantly** *adv.* **superabundance** *n.*

su·per·an·nu·ate (sōó·per·an′·yoo·āt) *v.t.* to pension off because of age or infirmity. **superannuation** *n.* pension [L. *super*, above; *annus*, year].

su·perb (soo·purb′) *a.* grand; splendid; magnificent; stately; elegant. **-ly** *adv.* **-ness** *n.* [L. *superbus*, proud].

su·per·car·go (sōó·per·kár′·gō) *n.* ship's officer who takes charge of cargo.

su·per·charge (sōó′·per·charj) *v.t.* to charge or fill to excess. **-r** *n.* in internal-combustion engine, device for forcing extra supply of gasoline mixture into cylinders.

su·per·cil·i·ar·y (sōó·per·sil′·i·er·i·) *a.* pert. to eyebrow. **supercilious** *a.* lofty with pride; haughty and indifferent. **superciliously** *adv.* [*supercilium*, the eyebrow].

su·per·cool (sōó·per′kool′) *v.t.* (*Chem.*) to cool (liquid) below its freezing point without solidifying it. **-ing** *n.*

su·per·e·go (sōó·per·ē′·gō) *n.* in psychoanalysis, that unconscious morality which directs action of censor.

su·per·er·o·ga·tion (sōó·per·er·a·gā′·shąn) *n.* doing more than duty or necessity requires.

[L. *super*, above; *erogare*, to expend].

su·per·fi·cial (sŏŏ·pẽr·fish′·al) *a.* on surface; not deep; shallow; understanding only what is obvious. **-ly** *adv.* **-ity** (fish·i·al′·a·ti·) [L. *super*, above; *facies*, the face].

su·per·fine (sŏŏ′·pẽr·fīn) *a.* fine above others; of first class quality; very fine.

su·per·flu·ous (soo·pur′·floo·as) *a.* more than is required or desired; useless. **-ly** *adv.* **superfluity** *n.* state of being superfluous; quantity beyond what is required; a superabundance. **-ness** *n.* [L. *super*, over; *fluere*, to flow].

su·per·heat (sŏŏ·pẽr·hēt′) *v.t.* to heat (steam) above boiling point of water, done under a pressure greater than atmospheric; to heat (liquid) above its boiling point.

su·per·het·er·o·dyne (sŏŏ·pẽr·het′·ar·a·dīn) *n.* (*Radio*) receiving set of great power and selectivity. *abbrev.* **superhet**.

su·per·hu·man (sŏŏ·pẽr·hū′·man) *a.* more than human; divine; excessively powerful.

su·per·im·pose (sŏŏ·pẽr·im·pōz′) *v.t.* to lay upon another thing. **superimposition** *n.*

su·per·in·tend (sŏŏ·pẽr·in·tend′) *v.t.* to manage; to supervise; to direct; to control; *v.i.* to supervise. **-ence, -ency** *n.* **-ent** *a.* superintending; *n.* one who superintends [L. *superintendere*].

su·pe·ri·or (sa·pi′·ri·ẽr) *a.* upper; higher in place, position, rank, quality, etc.; surpassing others; being above, or beyond, power or influence of; too dignified to be affected by; supercilious; snobbish; *n.* one who is above another, esp. in rank or office; head of monastery or other religious house. **superiority** (sa·per·i·ar′·i·ti·) *n.* [L. *superior*, higher].

su·per·la·tive (sa·pur′·la·tiv) *a.* of or in the highest degree; surpassing all others; supreme; (*Gram.*) denoting, as form of adjective or adverb, highest degree of quality; *n.* superlative degree of adjective or adverb. **-ly** *adv.* [fr. L. *super*, above; *ferre, latum*, to carry].

su·per·man (soo′·pẽr·man) *n.* ideal man; one endowed with powers beyond those of the ordinary man.

su·per·nal (sŏŏ·pur′·nal) *a.* pert. to things above; celestial; heavenly; exalted.

su·per·nat·u·ral (sŏŏ·pẽr·nach′·a·ral) *a.* beyond powers or laws of nature; miraculous.

su·per·nu·mer·a·ry (sŏŏ·pẽr·nū′·mer·er·i·) over and above; extra; *n.* person or thing in excess of what is necessary or usual; actor with no speaking part [L. *super*, above; *numerus*, a number].

su·per·scribe (sŏŏ·pẽr·skrīb′) *v.t.* to write or engrave on outside or top of. **superscription** *n.* act of superscribing; words written or engraved on top or outside of anything.

su·per·sede (sŏŏ·pẽr·sēd′) *v.t.* to set aside; to replace by another person or thing; to take the place of. **supersession** *n.* [L. *super*, above; *sedere*, to sit].

su·per·son·ic (sŏŏ·pẽr·sán′·ik) *a.* pert. to soundwaves of too high a frequency to be audible; denoting a speed greater than that of sound, i.e. more than 750 miles per hour.

su·per·sti·tion (sŏŏ·pẽr·stish′·an) *n.* belief in, or fear of, what is unknown, mysterious, or supernatural; religion, opinion, or practice based on belief in divination, magic, omens, etc. **superstitious** *a.* pert. to, believing in, or based on, superstition. **superstitiously** *adv.* [L. *superstitio*, excessive fear of the gods].

su·per·struc·ture (sŏŏ·pẽr·struk′·cher) *n.* structure built on top of another; the part of building above foundation. **superstructive, superstructural** *a.*

su·per·vene (sŏŏ·pẽr·vēn′) *v.i.* to happen in addition, or unexpectedly; to follow closely upon. **supervenient** *a.* **supervenience, supervention** *n.* act of supervening [L. *super*, above; *venire*, to come].

su·per·vise (sŏŏ·pẽr·vīz′) *v.t.* to oversee; to superintend; to inspect; to direct and control. **supervision** (vizh′·an) *n.* act of supervising; superintendence; inspection. Also **supervisal** *n.* **supervisor** (vī′·zer) *n.* **supervisory** *a.* [L. *super*, over; *videre, visum*, to see].

su·pine (sŏŏ′·pīn) *a.* lying on one's back; indolent; inactive [L. *supinus*, fr. *sub*, under].

sup·per (sup′·per) *n.* the last meal of the day [Fr. *souper*, to sup].

sup·plant (sa·plant′) *v.t.* to displace (person) esp. by unfair means; to take the place of. **-er** *n.* [L. *supplantare*, to trip up, fr. *planta*, the sole of the foot].

sup·ple (sup′·l) *a.* easily bent; flexible; limber; obsequious; *v.t.* and *v.i.* to make or become supple. **-ly** *adv.* **-ness** *n.* [L. *supplex*, suppliant].

sup·ple·ment (sup′·la·mant) *n.* something added to fill up or supply deficiency; appendix; special number of newspaper; extra charge; (*Geom.*) number of degrees which must be added to angle or arc to make 180° or two right angles. **supplement** (sup′·la·ment) *v.t.* to fill up or supply deficiency; to add to; to complete. **-al** *a.* **-ary** *a.* added to additional [L. *supplementum*, fr. *supplere*, to fill up].

sup·pli·ant (sup′li·ant) *a.* supplicating; asking humbly and submissively; beseeching; *n.* one who supplicates. **-ly** *adv.* **supplicant** *a.* supplicating; *n.* one who supplicates; suppliant. **supplicate** *v.t.* and *v.i.* to ask humbly; to beg earnestly; to petition. **supplication** *n.* [L. *supplicare*, to kneel down, fr. *plicare*, to fold].

sup·ply (sa·plī′) *v.t.* to provide what is needed; to furnish; to fill the place of; *n.* act of supplying; what is supplied; stock; store; **supplies** *n.pl.* food or money. **supplier** *n.* [L. *supplere*, to fill up].

sup·port (sa·pōrt′) *v.t.* to keep from falling; to bear weight of; to sustain; to bear or tolerate; to encourage; to furnish with means of living; *n.* act of sustaining; advocacy; maintenance or subsistence; one who, or that which, supports. **-er** *n.* [L. *sub*, under; *portare*, to carry].

sup·pose (sa·pōz′) *v.t.* to assume as true without proof; to advance or accept as a possible or probable fact, condition, etc.; to imagine. **-d** *a.* imagined; accepted; put forward as authentic. **supposedly** (sa·pōz′·id·li·) *adv.* **supposable** *a.* [Fr. *supposer*].

sup·po·si·tion (sup·a·zish′·an) *n.* act of supposing; assumption; that which is supposed; **-ally** *adv.* **supposititious** (sa·páz·a·tish′·as) [L. *sub*, under; *ponere, positum*, to place].

sup·pos·i·to·ry (sa·páz′·a·tōr·i·) *n.* medicinal substance, cone-shaped, introduced into a body canal [L. *sub*, under; *ponere, positum*, to place].

sup·press (sa·pres′) *v.t.* to put down or subdue; to overpower and crush; to quell; to stop. **suppression** (sa·presh′·an) *n.* **-ive** *a.* **-or** *n.* [L. *sub*, under; *premere, pressum*, to press].

sup·pu·rate (sup′·ya·rāt) *v.i.* to form pus; to fester. **suppurative** *a.* tending to suppurate. **suppuration** *n.* [L. *sub*, under; *pus*, matter].

su·pra- (sŏŏ′·pra) L. *prefix*, meaning above.

su·preme (sa·prēm′) *a.* holding highest authority; highest or most exciting; greatest possible; uttermost. **-ly** *adv.* **-ness** *n.* **supremacy** (sa·prem′·a·si·) *n.* state of being highest in power and authority; utmost excellence [L. *supremus*].

sur- *prefix*, meaning over, above, upon, in addition [Fr. fr. L. *super*, over].

sur·cease (sur·sēs′) *v.t.* (*Arch.*) to cause to cease; *v.i.* to cease; *n.* cessation [L. *supersedere*, to refrain from].

sur·charge (sur·chárj′) *v.t.* to make additional

charge; to overload or overburden. **surcharge** (sur'·chàrj) *n.* excessive charge, load, or burden; additional words or marks superimposed on postage stamp.

sur·cin·gle (sur'·sing·gl) *n.* belt, band, or girth for holding something on a horse's back [L. *super*, over; *cingulum*, a belt].

sur·coat (sur'·kōt) *n.* long and flowing cloak worn by knights over armor [O.Fr. *surcote*].

surd (surd) *a.* (*Math.*) not capable of being expressed in rational numbers; radical; (*Phon.*) uttered with breath alone, not voice, as *f*, *p*, *k*, etc.; *n.* (*Math.*) quantity that cannot be expressed by rational numbers, or which has no root [L. *surdus*, deaf].

sure (shoor) *a.* certain; positive; admitting of no doubt; firmly established; strong or secure. **-ly** *adv.* certainly; undoubtedly; securely. **-ness** *n.* **-ty** (shoor'·a·ti·) *n.* certainty; that which makes sure; security against loss or damage; one who makes himself responsible for obligations of another [L. *securus*, sure].

surf (surf) *n.* foam or water of sea breaking on shore or reefs, etc.

sur·face (sur'·fis) *n.* external layer or outer face of anything; outside; exterior; *a.* involving the surface only; *v.t.* to cover with special surface; to smooth; *v.i.* to come to the surface [L. *super*, over; *facies*, the face]

sur·feit (sur'·fit) *v.t.* to overfeed; to fill to satiety; *n.* excess in eating and drinking; oppression caused by such excess. **-er** *n.* **-ing** *n.* [Fr. *surfaire*, to overdo].

surge (surj) *n.* rolling swell of water, smoke, people; large wave or billow; *v.i.* to swell; to rise high and roll, as waves. **surging** *a.* [L. *surgere*, to rise].

sur·geon (sur'·jan) *n.* medical man qualified to perform operations; one who practices surgery. **surgery** *n.* branch of medicine dealing with cure of disease or injury by manual operation; operating room. **surgical** *a.* **surgically** *adv.* [Fr. *chirurgien*].

sur·ly (sur'·li·) *a.* of unfriendly temper; rude; uncivil; sullen. **surlily** *adv.* **surliness** *n.*

sur·mise (ser·mīz') *v.t.* to imagine or infer something without proper grounds; to make a guess; to conjecture; *n.* supposition; a guess or conjecture [O.Fr. *surmise*, accusation].

sur·mount (ser·mount') *v.t.* to rise above; to overtop; to conquer or overcome. **-able** *a.* [Fr. *sur*, over; *monter*, to mount].

sur·name (sur'·nām) *n.* family name [Fr. *surnam*].

sur·pass (ser·pas') *v.t.* to go beyond; to excel; to outstrip. **-ing** *a.* excellent; in an eminent degree; exceeding others [Fr. *sur*, beyond; *passer*, to pass].

sur·plice (sur'·plis) *n.* white linen vestment worn over cassock by clergy [L.L. *superpellicium*, overgarment].

sur·plus (sur'·plus) *n.* excess beyond what is wanted; excess of income over expenditure; *a.* more than enough [L. *super*, over; *plus*, more].

sur·prise (se(r)·prīz') *v.t.* to fall or come upon unawares; to capture by unexpected attack; to strike with astonishment; *n.* act of coming upon unawares; astonishment; unexpected event, piece of news, gift, etc. **surprisal** *n.* act of surprising or state of being surprised. **surprising** *a.* **surprisingly** *adv.* [L. *super*, over; *prehendere*, to catch].

sur·re·al·ism (sa·rē'·al·iz·am) *n.* 20th cent. phase in art and literature of expressing subconscious in images without order or coherence, as in dream. **surrealist** *n.* **surrealistic** *a.* [Fr. *sur*, over; *realism*].

sur·ren·der (sa·ren'·der) *v.t.* to yield or hand over to power of another; to resign; to yield to emotion, etc.; *v.i.* to cease resistance; to give oneself up into power of another; to capitulate; *n.* act of surrendering. **-er** *n.* [L. *super*, over; *reddere*, to restore].

sur·rep·ti·tious (sur·ap·tish'·as) *a.* done by stealth; furtive; clandestine. **-ly** *adv.* [L. *surripere*, fr. *sub*, under; *rapere*, to seize].

sur·rey (sur'·i.) *n.* lightly-built, four-wheeled carriage [prob. fr. proper name].

sur·ro·gate (sur'·a·gāt) *n.* deputy or delegate; deputy who acts for bishop or chancellor of diocese. **-ship** *n.* [L. *sub*, under; *rogare*, to ask].

sur·round (sa·round') *v.t.* to be on all sides of; to encircle; (*Mil.*) to cut off from communication or retreat; **-ings** *n.* that which surrounds; *pl.* things which environ; neighborhood [L. *superundare*, to overflow].

sur·tax (sur'·taks) *n.* additional tax; *v.t.* to impose extra tax on.

sur·veil·lance (ser·vā'·lans) *n.* close watch; supervision [Fr. fr. *surveiller*, to watch over].

sur·vey (ser·vā') *v.t.* to look over; to view as from high place; to take broad, general view; to determine shape, extent, position, contour, etc. of tract of land by measurement. **survey** (sur'·vā) *n.* general view, as from high place; attentive scrutiny; measured plan or chart of any tract of country. **-or** *n.* one who surveys [L. *super*, over; *videre*, to see].

sur·vive (ser·vīv') *v.t.* to live longer than; to outlive or outlast; *v.i.* to remain alive. **survival** *n.* living longer than, or beyond life of another person, thing, or event; any rite, habit, belief, etc. remaining in existence after what justified it has passed away. **survivor** *n.* **surviving** *a.* [L. *super*, over; *vivere*, to live].

sus·cep·ti·ble (sa·sep'·ta·bl) *a.* capable of; readily impressed; sensitive **susceptibly** *adv.* **-ness** *n.* **susceptibility** *n.* capacity for catching disease, for feeling, or emotional excitment; sensitiveness; *pl.* sensitive spots in person's nature. **susceptive** *a.* receptive **susceptivity, susceptiveness** *n.* [L. *suscipere*, to take up, receive].

suspect (sa·spekt') *v.t.* to imagine existence or presence of; to imagine to be guilty; to conjecture; to mistrust. **suspect** (sus'·pekt) *n.* suspected person; *a.* inspiring distrust. **-er** *n.* [L. *suspicere*, to look at secretly].

sus·pend (sa·spend') *v.t.* to cause to hang; to bring to a stop temporarily; to debar from an office or privilege; to defer or keep undecided. **er** *n.* one who suspends; *pl.* pair of straps for holding up trousers, skirt, etc. **suspense** *n.* state of being suspended; state of uncertainty or anxiety; indecision. **suspension** *n.* act of suspending or state of being suspended; delay or deferment; temporary withdrawal from office, function or privilege. **suspensive** *a.* **suspensively** *adv.* **suspensor** *n.* **suspensory** *a.* [L. *sub*, under; *pendere*, to hang].

sus·pi·cion (sa·spish'·an) *n.* act of suspecting; imagining of something being wrong, on little evidence; doubt; mistrust; slight trace or hint. **suspicious** *a.* feeling suspicion; mistrustful; arousing suspicion. **suspiciously** *adv.* [L. *suspicere*, to look at secretly].

sus·tain (sa·stān') *v.t.* to keep from falling or sinking; to nourish or keep alive; to endure or undergo; (Law) to allow the validity of. **-able** *a.* **-er** *n.* **sustenance** (sus'·ta·nans) *n.* that which sustains (life); food, nourishment. **sustentation** *n.* **sustentative** *a.* **sustention** *n.* [L. *sustinere*, to support].

sut·ler (sut'·ler) *n.* formerly person who followed army and sold provisions, liquors, etc., to troops [Dut. *zoetelaar*, a small tradesman].

su·ture (sòò'·cher) *n.* sewing up of wound; a stitch; connection or seam, between bones of skull; *v.t.* to join by stitching. **sutural** *a.* united by sutures [L. *suere*, *sutum*, to sew].

su·ze·rain (sòò'·za·ran, ·rān) *n.* feudal lord;

paramount ruler. **-ty** *n.* authority or dominion of **suzerain** [Fr. *suzerain*, paramount].

svelte (svelt) *a.* supple; lithe; slender [Fr.].

swab (swȧb) *n.* mop for rubbing over floors, decks, etc.; bit of cotton on stick for applying medicine, cleaning parts of body, etc. *v.t.* to clean with mop or swab. *pr.p.* **-bing.** *pa.t.* and *pa.p.* **-bed. -ber** *n.* [Dut. *zwabber*, ship's drudge].

swad·dle (swȧd'·l) *v.t.* to bind or wrap as with bandages; *n.* the cloth wrapping [O.E. *swathy* a bandage].

swag (swag) *n.* (*Colloq.*) bundle; stolen goods or booty; [O.N. *swagga*, to walk unsteadily].

swage (swāj) *n.* tool for bending, marking, or shaping metal. *v.t.* [L.L. *soca*, a rope].

swag·ger (swag'·er) *v.i.* to walk with a conceited or defiant strut; to boast or brag; *n.* defiant or conceited bearing; boastfulness. **-er** *n.* **-ing** *a.* [perh. fr. *swag*].

Swa·hi·li (swȧ·hē'·li·) *n.* people of mixed Bantu and Arab stock, occupying Zanzibar and adjoining territory; their language. (Poetic) **-an** *a.* [Ar. = coast-man].

swain (swān) *n.* (*Poetic*) country lad; rustic lover; suitor [O.N. *sveinn*, a boy, a servant].

swal·low (swȧl'·ō) *n.* small migratory, passerine, insectivorous bird. **-tail** *n.* forked tail; kind of butterfly [O.E. *swealwe*].

swal·low (swȧl'·ō) *v.t.* to receive into stomach through mouth and throat; to absorb; (*Colloq.*) to accept without criticism or scruple; *v.i.* to perform act of swallowing; *n.* act of swallowing; amount taken down at one gulp. **-er** *n.* [O.E. *swelgan*].

swam (swam) *pa.t.* of **swim**.

swamp (swȧmp, swawmp) *n.* tract of wet, spongy, low-lying ground; marsh; *v.t.* to cause to fill with water, as boat; *v.i.* to overwhelm; to sink. **-y** *a.* [Scand.].

swan (swȧn) *n.* large, web-footed bird of goose family, having very long, gracefully curving neck. **-nery** *n.* place where swans are bred. **-'s-down** *n.* fine, soft feathers on swan, used for powder puffs, etc.; thick cotton or woolen cloth with soft nap on one side.. **-song.** song which, according to myth, swan sings before dying; [O.E.].

swank (swangk) *v.i.* (*Slang*) to show off; to swagger; *n.* (*Slang*) style; swagger; *a.* (*Slang*) ostentations; showy. **-y** *a.*

swap (swȧp) *v.t.* and *v.i.* to exchange; to barter; *n.* exchange. *pr.p.* **-ping.** *pa.p.* and *pa.t.* **-ped.** Also **swop** [M.E. *swappe*, strike].

sward (swawrd) *n.* land covered with short green grass; turf; *v.t.* to cover with sward. **-ed** *a.* [O.E. *sweard*, skin of bacon].

swarm (swawrm) *n.* large number of insects esp. in motion; crowd; throng; great multitude or throng; *v.i.* to collect in large numbers [O.E. *swearm*].

swarm (swawrm) *v.i.* to climb with arms and legs [etym. uncertain].

swarth·y (swawr'·THi·) *a.* dark in hue; of dark complexion [O.E. *sweart*].

swash·buck·ler (swȧsh'·buk·ler) *n.* swaggering bully. **swashbuckling** *a.* [imit.].

swas·ti·ka (swȧs'·ti·kȧ) *n.* symbol in form of Greek cross with ends of arms bent at right angles, all in same direction, thus 卐; used as badge of Nazi party [Sans. *svasti*, well being].

swat (swȧt) *v.t.* (*Colloq.*) to hit smartly; to kill, esp. insects. *pr.p.* **-ting.** *pa.t.*, *pa.p.* **-ted.**

swatch (swȧch) *n.* piece of cloth, cut as a sample of quality [var. of *swath*].

swath (swȧth, swawth) *n.* line of hay or grain cut by scythe or mowing machine; Also **swathe** (swāTH) [O.E. *swaeth*, a track].

swathe (swāTH) *v.t.* to bind with bandage; to envelop in wraps; *n.* bandage; folded or draped band [O.E. *swathian*].

sway (swā) *v.t.* to cause to incline to one side

or the other; to influence or direct; *v.i.* to incline or be drawn to one side or the other; to swing unsteadily; to totter; *n.* swaying or swinging movement; control. **-er** *n.* **-back** *a.* having inward curve of the spine [M.E. *sweyen*].

swear (swār) *v.t.* to utter, affirm or declare on oath; *v.i.* to utter solemn declaration with appeal to God for truth of what is affirmed; (*Law*) to give evidence on oath; to use name of God or sacred things profanely; to curse. *pa.p.* **sworn.** *pa.t.* **swore. -er** *n.* **-ing** *n.* **to swear by**, (*Colloq.*) to have great confidence in [O.E. *swerian*].

sweat (swet) *n.* moisture excreted from skin; perspiration; moisture exuding from any substance; state of sweating; (*Colloq.*) state of anxiety; *v.t.* to cause to excrete moisture from skin; to employ at wrongfully low wages; *v.i.* to excrete moisture; (*Colloq.*) to toil or drudge at. **-er** *n.* warm knitted jersey or jacket. **-y** *a.* damp with sweat; causing sweat; like sweat. **-ily** *adv.* **-iness** *n.* [O.E. *swat*].

Swede (swēd) *n.* native of Sweden. **Swedish** *a.* pert. to Sweden; *n.* language of Swedes.

sweep (swēp) *v.t.* to pass brush or broom over to remove loose dirt; to pass rapidly over, with brushing motion; to scan rapidly; *v.i.* to pass with swiftness or violence; to move with dignity; to extend in a curve; to effect cleaning with a broom; *n.* act of sweeping; reach of a stroke; curving or wide-flung gesture, movement, or line; powerful drive forward, covering large area; long, heavy oar, used either to steer or to propel. *pa.p.* and *pa.t.* **swept. -er** *n.* **-ing** *a.* moving swiftly; of great scope; comprehensive. **-ingly** *adv.* — **stake(s)** *n.* gambling on race or contest, in which participators' stakes are pooled, and apportioned to drawers of winning horses [O.E. *swapan*].

sweet (swēt) *a.* tasting like sugar; having agreeable taste; fragrant; melodious; pleasing to eye; gentle; affectionate; dear or beloved; likeable; *n.* sweetness; darling; *pl.* confections. **-en** *v.t.* to make sweet, pleasing, or kind. **-ening** *n.* act of making sweet; ingredient which sweetens. **-ly** *adv.* **-ness** *n.* **-bread** *n.* pancreas or thymus of animal, as food. **-heart** *n.* lover or beloved person; darling. **meat** *n.* confection; candy. **-pea** *n.* climbing plant with fragrant flowers. **-potato** *n.* sweet, starchy tuber [O.E. *swete*].

swell (swel) *v.t.* to increase size, sound, etc.; to dilate; to augment; *v.i.* to grow larger; to expand; to rise in waves; to grow louder; to be filled to bursting point with some emotion. *n.* act of swelling; increase in bulk, intensity, importance, etc.; slight rise in ground level; slow heaving and sinking of sea after storm; *pa.p.* **swollen** or **swelled.** *pa.t.* **-ed. -ing** *n.* act of swelling; state of being swollen; prominence or protuberance; (*Med.*) enlargement [O.E. *swellan*].

swel·ter (swel'·ter) *v.i.* to be oppressive, or oppressed, with heat; to perspire profusely; *n.* heated or sweaty state. **-ing** *a.* **sweltry** *a.* [O.E. *sweltan*, to swoon or perish].

swept (swept) *pa.t.* and *pa.p.* of **sweep**.

swerve (swurv) *v.i.* to depart from straight line; to deviate; *v.t.* to cause to bend or turn aside; *n.* act of swerving [O.E. *sweorfan*, to rub, file].

swift (swift) *a.* quick; rapid; prompt; moving quickly. **-ly** *adv.* **-ness** *n.* speed; *a* quick-flying migratory bird, resembling swallow; common newt [O.E. *swifan*, to move quickly].

swig (swig) *v.t.* and *v.i.* (*Colloq.*) to gulp down; to drink in long drafts; *n.* long draft *pr.p.* **-ging.** *pa.p.*, *pa.t.* **-ged** [O.E. *swelgan*, to swallow].

swill (swill) *v.t.* and *v.i.* to drink greedily;

n. act of swilling; pig food; hogwash slops. **-er** *n.* [O.E. *swilian*, to wash].

swim (swim) *v.i.* to propel oneself in water by means of hands, feet, or fins, etc.; to float on surface; to move with gliding motion, resembling swimming; *v.t.* to cross or pass over by swimming; to cause to swim; *n.* act of swimming; spell of swimming. *pr.p.* **-ming**. *pa.p.* **swum**. *pa.t.* **swam. -mer** *n.* **-mingly** *adv.* easily, successfully [O.E. *swimmen*, to be in motion].

swim (swim) *v.i.* to be dizzy or giddy; *n.* dizziness or unconsciousness *pr.p.* **-ming**. *pa.p.* **swum**; *pa.t.* **swam**. [O.E. *swima*, to faint].

swin·dle (swin'·dl) *v.t.* and *v.i.* to cheat or defraud; to obtain by fraud; *n.* act of defrauding [Ger. *schwindeln*, to cheat].

swine (swīn) *n. sing.* and *pl.* thick-skinned domestic animal, fed for its flesh; pig; hog. **—herd** *n.* one who tends swine. **swinish** *a.* like swine; gross, brutal [O.E. *swin*].

swing (swing) *v.i.* to move to and fro, esp. as suspended body; to sway; to turn on pivot; to progress with easy, swaying gait; (*Colloq.*) to be executed by hanging; to wheel around; *v.t.* to attach so as to hang freely; to move to and fro; to cause to wheel about a point; to brandish; *n.* act of swinging or causing to swing; extent, sweep, or power of anything that is swung; motion to and fro; seat suspended by ropes, on which one may swing. *pa.p.* and *pa.t.* **swung. -er** *n.* **-ing** *a.* moving to and fro; moving with vigor and rhythm. **-ingly** *adv.* [O.E. *swingan*, to swing, whirl].

swing (swing) *n.* (*Mus.*) kind of jazz music [O.E. *swingan*].

swipe (swīp) *v.t.* and *v.i.* to strike with a wide, sweeping blow, as with a bat, racket, etc.; (*Slang*) to steal; *n.* sweeping stroke [O.E. *swipian*, to beat].

swirl (swurl) *n.* eddy of wind or water; whirling motion; a twist of something; *v.i.* to whirl; *v.t.* to carry along with whirling motion [O.N. *svirla*, to whirl round].

swish (swish) *n.* whistling or hissing sound; *v.i.* to move with hissing or rustling sound.

Swiss (swis) *n. sing.* and *pl.* native of Switzerland; people of Switzerland; *a.* pert. to Switzerland or the Swiss [O. Ger. *Swiz*].

switch (swich) *n.* flexible twig or rod; tress of false hair; on railway, movable rail for transferring train from one set of tracks to another; (*Elect.*) device for making, breaking, or transferring, electric current; act of switching; *v.t.* to strike with switch; to wisk; to shift or shunt (train) to another track; (*Elect.*) to turn electric current off or on with switch; to transfer one's thoughts to another subject; to transfer. **-er** *n.* **—like** *a.* **-back** *n.* zigzag method of ascending slopes, **-board** *n.* set of switches at telephone exchange [Old Dut. *swick*, a whip].

swiv·el (swiv'·l) *n.* ring turning on pivot, forming connection between two pieces of mechanism and enabling one to rotate independently of the other; *v.i.* to swing on pivot; *v.t.* to turn as on pivot [O.E. *swifan*, to revolve].

swol·len (swōl'·an) *a.* swelled. *pa.p.* of **swell**.

swoon (swóón) *v.i.* to faint; *n.* fainting fit [O.E. *swogan*, to sigh deeply].

swoop (swóón) *v.t.* to catch up with sweeping motion (with 'up'); *v.i.* to sweep down swiftly upon prey, as hawk or eagle; *n.* sweeping downward flight [O.E. *swapan*, to rush].

swop. See **swap**.

sword (sōrd, sawrd) *n.* weapon for cutting or thrusting, having long blade; emblem of judicial punishment or of authority. **-fish** *n.* large fish with sword-like upper jaw. **-play** *n.* fencing. **-sman** *n.* one skillful with sword.

—smanship *n.* [O.E. *sword*].

swore (swōr) *pa.t.* of **swear**.

sworn *pa.p.* of **swear**.

swum (swum) *pa.p.* of **swim**.

swung (swung) *pa.p.* and *pa.t.* of **swing**.

syb·a·rite (sib'·a·rīt) *n.* person devoted to luxury and pleasure. **sybaritic, sybaritical** *a.* [L. *Sybaris*, Greek city].

syc·a·more (sik'·a·mōr) *n.* tree with broad leaves, allied to plane tree and maple; kind of fig tree of Egypt and Asia Minor [Gk. *sukon*, fig; *moron*, black mulberry].

syc·o·phant (sik'·a·fant) *n.* flatterer, or one who fawns on rich or famous; parasite; *a.* servile; obsequious. **sychophancy, -ism** *n.* **-ic, -ical, -ically** *adv.* **-ish** *a.* [Gk. *sukophantēs*, to show].

syl·la·ble (sil'·a·bl) *n.* sound uttered at single effort of voice, and constituting word, or part of word; *v.t.* to utter in syllables; to articulate. **syllabic, syllabical** *a.* pert. to, or consisting of, a syllable(s). **syllabically** *adv.* **syllabicate, syllabify, syllabize**, *v.t.* to divide into syllables [Gk. *sullabē*, that which is held together].

syl·la·bus (sil'·a·bas) *n.* outline or program of main points in a course of lectures, etc. [Gk. *sun*, together; *lambanein*, to take].

syl·lo·gism (sil'·a·jizm) *n.* formal statement of argument, consisting of three parts, major premise, minor premise, and conclusion, conclusion following naturally from premises. **syllogize** *v.t.* and *v.i.* to reason by means of syllogisms. **syllogization** *n.* **syllogizer** *n.* **syllogistic, syllogistical** *a.* [Gk. *sullogismos*, a reckoning together].

sylph (silf) *n.* elemental spirit of the air; fairy or sprite; graceful girl. **-id** *n.* little sylph. **-like** *a.* graceful [Fr. *sylphe*].

syl·van (sil'·van) *a.* forest-like; abounding in forests; pert. to or inhabiting the woods [L. *silva*, a wood].

sym·bi·o·sis (sim·bī·ō'·sis) *n.* (*Biol.*) living together of different organisms for mutual benefit, as in the lichens. **symbiotic** *a.* **symbiont** *n.* organism living in symbiosis [Gk. *sun*, together; *bios*, life].

sym·bol (sim'·bal) *n.* something that represents something else, esp. concrete representation of moral or intellectual quality; emblem; type character or sign used to indicate relation or operation in mathematics; in chemistry, letter or letters standing for atom of element. **-ic, -ical, -ically** *adv.* **-ize** *v.t.* to stand for, or represent; to represent by a symbol or symbols. **-ism** *n.* representation by symbols; system of symbols; in art and literature, tendency to represent emotions by means of symbols, and to invest ordinary objects with imaginative meanings. **-ist** *n.* one who uses symbols; adherent of symbolism in art and literature [Gk. *sumbolon*, a token].

sym·me·try (sim'·a·tri·) *n.* due proportion between several parts of object; exact correspondence of opposite sides of an object to each other. **symmetric, symmetrical** *a.* **symmetricalness** *n.* **symmetrize** *v.t.* [Gk. *sun*, together; *metron*, measure].

sym·pa·thy (sim'·pa·thi·) *n.* fellow feeling, esp. feeling for another person in pain or grief; sharing of emotion, interest, desire, etc.; compassion or pity. **sympathetic(al)** *a.* exhibiting or expressing sympathy; compassionate; congenial; (*Med.*) denoting a portion of the nerve system in body. **sympathetically** *adv.* **sympathize** *v.i.* **sympathizer** *n.* [Gk. *sun*, together; *pathos*, feeling].

sym·pho·ny (sim'·fa·ni·) *n.* (*Mus.*) composition for full orchestra, consisting of four contrasted sections or movements. **symphonic** *a.* **symphonist** *n.* composer of symphonies. [Gk. *sun*, together; *phōnē*, sound].

WEBSTER Q–S

sym·po·si·um (sim·pō'·zi·ạm) *n.* gathering, esp. one at which interchange or discussion of ideas takes place; series of short articles by several writers dealing with common topic. *pl.* **symposia** [Gk. *sun*, together; *posis*, a drinking].

symp·tom (simp'·tạm) *n.* (*Med.*) perceptible change in body or its functions, which indicates disease; sign of the existence of something. **-atic, -atical** *a.* [Gk. *sun*, together; *ptōma*, a fall].

syn- (sin) *prefix* from Gk. *sun*, meaning with, together, at the same time; becomes *sym-*, before *p, b*, and *m*, and *syl-* before *l*.

syn·a·gogue (sin'·ạ·gȧg) *n.* congregation of Jews met for worship; Jewish place of worship. **synagogical** (sin·ạ·gȧj'·ạ·kạl) *a.* [Gk. *sun*, together; *agein*, to lead].

syn·chro·nize (sing'·krạ·nīz) *v.i.* to agree in time; to be simultaneous; *v.t.* to cause to occur at the same time; to run machines at exactly the same speed. **synchronization** *n.* **synchronism** *n.* concurrence of events in time; simultaneousness. **synchronal** *a.* **synchronous** *a.* [Gk. *sun*, together; *chrones*, time].

syn·chro·tron (sing'·krạ·trȧn) *n.* scientific machine, used in atom research, for accelerating electrons to very high speeds [Gk. *sun*, together; *chronos*, time].

syn·co·pate (sing'·kạ·pāt) *v.t.* (*Gram.*) to contract, as a word, by taking one or more sounds or syllables from middle; in music, to alter rhythm by accenting a usually unaccented note, or causing the accent to fall on a rest, or silent beat. **syncopation** *n.* [Gk. *sun*, together; *kopē*, a cutting].

syn·cope (sing'·kạ·pē) *n.* the omission of one or more letters from the middle of a word; (*Med.*) a fainting or swooning. **syncopal, syncopic** *a.* [see **syncopate**].

syn·dic (sin'·dik) *n.* magistrate or government official having different duties in different countries; legal representative chosen to act as agent for corporation or company. **-ate** *n.* council of syndics; body of persons associated to carry out enterprise; association of industrialists or financiers formed to carry out industrial project, or to acquire monopoly in certain goods; *v.t.* to control by a syndicate; to publish news, etc. simultaneously in several periodicals owned by one syndicate [Gk. *sundikos*, an advocate].

syn·ec·do·che (si·nek'·dạ·kē) *n.* (*Rhet.*) figure of speech by which the whole is put for the part, or a part for the whole. **synecdochic, synecdochical** *a.* [Gk.].

syn·od (sin'·ạd) *n.* an assembly of ecclesiatus; convention or council. **-al, -ic, -ical,** *a.* **-ically** *adv.* [Gk. *sunodos*, assembly].

syn·o·nym (sin'·ạ·nim) *n.* word which has same meaning as another. **-ous** *a.* **-ously** *adv.* [Gk. *sun*, together; *onoma*, name].

syn·op·sis (si·nȧp'·sis) *n.* general outlook, view; summary. *pl.* **synopses** (sēz). **synoptic, synoptical** *a.* **synoptically** *adv.* [Gk. *sun*, together; *opsis*, view].

syn·tax (sin'·taks) *n.* rules governing sentence construction. **syntactic, syntactical** *a.* **syntactically** *adv.* [Gk. *sun*, together; *tassein*, to put in order].

syn·the·sis (sin'·thạ·sis) *n.* combination or putting together; combining of parts into whole (opp. to *analysis*); (*Chem.*) uniting of elements to form compound; (*Gram.*) building up of words into sentences, and of sentences into one of a more complex nature. *pl.* **syntheses** (·sēz). **synthetic, synthetical** *a.* pert. to, consisting in synthesis; not derived from nature; artificial; spurious. **synthetically** *adv.* **synthesize, synthetize** *v.t.* **synthesist, synthetist** *n.* [Gk. *sun*, together; *thesis*, a placing].

syph·i·lis (sif'·ạ·lis) *n.* contagious venereal disease. **syphilitic** *a.* [fr. *Syphilus*, shepherd in Latin poem (1530)].

sy·phon. See **siphon.**

Syr·i·a (sir'·i·ạ) *n.* country in W. Asia. **-c** *n.* language of Syria. **-n** *n.* native of Syria; *a.* pert. to Syria.

syr·inge (sạ·rinj' sir'·inj) *n.* tube and piston serving to draw in and then expel fluid; *v.t.* to inject by means of syringe [Gk. *surinx*, a pipe or reed].

syr·inx (sir'·ingks) *n.* (*Mus.*) Pan-pipe; (*Anat.*) the Eustachian tube; vocal organ of birds. *pl.* **-es, syringes** (gēz). **syringeal** (si·rin'·je·ạl) *a.* [Gk.*surinx*, a reed or pipe].

syr·up, sirup (sir'·ạp) *n.* fluid separated from sugar in process of refining. **-y** *a.* [O.Fr. *syrop*, fr. Ar. *sharab*, a beverage].

sys·tem (sis'·tạm) *n.* assemblage of objects arranged after some distinct method, usually logical or scientific; whole scheme of created things regarded as forming one complete whole; universe; organization; classification; set of doctrines or principles; the body as functional unity. **-atic, -atical** *a.* **-atically** *adv.* **-atize, -ize** *v.t.* to reduce to system; to arrange methodically. **-atization, -ization** *n.* [L.L. *systema*, organized whole].

sys·to·le (sis'·tạ·lē) *n.* contraction of heart and arteries for expelling blood and carrying on circulation. opp. to *diastole;* (*Gram.*) shortening of long syllable. **systolic** *a.* contracting [Gk. fr. *sun*, together, *stellein*, to place].

T

tab (tab) *n.* small tag or flap; a label [fr. *tape*].

tab·ard (tab'·erd) *n.* sleeveless tunic worn over armor by knights; tunic emblazoned with royal arms, worn by heralds. Also **taberd.**

tab·by (tab'·i·) *n.* stout kind of watered silk; striped cat, esp. female; old maid; a malicious gossip; *a.* striped; *v.t.* to give watered finish to, as silk [Ar. *attabi*, a watered silk].

tab·er·nac·le (tab'·er·nak·l) *n.* movable shelter esp. for religious worship by Israelites; place for worship; human body [L. *tabernaculum*, a small tent].

tab·la·ture (tab'·lạ·cher) *n.* painting on ceiling or wall; mental picture [fr. *table*].

ta·ble (tā'·bl) *n.* smooth flat surface of wood, etc. supported by legs, as article of furniture for working at, or serving meals; any flat surface, esp. slab bearing inscription; food served on table; systematic arrangement of figures, facts, etc. as *multiplication table;* index, scheme, or schedule; synopsis; one of the divisions of decalogue; upper, flat surface of gemstone; *a.* pert. to or shaped like a table; *v.t.* to form into a table or catalogue; to lay down, as money in payment of a bill; to postpone for subsequent consideratioon. **-spoon** *n.* a large spoon for serving, measuring, etc., holding ½ fluid ounce. — **tennis** *n.* game of indoor tennis played on a table; ping-pong; **-ware** *n.* utensils (incl. china, glass and silver) for table use [L. *tabula*, a board].

tab·leau (tab'·lō) *n.* vivid representation of scene in history, literature, art, etc. by group of persons appropriately dressed and posed. *pl.* **tableaux** (tab'·lōz). — **vivant** (tab'·lō·vē'·vȧnt) *n.* living picture; tableau [Fr. *tableau*, a picture].

tab·let (tab'·lit) *n.* anything flat on which to write; pad; slab of stone with inscription;

small, compressed solid piece of medication, detergent, etc. [dim. of *table*].

tab·loid (tab'·loid) *n.* illustrated newspaper, giving topical and usually sensational events in compressed form; compressed lozenge.

ta·boo (ta·bóo) *n.* system among natives of the Pacific islands by which certain objects and persons are set aside as sacred or accursed; political, social, or religious prohibition; *a.* prohibited; proscribed; *v.t.* to forbid the use of; to ostracize [Polynesian *tapu*, consecrated].

ta·bor (tā'·ber) *n.* small drum like a tambourine. **-et** *n.* small tabor; embroidery frame; low cushioned stool [O.Fr. *tabour*, a drum].

tab·u·lar (tab'·ya·ler) *a.* pert. to, or resembling, a table in shape; having a broad, flat top; arranged systematically in rows or columns. **-ize** *v.t.* to tabulate. **-ly** *adv.* **tabulate** *v.t.* to put or form into a table, scheme or synopsis [L. *tabula*, a table].

ta·chom·e·ter (ta·kăm'·a·ter) *n.* instrument for measurement of speed [Gk. *tachus*, swift; *metron*, a measure].

tac·it (tas'·it) *a.* implied, but not expressed; silent; **-ly** *adv.* **-urn** *a.* silent; reserved of speech. **-urnity** *n.* **-urnly** *adv.* [L. *tacitus*].

tack (tak) *n.* small sharp-pointed nail; long stitch; ship's course in relation to position of her sails; course of action; *v.t.* to fasten with long, loose stitches; to append; to nail with; *v.t.* to change ship's course by moving position of sails; to change policy. **-er** *n.* **-iness** *n.* stickiness. **-y** *a.* sticky; viscous [O.Fr. *tache*, nail].

tack (tak) *n.* food; fore.

tack·le (tak'·l) *n.* mechanism of ropes and pulleys for raising heavy weights; rigging, etc. of ship; equipment or gear; (*Football*) move by player to grasp and stop opponent; *v.t.* to harness; to lay hold of; to undertake; (*Football*) to seize and stop. **tackling** *n.* gear; rigging of a ship. — **block** *n.* pulley [Scand. *taka*, to grasp].

tact (takt) *n.* intuitive understanding of people; awareness of right thing to do or say to avoid giving offense. **-ful** *a.* **-fully** *adv.* **-ile** *a.* pert. to sense of touch; capable of being touched or felt; tangible. **-less** *a.* wanting in tact. **-ual** *a.* pert. to sense of touch [L. *tangere*, *tactum*, to touch].

tac·tics (tak'·tiks) *n. sing.* science of disposing of military, naval, and air units to the best advantage; adroit management of situation. **tactic, -al** *a.* **tactically** *adv.* **tactician** *n.* [Gk. *taktika*, tactics].

tad·pole (tad'·pōl) *n.* young of frog in its first state before gills and tail are absorbed [O.E. *tad*, a toad; and *poll*].

taf·fe·ta (taf'·a·ta) *n.* light-weight glossy silk of plain weave. Also **taffety** [Pers. *taftah*, woven].

tag (tag) *n.* metal point at end of a shoelace, etc.; tab on back of boot; tie-on label; appendage; catchword; hackneyed phrase; ragged end; refrain; game in which one player chases and tries to touch another; *v.t.* to fit with tags; to add on; (*Colloq.*) to follow behind. *pr.p.* **-ging.** *pa.t.* and *pa.p.* **ged.** [Scand. *tagg*, a spike].

Ta·hi·tian (ta·hē'·ti·an, shan) *a.* pert. to island of Tahiti or its inhabitants.

Ta·ic (tä'·ik) *a.* pert. to inhabitants of Indo-China or their language; *n.* [Chin.].

tail (tāl) *n.* (*Law*) a limitation of ownership; entail; *a.* being entailed. **-age** *n.* [Fr. *taille*, cutting].

tail (tāl) *n.* flexible prolongation of animal's spine; back, lower, or inferior part of anything; (*Colloq.*) *pl.* reverse side of coin; queue; train of attendants; (*Aero.*) group of stabilizing planes or fins at rear of airplane;

pl. tail-coat; *v.t.* to furnish with tail; to extend in line; to trail. **-board** *n.* movable board at back of cart. **-coat** *n.* man's evening dress coat with tails. **-ed** *a.* **-less** *a.* **-light** *n.* usu. red rear light of vehicle. **-piece** *n.* ebony strip below bridge of violin to which strings are attached; ornamental design marking close of chapter in book. **-plane** *n.* (*Aero.*) stabilizing surface at rear of aircraft [O.E. *taegl*, a tail].

tai·lor (tāl'·er) *n.* one who makes clothes; *v.t.* and *v.i.* to make men's suits, women's costumes, etc. **-ing** *n.* work of a tailor. **-less** *a.* **-made** *a.* made by tailor; plain in style and fitting perfectly [O.Fr. *taillier*, to cut].

taint (tānt) *v.t.* to impregnate with something poisonous; to contaminate; *v.i.* to be infected with incipient putrefaction; *n.* touch of corruption; (*Fig.*) moral blemish [L. *tingere*, *tinctum*, to dye].

take (tāk) *v.t.* to grasp; to capture; to receive; to remove; to win; to inhale; to choose; to assume; to suppose; to photograph; *v.i.* to be effective; to catch; to please; to go; to direct course of; to resort to; *pr.p.* **taking.** *pa.t.* **took.** *pa.p.* **-n.** *n.* quantity of fish caught at one time; one of several movie shots of same scene; act of taking; receipts *n.* (*Slang*) fraud; hoax. —**off** *n.* (*Colloq.*) mimicry; caricature; (*Aero.*) moment when aircraft leaves ground. *n.* **taking** *n.* act of taking or gaining possession; agitation; *pl.* cash receipts of shop, theater, etc.; *a.* attractive; infectious. **takingly** *adv.* **takingness** *n.* quality of being attractive [Scand. *taka*, to seize].

talc (talk) *n.* hydrated silica of magnesia; fine, slightly perfumed powder; mineral with soapy feel. **-ose** *a.* pert. to or composed of talc. **-um** *n.* powdered talc, as toilet powder [Ar. *talq*.]

tale (tāl) *n.* narrative; story; what is told; false report; gossip; **-bearer** *n.* one who spitefully informs against another [O.E. *talu*, a reckoning].

tal·ent (tal'·ant) *n.* ancient weight and denomination of money; faculty; special or outstanding ability. **-ed** *a.* gifted [Gk. *talanton*].

tal·is·man (tal'·is·man) *n.* object endowed with magical power of protecting the wearer from harm; lucky charm. **-ic, -al** *a.* [Gk. *telesma*, payment].

talk (tawk) *v.t.* and *v.i.* to converse; to speak; to discuss; to persuade; *n.* conversation; short dissertation; rumor; gossip. **-ative** *a.* loquacious; chatty. **-atively** *adv.* **-ativeness** *n.* **-er** *n.* **-ie** *n.* (*Colloq.*) a sound film. **-ing** *a.* capable of speaking [M.E. *talken*, to speak].

tall (tawl) *a.* high in stature; lofty; (*Slang*) excessive; exaggerated. **-ness** *n.*

tal·low (tal'·ō) *n.* animal fat melted down and used in manufacture of candles, etc.; *v.t.* to smear with tallow. **-ish** *a.* pasty; greasy. **-like, -y,** *a.* [M.E. *talgh*, tallow].

tal·ly (tal'·i·) *n.* something on which a score is kept; the score; business account; match; identity label; *v.t.* to score; to furnish with a label; *v.i.* to correspond; to agree. *pa.t.* and *pa.p.* **tallied. tallier** [L. *talea*, a slip of wood].

Tal·mud (tal'·mud) *n.* standard collection of texts and commentaries on Jewish religious law. **-ic(al)** *a.* **-ist** *n.* student of the Talmud. **-istic** *a.* [Aramaic *talmud*, instruction].

tal·on (tal'·an) *n.* hooked claw of bird of prey. **-ed** *a.* having talons [L. *talus*, the heel].

tam·a·risk (tam'·a·risk) *n.* evergreen shrub with pink and white flowers [L. *tamarix*].

tam·bour (tam'·boor) *n.* small flat drum; circular embroidery-frame; piece of embroidery worked in metal threads on tambour [Fr. = a drum].

tam·bour·ine (tam·ba·rēn') *n.* round, shallow, single-sided drum with jingling metal disks, used to accompany Spanish dances [Fr.].

tame (tām) a. domesticated; subdued; insipid; dull; cultivated; v.t. to domesticate; to discipline; to curb; to reclaim. **-ability, tamability, -ableness** n. **-able** a. **-ly** adv. **-ness** n. **-r** n. [O.E. tam, tame].

tam o' shan·ter (tam'·a·shan'·ter) n. round flat cap, abbrev. **tam** [fr. Burns's poem].

tamp (tamp) v.t. to ram down; to plug a shot-hole with clay during blasting operations.

tam·per (tam'·per) v.i. to meddle; to interfere with; to alter or influence with malicious intent. **-er** n. [var. of temper].

tam·pon (tam'·pan) n. (surg.) a plug of cotton, etc. to close a wound, retard bleeding [Fr.].

tan (tan) n. bark of oak, etc. bruised to extract tannic acid for tanning leather; yellowish brown color; sunburn; v.t. to convert skins into leather by soaking in tannic acid; to make bronze-colored; (Colloq.) to thrash; v.i. to become sunburned. pr.p. **-ning.** pa.t. and pa.p. **-ned. -nate** n. (Chem.) salt of tannic acid. **-ner** n. one who works in tannery. **-nery** n. place where leather is made. **-nic** a. pert. to tannin. **-nin** n. now called **tannic acid.** **-ning** n. [Fr. tannique fr. tannin, tan].

tan·dem (tan'·dam) adv. one behind the other; n. pair of horses so harnessed; a bicycle for two people [L. tandem, at length].

tang (tang) n. a projection or prong (of a tool) which connects with the handle; a pungent smell or taste; a distinctive flavor; v.t. to furnish (a tool) with a tang. **-ed, -y** a. [Scand. tange, a point].

tan·gent (tan'·jant) n. (Geom.) line which touches curve but, when produced, does not cut it; a. touching but not intersecting. **tangency, tangence** n. state of touching. **tangential** a. pert. to, or in direction of, a tangent; digressing. **tangentially** adv. [L. tangere, to touch].

tan·ge·rine (tan·ja·rēn') n. small sweet orange originally grown near Tangiers.

tan·gi·ble (tan'·ji·bl) a. perceptible by the touch; palpable; concrete. **tangibility** n. **tangibility** adv. [L. tangere, to touch].

tan·gle (tang'·gl) n. knot of raveled threads, hair, etc.; confusion; v.t. to form into a confused mass; to muddle.

tan·go (tang'·gō) n. S. American dance of Spanish origin in two-four time [Sp.].

tank (tangk) n. large basin, cistern, or reservoir for storing liquids or gas; part of a railway engine, car, etc. where water, gas, etc. is stored; a mechanically propelled bullet-proof heavily armored vehicle with caterpillar treads; v.t. to store or immerse in a tank. **-age** n. storage of water, oil, gas, etc. in a tank; cost of this; liquid capacity of tank; fertilizing agent from refuse. **-er** n. vessel designed to carry liquid cargo [L. stagnum, a pool].

tank·ard (tang'·kerd) n. large drinking vessel, with lid and handle [O.Fr. tancquard, drinking-vessel].

tan·nin See tan.

tan·sy (tan'·si·) n. common perennial plant used in medicine [athanasia, immortality].

tan·ta·lize (tan'·ta·līz) v.t. to torment by keeping just out of reach something ardently desired; to tease. **tantalizing** a. provocative; teasing [fr. Tantalus, Gr. Myth.].

tan·ta·lum (tan'·ta·lam) n. (Chem.) rare metallic element, symbol **Ta,** used for filaments of electric lamps, chemical apparatus, and surgical instruments [fr. Tantalus].

tan·ta·mount (tan'·ta·mount) a. equivalent in value or significance [L. tantus, so much].

tan·trum (tan'·tram) n. fit of bad temper.

Tao·ism (tou·izm) n. a Chinese philosophical and religious system founded on the doctrines of Lao-tsze. **Taoist** n. **Taoistic** a. [Chin. tao, a way].

tap (tap) v.t. to strike lightly; to fix patch of leather or metal on shoe; v.i. to strike gentle blow. pr.p. **-ping.** pa.p. **-ped.** n. a rap; pl. military signal for lights out; leather patch or piece of metal on shoe sole. — **dance** n. a dance step audibly tapped out with the feet. **-dance** v.i. [imit.].

tap (tap) n. hole, pipe, or screw device with valve, through which liquid is drawn; liquor of particular brewing in a cask; instrument of hardened steel for cutting internal screwheads; (Elect.) connection made at intermediate point on circuit; v.t. to pierce to let fluid flow out, as from a cask, tree, etc.; to furnish (cask) with tap; (Surg.) to draw off fluid from body, as from lung, abdomen, etc.; to listen in deliberately on telephone conversation; pr.p. **-ping.** pa.p. **-ped. -per** n. one who taps. **-room** n. bar, of inn or hotel, for sale of liquor. **-root** n. the root of a plant which goes straight down into earth without dividing. **on tap,** of liquor, drawn from cask, not bottled; (Fig.) at hand [O.E. taeppa].

tape (tāp) n. narrow piece of woven material used for tying, fastening clothes, etc.; strip of this marking finish line on racetrack; strip of paper used in a printing telegraph instrument, etc., strip of paper or linen marked off in inches used for measuring; v.t. to tie or fasten with tape; to measure. — **measure** n. strip marked in inches. **-worm** n. parasite found in alimentary canal of vertebrates [O.E. taeppe, a band].

ta·per (tā'·per) n. long wick for lighting candles; a slender candle; v.i. to narrow gradually toward one end; v.t. to cause to narrow. **-ing** a. narrowing gradually [O.E. tapor].

tap·es·try (tap'·as·tri·) n. fabric covering for furniture, walls, etc. woven by needles, not in shuttles [Fr. tapis, carpet].

tap·i·o·ca (tap·i·ō'·ka) n. starchy gramular substance used for desserts, thickening, etc. [Braz. tipi, residue; ok, to press out].

ta·pir (tā'·per) n. ungulate mammal with piglike body and flexible proboscis [Braz.].

tap·is (tap'·ē, tap'·is) n. carpeting; tapestry [Fr. tapis, carpet].

tap·pet (tap'·it) n. small lever [O.Fr. tapper, to rap].

tar (tar) n. (Colloq.) sailor [fr. tarpaulin].

tar (tår) n. dark-brown or black viscid liquid, a by-product in destructive distillation of wood (esp. pine), coal, etc., used for waterproofing, road-laying, and as antiseptic and preservative; v.t. to smear, cover, or treat with tar. pr.p. **-ring.** pa.t. and pa.p. **-red. -ry** a. pert. to, smeared with, or smelling of, tar [O.E. teru, pitch].

tar·an·tel·la (tar'·an·tel'·a) n. Italian dance with rapid, whirling movements; music for it [fr. Taranto, in S. Italy].

ta·ran·tu·la (ta·ranch'·a·la) n. large, hairy, venomous spider [fr. Taranto].

tar·boosh (tår'·bòosh) n. cap resembling a fez, usually red with dark blue tassel [Ar.].

tar·dy (tår'·di·) a. slow; dilatory; late. **tardily** adv. **tardiness** n. [L. tardus].

tare (ter) n. plant grown for fodder; a weed.

tare (ter) n. allowance made for weight of container, such as cask, crate, etc. in reckoning price of goods [Ar. tarhah, to reject].

tar·get (tår'·git) n. mark to aim at in shooting, esp. flat circular board with series of concentric circles; circular railway signal near switches; butt; object of attack [fr. targe].

tar·iff (ta'·rif) n. list of goods (imports and exports) on which duty is payable; the duty imposed. [Ar. ta'rif, giving information].

tarn (tårn) n. (Literary) small lake among

mountains [Scand.].

tar·nish (tàrnish) v.t. to lessen luster of; to sully, as one's reputation; v.i. to become dull, dim, or sullied [Fr. *ternir*, to tarnish].

ta·ro (tá'·rō) n. plant of Pacific islands, cultivated for edible leaves and root [Native].

tar·pau·lin (tàr·paw'·lin) n. canvas sheet treated with tar to make it waterproof; oilskin coat, hat, etc. [fr. *tar* and *pauling*, a covering].

tar·pon (tàr'·pan) n. large edible fish of herring family.

tar·ra·gon (tar'·a·gàn) n. perennial herb cultivated for its aromatic leaves [Gk. *drakon*, a dragon].

tar·ry (tar'·i·) v.i. to stay; to linger; to delay; to stay behind [L. *tardus*, slow].

tar·sus (tàr'·sas) n. ankle. pl. **tarsi. tarsal** a. [Gk. *tarsos*, the sole of the foot].

tart (tàrt) a. sour to taste; acid; (*Fig.*) caustic; severe. **-ish** a. rather sour. **-ly** adv. **-ness** n. [O.E. *teart*, acid].

tart (tàrt) n. small pastry cup containing fruit or jam; (*Slang*) girl; prostitute [O.Fr. *tarte*].

tar·tan (tàr'·tan) n. woolen cloth of colored plaids, each genuine Scottish clan possessing its own pattern; a. made of tartan.

Tar·tar (tàr'·ter) n. native of Tartary. Also **Tatar. tartar** n. irritable, quick-tempered person [fr. *Tatar*, a Mongol tribe].

tar·tar (tàr'·ter) n. crude potassium tartrate; crust deposited in wine cask during fermentation (purified, it is called **cream of tartar;** in crude form, **argol);** acid incrustation on teeth. **-ous** a. consisting of tartar; containing tartar. **-ic** a. pert. to, or obtained from, tartar. **tartrate** n. a salt of tartaric acid. **-ic acid,** organic hydroxy-acid found in many fruits; in powder form used in manufacture of cooling drinks. **cream of tartar,** purified form of tartar used medicinally and as raising agent in baking [Fr. *tartre*].

task (task) n. specific amount of work apportioned and imposed by another; set lesson; duty; v.t. to impose task on; to exact. **-er** n. — **force** n. body of soldiers sent to do specific operation. **-master** (*fem.* **-mistress**) n. overseer [L. *taxare*, to rate].

Tas·ma·ni·an (taz·mā'·ni·an) a. pert. to or belonging to Tasmania, island south of Australia; n. native of Tasmania. [fr. *Tasman*, discoverer].

Tass (tàs) n. official news agency of the U.S.S.R. [Russ. *Telegrafnoje Agentstvo Sovjetskovo Sojuza* = Soviet Telegraphic Agency].

tas·sel (tas'·l) n. ornamental fringed knot of silk, wool, etc.; pendent flower of some plants. **-ed** a. [L. *taxillus*, a small die].

taste (tāst) v.t. to perceive or test by tongue or palate; to appraise flavor of by sipping; to experience; v.i. to try food with mouth; to eat or drink very small quantity; to have specific flavor; n. act of tasting; one of five senses; flavor; predilection; aesthetic appreciation; judgment; small amount. **-ful** a. having or showing good taste. **-fully** adv. **-fulness** n. **-less** a. insipid. **-lessly** adv. **-lessness** n. **-r** n. one whose palate is trained to discern subtle differences in flavor, as *tea-taster.* **tastily** adv. with good taste. **tasty** a. savory [L. *taxare*, to estimate].

tat (tat) v.i. to make tatting. pr.p. **-ting.** pa.t., pa.p. **-ted. -ting** n. lace-like edging made from fine crochet or sewing thread [prob. Scand. *taeta*, shreds].

tat·ter (tat'·er) n. shred of cloth or paper hanging loosely; v.t. and v.i. to tear or hang in tatters. **-demalion** n. ragged fellow. **-ed** a. **-y** a. [Scand. *toturr*, rag].

tat·tle (tat'·l) v.i. to prattle; to gossip; to tell a secret; n. chatter. **-r** n. [imit.].

tat·too (ta·tōó') n. beat of drum or bugle as signal to return to quarters; a rapping sound; v.i. to beat tattoo [Dut. *taptoe*].

tat·too (ta·tōó') v.t. to prick colored designs, initials, etc. into skin with indelible colored inks; n. such design. **-er** n. [Tahitian *tatau*].

tau (tou, taw) n. Greek letter T.

taught (tawt) pa.t. and pa.p. of verb teach.

taunt (tawnt) v.t. to reproach with insulting words; to gibe at; to sneer at; n. gibe; sarcastic remark. **-er** n. **-ing** a. [O.Fr. *tanter*, to provoke].

tau·rus (tawr'·as) n. Bull, 2nd sign of Zodiac, which sun enters about April 21st. **taurian** a. pert. to a bull. **taurine** a. bovine. [Gk.].

taut (tawt) a. tight; fully stretched; (of a ship) trim. **-en** v.t. to make tight or tense. **-ness** n. [a form of tight].

tau·tol·o·gy (taw·tál'·a·ji·) n. needless repetition of same idea in different words in same sentence. **tautologic, -al** a. **tautologically** adv. **tautologism** n. superfluous use of words [Gk. *tauto*, the same; *logos*, a word].

tav·ern (tav'·ern) n. licensed house for sale of liquor; inn [L. *taberna*, booth].

taw (taw) n. large marble for children's game; the line from which the marble is shot; a game of marbles [Gk. letter T.].

taw·dry (taw'·dri·) a. showy but cheap; gaudy. **tawdrily** adv. **tawdriness** n. [fr. *St. Audrey*, cheap laces sold at her fair].

taw·ny (taw'·ni·) a. of yellow-brown color. **tawniness** n. [O.Fr. *tanné*, tanned].

tax (taks) n. levy imposed by state on income, property, etc.; burden; severe test; v.t. to impose tax on; to subject to severe strain; to challenge or accuse; (*Law*) to assess cost of actions in court. **-able** a. **-ness,** **-ability** n. **-ably** adv. **-ation** n. act of levying taxes; assessing of bill of costs; aggregate of particular taxes. [L. *taxare*, to rate].

tax·i (tak'·si·) n. (*abbrev.* of **taximeter cab**) an automobile for hire, fitted with a taximeter; any car plying for hire; v.i. to travel by taxi; of aircraft, to travel on ground (or surface of water) under its own power. pr.p. **-ing.** pa.p. **-ed, -cab** n. automobile for public hire. — **driver,** — **man** n. **-meter** n. instrument which automatically registers mileage and corresponding fare of journey by taxi.

tax·i·der·my (tak'·sa·dur·mi·) n. art of preparing and preserving pelts of animals and stuffing them for exhibition. **taxidermist** n. **taxidermal, taxidermic** a. [Gk. *taxis*, an arrangement].

tea (tē) n. dried and prepared leaf of tea plant, native to China and Japan, and grown in India, Ceylon, etc.; infusion of dry tea in boiling water; any infusion of plant leaves, etc. or of chopped meat; reception at which tea is drunk. — **service** n. — **set** n. cups, saucers, plates, etc. for use at tea. **-spoon** n. small-sized spoon used with the teacup. **-spoonful** n. ⅓ tablespoon. **black tea,** tea allowed to ferment between two processes of rolling and firing. **green tea,** tea left exposed to air for only short time before firing. **Russian tea,** tea served in glasses with slice of lemon and sugar [Chin.].

teach (tēch) v.t. to instruct; to educate; to discipline; to impart knowledge of; v.i. to follow profession of a teacher. pa.t. and pa.p. **taught** (tawt). **-ability** n. **-able** a. capable of being taught; willing to learn. **-ableness** n. **-er** n. one who instructs [O.E. *taecan*].

teak (tēk) n. tree of E. Indies yielding very hard, durable timber [Malay].

team (tēm) n. two or more oxen, horses, or other beasts of burden harnessed together; group of people working together for common purpose; side of players in game, as *football team.* **-ster** n. one who drives team or a truck, as an occupation. **-work** n. co-operation among members of a group [O.E. *team*, off-spring].

tear (tir) *n*. small drop of fluid secreted by lachrymal gland, appearing in and flowing from eyes, chiefly due to emotion; any transparent drop; *pl*. grief; sorrow. **drop** *n*. tear. **-ful** *a*. weeping. **-fully** *adv*. **-fulness** *n*. **— gas** *n*. irritant gas causing abnormal watering of eyes and temporary blindness. **-less** *a*. dryeyed [O.E. *tear*, a tear]

tear (ter) *v.t.* to pull apart forcibly; to rend; *v.i.* to become ripped or ragged; (*Colloq*.) to move violently; to rush; to rage. *pr.p.* **-ing**. *pa.t.* **tore**. *pa.p.* **torn**. *n*. rent; fissure. **-er** *n*. [O.E. *teran*, to tear].

tease (tēz) *v.t.* to comb or card wool, hair, etc.; to raise pile of cloth; to harass; to annoy in fun; to chaff. **-r** *n*. **-teasing** *a*. [O.E. *taesan*, to pluck].

teat (tit) *n*. nipple of female breast; dug of animal; rubber nipple of baby's feeding bottle [O.E. *tit*].

tech·nic·al (tek'·ni·kal) *a*. pert. to any of the arts, esp. to useful or mechanical arts; connected with particular art or science; accurately defined; involving legal point. **-ity** *n*. state of being technical; term peculiar to specific art; point of procedure. **-ly** *adv*. **-ness** *n*. **technician** *n*. expert in particular art or branch of knowledge. **technics** *n.pl.* arts in general; industrial arts. **technique** (tek·nēk') *n*. skill acquired by thorough mastery of subject; method of handling materials of an art. **technologic, -al** *a*. pert. to technology. **technologically** *adv*. **technologist** *n*. **technology** *n*. science of mechanical and industrial arts, as contrasted with fine arts; technical terminology [Gk. *technē*, art].

Tech·ni·col·or (tek'·ni·kul·er) *n*. trade name for color movie photography.

tec·ton·ic (tek·tán'·ik) *a*. pert. to building; (*Geol*.) pert. to earth's crust [Gk. *tekton*, builder].

te·di·ous (tē'·di·as) *a*. wearisome; protracted; irksome. **-ness** *n*. **-ly** *adv*. **tedium** *n*. wearisomeness [L. *taedium*, weariness].

tee (tē) *n*. tiny cone of sand, wooden peg, etc. on which golf ball is placed for first drive of each hole; teeing ground which marks beginning of each hole on golf course. *v.t.* to place (ball) on tee [etym. uncertain].

tee (tē) *n*. the letter T; anything shaped like a T; *a*. having the form of a T.

teem (tēm) *v.i.* to bring forth, as animal; to be prolific; to be stocked to overflowing. **-ing** *a*. prolific [O.E. *team*, offspring].

teens (tēnz) *n.pl.* the years of one's age, thir*teen* through nine*teen*. **teen-ager** *n*. a young person of this age.

tee·ny (tēn'·i·) (*Colloq*.) very small [*tiny*].

tee·ter (tē'·ter) *v.i.* (*Colloq*.) to seesaw; vacillate; *n*. a seesaw or motion of seesaw [fr. *titter*].

teeth. See **tooth**.

teeth·ing (tēTH'·ing) *n*. the process, in babyhood, of cutting the first teeth. **teethe** *v.i.* to cut the first teeth [fr. *tooth*].

tee·to·tal (tē·tō'·tal) *a*. pert. to teetotalism; abstemious. **-er** *n*. one who abstains from intoxicating liquors. **-ism** *n*. [redupl. of initial letter of *total*].

teg·u·ment (teg'·ya·mant) *n*. covering, esp. of living body; skin; integument. **-al, -ary** *a*. [L. *tegere*, to cover].

tel·e·cast (tel'·a·kast) *v.i.* to transmit program by television [Gk. *tēle*, far; and *cast*].

tel·e·gram (tel'·a·gram) *n*. message sent by telegraph. **-mic** *a*.

tel·e·graph (tel'·a·graf) *n*. electrical apparatus for transmitting messages by code to a distance; a message so sent; *v.i.* to send a message by telegraph. **-er** (or ta·leg'·ra·fer)

-ist (or ta·leg'·) *n*. one who operates telegraph, **-ic(al)** *a*. **-ically** *adv*. **telegraphy** *n*. electrical transmission of messages to a distance. [Gk. *tēle*, far; *graphein*, to write].

tel·e·ol·o·gy (tel·i·ál'·a·ji·) *n*. science or doctrine of final causes. **teleologic, -al** *a*. **teleologically** *adv*. **teleologist** *n*. [Gk. *telos*, end; *logos*, discourse].

te·lep·a·thy (ta·lep'·a·thi·) *n*. occult communication of facts, feelings, impressions between mind and mind at a distance; thought-transference. **telepathic** *a*. [Gk. *tēle*, far; *pathos*, feeling].

tel·e·phone (tel'·a·fōn) *n*. electrical instrument by which sound is transmitted and reproduced at a distance; *v.t.* and *v.i.* to communicate by telephone. **telephonic** *a*. **telephonically** *adv*. **telephonist** *n*. telephone operator, esp. at switchboard of exchange. **telephony** *n*. art or process of operating telephone [Gk. *tēle*, far; *phonē*, a sound].

tel·e·pho·to (tel·a·fō'·tō) *a*. pert. to a camera lens which makes distant objects appear close.

Tel·e·promp·ter (tel'·a·prámp'·ter) *n*. in television, a device to enable the speaker to refer to his script out of sight of the cameras, thus giving viewers the impression of a talk without script [Trademark].

tel·e·scope (tel'·a·skōp) *n*. optical instrument for magnifying distant objects; *v.t.* to slide or drive together, as parts of telescope; *v.i.* to be impacted violently, as cars in railway collision. **telescopic, -al** *a*. pert. to or like a telescope. [Gk. *tēle*, afar; *skopein*, to see].

tel·e·type (tel'·a·tīp) *n*. automatically printed telegram; the apparatus by which this is done [Gk. *tēle*, far; and *type*; Trademark.]

tel·e·vi·sion (tel'·a·vizh'·an) *n*. transmission of scenes, persons, etc. at a distance by means of electro-magnetic radio waves. **televise** *v.t.* [Gk. *tēle*, far, and *vision*].

tell (tel) *v.t.* to recount or narrate; to divulge; to inform; to count; *v.i.* to produce marked effect; to betray (as secret); to report. *pa.t.* and *pa.p.* **told**. **-er** *n*. narrator; bank clerk who pays out money; one who counts votes; enumerator. **-ing** *a*. effective; striking. **-ingly** *adv*. **-tale** *n*. one who betrays confidence; an informer; *a*. warning; tending to betray [O.E. *tellan*, to count].

te·mer·i·ty (ta·mer'·a·ti·) *n*. rashness; audacity [L. *temere*, rashly].

tem·per (tem'·per) *v.t.* to mingle in due proportion; to soften, as clay, by moistening; to bring (metal) to desired degree of hardness and elasticity by heating, cooling, and reheating; to regulate; to moderate; *n*. consistency required and achieved by tempering; attitude of mind; composure; anger; irritation. **-ed** *a*. having a certain consistency, as clay, or degree of toughness, as steel; having a certain disposition, as *good-tempered, bad-tempered*. **-edly** *adv*. **-ing** *n*. **-er** *n*. [L. *temperare*, to combine in due proportion].

tem·per·a (tem'·per·a) *n*. process of painting using pigments mixed with size, casein, or egg instead of oil. also **tempora** [It. = to temper].

tem·per·a·ment (tem'·per(a)mant) *n*. natural disposition; physical, moral and mental constitution peculiar to individuals; (*Mus*.) system of adjusting tones of keyboard instrument, such as a piano, so as to adapt the scale for all keys. **-al** *a*. liable to moods; passionate **-ally** *adv*. [L. *temperamentum*, disposition].

tem·per·ance (tem'·per·ans) *n*. moderation; self-discipline, esp. of natural appetites; total abstinence from, or modification in, consumption of intoxicating liquors; sobriety [L. *temperantia*, moderation].

tem·per·ate (tem'·per·it) *a*. moderate; abstemious; (of climate) equable; not extreme. **-ly** *adv*. **-ness** *n*. **temperative** *a*. **tempera-**

ture *n.* degree of heat or cold of atmosphere or of a human or living body; fevered condition. — **zones,** areas of earth between polar circles and tropics. [L. *temperare*, to moderate].

tem·pest (tem′·pist) *n.* wind storm of great violence; any violent commotion. **-uous** *a.* pert. to tempest; violent. **-uously** *adv.* **-uousness** *n.* [L. *tempestas*, weather, storm].

tem·ple (tem′·pl) *n.* place of worship; place dedicated to pagan deity; a building devoted to some public use. [L. *templum*, a sacred place].

tem·ple (tem′·pl) *n.* part of forehead between outer end of eye and hair. **temporal** *a.* [L. *tempora*, the temples].

tem·plet, tem·plate (tem′·plit) *n.* pattern of wood or metal cut to shape required for finished flat object [prob. fr. L. *templum*, small rafter].

tem·po (tem′·po) *n.* (*Mus.*) time; degree of speed or slowness at which passage should be played or sung; the degree of movement, as in the plot of a drama [It.].

tem·po·ral (tem′·pa·ral) *a.* pert. to time or to this life; transient; secular; **temporality** *n.* concept of time; state of being temporal or temporary; *pl.* material possessions, esp. ecclesiastical revenues. **-ly** *adv.* **temporariness** *n.* **temporarily** *adv.* only for a time. **temporariness** *n.* **temporary** *a.* lasting only for a time; fleeting. **temporization** *n.* **temporize** *v.i.* to act so as to gain time; to hedge; to compromise. **temporizer** *n.* **temporizing** *n.* [L. *tempus*, time].

tempt (tem(p)t) *v.t.* to induce to do something; to entice. **-ation** *n.* act of tempting; that which tempts; inducement to do evil; **-er** *n.* (*fem.* **-ress**) one who tempts, esp. Satan. **-ing** *a.* attractive; seductive. **-ingly** *adv.* **-ingness** *n.* [O.Fr. *tempter*, to entice].

ten (ten) *a.* twice five; one more than nine; *n.* the number nine and one; the figure or symbol representing this, as 10, X. **-fold** *a.* ten times repeated; *adv.* ten times as much. **-th** *a.* next after the ninth; being one of ten equal divisions of anything; *n.* one of ten equal parts; tenth part of anything; tithe. **-thly** *adv.* [O.E. *ten*, ten].

ten·a·ble (ten′·a·bl) *a.* capable of being held, defended, or logically maintained. **-ness, tenability** *n.* [L. *tenere*, to hold].

te·na·cious (ta·nā′·shas) *a.* holding fast; adhesive; retentive; pertinacious. **-ly** *adv.* **-ness, tenacity** *n.* [L. *tenax*, holding fast].

ten·ant (ten′·ant) *n.* (Law) one who has legal possession of real estate; one who occupies property for which he pays rent; *v.i.* to hold or occupy as tenant. **tenancy** *n.* act and period of holding land or property as tenant; property held by tenant. **-able** *a.* fit for occupation. **-ry** *n.* tenants or employees collectively on estate [L. *tenere*, to hold].

tend (tend) *v.i.* to hold a course; to have a bias or inclination. **-ency** *n.* inclination; bent. **-entious** *a.* (of writings) having a biased outlook [L. *tendere*, to stretch].

tend (tend) *v.t.* to look after; to minister to. **-er** *n.* one who tends; small vessel supplying larger one with stores, etc., or landing passengers; car attached to locomotive, carrying water and fuel [contr. of *attend*].

ten·der (ten′·der) *v.t.* to offer in payment or for acceptance; *n.* an offer, esp. contract to undertake specific work, or to supply goods at fixed rate. **legal tender,** currency recognized as legally acceptable in payment of a debt [L. *tendere*, to stretch out].

ten··der (ten′·der) *a.* soft; delicate; expressive of gentler passions; considerate; immature; sore; not tough (of meat). **-foot** *n.* one not yet hardened to ranching or mining life;

novice. **-ly** *adv.* **-ness** *n.* [L. *tener*, delicate].

ten·der·loin (ten′·der·loin) choice cut of beef between loin and ribs; (*Cap.*) district in a city noted for vice and police corruption.

ten·don (ten′·dan) *n.* a tough fibrous cord attaching muscle to bone. **tendinous** *a.* [L. *tendere*, to stretch].

ten·dril (ten′·dril) *n.* spiral shoot of climbing plant by which it clings to another body for support; curl, as of hair. **-lar, -ous** *a.* [Fr. *tendrille*].

ten·e·brous (ten′·a·bras) *a.* dark; obscure; **tenebrosity** *n.* [L. *tenebrae*, darkness].

ten·e·ment (ten′·a·mant) *n.* building divided into separate apartments, usu. of very poor quality, and let to different tenants. **-al, tenementary** *a.* [L. *tenere*, to hold].

ten·et (ten′·it) *n.* any opinion, dogma, or principle which a person holds as true [L. *tenere*, to hold].

ten·nis (ten′·is) *n.* game for two or four players, played on a court by striking a ball with rackets, across a net; a version of this played on a grass called *lawn tennis.* — **court** *n.* specially marked enclosed court for tennis.

ten·on (ten′·an) *n.* end of piece of wood shaped for insertion into cavity (*mortise*) in another piece to form a joint; *v.t.* to join with tenons. [L. *tenere*, to hold].

ten·or (ten′·er) *n.* general drift, course, or direction, of thought; purport; (*Mus.*) highest male adult voice; one who sings tenor; *a.* pert. to tenor voice [L. *tenere*, to hold]

tense (tens) *n.* (*Gram.*) form of verb which indicates *time* of action, as *present, past* or *future tense* [L. *tempus*, time].

tense (tens) *a.* stretched; strained almost to breaking point; unrelaxed; (of vowel) made by tongue tensed, as *ē.* **-ly** *adv.* **-ness** *n.* **tensibility, -ness** *n.* the quality of being **tensile. tensible, tensile** *a.* capable of being stretched or subjected to stress, as metals; capable of being made taut, as violin strings. **tension** *n.* act of stretching; strain; a state of being nervously excited or overwrought; (of metals) *pulling* stress as opposed to *compressive* stress; (*Elect.*) potential. **tensor** *n.* body muscle which stretches [L. *tendere*, to *stretch*].

tent (tent) *n.* portable canvas shelter stretched and supported by poles and firmly pegged ropes; small plug of compressed absorbent gauze, or lint, which swells when moistened, used to keep open a wound, etc.; *v.i.* to live in tent; to pitch tent; *v.t.* to keep open, as wound, with tent. **-ed** *a.* covered with tents. [L. *tendere*, to stretch].

ten·ta·cle (ten′·ta·kl) *n.* long flexible appendage of head or mouth in many lower animals for exploring, touching, grasping, and sometimes moving; feeler. **tentacular** *a.* **—like** *a.* [L. *tentare*, to feel].

ten·ta·tive (ten′·ta·tiv) *a.* experimental; done or suggested as a feeler or trial. **-ly** *adv.* [L. *tentare*, to try].

ten·ter (ten′·ter) *n.* machine for stretching cloth by means of hooks; *v.t.* to stretch on hooks. **-hook** *n.* one of the sharp hooks by which cloth is stretched on a tenter. **on tenterhooks,** state of anxiety [L. *tendere*, to stretch].

ten·u·i·ty (ten·ū·i·ti·) *n.* smallness of diameter; thinness. **tenuous** *a.* slender; gossamerlike; unsubstantial. **tenuously** *adv.* **tenuousness** *n.* [L. *tenuis*, thin].

ten·ure (ten′·yer) *n.* holding of office, property, etc.; condition of occupancy [L. *tenere*, to hold].   [tent. Also **teepee.**

te·pee (tē′·pē) *n.* Indian wigwam or conical

tep·e·fy (tep′·a·fī) *v.t.* to make moderately warm. **tepefaction** *n.* [L. *tepere*, to be warm; *facere*, to make].

tep·id (tep′·id) *a.* moderately warm; luke-warm. **-ity, -ness** *n.* [L. *tepidus*, warm].

ter·cel (tur′·sal) *n.* a young male falcon [dim. of L. *tertius*, third].

ter·cen·te·nar·y (tur·sen′·ta·ne·ri· or tur′·sen·ten·a·ri·) *n.* the 300th anniversary of an event; *a.* pert. to a period of 300 years [L. *ter*, thrice; *centum*, a hundred].

ter·cet (tur′·set) *n.* (*Mus.*) triplet; (*Pros.*) group of three lines or verses [L. *ter*, thrice].

ter·gi·ver·sate (tur′·ji·ver·sāt) *v.i.* to make use of subterfuges; to be shifty or vacillating; to apostatize. **tergiversation** *n.* **tergiversator** *n.* [L. *tergum*, the back; *vertere*, to turn].

term (turm) *n.* limit, esp. of time; period during which law courts are sitting, schools, universities, etc. are open; fixed day when rent is due; word or expression with specific meaning; (*Math.*) member of compound quantity; *pl.* stipulation; relationship, as *on friendly terms*; charge as for accommodation, etc. as *hotel terms*; *v.t.* to give name to; to call. **-inological** *a.* pert. to terminology. **-inologically** *adv.* **-inologist** *n.* **-inology** *n.* technical words; nomenclature [L. *terminus*, end].

ter·ma·gant (tur′·ma·gant) *n.* quarrelsome, shrewish woman; *a.* scolding; quarrelsome. [*Tervagan*, Mohammedan diety].

ter·mi·nate (tur′·ma·nāt) *v.t.* to set limit to; to end; to conclude; *v.i.* to come to an end; to finish. **terminable** *a.* capable of being terminated; liable to cease. **terminal** *n.* extremity; large railroad station with yards, shops, etc. (*Elect.*) metal attachment such as screw, block, clamp for connecting end of circuit; *a.* pert. to end; belonging to terminus or terminal; occurring in, or, at end of, a term; (*Bot.*) growing at tip. **terminally** *adv.* **termination** *n.* act of terminating; finish; conclusion; ending of word. **terminational** *a.* **terminative** *a.* **terminatively** *adv.* **terminus** *n.* end; farthest limit; railway station, airport, etc., at end of line; *pl.* **termini, terminuses** [L. *terminus*, the end].

ter·mite (tur′·mīt) *n.* insect, very destructive to wood [L. *termes*, a wood worm].

tern (turn) *n.* sea bird allied to gull [Scand.].

tern (turn) *n.* that which consists of three; *a.* threefold. **-al, -ary** *a.* consisting of three; proceeding by threes; (*Chem.*) comprising three elements, etc. **-ate** *a.* arranged in threes; (*Bot.*) having three leaflets. **-ion** *n.* group of three [L. *terni*, three each].

Terp·sich·o·re (turp·sik′·a·rē) *n.* (*Myth.*) Muse of choral song and dancing. **-an** *a.* pert. to Terpsichore or to dancing [Gk. *Terpsichorē*, fond of dancing].

ter·ra (ter′·a) *n.* earth as in various Latin phrases. **— cotta** *n.* reddish, brick-like earthenware, porous and unglazed. **— firma** *n.* dry land. **— incognita** *n.* unexplored territory. **terranean** *a.* belonging to surface of earth. **-neous** *a.* growing on land. **terraqueous** (ter·ā′·kwe·as) *a.* comprising both land and water, as the globe [L. *terra*, the earth].

ter·race (ter′·as) *n.* level shelf of earth, natural or artificial; flat roof used for open-air activities; *v.t.* to form into terraces [L. *terra*, the earth].

ter·rain (ter′·ān, ta·rān′) *n.* tract of land, esp. as considered for suitability for various purposes [L. *terra*, the earth].

ter·ra·pin (ter′·a·pin) *n.* edible tortoise found in eastern U.S. [Amer.-Ind.].

ter·raz·zo·pav·ing (ta·rat′·tsō·pāv′·ing) *n.* kind of mosaic paving in concrete chips [It.].

ter·rene (te·rēn′) *a.* pert. to earth; earthy; terrestrial [L. *terra*, the earth].

ter·res·tri·al (ta·res′·tri·al) *a.* pert. to earth; existing on earth; earthly, as opp. to

celestial; *n.* inhabitant of earth [L. *terra*, the earth].

ter·ri·ble (ter′·a·bl) *a.* calculated to inspire fear or awe; frightful; dreadful; formidable; (*Colloq.*) very bad. **-ness** *n.* **terribly** *adv.* [L. *terrere*, to frighten].

ter·ri·er (ter′·i·er) *n.* breed of small or medium-sized dog, originally trained for hunting foxes, badgers, etc. [M.E. *terrere*, a burrowing dog].

ter·ri·fy (ter′·a·fī) *v.t.* to frighten greatly; to inspire with terror. *pa.t.* **terrific** *a.* causing terror or alarm; (*Colloq.*) tremendous. **terrifically** *adv.* [L. *terrere*, to terrify; *facere*, to make].

ter·ri·to·ry (ter′·a·tōr·i·) *n.* large tract of land, esp. under one governmental administration; part of country which has not yet attained political independence. **territorial** *a.* pert. to territory; limited to certain district. **territoriality** *n.* [L. *terra*, the earth].

ter·ror (ter′·er) *n.* extreme fear; violent dread; one who or that which causes terror. **-ization** *n.* **-ize** *v.t.* to fill with terror; to rule by intimidation. **-izer** *n.* **-ism** *n.* mass-organized ruthlessness. **-ist** *n.* one who rules by terror [L. *terrere*, to frighten].

ter·ry cloth (ter′·i·klath) *n.* cotton fabric with pile of uncut loops on both sides.

terse (turs) *a.* (of speech, writing, etc.) concise; succinct; brief. **-ly** *adv.* **-ness** *n.* [L. *terpere*, *tersum*, to smooth].

ter·tian (tur′·shan) *a.* (*Med.*) occurring every other day; *n.* fever, such as malaria, with paroxysms occurring at intervals of forty-eight hours [L. *textius*, third].

ter·ti·ar·y (tur′·she·ri·) *a.* of third formation or rank; (*Geol.*) (*Cap.*) pert. to era of rock formation following Mezozoic; *n.* (*Geol.*) (*Cap.*) the tertiary era [L. *tertius*, third].

ter·za·ri·ma (ter′·tsare̅′·ma) *n.* form of stanza arrangement of iambic pentamenter lines in groups of three, rhyming aba, bcb, cdc [It. *terza*, third; *rima*, rhyme].

tes·sel·late (tes′·a·lāt) *v.t.* to pave with tesserae; to make mosaic paving with square-cut stones. **tessella, tessera** *n.* (*pl.* **tessellae, tesserae**) one of the square stones etc. used in tessellated paving. **tessellation** *n.* [L. *tessera*, a square block].

test (test) *n.* critical examination; grounds for admission or exclusion; (*Chem.*) reagent; substance used to analyze compound into its several constituents; a touchstone; vessel in which metals are refined; *v.i.* to make critical examination of; to put to proof; (*Chem.*) to analyze nature and properties of a compound. **— case** *n.* (*Law*) case tried for purpose of establishing a precedent. **-er** *n.* **-ing** *n.* *a.* demanding endurance. **— paper** *n.* examination paper; litmus or other impregnated paper used to test acid or alkaline content of chemical solution. **— pilot** *n.* experienced pilot engaged in testing flying qualities of new types of aircraft. **— tube** *n.* glass tube rounded and closed at one end, used in chemical tests [L. *testa*, earthen pot].

tes·ta·ment (tes′·ta·mant) *n.* solemn declaration of one's will; one of the two great divisions of the Bible, as the *Old Testament*, or the *New Testament*. **testamental, testamentary** *a.* pert. to testament or will; bestowed by will [L. *testari*, to witness].

tes·tate (tes′·tāt) *a.* having left a valid will. **testacy** *n.* state of being testate. **testator** *n.* (*fem.* **testatrix**) one who leaves a will [L.*testari*, to witness].

tes·ter (tes′·ter) *n.* flat canopy, esp. over a bed [O.Fr. *teste*, the head].

tes·ti·cle (tes′·ti·kl) *n.* one of the two male reproductive glands. **testicular** *a.* **testic-**

ulate, -d *a.* having testicles; resembling testicle in shape. **testis** *n.* a testicle. *pl.* **testes** [L. *testis* testicle].

tes·ti·fy (tes′·tạ·fī) *v.i.* to bear witness; to affirm or declare solemnly; to give evidence upon oath. *v.t.* to bear witness to; to manifest. **testifier** *n.* [L. *testis,* a witness; *facere,* to make].

tes·ti·mo·ny (tes′·tạ·mō·ni·) *n.* solemn declaration or affirmation; proof of some fact; in Scripture, the two tables of the law; divine revelation as a whole. **testimonial** *a.* containing testimony; *n.* written declaration testifying to character and qualities of person, esp. of applicant for a position; a tribute to person's outstanding worth [L. *testimonium*].

tes·ty (tes′·ti·) *a.* fretful; irascible [O.Fr. *teste,* head].

tet·a·nus (tet′·ạ·nạs) *n.* a disease in which a virus causes spasms of violent muscular contraction; lockjaw; spasmodic muscular contraction or rigidity caused by intake of drugs. **tetanic** *a.* [Gk. *tetanos,* stretched].

tetch·y (tech′·i·) *a.* peevish; fretful. **tetch·ily** *adv.* Also **techy** [Fr. *tache,* blemish].

teth·er (teTH′·ẹr) *n.* rope or chain fastened to grazing animal to keep it from straying; *v.t.* to confine with tether; to restrict movements of [Scand.].

te·tre- (tet′·rạ) *prefix* meaning *four* [Gk.].

tet·rad (tet′·rad) *n.* the number four; group of four things [Gk. *tetras*].

tet·ra·gon (tet′·rạ·gȧn) *n.* a plane figure, having four angles. **tetragonal** *a.*

tet·ra·gram (tet′·rạ·gram) *n.* word of four letters; (*Geom.*) figure formed by four right angles.

tet·ra·he·dron (tet·rạ·hē′·dṛan) *n.* solid figure enclosed by four triangles; triangular-based pyramid. **tetrahedral** *a.* [Gk. *tetra-,* four; *hedra,* a base].

te·tral·o·gy (te·tral′·ạ·ji·)*n.* group of four dramas or operas connected by some central event or character [Gk. *tetra-,* four; *logos,* a discourse]. [four measures.

te·tram·e·ter (te·tram′·ạ·tẹr) *n.* verse of

te·trarch (tet′·rȧrk) *n.* Roman governor of fourth part of a province. **-ate, -y** *n.* office of tetrarch; province ruled by tetrarch. **-ic, -al** *a.* [Gk. *tetra-,* four; *archos,* ruler].

tet·ter (tet′·ẹr) *n.* skin disease; ringworm; *v.t.* to affect with this. **-ous** *a.* [O.E. *teter,* ringworm].

Teu·ton (tū′·tạn) *n.* member of one of Germanic tribes; (*Colloq.*) a German. **Teutonic** (tū·tȧn′·ik) *a.* pert. to Teutons or their language. [L. *Teutones*].

text (tekst) *n.* original words of author, orator, etc. as distinct from paraphrase or commentary; verse or passage of Scripture chosen as theme of sermon. **-book** *n.* manual of instruction. **-ual** *a.* pert. to text or subject matter; based on actual text or wording; literal. **-ually** *adv.* [L. *texere,* to weave].

tex·tile (teks′·tīl, tạl) *a.* pert. to weaving; capable of being woven; *n.* fabric made on loom [L.*texere,* to weave].

tex·ture (teks′·chẹr) *n.* quality of surface of a woven material; disposition of several parts of anything in relation to whole; surface quality; that which is woven [L. *texere*].

Thai·land (tī′·land) *n.* Siam.

tha·las·sic (tha·las′·ik) *a.* pert. to the sea; living in the sea [Gk. *thalassa,* the sea].

thal·lus (thal′·ạs) *n.* simple plant organism which shows little or no differentiation into leaves, stem, or root as in *fungi, algae,* etc. *pl.* **thalli** [Gk. *thallos,* green shoot].

than (THan) *conj.* introducing adverbial clause of comparison and occurring after comparative form of an adjective or adverb [O.E. *thonne,* than].

thane (thān) *n.* in Anglo-Saxon community, member of class between freemen and nobility. **-dom** *n.* property held by a thane [O.E. *thegn,* soldier].

thank (thangk) *v.t.* to express gratitude to *n.* expression of gratitude (usually in *pl.*). **-fulness** *n.* **-less** *a.* ungrateful; unappreciated by others. **-lessly** *adv.* **-lessness** *n.* **-sgiving** *n.* act of rendering thanks; service held as expression of thanks for Divine goodness. **-sgiving Day,** day, fourth Thursday in November set apart for rendering thanks to God for blessings granted to nation [O.E. *thanc,* thanks].

that (THat) *demons. pron.* or *a.* (*pl.* **those**) pointing out a person or thing, or referring to something already mentioned; not this but the other; *rel. pron.* who or which; *conj.* introducing a noun clause, adjective clause, or adverbial clause of purpose, result, degree or reason [O.E. *thaet*].

thatch (thach) *n.* straw, rushes, heather, etc. used to roof cottage, or cover stacks of grain; (*Colloq.*) hair; *v.t.* to roof with thatch. **-er** *n.* **-ing** *n.* [O.E. *thaec,* a roof, thatch].

thaw (thaw) *v.t.* to cause to melt by increasing temperature; to liquefy; *v.i.* to melt, as ice, snow, etc.; to become warmer; (*Fig.*) to become genial; *n.* melting of ice or snow [O.E. *thawian,* to melt].

the (THạ, emphatic THē) *a.* or *definite article,* placed before nouns, and used to specify general conception, or to denote particular person or thing; *adv.* by so much; by that amount, as *the more, the merrier* [O.E.].

the·ar·chy (thē′·ȧr·ki·) *n.* theocracy; government by gods **thearchic** *a.* [Gk. *theos,* a god; *archē,* rule].

the·a·ter (thē′·ạ·tẹr) *n.* in Ancient Greece, a large, open-air structure used for public assemblies, staging of dramas, etc.; building for plays or motion pictures; lecture or demonstration room for anatomy studies; field of military, naval, or air operations. **theatric, -al** *a.* **theatrically** *adv.* **theatricals** *n.pl.* dramatic performances, esp. by amateurs [Gk. *theatron*]. [thou.

thee (THē) (*Arch.*) *pron.* objective case of

theft (theft) *n.* act of stealing [O.E. *theof,* a thief].

their (THer) *a.* and *pron.* of them; possessive case of **they. theirs** *poss. pron,* form of *their* used absolutely [Scand. *theira,* their].

the·ism (thē′·izm) *n.* belief in existence of personal God who actively manifests Himself in world. **theist** *n.* **theistic, -al** *a.* [Gk. *theos,* a god].

them (THem) *pron.* objective and dative case of **they** [O.E. *thaem*].

theme (thēm) *n.* subject of writing, discourse, or discussion; brief essay; (*Mus.*) groundwork melody recurring at intervals and with variations. **thema** *n.* subject. **thematic** *a.* **thematically** *adv.* — **song** *n.* recurring melody in play, film [Gk. *thema,* something laid down].

them·selves (THem·selvz′) *pron. pl.* of **himself, herself,** and **itself;** emphatic form of **them** or **they;** reflexive form of them.

then (THen) *adv.* at that time (past or future); immediately afterwards; thereupon; that being so; for this reason; in consequence of; *conj.* moreover; therefore; *a.* existing or acting at particular time. **now and then,** occasionally [doublet of *than*].

thence (THens) *adv.* from that place; from that time; for that reason. **-forth** *adv.* from that time on. [M.E. *thennes*].

the·oc·ra·cy (thē·ȧk′·rạ·si·) *n.* government of state professedly in the name, and under direction, of God; government by priests.

theocrat, theocratist *n.* ruler under this system. **theocratic, -al** *a.* **theocratically** *adv.* [Gk. *theos*, a god; *kratos*, power].

the·od·o·lite (thē·ǎd'·ạ·līt) *n.* instrument for measuring angles, used in surveying.

the·ol·o·gy (thē·ǎl'·ạ·ji·) *n.* science which treats of facts and phenomena of religion, and relations between God and man. **theologian** *n.* one learned in theology. **theologic, -al** *a.* pert. to theology. **theologically** *adv.* **theologize** *v.t.* to render theological; to theorize upon theological matters. **theologist** *n.* [Gk. *theos*, god; *logos*, discourse].

the·oph·a·ny (thē·ǎf'·ạ·ni·) *n.* manifestation of God to men, in human form. **theophanic** *a.* [Gk. *theos*, a god; *phainesthai*, to appear].

the·o·rem (thē'·ạ·rạm) *n.* established principle; (*Math.*) proposition to be proved by logical reasoning; algebraical formula. **-atic, -al** *a.* [Gk. *theorēma*, speculation].

the·o·ry (thē'·ạ·ri·) *n.* supposition put forward to explain something; speculation; exposition of general principles as distinct from practice and execution; (*Colloq.*) general idea; notion. **theoretic, -al** *a.* pert. to or based on theory; speculative as opp. to *practical*. **theoretics** *n.pl.* speculative side of science. **theorize** *v.t.* to form a theory; to speculate. **theorizer, theorist** *n.* **theorization** *n.* [Gk. *theoria*, speculation].

ther·a·peu·tic (ther·ạ·pū'·tik) *a.* pert. to healing. **-ally** *adv.* **-s** *n.* branch of medicine concerned with treatment and cure of diseases. **therapeutist** *n.* [Gk. *therapeuein*, to attend (medically)].

ther·a·py (ther'·ạ·pi·) *n.* remedial treatment, as *radio-therapy* for cure of disease by radium [Gk. *therapeia*, (medical) attendance].

there (THer) *adv.* in that place; farther off opp. to *here;* as an introductory adverb it adds little to the meaning of the sentence as 'There is someone at the door'; *interj.* expressing surprise, consolation, etc. **-about,** **-abouts** *adv.* near that place, number or quantity. **-after** *adv.* after that time. **-by** *adv.* by that means; in consequence. **-fore** *conj.* and *adv.* consequently; accordingly. **-in** *adv.* in that, or this place, time, or thing; in that particular. **-inafter** *adv.* afterwards in same document. **-of** *adv.* of that or this. **-to** *adv.* to that or this. **-upon** *adv.* upon that or this; consequently; immediately. **-with** *adv.* with that or this; straightway. [O.E. *thaer*, there].

therm (thurm) *n.* a unit of heat; the large calorie, also small calorie; unit of 1.000 large calories. **-ae** *n.pl.* hot springs; Roman baths. **-al** *a.* pert. to heat. **-ic** *a.* caused by heat. [Gk. *thermē*, heat].

therm·i·on (thur'·mi·ạn) *n.* positively or negatively charged particle emitted from incandescent substance. **thermionic** *a.* pert to thermions. **thermionic current** (*radio*) flow of electrons from filament to plate of thermionic valve. **thermionics** *n.* branch of science dealing with thermions [Gk. *thermē*, heat; *ion*, going].

ther·mo·chem·is·try (thur·mō·kem'·is·tri·) *n.* branch of science which deals with heat in relation to chemical processes.

ther·mo·dy·nam·ics (thur·mō·dī·nam'·iks) *n.* branch of science which deals with the conversion of heat into mechanical engery.

ther·mo·e·lec·tric·i·ty (thur·mō·i·lek·tris'·ạ·ti·) *n.* electricity developed by action of heat alone on two different metals. **thermoelectric, -al** *a.* [Gk. *thermē*, heat; and *electricity*].

ther·mo·gen·e·sis (thur·mō·jen'·ạ·sis) *n.* production of heat, esp. in body. **thermogenetic, thermogenic** *a.*

ther·mom·e·ter (ther·mǎm'·ạ·ter) *n.* instrument for measuring temperature, usually consisting of graduated and sealed glass tube with bulb containing mercury. **thermometric, -al** *a.* **thermometrically** *adv.* **thermometry** *n.* [Gk. *thermē*, heat; *metron*, measure].

ther·mo·mo·tor (thur·mạ·mō'·ter *n.* engine worked by heat or hot air.

ther·mo·pile (thur'·mạ·pīl) *n.* instrument for measuring minute variations in temperature.

ther·mo·scope (thur'·mạ·skōp) *n.* instrument for detecting fluctuations in temperature without actual measurement.

Ther·mos (thur'·mạs) *n.* double-walled bottle or the like which substantially retains temperature of liquids by the device of surrounding interior vessel with a vacuum jacket [Trade Name].

ther·mo·stat (thur'·mạ·stat) *n.* instrument which controls temperature automatically. **thermostatic** *a.* **thermostatics** *n.* science dealing with equilibrium of heat [Gk. *thermē*, heat; and *static*].

ther·mot·ic (ther·mǎt'·ik) *a.* pert. to heat, Also **-al** *n.* the science of heat [Gk. *thermotēs*, heat].

the·sau·rus (thi·sawr'·ạs) *n.* treasury of knowledge, etc.; lexicon; encyclopedia [Gk. *thēsauros*, treasure-house].

these (THēz) *demons. a.* and *pron. pl.* of this.

the·sis (THē'sis) *n.* what is laid down as a proposition; dissertation *pl.* **theses. thetic** *a.* dogmatic [Gk. *thesis*, placing].

Thes·pis (thes'·pis) an Athenian of 6th cent. B.C. supposed inventor of trageday. **Thespian** *a.* pert. to drama; *n.* an actor; a tragedian.

the·ur·gy (thē'·ur'·ji·) *n.* art of working so-called miracles by supernatural agency. **theurgic, -al** *a.* **theurgically** *adv.* **theurgist** *n.* [Gk. *theos*, god; *ergon*, a work].

thew (thū) *n.* muscle; sinew; brawn (usually *pl.* [O.E. *theaw*, manner, or strength].

they (THā) *pron. pers. pl.* of **he, she, it**; indefinitely, for a number of persons.

thi·a·mine (thī'·ạ·mēn, mạn) *n.* Vitamin B, complex compound, deficiency of which causes beriberi also **thiamin** [Gk. *theion*, sulphur, and *amine*].

thick (thik) *a.* dense; foggy; not thin; abundant; packed; muffled, as *thick voice*; mentally dull; (*Slang*) intimate; *n.* thickest part; *adv.* thickly; to a considerable depth. **-en** *v.t.* to make thick; *v.i.* to become thick. **-ening** *n.* something added to thicken. **-et** *n.* dense growth of shrubs, trees, etc. **-headed** *a.* dull mentally. **-ly** *adv.* **-ness** *n.* quality of being thick; measurement of depth between opposite surfaces; layer. **—set** *a.* closely planted; sturdily built [O.E. *thicce*, thick].

thief (thēf) *n.* (*pl.* **thieves**) one who steals the goods and property of another. **thieve** *v.t.* to take by theft; *v.i.* to steal. **thievery** *n.* **thievish** *a.* addicted to stealing. **thievishness** *n.* [O.E. *theof*].

thigh (thī) *n.* fleshy part of leg between knee and trunk [O.E. *theoh*, thigh].

thim·ble (thim'·bl) *n.* metal or bone cap for tip of middle finger, in sewing; anything shaped like a thimble. **-ful** *n.* the quantity contained in a thimble; very small amount [O.E. *thymel*, thumb].

thin (thin) *a. comp.* **-ner.** *superl.* **-nest.** having little depth or thickness; slim; lean; flimsy; sparse; fine; *adv.* sparsely; not closely packed *v.t.* to make thin; to rarefy; *v.i.* to grow or become thin. *pr.p.* **-ning.** *pa.p., pa.t.* **-ned. -ly** *adv.* **-ness** *n.* **-ning** *n.* [O.E. *thynne*, thin].

thine (THīn) *pron. poss.* form of **thou** (*Arch.*) belonging to thee; thy [O.E. *thin*].

thing (thing) *n.* material or inanimate object;

entity; specimen; commodity; event; action; person (in pity or contempt); *pl.* belongings; clothes, furniture [O.E. *thing*, an object].

think (thingk) *v.t.* to conceive; to surmise; to believe; to consider; to esteem; *v.i.* to reason; to form judgment; to deliberate; to imagine; to recollect. *pa.t.* and *pa.p.* **thought** (thawt). **-able** *a.* **-ing** *a.* reflective; rational [O.E. *thencan*].

thi·o (thī'.ō) word element used in chemistry to illustrate the replacement by sulfur of part or all of the oxygen atoms in a compound. Also **thi-**.

third (thurd) *a.* next after the second; forming one of three equal divisions; *n.* one of three equal parts; (*Mus.*) interval of three diatonic degrees of the scale. **-class** *a.* pert. to accommodation for passengers not traveling first or second class; inferior. — **estate**, the commons. **-ly** *adv.* —**rate** *a.* of third-class quality; inferior [O.E. *thridda*, third].

thirst (thurst) *n.* desire to drink; suffering endured by too long abstinence from drinking; craving; *v.i.* to crave for something to drink; to wish for earnestly. **-er** *n.* **-ily** *adv.* **-iness** *n.* **-y** *a.* having a desire to drink; dry; parched; eager for [O.E. *thurst*, thirst].

thir·teen (thur'·tēn) *a.* ten and three; *n.* sum of ten and three; symbol representing thirteen units, as 13, XIII. **-th** *a.* next in order after twelfth; being one of thirteen equal parts; *n.* one of these parts [O.E. *threo*, three; *tyn*, ten].

thir·ty (thur'·ti·) *a.* three times ten; *n.* sum of three times ten; symbol representing this, as 30, XXX. **thirtieth** *a.* next in order after twenty-ninth; being one of thirty equal parts; *n.* thirtieth part [O.E. *thritig*, thirty].

this (THis) *demons. pron.* and *a.* denoting a person or thing near at hand, just mentioned, or about to be mentioned [O.E.].

this·tle (this'·l) *n.* one of the numerous prickly plants of the genus *Carduus*, with yellow or purple flowers; national emblem of Scotland. —**down** *n.* feathery down of thistle seeds. **thistly** *a.* [O.E. *thistel*, a thistle].

thith·er (thiTH'·er) *adv.* to that place; to that point, end, or result. **-ward** *adv.* toward that place [O.E. *thider*].

thole (thōl) *v.t.* pin in gunwale of boat to keep oar in rowlock. Also **-pin** [O.E. *thol*, a rowlock].

Tho·mism (tō'·mizm) *n.* doctrines expounded in theology of *Thomas Aquinas* (1226-74). **Thomist** *n.* adherent of Thomism.

thong (thawng) *n.* narrow strap of leather used for reins, whiplash, etc.; long narrow strip of leather used in leathercraft [O.E. *thwang*, a thong].

tho·rax (thōr'·aks) *n.* part of body between neck and abdomen; chest cavity containing heart, lungs, etc. **thoracic** *a.* [Gk. *thorax*].

thorn (thawrn) *n.* sharp, woody shoot on stem of tree or shrub; prickle; hawthorn; (*Fig.*) anything which causes trouble or annoyance; name in O.E. of the rune for *th*. **-y** *a.* full of thorns; prickly; beset with difficulties [O.E. *thorn*, a prickle].

thor·ough (thur'·ō) *a.* complete; absolute. **-bred** *a.* (of animals) pure bred from pedigree stock; (of people) aristocratic hence, high-spirited; mettlesome; *n.* animal (esp. horse) of pure breed. **-fare** *n.* passage through; highway. **-ly** *adv.* **-ness** *n.* [form of *through*].

those (THōz) *a.* and *pron. pl.* of **that**.

thou (THou) *pron. pres.*, 2nd *sing.* denoting the person addressed (used now only in solemn address, and by the Quakers).

though (THō) *conj.* granting; admitting; even if; notwithstanding; however [O.E. *theah*].

thought (thwat) *pa.t.* and *pa.p.* of **think**.

thought (thawt) *n.* act of thinking; that which one thinks; reflection; opinion; serious consideration. **-ful** *a.* contemplative; attentive; considerate. **-fully** *adv.* **-fulness** *n.* **-less** *a.* without thought; heedless; impulsive; inconsiderate. **-lessly** *adv.* **-lessness** *n.* [O.E. *gethoht*, thought].

thou·sand (thou'·zand) *a.* consisting of ten hundred; used indefinitely to express large number; *n.* the number ten hundred; symbol for this, 1,000 or M; any large number. **-fold** *a.* multiplied by a thousand. **-th** *a.* constituting one of thousand equal parts; next in order after nine hundred and ninety-nine; *n.* thousandths part [O.E. *thusend*].

thrall (thrawl) *n.* slave; bondsman; servitude. **-dom, thraldom** *n.* bondage [O.N. *thrael*, bondage].

thrash (thrash) *v.t.* to thresh; to flog; to defeat soundly. **-er** *n.* **thrashing** *n.* act of thrashing; corporal punishment; flogging. [var. of *thresh*].

thra·son·i·cal (thra·sán'·i·kal) *a.* boastful; bragging. **-ly** *adv.* [fr. *Thraso*, a braggart].

thread (thred) *n.* very thin twist of wool, cotton, linen, silk, etc.; filament as of gold, silver; prominent spiral part of screw; consecutive train of thought; *v.t.* to pass thread through eye of needle; to string together, as beads; to pick one's way with careful deliberation. **-bare** *a.* worn away with wear; shabby; hackneyed; trite. **-worm** *n.* thread-like parasitic worm often found in intestines of children. **-y** *a.* [O.E. *thrawan*, to twist].

threat (thret) *n.* declaration of determination to harm another; menace. **-en** *v.t.* to menace; to declare intention to do harm to; to portend. **-ener** *n.* **-ening** *a.* menacing; portending something undesirable; (of clouds or sky) lowering [O.E. *threatnian*, to urge].

three (thrē) *a.* two and one; *n.* sum of two and one; symbol of this sum, 3 or iii. **-fold** *a.* triple. —**ply** *a.* having three layers or thicknesses; having three strands twisted together, as wool. **-score** *a.* and *n.* sixty. **-some** *n.* game (as golf) played by three players; group of three people. **the three R's,** reading, riting, rithmetic [O.E. *threo*, three].

thren·o·dy (thren'·a·di·) *n.* song of lamentation; dirge. Also **threnode. threnodial, threnodic** *a.* pert. to threnody; funereal. [Gk. *thrēnos*, lament; *odē*, song].

thresh *v.t.* to separate grain from chaff by use of flail or machine; to beat. **-er** *n.* [O.E. *therscan*, to beat].

thresh·old (thresh'·ōld) *n.* door sill; point of beginning [O.E. *therscan*, to thresh; *wald*, wood].

threw (throo) *pa.t.* of **throw**.

thrice (thrīs) *adv.* three times; repeatedly; much, as in *thrice blessed* [O.E. *thriwa*].

thrift (thrift) *n.* economical management; frugality; plant, the sea pink. **-ily** *adv.* **-iness** *n.* frugality. **-less** *a.* extravagant; wasteful. **-lessly** *adv.* **-y** *a.* [fr. *thrive*].

thrill (thril) *n.* emotional excitement; quivering sensation running through nerves and body; *v.t.* to stir deeply; to arouse tingling emotional response; *v.i.* to feel a glow of excitement, enthusiasm, etc. **-er** *n.* (*Colloq.*) sensational novel, play, or film, etc. **-ing** *a.* **-ingly** *adv.* [O.E. *thyrlian*, to bore a hole].

thrive (thrīv) *v.i.* to prosper; to grow abundantly; to develop healthily. *pa.t.* **throve** and **-d.** *pa.p.* **thriven** (thriv'·n) **-d. thriving** *a.* **thrivingly** *adv.* [O.N. *thrifa*, to grasp].

throat (thrōt) *n.* forepart of neck; passage connecting back of mouth with lungs, stomach, etc.; narrow entrance. **-iness** *n.* quality of having throaty or muffled voice. **-y** *a.* guttural; muffled [O.E. *throte*, the throat].

throb (thrab) *v.i.* to pulsate; to beat, as heart,

with more than usual force. *pr.p.* **-bing.** *pa.t.* and *pa.p.* **-bed.** *n.* pulsation; palpitation (of heart, etc.); beat [etym. doubtful].

throe (thrō) *n.* suffering; pain; *pl.* pains of childbirth [O.E. *thrawa*, suffering].

throm·bo·sis (thrȧm·bō'·sis) *n.* formation of blood clot in vein or artery [Gk. *thrombos*].

throne (thrōn) *n.* chair of state; royal seat; bishop's seat in his cathedral; sovereign power and dignity; *v.t.* to place on royal seat; to exalt. *pr.p.* **throning.** *pa.p.* **-d** [Gk. *thronos*, a seat].

throng (thrawng) *n.* multitude; crowd; *v.t.* to mass together; to press in crowds [O.E. *thringan*, to press].

throt·tle (thrȧt'·l) *n.* windpipe; valve controlling amount of vaporized fuel delivered to cylinders in internal-combustion engine, or pressure of steam in steam engine; *v.i.* to choke by external pressure on windpipe; to obstruct steam in steam engine; (*Fig.*) to suppress; to silence; *v.i.* to pant for breath, as if suffocated [dim. of *throat*].

through (throo) *prep.* from end to end of; going in at one side and out the other; by passing between; across; along; by means of; as consequence of; *adv.* from one end or side to the other; from beginning to end. *a.* (of railway train) passing from one main station to another without intermediate stops; unobstructed, as *through-road*. **through and through**, completely. **-ly** (*Arch.*) *adv.* thoroughly. **-out** *adv.* and *prep.* wholly; completely; during entire time of [O.E. *thurh*, through].

throv (thrōv) *pa.t.* of **thrive.**

throw (thrō) *v.t.* to fling, cast, or hurl; to propel; to send; to twist into thread, as silk; to mold on potter's wheel; to unseat, as of a horseman; to shed, as snake's skin; to produce offspring, as animal; to spread carelessly; *v.i.* to cast, to hurl. *pr.p.* **-ing.** *pa.t.* **threw.** *pa.p.* **-n.** *n.* the act of throwing; distance something can be thrown; light blanket. **-er** *n.* **-n** *a.* [O.E.*thrawan*].

thrum (thrum) *n.* fringe of threads left on loom after web is cut off [O.N. *thromr*, edge].

thrum (thrum) *v.t.* to strum on instrument; to play carelessly; to drum with fingers *pr.p.* **-ming.** *pa.p.*, *pa.t.* **-med.** [O.N. *thruma*, rattle].

thrush (thrush) *n.* song bird [O.E. thrysce].

thrush (thrush) *n.* (*Med.*) inflammatory disease affecting mouth, tongue and lips, commonly found in young children; a disease affecting the feet of horses, etc. [O.E. *thyrre*, dry].

thrust (thrust) *v.t.* to push or drive with sudden force; to pierce; *v.i.* to make a push; to attack with a pointed weapon; to intrude; to push way through. *pa.t.* and *pa.p.* **thrust.** *n.* push; stab; assault; horizontal outward pressure as of arch against its abutments; stress acting horizontally, as in machinery; (*Geol.*) upward bulge of layer of rock due to lateral pressure. **-er** *n.* [Scand. *thrysia*, to press].

thud (thud) *n.* dull sound made by blow or heavy fall; *v.i.* to make sound of thud; [O.E. *thoden*, noise].

thug (thug) cutthroat; ruffian; gangster. **-gery** *n.* [Hind. *thag*].

Thule (thū'·lē) *n.* name in ancient times for most northerly part of world. Orkneys, Shetlands, Iceland, etc. [Gk. *Thoulē*].

thumb (thum) *n.* short, thick finger of human hand; part of glove which covers this; *v.t.* to manipulate awkwardly; to soil with thumb marks; (*Slang*) to hold up thumb, to solicit lift in automobile. **-ed** *a.* having thumbs; soiled with thumb marks. **-less** *a.* **-like** *a.* **-nail** *n.* nail on human thumb. **-nail**

sketch, miniature; succinct description. **-screw** *n.* old instrument of torture by which thumb was compressed till the joint broke. **by rule of thumb**, by rough estimate [O.E. *thuma*, a thumb].

thump (thump) *n.* blow of fist; sudden fall of heavy body or weight; thud; *v.t.* to beat with something heavy; *v.i.* to strike or fall with a thud. **-er** *n.* **-ing** *a.* very large; much exaggerated [imit.].

thun·der (thun'·der) *n.* rumbling sound which follows lightning flash; any very loud noise; *v.t.* to declaim or rage with loud voice; *v.i.* to rumble with thunder; to roar. **-bolt** *n.* flash of lightning followed by peal of thunder; anything totally unexpected and unpleasant. **-clap** *n.* a peal of thunder. **the thundered,** the god Jupiter; **-ing** *n.* thunder; booming, as of guns. *a.* making a loud noise; (*Colloq.*) outstanding; excessive. **-ous** *a.* **-ously** *adv.* **-storm** *n.* storm of thunder and lightning with torrential rain **-struck** *a.* speechless with amazement. **-y** *a.* **to steal someone's thunder,** to win applause expected by someone else; to expose or use first someone else's chief point(s) [O.E. *thunian*, to rattle].

thu·ri·ble (thyoo'·rạ·bl) *n.* a metal censer. **thurifer** *n.* one who carries and swings a thurible [L. *thus, thuris*, frankincense].

Thurs·day (thurz'·dē) *n.* fifth day of week, after *Thor*, Scandinavian god of thunder.

thus (THus) *adv.* in this or that manner; to this degree or extent; so; in this wise. **thus far,** so far [O.E. *thus*, by this].

thwack (thwak) *v.t.* to beat; to flog; *n.* heavy blow; a hard slap [O.E. *thaccian*, to stroke].

thwart (thwawrt) *a.* lying across; transverse; athwart; *v.t.* to hinder; to frustrate; to stop; *n.* seat across or athwart a row boat; *adv.* and *prep.* across. **-er** *n.* **-ing** *a.* [O.N. *thvert*, across].

thy (THī) *poss. a.* of thee; belonging to thee [contr. fr. *thine*].

thyme (tīm) *n.* small flowering shrub cultivated for its aromatic leaves for use as flavoring in cookery [Gk. *thumon*].

thy·mus (thī'·mạs) *n.* small ductless gland in upper part of the chest [Gk.].

thy·roid (thī'·roid) *a.* signifying cartilage of larynx or a gland of trachea. **— gland,** ductless gland situated in neck on either side of trachea, secreting hormone which profoundly affects physique and temperament of human beings [Gk. *thureos*, a shield; *eidos*, a form].

thy·self (THī·self') *pron. reflex.* or *emphatic,* of a person, thou or thee.

ti·ar·a (tī·or'·a, ti·ȧr'·a) *n.* lofty turban worn by ancient Persian kings and dignitaries; triple, gem-studded crown worn by Pope on ceremonial occasions; gem-studded coronet worn by ladies [Gk. *tiara*, headdress].

tib·i·a (tib'·i·a) *n.* shinbone; inner and usually larger of two bones of leg, between knee and ankle. *pl.* **-s, tibiae. -l** *a.* [L. *tibial*].

tic (tik) *n.* spasmodic twitching of muscle, esp. of face [Fr. *tic*, twitching].

tick (tik) *n.* a parasitic bloodsucking insect [M.E. *teke*].

tick (tik) *n.* cover of mattress, pillow, etc. **-ing** *n.* specially strong material used for mattress covers, etc. [Gk. *thēkē*, a case].

tick (tik) *v.i.* to make small, recurring, clicking sound, as watch; *n.* sound made by watch. **-er** *n.* anything which ticks regularly; machine which records on tape; (*Colloq.*) watch or clock; the heart [imit.].

tick (tik) *v.t.* to mark or dot lightly; *n.* small mark placed after word, entry, etc., esp. in checking; [M.E. *tek*, a touch].

tick·et (tik'·it) *n.* piece of cardboard or paper entitling admission to anything, to travel by public transport, to participate in function, etc.; price tag; label; (*U.S.*) list of candidates in an election; *v.t.* to mark with ticket. **season ticket,** ticket entitling holder to attend a series of concerts, lectures, etc. or to travel daily between certain specified stations over a certain period of time [O.Fr. *etiquet,* label].

tick·le (tik'·l) *v.t.* to touch skin lightly so as to excite nerves and cause laughter; to titillate; to amuse; *v.i.* to feel sensation of tickling; to be gratified. **-r** *n.* **ticklish** *a.* easily tickled; requiring skillful handling. **ticklishly** *adv.* **ticklishness** *n.* [freq. of *tick.* to touch lightly].

tid·bit (tid'·bit) *n.* choice morsel. Also **titbit** [Scand. *titto,* small bird].

tid·dly·winks (tid'·li·wingks) *n.pl.* game in which players try to snap small disks into cup.

tide (tīd) *n.* time; season, as in *eventide, Eastertide;* periodical rise and fall of ocean due to attraction of moon and sun; (*Fig.*) trend. **to tide over,** to manage temporarily; to surmount meantime. **tidal** *a.* pert. to tide. **tidal basin,** harbor which is affected by tides. **tidal wave,** mountainous wave as caused by earthquake, atom bomb explosion, etc. **-less** *a.* having no tides. **ebb,** or **low, tide,** the falling level of the sea. **flood,** or **high, tide,** the rising level of the sea. **neap tide,** minimum tide. **spring tide,** maximum tide [O.E. *tid,* time].

ti·dings (tī'·dingz) *n.pl.* news; information [O.N. *tithindi,* to happen].

ti·dy (tī'·dy·) *a.* neat; orderly; (*Colloq.*) comfortable; of fair size; *n.* chair-back cover; *v.t.* to put in order [M.E. tidy, timely].

tie (tī) *v.t.* to fasten by rope, string, etc.; to fashion into knot; to bind together, as rafters, by connecting piece of wood or metal; to hamper; (*Mus.*) to connect two notes with tie; *v.t.* (*Sport*) to make equal score, etc. *pr.p.* **tying.** *pa.t.* and *pa.p.* **tied.** *n.* knot; necktie; fastening; connecting link; equality of score; (*Mus.*) curved line connecting two notes indicating that sound is sustained for length of both notes; traverse supports for railroad tracks. — **beam** *n.* horizontal timber connecting two rafters. **-r** *n.* [O.E. *teah,* a rope].

tier (tir) *n.* row or rank, esp. when two or more rows are arranged behind and above the other [Fr. *tirer,* to draw].

tierce (tirs) *n.* cask containing third of pipe or 42 wine gallons; third of canonical hours, or service at 9 a.m.; in fencing, particular thrust (third position) [Fr. *tiers,* third].

tiff (tif) *n.* slight quarrel; *v.i.* to quarrel

ti·ger (tī'·ger) *n.* (fem. **tigress**) fierce carnivorous quadruped of cat tribe, with tawny black-striped coat. **-cat** *n.* wild cat; ocelot or margay. — **lily** *n.* tall Chinese lily with flaming orange flowers spotted with black [Gk. *tigris*].

tight (tīt) *a.* firm; compact; compressed; not leaky; fitting close or too close to body; tense; (*Colloq.*) restricted for want of money; (*Slang*) drunk; *adv.* firmly. **-en** *v.t.* to make tight or tighter; to make taut; *v.i.* to become tight or tighter. **-ener** *n.* **-ly** *adv.* **-ness** *n.* **-rope** *n.* a strong, taut rope, or steel wire on which acrobats perform. *n.pl.* close-fitting woven hose and trunks worn by acrobats, dancers, etc. [O.N. *thettr,* watertight].

til·de (til'·da) *n.* the mark (~) placed over the letter *n* in Spanish, to indicate a following *y* sound, as in cannon (canyon).

tile (tīl) *n.* a thin piece of slate, baked clay, plastic, asphalt, etc. used for roofs, walls, floors, drains, etc.; (*Slang*) a silk top-hat; *v.t.* to cover with tiles. **-r** *n.* **tiling** *n.* [L. *tegula*].

till (til) *n.* a money box or drawer in a shop counter; a cash register [etym. doubtful].

till (til) *prep.* as late as; until; *conj.* to the time when [M.E. *til,* up to].

till (til) *v.t.* to cultivate; to plow the soil, sow seeds, etc. **-age** *n.* the act of preparing the soil for cultivation; the cultivated land. **-er** *n.* [O.E. *tilian,* to till].

till (til) *n.* boulder clay or glacial drift.

til·ler (til'·er) *n.* a bar used as a lever, esp. for turning a rudder [O.Fr. *tellier,* weaver's beam].

tilt (tilt) *v.t.* to raise one end of; to tip up; to thrust, as a lance; to forge with a tilt hammer; *v.i.* to charge on horseback with a lance, as in a tournament; to slant; *n.* a thrust, as with a lance; a medieval sport in which competitors armed with lances charged each other; inclination. **-er** *n.* — **hammer** *n.* a heavy hammer used in iron works and tilted by a lever [O.E. *tealt,* tottering].

tilt (tilt) *n.* canvas covering of a cart; a small canvas awning; *v.t.* to cover with a tilt [O.E. *teld,* a tent].

tim·bal (tim'·bal) *n.* kettledrum [Sp. *timbal,* a kettledrum.

tim·ber (tim'·ber) *n.* trees or wood suitable for building purposes; trees collectively; single unit of wooden framework of house; rib of ship; *v.t.* to furnish with timber. **-ed** *a.* — **line** *n.* tree line, above which altitude trees will not grow [O.E. *timber,* material for building a house].

tim·bre (tim'·ber, tan'·br) *n.* special tone quality in sound of human voice or instrument [Fr. *timbre*].   [bourine [O.Fr. *timbre*].

tim·brel (tim'·bral) *n.* kind of drum, or tam-

time (tīm) *n.* particular moment; period of duration; conception of past, present, and future, as sequence; epoch; system of measuring duration, as *Greenwich time;* opportunity; occasoin; (*Mus.*) rhythmical arrangement of beats within measures or bars; *pl.* period characterized by certain marked tendencies, as *Victorian times;* term indicating multiplication, as *four times four; v.t.* to ascertain time taken, as by racing competitor; to select precise moment for; (*Mus.*) to measure; *v.i.* to keep or beat time. — **bomb** *n.* delayed-action bomb. —**honored** *a.* revered because of age; venerable. **-keeper** *n.* one who keeps a record of men's hours of work; clock or watch. **-less** *a.* eternal; unending. **-lessly** *adv.* **-liness** *n.* **-ly** *a.* opportune. **-piece** *n.* clock. **-r** *n.* a stop watch. **-server** *n.* **-serving** *n.* selfish opportunism. **-table** *n.* booklet containing times of departure and arrival of trains, buses, steamers, etc. **-worn** *a.* aged; decayed. **timing** *n.* control of speed of an action or actions for greatest effect. **Greenwich time,** British standard time as settled by passage of sun over meridian at Greenwich [O.E. *tima,* time].

tim·id (tim'·id) *a.* lacking courage or self-confidence; shy. **-ness, -ity** *n.* **-ly** *adv.* **timorous** *a.* frightened; very timid. **timorously** *adv.* **timorousness** *n.* [L. *timidus*].

ti·moc·ra·cy (tī·mak'·ra·si·) *n.* government in which possession of property is necessary qualification for holders of offices [Gk. *time,* honor; *kratos,* power].

tim·o·thy (tim'·a·thi·) *n.* grass grown for hay, and valued as fodder.

tim·pa·no (tim'·pa·nō) *n.* kettledrum, esp. as part of percussion section of orchestra. *pl.* **timpani. timpanist, tympanist** *n.* [Gk. *tumpanon,* a kettledrum].

tin (tin) *n.* soft, whitish-gray metal, very malleable and ductile, used for plating, as constituent of alloys (e.g. pewter, bronze) and for food containers in canning industry; tin can; (*Slang*) money; *a.* made of tin or plated with tin; *v.t.* to plate with tin. *pr.p.* **-ning.** *pa.p.* and *pa.t.* **-ned.** — **foil** *n.* wafer-thin sheets of tin; **-ned** *a.* preserved in a tin; plated with tin. **-ner, -man** *n.* a tin miner; one who makes tin plate. **-ning** *n.* **-ny** *a.* like tin; making a sound like tin when struck.

-type n. (*Photog.*) ferrotype; positive on varnished tin plate. **-ware** n. utensils, etc. made of tin plate [O.E. *tin*, tin].

Tin Pan Alley (tin'·pan·a'·li·) (*Slang*) the world of the composers of popular music.

tinc·ture (tingk'·cher) n. tinge or shade of color; faint trace; (*Pharm.*) solution of a substance in alcohol; v.t. to tinge; to imbue; to affect to a small degree [L. *tinctura*, dyeing].

tin·der (tin'·der) n. anything inflammable used for kindling fire from a spark [O.E. *tynder*, tinder].

tine (tīn) n. tooth or prong of fork; spike of harrow; branch of deer's antler. a. [O.E. *tind*, point].

ting (ting) n. sharp, ringing sound, as of bell; tinkle; v.t. and v.i. to tinkle. [imit.].

tinge (tinj) v.t. to color or flavor slightly; to temper. n. a faint touch [L. *tingere*].

tin·gle (ting'·gl) v.i. to feel faint thrill or pricking sensation; n. pricking sensation [prob. freq. of *ting*].

tink·er (tingk'·er) n. mender of pots, kettles, etc., esp. one who travels round countryside; jack of all trades; v.i. to do the work of a tinker; to attempt to mend [M.E. *tinker*, one who makes a sharp sound].

tin·kle (tingk'·l) v.t. to cause to make small, quick, metallic sounds; v.i. to make series of quick, sharp sounds; to jingle; n. small, sharp, ringing sound. **tinkling** n. a. [M.E. *tinken*, to chink].

tin·sel (tin'·sal) n. very thin, glittering, metallic strips for decorations, etc.; (*Fig.*) anything showy or flashy; a. gaudy; showy and cheap; v.t. to decorate with tinsel; to make gaudy. **—like** a. [Fr. *étincelle*, a spark].

tint (tint) n. hue or dye; faint tinge; color with admixture of white; v.t. to give faint coloring to; to tinge **-er** n. [L. *tinctus*, dyed].

tin·tin·nab·u·la·tion (tin·ti·nab·ya·lā'·shạn) n. tinkling sound of bells pealing. **tintinnabular, tintinnabulary, tintinnabulous** a. [L. *tintinnare*, to jingle].

ti·ny (tī'·ni·) a. very small; diminutive. Also **teeny**.

tip (tip) n. point of anything slender; end; top; v.t. to form a point on; to cover tip of. pr.p. **-ping.** pa.p. **-ped. -toe** adv. on tips of toes; v.t. to walk on tips of toes; to walk stealthily. [var. of *top*].

tip (tip) v.t. to touch lightly; to tap; to tilt; to overturn; to weigh down, as scales; (*Slang*) to give useful hint to, esp. about betting odds; to recompense with small gratuity; v.i. to fall to one side; to give gratuity; n. light stroke; private information; advice; gratuity; n. **-ping** n. **-ster** n. one who sells tips regarding horse-racing, etc. [M.E. *tipen*, to overthrow].

tip·pet (tip'·it) n. scarf or cloth of fur [L. *tapete*, tapestry].

tip·ple (tip'·l) v.i. to drink small quantities of intoxicating liquor frequently; v.t. to drink excessively. n. strong drink. **-r** n. [Scand. *tipla*, to drink little and often].

tip·sy (tip'·si·) a. intoxicated; staggering. **tipsily** adv. **tipsiness** n. [fr. *tipple*].

ti·rade (tī·rād') n. long denunciatory speech; volley of abuse [It. *tirata*, a drawing out].

tire (tīr) v.t. to weary or fatigue; v.i. to become wearied, bored, or impatient. **-d** a. wearied; bored. **-dness** n. **-less** a. **-lessly** adv. **-some** a. [O.E. *tiorian*, to be tired].

tire (tīr) n. hoop of iron, rubber, or rubber tube, etc. placed around a wheel [form of *attire*].

tir·o See **tyro**.

tis·sue (tish'·ōō) n. (*Biol.*) any of cellular structures which make up various organs of plant or animal body; unbroken series; web; fine cloth interwoven with gold or silver; a. made of tissue. **-d** a. made of or resembling

tissue. **— paper** n. very thin, white or colored semi-transparent paper [Fr. *tissu*, fr. L.*texere*, to weave].   [a little bird.

tit (tit) n. small bird, e.g. titmouse [O.N. *tittr*, **tit** (tit) n. teat [O.E. *tit*, a nipple].

Ti·tan (tī'·tạn) n. (*Gk. Myth.*) one of sons of Uranus and Gaea (Heaven) and Earth); (*l.c.*) person of magnificent physique or of brilliant intellectual capacity; a. pert. to Titans; (*l.c.*) colossal; mighty. **Titanic** a. pert. to Titans; colossal.

tithe (tīTH) n. tenth part; orig. tenth part of produce of land and cattle given to the church, later paid in form of tax; small portion; v.t. to levy a tithe; v.i. to give a tithe. **-r** n. **-less** a. [O.E. *teotha*, tenth].

tit·ian (tish'·ạn) a. rich auburn; from color of hair in many portraits by Titian, Italian painter.

tit·il·late (tit'·ạ·lāt) v.t. to tickle, usually in sense of stimulating mind, palate, etc.—**titillation** n. process of titillating; any pleasurable sensation. **titillative** a. [L. *titillare*, to tickle].

tit·i·vate (tit'·ạ·vāt) v.i. and v.t. (*Slang*) to put finishing touches to one's general appearance **titivator** n. [perh. fr. *tidy*].

ti·tle (tī'·tl) n. inscription put over, or under, or at beginning of, anything; designation; appellation denoting rank or office; that which constitutes just claim or right; (*Law*) legal proof of right of possession; title deed. **-d** a. having title, esp. aristicratic title. **— deed** n. document giving proof of legal ownership of property. **— page** n. page of book on which is inscribed name of book, author and publication data. **— role** n. part in play from which it takes its name [L. *titulus*, title].

tit·mouse (tit'·mous) n. small bird which builds in holes of trees; tit; tomtit. pl. **titmice** [M.E. *tit*, small; *mase*, name for several small birds].

ti·trate (tī'·trāt) v.t. to determine amount of ingredient in solution by adding quantities of standard solution until required chemical reaction is observed. **titration** n. [Fr. *titre*, title].

tit·ter (tit'·er) v.i. to give smothered laugh; to giggle; n. **-er** n. [imit.].

tit·tle (tit'·l) n. minute particle; whit; jot [L. *titulus*, superscription, small stroke to indicate contraction].

tit·u·lar (tich'·(y)ạ·ler) a. pert. to or having a title; nominal; ruling in name but not in deed. **titularity** n. **-y** a. titular; n. nominal holder of title [L. *titulus*, a title].

tme·sis (mē'·sis) n. separation of two parts of compound word by one or more interpolated words, as 'from *what* direction *soever*' [Gk. fr. *temnein*, to cut].

to (tōō) prep. expressing motion towards; as far as; regarding; unto; upon; besides; compared with; as to; expressing purpose, as in gerundial infinitive indicating dative case or indirect object; preceding infinitive mood of the verb; adv. forward; into customary position [O.E. *to*, to].

toad (tōd) n. amphibian resembling frog, but brownish with dry warty skin and short legs; mean, detestable person. **-stool** n. fungus resembling mushroom, but poisonous. **-y** n. obsequious flatterer; social parasite; v.i. to flatter excessively; to fawn on. pr.p. **-ying.** pa.t. and pa.p. **-ied. -yish** a. **-yism** n. sycophancy [O.E. *tadige*, a toad].

toast (tōst) v.t. to dry or warm by exposure to fire; to crisp and brown (as bread) before fire, under grill, etc.; to drink to health of, or in honor of; v.i. to drink a toast; n. slice of bread crisped and browned on both sides by heat; person in whose honor toast is drunk; the drink itself. **-er** n. **-master** n. one who presides at luncheon or dinner, proposes toasts, introduces speakers, etc. [L. *tostus*, roasted].

to·bac·co (tạ·bak'·ō) *n.* plant, dried leaves of which are used for chewing, smoking, or as snuff. *pl.* **-s, -es** [Sp. *tabaco*].

to·bog·gan (tạ·bȧg'·ạn) *n.* flat-bottomed sled used for coasting down snow-clad hill slopes; *v.i.* to slide down hills on toboggan. **-ing** *n.* [Amer.-Ind.].

to·by (tō'·bi·) *n.* small jug in shape of an old man wearing a three-cornered hat [fr. *Toby*, personal name].

toc·ca·ta (tạ·kȧ'·ta) *n.* (*Mus.*) composition for organ or piano which tests player's technique and touch [It.]. [sound [Fr.

toc·sin (tȧk'·sin) *n.* alarm bell or its ringing

to·day, to-day (tạ·dā') *n.* this day; present time; *adv.* on this day; at the present time [O.E. *to-daege*, today].

tod·dle (tȧd'·l) *v.i.* to walk with short, hesitating steps. *n.* unsteady gait. **-r** *n.* child just learning to walk [prob. form of *totter*].

tod·dy (tȧd'·i·) *n.* fermented juice of certain E. Indian palm trees; drink of whisky, sugar, and hot water [Hind. *tari*, juice of palm tree].

to·do (tạ·dòó') *n.* a commotion; a fuss [fr. *to* and *do*].

toe (tō) *n.* one of five small digits of foot; forepart of hoof; part of boot, shoe, or stocking covering toes; outer end of head of golf club; *v.t.* to touch or reach with toe; *v.i.* to tap with toes. **-d** *a.* having toes [O.E. *ta*, the toe].

tof·fee, tof·fy (tȧf'·i·) *n.* hard candy made of sugar, butter, flavoring, etc. boiled together. Also **taffy** [etym. uncertain].

tog (tȧg) *n.* (*Slang*) clothes. usu. in *pl.* *v.i.* to dress *pr.p.* **-ging.** *pa.p., pa.t.* **-get** [prob. fr. L. *toga*, a robe].

to·ga (tō'·gạ) *n.* loose outer garment worn by Roman citizens. **-ed, togated** *a.* wearing a toga [L. fr. *tegere*, to cover].

to·geth·er (tạ·geTH'·er) *adv* in company; in or into union; simultaneously; in same place [O.E. *to*, to; *geador*, together].

toil (toil) *v.i.* to labor; to move with difficulty; *n.* exhausting labor; drudgery; task. **-er** *n.* **-ful, -some** *a.* laborious. **-somely** *adv.* **-someness** *n.* **-worn** *a.* weary with toil; (of hands) hard and lined with toil [O.Fr. *touiller*, to entangle].

toil (toil) *n.* a net or snare; mesh. usu. *pl.* [Fr. *toile*, cloth].

toi·let (toi'·lit) *n.* process of dressing; mode of dressing; a lavatory. Also **toilette** (twạ·let'). — **articles** *n.pl.* objects used in dressing, as comb, brush, mirror, toothbrush, etc. — **paper** *n.* thin paper for lavatory use. — **powder** *n.* talcum powder [Fr. *toilette*, dim. of *toile*, cloth].

to·ken (tō'·kạn) *n.* sign; symbol; concrete expression of esteem; coin-like piece of metal for special use, as *bus token, etc.* — **payment** *n.* deposit paid as token of later payment of full debt [O.E. *tacen*, symbol].

told (tōld) *pa.t.* and *pa.p.* of verb **tell.**

tol·er·ate (tȧl'·ạ·rāt) *v.t.* to permit to be done; to put up with. **tolerable** *a.* endurable; supportable; passably good. **tolerability, tolerableness** *n.* **tolerably** *adv.* **tolerance** *n.* forbearance. **tolerant** *a.* forbearing; broadminded. **tolerantly** *adv.* **toleration** *n.* act of tolerating; practice of allowing people to worship as they please; granting to minorities political liberty. **tolerationist** *n.* **tolerator** *n.* [L. *tolerare*, to bear].

toll (tōl) *n.* tax, esp. for right to use bridge, ferry, public road. etc.; charge for long-distance telephone call. *v.i.* to exact toll. — **bar** *n.* formerly bar which could be swung across road to stop travelers to pay toll. [O.E. *toll*, tax].

toll (tōl) *v.t.* to cause to ring slowly, as bell, esp. to signify death; *v.i.* to peal with slow, sonorous sounds; *n.* [M.E. *tollen*, to pull].

tom (tȧm) *n.* used to denote male animal as tomcat. **-boy** *n.* girl of boyish behavior; hoyden, romping, mischievous girl. **-fool** *n.* complete fool. **-foolery** *n.* nonsensical behavior. [fr. *Thomas*].

tom·a·hawk (tȧm'·ạ·hawk) *n.* war hatchet used by N. American Indians; *v.t.* to wound or kill with tomahawk [Amer.-Ind.].

to·ma·to (tạ·mā'·tō) *n. pl.* **-es.** plant with red or yellow fruit much used in salads. [Sp. *tomate*].

tomb (tòom) *n.* a grave; underground vault; any structure for a dead body. **-stone** *n.* stone erected over grave [Gk. *tumbos*, a sepulchral mound].

tome (tōm) *n.* a book; a large, heavy volume [Gk. *tomos*, a piece cut off].

to·mor·row (tạ·mawr'·ō) *n.* day after today; *adv.* on the following day [O.E. *to*, and *morgen*, morning].

tom·tit (tȧm'·tit) *n.* a small bird [fr. *tit* as in *titmouse*].

tom-tom (tȧm'·tȧm) *n.* small drum used by Indian and African natives. Also **tam-tam** [Hind.]

ton (tun) *n.* weight consisting of 20 cwt. or 2000 lb.; measure of capacity varying according to article being measured; *pl.* (*Colloq.*) great amount or number. **-nage** *n.* cubical content (100 cub. ft.) or burden (40 cub. ft.) of ship in tons; duty on ships estimated per ton; shipping collectively assessed in tons. Also **tonnage** [O.E. *tunne*, vat].

ton (tȧn) *n.* fashion; latest mode [Fr.].

tone (tōn) *n.* quality or pitch of musical sound; modulation of speaking or singing voice; color values of picture; (*Mus.*) one of larger intervals of diatonic scale, smaller intervals being called *semitones;* (*Med.*) natural healthy functioning of bodily organs; general character, as of manners, morals, or sentiment; (*Gram*). pitch on one syllable of word; *v.t.* to give tone or quality to; to modify color or general effect of, as in photograph; to tune (instrument); *v.i.* to blend (with). **tonal** *a.* **tonality** *n.* quality of tone or pitch; system of variation of keys in musical composition; color scheme of picture. **tonally** *adv.* — **deaf** *a.* unable to distinguish musical intervals. *a.* having tone etc. [Gk. *tonos*, tension].

ton·ga (tȧng'·ga) *n.* a light, two-wheeled vehicle used in India [Hind.].

tong (tȧng, tawng) *n.* (in *U.S.*) an association exclusively for Chinese people [Chin. *t'ang*, meeting-place].

tongs (tȧngz, tawngz) *n.pl.* implement consisting of pair of pivoted levers, for grasping e.g. pieces of coal [O.E. *tange*, tongs].

tongue (tung) *n.* flexible muscular organ in mouth used in tasting, swallowing, and for speech; facility of utterance; language; anything shaped like a tongue; clapper of bell; narrow spit of land; slip of wood fitting into groove; *v.t.* to modulate with tongue as notes of flute; to chide; *v.i.* to use tongue as in playing staccato passage on flute; to chatter. **-d** *a.* having a tongue. —**tied** *n.* having tongue defect causing speech impediment; speechless through shyness [O.E. *tunge*].

ton·ic (tȧn'·ik) *a.* pert. to tones or sounds; having an invigorating effect bodily or mentally; *n.* a medicine which tones up the system; anything invigorating; (*Mus.*) a key note **-ally** *adv.* **tonicity** (tō·nis'·a·ti·) *n.* — **sol-fa,** a system of musical notation in which sounds are represented by syllables as do, ray, me, fah, etc. [Gk. *tonos*, act of stretching].

to·night, to-night (tạ·nīt') this night; night

following this present day; *adv.* on this night [fr. *to* and *night*].

ton·nage *n.* See **ton.**

ton·sil (tàn′·sil) *n.* one of two oval-shaped lymphoid organs on either side of pharynx. **-(l)itis** *n.* inflammation of the tonsils [L. *tonsillae*, tonsils].

ton·sure (tàn′·shẹr) *n.* act of shaving part of head as token of religious dedication; shaved crown of priest's head. **tonsor** *n.* barber. **tonsorial** *a.* pert. to a barber or his work (usu. humorous) [L. *tonsura*, clipping].

ton·tine (tàn′·tēn) *n.* shared annuity [fr. *Lorenzo Tonti*, the originator].

too (tòò) *adv.* in addition; more than enough; moreover [stressed form of *to*].

took (took) *pa.t.* of **take.**

tool (tòòl) *n.* implement or utensil operated by hand, or by machinery; cutting or shaping part of a machine; means to an end; *v.t.* to cut, shape, or mark with a tool; to indent a design on leather book cover, etc. with pointed tool. **-ing** *n.* [O.E. *tol*, a tool].

toot (tòòt) *v.t.* to cause to sound, as an automobile horn or wind instrument; *n.* sound of horn, etc.; hoot. [imit.].

tooth (tòòth) *n.* hard projection in gums of upper and lower jaws of vertebrates, used in mastication; prong as of comb, saw, rake; cog of wheel. *pl.* **teeth.** *v.t.* to provide with teeth; to indent; *v.i.* to interlock. **-ache** *n.* pain in tooth. **-brush** *n.* small brush for cleaning teeth. **-ed** *a.* **-some** *a.* palatable; pleasant to taste. **-y** *a.* having prominent teeth; toothed [O.E. *toth*, a tooth].

top (tàp) *n.* highest part of anything; upper side; highest rank; first in merit; green part of plants above ground; (*Naut.*) platform surrounding head of lower mast. *a.* highest; most eminent; best; *v.t.* to cover on the top; to rise above; to cut off top of; to hit, as golf ball, above center; to surpass; *v.i.* to be outstanding. **-coat** *n.* overcoat. **— hat** *n.* tall silk hat. **—heavy** *a.* unbalanced; having top too heavy for base. **-most** *a.* supreme; highest. **-notch** *a.* describing persons of high ability or anything which is super-excellent. **-per** something placed on the top; (*Slang*) top hat; topcoat. **-ping** *n.* act of lopping off top of something, as highest branches of tree; what is cut off; something put on top of a thing as decoration, to complete it, etc. *a.* **-pingly** *adv.* **-sail** *n.* square sail on top-mast. **-soil** *n.* surface layer of soil [O.E. *top*, summit]. [pointed end.

top (tàp) *n.* child's toy made to spin on its

to·paz (tō′·paz) *n.* gem stone, translucent and of varied colors [etym. uncertain].

tope (tōp) *v.i.* to drink hard or to excess. **-r** *n.* [Fr. *toper*, to clinch bargain].

to·pee (tō·pē′) *n.* pith helmet worn by Europeans in tropical climates. Also **topi** [Hind. *topi*, hat].

to·pi·a (tō′·pi·ạ) *n.* mural decoration comprising landscapes, popular in Roman houses. **topiary** *a.* cut into ornamental shapes, as trees, hedges, etc. *n.* topiary work or art; a garden or single shrub so trimmed. **topiarist** *n.* [L. *topia*, ornamental gardening].

top·ic (tàp′·ik) *n.* subject of essay, discourse, or conversation; branch of general subject. **-al** *a.* pert. to a place; up-to-date; concerning local matters. **-ally** *adv.* [Gk. *topos*, a place].

to·pog·ra·phy (tạ·pàg′·rạ·fi·) *n.* description of a place; scientific or physical features of region. **topographer** *n.* **topographic, -al** *a.* [Gk. *topos*, a place; *graphein*, to write].

top·ple (tàp′·l) *v.t.* to throw down; to overturn; *v.i.* to overbalance [freq. of *top*].

top·sy-tur·vy (tàp′·si·tur′·vi·) *adv.* upside down; *a.* turned upside down; *n.* disorder; chaos [prob. O.E. *top*, and *tearflian*, to roll].

toque (tōk) *n.* brimless woman's hat [Fr.].

To·rah (tōr′·ạ) *n.* the Pentateuch; (*l.c.*) whole scripture of Judaism [Heb. law].

torch (tawrch) *n.* piece of wood with some substance at the end soaked in inflammable liquid, and used as portable light. **-bearer** *n.* [L. *torquere*, to twist].

tore (tōr) *pa.t.* of **tear.**

tor·e·a·dor (tawr′·i·a·dawr) *n.* bull fighter [Sp. fr. L. *taurus*, a bull].

tor·ment (tawr′·ment) *n.* extreme pain of body; anguish of mind; misery; cause of anguish. **torment** *v.t.* to inflict pain upon; to torture; to vex; to tease. **tormenting** *a.* **tormentingly** *adv.* **tormentor, tormenter** *n.* [L. *tormentum*, instrument of torture].

torn (tōrn) *pa.p.* of **tear.**

tor·na·do (tawr·nā′·dō) *n.* whirling progressive windstorm causing wide-spread devastation. [Sp. *tronada*, thunderstorm].

tor·pe·do (tawr·pē′·dō) *n.* cigar-shaped underwater projectile with high explosive charge; type of explosive mine; electric ray fish which electrocutes its prey. *pl.* **-es.** *v.t.* to attack, hit, or sink with torpedoes. **-ist** *n.* expert in handling and firing torpedoes [L. *torpere*, to be numb].

tor·pid (tawr′·pid) *a.* dormant, as hibernating animal; lethargic; physically or mentally inert. **-ity** *n.* inactivity; lethargy. **-ly** *adv.* **-ness** *n.* **torpor** *n.* sluggishness; inertia. **torporific** *a.* [L. *torpere*, to be numb].

torque (tawrk) *n.* collar of gold wires twisted together, worn by ancient Britons, Gauls, etc. Also **torc;** (*Mech.*) rotating power in mechanism. **-d** *a.* [L. *torquere*, to twist].

tor·re·fy (tawr′·a·fī) *v.t.* to scorch; to parch; to roast, as metals. **torrefaction** *n.* [L. *torrere*, to burn; *facere*, to make].

tor·rent (tawr′·ạnt) *n.* swift-flowing stream; downpour, as of rain; rapid flow, as of words. **-ial** *a.* pert. to, resembling torrent; overwhelming [L. *torrens*, a boiling stream].

tor·rid (tawr′·id) *a.* extremely hot, dry or burning; passionate. **-ness, torridity** *n.* **-ly** *adv.* **— zone,** broad belt lying between Tropics of Cancer and Capricorn [L. *torrere*, to burn].

tor·sion (tawr′·shạn) *n.* act of turning or twisting; (*Mech.*) force with which twisted wire or similar body tends to return to original position. *a.* **— balance,** delecate scientific instrument for measuring minute forces by means of small bar suspended horizontally at end of very fine wire [L. *torquere*, to twist].

tor·so (tawr′·sō) *n.* trunk of human body; statue with head and limbs cut off [It.].

tort (tawrt) *n.* (*Law*) private injury to person or property for which damages may be claimed in court of law. **-ious** *a.* **-iously** *adv.* [L. *torquere*, to twist].

tor·til·la (tawr·tē′·(y)ạ) *n.* round, thin cake of corn meal [Sp. dim. of *torta*, a tart].

tor·toise (tawr′·tạs) *n.* land reptile or turtle; a very low person or thing; **-shell** *n.* horny mottled brown outer shell of tortoise used commercially for combs, etc.; *a.* mottled like tortoise shell [L. *tortus*, twisted].

tor·tu·ous (tawr′·choo·ạs) *a.* full of twists; crooked; devious; circuitous; deceitful. **-ity** *n.* **-ly** *adv.* **-ness** [L. *tortuosus*].

tor·ture (tawr′·chẹr) *n.* act of deliberately inflicting extreme pain as punishment or repraisal; anguish; torment; *v.t.* to put to torture; to inflict agony. *n.* **torturing** *a.* **torturous** *a.* [L. *tortura*, twisting].

to·ry (tōr′·i·) *a.* supporter of Britain in the American Revolution; (*Brit.*) a member of the Conservative party. **-ism** *n.* [Ir. *toruighe*, a pursuer].

toss (taws) *v.t.* to throw upwards with a jerk; to cause to rise and fall; to agitate violently; *v.i.* to be tossed; to roll and tumble; to be restless; *n.* fling; sudden fall from horseback; distance anything is tossed. **-er** *n.* **-ing** *n.* **-up,** tossing of coin to decide issue; (*Colloq.*) even chance [W. *tosio,* to jerk].

tot (tåt) *n.* anything small, esp. a child; [Scand. *tottr,* dwarf].

to·tal (tō·tạl) *a.* full; complete; utter; absolute; *n.* the whole; sum; aggregate; *v.t.* to sum; to add; *v.i.* to amount to. **-izator,** *n.* machine which registers totals. **-ity** *n.* whole sum; entirety. **-ly** *adv.* **-ness** *n.* [L. *totus* whole].

to·tal·i·tar·i·an (tō·tạl·ạ·tar′·i·ạn) *a.* relating to open-party dictorial form of government. **totalitarianism** *n.*

tote (tōt) *v.t.* (*Colloq.*) to carry; to bear; to transport.

to·tem (tō′·tạm) *n.* natural object, such as animal or plant, taken by primitive tribe as emblem of hereditary relationship with that object; image of this. **-ic** *a.* **-ism** *n.* **-ist** *n.* member of tribe. **-istic** *a.* — **pole** *n.* pole with totems carved on it, one above the other [Amer.-Ind.].

tot·ter (tåt′·ẹr) *v.i.* to walk with faltering steps; to sway; to shake; to reel. **-er** *n.* **-ing** *a.* **-ingly** *adv.* **-y** *a.* unsteady [O.E. *tealt,* unsteady].

tou·can (tòò′·kan, too·kån′) *n.* bird of tropical Am. [Braz.].

touch (tuch) *v.t.* to come in contact with; to finger; to reach; to attain; to treat of, superficially; to move deeply; to equal in merit; to play on; (*Slang*) to borrow from; *v.i.* to be in contact; to take effect on; *n.* contact; sense of feeling; quality of response in handling of instrument or color; individual style of execution; unique quality; trace or tinge; test; mild attack. **-able** *a.* **-ableness** *n.* — **and go,** precarious situation. — **down** (*Football*) scoring by having ball behind goal line. **-ed** *a.* (*Slang*) crazy. **-er** *n.* **-ily** *adv.* **-iness** *n.* **-ing** *a.* emotionally moving; pathetic; *prep.* concerning; referring to. **-ingly** *adv.* **-ingness** *n.* **-stone** *n.* variety of compact, siliceous stone, used for testing purity of gold and silver; criterion; standard of judgment. **-y** *a.* easily offended; hypersensitive. [Fr. *toucher*].

tough (tuf) *a.* flexible but not brittle; not easily broken; firm; difficult to chew; stouthearted; vigorous; hardy; difficult to solve; (*Slang*) vicious; *n.* a bully; a ruffian. **-en** *v.t.* to make tough, or hardy; *v.i.* to become tough. **-ly** *adv.* **-ness** *n.* [O.E. *toh,* tough].

tou·pee (tòò·pā′) *n.* wig or artificial lock of hair [Fr. *toupet,* a tuft of hair].

tour (toor) *n.* journey from place to place in a country; excursion; spell of duty; *v.t.* to travel round; to visit as part of tour. **-ism** *n.* **-ist** *n.* one who makes a tour; sightseer [Fr. *tour,* a turn].

tour·ma·lin(e) (toor′·mạ·lin) *n.* crystalline mineral [fr. Singh. *toramalli,* cornelian].

tour·na·ment (tur·, toor′·nạ·mạnt) *n.* mock fight, common form of contest and entertainment in medieval times; any sports competition or championship. **tourney** *n.* a tournament [O.Fr. *tournoiement,* a turning].

tour·ni·quet (toor′·ni·ket) *n.* surgical device for arresting hemorrhage by compression of a blood vessel, as a bandage tightened by twisting [Fr. fr. *tourner,* to turn].

tous·le (tou′·zạl) *v.t.* to make untidy by pulling, as hair; to dishevel. *a.* untidy [conn. with *tussle*].

tout (tout) *v.i.* and *v.t.* to solicit business, etc.; to give a tip on a race horse; to praise highly *n.* one who pesters people to be customers; hanger-on at racing stables. **-er** *n.* [O.E. *totian,* to peep out].

tow (tō) *v.t.* to drag through water by rope or chain; to pull along; *n.* act of pulling; rope or chain used for towing; course fiber of hemp used in rope making. **-age** *n.* act of or charge for towing. **-(ing)-path** *n.* path alongside canal used by horses towing canal barge. **to take in tow,** to pull along; (*Fig.*) to take charge of [O.E. *togian,* to pull].

to·ward(s) (tōrd(z), tawrd(s)) *prep.* in direction of; near (of time); with respect to; regarding [O.E. *toweard,* future].

tow·el (tou′·ạl) *n.* cloth or paper for drying skin, or for domestic purposes. **-ing** *n.* soft fabric for making towels. [O.H. Ger. *twahan,* to wash].

tow·er (tou′·ẹr) *n.* lofty, round or square structure; *v.i.* to be lofty or very high; to soar; to excel. **-ed** *a.* having towers. **-ing** *a.* lofty; violent [L. *turris,* tower].

town (toun) *n.* collection of houses etc., larger than village; inhabitants of town; *a.* pert. to town. — **clerk** *n.* official in charge of administrative side of a town's affairs. **-ship** *n.* a division of a county **-speople** *n.* inhabitants of town [O.E. *tun,* an enclosure].

tox·i·col·o·gy (tåk·sạ·kål′·ạ·ji·) *n.* science of poisons, their effects, nature, etc. **toxemia,** *n.* bloodpoisoning. **toxemic** *a.* **toxic, -al** *a.* poisonous. **toxically** *adv.* **toxicant** *a.* poisonous; *n.* poison. **toxicological** *a.* **toxicologist** *n.* **toxin** *n.* poison usually of bacterial origin [Gk. *toxikon,* poison].

tox·oph·i·lite (tåk·såf′·ạ·līt) *n.* student of, or expert in, archery. **toxophilitic** *a.* [Gk. *toxon,* bow; *philos,* fond of].

toy (toi) *n.* child's plaything; bauble; trifle; *v.i.* to daily; to trifle [Dut. *tuig.* tool].

trace (trās) *n.* mark; footprint; vestige; minute quantity; remains; outline; barely perceptible sign; *v.t.* to copy or draw exactly on a superimposed sheet; to follow track or traces of; to work out step by step; *v.i.* to move. **-able** *a.* capable of being traced or detected; attributable. **-ableness** *n.* **-ably** *adv.* **-er** *n.* **tracing** *n.* traced copy of drawing. **tracing-paper** *n.* specially prepared, transparent paper for tracing design, etc. [L. *trahre,* to draw].

trace (trās) *n.* strap, rope, chain, by which horse pulls vehicle [L. *trahere,* draw].

tra·che·a (trā′·ki·a, trạ·kē′·ạ) *n.* windpipe between lungs and back of throat. *pl.* **tracheae, -l** *a.* **tracheotomy** *n.* (*Surg.*) operation by which opening is made in windpipe [Gk. *tracheia* (*artēria*), windpipe, and *trachēlos,* neck].

track (trak) *n.* mark left by something; footprint; pathway trodden out by usage; laid-out course for racing; (or railway) metal rails forming a permanent way; (of motor vehicles) distance between wheels on one axle; (of aircraft) actual direction along which airplane is passing over ground; wheelband of tank or tractor; (*Fig.*) evidence; trace; *v.t.* to follow trail or traces of; to make a track of footprints on; *v.i.* to follow a trail; to run in the same track (of wheels); to be in alignment. **-er** *n.* — **meet,** athletic contest in sports held on a track, racing, jumping, etc. [O.Fr. *trac,* track of horse].

tract (trakt) *n.* region of indefinite extent; continuous period of time; short treatise, esp. on practical religion. **-ability** *n.* quality or state of being tractable. **-able** *a.* docile; amenable to reason. **-ableness** *n.* **-ably** *adv.* **-ile** *a.* capable of being drawn out; (of metals) ductile. **-ility** *n.* **traction** (trak′·shạn) *n.* act of drawing or pulling; gripping power, as of a wheel on a road. **tractional** *a.* **traction-engine** *n.* locomotive, steam-driven, for haulage. **-ive** *a.* having power to haul heavy loads; pulling. **-or** *n.* motor vehicle for drawing agricultural machinery [L. *trahere, tractum,* to draw].

trade (trād) *n.* the business of buying and selling; commerce; barter; occupation, esp. in industry, shopkeeping, etc.; employees collectively in a particular trade; vocation; *v.t.* to carry on a trade; to engage in commerce; *v.t.* to exchange. **-mark** *n.* registered name or device on maker's goods. — **name** *n.* name given by manufacturer to proprietary article. **-r** *n.* merchant (wholesale or retail); trading vessel. — **union** *n.* legally recognized association of workmen; a labor union. — **unionist** *n.* member of trade union. — **wind** *n.* one of two prevailing winds which blow steadily between the tropics and the Equator. **trading** *n.* [O.E. *tredan*, to tread].

tra·di·tion (trạ·dish'·ạn) *n.* belief, custom, narrative, etc. transmitted by word of mouth from age to age; religious doctrine preserved orally from generation to generation. **-al**, **-ary** *a.* **-alism** *n.* **-alist** *n.* **-alistic** *a.* [L. *tradere*, to hand over].

tra·duce (trạ·dūs') *v.t.* to defame the character of; to calumniate. **-r** *n.* a slanderer [L. *traducere*, to lead along].

traf·fic (traf'·ik) *n.* commerce; business dealings; illegal buying and selling, as *drug traffic*; movement of people, vehicles, etc. to and fro, in streets; coming and going of ships, trains, aircraft, etc.; people, vehicles, etc. collectively in any given area; *v.i.* to carry on trade; to do business, esp. illegally; *pr.p.* **—king.** *pa.t.* and *pa.p.* **-ked. -ker** *n.* [Fr. *trafiquer*, to traffic].

trag·e·dy (traj'·ạ·di·) *n.* serious and dignified dramatic composition in prose or verse with unhappy ending; sad or calamitous event. **tragedian** (trạ·jēd'·i·an) *n.* actor in or writer of tragedy. **tragedienne** *n. fem.* **tragic, -al** *a.* pert. to tragedy; distressing; calamitous. **tragically** *adv.* **tragicalness** *n.* **tragic irony,** use in tragedy of words which convey a deeper meaning to audience than to speaker—form of *dramatic irony.* **tragicomedy** *n.* drama combining tragedy and comedy [Gk. *tragōidia*, goat-song (reason for name variously explained)].

trail (trāl) *v.t.* to draw along ground or through water; to follow track of; (*Colloq.*) to follow behind; to carry rifle in hand at an angle, with butt close to the ground; to make a track by treading the ground; *v.i.* to dangle loosely, touching ground; to grow to great length as plant; to drag one foot wearily after other; *n.* track followed by hunter; visible trace left by anything; scent of hunted animal; something drawn behind; part of gun-carriage which rests on ground during firing. **-er** *n.* vehicle towed by another. **-less** *a.* [O.Fr. *trailer*, to tow a boat].

train (trān) *v.t.* to discipline; to instruct or educate; to submit person to arduous physical exercise, etc. for athletics; to teach animal to be obedient, to perform tricks, or compete in races; to cause plant to grow in certain way; to aim, as gun, before firing; *v.i.* to exercise body or mind to achieve high standard of efficiency; *n.* retinue; procession of people; line of cars drawn by locomotive on railway track; trailing folds of lady's evening dress; strong of pack animals; sequence of events, ideas, etc.; trail of gunpowder to lead fire to explosive charge. **-ed** *a.* **-ee** *n.* one who is training. **-er** *n.* **-ing** *n.* [O.Fr. *trahiner*, to drag].

trail oil (trā'·oil) *n.* oil extracted from blubber of whales [O.Dut. *traen*, whale oil].

traipse (trāps) *v.i.* (*Colloq.*) to walk aimlessly.

trait (trāt) *n.* distinguishing feature, esp. in character [Fr. *trait*, a feature].

trai·tor (trā'·tẹr) *n.* (*fem.* **traitress**) one who betrays person, country, or cause. **-ous**

a. guilty of treachery; pert. to treason or to traitors. **-ously** *adv.* [L. *tradere*,, to hand over].

tra·jec·to·ry (trạ·jek'·tạ·ri·) *n.* curve of projectile in its flight through space [L. *trans*, across; *facere*, to throw].

tram·mel (tram'·ạl) *n.* long net for catching birds or fish; shackle for training horse to walk slowly; anything which impedes movement; *v.t.* to impede; to hinder; to confine. **-er,** *n.* [O.Fr. *tramail*, a net].

tramp (tramp) *v.t.* to tread heavily; to hike over or through; *v.i.* to go on a walking tour; to plod; to wander as vagrant; *n.* homeless vagrant; a long walk; cargo boat with no regular route. **-er** *n.* [M.E. *trampen*].

tram·ple (tram'·pl) *v.t.* to tread heavily underfoot; to oppress; to treat with contempt; *v.i.* to tread heavily; *n.* act of trampling. **-r** *n.* [freq. of *tramp*].

tram·po·line (tram'·pạ·lēn) *n.* canvas springboard. **trampolinist** *n.* [It. *trampolino*, a springboard].

trance (trans) *n.* state of insensibility; a fit of complete mental absorption; (*Spiritualism*) condition in which medium is supposedly controlled by outside agency; semi-conscious condition [O.Fr. *transe*, a swoon].

tran·quil (trang'·kwil) *a.* calm; serene; undisturbed. **-ly** *adv.* **tranquillity** *n.* **-ness** [L. *tranquillus*].

trans- (tranz, trans) *pref.* meaning across, beyond, on the other side of [L. *trans*, across].

trans·act (tranz·, trans·akt') *v.t.* to carry through; to negotiate; *v.i.* to do (business). **-or** *n.* **-ion** *n.* act of transacting business; *pl.* records of, or lectures delivered to, a society. **-ional** *a.*

trans·al·pine (tranz·, trans·al'·pīn) *a.* north of Alps (as from Rome). [the Atlantic.

trans·at·lan·tic (trans·at·lan'·tik) *a.* across

tran·scend (tran·send') *v.t.* to go beyond; to excel; to surpass. **-ence, -ency** *n.* quality of being transcendent; (*Theol.*) supremacy of God above all human limitations. **-ent** *a.* supreme in excellence; surpassing all; beyond all human knowledge. **-ently** *adv.* **-entness** *n.* **-ental** *a.* abstruse; supernatural; intuitive. **-entalism** *n.* **-entalist** *n.* **-entally** *adv.* [L. *trans*, across; *scandere*, to climb].

trans·con·ti·nen·tal (trans·kȧn·tạ·nen'·tạl) *a.* crossing a continent.

tran·scribe (tran·skrīb') *v.t.* to copy out; to write over again; to reproduce in longhand or typescript notes taken in shorthand; (*Mus.*) to rearrange composition for another instrument or voice. **-r** *n.* **transcript** *n.* that which is transcribed; written copy. **transcription** *n.* act of copying; transcript.

tran·sect (tran·sekt') *v.t.* to cut transversely.

tran·sept (tran'·sept) *n.* transverse portion of church at right angles to nave. **-al** *a.* **-ally** *adv.* [L. *septum*, enclosure].

trans·fer (trans·fur') *v.t.* to move from one place to another; to transport; to remove; to pass an impression from one surface to another, as in lithography, photography, etc.; to convey, as property, legally to another. *pr.p.* **-ring.** *pa.t.* and *pa.p.* **-red. transfer** (trans'·fẹr) *n.* removal from one place to another; ticket allowing change of vehicle during single trip without further charge; design to be, or which has been transferred. **-ability** *n.* **-able** *a.* capable of being transferred; valid for use by another. **-ence** *n.* the act of transferring; in psychoanalysis, redirection of emotion, when under, analytical examination, towards someone else. **thought transference** *n.* telepathy. **-or, -rer** *n.* [L. *trans*, across; *ferre*, to bear].

trans·fig·ure (trans·fig'·yẹr) *v.t.* to change outward appearance of; to make more beautiful or radiant. **-ment** n. **transfiguration** n. change of appearance.

trans·fix (trans·fiks′) v.t. to pierce through; to impale; to astound; to stun. **-ion** n.

trans·form (trans·fawrm′) v.t. to change form, nature, character, or disposition of; to transmute; v.i. to be changed. **-able** a. **-ation** n. change of outward appearance or inner nature. **-ative** a. **-er** n. one who or that which transforms; an electrical device for changing voltage up or down. **-ing** a. [L. transformare, to change].

trans·fuse (trans·fūz′) v.t. to pour, as liquid, from one receptacle into another; (Med.) to transfer blood from one person to vein of another. **-r** n. **transfusible** a. **transfusive** a. **transfusion** n. [L. trans, across; fundere, fusum, to pour].

trans·gress (tranz·, trans·gres′) v.t. to overstep a limit; to violate law or commandment; v.i. to offend by violating a law; to sin. **transgression** n. act of violating civil or moral law; offense. **-ive** a. **-ively** adv. **-or** n. [L. transgressus, to step across].

tran·sient (tran′·shant) a. fleeting; ephemeral; momentary; not permanent; **transience, transiency** n. **-ly** adv. **-ness** n. [L. trans, across; ire, to go].

trans·it (tran′·sit, ·zit) n. the act of conveying; conveyance; (Astron.) apparent passage of celestial body across meridian of a place, or of a smaller planet across disc of larger; a surveyor's instrument for measuring angles. **transition** n. passage from one place to another; change from one state or condition to another; (Mus.) passing directly from one key to another. **transitional, transitionary** a. **transitionally** adv. **transitive** a. having power of passing across; (Gram.) denoting verb, the action of which passes on to direct object, as he broke his leg. **-ively** adv. **-iveness** n. **-orily** adv. **-oriness** n. state of being transitory. **-ory** a. [L. transitus, a passing across].

trans·late (tranz·, trans·lāt′) v.t. to turn from one language into another; to change from one medium to another; to remove from one place to another; to appoint bishop to different see; to convey to heaven without death; v.i. to be capable of translation. **translatable** a. **translation** n. **translator** n. [L. transferre, translatum, to carry over].

trans·lit·er·ate (tranz·, trans·lit′·a·rāt) v.t. to write words of language in alphabetic symbols of another. **transliteration** n. **transliterator** n.

trans·lu·cent (tranz·, trans·lōō′·sant) a. semitransparent; diffusing light but not revealing definite contours of object, as frosted glass. **translucence, translucency** n. **-ly** adv. **translucid** a. translucent [L. trans, across; lucere, to shine].

trans·mi·grate (tranz·, trans·mī′·grāt) v.i. to pass from one country to another as permanent residence; (of soul) to pass at death into another body or state. **transmigration** n. **transmigrator** n. **transmigratory** a.

trans·mit (trans·mit′) v.t. to send from one person or place to another; to communicate; to pass on, as by heredity. pr.p. **-ting.** pa.t. and pa.p. **-ted. transmissibility** n. **transmissible, transmittible** a. capable of being transmitted. **transmission** n. act of transmitting; in motoring, gear by which power is transmitted from engine to axle; (Radio.) radiation of electromagnetic waves by transmitting station. **-tal** n. transmission. **-tance** n. **-ter** n. one who or that which transmits; apparatus for transmitting radio waves through space [L. trans, across; mittere, to send].

trans·mute (tranz·, trans·mūt′) v.t. to change from one nature, species, form, or substance into another. **transmutable** a. **transmutableness** n. **transmutability** n. **transmutably** adv. **transmutant** a. **transmutation** n. act or process of transforming; alteration, esp. biological transformation of one species into another; in alchemy, supposed change of baser metals into gold. **transmutative** a. **-r** n. [L. trans, across; mutare, to change].

tran·som (tran′·sam) n. window over a doorway; lintel separating it from door; horizontal crossbar in window; transverse beam across sternpost of ship [L. transtrum, crossbeam].

trans·par·ent (trans·par′·ant) a. that may be distinctly seen through; pervious to light; clear; ingenuous; obvious. **transparence, transparency** n. **-ly** adv. **-ness** n. [L. trans, across; parere, to appear].

tran·spire (tran·spīr′) v.t. to emit through pores of skin; v.i. to exhale; (Bot.) to lose water by evaporation; to come out by degrees; to become known; loosely used as a synonym for to happen. **transpiration** n. **transpiratory** a. [L. trans, across; spirare, to breathe].

trans·plant (tranz·plant′) v.t. to remove and plant elsewhere; (Surg.) to graft live tissue from one part of body to another. **-able** a. **-ation** n. **-er** n.

trans·port (trans·pōrt′) v.t. to convey from one place to another; to banish, as criminal, to penal colony; to overwhelm emotionally. **transport** n. vehicles collectively used in conveyance of passengers; a troopship; passion; ecstasy. **-able** a. **-ability** n. **-er** n. **-ation** n. act or means of transporting from place to place; banishment, for felony. **-ted** a. [L. trans, across; portare, to carry].

trans·pose (trans·pōz′) v.t. to change respective place or order of two things; to alter order of words; (Mus.) to change key of a composition. **transposable** a. **transposal** n. change of order. **transposition** n. **transpositional** a. [L. trans, across; ponere, positum, to place].

tran·sub·stan·ti·ate (tran·sab·stan′·shi′·āt) v.t. to change into another substance. **transubstantiation** n. doctrine held by R.C. Church that the 'whole substance' of the bread and wine in the Eucharist is, by reason of its consecration, changed into flesh and blood of Christ, the appearance only of the bread and wine remaining the same [L. trans, across; substantia, substance].

tran·sude (tran·sūd′) v.i. to pass through pores of substance [L. trans, across; sudare, to sweat].

trans·verse (trans·vurs′) a. lying in crosswise direction. **transversal** n. line which cuts across, two or more parallel lines. **-ly** adv. [L. trans, across; vertere, versum, to turn].

trap (trap) n. device, mechanical or otherwise, for catching animals, vermin, etc.; snare; U-shaped bend in pipe which, by being always full of water, prevents foul air or gas from escaping; stratagem; plot to catch person unawares; v.t. to catch in a trap, or by stratagem. pr.p. **-ping.** pa.p., pa.t. **-ped.** **-door** n. hinged door in floor or ceiling. **-per** n. [O.E. traeppe].

trap (trap) n. one of several dark-colored igneous rocks. **-pean, -pose, -py** a. [Scand. trappa, stairs].

trap (trap) pl. (Colloq.) one's belongings, luggage, etc.; v.t. to adorn. pr.p. **-ping.** pa.p., pa.t. **-ped. -pings** n.pl. ornaments, gay coverings [Fr. drap, cloth].

tra·pe·zi·um (tra·pē′·zi·am) n. quadrilateral with no parallel sides; (Anat.) one of wrist bones pl.s. **trapezia. trapeze** n. apparatus comprising horizontal crossbar swing for gym-

nastics, acrobatic exhibitions, etc. **trapezoid**
n. quadrilateral with only two of its sides
parallel. **trapezoidal** *a.* [Gk. *trapezion*, a
little table].

trash (trash) *v.t.* to lop off, as branches,
leaves, etc.; *n.* worthless refuse; rubbish;
loppings of trees, bruised sugar canes, etc.
-ily *adv.* **-iness** *n.* **-y** *a.* worthless; cheap;
shoddy [prob. Scand. *tros.* twigs for fuel].

trass (tras) *n.* volcanic material used in
making cement [Dut. *tras*].

trau·ma (traw′·mạ) *n.* (*Med.*) bodily injury
caused by violence; emotional shock (psychic
trauma) with a lasting effect. *pl.* **-ta. -tic**
a. [Gk. *trauma*, a wound].

trav·ail (trav′·āl) *n.* painful, arduous labor;
pains of childbirth; *v.i.* (*Arch.*) to labor with
difficulty; to suffer pangs of childbirth [Fr.
travail, labor].

trave (trāv) *n.* beam; frame in blacksmith's
shop to keep horse steady [L. *trabs*, beam].

trav·el (trav′·ạl) *v.t.* to journey over; to pass;
v.i. to move; to journey on foot or in a
vehicle; to tour, esp. abroad. *n.* act of traveling; journey; touring, esp. abroad; (*Mach.*)
distance a component is permitted to move;
pl. prolonged journey, esp. abroad; book describing traveler's experiences and observa-
tions. **-ed** *a.* **-er** *n.* **-er's check,** check issued
by bank, express company, etc. which may be
cashed by anyone in whose presence it is endorsed. **-ing** *a.* **-ogue** *n.* travel lecture illustrated by slides, film, etc.; geographical film
[a form of *travail*].

tra·verse (trav′·ẹrs) *a.* lying across; built
crosswise; anything set across; a partition;
(*Archit.*) barrier, movable screen, or curtain;
gallery across church; zigzag course of a
ship; lateral movement; *v.t.* to cross; to
thwart; to obstruct; to survey across a plot
of ground; to rake with gun fire from end to
end; to pivot laterally; to discuss, as topic,
from every angle; to deny formally, in pleading at law; *v.i.* to turn, as on pivot; to move
sideways. **traversable** *a.* **-r** *n.* [L. *trans*,
across; *vertere, versum*, to turn].

trav·es·ty (trav′·is·ti·) *n.* burlesque imitation of a work; parody; *v.t.* to make a burlesque of; to caricature [Fr. *travestir*, to
disguise].

trawl (trawl) *v.t.* to catch fish with a trawl;
v.i. to drag with a trawl; *n.* a strong fishing
net, shaped like a large bag with one end
open. **-er** *n.* who fishes with a trawl; fishing
vessel. **-ing** *n.* [O.Fr. *trauler*, to drag].

tray (trā) *n.* flat, shallow, rimmed vessel used
for carrying dishes, food, etc. [O.E. *trog*, a
trough].

treach·er·y (trech′·ẹr·i·) *n.* violation of allegiance or faith; treason; perfidy. **treacherous** *a.* **treacherously** *adv.* [O.Fr. *trechier*,
to deceive].

tread (tred) *v.i.* to walk; to move with stately
or measured step; (of fowls) to copulate; to
crush; *v.t.* to step or walk one; to crush with
foot; to oppress; to operate with foot, as
treadle. *pa.t.* **trod.** *pa.p.* **trod** or **trodden.** *n.*
act of stepping; pace; that which one steps
on, as surface of horizontal step of flight of
stairs; sole of boot or shoe; part of a rubber
tire in contact with ground. **-ing** *n.* **-le,** *n.*
part of machine operated by foot pressure as
sewing machine, etc.; pedal; *v.i.* to work
treadle. **-ler** *n.* **-mill** *n.* mill worked by persons or animals treading upon steps on periphery of a wheel; drudgery [O.E. *tredan*,
to tread].

trea·son (trē′·zn) *n.* disloyalty to country;
act of betrayal. **-able** *a.* treason. **-ableness**
n. **-ably** *adv.* **-ous** *a.* [O.Fr. *traison*, be-
trayal].

treas·ure (trezh′·ẹr) *n.* accumulated wealth;
hoard of valuables; that which has great

worth; *v.t.* to hoard; to value; to cherish, as
friendship. **— chest** *n.* box for storing valuables. **-r** *n.* person appointed to take charge of
funds of society, church, club, etc. **-ship** *n.*
—trove *n.* any money, bullion, treasure, etc.,
of unknown ownership, which one finds.

treasury *n.* place where treasure, hoarded
wealth, or public funds are deposited; storehouse of facts and information; anthology.
Treasury *n.* government department which
controls management of public revenues.
treasury note *n.* currency note isued by the
United States Treasury [Fr. *trésor*, treasure].

treat (trēt) *v.t.* to entertain with food or
drink; to pay for another's entertainment or
refreshment; to behave towards; to apply a
remedy to; to subject, as a substance, to
chemical experiment; to consider as a topic
for discussion; to discourse on; *v.i.* to discourse; to come to terms of agreement, as
between nations; to give entertainment; *n.*
entertainment given as a celebration or expression of regard; (*Colloq.*) something that
gives special pleasure; one's turn to pay for
another's entertainment. **-er** *n.* **-ing** *n.* act
of standing treat. **-ise** *n.* dissertation on particular theme. **-ment** *n.* act or mode of treating person, subject, artistic work, etc.;
method of counteracting disease or of applying remedy for injury. **-y** *n.* a negotiated
agreement betwen states; a pact [L. *tracture*,
to handle].

tre·ble (treb′·l) *a.* threefold; triple; (*Mus.*)
playing or singing highest part; *n.* highest
part; *n.* highest of four principal parts in
music; soprano part or voice; *v.t.* to multiply
by three; *v.i.* to become three times as much.
trebly *adv.* [L. *triplus*].

tree (trē) perennial plant, having trunk,
bole, or woody stem with branches; any plant
resembling form of tree; (*Arch.*) cross of
Christ; *v.t.* to chase up a tree; to corner.
-less *a.* **-lessness** *n.* **-top** *n.* uppermost
branches of tree. **family tree,** genealogical
table of ancestry [O.E. *treow*, tree].

tre·foil (trē′·foil) *n.* plant of genus *Trifolium*,
with leaves comprising three leaflets; clover;
(*Archit.*) ornament of three cusps in circle
resembling three-leaved clover [L. *tres*, three;
folium, leaf].

trek (trek) *v.i.* to migrate; *pr.p.* **-king.** *pa.p.*,
pa.t. **-ked.** *n.* journey by wagon; mass-migra-
tion. **-ker** *n.* [Dut. *trekken*, to draw].

trel·lis (trel′·is) *n.* light-weight lattice structure esp. as frame for climbing plants. **-ed** *a.*
-work *n.* lattice work [L. *trilix*, three-ply].

trem·ble (trem′·bl) *v.i.* to shake involuntarily
to quiver; to quake; *n.* involuntary shaking;
quiver; tremor. **-r** *n.* **trembling** *n.* **trembling** *adv.* **trembly** *a.* shaky; **tremulant,
tremulous** *a.* quivering; quaking; fearful.
tremulously *adv.* **tremulousness** *n.* [L.
tremere, to shake].

tre·men·dous (tri·men′·dạs) *a.* awe-inspir-
ing; formidable; (*Colloq.*) great. **-ly** *adv.*
-ness *n.* [L. *tremere*, to tremble].

tre·mo·lan·do (trem·ạ·lán′·dō) *a.* (*Mus.*)
tremulous. **tremolo** *n.* quivering of singing
voice; device on organ to produce similar
sound. [It.].

trem·or (trem′·ẹr) *n.* involuntary quiver; a
nervous thrill; shaking, as caused by earthquake. **-less** *a.* steady [L.].

trem·u·lous See **tremble.**

trench (trench) *v.t.* to cut or dig, as a ditch;
to turn over soil by digging deeply; to fortify
with ditch using earth dug out for rampart;
v.i. to encroach; *n.* ditch; deep ditch to protect soldiers from enemy fire. **-ancy** *n.* quality
of being trenchant. **-ant** *a.* penetrating; keen;
clear-cut; **— coat** *n.* waterproof coat. **-ing** *n.*
[O.Fr. *trenchier*, to cut].

trench·er (tren′·chẹr) *n.* (*Arch.*) wooden plate

for holding food [O.Fr. *trenchoir*, platter].

trend (trend) *v.i.* to stretch in a certain direction; *n.* inclination; tendency; general direction [O.E. *trendln*, to make round].

tre·pan (tri·pan′) *n.* heavy tool for boring shafts; (*Surg.*) obsolete cylindrical saw (improved version called **trephine** (tri·fin′) *v.t.* to cut disks out of metal plates, etc.; to operate with trepan. *pr.p.* **-ning**. *pa.p., pa.t.* **-ned.** **-ation, -ning** *n.* [Gk. *trupanon*, borer].

trep·id (trep′.id) *a.* quaking. **-ation** *n.* involuntary trembling; alarm; fluster [L. *trepidus*].

tres·pass (tres′.pas, pas) *v.i.* to cross boundary line of another's property unlawfully; to intrude; to encroach; to violate moral law; *n.* **-er** *n.* [L. *trans*, across; *passus*, a step]

tress (tres) *n.* long lock, curl, braid or strand of hair; ringlet. **-ed** *a.* [O.Fr. *tresse*].

tres·tle (tres′.l) *n.* frame consisting of two pairs of braced legs fixed underneath horizontal bar, used as support; similar construction supporting a bridge [O.Fr. *trested*, a cross-beam].

tri- (trī) *prefix* meaning three, thrice, three-fold [L. *tres*, Gk. *treis, tria*, three].

tri·ad (trī′.ad) *n.* union of three; (*Chem.*) trivalent atom; (*Mus.*) the common chord, one of three notes; poem with triple grouping, common in Celtic literature. **-ic** *a.* **-ist** *n.* writer of triads [Gk. *trias*, group of three].

tri·al (trī′al) *n.* act of trying, testing, or proving properties of anything; experimental examination; affliction; judicial examination in law court of accused person [fr. *try*].

tri·an·gle (trī′.ang·gl) *n.* (*Math.*) figure bounded by three lines and containing three angles; anything shaped like a triangle; (*Mus.*) small percussion instrument consisting of a bar of steel bent in shape of triangle and struck with small steel rod. **-d** *a.* **triangular** *a.* **triangularity** *n.* **triangularly** *adv.*

tri·ar·chy (trī′.ar·ki·) *n.* government by three persons; a state so governed.

tri·a·tom·ic (trī·a·tăm′.ik) *a.* consisting of three atoms; having valency of three.

tribe (trīb) *n.* family, race, or succession of generations descending from same progenitor; nation of barbarian clans each under one leader; group of plants or animals within which members reveal common characteristics; (*Colloq.*) very large family. **tribal** *a.* **tribalism** *n.* tribal feeling; tribal life. **tribally** *adv.* **-sman** *n.* one of a tribe [L. *tribus*, one of *three* divisions of Roman people].

trib·u·la·tion (trib·ya·lā′.shan) *n.* severe affliction; prolonged suffering, esp. of mind [L. *tribulum*, instrument for threshing corn].

trib·une (trib′.ūn) *n.* in ancient Rome, magistrate chosen by the people to defend their rights; champion of the masses; a raised platform or pulpit. **tribunal** *n.* bench on which judge or magistrates sit; court of justice. **tribunate, tribuneship** *n.* office or functions of tribune [L. *tribus*, a tribe].

trib·ute (trib′.ūt) *n.* personal testimony to achievements or qualities of another; pre-arranged payment made at stated times by one state to another as price of peace and protection; tax. **tributarily** *adv.* **tributary** *a.* paying tribute; subordinate; contributory; (of river) flowing into main river; *n.* one who pays tribute; stream flowing into larger river [L. *tribuere*, to assign].

trice (trīs) *n.* moment; a very short time [O.Dut. *trisen*, to hoist].

tri·ceps (trī′.seps) *a.* three-headed; *n.* three-headed muscle as at back of upper arm [L. *tres*, three; *caput*, the head].

trich·i·no·sis (trik·a·nō′.sis) *n.* disease due to the presence of the nematode worm **trichina** in the intestines and muscular tissue [Gk. *trichinos*, hair].

tri·cho- *pref.* fr. Gk. *thrix, trichos*, hair.

tri·chol·o·gy (tri·kal′.a·ji·) *n.* study of hair and diseases affecting it. [ing the hair.

tri·cho·sis (tri·kō′.sis) *n.* any disease affect-

tri·chot·o·mous (tri·kat′.a·mas) *a.* divided into three or threes. **trichotomy** *n.* [Gk. *tricha*, in three; *tomē*, a cutting].

trick (trik) *n.* artifice or stratagem designed to deceive; conjurer's sleight of hand; prank for mischief, or to annoy; mannerism; dexterity; cards played out in one round, and taken by player with winning card; spell at the helm of ship; *v.t.* to deceive; to hoax; to mystify; to dress, trim, or decorate. **-er** *n.* **-ery** *n.* practice of playing tricks; fraud. **-ily** *adv.* **-iness** *n.* **-sy** *a.* tricky; ingenious; neat. **-ster**, *n.* cheat; swindler. **-y** *a.* full of tricks; crafty; requiring great dexterity; intricate [O.Fr. *tricher*, to beguile].

trick·le (trik′.l) *v.i.* to flow gently in a slow, thin stream; to move slowly, one by one; *n.* thin flow of liquid; slow movement of anything.

tri·col·or (trī′.kul·er) *n.* national flag of three colors, esp. French national flag. **-ed** *a.*

tri·corn (trī′.kawrn) *a.* having three horns, or points; *n.* three-cornered hat [L. *tricornis*].

tri·cot (trē·cot) *n.* fabric of wool; machine-made knitwear fabric. **-tine** *n.* a ribbed, fine woolen fabric, machine-made [Fr. *tricot*, knitting].

tri·cus·pid (trī·kus′.pid) *a.* having three cusps or points, as certain teeth, or a valve of the right ventricle of the heart.

tri·cy·cle (trī′.si·kl) *n.* three-wheeled cycle, esp. for children's use; *v.t.* to ride a tricycle. **tricyclist** *n.* [Gk. *treis*, three; *kuklos*, a circle].

tri·dent (trī′.dant) *n.* three-pronged scepter, symbol of Neptune; any three-pronged instrument, such as fish-spear. **-ate**, *a.* having three prongs [L. *tres*, three; *dens*, a tooth].

tried See **try**.

tri·en·ni·al (trī·en′.i.al) *a.* lasting for three years; happening once every three years. **-ly** *adv.* [L. *tres*, three; *annus*, a year].

tri·fle (trī′.fl) *n.* anything of little value or importance; paltry amount; pewter; *v.i.* to speak or act lightly; to be facetious; to toy, or waste time. **-r** *n.* **trifling** *a.* trivial. **trifling, -ly** *adv.* [O.Fr. *trufle*, mockery].

tri·form (trī′.fawm) *a.* having a triple form. Also **-ed. -ity** *n.*

tri·fur·cate (trī·fer′.kāt) *a.* having three branches **trifurcation** *n.* [L. *tres*, three; *furca*, a fork]. firm].

trig (trig) *a.* trim; neat; strong [O.N. *tryggr*.

trig·ger (trig′.er) *n.* catch of firearm which, when pulled, releases hammer of lock [Dut. *trkken*, to pull].

tri·glyph (trī′.glif) *n.* grooved rectangular block in Doric frieze, repeated at equal intervals. **-ic, -al** *a.* [Gk. *treis*, three; *gluphein*, to carve].

trig·o·nom·e·try (trig·a·nam′.at·ri·) *n.* branch of mathematics which deals with relations between sides and angles of triangle. **trigonometer** *n.* instrument for solving plane right-angled triangles by inspection. **trigonometric, -al** *a.* **trigonometrically** *adv.* [Gk. *trigonon*, a triangle; *metron*, a measure].

tri·he·dral (trī·hē′.dral) *a.* (*Math.*) having three sides or faces. **trihedron** *n.* [Gk. *treis*, three; *hedra*, seat].

tri·lat·er·al (trī·lat′.er.al) *a.* having three sides; arranged by three parties, as *trilateral pact.* **-ly** *adv.*

tri·lin·e·ar (trī·lin′.ē.er) *a.* consisting of three lines [L. *tres*, three; *linea*, a line].

tri·lin·gual (trī·ling′.gwal) *a.* expressed in three languages; speaking three languages.

trill (tril) *v.t.* and *v.i.* to sing or play (instrument) with vibratory quality; to pronounce, as letter 'r'; *n.* shake or vibration of voice, in singing; consonant, such as 'r' pronounced with trill [It. *trillare*, to shake].

tril·lion (tril′·yạn) *n.* million million million (British) i.e. 1 with 18 ciphers; a million million (U.S.) i.e. 1 with 12 ciphers.

tril·o·gy (tril′·a·ji·) *n.* group of three plays, novels, etc. with common theme, or common central character [Gk. *treis*, three; *logos*, a speech or discourse].

trim (trim) *a.* (*compar.*) **-mer.** (*superl.*) neat; in good order; to dress; to decorate, as hat; to clip shorter; to supply with oil and adjust wick, as lamp; (*Naut.*) to arrange sails according to wind direction; *v.i.* to balance; to fluctuate between two parties, so as to appear to favor each. *pr.p.* **-ming.** *pa.t.* and *pa.p.* **-med.** *n.* dress; decoration; order; anything trimmed off; **-ly** *adv.* **-mer.** one who trims; instrument for clipping; **-ming** *n.* that which trims, edges, or decorates; a beating; **-ness** *n.* neatness; compactness; readiness for use [O.E. *trymian*, to strengthen].

trim·e·ter (trim′·a·ter) *n.* verse containing three measures; *a.* **trimetric, -al** *a.*

tri·nal (trī′·nal) *a.* threefold; of three, as *trinal unity*, three in one. **trinary** *a.* consisting of three parts; ternary. **trine** *a.* threefold; *n.* group of three; aspect of two planets distant from each other 120°, or one-third of the zodiac [L. *trinus*]...

tri·ni·tro·tol·u·ene (trī·ni·trō·tál′·yoo·ēn) *n.* (*abbrev.* **T.N.T.**) high explosive.

Trin·i·ty (trin′·a·ti·) *n.* union of one Godhead of Father, Son, and Holy Ghost; (*l.c.*) any combination of three people or things as one. **Trinitarian** *a.* pert. to doctrine of the Trinity; *n.* one who believes in this doctrine. **Trinitarianism** *n.* [L. *trinitas*, three].

trin·ket (tring′·kit) *n.* small ornament worn as ring, brooch, etc.; ornament of little value. **-ry** *n.* [prob. fr. M.E. *trenket*, small knife].

tri·no·mi·al (trī·nō′·mi·al) *a.* (*Bot. Zool.*) having three names as of *order*, *species* and *subspecies*; (*Math.*) consisting of three terms connected by sign + or −; *n.* a trinomial quantity [L. *tres*, three; *omen*, a name].

tri·o (trē′·ō) *n.* group of three persons or things; (*Mus.*) composition arranged for three voices, or instruments. [It. fr. L. *tres*, three].

tri·ode (trī′·ōd) *n.* (*Radio*) three-electrode thermionic valve .[Gk. *treis*, three; *hodos*, a way].

tri·o·let (trī′·ō·lit) *n.* a short poem of eight lines with rhyme pattern abaaabab [Fr. *triolet*, a little trio].

tri·ox·ide (trī·ak′·sīd) *n.* (*Chem.*) compound comprising three atoms of oxygen with some other element [*tri-*, and *oxide*].

trip (trip) *v.t.* to cause to stumble; to frustrate; to loose, as ship's anchor; to start up, as machine, by releasing clutch; *v.i.* to walk or dance lightly; to stumble over an obstacle; to make a false step; (with *up*) to detect an error in another's statement. *pr.p.* **-ping.** *pa.p.* **-ped.** *n.* quick, light step; a journey; false step; indiscretion in speech or conduct. **-per** *n.* one who trips; device to start a mechanism. **-ping** *a.* light-footed. **-pingly** *adv.* [M.E. *trippen*, to tread on].

tri·par·tite (trī·pár′·tīt) *a.* divided into three parts; having three corresponding parts; arranged or agreed to, by three parties or nations, as *tripartite pact*. **tripartition** *n.*

tripe (trīp) *n.* large stomach of ruminating animal, prepared for food; (*Slang*) rubbish.

triph·thong (trif′·thawng) *n.* a syllable containing three vowels together as in *beauty* [Gk. *treis*, three; *phthongos*, a sound].

tri·ple (trip′·l) *a.* consisting of three united; three times repeated; *v.t.* to make three times as much or as many; *v.i.* to become trebled. **-crown** *n.* papal tira. **triplet** *n.* three of a kind; three consecutive verses rhyming to-

gether; (*Mus.*) three notes played in the time of two; one of three children born at a birth. **triplex** *a.* threefold; *n.* (*Mus.*) triple time. **triplicate** *a.* threefold; made three times as much; *n.* third copy corresponding exactly to two others; *v.t.* to treble; to make three copies of. **triplication** *n.* [L. *triplex*, threefold].

tri·pod (trī′·påd) *n.* stool, vessel, etc. on three-legged support; three-legged, folding stand for for a camera, etc.; *a.* having three legs. **tripodal, tripodic** *a.* [Gk. *treis*, three; *pous*, a foot].

trip·o·li (trip′·a·li·) *n.* mineral substance used for polishing metals, stones, etc.; originally brought from *Tripoli*.

trip·tych (trip′·tik) *n.* writing tablet in three parts; altarpiece or picture in three panels, [Gk. *treis*, three; *plux*, *pluchos*, a fold].

tri·sect (trī·sekt′) *v.t.* to divide into three equal parts, as a line or angle. **-ion** *n.*

triste (trēst) *a.* sad; melancholy [Fr.].

tri·sul·fide (trī·sul′·fīd) *n.* (*Chem.*) chemical compound containing three sulfur atoms.

tri·syl·la·ble (tri·sil′·a·bl) *n.* word of three syllables. **trisyllabic, -al** *a.* **trisyllabically** *adv.* [Gk. *treis*, three; *sullabē*, syllable].

trite (trīt) *a.* made stale by use; hackneyed; banal. **-ly** *adv.* **-ness** *n.*[L.*tritus*, rubbed away].

Tri·ton (trī′·tạn) *n.* (*Gk. Myth.*) god of the sea. **triton** *n.* (*Zool.*) marine mollusk with spiral shell.

trit·u·rate (trich′·a·rāt) *v.t.* to rub or grind to a very fine powder. **triturable** *a.* **trituration** *n.* [L. *triturare*, to pulverize].

tri·umph (trī′·amf) *n.* victory; conquest; rejoicing; great achievement; *v.i.* to celebrate victory with great pomp and ceremony; to achieve success; to prevail; to exult. **-al** *a.* pert. to triumph; expressing joy for success. **-antly** *adv.* [L. *triumphus*, a solemn procession].

tri·um·vir (trī·um′·ver) *n.* one of three men sharing governing power in ancient Rome. *pl.* **-i, -s. -al** *a.* **-ate** *n.* coalition of three men in office or authority [L. *tres*, three; *vir*, a man].

tri·une (trī′·ūn) *a.* three in one. **triunity** *n.* [L. *tres*, three; *unus*, one].

tri·va·lent (trī′·vā·lant) *a.* (*Chem.*) having valency of three; capable of combining with or replacing three atoms of hydrogen. **tri·valence** *n.*

triv·et (triv′·it) *n.* three-legged stool or support; iron tripod for standing a pot or kettle over fire; short-legged metal rack to put under a hot platter, etc. [L. *tres*, three; *pes*, foot].

triv·i·al (triv′·i·al) *a.* paltry; of little consequence. **-ism** *n.* **triviality** *n.pl.* trifles; insignificant matters. **-ly** *adv.* **-ness** *n.* [L. *trivalis*, pert. to crossroads, hence commonplace].

tro·che (trō′·kē) *n.* medicinal lozenge [Gk. *trochos*, pill].

tro·chee (trō′·kē) *n.* in English prosody, metrical foot of two syllables, first one accented, as *ho′·ly*. **trochaic** *n.* trochaic foot or verse. **trochaic, -al** *a.* [Gk. *trochaios*, running].

trod, trodden *pa.t.*, *pa.p.* of **tread.**

trog·lo·dyte (trág′·la·dīt) *n.* cave dweller; a hermit. [Gk. *troglē*, a cave; *duein*, to enter].

troi·ka (troi′·ka) *n.* Russian carriage or sledge drawn by three horses abreast; triunal.

Tro·jan (trō′·jan) *a.* pert. to ancient Troy; *n.* inhabitant of Troy.

troll (trōl) *n.* (*Scand. Myth*) a giant; mischievous hump-backed cave-dwelling dwarf.

troll (trōl) *v.t.* and *v.i.* to roll; to sing in a rich, rolling voice; to sing in succession the parts of a round; to fish with baited line trailing behind boat; *n.* a round or catch; act of trolling. **-er** *n.*

trol·ley (trál′·i·) *n.* form of truck, body of

which can be tilted over; device to connect electric streetcar with wires. — **bus**, passenger bus not operating on rails but drawing powers from overhead wires. — **car** *n.* electric streetcar.

trol·lop (trăl′·ạp) *n.* a slattern; a prostitute; **-y** *a.* slovenly; tawdry [prob. fr. *troll*].

trom·bone (trăm′·bōn) *n.* deep-toned brass musical instrument. **trombonist** *n.* [It. *tromba*, a trumpet].

troop (tròóp) *n.* large assembly of people; body of cavalry; *pl.* soldiers collectively; an army; *v.i.* to flock; to gather in a crowd. **-er** *n.* mounted policeman; state policeman; horse cavalryman. **-ship** *n.* vessel for transporting soldiers [Fr. *troupe*].

trope (trōp) *n.* word or phrase used metaphorically. **tropical** *a.* figurative. **tropically** *adv.* **tropist** *n.* one who uses figurative language. **tropological, -al** *a.* containing figures of speech. **tropology** *n.* figurative language; study of such language; a metaphorical interpretation of the Bible [Gk. *tropos*, a turn].

troph·ic, -al (trăf′·ik, -ạl) *a.* pert. to nutrition. **trophi** *n.pl.* masticating organs of insect. **trophology** *n.* the scientific study of nutrition [Gk. *trophē*, feeding].

tro·phy (trō′·fi·) *n.* orig. pile of arms taken from vanquished enemy; memorial of victory; memento; mural decoration, as stag's antlers; prize, esp. for sports, etc. [Gk. *tropaion*].

trop·ic (trăp′·ik) *n.* one of the two circles of celestial sphere, situated 23½° N. (*Tropic of Cancer*) and 23½° S. (*Tropic of Capricorn*) of equator, and marking the point reached by the sun at its greatest declination north and south; one of the two corresponding parallels of latitude on terrestrial globe. *pl.* region (*torrid zone*) between tropics of Cancer and Capricorn. **tropic, -al** *a.* pert. to or within tropics; (of climate) very hot. **-ally** *adv.* [Gk. *tropos*, a turn].

trop·o·sphere (trŏpŏp′·ạ·sfir) *n.* lower layer of atmosphere below stratosphere [Gk. *tropos*, a turn; *sphaira*, sphere].

trop·po (trăp′·ō) *adv.* (*Mus.*) too much. **non troppo**, moderately [It.].

trot (trăt) *v.i.* (of horse) to move at sharp pace; (of person) to move along fast; *v.t.* to cause to trot. *pr.p.* **-ting**. *pa.p.*, *pa.t.* **-ted**. *n.* brisk pace of horse; quick walk. **-ter** *n.* one who trots; horse which trots; foot of an animal [O.Fr. *troter*].

troth (trawth, trăth, trōth) *n.* (*Arch*). truth; fidelity. **to plight one's troth**, to become engaged to be married [O.E. *treowth*, truth].

trou·ba·dour (tròó′·bạ·dōr) *n.* one of school of Provençal poets between 11th and 13th cents., whose poems were devoted to lyrical and amatory subjects [Prov. *trobador*, poet].

trou·ble (trub′·l) *v.t.* to stir up; to vex; to distress; to bother; *v.i.* to take pains; to feel anxiety; *n.* disturbance; agitation of mind; unrest; ailment; inconvenience. **-r** *n.* **-some** *a.* difficult; vexatious; irksome. **-somely** *adv.* **-someness** *n.* **—shooter** *n.*, expert in discovering and eliminating trouble [L. *turbulare*, to disturb].

trough (trawf) *n.* long, open vessel for water or fodder for animals; channel; depression, as between waves; part of cyclone where atmospheric pressure is lowest [O.E. *trog*, hollow vessel of wood].

trounce (trouns) *v.t.* to punish or beat severely; (*Colloq.*) to defeat completely [Fr. *tronce*, a stump].

troupe (tròóp) *n.* company or troop, esp. of actors, acrobats, etc. **-r** *n.* member of a theatrical troupe [Fr.].

trou·sers (trou′·zẹrz) *n.pl.* a man's two-legged outer garment extending from waist to ankles; slacks. **trousered** *a.* wearing trousers. **trou-**serless *a.* [O.Fr. *trousses*, breeches].

trous·seau (tròó′·sō) *n.* bride's outfit of clothes, etc. *pl.* **trousseaux** or **trousseaus** [Fr.]

trout (trout) *n.* fish resembling salmon [O.E. *truht*, trout].

trow·el (trou′·ạl) *n.* mason's tool for spreading and dressing mortar; garden tool for scooping out earth, plants, etc.; *v.t.* to smooth or lift with trowel [L. *trulla*, a small ladle].

troy weight (troi′·wāt) *n.* system of weight for precious metals and gems [fr. *Troyes*, in France].

tru·ant (tròó′·ạnt) *n.* one who shirks his duty; pupil who absents himself from school; *a.* wandering from duty; idle; *v.i.* to play truant. **truancy** *n.* [O.Fr. *truant*, vagrant].

truce (tròós) *n.* temporary cessation of hostilities; armistice; lull [O.E. *treow*, faith].

truck (truk) *v.t.* to exchange; to barter; *v.i.* to deal with by exchange; *n.* exchange of commodities; (*Colloq.*) dealings; (*Colloq.*) rubbish; junk; (*U.S.*) garden produce. **-er** *n.* — **farm** *n.* a small farm on which vegetables are grown for market [Fr. *troquer*, to truck].

truck (truk) *n.* horsedrawn or automotive vehicle for hauling. small wooden wheel; porter's barrow for heavy luggage. **-age** *n.* transport by trucks; cost of such transport. **-le** *n.* small wheel or castor; truckle bed; *v.i.* to fawn on. — **bed** *n.* low bed on castors which may be pushed beneath another [Gk. *trochos*, a wheel].

truc·u·lent (truk′·yạ·lạnt) *a.* fierce; aggressive; ruthless. **truculence, truculency** *n.* **-ly** *adv.* [L. *trux*, fierce].

trudge (truj) *v.t.* to go on foot; to plod along; *n.* wearisome walk.

trudg·en (truj′·ạn) *n.* fast racing stroke in swimming. [fr. *J. Trudgen*, English swimmer].

true (tròó) *a.* conformable with fact; genuine; exact; loyal; trustworthy; *v.t.* to adjust accurately, as machine; to straighten; *adv.* truly conforming to type (of plants, etc.). **—blue** *a.* unchanging; stanch; true. **-ness** *n.* **truism** *n.* self-evident truth. **truly** *adv.* [O.E. *treowe*, true].

truf·fle (truf′·l) *n.* tuber-shaped edible underground fungus with unique flavor [prob. L. *tuber*, swelling, truffle].

tru·ism See **true**.

trull (trul) *n.* a trollop [var. of *troll*].

trump (trump) *n.* (*Arch.*) trumpet; its sound. **-et** *n.* wind instrument of brass, consisting of long tube bent twice on itself, ending in wide bell-shaped mouth, and having finger stops; powerful reed stop of pipe organ with full trumpet-like sound; call of the elephant; *v.t.* to proclaim by trumpet; to bellow; (*Fig.*) to praise loudly; *v.i.* to play on trumpet; (of elephant) to utter characteristic cry through trunk. **-eter** *n.* one who plays on trumpet; kind of domestic pigeon; long-necked S. American bird, resembling crane; wild swan of N. America. **-eting** *n.* [Fr. *trompe*].

trump (trump) *n.* one of the suit of cards, declared by cutting, dealing, or bidding which takes any card of another suit; (*Colloq.*) excellent fellow; *v.t.* and *v.i.* to play trump card; to take a trick with trump. [Fr. *triomphe*, triumph, game of cards].

trump (trump) *v.t.* to fabricate; to deceive. **-ery** *n.* anything showy but of little value; rubbish [Fr. *tromper*, to deceive].

trun·cate (trung′·kāt) *v.t.* to cut off; to lop; to maim. **truncate, -d, truncation** *a.* appearing as if cut off at tip; blunt [L. *truncare*].

trun·dle (trun′·dl) *n.* anything round or capable of being rolled; a small wheel or castor; act of roliing; *v.t.* to roll on little wheels; to bowl, as child's hoop, barrel, etc. *v.i.* to roll. — **bed** *n.* a truckle bed [O.E. *trendel*, a wheel].

trunk (trungk) *n.* stem of tree, as distinct

from branches and roots; body minus head and limbs; torso; shaft of column; main part of anything; main lines of railway, bus, or telephone system; large box of metal, hide, etc., with hinged lid, for storage or as luggage; proboscis of elephant; *pl.* short, tight-fitting pants, esp. for swimming.

truss (trus) *n.* bundle; as hay or straw; tuft of flowers on top of a long stem; framework of beams or girders constructed to bear heavy loads; (*Med.*) appliance to keep hernia in place; (*Naut.*) iron clamp fixing lower yards to masts; *v.t.* to bind or pack close; to support, as a roof, or bridge span, with truss; to skewer, as fowl, before cooking [Fr. *trousse*].

trust (trust) *n.* confidence; reliance; implicit faith; moral responsibility; property used for benefit of another; combine of business firms in which shareholders turn over stock to board of trustees; *v.t.* to rely upon; to have implicit faith in; to give credit; to entrust; to hope; to believe; *v.i.* to be confident or to confide in; *a.* held in trust. **-ee** *n.* person or group which manages the business affairs of another; **-eeship** *n.* **-er** *n.* **-ful** *a.* **-fully** *adv.* **-fulness** *n.* **-ily** *adv.* **-iness** *n.* quality of being trusty. **-ing** *a.* confiding. **-ingly** *adv.* **-worthiness** *n.* **-worthy** *a.* **-y** *a.* reliable; *n.* reliable prisoner given special privileges [O.N. *traust*, confidence].

truth (trooth) *n.* honesty; conformity to fact or reality; veracity; constancy; true statement; undisputed fact. **-ful** *a.* **-fully** *adv.* **-fulness** *n.* **-less** *a.* [O.E. *treowe*, true].

try (trī) *v.t.* to test; to attempt; (*Law*) to examine judicially; to purify or refine, as metals; *v.i.* to endeavor; to make effort. *pa.t.* and *pa.p.* **tried.** *n.* trial; effort; (*Colloq.*) attempt. **tried** *a.* **trier** *n.* [O.Fr. *trier*, to pick out].

tryst (trist) *n.* appointment to meet; place appointed for meeting. **-er** *n.* [var. of *trust*].

Tsar (tsär) *n.* same as **Czar.**

tset·se (tset'·sē) *n.* African fly, its bite causing sleeping sickness [S. Afr.].

T square (tē·skwer) *n.* ruler with crossbar at one end for drawing parallel lines.

tub (tub) *n.* vessel to bathe in; open, wooden vessel formed of staves, heading and hoops, as used for washing clothes, etc.; small cask; (*Colloq.*) slow, cumbersome boat. **-by** *a.* shaped like a tub; (of persons) squat and portly. [M.E. *tubbe*, a tub].

tu·ba (tū'·ba) *n.* (*Mus.*) largest brass instrument of orchestra; organ stop. *pl.* **-s, tubae** [L. *tuba*, trumpet].

tube (tūb) *n.* long hollow cylinder for conveyance of liquids, gas, etc.; pipe; siphon; *abbrev.* for tube-railway where rails are laid through immense steel tubes; (*Anat.*) cylindrical-shaped organ; small container with screw cap; stem of plant; inner rubber tire of bicycle or automobile wheel; **tubing** *n.* **tubular** *a.* **tubulate, -d, tubulous, tubulose** *a.* **tubule** *n.* a small tube [L. *tubus*, a tube].

tub·er (tū'·ber) *n.* fleshy, rounded underground stem or root, containing buds for new plant; (*Med.*) a swelling. **-ous, -ose** *a.* [L. *tuber*, a swelling].

tu·ber·cle (tū'·ber·kl) *n.* small swelling; nodule; (*Med.*) morbid growth, esp. on lung causing *tuberculosis.* *a.* having tubercles. **tubercular, tuberculate, -d, tuberculose, tuberculous** *a.* pert. to tubercles; nodular; affected with tuberculosis. **tuberculin** *n.* liquid extract from tubercle bacillus used as injection in testing for, or in treatment of, tuberculosis. **tuberculosis** *n.* (*Colloq. abbrev.* **T.B.**) consumption; phthisis, disease caused by infection with the tubercle bacillus. **tuberculum** *n.* tubercle [L. *tuberculum*, a small tuber].

tuck (tuk) *v.t.* to make fold(s) in cloth before stitching down; to roll up, as sleeves; to make compact; to enclose snugly in bed clothes; *n.* flat fold in garment to shorten it, or as ornament; **-er** *n.* tucked linen or lace front worn by women; *v.t.* (*slang*) to exhaust [M.E. *tukken*, to pull].

Tu·dor (tū'·der) *a.* pert. to period of Tudors (1485-1603) or to style of architecture in that period.

Tues·day (tūz'·di·) *n.* third day of week [O.E. *Tiwesdaeg*, day of *Tiw*, god of war].

tuft (tuft) *n.* cluster; bunch of something soft, as hair, feathers, threads, etc.; *v.t.* to adorn with, arrange in tufts. **-ed, -y** *a.*

tug (tug) *v.t.* to pull with effort; to haul along; *v.i.* to pull with great effort; to comb, as hair, with difficulty. *pr.p.* **-ging.** *pa.t.* and *pa.p.* **-ged.** *n.* strong pull; tussle; tugboat. **-boat** *n.* a small but powerful boat used for towing larger vessel. **tug of war** *n.* sports contest, in which two teams pull at either end of rope, until losing team is drown over center line [O.N. *toga*, to pull].

tu·i·tion (tū·ish'·an) *n.* the price for instruction; teaching. **-al, -ary** *a.* [L. *tueri*, to watch].

tu·lip (tū'·lap) *n.* bulbous plant popular in Holland [Turk. *tulbend*, turban].

tulle (tool) *n.* fine silk net used for dresses, hats, etc. [fr. *Tulle*, France].

tum·ble (tum'·bl) *v.i.* to fall heavily; to trip over; to toss from side to side; to turn head over heels; to perform acrobatic tricks; to slump, as prices; *v.t.* to overturn; to rumple, as bedclothes; to toss about, as contents of drawer; *n.* act of tumbling; fall; confusion. **—down** *a.* ramshackle; derelict. **-er** *n.* one who tumbles; acrobat; kind of pigeon; glass drinking vessel; spring catch of a lock. **tumbling** *n.* act of falling or turning somersault [O.E. *tumbian*, to dance].

tum·brel, tumbril (tum'·bral) *n.* cart used for carrying dung; low open cart in which victims of French Revolutionists were conveyed to guillotine [Fr. *tomber*, to fall].

tu·me·fy (tū'·ma·fī) *v.t.* to cause to swell; *v.i.* to swell; to develop into a tumor. **tumefaction** *n.* a swelling; a tumor [L. *tumere*, to swell; *facere*, to make].

tu·mid (tū'·mid) *a.* swollen; turgid; pompous. **tumescence** *n.* **tumescent** *a.* **-ness, tumidity** *n.* **-ly** *adv.* [L. *tumere*].

tu·mor (tū'·mer) *n.* (*Med.*) morbid overgrowth of tissue, sometimes accompanied by swelling. **-ous** *a.* Also **tumour** [L. *tumere*, to swell].

tu·mult (tū'·mult) *n.* commotion as of a crowd; violent uproar; mental disturbance. **-uary, -uous** *a.* confused; uproarious; disturbing. **-uously** *adv.* **-uousness** *n.* [L. *tumultus*, uproar].

tu·mu·lus (tū'·mya·las) *n.* artificial burial mound, erected by primitive peoples; barrow. *pl.* **-es, tumuli. tumulous** *a.* [L. fr. *tumere*, to swell].

tun (tun) *n.* large cask; measure of liquid, as for wine, usually equivalent to 252 gallons; *v.t.* to store in casks [O.E. *tunne*, a cask].

tu·na (too'·na) *n.* large oceanic food and game fish. [Sp.].

tun·dra (tun'·dra) *n.* one of vast treeless plains of Arctic Circle [Russ. *tundra*, a marsh].

tune (tūn) *n.* melody; rhythmical arrangement of notes and chords in particular key; quality of being in pitch; mood; unison; harmony; *v.t.* to adjust to proper pitch; to harmonize; to adapt or make efficient, esp. part of machine; (*Radio*) to adjust circuit to give resonance at desired frequency. **tunable** *a.* **tunableness** *n.* **tunably** *adv.* **-ful** *a.* melodious; harmonious. **-fully** *adv*. **-fulness** *n*. **-less** *a*. without melody; discordant; silent. **-r** *n*. **tuning fork** *n*. steel two-pronged instrument giving specified note when struck. **in tune** (*Fig.*) mentally and emotionally adjusted, as to one's company or environment. **out of tune**, at variance with. **to tune in** (*Radio*) to adjust radio set to desired wavelength [O.Fr. *ton*, a tone].

tung·sten (tung'.stạn) *n*. hard grey metallic element used in alloys, special forms of steel, and for filaments in electric lamps [Scand. *tung*, heavy; *sten*, a stone].

tu·nic (tū'.nik) *n*. short-sleeved knee-length garment worn by women and boys in ancient Greece and Rome; short-sleeved eccles. vestment; blouselike outer garment extending to hips [L. *tunica*, undergarment of both sexes].

tun·nel (tun'.ạl) *n*. subterranean passage; burrow of an animal; *v.t.* and *v.i.* to cut tunnel through; to excavate. **-er** n. [O.Fr. *tonne*, tun or cask].

tun·ny (tun'.i.) *n*. edible fish of mackerel family; tuna fish [Gk. *thunnos*].

tur·ban (tur'.bạn) *n*. Oriental male headdress comprising long strip of cloth swathed round head or cap; close-fitting cap or scarf headdress worn by women. **-ed** *a*. **-like** *a*. [Turk. *tulbend*].

tur·bid (tur'.bid) *a*. having dregs disturbed; muddy; thick; dense. **-ly** *adv*. **-ness, -ity** *n*. [L. *turbidus*, fr. *turbare*, to disturb].

tur·bine (tur'.bin or .bīn) *n*. rotary engine driven by steam, hot air, or water striking on curved vans of wheel, or drum; high speed prime mover used for generating electrical energy. **turbinal, turbinate** *a*. coiled like a spiral. **turbojet** *n*. jet propelled gas turbine. **turboprop**, jet engine in which turbine is coupled to propeller [L. *turbo*, whirl].

tur·bot (tur'.bạt) *n*. large flat sea fish [L. *turbo*, a top].

tur·bu·lent (tur'.byạ.lạnt) *a*. disturbed; in violent commotion; refractory. **-ly** *adv*. **turbulence, turbulency** *n*. [L. *turbare*, to disturb].

tu·reen (tòò.rēn' or tyoo.rēn') *n*. large, deep dish with removable cover, for serving soup [Fr. *terrine*, an earthen vessel].

turf (turf) *n*. surface soil containing matted roots, grass, etc.; sod; peat; a race-course. *v.t.* to cover with turf, as lawn. **-like** *a*. **the turf**, track over which horse races are run. **-man** *n*. one interested in horse racing. **-y** *a*. covered with turf [O.E. *turf*, turf].

turgent (tur'.jạnt) *a*. (*obs.*) swelling; puffing up like a tumor; pompous; bombastic. **-ly** *adv*. **turgescence, turgescency** *n*. swelling caused by congestion; empty bombast. **turgid** *a*. swollen; distended abnormally; bombastic. **turgidity, turgidness** *n*. **-ly** *adv*. [L. *turgere*, to swell].

Turk (turk) *n*. native of *Turkey*; Ottoman; a fierce person; a Mohammedan. **-ish** *a*. pert. to Turks or Turkey. **-ish bath**, steam or hot air bath after which person is rubbed down, massaged, etc. **-ish towel**, an absorbent towel.

tur·key (tur'.ki.) *n*. large bird, bred for food; guinea fowl. — **trot** *n*. an eccentric ragtime dance [fr. *Turkey*].

tur·mer·ic (tur'.mẹr.ik) *n*. E. Indian plant; powder prepared from it used as a condiment, dye, medicine [L. *terra merita*, deserving earth].

tur·moil (tur'.moil) *n*. commotion; tumult.

turn (turn) *v.t.* to move round; to cause to revolve; to deflect; to form on lathe; to change direction of; to convert; to upset or nauseate; to blunt; *v.i.* to rotate; to move as on a hinge; to depend; to become giddy, nauseated, or upset; (of tides) to change from ebb to flow or the reverse; to become

sour, as milk; *n*. act of turning; change of bend; an action, as *good turn*; action done in rotation with others; short walk; a subtle quality of expression, as *turn of phrase*; crisis. **-about** *n*. merry-go-round; reversal of position, opinion. **-coat** *n*. renegade; one who betrays party or other principles. **-ing** *n*. act of turning; deflection; winding; juncing and two roads or streets; process of shaping and rounding articles with lathe. **-ing point** *n*. decisive moment; crisis. **-key** *n*. one in charge of prison keys; warder. **—out** *n*. act of coming forth; production, as of factory; number of people at any gathering. **-over** *n*. total sales made by a business in certain period; rate at which employees of factory are replaced by others; tart of pastry folded over a filling of jam, or fruit. **-pike** *n*. **-pike road**, main highway with tollgate. **-spit** *n*. one who turns a spit. **-stile** *n*. revolving gate for controlling admission of people. **-table** *n*. revolving circular platform for turning locomotives on to another line or in opposite direction; relvolving disk of a phonograph. **— about** alternately. **to turn down,** to decline, as offer; to reject, as application. **to turn in**, to bend inwards; to hand in; to go to bed [O.E. *tyrnan*, to turn].

tur·nip (tur'.nip) *n*. plant of mustard family.

tur·pen·tine (tur'.pạn.tīn) *n*. oily liquid extracted by distillation of resin exuded by pine and other coniferous trees [Gk. *terebinthos*].

tur·pi·tude (tur'.pạ.tūd) *n*. revolting baseness; lewdness; infamy [L. *turpis*, baese].

tur·quoise (tur'.kwoiz, .koiz) *n*. bluish-green gem stone [Turkish (stone)].

tur·ret (tur'.it) *n*. small tower on buliding; revolving gun tower on ship, tank, or aircraft. **-ed** *a*. having turrets [O.Fr. *tourete*, a little tower].

tur·tle (tur'.tl) *n*. marine tortoise with hard shell and limbs like paddles.

tur·tle·dove (tur'.tl.duv) kind of pigeon, noted for its soft cooing and its affection for its mate [L. *turtur*, a dove].

Tus·can (tus'.kạn) *a*. pert. to Tuscany in Italy; (*Archit.*) denoting the simplest of the five classical styles in architecture.

tusk (tusk) *n*. the long, protruding side tooth of certain animals such as elephant, wild boar, walrus. **-ed** *a*. **-er** *n*. animal with fully developed tusks. **-y** *a*. **-less** *a*. **-like** *a*. [O.E. *tusc*, tooth].

tus·sle (tus'.l) *n*., *v.t.* struggle; scuffle.

tus·sock (tus'.ạk) *n*. (*Poet.*) clump, tuft, or hillock of growing grass [etym. doubtful].

tut (tut) *interj*. exclamation of irritation.

tu·te·lage (tū'.tạ.lij) *n*. guardianship; instruction state or period of being under this. **tutelar, tutelary** *a*. having protection over a person or place; protective [L. *tutela*].

tu·tor (tū'.ter) *n*. (*Law*) one in charge of minor; private teacher; (*Brit*.) university lecturer who directs and supervises studies of undergraduates; *v.t.* to teach; to prepare another for special examination by private coaching; to have guardianship of. **-ial** *a*. pert. to tutor. **-ially** *adv*. **-ing** *n*. **-ship** *n*. [L. *tutor*, a guardian].

tut·ti-frut·ti (tòò'.ti.-fròò'.ti) *n*. preserve of fruits; ice cream sundae with fruit, nuts, etc.; ice cream made with mixed fruits [It. = all fruits].

tu·tu (tòó'.tòó) *n*. ballet dancer's skirt [Fr.].

tux·e·do (tuk.sē'.dō) *n*. semiformal dinner jacket [fr. *Tuxedo Park*, country club near New York].

twad·dle (twȧd'.l) *n*. inane conversation; non-sensical writing; *v.i.* to talk inanely. **-r** *n*. **twaddling** *n*. twaddle. **twaddly** *a*. silly.

twain (twān) *a*., *n*. (*Arch*.) two [O.E. *twegin*].

WEBSTER T–Z

twang (twang) *n.* sharp, rather harsh sound made by tense string sharply plucked; nasalized speech; *v.t.* to pluck tense string of instrument; *v.i.* to speak with a twang [limit.].

tweak (twēk) *v.t.* to twist and pull with sudden jerk; *n.* sharp pinch or jerk [var. of *twitch*].

'twas (twóz) *contr.* of *it was*.

tweed (twēd) *n.* heavy woolen fabric esp. for costumes, coats, suits; *a.* of tweed [fr. mistaken reading of *'tweel'*].

'tween (twēn) *contr.* of **between. 'tween deck,** between upper and lower decks.

tweez·ers (twē'·zẹrz) *n. sing.* small pair of pincers, esp. for pulling superfluous hairs.

twelve (twelv)*a.* one more than eleven; two and ten; dozen; *n.* sum of ten and two; symbol representing twelve units, as 12, xii. **twelfth** *a.* next after eleventh; constituting one of twelve equal parts; *n.* one of twelve equal parts. **Twelfth Day,** January 6th, twelfth day after Christmas; Feast of Epiphany. **twelfthly** *adv.* **Twelfth Night,** evening of, or before, Twelfth Day, when special festivities were held. **the Twelve,** twelve Apostles [O.E. *twelf*, twelve].

twen·ty (twen'·ti·) *a.* twice ten; nineteen and one; *n.* number next after nineteen; score; symbol representing twenty units, as 20, xx. **twentieth** *a.* next after nineteenth; *n.* one of twenty equal parts. —**fold** *adv.* twenty times as many [O.E. *twentig*].

'twere (twur) *cont.* of *it were*.

twice (twīs) *adv.* two times; doubly [O.E. *twa*, two].

twid·dle (twid'·l) *v.t.* to play with; to twirl idly; *v.i.* to spin round; to trifle with. **-r** *n.* **to twiddle one's thumbs,** to have nothing to do [etym. doubtful].

twig (twig) *n.* small shoot or branch of tree. **-gy** *a.* covered with twigs [O.E. *twig*, branch].

twi·light (twī'·līt) *n.* half-light preceding sunrise or, esp., immediately after sunset; faint, indeterminate light; *a.* pert. to or like twilight. — **sleep,** in obstetrics, modern method of inducing state of partial insensibility in woman in childbirth by use of drug, scopolamine-morphine [lit, 'between-light'; O.E. *twa*, two; *leoht*, light].

twill (twil) *n.* fabric woven with diagonal ribbing; *v.t.* to weave with twill [O.E. *twilic*, two-threaded].

twin (twin) *n.* one of two born at birth; exact counterpart; *a.* being one of two born at birth; consisting of two identical parts; growing in pairs. **-ned** *a.* — **beds** *n.pl.* two single beds of identical size. —**born** *a.* born at the same birth. — **brother, sister** *n.* —**screw** *a.* of a vesel having two propellers on separate shafts [O.E. *twinn*, double].

twine (twīn) *n.* cord composed of two or more strangs twisted together; spring; tangle; *v.t.* to twist together; to entwine; to encircle; *v.i.* to wind; to coil spirally, as tendrils of plant; to follow circuitous route. **twining** *a.* winding; coiling [O.E. twin, double-thread].

twinge (twinj) *n.* sudden, acute spasm of pain; pang; *v.t.* (*Dial*) to tweak; to effect momentarily with sudden pain [O.E. *twengan*, to pinch].

twin·kle (twing'·kl) *v.i.* to sparkle; (of eyes) to light up; of feet to move quickly and neatly; *n.* act of twinkling; gleam of amusement in eyes; flicker; quick movement of feet, esp. in dancing;: sparkle. *n.* **twinkling** *n.* twinkle; an instant [O.E. *twinclian*, to sparkle].

twirl (turl) *v.t.* to whirl around; to flourish; to twiddle; *v.i.* to turn round rapidly; *n.* a rapid, rotary motion; a flourish; curl; convolution. **-er** *n.* one who or that which twirls; (*Colloq.*) baseball pitcher. [O.E. *thwiri*, a whisk for beating milk].

twist (twist) *v.t.* to contort; to coil spirally; to wind; to encircle; to distort; to form, as cord, from several fibers wound together; *v.i.* to become tangled or distorted; to wriggle; to be united by winding around each other; to coil; to follow a roundabout course; *n.* turning movement; curve; bend; act of entwining; a turn in meaning; a heavy silk thread; small roll of tobacco; **-ed** *a.* **-er** *n.* one who, or that which, twists; swindler. **-ability** *n.* **-able** *a.* **-ingly** *adv.* [O.E. *twist*, rope].

twit (twit) *v.t.* to taunt; to reproach; to tease. *pr.p.* **-ting.** *pa.t.* and *pa.p.* **-ted.** *n.* taunt [O.E. *twiccian*, to pluck].

twitch (twich) *v.t.* to pull suddenly with a slight jerk; to snatch; *v.i.* to be suddenly jerked; to contract with sudden spasm, as a muscle; to quiver; *n.* sudden spasmodic contraction of fiber or muscle. **-ing** *n.* [O.E. *twiccian*, to pluck].

twitch-grass (twich'·gras) *n.* prolific weed, couch grass or quitch grass.

twit·ter (twit'·ẹr) *n.* chirping sound; slight trembling of nerves; half-suppressed laugh; *v.i.* to make succession of small light sounds; to chirp; to talk rapidly and nerviously; to titter. **-ing** *n.* **-y** *a.* [imit.].

'twixt (twikst) *prep.* contr. of **between.**

Two (tòo) *a.* one and one; *n.* sum of one and one; symbol representing two units, as 2, ii; a pair. —**edged** *a.* having two sharp edges, as a sword; (*Fig.*) ambiguous. —**faced** *a.* having two faces; hypocritical; double-dealing. **-fold** *a.* double; doubly. —**handed** *a.* requiring two hands or two players; ambidextrous. **-penny** (tup'·an·i·) (*Brit.*) *a.* costing two pennies; (*Colloq.*) worthless; *n.* kind of ale. —**ply** *a.* having two strands twisted together, two layers, etc. —**seater** *n.* small automobile designed for two people . only. —**sided** *a.* having two surfaces or aspects; (of cloth) reversible; (*Fig.*) double-dealing.

ty·coon (tī·kòon') *n.* former title of a Japanese official; head of great business combine; a magnate [Jap. *taikun*, great prince].

tyke (tīk) *n.* a cur; boor; (*Colloq.*) small child [Sc. *tīk*, bitch].

tym·pa·num (tim'·pa·nam) *n.* a drum (*Anat.*) cavity of the middle ear; ear drum; (*Archit.*) flat, triangular space between sides of pediment; similar space over door between lintel and arch. *pl.* **-s, tympana. tympanal, tympanic** *a.* like a drum; pert. to middle ear. **tympanist** *n.* one who plays drum or any percussion instrument [Gk. *tumpanon*, a kettle-drum].

type (tīp) *n.* model; pattern; class or group; person or thing representative of group or of certain quality; stamp on either side of a coin; (*Chem.*) compound which has basic composition of other more complex compounds; (*Biol.*) individual specimen representative of species; (*Print.*) metal block on one end of which is raised letter, etc.; such blocks collectively; similar block in typewriter; style or form of printing; *v.t.* to typify; to represent in type; to reproduce by means of typewriter; to classify; *v.i.* to use a typewriter. **typal** *a.* — **cutter** *n.* one who engraves blocks for printing types. — **founder** *n.* one who casts type for printing. — **metal** *n.* alloy of lead, antimony,and tin used for casting type. **-script** *n.* a typewritten document. **-setting** *n.* process or occupation of preparing type for printing. **-writer** *n.* machine with keyboard operated by fingers, which produces printed characters on paper; typist **-writing** *n.* **-written** *a.* **typical** (tip'·a·kal) *a. pert.* to type; symbolic; true bolize; to exemplify. **typing** *n.* act of typing; script typed. **typist** *n.* one who operates typewriter. **typographer** *n.* printer. **typographic, -al** *a. pert.* to printing. **typography** *n.* art of printing; style or mode of printing [Gk. *tupos*, mark of a bowl].

ty·phoid (tī'·foid) *a.* resembling typhus; *pert.* to typhoid fever; — **fever** *n.* infectious disease characterized by severe diarrhea, profound weakness, and rash. **-al** *a.* [Gk. *tuphos*, fever; *eidos*, form].

ty·phoon (tī·fòòn') *n.* cyclonic hurricane occurring in China seas. **typhonic** *a.* [Ar. *tufan*].

ty·phus (tī'·fas) *n.* highly contagious disease caused by virus conveyed by body lice and characterized by purplish rash, prostration, and abnormally high temperature. **typhous** *a.* [Gk. *tuphos*, fever].

ty·rant (tī'·rant) *n.* in ancient Greece, usurper; harsh, despotic ruler; any person enforcing his will on others, cruelly and arbitrarily. **tyrannic, -al, tyrannous** (tir'·an·as) *a.* **tyrannically** *adv.* **tyrannously** *adv.* **tyrannicalness** *n.* **tyrannize** *v.i.* to rule tyrannically; to exert authority ruthlessly; *v.t.* to subject to tyrannical authority. **tyrannizer** *n.* **tyrannizingly** *adv.* **tyranny** (tir'·a·nē) *n.* despotic government; cruelly harsh enforcement of authority [Gk. *turannos*, an unconstitutional ruler].

ty·ro (tī'·rō) *n.* beginner; novice. Also **tiro** [L. *tiro*, recruit].

Tzar, Tzarina Same as **Czar, Czarina.**

U

u·biq·ui·ty (ū·bik'·wa·ti·) *n.* existing in all places at same time; omnipresence. **ubiquitous, ubiquitary** *a.* existing or being everywhere. **ubiquitously** *adv.* **ubiquitousness** *n.* omnipresence [L. *ubique*, everywhere].

U-boat (ū'·bōt) *n.* German submarine [Ger. *untersee*, under the sea, and *boat*].

ud·der (ud'·er) *n.* milk gland of certain animals, as cow [O.E. *uder*, udder].

u·dom·e·ter (ū·dàm'·a·ter) *n.* instrument for measuring rainfall. **udometry** *n.* **udometric** *a.* [L.*udus*, moist; *metron*, measure].

ug·ly (ug'·li·) *a.* offensive to the sight; of disagreeable aspect; dangerous, of situation. **uglify** *v.t.* to make ugly. **uglification** *n.* **ugliness** *n.* **uglily** *adv.* [O.N. *uggr*, fear].

u·kase (ū'·kās) *n.* official Russian decree [Russ. *ukaz*, edict].

U·krain·i·an (ū·krā'·ni·an) *n.* citizen of Ukraine in S.W. Russia; Slavic language related to Russian. *a. pert.* to Ukraine.

u·ku·le·le (ū·ka·lā'·li·) *n.* small four-stringed instrument like guitar [Hawaiian].

ul·cer (ul'·ser) *n.* superficial sore discharging pus; (*Fig.*) source of corruption. **-ate** *v.i.* to become ulcerous. **-ated, -ative** *a.* **-ation** *n.* **-ed** *a.* having ulcers. **-ous** *a.* having ulcers; like an ulcer. **-ously** *adv.* **-ousness** *n.* [L. *ulcus*].

ul·lage (ul'·ij) *n.* amount which cask lacks of being full; loss of wine, grain, etc. by leakage [O.Fr. *eullage*, the filling up of a cask].

ul·na (ul'·na) *n.* the larger of two bones of forearm. *pl.* **-s, ulnae. -r** *a.* [L. *ulna*, elbow].

ul·ster (ul'·ster) *n.* long loose overcoat originally made in *Ulster*, Ireland. **-ed** *a.*

ul·te·ri·or (ul·tir'·i·er) *a.* situated on the farther side; beyond; (of motives) undisclosed; not frankly stated. **-ly** *adv.* [L. *ulterior*, farther].

ul·ti·mate (ul'·ta·mit) *a.* farthest; final; primary; conclusive. **-ly** *adv.* **-ness** *n.* **ultimatum** (ul·ta·mā'·tam) *n.* final proposition; final terms offered as basis of treaty. *pl.* **ultimatums,** or **ultimata. ultima** *n.* last syllable of a word. **ultimo** *a.* in the month preceding current one (*abbrev.* **ult.**) [L. *ultimus*, last].

ul·tra (ul'·tra) *a.* beyond; extreme; in combination words with or without hyphen, as **ultra modern** [L. *ultra*, beyond].

ul·tra·ma·rine (ul·tra·ma·rēn') *a.* situated beyond the sea; *n.* bright blue pigment obtained from powdered lapis lazuli, or produced synthetically [L. *ultra*, beyond; *mare*, the sea].

ul·tra·mon·tane (ul·tra·màn'·tān) *a.* being beyond the mountains, esp. the Alps; used of Italians by those on northern side of Alps, and vice versa; *pert.* to absolute temporal and spiritual power of Papacy or to party upholding this claim; *n.* advocate of extreme or ultra-papal views. **ultramontanism** *n.* **ultramontanist** *n.*

ul·tra·vi·o·let (ul·tra·vī'·a·lit) *a.* beyond limit of visibility at violet end of the spectrum.

ul·u·lant (ūl'·ya·lant) *a.* howling. **ululate** *v.i.* to howl; to lament. **ululation** *n.* [L.].

um·bel (um'·bal) *n.* (*Bot.*) flower clusters, the stalks of which rise from a common center on main stem, forming a convexed surface above, as in carrot, parsley, etc. **-lar, -late, -d** *a.* having umbels. **-liferous** *a.* bearing umbels. **-liform** *a.* having shape of umbel [L. *umbella*, little shade].

um·ber (um'·ber) *n.* natural earth pigment, yellowish-brown in color when raw, reddish-brown when calcined or burnt [fr. *Umbria*, in Italy].

um·bil·i·cal (um·bil'·a·kal) *a. pert.* to umbilicus or umbilical cord. — **cord** (*Anat.*) fibrous cord joining fetus to placenta. **umbilicus,** the navel **umbiliform** *a.* [L. *umbilicus*].

um·bra (um'·bra) *n.* shadow; (*Astron.*) complete shadow cast by earth or moon in eclipse, as opposed to *penumbra*, partial shadow in eclipse. **-l** *a.* [L. *umbra*, shadow].

um·brage (um'·brij) *n.* (*Poetic*) shadow; feeling of resentment. **umbrageous** *a.* shady. **umbrageously** *adv.* **to take umbrage,** to feel resentful [L. *umbra*, shadow].

um·brel·la (um·brel'·a) *n.* light-weight circular covering of silk or other material on folding framework of spokes, carried as protection against rain (or sun). **-less** *a.* **-like** *a.* — **stand** *n.* stand for holding umbrellas [It. *ombrella*, dim. of *ombra*, shade].

um·laut (òòm'·lout) *n.* term used to denote mutation, e.g., caused by influence of vowel *i* (earlier *j*) on preceeding vowel such as a, o, u; in Modern German this vowel mutation is indicated by diaeresis over vowel, as in Führer (Fuehrer); in English it is seen in plural forms of man (*men*), mouse (*mice*), foot (*feet*). Also called **imutation** [Ger. *um*, about; *laut*, sound].

um·pire (um'·pīr) *n.* person chosen to arbitrate in dispute; impartial person chosen to see that rules of game are properly enforced; referee; *v.t.* and *v.i.* to act as umpire [orig. *numpire*, fr. O.Fr. *nomper*, peerless].

un- *prefix* before nouns, adjectives, and adverbs adding negative force; before verbs, expressing reversal of the action, separation, etc.

un·a·bashed a. (abash)
un·a·bat·ed a. (abate)
un·a·ble a. (able)
un·a·bridged a. (abridge)
un·ac·cent·ed a. (accent)
un·ac·cept·a·ble a. (accept)
un·ac·com·mo·dat·ing a. (accommodate)
un·ac·com·pa·nied (un·a·kum′·pạ·nēd) a. not accompanied; sung or played on instrument without piano, organ, or orchestral accompaniment.
un·ac·count·a·ble a. (account)
un·ac·cus·tomed a. (accustom)
un·ac·quaint·ed a. (acquaint)
un·a·dorned a. (adorn)
un·a·dul·ter·at·ed a. (adulterate)
un·ad·vised a. (advise)
un·af·fect·ed (un·ạ·fek′·tid) a. not affected unmoved; straightforward; sincere. **-ly** adv. simply; void of affection.
un·a·fraid a. (afraid)
un·aid·ed a. (aid)
un·al·loyed a. (alloy)
un·al·ter·a·ble (un·awl′·tẹr·ạ·bl) a. not capable of alteration; fixed; permanent. **-ness unalterability** n. **unalterably** adv. **unaltered** a. unchanged.
un·am·bi·tious a. (ambition)
u·nan·i·mous (yȯȯ·nan′·ạ·mạs) a. all of one mind; agreed to by all parties. **unanimity** (ū′·nạ·nim·ạ·ti·) n. **-ly** adv. **-ness** n. [L. unus, one; animus, mind].
un·an·nealed a. (anneal)
un·an·nounced a. (announce)
un·an·swer·a·ble. unanswerability, -ness n. (answer)
un·ap·pre·ci·at·ed a. **unapprecaitive** a. (appreciate)
un·ap·proach·a·ble a. **-ness** n. **unapproachably** adv. (approach)
un·arm (un·ảrm′) v.t. to disarm; to render harmless; v.i. to lay down arms. **-ed** a. defenseless. **-ored** a. without weapons; (of ships, etc.) not protected by armor plating.
un·a·shamed a. (ashamed)
un·asked a. (ask)
un·as·sail·a·ble (un·a·sāl′·ạ·bl) a. not assailable; irrefutable; invincible. **unassailed** a.
un·as·sim·i·la·ted a. **unassimilable** a. **unassimilating** a. (assimilate)
un·as·sist·ed a. (assist)
un·as·sum·ing (un·ạ·sȯȯm′·ing) a. not assuming; modest; not overbearing.
un·at·tached (un·ạ·tacht′) a. not attached; dangling; not posted to a particular regiment; not married or engaged.
un·at·tain·a·ble a. **unattainably** adv. (attain)
un·at·tend·ed a. **unattending** a. **unattentive** a. (attend)
un·at·test·ed a. (attest)
un·at·trac·tive (un·ạ·trak′·tiv) a. not attractive; repellent; plain; not prepossessing. **-ly** adv. **-ness** n.
un·au·thor·ized a. **unauthoritative** a. (authorize)
un·a·vail·ing (un·ạ·vāl′·ing) a. not availing; fruitless; having no result. **unavailability** n. **unavailable** a. not procurable; not at one's disposal. **-ly** adv. fruitlessly.
un·a·void·a·ble a. **-ness, unavoidability** n. **unavoidably** adv. **unavoided** a. (avoid)
un·a·ware (un·ạ·wār′) a. having no knowledge of; adv. unawares. **-s** adv. unexpectedly; without previous warning.
un·baked a. (bake)
un·bal·ance (un·bal′·ạns) v.t. to upset. **-d** a. not balanced; lacking equipoise, or mental stability; not adjusted or equal on credit and debit sides (of ledger). **unbalance** n.
un·bar v.t. and i. (bar)
un·bear·a·ble (un·ber′·ạ·bl) a. not bearable; intolerable; (of pain) excruciating. **-ness** n. **unbearably** adv.

un·beat·en a. (beat)
un·be·com·ing (un·bi·kum′·ing) a. not becoming; not suited to the wearer; (of behavior) immodest; indecorous. **-ly** adv.
un·be·fit·ting a. (befit)
un·be·known (un·bi·nōn′) a. not known. **-st** adv. without the knowledge of.
un·be·lief n. **unbelievability** n. **unbelievable** a. **unbelieving** a. **unbelievingly** adv. (believe)
un·belt v.t. (belt)
un·bend (un·bend′) v.t. to free from bend position; to straighten; to relax; to loose, as anchor; v.i. to become relaxed; to become more friendly. pa.t., pa.p. **bent** or **-ed. ing** a. not pliable; rigid; (Fig.) coldly aloof; resolute. **-ingly** adv. **unbent** a. straight.
un·bi·ased v.t. (bias)
un·bid·den a. (bid)
un·bind v.t. (bind)
un·bit·ten a. (bite)
un·blamed a. (blame)
un·bleached a. (bleach)
un·blem·ished (un·blem′·isht) a. not blemished; faultless; (of character) pure; perfect. **unblemishable** a.
un·blessed or **unblessed** a. (Bless)
un·blink·ing a. (blink)
un·blush·ing·ly adv. (blush)
un·bod·ied (un·bảd′·id) a. free from the body; incorporeal.
un·bolt v.t. **-ed** a. (bolt)
un·bolt·ed (un·bōl′·tid) a. (of grain) unsifted; not fastened with a bolt. **unbolt** v.t.
un·born (un·bawrn′) a. not yet born; future, as unborn generations.
un·bos·om (un·booz′·ạm) v.t. to disclose freely; to reveal one's intimate longings.
un·bound (un·bound′) a. not bound; free; without outer binding, as a book; pa.p., pa.t. of **unbind. -ed** a. illimitable; abundant; irrepressible. **-edly** adv.
un·bowed a. (bow)
un·break·a·ble a. (break)
un·bri·dle (un·brī′·dl) v.t. to remove the bridle from, as a horse. **-d** a. unrestrained; voilently passionate.
un·bro·ken (un·brō′·kn) a. complete; whole; (of horse) untamed; inviolate; continuous. **-ly** adv. **-ness** n.
un·buck·le v. **-d** a. (buckle)
un·bur·den (un·bur′·dn) v.t. to relieve of a burden; (Fig.) to relieve the mind of anxiety. **-ed** a. **-ing** n.a.
un·bur·ied a. (bury)
un·burned a. (burn)
un·busi·ness·like a. (business)
un·but·ton v.t. (button)
un·cage v.t. (cage)
un·cal·cu·la·ted v.t. (calculate)
un·called (un·kawld′) a. not summoned. **uncalled for,** unnecessary or without cause.
un·can·ny (un·kan′·i·) a. weird; unearthly. **uncannily** adv. **uncanniness** n.
un·caused a. (cause)
un·ceas·ing a. **-ly** adv. (cease)
un·cer·e·mo·ni·ous (un·ser·ạ·mō′·ni·ạs) a. not ceremonious; informal; abrupt. **-ly** adv. **-ness** n.
un·cer·tain (un·sur′·t(i)n) a. not certain; not positively known; unreliable; insecure. **-ly** adv. **-ness** n. **-ty** n. state of being or that which is uncertain; lack of assurance.
un·chain v.t. (chain)
un·change·a·ble a. **unchangeability, -ness** n. **unchangeably** adv. **unchanged** a. **unchanging** a. **unchangingly** adv. (change)
un·char·i·ta·ble a. **-ness** n. **uncharitably** adv. (charity)
un·chart·ed (un·chảr′·tid) a. not shown on a map; unexplored.
un·checked a. (check)
un·chris·tian a. **-ly** adv. (christian)
un·church (un·church′) v.t. to excommuni-

cate; to deprive of name and status of a church.

un·ci·al (un'·shạl) *a.* pert. to a type of rounded script, found in ancient MSS from 4th-9th cents.; *n.* uncial letter or manuscript. **-ly** *adv.* [L. *uncia,* inch; (*lit.*) letters, an inch high].

un·ci·form (un'·si·fawrm) *a.* shaped like a hook. **uncinal, uncinate** *a.* hooked; having hook-like prickles. [L. *uncus,* a hook].

un·cir·cum·cised (un·sur'·kạm·sīzd) *a.* not circumcised; Gentile. **uncircumcision** *n.*

un·civ·il *a.* **-ity** *a.* **ness** *n.* **-ized** *a.* **-ly** *adv.* (civil, civilize)

un·claimed *a.* (claim)

un·clasped *a.* (clasp)

un·clear *a.* (clear)

un·cloud·ed *a.* (cloud)

un·cle (ung'·kl) *n.* brother of one's father or mother; any elderly man; (*Slang*) pawnbroker. [L. *avunculus,* mother's brother].

un·clean (un·klēn') *a.* not clean; filthy; ceremonially unsanctified; obscene. **uncleanliness** *n.* (un·klen'·li·nạs). **-ly** (un·klēn'·li·, or un·klen·li··) *a. adv.* **-ness** *n.*

un·clench *v.t.* (clench)

un·clothe *v.t.* **-d** *a.* (clothe)

un·cock (un·kåk') *v.t.* to let down hammer of gun without exploding charge.

un·coil *v.t.* (coil)

un·come·ly (un·kum'·li·) *a.* not comely; unprepossessing; ugly; obscene.

un·com·fort·a·ble *a.* **-ness** *n.* **uncomfortably** *adv.* **uncomforted** *a.* (comfort)

un·com·mer·cial *a.* (commerce)

un·com·mit·ted *a.* (commit)

un·com·mon *a.* **-ly** *adv.* **-ness** *n.* (common)

un·com·mu·ni·ca·tive (un·kạ·mū'·nạ·kā'·tiv) *a.* not communicative; discreet; taciturn. **-ly** *adv.* **-ness** *n.* **uncommunicable** *a.* not capable of being shared or communicated. **uncommunicableness** *n.* **uncommunicated** *a.*

un·com·plain·ing (un·kạm·plān'·ing) *a.* not complaining; resigned. **-ly** *adv.* without complaint.

un·com·plet·ed *a.* (complete)

un·com·pli·men·ta·ry *a.* (compliment)

un·com·pro·mis·ing (un·kảm·prạ·mī'·zing) *a.* not compromising; making no concession; rigid. **-ly** *adv.*

un·con·cealed *a.* (conceal)

un·con·cern (un·kạn·surn') *n.* lack of concern; apathy. **-ed** *a.* not concerned; disinterested; apathetic; not involved. **-edly** *adv.* **-edness** *n.*

un·con·di·tioned (un·kạn·dish'·ạnd) *a.* not subject to conditions; absolute; instinctive. **unconditional** *a.* complete; absolute; without reservation. **unconditionally** *adv.* — **reflexes,** the instinctive responses of an animal to external stimuli.

un·con·firmed *a.* (confirm)

un·con·gen·i·al *a.* (congenial)

un·con·nect·ed *a.* (connect)

un·con'quer·a·ble *a.* **unconquerably** *adv.* (conquer)

un·con·scion·a·ble (un·kán'·shạn·ạ·bl) *a.* beyond reason; unscrupulous; excessive. **-ness** *n.* **unconscionably** *adv.*

un·con·scious (un·kán'·shạs) *a.* not conscious; unaware; deprived of consciousness; involuntary. **-ly** *adv.* **-ness** *n.* state of being insensible. **the unconscious,** in psychoanalysis, part of mind which appears to act without a conscious effort of will.

un·con·sti·tu·tion·al (un·kán·sti·tū'·shạn·ạl) *a.* not constitutional; contrary to the constitution, as of a society or state. **constitutionality** *n.* **-ly** *adv.*

un·con·strained *a.* **-ly** *adv.* **unconstraint** *n.* (constrain)

un·con·trol·la·ble (un·kạn·trōl'·ạ·bl) *a.* not capable of being controlled; unmanageable;

irrepressible. **-ness** *n.* **uncontrollably** *adv.*

uncontrolled *a.* not controlled; (of prices) not restricted by government regulations. **uncontrolledly** *adv.*

un·con·ven·tion·al (un·kạn·ven'·shạn·ạl) *a.* **-ity** *n.* **-ly** *adv.* not conforming to convention, rule or precedent.

un·con·ver·sant *a.* (**converse** *v.*)

un·con·vert·ed (un·kạn·vur'·tid) *a.* not converted; unchanged in heart; heathen; not changed in opinion; **unconversion** *n.* **unconvertible** *a.* not convertible.

un·con·vinced *a.* **unconvincing** *a.* (convince)

un·cooked *a.* (cook)

un·cork *v.t.* (cork)

un·cor·rupt·ed *a.* (corrupt)

un·count·ed *a.* not counted; innumerable.

un·cou·ple (un·kup'·l) *v.t.* to loose, as a dog from a leash; to disjoin, as railway carriages. **-d** *a.* not mated; not joined.

un·couth (un·kooth') *a.* awkward in manner; strange; unpolished; unseemly. **-ly** *adv.* **-ness** *n.* [O.E. *cuth,* known].

un·cov·a·nant·ed (un·kuv'·ạ·nạn·tid) *a,* not agreed to by covenant.

un·cov·er *v.t.* (cover)

un·crowned *a.* (crown)

unc·tion (ungk'·shạn) *n.* act of anointing with oil, as in ceremony of consecration or coronation; (*Med.*) ointment; act of applying ointment; that which soothes; insincere fervor. **unctuosity** *n.* **unctuous** *a.* oily; excessively suave. **unctuously** *adv.* **unctuousness** *n.* **extreme unction,** R.C. rite of anointing the dying [L. *unguere, unctum,* to anoint].

un·cul·ti·va·ble (un·kul'·ti·vạ·bl) *a.* not capable of being cultivated; waste. **uncultivated** *a.* not cultivated; not tilled; (*Fig.*) undeveloped. **uncultured** *a.* not cultured; not educated; crude.

un·cured *a.* (cure)

un·cut *a.* (cut)

un·damped (un·dampt') *a.* not damped; dry; (*Fig.*) not downhearted or dispirited.

un·dat·ed *a.* (date)

un·daunt·ed *a.* **-ly** *adv.* (daunt)

un·de·ceive (un·di·sēv') *v.t.* to free from deception. **-d** *a.*

un·de·cid·ed (un·di·sī'·did) *a.* not settled; irresolute; vacillating. **undecidable** *a.* not capable of being settled. **-ly** *adv.*

un·de·ci·pher·a·ble *a.* (decipher)

un·de·clared (un·di·klård') *a.* not declared; (of taxable goods at customs) not admitted as being in one's possession during customs' examination.

un·de·fen·ded *a.* (defend)

un·de·filed *a.* (defile *v.*)

un·de·fined *a.* **undefinable** *a.* (define)

un·dem·o·crat·ic (un·dem·ạ·krat'·ik) *a.* not according to the principlesa of democracy. **undemocratize** *v.t.* to make undemocratic.

un·de·mon·stra·tive *a.* **-ly** *adv.* **-ness** *n.* (demonstrate)

un·de·ni·a·ble *a.* **undeniably** *adv.* (deny)

un·de·nom·i·na·tion·al *a.* (denomination)

un·de·pend·a·ble *a.* (depend)

un·der (un'·dẹr) *prep.* below; beneath; subjected to; less than; liable to; included in; in the care of; during the period of; bound by; *adv.* in a lower degree or position; less; *a.* subordinate; lower in rank or degree. **under age,** younger than 21 years [O.E. *under*].

un·der·act (un·dẹr·akt') *v.t.* or *v.i.* to act a part in a play in a colorless, ineffective way.

un·der·arm (un'·dẹr·ȧrm) *a.n.* under the arm; armpit; *adv.* from below the shoulder (as a throw); *v.t.* to arm insufficiently. **-ed** *a.*

un·der·bid (un·dẹr·bid') *v.t.* to bid lower than another for a contract, etc.; to make lower bid at bridge than one's cards justify.

pr.p. **-ding.** *pa.p.*, *pa.t.* **underbid. -der** *n.*

un·der·bred (un·der·bred') *a.* of inferior manners; not thoroughbred.

un·der·brush (un'·der·brush) *n.* undergrowth of shrubs and bushes.

un·der·car·riage (un'·der·kar·ij) *n.* (*Aero.*) landing gear of aircraft.

un·der·charge (un·der·chárj·) *v.t.* to charge less than true price; *n.* price below the real value.

un·der·clothes (un'·der·klō(TH)z) *n.pl.* garments worn below the outer clothing, esp. next the skin; underclothing; lingerie. **underclothed** *a.* **underclothing** *n.*

un·der·cov·er (un'·der·kuv'·er) *a.* (*Colloq.*) secret; used esp. of secret service agents.

un·der·cur·rent (un'·der·kur·ant) *n.* current under surface of main stream, sometimes flowing in a contrary direction; hidden tendency.

un·der·cut (un·der·kut') *v.t.* to cut away from below, as coal seam; to strike from beneath; to sell goods cheaply in order to capture a market or monopoly; (*Golf*) to hit ball so it backspins. *pr.p.* **-ting.** *pa.p.*, *pa.t.* **undercut.** *a.* produced by cutting away from below. (un'·der·cut) *n.* act of cutting away from below; (*Boxing*) punch from underneath.

un·der·de·vel·op (un·der·di·vel'·ap) *v.t.* (*Photog.*) to develop insufficiently so that the photographic print is indistinct. **-ed** *a.* not developed physically; (of film) not sufficiently developed.

un·der·dog (un'·der·dawg) *n.* (*Colloq.*) dog which is beaten in fight; person who fares badly in any struggle.

un·der·dose (un·der·dōs') *v.t.* to give an insufficient dose (of medicine) to; (un'·der·dōs) *n.* an insufficient dose.

un·der·es·ti·mate (un·der·es'·ta·māt) *v.t.* to miscalculate the value of; to rate at too low a figure; *n.* an inadequate valuation.

un·der·ex·posed (un·der·iks·pōzd') *a.* (*Photog.*) insufficiently exposed to the light to impress details on a sensitive surface with clarity of outline. **underexposure** *n.*

un·der·feed (un·der·fēd') *v.t.* to feel insufficiently; to undernourish. **underfed** *a.*

un·der·foot (un·der·foot') *adv.* beneath the feet; *a.* lying under the foot; in subjection.

un·der·gar·ment (un'·der·gar·mant) *n.* a garment worn underneath the outer clothes.

un·der·go (un·der·gō') *v.t.* to bear; to suffer; to sustain; to participate in. *pr.p.* **-ing.** *pa.t.* **underwent.** *pa.p.* **undergone.**

un·der·grad·u·ate (un·der·graj'·oo·it) *n.* student attending classes for his first degree at a university or college; *a.* pert. to such student or university course.

un·der·ground (un'·der·ground) *a.* under the ground; subterranean; secret; *n.* (*chiefly Brit.*) a subway; (*Fig.*) secret organization or resistance movement; *adv.* below surface of earth; secretly.

un·der·growth (un'·der·grōth) *n.* small trees, shrubs, or plants growing beside taller trees.

un·der·hand (un'·der·hand) *adv.* by secret means; fraudulently; *a.* (*Sports*) served or thrown, as a ball, with hand underneath and an upward swing of the arm from below the waist; sly and dishonorable. **-ed** *a.* **-edly** *adv.* **-edness** *n.*

un·der·hung (un·der·hung') *a.* projecting beyond upper jaw, as lower jaw.

un·der·lay (un·der·lā) *v.t.* to lay underneath; to support by something put below; *n.* something placed under another thing; piece of paper, cardboard, etc. used by printers to raise type plate; floor covering laid underneath a carpet. *pa.p.*, *pa.t.* **underlaid.**

un·der·lie (un·der·lī') *v.t.* to lie underneath; to be the basis of. *pr.p.* **underlying.** *pa.p.*

underlain or **underlaid.** *pa.t.* **underlay.**

underlying *a.* basic; placed beneath; obscure.

un·der·line (un·der·līn') *v.t.* to mark with line below, for emphasis; to emphasize. (un'·der·līn) *n.* **-d** *a.*

un·der·ling (un'·der·ling) *n.* one who holds inferior position; subordinate member of a staff; a weakling.

un·der·manned (un·der·mand') *a.* supplied (as a ship) with too small a crew; having too small a staff.

un·der·mine (un·der·mīn) *v.t.* to excavate for the purpose of mining, blasting, etc.; to erode; to sap, as one's energy; to weaken insidiously.

un·der·neath (un·der·nēth') *adv.* and *prep.* beneath; below; in a lower place.

un·der·nour·ished (un·der·nur'·isht) *a.* insufficiently nourished. **undernourishment** *n.*

un·der·pass (un'·der·pas) *n.* road or passage (for cars, pedestrians) under a highway or railroad.

un·der·pay (un·der·pā') *v.t.* to pay inadequately for the work done; to exploit. *pa.p.*, *pa.t.* **underpaid. -ment** *n.*

un·der·pin·ning (un·der·pin'·ing) *n.* a support; *pl.* the legs.

un·der·priv·i·leged (un·der·priv'·a·lijd) *a.* deficient in the necessities of life because of poverty, discrimination, etc.

un·der·proof (un'·der·proof) *a.* containing less alcohol than proof spirit.

un·der·rate (un·der·rāt') *v.t.* to rate too low; to underestimate.

un·der·score (un·der·skōr) *v.t.* to underline for emphasis. **-d** *a.*

un·der·sec·re·tar·y (un'·der·sek'·ra·ter·i·) *n.* secretary who ranks below the principal secretary., esp. of government department.

un·der·sell (un·der·sel') *v.t.* to sell more cheaply than another. *pa.p.*, *pa.t.* **undersold. -er** *n.*

un·der·set (un'·der·set) *n.* (*Naut.*) an ocean undercurrent.

un·der·shot (un'·der·shát) *a.* (of mill-wheel) turned by water flowing under; having a protruding lower jaw.

un·der·side (un·der·sīd) *n.* the surface underneath.

un·der·sign (un·der·sin') *v.t.* to write one's name at the foot of or underneath. **-ed** *a.*

un·der·sized (un'·der·sīzd) *a.* smaller than normal size; dwarf. Also **undersize.**

un·der·skirt (un'·der·skurt) *n.* petticoat; skirt worn or placed under another.

un·der·stand (un·der·stand') *v.t.* to comprehend; to grasp the significance of. *pap.*, *pat.* **understood. -able** *a.* **-ably** *adv.* **-ing** *n.* **-ingly** *adv.* [O.E. *understandan*].

un·der·state (un·der·stāt') *v.t.* to state less strongly than truth warrants; to minimize deliberately. **-ment** *n.*

un·der·stud·y (un'·der·stud·i·) *n.* one ready to substitute for principal actor (or actress) at a moment's notice; *v.t.* to study theatrical part for this purpose.

un·der·take (un·der·tāk') *v.t.* to take upon oneself as a special duty; to agree (to do); to warrant; *v.i.* to be under obligation to do something; (*Colloq.*) to make arrangements for burial. *pa.t.* **undertook.** *pa.p.* **-n. -r** *n.* one who undertakes; one who manages a burial. **undertaking** *n.* project; guarantee.

un·der·tone (un'·der·tōn) *n.* low, subdued tone of voice or color.

un·der·tow (un'·der·tō) *n.* undercurrent or backwash of a wave after it has reached the shore.

un·der·val·ue (un·der·val'·ū) *v.t.* to set too low a price on; to esteem lightly; to underestimate; *n.* an underestimate. **undervaluation** *n.*

un·der·wear (un′·der·wer) n. underclothes.

un·der·went (un·der·went′) pa.t. of **undergo.**

un·der·wood (un′·der·wood) n. small trees growing among larger trees.

un·der·world (un′·dēr·wurld) n. the nether regions; Hades; the antipodes; section of community which lives by vice and crime.

un·der·write (un·der·rīt′) v.t. to write under something else; to subscribe; to append one's signature, as to insurance policy; to undertake to buy shares not bought by the public, and thereby guarantee success of issue of business capital. pa.t. **underwrote.** pa.p. **underwritten.** n.

un·der·wrought (un·der·rawt′) pa.t. and pa.p. of **underwork.**

un·de·served a. **undeserving** a. **undeservingly** adv. (deserve)

un·de·sir·a·ble (un·di·zīr′·a̱·bl) a. not desirable; having no appreciable virtues; n. person of ill-repute. **undesirability. undesirably** adv. **undesiring, undesirous** a. not desirous.

un·de·ter·mined a. **undeterminable** a. **undeterminate** a. (determine)

un·de·terred a. (deter)

un·de·vel·oped a. (develop)

un·de·vi·at·ing (un·dē′·vi·a̱·ting) a. not deviating; resolute in pursuing a straight course; (Fig.) resolute of purpose.

un·did (un·did′) pa.t. of **undo.**

un·dies (un′·dēz) n.pl. (Colloq. abbrev.) women's underwear.

un·dif·fer·en·ti·at·ed a. (differ)

un·di·gest·ed a. (digest)

un·di·lut·ed a. (dilute)

un·di·min·ished a. (diminish)

un·dine (un·dēn′) n. water sprite; [L. unda, a wave].

un·di·rect·ed a.

un·dis·ci·plined a. (discipline)

un·dis·crim·i·nat·ing a. (discriminate)

un·dis·guised a. (disguise)

un·dis·mayed a. (dismay)

un·dis·posed a. (dispose)

un·dis·put·ed a. **undisputable** a. **undisputableness** n. **-ly** adv. (dispute)

un·dis·solved a. (dissolve)

un·dis·tin·guished a. **distinguishable** a. **undistinguishableness** n. (distinguished)

un·dis·turb·ed a. (disturb)

un·di·vid·ed a. (divide)

un·do (un·dōō′) v.t. to reverse what has been done; to annul; to loose; to unfasten; to damage character of. pa.t. **undid.** pa.p. **undone. undoer** n. **-ing** n. act of reversing what has been done; ruin, esp. of reputation. **undone** a. ruined; not done; not completed.

un·do·mes·tic a. **-ated** a. (domestic)

un·doubt·ed a. **-ly** adv. **undoubtably** adv. **undoubtful** a. (doubt)

un·dress (un′·dres) n. informal dress; off-duty military uniform. (un·dress′) v.t. and i. **-ed** a.

un·due (un·dū′) a. not yet payable; unjust; immoderate; not befitting the occasion. **-ness** n.

un·du·late (un′·dya̱·lāt) v.t. to move up and down like waves; to cause to vibrate; v.i. to move up and down; to vibrate; to have wavy edge; a. (un′·dya̱·lit) wavy. **undulant** a. undulating; wavy. **-ly** adv. **undulating** a. wavy; having series of rounded ridges and depressions, as surface of landscape. **undulatingly** adv. **undulation** n. wave; fluctuating motion, as of waves; wave-like contour of stretch of land; series of wavy lines; vibratory motion. **undulatory** a. pert. to undulation; moving like a wave; pert. to theory of light which argues that light is transmitted through ether by wave motions. [L. unda, a wave].

un·du·ly (un·dōō′·li·) adv. unjustly; improperly; excessively.

un·dy·ing a. not dying; immortal; everlasting. **-ly** adv. **-ness** n.

un·earned (un·urnd′) a. not earned by personal labor. — **income,** income derived from sources other than salary, fees, etc. — **increment,** increased value of property, land, etc. due to circumstances other than owner's expenditure on its upkeep.

un·earth (un·urth′) v.t. to dig up; to drive as a fox, rabbit, etc. from its burrow; to bring to light. **-liness** n. **-ly** a. not of this world; supernatural.

un·eas·y (un·ē′·zi·) a. anxious; awkward; uncomfortable. **uneasiness** n. **uneasily** adv. (ease)

un·e·co·nom·ic a. (economy)

un·ed·i·fy·ing a. (edify)

un·ed·u·cat·ed a. (education)

un·em·ploy·ment (un·im·ploi′·mant) n. state of being unemployed. — **benefit,** money received by unemployed workers according to conditions laid down by insurance regulations. — **insurance,** insurance against periods of unemployment contributed to by workers, employers, etc. **unemployed** n.a.

un·end·ing a. **unended** a. **-ly** adv. (end)

un·en·dur·a·ble a. (endure)

un·en·light·ened a. (enlighten)

un·e·qual a. **-led** a. **-ly** adv. **-ness** n. (equal)

un·e·quiv·o·cal a. **-ly** adv. (equivocal)

un·er·ring (-ly). a. and adv. (err)

U·nes·co (ū·nes′·kō) n. coined word from initial letters of United Nations Educational, Scientific and Cultural Organization, established in November, 1945.

un·es·sen·tial a. (essential)

un·e·ven a. **-ly** adv. (even)

un·e·vent·ful a. (event)

un·ex·cep·tion·a·ble a. **unexceptional** a. (except)

un·ex·e·cut·ed a. (execute)

un·ex·pect·ed (un·iks·pek′·tid) a. not expected; sudden; without warning. **-ly** adv. **-ness** n.

un·ex·pired a. (expire)

un·ex·plained a. (explain)

un·ex·plored a. (explore)

un·ex·pressed a. (express)

un·ex·tin·guished a. (extinguish)

un·ex·tir·pat·ed a. (extirpate)

un·fad·a·ble a. **unfaded** a. **unfading** a. (fade)

un·fail·ing (un·fāl′·ing) a. not liable to fail; ever loyal; inexhaustible. **-ly** adv. **-ness** n.

un·fair (un·fār′) a. not fair; unjust; prejudiced; contrary to the rules of the game. **-ly** adv. **-ness** n.

un·faith·ful a. **-ly** adv. **-ness** n. (faith)

un·fal·ter·ing a. (falter)

un·fa·mil·iar a. **-ity** n. **-ly** adv. (familiar)

un·fash·ion·a·ble a. **-ness** n. **unfashionably** adv. (fashion)

un·fas·ten v.t. **-ed** a. (fasten)

un·fath·om·a·ble a. **-ness** n. **unfathomably** adv. **unfathomed** a. (fathom)

un·fa·vor·a·ble a. (favor)

un·feel·ing (un·fēl′·ing) a. void of feeling; callous; unsympathetic. **-ly** adv.

un·feigned a. **-ly** adv. **-ness** n. (feign)

un·fet·ter v.t. **-ed** a. (fetter)

un·fil·i·al a. (filial)

un·fin·ished (un·fin′·isht) a. not finished; roughly executed; not published. **unfinish** n. **unfinishable** a.

un·fit a. **-ly** adv. **-ness** n. **-ting** a. **-tingly** adv. (fit)

un·fledged (un·flejd′) a. not yet covered with feathers; immature.

un·fleshed (un·flesht′) a. (of sword) not yet used in fighting; not having tasted blood.

unfleshly *a.* uncorporeal. **unfleshy** *a.* having no flesh.

un·flinch·ing *a.* **-ly** *adv.* (flinch)

un·fold (un·fōld′) *v.t.* to open the folds of; to spread out; to disclose; *v.i.* to expand. **-er** *n.* **-ing** *n.* **-ment** *n.* **-ed** *a.*

un·fore·seen (un·fōr·sēn′) *a.* unexpected. **unforeseeable** *a.* not capable of being foreseen; unpredictable. **-unforeseeing** *n.*

un·for·get·ta·ble *a.* **unforgettably** *adv.* (forget)

un·for·giv·a·ble *a.* **unforgiving** *a.* **unforgivingness** *n.* **unforgotten** *a.* (forgive)

un·formed (un·fawrmd′) *a.* not formed; amorphous; immature.

un·for·tu·nate *a.* **-ly** *adv.* **-ness** *n.* (fortune)

un·found·ed (un·foun′·did) *a.* not based on truth; not established. **-ly** *adv.* **-ness** *n.* (found)

un·fre·quent·ed *a.* **unfrequent** *a.* (frequent)

un·friend·ly *a.* **unfriended** *a.* **unfriendedness** *n.* **unfriendliness** *n.* (friend)

un·frock (un·fråk) *v.t.* to deprive of a frock, esp. to deprive of the status of a monk or priest. **-ed** *a.*

un·fruit·ful (un·frŏŏt′·fạl) *a.* not productive; not profitable.

un·furl (un·furl′) *v.t.* and *i.* to open or spread out.

un·fur·nished *a.* **unfurnish** *v.t.* (furnish)

un·gain·ly (un·gān′·li·) *a.* clumsy; awkward; *adv.* in a clumsy manner. **ungainliness** *n.* [M.E. *ungein*, awkward].

un·gar·nished *a.* (garnish)

un·gen·er·ous *a.* (generous)

un·gen·tle *a.* **-manly** *adv.* (gentle)

un·glaze *v.t.* **-d** *a.* (glaze)

un·god·ly (un·gåd′·li·) *a.* not religious; sinful; (*Colloq.*) outrageous(ly). **ungodliness** *n.*

un·gov·ern·a·ble *a.* **-ness** *n.* **ungovernably** *adv.* **ungoverned** *a.* (govern)

un·grace·ful *a.* **-ly** *adv.* **-ness** *n.* (graceful).

un·gra·cious *a.* **-ly** *adv.* (grace)

un·gram·mat·i·cal *a.* **-ly** *adv.* (grammar)

un·grate·ful *a.* **-ly** *adv.* **-ness** *n.* (grateful)

un·ground·ed (un·groun′·did) *a.* having no foundation; false.

un·grudg·ing *a.* **ungrudged** *a.* **-ly** *adv.* (grudge)

un·gual (ung·gwạl) *a.* having nails, hooves, or or claws. **ungulate** (ung′·gvạ·lit) *a.* having hoofs, one of the hoofed mammals [L. *unguis*, a nail].

un·guard·ed *a.* **-ly** *adv.* **-ness** *n.* (guard)

un·guent (ung′·gwạnt) *n.* ointment. **-ary** *a.* pert. to unguents. **unguinous** *a.* oily [L. *unguere*, to anoint].

un·hal·lowed (un·hal′·ōd) *n.* unholy; not consecrated; wicked. **unhallowing** *n.*

un·hamp·ered *a.* (hamper)

un·hand (un·hand′) *v.t.* to let go. **-ily** *adv.* awkwardly. **-iness** *n.* **-led** *a.* not handled. **-y** *a.* not handy; inconvenient; lacking skill.

un·hap·py *a.* **unhappily** *adv.* **unhappiness** *n.* (happy)

un·harmed *a.* (harm)

un·har·ness *a.* (harness)

un·health·y *a.* **unhealthful** *a.* **unhealthfully** *adv.* **unhealthfulness** *n.* **unhealthily** *adv.* **unhealthiness** *n.* (health)

un·heard (un·hurd′) *a.* not heard; not given hearing. **unheard of,** unprecedented.

un·heed·ed *a.* (heed)

un·hes·i·tat·ing (un·hez′·ạ·tā·ting) *a.* not hesitating; spontaneous; resolute. **-ly** *adv.* without hesitation.

un·hinge (un·hinj′) *v.t.* to take from the hinges; (*Fig.*) to cause mental instability. **-d** *a.* (of the mind) unstable; distraught.

un·hitch *v.* (hitch)

un·ho·ly (un·hō′·li·) *a.* not sacred; (*Colloq.*) dreadful. **unholily** *adv.* **unholiness** *n.* (holy)

un·hon·ored *a.* (honor)

un·hook *v.t.* (hook)

un·horse (un·hawrs′) *v.t.* to throw from a horse; to cause to fall from a horse.

un·hur·ried *a.* (hurry)

un·hurt *a.* **-ful** *a.* (hurt)

un·hy·gi·en·ic (un·hī·ji·en′·ik) *a.* not hygienic; unsanitary; unhealthy.

u·ni-, (ūni) *prefix* denoting one or single [fr. L. *unus*, one].

u·ni·ax·i·al (ū·ni·ak′·si·ạl) *a.* having a single axis; having one direction along which ray of light can travel without bifurcation. **-ly** *adv.*

u·ni·cam·er·al having one legislative chamber.

u·ni·cel·lu·lar (ū·ni·sel′·yạ·lẹr) *a.* having a single cell; monocellular.

u·ni·corn (ū′·ni·kawrn) *n.* (*Myth.*) horselike animal with a single horn protruding from forehead [L. *unus*, one; *cornu*, horn].

un·i·de·al (un·ī·dē′·ạl) *a.* realistic; prosaic. **-ism** *n.*

u·ni·form (ū′·nạ·fawrm *a.* having always same form; conforming to one pattern; regular; consistent; not varying, as temperature; *n.* official dress, as a livery, etc. **-ed** *a.* wearing uniform. **-ity** *n.* conformity to pattern or standard. **-ly** *adv.* **-ness** *n.* [L. *unus*, one; *forma*, form].

u·ni·fy (ū′·nạ·fī) *v.t.* to make into one; to make uniform. **unifiable** *a.* capable of being made one. **unification** *n.* act of unifying; state of being made one; welding together of separate parts. **unifier** *n.* [L. *unus*, one; *facere*, to make].

u·ni·lat·er·al (ū·ni·lat′·ẹr·ạl) *a.* one-sided; binding one side only, as in party agreement. **-ity** *n.* **-ly** *adv.*

u·ni·loc·u·lar (ū·ni·lạk′·ū·lạr) *a.* having single chamber or cavity.

un·im·ag·i·na·ble (un·i·maj′·i·nạ·bl) *a.* not imaginable; inconceivable. **-ness** *n.* **unimaginably** *adv.* **unimaginative** *a.* not imaginative; dull; uninspired. **unimaginatively** *adv.* **unimaginativeness** *n.* **unimagined** *a.* not imagined.

un·im·paired *a.* (impair)

un·im·peach·a·ble (un·im·pēch′·ạ·bl) *a.* not impeachable; irreproachable; blameless. **-ness, unimpeachability** *n.* **unimpeachably** *adv.* **unimpeached** *a.*

un·im·por·tant *a.* **unimportance** *n.* (import)

un·im·proved *a.* (improve)

un·in·flect·ed *a.* (inflect)

un·in·formed (un·in·fawrmd′) *a.* having no accurate information; ignorant; not expert.

un·in·hab·it·able *a.* **uninhabitability** *n.* **uninhabited** *a.* (inhabit)

un·in·jured *a.* (injure)

un·in·spired (inspire)

un·in·sured *a.* (insure)

un·in·tel·li·gent *a.* **unintelligence** *n.* **unintelligently** *adv.* **unintelligibility** *n.* **unintelligible** *a.* **unintelligibleness** *n.* **unintelligibly** *adv.* (intelligent)

un·in·ten·tion·al *a.* **-ly** *adv.* (intent)

un·in·ter·est·ed *a.* **-ly** *adv.* **-ness** *n.* **uninteresting** *a.* **uninterestingly** *adv.* (interest)

un·in·ter·rupt·ed *a.* **-ly** *adv.* (interrupt)

un·in·vit·ed *a.* **uninviting** *a.* **uninvitingly** *adv.* (invite)

un·ion (ūn′·yạn) *n.* act of joining two or more things into one; federation; marriage; harmony; combination of administrative bodies for a common purpose; trade union; **-ed** *a.* joined. **-ist** *n.* one who supports union. **Union Jack,** national flag of United Kingdom [Fr. *union*, fr. L. *unus*, one].

u·nip·a·rous (ū·nip′·a·ras) *a.* producing normally just one at a birth; (*Bot.*) having single stem [L. *unus*, one; *parere*, to bring forth].

u·nique (ū·nēk′) *a.* single in kind; having no like or equal; unusual; different. **-ly** *adv.* **-ness** *n.* [L. *unicus*, one].

u·ni·sex·u·al (ū·ni·sek′·shoo·al) *a.* of one sex only, as a plant; not hermaphrodite or bisexual. **-ity** *n.* **-ly** *adv.*

u·ni·son (ū′·na·san) *n.* harmony; concord; (*Mus.*) identity of pitch. **in unison**, with all voices singing the same note at the same time; sounding together; in agreement.

u·nit (ū′·nit) *n.* single thing or person; group regarded as one; standard of measurement; (*Math.*) the least whole number. **-ary** *a.* pert. to unit(s); whole [L. *unus*, one].

U·ni·tar·i·an (ū·ni·ter′·i·an) *n.* one who rejects doctrine of the Trinity and asserts the oneness of God and the teachings of Jesus. **-ism** *n.* [L. *unus*, one].

u·nite (ū·nīt′) *v.t.* to join; to make into one; to form a whole; to associate; to cause to adhere; *v.i.* to be joined together; to grow together; to act as one; to harmonize. **united** *a.* joined together; harmonious; unanimous. **unitedly** *adv.* **-r** *n.* **unity** *n.* state of oneness; agreement; coherence; combination of separate parts into connected whole, or of different people with common aim; (*Math.*) any quantity taken as one. **unitive** *a.* **United Nations,** international organization, formed 1942. **United Nations Organization,** international organization set up after *World War* 2 with Security Council as chief executive body. *Abbrev.* **UN. United States,** N. Amer. country; federal union of 50 states U.S.A. [L. *unus*, one].

u·ni·va·lent (u·ni·vā′·lant) *a.* (*chem.*) having a valence of one; (*Bot.*) unpaired. **univalence, univalency** *n.*

u·ni·valve (ū′·ni·valv) *a.* having only one valve; *n.* a single-shelled mollusk. Also **univalvular** *a.*

u·ni·verse (ū′·ni·vurs) *n.* all created things regarded as a system or whole; the world. **universal** *a.* pert. to universe; embracing all created things; world-wide; general (as opp. of *particular*); *n.* universal proposition; general concept; (in motoring) universal joint. **-ize** *v.t.* to make universal. **-ization** *n.* **Universalism** *n.* theological doctrine of the ultimate salvation of all mankind. **Universalist** *n.* **universalistic** *a.* **-ity** *n.* — **joint** (in motoring device whereby one part of machine has perfect freedom of motion in relation to another. **-ly** *adv.* **-ness** *n.* [L. *unus*, one; *vertere, versum*, to turn].

u·ni·ver·si·ty (ū·ni·vur′·sa·ti·) *n.* institution for educating students in higher branches of learning, and having authority to confer degrees [L. *universitas*, a corporation].

un·just *a.* **-ifiable** *a.* **-ifiably** *adv.* **-ly** *adv.* **-ness** *n.* (**just**)

un·kempt (un·kempt′) *a.* dishevelled; rough [O.E. *un-*, not; *cemban*, to comb].

un·kind (un·kīnd) *a.* not kind, considerate, or sympathetic; cruel. **-liness** *n.* **-ly** *a.* **-ness** *n.* (**kind**)

un·know·a·ble (un·nō′·a·bl) *a.* not capable of being known; *n.* that which is beyond man's power to understand; the absolute. **-ness** *n.* **unknowably** *adv.* **unknowing** *a.* ignorant. **unknowingly** *adv.* **unknown** *a.* not known; incalculable; *n.* unknown quantity; unexplored regions of mind; part of globe as yet unvisited by man.

un·lace *n.* (**lace**)

un·lament·ed *a.* (**lament**)

un·latch *v.* (**latch**)

un·law·ful *a.* **-ly** *adv.* **-ness** *n.* (**law**)

un·learn *v.t.* **-ed** *a.* (**learn**)

un·leash *v.t.* **-ed** *a.* (**leash**)

un·leav·ened (un·lev′·and) *a.* not leavened; made without yeast, as *unleavened bread.*

un·less (un·les′) *conj.* except; if not; supposing that; *prep.* except.

un·let·tered (un·let′·erd) *a.* illiterate.

un·li·censed *a.* (**license**)

un·like (un·līk′) *a.* not like; dissimilar; *prep.* different from; *adv.* in a different way from. **-lihood, -ness** *n.* **-ly** *a.* improbable; unpromising; *adv.* improbably. **-liness** *n.*

un·lim·it·ed *a.* **-ly** *adv.* (**limit**)

un·load (un·lōd′) *v.t.* to remove load from; to remove charge from, as gun; to sell out quickly, as stocks, shares, etc. before slump; (*Fig.*) to unburden, as one's mind; *v.i.* to discharge cargo. **-ed** *a.* not containing a charge, as gun; not containing a plate or film, as camera.

un·lock *v.t.* (**lock**)

un·looked-for (un·lookt′·fawr) *a.* unexpected, unforeseen.

un·loose (un·loos′) *v.t.* to set free. **-n** *v.t.*

un·lov·a·ble *a.* **unloved** *a.* **unloving** *a.* (**love**)

un·love·ly *a.* **unloveliness** *n.* (**lovely**)

un·luck·y *a.* **unluckily** *adv.* **unluckiness** *n.* (**lucky**)

un·make (un·māk′) *v.t.* to destroy what has been made; to annul; to ruin, destroy; to depose. *pa.p.*, *pa.t.* **unmade. -r** *n.* **unmade** *a.* not made. **unmakable** *a.* **unmaking** *n.*

un·man *v.t.* **—like** *a.* **-liness** *n.* **-ly** *a.* **-ned** *a.* (**man**)

un·man·age·a·ble *a.* **-ness** *n.* **unmanageably** *adv.* **unmanaged** *a.* (**manage**)

un·man·ner·ly *a.* **unmannered** *a.* **unmannerliness** *n.* (**manner**)

un·marked (un·markt′) *a.* without a mark.

un·mar·ried *a.* **unmarriageable** *a.* **unmarriageableness** *n.* (**marry**)

un·mask *v.t.* **-ed** *a.* (**mask**)

un·mean·ing (un·mēn′·ing) *a.* without meaning; unintentional; insignificant. **-ly** *adv.* **unmeant** (un·ment′) *a.* not intended; accidental.

un·meas·ured *a.* **unmeasurable** *a.* **unmeasurably** *adv.* (**measure**)

un·men·tion·a·ble (un·men′·shan·a·bl) *a.* not worthy of mention; not fit to be mentioned. **-ness** *n.* **-s** *n.pl.* facetious synonym for undergarments.

un·mer·ci·ful (un·mur′·si·fal) *a.* having or showing no mercy; cruel. **-ly** *adv.*

un·mind·ed (un·mīn′·did) *a.* not remembered **unmindful** *a.* forgetful; regardless. **unmindfully** *adv.* **unmindfulness** *n.*

un·mis·tak·a·ble (un·mis·tāk′·a·bl) *a.* clear; plain; evident. **unmistakably** *adv.*

un·mit·i·gat·ed (un·mit′·i·gāt·id) *a.* not softened or lessened; absolute; unmodified.

un·mixed *a.* (**mix**)

un·mo·lest·ed *a.* (**molest**)

un·moor *v.t.* (**moor**)

un·mor·al (un·mar′·, un·mawr′·al) *a.* not concerned with morality or ethics. **-izing** *a.* not given to reflecting on ethical values. **-ity** *n.* **-ly** *adv.*

un·mount·ed *a.* (**mount**)

un·moved *a.* **unmovable, unmoveable** *a.* **unmoving** *a.* (**move**).

un·mu·si·cal *a.* **-ity** *n.* **-ly** *adv.* (**music**)

un·named *a.* (**name**)

un·nat·u·ral *a.* **-ize** *v.t.* **-ized** *a.* **-ly** *adv.* (**natural**)

un·nav·i·ga·ble *a.* **unnavigability** *n.* **unnavigated** *a.* (**navigate**)

un·nec·es·sar·y *a.* **unnecessarily** *adv.* **unnecessariness** *n.* (**necessary**)

un·nerve (un·nurv′) to deprive of courage, strength; cause to feel weak. *v.t.* **-d** *a.*

un·no·ticed *a.* (**notice**)

un·num·bered (un·num′·bẹrd) *a.* not counted; innumerable.
un·ob·served *a.* (observe)
un·ob·struct·ed *a.* (obstruct)
un·ob·tru·sive *a.* -ly *adv.* -ness *n.* (obtrude)
un·oc·cu·pied (un·ȧk′·yȧ·pīd) *a.* not occupied; untenanted; not engaged in work; not under control of troops.
un·of·fi·cial *a.* (official)
un·o·pened *a.* (open)
un·or·gan·ized (un·ȯr′·gȧ·nīzd) *a.* without organic structure; having no system or order; not belonging to a labor union.
un·op·posed *a.* (oppose)
un·or·tho·dox *a.* (orthodox)
un·os·ten·ta·tious *a.* -ly *adv.* (ostentation)
un·pack (un·pak′) *v.t.* to remove from a pack or trunk; to open by removing packing; *v.i.* to empty contents of. -ed *a.* -er *n.*
un·paid *a.* (pay)
un·pal·at·a·ble *a.* (palate)
un·par·al·leled (un·par′·ȧ·leld) *a.* having no equal; unprecedented.
un·par·don·a·ble *a.* **unpardonably** *adv.* **unpardoned** *a.* (pardon)
un·par·lia·men·ta·ry *(un·par·lạ·men′·tạ·ri·)* *a.* contrary to parliamentary law or usage.
un·peo·ple *v.t.* (people)
un·per·turbed *a.* -ness *n.* (perturb)
un·pick *v.t.* -ed *a.* (pick)
un·placed *a.* **unplace** *v.t.* (place)
un·pleas·ant *a.* -ly *adv.* -ness *n.* **unpleasing** *a.* **unpleasingly** *adv.* **unpleasurable** *a.* (please)
un·pol·ished *a.* (polish)
un·pop·u·lar *a.* **unpopularity** *n.* (popular)
un·prec·e·dent·ed (un·pres·ạ·den′·tid) *a.* without precedent; having no earlier example; novel. -ly *adv.*
un·pol·lut·ed *a.* (pollute)
un·pre·dict·a·ble *a.* (predict)
un·pre·med·i·tat·ed *a.* **unpremeditable** *a.* -ly *adv.* -ness, **unpremeditation** *n.* (premeditate)
un·pre·pared *a.* -ly *adv.* -ness *n.* (prepare)
un·pre·pos·sess·ing *a.* **unprepossessed** *a.* (prepossess)
un·pre·ten·tious *a.* (pretend)
un·prin·ci·pled *a.* (principle)
un·print·a·ble (un·print′·ạ·bl) *a.* not printable; too shocking to be set down in print.
un·pro·duc·tive *a.* -ly *adv.* -ness *n.* (product)
un·pro·fes·sion·al (un·prạ·fesh′·ạn·l) *a.* not professional; contrary to professional ethics. -ly *adv.* (profess)
un·prof·it·a·ble *a.* -ness *n.* **unprofitably** *adv.* (profit)
un·prom·is·ing *a.* (promise)
un·pro·nounce·a·ble *a.* (pronounce)
un·pro·tect·ed *a.* (protect)
un·pro·vid·ed *a.* (provide)
un·pro·voked *a.* (provoke)
un·pruned *a.* (prune *v.*)
un·pub·lished *a.* (publish)
un·pun·ished *a.* **unpunishable** *a.* (punish)
un·qual·i·fied (un·kwạl′·ạ·fid) *a.* not qualified; not having proper qualifications; not modified; absolute. **unqualifying** *a.*
un·quench·a·ble *a.* (quench)
un·ques·tion·a·ble *a.* **unquestionability**, -ness *n.* **unquestionably** *adv.* **unquestioned** *a.* **unquestioning** *a.* (question)
un·qui·et *a.* (quiet)
un·quote (un·kwōt) *v.t.* and *i.* to end a quotation.
un·rav·el *v.t.* -ed *a.* (ravel)
un·read (un·red′) *a.* (of a book) not read; not having gained knowledge by reading. -able (un·rēd′·ạ·bl) *a.* not readable—illegible, uninteresting or unsuitable.

un·read·y *a.* **unreadily** *adv.* (ready)
un·re·al (un·rēl′) *a.* not real; insubstantial; illusive. -izable *a.* not realizable. -izableness *n.* -ized *a.* not realized; unfulfilled. **unreality** *n.* want of reality. -ly *adv.* -ity *n.*
un·rea·son (un·rē′·zn) *n.* lack of reason; irrationality. -able *a.* immoderate; impulsive; exorbitant (of prices). -ableness *n.* -ably *adv.* -ed *a.* not logical. -ing *a.* irrational.
un·rec·og·nized *a.* **unrecognizable** *a.* -izably *adv.* (recognize)
un·re·cord·ed *a.* (record)
un·rec·ti·fied *a.* (rectify)
un·reeve *v.t.* (reeve *v.*)
un·re·fined *a.* (refine)
un·re·gen·er·ate *a.* **unregeneracy, unregeneration** *n.* -ly *adv.* (regenerate)
un·re·lat·ed (un·ri·lāt′·id) *a.* not related; having no apparent connection; diverse.
un·re·lent·ing *a.* -ly *adv.* (relent)
un·re·li·a·ble *a.* **unreliability**, -ness *n.* (reliable)
un·re·lieved *a.* (relieve)
un·re·mem·bered *a.* (remember)
un·re·mit·ting (un·ri·mit′·ing) *a.* not relaxing; incessant; persistent. **unremitted** *a.* not remitted. **unremittedly**, -ly *adv.*
un·re·proved *a.* (reproof)
un·re·quit·ed *a.* **unrequitable** *a.* -ly *adv.* (requite)
un·rest (un·rest′) *n.* want of rest; disquiet; political or social agitation. -ful *a.* -fulness *n.* -ing *a.* *not resting.* -ingly *adv.*
un·re·strained *a.* (restrain)
un·re·strict·ed *a.* -ly *adv.* (restrict)
un·right·eous *a.* -ly *adv.* -ness *n.* **unrightful** *a.* **unrightfully** *adv.* -fulness *n.* (righteous, right)
un·ripe *a.* -ned *a.* -ness *n.* (ripe)
un·robe *v.t.* and *v.i.* (robe)
un·ri·valed *a.* (rival)
un·roll *v.* (roll)
un·ruf·fled (un·ruf′·ld) *a.* not ruffled; placid. **unruffle** *v.i.* to become placid.
un·ruled (un·rōȯld′) *a.* not ruled; ungoverned; (of paper) blank; unrestrained. **unruliness** *n.* state of being unruly. **unruly** *a.* lawless; disobedient.
un·sad·dle *v.* (saddle)
un·safe *a.* -ly *adv.* -ness *n.* -ty *n.* (safe)
un·sale·a·ble *a.* **unsalability** *n.* (sale)
un·san·i·tar·y *a.* (sanitary)
un·sat·is·fac·to·ry *a.* **unsatisfactorily** *adv.* **unsatisfactoriness** *n.* **unsatisfied** *a.* **unsatisfying** *a.* (satisfy)
un·sa·vo·r·y *a.* **unsavorily** *adv.* **unsavoriness** *n.* (savory)
un·say (un·sā′) *v.t.* to retract (what has been said). *p.pa., pa.t.* **unsaid.**
un·scathed (un·skāTHd′) *a.* unharmed; without injury.
un·schooled *a.* (school)
un·sci·entif·ic *a.* -ally *adv.*
un·scram·ble (un·skram′·bl) *v.t.* to decode a secret message; to straighten out.
un·scru·pu·lous (un·skrōȯ′·pyạ·lạs) *a.* not scrupulous; ruthless; having no moral principles. -ly *adv.* -ness *n.*
un·seal *v.t.* -ed *a.* (seal *n., v.t.*)
un·sea·son·a·ble (un·sē′·zạn·ạ·bl) *a.* untimely; out of season. -ness *n.* **unseasonably** *adv.* **unseasoned** *a.*
un·seat (un·sēt′) *v.t.* to throw from a horse; to deprive of official seat.
un·seem·li·ness *n.* **unseemly** *a.* and *adv.* (seem)
un·seen *a.* (see)
un·self-con·scious (un·self·kȧn′·shạs) *a.* not self-conscious; natural. -ly *adv.* -ness *n.*
un·self·ish *a.* -ly *adv.* -ness *n.* (self)
un·set·tle (un·set′·l) *v.t.* to move or loosen

from a fixed position; to disturb mind; to make restless or discontented. **-d** *a.* not settled; changeable, as weather; unpaid, as bills; not allocated; not inhabited. **-dly** *adv.* **-dness, -ment** *n.* **unsettling** *a.* disturbing.

un·shack·le *v.t.* **-d** *a.* **(shackle)**

un·shad·ed *a.* **(shade)**

un·shak·en *a.* **(shake)**

un·shav·en *a.* **(shave)**

un·sheathe *n.* **(sheath)**

un·shed *a.* **(shed)**

un·shod (un·shȯd') *a.* barefoot.

un·sight·ed (un·sī'·tid) *a.* not sighted; not observed; (of gun) without sights; (of shot) aimed blindly. **unsightable** *a.* invisible. **unsightliness** *n.* ugliness. **unsightly** *a.* ugly; revolting to the sight.

un·skill·ful *a.* **-ly** *adv.* **-ness** *n.* **unskilled** *a.* **(skill)**

un·sling (un·sling') *v.t.* (*Naut.*) to remove slings from, as from cargo; to take down something which is hanging by sling, as a rifle. *pa.p., pa.t.* **unslung.**

un·smil·ing *a.* **-ly** *adv.* **(smile)**

un·so·cia·ble *a.* **unsociability, -ness** *n.* **unsociably** *adv.* **(sociable)**

un·smirched *a.* **(smirch)**

un·so·lic·i·ted (un·sa·lis'·i·tid) *a.* not solicited; gratuitous. **unsolicitous** *a.* unconcerned.

un·so·phis·ti·cat·ed (un·sa·fis'·ti·kāt·id) *a.* not sophisticated; ingenuous; simple. **-ly** *adv.* **-ness, unsophistication** *n.*

un·sound (un·sound') *a.* imperfect; damaged: decayed; (of the mind) insane; not based on reasoning; fallacious. **-ly** *adv.* **-ness** *n.*

un·speak·a·ble (un·spēk'·a·bl) *a.* beyond utterance or description (in good or bad sense); ineffable. **unspeakably** *adv.* **unspeaking** *a.* dumb.

un·spoiled *a.* Also **unspoilt** **(spoil)**

un·sport·ing (un·spȯr'·ting) *a.* (*Colloq.*) not like sportsman; unfair. **unsportsmanlike** *a.* not in accordance with the rules of fair play.

un·spot·ted *a.* **(spot)**

un·sprung (un·sprung') *a.* not fitted with springs, as a vehicle, chair, etc.

un·sta·ble (un·stā'·bl) *a.* unsteady; wavering; not firm; unreliable; (*Chem.*) applied to compounds which readily decompose or change into other compounds. **unstability, -ness** *n.* **unstably** *adv.* **(stable** *a.***)**

un·stained *a.* **(stain)**

un·stead·y *a.* **unsteadily** *adv.* **unsteadiness** *n.* **(steady)**

un·stead·fast *a.* **unsteadfastly** *adv.* **unsteadfastness** *n.* **(steadfast)**

un·stop (un·stȧp') *v.t.* to open by removing a stopper, as a bottle; to clear away an obstruction; to open organ stops. *pr.p.* **-ping.** *pa.p., pa.t.* **-ped.** *a.* not stopped; having no cork or stopper.

un·strained (un·strānd') *a.* not strained, as through a filter; (*Fig.*) relaxed; friendly.

un·stuck (un·stuk') *a.* not glued together.

un·sub·dued *a.* **(subdue)**

un·sub·stan·tial *a.* **(substantial)**

un·suc·cess·ful (un·sak·ses'·fal) *a.* not succeeding; unfortunate; incomplete. **-ly** *adv.* **-ness** *n.*

un·suit·a·ble *a.* **unsuitability** *n.* **unsuited** *a.*

un·sul·lied *a.* **(sully)**

un·sung (un·sung') *a.* not sung or spoken; not celebrated.

un·sup·port·ed (un·sa·pȯr'·tad) *a.* not supported; without backing. **unsupportable** *a.* not supportable; intolerable.

un·sure *a.* **-ness** *n.* **(sure)**

un·sur·passed *a.* **(surpass)**

un·sus·pect·ed *a.* **(suspect)**

un·sus·pi·cious *a.* **(suspicious)**

un·sweet·ened *a.* **(sweeten)**

un·swept *a.* **(sweep)**

un·swerv·ing *a.* **-ly** *adv.* **(swerve)**

un·sym·pa·thet·ic *a.* **-ally** *adv.* **unsympathizable** *a.* **unsympathizing** *a.* **(sympathy)**

un·taint·ed *a.* **(taint)**

un·tan·gle *v.* **(tangle)**

un·tar·nished *a.* **(tarnish)**

un·taught (un·tawt') *a. pa.p., pa.t.* of **unteach**; uneducated; ignorant; natural, without teaching.

un·ten·a·ble *a.* **(tenable)**

un·thank·ful (un·thangk'·fal) *a.* ungrateful.

un·tamed *a.* **untamable** *a.* **(tame)**

un·think·ing (un·thingk'·ing) *a.* thoughtless; heedless. **-ly** *adv.* **unthinkable** *a.* **(think)**

un·ti·dy *a.* **untidily** *adv.* **untidiness** *n.*

un·tie *v.t.* **-d** *a.* **(tie)**

un·til (un·til') *prep.* till; to; as far as; as late as; *conj.* up to the time that; to the degree that.

un·time·ly (un·tīm'·li.) *a.* not timely; premature; inopportune. **untimeliness** *n.*

un·tir·ing *a.* **untirable** *a.* **untired** *a.* **-ly** *adv.* **(tire** *v.***)**

un·to (un'·tȯȯ) *prep.* (*Poet.*) to; until [M.E. *und to*, up to, as far as].

un·touch·a·ble (un·tuch'·a·bl) *a.* incapable of being touched; unfit to be touched; out of reach; belonging to non-caste masses of India; *n.* non-caste Indian whose touch or even shadow was regarded as defiling. **-untouchability** *n.* **untouched** *a.*

un·to·ward (un·tȯrd') *a.* unlucky; inconvenient; hard to manage.

un·trained *a.* **(train)**

un·trav·eled (un·trav'·eld) *a.* not having traveled; unexplored.

un·tried (un·trīd') *pa.p., pa.t.* of **try**; not proven, attempted or tested, not tried in court.

un·trimmed *a.* **(trim)**

un·true (un·trȯȯ') *a.* not true; false; disloyal; not conforming to a requisite standard. **-ness** *n.* **untruly** *adv.* falsely. **untruth** *n.* **untruthful** *a.* dishonest; lying. **untruthfully** *adv.* **untruthfulness** *n.*

un·turned *a.* **(turn)**

un·twist *v.* **(twist)**

un·tu·tored *a.* **(tutor)**

un·used (un·ūzd') *a.* not used; not accustomed. **unusual** *a.* not usual; uncommon; strange. **unusually** *adv.* **unusualness** *n.*

un·ut·ter·a·ble (un·ut'·er·a·bl) *a.* unspeakable beyond utterance; **unutterability** *n.* **unutterably** *adv.* **unuttered** *a.* unspoken.

un·var·nished *a.* **(varnish)**

un·vary·ing *a.* **(vary)**

un·veil *v.t.* **(veil)**

un·ver·i·fied *a.* **(verify)**

un·vexed *a.* **(vex)**

un·vis·it·ed *a.* **(visit)**

un·want·ed *a.* **(want)**

un·war·rant·a·ble (un·war'·ant·a·bl) *a.* justifiable; improper. **-ness** *n.* **unwarrantably** *adv.* **unwarranted** *a.* **unwarrantedly** *adv.* **(warrant)**

un·war·y *a.* **unwarily** *adv.* **unwariness** *n.* **(wary)**

un·washed (un·washt') *a.* not washed; dirty; not reached by the sea.

un·well (un·wel') *a.* ill; ailing.

un·wept (un·wept') *a.* not mourned or regretted.

un·whole·some *a.* **-ly** *adv.* **-ness** *n.* **(wholesome)**

un·wield·y *a.* **unwieldily** *adv.* **unwieldiness** *n.* **(wield)**

un·will·ing (un·wil'·ing) *a.* loathe; reluctant. **-ly** *adv.* **-ness** *n.* **(will)**

un·wind (un·wīnd') *v.t.* to wind off; to loose what has been wound; to roll into a ball from a skein, as wool, silk, etc.; *v.i.* to become un-

WEBSTER
T–Z

wound. *pa.p.*, *pa.t.* **unwound.**

un·wit·ting (un·wit′·ing) *a.* unawares; not knowing. **-ly** *adv.*

un·wont·ed (un·wunt′·ad, un·wŏnt′·ad) *a.* unaccustomed; unusual. **-ly** *adv.* **-ness** *n.*

un·work·a·ble *a.* (work)

un·world·ly *a.* **unworldliness** *n.* (worldly)

un·wor·thy *a.* **unworthily** *adv.* **unworthiness** *n.* (worthy)

un·writ·ten (un·rit′·n) *a.* not written; oral; not expressed in writing. **unwritten Law,** law originating in custom, usage, or court rather than

un·yield·ing (un·yēl′·ding) *a.* not yielding; stubborn; implacable; not flexible. *adv.* **-ness** *n.*

un·yoke *v.* (yoke)

up (up) *adv. prep.* to or toward a higher place or degree; on high; on one's legs; out of bed; above horizon; in progress; in revolt; as far as; of equal merit or degree; thoroughly well versed in; competent. Also used as a verb intensifier. *a.* advanced; standing; reaching; tending toward; higher; even with; finished; *v.t.* and *i.* to put, left or take up; to raise; to bet more. *pr.p.* **-ping.** *pa.p.*, *pa.t.* **-ped.** **up-and-coming,** alert; enterprising.

u·pas (ū′·pas) *n.* tree of E. Indian islands, yielding sap of deadly poison [Malay = poison].

up·braid (up·brād′) *v.t.* to reprove severely; to chide; *v.i.* to voice a reproach. **-ing** *n.* reproach; *a.* reproachful [O.E. *up*, on; *bregdan*, to braid].

up·bring·ing (up′·bring·ing) *n.* the process of rearing and training a child; education.

up-coun·try (up′·kun·tri·) *adv.* inland; *a.* away from the sea.

up·date (up′·dāt) *v.t.* bring up-to-date.

up·end (up·end′) *v.t.* to stand on end.

up·grade (up′·grād′) *a.*, *adv.* uphill; *n.* incline; *v.t.* to raise to a higher level.

up·heave (up·hēv′) *v.t.* to lift up, as heavy weight. **upheaval** *n.* raising up, as of earth's surface, by volcanic force; (*Fig.*) any revolutionary change in ideas, etc.

up·held (up·held′) *pa.t.* and *pa.p.* of **uphold.**

up·hill (up′·hil) *a.* going up; laborious; difficult; *adv.* towards higher level.

up·hold (up·hōld′) *v.t.* to hold up; to sustain; to approve; to maintain, as verdict in law court. *pa.p.*, *pa.t.* **upheld. -er** *n.*

up·hol·ster (up·hōl′·ster) *v.t.* to stuff and cover furniture. **-y** *n.* craft or stuffing and covering furniture, etc.; material used. **-er** *n.*

up·keep (up′·kēp) *n.* maintenance; money required for maintenance, as of a home.

up·land (up′·land) *n.* high land or region. *a.* pert. to or situated in higher elevations.

up·lift (up·lift′) *v.t.* to lift up; to improve conditions of, morally, socially etc.; to exalt. **-er** *n.* **-ment** *n.* (up′·lift) *n.* emotional or religious stimulus; moral and social improvement; a brassiere.

up·on (a·pàn′) *prep.* on [O.E. *uppon*, on].

up·per (up′·er) *a.* higher in place, rank, or dignity; superior; more recent; *n.* the part above; (*Colloq.*) upper berth; *n.pl.* (*Colloq.*) upper teeth. **—most. —case** *n.* (*Print.*) case containing capital letters. **-cut** *n.* (*Boxing*) blow struck upwards inside opponent's guard; *v.t.* to deliver such blow. **—hand** *n.* superiority; advantage over another. **uppish** or **uppity** (*Colloq.*) *a.* arrogant; affectedly superior in manner or attitude. **uppishly** *adv.* **uppishness** *n.* **-most** *a.*, *adv.* [fr. *up*].

up·right (up′·rīt) *a.* standing, pointed straight up; honest; *adv.* in such a position; *n.* a vertical part.

up·rise (up·rīz′) *v.i.* to rise up; to revolt. *pa.p.* **-n** (up·rī′·zan). *pa.t.* **uprose. up·rising** *n.* insurrection; revolt; a slope.

up·roar (up′·rōr) *n.* tumult; violent, noisy disturbance. **-ious** *a.* **-iously** *adv.* **-iousness** *n.* [Dut. *oproer*].

up·root (up·rōōt′) *v.t.* to tear up by the roots; to eradicate. **-al** *n.* **-er** *n.*

up·set (up·set′) *v.t.* to turn upside down; to knock over; to defeat; to disturb or distress. *pr.p.* **-ting** *pa.p.*, *pa.t.* **upset;** (up′·set) *n.* an overturn; overthrow; confusion; *a.* disordered; worried; overturned. **— price,** lowest price at which goods will be sold by auction.

up·shot (up′·shat) *n.* final issue; conclusion.

up·side (up′·sīd) *n.* the upper side. **—down** *adv.* with the upper side underneath; inverted; in disorder.

up·stage (up′·stāj′) *a.*, *adv.* of or toward rear of stage; *v.t.* to act on stage so as to minimize another actor.

up·stairs (up·sterz′) *adv.* in the upper story; on the stairs; *a.* pert. to upper story; *n.* upper story.

up·stand·ing (up·stan′·ding) *a.* erect; honorable.

up·start (up′·start) *n.* one who has suddenly risen to wealth, power, or honor; parvenu; *v.i.* to rise suddenly.

up·stream (up′·strēm) *adv.* in direction of source (of stream).

up·stroke (up′·strōk) *n.* the upward line in handwriting; upward stroke.

up·surge (up·surj′) *v.t.* to surge upwards. (up′·surj) *n.* welling, as of emotion.

up·sweep (up′·swēp) *n.* a curve upward; an upswept hair-do.

up·swing (up′·swing) *n.* a trend upward.

up·thrust (up′·thrust) *n.* upward thrust.

up-to-date (up′·ta·dāt′) *a.* modern; most recent; extending up to, pert. to, the present time.

up·town (up′·toun) *a.* pert. to, or in upper part of, town; *adv.*

up·turn (up·turn′) *v.t.* to turn up. (up′·turn) *n.* an upward turn for the better. **-ing** *n.*

up·ward (up′·werd) *a.* directed towards a higher place; *adv.* upwards. **-s, -ly** *adv.* towards higher elevation or number [O.E. *upweard,* upward].

u·ran·i·nite (yoo·rān′·a·nīt) *n.* pitchblende, in which uranium was first found in 1789.

u·ra·nite (yoor′·a·nīt) *n.* an almost transparent ore of uranium. **uranitic** *a.*

u·ra·ni·um (yoo·rā′·ni·am) *n.* radio-active metallic element (symbol U), used as an alloy in steel manufacture and in the production of atom bomb. **uranic, uranous** *a.* [fr. *Uranus,* the planet].

u·ra·nog·ra·phy (yoor·a·nág′·ra·fi·) *n.* descriptive astronomy. **uranographer, uranographist** *n.* **uranographic, uranographical** *a.* **uranometry** *n.* measurement of heavens; chart of heavens [Gk. *ouranos,* heaven].

ur·ban (ur′·ban) *a.* pert, to, or living in, city or town. **urbane** *a.* refined; suave; courteous. **urbanely** *adv.* **urbanity** *n.* **-ize** *v.t.* to make urban; to bring town conditions and advantages to rural areas. [L. *urbs,* a city].

ur·chin (ur′·chin) *n.* sea urchin; (*Arch.*) hedgehog (*Arch.*) goblin; mischievous child; a child [L. *ericius,* hedgehog].

Ur·du (oor·dōō′) *n.* a language form of Hindustani, mixture of Persian, Arabic, and Hindi [Hind. *urdu,* camp].

u·re·a (ū′·rē·a) *n.* crystalline solid, the principle organic constituent of urine [Gk. *ouron,* urine].

u·re·ter (ū·rē′·ter) *n.* one of two ducts of kidney conveying urine to bladder. **urethra** *n.* duct by which urine passes from bladder. *pl.* **urethrae. urethral** *a.* [Gk. *ouron,* urine].

urge (urj) *v.t.* to press; to drive; to exhort;

to simulate; to solicit earnestly; *v.i.* to press onward; to make allegations, entreaties, etc. *n.* act of urging; incentive; irresistible impulse. **-ncy** *n.* quality of being urgent; compelling necessity; importunity. **-nt** *a.* calling for immediate attention; clamant; importunate. **-ntly** *adv.* **-r** *n.* [L. *urgere*, to press].

u·rine (ū'·rin) *n.* yellowish fluid secreted by kidneys, passed through ureters to bladder from which it is discharged through urethra. **uremia** *n.* toxic condition of the blood caused by insufficient secretion of urine. **uremic** *a.* **uric** *a.* pert. to or produced from urine. **urinal** *n.* vessel into which urine may be discharged; a place for urinating. **urinary** *a.* pert. to urine. **urinate** *v.i.* to pass urine. **urination** *n.* **urinogenital** *a.* pert. to urinary and genital organs. **urology** *n.* branch of Med. dealing with urinogenital system. **urologist** *n.* [Gk. *euron*, urine].

urn (urn) *n.* vase-shaped vessel of pottery or metal with pedestal, and narrow neck, as used for ashes of dead after cremation; vessel of various forms usually fitted with tap, for liquid in bulk, as *tea urn*. **-al** *a.* [L. *urna*].

ur·sine (ur'·sin) *a.* pert. to or resembling a bear. **ursiform** *a.* resembling bear in shape [L. *ursus*, a bear].

us (us) *pron. pl.* the objective form of **we**.

use (ūz) *v.t.* to make use of; to employ; to consume or expend (as in material); to practice habitually; to accustom; to treat; *v.i.* to be accustomed (only in past tense). **use** (ūs) *n.* act of using or employing for specific purpose; utility; custom; (*Law*) profit derived from trust. **usable** *a.* fit for use. **usability** *n.* **usage** *n.* mode of using; treatment; long-established custom. **usance** *n.* usual time allowed for payment of foreign bills of exchange. **-ful** *a.* of use; handy; profitable; serviceable; **-fully** *adv.* **-fulness** *n.* **-less** *a.* of no use; inefficient; futile. **-lessly** *adv.* **-lessness** *n.* **-r** *n.* [L. *uti, usus*, to use].

ush·er (ush'·er) *n.* doorkeeper; one who conducts people to seats in church, theater, etc.; official who introduces strangers or walks before person of high rank; *v.t.* to act as usher. **-ette** *n.* girl employed, as in theater to show patrons to seats. **to usher in**, to precede [O. Fr. *ussier*, fr. L. *ostiarius*, a doorkeeper].

us·que·baugh (us'·kwi·baw) *n.* whiskey [Gael. *uisge*, water, *beatha*, life].

u·su·al (ū'·zhoo·al) *a.* customary; ordinary. **-ly** *adv.* **-ness** *n.* [L. *usus*, to use].

u·su·fruct (ū'·za·frakt) *n.* right of using and enjoying produce benefit, or profits of another's property provided that the property remains undamaged. **-uary** *a.* pert. to usufruct; *n.* one who has the use of another's property by usufruct [L. *usus*, use; *fructus*, fruit].

u·surp (ū·surp', zurp') *v.t.* to take possession of unlawfully or by force. **-ation** *n.* act of usurping; violent or unlawful seizing of power [L. *usurpare*, to seize].

u·su·ry (ū'·zha·ri·) *n.* charging of exorbitant interest on money lent. **usurer** *n.* money lender who charges exorbitant rates of interest **usurious** *a.* **usuriously** *adv.* **usuriousness** *n.* [L. *usura*, use].

u·ten·sil (ū·ten'·sal) *n.* vessel of any kind which forms part of domestic, esp. kitchen, equipment [L. *utensilis*, fit for use].

u·ter·ine (ū'·ter·in) *a.* pert. to uterus or womb; born of the same mother but by a different father. **uterus** *n.* womb [L. *uterus*].

u·til·i·tar·i·an (ū·til·a·ter'·i·an) *a.* pert. to utility or utilitarianism; of practical use. *n.* one who accepts doctrines of utilitarianism. **-ism** *n.* ethical doctrine, the ultimate aim and criterion of all human actions must be 'the greatest happiness for the greatest number' [L. *utilis*, useful].

u·ti·lize (ū·ta·līz) *v.t.* to put to use; to turn to profit. **utilizable** *a.* **utilization** *n.* **-r** *n.* **utility** *n.* usefulness; quality of being advantageous; *pl.* public services, as gas, electricity, telephone, etc. [L. *utilis*, useful].

ut·most (ut'·mōst) *a.* situated at farthest point or extremity; to highest degree; *n.* most that can be; greatest possible effort [O.E. *utemest*, superb. of *ut*, out].

u·to·pi·a (ū·tō'·pi·a) *n.* any ideal state, constitution, system, or way of life. **-n** *a.* ideally perfect but impracticable; visionary [=nowhere; Gk. *ou*, not; *topos*, place].

u·tri·cle (ū'·tri·kl) *n.* (*Bot.*) little bag or bladder, esp. of aquatic plant; (*Anat.*) a sac in inner ear influencing equilibrium. **utricular, utriculate** *a.* [L. *utriculus*, small bag].

ut·ter (ut'·er) *a.* total; unconditional. **-ly** *adv.* **-ness** *n.* [O.E. *utor, outer*].

ut·ter (ut'·er) *vt.* to speak; to disclose; to put into circulation. **-able** *a.* **-ableness** *n.* **-ance** *n.* act of speaking; manner of delivering speech; something said; a cry. **-er** *n.* [O.E. *utian*, to put out].

ut·ter·most (ut'·er·mōst) *a.* farthest out; utmost; *n.* the highest degree.

u·vu·la (ū'·vya·la) *n.* fleshy tag suspended from middle of lower border of soft palate. **-r** *a.* [L. *uva*, grape].

ux·o·ri·ous (uk·sōr'·i·as) *a.* foolishly or excessively fond of one's wife. **uxorial** *a.* pert. to wife. **-ly** *adv.* **-ness** *n.* [L. *uxor*].

V

va·cant (vā'·kant) *a.* empty; void; not occupied; unintelligent. **-ly** *adv.* **vacancy** *n.* emptiness; opening; lack of thought; place or post, unfilled. **vacate** (vā'·kāt) *v.t.* to leave empty or unoccupied; to quit possession of; to make void. **vacation** *n.* act of vacating; intermission of stated employment; recess; holidays. **vacational** *a.* **vacationist** *n.* [L. *vacare*, to be empty].

vac·cine (vak·sēn'·, vak'·sēn) *a.* pert. to, or obtained from cows; *n.* virus of cowpox, used in vaccination; any substance used for inoculation against disease. **vaccinate** *v.t.* to inoculate with cowpox, to ward off smallpox or lessen severity of its attack. **vaccination** *n.* act or practice of vaccinating; the inoculation. **vaccinator** *n.* [L. *vacca*, cow].

vac·il·late (vas'·a·lāt) *v.i.* to move to and fro; to waver; to be unsteady; to fluctuate in opinion. **vacillating, vacillatory** *a.* **vacillation** *n.* [L. *vacillare*].

vac·u·um (vak'·yoom) *n.* space devoid of all matter; space from which air, or other gas, has been almost wholly removed, as by air pump. **vacuous** *a.* empty; vacant; expressionless; unintelligent. **-ly** *adv.* **-ness** *n.* **vacuity** (va·kū'·a·ti·) *n.* emptiness; empty space; lack of intelligence. **— cleaner** *n.* apparatus for removing dust from carpets, etc. by suction. **— bottle** *n.* double-walled flask with vacuum between walls, for keeping contents at temperature at which they were inserted. **— tube** used in Radio, TV, and electronic equipment; a sealed tube containing metallic electrodes but (almost) no air or gas. [L. *vacuus*, empty].

va·de·me·cum (vā'·dē·mē'·kam) *n.* small handbook or manual for ready reference [L. =go with me].

vag·a·bond (vag'·a·band) *a.* moving from place to place without settled habitation; wandering; *n.* wanderer or vagrant, having

WEBSTER T–Z

no settled habitation; idle scamp; rascal. **-age ism,** *n.* [L. *vagari,* to wander].

va·gar·y (vā'.ga.ri., va.ger'.i.) *n.* whimsical or freakish notion; unexpected action; caprice. **vagarious** *a.* [L. *vagari,* to wander].

va·gi·na (va.jī'.na) *n.* (*Anat.*) canal which leads from uterus to external orifice; (*Bot.*) sheath as of leaf **-l** *a.* [L.].

va·grant (vā'.grant) *a.* wandering from place to place; moving without certain direction; roving; *n.* idle wanderer; vagabond; disorderly person; beggar. **-ly** *adv.* **vagrancy** *n.* [L. *vagari,* to wander].

vague (vāg) *a.* uncertain; indefinite; indistinct; not clearly expressed. **-ly** *adv.* **-ness** *n.* [L. *vagus,* wandering].

vain (vān) *a.* useless; unavailing; fruitless; empty; worthless; conceited; **-ly** *adv.* **-ness** *n.* **vanity** (van'.a.ti.) *n.* conceit; something one is conceited about; worthlessness; dressing table. **vanity case** *n.* lady's small handbag or case, fitted with powder puff, mirror, lipstick, etc. [L. *vanus,* empty].

vain·glo·ry (vān.glō'.ri.) *n.* excessive vanity; boastfulness. **vainglorious** *a.* **vaingloriously** *adv.* **vaingloriousness** *n.* [*vain* and *glory*].

val·ance (val'.ans) *n.* short drapery across the top of a window, bed, etc.; similar facing of wood or metal. **-d** *a.* [O.Fr. *avalant* to hang].

vale (vāl) *n.* valley [L. *vallis,* valley].

val·e·dic·tion (val.a.dik'.shan) *n.* farewell; a bidding farewell. **valedictory** *a.* bidding farewell; suitable for leave-taking; *n.* a valedictory address, esp. by a school valedictorian. **valedictorian** *n.* student in a graduating class with the highest scholastic standing who gives the valedictory at graduation exercises. [L. *valedicere,* to say farewell].

va·lence, va·len·cy (vā'.lans, vā'.lan.si.) *n.* (*Chem.*) the combining power of an element or atom as compared with a hydrogen atom [L. *valere,* to be strong].

Va·len·ci·ennes (va.len(t).sē.enz') *n.* rich lace, made orig. at *Valenciennes,* in France.

va·len·tine (val'.an.tīn) *n.* sweetheart chosen on *St. Valentine's* day; card containing profession of love, sent on *St. Valentine's* day, Feb. 14th [L. proper name *Valentinus*].

va·le·ri·an (va.lir'.i.an) *n.* flowering herb with strong odor; its root, used as sedative drug [O.Fr. *valeriance*].

val·et (val'.it, val'.ā) *n.* manservant who cares for clothing, etc. of his employer [Fr. *valet,* a groom, Doublet of *varlet*].

val·e·tu·di·nar·i·an (val.a.tū.da.ner'.i.an) *a.* sickly; infirm; solicitous about one's own health; *n.* person of sickly constitution; person disposed to live life of an invalid. **-ism** *n.* **valetudinary** *a.* [L. *valetudo,* health].

Va·hal·la (val.hal'.a) *n.* (*Norse myth.*) hall of immortality where Odin received souls of heroes slain in battle [O.N. *valr,* slain; *holl,* hall].

val·iant (val'.yant) *a.* brave; heroic; courageous; intrepid. **-ly** *adv.* **-ness** *n.* **valiance, valiancy** *n.* valor; courage [L. *valere,* to be strong].

val·id (val'.id) *a.* sound or well-grounded; capable of being justified; (*Law*) legally sound; executed with proper formalities. **-ly** *adv.* **-ate** *v.t.* to make valid; to ratify. **-ation** *n.* **-ness, -ity** *n.* [L. *validus,* strong].

va·lise (va.lēs') *n.* suitcase [Fr.].

Val·kyr (val'.kir) *n.* (*Norse myth.*) one of Odin's nine handmaidens. who conduct the souls of slain heroes to Valhalla. Also **Valkyrie** (val.wir'.i.) **Valkyria** (val.kir'.ya). **Valkyrian** *a.*

val·ley (val'.i.) *n.* low ground between hills; river basin [L. *vallis,* vale].

val·or (val'.er) *n.* bravery; prowess in war; courage. **-ous** *a.* brave; fearless. **-ously** *adv.* **-ousness** *n.* [L. *valere,* to be strong].

valse (vals) *n.* waltz, esp. one played as concert piece [Fr.].

val·ue (val'.ū) *n.* worth; utility; importance; estimated worth or valuation; precise significance; equivalent; (*Mus.*) duration of note; *v.t.* to estimate worth of; to hold in respect and admiration; to prize. **-r** *n.* **-less** *a.* **valuable** *a.* precious; worth a good price; worthy; *n.* thing of value (generally *pl.*) **valuableness** *n.* **valuably** *adv.* **valuate** *v.t.* to set value on; to appraise. **valuation** *n.* value estimated or set upon a thing; appraisal. **-d** *a.* **valuator** *n.* [L. *valere,* to be worth].

valve (valv) *n.* device for closing aperture (as in pipe) in order to control flow of fluid, gas, etc. (*Anat.*) structure (as in blood-vessel) which allows flow of fluid in one direction only; (*Zool.*) either of two sections of shell of mollusk; (*Mus.*) device in certain instruments (as horn, trumpet, etc.) for changing tone. **-less, -like** *a.* **valvular** *a.* **-let, valvule** *n.* small valve [L. *valva,* leaf of folding door].

va·moose (va.mòòs') *v.i., t.* (*Slang*) to depart quickly; to leave; to decamp [Sp. *vamos,* let us go].

vamp (vamp) *n.* upper leather of shoe or boot; new patch put on old article; (*Mus.*) improvised accompaniment; *v.t.* to provide (shoe, etc.) with new upper leather; to patch; (*Mus.*) to improvise accompaniment to [Fr. *avant-pied,* front of foot].

vamp (vamp) *n.* (*Slang*) woman who allures and exploits men; adventuress; *v.t.* and *v.i.* (*Slang*) to allure and exploit; to flirt unscrupulously [contr. of *vampire*].

vam·pire (vam'.pīr) *n.* reanimated body of dead person who cannot rest quietly in grave, but arises from it at night and sucks blood of sleepers; one who lives by preying on others; extortioner; a vamp. **— bat** *n.* of several species of bat of S. America which sucks blood of animals. **vampiric, vampirish** *a.* **vampirism** *n.* [Fr fr. Serbian *vampir*].

van (van) *n.* covered wagon or motor truck for goods [contr. of *caravan*].

van (van) *n.* leaders of a movement. **-guard** *n.* detachment of troops who march ahead of army [Fr. *avant,* before; *garde,* a guard].

va·na·di·um (va.nā'.di.am) *n.* a metallic element (the hardest known) used in manufacture of hard steel [fr. *Vanadis,* Scand. goddess].

van·dal (van'.dal) *n.* one who wantonly damages or destroys property of beauty or value; **-ic** *a.* **-ism** *n.* [L. *Vandalus,* Vandau, tribe which ravaged Europe in 5th cent.].

van·dyke (van.dīk') *n.* one of the points forming an edge, as of lace, ribbon, etc.; broad collar with deep points of lace as worn in portraits by *Van Dyck;* painting by Van Dyck. **— beard,** pointed beard. **— brown,** dark brown [*Van Dyck,* Flemish painter].

vane (vān) *n.* a device on a windmill, spire, etc. to show the direction of the wind; a weathercock; the blade of a propeller, of a windmill, etc.; a fin on a bomb to prevent swerving **-d** *a.* **-less** *a.* [O.E. *fana,* a banner].

van·guard (van'.gàrd) *n.* See **van** (2).

va·nil·la (va.nil'.a) *n.* tropical American plant of orchid family; long pod of plant, used as flavoring. **vanillic** *a.* **vanillin** *n.* [dim. fr. Sp. *vaina,* sheath].

van·ish (van'.ish) *v.i.* to pass away; to be lost to view; to disappear; (*Math.*) to become zero. **-er** *n.* **-ing** *a.* disappearing. **-ingly** *adv.* [L. *evanescere,* fr. *vanus,* empty].

van·i·ty. See **vain.**

van·quish (vang'.kwish) *v.t.* to conquer in battle; to defeat in any contest; to get the better of; **-able** *a.* **-er** *n.* [Fr. *vaincre,* fr. L. *vincere*].

van·tage (van'.tij) *n.* better situation or opportunity; advantage; in tennis, same as 'advantage.' Used esp. in — **ground,** position of advantage [M.E. *avantage,* advantage].

vap·id (vap'·id) *a.* having lost its life and spirit; flat; insipid; dull. **-ly** *adv.* **-ness, vapidity** *n.* [L. *vapidus,* state].

va·por (vā'·pẹr) *n.* any light, cloudy substance which impairs clearness of atmosphere, as mist, fog, smoke, etc.; a substance converted into gaseous state; anything unsubstantial; *pl.* (*Arch.*) disease of nervous debility; depression; melancholy; *v.i.* to pass off in vapor; (*Fig.*) to talk idly; to brag. **-ize** *v.t.* to convert into vapor; *v.i.* to pass off in vapor. **-izable** *a.* **-ization** *n.* **-izer** *n.* mechanism for splitting liquid into fine particles. **-ish** *a.* full of vapor; prone to depression. **-ishness** *n.* **-ous** *a.* like vapor; unsubstantial; full of fanciful talk. **-ously** *adv.* **-ousness** *n.* **-ings** *n.pl.* boastful talk. **-y** *a.* full of vapor; depressed [L. *vapor*].

var·i·a·ble (ver'·i·ạ·bl) *a.* changeable; capable of being adapted; unsteady or fickle; *n.* that which is subject to change; symbol that may have infinite number of values; indeterminate quantity; shifting wind. **variably** *adv.* **-ness** *n.* **variability** *n.* (*Biol.*) tendency to vary from average characteristics of species. **variant** *a.* different; diverse; *n.* different form or reading. **variance** *n.* difference that produces controversy; state of discord or disagreement. **variation** (ver'·i·ā'·shạn) *n.* act of varying; alteration; modification; extent to which thing varies; (*Gram.*) change of termination; in magnetism, deviation of magnetic needle from true north; (*Mus.*) repetition of theme or melody with various embellishments and elaborations. **at variance,** not in harmony or agreement [L. *variare,* to change, vary].

var·i·col·ored (ver'·i·kul·ẹrd) *a.* having various colors.

var·i·cose (var'·i·kōs) *a.* enlarged or dilated, as veins, esp. in legs [L. *varix,* a dilated vein; fr. *varus,* crooked].

var·ied *a.* See **vary.**

var·i·e·gate (ver'·i·ạ·gāt, ver'·i·gāt) *v.t.* to diversify by patches of different colors; to streak, spot, dapple, etc. **variegation** *n.* **-d** *a.* [L. *varius,* various; *agere,* to make].

va·ri·e·ty (vạ·rī'·ạ·ti·) *n.* state of being varied; diversity; collection of different things; many-sidedness; different form of something; subdivision of a species. — **show** *n.* mixed entertainment, consisting of songs, dances, short sketches, juggling, etc. [L. *varietas,* variety, fr. *varius,* various].

var·i·o·rum (ver·i·ō'·rạm, var·i·ō'·rạm) *n.* an edition of a work with notes by various commentators [L. = of various men].

var·i·ous (ver'·i·ạs, var'·i·ạs) *a.* different; diverse; manifold; separate; diversified. **-ly** *adv.* **-ness** *n.* [L. *varius*].

var·let (vàr'·lit) *n.* (*Arch.*) page or attendant; scoundrel. **-ry** *n.* [O.Fr. *varlet,* var. of *vaslet,* fr. L.L. *vassalus,* vassal].

var·nish (vàr'·nish) *n.* clear, resinous liquid laid on work to give it gloss and protection; glossy appearance; outward show; *v.t.* to lay varnish on; to conceal something with fair appearance **-ed** *a.* [Fr. *vernis,* varnish].

var·si·ty (vàr'·sạ·ti·) *n.* team, usu. athletic, representing a university, school, etc. in competition; *a.* designating such a team [contr. of *university*].

var·y (ver'·i·, var'·i·) *v.t.* to change; to make different or modify; to diversify; *v.i.* to alter, or be altered; to be different; **varied** *a.* various; diverse; diversified. **varier** *n.* **-ingly** *adv.* [L. *variare,* to vary].

vas (vas) *n.* (*Anat.*) vessel or duct. **-cular** (vas'·kyạ·lạr) *a.* pert. to vessels or ducts for conveying blood, lymph, sap, etc. **-culum** *n.* botanist's collecting box. **-omotor** *a.* pert. to nerves controlling tension of blood vessels and thus the flow of blood. *n.pl.* **vasa** [L.].

vase (vās, vāz) *n.* vessel for flowers or merely for decoration; large sculptured vessel, used as ornament, in gardens, on gateposts, etc. [L. *vas,* vessel].

vas·e·line (vas'·ạ·lēn) *n.* brand of petroleum used in ointments, pomades, as lubricant, etc. (*Cap.*) trademark for this [Ger. *Wasser,* water; Gk. *elaion,* oil].

vas·sal (vas'·ạl) *n.* one who holds land from superior, and vows fealty and homage to him; dependant; retainer. **-age** *n.* state of being a vassal [Fr. fr Celt. *gwaz,* servant].

vast (vast) *a.* of great extent; very spacious; very great in numbers or quantity; *n.* (*Poet.*) boundless space. **-ly** *adv.* **-ness** *n.* **-itude** *n.* [L. *vastus,* very great].

vat (vat) *n.* large vessel, tub, for holding liquids [O.E. *foel,* a vessel, cask].

vat·ic (vat'·ik) *a.* prophetic; oracular. Also **-al** *a.* **-inal** (vạ·tis'·i·nạl) *a.* **-inate** (vạ·tis'·i·nāte) *v.t.* and *i.* to prophesy. **-ination** (vat·ạ·si·nā'·shạn) *n.* [L. *vates,* a prophet].

Vat·i·can (vat'·i·kạn) *n.* palace and official residence of Pope on Vatican Hill (L. *Mons Vaticanus*), in Rome; papal authority.

vaude·ville (vawd'·(ạ)vil, vōd'·vil) *n.* stage show with mixed specialty acts; variety show [fr. *Vau de Vire* in Normandy].

vault (vawlt) *n.* arched roof; room or passage covered with vault, esp. subterranean; cellar; sky; anything resembling a vault; *v.t.* to cover with arched roof; to form like vault. **-ed** *a.* arched [L. *volutus,* turned].

vault (vawlt) *v.i.* to spring or jump with hands resting on something; to leap or spring, as horse; *v.t.* to spring or jump over; *n.* such a spring [Fr. *volte,* turn; fr. L. *volutus*].

vaunt (vawnt, vànt) *v.t.* to boast of; to make vain display of; *n.* boast; vainglorious display. **-er** *n.* **-ingly** *adv.* [O.Fr. *vanter;* fr. L. *vanitas,* vanity].

veal (vēl) *n.* flesh of a calf killed for the table [O.Fr. *veel,* fr. L. *vitellus,* calf].

vec·tor (vek'·tẹr) *n.* (*Math.*) any quantity requiring direction to be stated as well as magnitude in order to define it properly; disease-carrying insect. **vectorial** *a.* [L. *vehere, vectum,* to convey].

Ve·da (vē'·dạ) *n.* most ancient sacred literature of Hindus. **Vedic** *a.* pert. to the Vedas [Sans. *veda,* knowledge].

ve·dette (vạ·det') *n.* mounted sentinel placed in advance of outposts to give notice of danger [It. *vedetta,* fr. *vedere,* to see, fr. L. *videre*].

veer (vēr) *v.t.* and *v.i.* to turn; of wind, to change direction, esp. clockwise; (*Naut.*) to change ship's course; (*Fig.*) to change one's opinion or point of view [Fr. *virer*].

veg·e·ta·ble (vej'·(ạ)·tạ·bl) *a.* belonging to plants; having nature of plants; *n.* plant, esp. plant used as food, e.g. potato, carrot, cabbage, bean. **vegetal** *a.* **vegetarian** (vej·ạ·ter'·i·ạn) *n.* one who abstains from animal flesh and lives on vegetables, eggs, milk, etc.; *a.* pert. to vegetarianism; consisting of vegetables. **vegetarianism** *n.* **vegetate** *v.i.* to grow as plant does; to lead idle, unthinking life. **vegetation** *n.* process of vegetating; vegetable growth; plants in general. **vegetational** *a.* **vegetative** *a.* **vegetatively** *adv.* **vegetativeness** *n.* [L. *vegetare,* to enliven].

ve·he·ment (vē'·ạ·mạnt) *a.* acting with great force; impetuous; vigorous; passionate. **-ly** *adv.* **vehemence, vehemency** *n.* impetuosity; fury; violence; fervor [L. *vehemens,* eager].

ve·hi·cle (vē'·(h)ạ·kl) *n.* any means of conveyance (esp. on land) as carriage, etc.; liquid medium in which drugs are taken, or pigments applied; means or medium of expression or communication. **vehicular** (vē·hik′·yą·ler) *a.* Also **vehiculatory** (L. *vehiculum,* fr. *vehere,* to carry].

veil (vāl) *n.* piece of thin, gauzy material worn by women to hide or protect face; covering; curtain; disguise; *v.t.* to cover with veil; to conceal. **-ed** *a.* **-less** *a.* **-like** *a.* **-ing** *n.* act of covering with veil; material from which veil is made. **to take the veil,** to become a nun [L. *velum*].

vein (vān) *n.* each of the vessels or tubes which receive blood from capillaries and return it to heart; (loosely) any blood vessel; (*Biol.*) one of the small branching ribs of leaf or of insect's wing; layer of mineral intersecting a stratum of rock; streak or wave of different color appearing in wood, marble, etc.; distinctive tendency; mood or cast of mind; *v.t.* to mark with veins. **-ed** *a.* **-less** *a.* surface. **-ous, -y** *a.* **venation** *n.* [L. *vena*].

veld, veldt (felt, velt) *n.* in S. Africa, open grass country [Dut. *veld,* a field].

vel·lum (vel′·ąm) *n.* fine parchment made of skin; paper of similar texture; *a.* [O.Fr. *velin,* fr. L. *vitulus,* calf].

ve·loc·i·pede (vą·làs′·ą·pēd) *n.* a vehicle propelled by the rider, early form of bicycle or tricycle [L. *velox,* swift; *pes,* the foot].

ve·loc·i·ty (vą·làs′·ą·ti·) *n.* rate of motion; swiftness; speed; distance traversed in unit time in a given direction [L. *velox,* swift].

ve·lours (vą·loor′) *n. sing.* and *pl.* fabric resembling velvet or plush. Also **velour** [Fr.].

vel·vet (vel′·vit) *n.* soft material of silk with thick short pile on one side; *a.* made of velvet; soft and delicate. **-y** *a.* soft as velvet. **-een** *n.* a pile fabric made of cotton, or of silk and cotton mixed [L.L. *vellutum,* fr. L. *villus,* shaggy hair].

ve·nal (vē′·nąl) *a.* to be obtained for money; prepared to take bribes; mercenary. **-ly** *adv.* **venality** *n.* quality of being purchaseable [L. *venalis,* fr. *venus,* sale].

ve·nat·ic, ve·nat·i·cal (vi·nat′·ik, ·i·kąl) *a.* relating to hunting. **-ally** *adv.* [L. *venari,* to hunt].

vend (vend) *v.t.* to sell; to dispose of by sale. **-ible** *a.* **-ibly** *adv.* **-ibility, -ibleness** *n.* the quality of being saleable. **-or** *n.* person who sells. **-ue** *n.* public auction [L. *vendere*].

ven·det·ta (ven·det′·ą) *n.* blood feud, in which it was the duty of the relative of murdered man to avenge his death by killing murderer or relative of murderer; any bitter feud [It. fr. L. *vindicta,* revenge].

ve·neer (vą·nēr′) *n.* thin layer of valuable wood glued to surface of inferior wood; thin coating of finer substance; superficial charm or polish of manner; *v.t.* to coat or overlay with substance giving superior surface; to disguise with superficial charm. **-ing** *n.* act of treating with veneer; thin layer used in this process [Fr. *fournir,* to furnish].

ven·er·ate (ven′·ą·rāt) *v.t.* to regard with respect and reverence. **venerator** *n.* **veneration** *n.* respect mingled with awe; worship. **venerable** *a.* worthy of veneration; deserving respect by reason of age, character, etc.; sacred by reason of religious or historical associations, aged. **venerability, venerableness** *n.* **venerably** *adv.* [L. *venerari,* to worship].

ve·ne·re·al (vą·nir′·i·ąl) *a.* pert. to sexual intercourse; arising from sexual intercourse with infected persons [L. *Venus, Veneris,* goddess of Love].

ven·er·y (ven′·ą·ri·) *n.* (*Arch.*) hunting; sports of the chase [L. *venari,* to hunt].

Ve·ne·tian (vą·nē′·shąn) *a.* pert. to city of Venice, Italy; *n.* native, inhabitant of Venice. **— blind,** blind made of thin, horizontal slats, so hung as to overlap each other when closed.

venge·ance (ven′·jąns) *n.* infliction of pain or loss on another in return for injury or offense. **vengeful** *a.* disposed to revenge; vindictive. **vengefully** *adv.* **vengefulness** *n.* [L. *vindicare,* to avenge].

ve·ni·al (vē′·ni·ąl) *a.* capable of being forgiven; excusable. **-ly** *adv.* **-ness, -ity** *n.* [L. *venialis,* pardonable, fr. *venia,* forgiveness].

ven·i·son (ven′·ą·zn) *n.* flesh of the deer [Fr. *vendison,* fr. L. *venari,* to hunt].

ven·om (ven′·ąm) *n.* poison, esp. that secreted by serpents, bees, etc.; spite; malice. **-ous** *a.* poisonous; spiteful; malicious. **-ously** *adv.* **-ousness** *n.* [L. *veneum,* poison].

ve·nous, ve·nose (vē′·nąs) *a.* pert. to veins or the blood in veins. **venosity** *n.* [L. *venosus,* fr. *vena,* vein].

vent (vent) *n.* small opening; outlet; flue or funnel of fireplace; touch hole of gun; utterance; emission; voice; escape; anus of certain lower animals; slit in back of coat; *v.t.* to give opening or outlet to; to let escape; to utter or voice; to publish. **-age, -er** *n.* **-less** *a.* **to give vent to,** to pour forth [Fr. *fendre,* fr. L. *findere,* to cleave].

ven·ti·late (ven′·tą·lāt) *v.t.* to remove foul air from and supply with fresh air; to expose to discussion; to make public. **ventilation** *n.* replacement of stale air by fresh air; free exposure to air; open discussion. **ventilator** *n.* contrivance for keeping air fresh [L. *ventilare,* fr. *ventus,* wind].

ven·tral (ven′·trąl) *a.* belonging to belly; abdominal; opp. of *dorsal; n.* one of the pair of fins on belloy of fish. **ventricle** *n.* (*Anat.* or *Zool.*) small cavity in certain organs, esp. one of chambers of heart. **ventricular** *a.* [L. *ventralis,* fr. *venter,* belly].

ven·tril·o·quism (ven·tril′·ą·kwizm) *n.* art of speaking in such a way that words or sounds seem to come from some source other than speaker. Also **ventriloquy. ventriloquist** *n.* **ventriloquistic** *a.* **ventriloquize** *v.i.* to practice ventriloquism [L. *venter,* belly; *loqui,* to speak].

ven·ture (ven′·cher) *n.* undertaking of chance or danger; business speculation; *v.t.* to expose to hazard; to risk; *v.i.* to run risk; to dare; to have presumption to. **-r** *n.* **venturous** *a.* daring; risky. **venturously** *adv.* **venturousness** *n.* **-some** *a.* bold; dangerous. **-someness** *n.* [contr. of *adventure*].

ven·ue (ven′·ū) *n.* (*Law*) district in which case is tried; scene of an event [L. *venire,* to come].

ven·ule (ven′·ūl) *n.* small vein.

Ve·nus (vē′·nąs) *n.* (*Myth.*) Roman goddess of love and beauty; brightest planet of solar system; beautiful woman [L.].

ve·ra·cious (vą·rā′·shąs) *a.* truthful; true. **-ly** *adv.* **-ness** *n.* **veracity** (vą·ras′·ą·ti·) *n.* quality of being truthful; truth; correctness [L. *verax, veracis,* fr. *verus,* true].

ve·ran·da, verandah (vą·ran′·dą) *n.* open porch or gallery, along side of house, often with roof [Sp. *veranda,* balcony].

verb (vurb) *n.* (*Gram.*) part of speech which expresses action or state of being. **-less** *a.* **-al** *a.* pert. to words; expressed in words, esp. spoken words; literal or word for word; pert. to verb; derived from verb. **-ally** *adv.* **-alize** *v.t.* and *v.i.* to put into words; to turn into verb. **-alization** *n.* **-alism** *n.* something expressed orally; over-attention to use of words; empty words. **-alist, -alizer** *n.* **-atim** (ver·bā′·tim) *a.* and *adv.* word for word [L. *verbum,* a word].

ver·be·na (ver·bē′·ną) *n.* genus of plants of

family Verbenaceae, used in ornamental flower beds. Also called **vervain** [L.].

ver·bi·age (vur′·bi·ij) *n.* excess of words; use of many more words than are necessary; wordiness. **verbose** (ver·bōs′) *a.* prolix; tedious because of excess of words. **verbosely** *adv.* **verboseness, verbosity** (ver·bàs′·a·ti·) *n.* [L. *verbum*, a word].

ver·bo·ten (fer·bō′·tan) *a.* forbidden [Ger.].

ver·dant (vur′·dant) *a.* green or fresh; flourishing; ignorant or unsophisticated. **-ly** *adv.* **verdancy** *n.* **verdure** (vur′·jer) *n.* greenness or freshness; green vegetation. **-less** *a.* [O.Fr. *verd*, fr. L. *viridis*, green].

ver·dict (vur′·dikt) *n.* decision of jury in a trial; decision or judgment [O.Fr. *verdit*, fr. L. *vere dictum*, truly said].

ver·di·gris (vur′·di·grēs) *n.* green rust on copper, bronze, etc.; basic acetate of copper, used as pigment, etc. [O.Fr. *verd de Gris*, Greek green].

verge (vurj) *n.* border, or edge; brink; a rod of office; mace of bishop, etc. **-r** *n.* one who carries verge or emblem of authority; caretaker of church [L. *virga*, slender twig].

verge (vurj) *v.i.* to tend; to slope; to border upon [L. *vergere*, to tend towards].

ver·i·fy (ver′·a·fī) *v.t.* to prove to be true; to confirm truth of; **verifier** *n.* **verifiable** *a.* **verifiability** *n.* **verification** *n.* act of verifying or state of being verified; confirmation [L. *versus*, true; *facere*, to make].

ver·i·ly (ver′·i·li·) *adv.* (*Arch.*) truly; certainly.

ver·i·sim·i·lar (ver·a·sim′·a·ler) *a.* having the appearance of truth; probable; likely. **-ly** *adv.* **verisimilitude** *n.* appearance of truth; probability; likelihood [L. *verus*, true; *similis*, like].

ver·i·ta·ble (ver′·a·ta·bl) *a.* actual; genuine. **-ness** *n.* **veritably** *adv.* [L. *veritas*, truth].

ver·i·ty (ver′·a·ti·) *n.* quality of being true; truth; reality [L. *veritas*].

ver·juice (vur′·jòòs) *n.* sour juice of crabapples, unripe grapes, etc. used in cooking; sourness of disposition [Fr. *verjus*, fr. L. *viridis*, green; *jus*, juice].

ver·mi- (vur′·mi) *prefix.* fr. L. *vermis*, worm. **-an** *a.* worm-like; pert. to worms, **-celli** (·sel′·i·, ·chel′·i·) *n.* paste made from same ingredients as macaroni, and formed into slender worm-like threads. **-cide** *n.* any substance that destroys worms. **-icidal** *a.* **-icular** *a.* pert. to worm; like a worm in shape or movement; vermiculate. **-cularly** *adv.* **-culate** *a.* *v.t.* to ornament in pattern like worm tracks. **-culation** *n.* **-form** *a.* having shape of a worm.

ver·mil·ion (ver·mil′·yan) *n.* prepared red sulfide of mercury; brilliant red color; *v.t.* to color with red. Also **vermeil** [L. *vermiculus*, little worm].

ver·min (vur′·min) *n.* collectively noxious or troublesome small animals or insects, e.g. squirrels, rats, worms, lice, etc.; low contemptible persons. **-ous** *a.* infested by vermin; caused by vermin; tending to breed vermin. **-ously** *adv.* **-ousness** *n.* [L. *vermis*, worm].

ver·mouth, vermuth (ver·mòòth′, vur′·mòòth) *n.* cordial of white wine flavored with wormwood, used as aperitif [Ger.].

ver·nac·u·lar (ver·nak′·ya·ler) *a.* belonging to country of one's birth; native (usu. applied only to language or idiom); *n.* native idiom of place; mother tongue; common name for a plant, animal, etc. [L. *vernaculus*, native, fr. *verna*, home-born slave].

ver·nal (vur′·nal) *a.* belonging to, or appearing on, spring; youthful. **-ly** *adv.* **equinox**, equinox occurring about March 21 [L. *ver*, spring].

ver·ni·er (vur′·ni·er) *n.* short, graduated-

scale instrument, for measuring fractional parts [fr. P. *Vernier*, inventor].

Ver·o·nal (ver′·a·nal) *n.* hypnotic or sedative drug [Protected Trade Name].

ve·ron·i·ca (va·ràn′·i·ka) *n.* genus of plants, including speedwell [L. *vettonica*, betony].

ver·ru·ca (va·ròò′·ka) *n.* wart or wart-like elevation. *pl.* **verrucae** (·sē), **verrucose, verrucous** *a.* **verrucosity** *n.* [L.].

ver·sa·tile (vur′·sa·til) *a.* having aptitude in many subjects; liable to change; capable of moving freely in all directions. **-ly** *adv.* **-ness, versatility** *n.* [L. *versatilis*, fr. *versare*, fr. *vertere*, to turn].

verse (vurs) *n.* metrical line containing certain number of feet; metrical arrangement of language; short division of any literary composition; stanza; piece of poetry. **-d** (vurst) *a.* skilled; experienced (foll. by 'in'); practiced. **versicle** *n.* little verse. **versify** (vur′·sa·fī) *v.t.* to turn prose into verse; to express in verse. *v.i.* to make verses. **versification** *n.* **versifier** *n.* [L. *vertere*, *versum*, to turn].

ver·sion (vur′·zhan) *n.* translation; account from particular point of view **-al** *a.* [L. *versio*, fr. *vertere*, to turn].

vers li·bre (ver′ lē′·br) *n.* free verse [Fr.].

ver·so (vur′·sō) *n.* left-hand page; reverse side of coin or medal [L.].

ver·sus (vur′·sas) *prep.* (*Law, Games*) against; contrasted with [L.].

ver·te·bra (vur′·ta·bra) *n.* one of the small bony segments of spinal column. *pl.* **-e. -l** *a.* pert. to vertebrae or spine. **vertebrate** *a.* having backbone; *n.* vertebrate animal [L.].

ver·tex (vur′·teks) *n.* highest point; summit; top of head; (*Astron.*) zenith; (*Geom.*) angular point of triangle etc. *pl.* **-es, vertices** (vur′·ta·sēz). **vertical** *a.* situated at vertex; directly overhead or in the zenith; upright or perpendicular; *n.* vertical line. **vertically** *adv.* **verticalness** *n.* **verticality** *n.* [L.].

ver·ti·go (vur′·ti·gō) *n.* sensation of whirling or swimming of head, with loss of equilibrium; dizziness. **vertiginous** (ver·tij′·a·nas) *a.* revolving; giddy; causing giddiness. **vertiginously** *adv.* **vertiginousness** *n.* [L. *vertigo*, whirling, fr. *vertere*, to turn].

ver·tu. See **virtu.**

ver·vain (vur′·vān) *n.* plant of genus *Verbena* [L. *verbena*].

verve (vurv) *n.* enthusiasm or vigor; energy; spirit [Fr.].

ver·y (ver′·i·) *a.* true; real; actual; genuine; now used chiefly to emphasise word following. *adv.* in a high degree; extremely. **verily** *adv.* truly [L. *versus*, true].

ves·i·cal (ves′·i·kal) *a.* (*Med.*) pert. to bladder. **vesicant** *a.* tending to raise blisters; *n.* blistering application. **vesicate** *v.t.* to raise blisters on. **vesication** *n.* process of blistering. **vesicle** *n.* small bladder-like structure; blister; cyst. **vesicular** (va·sik′·ya·ler) *a.* pert. to vesicles. **vesiculate, vesiculose, vesiculous** *a.* vesicular **vesiculation** *n.* [L. *vesica*, bladder].

Ves·per (ves′·per) *n.* the evening star, Venus; (*l.c.*) evening; *a.* (*l.c.*) pert. to evening or vespers. **-s** *n.pl.* an evening prayer; evensong; late afternoon or evening service.

ves·pi·ar·y (ves·pi·er′·i·) *n.* paperlike wasps' nest. **vespid** *n.* social wasp or bee [L. *vespa*, wasp].

ves·sel (ves′·al) *n.* utensil for holding either liquids or solids; large ship; (*Anat.*) tube or canal; recipient or means of conveying something [L. *vas*].

vest (vest) *n.* short, sleeveless garment worn under a man's suit coat; undergarment; *v.t.* to clothe; to cover; to put in possession; to endow; to furnish with authority. **-ed** *a.* that cannot be transferred or taken away; robed.

-ment *n.* ceremonial or official garment. **-ure** *n.* (*Arch.*) clothing. **-ee** *n.* a vest. **—pocket** *a.* relatively small (as a book) [L. *vestis*, garment].

ves·tal (ves'·tal) *a.* chaste; pure. *n.* nun; chaste woman [fr. Rom. Myth. *Vesta*, goddess of the hearth].

ves·ti·bule (ves'·ta·būl) *n.* small room or hall between outer and inner doors at entrance to house or building [L. *vectibulum*, entrance].

ves·tige (ves'·tij) *n.* trace or sign; mark of something that has been; remains; (*Biol.*) trace of some part or organ formerly present in body. **vestigial** *a.* **vestigially** *adv.* [L. *vestigium*, a footprint].

ves·try (ves'·tri·) *n.* room attached to church for holding ecclesiastical vestments, prayer meetings, etc.; committee of parishioners to deal with parochial affairs. **-man** *n.* [L. *vestiarium*, fr. *vestis*, garment].

vet (vet) *n.* (*Colloq. abbrev.*) veterinary surgeon or a veteran.

vetch (vech) *n.* plant of bean family used for fodder [L. *vicia*].

vet·er·an (vet'·er·an) *n.* person who has served a long time; *a.* long practiced [L. *veteranus*, fr. *vetus*, old].

vet·er·i·nar·y (vet'·er·a·ner·i·) *a.* pert. to healing diseases and surgical treatment of domestic animals. **veterinarian** *n.* one skilled in medical and surgical treatment of animals [L. *veterinarius*, pert. to beasts of burden].

ve·to (vē'·tō) *n.* power or right of forbidding. *pl.* **-es.** *v.t.* to withhold assent to; to reject. **-er** *n.* **-less** *a.* [L. *veto*, I forbid].

vex (veks) *v.t.* to make angry; to irritate; to distress. **-ation** *n.* **-atious** *a.* causing vexation; distressing. **-atiously** *adv.* **-atiousness** *n.* **-ed** *a.* [L. *vexare*, to harass].

vi·a (vī·a, vē'·a) *prep.* by way of [L.].

vi·a·ble (vī'·a·bl) *a.* born alive and sufficiently developed to be able to live; capable of living or growth. **viability** *n.* [L. *vita*, life].

vi·a·duct (vī'·a·dukt) *n.* high bridge or series of arches for carrying road or railway over valley etc. [L. *via*, way; *ducere*, to lead].

vi·al (vī'·al) *n.* small glass bottle; phial; *v.t.* to put into a vial [Gk. *phialē*, shallow bowl].

vi·and (vī'·and) *n.* article of food; chiefly *pl.* food, victuals, provisions [L. *vivenda*, provisions, fr. *vivere*, to live].

vi·at·i·cum (vī·at'·i·kam) *n.* supplies for a journey; Communion or Eucharist given to dying person. *pl.* **-s, viatica** [L. *via*, a way].

vi·brate (vī'·brāt) *v.t.* to move to and fro; to cause to quiver; to measure by vibrations or oscillations; *v.i.* to swing or oscillate; to quiver; to thrill or throb; of sound, to produce quivering effect; to sound tremulous. **vibration** *n.* **vibrator** *n.* **vibratory** *a.* vibrating; causing vibration. **vibrant** *a.* vibrating; thrilling or throbbing; powerful. **vibrancy** *n.* **vibrantly** *adv.* [L. *vibrare*, to swing or shake].

vi·bur·num (vī·bur'·nam) *n.* any of a group of shrubs of honeysuckle family [L.].

vic·ar (vik'·er) *n.* a deputy; clergyman. **-age** *n.* residence of vicar. **-ial** (vī·ker'·i·al) *a.* pert. to, acting as, vicar. **-ship** *n.*

vi·car·i·ous (vī·kar'·i·as) *a.* delegated; substituted; done or suffered for another. **-ly** *adv.* **-ness** *n.* [L. *vicarius*, deputy].

vice (vīs) *n.* depravity or immortal conduct; blemish or defect in character, etc.; failing or bad habit. **vicious** (vish'·as) *a.* depraved; wicked; spiteful; not well broken, as horse. **viciously** *adv.* **viciousness** *n.* **vicious circle,** describes state in which remedy for evil produces second evil, which when remedied in its turn leads back to first [L. *vitium*, blemish, fault].

vice See **vise.**

vice- (vīs) *prefix* in words signifying persons, denoting one who acts in place of another, or one who is second in authority, as **vice-admiral, vice-chairman, vice-president, vice-principal,** etc. [L. *vice*, in place of].

vice-ge·rent (vīs·jir'·ant) *a.* exercising delegated power; *n.* holder of delegated authority [L. *vice*, in place of; *gerere*, to act].

vice-roy (vīs'·roi) *n.* governor of country or province who rules as representative of his king; red and black butterfly [L. *vice*, in place of; *roi*, king].

vi·ce ver·sa (vī'·si·ver'·sa) *adv.* the order being reversed; the other way round [L.].

vi·chy·ssoise (vē·shē·swàz') *n.* thick cream soup of potatoes [Fr.].

vi·cin·i·ty (va·sin·a·ti·) *n.* neighborhood; nearness or proximity. **vicinage** (vis'·n·ij) *n.* neighborhood [L. *vicinus*, near].

vi·sious See **vice.**

vi·cis·si·tude (va·sis'·a·tūd) *n.* regular change or succession; alteration; *pl.* ups and downs of fortune. **vicissitudinary, vicissitudinous** *a.* [L. *vicissitudo*, alteration].

vic·tim (vik'·tim) *n.* living creature sacrificed in performance of religious ceremony; person, or thing, destroyed or sacrificed; person who suffers; dupe or prey. **-ize** *v.t.* to make victim of. **-ization** *n.* **-izer** *n.* [L. *victima*].

vic·tor (vik'·ter) *n.* one who defeats enemy in battle; conqueror; winner in contest. **-y** *n.* defeat of enemy in battle, or of antagonist in contest; conquest; triumph. **-ious** (vik·tōr'·i·as) *a.* having conquered; indicating victory; triumphant; winning. **-iously** *adv.* **-iousness** *n.* [L. *victor*, fr. *vincere* to conquer].

vic·to·ri·a (vik·tōr'·i·a) *n.* low four-wheeled carriage with folding top; early touring car with folding top [fr. Queen *Victoria*].

Vic·to·ri·an (vik·tōr'·i·an) *a.* of or characteristic of time of Queen *Victoria*; prudish; easily shocked; (of style) ornate, flowery.

vic·tro·la (vik·trō'·la) *n.* a phonograph [Trade Mark].

vict·ual (vit'·l) *v.t.* to supply with provisions; *v.i.* to take in provisions. **-s** *n.pl.* (*Colloq.*) food. **-er** (vit'·ler) *n.* one who supplies provisions. **-ess** *a.* [L. *victualis*, of food].

vi·cu·na (vi·kū'·na) *n.* S. Amer. animal; soft shaggy wool or fabric made from it [Sp.].

vid·e·o (vid'·i·ō *n.* television; *a.* of picture phase of television (opp. to *audio*) [L. = I see].

vi·dette. See **vedette.**

vie (vī) *v.i.* to strive for superiority; to contend. *pr.p.* **vying.** *pa.p.* and *pa.t.* **-d** (vīd) [O.Fr. *envier*, to challenge].

view (vū) *n.* sight; inspection by eye or mind; power of seeing; range of sight; what is seen; pictured representation of scene; manner of looking at anything, esp. mental survey; opinion; aim or intention. *v.t.* to see; to look at; to survey mentally; to consider. **-er** *n.* **-less** *a.* **— finder** *n.* device in camera for showing limits of picture. **-point** *n.* attitude or standpoint. **on view,** displayed. **in view of,** taking into consideration [L. *videre*, to see].

vig·il (vij'·il) *n.* staying awake at night, either for religious exercises, or to keep watch; a watch or watching; *pl.* nocturnal devotions. **-ant** *a.* watchful; alert; corcumspect. **-ante** (an'·ti·) *n.* a member of an unlawful group which sets itself up to control and punish crime. **-antly** *adv.* **-ance** *n.* wakefulness; watchfulness [L. *vigilia*, a watch].

vigilia, a watch].

vi·gnette (vin·yet') *n.* orig. running ornament of leaves or tendrils; small designs used as headings or tail pieces in books; any engraving, woodcut, etc. not enclosed within border; photograph or portrait showing only head or quarter-length likeness against shaded background; short, neat description in words [Fr. dim. of *vigne*, vine].

vig·or (vig′.ẹr) *n.* active strength; capacity for exertion; energy; vitality; forcefulness of style, in writing. **-ous** *a.* full of physical or mental strength; powerful. **-ously** *adv.* **-ousness** *n.* **-oso** *a. Mus.* direction. (*Brit.*) **vigour** [L.]

vi·king (vī′.king) *n.* Scand. sea rover or pirate who ravaged the northwest coast of Europe (8th 10th cent.) [O.N. *vikingr*].

vile (vīl) *a.* mean; worthless; base; depraved; repulsive; shockingly bad. **-ly** *adv.* **-ness** *n.*

vilify (vil′.ạ.fī) *v.t.* to speak ill of; to try to degrade by slander; to defame or traduce. **vilifier** *n.* **vilification** *n.* [L. *vilis*, base].

vil·la (vil′.ạ) *n.* country seat; large suburban residence [L. = a farm-house].

vil·lage (vil′.ij) *n.* assemblage of houses, smaller than town and larger than hamlet; *a.* pert. to village; rustic. **-r** *n.* an inhabitant of a village [L. *villaticus*, of a villa].

vil·lain (vil′.ạn) *n.* wicked, depraved or criminal person. **-ous** *a.* wicked; vile. **-ously** *adv.* **-ousness** *n.* **-y** *n.* extreme wickedness; an act of great depravity [L.L. *villanus*, farm servant].

vil·la·nelle (vil.ạ.nel′) *n.* poem of 19 lines on 2 rhymes having 5 three-lined stanzas, followed by one of four lines [It. *villanella*].

vil·lein (vil′.in) *n.* serf who was slave to his lord but free with respect to others. **-age** *n.* serfdom [fr. *villain*].

vil·lus (vil′.ạs) *n.* one of the small, fine, hairlike processes which cover certain membranes; any of the fine soft hairs covering certain fruits, flowers, or plants. *pl.* **villi** (vil′.ī) **villous** *a.* [L. *villus*, shaggy hair].

vim (vim) *n.* force; energy; vigor [L. *vis*, force].

vin·ai·grette (vin.ạ.gret′) *n.* small box, containing sponge saturated with aromatic vinegar salts, etc.; a savory sauce [Fr. dim. fr. *vinaigre*, vinegar].

vin·ci·ble (vin′.sạ.bl) *a.* that may be conquered. **vincibility** *n.* [L. *vincere*].

vin·cu·lum (ving′.kyạ.lạm) *n.* bond of union; (*Alg.*) straight, horizontal mark placed over several members of compound quantity to be treated as one quantity. *pl.* **vincula** [L. = bond, fr. *vincire*, to bind].

vin·di·cate (vin′.dạ.kāt) *v.t.* to justify; to maintain as true and correct; to clear of suspicion, dishonor, etc. **vindicable** *a.* **vindicability** *n.* **vindication** *n.* justification; defense of statement against denial or doubt. **vindicator** *n.* **vindicatory** *a.* [L. *vindicare*, to claim].

vin·dic·tive (vin.dik′.tiv) *a.* given to revenge; revengeful. **-ly** *adv.* **-ness** *n.* [L. *vindicta*, vengeance].

vine (vīn) *n.* woody, climbing plant that produces grapes; any plant which trails or climbs. **vinery** *n.* greenhouse for rearing vines. **-yard** (vin′.yẹrd) *n.* plantation of grapevines. **vinic** *a.* pert. to, or obtained from, wine; alcoholic. **viniculture** *n.* cultivation of vines. **vinicultural** *a.* **viniculturist** *n.* **vinaceous, vinous** *a. pert.* to, or like, wine [L. *vinea*, vine; *vinum*, wine].

vin·e·gar (vin′.ạ.gẹr) *n.* acid liquor obtained from malt, wine, cider, etc. by fermentation, and used as condiment or in pickling. *a.* like vinegar; sour. **-y** *a.* [Fr. *vinaigre*, fr. L. *vinum*, wine; *acer*, sour].

vin·tage (vin′.tij) *n.* gathering of grapes; season's yield of grapes or wine; wine of

particular year (*Colloq.*) any output of a season — **wine**, wine made from grapes of particularly good year [L. *vindermia*, vintage].

vi·nyl (vī′.nil, vin′.il) *n.* man-made plastic material.

vi·ol (vī′.ạl) *n.* medieval stringed musical instrument like violin but larger. **bass-viol** *n.* predecessor of violoncello. **-ist** *n.* one who plays viol [Fr. *viole*].

vi·o·la (vī.ō′.lạ) *n.* instrument larger than violin, but smaller than violoncello; alto or tenor violin [It.].

vi·o·la (vī′.ō.lạ) *n.* (*Bot.*) genus of plants including violet and pansy [L.].

vi·o·late (vī′.ạ.lāt) *v.t.* to infringe or break a promise; to treat with disrespect; to outrage or rape. **violation** *n.* transgression; profanation; ravishment; infringement. **violative** *a.* **violator** *n.* **violability** *n.* **violable** *a.* [L. *violare*].

vi·o·lence (vī′.ạ.lạns) *n.* force; vehemence; intensity; assault or outrage. **violent** *a.* characterized by physical force, esp. improper force; forcible; furious; passionate. **violently** *adv.* [L. *violare*, fr. *vis*, force].

vi·o·let (vī′.ạ.lit) *n.* flower of genus Viola, generally of bluish-purple color; color produced by combining blue and red; *a.* bluish or purple [Fr. fr. L. *viola*].

vi·o·lin (vī.ạ.lin′) *n.* modern musical instrument of viol family, with four strings, played with bow; fiddle. **-ist** *n.* [It. *violino*].

vi·o·lon·cel·lo (vī.ạ.lau.chel′.ō) *n.* bass violin, much larger than violin, held between player's knees; usually *abbrev.* **cello. violoncellist** *n.* [It. dim of *violone*].

vi·per (vī′.pẹr) *n.* a venomous snake; malicious person. **-ish** *a.* like a viper. **-ine, -ous** *a. venomous* [L. *vipera*].

vi·ra·go (vi.rā′.gō) *n.* turbulent or scolding woman [L.].

vi·res·cent (vi.res′.ạnt) *a.* turning green. **virescense** *n.* **viredescent** *a.* **viredity** *n.* greeness, freshness [L. *virescere* fr. *viridis*, green].

vir·gin (vur′.jin) *n.* girl or woman who has not had sexual intercourse; maiden; *a.* without experience of sexual intercourse; unsullied; chaste; fresh; untilled (of land). **-al** *a.* pert. to virgin; maidenly; fresh and pure; *n.* old musical instrument like spinet. **-ity** *n.* **the Vigin**, mother of Christ [L. *virgo*, *virginis*, maiden].

Vir·gin·ia creep·er (vẹr.jin′.yạ krēp′.ẹr) climbing vine whose leaves turn bright red in autumn. **Virginia reel**, a country dance.

Vir·go (vur′.gō) *n.* (*Astron.*) the Virgin, one of the signs of Zodiac [L. *virgo*, virgin].

vir·gule (vur′.gūl) *n.* short diagonal line (/) between 2 words indicating either may be used [L. *verga*, slender twig].

vir·i·des·cent, viridity See **virescent**.

vir·ile (vir′.il) *a.* pert. to man; masculine; strong; having vigor. **virility** *n.* manliness; power of procreation [L. *vir*, man].

vir·tu (vur.tōō′) *n.* objects of art or antiquity, collectively; taste for objects of art [It. fr. L. *virtus*, excellence].

vir·tu·al (vur′.choo.ạl) *a.* being in essence or effect, though not in fact; potential. **-ly** *adv.* to all intents and purposes. **-ity** *n.* [L. *virtus*, excellence].

vir·tue (vur′.chóò) *n.* moral excellence; merit; good quality; female chastity; power or efficacy. **virtuous** *a.* upright; dutiful; chaste. **virtuously** *adv.* **virtuousness** *n.* [L. *virtus*, manly excellence].

vir·tu·o·so (vur.chóò.ō′.sō) *n.* one with great knowledge of fine arts; highly skilled musician, painter, etc. *pl.* **-s, virtuosi. virtuosity** (vur.chóò.ás′.ạ.ti.) *n.* great technical skill in fine arts, esp. music [It.].

vir·u·lent (vir'·ya·lant) *a.* extremely poisonous; bitter in enmity; malignant; deadly. **-ly** *adv.* **virulence** *n.* acrimony; rancor; malignity; bitterness. **virulency** *n.* **virus** (vī'·ras) *n.* organism causing disease; corrupting influence [L. *virus*, poison].

vi·sa (vē'·za) *n.* official endorsement, as on passport, in proof that document has been examined and found correct, granting entry into that country [Fr. fr. L. *videre, to see*].

vis·age (viz'·ij) *n.* face; countenance; look or appearance. **-d** *a.* [Fr.].

vis·a·vis (vē'·za·vē) *adv.* face to face; *n.* person facing another [Fr. = face to face].

vis·cer·a (vis'·a·ra) *n.pl.* internal organs of body; intestines; entrails. **-l** *a.* [pl. of L. *viscus*].

vis·cid (vis'·id) *a.* glutinous; sticky; tenacious.**-ity** *n.* **viscose** (vis'·kōs) *n.* viscid solution of cellulose, drawn into fibers and used in making rayon, cellophane. **viscous** (vis'·kas) *a.* glutinous; tenacious; thick. **viscosity** *n.* [L. *viscidus*, sticky, fr. *viscum*, birdlime].

vis·count (vī'·kount) *n.* (*fem.* **-ess**) a degree or title of nobility next in rank below earl [L. *vice*, in place of; *comes*, companion].

vise (vīs) *n.* device with two jaws that can be brought together with screw, for holding steady anything which needs filing, etc. Also **vice** [Fr. *vis*, a screw].

vis·i·ble (viz'·a·bl) *a.* that can be seen; perceptible; in view. **visibly** *adv.* **visibility** *n.* degree of clarity of atmosphere, esp. for flying [L. *visibilis*, fr. *videre*, to see].

vi·sion (vizh'·an) *n.* act or faculty of seeing external objects; sight; thing seen; imaginary sight; phantom; imaginative insight or foresight. **-ary** *a.* apt to see visions; indulging in fancy or reverie; impractical; existing only in the imagination; *n.* one prone to see visions. **-al** *a.* [L. *visio*, sight, fr. *videre*, to see].

vis·it (viz'·it) *v.t.* to go, or come, to see; to punish; *v.i.* to be a guest; *n.* act of visiting or going to see; stay or sojourn; official or formal inspection. **-ant** *a.* visiting. *n.* one who visits; migratory bird. **-ation** *n.* act of visiting; formal or official inspection; visit of inordinate length; dispensation of divine favor or anger. **-or** *n.* one who visits. **-orial**, **-atorial** *a.* pert. to official visit or visitor **-ing** *n.a.* [L. *visitare*, fr. *videre*, to see].

vi·sor (vī'·zer) *n.* front part of helmet which can be lifted to show face; propecting from brim of cap; similar protective device on car windshield. **-ed** *a.* **-less** *a.* [Fr. *visière*, fr. O.Fr. *vis*, face].

vis·ta (vis'·ta) *n.* view, esp. distant view, as through avenue of trees; mental view [It. fr. L. *videre*, to see].

vis·u·al (viz'·, vizh'·oo·al) *a.* relating to sight; used in seeing; visible. **-ly** *adv.* by sight; with reference to vision. **-ize** *v.t.* to make visual; to call up mental picture of. **-ization** *n.* **-izer** *n.* [L. *visualis*].

vi·tal (vī'·tal) *a.* necessary to or containing life; very necessary. **-s** *n.pl.* essential internal organs, as lungs, heart, brain. **-ly** *adv.* **-ize** *v.t.* to give life to; to lend vigor to. **-ization** *n.* **-ity** *n.* the principle of life; vital force; vigor. — **statistics** data concerning births, deaths, etc. [L. *vitalis*, belonging to life].

vi·ta·min (vī'·ta·min) *n.* any of a group of chemical substances present in various foods and indispensable to health and growth [L. *vita*, life].

vi·ti·ate (vish'·i·āt) *v.t.* to make faulty or impure; to corrupt; to impair; to invalidate. **vitiation** *n.* **vitiator** *n.* [L. *vitium*, vice].

vit·i·cul·ture (vit'·a·kul'·cher) *n.* cultivation

of grapevines [L. *vitis*, vine].

vit·re·ous (vit'·ri·as) *a.* pert. to, or resembling, glass; glassy; derived from glass. **-ness** *n.* **vitrescent** *a.* tending to become like glass; capable of being formed into glass. **vitrescence** *n.* **vitric** *a.* [L. *vitrum*, glass].

vit·ri·fy (vit'·ra·fī) *v.t.* to convert into glass or glassy substance; *v.i.* to be converted into glass. **vitrifiable** *a.* **vitrifiability** *n.* **vitrifaction, vitrification** *n.* [L. *vitrum*, glass; *facere*, to make].

vit·ri·ol (vit'·ri·al) *n.* sulfuric acid. **-ic** *a.* pert. to, resembling, derived from, vitriol; sarcastic, caustic; bitter. **-ize** *v.* **-ization** *n.* [L. *vitreolus*, of glass].

vi·tu·per·ate (vī·tōō'·pa·rāt) *v.t.* to abuse in words; to revile; to berate. **vituperative** *a.* abusive; scolding. **vituperatively** *adv.* **vituperator** *n.* **vituperation** *n.* [L. *vituperare*, to blame].

vi·va (vē'·va) *interj.* long live [It.].

vi·va·ce (vē·va'·chi) *adv.* (*Mus.*) with spirit [It.].

vi·va·cious (vī·vā'·shas) *a.* lively; sprightly; animated; having great vitality. **-ly** *adv.* **vivacity** (vī·vas'·a·ti) *n.* liveliness [L. *vivax*, fr. *virere*, to live].

vi·var·i·um (vī·ver'·i·am) *n.* place for keeping or raising living animals or plants [L.].

vi·va vo·ce (vī'·va vō'·si·) *adv.* orally; *a.* oral [L. = with the living voice].

viv·id (viv'·id) *a.* animated; lively; clear; evoking brilliant images; (of color) bright; glaring. **-ly** *adv.* **-ness** *n.* [L. *vividus*, lively, fr. *vivere*, to live].

viv·i·fy (viv'·a·fī) *v.t.* to endue with life; to animate; to make vivid. **vivification** *n.* **vivifier** *n.* [L. *vivus*, living; *facere*, to make].

vi·vip·a·rous (vī·vip'·a·ras) *a.* producing young in living state, instead of eggs. **-ly** *adv.* **-ness, viviparity** *n.* [L *vivus*, living; *parere*, to give birth].

viv·i·sec·tion (viv·a·sek'·shan) *n.* dissection of, or experimenting on, living animals for purpose of physiological investigations **-al** *a.* **-ist** *n.* [L. *vivus*, alive; *secare*, to cut].

vix·en vik'·en) *n.* she-fox; cross bad-tempered woman. **-ish** *a.* [O.E. *fyxen*, a she-fox].

vi·zier, vi·zir (vi·zir') *n.* high executive officer in Turkey and other Oriental countries. **-ate, -ship** *n.* **-ial** *a.* [Ar. *wazir*].

vo·ca·ble (vō'·ka·bl) *n.* a word esp. with ref. to sound rather than meaning; term [L. *vocabulum*, an appellation].

vo·cab·u·lar·y (vō·kab'·ya·ler·i·) *n.* list of words, usu. arranged in alphabetical order and explained; wordbook; stock of words used by language, class, or individual [L. *vocabulum*, a word].

vo·cal (vō'·kal) *a.* pert. to voice or speech; having voice; uttered by voice; (*Phon.*) sounded; having character of vowel. **-ly** *adv.* **-ize** *v.t.* to make vocal; to utter with voice, and not merely with breath; *v.i.* to make vocal sounds. **-ist** *n.* [L. *vox*, the voice].

vo·ca·tion (vō·kā'·shan) *n.* divine call to religious career; profession, or occupation. **-al** *a.* **-ally** *adv.* [L. *vocare*, to call].

voc·a·tive (vàk'·a·tiv) *a.* relating to, used in, calling or address; *n.* (*Gram.*) case used in direct address. [L. *vocare*, to call].

vo·cif·er·ate (vō·sif'·a·rāt) *v.t.* to utter noisily or violently; to bawl; *v.i.* to cry with loud voice. **vociferation** *n.* **vociferator** *n.* **vociferous** *a.* making loud outcry; noisy or clamorous. **vociferously** *adv.* **vociferousness** *n.* [L. *vox, vocis*, the voice; *ferre*, to carry].

vod·ka (vàd'·ka) *n.* in Russia and Poland alcoholic liquor distilled from cereals or potatoes [Russ. = little water].

vogue (vōg) *n.* prevailing fashion; mode; style; current usage [Fr.].

voice (vois) *n.* faculty of uttering audible sounds; sound produced by organs of respiration; utterance; quality of utterance; expression of feeling or opinion; vote; share in discussion; (*Gram.*) mode of inflecting verbs to show relation of subject to action, as *active, passive voice; v.t.* to give expression to; to announce. **-d** (voist) *a.* furnished with voice or with expression; (*Phon.*) uttered with vocal tone. **-ful** *a.* **-less** *a.* **-lessly** *adv.* **-lessness** *n.* [L. *vox*, voice].

void (void) *a.* empty; being without; not legally binding; *n.* an empty space; *v.t.* to make vacant; to empty out; to make ineffectual or invalid. **-er** *n.* **-ness** *n.* **-able** *a.* **-ance** *n.* act of voiding; state of being void; (*Eccles.*) ejection from benefice [O.Fr. *voit*].

voile (voil, vwàl) *n.* thin cotton, woolen, or silk material [Fr. = veil].

vo·lant (vō'·lạnt) *a.* borne through the air; capable of flying [L. *volare*, to fly].

Vo·la·puk (vō'·lạ·pook') *n.* artificial language invented in 1879 [= world's speech].

vol·a·tile (vàl'·ạ·tạl) *a.* evaporating quickly; easily passing into a vapor state; fickle; changeable. **volatilize** *v.t.* and *v.i.* to render or become volatile; to cause to pass off in vapor. **volatilizable** *a.* **volatilization** *n.* **volatizer** *n.* **volatility** *n.* [L. *volatilis*, flying].

vol·ca·no (vàl·kā'·nō) *n.* opening in crust of earth, from which heated solid, liquid, and gaseous matters are ejected. **volcanic** (vàl·kan'·ik) *a.* **volcanically** *adv.* **volcanicity** [It. fr. L. *Vulcanus*, god of fire, whose forge was supposed to be below Mt. Etna].

vole (vōl) *n.* mouse-like rodent living out-of-doors [Scan. *voll*, field].

vol·i·tant (vàl'·ạ·tạnt) *a.* volant; flying; having power of flight. **volitation** *n.* flight. **volitational** *a.* [L.*volare*, to fly].

vo·li·tion (vō·lish'·ạn) *n.* act of willing or choosing; exercise of will. **-al** *a.* **-ally** *adv.* **volitive** *a.* [L. *volo, velle*, to be willing].

vol·ley (vàl'·i·) *n.* discharge of many shots or missiles at one time; missiles so discharged; rapid utterance; (*Tennis*) return of ball before it touches ground; *v.t.* to discharge in a volley; *v.i.* to fly in a volley; to sound together; (*Tennis*) to return ball before it touches ground. **-er** *n.* **-ball** *n.* team game played with ball and net. [L. *volare*, to fly].

volt (vōlt) *n.* practical unit of electro-motive force, being the pressure which causes current of one ampere to flow through resistance of one ohm. **-age** *n.* electro-motive force reckoned in volts. **-aic** *a.* **-meter** *n.* instrument used for measuring electro-motive force in volts [*Volta*, Italian scientist].

volt, volte (vōlt) *n.* in fencing, sudden turn or movement to avoid thrust; gait, or track, made by horse going sideways round center; circle so made [Fr. fr. L. *volvere*, to roll].

volte·face (vawlt·fás') *n.* turning round; sudden reversal of opinion or direction [Fr.].

vol·u·ble (vàl'·yạ·bl) *a.* having flowing and rapid utterance; fluent in speech; glib. **volubly** *adv.* **-ness, volubility** *n.* [L. *volubilis*, fr. *volvere*, to roll].

vol·ume (vàl'·yạm) *n.* formerly, roll or scroll; book; part of a work which is bound; bulk or compass; cubical content; power, fullness of voice or musical tone. **volumetric** *a.* pert. to measurement by volume. **volumetrically** *adv.* **voluminal** *a.* pert. to cubical content. **voluminous** *a.* consisting of many volumes; bulky. **voluminousness** *n.* **voluminosity** *n.* [L. *volumen*, roll or scroll, fr. *volvere*, to roll].

vol·un·tar·y (vàl'·ạn·ter·i·) *a.* proceeding from choice or free will; unconstrained; spontaneous; subject to the will; *n.* organ solo played during, or after, church service. **voluntarily** *adv.* **voluntariness** *n.* [L. *voluntas*, will].

vol·un·teer (vàl·ạn·tēr') *n.* one who enters service, esp. military, of his own free will; *a.* serving as a volunteer; composed; pert. to volunteers; *v.t.* to offer or bestow voluntarily; *v.i.* to enter into of or of one's own free will [L. *voluntas*, free will].

vo·lup·tu·ar·y (vạ·lup'·chòo·er·i·) *n.* one addicted to luxurious living or sensual gratification; sensualist; *a.* concerned with, or promoting, sensual pleasure. **voluptuous** *a.* **voluptuously** *adv.* **voluptuousness** *n.* [L. *voluptas*, pleasure].

vo·lute (vạ·lòot') *n.* (*Archit.*) spiral scroll used in Ionic, Corinthian, and Composite capitals; (*Zool.*) tropical spiral shell; *a.* rolled up spiraled. **-d** *a.* **volution** *n.* [L. *volvere, volutum*, to roll].

vom·it (vàm'·it) *v.t.* to eject from stomach by mouth; to spew or disgorge; *v.i.* to eject contents of stomach by mouth; *n.* matter ejected from stomach. **-er** *n.* **-ive, -ory** *a.* provoking vomiting; *n.* emetic; an opening through which matter is discharged [L. *vomere*, to throw up].

voo·doo (vòo'·dòo) *n.* body of primitive rites and practices; one who practices such rites; evil spirit; *a.* belonging to, or connected with, system of voodoo. **-ism** *n.* [Creole Fr. *vaudoux*, a sorcerer].

vo·ra·cious (vō·rā'·shạs) *a.* greedy in eating; eager to devour; ravenous. **-ly** *adv.* **-ness, voracity** (vō·ras'·i·ti·) *n.* [L. *vorax*, greedy to devour].

vor·tex (vawr'·teks) *n.* whirling motion of any fluid, forming depression in center of circle; whirlpool; whirling mass of air, fire, etc. which draws with irresistable power. *pl.* **-es, vortices** (vawr'·ti·sēz) **vortical, vorticose** *a.* **vortically** *adv.* [L.].

vo·ta·ry (vō'·tạ·ri·) *a.* consecrated by vow; devoted to any service, study, etc. **votaress** or promise; *n.* one engaged by vow; one *n.(fem.)* [L. *votum*, vow].

vote (vōt) *n.* formal expression of wish, choice, or opinion, of individual, or a body of persons; expression of will by a majority; right to vote; suffrage; what is given or allowed by vote; *v.t.* to declare by general consent; *v.i.* to express one's choice, will, or preference. **-r** *n.* [L. *votum*, vow].

vo·tive (vō'·tiv) *a.* offered or consecrated by vow; given in fulfillment of vow. **-ly** *adv.* **-ness** *n.* [L. *votivus*, promised by vow].

vouch (vouch) *v.t.* to warrant; to attest; to affirm; *v.i.* to bear witness; to be guarantee (for). **-er** *n.* one who bears witness or attests to anything; paper or document that serves to vouch truth of accounts, or to establish facts; receipt [L. *vocare*, to call].

vouch·safe (vouch·sāf') *v.t.* to condescend to grant or do something; *v.i.* to deign. **-ment** *n.*

vow (vou) *n.* solemn promise made esp. to deity; *v.t.* to consecrate or dedicate by solemn promise; to devote; *v.i.* to make vow or solemn promise [L. *votum*, vow].

vow·el (vou'·ạl) *n.* any vocal sound (such as *a, e, i, o, u*) produced with least possible friction or hindrance from any organ of speech; letter or character that represents such sound; *a.* pert. to vowel. **-less** *a.* **-ize** *n.* **-ization** *n.* [L. *vocalis*, fr. *vox*, voice].

voy·age (voi'·ij) *n.* journey esp. by sea; *v.i.* to sail or traverse by water. **-r** *n.* one who makes voyage [Fr. fr. L. *viaticum*, traveling money, fr. *via*, way].

Vul·can (vul'·kạn) n. (Myth.) Roman god of fire and of metal working. **vulcanize** v.t. to treat rubber with sulfur at high temperature to increase durability and elasticity. **vulcanization** n. **vulcanite** n. rubber hardened by vulcanizing. **vulcanizable** a. **vulcanizer** n. [L. Vulcanus, god of fire].

vul·gar (vul'·gẹr) a. of common people; in common use; coarse or offensive; rude; boorish. **-ly** adv. **-ian** n. vulgar person, esp. rich and unrefined. **-ize** v.t. to make vulgar. **-izer** n. **-ization** n. **-ism** n. vulgar expression; grossness of manners. **-ness, vulgarity** n. commonness; lack of refinement in manners; coarseness of ideas or language [L. vulgaris, fr. vulgus, the common people].

vul·ner·a·ble (vul'·nẹr·(ạ)·bl) a. capable of being wounded; offering open to criticism; assailable; in contract bridge, denoting side which has won first game in rubber and is subject to increased honors and penalties. **-ness, vulnerability** n. **vulnerably** adv. [L. vulnus, wound].

vul·pine (vul'·pīn) a. pert. to fox; cunning; crafty [L. vulpes, fox].

vul·ture (vul'·chẹr) n. large, rapacious bird of prey; rapacious person. **vulturine, vulturish, vulturious** a. characteristic of vulture; rapacious [L. vultur].

vul·va (vul'·vạ) n. fissure in external organ of generation in female [L.].

vy·ing (vī'·ing) pr.p. of **vie.**

W

wad (wȧd) n. little tuft or bundle; soft mass of loose, fibrous substance, for stuffing, etc., roll of bank notes; v.t. to form into wad; to line with wadding; to pad; pr.p. **-ding.** pa.t. and pa.p. **-ded. -ding** n. soft material for wads [Scand.].

wad·dle (wȧd'·l) v.i. to walk like duck, with short swaying steps; n. slow, rocking gait [freq. of wade].

wade (wād) v.i. to walk through something which hampers movement, as water, mud, etc.; to cope with, as accumulation or work; v.t. to cross (stream) by wading; n. a wading. **-r** n. one who wades; long-legged bird, e.g. stork, heron. **-rs** n.pl. high waterproof boots [O.E. wadan].

wa·di, wa·dy (wȧd'·i·) n. channel or stream which is dry except during rainy season [Ar. wadi, ravine].

wa·fer (wā'·fẹr) n. very thin biscuit; thin disk of unleavened bread, used in Eucharist service of R.C. Church; thin, adhesive disk for sealing letters; v.t. to seal or close with wafer. **-y** a. [O.Fr. waufre].

waf·fle (wȧf'·l) n. a thin cake of batter with criss-cross pattern. — **iron** n. hinged metal utensil for baking both sides of waffle at once [Dut. wafel, a wafer].

waft (wȧft, waft) v.t. to impel lightly through water or air; v.i. to float gently; n. breath or slight current of air or odor; puff. **-ure** n. [O.E. wafian, to wave].

wag (wag) v.t. to cause to move to and fro; v.i. to shake; to swing; to vibrate. pr.p. **-ging.** pa.p., pa.t. **-ged.** n. swinging motion, to and fro [O.E. wagian].

wag (wag) n. droll, witty person; humorist, **-gery** n. pleasantry; prank; jocularity. **-gish** a. frolicsome; droll. **-gishly** adv. **-gishness** n. [orig. E. wag-halter, one who deserves hanging—jocularly].

wage (wāj) v.t. to carry on; n. (usu. pl.) payment paid for labor or work done; hire; reward; pay [O.Fr. wagier].

wa·ger (wā'·jẹr) n. something staked on issue of future event or of some disputed point; bet; stake; v.t. to bet; to lay wager. **-er** n. [O.Fr. wageure, fr. Gothic, wadi, pledge].

wag·gle (wag'·l) v.t. and v.i. to move one way and the other; to wag [freq. of wag].

wag·on (wag'·ạn) n. four-wheeled vehicle or truck, for carrying heavy freight; (Brit.) railway freight car. (Colloq.) station wagon; police wagon. **-er** n. one who drives wagon. **-ette** n. four-wheeled open carriage with two lengthwise seats facing one another behind driver's seat. **-less** a. **-load** n. [Dut. wagen].

wag·tail (wag'·tāl) n. bird distinguished by long tail almost constantly in motion.

waif (wāf) n. homeless person, esp. neglected child; stray article or animal [Ice. veif].

wail (wāl) v.t. and v.i. to lament (over); to express sorrow audibly; to weep; to bewail; to bemoan; to cry loudly; n. loud weeping; great mourning; doleful cry. **-er** n. **ing** n. **-ingly** adv. [O.N. vaela].

wain (wān) n. (Poetic) wagon, esp. in farm use. **wainwright** n. wagon maker [O.E. waegen].

wain·scot (wān'·skạt) n. paneling of wood or other material used as lining for inner walls of building; lower part of a wall; v.t. to line with wainscoting. **-ing** n. wall paneling material [Low, Ger. wagenschot, oak wood].

waist (wāst) n. part of human body immediately below ribs and above hips; garment or part of woman's dress covering from neck to waist; middle part of anything; part of upper deck of ship which lies between quarter-leck and forecastle. **-band** n. part of dress or trousers which fits round waist [M.E. waste, growth, fr. wax, to grow].

wait (wāt) v.t. to stay for; v.i. to stop until arrival of some person or event; to be temporarily postponed; to be expecting; to serve at table; to attend (on); n. act, period of waiting. **-er** n. one who waits; a man who waits on table; tray. **-ing** n. and a. **-ing-list** n. list of names of those wishing some article, etc. in short supply. **-ing room** n. room set aside for use of people waiting in public place, office, etc. **-ress** n. female waiter [O.Fr. waiter, to lurk]

waive (wāv) v.t. to give up claim to; to forgo; (Law) to relinquish a right, etc. **-r** n. (Law) relinquishment, or statement of such [O.N.Fr. weyver, to renounce].

wake (wāk) v.t. to rouse from sleep; to waken; to excite; to kindle; to provoke; v.i. to awaken; to be stirred up or roused to action. pa.t. and pa.p. **-d** or **woke.** pr.p. **waking.** n. vigil; act of sitting up overnight with corpse. **-ful** a. indisposed to sleep; sleepless; watchful; wary. **-fully** adv. **-n** vt., i. **-ner** n. **waking** a. as in waking hours, period when one is not asleep [O.E. wacian].

wake (wāk) n. that part of track immediately astern of ship; air disturbance caused in rear of airplane in flight. **in the wake of,** following behind; in rear of [Dut. wak].

wale (wāl) n. mark left on flesh by rod or whip; ridge in the weave of a fabric; v.t. to mark with wales. **waling** n. wale, piece of heavy timber fastened horizontally to tie together boards supporting sides of trench or vertical pieces of jetty [O.E. walu].

walk (wawk) v.t. to pass through, along, upon; to cause to step slowly; to lead, drive, or ride (horse) at a slow pace; v.i. to go on foot; to appear as specter; to conduct oneself; n. act of walking; slowest pace of quadruped; characteristic gait or style of walking; path for pedestrians; avenue set with trees; stroll; distance walked over; sphere of life; conduct. **-er** n. **-ie-talkie** n. portable wireless combined transmitting and receiving set. **-out** n. a strike. **—over** n. in sporting contests, easy victory. **—on** minor role in a play. **—up** apartment house without an elevator. [O.E. *wealcan*, to roll].

wall (wawl) n. structure of brick, stone, etc. serving as fence, side of building, etc.; surface or side; anything resembling a wall; pl. fortifications; works for defense; v.t. to enclose with wall; to block up with wall. **—board** n. lining of various materials for applying to or making walls. **-ed** a. provided with walls; fortified. **-flower** n. garden plant, with sweet-scented flowers; lady left sitting at dance for lack of partners. **-less** a. **-like** a. [L. *vallum*].

wal·la·by (wȧl'.ȧ.bi.) n. a small kangaroo [Austral. native name].

wal·la·roo (wȧl·ȧ·róó') n. large kangaroo [Austral.].

wal·let (wȧl'.it) n. folding pocketbook for paper money identification, cards, etc.

wall-eye (wawl'.ī) n. variety of fish having large eyes. affection of the eye due to opacity of cornea; an eye turned outward. **-d** a. glary-eyed [Scand.].

Wal·loon (wȧ·lóòn') n. descendant of ancient Belgae, race of mixed Celtic and Roman stock, now French speaking population of Belgium; their dialect; a. of, or pert, to, Walloons [O.Fr. *Wallon*, fr. L. *Gallus*, a Gaul].

wal·lop (wȧl'.ȧp) v.t. (*Colloq.*) to beat soundly; to strike hard; n. stroke or blow. **-ing** n. a thrashing; a. tremendous; big.

wal·low (wȧl'.ō) v.i. to roll about (in mud, etc.); to thrive or revel in filth, vice, luxury, etc. [O.E. *wealwian*, to roll round].

wal·nut (wawl'.nut) n. large tree producing rich, dark-brown wood of fine texture; fruit of tree, large nut with crinkled shell [O.E. *wealh*, foreign; *knutu*, nut].

wal·rus (wawl'.rȧs) n. mammal closely related to seal but with down-turned tusks [Dan. *hvalros* = whale-horse].

waltz (wawlts) n. ballroom dance in three-four time; music for this dance; v.i. to dance a waltz; to skip about, from joy, etc. **-er** n. **-ing** n. [Ger. *walzer*, fr. *walzen*, to roll].

wamp·pum (wȧm'.pȧm) n. strings of shells, strung like beads, used as money and for ornament by N. American Indians [Native, *wanpanpiak*, string of white shell beads].

wan (wȧn) a. having a sickly hue; pale; pallid; ashy; gloomy. **-ly** adv. **-ness** n. [O.E.].

wand (wȧnd) n. long, slender, straight rod; rod used by conjurers or as sign of authority [O.N. *vondr*, switch].

wan·der (wȧn'.der) v.i. to ramble; to go astray; to be delirious; to depart from subject. **-er** n. **-ing** a. rambling; unsettled; n. journeying here and there, usually in pl. **-ingly** adv. **-lust** (wȧn'.der.lust) n. urge to wander or travel [O.E. *wandrian*].

wane (wȧn) v.i. to decrease; to fail; n. decrease of illuminated part of moon; decline; diminution [O.E. *wanian*, fr. *wan*, wanting].

wan·gle (wang'.gl) v.t. (*Colloq.*) to obtain by deception or trickery; v.i. to manage with difficulty. **-r** n. (*Colloq.*) trickery; artifice.

want (wawnt) n. scarcity of what is needed; poverty; v.t. to be without; lack; v.t. to be without; to lack; to need; to crave; v.i. to be lacking; to have need. **-ed** a. desired; required; sought after; searched for (by police). **-er** n. **-less** a. **-ing** a. lacking; deficient. prep. without; minus. **-s** n.pl. requirements [O.N. *vant*].

wan·ton (wawn'.tȧn) a. dissolute; unre-

strained; recklessly arrogant, malicious; n.; v.i. **-ly** adv. **-ness** n. [M.E. *wantowen*].

wap·i·ti (wȧp'.ȧ.ti.) n. N. American elk related to red deer [Amer.-Ind.].

war (wawr) n. armed conflict between two (groups of) states; state of opposition or hostility; profession of arms; art of war; v.i. to make war; to carry on hostilities; to contend. pr.p. **-ring**. pa.t. and pa.p. **-red. — cry** n. wild whoop or battle cry uttered by attacking troops; slogan. **— dance** n. wild dance, among savages, preliminary to entering battle. **-fare** n. hostilities. **—head** n. explosive cap on missile. **—horse** n. charger. **-like** a. disposed for war; martial; hostile; **-monger** n. advocator of war. **—paint** n. special adornment of Indians when on warpath; (*Slang*) full dress or regalia. **-path** n. military foray, esp. among Amer. Indians on scalping expedition. **-ship** n. vessel equipped for war. Also **man·of·war. civil war,** war between citizens of same country. **cold war,** state of international hostility short of actual warfare [O.N.Fr. *werre*, Fr. *guerre*].

war·ble (wawr'.bl) v.t. to sing in quavering manner; to trill; to carol; v.i. to sound melodiously; n. soft, sweet flow of melody; carol; song. **-r** n. one that warbles; bird with pleasant trilling song [O. Fr. *werbler*].

war·ble (wawr'.bl) n. hard tumor on back of horse. **— fly,** fly which lays its eggs in skin of cattle, horses, etc.

ward (wawrd) v.t. to repel; to turn aside; n. division of city; room for patients in hospital; guardianship; minor legally in the care of a guardian; divisions of a prison; custody; district of city or town for purposes of administration, voting, etc. slot in key; defensive movement in fencing, parry. **-en** n. civil defense officer; keeper; supervisor of prison. **-er** n. watchman; staff of authority. **-robe** n. cupboard for holding clothes; wearing apparel in general. **-room** n. mess room on liner or battleship for senior officers. **-ship** n. office of guardian; state of being under guardian [O.E. *weard*, protection].

ware (wer) n. article of merchandise; pottery; usually in combinations as, *earthenware, hardware*, etc.; pl. goods for sale; commodities; merchandise. **-house** n. storehouse for goods; v.t. to store in warehouse [O.E.*waru*].

ware (wer) a. aware; cautious; v.t. to beware of [A.S. *warian*]

war·i·ly, war·i·ness See **wary.**

warm (wawrm) a. having heat in moderate degree; not cold; hearty; lively; of colors, suggesting heat, as red, orange, yellow; excited; passionate; affectionate; v.t. to communicate moderate degree of heat to; to excite interest or zeal in; v.i. to become moderately heated; to become animated. **—blooded** a. of animals with fairly high and constant body-temperature; passionate; generous.**—hearted** a. affectionate; kindly disposed; sympathetic. **-ly** adv. **-ness, -th** n. slight heat; cordiality; heartiness; enthusiasm [O.E.*wearm*].

warn (wawrn) v.t. to notify by authority; to caution; to admonish; to put on guard. **-ing** n. advance notice of anything; admonition; caution; notice to leave premises, situation, etc.; a. cautioning [O.E.*warnian*].

warp (wawrp) v.t. to twist permanently out of shape; to bend; to pervert; to draw vessel or heavy object along by means of cable coiled on windlass; v.i. to turn, twist, or be twisted; n. distortion of wood due to unequal shrinkage in drying; system of spun threads extended lengthwise in loom on which woof is woven; a towing line. **-ed** a. twisted by unequal shrinkage; perverted; depraved. **-er** n. one who, or that which, warps. **-ing** n. [O.E. *weorpan*, to throw, to cast].

war·rant (wàr'., wawr'.ant) *v.t.* to give justification for; to authorize or sanction with assurance of safety; to guarantee to be as represented; to vouch for; to assure; to indemnify against loss; *n.* (*Law*) instrument which warrants or justifies act otherwise not permissible or legal; instrument giving power to arrest offender; authorization; guarantee; naval or military writ inferior to commission. **-able** *a.* **-ably** *adv.* **-ableness** *n.* **-ed** *a.* guaranteed. **-er, -or** *n.* **-y** *n.* security; guarantee. — **officer,** officer in Navy and Army intermediate between non-commissioned and commissioned officer [O.Fr. *warantir*].

war·ren (wawr'.an) *n.* enclosure for breeding rabbits and other game; overcrowded slum [O.Fr. *warenne*, Fr. *garenne*].

war·ri·or (wawr'.i.er) *n.* soldier; fighting man; brave fighter [*war*].

wart (wawrt) *n.* small hard conical excrescence on skin; (*Bot.*) hard, glandular protuberance on plants and trees. — **hog** *n.* African mammal of pig family with large warty protuberances on face. **-y** *a.* [O.E. *wearte*].

war·y (war'.i., wer'.i.) *a.* cautious; heedful; careful; prudent. **warily** *adv.* **wariness** *n.* [*ware*].

was (wuz) *pa.t.* of verb **to be** [O.E. *waes*].

wash (wash, wawsh) *v.t.* to free from dirt with water and soap; to tint lightly and thinly; to separate, as gold, by action of water; *v.i.* to perform act of ablution; to cleanse clothes in water; to be washable; *n.* clothes, etc. washed at one time; liquid applied to surface as lotion or coat of paint; flow of body of water; rough water left behind by vessel in motion; marsh or fen; shallow bay or inlet **-able** *a.* **-board** *n.* baseboard; board with a corrugated surface for washing clothes on; board above gunwale of boat to keep waves from washing over. **-er** *n.* one who washes; flat ring of metal, rubber, etc to make a tight joint, distribute pressure from nut or head of bolt, prevent leakage, etc. **-erman, -erwoman** *n.* **-basin, -bowl, -tub** *n.* for washing purposes. **-iness** *n.* state of being washy, weak, or watery. **-ing** *n.* act of one who washes; ablution; clothes washed at one time; *a.* used in, or intended for, washing. **-ing soda,** form of sodium carbonate used in washing. **-out** *n.* cavity in road, etc. caused by action of flood water; (*Colloq.*) failure or fiasco. **-y** *a.* watery; weak; thin; insipid. **-ed out,** exhausted; faded [O.E. *wascan*].

wasp (wasp, wawsp) *n.* stinging insect like bee with longer body and narrow waist; an ill-natured, irritable person. **-ish** *a.* like wasp; irritable; snappy. **-ishly** *adv.* **-ishness** *n.* **—waisted** *a.* having slender waist [O.E. *waesp, waeps*].

was·sail (was'.al) *n.* ancient salutation in drinking of health; celebration or festivity; spiced ale; *v.i.* to carouse; to drink wassail; **-er** *n.* [O.E. *wes hal*, be hale = 'your health'].

waste (wāst) *v.t.* to expend uselessly; to use extravagantly; to squander; to neglect; to lay waste; to spoil; *v.i.* to wear away by degrees; to become worn and emaciated; to decrease; to wither; *a.* lying unused; of no worth; desolate; unproductive; *n.* act of wasting; that which is wasted; refuse; uncultivated country; loss; squandering. **wastage** *n.* loss by use, leakage, or decay. **-basket** *n.* container for waste materials. **-ful** *a.* full of waste; destructive; prodigal; extravagant. **-fully** *adv.* **-fulness** *n.* **-land** *n.* barrenland. — **pipe** *n.* discharge pipe for drainage water. **-r** *n.* **wastrel** *n.* waster; profligate; spendthrift. **to waste away,** to be in state of decline. **to lay waste,** to devastate [O.Fr. *waster;* L. *vastare*, to lay waste].

watch (wach) *n.* state of being on the lookout; close observation; vigil; one · who watches; watchman; sentry; city night patrol of earlier times; portable timekeeper for pocket, wrist, etc.; one of the divisions of working day on ship; sailors on duty at the same time; division of the night; *v.t.* to give heed to; to keep in view; to guard; to observe closely; *v.i.* to be vigilant; to be on watch; to keep guard; to be wakeful; to look out (for); to wait (for). **-dog** *n.* guard dog; any watchful guardian. **-er** *n.* **-ful** *a.* vigilant; attentive; cautious. **-fully** *adv.* **-fulness** *n.* **-maker, -making** *n.* **—man** *n.* man who guards property. **—night,** New Year's Eve. **—word** *n.* password; a slogan; rallying cry [O.E. *waecce*].

wa·ter (waw'.ter, wa'.ter) *n.* transparent, tasteless liquid, substance of rain, rivers, etc.; body of water; river; lake; sea; saliva; tear; urine; serum; transparency of gem; *v.t.* to wet or soak with water; to put water into; to cause animal to drink; to irrigate; to give cloth wavy appearance; *v.i.* to shed water; to issue as tears; to gather saliva in mouth as symptom of appetite; to take in or obtain water. — **closet** *n.* sanitary convenience flushed by water. **—color** *n.* artist's color ground up with water; painting in this medium. **—colorist** *n.* **-course** *n.* channel worn by running water; canal. **—cress** *n.* aquatic plant with succulent leaves. **-ed** *a.* diluted with water; of silk fabrics upon which wavy pattern has been produced. **-fall** *n.* fall or perpendicular descent of water of river; cascade; cataract. **-fowl** *n.* any aquatic bird with webbed feet and coat of closely packed feathers or down. — **gauge** *n.* instrument for measuring height of water in boiler, etc. **—glass** *n.* mixture of soluable silicates of potash and soda, used in storing eggs or for preserving stone work; glass for drinking water. **-iness** *n.* state of being watery. **-ing place** *n.* a place where water may be obtained. **-ish** *a.* containing too much water; watery; thin. **-less** *a.* — **level** *n.* level formed by surface of still water; leveling instrument in which water is employed. **-lily** *n.* aquatic plant with fragrant flowers and large floating leaves. **—line** *n.* line on hull of ship to which water reaches. **—logged** *a.* saturated or full of water. — **main** *n.* large pipe running under streets, for conveying water. **—man** *n.* man who manages water craft; ferryman. — **mark** *n.* in paper making, faint translucent design stamped in substance of sheet of paper and serving as trademark. **-melon** *n.* large fruit with smooth, dark-green rind and red pulp. — **moccasin** *n.* poisonous semiaquatic pit viper of southern U.S., related to copperhead. — **polo** *n.* ball game played in water. — **power** *n.* power of water used as prime mover. **-proof** *a.* impervious to water; *v.t.* to make impervious to water. **-shed** *n.* area drained by a river. **-spout** *n.* whirlwind over water, producing vortex connecting sea and cloud, resulting in moving gyrating pillar of water; drain carrying rain water down side of building. **-tight** *a.* so fitted as to prevent water escaping or entering. — **tower** *n.* raised tank for water storage. **-way** *n.* fairway for vessels; navigable channel. — **wings** *n.pl.* small rubber floats filled with air to support learners at swimming. **-works** *n.pl.* reservoirs, etc. for the purification, supply and distribution of water; (*Slang*) tears. **-y** *a.* resembling water; thin or transparent, as a liquid. **above water,** financially sound; solvent. **heavy water,** deuterium oxide, differing from ordinary water in its density, boiling-point, and physiological actions. **high (low) water,**

highest (lowest) elevation of tide; maximum (minimum) point of success, etc. **mineral water,** water impregnated with mineral matter and possessing specific medicinal properties; artificially aerated water. **in hot water,** involved in trouble. **in low water,** financially embarrassed. **of the first water,** of finest quality. **to hold water,** of statement, to be tenable or correct. **to water down,** to moderate [O.E. *waeter*].

watt (wȧt) *n.* unit of power represented by current of one ampere produced by electromotive force of one volt (746 watts = 1 horsepower) [fr. James *Watt*, 1736-1819].

wat·tle (wȧt'·l) *n.* fleshy excrescence, usually red, under throat of cock or turkey; one of numerous species of Australian acacia; woven work made of sticks and twigs for roofs, fences, etc. **-d** *a.* [O.E. *watel, watul*, hurdle].

wave (wāv) *n.* waving movement or gesture of hand; advancing ridge or swell on surface of liquid; surge; undulation; unevenness; extended group of attacking troops or planes; rise of enthusiasm, heat, etc.; wavelike style of hair dressing; spatial form of electrical oscillation propagated along conductor or through space; passage of sound or light through space; *pl.* (*Poet.*) the sea; *v.t.* to raise into inequalities of surface; to move to and fro; to give the shape of waves; to brandish; *v.i.* to wave one way and the other; to flap; to undulate; to signal. **—band** *n.* range of wave lengths allotted for broadcasting, morse signals, etc. **-d** *a.* undulating. **wavily** *adv.* — **length** *n.* distance between maximum positive points of two successive waves; velocity of wave divided by frequency of oscillations. **—let** *n.* ripple. **—like** *a.* **waviness** *n.* **waving** *a.* moving to and fro. **wavy** *a.* [O.E. *wafian*, to brandish].

wa·ver (wā'·ver) *v.i.* to move to and fro; to fluctuate; to vacillate; to tremble; to totter. **-er** *n.* **-ing** *n.* and *a.* **-ingly** *adv.* [M.E. *waveren*, to wander about].

wax (waks) *n.* a fatty acid ester of a monohydric alcohol; an amorphous, yellowish, sticky substance derived from animal and vegetable substances; beeswax; sealing wax, cerumen, waxy secretion of ear; *v.t.* to smear, rub, or polish with wax. **-bill** *n.* name given to several small, seed-eating cage birds. **-en** *a.* made of or resembling wax; plastic; impressionable. **-er** *n.* **-iness** *n.* **-ing** *n.* **—paper** *n.* paper coated with wax, used for airtight packing. **-wing** *n.* hook-billed bird of chatterer family with quills tipped with red hornlike appendages resembling sealing wax. **-work** *n.* figure modeled in wax. *pl.* exhibition of wax figures. **-y** *a.* made of or like wax [O.E. *weax*, beeswax].

wax (waks) *v.i.* to increase in size; to grow; opposite of *wane* [O.E. *weaxan*].

way (wā) *n.* street; highway; passage; path; lane; route; progress; distance; method; mode; custom; usage; habit; means; plan; desire; momentum; movement of ship through water; state or condition. **-bill** *n.* list of passengers or articles carried by vehicle. **-farer** *n.* wanderer on foot. **-faring** *a.* and *n.* **-lay** *v.t.* to lie or wait in ambush for; *pa.t.* and *pa.p.* **-laid. -layer** *n.* **-side** *n.* border of road or path; *a.* adjoining side of road. **-ward** *a.* liking one's way; perverse; refractory. **-wardly** *adv.* **—wardness** *n.* **ways and means,** methods; resources. **by the way,** as we proceed; incidentally. **right-of-way** *n.* right to use path through private property; such a path. **under way,** of vessel when moving. **to make way,** to step aside [O.E. *weg*].

we (wē) *pron.* plural form of **I;** another person, or others, and I [O.E.].

weak (wēk) *a.* feeble; frail; delicate; fragile; easily influenced; simple; low; faint; thin; watery; diluted; inconclusive; (*Gram.*) of verb, forming past by addition of *d* or *t.* **-en** *v.t.* to make weak; *v.i.* to become weak or less resolute. **—minded** *a.* indecisive. **—kneed** *a.* irresolute. **-liness** *n.* **-ling** *n.* feeble person, physically or mentally. **-ly** *adv.* **-ness** *n.* **-er sex,** women [O.N. *veikr*].

weal (wēl) *n.* streak left on flesh by blow of stick or whip; wale [fr. *wale*].

weal (wēl) *n.* (*Arch.*) prosperity; welfare. **the common weal,** well-being and general welfare of state or community [O.E. *wela*].

weald (wēld) *n.* (*Poetic*) woodland; open country. [O.E. *weald*, forest].

wealth (welth) *n.* riches; affluence; opulence; abundance. **-iness** *n.* **-y** *a.* [O.E. *wela*, well-being].

wean (wēn) *v.t.* to discontinue breast-feeding of infant gradually; to detach or alienate. **-ling** *n.* newly-weaned infant [O.E. *wenian*, to accustom].

weap·on (wep'·an, wep'·n) *n.* instrument to fight with [O.E. *waepen*].

wear (wer) *v.t.* to carry clothes, decorations and the like, upon the person; to consume or impair by use; to deteriorate by rubbing; *v.i.* to last or hold out; to be impaired gradually by use or exposure. *pa.t.* **wore.** *pa.p.* **worn.** *n.* act of wearing; impairment from use; style of dress; fashion; article worn. **-able** *a.* **-er** *n.* **-ing** *a.* intended for wearing; exhausting; exhausting to mind and body. **-ing-apparel** *n.* dress in general. **wear and tear,** loss or deterioration due to usage. **to wear off,** to disappear slowly. **wear out,** become useless [O.E. *werian*].

wear (wer) *v.t., i.* to bring ship on the other tack by presenting stern to wind; opposite to *tack.* *pa.t.* **wore.** *pa.p.* **worn** [var. of *veer*].

wear·y (wir'·i·) *a.* fatigued; tired; bored; exhausted; tiresome; *v.t.* to exhaust one's strength or patience; to make weary; *v.i.* to become weary; to become dissatisfied with. **wearily** *adv.* **weariless** *a.* tireless. **weariness** *n.* **wearisome** *a.* tedious; causing annoyance or fatigue. **wearisomely** *adv.* **wearisomeness** *n.* [O.E. *werig*].

wea·sel (wē'·zl) *n.* small, long-bodied, short-legged, bloodthirsty carnivor [O.E. *wesle*].

weath·er (weTH'·er) *n.* combination of all atmospheric phenomena existing at one time in any particular place; *v.t.* to expose to the air; to season by exposure to air; to sail to windward of; to endure; *v.i.* to decompose or disintegrate, owing to atmospheric conditions. **—beaten** *a.* seasoned, marked, or roughened by continual exposure to rough weather. **Weather Bureau** (bū·rō') *n.* meteorological office directed by U.S. Department of Commerce. **— chart** *n.* synoptic chart, an outline map on which lines are plotted to indicate areas of similar atmospheric pressure along with other meteorological conditions. **—cock** *n.* pivoted vane, commonly in shape of cock, to indicate direction of wind; one who changes his mind repeatedly. **— forecast** *n.* prediction of probable future weather conditions based on scientific data collected by meteorological office. **— gauge** *n.* bearing of ship to windward of another. **—glass** *n.* instrument to indicate changes in atmospheric pressure; barometer. **-ing** *n.* process of decomposing of rocks, wood, etc. exposed to elements. **— report,** daily report of meteorological conditions. **—strip** *v.t.* to fit with weather stripping (strips used to keep out draft around doors, windows). **—vane** *n.* weather cock. **under the weather,** (*Colloq.*) ill; drunk [O.E. *weder*].

weave (wēv) v.t. to cross the warp by the woof on loom; to interlace threads, etc.; to construct, to fabricate, as a tale; v.i. to practice weaving; to move from side to side. pa.t. **wove**. pa.p. **woven**. n. style of weaving. **-r** n. [O.E. wefan].

web (web) n. that which is woven; whole piece of cloth woven in loom; weaver's warp; membrane which unites toes of water fowls; network spun by spider; anything as plot, intrigue, cunningly woven. **-bed** a. having toes united by membrane of skin. **-bing** n. strong, hemp fabric woven in narrow strips, used for chairs, etc. —**footed** a. [O.E. webb].

wed (wed) v.t. to take for husband or wife; to marry; to join closely; v.i. to contract matrimony. pr.p. **-ding**. pa.t. and pa.p. **-ded** or **wed**. **-ded** a. married; wholly devoted (to art, etc.) **-ding** n. nuptial ceremony; nuptials; marriage. [O.E. weddian].

wedge (wej) n. piece of wood or metal, tapering to thin edge at fore end, used for splitting, lifting heavy weights, or rendering rigid two parts of structure; anything shaped like wedge; something used for dividing; v.t. to jam; to compress; to force (in); to squeeze (in); to fasten with wedge. **-d** a. cuneiform or wedge-shaped; jammed tight [O.E. wecg].

Wedg·wood (wej'·wood) n. and a. fine Eng. pottery [fr. Josiah Wedgwood].

wed·lock (wed'·lȧk) n. marriage; married state [O.E. wedd, a pledge; lac, a gift].

Wednes·day (wenz'·di·) n. fourth day of week [O.E. Wodnesdaeg, day of Woden, Norse god].

wee (wē) n. small; tiny [M.E. we, wei, bit].

weed (wēd) n. plant growing where it is not desired; sorry, worthless person or animal; (Colloq.) cigar; tobacco; v.t. to free from weeds; to remove (something undesirable). —**killer** n. preparation for killing weeds. **-y** a. full of weeds; lanky and weakly. **to weed out**, to eliminate [O.E. weed].

weed (wēd) n. (Arch.) garment; mourning garb, as of widow (usu. pl.) [O.E. waed].

week (wēk) n. seven successive days, usually Sunday to Sunday. —**day** n. any day of week except Sunday. —**end** n. Friday or Saturday to Monday; holiday for this period. **-ly** a. pert. to a week; happening once a week. n. publication issued weekly; adv. once a week. **Holy Week, Passion Week**, week preceding Easter Sunday [O.E. wicu].

weep (wēp) v.i. to grieve for by shedding tears; to cry; to drip; to exude water; v.t. to lament; to bewail. pa.t. and pa.p. **wept**. **-er** n. one who weeps; crepe band worn by men at funerals; male professional mourner; mourning sleeve, sash, or veil. **-ing** a. of trees whose branches droop, as weeping willow. **-y** a. [O.E. wepan].

wee·vil (wē'·vȧl) n. common name given to thousands of different kinds of small beetles, all distinbuished by heads lengthened out to resemble beaks—larvae attack plants and stored grain [O.E. wifed].

weft (weft) n. filling thread carried by shuttle under and over the warp in a weaving loom. Also **woof** [O.E. wefta].

weigh (wā) v.t. to find weight of; to deliberate or consider carefully; to oppress; to raise (anchor, etc.); v.i. to have weight; to be considered as important; to press hard; to bear heavily (on). **-er** n. **-t** n. gravity as property of bodies; heavy mass; object of known mass for weighing; importance; power and influence; v.t. to make more heavy. **-tily** adv. **-tiness** n. **-ty** a. having great weight; important; momentous; forcible. **dead weight** n. heavy burden [O.E. wegan].

weir (wir) n. fence of stakes set in stream

for taking fish; a dam [O.E. wer].

weird (wird) a. unearthly; uncanny; (Colloq.) odd. **-ly** adv. **-ness** n. [O.E. wyrd, fate].

welch (welch) v.t., i. (Slang) to welsh. **-er** n.

wel·come (wel'·kȧm) a. received gladly; causing gladness; free to enjoy or use; n. kind or hearty reception; v.t. to greet with kindness and pleasure.

weld (weld) v.t. to join pieces of heated, plastic metal by fusion without soldering materials, etc.; to unite closely; n. homogeneous joint between two metals. **-er** n. [var. of well, to boil up].

wel·fare (wel'·fār) n. well-doing or well-being; prosperity.

well (wel) n. shaft or tube sunk deep in ground to obtain water, oil, etc.; spring; fountain; source; bottom of elevator shaft; cavity or pit below ground level; chamber for catching surplus water or oil; enclosure in hold of fishing vessel, for preservation of fish; v.i. to issue forth in volume, as water [O.E. wella].

well (wel) a. comp. **better**. superl. **best**. in good health; fortunate; comfortable; satisfactory; adv. agreeably; favorably; skillfully; intimately; satisfactorily; soundly; interj. exclamation of surprise, interrogation, resignation, etc. —**advised** a. prudent; sensible. —**appointed** a. handsomely furnished or equipped. —**balanced** a. eminently sane. —**being** n. welfare. **-born** a. of good family. —**bred** a. courteous and refined in manners; of good stock. —**favored** a. good-looking; pleasing to the eye. —**informed** a. knowing inner facts; possessing wide range of general knowledge; having considerable knowledge. —**meaning** a. having good intentions. —**nigh** adv. nearly; almost. —**spoken** a. cultured in speech; favorably commented on; speaking easily, fluently, graciously. —**timed** a. opportune. —**to-do** a. wealthy. **as well as**, in addition to; besides; **-spring**, source of stream, knowledge [O.E. wel].

Welsh, Welch (welsh, welch) a. relating to Wales or its inhabitants; n. language or people of Wales. —**man, —woman** n. — **rabbit**, or **rarebit**, savory dish consisting of melted cheese on toast [O.E. waelisc, foreign].

welsh, welch (welsh, welch) v.t. and v.i. (Slang) to cheat by failing to pay a debt or meeting an obligation. **-er** n. [perh. fr. Ger. welken, to fade].

welt (welt) n. cord around border or seamline of upholstery, etc.; a flat, overlapping seam; narrow strip of leather between upper and sole of shoe; weal; (Colloq.) ridge on flesh from whiplash, etc. v.t. to furnish with welt; (Colloq.) beat soundly. **-ed** a. **-ing** n.

welt·er (wel'·ter) v.i. to roll about; to wallow in slime, blood, etc.; n. confusion; turmoil. **-ing** a. [O.E. wealt, unsteady].

wel·ter·weight (wel'·ter·wāt) n. in boxing or wrestling, class of contestants weighing between 135lb. and 147lb.; boxer or wrestler of this weight.

wen (wen) n. small superficial tumor or cyst, esp. on scalp. **-nish** a. [O.E. wenn].

wench (wench) n. girl; maid; (Arch.) lewd woman; v.i. (Arch.) to associate with wenches. (Arch.) **-ing** n. fornication [O.E. wencel].

wend (wend) v.t. (Arch.) to direct; to betake (one's way); v.i. to go [O.E. wendan, to turn].

went (went) pa.t. of **wend**; pa.t. of **go**.

wept (wept) pa.t. and pa.p. of **weep**.

were (wur) pa.t. plural, and subjunctive singular and plural, of **be** [O.E. waeron].

were·wolf, wer·wolf (wir'·woolf) n. human being who, at will, could take form of wolf while retaining human intelligence [O.E. wer, a man; *wulf*, a wolf].

Wes·ley·an (wes'·li·ạn) *n.* pert. to Wesley or Wesleyanism. **-ism** *n.* Wesleyan Methodism, i.e. religion practiced in methodical manner [John *Wesley*, (1703-1791)].

west (west) *n.* point in heavens where sun sets; one of four cardinal points of compass; region of country lying to the west; *a.* situated in, facing, coming from the west; *adv.* to the west. **-erly** *a.* situated in west; of wind, blowing from west; *adv.* in west direction; *n.* wind blowing from west. **-ern** *a.* situated in west; coming from west; *n.* inhabitant of western country or district; film featuring cowboys in western states of U.S. **-erner** *n.* native of the west. **-ernmost, -most** *a.* farthest to west. **-ward** *a.* and *adv.* toward west. **-ward(s)** *adv.* **-bound** *a.* going west [O.E.].

wet (wet) *a. comp.* **-ter** *superl.* **-test.** containing water; full of moisture; humid; dank; damp; rainy; *n.* water; moisture; rain; *v.t.* to make wet; to moisten; *pr.p.* **-ting.** *pa.p.* **wet** or **ted. -blanket** *n.* a kill-joy. **-ness** *n.* **—nurse** *n.* woman who suckles child of another. **-tish** *a.* humid; damp [O.E. *waet*].

weth·er (weTH'·ẹr) *n.* castrated ram [O.E.].

whack (hwak) *v.t.* to hit, esp. with stick; to beat; (*Slang*) to share; *v.i.* to strike with smart blow; *n.* blow; (*Slang*) chance; good condition; share. **-y** *a.* [fr. *thwack*].

whale (hwāl) *n.* large fishlike mammal; (*Slang*) something huge; *v.i.* to hunt for whales. **-back** *n.* type of freight vessel on Great Lakes in N. America with covered, rounded deck. **-boat** *n.* long boat with sharp bow at each end. **-bone** *n.* baleen, an elastic, flexible, horny product of jaws of baleen whale. **— oil** *n.* lubricating oil extracted from blubber of sperm whale. **-r** *n.* man or ship engaged in whaling industry. [O.E. *hwael*].

whale (hwāl) *v.t.* (*Slang*) to thrash. **whaling** *n.* a thrashing.

wharf (hwawrf) *n.* structure on bank of navigable waters at which vessels can be loaded or unloaded; quay. *pl.* **-s, wharves.** *v.t.* to moor at, or place on, wharf. **-age** *n.* charge for use of wharf; wharf accommodation. **-inger** (hwawr'·fin·jẹr) *n.* one who owns or has charge of wharf [O.E. *hwearf*].

what (hwȧt, hwut) *pron.* interrogative pronoun (used elliptically, in exclamation, or adjectively); relative pronoun, meaning that which (used adjectively); *a.* which; which kind; *conj.* that; *interj.* denoting surprise, anger, confusion, etc.; *adv.* to what degree? **-ever** *pron.* anything that; all that. **-soever** *pron.* whatever [O.E. *hwaet*].

what·not (hwut'·nȧt) *n.* piece of furniture, having shelves for books, bric-a-brac, etc.; indescribable thing.

wheal (hwēl) *n.* raised spot or ridge on skin due to mosquito bite, hives, etc. [O.E. *hwele*].

wheat (hwēt) *n.* edible portion of annual cereal grass providing most important bread food of the world. **-en** *a.* made of wheat or whole flour [O.E. *hwgete*].

whee·dle (hwē'·dl) *v.t.* to cajole; to coax.

wheel (hwēl) *n.* solid disk or circular frame with spokes. *pl.* controlling forces; circular frame used for punishing criminals; (*Colloq.*) bicycle; steering wheel; wheeling movement; *v.t.* to convey on wheels; to furnish with wheels; *v.i.* to turn on, or as on, axis; to change direction by pivoting about an end unit, as in marching; to roll forward; to revolve. **-barrow** *n.* conveyance with a single wheel and two shafts for pushing. **-er** *n.* one who wheels; maker of wheels; hindmost horse, nearest wheels of carriage. **-house** *n.* (*Naut.*) a deckhouse to shelter steersman. **-ing** *n.* **-wright** *n.* one who makes and repairs wheels [O.E. *hweol*].

wheeze (hwēz) *v.i.* to breathe audibly and with difficulty; *n.* the sound or act of wheezing; (*Colloq.*) joke. **-r** *n.* **wheezingly** *adv.* **wheezy** *a.* **wheezily** *adv.* **wheeziness** *n.* [O.N. *hvaesa*, to hiss].

whelk (hwelk) *n.* spiral-shelled sea snail used as bait and food [O.E. *weoloc*].

whelm (hwelm) *v.t.* to cover completely; to submerge; to overpower.

whelp (hwelp) *n.* young dog, lion, seal, wolf, etc.; a youth (contemptuously); *v.i.* and *v.t.* to bring forth young [O. E. *hwelp*].

when (hwen) *adv.* and *conj.* at what time? at the time that; whereas; at which time. **-ce** *adv.* and *conj.* from what place; from what, or which, cause, etc. **-cesoever** *adv.* and *conj.* from whatsoever place, source, or cause. **-e'er** or **-ever** *adv.* and *conj.* at whatever time. **-soever** *adv.* and *conj.* whenever [O.E. *hwaenne*].

where (hwer) *adv.* and *conj.* at what place?; in what circumstances? at or to the place in which. **-abouts** *adv.* and *conj.* about where; near what or which place? *n.* place where one is. **-as** *conj.* considering that; when in fact. **-at** *adv.* and *conj.* at which; at what. **-by** *adv.* and *conj.* by which; how. **-fore** *adv.* for which reason? why? *conj.* accordingly; in consequence of which; *n.* the cause. **-in** *adv.* in which; in which, or what, respect, etc.; in what. **-of** *adv.* of which; of what. **-on** *adv.* on which; on what. **-soever** *adv.* in, or to, whatever place. **-to** *adv.* to which; to what; to what end. **-upon** *adv.* upon which; in consequence of which. **-'er, -ver** *adv.* at whatever place. **-with** *adv.* with what. **the wherewithal,** the money; the means [O.E. *hwaer*].

wher·ry (hwer'·i·) *n.* a light rowboat; skiff. (*Brit.*) vessel used in fishing; light barge.

whet (hwet) *v.t.* to sharpen by rubbing; to make sharp, keen, or eager; to stir up; *n.* act of sharpening. *pr.p.* **-ting.** *pa.t.* and *pa.p.* **-ted. -stone** *n.* fine-grained stone used for sharpening cutlery and tools; sharpener. **-ter** *n.* [O.E. *hwettan*].

wheth·er (hweTH'·ẹr) *conj.* used to introduce the first of two or more alternative clauses, the other(s) being connected by *or* [O.E. *hwaether*].

whew (hwū) *n.* or *interj.* whistling sound, expressing astonishment, dismay, or pain.

whey (hwā) *n.* clear liquid left as residue of milk after separation of fat and casein (curd). **—face** *n.* palefaced person. **—faced** *a.* **-ey** *a.* [O.E. *hwaeg*].

which (hwich) *pron.* as interrogative, signifying *who,* or *what one,* of a number; as relative, used of things; a thing or fact that; whatever. **-ever, -soever** *pron., a.* whether one or the other [O.E. *hwile*].

whiff (hwif) *n.* puff of air, smoke, etc.; an odor; *v.t.* to throw out in whiffs; to blow; *v.i.* to emit whiffs, as of smoke [imit.].

whif·fle (hwif'·l) *v.t.* to disperse, as by a puff; *v.i.* to veer, as wind; to be fickle [fr. *whiff*].

Whig (hwig) *n.* (*U.S.*) supporter of American Revolution; member of early political party (1834-1955); (*Brit.*) political party supporting Hanoverian succession but after 1832 replaced by term, 'Liberal'; *a.* pert. to Whigs. **-gish** *a.* **-gism** *n.* [contr. fr. Scots *whiggamore*].

while (hwīl) *n.* space of time; *conj.* during time when; as long as; whereas; *adv.* during which. **whilom** (hwīl'·ạm) *adv.* (*Arch.*) formerly; *a.* former. **to while away,** to pass time (usually idly) [O.E. *hwil*, time].

whim (hwim) *n.* passing fancy; caprice; fad. **-sical** *a.* capricious; freakish; fanciful; quaint. **-sicality** *n.* fanciful idea; whim. **-sically** *adv.* **-sicalness** *n.* **-sy** *n.* caprice; fancy [O.N. *hvima*, to have straying eyes].

whim·brel (hwim′·brạl) *n.* bird resembling, but small than, curlew [imit.].

whim·per (hwim′·pẹr) *v.i.* and *v.t.* to cry, or utter, with low, fretful, broken voice; *n.* low peevish, or plaintive cry. **-er** *n.* **-ing** *n.*

whin (hwin) *n.* whinstone; low, coarse evergreen.

whine (hwīn) *n.* drawing, peevish wail; unmanly complaint; *v.i.* to utter peevish cry; to complain in childish way. *n.* **whining** *n.* **whiningly** *adv.* **whiny** *a.* [O.E. *hwinan*].

whinny (hwin′·i·) *v.i.* to neigh; *n.* sound made by horse [O.E. *hwinan*, to whine].

whin·stone (hwin′·stōn) *n.* basaltic or hard unstratified rock. Also **whin.**

whip (hwip) *v.t.* to strike with lash; to flog; to overcast edges of seam, etc.; to bind ends of rope with twine; to snatch or jerk (away); to beat into froth, as **cream** or **eggs**; (*Colloq.*) to defeat decisively; *v.i.* to start suddenly. *pr.p.* **-ping.** *pa.t.* and *pa.p.* **-ped.** *n.* lash attached to handle for urging on or correction; legislative manager appointed to ensure fullest possible attendance of members of his party at important debates, etc. **-cord** *n.* worsted fabric with bold, diagonal ribbing. **— hand** *n.* hand which holds whip; mastery, upper hand. **-like** *a.* **-per** *n.* **-per-snapper** *n.* *n.* insignificant person; impertinent young fellow. **-ping** *n.* flogging. [M.E. *whippen*].

whip·pet (hwip′·it) *n.* cross-bred dog of greyhound type, for racing [prop. fr. *whip*].

whip·poor·will (hwip′·pẹr·wil) *n.* nocturnal American bird [echoic].

whir (hwur) *v.i.* to dart, fly, or revolve with buzzing or whizzing noise. *pr.p.* **-ring.** *pa.t.* and *pa.p.* **-red.** *n.* buzzing or whizzing sound [Dan. *hvirre*, to twirl].

whirl (hwurl) *v.t.* to turn round rapidly; to cause to rotate; *v.i.* to rotate rapidly; to spin; to gyrate; to move very rapidly; *n.* rapid rotation; anything which whirls; bewilderment. **-igig** *n.* spinning toy; merry-go-round. **-ing** *n.* and *a.* **-pool** *n.* vortex or circular eddy of water. **-wind** *n.* forward-moving column of air revolving rapidly and spirally around low-pressure core [ON. *hvirfila*, ring].

whish (hwish) *v.i.* to move with soft, rustling sound; *n.* such a sound [echoic].

whisk (hwisk) *n.* rapid, sweeping motion; small bunch of feathers, straw, etc. used for brush; instrument for beating eggs, etc. *v.t.* to sweep with light, rapid motion or with a whisk. **-er** *n.* thing that whisks; *pl.* hair on a man's face; long stiff hairs at side of mouth of cat or other animal. **-ered** *a.* [Scand. *visk*, wisp].

whis·key (hwis′·ki·) *n.* distilled alcoholic liquor made from various grains. Also **whisky** [Gael. *uisge beatha*, water of life].

whis·per (hwis′·pẹr) *v.t.* to utter in low, sibilant tone; to suggest secretly or furtively; *v.i.* to speak in whispers, under breath; to rustle; *n.* low, soft, sibilant remark; hint or insinuation. **-er** *n.* **-ing** *n.* **-ingly** *adv.* [O.E. *hwisprian*].

whist (hwist) *n.* card game for four players (two a side) [fr. *whisk*].

whis·tle (hwis′·l) *n.* sound made by forcing breath through rounded and nearly closed lips; instrument or device for making a similar sound; form of horn; *v.i.* to make such sound; *v.i.* and *v.t.* to render tune by whistling; to signal, by whistling. **-r** *n.* one who whistles. **whistling** *n.* [O.E. *hwistlian*].

whit (hwit) *n.* smallest part imaginable; bit [O.E. *wiht*].

white (hwīt) *a.* of the color of snow; light in color; hoary; pale; pure; clean; bright; spotless; (*Colloq.*) honest; just; *n.* color of pure snow; albuminous part of an egg; white

part of eyeball surrounding iris. **— alloy, — metal** *n.* alloy containing lead or tin, as pewter, resembling silver. **—ant** *n.* termite. **-bait** *n.* newly hatched young of sprat, herring, and related fishes, used as table delicacy. **-cap** *n.* wave with crest of white foam. **—collar** *a.* of clerical or professional workers. **— corpuscle**, leucocyte. **— elephant**, sacred elephant of Siam; gift entailing bother and expense; object valueless to the owners. **— feather** *n.* symbol of cowardice. **—fish** *n.* non-oily food fish. **— flag**, sign of truce or surrender. **— gold** alloyed gold with platinum appearance. **—heat** *n.* temperature at which substances become incandescent; state of extreme excitement or passion. **—hot** *a.* **—lead** *n.* compound of lead carbonate and hydrated oxide of lead, used as base and pigment for paint. **— lie**, harmless fib. **-n** *v.t.* and *v.i.* to make or turn white. **-ner** *n.* **-ening** *n.* making white. **-ness** *n.* **— slave**, woman or girl enticed away for purposes of prostitution. **-wash** *n.* mixture of whiting, water, and size, for coating walls; *v.t.* to cover with whitewash; to clear reputation of; to conceal errors, faults, etc. **whitish** *a.* somewhat white [O.E. *hwit*].

whith·er (hwiTH′·ẹr) (*Poetic*) *adv.* to which, or what, place? [O.E. *hwider*].

whit·ing (hwīt′·ing) *n.* edible seafish; pulverized chalk, for making putty and whitewash [fr. *white*].

whit·low (hwit′·lō) *n.* inflammatory sore affecting fingernails; [for *whickflaw* i.e. *quick*, sensitive part under fingernail, *flaw*, crack].

Whit·sun·day (hwit′·sun·di·) *n.* seventh Sunday after Easter, festival day of Church, kept in commemoration of descent of Holy Ghost. **Whitsun, Whitsuntide,** week containing Whitsunday [so called because newly baptized appeared in white garments].

whit·tle (hwit′·l) *v.t.* and *v.i.* to cut off thin slices or shavings with knife; to pare away [O.E. *thwitan*, to cut].

whiz, whizz (hwiz) *v.i.* to make hissing sound, as arrow flying through air. *pr.p.* **-zing.** *pa.t.* and *pa.p.* **-zed.** *n.* violent hissing and humming sound; person or thing regarded as excellent. **-zingly** *adv.* **—bang** *n.* (*Slang*) high-velocity, light shell whose explosion occurs almost immediately after its flight through the air is first heard [imit.].

who (hòò) *pron.* relative or interrogative, referring to persons. **-ever** *pron.* whatever person; any one, without exception. **-m** *pron.* objective case of *who.* **-msoever** *pron.* objective of **-soever** *pron.* any person, without exception. **-se** (hòòz) *pron.* possessive case of *who* or *which.* **-dunit** (hòò·dun′·it) *n.* (*Slang*) a detective story [O.E. *hwa*].

whoa (wō, hwō) *interj.* stop! [var. of *ho*].

whole (hōl) *a.* entire; complete; not defective or imperfect; unimpaired; healthy; sound; *n.* entire thing; complete system; aggregate; gross; sum; totality. **-hearted** *a.* earnest; sincere. **-heartedly** *adv.* **-heartedness** *n.* **—hog** *n.* completeness; without any reservations. **-ness** *n.* **-sale** *n.* sale of goods in bulk to retailers; *a.* selling or buying in large quantities; extensive; indiscriminate. **-saler** *n.* **-some** *a.* tending to promote health; healthy; nourishing; beneficial. **-someness** *n.* **wholly** *adv.* completely [O.E. *hal*].

whom See **who.**

whoop (hwòòp, hòòp) *n.* loud cry or yell; hoot, as of owl; convulsive intake of air after cough; *v.i.* to utter loud cry; to hoot; to make the sound characteristic of whooping cough. **-ee** *interj.* exclamation of joy or abandonment. **-er** *n.* one who whoops; bird with a loud harsh note. **-ing cough** *n.* infectious disease marked by fits of convulsive coughing, followed by characteristic loud whoop or indrawing of breath. **to make whoopee** (*Slang*) to celebrate uproariously [O.Fr. *houper*, to shout].

whop (hwáp) *v.t.* (*Arch.*) to beat severely. *pr.p.* **-ping**. *pa.p.*, *pa.t.* **-ped**. **-per** *n.* (*Colloq.*) anything unusually large; monstrous lie. **-ping** *a.* (*Colloq.*) very big [fr. *whip*].

whore (hōr) *n.* harlot; prostitute; *v.i.* to have unlawful sexual intercourse [O.N. *hora*].

whorl (hwurl, hwawrl) *n.* spiral of univalve shell; ring of leaves, petals, fingerprints, etc. **-ed** *a.* [O.E. *hweorfan*, to turn].

whor·tle·ber·ry (hwurt′·al·ber·i·) *n.* huckleberry [O.E. *wyrtil*, dim. of *wurt*, wort].

whose (hōóz) *poss.* of *who, which*. **whosoever, whomsoever** See **who.**

why (hwī) *adv.* and *conj.* for what reason? on which account? wherefore? *interj.* expletive to show surprise, indignation, protest; *n.* reason; cause; motive [O.E. *hwi*].

wick (wik) *n.* cotton cord which draws up oil or wax, as in lamp or candle, to be burned. **-less** *a.* [M.E. *wicke*, fr. O.E. *weoce*].

wick·ed (wik′·id) *a.* addicted to vice; evil; immoral; mischievous. **-ly** *adv.* **-ness** *n.* [M.E. *wikke*, evil].

wick·er (wik′·er) *n.* small flexible twig; wickerwork; withe; *a.* made of pliant twigs. **-work** *n.* basketwork [Cf. O.E. *wican*, to bend].

wick·et (wik′·it) *n.* small door or gate, adjacent to or part of larger door; arch; one of wire arches used in croquet; box-office window [O.Fr. *wiket*].

wide (wīd) *a.* broad; spacious; distant; comprehensive; missing the mark; *adv.* to a distance; far; astray; to the fullest extent. **—angle** *a.* of motion picture system using one or more cameras and projectors and a wide curved screen. **—awake** *a.* fully awake. **-ly** *adv.* **-n** *v.t.* to make wide or wider; *v.i.* to grow wide or wider; to expand. **-ness** *n.* width. **-spread** *a.* extending on all sides; diffused; circulating among numerous people. **width** *n.* wideness; breadth. **widthwise** *adv.* [O.E. *wid*].

widg·eon, wigeon (wij′·an) *a.* fresh-water duck [O.Fr. *vigeon*].

wid·ow (wid′·ō) *n.* woman who has lost husband by death; *v.t.* to bereave of husband; to be a widow to. **-er** *n.* man whose wife is dead. **-hood** *n.* **grass widow**, wife temporarily separated from husband; divorcee. [O.E. *widwe*].

width See **wide.**

wield (wēld) *v.t.* to use with full command or power; to swing; to handle; to manage; to control. **-able** *a.* **-er** *n.* **-iness** *n.* **-y** *a.* manageable; controllable [O.E. *gewieldan*, to govern].

wie·ner (wē′·ner) *n.* smoked sausage in casing; frankfurter. Also **weenie** [Ger. *Wiener wurst*, Vienna sausage].

wife (wīf) *n.* married woman; spouse; (*Colloq.*) woman. *pl.* **wives**. **-hood** *n.* **-less** *a.* **-lessness** *n.* without wife; unmarried. **-ly** *a.* as befits a wife [O.E. *wif*].

wig (wig) *n.* artificial covering for head which imitates natural hair. **-ged** *a.* [for *periwig*].

wig·gle (wig′·l) *v.i.* to waggle; to wriggle; *n.* a wriggling motion. **-r** *n.* wiggling thing; mosquito larva. [var. of *waggle*].

wig·wag (wig′·wag) *v.t.* to move back and forth; to signal with flags, etc. *pr.p.* **-ging**. *pa.p.*, *pa.t.* **-ged**. **-ger** *n.* [fr. *wag*].

wig·wam (wig′·wam) *n.* Amer. Ind. conical shelter [N. Amer. Ind. *Wigiwam*, their dwelling].

wild (wīld) *a.* living in state of nature; not domesticated or cultivated; native; savage; turbulent; *n.* uncultivated, uninhabited region. **-cat** *n.* medium-sized, undomesticated feline;

experimental oil well; *a.* reckless; financially unsound; highly speculative. **-fire** *n.* anything which burns rapidly or spreads fast; sheet lightning; **—goosechase** *n.* foolish, futile pursuit or enterprise. **-ly** *adv.* **-ness** *n.* **to sow wild oats**, to be given to youthful excesses [O.E. *wilde*].

wil·de·beest (wil′·da·bēst) *n.* gnu [Dut.].

wil·der (wil′·der) (*Arch.*) *v.t.* to cause to lose the way; to bewilder [fr. *bewilder*].

wil·der·ness (wil′·der·nas) *n.* tract of land uncultivated and uninhabited by human beings; waste; desert; state of confusion [O.E. *wildor*, wild animal].

wile (wīl) *n.* trick or stratagem practiced for ensnaring or alluring; artifice; lure; ruse; *v.t.* to entice; to pass (time) lazily. **wilily** *adv.* **wiliness** *n.* artfulness; guile; cunning. **wily** *a.* [O.E. *wil*].

will (wil) *n.* power of choosing what one will do; volition; determination; discretion; wish; desire; (*Law*) declaration in writing showing how property is to be disposed of after death; *v.t.* to determine by choice; to ordain; to decree; to bequeath; *v.i.* to exercise act of volition; to choose; to elect; *v.* used as an auxiliary, to denote futurity dependent on subject of verb, intention, or insistence. *pa.t.* **would**. **-able** *a.* **-er** *n.* **-ing** *a.* favorably inclined; minded; disposed; ready. **-ingly** *adv.* readily; gladly. **-ingness** *n.* **— power** *n.* strength of will. **at will**, at pleasure. **with a will**, zealously and heartily [O.E. *willan*].

will·ful (wil′·fal) *a.* governed by the will without yielding to reason; obstinate; intentional. **-ly** *adv.* **-ness** *n.* [fr. *will*].

will·o′·the·wisp (wil′·a·tha·wisp) *n.* ignis fatuus, flickering, pale-bluish flame seen over marshes; anything deceptive or illusive.

wil·low (wil′·ō) *n.* name of number of trees of genus Salix, having flexible twigs used in weaving; machine for cleaning cotton. **-er** *n.* **— pattern**, design used in decorating chinaware, blue on whte ground. **-ware** *n.* china of this pattern. **-y** *a.* abounding in willows; pliant; supple and slender. **weeping willow** *n.* tree with pendent branches [O.E. *welig*].

wil·ly·nil·ly (wil′·i·nil′·i·) *a.* indecisive; *adv.* whether or not [fr. *will I, nill I*].

wilt (wilt) *v.i.* to fade; to droop; to wither; *v.t.* to depress; *n.* weakness; plant disease.

Wil·ton (wil′·tn) *n.* velvet-pile carpet [*Wilton*, town in Wiltshire].

wil·y See **wile.**

wim·ble (wim′·bl) *n.* tool for boring; *v.t.* [O.Fr.].

wim·ple (wim′·pl) *n.* covering for neck, chin and sides of face, still retained by nuns; *v.i.* to ripple; to lie in folds [O.E. *wimpel*].

win (win) *v.t.* to gain by success in competition or contest; to earn; to obtain; to reach, after difficulty; *v.i.* to be victorious; *pr.p.* **-ning**. *pa.p.*, *pa.t.* **won**. *n.* (*Colloq.*) victory, success. **-ner** *n.* **-ning** *n.* act of gaining; *pl.* whatever is won in game or competition; *a.* attractive; charming; victorious. **-ningly** *adv.* [O.E. *winnan*, to strive].

wince (wins) *v.i.* to shrink or flinch, as from blow or pain; *n.* act of wincing. **-r** *n.* [O.Fr. *guinchir*, to shrink].

winch (winch) *n.* hoisting machine; a wheel crank; a windlass [O.E. *wince*, pulley].

Win·ches·ter (win′·ches·ter) *n.* lever action repeating rifle [fr. *maker*].

wind (wind) *n.* air in motion; current of air; gale; breath; power of respiration; flatulence; idle talk; hint or suggestion; (*Naut.*) point of compass; *pl.* wind instruments of orchestra; *v.t.* to follow by scent; to run, ride, or drive till breathless; to rest (horse) that it may recover wind; to expose to wind; *v.t.* (wind) to sound by blowing (horn, etc.). *pa.p.* **-ed.** **-bag** *n.* leather bag, part of bagpipe, filled with wind by mouth; (*Slang*) empty, pompous talker. **-breaker** *n.* a warm sports jacket. **ed** *a.* breathless. **-fall** *n.* anything blown down by wind, as fruit; unexpected legacy or other gain. **-flower** *n.* the anemone. **-ily** *adv.* **-iness** *n.* — **instrument** *n.* musical instrument played by blowing or air pressure. **-jammer** *n.* (*Colloq.*) merchant sailing ship; crew member. **-less** *a.* calm; out of breath. **-mill** *n.* mill worked by action of wind on vanes or sails. **-pipe** *n.* trachea; cartilaginous pipe admitting air to lungs. **—shield** *n.* protection against wind for driver or pilot. **— sock** (or **sleeve**) cone-shaped bag to show direction of wind. **-storm** *n.* — **tunnel** in aviation, tunnel-shaped chamber for making experiments with model aircraft in artificially created atmospheric conditions. **-ward** *n.* point from which wind blows; *a.* facing the wind; *adv.* toward the wind. **-y** *a.* consisting of, exposed to wind; tempestuous; flatulent; empty; **before the wind,** with the wind driving behind. **in the wind,** afoot; astir; in secret preparation. **second wind,** restoration of normal breathing. **to get wind of,** to be secretly informed of [O.E.].

wind (wīnd) *v.t.* to twist around; to coil; to twine, to wrap; to make ready for working by tightening spring; to meander; *v.i.* to twine; to vary from direct course—*pa.t.* and *pa.p.* **wound. -er** *n.* one who, or that which, winds; step, wider at one end than the other. **-ing** *a.* twisting or bending from direct line; sinuous; meandering; *n.* turning; twist. **-ing-sheet** *n.* sheet in which corpse is wrapped. **—up** *n.* conclusion; closing stages; baseball pitcher's preliminary swing of arm before delivery. **to wind up,** to coil up; to bring to conclusion. **wound-up** *a.* highly excited [O.E. *windan*].

wind·lass (wind′·lạs) *n.* form of winch for hoisting or hauling purposes, consisting of horizontal drum with rope or chain, and crank with handle for turning [O.N. *vindill,* winder; *ass,* pole].

win·dow (win′·dō) *n.* opening in wall to admit air and light, usually covered with glass. **— box** *n.* box for growing plants outside window. **— dressing** *n.* effective arrangement of goods in shop window. **— sill** *n.* flat portion of window opening on which window rests [O.N. *vindauga,* wind-eye].

wine (wīn) *n.* fermented juice of grape; similar liquor made from other fruits; *v.t.* to entertain by serving wine; *v.i.* to drink much wine at a sitting. **—bibber** *n.* one who drinks much wine. **— cellar,** stock of wine. **-press** *n.* apparatus for pressing juice out of grapes. **-ry** place where wine is made [O.E. *win,* fr. L. *vinum*].

wing (wing) *n.* organ of flight; one of two feathered fore limbs of bird; flight; main lifting surface of airplane; extension or section of a building; right or left division of army or fleet; section of team to right or left of center or regular scrimmage line; sidepiece; *pl.* the side parts of a stage; *v.t.* to furnish with wings; to enable to fly or hasten; to wound in wing, arm, or shoulder; *v.i.* to soar on the wing. **-ed** *a.* furnished with wings; wounded in wing; swift. **-less** *a.* **-spread** *n.* distance between tips of outstretched wings of bird or of airplane [O.N. *vaengr*].

wink (wingk) *v.t.* and *v.i.* to close and open eyelids; to blink; to convey hint by flick of eyelid; to twinkle; *n.* act of winking; hint conveyed by winking. **forty winks,** short nap. **to wink at,** to connive at; to pretend not to see [O.E. *wincian*].

win·kle See **periwinkle.**
win·ner, win·ning See **win.**
win·now (win′·ō) *v.t.* to separate grain from chaff by means of wind or current of air; to fan; to separate; to sift; to sort out. **-er** *n.* **-ing** *a.* and *n.* [O.E. *windwian*].
win·some (win′·sạm) *a.* cheerful; charming; attractive. **-ly** *adv.* **-ness** *n.* [O.E. *wynsum,* fr. *wynn,* joy].
win·ter (win′·tẹr) *n.* fourth season; (*Astron.*) in northern latitudes, period between winter solstice and vernal equinox (22nd Dec.—20th-21st March); any dismal, gloomy time; *a.* wintry; pert. to winter; *v.t.* to keep and feed throughout winter; *v.i.* to pass the winter. **-er** *n.* **-green** *n.* aromatic evergreen plant from which is obtained oil of wintergreen, used in medicine and flavoring. **-ize** *v.t.* ready for winter. **-ly** *adv.* **wintriness** *n.* **wintry** *a.* of or like winter [O.E.].
wipe (wīp) *v.t.* to rub lightly, so as to clean or dry; to remove gently; to clear away; to efface; *n.* act of wiping. **-r** *n.* one who, or that which, wipes; in motoring, automatically operated arm to keep part of windshield free from rain or dust. **wiping** *n.* act of wiping. **to wipe out,** to erase; to destroy utterly [O.E. *wipian*].
wire (wīr) *n.* metal drawn into form of a thread or cord; a length of this; telegraphy; a telegram; string of instrument; a rabbit snare; *v.t.* to bind or stiffen with wire; to pierce with wire; to fence with wire; to install (building) with wires for electric circuit; (*Colloq.*) to telegraph; to snare; *a.* formed of wire. **-d** *a.* **—gauze** *n.* finely woven wire netting. **—haired** *a.* having short, wiry hair. **-less** *a.* without wires; pert. to several devices operated by electromagnetic waves. *n.* wireless telegraphy or telephony; (*Brit.*) a radio; *v.t.* and *v.i.* to communicate by wireless. **-less operator** *n.* one who receives and transmits wireless messages. **— netting** *n.* galvanized wire woven into net. **-photo** *n.* method of sending photographs by means of electric impulses; the photograph so reproduced. **-puller** *n.* one who exercises influence behind scenes, esp. in public affairs. **-r** *n.* one who installs wire. **— tapping** act of tapping telephone wires to get information. **-worm** *n.* larva of various click beetles, very destructive to roots of plants. **wirily** *adv.* **wiriness** *n.* **wiring** *n.* system of electric wires forming circuit. **wiry** *n.* stiff (as hair); lean, sinewy and strong, **a live wire,** wire charged with electricity; enterprising person [O.E. *wir*].
wis·dom (wiz′·dạm) *n.* quality of being wise; knowledge and the capacity to make use of it; judgment. **— tooth** *n.* posterior molar tooth, cut about twentieth year [O.E.].
wise (wīz) *a.* enlightened; sagacious; learned; dictated by wisdom. **-acre** *n.* a foolish know-it-all. **-crack** *n.* concise flippant statement; *v.i.* to utter one. **-ly** *adv.* **-ness** *n.* [O.E. *wis*].
wise (wīz) *n.* way; manner [O.E. *wise*].
wise (wīz) *adv. suffix.* in the way or manner of, arranged like, as in *clockwise, likewise, crosswise,* etc.
wish (wish) *v.t.* to desire; to long for; to hanker after; to request; *v.i.* to have a desire; to yearn; *n.* expression or object of desire; longing; request. **(ing)-bone** *n.* forked bone of fowl's breast. **-er** *n.* **-ful** *a.* desirous; anxious; longing; wistful. **-fully** *adv.* **-fulness** *n.* [O.E. *wyscan*].
wish·wash (wish′·wȯsh) *n.* thin, weak, insipid drink. **-y** *a.* morally weak; watery; diluted [redupl. of *wash*].
wisp (wisp) *n.* twisted handful, usually of hay; whisk or small broom; stray lock of hair. **-like** *a.* **-y** *a.* [M.E. *wisp, wips,* Cf. **wipe**].
wis·te·ri·a (wis·tir′·i·ạ) *n.* hardy climbing

leguminous shrub, with blue, purple, white or mauve flower clusters [*Wistar*, Amer. anatomist, 1761-1818].

wist·ful (wist'.fəl) *a.* pensive; sadly contemplative; earnestly longing. **-ly** *adv.* **-ness** *n.* [*var.* of wishful].

wit (wit) *n.* intellect; understanding; (one with) ingenuity in connecting amusingly incongruous ideas; humor; pleasantry; *pl.* mental faculties. **-less** *a.* lacking wit or understanding; silly; stupid. **-lessly** *adv.* in all innocence. **-lessness** *n.* **-ticism** *n.* witty remark. **-tily** *adv.* **-tiness** *n.* **-tingly** *adv.* with foreknowledge or design; knowingly; of set purpose. **-ty** *a.* possessed of wit; amusing. **at one's wits' end**, baffled; perplexed what to do. **to wit**, namely [O.E. *witan*, to know].

wit·an (wit'.ən) *n.pl.* members of the witenagemot [O.E. *wita*, wise man].

witch (wich) *n.* woman who was supposed to practice sorcery; ugly old woman; hag; crone; *v.t.* to bewitch; to enchant. **-craft** *n.* black art; sorcery; necromancy. — **doctor** *n.* medicine man of a savage tribe. **-ery** *n.* arts of a witch; sorcery. **—hunt** search for, and trial of subversives. **-ing** *a.* fascinating. **-ingly** *adv.* [O.E. *wicca*].

witch haz·el (wich·hā'.zəl) *n.* shrub with yellow flowers and edible seeds; of dried bark and leaves of the tree used, in distilled form, as astringent drug [O.E. *wice*, drooping].

wit·e·na·ge·mot (wit'.a.na.ga.mōt) *n.* national council of England in Anglo-Saxon times [O.E. *wita*, wise man; *gemot*, meeting].

with (wiTH, with) *prep.* in company or possession of; in relation to; against; by means of; denoting association, cause, agency, comparison, immediate sequence, etc. [O.E.].

with·al (wiTH·awl') *adv.* (*Arch.*) besides.

with·draw (wiTH·draw') *v.t.* to take away; to recall; to retract; *v.i.* to go away; to retire; to retreat; to recede. *pa.t.* **withdrew.** *pa.p.* **-n, -al** *n.* **-ment** *n.*

withe (with, wiTH) *n.* tough, flexible twig, esp. willow, reed, or osier. Also **withy.** **withy** *a.* (*Chiefly Brit.*) made of withes; flexible and tough [O.E. *withig*, willow].

with·er (wiTH'.er) *v.t.* to cause to fade and become dry; to blight; to rebuff; *v.i.* to fade; to decay; to languish. **-ing** *a.* **-ingly** *adv.* scathingly; contemptuously [var. of *weather*].

with·ers (wiTH'.erz) *n.pl.* ridge between horse's shoulder blades [O.E. *wither*, resistance].

with·hold (with·hōld') *v.t.* to hold or keep back. *pa.p.*, *pa.t.* **withheld.**

with·in (wiTH·in') *prep.* in the inner or interior part of; in the compass of; *adv.* in the inner part; inwardly; at home.

with·out (wiTH·out') *prep.* on or at the outside of; out of; not within; beyond the limits of; destitute of; exempt from; all but; *adv.* on the outside; out of doors.

with·stand (with·stand') *v.t.* to oppose; to stand against; to resist. *pa.t.* and *pa.p.* **withstood. -er** *n.*

with·y See **withe.**

wit·ness (wit'.nis) *n.* testimony; one who, or that which, furnishes evidence or proof; one who has seen or has knowledge of incident; one who attests another person's signature to document; *v.t.* to be witness of or to; *v.i.* to give evidence; to testify. — **stand** *n.* place where witness gives testimony in court of law. **-er** *n.* [O.E. *witnes*, evidence].

wit·ti·cism, wit·ty, etc. See **wit.**

wive (wīv) *v.t.* to provide with or take for a wife; *v.i.* to take a wife [fr. *wife*].

wi·vern (wī'.vern) *n.* (*Her.*) imaginary monster, with two clawed feet, two wings and serpent's tail [O.Fr. *wivre*, viper].

wives (wīvz) *pl.* of **wife.**

wiz·ard (wiz'.erd) *n.* one devoted to black art; sorcerer; magician; conjurer; a skillful person; *a.* with magical powers. **-like** *a.* **-ly** *a.* **-ry** *n.* magic [fr. *wise*].

wiz·en, wiz·ened (wiz'.n, wiz'.nd) *a.* dried up; withered [O.E. *wisnian*, to wither].

woad (wōd) *n.* plant yielding blue dye derived from pounded leaves [O.E. *wad*].

wob·ble, wab·ble (wàb'.l) *v.i.* to rock from side to side; (*Colloq.*) to vacillate; to be hesitant; *n.* rocking; unequal motion. **-r,** *n.* **wobbly, wabbly** *a.* shaky; unsteady.

woe, wo (wō) *n.* grief; heavy calamity; affliction; sorrow. **-begone** *a.* overwhelmed with woe; sorrowful; **-ful** *a.* sorrowful; pitiful; paltry. **-fully** *adv.* [O.E. *wa*].

woke. alt. *pa.t.* of **wake.**

wold (wōld) *n.* wood; open tract of country; low hill [O.E. *weald, wald*, a forest].

wolf (woolf) *n.* carnivorous wild animal, allied to dog; rapacious, cruel person; (*Slang*) lady-killer. *pl.* **wolves** (woolvz). *v.t.* (*Colloq.*) to devour ravenously. — **dog** *n.* animal bred from wolf and dog; large dog for hunting wolves. **-hound** *n.* dog bred for hunting wolves. **-ish** *a.* rapacious, like wolf; voracious; fierce and greedy. **-ishly** *adv.* **-ishness** *n.* [O.E. *wulf*].

wolf·ram·ite (wool'.fram.īt) *n.* the mineral, ferrous tungstate, the chief source of the metal tungsten. Also **wolfram** [Ger].

wol·ver·ine, wol·ver·ene (wool.va.rēn') *n.* a carnivorous mammal inhabiting northern region; the glutton [fr. *wolf*].

wolves *pl.* of **wolf.**

wo·man (woom'.an) *n.* adult human female; the quality of being a woman. *pl.* **women** (wim'.in). **-hood** *n.* adult stage of women; the qualities of women. **-ish** *a.* like a woman; effeminate. **-ishness** *n.* **-kind, womenkind** *n.* female sex. **-like** *a.* like, or characteristic of, a woman. **-liness** *n.* **-ly** *a.* befitting a mature woman; essentially feminine; *adv.* in manner of a woman [O.E. *wifmann*].

womb (woom) *n.* female organ of conception and gestation; uterus [O.E. *wamb*, belly].

wom·bat (wàm'.bat) *n.* group of Australian and Tasmanian fur-bearing, burrowing marsupial animals [Austral. *womback*].

wo·men (wim'.in) *pl.* of **woman.**

won (wun) *pa.t.* and *pa.p.* of **win.**

won·der (wun'.der) *n.* astonishment; surprise; amazement; admiration; prodigy; miracle; *v.i.* to feel wonder; to marvel; to speculate. **-er** *n.* **-ful** *a.* very fine; remarkable; amazing. **-fully** *adv.* **-fulness** *n.* **-ing** *a.* **-ingly** *adv.* in a wondering and expectant manner. **-land** *n.* land of marvels; fairyland. **wondrous** *a.* wonderful. **wondrously** *adv.* **wondrousness** *n.* [O.E. *wundor*].

custom; use; *v.i.* fe·alrfl·fl,

wont (wawnt, wunt) *a.* accustomed; used; *n.* habit; custom; use; *v.i.* (*Poetic*) to be accustomed. **-ed** *a.* accustomed; habitual; usual. **-edness** [O.E. *gewun*, usual].

won't (wōnt) *v.i.* a contr. of **will not.**

woo (woo) *v.t.* to make love to; to court; to endeavor to gain (sleep, etc.) **-er** *n.* **-ing** *n.* [O.E. *wogian*].

wood (wood) *n.* (usu. *pl.*) land with trees growing close together; grove; forest; hard, stiffening tissue in stem and branches of tree; timber; wood-wind instrument; *v.t.* to supply with wood; to plant with trees; *v.i.* to take in good. — **alcohol** *n.* methyl alcohol, product of dry distillation of wood, esp. beech and birch. **-bine,** *n.* wild honeysuckle; Virginia creeper. *n.* **-chuck** *n.* small burrowing rodent; ground hog. — **coal** *n.* wood charcoal; lignite or brown coal. **-cock** *n.* migrant gamebird of snipe family. **-craft** *n.* expert knowledge of woodland conditions; art of making objects of wood. **-cut** *n.* engraving on wood; impression from such engravings. **-cutter** *n.* a woodsman. **-ed** *a.* covered with trees. **-en** *a.* made of wood; expressionless; stiff; stupid. — **engraver** *n.* — **engraving** *n.* art or process of cutting design on wood for printing; impression from this; woodcut. **-enhead** *n.* (*Colloq.*) a numbskull; a blockhead.**-enly** *adv.* stiffly. **-enness** *n.* **-enware** *n.* articles of wood. **-iness** *n.* **-land** *n.* and *a.* (of) wooded country. — **louse** *n.* the slater, prolific in damp places, esp. under decaying timber. **-man** *n.* or **-sman.** — **nymph** *n.* goddess of woods, a dryad; a moth. **-pecker** *n.* bird which taps and bores with bill the bark of trees in search of insects. — **pulp** *n.* wood crushed and pulped for paper making. **-sman** *n.* forest dweller; forester; woodcutter. — **sorrel** *n.* perennial herb of geranium order with small white flowers and acid leaves. **-shed** *n.* firewood storage place. **-sy** *a.* like the woods. —**wind** *n.* wooden musical instrument, as flute, oboe, clarinet, bassoon, etc. **-work** *n.* fittings made of wood, esp. interior moldings of a house. **-y** *a.* abounding with trees or wooded growth. **not out of the woods,** still in jeopardy [O.E. *wudu,* forest]. **woo·er** See **woo.**

woof (woof) *n.* threads which cross warp in weaving; texture [O.E. *owef*].

woof·er (woof'·er) *n.* large loud-speaker that reproduces low frequency sound waves (opp. of *tweeter*).

wool (wool) *n.* soft, curled hair of sheep, goat, etc.; yarn or cloth of this; **-gather-ing** *n.* day dreaming.**-(l)en** *n.* cloth made of wool; *pl.* woolen goods; *a.* made of, pert. to, wool.**-liness** *n.* **-ly** *a.* of, or like wool; muddled and confused. **-pack** *n.* a pack of wool; a cumulus cloud resembling a fleecy woolen ball. **dyed-in-the-wool,** become inherent; unchangeable [O.E. *wull*].

word (wurd) *n.* spoken or written sign of idea; term; oral expression; message; order; password; promise; brief remark or observation; *pl.* speech; language, esp. contentious; wordy quarrel; *v.t.* to express in words; to phrase. **-ed** *a.* phrased; expressed.**-ily** *adv.* verbosely; pedantically. **-iness** *n.* verbosity; **-ing** *n.* precise words used; phrasing; phraseology. **-less** *a.* **-ly** *a.* verbose; prolix. **word for word,** literally; verbatim. **by word of mouth,** orally [O.E. *word*].

wore (wor) *pa.t.* of **wear.**

work (wurk) *n.* exertion of strength; effort directed to an end; employment; toil; labor; occupation; production; achievement; manufacture; that which is produced; (*Phys.*) result of force overcoming resistance over definite distance; *pl.* structures in engineering; manufacturing establishment; good deeds; artistic productions; mechanism of a watch, etc.; fortifications; *v.i.* to exert oneself; to labor; to be employed; to act; to be effective; to have influence (on, upon); *v.t.* to produce or form by labor; to operate; to perform; to effect; to embroider. **-able** *a.* **-aday** *a.* commonplace. **-bag, -basket, -box** *n.* receptacle for holding work implements, esp. for needlework. —**day** *n.* day when work is done; week-day. **-er** *n.* —**house** *n.* house of correction. **-ing** *n.* act of laboring or doing something useful; mode of operation; fermentation; *pl.* a mine as a whole, or a part of it where work is being carried on, e.g. level, etc.; *a.* laboring; fermenting. **-man** *n.* one actually engaged in manual labor; craftsman. **-manlike** *a.* befitting skilled workman; skillful. **-manship** *n.* skill. **-out** *n.* practice; performance; training. **-shop** *n.* place where things are made or repaired; people meeting

for intensive study in some field. **to work off,** to get rid of gradually. **to work out,** to solve (problem); to plan in detail; to exhaust (mine, etc.). **to work up,** to excite unduly; to study intensively; to advance [O.E. *weorc*].

world (wurld) *n.* earth and its inhabitants; whole system of things; universe; any planet or star; this life; general affairs of life; society; human race; mankind; great quantity or number. **-liness** *n.* state of being worldly. **-ling** *n.* one who is absorbed in the affairs, interests, or pleasures of this world. **-ly** *a.* relating to the world; engrossed in temporal pursuits; earthly; mundane; carnal; not spiritual. **-ly-wise** *a.* experienced in the ways of people. —**weary,** —**wearied** *a.* tired of worldly affairs. —**wide** *a.* extending to every corner of the globe. —**man (woman) of the world,** one with much worldly experience. **old-world** *a.* old-fashioned; quaint. **the New World,** N. and S. America. **the Old World,** Europe, Africa, and Asia [O.E. *weorold*].

worm (wurm) *n.* small, limbless, invertebrate animal with soft, long, and jointed body; spiral thread; small, metal screw that meshes with the teeth of a worn wheel; spiral pipe through which vapor passes in distillation; emblem of corruption, of decay, or remorse; groveling, contemptible fellow; *pl.* disease of digestive organs or intenstines of humans and animals due to parasite worms; *v.i.* to work (oneself) in insidiously; to move along like a worm; *v.t.* to work slowly and secretly; to free from worms. — **drive** *n.* system in which power is communicated by means of worm, through worm wheel. —**eaten** *a.* of wooden furniture, etc., full of holes gnawed by worms; old; antiquated. **-er** *n.* **-less** *a.* **-like** *a.* — **wheel** *n.* cogged wheel whose teeth engage smoothly with coarse threaded screw or worm. **-y** *a.* worm-like; abounding with worms; groveling [O.E. *wyrm,* serpent].

worm·wood (wurm'·wood) *n.* bitter plant, Artemisia, used in making absinthe, vermouth, etc.; bitterness [O.E. *wermod*].

worn (worn) *pa.p.* of **wear.** —**out** *a.* no longer serviceable; exhausted; tired.

wor·ry (wur'·i·)*v.t.* to cause anxiety; to torment; to vex; to plague; to tear or mangle with teeth; *v.i.* to feel undue care and anxiety; *n.* mental disturbance due to care and anxiety; trouble; vexation. **worrier** *n.* **worrisome** *a.* causing trouble, anxiety, or worry. **-ing** *a.* [O.E. *wyrgan,* to strangle].

worse (wurs) *a. comp.* of **bad, ill;** more unsatisfactory; of less value; in poorer health; *adv.* in a manner more evil or bad. **worsen** *v.t.* to make worse; to impair; *v.t.* and *i.* to make or become worse; to deteriorate. **worsening** *n.* [O.E. *wyrsa*].

wor·ship (wur'·ship) *n.* religious reverence and homage; act or ceremony of showing reverence; adoration; *v.t.* to adore; to pay divine honors to; *v.i.* to perform religious service; to attend church. **-ful** *a.* **-fully** *adv.* **-fulness** *n.* **-er** *n.* [O.E. *weorthscipe* = worth-ship].

worst (wurst) *a. superl.* of **bad, ill;** most evil; of least value or worth; *adv.* in most inferior manner or degree; *n.* that which is most bad or evil; *v.t.* to get the better of; to defeat [O.E. *wyrst, wyrsta*].

wor·sted (woos'·tid, woor'·stid) *n.* yarn spun from long-fibred wools which are combed, not carded; cloth of this yarn; *a.* made of worsted [*Worstead,* England].

wort (wurt, wawrt) *n.* plant, herb—usually appearing as the last element of a compound term, e.g. *milkwort,* etc. [O.E. *wyrt*].

wort (wurt) *n.* in brewing of beer, liquid portion of mash of malted grain produced during fermenting process before hops and yeast are added; malt extract used as a medium for culture of micro-organisms [O.E. *wyrt*, a plant].

worth (wurth) *n.* quality of thing which renders it valuable or useful; relative excellence of conduct or of character; value, in terms of money; merit; excellence; *a.* equal in value to; meriting; having wealth or estate to the value of. **-ily** *adv.* **-iness** *n.* **-less** *a.* of no worth or value; useless. **-while** *a.* **-lessly** *adv.* **-lessness** *n.* **-y** (wur'THi.) *a.* having worth or excellence; deserving; meritorious; *n.* man of eminent worth; local celebrity. *pl.* **worthies** [E. *weorth*].

wot (wǎt) (*Arch.*) *v.i.* to know; to be aware [O.E. fr. *witan*, to know].

would (wood) *pa.t.* of **will;** expresses condition, futurity, desire. **—be** *a.* desiring or intending to be.

wound (wound) *pa.t.* and *pa.p.* of **wind.**

wound (woond) *n.* injury; cut, stab, bruise, etc.; hurt (to feelings); damage; *v.t.* to hurt by violence; to hurt feelings of; to injure. **-er** *n.* **-less** *a.* [O.E. *wund*].

wove (wōv) *pa.t.* of **weave.** **-n** *pa.p.* of **weave. — paper** *n.* paper with no marks of wire as in laid paper.

wow (wou) *interj.* exclamation of astonishment; *n.* (*Slang*) great success.

wrack (rak) *n.* seaweed thrown ashore by waves; shipwreck; ruin. Also **rack** [var. of *wreck*].

wraith (rāth) *n.* apparition of person seen shortly before or after death; specter; ghost. **-like** *a.* [O.N. *vorthr*, guardian].

wran·gle (rang'·gl) *v.i.* to dispute angrily; to bicker; to tend horses; *n.* angry dispute; an argument. *n.* angry disputant; ranch hand who rounds up cattle. **-r** *n.* [M.E. *wranglen*, to dispute].

wrap (rap) *v.t.* to cover by winding or folding something around; to roll, wind, or fold together; to enfold; to envelop; to muffle. *pr.p.* **-ping.** *pa.t.*, *pa.p.* **-ped** (or **-t**) *n.* a loose garment; a covering. **-per** *n.* one who, or that which, wraps; loose dressing-gown worn by women; negligee. **-ping** *n.* wrapping material [earlier *wlap*, etym. uncertain].

wrapt (rapt) *a.* alt. *pa.p.*, *pa.t.* of wrap; rapt; ecstatic; transported.

wrath (rath) *n.* violent anger; indignation; rage; fury. **-ful** *a.* **-fully** *adv.* **-fulness** *n.* [O.E. *wrath*, angry].

wreak (rēk) *v.t.* to inflict (vengeance, etc.) **-er** *n.* [O.E. *wrecan*, to avenge].

wreath (rēth) *n.* circular garland or crown of flowers, leaves, etc. entwined together; chaplet; a similar formation, as of smoke. **wreathe** (rēTH) *v.t.* to surround; to form into a wreath; to wind round; to encircle; *v.i.* to be interwoven or entwined [O.E. *wraeth*, a fillet].

wreck (rek) *n.* destruction of vessel; hulk of wrecked ship; remains of anything destroyed or ruined; desolation; *v.t.* to destroy, as vessel; to bring ruin upon; to upset completely. **-age** *n.* remains of something wrecked. **-er** *n.* one who wrecks; one employed in tearing down buildings, salvaging or recovering cargo from, wreck [O.E. *wraec*, punish].

wren (ren) *n.* tiny song-bird about 4 in. long, with reddish-brown plumage [O.E. *wrenna*].

wrench (rench) *v.t.* to wrest, twist, or force by violence; to distort; *n.* sudden, violent twist; tool with fixed or adjustable jaws for holding or adjusting nuts, bolts, etc. [O.E. *wrenc*, twist].

wrest (rest) *v.t.* to pull or force away by violence; to extort; to get with difficulty; to twist from its natural meaning; to distort; *n.* violent pulling or twisting [O.E. *wraestan*].

wres·tle (res'·l)) *v.i.* to contend by grappling

and trying to throw another down; to struggle; to strive (with). **-r** *n.* **wrestling** *n.* sport in which contestants endeavor to throw each other to the ground in accordance with rules [O.E. *wraestlian*, fr. *wraestan*, to twist about].

wretch (rech) *n.* miserable creature; one sunk in vice or degradation; one profoundly unhappy. **-ed** (rech'·id) *a.* very miserable; very poor or mean; despicable. **-edly** *adv.* **-edness** *n.* [O.E. *wraecca*, an outcast].

wrig·gle (rig'·l) *v.i.* to move sinuously, like a worm; to squirm; *v.t.* to cause to wriggle; *n.* act of wriggling; wriggling motion. **-r** *n.* **wriggling** *n.* **wriggly** *a.* [Dut. *wriggelen*, to move].

wright (rīt) *n.* one who fashions articles of wood, metal, etc., as *wheelwright* [O.E. *wyrhta*].

wring (ring) *v.t.* to twist and compress; to turn and strain with violence; to squeeze or press out; to pain; to extort; *v.i.* to turn or twist, as with pain. *pa.t.* and *pa.p.* **wrung.** **-er** *n.* one who wrings; machine for pressing out water from wet clothes, etc. **-ing wet,** absolutely soaking [O.E. *wringan*].

wrin·kle (ring'·kl) *n.* ridge or furrow on surface due to twisting, shrinking, or puckering; crease in skin; fold; corrugation; *v.i.* to make ridges, creases, etc. *v.i.* to shrink into wrinkles. **-ling** *n.* **wrinkly** *a.* [O.E. *wrincle*].

wrin·kle (ring'·kl) *n.* (*Colloq.*) valuable hint; novel method or approval [O.E. *wrenc*, trick].

wrist (rist) *n.* joint connecting the forearm and hand; the carpus. **-band** *n.* part of shirt sleeve covering wrist; elastic band to give support to injured wrist. **-let** *n.* band clasping wrist fairly tightly; bracelet; (*Slang*) handcuff. **-lock** *n.* wrestling hold [O.E.].

writ (rit) *n.* that which is written; in law, mandatory precept issued by a court; **Holy Writ,** the Scriptures [fr. *write*].

write (rīt) *v.t.* to set down or express in letters or words on paper, etc.; to compose, as book, song, etc.; *v.i.* to form characters representing sounds or ideas; to be occupied in writing; **to express ideas in writing.** *pr.p.* **writing.** *pa.t.* **wrote.** *pa.p.* **written. -r** *n.* one who writes; scribe; clerk; author. **-r's cramp** *n.* neurosis of muscles of hand. **-up** *n.* (*Colloq.*) favorable press criticism or report.

writing *n.* mechanical act of forming characters on paper or any other material; anything written; style of execution or content of what is written; *pl.* literary or musical works; official papers, etc. **written** *a.* expressed in writing. **to write off,** to cancel, as bad debts [O.E. *writan*].

writhe (rīTH) *v.t.* to twist or distort; to turn to and fro; *v.i.* to twist or roll about (as in pain) [A.S. *writhen*, to twist].

writ·ten *pa.p.* of **write.**

wrong (rawng) *a.* not right; incorrect; mistaken; evil; immoral; injurious; unjust; illegal; unsuitable; improper; *n.* harm; evil; injustice; trespass; transgression; error; *adv.* not rightly; erroneously; *v.t.* to treat with injustice; to injure; to impute evil to unjustly. **-doer** *n.* one who injures another; one who breaks law; offender; sinner. **-ful** *a.* **-fully** *adv.* **-fulness** *n.* **-headed** *a.* obstinate; stubborn; perverse. **-headedly** *adv.* **-headedness** *n.* **-ly** *adv.* **-ness** *n.* **in the wrong,** at fault; blameworthy [O.E. *wrang*, injustice].

wrote (rōt) *pa.t.* of **write.**

wroth (rawth) *a.* full of wrath; angry; incensed [fr. *wrath*].

wrought (rawt) *pa.t.* and *pa.p.* of **work.** *a.* hammered into shape, as metal products. **—iron** *n.* purest form of commercial iron, fibrous, ductile, and malleable, prepared by puddling. **—up** *a.* excited; frenzied [O.E. *worhte*, worked].

wrung (rung) *pa.t.* and *pa.p.* of **wring**.

wry (rī) *a.* turned to one side; twisted; distorted; crooked; askew. **-ly** *adv.* **-neck** *n.* condition in which head leans permanently towards shoulders. **-necked** *a.* **-ness** *n.* [O.E. *wrigian*, to twist].

wy·an·dotte (wī'·an·dåt) *n.* breed of domestic fowls [name of N. Amer. tribe].

X

xan·tip·pe (zan·tip'·ē) *n.* a scolding, shrewish woman [*Xantippē*, wife of Socrates].

X chro·mo·some (eks'·krōma·sōm) *n.* (*Biol.*) chromosome which determines the sex of the future organism.

xe·bec (zē'·bek) *n.* small three-masted vessel with lateen and square sails, used formerly in the Mediterranean by pirates [Fr. *chebec*].

xe·nog·a·my (zi·någ'·a·mi·) *n.* (*Bot.*) cross-fertilization. **xenogamous** *a.* [Gk. *xenos*, stranger; *gamos*, marriage].

xen·o·gen·e·sis (zen·a·jen'·a·sis) *n.* fancied generation of organism totally unlike parent. **xenogenetic** *a.* [Gk. *xenos*, stranger; *gamos*].

xe·non (zē'·nån) *n.* non-metallic element belonging to group of rare or inactive gases [Gk. *xenos*, a stranger].

xen·o·pho·bi·a (zen·a·fō'·bi·a) *n.* fear or hatred of strangers or aliens [Gk. *xenos*, strange; *phobos*, fear].

xe·rog·ra·phy (zē·råg'·ra·fi·) *n.* a process similar to photography, but not requiring specially sensitized paper or plates, using instead a special photoconductive plate.

X rays (eks'·rāz) *n.pl.* Röntgen rays—electromagnetic rays of very short wave length, capable of penetrating matter opaque to light rays and imprinting on sensitive photographic plate picture of objects; the picture so made. *v.t.* to treat, examine, or photograph with X-rays.

xy·lo·graph (zī'·la·graf) *n.* a wood engraving; impression from wood block. **-er** *n.* **-ic** *a.* **-ical** *a.* **-y** *n.* the art of wood engraving. [Gk. *xylon*, wood; *graphein*, to write].

xy·loid (zī'·loid) *a.* of the nature of wood; resembling wood; ligneous [Gk. *xylon*, wood].

xy·lol (zī'·lawl) *n.* commercial name for **xylene**, dimethyl benzene—hydrocarbon defrom coal tar used medicinally and as solvent for fats [Gk. *xylon*, wood; L. *oleum*, oil].

xy·lo·phone (zī'·la·fōn) *n.* musical instrument consisting of blocks of resonant wood, notes being produced by striking blocks with two small hammers. **xylophonist** *n.* [Gk. *xulon*, wood; *phonē*, a voice].

xy·lo·py·rog·ra·phy (zī·lō·pī·råg'·ra·fi·) *n.* production of designs in wood by charring with hot iron [Gk. *xulon*, wood; *pur*, fire; *graphein*, to write].

xys·ter (zis'·ter) *n.* surgical instrument for scraping bones [Gk. fr. *xuein*, to scrape].

Y

yacht (yåt) *n.* light sailing or power-driven vessel, for pleasure or racing; *v.i.* to sail in a yacht. **-ing** *n.* art or act of sailing a yacht; *a.* pert. to yacht. **-sman** *n.* **-smanship** *n.* [Dut. *jagt*].

yah (yå) *interj.* exclamation of derision, defiance or disgust.

yak (yak) *n.* species of ox found in C. Asia, with a hump and long hair [Tibetan, *gyag*].

yam (yam) *n.* tuber of tropical climbing-plant; sweet potato [Port. *inhame*].

yam·mer (yam'·er) *v.i.* (*Colloq.*) to whine; to wail; to shout; complain [O.E. *geomor*, sad].

yank (yangk) *v.t.* and *v.i.* (*Colloq.*) to jerk; to tug; to pull quickly; *n.* quick tug.

Yank (yangk) *n.* (*Slang*) Yankee.

Yan·kee (yang'·kē) *n.* (in U.S.A.) citizen of New England, or of Northern States; (outside U.S.A.) an American; *a.* American. **-dom** *n.*

yap (yap) *v.i.* to yelp; (*Slang*) to chatter incessantly; *n.* yelp. *pr.p.* **-ping**. *pa.p.* and *pa.t.* **-ped** [imit. origin].

yapp (yap) *n.* style of bookbinding in limp leather projecting beyond edges of book [Fr. *Yapp*, the inventor].

yard (yård) *n.* standard measure of length, equal to three feet or thirty-six inches; (*Naut.*) spar set crosswise to mast, for supporting a sail. **-age** *n.* measurement in yards; amount to be measured. **-arm** *n.* either half of a ship's yard. **-stick** *n.* measuring stick 36 inches long; (*Fig.*) standard of measurement [O.E. *gyrd*, a rod].

yard (yård) *n.* grounds surrounding a building; enclosed space used for specific purpose as *brickyard*, a *railroad yard*, etc. [O.E. *geard*, enclosure].

yarn (yårn) *n.* spun thread, esp. for knitting or weaving; thread of rope; (*Colloq.*) imaginative story; *v.i.* to tell a story. [O.E. *gearn*].

yar·row (yar'·ō) *n.* plant having strong odor and pungent taste [O.E. *gearwe*].

yash·mak (yash'·mak) *n.* veil worn by Mohammedan women, covering the face from beneath the eyes down [Ar.].

yat·a·ghan (yat'·a·gan) *n.* Turkish dagger, without a guard and usually curved [Turk.]

yaw (yaw) *v.i.* of ship or aircraft, to fail to keep steady course; *n.* act of yawing; temporary deviation from a straight course [O.N. *jaga*, to bend].

yawl (yawl) *n.* small, two-masted sailing boat, with smaller mast at stern; ship's small boat [Dut. *jol*].

yawn (yawn) *v.i.* to open mouth involuntarily through sleepiness, etc.; to gape; *n.* involuntary opening of mouth through sleepiness, etc. a gaping space. **-ing** *a.* gaping [O.E. geonian].

yaws (yawz) *n.* tropical contagious disease of the skin, usually chronic; (*Med.*) frambesia [Afr. *yaw*, a raspberry].

y·clept (i·klept') *a.* (*Arch.*) called [O.E. *clipian*, to call].

ye (yē) *pron.* (*Arch.*) **you** [O.E. *ge.*].

ye (yē) *a.* an *Arch.* spelling of article **the**.

yea (yā) *n.* yes; *adv.* indeed [O.E. *eag.*].

yean (yēn) *v.t.* and *v.i.* to bring forth young; as sheep or goat. **-ling** *n.* a lamb; kid [O.E. *eanian*].

year (yir) *n.* time taken by one revolution of earth round sun, i.e. about 365¼ days; twelve months; scholastic session in school, university, etc.; *pl.* age; old age. **-ly** *a.* and *adv.* happening every year; annual. **-ling** *n.* young animal, esp. horse, in second year; *a.* being a year old. **-long** *a.* **-book** *n.* reference book of facts and statistics published yearly. **leap year**, year of 366 days, occurring every fourth year. [O.E. *gear*]

yearn (yurn) *v.i.* to seek earnestly: to feel longing or desire; to long for. **-ing** *n.* earnest desire; longing; *a.* desirous. **-ingly** *adv.* [O.E. *gyernan*].

yeast (yēst) *n.* froth that rises on malt liquors during fermentation; frothy yellow fungus growth causing this fermentation, used also in bread making, as leavening agent to raise dough. **-y** *a.* frothy; fermenting. **-cake** *n.* yeast mixed with meal and formed into small cakes for use in baking. [O.E. *gist*].

yegg (yeg) *n.* (*Slang*) criminal.

yell (yel) *v.i.* to cry out in a loud, shrill tone; to scream; to shriek; *n.* a loud, shrill cry. **-ing** *n.* [O.E. *gellan*].

yel·low (yel'·ō) *n.* primary color; color of gold, lemons, buttercups, etc.; *a.* of this color; (*Colloq.*) cowardly; mean; despicable; of newspaper, sensational; *v.t.* to make yellow; *v.i.* to become yellow. **-ish, -y** *a.* somewhat yellow. **-ishness** *n.* **-ness** *n.* — **fever** *n.* infectious, tropical disease, characterized by a yellow skin, vomiting, etc. — **jack** *n.* (*Colloq.*) yellow fever; yellow flag flown by ships, etc. in quarantine. — **jacket** *n.* a bright yellow wasp [O.E. *geolu*].

yelp (yelp) *n.* sharp, shrill bark or cry; *v.i.* to utter such a bark or cry. **-er** *n.* [O.E. *gilpan*, to boast].

yen (yen) *n.* (*Colloq.*) longing; urge.

yeo·man (yō'·man) *n.* (*Arch.*) officer of royal household; (*Navy*) petty officer. *pl.* **yeomen. -ly** *a.* **-ry** *n.* yeomen collectively. — **service,** long and faithful service; effective aid [*contr.* of *young man*].

yes (yes) *interj.* word expressing affirmation or consent. —**man** *n.* servile and obedient supporter [O.E. *gese*].

yes·ter (yes'·ter) *a.* (*Arch.*) pert. to yesterday; denoting period of time just past, esp. in compounds, e.g. 'yester-eve.' **-day** *n.* day before today. **-year** *n.* last year [O.E. *geostran*].

yet (yet) *adv.* in addition; at the same time; still; at the present time; now; hitherto; even; *conj.* nevertheless; notwithstanding. **as yet,** up to the present time [O.E. *giet*].

yew (ū) *n.* cone-bearing evergreen tree; its fine-grained wood, formerly used for making bows for archers [O.E. *iw*].

Yid·dish (yid'·ish) *n.* a mixture of dialectal German, Hebrew and Slavic, spoken by Jews; *a.* to or in this language [Ger. *Judisch*, Jewish].

yield (yēld) *v.t.* to produce; to give in return, esp. for labor, investment, etc.; to bring forth; to concede; to surrender; *v.i.* to submit; to comply; to give way; to produce; to bear; *n.* amount produced; return for labor, investment, etc.; profit; crop. **-ing** *a.* **-ingly** *adv.* [O.E. *gieldan* to pay].

yo·del, yo·dle (yō'·dl) *v.t.* and *v.i.* to sing or warble, with frequent changes from the natural voice to falsetto tone; *n.* falsetto warbling. **-er, yodler** *n.* [Ger. *jodeln*].

yo·ga (yō'·ga) *n.* system of Hindu philosophy; strict spiritual discipline practiced to gain control over forces of one's own being, to gain occult powers, but chiefly to attain union with the Deity or Universal Spirit. **yogi** *n.* one who practices yoga [Sans. = union].

yo·gurt (yō'·goort) *n.* a thick liquid food made from fermented milk [Turk. *yoghurt*].

yoicks (yoiks) *interj.* old fox-hunting cry.

yoke (yōk) *n.* wooden framework fastened over necks of two oxen, etc. to hold them together, and to which a plough, etc. is attached; anything having shape or use of a yoke; separately cut piece of material in garment, fitting closely over shoulders; bond or tie; emblem of submission, servitude, bondage; couple of animals working together; *v.t.* to put a yoke on; to couple or join, esp. to unite in marriage; to attach draft animal to vehicle; *v.i.* to be joined [O.E. *geoc*].

yo·kel (yō'·kl) *n.* rustic; country bumpkin.

yolk (yōk, yōlk) *n.* yellow part of egg. **-less** *a.* **-y** *a.* [O.E. *geolu*, yellow].

yon (yan) (*Arch.*) *a.* and *adv.* yonder. **-der** *a.* that or those there; *adv.* at a distance [O.E. *geon*].

yore (yōr) *n.* the past; old times [O.E. *geara*, fr. *gear*, year].

York·shire (yawrk'·sher) *n.* county in north of England. — **pudding,** batter baked in roasting tin along with meat. — **terrier,** small, shaggy terrier, resembling Skye terrier.

you (ū) *pron. sing., pl.* of second person in nominative or objective case, indicating person or persons addressed; also used indefinitely meaning, one, they, people in general. **your, yours** *a.* possessive form of *you*, meaning belonging to you, of you, pert. to you. **yourself** *pron.* your own person or self (often used for emphasis or as a reflexive). *pl.* **yourselves** [O.E. *eow, eower*].

young (yung) *a.* not far advanced in growth, life, or existence; not yet old; vigorous; immature; *n.* offspring of animals. **-ish** *a.* somewhat young. **-ling** *n.* young person or animal. **-ster** *n.* young person or animal; child. **with young,** pregnant [O.E. *geong*].

youth (yōōth) *n.* state of being young; life from childhood to manhood; lad or young man; young persons collectively. **-ful** *a.* possessing youth; pert. to youth; vigorous. **-fully** *adv.* **-fulness** *n.* [O.E. *geoguth*].

yowl (youl) *v.i.* to howl; *n.* cry of a dog; long, mournful cry [M.E. *yowlen*].

yo-yo (yō'·yō) *n.* toy consisting of flat spool with string wound round in the deep groove in its edge, which when released from hand spins up and down string. [Trade Name].

yuc·ca (yuk'·a) *n.* genus of lilaceous plants, having tall, handsome flowers [W. Ind. name].

Yu·go·slav (yōō'·gō·slav) *a.* pert. to *Yugoslavia*, the country of the Serbs, Croats, and Slovenes, in the N.W. of the Balkan Peninsula; *n.* a native of Yugoslavia. Also **Jugoslav.** [Slav. *jug*, the south].

yule (yōōl) *n.* feast of Christmas. **-tide** *n.* season of Christmas. — **log** *n.* log of wood to burn on the open hearth at Christmas time [O.E. *geol*].

Z

za·min·dar (za·mēn·dàr') *n.* in India, landowner paying revenue to government. Also **zemindar** [Pers. = a landowner].

za·ny (zā'·ni·) *n.* formerly, buffoon who mimicked principal clown; simpleton. *a.* comical. **-ism** *n.* [corrupt. of It. *Giovanni*].

za·re·ba (za·rē'·ba) *n.* in Sudan, stockade of thorny bushes to protect against enemies and wild animals [Ar. *zaribah*, an enclosure].

zeal (zēl) *n.* intense enthusiasm for cause or person; passionate ardor. **zealot** (zel'·at) *n.* fanatic; enthusiast. **zealotry** *n.* fanaticism. **zealous** (zel'·as) *a.* ardent; enthusiastic; earnest. **zealously** *adv.* **zealousness** *n.* [Gk. *zēlos*, ardor].

ze·bec Same as **xebec.**

ze·bra (zē'·bra) *n.* genus of African quadrupeds of horse family, with tawny coat striped with black [W. Afr.].

ze·brass (zē'·bras) *n.* offspring of male zebra and she-ass.

ze·bu (zē'·bū) *n.* the humped Indian ox [Fr.].

zed (zed) *n.* name for letter z.

ze·na·na (ze·na'·na) *n.* women's apartments in Hindu household [Pers. *zan*, woman].

Zend (zend) *n.* interpretation of the *Avesta*, sacred writings of Zoroastrians; Iranian language in which Zend-Avesta is written. —**Avesta** *n.* sacred writings and commentary thereon (Zend) of Zoroastrians [Pers. *Avistak va Zand*, text and commentary].

ze·nith (zē′·nith) *n.* point of heavens directly above observer's head; summit; height of success; acme; climax. **-al** *a.* [Ar. *samt.* path].

zeph·yr (zef′·ẹr) *n.* west wind; gentle breeze; fine, soft woolen fabric [Gk. *zephuros*, west wind].

zep·pe·lin (zep′·(ạ)·lin) *n.* cigar-shaped long-range dirigible [fr. Count *Zeppelin*, inventor].

ze·ro (zē′·rō) *n.* nought; cipher; symbol, 0; neutral fixed point from which graduated scale is measured, as on thermometer, barometer, etc.; lowest point. *pl.* **-s, -es.** *v.t.* to adjust instrument to a fixed point. — **hour**, precise moment at which military offensive, etc. is timed to begin; crucial moment. — **in**, *v.i.* to adjust gun fire to a specific point [Ar. *cifr.* a cipher].

zest (zest) *n.* relish; fillip; stimulus; keen pleasure. **-ful** *a.* [O.Fr. *zeste*, lemon peel].

zeug·ma (zoog′·mạ) *n.* condensed sentence in which word, such as a verb, is used with two nouns to only one of which it applies. **-tic** *a.* [Gk. *zeugnunai*, to yoke].

Zeus (zòòs) *n.* in Greek mythology, chief deity and father of gods and men, his seat being Mt. Olympus [Gk.].

zig·zag (zig′·zag) *n.* line, with short sharp turns; *a.* forming zigzag; *v.t.* and *v.i.* to form, or move with, short sharp turns. *pr.p.* **-ging.** *pa.p.*, *pa.t.* **-ged.** *adv.* [Ger. *zacke*, sharp point].

zil·lion (zil′·yạn) *n.* (*Colloq.*) inconceivably large number [coined word].

zinc (zingk) *n.* hard bluish-metal used in alloys, esp. brass, and because of its resistance to corrosion, for galvanizing iron; *v.t.* to coat with zinc, to galvanize. — **alloys** (*Met.*) alloys containing percentage of zinc, as brass, etc. **-ic** *a.* **-iferous** *a.* containing zinc. **-ify** *v.t.* **-ograph** *n.* waxed-zinc engraving plate for etching; print of this. **-ographer** *n.* **-ographic** *a.* **-ographical** *a.* **-ography** *n.* process of engraving on zinc. **-oid** *a.* resembling zinc. **-ous** *a.* pert. to zinc [Ger. *Zink*, zinc].

zing (zing) *n.* the high-pitched sound of something moving at great speed; pep [echoic].

zin·ga·ro (tsing′·gạ·rō) *n.* Italian name for Gypsy. *fem.* **zingara**, *pl.* **zingari**, **zingare.**

zin·ni·a (zin′·i·a) *n.* plant with bright-colored flowers [fr. *Zinn*, a German botanist].

Zi·on (zī′·ạn) *n.* hill in Jerusalem; town of Jerusalem; the Jewish people; Church of God; heaven. **-ism** *n.* movement among Jews to further the Jewish national state in Palestine. **-ist** *n.* advocate of Zionism [Heb. *tsiyon*, a hill].

zip (zip) *n.* whizzing sound, as of bullet in air; (*Slang*) energy; *v.t.* to shut with a zipper; *v.i.* to move with great speed. *pr.p.* **-ping.** *pa.p.*, *pa.t.* **-ped**, **-per** *n.* device of interlocking, flexible teeth opened and shut by sliding clip. (*Cap.*) trademark for this. **-py** *a.* lively [imit.].

zir·con (zur′·kạn) *n.* silicate of zirconium occurring in crystals; transparent ones used as gems. **zirconium** (zẹr·kōn′·i·ạm) *n.* metal obtained from zircon, and resembling titanium **-ic** *a.* [Ar. *zargun*].

zith·er (ziTH′·ẹr, zith′·ẹr) *n.* flat, stringed instrument comprising resonance box with strings. Also **zithern. -ist** *n.* [Ger.].

zlo·ty (zlȧ′·ti·) *n.* Polish coin and monetary unit [Pol.].

zo·an·thro·py (zō·an′·thrạ·pi·) *n.* form of mental disorder in which man believes himself to be one of the lower animals [Gk. *zōon*, animal; *anthropos*, man].

zo·di·ac (zō·di·ak) *n.* (*Astron.*) imaginary belt in heavens following path of sun, and divided into twelve equal areas containing twelve constellations, each represented by appropriate symbols, called the *signs of the*

zodiac; namely Aries (*Ram*), Taurus (*Bull*), Gemini (*Twins*), Cancer (*Crab*), Leo (*Lion*), Virgo (*Virgin*), Libra (*Balance*), Scorpio (*Scorpion*), Sagittarius (*Archer*), Capricornus (*Goat*), Aquarius (*Water-bearer*), Pisces (*Fishes*); a circular chart representing these signs **-al** *a.* [Gk. *zōdiakos*, fr. *zōon*, animal].

zom·bi, zom·bie (zȧm′·bi·) *n.* orig. in Africa, deity of the python; in West Indies, corpse alleged to have been revived by black magic; the power which enters such a body; human being without will or speech but capable of automatic movement; intoxicating drink made with rum [W. African *zumbi*, fetish].

zone (zōn) *n.* girdle; climatic or vegetation belt; one of five belts into which earth is divided by latitude lines, as *frigid zone* of Arctic and Antarctic, *torrid zone* between Tropics of Cancer and Capricorn, *temperate zone* north of Tropic of Cancer and south of Tropic of Capricorn; division of a city, etc., for building or other purposes; *v.t.* to enclose; to divide into zones; to divide country into regional areas. **zonal** *a.* pert. to or divided into zones. **-d** *a.* having zones; distributed regionally. **zonate** *a.* striped [Gk. *zonē*].

zoo (zòò) *n.* zoological garden; place where wild animals are kept for showing.

zo·o (zō′·a) *prefix* (from Greek word *zōon*, animal) used in compound words, such as *zoochemistry, zoogeny*, etc.

zo·o·chem·is·try (zō·a·kem′·is·tri·) *n.* chemistry of constituents of animal body [Gk. *zōon*, animal; and *chemistry*].

zo·o·ge·og·ra·phy (zō·a·jē·ȧg′·rạ·fi·) *n.* science which treats of the regional distribution of animals in the world. **zoogeographer** *n.* **zoogeographic, -al** *a.*

zo·oid (zō′·oid) *a.* resembling an animal; *n.* organism capable of relatively independent existence; a compound organism [Gk. *zōon*, an animal; *eidos*, a form].

zo·ol·a·try (zō·ȧl′·ạ·tri·) *n.* animal worship. **zoolater** *n.* **zoolatrous** *a.* [Gk. *zōon*, animal; *latreia*, worship].

zo·ol·o·gy (zō·ȧl′·ạ·ji·) *n.* natural history of animals, part of science of biology. **zoological** *a.* **zoologically** *adv.* **zoologist** *n.* one versed in zoology, **zoological gardens**, **zoo**, park where wild animals are kept for exhibition [Gk. *zōon*, animal; *logos*, discourse].

zoom (zòòm) *n.* *v.t.* (of prices) to become inflated; (of aircraft) to turn suddenly upwards at sharp angle; to move camera rapidly toward or away from an object which thus appears to move similarly [imit.].

zo·on (zō′·ȧn) *n.* individual part of compound animal; complete product of fertilized germ. *pl.* **zoa**, **zoons**, **-ic** *a.* [Gk. *zōon*, animal].

zo·oph·a·gous (zō·ȧf′·ạ·gạs) *a.* feeding on animals; carnivorous. Also **zoophagan** [Gk. *zōon*, animal; *phagein*, to eat].

zo·o·phyte (zō′·ạ·fīt) *n.* plant-like animal, such as sponge. **zoophytic, -al** *a.* pert. to zoophytes. **zoophytology** *n.* study of zoophytes [Gk. *zōon*, animal; *phuton*, plant].

zoot suit (zòòt′·sòòt) *n.* flashy type of man's suit, generally with padded shoulders, fitted waist, knee-length jacket and tight trousers.

Zo·ro·as·tri·an (zō·rō·as′·tri·ạn) *n.* follower of Zoroaster; *a.* pert. to Zoroaster or his religion; **-ism** *n.* ancient Persian religious doctrine taught by Zoroaster, principal feature of which is the recognition of the dual principle of good and evil; religion of the Parsees [fr. L. corrupt. of Persian *Zarathustra*].

zounds (zoundz) (*Arch.*) *interj.* of anger and surprise [corrupt. of *God's wounds*].

zuc·chet·to (zòò·ket′·ō, tsòòk·ket′·ō) *n.* skull cap worn by R.C. ecclesiastics, and differing in color according to rank of wearer. [It. *zucca*, a gourd].

zuc·chi·ni (zŏŏ·kē′·ni·) *n.* a long green-skinned squash [It. dim. of *zucca*, squash].

Zu·lu (zŏŏ′·lŏŏ) *n.* member of Bantu tribe of S. Africa; *a.* pert. to Zulus [Native].

zwie·back (swē′·bak, ·bák, swī′·bák)*n.* a dry crisp bread, usually sweetened, that has been baked, sliced and then toasted [G. = twice baked].

zyme (zīm) *n.* ferment; disease germ. **zymic** *a.* **zymogen** *n.* any substance producing an enzyme. **zymogenesis** *n.* **zymogenic** *a.* **zymoid** *a.* resembling ferment. **zymosis** *n.* fermentation. **zymotic** *a.* pert. to or caused by fermentation. **zymotically** *adv.* **zymotic disease,** infectious or contagious disease caused by germs introduced into body from without [Gk. *zumē*, leaven].

zy·mur·gy (zī′·mur·ji·) *n.* branch of chemistry dealing with fermentation process. [Gr. *zūme* leaven + *-ourgia*, working].

RULES OF SPELLING

The rules listed below are meant to guide you in spelling; but there are exceptions to these rules. The most common exceptions are noted.

Drop the silent "e" at the end of a word when adding a termination that begins with a vowel (*Ex: shade, shading; move, movable*). Exceptions: words ending in *ce* or *ge* before terminations beginning with *a* or *o* (*Ex: change, changeable; notice, noticeable*); where confusion would result (*Ex: dye, dyeing [dying]*).

Keep the silent "e" at the end of a word when adding a termination that begins with a consonant (*Ex: bare, bareness; hate, hateful*). Exceptions: *acknowledge, acknowledgment; whole, wholly.*

Repeat the final consonant at the end of a single syllable or last syllable accented word if it is preceded by a single vowel when adding a terminal beginning with a vowel (*Ex: hit, hitting; begin, beginning*).

Do not repeat the final consonant at the end of a word if it is preceded by a consonant, two vowels, or if the last syllable is unaccented when adding a terminal beginning with a vowel (*Ex: art, artful; troop, trooping; profit, profiting*).

Keep the double consonant at the end of a word when adding a terminal (*Ex: fall, falling; stiff, stiffen*). Exception: where the terminal begins with the same letter as the double consonant (*Ex: full, fully*).

Add "k" to words ending in "c" when adding a terminal beginning with *e, i,* or *y* (*Ex: picnic, picnicked; shellac, shellacking; panic, panicky*).

Drop one "e" of an "ee" ending when adding a terminal beginning with *e* (*Ex: agree, agreed*).

Change "ie" to "y" before adding the terminal *-ing* (*Ex: die, dying*).

Change "y" to "i" before adding a terminal other than *-ing* (*Ex: racy, raciest; twenty, twentieth*). Exceptions: where a vowel precedes the *y* (*Ex: gay, gayest*).

USE OF CAPITALS

Capitals (denotes capitalization of the first letter of the word) are used: (1) at the beginning of each sentence; (2) for proper names and adjectives derived from these names; (3) for words referring to the Deity; (4) for official and honorary titles; (5) at the beginning of every line of poetry; (6) for each important word in a title (book, magazine, etc.); (7) for the pronoun "I" and the exclamation "O"; (8) for the days of the week and the months of the year; (9) at the beginning of each quotation; (10) for special words.

USE OF PUNCTUATION MARKS

Period (.) Used: (1) at the end of a sentence that is not a question or explanation; (2) after abbreviations; and (3) to mark off decimals.

Question Mark (?) Used: (1) at the end of a sentence that asks a question; and (2) to denote something questionable.

Exclamation Mark (!) Used at the end of a strong exclamatory word, phrase, or sentence.

Comma (,) Used: (1) to separate words, phrases and clauses of a series; (2) to set off parenthetical expressions, non-restrictive clauses, transitional words or phrases, appositives, and nouns of direct address from the rest of the sentence; (3) to separate words in a date or address; (4) before a quotation; (5) to separate independent clauses, containing no commas, that are joined by a simple conjunction; (6) denote the omission of a word; and (7) after the salutation of an informal letter.

Semi-colon (;) Used: (1) to separate parts of a complex series; (2) to separate independent clauses not connected by co-ordinating conjunction, or which already contain one or more commas; and (3) where a comma would not afford the proper clarity.

Colon (:) Use (1) to introduce a formal direct quotation; (2) after the salutation of a business letter; and (3) to introduce a long series.

Dash (—) Used: (1) to show an interruption or change of thought or sense; (2) to denote omission of a word or part of a word; and (3) to introduce a repetitious phrase.

Hyphen (-) Used: (1) to break a word between syllables when the word must be divided between the end of one line and the beginning of another; (2) to divide certain compound words; (3) to divide words which would be otherwise confusing; and (4) after a prefix that is before a proper noun.

Parentheses (()) Used to set off words, phrases, clauses, or sentences which are in the text as comment or explanation.

Brackets ([]) Used: (1) to show editorial comment; and (2) as parentheses containing parentheses.

Apostrophe (') Used: (1) to indicate possession; and (2) to replace the missing letters in a contraction.

Quotation marks (" ") Used: (1) to enclose direct quotations [quotations within quotations are enclosed by single quotation marks (' ')]; (2) to indicate titles of plays, books, etc.; and (3) to indicate the opposite meaning of the word used.

WEIGHTS AND MEASURES

Troy Weight
Used for weighing gold, silver and jewels.

3.086 grains = 1 carat.   20 pwts. = 1 ounce.
24 grains = 1 pwt.   12 ounces = 1 pound.

Apothecaries' Weight
The ounce and pound in this are the same as in troy weight.

20 grains = 1 scruple.   8 drams = 1 ounce.
3 scruples = 1 dram.   12 ounces = 1 pound.

Avoirdupois Weight
$27^{11}\!/_{32}$ grains = 1 dram. 4 quarters = 1 cwt.
16 drams = 1 ounce.   2,000 lbs. = 1 short ton.
16 ounces = 1 pound.   2,240 lbs. = 1 long ton.
25 pounds = 1 quarter.

Dry Measure
2 pints = 1 quart.   4 pecks = 1 bushel.
8 quarts = 1 peck.   36 bushels = 1 chaldron.

Liquid Measure
4 ounces = 1 gill.   4 quarts = 1 gallon.
4 gills = 1 pint. $31\frac{1}{2}$ gallons = 1 barrel.
2 pints = 1 quart.   2 barrels = 1 hogshead.

Time Measure
60 seconds = 1 minute. 24 hours = 1 day.
60 minutes = 1 hour.   7 days = 1 week.
28, 29, 30 or 31 days = 1 calendar month.
365 days = 1 year.   366 days = 1 leap year.

Linear Measure
12 inches = 1 foot.   40 rods = 1 furlong.
3 feet = 1 yard.   8 furlongs = 1 sta. mile.
$5\frac{1}{2}$ yards = 1 rod.   3 miles = 1 league.

Cloth Measure
$2\frac{1}{4}$ inches = 1 nail.   4 quarters = 1 yard.
4 nails = 1 quarter.

Square Measure
144 sq. inches = 1 sq. ft.   40 sq. rds. = 1 rood.
9 sq. ft. = 1 sq. yard.   4 roods = 1 acre.
$30\frac{1}{4}$ sq. yds. = 1 sq. rd.   640 acres = 1 sq. mile.

Surveyors' Measure
7.92 inches = 1 link.   4 rds. = 1 chain.
25 links = 1 rod.
10 sq. chains or 160 sq. rods = 1 acre.
640 acres = 1 sq. mile.
36 sq. miles (6 smiles sq.) = 1 township.

Cubic Measure
1,728 cu. in. = 1 cu. ft. 128 c. f. = 1 cord (wood)
27 cubic ft. = 1 cu. yd. 40 c. f. $\frac{1}{4}$ 1 ton (shpg.)
2,150.42 cubic inches = 1 standard bushel.
231 cubic inches = 1 standard gallon.
1 cubic ft. = about $\frac{4}{5}$ of a bushel.

pwt = pennyweight.   cwt = hundredweight.   sta = statute.

METRIC EQUIVALENTS

Linear Measure
1 centimeter = 0.3937 in.
1 decimeter = 3,937 in. = 0.328 feet.
1 meter = 39.37 inches = 1.0936 yards.
1 dekameter = 1.9844 rods.
1 kilometer = 0.62137 mile.
1 in. = 2.54 centimeters.
1 ft. = 3.048 decimeters.
1 yd. = 0.9144 meter.
1 rod = 0.5029 dekameter.
1 mile = 1.6093 kilometers.

Square Measure
1 sq. centimeter = 0.1550 sq. in.
1 sq. decimeter = 0.1076 sq. ft.
1 sq. meter = 1.196 sq. yds.
1 are = 3.954 sq. rds.
1 sq. inch = 6.452 sq. centimeters.
1 sq. ft. = 9.2903 sq. decimeters.
1 sq. yd. = 0.8361 sq. meter
1 sq. rd. = 0.2529 are.

1 hectare = 2.47 acres.
1 sq. kilometer = 0.386 sq. m.
1 acre = 0.4047 hectare.
1 sq. m. = 2.59 square kilometers.

Weights
1 gram = 0.03527 oz.
1 kilogram = 2.2046 lbs.
1 metric ton = 1.1023 English ton.
1 oz. = 28.35 grams.
1 lb. = 0.4536 kilogram.
1 English ton = 0.9072 metric ton.

Approximate Metric Equivalents
1 decimeter = 4 inches.
1 meter = 1.1 yards.
1 kilometer = $\frac{5}{8}$ of a mile.
1 hectare = $2\frac{1}{2}$ acres.
1 stere. or cu. meter = $\frac{1}{4}$ of a cord.
1 liter = 1.06 qts. liquid, 0.9 qt. dry.
1 hektoiler = $2\frac{1}{2}$ bushels.
1 kilogram = $2\frac{1}{5}$ lbs.
1 metric ton = 2,200 lbs.

KITCHEN WEIGHTS, MEASURES

Usual Weights and Measures
1 tablespoonful = 1 fl. ounce
4 large tablespoonsful = $\frac{1}{2}$ gill
1 teacup = 1 gill
1 common sized tumbler = $\frac{1}{2}$ pint
2 cups = 1 pint
2 pints = 1 quart
1 tablespoonful = $\frac{1}{2}$ ounce
1 large wine glass = 2 ounces
8 quarts = 1 peck
4 cups flour = 1 pound
2 cups solid butter = 1 pound
4 quarts = 1 gallon
2 cups granulated sugar = 1 pound
3 cups cornmeal = 1 pound
$2\frac{2}{3}$ cups brown sugar = 1 pound
2 cups solid meat = 1 pound
$2\frac{2}{3}$ cups powdered sugar = 1 pound
16 ounces = 1 pound
2 tablespoons butter, sugar, salt = 1 ounce
4 tablespoons flour = 1 ounce
16 tablespoonsful = 1 cupful
60 drops = 1 teaspoonful
8 saltspoonsful = 1 teaspoonful
3 teaspoonsful = 1 tablespoonful
4 tablespoonsful = $\frac{1}{4}$ cupful
1 cup shelled almonds = $\frac{1}{4}$ pound
$\frac{1}{4}$ pound cornstarch = 1 cupful

Approximate Cup Measures
1 cup granulated sugar	= $\frac{1}{2}$ pound
1 cup butter	= $\frac{1}{2}$ pound
1 cup lard	= $\frac{1}{2}$ pound
1 cup flour	= $\frac{1}{4}$ pound
1 cup rice	= $\frac{1}{2}$ pound
1 cup cornmeal	= 5 ounces
1 cup raisins (stemmed)	= 6 ounces
1 cup currants (cleaned)	= 6 ounces
1 cup bread crumbs (stale)	= 2 ounces
1 cup chopped meat	= $\frac{1}{2}$ pound
3 teaspoons	= 1 tablespoon
$\frac{1}{2}$ fluid ounce	= 1 tablespoon
16 tablespoons	= 1 cup
2 gills	= 1 cup
$\frac{1}{2}$ liquid pint	= 1 cup
8 fluid ounces	= 1 cup
1 liquid pint	= 2 cups
16 fluid ounces	= 2 cups

PRESIDENTS OF THE UNITED STATES

Name (and party)	State of Birth	Born	Term	Died
George Washington (F)	Va.	1732	1789-97	1799
John Adams (F)	Mass.	1735	1797-1801	1826
Thomas Jefferson (D-R)	Va.	1743	1801-09	1826
James Madison (D-R)	Va.	1751	1809-17	1836
James Monroe (D-R)	Va.	1758	1817-25	1831
John Quincy Adams (D-R)	Mass.	1767	1825-29	1848
Andrew Jackson (D)	S.C.	1767	1829-37	1845
Martin Van Buren (D)	N.Y.	1782	1837-41	1862
William Henry Harrison (W)	Va.	1773	1841	1841
John Tyler (W)	Va.	1790	1841-45	1862
James Knox Polk (D)	N.C.	1795	1845-49	1849
Zachary Taylor (W)	Va.	1784	1849-50	1850
Millard Fillmore (W)	N.Y.	1800	1850-53	1874
Franklin Pierce (D)	N.H.	1804	1853-57	1869
James Buchanan (D)	Pa.	1791	1857-61	1868
Abraham Lincoln (R)	Ky.	1809	1861-65	1865
Andrew Johnson (R)	N.C.	1808	1865-69	1875
Ulysses Simpson Grant (R)	Ohio	1822	1869-77	1885
Rutherford Birchard Hayes (R)	Ohio	1822	1877-81	1893
James Abram Garfield (R)	Ohio	1831	1881	1881
Chester Alan Arthur (R)	Vt.	1830	1881-85	1886
Grover Cleveland (D)	N.J.	1837	1885-89	1908
Benjamin Harrison (R)	Ohio	1833	1889-93	1901
Grover Cleveland (D)	N.J.	1837	1893-97	1908
William McKinley (R)	Ohio	1843	1897-1901	1901
Theodore Roosevelt (R)	N.Y.	1858	1901-1909	1919
William Howard Taft (R)	Ohio	1857	1909-13	1930
Woodrow Wilson (D)	Va.	1856	1913-21	1924
Warren Gamaliel Harding (R)	Ohio	1865	1921-23	1923
Calvin Coolidge (R)	Vt.	1872	1923-29	1933
Herbert Clark Hoover (R)	Iowa	1874	1923-33	1965
Franklin Delano Roosevelt (D)	N.Y.	1882	1933-45	1945
Harry S. Truman (D)	Mo.	1884	1945-53	1972
Dwight David Eisenhower (R)	Tex.	1890	1953-61	1969
John F. Kennedy (D)	Mass.	1917	1961-63	1963
Lyndon B. Johnson (D)	Tex.	1908	1963-69	1973
Richard M. Nixon (R)	Calif.	1913	1969-74 (r)	
Gerald R. Ford (R)	Nebr.	1913	1974-77	
James Earl Carter, Jr. (D)	Ga.	1924	1977-	

VICE-PRESIDENTS OF THE UNITED STATES

Name (and party)	State of Birth	Born	Term	Died
John Adams (F)	Mass.	1735	1789-97	1826
Thomas Jefferson (D-R)	Va.	1743	1797-1801	1826
Aaron Burr (R)	N.J.	1756	1801-05	1836
George Clinton (R)	N.Y.	1739	1805-12	1812
Elbridge Gerry (R)	Mass.	1744	1813-14	1814
Daniel D. Tompkins (R)	N.Y.	1774	1817-25	1825
John U. Calhoun (R)	S.C.	1782	1825-32	1850
Martin Van Buren (D)	N.Y.	1782	1833-37	1862
Richard M. Johnson (D)	Ky.	1780	1837-41	1850
John Tyler (W)	Va.	1790	1841	1862
George M. Dallas (D)	Pa.	1792	1845-49	1864
Millard Fillmore (W)	N.Y.	1800	1849-50	1874
William R. King (D)	N.C.	1786	1853	1853
John C. Breckinridge (D)	Ky.	1821	1857-61	1875
Hannibal Hamlin (R)	Me.	1809	1861-65	1891
Andrew Johnson (R)	N.C.	1808	1865	1875
Schuyler Colfax (R)	N.Y.	1823	1869-73	1885
Henry Wilson (R)	N.H.	1812	1873-75	1875
William A. Wheeler (R)	N.Y.	1819	1877-81	1887
Chester A. Arthur (R)	Vt.	1830	1881	1886
Thomas A. Hendricks (D)	Ohio	1819	1885	1885
Levi P. Morton (R)	Vt.	1824	1889-93	1920
Adlai E. Stevenson (D)	Ky.	1835	1893-97	1914
Garrett A. Hobart (R)	N.J.	1844	1897-99	1899
Theodore Roosevelt (R)	N.Y.	1858	1901	1919
Charles W. Fairbanks (R)	Ohio	1852	1905-09	1918
James S. Sherman (R)	N.Y.	1855	1909-12	1912
Thomas R. Marshall (D)	Ind.	1854	1913-21	1925
Calvin Coolidge (R)	Vt.	1872	1921-23	1933
Charles G. Dawes (R)	Ohio	1865	1925-29	1951
Charles Curtis (R)	Kan.	1860	1929-33	1936
John N. Garner (D)	Tex.	1869	1933-41	1967
Henry A. Wallace (D)	Ia.	1888	1941-45	1965
Harry S. Truman (D)	Mo.	1884	1945	1972
Alben W. Barkley (D)	Ky.	1877	1949-53	1956
Richard M. Nixon (R)	Calif.	1913	1953-61	
Lyndon B. Johnson (D)	Tex.	1908	1961-63	1973
Hubert H. Humphrey (D)	S.D.	1911	1965-69	
Spiro T. Agnew (R)	Md.	1918	1969-73 (r)	
Gerald R. Ford (R)	Nebr.	1913	1973-1974	
Nelson A. Rockefeller (R)	Me.	1908	1974-77	
Walter F. Mondale (D)	Minn.	1928	1977-	

F—Federalist; D—Democratic; R—Republican; W—Whig; (r)— resigned

CHIEF JUSTICES OF THE UNITED STATES SUPREME COURT

Name	State of Birth	Born	Term	Died
John Jay	N.Y.	1745	1789–95	1829
John Rutledge	S.C.	1739	1795	1800
Oliver Ellsworth	Conn.	1745	1796–99	1807
John Marshall	Va	1755	1801–35	1835
Roger B. Taney	Md	1777	1836–64	1864
Salmon P. Chase	Ohio	1808	1864–73	1873
Morrison R. Waite	Ohio	1816	1874–88	1888
Melville W. Fuller	Ill.	1833	1888–1910	1910
Edward D. White	La	1845	1910–21	1921
William H. Taft	Conn.	1857	1921–30	1930
Charles E. Hughes	N.Y.	1862	1930–41	1948
Harlan F. Stone	N.Y.	1872	1941–46	1946
Fred M. Vinson	Ky.	1890	1946–53	1953
Earl Warren	Calif.	1891	1953-68	1974
Warren E. Burger	Minn.	1907	1970	

DIMENSIONS OF THE WORLD

Equatorial Diameter	7,926.68	Miles
Polar Diameter	7,899.99	Miles
Difference	26.69	Miles
Mean Diameter	7,918.00	Miles
Equatorial Circumference	24,902.37	Miles
Meridional Circumference	24,860.44	Miles
Area of Surface	196,950,284	Square Miles
Water Area	139,950,284	Square Miles
Land Area	57,000,000	Square Miles
Volume of Land	29,300,000	Cubic Miles
Volume of Water	320,000,000	Cubic Miles

DIMENSIONS OF CONTINENTS.

Africa	11,500,000	Square Miles
Asia	17,000,000	Square Miles
Europe	3,750,000	Square Miles
North America	8,000,000	Square Miles
Oceania	4,000,000	Square Miles
Polar Regions	6,205,000	Square Miles
South America	6,800,000	Square Miles

The latest estimates of the earth's area place the fertile regions at 33,000,000 square miles, steppes at 19,000,000 miles; deserts at 5,000,000 square miles.

Asia, the largest continent, is about 6,000 miles from East to West, and over 5,300 miles from North to South. Africa is 5,000 miles from North to South. Europe is 2,400 miles from North to South, and 3,300 miles from East to West. South America is 4,600 miles from North to South and 3,200 miles from East to West. North America is 4,900 miles from North to South and over 4,000 miles from East to West.

AREAS AND DEPTHS OF THE OCEAN

Oceans	Greatest Depth (Feet).	Area (Square Miles)
Pacific	30,000	68,634,000
Atlantic	27,366	41,321,000
Indian	18,582	29,340,000
Antarctic	25,200	7,500,000
Arctic	9,000	4,000,000

State	Land Area (Sq. Miles)	July 1, 1960 Population	Capital	State	Land Area (Sq. Miles)	July 1, 1960 Population	Capital
Alabama	51,078	3,226,740	Montgomery	Missouri	69,270	4,319,813	Jefferson City
Alaska	571,065	226,167	Juneau	Montana	146,316	647,767	Helena
Arizona	113,580	1,302,161	Phoenix	Nebraska	76,653	1,411,330	Lincoln
Arkansas	52,725	1,786,272	Little Rock	Nevada	109,802	285,278	Carson City
California	156,803	15,717,204	Sacramento	New Hampshire	9,024	606,921	Concord
Colorado	103,967	1,753,947	Denver	New Jersey	7,522	6,066,782	Trenton
Connecticut	4,899	2,535,234	Hartford	New Mexico	121,511	951,023	Santa Fe
Delaware	1,978	446,292	Dover	New York	47,929	16,782,304	Albany
Dist. of Columbia	61	763,956		North Carolina	49,142	4,556,155	Raleigh
				North Dakota	70,054	632,446	Bismarck
Florida	54,262	4,051,560	Tallahassee	Ohio	41,122	9,328,284	Columbus
Georgia	58,518	3,943,116	Atlanta	Oklahoma	69,283	2,328,284	Oklahoma City
Hawaii	6,420	632,772	Honolulu	Oregon	96,350	1,768,687	Salem
Idaho	82,808	667,191	Boise	Pennsylvania	45,045	11,319,366	Harrisburg
Illinois	55,947	10,081,158	Springfield	Rhode Island	1,058	859,488	Providence
Indiana	36,205	4,662,498	Indianapolis	South Carolina	30,594	2,382,594	Columbia
Iowa	55,985	2,757,537	Des Moines	South Dakota	76,536	680,514	Pierre
Kansas	82,113	2,178,611	Topeka	Tennessee	41,961	3,568,089	Nashville
Kentucky	40,109	3,038,156	Frankfort	Texas	263,644	9,579,677	Austin
Louisiana	45,177	3,257,022	Baton Rouge	Utah	82,346	890,627	Salt Lake City
Maine	31,040	949,265	Augusta	Vermont	9,278	389,881	Montpelier
Maryland	9,887	3,100,689	Annapolis	Virginia	39,899	3,966,949	Richmond
Massachusetts	7,907	5,148,578	Boston	Washington	66,977	2,853,214	Olympia
Michigan	57,022	7,823,194	Lansing	West Virginia	24,090	1,860,421	Charleston
Minnesota	80,009	3,413,864	St. Paul	Wisconsin	54,715	3,951,777	Madison
Mississippi	47,420	2,178,141	Jackson	Wyoming	97,506	330,066	Cheyenne

LARGEST CITIES OF THE UNITED STATES
1960 Census—35,000 and Over

ALABAMA
Birmingham....340,887
Gadsden.........58,088
Huntsville......72,365
Mobile.........202,779
Montgomery....134,393
Prichard........47,371
Tuscaloosa......63,370
ALASKA
Anchorage........44,237
ARIZONA
Phoenix.........439,170
Tucson.........212,892
ARKANSAS
Fort Smith......52,991
Little Rock....107,813
N. Little Rock....58,032
Pine Bluff........44,037
CALIFORNIA
Alameda.........61,316
Alhambra........54,807
Anaheim........104,184
Arcadia........41,005
Bakersfield......56,848
Bellflower......44,846
Berkeley.......111,268
Buena Park.....46,401
Burbank........90,155
Chula Vista.....42,034
Compton........71,812
Concord........36,208
Costa Mesa......37,550
Daly City.......44,791
Downey.........82,505
El Cajon........37,618
Fremont........43,790
Fresno.........133,929
Fullerton........56,180
Gardena........35,943
Garden Grove....84,238
Glendale.......119,442
Hayward........72,700
Inglewood.......63,390

Lakewood........67,126
Long Beach....344,168
Los Angeles....2,479,015
Modesto........36,585
Monterey Park....37,821
Norwalk........88,739
Oakland.......367,548
Ontario........46,617
Oxnard.........40,265
Palo Alto........52,287
Pasadena.......116,407
Pico Rivera......49,150
Pomona........67,157
Redondo Beach....46,986
Redwood City....46,290
Richmond........71,854
Riverside.......84,332
Sacramento.....191,667
San Bernardino....91,922
San Diego......573,224
San Francisco....742,855
San Jose......204,106
San Leandro.....65,962
San Mateo......69,870
Santa Ana.....100,350
Santa Barbara....58,786
Santa Clara.....58,880
Santa Monica....83,249
South Gate......53,831
S. San Francisco..39,418
Stockton........86,321
Sunnyvale......52,899
Torrance.......100,991
Vallejo.........60,877
West Covina.....50,645
COLORADO
Aurora.........45,548
Boulder.........37,718
Colorado Springs..70,194
Denver.........493,887
Pueblo.........91,181
CONNECTICUT
Bridgeport.....156,748
Bristol.........45,499

Hartford.......162,178
Meriden........51,850
Millford........41,662
New Britain.....82,201
New Haven.....152,048
Norwalk........67,775
Norwich........38,506
Stamford.......92,713
Waterbury.....102,130
DELAWARE
Wilmington.....95,827
District of Columbia
Washington.....763,956
FLORIDA
Daytona Beach...37,395
Fort Lauderdale..83-648
Hialeah........66,972
Hollywood......35,237
Jacksonville...201,030
Lakeland........41,350
Miami.........291,688
Miami Beach.....63,145
Orlando........88,135
Pensacola......56,752
St. Petersburg..181,298
Tallahassee.....48,174
Tampa.........274,970
West Palm Beach.56-208
GEORGIA
Albany.........55,890
Atlanta........487,455
Augusta........70,626
Columbus......146,779
East Point......35,633
Macon.........69,764
Savannah......149,245
HAWAII
Honolulu.......294,179
ILLINOIS
Alton.........43,047
Aurora........63,715
Belleville......37,264
Berwyn........54,224
Bloomington.....36,271

Champaign......49,583
Chicago......3,550,404
Cicero.........69,130
Danville........41,856
Decatur........78,004
East St. Louis....81,714
Elgin..........49,447
Elmhurst........36,991
Evanston........79,283
Galesburg.......37,243
Granite City.....40,073
Joliet..........66,780
Moline.........42,705
Oak Park.......61,093
Peoria.........103,162
Quincy.........43,793
Rockford.......126,706
Rock Island.....51,863
Skokie.........59,364
Springfield......83,271
Waukegan.......55,719
INDIANA
Anderson........49,061
East Chicago....57,669
Elkhart.........40,274
Evansville......141,843
Fort Wayne.....161,776
Gary..........178,320
Hammond......111,698
Indianapolis....476,258
Kokomo........47,197
Lafayette.......42,330
Marion.........37,854
Michigan City....36,653
Muncie.........68,603
New Albany.....37,812
Richmond.......44,149
South Bend.....132,445
Terre Haute.....72,500
IOWA
Cedar Rapids....92,035
Council Bluffs....59,361
Davenport......88,981
Des Moines.....208,892

Dubuque..........56,606	Duluth..........106,884	White Plains.....50,485	Columbia.........97,433
Sioux City.......89,159	Minneapolis.....482,872	Yonkers.........190,634	Greenville.......66,181
Waterloo.........71,755	Richfield........42,523	**NORTH CAROLINA**	Spartanburg......44,352
KANSAS	Rochester........40,663	Asheville........60,192	**SOUTH DAKOTA**
Hutchinson......37,574	St. Louis Park....43,310	Charlotte.......201,564	Rapid City.......42,399
Kansas City....121,901	St. Paul........313,411	Durham..........78,302	Sioux Falls......65,466
Salina...........43,202	**MISSISSIPPI**	Fayetteville......47,106	**TENNESSEE**
Topeka.........119,484	Biloxi...........44,053	Gastonia........37,276	Chattanooga....130,009
Wichita........254,698	Greenville.......41,502	Greensboro.....119,574	Knoxville.......111,827
KENTUCKY	Jackson.........144,422	High Point......62,063	Memphis.......497,524
Lexington.......62,810	Meridian........49,374	Raleigh.........93,931	Nashville.......170,874
Louisville......390,639	**MISSOURI**	Wilmington......44,013	**TEXAS**
Owensboro.......42,471	Columbia........36,650	Winston-Salem...111,135	Abilene.........90,368
LOUISIANA	Florissant.......38,166	**NORTH DAKOTA**	Amarillo.......137,969
Alexandria.......40,279	Independence.....62,328	Fargo...........46,662	Arlington........44,775
Baton Rouge....152,419	Joplin..........38,958	**OHIO**	Austin.........186,545
Lafayette........40,400	Kansas City.....475,539	Akron..........290,351	Beaumont......119,175
Lake Charles.....63,392	St. Joseph.......79,673	Canton.........113,631	Brownsville......48,040
Monroe..........52,219	St. Louis.......750,026	Cincinnati.......502,550	Corpus Christi..167,690
New Orleans....627,525	Springfield.......95,865	Cleveland......876,050	Dallas.........679,684
Shreveport.....164,372	University City...51,249	Cleveland Heights.61,813	El Paso........276,687
MAINE	**MONTANA**	Columbus.......471,316	Fort Worth.....356,268
Bangor..........48,912	Billings.........52,851	Dayton.........262,332	Galveston.......67,175
Lewiston........40,804	Great Falls......55,357	East Cleveland...37,991	Garland.........38,501
Portland.........72,566	**NEBRASKA**	Elyria..........43,782	Harlingen........41,207
MARYLAND	Lincoln........128,521	Euclid..........62,998	Houston.......938,219
Baltimore......939,024	Omaha.........301,598	Garfield Heights..38,455	Irving..........45,985
Hagerstown......36,660	**NEVADA**	Hamilton........72,354	Laredo.........60,678
MASSACHUSETTS	Las Vegas.......64,405	Kettering.......54,462	Longview........40,050
Beverly.........36,108	Reno...........51,470	Lakewood.......66,154	Lubbock.......128,691
Boston.........697,197	**NEW HAMPSHIRE**	Lima...........51,037	Midland.........62,625
Brockton........72,813	Manchester......88,282	Lorain..........68,932	Odessa.........80,338
Cambridge......107,716	Nashua.........39,096	Mansfield........47,325	Pasadena........58,757
Chicopee........61,553	**NEW JERSEY**	Marion..........37,079	Port Arthur......66,667
Everett..........43,544	Atlantic City.....59,544	Middletown......42,115	San Angelo......58,815
Fall River.......99,942	Bayonne.........74,215	Newark..........41,790	San Antonio....587,718
Fitchburg.......42,021	Belleville........35,005	Parma..........82,834	Tyler..........51,230
Haverhill........46,346	Bloomfield.......51,876	Shaker Heights...36,460	Waco...........97,808
Holyoke.........52,689	Camden........117,159	Springfield......82,723	Wichita Falls....101,724
Lawrence........70,933	Clifton.........82,084	Toledo.........318,003	**UTAH**
Lowell..........92,107	East Orange......77,259	Warren.........59,648	Ogden.........70,197
Lynn...........94,478	Elizabeth.......107,698	Youngstown.....166,689	Provo...........36,041
Malden..........57,676	Fair Lawn.......36,421	Zanesville.......39,077	Salt Lake City...180,454
Medford.........64,971	Hoboken.........48,441	**OKLAHOMA**	**VERMONT**
New Bedford....102,477	Irvington........59,379	Enid............38,859	Burlington.......35,531
Pittsfield........57,879	Jersey City.....276,101	Lawton..........61,697	**VIRGINIA**
Quincy..........87,409	Kearny.........37,472	Midwest City.....36,058	Alexandria.......91,023
Revere..........40,080	Linden..........39,931	Muskogee........38,059	Danville.........46,577
Salem...........39,211	Montclair........43,129	Oklahoma City..324,253	Hampton.........89,258
Somerville.......94,697	Newark........405,220	Tulsa..........261,685	Lynchburg.......54,790
Springfield.....174,463	New Brunswick...40,139	**OREGON**	Newport News...113,662
Taunton.........41,132	Orange..........35,789	Eugene.........50,977	Norfolk........305,872
Waltham.........55,413	Passaic.........53,963	Portland.......372,676	Petersburg......26,750
Worcester......186,587	Paterson.......143,663	Salem..........40,142	Portsmouth.....114,773
MICHIGAN	Perth Amboy.....38,007	**PENNSYLVANIA**	Richmond......219,958
Allen Park.......37,052	Plainfield........45,330	Allentown......108,347	Roanoke.........97,110
Ann Arbor......67,340	Trenton........114,167	Altoona.........69,407	**WASHINGTON**
Battle Creek.....44,169	Union City......52,180	Bethlehem.......75,408	Everett.........40,304
Bay City........53,604	Vineland........37,685	Chester.........63,658	Seattle........557,087
Dearborn......112,007	West New York...37,685	Erie...........138,440	Spokane.......181,608
Detroit.......1,670,144	West Orange.....39,895	Harrisburg.......79,697	Tacoma.......147,979
East Detroit......45,756	**NEW MEXICO**	Johnstown.......53,949	Yakima.........43,284
Flint..........196,940	Albuquerque....201,189	Lancaster.......61,055	**WEST VIRGINIA**
Grand Rapids...177,313	Roswell.........39,593	McKeesport......42,489	Charleston.......85,796
Highland Park....38,063	Santa Fe........34,676	New Castle......44,790	Huntington......83,627
Inkster.........39,097	**NEW YORK**	Norristown......38,924	Parkersburg......44,797
Jackson.........50,720	Albany.........129,726	Philadelphia...2,002,512	Wheeling........53,400
Kalamazoo......82,089	Auburn.........35,249	Pittsburgh......604,332	**WISCONSIN**
Lansing........107,807	Binghamton......75,941	Reading.........98,177	Appleton........48,411
Lincoln Park.....53,933	Buffalo........532,759	Scranton.......111,443	Eau Claire.......37,987
Livonia.........66,703	Elmira..........46,517	Wilkes-Barre.....63,551	Green Bay.......62,888
Muskegon........46,485	Jamestown.......41,818	Williamsport.....41,967	Janesville.......35,164
Oak Park........36,632	Mt. Vernon......76,010	York...........54,504	Kenosha.........67,899
Pontiac.........82,233	New Rochelle.....76,812	**RHODE ISLAND**	La Crosse.......47,574
Port Huron.......36,084	New York City.7,781,984	Cranston........66,767	Madison........126,706
Roseville........50,195	Niagara Falls....102,394	East Prov dence..41,955	Milwaukee......741,324
Royal Oak.......80,612	Poughkeepsie.....38,330	Newport.........47,049	Oshkosh........45,110
Saginaw.........98,265	Rochester.......318,611	Pawtucket.......81,001	Racine.........89,144
S. Clair Shores....76,657	Rome...........51,646	Providence......207,498	Sheboygan.......45,747
Warren.........89,246	Schenectady......81,682	Warwick.........68,504	Wauwatosa......56,923
Wyandotte.......43,519	Syracuse.......216,038	Woonsocket......47,080	West Allis.......68,157
Wyoming.........45,829	Troy...........67,492	**SOUTH CAROLINA**	**WYOMING**
MINNESOTA	Utica..........100,410	Anderson........41,316	Casper.........38,930
Bloomington.....50,498	Valley Stream....38,629	Charleston.......65,925	Cheyenne.......43,505

Motions arranged in their order of precedence as they relate to each other.

Modifying or Amending. Rules

To amend, substitute, or to divide
the question ....K

To refer to committee.

To commit (or recommit)............D

Deferring Action.

To postpone to a fixed time..........C

To lay on the table..............A E G

Suppressing or extending debate.

For the previous question........A E M

To limit, or close debate...........A M

To extend limits of debate............A

Supressing the question.

Objection to consideration.....A H M N

To postpone indefinitely............D H

To lay upon the table............A E G

Raising a question the second time.

To reconsider debatable question..E F I

To reconsider undebatable
question ....A E F I

Orders, rules, etc.

For the orders of the day......A E H N

To make subject a special order......M

To amend the rules.................M

To suspend the rules.........A E F M

To take up a question out of order..A E

To take from the table.........A E G

Touching priority of business........A

Questions of privilege.

Asking leave to continue speaking
after in decorum...................A

Appeal from chair's decision
touching indecorum ....A E H L

Appeal from chair's decision
generally ....E H L

Question upon reading of papers.....A E

Adjournment.

To adjourn, or to take a recess,
without limitation ....A E F

To fix the time at which to adjourn....B

RULES

RULE A. Undebatable, but remarks may be tacitly allowed.

RULE B. Undebatable if another question is before the assembly.

RULE C. Limited debate allowed on propriety of postponement only.

RULE D. Opens the main question to debate. Motions not so marked do not allow of reference to main question.

RULE E. Cannot be amended. Motion to adjourn can be amended when there is no other business before the house.

RULE F. Cannot be reconsidered.

RULE G. An affirmative vote cannot be reconsidered.

RULE H. In order when another has the floor.

RULE I. A motion to reconsider may be moved and entered when another has the floor, but the business then before the house may not be set aside. This motion can only be entertained when made by one who voted originally with the prevailing side. When called up it takes precedence of all others which may come up, excepting only motions relating to adjournment.

RULE K. A motion to amend an amendment cannot be amended.

RULE L. When an appeal from the chair's decision results in a tie vote, the chair is sustained.

RULE M. Requires a two-thirds vote unless special rules have been enacted.

RULE N. Does not require to be seconded.

GENERAL RULES

No motion is open for discussion until it has been stated by the chair.

The maker of a motion cannot modify it or withdraw it after it has been stated by the chair except by general consent.

Only one reconsideration is permitted.

A motion to adjourn, to lay on the table, or to take from the table, cannot be renewed unless some other motion has intervened.

On motion to strike out the word, "Shall the words stand part of the motion?" Unless a majority sustains, the words are struck out.

On motion for previous question, the form to be observed is, "Shall the main question be now put?" This if carried, ends debate.

On an appeal from the chair, "Shall the decision be sustained as the ruling of the house?" The chair is generally sustained.

On motion for orders of the day, "Will the house now proceed to the orders of the day?" This, if carried, supersedes intervening motions.

On objection raised to considering questions, "Shall the question be considered?" Objections may be made before debate has commenced, but not subsequently.

1. Division of words should be minimized in leaded matter and avoided in double-leaded matter.

2. Wordbreaks should be avoided at the ends of more than two consecutive lines.

3. In centerheads and in display lines making two lines, wordbreaks should be avoided. The first line should be centered and set as full as possible, but it is not set to fill the measure by unduly wide spacing. If unavoidable, flush sideheads may be divided at the end of a line, but lines are not set ragged to avoid a division.

4. The final word of a last full line of a paragraph should not be divided.

5. Words should preferably be divided according to pronunciation; and to avoid mispronunciation, they should be divided so that the part of the word left at the end of the line will suggest the whole word: *capac-ity*, not *capa-city*; *extraor-dinary*, not *extra-ordinary*; *Wednes-day*, not *Wed-nesday*; *deteri-orate*, not *deter-iorate*; *physi-cal*, not *phys-ical*; *service-man*, not *serv-iceman*.

6. Although WORD DIVISION lists beginning and ending one-letter syllables for pronunciation purposes, under no circumstances are words to be divided on a single letter (e.g., *usu-al-ly*, not *u-su-al-ly*; *imag-i-nary*, not *i-mag-i-nar-y*).

7. Division of short words (of five or fewer letters) should be avoided; two-letter divisions, including the carry-over of two-letter endings (*ed, el, en, er, es, et, fy, ic, in, le, ly, or,* and *ty*), should also be avoided. In narrow measure, however, a sounded suffix or syllable of two letters may be carried over—only if unavoidable; e.g., *re-lat-ed*; not *cancel-ed*. (See rule 10.)

8. Words of two syllables are split at the end of the first syllable: *dis-pelled, con-quered*; words of three or more syllables, with a choice of division possible, divide preferably on the vowel: *particu-lar, sepa-rate*.

9. In words with short prefixes, divide on the prefix; e.g., *ac, co, de, dis, ex, in, non, on, pre, pro, re, un,* etc. (e.g., *non-essential*, not *nones-sential; pre-selected*, not *prese-lected*).

If possible, prefixes and combining forms of more than one syllable are preserved intact: *anti, infra, macro, micro, multi, over, retro, semi,* etc. (e.g., *anti-monopoly*, not *antimo-nopoly; over-optimistic*, not *overop-timistic*). (For chemical prefixes, see rule 30.)

10. *Words ending in* -er.—Although two-letter carryovers are to be avoided (rule 7), many -er words which are derived from comparatives (*coarse, coarser; sharp, sharper*) have been listed to prevent a wrong wordbreak; e.g., *coars-er*, not *coar-ser*.

Nouns ending in -er (*adviser, bracer, keeper, perceiver, reader*) derived from action verbs are also listed to prevent a wrong division; e.g., *perceiv-er*, not *percei-ver*.

Except in narrow measure and if unavoidable, the above -er words are not divided unless division can be made on a prefix; e.g., *per-ceiver*.

11. *Words ending in* -or.—Generally, -or words with a consonant preceding are divided before the preceding consonant; e.g., *advi-sor* (legal), *fabrica-tor, guaran-tor, interve-nor, simula-tor, tai-lor*; but *bail-or, bargain-or, con-sign-or, grant-or*.

12. The following suffixes are not divided: *ceous, cial, cient, cion, cious, scious, geous, gion, gious, sial, tial, tion, tious,* and *sion*.

13. The suffixes -able and -ible are usually carried over intact; but when the stem word loses its original form, these suffixes are divided according to pronunciation: *comfort-able, corrupt-ible, manage-able*; but *dura-ble, com-prehensi-ble*.

14. Words ending in -ing, with stress on the primary syllable, are preferably divided on the base word; e.g., *appoint-ing, combat-ing, danc-ing, engineer-ing, process-ing, program-ing, stencil-ing, trac-ing,* etc. However, present participles, such as *control-ling, forbid-ding, refer-ring,* with stress placed on the second syllable, divide between the doubled consonants (see also rule 16).

15. When the final consonant sound of a word belongs to a syllable ending with a silent vowel, the final consonant or consonants become part of the added suffix: *chuck-ling, han-dler, han-dling, crum-bling, twin-kled, twin-kling*; but *rollick-ing*.

16. When the addition of -ed, -er, -est, or of a similar ending, causes the doubling of a final consonant, the added consonant is carried over: *pit-ted, rob-ber, thin-nest, glad-den, control-lable, transmit-table*; but *bless-ed* (adj.), *dwell-er, gross-est*.

17. Words with doubled consonants are usually divided between these consonants: *clas-sic, ruf-fian, neces-sary, rebel-lion*; but *call-ing, mass-ing*.

18. If formation of a plural adds a syllable ending in an *s* sound, the plural ending should not be carried over by itself: *hor-ses, voi-ces*; but *church-es, cross-es*, thus not breaking the base word (see also rule 7).

19. The digraphs *ai, ck, dg, gh, gn, ng, oa, ph, sh, tch,* and *th* are not split.

20. Do not divide contractions: *doesn't, haven't*.

21. Solid compounds should preferably be divided between the members: *bar-keeper, hand-kerchief, proof-reader, humming-bird*.

22. Avoid a division which would add another hyphen to a hyphened compound: *court-martial*, not *court-mar-tial; tax-supported*, not *tax-sup-ported*.

23. A word of one syllable is not split: *tanned, shipped, quenched, through, chasm, prism*.

24. Two consonants preceded and followed by a vowel are divided on the first consonant: *abun-dant, advan-tage, struc-ture*; but *attend-ant, accept-ance, depend-ence*.

25. When two adjoining vowels are sounded separately, divide between them: *cre-ation, gene-alogy*.

26. In breaking homonyms, distinction should be given to their relative functions: *pro-ject* (v.), *proj-ect* (n.); *pro-duce* (v.), *prod-uce* (n.); *stran-ger* (n.), *strang-er* (comparative adjective); *rec-ollect* (recall), *re-collect* (collect again); but *proc-ess* (n., v.); *pro-test* (n., v.).

27. *Words ending in* -meter.—In the large group of words ending in -meter, distinction should be made between metric system terms and terms indicating a measuring instrument. When it is necessary to divide metric terms, preserve the combining form -meter; e.g., *centi-meter, deca-meter, hecto-meter, kilo-meter*. But measuring instruments divide after the *m: al-tim-e-ter, ba-rom-e-ter, mi-crom-e-ter, mul-tim-e-ter,* etc. Derivatives of these -meter terms follow the same form; e.g., *mul-tim-e-ter, mul-tim-e-try*.

For orthographic reasons, however, several measuring instruments do not lend themselves to the general rule; e.g., *flow-meter, flux-meter, gauss-meter, taxi-meter, torque-meter, volt-meter, water-meter, watt-meter,* etc.

28. *Foreign languages.*—Rules for word division in foreign languages, by language, are printed in the 1959 GPO Style Manual (unabridged), pages 376–476.

29. *Chemical formulas.*—In chemical formulas, the hyphen has an important function. If a break is unavoidable in a formula, division is preferably made after an original hyphen to avoid the introduction of a misleading hyphen. If impractical to break on a hyphen, division may be made after an

original comma, and no hyphen is added to indicate a runover. The following formula shows original hyphens and commas where division may be made. No letterspacing is used in a chemical formula, but to fill a line, a space is permitted on both sides of a hyphen.

$$1-(2,6,6\text{-trimethylcyclohex-}1\text{-en-}1\text{-yl})-3,7,12,16$$

30. *Chemical combining forms, prefixes, and suffixes.*—If possible, and subject to rules of good spacing, it is desirable to preserve as a unit such combining forms as follows:

aceto, anhydro, benzo, bromo, chloro, chromo, cincho, cyclo, dehydro, diazo, flavo, fluoro, glyco, hydroxy, iso, keto, methyl, naphtho, phospho, poly, silico, tetra, triazo.

The following suffixes are used in chemical printing. For patent and narrow measure composition, two-letter suffixes may be carried over.

al, an, ane, ase, ate, ene, ic, id, ide, in, ine, ite, ol, ole, on, one, ose, ous, oyl, yl, yne.

31. *Mineral elements.*—When it is necessary to break mineral constituents, division should preferably be made before a center period and beginning parenthesis, and after inferior figures following a closing parenthesis; but elements within parentheses are not separated. In cases of unavoidable breaks, a hyphen is not added to indicate a runover.

$$Mg(UO_2)_2(SiO_3)_2(OH)_2 \cdot 6H_2O$$

32. The em dash is not used at the beginning of any line of type, unless it is required before a credit line or signature, or in lieu of opening quotation marks in foreign languages. (See rules 9.51, 9.52, p. 138, 1959 GPO Style Manual.)

33. Neither periods nor asterisks used as an ellipsis are overrun alone at the end of a paragraph. If necessary, run over enough preceding lines to provide a short word or part of a word to accompany the ellipsis. If a runback is possible, subject to rules of good spacing and word division, this method may be adopted.

34. Abbreviations and symbols are not broken at the end of a line: *A.F. of L., A.T. & T., C. Cls. R., f.o.b., n.o.i.b.n., R. & D., r.p.m., WMAL.*

35. Figures of less than six digits, decimals, and closely connected combinations of figures and abbreviations should not be broken at the end of a line: *$15,000, 34,575, 0.31416, £8 4s. 7d., $10.25, 5,000 kw.-hr., A.D. 1952,*

9 p.m., 18° F., NW¼. If a break in six digits or over is unavoidable, divide on the comma, retain it, and use a hyphen.

36. Closely related abbreviations and initials in proper names and accompanying titles should not be separated, nor should titles, such as *Rev., Mr., Esq., Jr., 2d,* be separated from surnames.

37. Avoid dividing proper names, but if inescapable, follow general rules for word division.

38. Divisional and subdivisional paragraph reference signs and figures, such as *§18, section (a)(1), page 363(b),* should not be divided, nor should such references be separated from the matter to which they pertain.

In case of an unavoidable break in a lengthy reference (e.g., *7(B)(1)(a)(i)*), division will be made after elements in parentheses, and no hyphen is used.

39. In dates, do not divide the month and day, but the year may be carried over.

40. In case of an unavoidable break in a land-description symbol group at the end of a line, use no hyphen, and break after a fraction.

41. Avoid breaking longitude and latitude figures at the end of a line; space out the line instead. In case of an unavoidable break at end of line, use hyphen.

SYNONYMS
ANTONYMS
&
HOMONYMS

WEBSTER'S SYNONYMS ANTONYMS&HOMONYMS

DEFINITIONS

Synonyms—Words that have the same meaning.
Example: big, large.

Antonyms—Words that have opposite meanings.
Example: large, small.
Note: Antonyms appear in parentheses ( ) following the synonyms.

Homonyms—Words that sound alike, but are spelled differently and have different meanings.
Example: one, won.

A

abandon—leave, forsake, desert, renounce, cease, relinquish, discontinue, cast off, resign, retire, quit, forgo, forswear, depart from, vacate, surrender, abjure, repudiate. (*pursue, prosecute, undertake*)

abandoned—profligate, wicked, vicious, unprincipled, reprobate, incorrigible, sinful, graceless, demoralized, dissolute, depraved, bad, licentious, corrupt. (*virtuous, conscientious, correct, upright*)

abbreviate—shorten, reduce, abridge, contract, curtail, epitomize, condense, prune, compress. (*lengthen, prolong, extend, enlarge, produce, elongate*)

abdicate—abandon, relinquish, resign, surrender, vacate. (*retain, maintain, claim, occupy, assert*)

abet—aid, support, promote, countenance, uphold, assist, instigate, encourage, incite, advocate, sanction, subsidize, embolden. (*thwart, contradict, obstruct, oppose, baffle, confound, discourage, disapprove, disconcert, counteract, deter, dissuade, frustrate*)

abeyance—suspension, reservation, dormancy, expectation, intermission. (*revival, renewal, operation, resuscitation, action, enjoyment, possession*)

abhor—hate, abominate, detest, loathe, despise, dislike, eschew, nauseate. (*love, admire, enjoy*)

abide—dwell, stay, inhabit, continue, rest, tarry, lodge, reside, live, wait, sojourn, remain, expect, endure, tolerate, anticipate, confront, await, bear, face, watch. (*deport, migrate, move, journey, proceed, resist, mislike, forfend, avoid, shun, reject, abandon, forfeit*)

ability—power, cleverness, faculty, skill, capacity, talent, expertness, aptitude, dexterity, efficiency, competency, qualification. (*weakness, incapacity, imbecility, inability, unreadiness, maladroitness*)

abject—degraded, outcast, miserable, vile, pitiable, worthless, despicable, groveling, fawning, squalid, base-minded, slavish, beggarly, servile, cringing, low, wretched, sordid. (*honorable, dignified, eminent, exalted, esteemed, worthy, venerable, noble, princely, illustrious, independent, self-assertive, self-reliant, vain, arrogant, insolent, haughty*)

abjure—renounce, deny, apostatize, discard, recant, disclaim, disavow, repudiate, revoke, retract, disown. (*profess, assert, demand, vindicate, claim, cherish, advocate, retain, acknowledge, appropriate, hug*)

able—strong, powerful, clever, skillful, talented, capable, fitted, efficient, effective, learned, gifted, masterly, telling, nervous, vigorous. (*weak, inefficient, unskillful, incapable, ineffective, unqualified*)

abnormal—irregular, erratic, peculiar, unusual, exceptional, monstrous, aberrant, devious, divergent, eccentric, strange. (*typical, normal, regular, ordinary, usual, natural, customary, illustrative*)

abode—home, stay, place, residence, domicile, habitation, lodgings, berth, quarters. (*halt, perch, tent, bivouac, caravansary: with the idea of transience*)

abolish—destroy, eradicate, invalidate, make void, obliterate, extirpate, abrogate, annul, subvert, cancel, revoke, quash, nullify, overthrow, annihilate, supersede, suppress, expunge. (*support, sustain, cherish, promote, continue, confirm, restore, repair, revive, reinstate, enact, institute, re-enact*)

abominable—abhorrent, foul, accursed, detestable, hateful, horrible, loathsome, odious, offensive, execrable, nauseous, impure. (*delectable, desirable, admirable, enjoyable, lovable, charming, delightful, grateful, pure*)

abortion—failure, miscarriage, misadventure, downfall, mishap, misproduction, defect, frustration, blunder, mess. (*success, consummation, completion, achievement, realization, perfection, exploit, feat, development*)

abound—stream, swell, flow, increase, overflow, superabound, luxuriate, teem, swarm, flourish, prevail, be plentiful, wanton, revel, multiply. (*fall, waste, dry, lack, wane, evaporate, drain, die, decay, vanish, lessen, decrease*)

about—almost, with respect to, near, nearly, touching, concerning, surrounding, relative to, relating to, in relation to, approximately, touching, roughly, generally. (*afar, away from, precisely, exactly*)

above—over, beyond, exceeding. (*below, within, beneath*)

abridge—abbreviate, diminish, shorten, lessen, curtail, restrict, contract, condense, epitomize, compress. (*amplify, expand, spread out*)

abrupt—sudden, steep, precipitous, craggy, coarse, curt, blunt, violent, harsh, unceremonious, rugged, rough. (*undulating, easy, gliding, polished, smooth, blending, courteous*)

absent—*a.* not present, gone away, elsewhere, inattentive, thoughtless, listless, preoccupied. (*present, in this place, here, attentive*)

absent—*v.* keep away, depart, withdraw. (*be present, stay, remain*)

absolute—perfect, complete, unconditional, irrelative, irrespective, supreme, despotic, autocratic, certain, authoritative, unqualified, unequivocal, irresponsible, arbitrary. (*imperfect, incomplete, conditional, conditioned, contingent, relative, dependent, constitutional, dubious, accountable, responsible*)

absorb—swallow, drown, consume, imbibe, engross, drink in, suck up, engulf, monopolize, exhaust. (*eject, emit, exude, disgorge, dissipate, distract, distil, disperse*)

abstain—refrain, forbear, refuse, demur, avoid, cease, stop, keep back, desist, discontinue, withhold, scruple. (*indulge, exceed, reveal, wanton*)

abstemious—abstinent, moderate, self-denying, sober, temperate, sparing, frugal. (*sensual, self-indulgent, gluttonous, greedy, intemperate*)

abstract—separate, detach, part, eliminate, draw away, remove, take away, appropriate, purloin, steal, thieve, draw from. (*add, unite, conjoin, adduce, impose, restore, surrender, return*)

absurd—irrational, ridiculous, monstrous, senseless, asinine, stupid, chimerical, unreasonable, preposterous, silly, nonsensical, foolish. (*sensible, rational, reasonable, consistent, sound, substantial, logical, wise, sagacious, reflective, philosophical*)

abundant—plentiful, copious, plenteous, large, ample, overflowing, teeming, full, lavish, luxuriant, liberal, rich. (*rare, scarce, scant, deficient, short, insufficient, niggardly, sparing, dry, drained, exhausted, impoverished*)

abuse—*v.* injure, damage, spoil, maltreat, treat ill, ill-use, ill-treat, revile, scandalize, disparage, reproach, upbraid, asperse, malign, slander, vituperate, prostitute, defame, pervert, misuse, misemploy, vilify. (*tend, protect, conserve, consider, regard, shield, cherish, praise, extol, laud, vindicate, panegyrize, respect*)

abuse—*n.* mistreatment, invective, ill-treatment, opprobium, scurrility, vituperation, ribaldry, obloquy, reproach, insolence, misusage, ill usage. (*good usage, good treatment, kindness, praise, deference, respect*)

accelerate—hasten, urge, expedite, quicken, speed, urge on, press forward, hurry, promote, dispatch, facilitate. (*delay, obstruct, impede, clog, retard, hinder, shackle, drag*)

accent—stress, rhythm, pulsation, beat, emphasis. (*smoothness, inaccentuation, monotony, equableness, babble, flow*)

accept—welcome, hail, admit, recognize, avow, acknowledge, take, accede to, receive, assent to. (*refuse, decline, reject, disown, disavow, ignore, repudiate*)

acceptable—grateful, pleasant, welcome, agreeable, pleasurable, seasonable, gratifying.

accessory—assistant, additive, additional, auxiliary, supplementary, conducive, accomplice, ally, associate, abettor, colleague, confederate, helper. (*essential, inherent, immanent, incorporate, superfluous, irrelevant, malapropos, obstructive, cumbersome*)

accident—chance, fortuity, disaster, incident, adventure, casualty, hazard, contingency, calamity, misadventure, mishap. (*law, purpose, appointment*)

accommodate—convenience, oblige, adapt, supply, reconcile, suit, fit, adjust, furnish, serve, harmonize. (*inconvenience, disoblige, disturb, misfit*)

accommodating—kind, unselfish, obliging, polite, considerate, yielding, conciliatory. (*disobliging, selfish, churlish, rude, imperious, dictatorial, exacting*)

accomplice—abettor, confederate, accessory, ally, associate, partner, colleague, coadjutor, assistant, *particeps criminis.* (*rival, foe, adversary, antagonist*)

accomplish—execute, perfect, perform, fulfil, do, carry out, attain, realize, consummate, achieve, finish, complete. (*fail of, frustrate, defeat, disconcert, destroy, baffle, mar, spoil*)

accord—agree, consent, harmonize, tally, answer, comport, consist, conform, grant, concede, surrender, allow. (*disagree, differ, misfit, miscomport*)

accordingly—agreeably, suitably, conformably, hence, consequently.

account—*n.* narration, report, rehearsal, story, statement, narrative, recital, relation, description, motive, value, importance, advantage, ground, reason, profit. (*silence, suppression, disadvantage, concealment*)

account—*v.* deem, esteem, consider, regard, hold, judge, rate, estimate, value, reckon, explain, solve. (*disesteem, misestimate, mystify, underrate, undervalue, perplex, darken*)

accountable—responsible, liable, amenable, punishable, answerable, accredited, delegated, subordinate. (*autocratic, independent, irresponsible*)

accredit—believe, trust, entrust, delegate, depute, commission, authorize. (*disbelieve, distrust*)

accumulate—collect, garner, grow, mass, heap, store, bring together, hoard, gather, agglomerate, husband, augment, amass, increase. (*dissipate, disperse, diminish, scatter, expend, waste*)

accumulation—heap, collection, store, mass, aggregation, hoard, pile. (*segregation, separation*)

accurate—careful, exact, faithful, precise, correct, close, truthful, strict, just, actual, nice. (*careless, inexact, faulty, incorrect, inaccurate, loose, defective*)

accuse—charge, incriminate, impeach, arraign, tax, taunt, censure, cite, summon, criminate. (*defend, vindicate, discharge, acquit, absolve, condone*)

accustom—habituate, familiarize, form, inure, train, reconcile. (*disaccustom, dishabituate, estrange, wean, alienate*)

achieve—accomplish, do, gain, perform, execute, effect, fulfil, finish, attain, win. (*fail, lose, miss*)

achievement—exploit, feat, attainment, accomplishment, performance. (*failure, lack in completion*)

acknowledge—avow, admit, recognize, own, accept, profess, endorse, grant, concede, concern. (*disavow, disclaim, disown, repudiate, ignore, deny*)

acme—summit, zenith, climax, apex, pitch, culmination, meridian. (*base, floor, ground, foundation, nadir, depth, depression, foot, root*)

acquaint—advertise, inform, impart, make known, divulge, teach, notify, apprize, advise, tell. (*misinform, deceive, delude, mislead, misguide*)

acquaintance—knowledge, intimacy, familiarity, experience, companionship. (*ignorance, unfamiliarity, inexperience*)

acquiesce—assent, concur, repose, agree, yield, be resigned, comply. (*dissent, demur, object*)

acquit—discharge, exonerate, absolve, exculpate, release, dismiss, liberate, pardon. (*charge, accuse, impeach, constrain, implicate, bind, compel, condemn*)

acquittance—release, receipt, discharge. (*bond, claim, charge, obligation*)

across—athwart, against, transversely, opposed. (*lengthwise, along, concurrently, parallel*)

act—deed, performance, action, movement, proceeding, exercise, operation, play. (*inaction, rest, repose, cessation, suspension, quiet, immobility*)

active—nimble, agile, lively, sprightly, brisk, quick, expert, dexterous, supple, wide-awake, prompt, busy, industrious, diligent. (*slow, inactive, indolent, sluggish, heavy*)

actual—developed, positive, unquestionable, demonstrable, certain, real, authentic. (*potential, undeveloped, hypothetical, supposititious, possible, virtual*)

acute—pointed, penetrating, sagacious, perspicacious, keen, astute, piercing, sharp, shrewd, keen-sighted, severe, distressing. (*dull, blunt, obtuse*)

adapt—fit, accommodate, suit, adjust, conform, admeasure, harmonize, attune. (*misfit, misconform, misapply*)

add—adduce, adjoin, increase, extend, enlarge, sum up, cast up, subjoin, amplify, annex. (*deduct, subtract, dissever, abstract*)

addicted—given, accustomed, prone, inclined, disposed, habituated. (*unaddicted, disinclined, unaccustomed, indisposed, averse, free*)

addition—accession, enlargement, increase, extension, accretion, appendage. (*deduction, detraction, drawback, decrement, deterioration*)

address—*n.* tact, manners, speech, abode. (*awkwardness, unmannerliness*)

address—*v.* accost, greet, salute, approach, apostrophize, appeal, hail, woo, court. (*elude, avoid, shun, ignore, pass*)

adept—expert, adroit, handy, master, performer, professor, artist. (*awkward, clumsy, inexpert, tyro*)

adequate—equal, sufficient, fit, satisfactory, full, competent, capable, able. (*unequal, insufficient*)

adherence—adhesion, attachment, devotion, fidelity, cleaving to, constancy, endearment. (*separation, disunion, unfaithfulness, desertion, treachery*)

adherent—follower, supporter, ally, disciple, admirer, backer, aid, partisan. (*opponent, deserter, adversary, renegade, antagonist*)

adieu—good-bye, farewell, leavetaking, parting, valediction. (*greeting, welcome, recognition, salutation*)

adipose—obese, corpulent, sebaceous, oleaginous. (*leathery, skinny, bony, thin*)

adjacent—near, neighboring, contiguous, close, bordering, conterminous. (*remote, distant*)

adjoin—annex, add, connect, append, supplement, attach, unite, border, neighbor, touch, abut, approximate, verge, trench. (*disjoin, dismember, disconnect, detach, disintegrate, disunite, part, separate, recede, return, diverge, be distant, removed*)

adjourn—postpone, suspend, defer, prorogue, delay, protract, put off. (*expedite, dispatch, urge*)

adjunct—addition, additament, attachment, appendage, auxiliary, appurtenance, aid, acquisition, advantage, help. (*essence, substance, body, clog*)

adjust—harmonize, collocate, arrange, localize, adapt, affix, right, suit, classify, set in order, reconcile, accommodate, compose. (*dislocate, disarrange, disturb, confound, dismember, disorder*)

administer—distribute, award, accord, dole, give, impart, afford, discharge, dispense, execute, perform, furnish, contribute, conduct. (*withdraw, withhold, refuse, retain, assume, resume, resign, deny*)

admirable—wonderful, excellent, surprising, astonishing, praiseworthy, pleasing. (*commonplace, mediocre, ridiculous, abominable, displeasing*)

admissible—allowable, permissible, probable, reasonable, just, proper, fair, right, qualified. (*unallowable, inadmissible, improper, unreasonable*)

admit—receive, pass, permit, accept, grant, concede, allow, acknowledge, confess, own, avow, suffer. (*exclude, debar, disallow, reject, deny, discharge, dismiss, eject, extrude, repudiate, disavow*)

admonish—remind, forewarn, advise, warn, dissuade, caution, counsel, reprove, censure, rebuke. (*encourage, instigate, abet, incite, urge, applaud*)

adopt—assume, select, affiliate, take, elect, arrogate, choose, endorse, avow, appropriate. (*reject, decline, repudiate, disavow, discard, renounce*)

adore—admire, hallow, glorify, praise, venerate, reverence, worship, idolize. (*abhor, despise, disesteem, abominate, execrate, blaspheme*)

adulation—flattery, compliment, sycophancy, courtship, incense, praise, blandishment, fawning, cringing. (*detraction, obloquy, defamation, calumny, traducement, sarcasm, ridicule, satire, bespatterment*)

advance—propel, elevate, promote, further, lend, propagate, progress, increase, prosper, rise. (*retard, hinder, withhold, withdraw, recall, depress, degrade*)

advantage—gain, success, superiority, help, assistance, benefit, good, avail, interest, utility, service, profit, acquisition. (*loss, disappointment, defeat, frustration, inferiority, obstacle, obstruction*)

adventurous—bold, brave, daring, enterprising, courageous, gallant, fearless, venturesome, rash, chivalrous, hazardous. (*timid, unenterprising, inadventurous, cowardly, nervous, hesitating, cautious*)

adversary—antagonist, foe, enemy, rival, assailant. (*accessory, abettor, aider, friend, helper, assistant, ally, accomplice*)

adversity—ill luck, misfortune, misery, calamity, disaster, distress, unsuccess, failure, ruin, trouble, affliction, sorrow. (*good luck, prosperity, happiness*)

advertent—attentive, regardful, mindful, watchful, thoughtful, observant, considerate. (*inattentive, inadvertent, casual, thoughtless, heedless, inobservant, inconsiderate*)

advertise—publish, inform, advise, circulate, announce, notify, proclaim, promulge. (*suppress, hush, conceal, ignore, hoodwink, misguide, mislead*)

advise—admonish, warn, deliberate, counsel, persuade, urge, prompt, instigate, incite, instruct, acquaint, inform. (*dissuade, deter, expostulate, remonstrate, prohibit, inhibit, restrain, curb, mislead, misadvise, hoodwink, deceive, delude, misinform*)

advocate—pleader, counselor, upholder, propagator, promoter, supporter, countenancer, defender, maintainer. (*opponent, adversary, discountenancer*)

affable—courteous, accessible, condescending, conversable, gracious, sociable, gentle, complaisant, urbane, polite, easy, approachable. (*exclusive, discourteous, distant, inaccessible, unapproachable, inconversable, haughty, contemptuous, supercilious*)

affect—like, desire, favor, seek, assume, move, influence, concern, interest, feign, pretend. (*dislike, eschew, shun, repel, repudiate*)

affectation—pretense, artifice, hypocrisy, assumption, simulation, mannerism, euphuism, airs. (*genuineness, naturalness, unaffectedness, simplicity, artlessness*)

affection—influence, condition, state, inclination, bent, mood, humor, feeling, love, desire, propensity. (*insensibility, indifference, repugnance, disaffection*)

affinity—relationship, relation, kindred, conformity, connection, alliance, similarity, analogy, homogeneity, harmony, correlativeness, sympathy, interdependence, interconnection, intercommunity. (*dissimilarity, discordance, disconnection, independence, antagonism, antipathy, repugnance, interrepulsiveness*)

affirm—assert, swear, testify, tell, aver, propound, asseverate, depose, state, declare, endorse, maintain. (*deny, dispute, doubt, demur, negative*)

affliction—trouble, trial, grief, pain, disease, misery, hardship, sorrow. (*consolation, relief, alleviation, assuagement, boon, blessing, gratification, pleasure*)

afford—produce, supply, give, yield, grant, confer, bestow, impart, administer, extend. (*withhold, deny, withdraw, retain, stint, grudge*)

affront—outrage, provocation, insult, ill-treatment, abuse, wrong, offense, indignity. (*homage, salutation, courtesy, apology, amends, compliment*)

afloat—adrift, abroad, at sea, abroach, loose, distracted, dazed. (*ashore, snug, tight, close, fast, collected, concentrated*)

afoot—working, launched, afloat, agoing, inaugurated, started, instituted, established. (*uncommenced, incomplete, projected, proposed, contemplated, designed*)

afraid—fearful, apprehensive, timid, timorous, cowardly, fainthearted, cautious, careful, frightened, alarmed, terrified, suspicious, distrustful, anxious. (*fearless, inapprehensive, unsolicitous*)

afresh—anew, again, frequently, repeatedly, intermittently. (*continuously, uniformly, uninterruptedly, unintermittently, connectedly*)

after—behind, following, succeeding. (*before, afore, introducing, preceding*)

again—anew, afresh, repeatedly, frequently. (*continuously, uniformly, uninterruptedly, unintermittently, once*)

against—over, opposite, abutting, opposing, resisting, despite, across, athwart, counter. (*with, for, accompanying, aiding, suiting, promoting*)

age—period, generation, era, epoch, date, century, antiquity, senility, eldership, seniority. (*youth, infancy, boyhood, childhood, moment, instant*)

agent—doer, performer, actor, force, means, instrument, influence, cause, promoter, operator. (*counteragent, counteractor, counteraction, opponent*)

aggravate—exasperate, provoke, wound, heighten, intensify, irritate, make worse, increase, enhance, embitter, magnify. (*soothe, conciliate, assuage, diminish, palliate, neutralize, soften, lessen*)

agile—nimble, active, fleet, brisk, alert, featly, lithe, prompt, ready, quick, supple, swift, sprightly. (*slow, heavy, awkward, inert, clumsy, bulky, ponderous, elephantine*)

agitate—disturb, trouble, excite, ruffle, stir, fluster, oscillate, instigate, convulse, shake. (*calm, compose, allay, pacify, smooth*)

agony—pain, torture, torment, distress, woe, throe, suffering, pang, excruciation. (*assuagement, comfort, peace, ease, relief, gratification, enjoyment*)

agree—suit, tally, accord, fit, harmonize, combine, assent, concur, acquiesce, admit, consent, conform, consort, comport, coincide. (*differ, disagree, revolt, protest, decline, refuse, dissent, demur*)

agreeable—obliging, pleasant, accommodating, grateful, acceptable, welcome, suitable, consistent, consonant, amiable, gratifying, pleasing, good-natured, complaisant. (*disobliging, unpleasant, unaccommodating, disagreeable, obnoxious, ungrateful*)

agreement—contract, compact, bond, concord, concurrence, conformity, harmony, unison, consonance, bargain, covenant, obligation, undertaking, treaty. (*disagreement, informal understanding or promise, parole*)

aid—help, assist, succor, support, befriend, cooperate, contribute, favor, foster, protect, abet, encourage, instigate, subsidize. (*oppose, resist*)

ailment—complaint, sickness, illness, disease. (*recovery, convalescence, sanity, health, robustness*)

aim—n. tendency, intent, aspiration, bent, drift, object, scope, goal, purpose, mark, end, design, intention. (*shunning, disregarding, disaffecting*)

aim—v. seek, level, propose, design, affect, intend, mean, purpose. (*shun, disregard, disaffect, ignore*)

akin—related, agnate, cognate, homogeneous, similar, consanguineous, congenial, allied, sympathetic. (*unrelated, unconnected, foreign, alien, heterogeneous, uncongenial, hostile, unallied, antagonistic*)

alacrity—quickness, readiness, briskness, activity, cheerfulness, compliance, willingness, promptitude. (*slowness, reluctance, repugnance*)

alarming—terrible, fearful, frightful, portentous, ominous, threatening. (*soothing, assuring, encouraging, inviting, propitious, hopeful, alluring*)

alert—active, brisk, nimble, prepared, prompt, vigilant, ready, wakeful, watchful, on the watch, lively. (*slow, sleepy, lazy, absent, unready, oblivious*)

alien—foreign, strange, undomesticated, inappropriate, irrelevant, impertinent. (*pertinent, essential, proper, appropriate, relevant, germane, akin*)

alike—resembling, similar, together, twin-fellow, analogous, identical, equal, equivalent, same, homogeneous, akin, equally. (*unlike, heterogeneous*)

alive—quick, living, breathing, warm, lively, vivacious, alert, existing, existent, safe, subsisting, active, brisk, animated. (*dead, departed, cold, lifeless, defunct, inanimate, dispirited, dull*)

allege—declare, affirm, assert, asseverate, depose, plead, cite, quote, assign, advance, maintain, say.

(*contradict, gainsay, refute, deny, disprove, neutralize*)

allegiance—subjection, obedience, loyalty, fealty, homage. (*disloyalty, rebellion, resistance, disaffection, malcontentment, treason*)

alleviate—lighten, lessen, assuage, mitigate, soothe, moderate, relieve, remit, diminish. (*aggravate, enhance, increase, embitter, augment*)

alliance—compact, treaty, cooperation, union, connection, partnership, league, combination, coalition, confederation, friendship, relation, relationship. (*disunion, enmity, divorce, discord, disruption*)

allot—assign, grant, award, give, apportion, deal, dispense, parcel, distribute, divide, mete out, portion out. (*refuse, withhold, retain, appropriate*)

allow—concede, apportion, allot, assign, afford, tolerate, authorize, grant, remit, recognize, acknowledge, avow, confess, admit, permit, suffer, sanction, yield. (*withhold, withdraw, resume, refuse*)

alloy—admixture, deterioration, adulteration, drawback, diminution, decrement, impairment, debasement, depreciation, disparagement. (*purity, genuineness, enhancement, integrity*)

allude—point, indicate, suggest, hint, signify, insinuate, refer, imply, intimate. (*specify, demonstrate, declare, mention, state*)

ally—friend, companion, supporter, aider, abettor, accomplice, assistant, confederate, helper, associate, accessory, colleague, coadjutor. (*foe, enemy, opponent, adversary, baffler, counteractor*)

aloud—audibly, loudly, clamorously, sonorously, vociferously, obstreperously. (*softly, silently, inaudibly, suppressedly*)

alter—substitute, change, vary, modify, exchange, diversify, remodel. (*retain, perpetuate, conserve, stereotype, arrest, solidify, stabilitate*)

alternative—choice, resource, opinion. (*compulsion, quandary, necessity, fix*)

altogether—collectively, combined, in one, totally, entirely, wholly, fully, completely, utterly, thoroughly. (*separately, individually, partially*)

amass—collect, accumulate, aggregate, heap, gather, store up, hoard, pile up. (*divide, dissipate, waste, scatter, disperse, parcel, portion, spend*)

amazement—astonishment, awe, wonder, bewilderment, surprise, stupefaction, marvel. (*expectation, preparation, anticipation, familiarity*)

ambiguous—equivocal, vague, doubtful, enigmatical, uncertain, obscure, unintelligible, perplexing, indistinct, dubious. (*univocal, obvious*)

ameliorate—improve, raise, better, advantage, promote, advance, amend, rectify, meliorate. (*debase, depress, deteriorate, injure, impair, vitiate*)

amend—improve, mend, repair, correct, rectify, better, ameliorate, reform. (*deteriorate, degenerate, neglect, aggravate, tarnish, blemish, spoil, corrupt*)

amiable—lovable, good, kind, benevolent, charitable, delectable, engaging, fascinating, agreeable, lovely, pleasing, charming, attractive. (*churlish, disagreeable, hateful, abominable, ill-natured, ill-conditioned, unamiable*)

amiss—wrong, untrue, wide, bad, false, defective, short, inappropriate, inopportune, injudicious, untimely, abortive. (*right, true, good, complete, effective, successful, satisfactory, consummate, expedient, appropriate, opportune*)

amnesty—pardon, acquittal, remission, condonation, oblivion, dispensation, absolution. (*penalty, retaliation, punishment, retribution, requital, visitation, infliction, exaction, trial, account*)

ample—large, bountiful, liberal, copious, spacious, roomy, diffusive, full, complete, sufficient, plentiful, abundant. (*narrow, niggardly, insufficient, stingy, scant, mean, stint, bare*)

amplify—enrich, enlarge, increase, augment, multiply, dilate, develop, swell, expatiate, expand, discuss, unfold, extend. (*retrench, amputate, curtail, condense, abbreviate, epitomize, gather, collect*)

analogy—relation, resemblance, proportion, similarity, similitude, coincidence, affinity, comparison, parity. (*disproportion, dissimilarity, disharmony*)

analysis—dissection, separation, anatomy, segregation, decomposition, resolution, partition. (*composition, synthesis, aggregation, combination, coalition, amalgamation, coherence*)

anarchy—disorder, tumult, rebellion, riot, misgovernment, insubordination. (*order, subjection*)

anatomy—dissection, division, segregation, analysis, resolution, dismemberment. (*synthesis, collocation, organization, union, construction, structure*)

ancient—old, antiquated, old-fashioned, antique, obsolete, old-time, aged, primeval, primordial, immemorial, time-honored. (*new, young, modern*)

anger—*n.* ire, incensement, vexation, grudge, pique, exasperation, indignation, enmity, displeasure, irritation, passion, spleen, gall, resentment, rage, animosity, fury, choler, wrath. (*peace, peacefulness, peaceableness, appeasement, forgiveness*)

anger—*v.* enrage, vex, kindle, fret, ruffle, chafe, infuriate, exasperate, provoke, irritate, incense, wound, inflame, embitter. (*appease, compose, forbear, allay, soothe, calm, conciliate, heal*)

animosity—hatred, antipathy, dissension, aversion, acrimony, feud, strife, rancor, antagonism, bitterness, acerbity, hostility, enmity, malice, anger, malevolence, ill will, malignity, feeling against. (*congeniality, companionship, friendship*)

annex—add, attach, fasten, affix, subjoin, append, connect, unite. (*withdraw, detach, disconnect*)

annihilate—abolish, destroy, bring to naught, uproot, eradicate, nullify, exterminate, end, extinguish, demolish, obliterate, efface. (*keep, conserve, preserve, foster, tend, protect, cherish, develop*)

announce—declare, propound, give notice, enunciate, advertise, publish, report, notify, make known, give out, reveal, herald, proclaim, intimate, promulge. (*conceal, suppress, hush, stifle, withhold*)

annoy—tease, vex, irritate, disturb, affront, molest, pain, disquiet, incommode, tantalize, bother, weary, inconvenience, plague, discommode, harass, chafe, trouble. (*soothe, conciliate, appease, regard*)

anomaly—irregularity, abnormity, exception, informality, peculiarity, eccentricity. (*conformity, regularity, illustration, conformance, exemplification*)

anonymous—nameless, unattested, authorless, unidentified, unauthenticated. (*authenticated, attested, identified, authorized, verified, signed*)

answer—reply, response, counterargument, confutation, acceptance (as of a challenge), tally counterpart, solution, vindication, apology, exculpation, defense, rejoinder, repartee, retort. (*challenge, question, defiance, summons, interrogation*)

Synonym
Ant/Hom

antecedent—prior, foregoing, previous, precursive, precedent, earlier, introductory, preliminary, former. (*posterior, later, subsequent, consequent*)

anticipate—forestall, prejudge, expect, foretaste, apprehend, prevent, prearrange, prepare, meet, obviate, intercept, forecast. (*remember, recollect, remedy, recall, undo, cure, misapprehend*)

anticipation—expectation, awaiting, preoccupation, preconception, foresight, forethought, foretaste, prevention, forestallment, contemplation, hope, trust, prospect, forecast, provision. (*surprise, unpreparedness, unexpectedness*)

anxiety—care, trouble, eagerness, disquiet, apprehension, carefulness, diffidence, solicitude, misgiving. (*carelessness, ease, confidence, contentment*)

anxious—solicitous, careful, uneasy, concerned, restless, watchful, disturbed, unquiet. (*without care, careless, inert, ease, unconcerned, calm, composed*)

apathy—indifference, insensibility, unfeelingness in company, insusceptibility, unconcern, sluggishness, hebetude. (*anxiety, care, eagerness, interestedness, sensibility, susceptibility, sensitiveness, irritability, curiosity*)

ape—mimic, imitate, simulate, personate, represent. (*not to imitate, vary, modify, change*)

apiece—distributively, individually, separately, severally, analytically. (*collectively, together, accumulatively, indiscriminately, confusedly, synthetically*)

apology—defense, justification, plea, exculpation, excuse, vindication, acknowledgment, confession. (*charge, imputation, impeachment, offense, incrimination, injury. accusation, wrong, insult*)

appall—affright, alarm terrify, scare, daunt, cow, shock, frighten, discourage, dishearten, horrify, dismay, astound. (*encourage, rally, assure, embolden*)

apparel—clothes, robes, vesture, vestments, raiment, garniture, habiliments, habit, dress, clothing, caparison, trappings, housings. (*nudity, divestiture, dishabille, tatters, rags*)

apparent—obvious, plain, conspicuous, manifest, appearing, unmistakable, clear, probable, seeming, presumable, likely, patent, ostensible, visible, evident, indubitable, notorious, certain. (*uncertain, dubious, inapparent, minute, unobservable, improbable, insupposable, hidden, real*)

appeal—accost, address, apostrophize, invite, cite, invoke, urge, refer, call upon, entreat, request, resort. (*deprecate, repudiate, protest, disavow, disclaim, defy, abjure*)

appearance—advent, coming, arrival, presence, apparition, aspect, manifestation, probability, likeness, exhibition, mien, manner, semblance, air, show, look, pretense, likelihood, presumption. (*departure, disappearance, unlikelihood, nonappearance, concealment, evanition*)

append—affix, supplement, subjoin, attach. (*separate, disengage, disconnect, detach*)

appetite—passion, desire, propensity, proclivity, inclination, propension, appetency, want, craving, disposition, tendency, proneness. (*repugnance, aversion, antipathy, loathing, indifference, apathy*)

applause—praise, plaudit, laudation, encomium, commendation, approbation, acclamation, approval, eulogy, acclaim. (*obloquy, condemnation, denunciation, dissatisfaction, contempt, censure, blame*)

applicable—available, ancillary, convenient, useful, pertinent, conducive, appropriate. (*useless, unavailable, inconducive, inapplicable, irrelevant*)

appoint—fix, determine, install, allot, order, prescribe, institute, employ, apportion, apply, designate, assign, intrust, invest, ordain, arrange. (*reverse, cancel, recall, withdraw, reserve, withhold*)

apportion—assign, deal, allot, grant, share, divide, dispense, administer, distribute, appoint. (*reserve, retain, refuse, withhold, assume, resume*)

appreciate—esteem, recognize, acknowledge, respect, value, prize, regard, reckon, estimate. (*undervalue, misconceive, misjudge, ignore, misappreciate*)

apprehend—comprehend, understand, take, expect, seize, conceive, arrest, fancy, dread, imagine, presume, anticipate, fear, conjecture. (*ignore, miss, lose, misconjecture, misconceive, misapprehend*)

approach—access, avenue, entrance, adit, vestibule, arrival, approximation, advent, nearing, admission, appropinquation, admittance, mode, path, way, advance, similarity. (*exit, egress, debouchure, outlet, departure, recession, distance*)

approve—like, comment, sanction, praise, support, second, promote, encourage, authorize. (*disapprove, dislike, censure, blame, disown, disavow*)

approximate—approach, resemble, border, abut, near, trench. (*separate, differ, vary, recede, diverge*)

apt—fit, apposite, clever, meet, liable, becoming, appropriate, ready, fitting, suitable, pertinent, qualified, prompt, adapted, likely. (*unfitted, ill-timed, awkward, unlikely, inapt*)

arbitrary—tyrannical, despotic, harsh, dictatorial, imperious, unforbearing, overbearing, selfish, absolute, irresponsible, tyrannous, domineering, peremptory. (*mild, modest, lenient, considerate*)

arbitrate—settle, adjust, compose, decide, determine, accommodate, adjudicate. (*dispute, claim*)

ardent—longing, passionate, aspiring, warm, eager, fervent, excited, fiery, glowing, zealous, fervid, fierce, keen, vehement, hot, affectionate, impassioned, burning, heated. (*cool, cold, indifferent, dispassioned, apathetic, passionless, unimpassioned, phlegmatic, platonic*)

argue—discuss, debate, prove, question, evidence, establish, imply, sift, dispute, persuade, controvert, contend, demonstrate, reason. (*dictate, assert, propound, command*)

argument—reasoning, controversy, evidence, discussion, topic, dispute. (*assertion, assumption*)

arid—dry, parched, sterile, unproductive. (*moist, dewy, watered, fertile, luxuriant, exuberant, verdant*)

aright—right, well, rightly, correctly, truly, properly, uprightly, unexceptionably, justly, suitably, appropriately. (*wrongly, awry, incorrectly, improperly, defectively, erroneously*)

arouse—stir, excite, disturb, animate, wake up, stimulate, alarm, provoke, cheer. (*allay, assuage*)

arraign—summon, accuse, censure, indict, charge, impeach. (*acquit, condone, discharge, release*)

arrange—order, put in order, group, array, place, adjust, range, locate, dispose, assort, deal, sort, parcel, classify. (*derange, disarrange, confuse, disturb, disperse, jumble, disorder*)

array—*v.* vest, deck, equip, decorate, rank, adorn, dress, accoutre, invest, attire, place, arrange, draw up, marshal, set in order, dispose. (*disarray, disarrange, confuse, jumble, divest, denude, strip*)

array—*n.* arrangement, order, disposition, sight, exhibition, show, parade. (*disarray, disorder, confusion, confusedness, jumble*)

arrest—seize, take, stop, capture, withhold, restrain, hold, detain, apprehend. (*release, dismiss*)

arrive—reach, attain, come to, enter, get to, land. (*embark, depart, start*)

arrogance—haughtiness, overbearingness, contemptuousness, hauteur, browbeating, loftiness, self-conceit, stateliness, vainglory, insolence, self-importance, assumption, discourtesy. (*bashfulness, servility, considerateness, deference, courtesy, modesty, shyness, diffidence, politeness*)

artful—cunning, designing, maneuvering, sharp, knowing, subtle, sly, crafty, wily, shrewd. (*simple, undesigning, artless, open, innocent, unsophisticated*)

artificial—invented, fabricated, fictitious, constructed, manufactured, pretended, simulated, false, assumed, concocted, contrived, deceptive, artful, affected, unnatural, constrained. (*natural, inartificial, genuine, spontaneous, transparent, artless, unaffected*)

ascertain—prove, verify, find out, discover, confirm, detect, determine, learn, discern. (*guess, conjecture, surmise, suppose, presume*)

ascribe—assign, attribute, impute, refer, render, allege, charge. (*deny, refuse, exclude, dissociate*)

aspiration—longing, desire, aim, wish, craving, ambition, endeavor, hope, effort, eagerness. (*apathy, indifference, aimlessness, dullness, inertia, callousness, carelessness, aversion, avoidance*)

assembly—meeting, concourse, assemblage, multitude, group, synod, conclave, conference, convocation, unison, company, congregation, collection, crowd, gathering, convention, aggregate. (*dispersion, dissipation, disunion, disruption*)

assent—coincidence, agreement, concert, acknowledgment, consent, acquiescence, approval, concurrence, approbation, compliance. (*dissent, disagreement, difference, disavowal, repudiation*)

assign—attribute, apportion, allege, refer, specify, consign, entrust, commit, point out, allot to, adduce, advance, appoint, convey. (*withhold, withdraw, resume, retain, refuse, disconnect, dissociate*)

assist—help, succor, aid, support, relieve, befriend, second, cooperate with, back, benefit, further. (*hinder, resist, oppose, antagonize, counteract, clog, prevent*)

assistant—helper, aider, attendant, coadjutor, auxiliary, ally, associate, contributor, partner, confederate. (*hinderer, opposer, rival, foe, antagonist*)

association—union, connection, conjunction, consortment, companionship, alliance, familiarity, community, membership, society, company, denomination, partnership, fellowship, fraternity, friendship. (*disunion, disconnection, estrangement*)

assortment—collection, disposition, distribution, class, quantity, selection, stock, miscellany, lot, variety. (*misarrangement, disarrangement, displacement, misplacement*)

assume—take, appropriate, arrogate, wear, exhibit, postulate, suppose, presume, usurp, claim, pretend, feign, affect. (*waive, allow, doff, render, surrender, concede, grant, demonstrate, abandon*)

assure—advise, advertise, promise, inform, rally, console, encourage, countenance, aid, support, convince, uphold, certify. (*misinform, misadvise*)

astonish—startle, surprise, confound, amaze, astound, fill with wonder, stupefy, alarm, terrify, electrify, scare, dumfound. (*rally, encourage*)

astray—loose, abroad, missing, about, at large, wrong, erring, wandering. (*right, close, at home*)

athletic—strong, vigorous, powerful, stalwart, brawny, muscular, ablebodied, lusty, sinewy, robust. (*weak, puny, effeminate, nerveless, strengthless, unbraced*)

atrocious—monstrous, nefarious, wicked, outrageous, villainous, enormous, shameful, heinous, cruel, flagrant, facinorous, flagitious. (*laudable, noble, honorable, generous, humane, admirable*)

attach—fasten, apply, append, add, fix, subjoin, annex, unite, conciliate, tie, connect, conjoin, attract, win, bind. (*unfasten, loose, disunite, untie*)

attack—*v.* assail, assault, invade, encounter, charge, besiege, impugn, contravene. (*defend, resist, repel, protest, withstand on one's own part or for another, support, aid, shield, uphold, vindicate*)

attack—*n.* invasion, assault, onset, aggression, onslaught. (*defense, resistance, repulse, protection*)

attain—reach, extend, master, arrive at, earn, win, achieve, accomplish, get, obtain, acquire, gain, secure. (*lose, fail, forfeit, miss, abandon, resign*)

attempt—try, endeavor, strive, undertake, seek, essay, attack, violate, force. (*disregard, abandon, pretermit, dismiss, neglect, shun, drop*)

attend—listen, heed, notice, observe, wait on, serve, mind, watch, accompany, consort, follow, imply, involve. (*wander, disregard, leave, forsake*)

attention—observation, notice, regard, watchfulness, heed, consideration, circumspection, study, vigilance, care. (*disregard, inadvertence, remission, indifference, carelessness, abstraction, distraction*)

attest—vouch, aver, assert, certify, witness, vouch for, affirm, testify, evidence, support, confirm, suggest, prove, involve, demonstrate, establish, imply, bespeak. (*deny, controvert, contradict, contravene, disprove, disestablish, exclude, neutralize*)

attire—robes, garment, clothing, vestments, habiliment, habit, raiment, clothes, garb, apparel, accoutrements, livery, uniform, costume. (*nudity, divestment, exposure, denudation, bareness, disarray*)

attract—influence, induce, dispose, incline, tempt, prompt, allure, charm, fascinate, invite, entice. (*repel, deter, indispose, disincline, estrange, alienate*)

attractive—winning, alluring, tempting, inviting, engaging, captivating, fascinating, enticing, interesting, charming, pleasant, beautiful, agreeable. (*unattractive, repugnant, repulsive, uninteresting, disagreeable, unpleasant, deformed, ugly, deterrent*)

attribute—*v.* refer, assign, associate, apply, ascribe, charge, impute, connect. (*divorce, disconnect, dissociate, dissever*)

attribute—*n.* property, quality, characteristic, attainment, sign, mark, indication, manifestation, symbol.

attrition—sorrow, repentance, affliction, penitence, compunction, remorse, self-reproach. (*im-*

penitence, callousness, obduracy, reprobation, relentlessness)

audacious—insolent, adventurous, presumptuous, valiant, rash, bold, daring, reckless, enterprising. *(timid, cowardly, cautious, inadventurous, unventuresome, unenterprising)*

audacity—boldness, rashness, temerity, recklessness, hardihood. *(caution, self-preservation, timidity, calculation, forethought, foresight, diffidence, inadventurousness)*

augment—increase, enlargement, amplification, enrichment, supply, enhancement, addition, acquisition, improvement. *(deduction, detraction, diminution, contraction, withdrawal, reservation, expenditure, loss, waste, detriment, deterioration, impoverishment, reduction, curtailment)*

augury—prophecy, prediction, divination, conjecture, omen, prognostication. *(experience, science)*

august—majestic, dignified, stately, noble, pompous, imposing, grand, solemn, exalted. *(mean, undignified, unimposing, common, vulgar, despicable, paltry, unnoticeable, beggarly, commonplace)*

auspicious—propitious, lucky, favorable, encouraging, satisfactory, successful, hopeful, promising, happy, golden, fortunate, opportune, prosperous. *(unpropitious, unfavorable, discouraging, unsatisfactory, inauspicious, unpromising, abortive)*

austere—hard, rigid, stern, severe, morose, unrelenting, unyielding, strict, rigorous, harsh, sour, relentless. *(mild, affable, kindly, tender feeling)*

authentic—genuine, veritable, reliable, real, original, trustworthy, not spurious, true, legitimate, certain, accepted, current, received. *(unreliable, spurious, false, apocryphal, disputed, exploded, rejected, counterfeit, unfounded, unauthorized, baseless)*

authoritative—decisive, sure, conclusive, authentic, powerful, firm, potent, dictatorial, imperious, arbitrary, arrogant, imperative, dogmatic, commanding. *(weak, inconclusive, vague, indeterminate, indefinite, vacillating, undecisive, bland, conciliatory)*

authority—ground, justification, authenticity, genuineness, conclusiveness, decisiveness, control, direction, jurisdiction, government, regulation, power, right, rule, sway, sufferance, supremacy, dominion. *(groundlessness, spuriousness, indecision, inconclusiveness, inoperativeness, incompetency, weakness, usurpation, wrong)*

autocratic—independent, arbitrary, despotic, irresponsible, absolute. *(dependent, subordinate, responsible, constitutional, limited)*

auxiliary—helpful, abetting, aiding, accessory, promotive, conducive, assistant, ancillary, assisting, subsidiary, helping. *(unassisting, unconducive, unpromotive, redundant, superfluous, obstructive)*

avail—suffice, hold, stand, endure, answer, tell, profit, help, benefit, advantage, service, use, utility. *(fail, fall, disappoint, betray)*

available—useful, appropriate, convertible, attainable, handy, conducive, applicable, procurable, advantageous, helpful, profitable, suitable, serviceable. *(useless, inappropriate, inapplicable, unprocurable, inconducive, irrelevant, inoperative, unavailable)*

avarice—greed, cupidity, rapacity, penuriousness, niggardliness, miserliness, stinginess, covetousness, acquisitiveness, griping, greediness. *(largeheartedness, unselfishness, liberality, bountifulness)*

aver—assert, asseverate, affirm, depose, avouch, protest, oblige, declare. *(deny, contradict, contravene, disavow, disclaim, repudiate, gainsay, oppugn)*

avidity—cupidity, avarice, desire, greed, longing, rapacity, eagerness. *(coldness, indifference, apathy, insensibility, antipathy, nausea, aversion, repugnance, loathing)*

avoid—quit, shun, abandon, desert, forsake, relinquish, fly, eschew, elude, dodge, escape, shirk. *(seek, court, approach, accost, address, affect)*

award—assign, apportion, attribute, accord, grant, distribute, divide, allot, give, determine, decree, order, adjudge. *(refuse, withhold, withdraw)*

aware—conscious, sensible, informed, certified, assured, known, apprized, cognizant. *(unconscious, insensible, ignorant, unaware, uninformed)*

awful—fearful, direful, appalling, terrible, alarming, dreadful, horrible, solemn, portentous, horrific. *(inocuous, informidable, unimposing, unastonishing)*

awkward—ungainly, clownish, clumsy, maladroit, unhandy, uncouth, rough, boorish, bungling, gawky. *(neat, clever, dexterous, skillful, adroit)*

axiom—self-evident truth, aphorism, truism, apophthegm, maxim. *(nonsense, absurdity, stultiloquy, absurdness)*

B

babble—prate, prattle, dribble, chatter, gabble, twaddle, blab, cackle. *(enunciate, vociferate, hush)*

babel—hubbub, confusion, clamor, jargon, din, discord, clang. *(elocution, articulation, monotony, distinctness, consecutiveness, intonation, enunciation)*

baffle—frustrate, counteract, estop, disconcert, elude, mock, thwart, confound, defeat, perplex, restrain, upset, foil, mar, balk, neutralize, dodge, counterfoil. *(point, aid, abet, enforce, promote)*

bait—morsel, snare, decoy, enticement, allurement, inducement. *(warning, scarecrow, dissuasive, deterrent, prohibition, intimidation, threat)*

balance—weigh, poise, pit, set, counterpoise, counteract, neutralize, equalize, estimate, redress, adjust. *(upset, tilt, cant, subvert, mispoise, overbalance)*

balderdash—gasconade, flummery, rhodomontade, bombast, fustian, froth. *(sense, wisdom)*

balk—estop, bar, thwart, frustrate, foil, stop, prevent, hinder, neutralize, nullify, mar, counteract, disappoint, defeat, baffle. *(aid, abet, promote)*

banish—expel, abandon, dispel, eject, extrude, exclude, relegate, expatriate, repudiate, disclaim. *(cherish, foster, protect, consider, encourage, locate)*

banquet—feast, festivity, treat, entertainment, festival, carousal, carouse, regalement, cheer. *(fast, abstinence, starvation)*

banter—badinage, chaff, mockery, derision, ridicule, irony, jeering, raillery. *(discussion, discourse)*

bargain—transaction, negotiation, business, profit, speculation, higgling, gain, hawking, chaffer, haggling. *(loss, misprofit)*

base—vile, dishonorable, low, sordid, ignoble, worthless, mean, infamous, shameful, groveling, disingenuous, disesteemed, cheap, corrupt, deep. *(lofty, exalted, refined, noble, esteemed, honored)*

bashful—modest, diffident, shy, retiring, reserved. (*bold, impudent, forward, unreserved, pert, conceited, ostentatious, egotistic*)

battle—fight, conflict, contest, combat, engagement, encounter, action. (*peace, truce, pacification, arbitrament, council, mediation*)

bawl—shout, vociferate, halloo, roar, bellow. (*whisper, mutter, babble, mumble*)

beach—shore, coast, strand, seacoast, seaboard, seashore. (*sea, ocean, deep, main*)

beaming—shining, gleaming, bright, radiant, beautiful, transparent, translucid. (*dull, opaque, dingy, beamless, wan*)

bear—carry, lift, transport, convey, maintain, uphold, suffer, undergo, support, tolerate, waft, yield, sustain, hold, harbor, entertain, fill, enact, endure, admit, produce, generate. (*drop, refuse*)

beat—strike, pound, batter, surpass, thrash, cudgel, overcome, defeat, conquer, worst, whack, belabor, vanquish. (*defend, protect, shield, fail*)

beauty—loveliness, grace, fairness, seemliness, comeliness, picturesqueness, exquisiteness, adornment, embellishment. (*foulness, ugliness, deformity, hideousness, bareness, unattractiveness*)

because—owing, consequently, accordingly. (*irrespectively, independently, inconsequently, unconnectedly*)

beck—nod, sign, signal, symbol, token, indication, authority, orders, instruction, subserviency, influence, call, command, control, mandate. (*independence, unsubservience*)

becoming—beseeming, neat, fit, proper, decorous, comely, seemly, befitting, graceful, decent, suitable, improving. (*unbeseeming, unseemly, uncomely, unbecoming, unbefitting, ungraceful, indecent*)

befitting—fitting, decent, becoming, suitable, appropriate, proper, consistent, expedient, desirable. (*obligatory, compulsory, unbefitting, indecent*)

before—precedently, anteriorly, antecedently. (*after, afterward, subsequently, posteriorly, later*)

beg—ask, request, entreat, supplicate, beseech, implore, pray, petition, crave. (*insist, exact, extort, require, demand*)

beggarly—miserable, poor, stinted, wretched, niggardly, stingy, scant, illiberal. (*noble, princely, stately, prodigal, sumptuous, liberal, profuse, gorgeous, magnificent*)

begin—initiate, commence, prepare, start, originate, arise, inaugurate. (*achieve, complete, terminate, conclude, consummate, finish, close, end*)

beginning—commencement, start, origin, rise, initiation, preparation, preface, prelude, inauguration, inception, threshold, opening, source, outset, foundation. (*end, close, termination, conclusion, consummation, completion*)

behavior—conduct, bearing, demeanor, proceeding, comportment, action, manner, deportment. (*misdemeanor, misbehavior, misconduct*)

belief—assent, faith, trust, credence, avowal, assurance, admission, conviction, opinion, permission, creed, reliance, concession, confidence. (*dissent, unbelief, distrust, denial, misgiving, disavowal*)

belonging—related, connected, appertaining, cognate, congenial, obligatory, accompanying. (*unrelated, unconnected, irrelevant, impertinent, alien*)

bend—curve, deviate, incline, tend, swerve, diverge, mold, persuade, influence, bias, dispose, direct, lower, subordinate to, lean, deflect, bow, condescend, yield, stoop, submit. (*proceed, continue, extend, advance, stand, stiffen, break, crush*)

benediction—blessing, commendation, approval, benison, gratitude, thankfulness, thanksgiving. (*curse, malediction, disapproval, censure, obloquy*)

benefactor—friend, supporter, contributor, upholder, well-wisher, favorer, well-doer, patron. (*foe, opponent, disfavor, antagonist, rival, backfriend, oppressor*)

beneficial—profitable, salutary, advantageous, wholesome, salubrious. (*prejudicial, noxious, hurtful, unprofitable, detrimental*)

benefit—boon, behoof, service, utility, avail, use, good, advantage, profit, favor, blessing. (*evil, loss, disadvantage, detriment, damage, calamity*)

bequeath—give, grant, will to, bestow, impart, leave to. (*withhold, alienate, transfer, disinherit, dispossess*)

bereavement—destitution, affliction, deprivation, loss. (*gift, blessing, donation, benefaction, compensation, reparation, restoration, reinstatement*)

besotted—intoxicated, steeped, stupefied, drunk, drenched, doltish, gross, prejudiced. (*sober, temperate, clear, unbiased, unprejudiced, enlightened*)

bespeak—betoken, foreorder, forestall, provide, prearrange, indicate, evidence. (*belie, resign*)

betimes—early, beforehand, prepared, readily. (*behindhand, slowly, sluggishly, belatedly*)

betray—deceive, delude, dupe, circumvent, ensnare, dishonor, manifest, indicate, reveal. (*protect, preserve, guard, conserve, foster, cherish, fence*)

better—meliorate, improve, amend, emend, ameliorate, rectify, reform. (*make worse*)

beware—care, refrain, consider, heed, look, fear, avoid. (*ignore, overlook, neglect, incur, brave, dare*)

bewilder—daze, dazzle, confound, mystify, puzzle, embarrass, astonish, perplex, confuse, mislead. (*guide, inform, lead, instruct, enlighten*)

bewitch—enchant, fascinate, charm, captivate, entrance. (*exorcise, disillusionize, disenchant*)

bid—tell, request, instruct, direct, order, proffer, charge, command, propose, offer. (*forbid, deter*)

bide—wait, remain, tarry, stay, await, expect, anticipate, continue, bear, abide, endure. (*quit, depart, migrate, move, resist, resent, repel, abjure*)

big—large, great, wide, huge, bulky, proud, arrogant, pompous, fat, massive, gross. (*little, small, narrow, minute, slight, lean, affable, easy*)

binding—restrictive, obligatory, restraining, stringent, styptic, costive, astringent. (*loosening, opening, enlarging, distending*)

birth—parentage, extraction, nativity, family, race, origin, source, rise, lineage, nobility. (*death, extinction, plebeianism*)

bitter—harsh, sour, sharp, tart, acrimonious, sarcastic, severe, sad, afflictive, intense, stinging, pungent, acrid, cutting. (*sweet, mellow, pleasant*)

blacken—bespatter, befoul, bedaub, defame, decry, calumniate, dishonor, asperse, traduce, vilify, slander, malign. (*vindicate, clear, eulogize*)

blackguard—scoundrel, rascal, rapscallion, blackleg, villain. (*gentleman*)

blame—censure, chide, rebuke, reproach, vituperate, dispraise, disapprove, condemn, reprehend, reprobate, reprove. (*acquit, exculpate, exonerate, encourage, praise, approve*)

bland—soft, mild, gentle, complaisant, courteous, affable, gracious, tender, benign. (*harsh, abrupt*)

blast—*n.* breeze, efflation, explosion, blight, burst, blaze, frustration, destruction, squall, gale, tempest, hurricane. (*zephyr, gentle breeze*)

blast—*v.* blight, shrivel, destroy, wither. (*restore, expand, swell*)

bleak—blank, bare, open, cold, exposed, stormy, nipping. (*warm, sheltered, verdant, luxuriant*)

blemish—spot, blur, blot, flaw, speck, fault, imperfection, stain, daub, tarnish, defacement, discoloration, disfigurement, disgrace, dishonor, defect. (*purity, unsulliedness, honor, intactness*)

blend—mix, harmonize, unite, combine, fuse, merge, amalgamate, mingle, commingle, coalesce. (*run, separate, divide, dissociate, confound*)

bless—felicitate, endow, enrich, gladden, rejoice, cheer, thank. (*deprive, sadden, impoverish, ignore*)

blind—sightless, unseeing, eyeless, depraved, undiscerning, ignorant, prejudiced, uninformed, unconscious, unaware. (*farsighted, penetrating, sensitive, keen, discriminating, clear-sighted, pure-minded, aware, conscious*)

blink—wink, ignore, connive, overlook. (*notice, visit, note, mark*)

bliss—blessedness, joy, ecstasy, rapture. (*condemnation, accursedness, suffering, misery, woe*)

blithe—light, merry, joyous, happy, bright, elastic, gladsome, bonny, vivacious, lively, cheerful, blithesome, gay. (*heavy, dull, dejected, sullen*)

blockhead—dolt, dunderhead, jolterhead, dunce ninny, numskull, dullard, simpleton, booby, loggerhead, ignoramus. (*sage, adept, luminary, schoolman, philosopher, savant*)

blooming—flourishing, fair, flowering, blossoming, young, beautiful. (*fading, waning, blighted*)

blot—obscure, tarnish, spoil, sully, spot, discolor, pollute, obliterate, erase, blur, stain, blotch, smear, smutch. (*elucidate, clear, absterge, perpetuate*)

blow—puff, blast, breath, stroke, infliction, wound, disappointment, affliction, knock, shock, calamity, misfortune. (*assuagement, consolation, relief, comfort, blessing, sparing*)

bluff—bare, open, bold, abrupt, frank, plain-spoken, blunt, surly, rude, blustering, swaggering, brusque, hectoring, coarse, discourteous, rough, bullying. (*undulating, inclined, inabrupt, courteous*)

blunder—error, mistake, misunderstanding, fault, oversight, inaccuracy, delusion, slip. (*accuracy, truthfulness, exactness, correctness, faultlessness*)

blush—bloom, color, carnation, complexion, aspect, shame, confusion, guiltiness, self-reproach. (*innocence, purity, guiltlessness, unconsciousness*)

boast—vaunt, brag, swagger, swell, bluster, vapor, triumph, glory.

body—substance, mass, whole, substantiality, collectiveness, assemblage, collection, matter, association, organization. (*spirit, soul, individual*)

boggle—halt, hesitate, dubitate, falter, blunder, blotch, botch, spoil, mar. (*encounter, face, advance*)

bold—courageous, fearless, adventurous, brave, self-confident, forward, intrepid, dauntless, valiant, daring, audacious, lionhearted, doughty. (*timid, fearful, inadventurous, shy, bashful, retiring*)

bombast—bluster, inflatedness, pomposity, boastfulness, exaggeration, fustian. (*truthfulness, moderation, restraint, modesty, humility*)

bond—tie, fastening, chain, association, manacle, fetter, compact, obligation, security. (*freedom, option, discretion, honor, parole*)

bondsman—slave, serf, prisoner, captive, vassal. (*freeman, yeoman, gentleman, lord, master*)

bonny—fair, pretty, pleasant, lively, cheerful, shapely, buxom. (*dull, unseemly, ill-favored*)

border—limit, boundary, brink, rim, verge, brim, edge, edging, band, hem, enclosure, confine. (*land, tract, interior, substance, space, center*)

border on—be contiguous to, be adjacent to, conterminous with, adjoin, adjacent to. (*remote from, away from*)

botch—patch, cobble, blunder, clump, disconcert, spoil, jumble, mess, bungle, mar, blacksmith. (*finedraw, trim, harmonize, mend, beautify, embroider*)

bother—fuss, worry, pester, excitement, stir, plague, vex, annoy, tease, confusion, vexation, flurry, trouble. (*calm, composure, orderliness*)

boundless—unbounded, immeasurable, infinite, unlimited, illimitable, unmeasurable. (*narrow, restricted, limited, confined, circumscribed*)

bounty—liberality, bounteousness, benevolence, munificence, donation, gift, generosity, charity, benignity. (*illiberality, closeness, hardness, churlishness, stinginess, niggardliness*)

brag—boast, vaunt, swagger, bully. (*cringe, whine, whimper*)

branch—member, bifurcation, bough, limb, offspring, shoot, spray, sprig, twig, ramification, offshoot, relative, scion. (*trunk, stock, stem, race*)

break—fracture, rupture, shatter, shiver, destroy, tame, curb, demolish, tear asunder, rend, burst, sever, smash, split, subdue, violate, infringe. (*heal, piece, conjoin, protect, conserve, encourage*)

breath—respiration, inspiration, expiration, inhalation, exhalation. (*cessation, passing, departure*)

breeding—nurture, education, training, discipline, instruction, manners, air, demeanor, decorum. (*ill manners, ill training, ill behavior, ignorance*)

brevity—shortness, closeness, conciseness, succinctness, terseness, compendiousness, pointedness, abbreviation, abridgment. (*length, protraction, elongation, extension, prolixity, diffuseness, interminableness, tediousness*)

bright—shining, brilliant, burnished, luminous, lucid, sparkling, limpid, clever, happy, witty, joyous, cheerful, radiant. (*opaque, dull, dead, muddy*)

brilliant—flashing, radiant, shining, lustrous, highly intelligent, sparkling. (*dull, stupid*)

bring—fetch, procure, convey, carry, bear, adduce, import, produce, cause, induce. (*export, remove, abstract, subtract, prevent, exclude, debar*)

brisk—quick, lively, vivacious, active, alert, nimble, sprightly, spirited, animated, prompt, effervescent. (*slow, heavy, dull, inactive, indolent*)

broad—wide, extensive, expansive, ample, liberal, comprehensive, unreserved, indelicate, coarse, generic. (*narrow, restricted, confined, limited*)

brotherhood—fraternity, association, fellowship, society. (*division, disunity, individual*)

brutal—savage, inhuman, rude, unfeeling, merciless, ruthless, brutish, barbarous, sensual, beastly, ignorant, stolid, dense, cruel, violent, vindictive, bloodthirsty, intemperate. (*humane, civilized, generous, intelligent, polished, chivalrous, conscientious*)

bubble—trifle, toy, fancy, conceit, vision, dream, froth, trash. (*acquisition, prize, treasure, reality*)

bugbear—hobgoblin, goblin, gorgon, ghoul, spirit, spook, specter, ogre, scarecrow.

building—edifice, architecture, construction, erection, fabric, structure. (*ruin, dilapidation, dismantlement, demolition*)

bulk—mass, whole, entirety, integrity, majority, size, magnitude, extension, body, volume, bigness, largeness, massiveness, dimension. (*tenuity, minority, dismemberment, disintegration, diminution, portion, contraction, section, atom, particle*)

bungler—botcher, clown, lubber, fumbler, novice. (*adept, adroit, master, artist, workman, proficient, professor*)

buoyant—sprightly, spirited, vivacious, lively, light, floating, hopeful, cheerful, elastic, joyous. (*heavy, depressed, cheerless, joyless, dejected, moody*)

burden—load, weight, incubus, obstruction, oppression, grief, difficulty, affliction. (*ease, lightness, airiness, expedition, facility, acceleration, abjugation, liberation, lightheartedness, alleviation*)

burn—ignite, kindle, brand, consume, cauterize, rage, glow, smoulder, blaze, flash, cremate, incinerate. (*extinguish, stifle, cool, wane, subside*)

bury—inter, inhume, conceal, repress, suppress, obliterate, cancel, entomb, compose, hush. (*disinter, exhume, bruit, excavate, expose, resuscitate*)

business—occupation, profession, vocation, transaction, trade, calling, office, employment, interest, duty, affair, matter, concern. (*stagnation, leisure, inactivity*)

bustle—business, activity, stir, commotion, energy, excitement, haste, hurry, eagerness, flurry. (*idleness, vacation, inactivity, indolence, indifference*)

busy—industrious, diligent, assiduous, engaged, occupied. (*idle, slothful, lazy, indolent, unoccupied*)

but—save, except, barring, yet, beside, excluding, still, excepting, notwithstanding. (*with, including, inclusive, nevertheless, however, notwithstanding*)

C

calamity—disaster, misfortune, mishap, catastrophe, misadventure, trouble, visitation, affliction, reverse, blight. (*godsend, blessing, boon*)

calculate—estimate, consider, weigh, number, count, apportion, proportion, investigate, reckon, rate, compute. (*guess, conjecture, hit, chance, risk*)

calculation—estimation, consideration, balance, apportionment, investigation, reckoning, computation, anticipation, forethought, regard, circumspection, watchfulness, vigilance, caution, care. (*inconsiderateness, inconsideration, incaution, indiscretion, miscalculation, misconception, exclusion, exception, omission, carelessness, supposition*)

caliber—gauge, diameter, ability, capacity, force, quality, character. (*weakness, incapacity*)

called—named, designated, denominated, yclept, termed. (*unnamed, undesignated, misnamed, misdesignated*)

calm—smooth, pacify, compose, allay, still, soothe, appease, assuage, quiet, tranquilize. (*stir, excite, agitate, disconcert, ruffle, lash, heat, discompose*)

calumny—slander, defamation, detraction, libel, traducement, backbiting, opprobrium, aspersion. (*vindication, clearance, eulogy, panegyric*)

cancel—efface, blot out, annul, expunge, nullify, quash, rescind, repeal, revoke, abrogate, obliterate, discharge, erase, abolish, countervail. (*enforce, enact, re-enact, confirm, perpetuate, contract*)

candid—fair, honest, open, sincere, frank, artless, impartial, plain, straightforward, aboveboard, transparent, unreserved, ingenious. (*unfair, close*)

candidate—aspirant, petitioner, canvasser, applicant, claimant, solicitor. (*waiver, decliner, abandoner, resigner, abjurer, noncompetitor*)

canvass—question, investigate, challenge, test, dispute, solicit, sift, examine, discuss, apply for, request. (*pretermit, allow, ignore, disregard, admit*)

capacity—space, size, volume, tonnage, caliber, ability, faculty, capability, cleverness, talents, magnitude, parts, competency, comprehensiveness, accommodation. (*narrowness, restriction, incapacity, coarctation, contractedness*)

capital—chief, excellent, important, cardinal, principal, consummate, high. (*inferior, unimportant, subordinate, minor, defective, mean*)

capricious—wayward, uncertain, fanciful, freakish, fitful, fickle, changeful, whimsical, humorsome, inconstant, crotchety. (*firm, unchanging, inflexible, decided, unswerving, constant*)

captivated—taken, charmed, smitten, fascinated, enslaved, captured, enthralled. (*free, unaffected, uninfluenced, unscathed, insensible, insensitive*)

care—attention, pains, anxiety, concern, trouble, circumspection, regard, solicitude, caution, prevention, custody, preservation, thrift, heed, foresight, wariness, economy, prudence. (*inattention, neglect*)

career—course, success, walk, line, progress, history, way of life, passage, race. (*misproceeding, misdeportment, unsuccess, miscarriage*)

caress—endearment, blandishment, wheedling, fondling, stroking. (*vexation, irritation, annoyance*)

caricature—mimicry, parody, travesty, burlesque, extravagance, exaggeration, hyperbole, monstrosity, farce. (*portraiture, representation, resemblance, justice, fidelity, truthfulness*)

carnival—revel, rout, festivity, masquerade. (*fast, mortification, lent, retirement*)

carpet—table, board, consideration, consultation. (*shelf, rejection, disposal, oblivion*)

carriage—transportation, conveyance, bearing, manner, conduct, demeanor, walk, gait, mien, behavior, deportment, vehicle. (*misconveyance, miscarriage, misconduct, misconsignment*)

case—occurrence, circumstance, contingency, event, plight, predicament, fact, subject, condition, instance. (*hypothesis, supposition, fancy, theory*)

cast—*v.* hurl, send down, throw, fling, pitch, impel, project, construct, mold, frame. (*raise, elevate*)

cast—*n.* mold, stamp, kind, figure, form, aspect, mien, air, style, manner, character. (*malformation, deformity, abnormity*)

caste—order, class, rank, lineage, race, blood, dignity, respect. (*degradation, taboo, disrepute*)

Synonym
Ant/Hom

casual—accidental, occasional, incidental, contingent, unforeseen, fortuitous. (*regular, ordinary*)

catastrophe—revolution, disaster, calamity, misfortune, misadventure, reverse, blow, visitation. (*blessing, victory, triumph, felicitation, achievement*)

cause—source, origin, producer, agent, creator, purpose, inducement, reason, account, principle, motive, object, suit, action. (*effect, result, accomplishment, end, production, issue, preventive*)

cease—intermit, stop, desist, abstain, discontinue, quit, refrain, end, pause, leave off. (*ceaseless, never-ending, everlasting, constant, incessant*)

celebrated—famed, renowned, illustrious, eminent, glorious, famous, noted, distinguished, notable, exalted. (*unrenowned, obscure, undistinguished*)

celebrity—fame, honor, glory, star, reputation, distinction, renown, notability, eminence, notoriety. (*obscurity, meanness, ingloriousness, ignominy, disgrace, contempt, cipher, nobody*)

celestial—heavenly, ethereal, atmospheric, supernal, angelic, radiant, eternal, immortal, seraphic, divine, godlike, elysian. (*earthly, terrestrial, terrene*)

censure—blame, stricture, reproach, reprobate, inculpate, reprove, condemn, reprehend, chide, berate, scold, upbraid, disapproval, remonstrance, rebuke, reprimand, dispraise. (*praise, eulogy, approbation, encouragement, commendation*)

ceremonial—official, ministerial, functional, pompous, imposing, sumptuous, scenic. (*ordinary, private, unimposing, unostentatious, undramatic*)

certain—true, fixed, regular, established, incontrovertible, undoubtful, indubitable, infallible, unmistakable, sure, unfailing, real, actual, undeniable, positive, convinced, assured. (*uncertain, dubious, exceptional, irregular, casual, occasional*)

certify—acknowledge, aver, attest, vouch, avow, avouch, testify, protest, declare, demonstrate, prove, evidence, inform, assure. (*disprove, disavow, misinform, misadvise*)

challenge—defy, summon, dare, question, investigate, brave, canvass. (*pass, allow, grant, concede*)

chance—accident, fortuity, hazard, haphazard, fortune, random, casualty, befallment, luck. (*law, rule, sequence, consequence, causation, effectuation*)

changeless—regular, settled, steady, firm, stationary, consistent, resolute, reliable, undeviating, uniform, immutable, immovable. (*irregular, unsettled, unsteady, wavering, fluctuating, capricious*)

character—symbol, letter, nature, type, disposition, genius, temperament, cast, estimation, repute, office, reputation, part, capacity, class, order, sort, stamp, kind, quality, species, sign, tone, mark, figure, record. (*vagueness, anonymousness, nondescription, disrepute*)

characteristic—distinction, peculiarity, diagnosis, idiosyncrasy, specialty, individuality, personality, singularity. (*nondescription, abstractedness, generality, miscellany*)

charitable—kind, benign, benevolent, beneficent, liberal, considerate, forgiving, compassionate, placable, inexacting, inextreme. (*uncharitable, unkind, harsh, selfish, churlish, illiberal, censorious*)

charm—*v.* bewitch, enchant, fascinate, lay, soothe, mesmerize, delight, enrapture, transport, entice, allure, entrance, captivate, subdue. (*disenchant, rouse, disturb, annoy, irritate*)

charm—*n.* spell, incantation, enchantment, fascination, attraction, allurement. (*disenchantment, repulsion, fear*)

chaste—pure, modest, uncontaminated, spotless, immaculate, undefiled, virtuous, incorrupt, simple, unaffected, nice. (*impure, corrupt, meretricious*)

cheap—common, inexpensive, uncostly, mean, vile, worthless, low-priced. (*rare, costly, worthy*)

cheat—*v.* overreach, fleece, silence, trick, gull, cozen, juggle, defraud, swindle, dupe, beguile, deceive, deprive, hoodwink, prevaricate, dissemble, shuffle, inveigle. (*enlighten, guide, remunerate*)

cheat—*n.* deception, fraud, imposition, trick, artifice, illusion, impostor, swindle, finesse, deceit, lie, fiction. (*truth, reality, verity, fact, certainty*)

cheer—hope, happiness, comfort, hospitality, plenty, conviviality. (*dejection, sullenness, gloom, starvation, niggardliness, dearth, inhospitableness*)

cheerful—lively, gay, bright, happy, bonny, merry, joyful, pleasant, buoyant, sunny, enlivening, in good spirits, sprightly, blithe, joyous. (*lifeless, dull, gloomy, unhappy, dejected, depressed, sullen*)

childish—weak, silly, puerile, infantile, imbecile, foolish, trifling, paltry, trivial. (*strong, resolute, manly, wise, judicious, sagacious, chivalrous*)

chivalrous—courageous, generous, knightly, gallant, heroic, adventurous, valiant, spirited, handsome, high-minded. (*unhandsome, dirty, sneaking*)

choice—option, adoption, selection, election, preference, alternative. (*compulsion, necessity, rejection, refusal, unimportance, indifference, refuse*)

chuckle—grin, crow, cackle. (*cry, wail, grumble, whimper, whine*)

cipher—nonentity, dot, nothing, trifle, button (*fig.*), straw, pin, rush, molehill. (*somebody, bigwig, something, notability, celebrity, triton, colossus*)

circumstance—detail, feature, point, event, occurrence, incident, situation, position, fact, topic, condition, particular, specialty. (*deed, case, transaction*)

civil—well-mannered, political, courteous, well-bred, complaisant, affable, urbane, polite, obliging, accommodating, respectful. (*disobliging, unaccommodating, disrespectful, boorish, clownish, churlish*)

claim—*v.* demand, ask, require, insist, pretend, request, maintain. (*forgo, waive, disclaim, abjure, disavow, abandon*)

claim—*n.* assertion, vindication, pretension, title, right, privilege, arrogation, demand. (*waiver, abjuration, disclaimer, surrender*)

claimant—assertor, vindicator, appellant, litigant. (*relinquisher, resigner, conceder, waiver*)

classification—order, species, nature, character, cast, stamp, group, kind, section, sect, category, assortment, designation, description, genus. (*individuality, specialty, isolation, alienation, division*)

clause—portion, paragraph, stipulation, provision, article, condition, chapter, section, passage. (*document, instrument, muniment*)

clear—*v.* clarify, disencumber, disentangle, disembarrass, vindicate, liberate, set free, release, exonerate, exculpate, justify, retrieve, acquit, absolve, whitewash, extricate, eliminate. (*befoul, contaminate, pollute, clog, encumber, embarrass*)

clear—*a.* open, pure, bright, transparent, free, disencumbered, disentangled, disengaged, absolved, acquitted, serene, unclouded, evident, apparent, distinct, manifest, conspicuous, unobstructed, plain, obvious, intelligible, lucid. (*thick, muddy*)

clever—able, ready, talented, quick, ingenious, dexterous, adroit, expert, gifted, quick-witted, skillful, well-contrived. (*weak, dull, stupid, slow*)

cling—fasten, hold, adhere, embrace, stick, cleave, hang, twine, hug. (*drop, recede, secede, apostatize, abandon, relax, forgo, swerve, surrender*)

cloak—conceal, disguise, mask, veil, hide, cover, palliate, screen, mitigate, extenuate. (*exhibit, propound, promulge, portray, aggravate, expose, demonstrate, reveal*)

close—narrow, limited, restricted, condensed, packed, secret, compressed, solid, firm, compact, reserved, niggardly, shut, fast, dense. (*wide, open*)

clownish—rustic, boorish, bucolic, foolish, awkward, clumsy, cloddish, untutored, rude. (*polite, civil, urbane, affable, graceful, polished, refined*)

clumsy—awkward, inexpert, uncouth, maladroit, botching, bungling, unskillful, unwieldy, unhandy, ill-shaped. (*neat, workmanlike, artistic, handy*)

coarse—common, ordinary, indelicate, vulgar, gross, unrefined, immodest, rough, rude, unpolished. (*fine, refined, gentle, polished, delicate, choice*)

cognizance—notice, observation, recognition, knowledge, experience. (*inadvertence, neglect, ignorance, inexperience, oversight, connivance*)

coherent—consecutive, consistent, complete, sensible, compact, logical, close. (*inconsecutive, rambling, disunited, inconsistent, discursive, loose*)

coincidence—chance, fortuity, casualty, concurrence, correspondence, contemporaneousness, commensurateness, harmony, agreement, consent. (*design, purpose, adaptation, asynchronism, anachronism, disharmony, incommensurateness, discordance, variation, difference*)

colleague—helper, companion, associate, ally, confederate, coadjutor, partner, assistant, adjutant, assessor. (*co-opponent, corival, counteragent, co-antagonist, competitor*)

collect—collate, gather, glean, sum, infer, learn, congregate, assemble, convoke, convene, muster, amass, garner, accumulate. (*classify, arrange, distribute, dispose, dispense, divide, sort, deal*)

collection—assembly, assemblage, store, gathering, collation. (*dispersion, distribution, dispensation, division, arrangement, disposal, classification*)

color—hue, tint, complexion, pretense, speciousness, tinge, garbling, falsification, distortion, perversion, varnish. (*achromatism, paleness, nakedness, openness, genuineness, transparency, truthfulness*)

combination—union, association, consortment, concert, confederacy, alliance, league, coalition, cabal, synthesis, cooperation. (*division, disunion*)

comfortable—snug, satisfied, pleasant, agreeable, cozy, commodious, convenient, consoled. (*uncomfortable, dissatisfied, troubled, miserable, wretched*)

commerce—trade, traffic, merchandise, barter, exchange, business, communication, dealing, intercourse. (*stagnation, exclusion, inactivity, interdict*)

commodious—ample, easy, convenient, spacious, suitable, comfortable. (*inconvenient, incommodious, narrow, ill-contrived, incommensurate, discommodious*)

common—ordinary, familiar, habitual, everyday, frequent, coarse, vulgar, low, mean, universal. (*unusual, exceptional, scarce, rare, uncommon, refined, partial, infrequent, sporadic, egregious, excellent*)

community—aggregation, association, commonwealth, coordination, society, sympathy, order, class, brotherhood, fraternity, polity, unity, nationality, similarity, homogeneity. (*segregation, secession, independence, dissociation, disconnection*)

company—aggregation, association, union, sodality, order, fraternity, guild, corporation, society, community, assemblage, assembly, crew, posse, gang, troop, audience, congregation, concourse. (*rivalry, opposition, disqualification, antagonism*)

compass—encompass, surround, enclose, environ, circumscribe, embrace, achieve, effect, effectuate, consummate, complete, circumvent. (*expand, dispand, unfold, amplify, display, dismiss, liberate, discard, fail, bungle, botch, misconceive, mismanage*)

compatible—consistent, consentaneous, harmonious, coexistent, correspondent, congruous, accordant, agreeable, congenial, consonant. (*incompatible, impossible, insupposable, inconsistent, discordant, hostile, adverse, antagonistic, incongruous*)

compel—force, oblige, drive, constrain, necessitate, make, coerce, bind. (*persuade, convince, coax*)

compensation—remunerative, equivalent, wages, pay, allowance, restoration, restitution, satisfaction, atonement, expiation, indemnification, amercement, damages. (*deprivation, injury, nonpayment, gratuity, donation, fraudulence, damage*)

competition—rivalry, emulation, race, two of a trade. (*association, colleagueship, alliance, joint-stock, copartnership, confederation*)

complacent—pleased, satisfied, content, pleasant, affable, kind, mannerly, acquiescent, amiable. (*dissatisfied, irritated, churlish, unmannerly, morose*)

complaint—murmur, discontent, repining, grievance, annoyance, remonstrance, expostulation, lamentation, sickness, disease. (*congratulation, rejoicing, approbation, complacency, boon, benefit*)

complement—completion, fulfilment, totality, supply, counterpart, correlative. (*deficiency, deficit, insufficiency, abatement, detraction, defalcation*)

complete—full, perfect, finished, adequate, entire, consummate, total, exhaustive, thorough, accomplished. (*incomplete, partial, imperfect, unfinished, inadequate*)

complexion—face, aspect, color, look, feature, appearance, character, hue, interpretation, indication. (*unindicativeness, concealment, reticence, inexpression, heart, core*)

complicated—confused, intricate, involved, perplexed, entangled. (*clear, simple, uninvolved, lucid*)

compliment—homage, courtesy, flattery, praise. (*insult, discourtesy, contempt*)

complimentary—commendatory, laudatory, panegyrical, eulogistic, encomiastic, lavish of praise. (*disparaging, condemnatory, damnatory, denunciatory, reproachful, abusive, objurgatory, vituperative*)

composition—compound, conformation, structure, mixture, combination, compromise, adjustment, settlement, commutation. (*analysis, segregation, examination, criticism, discussion, disturbance, aggravation, perpetuation*)

Synonym Ant/Hom

comprehend—comprise, embody, grasp, understand, conceive, apprehend, enclose, include, involve, embrace. (*exclude, except, misunderstand*)

comprehensive—wide, ample, general, extensive, large, broad, all-embracing, generic, significant, capacious, inclusive, compendious, pregnant. (*narrow, restricted, shallow, exclusive, adversative*)

compromise—arbitrate, adjust, compose, settle, endanger, implicate, involve. (*aggravate, excite, foster, perpetuate, exempt, enfranchise, disengage*)

conceal—hide, secrete, disguise, keep secret, dissemble, screen, suppress. (*reveal, manifest, exhibit, avow, confess, expose, promulgate, publish*)

concentrate—assemble, converge, muster, congregate, convene, draw, conglomerate, condense, localize, centralize. (*disperse, scatter, dismiss, decentralize*)

concerning—about, of, relating, regarding, touching, in relation to, respecting, with respect to, with regard to, with reference to, relative to. (*omitting*)

concert—union, combination, concord, harmony, agreement, association, cooperation. (*dissociation, counteraction, opposition*)

condescension—affability, graciousness, favor, stooping. (*haughtiness, arrogance, pride, superciliousness, disdain, scorn*)

condition—state, case, mood, term, mode, qualification, requisite, stipulation, predicament, proviso, situation, circumstances, plight. (*relation*)

conditionally—provisionally, relatively, provided, hypothetically, contingently. (*absolutely, unconditionally, categorically, positively*)

conducive—contributive, promotive, subsidiary, causative, effective, productive. (*preventive, counteractive, contrariant, repugnant, destructive*)

conduct—lead, bring, carry, transfer, direct, guide, control, manage, administer. (*mislead, miscarry, mismanage, misconduct, misadminister*)

confer—compare, collate, discuss, deliberate, converse, consult, give, present. (*dissociate, contrast, hazard, conjecture, withhold, withdraw*)

confession—creed, catechism, articles, doctrine, tenets, profession, declaration, subscription. (*heresy, apostasy, protest, condemnation, refutation*)

confidant—confessor, adviser, confederate. (*traitor, betrayer, rival*)

confident—positive, assured, sure, certain, impudent, bold, sanguine. (*unsure, afraid, timid*)

confidential—private, secret, trustworthy, intimate. (*public, open, patent, official, treacherous*)

confirm—strengthen, stabilitate, establish, substantiate, settle, prove, fix, perpetuate, sanction, corroborate, ratify. (*weaken, shake, upset, cancel*)

confront—oppose, face, encounter, resist, intimidate, menace. (*rally, encourage, abet, countenance*)

confused—abashed, embarrassed, perplexed, disconcerted, disorganized, promiscuous, chaotic, complex, involved, disarranged, disordered. (*unabashed, unembarrassed, systematic, unconfused*)

congress—parliament, council, conclave, assembly, synod, legislature, convention. (*cabal, conclave, mob*)

conjecture—guess, divination, hypothesis, theory, notion, surmise, supposition. (*computation, calculation, inference, reckoning, proof, deduction*)

connection—junction, conjunction, union, association, concatenation, relation, affinity, relevance, intercourse, communication, kinsman, relationship, kindred. (*disconnection, disjunction, dissociation*)

conquer—subdue, vanquish, surmount, overcome, overpower, overthrow, defeat, crush, master, subjugate, prevail over. (*fail, fall, retreat, succumb, fly, submit, surrender, lose, forfeit, sacrifice*)

conscious—aware, cognizant, sensible. (*unaware, unconscious, insensible*)

consecutive—orderly, arranged, coherent, continuous. (*disordered, undigested, incoherent*)

consent—submit, agree, acquiesce. (*resist, disagree, dissent, decline, refuse*)

consequence—effect, issue, result, inference, coherence, deduction, conclusion, outcome, importance, note, moment, dignity. (*cause, causation, antecedence, premise, origin, datum, postulate*)

consider—attend, revolve, meditate, think, reflect, investigate, regard, observe, judge, opine, infer, deduce, weigh, cogitate, deliberate, ponder, deem. (*disregard, ignore, pretermit, despise, guess*)

considerate—thoughtful, attentive, forbearing, unselfish, judicious, serious, prudent, circumspect, reflective, careful, cautious. (*thoughtless, inconsiderate, inattentive, rude, overbearing, selfish, injudicious, rash, careless*)

consistency—consistence, congruity, composition, substance, material, amalgamation, compound, mass, density, solidity, closeness, compactness, coherence, uniformity, harmony, analogy, proportion. (*volatility, vaporousness, subtility, tenuity, sublimation, incoherence, inconsistency, incongruity, disproportion, contrariety, contradiction*)

consistent—congruous, accordant, consonant, agreeing, compatible, harmonious. (*incongruous, at variance with, not agreeing with, incompatible*)

conspicuous—visible, easily seen, prominent, distinguished, manifest, eminent, famous, noted, salient, observable, noticeable, magnified. (*invisible, inconspicuous, inobservable, noticeable, microscopic*)

constant—uniform, regular, invariable, perpetual, continuous, firm, fixed, steady, immutable, faithful, true, trustworthy. (*irregular, exceptional*)

constitution—temperament, frame, temper, character, habit, nature, government, polity, state, consistence, composition, substance, organization, structure, regulation, law. (*accident, habituation, modification, interference, anarchy, despotism, tyranny, rebellion, revolution, dissipation, disorganization, demolition, destruction*)

construction—composition, fabrication, explanation, rendering, erection, fabric, edifice, reading, understanding, interpretation, view. (*dislocation, dismemberment, demolition, displacement, misplacement, misconstruction, misunderstanding, misconception, misinterpretation*)

consult—interrogate, canvass, question, deliberate, confer, advise with, regard, consider, ask advice of, care for, promote. (*resolve, explain, expound, direct, instruct, dictate, counteract, contravene*)

consumption—decline, decay, expenditure, waste, decrement, lessening, decrease. (*growth, development, enlargement, augmentation*)

contact—touch, contiguity, continuity, apposition, adjunction. (*proximity, adjacence, interrup-*

tion, disconnection, separation, distance, isolation)

contagious—catching, epidemic, infectious, pestilential, communicated, transferred, transmitted, infectious. (*sporadic, endemic, preventive, antipathetic*)

contaminate—defile, taint, corrupt, sully, befoul, soil. (*purify, cleanse, lave, clarify, sanctify, chasten*)

contemplate—meditate, behold, observe, ponder, study, purpose, design, intend, project. (*ignore, overlook, waive, abandon*)

contemptible—despicable, mean, vile, pitiful, disreputable, paltry, trifling, trivial. (*important, grave, weighty, honorable, respectable, venerable*)

content—full, satisfied, pleased, gratified, contented, willing, resigned. (*unsatisfied, dissatisfied*)

contentious—litigious, perverse, wayward, splenetic, cantankerous, exceptious. (*pacific, obliging*)

contingent—dependent, incidental, resultant, coefficient, hypothetical, uncertain, conditional. (*positive, absolute, independent, unmodified, unaffected, uncontrolled, irrespective*)

continually—constantly, persistently, always, ever, perpetually, unceasingly, repeatedly, frequently, continuously. (*casually, occasionally, contingently, sometimes, rarely, fitfully, intermittently*)

contract—*n.* covenant, agreement, compact, bond, pact, stipulation, bargain. (*promise, assurance, parole*)

contract—*v.* abridge, abbreviate, narrow, lessen, reduce, compress, decrease, retrench, curtail, form, agree. (*expand, amplify, dilate, elongate*)

contradict—oppose, dissent, negative, controvert, deny, disprove, confute, refute, gainsay, contravene. (*state, propound, maintain, argue, confirm, affirm*)

contrary—opposed, opposite, repugnant, antagonistic, adverse, incompatible, inconsistent. (*agreeing, consentaneous, compatible, kindred, coincident*)

contribute—conduce, add, subscribe, give, cooperate, assist, tend, supply. (*refuse, withhold*)

contrive—plan, design, arrange, fabricate, adapt, manage, scheme, devise, concert, adjust. (*hit, hazard, run, chance, venture, bungle, over-vault*)

control—check, curb, moderate, repress, guide, regulate, restrain, coerce, manage, administer, govern. (*neglect, abandon, license, liberate, mismanage, misconduct*)

convenient—handy, apt, adapted, fitted, suitable, helpful, commodious, useful, timely, seasonable, opportune. (*inconvenient, awkward, obstructive, useless, superfluous, unseasonable, untimely*)

conventional—customary, usual, ordinary, stipulated, prevalent, social. (*unusual, unsocial, legal*)

conversant—familiar, acquainted, proficient, experienced, versed, learned. (*unfamiliar, unacquainted, ignorant, unversed, unlearned, strange*)

convertible—identical, commensurate, conterminous, equivalent, equipollent. (*variant, incommensurate, unequivalent, contrary, contradictory*)

conviction—assurance, persuasion, belief. (*doubt, misgiving, disbelief*)

cooperate—assist, abet, contribute, concur, work together, help, conspire. (*thwart, oppose*)

copy—imitation, portraiture, facsimile, counterfeit, duplicate, image, likeness, transcript. (*original, prototype, model, example, pattern*)

cordial—warm, earnest, sincere, reviving, invig-

orating, affectionate, hearty. (*cold, distant, formal*)

corner—cavity, hole, nook, recess, retreat. (*coin, abutment, prominence, salience, angle, protrusion, elbow, protection, convexity*)

corpulent—stout, burly, fat, portly, gross, lusty, plethoric, fleshy. (*lean, thin, attenuated, slight*)

correct—*a.* true, exact, faultless, accurate, proper, decorous, right. (*false, untrue, incorrect*)

correct—*v.* chasten, punish, rectify, amend, reform, emend, redress, set right, improve. (*spare, falsify, corrupt*)

correction—amendment, discipline, emendation, chastisement, punishment. (*deterioration, debasement, retrogradation, reward, recompense*)

correspond—match, tally, fit, answer, agree, suit, harmonize. (*vary, differ, disagree, jar, clash*)

correspondence—fitness, agreement, adaptation, congruity, answerableness, match, congeniality, communication, letter, writing, dispatches. (*conversation, colloquy, confabulation, reservation, withdrawal, withholding, nonintercourse, difference*)

corrupt—defiled, polluted, vitiated, decayed, depraved, putrid, rotten, infected, tainted, profligate, contaminated. (*pure, uncorrupt, undefiled*)

corruption—decomposition, decay, putrescence, adulteration, depravity, rottenness, defilement, deterioration, perversion, debasement, taint, contamination, putrefaction. (*vitality, organization*)

cost—*v.* require, consume, absorb. (*bring, produce, yield, afford, fetch, return*)

cost—*n.* expenditure, outlay, disbursement, payment, compensation, price, worth, expense, charge, outgoings. (*receipt, income, emolument*)

costly—valuable, expensive, high-priced, rich, precious, sumptuous. (*valueless, cheap, low-priced, mean, worthless, beggarly, paltry*)

council—cabinet, bureau, chamber, consultation, conclave, parliament, congress, synod, company, assembly, meeting, conference, convention, convocation. (*league, conspiracy, cabal, intrigue, mob*)

counsel—advice, instruction, monition, admonition, warning, recommendation. (*misguidance, misinstruction, betrayal*)

count—compute, reckon, enumerate, estimate, number, sum, calculate. (*hazard, conjecture, guess*)

countenance—*v.* help, aid, abet, favor, sanction, patronize, support, encourage. (*oppose, confront, discourage, discountenance, browbeat*)

countenance—*n.* aid, abet, encourage, support. (*discountenance*)

counteract—counterinfluence, counterfoil, foil, baffle, neutralize, oppose, rival, thwart, hinder. (*aid, help, abet, promote, conserve, cooperate, subserve*)

counterpart—match, fellow, tally, brother, twin, copy, correlative, complement, supplement. (*opponent, counteragent, reverse, obverse, opposite, antithesis, contrast, contradiction*)

countryman—rustic, clown, boor, compatriot, swain, yeoman, husbandman, farmer, agriculturist, laborer, peasant, fellow countryman, fellow subject, fellow citizen, subject, citizen, inhabitant, native. (*oppidan, townsman, cockney, foreigner, alien*)

couple—bracket, link, conjoin, unite, splice, buckle, button, clasp, pair, yoke, connect, tie, brace. (*loose, part, isolate, separate, detach, divorce, uncouple*)

Synonym Ant/Hom

courage—bravery, boldness, valor, pluck, fortitude, resolution, gallantry, fearlessness, intrepidity. (*timidity, cowardice, pusillanimity, poltroonery, dastardliness*)

course—order, sequence, continuity, direction, progress, line, way, mode, race, career, road, route, series, passage, succession, round, manner, plain, conduct, method. (*disorder, discursion, solution, interruption, deviation, hindrance, error, conjecture*)

courtly—dignified, polished, refined, aristocratic, high-bred, mannerly. (*undignified, rough, unpolished, coarse, unrefined, plebeian, awkward, boorish, rustic, unmannerly*)

covetous—acquisitive, avaricious, greedy, grasping, rapacious. (*unselfish, liberal, self-sacrificing*)

coward—craven, dastard, recreant, poltroon, renegade. (*champion, hero, daredevil, desperado*)

coxcomb—fop, dandy, puppy, prig, pedant. (*genius, savant, authority, celebrity, philosopher, sage*)

coy—shy, reserved, bashful, shrinking, retreating, modest. (*bold, forward, rompish, hoydenish*)

crabbed—sour, morose, cross-grained, petulant, churlish, irritable, crusty. (*pleasant, open, easy, genial, conversable, warm, cordial, hearty*)

craft—art, artifice, cunning, guile, stratagem, maneuver, wiliness, trickery, duplicity, chicanery, intrigue, underhandedness, dodge. (*openness, fairness, candor, honesty, frankness, sincerity, artlessness*)

cram—stuff, choke, squeeze, ram, pack, gorge. (*disgorge, vent, discharge, unload, unpack, eviscerate*)

crash—jar, clang, clash, resonance. (*murmur, whisper, babble, rumbling, reverberation, din*)

cream—marrow, pith, gist, acme. (*refuse, offal, dregs, dross, garbage*)

credential, or **credentials**—missive, diploma, title, testament, seal, warrant, letter, vouchers, certificates, testimonials. (*self-license, self-constitution, self-appointment, autocracy*)

credit—relief, trustworthiness, reputation, security, honor, praise, merit, confidence, faith. (*disbelief, distrust, untrustworthiness, shame, insecurity*)

creed—belief, catechism, articles, confession, subscription. (*protest, abjuration, recantation, retractation, disbelief, nonsubscription*)

criminal—illegal, felonious, vicious, culpable, wrong, iniquitous, sinful, immoral, guilty, nefarious, flagitious. (*lawful, virtuous, right, just, innocent*)

critical—nice, delicate, exact, fastidious, discriminating, censorious, accurate, dubious, precarious, ticklish, crucial, important, momentous, hazardous. (*inexact, popular, loose, easy, undiscriminating, safe, determined, decided, settled, retrieved, redressed*)

criticism—stricture, censure, animadversion. (*approval, praise*)

cross-grained—perverse, wayward, peevish, morose, cantankerous, ill-conditioned. (*genial, pleasant, agreeable, jolly, obliging, accommodating*)

crude—raw, undigested, unconsidered, halfstudied, harsh, unshaped, unchastened, unfinished, unrefined, ill-prepared. (*well-prepared, well-digested, well-considered, well-studied, ripe, welladapted, well-proportioned, well-expressed, classical*)

cruel—savage, barbarous, pitiless, inexorable, unrelenting, ruthless, truculent, hardhearted, harsh,

unmerciful, brutal, inhuman, maleficent, malignant. (*humane, forbearing, generous, merciful, forgiving, benevolent, beneficent*)

crush—pulverize, triturate, pound, bray, crumble, overpower, demolish. (*consolidate, compact*)

cuff—slap, box, smack, punch, pummel, hustle buffet. (*cudgel, flagellate, thrash, cane, strap, lash*)

cultivate—promote, foster, study, improve, fertilize, till, advance, refine, improve, civilize, nourish, cherish. (*neglect, desert, abandon, stifle, prevent*)

cupidity—avarice, acquisitiveness, covetousness, stinginess. (*prodigality, extravagance, liberality*)

cure—remedy, alleviation, restorative, heal-all, amelioration, reinstatement, restoration, renovation, convalescence. (*aggravation, confirmation*)

curiosity—inquisitiveness, interest, wonder, marvel, interrogativeness, rarity, phenomenon, celebrity, oddity, lion. (*indifference, heedlessness, disregard, abstraction, absence, weed, drug, dirt, cipher*)

curious—inquiring, inquisitive, scrutinizing, prying, meddling, singular, searching, interrogative, peeping, peering, rare, unique, odd, recondite. (*indifferent, uninquiring, incurious, uninterested*)

current—running, prevalent, ordinary, present, popular, general, floating, exoteric, vulgar. (*rejected, obsolete, exploded, confined, private, secret*)

custody—keeping, guardianship, conservation, care. (*neglect, betrayal, exposure, abandonment*)

cynical—sarcastic, snarling, snappish, sneering, cross-grained, currish, carping. (*genial, lenient*)

D

daft—silly, innocent, idiotic, lunatic, lightheaded, cracked. (*sane, sound, sensible, practical*)

dainty—choice, rare, refined, tasty, exquisite, luxurious, epicurean. (*common, coarse, unrelishing, nasty, dirty, omnivorous, greedy, gluttonous*)

damp—cool, blunt, dishearten, quench, slack, moderate, humid, wet, moist, discourage, discountenance, repress. (*urge, inflame, incite, fan*)

dapper—spruce, neat, natty, smart. (*slovenly, awkward, unwieldy, untidy*)

daring—adventurous, dashing, bold, courageous, venturesome, dauntless, foolhardy, fearless, brave, intrepid, valorous. (*cautious, timid, inadventurous*)

dark—black, dusky, sable, swarthy, opaque, obscure, enigmatical, recondite, abstruse, unintelligible, blind, ignorant, besotted, benighted, dim, shadowy, inexplicable, secret, mysterious, hidden, murky, nebulous, cheerless, dismal, dim, gloomy, somber, joyless, sorrowful. (*white, fair, cheerful*)

dash—hurl, cast, throw, subvert, detrude, drive, rush, send, fly, speed, dart, scatter, strike, course. (*raise, reinstate, erect, creep, crawl, lag, hobble*)

daunt—terrify, scare, frighten, cow, dishearten, appall, intimidate, confront. (*countenance, encourage, rally, inspirit*)

dawdle—lag, dally, idle. (*haste, speed, dash*)

dead—defunct, deceased, departed, gone, inanimate, lifeless, insensible, heavy, unconscious, dull, spiritless, cheerless, deserted, torpid, still. (*vital, living, animate, vivacious, susceptible, alive, joyous*)

deadly—mortal, fatal, malignant, baleful, pernicious, noxious, venomous, destructive, baneful, implacable. (*vital, life-giving, healthful, wholesome*)

deaf—surd, hard of hearing, disinclined, averse,

inexorable, insensible, rumbling, inaudible, heedless, dead. (*acute, listening, disposed, interested*)

dear—high-priced, costly, expensive, beloved, precious, loved. (*cheap, inexpensive, misliked, vile*)

death—departure, demise, decease, dissolution, mortality, fall, failure, termination, cessation, expiration, release, exit. (*birth, rise, life, growth*)

debatable—dubious, doubtful, inestimable, uncertain, problematical, floating, unsettled, disputable. (*certain, sure, unquestionable, indisputable*)

debauchery—riot, revel, excess, orgies, gluttony. (*moderation, frugality, asceticism*)

debt—debit, liability, default, obligation, claim, score, something due. (*liquidation, assets, credit, trust, grace, favor, obligation, accommodation, gift*)

decay—*v.* decline, wane, sink, dwindle, rot, wither, perish, waste, ebb, decrease. (*rise, grow, increase*)

decay—*n.* declension, waning, sinking, wasting, decrease, corruption, decadence, putrefaction, rottenness, dry rot, consumption, decline. (*rise, growth, birth, increase, fertility, exuberance, luxuriance, prosperity*)

deceit—cheat, imposition, trick, fraud, deception, double dealing, delusion, circumvention, guile, beguilement, treachery, sham, insidiousness, indirection, duplicity, cunning, artifice. (*enlightenment, instruction, guidance, reality, verity, fair dealing, honesty, openness*)

deceitful—deceptive, delusive, fraudulent, fallacious. (*open, fair, honest, truthful, veracious*)

deceive—trick, cheat, beguile, delude, gull, dupe, take in, overreach, mislead, betray, ensnare, entrap, circumvent. (*enlighten, advise, illumine, guide, disabuse, undeceive, deliver*)

decide—determine, fix, settle, adjudicate, terminate, resolve. (*waver, raise, moot, drop, doubt*)

decipher—read, spell, interpret, solve, unravel, explain, unfold. (*cipher, symbolize, mystify*)

declaration—avowal, exhibition, manifestation, statement, ordinance, assertion, affirmation, profession. (*denial, concealment, suppression*)

decompose—analyze, segregate, individualize, resolve, dissolve. (*compound, concoct, mix, organize*)

decorum—seemliness, propriety, dignity, order, decency, good manners, good behavior, modesty. (*impropriety, bad manners or behavior*)

decrease—diminish, lessen, subside, abate, lower, decline, retrench, curtail, reduce, wane. (*increase, grow, amplify, expand, augment, extend*)

decrepit—infirm, weak, crippled, superannuated, effete, broken down, enfeebled, tottering, aged. (*strong, straight, young*)

dedicate—devote, consecrate, offer, set, apportion, assign, apply, separate, hallow, set apart. (*alienate, misapply, desecrate, misconvert, misuse*)

deed—act, action, commission, achievement, perpetration, instrument, document, muniment, exploit, feat. (*omission, failure, abortion, false witness, innocent, canceling, disproof, invalidation*)

deep—profound, subterranean, submerged, designing, abstruse, recondite, learned, low, sagacious, penetrating, thick, obscure, mysterious, occult, intense, heartfelt. (*shallow, superficial, artless*)

deface—mar, spoil, injure, disfigure, deform, damage, mutilate, destroy. (*decorate, adorn*)

default—lapse, forfeit, omission, defect, delin-

quency, absence, want, failure. (*maintenance, appearance, plea, satisfaction, forthcoming, supply*)

defeat—*n.* frustration, overthrow, discomfiture. (*victory, triumph, success*)

defeat—*v.* conquer, overcome, worst, beat, baffle, rout, overthrow, vanquish, frustrate, foil. (*secure, promote, insure, speed, advance, establish*)

defect—shortcoming, omission, fault, imperfection, flaw, blemish, want. (*supply, sufficiency*)

defective—faulty, imperfect, insufficient, deficient, wanting, short. (*correct, complete, sufficient*)

defense—resistance, protection, vindication, plea, justification, excuse, rampart, bulwark, apology, shelter, excuse. (*abandonment, surrender*)

defer—delay, postpone, waive, adjourn, prorogue, put off, retard, procrastinate, protract, hinder, prolong. (*expedite, hasten, quicken, press*)

deference—respect, consideration, condescension, contention, regard, honor, veneration, submission, reverence, obedience, homage, allegiance. (*disrespect, contumely, contumacy, disregard, slight*)

definite—clear, specified, determined, definitive, restricted, specific, certain, ascertained, precise, exact, fixed, limited, bounded, positive. (*vague, unspecified, undetermined, indefinite, obscure, confused, intermingled*)

definition—determination, limitation, specification, restriction. (*confusion, vagueness, acceptation*)

defray—meet, liquidate, pay, settle, bear, discharge, quit. (*dishonor, repudiate, dissatisfy, misappropriate, embezzle*)

defy—scorn, challenge, provoke, oppose, brave. (*accept, give in, concede*)

degree—grade, rank, stage, step, extent, measure, mark, rate, position, quality, class, station, range, quantity, amount, limit, order. (*space, mass, magnitude, size, numbers*)

deliberate—*v.* consider, meditate, consult, weigh, reflect, ponder, debate, perpend. (*shelve, burke, discard, hazard, chance, risk*)

deliberate—*a.* grave, purposed, intentional, designed, determined, resolute, earnest, unbiased, unprejudiced. (*playful, jocose, facetious, irresolute*)

delicious—exquisite, luxurious, delightful, dainty, choice. (*coarse, common, unsavory, unpalatable, nauseous, loathsome*)

delight—enjoyment, pleasure, happiness, transport, ecstasy, joy, gratification, gladness, rapture, bliss. (*pain, suffering, sorrow, trouble, misery, displeasure, dissatisfaction, disappointment, discomfort*)

delinquent—criminal, culprit, offender. (*worthy, paragon, pattern*)

deliver—liberate, free, save, utter, set free, surrender, yield, transmit, concede, give up, rescue, pronounce, hand, give, entrust, consign. (*confine, capture, suppress, retain, betray, withdraw, assume*)

democratic—popular, leveling, radical, subversive, unlicensed, anarchical, destructive, republican. (*regal, imperial, aristocratic, oligarchical, constitutional, conservative, tyrannical, despotic, autocratic*)

demonstrate—prove, show, exhibit, manifest, evince, illustrate. (*disprove, conceal, misdemonstrate, misexemplify*)

demure—sedate, staid, grave, modest, downcast, sober, dispassionate, prudish, discreet. (*lively,

Synonym
Ant/Hom

vivacious, facetious, wanton, wild, noisy, boisterous)

denomination—name, designation, description, kind, class, order. (*nondescription, misnomer*)

dense—slow, thick, stupid, stolid, solid, stout, compact, consolidated, condensed, close, thickset. (*quick, clever, intelligent, rare, rarefied, sparse*)

deny—refuse, reject, withhold, negative, contradict, gainsay, disclaim, disavow, disown, oppose. (*grant, accept, concede, admit, affirm, confirm, afford*)

department—section, division, portion, function, office, branch, province, line. (*institution, establishment, art, science, literature, service, state, whole*)

dependent—hanging, resting, contingent, trusting, relying, subject, relative. (*independent, irrelative, irrespective, absolute, free*)

depression—lowering, degradation, debasement, dejection, discouragement, hollow, valley, dip. (*raising, elevation, exaltation, promotion, preferment*)

deprive—strip, bereave, despoil, rob, divest, dispossess, abridge, depose, prevent, hinder. (*invest, endow, compensate, enrich, supply, present, reinstate*)

derision—scorn, contempt, mockery, irony, sarcasm, contumely, disrespect. (*respect, regard, admiration, reverence*)

descendant—offspring, progeny, stock, scion, seed, branch, issue, house, family, lineage. (*author, founder, parent, ancestor, progenitor, stock, root*)

describe—draw, delineate, portray, explain, illustrate, define, picture, depict, represent, relate, narrate, recount. (*confound, confuse, mystify, misrepresent, caricature, distort*)

desert—wild, waste, wilderness, solitude, void. (*inclosure, field, pasture, garden, oasis*)

design—*v.* contemplate, purpose, intend, plan, prepare, project. (*hit, risk, guess, conjecture*)

design—*n.* contemplation, purpose, intention, plan, preparation, draft, delineation, sketch, drawing, artifice, cunning, artfulness, guile, contrivance, intent, project, scheme. (*execution, performance, result, issue, construction, structure, candor, fairness*)

desirable—expedient, advisable, valuable, acceptable, proper, judicious, beneficial, profitable, good, enviable, delightful. (*undesirable, inadvisable, inexpedient, objectionable, improper, injudicious, unprofitable, evil*)

desire—longing, affection, propension, craving, concupiscence, appetency. (*loathing, hate, repugnance, disgust, aversion, abomination, horror*)

despair—hopelessness, despondency, desperation. (*hopefulness, elation, anticipation, hilarity, confidence, sanguineness, expectation*)

desperate—wild, daring, audacious, determined, reckless, abandoned, rash, furious, frantic, despairing, regardless, mad, desponding, hopeless, inextricable, irremediable. (*cool, calm, cautious*)

despotic—autocratic, domineering, arbitrary, arrogant, imperious, self-willed, irresponsible, absolute, cruel, tyrannical. (*limited, constitutional*)

destination—purpose, intention, design, consignment, object, end, fate, doom, arrival, application, use, scope, appointment, point, location, goal, aim. (*operation, tendency, exercise, action, movement, design, initiation, project, effort*)

destiny—fate, decree, lot, fortune, predestination, necessity, doom, end. (*will, volition, choice, deliberation, freedom, free will*)

destroy—demolish, annihilate, subvert, ruin, overthrow, undo, waste, consume. (*restore, reinstate, repair, fabricate, make, construct, create*)

destructive—detrimental hurtful, noxious, injurious, deleterious, baleful, baneful, ruinous, subversive. (*wholesome, conservative, preservative, beneficial, reparatory, subsidiary, restorative*)

detraction—diminution, deterioration, depreciation, slander, backbiting, derogation. (*augmentation, improvement, enhancement, eulogy, compliment*)

detriment—loss, harm, hurt, injury, deterioration, impairment, disadvantage, prejudice, damage, inconvenience. (*enhancement, improvement, remedy, reinstatement, repair, augmentation*)

detrimental—injurious, hurtful, pernicious. (*beneficial, profitable, augmentative*)

develop—educe, enucleate, eliminate, enunciate, lay open, disclose, unravel, unfold, clear, amplify, expand, enlarge. (*envelop, wrap, obscure, mystify*)

device—artifice, expedient, design, plan, stratagem, project, symbol, emblem, show, invention, contrivance, cognizance. (*fair dealing, openness*)

devil—satan, lucifer, fiend, arch-fiend, foul fiend, demon. (*archangel, angel, seraph, cherub*)

devise—contrive, plan, maneuver, concert, manage. (*miscontrive, mismanage*)

devoid—void, wanting, destitute, unendowed, unprovided. (*furnished, supplied, replete, provided*)

devotion—piety, devoutness, religiousness, dedication, self-abandonment, consecration, ardor, self-surrender, self-sacrifice, love, attachment. (*impiety, profanity, selfishness, aversion, alienation*)

devour—eat, consume, swallow, gorge, gobble, bolt, absorb. (*disgorge, vomit*)

dictate—prompt, suggest, enjoin, order, direct, prescribe, decree, instruct, propose, command. (*follow, repeat, obey, echo, answer*)

dictation—imperative, imperious, domineering, arbitrary. (*condescending, affable, indulgent, modest, unassuming, suppliant, supplicatory, precatory*)

die—expire, depart, perish, decline, decease, disappear, wither, languish, wane, sink, fade, decay, cease. (*begin, originate, rise, live, develop*)

difference—separation, destruction, dissimilarity, unlikeness, disagreement, dissonance, discord, contrariety, dissent, distinction, dissimilitude, estrangement, variety. (*community, consociation*)

difficult—hard, intricate, involved, perplexing, enigmatical, obscure, trying, arduous, troublesome, uphill, unmanageable, unamenable, reserved, opposed. (*easy, plain, straight, simple, lucid, categorical, tractable, amenable, unreserved, favorable*)

digest—sort, arrange, dispose, order, classify, study, ponder, consider, prepare, assimilate, incorporate, convert, methodize, tabulate. (*displace, confound, complicate, derange, disorder, discompose*)

dilemma—fix, hobble, quandary, doubt, difficulty, scrape. (*extrication, rebutment, freedom, advantage, superiority, escape, solution, retort*)

diligence—care, assiduity, attention, application, heed, industry. (*indifference, carelessness, neglect*)

dingy—dull, dusky, rusty, bedimmed, soiled, tarnished, dirty, dim, colorless, obscure, dead, somber. (*bright, burnished, glossy, high-colored*)

diplomacy—embassage, ministry, ambassadorship, representation, tact, contrivance, management, negotiation, outwitting, circumvention. (*cancel, recall, conge, miscontrivance, mismanagement*)

diplomatic—judicious, knowing, wise, prudent, well-contrived, clever, astute, politic, discreet, well-planned, well-conceived, sagacious, well-managed. (*injudicious, bungling, stultifying, ill-managed, undiplomatic*)

direction—course, tendency, inclination, line, control, command, bearing, superscription, order, address. (*misdirection, deviation, miscontrol, misinstruction, aberration*)

directly—straightly, straightaway, immediately, undeviatingly, at once, promptly, quickly, instantly. (*indirectly, by-and-by, interveniently*)

disability—disqualification, impotency, unfitness, incapacity, forfeiture, incompetency. (*qualification, recommendation, fitness, deserving, merit*)

disappoint—betray, deceive, frustrate, baffle, delude, vex, mortify, defeat, foil. (*realize, justify*)

discernible—visible, conspicuous, manifest, palpable, apparent, plain, perceptible, evident. (*invisible, inconspicuous, obscure, indiscernible, impalpable, microscopic, minute*)

discipline—order, strictness, training, government, instruction, drilling, control, coercion, punishment, organization. (*disorder, confusion, rebellion, mutiny, encouragement, reward, disorganization*)

discomfort—disquiet, vexation, annoyance, trouble, unpleasantness, disagreeableness. (*comfort, ease, pleasantness, agreeableness*)

disconcert—abash, confuse, confound, upset, baffle, derange, discompose, thwart, disturb, defeat, fret, interrupt, vex, ruffle, disorder, unsettle, frustrate, discomfit. (*encourage, rally, countenance*)

discreet—discerning, wise, prudent, circumspect, cautious, wary, regulative, sensible, judicious. (*undiscerning, blind, foolish, imprudent, indiscreet, unrestrained, reckless*)

discrimination—penetration, sagacity, acuteness, nicety, shrewdness, judgment, discernment, insight, distinction. (*dullness, confusedness, indiscriminateness, shortsightedness, hebetude, indiscernment*)

disease—complaint, disorder, illness, indisposition, distemper, ailment, malady, sickness. (*health, convalescence, sanity, salubrity*)

disgust—nausea, loathing, abomination, aversion, dislike, repugnance, abhorrence, distaste. (*desire, liking, partiality, predilection, relish, fondness, longing, avidity*)

dismal—dreary, ominous, foreboding, lonesome, cheerless, gloomy, sad, depressed, lugubrious, funereal, sorrowful, melancholy, tragic, blank. (*gay, propitious, promising, cheerful, lively, elated*)

dispatch—expedite, send, accelerate, hasten, execute, conclude, get rid of. (*retard, detain, obstruct, impede, retain*)

dispel—disperse, scatter, dissipate, drive away, dismiss. (*collect, recall, summon, convene, congregate, conglomerate, mass, accumulate*)

disperse—dispel, scatter, disseminate, separate, break up, spread abroad, deal out, distribute, dissipate. (*collect, summon, recall, gather, concentrate*)

dispute—argue, question, canvass, contest, contend, challenge, debate, controvert, controversy, difference, gainsay, impugn, quarrel, altercation. (*waive, concede, allow, forgo*)

dissemble—disguise, conceal, repress, smother, restrain, cloak. (*exhibit, manifest, protrude, vaunt*)

disseminate—spread, propagate, preach, proclaim, publish, promulgate, scatter, circulate. (*repress, suppress, stifle, discountenance, extirpate*)

dissolute—abandoned, profligate, loose, licentious, wanton, vicious. (*upright, conscientious*)

distance—interval, removal, separation, interspace, remoteness, absence, space, length. (*proximity, nearness, adjacency, contiguity, neighborhood*)

distinct—separate, independent, unconnected, detached, disjoined, unlike, definite, obvious, different, dissimilar, clear, conspicuous, plain, perspicuous. (*united, consolidated, conjoined, one*)

distinction—difference, separation, dignity, eminence. (*unity, identity, debasement, insignificance*)

distinguish—discern, descry, perceive, characterize, make famous, know, discriminate, see, discover, separate, divide, dissimilate, differentiate. (*miss, overlook, confound, confuse*)

distinguished—illustrious, noted, celebrated, conspicuous, eminent, marked, famous. (*obscure, inconspicuous, hidden, not famous*)

distress—harass, embarrass, trouble, grieve, annoy, vex, mortify, pain, disturb, afflict, worry. (*soothe, compose, please, gratify, gladden, console*)

disturb—derange, discompose, disorder, discommode, plague, confuse, rouse, agitate, annoy, trouble, interrupt, incommode, worry, vex, molest, disquiet. (*order, collocate, arrange, pacify, soothe*)

diversion—detour, divergence, deviation, recreation, amusement, pastime, sport, enjoyment. (*continuity, directness, procedure, business, task*)

divide—separate, dissect, bisect, portion, part, divorce, segregate, sever, sunder, deal out, disunite, keep apart, part among, allot, distribute, multiply. (*unite, collocate, classify, convene, congregate, conglomerate, conglutinate, commingle, join, consociate*)

divorce—separate, disconnect, dissever, divert, alienate. (*conjoin, unite, connect, apply, reconcile*)

do—work, act, accomplish, execute, achieve, transact, finish, enact, perform, produce, complete. (*undo, mar, neglect, omit*)

docile—compliant, amenable, easily managed, yielding, gentle, quiet, pliant, tractable, teachable, tame. (*intractable, stubborn, obstinate, self-willed*)

dogmatic—doctrinal, theological, imperious, dictatorial, authoritative, arrogant, magisterial, self-opinionated, positive. (*practical, active, moderate*)

doleful—dolorous, rueful, melancholy, piteous, somber, sorrowful, woebegone, dismal. (*merry, joyful, gay, blithe, beaming*)

dominion—power, authority, rule, tyranny, despotism, government, control, empire, sway, realm, territory, jurisdiction. (*weakness, submission, subjugation, inferiority, servitude*)

dormant—sleeping, slumbering, latent, undeveloped, quiescent, inert. (*vigilant, wakeful, active*)

doubt—dubiousness, dubitation, scruple, hesitation, suspense, distrust, suspicion, perplexity, uncertainty, ambiguity, difficulty, indecision. (*certainty, clearness, precision, determination, decision*)

drain—draw, strain, drip, percolate, drop, exhaust, empty, dry. (*replenish, fill, supply, pour*)

draw—drag, pull, attract, induce, haul, entice, inhale, sketch, delineate, describe. (*push, carry,

Synonym
Ant/Hom

propel, throw, repel, drive, compel, impel, thrust)

dreadful—fearful, shocking, monstrous, dire, terrible, frightful, terrific, horrible, alarming, awful. (*encouraging, inspiriting, assuring, promising*)

dreamy—fanciful, visionary, speculative, abstracted, absent, foggy. (*collected, earnest, attentive, awake, active, energetic, practical*)

dregs—refuse, sediment, offal, lees, off-scouring, dross, trash. (*cream, flower, pink, pickings, bouquet*)

dress—garniture, preparation, arrangement, clothing, habiliments, accoutrements, vestments, uniform, raiment, apparel, attire, clothes, array, garments, livery, costume, garb, investiture. (*nudity, disorder, disarrangement, undress, deshabille*)

drift—tendency, direction, motion, tenor, meaning, purport, object, intention, purpose, scope, aim, result, issue, inference, conclusion, end, course. (*aimlessness, pointlessness, vagueness, unmeaningness, indefiniteness, confusedness, aberrancy*)

drink—imbibe, swallow, quaff, absorb, drain, draught. (*disgorge, replenish, pour, exude, water*)

drivel—fatuity, nonsense, trifling, snivel, babble. (*soundness, coherence, substance, solidity*)

droll—whimsical, comical, odd, queer, amusing, laughable, funny, comic, fantastic, farcical. (*sad, lamentable, tragic, lugubrious, funereal*)

drop—ooze, emanate, distill, percolate, fall, decline, descend, faint, droop. (*evaporate, rally, rise*)

drown—sink, immerse, swamp, overwhelm, engulf, deluge, inundate, submerge. (*dry, drain*)

dry—arid, parched, moistureless, juiceless, barren, tame, sarcastic, vapid, lifeless, dull, tedious, uninteresting, monotonous. (*moist, fresh, juicy*)

dull—stupid, stolid, doltish, insensible, callous, heavy, gloomy, dismal, cloudy, turbid, opaque, dowdy, sluggish, sad, tiresome, commonplace, dead. (*sharp, clever, lively, animated, sensible, cheerful*)

durable—lasting, permanent, stable, persistent, abiding, constant, continuing. (*evanescent, transient, impermanent, unstable*)

duty—obligation, part, business, responsibility, allegiance, function, office, province, calling, trust, commission, service. (*freedom, exemption, immunity, license, dispensation, desertion, dereliction*)

dwindle—pine, waste, diminish, decrease, fall off, decline, melt. (*expand, enlarge, increase, grow*)

early—soon, betimes, forward, shortly, quickly, erelong, anon, matutinal, beforehand. (*late, tardily, backward, vespertinal, belated*)

earn—merit, acquire, achieve, obtain, win, gain, deserve. (*forfeit, forgo, waste, lose, spend, squander*)

earnest—eager, serious, intent, determined, strenuous, solemn, grave, warm, fervent, intense, ardent. (*indifferent, idle, playful, desultory, irresolute, unearnest, sportive, jesting, flippant*)

easy—quiet, comfortable, manageable, indulgent, facile, lenient, unconstrained, gentle, not difficult, unconcerned, self-possessed. (*uneasy, disturbed, uncomfortable, difficult, unmanageable, hard, exacting*)

economy—administration, dispensation, management, rule, arrangement, distribution, husbanding. (*maladministration, waste, misrule, mismanagement*)

ecstasy—rapture, inspiration, fervor, frenzy, transport, emotion, joy, delight, enthusiasm, happiness. (*indifference, coolness, dullness, weariness*)

edifice—structure, building, tenement, fabric. (*ruin, heap, demolition, dismantlement*)

educate—instruct, nurture, discipline, train, teach, develop, ground, school, initiate. (*miseducate, misinstruct, misnurture*)

effective—powerful, conducive, operative, cogent, telling, able, potent, talented, efficacious, efficient, serviceable, effectual. (*weak, ineffective*)

effort—trial, attempt, endeavor, exertion. (*failure, misadventure, unsuccess, frustration, futility*)

egotism—conceit, vanity, self-assertion, self-conceit, self-praise, self-exaltation, conceitedness. (*considerateness, deference, self-abnegation*)

ejaculation—exclamation, utterance, cry. (*silence, speechlessness*)

elastic—ductile, extensile, alterable, resilient, modifiable, flexible, buoyant, springy. (*tough, unchangeable, rigid, unflexible, inelastic, crystallized*)

elated—cheered, joyed, inspirited, overjoyed, proud, inflated. (*depressed, dispirited, disappointed*)

elegance—beauty, grace, refinement, symmetry, gracefulness, taste. (*deformity, awkwardness, inelegance, disproportion, ungracefulness, coarseness*)

elegant—graceful, lovely, well formed, well made, symmetrical, accomplished, polished, refined, handsome. (*inelegant, deformed, unsymmetrical, ill-proportioned, ungraceful, coarse, rude*)

elementary—physical, material, natural, primary, rudimentary, simple, inchoate, component, constituent, ultimate. (*immaterial, incorporeal, impalpable, compound, collective, aggregate*)

eligible—capable, suitable, worthy, desirable, preferable, choice, prime. (*undesirable, worthless*)

elude—escape, avoid, baffle, shun, eschew, evade, parry, fence, mock, frustrate. (*encounter, meet, confront, court, dare, defy*)

embalm—conserve, preserve, treasure, store, enshrine, consecrate. (*expose, desecrate, abandon*)

embarrass—entangle, disconcert, trouble, perplex, confuse, hamper, clog, distress, puzzle, encumber. (*extricate, liberate, expedite, facilitate*)

embezzle—appropriate, confuse, falsify, peculate, misappropriate. (*square, balance, clear*)

embody—express, methodize, systematize, codify, incorporate, aggregate, integrate, compact, introduce, enlist, combine. (*eliminate, segregate*)

embrace—clasp, comprehend, include, hug, comprise, contain, close, embody, incorporate. (*exclude, reject, except*)

emergency—crisis, conjuncture, pitch, embarrassment, strait, necessity, exigency, casualty, difficulty. (*rescue, deliverance, solution, subsidence*)

emotion—passion, feeling, excitement, agitation, perturbation, trepidation, tremor. (*indifference, lack of feeling*)

emphatic—earnest, forcible, strong, energetic, impressive, positive, important, special, egregious, consummate. (*mild, unemphatic, cool, unimpassioned, unimportant, ordinary, unnoticeable*)

employ—use, apply, economize, occupy, engage, engross. (*discard, dismiss, misuse, misemploy*)

empower—enable, commission, encourage, qualify, delegate, warrant, sanction, direct, authorize. (*hinder, prevent, discourage, disable, disqualify*)

empty—vacant, void, unencumbered, unobstructed, unoccupied, waste, uninhabited, unfrequented, devoid, vacuous, destitute, unfilled, unfurnished, untenanted, evacuated, deficient, weak, silly, idle, senseless. (*full, occupied, encumbered, obstructed, cultivated, colonized, inhabited, informed, well-instructed, experienced, sensible, significant, forcible, important, substantial*)

enamor—captivate, fascinate, enslave, charm, endear, bewitch, enchain. (*repel, disgust, estrange*)

enclose—shut, encircle, environ, include, circumscribe, envelop, wrap, afforest. (*open, disclose, exclude, bare, disencircle, expose, develop, disafforest*)

encourage—embolden, rally, enhearten, cheer, incite, stimulate, foster, cherish, promote, urge, impel, advance, countenance, forward, reassure, animate, inspirit, prompt, abet. (*deter, discourage*)

endanger—imperil, expose, peril, jeopardize, hazard, risk. (*cover, defend, protect, shield, screen*)

endear—attach, conciliate, gain. (*estrange, alienate, embitter*)

endless—interminable, illimitable, unending, unceasing, boundless, deathless, imperishable, everlasting, perpetual, eternal, infinite. (*terminable*)

endorse—sanction, approve, subscribe, accept. (*protest, repudiate, cancel, abjure, renounce*)

endowment—gift, provision, benefit, benefaction, capacity, attainment, qualification. (*impoverishment, spoliation, disendowment, incapacity*)

enforce—urge, compel, require, exact, exert, strain. (*relax, waive, forgo, remit, abandon*)

engage—promise, undertake, vouch, employ, occupy, hire, gain, attract, enlist, stipulate, pledge, agree, buy, adopt, involve. (*decline, refuse, withdraw, dismiss, discard, extricate, disengage*)

enigmatical—puzzling, perplexing, obscure, mystic. (*lucid, explanatory, plain, self-evident*)

enlarge—amplify, expand, augment, broaden, swell, stretch out, extend, stretch, dilate, increase. (*narrow, lessen, contract, restrict, diminish, curtail*)

enlighten—illumine, edify, instruct, illuminate, inform, teach. (*mislead, darken, confound, obscure*)

enlist—enter, register, enroll, incorporate, embody. (*withdraw, erase, expunge, dismiss, disband*)

enmity—discord, hate, hostility, malevolence, maliciousness, aversion, malignity, ill-feeling, animosity, opposition, bitterness, acrimony, asperity. (*friendship, love, affection, esteem, friendliness, cordiality*)

enormous—huge, immense, gigantic, colossal, elephantine, vast, gross, monstrous, prodigious. (*diminutive, insignificant, trivial, venial, average*)

enough—sufficient, ample, plenty, abundance. (*bare, scant, insufficient, inadequate, short*)

ensue—follow, accrue, supervene, befall. (*precede, threaten, premonish, forewarn*)

ensure—fix, determine, secure, seal. (*imperil, hazard, jeopardize, forfeit*)

enterprising—active, bold, daring, adventurous, speculative, dashing, venturesome. (*inactive, timid, inadventurous, cautious*)

entertain—harbor, maintain, conceive, foster, receive, recreate, amuse. (*eject, exclude, deny, debar, annoy, weary, bore, tire.*)

enthusiasm—excitement, frenzy, sensation, inspiration, transport, rapture, warmth, fervor, fervency, zeal, ardor, vehemence, passion, devotion. (*coldness, callousness, indifference, disaffec-*

tion, repugnance, alienation, contempt*)

entire—whole, complete, unimpaired, total, perfect, all, full, solid, integral, undiminished. (*partial*)

entitle—qualify, empower, fit, enable, name, style, denominate, designate, characterize. (*disqualify, disentitle, disable, not designate, not characterize*)

entreat—implore, obsecrate, beg, beseech, importune, crave, solicit, supplicate, pray, ask, urge. petition. (*command, insist, bid, enjoin*)

enumerate—specify, name, number, recount, detail, reckon, compute, calculate, call over. (*confound, miscount, misreckon*)

ephemeral—transient, evanescent, fleeting, fugacious, fugitive, momentary. (*abiding, persistent*)

equable—uniform, regular, proportionate, even, smooth, easy. (*irregular, desultory, variable, fitful,*

equal—uniform, commensurate, coordinate, adequate, alike, equivalent, even, equable, sufficient, impartial, coextensive, smooth. (*unequal, incommensurate, incoordinate, inadequate, disparate*)

equitable—fair, just, proportionate, impartial, upright, proper, reasonable, evenhanded, honest. (*unfair, unjust, disproportionate, partial*)

erase—obliterate, efface, expunge, blot, cancel. (*mark, write, delineate*)

erect—elevate, raise, establish, plant, uplift, construct, build, found, institute, set up. (*lower, supplant, subvert, depress, remove, destroy, demolish*)

erratic—desultory, aberrant, abnormal, flighty, changeful, capricious. (*regular, normal, methodical, calculable, unalterable, steady, undeviating*)

error—fault, mistake, blunder, falsity, deception, fallacy, untruth, hallucination. (*correction, correctness, truth, accuracy, soundness, rectification*)

escape—elude, decamp, abscond, fly, flee, evade, avoid. (*incur, confront, encounter, meet, suffer*)

essential—innate, inherent, requisite, necessary, vital, immanent, indispensable, leading. (*accidental, qualitative, quantitative, promotive, regulative, induced, imported, adventitious*)

establish—plant, fix, settle, found, demonstrate, organize, confirm, institute, prove, substantiate. (*supplant, unsettle, break up, disestablish*)

esteem—price, value, consider, deem, judge, believe, estimate, think, regard, affect, appreciate, revere, honor, respect, admire, venerate, prize, love, like. (*disregard, disconsider, disaffect, dislike, undervalue, underrate, decry, deprecate*)

eternal—infinite, endless, everlasting, deathless, imperishable, never-dying, ceaseless, ever-living, perpetual, undying, unceasing. (*ephemeral, transient, temporal, fleeting, evanescent, sublunary*)

etiquette—manners, breeding, fashion, conventionality. (*boorishness, rudeness, misobservance*)

evaporate—melt, colliquate, liquefy, vaporize, disappear, dissolve, exhale, distill. (*consolidate, compact, solidify, indurate, crystallize*)

event—occurrence, circumstance, episode, adventure, issue, accident, result, fact, incident. (*cause, antecedent, operation, inducement, contribution, convergence, predisposition, tendency*)

eventful—remarkable, memorable, signal, important, marked, noted, critical, stirring, notable. (*ordinary, unmarked, unimportant, eventless, uninteresting, characterless, trivial*)

Synonym
Ant/Hom

evidence—manifestation, attraction, averment, testimony, disposition, declaration, appearance, sign, token, proof, indication, exemplification, illustration. (*surmise, conjecture, counterevidence, disproof, refutation, concealment, suppression, misindication, fallacy*)

evident—plain, visible, conspicuous, manifest, indisputable, obvious, clear, palpable, incontrovertible. (*doubtful, obscure, questionable, uncertain, dubious*)

evil—ill, noxious, deleterious, wrong, bad, mischievous, hurtful, sinful, unhappy, adverse, unpropitious, wicked, corrupt, harmful, unfair, notorious, miserable, sorrowful. (*wholesome, beneficial, right, virtuous, holy, pure, happy, fortunate*)

exactly—precisely, accurately, correspondently. (*loosely, inadequately, incorrectly, differently, otherwise*)

exaggerate—amplify, enlarge, heighten, magnify, overstate, overdraw, strain, overpaint, overestimate. (*disparage, attenuate, palliate, understate*)

examine—weigh, ponder, investigate, perpend, test, scrutinize, criticize, prove, study, discuss, inquire, search, overhaul, explore, inspect. (*discard, conjecture, guess, slur, misconsider, misinvestigate*)

example—sample, specimen, pattern, model, copy, illustration, instance, issue, development. (*stock, material, substance, law, rule, character*)

except—exclude, save, bar, segregate, negative. (*count, include, reckon, state, classify, propound*)

exceptional—rare, peculiar, uncommon, irregular, unusual, abnormal. (*common, regular, normal, usual, ordinary*)

excessive—enormous, undue, exorbitant, overmuch, superabundant, superfluous, unreasonable, immoderate, inordinate, extravagant. (*insufficient, scant, inadequate*)

excuse—exculpate, absolve, pardon, forgive, overlook, condone, remit, indulge, justify, vindicate, defend, acquit, mitigate, extenuate, release, exempt, exonerate. (*charge, inculpate, condemn*)

execrable—detestable, loathsome, accursed, cursed, villainous, diabolical, hateful, abominable, damnable. (*desirable, eligible, respectable, laudable*)

exemplary—laudable, praiseworthy, conspicuous, honorable, wary, meritorious, worthy, excellent. (*detestable, objectionable, exceptionable*)

exempt—free, irresponsible, unamenable, clear, liberated, privileged, absolved. (*subject, responsible, liable, amenable*)

exercise—exertion, use, practice, application, training, employment, drill. (*rest, ease, relaxation*)

exhaust—empty, spend, consume, debilitate, waste, void, drain, weaken, weary. (*fill, replenish*)

existence—being, entity, creature. (*nonentity, nonexistence, chimera*)

expand—swell, dilate, spread, extend, open, diffuse, develop, unfold, enlarge, amplify. (*contract, curtail, attenuate, restrict, condense*)

expect—anticipate, await, forecast, forebode, wait for, rely on, look for, foresee. (*welcome, hail, recognize, greet, realize*)

expediency—utility, advantage, interest. (*inexpediency, disadvantage, inutility, detriment*)

expend—spend, disburse, lay out, waste, consume, use. (*save, husband, economize*)

expense—price, cost, charge, payment, expenditure, outlay. (*income, profit, receipt*)

experience—*n.* experiment, trial, test, proof, habit, knowledge. (*ignorance, inexperience*)

experience—*v.* try, feel, undergo, encounter, endure. (*evade, escape, miss, lose*)

explain—expound, teach, illustrate, clear up, interpret, elucidate, decipher. (*mystify, obscure*)

explanation—exposition, explication, interpretation, sense, description. (*mystification, obscuration, confusion, misinterpretation*)

explicit—plain, detailed, inobscure, declaratory, categorical, stated, distinctly stated, express, definite, determinate. (*implicit, implied, hinted*)

expression—countenance, look, indication, phrase, term, face, feature, lineament. (*falsification, misstatement, solecism, enigma, suppression*)

exquisite—choice, rare, refined, delicate, perfect, matchless, intense, consummate, delicious. (*common, coarse, ordinary*)

extend—prolong, stretch, expand, enlarge, increase, augment, reach, spread, amplify, avail, apply. (*curtail, contract, restrict, narrow, limit*)

extent—degree, distance, quantity, space, size. (*diminution, restriction, limitation*)

extinguish—abolish, destroy, extirpate, eradicate, kill, quench, annihilate, put out. (*implant, replenish, cherish, promote, invigorate, propagate, establish, confirm, secure*)

extortionate—hard, closefisted, severe, rigorous, exorbitant, preposterous, monstrous, exacting. (*liberal, indulgent, bountiful, reasonable, fair, moderate*)

extraordinary—unwonted, uncommon, peculiar, unusual, unprecedented, wonderful, marvelous, prodigious, monstrous, remarkable, strange, preposterous. (*wonted, common, usual, ordinary*)

extravagant—wild, monstrous, preposterous, absurd, prodigal, wasteful, reckless, excessive, lavish, profuse, abnormal. (*sound, sober, consistent, rational, fair, economical, frugal, careful*)

extreme—terminal, final, remote, utmost, farthest, last, extravagant, immoderate, most violent, distant, ultimate. (*initial, primal, moderate, judicious*)

F

fable—apologue, fiction, parable, allegory, romance, invention, fabrication, untruth, novel, falsehood. (*history, narrative, fact*)

facetious—witty, funny, humorous, jocular, waggish, playful, droll, jocose. (*heavy, matter-of-fact, dull, grave, serious, lugubrious, somber, saturnine*)

facile—docile, tractable, manageable, indulgent, weak, irresolute, easy, affable, flexible, characterless, pliable. (*sturdy, obstinate, determined, resolute, pigheaded, crusty, inflexible, self-willed, independent, self-reliant*)

facility—ease, address, readiness, quickness, adroitness, dexterity, pliancy. (*labor, awkwardness, difficulty*)

fact—truth, deed, occurrence, certainty, circumstance, event, reality. (*fiction, supposition, falsehood, unreality, lie, delusion, chimera, inven-*

tion, romance)

fade—fall, fail, decline, sink, droop, dwindle, vanish, change, pale, bleach, set, etiolate. (*rise, increase, grow, bloom, flourish, abide, stand, last*)

fag—work, toil, slave, drudge. (*bask, idle, lounge, dawdle, strike*)

faint—weak, languid, fatigued, unenergetic, timid, irresolute, feeble, exhausted, halfhearted, obscure, dim, pale, faded, inconspicuous. (*strong, vigorous, energetic, fresh, daring, resolute, prominent*)

fair—open, clear, spotless, unspotted, untarnished, reasonable, unblemished, serene, beautiful, just, honorable, equitable, impartial. (*lowering, dull, foul, disfigured, ugly, unfair, dishonorable*)

faithful—true, firm, attached, loyal, accurate, close, consistent, correspondent, exact, equivalent, staunch, incorruptible. (*false, fickle, capricious*)

fallacy—sophistry, error, blunder, misconception, bugbear, fiction, delusion, chimera. (*truth, verity*)

false—untrue, erroneous, fallacious, sophistical, spurious, deceptive, fabrication, counterfeit, mendacious, sham, mock, bogus, unfaithful, fib, falsity, fiction, dishonorable, faithless. (*true, correct*)

falsify—mistake, misinterpret, misrepresent, belie, betray, garble, cook. (*verify, correct, rectify*)

falter—halt, hesitate, hobble, slip, dubitate, stammer, demur, waver, flinch, vacillate. (*proceed, run, speed, flow, discourse, determine, persevere, resolve, career*)

familiar—household, common, free, frank, affable, everyday, well-acquainted, accustomed, conversant, intimate. (*uncommon, rare, strange*)

famous—renowned, glorious, celebrated, illustrious, far-famed. (*unknown, obscure, unsung, inglorious*)

fanciful—grotesque, chimerical, unreal, imaginary, quaint, eccentric, freakish, humorous, erroneous, capricious, whimsical, erratic, absurd, fitful. (*natural, literal, regular, real, sober, ordinary, truthful, accurate, correct, orderly, calculable*)

fancy—thought, belief, idea, supposition, imagination, caprice, notion, conceit, vagary, inclination, whim, humor, predilection, desire. (*object, subject, fact, reality, order, law, truth, system, verity*)

fashion—form, shape, guise, style, appearance, character, figure, mold, mode, custom, practice, usage, manner, way, ceremony. (*person, work, dress, speech, formlessness, shapelessness, derangement, eccentricity, strangeness, outlandishness*)

fast—firm, secure, fixed, constant, steadfast, stable, unyielding, unswerving, rapid, accelerated, wild, reckless, dissipated, gay. (*loose, insecure*)

fastidious—critical, overnice, overrefined censorious, punctilious, particular, squeamish, dainty. (*easy, indulgent, uncritical, coarse, omnivorous*)

fat—corpulent, fleshy, brawny, pursy, rich, luxuriant, portly, stout, fertile, unctuous, obese, oleaginous. (*lean, slender, attenuated, emaciated*)

fatal—calamitous, deadly, destructive, mortal, lethal. (*beneficial, wholesome, nutritious, vitalizing, salubrious, restorative, slight, superficial, harmless.*)

fate—necessity, destiny, lot, end, fortune, doom. (*will, choice, decision, freedom, independence*)

fault—defect, error, imperfection, flaw, misdeed,

failure, omission, want, drawback. (*sufficiency, correctness, completeness, perfection*)

favor—permission, grace, concession, predilection, gift, civility, benefit, kindness, good will, regard, condescension, preference, boon, countenance, patronage. (*refusal, denial, prohibition*)

favorable—permissive, indulgent, propitious, concessive, partial, fond, liberal, advantageous, auspicious, friendly. (*reluctant, unpropitious, unfavorable, impartial*)

fear—apprehension, solicitude, alarm, fright, dread, terror, trepidation, dismay, consternation, misgiving, horror, timidity, awe. (*assurance, confidence, courage, fearlessness, trust, boldness*)

feeble—wretched, weak, poor, frail, debilitated, dull, forceless, puny, nerveless, enfeebled, enervated, faint, infirm, incomplete, vain, fruitless, scanty, pitiable. (*strong, robust, active, effective*)

feeling—touch, sensation, contact, pathos, tenderness, impression, consciousness, sensibility, emotion, sentiment, passion, sensitiveness. (*insensibility, callousness, imperturbability, inexcitability, coldness, insensateness*)

felicitous—happy, timely, successful, opportune, joyous. (*unfortunate, unhappy, untimely, unsuccessful, disastrous, inopportune, sad*)

feminine—delicate, womanly, tender, modest, soft. (*robust, manly, indelicate, rude, rough, unfeminine*)

fertile—rich, luxuriant, teeming, productive, exuberant, causative, conducive, pregnant, fraught, prolific, fecund, fruitful, ingenious, inventive. (*poor, sterile, barren, unproductive, ineffective, inconducive, fruitless, inoperative, uninventive, unimaginative*)

fickle—fanciful, fitful, capricious, irresolute, changeable, vacillating, mutable, unreliable, veering, shifting, variable, restless, inconstant, unstable. (*sober, orderly, reliable, well-regulated, calculable, trustworthy, steady, uniform*)

fiction—invention, fabrication, creation, figment, fable, falsehood, romance, myth. (*fact, truth*)

fidelity—fealty, attachment, truthfulness, allegiance, accuracy, closeness, exactness, faithfulness, integrity, loyalty, honesty. (*treachery, disloyalty*)

fiery—hot, vehement, ardent, fervent, fierce, passionate, irascible, choleric, excited, enkindled, glowing, fervid, impassioned, irritable, hot-brained, (*cold, icy, indifferent, phlegmatic, passionless, unimpassioned, mild, quenched, extinguished, tame*)

fight—battle, contention, struggle, conflict, combat, contest, action, engagement, encounter, (*pacification, reconciliation*)

figure—aspect, shape, emblem, type, image, condition, appearance, form, symbol, metaphor, likeness, delineation, illustration. (*misrepresentation, deformity, disfigurement*)

fill—replenish, content, supply, satisfy, gorge, glut, occupy, appoint, stuff, store, rise, swell, glow, expand, increase. (*exhaust, deprive, drain, dissatisfy, stint, vacate, misappoint, subside, shrink*)

final—terminal, last, latest, conclusive, definite, developed, ultimate, decisive. (*initiative, open*)

find—meet, confront, ascertain, experience, perceive, discover, furnish, invent. (*miss, elude, over-*

look, lose, withhold, withdraw, miscontrive)

fine—thin, minute, slender, delicate, pure, smooth, filmy, gauzy, keen, artistic, choice, finished, high, grand, noble, sensitive, refined, generous, honorable, excellent, superior, pretentious, handsome, pretty, beautiful, showy, elegant, ostentatious, presumptuous, nice, casuistical, subtle, *(coarse, large, rough, blunt, rude, unfinished, mean)*

finical—affected, overnice, dandyish, dallying, foppish, spruce, factitious, euphuistic. *(unaffected, effective, practical, energetic, real, genuine, natural)*

finish—complete, perfect, accomplish, conclude, achieve, end, shape, terminate. *(begin, commence, start, undertake, fail, miscontrive, mismanage, botch)*

first—leading, primary, pristine, original, foremost, primitive, principal, primeval, highest, chief, earliest, onmost. *(subsequent, secondary)*

fit—decent, befitting, meet, apt, fitting, adapted, seemly, appropriate, becoming, decorous, qualified, congruous, peculiar, particular, suitable, prepared, adequate, calculated, contrived, expedient, proper, ripe. *(awkward, ungainly, misfitting, ill-suited)*

fix—place, settle, fasten, link, locate, attach, consolidate, tie, plant, root, establish, secure, determine, decide. *(displace, unsettle, disarrange, remove, uproot, transfer, transplant, disestablish)*

flat—dull, tame, insipid, vapid, spiritless, level, horizontal, absolute, even, downright, mawkish, tasteless, lifeless. *(exciting, animated, interesting)*

flexible—pliant, lithe, supple, elastic, easy, indulgent, ductile, flexible, yielding, pliable. *(tough, rigid, inelastic, inflexible, hard, inexorable)*

flimsy—gauzy, poor, thin, transparent, trifling, trivial, puerile, insane, slight, superficial, weak, shallow. *(solid, sound, irrefragable, substantial)*

flippant—pert, forward, superficial, thoughtless, saucy, malapert. *(flattering, servile, obsequious)*

flock—herd, congregate, throng, assemble, crowd. *(disperse, scatter, separate, segregate)*

flood—deluge, inundation, abundance. *(drought, drain, ebb, scarcity, subsidence)*

florid—rubicund, flowery, sanguine, ornate, overwrought, meretricious. *(pallid, exsanguineous, bare, unadorned, nude, sober, chaste)*

flounder—roll, blunder, bungle, boggle, wallow, tumble. *(emerge, flow, course, career, speed, rise)*

flourish—prosper, thrive, speed, triumph, brandish, wave. *(fail, fade, decline, miscarry, founder)*

flow—stream, issue, progress, glide, course, career, run. *(halt, stick, stickle, stop, hesitate, fail)*

flurry—agitate, excite, worry, ruffle, fluster. *(soothe, compose, quiet, calm, mesmerize)*

foible—peccadillo, failing, fault, weakness, infirmity. *(crime, atrocity, enormity, sin)*

follow—pursue, chase, accompany, obey, imitate, succeed, result, ensue, attend, shadow, observe, copy. *(avoid, elude, quit, disobey, precede)*

folly—madness, nonsense, misconduct, imprudence, silliness, foolishness, weakness, absurdity, imbecility. *(sense, wisdom, sanity, judgment, prudence, sobriety)*

foment—excite, cherish, fan, propagate, encourage. *(allay, extinguish, discourage, extirpate)*

fond—loving, attached, affectionate, foolish, silly, weak, doting, empty, enamored, devoted. *(unloving, averse, unaffectionate, strong-minded)*

foolish—senseless, idiotic, crazed, shallow, weak, silly, injudicious, irrational, absurd, contemptible, objectionable, witless, brainless, imbecile, preposterous, ridiculous, nonsensical, simple. *(sensible, sane, deep, clearsighted, sound, sagacious)*

forbidding—repulsive, deterrent, prohibitory, offensive. *(attractive, encouraging, alluring, seductive, permissive)*

force—power, strength, agency, instrumentality, compulsion, cogency, vigor, might, dint, vehemence, pressure, host, army, coercion, validity, violent, *(feebleness, weakness, counteraction, neutralization)*

foreign—strange, exotic, outlandish, alien, irrelevant, extraneous. *(domestic, native, congenial, pertinent, germane)*

forfeit—fine, penalty, mulct, amercement, damages, loss. *(premium, bribe, douceur, remuneration, compensation, reward, gratuity)*

forge—work, frame, produce, elaborate, fabricate, counterfeit, feign, falsify, form, shape, make falsely. *(shatter, batter, shiver, blast, fuse, detect)*

forget—lose, pretermit, unlearn, obliviate, overlook. *(acquire, learn, remember, recollect, mind)*

form—shape, mold, fashion, constitute, arrange, frame, construct, contrive, make, produce, create, devise. *(deform, dislocate, distort, dissipate)*

formal—regular, complete, shapely, sufficient, correct, stately, dignified, ceremonious, pompous, stiff, precise, explicit, exact, affected, methodical. *(irregular, incomplete, informal, inadequate, incorrect, easy, unassuming, unceremonious)*

formality—ceremony, parade, affectation, stateliness, punctiliousness, etiquette. *(informality, casualness, simplicity)*

former—preceding, antecedent, previous, prior, earlier, ancient, bygone, anterior, first-mentioned, foregoing. *(succeeding, subsequent, posterior, latter, modern, coming, future)*

fortunate—lucky, propitious, happy, felicitous, prosperous, auspicious, providential, successful. *(unlucky, unfortunate, unhappy, infelicitous)*

forward—advanced, ready, eager, anxious, obtrusive, self-assertive, impertinent, progressive, onward, confident, bold, presumptuous. *(tardy, backward, reluctant, indifferent, slow, modest)*

found—establish, institute, fix, set, build, set up, base, endow, rest, ground, plant, root. *(disestablish, subvert, supplant, uproot)*

foundation—institution, establishment, footing, base, basis, origin, ground, groundwork, rudiments, substratum, underlying principle. *(disestablishment, superstructure)*

fragrant—odorous, scented, perfumed, balmy, sweet-smelling, aromatic, sweet-scented, odoriferous, spicy. *(inodorous, scentless, fetid)*

frail—irresolute, erring, mutable. *(resolute, virtuous, lasting)*

frank—ingenuous, candid, open, unreserved, artless, free, familiar, honest, easy, sincere, outspoken, plain. *(disingenuous, close, reserved)*

freakish—sportful, frisky, whimsical, fanciful, capricious, erratic. *(steady, sober, demure, unwhimsical, unfanciful, reliable, consistent, uniform)*

free—detached, playing, operating, open, unoccupied, unobstructed, unimpeded, permitted, unhindered, exempt, gratuitous, unconditional, at liberty, clear, liberal, untrammeled, unconfined, careless, loose, easy, munificent, unreserved, frank, bountiful, generous, bounteous. (*subservient*)

frequent—many, repeated, numerous, recurrent, general, continual, usual, common. (*few, solitary, rare, scanty, casual*)

fresh—new, young, vigorous, cool, recent, renewed, unimpaired, untarnished, unfaded, blooming, ruddy, novel, untried, modern, unskilled. (*old, stale, jaded, weary, former, stagnant, ordinary*)

fretful—irritable, fractious, peevish, impatient, petulant, waspish. (*patient, forbearing, contented*)

friction—rubbing, grating, attrition, abrasion, contact. (*lubrication, detachment, isolation*)

friend—associate, companion, acquaintance, familiar, ally, chum, messmate, coadjutor, confidant, adherent. (*opponent, foe, adversary, antagonist, enemy*)

friendly—well-inclined, well-disposed, amicable, kindly, social, neighborly, sociable, affectionate, favorable, cordial. (*ill-inclined, ill-disposed, hostile, inimical, adverse, antagonistic*)

frightful—terrible, horrible, alarming, ugly, hideous, monstrous, dreadful, direful, awful, shocking, horrid, terrific. (*pleasing, attractive, beautiful*)

frivolous—trifling, silly, trivial, petty, worthless. (*serious, earnest, important, grave*)

frolic—play, game, sport, festivity, entertainment, gambol, gaiety, lark, spree, merrymaking, prank. (*study, undertaking, purpose, engagement*)

frugal—sparing, economical, parsimonious, abstinent, abstemious, temperate, saving, thrifty, provident. (*profuse, luxurious, extravagant, prodigal, self-indulgent, intemperate*)

fruitful—productive, prolific, pregnant, fraught, causative, effectual, useful, successful, fertile, abundant, plenteous, fecund, plentiful. (*unproductive, sterile, barren, fruitless, ineffectual, useless*)

fulfill—fill, complete, discharge, verify, accomplish, achieve, execute, effect. (*neglect, ignore*)

fulsome—excessive, gross, loathsome, nauseous, sickening, fawning, offensive. (*chaste, sober, nice*)

function—office, part, character, capacity, business, administration, discharge, operation, exercise, power, duty, employment. (*usurpation, maladministration, misconduct, misdemeanor*)

fundamental—primary, important, indispensable, essential. (*secondary, unimportant, adventitious, ascititious, nonessential*)

funny—sportive, droll, comical, laughable, humorous, jocose, ridiculous, ludicrous, diverting. (*dull, tedious, mournful, lugubrious, dismal, grave*)

furnish—supply, provide, equip, afford, yield, bestow, purvey, give. (*withhold, withdraw, dismantle*)

fuss—stir, excitement, tumult, worry, ado, bustle, flurry, fidget. (*quiet, peace, sedateness, tranquillity*)

future—forthcoming, coming, advenient. (*gone, bygone, past*)

G

gabble—prate, jabber, jargon, stuff, babble, rattle, twaddle, gibber, chatter, gibberish. (*conversation, speech, eloquence, reticence, taciturnity*)

gain—acquire, get, win, procure, obtain, profit, benefit, earn, attain, realize, achieve, reap, reach. (*lose, forfeit, suffer*)

gallant—brave, chivalrous, intrepid, courteous, heroic, fearless, courageous, valiant, bold, splendid, showy, gay. (*cowardly, churlish, discourteous*)

game—sport, recreation, pastime, amusement, frolic, diversion, play. (*study, toil, labor, business*)

garble—misrepresent, misquote, mutilate, cook, dress, color, falsify, pervert, distort. (*quote, cite*)

gaudy—tawdry, fine, meretricious, bespangled, glittering, showy, gay, garish. (*rich, simple*)

gauge—measure, fathom, probe. (*survey, conjecture, view, scan, guess, observe, mismeasure*)

gawky—awkward, ungainly, uncouth, clumsy, clownish. (*neat, handy, graceful, handsome*)

gay—merry, blithe, lively, jolly, sportive, sprightly, smart, festive, gladsome, pleasuresome, cheerful. (*heavy, melancholy, grave, sad, somber*)

generous—noble, chivalrous, liberal, disinterested, bountiful, magnanimous, openhearted, munificent, honorable. (*mean, ignoble, illiberal*)

genial—warm, cordial, balmy, cheering, merry, festive, joyous, hearty, revivifying, restorative. (*cold, cutting, harsh, deleterious, noxious, deadly*)

genteel—polite, well-bred, refined, courteous, fashionable, elegant, aristocratic, polished, graceful. (*rude, boorish, ill-bred, clownish, unfashionable, unpolished, inelegant, plebeian*)

gentle—courteous, polite, high-bred, mild, bland, tame, docile, amiable, meek, soft, placid, tender. (*rough, rude, coarse, fierce, savage*)

genuine—authentic, true, real, pure, unalloyed, natural, unaffected, sincere, unadulterated, veritable, sound. (*spurious, fictitious, adulterated*)

get—gain, procure, acquire, earn, obtain, attain, secure, achieve. (*lose, forfeit, surrender, forgo*)

ghastly—deathlike, wan, grim, cadaverous, spectral, pallid, hideous, shocking. (*blooming, fresh*)

giddy—whirling, vertiginous, thoughtless, inconstant, unsteady, lofty, beetling, dizzy, harebrained, flighty. (*stationary, slow, ponderous, thoughtful*)

gift—donation, present, grant, boon, gratuity, benefaction, endowment, talent, faculty, alms, douceur. (*reservation, refusal, wages, purchase*)

gist—essence, pith, marrow, substance, kernel, force, main point. (*surplusage, redundancy, additament, environment, accessories, garb, clothing*)

give—bestow, grant, confer, impart, yield, produce, surrender, concede, present, afford, communicate, furnish. (*withhold, withdraw, refuse*)

glad—happy, joyous, pleased, gratified, blithesome, gleeful, gladsome, delighted, cheerful, elated, joyful. (*unhappy, sorrowful, disastrous*)

glare—beam, shine, gleam, ray, radiate, glow. (*shimmer, scintillate, glitter, smolder, glimmer*)

glassy—vitreous, smooth, polished, glacial, glabrous, brittle, transparent, crystalline, pellucid, limpid, glossy, silken. (*rough, uneven, rugged*)

glory—brightness, radiance, effulgence, honor, fame, celebrity, pomp, luster, magnificence, splendor, renown. (*obscurity, ignominy, cloud, dishonor*)

glut—*v.* gorge, fill, stuff, cram, satiate, cloy, surfeit. (*disgorge, empty, void*)

glut—*n.* surplus, redundancy, superfluity, overstock. (*scarcity, drainage, exhaustion, dearth*)

go—move, depart, pass, travel, vanish, reach, extend, proceed, stir, set out, budge. (*stand, stay*)

good—*a.* right, complete, virtuous, sound, pious,

benevolent, propitious, serviceable, suitable, efficient, sufficient, competent, valid, real, actual, considerable, honorable, reputable, righteous, proper, true, upright, just, excellent. (*wrong, imperfect, unsound, vicious, profane, niggardly*)

good—*n.* boon, benefit, advantage, gain, blessing, mercy, virtue, prosperity, weal, profit, interest, welfare. (*hurt, injury, loss, detriment*)

goodly—pleasant, desirable, excellent, fair, comely, considerable, graceful, fine. (*unpleasant*)

gorgeous—magnificent, splendid, costly, rich, superb, grand, strong. (*poor, naked, bare, cheap*)

govern—rule, direct, control, moderate, guide sway, supervise, manage, command, conduct (*misrule, misdirect, miscontrol*)

grace—favor, beauty, condescension, kindness, elegance, charm, excellence, pardon, mercy. (*disfavor, deformity, unkindness, pride, inelegance*)

gracious—affable, courteous, benignant, kind, civil, condescending, merciful, friendly, tender, gentle, beneficent. (*haughty, discourteous, illdisposed, ungracious, churlish*)

gradual—slow, continuous, unintermittent, gradational, regular, step by step, progressive. (*sudden, momentary, instantaneous, periodic, recurrent*)

grand—large, dignified, imposing, important, eventful, magnificent, grandly, majestic, august, exalted, stately, splendid, lofty, elevated, pompous, gorgeous, sublime, superb. (*little, undignified*)

graphic—picturesque, illustrative, descriptive, pictorial, forcible, vivid, feeling, described, picturesquely. (*unpicturesque, unillustrative, undescriptive*)

grateful—pleasant, acceptable, agreeable, thankful, obliged, welcome. (*unpleasant, disagreeable*)

gratify—please, satisfy, indulge, humor. (*displease, dissatisfy, disappoint, stint, discipline, inure*)

gratitude—thankfulness, gratefulness. (*unthankfulness, ingratitude, thanklessness, oblivion*)

grave—sad, serious, momentous, weighty, pressing, sedate, demure, thoughtful, sober, somber, solemn, important, aggravated, heavy, cogent. (*joyous, merry, facetious, unimportant, ridiculous*)

great—big, wide, huge, numerous, protracted, excellent, large, immense, bulky, majestic, gigantic, vast, grand, sublime, august, eminent, magnanimous, noble, powerful, exalted, noticeable. (*little, narrow, puny, scanty, few, short, mean, ignoble, weak, unimportant*)

greedy—gluttonous, voracious, hungry, desirous, avaricious. (*abstemious, abstinent, indifferent, contented*)

grief—trouble, tribulation, woe, mourning, regret, affliction, sorrow, sadness. (*joy, exultation*)

grieve—trouble, burden, annoy, distress, bewail, wound, pain, sorrow, hurt, afflict, mourn, lament, complain, deplore. (*ease, console, soothe, please*)

grim—fierce, ferocious, terrible, hideous, ugly, ghastly, sullen, stern. (*mild, docile, attractive*)

groan—moan, whine, growl, grumble. (*giggle*)

groundless—vain, suppositious, unfounded, baseless, fanciful, gratuitous, chimerical, false. (*wellfounded, substantial, authoritative, actual, authentic*)

group—cluster, bunch, knot, assemblage, collocation, class, collection, clump, order, assembly. (*isolation, individual, crowd, confusion, medley*)

grudge—*v.* spare, retain, covet, envy, withhold. (*spend, impart, welcome, satisfy, gratify*)

grudge—*n.* spite, grievance, aversion, rancor, hatred, pique, dissatisfaction, discontent, refusal. (*welcome, satisfaction, approval, contentment, complacency, bestowal, benefaction*)

gruff—rough, surly, bearish, harsh, rude, blunt. (*smooth, mild, affable, courteous*)

guess—conjecture, surmise, divine, suppose, suspect, fancy, imagine. (*examine, prove, investigate, establish, demonstrate, elaborate, deduce*)

guide—lead, direct, conduct, pilot, regulate, superintend, influence, train, manage. (*mislead*)

gush—burst, stream, flow, gush, spout, rush, pour out, flow out. (*drip, drop, dribble, trickle*)

H

habit—habituation, custom, familiarity, association, inurement, usage, practice, way, manner. (*dishabituation, inexperience, inconversance, desuetude*)

habitual—regular, ordinary, perpetual, customary, usual, familiar, accustomed, wonted. (*irregular, extraordinary, occasional, unusual, exceptional, rare*)

half—moiety, bisection, dimidiation. (*integrity, entirety, totality, whole*)

halt—stop, rest, limp, falter, hammer, stammer, demur, dubitate, pause, hold, stand still, hesitate. (*advance, decide, determine, speed, flow, career*)

handsome—comely, good-looking, generous, liberal, beautiful, ample, pretty, graceful, lovely, elegant. (*uncomely, ill-looking, ungenerous, illiberal, unhandsome*)

handy—near, convenient, useful, helpful, manageable, dexterous, ready, expert. (*remote, inconvenient, awkward, useless, cumbrous, unwieldy*)

happy—lucky, fortunate, felicitous, successful, delighted, joyous, merry, blithesome, prosperous, glad, blissful. (*unlucky, unfortunate, infelicitous*)

hard—firm, dense, solid, compact, unyielding, impenetrable, arduous, difficult, grievous, distressing, rigorous, oppressive, exacting, unfeeling, stubborn, harsh, forced, constrained, inexplicable, flinty, severe, cruel, obdurate, hardened, callous. (*soft, fluid, liquid, elastic, brittle, penetrable, easy*)

hardship—trouble, burden, annoyance, grievance, calamity, infliction, endurance, affliction. (*pleasure, amusement, alleviation, recreation, gratification, relief, assuagement, facilitation, boon*)

hardy—inured, robust, strong, resolute, stouthearted, vigorous, intrepid, brave, manly, valiant. (*weak, uninured, delicate, irresolute, enervated, debilitated, tender, fragile*)

harm—hurt, mischief, injury, detriment, damage, evil, wrong, misfortune, ill, mishap. (*benefit, boon, amelioration, improvement, reparation*)

harmonious—congruous, accordant, proportioned, uniform, melodious, musical, dulcet, tuneful, consistent, peaceful, agreeable, amicable, friendly, concordant. (*incongruous, discordant*)

hasty—speedy, rapid, superficial, hurried, irascible, impetuous, reckless, headlong, crude, incomplete, undeveloped, immature, swift, precipitate, fiery, passionate, slight, quick, excitable, rash, cursory. (*slow, leisurely, careful, close, reflective, developed, matured, complete, elaborate*)

hateful—abominable, detestable, vile, odious, heinous, execrable, loathsome, repulsive. (*lovable*)

have—own, possess, feel, entertain, accept, bear, enjoy, keep. (*want, need, lose, forgo, discard, reject, miss, desiderate, covet, desire*)

hazard—peril, risk, jeopardy, danger, chance, imperil, dare. (*safety, security, protection, warrant, certainty, calculation, law*)

hazy—foggy, nebulous, misty, filmy, gauzy, cloudy, murky, caliginous. (*diaphanous, clear*)

head—top, crown, chief, leader, ruler, mind, source, section, division, topic, gathering, culmination, crisis, leadership, guide, commander, acme, summit. (*tail, bottom, follower, servant, retainer*)

heart—core, nucleus, kernel, interior, center, character, disposition, courage, hardihood, nature, life, feeling, benevolence. (*exterior, hand, action*)

hearty—healthy, robust, cordial, sound, warm, honest, earnest, genuine, well, sincere, heartfelt, hale. (*unhealthy, delicate, infirm, cold, insincere*)

heat—warmth, ardor, passion, excitement, fever, ebullition, intensity. (*coolness, indifference, subsidence, calmness, composure, reflection*)

heavy—weighty, ponderous, inert, slow, stupid, dull, impenetrable, stolid, cumbrous, grievous, afflictive, oppressive, burdensome, sluggish, laborious, depressed. (*light, trifling, trivial, agile, active, quick, joyous, alleviative, consolatory, inspiriting, animating, buoyant*)

heighten—exalt, increase, enhance, intensify, color, vivify, aggravate, raise, exaggerate, lift up, amplify. (*lower, depress, diminish, deteriorate*)

heinous—hateful, flagrant, detestable, flagitious, atrocious, odious, abominable, execrable, enormous. (*excellent, laudable, meritorious, praiseworthy, distinguished, justifiable, excusable, palliable*)

help—aid, succor, remedy, prevent, avoid, assist, promote, cooperate, relieve, second. (*oppose*)

hereditary—inherited, ancestral, lineal. (*conferred, acquired, won*)

hesitate—dubitate, waver, demur, scruple, falter, stammer, pause, doubt. (*decide, determine*)

hide—conceal, secrete, mask, dissemble, store, protect, disguise, ensconce, screen, cover, burrow. (*expose, discover, exhibit, manifest, betray, strip*)

hideous—frightful, unshapely, monstrous, horrid, horrible, ugly, grisly, grim, ghastly. (*graceful*)

high—elevated, lofty, tall, eminent, excellent, noble, haughty, violent, proud, exalted. (*depressed, low, stunted, ignoble, mean, base, affable*)

hinder—prevent, interrupt, obstruct, retard, debar, embarrass, impede, thwart, block, stop. (*accelerate, expedite, enable, promote, facilitate*)

hoarse—harsh, grating, husky, raucous, rough, gruff. (*mellifluous, mellow, rich, sweet, melodious*)

hold—keep, grasp, retain, support, restrain, defend, maintain, occupy, possess, sustain, regard, consider, cohere, continue, have. (*drop, abandon*)

hollow—empty, concave, foolish, weak, faithless, insincere, artificial, unsubstantial, void, flimsy, transparent, senseless vacant, unsound, false. (*full, solid, well-stored, strong, firm, sincere, true*)

homely—plain, coarse, uncomely. (*handsome, beautiful, refined, courtly*)

honest—honorable, upright, virtuous, proper, right, sincere, conscientious. (*dishonest, dishonorable, vicious, improper, wrong, insincere*)

honor—respect, reverence. nobility. dignity. eminence, reputation, fame, high-mindedness, spirit, self-respect, renown, grandeur, esteem. (*disrespect, contempt, irreverence, slight, obscurity*)

honorary—gratuitous, unofficial, unremunerative, nominal, titular. (*official, remunerative, professional, jurisdictional*)

hope—anticipation, prospect, vision, longing, confidence, desire, expectation, trust. (*despair, despondency, distrust, disbelief, abandonment, abjuration*)

horrible—abominable, detestable, dreadful, fearful, hideous, ghastly, terrific, hateful, direful, horrid, awful, frightful. (*lovely, desirable, enjoyable*)

huge—enormous, monstrous, colossal, vast, bulky, large, great, prodigious, immense, stupendous, gigantic. (*petty, undersized, pigmy, puny*)

humane—benign, kind, tender, merciful, benevolent, compassionate. (*unkind, cruel, unmerciful*)

humble—low, lowly, obscure, meek, modest, unassuming, unpretending, submissive. (*high, lofty, eminent, proud, boastful, arrogant, assuming, pretentious*)

humor—disposition, temper, mood, caprice, jocoseness, pleasantry, frame, drollery, fun. (*nature, personality, mind, will, purpose, seriousness*)

hurt—*v.* wound, bruise, harm, injure, damage, pain, grieve. (*heal, soothe, console, repair, reinstate, compensate, benefit*)

hurt—*n.* harm, injury, damage, wound, detriment, mischief. (*benefit, pleasure*)

hurtful—mischievous, injurious, pernicious, baleful, deleterious, baneful, noxious, detrimental, prejudicial. (*helpful, remedial*)

hypocritical—pharisaical, sanctimonious, smug, smooth, mealy, unctuous, mincing. (*plain-spoken, candid, truthful, sincere, genuine, transparent*)

I

idea—image, notion, conception, belief, doctrine, supposition, understanding, fiction, fancy, thought, opinion, impression, sentiment. (*object*)

ideal—mental, notional, conception, intellectual, creative, spiritual, poetical, supposititious, fictitious, unreal, imaginary, chimerical, fanciful, imaginative. (*physical, visible, material, tangible*)

idle—void, unoccupied, waste, vain, empty, unemployed, useless, inactive, lazy, indolent. (*tilled, occupied, populated, filled, employed, assiduous, industrious*)

ignoble—mean, base, dishonorable, humble, plebeian, lowly. (*honorable, noble, eminent, exalted, lordly, grand, notable, illustrious*)

ignominious—shameful, scandalous, dishonorable, infamous. (*honorable, reputable, creditable*)

ignorant—untaught, uneducated, uninformed, unlearned, illiterate, unlettered. (*wise, learned*)

illusion—dream, mockery, deception, delusion, hallucination, phantasm, vision, myth, false show, error, fallacy. (*form, reality, body, substance*)

illustrious—renowned, glorious, brilliant, death-

Synonym Ant/Hom

less, eminent, distinguished, celebrated, conspicuous, noble, famous. (*ignominious, disgraceful*)

ill will—antipathy, hatred, malevolence, dislike, aversion. (*good will, beneficence*)

imaginative—creative, conceptive, ideal, poetical, romantic, inventive, original. (*unimaginative, unpoetical, unromantic, prosaic, matter-of-fact*)

imagine—conceive, suppose, surmise, understand, fancy, fabricate, deem, presume, think, apprehend. (*represent, exhibit, demonstrate, prove*)

imitate—represent, copy, resemble, follow, portray, depict, repeat, pattern after, mock, ape, counterfeit, mimic. (*misrepresent, caricature, alter*)

immediate—proximate, contiguous, present, direct, instant, next. (*distant, remote, future, mediate*)

impair—deteriorate, injure, reduce, damage, enfeeble, vitiate, diminish, lessen. (*enhance, improve, augment, repair*)

impassible—immaterial, immortal. (*passible*)

impediment—hindrance, obstacle, obstruction, stumbling block. (*aid, aidance, help, assistance*)

imperative—urgent, irresistible, dictatorial, inexorable, peremptorily, compulsory, obligatory. (*indulgent, lenient, mild, entreative, supplicatory*)

imperious—arrogant, exacting, dictatorial, authoritative, domineering, haughty, lordly. (*yielding, submissive, compliant, docile, ductile, lenient*)

implement—instrument, utensil, tool, appliance. (*labor, work, science, art, manufacture, agriculture*)

implicate—connect, associate, charge, criminate, involve, entangle, infold, compromise. (*disconnect, dissociate, acquit, extricate*)

imply—involve, mean, indicate, suggest, hint, import, denote, include. (*express, declare, state*)

importance—weight, moment, consequence, significance, signification, avail, concern. (*unimportance, insignificance, nothingness, immateriality*)

important—significant, expressive, relevant, main, leading, considerable, great, dignified, influential, weighty, momentous, material, grave, essential. (*insignificant, trivial, inexpressive, irrelevant, inconsiderable, petty, mean, uninfluential*)

impotent—weak, powerless, useless, feeble, helpless, nerveless, enfeebled. (*strong, vigorous, powerful, virile*)

impressive—forcible, solemn, affecting, imposing, important. (*weak, unimpressive, feeble, tame, jejune, dry, vapid, unimportant, insignificant*)

improvement—advancement, amendment, progress, increase, correction, proficiency. (*degeneracy, deterioration, debasement, retrogression*)

impudent—impertinent, insolent, saucy, shameless, brazenfaced, rude, bold, immodest. (*servile*)

impulse—incentive, push, incitement, force, influence, instigation, feeling, sudden thought, motive. (*rebuff, premeditation, deliberation*)

inadvertence—oversight, negligence, inattention, carelessness, blunder. (*carefulness, exactness, meticulousness*)

inaudible—low, inarticulate, suppressed, muttering, mumbling, stifled, muffled. (*audible, outspoken, sonorous, articulate, clear, ringing, loud*)

incapable—unqualified, unable, unfitted, weak, incompetent, feeble, disqualified, insufficient.

(*qualified, able, fitted, strong, clever*)

incidental—casual, occasional, appertinent, concomitant, concurrent, accidental, fortuitous. (*systematic, regular, independent, disconnected*)

incivility—discourtesy, ill-breeding, ill-manners, uncourteousness. (*civility, urbanity, good manners*)

inclement—harsh, tyrannical, cruel, unmerciful, severe, stormy, rough, rigorous. (*mild, benign*)

inclination—leaning, slope, tendency, disposition, proneness, aptness, predilection, bias, bent, attachment, affection, liking, wish. (*inaptitude*)

incoherent—unconnected, incongruous, inconsequential, loose. (*coherent, connected*)

incomparable—matchless, unique, consummate, transcendent. (*common, ordinary, average*)

inconsolable—cheerless, joyless, spiritless, melancholy, gloomy, disconsolate, comfortless, forlorn, heartsick, in despair. (*cheerful, hopeful, consolable*)

inconstant—fickle, mutable, variable, fitful, unstable, undependable, changeable, capricious. (*stable, steadfast, dependable*)

incontestable—indisputable, unquestionable, unassailable, impregnable. (*dubious, questionable*)

inconvenience—incommode, discommode, distrust, molest. (*suit, aid, benefit, subserve, assist*)

increase—advance, heighten, dilate, enhance, aggregate, pile up, raise, magnify, spread. (*lessen*)

incredible—surpassing belief, fabulous, marvelous. (*credible, believable*)

inculcate—impress, urge, enforce, infuse, instill, implant, press, teach. (*insinuate, suggest, disavow, abjure, denounce*)

incumbent—pressing, binding, coercive, indispensable, urgent, devolvent, obligatory. (*optional, discretional*)

incurable—irremediable, irredeemable, terminal. (*tractable, removable, remediable*)

indecent—indelicate, immodest, improper.

indelible—indestructible, indefeasible, ineffaceable, persistent, irreversible. (*mutable, evanescent, transient, effaceable*)

indescribable—unaccountable, inexpressible, ineffable, unutterable. (*familiar, ordinary*)

indestructible—imperishable, indiscerptible. (*perishable, destructible, dissoluble*)

indicate—show, evidence, betray, evince, manifest, declare, specify, denote, point out, betoken, designate, mark. (*conceal, contradict, negative*)

indifference—triviality, unimportance, insignificance, coolness, carelessness, apathy, insensibility, composure. (*importance, significance, weight, gravity, eagerness, interest, affection, ardor*)

indiscriminate—mixed, confused, medley, promiscuous, ill-assorted, undiscerning, undistinguishing, undiscriminating. (*careful, sorted, select*)

indispensable—necessary, essential, requisite, needful, expedient. (*unnecessary, unessential, inexpedient, dispensable*)

individual—personal, specific, peculiar, indivisible, identical, singular, idiosyncratic, special, single, separate, particular. (*general, common*)

indivisible—minute, atomic, ultimate. (*divisible*)

induce—produce, cause, prompt, persuade, instigate, impel, actuate, urge, influence, move, prevail on. (*slave, prevent, disincline, dissuade*)

indulge—spoil, pamper, humor, gratify, cherish, bask, revel, grovel, foster, favor, allow. (*thwart*)

indulgent—compliant, tender, tolerant. (*harsh*)

industrious—diligent, laborious, busy, assiduous, active, hardworking. (*lazy, shiftless, idle*)

ineffable—inexpressible, inconceivable, insurpassable, indeclarable, indescribable, exquisite, perfect. (*common, trivial, superficial, vulgar, conversational, colloquial, obvious, commonplace*)

ineffectual—fruitless, useless, vain, idle, unavailing, abortive, inoperative, ineffective. (*effective, effectual, successful*)

inexcusable—unmitigated, unpardonable, indefensible, unjustifiable. (*mitigable, pliable, justifiable, vindicable, defensible, pardonable*)

inexhaustible—incessant, unwearied, indefatigable, perennial, illimitable. (*limited, scant, poor*)

inexpedient—undesirable, inadvisable, disadvantageous. (*advisable, profitable, expedient*)

infamy—despair, degradation, disgrace, ignominy, obloquy, extreme vileness, dishonor. (*honor*)

infatuation—fatuity, hallucination, madness, self-deception. (*clear-sightedness, sagacity, wisdom*)

inference—deduction, corollary, conclusion, consequence. (*statement, proposition, enunciation*)

inferiority—subordination, minority, poverty, mediocrity, subjection, servitude, depression. (*superiority, majority, excellence, eminence, independence, mastery, exaltation, elevation*)

infidel—skeptic, unbeliever, heretic, freethinker. (*believer, Christian, devotee, pietist*)

inflame—fire, kindle, excite, rouse, fan, incense, madden, infuriate, exasperate, irritate, embitter, anger, enrage. (*quench, extinguish, allay, cool*)

influence—effect, control, causation, affection. impulse, power, credit, character, sway, weight, ascendancy, prestige, authority. (*inefficiency, ineffectiveness, inoperativeness, nullity, neutrality*)

influential—potent, powerful, efficacious, forcible, persuasive, controlling, guiding, considerable. (*weak, ineffective, inoperative, unpersuasive*)

information—instruction, advice, counsel, notice, notification, knowledge. (*concealment, hiding, occultation, mystification, ignorance*)

infringe—break, violate, transgress, contravene. (*observe, conserve, preserve, keep within bounds*)

ingenious—skillful, adept, clever, inventive, ready, frank, sincere. (*unskillful, slow, uninventive, unready*)

ingenuous—noble, candid, generous, frank, sincere, straightforward, honorable, open, artless, honest. (*mean, reserved, sly, disingenuous*)

ingredient—element, component, constituent. (*noningredient, refuse, residuum, counteragent*)

inherent—innate, congenial, immanent, ingrained, inborn, intrinsic, natural, inbred. (*foreign, ascititious, temporary, separable, extraneous*)

initiative—start, leadership, commencement, example. (*wake, rear, prosecution, termination*)

injunction—mandate, order, command, exhortation, precept. (*disobedience, insubordination*)

injurious—hurtful, deleterious, prejudicial, noxious, detrimental, baleful, pernicious, wrongful, mischievous, damaging, baneful. (*helpful, beneficial, advantageous*)

innocence—innocuousness, inoffensiveness, guile-lessness, guiltlessness, simplicity, purity, sinlessness. (*hurtfulness, offensiveness, guile, guilt, contamination, corruption, impurity, sinfulness*)

innocuous—inoffensive, harmless, wholesome. (*obnoxious, hurtful, deleterious, insidious*)

inquiry—interrogation, question, asking, investigation, search, examination, research, scrutiny, exploration. (*conjecture, guess, intuition, hypothesis, assumption, supposition*)

insatiable—voracious, unappeasable, omnivorous, ravenous, rapacious, greedy. (*moderate, delicate, fastidious, dainty, squeamish*)

insidious—wily, treacherous, designing, dangerous, deceitful, sly, crafty, artful. (*straightforward*)

insinuate—introduce, insert, worm, ingratiate, intimate, suggest, infuse, hint. (*withdraw, retract*)

insipid—tasteless, vapid, uninteresting, characterless, flavorless, flat, insulse, lifeless, prosy, stupid. (*tasty, sapid, relishing, racy, interesting*)

insist—stand, demand, maintain, contend, persist, persevere, urge. (*abandon, waive, concede*)

insolent—haughty, overbearing, contemptuous, abusive, saucy, impertinent, opprobrious, offensive. (*meek, polite, well-mannered*)

insolvent—bankrupt, ruined, penniless, beggared. (*flush, flourishing, monied, thriving*)

inspire—animate, inspirit, inflame, imbue, impel, encourage, inhale, enliven, cheer, breathe in, infuse, exhilarate. (*depress, dispirit, discourage, deter*)

instance—entreaty, request, prompting, persuasion, example, solicitation, case, illustration, exemplification, occurrence, point, precedence. (*dissuasion, depreciation, warning, rule, statement*)

instill—pour, infuse, introduce, import, implant, insinuate, inculcate. (*drain, strain, extract, eradicate, eliminate, remove, extirpate*)

instinctive—natural, voluntary, spontaneous, intuitive, impulsive. (*cultivated, forced, reasoning*)

instruction—teaching, education, information, counsel, advice, direction, order, command. (*misteaching, misinformation, misguidance*)

insufferable—intolerable, unpermissible, unallowable, unendurable, unbearable. (*tolerable, allowable, endurable, supportable*)

insupportable—unbearable, intolerable, insufferable, unendurable. (*endurable, comfortable*)

integrity—uprightness, honor, honesty, probity, truthfulness, candor, single-mindedness, conscientiousness, entireness, rectitude, completeness, parity. (*unfairness, sleight, underhandedness, meanness, chicanery, duplicity, fraud, roguery, rascality*)

intellectual—mental, metaphysical, psychological, inventive, learned, cultured. (*unintellectual*)

intelligence—understanding, apprehension, comprehension, conception, announcement, report, rumor, tidings, news, information, publication, intellectual capacity, mind, knowledge, advice, notice, instruction, intellect. (*misunderstanding, misinformation, misconception, stupidity, dullness*)

intensity—tension, force, concentration, strain, attention, eagerness, ardor, energy. (*laxity, debility, relaxation, languor, indifference, coolness, hebetude, diminution*)

intentional—purposed, designed, deliberate, intended, done on purpose, contemplated, premeditated, studied. (*undesigned, casual, unintentional*)

Synonym
Ant/Hom

intercourse—correspondence, dealing, intercommunication, intimacy, connection, commerce. (*reticence, suspension, cessation, disconnection, interception, interpellation*)

interest—concern, business advantage, profit, attention, curiosity, behalf, cause, share. (*unconcern, disconnection, repudiation, disadvantage, loss*)

intermediate—intervening, included, interposed, comprised, middle, moderate, interjacent. (*circumjacent, surrounding, enclosing, embracing, outside, extreme, excluded, exclusive*)

interpret—translate, render, construe, explain, expound, expone, represent, declare, understand, elucidate, decipher, solve. (*misinterpret, misunderstand, mistake, misconceive, falsify, distort, misdeclare, misrepresent*)

interrupt—break, disconnect, discontinue, intersect, disturb, stop, hinder. (*continue, prosecute*)

interval—interim, meantime, period, gap, intermission, interspace, cessation, space between, season. (*continuity, simultaneousness, uninterruptedness*)

intimate—impart, communicate, announce, declare, tell, suggest, hint, insinuate, mention briefly. (*reserve, repress, withhold, conceal*)

intoxication—venom, poison, obfuscation, bewilderment, delirium, hallucination, ravishment, ecstasy, inebriation, drunkenness, inebriety. (*antidote, clarification, sobriety, sanity, ebriety, melancholy, depression*)

intricate—complicated, involved, mazy, labyrinthine, entangled, tortuous. (*simple, uninvolved*)

introduction—induction, importation, leading, taking, presentation, insertion, commencement, preliminary, preface, initiative, portico, vestibule, entrance, gate, preamble, prelude. (*eduction, extraction, exportation, elimination, ejection, estrangement, conclusion, completion, end, egress*)

introductory—prefatory, initiatory, commendatory, precursory, preliminary, preparatory. (*completive, final, conclusive, alienative, supplemental*)

intuition—instinct, apprehension, recognition, insight. (*information, learning, instruction, elaboration, acquirement, induction, experience*)

invalid—infirm, sick, weak, frail, feeble. (*strong, vigorous, healthy, well*)

invent—discover, contrive, concoct, imagine, elaborate, conceive, design, devise, fabricate, originate, find out, frame, forge, feign. (*imitate*)

invincible—impregnable, immovable, inexpugnable, unsubduable, irresistible, indomitable, unconquerable, insuperable, insurmountable. (*weak, spiritless, powerless, puny, effortless*)

involve—implicate, confound, mingle, envelop, compromise, include, complicate, entangle. (*separate, extricate, disconnect*)

irreligious—undevout, ungodly, godless, profane, impious. (*religious, godly, reverent, reverential, pious, devout*)

irrepressible—unrepressible, ungovernable, uncontrollable, insuppressible, free, unconfined, excitable. (*repressible, governable, controllable, calm*)

irresponsible—unbound, unencumbered, unaccountable, not answerable, excusable, lawless.

J

jealous—envious, self-anxious, covetous, in-

vidious, suspicious. (*unenvious, liberal, genial*)

jingle—rhyme, chime, tinkle, tingle. (*euphony*)

join—unite, adhere, adjoin, add, couple, connect, associate, annex, append, combine, link, accompany, confederate. (*separate, disjoin, subtract, disconnect*)

jollification—revelry, festivity, conviviality, fun, carnival, merrymaking. (*weariness, tediousness*)

jolly—gay, joyful, gladsome, mirthful, genial, jovial, jubilant, robust, lively, plump, merry. (*sad*)

jostle—hustle, push, thrust, jog, jolt, incommode. (*clear, lead, extricate, convoy, escort, precede, pilot, attend*)

joy—gladness, pleasure, delight, happiness, exultation, transport, felicity, ecstasy, rapture, bliss, gaiety, mirth, merriment, festivity, hilarity, charm, blessedness. (*sorrow, pain, trouble, misery*)

jubilant—joyous, triumphant, festive, congratulatory, exultant. (*doleful, mournful, sorrowful, wailing, penitent, penitential, lugubrious, remorseful*)

judgment—decision, determination, adjudication, sagacity, penetration, judiciousness, sense, intellect, belief, estimation, opinion, verdict, sentence, discernment, discrimination, intelligence, prudence, award, condemnation. (*argument, consideration, inquiry, speculation, proposition*)

judicious—wise, sagacious, expedient, sensible, prudent, discreet, well-judged, well-advised, polite, discerning, thoughtful. (*foolish, unwise, silly*)

juggle—conjure, cheat, bamboozle, shuffle, trick, beguile, circumvent, swindle, overreach, mystify, mislead. (*expose, correct, enlighten, guide, lead, undeceive, disillusionize, detect*)

just—exact, fitting, true, fair, proportioned, harmonious, honest, reasonable, sound, honorable, normal, impartial, equitable, upright, regular, orderly, lawful, right, righteous, proper. (*inexact*)

justice—equity, impartiality, fairness, right, reasonableness, propreity, uprightness, desert, integrity. (*injustice, wrong, partiality, unfairness*)

juvenile—youthful, young, infantile, boyish, girlish, early, immature, adolescent, pubescent, childish, puerile. (*mature, later, manly, womanly*)

K

keen—eager, vehement, sharp, piercing, penetrating, acute, cutting, biting, severe, sarcastic, satirical, ardent, prompt, shrewd. (*indifferent*)

keep—hold, restrain, retain, detain, guard, preserve, suppress, repress, conceal, tend, support, maintain, conduct, continue, obey, haunt, observe, frequent, celebrate, protect, adhere to, practice, hinder, sustain. (*release, acquit, liberate, send, dismiss*)

kind—*n.* style, character, description, designation, denomination, genus, species, sort, class, nature, set, breed. (*dissimilarity*)

kind—*a.* benevolent, benign, tender, indulgent, humane, clement, lenient, compassionate, gentle, good, gracious, forbearing, kindhearted. (*unkind, harsh, severe, cruel, hard, illiberal*)

knot—tie, bond, intricacy, difficulty, perplexity, cluster, collection, band, group, protuberance, joint. (*loosening, unfastening, dissolution, solution, explication, unraveling, dispersion, multitude*)

knowing—shrewd, astute, discerning, sharp, acute, sagacious, penetrating, proficient, skillful, intelligent, experienced, well-informed, accomplished. (*simple, dull, innocent, gullible, undiscerning, stolid, silly*)

knowledge—apprehension, comprehension, recognition, understanding, conversance, experience, acquaintance, familiarity, cognizance, notice, information, instruction, learning, enlightenment, scholarship, attainments, acquirements. (*misapprehension, inobservance, incomprehension, misunderstanding, misconception, inconversance, inexperience, ignorance, unfamiliarity, incognizance*)

L

laborious—assiduous, diligent, painstaking, indefatigable, arduous, burdensome, toilsome, wearisome, industrious, hard-working, active, difficult, tedious. (*idle, indiligent, lazy, indolent, easy*)

laconic—terse, curt, epigrammatic. (*prolix*)

lame—weak, faltering, hobbling, hesitating, ineffective, impotent, crippled, halt, defective, imperfect. (*robust, agile, potent, efficient, satisfactory*)

language—speech, talk, conversation, dialect, discourse, tongue, diction, phraseology, articulation, accents, vernacular, expression. (*jargon, jabber, gibberish, babel, gabble, cry, whine, bark, howl*)

languid—faint, weary, feeble, unnerved, unbraced, pining, drooping, enervated, exhausted, flagging, spiritless. (*strong, healthy, robust, vigorous, active, braced*)

large—big, bulky, extensive, abundant, capacious, ample, liberal, comprehensive, enlightened, catholic, great, vast, wide. (*small, mean, narrow*)

last—*v.* continue, remain, hold, endure, abide, live. (*cease, fail, fade, fly, wane, depart, disappear*)

last—*a.* latest, ending, final, concluding, hindmost, past, extreme, lowest, remotest, ultimate. (*first, introductory, initiatory, opening, foremost*)

laughter—merriment, glee, derision, ridicule, cachinnation, contempt. (*weeping, tears, mourning, sorrow, admiration, veneration, respect*)

law—rule, edict, regulation, decree, command, order, statute, enactment, mode, method, sequence, principle, code, legislation, adjudication, jurisdiction, jurisprudence. (*misrule, disorder, anarchy*)

lawful—legal, permissible, orderly, right, allowable, fair, constitutional, rightful, legitimate. (*illegal, impermissible, unlawful, wrong, lawless, unfair*)

lay—place, establish, deposit, allay, prostrate, arrange, dispose, put, spread, set down. (*erect*)

lead—*v.* conduct, guide, precede, induce, spend, pass, commence, inaugurate, convoy, persuade, direct, influence. (*misconduct, mislead, follow*)

lead—*n.* priority, pre-eminence, initiative, guidance, control. (*subordination, inferiority, submission*)

lean—*a.* meager, lank, tabid, emaciated, shriveled, bony, thin, scraggy, skinny, slender, scanty. (*fat, brawny, plump, well-conditioned*)

lean—*v.* incline, rest, support, tend, bend, depend, hang, repose, confide, slope. (*stabilitate*)

learned—conversant, erudite, read, skilled, scholarly, literary, knowing, well-informed, versed. (*inconversant, illiterate, ignorant, unlearned, unscholarly*)

learning—knowledge, erudition, literature, lore, letters, acquirements, attainments, scholarship, education, tuition, culture. (*ignorance, boorish-

ness, illiterateness, emptiness, sciolism, intuition*)

leave—liberty, permission, license, concession. (*restriction, prohibition, prevention, inhibition, refusal*)

legend—myth, fable, marvelous story, fiction. (*history, fact, actual occurrence*)

lengthy—diffuse, prolix, tedious, long-drawn, verbose. (*concise, compendious, curt, short, brief*)

lesson—precept, warning, instruction, lecture, homily, information. (*misinstruction, misguidance, misinformation*)

level—*n.* plane, surface, floor, equality, aim, platform, ground, coordinateness, horizontalness. (*unevenness, acclivity, declivity, inequality, incoordinateness, verticality*)

level—*v.* plane, smooth, roll, flatten, equalize, raze. (*roughen, furrow, disequalize, graduate*)

level—*a.* horizontal, plain, flat, even, smooth. (*rough, uneven, broken, rolling*)

libel—defamation, detraction, traducement, calumny, slander, defamatory publication, lampoon. (*retraction, vindication, apology, eulogy, panegyric*)

liberal—free, gentle, refined, polished, generous, bountiful, catholic, enlarged, copious, ample, profuse, large, handsome, munificent, abundant, noble-minded, bounteous, tolerant, plentiful. (*churlish*)

liberty—freedom, leave, independence, permission, privilege, license, franchise, immunity, insult, impropriety, volition, voluntariness, exemption, (*slavery, servitude, restraint, constraint, submission*)

licentious—voluptuous, dissolute, rakish, debauched, self-indulgent, lax, profligate, loose, unbridled. (*temperate, strict, sober, self-controlled*)

lie—*n.* falsehood, untruth, fabrication, subterfuge, evasion, fib, fiction, falsity. (*truth, fact, veracity*).

lie—*v.* rest, repose, be, remain. (*rise, move, stir*)

life—vitality, duration, existence, condition, conduct, animation, vivacity, personality, state, society, morals, spirit, activity, history, career. (*mortality, decease, death, nonexistence, dullness*)

lift—raise, elevate, upraise, upheave, exalt, hoist, elate, erect. (*lower, sink, depress, crush, overwhelm*)

light—*n.* luminosity, radiance, beam, gleam, phosphorescence, scintillation, coruscation, flash, brightness, brilliancy, effulgence, splendor, blaze, candle, lamp, lantern, explanation, instruction, illumination, understanding, interpretation, day, life. (*darkness, dimness, obscurity, shade, duskiness, gloom, extinction, misinterpretation, ignorance*)

light—*a.* imponderous, portable, unweighty, buoyant, volatile, easy, digestible, scanty, active, unencumbered, empty, slight, gentle, unsteady, capricious, vain, frivolous, characterless, thoughtless, unthoughtful, unconsidered, inadequate, incompact, unsubstantial, inconsiderable, not difficult, bright, whitish, trifling. (*heavy, ponderous*)

likeness—similarity, resemblance, correspondence, similitude, parity, copy, imitation, portrait, representation, image, effigy, carte de visite, picture. (*dissimilarity, dissimilitude, disparity, inequality, unlikeness, original*)

line—cord, thread, length, outline, row, direction, verse, course, method, succession, sequence, continuity. (*breadth, contents, space, divergency*)

liquid—fluid, liquescent, melting, **running**,

watery, fluent, soft, mellifluous, limpid, flowing, clear, smooth. (*solid, solidified, concrete, congealed*)

listen—hear, attend, hearken, incline, give ear, heed. (*disregard, ignore, refuse, repudiate*)

literal—exact, grammatical, verbal, close, real, positive, actual, plain. (*general, substantial, metaphorical, free, spiritual*)

literary—erudite, scholarly, studious. (*illiterate*)

literature—lore, erudition, reading, study, learning, attainment, scholarship, literary works. (*genius, intuition, inspiration*)

little—small, tiny, pigmy, diminutive, short, brief, scanty, unimportant, insignificant, slight, weak, inconsiderable, trivial, illiberal, mean, petty, paltry, dirty, shabby, dwarf. (*big, bulky, large*)

live—*v.* vegetate, grow, survive, continue, abide, dwell, last, subsist, behave, act, breathe, exist. (*die, perish, wither, demise, migrate, vanish, fade*)

live—*a.* animate. (*inanimate, defunct*)

load—*n.* weight, lading, cargo, oppression, incubus, drag, burden. (*refreshment, support, solace*)

load—*v.* burden, charge, lade, cargo, cumber, oppress. (*disburden, unload, disencumber, lighten*)

loan—advance, mortgage, hypothecation. (*recall, resumption, foreclosure*)

locate—place, establish, settle, fix, dispose, lodge. (*displace, disestablish, dislodge, remove*)

lofty—elevated, towering, high, dignified, eminent, stately, haughty, majestic, airy, tall. (*depressed, low, stunted, undignified, ordinary, unstately, mean, unimposing, unassuming, affable*)

logical—close, argumentative, sound. (*inconclusive, illogical, fallacious*)

lonesome—forlorn, dreary, forsaken, wild, solitary, desolate, lonely. (*cheerful, befriended, festive*)

long—protracted, produced, dilatory, lengthy, tedious, prolix, extensive, diffuse, far-reaching. (*short, curt, curtailed, brief, speedy, quick, concise*)

loose—*v.* untie, unfasten, let go. (*tie, fasten, hold*)

loose—*a.* unbound, detached, flowing, scattered, sparse, incompact, vague, inexact, rambling, dissoluted, licentious. (*bound, tied, fastened, tight*)

lose—miss, drop, mislay, forfeit. (*keep, retain*)

loss—mislaying, dropping forfeiture, missing, privation, waste, detriment, damage. (*preservation, recovery, earning, satisfaction, restoration, economy, augmentation, advantage, gain*)

lot—chance, fortune, fate, hazard, ballot, doom. (*law, provision, arrangement, disposal, design, purpose, plan, portion, allotment*)

loud—sounding, sonorous, resonant, noisy, audible, vociferous, clamorous, obstreperous. (*soft*)

love—affection, attachment, passion, devotion, benevolence, charity, kindness. (*hatred, dislike*)

lovely—amiable, lovable, enchanting, beautiful, pleasing, delightful, charming. (*unamiable, unlovable, hateful, hideous, plain, homely, unattractive*)

lover—suitor, wooer, sweetheart, swain, beau. (*husband, wife, mate*)

low—abated, sunk, depressed, stunted, declining, deep, subsided, inaudible, cheap, gentle, dejected, degraded, mean, abject, base, unworthy, lowly, feeble, moderate, frugal, repressed, subdued, reduced, poor, humble. (*elevated, lofty, tall*)

lower—*v.* depress, decrease, reduce, bate, abate, drop, humiliate, sink, debase, humble, diminish,

(*hoist, raise, heighten, exalt, increase, aggrandize*)

lower—*a.* inferior. (*higher, superior*)

loyal—submissive, obedient, faithful, allegiant, true, constant. (*insubmissive, insurgent, malcontent, rebellious, disobedient, unfaithful, unallegiant*)

lucky—fortunate, auspicious, prosperous, successful, favorable. (*unlucky, unfortunate, inauspicious*)

ludicrous—ridiculous, farcical, laughable, comic, droll, funny, comical. (*serious, momentous, grave*)

lunatic—mad, maniacal, crazy, wild, unthinking. (*sane, levelheaded, intelligent*)

lurid—murky, lowering, wan, dismal, gloomy. (*bright, luminous*)

luscious—sweet, delicious, sugary, honied, delightful, toothsome, delightsome. (*sour, sharp*)

luxurious—voluptuous, self-indulgent, pleasurable, sensual, pampered. (*hard, painful, self-denying, ascetic, hardy*)

luxury—effeminacy, epicurism, voluptuousness, wantonness, self-indulgence, softness, animalism, delicacy, dainty, profuseness. (*hardness, asceticism, stoicism, self-denial, hardship*)

lying—mendacious, false, untrue, untruthful. (*true, veracious*)

M

mad—insane, demented, furious, lunatic, infuriated, crazy, maniacal, frantic, rabid, wild, distracted. (*sane, sound, sensible, quiet, composed*)

madden—infuriate, enrage, exasperate, inflame. (*calm, pacify, assuage, mesmerize, lay*)

magnanimous—noble, high-minded, exalted, high-souled, great-souled, lofty, honorable. (*mean*)

magnificent—grand, magnanimous, noble, splendid, superb, august, imposing, gorgeous, stately, majestic, dignified, sublime, pompous. (*petty*)

maid—maiden, girl, damsel, lass, virgin. (*matron, married woman*)

main—bulk, majority, body, principal, trunk, chief, leading, most important, first. (*portion, section, minority, branch, limb, tributary, member*)

majority—superiority, eldership, priority, bulk, preponderance, seniority. (*inferiority, juniority*)

make—create, produce, fashion, frame, fabricate, construct, effect, do, perform, execute, find, gain, compel, establish, constitute, reach, mold, shape, form, bring about. (*annihilate, unmake, undo, dismember, disintegrate, destroy, defeat, miss, lose, mar*)

manage—handle, manipulate, control, conduct, administer, mold, regulate, contrive, train, husband, direct, wield. (*mismanage, misconduct, upset, derange, misuse*)

manageable—easy, feasible, possible, docile, tractable, practicable. (*difficult, impracticable, impossible, unmanageable, intractable, refractory*)

management—treatment, conduct, administration, government, address, skill, superintendence, skillful treatment. (*maltreatment, misconduct, maladministration, misgovernment, maladroitness*)

manifest—visible, obvious, distinct, conspicuous, indubitable, clear, plain, patent, apparent, evident, open. (*invisible, dubious, inconspicuous, indistinct*)

manly—bold, courageous, generous, open, chivalrous, frank, firm, noble, stately, fine, mature, masculine, brave, fearless, hardy, vigorous, manlike, manful, dignified. (*womanish, childish, timid, unmanly, dastardly, weak, puny, ungrown, boyish*)

manner—mode, method, style, form, fashion, carriage, behavior, deportment, habit, sort, kind. (*work, project, design, performance, life, action, proceeding, appearance, being*)

manners—deportment, behavior, carriage, courtesy, politeness, intercourse, demeanor. (*misdemeanor, misbehavior, unmannerliness*)

manufacture—make, production, fabrication, composition, construction, manipulation, molding. (*use, employment, consumption, wear*)

many—numerous, abundant, frequent, manifold, divers, sundry, multifarious. (*few, scarce, rare*)

mark—*n.* trace, token, sign, symptom, impression, vestige, indication, note. (*erasure, obliteration, effacement, unindicativeness, plainness*)

mark—*v.* stamp, label, sign, indicate, decorate, brand, stigmatize, signalize, note, observe, regard, heed, specify, specialize. (*ignore, overlook, omit*)

martial—military, brave, warlike. (*unmartial, unmilitary, peaceful*)

marvel—wonder, prodigy, admiration, portent, miracle, astonishment, amazement, phenomenon. (*incuriosity, unconcern, joke, trifle, farce, bagatelle*)

masculine—male, manly, manful, hardy, courageous, virile. (*female, feminine, womanish, womanly, effeminate*)

mask—*n.* pretext, screen, pretense, ruse, cover, hypocrisy. (*truth, nakedness, detection, exposure*)

mask—*v.* hide, screen, blink, cloak, disguise. (*expose, unmask, detect*)

master—*n.* lord, ruler, governor, owner, possessor, proprietor, teacher, professor, adept, chief. (*servant, slave, subject, property, learner, pupil, tyro*)

master—*v.* conquer, overcome, subdue, overpower. (*yield, fail, surrender, succumb*)

masterly—finished, artistic, consummate, skillful, clear, dexterous, expert. (*clumsy, rude, bungling, unskilled, botchy, maladroit*)

match—*n.* equal, mate, companion, contest, competition, tally, equality, pair. (*superior, inferior*)

match—*v.* equal, compare, oppose, pit, adapt, sort, suit, mate. (*fail, exceed, predominate, surpass, mismatch, dissociate, separate, misfit, misadapt, missort*)

matchless—consummate, incomparable, peerless, surpassing, inimitable. (*common, ordinary*)

matter—substance, stuff, subject, body, importance, (or, prefixing the definite article) the visible, tangible, substantial, corporal, physical, ponderable. (*immateriality, spirituality, mind, intellect*)

meager—thin, lean, lank, scanty, barren, dry, tame. (*stout, fat, brawny, abundant, fertile, copious*)

mean—*a.* common, low, base, spiritless, dishonorable, contemptible, despicable, beggarly, sordid, vulgar, niggardly, vile, middle, intermediate, average. (*high, exalted, eminent, spirited, honorable*)

mean—*n.* medium, moderation, balance, average. (*extreme, excess, preponderance, disproportion*)

mean—*v.* intend, purpose, design, signify, denote, indicate, hint, suggest. (*say, state, enunciate*)

meanness—penuriousness, littleness, selfishness, baseness, smallness, illiberality, ungenerousness, sordidness. (*nobleness, unselfishness, liberality*)

means—resources, instrument, media. (*end, purpose, object*)

mechanical—habitual, automatic, unreflective,

self-conscious, feeling, forced, spirited, appreciative)

meddlesome—officious, obtrusive, intrusive, interfering. (*unofficious, inobtrusive, unmeddlesome*)

mediocrity—mean, commonplace, medium, average, sufficiency. (*excellence, superiority, rarity*)

meek—mild, gentle, submissive, modest, yielding, unassuming. (*bold, arrogant, self-asserting*)

melancholy—gloomy, sad, dejected, disconsolate, dismal, moody, hypochondriacal, cast down. (*lively, sprightly, gladsome, gleesome, blithesome*)

mellow—ripe, rich, full-flavored, jovial, mature, soft. (*unripe, harsh, sour, acid, acrid, crabbed*)

memorable—great, striking, remarkable, conspicuous, prominent, noticeable, illustrious, extraordinary, famous, distinguished. (*petty, trifling*)

memory—remembrance, reminiscence, perpetuation, recollection, retention, retrospect, fame. (*forgetfulness, oblivion*)

mend—repair, restore, correct, promote, improve, rectify, reform, amend, ameliorate, better. (*damage, impair, pervert, retard, deteriorate, falsify*)

menial—domestic, attendant, dependent, servile, drudge. (*paramount, sovereign, supreme, lordly*)

mental—intellectual, subjective, metaphysical, psychical, psychological. (*corporal, objective, physical, bodily*)

mention—declaration, notice, announcement, observation, remark, hint, communication. (*silence, suppression, forgetfulness, omission*)

mercantile—commercial, interchangeable, wholesale, retail, marketable. (*stagnant, unmarketable*)

merchant—trader, dealer, importer, tradesman, trafficker. (*shopman, salesman, hawker, huckster*)

merciful—compassionate, kindhearted, clement, gracious, kind. (*pitiless, unrelenting, remorseless*)

mere—pure, unmixed, absolute, uninfluenced, unadulterated, unaffected, simple. (*mixed, compound, impure, biased*)

merit—goodness, worth, worthiness, desert, excellence. (*badness, demerit, unworthiness, worthlessness, weakness, imperfection, error, defect, fault*)

meteoric—momentary, flashing, displosive, phosphorescent, pyrotechnic, coruscant, volcanic. (*permanent, beaming, burning, steady, persistent, enduring*)

method—order, system, rule, way, manner, mode, course, process, regularity, arrangement. (*disorder, conjecture, quackery, empiricism, experimentation, assumption, guesswork*)

methodical—methodic, orderly, systematical, systematic, regular. (*disorderly, unmethodical, unsystematical, irregular*)

middling—ordinary, average, pretty well, not bad, well enough.

midst—middle, center, thick, throng, heart. (*outskirt, confine, edge, limit, extreme, purlieu, margin*)

might—strength, force, power, ability. (*weakness, infirmity, feebleness*)

mild—moderate, lenient, calm, gentle, genial, tempered, soft, meek, tender, placid. (*violent, wild, fierce, savage, strong, severe, merciless, harsh*)

mind—soul, spirit, intellect, understanding, opinion, sentiment, judgment, belief, choice, inclination, desire, will, liking, purpose, spirit, impetus, memory, remembrance, recollection. (*body,*

Synonym Ant/Hom

limbs, organization, action, proceeding, conduct)

mindful—regardful, attentive, thoughtful, careful, recollective. (*regardless, inattentive, mindless*)

mingle—mix, compound, blend, confound, confuse, intermingle, associate, amalgamate. (*separate, segregate, sift, sort, analyze, discompound, eliminate, classify, unravel, avoid*)

minister—servant, officer, delegate, official, ambassador, subordinate, ecclesiastic, clergyman, priest, parson, divine, preacher, pastor, shepherd, reverend, curate, vicar. (*monarch, government, master, superior, principal, head, layman, fold, flock*)

minute—diminutive, microscopic, tiny, exact, searching, specific, detailed. (*monstrous, enormous, huge, inexact, superficial, general, broad, comprehensive*)

mischief—damage, hurt, detriment, disservice, annoyance, injury, ill turn, damage, harm. (*compensation, good turn, benefit, gratification*)

mischievous—detrimental, injurious, spiteful, wanton. (*beneficial, advantageous, reparatory, conservative, careful, protective*)

miser—niggard, churl, skinflint, curmudgeon, screw, scrimp, hunks. (*prodigal, spendthrift, rake*)

miserable—abject, forlorn, pitiable, wretched, worthless, despicable, disconsolate. (*respectable, worthy, happy, contented, comfortable*)

misery—wretchedness, heartache, woe, unhappiness. (*happiness, glee*)

mock—jeer, ridicule, flout, mimic, insult, ape, deride, deceive, imitate. (*salute, welcome, respect, admire, compliment*)

model—standard, pattern, example, type, mold, design, kind. (*imitation, copy, production, execution, work*)

moderate—*v.* control, soften, allay, regulate, repress, govern, temper. (*disturb, disorganize, excite, misconduct*)

moderate—*a.* limited, temperate, calm, dispassionate, sober, abstinent, sparing, steady, ordinary. (*extravagant, intemperate, rigorous, excessive, violent, extraordinary*)

modern—present, existent, new, newfangled, new-fashioned, recent, late, novel, later. (*past, bygone, former, older, ancient, old-fashioned, antiquated, obsolete*)

modesty—sobriety, diffidence, bashfulness, humility, pure-mindedness. (*vanity, conceit, self-sufficiency, self-admiration, foppery, coxcombry, wantonness, shamelessness, effrontery*)

moment—instant, second, importance, twinkling, trice, weight, force, gravity, consequence, avail. (*age, period, century, generation, triviality, insignificance, worthlessness, unimportance, inefficacy*)

monopoly—privilege, engrossment, appropriation, exclusiveness, preoccupancy, impropriation. (*participation, partnership, community, competition*)

monotonous—uniform, unvaried, dull, humdrum, undiversified, tedious. (*varying, changing*)

monstrous—prodigious, portentous, marvelous, deformed, abnormal, hideous, preposterous, intolerable. (*ordinary, familiar, unnoticeable, fair, comely, shapely, regular, natural, reasonable, just*)

moral—mental, ideal, intellectual, spiritual, ethical, probable, inferential, presumptive, analogous, virtuous, well-conducted. (*physical, material, practical, demonstrative, mathematical, immoral, vicious*)

mortal—human, ephemeral, sublunary, short-lived, deadly, fatal, perishable, destructive. (*immortal, divine, celestial, life-giving, venial, superficial*)

motive—inducement, purpose, design, prompting, stimulus, reason, impulse, incitement. (*execution, action, effort, deed, attempt, project, preventive*)

move—change, go, progress, stir, affect, agitate, actuate, impel, propose, advance, propel, instigate, provoke. (*stand, stop, lie, rest, stay, allay, deter*)

movement—motion, move, change of place. (*stop, rest, pause, stillness, quietness*)

much—abundant, plenteous, greatly, abundantly, far, considerable, ample. (*little, scant, slightly, shortly, short, near*)

muddle—fail, waste, fritter away, confuse, derange, misarrange. (*clarify, manage, economize*)

muggy—foggy, misty, dank, damp, murky, dim, vaporous, cloudy. (*clear, bright, vaporless*)

multitude—crowd, swarm, accumulation, throng, concourse, number, host, mob, rabble. (*paucity, scantiness, sprinkling*)

munificent—liberal, princely, bounteous, generous. (*niggardly, beggarly*)

murmur—undertone, whisper, mutter, grumble, complaint, repining. (*clamor, vociferation, bawling*)

muscular—powerful, brawny, robust, sinewy, strong, stalwart, athletic, lusty, sturdy. (*debile, flabby, feeble, lanky*)

musical—melodious, harmonious, dulcet, concordant, rhythmical, tuneful, mellifluous. (*unmelodious, inharmonious, harsh, discordant*)

musty—fusty, rank, moldy, frowzy, stale, sour, fetid, mildewed. (*fragrant, fresh, balmy, aromatic*)

mutter—murmur, mumble. (*enunciate, exclaim, pronounce, vociferate*)

mysterious—dim, obscure, unrevealed, unexplained, unaccountable, reserved, veiled, hidden, secret, incomprehensible, mystic, inexplicable. (*clear, plain, obvious, explained, understood, easy*)

mystery—enigma, puzzle, obscurity, secrecy, veil, shroud, arcanum. (*publication, solution, commonplace, truism, matter of fact*)

mystify—confuse, bamboozle, hoodwink, puzzle, confound, mislead, obfuscate. (*illumine, enlighten, inform, guide*)

N

naked—nude, bare, unclothed, denuded, undraped, defenseless, destitute, unqualified, uncolored, unvarnished, mere, simple. (*dressed, robed, draped, muffled, protected, qualified, veiled, shrouded*)

name—*n.* designation, cognomenation, appellation, title, fame, reputation, authority, appointment, stead, representation. (*namelessness, anonymity, misnomer, pseudonym, obscurity, ingloriousness, disrepute, individuality, person*)

name—*v.* specify, designate, call, indicate. (*misname, miscall, misdesignate, misindicate, hint, suggest, shadow, adumbrate*)

narrow—straight, straightened, slender, thin, spare, contracted, limited, cramped, pinched, scant, close, scrutinizing, near, bigoted, niggardly, tight. (*wide, broad, ample, thick, expanded, easy, liberal*)

nasty—foul, offensive, odious, disagreeable, indelicate, impure, gross, unclean, obscene. (*nice, _pleasant, sweet, savory, agreeable, pure)_

natural—intrinsic, essential, regular, normal, cosmical, true, probable, consistent, spontaneous, artless, original. (_ascititious, adventitious, abnormal_)

nature—essence, creation, constitution, structure, disposition, truth, regularity, kind, sort, character, species, affection, naturalness. (_thing, object, subject, man, being, creature, monstrosity, unnaturalness, art, fiction, romance, invention_)

near—nigh, close, adjacent, neighboring. (_far away, distant, remote_)

necessary—certain, inevitable, indispensable, requisite, essential, compulsory, needful, expedient. (_contingent, casual, optional, discretional, unnecessary, unessential, free_)

necessity—indispensableness, inevitableness, need, indigence, requirement, want, fate, destiny. (_dispensableness, uncertainty, superfluity, uselessness, competence, affluence, casualty, contingency_)

neglect—_v._ slight, overlook, omit, disregard, disesteem, despise, contemn. (_consider, respect, notice, observe, regard, esteem, tend, attend, foster, study_)

neglect—_n._ negligence, disregard, omission, failure, default, slight, carelessness, remissness. (_attention, consideration, respect, notice, regard, esteem_)

nerve—strength, firmness, resolution. (_nerveless, forceless, feeble, weak, enfeebled, impotent, palsied_)

new—novel, recent, fresh, modern. (_old, ancient, antique, antiquated, obsolete_)

nice—fastidious, scrupulous, accurate, neat, discerning, dainty, pleasant, agreeable, exact, fine, finished, particular. (_coarse, unscrupulous, inaccurate, rude, rough, undiscriminating, nasty, nauseous, disagreeable_)

nobility—distinction, dignity, rank, peerage, lordship, loftiness, generosity, rank, aristocracy. (_obscurity, meanness, commonalty, serfdom, paltriness, contemptibleness, plebeianism_)

noble—grand, aristocratic, generous, illustrious, exalted, worthy, magnanimous, dignified, excellent, lofty-minded, honorable, fine. (_mean, plebeian, ignoble, paltry_)

noisome—hurtful, harmful, nocuous, pestilential. (_wholesome, salutary, salubrious, beneficial_)

noisy—loud, clamorous, stunning. (_still, soft, inaudible, whispering, soothing, musical, melodious_)

nominal—trifling, supposititious, ostensible, professed, pretended, formal. (_real, deep, serious, important, grave, substantial, actual, intrinsic, veritable_)

nonsense—absurdity, trash, folly, pretense, jest, balderdash. (_sense, wisdom, truth, fact, gravity_)

notice—observation, cognizance, heed, advice, news, consideration, visitation, mark, note. (_oversight, disregard, misinformation, mistidings, neglect_)

notion—apprehension, idea, conception, judgment, opinion, belief, expectation, sentiment. (_misapprehension, falsification, misbelief, misjudgment, frustration, misconception_)

notorious—known, undisputed, recognized, allowed. (_suspected, reported, reputed_)

nuisance—offense, annoyance, plague, pest, trouble. (_gratification, blessing, pleasure, delight_)

O

obedience—submission, compliance, subservience. (_resistance, rebellion, violation, transgression_)

obesity—fatness, fleshiness, corpulence, plumpness, corpulency, embonpoint. (_leanness, thinness_)

obey—submit, comply, yield. (_resist, disobey_)

object—appearance, sight, design, end, aim, motive, intent, view, goal. (_idea, notion, conception, fancy, subject, proposal, purpose, effect_)

object to—oppose, contravene, obstruct, demur to, except to, gainsay, disapprove. (_approve, approve of_)

oblige—compel, coerce, necessitate, force, benefit, favor, accommodate, gratify, bind, constrain. (_release, acquit, induce, persuade, annoy, disoblige_)

obliging—kind, considerate, compliant, complaisant, accommodating. (_discourteous, rude, crossgrained, perverse, unaccommodating, disobliging_)

obscene—impure, immodest, indecent, lewd, foul, indelicate, filthy, disgusting, foulmouthed. (_pure, modest, decent_)

obscure—dark, dim, lowering, indistinct, enigmatical, uncertain, doubtful, unascertained, humble, unintelligible, mean. (_bright, luminous, distinct, lucid, plain, plain-spoken, intelligible, unambiguous, ascertained, eminent, prominent_)

observance—attention, fulfillment, respect, celebration, performance, ceremony, custom, form, rule, practice. (_inobservance, inattention, breach, disrespect, disregard, desuetude, disuse, nonperformance, informality, unceremoniousness, omission_)

observant—regardful, attentive, mindful, obedient, watchful, heedful. (_disregardful, neglectful_)

observation—contemplation, study, remark, attention, notice, comment. (_disregard, oversight_)

obstacle—impediment, obstruction, hindrance, objection, bar, difficulty, check. (_course, proceeding, career, advancement_)

obstinate—headstrong, stubborn, refractory, self-willed, pertinacious, obdurate, perverse, intractable. (_amenable, complaisant, yielding, docile, ductile, characterless, irresolute, wavering_)

obvious—plain, self-evident, manifest, explicit, apparent, open, patent. (_remote, obscure, far-fetched, involved, latent_)

occasion—conjuncture, opportunity, occurrence, cause, need, event, reason, necessity, opening, ground. (_untimeliness, unseasonableness, frustration_)

occult—latent, hidden, unrevealed, mysterious, secret, dark, unknown. (_developed, plain, patent_)

occupation—employment, avocation, possession, usurpation, encroachment, tenure, calling, pursuit, trade, business, holding. (_idleness, vacancy, leisure_)

odd—alone, sole, unmatched, remaining, over, fragmentary, uneven, singular, peculiar, queer, quaint, fantastical, uncommon, nondescript. (_aggregate, consociate, matched, balanced, squared, integrant, even, common, usual, regular, normal_)

odious—hateful, offensive, detestable, abominable, hated. (_delectable, grateful, acceptable_)

offense—attack, sin, crime, umbrage, transgression, misdeed, injury, wrong, affront, outrage, insult, trespass, indignity, misdemeanor. (_defense, innocence, guiltlessness_)

offensive—aggressive, obnoxious, distasteful, displeasing, foul, fetid, unsavory. (_defensive, grateful, pleasant, savory_)

offer—propose, exhibit, proffer, present, tender, extend, adduce, volunteer. (_withhold, withdraw_)

office—service, duty, appointment, function, employment, station, business, post. (*leisure, vacancy*)

officious—meddling, interfering, pushing, forward, intrusive, intermeddling. (*backward, negligent, remiss, unofficious, retiring, modest, backward*)

often—frequently, repeatedly. (*infrequently*)

old—aged, pristine, long-standing, ancient, preceding, antiquated, obsolete, senile, antique. (*youthful, young, recent, fresh, modern, subsequent*)

ominous—portentous, suggestive, threatening, foreboding, premonitory, unpropitious. (*auspicious, propitious, encouraging*)

open—*v.* unclose, lay open, lay bare, expose, explain, disclose, initiate, begin, commence. (*close, shut up, conceal, enclose, mystify, misinterpret, conclude, cover*)

open—*a.* accessible, free, available, unshut, unfolded, public, free, unrestricted, unreserved, unaffected, genuine, barefaced, undisguised, aboveboard, liberal, unclosed, candid, frank, ingenuous, unsettled, undetermined. (*inaccessible, closed, barred, unavailable, shut, close, secretive, reserved*)

opening—aperture, gap, opportunity, space, commencement, initiation, start, inauguration, hole, fissure, chink, beginning. (*occlusion, obstruction, stopgap, unreasonableness, contretemps, inopportuneness, enclosure, termination, close, end, conclusion*)

operation—agency, action, exercise, production, influence, performance. (*cessation, inaction, rest*)

opinion—conviction, view, judgment, notion, idea, impression, estimation, theory.

opportunity—occasion, turn, opening, convenience. (*inopportuneness, unseasonableness, lapse*)

opposite—facing, adverse, repugnant, inconsistent, irreconcilable, contrary, antagonistic, counter, contradictory. (*agreeing, coincident, consentaneous*)

opposition—resistance, hostility, obstacle, obstruction.

oppressive—heavy, overpowering, unjust, galling, extortionate, grinding. (*light, just, compassionate*)

order—*n.* arrangement, condition, sequence, direction, rank, grade, class, decree, succession, series, method, injunction, precept, command. (*disarrangement, confusion, disorder*)

order—*v.* arrange, dispose, regulate, adjust, direct, command, classify, ordain, enjoin, prescribe, appoint, manage. (*disarrange, confuse, unsettle, disorganize*)

ordinary—settled, wonted, conventional, plain, inferior, commonplace, humdrum, matter of fact. (*extraordinary, unusual, uncommon, superior*)

organization—structure, form, construction. (*disorganization*)

origin—source, commencement, spring, cause, derivation, rise, beginning. (*termination, conclusion, extinction*)

original—primary, initiatory, primordial, peculiar, pristine, ancient, former, first. (*subsequent, terminal, modern, later, derivative*)

oust—eject, dispossess, deprive, evict, eject, dislodge, remove. (*install, reinstate, readmit, restore*)

outcast—castaway, reprobate, vagrant, vagabond, exiled.

outlandish—strange, queer, grotesque, foreign, rustic, barbarous, rude. (*fashionable, modish*)

outline—delineation, sketch, contour, draft, plan. (*form, substance, figure, object, subject, field*)

outrage—outbreak, offense, wantonness, mischief, abuse, ebullition, violence, indignity, affront, insult. (*moderation, self-control, self-restraint, subsidence, coolness, calmness*)

outrageous—excessive, unwarrantable, unjustifiable, wanton, flagrant, nefarious, atrocious, violent. (*moderate, justifiable, reasonable*)

outset—opening, start, commencement, exordium, beginning, inauguration, preface. (*close, termination, conclusion, peroration*)

outward—external, apparent, visible, sensible, superficial, ostensible, forthcoming, extrinsic, extraneous. (*internal, intrinsic, withdrawn, inapparent, inward*)

overcome—vanquish, conquer, surmount, exhaust, defeat.

overflow—redundancy, exuberance, superabundance, deluge, inundation. (*deficiency, exhaustion*)

overlook—condone, connive, disregard, oversee, supervise, inspect, survey, review, excuse, pardon, forgive, neglect. (*visit, scrutinize, investigate, mark*)

oversight—error, omission, mistake, neglect, slip, inadvertence, inspection, superintendence. (*scrutiny, correction, emendation, attention, mark*)

overthrow—destroy, subvert, upset, overturn, ruin, demolish, defeat, rout, overcome, discomfit, invert, overset, reverse. (*restore, reinstate, construct, regenerate, redintegrate, revive, re-edify*)

overwhelm—crush, quell, extinguish, drown, subdue, swamp. (*raise, reinvigorate, reinstate*)

owing—due, imputable, ascribable, attributable. (*casually, perchance, by chance, by accident*)

own—possess, hold, have, acknowledge, avow, admit, confess. (*alienate, forfeit, lose, disclaim*)

P

pacify—appease, conciliate, calm, still, soothe, quiet, tranquilize. (*exasperate, agitate, excite, irritate, rouse, provoke*)

pack—*n.* burden, bundle, package, lot, parcel, load.

pack—*v.* stow, compact, compress, cook. (*unpack, unsettle, jumble, displace, misarrange, dissipate, neutralize*)

pain—*n.* penalty, suffering, distress, uneasiness, grief, labor, effort, anguish, torture, agony. (*reward, remuneration, ease, gratification, joy, pleasure*)

pain—*v.* hurt, grieve, afflict, torment, rack, agonize, trouble, torture, aggrieve, annoy, distress. (*gratify, please, delight, rejoice, charm, relieve, ease*)

painful—afflicting, distressful, grieving, grievous, excruciating, hurting.

painstaking—careful, attentive, diligent, laborious. (*careless, negligent*)

palatable—tasteful, savory, appetizing, delicious, toothsome.

pale—pallid, wan, faint, dim, undefined, etiolated, sallow, cadaverous. (*ruddy, high-colored*)

palmy—prosperous, glorious, distinguished, victorious, flourishing. (*depressed, inglorious, undistinguished, unflourishing*)

paltry—mean, shabby, shuffling, trifling, prevaricating, shifty, contemptible, pitiable, vile, worthless, beggarly, trashy. (*noble, honorable, candid, conscientious, determined, straightforward*)

pang—paroxysm, throe, agony, convulsion, smart, anguish, pain, twinge. (*pleasure, enjoyment, gratification, delight, delectation, fascination*)

paradox—contradiction, enigma, mystery, absurdity, ambiguity. (*precept, proposition, axiom*)

parallel—correspondent, congruous, correlative, analogous, concurrent, equidistant. (*different, opposed, incongruous, irrelative, unanalogous, divergent*)

paralyze—deaden, benumb, prostrate, enervate, debilitate, enfeeble. (*give life, strengthen, nerve*)

pardon—forgive, condone, absolve, acquit, remit, excuse, overlook. (*condemn, punish, visit*)

pardonable—venial, excusable. (*inexcusable, unpardonable*)

parsimonious—sparing, close, penurious, frugal, niggardly, illiberal, stingy. (*liberal, unsparing, profuse, extravagant*)

part—portion, piece, fragment, fraction, division, member, constituent, element, ingredient, share, lot, concern, interest, participation, side, party, interest, faction, behalf, duty. (*whole, completeness, entirety, integrity, totality, mass, bulk, body*)

partake—share, participate, accept, derive. (*forfeit, relinquish, forego, cede, yield, afford*)

partial—restricted, local, peculiar, specific, favoring, inequitable, unfair, biased, particular. (*unrestricted, total, universal, general, impartial, equitable, just, fair, unbiased*)

particular—local, specific, subordinate, detailed, partial, special, fastidious, minute, scrupulous, careful, accurate, exact, circumstantial, precise, delicate, nice. (*universal, general, unspecial, comprehensive, unscrupulous, uncareful, inaccurate, inexact, rough, coarse, indiscriminate, undiscriminating*)

partisan—adherent, follower, party man, henchman, clansman, supporter, disciple

partition—barrier, division, enclosure, compartment, interspace, separation, distribution, allotment, screen. (*nonpartition, nondistinction, nonseparation, inclusion, comprehension, combination*)

partner—associate, sharer, participator, colleague, coadjutor, confederate, accomplice, partaker, companion, spouse. (*rival, alien, competitor*)

passable—traversable, navigable, penetrable, admissible, tolerable, ordinary. (*impassable, impervious, impenetrable, inadmissible, excellent*)

passage—journey, thoroughfare, road, course, avenue, route, channel, clause, phrase, sentence, paragraph.

passive—inactive, inert, quiescent, unresisting, unquestioning, negative, enduring, patient. (*active, alert, resistant, positive, unsubmissive, malcontent, vehement, impatient*)

pastime—recreation, entertainment, amusement, diversion, play, sport. (*business, study, labor, task*)

patent—obvious, evident, indisputable, plain. (*dubious, ambiguous, questionable*)

pathetic—affecting, moving, emotional, tender, melting. (*ludicrous, unimpassioned, farcical, unaffecting*)

patience—endurance, resignation, submission, perseverance. (*resistance, unsubmissiveness, repining, rebellion, inconsistency, impatience*)

pattern—model, sample, archetype, exemplar, specimen, shape, precedent, mold, design, shape. (*monstrosity, caricature, perversion, misrepresentation*)

pause—*n.* stop, cessation, suspension, halt, intermission, rest. (*continuance, advancement, perseverance*)

pause—*v.* cease, suspend, intermit, forbear, stay, wait, hesitate, demur, stop, desist. (*continue, proceed, advance, persist, persevere*)

peace—quiet, tranquility, calm, repose, pacification, order, calmness, reconciliation, harmony, concord. (*noise, disturbance, tumult, agitation, hostility*)

peaceable—unwarlike, inoffensive, quiet, peaceful, innocuous, mild, unquarrelsome, serene, placid. (*pugnacious, warlike, litigious, quarrelsome, savage*)

peculiar—private, personal, characteristic, exceptional, exclusive, special, specific, particular, unusual, singular, uncommon, strange, rare, odd. (*public, common, general, universal, unspecial, ordinary*)

peculiarity—speciality, individuality, distinctiveness, idiosyncrasy. (*generality, universality, community, uniformity, homology, homogeneity*)

people—nation, community, populace, mob, crowd, vulgar, herd, mass, persons, inhabitants, commonalty, fellow creatures, tribe, race, group. (*aristocracy, nobility, government, ruler, oligarchy*)

perceive—discern, distinguish, descry, observe, feel, touch, see, recognize, understand, know. (*miss, misobserve, overlook, misunderstand, misconceive, misperceive*)

perception—cognizance, apprehension, sight, understanding, discernment. (*incognizance, ignorance, imperception, misapprehension, misunderstanding*)

peremptory—decisive, express, absolute, authoritative, dictatorial, dogmatic, imperious, despotic, positive. (*suggestive, entreative, mild, postulatory*)

perfect—consummate, complete, full, indeficient, immaculate, absolute, faultless, impeccable, infallible, unblemished, blameless, unexceptionable, mature, ripe, pure. (*incomplete, meager, faulty, scant, short, deficient, defective, imperfect, peccable*)

perfectly—fully, wholly, entirely, completely, totally, exactly, accurately. (*imperfectly, incompletely, partially, inaccurately*)

perform—accomplish, do, act, transact, achieve, execute, discharge, fulfill, effect, complete, consummate, enact. (*miss, mar, misperform, misexecute*)

perhaps—possibly, peradventure, perchance, maybe. (*certainly, inevitably*)

perilous—hazardous, dangerous. (*safe, secure*)

period—time, date, epoch, era, age, duration, continuance, limit, bound, end, conclusion, determination. (*eternity, datelessness, immemoriality, infinity, perpetuity, illimitability, endlessness, indefiniteness, indeterminateness*)

periodic—stated, recurrent, regular, systematic, calculable. (*indeterminate, eccentric, irregular, incalculable, spasmodic, fitful*)

permeable—penetrating, pervading. (*impenetrable, ineffective*)

perpetual—constant, unceasing, endless, eternal, everlasting, unfailing, perennial, continual, enduring, incessant, uninterrupted. (*inconstant, periodic, recurrent, temporary, transient, falling, exhaustible*)

perplex—embarrass, puzzle, entangle, involve,

Synonym Ant/Hom

encumber, complicate, confuse, bewilder, mystify, harass, entangle. (*clear, enlighten, explicate, disentangle, simplify, elucidate, disencumber*)

perseverance—persistence, steadfastness, constancy, indefatigability, resolution, tenacity. (*inconstancy, unsteadfastness, fitfulness, caprice, irresoluteness, vacillation, wavering, indecision, variableness, levity, volatility*)

persuade—induce, influence, incline, convince, dispose, urge, allure, incite. (*deter, disincline, indispose, mispersuade, misinduce, coerce, compel*)

perverse—forward, untoward, stubborn, fractious, wayward, unmanageable, intractable, crochety. (*docile, ductile, amenable, governable, complacent, accommodating, pleasant, obliging*)

pet—darling, fondling, favorite, cosset, jewel, minion, idol. (*horror, bugbear, aversion, scarecrow*)

petition—supplication, entreaty, craving, application, appeal, salutation, prayer, request, instance. (*deprecation, expostulation, protest, command, injunction, claim, demand, requirement*)

petty—small, mean, paltry, ignoble, trifling, narrow, trivial, contemptible. (*large, bighearted, noble, generous, chivalrous, magnificent, liberal*)

philanthropy—humanity, love of mankind, generosity, charity, benevolence. (*misanthropy, hatred of men. selfishness, stinginess*)

philosopher—doctor, savant, teacher, master, schoolman. (*ignoramus, sciolist, freshman, tyro, greenhorn, fool, booby, dunce*)

philosophical—wise, sound, conclusive, scientific, accurate, enlightened, rational, calm, unprejudiced. (*unsound, crude, vague, loose, inaccurate, popular*)

physical—natural, material, visible, tangible, substantial, corporeal. (*mental, moral, intellectual, spiritual, immaterial, invisible, intangible, unsubstantial, supernatural, hyperphysical*)

picture—likeness, resemblance, drawing, painting, representation, image, engraving. (*original*)

picturesque—comely, seemly, graceful, scenic, artistic, pictorial, graphic. (*unseemly, uncouth, rude, unpicturesque, ugly, flat, tame, monotonous*)

pinch—squeeze, grip, press, compress, nip, distress.

piquant—pungent, sharp, lively, racy, severe, biting, cutting, smart, stimulating, keen, stinging, tart. (*tame, dull, flat, characterless, insipid*)

pithy—terse, forceful, laconic, expressive, concise. spongy. (*weak, characterless, diluted, pointless*)

pity—mercy, compassion, tenderness, commiseration, ruth, sympathy, condolence. (*cruelty, hardheartedness, relentlessness, pitilessness, ruthlessness*)

place—locate, assign, fix, establish, settle, attribute, situate, put, set. (*disturb, remove, unsettle, disarrange, disestablish, misplace, misattribute, misassign, uproot, transplant, extirpate, eradicate, transport*)

plain—level, even, flat, smooth, open, clear, unencumbered, unobstructed, uninterrupted, manifest, evident, obvious, unmistakable, simple, easy, natural, unaffected, homely, unsophisticated, open, unvarnished, unembellished, unreserved, artless. (*uneven, undulating, rugged, rough, abrupt, broken, confused, encumbered, obstructed, interrupted, questionable, uncertain, dubious, ambiguous, enigmatical*)

plan—*n.* design, drawing, sketch, draft, scheme, project, contrivance, stratagem, device.

plan—*v.* contrive, devise, sketch out, design, hatch.

platonic—cold, intellectual, unsensual, mental, philosophical. (*ardent, animal, sensual, passionate*)

plausible—specious, superficial, passable, unctuous, fair-spoken, pretentious, ostensible, right, apparent, colorable, feasible, probable. (*genuine, sterling, unmistakable, profound*)

playful—lively, sportive, jocund, frolicsome, gay, vivacious, sprightly. (*somber, dull*)

plea—excuse, vindication, justification, ground, defense, apology, entreaty, request. (*charge, accusation, impeachment, action*)

pleasant—grateful, agreeable, acceptable, pleasurable, desirable, gratifying, cheerful, enlivening, sportive, delicious, delectable, jocular, satisfactory, exquisite, merry. (*unpleasant, ungrateful, disagreeable, obnoxious, unacceptable, offensive, unlively*)

pleasure—enjoyment, gratification, sensuality, self-indulgence, voluptuousness, choice, preference, will, inclination, purpose, determination, favor, satisfaction, indulgence. (*pain, suffering, affliction, trouble, asceticism, self-denial, abstinence, disinclination, aversion, indisposition, denial, refusal*)

plebeian—low, vulgar, low-born, low-bred, coarse, ignoble. (*patrician, noble, aristocratic, refined, high-born, high-bred*)

plodding—painstaking, industrious, persevering, laborious, studious. (*indiligent, unindustrious, distracted, inattentive, impatient, unpersevering, flighty, fitful*)

plot—*n.* scheme, plan, stratagem, conspiracy, machination.

plot—*v.* devise, concoct, conspire, contrive, frame, hatch, plan, scheme.

plump—well-conditioned, well-rounded, chubby, strapping, bouncing, fleshy, brawny, full, fat, round, massive, portly. (*ill-conditioned, lean, emaciated, scraggy, weazen, macilent, lank, rawboned, shriveled, flaccid, tabid*)

plunge—dip, dive, douse, duck, submerge, immerse, precipitate, sink, overwhelm, thrust under, pitch headlong. (*emerge, issue, soar, raise, extricate*)

poetical—metrical, rhythmic, versified, lyric, rhyming, imaginative, creative, romantic, fictitious, dreamy, flighty. (*unmetrical, unrhythmical, prosaic, unpoetical, unversified, unimaginative, commonplace, historical, mathematical, logical, matter-of-fact, veracious, sober*)

poisonous—venomous, infectant, vicious, corruptive, vitiative, noxious, baneful, malignant, morbific, virulent, pestiferous, deleterious. (*wholesome, genial, beneficial, sanative, invigorative, healthful, innoxious, restorative, remedial, hygienic*)

polite—elegant, refined, well-bred, courteous, obliging, complaisant, civil, courtly, polished, genteel, accomplished. (*awkward, rude, uncouth, illbred, discourteous, boorish, clownish, disobliging*)

politic—prudent, wise, sagacious, provident, diplomatic, judicious, cunning, wary, well-devised, discreet. (*imprudent, unwise, improvident, undiplomatic, impolitic*)

pompous—magnificent, gorgeous, splendid, showy, sumptuous, ostentatious, stately, lofty, grand, bombastic, turgid, stiff, inflated, pretentious, coxcombical, assuming. (*unpretending, unobtrusive, modest, unassuming, plain-mannered, humbleminded*)

ponder—think over, meditate on, weigh, consider, cogitate, deliberate, ruminate, reflect, amuse, study, resolve.

poor—indigent, moneyless, impecunious, penniless, weak, meager, insufficient, deficient, faulty, unsatisfactory, inconsiderable, thin, scanty, bald, (*rich, wealthy, copious, affluent, abundant, liberal*)

popular—common, current, vulgar, public, general, received, favorite, beloved, prevailing, approved, widespread, liked. (*exclusive, restricted, scientific, esoteric, unpopular, odious, detested*)

positive—real, actual, substantial, absolute, independent, unconditional, unequivocal, explicit, fixed, settled, definitive, indisputable, decisive, express, enacted, assured, confident, direct, dogmatic, overbearing, dogmatical. (*negative, insubstantial, unreal, fictitious, imaginary, relative, contingent, dependent, conditional, implied, dubious, questionable*)

possess—occupy, enjoy, have, hold, entertain, own. (*abandon, renounce, abjure, surrender, lose, forfeit, resign*)

possible—practicable, feasible, likely, potential, (*impracticable, impossible*)

postpone—defer, delay, prorogue, procrastinate, (*expedite, dispatch, accelerate*)

poverty—want, need, indigence, destitution. (*abundance, wealth, affluence*)

power—faculty, capacity, capability, potentiality, ability, strength, force, might, energy, susceptibility, influence, dominion, sway, command, government, agency, authority, rule, jurisdiction, effectiveness. (*incapacity, incapability, impotence, inability, weakness, imbecility, inertness, insusceptibility, subjection, powerlessness, obedience, subservience, ineffectiveness*)

powerful—strong, potent, puissant, masterful, mighty. (*weak, poor*)

practice—*n.* usage, habit, exercise, experience, exercitation, action, custom, manner, performance. (*disuse, dishabituation, inexperience, theory, speculation, nonperformance*)

practice—*v.* perform. exercise. deal in. carry on.

praise—eulogize, laud, commend, honor, glorify, compliment, celebrate, puff, extol, applaud, panegyrize. (*blame, censure, discommend, reprove*)

pray—beg, beseech, entreat, implore, solicit, supplicate, adjure, invoke, crave.

prayer—petition, supplication, entreaty, orison, benediction, suit, request.

precaution—forethought, provision, premonition, anticipation, prearrangement, care, providence. (*carelessness, thoughtlessness, improvidence*)

preceding—precedent, former, forgoing, prior, previous, antecedent, anterior. (*following, subsequent, posterior*)

precious—dear, valuable, costly, cherished, treasured, beloved, estimable, of great value. (*cheap, valueless, worthless, unvalued, disesteemed*)

precise—definite, exact, nice, pointed, accurate, correct, particular, formal, explicit, scrupulous, terse, punctilious, ceremonious, formal. (*indefinite, vague, inexact, rough, inaccurate, loose, circumlocutory, ambagious, tortuous, informal, unceremonious*)

predict—prophesy, foretell, forecast, prognosticate, forebode, foreshadow.

prediction—prophecy, prognostication, vaticina-

tion, foreannouncement, premonstration, foretelling, forebodement, presage, augury, foreshowing. (*narration, relation, history, account, report*)

preface—introduction, proem, prelude, prologue, preamble, premiss. (*peroration, sequel, appendix, epilogue, postscript*)

prefer—choose, elect, select, fancy, promote, advance, further. (*reject, postpone, defer, withhold*)

prejudice—prepossession, prejudgment, predisposition, bias, unfairness, injury, harm, impairment, detriment, partiality, disadvantage, damage. (*judgment, fairness, impartiality, advantage*)

premature—hasty, crude, unauthenticated, untimely, precocious, precipitate, too early, rash, unseasonable. (*ripe, timely, seasonable, opportune*)

premium—reward, guerdon, encouragement, douceur, enhancement, bribe, recompense, bonus, prize, bounty. (*penalty, fine, amercement, mulct, forfeit, depreciation*)

preparation—provision, readiness. (*unpreparedness, without provision*)

prepare—fit, adapt, qualify, adjust, provide, arrange, order, lay, plan, equip, furnish, ready. (*misfit, misadapt, misprovide, derange, disarrange*)

prepossessing—attractive, alluring, charming, winning, taking, engaging. (*repulsive, unattractive*)

preposterous—monstrous, exorbitant, unreasonable, absurd, irrational, foolish, ridiculous. (*just, due, fair, reasonable, moderate, right, judicious*)

presence—nearness, influence, intercourse, closeness. (*remoteness, absence, separation, distance*)

preserve—defend, guard, save, keep safe, uphold, protect, maintain, rescue, spare. (*ruin, destroy*)

president—chairman, moderator, principal, superintendent. (*member, subordinate, constituent, corporation, society, ward, institution*)

press—urge, crowd, compel, force, squeeze, crush, compress, express, constrain, hurry, instigate, inculcate, impress, throng, encroach, lean, weigh, harass. (*relax, inhibit, persuade, entice, allure, solicit, touch, skim, graze, free, liberate, ease*)

presume—suppose, anticipate, apprehend, venture, take for granted, conjecture, believe, deem, assume. (*infer, deduce, prove, argue, retire, withdraw, hesitate, distrust*)

pretend—feign, simulate, offer, allege, exhibit, propound, affect, profess. (*verify, unmask, detect*)

pretense—excuse, pretext, fabrication, simulation, cloak, mask, color, show, garb, plea, assumption, make-believe, outside show, pretension. (*verity, reality, truth, simplicity, candor, guilelessness, openness, veritableness, actuality, fact*)

pretty—handsome, attractive, neat, trim, tasteful, pleasing, beautiful, fine, comely. (*ugly, grotesque*)

prevailing—controlling, ruling, influential, operative, predominant, prevalent, rife, ascendant, most general, most common. (*mitigated, diminishing, subordinate, powerless*)

prevent—hinder, obstruct, bar, neutralize, nullify, thwart, intercept, anticipate, forefend, frustrate, obviate, checkmate. (*promote, aid, facilitate, expedite, encourage, advance, accelerate, induce*)

price—cost, figure, charge, expense, compensation, value, appraisement, worth. (*donation, dis-

Synonym Ant/Hom

count, allowance, remittance, abatement)

pride—loftiness, haughtiness, lordliness, self-exaltation, arrogance, conceit, vainglory. (*lowliness, meekness, modesty, self-distrust*)

priggish—coxcombical, dandified, foppish, affected, prim, conceited. (*plain, sensible, unaffected, simple-minded, simple-mannered*)

prim—formal, precise, demure, starched, stiff, self-conscious, unbending, priggish. (*unformal, easy, genial, unaffected, natural, free, naive*)

primary—first, original, earliest, elementary, main, chief, principal, important, leading, primitive, pristine. (*secondary, subordinate, posterior, unimportant, inferior, subsequent, later*)

primitive—old-fashioned, primeval, quaint, simple, unsophisticated, archaic, pristine. (*modern, newfangled, sophisticated, modish*)

princely—imperial, munificent, magnificent, superb, august, regal, royal, supreme. (*beggarly, mean, niggardly, poverty-stricken*)

principal—highest, first, main, leading, chief, primary, foremost, pre-eminent, prominent. (*inferior, subordinate, secondary, supplemental, subject, auxiliary, minor*)

principle—source, origin, motive, cause, energy, substance, element, power, faculty, truth, tenet, law, doctrine, axiom, maxim, postulate, rule. (*exhibition, manifestation, application, development*)

private—special, peculiar, individual, secret, not public, retired, privy. (*general, public, open, unconcealed*)

privilege—prerogative, immunity, franchise, right, liberty, advantage, claim, exemption. (*disfranchisement, disqualification, exclusion, prohibition, inhibition*)

prize—booty, spoil, plunder, prey, forage, trophy, laurels, guerdon, premium, honors, ovation, palm. (*loss, forfeiture, fine, penalty, amercement, sacrifice, disappointment, failure, brand, stigma*)

probability—likelihood, presumption, verisimilitude, chance, appearance. (*unlikelihood, improbability, impossibility, inconceivableness*)

probable—likely, presumable, credible, reasonable. (*unlikely, unreasonable, incredible*)

proceed—move, pass, advance, progress, continue, issue, emanate, flow, arise. (*recede, deviate, retreat, stand, stop, stay, desist, discontinue, ebb, retire*)

procession—train, march, caravan, file, cortege, cavalcade, retinue. (*rabble, herd, rush, disorder, mob, confusion, rout*)

prodigal—lavish, profuse, extravagant, reckless, wasteful, squandering, improvident. (*frugal, saving, hoarding, economical, niggardly, miserly, close*)

prodigious—marvelous, portentous, wonderful, astounding, enormous, monstrous, amazing, surprising, remarkable, extraordinary, huge, vast. (*ordinary, commonplace, everyday, usual, familiar, moderate*)

produce—*v.* exhibit, bear, furbish, afford, cause, create, originate, yield, extend, prolong, lengthen. (*withdraw, retain, stifle, withhold, neutralize, destroy, annihilate, curtail, shorten, contract, reduce*)

produce—*n.* product, yield, fruit, profit, effect, consequence, result, amount.

product—fruit, result, issue, consequence, effect,

emanation, work. (*cause, principle, power, motive, energy, operation, action, tendency, law*)

production—origination, evolution, formation, genesis, manufacture.

profane—unconsecrated, secular, temporal, unsanctified, unholy, irreligious, irreverent, ungodly, wicked, godless, impious, blasphemous. (*holy, consecrated, sacred, spiritual, sanctified, reverent*)

profess—declare, avow, acknowledge, own, confess, pretend, proclaim, lay claim to. (*conceal, suppress, disown, disavow, repudiate, renounce, abjure*)

profit—gain, emolument, advantage, avail, acquisition, benefit, service, use, improvement. (*loss, detriment, damage, disadvantage, waste*)

profitable—gainful, advantageous, desirable, beneficial, useful, productive, remunerative, lucrative. (*unprofitable, disadvantageous, undesirable, detrimental, unbeneficial, unprofitable, useless, vain, fruitless, unproductive, unremunerative*)

program—advertisement, notice, plan, catalogue, schedule, performance. (*review, rehearsal, repetition, resume, analysis, précis*)

progress—advancement, advance, movement, proceeding, way, journey, proficiency, speed, growth. (*delay, stoppage, retreat, stay, retrogression, failure, relapse*)

project—plan, purpose, design, scheme, contrivance, device, venture. (*hazard, chance*)

prominent—jutting out, protuberant, embossed, extended, manifest, conspicuous, eminent, distinguished, main, important, leading, characteristic, distinctive. (*receding, concave, rebated, indented, hollowed, engraved, entailed, withdrawn*)

promiscuous—mingled, confused, undistinguished, unselected, unarranged, undistributed, unassorted, common, unreserved, casual, disorderly, unordered. (*sorted, select, orderly, arranged, distributed, reserved, assorted, exclusive, nice*)

promise—*v.* pledge, engage, assure, covenant, pledge, stipulate.

promise—*n.* engagement, assurance, word, pledge, oath, covenant.

promote—aid, further, advance, excite, exalt, raise, elevate, prefer. (*discourage, repress, hinder, check, allay, depress, degrade, dishonor*)

prompt—ready, alert, responsive, active, quick, brisk, apt, unhesitating. (*unready, sluggish, irresponsive, inactive*)

pronounce—articulate, utter, declare, propound, deliver, assert, affirm, enunciate, express. (*mispronounce, mispropound, misaffirm, suppress, stifle, silence, choke, swallow, gabble, mumble*)

proof—test, trial, examination, criterion, essay, establishment, comprobation, demonstration, evidence, testimony, scrutiny. (*disproof, failure, invalidity, shortcoming, fallacy, undemonstrativeness, reprobation*)

proper—peculiar, appertinent, personal, own, constitutional, special, befitting, adapted, suited, suitable, appropriate, just, fair, equitable, right, decent, becoming, fit. (*common, inappertinent, alien, universal, nonspecial, unbefitting, unadapted*)

property—quality, attribute, peculiarity, nature, characteristic, possessions, goods, wealth, estate, gear, resources, ownership.

proportion—adaptation, relation, rate, distribution, adjustment, symmetry, interrelationship, uniformity, correlation. (*misproportion, misadjustment, incongruity, disparity, disharmony, disorder, irrelation, disproportion*)

propose—offer, tender, proffer, bring forward, purpose, intend, mean, propound, move, design.

prosaic—dull, matter-of-fact, tedious, prolix. (*poetic, animated, interesting, lively, fervid, eloquent*)

prospect—view, vision, field, landscape, hope, anticipation, probability. (*viewlessness, dimness, obscurity, darkness, cloud, veiling, occultation, hopelessness, improbability*)

prospectus—program, plan, catalogue, announcement, bill, scheme, compendium, brochure. (*subject, transaction, proceeding*)

prosperity—success, wealth, welfare, good fortune, well-being, good luck. (*unsuccess, woe, adversity, failure, reverse*)

protect—defend, fortify, guard, shield, preserve, cover, secure, save, vindicate. (*betray, endanger, imperil, abandon, expose*)

proud—arrogant, haughty, imperious, supercilious, presumptuous, boastful, vainglorious, vain, ostentatious, elated, self-satisfied, lofty, imposing, magnificent, self-conscious. (*deferential, humble, affable, unpresuming, meek, lowly, ashamed, unimposing, mean*)

prove—try, assay, test, establish, demonstrate, ascertain, argue, show, confirm, examine, substantiate, make trial of, verify, ascertain. (*pass, pretermit, misdemonstrate, misindicate, refute, disprove, contradict, disestablish, neutralize*)

proverbial—notorious, current, acknowledged, unquestioned. (*dubious, unfounded, suspicious, suspected, questionable*)

provide—prepare, arrange, procure, afford, supply, contribute, yield, cater, furnish, get, agree, produce, collect, stipulate. (*misprovide, neglect, overlook, withhold, retain, appropriate, refuse, deny*)

province—tract, region, department, section, sphere, domain. territory. (*metropolis, center, capital*)

provision, provisions—preparation, arrangement, produce, supply, anticipation, food, supplies, victuals, edibles, eatables. (*neglect, misprovision, forgetfulness, thoughtlessness, oversight, destitution*)

provoke—educe, summon, rouse, irritate, excite, challenge, vex, impel, offend, exasperate, anger, tantalize. (*allay, relegate, pacify, soothe, conciliate*)

proxy—agency, substitution, representation, agent, substitute, representative, deputy, commissioner, lieutenant, delegate. (*principalship, personality, principal, person, authority, deputer*)

prudent—wise, wary, cautious, circumspect, discreet, careful, judicious. (*foolish, unwary, incautious, uncircumspect, indiscreet, rash, imprudent*)

prudish—coy, overmodest, overnice, squeamish, reserved, demure. (*promiscuous*)

public—open, notorious, common, social, national, exoteric, general, generally known. (*close, secret, private, domestic, secluded, solitary, personal*)

pull—draw, drag, adduce, extract, tug, haul, pluck. (*push, eject, extrude, propel*)

punch—perforate, poke, pierce, puncture, terebrate, bore. (*stop, plug, seal, bung*)

punish—chastise, castigate, chasten, correct, whip, scourge, discipline. (*reward, recompense, remunerate, indemnify*)

pupil—scholar, learner, student, tyro, novice, ward. (*teacher, master, proficient, adept, guardian*)

puppy—youth, fop, coxcomb, prig. (*boor, clown, lout*)

pure—clear, unmixed, simple, genuine, sheer, mere, absolute, unadulterated, uncorrupted, unsullied, unblemished, chaste, real, clean, spotless, immaculate, undefiled, unspotted, guileless, innocent, guiltless. (*foul, turbid, impure, adulterated, corrupt, sullied, stained, tarnished, defiled, mixed*)

purpose—*v.* intend, determine, design, resolve, mean, propose. (*chance, risk, hazard, revoke, miscalculate. venture. stake*)

purpose—*n.* intention, design, mind, meaning, view, object, aim, end, scope, point, resolve. (*chance, fortune, fate, accident, hazard, lot, casualty, lottery, hit*)

push—press, drive, impel, shove, press against, propel, butt, thrust, urge, expedite, accelerate, reduce. (*pull, draw, drag, adduce*)

put—place, lay, set, propose. (*remove, raise, displace, transfer, withdraw*)

puzzle—*v.* pose, perplex, embarrass, bewilder, confound, mystify, confuse. (*enlighten, instruct*)

puzzle—*n.* embarrassment, bewilderment, enigma, confusion, conundrum, intricacy, labyrinth. (*disentanglement, solution, explanation. extrication*)

Q

quack—empiric, mountebank, charlatan, impostor, pretender, humbug. (*dupe, gull, victim*)

quaint—curious, recondite, abstruse, elegant, nice, affected, whimsical, odd, antique, archaic, fanciful, singular, old-fashioned. (*commonplace, ordinary, usual, coarse, common, modern, modish, fashionable, dowdy*)

qualified—fitted, adapted, competent, suitable. (*unsuited, inappropriate, ineligible*)

quality—condition, character, property, attribute, peculiarity, disposition, temper, sort, kind, description, capacity, power, virtue, nature, tendency. (*anomalousness, heterogeneousness, nondescript, incapacity, weakness, indistinctiveness, ineffectiveness, disqualification, negation, disability*)

quantity—measure, amount, bulk, size, sum, portion, aggregate, muchness, part, share, division. (*margin, deficiency, deduction, want, inadequacy, scantiness, insufficiency, loss, deterioration, diminution, waste, wear, leakage*)

quarrel—brawl, altercation, affray, squabble, feud, tumult, dispute, wrangle, variance, disagreement, misunderstanding, hostility, quarreling, embroilment, bickering, broil. (*confabulation, conversation, pleasantry, conciliation, friendliness*)

quarrelsome—choleric, irascible, petulant, litigious, pugnacious, brawling, fiery, hot-tempered, contentious, irritable. (*peaceable, amenable, genial, unquarrelsome, inoffensive, mild, meek, conciliatory*)

quarter—region, district, locality, territory, mercy, forbearance, pity. (*extermination, mercilessness, unsparingness, pitilessness, ruthlessness*)

queer—odd, whimsical, quaint, cross, strange, crochety, singular, eccentric. (*ordinary, common,*

Synonym
Ant/Hom

usual, familiar, customary)

question—*v.* ask, inquire, interrogate, doubt, investigate, dubitate, controvert, dispute. (*dictate, state, assert, pronounce, enunciate, concede, endorse*)

question—*n.* inquiry, interrogation, doubt, scrutiny, investigation, topic. (*reply, response, solution, answer, explanation, admission, concession*)

questionable—doubtful, dubious, problematical, disputable, debatable, uncertain, suspicious. (*certain, evident, self-evident, obvious, indisputable*)

quick—fast, rapid, speedy, expeditious, swift, hasty, prompt, ready, clever, sharp, shrewd, adroit, keen, fleet, active, brisk, nimble, lively, agile, alert, sprightly, transient, intelligent. irascible. (*slow, tardy, sluggish, inert, inactive, dull, insensitive*)

quiet—*n.* rest, repose, stillness, calm, appeasement, pacification, silence, peace. (*unrest, motion, noise, agitation, excitement, disturbance, turmoil*)

quiet—*v.* allay, appease, still, pacify, hush, lull, tranquilize, soothe, calm. (*rouse, excite, disturb, agitate, stir, urge, goad*)

quit—leave, resign, abandon, relinquish, discharge, release, surrender, give up, depart from, forsake. (*seek, occupy, invade, bind, enforce, haunt*)

quite—perfectly, entirely, completely, wholly, truly, altogether, totally. (*partially, imperfectly, barely, insufficiently, hardly*)

quote—cite, name, adduce, plead, allege, note, repeat. (*disprove, refute, retort, oppose, contradict*)

R

racy—fine-flavored, fresh, rich, pungent, piquant, spirited, smart, lively, vivacious, spicy. (*flavorless, dull, stupid*)

radical—original, fundamental, thoroughgoing, unsparing, extreme, entire, innate, natural, essential, immanent, ingrained, underived, deep-seated. (*derived, ascititious, adventitious, superficial, extraneous, partial, moderate, conservative, acquired*)

rage—*n.* fury, rabidity, choler, indignation, frenzy, anger, ire, dudgeon, mania, passion, madness, ferocity. (*reason, moderation, gentleness, temperateness, calmness, quiescence, mitigation, assuagement, tranquillity, mildness, softness*)

rage—*v.* rave, storm, fume, be furious, be violent. (*be calm, be composed, be peaceful*)

raise—lift, heave, elevate, exalt, advance, promote, heighten, enhance, awaken, rouse, excite, call forth, cultivate, rear, produce, collect, summon, erect, originate, propagate. (*lay, cast, depress, degrade, retard, dishonor, lower, depreciate, lull, compose, quiet, calm, blight, destroy, disperse, disband*)

range—rank, dispose, class, place, order, collocate, file, concatenate, ramble, stroll, rove. (*disturb, disconnect, disorder, derange, intermit, disconnect, remain, be stationary*)

rank—*a.* luxuriant, exuberant, extreme, excessive, rampant. (*meager, sparse, thin*)

rank—*n.* row, line, tier, order, degree, grade, dignity. (*disconnection, disorder, incontinuity, intermission, hiatus, plebeianism, meanness*)

rankle—fester, smolder, burn, irritate, gall, disquiet. (*heal, cool, close, calm, quiet, compose*)

rapid—quick, swift, speedy, accelerated, flying (*slow, tardy, retarded, cumbrous, lazy*)

rare—scarce, choice, infrequent, excellent, few,

exceptional, sparse, unusual, singular, uncommon, incomparable, extraordinary, unique, dispersed, valuable, precious, thin, volatile. (*common, frequent, abundant, numerous, mean, ordinary, usual, regular, crowded, dense, vulgar, worthless, cheap*)

rash—headstrong, audacious, hasty, precipitate, reckless, foolhardy, careless, adventurous, thoughtless, indiscreet, venturesome, overventuresome, incautious, unwary, heedless. (*wary, cautious, calculating, discreet, unventuresome, dubitating, hesitating, reluctant, timid*)

rashness—hastiness, precipitancy, recklessness, venturesomeness, temerity, indiscretion. (*slowness, carefulness, cautiousness, discretion*)

rate—*n.* tax, impost, assessment, duty, standard, allowance, ratio, quota, worth, price, value.

rate—*v.* compute, calculate, estimate, value, scold, abuse, appraise.

rational—sane, sound, intelligent, reasoning, reasonable, judicious, sober, sensible, probable, equitable, moderate, fair. (*insane, unsound, weak, silly, unintelligent, absurd, injudicious, fanciful, extravagant, preposterous, unreasoning, unreasonable*)

ravel—separate, undo, untwist, unwind, disentangle. (*entangle, complicate, confuse*)

ravish—entrance, transport, enchant, enrapture, charm, violate, outrage, debauch.

raw—uncooked, unprepared, unfinished, unripe, crude, unseasoned, inexperienced, fresh, green, unpracticed, untried, bare, bald, exposed, galled, chill, bleak, piercing. (*cooked, dressed, prepared, finished, ripe, mature, mellow, seasoned, experienced, expert, adept, habituated, familiar, practiced, trained, tried*)

reach—extend, thrust, stretch, obtain, arrive at, attain, gain, grasp, penetrate, strain, aim. (*fail, stop, cease, revert, rebate, miss, drop*)

read—peruse, interpret, decipher, unravel, discover, recognize, learn. (*misread, misinterpret, overlook, misobserve*)

ready—prompt, alert, expeditious, speedy, unhesitating, dexterous, apt, skillful, handy, expert, facile, easy, opportune, fitted, prepared, disposed, willing, free, cheerful, compliant, responsive, quick. (*unready, tardy, slow, hesitating, reluctant, dubitating, awkward, unhandy, clumsy, remote, inaccessible, unavailable, inopportune, unsuited, unfitted, unprepared, indisposed, unwilling, constrained, grudging*)

real—actual, veritable, existent, authentic, legitimate, true, genuine, developed. (*fictitious, imaginary, unreal, nonexistent, untrue, false, artificial, adulterated, assumed, pretended, potential, possible*)

really—veritably, truly, indeed, unquestionably, (*questionably, possibly, perhaps, falsely, untruly*)

reason—*n.* ground, account, cause, explanation, motive, proof, apology, understanding, reasoning, rationality, right, propriety, justice, order, object, sake, purpose. (*pretext, pretense, misinterpretation, falsification, misconception, disproof, unreasonableness, absurdity, fallacy, irrationality, wrong, unreason, impropriety, unfairness, folly, aimlessness*)

reason—*v.* debate, discuss, argue, infer, deduce, conclude.

reassure—rally, restore, encourage, inspirit, animate, countenance. (*discourage, cow, browbeat, intimidate, discountenance*)

rebuff—*n.* rebuke, discouragement, repulsion,

check. (*welcome, acceptance, encouragement*)

rebuff—*v.* rebuke, repel, repulse, check, snub, oppose.

rebuke—reprove, chide, rebuff, reprimand, censure. (*approve, encourage, eulogize, applaud, incite*)

receipt—acknowledgment, reception, voucher.

receive—take, accept, admit, hold, entertain, assent to. (*give, impart, afford, reject, discharge*)

reception—admission, admittance, acceptance, acceptation, entertainment. (*denial, protest, repudiation, rejection, nonacceptance, dismissal, discardment, renunciation, abjuration*)

recess—cavity, nook, withdrawal, retirement, retreat, seclusion, privacy, vacation, holiday. (*promontory, protrusion, projection, publicity, worktime*)

reckless—careless, heedless, incautious, foolhardy, thoughtless, rash, overventuresome, regardless, inconsiderate, improvident. (*careful, heedful, cautious, timid, chary, thoughtful, calculating, provident, considerate, wary, circumspect*)

reckon—compute, calculate, count, regard, estimate, value, account, consider, argue, infer, judge. (*miscompute, miscalculate, misestimate, misreckon*)

recognize—identify, acknowledge, concede, know again, avow, own, allow. (*ignore, overlook, misobserve, repudiate, disavow, disown, disallow*)

recollect—recover, recall, remember, bethink, bring to mind, call up, think of. (*forget, lose*)

recommend—commend, confide, praise, applaud, approve, advise. (*discommend, disapprove, warn*)

recompense—*n.* reward, indemnification, satisfaction, remuneration, amends.

recompense—*v.* requite, remunerate, reward, indemnify, satisfy, repay, reimburse, compensate. (*damnify, injure, misrequite, dissatisfy*)

reconcile—unite, conciliate, propitiate, pacify, harmonize, adjust, adapt, suit, reunite. (*separate, sever, dissever, estrange, disharmonize, derange*)

record—registry, entry, enrollment, list, index, catalogue, register, schedule, roll, scroll, enumeration, inventory, muniment, instrument, archive, memorandum, rememberance. (*obliteration, oblivion, nonregistration, desuetude, obsolescence*)

recover—regain, repossess, resume, retrieve, recruit, heal, cure, revive, restore, reanimate, save. (*lose, forfeit, miss, sacrifice, deteriorate, impair, decay, decline, relapse*)

recovery—repossession, regaining, reinstatement, vindication, renovation, restitution, re-establishment, retrieval, rectification, replacement, reanimation, resuscitation, revival, redemption. (*lcss, forfeiture, privation, deprival, sacrifice, abandonment, relapse, retrogression, decay, declension, incurableness, ruin*)

recreation—refreshment, cheer, reanimation, amusement, diversion, revival, holiday, sport, pastime, relaxation. (*weariness, toil, lassitude, labor, fatigue, employment, assiduity, work*)

redeem—repurchase, regain, retrieve, make amends for, recompense, ransom, liberate, rescue, recover, satisfy, fulfill, discharge. (*pledge, lose, forfeit, abandon, betray, surrender, sacrifice*)

reduce—lessen, diminish, curtail, attenuate, impoverish, narrow, contract, weaken, impair, sub-

due, subjugate, bring, refer, subject, classify, convert. (*enlarge, magnify, increase, augment, produce, extend, amplify, broaden, expand, renovate, invigorate, restore, repair, liberate, free, except, dissociate, transform*)

refer—attribute, associate, assign, advert, connect, relate, point, belong, allude, apply, appeal, (*disconnect, dissociate, misapply, misappertain, alienate, misbeseem, disresemble*)

reference—relation, regard, intimation, allusion.

refinement—clarification, purification, filtration, sublimation, polish, elegance, cultivation, civilization, subtility, finesse, sophistry. (*turbidity, grossness, foulness, coarseness, impurity, unrefinement, rudeness, inelegance, boorishness, broadness, bluntness, unsophisticatedness*)

reflect—return, image, mirror, exhibit, consider, think, cogitate, meditate, contemplate, ponder, muse, ruminate, heed, advert, animadvert. (*divert, dissipate, idle, dream, wander, rove, stargaze, woolgather, connive, disregard, overlook*)

reform—amend, ameliorate, correct, rectify, better, reclaim, regenerate, remodel, reconstitute, reorganize, improve. (*corrupt, vitiate, worsen, deteriorate, perpetuate, stabilitate, confirm, impair, deform*)

refresh—cool, refrigerate, invigorate, revive, reanimate, renovate, recreate, renew, restore, cheer, freshen, brace. (*heat, oppress, weary, burden, afflict, annoy, tire, fatigue, exhaust, debilitate, enervate*)

refuse—*v.* deny, withhold, reject, decline, repudiate. (*grant, afford, yield, concede, acquiesce*)

refuse—*n.* offal, scum, dregs, sediment, recrement, sweepings, trash, offscourings, debris, remains, dross. (*cream, pickings, first fruits, flower*)

regard—behold, view, contemplate, esteem, consider, deem, affect, respect, reverence, revere, value, conceive, heed, notice, mind. (*miss, overlook, disregard, despise, dislike, contemn, hate, loathe, misconsider, misconceive, misestimate, misjudge*)

regardless—heedless, inconsiderate, careless, unmindful, inattentive, unobservant, disregarding, indifferent, despising. (*careful, considerate, regardful, attentive, prudent, cautious, circumspect, scrupulous*)

regret—*n.* sorrow, grief, concern, remorse, lamentation, repentance. (*see* **grief**)

regret—*v.* grieve, lament, repent, miss, desiderate, deplore. (*welcome, hail, approve, abandon, abjure, forget, disregard*)

regular—customary, normal, ordinary, orderly, stated, recurrent, periodical, systematic, methodic, established, recognized, formal, symmetrical, certain. (*unusual, exceptional, abnormal, capricious, rare, irregular, disordered, fitful, unsymmetrical, variable, eccentric, erratic, uncertain*)

regulation—rule, law, adjustment, disposal, method, government, order, control, arrangement. (*misrule, disorder, anarchy, misgovernment, maladministration, disarrangement, nonregulation, caprice, license, insubjection, uncontrol*)

reject—repel, renounce, throw by, cast away, repudiate, decline, discard, refuse, exclude. (*hail, welcome, accept, appropriate, choose, select, admit*)

rejoice—delight, glory, exult, joy, triumph, gladden, delight, revel, be glad, cheer, please, enliven, gratify. (*mourn, grieve, lament, weep, sorrow, repent, trouble, afflict, oppress, weary, depress, disappoint.*

Synonym Ant/Hom

burden, darken, distress, pain, sadden, vex, annoy)

relation—reference, aspect, connection, narration, proportion, bearing, affinity, homogeneity, association, relevancy, pertinency, fitness, harmony, ratio, relative, agreement, kinsman, kindred, appurtenancy. (*irrelation, disconnection, dissociation, irrelevancy, impertinency, disproportion, misproportion, unfitness, unsuitableness, heterogeneity, disharmony, disagreement, alien*)

release—free, loose, liberate, discharge, quit, acquit, exempt, extricate, disengage, indemnify. (*bind, constrain, confine, shackle, fetter, yoke*)

reliance—confidence, trust, dependence, assurance. (*distrust, misgiving, suspicion, diffidence*)

relief—succor, support, release, extrication, alleviation, mitigation, aid, help, assistance, remedy, redress, exemption, deliverance, refreshment, comfort. (*oppression, aggravation, intensification, burdensomeness, trouble, exhaustion, weariness, discomfort*)

religion—faith, creed, theology, belief, profession, piety, sanctity, godliness, holiness. (*unbelief, irreligion, godlessness, atheism, impiety, sacrilege, scoffing, blasphemy, skepticism, profanity, hypocrisy, sanctimoniousness, pharisaism*)

religious—pious, godly, devout, devotional, divine, holy, sacred. (*impious, ungodly, undevout, sacrilegious, blasphemous, skeptical, profane*)

relish—zest, recommendation, enhancement, flavor, savor, gusto, taste, appetite, piquancy sapidity. (*drawback, disflavor, disrecommendation nauseousness, disrelish, insipidity, unsavoriness*)

remain—stay, continue, wait, stop, tarry, halt, sojourn, rest, dwell, abide, last, endure, accrue, survive. (*fly, vanish, remove, depart, speed, hasten press, flit, disappear, pass*)

remarkable—observable, noticeable, extraordinary, unusual, rare, striking, noteworthy, notable, distinguished, famous, peculiar, prominent, singular. (*unremarkable, unnoticeable, ordinary, mean, commonplace, everyday, undistinguished*)

remedy—cure, restorative, counteraction, reparation, redress, relief, help, specific. (*evil, disease, hurt, infection, plague, ill, impairment, deterioration, aggravation, provocation*)

remember—recollect, recall, retain, bear in mind, mind. (*forget, obliviate, disregard, overlook*)

remembrance—recollection, memory, memorial, token, souvenir, memento, reminiscence, (*forgetfulness, oblivion*)

remiss—slack, careless, negligent, inattentive, wanting, slow, slothful, idle, lax, dilatory, tardy, remissful. (*energetic, careful, attentive, active, assiduous, alert, painstaking, diligent, strict*)

remit—relax, pardon, absolve, forgo, discontinue, surrender, forgive, resign. (*increase, intensity, enforce, exact*)

remorse—compunction, anguish, self-condemnation, penitence, sting of conscience. (*complacency, self-approval, self-congratulation*)

remote—distant, indirect, unconnected, unrelated, foreign, alien, heterogeneous, separate, contingent. (*near, close, direct, connected, related, homogeneous, immediate, proximate, essential, present, pressing, urgent, actual*)

remove—displace, separate, abstract, transport, carry, transfer, eject, oust, dislodge, suppress, migrate, depart. (*restore, conserve, stabilitate, perpetuate, establish, reinstate, reinstall, install, fix*)

render—give, present, return, restore, give up, apportion, assign, surrender, pay, requite, deliver. (*keep, retain, withhold, appropriate, alienate, misapportion, misappropriate, misrequite*)

renew—recreate, restore, refresh, renovate, rejuvenate, furbish, recommence, repeat, reiterate, reissue, regenerate, reform, transform. (*impair, wear, deteriorate, vitiate, exhaust, discontinue, corrupt, weaken, defile, deprave*)

renounce—reject, abjure, disclaim, disown, forgo, disavow, deny, quit, resign, abandon, recant, relinquish, repudiate. (*acknowledge, recognize, claim, maintain, assert, propound, own, vindicate, avow, profess, hold, retain, defend*)

renowned—famous, celebrated, wonderful, illustrious.

repay—remunerate, reimburse, recompense, reward, retaliate, requite, refund. (*defraud, misappropriate, embezzle, waste, alienate, extort, confiscate*)

repeal—*v.* abolish, revoke, rescind, cancel, annul, recall, abrogate, reverse, discontinue, make void. (*continue, establish, pass, institute, sanction, enact, perpetuate, confirm*)

repeal—*n.* abrogation, rescisson, revocation, annulment. (*continuance, establishment, perpetuation*)

repeat—reiterate, iterate, renew, cite, quote, relate, rehearse, recapitulate, reproduce. (*discontinue, drop, discard, abandon, ignore, suppress, misrepeat, misquote, misrecite, misrepresent, misinterpret, misconvey*)

repeatedly—frequently, again and agian, often. (*seldom, rarely*)

repentance—penitence, contrition, compunction, regret, remorse, sorrow, self-reproach, self-condemnation. (*impenitence, obduracy, recusancy, hardness, reprobation, self-approval*)

repetition—iteration, reiteration, dwelling upon, diffuseness, verbosity, relation.

replace—restore, supply, substitute, reinstate, rearrange, re-establish. (*move, abstract, withdraw, remove, damage, deprive*)

reply—*n.* answer, rejoinder, response, replication. (*passing by, ignoring*)

reply—*v.* replicate, answer, respond, rejoin. (*ignore, drop, pretermit, pass, disregard*)

report—*v.* announce, relate, tell, circulate. notify, narrate, recite, describe, detail, communicate, declare. (*silence, hush, suppress, misreport, misrepresent, misrelate, falsify*)

report—*n.* tidings, announcement, relation, narration, recital, description, communication, declaration, news, rumor, fame, repute, noise, reverberation. (*silence, suppression, misannouncement, fabrication, noiselessness*)

represent—portray, delineate, reproduce, exhibit, personate, state, describe, indicate, embody, enact, illustrate, denote, play, dramatize, resemble. (*misportray, misdelineate, distort. falsify, caricature*)

representative—agent, commissioner, proxy, deputy, substitute, embodiment, personation, delegate, vicar, vicegerent, principal, sovereign. (*autocrat, dictator*)

reproach—blame, censure, taunt, rebuke, upbraid, reprobate, reprove. (*laud, praise, approve, commend*)

reprobate—castaway, villain, ruffian, miscreant, scapegrace, scalawag. (*example, pattern, mirror, model, paragon*)

repudiate—disavow, disown, discard, cast off, abjure, renounce, disclaim, divorce. (*avow, own, vindicate, assert, retain, vaunt, claim, profess, recognize, acknowledge, accept*)

repulsive—forbidding, deterrent, ungenial, odious, ugly, unattractive, disagreeable, revolting. (*charming, agreeable, attractive, winning, captivating, fascinating, alluring, seductive, pleasant*)

reputable—respectable, creditable, honorable, estimate. (*unrespectable, discreditable, dishonorable, disgraceful, disreputable*)

rescue—retake, recover, recapture, liberate, extricate, save, deliver, preserve. (*endanger, imperil, betray, surrender, abandon, expose*)

resemblance—likeness, similarity, similitude, semblance, representation, portrait, reflection, image. (*unlikeness, dissimilarity, disresemblance, difference, contrariety*)

resent—repel, resist, rebel, recalcitrate, take ill. (*acquiesce, submit, condone, pardon, overlook*)

reserve—reservation, retention, limitation, backwardness, coldness, shyness, coyness, modesty. (*boldness, rashness, recklessness, immodesty*)

residence—sojourn, stay, abode, home, habitation, domicile, mansion.

resist—withstand, oppose, hinder, check, thwart, baffle, disappoint. (*weaken, yield, give up, surrender*)

resolute—determined, decided, fixed, steadfast, steady, constant, persevering, bold, firm, unshaken. (*weak, infirm, shy, cowardly, inconstant*)

resource—material, means, supplies, expedients, wealth, riches. (*destitution, exhaustion, lack, drain, nonplus, poverty*)

respect—regard, esteem, honor, revere, venerate.

respond—answer, reply, rejoin.

rest—remainder, overplus, remnant, residue, others.

restless—unquiet, uneasy, disturbed, disquieted, sleepless, agitated, anxious, unsettled, roving, wandering. (*steady, quiet, settled*)

restrain—check, hinder, stop, withhold, repress, curb, suppress, coerce, restrict, abridge, limit, confine. (*give full rein to, let go, release, free*)

result—effect, consequence, conclusion, inference, issue, event.

retain—keep, hold, restrain. (*yield, give up*)

retire—withdraw, leave, depart, secede, recede.

retort—repartee, answer.

retreat—retirement, departure, withdrawment, seclusion, solitude, privacy, asylum, shelter, refuge. (*advance, forward march*)

return—restore, requite, repay, recompense, render, remit, report.

reveal—communicate, disclose, divulge, unveil, uncover, open, discover, impart, show. (*keep secret, withhold, cover, conceal, hide*)

revengeful—vindictive, resentful, spiteful, malicious. (*open, ingenuous, frank, hearty, generous, kind, cordial*)

revenue—receipts, returns, income, proceeds, wealth, result. (*expense, outgo*)

reverence—awe, honor, veneration, adoration.

review—re-examination, resurvey, retrospect, survey, reconsideration, revise, revision

reward—recompense, compensation, remuneration, pay, requital, retribution, punishment.

rich—wealthy, affluent, opulent, ample, copious, abundant, fruitful, costly, sumptuous, precious, generous, luscious. (*poor, weak, straitened, cheap, scanty, sordid*)

ridicule—derision, twit, banter, raillery, burlesque, mockery, sarcasm, gibe, jeer, sneer.

ripe—mature, mellow, complete, finished. (*green, young, incomplete, unfinished*)

rise—arise, mount, ascend, climb, scale.

risk—danger, hazard, peril, jeopardy, exposure.

rival—competitor, emulator, antagonist.

road—way, highway, street, lane, pathway, route, passage, course.

robbery—theft, depredation, spoliation, despoilation, despoilment, plunder, pillage, freebooting, piracy.

romance—fable, novel, fiction, tale.

romantic—sentimental, fanciful, fictitious, extravagant, wild, chimerical.

room—space, compass, scope, latitude.

round—circular, spherical, globular, globose, orbicular, orbed, cylindrical, full, plump, rotund. (*square, oblong, angular, lean, thin*)

rout—defeat, smite, conquer. (*victory*)

route—roadway, path, track.

royal—kingly, regal, monarchical, imperial, kinglike, princely, august, majestic, superb, splendid, illustrious, noble, magnanimous.

ruin—destruction, downfall, perdition, fall, overthrow, subversion, defeat, bane, pest, mischief.

rule—regulation, law, precept, maxim, guide, canon, order, method, direction, control, government, sway, empire.

rustic—rural, rude, unpolished, inelegant, untaught, awkward, rough, coarse, plain, unadorned, simple, artless, honest.

S

sacred—holy, divine, hallowed, consecrated, dedicated, devoted, religious, venerable, reverend.

sad—sorrowful, mournful, gloomy, dejected, depressed, cheerless, downcast, sedate, serious, grave, grievous, afflictive, calamitous. (*gay, lively, happy, spirited, sprightly, jolly, fortunate, seductive*)

safe—secure, unendangered, sure. (*in danger, dangerous, exposed, risky*)

sagacity—penetration, shrewdness, judiciousness. (*stupidity, thickheadedness, dullness, foolishness*)

salutary—wholesome, healthful, salubrious, beneficial, useful, advantageous, profitable. (*unhealthy, infectious, tainted*)

sample—specimen, example, illustration.

sanction—ratify, support, endorse.

satire—lampoon, sarcasm, irony, ridicule, burlesque, wit, humor.

satisfaction—contentment, content, gratification, pleasure, recompense, compensation, amends, remuneration, indemnification, atonement.

satisfy—satiate, content, please, gratify, recom-

Synonym
Ant/Hom

pense, compensate, remunerate, indemnify.

saucy—impertinent, insolent, rude, impudent.

savage—ferocious, wild, uncultivated, untaught, uncivilized, unpolished, rude, brutish, brutal, heathenish, barbarous, cruel, inhuman, fierce, pitiless, merciless, unmerciful, murderous. (*cultured, refined, kind, gentle, merciful, humane, human, tame*)

save—preserve, rescue, deliver, protect, spare, reserve, prevent. (*abandon, expose, give up, throw away*)

saying—declaration, speech, adage, maxim, aphorism, apothegm, saw, proverb, byword.

scandal—defamation, detraction, slander, calumny, opprobrium, reproach, shame, disgrace. (*honor, glory, respect*)

scanty—deficient, gaunt, meager, scarce. (*full, ample, plenty*)

scarce—rare, infrequent, deficient, uncommon. (*common, general, usual, frequent*)

scatter—disperse, dissipate, spread, strew, sprinkle. (*gather, keep together, collect, preserve*)

scheme—plan, project, design, contrivance, purpose, device, plot.

scholar—pupil, learner, disciple, learned man, sage.

science—literature, art, knowledge.

scorn—contempt, disdain, derision, contumely, despite, slight, dishonor, contempt. (*love, respect, honor, admiration, flattery*)

scrupulous—cautious, careful, conscientious, hesitating. (*unscrupulous, careless, scatterbrained, reckless, daring, dishonest*)

scurrilous—opprobrious, abusive, reproachful, insulting, insolent, offensive, gross, vile, vulgar, low, foul, foul-mouthed, indecent, mean.

seasonable—opportune, timely, fit convenient.

secret—hidden, concealed, secluded, unseen, unknown, private, obscure, recondite, latent, covert, clandestine, privy. (*open, free, known, public*)

sectarian—heretic, partisan, schismatic.

section—part, division, portion.

security—protection, defense, guard, shelter, safety, certainty, ease, assurance, carelessness, confidence, surety, pledge. (*danger, exposure, doubt, uncertainty*)

sedate—sober, demure, serious, calm, grave, settled, serene, passive, quiet. (*flighty, frolicsome, indiscreet, ruffled, agitated, disturbed*)

seem—appear, look.

seemly—becomingly, fit, suitable, proper, appropriate, congruous, meet, decent, decorous. (*improper, immodest, unconventional, gross, rude*)

seize—catch, grasp, clutch, snatch, append, arrest, take, capture.

sense—understanding, reason, perception, sensation, feeling, meaning, import, signification, notion, opinion, judgment.

sensible—intelligent, wise, cognizant, satisfied, persuaded. (*scatterbrained, foolish, ignorant of*)

sentiment—thought, opinion, sensibility, feeling.

serious—grave, solemn, important, weighty. (*gay, lively, happy, light, unimportant*)

serve—obey, minister to, subserve, promote, aid, help, assist, benefit, succor.

set—*v.* sink, settle, subside, decline, compose, consolidate, harden. (*rise, ascend, soar, mount, stir,*

agitate, loosen, run, soften, melt, mollify, fuse, flow)

set—*a.* fixed, established, firm, determined, regular, formal.

settle—fix, establish, regulate, arrange, compose, adjust, determine, decide, adjudicate, quiet, allay, still, sink, fall, subside, lower, calm, acquiesce, abate, agree. (*remove, disestablish, misregulate, derange, discompose, aggravate, disorder, disturb, confuse, misdetermine, misarrange, misplace, unsettle, rise, ascend, move, disagree, increase, heighten*)

settlement—subsidence, dregs, residuum, precipitation, colonization, location, colony. (*excitement, perturbation, turbidity, fluctuation*)

several—separate, distinct, diverse, sundry, divers, various, different. (*one, same, identical, indistinguishable, inseparable, united, total, integral*)

severe—serious, austere, stern, grave, strict, harsh, rigid, rigorous, sharp, afflictive, distressing, violent, extreme, exact, critical, censorious, caustic, sarcastic, cutting, keen, better, cruel. (*gay, smiling, cheerful, relaxed, jocose, jocund, joyous, mild, genial, indulgent, light, trivial, trifling, inconsiderable, inexact, loose, uncritical, lenient, inextreme, moderate, kind, considerate, feeling, tender, gentle*)

shabby—ragged, threadbare, contemptible, beggarly, paltry.

shadowy—dim, cloudy, obscure, dark, murky, gloomy, mysterious.

shallow—shoal, slight, flimsy, trifling, simple, superficial, unprofound. (*deep, profound*)

sham—phantom, ghost, delusion, illusion, mockery, shadow, pretense, counterfeit, unreality. (*substance, reality, verity, substantiality, truth*)

shame—abashment, humiliation, modesty, shamefacedness, decency, decorum, reproach, dishonor, ignominy, contempt, degradation, discredit, dispraise. (*shamelessness, barefacedness, immodesty, impudence, indecency, indecorum, impropriety, honor, glory, exaltation, renown, credit*)

shameful—disgraceful, degrading, scandalous, outrageous, dishonorable, indecent, unbecoming.

shape—*v.* form, mold, figure, adapt, delineate, adjust, contrive, create, execute, make. (*pervert, distort, misadapt, misdelineate, derange, discompose, miscontrive, misproduce, caricature*)

shape—*n.* figure, form, outline, mold, fashion, pattern, cast, model.

share—portion, apportionment, lot, division, participation, allowance, quota, contingent, allotment. (*whole, mass, aggregate, entirely*)

sharp—thin, fine, keen, shrewd, discerning, clever, sarcastic, acute, pointed, aculeated, penetrating, pungent, acid, shrill, piercing, afflictive, distressing, harsh, severe, cutting, eager, active, ardent, sore, hard, animated, spirited. (*thick, blunt, dull, obtuse, knobbed, rounded, bluff, mellow, bass, hollow, deep, light, trifling, trivial, mild, gentle, soft, tender, lenient, sluggish, inactive, indifferent, careless, spiritless, tame*)

shatter—split, dissipate, disrupt, derange, break in pieces, rend, demolish, shiver, dismember, disintegrate. (*construct, organize, collocate, fabricate, compose, rear, constitute*)

sheer—pure, mere, unmixed, unqualified, unmitigated, absolute, simple, unadulterated. (*mixed, qualified, adulterated, modified, partial*)

shelve—dismiss, discard, swamp, stifle, shift. (*start, prosecute, pursue, revive, agitate*)

shift—*v.* change, alter, transfer, shelve, displace, remove. (*fix, fasten, locate, insert, pitch, plant, place*)

shift—*n.* contrivance, expedient, substitute, pretext, motive, change, evasion, device, artifice, resource, transference. (*miscontrivance, fixity, steadiness, retention, location, permanence*)

shocking—sad, horrible, disgraceful, hateful, revolting, abominable, loathsome, foul. (*pleasing, honorable, charming, delightful, creditable, edifying, exemplary, attractive, alluring, enticing*)

short—brief, limited, scanty, inadequate, insufficient, lacking, deficient, defective, imperfect, incomplete, soon, near, narrow, weak, incomprehensive, inextensive, less, abrupt, blunt, concise, condensed. (*long, protracted, extended, unlimited, plentiful, ample, abundant, adequate, sufficient, exuberant, liberal, large, copious, complete, distant, deferred, wide, strong, comprehensive, extensive, exceeding, bland, courteous, inabrupt, expanded, diffuse*)

show—*n.* appearance, exhibition, demonstration, parade, pomp, semblance, likeness, pretext, profession, pretense, illusion. (*nonappearance, disappearance, concealment, suppression, secrecy, disguise, dissimilarity, unlikeness, ungenuineness, reality, sincerity, substance*)

show—*v.* exhibit, present, demonstrate, unfold, reveal, teach, inform, conduct, manifest, evince, evidence, prove, explain. (*conceal, suppress, hide, withhold, obscure, mystify, wrap, misdemonstrate, misdeclare, contradict, refute, deny, disprove, misinterpret, falsify, misexplain*)

showy—gay, gaudy, high-colored, gorgeous, flashy, tinsel. (*inconspicuous, unnoticeable, quiet, subdued*)

shrewd—sagacious, penetrating, astute, discriminating, intelligent, discerning, acute. (*stolid, undiscerning, unsagacious, stupid, dull*)

shrink—contract, shrivel, withdraw, retire, recoil, revolt. (*stretch, expand, dilate, venture, dare*)

shrivel—contract, dry up, wither, wrinkle, corrugate, decrease. (*expand, flatten, develop, unfold, spread, dilate*)

shuffle—confuse, interchange, shift, intershift, intermix, derange, agitate, evade, prevaricate, equivocate, quibble, cavil, sophisticate, mystify, palter, dissemble. (*deal, distribute, order, arrange, compose, confess, propound, declare, explain, elucidate, reveal*)

shy—timid, reserved, modest, bashful, suspicious, shrinking, chary. (*bold, brazenfaced, impudent, audacious, reckless*)

sick—diseased, ill, disordered, distempered, indisposed, weak, ailing, feeble, morbid, nauseated, disgusted, corrupt, impaired, valetudinarian. (*whole, well, healthy, sound, robust, strong, well conditioned, salubrious*)

sickly—weak, diseased, disordered, ailing, feeble, pining, drooping, morbid, unhealthy, vitiated, delicate, tainted, valetudinary. (*strong, healthy, vigorous, flourishing, salubrious, sound, robust*)

side—margin, edge, verge, border, laterality, face, aspect, plane, party, interest, cause, policy, behalf. (*center, body, core, interior, essence, neutrality, disconnection, severance, secession, opposition*)

sight—seeing, perception, view, vision, visibility, spectacle, show, inspection, examination, representation, appearance. (*nonperception, invisibility, blindness, obscuration, disappearance, oversight, nonappearance, undiscernment*)

sign—token, indication, proof, memorial, expression, symbol, emblem, prefiguration, badge, type, premonition, symptom, prognostic, mark, wonder, presage, signal. (*misindication, misrepresentation, misleader*)

signal—eminent, conspicuous, remarkable, extraordinary, notable, memorable, illustrious, important, salient, distinguished. (*ordinary, common, unnoticeable, mediocre, unmemorable, unimportant*)

signify—portend, purport, prognosticate, mean, represent, indicate, communicate, denote, betoken, declare, utter, forebode, presage. (*conceal, suppress, misindicate, misdenote, nullify, refute, neutralize, preclude*)

silence—taciturnity, stillness, calm, peace, hush, muteness, secrecy, oblivion. (*garrulity, loquacity, talkativeness, chatter, noise, brawl, clamor, clatter, din, babel, tumult, agitation, restlessness, storm, unrest, roar, bruit, reverberation, resonance, commotion, cackling, proclamation, publicity, fame, rumor, remembrance, repute, celebrity*)

silly—simple, foolish, weak, shallow, witless, unwise, indiscreet, imprudent, absurd. (*sagacious, intelligent, astute, wise, deep, discreet, prudent, sound, rational*)

similar—correspondent, resembling, alike, common, homogeneous, concordant, harmonious, congruous. (*different, unlike, dissimilar, alien, heterogeneous, discordant, incongruous*)

simple—single, incomplex, uncompounded, unblended, isolated, pure, unmixed, mere, absolute, plain, unadorned, unartificial, artless, sincere, undesigning, single-minded, unaffected, silly, weak, unsophisticated, humble, homely, lowly, elementary, ultimate, primal, rudimentary. (*double, complex, compounded, blended, mixed, fused, multiform, multigenerous, various, compound, articulated, subdivided, organized, connected, modified, complicated, elaborate, artificial, artful, designing, insincere, double-minded, affected, self-conscious, sagacious, sophisticated, great, eminent, illustrous, complete, developed, perfect*)

simultaneous—synchronous, concomitant, concurrent. (*separate, apart, intermittent, periodic*)

sin—transgression, iniquity, unrighteousness, ungodliness, wickedness, evil, impurity, crime, wrongdoing. (*sinlessness, obedience, holiness, righteousness, purity, godliness, goodness*)

sincere—pure, unmixed, genuine, unadulterated, hearty, honest, unaffected, unvarnished, candid, cordial, frank, unfeigned, true. (*impure, adulterated, dishonest, insincere, hypocritical, feigned, false*)

single—one, unique, only, individual, sole, solitary, separate, uncombined, unmarried, uncompounded. (*plural, many, collective, united, numerous, frequent, married*)

singular—single, individual, unique, eminent, extraordinary, conspicuous, consummate, unusual, uncommon, odd, whimsical quaint, peculiar, unexampled, unprecedented, solitary, sole, eccentric, fantastic, exceptional, particular, remarkable,

Synonym Ant/Hom

curious, queer. (*common, frequent, numerous, ordinary, usual, unnoticeable, everyday, customary, general, regular*)

situation—locality, position, topography, state, seat, post, place, condition, residence, aspect, footing, office, birth, plight, predicament, standing. (*nonsituation, nonlocation, absence, nonassignment, unfixedness, displacement, dislodgement*)

slender—thin, narrow, slight, slim, small, trivial, spare, inadequate, fragile, feeble, flimsy, meager, inconsiderable, superficial. (*stout, thick, broad, robust, massive, considerable, ample, deep*)

slow—sluggish, inactive, inert, lazy, unready, tardy, late, gradual, tedious, dull, dilatory, lingering, slack. (*active, quick, fast, rapid, alert, ready, prompt, early, sudden, immediate*)

sly—cunning, subtle, crafty, artful, wily, underhanded, astute, stealthy. (*open, frank, artless, undesigning*)

small—little, diminutive, slight, minute, feeble, trivial, insignificant, paltry, narrow, mean, weak, slender, fine, inferior. (*great, large, big, considerable, bulky, extensive, ample, spacious, stout, strong, important, broad, liberal*)

smart—keen, pungent, piercing, quick, vigorous, sharp, severe, active, clever, brilliant, vivacious, witty, ready, spruce, brisk, fresh, dressy, showy. (*dull, heavy, aching, slow, inactive, stupid, sluggish, unready, slow-minded, unwitty, dowdy, shabby, clownish*)

smooth—even, plain, level, flat, polished, glossy, sleek, soft, unruffled, unobstructed, bland, oily, suave. (*uneven, rough, rugged, abrupt, precipitous, unpolished, harsh, blunt*)

smother—suffocate, stifle, repress, gag, conceal, suppress, choke, strangle, allay, swallow. (*fan, ventilate, foster, cherish, nurture, publish, promulgate, divulge, spread, excite, vent*)

sneer—scoff, gibe, jeer, taunt, disparagement, contempt, scorn, superciliousness, disdain. (*compliment, eulogy, commendation, deference*)

snub—mortify, check, rebuke, reprimand.

snug—close, housed, compressed, compact, comfortable, sheltered. (*exposed, loose, disordered, incompact, uncomfortable, bare, shivering*)

sober—temperate, unintoxicated, cool, dispassionate, reasonable, calm, self-possessed, sound, unexcited, serious, grave, sedate, steady, abstemious, moderate. (*intemperate, drunk, intoxicated, heated, excited, impassioned, unreasonable, agitated, furious, passionate, extravagant, extreme, exorbitant, immoderate, flighty, erratic, eccentric*)

society—community, polity, association, collection, companionship, fellowship, connection, participation, company, sociality, communion, intercourse, sodality. (*individuality, personality, segregation, separation, solitariness, unsociality, privacy, dissociation, disconnection*)

soft—yielding, pressible, impressible, smooth, delicate, fine, sleek, glossy, mild, gentle, balmy, kind, feeling, flexible, effeminate, luxurious, unmanly, tender, irresolute, undecided. (*hard, tough, stubborn, unyielding, rigid, unimpressible, rough, coarse, harsh, abrupt, ungentle, rigorous, cutting, severe, unkind, unfeeling, sharp, inflexible, stern, austere, ascetic, self-denying, resolute, determined*)

soften—mollify, palliate, compose, mitigate, assuage, dulcify, lenify, yield, macerate, humanize, abate, moderate. (*harden, indurate, aggravate, excite, infuriate, consolidate*)

solemn—sacred, formal, devotional, reverential, ritual, ceremonial, impressive, religious, grave, serious. (*profane, undevotional, secular, light, gay, trivial, unceremonial, informal, unsolemn*)

solid—hard, firm, compact, resistant, dense, substantial, weighty, strong, valid, just, sound, impenetrable, stable, cubic. (*soft, hollow, yielding, frail, brittle, flimsy, elastic, resilient, malleable, impressible, fluid, liquid, frivolous, light, trifling, weak, invalid, unsound, fallacious, weakly*)

solitude—loneliness, remoteness, seclusion, retirement, isolation, wildness, desertion, barrenness, wilderness, privacy. (*publicity, populousness, society, frequentedness, intercourse, resort, meeting, reunion, throng, crowd*)

solution—separation, discerption, disruption, breach, discontinuance, disconnection, disentanglement, elucidation, explanation, key, answer, resolution, disintegration. (*union, combination, amalgamation, continuity, connection, conjunction, entanglement, complication, confusion, mystification, obscurity, integration*)

sore—painful, irritated, susceptible, excoriated, raw, scarified, ulcerous, grievous, afflictive, heavy, burdensome. (*painless, sound, whole, healthful, healed, unbroken, unscarified, light, trivial, unburdensome, pleasant, untroublesome, grateful*)

sorry—grieved, pained, hurt, afflicted, woebegone, doleful, downhearted, mortified, vexed, dejected, poor, mean, vile, shabby, worthless. (*glad, rejoiced, delighted, pleased, gratified, fine, choice, handsome*)

sort—kind, species, nature, class, order, character, rank, manner, quality, condition, description, designation, genus. (*nondescription, solitariness, uniqueness, nonclassification, heterogeneity*)

sound—entire, unbroken, whole, perfect, unhurt, well-grounded, uninjured, unimpaired, healthy, firm, strong, vigorous, weighty, solid, irrefragable, irrefutable, thorough, valid, wholesome, correct, substantial. (*partial, broken, injured, impaired, unhealthy, unsound, weak, frail, fragile, light, trivial, unfounded, hollow, fallacious, imperfect, unwholesome, incorrect, unsubstantial, invalid*)

sour—tart, rancid, coagulated, turned, harsh, crabbed, austere, morose, pungent, crusty, acid, churlish, bitter, acetous, acrimonious, peevish. (*sweet, wholesome, untainted, mellow, genial, kindly*)

spacious—ample, extensive, broad, vast, capacious, large, wide, roomy, expansive. (*narrow, restricted, limited, cramped, confined, inextensive*)

spare—*a.* scanty, unplentiful, inabundant, meager, economical, frugal, stinted, restricted, parsimonious, niggardly, chary, superfluous, disposable, available, lean, thin, ill-conditioned. (*ample, plentiful, abundant, profuse, liberal, unrestricted, generous, bountiful, unsparing, unstinted, unbounded, available, well-conditioned*)

spare—*v.* save, afford, grant, reserve, do without, husband, economize, retain, store, grudge, discard, omit, forbear, withhold, refrain, abstain. (*spend, squander, waste, lavish, scatter, expend, indulge, vent*)

special—particular, specific, peculiar, appropriate, proper, distinctive, extraordinary, especial, exceptional. (*general, universal, common, generic*)

speculation—contemplation, consideration, view, weighing, thought, theory, scheme, hypothesis, conjecture. (*realization, proof, fact, verification, certainty*)

speed—dispatch, expedite, accelerate, urge, hasten, hurry, press. (*retard, delay, postpone, obstruct, drag, loiter, dawdle, linger, lag, stay*)

spend—bestow, waste, exhaust, squander, expend, lay out, consume, disburse, lavish. (*retain, save, hoard, accumulate, husband, economize*)

spirit—air, breath, life, soul, vital, force, essential quality, essence, immateriality, intelligence, disembodiment, specter, apparition, ghost, energy, ardor, enthusiasm, activity, earnestness, courage, zeal, disposition, temper, principle, motive, distillation. (*substance, body, corporeity, materiality, flesh, organization, frame, embodiment, spiritlessness, listlessness, soullessness, lifelessness, torpor, deadness, timidity, dejection, slowness, sluggishness*)

spirited—animated, lively, vivacious, ardent, buoyant, sprightly, courageous. (*dull, dispirited, depressed, cowardly*)

spiritual—divine, religious, holy, ghostly, ethical, immaterial, incorporeal, intellectual. (*carnal, fleshy, unspiritual, gross, material, sensuous*)

spite—malice, malevolence, grudge, pique, hatred, ill will, vindictiveness, rancor, spleen. (*good will, benevolence, kindness*)

splendid—brilliant, showy, magnificent, sumptuous, gorgeous, glorious, pompous, imposing, illustrious, superb, famous, heroic, grand, signal. (*dull, obscure, tame, somber, poor, beggarly, unimposing, ordinary, ineffective, inglorious*)

split—divide, separate, rive, cleave, crack, splinter, burst, rend, sunder, disagree, secede, disunite. (*cohere, unite, amalgamate, coalesce, conform, agree, splice, consolidate, integrate*)

spoil—plunder, strip, rob, devastate, pillage, denude, corrupt, vitiate, mar, deteriorate. (*invest, enrich, endow, replenish, renovate, improve, better, ameliorate, rectify, preserve*)

spontaneous—voluntary, self-generated, self-originated, willing, unbidden, gratuitous. (*involuntary, imposed, compulsory, unwilling, necessitated*)

sport—play, frolic, wantonness, joke, diversion, merriment, gaiety, fun, amusement, recreation, game, pastime. (*work, seriousness, business, earnestness*)

spread—extend, stretch, expand, open, unfurl, divulge, propagate, publish, disperse, diffuse, overlay, distribute, scatter, circulate, disseminate, ramify. (*contract, furl, gather, fold, close, shut, secrete, suppress, confine, restrict, repress, hush, conceal, recall, collect, stagnate, concentrate, localize*)

spring—leap, bound, jump, start, emerge, issue, proceed, orginate, rise, emanate, germinate, burst, flow. (*settle, alight, land, drop, arrive, issue, eventuate, end, terminate, debouch, disembogue*)

staid—grave, demure, steady, sober, sedate. (*unsteady, flighty, indiscreet, wanton, insedate, erratic, eccentric, agitated, discomposed, ruffled*)

stammer—stutter, hesitate, falter. (*speak clearly, speak unhesitatingly*)

stamp—genus, kind, description, make, mark, impression, imprint, print, brand, cast, mold, character, type. (*heterogeneity, nondescription, formlessness*)

stand—rest, remain, stop, be, exist, keep one's ground, insist, depend, await, consist, hold, continue, endure, pause, halt. (*progress, move, proceed, advance, fall, fail, yield, succumb, drop, lie, vanish, fade, run, depart*)

standard—measure, gauge, criterion, test, rule, exemplar, banner, flag, type, model, scale, plummet, touchstone. (*mismeasurement, misrule, misadjustment, miscomparison, inconformity, misfit, incommensurateness, noncriterion*)

state—*n.* position, condition, situation, circumstances, plight, predicament, case, province.

state—*v.* say, declare, propound, aver, set forth, narrate, specify, avow, recite. (*suppress, repress, suppose, imply, deny, contradict, retract*)

stately—dignified, imposing, lofty, elevated, lordly, proud, majestic, pompous, magnificent, grand. (*undignified, unimposing, unstately, commonplace, mean*)

stay—hold, stop, restrain, withhold, arrest, hinder, delay, obstruct, support, rest, repose, remain, continue, dwell, await, halt, abide, wait, tarry, confide, trust, lean. (*loose, liberate, send, expedite, speed, free, accelerate, hasten, oppress, depress, burden, fail, fall, proceed, move, depart, overthrow, mistrust*)

steady—firm, fixed, constant, uniform, consistent, equable, regular, undeviating, well-regulated. (*infirm, variable, unsteady, inconstant, changeable, wavering, ill-regulated*)

step—advance, pace, space, grade, remove, degree, gradation, progression, track, trace, vestige, walk, gait, proceeding, action, measure. (*retreat, recession, halting, station, standing, nongraduation, nonprogression, standstill, stop, tracklessness, untraceableness, nonimpression, desinence, desistance, inaction*)

stern—severe, austere, rigid, harsh, strict, rigorous, unrelenting, unyielding, forbidding. (*lenient, genial, kindly, easy, flexible, encouraging*)

stiff—unbending, inflexible, rigid, unyielding, unpliant, strong, stubborn, obstinate, pertinacious, constrained, affected, starched, formal, ceremonious, difficult. (*pliant, flexible, flaccid, yielding, easy, unaffected, genial, affable, unceremonious*)

still—quiet, calm, noiseless, hushed, silent, pacific, serene, motionless, stagnant, peaceful, quiescent, tranquil, stationary. (*unquiet, disturbed, agitated, moved, noisy, resonant, turbulent, moving, transitional*)

stingy—close, avaricious, mean, niggardly, close-fisted, hidebound, parsimonious, sparing, sordid, penurious. (*liberal, generous, large, handsome, lavish, bountiful, unsparing*)

stop—close, obstruct, plug, cork, bar, seal, arrest, suspend, end, rest, halt, hinder, suppress, delay, cease, terminate. (*open, expedite, clear, broach, unseal, promote, advance, further, continue, proceed, speed, hasten*)

stout—strong, lusty, vigorous, robust, sturdy,

Synonym
Ant/Hom

brawny, corpulent, resolute, brave, valiant, redoubtable. (*weak, debile, frail, attenuated, thin, slender, lean, irresolute, feeble, cowardly, timid*)

straight—direct, rectilinear, undeviating, unswerving, right, nearest. (*indirect, winding, incurved, tortuous, sinuous, serpentine, circuitous, waving, crooked*)

strange—foreign, alien, exotic, unfamiliar, unusual, odd, irregular, abnormal, exceptional, surprising, wonderful, marvelous, astonishing, uncommon, peculiar. (*home, domestic, familiar, usual, ordinary, common, regular, customary, commonplace, unsurprising, universal, general*)

strength—force, vigor, power, security, validity, vehemence, intensity, hardness, soundness, nerve, fiber, sinew. (*weakness, imbecility, feebleness, insolidity, insecurity, invalidity, frailty, delicacy, softness, flimsiness, hollowness*)

strenuous—strong, resolute, determined, earnest, vigorous, ardent, bold, energetic, vehement. (*weak, irresolute, undetermined, unearnest, debile, feeble, emasculate*)

strict—close, exact, accurate, rigorous, severe, stringent, nice, precise. (*loose, inexact, inaccurate, lenient, mild, indulgent, lax*)

striking—impressive, affecting, admirable, wonderful, surprising.

strong—powerful, vigorous, solid, secure, fortified, forcible, impetuous, hale, hearty, brawny, sinewy, sound, robust, cogent, influential, zealous, potent, pungent, muscular, hardy, stanch, tenacious. (*powerless, weak, frail, insecure, defenseless, feeble, mild, calm, gentle, delicate, sickly, inefficacious, unsatisfactory, unconvincing, unimpressive, vapid, impotent, unavailing, lukewarm, debile, flaccid, nerveless, tender, moderate, indifferent*)

stubborn—tough, unbending, unyielding, hard, obstinate, intractable, obdurate, stiff, harsh, inflexible, headstrong, refractory, heady, contumacious, pigheaded. (*docile, tractable, manageable, pliant, pliable, malleable, flexible*)

studious—literary, diligent, desirous, attentive, careful, thoughtful, assiduous, reflective. (*unliterary, illiterate, idle, indulgent, careless, regardless, indifferent, inattentive, negligent, thoughtless*)

stupid—dull, senseless, stolid, doltish, besotted, insensate, obtuse, prosy, addlepated, dull-witted. (*quick, sharp, bright, sensible, sagacious, penetrating, clever*)

subdue—conquer, reduce, overpower, break, tame, quell, vanquish, master, subjugate. (*aggrandize, exalt, fortify, strengthen, empower, liberate, enfranchise*)

subject—subordinate, subservient, exposed, liable, prone, disposed, obnoxious, amenable. (*superior, independent, exempt, indisposed, unliable, unamenable*)

submissive—obedient, compliant, yielding, obsequious, humble, docile, modest, passive, acquiescent, subservient. (*disobedient, incompliant, unyielding, inobsequious, recalcitrant, refractory, proud, resistant, renitent, malcontent, recusant*)

substantial—existing, real, solid, true, corporeal, material, strong, stout, massive, bulky, tangible. (*imaginary, unreal, insubstantial, fictitious, sup-*

positious, incorporeal, chimerical, visionary, immaterial, weak, frail, airy, disembodied, spiritual)

subtle—sly, artful, cunning, insinuating, wily, astute, nice, discriminating, crafty, fine, shrewd, sophistical, jesuitical. (*open, frank, honest, artless, undiscriminating, rough, blunt, undiscerning, unsophisticated, simple*)

success—achievement, luck, consummation, prosperity, victory, good fortune. (*failure, defeat, disaster, ruin*)

succession—following, supervention, consecutive, sequence, order, series, rotation, continuity, supply, suite. (*precedence, anticipation, prevention, antecedence, irregularity, disorder, nonsequence, solution, failure, intermission, break, gap, inconsecutiveness*)

suffer—bear, endure, sustain, undergo, let, permit, allow, admit, tolerate, experience, support. (*resist, repel, expel, reject, disallow, repudiate, forbid, ignore*)

sufficient—adequate, equal, competent, satisfactory, fit, qualified, adapted, suited, enough, ample. (*inadequate, unequal, incompetent, unqualified, unadapted, insufficient, unsuited, meager, bare, scanty, short, deficient*)

suit—fit, adapt, match, adjust, harmonize, apportion, befit, beseem, tally, correspond, answer, comport, please, serve, agree, become, accord. (*misfit, misadapt, mismatch, misapportion, unbeseem, vary, differ, disagree, miscomport*)

summary—analysis, tabulation, abridgment, résumé, compendium, digest, epitome, abstract. (*dilatation, expansion, dilution*)

superb—grand, magnificent, elegant, princely, splendid, showy, proud, august, stately, gorgeous. (*mean, common, commonplace, unimposing, shabby*)

supercilious—haughty, contemptuous, disdainful, arrogant, insolent. (*affable, courteous, respectful, modest, bashful*)

superficial—light, slight, imperfect, showy, external, flimsy, surface, shallow, smattering, skindeep. (*deep, profound, abstruse, recondite, accurate, exact, deep-seated*)

superior—higher, upper, better, preferable, surpassing, loftier, excellent, remarkable, eminent, conspicuous. (*inferior, lower, worse, subordinate, ordinary, common, unremarkable, average, mean, mediocre*)

supple—pliant, bending, yielding, flexible, elastic, servile, fawning, cringing, adulatory, sycophantic, lithe, limber, compliant. (*firm, unbending, unyielding, stiff, stubborn, inflexible, inelastic, independent, self-assertive, supercilious*)

supply—furnish, afford, provide, accouter, give, minister, yield, contribute. (*expend, use, consume, waste, exhaust, absorb, demand, withhold, withdraw, retain*)

support—*n.* prop, stay, foundation, buttress, help, aid, assistance, influence, maintenance, living, patronage, subsistence, livelihood, food.

support—*v.* bear, uphold, sustain, underlie, befriend, assist, second, promote, further, suffer, defend, foster, nurture, nourish, cherish, endorse, maintain, continue, countenance, patronize, subsidize, help, back, stay, favor, prop. (*drop, betray,* surrender, abandon, discontinue, oppose, discourage, weaken, exhaust, thwart, discountenance, disfavor, subvert, suppress)

suppose—assume, presume, believe, divine, deem, fancy, think, regard, conceive, imagine, imply, presuppose, conjecture, guess, conclude, judge, consider. (*prove, demonstrate, substantiate, realize, disbelieve, negative, deny*)

sure—certain, secure, safe, assured, unmistakable, stable, firm, knowing, believing, confident, trusting, unquestioning, positive, unfailing, strong, permanent, abiding, enduring, infallible, indisputable, fast. (*uncertain, ignorant, dubious, doubtful, hesitating, distrustful, questioning, vacillating, weak, untrustworthy, precarious, insecure, impermanent, transient, evanescent, fallible, disputable, loose*)

susceptible—capable, impressible, tender, sensitive. (*incapable, unimpressible, insensitive, insusceptible, impassible*)

suspense—protraction, uncertainty, doubt, solicitude, cessation, pause, waiting, intermission, discontinuance, abeyance, stoppage, indetermination, incertitude, indecision. (*determination, settlement, execution, continuance, uninterruption, revival, decision, finality*)

sway—*n.* wield, influence, rule, authority, government, superiority, bias, dominion, control, preponderance, domination, supremacy, mastery, ascendancy, weight, force, power. (*weakness, inferiority, subordination, irresistance, obedience, subservience, subjection*)

sway—*v.* influence, govern, rule, bias, wave, swing, wield.

sweet—saccharine, luscious, fragrant, dulcet, melodious, harmonious, musical, beautiful, lovely, wholesome, pleasing, pure, mild, winning, agreeable, fresh, gentle, amiable. (*sour, bitter, unsweet, fetid, offensive, nauseous, olid, stinking, nasty, inharmonious, discordant, unlovely, repulsive, unwholesome, putrid, tainted, ungentle, unamiable*)

swell—dilate, extend, enlarge, heighten, heave, enhance, rise, expand, increase, augment, protuberate, aggravate, amplify, distend. (*contract, curtail, shrivel, diminish, lessen, retrench, reduce, collapse, fold, narrow, condense, concentrate*)

sympathy—fellow feeling, congeniality, commiseration, compassion, pity, concert, tenderness, agreement, condolence. (*antipathy, antagonism, incongeniality, pitilessness, mercilessness, compassionlessness, unkindness, harshness, unkindliness*)

system—method, scheme, order, regularity, classification, arrangement, rule, plan. (*disorder, derangement, confusion, fortuity, chance, medley, haphazard, incongruity, nonarrangement, nonclassification*)

T

take—seize, grasp, catch, capture, siege, use, obtain, pursue, employ, follow, assume, procure, captivate, engage, interest, charm, choose, select, admit, accept, receive, conduct, transfer. (*drop, reject, abandon, surrender, lose, miss, repel*)

tall—high, lofty, towering, elevated. (*low*)

tame—domesticated, reclaimed, tamed, subjugated, broken, gentle, mild, docile, meek, spiritless, tedious, dull, flat. (*undomesticated, unre-*

claimed, untamed, unbroken, savage, wild, fierce, spirited, animated, ferine, interesting, exciting, stirring, lively)

task—work, function, labor, job, operation, business, undertaking, drudgery, toil, lesson. (*relaxation, leisure, amusement, hobby*)

taste—gustation, savor, flavor, sapidity, relish, perception, judgment, discernment, nicety, critique, sensibility, choice, zest, predilection, delicacy, elegancy, refinement. (*nongustation, illsavor, insipidity, disrelish, nonperception, indiscrimination, indiscernment, indelicacy, coarseness, inelegancy*)

tasteful—sapid, relishing, savory, agreeable, tasty, toothsome, palatable, elegant, refined. (*insipid, unrelishing, unsavory, unpalatable, nauseous, inelegant, tasteless, unrefined, vapid*)

teach—impart, tell, direct, instruct, inform, counsel, admonish, educate, inculcate, enlighten, advise, indoctrinate, train. (*withhold, misteach, misdirect, misinstruct, misinform, misguide, mislead*)

teacher—instructor, schoolmaster, preceptor, tutor, professor, pedagogue, educationist, educator, schoolmistress. (*pupil, scholar, disciple, learner*)

tedious—wearisome, tiresome, monotonous, dilatory, dreary, sluggish, irksome, dull, flat, prolix. (*interesting, exciting, stirring, charming, fascinating, delightful, amusing*)

tell—mention, number, enumerate, count, recount, utter, recite, state, narrate, disclose, publish, betray, divulge, promulgate, acquaint, teach, inform, explain, communicate, report, rehearse, discern, judge, discriminate, ascertain, decide, describe. (*repress, suppress, misrecount, misnarrate, miscommunicate, misdeclare, misrecite, misjudge, misdescribe*)

temporary—present, immediate, partial, limited, transient, impermanent. (*perpetual, lasting, confirmed, complete, final, perfect, permanent, entire*)

tendency—vergency, proneness, bias, gravitation, drift, scope, aim, disposition, predisposition, proclivity, leaning, inclination, attraction, conduciveness, course. (*disinclination, aversion, repulsion, contravention, deviation, divergency, tangency, divarication, opposition, renitency, reluctance, prevention, neutralization, termination*)

tender—*v.* offer, proffer, propose, bid, produce, present. (*withhold, withdraw, retain, appropriate*)

tender—*a.* delicate, frail, impressible, susceptible, yielding, soft, effeminate, weak, feeble, compassionate, affectionate, careful, jealous, gentle, mild, meek, pitiful, merciful, pathetic. (*strong, sturdy, hardy, robust, tough, iron, pitiless, unmerciful, cruel, hard-hearted, careless, liberal, lavish, unchary, ungentle, rough, rude, coarse, unsentimental, unmoving, unfeeling, unimpressive, unimpassioned, unimpressed, vigorous, tenacious*)

term—limit, boundary, condition, time, season, period, expression, designation, word, name, article, proviso, stipulation.

terrible—awful, fearful, dreadful, formidable, terrific, frightful, tremendous, horrible, shocking. (*unimpressive, not startling or astonishing*)

terror—fear, dread, alarm, fright, consternation, horror, dismay. (*confidence, fearlessness, boldness, reassurance*)

test—cupel, trial, examination, proof, criterion,

standard, experiment, touchstone, experience, ordeal. (*misindication, misjudgment, misproof*)

testimony—witness, evidence, attestation, affirmation, corroboration, confirmation, proof. (*refutation, contradiction, disproof, confutation, contravention, invalidation*)

theatrical—dramatic, scenic, melodramatic, showy, ceremonious, gesticulatory, pompous, meretricious, tinsel. (*chaste, genuine, simple, unaffected, quiet, subdued, mannerless, plain*)

thick—dense, condensed, inspissated, close, compact, turbid, luteous, coagulated, muddy, dull, misty, foggy, vaporous, crowded, numerous, solid, bulky, deep, confused, inarticulate. (*race, fine, thin, sparse, strained, pure, percolated, limpid, crystalline, scanty, incompact, slight, shallow, laminated, clear, articulate, distinct*)

thicken—condense, inspissate, incrassate, compact, solidify, befoul, obscure, bemire, becloud, increase, coagulate, amalgamate, commingle, intermix, crowd, multiply, enlarge, expand, extend, broaden, deepen, obstruct, confuse. (*rarify, dissipate, refine, attenuate, clear, purify, strain, percolate, clarify, defecate, depurate, brighten, lighten, open, filtrate, diminish, separate, reduce, narrow, contract, liberate, free, extricate, unravel, disentangle, loosen*)

thin—slim, slender, flimsy, attenuated, diluted, watery, meager, unsubstantial, lean.

think—ponder, meditate, consider, reflect, contemplate, conceive, imagine, apprehend, fancy, hold, regard, believe, deem, opine, purpose, judge, reckon.

thought—reflection, reasoning, cogitation, supposition, view, sentiment, meditation, conception, idea, opinion, judgment, conceit, fancy, design, purpose, intention, deliberation, care, provision. (*vacuity, incogitation, thoughtlessness, dream, hallucination, aberration, misconception, incogitancy, carelessness, improvidence, unreflectiveness*)

threatening—menacing, intimidating, minatory, comminatory, minacious, foreboding, unpromising, imminent, impending. (*encouraging, promising, reassuring, enticing, passed, overpast, withdrawn*)

tide—flow, course, current, rush, inundation, influx, stream, movement, flood. (*stagnation, arrestation, stoppage, cessation, motionlessness, subsidence*)

tight—firm, compact, fast, close, tidy, neat, smart, natty, tense, stretched. (*loose, incompact, open, flowing, loose-fitting, large, untidy, lax, relaxed*)

time—period, duration, season, interval, date, opportunity, age, era, occasion, term, space, span, spell. (*neverness, eternity, nonduration, indetermination, indeterminableness*)

timid—fearful, pusillanimous, shy, diffident, coy, timorous, afraid, cowardly, fainthearted, inadventurous. (*bold, confident, venturesome, courageous, overventuresome, rash, audacious*)

tint—color, hue, tinge, dye, complexion. (*achromatism, decoloration, paleness, pallor, bleaching, etiolation, colorlessness, sallowness, wanness, cadaverousness, exsanguineousness*)

title—inscription, heading, denomination, style, designation, appellation, distinction, address, epithet, name. (*nondesignation, indistinction, nondescript, namelessness, indenomination*)

together—unitedly, conjointly, contemporaneously, concertedly, simultaneously, coincidently, concomitantly, concurrently. (*separately, disconnectedly, independently, variously, incoincidently, inconcurrently*)

tolerable—endurable, bearable, supportable, sufferable, allowable, permissible, sufficient, passable. (*unendurable, unbearable, insupportable, insufferable, unallowable, impermissible, insufficient, intolerable*)

tongue—discourse, speech, language, dialect, idiom.

tool—utensil, implement, machine, instrument, dupe, cat's-paw, hireling.

topic—question, theme, subject, subject matter.

tough—resistant, stubborn, lentous, fibrous, difficult, refractory, hard, unmanageable, tenacious, firm, strong. (*yielding, tender, soft, brittle, fragile, frangible, friable*)

tragedy—disaster, calamity, affliction, adversity, catastrophe, grief. (*joy, delight, boon, prosperity, comedy*)

train—*n.* suite, procession, retinue, cortege, course, series.

train—*v.* lead, rear, accustom, habituate, inure, drill, exercise, practice, discipline, instruct, bend, educate. (*force, break, trail, disaccustom, dishabituate, miseducate, disqualify*)

transfer—convey, transport, remove, sell, assign, remand, make over, transplant, give, alienate, translate, transmit, forward, exchange. (*retain, withhold, fix, appropriate, keep*)

transient—fleeting, fugitive, transitory, temporary, passing, evanescent, ephemeral, momentary, brief. (*abiding, permanent, perpetual, persistent, lasting, enduring*)

transparent—pellucid, crystalline, translucent, limpid, diaphanous, obvious, clear, indisputable, self-evident. (*thick, turbid, opaque, intransparent, mysterious, dubious, questionable*)

travel—journey, wandering, migration, pilgrimage, excursion, tramp, expedition, trip, ramble, voyage, tour, peregrination. (*rest, settlement, domestication*)

treatise—tract, essay, paper, pamphlet, disquisition, brochure, dissertation, monograph, article. (*jottings, notes, adversaria, memoranda, effusion, ephemera*)

treaty—contract, agreement, league, covenant, alliance, negotiation, convention. (*neutrality, noninterference, nonalliance, nonagreement, nonconvention*)

tremble—shake, quake, quiver, totter, shiver, shudder, vibrate, jar. (*stand, steady, settle, still, calm*)

tremendous—terrible, dreadful, awful, fearful, appalling. (*unimposing, unappalling, inconsiderable*)

trial—test, gauge, experiment, temptation, trouble, affliction, grief, burden, suffering, attempt, endeavor, proof, essay, criterion, ordeal, tribulation, verification. (*nontrial, nonprobation, mismeasurement, miscalculation, misestimate, trifle, triviality, alleviation, relief, disburdenment, refreshment, nonattempt, pretermission, oversight, disregard, nonverification*)

trick—artifice, contrivance, machination, guile, stratagem, wile, fraud, cheat, juggle, antic, vagary, finesse, sleight, deception, imposition, delusion, legerdemain. (*blunder, exposure, bungling, mishap, botch, fumbling, inexpertness, maladroitness, genuineness, openhandedness, artlessness*)

trifle—bauble, bagatelle, toy, straw, nothing, triviality, levity, joke, cipher, bubble, gewgaw, kickshaw, rush. (*treasure, portent, phenomenon, crisis, conjuncture, importance, urgency, weight, necessity, seriousness*)

triumph—victory, success, ovation, achievement, conquest, exultation, trophy. (*defeat, discomfiture, failure, unsuccess, abortion, baffling, disappointment*)

trivial—trifling, trite, common, unimportant, useless, nugatory, paltry, inconsiderable. (*important, weighty, critical, original, novel*)

trouble—*v.* disturb, vex, agitate, confuse, perplex, distress, annoy, harass, tease, molest, grieve, mortify, oppress. (*compose, calm, allay, appease, please, soothe, delight, gratify, recreate, entertain, relieve, refresh*)

trouble—*n.* affliction, disturbance, annoyance, perplexity, molestation, vexation, inconvenience, calamity, distress, uneasiness, tribulation, disaster, torment, misfortune, adversity, anxiety, embarrassment, sorrow, misery, grief, depression, difficulty, labor, toil, effort. (*alleviation, composure, pleasure, appeasement, delight, assuagement, happiness, gratification, boon, blessing, exultation, joy, gladness, ease, facility, luck, recreation, amusement, carelessness, indifference, indolence, inertia, indiligence*)

troublesome—tiresome, irksome, difficult, tedious, arduous, laborious, grievous, importunate, vexatious. (*easy, pleasant, amusing, facile, light, unlaborious, untroublesome*)

true—veritable, veracious, exact, precise, accurate, faithful, actual, loyal, genuine, pure, real. (*fictitious, unreliable, unhistorical, untrustworthy, inveracious, false, inaccurate, unfaithful, faithless, fickle, treacherous, erroneous, spurious, perfidious, counterfeit, adulterated*)

trust—*v.* confide, rely, credit, believe, charge, deposit, entrust, repose, hope. (*distrust, suspect, discredit, doubt, disbelieve, withdraw, despair*)

trust—*n.* faith, confidence, reliance, belief, hope, expectation, credit, duty, commission, charge.

try—attempt, endeavor, strive, aim, examine, test, sound, gauge, probe, fathom. (*ignore, pretermit, reject, abandon, discard, misexamine, misinvestigate*)

turn—*n.* revolution, rotation, recurrence, change, alteration, vicissitude, winding, bend, deflection, curve, alternation, opportunity, occasion, time, deed, office, act, treatment, purpose, requirement, convenience, talent, gift, tendency, character, exigence, crisis, form, cast, shape, manner, mold, fashion, cut. (*stability, fixity, immobility, stationariness, unchangeableness, uniformity, rectilinearity, indeflection, continuity, untimeliness, incognizance, oversight, independence, nonrequirement, malformation, shapelessness*)

turn—*v.* round, shape, mold, adapt, spin, reverse, deflect, alter, transform, convert, metamorphose, revolve, rotate, hinge, depend, deviate, incline, diverge, decline, change. (*misshape, perpetuate, stabilitate, stereotype, fix, arrest, continue, proceed*)

turncoat—trimmer, deserter, renegade.

tutor—guardian, governor, instructor, teacher,

preceptor, professor, master, savant. (*ward, pupil, scholar, student, disciple, learner, tyro*)

twine—twist, wind, embrace, entwine, wreath, bind, unite, braid, bend, meander. (*untwist, unwind, separate, disunite, detach, unwreath, unravel, disentwine, continue, straighten*)

twist—contort, convolve, complicate, pervert, distort, wrest, wreath, wind, encircle, form, weave, insinuate, unite, interpenetrate. (*straighten, untwist, rectify, verify, represent, reflect, render, preserve, express, substantiate, unwreath, unwind, detach, disengage, separate, disunite, disentangle, disincorporate, unravel*)

type—mark, stamp, emblem, kind, character, sign, symbol, pattern, archetype, form, model, idea, image, likeness, expression, cast, mold, fashion. (*nondescription, nonclassification, inexpression, misrepresentation, misindication, falsification, abnormity, deviation, caricature, monstrosity*)

U

ugly—loathesome, hideous, hateful, frightful, uncouth, ill-favored, unsightly, ill-looking, plain, homely, deformed, monstrous, ungainly. (*attractive, fair, seemly, shapely, beautiful, handsome*)

ultimate—last, final, extreme, conclusive, remotest, farthest. (*prior, intermediate, proximate, preliminary*)

unanimous—of one mind, agreeing, like-minded. (*discordant, disagreeing*)

unanswerable—unquestionable, indisputable, undeniable, incontrovertible.

uncertain—doubtful, dubious, questionable, fitful, equivocal, ambiguous, indistinct, variable, fluctuating.

undeniable—incontestable, indisputable, unquestionable, incontrovertible.

undergo—bear, suffer, endure, sustain, experience. (*evade, shun, elude*)

underhand—clandestine, furtive, dishonest, unfair, fraudulent, surreptitious. (*openhanded, straightforward, fair, honest, undisguised*)

understand—apprehend, comprehend, know, perceive, discern, conceive, learn, recognize, interpret, imply. (*misapprehend, miscomprehend, ignore, misinterpret, declare, state, enunciate, express*)

understanding—knowledge, discernment, interpretation, construction, agreement, intellect, intelligence, mind, sense, conception, reason, brains, (*ignorance, misapprehension, misunderstanding, misinterpretation, misconstruction, mindlessness, irrationality*)

unfit—*a.* improper, unsuitable, inconsistent, untimely, incompetent.

unfit—*v.* disable, incapacitate, disqualify, render unfit.

unfortunate—calamitous, ill-fated, unlucky, wretched, unhappy, miserable.

uniform—unvarying, invariable, conformable, homogeneous, consistent, equal, even, alike, unvaried, regular, symmetrical, equable. (*varying, variable, inconformable, incongruous, diverse, heterogeneous, inconsistent, irregular, unsymmetrical, multifarious, multigenous, polymorphic, bizarre, eccentric, erratic*)

union—junction, coalition, combination, agreement, harmony, conjunction, concert, league, connection, alliance, confederacy, concord, confederation, consolidation. (*disjunction, separation, severance, divorce, disagreement, discord, disharmony, secession, disruption, multiplication, diversification, division*)

unit—ace, item, part, individual. (*total, aggregate, collection, sum, mass*)

unite—join, combine, link, attach, amalgamate, associate, coalesce, embody, merge, be mixed, conjoin, connect, couple, add, incorporate with, cohere, concatenate, integrate, converge. (*disjoin, sever, dissociate, separate, disamalgamate, resolve, disconnect, disintegrate, disunite, disrupt, divide, multiply, part, sunder, diverge*)

unity—oneness, singleness, individuality, concord, conjunction, agreement, uniformity, indivisibility. (*plurality, multitude, complexity, multiplicity, discord, disjunction, separation, severance, variety, heterogeneity, diversity, incongruity, divisibility*)

universal—all-embracing, total, unlimited, boundless, comprehensive, entire, general, whole, exhaustive, complete. (*partial, local, limited, incomplete, exclusive, particular, inexhaustive, exceptional, narrow, special, only*)

unreasonable—foolish, silly, absurd, preposterous, immoderate, exorbitant, ridiculous.

upright—vertical, erect, perpendicular, honest, honorable, pure, principled, conscientious, just, fair, equitable. (*inverted, inclined, dishonest, dishonorable, corrupt, unprincipled, unconscientious*)

urge—press, push, drive, impel, propel, force, importune, solicit, animate, incite, instigate, stimulate, hasten, expedite, accelerate, dispatch. (*repress, hold, retain, inhibit, coerce, restrain, cohibit, hinder, retard, discourage, damp, obstruct*)

urgent—pressing, imperative, immediate, importunate, forcible, strenuous, serious, grave, momentous, indeferrable. (*unimportant, insignificant, trifling, trivial, deferrable*)

use—*n.* advantage, custom, habit, practice, service, utility, usage.

use—*v.* employ, exercise, treat, practice, accustom, habituate, inure. (*discard, suspend, ignore, avoid, dishabituate, disinure*)

useful—advantageous, profitable, helpful, serviceable, beneficial, available, adapted, suited, conducive. (*disadvantageous, unprofitable, obstructive, retardative, preventative, antagonistic, hostile, cumbersome, burdensome, unbeneficial, unavailable, inconducive, useless, fruitless, ineffectual*)

usual—common, customary, ordinary, normal, regular, habitual, wonted, accustomed, general. (*uncommon, rare, exceptional, uncustomary, extraordinary, abnormal, irregular, unusual*)

utter—*a.* extreme, perfect, complete, unqualified, absolute, thorough, consummate, entire, sheer, pure. (*imperfect, incomplete, impure*)

utter—*v.* circulate, issue, promulgate, express, articulate, pronounce, speak. (*recall, suppress, repress, hush, stifle, check, swallow*)

utterly—totally, completely, wholly, quite, altogether, entirely.

V

vacant—empty, leisure, unemployed, unencum-

bered, unoccupied, void, unfilled, mindless, exhausted. (*full, replenished, business, employed, engaged, occupied, filled, thoughtful*)

vague—general, lax, indefinite, undetermined, popular, intangible, equivocal, unsettled, uncertain, ill-defined, pointless. (*strict, definite, determined, limited, scientific, pointed, specific*)

vain—empty, worthless, fruitless, unsatisfying, unavailing, idle, ineffectual, egotistic, showy, unreal, conceited, arrogant. (*solid, substantial, sound, worthy, efficient, effectual, cogent, potent, unconceited, modest, real*)

valid—strong, powerful, cogent, weighty, sound, substantial, available, efficient, sufficient, operative, conclusive. (*weak, invalid, powerless, unsound, unsubstantial, unavailable, inefficient, insufficient, inoperative, obsolete, effete, superseded, inconclusive*)

value—appreciate, compute, rate, estimate, esteem, treasure, appraise, prize. (*miscompute, misestimate, disesteem, disregard, vilipend, underrate*)

vanity—emptiness, unsubstantiality, unreality, falsity, conceit, self-sufficiency, ostentation, pride, worthlessness, triviality. (*substance, solidity, substantiality, reality, truth, modesty, self-distrust, simplicity, unostentatiousness, humility*)

variable—changeable, mutable, fickle, capricious, wavering, unsteady, inconstant, shifting. (*unchanging, unchangeable, immutable, constant, firm*)

variation—deviation, alteration, mutation, diversity, departure, change, abnormity, exception, discrepancy. (*continuance, fixity, indivergency*)

variety—difference, diversity, medley, miscellany, multiplicity, multiformity, abnormity. (*uniformity, species, type, specimen*)

various—different, diverse, multiform, multitudinous, several, sundry, uncertain, manifold, diversified. (*one, same, identical, uniform, few*)

vast—waste, wild, desolate, extensive, spacious, widespread, gigantic, wide, boundless, measureless, enormous, mighty, huge, immense, colossal, prodigious, far-reaching. (*narrow, close, confined, frequented, populated, cultivated, tended, tilled, limited*)

vehement—violent, impetuous, ardent, burning, fervent, raging, furious, passionate, fervid, urgent, forcible, eager. (*mild, feeble, inanimate, subdued*)

vengeance—retribution, retaliation, revenge. (*forgiveness, pardon, condonation, amnesty, grace, remission, absolution, oblivion, indulgence, reprieve*)

venture—speculation, risk, chance, hazard, stake, undertaking, luck experiment, throw. (*nonspeculation, caution, reservation, calculation, certainty, law*)

veracity—truth, truthfulness, credibility, exactness, accuracy.

verdict—finding, judgment, answer, opinion, decision, sentence. (*nondeclaration, indecision, indetermination*)

verge—tend, bend, slope, incline, approach, approximate, trend, bear. (*decline, deviate, revert, depart, recede, return, back, retrocede*)

verify—establish, confirm, fulfill, authenticate, substantiate, identify, realize, test, warrant, demonstrate. (*disestablish, subvert, fail, falsify, mistake*)

versed—skilled, practiced, conversant, acquainted, initiated, indoctrinated, clever, familiar, thoroughly acquainted, proficient. (*unskilled, illversed, unpracticed, inconversant, unfamiliar, un-*

initiated, ignorant, awkward, strange, unversed, untaught)

vex—tease, irritate, provoke, plague, torment, tantalize, bother, worry, pester, trouble, disquiet, afflict, harass, annoy. (soothe, appease, gratify, quiet)

vice—corruption, fault, defect, evil, crime, immorality, sin, badness. (purity, faultlessness, perfection, virtue, immaculateness, goodness, soundness)

vicious—corrupt, faulty, defective, bad, morbid, peccant, debased, profligate, unruly, impure, depraved. (pure, sound, perfect, virtuous, healthy)

victory—conquest, triumph, ovation, success. (failure, defeat, frustration, disappointment, abortion)

view—v. behold, examine, inspect, explore, survey, consider, contemplate, reconnoiter, observe, regard, estimate, judge. (ignore, overlook, disregard)

view—n. sight, vision, survey, examination, inspection, judgment, estimate, scene, representation, apprehension, sentiment, conception, opinion, object, aim, intention, purpose, design, end, light, aspect. (blindness, occultation, obscuration, darkness)

vile—cheap, worthless, valueless, low, base, mean, despicable, hateful, bad, impure, vicious, abandoned, abject, sinful, sordid, ignoble, wicked, villainous, degraded, wretched. (costly, rare, precious, valuable, high, exalted, noble, honorable, lofty)

villain—scoundrel, ruffian, wretch.

villainous—base, knavish, depraved, infamous.

vindicate—assert, maintain, uphold, clear, support, defend, claim, substantiate, justify, establish. (waive, abandon, surrender, forgo, disprove, disestablish, neutralize, nullify, destroy, subvert, annul)

violate—ravish, injure, abuse, disturb, hurt, rape, outrage, debauch, break, infringe, profane, transgress, disobey. (respect, foster, observe, regard)

violence—vehemence, impetuosity, force, rape, outrage, rage, profanation, injustice, fury, infringement, fierceness, oppression. (lenity, mildness, self-restraint, feebleness, gentleness, respect, forbearance)

virtue—power, capacity, strength, force, efficacy, excellence, value, morality, goodness, uprightness, purity, chastity, salubrity. (weakness, incapacity)

visible—perceptible, apparent, clear, plain, obvious, conspicuous, observable, discernible, palpable, manifest, distinguishable, evident. (imperceptible)

visionary—fanciful, dreamy, chimerical, baseless, shadowy, imaginary, unreal, fabulous, romantic. (actual, real, truthful, sound, substantial, palpable)

vivid—bright, brilliant, luminous, resplendent, lustrous, radiant, graphic, clear, lively, animated, stirring, striking, glowing, sunny, bright, scintillant. (dull, opaque, nonluminous, obscure, rayless, lurid)

volume—size, body, bulk, dimensions, book, work, tome, capacity, magnitude, compass, quantity. (diminutiveness, tenuity, minuteness, smallness)

voluntary—deliberate, spontaneous, free, intentional, optional, discretional, unconstrained, willing. (compulsory, coercive, necessitated, involuntary)

volunteer—offer, proffer, tend, originate. (withhold, refuse, suppress)

voluptuous—sensual, luxurious, self-indulgent, licentious, highly pleasant. (unsensual, abstinent)

vulgar—popular, general, loose, ordinary, public, vernacular, plebeian, uncultivated, unrefined, low, mean, coarse, underbred. (strict, scientific, philo-

sophical, restricted, technical, accurate, patrician, select, choice, cultivated, refined, polite, high-bred, stylish, aristocratic)

W

wages—remuneration, hire, compensation, stipend, salary, allowance. (gratuity, douceur, premium, bonus, grace)

wander—ramble, range, stroll, rove, expatiate, roam, deviate, stray, depart, err, swerve, straggle, saunter, navigate, circumnavigate, travel. (rest, stop, perch, bivouac, halt, lie, anchor, alight, settle)

want—deficiency, lack, failure, insufficiency, scantiness, shortness, omission, neglect, nonproduction, absence. (supply, sufficiency, provision)

wanton—wandering, roving, sportive, playful, frolicsome, loose, unbridled, uncurbed, reckless, unrestrained, irregular, licentious, dissolute, inconsiderate, heedless, gratuitous. (stationary, unroving, unsportive, unplayful, unfrolicsome, joyless, thoughtful, demure, sedate, discreet, staid, self-controlled)

warm—blood-warm, thermal, genial, irascible, hot, ardent, affectionate, fervid, fiery, glowing, enthusiastic, zealous, eager, excited, interested, animated. (frigid, cold, tepid, starved, indifferent)

warmth—ardor, glow, fervor, zeal, heat, excitement, intensity, earnestness, cordiality, animation, plait, complicate, intersect. (unravel, untwist, disunite, disentangle, extricate, simplify, enucleate)

waste—ruin, destroy, devastate, impair, consume, squander, dissipate, throw away, diminish, lavish, desolate, pine, decay, attenuate, dwindle, shrivel, wither, wane. (restore, repair, conserve, preserve, perpetuate, protect, husband, economize, utilize, hoard, treasure, enrich)

watchful—vigilant, expectant, wakeful, heedful, careful, observant, attentive, circumspect, wary, cautious. (unwatchful, invigilant, unwakeful, slumbrous, drowsy, heedless, careless, inobservant, inattentive, uncircumspect, unwary, incautious, distracted)

weak—feeble, infirm, enfeebled, powerless, debile, fragile, incompact, inadhesive, pliant, frail, soft, tender, milk and water, flabby, flimsy, wishy-washy, destructible, watery, diluted, imbecile, inefficient, spiritless, foolish, injudicious, unsound, undecided, unconfirmed, impressible, wavering, ductile, easy, malleable, unconvincing, inconclusive, vapid, pointless. (strong, vigorous, robust, muscular, nervous, powerful, sturdy, hard)

weaken—debilitate, enfeeble, enervate, dilute, impair, paralyze, attenuate, sap. (strengthen, invigorate, empower, corroborate, confirm)

wealth—influence, riches, mammon, lucre, plenty, affluence, abundance, opulence. (indigence, poverty, scarcity, impecuniosity)

wear—carry, bear, exhibit, sport, consume, don, waste, impair, rub, channel, groove, excavate, hollow, diminish. (doff, abandon, repair, renovate, renew, increase, swell, augment)

weary—fatigued, tired, exhausted, worn, jaded, debilitated, spent, toil-worn, faint. (fresh, vigorous, recruited, renovated, hearty)

weave—interlace, braid, intertwine, intermix, eagerness, vehemence, geniality, sincerity, passion, irascibility, emotion, life. (frigidity, frost, congelation, iciness, coldness, calmness, coolness, indiffer-

Synonym Ant/Hom

ence, torpidity, insensitiveness, apathy, slowness, ungeniality, insincerity, passionlessness, hypocrisy)

weight—gravity, ponderosity, heaviness, pressure, burden, importance, power, influence, efficacy, consequence, moment, impressiveness. *(lightness, levity, portableness, alleviation, unimportance, insignificance, weakness, inefficacy, unimpressiveness)*

well—rightly, thoroughly, properly, hale, sound, healthy, hearty. *(wrongly, imperfectly, improperly)*

white—colorless, pure, snowy, umblemished, unspotted, stainless, innocent, clear. *(black, impure)*

whole—total, entire, all, well, complete, sound, healthy, perfect, unimpaired, undiminished, integral, undivided, gross. *(partial, imperfect, incomplete, unsound, sick, impaired, diminished, fractional)*

wholesome—healthful, salubrious, salutary, salutiferous, beneficial, nutritious, healing. *(unhealthy, unhealthful, insalubrious, insalutary, prejudicial, unwholesome, deleterious, detrimental, morbific)*

wicked—evil, bad, godless, sinful, immoral, iniquitous, criminal, unjust, unrighteous, irreligious, profane, ungodly, vicious, atrocious, black, dark, foul, unhallowed, nefarious, naughty, heinous, flagitious, abandoned, corrupt. *(good, virtuous, just, moral, honest, pure)*

wild—untamed, undomesticated, uncultivated, uninhabited, desert, savage, uncivilized, unrefined, rude, ferocious, untrained, violent, ferine, loose, disorderly, turbulent, ungoverned, inordinate, disorderly, chimerical, visionary, incoherent, raving, distracted, haggard. *(tame, domesticated, cultivated coherent, mild, orderly, sane, calm)*

willful—purposed, deliberate, designed, intentional, prepense, premeditated, preconcerted, wayward, refractory, stubborn, self-willed, headstrong. *(undesigned, accidental, unintentional, unpremeditated, docile, obedient, amenable, manageable, deferential, considerate, thoughtful)*

wisdom—knowledge, erudition, learning, enlightenment, attainment, information, discernment, judgment, sagacity, prudence, light. *(ignorance, illiterateness, sciolism, indiscernment, injudiciousness, folly, imprudence, darkness, empiricism, smattering, inacquaintance)*

wit—mind, intellect, sense, reason, understanding, humor, ingenuity, imagination. *(mindlessness, senselessness, irrationality, dullness, stolidity, stupidity, inanity, doltishness, wash, vapidity, platitude)*

withhold—retain, keep, inhibit, cohibit, stay, restrain, refuse, stint, forbear, detain. *(grant, afford, furnish, provide, allow, permit, encourage, incite)*

withstand—oppose, resist, confront, thwart, face. *(yield, surrender, submit, acquiesce, countenance, support, encourage, aid, abet, back)*

witness—attestation, testimony, evidence, corroboration, cognizance, corroborator, eyewitness, spectator, auditor, testifier, voucher, earwitness. *(invalidation, incognizance, refutation, ignorance)*

wonder—amazement, astonishment, surprise, admiration, phenomenon, prodigy, portent, miracle, sign, marvel. *(inastonishment, indifference, apathy, unamazement, anticipation, expectation, familiarity, triviality)*

wonderful—amazing, astonishing, wondrous, admirable, strange, striking, surprising, awful, prodigious, portentous, marvelous, miraculous, supernatural, unprecedented, startling. *(unamazing, unastonishing, unsurprising, common, everyday, regular, normal, customary, usual, expected, anticipated, calculated, current, natural, unwonderful, unmarvelous)*

word—term, expression, message, account, tidings, order, vocable, signal, engagement, promise. *(idea, conception)*

work—exertion, effort, toil, labor, employment, performance, production, product, effect, result, composition, achievement, operation, issue, fruit, *(effortlessness, inertia, rest, inoperativeness, nonemployment, nonperformance, nonproduction, abortion, miscarriage, frustration, neutralization, fruitlessness)*

worldly—terrestrial, mundane, temporal, secular, earthly, carnal. *(heavenly, spiritual)*

worry—harass, irritate, tantalize, importune, vex, molest, annoy, tease, torment, disquiet, plague, fret. *(soothe, calm, gratify, please, amuse, quiet)*

worth—value, rate, estimate, cost, price, merit, desert, excellent, rate. *(inappreciableness, cheapness, worthlessness, demerit)*

worthless—cheap, vile, valueless, useless, base, contemptible, despicable, reprobate, vicious. *(costly, rich, rare, valuable, worthy, useful, honorable, estimable, excellent, noble, precious, admirable, virtuous)*

wrench—wrest, twist, distort, strain, extort, wring.

wretched—miserable, debased, humiliated, fallen, ruined, pitiable, mean, paltry, worthless, vile, despicable, contemptible, sorrowful, afflicted, melancholy, dejected. *(flourishing, prosperous, happy, unfallen, admirable, noble, honorable, worthy, valuable, enviable, joyous, felicitous, elated)*

wrong—unfit, unsuitable, improper, mistaken, incorrect, erroneous, unjust, illegal, inequitable, immoral, injurious, awry. *(fit, suitable, proper, correct, accurate, right, just, legal, equitable, fair, moral, beneficial, straight)*

Y

yearn—long, hanker, crave, covet, desire. *(loathe, revolt, recoil, shudder)*

yet—besides, nevertheless, notwithstanding, however, still, eventually, ultimately, at last, so far, thus far

yield—furnish, produce, afford, bear, render, relinquish, give in, let go, forgo, accede, acquiesce, resign, surrender, concede, allow, grant, submit, succumb, comply, consent, agree. *(withdraw, withhold, retain, deny, refuse, vindicate, assert, claim, disallow, appropiate, resist, dissent, protest, recalcitrate, struggle, strive)*

yielding—conceding, producing, surrendering, supple, pliant, submissive, accommodating, unresisting. *(firm, defiant, stiff, hard, unyielding, resisting, unfruitful)*

yoke—couple, conjoin, connect, link, enslave, subjugate. *(dissever, divorce, disconnect, liberate, release, manumit, enfranchise)*

youth—youngster, young, person, boy, lad, minority, adolescence, juvenility.

youthful—juvenile, young, early, fresh, childish, unripe, puerile, callow, immature, beardless. *(aged,* senile, *mature, decrepit, decayed, venerable, antiquated, superannuated*)

Z

zeal—ardor, interest, energy, eagerness, engagedness, heartiness, earnestness, fervor, enthusiasm.

(*apathy, indifference, torpor, coldness, carelessness, sluggishness, incordiality*)

zenith—height, highest point, pinnacle, acme, summit, culmination, maximum. (*nadir, lowest point, depth, minimum*)

zest—flavor, appetizer, gusto, gust, pleasure, enjoyment, relish, sharpener, recommendation, enhancement. (*distaste, disrelish, detriment*)

HOMONYMS

A

able, strong, skillful. **Abel**, a name.
accidence, rudiments. **accidents**, events.
acclamation, applause. **acclimation**, used to climate.
acts, deeds. **ax** or **axe**, a tool.
ad, advertisement. **add**, to increase.
adds, increases. **adze** or **adz**, a tool.
adherence, constancy. **adherents**, followers.
ail, pain, trouble. **ale**, a liquor.
air, atmosphere. **ere**, before. **heir**, inheritor.
aisle, passage. **isle**, island. **I'll**, I will.
ait, an island. **ate**, devoured. **eight**, a number.
ale, liquor. **ail**, pain, trouble.
all, everyone. **awl**, a tool.
allegation, affirmation. **allegation**, uniting.
aloud, with noise. **allowed**, permitted.
altar, for worship. **alter**, to change.
amend, to make better. **amende**, retraction.
anker, a measure. **anchor**, of a vessel.
Ann, a name. **an**, one.
annalist, historian. **analyst**, analyzer.
annalize, to record. **analyze**, to separate.
ant, insect. **aunt**, relative.
ante, before. **anti**, opposed to.
arc, part of a circle. **ark**, chest, boat.
arrant, bad. **errant**, wandering.
ascent, act of rising. **assent**, consent.
asperate, make rough. **aspirate**, give sound of "h."
asperation, making rough. **aspiration**, ambition.
assistance, help, aid. **assistants**, helpers.
ate, consumed or devoured. **ait**, an island. **eight**, a number.
Ate, a goddess. **eighty**, a number.
attendance, waiting on. **attendants**, those who attend, are in attendance.
aught, anything. **ought**, should.
augur, to predict. **auger**, a tool.
aune, a cloth measure. **own**, belonging to oneself.
aunt, relative. **ant**, insect.
auricle, external ear. **oracle**, counsel.
awl, a tool. **all**, everyone.
axe, a tool. **acts**, deeds.
axes, tools. **axis**, turning line.
aye, yes. **eye**, organ of sight. **I**, myself.

B

bacon, pork. **baken**, baked.
bad, wicked. **bade**, past tense of the verb TO BID.
bail, security. **bale**, a bundle.
bait, food to allure. **bate**, to lessen.
baize, cloth. **bays**, water, garland, horses.
bald, hairless. **bawled**, cried aloud.
balks, frustrates, refuses to proceed. **box**, case tree.
ball, round body, dance. **bawl**, to cry aloud.
bare, naked. **bear**, animal, to carry.
bard, poet. **barred**, fastened with a bar.
bark, cry of dog, rind of tree. **barque**, vessel.
baron, nobleman. **barren**, unfruitful.
baroness, baron's wife. **barrenness**, sterility.
base, mean. **bass**, musical term.
bask, to lie in warmth. **basque**, fitted tunic.
bass, musical term. **base**, mean.
batten, a board, to fatten. **baton**, a staff, a rod
bay, water, color, tree. **bey**, governor.
beach, seashore. **beech**, a tree.
bear, an animal, to carry. **bare**, naked.
beat, to strike. **beet**, vegetable.
beau, man of dress. **bow**, archery term.
bee, insect. **be**, to exist.
been, past participle of the verb TO BE. **bin**, container for grain.
beer, malt liquor. **bier**, carriage for the dead.
berry, fruit. **bury**, to inter.
berth, sleeping place. **birth**, act of being born.
better, superior. **bettor**, one who bets.
bey, governor. **bay**, sea, color, tree.
bier, carriage for the dead. **beer**, malt liquor.
bight, of a rope. **bite**, with the teeth.
billed, furnished with a bill. **build**, to erect.
bin, for grain. **been**, of the verb TO BE.
binocle, telescope. **binnacle**, compass box.
birth, being born. **berth**, sleeping place.
blew, did blow. **blue**, a color.
bloat, to swell. **blote**, to dry by smoke.
boar, swine. **bore**, to make a hole.
board, timber. **bored**, pierced, worried.
bold, courageous. **bowled**, rolled balls.
boll, a pod, a ball. **bowl**, basin. **bole**, earth, trunk of tree.
border, outer edge. **boarder**, lodger.

bourn, a limit, stream. borne, carried.
borough, a town. burrow, hole for rabbits.
bow, in archery. beau, a man of dress.
bow, to salute, part of ship. bough, branch of tree.
bowl, basin. bole, earth, trunk of tree. boll, a pod, a ball.
boy, male child. buoy, floating signal.
braid, to plait. brayed, did bray.
brake, device for retarding motion, a thicket. break, opening, to part.
bray, harsh sound. brae, broken ground.
breach, a gap, a break. breech, part of a gun.
bread, food. bred, brought up.
brewed, fermented. brood, offspring.
brews, to make malt liquor. bruise, to crush.
bridal, belonging to a wedding. bridle, a curb.
Briton, native of Briton. Britain, England, Scotland, Wales, Northern Ireland.
broach, to utter. brooch, a jewel.
brows, edges. browse, to feed.
bruit, noise, report. brute, a beast.
build, to erect. billed, furnished with a bill.
bun, small cake or bread. bonne, a nurse.
buoy, floating signal. boy, male child.
burrow, hole for rabbit. borough, a town.
bury, to cover with earth. berry, a fruit.
but, except, yet. butt, a cask, to push with head.
by, at, near. buy, to purchase.

C

cache, hole for hiding goods. cash, money.
caddy, a box. cadi, a Turkish judge.
Cain, man's name. cane, walking stick.
calendar, almanac. calender, to polish.
calk, to stop leaks. cauk or cawk, mineral.
call, to name. caul, a membrane.
can, could, tin vessel. Cannes, French city.
cannon, large gun. canon, a law, a rule.
canvas, cloth. canvass, to solicit, to examine.
capital, upper part, principal. capitol, statehouse.
carat, weight. caret, mark. carrot, vegetable.
carol, song of joy. Carroll, a name.
carrot, vegetable. carat, weight. caret, mark.
cash, money. cache, hole for hiding goods.
cask, wooden vessel. casque, a helmet.
cast, to throw, to mold. caste, rank.
castor, a beaver. caster, frame for bottles, roller.
caudal, tail. caudle, drink.
cause, that which produces. caws, cries of crows.
cede, to give up. seed, germ of plants.
ceiling, of a room. sealing, fastening.
cell, small room. sell, to part for price.
cellar, a room under house. seller, one who sells.
censor, critic. censer, vessel.
cent, coin. sent, caused to go. scent, odor.
cerate, a salve. serrate, shaped like a saw.
cere, to cover with wax. sear, dry. seer, a prophet.
cession, yielding. session, a sitting.
cetaceous, whale species. setaceous, bristly.
chagrin, ill-humor. shagreen, fish skin.
chance, accident. chants, melodies.
champaign, open country. champagne, a wine.

chaste, pure. chased, pursued.
cheap, inexpensive. cheep, a bird's chirp.
chews, masticates. choose, to select.
choir, singers. quire, of paper.
choler, anger. collar, neckwear.
chord, musical sound. cord, string. cored, taken from center.
chronical, a long duration. chronicle, history.
chuff, a clown. chough, a sea bird.
cilicious, made of hair. silicious, flinty.
cingle, a girth. single, alone, only one.
cion or scion, a sprout. sion or zion, mountain.
circle, round figure. sercle, a twig.
cit, a citizen. sit, to rest.
cite, to summon, to quote, to enumerate. site, situation. sight, view.
clause, part of a sentence. claws, talons.
climb, to ascend. clime, climate.
coal, fuel. cole, cabbage.
coaled, supplied with coal. cold, frigid, not hot.
coarse, rough. course, route. corse or corpse, dead body.
coat, garment. cote, sheepfold.
coddle, to fondle. see caudal.
codling, apples. coddling, parboiling.
coffer, money chest. cougher, one who coughs.
coin, money. quoin, wedge.
colation, straining. collation, a repast.
collar, neckwear. see choler.

colonel, officer. kernel, seed in a nut.
color, tint. culler, a chooser.
complacence, satisfaction. complaisance, affability, compliance.
complacent, civil. complaisant, seeking to please.
compliment, flattery. complement, the full number.
confidant, one trusted with secrets. confident, having full belief.
consonance, concord. consonants, letters which are not vowels.
consequence, that which follows. consequents, deduction.
consession, a sitting together. concession, a yielding.
coolly, without heat, calmly. coolie, East Indian laborer.
coom, soot. coomb, a measure.
coquet, to deceive in love. coquette, vain girl.
coral, from the ocean. corol, a corolla.
cord, string. chord, musical sound. cored, taken from center.
cores, inner parts. corps, soldiers.
correspondence, interchange of letters. correspondents, those who correspond.
council, assembly. counsel, advice.
cousin, relative. cozen, to cheat
coward, one without courage. cowered, frightened.
creak, harsh noise. creek, stream.
crewel, yarn. cruel, savage.
crews, seamen. cruise, voyage. cruse, a cruet.
cue, hint, rod, tail. queue, pigtail, waiting line.
culler, a selecter. color, a tint.
currant, fruit. current, flowing stream.
cygnet, a swan. signet, a seal.
cymbal, musical instrument. symbol, sign.
cypress, a tree. Cyprus, an island.

D

dam, wall for stream. damn, to doom or curse.
dammed, confined by banks. damned, doomed.
Dane, a native of Denmark. deign, condescend.
day, time. dey, a governor.
days, plural of day. daze, to dazzle.
dear, beloved, costly. deer, an animal.
deformity, defect. difformity, diversity of form.
deign, to condescend. Dane, native of Denmark.
demean, to behave. demesne, land.
dents, marks. dense, close, compact.
dependents, subordinates. dependence, reliance.
depravation, corruption. deprivation, loss.
descent, downward. dissent, disagreement.
descendent, falling. descendant, offspring.
desert, to abandon. dessert, last course of a meal.
deviser, contriver. divisor, a term in arithmetic.
dew, moisture. do, to perform. due, owed.
die, to expire, a stamp. dye, to color.
dire, dreadful. dyer, one who dyes.
discous, flat. discus, quoit.
discreet, prudent. discrete, separate.
doe, female deer. dough, unbaked bread.
does, female deer. doze, to slumber.
done, performed. dun, a color.
dost, from verb TO BE. dust, powdered earth.
drachm, weight. dram, small quantity.
draft, bill. draught, a drink, a potion.
dual, two. duel, combat.
due, owed. dew, moisture. do, to perform.
dun, color, ask for debt. done, finished.
dust, powdered earth. dost, from verb TO BE.
dye, to color. die, to expire, a stamp.
dyeing, staining. dying, expiring.
dyer, one who dyes. dire, dreadful.

E

earn, to gain by labor. urn, a vase.
eight, a number. ate, consumed or devoured.
eighty, a number. Ate, a goddess.
ere, before. air, atmosphere. heir, inheritor.
errant, wandering. arrant, bad.
ewe, female sheep. yew, tree. you, *pronoun*.
ewes, sheep. yews, trees. use, employ.
eye, organ of sight. I, myself. aye, yes.

F

fain, pleased. fane, temple. feign, pretend.
faint, languid. feint, pretense.
fair, beautiful, just. fare, price, food.
falter, to hesitate. faulter, one who commits a fault.
fane, temple. fain, pleased. feign, to pretend.
fare, price, food. fair, beautiful, just.
fate, destiny. fete, a festival.
faulter, one who commits a fault. falter, to hesitate.
fawn, young deer. faun, woodland deity.
feat, deed. feet, plural of foot.
feign, pretend. fain, pleased. fane, temple.
feint, pretense. faint, languid.
felloe, rim of wheel. fellow, companion.
feod, tenure. feud, quarrel.
ferrule, metallic band. ferule, wooden pallet.

feted, honored. fated, destined.
feud, quarrel. feod, tenure.
fillip, jerk of finger. Philip, man's name.
filter, to strain. philter, love charm.
find, to discover. fined, punished.
fir, tree. fur, animal hair.
fissure, a crack. fisher, fisherman.
fizz, hissing noise. phiz, the face.
flea, insect. flee, to run away.
flew, did fly. flue, chimney. flu, influenza.
flour, ground grain. flower, a blossom.
flue, chimney. flu, influenza. flew, did fly.
for, because of. fore, preceding. four, cardinal
    number.
fort, fortified place. forte, peculiar talent.
forth, forward. fourth, ordinal number.
foul, unclean. fowl, a bird.
four, cardinal number. for, because of. fore, pre-
    ceding.
fourth, ordinal number. forth, forward.
franc, French coin. Frank, a name, generous.
frays, quarrels. phrase, parts of a sentence.
freeze, to congeal with cold. frieze, cloth. frees,
    to set at liberty.
fungus, spongy excresence. fungous, as fungus.
fur, hairy coat of animals. fir, a tree.
furs, skins of beasts. furze, a shrub.

G

gage, a pledge, a fruit. gauge, a measure.
gait, manner of walking. gate, a door.
gall, bile. Gaul, a Frenchman.
gamble, to wager. gambol, to skip.
gantlet, punishment. gauntlet, a glove.
gate, a door. gait, manner of walking.
gauge, a measure. gage, a pledge, a fruit.
Gaul, a Frenchman. gall, bile.
gild, to overflow with gold. guild, a corporation.
gilt, gold on surface. guilt, crime.
glare, splendor. glair, white of an egg.
gneiss, rock similar to granite. nice, fine.
gnu, animal. new, not old. knew, understood.
gourd, a plant. gored, pierced.
grate, iron frame. great, large.
grater, a rough instrument. greater, larger.
great, large. grate, iron frame.
greater, larger. grater, a rough instrument.
Greece, country in Europe. grease, fat.
grisly, frightful. grizzly, an animal, gray.
groan, deep sigh. grown, increased.
grocer, merchant. grosser, coarser.
grown, increased. groan, deep sigh.
guessed, conjectured. guest, visitor.
guild, a corporation. gild, to overflow with gold.
guilt, crime. gilt, gold on surface.
guise, appearance. guys, ropes.

H

hail, ice, to salute. hale, healthy.
hair, of the head. hare, a rabbit.
hale, healthy. hail, ice, to salute.

hall, large room, a passage. **haul,** to pull.
hare, a rabbit. **hair,** of the head.
hart, an animal. **heart,** seat of life.
haul, to pull. **hall,** a large room, a passage.
hay, dried grass. **hey,** an expression.
heal, to cure. **heel,** part of foot or shoe, the end of a loaf of bread, a scoundrel.
hear, to hearken. **here,** in this place.
heard, did hear. **herd,** a drove.
heart, seat of life. **hart,** an animal.
heel, part of foot or shoe, the end of a loaf of bread, a scoundrel. **heal,** to cure.
heir, inheritor. **air,** atmosphere. **ere,** before.
herd, a drove. **heard,** did hear.
here, in this place. **hear,** to hearken.
hew, to cut down. see **hue.**
hey, an expression. **hay,** dried grass.
hide, skin, to conceal. **hied,** hastened.
hie, to hasten. **high,** lofty, tall.
hied, hastened. **hide,** skin, to conceal.
higher, more lofty. **hire,** to employ.
him, that man. **hymn,** sacred song.
hire, to employ. **higher,** more lofty.
hoa, exclamation. **ho,** cry, stop. **hoe,** tool.
hoard, to lay up. **horde,** tribe.
hoarse, rough voice. **horse,** animal.
hoe, tool. **ho,** cry, stop. **hoa,** exclamation.
hoes, tools. **hose,** stockings, tubing.
hole, cavity. **whole,** all, entire.
holm, evergreen oak. **home,** dwelling.
holy, pure sacred. **wholly,** completely.
home, dwelling. **holm,** evergreen oak.
horde, tribe. **hoard,** to lay up.
horse, animal. **hoarse,** rough voice.
hose, stockings, tubing. **hoes,** tools.
hour, sixty minutes. **our,** belonging to us.
hue, color. **hew,** to cut down. **Hugh,** man's name.
hymn, sacred song. **him,** that man.

I

idol, image. **idle,** unemployed. **idyl,** poem.
I'll, I will. **isle,** island. **aisle,** passage.
in, within. **inn,** a tavern.
indict, to accuse. **indite,** to dictate, write, compose.
indiscreet, imprudent. **indiscrete,** not separated.
indite, to dictate. **indict,** to accuse.
inn, a tavern. **in,** within.
innocence, purity. **innocents,** harmless things.
instants, moments. **instance,** example.
intense, extreme. **intents,** designs.
intention, purpose. **intension,** energetic use or exercise.
intents, designs. **intense,** extreme.
invade, to infringe. **inveighed,** censured.
irruption, invasion. **eruption,** bursting forth.
isle, island. **I'll,** I will. **aisle,** passage.

J

jail, prison. **gaol,** prison.
jam, preserves. **jamb,** side of door.

K

kernel, seed in nut. **colonel,** officer.
key, for a lock. **quay,** wharf.
knag, knot in wood. **nag,** small horse.
knap, protuberance, noise. **nap,** short sleep.
knave, rogue. **nave,** center, hub.
knead, work dough. **need,** want. **kneed,** having knees.
kneel, to rest on knee. **neal,** to temper.
knew, understood. **gnu,** animal. **new,** not old.
knight, title of honor. **night,** darkness.
knit, unite, weave, frown. **nit,** insect's egg.
knot, tied. **not,** word of refusal.
know, understand. **no,** not so.
knows, understands. **nose,** organ of smell.

L

lack, to want. **lac,** gum.
lacks, wants, needs. **lax,** loose, slack.
lade, to load. **laid,** placed, produced eggs.
lane, a road. **lain,** rested.
Latin, language. **latten,** brass.
lax, loose, slack. **lacks,** wants, needs.
lea, meadow. **lee,** shelter place.
leach, to filtrate. **leech,** a worm.
lead, metal. **led,** guided.
leaf, part of a plant. **lief,** willingly.
leak, a hole. **leek,** a plant.
lean, not fat, to rest, to slant. **lien,** mortgage.
leased, rented. **least,** smallest.
led, guided. **lead,** metal.
lee, shelter, place. **lea,** meadow.
leech, a worm. **leach,** to filtrate.
leek, a plant. **leak,** a hole.
lesson, task. **lessen,** to diminish.
levee, bank, visit. **levy,** to collect.
liar, falsifier. **lyre,** musical instrument. **lier,** one who lies down.
lie, falsehood. **lye,** liquid.
lief, willingly. **leaf,** part of a plant.
lien, legal claim. **lean,** not fat, to rest, to slant.
lightning, electricity. **lightening,** unloading.
limb, branch. **limn,** to draw.
links, connecting rings. **lynx,** an animal.
lo, look, see. **low,** not high, mean.
loan, to lend. **lone,** solitary.
lock, hair, fastening. **loch** or **lough,** lake.
lone, solitary. **loan,** to lend.
low, not high, mean. **lo,** look, see.
lusern, a lynx. **lucerne,** clover.
lye, liquid. **lie,** falsehood.
lynx, animal. **links,** connecting rings.
lyre, musical instrument. **liar,** falsifier. **lier,** one who lies down.

M

made, created. **maid,** unmarried woman.
mail, armor, post bag. **male,** masculine.
main, principal. **mane,** hair. **Maine,** a state.
maize, corn. **maze,** intricate.
male, masculine. **mail,** armor, post bag.

mall, hammer, walk. **maul**, to beat.

manner, method. **manor**, landed estate.

mantel, chimney piece. **mantle**, a cloak.

mark, visible line. **marque**, a pledge.

marshall, officer. **martial**, warlike.

marten, an animal. **martin**, a bird.

martial, warlike. **marshall**, officer.

maul, to beat. **mall**, hammer, walk.

mead, drink. **meed**, reward. **Mede**, native of Media.

mean, low. **mien**, aspect.

meat, food. **meet**, to encounter, a match, suitable.

Mede, native of Media. **mead**, drink. **meed**, reward.

meddle, interfere. **medal**, a token.

meddler, one who meddles. **medlar**, a tree.

meed, reward. **mead**, drink. **Mede**, native of Media.

meet, to encounter a match, suitable. **meat**, food.

mettle, spirit, courage. **metal**, mineral.

mew or **mue**, to melt. **mew**, fowl enclosure.

mewl, to cry. **mule**, an animal.

mews, cat cries. **muse**, deep thought.

mien, look aspect. **mean**, low.

might, power. **mite**, insect.

mighty, powerful. **mity**, having mites.

mince, to cut. **mints**, coining places.

miner, worker in mines. **minor**, one underage.

mints, coining places. **mince**, to cut.

missal, book. **missel**, bird. **missile**, weapon

mite, insect, small. **might**, power.

mity, having mites. **mighty**, powerful.

moan, lament. **mown**, cut down.

moat, ditch. **mote**, small particle.

mode, manner. **mowed**, cut down.

morning, before noon. **mourning**, grief.

mote, small particle. **moat**, ditch.

mowed, cut down. **mode**, manner.

mucous, slimy. **mucus**, a fluid.

mue, to molt. **mew**, fowl enclosure.

mule, an animal. **mewl**, to cry.

muscat, grape. **musket**, gun.

muse, deep thought. **mews**, cat cries.

mustard, plant. **mustered**, assembled.

N

nag, small horse. **knag**, knot in wood.

nap, short sleep. **knap**, protuberance, noise.

naval, nautical. **navel**, center of abdomen.

nave, center, hub. **knave**, rogue.

navel, center of abdomen. **naval**, nautical.

nay, no. **neigh**, whinny of a horse.

neal, to temper. **kneel**, to rest on knee.

need, necessity, want. **knead**, work dough. **kneed**, having knees.

neigh, whinny of a horse. **nay**, no.

new, not old. **gnu**, animal. **knew**, understood.

nice, fine. **kneiss**, rock similar to granite.

night, darkness. **knight**, title of honor.

nit, insect's egg. **knit**, to unite, to form.

no, not so. **know**, to understand.

none, no one. **nun**, female devotee.

nose, organ of smell. **knows**, understands.

not, word of refusal. **knot**, a tie.

nun, female devotee. **none**, no one.

O

oar, rowing blade. **o'er**, over. **ore**, mineral.

ode, poem. **owed**, under obligation.

o'er, over. **oar**, paddle. **ore**, mineral.

oh, denoting pain. **O!** surprise. **owe**, indebted.

one, single unit. **won**, gained.

onerary, fit for burdens. **honorary**, conferring honor.

oracle, counsel. **auricle**, external ear.

ordinance, a law. **ordnance**, military supplies.

ore, mineral. **o'er**, over. **oar**, paddle.

ottar, oil of roses. **otter**, an animal.

ought, should. **aught**, anything.

our, belonging to us. **hour**, sixty minutes.

owe, to be indebted. **oh**, denoting surprise. **O!** surprise.

owed, under obligation. **ode**, poem.

P

paced, moved slowly. **paste**, flour and water mixed.

packed, bound in a bundle. **pact**, contract.

pail, bucket. **pale**, whitish.

pain, agony. **pane**, a square of glass.

pair, a couple, two. **pare**, to peel. **pear**, a fruit.

palace, princely home. **Pallas**, heathen deity.

palate, organ of taste. **pallette**, artist's board. **pallet**, a bed.

pale, whitish. **pail**, bucket.

pall, covering for the dead. **Paul**, man's name.

pare, to peel. **pair**, a couple, two. **pear**, a fruit.

passable, tolerable. **passible**, with feeling.

paste, flour and water mixed. **paced**, moved slowly.

patience, calmness. **patients**, sick persons.

paw, foot of a beast. **pa**, papa.

paws, beasts' feet. **pause**, stop.

peace, quiet. **piece**, a part.

peak, the top. **pique**, grudge. **peek**, to peep.

peal, loud sound. **peel**, to pare.

pealing, sounding loudly. **peeling**, rinds.

pear, a fruit. **pair**, a couple, two. **pare**, to peel.

pearl, a precious substance. **purl**, a knitting stitch.

pedal, for the feet. **peddle**, to sell.

peek, to peep. **peak**, the top. **pique**, grudge.

peer, nobleman. **pier**, column, wharf.

pencil, writing instrument. **pensile**, suspended.

pendant, an ornament. **pendent**, hanging.

philter, love charm. **filter**, to strain.

phiz, the face. **phizz**, hissing noise.

phrase, expression. **frays**, quarrels.

piece, a part. **peace**, quiet.

pier, a column, wharf. **peer**, nobleman.

pique, grudge. **peak**, the top. **peek**, to peep.

pistil, part of a flower. **pistol**, firearm.

place, situation. **plaice**, a fish.

plain, clear, simple. **plane**, flat surface, tool.

pleas, arguments. **please**, to delight.

plum, a fruit. **plumb**, perpendicular, leaden weight.

pole, stick. **poll**, the head.

pool, water. **poule** or **pool**, stakes played for.

pore, opening. **pour**, cause to flow.

poring, looking intently. **pouring**, raining, flowing.

port, harbor. **porte**, Turkish court.

praise, commendation. **prays**, entreats, petitions. **preys**, feeds by violence, plunders.

pray, to supplicate. **prey**, plunder.

presence, being present. **presents**, gifts.

pride, self-esteem. **pried**, moved by a lever.

prier, inquirer. **prior,** previous.
pries, looks into. **prize,** reward.
prints, impressions. **prince,** king's son.
principal, chief. **principle,** an element.
prior, previous. **prier,** inquirer.
prize, reward. **pries,** looks into.
profit, gain. **prophet,** a foreteller.
purl, a knitting stitch. **pearl,** precious substance.

Q

quarts, measure. **quartz,** rock crystal.
quay, wharf. **key,** lock fastener.
queen, king's wife. **quean,** worthless woman.
queue, pigtail, waiting line. **cue,** hint, rod.
quire, package of paper. **choir,** church singers.
quoin, a wedge. **coin,** money.

R

rabbet, a joint. **rabbit,** small animal.
radical, of first principles. **radicle,** a root.
rain, water. **reign,** rule. **rein,** bridle.
raise, to lift. **rays,** sunbeams. **raze,** to demolish.
raised, lifted. **razed,** demolished.
raiser, one who raises. **razor,** shaving blade.
rancor, spite. **ranker,** stronger, more immoderate.
rap, to strike. **wrap,** to fold.
rapped, quick blows. **wrapped,** enclosed.
rapping, striking. **wrapping,** a cover.
rays, sunbeams. **raise,** to lift. **raze,** to demolish.
raze, to demolish. **raise,** to lift. **rays,** sunbeams.
razed, demolished. **raised,** lifted.
razor, shaving blade. **raiser,** one who raises.
read, to peruse. **reed,** a plant.
real, true. **reel,** winding machine, to stagger.
receipt, acknowledgment. **reseat,** to sit again.
reck, to heed. **wreck,** destruction.
red, color. **read,** perused.
reek, to emit vapor. **wreak,** to inflict.
reel, winding machine, to stagger. **real,** true.
reign, rule. **rein,** bridle. **rain,** water.
reseat, to seat again. **receipt,** acknowledgment.
residence, place of abode. **residents,** citizens.
rest, quiet. **wrest,** to twist.
retch, to vomit. **wretch,** miserable person.
rheum, thin, water matter. **room,** space.
Rhodes, name of an island. **roads,** highways.
rhumb, point of a compass. **rum,** liquor.
rhyme, harmonical sound. **rime,** hoar frost.
rigger, rope fixer. **rigor,** severity.
right, correct. **rite,** ceremony. **write,** to form letters.
rime, hoar frost. **rhyme,** harmonical sound.
ring, circle, sound. **wring,** to twist.
road, way. **rode,** did ride. **rowed,** did row.
roads, highways. **Rhodes,** name of an island.
roan, color. **rown,** impelled by oars. **Rhone,** river.
roe, deer. **row,** to impel with oars, a line.
roes, eggs, deer. **rows,** uses oars. **rose,** a flower.
Rome, city in Italy. **roam,** to wander.
rood, a measure. **rude,** rough.
rote, memory of words. **wrote,** did write.
rough, not smooth. **ruff,** plaited collar.
rouse, stir up, provoke. **rows,** disturbances.
rout, rabble, disperse. **route,** road.
row, to impel with oars, a line. **roe,** a deer.

rowed, did row. **road,** way. **rode,** did ride.
rows, uses oars. **roes,** deer. **rose,** a flower.
rude, rough. **rood,** measure.
ruff, collar. **rough,** not smooth.
rum, liquor. **rhumb,** point of a compass.
rung, sounded, a step. **wrung,** twisted.
rye, grain. **wry,** crooked.

S

sail, canvas of a ship. **sale,** traffic.
sailer, vessel. **sailor,** seaman.
sale, traffic. **sail,** canvas of a ship.
sane, sound, in mind. **seine,** fish net.
saver, one who saves. **savor,** taste, scent.
scene, a view. **seen,** viewed.
scent, odor. **sent,** caused to go. **cent,** coin.
scion or **cion,** sprout. **sion** or **zion,** a mountain.
scull, oar, boat. **skull,** bone of the head.
sea, ocean. **see,** to perceive.
seal, stamp, an animal. **seel,** to keel over, **to close** the eyes.
sealing, fastening. **ceiling,** top of a room.
seam, a juncture. **seem,** to appear.
seamed, joined together. **seemed,** appeared.
sear, to burn. **cere,** wax.
seas, water. **sees,** looks. **seize,** take hold of.
seed, germ of a plant. **cede,** to give up.
seen, viewed. **scene,** a view.
seine, a net. **sane,** sound in mind.
sell, to part for price. **cell,** small room.
seller, one who sells. **cellar,** room.
senior, elder. **seignoir,** a title.
sense, feeling. **scents,** odors. **cents,** coins. **cense,** tax.
sent, caused to go. **scent,** odor. **cent,** coin.
serf, a slave. **surf,** of the sea.
serge, a cloth. **surge,** a billow.
serrate, notched, like a saw. **cerate,** salve.
session, a sitting. **cession,** a yielding.
setaceous, bristly. **cetaceous,** whale species
sew, to stitch. **sow,** to scatter seed. **so,** in this manner.
sewer, one who uses a needle. **sower,** one who scatters seed.
sewer, a drain. **suer,** one who entreats.
shear, to clip. **sheer,** to deviate, pure.
shoe, covering for foot. **shoo,** begone.
shone, did shine. **shown,** exhibited.
shoo, begone. **shoe,** covering for foot.
shoot, to let fly, to kill. **chute,** a fall.
shown, exhibited. **shone,** did shine.
side, edge, margin. **sighed,** did sigh.
sigher, one who sighs. **sire,** father.
sighs, deep breathings. **size,** bulk.
sight, view. **site,** situation. **cite,** to summon.
sign, token, mark. **sine,** geometrical term.
signet, a seal. **cygnet,** a swan.
silicious, flinty. **cilicious,** made of hair.
silly, foolish. **Scilly,** name of islands.
single, alone. **cingle,** a girth.
sit, to rest. **cit,** a citizen.
skull, bone of the head. **scull,** oar, boat.
slay, to kill. **sley,** weaver's reed. **sleigh,** vehicle.
sleeve, cover for arm. **sleave,** untwisted silk.

slew, killed. **slue**, to turn about. **slough**, bog.

slight, neglect, small. **sleight**, artful trick.

sloe, fruit, animal. **slow**, not swift.

soar, to rise high. **sore**, painful.

soared, ascended. **sword**, a weapon.

sold, did sell. **soled**, furnished with soles. **souled**, instinct with soul or feeling.

sole, part of foot, only. **soul**, spirit of man.

some, a part. **sum**, the whole.

son, a male child. **sun**, luminous orb.

sow, to scatter seed. **sew**, to stitch.

sower, one who scatters seed. **sewer**, one who uses a needle.

staid, sober, remained. **stayed**, supported.

stair, steps. **stare**, to gaze.

stake, a post, a wager. **steak**, meat.

stare, to gaze. **stair**, steps.

stationary, motionless. **stationery**, paper, etc.

steel, metal. **steal**, to thieve.

sticks, pieces of wood. **Styx**, a fabulous river.

stile, stairway. **style**, manner.

straight, not crooked. **strait**, narrow pass.

style, manner. **stile**, stairway.

Styx, a fabulous river. **sticks**, pieces of wood.

subtle, cunning. **suttle**, net weight.

subtler, more cunning. **sutler**, trader.

succor, aid. **sucker**, a shoot of a plant, a fish.

suer, one who entreats. **sewer**, a drain.

suite, train of followers. **sweet**, having a pleasant taste, dear.

sum, the whole. **some**, a part.

sun, luminous orb. **son**, a male child.

surcle, a twig. **circle**, a round figure.

surf, dashing waves. **serf**, a slave.

surge, a billow. **serge**, cloth.

sutler, trader. **subtler**, more cunning.

suttle, net weight. **subtle**, cunning.

swap, to barter. **swop**, a blow.

symbol, emblem, representative. **cymbal**, musical instrument.

T

tacked, changed course of ship. **tact**, skill.

tacks, small nails. **tax**, a tribute.

tale, story. **tail**, the hinder part.

taper, a wax candle. **tapir**, an animal.

tare, a week, allowance. **tear**, to pull to pieces.

taught, instructed. **taut**, tight.

teal, a water fowl. **teil**, a tree.

team, two or more horses. **teem**, to be full.

tear, moisture from eyes. **tier**, a rank, a row.

tear, to pull to pieces. **tare**, weed, allowance.

teas, different kinds of tea. **tease**, to torment.

tense, rigid, form of a verb. **tents**, canvas houses.

the, adjective. **thee**, thyself.

their, belonging to them. **there**, in that place. **they're**, they are.

threw, did throw. **through**, from end to end.

throne, seat of a king. **thrown**, hurled.

throw, to hurl. **throe**, extreme pain.

thrown, hurled. **throne**, seat of a king.

thyme, a plant. **time**, duration.

tide, stream, current. **tied**, fastened.

tier, a rank, a row. **tear**, moisture from eyes.

timber, wood. **timbre**, crest, quality.

time, duration. **thyme**, a plant.

tire, part of a wheel, weary. **Tyre**, city. **tier**, one who ties.

toad, reptile. **toed**, having toes. **towed**, drawn.

toe, part of foot. **tow**, hemp, to drag.

told, related. **tolled**, rang. **toled**, allured.

tole, to allure. **toll**, a tax.

ton, a weight. **tun**, a large cask.

too, denoting excess. **to**, toward. **two**, couple.

tracked, followed. **tract**, region.

tray, shallow vessel. **trey**, three of cards.

tun, a large cask. **ton**, a weight.

two, a couple. **to**, toward. **too**, denoting excess.

U

urn, a vase. **earn**, to gain by labor.

use, to employ. **yews**, trees. **ewes**, sheep.

V

vain, proud, delusive. **vane**, weathercock. **vein**, blood vessel.

vale, valley. **vail**, a fee. **veil**, to cover.

vane, weathercock. **vein**, blood vessel. **vain**, proud, delusive.

veil, a covering for face. **veil**, to cover. **vail**, a fee.

vein, blood vessel. **vane**, weathercock. **vain**, proud, delusive.

Venus, planet. **venous**, relating to the veins.

vial, a bottle. **viol**, violin. **vile**, wicked.

vice, sin. **vise**, a press.

W

wade, to ford. **weighed** balanced.

wail. to moan. **wale**, a mark. **whale**, a sea animal.

waist, part of the body. **waste**, destruction.

wait, to stay for. **weight**, heaviness.

waive, to relinquish. **wave**, a billow.

wall, a fence. **wawl**, wail, bowl.

wane, to decrease. **wain**, a wagon.

want, desire. **wont**, custom, habit.

ware, merchandise. see **wear**.

wart, hard, excrescence. **wort**, beer.

way, road, manner. **whey**, curdled milk. **weigh**, to balance.

weak, not strong. **week**, seven days.

weal, happiness. **wheal**, a pustule. **wheel**, circular body.

wear, to impair by use. **ware**, merchandise.

weasel, an animal. **weazel**, thin, weasen.

ween, to think. **wean**, to alienate.

weigh, to balance. **way**, road. **whey** of milk.

weighed, balanced. **wade**, to ford.

weight, heaviness. **wait**, to stay for.

wen, a tumor. **when**, at what time.

wether, a ram. **weather**, state of air.

what, that which. **wot**, to know.

wheel, circular body. **wheal**, a pustule.

whey, thin part of milk. **way**, road, manner. **weigh**, to balance.

Whig, name of a party. **wig**, false hair.

whist, a game of cards. **wist**, thought, knew.

whole, all, entire. **hole**, a cavity.

wholly, completely. **holy**, sacred, pure.

wig, false hair. **Whig**, name of a party.

Synonym Ant/Hom

wight, a person. **wite,** blame.
wist, thought, knew. **whist,** a game of cards.
won, gained. **one,** single, unit.
wont, custom, habit. **want,** desire.
wood, substance of trees. **would,** was willing.
wort, beer, herb. **wart,** hard excrescence.
wot, to know. **what,** that which.
wrap, to fold. **rap,** to strike.
wrapped, covered. **rapped,** struck with quick blows.
wrapping, a cover. **rapping,** striking.
wreak, to inflict. **reek,** to emit vapor.
wrest, to twist. **rest,** quiet.
wretch, miserable person. **retch,** to vomit.
wring, to twist. **ring,** a circle, a sound.

write, to form letters. **wright,** workman. **right,** correct.
wrote, did write. **rote,** a memory of words.
wrung, twisted. **rung,** sounded.
wry, crooked. **rye,** a grain.

Y

yew, a tree. **you,** person spoken to. **ewe,** a sheep.
yews, trees. **use,** employ. **ewes,** sheep.
yolk, yellow of egg. **yoke,** collar for oxen.
your, belonging to you. **you're,** you are.

CROSSWORD
PUZZLE
DICTIONARY

CROSSWORD PUZZLE DICTIONARY

BY

BETTYE F. MELNICOVE

ABBREVIATIONS

ab.—abbreviation
alch.—alchemy
Amer.—American
anat.—anatomical
arch.—archaic
bacteriol.—bacteriological
bldg.—building
Calif.—California
co.—company
colloq.—colloquial
comb. form—combined form

contr.—contraction
Dep.—Deputies
dept.—department
dial.—dialectic
E.—East
Eng.—English
Fr.—French
gram.—grammatically
her.—heraldry
imp.—imperial
internat.—international

isl.—island
Jan.—January
Jap.—Japanese
L.—Latin
lang.—language
Mass.—Massachusetts
math.—mathematical
med.—medical
Mex.—Mexican
mt.—mountain
mus.—musical

N.—North
naut.—nautical
obs.—obsolete
Pa.—Pennsylvania
pert. to—pertaining to
Phil.—Philippine
Phoen.—Phoenician
poet.—poetical
rel.—reluctance
rep.—republic
rev.—reverential

S.—South
Scand.—Scandinavian
Scot.—Scotch
Shosh.—Shoshone
ter.—territorial
Test.—Testament
trig.—trigonomical
Tues.—Tuesday
var.—variant
vest.—vestment
W.—West

X–WORD DICT

A

abaft: aft, astern, behind
abandon: despair, forsake, leave, desolate, desert
abase: lower, discredit, humble, degrade, dishonor
abash: shame, disconcert, humiliate, chagrin, ashame, confuse
abate: lessen, diminish, subside, moderate
abbess: amma
abbey superior: abbot
abbot: abbe [quish
abdicate: demit, relin-
Abraham's birthplace: Ur
" **nephew:** Lot
" **wife:** Sarah
abet: aid assist, urge, instigate, egg, incite, encourage, promote, foment, help, sanction, uphold, second
abhor: hate, detest, loath
abide: wait, remain, sojourn, dwell, tarry
ability: competence, talent, power
abjure: disavow, renounce, recant
able: competent, could, clever, capable
" **to pay:** solvent
abnormal: aberrant
abode: residence, lodge, home, habitat, habitation, lodging
" **of ancient harp:** tara
" **of the dead:** aralu, aaru
abolish: repeal
abominate: hate, execrate, loathe
aborigine: native [ate
abound: teem, exuber-

abounding: replete, rife
about: of, on, anent, around, at
above: over, up, atop
" **(poet.) oer** [ra
" **(prefix):** super, sup-
" **& touching:** onto, on, upon
abrade: wear, grate, rasp, excoriate
abrasive material: emery, bort
abridgement: epitome
abridge (var.): rasee
abroad: overseas, afar
abrogate: repeal, rescind, annul, cancel
abrupt: steep, sudden, hasty, unexpected, short [eloin
abscond: elope, desert,
absent minded: distrait, away
absolute: utter, sheer, stark, implicit, mere, total, pure
" **monarch:** despot
" **superlative:** elative
absolve: free, remit, pardon
absorb: merge, imbib
absorbed: rapt
abstain from: avoids, eschew, refrain
" " **food:** fast
" **being:** ens [condite
abstruse: complex, re-
absurd: inept
abundance: plenitude, plenty, galore, store flow
abundant: ample, galore, plentiful, copious
abuse: revile, maltreat, maul, outrage, mistreat [project
abut: border, adjoin,
abyss: pit, chasm, deep, gulf
Abyssinian: Ethiop

" **herb:** ramtil
" **title or governor:** ras, negus [comply
accede: consent, agree,
accent: stress, emphasize, tone
accept: take
" **as one's own:** adopt
" **as true:** credits, believe [entry, adit
access: entree, door,
accessible: open [hap
accident: chance, mis-
acclaim: praise, clap, ovation, applause
accommodate: adapt, suit, please, oblige
accompany: escort, attend
accomplice: tool, pal
accomplish: do, realize, execute [deed
accomplishment: feat,
accost: hail, greet, assail, address [tab
account: report, recital,
" **entry:** item
accountable: liable
accumulate: store, pile, amass, collect [true
accurate: exact, correct,
accuse: censure, blame, charge, arraign
accustom (var.): enure, inure [ured
accustomed: used, inace: top, unit, expert, jot, particle
" **of clubs:** basto
acerb: bitter, harsh, sour, tart
acetic: sour
ache: ail, pain, pang
achieve: win, earn, do, gain, attain
achievement: deed, act, record, feat, gest
acid: sour, biting
" **of apples:** malic
" **chemical:** amide

" **condiment:** vinegar
" **neutralizer:** alkali
acidity: acor
acknowledge: own, admit, avow, confess, concede
acknowledgement of a wrong: apology
acme: apex, top
aconite: atis
acquaint: apprise
acquiesce: assent, consent, agreement, agree
acquire: gain, learn, secure, win, get, attain, earn
" **with difficulty:** eke
acquit: exonerate, clear, free
acre (¼): rood
acrid: sour, bitter, pungent, tart [beyond
across: astride, over,
" **(poet.):** oer
act: deed, feat, behave, do, feign, simulate, law
" **out of sorts:** mope
" **wildly:** rave
action: deed, act
" **in law:** res, re
active: spry, alive, astir, nimble, brisk, quick
actor: player, thespian, doer
actual: real
" **being:** esse
actuality: fact
actuate: incite, move, arouse, impel, urge, impell [gacity
acumen: sharpness, sa-
acute: keen, intense, pointed, tart, shrewd, poignant, critical
adage: saw, proverb, saying, maxim, motto
adamant: hard, firm, immovable [form, fit
adapt: adjust, suit, con-
add: append, increase, total, augment, at-

517

tach, annex, affix
addicted: prone
addition: also, besides, aside, plus, yet, more, too, else, and
" **to a bill:** rider
" " " **building:** ell
" " " **document:** rider
additional: extra, other, more, plus
" **allowance:** bonus
address: sermon, direct, oration, talk, apply, accost, greet
adduce: cite, allege
adept: expert, proficient, skilled [equal
adequate: sufficient, fit,
adhere: stick, persist, cling
adherent of the crown: Tory
" **(suffix):** ite
adhesive: glue, paste, mucilage, gum
adipose: fatty, fat
adit: entrance, access approach
adjective (suffix): ile, ent, ian, ive, ic
adjoin: abut, touch

adjudge: opine, deem, award, decree
adjudged unfit for use: condemned
adjunct: accessory
adjust: adapt, set, arrange, deem, regulate, fix, range, frame, settle, align
administer: manage
admirable: good, fine
admire: revere, approve
admission: entree, access
admit: concede, allow, confess, own [mand
admonish: warn, repriado: fuss, bustle [sume
adopt: pass, take, as-
adore: venerate, worship [nament
adorn: crest, trim, deck, grace, drape, ornate, bedeck, decorate, or-
Adriatic island: Eso, Lido.
" **seaport:** Trieste
" **winter wind:** bora
adrift: afloat [deft
adroit: skillful, neat,
adulate: flatter
adulation: praise
adult: grown [imago
" **form of insect:**
" **steer:** beeve
advance: gain, progress, promote
" **guard:** van
" **notice:** warning
advantage: stead, behoof, profit [enemy
adversary: foe, rival,
" **of man:** satan
adversity: ill

advocate: proponent, plead, pleader [dea
Aetes's daughter: Me-
Aegean Island: Psara, Nio, Los, Samos, De-
aerial: airy [los
aeriform matter: gas
aeronaut: aviator
aery: lofty
affairs: matters
" **of chance:** lottery
affect: rasp, influence
" **deeply:** penetrate, impress
affection: love, ardor, pretension, pretence
affidavit: oath
affirm: allege, assert, asseverate, aver, declare
affirmative: yes, aye, yep, yea
affix: append, add
affliction: ill, sore, distress, pain, woe, sor-
affluence: wealth [row
afford: supply, lend, furnish, provide
" **aid:** help
affray: melee, feud
affront: insult, displease
Afghan coin: amania
" **prince:** amir, ameer
afire: eager, blazing, flaming [awash
afloat: buoyed, adrift,
afraid: timorous, fearful, fear
afresh: anew
African: Negro, Taal
" **animals:** ayeayes, okapi, giraffes
" **antelope:** gnu, eland, addax, peele, bongo
" **city:** Tripoli
" **cony:** dassie, das
" **desert:** Gobi
" **fly:** tsetse
" **gazel:** ariel, cora
" **giraffe:** okapi
" **hartebeest:** tora
" **hemp:** ife
" **hottentot:** nama
" **hunting expedition:** safari
" **lake:** Chad, Tana
" **monkey (small):** grivet
" **mountain:** Cameroon
" **native:** Zulu, ibo
" **tribe:** Kabonga, Krepi, Nuba
" **Portuguese territory:** Angola
" **region:** Sudan
" **republic:** Liberia
" **river:** Nile, Congo, Niger, Bia, Calabar, Nun, Senegal
" **seaport:** Tunis

" **soup ingredient:** lalo
" **tree:** shea, cola, tarfa, baobab

" **tribesman:** bantu
" **village:** stad
" **wild hog:** wart
" **wildcat:** serval
" **wood:** ebony
" **worm:** loa
aft: astern, stern
after: behind, later
" **awhile:** anon, later
aftersong: epode
again: anew, over, encore, moreover
" **(Latin):** iterum
" **(prefix):** ob, anti, re
against: con, versus
" **(prefix):** anti
agalloch: agar, aloes
agape: open, staring
agave: aloe
age: seniority, era, eon, epoch, century, lifeaged: senile, old [time
agent: consignee, doer, broker, factor, deputy, promoter, representative
aggravate: tease, nag, intensify
aggregate: sum
aggregation: tribe, mass
agile: spry, nimble, alert, lithe, lively
agitate: stir, roil, rile, fret, disturb, vex, perturb, flurry, move
ago: past, since
" **(poet.)** agone
agog: eager [tering
agony: pain, pang, suf-
agree: consent, accede, assent, accept, coincide, concur, comport, gibe, homologate, conform [ant
agreeable: nice, pleasagreement: covenant, yes, pact, consent, unity, assent, treaty, unison, contract, coincidence, unity
agriculturist: farmer, gardener
ahead: on forward
aid: abet, assist, befriend, sustain, succor
ail: suffer, bother
ailment: malady
aim: point, goal, ambition, purpose, end, intent, ideal, objective, aspiration, target, direct, object
" **high:** aspire
air: tone, aria, breeze, tune, carriage, manner, mien, display, atmosphere, song, melody, vapor
" **(comb. form):** aeri, aero, aer
" **(pert. to):** aural, ariel
" **hero:** ace
aircraft: aeri, aero, blimp

" **shelter:** hangar, nacelle
airy: ethereal, light, sprightly, aerial
aisle: passage
akin: related, alike, sib, similar, allied
alackaday: alas
alarm: alert, frighten, arouse, startle, scare
" **whistle:** siren
alas: ay
Alaska auks: arries
" **cape:** Nome
" **capital:** Juneau
" **city & town:** Nome
" **district:** Sitka
" **garment:** parkas
" **Mt.:** Ada,
" **native:** Aleut
" **river:** Yukon
Albanian coin: lek
alcohol: spirits
alcoholic beverage: gin, mead, posset, wine, rum
alder tree (Scot.): arn
alert: ready, agile, vigilant, prepared, nimble, awake, aware
alfalfa: lucerne
alga: seaweed
Algerian cavalryman: spahs, spahee
" **city:** Oran
" **governor:** Dey
" **seaport:** Oran, Bone
Algonquin Indian: Cree, Sac, Lenape
alienate: separate, disaffect, estrange, wean
alike: equally, similar, akin, analogous, same
aliment: food
alive: rank, active, animate, swarming
alkaline compound: soda
" **solution:** lye
alkaloid in bean: eserin
" **in tea plant:** theine
all: entire, wholly, totally, total, every, individually, solely, quite
" **(comb. form):** pan
allay: ease, relieve, mitigate, assuage, mollify, calm, quell, slake
allege: adduce, affirm, maintain, cite, assert, aver, quote [elod
alleged electric force:
alleviate: allay, ease, mitigate, relieve
alliance: treaty, union
allied: cognate, agnate, akin
alligator pear: avocado
allot: mete, destine, assign, ration
allow: let, permit, grant, admit
" **to remain:** leave
" **free use of:** lend
allowance: ration
" **for past services:**

pension

" " **waste:** tret, stet, tare

" " **weight or wt. of container:** tare

alloy of copper & zinc: brass

" **for domestic utensils:** pewter

" **of gold & silver:** asem

" " **iron:** steel

" " **tin & zinc:** oroide [tion

allude to: refer, men-

allure: tempt, win, entice, lead, decoy

ally: helper, unite

almanac: yearbook, calendar

almost: nearly

" (arch.): anear

alms: dole, doles, char- [ity

" **box:** arca

almsgiving: charity

alone: solo, singly, unique, solitary, only

along: ever, on, forward, onward

aloud: oral, audibly

alphabetic character: letter, rune

alps: alpine, mountains

also: and, too, withal

" (arch.): eke

" **called:** alias

" (poet.): eke

altar screen: reredos

" **slab:** mensa

alter: change, modify, amend, vary, mutate, emend

alternate: other, rotate

alternative: or

always: ever, evermore, aye

" (contr. or poet.): eer

amalgamate: fuse, unite

amaryllis plant: agave

amass: heap, collect

amateur: dabbler, dilettante

amaze: surprise, astound, astonish

Amazon estuary: Para

ambary: da

ambassador: legate

ambiguous: delphic, indefinite, oracular

ambition: aim, goal, target, aspiration

ambrosia: nectar

ambush: trap

amend: alter, rectify, repeal, revise, improve, better

amerces: fines, mulcts, deprives [dian

American aborigine: In-

" **actor:** Drew

" **admiral:** Evans, Sims, Dewey

" **artist:** Pyle, Peale

" **author:** Harte, Reo, Grey, Paine, Alden, Roe

" **canal:** Panama

" **capitalist:** Astor, Rascob

" **caricaturist:** Nast

" **cartoonist:** Arno, Dorgan

" **cataract:** Niagara

" **clergyman:** Olin

" **composer:** Paine, Nevin, Speaks

" **critic:** Ayres [Grew

" **diplomat:** Reid,

" **divine:** Olin

" **editor:** Bok [Fisk

" **educator:** Hume,

" **engineer:** Eads

" **essayist:** Mabie

" **explorer:** Peary, Lewis, Byrd

" **feminist:** Catt

" **financier:** Biddle

" **general:** Otis, Lee, Ord

" **geologist:** Dana

" **herb:** sego, leafcup

" **humorist:** Ade, Nye, Twain, Lardner, Artemus, Cobb, Day

" **illustrator:** Newell

" **inventor:** Morse, Hoe, Howe

" **isthmus:** Panama

" **journalist:** Bigelow, Holt, Reid

" **jurist:** Moore, Paine

" **lawyer:** Paine, Ellery

" **machinist:** Howe

" **monetary unit:** dollar

" **novelist:** Steele, Roe, Harte

" **operatic singer:** Farrar

" **painter:** Peters

" **pathologist:** Ewing

" **patriot:** Paine, Otis, Ross

" **philanthropist:** Riis

" **pioneer:** Boone

" **pirate:** Kidd

" **poet:** Riley, Lanier, Tate, Poe

" **statesman:** Blaine, Logan, Dawes, Jay

" **writer:** Bok, Pyle

amical: friendly

amid: among, amist

amiss: awry, faultily, wrong, faulty, astray improper

ammonia derivative: amine, amide, amin, anilide [son

ammunition wagon: cais-

among: in, amid, mid, amidst

" (poet.): mid, amid

amorous look: leer, ogle

amort: lifeless, spiritless

amount: sum, quantity

" **offered:** bid

amphibia order: anura

amphibian: toad, frog

amphibole: edenite

ample: plenty, abundant, full, plenteous

" (poet.): enow

amplify: add, widen, enlarge

amulet: charm, talisman

amuse: entertain, divert [game

amusement: sport,

anaconda: boa

analyze gram.: parse

anarchist: red [ban

anathematize: curse,

Anatolian goddess: Ma

ancestor: sire, elder, forbear, forefather, forebear

ancestral: avital

anchor: moor, cat, kedge

" **bill:** pee

" (small): grapnel

" **tackle:** cat

ancient: early, olden, old, aged, archean— *see also early, olden*

" **alloy:** asem

" **Arabian measure:** saa

" **ascetic people:** essene

" **Caucasian race:** Aryans

" **chariot:** essed

" **Chinese:** Seres

" **city:** Nineveh, Tyre

" **country:** Media,

" **court:** eyre [Aram

" **Danish legal code:** danelaw

" **drink:** morat

" **Egyptian City:** No, Thebes

" " **scroll:** papyri

" " **title:** Soter

" " **wt.:** kat

" **English court:** Leet

" **king:** Canute

" **fine for homicide:** cro

" **firearm:** dag

" **form for shaping objects:** ame [Erin

" **Gaelic capital:** Tara,

" **galley:** trireme, bi-

" **game:** mora [reme

" **Genoa coin:** jane

" **tribesmen:** Teuton

" **gold coin:** rial

" **Greek:** Ionian

" " **city:** Argos, Corinth, Elis

" " **contest:** agon

" " **country:** Epirus, Elis, Aeolia

" " **invader:** Dorian

" " **judge:** dicast

" " **kingdom:** Attica

" " **marker:** stela

" " **milestone:** stele

" " **platform:** bema

" " **warship:** trireme

" **hammering form:** ame

" **headdress:** mite

" **Hebrew measure:** bath

" " **notes on old Test.:** masora [far

" " **ram's horn:** sho-

" **Hindu scripture:** veda

" **implement of war:** onager, celt

" **instrument of torture:** cross, rack

" **Irish chieftain:** Tanist

" " **clan:** Sept

" " **fort:** Lis, Liss

" " **party:** sept

" " **priest:** Druid

" **Jap race:** Ainu

" **Jewish cabalistic book:** Zohar

" " **measure:** homer

" " **sacred objects:** urim

" " **title:** abba

" **lang.:** pali, sanskrit, Latin

" **Latin grammar:** Donat

" **manuscript:** codex

" **Media people:** Medes

" **Mexican:** Aztec

" **military machine:** onager, catapult

" **money:** aes

" " **unit:** talent

" **musical character:** neume

" **Norse minstrel:** Scald

" **Norwegian king:** Olaf

" **Palestinian city:** Gilead

" " **cry:** jericho

" " **lang.:** aramaic

" " **town:** Eire

" " **village:** Endor

" **persecutor of Christians:** Nero

" **Persian coin:** daric

" " **priests:** magi

" **Peruvian title:** inca

" **Phoenicia capital:** Tyre

" **Pilgrim's protector:** Templar

" **pillarlike monument:** stela

" **playing card:** tarot

" **race:** Medes, Goth

" **Roman citadel:** Arx

" " **coin:** sesterce

" " **diety:** Ianus

" " **festivals:** cerealia

" " **measure:** wina

" " **port:** Ostia

" " **priestess:** vestal

" " **seats:** sellae

" " **shield:** clypeus

" " **wall:** spina

" **Sc. minstrel:** scald

" **Scottish fine:** cro

" " **name:** Alba

" " **tax:** cro

" **Semitic god:** Baal

" **sepulchral slab:** stela
" **spice:** stacte
" **story teller:** Aesop
" **stringed instrument:** lute, nebel, asor, rebec
" **Syrian country:** Aram
" **tax:** cro
" **temple:** naos
" **Toltec capital:** Tula
" **trading vessel:** nef
" **Troy:** Iliac, Troas, Ilion
" **region:** Troad
" **Turkish title:** Dey
" **vehicle:** chariot
" **war machine:** onager
" **warship:** galleon
" **weapon:** dag, celt, lance, sling, spear, pike, mace
" **weight:** talent
" **wicked city:** Sodom
" **wine pitcher:** olpe
" " **receptacle:** ama
and: also
andiron: firedog
anecdotes: ana, tales
anesthetic: ether, gas
anet: dill, dillseed
anew: again, afresh
angel: seraph
" **of light:** cherub [ly
angelic: cherubic, saint-
anger: enrage, ire, wrath, rage, irritate, fury, choler, exasperate, animosity
" **(colloq.):** rile
angle: corner, fish, nook
" **iron:** lath
" **of leaf & stem:** axil
angler: fisher
" **'s basket:** creel
" **'s hope:** bite
Anglo-Indian monetary unit & coin: anna
" " **number:** crore
" " **nurse:** amah
" " **title of address:** babu
" " **weight:** tola, ser
" **Saxon coin & money of account:** ora
" " **consonant:** eth
" " **free servant:** thane [tul, mad
angry: irate, sore, ire
anguish: pain, travail, remorse, dolor
animal: brute, beast, sloth, genet, creature, boar
" **'s backbone:** chine
" **body:** soma [lage
" **coat:** hair, fur, pedisease:** mange
" **fat:** adeps, suet, wax, ester, lard, tallow, grease
" **food:** flesh, meat
" **inclosure:** corral,

cage, pen
" **neck hair:** mane
" **skin:** hide, fur
" **stomach:** maw, craw
" " **part:** tripe
" **thigh:** ham
" **track:** trail, spoor
" **trail:** run, track
animate: liven, alive, invigorate, enliven
animation: life, pep, vivacity, spirit
animosity: anger, spite,
ankle: talus [rancor
" **(of the):** tarsal
Annamese measure: sao, quo, tao
anneal: temper, fuse
annex: add, attach, subjoin, extension, join
announcement: notice
annoy: pester, irk, nag, harass, bless, vex, disturb, harry, irritate, exasperate, tease, rile, molest, peeve, nettle
annoyance: bore, pest, peeve
annul: revoke, rescind, elide, repeal, abolish, nullify, cancel, undo, abrogate
anoint: oil, anele
anon: later, soon
anonymous: nameless
another time: again
answer: reply, retort, respond, response, solution [do
" **the purpose:** serve,
antagonist: enemy
Antarctic bird: penguin
" **sea:** Ross
ante: stake [prior
antecedent: precedent,
" **period:** past
antelope (female): doe
" **(kind):** serow, gnu, addax, eland, bongo
" **(male):** buck
antenna: feeler, aerial
anterior: forward, previous, prior, before
anthem: motet
anthropoid: ape
" **ape:** orang
antic: caper, dido
anticipate: antedate, expect, hope, devance
antipathy: aversion, distaste, dislike [ish, old
antiquated: passe, old-
antiquity (arch. & poet.): eld [sera (pl.)
antitoxin: serum (sg.),
antlered animal: stag, deer, moose
antrum: cavern
anvil: teest
anxiety: care, concern
anxious: eager, concerned
apace: swiftly, fast, rapidly, quick

apart: aside, separate, borders, asunder, separately
" **(prefix):** dis
apartment: suite, flat
ape: lar, mimic, simian, simulate, copy, imitator, gorilla, monkey, imitate
apelike: simian
aperture: slot, gap, leak, mouth, hole, vent
apex: point, acme, summit, top, vertex
aphorism: adage, saw
apogee: climax
Apollo's mother: Leto
" **oracle:** delos [mis
" **sister:** Diana, Arte-
" **son:** Iamus
apostate: renegade
apostle: Paul, Peter, disciple, Mark
apothecaries wt.: dram, grain
appal: awe, astonish, horrify, shock, dismay, overcome
appall: dismay
apparatus for heating liquids: etna
apparel: raiment, gear, attire, garb
apparent: evident, patent, plain
apparition: shape, specter, ghost, idolon
appeal: plead, request, entreaty, refer
appear: seem, arise, look
" **again:** recur
appearance: aspect, mien, guise, phase, look
appearing gnawed: erose
appease: placate, atone, propitiate, conciliate, pacify
appellation: title, name, epithet
Appellation of Athena: Alea, Palea
append: add, attach, affix
appendages: tails, addenda, tabs, arista, tags
appertain: relate, belong
appetite: stomach, longing, craving
appetizer: canape, aperitif
applaud: clap, cheer
apple: pome, pippin, crab, winesap, russet,
" **acid:** malic [esopus
" **juice:** cider
" **seed:** pit, pip
application: use, term
apply: devote, address, treat
appoint: ordain, detail, commission, nominate,

assign,
" **as agent:** depute
appointment: tryst date,
apportion: mete, dele, ration, deal, allot, dole, lot, allocate
apposite: relative, relevant
appraise: rate, evaluate, price, estimate, value, gauge
appreciate: value
apprehend: nab, arrest, grasp, perceive
" **clearly:** realize
" **thru the senses:** sensate
apprehension: fear
apprise: inform
approach: verge, come, near, adit
appropriate: fit, proper, suit, apt, suitable, becoming
approval: endorsement, consent, sanction
approve: admire, pass, O. K. [aptly
approximate: approach,
apron: pinafore
" **(dial.):** brat
" **top:** bib
apt: fit, pat, liable talented, clever, fitting, timely, skilled, dextrous
aptitude: art, talent, bent
aquatic animal: otter, fish, polyp, newt
" **bird:** dabchick, flamingo, goose, gull, coot, swan, duck, smew
" **mammal:** sirenian, whale, otter, seal
" **worm:** cadew
Arab: Saracen, tad, gamin, bedouin, semite, urchin
Arabia (poet.): Araby
Arabian capital: Sana
" **chieftain:** Emir
" **city:** Aden [emeer
" **cloth:** aba
" **commander:** Emir, Emeer, ameer, amir
" **country:** Yemen
" **garment:** aba
" **gazelle:** ariel
" **gulf:** Aden
" **jasmine:** bela
" **judge:** cadi
" **kingdom:** Irak, Iraq
" **language:** arabic
" **Moslem:** Wahabi
" **Night bird:** roc
" **peninsula:** Aden, Sinai
" **prince:** sherif
" **river bed:** wadi
" **seaport:** Aden
" **shrub:** kat
" **state:** Oman
" **sultanate:** Oman

" **tambourine:** taar,
" **title:** emir [daira
" **wind:** simoon
arachnid: spider, mite, acarus, tick
arbiter: judge, umpire, referee [cide
arbitrate: mediate, de-
arbor: bower, pergola
arboreal mammal: lemur, opossum, raccoon
arc: bow, arch [coon
arch: curve, chief, arc, bend, sly, bow, span, waggish, roguish
" **over:** cove, span
archaic pronoun: ye, thy, thine
archer: bowman
archetype: ideal
architectural column: pilaster
" **design:** spandrel
" **ornament:** dentil,
" **pier:** anta [corbeil
" **screen:** spier
Arctic: Polar, frigid
" **exploration base:** Etah
" **explorer:** Kane
" **lawyer:** Hyde
" **native:** Eskimo
ardent: intense, zealous, fervid, eager, flery, fiery
" **partison:** devotee
ardor: elan, fervor, affection, zeal
area: space, extent, site, tract, section, range, scope, region
" **(small):** areola, plot
arena: oval, stadium, field, ring
arenaceous: sandy
Ares's sister: Eris
argent: silvery, silver
Argonaut's leader: Jason [jargon, cant
argot: slang, dialect,
argue: debate, reason, dispute, discuss
argument: debate, spat, row, add
" **against:** con
" **in favor of:** pro
aria: tune, song, solo
arid: barren, waterless, dry, parched
" **region:** Sahara
Aries: ram
arise: emanate, ascend originate, mount, issue, spring
arista: beard, awn
Arius's follower: Arian
ark's builder (var.): Noe
" **landing place:** Ararat
arm: fortify, might, branch
" **covering:** sleeve
" **of sea:** inlet, bay,

firth, gulf
armadillo: apara, apar, peba, tatou
armed band: posse
" **conflict:** war, battle
" **fleet:** navy [ment
" **force:** army, regi-
" **galley of Northmen:** Aesc [nel
" **guard:** sentry, senti-
" **merchant man:** raider
" **power:** armament
armistice: truce
armor: mail [quire
" **bearer:** squire, es-
" **splint:** tace
" **for the thigh:** taslet, tace
armpit: ala
army: host, horde
" **follower:** sutler
" **section:** corps
" **unit:** brigade
aroma: fragrance, odor, scent, flavor [rant,
aromatic: spicy, frag-
" **condiment:** spice
" **gum resin:** myrrh
" **herb:** anise, mint, thyme, spearmint, caraway
" **plant:** mint, nard, basil, herb, tansy, angelica
" **principal of violet root:** irone
" **seasoning:** spice
" **seed:** anise
" **smoke:** fume
" **spice:** mace
" **tree gum:** balsam
" **wood:** cedar
arouse: actuate, excite, stir, alarm
" **to action:** rally
arraign: indict, denounce
arrange: prepare, adjust, plan, fettle, dispose, place
" **for exhibition:** stage
" **in folds:** drape
" **in layers:** tier, laminate
" **side by side:** appose
" **in succession:** seriate
" " **thin layers:** laminal
arrangement: plan, system, setup, order, disposal
" **of interwoven parts:** web
" " **sails:** rig
array: dress, garb, clothe, deck, robe, attire, restrain, capture, stop, apprehend
arrest: halt, stem, check, rein, hinder, seizure, detain
arrive: come, reach
arrogant: haughty, proud

arrow: dart, barb
" **body:** stele
" **case:** quiver [rare
" **poisoning:** inee, cu-
art: knack, aptitude, science, wile, facility
Artemis's mother: Leto
Artemis's twin: Apollo
artery (large): aorta
artful: sly, wily [a, the
article: thing, item, an,
" **of apparel:** gaiter
" **(arch.):** ye [creed
" **of belief:** tenet,
" " **commerce.** staple
" **in a document:** clause
artifice: guile, trickery, ruse, finesse, wile, dodge, stratagem, art
artificial: unreal, paste,
" **butter:** oleo [sham
" **as jewels:** paste
" **lang.:** ide, ido, ro, esperanto
" **light:** lamp
" **manners:** airs
" **teeth:** denture
artificial waterway: canal, sluice
artists medium: oil
" **mixing board:** palette
artless: naive, naif
" **woman:** ingenue
artlessness: naivete
arum plant: arad, aroid, lily
Aryan: Slav, Mede
as before: ditto
" **compared with:** than
" **far as:** unto, to
" **it stands (mus.):** sta
" **long as:** while
" **well:** also, and
ascend: arise, mount, up, climb, scale
ascertain: learn, see
" **the bearings of:** orient [sene
ascetic: stoic, yogi, es-
ascribable: due
ascribe: refer, impute, attribute
ashes (Scot.): ase
ashy: pale, wan, white, ashen, livid, grey
Asia Minor Island: Samos
" " **Mt.:** Ida
" " **republic:** Syria
Asiatic: Asian, Tatar, Hun, Korean, Turk
" **animal:** rasse, tiger,
" **bean:** soy [serow
" **bird:** minivet, myna serow
" **coast wind:** monsoon
" **country:** Siam, India, Tibet, Korea, Nepal, Irak, Arabia, Russia, Anam, Syria, Burma, China

" " **(ancient):** Medea, Elam, Eolis
" **domestic cattle:** zobo
" **gazelle:** Cora, ahu
" **isthmus:** kra
" **kingdom:** Nepal, Irak, Annam, Iraq, Anam, Siam
" **lemur:** loris
" **mountains:** Altai
" **native:** arab
" **nomad:** arab
" **palm:** areca, nipa, betel [Arabia
" **peninsula:** Korea,
" **perennial:** ramie
" **plant:** odal
" **river:** Amur, Indus, Ob, Tigris, Lena
" **ruminant:** camel,
" **sea:** Aral [yak
" **tea:** cha
" **tree:** siris, dita
" **tribeman:** tatar
" **vine:** betel
" **weight:** catty, tael
" **wild ass:** onager
" " **sheep:** rasse, argali [arate
aside: apart, away, separ
ask: inquire, invite, bid, solicit, request, beg
" **payment:** dun
" **(Scot.):** spere
askew: wry, atilt, awry, crooked
asleep: abed, dormant
asp: viper, reptile, snake
aspect: phase, guise, appearance, side, mien
aspen: poplar, shaking
asperation: slur
asperse: slander, vilify, villify, traduce, caluminate
aspiration: aim, desire, ambition
aspire: pretend, desire, seek, reach
assail: beset, attack, scathe, assault, ac-
Assam silk: eri [cost
Assamese tribe: Ao
assault: assail, onset, attack, raid, on-
assay: test [slaught
assaying vessel: cupel
assemblage: meeting, host
assemble: meet, convene, mass, convoke, congregate, muster
assembly: diet, agora
assent: agree, agreement, consent, concur, sanction
assert: state, aver, allege, attest, avow, predicate, affirm, maintain, avouch, declare, contend, pronounce
" **as fact:** posit [mate
assess: tax, levy, esti-

asset: estate [laver
asseverate: affirm, vow,
assign: relegate, award,
designate, label, appoint, allot
" **parts:** cast
" **to:** refer, class
assignment: task
assimilate: digest
assist: befriend, aid,
help, abet
assistance: help, succor
associate: partner, fellow, ally, mix, herd,
assort: classify [consort
assuage: relieve, slake,
mitigate, allay
assume: don, wear,
suppose, adopt, pretend
" **an attitude:** pose
" **as fact:** posit
assumed character: role
assurance: aplomb
assure: convince, confirm, vouch.
Assyrian deity: Ashur,
Ira
asterisk: stars, star
astern: aft, abaft, backward, behind
astir: agog, active
astonish. awe, appal,
amaze, surprise
astound: amaze, awe,
stun
astraddle: astride

astral: starry, stellar
astray: amiss
astride: astraddle [nin
astringent: alum, tan-
astronomical: uranian
astute: shrewd, crafty,
sly, cunning
asunder: apart
at: near, by, about,
during, in [studio
atelier: workshop,
Athama's wife: Ino
Athena lawgiver: solon
" **statesman:** Pericles
" **title:** alea
atilt: askew, aslant,
slanting
atmosphere: aura, air,
ether [airy
atmospheric: aerial,
" **conditions:** climate
" **disturbance:** storm,
fog
atom: particle, iota, ion,
jot, proton
atomic: tiny
atone: expiate, appease,
reparation, redeem,
reconcile
atop: above, upon
attach: annex, append,
add, fasten, link
attachment: adherence,
devotion, adhesion
attack: assail, assault,
onset, onslaught, raid
attain: gain, achieve,
reach, earn, compass,
acquire

" **success:** arrive, win
attempt: trial, effort,
essay, strive, try, endeavor, stab
" **(colloq.):** go, stab
" **(Scot.):** ettle
attend: await, escort,
wait, minister
" **to:** heed, listen,
nurse
attendant: aide, helper,
ministering, clerk,
server
attention: ear, diligence, observance,
heed
attenuated: rarefied,
thin, diluted, weakened

attest: assert, witness,
confirm, testify, cer-
attic: garret, loft [tify
attire: garb, dress, raiment, equip, rig,
robe, habit, array
attitude: pose, mien,
posture [charm, lure
attract: draw, allure,
attractive: taking, engaging
" **(colloq.):** cute
attribute: refer, ascribe
auction: sale
audacious: bold
audacity: nerve, cheek
audibly: aloud
audience: ear
audition: hearing
auditor: listener, hearer
auditory: otic
augment: eke, add
augur: bode, portend,
forebode
augury: omen
auk: murre
aural: aricular, otic
aureola: halo
aureole: halo
auricle: ear, pinna
auricular: otic, aural
auriferous: golden
aurora: dawn, eos
auroral: eoan
austere: severe, granitic, stern, hard,
frosty
Australian aborigine:
mara
" **badger:** wombat
" **bear:** koala
" **bird:** emu
" **boomerang:** kylie
" **brushwood:** mallee
" **cape:** Howe
" **city:** Perth, Sydney
" **clover fern:** nardoo
" **insect:** lerp
" **lake:** Eyre [tait
" **marsupial:** koala,
" **ostrich:** emu
" **resin:** damar
" **soldier:** anzac
" **tree:** billa
" **tribe:** Mara
" **wild dog:** dingo

Austrian botanist: Mendel
" **capital:** Vienna
" **coin:** florin
" **composer:** Mozart
" **province:** Tyrol,
" **wt.:** saum [Tirol
authentic: real, true
author: writer, creator
authoritative: assertive,
official
" **answer:** oracle
" **requirement:** mandate
authority: expert, dominance, dominion
authorize: accredit, delegate, license
autocrat: despot, mogul
automaton: robot, golem
auxiliary: ancillary, ally, alar, helping, assistant
avail: stead, benefit,
profit, use, boot
avalanche: slide
avarice: greed, cupidity, grasping [etous
avaricious: greedy, cov-
avenaceous: oaten
avenge: revenge, retaliate, requite
aver: state, varify, assert, allege, affirm,
avouch, say, declare,
vouch
average: mean, ordinary, usual, medium,
medial
averse: reluctant, loath,
opposed, inimical, unwillin
aversion: dislike, distaste, hate, hatred
avert: prevent, avoid
aviator: ace, pilot, flier,
flyer, aeronaut
avid: eager, greedy
avoid: shun shirk,
evade, avert, elude,
sidestep, escape, eschew, beware
avouch: aver, assert
avow: aver, acknowledge, a sert, testify,
own, confess, profess
await: expect, attend,
bide
" **settlement:** pend
awake: vigilant, alert
awaken: rouse, arouse
award: mete, assign
bestow, prize
" **of valor:** medal
aware cogniza t, informed, alert, know,
knowing, vigilant
away: off, fro, begone,
out, removed, far,
aside, absent
" **from:** off, fro
" **(prefix):** apo
" **(Scot.):** awa
awe: appal, dread, fear
awful: dire terrible

awkward: clumsy, ungainly [arista
awn: beard, bristle.
awry: amiss, askew,
crooded, askance ob-
ax handle: helve [lique
axillary: alar
axiom: maxim
aye: yes, ever, always
Azores town: Horta

B

**Babylonian abode of
the dead:** aralu
" **chief priest:** En
" **god:** el, ea, bel,
anu, adad, hea, baal
" **hero:** Etana
" **numeral:** sar
" **storm god:** Adad
babble: prattle, prate,
jabber, blather
baby: infant, humor
" **carriage:** stroller,
pram, gocart [A.B.
Baccal. degree: B.A.,
Bacchan cry: evoe
back: rear, fro, support,
uphold
" **of animal:** dorsum
" **gate:** postern
" **of neck:** nape
" **payment:** arrear
" **(prefix):** un, ana
backbone: spine
" **of animal:** chine
backer: sponsor
backward: astern, arear
bacon cut: rasher
bacteriol. culture: agar
" **wire:** oese
bad: spoiled, harmful,
baleful, inferior, ill,
poor, faulty
" **habits:** vice
badge: pin, token
" **of honor:** medal
badgerlike mammal:
ratel
badinage: banter
badly: illy
" **(prefix):** mal
baffle: pose, elude,
poise, evade
baffling question: poser
bag: sack, pouch, satchel, valise, entrap, cap-
bagpipe: drone [ture
Bahama Isl. Capital:
Nassau
bail: lade, security,
replevin, hoop
bait: lure, harass, torment, worry
baked clay: tile
baker's implement: peel
baking dish: ramekin
" **soda:** saleratus
balance: scales, poise,
remainder, par, even
baleful: bad [let
ball: dance, globe, pel-
" **of thread or yarn:**
clew

ballad: song, lay, derry
balloon basket: car
ballot: vote   [balm
balsam (kind of): tolu,
balustrade: railing
bamboo shoot: achar
ban: forbid, curse, ex-
    clude
banal: trite, trivial
band: belt, company,
    group, strip, troop,
    strap, girdle, crew,
    fetter, unite, stripe
" **across an escutch-**
    eon: fess
" **for hair:** fillet
bandage: ligate
bandit: brigand
bandy: exchange, cart
bane: harm, poison,
    ruin, mischief, woe
baneful: ill, bad
bang: slam, thump
banish: exile, deport,
    oust, evict, expel,
    expatriate
banister: baluster
bank: tier, brink
bankrupt: ruin [pennon
banner: flag, ensign,
banquet: feast
banteng: tsine
banter: badinage, rail-
    lery, chaff, wit, pleas-
    antry
Bantu lang.: ila, ronga
" **tribesman:** zulu
baptismal vessel: font
" **water:** laver
bar: exclude, cake, ex-
    cept, rail, stripe,
    estop
" **of balance:** beam
" " **cast metal:** ingot
" **legally:** estop
" **in a loom:** easer
" **of a soap frame:**
    sess
" **to transmit force:**
    lever
barb: dart, arrow
barbarian: Hun, Goth
barbarity: savagery,
    ferity
bard: poet, minstrel
bare: open, plain, ex-
    posed, expose, mere,
    meager, stark, de-
    nude, nude, strip,
    bald, blank, naked
bargain: deal, sale
barge: tow, scow
bark: yap, yelp, bay,
    clamor, rind
" **cloth:** tapa
" **exterior:** ross
" **of paper mulberry:**
    tapa
baronet's title: sir
barracks: etape, casern
barracuda: spet
barrel: cask, keg, tun
" **hook side piece &**
    slat: stave
" **maker:** cooper

barren: sterile, fallow,
    arid, effete
barrier: dam, hedge,
    barricade, hurdle
barrister: lawyer
barter: sell, trade, ex-
    change, truck
base: low, mean, sor-
    did, station, bed,
    pedestal, ignoble, ab-
    ject, vile, establish,
    snide
" **forming element:**
    metal
" **for a statue:** plinth
bashful: shy, coy
basin: vessel, laver
basis: root
" **of assessment:**
    ratal
" " **a conclusion:**
    premise
" " **fruit jellies:** pec-
    tin
" " **quartz:** silica
basket: hamper
basque cap: beret
bass horn: tuba
basswood: linden
bast: fiber
bat: cudgel, club
bate: restrain, reduce,
    lower, lessen
bathe: lave
batter: hitter, bombard,
    ram, bruise
battle: fight, conflict,
    war   [gaw
bauble: trinket, gew-
bawl out: berate, scold
bay: cove, sinus, inlet,
" **(scot.):** loch [bark
" **tree:** laurel [ador
" **window:** oriel, mir-
bazaar: fair
be enough: do
" **expected:** natural
" **in harmony:** agree,
    chord
" **of the opinion:** feel
" **situated:** lie [rue
" **sorry for:** repent,
" **in store for:** await
" **undecided:** doubt,
" **of use:** avail [pend
beach: strand, sand,
    shore
bead: globule, drop
beak: neb, nib, bill
beam: ray, shine, rafter,
    radiate [goa, legume
bean: soya, lima, soy,
bear: endure, stand,
    carry, bruin
" **(the):** Ursa
" " **(female):** ursa
" **weapons:** arm
" **witness to:** attest,
    depone   [awn
beard: arista, goatee,
" **of grains & grass-**
    es: awns, avels,
    aristae
bearded: aristate
bearer: carrier

bearing: air, mien, orle,
    carriage
" **(her.):** ente
" **spines:** spinate
bearlike: ursine
beast: animal
" **of burden:** onager,
    ass, camel, yak, don-
    key, mule, llama
beat: thrash, hammer,
    defeat, lash, drub,
    flay, lam, best, flog,
    pulsate, swinge, pul-
    sation, pummel, con-
    quer, flail, drum, sur-
    pass
" **back:** repel, repulse
" **hard:** hammer
beater: dasher, rab
beatify bless
beau: dandy, suitor
because: since, for, as,
    that
beck: nod, command
becloud: bedim, darken
become: grow, wax,
    get, suit, befit
" **buoyant:** levitate
" **exhausted:** peter
" **less severe:** relent
" **operative:** inure,
    enure
" **visible:** appear
" **void:** lapse
bed: stratum, matrix,
    couch, base
" **canopy & drapery:**
    tester   [spread
" **coverlet:** quilt,
" **of straw:** pallet
bedaub: smear
bedeck: adorn
bedim: becloud, mist
bee (male): drone

beef on hoof: steer,
beer: lager, ale [cattle
" **ingredient:** malt
" **mug:** stein, seidel
bees: apian, drones
Beethoven's birthplace:
    Bonn
beetle: dor, overhang,
    elater, scarab [tide
befall: happen, hap,
befit: become, suit
befitting: proper, suit-
befog: confuse   [able
befool: delude, deceive
before: pre, ere, ante,
    di, anterior, prior,
    previously
" **all others:** first
" **long:** presently,
    soon, non
" **(naut.):** afore
" **(prefix):** pro, pre,
    ante
" **this:** erenow
befriend: aid, help
befuddle: addle
beg: plead, implore, be-
    seech, entreat, peti-
    tion
beget: sire, father, en-
    gender

[cant
beggar: rogue, mendi-
begin: open, start, com-
    mence, initiate, lead
beginner: novice, en-
    trant, neophyte, tyro
beginning: onset, open-
    ing, first, origin, in-
    ceptive, genesis, start,
    outset, dawn
begone: avaunt, out,
    off, scat
begrudge: envy   [tain
beguile: delude, enter-
behalf: sake   [react
behave: act, demean,
behavior: manners,
    treatment, demeanor
behead: decapitate
behind: rear, after,
    abaft, astern
" **(naut.):** abaft, aft
" **a vessel:** astern, aft
behold: lo, see   [ence
being: esse, ens, exist-
belabor: drub, flog,
belate: delay   [thrash
beldam: hag   [seige
beleaguerment: siege,
Belgian canal: Yser
" **city:** Ans, Schent,
    Ghent, Arlon, Ypres,
" **coin:** belga   [Spa
" **commune:** Ans
" **Congo river:** Uele
" **marble:** rance
" **province:** Namur
" **resort:** spa
" **river:** Yser, Lys
" **seaport:** Ostend
" **town:** Spa, Ypres
" **violinist:** Ysaye
belie: slander, calum-
    niate
belief: ism, faith, creed,
    tenet, creedence, cre-
    dence, credo, idea,
    trust, doctrine
believe: credit, opine,
    think suppose
believer in God: Deist
belittled: derided, de-
    cried, disparaged
bell: gong
" **clapper:** tongue
" **tower:** belfry   [tain
belong: appertain, per-
belonging to: of
" " **neither neuter**
" " **spring:** vernal
belongings: traps, gear
below: infra, under,
    beneath
" **(poet.):** neath
belt: girdle, sash, band,
    encircle, zonic, strap,
    zone, surround
bemoan: lament, be-
    wail, wail
bend: stoop, trend,
    lean, crook, curve,
    flex, nod, bow, arch,
    sag
" **in timber:** sny
benediction: blessing
beneath: below, under

benefactor: patron, donor, giver
beneficent gift: blessing, boon [good
beneficial: salutary,
benefit: avail, profit, interest [charity
benevolence: mercy,
benevolent: kind

bent: trend, proneness, inclination, aptitude, tendency
bequeathed: demised, left, willed
berate: scold, rail, lash
bereave: deprive
bereft: lorn, forlorn
beseech: pray, plead, entreat, beg [siege
beset: harass, assail,
beside (prefix): par, para [moreover, and
besides: also, yet, else,
besiege: beleaguer, storm [mar
besmirch: soil, smear,
besom: broom
bespangle: star [dy
bespatter: splash, mud
best: finest, overcome, defeat, cream
" **of its kind:** ace
bestial: brutish, depraved
bestow: grant, give, confer, render, award, impart
" **approval:** smile
" **as due:** award
" **income upon:** endow
bet: wager, stake, gamble
" **in roulette:** bas
betel: siri
" **palm:** areca
betide: happen, befall
betimes: early
betoken: foreshow, indicate, bode, augur
betrayer: traitor
between: amid, betwixt [meta
" **(prefix):** dia, inter,
" **two extremes:** mesne
bevel: slope, slant
beverage: lager, porter, drink, cocoa, lemonade, tea, ale
bevy: group, flock, galaxy [bemoan
bewail: lament, weep,
bewilder: daze, stun, fog, dazzle
bewitch: enchant, hex
beyond: over, across, farther, past [sur
" **(prefix):** eg, para,
bias: influence, slant, diagonal, ply [sided
biased: partial, one-
Biblical city: Aven, Tyre, Nain, Ivah, Sidon, Nob, Sodon,

Sodom, Ono
" **country:** Edam, Edom, Elam, Ophir, Sodom, Seba, Moab
" " **native:** Elamite, Edomite
" **expression:** selah
" **food:** manna
" **giant:** Goliath
" **hunter:** Nimrod
" **judge:** elon
" **king:** Asa, Evi, Amon, Agag, Reba, Herod
" **kingdom:** Sheba
" **land:** Tob, Nod
" **Mt.:** Horeb, Ararat, Olivet, Peor
" **name:** Caleb, Eri, Ater, Adah, Leah, Pelleg, Ari, Iri
" **passage:** text
" **patriarch:** Abraham, Israel, Noah
" **people:** Moabite
" **plain:** Sharon
" **pool:** Siloam
" **priest:** Eli, Aaron
" **prophet:** Elisha, Elias [enon
" **region:** Enom,
" " **of darkness:** Rahab
" **sign:** selah
" **site:** Ophir
" **spice:** stacte
" **tower:** Edar, Babel
" **town:** Cana, Nain, Bethel, Endor
" **tribe:** Amon
" **vessel:** ark
" **weed:** tare
" **wise men:** magi
" **word:** selah, mene
bid: offer, summon, order, invite, obey, enjoin, command
bide: tarry, tolerate, await [narrow
bigoted: intolerant,
bilk: cheat
bill: beak, poster
" **of fare:** carte, menu
billiard cue: mace
" **player & writer:** Hoppe
" **shot:** carom, masse
" **stick:** cue
billow: wave, surge, sea
bin: crib
binary: double
bind: tape, truss, tie, restrain, fasten, obligate
biographical fragment: anecdote
biography: memoir, life
biological factor: id, genes (pl.)
" **group:** species
bird dog: setter
" **food:** seed
" **of gull family:** tern
" **house:** aviary,

nest, sea [can
" **(large):** emu, pelican
" **of peace:** dove
" **(pert. to):** avine, avian
" **plumage:** heron
" **of prey:** eagl, kite, vulture, erne, owl, elanet, hawk, ern
" " **a region:** ornis
" **(small):** tody, serin, tit, wren, pewee, finch, tontit, virec
" **wing part:** alula
birdling: nestling
birth (pert. to): natal
birthright: heritage
biscuit: roll, bun, rusk, cracker [ter, mitre
Bishop's headress: mi-
" **jurisdiction:** diocese
" **office:** see [cese
bit: scrap, morsel, piece
bite: sting, chop, morsel, corrode, snap, nip [champ
" **noisily:** gnaw,
biting: sharp, acid, sarcastic

bitter: virulent, poignant, gall, acerb, acrid, painful
" **cynic:** timon
" **flavoring agent:** asarum
" **herb:** rue, aloe
" **nut:** cola
" **vetch:** ers
bivalve: oyster, clam
bivouac: camp, encamp
bizarre: odd, outre
Bizet's pera: Carmen
black: ebon, melanic, inky, sooty, sable, jet
" **& blue:** livid
" **covering:** pall
" **gum:** tupelo
" **magic:** witchcraft
" **mineral:** jet
" **nightshade:** morel
" **pipe of Otago:** Miro
" **powdery substance:** soot
" **rock:** basalt
" **Sea peninsula:** Crimea
" **Seaport:** Odessa
" **substance:** tar, soot
" **swan:** trumpeter
" **& white mixture:** gray, grey
" **wood:** ebony, jackdaw
blackbird: daw, crow, ani, raven, merl, starling, jackdaw
blacken: sooty, ink denigrate
blackfish: tautog [work
blacksmith's art: smith-
" **tool:** anvil [ter
blacksnake (kind): rac-
blackthorn fruit: sloe
blade of grass: spear

blame: censure, accuse, reproach
blameless: innocent
blanch: pale, whiten
bland: mild, balmy, open, gentle
blandish: flatter [tara
blare of trumpet: tan-
blarney: flattery
blase: bored, sated
blaspheme: swear
blast: sere, sear, blight, shrivel
" **furnace:** smelter
blatant: noisy
blaze: flame, flare
bleach: whiten, etiolate
bleak: drear, raw, dismal
bleat: baa
blemish: stain, mar, spot, speck, fault, scar, taint, blot
blend: mix, mingle, merge
bless: anele, glorify, hallow, protect, beatify, concentrate
blessing: benison, boon
blight: nip, blast
blind: seel, sightless, shutter
" **fear:** panic
blissful: edenic, paradisiac
blister: scorch
blithe: gay, riant, cheerful, joyful
block: dam, bar, prevent, chump, stoppage
blockade: siege [lout
blockhead: dolt, oaf,
" **(arch.):** mome
blood: gore
" **(comb. form):** hem
" **of the gods:** ichor
" **kindred:** gens
" **sucking animal:** leech
" **vessel:** artery, vein
bloody: gory [glow
bloom: flower, blossom,
blossom: bud, flower, bloom, flourish
blot: spot, sully blemish, stain [cancel
" **out:** erase, delete,
blotch: mess, stain, mottle, blob
blow: rap, stroke, slap, thump, inflate
" **air forcibly thru nose:** snort
" **on head:** nob
" **up:** inflate
blowgun missile: dart
blue: azure, perse, depressed
" **bird:** jay
" **grass:** poa
bluish gray: merle, pearl, slate [take
blunder: err, error, mis-
blunt: dull, outspoken, obtuse, deaden, heb-
" **end:** stub [etate

blur: blear, dull
blushing: rosy, red
bluster: roister
board: plank
" **a ship**: embark
boast: vaunt, brag, praise, extol
boat: barge, scow, tug, punt, vessel, dory freighter, canoe, coracle, skiff
" **marker**: buoy
" **part**: prow, aft
bobbin: reel, spool
bode: indicat , portend, augur, presage
bodice: waist
" **posy**: corsage
bodily appetite: lust
body of advisers: cabinet
" " **armed men**: posse
" **bones**: ribs
" **of church**: nave
" **(comb. form)**: soma
" " **Jewish law** Talmud, Tora, Torah
" " **laws**: code
" " **learning**: lore
" **organ**: lung, liver, gland
" **(pert. to)**: somal
" **of printed matter**: text [maid
" **servant**: valet,
" **of solar system**: planet
" " **soldiers**: platoon, corps, militia, troop, regiment
" " **tree**: bole
bog: fen, moor, mire, morass, syrt, muskeg, marsh, swamp
" **substance**: peat
bogus: spurious
Bohemia city: Pilsen
" **dance**: redowa
" **religious reformer**: Huss
" **river**: Iser [mer
boil: stew, seethe, sim-
" **on eyelid**: stye
boisterous play: romp
bolar: clayey
bold: pert, daring, keep
Bolivian Indian: Uro, Uru, Iten
" **product**: tin
bolster: support, crop
bolt: rivet, lock, dart, pin, fasten, fastener, sift
bomb (kind): petard, grenade, atom, shell
bombard: batter, shell
" **fiercely**: strafe
bombast: rant, rave
bombastic: stilted
" **talk**: rant
bombproof chamber: casemate [eggers
bombycid moths: ios,

bond: tie, security, covenant, ligament [ery
bondage: serfage, slav-
bondman: slave, thrall, vassal, serf
bone: os, rib, ilia, talus
" **of arm**: ulna
" **cavity**: antrum
" **(comb. form)**: osteo [ulnar
" **of forearm**: ulna,
" " **hard palate**: palatine [one, fibula
" " **leg**: tibia, per-
" **(prefix)**: oste [mur
" **of thigh**: tibia, fe-
bones: ossa
bony: osteal, thin
book: mo
" **of accounts**: ledger
" " **Bible**: Jonah, Kings, Amos, Genesis, Lev, Titus, Romans, Micah, Luke, Psalms, Hosea, Ezra, Exodus, Acts, Mark
" " **devotions**: missal
" " **gospel**: Mark
" **(large)**: tome
" **of Jewish law**: Talmud
" " **Old Testament**: Hosea, Isaiah, Daniel, Amos, Ezra
" **palm**: tara
" **of psalms**: psalter
" " **runrics**: ordo
boon: blessing
boor: churl, kern, rustic
boost: hoist, raise
booth: stall, loge, stand
booty: prey, swag, spoils, spoil, loot
border: abut, skirt, fringe, hem, margin, side, edge, brink, verge
" **for a picture**: mat
bore: pall, drill, weary
" **into**: eat
boredom: ennui
boring: dull, tiresome
" **tool**: awl, drill, bit, auger, wimble, gimlet
born: natural, nee
boron with another element: bo ide
bother: molest, pester, harass, trouble, ado, bore, fuss, a l, perplex
bottle for liquids: car-
" **(small)**: vial [boy
" **stopper**: cork
bottom: root
" **of ship**: keel
bottomless: abysmal
bough: limb, branch
" **of tree**: ramage
bound: dart, obligated, tied, base, leap, limit, ambit
boundary: terminus, limit, mete, line, side,
" **line**: mete

" **(outer)**: perimeter
bounder: cad [profuse
bountiful: generous,
bouquet: corsage, aroma bunch, spray, posy
bout: setto, contest
bovine animal: cow, ox, cattle (pl.)
" **(male)**: steer, bull
bow: nod, arc, bend, prow, submit, stoop, yield, curve, arch
" **of vessel**: prow
bower: arbor
bowfin: amia
bowman: archer
box: crate, spar, case, chest, stow, loge
" **for live fish**: car
" " **packing**: kit
boy attendant: page
" **(small)**: tad
brace: pair, prop, support, strut
braced framework: trestle
bracing: tonic
brad: nail
brag: cite, crow, boast
braid: plait, lacet, cue, tress, interlace, pat
brain: thwart, intellect, mind
" **passage**: iter [ly
brambly: thorny, prick-
branch: bough, limb, arm [art
" **of learning**: arts,
" " **math.**: calculus
" **off**: diverge, fork
" **(small)**: sprig, twig
branched: ramose
brand: stamp, mark
brandish: swing, flourish
brash: bold, brittle, impudent, saucy
brave: valiant, intrepid, dare, spartan, daring, defy, stout, gallant, heroic
" **& enduring person**: spartan
bravery: valor [fracas
brawl: riot melee, row,
braying instrument: pestle
Brazilian bird: agami, ara, seriema
" **city**: Para, Rio
" **coin**: rei
" **drink**: assai
" **estuary**: para
" **money**: rei
" **palm**: jupati
" **parrot**: ara
" **river**: Ica, Apa
" **rubber tree**: para
" **seaport**: Para, Natal, Santos
" **state**: Bahia, Para
" **tapir**: anta, antae
" **tree**: araroba [gap
breach: strand, rent,
bread basket: pannier

" **& milk**: panada
break: snap, fracture, destroy, rent, rift, sever, rend
" **away**: escape
" **in continuity**: gap
" **a hole in**: stave
" **off**: end
" **one's sword**: renig
" **into pieces**: shatter, crumble
" **suddenly**: pop
" **up**: disband
" **violently**: burst
" **without warning**: snap [tive
breaking forth: erup-
breakwater: pier, m le,
breastplate: armor [cob
breastwork: parapet
breathe: respire
" **convulsively**: gasp
" **in**: inhale
" **noisily**: snort
" **quickly**: pant
breathing: rale
" **orifice**: spiracle
breed: progeny, ilk, originate, propagate
" **of cattle**: devon
" **chickens**: shanghai, bantam
" " **pigeons**: nun
" " **Scottish terriers**: skye [zephyr
breeze: aura, air,
breezy: airy, windy
brew: ale, gather
brewing agent: malt
bribe: s p, grease
bric a brac stand: etagere, whatnot
brick: tile
" **carrier**: hod
brickbat: missile
bridge: span
" **over gorge**: viaduct
bridle: restrain, rep ess
" **bit without curb**: snaffle
" **part**: bi
" **strap**: rein
brief: short, curt, curtal, transitory, terse
" **extract**: scrap
" **notice**: mention
" **period**: spurt
" **remark**: word
brier: thorn, pipe
brigand: pirate
bright: garnish, smart, sunny, rosy, nitid,
" **saying**: mot [riant
" **star**: nova
brighten: light [lucida
brightest star: cor, sun,
brightness sunniness, sheen, sunshine
brilliancy of achievement: eclat
brilliant: refulgent
brim: lip, edge, margin
brimless cap: tam, fez
bring: fetch
" **back**: restore
" **charge against**: ac-

cuse, delate
" down: lower
" forth (Scot.): ean
" forward: adduce
" into being: create
"   " confict: engage
"   " court: arraign
"   " harmony: at-
tune   [align
"   " row: aline,
" on: induce, incur
" to life again: revive
"   " light: unearth,
elicit
"   " memory: re-
mind, recall
"   " standstill: stall
" together: compile
" up: rear
bringer of misfortune:
jonah, jinx
brink: edge, verge, border, rim, bank
briny: salty
brisk: lively, live, spry,
snappy, fresh, active,
brightly
bristle: seta, tela, awn
" like appendage:
arista
bristly: setose, seta
British bar: pub
" colony in Arabia:
Aden
" gasoline: petrol
" Indian coin: anna
"   " district: Banda,
Bengal
"   " monetary unit:
anna rupee
" legislature: parlia-
ment
" mining truck: corf
" oak: robur
" parliament mem-
bers: commons
" territorial division:
shire
" territory in Africa:
Nigeria
brittle: crisp, brash,
fragile   [liberal
broad: wide, spacious,
" thick piece: slab
" thin piece: sheet
" topped hill: loma
brokerage: agio
bronze: tan
" money: aes
brood: incubate, sit,
set, team, ponder
" of pheasants: nyes,
nide, nye, ni i
"   " young fishes:
fry
brook: run, stomach
" (small): rill, rillet,
rivulet
broom: besom, barsom
brother: fra
brown: toast
" apple: russet
" color: sepia, pablo,
umber, tenne
brownie: nis
bruise: pommel, batter,

contuse, contusion
brush: sweep, skirmish
brute: animal
brutish: coarse, bestial,
stolid, gross
bryophictic plant: moss
bubble: bleb, bead
" up: boil
buccaneer: pirate
bucket: pail
" used in mining:
tub
buckwheat tree: titi,
teetee
bucolic: rustic, rural
bud: sprout, scion, burgeon, blossom, cion
**Buddhist church in Ja-
pan:** Tera
" column: lat
" mound: stupa
" pillar: lat
" priest: lama, bo
" scripture lang.: pali
" temple approach:
toran
buddy: crony, pal
buffoon: mime, clown,
mimer, droll
build: erect, create,
construct   [fice
building: erection, edi-
" lot: site
" material: mortar,
concrete, laterite
" part: wing, apse
Bulgarian coi: 'ev
bulging pot: olla
bulk: mass, size
bulky: big, large
bull toro, taurus
bullet: shot, slugs
bullfighter: toreador,
matador, torero,
picador
bullfinch: olp
bully: hector
bulrush: tule
bulwark: rampart, de-
fense, fence
bunch: wad, tuft, wisp
bundle: parcel, bale,
package
" of grain: sheaf
" sticks: fagot
bundling machine:
baler
bungle: botch
bunting: etamine
buoy: float
buoyant: elastic, levitate, sprightly
burden: lade, load, laden, saddle, onus
burdensome: grievous,
heavy, onerous
bureau: d esser
burglar: thief
" (slang): yegg
" 's tool: jimmy [ire
burlesque: parody, sat-
Burmese city: Rangoon
" demon: nat
" native: wa, lai
" town: Mandalay

" tribe: Tai, Lai
" umbrella finial: tee
burn: scald, sear, char,
smart, singe
" to ashes: cremate,
incinerate
" brightly: flame
" slowly: smoulder
" unsteadily: flicker,
flare   [torrid
burning: afire, ablaze,
" pile: pyre
burr in wood: knar
burrow: dig, mine
burrowing animal:
mole, gopher, mar-
mot, rabbit   [plode
burst: spurt, rend, ex-
" asunder: disrupt
" of cheers: salvo
" forth: pop, sally,
bury: inter   [erupted
bush: shrub, tod
bushy: shaggy
" clump: tod
" herb: rue
business getter: ad
" house: firm
bustle: ado, tod , stir,
bother, fuss
busy: engaged, diligent,
occupied
" place: hive
busybody: meddler
but: yet, save, merely,
butt: ram, target [mere
butter: oleo
butterfly: io
" (kind): diana, skip-
per, ursula
button: stud
buttress: prop
buy: purchase
" back: redeem
buzz: drone, hum
by: per, at, past, alongside, near, via
" means of: per
" oneself (comb.
form): aut
" passes: tunnels
" side of: beside,
along
" way of: via, per
bypath: lane

C

caama: asse   [taxi
cab: hack, hansom,
cabal: plot
cabbage: kale
" like plant: cole
" (var.): cale, kale
cabin: hut, lodge
cache: hide
cachet: seal
cactus (small): mescal
caddis worm: cadew
cadillo: burdock
cadis worm: cadew
Cadmus's daughter:
Temple, Ino, Semele
cadre: framework
cage: confine, imprison

cajole: flatter, wheedle,
cake: scone, bar [coax
" (small): bun
calabash: gourd
calamitous: dire, evil,
tragic, fatal
calculate: rate, estimate, figure, reckon
" means of: average
calculating instrument:
abacus
Caledonian: Scot
calendar: almanac
calf flesh: veal
" of leg (of the):
sural
caliber: bore
Calif. bulrush: Tule
" holly: toyon
" lake: Tahoe
" laurel: myrtle
" mt.: Sierras
"   " peak: Shasta
" volcano: Shasta
call: dub, term, name,
page, entitle, style,
summon, denomi-
nate, visit
" for aid: appeal
" boy: page
" forth: evoke, elict
" loudly: cry, hail
" together: convoke
caller: visitor, guest
calloused: horny
calm: serene, mild, allay, soothe, com-
posed, cool, peace
calorie: therm
calumniate: asperse,
slur, belie, slander
calyx leaf: sepal, petal
came to rest: lit, alit,
sat
camel driver: sarwan
" hair cloth: aba
camelopard: giraffe
camera stand: tripod
Cameron native: Sara,
Abo
can: able, tin, preserve
Canadian city: Saskat,
Levis, Banff
" emblem: maple
" lake: Reindeer
" national park: Yoho
" peninsula: Gaspe
" province: N.S., On-
tario, Manitoba, Alta
" river: Yukon
canal: passage, duct,
Suez, Panama
canard: hoax
cancel: delete, dele,
revoke, rescind, re-
mit, erase, annul
candid: frank
candidate: aspirant,
nominee
" list: slate
candle: taper, luminary,
dip
candlenut tree: ama
candy: sweets, caramel
cane: flog, rattan, flay
canine disease: rabies,

canoe: proa [mange
canon: law
canonize: saint [dais
canopy: finial, tester,
cant: slant, tip, tilt,
slope, heel, argot
canter: lope
canticle: song [py
canvas covering: cano-
canyon: valley, ravine
Caoutchouc tree: ule
cap: beret, fez, tam
crown, cover, excel,
top, coif, complete
capable: able, compe-
tent, efficient
" of being extended:
tensile
" " " maintain-
ed: tenable

capacious: ample, large
cape: ness, ras
Cape Verde Island:
Fogo, Sal
caper: prank, antic,
prance, dido, gambol,
frisk [uent
capital: chief, preemi-
caprices: whimsies, va-
garies, fancies, whims
captain's boat: gig
captivate: enamor,
charm, enthrall
capture: bag, take, ar-
rest, catch
Capuchin monkey: sai
caravansary: serai, ho-
carbon: soot [tel
carborundum: emery
card in faro: soda
" game: skat, whist,
monte, bezique, pam,
ecarte, faro, vint,
stuss, lu, hearts,
pedro, casino, brag,
cassino, fantan, pi-
nochle, nullo
" " (old): pam, loo
" holding: tenace
" (as wool): tease,
rove
care: concern, desire,
vigilance, worry,
heed, mind, caution,
anxiety, tend
" for: tend, attend,
mind, nurse
careen: list, lurch
career: course, vocation
careful: provident, dis-
creet
careless: heedless, re-
miss, neglectful, slack
caress: fondle, pet
cargo: load, lading,
freight
" cast overboard:
jetsam
caribou: reindeer
caricature: cartoon
carnelian: sard
carvivore: civet, genet,
ratel, cat, lion
carnivorous insect:
mantis

carol: sing, warble
Caroline Island: Yap
carom: rebound [orgy
carousal: spree, revel,
carouse: revel
carp fish: dace
carpenter's tool: saw,
plane
carpet: mat
carriage: phaeton, mien,
poise, shay, rig, gig,
air, clarence, chariot,
bearing
carried: borne
carry: sustain, tote,
convey, bear
" across water: ferry
" away as property:
eloin [prosecute
" on: wage, transact,
" out: execute
" again: reenact
" too far: overdo
carrying charge: cart-
age [van
cart: wagon, haul, dray,
cartridge: shot, shell
carve: cut, slice
carved gem & stone:
cameo [statues
" images: statuary,
carving tool: chisel
cascade: waterfall
case: instance, crate,
chest, encase, box,
container, example,
plight
" for small toiletries:
etui
cash: specie, money
" box: till
cask: tun, barrel, keg,
tierce, tub, vat,
bareca
casket for valuables:
coffer
cast: shade, throw,
heave, hove
" down: abase
" forth: heave, hove
" metal mass: pig,
ingot
" off: shed, molt
" out: expel [leer
" sidelong glances:
castaway: waif
caste: class
caster: cruet
castigate: punish
castle: fort, palace,
fortress
Castor & Pollux's
mother: Leda
cat: feline, felid, gri-
malkin, puss, manx,
anchor
" cry: mew, pur, purr
" (kind): angora,
maltese, ocelot
catalogue: list
catapult (kind): onager
catch: nab, snare, seize,
detent, hasp, over-
take, trap
" the breath: gasp

" of game: bag
" for a hook: eye
" sight of: espy
" (slang): cop, nab
catching device: net
catchword: cue, slogan
category: genre
catena: chain
cater: purvey
" to base desires:
pander
catkin: ament
catlike: feline
catnip: nep
cattle: kine, cows
" dealers: drovers
caudal appendage: tail
cause: reason, produce,
motive, provoke
" to adhere: cement,
unite
" to branch: ramify
" to coalesce: merge
" emotion: emote
" exhaustion of:
drain
" to float gently:
waft
" to go: send [mind
" to remember: re-
" to revolve: trundle
" of ruin: bane
" (Scot.): gar
" sudden surprise &
fear: startle
caustic: acrid, erodent,
lye, tart
" compound: lye,
erodent, lime
cauterize: scar, sere,
sear, burn

caution: warn, care,
wariness
" in advance: fore-
warn
cautious: careful, wary,
canny
cavalier: knight
cavalry soldier: lancer
cave: grotto, cavern,
den, lair
" (arch.): antre
cavil: carp
cavities: atria, antra
cavity: sinue, sac, ora-
ter, pit, hole
cavort: play, prance
cease: desist, cessate,
pause, stop, quit
" (naut.): avast
cebine monkey: sai
cede: yield, grant
celebration: gala, fes-
tivity, fete
celestial: uranic
" beings: angles, ser-
aphs, seraphim
" body: comet, star,
sun, moon [ula
" phenomenon: neb-
" region: sky
" sphere: orb
celibate: unmarried
cellulose fiber: rayon
Celtic: Irish

" lang.: Gael, Erse,
Welsh, Irish
cement: paste, lime,
mastic, solder, lute,
unite
censure: asperse, slate,
accuse, taunt, blame,
reprove, condemn
center: core, middle
centerpiece: epergne
central: eboe, mid,
chief, hub
Central Amer. Indian:
Ona, Carib, Inca,
Nahua
" " republic: Pan-
ama
" " rodent: paca
" " tree: ule, Eboe,
Ebo
" cylinder of plants:
stela, stele
" part: core
" point: focus, hub
" " (pert. to): focal
century: age [pita
" plant: aloe, agave,
ceratoid: horny
cere: wax
cereal: rice, grain
" grass: oat
" husk: bran
" spike: ear
ceremonial dance: pa-
vane, pavan [pomp
ceremony: rite, fete,
certain: sure, positive
certificate in lieu of
cash: scrip
certify: attest
cess: tax
cessation: pause, fail-
ure, stop, lull
" of being: desition
cetacean: inia
chafe: fret, grate, rub,
gall, irk
chaff: banter, guy
chaffy part of grain:
brain, bran
chagrin: abash, shame,
vexation
chain: catenae, catena,
fetter, restrain
" part & ring: link
chainlike: catenate
chair: seat
" back piece: splat
chalcedony (var.): sard,
agate
Chaldea city: Ur
chalice: grail, grill, ama,
goblet
" cover: pall
chalk: crayon, whiten
challenge: dare, cartel,
stump, defy
chamber: room
champagne (kind): ay
chance: odd, hap, ran-
dom, fortune, risk,
happen, accident,
luck
chancel part: bema
change: revise, alter,
shift, mutation, mu-

tate, convert, transmute, transfer, emend, amend, vary, revision
" **color of:** dye
" **course:** reverse
" **direction:** veer, turn
" **form:** remodel
" **the title:** rename
changeless: constant
changeling: oaf
channel: chute, flume, vale, strait, gat, way, passage
chant: intone, chortle, sing
chap: fellow, split, crack
chaplet: anadem
char: scorch, burn
character: role, nature, quality, tone, stamp
" **of a people:** ethos
characteristic: mark, trait, typical, feature
" **form of expression:** idiom
" **mark:** stamp
" **taste:** smack
characterization: role
characterless: inane
charge: cost, rate, load, debit, fee, accusation, fare, rush, price, ac-
" **per unit:** rate [cuse
" **on property:** lien,
" **a sum:** debit [tax
" **for using a road:** toll
" **with crime:** indict
" " **gas:** aerate
" **with electricity:** alive, live
charger: steed
chariot: essed, carriage
charioteer: Hur
charity: alms, love, benevolence
charlatan: quack
Charles Dickens: Boz
charm: grace, attract, captivate, amulet, talisman, spell, entrance, entice, enchant
chart: plan, map, plot, graph, plat
chary: frugal, sparing, prudent [hunt
chase: pursue, follow,
chasm: abyss, gulf, cleft
chaste: pure, modest

chasten: smite, train, chastize [reprove
chastise: berate, swinge,
chat: talk, converse
chatter: prate, gab, gabble
cheat: dupe, cozen, fraud, hocus, fleece, defraud, mulct, fob, bilk, swindler
" (**colloq.**): stick
" (**slang**): welsh, bam

check: repress, stem, rein, arrest, test, curb, inhibit, restrain
" **growth:** stunt, nip
checkered cloth: tartan,
cheek: gena [plaid
" **bone:** malar
" (**of the**): molar, malar, genal
cheer: gladden, elation, rah, encourage, hearten, applaud, inspirit
cheerful: genial, blithe, joyful, sunny
" **tune:** lilt
cheerless: dreary
cheese dish: rarebit
" (**kind**): edam, brie, gruyere, parmesan, cheddar, stilton
chemical compound: ester, amine, water, amide, sucrate
" **suffix:** ine, yl, al, ol, ite, ose, olid
" **vessel:** udell, aludel
herish: bosom, nurse, foster
cherry color: cerise
chess opening: gambit
" **pieces:** men, pawns, rooks, knights, castles, queens
chest: safe, thorax, case, coffer
" **bone:** rib
" **noise:** rale
chestnut & grey: roan
chevrotain: napu
chew: manducate, masticate
" **audibly:** crunch
chic: modish, smart
chick pea: gram [tam
chicken (small): ban-

chickory like herb: endive [rebuke
chide: scold, berate,
chief: headman, head, principal, staple, primal, arch, main, prime, capital, paramount, first, central
" **of clan:** Thane
" **commodity of region:** staple
child (comb. form): ped
" (**small**): tot, tad
childish: puerile, anile
Chile city: Talca, Arica
" **timber tree:** muermo, rauli [frost
chill: ice, cool, ague,
" **'s & fever:** ague, malaria
chimes: bells
chimney: flue, stack
" **passage:** flue
Chinese animal: rasse
" **antelope:** tserin
" **boat:** sampan
" **building:** pagoda
" **bushy plant:** udo
" **card game:** lu, loo
" **city:** Amoy, Ude,

Nom, Pekin
" **civet cat:** rasse
" **coin:** tael, tsien, pu
" (**comb. form**): sino
" **dependency:** Tibet
" **dialect:** wu
" **dynasty:** Ming, Han Yin, Tang
" **herb:** ginseng, tea
" **laborer:** coolie
" **measure:** tua, li, tael, tu, ri
" **medium of exchange:** sycee
" **mile:** li
" **monetary unit:** tael
" **money:** sycee
" " **of account:** tiao
" **obeisance (var.):** salam
" **official:** Mandarin
" **pagoda:** taa, ta
" **philosopher:** Confucius
" **plant:** tea
" **pound:** catty
" **puzzle:** tangram
" **religion:** taoism

" **river:** Peh, Gan, Tung
" **secret society:** tong
" **shrub:** tea
" **skiff:** sampan
" **statesman:** Koo
" **tea:** tsia
" **temple:** pagoda
" **treaty port:** Amoy, Wenchow
" **unit of value:** tael
" **wax:** pela [li
" **weight:** liang, tsien,
chip: fragment, flake
chirp: peep, twitter, tweet
chisel to break ore: gad
chloroform substance: acetone [best, option
choice: elite, prime,
" **morsel:** titbit
choicest: best
" **part:** marrow
choose: select, prefer, elect, opt
" **for office:** slate
chop: hew, mince, lop, bite, hack
chord of 3 tones: triad
chore: stint, task
Christmas: Yule, Noel
chronicle: record, annal
chrysalis: pupa, pupae
chum: friend, crony, pal
church: chapel, basilica
" **body:** nave
" **caretaker:** sexton
" **chancel:** bema
" **congregation:** synaxis
" **council:** synod
" **dignitary:** canon, prelate, pope
" **land:** glebe
" **officer:** trustee, bishop, elder, sexton
" **official:** elder, pope, deacon, beadle, pas-

tor, priest
" **part:** apse, nave, chancel, steeple, altar, transept
" **service:** mass
" **sitting:** pew
" **vault:** crypt
churl: boor, thane
cicada: locust
cicatrix: scar
cigar: panetela, cheroot, stogie, stogy
" **fish:** scad
" (**long**): corona
cigarette (slang): fag
cinder: ash
cion: sprout, twig, bud
cipher: zero, code, null, naught,
Circe's sister: Medea
circle: arc, ring, orb, loop
" **around the moon:** corona
" **of light:** halo
" **part:** sector
circlet: ring, wreath
circuit: tour, cycle, lap, ambit
" **court:** Eyre
circular: round
" **band:** hoop
" **disc:** plate
" **indicator:** dial
" **plate:** disc, disk
circumscribed: narrow, limited [event
circumstance: fact
cistern: bac, tank, vat
citadel: tower, stronghold [lin
" **of Moscow:** Krem-
cite: adduce, allege, quote, summon
citizen: resident
citron: cedrat
city official: mayor, alderman
" (**pert. to**): civic, urban, municipal
civet: rasse
" **like animal:** genet
civil injury & wrong: tort
" **law term:** aval
clad: garbed, dressed, drest
claim: maintain, require, title, demand, lien
" **on property:** lien
claimant: pretender
clamor: din, noise, outcry, bark
clamorous: loud, noisy
clamp: nip, fastener
clamping device: vise
clan: sept, tribe, sect, gens, clique
clandestine: secret
clarify: define, clear
clash: jar, conflict
clasp: grasp, fastener, hold, hook, seize
" **pin:** broach

class: sect, grade, caste, genue, group, sort, rank, genus
class jargon: argot
classify: rate, sort, arrange, assort, label, grade   [din
clatter: rattle, clack,
claw: talon, scratch
clay: loam, laterite, marl, pug, earth
" (pert. to): bolar
clayey: bolar, loamy
" **earth**: loess, loam, marl
clean: pure, neat, spotless, purify, fair, wipe
cleanse: bathe, rinse, scrub, scour, deterge
" **wool**: card
clear: pure, exonerate, net, serene, rid, clarify, plain, evident, crystal, lucid
" **sky**: ether   [glade
cleared woods: grove,
cleave: cut, rend, tear, rive, split, hew
cleft: divided, riven, chasm, fissure, cut, rift, gap   [niency
clemency: mercy, le-
clement: mild, lenient
Cleopatra's attendant: Iras
" **pet**: asp   [tor
clergyman: vicar, priest, cleric, rector, parson, minister, curate, pas-
clerical collar: rabat
" **dress**: vestment
" **title**: reverend, abba, abbe
" **vestment**: alb
clever: astute, smart, talented, cute, apt, able, dexterous, shrewd, slick
cleverness: wit, art
click beetle: elater, dor
cliff: crag, precipice
climax: apogee, top, end   [rise, shin
climb: scale, ascend,
climbing herb: hop, pea
" **palm**: rattan
" **pepper**: betel [ivy
" **plant**: vine, liane, liana, bine, creeper,
" **stem**: bine
clime: region
clinch: nail, grapple
cling: cohere, adhere
clinging fish: remora
clip: shear, snap, curtail, snip, nip, mow
cloak: robe, wrap, mantle, disguise, hide
clock: time
" **face**: dial
" **part**: pendulum
" **in shape of ship**: nef
clog: impede   [ory
cloister: hermitage, pri-
close: end, near, shut,

dense, finale, seal
" **bond**: tic
" **by**: nigh   [sunset
" **of day**: eventide,
" " " (**Poet.**): een, eve   [cloche
" **fitting cap**: coif,
" **mouthed**: clam
" (poet.): anear
" **ties**: bonds
" **to**: near, at
closing chord: cadence
cloth: denim, serge, marl, baize, satinet, rep, satin, melton, tweed, worsted, leno
" **fibers**: nap
" **measure**: ell
" **strainer**: tamis
clothed: clad, garbed, attired, dressed, arrayed   [toggery
clothes: togs, apparel,
" **basket**: hamper
" **brush**: whisk   [er
" **dryer**: airer, wring-
" **moth**: tinea
" **rack**: tree, airer
cloud: cumulus, cirrus
cloudless: clear
cloudlike mass: nebula
cloudy: nebulous, dim, nebular
cloverlike plant: melitot
clown: loon, mime, buffoon, bumpkin
cloy: sate, pall, surfeit
club: mace, bat
" **shaped**: claviform clavate,
clue: hint, tip
clump: tuft
" **of earth**: clod
clumsy: inept, awkward
" **boat**: ark
" **fellow**: lout, lubber, oaf, gawk
" **work**: botch
cluster of spore cases: sori, sorus   [grove
" " **trees**: thicket,
clutch: grasp, hold, grab, seize, grip
coach: trainer, train
coachman: driver [gel
coagulate: clot, curdle,
coal box: hod
" **fragment**: ember
" **lifter**: shovel
" **mine shaft**: pit
" **miner**: collier
" **product**: tar
" **shuttle**: hod
" **wagon**: tram
coalesce: unite
coalition: fusion, union
coarse: brutish, ribald, thick, crass
" **cloth**: manta, burlap, leno, scrim
" **fiber**: tow, adad
" **hominy**: samp, grits   [ecru
" **linen fabric**: crash,
" **matted wool**: shag
" **of procedure**: proc-

ess   [bristle
" **rigid hair**: seta,
coast: shore, slide
coat: cover, layer
" **of animal**: fur, pelage   [heraldic
" " **arms**: crest,
" " **certain alloy**: tern, terne
" " **gold**: gild
" **with icing**: glace
" " **metal**: plate
coax: tease, cajole
cocoanut fiber: coir
code: cipher, law
coffee bean: nib
" **cake**: stollen [java
" (**kind**): mocha,
coffer: chest, ark
coffin: bier
cog: tooth, pawl, gear
cogent: valid, conclusive, convincing
cogitate: think, ponder, muse, mull
cognizance: ken
cognizant: aware
cogwheel: gear   [wind
coil: twist, twine, curl,
" **into a ball**: clew
coin: mint, money, originate, pence   [spond
coincide: agree, corre-
cold: icy, frigid, gelid, chilly, frosty
" **dish**: salad
collarbone: clavicle
colleague: ally, partner, confrere
collect: gather, levy, amass, garner, pool, accumulate, compact
" **& keep**: hoard
" **to a point**: center
collection: set
" **of cattle**: drove
" " **facts**: ana
" " **implements**: kit
collector's item: curio
college dance: prom
" **officer**: proctor
" **official**: regent
" **session**: seminar
" **song**: glee
collide with: ram, bump
colonist: settler, planter
" **greeting to Indian**: netop   [sepia, red
color: tint, dye, roan, paint, stain, puce, tinge, bice, hue, olive,
" **lightly**: tinge
" **matter**: dye
" **quality**: tone, hue
Colorado Indian: Ute
" **Mt.**: Owen, Oso
coloring agent: dye, paint   [pallid
colorless: wan, pale,
" **liquid**: olein
Columbus's birthplace: Genoa
" **ship**: Nina, Pinta
column: pillar, pilaster
coma: stupor, lethargy

comb wool: card, tease
combat: duel, struggle, fight
" **place**: arena
combine: unite, merge
" **resources**: pool
combustible heap: pyre
combustion: fire
" **product**: smoke, soot, ash   [approach
come: arrive, reach,
" **ashore**: land
" **before**: precede
" **forth**: emerge, issue
" " **operation**: enure   [emerge, loom
" " **view**: appear,
" **to pass**: transpire, befall, happen
" " **rest**: lodge, light   [meet
" **together**: clash,
comedy: farce
comely: fair, pretty
comestible: edible
comfort: wry, ease, rest, solace, console
comical: funny, ludicrous   [join, edict
command: order, bade, behest, bid, fiat, beck, mandate, dictate, en-
" **to a horse**: gee, wo
commander: leader, chief   [orial
commemorative: mem-
" **disc**: medal
commence: open, start
commend: praise, order
commerce: trade, start
commission (honorary): brevet
commit: intrust, entrust, consign
" **to memory**: con
common: usual
" **fund**: pool
" **level**: par   [demos
" **people**: populace,
" **sayings**: dicta
" **talk**: rumor
commonplace: banal, trite, stale, usual, prosaic   [state
commonwealth: demos,
commotion: stir, todo, noise, welter, ado, fray   [sage, word
communication: mes-
communion cup: ama
" **plate**: paten
" **table**: altar
compact: tight, solid, terse, condense
" **mass**: wad   [friend
companion: mate, playmate, comrade, pal,
companionship: society
company: band, troop
" **of players**: team, troupe
" " **seamen**: crew
comparative: relative
" **suffix**: er   [trast

compare: liken, con-
" **critically:** collate
" **with fixed stand-
ard:** measure [alogy
comparison: simile, an-
compass: attain
compassion: pity
compel: oblige, force,
impel, coerce, drive
compendium: digest
compensate: redeem,
requite, pay, remu-
nerate [ment
compensation: fee, pay-
compete: vie, race
competent: able, capable, fit
compile: edit
complacement: smug
complain: repine, moan,
grunt, grumble, kick,
whine, beef
complement of bolt: nut
" " **a hook:** eye
complete: plenary, entire, finish, end, utter,
perfect, fulfill, total,
entire, cap, intact
" **disorder:** chaos
completed: over
" **(poet):** oer
completely: all, quite
" **developed:** mature
complex: abstruse, intricate [node
complication: nodus,
comply: adapt, obey,
accede, conform
component: element,
material, ingredient
" **of molecule:** atom
comport: agree [repose
compose: write, frame,
composed: calm
" **of:** consist
" " **different parts:**
compound [lar
" " **grains:** granu_

" " **hackled flax:**
towy, toury
" " **two elements:**
binary [say, opus
composition: theme, es-
" **for nine:** nonet
" " **two:** duet
" **in verse:** poem
composure: poise [ken
comprehension: grasp,
comprehensive: wide,
compress: squeeze,
wring, stupe [ess
compulsion: stress, dur-
compunction: penitence,
remorse
compute: add, reckon
conceal: hide, mask,
veil, mew, secrete,
palliate [yield, admit
concede: grant, hide,
conceited: vain, prided,
opinioned, egotistic
" **nature:** ego [tist
" **person:** snob, ego-
conceive: ideate, realize
concentrate: bless, center, focus, mass

concept: notion, idea,
opinion
concern: pertain, care,
matter, anxiety, in-
terest [about, on, of
concerning: anent, re,
conciliate: propitiate,
appease, mollify
conciliatory: irenic
concise: terse, curt
conclude: end, deter-
mine, infer, termi-
nate
concluding passage:
coda, epilogue
conclusion: end, finis,
upshot
concoct: brew, hatch
concord: peace, unison
concrete: beton, spe-
cific, real
concur: agree, assent
condemn: doom, cen-
sure, denounce, sen-
tence
condense: compact
condensed moisture:
dew
" **vapor:** fog
condescend: deign
condiment: vinegar,
curry, spice, mustard,
salt, pepper
" **cruet:** caster
condition: state, status,
if, estate, term, situa-
tion, fettle
" **barley:** malt
" **of payment:** terms
conduct: lead, wage,
direct, run, preside,
transact, deportment,
demean, escort
conduct oneself: be-
have, demean
conductor: maestro,
leader, guider
" **of electricity:** metal
conduit: main
cone: pina
" **bearing trees:** firs,
pines, coniferae
" **shaped:** conic
confectionary: candy,
sweets
confederacy: league
confederate: ally, band
confer upon: endow,
dub, grant, bestow
conference: powwow,
parley [avow
confess: admit, own,
confession of faith: credo, creed [entrust
confide: intrust, trust,
confidence: secret,
trust, faith
confident: sure, reliant
confine: stint, pend,
seal, pen, coop, mew,
cage, restrict, tether,
limit, imprison, in-
tern [ratify, attest
confirm: assure, seal,
conflict: war, clash, contest, battle [ply

conform to: adapt, com-
" **to the shape:** fit
confuse: befog, fluster,
bemuddle, muddle,
distract, abash
confused: chaotic
" **lang.:** jargon
" **murmur:** bizz, buzz
confusion: bother, mess,
turmoil
congeal: freeze, set
congenial: boon
congregate: mass, meet,
swarm, assemble
conic section: parabola,
ellipse
coniferous tree: yew,
cedar, fir, pine [ween
conjecture: opine, guess,
imagine, speculate,
conjurer: mage
" **'s rod:** wand
connect: unite, join
connected: coherent
" **sequence:** series
**connecting body of wa-
ter:** strait
" **link:** liaison, bond
" **pipe:** tee [relation
connection: link, nexus,
connective: and, that
connoisseur: judge
" **of food:** epicure
connubial: marital
conquer: master, defeat,
overcome, tame, beat
conqueror: victor, hero
conquest: victory
consecrate: bless, devote, dedicate
consent: agree, assent,
approval, permission
consequence: end, re-
sult [thus
consequently: so, hence,
conservative: Tory
conserve: save
consider: rate, ponder,
deem, regard, opine,
esteem, judge, think
consideration: reason,
price, attention, re-
gard [mit
consign: relegate, com-
console: solace, com-
fort, condole
consolidate: unite, knit
conspiracy: plot, cabal
conspire: plot, scheme,
collude
constant: invariant
" **desire:** itch
constantly: ever
constellation: aries, leo,
bootes, ara, ram,
orion, ursa, gemina,
argo, lyra, dipper,
mensa, draco, sirius
consternation: terror,
dismay [part
constituent: element,
constrain: astrict, manacle, force tie, oblige,
impel
constrict: cramp [rear

construct: build, erect,
construe: translate, interpret [fect
consummate: end, per-
contact: touch
contain: hold, embrace
container: case, pail,
basket, crate, pot,
box, holder, urn, can,
crate, sack, tub, vat,
con aining iron: ferric
" **lumps:** nodular
" **maxims:** gnomic
" **salt:** saline [file
contaminate: taint, de-
contemn: scorn
contemplate: meditate,
ponder [able
contemptible: cheap,
mean, base, despic-
contend: vie, cope,
strive, maintain, mili-
tate, assert
content: fain, satisfy
contention: strife
contest: game, dispute,
race, conflict, vie,
argue, strife, bout,
struggle [gate
" **law:** deraign, liti-
contiguous: near
continent: mainland
contingency: event, case
contingent: dependent
continual: endless, incessant [ceed
continue: last, resume,
remain, persist, pro-
continued knocking:
ratatat [twist
contorted: wry, warped,
contour: shape, line,
outline
contract: narrow, incur,
shrink, agreement,
knit, lease, covenant,
contradict: negate, belie,
rebut, deny
**contradictory state-
ment:** paradox
contrary: reverse
" **to rules:** foul
contrast: compare
contribute: redound,
render, tend
contribution: scot
contrite: penitent, sorry,
repentant, sorrowful
contrivance: device, engine [weave
contrive: devise, in-
vent, manage, plan,
control: rein, dominate,
govern, steer, man-
age, demean
controversial: polemic,
polemical, eristical
contuse: bruise
conundrum: riddle
convene: meet, sit
convenient: handy
conversation: speech,
talk, chat
convert: change, proselyte, transmute

convex molding: ovolo boltel, torus, reed
convey: sell, impart, remove, bring, ride, bear, carry, move, transfer, transport
" **beyond jurisdiction (law):** eloin [vehicle
conveyance: transit, car,
" **charge:** fare
" **for dead:** hearse
convince: assure
convincing: cogent
convoke: assemble
convulsion: spasm, fit
convulsive cry: sob
cooking term: rissole
" **pot:** olla
cooky: snap
cool: ice, sober, calm, fan   [frigerant
cooling device: fan, re-
coop up: pent, pen, corral, confine
copious: abundant
copper: CU, cent, penny
" **money:** aes
copy: imitate, ape, mimic, replica, image, transcribe
copyright: patent
coquettish: coy
Coral Islands: Atolls, Keys, Atoll   [rope
cord: line, twine, string,
corded cloth: rep, poplin   [ame
core: heart, gist, pith,
cork: stopper, suberic
corn: pickle, callus
" **bread:** pone
" **lily:** ixia
" **meal mush:** atole
corner: angle, nook, tree, niche, coign, in
" **of a sail:** clew
cornucopia: horn
corolla leaf: petal
coronet: tiara, crown
corpulent: fat, obese
correct: amend, emend, right, accurate, fit, OK
correlative: nor
correspond: tally, coincide   [rust
corrode: bite, eat, gnaw,
corrosion: erosion, rust
corrupt: taint, degrade, poison, deprave, pervert, evil, attaint
corsair: pirate, privateer
corundum: emery
corvine bird: crow, raven, rook
cosmetic: paint, rouge
Cossack chief: Ataman
cosset: fondle, pamper, pet   [price, rate
cost: expense, charge,
costly: dear, expensive, high, valuable
costume: attire, getup
cote: shed
coterie: clique, set
cotton fabric: percale,

denim, leno, pima, surat, silesia, muslin, satinet, calico, khaki
" **seed capsule:** boll
" " **machine:** gin
couch: bed, divan, sofa
cougar: puma
counsel: advice
" **(arch.):** rede
count: number   [visage
countenance: abet, face,
counterfeit: pretend, base, sham, simulate, fake, forge   [twin
counterpart: parallel,
countrified: rural   [soil
country: land, nation,
" **gallant:** swain
county: shire, parish
coup: upset   [link
couple: pair, yoke, two,
courage: valor, nerve, mettle, dares, heart, grit, sand
courageous: bold, brave
course: way, trail, route, career, path, direction, tenor, road
" **of action:** trend, routine, habit
" " **eating:** diet
" " **operation:** run
" " **travel:** route
court: woo, solicit, patio
" **crier:** beadle
" " **'s call:** oyes
" **hearings:** oyers
" **of justice:** bar
" **officer:** crier
" **order:** writ, mem-
courtly: aulic   [damus
courtyard: patio   [bond
covenant: promise, testament, contract,
cover: sheathe, lid, screen, cap, coat, tree, pretext, envelop, shelter, hide
" **for the face:** mask
" **the inside:** line
" **the top:** cap
" **with asphalt:** pave
" " **cloth:** drape
" " **dots:** bedot, stipple
" " **first plain coat:** prime   [gild, engild
" " **gold:** plate,
" " **jewels:** begem
covered cloister: stoa
" **colonade:** stoa
" **walk:** arcade
" **with hair:** pilar
" " **vine:** ivied
" " **water:** awash
covering of head: scalp
covert: thicket, sheltered, secret, hidden
covet: desire, envy, crave, wish
covetousness: avarice
cow: daunt, overawe
" **barn:** byre
" **headed deity:** Isis
coward: recreant, cra-

ven, dastard, sneak, poltroon   [tardly
cowardly: craven, das-
" **carnivore:** hyena
cower: cringe, shrink, quail
cowfish: toro
coy: shy, demure, reserved, bashful
cozenage: deceit
cozy: snug
" **retreat:** nest
crackle: snap, crepitate
crack: snap, fissure, chap
craft: art, trade, vessel
crafty: sly, astute
crag: cliff, tor
cram: wad, stuff, crowd
cramp: restrain, constrict, hinder
cranium: skull
cranny: fissure
crash: smash
cravat: tie, ascot
carve: seek, covet, desire, long, entreat
craven: coward, cowardly   [imia
craving: yen, desiring, appetite, thirst, bul-
craw: crop, maw
crawl along: slither, creep   [worm
crawling animal: reptile,
crayon: chalk, pencil
" **picture:** pastel
craze: mania, fad, derange, furor, madden
crazy: daft, loco, loony, demented, daffy
cream (the): elite   [ruga
crease: wrinkle, fold,
create: originate, generate, make, form, produce, devise
" **force:** nature
creator: author
credence: belief
credible: likely   [honor
credit: trust, believe,
credo: creed, belief
creed: credo, tenet
creek: rivulet, stream, bayou, ria, cove
creep away: slink   [liana
" **plant:** ipecac, vine,
crepitate: crackle
cresent shaped: moony, lunate   [nate, lunette
" " **figure:** lune, lu-
crest: peak, top, crown, plume, tuft, summit
" **of a wave:** comb
Crete Mt. Ada, Ida
crew: gang, band
crib for storage: bin
cribbage pin; peg
" **score:** peg
" **term:** nob
cricket play: twister
" **position:** slip
" **side:** eleven
" **sound:** chirp
crime: felony, iniquity
Crimea river: Alma   [ado
criminal: felon, desper-

crimp: wrinkle, crinkle
cringe: cower, grovel, fawn   [wrinkle
crinkle: crumple, crimp,
cripple: maim, lame
crisp: brittle, curt
" **cookie:** snap
criterion: test, standard
critic: censor, caviler
critical: acute
" **moment:** crisis   [sor
criticize officially: cen-
" **severely (colloq.):** roast, pan, rap
Croatian: Croat   [loop
crochet stitch: tricot,
crocodile: mugger, goa
crone: hag   [pal, chum
crony: friend, buddy,
crook: curve, bend
crooked: awry, wry, bent, askew
" **(Scot.):** agee   [duce
crop: sprout, craw, pro-
cross: traverse, rood, angry, span, intersect, surly, peevish
" **rib:** lierne
" **shaped:** cruciate
" **stroke:** serif
" **timber:** spale
" **by wading:** ford
crossbeam: trave
crossbreed: hybrid
crow: brag, rook, raven
crowbar: lever
crowd: mob, gathering, horde, serry, press, throng, cram, jam, pack, herd
crowfoot flower: anemone, peony   [raven
crowlike bird: oriole, rook, daw, jackdaw,
crown: tiara, crest, diadm, coronet, cap
crucifix: rood
crude: raw, crass
" **dwelling:** hut
" **metal:** ore   [mean
cruel: pitiless, ogrish,
cruet: caster
crus: shank, leg
crush: mash, grind
" **(colloq.):** scrunch
crustacean: crab, lobster, prawn, isopod
cry: weep, moan, snivel, sob, hue, shout, wail
cryptic: occult
cryptogamous plant: moss
crystal: clear
" **gazer:** seer
crystalline compound: elaterin, alanine, parillin   [spar
" **mineral:** spinelle,
" **salt:** borax, niter
Cuban measure: tarea
" **tobacco:** capa
cube: die, dice
cubic content: volume
" **decimeter:** liter
" **measure:** cord
" **meter:** stere

cuckoo: ani
cuckoopint: arum
cud: rumen
cuddle: nestle, snuggle
cudgel: bat, staff, drub
cue: hint, braid
cuirass: lorica
cull: sift, sort, assort
culmination: acme, end, climax, zenith
culpable: guilty
culprit: criminal
cultivate: till, farm, hoe, garden, foster, [do
cultivated ground: ara-
culture: refinement
culture media: agar
cunning: astute, cute, craft, sly, foxy
Cupid: Eros, Amor
" 's love: Psyche
cupidity: avarice, greed
cupola: dome, turret
curate: clergyman
curb: repress, restrain, rein, check
cure: heal, vulcanize, remedy, preserve
" all: panacea, elixir
curl: tress, ringlet, coil, twine [rife, torrent
current: tide, stream,
" of air: draft
" (comb. form): rheo
curse: oath, ban, anathema [cise, brusk, crisp
curt: short, brief, con-
curtail: shorten, clip
curtain: drape, veil

curve: arc, bend, wind, arch, loop, bow
curved structure: arch
" support: rib
cushion: pad, mat
custom: usage, habit, wont, use, manner
customary: habitual, wonted, usual [cleft
cut: clip, bob, snip, hew, slash, gash, nip, incision, shear, sunder, mow, lop, slit, saw, carve, cleave, lance, fell, incise, shorten, slice, sever, reap, snee, sawed,
" after terms with snick: snee [slit
" lengthwise: slitted,
" of meat: loin, rump, steak
" out: elide, excide
" roughly: hack
" in small pieces: mince, dice, hash
" in thin slices: shave
" through: intersect
" in two: sever, bisect
cute: clever
cutting implement: razor, knife, jackknife, scissors, shears, mower, slicer, ax, adz
" off of a vowel: elision

" wit: satire
cuttlefish: sepia, spirula
Cyclades Isl.: Samos, Delos, Syra, Nio
cylinder: spool, roller, roll, tube
" disk: piston
cylindral: terete
cylindrical & hollow: tubular
Cymric: Welsh
" sun god: Lleu
cyprinoid fish: id, ide
cyst: wen

D

dabble: mess
daft: idiotic
dagger: snee, dirk, stiletto, poniard
daily: diurnal, aday
" fare: diet
" food & drink: fare
" record: diary
dairymaid (Scot.): dey
daisy (kind): oxeye
" (Scot.): gowan
dale: glen, vale
dally: trifle, toy
dam: obstacle, millpond, barrier, restrain
damage: loss, hurt, mar, scathe, harm, injure, impair
damp: moist, humid
" & cold: dank, raw
dampen: wet, depress, moisten [ball, frisk
dance: ballet, dandle,
" (kind): galop, jig, reel, redowa, polka, pavan, adagio, minuet
" step: pas
dancing shoes: pumps
dandy: dude, fop
danger: peril, harm, hazard, risk [ous
dangerous: risky, perilDanish coin: ore, krone
" composer: Gade
" divisions: amt
" fiord: ise [Faroe
" island: Aero, Als,
" king: Canute
" measure: alen, rode
" money: ora
" wt.: eser, lod
dap: dib, dip, dibble
dapple: spot, spotting
dared: durst, defied, risked, ventured, braved [brave
daring: fearless, bold,
dark: deep, gloomy, unlighted, dusky, ebon
darkened: clouded, deepened, shadowed, murk, obscured
darkness: murk, gloom
dart: flit, arrow, bolt, spear, bound, darb, barb, javelin, shoot
" (colloq.): scoot
" forth: spurt

" suddenly: dash
dash: spirit, elan, dart, shatter, sprint
dastardly: cowardly
data: facts
dating from birth: natal
daub: smear, plaster
David's son: Solomon
dawdle: poke, linger
dawn: daybreak, aurora
" (comb. form): eo
" (pert. to): eoan
" (poet.): morn
day before: eve
daydream: reverie
days march: etape [muse
daze: trance, stun, bedazzle: glare
dead: adead, extinct lifeless [mute
deaden: stun, blunt,
deadly: lethal, fatal
deal: bargain, trade
" in: sell
" out: dole [cope
" with: handle, trade,
dealer in cloth: draper
dear: beloved, darling, costly, precious, loved
dearth: lack, famine
death: decease
" notice: obit
" " (var.): obet
" rattle: rale [clude
debar: preclude, exdebark: land
debase: demean, traduce, degrade, sink, reduce, lower, defile
debatable: moot
debate: reason, argue, discuss, discussion, moot, palaver
debit: charge [trash
debris: ruins, rubbish,
decade: ten
decay: rot, decompose
deceit: fraud, guile, imposture [hoodwink
deceive: betray, delude, dupe, entrap, mislead, fool, befool
decent: modest, proper
deceptive: illusive
decide: determine, resolve, settle, opt
decide upon: elect
decimal unit: ten
decipher: decode
deck out: tog, array
declaim: orate, rant
declare: aver, assert, state, proclaim, avow, affirm, pronounce
decline: fall, droop, deteriorate, die, refuse, ebb, dip, wane
decompose: rot, decay
decorate: deck, embellish, adorn, festoon, ornate, trim, paper
decoration for valor: medal [mure
decorous: decent, dedecoy: entrap, lure, entice, allure [ebb

decrease: lower, wane,
decree: tenet, ordain, law, ukase, enact, fiat, adjudge, rescript, edict, arret
dedicate: devote, inscribe, consecrate
deduce: infer, derive, evolve [subtract
deduct: bate, rebate,
deduction: rebate, inference [exploit
deed: act, feat, action, event, remise, escrow,
deem: consider, regard, think, judge
deep: dark, profound, obscure, hidden
deepen: thicken, intensify, dredge
deer: stag, doe, hart, hind, elk, moose
" flesh: venison
defamation: libel
defame: slander, malign
default: failure, neglect
defeat: beat, best, foil, rout, overcome, conquer, frustrate, frustration, loss, vanquish, worst
" at chess: mate
defect: flaw, fault
defective: bad
" explosive: dud
defense: protection, bulwark [mail
defensive armor: egis,
" bastions: forts
" enclosure: boma
" head covering: helmet
" plating: armor
defer: postpone, prolong, adjourn [spect
deference: homage, re
deficiency: want, shortage, lack, scarcity
defile: moil, pollute, soil, pass, ubra, abra, taint, debase

deflect: divert [rob
defraud: trick, cheat,
defy: dare, beard, brave, handy
" (colloq.): stump
degrade: corrupt, debase, lower, abase, depose, demean
degree: extent, stage, step, rank, grade
dehydrate: dry
deity: God, divinity
dejected: low, spiritless, sad, glum, depressed
Delaware town: Lewes
delay: stall, retard, demur, belate, wait, linger, lag, remora, hinder, loiter, demurral, detain
" (law): mora
delegate: depute, deputize, authorize
delete: dele, remove, erase [sider, ponder

deliberate: slow, con-
delicacy: cate, caviar
  tact   [fragile, frail
delicate: tender, fine,
" **fabric:** lace
" **perception:** tact
delight: regale, elate,
  please, entrance, rev-
  el, delectate
delineate: limn, draw,
  picture, depict, por-
  tray, describe
delirium: frenzy
deliver: rid, send, free,
  render, rescue, re-
  lease, redeem
dell: dene, ravine, glen
delude: mislead, trick,
  beguile,
deluge: flood, inundate
delve: dig, fathom
demand: exact, insist,
  require, claim, need
" **as due:** claim
demean: degrade, low-
  er, conduct, control,
  behave   [behavior
demeanor: mien, air,
demented: mad, insane,
  crazy   [die
demise: death, decease
demit: abdicate, dis-
  miss, oust, resign
deminish: rase, destroy,
  raze, ruin
demon: imp, ogre, fiend,
  devil, rahu   [evince
demonstrate: prove,
demur: protest, delay,
  object, hesitate
demure: serious, sober,
  prim, coy, staid, se-
  date, grave, decorous
den: lair, dive, nest,
  hunt, cave, sanctum,
  cavern   [rejection
denial: negative, negation, refusal, nay, no,
Denmark: see under
  "Danish"   [title
denominate: call, en-
denomination: sect
denote: indicate, signify, show, mean,
  mark
" **a final purpose:**
  telic   [arraign
denounce: condemn,
dense: crass, close, obtuse, thick
" **growth of trees:**
  forest, jungle
" **smoke:** smudge
dent: hollow, dint, indent, notch, tooth
dentine: ivory
dentist's drill: burr
denude: bare, strip,
  scalp   [ban
denunciation: threat,
deny: negate, gainsay,
  disown, refuse, dis-
  avow, renege, ab-
  negate, renounce
depart: go, leave [mose
" **quickly (slang):** va-

" **secretly:** decamp,
  abscond   [drawal
departure: exit, with-
depend: rely, hinge,
  lean, trust
depict: picture, delineate, draw, portray
deplete: drain, lessen,
  exhaust, empty
depone: testify
deport: banish, **exile**
department: conduct
" **(arch.):** geste, gest
depose: degrade, de-
  throne   [set
deposit: lay, leave, put,
depot: station, entrepot,
  storehouse

depraved: bad, corrupted, bestial   [sen
depreciate: belittle, les-
depress: sadden, lower,
  discourage, dispirit,
  dampen, deject
depression: dent, pit,
  dip, dint
" **between mt. peak:**
  col, dip
" **in golf green:** cup
" **worn by running**
  water: ravine, gully
deprive: bereave, di-
  vest, dispossess
" **of:** lose
" " **moisture:** drain
" " **reason:** dement
depute: delegate, send
deputy: agent, surro-
  gate
deride: taunt, sneer,
  ridicule, mock, scoff,
  scorn, gibe, belittle
" **(slang):** rag
derisive cry: hoot, hiss
derive: deduce, evolve,
  obtain, infer, get,
  trace   [sebacic
derived from fat: adipic,
" **oil:** oleic
dervish's cap: taj
descend: sink
" **abruptly:** plunge
descendant: scion, son
" **of Jacob:** Levite
" " **Shem:** Semite
describe: relate, delineate
" **gram.:** parse
descry: espy, see
desert: abandon, ab-
  scond, forsake, ice,
  wasteland   [Arab
" **dweller:** bedouin,
" **plant:** cactus
" **train:** caravan
" **wind:** simoom, si-
  rocco
deserter: turncoat, renegade, absconder, rat
deserve: merit, mete,
  earn   [pose
design: intention, plan,
  pattern, model, pur-
" **of scattered ob-**

jects: seme   [name
designate: signate, assign, label, dub, term,
  distinguish, connote,
  appoint, entitle,
desire: crave, lust,
  want, yen, wish, care,
  longing, hope, thirst,
  covet, aspire, yearn
" **(colloq.):** yen
" **wrongfully:** covet
desirous: eager
desist: cease, forbear,
  stop, spare, rest, end
despairing: hopeless
desperado: ruffian
despicable: vile, sordid
despise: hate, disdain,
  contemn, detest
despoil: spoil, plunder,
  fleece
despoiled (arch.): reft
despondent: blue, sad
despot: tyrant, satrap
despotism: tyranny
destine: allot
destiny: fate, lot, doom
destitude: devoid [raze
destroyed: rase, ruined,
  extirpated, broke, de-
  molished, perish,
destruction: loss, demolition, ruin, death
desultory: aimless
detach: disengage, isolate, disunite [tion
detached state: isola-
detail: item, appoint
detain: halt, hinder,
  retard, harass, delay,
  deter, arrest, with-
  hold, intern [spy, nose
detect: discover, espy,
detective: sleuth
" **(slang):** tec, dick
detent: pawl, catch
deter: restrain, hinder,
  prevent, retard
deterge: cleanse
detergent: soap
deteriorate: fail, degenerate, decline, wear
determine: conclude,
  destine, settle, will,
  decide, resolve
detest: despise, loathe
detonate: explode [draw
detract: derogate, with-
devastate: rase
devastation: havoc
develop: volve, grow
deviate: stray, lapse,
  err, digress, swerve

device to hoist large
  stones: lewis
device for raising
  chicks: brooder
" **to spread lamp**
  flame: cric [mon, imp
devil: satan, fiend, de-
devilfish: manta
devilish: infernal
devise: plan, contrive,
  invent, frame, create
devote: apply, dedicate

devoted: liege, faithful
devotee: fan, partisan
devoutness: piety
dewy: roric, wet, moist
dexterity: art, ease
dexterous: clever, deft
diabolical: infernal
diadem: tiara, crown
diagonal: bias
dialect: patoic, argot,
  speech, patois, idiom
diameter: caliper
diamond cutter: dop
dibble: dap, dib
dice: cube
Dicken's pen name:
  Boz   [prank
dido: antic, caper,
die: perish, demise, decline, expire, mold,
  stamp, print
" **to make pipe:** dod
diet: fast, fare
different: diverse, another, other, variant,
  novel   [rub
difficult: hard, knotty,
" **(prefix):** dys
" **question:** poser
difficulty: snag, strait
diffident: coy, shy
diffuse: radiate, strew,
  disperse, spread
dig: mine, delve, burrow, spade
" **up:** unearth
digit: toe, figure, number, finger
dignify: ennoble
digress: deviate
dike: levee, causeway
dilate: swell, enlarge,
  expand, distend
dilatory: remiss, slow
diligent: busy, sedulous
dillseed: anet, anise
dilute: water, weaken,
  thin [faint, faded, pale
dim: obscure, blear,
diminish: fade, lessen,
  wave, bate, abate, de-
  crease, wane, lower,
  moderate, taper, ebb
" **strength of:** dilute
diminutive: small, petite, dwarf
" **ending:** ie, ette
" **suffix:** ile, ot, ole,
  ie, et, ule
din: noise, clamor
dine: eat, sup
dingy: dull, soiled [grill
dining room: cenacle,
dinner course: entree
dip: immerse, decline,
  sink, incline, lade,
  plunge, dap
dip out: bail
diplomacy: tact
dipthong: ae, ea
dire: fatal, dreadful
direct: lead, drive,
  steer, manage, aim,
  address, refer, im-
  mediate, guide, man-
  age, straight, govern

X-WORD DICT

" **course:** pilot
" **one's way:** wend
" **proceedings:** preside
direction: trend, course
director: stager, manager, head, leader
dirk: poniard, dagger, snee
dirt: grime, sod, trash, refuse, soil, loam
dirty: soil, grimy, foul
disagree: dissent, differ
disagreeable: nasty, mean, vile
disappoint: fail
disaster: woe, calamity, misfortune [abjure
disavow: retract, deny,
disburden: ease, rid
disburse: pay, spend
discard: shed, scrap
discern: espy, see, look, spy [sagacious
discerning: astute, nice,
discharge: shoot, emit, exude, pay, payment
disciple: apostle
discipline: train, chasten, ferule
disclaim: disavow, repudiate, deny
disclose: reveal, bare, open, unearth, unveil, tell
discolor: stain, spot
discompose: upset
disconcert: abash, rattle, upset, jar, faze
disconnect: sever, separate [desist, quit
discontinue: suspend,
discordant: harsh
discount: rebate, agio
discourage: appal, depress, deter
discover: spy, espy, detect, invent, find, locate [dent
discreet: careful, prudiscretion: tact
discriminating: astute, nice, judicial
discrimination: acumen
discuss: debate, argue
disdain: pooh, scorn, despise, spurn [pox
disease: malady, gout,
" **of animals:** mange
" " **cattle & horses:** hoove [ergot
" " **cereals:** smut,
" " **fowl:** pip
disembark: land
disencumber: rid
disengage: ravel, free, detach [evolve
disentangle: ravel,
" **wool:** card
disfigure: mar, deface
disgrace: sham, humble, shame, ignominy
disguise: veil, mash, cloak, incognito
disgust (Scot.): ug
dish: tureen, platter, plate, bowl

" **of crackers & water:** panada
" " **eggs & milk:** custard [averse
disincline: indispose,
disjoin: sever, separate
dislike: aversion, hatred, antipathy, mind
dismal: bleak, drear, gray, triste, mournful, dreary, lurid
dismay: dread, appall, fear, appal, terrify
dismiss: oust, demit
" **from office (law):** amove
dismounted: alit
disorder: chaos, mess
disown: repudiate, deny
disparage: belittle, slur
dispatch: send, message, haste
" **boat:** aviso [pate
dispel: disperse, dissi-
disperse: scatter, dispel, spread, diffuse
dispirit: depress, mope
display: pomp, parade, show, wear, evince, manifest, air, expose
displease: offend
displeasure: anger
dispose: divest, settle, arrange [ture, mood
disposition: mien, na-
dispossess: deprive, divest [rebuttal
disprove: refute, rebut,
dispute: contest, argue, chaffer, wrangle
" **(colloq.):** spat
disregard: waive, override, ignore, neglect
disrupt: split
disseminate: sow, propagate, scatter, strew, spread [test
dissent: disagree, pro-
dissenter: heretic
dissipate: waste, squander, dispel
distance: space
distant: formal, remote, yon, far, afar, aloof
" **(prefix):** tel, tele
distaste: aversion, dislike [expand, swell
distend: inflate, dilate,
distilling vessel: retort
distinctive mark: badge
distinguish: discern
distinguished: eminent
distort: warp, screw
distress: pain, grief
distributed: dole, dealt, meted, allotted, dele, assort, dispensed
disturb: roil, rile, unsettle, agitate, ail, molest, annoy, ruffle, heckle, stir, violate
" **the peace:** riot
disunite: detach, sever
ditch: trench, moat, rut
diurnal: daily [sofa

divan: couch, canape,
dive: plunge [various
divers: several, sundry,
diverse: unlike, different
diversify: vary
diversion: sport, game
divert: entertain, amuse, deflect, sport, recreate, distract
divest: dispossess, disposes, deprive [cleft
divide: share, sunder, apportion, separate, fork, halve, bisect,
dividing wall: septum
diving bird: loon, tern, smew, auk, grebe
divinity: deity
division: share, class, squadron, partition, schism, game, section, part
" **of Ancient Greece:** Demes, Deme [cinct
" " **city:** ward, pre-
" " **Greece:** Nomes
" " **Israelites:** tribe
" " **mankind:** race
" " **music:** bar
" " **opera:** scena
" " **poem:** canto, verse, stanza
" " **stock:** shares
do: perform, act, fare, achieve,
" **again:** iterate
" **without:** spare
docile: tractable, gentle, tame
dock: pier
doctrine: dogma, tenet, creed, ism, belief, gospel, hedonism
document: paper, script
dodge: elude, evade
doer: actor, agent
doff: remove
dog: canine, pug, terrier hound, beagle
" **(large):** alan, dane
" **of mixed breed:** mongrel [sept
dogfish: rosset, tope,
dogma: tenet, doctrine
doily: mat
dole: alms, gratuity, mete, share, grief
" **out:** ration

doleful: sad [sorrow
dolor: grief, mourning,
dolphin: porpoise, inia
dolt: ass, clod, dunce, oaf, simpleton, fool
domain: realm, empire
dome: edifice, cupola
domestic: maid, menial
domesticate: tame
domicile: house, menage
dominate: control, rule
" **(colloq.):** boss
domineer: lord [empire
dominion: sway, reign,
domino: tile
Don Juan's mother: Inez
donate: present, give,

bestow
" **(Scot.):** gie [ass
donkey: onager, burro,
" **call:** bray
doom: fate, condemn, lot, sentence, destiny
door: portal, access, stoa [latch
" **fastening:** hasp,
" **knocker:** rapper
doorkeeper: porter, ostiarius, tiler [asleep
dormant: latent, torpid,
dormouse: lerot, loir
dose of medicine: potion [stipple
dot: dowry, period, iota, speck, scatter, point,
double: dual, twin, binary, duplex, twain
" **(prefix):** di, dis
doubly: twice
doubt: mistrust
doubter: skeptic
doughy: pasty
dove: pigeon, cushat
" **'s home:** cote
dower: dos, endowment
" **(pert. to):** dotal
down (prefix): de
downcast: sad [spill
downpour: rainstorm,
downright: stark
downy surface: nap
dowry: dos, dot
" **(pert. to):** dotal
doze: nap, sleep
draft: potion, sketch, conscript [ox
" **animal:** mule, oxen,
drag: lug, haul, trail
drain: sewer, deplete, milk, sump

dramatic piece: skit, monodram
" **portrayal:** acting
drape: curtain, adorn
draw: extract, attract, portray, haul, drag, delineate, tie, tow, pull, lure, limn, depict, stipple [rive
" **as conclusion:** de-
" **forth:** educe, elicit, extract, evoke
" **off:** drain
" " **thru a bent tube:** siphon
" **out:** lengthen, extract, educe, lade
" **sap:** bleed
" **tight:** taut, frap
" **to:** attract
" " **a point:** taper
" **up shoulders:** shrug [ror, terror
dread: fear, awe, hor-
dreadful: dire, horrid, terrible, frightful
dream: reverie, imagine, vision, romance, fancy
drear: bleak, dismal, gloomy [remnant
dreg: lee, lea, settling,
drench: saturate, souse,

douse, soak, hose
dress: attire, garb, tog, frock, gown, align, rig, clothe, array
" **ornament:** sash
" **stone:** nig
" **trimming:** ruche, ruching, piping, gimp
" **up:** tog, rig, primp
" **with beak:** preen
dresser: bureau
dressing gown: kimono
dressmaker: modiste
dried: sere
" **brick:** adobe
" **grape:** raisin
" **grass:** hay
drift: tenor, trend, sag
drill: bore, train, practice, perforate, anet
" **hall:** armory
drink: beverage, gin, potation, nectar, imbibe, swig
" **anothers health:** pledge, toast
" **heavily:** tope
" **made from molasses:** rum [nip
" **(small):** dram, sip,
drinker: toper [ard
" **vessel:** gourd, cup, beaker, stein, mug, goblet, tumbler, tankard
drip: drop, trickle [urge
drive: impell, impel, ride, propel, force,
" **away:** repel, banish, dispel, scat, shoo
" **back:** repulse
" **nail at angle:** toe
drivel: dote, slaver
droll: whimsical, comic
dromedary: camel
drone: idler, hum, snail
drool: slaver
droop: sag, wilt, decline, languish, lop, loll, flag, slouch
drooping: nutant [bead
drop: drip, fall, plummet, trapdoor, sink,
" **gently:** dap
dropsy: edema
dross: scum, waste
" **of a metal:** slag
drove: herd, horde
drowse: nod, nap
drudge: moil, slave, plod, fag [ural
drug: heroin, stupefy, dope, opium, aloes,
" **plant:** aloe [bour
drum: beat, snare, tam-
" **(small):** tabor
drunkard: sot
dry: sec, arid, ted, sere, thirsty, parch, dull
" **(poet.):** sere
" **by rubbing:** wipe
" **as wine:** sep, brut
drying cloth: towel
duck (kind): pintail, tern, eider, teal, mallard, goldeneye, smew
" **(male):** drake

duct: vas, passage, canal
ductile: tensile
dude: dandy, fop
due: payable, toll, owing
duel: combat
duet: duo [glassy
dull: dim, blunt, slow, sluggish, mope, stolid, stodgy, vapid, drab, dry, blur, tarnish, dingy, stupid, leaden,
" **color:** drab, dun
" **finish:** matte, mat
" **sound:** thud
" **& tedious:** prosy
Dumas character: Athos [pid
dumb: mute, still, stu-
dunce: dolt, fool, ninny
dupe: tool, victim, deceive, gull, fool
duplicate: bis, replica
" **(colloq.):** ditto
duarble: lasting
duration: time, space, term, eternity
dusk: gloom
Dutch admiral: Tramp
" **cheese:** edam
" **city:** Ede
" **coin:** doit
" **commune:** Ede
" **E. Indies Isl.:** Java, Timor, Moena,
" **food:** eel
" **geographer:** Aa
" **island:** Aruba [kop
" **measure:** vat, aam,
" " **of length:** roede
" **meter:** el [Steen
" **painter:** Dow, Hals,
" **S. African:** Boer
" **village:** Doorn
" **weight:** aam
duty: task, chore, tariff, devoir, impost, tax
dwarf: stunt, pygmy, troll, runt
" **negrito of Mindaneo:** aeta [side
dwell: live, abide, re-
" **on:** harp
" **upon:** brood [dent
dweller: tenant, resident
dwelling: home, hovel, tenement, mansion, abode [anil
dye: color, stain, henna,
" **indigo:** anil
dynamite inventor: Nobel
dynamo: generator
" **part:** armature
dynasty: realm

E

eager: anxious, avid, keen, earnest, agog, intent, desirous, afire, ardent, athirst
eagerness for action: elan
eagle: ern, erne [aery
" **'s nest:** aerie, eyrie,

eaglestone: etite [lug
ear: auricle, barken, pinna, heed, spike,
" **covering:** earlap
" **lobe:** lug, earlop
" **part:** pinna, lobe
" **(pert. to):** aural, otic
earache: otalgia
early: betimes, soon
" **alphabetic character:** rune
" " " **(pert. to):** runic
" **Briton:** Pict
" **Christian champion:** Cid
" **Eng. money:** ora
" **Irish tenant:** Saer
" **Norse gods:** Vanir
" **physician:** Galen
" **(poet.):** rath
" **prohibitionist:** Dow
" **Scots:** Picts
" **theologian:** Arius
" **(pert. to):** Arian
" **Venetian coin (var.):** betso
earn: gain, merit, deserve, attain, achieve
" **profit:** net
" **with difficulty:** eke
earnest: serious, eager, pledge, zealous
earnings: salary
earth: terra, soil, geal, dirt, loam, world, sod, globe, clay, land
" **(comb. form):** geo, ge, gea
" **(dial.):** erd
" **(latin):** terra
" **mound:** rideau
" **(poet.):** marl [jug
earthenware: crockery, faience, crock, pot,
earthnut: peanut
earthquake: seism [rene
earthy: temporal, ter-
" **deposit:** marl
" **iron ore:** ocher
" **material:** mold, clay, marl
ease: comfort, allay, relieve, repose, rest, facility, lighten, relief
easily: readily, smoothly [irascible
" **angered:** iracund,
" **bent:** limp [frail
" **broken:** crumbly,
" **frightened:** timid
" **moved:** mobile
" **tempted:** frail
" **vaporized:** volatile
East: occident, orient, levant
E. African coin: pesa
" **hartebeest:** tora
" " **ascetic:** fakir
" " **cart:** tonga
" " **caste:** dom
" " **cavalryman:**

Sowar
" " **cedar:** deodar
" " **cereal grass:** ragee, ragi
" " **chief of police:** daroga, darogah [pee
" " **coin:** anna, ru-
" " **cymbals:** tal
" " **fiber plant:** da
" " **food staple:** ragi
" " **gateway:** Toran
" " **granary:** gola
" " **grass:** glagah, kasa, rice
" " **harvest:** rabi
" " **hat plant:** sola
" " **helmet:** topee
" " **herb:** pia, sola, sesame, rea
" " **language:** tamil
" " **litter:** doolie
" " **money:** anna
" " **palm:** nipa [ang
" " **civet:** mus-
" " **peasant:** ryot
" " **perennial:** ramie [al
" " **pheasant:** mon-
" " **plant:** ramie, benne, sola
" " **poet:** Tagore
" " **sailor:** lascar
" " **soldier:** sepoy
" " **sword:** pata
" " **temple:** pagoda
" " **tent:** pawl
" " **timber tree:** sal, dar, salai, teak
" " **title:** aya, sahib, mian
" " **tree:** banyan, ach, niepa, sal, salai palay, khair, teak
" " **vehicle:** tonga
" " **vine:** odal
" " **water vessel:** lota [ser tola
" " **weight:** bahar,
" " " **sheep:** urial
" " **wood:** eng, aloe
Eastern inhabitant: Asian
" **Mediterranean:** Levant [emir
" **potentate:** ameer,
easy: comfortable, gentle, facile, simple
" **chair:** rocker
" **to do:** facile
" **job:** sinecure
" **to manage:** docile
" **task (slang):** snap
eat: dine, corrode, devour, sup, gnaw, rust, feed [gnaw
" **away:** erode, erose,
" **sparingly:** diet [ed
eaten away: erose, erod-
eating (pert. to): dietary
" **regimen:** diet
ebb: recede, decline, subside, reflux, wane, decrease, sink
" **tide:** neap
ebbing & flowing: tidal
eccentric wheel por-

tion: cam
Ecclesiast: fra
Ecclesiastical council: synod
" **court:** rota
" **headdress:** miter
" **linen cloth:** fanon
" **plate:** paten
" **residence:** manse
" **scarf & vest:** orale
" **service:** matin
" **unit:** parish
" **vest:** amice, orale, alb, stole   [gal
economical: sparing, fru-
economize: scrimp
ecstasy: rapture, bliss
Ecuador province: Oro
eddy: swirl, whirlpool, pool, vortex
edge: lip, brim, rim, brink, sharpen, margin, verge, border, sharpness, sidle, hem
" **of crater:** lip
" **(poet.):** marge
edged tool: axe, edger, ax, sword
edible: esculent
" **bulb:** onion
" **fruit portion:** pulp
" **fungus:** morel
" **grain:** cereal
" **mollusk:** asi, clam,
" **root:** garlic, carrot, beet, parsnip, yam, radish, potato
" " **stock:** taro
" **seaweed:** agar laver, dulse   [pea
" **seed:** lentil, bean,
" **tuber:** oca, taro
edict: decree, arret
edify: construct
edit: revise, redact, compile publish, issue,
educated: liberate, literate, trained, taught instructed, lettered,
educe: elicit, evolve evoke   [ger, siren
eel (kind): moray, con-
" **trap:** eelpot
eerie: uncanny, weird, macabre, scary
efface: erase, sponge
effect: result, do
effective as an agent: causal   [womanish
effeminate: epicene,
efficacy: dint
efficient: able, capable
effigy: image, doll
effort: attempt, exertion, struggle, nisus, essay
effortless: easy
eft: newt
egest: excrete
egg: ovum, urge, incite, ova (pl)   [lette
egg dish: omelet, ome-
" **shaped:** ovate, ovoid, ovated, ooidal,
egis: shield
ego: self, past
egress: exit

Egyptian: Copt
" **city:** Cairo
" **cotton:** pima
" **crown:** atef
" **dancing girl:** Alme
" **deity:** Bes, Amon, Min, Ptah, Isis, Ra, Dera, Osiris, Apet Thoth, Serapis, Maat, Sati, Geb
" **gold or silver alloy:** asem
" **king:** Rameses
" **lizard:** adda
" **measure:** dera, ket
" **monarch:** Rameses Tut
" **month:** Apap
" **queen of the gods:** Sati
" **religious body:** ka
" " **heart:** Ab
" " **soul:** Ba
" **river:** Nile
" **sacred bull:** apis
" **singing girl:** Alme, Alma
" **snake:** asp
" **structure:** pyramid
" **sun disk:** aten
" " **God:** Ra, Tem, Ammon, Amon
" **symbolic eye:** uta
eidolon: icon, image
eight: octet, octave, octa
eire: erin
ejaculation: alas
eject: emit, oust, evict eliminate, expel, out
" **in a jet:** spout
elan: dash, zeal, ardor impulse, spirit
elapse: pass, expire
elastic: resilient, springy
elate: gladden excite, exalt
elation: joy
elbow: ancon
elder: senior, prior
elect: choose, chosen, prefer, decide
electric catfish: raad
" **circuit:** loop
" **current:** A.C., D.C.
" **generator:** dynamo
" **light (kind):** arc
" **od:** elod
electrical degree: ee
" **devise:** coder, reverser, generator
" **particle:** ion, ian
" **transmission:** radio
" **unit:** farad, watt, volt, ampere, ohm, rel
electricity (kind): static
" **(pert. to):** voltaic
elegance: grace, polish, refined   [ponent
element: neon, factor, arsenic, silver, constituent, barium, com-
" **of borax:** boron
" " **the earth's crust:** silicon
elemental: primal, pri-

mary, simple
elementary substance: metal
elephant's ear: taro
" **goad:** ankus,
" **jockey:** mahout
elevate: heighten, rear, lift, raise, exalt
elevated: lofty, high
" **line:** el [mountain
elevation of land: hill,
elevator carriage: car
elf: gnome, sprite, fay, peri, fairy
elflike creature: peri
elicit: educe, evoke
elide: dele, ignore, annul, suppress, omit
eliminate: remove, exclude, eradicate, eject
elite: pick
elk: eland, moose, stag, wapiti
elliptical: oval, ovate
elocutionist: reader
elongate: lengthen, stretch
elope: abscond
eloquence: oratory
else: other, besides
elude: evade, avoid, dodge, escape, baffle
elusive: evasive
elysium: eden, paradise
emanation: aura
emancipate: deliver
embankment: levee
embellish: adorn
ember: coal, cinder
embezzle: steal   [ard
emblem: badge, image-symbol, type, stand-
" **of authority:** baton, mace   [dent
" " **Neptune:** Triembrace: clasp, adopt, hug, comprise, fold, contain   [taboret
embroidery frame:
amend: reform, amend, rectify, revise

Emerald Isle: Erin
emery: corundum
eminence: fame, height, hill   [nent, great
eminent: noted, promi-
emissary: agent
emit: eject, erupt, exude, discharge, voice, issue, shed, radiate
" **light & heat:** glow
" **ray:** eradiate, radiate, beam
emmet: ant   [ary
emolument: profit sal-
emotion: feeling
emperor (former): tsar
emphasis: salience stress, accent   [use
employ: hire engage,
emporium: mart
empty: void, inane, bare, vain, deplete
" **form:** blank
emulate: vie, rival
enact: decree, perform,

play, pass
" **law:** legislate
enamored: captivated, smit, fond
encamp: bivouac, tent
encase: case, ensheath, wrap, surround
enchanted: bewitched, charmed, rapt
enchantress: Medea, siren, Circe   [environ
encircle: ring, enclasp, surround, belt, hoop,
encircled: girt
enclose: case, surround, hem, pen, insert
enclosed: internal
enclosure: pen, yard, cage, coop   [corral
" **for cattle:** kraal,
encore: bis, again
encourage: abet, hearten, egg, cheer, impel
encroach: trespass, invade, intrude   [per
encumber: load, ham-
end: terminate, finis, omega, cease, outcome, tip, close, purpose, terminal, finale, climax, limit, desist
" **aimed at:** goal
endeavored: striven, tried, aimed, essayed, assayed, attempted

endings: finales, finises
endless: eternal, everlasting, continual, infinite, perpetual
" **time:** eternity
endorse: sanction, OK, ratify, back
endow: dower, invest, furnish, vest, gift
endowment: fund, dos
endue: invest
endure: bear, tolerate, abide, stand, sustain, last, withstand
endure (Scot.): dree
enemy: foe   [vim, force
energy: vigor, power,
" **(colloq.):** pep
enervate: weaken, sap
enfold: wrap, lap
enforce: compel
engage: hire, employ, retain, betroth
" **in:** wage
engender: breed, produce, exite, occasion, beget, gender   [tive
engine: motor, locomo-
engineer: manage
" **'s shelter:** cab   [CE
engineering degree: EE,
" **unit:** bel
engirdle: zone
English: Saxon — see also British
" **actor & manager:** Tree
" **architect:** Wren
" **author:** Dickens, Milne, Roget, Ramee, Sterne, Reade, Caine,

Bronte, Hardy, Opie
" **baby carriage:**
pram   [ers
" **banker poet:** Rog-
" **bishop:** Ken
" **borough:** Leeds
" **cathedral:** Ely
" " **city:** Truro
" " **passage:** Slype
" **cheese:** stilton
" **chemist & psysi-
cist:** Faraday
" **city:** Leeds, Ches-
ter, Wallsend
" **clergyman:** Sterne
" **coins:** pence, shil-
lings, farthings, guin-
eas   [Elgar
" **composer:** Arne,
" **country:** Shire, Do-
set, Kent, Essex
" **dance:** morris
" **dean:** Inge
" **diarist:** Pepys
" **divine:** Inge, Donne
" **dramatist:** Pinero,
Udal, Marlowe, Peele,
Kyd, Lyly
" **essayist:** Lamb
" **forest tract:** Arden
" **hedgerow:** rew
" **historian:** Grote
" **humorist:** Sterne
" **hymn writer:** Lyte
" **journalist:** Henty
" **law court:** Leet
" **monk:** Bede, Beda
" **murderer:** Aram
" **musician:** Arne
" **nat. emblem:** rose
" **painter:** Turner
" **philologist:** Aram
" **philosopher:** Bacon
" **physician:** Ross
" **poet:** Keats, Spen-
ser, Donne, Blake
" **policeman:** bobby
" **political party:** Tory
" **port:** Preston
" **quaker:** Penn
" **race course & race
horse:** Ascot
" **river:** Ure, Avon,
Exe, Dee, Thames,
Tee, Usk, Aire, Ouse,
Tyne, Wye, Tees,
Trent, Mersey, Sev-
ern   [dor, Stuart
" **royal family:** Tu-
" " **stables:** Mews
" **sandy tract of land:**
dene   [Eton, Rugby
" **school:** Harrow,
" **schoolmaster:**
Aram   [Deal
" **seaport:** Dover,
" **spy:** Andre
" **stage:** plateau
" **statesman:** Grey,
Pitt   [tram
" **streetcar:** tramcar,
" **surgeon:** Lister
" **title:** baronet [Ely
" **town:** Eton, Leeds,
" **weight:** stone [ver
" **wood pigeon:** cul-

engrave by dots: stipple
" " **a needle:** etch
engraving: cut [rapt
engrossed: engaged,
enigma: mystery, rid-
dle, charade, puzzle,
enjoin: command, bid,
press, forbid [ure
enjoyment: fun, pleas-
enlarge: spread, mag-
nify, dilate, increase,
expand, amplify, grow
enlist: enroll, recruit
enliven: animate, ex-
hilarate, quicken
enmesh: tangle, en-
tangle, enlace,
enmity: hatred, rancor
ennead: nine
ennoble: elevate, honor
ennui: boredom
enormous: huge, large
Enos's father: Seth
enough (poet.): enow
enrage: madden, anger,
inflame
enrich: fatten, lard
enroll: enlist, record,
poll, enter, join
ensconce: hide
ensemble: whole, decor
ensign: banner
ensnare: tangle, trap,
entrap, net [result
ensue: succeed, follow,
entangle: mat, embroil,
snare, ravel, mesh,
ensnarl, knot, web
enter: pierce, record,
penetrate, register, en-
roll, insert, join
enterprise: venture
entertain: amuse, treat,
regale, beguile, fete,
divert, harbor
" **royally:** regale, fete
enthusiasm: pep spirit,
elan, ardor, verve
enthusiast: zealot
enthusiastic: eager, ardor, keen
entice: inveigle, attract,
tempt, allure, charm,
invite, lure, decoy, win
" **(var.):** tole
enticement: lure, bait
entire: total, complete,
whole, integral, all
" **man:** egos, ego
entitle: name, dominate,
designate, qualify, dub
entity: ens, unit
entomb: inter
entrance: charm, adit,
entry, portal, ingress,
doorway, gate, inlet,
gateway, door, trans-
port, delight
" **halls:** atria, foyers
entranced: rapt
entrap: noose, deceive,
decoy, trepan, en-
snare, bag
entreat: pray, beseech,
supplicate, crave, im-
plore, plead, request,

adjure, woo, beg
entrepot: depot
entrust: consign, confide, commit
entry: entrance, access
engress, passage, item
" **in an account:**
item, debit
entwined: vove, laced
environ: surround, encircle   [medium
environment: setting,
envoy: legate
envy: covet, jealousy
enwrap: roll
enzyme: ase
eon: age [noble, grand
epic: heroic, poem,
" **poem:** epos, epo,
epopee   [gourmet
epicure: gourmand,
epidemic: pest
Episcopal pastor: rector
episode: event, scene,
incident
epistle: letter, missive
epithet: name [mary
epitome: synopsis, sum-
epoch: age, era, event
epochal: eral
equal: peer, iso, even,
equitable, co ipeer,
coordinate, tie, same,
adequate, par [iso
" **(comb. form):** pari,
equality: par, parity
equalize: even
equally: alike, as
equilibrium: poise
equine: horse, mare, ass
equip: rig, attire, gear
" **with crew:** man
equipment: tackle, rig,
gear   [fair
equitable: even, equal,
" **part:** share
era: age, period, time,
epoch, date
" **(pert. to):** eral
eradicate: eliminate, uproot, remove, erase
erase: lelete, dele, efface expunge, cancel
eraser: rubber
ere: soon, anon
erect: rear, construct,
raise, upright, build
eremite: hermit, recluse
Erin: Eire
ermine: stoat
eroded: eat, corroded
err: blunder, sin, s ip,
stray
errand: mission
errant: arrant, erratic
erroneous: mistaken,
false
error: misstep, mistake,
blunder, slip, fallacy
" **in printing:** erra-
tum, errata (pl.)
Erse: Gaelic
erudite critic: pundit
erudition: lore, wisdom,
learning
escape: evade, leakage,
flee, elude, avoid

" **(slang):** lam
eschew: avoid, shun
escort: convoy, usher,
accompany, squire,
conduct, attend
esker: asar, osar, os
Eskimo canoe: kayak,
umiak
" **hut:** iglu, igloo
" **settlement:** Etah
esne: serf
esoteric: inner
espy: detect, descry
essays: theses, tries,
tests, efforts, papers,
attempts, themes
essence: attar, sub-
stance, pith, perfume,
yolk, nature, soul
essential: vital, virtual,
necessary, needful
" **part:** element, fac-
tor, vital, pith
establish: settle, rear,
base, instate, set,
institute, plant
" **ownership:** claim
estate: manor, property
esteem: regard, revere,

estimate, value, hon-
or, prize, respect, con-
sider [judge, appraise
estimate: rate, calculate, measure gage,
rank, esteem, assess,
estimation: repute
estop: plug, bar, im-
pede, hinder, obstruct
estrange: alienate
eternal: deathless, endless, everlasting, time-
less, ceaseless, infinite
ether: ester
ethereal: airy, aerial
ethereal salt: ester
ethical: moral [ras
Ethiopian title: negus,
ethnic: pagan [lars
Etruscan gods: lares,
eulogy: eloge, praise
euphony: meter
European: Pole, Dane,
Finn, Swede, Slav,
Lapp, Lett, Serb,
Slovak, Croat
" **bass:** brasse
" **bird:** serin, motacil,
ortolan, pie
" **bison:** aurochs
" **blackbird:** merle,
ousel
" **capital city:** Riga
" **cavalryman:** Hus-
sar   [ant, peasandry
" **countryman:** peas-
" **deer:** roe
" **dormouse:** lerot
" **finch:** serin, terin,
citril, tarin
" **fish:** id
" **gulf:** Riga, Aden
" **gull:** mew
" **herring:** sprat
" **juniper:** cade
" **kite:** glede
" **lime:** teil [Alps

" **mts.:** alpine, ural,
" **native:** Serb, Croat
" **oriole:** loriot
" **rabbit:** cony
" **river:** Saar, Bug
" **thrush:** mavis, ousel
" **tree:** sorb, lentisk
Eva's friend: Topsy
evade: elude, dodge, shun, escape, baffle, shirk, avoid, gee
evanescent: fleety
evangel: gospel

evasive: shifty, deceitful, elusive
even: unvaried, smooth, equalize, flush, qual, balance, level
   (poet.): een
evening party: soiree
" (poet.): een, eve
" **song:** serenade
" **star:** vesper
event: episode, incident, deed, epoch, fact
ever: once, aye
" (poet.): eer [myrtle
evergreen shrub: box, furze, holly, oleander,
" **tree:** pine, cedar, fir carob, spruce, olive, yew, holly, balsam
everlasting: eternal, endless, agelong, unending   [etern
" (poet.): eterne,
eve y: each, complete
everyone: each, all
evict: object, banish, expel, eject, oust
evidence: proof, show
evident: patent apparent, clear, plain, manifest, obvious
evil: bad, banc, sin, ill, iniquity, sinful, harm, corrupt, vice
" **act:** crime
" **intent:** malice
" (prefix): mal
" **spir t:** demon, devil, satan, fiend
evince: show, manifest, display, exhibit
evoke: educe, elicit
evolve: educe, develop, derive
ewer: jug   [literal
exact: demand, accurate, precise, wreak,
" **counterpart:** match
" **likeness:** image
" **reasoning:** logic
" **satisfaction:** avenge, revenge
exaggerate: overtell, overstate, overdo
exalt: laud, raise, elevate, honor
" **the spirits of:** elate
examination: test
" **of accounts:** audit
examine: test, scrutinize, inspect, scan, overhaul [sift, probe

" **critically:** censor,
example: norm, case
exasperate: anger, irritate   [anger
exasperation: ire, heat,
excavation: pit, hole, cut, mine
" **for extracting ore:** stope   [pass
exceed: surpass, better, transcend, overstep,
exceedingly: extremely, greatly, very
excel: top, surpass, cap, outdo   [tue
excellence: merit, vir-
excellent: fine, capital
" (slang): super [bar
except: but, save, exclude, unless, omit,
excess of solar over lunar year.: epact
exchange: trade, swap, barter
" **for money:** sell
" **premium or discount:** agio
excite: elate, arouse, stir, startle
excited: agog, nervous
exclamation: ahem, ah, ho, alas, fie, tut, wow, rats, expletive, ouch
" **of contempt:** pah, foh [bah, tush, ugh
" " **disgust:** aw, fie,
" " **pity:** ay
exclude: debar, eliminate, bar, ban, except
exclusive: select
" **person:** snob [only
exclusively: solely, all,
excrete: egest   [jaunt
excursion: tour, tramp,
excuse: apology, plea, alibi, pardon, pretext, extenuate
" **for not appearing in court:** essoin
exercise: lesson, use
" **control:** dominate, preside
" **sovereign power:** reign   [steam
exhalation: breathe,
exhale: emit
exhaust: deplete, spend, sap, fag, waste

exhibit: evince, display, show, stage, wear
" **malign satisfaction:** gloat   [eant
exhibition: show, pag-
exigency: need, demand
exile: deport, banish
exist: live
existence: esse, alive, ens, life, being, entity
existing in name only: titular
exit: egress, door
exonerate: clear, acquit
exorbitant interest: usury
exotic: foreign
expand: dilate stretch,

grow, distend, open, enlarge,   [tract
expanse: room, area,
expansive: wide
expatriate: banish
expect: hope, await, anti ipate
expectation: hope
expectorate: spit
expedient: politic
expedition: trek, safari
e pel: oust, eject, evict, banish, deport [bar
" **from the bar:** dis-
expend: spend, pay
expense: cost, outlay
expensive: dear, costly
experience: feel, undergo, live
experiences regret: repent
experiment: test [ace
expert: skilled, adept,
expiate: atone
expiration: end   [die
expire: perish, elapse,
explain: i terpret, lefine, solve [gosh, gee
expletive (mild): egad,
explode: blast, detonate, burst [bolide
exploding meteor: bolis,
exploit: feat, deed, gest, act, geste (var.)
explosion: blast, pop
" **devise:** cap, petard, torpedo
explosive: TNT, tonite
expose: bare, detect, open, display, reveal
" **to moisture:** ret
" " **ridicule:** pillory

exposition: fair
expostulate: protest
express: voice
" **disapproval:** deprecate, rebuke
" **displeasure:** resent
" **gratitude:** thank
" **official disapproval:** veto   [term
expression: phrase,
" **of approval:** smile
" " **contempt:** pish, sneer, hiss
" " **inquiry:** eh
" **peculiar to a lang.:** idiom
" **of pity:** ay
" " **sorrow:** alas
expressive action: gesture   [erase, sponge
expunge: delete, dele,
exquisite: fine, elegant, lovely   [prolong
extend: spread, lie, stretch, run, reach,
" **the depth:** deepen
" **over:** lap, span, cover   [spread, ran
extended: long, lengthy,
" **view:** panorama
extent: area, ambit, degree, scope, span, length, size, limit, range [igate, excuse

extenuate: palliate, mit-
exterior: surface, out, outer
" **of bark:** ross
" (anat.): ectal
external: outer, cortical, out, outside
" **appearance:** face, mien, guise
" (comb. form): ecto
extinct: dead
" **bird:** moa, dodo
" **reptile:** dinosaur
extinguish: quench
extirpate: root, destroy
extol: praise, laud, boast
extra: spare, more, over
" **payment:** bonus
" **supply:** relay, reservoir [wring, educt
extract: draw, excerpt,
" **fat:** render
extravagant: wasteful, prodigal, outre
extreme: limit, dire,

exhibit: evince, display, show, stage, wear
" **malign ' satisfaction:** gloat   [eant
exhibition: show, pag-
exigency: need, demand
exile: deport, banish
exist: live
existence: esse, alive, ens, life, being, entity
existing in name only: titular
exit: egress, door
exonerate: clear, acquit
exorbitant interest: usury
exotic: foreign
expand: dilate stretch, grow, distend, open, enlarge,   [tract
expanse: room, area,
expansive: wide
expatriate: banish
expect: hope, await, anticipate
expectation: hope
expectorate: spit
expedient: politic
expedition: trek, safari
e pel: oust, eject, evict, banish, deport [bar
" **from the bar:** dis-
expend: spend, pay
expense: cost, outlay
expensive: dear, costly
experience: feel, undergo, live
experiences regret: repent
experiment: test [ace
expert: skilled, adept,
expiate: atone
expiration: end   [die
expire: perish, elapse,
explain: i terpret, lefine, solve [gosh, gee
expletive (mild): egad,
explode: blast, detonate, burst [bolide
exploding meteor: bolis,

exploit: feat, deed, gest, act, geste (var.)
explosion: blast, pop
" **devise:** cap, petard, torpedo
explosive: TNT, tonite
expose: bare, detect, open, display, reveal
" **to moisture:** ret
" " **ridicule:** pillory
exposition: fair
expostulate: protest
express: voice
" **disapproval:** deprecate, rebuke
" **displeasure:** resent
" **gratitude:** thank
" **official disapproval:** veto [term
expression: phrase,
" **of approval:** smile
" " **contempt:** pish, sneer, hiss
" " **inquiry:** eh
" **peculiar to a lang.:** idiom
" **of pity:** ay
" " **sorrow:** alas
expressive action: gesture [erase, sponge
expunge: delete, dele,
exquisite: fine, elegant, lovely [prolong
extend: spread, lie, stretch, run, reach,
" **the depth:** deepen
" **over:** lap, span, cover [spread, ran
extended: long, lengthy,
" **view:** panorama
extent: area, ambit, degree, scope, span, length, size, limit, range [igate, excuse
extenuate: palliate, mit-
exterior: surface, out, outer
" **of bark:** ross
" **(anat.):** ectal
external: outer, cortical, out, outside
" **appearance:** face, mien, guise
" **(comb. form):** ecto
extinct: dead
" **bird:** moa, dodo
" **reptile:** dinosaur
extinguish: quench
extirpate: root, destroy
extol: praise, laud, boast
extra: spare, more, over
" **payment:** bonus
" **supply:** relay, reservoir [wring, educt
extract: draw, excerpt,
" **fat:** render
extravagant: wasteful, prodigal, outre
extreme: limit, dire, radical, intense, ultra, rank [ing, end, very
extremely: so, exceed-
exude: emit, discharge, ooze, seep [elate
exult: rejoice, crow,

eye: ogle, orb, observe, watch, view, optic, vision, regard, sight
" **of bean:** hilum
" **coat:** retina
" **part:** retina, uvea, irian, pupil, lens, iris, cornea, eyeball
" **(pert. to):** optic
" **(Scot.):** ee, een (pl.)
" **so:ket (anat.):** orbit
eyeglass: monocle, lens
eyelashes: cilia
eyelid infection: sty
eyes: peepers

F

fable: story, myth
" **maker:** Aesop
fabric: material, voile, moire, rayon, terry, web, leno, etoile
" **filling:** welt, weft
" **(glossy):** satin
fabricate: make
fabulous bird: roc [front
face: confront, prestige,
" **of a coin:** head
" **downward:** prone
" **of a gem:** facet
" **hair:** beard
" **on hewn stone:** panel
" **up a glacier:** stoss
" **value:** par
" **with stone:** revet
facetious: witty, jocose
facial bone: jaw [grin
" **expression:** pout,
facility: ease, art
facing direction of glacier's move: stoss
fact: reality, datum, truth [clique
faction: side, sect, party,
factor: manager, agent, gene, element
factory: mill, plant
facts: data [hobby
fad: whim, fancy, craze,
fade: wane, vanish, pale
Faerie Queen: Una
" **author:** Spenser [Amoret, Alma
" " **character:** Ate,
fag: tire, fatigue, weary
fail: peter, miss, disappoint, default
" **in duty:** lapse
" **to follow suit:** reneg [get
" " **remember:** for-
" **(slang):** flunk
failure (slang): dud, flop [weak
faint: dim, swoon, pale,
fainting spell: syncope
fair: blond, decent, just, impartial, comely, bazaar
fairy: elf, sprite, fay
" **chief:** Puck

" **queen:** Titania, Una, Mab
fairylike: elfin
faith: troth, belief, credit, confidence, trust
faithful: liege, true, leal, loyal, devoted
" **(poet.):** leal [falsify
fake: fraud, feign, sham
fakir: yogi
falcon: lanneret, peregrine, eagle, hawk
fall: drop, tumble, subside, plummet, slip
" **back:** retreat
" **in former state:** relapse [drip
" **in drops:** patter,
" " " **(obs.):** drib
" **forward:** topple
" **from power:** wane
" **headlong:** pitch
" **into disuse:** lapse
" **profusely:** pour
" **short:** lack, fail
" **suddenly:** plop
" **upon:** assail
falling: cadent
" **star:** meteor
false: erroneous, lie, untrue, sham, spurious, fake
" **gods:** idols
" **idea:** fallacy
" **jewelry:** paste
" **move:** misstep
" **report:** canard
falsehood: tale, lie, fib
falsify: forge, fake
falter: waver, fail, hesitate, lag [household
family: genus, kindred,
famous: noble, noted, renowned, eminent
" **murder & murderer:** Aram
" **soprano:** Patti, Lind
" **uncle:** Sam
fan: winnow, devotee, rooter, cool
fanatical: rabid
" **partisan:** zealot
fanciful: unreal, dreamy
fancy: fad, whim, idea, dream, caprice, vagary, ideate
" **(poet.):** ween
fane: temple, sanctuary
fanon: orale
fantasy: dream
far: remote, away, advanced, widely
" **across:** wide
" **down:** deep, low
" **off:** remote, distant
" " **(comb. form):** tele
" **reaching:** long
farce: comedy, mockery [do, prosper
fare: passenger, diet,
farewell: ave, adieu, tata, adios
farinaceous: mealy
" **food:** sago
farm: till, plow [shed

" **bldg.:** silo, barn,
farmer: planter, cultivator
Faroe Isl. Windstorm: Oe
farther than: beyond
farthest: endmost
" **in:** inmost
fascinating woman: siren, charmer
fascination: spell
fashion: style, mode, shape, mold, vogue, fad, frame
" **follower:** modist
fast: rapid, fleet, firm, speedy, securely, secure, diet, apace, firmly [brace
fasten: nail, lace, tie, pin, seal, glue, tether, bolt, secure, rivet,

bind, paste, moor, attach, lock, clamp
fastener: hasp, snapper, snap, pin, lock, bolt, dowel, strap, clamp, clasp, rivet, cleat
fastidious: finical, elegant, refined, nice, dainty
fat: obese, obesity, suet, plane, fleshy, plump, portly, oily, lard
fatal: lethal, dire, mortal, deadly
fate: doom, lot, destiny, kismet
father: sire, papa, abbe, abba, parent, dad, pa, padre, beget,
" **(Arabic):** abu
" **of engraving:** Pye
fathom: delve
fatigue: overdo, harass, tire, weary, irk, fag
fatty: adipose
" **fruit:** olive
fatuous: inane, insensate, silly
faucet: tap, spigot
fault: defect, foible, slip, blemish, offense
" **finding:** captious
faultless: ideal [bad
faulty: wrong, amiss
faun: satyr
favor: boon, prefer
favorable: good
favorite: pet, dear
fawn: cringe
fawning: servile
fay: elf, sprite
fear: awe, terror, dread, panic [timid, afraid
fearful: dire, nervous,
fearless: daring
feast: regale, fete, banquet, repast, fiesta
feat: deed, act, exploit, stunt
feather: pennas, plumage, plume, pinna
" **shaft:** scape
featherlike: pinnate

federation: league, union

fee: hire, charge, payment, price

feeble: anile, lame, infirm, weak

feebleminded: anile

feed: nourish, nurture, eat, graze, subsist

" **to the full:** sate

feeding box: manger

feel: sense, touch, grope

" **discontent:** repine

" **indignant at:** resent [regret

" **sorry for:** repent,

" **sympathy or pity:** yearn

" **want of:** miss

feeler: tentacle, antenna, palp

feet (having): pedate

" **(of the):** pedal

feign: pretend, sham, simulate, act, fake

" **sickness:** malinger

felicity: bliss, happiness

felony: crime

female demon: ogress

" **elephant:** cow

" **ruff:** ree, reeve

" **saint:** ste

" **sandpiper:** ree

" **singer:** diva

" **warrior:** amazon

fen: swamp, moor, bog, marsh, morass

fence: rail, bulwark

" **barrier:** bars

" **picket:** pale, paling

" **steps:** stiles

fencer cry: sasa, touche

" **dummy:** pel

fencing leaping movement: volt [tierce

" **position:** carte,

" **term:** touche, riposte

" **weapon:** rapier, foil, epee, sword

fend: guard, parry

feral: savage, wild

ferine: wild [wine

fermented drink: mead,

" **liquor:** ale, beer

fern leaf: frond [wild

ferocious: grim, savage,

fertile spot: oasis, oases

fertilizer: marl

fervent: warm, eager

fervid: ardent, intense

fervor: ardor, zeal

fester: rankle

festival: fete, gala, fair, carnival, fiesta

festive: joyous, gala

festivity: gala

fetch: bring

fetid: olid

fetish: obi

fetter: bind, iron, band, shackle, chain

feudal estate: feod, fief

fiat: decree [thread

fiber: hemp, bast, ramie,

" **of Amer. aloe:** pita

" " **peacock feathers:** marl

" **plant:** aloe, ramie, sisal, cotton, flax, istle, hemp [fealty

fidelity: constancy,

fidgety: restive

field: lea, arena

" **of activity:** terrain

" **(arch.):** glebi

" **of granular snow:** neve

fiend: satan, devil [wild

fierce: grim, savage,

fiery: hot, intense

fiesta: holiday, festival

fig (kind): eleme, elemi

fight: scrap, battle, fray, melee, strive, combat

" **against:** resist

" **(general):** melee

fighter: warrior

figure: digit, calculate

" **out (slang):** dope

" **of speech:** trope, metaphor, simile,

filament: hair, thread

file: rasp, row

fill: sate, saturate

" **with air:** aerate

" " **mud:** silt

" " **rev. fear:** awe

filled pastry shell: dariole, eclair

fillet for hair: snood

" **at top of column:** orle

filly: foal

film: negative

" **on copper:** patina

" " **liquid:** scum

filter: purify, strain, sieve [timate

final: last, decisive, ul-

finale: end, termination, finish, close, ending, coda

financial: monetary

" **instrument:** mortgage [teri

finch: serin, linnet,

find: locate, discover

" **fault:** nag, carp

" **out:** detect, learn, see

fine: dainty, thin, nice, mulct, amerce, keen,

" **for murder:** cro

" **& delicate:** lacy

" **dirt:** dust

" **ravelings:** lint

finger game: mora

finger or toe: digit

finial: epi, canopy

" **on pagoda:** tee

finical: fussy, nice

finis: nding, end

finished: over, done, closed, completed

" **(poet.):** oer

Finnish city: Abo

fire: shoot, ignite, kindle, inflame

" **basket:** cresset

" **(comb. form):** yr, Igni

" **feeder:** stoker

" **particle:** spark

" **worshipper:** parsee

firearm: pistol, weapon, gun, piece, shotgun, repeater, rifle

firecracker: petard, retard

fired clay: tile

firedog: ardiron

fireman: stoker [grate

fireplace: ingle (Scot),

" **facing:** mantel [hob

" **part:** spit, grate,

fireside: hearth

firm: stable, solid, immutable, steady, iron, adamant, secure, fast

firmament: sky, heaven

first: erst, prime, foremost, original, initial, primary, chief, primal, preeminent

" **high priest:** Aaron

" **king of Israel:** Saul

" **letter:** initial

" **magnitude star:** altair, vega

" **man (pert. to):** adamic, adamical

" **name:** forename

" **Pope:** Peter [seed

" **principle:** arche,

" **team (colloq.):** varsity [snapper, ide

fish: perch, gar, shad, par, scrod, hake, ray, id, carp, dace, bass, sprat, ray, sturgeon, darter, opah, wrasse, tarpon, ling, eelpout, chub, sennet, angle,

" **basket:** creel

" **eggs:** roe

" **like vertebrate:** ray

" **hawk:** osprey

" **from moving boat:** troll

" **net:** trawl, seine

" **part:** fin, scale

" **sauce:** alec

" **(small):** sparat, id, sardine, shiner, dace, minnow, smelt darter, fry, ide

" **spear:** gig, gaff

" **trap:** eelpot

" **which clings to another fish:** remora

fisherman: seiner, angler

fishhook: angle

fishline: snell

" **(part):** barb

fishing device: net

fissile rock: shale

fissure: rime, rent, cleft, rima, seam, cranny rift, crack,

fit: adapt, proper, prepared, correct, adapted, apt, suit, ready

" **of anger:** rage

" **one inside another:**

nest

" **of passion:** tantrum

" **for plowing:** arable

" **together:** mesh, piece, nest

five sided figure: pentagon [tad, lustrum

" **year period:** pen-

fix: repair, mend, correct, set, adjust, settle [anchor

" **firmly:** brace, root,

" **grade of:** rate [dow

" **income upon:** en-

fixed: stationary, stable, steady

" **allowance:** ration

" **charge:** rate, fee

" **course:** rote

" **ratio:** rate

" **time:** term

" **value on:** assess

flaccid: limp

flag: standard, banneret banner, sag, streamer, iris, pennon, pennant, lanquish, droop

flail: beat

flaky: scaly, laminar

" **mineral:** mica

flambeau: torch

flamboyant: ornate

flame: blaze, flare

flaming: aglow, afire

flap: tab, fold [glint

flash: spark, sparkle

flashy: sporty, gaudy

flat: level, tenement, plane, insipid, tame, vapid, apartment

" **bodied fish:** skate

" **bottle:** flask

" **bottom boat:** bateau, scow, punt, barge, keel, ark

" **disc:** plate

" **piece:** slab, fin

" **stick:** ferule

" **stone:** flag, slab

" **surface:** area, plane

flatfish: dab, sole, skate, ray, turbot

flatter: adulate

flattery: blarney

flaunt: parade

flavor: salt, sapor, aroma, savor, taste, anise

flawless: perfect

flax (dial): lin

flax fiber: tow

flaxen fabric: linen

flaxseed: linseed

flay: beat, skin, cane, reprove [escape, shun

flee: vanish, hasten,

" **(slang):** lam

fleece: despoil, swindle, shear, cheat

fleer: mock, scoff

flesh: meat

" **of calf:** veal

fleshy: fat [date, drupe

" **fruit:** pome, pear,

fleur delis: lis, iris

flexible: lithe, elastic, limber, pliable, willowy, pliant

" **branch:** withe
" **pipe:** hose

" **shoot:** bine
" **& tough:** withy
flicker: flare, waver
flight: aviation
flightless bird: moa
flinch: wince [hurl
fling: sling, throw, toss,
flip: toss, snap, fillip
flippant: glib
flit: dart, skim, flutter
float: raft, drift, waft,
swim, ride, buoy, sail
floating fish box: car
" **in water:** natant
flock: herd, troop, bevy
" **of seals:** pod
flog: lash, tan, beat,
cane, trounce
flood: deluge, torrent,
inundate, overflow,
spate
floor: story, down
floral leaf: petal, sepal
" **organs:** stamens
florid: ruddy, ornate
Florida bird: ani [do
" **city:** Tampa, Orlan-
" **Indian:** Seminole
floss silk: sleave
flounder: dab, grovel
flour receptacle: bin
flourish: wield, prosper,
blossom, brandish
flout: deride, sneer,
mock, gibe, jeer
flow: run, stream, pour,
abundance, recover
" **against:** lap
" **back:** ebb
" **(comb. form):** rheo
" **forth:** emanate
" **off:** drain
" **out:** emit
" **through:** seep
" **of water:** flood
flower: blossom, bloom
" **border:** platband
" **cluster:** corymb,
raceme, cyme
" **part:** stamen, petal,
sepal, corolla, spadix,
anther, pericarp
flowering plant: arum,
lupin, canna, fern,
yucca, lupine, spirea,
geranium
" **shrub:** lilac, wara-
tah, japonica, sumac,
oleander, azalea, ole-
aster, spirea
" **water plant:** lotus
flowerless plant: fern,
lichen, moss
fluctuate: waver, veer,
vary, sway
flue: chimney, pipe
fluent: glib
fluid: liquid
" **rock:** lava [agitate
flurry: ado, agitation,
flush: even, redden
" **success:** elate
flutter: wave, flit [flit
fly: tsetse, bot, gnat,

soar, hasten, aviate,
**flying Dutchman he-
roine:** Senta
" **water:** spray
foal: filly [er, spume
foam: froth, suds, lath-
fob: pendent, cheat
focus: center, concentrate [grass, silage
fodder: hay, ensilage,
" **pit & tank:** silo
fog: vapor, mist, ob-
scure, haze
foible: fault, weakness
foil: frustrate, outwit
fold: plait, ply, plicate,
flap, ruga, rimple, lap,
crease, loop, embrace,
pleat, seam
" **on animal's throat:**
dewlap
" **of coat:** lapel
" **over & stitch:** hem
" **of sail:** reef
foliage: leaves
follow: ensue, trace, result, trail, chase, tail
" **closely:** dog, heel,
tag
follower: adherent, fan
" **of (suffix):** ite [next
following: after, sect,
foment: incite, abet
fond: attached, loving,
doting, dote
fondle: caress, nestle,
pet cosset
food: aliment, meat
" **fish:** salema, tuna,
ling, cero, mackerel,
pompano, trout, shad,
smelt, mullet, ale-
wife, salmon, robalo,
spot cod
" **of the gods:** am-
brosia [na
" **from heaven:** man-
" **medium for bac-
teria:** agar [grub
" **(slang):** eats, chow,
fool: ninny, dolt, deceive, dupe, dunce,
jester, ass
foolish: daft, mad, unwise, daffy [tard
" **person:** simp, do-
foolishness: folly
foot: iamb
" **(comb. form):** podo
" **like part:** pes [step
" **part:** toe, sole, in-
" **pedal:** treadle, lever
" **(pert. to):** pedal
" **traveler:** tramp
footless: apod, apodal
" **animal:** apod, apo-
da (pl.) [track
footprint: step, trace,
fop: dude, dandy
for: pro, since, per, to
" **example:** as
" " **(abbr.):** eg, ec
" **fear that:** lest
foray: raid, pillage
forbear: parent, an-

cestor, desist
fo bear ng: patient
forbid: ban, tabu, prohibit, veto, vote, en-
join [banned
forbidden: taboo, tabu,
forbidding: grim
forbode: portend, omen
force: vis, power, dint,
pressure, compel, im-
pel, constrain, drive,
vim, urge, violence,
energy
" **air thru nose:** snort
" **back:** repel
" **of a blow:** brunt
" **down:** ram
" **(Latin):** vis
" **of men:** posse
forceful: dynamic, energetic [lent, emphatic
forcible: cogent, vio-
forcibly: amain
ford: wade
fore: front
" **limbs:** wings, arms
forebear: spare, parent,
ancestor
forebode: augur
foreboding: omen, dire
forefather: elder, ancestor
forego: waive, remit
forehead: brow [strange
foreign: alien, exotic,
" **(comb. form):**
xeno
foreman: boss
foremost: first, front,
prime, main [ing,
forenoon: morn morn-
forerun: precede, usher
forerunner: herald
forest: trees, woods,
woodland, wood
" **divinity:** nymph
" **warden:** ranger
" **(pert. to):** sylvan
forestless tract: steppe
foretell: predict, presage, prophesy
" **(Scot.):** spae
foretoken: omen [aye
forever: eternally, ay,
forewarning: portent
forfeit: lose
forge: falsify, frame
forgive: pardon, remit
fork: divide
forlorn: bereft, lorn
form: shape, ceremony,
mold, create, frame,
make, variety, style
" **of architect.:** ionic
" " **croquet:** roque
" " **Esperanto:** ido
" **into groove:** chan-
nel
" **hollows in:** pit
" **into jelly:** gel [ate
" " **league:** feder-
" **in the mind:** ideate
" **(pert. to):** modal
" **in small grains:**
pearl [bank
" **into a terrace:** em-
" **of worship:** ritual,

liturgy [precise
formal: distant, stiff,
" **address:** lecture
" **choice:** election
" **dance:** ball, hop,
prom
formative: plastic
former: erst, quondam,
sometime, previous,
whilim, old, ex
" **autocrat:** tsar
" **czar:** Ivan
" **days:** pasts, past
" **English coin:** groat,
ryal
" **European coin:** ecu
" **German monetary
unit:** taler
" **public conveyance:**
stage
" **Roman emperor:**
Otto, Nero
" **Russian ruler:** tsar,
Lenin, Paul
" **Span. coin:** real,
peseta, pistole
" **times:** yore
" " **(poet.):** eld
formerly: erst, once, ere-
while, onetime, ago
" **(prefix):** ex
forsaken: lorn
fort: castle
fortification: redan, ravelin, abatis, redoubt
fortify: arm, strengthen,
man
fortress: castle, citadel,
rampart, stronghold
fortune: lot, fate, hap,
chance [ist, sibyl
" **teller:** seer, palm-
forward: ahead, on, anterior, to, along, send,
front, transmit
" **part:** front, fore
foster: nurse, cultivate,
cherish, rear, promote
foul: dirty, unfair, rank
foundation: base, basis,
root, bottom, bed
" **timber:** sill
fountain: well
four (comb. form): tetra
fourscore & ten: ninety
fourth calif: ali, uli
fowl: hen, goose, bird
fox: tod
" **(female):** vixen
" **(Scot.):** tod
" **(var.):** renard
foxy: sly, wily [brawl
fracas: melee, quarrel,
fracture: break [brittle
fragile: frail, delicate,
fragment: shread, bit,
scarp, tatter, crumb,
relic, shard, chip, snip
" **of cloth:** rag
" **left at a meal:** ort
" **ointment:** spiken-
ard
" **of pottery:** sherd
fragrance: aroma [ous
fragrant: olent, redolent,
sweet, aromatic, odor-

" oil: attar
" seed: anise [tiara
" shrub: rosemary,
frail: fragile, slender, puny, weak, delicate
frame: forge, compose, adjust, fashion, devise, shape, form
" of bed: bedstead
" " a car: chassis
" " mind: mood
" " vessel: hull
" " bars: grate
" " crossing laths: lattice
" " slats: crate
" " a window: casing [trestle
framework: cadre, rack,
frank: candid, honest, open
frankness: candor
frantic: desperate, frenzied, mad, furious
fraternal: brotherly
fraud: cheat, swindle, faker, fake, trickery, humbug, deceit, jape
fray: melee, fight, setto
free: rid, clear, release, gratis, deliver, independent, unchecked, loose, rescue, liberate
" of impurities: refine, cleanse, clean
" from restraint: loosen, unbend
freedom: liberty
" of access: entree
freeholder: yeoman
freeze: ice, refrigerate, congeal, gelate
freight: lade, cargo
" boat: barge, ark, flatboat [boose
" car: gondola, ca-
French: Gallic
" African capital city: Tunis
" annuity & security: rente
" article: le, un, la
" artist: Dore
" astronomer: Pons
" author: Loti, Gide, Dumas, Verne, Hugo, Renan
" bond: rente
" brandy: cognac
" cheese: Sens
" city: Nantes, Arles, Nancy, Rennes, Sens, Caen, Lyons, Ariens, Ay, Sevres, Cannes, Amiens, Lille, Nice, Limoges, Aix, Reims
" clergyman: abbe
" coin: centime, sou, franc, ecu, obole
" composer: Widor, Lalo, Ravel
" dept.: Orne, Nord, Somme, Eure, Isere, Oise, Ain
" dugout: abri
" emperor: Napoleon

" illustrator: Dore
" income: rente
" Indo China capital: Hanoi [Ney
" marshall: Murat,
" painter: Tissot, Dore, Corot, Degas, Manet, Gelee, Monet
" parliament: senat
" poet: Verlaine,
" porcelain: limoges
" priest: abbe [at
" revolutionist: Marriver: Isere, Oise, Marne, Lys, Meuse, Saar, Saone, Ain, Rhone, Loire, Seine, Vesle, Scarpe, Yser, Somme, Orne
" scientist: Curie
" sculptor: Rodin
" shooting match: tir
" soldier: poilu, chasseur
" symbol: lily
" theologian: Calvin
" town: Valence, Nerac, Bareges, Lens, Ay, Laon
" village: Ham
Frenchman: Gaul
frenzied: frantic, berserk, frenetic [amok
" manner: amuck,
frenzy: furor, delirium rage
frequent: haunt [sort
frequented place: re-
frequently: oft, often
fresh: modern, new, brisk, recent
" supply: relay
" water fish: dace, bass, id, ide, roach, ellpout, burbot
" " porpoise: inia
freshet: flood, spate
fret: stew, nag, worry, chafe, agitate, repine, irritate, fuss, annoy, vex [pettish, petulant
fretful: peevish, testy,
friar: monk, fra
fried meatball: rissole
friend: ally, crony, ami, chum, companion
" (greeting to Indian): netop
friendly: amicable, kind
" associate: ally
friendship: amity
fright: terror, panic, awe
frighten: alarm, startle, scare [stiff
frigid: cold, icy, arctic,
frisk: gambol, sport, caper, frolic, romp
frivolous: inane, gay
frog: rana, rama, anuran, anura
froglike: ranine
frolic: caper, spree, fun, romp, play, gambol, prank, sport, frisk, lark [sportive
frolicsome: gay, merry,

from (prefix): de
" that place or there: thence, since
" what place: whence
" within: out [formost
front: fore, van, face,
" of bldg.: facade
" " hoof: toe
" " mouth: preoral
" part of helmet: visor
" of ship: bow, prow
frost: ice, chill, cold, rime, foam [cold
frosty: rimy, austere,
froth: yeast, spume, foam
frowning: glum, scowling
frozen: icy, gelid, glace
" desserts: mousses
" dew: rime

frugal: sparing, economical, provident, thrifty, chary [ade
fruit drink: ade lemon-
" of fir: cone
" " gourd: pepo
" " hawthorn: haw
" kernel: pit
" of nut: kernel
" " palm: date
" part: core, rind
" pulp: pap
" seed: pip [tive
fruitless: useless, abor-
frustrate: foil, defeat, balk, thwart
fry quickly: saute [der
frying pan: skillet, spi-
fuddled: tipsy, flustered
fuel: peat, stoke, charcoal, gas, coke
fulfill: complete
full: plenary, ample, replete, laden [ted
" of depressions: pit-
" dress: tails
" of fissures: rimose
" force: amain
" grown: adult
fume: rave, smoke, reek, incense, rage
fun: sport, play
fundamental: essential, basic, basal, organic
" mass of life tendencies: id
funeral announcement: obit
" car: hearse
" hymn: dirge
" oration: eloge
" pile: pyre
fungi (kind): rust
" (pert. to): agaric
fungus: agaric, yeast
" disease: ergot
" growth: mildew, mold [ous, comic
funny: comical, humor-
fur: pelt
" animal: otter, sable, seal, genet, mink, marten, calabar
" of coypu: nu ria
" scarf: tippet

furious: rabid, raving, frantic [kiln
furnace: heater, oven,
" tender: stoker [rig
furnish: provide, lend, indue, afford, equip, endow, render, cater
" a crew: man
" with authority: vest
" " feathers: fledge
" " money: endow
furniture wheel: caster
furor: rage, frenzy, craze [groove, plow
furrow: line, stria, rut,
further: promote, abet, yet, remote
furthersome: also
furtive: sly, stealthy, sneaky [anger, wrath
fury: rage, ire, violence,
fuse: melt, anneal
fused metal & refuse: slag
fusible alloy: solder
" substance: metal
fuss: ado, bother, todo, fret, bustle
futile: useless, idle

G

Gael: Celt, Scot
Gaelic: Erse
" sea god: Ler
gag: joke, silence
gaiety: mirth, glee
gaily: merrily [gress
gain: net, win, profit, attain, advance, improve, acquire, obtain, lucre, earn, pro-
" advantage over: worst [tort
" by compulsion: ex-
" control over: master
" success: prosper
" superiority: master
gainsay: deny [gallop
gait: lope, step, pace, stride, trot, amble
gaiter: spat
gala: festive, festivity
Galatea's lover: Acis
gale: wind, gust [chafe
gall: harass, irritate,
gallant: cavalier, spark, brave, knight
Gallic: French [game
gamble: frolic, bet, dice,
gambler's capital: stake
gambling: gaming
" house: casino

gambol: frisk, caper, romp, frolic
game: sport, contest, plucky, jest, mockery, diversion, gamble
" bird: grouse, snipe
" of chance: loo, bingo, keno, lotto
" fish: tarpon, bass, cero, trout, marlin
" like Napoleon: Pam

" of skill: chess
gamin: arab, tad, urchin
gaming cube: dice, die
gamut: scale
gang: crew, squad
gannet: solan
ganoid fish: amia
gap: breach, hiatus, notch, opening, cleft
" in mt. ridge col
garb: attire, dress, clothe, array, apparel
garden: cultivate, hoe
" bed: plot
" implement: trowel, hoe, weeder, rake
garish: gaudy, showy
garland: lei, anadem, wreath [aba, stole
garment: robe, vesture,
garner: reap, glean, gather, collect [loft
garret: attic, mansard,
gaseous (comb. form): aeri
" compound: ethane
" element: neon, oxygen
" mixture: air
gash: slit, cut, slash
gastropod: snail, slug
gate: entrance, portal, passageway
gather: amass, assemble, mass, shirr, brew, congregate, collect, reap, collect, garner, glean, muster
" after a reaper: glean
gathering: bee, crowd, harvest, reunion
" implement: rake
gaudy: tawdry, garnish, garish, flashy
" ornament: tinsel
gaunt: rawboned, lean, lank, thin, spare
gauntlet: glove
gauzy fabric: tulle, chiffon, tissue
gay: merry, blithe, riant, sportive [glare
gaze: stare, look, peer,
" askance: leer
" with close attention: pore
" " satisfaction: gloat, admire
gazelle: cora, goa
gazing: astare
gear: harness, outfit, clothing, rig, tackle, trappings
" tooth: cog
gelatinous matter: agar
gelid: frozen, icy, cold
gem: muffin, stone
" carved in relief: cameo
" weight: carat
gemel: coupled, twin
gender: sex, engender
genealogical record: tree
general character: ten-

or, nature
" course of action: career, trend
" fight: melee
" type: average
generate: gender, produce, create, develop
generation: age
generator: dynamo
genteel: nice, polite
gentle: soft, docile, tame, kind, mild, tender, meek, easy
" blow: dab, pat
gentleman: sir
genuflect: kneel
genuine: sincere, sterling, real, true
genus: kind, class, variety [weed
" of ambrosia: rag-
" " auks: alle, alca
" " beet: beta
" " birds: otis
" " burbots: lota
" " cabbage: brassica, cos, kale [ris
" " candytuft: ibe-
" " cattle: bos
" " cetaceans: inia
" " cow: bos
" " dogs: canis
" " ducks: anas, anser
" " flowering shrubs: acacia [rana
" " frog: anura,
" " garter: elaps
" " gastropods: triton [solar
" " geese: anser,
" " goose barnacles: lepas [poa
" " grasses: avena,
" " herbs: ruta, arum, liatria
" " honey bee: apis
" " insect: nepa
" " kites: elanus
" " lily: aloe
" " lindens: tilia
" " lizards: iguana, uta
" " man: homo
" " maples: acer
" " mollusks: eolis
" " moose: alces
" " moth: tinea
" " mouse: mus
" " myrtle trees: pimenta [ta
" " nuthatches: sit-
" " oak: quercus
" " oat: avena
" " olive tree: olea
" " orchids: laelia
" " palms: areca
" " peacock: pavo
" (pertaining to): generic
" of pickerel: esox
" " pig: sus
" " pineapple: ananas
" " plants: aloe

" " rails: sora
" " rye: secale
" " S. Amer. & S. African garter snakes: elaps [pa
" " sac fungi: ver-
" " sea birds: sula
" " shad: alosa
" " sheep: ovis
" " shrubs: itea, rosa, olea, erica
" " spider monkeys: ateles
" " sticklike insects: emesa
" " succulent plants: aloe
" " sumac: rhus
" " swan: olor
" " toad: anura
" " trees & shrubs: acer
" " turtle: emy
" " vipers: echis
" " Virginia willow: ites, itea
" " wasp: vespa
geological age: era
" direction: stoss
" formation: lias
" period: eocene
geometrical curve: parabola, spiral, polar
" figure: cone, prism, ellipse, circle, rhomb, rhombus, lune [rem
" proportion: theo-
" ratio: pi
Geraint's wife: Enid
germ: seed, spore, microbe
" cells: ova, eggs
German: Teuton, Hegel
" admiral: Spee
" article: der
" author: Mann
" beer: mum
" city: Ulm, Essen, Emden, Ems, Trier
" coin: taler, mark
" composer: Abt, Bach
" district: Saar, Ruhr
" doctor: Kant
" E. African coin: pesa
" emperor's title: kaiser
" engraver: Stoss
" hall: sala
" inventor: Otto
" kobold: nis
" mathematician: Klien [Marc
" painter: Durer,
" philosopher: Hegel, Kant
" physicist: Ohm
" poet: Heine
" port: Stettin
" religious reformer: Luther [Ruhr, Saar
" river: Eser, Oder, Eder, Elbe, Weser, Ems, Rhine, Isar,
" ruler: kaiser
" sculptor: Stoss

" socialist: Marx
" soldier: uhlan [ony
" state: lesse, Sax-
" title: herr, von
" watering place: Ems
germinate: sprout
germinated grain: malt
gest: exploit, gesture
gesture: motion, gest
" of affection: caress
get: obtain, receive, secure, procure, win, become, acquire, derive
" along: fare
" away: scat, escape
" back: recover, regain
" out (colloq.): scram
" ready: prepare
" to in time: catch
" up: gee, arise
ghastly: lurid, wan
ghost: specter, shade, spook, apparition, phantom, spirit
giant: titan, huge, ogre
" killer: David
gibbon: lar
gibe: sneer, quip, deride, agree, jape, taunt, flout
gift: grant, present, endow, donation, talent
" to bride: dower
" to employe: bonus
gigantic: mammoth, titan, immense, huge
giggle: snicker, tehee, snickerer, titter
gilded bronze: ormolu
gin: snare, trap
" (kind): sloe
giraffelike animal: okapi
girdle: sash, belt, cest, band, cincture, zone
girl: maid, lassie, damsel, maiden, damosel
" (dial.): gal [point
gist: pith, core, pitch,
give: donate, render, contribute, present, proffer, hand, bestow, impart
" an account of: report [power
" authority to: em-
" away: betray [turn
" back: restore, re-
" bevel to: cant [sure
" confidence to: as-
" courage to: nerve
" ear to: heed
" expression to: voice
" forth: emit, utter
" a grant: charter
" high value to: idealize [date
" legal force to: vali-
" the meaning: define
" nourishment: feed
" off: emit
" " fumes: reek

" one's word: promise [emit
" out: mete, issue,
" permission: consent
" pleasure: delight
" reluctantly: begrudge, grudge
" right to: entitle
" rise to: gender
" (Scot.): gie
" sloping edge to: bevel
" up: resign, cede, yield, despair [sify
" variety to: diver-
" way: yield
" zest to: sauce
given to jesting. jocular, jocose [moraines
glacial deposits: eskers,
" direction: stoss
" fissure: crevass
" ice pinnacle: serac
" ridges: osar, eskers, eskars
" snowfields: neves
glad: elated, happy, joyful, gratified, delighted, pleased
gladden: cheer, elate, please
glaring light: flare
glass: tumbler, mirror
" for artificial gems: strass
" container: phial, jar, cruet, ampule
" " (small): vial
" tube for blowpipe: matrass
glassy: smooth, dull
glaze: enamel
gleam: shine, glow, radiate, light, glint, glimmer, sparkle
glean: garner, gather
glee: mirth, joy, gaiety
glib: smooth, fluent, flippant [slither
glide: slide, sail, slip,
" hurriedly: skitter
" over: skim
" smoothly: flow [ter
glint: gleam, flash, glit-
glisten: sparkle, shine
glitter: shine, glint, spangle, sparkle
globe: orb, ball, sphere, earth, steer
globule: bead, drop
gloom: melancholy, murk, dusk
gloomy: dreary, lurid, glum, drear, sad, morose, saturnine, stygian, dark, tenebrous
glorify: bless, exalt, laud [pride, renown
glory: splendor, eclat,
gloss: luster, palliate, sheen, lustre
glossy: sleek, silken, nitid, lustrous, shiny

" fabric: silk, sateen, satin, rayon, satinet
" paint: enamel
glove: mit, gauntlet, mitt [bloom
glow: gleam, shine
glowing: radiant
glue: paste, fasten
glut: sate, satiate
glutinous: viscid
gnar: snarl, growl
gnarl: twist distort
gnat: midge [corrode
gnaw: eat, nibble, peck,
" away: erose
gnawing animal: rodent
gnome: elf, goblin
go: proceed, precede, depart, leave, went, wend, betake [embark
" abroad: entrain,
" against: oppose
" ahead: lead
" aloft: ascend
" around: bypass
" astray: err
" away: scat, shoo, depart, begone, leave
" back: retreat, revert, ebb [lead
" before: precede,
" by: pass [sink, set
" down: descend,
" easily: amble, lope
" frequently: resort
" furtively: sneak, steal
" and get: fetch
" heavily: lumber
" hunting: gun [tire
" into seclusion: re-
" on: gee, proceed
" " with: resume
" (poet.): wend
" quickly: scoot, dart
" rapidly: race, tear
" the rounds: patrol
" (Scot.): gae
" silently: steal
" to: attend
" " law: sue
" too far: overstep
" up in rank: rise
" without food: fast
" wrong: err [sting
goad: spur, prod, incite,
goal: end, aim, target, ambition, mecca
goat cry: maa, bleat
" (kind): alpaca, ibex
" (wild): ibex
gob: mass
goblet: chalice, hanap
goblin: sprite, gnome
god: idol, deity
God of altar fire: Agni
" " Ancient Memphis: Ptah
" " Fields & Herds: Faun
" " Flocks & pastures: Pan
" " Gates: Janus
" " Love: Amor, Eros, Cupid

" " manly youth: Apollo
" " metal working: Vulcan
" " mirth: Comus
" " mischief: Loki
" " pastures: Pan
" " revelry (class myth): Comus
" " Sea: Poseidon, Neptune, Ler
" " Shepherds: Pales [Thor
" " Thunder: Dis,
" " Underworld: Dis
" for whom Jan. is named: Janus
" " " " Tues. is named: Tyr
" of War: Ares, Tyr, Mars, Ira, Odin, Thor
" wearing the solar disk: Ra
" of Winds: Aeolus
goddess: dea, ge
Goddess of Agriculture: Ops, Demeter, Ceres
" " Arts & Sciences: Athena
" banished from Olympus: Ate
" of Dawn: Eos
" " Destiny: Fate
" " Discord: Eris, Ate [Ge
" " Earth: Erda,
" " Fertility: Ma, Ops
" " Grain: Ceres
" " Harvest: Ops Ceres
" " Healing: Eir
" " Hearth: Vesta
" " Hope: Spes
" " Horses: Epons
" " Hunt: Diana
" " Infatuation: Ate [traea
" " Justice: As-
" " Love: Venus, Eros
" " Marriage: Hera
" " Mischief: Eris, Ate [Selene Selena
" " Moon: Luna,
" " Morning: Aurora [Irine
" " Peace: Irene,
" " Plenty: Ops
" " Rainbow: Iris
" " Retribution: Ara
" " sea: Ran
" " seasons: Horae
" " sorrow: Mara
" " vegetation: Ceres
" " vengeance: Ara
" " victory: Nike
" " war: Alca
" " wisdom: Minerva [ana, nymph
" " the wood: Di-
" " youth: Hebe

godlike: deific, divine
godly person: saint
gold (alchem.): sol
" bar: ingot
" (heraldry): or
" in Latin Amer. countries: oro
" paint: gilt
" symbol: A.U.
golden: precious, aureate [mashie
golf club: cleek, spoon, putter, brassy, driver, midiron, iron, brassie,
" " nose: toe
" course: links
" " depression: cup
" " parts: greens, fairways, tees
" hazard: trap
" holes unplayed: bye
" mound: tee:
" position: stance
" score: par, bogey, stroke [chip
" stroke: putt, drive,
" turf: divot
golfer's target: cup
" warning cry: fore
Goliath's home: Gath
gone: past, lost [past
" by: ago, agone,
goober: peanut
goodbye: adieu, tata
good fortune: hap
" luck charm: mascot
" manners: breeding
" name: honor
" (prefix): eu
" promise: hope
" turn: favor [ness
" will: amity, kind-
goods cast adrift: ligan, lagan
" on hand: stock
" for sale: wares
" as shipped: invoice
" shipped by public carrier: freight
" thrown overboard jetsam [brant
goose (kind): solan,
" (male): gander
gore: stab, blood
gorge: ravine, chasm, glut, abides, stuff
gorse: furze [trine
gospel: evangel, doc-
gossip: tattle, rumor
" (dial.): norate
Gounod opera: Faust
gourd plant: squash, melon, pepo
gourmand: epicure
govern: rule, control, regulate, direct, reign
government duty: tariff
" grant: patent
" levy: tax
" rep.: consul
governor: regent
grab: seize, collar, trap, snatch, clutch
grace: charm, adorn

graceful: elegant
" woman: sylph [fair
gracious: polite, benign,
grade: incline, standing, rank, degree, sort, rate, rating, class
grafted: ente [nel, cereal
grain: granulate, ker-
" (artificial): malt
" beating instrument: flail
" of a cereal: oat
" fungus: ergot
" grinder: miller
" for gringing: grist
" (pert. to): oaten
" stalk: straw [tor
" warehouse: eleva-
grampus: orc, orca
grand: august, great, epic
" slam at cards: vole
grandchild (Scot.): oe
grandeur: eclat
grandparents: aval
grant: concede, cede, bestow, allow, confer, yield gift, lend
grape: uva, rasp, acini, acinus
" (dried): raisin
" drink: wine
" (kind): malaga, tokay, niagara
" pomace: rape
" preserve: uvate
" refuse: marc
graphic: vivid
" symbol: character

grasp: apprehend, seize, clutch, take, clasp
grass: graze, pasture
" covered earth: sod
" flower part: palea
" (kind of): rie, reed, sedge, fodder, poa, sward, grama
" like herb: sedge
" mowed & cured: hay
" stem: reed
grassland: lea, meadow
grassy land surface: sward
grate: rub, rasp, grill, abrade, irritate. grit grind, scrape,
gratified: glad
gratify: please, humor, sate, wreak
grating: grid, grille, raspy, grate, grill
gratitude: thanks
gratuity: tip, dole, fee
grave: solemn, sober, demure, somber
" robber: ghoul
gravel: grit, sand
gravy: sauce
" dish: boat [dismal
gray: ashen, leaden, ashy, hoary, taupe,
" cloth: trab
" with age: hoar
grayish-green: reseda

" -white: ashen
graze: pasture, grass, browse, feed
grazing tract: range, pasture, pasturage
grease: lard, oil, fat. lubricate, lubricant, bribe
great: vast, immense, eminent, large, grand
" age: ancient
" Britain: Albion
" deal: lots, lot, much
" desert: Sahara
" Lake: Erie, Huron, Ontario, Superior
" number: multitude
" personage: mogul
greatest: largest, most, supreme
" age: oldest
Greece: Hellas
" (division of): Deme
" (pert. to): Greco

greed: avarice, cupidity
greedy: avid
" person: Midas, pig
Greek: Argive
" assembly: agora
" capital: Athens
" city: Arta
" coin: obol, obolo, lepton [ter
" " (ancient): sta-
" communes: demes
" country: Elis
" deity: Eos
" dialect: eolic, ionic
" district: Argolis
" enchantress: Medea [odyssey
" epic poem: iliad,
" festival: delia
" fury: erinys, alecto
" garment: tunic
" ghost: Ker
" god: Leto, Apollo, Eros, Ares
" goddess: Athena
" gravestone: stela, stele
" hall: saal
" hero: Ajax [phon
" historian: Xeno-
" Island: Melos, Ios, Samos, Nio, Rhodes, Crete, Milo Delos
" legendary hero: Idas
" market place: agore, agora
" measure: stadium
" " of length: bema
" mountain: Ossa
" nome: elis
" patron: Pan
" peninsula: Morea
" philosopher: Plato, Galen, stoic, Aristotle, Zeno
" " school: Ionian
" physician: Galen
" poet: Homer, Pindar, Arion, Hesiod
" portico: stoa
" priestess: Hero

" province: Nome
" room: saal
" sea: Ionian
" seaport: Enos, Volo
" sylvan deity: satyr
" tense: aorist
" theater: odeon
" warrior: Ajax
green: verdant, wreath
" film on copper: patina
" mineral: erinite
" Mt. Boys leader: Allen
" pigment: bice
" plum: gage
" tea: hyson
greenish yellow: olive
Greenland Eskimos: Ita
" settlement: Etah
greet: salute, hail, welcome, address
greeting: hi, salutation, bow, hello, salute
gregarious: social
griddle cake: scone
gridiron: grill
grief: dolor, woe, distress, dole, sorrow
" (poet.): dolor
grieve: sigh, lament, mourn, pine, sorrow
grievously afflicted: smitten [broil
grill: gridiron, grate,
" with pepper: devil
grim: fierce, stern, terrible, gaunt
grime: dirt, sully [bray
grind: grate, crush,
" together: gnash, crunch, grit [ting
grinding: molar, grit-
grip: valise, seize, grasp, handbag, clutch
gripping device: clamp, vise [pluck, courage
grit: sand, grind, gravel,
groove: rut, slot, score, stria
" part of joint: rabbet
grope: fumble, feel
grotto: cave [land
ground: soil, terrain,
" grain: grist, meal
groundless: baseless
groundwork: base, basis
group: band, set, class, bevy, squad, team
" of animals or plants: genus
" " bees: swarm
" " horses: dorp
grow: wax, increase, become, expand, mature, raise, enlarge, develop, thrive [mose
" in clusters: race-
" dim: fade, blear
" less: wane
" severe: relent
" out: enate
" rich: fatten
" uninteresting: pall
growl: snarl, gnarl, gnar
growth: tumor, stature

grub: larva [plain
grumble: mutter, com-
Guam capital: Agana
guarantee: insure, avouch, bail, assure, pledge, endorse
guaranty: pledge, warranty, security
guard: protect, keeper, fend, tend, sentinel
guardian: patron, warden
" deities: genii
" spirit: angel
Gudrun's husband: Atli
guerdon: reward
guest: visitor, caller, patron, visitant, lodger
guide: steer, pilot, direct, lead, clue, leader
guiding light: beacon
Guildo's high note: ela
" low note: ut
" note: alamire
" second note: are
guile: deceit
guileless: naive
guinea pig: cavy
gulch: canyon, ravine
gulf: chasm, abyss
Gulf in Baltic Sea: Riga
" of New Guinea: Huon
gull: dupe, cob [ternes
" like bird: tern,
gully: ravine
gum resin: elemi, copal, damar, sandarac, ava
gumbo: okra
" (var.): ocra
gun: rifle, cannon
" dog: setter, pointer
" (slang): gat, rod
gush: pour, jet, spurt, spout
gust: gale, waft, wind
guy: chaff, josh
gymnastic bar: trapeze
gypsum: selenite
gypsy: rom, romany
" book: lil

H

habit: usage, custom, routine, attire, wont
habitation: abode, lair
habitual: customary
habituate: inure
" (var.): enure
hackle: comb
hackneyed: trite, banal
Hades river: Lethe, Styx
haft: handle, hilt
haggard: gaunt
hail: ave, greet, call, salute. accost
hair braid: pigtail
" cloth: aba
" (comb. form): pil
" disease: xerasia, mange
" dye: henna
" fellet, covering & ribbon: snood

" line (var.): cerif
" ointment: pomade
" ornament: comb
" roll: rat
hairy: pilary, hirsute, pilar, comate
hale: strong, robust, hearty, vigorous, pull
half boot: pac   [tee
" breed: metis, mes-
" diameters: radii
" an em: en
" a farthing: mite
" man, half goat: faun   [taur
" " " horse: cen-
" mask: domino
" note: minim
" penny: mag   [demi
" (prefix): semi, hemi,
" score: ten
" sole: tap
" tone: semitone
" woman, half bird: siren
hall: aula, corridor
hallow: holy, bless
hallowed place: shrine
halo: areola, nimbus, aureole, aureola
halt: stem, pause, lame, arrest, hesitate
halting place: etape
hammer: sledge, maul, pound, beat, mallet, oliver   [poll
" head (end): peen,
" out: anvil
hamper: trammel, crate, cramp, basket, hinder, hanaper, encumber   [proffer
hand: give, pointer,
" (arch.): nieve
" propellor: oar
" pump: syringe
" (slang): fin
handbag: grip, reticule, satchel, valise
handful: wisp   [wield
handle: ansa, hilt, haft, treat, manage, helve,
" of a pail: bail
" roughly: paw, maul
hands on hips: akimbo
handsome (Scot.): braw
handwriting: script
handy: convenient, deft
hang: pend, drape, suspend, hover, cling
" about: hover
" down: sag, droop, lop, slouch   [dangle
" loosely: drape, loll,
hanger on: parasite
hanging: drape, pensile, pendent [dossal
" for back of altar:
" mass of ice: icicle
" ornament: tassel, pendant
hangman's loop: noose
hanker: long
hap: luck, chance, befall, fortune   [casual
haphazard: random,

happen: occur, betide, befall, chance
" again: recur
happenings: events, news, incidents
happiness: bliss, joy, felicity   [blest
happy: glad, elate,
harangue: nag, tirade, orate, screed, spiel
harass: nag, beset, fret, bother, gall, perplex, plague, vex, annoy, gripe, pester, bait, irk, tease, distract
" with clamor: din
harbor: cove, port, hold
" boat: tug   [severe
hard: austere, renitent, callous, set, adamant, arduous, solid, iron,
" drawn: taut, tense
" finish: enamel
" to manage: ornery
" metal: steel [spinel
" mineral: emery,
" (prefix): dys
" question: poser
" rock: flint
" rubber: ebonite
" substance: adamant
" tissue: bone
" wood: ash, teak, oak, lana, ebony, elm
harden: gel, set, enure, ossify, steel, inure
" sails: tan
hardness: adamant
hardship: trial, rigor
hardwood tree: ash, oak, hickory
hardy: hale, spartan, robust, well
Hardy heroine: Tess
harem: seraglio
" room: oda
harken: listen, hear, ear
harm: bane, damage, injure, evil, hurt
harmonious: musical
harmonize: attune, agree, tone, blend, tune, chime
" (colloq.): gee
harmony: peace, union, unison
harness: gear   [halter
" part: hame, reins, trace, bridle, rein,
harsh: stern, severe, acerb, rasping, raucous, rigorous
" cry: bray   [acerb
" tasting: bitter,
hart: stag   [caama
hartebeest: lecama,
harvest: reap, crop, gathering
haste: speed, hurry, dispatch, quickness
hasten: hie, run, hurry, fly, scurry, race
" away: scamper

hasty: rash, sudden, impatient, brash, abrupt, impulsive
" (colloq.): brash
" pudding: hash, mush   [fedora, cap
hat: bonnet, headgear,
" crown: poll [loathe
hate: detest, abhor,
hateful: crused, odious
hatred: rancor, dislike, odium, aversion, enmity
haughty: arrogant, proud, lofty   [tug
haul: tow, lug, pull, cart draw, drag, hale,
" (naut.): hea e [dive
haunt: den, resort, visit, lair, frequent, nest,
hautboy: oboe
have: own, possess
" ambitions: aspire
" confidence: hope, trust   [ate
" impression of: ide-
" life: be
" meter: scan
" recourse to: betake, refer, resort
" weight or effect: militate   [shelter
haven: port, refuge,
having ability: able
" branches: ramose, ramulose
" feeling: sentient
" a handle: ansate
" hoofs: ungulate
" a large nose: nasute
" limits: finite
" made & left a will: testate
" no feet: apodal
" " interest or care: supine   [free
" " worries: care-
" offensive smell: olid
" raised strips: ridgy
" retired: abed
" ribs: costate
" risen: up
" spikes: tined
" supports: piered
" toothed margin: erose
" two horns: bicorn
" wings: alated, alate
Hawaiian bird: oo, io, ooaa
" cloth: tapa
" dance: hula
" district: Puna
" farewell: aloha
" fish: lania, ahi
" food: poi
" goose: nene
" hawk: io
" herb: hola   [aloha
" salutation: aloaa,
" taro paste: poi
" town: Hilo
" tree: koa, aalii

" valley: Manoa
" wreath: lei
hawk's cage: mew
" headed deity: Ra
" (kind): kestrel, elanet, falcon, io, harrier
" leash: lune
" like bird: kite
" nest: aerie
" parrot: hia
hawser: rope
hay storage compartment: mow, loft
haying machine: tedder
haystack: rick
hazard: risk, peril, lot, stake, danger, dare
hazardous: unsafe
haze: fog, mist
head: pate, lead, poll, director, leader, cop
" of convent: abess
" covering: hood, hair
" part: scalp
headdress: tiara, hat
heading: caption, title
headland: cape, ness, ras, hook
headliner: star
heal: cure
healthy: hale, well, sane
heap: pile, mass, stack, amass
" adulation on: praise   [cairn
" of stones: scree,
hear: harken, regard, heed, listen   [hear
" by accident: over-
" ye: oyez
hearing: audition, mien
" (pert. to): otic
hearsay: rumor
heart: cor, core, spirit
" chamber: camera, auricle
" (pert. to): cardiac
" shaped: cordate
hearty: hale, sincere
heat: warmth
" excessively: toast
" (pert. to): caloric
" producer: fuel
heated: hot
heath: erica, moor
Heathen: pagan
" diety: idol
heather: gorse, erica
heating implement: stove, etna, radiator, boiler   [lift, hoist
heave: cast, surge, raise, strain, throw,
heaven: firmament, sky
heavenly: celestial, supernal
" being: angel planet
" body: star, sun, comet, meteor, luminary, moon, lamp,
" bread: manna
" food: manna
heavy: leaden, stolid
" blow (slang): oner

" impact: slam
" & sweet: sirupy
Hebrew: see also Jewish
" diety: Baal, El
" judge: Elon, Eli
" king: Saul, David
" kingdom: Israel
" letter: tav, ab, pe daleth, mem, ayin, resh, teth
" lyre: asor
" measure: omer, cab, hin, kab
" musical instrument: Asor
" name for God: El
" plural ending: im
" prophet: Jeremiah, Amos, Hosea, Elias, Daniel, Isaiah, Elisha
" proselyte: Ger
" vowel point: tsere
Hebrides Isl.: Iona
hector: tease, bully
heed: notice, note, attention, mind, ear, care, hear
heedless: careless, rash
heel: cant [reen
" over: tip, tilt, careen
height: altitude, stature, elevation
heir: legatee, scion

Helen of Troy's mother: Leda
helical: spiral
helix: spiral
hell: inferno
helm: steer, tiller
helmet shaped organ: galea [man
helmsman: pilot, steersman
help: aidance, benefit, stead, attend, abet, aid, assist, succor
helper: ally, aide [border
hem: restrict, margin,
" in: beset
hematite: ore
hemp fiber: tow, sisal
hence: ergo, so, therefore
[engist's brother: Horsa
heraldic bearing: orle
" cross: patee, patte
" grafted: ente [dill
herb: sage, sedum, catnip, anise, moly, rue,
" of aster family: arnica
" (cloverlike): medic
" dill: anet
" eve: iva
herbage: grass
herd: drove, flock
hereditary: lineal
" factor: gene
heretic: dissenter [cluse
hermit: eremite, re-
Herod's granddaughter: Salome
heroic: epic, brave, epical, valiant, issustrate [saga
" tale: sage, gest,

heroism: valor
heron: egret, crane, aigret, bittern, rail
herring like fish: sprat, lile, shad, alewives
hesitate: haw, demur, falter, halt, pause, waver [mer
" in speech: stammew: chop, cut, cleave
hewing tool: axe, ax
hiatus: gap, opening
hibernian: Irish
hickory: pecan [covert
hidden: inner, secret, latent, perdu, deep.
" obstacle: snag
hide: stow, pelt, secrete, conceal, skin, cache, cover, veil, concede, ensconce, cloak, screen
hideous: ugly, horrible [niche
hiding place: cache,
high: tall, up, lofty, costly, elevated
" (comb. form): alti
" hill: tor
" honor: homage
" mts.: Andes
" note: ela, ala
" priest: Eli
" temperature: heat
" volley: lob
" waters: floods
higher: up, above
highest: upmost, supreme
" Mt.: Everest, peak
" note of gamut: ela pinnacle, noon, apex
highlander: Scot
" costume: kilt
" purse: sporran
" seasoned dish: olla, ragout
highway: pike, avenue
" division: lane
highwayman: bandit, ladrone, footpad
hill (flat): mesa
hilt: handle, haft
Himalayan animal: panda [goral
" antelope: serow,
" monkshood: atis
" peak: Everest
" wild sheep: nahoor
hinder: impede, obstruct, arrest, let, delay, hamper, estop, deter, bar, retard, harass, detain, cramp
hindrance: bar, rub, restraint, let, balk
Hindu acrobat: nat
" army man: Sepoy
" ascetic: Yogi
" avatar: rama
" charitable gift: enam
" cymbals: dal, tal
" deity: siva, rama, uma, deva, varuna
" " with 7 arms: Agni

" demon: asura, rahu
" game: rance
" garment: sari
" god: siva
" " (unknown): ka
" goddess: devi
" gods abode: meru
" guitar: sitar [abar
" handkerchief: malhero: rama
" holy city: Benares
" measure: ryots
" merchant: banian
" month: pus, asin
" peasant: ryot
" pillar: lat [thana
" police station:
" policeman: sepoy
" political leader: Gandhi
" prayer rug: asan
" prince: raja, rajah, rana [ranee
" princess: rani,
" progenitor: Manu
" proprietor: malik
" queen: rance, rani
" red dye: alta
" sacred literature: veda
" social class: caste
" symbals: tal [rajah
" title: mir, sahib,
" " " respect: swami
" trinity: siva
" weight: tola, ser
" word (sacred): om
Hindustan: India
" hill dweller: toda
" (poet.): Ind. [pivot
hinge: joint, depend,
hint: clue, cue, trace, clew, suggest, intimate, tip, imply, allusion, intimation
hire: charter, engage, rent, fee, employ, let, contract, lease
hireling: slave, esne
hirsute: hairy [hair
" adornment: beard,
hiss: siss, boo
hissing: sibilant, sis
historical period (pert. to): erol, eral
history: annals
hit: swat, batted, strike, bat, smite
" aloft: lob
" gently: tap
" (slang): swat, lam
hoar: white
" frost: rime
hoarder: miser
hoax: canard
" (slang): kid, spoof
hobby: fad, avocation
hocus: cheat
hod: scuttle
hodgepodge: olio
hoist: boost, cat, raise, winch, heave [davit
hoisting apparatus: gin, derrick, cage, crane, elevator, capstan,

hold: have, retain, clutch, harbor, keep
" in affection: endear
" attention: interest
" back: dam, retard, deter, restrain, stem, hinder, delay, resist, detain, refrain
" balance: poise
" in common: joint
" dear: love, cherish
" fast: cling, anchor, pin
" firmly: grip
" in greater favor: prefer
" ones ground: stand
" in respect: awe
" a session: sit
" in suspense: hang
" together: cohere, clamp
" under spell: charm
holder: container, owner
" of a lease: lessee
holding: tenure, property
" at bridge: tenace
" device: vise
hole: orifice, aperture, opening, cavity, perforation, eyelet
" in one (slang): ace
" repairer: darner
holidays: fiestos, vacations, feria
Holland city: Ede
" seaport: Edam
hollow: depression, concave, cavernous, dent
holly: ilex
holy: sacred, blessed, hallow
" person: saint

" picture: icon
" scriptures: Bible
home: abode
" coming: return
homeless child: waif
" outcast: arab
Homer's epic: Iliad, Odyssey
homicide: murder
homily: sermon
hominy: samp [upright
honest: se, true, frank,
honey: mel
" badger: ratel
" buzzard: pern
" container: comb
honeyed: sugary
honor: venerate, revere, credit, esteem, reputation, renown, exalt, ennoble, respect
hooded cloak: capote
hoo wink: deceive
hooligan: ruffian
hoop: encircle, ring, bail
Hoosier humorist: Ade
" poet: Riley
" state (abbr.): Ind.
hop: leap, spring, vine
" kiln: oast
hop stem: bine
hope: desire, reliance,

anticipate, trust, wish, expectation
hopelessness: despair
horde: crowd, drove, swarm, throng, army, host
horizontal: flat, level
" **beam over door:** lintel
horned horse: unicorn
" **quadruped:** ibex
horrify: appal
horror: dread, terror
horse: nag, steed, hunter, miler, arab, pacer
" **blanket:** manta
" **color:** roan, pinto
" **disease:** glander
" **fodder:** oats
" **'s foot part:** pastern
" **of a gait:** gaiter, pacer, trotter
" **'s gait:** rack
" **headstall flap:** blinder [nag, pacer
" **(kind):** roan, padleg: fetlock
" **leg:** fetlock
" **in a race:** entry
" **(small):** tit, pony, bidet, cob
" **tender:** groom
" **'s working gear:** harness [horde
host: army, throng,
hostelry: inn
hostile feeling: animus
hostler: groom
hot: torrid, peppery, fiery, heated
" **wind:** sirocco
hotel: inn [pursus
hound: dog, basset,
hourly: horal
house: lodge, domicile
" **(pert. to):** domal
" **plant:** calla [tage
" **(small):** cabin, cot-
houseboat: barge
household: menage family [lars
" **gods:** penates, di,
hover: poise, linger
however: yet, but
howl: ululate, wail, roar
hoyden: tomboy
hub: nave
hubbub: clamor, tumult, noise, uproar
hue: color, tint, cry, shade, tinge [vast
huge: giant, enormous, massive, gigantic,
" **(poet.):** enorm
hulled corn: samp
hum: croon, drone, boom, buzz [mortal
human: man, adamite,
" **affairs:** lives
" **trunk:** torso
humble: abase, low, disgrace, lower
humbug: fraud, imposture [moist
humid: damp, wet,
humiliate: shame, mortify, abase, debase,

abash [ava
hummingbird: colibri,
humor: wit, mood, indulge, baby, whim, comicality, gratify
humorist (colloq.): wag
humorous: funny, droll
" **play:** farce, bigwig
Hun: Asiatic, vandal
hunt: en, chase, trail, search, pursue, seek
hunter: nimrod [basset
hunting dog: setter, hound, aland, beagle,
" " **(arch.):** alan
" **expedition:** safari
hurl: cast, sling, toss, throw, fling, pelt
" **(poet.):** evance
hurry: speed, rush, haste, hasten, hie
hurt: pain, pained, damage, dere, injury, harm, injure
hurtful: malefic, sore
husband or wife: spouse
husk: shell, shuck
husks of fruit: lemma, hulls [straw, bran
" " **grain:** chaff,
hut: hovel, cabin, shack, shanty
hydraulic pump: ram
hydrophobia: rabies
hymn: psalm
" **of praise:** paean
" **tune:** choral
hynotic state: trance
hypocritical talk: cant
hypothetical force: od
" **maiden:** io
" **structural unit:** id

I

Ibsen character: Ase, Nora, Hedda
ice: sleet, chill, dessert, frost, frosting, sherbet [conc
" **cream container:** crampon
" **creeper:** crampon
" **crystals:** snow
" **(floating mass):** floe, berg, iceberg
" **runner:** skate
" **sheet:** glacier
Icelandic giant: Atli
" **lang.:** Norse
" **literary work:** edda
" **measure of length:** lina
" **story:** saga
icy: frigid, gelid
Idaho capital: Boise
" **county:** Ada
idea: opinion, concept, notion, theory, impression, belief, fancy, thought, intention
ideal: aim, pattern, standard, faultless, perfect, mental
" **place:** Utopia [same

identical: same, self-
identification mark: tag, marker [pleton
idiot: moron, oaf, simidiotic: daft
idiotic: daft [otiose, laze
idle: inactive, loiter, loaf, useless, lazy, indolent, vacant, sluggish, vain, futile,
" **(colloq.):** laze
" **fancy:** dream
" **talk:** patter, gab, gossip, prate, palaver
idler: rounder, drone, dawdler, lazer, loafer
idol: image [porphyry
igneous rock: basalt,
ignite: fire, kindle, light
ignoble: mean, base
ignorant: nescient, unaware, unlearned
Igorot town division: Ato
Iliad character: Ajax
ilk: sort, breed, kind
ill: baneful, evil, bad, harmful, unkind, woe, poorly, ailing
" **boding:** dire
" **bred person:** boor, cad, churl
" **gotten gain:** pelf
" **humored:** morose
" **natured:** nasty
" **(prefix):** mal
" **tempered woman:** virago, shrew
" **will:** rancor, malice, animus
illness: malady
illuminant: gas
illusion: mirage [liant
illustrious: noble, brilimage: idol, emblem,
image: idol, emblem, likeness, statue, icon, copy, picture, effigy
imaginative: poetic
imagine: ideate, dream, fancy, conjecture
imbecile: cretin, anile
imbibed: drank, absorbed
imbue: ingrain, leaven, steep, infuse, tincture, pervade, permeate
" **with vigor:** nerve
imitate: ape, emulate, simulate, min, copy, echo, mock, mimic
imitation: paste, sham
" **gold:** oroide
" **pearl:** olivet
immature: unripe
immediate: direct
immediately: anon, presto, now [vasty
immense: vast, enormous, gigantic, great,
immerse: souse, dip, submerge, douse
immigration center: Ellis [still
immovable: adamant,
immutable: firm
imp: sprite, demon

impair: mar, wear, damage, sap, ruin
" **by time:** rust
impart: instil, tell, convey, inspire, give
impartial: unbiased, fair, just
impassive: stolid
impatient: restive, hasty, tolerant
impede: obstruct, hinder, estop, clog [bar
impediment: remora,
impel: urge, send, induce, constrain, force, drive, compel, incite, spur
imperative: urgent
imperfection: blemish
imperfect (prefix): mal
imperial: regal, majestic
" **domains:** emperies, empires [saucy, sassy
impertinent: officious,
" **(colloq.):** sass
impetuous: rash, eager, abrupt, fiery [lodged
implanted: rooted, inculcated, infixed,
implement: tool, spade, utensil, fulfill
" **for bruising:** pestle
implicate: involve
implied: tacit
implore: beg, entreat, plead, pray
imply: mean, hint
import: interest, sense, matter
importance: stress
importune: solicit, pray, tease, dun
impose: obtrude, lay
" **as necessary result:** entail
impost: duty, toll, tax
imposture: deception, sham, humbug, deceit [curse
imprecation: oath,
impress: print, stamp, mark, awe [affect
" **deeply:** engrave,
impression: dent, idea
" **of type:** print
imprint: stamp, dint
imprison: cage, inter, sconce, incarcerate, jail, confine
imprisonment: durance
improve: better, amend, emend, gain, revise
impudent: saucy, rude, brash, pert, sassy
impure from ore: ocher
impute: ascribe
in: at, among, into
" **advance:** ahead, before
" **any degree:** ever
" **behalf of:** pro, for
" **the capacity of:** as, qua [with
" **company:** along,
" **direction of:** to, axial, toward, on

" existence: extant
" fact: indeed, truly
" favor of: pro, for
" front: ahead, aface
" high spirits: elated, exulted
" the lead: ahead
" like manner: so
" a line: arow
" the main: generally
" name only: nominal [noways
" no matter: not,
" order that: lest
" passing: obiter
" the past: ago
" place of: for, else, stead, instead
" (prefix): en
" progress: afoot
" pursuit of: after
" quick time: presto
" reality: indeed
" a row: alinement
" same degree: so
" " place: ibidem, ibid, ib
" " state: so
" so far as: qua
" store for: await
" such a manner: so
" that case: so, then
" this: herein
" " matter: so
" " place: here
" " way: thus
" time of: during
" " (mus.): train
" a trice: anon
" truth: verily
" what place: where
" " way: how
inactive: inert, indolent, idle, inanimate, otiose, passive, resting, retired [stupid
inane: empty, silly, fatuous, vacuity,
inappropriate: inept
inaugurate: open
inborn: innate, inbred, natural, native
inbred: inborn, innate
incantation: spell
incarnation: avator
incase: case, surround
incendiarism: arson
incensed: irate, enraged, wroth
incentive: motive, spur
ncident: episode, event, happening, act
incidental: bye, stray
incinerate: cremate
incipient: initial
" laugh: smile
incision: cut
incite: egg, exhort, edge, urge, abet, goad, spur, forment, stimulate, impel
" to activity: prod
inclination: trend, bent, penchant, slant, rake, grade, tilt, will, bevel
" of the head: bow

incline: lean, grade, dip, slope, slant, tend, tilt, trend
inclined: prone
" (arch.): fain
" (poet.): leant
" railway: ramp
" trough: chute [yard
inclosure: cage, pen,
income: revenue
incomparable: rare
incomplete: broken, partial
incongruous: alien
incorporate: blend, mix, embody
increase: grow, enhance, raise, enlarge,-deepen, add, spread, rise, wax [rich
" knowledge of: en-
incrustation: scar
" on teeth: tartar
inculcate: implant, instil, instill
incursion: raid [truly
indeed: really, yea,
indefinite: vague [one
" pronoun: one, any-
" quantity: some, many, any
indemnify: pay [dent
indent: depress, notch,
independent: free
India (poet.): Ind.
Indian: Amerind, Delaware, Erie, Ute, Otee, Kaw, Mohave, Oto, Otoe, Osage, Keres, Ewers, Cree, Hopi, Mohawk, Seminole, Sac, Oneida, Redskin, Apache, Serrano, Aht
" antelope: nilgai
" arrow poison: curare
" boat: canoe
" building material: laterite
" carpet: agra
" city: Agra, Benares, Lahore, Madira
" class society: caste
" coin: anda, rupee, anna, paisa, spare, annas
" (comb. form): indo
" corn: samp, maize
" currency: wampum
" divisions: tribal, tribals, agras
" festival: mela
" fetish: totem
" god: manitou
" groom: sice, syce
" harvest: rabi
" hemp: ramie, kef
" hut: lodge

" jungle: Saola
" landing place: Ghat
" lodge: teepee, tepee
" madder: el, aal
" measure: kos
" memorial post: Xat
" moccasin: pac

" monetary unit: anna
" mountain pass: Ghat [ash, ach
" mulberry: al, aal,
" noble title: Raia
" nurse: amah [bian
" Ocean Sea: Ara-
" " vessel: dhow
" peace pipe: calumet
" peasant: ryot
" poll: totem
" pony: cayuse
" prince: ameer
" province: Assam
" race: Jat, Tamil
" river: Ul, Ganges, Deo
" robber: dacoit
" seaport: Surat
" silk: eri
" snake: krait
" soldier: sepoy
" song bird: shama
" sovereign: raj
" spirit: manitou
" spring crop: rabi
" symbol: totem
" tent: tepee
" thorny tree: bel
" title of address: sahib
" town: Patan, Arcot
" tree: dar
" tribe: Ao
" utterance: ugh
" village: Pueblo
" war cry: whoop
" " trophy: scalp
" warrior: brave
" weight: tola, ser
" woman: squaw
indicate: dominate, denote, connote, bode, betoken, read, signify
indicating succession: ordinal [dence, note
indication: sign, evi-
indicator: pointer, dial
indifference: apathy

indifferent: supine, cool, apathetic [stoic
" to pain or pleasure:
indigence: want, poverty [natural
indigenous: native,
indigent: poor, needy
indignation: wrath
indigo dye & plant: anil
indisposed: ails, ail, ill
indisposition: ailment
" to motion: inertia
indistinct: dim, blur, obscure
indite: write, pen
individual: one, person, self, ego, sole
" (comb. form): idio
" performance: solo
Indo Chinese city: Hanoi
" " kingdom: Anam

" " language: bama, tai [Tai
" " race: Naga,
indolence: sloth
indolent: inert, otiose, lazy, idle
Indonesian: Ata
induce: urge, prevail, lead, make, persuade
indulge: humor, pamper, please
indulgent: easy
industrialist: magnate
ineffectual: weak, futile
inequality: odd, odds
inert: inactive, lifeless, sluggish, torpid, indolent [lay
inexperienced: callow,
infatuation: ate
infect: taint [derive,
infer: deduce, conclude
inferior: worse, low, bad
" cloth: surat, shoddy
" horse: tit, plater
" (prefix): sub
" wares: seconds
infernal: devilish
inferno: hell
infinite: endless, boundless, eternal
infinitive part: to [lame
infirm: anile, feeble,
inflame: rankle, fire, enrage [den
" with passion: mad-
inflexible: rigid, iron

inflict: wreak, deal
influence: interest, affect, prestige
" corruptly: bribe
influx: inflow, inset
infold: lap, wrap
inform: apprise, tell
informal conversation: chat
" gathering: social
information: data, word
informed: aware, hep
informer: spy [dom
infrequent: rare, sel-
infuriate: madden, enrage
infuse: imbue, instill
ingenuity: art, wit
ingenuous: naive
ingrained: innate
ingredient: materials, component, element
ingress: entry, entrance
inhabitant: inmate, denizen
" of city: cit [otes
" 's of (suffix): ites,
inhibit: check
inhume: inter
inimical: hostile, averse
iniquity: crime, sin, evil, vice [begin
initiate: institute, start,
injunction: order, precept, mandate
injure: harm, damage, maim, hurt, mar, wrong [damage, hurt
injury: lesion, harm,

X-WORD DICT

inky: black
inland body of water: river, pond, brook
inlay: insert, inset
inlet: ria, bay, cove, slew, entrance or ´fice
" **from sea**: arm, bayou
inn: hotel, tavern, hostel, hostelry
innate: hidden, natural, inherent, ingrained, inborn   [scure
inner: hidden, internal, within inside, ob-
" **bark**: bast [heart
" **part**: inside, core,
" **point**: into [gestion
innuendo: slur, sug-
inorganic: mineral
inquiry: search

" **for lost goods**: tracer   [ing
inquisitive: nosy, pry-
" **(colloq.)**: snoopy, nosey   [luny
insane: demented, mad,
inscribe: write, dedicate, letter
insect: mantis, flea, fly, termite, gnat, ant, aphis, bee, bug, moth, wasp, mite, midge, aphid, nit, earwig, dor, cricket, beetle
" **egg**: nit
" **exudation**: lac
" **feeler**: antenna
insectivorous mammal: tenrec
insecure: risky, unsafe, perilous   [put
insert: enter, enclose,
inset: inlay, influx
inside: into, interior, within, inner, internal
insight: ken
insignia: regalia, badge
insignificant: trivial, null, tiny
" **par**: iota
" **person**: snip
insipid: vapid, flat, stale
insist: persist, demand, urge
inspect: pry, examine
inspector of electric lamps: ager
" " **wts. & measures**: sealer   [stir
inspire: uplift, impart,
inspirit: cheer, liven
install: seat, invest
instance: case
instant: moment, trice
instead: else   [egg
instigate: abet, foment,
instill: infuse   [tiate
institute: establish, ini-
" **suit**: sue
instruct: train, teach, educate, school, edify
instrument: tool, organ
" **board**: panel
" **to record time**: dater   [cy, mean

instrumentality: agen-
insufficient: scanty
insulate: isle, isolate
insult: affront, offend, slap
insurgent: rebel   [tire
integral: composite, en-
integrity: honor
intellect: mind, brain
" **(pert. to)**: noetic
intellectual: mental
intelligence: sense, wit, mind, wants, reason
intend: mean, purpose, propose, aim
intense: ardent, extreme, acute, fierce, fervid, deep   [rapt
intent: purpose, eager,
intention: aim, purpose, idea
inter: inhume, entomb
intercede: mediate
interdict: ban, bar
interdiction: veto, ban
interfere: meddle
interim: meantime
interior: inside, inner
" **(comb. form)**: ento
interjection: ha, ho, oh, ah, ahem
interlace: braid, weave
interlock: knit [between
intermediate: mesne,
intermix: mingle
internal: inner, enclosed, inside
" **fruit decay**: blet
internat. agreement: treaty, cartel
" **lang.**: ro   [tente
" **understanding**: en-
interprets: decodes, renders, construes, rede, reads
interrogate: ask, inquire
interruption: hiatus, gap, break   [join
intersect: meet, cross,
intersecting: secant [ola
interstice: crevice, are-
intertwine: lace
interval: space, time, respite, span, gap
intervening: between
" **(law)**: mesne
interweave: braid, mat, plait, lace, raddle
intimate: hint, near, suggest   [homey
" **(colloq.)**: homy,
intimation: cue, hint
intimidate: cow, awe, deter, daunt, overawe
into: within, inside, in

intolerant: bigoted
intone: chant, sing
intransitive: neuter
intrepid: bold, dreadless, brave, dauntless
intrepidity: nerve
intricate: dedal, gordian, complex
intrigue: cabal, plot
intrinsic nature: essence

introduce: herald, insert, present, usher
introduction: entree, prelude, preamble, debut, prologue, preface, insertion
inundate: flood, deluge
inure: harden, season, accustom, use
inutile: useless
invade: raid, encroach
invalid: null
invaluable: priceless
invariable: steady
invariant: constant
invent: create, feign, coin, originate, devise, discover
inventor of sewing machine: Howe
" " **telegraph**: Morse   [verse
invert: transpose, re-
invest: instate, install, envelop, endue, vest, endow   [quire
investigate: probe, in-
invigorate: renew, strengthen
invisible emanation: aura
invite: bid, ask, entice
involve: tangle, entail, implicate, engage
inward: secret   dot
iota: jot, atom, whit,
Iowa college: Coe
" **town**: Ames
Ipecac plant: ever
Iranian: Persian
Iraq capital: Bagdad
irascible: touchy, testy
irate: wroth, wrath, angry, mad
ire: rage, anger, wrath, fury, passion
Ireland: Eire, Erin
irenic: peaceful, serene
iridescent: opaline, irised
" **gem**: opal
iris: flag
" **of the eye (pert. to)**: irian
" **(heraldry)**: lis
" **(kind)**: orris
" **layer**: uvea
" " **(pert. to)**: uveal   [flag
" **plant**: irid, ixia,
Irish: celtic
" **ancient capital**: Tara
" **author**: Shaw
" **battle cry**: abu
" **bay**: Sligo
" **Chamber of Dep.**: Dail
" **city**: Cork
" **coin**: rap
" **cudgel**: alpeen
" **dramatist**: Steele Shaw
" **epic tale**: tana [rah
" **expletive**: arra, ar-
" **fish**: pollan

" **floral emblem**: shamrock
" **lassie**: colleen
" **Neptune**: Ler
" **peasant**: kern
" **poet**: Wildé, Moore, Yeats
" **river**: Nore, Lagan
" **sea god**: Ler
irk: annoy, chafe
irksome: tedious
iron: F.E., fetter, ferrum, firmness, hard, smooth, manacle, firm, press
" **alloy**: steel
ironic: sarcastic, satirical, satiric
iroquois tribe: Oneida
irredescent jewels: opals   [erose
irregular: abnormal,
irrigate: water
irritable: testy, edgy
irritate: gall, fret, rile, peeve, grate, nettle, tease, provoke, vex, anger, exasperate
irritation: itch, pique
isinglass: mica
island: ait, alt
" **(Fr.)**: ile   [moa
" **group**: Faroe, Sa-
" **off Ireland**: Aran

" " **Tuscany coast**: Elba
" **(poet.)**: isle
" **of Saints**: Erin
" **(small)**: isle, islet
islet: cay, bay, ait, alt
isolated: singular, alone, detached
Israelite: see "Hebrew" & "Jewish"
" **tribe**: Gad, Dan, Asher, Levi, Aser
issue: print, outcome, emerge, emit, arise
" **forth**: emanate
Italian: Roman, Latin
" **actress**: Duse
" **anatomist**: Aselli
" **article**: il
" **astronomer**: Secchi, Galileo
" **building**: Casa
" **chief magistrate**: doge
" **city**: Taranto, Pisa, Asti, Milan, Nola, Venice, Trieste, Alba, Ferrara, Bra, Teano, Rome, Trent, Turin, Este, Genoa, Sassari
" **coins**: lire, lira, soldos
" **(comb. form)**: Italo
" **composer**: Verdi
" **condiment**: tamara
" **dept.**: Calabria
" **family**: Este
" " " **health**: Salus
" **house**: casa
" **island**: Cos, Lido, Elba, Capri

" lake: Como
" legislative **chamber**: camera
" measure: stero
" millet: tenai
" music **reformer**: Guido
" novelist: Serao [ma
" opera: Aida, Nor-
" painter: Reni, Titian, Raphael
" physicist: Volta
" poet.: Dante, Tasso
" princely **house**: este
" province: Mantua, Parma, Este, Como, Pisa [Tiber, Piave
" river: Po, Arno
" saint: Neri
" seaport: Pola, Trieste, Genoa
" seaside **resort**: Lido
" soprano: Patti [dra
" statesman: Salanti
" tenor: Caruso
" title: donna
" violin: amati
" wine: asti
" woodwork: tarsia
" writer: Cellini
" for yes: si [maxim
item: detail, entry,
" of property: asset
itemize: list
iterate: repeat
ivory: dentine

J

jab: poke
jabber: babble, sputter
jackdaw: daw
jacket: reefer, eton
Jacob's brother: Esau, Edom [ban
" father-in-law: Laban
" son: Dan, Levi, Reuben, Gad
" wife: Leah [lockup
jail: prison, imprison,
Jap: Nip [aino, aeta
" aborigine: ainu,
" admiral: Ito, Togo
" boxes: inro
" church: tera
" city: Osaka, Ujina, Nagasaki, Kobe [rin
" coin: sen, yen, ril,
" dancing girl: geisha
" drink: sake, saki
" emperor: Mikado, Hirohito
" family badge: mon
" festival: bon
" fortress: truk [cho
" measure: ri, se, rin,
" money: sen
" mt.: Usu
" pagoda: taa
" peninsula: Corea
" plane: zero
" plant: udo
" porgy: tai

" rice paste: ame
" sash: obi
" statesman: Ito
" wt.: mo, shi [trick
jape: gibe, fraud, jest,
jar: jolt, shock, disconcert, shake, clash, discord olla, urn
jargon: cant, slang, patter, lingo, argot
Jason's follower: Argonaut
" helper: Medea
" ship: Argo, Argonaut
jaunt: sally, trip [upas
Java poisonous tree:
javelin: dart, spear
jealousy: envy [taunt
jeer: scoff, flout, boo,
jejune: dry, arid
jellyfish: medusa
jellylike material: gel
jeopardy: danger, peril
jerk: yank, bob
Jerusalem hill: Zion
" mosque: Omar
" oak: ambrose
jest: joke, game, jape
jet: spout, gush, jut, black
" black: raven, ebon
jewel: stone, gem, opal
" mounting: setting
jeweler's weight: carat
jewelry alloy: oroide
Jewish: see also Hebrew
" festival: seder [Eli
" high priest: Ezra,
" law: torah, talmud
" leader: Moses
" month: Nisan, Adar, Tisri, Elul, Ab, Sebat, Tebet, Shebat
" ram's horn: shofar
" teacher: rabbi
" weight: gerah, omer
jib: gib, balk
jocularity: wit
jog: nudge, trot
John (Scot.): Ian
johnnycake: pone
join: unite, meet, team, connect, mortise, ally, enter, intersect, annex, yoke, engage, add, meld, merge
" closely: weld, enlink
joint: hinge, tenon, seam [wrist
" of arm: elbow,
" " door: hinge
" " leg: knee
" legatee: coheir
" of stem: node
joke: jest, gag
joker: wit, wag
jolly: jovial, merry
jolt: jar, bump
josh: guy
Joshua's father: Nun
jostle rudely: elbow
jot: iota, mite, speck, whit, atom, ace, par-

ticle [trip, trek, tour
journey: fare, travel,
joust: tilt
jovial: jolly[ness, elation
joy: bliss, glee, glad-
joyful: cheerful, blithe
joyous: glad, happy, riant, festal, festive
jubilant: elated
Judah's son: Er
judge: consider, arbiter, decide, deem, opine, arbitrator, referee, estimate
" chamber: camera
" circuit (arch.): iter
" court bench: banc
" gavel: mace
" robe: gown
judgement: doom, sense, award, verdict, opinion, sentence
judicial command: mandate
" order: writ
" writ: elegit
jug: ewer, cruse
juice of plant: sap
juicy plant: uva
Jules Verne character: Nemo
jumble: displace, pie
jumbled type: pi
jump: leap, hop [per
" about: prance, cajumping
jumping stick: pogo
junction: union, meeting
" lines: suture, seam
june bug: dor
juniper (kind of): Cade
Jupiter: Zeus, Jove
" 's son: Caster
jurisdiction (law): soc
jurisprudence: law
jury: panel
just: fair, impartial

" clear the ground (naut.): atrip, aweigh
justice: law, fairness
jutting rock: tor, crag
juvenile: young, youthful

K

Kaffir warriors: Impi
kaka: parrot
kava: ava
keen: sharp, nice, fine, acute, shrewd, pungent [zest
" enjoyment: gusto,
keeness of mind: acumen [maintain
keep: retain, hold,
" afloat: buoy [clude
" apart: separate, seaway
" away from: avoid
" back: detain, hinder, stifle, deter
" close to: hug
" company: consort
" from action: deter
" intact: preserve

King Arthur's abode: Camelot, Avalon
" " father: Uther
" " lance: ron
" of Bosham: Og
" David's ruler: Ira
" of England & Denmark: Canute, Cnut
" " fairies: Oberon
" fish: barb
" " Huns: Attila
" " Israel: Saul, Omri, Ahab, David
" " Judah: Asa, Ahaz, Herod
" (latin): rex [das
" " Phrygia: Midas
" " Troy: Priam
" " Tyre: Hiram
" " underground: Satan [ric
" " Visigoths: Alakingdom: realm, empire
kingly: regal [relative
kinsman: relation, sib,
kiss: buss, osculate
kite: elanet
kittenish: playful
kiwi: roa
knack: art [varlet
knave: rascal, rogue,
" of clubs: pam
" in cribbage: nob
knead: massage, elt
kneecap: patella [vet
" to cut loops: tre-
" (large): machete, snee, bolo
knifelike instrument: spatula
knight: cavalier, gallant
" 's cloak: tabard
knighterrant: paladin
knit: contract, unite
knob: node, nub, lump
knock lightly: tap [ko
knockout (slang): kayo,
knot: node, noose, tie, gnarl, entangle, nodule, mat
" of hair: chignon
" (pert. to): nodal
" in wood: gnarl, burl, knar, gnar
" of wool: noil
" " yarn: skein
knotted lace: tatting
knotty: gnarly, gnarled, nodal, nodose
know: ken
" order: police
" from progressing: delay
" from shaking: steady [warden
keeper: custodian,
keeve: tub, vat
keg: cask, barrel
Kentucky bluegrass: poa [barrel
kernel: nut, grain,
kettledrum: atabal, typani, timbal
key: cay, wharf, pitch, solution
" note in music:

tonic
Keystone state: Pa.
kick a football: punt
killer whale: orc, orca
kiln: ost, oven, oast, osier, furnace, stove
kind: sort, ilk, genus, humane, gentle, genre, friendly, type
kindle: fire, fume, lume, ignite, light
kindly: benign
kindness: favor, tenderness   [family, sib
kindred: gens, kinship,
" **(arch.):** wot, wis
" **(Scot.):** ken [aware
knowing: shrewd, wise,
knowledge: lore, ken, cognition, wisdom
" **gained:** lesson
" **(pert. to):** gnostic, gnostical
known facts: data
kobold: nisse, nis

L

Laban's daughter: Leah
label: designate, brand, docket, stamp, mark, classify, tag, tab
labor: toil
" **hard:** strive
" **organization:** union
labored breath: gasp, pant
laborer: peon, serf
Labrador tea: ledum [tie
lace: thread, embroider,
" **collar:** bertha
" **edging:** frill
" **pattern:** toile
lacelike: lacy [mangle
lacerate: rend, tear,
lacet: braid
lachrymal drop: tear
lack: need, dearth
" **of good qualities:** badness   [cord
" " **harmony:** disvigor: atony
" " **vigor:** atony
lackadaisical: blah
lacking: destitute, shy
Laconia capital: Sparta
laconic: terse
lacquer: lac
lacteal fluid: milk
lad: stripling, boy
ladderlike: scalar
lade: load, bail, burden, freight, dip
ladle: scoop, dipper
lag: trail, linger, falter, loiter, delay, tarry
laggard: loiterer, remiss
lair: den, tier, row, haunt, amass, cave
laity: people
" **(pert. to):** laic
lake (small): mere
lamb: tag
Lamb's mother: Ewe
" **pen name:** Elia

lame: halt, infirm, feeble   [cry
lament: deplore, bemoan, sigh, grieve, bewail, regret, wail, beweep, pine, moan,
lamentation: moan
lamia: witch
lamina: leaf
laminar: scaly, flaky
laminated: slaty
" **rock:** shale [tern
lamp: torch, light, lan-
" **cord:** wick
" **fuel:** kerosene
" **iron frame:** cresset
" **part:** burner
" **(slang):** glim
lampoon: satire, ridicule, squib, skit
lamprey: eel
lanate: wooly
lance: spear, open, pierce, dart
land: terra, soil, ground, shore, earth, country, debark, alight
" **conveyance:** deed
" **held absolutely:** alod   [decare
" **measure:** are, rod, acre, ar, meter, rood,
landed: alit
" **estate:** manor
" **property:** estate
landing place: quay, wharf   [ery
landscape: scene, scen-
lane: path
language: tongue, ro
" **peculiar to a people:** idiom
languid: wan, listless
languish: pine, droop, flag   [slander
lank: lean, gaunt,
lanneret: falcon
lap: circuit, fold, unfold, enfold, truncate
lapped joint: scarf
lapse: slip
lapwing: pewit
lard: adeps, fat
larded: enriched
larder: pantry [bulky
large: huge, great, big,
" **amount:** plenty
" **animal:** behemoth
" **body of land:** continent   [cro
" **(comb. form):** ma-
" **fish:** shark, tuna, skate, snapper
" **number:** score, host, billion, myriad
" " **(colloq.):** raft
" " **(slang):** slew
lariat: riata, lasso
larva: grub, loa
" **of fly:** maggot
lash: flog, tie, whip, satirize, berate [girl
lass: maid, maiden,

lassitude: inertia, languor, debility [lariat
lasso: riata, reata, rope,
last: final, endure, continue, omega, ultimate
" **act:** finale
" **(arch.):** dure
" **month:** ultimo
" **state of insect:** imago
" **traces:** ashes
late: recent, tardy, delayed
" **afternoon service:** vespers
" **(comb. form):** neo
" **information:** news
latent: hidden, dormant, potential quiescent   [newer
later: after, tardier,
lateral boundry: side
lath: slat
lather: suds, soap, foam
Latin: Roman, Italian
" **greeting:** ave
" **poet:** Ovid
latite: lava
lattice structure: trellis
Latvian: Lett, Lettic
" **capital:** Riga
" **coin:** lat
" **river:** Aa [glorify
laud: praise, extol, exalt,
laugh: chorlte
" **loudly:** snort [fleer
" **to scorn:** deride,
laughing: riant
laurel tree: bay
lava: latite
" **(cooled):** aa
lave: bathe, wash
lavender: aspic   [ta
Lavinia's mother: Amalavish: profuse
lavish: profuse
" **fondness on:** dote
law: canon, code, justice, statute, rule, act
" **(delay):** mora
" **(intervening):** mesne
" **(Latin):** ius, lex
" **note:** ut
lawful: legal, licit
lawless: unruly, disorderly
lawmaker: solon
lawn (fine): batiste [ter
lawyer: legalist, barris-
lax: slack, loose, remiss
lay: put, song, ballad
" **away:** store, reposit
" **hidden:** lurked
" **siege to:** invest
" **waste:** ravage, desolate, devastate
layers: coats, strata, beds, rows, tiers, thickness, plies
" **of clay in coal:** sloam
" " **metal:** seam
" " **mineral:** vein

laymen: laics, seculars
leaf: tendril, spathe, petal, lamina, page
" **part:** blade
" **vein:** rib
leafy shelter: bower
" **stemmed herb:** aster   [union
league: federation,
leak: drip, seep [trust
lean: lank, gaunt, tip, incline, tilt, rest, spare, slant, depend,
" **on one side:** heel
" **to:** shed
Leander's love: Hero
leap: spring, hop, bound, vault, jump
" **(dial.:)** lep
" **over:** skip
" **playfully:** gambol
learn: acquire, memorize, ascertain, con
learned: erudite, wise, erudition, scholarly
" **man:** pundit
learning: lore
lease: charter, let, hire, rent, contract, tenure
least: minimum, slightest, fewest   [nery
leather factory: tan-
" **on football shoe:** cleat
" **(kind):** napa, oxhide, levant, kid, calf, roan, cowhide
" **(long piece):** strap
" **(soft):** suede, napa, roan   [quit
leave: depart, vacate, retire, permission, go,
" **country:** emigrate
" **helpless:** strand, maroon   [miss
" **out:** omit, elide
leaven: yeast
leaves: foliage
leaving: ort
" **a will:** testate
ledge: shelf
ledger entry: item
leer: ogle, mock, entice
left after expenses: net
" **hand page:** V.O.
" " **side of an account:** debtor
" **side:** aport
leg: crus, support
" **joint:** ankle, knee
" **part:** shin, shank
legacy recipient: legatee
legal: lawful, dominate, valid, licit   [levin
" **action:** res, rep-
" **charge:** due, fee
" **claim:** lien
" **defense:** alibi
" **hearing:** trial
" **offense:** crime
" **official:** notary
" **order:** writ
" **paper:** deed

" profession: bar
" records: acta
" suffix: ee   [lars
" tender notes: dol-
" wrong: tort
legate: envoy [recipient
legatee: heir, heiress,
legend: saga, myth
legendary bird: roc
" founder of Rome:
Remus
legislate: enact
legislative body divi-
sion: house   [tor
legislator: solon, sena-
legume: pod, bean, uva,
lentil, pea, loment
leguminous plant: len-
til, peas, pulse, pea
lei: wreath
leisure: time
lemur: loris, lori [nish
lend: loan, afford, fur-
lengthen: extend, elon-
gate, prolong
lengthwise of: along
lengthy: long, extended
lenient: clement, merci-
ful
lens (type of:) toric
leonine: lionlike
leopard: panther, chetah
leper: lazar, outcast
"Les Miserables" au-
thor: Hugo
less: minus, minor,
fewer, smaller [rarer
" common: rare,
" (musical): meno
" (prefix): mis
" ripe: greener
" severe: relent
lessee: tenant, renter
lessen: bate, abate, re-
duce, wane, ease, low-
er, taper, diminish,
shrink, deplete [hire
lesser: smaller, minor
let: lease, rent, hinder,
" air out of: deflate
" the bait bob: dib
" down: lower
" " tension: relax
" go: release
" in: admit
" slip by: lapse
" stand: stet
" " (mus.): sta
lethal: fatal, deadly
lethargic: dull, sleepy
" sleep: sopor
" state: coma
lethargy: stupor, tor-
por, apathy, coma
letter: epistle, missive,
inscribe
" of defiance: cartel
lettered: literate, edu-
cated
lettuce: cos, romaine
Levantine: oriental
" ketch: saic, proa
levee: dike, quay [aim
level: even, flat, plane,
lever: pry, crowbar

" in a loom: lam
levy: tax, assess, collect
liable: apt
" to punishment:
guilty   [malign
libel: slander, calumny,
liberal: generous, broad
" gift: largess
liberate: redeem, re-
lease, free
Libyan seaport: Derna
license: permit, author-
ity
lichen: moss   [legal
licit: lawful, permitted
lick up: lap
lid: cover, top
lie: fib, falsehood
" in ambush: lurk
" at anchor: moor
" dormant: sleep
" at ease: bask, loll
" in warmth: bask
liege: devoted, loyal,
faithful, vassal
lien: claim, mortgage
lieu: place, stead
life: vitality, existence
" of business: sales
" fluid: blood
" insurance tontine
lifeboat crane: davit
lifeless: inert, amort,
dead   [exalt
lift: hoist, raise, elevate,
heave, elevator, pry,
" price: up
" in spirits: elate
lifting implement: tongs
light: lamp, gleam, pale,
ignite, airy, leger
" brushing sound:
swish
" carriage: gig, shay,
phaeton, surrey
" colored: claro
" of day: sun
" " evening: star
" & fine: leger
" hasty lunch: snack
" helmet: sallet
" (kind): arc   [tion
" meal: tea, colla-
" material: gauze
" rain: shower
" repast: tea
" sketch: pastel
" substance: cork
" tan: almond
" up: illume
lightheaded: gay
lighthouse: pharos
like: admire, as, similar,
enjoy, relish, prefer
likelihood: chance
likely: probable, veri-
similar, credible
likewise: too, also
" (poct.): eke
lilac color: mauve
lily, the: lis
" (day): niobe
" (kind): calla, sego,
aloe, onion, yucca,
tulip, arum
limb: bough, branch

limber: limp, pliant
lime tree: teil, linden
limit: term, solstice,
end, restrict, bounda-
ry, confine, extent
limited: finite, few
" to small area: local
limn: paint, sketch,
draw
limp: limber, clop
linden tree: lin, teil
line: row, streak, rein,
cord, boundry, mark,
course, string, rule
" of descent: strain
" " juncture: seam
" " persons: cue
" " poetry: verse
" " revolution: axis
" the roof of: ceil
" with ridges: rib
lineage: race, pedigree
lineament: feature, line
linen clothes: napery
" fabric: crash
" (fine): damask,
lawn, cambric
" fluff: lint
" plant: flax
" (sheer): toile
" vestment: alb   [er
liner: steamship, steam-
linger: hover, lag, loiter,
tarry, dawdle, stay,
delay, wait
lingo: jargon
lining of a well: steen
link: yoke, nexus, cou-
ple, unite, tie, attach
" together: catenate,
couple
linseed: flaxseed
lionlike: leonine
lip: labium, edge, brim
lips (pert. to): labial
liqueur: creme
liquid: fluid
" compound: oleir.
" container: pail,
tank
" dose: potion
" fat (var.): elaine,
elain, olein
" measure: gallon,
minim, pint
" particle: drop
liquify by heat: melt
liquor: rum, noyau,
anisette, ale, grog,
tipple, hydromel
lissome: lithe, supple,
nimble
list: rota, roll, roster,
itemize, agendum,
careen, register, cata-
log, catalogue
" of electors: poll
" " errors: errata
" " things to be
done: agenda
listen: harken, hark,
attend, hear
listless: languid
literal: exact
literary: literate [thesis

" composition: pa-
per, tragedy, essay,
" fragments: ana
" supervisor: editor
" " (abbr.): ed
literate: educated, literary, lettered
lithe: supple, pliant,
lissome, agile, flexible
litter: bier, clutter
little: bit, small, petty
live: reside, are, be,
brisk, subsist, quick
" coal: ember
" in a tent: camp
lively: brisk, nimble,
animated, pert, agile
" dance: reel
" song: lilt
liven: animate, acti-
vate, inspirit
liver secretion: bile, gall
livid: ashen
living: alive
lixivium: lye [monitor
lizard: agama, gila,
iguana, lacerta, eft,
adda, skink, seps

" like amphibian:
salamander, newt
llama (kind): alpaca
load: lade, burden, car-
go, saddle
loadstone: magnet
loaf: idle, loiter, lounge
loam: soil, earth, marl,
dirt, clay
" deposit: loess
loath: abhor, hate,
averse, detest, reluc-
tant, abominate
loathsome: foul
lobby: foyer, vestibule
lobster chela: pincer
" claw: chela
" row: coral
local ordinance: bylaw
locale: position, place
localities: loci, sites,
spots, regions, places
located: situate, stands
location: site, seat, spot,
place
lock: bolt, hasp, fasten
" of hair: tress, ring-
let
lockup: jail
locomotive: engine
" part: cab
" service car: tender
locus: place
locust: cicada, acacia
lodge: room, cabin, lie,
house, implant, lay
" doorkeeper: tiler
lodger: guest
lodging: abode
loft: attic
lofty: elevated, aerial,
tall, eminent, haugh-
ty, aery, high
" in style: epic
log: record
" float: raft
" from which shin-

gles are cut: spalt
loge: booth, box
logger's boot: pac
logograph: anagram
Lohengrin's wife: Elsa
loiter: linger, lag, idle, tarry, saunter, delay
loll: recline, droop, sprawl, laze
London district: Soho
lone: solo, solitary, sole
long: tall, hanker, lengthy, crave, yearn
" distance runner: miler
" fish: eel
" for: pine, crave, desire, yearn, hanker
" handled implement: hoe, poleax
" hill: ridge
" intently: pant
" leg bird: steve, stilt, wader, egret, stork, avocet, curlew, crane, rail, heron
" low seat: settee
" since: yore [reedy
" & slender: spindle,
" space of time: eon
" standing: old
longing: yen, appetite, desire [leer
look: gaze, search, see, discern, peer, eye, seem, appearance, appear, glance, lo,
" after: tend, attend
" aimlessly: grope
" angrily: glare
" approvingly: smile
" askance: leer, ogle
" at: view
" attentively: pore
" of contempt: sneer
" despondent: gloom
" for: crave, seek
" at intently: stare
" into: pry
" joyous: smile
" on with contempt: despise
" out: beware [ogle
" slyly: peek, peep,
" sullen: pout, lower
" upon: regard
" well on: become
loom part: reed
loop: noose, curve, circle, fold, tab, picot
" on edge of lace or ribbon: picot
loophole: eyelet
loose: free, slack, release, unbound, lax
" end: tag, dag
" fragments of rock: gravel
loosen: relax, slacken, untie, release, free
loot: sack, rob, plunder, booty, pillage, spoil
lop: pendent, chop, trim, droop
" off: prune

lope: canter
lopsided: alop
loquacity (colloq.): gab
lord's chief manor place: demesne
lore: learning
lose: waste, stray, misplace, miss, spill
" color: pale, fade
" freshness: wilt, stale, fade
" heat: cool [spond
" hope: despair, de-
" luster: fade, tarnish
" vigor: flag [damage
loss: defeat, failure,
" of hope: despair
lot: fate, destiny, portion, hazard, share, fortune
lottery (form of): raffle
lotto (form of): keno
loud: noisy, clamorous
" call: cry
" cry: howl, yawp
" lamentation: wail
" noise: bang, din, roar, clang
" sound: noise [tor
" voice person: sten-
Louisiana court decree: arret
lounge: loll, sofa, loaf
louse egg: nit
lout: boor, yahoo, oaf, bumpkin, blockhead
love: fondness, charity, affection, gra
" apple: tomato
" greatly: dote
" missive: valentine
" (pert. to): erotic, amatory
" potion: philter
" story: romance
lover: swain, ami
" of one's country: patriot [ly, bellow
low: moo, base, soft, humble, inferior, soft-
" bow: salaam
" cloud: nebula
" deck of ship: orlop
" form of animal life: amoeba
" island: key
" necked: decollete
" noise: hum
" note: ut
" sound: hum, murmur, drone, rumble
" spirits: dumps, blues
" tree: shrub
" tufted plant: moss
lower: reduce, lessen, abase, nether, frown, diminish, sink, debase, humble, demean, depress, degrade, bate
" the bottom: deepen
" end of mast: heel
" region: Hades
" in value: debase

lowest: see also "low"
" ebb: neap
" form of wit: pun
" of high tides: neap
" limit: minimum
" part: bottom
" " in music: bass
" point: nadir
lowing sound: moo
loyal: leal, true, liege, faithful
loyalist: Tory
lozenge: pastil [graphite
lubricate: oil, grease,
lucent: shining
lucerne: alfalfa
lucid: clear, sane
luck: hap, chance
lucre: gain [comic
ludicrous: comical,
lug: drag, haul, ear
lukewarm: tepid
lull: quiet, respite
lumber: timber
luminous body: star
lump: mass, nodule, nub, piece, knob, gob
" of earth: clod
lunar creator: linne
" months: moons
lure: bait, entice, decoy, tempt, draw, attract
lurk: prowl [shine
luster: sheen, gloss,
lustrous mineral: spar
lusty: robust
luxuriant: lush
luxuriate: bask [Igorot
Luzon native & savage: Atta, Ata, Aeta,
Lyra star: Vega
lyrelike instrument: asor
lyric: poem, musical

M

macabre: eerie [parrot
macaw: ara, arara, arar,
macebearer: beadle
macerate: steep
machine: engine, motor
" bar: rod
" to compress: baler
" " cut hay: mower
" " grind grain: mill
" " move heavy wts.: gin
" " notch girders: coper [et
" part (slang): gadg-
" to raise pile on cloth: napper
" " spread hay: tedder
" tool: lathe [irate
mad: insane, frantic,
madagascar animals: ayeayes, tenrecs
madden: enrage, craze
made of cereal: oaten
" " grain: cereal
" " flowers: floral
" " tile: tegular

" " wood: treen
madness: mania
magazine: arsenal, store
mage: wizard
maggot: larva
magic: rune, sorcery
magician: Houdini
" 's word: presto
magnesia: talc
magnet: loadstone
" end: pole
magnificence: pomp, splendor, grandeur
magnificent: splendid, grand, palatial, superb
magnitude: size
mahognany pine: totara
maid: lass, nymph, girl, domestic
mail: post, armor
maim: cripple, lame, injure, disable
main: ocean, principal, chief, foremost
" blood stream: aorta
" body: trunk, mass
" course: entree
" idea: gist
Maine capital: Augusta
" lake: Sebago
" town: Orono, Milo, Bangor, Hiram [tend
maintain: keep, preserve, claim, assert, vindicate, allege, con-
" order: police
maize: corn
majestic: leonine, stately, imperial, superb, glorious [render
make: fabricate, construct, create, form, manufacture, induce,
" additions to: eke
" allegations against: accuse [tion
" allusion to: men-
" amends: atone, redress, redeem
" angry: rile
" ashamed: abash
" believe: sham, pretend, feign
" beloved: endear
" a botch of: flub
" certain: assure, insure
" choice: opt [cus
" clear: explain, fo-
" cloth: weave
" complicated: snarl
" dejected: mope
" designs by lines: etch [bereave
" destitute: bereft,
" dizzy: stun
" an edging: tat
" an end of: destroy
" enduring: anneal
" equal: equate
" ethereal: aerate
" evident: evince
" excuses: stall
" explanation: atone
" faint: bedim [belay

`"` **fast:** secure, gird,
`"` **finer:** strain
`"` **firm:** fix
`"` **first move:** lead
`"` **fleshy:** fatten
`"` **fun of:** guy
`"` **glossy:** sleek
`"` **of goods:** brand
`"` **a hedge:** plash
`"` `"` **hole:** bore
`"` **ill:** ail
`"` **an imitation of:** pattern   [knit
`"` **into fabric:** weave,
`"` `"` **law:** enact [taw
`"` `"` **leather:** tan,
`"` `"` **thread:** spin
`"` **knotted lace:** tat
`"` **known:** notify, impart
`"` **late:** belate
`"` **laws:** legislate
`"` **lean:** emaciate
`"` **dense:** rarefy
`"` **lustrous:** gild
`"` **muddy:** roil
`"` **necessary:** entail
`"` **note of:** jot
`"` **obeisance:** kneel
`"` **out:** discern [vate
`"` **over:** remodel, reform, remake, reno-
`"` **petulant:** peeve
`"` **possible:** enable
`"` **precious:** endear
`"` **proud:** elate
`"` **public:** delate, air
`"` **quiet:** husb
`"` **quilt:** piece [atone
`"` **reparation:** expiate,
`"` **requital for:** repay
`"` **resolute:** steel
`"` **(Scot.):** gar
`"` **sleek:** preen [pall
`"` **spiritless:** mope,
`"` **suitable:** adapt, fit
`"` **too small:** scrimp
`"` **turbid:** roil, mud
`"` **untidy:** litter
`"` **unyielding:** steel
`"` **up:** compromise
`"` `"` **for:** atone
`"` **vapid:** pall [liven
`"` **vigorous:** energize,
`"` **well:** cure, heal
`"` **wine:** vint
maker of roofing material: tiler
`"` `"` **wills:** testator
malady: disease
malaria & malarial fever: ague
Malay animal: napu
`"` **ape:** lar
`"` **canoe:** proa
`"` **coin:** tra, ora
`"` **dagger:** kris
`"` **disease:** amok
`"` **fan palm:** gebang
`"` **garment:** sarong
`"` **gibbon:** lar [Java
`"` **island:** Sumatra, Timor, Borneo, Oma,
`"` **isthmus:** kra
`"` **vessel:** proa

male: mas, man
`"` **ancestry:** paternity
`"` **attendant:** page
`"` **figure for supporting column:** telamon
`"` **forbears:** sires
malediction: curse
malevolent: evil, ill
malice: spite
malicious: spiteful, leer, carry, felonious, evil
`"` **damage:** sabotage
malign: evil, defame, libel, revile
malignity: rancor, hate
malleable: soft
`"` **metal:** tin
mallet: gravel, maul, gavel, hammer
malodorous: fetid
malt hop drink: beer
`"` **liquor:** alt, porter, stout, ale   [ery
`"` `"` **factory:** brewman
of courage: lion
`"` **of great strength:** Samson   [bob
`"` `"` `"` **wealth:** Na-
`"` `"` `"` **learning:** savant, pundit
`"` **leaving a will:** testator
`"` **'s arch enemy:** satan   [fetter
manacle: iron, shackle
manage: contrive, regulate, handle, wield, direct, manipulate, administer, control, operate, engineer
manager: steward, director, factor, boss
mandate: order, command, injuction
mandatory precept: writ
manducate: chew
manger: stall
mangle: 1 cerate, mutilate, ironer
mania: craze, madness
manifest: patent, signify, plain, display, evident, evince, clear, overt, palpable
manifesto: edict
Manila hemp: abaca
manipulate: handle, use, treat, manage, wield
mankind: world
manly: virile, resolute
manner: mien, air, custom, style, sort, way, mode, means
mannerly: polite
manor: estate, mansion
`"` **court (kind):** leet
mansion: palace, manor
mantle: cloak, robe
manual art: craft
`"` **digit:** finger, thumb
`"` **vocation:** trade
manufacture: make
many: several, multiple, numerous, various
map: plat, chart, sketch

`"` **(kind):** relief
`"` **out:** plan
`"` **of solar system:** orrery
maples: acer
mar: deface, damage, spoil, impair, tarnish, injure   [agate, mib
marble: taw, mig, alley,
march: parade
`"` **king:** Sousa
`"` **on:** troop
marching cry: hep
margin: lip, border, edge, hem, verge, scope, brim
marginal note: apostil
marinate: pickle
marine: maritime, oceanic, nautical
`"` **animal:** coral
`"` **carnivore:** otter
`"` **fish:** opah, scaroid, ling, eelpout
`"` **gastropod:** trition, yet, limpet, nerite
`"` **mammal:** seal
`"` **plant:** moss, seaweed, enalid
mariner: sailor, seaman, navigator
maritime: marine, naval, nautical
mark: trace, track, lane, target, label, brand, note, tab
`"` **aimed at in curling:** tee   [dint
`"` **of a blow:** dent,
`"` `"` **infamy:** stigma
`"` `"` **injury:** scar
`"` **the limits:** define
`"` **of omission:** caret, dele, apostrophe
`"` **paid:** receipt
`"` **of pronunciation:** tilde
`"` **to retain:** stet
`"` **the skin:** tattoo
`"` **with asterisk:** star
`"` `"` **cuts:** score
`"` `"` **ridges:** rib
`"` `"` **spots:** dapple, notate, mottle   [er
`"` `"` **squares:** check-
`"` `"` **streaks:** line
`"` **of wrinkle:** crease
marker: peg
market: store, sell, mart
`"` **place:** mart, agora
`"` **town:** bourg
marksman: shot
marl: loam
marriage: marital, connubial, matrimony, union, wedlock
`"` **(comb. form):** gamo
`"` **dot:** dower
marry: mate, espouse, wed
marsh: swamp, morass, swale, bog, fen [sora
`"` **bird:** snipe,- rail,
`"` **crocodile:** goa

`"` **elder:** iva   [sedge
`"` **grass (tall):** reed,
`"` **marigold:** cowslip
`"` **plant:** cattail
`"` **(soft):** salina
marshy: paludic
`"` **place:** slew
martial: warlike
Martinique volcano: Pelee   [igy, miracle
marvel: wonder, prod-
masculine: male, luis
mash: crush
`"` **down:** stomp, rice
mask: visor, disguise, veil, conceal
mason's hammer point: peen
Masonic doorkeeper: tiler   [gob, heap
mass: wad, bulk, lump, throng, pat, assemble,
`"` **book:** missal
`"` **of bread:** loaf
`"` `"` **butter:** pat
`"` **(comb. form):** mas
`"` **of floating ice:** floe, berg
`"` `"` `"` **logs:** drive
`"` `"` **hay:** mow
`"` `"` **ice:** berg, serac
`"` **meeting:** rally
`"` **of untidy hair:** mop
`"` `"` **water:** eddy
`"` `"` **yarn:** cop
Mass. cape: Ann, Cod
`"` **city:** Salem
`"` **mt.:** Tom
`"` **town:** Lee
massage: kneed, rub
mast: spar   [due
master: conquer, sub
`"` **stroke:** coup
masticate: chew
mat: carpet, knot, cushion, doily, entangle
match: mate, pair, twin, cope, peer, tally, team   [stance
material: real, data, corporeal, fabric, sub-
math. arc: radian
`"` **function & ratio:** sine, pi, cosine
`"` **instrument:** sector
`"` **line in space:** vector
`"` **quantity:** surd
matrix: mold, bed
matron: dame [import
matter: substance, affair, concern, signify,
`"` **(arch.):** reck
`"` **of fact:** literal
mattress covering: tick
mature: age, ripen, mellow, ripe, season, grow   [mallet
maul: abuse, gavel,
mauser: rifle
maw: craw
maxim: adage, moral, motto, tenet, item, precept, axiom, saw, proverb, principle

May apple: mandrake
meadow: lea, grassland
"   **mouse**: vole
"   **(poet.)**: mead [bare
meager: scant, scanty,
meal: repast
"   **(fine)**: farina
"   **to be ground**: grist
mean: intend, brutal, average, signify, base, cruel, stingy, shabby, snide, imply, denote
meaning: sense, intending   [poses, wealth
means: resources, pur-
" " **crossing fence**: stile   [ment, abatis
" " **defense**: muni-
" " **education**·travel   [hole
" " **escape**: loop-
" " **livelihood**: trade
" " **transmitting force**: lever
" " " **power**: belt
meantime: interim
measure: mete, gage, estimate, are, acre, meter, ton
"   **of capacity**: pint, liter, bushel, peck, gill, litre, stere, quart,
" " **extent**: acre
" " **length**: ell meter, mile, metre, rod, cubit, pik, dra, foot, yard
"   **(pert. to)**: metric
"   **thickness of**: caliper
"   **(var.)**: gazer
"   **of wire**: mil
" " **weight**: carat, ounce, grain
"   **for wood**: cord
"   **of yarn**: lea
measurement: metric, dimension
measuring instrument: altimeter, meter, caliper   [yardwand
"   **stick**: ellwand, pole,
meat: flesh
"   **ball**: rissole
"   **in dough shells**: ravioli
"   **jelly**: aspic
"   **paste**: pate
"   **pie**: pasty
"   **pin**: skewer
"   **& vegetable dish**: ragout
meaty: pithy
mecca shrine: Caaba
mechanical device: lever, wheel, machine, pump, robot
mechanism: action
meddle: tamper, mess
medial: average
mediate: arbitrate, intercede, muse
medical fluids: sera
medicinal herb: senna

aloe, arnica
"   **nut**: cola [na, tansy
"   **plant**: herb, aconite, ephedra, aloe, ipecac, camomile, sen-
"   **root**: jalap
medicine: drug, tonic
medieval: see also under ancient, old, etc.
"   **dagger**: anlace
"   **fabric**: samite [tle
"   **fortified bldg.**: cas-
"   **French kingdom**: Arles
"   **hat**: abacot
"   **knight**: pennon
"   **romantic island**: Avalon
"   **shield**: ecu
"   **ship**: nef
"   **silk fabric**: samite
"   **sport**: tilt
"   **sword**: estoc
"   **tale**: lai [templ te
meditate: muse, ponder, study, brood, mu l, ruminate, con-
Mediterranean island: Malta, Crete, Capri, Elba, Sardinia, Sicily
"   **sailing vessel**: saic, setee, mistic, tartan, xebec polacre, felucca
medium: average
medley: olio, melange
meek: tame, gentle
meet: confer, assemble, encounter, join, convene, intersect, proper, confront
meeting: trysting, tryst, assemblage, conclave, parley, junct on
"   **room for students**: seminar
"   **of spiritualists**: seance
mel: honey
melancholy: sad, gloom, rueful, blue
melange: mixture
melee: skirmish, battle, feud, affray, fray, brawl   [soft
mellow: age, mature, ripe, ripen, soften,
melodious: ariose, tuneful, dulcet, musical
melody: tune, aria, air, strain, lay song, music   [solve, liquify
melt: fuse, thaw, dis-
"   **down**: render
member of governing board: regent   [laic
" " **laity**: layman,
" " **religious order**: monk
membership: seat
"   **charges**: dues
membrane: tela
memento: relic
memoir: eloge
memorandum: notes, note, memo
memorial post: Xat

"   **stones**: cairn
memorize: learn, rote
Memphis divinity: Ptah
menace: threat, threaten, imperil [domicile
menage: household,
menagerie: zoo
mend: repair, darn, fix heal, patch, sew
mendicant: beggar
menial: servile, domestic, varlet servant
mental: ideal, intellectua
"   **concept**: idea
"   **confusion**: fog
"   **function**: power
"   **perception**: tact
"   **power**: w t [rale
"   **state**: mood, mo-
menthyl ketol: acetol
mention: name, cite
menu card: carte
mephistopheles: Satan, devil   [ling
mercenary: venal, hire-
merchandise: ware, goods
merchant: dea er, trader se ler, vender
"   **of Bagdad**: Sindbad
"   **ship**: argosy
"   **of Venice**: Port a
mercurous chloride: calomel   [duceus
Mercury's wand: ca-
"   **winged shoes**: talaria   [pond
mere: bare, simple, only, absolute, pool,
merely: only, but
merganser: smew
merge: fuse, sink, join, combine, unite, absorb, blend
meridian: noonday
merit: earn, warrant, worth, deserve, rate
mermaid: siren
merriment: glee, fun, hilarity, gayety
merry: gay, sunny, hilarious, jolly
"   **go round**: carousel
"   **makings**: revel
"   **song**: lilt
"   **Widow" composer**: Lehar
mesa: plateau
meshed fabric: lace, net, netting, web, tulle   [er
"   **instrument**: strain-
Mesopotamia: Iraq
mess: botch, meddle
message: word, note
messenger: carrier, page, herald
"   **of the gods**: Hermes
metal: steel, lead, ore, silver, tin
"   **bar**: rivet, rod, rail
"   **bearing vein**: lode

"   **disk**: paten, sequin, medal, gong   [nail
"   **fastener**: rivet, nut,
"   **flask**: canteen
"   **mass**: pig, ingot
"   **plate**: disc, paten, platen
"   **tag of a lace**: aglet
"   **thread**: wire [eter
"   **worker**: smith, riv-
"   **working tool**: swage
metallic alloy: brass
"   **bracelet**: bangle
"   **cloth**: tinsel
"   **element**: zinc, iridium, silver, iron, lead
"   **mixture**: alloy
metamere: somite
mete: allot, dole, distribute   [ure
meter: rhythm, measure
method: system, plan, way, order, technique, process, rule
"   **(pert. to)**: modal
metric measure: liter, stere, decare, are, gram
metrical beat: ictus
"   **composition**: verse, poem [pest, anapaest
"   **foot**: iambs, ana-
"   **land measure**: ar, are, meter
"   **units of verses**: feet   [rape
Mexican blanket: se-
"   **cake**: tortilla
"   **city**: Tampico
"   **coin**: peso, rei
"   **conquerer**: Cortes
"   **corn mush**: atole
"   **cotton cloth**: manta
"   **cottonwood**: alamo
"   **dish**: tamale [cal
"   **drink**: pulque, mes-
"   **fiber**: istle
"   **guardian spirit**: Nagual
"   **hero**: Jaurez
"   **hut**: jacal [Maya
"   **Indian**: Tlascalan, Alais, Aztec, Cora,
"   " **(var.)**: xova
"   **mammal**: ocelot
"   **peasant**: peon
"   **president**: Aleman
"   **race (early)**: Toltec
"   **ranch**: hacienda
"   **stirrup hood**: tapadero
"   **tea**: apasote
"   **town**: Tula
"   **wt.**: arroba
microbe: germ
microscopic: little
"   **animal**: amoeba
"   **fungi**: yeast
middle: mesne, center, mid, median
"   **ages (pert. to)**: mediaeval, medieval
"   **(law)**: mesne
midshipman: plebe,

reefer
midst of: among [pect
mien: bearing, air, as-
might: power, arm
mighty: strong, potent
mignonette color: reseda
migration: trek
migratory worker: hobo
mild: tame, gentle soft,
bland
" **& easy:** facile
**military artifice (use
of):** strategy
" **assistant:** aide
" **barrier:** abattis
" **chaplain (slang):**
padre [vet
" **commission:** bre-
front: sector
" **group:** corps, troop
" **hat:** shako, kepi
" **nspect on:** review
" **post:** station, base
" **signal:** taps
" **spectacles:** parades
" **storehouse:** arsenal
" **truck:** camion
" **vehicle:** caisson
" **warehouse:** etape
milk (comb. form):
lacto, lact
" **curdler:** rennet
" **farm:** dairy
" **(pert. to):** lactic
" **(pharm.):** lac
" **protein:** casein
milkfish: awa
Milky Way: Galaxy
mill: factory
millstone support: rynd
milt: spleen
mime: clown, buffoon
mimic: ape, aper, imitate, mime
mince: chop
minced dish: hash
" **oath:** ecod, egad
mind: care, obey, tend,
heed, mentality, dis-
like, brain, sentient
" **(of the):** mental
Mindanao Indonesian:
Ata
" **lake:** lanao
" **language:** ata
mine: burrow
" **division:** panel
" **entrance:** adit
" **vein:** lode
mineral: metal, iolite,
ore, erinite, spinel
" **bed:** seam [er
" **deposit:** lode plac-
" **(kind of):** edenite,
egeran, epidote, irite,
uralite, galactite, cal,
rutile, aragonite
" **pitch:** asphalt
" **salt:** alkali, alum
" **(soft):** talc
" **spring:** spa
mingle: mix, blend
minister: pastor, cleric
priest, divine, preach-
er, parson, attend,

serve, tend
" **'s home:** parson-
age, manse
Minnesota city: Ely
" **inhabitant:** gopher
minor: lesser, smaller,
minority: nonage
minstrel: bard, harper
" **show (part):** olio
mint: coin
" **plant:** basil, catnip
minus: less [mite
minute: wee, small,
" **difference:** shade
" **distinction:** nicety
" **groove or channel:**
stria
" **organism:** spore
" **orifice:** stoma, pore
" **particle:** molecule,
mote, atom [der
miracle: marvel, won-
" **man:** fakir
mirage: illusion, serab
mire: mud, muck, stall,
bog, muddy, ooze
mirror: glass, reflect
mirth: glee, gaiety, jollity
miry: muddy, boggy
miscellany: ana
mischievous: evil, elfish, elfin, sly, arch,
devilish
" **spirit:** imp, pixie,
elf [trip
" **trick:** prank, can-
miscreant: villain
misdeed: crime, sin
miser: niggard, hoarder
miserable: wretched
miserly: stingy, pain
misery: woe
misfortune: ill, disaster
blow, evil, woe
misgiving: fear, qualm
misjudge: err

mislead: delude, mis-
direct, deceive
misleading argument:
fallacy
misrepresent: belie
miss: omit, fail, lose,
overlook, skip, err
missile: dart, bullet,
brickbat, arrow, bol-
as, spear, shaft
mission: errand, pur-
pose, delegation
missive: note, letter
misstep: trip
mist: fog, haze, bedim
mistake: err, boner,
blunder
**mistakes in published
work:** errato, errata
misuse: abuse [acarus
mite: tick, acarid,
mix: stir, blend, mingle
" **up:** melee
" **when wet:** pug
mixed dish: salad
" **drink:** nog
" **type:** pi
mixture: olio, melange,

hash, blend
" **of spirits & wa-
ter:** grog, toddy
moan: complain, wail,
lament
moat: ditch, fosse, foss
mob: rabble, populace,
crowd
moccasin: pac, larrigan
mock: taunt, deride,
sneer, gibe, mow, leer,
fleer, imitate, flout
" **orange:** syringa
mockery: farce, game,
crony [style
mode: fashion, manner
model: norm, type, pattern, shape, paragon,
paradigm, design
" **of perfection:** paragon, standard
moderate: bate, abate,
restrain, cool, some,
temperate, diminish
modern: new, recent
modest: retiring, de-
mure, decent, prim
modish: chic
Mohammedan: also see
Moslem: Islam
" **adopted son:** ali
" **Ali's son:** Ahmed

" **ascetic:** fakir
" **caravan.:** imaret
" **chieftan:** emir
" **cleric:** imam, iman
" **daughter:** Fatima
" **decree:** irade
" **descendant:** Emir
" **festival:** bairam
" **Filipino:** Moro
" **God:** Allah
" **judge:** cadi, mollah
" **leader:** aga, ata
" **month:** Safar, ram-
adan
" **name:** ali
" **nature spirit:** genie
" **noble:** amir, ameer
" **nymph:** houri
" **prayer:** salat
" **call:** azan
" **priest:** imam
" **'s (body of):**
ulema [sultan
" **prince:** amir, emir,
ameer, amee, emeer,
" **princess:** emir
" **religion:** islam
" **teacher:** Alim
" **ruler:** aga, calif
" **saint:** Pir
" **tomb:** pir
" **scholars:** ulema
" **scriptures:** Koran
" **son:** ali
" **state head:** kalif
" **title:** ali, aga, calif
" **tribe:** arain
" **uncle:** Abbas
moil: toil, soil, drudge,
drudgery
moist: damp, humid,
wet, dewy, dank
moisture: dew
molar: tooth, grinding

molasses: treacle
mold: matrix, shape,
form, fashion, die,
must [torus listed
molding: ogee, ovolo,
mole: pier
moleskin color: taupe
molest: disturb, tease,
annoy, trouble
mollify: sleek, allay,
smooth, conciliate
mollusk: snail, clam,
abalone, mussel, scal-
lop shellfish,
molt: shed
molten glass: metal

" **lava:** aa
" **rock:** lava
moment: instant, trice,
jiff [important
momentous: weighty,
monarch: king, em-
peror, ruler, sover-
eign
monastery: abbey
" **room:** cell
monastic house: priory
monetary: financial
money: coin, cash, coinage, specie [ment
" **on account:** pay-
" **box:** till
" **due but not paid:**
arrears
" **matters:** economic
" **owed:** debt
" **paid:** scot
" **(slang):** moss, tin
Mongolian: tatar
" **desert region:** Gobi
mongoose: urva [mutt
mongrel: cur, mut,
monk: friar, fra
" **'s hood:** cowl, aco-
nite, atis
monkey: stentor, ta-
marin, mono, ape,
titi, sai, marmoset
" **like animals:** lem-
urs, ayeayes
monopoly: trust
monotonous: dreary,
humdrum
monster: ogre, giant,
centaur, sphinx
" **(med.):** tarata,
teras [Butte
Montana city: Helena,
month preceding: ul-
timo
moo: low
mood: tune, humor
moody: morose, peev-
ish [ana, lune
moon: luna, lunar, Di-
" **'s age at begin-
ning of year:** epact
" **crescent point:** cusp,
horn
" **in her first quarter:**
crescent [fen, heath
moor: anchor, fasten,
moorish drum: tabor
" **tabor:** atabal
moose: elk
mop: swap, swab, wipe

mope: sulk, pine
moral: ethical, teaching, maxim
" teachings: precepts
morass: bog, swamp, marsh, fen
moray: eel
more: extra, greater
" than: over
" " enough: too
moreover: besides
morindin dye: al [noon
morning: morn, fore-
" prayer: matin
" (relat. to): matinal
" star: daystar, venus
Moro chief: Dato
" high priest: sarip
Morocco cape: nun
" coin: okia, rial
" native: Moor
" seaport: Rabat
" tree: sandarac
morose: gloomy, glum, sullen, moody, sour
morsel: bite, bit, ort, tidbit, piece, crumb
mortal: fatal, human
mortar: cement, petard
" tray: hod
mortification: chagrin
" of tissue: gangrene
mortify: abash, spite, shame, humiliate
mortise (part of): tenon
Moslem: (also Moham.)
" gold coin: dinar
" javelin: jereed
" official: aga
" ruler: Nawab
Mosque tower: minaret
moss: rag, lichen
moth (kind): regal, lappet, egger, tinea
mother: matron, mama
" (Latin): mater
" of mankind: Eve
" " Pearl: nacre
" (Phil. Isl.): Ina
motion: gesture, movement
motion of horse in rearing: pesade
" of sea: tidal, tide
motionless: still, stagnant [incentive
motive: reason, cause,
motor: engine, machine
" car (colloq.): auto
" coach: bus
" part: cam [aviette
motorless plane: glider,
mottled: pinto, pied
" appearances in mahogany: roes
motto: saw, maxim, adage, slogan [dune
mound: hill, knoll, tee,
mt. aborigines: atis
" ash: rowan
" chain: range, sierra
" in Colorado: Owen
" (comb form): oro
" crest: arete
" gap: col
" lake: tarn [ad
" nymph: oread, dry-

" pass: ghat, col
" passage: tunnel
" pasture land: alp
" pool: tarn
" range: ridge, sierra, andes, alps, ural
" ridge: range, arete
" " (flat top): loma
" (Scot.): ben
" spinach: orach
" spur: arete
" near Troy: Ida
mourn: sorrow, grieve
mournful: plaintive, sad, sorrowful, funereal, dismal
" cry: wail [ting
mourning: dolor, regret-
" hymn: dirge
" poem: elegy
" sumbal: crepe
mouth: os
" (comb. form): oro
" (of the): oral
" organ: harmonica, lip, tongue
" of river: delta
" volcano: crater
mouthlike opening: stoma [door
movable barrier: gate,
" frame: sley
" part: rotor [tate
move: stir, budge, agi-
" ahead steadily: forge [treat, retire
" back: recede, re-
" " & forth: way, saw, wave, wag
" forward: progress
" with difficulty: wade [sneak, prowl
" furtively: steal,
" heavily: lug
" on: onrush, go
" rapidly: hurtle, fly, career, flit, dart
" sideways: sidle, slue
" slowly: lag, inch
" smoothly: glide, slide, sail
" vigorously: bestir
" on wheels: roll
movement: trend, motion
" of the feet: gait
" " " sea: tide
moving: astir, transient
" force: agent
" part: rotor
" power: motor
mud: mire, slime, slosh, sludge
" eel: siren
" volcano: salse
muddle: addle, mess, confuse [mire
muddled: asea
muddy: bespatter, roil, sludgy, miry, roily,
muddy ground: sog
mudworm: ipo
muffin: gem
muffle: deaden, mute
muffler: scarf, silencer

mug: stein, noggin
mulberry: al, ach, aal
mulct: bilk, amerce, cheat, fine
mule: ass
" cry: bray
multiform: diverse
multitude: host, legion
municipality: city
" (pert. to): civic
murder: homocide, slay
murk: gloom, darkness
murmur: repine, mutter
" softly: purl, coo, hum, purr
muscle: sinew, thew
muscle in arm: biceps, triceps
" band: tendon
" of mouth: lip [sor
" for stretching: ten-
muscular: torose, sinewed
muse: meditate, reve, cogitate, ponder
" of history: clio
" " music: euterpe
" " poetry: erato
mushroom: agaric, morel
music: melody
" (as it stands): sta
" (concluding passage): coda
" (high): alt
" (increase in volume): crescendo
" (melodious): arioso
" (moderately slow): andante
" (silent): tacet
" (slow): lento, adagio, largo
" (smooth & connected): legato
" (soft): piano
" (stately): largo
musical: melic, lyric, harmonious, melodious, lyrical song
" air: tune, melody,
" aria: solo
" bells: chimes
" character: rest, clef, sharp, note
" comedy: revue
" composition: song, rondo, oratorio, serenade, nocturne, cantata, sonata, ballade, opus, trio, glee, sextet, serenata, arioso, opera
" direction: tacet
" drama: cantata
" exercise: etude
" group: band
" half step: semitone
" instrument: rebec, gora, oboe, saxhorn, tuba, bugle, spinet, cornet, ocarina, marimba, uke, fife, lute, guitar, cello, lyre, viol, concertina, reed
" interval: rest, oc-

tave, tritone, second
" key: minor
" line: tie [tal, concert
" performance: reci-
" pipe: reed
" pitch: tone
" reed: pipe [molo
" shake: trill, tre-
" show: revue [note
" sound: tone, tonal,
" " (pert. to): tonal
" study: etude
" sylable: si, tra, re
" tone: chord
" triplet: tercet
" up beat: arsis
" wave: tremolo
" work: opus
" " (abbr.): O.P.
muss: rumple, crumple
mustang: bronco
mustard: sinapis
" plant: cress, radish
muster: assemble, gather
musty: moldy
mutation: change
mute: dumb, muffle, silent, speechless
" consonant: lene
mutilate: mangle
mutiny: revolt [ble
mutter: murmur, grum-
mysterious: sphinxine, occult, runic [enigma
mystery: cabala, secret,
mystic: epoptic
" ejaculation: om
myth: legend, saga, table
mythical: imaginary
" being: giant
" bird: ro, roc
" character: Pandora
" hero: Leander
" hunter: Orion
" king: Atli, Midas
" " of Britain: Lud, Lear, Bran
" " of Crete: Minos
" kingdom: Oz
" maiden: Io, Danae
" monster: ogree, giant, dragon
" mountain: Ossa
" swimmer: Leander
" Titan: Atlas
" world: Limbo

N

nab: catch, seize, trap, snatch,
nacre: pearl
nag: tease, horse, scold, pester, henpeck
nahoor sheep: sna
nail: brad, hob, stud, spike, spad, fasten, secure, tack, clinch
" driven obliquely: toed
" marker: spad
naive: artless, guileless
name: term, mention,

entitle, call, title, dub)
namesake: homonyon
nap: pile, siesta, doze, sleep, slumber
nape: scruff, nucha
napkin: bib, doily
Napoleonic marshall: Ney
Napoleon's exile: Elba
nappy: shaggy [opium
narcotic: opiate, dope,
" **drug:** hemp
" **shrub:** kat [tel!
narrate: relate, recite,
narrow: strait, contract
" **bar:** stripe
" **board:** lath, slat
" **(comb. form):** sten
" **fabric:** braid [listle
" **fillet (arch):** orle,
" **inlet:** ria
" **minded:** bigoted
" **opening:** rima, slit, slot
" **pass:** abra
" **passage:** gut, alley, strait, gorge, lane
" **piece:** strip
" **strip:** ribbon, strap
" **track:** lane
" **waterway:** inlet, ria
nasal: rhinal, narine
" **noise:** snort, whine
" **tone:** twang
nation: empire, country, people, realm
national emblem: eagle
" **guard:** militia
" **hymn:** anthem
" **park:** Estes
native: natal, son, inborn, indigenous
" **borax:** tincal
" **garment:** sarong
natty: dapper, neat, spruce
natural: normal, inborn, innate, lifelike
" **abode:** habitat
" **capacity:** talent
naturalness: ease
nature: creation, type, essence, character, sort [cipher
naught: zero, nothing,
nautical: marine, naval, maritime
" **command:** avast
" **fly:** burgee
nautical hazard: fog
" **instrument:** sextant
" **mile:** knot
" **term to cease:** avast [ahoy
" " **in hailing:** aloe,
Navajo Indian hut: hogan [maritime
naval: marine, nautical,
" **officer:** yeoman
" " **(var.):** bosun
" **weapons:** torpedo
nave: hub
navigate: sail
" **the air:** fly, aviate
near: at, close, nigh, by

" **the back:** dorsal
" **by:** beside
" **the center:** inner
" " **cheek:** malar
" " **ear:** otic
" **(poet.):** anear
" **(prefix):** be
" **(Scot.):** nar
" **the stern:** aft
nearer (dial.): nar
nearly: almost
nearsighted person: myope
neat: tidy, trim, trig, orderly, adroit, prim, natty, spruce, precise
neb: beak [Omaha
Nebraska city: Ord,
" **county:** Otoe
nebris: fawnskin
nebulous: misty
necessity: want, need
neckband: collar, scarf
neckpiece: boa, boas, stole, collar [scarf
necktie: cravat, ascot,
necromancy: magic, sorcery, conjuration
need: necessitate, lack, want, require, poverty, demand
" **(urgent):** exigency
needle shaped: acerose, acerate
needlefish: gar
needless: useless
needy: poor, indigent
negate: deny, nullify
negation: not, no, denial, blankness
negative: nay, not, film
" **particle:** non, anion
neglect: omit, disregard
neglected: untended undone, forgot, defaulted [careless
negligent: remiss, lax,
negotiate: treat, transact
negrito: ita
Negro of Fr. W. Africa: Habe
" " **Niger Delta:** Ibo [Edo, Vai, Ibo
" " **Negeria:** Aro,
neighborly gathering: bee [dent
Neptune's spear: trinerve: pluck [neuro
" **(comb. form):** neur,
" **of leaf:** vein
" **network (sg.):** rete, arete, plexus
" **substance:** alba
nervous: uneasy [tic
" **disorder:** chorea,
" **system (pert. to):** neural
" **twitching:** tic
nest: den, aerie, retreat, haunt, nide
nestle: cuddle, snuggle
nestling: bird, birdling, eyas [trap
net: clear, seine, mesh,

gain, yield, snare,
nether: lower, under
Netherlands measure: roede [tate, annoy
nettle: provoke, irri-
" **rash:** uredo
network: mesh, web, rete, plexus [tice
" **of thin strips:** lat-
" " **threads:** lace
networks: retia [tatic
neutral equilibrium: as-
Nevada city: Reno, Elko
" **lake:** Tahoe
new: recent, neoteric, fresh, late, unused, modern, untried
" **(comb. form):** neo
" **Guinea seaport:** Lae [ron
" " **tribesman:** Ka-
New Hampshire city: Keene
" " **river:** Saco,
" **Mex. co.:** Otero
" " **dollar:** sia [Sia
" " **Indian:** Taos,
" " **river:** Gila
" " **state flower:** yucca
" **(prefix):** neo, nea
" **star:** nova
" **start:** redeal
" **Test. part:** Gospel
" **World Rep.:** Haiti
" **York Canal:** Erie
" " **capital:** Albany
" " **Indian tribe:** Oneida
" " **island:** Ellis
" " **river:** Mohawk Niagara
" " **state city:** Troy, Utica, Olean, Elmira
" " " **county:** Yates, Tioga
" " " **flower:** rose
" " " **lake:** Seneca, Oneida, George
" " " **village:** Avon
" **Zealand aborigine:** maori [pork, moa
" " **bird:** kea, more-
" " **clan:** ati
" " **demon:** taipo
" " **district:** Otago
" " **food fish:** ihi
" " **hedge laurel:** Tarata
" " **mahogany pine:** Totara
" " **native:** maori
" " " **fort:** Pa
" " **parrot:** kea
" " **parson bird:** koko, poe
" " **plant:** karo
" " **soldier:** anzac
" " **tree:** ake, taro, rata, tawa, tarata
" " **woody vine:** aka
newcomer: entrant

newest: neo
news: tidings
" **monger:** gossip
" **stand:** kiosk [tion
newspaper issue: edi-
newspapers: press sheets, news
newt: triton, eft
nexus: link
nib: point, beak, prong
nibble: peck, gnaw
nice: finical, pleasant, genteel, agreeable, sociable, fine
niche: corner, recess
nick: notch
nickname: agname
nictitate: wink
niggard: miser
nigh: near, close
nightfall (poet.): eve, een, eventide
nimble: agile, active, spry, lissome, alert
nimbus: halo
nimrod: hunter
nine: nonet, ennead
" **(comb. form):** ennea [vena
" **days devotion:** no-
" **headed monster:** hydra
" **inches:** span
ninefold: nenary
ninny: fool, dunce
nip: bite, pincer, pinch, blight, peck, clamp, clip
nitid: glossy, bright
nitrogenous compound: kenatin, protein
no extent: not
Noah (N. Test. Spell.): Noe [Ahab
" **son:** Shem, Ham,
noble: epic, peer, sublime, epical, baron
nobleman: baron, peer, earl, prince, lord, grandee, marquis
nocturnal animal: coon
" **bird:** owl, bat
" **mammal:** weasel, lemur [beck, sway
nod: bow, drowse, bend,
nodding: nutant [by
nodose: knotty, knob-
nodule: knot
" **of stone:** geode
nog: pin
noise: din, sound, roar, hubbub, clamor, rattle, racket
noisy: loud, blatant, clamorous
" **bird:** pie [crial
" **condemnation:** de-
" **laugh:** guffaw
nom de plume: alias
nomad: bedouin, rover, wanderer
nominal stock value: par [point
nominate: name, ap-
non-professional: lay, laic, amateur

X-WORD DICT

" Semetic: Aryan
none (dial.): nin
nonentity: nobody
nonmetallic element: boron, silicon, iodine
nonsense: bah, bosh, fudge, falderal
nook: corner, in, angle, recess
noose: loop, entrap, snare [ard
norm: pattern, stand-
normal: sane, natural, same, standard, regular
" **state:** order
" **value:** par
Norse deities home: Asgard
" **fate:** Norn, Norm
" **fire demon:** Surtr
" **galley:** aesc [Eir
" **god:** Odin, Tyr, Thor, Aesir (pl), Ve,
" " **of dead:** Hel
" **goddess:** Eir, Norn
" **gods:** Aesir
" **literary work:** edda
" **myth. giant:** Atli
" **saint:** Olaf
" **sea deity:** Van
" **tale:** saga
" **ter. division:** amt
North African: see also African
" " **native:** eritrean, hamite
" " **plant:** anise
" " **seaport:** Oran, Derna
" " **wt.:** rotl [gan
" **American mt.:** Lo-
" " **Island:** Iceland
" **Carolina county:** Ashe
" " **river:** Tar
" **Pole discoverer:** Peary [star, polaris
" **star:** polestar, lode-
" **Syrian diety:** El

" **wind:** boreas
northern: boreal
" **bird:** loon, auk
" **European:** Finn, Slav, Lapp, Lett
Norwegian: Norseman, Norse
" **capital:** Oslo [sund
" **city:** Narvik, Ale-
" **county:** Amt
" **dramatist:** Ibsen
" **land division:** amt
" **measure:** alen
" **name:** Olaf, Olav
" **painter:** Dahl
" **river:** Oi, Nea, Ena
nose: sniff, scent, detect
" **(comb. form):** rhin
" **(pert. to):** rhinal, nasal
nostril: nare, nose
" **(pert. to):** narine
notable act: feat
notch: nick, gap, dent, serrate, indent

notched bar: ratch
" **wheel:** ratchet
note: observe, heed, remark
" **of chromatic scale:** ri, di, li
" **the speed:** time
noted: famed, eminent, marked, famous
notes: memoranda, memo [hil, nought
nothing: nil, zero, ni-
" **(colloq.):** nix
" **more than** or **nothing but:** mere
notice: heed, observe, see, sign, spot
notion: idea, fad, whim
" **(dial.):** idee
notoriety: eclat [rant
notorious: infamous, ar-
notwithstanding: despite, however, yet
nought: nothing, zero
noun suffix: ier, ac, ist, ite [alible, meaty
nourishing: alimental,
Nova Scotia: Acadia
" " **seaport:** Truro
novel: new, unusual, strange, romance, different [acolyte, tiro
novice: tyro, beginner,
now: here, forthwith
noxious: ill, miasmic

" **substance:** poison
nuance: shade
nub: pith, lump, knot
nucha: nape
nucleus of atom: proton
nudge: jog [valid
null: void, cipher, in-
nullify: negate
number: count, enumerate, digit
" **to be added to another:** addend
" **of Muses:** nine
numbness: torpor
numeral style: arabic
numerical: ten [tiful
numerous: many, plen-
nurse: nurture, foster, nana, tend
" **shark:** gat
nurture: breed, cherish, nurse, feed
nut: problem [nougats
" **confection:** praline
" **(kind):** kola, cola, almond [ing
nutant: nodding, droop-
nutriment: food, meat
nutritious: alimentary
Nyx's daughter: Eris

O

oaf: dolt, lout, idiot
oak: blackjack, alder
oar: paddle, row, rower
" **blade:** palm
" **fulcrum:** thole
" **part:** loom

oarsman: rower
oath: vow, curse
" **(mild):** drat, egad
" **(old):** ecod, egad
obedient: dutiful
obeisance: homage
obese: fat
obey: mind, comply, submit, yield
object: intention, demur, thing, aim, evict, protest, target
" **of alm:** butt
" " **bric a brac:** curio
" " **devotion:** idol
objective: goal, target, aim
objurgate: scold

obligation: debt, bond, duty, due, tie
oblique: lateral, slant, bevel, awry, skew, sidelong
obliterate: erase, efface, raze, rase, blot
oblivion: annesty, lethe
obscure: dim, shade, fog, deep, indistinct, see, darken, inner, blur [tion
observance: rite, atten-
observe: notice, note, regard, remark, eye, lo [hitch
obstacle: dam, snag, bar,
obstinate: stubborn, set
obstruct: dam, bar, deter, impede, clog, hinder, occlude, estop
obtain: derive, gain, get, procure, secure, win
" **control of:** take
" **aboriously:** eke
obtuse: crass, dense, blunt [evident
obvious: overt, patent,
" **facts:** truisms
occasion: once, nonce, time, breed, engender
" **(Scot):** sele
occasional (Scot.): orra
occident: west
occlude: obstruct, close
occult: cryptic
occultism: cabala [dent
occupant: tenant, resi-
occupation: career, tenure, business, metier, work, trade
occupied: rapt, busy
occupy: interest, use, engage, fill
" **a seat:** sit, preside
occur: happen, pass, betide
" **every year:** annual
" **at irregular intervals:** sporadic
" " **stated intervals:** regular [incident
occurrence: event, hap,
ocean: main, sea
" **(pert. to):** pelagic
" **route:** lane

" **vessel:** liner
oceanic: marine, pelagic
Octavia's husband: Nero
ocular: visual [unique
odd: strange, eccentric, queer, singular, uneven, quaint, rare,
" **(Scot.):** orra
odds: chances
Odin's brother: Ve
" **son:** Tyr
odious: hateful [smell
odor: aroma, scent,
" **(offensive):** olid
odorous: fragrant, redolent
odylic force: od
Odysseus's dog: Argos
of: about
" **(Dutch):** van
" **each (Med.):** ana
" **the matter:** re
" " **past:** yore
" **(prefix):** de
" **the side:** lateral
" **that kind:** such
" " **thing:** its
off: away, begone, mistaken [insult
" **hand:** impromptu
offend: pique, displease,
offense: crime, fault
" **against the law:** delict
offensiveness: odium
offer: bid, tender, proffer, propose, proposal
" **objections:** demur
" **to pay:** bid
" **for sale:** vend
" **solemnly:** pledge
" **to verify:** aver
offering: tribute
office head: manager
" **holders:** ins
official: magnate
" **decree:** ukase [ture
" **document:** inden-
" **endorsement:** visa
" **examiner:** censor
" **message:** brevet
" **paper:** document
" **proof of a will:** probate [roll, actum
" **record:** protocol,
" **sitting:** session
" **stamp:** seal
" **transactions:** acta
officiate: act [son
offspring: descendant,
often (poet.): oft
ogle: leer, eye, gaze
ogrish: cruel, monstrous
Ohio city: Xenia, Lima
" **county:** Ross, Erie
" **town:** Ada
oil: oleic, oleo, grease, lubricate, anoint, petroleum
" **based ointment:** ecrate
" **bottle:** cruet
" **can:** oiler
" **of orange:** neroli

" " of orris root: irone
" of roses (var.): atar, otto, attar, ottar
" ship: tanker
" (suffix): ol
" tree: eboe
" well: gusher [nut
" yielding herb: pea-
oilstone: hone
oily: fat, sebaceous
" ketone: irone
" substance: fat
ointment: cerate, salve, pomade, unguent, balsam, balm, nard
" of the ancients: nard
Okinawa capital: Naha
Oklahoma city: Enid, Tulsa, Ada
" nickname of natives: Sooners
okra: gumbo
old: stale, aged, ancient, former
" age: senile
" Dominion State (abbr.): Va
" Dutch measure: aam [groat
" English coin: ora,
" English rent: tac
" " tax: tallage, prisage [archaic
" fashioned: passe,
" " fellow: fogy
" love song: amoret
" maid: spinster
" military device: petard [it
" moneyer's wt.: per-
" Moslem coin: dinar
" musical instrument: rebec, lyre, citole, rota, asor, cithern, spinet [are
" " note: ela, fe, ut,
" Norse work: edda
" piano: spinet
" pronoun: thee
" rifle part: tige
" Roman chest: cyst
" salt: tar
" saying: saw [baubee
" Scot. coin: demy,
" " wt.: trone
" time beverage: posset
" " dance: carole
" times: yore
" vessel: galleon, frigate
" woman: crone, hag
" womanish: anile, senile
" World bird: starling, terek [genet
" " carnivore:
" " crow: rook
" " finch: serin
" " fish: loach
" " genus of herbs: paris
" " lizard: seps

" " plant: aloe
" " sandpiper: terek [der
" " shrub: olean-
olden: ancient [yore
" times (poet.): eld,
older: elder, senior, staler, sr
oldest member: dean
oldtimer: veteran
oleaginous: oily
olent: fragrant
oleo esin: elemi, anime
olfactory organ: nose
olive: relish, tawny, olea
" tree: ash
Oliver Twist character: Fagin
olla: pot, jug [temis
Olympian goddess: Ar-
omen: sign, presage, portent, forbode [ful
ominous: sinister, fate-
omission: elision
" of end of a word: afocope
" " letter from word: syncope
" mark: caret
omit: delete, skip, cut,

miss, spare, except, neglect, elide [elide
" from pronouncing:
on: above, along, about, upon, forward
" all sides: around, about
" board ship: asea
" condition that: so, if
" fire: ablaze
" the line of: along
" that account: thereat
" this: hereupon
" top of: atop, upon
" the way: enroute
onager: donkey, catapult
once: formerly, occasion, ever, singly
" again: over
" " (poet.): oer
" more: anew, encore
one: unit, unity, same, anybody, united, person, an, single
" before another: tandem [mono
" (comb. form): uni,
" devoted to monastic life: oblate
" of gigantic size: Titan
" given to a habit: addict
" horse carriage: shay
" impervious to pain or pleasure: stoic
" lately arrived: newcomer [maker
" in the lead: paceless than par:

birdie
" masted vessel: sloop
" of mixed breed: metis
" named after another: namesake [inee
" " for office: nom-
" omitted: out
" (prefix): mono, uni
" (Scot.): ane, ae
" skilled in colors: colorist [guist
" " in lang.: lin-
" spot: ace, pip
" " " Musketeers: Aramis
" of two: either
" " " equal parts: half, moiety [er
" unclean (bib.): lep-
oneness: unity
onion (variety): rare-ripe, leek, cibol
only: sole, mere, solely, alone [outset, dash
onset: attack, start,
onslaught: onset, attack, assault
onus: burden, weight
onward: along
ooze: exude, seep, mire, slime, spew
open: overt, accessible, unfold, unlock, bare, exposed, frank, start, unfurl, bland, agape, unstopped, expanded, lance, unclose, disclose, expand [patio
" court: area, hiatus,
" to general use: public [moor
" land: field, heath,
" shelved cabinet: etagere
" space in forest: glade
" to view: bare, overt
" wide: gape, yawn
opening: gap, fissure, aperture, vent, eyelet, hole, pore, rima, hiatus, rift [som
" above door: tran-
" in net: mesh
" " nose: nare
" wide: agape
openwork fabric: lace
opera: Aida [run
operate: work, manage,
" on a skull: trepan
operatic soprano: Eames, Melba
operative: artisan
ophidian: snake
opine: think, judge, suppose, consider
opinion: view, concept, credo, thought, idea, judgment, repute
opium: narcotic, drug
" paste: dope
" poppy seed: maw
opponent: foe, rival

opportune: apropos, pat, timely
opportunity: opening
oppose: face, withstand, repel, resist
opposed: averse, anti
" " stoss: lee
opposite: inverse, reverse [subtend
" to: against, reverse,
" of aweather: alee-
" " liabilities: assets [persecute
oppress: aggrieve, lade,
Op's daughter: Ceres
opt: choose, decide
optic: eye
" (comb. form): opto
optical glass: lens
" illusion & phenomenon: mirage
" instrument: prism, periscope, telescope
" " part: alidade
optimistic: roseate, rosy, sanguine
option: choice
optional: elective
opulent: rich, profuse, wealthy
opus: work, burden
oracle: mentor [vatic
oracular: ambiguous,
orage: tempest, storm
oral: spoken, parol, verbal, aloud, vocal
" utterance: parol
orange dye: mandarin, henna, chica
orangutan: mias, satyr
orate: declaim, speak, talk, harangue, say
oration: address, prayer, speech [globe
orb: circle, sphere, eye,
" of day: sun
orbed: round, lunar
orbit: path
orc: grampus, whale
orchid (kind): arethusa, pogonia, faham
" meal or root: salep
ordain: decree
ordeal: trial
order: command, mandate, method, bade, regulate, bid, system
" of aquatic mammals: cete, cetacea
" " architecture: doric, ionic
" back: remand [da
" of business: agen-
" " mammals: primate, cete
" " reptiles: sauria
" " whales: ceta
orderly: trim, neat, shipshape [tem, series
" arrangement: sys-
ordinary: usual, average, mediocre
ore: metal [nanza, bed
" deposit: lode, bo-
" of lead: galen

" **refiner**: smelter
" **vein**: lode
Oregon capital: Salem
organ bass note: pedal
" **desk**: console
" **pipe**: reed, flue
" **shrub**: salal
" **of speech**: lip, voice, throat, tongue
" **stop**: celeste, gamba, tremolo
organic unit: monad
organism living on another: parasite
" **(minute)**: spore
" **(simple)**: monad
organization: setup
orgy: carousal, frolic, lark [tine
oriental: Asian, eastern, asiatic, levan-
" **animal**: rasse
" **bird**: mino, mina
" **bow**: salaam
" **building**: pagoda
" **captain**: ras
" **caravansary**: serai
" **cart**: araba
" **case**: inro
" **coin**: rin, yen, sen
" **commander**: Ras
" **country**: India
" **dish**: pilaw, pilau
" **drums**: tomtoms
" **dwelling**: dar
" **food fish**: tai
" **garment**: aba
" **governor**: dey
" **greeting**: salam
" **guitar**: sitar, samisen
" **inn**: serai
" **laborer**: coolie
" **measure**: parah
" " **of capacity**: ardeb [Asian
" **native**: Korean,
" **nature spirits**: genii
" **nurse**: amah, ayah
" **obeisance**: salaam, salam
" **plant**: sesame
" **prince**: amir
" **receptacle**: inro
" **ruler**: ameer [goda
" **sacred tower**: pa-
" **sail**: lateen [salam
" **salutation**: salaam,
" **shrub**: tea, henna, oleander
" **tea**: cha
" **wagon**: araba
" **weight**: mo, cantar, tael, catty, rotl [let
orifice: hole, pore, in-
origin: root, source, parentage, genesis, beginning [emanate
originate: arise, invent, create, breed, coin,
originator of atomic theory: Dalton
Orion meteor: orionid
" **star**: rigel
orison: prayer

orle: bearing [ette
ornament: pin, trinket, amulet, adorn, ros-
ornamental: decorative, bow, bead, fancy
" **ball**: bead, pompon
" **device**: pin
" **ensemble**: decor
" **grass**: neti [tain
" **jet of water**: foun-
" **part of wall**: dodo, dado
" **tree**: almond, palm
ornamented leather: tooled [elaborate
ornate: florid, decorated, showy, adorn,
ort: morsel, scrap, bit
orthographer: speller
os: bone, mouth
oscilate: wag, rock, swing, vibrate, sway
osculate: kiss
osier: willow, wand, rod
Osiris's brother: Set
" **crown**: atef
" **wife**: Isis
ossified tissue: bone
ostentatious: pretentious, showy, gaudy
" **display**: pomp, parade, splurge
ostiole: stoma, pore
ostrich: rhea, emu
otalgia: earache
Othello's false friend: Iago [alternate
other: else, different,
otherwise: else, or, alias
otiose: indolent, inactive, idle [ish
Ottoman: Turk, Turk-
" **court**: Porte
" **standard**: alem
oust: remove, evict, expel, eject
out: ex, forth, eject, outside, external
out of: from [agasp
" **of breath**: winded,
" " **date**: passe, old
" **& out**: arrant
" " **(prefix)**: ec, de
" " " **way**: remote, afield, aside
outbreak: riot, eruption [steria
" **of enthusiasm**: hy-
outbuilding: shed, barn
outcast: leper, pariah
outclass: surpass, excel
outcome: issue, result, end, sequel
outcry: clamor [exceed
outdo: cap, excel, trump,
outer: external, exterior
" **boundary of plane figure**: perimeter
" **covering**: rind, hull, skin, shell, wrap, coat, husk, crust
" " **of tire**: shoe
" **grain husk**: bran
outfit: rig, equipment, gear, kit, tog [cost
outlay: price, expense,

outlet: vent [sis, sketch
outline: contour, synop-
" **of play**: scenario
outlook: aspect, prospect, vista
outmoded: passe, dated
outpouring: tirade, torrential, emitting, flood
outrage: abuse
outside: out
" **(comb. form)**: ecto
" **(prefix)**: ect
outspoken: blunt, candid, frank [salient
outstanding: notable,
outward: ectad, outer
oven: kiln, baker
over: above, again, past, across, finished, extra, completed, beyond, ended, done
" **again**: anew
" **(poet.)**: oer
overcoat: ulster, topcoat, paletot
overcome: rout, best, surmount, conquer, appal, defeat
overflow: flood, teem
overhang: beetle, jut
overhead: above, aloft
overlook: miss, skip
overly: too, careless
overpower: awe, master, repress, subdue
" **with sudden emotion**: stun
overseer: boss, censor, curator, taskmaster
overt: open, public, manifest, obvious
overtop: surpass, transcend
overture: prelude
overturn: upset, tip
overwhelm: swamp
ovule: seed, egg
ovum: egg, seed, spore
own: possess, confess, avow, have
" **(Scot.)**: ain
ownership: title
ox: bos, steer, yak
" **of Celebes**: Anoa, goa, noa
oxidize: rust
oxlike quadruped: yak, bison [ide
oxygen compound: ox-
" **(form of)**: ozone
oxygenate: aerate
oyster: bivalve, reefer
" **bed**: layer

P

pace: gait, stride, rate, amble, step, trot
Pacific: Irenic [salal
" **coast shrub**: salad,
" **Isl. aroid**: taro
" " **group**: Samoa, Saipan, Hawaii
" " **pine**: ei, ie

" " **tree**: ipio, ipil
pacify: pacate, placate, soothe, appease
pack: stow, cram
" **of cards**: deck
" **down**: tamp
package: carton, parcel, bundle
packing box: crate
" **ring**: gasket
pact: treaty, agreement
pad: cushion, tablet
paddle: oar, row
pagan: heathen, ethnic, idolater
page: folio, leaf
pageant: pomp
pagoda ornament & final: tee
" **top**: finial
pain: ache, pang, sting, throe, disquiet, misery, hurt, distress
painful: bitter, sore
paint: color, pigment, rouge, decorate, limn
painter: artist, limner
" **'s tablet**: palette
painting of Madonna: Sistine
" **on plaster**: fresco, secco, frescoing
" **style**: genre [dyad
pair: duo, team, brace, twain, match, two,
" **(var.)**: diad
paired (her.): gemel
palatable: savory, sapid
palate: taste
" **(soft)**: uvula
palatial: palatine, velar
pale: wan, stake, pallid, blanch, ashy, dim, white, picket, ashen, faint, fade
Palestine animal: daman [ia
" **city**: Haifa, Samar-
" **coin**: mil
" **mountain**: Carmel, Gilead, Sinai
" **plain**: Sharon
" **town**: Cana
paletot: overcoat
palliate: extenuate, mitigate, conceal, gloss, salve
palm: areca
" **cockatoo**: arara
" **of hand**: vola thenar
" **(kind)**: coco, assai
" **leaf**: ola, ole, frond
" **lily**: ti, titree
" **off**: foist
" **stem**: rattan
" **wine**: taree [ola
Palmyra palm: tal, ole,
palp: feeler [ifest
palpable: tangible, man-
pamper: coddle, spoil, pet, cosset
pamphlet: tract
panacea: elixir, cure
Panama Canal dam: Gatun

panel: jury   [throe
pang: agony, pain, ache,
pant: gasp, throb, beat,
    puff, yearn   [leopard
panther: puma, pard,
pantry: larder
pants: trousers, slacks
papal: apostolic
"   veil: orale   [quire
paper measure: ream,
parade: spectacle, dis-
    play, flaunt, march,
    review
Paradise: Eden
paragon: model, pat-
    tern, type
paragraph: item
Paraguay city: Ita
parallel: even
parallelogram (kind):
    rhomb   [preme
paramount: chief, su-
parasite: sponge
parasitic insect: flee,
    louse, lice (pl.)
parcel: package, packet
"   of land: lot, let
"   out: allot, mete
parched: thirsty, arid,
    seared
pard: panther
pardon: condone, for-
    give, reprieve, remit,
    remission, excuse, ab-
    solve, amnesty
pardonable: venial
pare: peel, remove, re-
    duce, cut, shave
parget: coat, whitewash,
    plaster
Paris's father: Priam
"   wife: Oenone
Park in Rockies: Estes
parlance: diction
parley: conference, con-
    fer, discuss
parliament: diet   [satire
parody: skit, travesty,
parol: unwritten, oral
paronomasia: pun
paroxysm: spasm, fit
parrot: macaw, kea
"   fish: lania, cotoro
"   (kind): lory, ara,
    macaw, kaka
parry: fend, avoid
parsimonious: stingy
parsley plant: dill
parson: pastor, min-
    ister
"   bird: tui, tue, poe
parsonage: manse, rec-
    tory
part: section, sever,
    portion, piece, side,
    sunder, role, bit
partake: share, use
partial: half, biased,
    favorable   [shadow
"   darkness: shade,
"   to: favor
participator: party
particle: iota, mite, jot,
    shred, atom, grain,
    speck, mote, ace
"   "   fire: spark, arc

particolored: pied
particular: special, espe-
    cial, fussy   [tion
partition: severance, di-
    vision, cell, wall, sec-
partly open: ajar
"   (prefix): semi   [ally
partner: mate, sharer,
party: sect, faction
pasquinade: lampoon
pass: elapse, fare, ap-
    prove, circulate, oc-
    cur, defile, adopt, de-
    volve, enact
"   around: skirt
"   away: elapse, per-
    ish, die   [file
"   between hills: de-
"   "   peaks: col
"   into use: enure
pass on: relay   [omit
"   over: elide, cross,
"   "   lightly: skim
"   a rope thru: reeve
"   slowly: drag, lapse
"   swiftly: sweep
"   through: penetrate,
    cross
"   "   cautiously:
    reeve
"   "   a sieve: sift
"   as time: spend
"   without touching:
    clear
passage: transit, aisle,
    aperture, alley, way,
    entry, alee, canal,
    channel, voyage
"   out: exit, egress
"   of Scripture: text
"   from shore inland:
    gat
passageway: arcade,
    ramp, aisle, gate
passe: obsolete
passenger: fare, rider,
    traveler, passer
passerine bird: star-
    ling, finch   [lust
passion: ire, feeling,
passive: inert, inactive
passport indorsement:
    visa, vise [gone, over
past: by, agone, ago,
"   (poet.): agone
"   tense: preterit
paste: cream, glue, arti-
    ficial, imitation, ce-
    ment, fasten, adhe-
    sive, dough, stick
pastime: sport, diver-
    sion   [keeper
pastor: rector, parson,
    minister, clergyman,
pastoral: rustic, rural,
    idyl, drama, poem
"   poem: idyll, idyl,
    eclogue
pastry: pie, tart
pasture: lea, grass, graze
"   grass: grama
"   for hire: agist
"   plant: clover
pasty cement: mastic
pat: apt, timely, trap,
    tap, stroke   [bos

Patagonian deity: sete-
patch: piece, mend
paten: disc   [right
patent: manifest, copy-
path: trail, lane, route,
    way, footway, track,
    course, orbit
patio: court
patriotic: national
patrol: scout, watch
patron: protector
    factor, guest
"   of cripples:
    Giles
"   "   "   Ireland:
    Patrick
"   "   "   lawyers:
    Ives
"   "   "   Norway:
    Olaf
"   "   "   sailors:
    Elmo
"   "   "   Wales:
    David   [digm
pattern: norm, model,
    ideal, design, para-
pause: rest, selah, re-
    spite, hesitate, stop
paving block: paver
pawl: detent, cog
pay: remunerate, de-
    fray, disburse, dis-
    charge, wages, sti-
    pend, compensate,
    expend, wage
"   attention: heed
"   back: retaliate, re-
    mit, render, reim-
    burse
"   homage to: honor
"   one's part: antes
"   out: spend
payable: due
payment: fee
peace: serenity, repose,
    concord, calm
"   (Latin): pax
"   pipe: calumet
peacock: moa, pawn
"   butterfly: io
peak: acme, crest, sum-
    mit, cusp
peal: ring, respond, toll
peanut: earthpea, earth-
    nut, mani, goober
pear: pome
"   shaped vessel:
    aludel
peart: frisky   [serf
peasant: ryot, rustic,
peat bog: moss, cess
pebbles (sand): gravel
pecan: hickory
peck: dot, dab, nip
peculiar: strange, sing-
    ular, queer, odd
"   saying: idiom
pedagogue: tutor
pedal digit: toe
"   extremity: foot
peddler: hawker   [anta
pedestal: support, base,
"   face: dado
pedigree: race, lineage
peduncle: pedicel, stem,
    scape

peek: peep, peer   [rind
peel: ring, bark, pare,
    remove, skin, strip,
peep: chirp, peek
"   show: raree
peepers: eyes
peer: pry, nobleman,
    look, match, noble,
    gaze, peek
Peer Gynt's author:
    Ibsen
"   "   mother: Ase
peeve: vex, annoyance,
    irritate, annoy, nettle
peevish: pettish, fret-
    ful, cross, testy,
    moody, techy
peg: dowel, pin, mar-
    ker, nob
pegu ironwood: acle
pelagic: oceanic
pellet: pill
pelt: fur, skin, hide,
    hurl, throw, pepper
pen: sty, quill, coop,
    indite, write, cage,
    confine, enclose
"   point: nib, neb
penalty: fine, loss
pend: hang
pendant: tassel, earring
pendent: lop fob, bob,
    hanging   [bore
penetrate: enter, pierce,
penetrating: acute, raw
penitent: repent, con-
    trite, repentant   [rere
penitential chant: mise-
"   period: Lent
pennant: streamer, flag
pennon: flag, banner
Penn. borough: Sayre,
    Etan
"   city & lake port:
    Erie, Easton
"   town: Ono, Avoca
penurious: poor, stingy,
    miserly, mean
people: demos, nation,
    populate, laity, folks,
    race, inhabit, ones
pepper: betel ava, kava
per: by, for

perceive: see, sense,
    realize, apprehend
"   by senses: sensate
perch: roost, seat, sit
percolate: seer, seep,
    filter
percussion instrument:
    gong, triangle, drum,
    trap   [eign
peregrine: falcon, for-
perennial herb: madder,
    pia, sedum   [plete
perfect: ideal, flawless,
    consummate, com-
"   (comb. form): teleo
perforate: punch, tere-
    brate, drill, bore
"   design: stencil
"   ornament: bead
perforation: hole
perform: do, act, play,
    enact   [tion
performance: act, rendi-

performer: doer
perfume: essence, attar, scent, cense
" **bag:** sachet
" **of flowers:** attar
" **(kind):** civet
" " **(var.):** atar
" **with odors:** cense
pergola: arbor
perhaps (arch.): mayhap, belike
peril: menace, danger, hazard, risk, jeopardy [time
period: age, dot, era,
" **of denial:** lent
" **just before:** eve
" " **time:** eral, eon, term, decade, epoch
perish: expire, die, ruin
permanent: durable, enduring
permeable by liquids: porous [bue
permeate: pervade, impermission:** leave, consent, license
" **to travel:** passport
permit: let, allow, license
pernicious: bane, evil, bad [sine
perpendicular: sheer,
perpetual: endless, constant, unceasing,
perpetually: ever
perplex: harass, bother
persecute: harry, badger, oppress
perserverance: grit
persevere: persist
Persia: Iran [Perse
Persian: Iranian, Mede,
" **angel:** mah
" **coin:** rial, kran
" **(ancient):** daric
" **fairy & elf:** peri
" **gazelle:** cora
" **governor:** satrap
" **judge:** cadi
" **king:** Xerxes
" **money:** dinar
" **poet:** Omar
" **race:** Lur
" **ruler:** Shah
" **title:** shah, mir
" **town:** Fao
" **water wheel:** noria
" **weight:** abbas, sang
persiflage: banter
persist: last, persevere, remain, insist, endure, continue
person: one, soul, being
" **a dressed:** you, ye
" **appointed to act as sheriff:** elisor
" **of foresight:** sage
" **named for office:** nominee
" **not in office:** out
" **of rank:** magnate
" **with loud voice:** stentor [lions
personal beliefs: opin-
" **belongings:** traps, gear

" **consideration & interest:** self
personality: ego, self
personification of rumor: fama
" **of truth:** una
perspicacity: acumen
perspiration: sudor
persuade: urge, influence, induce, coax, reason, convince
pert: lively, bold, impudent, short
" **girl:** minx [belong
pertain: relate, concern,
pertaining to: anent
" **to (suffix):** ar, ac, ile, ic [relevant
pertinent: relative, apt,
perturb: agitate

peruke: wig
perusal: reading
peruse: read, con, scan
Peruvian capital: Lima
" **chieftan:** Inca
" **coin:** diner, dinero
" **dance:** cueca
" **Indian:** Cana, Inca
" **plant:** oca
" **race:** Inca
" **seaport:** Calloa
" **tinamou:** yutu
" **volcano:** Misti
pervade: permeate, imbue, fill
perverse: froward
pest: bore, epidemic
pester: harry, harass, annoy, nag
pet: fondle, cosset
" **lamb:** cosset
petal: leaf
petiole: leafstalk, stem
petit: small
petition: sue, beg, plea, ask, solicit, suit
petty: small, trifle, little [satrap
petty officer: yeoman,
" " **(colloq.):** bosun
petulant: short, cross, fretful [eidolon
phantom: idolon, ghost,
phase: aspect, side, appearance, stage
phial: vial, bottle
philippic: screed, tirade
Philippine aborigine: aeta, ata, ita
" **archipelago:** sulu
" **dagger:** itac
" **dwarf race:** aeta
" **foe:** Samson
" **garment:** saya
" **group:** igorot
" **Island:** Mindanso, Leyte, Panay, Cebu, Samar [vite
" " **province:** Ca-
" **knife:** bolo
" **Moham.:** Moro
" **mountain:** Apo, Iba
" **native:** Ati, Ata Tagalog, Aeta, Moro
" **negrito:** iti, ita, at
" **peasant:** tao

" **rice:** macan
" **termite:** anay, ana
" **tree:** tua, ipil, dita dao, amaga
" " **(poisonous):** ligas
" **tribe:** Atas, Moros
" **weapon:** bolo
" **god:** Baal [tarte
Phoen. goddess: Asphosphorous compound source:** apatite [mug
photograph: print, snap,
" **bath:** reducer, developer, toner, fixer
physiognomy: face
piano keyboard: clavier
piazza: veranda
pick: pluck, select, elite
icket: pale, stake
pickle: marinate, corn, souse
pickpocket (slang): dip
picnic: outing
picture: depict, portrayal, photo, image, icon, pastel
" **frame:** easel
" **puzzle:** rebus [llic
picturesque: scenic, idy-
piece: patch, portion, fragment, section, chip, missel, part, bit, lump, stab, morsel, scrap
" " **log:** slab
" " **money:** coin
" **put in:** inset
" **of timber:** plank
" " **turf:** divot, sod, peat
" " **wastesilk:** noil
" " **work:** job
pieces out: eke
pier: anta, dock, mole, wharf, jetty
pierce: stab, penetrate, enter, gore, lance, puncture
" **with a stake:** impale, empale
pigeon: dove, pouter, barb, nun
" **food:** saltcat, pea
house: dovecot
" **pea:** tur, dal
pigment: paint
" **from plants:** etiolin
" **used in water color:** bistre
pigtail: queue
pike: highway, luce
" **like fish:** gara, gar, robalo
piker: tightwad
pilaster: anta, column
pile: heap, mass, stack, load, nap, spile
" **to be burnt:** pyre
" **of earth:** hill
" " **hay or straw:** rick, mow
" **up:** amass, stack
pilfer: rob, steal, plunder
pilgrim Father: Alden

" **from Holy Land:** Palmer
" **leader:** Standish
pill: pellet, bolus
" **bug:** slater
pillage: loot, ravage, rapine, plunder, sack, ransack, rifle, foray
pillar: obelisk, lat, post, shaft, stela
pillow: cover: sham
pilot: steer, steersman, guide, guider, steerer, aviator
" **fish:** romero
pin: fasten, bolt, peg, nog, badge, skittle
" **to fasten meat:** skewer
pinch: nip [grieve
pine: languish, mope, sulk, yearn, lament,
pineapple: pina, anana, nana, ananas
pink, rose, rosy
pinnacle: top, apex
" **of ice in a glacier:** serac
" **ornament:** finial
" **of rock:** needle
pinochle score & term: meld
pintail duck: smee
pipe: tube, flagolet, flue, hose, cinch, brier
" **to discharge liquid:** spout [zesty
piquant: racy, salty,
pique: offend, spite, resent, dudgeon, stir
piquet term: capot
pirate: corsair, rover, buccaneer, privateer
" **flag:** roger
pistol (old): dag
pit: hole, grave, excavate, abyss, cavity, gravity

pitch: tar, tone, key, toss, throw, gist
pitcher: ewer, toby, tosser
" **'s area:** box
pitfall: snare, trap
pith: core, gist, nub, essence
" **helmet:** topee
pithy: meaty, terse
" **saying:** mot
pitiable: forlorn, sorry
pitiless: cruel
pivot: turn, hinge, slue
" **pin:** pintle
placard: sign, poster
placate: appease
place: see also put
" **stead, station, put, set, locality, lay, spot, seat, locale, deposit, situate, locus, rank, lieu, arrange, position
" **of activity:** hive
" **alone:** isolate [sort
" **of amusement:** re-
" **to anchor:** moorage

" at an angle: skew
" of barter: mart
" bliss: paradise, Eden
" in charge: entrust
" (comb. form): gea
" in common fund: pool
" confinement: prison [bus
" " darkness: ere-
" in different order: transpose, rearrange
" elsewhere: relocate
" end for end: reverse
" of entry: port
" at intervals: spaces
" of justice: bar
" levy on: tax
" on a mound: tee
" in office: seat
" one inside another: nestle, nest
" opposite: appose
" (pl.): loci
" of refuge: ark, harbor [cess
" " retirement: re-
" in rows (var.): aline
" of safety: haven
" for storing corn: crib
" " " fodder: silo
" " " hay: mow
" of trade: mart
" trust in: repose
" of worship: chapel, altar [law
" under a ban: out-
" " " promise: obligate [tern
" " restraint: in-
" " " water: submerge [lam
" of uproar: bed-
" " wealth exists: Indies
placid: calm, serene
plague: tease, taunt, torment, harass
plaid: tartan [dent
plain: bare, clear, apparent, simple, evi-
plaintive: mournful, sad
plait: braid [method
plan: plot, intend, design, arrange, devise, contrive, diagram, plat, scheme, project,
" of action: idea
" future · procedure: program
plane: level
" handle: tote [giro
" (kind): router, jet,
" maneuver: loop
" surface: flat, level, area
planet: Mars, Saturn, Asteroid, Neptune, Uranus, Venus, Pluto
planetarium: orrery
plank: board
plant: seed, endogen,

embed, factory, sow sapling, shrub
" of abnormal development: ecad
" axis: stalk
" bearing aromatic seeds: cumin, anise
" disease: scab, rot
" embryo: seed
" exudation: resin
" " (var.): rosin
" of gourd family: melon
" life: flora
" of mustard family: cress
" not having woodey stem: herb
" organ: leaf, tendril, soma
" stem: bine
" substance: resin
plants of a region: flora
plash: puddle, pool
plaster: stucco, smear, daub, parget
" support: lath
plat: plot, plan, map, chart, braid
plate: dish, saucer
plateau: tableland, mesa [estrade
platform: stage, dais,
platinum loop: oese
play: sport, enact, perform, drama, toy, disport, cavort, frolic, romp [lick, romp
" boisterously: rol-
" carelessly: strum
" first card: lead
" the lead: star
" at love: flirt
" on words: pun
player: actor, gambler
playing card spot: pip
playlet: skit
plead: entreat, appeal, implore, solicit, beg, advocate, argue
pleasant: sweet, agreeable, nice, amiable
please: suit, gratify, delight, indulge
pledge: vow, truce, commit, earnest, seal, promise, token, guaranty, guarantee
plentiful: abound, numerous, abundant
plexus: rete, retia, network
pliable: soft, supple, flexible, plastic
pliant: lithe, limber, supple, flexible
plicate: fold, pleat
plot: plan, plat, scheme, conspire, chart, intrigue, cabal, conspiracy, bed
" of land: lot, parcel
plow: till, furrow
pluck: spunk, grit, nerve, pick

" or pull off: avulse
plucky: game
plug: estop, stopper
plum: gage, sloe
" kernel: pit
plume: preen, feather, crest, egret
plummet: fall, drop
plunder: despoil, loot, rob, raid, prey, gut, spoil, sack, steal, pillage, pilfer rapine, spoliate, maraud
" (Arch.): reave
plundered (arch.): reft
plunge: dive, dip
ply: bias, fold, layer, thickness, wield
poach: trespass
pocket case: etui
" in trousers: fob
pocketbook: purse, reticule, bag
Poe's heroine: Lenore
" poem: Lenore
poem: epic, sonnet, lay, epode, verse, epepee, lyric, elegy, ballade, ballad, epos
poet: lyrist, bard, rimer
poetical measure & rhythm: meter
poetry (arch.): poesy
poignant: acute
point: peak, neb, tip, apex, indicate, aim, cusp, sharpen, apice, gist, nib, dot, focus
" between extremes: mesne [rhumb, airth
" of compass: airt,
" " crescent moon: cusp [men
" " difference: li-
" " land: spit
" " magnet: pole
" opposite the zenith: nadir
" under discussion: issue
" where leaf branches: axil
pointed: cultrat acute
" arch: ogive
" end: cusp
" instrument: needle, awl, prod
" part: nib
" process: awn
" stick: stake [row
" weapon: spear, ar-
pointer: hand, tip
pointless: inane
poise: balance, hover, carriage, equipoise
poison: venom, bane, corrupt, virus, taint
poisonous: venomous, toxic
" element: arsenic
" tree: upas
" weed: loco [dle
poke: prod, jab, daw-
" around: root, probe
" fun at: josh

poker chip: dib
" stake: ante
polar: arctic
pole: rod, staff, stick, pike, stake
" (pert. to): nodal
" (Scot.): caber
polecat: skunk [sheen
polish: gloss, scour, elegance, rub, shine,
Polish cake: baba
" river: San, Narew, Bug, Seret
polishing material: rabat, emery
polite: courteous, gracious, mannerly, urbane, genteel, civil
political group: bloc, party [roll, head
poll: election, vote, en-
polliwog: tadpole
pollute: taint, defile
Pollux's twin: Castor
polo mount: pony
poltroon: coward
Polynesian apple: hevi
" baking pit: umu
" chestnut: rata
" cloth: tapa
" herb: pia
" island group: Samoa
" yam: uve, ube, ubi
pome: apple, pear
pompous: stilted
ponder: pore, cogitate, meditate, consider, brood, contemplate, ruminate, muse, reflect, deliberate
pony: nag, pinto
pool: puddle, mere
" (Scot.). dib
poor: indigent, needy, bad, scanty, penurious, inopulent
poorhouse: almshouse
poorly: ill, illy, badly
Pope (relating to): papal
" scarf,collar or veil: orale
" triple crown: tiara
poplar: alamo, aspen
" (white): abele
populace: mob, demos
popular: demotic
porch: plaza, veranda, stoop, portico [hog
porcine animal: pig,
pore: ponder, study, stoma, opening
porgy: scup
" (red): tai
porridge: gruel, atole
port: haven, harbor
portal: gate
portend: bode, augur, presage, forbode
portent: omen, sign
portentous: dire [redcap
porter: carrier, suisse,
Portia's maid: Nerissa
portico: stoa, porch
portion: piece, some, share, part, dole, bit

X—WORD DICT

whit, dab, lot, half, sample, taste
portly: fat
portray: paint, draw, picture, limn, depict, delineate [bon
Portuguese capital: Lis-
" **city**: Ovar
" **coin**: rei
" **money of account**: rei, escudo
" **poet & historian**: Melo
" **province**: Azores
" **river**: Soa, Sado
" **territory in India**: Goa
" **title**: dom [ture
pose: sit, attitude, pos-
Poseidon's son: Triton
position: locale, job, station, stand, post, stance, place
positive: sure, certain
" **terminal**: anode
possess: own, have [sin
possession (Law): sei-
post: mail, station, office, stake, mall, pil-lar, bitt
" **to secure haw-**
poster: bill, placard, ad
postpone: defer, delay
posture: stance, atti-tude, pose
pot: kettle, olla
potato: tuber, spud
" **masher**: ricer
potency: vis [mighty
potent: powerful, strong,
potential: latent
" **energy**: ergal
pother: bustle, ado
potpourri: olio [pallet
potter's wheel: lathe,
pottery fragment: shard
" **(kind)**: delft
" **(pert. to)**: ceramic
pouch: sac, bag
pound: beat, hammer, thump, ram
" **down**: tamp [cant
pour: stream, flow, de-
" **forth**: emit, gush
" **off liquid**: drain
" **oil upon**: anoint
pout: sulk, mope
poverty: penury, need, want, indigence
powder: talc, dust, pul-verize
power: energy, force, strength, ability, vis, might, steam, vigor
powerful: strong, po-tent
" **jokes**: pranks, hoaxes [use
practice: drill, rehearse,
prairie wolf: coyote
praise: laud, bless, com-mend, flatter, extol, acclaim, adulation, tribute
praiseworthy: laudable
prance: caper, cavort

prank: antic, escapade, trick, dido frolic,
prate: babble, prattle, gab [seech
pray: entreat, impor-tune, implore, be-
prayer: orison, ave, litany, plea, entreaty
" **(arch.)**: bene, ori-son
precarious: dubious
precede: lead, forerun
" **in time**: predate, antedate
precedence: priority
precpt: maxim [rare
precious: dear, golden,
" **stone**: garnet sard, opal, zircon, gem, lazuli, beryl, asteria,
precipice: cliff
precipitation: rainfall rain, mist
precipitous: steep
precis: summary
precise: exact, formal neat, prim, nice
preclude: debar, bar
predetermine: destine
predicament: dilemma, scrape, plight, pickle, fix, scrape [sert, base
predicate: connote, as-
predict: foretell, bode, prophesy [first, star
preeminent: capital,
preen: plume, trim
prefer: favor, choose
prejudiced: partial, bi-ased [ture
prelude: proem, over-
premature develop-ment: precocity
premier: principal
premium: bonus, agio
prepare: arrange, set, ready, prime
" **for action**: alert
" **leather**: taw, tan
" **for publication**: edit
presage: omen, bode, portend
prescribe: define, set
present: boon, gift **here**, attend, proffer, **give**, introduce, donate
" **occasion**: nonce, now
presently: anon
preserve: can, save, maintain, protect, cure, spare [cate
" **by drying**: desic-
press: iron, urge, im-pel, squeeze, crowd, enjoin [press
" **down**: tamp, de-
" **for payment**: dun
" **forward**: drive
" **into dough**: knead
pressure: stress, force, weight, urgency
presto: quickly, speed-ily [pose, impose
presume: venture, sup-
pretend: feign, sham,

simulate [terfuge
pretense: sham, plea, pretext, feint, sub-
pretentious: arty, elab-orate, showy
pretext: pretense, peg, cover, excuse
pretty: comely [win
prevail: triumph, reign,
" **upon**: lead, induce
prevalent: refe, spread, dominant, rife
prevent: stop, pre-clude, avert, deter, block, forestall
previous: anterior, pri-or, former, preceding
previously: erst, before, supra [quarry
prey: victim, booty,
" **upon**: raven
Priam's kingdom: Troy
" **son**: Paris
price: rate, cost, value, charge, outlay, fee
prickly envelope of fruit: bur, burr
" **herb**: teasel
" **pear**: nopal, tuna
" **plant**: thistle, acan-thus, nettle [briar
" **shrub**: rose, gorse,
pride: vanity, conceit, arrogance, vainglory, glory [mure
prim: neat, modest, de-
prima donna: diva
primal: elemental, first, chief
prime: first, chief, fore-most, prepare, choice
" **minister**: premier
primer: reader, text-book [can, pristine
primitive: early, pris-
prince of apostate an-gels: Eblis
" **darkness & evil**: Satan
principal: main, pre-mier, chief, cardinal
" **element**: staple
principle: reason, ideal, tenet, credo, maxim
print: publish, impress, die, stamp
printed defamation: libel
printer's apprentice: devil
" **(colloq.)**: typo [tum
" **error**: errato, erra-
" **mark**: stet [pica
" **measure**: em, en,
" **spacing block**: quad
printing: edition
" **form**: mat, type
" **need**: ink
" **press part**: platen
prior: anterior, before, elder, previous
" **to**: ere
priory: abbey, cloister
priscan: primitive
prison: gaol [tive

prisoner: captor, cap-
pristine: primitive, pri-meval, original
privacy: seclusion [rate
privateer: corsair, pi-
privately: aside
privation: loss
prize: treasure, esteem, value, award
" **in lottery**: tern
pro: for
probabilities: odds
probe: search [nut
problem: poser, task,
proboscis: nose, snout
proceed: go, continue
proceeds: starts, in-come, goes
process of decision: pend
procession: parade
proclaim: herald
proclamation: edict
proclivity: talent
procrastination: delay
procurator of Judea: Pilate [obtain
procure: get, provide,
prod: goad, punch, slog, poke, thrust, nudge
prodigal: lavish, waste-ful, extravagant
prodigious: marvelous
prodigy: marvel
produce: cause, gene-rate, engender, stage, yield, create, crop
produced by a river: fluvial
" **by the wind**: eolian
product: fruit
productive: rich, fer-tile, creative
proem: preface, prelude
profane: desecrate
profess: avow
profession: metier, vo-cation, trade
professional mourner: weeper, wailer [hand
proffer: bid, tender, of-fer, give, present,
proficient: adept, skill-ed, versed
profit: avail, gain, bene-fit, advantage
profound: deep, recon-dite, [ful, opulent
profuse: lavish, bounti-
" **talk**: palaver
progenitor: parent, sire
progeny: seed, breed, strain, issue
progress: gain, advance
" **with difficulty**: wade [bid
prohibit: bar, ban, de-bar, estop, veto, for-
prohibitionist: dry
project: scheme, plan
projecting crane arm: gib
" **member**: tenon
" **nose**: snout
" **part**: nob, apse
" **piece**: fin, shelf

" " **of a cap**: visor
" **point**: peak, jag
" **rim**: flange
" **rock**: crag
" **tooth**: snag
" **window**: dormer
prolong: lengthen, extend, defer, protract
prominence: salience
prominent: eminent, important, star
promise: pledge, vow, swear, word
promising: favonian
promontory: cape, ness
" **(var.)**: nase [vance
promote: abet, foster, serve, further, advance
promoter: agent
prone: apt, prostrate
prong: tine, nib, fork
pronounce: assert, utter, declare
" **holy**: bless

pronto: quickly
pronunciation mark: diacritic, tilde
proofreader: reviser
" **'s mark**: caret, stet
prop: stay, brace, shore, strengthen [row, urge
propel: drive, impel
propeller: driver, fan
proper: decent, meet, prim, fit, right
property: estate, realty, asset, holdings
" **charge**: lien
" **of a matter**: inertia, mass [tell
prophesy: predict, foreprophet**: seer, Amos, oracle, sage, seeress
prophetical: vatical, vatic [pease, conciliate
propitiate: atone, approportion**: ratio, rate
proposal: suggest, intend, offer
proposed act: bill
" **international lang.**: ro, ido, od
propound: premise, pose
propped up: shored
prorogue: adjourn
proscribe: ban
proselyte: convert, ger
prospect: outlook, vista
prosper: thrive, flourish, fare
prosperity: welfare, weal
prosperous times: ups, boom
prostrate: prone
prosy: dull, tedious
protect: shelter, shield, defend, armor, preserve, bless
" **against loss**: insure
protection: armor, egis, defense, aegis, lee
protective covering: armor, raincoat, paint
" **ditch**: moat, foss
" **garment**: apron,

duster, coverall [met
" **head covering**: helmet
" **influence**: aegis
" **railing**: parapet
protector: patron
protest: demur, complaint, dissent
proton: atom
protract: eke, prolong
proturberance: snag, wen, node, nub, lobe, bulge, wart
" **(pert. to)**: lobar
" **of skull**: inion
prove: test [fute
" **false**: betray, conproverb**: adage, saw, maxim
provide: store, purvey, furnish, afford
" **food**: cater, purvey
" **quarters for**: lodge
provided: if
" **that**: so
provident: careful, frugal thrifty, [tois
provincial speech: paprovision**: grist, store, ration [cause, irritate
provoke: nettle, ire,
prow: stem, bow
prowl about: lurk
proximity: nearness, presence [creet, chary
prudent: wise, sage, dis**prune**: trim [Anklam
Prussian city: Essen,
" **river**: Ruhr, Lena
" **seaport**: Emden, Stettin, Kiel
" **town**: Erna, Ems
" **watering place**: Ems
pry: lever, snoop, peep
pseudonym: alias
ptarmigan: ripa
public: universal, overt exoteric, national
" **announcement**: ad
" **announcer**: crier
" **estimation**: repute
" **guardian**: police
" **house**: tavern, inn, hotel
" **life**: career
" **meeting**: forum
" **notice**: edict
" **officer**: notary
" **performer**: artiste
" **recreation ground**: park
" **regard**: repute
" **room**: hall
" **storehouse**: etape
" **vehicle**: cab, bus
" **walk**: promenade, mall [print
publish: edit, issue,
" **without authority**: piratic, pirate
pucker: purse
puddle: pool, plash
Pueblo Indian: Hopi
puerile: childish
Puerto Rican city:

Lares, Ponce
puff: pant, waft [elate
" **up**: bloat, swell,
pugilist: pug, boxer
pule: whimper
pull: tug, tow, draw, lug, yank, hale, haul
" **apart**: tear, rend
" **off**: avulse
pulley wheel: sheave
pulpy fruit: uva, grape
pulsate: beat, throb
pulverize: grind, stamp powder, pestle, fine
pummel: beat
pump handle: swipe
punch: prod, perforate
" **(colloq.)**: pep
puncture: pierce, stab
pungent: bitter, acrid, keen, sharp, racy
punish: chastize, castigate, aveng
" **by fine**: amerce
punishing rod: ferule
" **(law)**: peine
punitive: penal
puny: weak, frail
pupil: student, scholar
puppet: doll, marionette
puppy: whelp
purchasable: venal
pure: chaste, clean, clear, absolute, vestal
purify: refine, cleanse, aerate, clean, filter, lustrate, purge
purple: tyrian, mauve
purplish brown: puce
purport: tenor
purpose: end, aim, design, intend, mission, mean, intention, intent, goal
purposive: telic
purse: wallet, pucker
pursue: bound, ply, con, trace, chase, steer, hunt
pursuit: chase
purvey: supply, provide, cater
push: jostle, shove, urge
" **gently**: nudge
put: see also place
put: deposit, place, set, lay, insert, laid
" **in action**: exert, bestir
" **aside**: fob, table
" **away**: store
" **back**: replace, restore [lade
" **burden on**: strain,
" **in circulation**: publish [case
" **container**: en" **in disordered condition**: litter [press
" **down**: deposit, lay, laid, deposited, de" **on file**: filed [rout
" **to flight**: routed,
" **in forgotten place**: mislaid
" **forth**: exert, issue

" " **effort**: strive
" **on guard**: warn
" **in**: insert, inserted
" **off**: postpone, defer
" **in order**: regulate, arrange, file [evict
" **out**: expel, oust,
" **to shame**: abash
" " **a strain**: tax
" **together**: frame, add
" **in type**: print, set
" **up**: can, post, erect
" " **with**: add, tolerated, tolerate [ply
" **to use**: applied, ap" **with**: add, tolerate
puzzle (kind): acrostic, riddle, enigma, rebus, charade
pygmy: dwarf
pylon: tower
pyramid builder: Cheops [dorra
Pyrenees republic: An**Pythias's friend**: Damon

Q

quack: charlatan
" **medicine**: nostrum
quadruped: horse, deer, sheep, goat, beast
quagmire: bog, fen, lair
quail: cower, colin
quake: tremble, tremor
Quaker: friend
quaking: aspen
qualified: fit, able, apt
qualify: temper, entitle
quality of sound: tone
quantity: amount
" **of matter**: mass
" **of medicine**: dosage [hank
" **of yarn**: skein,
quarrel: affray, row, tiff, feud, spat, fracas
quarry: game, prey
quartz (kind of): prase ogate, flint, onyx
quaver: trill, shake
quay: levee, wharf
queen of beasts: Lioness [Titania, Una
" " **Fairies**: Mab,
" " **Gods**: Hera
queer: erratic, odd, singular, peculiar
quell: repress, allay, suppress
quench: slake
queue: pigtail [apace
quick: fast, rapid, active, speedy, sudden,
" **blow**: rap
" **to learn**: apt
" **movement**: dart
quicken: animate, urge, enliven [pronto
quickly: apace, presto,
quickness: haste

quid of tobacco: cud
quiescent: dormant, latent, static
quiet: still, serene, silence, static, allay, inert, silent, lull, stilly, soothe, peace
quill: pen, cop
quip: gibe
quirk: twist
quit: retire, cease, leave, vacate, stop [pletely
quite: entirely, all, com-
quiver: tremble, tremor
quivering: aspen
quoit: discus
quota: share
quote: cite, allege

R

Ra's wife: Mut [dent
rabbit: hare, cony, ro-
" (female): doe
" fur: lapin
" home: hutch
" tail: scut
rabble: raff, mob
rabid: mad, furious
raccoon: coon, coati
" like carnivore: panda
race: speed, contest, lineage, hasten, subspecies, people, run
" of animals: breed
" horse: trotter, arabian, mantis, plater
" (kind): relay [dash
" (short): sprint,
" track tipster: tout
Rachael's father: Laban
racing boat: shell
racket: noise
radiant: beaming, glowing [glow
radiate: shine, emit,
radical: red, organic, surd, extreme
radicel: rootlet
radio: wireless
" chain: network
" wire: aerial
radium emanation: niton, radon
radix: root
raft: float
rafter: beam [nant
rag: tatter, shred, rem-
rage: storm, rant, furor, ire, fury, wrath fume, violence, frenzy
ragout of lamb: haricot
raid: forage, maraud, foray, invade, incursion, attack
rail: fence, scold, heron, bar, scoff, sora, revile, scoff, berate, rant
railbird: crake, sora
railing: parapet
raillery: banter
railroad tie: sleeper
raiment: dress, attire
rain: shower

" cloud: nimbus
rainbow: iris
rainspout (Scot.): rone
rainstorm: downpour
rainy: wet [heft
raise: elevate, lift, exalt, rear, breed, hoist, emboss, boost, erect, grow, uplift, increase
" a nap: teasel, teasle
" spirits of: elate
" to third power: cube
raised lawns: terrace
" strip: ridge
" stripe: welt, rib
Rajah's wife: ranee, rani
rake: roue [batter
ram: butt, stuff, aries, tup, strike, tamp,
" down: tamp
" (the): Aries [roam
ramble: meander, gad, rove, range, stroll,
rampart: wall, redan, parapet bulwark
rancid: rank
rancor: enmity, spite,
range: scope, stove, sweep, ramble, rank, adjust, roam, area, gamut, extent
" of hills: ridge
" " knowledge: ken
rank: degree, caste, grade, rate, tier, row, foul, estimate, class, extreme, range, rancid, status, flagrant
rankle: inflame, fester
ransack: rake, pillage
ransom: redeem [bast
rant: rage, rail, bom-
rapier: sword
rapid: fleet, quick, fast, swift, speedy
rapine: pillage, plunder
rapt: absorbed, intent
rapture: bliss, ecstasy
rare: unique, odd, scarce, infrequent, unusual, tenuous
rascal: scamp, knave, rogue, scoundrel
rash: hasty, headstrong
rasp: grate, scrape, file, affect, abrade
rasping: harsh
rasse: civet [percent
rate: pace, value, grade, calculate, scold, degree, regard, price, charge, merit, cost
" of movement: pace, tempo
rather (Scot.): gey
" than: ere [dorse
ratify: seal, confirm, en-
ration: allowance, allot, share, apportion
rational: sane, sensible
rattan: reed, sega, cane
rattle: clatter, noise
raucous: hoarse, harsh

ravage: ruin [bast
rave: rant, fume, bom-
ravel: unknit, entangle
ravine: dell, gulch, dale, gorge, canyon
raw: crude, bleak,
ray: shine, beam
raze: obliterate, destroy, cut, demolish
razor billed auk: murre
" sharpener: strop
reach: attain, arrive, extend, aspire, span, come [minate
" highest point: cul-
react: respond, behave
read: peruse, pore
" metrically: scan
reading: perusal
ready: alert, prepared, willing, fit, ripe, apt
real: true, concrete, actual, factual, genuine [realty
" estate: property,
" " absolutely owned: alod
" " contract: lease
realize: sense, accomplish, conceive, perceive, see [empire
realm: domain, nation,
reap: gather, garner
rear: hind, posterior, elevate, behind, raise, erect, construct, back
" (in the): astern
" of vessel: aft
reason: cause, motive
reasoning: logic
rebel: rise, insurgent
rebellion: revolt
rebound: dap, carom
rebuff: slap, repell, snub, scorn, repulse
rebuke: snub, reprimand, chide

rebut: disprove, refute
recall: remember, retract, remind [revoke
recant: retract, abjure,
recede: ebb
receipt: recipe, stub
receive: get, accept, take [dern, fresh
recent: new, late, mo-
receptacle: bin, receiver, tray, box, tank
reception: tea
" room: parlor, salon
recess: niche, nook
" in seashore: bay, inlet
recipe: receipt
recipient: receiver, legatee [donee
" of gift: presentee,
reciprocal: mutual
recite: relate, narrate, report
" metrically: scan
" in musical monotone: intone, chant
reckless: rash, bold, mad, desperate
reckon: rate, date,

tally, compute, calculate [deem, rescue
reclaim: recover, re-
recline: repose, lie, loll, rest [mite
recluse: hermit, ere-
recoil: shrink, shy
recollect: recall
recollection: mind
recommence: resume
recommit: remand
recompense: pay, reward, meed, renew, fee [sign
reconcile: atone, re-
recondite: abstract, abstruse [scout
reconnoiter: pickeer,
record: annal, log, enter, enroll, pen
" book: ledger
" of proceedings: acta, actum
recount: tell, relate
recourse: resort
recover: restore, regain, reclaim, rally, retrieve, flow
recreation: play, sport
" area: park
rectangular: oblong
" inserts: panels
rectify: correct, amend, emend
rectory: parsonage
red: ruddy, vermilion, roset, crimson, rosy, carmen, flushed, roseate, scarlet, cerise
" cedar: savin
" dye: alta
" pepper: cayenne
" planet: Mars
" purple: claret
redact: edit
redcap: porter [flush
redden: blush, ruddle,
reddish: roseate
" brown: auburn, bay, henna, sepia, sorrel, chestnut
" color: peony, coral
" orange dye: henna
" yellow: orange, amber, totem, titian
redeem: reclaim, ransom [liverer
redeemer: savior, de-
redolent: fragrant, odorous [pare
reduce: lessen, abate, bate, lower, debase,
" to ashes: cremate
" in density: thin
" to fine state: refine
" " fluid state: liquefy [age
" " a means: aver-
" " a pulp: mash, crush
" in rank: demote
" " size: shrink
" to soft mass: macerate [ize
" " a spray: atom-
reducing medium: diet

reef: shoal, lode
reek: smoke, fume
reel: spin, stagger, spool, waver, sway, falter, bobbin, troll
refer: appeal, allude, ascribe, relegate, direct, cite, mention
referee: umpire, judge
reference: allusion
" table: index
refine: pure, nice, neat
refinement: polish, culture, elegance
reflect: mirror, ponder, ruminate
reflux of the tide: ebb
reform: amend, regenerate, correct
Reformation leader: Lutheran
refractory: unruly
refrain: chorus, abstain, forgo, ditty
refrigerate: ice, freeze
refuge: haven, retreat
refulgent: brilliant
refund: repay, rebate
refuse: deny, veto, marc, scum, reject, decline, waste, trash
" approval: veto
refute: deny, disprove, rebut
regain: recover, restore
regal: imperial, royal, kingly, stately
regale: treat, entertain
regard: observe, consider, eye, estimation, hear, care, rate
" favorably: approve
" highly: admire, esteem, honor, deem
" reverently: adore
" studiously: con
" with honor: venerate, respect
[form
regenerate: renew, reregent: ruler
region: clime, zone, tract, area, district-realm, territory, locality, terrain
" beyond Jordan: Perea, Enon [bus
" of darkness: Ere-
" in general: demesne [areal
regional: local, zonal,
register: enlist, slate, tally, roll, list, enter
regret: rue, repent, resent, mourn, lament, deplore, spurn
regretful: sorry
regular: stated, normal, canonic, periodic
regulate: settle, manage, order, adjust, govern, direct
regulation: rule, law
reign: rule, prevail,

govern
reigning beauty: belle
reimbue with courage: reman
reimburse: pay, repay
rein: restrain, line, curb, check
reindeer: caribou
reject: repel, deny, spurn, refuse
rejoinder: answer, repartee, retort, response
relate: recite, tell, pertain, appertain, narrate, recount, detail
related: kin, akin
" by blood: akin, sib
" on father's side: agnate
" by marriage: inlaw
" on mother's side: enate, enatic, enation
relative: pertinent, kin, kinsman, relation
relax: ease, loosen, unbend, slacken, remit
relaxation: rest
release: loose, free, deliver, relet, undo, unbind, loosen, liberate
" on honor: parole
relent: yield, soften
relevant: pertinent, germane [confidence
reliance: trust, hope,
relict: widow
relieve: lessen, ease, allay, mitigate, aid, spell, vent
religious awakening: revival
" belief: creed
" ceremony: mass
" class: sect
" composition: motet, anthem [ish
" congregation: par-
" discipline: penance
" faith: religion [rim
" festival: Easter, Pu-
" hermit: monk
" holiday: fiesta
" image: icons, ikon
" observance: rite
" pamphlet: tract
" poem: psalm
" song: chant, psalm
" talk: cant
" woman: nun
relinquish: cede, go, waive, resign, abdicate, leave
reliquary: arca, apsis
relish: flavor, zest, canape, savor, taste, olive, gusto, like
reluctant: averse, loath
rely: depend, trust, rest
remain: stay, abide, tarry, continue [rest
remainder: balance, recall, relic, monitor,
remaining: remanent, other, residual, left
remark: say, note, comment, observe, word

remedy: cure, repair
remind oneself: bethink, recall
remiss: negligent, laggard, lax
remit: send, forgive, absolve, forego, relax
remnant: rag, ort, dreg
" of fire: ash
remonstrate: protest
remote: far, distant, old, secluded
remove: elide, eliminate, dele, delete, rid, oust, peel, eradicate, doff, pare, convey
" afar off: eloin, eloign
" air: deflate
" beyond jurisdiction (law): eloin
" a cargo: unload
" cream: skim
" error: correct
" from high position: depose, unseat
" hair: epilate
" impurities: refine
" by light rubbing: wipe [rate, dry
" moisture: evapo-
" pits from: stone
" in printing: dele
" utterly: raze
remunerate: compensate, pay [break
rend: split, rive, tear, cleave, rupture, rip,
render: translate, contribute, transmit, deliver, give, bestow, sunder, make furnish
" accesible: open
" active: activate
" asunder: split, rive
" desolate: destroy
" enduring: anneal
" fat: lard [enervate
" ineffective: negate,
" muddy: roil
" senseless: stun
" suitable: adapt
" turbid: roil
" unconscious: stun
" useless: null
rendezvous: tryst
renegade: deserter, apostate, traitor
renege: revoke, deny, renounce
renew: restore, resale, resume, regenerate, renovate, revive
" wine: stum
renounce: repudiate, disown, deny, abjure, renege, waive
renovate: repair, restore, alter, cleanse, renew, clean, furnish
renown: glory, honor, fame [schism
rent: lease, hire, riven, let, breach, break,
renter: lessee, tenant
repair: mend, renovate, fix, redress, resort,

remedy [atonement
reparation: amends, redress, amend, atone,
" for injury: damages [retort
repartee: riposte, reply,
repast: meal, feast, reflection, dinner, lunch
repay: refund, requite
repeal: abrogate, annul, rescind, revoke, abolish [echo
repeat: iterate, parrot,
" mechanically: parrot [tatat
repeated knocking: ra-
repel: repulse, ward, reject, oppose
repent: atone, rue
repentant: penitent, contrite
repetition: encore, echo, rote, reiterate, iteration, iterance
repine: complain, fret
replaced: reset, restored
replenish: refill, fill
replete: rife, full
replica: copy, duplicate, facsimile [answer
reply: retort, respond,
report: rumor, recite, account [rest, peace
repose: compose, ease,
repository: safe, vault
representative: agent, delegate, legate
" example: type
repress: restrain, bridle
reprimand: admonish, rebuke, slate, lesson
" (Scot.): ston
reproach: blame, slur, upbraid, taunt
" abusively: revile
reprove: rebuke, censure, flay [asp
reptile: snake, turtle,
repudiate: renounce, disown, disclaim, recant, deny
repulse: repel, rejection, rebuff [prestige
reputation: repute, credit, stamp, honor
request: ask, entreaty, solicit, entreat, appeal [tition
request formally: peti-
" for payment: dun
require: need, demand claim
requisition: order
requite: repay, revenge, avenge, retaliate, reward [gate
rescind: repeal, retract, revoke, cancel, abro-
rescue: save, deliver, succor, free, reclaim
reserve: spare, reticence, retain
reserved: taken, aloof, offish, coy, shy, cold
" in speech: reticent [live
reside: abide, dwell,

resident: citizen, inherent, dweller, occupant [maining
residual: remanent, residue: ash, rest
resign: demit, relinquish, reconcile,
resilient: elastic
resin: lac, anime, copal, elemin
" (fragrant): aloe, elemi, nard
resist: rebel, oppose, repel, withstand
resistance to attack: defense [nitent
resisting pressure: re-
resolute: determined, manly [mine, rotate
resolve: decide, determine
resonant: ringing
resort: spa, haunt, recourse, repair
resound: ring, peal, echo, reverberate, clang, toll [sets
resources: means, as-
respect: esteem, awe, reverence, homage, deference, honor
respectable: decent
respiratory organ: lung
" sound: rale
respire: breathe
respite: rest, reprieve, pause, truce, interval, lull [golden
resplendent: aureate,
respond: react, answer, peal, reply
response: answer, reaction, rejoinder
rest: pause, repose, lean, sit, respite, ease, lair, desist, recline, rely, support
restless: uneasy, tossing, restive
restore: renew, replace, renovate, reinstate, return, revive
" to normal position: right
restrain: dam, stint, moderate, curb, bate, chain, check, repress, tether, bridle, cramp, bind, deter, confine, arrest, rule, rein
" thru fear: deter
restrict: limit, hem, resew, dam, stint
result: eventuate, outcome, ensue, follow, upshot, effect
" of an inquiry: findings [continue
resume: renew, reopen,
resuscitate: revive
ret: soak, steep
retain: save, hold, keep, engage, reserve
retaliate: avenge, requite, repay
retaliation: reprisal, revenge [hinder
retard: delay, slow,

reticence: reserve
reticent: secretive
reticule: handbag
retinue: suite, train
" of wives: harem
retire: retreat, quit, leave, resign, withdraw
retired: inactive, abed
" from the world: recluse [tus
" with honor: emeri-
retiring: shy
retract: recant, disavow, recall [nest
retreat: recess, retire, withdraw, refuge
retribution: revenge, avenge, nemesis, pay
retrieve: recover [recur
return: restore, revert,
" evil for evil: retaliate
" to office: reelect
" thrust: riposte
reveal: bare, disclose, show, unveil, expose
revel: feast, spree, delight, riot
revelry: riot, joy
revenge: requite, retaliate avenge,
revenue: income
reverberate: resound, echo, roll, ring
revere: adore, venerate, admire [honor
reverence: awe, revere,
reverie: dream, daydream
revert: reverse, recur, return
review: survey, consider, revise, parade, critique [scoff, vilify
revile: malign, abuse,
revise: amend, proofread, edit, review, change, emend
revive: freshen, resuscitate, rally, reanimate, renew [scind
revoke: repeal, cancel, renig, adeem, renege, reverse, recant, re-
" a legacy: adeem
revolt: rebel, mutiny, rise, rebellion, uprising
revolution: rotation
" hero: Hale, Revere, Allen
" traitor: Arnold
revolve: rotate, gyrate, spin, roll, turn, whirl,
revolving arrow: vire
" part: rotor [guerdon
reward: mend, prize, meed, medal, requite,
rhea: emu
rhetorical: oratorical
" device: aporia
Rhine affluent: Ruhr
rhythm: cadence, meter, tempo [rical
rhythmic: cadent, met-

" beat: pulse
" silence: rest
" swing: lilt
ria: inlet [gay blithe
riant: bright, smiling,
rib: vein, vertebra, purl
ribald: coarse
ribbed fabric: rep, twill, dimity [sette
ribbon decoration: ro-
rice in the husk: paddy
" liquor: sake
" paste: ame
rich: affluent, opulent
" man: nabob
" source: mine [om
richochet: glance, car-
rid: clear, free [bus
riddle: enigma, sift, re-
" in cloth: rib
" (colloq.): welt
" 's of drift: osar, eskar, esker
" of earth: rideau
" of rock: reed, reef
ridicule: deride, satire, satirize, lampoon, snort, banter, roast, scout, twit
" (Colloq.): roast, pan
ridiculous failure: fiasco [nege
riding academy: ma-
" whip: quirt, crop
rife: replete, current, abounding, widespread
rifle: garand, gun, pillage, ransack, mauser
rift: fissure, cleft, break
rig: attire, gear
Riga Island gulf: Oesel
right: proper, just, correct
" away: pronto
" hand page: recto
" " (Pert. to): dexter [ure
" to hold office: ten-
" of suffrage: vote
" of using another's property: easement
rigid: set, tense, stark, severe, stiff, strict
rigor: asperity
rigorous: severe, drastic, spartan, strait, inclement, stern
rile: vex, annoy, irritate
rill: streamlet, rillet
rim: border, edge, brink, edging
rima: fissure
rimple: fold, wrinkle
rind: peel, skin
ring: peal, circle, toll, knell, arena, hoop, encircle, ringlet [rona
" around moon: co-
" of chain: link
" to hold reins: terret
" shaped: annular
ringed boa: aboma
ringlet: trees, curl
ringworm: tinea [revel
riot: uproar, brawl, unsew, revelry, orgy,
rip: tear, rend [ready

ripe: mellow, mature,
riposte: repartee
ripple: wavelet
" against: lap [climb
rise: elevate, levitate, mount, soar, lift, ascent, rebel, revolt,
" & fall of sea: tide
" high: tower
" threateningly: loom
risible: funny
risk: dare, venture, hazard, stake, danger, chance, peril
rite: ceremony
rival: foe, emulate, competitor, emulator, competing [rent
rive: rend, cleave, split,
river: stream, run
" bank: ripa
" " (pert. to): riparian, riverain
" bed: wady, wadi
" boat: barge, ark
" bottom: bed
" dam: weir
" deposit: silt
" descent: rapids
" duck: teal
" embankment: dam
" of forgetfulness: Lethe
" god's daughter: Io
" of ice: glacier
" island: ait
" lowland: flat
" mouth: delta
" mussel: unio
" nymph: naiad, nais
" shore: bank
" tract: flat
" of underworld: Styx
rivet: bolt, fasten
rivulet: rill, streamlet, creek
road: course, way
roam: range
" about idly: gad
roar: bellow, scream, yell, boom, din, howl
" of surf: rote
roasting iron & stick: spit [burgle
rob: steal, loot, plunder, defraud, pilfer,
robbed: reft
robbery on high seas: piracy [ray, talar
robe: mantle, attire, ar-
Robinson Crusoe's author: Defoe
robust: strong, hardy, vigorous hale, rugged
rock: vibrate, totter, stone, ore, shake
" (kind): slate, spar, agate, stone, trap, besalt, prase, shale, gneiss, basalt
" (sharp): crag
rockfish: rena, reina
Rocky Mt. Park: Estes
" " Range: Teton
" pinnacle: tor

rod: staff, pole, wand, twig, ferule, baton, spindle, axle
" used in basketry: osier [bit, gnawer
rodent: paca, hare, marmot, mouse, rab-
rodeo: roundup
rogue: beggar, knave, rascal, scamp, pica-roon, scoundrel
roguish: sly, arch
roil: muddy [ter
roister: swagger, blus-
role: part
roll: rota, list, bun, re-volve, register, roster
" of cloth: bolt
" (dial): whelve
" " parchment: pell
" " thread: cop
" up: furl
romaine lettuce: cos
Roman: Latin
" bascilica: lateran
" boxing glove: ces-tus
" bronze: aes
" chariot: essed
" church cathedral: Lateran
" clan: gens
" coin: as, ae
" cuirass: lorica
" date: nones. ides
" emperor (old): Caesar, Otho, Nero, Otto
" fate: nona
" garment: stola, tu-nic, stolae, toga
" god: di, lare
" of under-world: Dis, Pluto
" goddess: Luna, Lua
" " of horses: Epona [Ceres
" " " vegetation:
" greeting: ave
" highway: iter
" hill: Viminal, Pala-tine [Livy
" historian: Nepos,
" house god: Lar, Lare, Penate
" magistrate: pretor, edile, tribune
" meal: cena
" monetary unit: ley
" money: aes
" naturalist: Pliny
" official: prefect, edile, tribune
" orator: Pliny
" palace: lateran
" patriot: Cato [eca
" philosopher: Sen-
" poet: Ovid, Horace
" priest: flamen
" room: atria (pl.)
" sock (ancient): udo
" statesman: Cato
" tribune: rienzi
" tyrant: Nero
" weight: as
" writer: Terence
romance: novel, dream

romp: frolic, gambol
romping girl: tomboy
rood: cross, crucifix
roof: slate, summit
" edge: eave [tile
" material: tile, pan-
" of mouth: palate
rook: chessman
" cry: caw
room: space, lodge, chamber, aula
" for pitchers & linens: ewery
" (small): cell
roost: set, sit, perch
root: radix, bottom, ori-gin, basis, source
" of certain plant: bulb [tirpate, stub
" out: eradicate, ex-
" word: etymon
rootlet: radicel [cable
rope: hawser, riata,
" fiber: sisal
" for hoisting a ships yard: tye
" to moor a boat: painter
rose (dial.): ris
" essence: attar
" fruit: hip
" red dye: eosin, eosine [rosette
" shaped ornament:
roseate: rosy, reddish
roster: list, rota, roll
rosy: blushing, roseate, red, blooming, pink
rot: decay, rubbish
rota: roll, list
rotary motor: turbine
rotate: turn, spin, re-volve, resolve, alter-nate, swirl [cam
rotating part: rotor,
" pin: spindle
roue: rake [aspirate
rough breathing: asper,
" house: shack [pid
" with bristles: his-
roughen: shag, nurl
roulade: run
roulette bet: bas
round: circular, orbed, spherical
" about way: detour
" & hollow: concave
" muscle: teres [nob
" projection: lob,
" room: rotunda
rounded appendage: lobe
" hill: knoll, knob
" molding: ovolo
roundup: rodeo
rouse: stir, bestir, waken, spur, awaken
" to vigilance: alarm
rout: defeat
route: way, course, line, trail, path [stroll
rove: prowl, wander,
" about: gad, range
rover: pirate, nomad
roving: errant, er-rantry, migrant

row: tier, line, oar, layer, spat, quarrel, brawl, rank, argument
rowan tree: sorb
rowboat: gig, caique
rower: oarsman, oar
royal: regal
rub: abrade, scrape, polish, chafe, scour
" gently: stroke, wipe
" hard: scrub
" out: erase, expunge
" with rough file: rasp [gum
rubber: para, eraser,
" jar ring: lute
" tree: ule
rubbish: trash, refuse, debris, rot
" (mining): attle
rude: borish, uncivil uncouth, impolite
" house: shack, hut, cabin, shed
" person: boor, cad
rue: regret, repent, herb
ruffian: desperado, thug
ruffle: roil, frill, dis-turb [ner
rug (small): mat, run-
ruga: wrinkle, crease
rugged: robust
" crest: tor
" rock: crag
ruin: wreck, undoing, impair, bankrupt, doom, destroy, deva-state, ravage, rase, demolish, undo, bane
rule: preside, reign, re-strain, dominate, for-mula, law, govern, regime, line
ruler: dynast, gerent, regent, monarch, ferule, oligarch, em-peror, sovereign
" in place of a king: viceroy
Rumanian coin: leu, ley
rumen: cud
ruminant: sheep, camel, goat, llama [tripe
" stomach: rumen,
ruminate: ponder, muse, meditate, reflect
rumor: report, gossip hearsay
" personified: fama
rumple: tousle, muss
run: flow, race, operate, extend, speed, sprint, conduct, brook
" after: chase [sand
" aground: strand,
" away: decamp
" between ports: ply
" (dial.): rin
" down: decry
" easily: lope, trot
" off: elope, bolt
" (colloq.): peter
" over: spill
" rapidly: scud
" (Scot.): rin
" slowly: trickle
" on wheels: roll

runagate: fugitive
rung of ladder: ratline, spoke fugitive
runner: miler, speeder, operator, racer, ski,
rural: pastoral, arca-dian, rustic, bucolic
" deity: faun
" poem: georgic
" residence: villa
ruse: trick, artifice
rush: hurry, cattail, charge, speed, surge
" headlong: bolt
" suddenly: hurtle sally, tear
rusk: bun, biscuit [Red
Russian: Slav, Soviet,
" antelope: saiga
" bay: Luga [sack
" cavalryman: cos-
" city: Tula, Grosny, Orel, Dno, Minsk, Osa, Samara, Ufa
" coin: kopeck, ko-pek, altin, rupee
" " (old): altin
" composer: Cui
" council: Duma, So-viet
" czar: Ivan
" emperor: Nicholas
" empress's title: Tsarina
" gulf: Ob
" hemp: rive, rine
" leader: Lenin
" measure: verst
" monarch: tsar
" money: ruble
" mountain: Ural
" name: Igor, Ivan
" news agency: Tass
" novelist: Gorki
" peninsula: Kola
" plain: steppe
" river: Ural, Neva, Don, Lena, Ros, Ob, Ner, Amur, Duna, Kara, Irtish, Volga, Ik, Ilet, Ai
" ruler: Ivan, Tsar
" sea & lake: Aral, Azof, Azov [ape
" stockade: etah, et-
" storehouse: etape
" sturgeon: sterlet
" tea urn: samovar
" town: Elista
" trade commune: artel
" union: artel
" village: Mir
" wagon: telega
rustic: rural, yokel, peasant, pastoral, bu-colic, sylvan, boor
" (colloq.): hodge
" dance: hay
" gallant: swain
" workman: peasant
rut: groove, ditch,
Ruth's husband: Boaz
" mother in law: Naomi

rye disease: ergot
" **drink:** gin

S

S shaped curve: ess
" " **molding:** ogee
sable: black
sacshaped: saccate
saccharine: sweet,
sugary [pillage
sack: loot, pouch, bag,
sacrament: rete, rite
sacred: holy, hallowed
" **beetle:** scarab
" **bull:** apis [dina
" **city of Islam:** Me-
" **image:** icon, idol
" " **(var.):** ikon
" **musical composition:** motet
" **picture:** icon, ikon
" **poem:** hymn,
psalm [choral
" **tune:** chorale,
" **vessel:** ark
" **work:** om
" **writing:** scripture
sad: plaintive, mournful, doleful, gloomy, downcast, dejected, despondent, woeful
saddle loop: stirrup
" **pad:** panel
sadness: sorrow
safe: secure
" **keeping:** storage
sag: droop, sink [end
saga: tale, myth, leg-
sagacious: wise, discerning
sagacity: acumen
sage: wise, seer, sapient, prophet, prudent, solon
said to be: reputed
sail: navigate, voyage, cruise, jib, lateen
" **upward:** soar [Rae
" **yard (Scot.):** Ra,
sailing race: regatta
" **vessel:** sloop, saic, ketch, yawl
sailor: tar, salt, mariner, gob, seaman
" **'s outfit:** kit [holy
saintly: pious, angelical,
salad plant: cress, endive [triton
salamander: newt, eft,
salary: wages, stipend, earnings, emolument
sale: auction, bargain
saline: salty
" **solution:** brine
sally: sortie, start
" **forth:** issue
salt: sal, season, marinate, alum [tate
" **of acetic acid:** ace-
" " **anisic acid:**
anisate [rate
" " **boric acid:** bo-
" **marsh:** salina
" **of nitric acid:** ni-

trate, nitrite [ate
" " **oleic acid:** ole-
" **solution:** brine
" **water:** brine
salted (Phil. Isl.): alat
saltpeter: niter, nitre
salty: saline, briny
salutation: ave, bow, greeting, hello
salute: greet, hail [ate
salve: ointment, pallisalver:** tray
Sambar deer: maha
same: similar, identical, equal, ditto, alike, one
" **(of) kind:** akin
" **(Lat. abbr.):** id
sameness: monotony
Samoan bird: iao
" **city:** Apia
" **mollusk:** asi
" **mudworm:** ipo
" **seaport:** Apia
" **warrior:** toa [men
sample: taste, speci-
" **of fabric:** swatch
Samuel's mentor: Eli
sanctify: bless [sent
sanction: approve, approval, fiat, abet, ratify, endorse, as-
sanctuary: fane, bema
sanctum: den [el
sand: grit, beach, grav-
" **bank:** shoal
" **bird:** snipe
" **clay mixture:** loam
" **hill:** dune, dene
" **ridge:** dune, reef
" **on sea bottom:**
paar
sandal: slipper [adar
sandarac tree: arar,
" **wood:** alerce
sandpaper: stib
sandpiper: ree, stint, reeve, ruff
sandy: arenose [sound
sane: lucid, rational,
sap: vitality, enervate, weaken, exhaust
sapidity: savor, taste
sarcasm: irony [dant
sarcastic: satiric, ironic, sardonic, biting, mor-
sash: scarf, belt, girdle
sartor: tailor [lucifer
satan: devil, tempter,
satchel: handbag, bag, valise [surfeit
sate: glut, satiate, fill,
sated with pleasure:
blasé
satellite: moon
" **of the sun:** planet
" " **Uranus:** Ariel
satire: lampoon, irony
satisfy: sate, suit, satiate, content, serve
saturate: soak, imbue, steep, drench, souse
satyr: faun
sauce: gravy, pertness
saucy: malapert, pert, insolent, brash
" **girl:** minx
saunter: stroll, loiter

savage: feral, fierce
savant: scientist, sage
save: rescue, but, spare, except, hoard, preserve, conserve
savior: redeemer
savor: sapidity, relish, smack, taste
savory: sapid, tasty
" **meat jelly:** aspic
sawlike edge: serrate
" **part:** serra
saxifrage: seseli
Saxon: English [voice
say: utter, aver, state,
" **further:** add
saying: adage
scabbard: sheath
scalawag: scamp [flake
scale: climb, gamut,
" **(comb. form):** lepis
scalloped: crenate
scaly: laminar
scamp: rascal, scalawag, rogue
scan: study
Scand.: Dane, Norse, Finn, Swede, Lapp
" **division:** amt
" **giant:** Troll
" **goddess:** Hel
" **lang.:** Norse
" **literary work:** edda
" **measure:** alen
" **mongoloid:** Lapp
" **myth:** saga
" **mythical monarch:**
Atli
" **navigator:** Eric
" **(pert. to):** Norse, Nordic
" **poet:** Scald [spare
scanty: meager, sparse, scarce, bare, poor,
scar: blemish
scarce: sparse, rare, scanty, deficient
scarcely: hardly
scarcity: dearth, famine, want [alarm
scare: frighten, startle,
scarf: ascot, necktie, sash, tippet, tie
" **of feathers:** boa
scarflike vestment:
orale
scarlet: red
scathe: damage
scatter: dispel, radiate, sow, disperse, strew, spread, disseminate, disband, bestrew, dot
" **carelessly:** litter
scene: view, vista, outlook, episode, landscape [stage
" **of action:** arena,
scenic view: scape
" **word enigma:** charade [aroma, smell
scent: perfume, nose,
" **bag:** sachet
" **of cooking:** nidor
scepter: wand, mace
scheme: plot, plan,

conspire, project
schism: rent, division
scholar: student, pupil, pedant, savant
scholarly: learned
school: train, tutor
" **of seals:** pod [inar
" **session:** term, sem-
" **of whales:** gam
schoolmaster: pedant, pedagogue
science: art
" " **government**
politics
" " **life:** biology
" " **plants:** botany
" " **reasoning:**
logic [spark, sparkle
scintillate: twinkle,
scion: bud, sprout, heir, descendant, son
scoff: sneer, scorn, rail, deride, mock, fleer, revile, jeer
scold: berate, rate, nag, rant, chide, rail, objurate
sconce: shelter
scoop: shovel [gin
scope: range, extent, latitude, area, mar-
scorch: blister, char, singe, sear, toast
score: tally, groove, twenty, scratch, goal
scoria: slag
scorn: scoff, spurn, disdain, rebuff, mock, deride, derision, contemn [donian
Scot: Gael, tax, Cale-
Scotch author: Milne
" **cake:** scone
" **child:** bairn [Perth
" **city & town:** Ayr,
" **dairymaid:** dey
" **dance:** reel
" **explorer:** Rae
" **girl:** lassie
" **highlander:** Gael
" " **lang.:** erse
" **hillside:** brae
" **island:** Iona
" **jurist:** Erskine
" **king:** Robert
" **landowner:** laird
" **mountain:** Nevis
" **music instrument:**
bagpipe
" **musician:** piper
" **negative:** nae
" **petticoat:** kilt
" **plaid:** tartan
" **poet:** Burns, Hogg
" **river:** Dee, Tay, Afton, Clyde, Devon
" **weighing machine:**
trone [Scot
Scotchman: Bluecap,
scoundrel: knave, cad, varlet, rogue, rascal
scour: scrub, rub
scourge: bane
scowl: frown, glower
scrap: bit, shred, fragment, fight, ort

scrape: grate, rasp
" off: abrade
" together: rake
" with something
    sharp: scratch, paw
scraped linen: lint
scratch: scrape, claw,
    rist, score
screed: tirade   [cover
screen: sift, shade, hide,
screw: distort, twist
scribe: write, writer
scrimp: stint   [son
scripture reading: les-
scrub: mop, scour
scruff: nape
scrutinize: scan, examine,
    eye, peruse, pry
scuffle: tussle
scull: oar, shoal
scum: dross, silt, refuse
scurrilous: abusive
scurry: run, scamper
scuttle: hod
scythe handle: snead,
    snath, snathe
sea: wave, ocean, main
" anemones: polyps
" animal: coral, orc
" bird: petrel, erne,
    tern, gull, solan, auk,
    ern, gannet
" cow: manatee
" cucumber: trepang
" demigod: triton
" duck: eider, coot
" eagle: erne, tern
" ear: abalone
" god: Ler, Neptune
" gull: cob, mew
" kale beet: chard
" mile: naut, knot
" nymph: nereid, naiad,
    siren   [naval
" (pert. to): marine,
" robbery: piracy
" shell: conch [ton
" swallow: tern, tri-
seal: stamp, cere, signet,
    ratify, confirm,
    sigil, pledge, cachet
seam: suture, stratum,
    juncture
" of ore: vein
seaman: sailor, mariner
sear: blast, scorch,
    burn, parch
search: ransack, hunt,
    seek, grope, ferret,
    inquiry, quest, probe
" for food: forage
seashore: coast
season: tide, weather,
    winter, inure, mature,
    autumn
" for use: age
seasoned: ripe   [spice
seasoning: spice, all-
" herb: sage, thyme,
    basil, parsley
seat: install, perch,
    chair, bench, settee
seaweed: alga, ore,
    laver, kelp, algae (pl)
" ashes: varec, kelp
" derivative: agar
secluded: private, re-

mote, lonely
seclusion: privacy
second: abet
" childhood: dotage
" growth crop: rowen
secondary: bye
" school: prep
secondhand: used
secret: private, hidden,
    covert, concealed
" agent: spy
" procedure: stealth
" writing: code
secretary: desk
secreting organ: gland
secretive: reticent
sect: cult, faction, party
section: division, part,
    piece, partition, area
secular: laic, layman
secure: safe, obtain,
    get, acquire, fast,
    nail, firm, fasten
security: pawn, guaranty,
    bond, tie, bail,
    warranty
" for payment: lien
sedate: staid, sober,
    settled, tranquil, matronly
       [lees
sediment: silt, dreg,
seductive woman:
    siren, vampire
sedulous: diligent
see: lo, behold, witness,
    notice, descry [corn
seed: germ, ovule, pip,
    plant, progeny, spore,
    source, sow, seedlet,
" of cereal: kernel
" coat (hard): testa
" container: pod, bur,
    loment
" covering: aril, testae,
    testa, pod
" of flowerless plant:
    spore
" integument: testa
" of leguminous
    plants: pulse
" " opium poppy:
    maw
" plant: herb [meg
" used as spice: nutmeg
" vessel: pod, legume
seedlike fruit: bean
seek: crave, search,
    aspire, hunt, court
" after: sue
seem: appear, look
seep: percolate, transude,
    ooze, leak
seer: prophet, sage
seesaw: teeter
seethe: boil, stew
segment of curve: arc
seine: net, trap
seize: grasp, grab, nab,
    catch, take, arrest,
    clasp, clutch, grip
seizure: arrest
select: choose, pick
" body: quorum
" group: elite

self: ego
" centered person:
    egoist, egotist
" (comb. form): auto
" conceit: egotism
" esteem: pride
" evident truth: axiom,
    truism
" exaltation: pride
" interested: egoist
" (pert. to): personal
" possessed: cool
" reproach: remorse
" satisfied: smug
" (Scot.): sel
" sufficient person:
    prig   [pose
sell: vend, trade, dis-
" to customer: retail
semi circular recess:
    apse   [dius
" diameter: radii, ra-
semiprecious stone:
    agate, olivin, onyx,
    garnet, sards
semite: arab
" language: arabic
send: dispatch, deliver,
    transmit, forward
" along: relay [mand
" back: remit, remand
" down: demit
" forth: emit
" out: emit, radiate
senile: aged   [doter
" person: dotard,
senior: eldest, elder
sensational: lurid
sense: feel, meaning,
    comprehend, wit
" of dignity: pride
" " guilt: shame
" " smell: olfactory,
    nose
" " taste: palate
senseless: inane, folly,
    unideaed, mad
sensible: rational
sensitive: sore, tender
sentence: doom, judgment,
    condemn
sentimental: romantic
sentinel: guard
sentry's greeting: halt
separate: divorce, part,
    apart, partitive, alienate,
    sever, divide,
    aside, disjoin, sort
" & classify: assort
" & divide: sleave
" entry: item
sepulcher: tomb
sepulchral: charnel
sequel: outcome, upshot
seraglio: harem
seraphic: angelic
Serbian: Serb, Slav
sere: dry, wither
serene: calm, placid,
    tranquil, irenic
serf: esne, slave, vassal,
    bondman, thrall, helot,
    villein, peasant
serfage: bondage
series: sets
" of ancestors: line

" " links: chains
" " meetings: session
" " names: list
" " rings: coil
" " stairs: flight
serious: sober, solemn,
    severe, grim, earnest,
    grave, demure, rapt
" attention: care
" discourse: sermon
sermon: address, oration,
    homily
" subject: text [sera
serous fluid: serum
serpent: aboma, asp,
    snake, adder, cobra,
    boa, python
serpentine: snaky
" fish: eel
serrate: notch   [ial
servant: servitor, men-
" 's garb: livery
serve: bestead, satisfy,
    minister, attend
" food: cater
" the purpose: do
server: tray, attendant
service: use   [abject
servile: menial, slavish,
" dependent: minion
sesame: til, semsem
session: seance
set: fix, coterie, series,
    clique, group, hard,
    adjust, rigid, appoint,
    mount, congeal, put
" apart: isolate, allocate,
    devote
" back: recess
" of boxes: nest
" fire to: burn, ignite,
    lit
" forth: sail
" of four: tetrad
" in from margin:
    indent
" of instruments: kit
" of jeweled ornaments:
    parure
" in motion: stir
" of nested boxes:
    inro
" of organ pipes:
    stop   [rure
" " ornaments: parure
" out: embark, start
    sail
" of players: team
" right: correct
" to rights: settled
" of signals: code
" solidly: embed
" the speed: pace
" of three: tierce
" to: bout
" of type: font
" up: rear
" upright: erect, rear
" value on appraise,
    rate
Seth's brother: Abel
" mother: Eve
" son: Enos
settle money on: endow

settled: sedate, sedentary, lit, determined, agreed, decided, adjusted, regulated, colonized, disposed
" **habit:** rut
settler: colonist
settling: dreg, lee
setto: bout, fray
seven (comb. form): hepta
" **part composition:** septet
sever: cut, disunite, part, disjoin, rend, separate, break
several: divers, many
severe: stern, strict, spartan, drastic, austere, crucial, rigid, hard, rigorous, disjoin, harsh [ness
severity: rigor, sternness
sew: plant, stitch, mend
" **loosely:** baste
sewer: ditch, drain
sex: gender
shack: hut [manacle
shackle: fetter, pinion,
shad: alose, alosa
shade: tone, shadow, hue, tint, screen, cast, ghost, nuance, tinge
" **of the dead:** mane
" **tree:** elm, lin, ash
shaded walk: mall
shadow: shade, darken
shaft: pole, missile
" " **vehicle:** thill
shaggy: bushy, nappy
shake: tremor, wag, jar, tremble, shiver, bob, dodder, convulse, rattle
" **up fire:** stoke
Shakesperian character: Salerio, Falstaff, Othello, Iras, Iago, Oberon [sius
" **conspirator:** Cas-
" **forest:** Arden
" **heroine:** Portia
" **king:** Lear
" **lord:** Bigot
" **river:** Avon
" **villain:** Iago
shaking: tremor, aspen
" **box:** tray
" **dish:** plate, saucer
" **vessel:** basin
sham: pretend, feign, false, imposture, artificial, fake
shame: mortify, abash, disgrace, chagrin, humiliate, abasement
shameless: arrant
shank: shin, crus [tour
shape: form, model, mold, frame, con-
" **conically:** cone
shaped like pine cone: pineal [hewn
" **with an ax:** hewed,
share: impart, portion, partake, quota, divide, bit, lot, dole

shark: gata, tope
sharp: tart, acute, keen, ration, pungent, edgy, edged, stern, nippy, biting, incisive, acerb
" **answer:** retort
" **cornered:** angular
" **cry:** yelp, yell
" **end:** point [twinge
" **pain:** pang, sting,
" **point:** barb, cusp
" **pointed:** acute, aculeate [ness
" **taste:** tang, tart-
" **to taste:** acid, tart
" **tempered:** edgy
sharpen: strop, whet, hone, point, edge
sharpening machine: grinder
" **stone:** hone
sharpshooter: sniper
shatter: smash, break
shave: shear, pare
" **head of:** tonsure
shawl: paisley, wrap
Shawnee's chief: Tecumseh [fleece, strip
shear: poll, clip, shave,
sheath: case, encase, scabbard
" **internally:** ceil
shed: leanto, spill, cote, molt, emit [molt
" **feathers:** moult,
sheen: luster, polish, gloss, brightness
sheep: ewe, ram, sna
" **(breed):** merino
" **coat:** fleece, wool
" **cry:** bleat
" **disease:** coe
" **dog:** collie
" **(female):** ewe
" **killing parrots:** keas
" **(male):** ram
" **two years old:** teg
" **shelter:** cote, fold
sheeplike: ovine
sheet of floating ice: floe [plate
" **of glass:** pane,
shelf: ledge
shell: shot, bomb
" **not exploding:** dud
shellac: varnish, lac
shellfish: clam, crab, abalones, mollusk
shelter: lee, haven, protect, shed, abri, tent, roof, sconce, cover, asylum [covert
sheltered: shady, lee,
" **side:** lee [ite
Shem descendant: sem-
sherbet: ice
sheriff's deputy: bailiff
" **group:** posse [ecus
shield: egis, protect, buckler, targe, ecu,
" **division (her.):** ente
shift: veer, tour, change
shine: gleam, radiate, beam, glitter, ray, polish, glisten, glow, luster, gloss

shining: radiant, lucent, aglow
Shinto temple: Sha
" **gateway:** Torii
ship: boat vessel
" **body:** hull
" **bow:** stem, prow
" **cabin:** saloon
" **channel:** gat
" **crane:** davit
" **cubical content:** tonnage
" **deck:** poop
" **employe:** steward
" **guns:** teeth
" **kitchen:** galley
" **line:** lanyard
" **load:** cargo
" **officer:** mate, purser, navigator
" **part:** keel, mast, rudder
" **personnel:** crew
" **(pert. to):** naval
" **(poet.):** keel, prow
" **prison:** brig
" **rear:** aft [spar
" **timber:** keel, bitt,
shipboard: asea
shipbuilding to bend upward: sny [shun
shirk: evade, avoid,
shirt (arch.): sark
" **button:** stud
shiver: shudder, shake, splinter, tremor
shoal: flat, shallow, reef
shock: appal, strike, jar, startle, brunt
shoe: boot, brogan
" **fastener:** latchet
" **form:** last, tree [per
" **(kind):** sandal, slip-
" **part:** rand, welt, insole, upper, vamp
" **store:** bootery
shoemaker tool: awl
shoestring: lace, lacet
shoot: cion, fire, sprout, discharge, dart, sprig
" **out:** dart [leonid
shooting star: meteor,
shore: coast, strand, land, beach, prop, support [ree
" **bird:** snipe, rail, stilt, avocet, plover,
short: curt, brief, succinct, pert, abrupt
" **contest:** setto
" **distance:** step, pace
" **letter:** billet, line
" **napped fabric:** ras
" **piece of pipe:** tee,
" **& to the point:** terse
" **race:** dash, sprint
" **rest:** siesta, nap
" **sentence:** clause
" **skirt:** kilt
" **stop:** pause
" **story:** anecdote
" **& thick:** stocky, dumpy
" **time:** spell
shortage: deficit
shorten: cut, curtail

shortening: lard
Shosh. Indian: Ute, Paiute, Piute
shoulder (comb. form): omo
" **ornament:** epaulet
" **pack:** knapsack
" **of road:** berm
shout: yell, hoot, cry, hooy, bawl, root
" **applause:** cheer
shove: push, thrust
shovel: spade, scoop
show: array, parade, evince, display, exhibit denote, reveal
" **approval:** smile
" **contempt:** sneer, hiss, boo [trast
" **difference:** con-
" **to be false:** belie, disprove
" **fondness:** dote
" **mercy:** spare
" **off:** parade
" **sorrow for:** pity
" **to be true:** prove
shower: rain
showy: ornate, garish
" **clothes:** regalia, finery [sy
" **(colloq.):** loud, dres-
" **display:** splurge
" **ornament:** tinsel
shred: rag, particle, scrap, tatter, wisp, fragment, snip
shrew: virago, vixen, termagant [clever
shrewd: canny, keen, astute, politic, smart, knowing, sly, acute,
" **(slang):** cagy
" **woman:** virago
shrewdness: acumen
shrill bark: yap, yelp
" **cry:** shriek, scream
shrink: wane, contract, cower, recoil, lessen, cringe, shrivel
shrivel: wither, wizen, blast, shrink
shroud: sheet
shrub: spirea, elder, alder, lilac, baretta, bush, laurel, sumac, plant, senna, bush
" **fence:** hedge
shudder: tremble, shiver [eschew, flee
shun: avoid, evade,
" **(archaic):** evite
shunt: switch
shut: close, closed
" **close:** seal
" **in:** hem
" **up:** pent
shutter: blind [orous
shy: timid, demure, coy, recoil, bashful, swerve, wary, reserved, retiring, tim-
" **(colloq.):** mim
Siamese: Thai
" **coin:** at, att, tical
" **Island group:** Tai
" **measure:** niu, rai,

sen
" race: tai
" river: Si
" twin: Eng, Chang
" wt.: pai
Siberian antelope :saiga
" **Mongoloid:** Tatar
" **mountain:** Altai
" **natives:** Sagai, Tatars
" **plains:** Steppes
" **river:** Ob, Lena, Amur, Onon, Om, Tom, Opus
" **squirrel:** miniver
" **sound:** hiss
Sicilian city: Palermo
" **mt.:** Etna   [sala
" **seaport:** Aci, Mar-
" **volcano:** Etna
sick: ail, abed
sickness: disease
side: party, lateral, faction, support, aspect, border, slope, part, flank, phase
" **away from the wind:** alee
" **of book leaf:** page
" " **bldg.:** wall
" **dish:** entree
" **(of the):** lateral
" **order:** rasher
" **piece:** rib
" " **of window or door:** jamb
" **portion:** rasher
" **road:** byway
" **shoots:** laterals
" **by side:** abreast, parallel
" **tracked:** shunted
" **of triangle:** leg
" **view:** profile
sidelong: oblique
" **glance:** leer, ogle
sideslip: skid
sidestep: avoid, duck
sidetrack: shunt
sidle: edge
siege: beset, blockade
siesta: nap   [strainer
sieve: sift, screen, filter,
sigh: groan, sob, lament, suspire   [otic
sight (pert. to): visual,
sigil: seal
sign: shingle, symbol, token, portent, trace, signal, notice, omen
" **of addition:** plus
" " **assent:** nod
" " **infinitive mood:** to
" " **omission:** caret
signal: sign, noticeable, warning, alarm
" **bell:** gong, curfew
signature of approval: visa, vise
signet: seal   [import
significance: meaning,
signification: sense
signify: denote, mean, matter, indicate
silence: gag, quiet, still, hush

[tacit, muted
silent :still, mum, mute, noiseless, taciturn,
silicate: wellsite
silk fabric: alamode, pongee, satin, surah, samite
" **fibers:** floss
" **filling:** tram
" **(kind):** eria, moire
" **net:** tulle
" **thread:** tram, floss
silken: seric, glossy
silkworm: eri, eria
" **'s envelope:** cocoon
silly: inane, asinine, fatuous
silver: splinter, argent
" **(symbol):** A. G.
silverweed: tansy
silvery: argent
simian: ape, apelike
similar: alike, same, like, akin, such
simper: smirk
simple: mere, elementary, plain, easy
" **animal:** amoeba, monad
" **song:** ballad, lay
simpleton: idiot, oaf, fool, ass, daw, dolt, goose, sap, ninny
simulate: pretend, imitate, ape, act, feign
sin: err, evil, iniquity, transgress   [cause
since: ago, as, for, be-
" **(arch.):** sith
" **(prefix):** cis
" **(Scot.):** syne
sincere: honest, genuine, gearty   [thew
sinew: muscle, tendon,
sinewy: wiry
sinful: evil, wicked
sing: chant, lilt, carol, warble, intone, croon, hum   [del, yodle
" **in Swiss style:** yo-
singe: burn
singers: choir, divas, vocalists, tenors
singing bird: robinet, wren, shama, lark, vireo, linnet, pipit, veery, redstart, bobolink, oriole
single: sporadic, lone, one, solo   [uni
" **(comb. form):** mon,
" **note:** monotone
" **thing:** unit
singly: alone, once
singular: odd, queer
sink: drain, settle, sag, merge, descend, dip, drop, debase, lower, ebb   [otoe
Siouan Indian: Osage,
sip: sup, taste
sister: nun [pose, perch
sit: roost, rest, brood,
site: locality, area, situs
sitting: session, sedent, seated   [place, lie
situate: locate, located,

situated at the back: postern   [dial
" **in the middle:** me-
situation: site, condition, seat   [sestet
six (group of): senary,
" **line stanza:** sestet
sixty sixties: sar, saros
size: area, extent, bulk
" **of book:** quarto
" " **coal:** pea, egg
" " **paper:** atlas, demy, cap
" " **shot:** T. T.
" " **type:** pica, gem, agate, diamond
skeleton: frame, remains
" **part:** bone, rib
skeptic: doubter
sketch: trace, draft, paint, drawing, limn, skit, map, outline
ski (var.): skee
skid: slide, slip, slue, sideslip
skiing race and term: slalom
skill: art, craft   [tor
skilled person: opera-
" **shot:** marksman
skillful: adept, deft, clever, adroit, apt
skin: peel, rind, pelt, flay, hide
" **(comb. form):** derm, derma
" **covering:** fur
" **disease:** psora, acne, tinea, rupia, hives
" " **of dogs:** mange
" **inflammation:** papula
" **layer:** enderon
" **(of the):** dermal
" **opening and orifice:** pore
" **protuberance:** wen, mole, wart, blister
" **of seal:** sculp
skink: lizard
skip: omit, trip, miss
" **about:** caper
" **over water:** dap
skirmish: feud, melee, battle, brush
skirt: border
" **of a suit of armor:** tasse
skit: parody, playlet, sketch, lampoon
skittle: pin
skoal: toast
skulk: hedge
skull: cranium
" **(pert. to):** cranial
skunk: conepate, polecat   [less
slack: loose, lax, care-
slacken: relax, loosen
slag: dross, scoria
slam: bang
" **at cards:** vole
slander: aperse, libel, defame, asperse, belie, caluminiate, as-

persion, calumniate
slang: argot, jargon
slant: bias, slope, cant, incline, tilt, lean, bevel, incline   [askew
slanting: alist, atilt
slap: hit, cuff, rebuff, blow, strike, insult
slash: slit, cut, gash
slate cutter's tool: sax
slattern: trollop
slaughter: massacre
" **house:** abattoir
slave: esne, serf, bondman, vassal, minion, thrall, helot, drudge
Slavic tribe: Serb
slay: murder, kill
sled: sleigh, sledge, tode
sleep: rest, nap, doze, slumber
sleeveless garment: aba, cape
slender: slim, thin, svelte, lank, frail
" **fish:** gar
" **graceful woman:** selph, sylph
" **prickle:** seta
slice: split, carve, out, shave, slab
slid: slipped   [coast
slide: skid, slip, slither,
slight :snub, scant, trivial, ignore
" **amount:** trace
" **breeze:** breath
" **coloring:** tint
" **sound:** peep
slighting remark: slur
slightly opened: ajar
slim: svelte, slender, spare, thin
slime: ooze, muck, mud
sling: fling, hurl, slue
slip: slide, lapse, skid, err, fault, glide, error
" **away:** elapse, elope
slipper: mule, sandal
slippery: eely, elusive
slit: gash, slash
slogan: motto
slop over: spill   [ramp
slope: slant, incline, declivity, side, cant, bevel, gradient, dip,
" **upward:** climb, rise
slot: groove [mal, unau
sloth: ai indolence, ani-
slothfully: idly
slough off: moult, molt
slovenly woman: trollop, slob, slattern
slow: deliberate, sluggish, dilatory, poky, gradual, retard
" **leak:** drip
" **moving person:** snail   [largo, ritard
" **(musical):** lento,
" " **(abbr.):** rit
slowed: retarded
slue: twist, swamp, veer, pivot, skid
sluggard: drone
sluggish: inert, leaden, slow, supine, dull, idle

slumber: nap, sleep
"   **music:** snore
slur: aspersion, traduce, soil, reproach
"   **over:** elide [shrewd
sly: foxy, cunning, furtive, roughish, crafty, artful, arch, wily,
"   **artifice:** wile
"   **look:** leer
"   **(Scot.):** slee
smack: strike, savor
small: petty, atomic, trivial, paltry, miniature, petite, wee, tiny, minute, little, few, petit, less
"   **amount:** trace, bit, mite, hair
"   **animal:** insect, genet, organism
"   **(colloq.):** teeny, weeny [cro, lepto
"   **(comb. form):** mi-
"   **(prefix):** micro
"   **(Scot.):** sma
smallest: least
"   **integer:** one
"   **particle:** whit
"   **planet:** Mercury
smart: trig, chic, clever, sting, shrewd, dashing, bright
smarten: spruce
smash: crash, shatter
smear: daub, bedaub, smudge, smirch, plaster, stain, soil
smell: olid, odor, scent
smile: grin, smirk
"   **foolishly:** simper
smiling: riant [stain
smirch: soil, smear,
smirk: simper, grin
smoke: smudge, reek
"   **flue:** funnel, stack
smooth: sleek, lene, sand, level, glib, even, plane, iron, glassy, greasy, pave, ease
"   **as with beak:** preen
"   **and glossy:** sleek
"   **over:** plaster
"   **and shining:** waxen
"   **spoken:** glib
smoothing implement: sadiron, planer, scraper, plane
smoothly polite: suave
smother: stifle [smear
smudge: blot, smoke,
Smyrna figs: eleme
snail (soft): slug, drone
snake: asp, reptile, boa, adder, serpent, viper
"   **bird:** darter
"   **(black):** racer
"   **in the grass:** enemy
snakelike fish: eel
snap: crack, clip, wafer, bite, fastener, cooky, crackle, flip, sneck
"   **with fingers:** fillip
snapper: fastener, turtle
snare: net, entrap, trap, entangle, pitfall, web,

springe, noose, benet, drum, gin   [growl
snarl: tangle, gnar,
snatch: nab, grab, wrest
"   **(slang):** swipe
sneaky: furtive
sneer: gibe, scoff, mock, taunt, deride
snide: mean, base
sniff: nose   [ment
snip: clip, shred, frag-
snood: fillet
snoop: pry, prowl, peer
snow: neve, whiten
"   **runner:** ski, skee
snub: slight, rebuff, rebuke
snug: cosy, cozy
"   **retreat:** den, nest
snuggle: nestle, cuddle
so: thus, ergo, hence
"   **be it:** amen
"   **(Scot.):** sic, sae
soak: ret, sop, sog, saturate, drench, steep
"   **flax:** ret
soap ingredient: lye
"   **frame part:** sess
"   **plant:** amole
soapstone: talc
soar: tower, rise, fly
sober: sedate, serious, staid, grave, solemn, abstinent, demure
social affair: tea, reception, dance, party
"   **class:** caste
"   **error:** boner
"   **group:** tribe [riah
"   **outcast:** leper, pa-
"   **unit:** clan, sept, tribe, caste
society bud (colloq.): deb   [tippe
Socrates wife: Xan-
sod: sward, dirt, turf, earth, soil, glebe
soda: pop
"   **ash:** alkali
sodium: N. A., sal
"   **carbonate:** trona
"   **chloride:** salt, sal
"   **nitrate:** niter
sofa: divan, settee, lounge
soft: tender, malleable, pliable, mild, mellow, low, yielding
"   **candy:** fudg
"   **cheese:** brie
"   **drink:** soda, pop
"   **fabric:** velvet, plush
"   **feathers:** down
"   **food:** pap
"   **fruit part:** pulp
"   **hematite:** ore
"   **limestone:** chalk
"   **mass:** pulp
"   **metal:** tin
"   **palate:** uvula
"   **shoe:** moccasin
"   **substance:** pap
soften: relent, mellow, mitigate, relent [ate
"   **by soaking:** macer-
"   **tone:** mute
softly: low

soggy: sodden
"   **mass:** sop
soil: mess, dirt, earth, begrime, smirch, sod, dirty, country, land, defile, moil, sully, slur, tarnish, mire
"   **(kind of):** marl, loam, clay
"   **(poet.):** glebe
sojourn: abide, stay
solace: comfort, console
solan: gannet
solar disc: aten, aton
"   **year excess:** epact
solder: cement
soldering flux: rosin
soldier: warrior
"   **cap:** baret, shako
"   **cloak:** capote
soldiers: troops
sole: one, only, lone
"   **of foot:** plantar
"   **" plow:** slade
solemn: sober, grave, serious, somber [vow
"   **assertion:** oath,
solicit: beg, ask, canvass, canvas, urge, court, woo, petition, request, plead
"   **(colloq.):** tout
solicitude: care
solid: hard, firm, compact, rigid, prism
"   **(C. form):** stereo
solidified mass: cake
solidify: set, harden, gel
solitary: lone, alone
"   **(form):** eremo
solo: aria, lone, single
solution: answer, key
somber: solemn, grave, lenten
some: one, any, few
something added: insert
"   **attached:** tag
"   **found:** trove
"   **new:** novelty
"   **owed:** debit
sometime: former, once
somewhat: rather
son: scion
sonance: sound
song: melody, ballad, ditty, air, lay, canticle, carol, lilt
"   **bird:** wren, robin
"   **of joy or praise:** paean, paeon
"   **" (var.):** pean
"   **thrush:** mavis
"   **verse:** lyric
soon: anon, early, ere, shortly, promptly
sooner than: ere
soot: carbon, smut
soothe: ease, allay, pacify, calm, quiet
soothing: balmy
"   **ointment:** balsam, balm   [diviner
soothsayer: seer, augur,
sora: rail
sorcerer: magi
"   **(plural):** mages

sorceress: witch
sorcery: magic
sordid: base   [tender
sore: painful, angry,
sorrow: dolor, woe, repine, mourn, pine, sadness, grieve, grief
sorrowful: sadden, contrite, mournful
"   **sinner:** penitent
"   **state:** woe [gretful
sorry: regret, pitiable, grieved, contrite, resort: sift, kind, ilk, variety, manner, seggregate, cull, class, classify, type, grade
sortie: sally   [son
soul: spirit, esprit, essence, pneuma, persound: valid, sonance, sane, noise, tone
"   **accompanying breathing:** rale
"   **of or as a bell:** ding, toll
"   **" distress:** moan
"   **to frighten:** boo
"   **loudly:** blare
"   **(relating to):** tonal
"   **resonantly:** ring
"   **of surf:** rote
soup: pottage, broth, puree, bisque
"   **basis:** okra
"   **dish, ladle, & vessel:** tureen   [acetose
sour: acid, acerb, tart, acetic, acrid, morose,
source: origin, font, fount, root, seed, rise
"   **" heat:** steam
"   **" & light:** gas
"   **" help:** recourse
"   **" iodine:** kelp
"   **" light:** sun, lamp
"   **" oil:** olive
"   **" ore:** mine
"   **" perfume:** musk
"   **" power:** motor
"   **" sugar:** cane
"   **" water:** well
S. African: Boer
"   **" animal:** suricate, ratel   [eland
"   **" antelope:** gnu,
"   **" Dutch:** taal, Boer
"   **" farmer:** Boer
"   **" fox:** asse, caama
"   **" grassland:** veld, veldt
"   **" legislative assembly:** raad [bantu
"   **" native:** kafir,
"   **" plateau:** Karoo
"   **" province:** Transvaal
"   **" thong:** riem
"   **" tribesman:** Bantu, Zulu
"   **" underground stream:** Aar
"   **" village:** Kraal
"   **American animal:** tapir, llama, tayra

" " **arrow poison:** curare
" " **bird:** screamer, seriema, rara, ara, tinamou, agami
" " **cape:** Horn
" " **hare:** tapeti
" " **Indian:** Ona, Carib, Ge, Caril, Mayan, Inca
" " **laborer:** peon
" " **linguistic family:** Onan [Andean
" " **mts.:** Andes,
" " **ostrich:** rhea
" " **plain:** Llano, Pampa
" " **wind:** Pampero
" " **rabbit:** tapeti
" " **republic:** Peru
" " **river:** Apa, Plata, Amazon, Orinoco, Acre, Para
" " **rodent:** paca, ratel, tapir [ma, boas
" " **serpents:** abo-
" " **tree:** Mora, Balsa, Carob
" " **snake:** lora [lu
" " **tribesman:** Zu-
" " **tuber:** oca[bolo
" " **weapon:** bolas;
" " **wood sorrel:** oca [erre
" **Dakota capital:** Pi-
" **Sea canoe:** proa
" **island:** Bali, Samoa
" **islander:** Kanaka, Samoan
southeast wind: eurus
southwest wind: aner, afer [lic
souvenir: memento, re-
sovereign: ruler, monarch [strew
sow: plant, seed, swine,
space: room, area, time, void, distance [ment
" **above door:** pedi-
" **surrounding castle:** ambit
" **theory:** plenism
spacious: roomy, broad, large [bridge, arch
span: cross, reach, extent, interval, team,
spangle: glitter
Spanish article: el, las
" **channel:** Cano
" **city:** Irun, Cadiz, Toledo
" **cloth:** leno
" **coin:** peseta, peso, centavo, real
" **commune:** irun
" **conquerer of Mexico:** Cortez [olla
" **cooking pot:** alla,
" **dance:** bolero, jota, tango
" **farewell:** adios
" **feast days:** fiestas
" **gentleman:** caballero, don
" **griddle cake:** arepa
" **head covering:**

mantilla
" **hero:** Cid
" **(var.):** Sid
" **horse:** genet
" **house:** casa
" **larait:** reata, riata
" **legislature chamber:** camera
" **mackerel:** bonita
" **measure:** cantara, vara
" **painter:** Goya
" **peninsula:** Iberia
" **priest:** cura, padre
" **river:** Ebro, Oro
" **room:** sala [manta
" **shawl:** serape,
" **title of address:** don, senor, senora
" **weapon:** bolas
" **wt.:** arroba [yard
spar: mast, sprit, box,
" **end:** arm
" **to stow:** steeve
spare: lean, disposable, save, desist, reserve, stint, omit, slim, extra, tire, gaunt
sparing: chary
sparkle: glisten, flash, glitter, gleam [tai
sparoid fish: gar, sar,
sparse: scanty, scarce, thin, scant [hardy
Spartan: Stoic, brave,
" **army:** Mora
" **bondsman:** helot
" **serf & slave:** helot
spasmodic breaths: gasps
" **exhalation:** sneeze
" **twitch:** tic
spat: gaiter, tiff, row
spate: freshet, flood
spatter: sprinkle, splash
speak: orate, utter
" **in defense:** plead
" **haltingly:** stammer
" **imperfectly:** lisp, stutter [cite
" **from memory:** re-
" **of:** mention
" **rhetorically:** declaim [parage
" **slightingly of:** dis-
" **in slow tone:** drawl
" **softly:** whisper
" **in surly manner:** snarl [arrow
spear: dart, harpoon, javelin, lance, pike,
special: particular
specify: mention, name
specimen: sample
speck: dot, spot, mote, jot, blemish, nit [play
spectacle: parade, dis-
spectator: observer
specter: ghost, spirit
speech: dialect, voice, oration [rade
" **(long, abusive):** ti-
" **(pert. to):** vocal
" **(slang):** lingo
speechless: mute [rush
speed: race, haste, hie, pace, rapidity, run,

speedily: apace, presto
speedy: fast, fleet, rapid
spell: trance, relieve, charm [Enid
Spencer character: Una,
spend: exhaust, disburse [laze
" **time idly:** loiter,
spendthrift: wastrel
sphere: orb, globe, ball, arena [ate
spherical: round, globular, orbicular, glob-
" **body:** orb, ball
spice: mace, ginger, seasoning, zest
spicy: aromatic
spider: arachnid, tarantula, spinner
spigot: tap
spike: nail
" **of cereal:** ear
" **flowers:** ament
" **fork:** prong, tine
spikenard: na, nard
spill: shed, tumble, slop, downpour [revolve
spin: reel, turn, whirl, rotate, twirl, weave,
spindle: axle
spinner: spider, top
spiral: coil, helical, coiled, helix [mit
spire: epi, steeple, sum-
spirit: elan, demon, elf, vim, soul, mettle, dash, heart, ghost, animation, specter
" **of air:** ariel
" " **the dead:** mane
" " **evil:** satan, mara, mora
" **lamp:** etna
" **of nature:** genie
" " **the people:** ethos
" **in Tempest:** Ariel
spirited: fiery, lively
" **horse:** steed, arab, courser
spiritless: amort, dull, dejected, vapid
spiritual beings: essences, angel
" **nourishment:** manna
" **session:** seance
spite: pique, venom, thwart, rancor
splash: splatter, spatter
splatter: splash, dab
splay: expand
spendid: superb
" **(Scot.):** braw
splendor: eclat, glory
splinter: sliver, shiver
split: rive, rivet, rend, riven, slice, tear, disrupt, chap, cleave
" **asunder:** riven
" **pulse:** dal
splotch: blot [pamper
spoil: addle, impair, rot, mar, taint, vitiate, plunder, loot, booty,
spoiled: bad
spoils: booty
spoken: oral, parol
spoliation: rapine

sponge: expunge, efface
spongy: porous
sponsor: backer
spook: ghost [inder
spool: bobbin, reel, cyl-
spoon (deep): ladle
spore: seed [divert
sport: game, play, fun, frisk, frolic, pastime,
" **group:** team
sportive: playful, gay
spot: stain, blemish, notice, blot, tarnish, locality, speck, dapple
" **on playing card or domino:** pip [ocelot
spotted cat: cheetah,
spout: gush, jet
" **to draw sap:** spile
sprawl lazily: loll
spread: scatter, unfurl, disseminate, ted, disperse, broaden, unfold, diffuse, extend
" **by rumor:** noise
" **out:** deploy
" **outward:** flare
spree: frolic
sprig: twig [per, pert
sprightly: alive, nimble, buoyant, airy, chip-
" **tune:** lilt
spring: leap, vault, spa, bolt, ramp, arise
" **back:** rebound [let
" **flower:** crocus, vio-
" **from:** derive
" **(old word):** ver
" **(pert. to):** vernal
" **up:** arise, rise
springe: snare
springy: elastic [zle, wet
sprinkle: spatter, driz-
" **with flour:** dredge
sprint: run, dash, race
sprite: elf, imp, goblin, fairy, fay [ate
sprout: bud, crop, cion, shoot, scion, germin-
spruce: dapper, neat, smarten, trim, trig, natty [ble, brisk
spry: agile, active, nim-
spud: potato
spume: froth, foam
spur: incite, goad, impel, urge, stimulus, rouse [false, fake
spurious: snide, bogus,
spurn: scorn, reject
spurt: dart, spout, gush, burst, squirt
spy: scout, discoverer, informer, detect, dissern [gang
squad: team, group,
squall: gust
squander: waste, spend, dissipate, misspend
squatter: nester
squeeze: press, crush, pinch, compress, hug
squelch: suppress
squib: lampoon
squire: escort
squirm: wring, wriggle
squirrel: gopher

" **shrew:** tana [ture
stab: gore, pierce, attempt, pink, punc-
stable: barn, stall, fixed
stableman: ostler, hostler [ney
stack: pile, heap, chim-
" **of corn:** shock
" " **hay or grain:** rick
stadium: arena [wand
staff: pole, rod, cudgel,
" **of life:** bread
" " **office:** mace
" **officer:** aide
stag: pollard, elk, hart
stage: produce, degree, dais, platform, phase
" **extra:** super
" **hangings:** scenery
" **part:** role
" **(pert. to):** scenic
" **show:** revue
" **speech & whisper:** aside [ter, waver
stagger: reel, stun, tot-
staid: sedate, demure
stain: dye, tax, discolor, color, spot, tinge, blemish, smirch, soil, stigma, smear, blot
stair: step
stair part: riser, tread
" **post:** newel
stake: post, wager, bet, picket, ante, hazard, risk, pole [insipid
stale: trite, vapid, old,
stalk: stem, stipe
" **of grain:** straw
stall: stable, booth, manger
stalwart: strong
stammer: stutter
stamp: postage, brand, impress, print
stamping form: die
stance: position
stanch: stem
stand: bear, endure, position, booth, tolerate
" **against:** oppose
" **for:** represent
" **opposite:** face
" **up:** rise
standard: flag, norm, ideal, normal, test, classic, criterion, emblem, streamer [norm
" **of conduct:** moral,
" " **excellence:** ideal
" **quality & quantity:** unit
standing: status, grade
" **as grain:** uncut
stannum: tin
stanza: verse, strophe
star: asterisk, feature, nova, celebrity, sun, vega, bespangle, giansar, mirak
" **(comb. form):** aster, astero [etamin
" **in Dragon:** adib,
" **flower:** aster
" **in heraldry:** etoile

" " **Orion:** rigel
" " **virgo:** spica
starch: sago, arrowroot, cassava, farina
stare: gaze, agape, gape, glare [absolute
stark: stiff, rigid, bare,
starry: astral, sparkling, stellar
start: initiate, begin, onset, open, commense
starting line: scratch
startle: surprise, shock, frighten, scare, alarm
starve: famish
state: declare, say, assert, aver, condition, nation, republic, assert [situation
" **of affairs:** pass,
" " **being equal:** par
" **of bliss:** eden
" **(comb. form):** stato
" **differently:** reword
" **house:** capitol
" **by items:** itemize
" **of lost soul:** perdition [spirits, mood
" **of mind:** morale,
" **on oath:** depose
" **policeman:** trooper
" **of relief:** easiness
" **treasury:** fisc
" **troops:** militia [lege
" **without proof:** al-
" **wrongly:** misstate
stately: majestic, regal
statement: assertion, fact [credo
" **of belief:** creed,
station: post, base, depot, degree
stationary part: stator
statue: image
statute: law, edict
stay: remain, wait, stop, linger
stead: avail, place, lieu
steadfast: staid, true
steady: firm, fixed, invariable [fer, filch
steal: rob, purloin, pil-
" **(arch.):** nim
" **as cattle:** rustle
stealthy: furtive
steam: vapor, power
steamer: liner
steed: horse, charger
steel: harden
steep: ret, brew, sop, imbue, hilly, soak, abrupt, macerate, sheer
" **descent:** escarp, scarp, bank
" **as flax:** ret
" **hill:** butte
" **in oil & vinegar:** marinate
steeple: spire, epi
steer: pilot, guide, ox, pursue, control, helm
" **wild:** yak, yaw
steering apparatus: rudder, helm, wheel
" **lever:** tiller
steeve: stow
stein: mug

stellar: astral, starry
stem: prow, arrest, stalk, check, peduncle, petiole, stanch
" **of an arrow:** shaft
" **from:** derive
step: pace, stride, race, stair, gait, tread, degree, walk [rime
" **of ladder:** rung,
sterotyped: trite
sterile: barren
stern: grim, harsh, severe, rigorous
" **of vessel:** aft [er
stevedore: loader, stow-
stew: ragout, worry, boil, seethe, simmer
stick: rod, stall, adhere, cohere, transfix, pole, paste, wand
stickler for perfect English: purist
sticky stuff: goo, glue, tar [formal, stilted
stiff: rigid, stark, frigid,
stifle: smother, strangle
stigma: brand, stain
still: yet, silent, quiet, dumb, silence, immobile, immovable
stimulate: fan, stir, incite, joy, sting, whet, exhilarate, innervate
stimulus: spur, incentive [ulate, goad
sting: bite, smart, stim-
stinging fish: ray [net
" **insect:** wasp, hornet
" **plant:** nettle
stingy: miserly, mean
stint: scrimp, task, chore, spare, restrict
stipend: salary, wages, pay [excitement
stir: mix, move, arouse, rouse, inspire, excite, stimulate, disturb, agitate, urge, bustle,
" **the air:** fan [foment
" **up:** agitate, rouse, roust, roil, provoke,
stitch: sew
" **bird:** ihi
stoat: ermine, weasel
stock: store
" **certificates:** scrip
stogie: cigar
stoker: fireman [ment
stole: garment, vest-
stolen goods: mainor
" **property:** pelf
stolid: dull, impassive, wooden, heavy
stomach of mammal: maw
stone: gem, lapis, agate, rock, flint, lapidate, jewel, pebble, marble
" **fruit:** drupe, plum
" **jar:** crock
" **(L.):** lapis
" **nodule:** geode
" **tablet:** stele
" " **(var.):** stela
" **writing tablet:** slate
stoneworker: mason

stony: rocky [bow
stoop: bend, submit,
stop: cease, prevent, rest, desist, ho, cessation, stay, pause, suspend, bar, arrest, avast, deter, quit
" **(naut.):** avast
" **seams of a boat:** calk
" **unintentionally:** stall
" **up:** dam, clog, plug
" **watch:** timer
stoppage: block
stopper: plug, cork
storage box: bin
" **place for arms:** arsenal
" " " **grain:** silo
store: mart, fund, shop, stock, provide, stow, supply, accumulate
" **attendant:** clerk
" **fodder:** ensile
" **for safety:** reposit, deposit
" **in a silo:** ensile
storehouse: depot, etape
storekeeper: merchant
storm: rave, rampage, tempest, wester, rain, orage, rage, besiege
story: tale, yarn, novel, floor, fable
stout: strong, brave
stove: range, etna, kiln, heater
" **part:** oven, grate
stow: store, pack, box, steeve, stuff
straddle: astride, bestride [gut
straight: direct, arow,
" **batted ball:** liner
straighten: aline, align
straightforward: candid, direct [exert
strain: tension, tax, sprain, strive, sift, stretch, filter, melody, progeny, trace,
" **(comb. form):** tono
" **forward:** press
strainer: sieve, sifter
strait: channel, narrow
strand: string, breach
strange: odd, alien, novel
" **C. (form):** xeno
stranger: odder, alien, foreigner
strangle: stifle
strap: belt, thong, strop
" **to lead:** halter, leash
" **shaped:** lorate
stratagem: ruse, wile, artifice [seam
stratum: layer, bed,
straw hat: panama
stray: divagate, wander, deviate, lose, err
streak: stripe, line, vein, trace, brindle
stream: freshet, tor-

rent, river, creek, pour, run, rill, flow
streamer: pennant, flag, standard [waif, arab
street urchin: gamin,
strength: vigor, power, soundness, stamina
strengthen: brace, fortify, invigorate, prop
stress: strain, accent, pressure, tension, emphasis [span
stretch out: eke, prolate, sprawl, expand, lie,
" **one's neck**: cran, crane
stretched: taut, extended, strained, reached
" **tight**: tense
stretcher: litter [sor
stretching muscle: ten-
strew: scatter, diffuse, sow [rigid
strict: stern, rigorous,
strictness: rigor
stride: pace, gait
strident: shrill [test
strife: feud, war, con-
strike: slap, beat, rap, smite, carome, swat, hit, ram, smack, bang
" **(arch.)**: smite
" **as a bell**: chime
" **breaker**: scab
" **(colloq.)**: lam [dab
" **gently**: pat, tap,
" **out**: dele, elide, fan, cancel, delete
" **& rebound**: carom
" **together**: collide
" **violently**: ram
striking effect: eclat
string: cord, rope, line, twine, strand
stringed instrument: viol, viola, rebec, lute, harp, lyre, piano, cello
stringent: strict, alum
strip: stripe, divest, band, denude, peel, shear, bare
" **of cloth**: tape
" **of leather**: welt, strop, thong, cleat
stripe: bar, streak
stripling: lad
strive: strain, struggle, attempt, vie, try, contend, endeavor, toil
" **after**: seek
" **to equal**: emulate
stroke: blow, pat
stroll: meander, saunter, ramble, rove
strong: potent, stout, hale, robust, sturdy, powerful, stalwart
" **box**: chest, safe
" **point**: forte
" **rope**: cable
" **scented**: redolent
" **smelling**: olid, sisal
" **tackle (naut.)**: cat
" **voiced person**: stentor

[ress, citadel
stronghold: fort, fort-
strop: hone, strap
structure: edifice, shed, frame [test, strive
struggle: cope, tussle, combat, wrestle, con-
stub: stump, receipt
stuck in the mud: mired, bemired
student: scholar, pupil
studio: atelier
study: con, pore, peruse, pon, scan, meditate
stuff: pad, sate, cram, fill, wad, ram, gorge
stulm: adit
stumble: trip
stump: stub, challenge
stun: daze, astound
stunt: feat, dwarf, trick
stupefy: stun, daze, drug, besot
stupid: crass, insipient, asinine, dumb, dull, inane, doltish
" **person**: dolt, ass, dunce, log, moron
" **(colloq.)**: ass
" **play (slang)**: boner
stupor: coma, trance
sturdy: strong
stutter: stammer
sty: pen
style: see also "type"
style: manner, mode, fashion
" **of architecture**: doric, ionic
" " **painting**: genre
" " **penmanship**: hand
" " **poetry**: epic
" " **sewing**: shirr
" **type**: italic, pica, italica, roman, gothic
stylish: chic, alamode, dressy [nifty, tony
" **(slang)**: classy,
suave: bland
subdue: master, overpower, tame
subject: topic, theme, vassal, text
subjoin: annex
subjugate: conquer
sublime: exalted, noble [immerse
submerge: sink, drown,
submissive: passive, meek, servile
submit: stoop, bow, yield, obey
" **to**: endure [minor
subordinate: secondary,
" **bldg.**: annex [ter
subsequently: later, af-
subside: abate, ebb, fall
subsist: live, feed [pith
substance: material, matter, gist, essence,
substantial: solid, real
substitute: alternate, ersatz, vicar, agent
subtle emanation: aura
success: go, hit, victory

[dina
succession: series, or-
" **of family sovereigns**: dynasty
succinct: terse, short
succor: aid, relief, rescue, help
succulent: juice
" " **fruit**: uva
" " **part**: pulp
" **plant**: herb, aloe
succumb: yield
sudden: quick, abrupt
" **attack**: raid
" **blast of wind**: gust
" **effort**: spurt, spasm
" **impulse**: start
" **sensation**: thrill
" **thrust**: lunge, jab
sue: woo, urge
suet: tallow, fat
suffer: ail, agonize, let, tolerate, ache
" **(Scot.)**: dree
suffering: agony, pain
suffice: do, avail [quate
sufficient: ample, ade-
" **(be:)** do
" **(poet.)**: enow
sugar (kind of): tetrose, ose, dextrose
" **plum**: bonbon
" **solution**: syrup
sugary: sweet, honeyed
suggest: intimate, hint, propose
suit: please, satisfy, adapt, become, fit, petition, befit
" **(colloq.)**: gee
" **at law**: case
suitable: pat, befitting, adapted, apt, fit, meet
suite: retinue
suited for song: lyric
suitor: beau, wooer
sulk: mope, pout [glum
sullen: morose, dour,
sully: defile, tarnish, soil, blot, grime
sulphur alloy: niello
sum: total, amount [cis
summary: epitome, pre-
" **pf principles**: credo
summer (of the): estival
" **(Fr.)**: ete
summit: tip, apical, apex, crest, roof, top, spire, peak [cite
summon: bid, call, page,
" **forth**: evoke
" **publicly**: page
" **together**: muster
" **up**: rally
sun: star, sol
" **(of the)**: solar [lio
" **(comb. form)**: he-
" **disk**: aton
" **dried brick**: adobe
" **god**: ra, Apollo
" **part**: corona
sunburnt: adust, tanned
sunder: part, rend, cut, rive, divide
sundry: divers

sung by a choir: choral
sunk fence: haha, aha
sunny: clear, bright, merry, cheerful
sunset: sundown
sunshade: parasol
sup: sip, eat
supercilious person: snob [shallow
superficial: outward,
superintendant: manager, overseer, boss
superior: finer, upper, above
" **mental endowment**: talent [niority
superiority in office: se-
supernatural being: fairy
" **event**: miracle
supersede: replace
supine: sluggish [vert
supplant: replace, sub-
supple: pliable, lithe, lissome, compliant, pliant
supplement: eke, add
supplicate: appeal, beg, plead, entreat, pray, implore
supply: afford, store, purvey, fund, cater
" **with fuel**: stoke
support: prop, behalf, abet, shore, second pedestal, stay, rest, brace, leg, aid, bear, side, guy, back, bolster, hinge
" **for plaster**: lath
" " **rails**: tie
" " **sail**: topmast, mast [tal
" " **statue**: pedes-
" **by timbers**: shore
" **for a vine**: trellis
supporter: booster, rooter [tron
" **of institution**: pa-
supporting beam: sleeper [easel
" **framework**: trestle,
" **member**: leg
" **rod**: rib
" **wires**: guys [deem
suppose: presume, believe, opine, assume,
" **(arch.)**: trow, wis
supposition: if [quell
suppress: elide, squelch,
suppression of a part: elision [est
supreme: highest, great-
surcease: balm, end
sure: certain, confident, positive
surety: bail, backer
surf duck: coot
surface of gem: facet
surfeit: sate, cloy, glut, satiate
surfeited with enjoyment: blase
surge: swell, heave, tide, billow

surgical compress: stupe
" sewing: suture
" thread: seton
surly: cross, gruff
surmise: guess
surmount: overcome, tide, hurdle, top
surmounting: above, atop [doe
surname: cognomen,
surpass: beat, exceed, best, transcend, top, cap, excel, outclass
surplice (short): cotta
surprise: startle, amaze
surrender: cede, cession [case
surround: beset, hem, encircle, envelop, environ, enclose, incase, belay, mew, belt, en-
surrounded: girt [mid
" by: amid, among,
survey: review
surveying instrument: aliner, transit
survival: relic
survive: outlive, live
suspend: hang, stop
suspicious (slang): leery
Sussex land: Laine
sustain: stand, prop, endure, aid [bread
sustenance: aliment,
suture: seam [thin
svelte: slender, slim,
swab: mop, wipe
swag: booty
swagger: strut, roister
swain: lover
swallow hurriedly: bolt, engorge, gulp, engulf, absorb [tern
" (kind): martin,
swamp: bog, fin, marsh, everglade, morass, slue, overwhelm
swan: leda, trumpeter
" (male): cob
swap: trade
sward: sod, turf, grass
swarm: teem, horde
" of bees: hive
" " " (Scot): byke, bike
swarming: alive
swarthy: dun
swat: hit
swathe: wrap [nod, wag
sway: totter, rock, reel, teeter, fluctuate,
" from side to side: careen, waddle
swear: vow
" falsely: perjure
sweat: perspire
Swedish chemist: Nobel [krona
" coin: ore, krone,
" nightingale: Lind
" province: Laen, Lan
" river: Klar
sweet: sugary
" cake: cruller
" clover: melilot
" drink: nectar

[cet
" to the ears: dul-
" potato: yam [rup
" solution: sirup, sysound: music
sweetbrier: eglantine
sweeten: sugar, candy
sweetheart: lover, inamorata, leman, amoret
" (Anglo. Ir.): gra
" (Scot.): jo]gat
sweetmeat: candy, nousweetsop: ates, atta
swell: dilate, bulb, surge, expand, distend [sea
" of water: surge,
swerve: veer, sheer, careen, shy, deviate
swift: rapid, fleet, fast
swiftly: apace [ity
swiftness: speed, celerswimming: natant [auk
" bird: loon, grebe,
" organ: fins, fin
swindle: wangle, dupe, fraud, bilk, fleece, cheat, gip, gyp [hog
swine: porcine, tapir,
" (female): sow
" (male): boar
swing: sway
swirl: eddy, whirl [gau
Swiss canton: Uri, Aar-
" capital: Bern, Berne
" city: Basle, Sion, Basel, Aarau
" commune: Sion
" cottage: chalet
" dialect: ladin
" lake: Uri, Lucerne
" measure: staab, elle
" mountain: rigi
" patriot: Tell
" poet: Amiel
" river: Aar
" song: yodel
switch: shunt
switchboard section: panel
swollen: tumid
swoon: faint, trance
sword: saber, epee, rapier, sabre, toledo
" handle: hilt, haft
" shaped: ensate, ensiform
swordsmen's dummystake: pels, pel
sycophant: parasite, toady
syllable of hesitation: er
" stress: tone
sylvan: wooded, rustic
" deity: satyr
symbol: sign, emblem
" of bondage: yoke
" " dead: orant
" " office: mace
" " peace: dove
" " power: sword
" " victory: palm
" " wedlock: ring
symetrical: regular

synopsis: outline, table, epitome
Syrian antelope: addax
" city: Aleppo
" deity: el
" garment: aba
system: order, method
" of management: regime [laws
" " rules: code,
" " signals: code
" " weights: Troy
" " worship: cult

T

tab: flap, label, tally, account, mark
table linen: napery
" (small): stand
" vessel: tureen teau
tableland: mesa, platablet: pad, troche
tabulation: calendar
tacit: implied, silent
taciturn: reticent
tack: brad, baste, gear
tadpole: polliwog
Tai race (branch): Lao
tailor: sartor
" 's iron: goose
taint: pollute, poison, infect, defile, blemish, corrupt, vitiate
Taj Mahal city: Agra
take: seize, accept, receive, capture, grasp
" as one's own: adopt
" away: adeem, deduct, detract, remove
" (law): adeem
" back: rescind, retract, recant [mind
" care: beward, tend,
" " (arch.): reck
" " horse: groom
" on cargo: lade
" charge: preside, attend [tice
" cognizance of: no-
" credit: pride
" delight: revel
" ease: rest [dine
" evening meal: sup,
" exception: demur
" from: wrest
" for granted: assume, presume
" illegally: steal, poach
" the initiative: lead
" into custody- arrest [gest
" into stomach: in-
" liberties: presume
" medicine: dose
" oath: swear
" off: doff, depart
" offense at: resent
" one's way: wend
" out: dele, delete
" place- happen
" " again: recur
" " of: supplant
" pleasure in: enjoy

" position: stand
" precedence: rank
" in sail: reef [rotate
" turns: alternate,
" umbrage: resent
" unawares: surprise
" up again: resume
tale: story, anecdote, legend
talebearer: tattler
talent: gift, aptitude, flair
talented: apt, clever
talisman: amulet
talk: chat, converse, orate, address
" childlessly: prattle [ture
" dogmatically: lec-
" effusively: gush
" foolishly: drivel, prate [ter
" glibly: prate, pat-
" hypocritically: cant
" idly: prate, gab, chatter, tattle
" imperfectly: lisp
" informally: chat
" (slang): spiel, gab, chatter, jabber
" tediously: prose
" vainly: prate [ter
" volubly: chin, pat-
" wildly or with enthusiasm: rave, rant
tall: long, high, lofty
" bldg: tower
" & thin: lane, lank
" timber: teak
tallow: suet
tally: score, count, reckon, register
" (colloq.): tab
talon: claw
tamarisk salt tree: atlee, atle, atli [subdued
tame: subdue, docile, gentle, flat, tractable, mild, conquer, meek,
tamper: meddle, tinker
tan: ecru, sunburn, bronze
tang: taste, trace [able
tangible: tactile, palptangle: snarl, mat, ravel, enmesh ensnare [shag, ravel
tangled mass: mop,
tank: cistern
tanned: tawny
" hide: leather [mac
tanning material: sutantalize: taunt, tease
Tantalus's daughter: Niobe
tantrum: rage
tap: pat, spigot
taper: candle, diminish
" a timber in shipbldg.: snape
tapering: terete [gusset
" piece: shim, gore,
" solid: cone
tapestry: arras, tapis
Tapuyan Indian: Ges
tar: sailor [late
tardy: belated, slow,

target: aim, mark, goal, object, ambition, butt
tariff: duty [spot
tarnish: mar, dull, soil,
Taro paste: poi
" **roots**: eddoes, eddo
tarry: wait, remain, lag, bide, linger, loiter, abide
tart: acute, acid, sour, acrid, sharp, caustic
tartan: plaid
Tartar: Turk
task: chore, stint, stent, job, duty, tax
taste: relish, penchant, savor, sip, flavor, palate, sapor, tang
tasteless: pall, sapid, vapid
tasty: savory, sapid
" (Scot): taver
tattle: gossip, blab
taunt: sneer, plague, censure, twit, gibe, reproach, mock, jibe
taut: tense, tight
tavern: inn, cabaret
" (slang): pub [gaudy
tawdry: cheap, tinsel,
tax: stent, assess, levy, toll, duty, scot, tribute, tariff, strain, assessment, exaction, cess, excise, impost, task
" (kind): poll
tea: cha
" (kind): oolong
" **tester**: taster
" **urn**: samovar
teacake: scone
teach: instruct, train
team: crew, overflow, squad, yoke, group
" **drivers**: teamsters
" **of horses**: span
teamster: carter [gee
" **'s command**: haw,
tear: rip, rend, lacerate, cleave, sever split
" **apart**: tatter, rend, rip [molish, raze
" **down**: rase, de-
tease: plague, annoy, molest, tantalize, pester, coax, nag
" (slang): rag
tedious: prose, irksome tiresome, fatiguing
tedium: ennui
teem: abound [sway
teeter: seesaw, jiggle,
teeth: fangs
" **coating**: enamel
" **incrustation**: tartar
" (pert to): dental
tela: web, tissue
telegraph: wire
" **code**: morse
tell: relate, narrate, impart, recount, inform, disclose
" **tales**: blab, tattle
teller's office: cage
temper: anneal, meddle, tone, qualify,

tantrum, mitigate
temperate: moderate,
tempest: storm, tumult
"The Tempest's" character: Ca'iban
"The Tempest's" spirit Ariel [violent
tempestuous: stormy,
temple: fane [rhythm
tempo: time, meter,
temporarily: nonce [tice
tempt: allure, lure, enten: decade, denary
" (comb. form): deca
" **thousand**: myriad
tenant: lessee, renter
tend: care, mind, trend, contribute, conduce, guard, incline, treat
" **to wear away**: abrasive, erosive
tendency: trend, bent
tender: sore, soft, gentle, proffer, offer, sensitive, kind
" **feeling**: sentiment
tendon: sinew
" (comb. form): teno
tenement: flat, dwelling [trine, dogma
tenet: belief, maxim, principle, creed, doc-
tenfold: denary
tennis point: ace [deuce
" **score**: set, all, love,
" **stroke**: lob, chop
Tennyson hero: Arden
" **heroine**: Enid, Elaine
tenor: trend, course, purport, drift [taut,
tense: rigid, strained
tensile: ductile
tension: strain, stress
tent: encamp, tepee
tentacle: feeler
tenth: tithe
tenuous: rare [term
tenure: lease, holding,
tepid: warm [duration
term: word, call, limit,
" **of holding**: tenure
" **in tag**: it
termagant: shrew
termination: ending, limit, finale
terpsichoreans: dancers
Terra del Fuego Indian: Ona
terrace: balcony
terrain: region
terrapin: turtle [earthy
terrestrial: terrene,
terrible: dire, awful, tragic, dreadful, grim
terrier (kind): skye
terrified: agast, aghast
terrify: dismay [ton
territorial division: can-
terror: dread, fright, fear, horror
terse: laconic, concise pithy, compact, brief
test: trial, try, tryout, essay, check, examine, prove, standard, assay, criterion

" **ore**: assay
testify: aver, depone, avow, attest [pone
" **under oath**: detestimony: evidence
testy: peevish, touchy
tether: fasten, restrain confine, try, tie
Teutonic alphabet character: rune
" **goddess**: Norm
" **god**: Aesirf Odin, Tyr, Er
Texas mission: Alamo
text: topic, subject
textbook: manual, primer
texture: wale, web
that (arch.): yon
" **is** (abbr.): ie, eg
" " **to say**: namely
" " **is kept**: retent
" " **is left**: remnant
the (Scot.): ta
theatrical: stagy
" **profession**: stage
theme: topic, subject, motif, essay
theoretical force: od
therefore: ergo, hense, so, thus, hence
thespian: actor
Thessaly mt.: Ossa
thick: dense, fat, coarse
thicken: deepen, gel
thicket: bush brake, hedge, covert, copse
thickness: ply, layer
thief: robber, looter
thin: slender, rarefied, lean, sparse, fine, sheer, dilute, watery, slim, bony, svelte, diluted, gaunt, lank
" **cake**: wafer [neer
" **coating**: film, velayer: lamella
" & **light**: papery
" **out**: peter
" **paper**: tissue
" **piece of stone**: slab
" **plate**: lamina, lamella, disc
" **scale**: lamina
" **strip of wood**: lath, splint, sliver
" & **vibrant**: reedy
thing: matter
" **in law**: res, les, re
" **lost**: losses
things to be added: addenda
" **be done**: agenda
" **done**: acta, actum
" **owned**: property
think: opine, ponder, cogitate, believe, deem, cerebrate, consider [ween
" (arch.): wis, trow,
" **logically**: reason
thinly scattered: sparse
third in degree: tertiary
" (mus.): tierce
" **power**: cube

thirsty: dry, parched
this place: here
" **springs eternal**: hope [amenta
thong: strap, lasso,
thorn: briar, brier, spine, seta [brambly
thorny: spinose, spinate,
" **shrub**: acacia, brier
thorough: arrant
those against: antis
" " **office**: ins
" **who ask alms**: beggars [opined
thought: opinion, idea,
thoughtful: pensive considerate
thousand: chiliad [mille
" (comb. form): kilo.
thrall: bondman, slave, serf [drub, whiplash
thrash: beat, belabor,
" (slang): lam
thread: lace, twine, lisle, fiber, reeve, filament
" (kind): linen, lisle, cotton, silk
" **of a story**: clue
threadlike: filose, filar
" **tissue**: fiber
threat: menace
threatening: lowery
three: triad, trio [teen
" **cornered sail**: ladimensional: cubic
" **joints**: trinodal
" **legged chair**: stool
" " **stand**: tripod, trivet, teapoy
" (mus.): ter
" **in one**: triune
" (prefix): tri
" **pronged weapon**: trident [enty
" **score & ten**: sev-
" **toed sloth**: ai
" **toned chord**: triad
threefold: trine, treble trinal, triple
threshing tool: flail
threshold: sill [tro
thrice (prefix): ter, tri,
thrifty: provident, frugal [grow
thrive: prosper, batten,
throat part: tonsil,
" (pert. to): gular
" **swelling**: goiter
throb: beat, pant, pulse
throe: pang [crowd
throng: mass, horde,
through: per, dia, by
throw: hurl, toss, cast, heave, fling, pitch
" **away**: discard
" **back**: repel [turb
" **into confusion**: dis-
" **of dice**: main
" **into disorder**: derange, pie, clutter
" **light on**: illume
" **lightly**: toss
" **off**: shed, emit
" **track**: derail
" **out**: eject
" **over**: jilt
" (poet.): elance

" **of six at dice:** sise
" **up:** retch
thrush: mavis, missel, robin, veery
thrust: poke, lunge, stab, prod, shove
thrusting weapon: lance
thump: bang, bump, blow, pound
thurible: censer [hence
thus: sic, therefore, so,
" **far:** yet
" **(Scot.):** sae
thwart: spite, frustrate, brain [frontlet
tiara: coronet, diadem,
Tibetian capital: Lassa
" **gazel:** goa
" **monk:** lama
" **ox:** yak
" **priest:** lama
tick: mite: acarid
tidal wave: eagre
tide: current, season, surge, befall, neap
tidings: news, word
tidy: trim, neat, trig
tie: draw, knot, bond, cravat, lace, bind, equal, tether, unite, link, scarf, **fasten**
" **game:** draw
Tierra del Friego Indian: Ona
tiff: spat
tight: taut, tense, snug
til: sesame
tile: domino, slate
till: plow, farm, cultivate, hoe
tillable: arable
tilled land: arada, arado
tilt: tip, lean, incline, cant, slant, name, joust [cedar, lumber
timber: wood, ash, oak,
" **bend:** sny
" **piece:** tenon
timberwolf: lobo
timbrel: tabor
time: tempo, era, schedule, leisure, period, duration, occasion
" **long ago:** yore
" **before event:** eve
" **(Scot.):** tid
timeless: ageless, eternal [apt
timely: opportune, pat,
timepiece: clock
times ten (suffix): ty
timid: shy
Timor coin: avo [trepid
timorous: afraid, shy,
tin: stannum, can, Sn
" **container:** canister
" **foil for mirrors:** tain [bue, tint
tincture: modicum, imtine: prong, spike
tinge: tint, imbue, hue, stain, trace, shade
tinkle: dingle, clink
tint: hue, tinge, dye, shade, tincture
tiny: small, atomic
tip: point, apical, cue,

careen, overturn, top, tilt, lean, cant, hint
" **of fox's tail:** tag
" **to one side:** careen, tilt, list
" **over:** overset, cant
" **of a pen:** neb
tippet: fur, scarf
tipping: atilt [sot
tippler: toper, drinker,
tipster: tout
tirade: screed, philippic
tire: exhaust, weary, fag [bored, weary
tired: jaded, fatigued,
tiresome: dreary, boring, tedious
" **person:** bore, pill
tissue: telo, tela, teca
Titania's husband: Oberon
tithe: tenth
title: name, sir, claim, ownership, heading
" **of Athena:** Alea
titmouse: tomtit
titter: giggle
to: unto, forward, into, toward, until, for
" **lee side:** alee
" **the left:** aport
" **other side:** over
" **a point on:** onto
" **(prefix):** ac
" **same degree:** as
" **(Scot.):** tae [even
" **such degree:** so,
" **this:** hereto [until
" **the time that:** till,
" **your health:** prosit
toad (Scot.): tade
toads: agua, anurans, anura
toady: truckle
toast: scorch, warm, prosit, brown, skoal
tobacco box: humidor
" **(kind of):** capa, caporal, snuff, latakia
" **roll:** cigar
' " **(var.):** segar
together: along
" **(prefix):** co
" **with:** and
toggery: clothes
toil: labor, ring, moil
token: relic, pledge, sign, badge
tolerable: soso, passable
tolerate: endure, stand, bide, digest [knell
toll: due, tax, impost, strive, resound, ring,
tomato sauce: catsup
tomboy: hoyden
tomcat: gib
tone: sound, accent, air
" **color:** timbre
" **down:** soften
tongue: language
tonic: bracer
too: overly
" **bad:** alas
" **late:** belated
tool: utensil, chaser, dupe, implement
" **to enlarge:** reamer

" " **flesh hides:** slater
tooth: molar, cog, fang
" **(comb. form):** denti
" **decay:** caries [dent
" **of gear wheel:** cog,
" **point:** cusp
" **substance:** dentine
" **wheel:** sprocket, gear, cog
toothed: serrate, dentate, cerose [comb
" **instrument:** saw,
" **, irregular:** erose
top: crest, ace, surmount, apex, head, cap, excel, surpass, tip, lid, acma, summit
" **of altar:** mensa
" **of doorway:** lint l
topaz hum. bird: ava
toper: sot, drinker [ject
topic: text, theme, subtopple: upset
Topsy's friend: Eva
torch: lamp, flambeau
torment: bait, torture, plague, tease, rack
tornado: twister
torpid: inert, dormant
torpor: coma, numbness
torrent: flood
torrid: tropical, hot
torture: torment [buffet
toss: hurl, pitch, flip,
total: add, sum, whole, entire, complete, tot, utter, absolute, all
totter: stagger, waver, toddle, rock
touch: contact, feel, adjoin, finger, nudge
" **at boundary line:** abut
" **lightly:** pat, dab
" **at one point:** tangent
touchwood: punk
tough: wiry
toupee: wig
tourist: traveler
tousle: rumple, dishevel
tout: tipster [barge
tow: drag, draw, pull,
toward: to, at, facing
" **the center:** entad, orad [ward
" **the inside:** into, in-
" " **left side:** aport
" " **mouth:** orad, entad [tern, aft
" " **rear of ship:** as-
" **(Scot.):** tae
" **the stern:** aft, abaft
tower: turret, soar, pylon, citadel
town (colloq.): burg
toy: dally, trifle, play
trace: track, sign, footprint, tinge, vestige, tail, mark, streak, follow, tang, derive
track: trail, rail, trace, path, mark, footprint
" **worn by a wheel:** rut [expanse, area
tract: treatise, region,

" **drained by river:** basin [easy
tractable: docile, tame,
trade: barter, sell, exchange, craft, deal, swap, traffic, strain
" **agreement:** cartel
trader: dealer, merchant [legend, folklore
traditional tale: saga,
traduce: debase, slur, revile, asperse
traffic: trade, barter
trail: path, track, route, way, course, lag, follow, drag, hunt
" **(slang):** tail
" **of wild animal:** spoor
train: educate, school, tame, instruct, drill, teach, retinue, coach
" **of wives:** harem
tramp: hike, slog, hobo, vagrant, tread
trample: tread, crush
trance: spell, stupor, daze, swoon [calm
tranquil: serene, sedate,
tranquility: peace
transact: conduct, negotiate [act, deed
transaction: deal, sale,
transcend: overtop, surpass, overpass
transcribe: copy, write
transfer: transmit, convey, transpose
transfix: pin, stick
transgress: violate, err, sin [poral
transitory: brief, temtranslate: render, decode, construe
translation: rendition, version
transmit: render, send, transfer, forward
transmute: transform, convert [crystal
transparent: laky, clear,
" **mineral:** mica
transport: convey, cart, ferry
transported: rapt
transpose: reverse, invert, transfer [nab
trap: gin, snare, tree, ensnare, pitfall, web, net, ambush, grab,
trap door: drop
trappings: gear [use
trash: rubbish, dirt, reftrashy: worthless
travel: tour, wend, ride, journey
" **by wagon:** trek
traveler: tourist, viator, passenger, wayfarer
traveling co.: caravan
traverse: cross, scour, run [parody
travesty: mime, satire
tray: server, salver
treachery: treason

treacle: molasses
tread: step, trample, walk, tramp [value
treasure: wealth, prize,
treasurer: bursar
treat: use, regale, tend, handle, negotiate
" **indulgently:** pamper
" **maliciously:** spite
" **unkindly:** mistreat
treatise: tract, discourse
treaty: pact, alliance
tree: catalpa, yew, ule, tamarack, rack, aspen, corner, myrtle
" **of antiquity:** olive
" **covering:** bark
" **exudation:** rosin, resin, gum
" **frog (young):** peeper
" **snake:** lora, lerot
" **trunk:** bole, log
" **yielding caucho:** ule
treeless plains: pampas, tundras
trees: forest
" **(pert. to):** arboreal
trellis: lattice, espalier
tremble: quiver, quake, dodder, shake, shiver,
tremulous: aspen
trench: ditch, moat
trend: tendency, movement, tend, tenor, incline, drift, bent
trepan: entrap
trespass: encroach, intrude, poach, venture
tress: braid, lock, ringlet, curl [ternary
triad: trine, trivalent,
trial: test, ordeal, attempt, hardship
triangle with unequal sides: scalene
" **piece:** gore, gusset
tribal sign: totem
tribe: clan, gens
tribulation: trial, woe
tribunal: bar
tributary: feeder
" **of the Amazon:** Napo
" " " **Colo.:** Gila
" " " **Elbe:** Iser
" " " **Missouri:** Osage, Platte
" " " **Ohio River:** Wabash [fering
tribute: tax, praise, of-
tricar: tricycle
trice: moment, instant
trick: stunt, jape, feint, prank, delude, ruse, antic, defraud, palter, wile, deceit, fraud
trickle: drip
tricky (slang): snide
trifle: dally, toy, petty, straw [spruce, smart
trig: trim, neat, tidy,
trig. function, ratio or figure: sine, secant, cosine
trill: warble, roll
trim: decorate, adoren,

prune, trig, spruce, neat, preen, lop
" **& simple:** tailored
" **with the beak:** preen [ing
trimming: ruche, edg-
trip: stumble, misstep, jaunt, tour
triple: trine, threefold
triste: dismal [stale
trite: banal, threadbare,
triton: newt, salamander [prevail, victory
triumph: pervail, win,
trivial: small, slight, banal

Trojan hero & defender: Eneas, Aeneas
" **warrior:** agenor
troop: band, company
tropical: torrid, sultry, warm [parrot
" **bird:** ani, toucan,
" **carnivore:** ratel
" **fruit:** papaw, date, bana, guava, mango
" **herb:** sida [taro
" **plant:** aloe, ipecac,
" **tree:** palm, tamarind, mabi, zorro
trot: jog [sore, woe
trouble: bother, aid, ail, agitate, molest, ado,
trough to cool: bosh
trousers: slacks, pants
truck: barter, van, lorry
truckle: toady
trudge: plod
true: honest, loyal, accurate, faithful
" **to fact:** literal
" **hearted:** leal
truly: indeed, yes, yea, verily, veritably
trump: ruff, outdo [oma
trumpet creeper: tec-
" **(small):** clarion
" **sound:** blare, blast
trumpeter bird: agami
trunk of statue: torso
trunkfish: toro
truss: bind
trust: monopoly, rely, credit, confide, believe, hope, lean, reliance, merger, faith, depend, belief
trustworthy: safe, honest, reliable [fact
truth: verity, veracity,
" **(arch.):** sooth
truthful: honest
try: test, sample, endeavor, essay, strive, attempt, teth r, undertake, trial
tub: keeve, cask, vat
tube: pipe
" **on which silk is wound:** cop [crest
tuft: bunch, clump,
tug: haul
tumble: spill, wilter
tumbler: glass
tumeric: rea

tumor: wen
tumult: bedlam, riot, din, tempest, hubbub
tun: cask [adapt
tune: aria, air, melody,
Tungsten ore: cal
Tunisia capital: Tunis
" **city:** Sfax
" **measure:** saa, saah
" **pasha:** dey
" **ruler:** Bey, dey
turban hat: moab
turbid: roily
turf: sod, sward
" **in golf:** divot
" **(poet.):** glebe
Turk: Tatar, Ottoman, Tartar
turkey buzzard: aura
" **(male):** tom
Turkish: Ottoman
" **bath:** hammam
" **capital:** Ankara
" **city:** Adana, Aintab
" **coin:** asper, para
" **commander:** aga
" **decree:** Irade
" **flag:** alem
" **government:** Porte
" **governor:** Pasha, Bey
" **hat:** fez
" **imp. standard:** alem
" **inn:** imaret
" **judge:** cadi, aga
" **measure of length:** arshin
" **mon. unit:** asper
" **money:** asper
" **mt. range:** Alai
" **name:** ala, ali
" **officer:** emir, aga, pasha
" **official (var.):** emeer
" **prince:** ameer
" **province:** Angora
" **regiment:** alai
" **ruler:** sultan
" **sailing vessel:** saic
" **soldier:** nizam
" **sultan:** Selim
" **title:** aga, emir, pasha, bey
" " **(var.):** amir
" **town:** Bir [tatar
" **tribesman:** tatir,
" **vilayet:** Adana
" **weight:** oka
turmeric: rea [whirl
turn: twist, rotate, revolve, bend, pivot,
" **aside:** shunt, deviate, wry, deter, divert, swerve, avert
" **away:** shy
" **back:** repel, revert
" **down:** reject, veto
" **the front wheels:** cramp
" **for help:** resort
" **inside out:** evert
" **into money:** cash
" **inward:** introvert
" **to left:** haw
" **out to be:** prove

" **outward:** extrovert, evert
" **over:** keel [form
" " **new leaf:** repages of: leaf [slue
" **on pivot:** swivel,
" **to right:** gee
" **the soil:** spade
" **white:** pale
turner: gymnast
turning: rotary
" **joint:** hinge
" **point:** pivot, crisis
turret: tower, cupola
turtle: terrapin, snapper, tortoise
" **shell:** carapace
tussle: struggle
Tutelary gods: lares
tutor: school
twelve dozen: gross
twice: bis, doubly
" **(prefix):** di, bi
twig: sprig, rod, cion
twilight: dusk, eve
twilled fabric: serge, silesia, denim, covert, surah [gemel
twin: match, double,
" **crystal:** macle
twine: wind, twist, coil, meander, string, encurl, cord, wreath
twining plant: smilax, winder, vine
" " **part:** tendril
twinkle: wink
The Twins: Gemini
twirl: turn, spin [screw
twist: contort, writh, warp, bend, turn, coil, twine, slue, wry, spiral, wrench, quirk, gnarl, skew, wring,
" **around:** slue, slew
" **out of shape:** contort, warp, distort
twisted: wry
" **cotton thread:** lisle
" **roll of wool:** slub
" **silk:** sleave
" **(var.):** slewed
twit: taunt, upbraid, ridicule
twitching: tic
two: pair, both, couple
" **edged:** ancipital
" **feet (having):** bipedal, dipode [ped
" **footed animal:** biheaded deity: Janus
" **(prefix):** di, bi
" **pronged instrument:** bident
" **(Scot.):** twa
" **toed sloth:** unau
" **wheeled cab:** hansom [essede
" " **chariot:** essed,
" " **conveyance:** bike, gig, cart
" **winged fly:** gnat
twofold: dual, twin
" **(prefix):** di
type: see also "style"

type: variety, sort, nature, kind, model, norm, emblem, genre
" **(kind):** italic
" **of lens:** toric
" **measure:** em, en
" **of molding:** torus
" " **perfection:** paragon
" **square:** em [en
typewriter roller: platen
typical example: norm
typographer: printer
tyrant: despot
tyro: novice [final

U

ultimate: eventual, last
ululant: howling
umbrella (colloq.): gamp
" **part:** rib
umpire: referee, arbiter
unaccompanied: alone, sole, lone [bald
unadorned: bare, stark,
unadulterated: pure
unaspirated: lene
unassumed: natural
unassuming: modest
unattached: loose, free
unbalanced: deranged, onesided
unbend: thaw, relax
unbiased: impartial
unbind: untie, release
unbleached: ecru
unbound: loose
unbounded: limitless
unbroken: intact [eerie
uncanny (var.): eery,
unceremonious: abrupt
uncertainty: doubt
unchanging: uniform
unchecked: rampant, free
uncivil: rude
uncivilized: savage
Uncle Remus creator: Harris
uncle (Scot.): eme
unclose: open, ope
uncommon: unusual, rare, odd
uncompromising: stern
unconcealed: open
unconfined: free
unconscious: unaware
uncouth: rude [lidless
uncovered: bare, open,
unctuous: oily [low
uncultivated: wild, fal-
uncultured: unrefined
undecided: pend
under: beneath, below
" **obligation:** indebted
" **part of auto:** chasis
" **(poet.):** neath
" **(prefix):** sub
underground bud: bulb
" **chamber:** cavern, cave [nel
" **passageway:** tunroom:** cellar
" **stem:** tuber
underhanded: sly

" **person:** sneak
underlings: slave, serfs
undermine: sap
underneath: below
understand: see, realize, know, comprehend
understanding: reason, entente, sense
understood: tacit [try
undertake: endeavor,
undertaking: venture
underwater ridge: reef
" **worker:** diver
underworld: Hades
undisclosed: ulterior
undivided: one, entire, whole, total [unclasp
undo: release, neglect, offset, annul, ruin,
undoing: ruin [wild
undomesticated: feral,
undressed calfskin: kip
" **kid:** suede
undulate: wave, roll
undulation: crimp, wave [close
unearth: uncover, dis-
unearthly: eerie
uneasy: restive, restless, nervous
unemployed: idle
unenclosed: fenceless
unencumbered: free
uneven: erose, odd
unexciting: tame
unexpected: abrupt
" **pleasure:** treat
" **result:** upset
unexplosive shell: dud
unfair: foul [known, new
unfamiliar: strange, un-
unfastened: ripped, loose, undid, untied, untethered [bad
unfavorable: averse, ill,
unfeeling: stony, insensate, marble, numb
unfeigned: sincere
unfettered: free
unfledged: callow
unfold: open, spread
" **gradually:** develop
unfounded: idle
unfriendly: inimical
unfruitful: sterile
unfurl: spread, open
ungainly: awkward
ungrateful person: ingrate [an, tapir
ungulate animal: dam-
unheeding: deaf
uniform: even, unchanging, consistent
unimaginative: literal
unimpaired: intact
uninhabited: deserted, desolate
uninteresting: dry dull
union: junction, coalition, fusion, league, merger, marriage, juncture, alliance
unique: odd, rare, alone
unison: harmony, agreement, accord, concord
unit: see "measure"

unit: ace, one, item
" **of acoustics:** Bel
" " **conduct.:** mho
" " **dis.:** word
" " **drymeas.:** peck
" " **electric capacity:** farad [ere
" " " **int.:** amp-
" " " **pow.:** watt
" " " **reluct.:** rel
" " " **resist.:** ohm
" " **elect.:** volt
" " **electrol.:** ion
" " **energy:** erg
" " **force:** dene, dyne
" " **germ plasm:** ids, id [therm
" " **heat:** calory,
" " **illum.:** phot
" " **inductance (elect.):** henry
" " **light:** lumen
" " **intensity:** pyr
" " **power:** watt [ad
" " **pressure:** bar-
" " **resist.:** ohm
" " **square measure:** acre, rod [day
" " **time:** month,
" " **velocity:** kine, kin [gram, ton, grain
" " **weight:** carat,
" " **wire measure:** mil [erg
" " **work:** erg, kil-
" " " **(pert. to):** ergal
unite: coalesce, link, tie, undo, merge, cement, add, band, connect, ally, knit, consolidate, combine, splice [fay
" **closely:** ally, weld,
" **by weaving:** splice
unity: one, oneness, agreement [acea
universal remedy: pan-
unkind: ill, cruel
unknit: ravel, unravel
unless (Latin): nisi
unlike: diverse
unmannerly person: cad
unmarried: celibate
unmarried girl: maid, spinster [sheer
unmitigated: arrant,
unmixed: pure
unnecessary: needless
unoccupied: idle, vacant
unpaid debt: arrear
unparalleled: alone
unprepared: raw
unproductive: barren, sterile
unreal: visionary
unrefined: crude, wild, uncultivated, inelegant, uncultured, raw
unrelenting: iron
unrestrained: free [cool
unruffled: serene, calm,
unruly: restive, law-

less, disorderly [lick
" **lock of hair:** cowperson:** rebel
unsafe: insecure
unsatisfactory: lame
unseal: open
unsettle: disturb
unshackled: free
unsightly: ugly
unskilled: inept
unsoiled: clean
unspoken: tacit [lish
unstable: erratic, tickunstitched glove:** trank
unsubstantial: airy, aery, flimsy
unsuitable: inept, inapt
untamed: wild, feral
untidy: messy, mussy
" **person:** sloven, slattern
untie: loosen, unfasten
until: unto, to, til
unto: until, to
untrammeled: free
untried: new
unused: untried, new
unusual: rare, odd, novel, uncommon
unvarying: even
unwilling: averse
unwritten: oral, parol
unyielding: grim, set stern, obdurate, hard adamant, rigid
up: aloft, above, higher, upon, atop
up (prefix): ana
" **to:** until
upbraid: reproach, twit
uphold: sustain, abet, back [erect
uplift: raise, inspire,
upon: atop, onto, on, up, above
" **(poet.):** oer
" **(prefix):** epi, ep
upper: high, higher, superior, top
" **air:** ether
" **house:** senate
" **room:** loft
upright: erect, honest, vertical
" **doorway piece:** jamb
uprightness: virtue, honesty [din, hubbub
uproar: tumult, riot,
upset: topple, keel, overthrow, coup, disconcert, discompose
upshot: result, sequel
upstart: parvenu, snob
upward movement of ship: scend
Uranus's daughter: Rhea
" **mother:** Ge
urbane: suave, polite
urchin: tad, elfin, arab, gamin [push, goad
urge: egg, press, spur, insist, prod, stir, incite, flagitate, impel, drive, actuate, sue, solicit, persuade, dun,
" **on:** abet, hurry,

incite, spur, egg
urial: sha
urn: vase [custom
usage: habit, manners,
use: exercise, worth,
  practice, avail, em-
  ploy, utility, custom,
  treat, service, manip-
  ulate, occupy, inure
" **diligently**: ply
" **frugally**: spare
" **a lever**: pry, prise
" **of new word**: ne-
  ology
" **trickery**: palter
" **up**: consume
used: secondhand
" **in flight**: volar
" **to be**: was
useful: utile [needless
useless: idle, inutile,
  futile, vain, fruitless,
usher: escort, intro-
  duce, forerun, fore-
  arm [age, customary
usual: common, aver-
Utah state flower: sego
utensil: tool, implement
utility: use
utmost: best
' **degrees**: tops
" **limit**: extreme
utopian: ideal [say
utter: state, speak,
  absolute, stark, pro-
  nounce, total, voice,

V

vacant: hollow, idle,
  empty
vacate: evacuate, quit
vacillate: waver, teeter
vagabond: bum, va-
  grant, tramp, hobo
vagary: fancy, caprice
vagrant: bum, tramp,
  vagabond [indefinite
vague: sketchy, hazy,
vain: empty, idle, useless, conceited
vale: glen, dale, channel
valiant: brave, heroic
valid: sound, cogent,
  legal [bag, satchel
valise: grip, bag, hand-
valley: dale, vale, glen,
  dell, dingle, canyon
valor: courage, heroism
valorous person: hero
value: prize, price,
  worth, rate, esteem,
  appraise, treasure
" **highly**: endear
valve: piston
Vandal: Hun [appear
vanish: flee, fade dis-
vanity: pride
vanquish: defeat, conquer, worst, beat
vapid: stale, spiritless,
  insipid, dull, taste-
  less, flat [mist
vapor: gas, steam, air,
" **in the air**: haze
" **(dense)**: fog

[nova
variable star: mira,
" " **in Perseus**:
  algol
variegated: pied, tis-
  sued, dappled, striped
variety: specie, sort,
  class, form, diversity,
  type, genus
various: many, diverse
varnish: lac, shellac
" **ingredient**: resin,
  lac [diverge
vary: change, alter,
vas: duct, vessel
vase: urn
vassal: subject, slave,
  serf, bondman, liege
vast: immense, huge,
  great
" **age**: eon
" **horde**: legion
" **number**: billion
" **(poet.)**: enorm
vat: tub, keeve, bac,
  cistern
vault: leap, crypt
vaunt: boast
Vedic fire god: Agni
veer: shift, slue, fickle,
  fluctuate, turn
vegetable exudation:
  resin [tree
" **organism**: plant,
vehemence: fury, rage,
  ardor, heat [dent
vehement: fervent, ar-
vehemently: amain
**vehicle carrying a dis-
  play**: float
" **for heavy loads**:
  lorry, dray [sledge
" **on runner**: cutter,
veil: curtain, disguise,
  conceal, hide
" **(silk)**: orale
vein: rib, vena, streak
velocity: speed
velvetlike fabric:
  panne, velure
vend: sell
venerable: august, aged
venerate: revere, honor,
  adore, worship, re-
  verse, reverence [ence
veneration: awe, rever-
Venetian bridge: Rialto
" **magistrate**: doge
" **painter**: Titian
" **red**: siena
Venezeula capital:
  Caracas
" **coin**: bolivar
" **tree snake**: lora
venom: spite, virus
vent: outlet, opening,
  aperture
" **in earth's crust**:
  volcano
venture: dare, presume,
  risk, enterprise
ventured: durst [bold
venturesome: daring,
Venus's love: Adonis
" **son**: Cupid
veracity: truth
veranda: porch, **piazza**

verb form: tense
verbal: oral
verdant: green
Verdi's opera: Aida
verge: brink, border,
  edge, margin, ap-
  proach [prove
verify: aver, collate,
verily: indeed, amen,
  yea, truly
veritable: real
verity: truth
vermilion: red [stave
verse: rime, poem,
  poetry, canto, stanza,
" **form**: tercet, poem,
  triolet, sonnet
" **pattern**: meter
" **of two feet**: di-
  meter
verso (ab.): vo
vertebral: spinal
vertical: upright
" **(naut.)**: apeak
" **pipe**: stack
" **support**: pillar
" **timber**: bitt, mast
verve: elan, ardor, pep
very (comb. form): eri
" **large (poet.)**: enorm
" **loud (Mus.)**: ff
" **(Scot.)**: vera
vessel: basin, craft,
  liner, settee, pot, vas,
  ship, sloop, tug, setee,
  can, yawl, boat, urn,
  barque, pan, tub
" **(abbr.)**: S. S.
" **curved planking**:
  sny
" **to heat liquid**: etna
" **to hold liquid**:
  cruse, teapot, vial
" **(large)**: tureen,
  vat, tankard [flask
" **for liquors**: flagon,
" **(poet)**: bark [hall
vestibule: entry, lobby,
vestige: trace, relic
vestment: cope, alb,
  stole
vetch: tare
veto: prohibit, forbid
vex: roil, irk, irritate,
  tease, harass, peeve,
  agitate, fret, annoy
" **(colloq.)**: rile
vexation: pest, pique,
  chagrin
viaduct: trestle
vial: phial
viator: traveler
vibration: tremor
vicarage: manse
vice: evil, sin, iniquity
vicious: cruel, mean
victim: prey, dupe
victor: winner, con-
  queror [cess, conquest
victory: triumph, suc-
victual: meat
vie: contend, emulate,
  contest, strive
view: scene, vista, eye
vigilance: care
vigilant: alert, aware,
  awake, watchful

vigor: pep, vim, energy,
  strength, power, vis
vigorous: energetic,
  sturdy, robust, hale,
  forcible, animated,
  virile, lusty
vile: filthy, vulgar, unclean, base
vilify: asperse, revile
village: hamlet, town,
  dorp [force
vim: pep, vigor, energy,
vindicate: justify, maintain, exculpate
vine: ivy, wistaria pea,
  creeper, hop
vinegar bottle: cruet
" **made from ale**:
  alegar
" **(pert. to)**: acetic
vineyard: cru [force
violence: fury, rage,
violent: rabid
" **woman**: virago
violently: hard, amain
violin (colloq.): strad
" **maker**: amati
" **(old)**: cremona,
  amati, rebec
" **(small)**: kit
viper: adder, snake, asp
Virgil's hero: Eneas
" **poem**: Aeneid
virile: vigorous, manly
virtuous: moral
viscous substance: tar,
  glue, grease
vise part: jaw
Vishnu's incarnation:
  rama
vision: dream eye
visionary: dreamer,
  idealist, ideal, aery,
  Utopian, unreal
visit: see, haunt, call
visitor: guest, caller
vista: view, outlook,
  scene, prospect
visual: ocular [pep
vitality: sap, tamina,
vitiate: deprave, taint,
  spoil [mated, airy
vivacious: gay, ani-
vivid: graphic
vixen: shrew
vocal: oral
" **inflection**: tone
vocation: calling, profession, career, trade
vociferated: clamored,
  roared, yelled
vociferous: blatant
vogue: fashion
voice: emit, divulge,
  say, speech, express,
  utter [phonetic
" **(pert. to)**: vocal,
voiceless: spirate, surd
void: space, annul,
  empty, null
" **space**: inanity
voided escutcheon: orle
volatile liquid: alcohol,
  ether, ligroin
volcanic cinder: scoria
" **deposit**: trass

X—WORD
DICT

" glass froth: pumice
" matter: lava
" rock: basalt, trass, tephrite, obsidian
volcano: Etna, Pelee
" mouth: crater, lava
volumn: mo
" (large): tome
volunteer: offer
vortex: eddy, gyre,
vote: ballot, poll, elect
vouch for: sponsor, attest, assure, aver
vouchsafe: deign
vow: oath, pledge
vowel mutation: umlaut
vulcanize: cure
vulgar: vile
" fellow: cad
vulture (large): condor

W

wad: stuff, cram
wade: ford
wader: snipe [sora, rail
wading bird: stilt, heron, flamingo, crane, jabiru, stork, ibis,
wafer: snap [sway
wag: wit, joker, shake,
wager: ante, bet, stake, parlay, wit [stipend
wages: salary, pay,
Wagnerian character: Hagen, Erda [Senta
" heroine: Elsa,
wagon: wain, cart, dray, lorry, tram truck
" track: rut
wail: howl, lament, moan, bemoan
wainscot: ceil
waist: bodice
waistcoat: vest [delsy
wait: stay, linger, tarry,
" for: bide
" on: attend, serve, tend, clerk, cater
walk: step, tread, stride, pace, hike, ambulate, tramp, plod
" feebly: totter
" lamely: limp
" leisurely: stroll
" on: tread [stalk
" pompously: strut,
" proudly: prance
" unsteadily: stagger, toddle, totter
" wearily: trudge, plod, trail [pogo
walking stick: cane, rattan, staff, stilt,
wall border: ogee, dado
" coating: plaster
" (pert. to): mural,
" section: panel
Wallaba: apa
walrus collection: pod
wampum: peag
wan: pale, pale, pallid, colorless, ashy, languid [osier, staff
wand: rod, scepter,

wander: err, roam, stray, rove, stroll, traipse, ramble, digress, gad, meander, divagate
wandering: errant, vagrant, astray, abberrant, nomadic, erring
" race: gypsy
wane: ebb, fade, decrease, shrink
wangle: wriggle
want: need, lack, poverty, desire, wish, scarcity, deficiency
Wapiti: elk [battle
war: conflict, strife,
" fleet: armada
" horse: steed
" (pert. to): martial
warble: yodel, sing, trill, carol
ward off: avert, fend, prevent, parry, repel, stave [ian
warden: keeper, guardwariness: caution
warm: thermal, toasty, tepid, tropical, toast
warmth: heat, ardor
warn: caution
warning: notice, alert, caveat, signal [alarm
" signal: tocsin, siren, alarum, alert,
warp yarn: abb
warriors: cohort, soldiers, fighters
wary: shy, cautious, watchful
" (colloq.): leery
wash: lave, launder, bathe, rinse
wasp: hornet
waste: emaciate, refuse, squander, lose, fritter, exhaust, dross
" allowance: tare
" away: repine
" land (Eng.): moor
" matter: dross
" pipe: sewer
" silk (piece): noil
" time: dally, idle
wasteland: desert, heath [vigil, tend
watch: patrol, eye,
" dog: mastiff
" pocket: fob
" secretly: spy
watchful: alert, vigilant, wary
watchman: sentinel
water: irrigate, aqua, eau, dilute
" barrier: dam
" bird: coot, swan
" bottle: carafe
" excursion: sail
" (flying): spray
" fowl: brant, egret (Fr.): eau
" jar: hydria
" jug: ewer, olla
" lily: lotus [strait
" passage: sound,

" pipe (large): main
" plant: lotus
" of the sea: brine
" spirit: Undine, Ariel
" wheel: noria
watercresses (dial.): ekers
watered appearance: moire [linn, cascade
waterfall: cataract, lin,
" (Scot.): lin [oasis
watering place: spa,
waterless: arid, dry
waterway: channel, stream, canal
watery: wet, thin
wave: sea, comber, surf, breaker, flutter, watt, crimp, roller, surge, undulate
" to & fro: flap, wag
wavelet: ripple
waver: falter, stagger, fluctuate, totter, reel, hesitate, flicker
wavy (heraldry): onde
wax: cere, grow, increase, cerate
" (obs.): cere
" (pert. to): ceral
way: manner, route, method, path, passage, course, road, lane [ble, faint
weak: puny, frail, fee-
" (arch.): seely
weaken: sap, enervate, dilute, unnerve, debiliate, attenuate
weakness: foible
wealthy: rich, affluent
wealthy person: nabob, midas
weapon: bomber, gun, spear, sword, pistol, arms, dagger, firearm
wear: exhibit, display
" away: erode, fray, abrade, eat, rub
" at the edge: fray
wearisomeness: tedium
weary: tire, irk fatigue, fag, bore [marten
weasel: ermine, stoat, otter, ferret, sable,
weather: season
" cock: vane
" conditions: climate
weave: spin, interlace
weaver's reed: sley
weaving machine: loom
web: network, fabric, trap, texture, snare, ply, tela
" footed bird: swan, goose, avocet, penguin, gannet
" like: telar [tela
" " membrane:
" " " (pl.): telae
wedge: cleat
" in: jam
" shaped: cuneated
weed: tare
weekly: aweek [boohoo
weep: moan, sob, cry,

weeping: tearful
weight: dram, ton, pressure, heft, onus, troy, carat, pound, mite
" allowance: tare
" on fishlines: sinkers
" for wool: tod
weighty: momentous
weir: dam [in
welcome: greet, pleas
welkin: sky, air
well: hardy, fit, healthy
" assured: confident
" bred: genteel
" " woman: lady
" grounded: valid
" known: familiar
" lining: steen
Welsh onion: cibol
West African baboon: mandrill, mandril
" " seaport: Dakar
" Indian bird: tody
" " fish: pelon, pega
" " fruit: genipap
" " Isl.: Bahamas, Antilles, Haiti, Cuba
" " lizard: arbalo
" " plant: anil
" " rodent: hutia
" " shark: gata
" " shrub: anil
" " sorcery: obi
" " tree: genip
" " vessel: droger
" Point freshman: pleb, plebe
" Saxon king: Ine
wet: moist, watery, rainy, humid, damp, dampen
" (Scot.): wat [soak
" thoroughly: souse,
whale: cete, sperm, orc
" (pert. to): cetic
" school: gam
" skin: rind
whalebone: baleen
wharf: pier, key, quay
whatnot: etagere
wheedle: cajole
wheel bar: axle
" braker: sprad
" of caster: roller
" groove: rut
" hub: nave [rim, tire
" part: cam, spoke,
" (pert. to): rotal
" (small): caster
" of spur: rowel
" tooth: cog [en
whet: stimulate, sharp-
whether: if
whetstone: hone
whey of milk: serum
while: yet, as [fad
whin: notion, caprice,
whimper: mewl, pule
whimsy: caprice
whine & cry: snivel
whinny: neigh
whip: beat, flay, defeat, scourge, cane, lash, flog, knout
" handle: crop
whirl: spu, spin, swirl, twirl, reel, eddy, re-

volve
whirlpool: eddy, vortex
whistle: pipe, siren
whit: doit, jot, iota
white: pale, hoar, ashy
  snowy   [glai
"   **animal:** albino
"   **of egg:** albumen
"   **man:** paleface
"   **substance:** ivory
"   **vestment:** amice,
  alb   [bleach
whiten: blanch, snow,
whither: where
whitish: chalky
whittle: cut
whole: all, entire, complete, aggregate, total
"   **number:** integer
wicked: evil, sinful
wide: broad
"   **awake:** alert
"   **mouth jar or jug:**
  olla, ewer
"   " " **(var.):** ola
widespread: prevalent,
  rife
widgeon: smee
widow: relict
"   **'s coin:** mite
"   " **dower (law):**
  terce
"   " **income:** dower
wield: manage, ply,
  handle
wife: spouse
wig: toupee, peruke,
  tete
wigwam: tepee, teepee
wild: ferocious, feral,
  ferine, fierce
"   **animal:** beast, polecat, elk, fox, tiger,
  lion, lynx, moose
"   **ass of Asia:** onager
"   **buffalo of India:**
  arna, arnee [ocelot
"   **cat:** eyra, lynx,
"   **cherry:** gean
"   **cry:** evoe
"   **duck:** mallard
"   **ox:** anoa, urus
"   **plant:** weed [urial
"   **sheep:** sha, argali,
"   **swine:** boar
"   **tract of land:** heath
wile: trick, art
will: bequeath, decree
"   **leaver:** testator
"   **left & made**
  testate
willing: lieve, ready
willow: osier, itea, salix
wilt: droop
wily: sly, foxy, artful
win: gain, acquire, entice, prevail, earn,
  triumph, get, obtain
"   **over:** defeat, persuade
wince: flinch
wind: gale, breath, coil
"   **blast:** gust
"   **indicator:** vane
"   **instrument:** reed,
  horn, clarinet, tuba,
  organ, bagpipe, flute,

bugle, accordion
windflower: anemone
winding: spiral, sinuous
windlass: winch
windmill arm: vane
window cover: shutter
wing: ala', pinion, alea
"   **of bldg.:** annex
"   **footed:** aliped
"   **of house:** ell
"   **shaped:** alary, alar,
  alate   [alated
winged: alate, flew,
"   **insect:** wasp, moth
"   **serpent:** dragon
"   **steed:** Pegasus
wingless: apteral
wink: nictate, nictitate
winner: victor
winnow: fan
winter (pert.to): hiemal
wipe: mop, clean, swab
wire: telegraph
"   **coil:** spring
"   **rope:** cable
wireman: wirer
wiry: sinewy
wisdom: lore, gnosis,
  erudition, knowledge
wise: sage, learned,
  erudite, prudent,
  knowing [mentor
"   **counselor:** nestor,
"   **men:** sage, magi,
  solomons, solons, nes-
  tors   [acle
"   **saying:** adage, or-
wisely: sagely
wiser: sager [covet
wish: hope, desire, want,
wisp of smoke: floc
wit: wag, humor, sense,
  satire, banter, wag-
  gery, cleverness, as
witch: hex, lamia, hag
witchcraft: sorcery
with might: amain [com
"   **(prefix):** syn, con,
"   **(Scot.):** wi [tract
withdraw: retreat, retract, retire, secede,
  seclude, recede, de-
wither: sere, sear, dry,
  shrink, droop, wilt,
  shrivel [detain
withhold: keep, deny,
within: into, inside,
  inner, in [endo
"   **(comb. form):** eso,
"   **(prefix):** intra
without elevations: flat
"   **feet:** apod
"   **(Fr.):** sans
"   **friends:** lorn
"   **life:** amort
"   **luster:** mat
"   **mate:** odd
"   **purpose:** aimless
"   **reserve:** freely
"   **teeth:** edentate
"   **title:** nameless
withstand: resist, oppose, endure
"   **use:** wears, wear
witness: attest, see
witnessing clause of a

writ: teste [sally
witticism: mot, joke,
witty: facetious [ster
"   **person:** wag, pun-
"   **reply:** repartee
"   **saying:** mot, quip
woe: ill, disaster, bane
woeful: sad
wolfhound: alan
wolframite: cal
woman's cloak: dolman
"   **club:** sorosis
"   **marriage (pert. to)**
  or portion: dotal
wonder: marvel, awe
wont: custom, habit
woo: sue, court, solicit
wood: ebony, teak,
  grove, timber, wal-
  nut, oak, fir, balsa
"   **ash substance:**
  potash
"   **deity:** faun [mite
"   **eating insect:** ter-
"   **(light):** balsa
"   **louse:** slater
"   **nymph:** sprite, dry-
  as, dryad
"   **(small):** grove
"   **sorrel:** oca, oxalis
woodchuck: marmot
woodcutter: sawyer
wooded hill: holt
wooden bench: settee
"   **container:** crate,
  box, barrel, case
"   **cup:** noggin
"   **joint:** tenon [nog
"   **pin:** peg, dowel, fid,
"   **shoe:** sabot
woods: trees, forest
woody corn spike: cob
"   **fiber:** bast
wool colored: beige
"   **(kind):** merino,
  challis, alpaca
woolen cluster: nep
"   **fabric:** tamis, serge,
  beige, ratine, tamine,
  moreen, delaine, chal-
  lis, tweed
"   **surface:** nap
wooly: lanate, fleecy
word: message, term,
  tidings, promise
"   **of assent:** amen
"   " **honor:** parole
"   " **lamentation:**
  alas
"   " **mouth:** parol
"   **for word:** literal
work: operate, opus,
  remark, toil
"   **for:** serve [drudge
"   **hard:** moil, ply,
"   **hard (Scot.):** tew
"   **out:** solve, elaborate [vamp, rework
"   **over:** rehash, re-
"   **party:** bee
"   **at steadily:** ply
"   **too hard:** overdo
"   **with hands:** knead
workman: laborer
workshop: atelier, studio, lab

world wide: global
worm: asp, cadew, ess,
  eis, loa, annelid
worn out: effete, passe,
  spent, old [harass
worry: fret, stew, care,
worship: idolize, revere,
  venerate, adoration
worstedcloth: serge
worth: value, merit,
  use, deserving
worthless: bad, trashy
"   **(Biblical):** raca
"   **(colloq.):** N G.
"   **leaving:** ort
"   **scrap:** ort
wound mark: scar, stab
woven cloth: fabric
"   **fabric:** tissue, texture, blanket, web
wrangle: bicker, dis-
  pute, spar [infold
wrap: envelop, swathe,
  cere, enswathe, shawl,
"   **round & round:**
  roll   [rage
wrath: anger, ire, fury,
wrathful: irate [green
wreath: twine, anadem,
  garland, lei, circlet,
"   **bearing a knight's
  crest:** orle
wreck: ruin [wrest
wrench: spanner, twist,
"   **out of shape:** distort   [snatch
wrest: wrench, wring,
"   **illegally:** extort
wretched: miserable, ill,
  forlorn
wriggle: squirm, wangle
wriggling: eely [twist
wring: extract, wrest,
wrinkled: rugate
wrinkles: creases, rugas,
  rugae, crimp, rimples,
  crinkles, crimps, fold
wrist: carpus
write: transcribe, pen,
  indite, compose, in-
  scribe, scribe
"   **carelessly:** scrawl
writer: author, scribe,
  penman [songster
"   **of verse:** poet,
writing instrument:
  stylus
written agreement:
  cartel
"   **instrument:** deed
"   **promise to pay:**
  note [injure, err
wrong: amiss, faulty,
"   **(prefix):** mal, mis
wrongdoing: sin, evil,
  crime
wrongful act: tort
wrongs: mala
wroth: irate [Teton
Wyoming Mt.: Moran,

Y

Yale: Eli
yam: uve, ube

yank: jerk
yap: yelp
yarn: tale, clew, crewel
yawn: gape
year: annum
" **'s record**: annal
yearbook: almanac
yearn: long, desire, pant, pine [ferment
yeast: leaven, froth,
" **(brewing)**: barm
yell: shout, roar
yellow bugle: iva
" **gray color**: drab
" **ocher**: sil
yelp: yap, yip
yeoman: freeholder
yes: yea, ay, aye [still
yet: besides, though, but, while, however,
yield: obey, cede, return, bow, succumb, net, concede, relent, submit, produce, give
yielding: soft
yogi: fakir, ascetic
yoke: servitude, link, team, couple, join
" **of beasts**: span

yonder (poet.): yon [ye
you (arch.): thee, thou,
young: juvenile
" **of animals**: brood
" **antelope**: kid
" **bird**: nestling
" " **of prey**: eaglet
" **bluefish**: snapper
" **branch**: shoot
" **cat**: kitten, kit
" **chicken**: fryer
" **child**: tad
" **cod**: scrod
" **deer**: fawn
" **dog**: pup
" **eel**: elver
" **fish**: fry
" **fowl**: bird
" **fox**: cub
" **frog**: tadpole
" **goat**: kid
" **hare**: leveret
" **hawk**: eyas [en
" **hen**: pullet, chick-
" **herring**: brit
" **hog**: shoat, shote
" **horse**: colt, foal
" **lady**: belle
" **lion**: lionet

" **man (Scot.)**: laddy
" **onion**: scallion
" **owl**: owlet
" **oyster**: spat
" **pig**: shote, shoat
" **plant**: seedling
" **rowdy**: hoodlum
" **salmon**: parr
" **screen star**: starlet
" **seal**: pup
" **sheep**: lamb
" **swan**: cygnet
" **swine**: pig
younger: tot, junior
youngster: lad, tot, tad, shaver
your (arch.): thy
yours (arch.): thine
youth: lad, stripling, boyhood [nile
youthful: young, juve-
Yugoslav: Serb
" **coin**: dinar
" **leader**: Tito

Z

Z (English form): zed

zeal: ardor, elan, fervor, interest [siast
zealot: fanatic, enthu-
zealous: ardent, earnest
zenith: top, meridian, acme [cipher, nought

zero: nothing, naught,
zest: spice
zesty: piquant

Zeus brother: Hades
" **first wife**: Metis
" **love**: Io
" **mother**: Rhea
" **sister**: Hera [Argus
" **son**: Ares, Hermes,
" **'s wife**: Hera

Zodiac's sign: Aries, Leo, Libra, Virgo
" **2nd sign**: Taurus
" **3rd sign**: Gemini
" **5th sign**: Leo

Zola's novel: Nana
zone: belt, area, region, engirdle, girdle
zoroastrian bible: avesta

Miscellaneous

1/6 drachma: obol.
1/8 mile: furlong [meter
1/10 of a meter: deci-
1/12 inch: en
1/16 of an ounce: dram
" " **a yard**: nail
.025 acre: are
1 kiloliter: stere
2: twain
" **ens**: em
" **quarts**: flagon
3 miles: league
4 inches: hand
" **rods**: acre
5 centimes: sou [pent
" **(comb. form)**: tent.
6 (prefix): hex
9 inches: span

10: X
12: dozen
" **dozen**: gross
16 annas: rupee
16-1/2 feet: rod
20: score
" **cwt.**: ton
" **quires**: ream
" **year sleeper**: rip
39.37 inches: meter
40: XL
49: IL
50: L
51: LI
55: LV
60 grains: dram
90: XC
99: IC

100: C
" **cubic feet**: ton
" **make a yen**: sen
" **sen**: yen [are
" **square meters**: ar,
110: CX
120 yards of silk: lea
144 units: gross
150: CL
160 Square rods: acre
200 milligrams: carat
220 yards: furlong
300 yards of linen: lea
320 rods: mile
433d asteroid: Eros
451: LDI
480 sheets: ream
501: DI

550: DL
600: DC
900: CM
1000: M
" **sq. meters**: decare
1001: MI
1050: ML
1100: MC
1196 sq. yds.: are, ar
1760 yds: mile
2000: MM
" **lbs.**: ton
4047 sq. meters: acre
4840 sq. yds.: acre
3.1416: pi
1,000,000 rupees: lac

MEDICAL
DICTIONARY

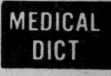

MEDICAL DICTIONARY

COMPILED BY
M. H. GUANDOLA

— A —

Abacterial, sterile, free of bacteria.
Abalienation, mental derangement.
Abarognosis, loss of sense of weight
Abarticular, not affecting a joint.
Abarticulation, dislocation.
Abasia, unable to walk because of loss of motor coordination.
Abatement, lessening of pain.
A.B.C. Process, purifying water or sewage by use of alum, blood and charcoal.
Abdomen, area of body between diaphragm and pelvic bones.
Abdominal, pertaining to the abdomen.
Abduce, abduct.
Abduct, movement of an extremity away from the body or of a part from the middle of the whole.
Aberration, different from normal action.
Abevacuation, incomplete evacuation.
Abeyance, condition of suspended activity.
Abiology, study of nonliving things.
Abionarce, insanity due to infirmity.
Abiosis, absence of life.
Abirritant, soothing.
Ablactation, weaning.
Ablation, removal.
Ablepsia, blindness.
Ablucent, detergent.
Ablution, a washing.
Abnormal, not normal.
Aborad, away from the mouth.
Abortion, termination of pregnancy before the child is able to exist outside the womb.   [arms.
Abrachia, congenital absence of
Abrade, chafe, roughen.
Abrasion, any injury which rubs off the surface skin.
Abscess, collection of pus enclosed anywhere in the body.
Abscission, surgical removal of a growth.
Absorb, to seep in.
Abstract, to take away from.
Abtorsion, turning outward of both eyes.
Abutment, anchorage tooth for a bridge.
Acampsia, rigidity of a part or limb.
Acapnia, decrease in carbon dioxide in the blood.
Acarbia, decrease of bicarbonate in the blood.
Acarid, tick, mite.
Acathexia, inability to retain bodily secretions.
Acceleration, increase the motion or speed.
Accident, unpleasant, unexpected happening.   [ate.
Acclimatize, to get used to a climate.
Accommodation, adjustment.
Accouchement, act of being delivered.
Accretion, accumulation of matter at a part.
Acedia, mental depression.
Acephalous, headless.
Acescence, sour.
Acetabulum, hollow area in the hip bone in which thigh bone fits.
Acetate, salt of acetic acid.
Acetic, sour like vinegar.
Acetone, a colorless, inflammable solvent.
Acetychlorine, hormone secreted by the nervous system.
Achalasia, inability of certain hollow, muscular organs to contract.
Achilles Tendon, the tendon at the back of the heel.
Achlorhydria, inability of the stomach wall to manufacture hydrochloric acid.
Achondroplasia, form of dwarfism in which the trunk is of normal size, the limbs are too short.
Achor, small skin elevation on hairy parts of body.
Achromyan, antibiotic.
Achoresis, diminution of the capacity of an organ.
Achroma, absence of color.
Achylia, absence of chyle, an emulsion of fat globules formed in the intestine.
Acicular, needle-shaped.
Acid, a sour substance that combines with metals, releasing hydrogen.
Acid-forming, applied to foods, which when digested, leave a residue that is acid.
Acidosis, condition in some diseases which causes more acid in the blood than normal.
Acidity, excess of the hydrochloric acid normally found in the stomach.
Acme, crisis
Acne, skin condition found usually in adolescents in which glands of skin become infected.
Acneform, resembling acne.
Acoria, insatiable appetite.
Acousma, hearing imaginary sounds.
Acoustic, relating to sound or hearing.
Acquired, obtained after birth.
Acral, affecting the extremities.
Acrid, irritating.
Acroarthritis, arthritis of the extremities.
Acromegaly, gigantism; state of excessive growth of the body caused by overactivity of the pituitary gland.
Acronyx, ingrowing nail.
Acropathy, disease of the extremities.
Acrophobia, fear of great heights.
Acrosphacelus, gangrene of the fingers or toes.
Acrotism, pulse defect.
A. C. T. H., Adreno-Cortico-Tropic-

Hormone; hormone that stimulates one part of the adrenal gland.
Actinic, applies to those rays of sunlight beyond the violet end of the spectrum, which produce chemical change.
Actinomycosis, disease of cattle that can be transmitted to man.
Acuity, sharpness, clearness.
Acute, illness which had a sudden beginning, a short course and severe symptoms.
Acyesis, female sterility.
Addiment, complement.
Addison's Disease, condition in which adrenal glands are underactive.
Adduct, movement of an extremity toward the body or parts toward the midline of the body.
Adenalgia, pain in a gland.
Adenase, enzyme.
Adenitis, inflammation of a gland.
Adenoidectomy, surgical removal of the adenoids.
Adenoids, lymph glands in back of nasal passage which function to trap germs and debris.
Adenoma, tumor consisting of glandular material.   [glands.
Adenopathy, any disease of the
Adhesions, abnormal growing together of tissue following injury or operation.
Adiaphanous, opaque.
Adicity, valance.
Adipose, fatty.
Adiposity, obesity.
Adjuvant, an auxiliary agent or medication.
Adneural, toward a nerve.
Adnexa, appendages or accessory parts of an organ.
Adrenal Gland, small gland immediately above each of the two kidneys.
Adrenalin, hormone secreted by the adrenal gland, with many properties.
Adtorsion, turning inward of both eyes.
Adult, fully developed.
Adventitious, accidental or acquired; pertaining to the tough outer coat of an organ or blood vessel; occurring in unusual places.
Aeriform, gaseous.
Aeropathy, decompression sickness.
Afebrile, without fever.
Affect, feeling, mood.
Afferent, conducting toward a center.
Affinity, attraction.
Afterbirth, material from womb after childbirth.   [tion.
Agalactia, absence of milk secre-
Agar, form of seaweed used in treating constipation.
Agenesia, sterility; imperfect development.
Ageusia, lack of sense of taste.

Agitation, restlessness; mental illness.

Aglutition, inability to swallow.

Aglycemia, lack of sugar in the blood.

Agnogenic, of unknown origin.

Agnosia, inability to perceive things.

Agonad, person having no sex glands.

Agony, extreme pain.

Agoraphobia, extreme fear of open places.

Ague, an old-fashioned name for malaria or other fevers.

Ahypnia, insomnia.

Air, the gaseous mixture which constitutes the atmosphere.

Air-sickness, sickness caused by high altitudes and motion during air travel.

Airway, instrument used to keep breathing passages open.

Akalamathesia, inability to understand.

Alae Nasi, nostril openings.

Alalia, speech impairment.

Alba, white.

Albinism, absence of pigmentation.

Albino, lack of pigment in the skin.

Albumen, protein.

Albuminuria, albumin in urine.

Alcoholism, drunkenness.

Alexia, unable to read.

Algesia, sensitivity to pain.

Algid, cold.

Algogenic, causing pain; lowering temperature.

Algophobia, extreme fear of pain.

Alienist, psychiatrist.

Alimentary, pertaining to nutrition.

Alimentation, act of nutrition.

Alkalosis, an excess of alkaline in the body and blood stream.

Allergen, that which produces an allergic reaction.

Allergist, specialist in allergies.

Allergy, abnormal sensitivity to any substance.

Allochroism, variation in color.

Allodromy, irregular heart rhythm.

Aloe, vegetable used as a laxative.

Alogia, inability to form words; senseless behavior.

Alopecia, baldness.

Alvine, pertaining to the belly.

Amaurosis, blindness.

Ambidextrous, proficient with each hand.

Amblyacusia, dullness of hearing.

Amblyopia, dimness of vision due to errors of refraction.

Ambulatory, able to walk.

Ambustion, burn, scald.

Amenia, amenorrhea.

Amenorrhea, stoppage of normal menstrual periods.

Amentia, mental impairment.

Amino Acids, a chemical radical in all proteins.

Amnesia, loss of memory.

Amorphous, shapeless.

Ampule, container for hypodermic solutions.

Ampulla, widened end of a small passageway.

Amputation, removal of a limb or appendage.

Amyasthenic, muscular weakness.

Amyloid, starchlike.

Amylophagia, Eating of starch.

Amylum, starch.

Amyotonia, flaccidity of muscles.

Amyotrophic Lateral Sclerosis, a disease causing paralysis because of degeneration of spinal cord.

Amyxia, absence of mucus.

Ana, of each.

Anadipsia, intense thirst.

Anal, pertaining to the anus.

Analgesia, lack of feeling any pain.   [pain.

Analgesic, drug used to relieve

Analysand, one undergoing psychoanalysis.

Anamnesis, patient's history.

Anandria, absence of male characteristics.

Anemic, pertaining to anemia.

Anmeophobia, extreme fear of winds and draughts.

Anepia, inability to speak.

Anesthesia, loss of sensation.

Anesthesiology, study and administration of anesthetics.

Anesthetic, drug or gas used to abolish pain.

Aneuria, deficiency of nervous energy.

Anaphia, lack of sense of touch.

Anaphrodisia, loss of sexual desire.

Anastattis, highly astringent.

Anastole, retraction.

Anatomy, science which deals with the structure of the body.

Ancipital, two-edged.

Anconal, pertaining to the elbow.

Androcyte, spermatid.

Androphobia, fear of men.

Anemia, condition in which the normal amount of red blood cells is reduced.

Aneurysm, swelling in a blood-vessel arising from the stretching of a weak place in the wall.

Anfractuous, convoluted.

Angina Pectoris, severe attacks of pain over the heart.

Angitis, inflammation of a vessel.

Anhelation, shortness of breath.

Anhematosis, defective blood formation.

Anhydrous, containing no water.

Anhypnosis, insomnia.

Anility, like an old woman.

Animation, liveliness.

Anisomastia, inequality of the breasts.

Ankle, region between the foot and lower leg.

Ankylosis, partial or complete rigidity of a joint produced either by disease, such as arthritis, or deliberately, by surgical operation.

Ankyroid, hooklike.

Annectent, connecting.

Annular, ring-shaped.

Annulus, circular opening.

Anodyne, pain reliever.

Anoia, idiocy.

Anomaly, abnormality.

Anopsia, defective vision.

Anorchism, absence of testes.

Anorexia, loss of appetite.

Anoscope, instrument used for rectal examination.

Anoscopy, examination of the anus.

Anosmia, lack of sense of smell.

Anostosis, defective formation of bone.

Anoxemia, reduction in the normal amount of oxygen in the blood.

Anoxia, insufficient supply of oxygen.

Ansa, looplike structure.

Antabuse, proprietary drug used in the treatment of alcoholism.

Antacid, substance that neutralizes acids.

Antebrachium, forearm.

Antemortem, before death.

Antenatal, before birth.

Ante-Partum, before maternal delivery.

Anterior, before.

Anteversion, forward displacement

of part of the body, particularly the womb.

Anthelmintic, drugs used to rid the body of worms.

Anthophobia, extreme dislike of flowers.

Anthorisma, swelling.

Anthracosis, inflammation of the lungs due to inhalation of carbon dust.

Anthrax, disease of man from animals; two forms exist, one on skin and other in lungs.

Antianemic Principle, substance which counteracts anemia.

Antiarthritic, that which relieves or cures arthritis.

Antibechic, relieving cough.

Antibiotics, the group of drugs usually prepared from molds or mold-like organisms, which are used in treatment of specific infections.

Antibody, a protein produced by body which reacts specifically with a foreign substance in the body.

Antibromic, deodorant.

Anticoagulants, a group of drugs which reduce the clotting tendencies of the blood.

Anticus, anterior.

Antidote, remedy given to counteract a poison.   [miting.

Antiemetic, remedy to prevent vo-

Antigen, any protein not normally present in the body and which stimulates the body to produce antibodies.

Antihistamine Drugs, a series of drugs used in the treatment of allergy.

Antilemic, counteracting plague.

Antipathic, opposite in nature.

Antipathy, dislike.

Antipyretic, anything that reduces fever.

Antirabic, counteracting rabies.

Antiseptic, substance used to inhibit growth or destroy germs.

Anti-Toxin, substance manufactured by the blood, which specifically neutralizes the poison (toxin) given off by a particular germ.

Antixerotic, preventing dryness.

Antrum, space within a bone, usually that in the maxilla or upper jaw.

Anuria, absence of urine flow.

Anus, outlet of the bowel.

Anxietas, anxiety, worry.

Aorta, main artery leaving the heart.

Aortitis, inflammation of the aorta.

Aortits, inflammation of the aorta.

Apandria, dislike of men.

Apanthropy, dislike of human society.

Apathic, not having sensation.

Aperient, mild laxative.

Aperture, opening.

Aphagia, inability to swallow.

Aphakia, absence of a lens behind the pupil of the eye.

Aphasia, inability to form words.

Aphephobia, fear of being touched.

Aphonia, inability to speak.

Aphrodisiac, drug which produces sexual excitement.

Aphtha, white spot.

Apogee, state of greatest severity of a disease.

Apoplexy, condition which is the result of decreased blood flow to part of brain, also called stroke.

Apostasis, abscess.

Apothecary, druggist.

Appendage, outgrowth.

Appendectomy, surgical removal of the appendix.

Appendicitis, inflammation of the appendix.

Appendix, fingerlike projection from the large intestine with no known function.

Appetite, desire for food.

Applicator, instrument used to make local application of medicine.

Approximal, close.

Apsychia, unconsciousness.

Aptyalism, lack of saliva

Aqua, water.

Aqueous, watery.

Arachnephobia, extreme fear of spiders.

Arachnidism, condition resulting from spider bite.

Arachnoid, fine, thin tissue.

Arcate, curved

Archepyon, very thick pus.

Arenoid, like sand.

Areola, ring of color around a particular point, e.g., the nipple.

Argentic, containing silver.

Ariboflavinosis, deficiency of riboflavin.   [bow.

Arm, region from shoulder to elbow.

Armamentarium, doctor's entire equipment.

Arrest, stopping; restraining.

Arrhenic, pertaining to arsenic.

Arrhythmia, disturbance of normal rhythm.

Arrowroot, nutrient starch.

Arsenic, poisonous chemical element.

Arteria, artery.

Arteriole, smallest sized artery.

Arterioplasty, operation in which the artery is reconstructed.

Arteriosclerosis, condition in which arteries of body become thickened and inelastic.

Arteriostenosis, constiction of an artery.   [tery.

Arteristis, inflammation of an artery.

Artery, vessel which carries blood away from the heart.

Arthralgia, pain in a joint.

Arthrifuge, remedy for gout.

Arthritis, inflammation of one or more joints.

Arthrocace, ulceration of a joint.

Arthronosos, any joint disease.

Arthropathy, any joint disease.

Arthrophyma, joint swelling.

Arthroplasty, an operation upon a joint to make it function.

Arthrosclerosis, stiffening of the joints.

Articulation, enunciation of speech; a joint.

Artificial, not natural.

Artificial Respiration, the act of restoring breathing, the best method being mouth to mouth respiration.

Asbestosis, lung disease occurring in those who inhale asbestos or asbestos-like material.

Ascariasis, invasion of the body by roundworms.

Ascites (Dropsy), an accumulation of body fluid in the abdomen.

Asepsis, absence of infected material or infection.

Asexual, without sex.

Asexualization, castration.

Asiderosis, iron deficiency.

Asitia, dislike of food.

Aspermatism, nonformation of sperm.

Asphyxia, stoppage of breathing due to obstruction of the air passages.

Aspirator, instrument for withdrawing fluids by suction.

Aspirin, Acetylsalicylic acid, commonly used to relieve headache.

Assay, examine.

Asteroid, shaped like a star.

Asthenia, lack or loss of strength.

Asthma, condition of lungs characterized by decrease in diameter of some air passages.

Astigmatism, a defect of eyesight caused by uneven curvature of the outside membrane of the eye.

Astringent, that which causes contraction and stops discharges.

Asynergy, lack of coordination.

Atactitia, loss of the sense of touch.

Ataxia, loss of co-ordinated movement caused by disease of the nervous system.

Atheroma, hardening of the arteries.

Atherosclerosis, form of hardening of the arteries.

Athetosis, repetitive, involuntary, slow movements.

Athlete's Foot, fungus infection of the foot.

Athrombia, defective blood clotting.

Atlas, topmost vertebra in the spinal column.

Atocia, sterility in the female.

Atomization, breaking up of a liquid into a fine spray.

Atony, lack of normal tone.

Atopy, allergy.

Atoxic, not poisonous.

Atresia, absence of a normal body opening.

Atrophy, decrease in size of a normally developed organ or tissue.

Atrichia, absence of hair.

Attack, the onset of illness.

Attenuation, weakening, thinning.

Audiograph, graph showing acuteness of hearing.

Audiology, science of hearing.

Audiometer, instrument for measuring acuteness of hearing.

Audiphone, hearing aid.

Aura, sensations experienced before the onset of a disease or convulsion.

Aural, pertaining to the ear or hearing.

Aureomycin, antibiotic.

Auris, ear.

Aurotherapy, treatment with gold salts.

Auscultation, part of physical examination which uses detection of sounds in body by use of stethescope to aid diagnosis.

Autism, morbid concentration.

Autoclave, sterilizer.

Autodigestion, self-digestion.

Autoerotism, sexual stimulation of self.

Autogenous, self, generated.

Autointoxication, poisoning by toxins formed within the body.

Autokinesis, voluntary motion.

Automatic, involuntary motion.

Autonomic, independent in action or function.   [tude.

Autophobia, extreme fear of solitude.

Autopsy, examination of a body after death to discover the cause of death.

Autonomic Nervous System, part of the central nervous system which supplies the internal organs. It is divided into two parts: the sympathetic and the parasympathetic nervous systems.

Avitamic Acid, vitamin C; ascorbic acid.   [body.

Autotoxin, toxin formed in the

Auxesis, increase in size.

Avitaminosis, disease resulting from a vitamin deficiency.

Avulsion, tearing away of a part.

Axilla, armpit.

Axillary, pertaining to the armpit.

Azoospermia, absence of sperm in the semen.

Azote, nitrogen.

— B —

Bacca, berry.

Baccate, berry-shaped.

Bacillary, pertaining to bacillus bacteria.

Bacillemia, presence of bacilli in the blood.

Baccilliform, similar to a bacillus in shape.

Bacilluria, presence of bacilli in the urine.

Bacillus, pl., **Bacilli,** one of the major forms of bacteria.

Bacitracin, an antibiotic drug.

Back, posterior part of the body from the neck to the pelvic girdle.

Backache, pain in spine or adjacent areas.

Bacteremia, bacteria in the blood

Bacteria, microscopic organisms.

Bactericide, that which destroys bacteria.

Bacteriuria, bacteria in the urine.

Bagassosis, Lung disease.

Balanitis, inflammation of the tip of the penis or clitoris.

Balanus, tip of the penis or clitoris.

Balbuties, stammering.

Baldness, lack of hair.

Ballistophobia, extreme fear of missiles.

Ballooning, distention of a cavity.

Ballottement, rebound of a part when pressure is released.

Balm, soothing ointment.

Balsam, an aromatic resin.

Bandage, piece of gauze or other material for wrapping any part of the body.

Barber's Itch, infection of the beard area, also known as sycosis.

Barbiturates, drugs used as a hypnotic or sleep producer.

Barium Sulfate, powder used in an emulsion which a patient drinks prior to X-rays of the stomach and intestines.

Barren, sterile.

Baryecois, deafness.

Basal Metabolism, the processes and/or measurement of vital cellular activity in the fasting and resting state based on oxygen usage.

Baseplate, plastic material for making dental trial plates.

Basic, opposite of an acid; fundamental.

Basilic Vein, large vein on the inner side of the upper arm.

Bastard, one born of an unwed mother.

Bath, method of cleansing; therapeutic treatment.   [objects.

Bathophoia, extreme fear of high

Battarism, stuttering.

Beaker, glass with a wide mouth.

Behavior, the observable activity of an individual.

Bearing Down, the expulsive effort of a woman in the second stage of labor.

Beat, throb due to the contraction of the heart or passage of blood through a vessel.

Bedsores, lesions over pressure areas on body of a bedridden patient.

Begma, cough.

Belch, escape of gas from the stomach through the mouth.

Belladonna, drug used to help spasmodic disorders.

Bell's Palsy, paralysis of the facial nerve; shown in weakness of one side of the face. The eye on the affected side will not close properly, and it becomes impossible to blow out the cheeks or whistle.

Belly, stomach.

Bends, decompression sickness.

Benign, non-repeating when referring to a disease.

Benignant, not recurrent.

Benzedrine, the proprietary name of a nervous stimulant.

Beriberi, disease, uncommon in this country, caused by eating food deficient in vitamin B.

Beryllosis, inflammation of the lungs due to beryllium oxide dust.   [mal.

Bestiality, intercourse with an ani-

Beta Rays, negatively charged particles emitted by radium.

Betalin S, synthetic vitamin B.

Bex, cough.

Bicameral, having two cavities.

Biceps, major muscle of the upper arm.

Bicarbonate, salt containing two parts carbonic acid and one part basic substance.

Bicellular, composed of two cells.

Bicuspid, premolar tooth.

Bifurcate, forked.

Bile, liver secretion.

Biliation, excretion of bile.

Biliousness, mild upset of the liver caused by dietary indiscretion.

Biliuria, bile in the urine.

Binder, broad bandage used to encircle and support.

Biochemistry, chemistry of living things.

Biologicals, medical preparations used in the treatment or prevention of disease.

Biology, science of life and living things.

Biolytic, able to destroy life.

Bion, any living organism.

Bionomy, science dealing with vital functions.

Biopsy, tissue taken from a living living person for study.

Biostatics, vital statistics.

Biotics, pertaining to the laws of living organisms.

Biotomy, vivisection.

Bipara, woman who has had two labors.

Birth, process of being born.

Birth Control, measures used to prevent pregnancy.

Birth Injury, any injury to an infant during the birth process.

Birth-Mark, blemish on skin of new born child, which is usually permanent.

Bisexual, both sexes in one person.

Bismuthosis, poisoning due to use of bismuth, a drug formerly used in the treatment of syphilis.

Bistoury, surgical knife.

Bite, cut with teeth; puncture by an insect.

Bitter, of disagreeable taste.

Black, absence of light; of dark pigmentation.

Blackblood, impure blood.

Black Death, bubonic plague.

Blackout, sudden temporary loss of sight and even consciousness.

Blackwater Fever, form of malaria.

Black Widow, poisonous spider.

Bladder, collecting pouch for urine from kidneys.

Bland, soothing; mild.

Blastoma, tumor.

Blear-eye, chronic inflammation of margins of eyelids.

Bleb, blister.

Bleeder, One suffering from hemophilia; an inborn incurable disease in which severe bleeding follows even a slight cut.

Bleeding, emitting blood.

Bleeding Time, time necessary for the natural stoppage of bleeding from a cut, about 3 minutes or less.

Blenna, mucus.

Blennagenic, producing mucus.

Blepharitis, inflammation of the eyelids shown by redness, crusting, swelling and infection of the eyelashes.

Blepharon, eyelid.

Blindness, inability to see.

Blister, collection of fluid under the skin.   [size.

Bloated, swollen beyond normal

Blood, fluid contained in arteries and veins of body that carries nutrients to and waste away from all tissues. Made up of cells and plasma.

Blood Bank, storing place for reserve blood.

Blood Clot, coagulated mass of blood.

Blood Count, a procedure that determines the number and type of red and white blood cells per cubic millimeter of blood.

Blood Groups, categories under which all human blood can be classified.   [blood.

Bloodshot, locally congested with

Blood-Pressure, this term refers to two different pressures in the blood system; the systolic pressure, which is that existing when the heart contracts and the diastolic pressure when the heart is in full relaxation.

Blood Type, classification of blood into different types.

Bloody Flux, dysentery.

Blue Baby, child born with a blue color due usually to a heart defect.

Blue Ointment, mercurial ointment.

Blushing, rush of blood to the face.

Body, the physical man; trunk.

Body Cavities, thorax, abdomen, pelvis.

Bolus, round mass; pill; food prepared for swallowing by mastication.

Boil, infection of the skin.

Bone Grafting, transplanting a healthy bone to replace missing or defective bone.

Bonelet, small bone.

Bone Onlay, portion of transplanted bone placed across a break in a bone.

Bones, framework of body, composed of calcium and elastic tissue.

Bone Wax, material used to pack bone in order to stop bone bleeding.

Boric Acid, an antiseptic used on skin to help infections.

Boss, protuberance at one side of a bone.

Botulism, the most dangerous form of food poisoning.

Bowel, intestine.

Box Splint, used for fractures below the knee.

Brachium, arm.

Bradycardia, slow heart rate.

Braidism, hypnotism.

Brain, the primary nervous structure which sends out and receives stimulations to and from the rest of the body.

Brain Fever, meningitis.

Breakbone Fever, acute epidemic febrile disease.

Breast, front of the chest; mammary gland.

Breath, air inhaled and exhaled in the respiratory process.

Breathe, to inhale and exhale air.

Breathing, act of taking in air to the body and exhaling carbon dioxide.

Bright's Disease, kidney disease.

Bromides, salts of bromine.

Bromidrosis, offensive body odor.

Bromide, any salt containing bromine.

Bronchiectasis, state in which the lung tissue around the end of the breathing tubes becomes infected with the formation of sac-like cavities which fill with infectious material.

Bronchiole, smallest subdivision of the breathing tubes within the lung.

Bronchitis, inflammation of the windpipe which divides and subdivides into narrower tubes making up the network of air passages within the lungs.

Brown Mixture, cough syrup containing opium and licorice.

Brucella, type of bacillus.

Bruise, any injury to the surface of the body in which the skin is discolored but not broken.

Bruit, abnormal sound or murmur.

Buerger's Disease, disease of the blood vessels, usually in the arms and legs, in which spasm of the arteries leads to numbness, coldness, pain in the muscles and change of color.

Bubonic Plague, fatal infectious disease.

Bucca, mouth.

Bug, small insect.

Buggery, sexual relations through the anus.

Bulimia, an insatiable appetite.

Bulla, large blister.

Bunion, thickened area of skin on skin on lateral side of big toe.

Bundle, group of fibers.

Burn, an injury to the body caused by high temperature.

Bursa, a sac like cavity usually found in or near joints.

Bursitis, inflammation of a bursa.

Buttonhole, straight cut through the wall of a cavity.

Bysma, plug; tampon.

Bythus, lower abdominal region.

Byssinosis, irritation of the air passages in the lung due to inhalation of cotton dust.

— C —

Cacation, defecation.

Cachet, capsule.

Cachexia, extreme wasting and weakness found in the later stages of a severe illness or starvation.

Cachinnation, hysterical laughter.

Cadaver, corpse.

Caduceus, symbol of the medical, i.e., the wand of Hermes.

Caffeine, stimulant found mainly in coffee.

Cainotophobia, extreme fear of anything new.

Caisson Disease, occurs in workers, such as divers, who work under high atmospheric pressure, occurs when the pressure is reduced too rapidly, and the nitrogen in the blood escapes in the form of bubbles.

Calamine, pink substance composed of zinc and iron oxides, used in the form of lotion to soothe the skin.

Calcaneus, heel bone.   [cium.

Calcareous, chalky; containing cal-

Calcicosis, inflammation of the lungs due to marble dust.

Calcification, calcium deposits within the tissues of the body.

Calcinosis, calcium deposit in the skin and its underlying tissue.

Calcium, element which is the basis of limestone, important in body skeleton and function.

Calculus, stone-like mass which may form in the body under abnormal conditions.

Calf, the fleshy part of the back of the leg.

Calibrator, instrument for measuring openings.

Callous, any thickening of the skin formed on the site of continual irritation, unusually on the feet or hands.

Callus, the new tissue formed at the site of fracture when a bone heals.

Calmant, Calmative, sedative.

Calomel, mercurous chloride; formerly used in the treatment of syphilis.

Calorie, measure of energy intake and output in the body.

Calvities, baldness.

Camphor, drug obtained from the camphor tree and used to stimulate the skin.

Camphorated, containing camphor.

Canal, passage, duct.

Cancer, any malignant tumor.

Cancroid, like cancer; a tumor; type of skin cancer.

Canine Teeth, four teeth (upper and lower) between the incisors and molars.

Canker, type of mouth ulceration.

Capillary, smallest blood vessel.

Capsule, tissue covering a part; soluble coating surrounding medication.

Caput, head.

Carbo, carbon, charcoal.

Carbohydrates, the scientific name for sugars, starches and cellulose.

Carbolic Acid, coal tar derivative used as an antiseptic and disinfectant.

Carbon, element which is the characteristic constituent of organic compounds.

Carbon Dioxide (CO_2), colorless, odorless gas used with oxygen to promote respiration.

Carbuncle, large boil.

Carcinogenic, causing cancer.

Carcinoma, particular type of cancer.

Cardiac, concerning the heart.

Cardiac Failure, heart failure.

Cardiogram, record of changes in electrical energy of heart cycle.

Cardiograph, apparatus for making a graph of heart cycle.

Cardiology, medical specialty dealing with the heart.

Cardiophobia, extreme fear of heart disease.

Cardiospasm, contraction of the muscles controlling the inlet to the stomach.

Cardiovascular, pertaining to the heart and blood vessels.

Caries, condition of decay, usually applied to decay of the teeth.

Carminative, drug to aid digestion and relieve flatulence, e.g., ginger, peppermint.

Carnal, pertaining to the flesh.

Carnal Knowledge, sexual knowledge.

Carnivorous, flesh-eating.

Carotid, major artery leading to the brain.

Carpal, relating to the wrist.

Carpus, wrist.

Carrier, one who harbors disease germs without suffering from the disease himself.

Car Sickness, illness due to motion of a car.

Cartilage, gristle.

Cascara, a laxative.

Case, particular example.

Caseation, conversion of tissue into a cheese-like substance by certain diseases.

Casebook, Physician's record book.

Casein, protein product of milk.

Cast, mold to hold bone rigid and straight.

Castor Oil, old-fashioned purgative.

Castrate, to remove the testicles or ovaries.

Castration Complex, extreme fear of injury to the sex organs.

Casualty, accidental injury.

Catabolism, the breaking down of complex compounds into simpler ones.

Catalepsy, general name to describe various states marked by loss of power to move the muscles.

Catalyst, agent which influences a chemical reaction without taking part in it.   [period.

Catemenia, onset of first menstrual

Cataract, clouding of the lens of the eye which prevents clear vision.

Catarrh, any illness which causes inflammation of membranes with a discharge of mucus.

Catatonia, type of schizophenia characterized by immobility.

Catgut, Sheep's intestine twisted for use as surgical thread.

Catharsis, purging.

Cathartic, purgative.

Catheter, tube for passage through body channels, usually to evacuate fluids.

Cathexis, emotional energy attached to an object.

Caustic, irritating, burning.

Cautery, application of a burning agent to destroy tissue.

Cauterization, application of heat or burning chemicals to the surface of the body.

Cavernous, having hollow spaces.

Cavity, hollow space.

Cecostomy, establishing an artificial opening into the large intestine near the appendix for evacuation.

Cecum, first part of the large intestine.   [egion.

Celiac, pertaining to the abdominal

Cell, small cavity; a mass of protoplasm containing a nucleus.

Cellular, composed of cells.

Cellulitis, deep inflammation of the tissues just under the skin caused by infection with germs.

Centrifugal, moving away from a center.

Cephalalgia, headache.

Cephalic, pertaining to the head.

Cerebellum, small part of the nervous system, situated at the back of the brain, which is concerned with co-ordination of movements and bodily functions such as respiration.

Cerebration, mental activity.

Cerebro-Spinal Fluid, the clear fluid which surrounds the brain and spinal cord as they lie inside the skull and in the canal of the spinal column; acts mainly as a shock absorber.

Cerebrum, the brain, especially the large frontal portion, as distinct from the cerebellum and the spinal cord.

Cerumen, Ear wax.

Cervix, the neck or that part of an organ resembling the neck.

Cervical, pertaining to the neck or mouth of womb.

Cesarean Operation, abdominal operation to remove a child from the womb of a pregnant woman.

Cestoid, resembling a tapeworm.

Chafing, irritation caused by the rubbing together.

Chalazion, tumor of the eyelid.

Chancre, the name given to the sore that appears on the body when infected with certain types of venereal disease organisms.

Change of Life, the menopause, usually occurring in women between the ages of forty and fifty-five, and about ten years later in men.

Chapped Skin, skin becomes dry and cracks due to decreased activity of glands in the area.

Charley Horse, bruised or torn muscle associated with cramping pain in the muscle.

Charting, recording the progress of a disease.

Check, slow down; stop, verify.

Cheek, side of the face below the eye.

Cheilitis, inflammation of the lips.

Cheilosis, lip disorder due to vitamin deficiency.   [sternum.

Chest, area enclosed by the ribs and

Chigger, mite whose bite causes severe inflammation.

Chilblains, painful swelling of fingers, toes and ears caused by exposure to cold.

Child, one in the period between infancy and youth.

Chill, symptoms that occur when one first becomes infected with any germs which cause fever; result of nervous stimulation.

Chin, area below lower lip.

Chirology, means of communicating with deaf mute by sign-language.

Chiropractic, system of treatment based on the belief that all disease is caused by pressure on the nerves as they leave the spinal column.

Chiropractor, one who specializes in bone manipulation.

Chloasma, brownish discoloration of the skin found in patches on any part of the body; particularly apparent in some pregnant women.

Chloremia, decrease of hemoglobin and red corpuscles of the blood.

Chloroform, heavy, clear, colorless liquid used as an anesthetic.

Chloromycetin, antibiotic.

Chlorosis, form of anemia.

Choke, obstruction of the pharynx or esophagus.

Cholecystectomy, removal of the

gall bladder.

Cholecystitis, inflammation of the gall bladder.

Cholelith, gallstone. ⌈blood.

Cholemia, presence of bile in the

Cholera, tropical intestinal disease.

Cholesteral, substance found in fats and oils.

Choleric, irritable.

Cholinesterase, an enzyme.

Chondral, pertaining to cartilage.

Chondroma, tumor of a resembling cartilage.

Chorda, string, tendon.

Chorea, also known as St. Vitus' dance or Sydenham's chorea; disease of the nervous system, usually considered to be related to rheumatism or rheumatic fever.

Choriomeningitis, inflammation of the coverings of the brain.

Chorion, outermost of the fetal membranes.

Chromatelopsia, color blindness.

Chromatic, pertaining to color.

Chromatosis, pigmentation.

Chromocyte, colored cell.

Chronic, of long duration.

Chronological, according to time sequence.

Chyme, food after digestion in the stomach.

Cicatrix, scar.

Circulation, flowing in a circular course.

Circulation Time, rate of blood flow.

Circumcision, operation of cutting off the foreskin of male penis.

Cirrhosis, hardening of any tissue, but particularly of the liver.

Cirsectomy, removal of a part of a varicose vein.

Clamp, surgical device for compressing a part or structure.

Claudication, lameness due to decreased blood flow.

Claustrophobia, extreme fear of enclosed spaces.

Clavicle, collar bone.

Clavus, corn.

Cleavage, division into distinct parts.

Cleft, fissure.

Cleft Palate, congenital fissure of the palate forming one cavity for the nose and throat.

Climacteric, change of life.

Clinic, bedside examination; center where patients are treated by a group of physicians practicing together.

Climax, period of greatest intensity.

Clinical, pertaining to bedside treatment.

Clitoris, small erectile organ of the femal genitalia.

Clot, to coagulate.

Club-Foot, congenital deformity of the feet of unknown cause.

Clunis, buttock.

Clyster, enema.

Coagulation, formation of a blood clot.

Coalescence, fusion of parts.

Cocaine, a local anesthetic.

Coccygodynia, pain in the area of the tail bone.

Coccyx, small bones at the end of the spine.

Cochlea, cavity in the internal ear.

Codeine, sedative.

Cod-Liver Oil, the chief outside source of vitamins A and D, obtained from oil of cod fish.

Cognition, processes involved in knowing.

Coitus, sexual intercourse.

Colchicine, drug which helps to relieve symptoms of gout.

Colds, common viral infection of man causing symptoms of nasal fullness, cough and fever.

Cold Sores, lesions particularly in and around mouth caused by herpes simplex virus.

Colectomy, removal of part of the large intestine.

Colic, severe abdominal pain caused by spasm of one of the internal organs, usually the intestines; pertaining to the colon or large intestine.

Collapse, to flatten; breakdown; prostration.

Colitis, inflammation of the large intestine.

Collodion, drug which, when painted on the skin, forms a thin transparent protective film.

Collyrium, local eye medication, e.g., eye wash.

Colon, large intestine.

Color Blindness, an inborn condition in which, while ordinary vision remains normal the individual is unable to distinguish between particular colors.

Colostrum, first milk from a mother's breast after childbirth.

Colpalgia, vaginal pain.

Colpatitis, vaginal inflammation.

Column, supporting part.

Coma, complete loss of consciousness, which may be the result of various causes.

Comatose, state of being in a coma.

Comedo, blackheads in glands of skin.

Comminution, breaking into small fragments.

Comminute, a bone shattered in several pieces.

Commitment, placing a patient in an institution.

Comparative Anatomy, human anatomy compared to that of animals.

Complication, added difficulty.

Compound, substance composed of different elements.

Compress, a pad for application of pressure or medication to a specific area.

Conception, fertilization.

Concha, shell-like organ.

Concussion, stunning; condition of dizziness, mental confusion and sometimes unconsciousness, due to a blow on the head.

Condom, rubber covering worn over the penis to prevent conception.

Conduction, conveyance of energy.

Condyloma, wartlike growth near the anus or genitals.

Congenital, existing at or before birth.

Congestion, excess accumulation of blood or mucus in any part of the body.

Conjunctivitis, inflammation of the transparent membrane which covers the eyeball.

Connective, that which binds together.

Connective Tissue, one of the four main tissues of the body which support bodily structures, bind parts together and take part in other bodily functions.

Consciousness, awareness.

Constipation, failure of bowels to excrete residue at proper intervals.

Consumption, tuberculosis.

Contagion, (see infection.)

Contagious, easily transmitted by contact.

Contagium, agent causing infection.

Continence, ability to control natural impulses.

Contraception, use of mechanical devices or medicines to prevent conception.

Contraction, a drawing together.

Contracture, a shortening of tissue, causing deformity or distortion, e.g., scar.

Contusion, bruise.

Convex, rounded and somewhat elevated.

Convulsant, medicine which causes convulsions.

Convolution, coil of tissue on the brain surface, separated by fissures.

Convulsion, temporary loss of consciousness with severe muscle contractions due to many causes; fit or generalized spasm.

Co-ordination, working together of various muscles.

Copulation, sexual intercourse.

Cord, Spinal, that portion of the central nervous system contained in the spinal canal.

Cord, Umbilical, cord which connects the umbilicus of the fetus to the placenta.

Cordate, heart-shaped.

Corium, layer of skin under the epidermis.

Corn, thickening of the skin, hard or soft, according to location on the foot.

Cornea, transparent membrane covering the eye and lying beneath the conjunctiva.

Corneum, outmost layer of skin.

Coronary Thrombosis, clotting of blood in the blood vessels which supply the heart.

Coroner, one who holds inquests over those dead from violent or unknown causes.

Corpus, principal part of an organ; mass.

Corpuscle, blood cell.

Corrosive, destructive; disintegrating.

Cortex, outer layer of the brain and other organs.

Cortisone, a hormone produced by the adrenal glands.

Corsucation, sensation of flashes of light before the eyes.

Coryza, nasal catarrh or common cold.

Costalgia, rib pains.

Costive, constipated.

Cough, an attempt on the part of the body to expel something causing irritation in the respiratory tract.

Coxa, hip; hip joint. ⌈tion.

Cramp, painful, spasmodic contrac-

Cranium, skull.

Crapulent, characterized by excessive eating and drinking.

Cremaster, muscle which draws up the testis.

Crest, ridge on a bone.

Cretinism, condition caused by the lack of or decreased secretion of the thyroid gland in a child.

Crevice, small fissure. ⌈ease.

Crisis, the turning point of a dis-

Critical, dangerous; severe.

Cross-eyes, condition in which eyes do not move together.

Cross-Knee, knock knee.

Croup, a disease of children characterized by coughing and difficult breathing.

Cryptogenic, of unknown or obscure origin.

-cule, -cle (suffix), little.

Culture, propagation of an organism.

Cumulative, increasing.

Cure, system of treatment; restoration to health.

Curettage, scraping the interior of a cavity with a curette.

Curette, a spoon-shaped instrument used for scraping away dead tissue.

Cusp, point of the crown of a tooth; pointed projection on a segment of a cardiac valve.

Cuspid, canine tooth.

Cutaneous, pertaining to the skin.

Cuticle, outermost layer of the skin.

Cyanosis, term used to describe blueness of the skin, generally caused by lack of oxygen.

Cycle, sequence.

Cyesis, pregnancy.

Cyst, any sac in the body filled with liquid or semi-liquid substance.

Cystitis, inflammation of the bladder.

Cystoscopy, process of examining the inside of the bladder with an instrument.

— D —

Dacryorrhea, excessive flow of tears.

Dactyl, digit.

Dactylion, webbing of the fingers and toes.

Dactylitis, inflammation of a finger or toe.

Dactylology. communication with the fingers, i.e., sign language.

Dactylus, finger; toe.

Daltonism, color blindness.

D. & C., dilation and curettage of uterus.

Dandruff, condition of the scalp characterized by dry scaling.

Dartos, fibrous layer under the skin of the scrotum.

Deaf-mutism, inability to hear or speak.

Deafness, complete or partial loss of hearing.

Dealbation, bleaching.

Dearterialization, conversion of arterial into venous blood.

Death Rate, number of people who die each year, compared with the total number of population.

Death Rattle, gurgling noise caused by passage of air through accumulated fluid in the windpipe.

Debility, weakness.

Decalcification, decrease in the normal mineral salts content of bone.

Decalvant, making bald.

Decerebration, removal of the brain.

Decidua, membranous lining of the uterus shed after childbirth or at menstruation.

Decompensation, failure of an organ to adjust itself to changing condition. [sure.

Decompression, removal of pres-

Decripitude, senile feebleness.

Decubitus, lying down posture.

Decubation, period of convalescence from an infectious disease.

Defecation, evacuation of the bowels.

Defective, imperfect.

Defemination, loss of female and assumption of male sex characteristics.

Deficiency Disease, any disease

caused by the lack of some essential part of the diet.

Defloration, loss in a woman of virginal characteristics, i.e., rupture of the hymen.

Defluvium, falling out of hair.

Deformity, distortion, malformation.

Degeneration, deterioration or breaking down of a part of the body.

Deglutition, act of swallowing.

Dehydration, loss of water.

Dejecta, excrement.

Dejection, melancholy.

Delactation, weaning, stopping of lactation.

Deliquesence, liquefaction of a salt by absorption of moisture from the air.

Delirium, mental disturbance, usually occuring in the course of some infectious disease, or under the influence of poisonous drugs.

Deliver, to aid in birth.

Deltoid, triangular.

Delusion, false belief.

Demented, insane. [gence.

Dementia, deterioration of intelli-

Demorphinization, treatment of morphine addiction by gradual withdrawal.

Demulcent, reducing irritation; a soothing substance.

Dengue, tropical disease carried by mosquitoes, causing fever and joint pain.

Denigration, process of becoming black.

Dens, tooth.

Dentagra, toothache; forceps for pulling teeth.

Dentalgia, toothache.

Dentifrice, any substance used for cleaning teeth.

Dentin, chief substance of teeth.

Dentistry, branch of medicine dealwith teeth.

Denture, complete unit of teeth.

Deodorant, that which destroys odors.

Deontology. medical ethics.

Deorsum, downward.

Depersonalization, loss of the sense of one's own reality.

Depilate, to remove hair.

Depilatory, substance used to remove hairs.

Deplete, to empty.

Depraved, perverted.

Depressant, that which retards any function.

Derangement, disorder.

Dermad, toward the skin.

Dermatitis, inflammation of the skin, eczema.

Dermatologist, skin specialist.

Dermatology, branch of medicine which deals with the skin and its diseases.

Dermatosis, any skin disease.

Dermoid, resembling skin.

Desiccant, a drying medicine; tendency to cause drying.

Desiccate, to dry.

Desmalgia, pain in a ligament.

Detergent, cleansing.

Deviation, variation from the normal condition.

Dexter, right.

Dextrocardia, position of the heart in the right side of the chest.

Dextrophobia, extreme fear of objects on the right side of the body.

Dextrose, form of sugar.

Diabetes, a disease which shows itself in an inability of the body to

handle glucose.

Diagnosis, determination of a patient's disease.

Diagnostician, one skilled in determining the nature of a disease.

Di- (prefix), two.

Diaphragm, large muscle which separates the inside of the chest from the inside of the abdomen; contraceptive device.

Diaphysis, shaft of a long bone.

Diarrhea, watery, loose bowel movements.

Diarticular, pertaining to two joints.

Diastole, period of relaxation of the heart during which it fills with blood.

Diastalsis, forward movement of the bowel contents.

Diastema, space, cleft.

Diathermy, treatment of disease or injury by use of heat.

Diathesis, type of constitution which makes one liable to a particular disease.

Dichotomy, division into two separate parts.

Dick Test, test to discover whether a patient is liable to or immune from scarlet fever.

Didymalgia, pain in a testis.

Diet, nutritional intake; prescription of food permitted to be eaten by a patient. [trition.

Dietetics, science of diet and nu-

Dietitian, specialist of diet in health and disease.

Dietotherapy, use of a diet regimen for cure.

Diffuse, widely spread.

Digestant, that which aids digestion.

Digestion, assimilation of food by the body.

Digit, finger; toe.

Digitalis, drug used in the treatment of heart diseases.

Dilatation, stretching; increase in diameter.

Dionism, homosexuality.

Diphasic, having two phases.

Diphtheria, disease causing the development of membrane in nose and throat.

Diploplia, double vision.

Dipsomania, excessive desire for drink.

Disarticulation, separation of bones at a joint.

Disc, Disk, platelike structure or organ.

Discharge, setting free; excretion.

Discrete, separate.

Disease, sickness; ailment.

Disengagement, liberation of the fetus from the vaginal canal.

Disinfection, killing germs by antiseptics or other methods.

Disinfectation, extermination of pests.

Dislocation, displacement of the bones in a joint.

Disseminated Schlerosis, disease of the nervous system in which small patches of hard tissue (sclerosis) develop throughout the spinal cord and brain.

Distention, widening; enlargement.

Dismemberment, amputation.

Dispensary, place which gives free or low cost medical treatment.

Dissection, cutting up.

Distillation, purification of a liquid by vaporizing it and then condensing it.

Distrix, the splitting of the hairs at the end.
Diuresis, frequent urination.
Dieuretic, medicine which increases the flow of urine.
Divagation, unintelligible speech.
Diverticulitis, inflammation of small pouches or diverticuli in large intestine.
Dizziness, sensation of spinning or off balance.
Dolorific, causing pain.
Domatophobia, extreme fear of being in a house.
Donor, one who gives blood or body tissue for the use of others.
Doraphobia, extreme fear of fur.
Dorsal, pertaining to the back or hind part of an organ.
Dorsalgia, pain in the back.
Dorsum, back.
Dose, amount of medication to be given at one time.
Dose, Lethal, dose large enough to to cause death.
Dossier, file containing a patient's case history.
Douche, stream of water directed into a body cavity or against the body itself.
Dowel, pin used to hold an artificial crown to a natural tooth root.
D.P.H., Department of Public Health.
Dragee, large, sugar-coated pill.
Drain, channel of exit for discharge from a wound.
Dramamine, drug commonly used for seasickness.
Dressing, protective covering placed over a wound to aid the healing process.
Drive, basic urge.
Drop Foot, state of inability to raise the foot upwards due to paralysis of the leg muscles.
Dropper, tube for giving liquid in drops.
Dropsy, generalized accumulation of fluid in body, edema.
Drowning, suffocation and death due to filling the lungs with liquid.
Drug, any medicinal substance.
Duct, tube or channel that conducts fluid, especially the secretion of a gland.
Duipara, woman who has had two children.
Dumb, unable to speak.
Duodenum, first eight to ten inches of the small intestine.
Dura Mater, outermost covering of the brain and spinal cord.
Dwarf, an undersized person.
Dynamia, energy.
Dys- (prefix), bad; difficult.
Dysarthria, stammering.
Dysarthrosis, dislocation; disease or deformity of a joint.
Dysbasia, difficulty in walking.
Dyschiza, painful bowel movement.
Dysemesia, painful vomiting.
Dysentery, name given to a group of disorders in which there is diarrhea, produced by irritation of the bowels. [tion.
Dysfunction, impairment of func-
Dysgenesis, malformation.
Dysgraphia, inability to write.
Dyskinesia, impairment of the ability to make any physical motion.
Dysmenorrhea, painful menstruation.
Dyspepsia, indigestion.
Dysphagia, difficulty in swallowing.
Dyspnea, labored breathing.

Dysomia, sleep disorder.
Dyspareunia, pain felt by the woman during sexual intercourse.
Dystithia, difficulty in breast feeding.
Dystocia, difficult childbirth.
Dystrophy, weakening of muscle due to abnormal development.
Dysuria, painful urination.

— E —

Ear, organ of hearing.
Earache, pain in ear usually due to inflammation.
Eat, to take solid food.
Ebullition, boiling.
Eburnation, hardening of teeth or bone.
Ecbolic, that which speeds up child birth or produces abortion.
Eccentric, peripheral, peculiar in ideas.
Ecchymosis, a discoloring of the skin caused by the seepage of blood beneath skin.
Eccyesis, extrauterine pregnancy.
Ecdemic, pertains to disease brought into a region from without.
Echinococcosis, infestation with a type of tapeworm.
Echo, reverbrating sound.
Echolalia, senseless repetition of words spoken by others.
Eclampsia, form of internal poisoning and convulsions which may occur in late pregnancy.
Ecouvillonage, cleansing of a wound or cavity.
Ecphuma, outgrowth.
Ecstasy, exaltation.
Ectal, external.
Ectasia, widening in diameter of a tubular vessel.
Ecthyma, inflammation of the skin, characterized by large pimples that rupture and become crusted.
Ectocardia, displacement of the heart.
Ectoderm, outermost layer of cells in a developing embryo.
-ectomy (suffix), excision.
Ectopic, abnormal position of an organ, part of a body; pregnancy outside the uterus.
Ectropion, the turning out of a part, particularly an eyelid.
Eczema, an itching disease of the skin.
Edema, an excessive accumulation of tissue fluid.
Edentate, without teeth.
Edeology, study of the genitalia.
Edible, suitable to be eaten.
Effemination, assumption of feminine qualities in a man.
Efferent, conducting away from a center.
Effluvium, foul exhalation.
Effusion, accumulation of fluid, or the fluid itself, in various spaces of the body, e.g., joints.
Egesta, body excretions or discharges.
Egg, ovum.
Ego, that part of the mind which possesses reality and attempts to bring harmony between the instincts and reality.
Egocentric, self-centered.
Egomania, morbid self-esteem.
Egotism, exaggerated evaluation of one's self.
Eiloid, coiled.
Ejaculation, ejection of semen.
Ejection, the act of expelling.
Elastic, able to return to normal shape after distortion.

Elation, joyful emotion.
Elbow, juncture at which the arm and forearm meet.
Electric Shock, burns with loss of consciousness.
Electricity, form of energy having magnetic, chemical and thermal effects.
Electrocardiography, a machine which records the electrical activity of the heart muscles.
Electrocogulation, the deterioration or hardening of tissues by high-frequency currents.
Electrode, an electric conductor through which current enters or leaves a cell, an apparatus or body.
Electroencepalogram, record of the electrical changes of the brain.
Electron, an elementary unit of electricity; negatively charged particle of the atom.
Electroshock, shock produced by electric current.
Electrotherapy, treatment of disease by use of electricity.
Electuary, soft, medicated confection.
Elephantiasis, tropical disease in which blocking of the lymph vessels by a parasite leads to great swelling of the tissues, especially in the lower part of the body.
Elimination, discharge of indigestible materials and waste products from the body.
Elixer, a sweetened, alcoholic liquid used to disguise unpleasant tasting medicines.
Emaciated, excessively thin.
Emasculation, castration.
Embalming, preservation of a corpse against decomposition.
Embolism, small clot or foreign substance detached from the inside of a blood vessel and floating free in the blood stream.
Embryo, earliest stage of development of a young organism; the human young through the third month of pregnancy.
Emedullate, to deprive of marrow.
Emesis, vomiting.
Emetic, drug that causes vomiting.
Emetine, drug that causes sweating and expectoration.
Emiction, urination.
Emission, sending forth; discharge of semen.
Emmenia, the menses.
Emmenology, that which is known about menstruation.
Emmenagogue, that which stimulates the menstrual flow.
Emollient, relaxing, soothing agent used to soften the skin or internally to soothe an irritated surface.
Emotion, mental attitude.
Empathy, understanding, sympathy.
Emphysema, lung disease characterized by the thinning and loss of elasticity of lung tissue.
Emphiric, based on experience.
Empyema, collection of pus in the lung.
Emulgent, draining out.
Emulsion, product made up of tiny globules of one liquid suspended in another liquid.
Enamel, the hard, white substance which covers and protects the tooth. [gion.
Encelialgia, pain in abdominal re-
Encephalic, pertaining to the brain.

Encephalitis, inflammation of the brain.

Encephalogram, brain x-ray.

Encephalomalacia, softening of the brain due to deficient blood supply.

Encephalon, the brain. [ium.

Encranial, located within the cran-

Endomoeba, a single-celled parasite that lives in humans.

Endeictic, symptomatic.

Endemic, disease prevalent in a particular area.

Endangium, membrane which lines blood vessels.

Endermic, administered through the skin.

Endoblast, cell nucleus.

Endocardial, pertaining to the interior of the heart.

Endocarditis, inflammation of the inner lining of the heart, especially the heart valves.

Endocardium, tissue lining the inside of the heart.

Endochrome, coloring matter of a cell.

Endocranial, within the cranium.

Endocrine Glands, ductless glands that secrete directly into the blood stream.

Endocrinology, study of ductless glands and their secretions.

Endoderm, inner layer of cells of an embryo.

Endodontitis, inflammation of the dental pulp.

Endometritis, inflammation of the lining of the womb.

Endometrium, tissue that lines the interior wall of the womb.

Endoplast, nucleus of a cell.

End-Organ, any terminal structure of a nerve.

End Pleasure, pleasure enjoyed at the height of the sexual act.

End Product, the final excretory product that passes from the system.

Endothermic, characterized by heat absorption.

Enema, an injection of liquid into the rectum, usually intended for the treatment of constipation.

Energy, ability to work.

Enervation, weakness.

Engorgement, excessive fulness.

Engram, the indelible impression which experience makes upon nerve cells.

Enomania, craving for alcoholic drink, delerium tremens.

Enstrophe, turning inward.

Ental, inner.

Enteralgia, pain in the intestine.

Enteric, pertaining to the intestines.

Enteritis, inflammation of the intestinal tract by infection or irritating food.

Enterocolitus, inflammation of the small and large intestines.

Enteron, the intestine.

Enthetic, introduced from without.

Entopic, located in the proper place.

Entropian, turning in of the edge of the eyelid so that the lashes rub against the eyeball.

Enucleate, to remove a tumor or an organ in its entirety.

Enuresis, bed wetting.

Environment, external surroundings.

Enzyme, a substance produced by living cells which, although not participating in a chemical reaction, promotes its speed.

Ephebic, pertaining to puberty.

Ephedrine, drug used to shrink the lining of the nose in colds and in the treatment of asthma.

Ephelis, freckle.

Ephidrosis, profuse sweating.

Epibular, upon the eyeball.

Epicutaneous, on the surface of the skin.

Epicyte, wall of a cell.

Epidemic, disease that affects many people at one time in the same area.

Epidemiology, study of the occurrence and distribution of disease.

Epidermis, outermost layer of the skin.

Epididymitis, inflammation of the epididymis, a structure which covers the upper end of the testicle.

Epiglottis, a lid which covers the opening to the windpipe and prevents food from getting into the voice box or lungs.

Epilation, removal of hair by the root.

Epilepsy, convulsive disorder.

Epinephrine, the active principle of one of the secretions of the adrenal gland.

Epiotic, located on or above the ear.

Epiphora, continuous overflow of tears.

Episiotomy, cutting of the wall of the vagina during childbirth to avoid tearing.

Epistasis, substance which rises to the surface instead of sinking.

Epistaxis, nose bleeding.

Epithelioma, cancer of the skin.

Epithelium, cellular substance of skin and mucous membrane.

Eponym, using the name of a person to designate a disease, organ, syndrome, etc.

Equilibrium, balance.

Equivalent, of equal value.

Erasion, abrasion.

Erection, becoming upright and rigid.

Eremophobia, extreme fear of being alone.

Erepsin, intestinal enzyme.

Erg, unit of work.

Ergasiatrics, psychiatry.

Ergophobia, extreme fear of work.

Ergosterole, substance found in the skin and elsewhere which, when exposed to sunlight, becomes converted to vitamin D.

Ergot, drug used to cause contraction of the uterus and control bleeding after childbirth.

Ergotamine, an alkaloid substance used in treatment of migraine and can produce contractions of the uterus.

Erode, wear away.

Erogenous, producing sexual excitement. [stance.

Erosion, wearing away of a sub-

Erotic, pertaining to sex.

Erotogenic, originating from sexual desire.

Erotogenic Zones, areas of the body, stimulation of which promote sexual feelings.

Erotophobia, extreme fear of sexual love.

Errhine, causing sneezing and nasal discharge.

Eructation, belching.

Eruption, rash; cutting of a tooth.

Erysipelas, infection of the skin with streptococci.

Erythema, rednes of the skin.

Erythrocytes, red blood cells.

Erythroderma, skin disturbance characterized by abnormal redness.

Esbach's Method, a method of estimating quantity of albumin in urine. [burn.

Eschar, sloughed tissue due to a

Esophagus, the tube that connects the stomach to the throat, about nine inches long.

Ester, compound formed by the combination of an organic acid with an alcohol.

Estrogens, the female sex hormone.

Estrus, female sexual cycle.

Estuarium, vapor bath.

Ether, organic liquid used as an anesthetic.

Ethics, Medical, system of moral principles governing medical conduct.

Ethnic, pertaining to the races of mankind.

Etiology, study of the causes of disease.

Eucalyptus, an oil used as an antiseptic in nasal solutions and mouth washes.

Eugenics, study of inheritance.

Eunuch, castrated male.

Eupepsia, normal digestion.

Euphonia, normal clear condition of the voice.

Euphoria, exaggerated sense of well-being.

Eupnea, normal respiration.

Eusitia, normal appetite.

Euthanasia, mercy killing.

Evacuant, medicine which empties an organ; laxative.

Evagination, protusion of a part or organ.

Eversion, turning outward.

Evisceration, removal of inner parts.

Evolution, gradual transition from one state to another.

Ex- (previx), out; away from.

Exacerbation, increase in the degree of sickness.

Examination, scrutiny of a patient's state of health.

Exanthema, any fever accompanied by a rash. [brain.

Excerebration, removal of the

Excise, surgical removal. [lation.

Excitability, susceptible to stimu-

Excitation, stimulation; irritation.

Excoriation, rubbing away of part of the skin by disease or injury.

Excrement, feces.

Ergrescence, abnormal out-growth upon the body.

Exenteration, evisceration.

Exercise, physical exertion.

Exhalation, expulsion of air from the lungs.

Exhaustion, extreme fatigue.

Exhibitionist, abnormal impulse to show one's genitals to a member of the opposite sex.

Exhilarant, cheering.

Exo- (prefix), outside; outward.

Exocardia, abnormal position of the heart.

Exodontia, tooth extraction.

Exophthalmos, bulging of the eyes, usually caused by over-activity of the thyroid gland.

Exostosis, outgrowth from the surface of a bone.

Expansion, increase in size.

Expectorant, drug supposed to have the effect of liquefying the sputum.

Expectoration, spittle.

Expire, exhale; die

Exploration, investigation.

Expression, the act of squeezing out; facial disclosure of feeling or emotion.

Exterior, outside.

Extern, medical student who works in a hospital but lives elsewhere.

Extima, outermost covering of a blood vessel.

Extirpation, complete surgical removal or destruction of a part.

Extra- (prefix), outside of; in addition.

Extract, to pull out; remove the active portion of a drug.

Extremity, terminal part of anything; a limb of the body.

Extrinsic, of external origin.

Extrovert, one interested in external objects and actions.

Eye, the organ of vision.

Eyebrow, hair ridge above the eye.

Eyelash, hair growing on the edge of an eyelid.

Eyestrain, eye fatigue.

Eyetooth, a cuspid or upper canine tooth.

— F —

F., Fahrenheit, one gauge of measuring temperature.

Face, anterior part of the head.

Facial, pertaining to the face.

Facies, appearance of the face.

Facilitation, hastening of a natural process.

Facioplegia, facial paralysis.

Factitious, artificial.

Faculty, normal power or function; mental attribute.

Farenheit Scale, boiling point of water 212 degrees, freezing point, 32 degrees.

Fahr., Fahrenheit.

Fainting, temporary loss of consciousness due to insufficient blood reaching the brain.

Fallopian Tubes, tubes which connect the ovaries with the womb.

Fallout, settling of radioactive dust from the atmosphere after a nuclear explosion.

False, not true.

False Ribs, lower five pairs of ribs.

Familial, pertaining to the same family.

Family, group descended from a common ancestor.

Fang, root of a tooth.

Farina, meal; flour.

Far Point, farthest point which an eye can see distinctly when completely relaxed.

Fastigium, acme; highest point.

Fat, obese; greasy deposits in body tissue.

Fatigue, exhaustion; weariness.

Fauces, space in the back part of the mouth, surrounded by the soft palate, the tonsil arches and the base of the tongue.

Favus, contagious skin disease.

F. D., fatal disease.

Fear, emotional response to danger.

Fear Reaction, emotional illness in which anxiety is shown by the conscious fear of a particular event or object.

Febricide, that which destroys fever.

Febrifacient, producing fever.

Febrile, pertaining to fever.

Febris, fever.

Fecal, pertaining to feces.

Feces, waste matter excreted by the bowels.

Fecundity, fertility.

Feeble-mindedness, state of low development of the intelligence.

Feeding, taking of food.

Fee Splitting, unethical practice of dividing the patient's charges between the referring physician and the consultant.

Feet, the extremities of the legs on which humans stand.

Fellatio, type of sexual perversion in which the male sex organ is placed in the mouth of another.

Felon, deep skin, infection on the far end and inner surface of a finger.

Female, woman; girl; pertaining to a woman.

Feminism, possession of female characteristics by a male.

Femur, thighbone.

Fenestration, surgical operation designed for the treatment of certain types of deafness.

Fermentation, decomposition of complex substances under the influence of enzymes.

Ferrule, metal band applied to a tooth to strengthen it.

Fertile, capable of reproduction.

Fester, to produce pus.

Fetal, pertaining to a fetus.

Fetation, pregnancy.

Feticide, killing of an unborn child.

Fetid, having a disagreeable odor.

Fetish, that which becomes attractive because of its association with sexual pleasure.

Fetus, an unborn child from the third month until birth.

Fever, elevation of the body temperature.

Fiber, threadlike structure.

Fibrillation, state of tremor in the muscles found in certain nervous, muscular and heart diseases.

Fibrin, protein substance produced by elements of the blood and tissues which forms a network as the base of clots.

Fibroid, benign tumor of the womb consisting of tough, fibrous tissue.

Fibroidectomy, surgical removal of a fibroid tumor.

Fibroma, benign tumor composed of fibrous tissue.

Fibula, bone of lower leg.   [ure.

Filament, small, threadlike struct-

Field, limited area.

Figure, body; shape; outline.

Filament, delicate fiber or thread.

Filariasis, tropical disease due to infection of the body with tiny worms which block the lymph vessels, causing swelling of the limbs, elephantiasis.

Filling, material inserted in the cavity of a tooth.

Filter, to pass a liquid through a porous substance to eliminate solid particles; device used in this process.

Filtrate, fluid which has passed through a filter.

Finger, digit of the hand.

First Aid, emergency, temporary medical care and treatment of an injured person.

Fission, division into parts.

Fissure, groove, cleft.

Fistula, abnormal passage leading from the surface of the body to an internal cavity.

Fit, convulsion; sudden attack.

Flaccid, flabby; weak; soft.

Flagellation, to beat or whip; beating as a means of satisfying sexual desires.   [sue.

Flap, mass of partly detached tis-

Flat, Foot, not having the normal arch of the sole of the foot.

Flatulence, gas in the stomach or intestines.

Flatus, stomach or intestinal gas.

Flaxseed, linseed.

Flesh, soft tissue and muscles of the animal body.

Fletcherism, thorough mastication of food.

Flex, to bend.

Flexion, bending.

Flexor, muscle that bends or flexes.

Floating, moving around; out of normal position.

Flora, plant life.

Florid, having a bright color.

Fl. Oz., fluid ounce.

Fluid, a non-solid, liquid or gaseous substance.

Fluoroscope, an X-ray instrument used to examine the interior of the body.

Flush, to blush; to clean with a stream of water.

Flutter, irregular, rapid motion; agitation, especially of the heart.

Flux, a large flow of any body excretion, particularly the bowel contents.

Fold, ridge; a doubling back.

Folie, mania; psychosis.

Follicle, small secretory sac or gland.

Folliculitis, inflammation of the follicles of the hair.

Fomentation, treatment of inflammation by applying heat and moisture to the affected part.

Fontanel, the soft spot of a baby's head that later is closed by the growth of bone.

Food, that which nourishes.

Food Poisoning, digestive disorder due to eating foods containing poisonous substances.

Foot, terminal part of the leg.

Foot Print; impucssion of the foot.

Foramen, any opening or perforation.

Forceps, two-pronged instrument for extracting.

Forearm, portion of the arm between the elbow and wrist.

Forefinger, first finger.

Forehead, portion of the head above the eyes; brow.

Forensic Medicine, aspects of medicine related to law.

Formation, structure; shape; figure.

Formula, rule prescribing the kind and quantity of ingredients in a preparation.

Fornication, sexual intercourse of persons not married to each other.

Fossa, pit; depression.

Fracture, breaking of a bone.

Fragilitas, brittleness.

Fragility, characteristic of being easily broken.

Frenum, fold of skin or lining tissue that limits the movement of an organ, e.g., tissue under the tongue.

Freckles, small patches of pigmented skin more commonly found in blonde or red-headed people.

Freezing, frigidity of a limb due to severe cold.

Frenzy, maniacal excitement.

Friable, easily broken into small pieces.

Friction, rubbing.

Fright, extreme, sudden fear.

Frigidity, absence of sexual desire in women, coldness.

Frons, forehead.

Frontal, relating to the front of the body or an organ; pertaining to the forehead.

Frost Bite, condition caused by long exposure to severe cold; freezing of a part of the body, usually nose, fingers, toes.

Frottage, rubbing, massage.

Frustration, the feeling aroused when physical or personal desides are thwarted.

Fugitive, wandering.

Fulguration, therapeutic destruction of tissue by means of electric sparks.

Fulling, kneading.   [nancy.

Full Term, normal end of pregnancy.

Fumes, vapors.

Fumigation, disinfecting.

Function, normal and specific action of a part.

Fundament, base; foundation.

Fundus, base of an organ.

Fungicide, an agent that destroys fungi.

Fungus, mold.

Funny Bone, outer part of the elbow which is crossed by part of the ulnar nerve.

Fur, deposit forming on the tongue.

Furfur, dandruff.

Furibund, maniacal.

Furor, rage.

Furuncle, boil.

Furunculosis, boils on skin.

Fusiform, spindle-shaped.

Fusion, uniting.

— G —

Gait, manner of walking.

Galactic, pertaining to milk.

Galactischia, suppression of the secretion of milk.   [milk.

Galactorrhea, excessive flow of

Galeophobia, extreme fear of cats.

Gall, secretion stored in the liver which helps in emulsifying fats.

Gall Bladder, sac beneath the liver which stores bile and secretes mucus.

Gall Stones, stone-like objects found in gall bladder and its drainage system, composed primarily of calcium.

Galvanism, uninterrupted electric current.

Gammacism, imperfect pronounciation of g and k sounds.

Gamogenesis, sexual reproduction.

Gamophobia, extreme fear of marriage.

Ganglion, cyst-like swelling found in the region of a joint or the sheath of a tendon; area between two nerve fibers.

Gangrene, death and deterioration of a part of the body, caused by interference with the blood supply.

Gapes, disease of fowls caused by a worm.

Gargle, mouth wash.

Gastralgia, stomach pain.

Gastric, pertaining to the stomach.

Gastritis, inflammation of the stomach walls.

Gastrobrosis, perforation of the stomach.

Gastrocnemius, calf muscle.

Gastroenteritis, inflammation of the stomach and intestine.

Gastroptosis, abnormal relaxation of stomach musculature.

Gastrorrhagia, stomach hemorrhage.

Gastrosis, any stomach disease.

Gatophilia, abnormal fondness for cats.

Gatophobia, extreme fear of cats.

Gauntlet, hand bandage.

Gavagi, liquid nourishment supplied through a tube inserted into the mouth, down the gullet and into the stomach.

Gelatin, body protein in a solid state, used in manufacture of drug capsules.

Gelatinous, like jelly.

Gelosis, hard, swollen mass.

Gelotolepsy, spontaneous loss of normal muscle tension.

Geminate, in pairs.

Gen., gene.

Genal, pertaining to the cheek.

Gender, sexual category; male or female.

Gene, biological unit which transmits hereditary characteristics.

Generation, reproduction; period of family history.

Generative, pertaining to reproduction.   [tinctive.

Generic, pertaining to genus; dis-

Genesis, origin and development.

Genetics, the science of natural differences and similarities in successive generations of living organisms.

Genetous, dating from fetal life.

Genial, pertaining to the chin.

Genicular, pertaining to the knee

Genital, pertaining to the sex organs.

Genitalia, reproductive organs.

Genocide, race destruction.

Genu, knee; knee-like structure.

Genus, biological classification.

Geophagy, eating of soil.

Geratic, pertaining to old age.

Geriatrics, medical study of old age.

Germ, organism that infects man; primitive beginning of a developing embryo.

German Measles, a viral infection characterized by high fever and skin rash.

Germicide, agent that destroys germs.

Geroderma, wrinking of the skin.

Gestation, pregnancy.

Gestosis, toxemia in pregnancy.

Gibbous, humpbacked.

Gigantism, abnormal height and size.

Gingiva, the gum that surrounds the tooth.

Gingivitis, inflamation of the gums.

Girdle, encircling structure.

Glabella, space between the eyebrows.

Glabrous, smooth.

Gladiolus, main portion of the sternum.

Glanders, contagious horse disease.

Glandilemma, outer covering of a gland.

Glandula, smal gland.

Glands, there are three main types of glands: the lymph glands, which are found mainly at various junctions in the body, such as the armpit and the groin, and also within the body and around the base of the neck, their function being to trap germs and prevent them from reaching vital areas; larger glands, such as the pancreas and liver which produce digestive agents such as bile, enzymes, etc. and which empty their products into the intestines through a duct or tube; the endocrine glands, which are also called ductless glands because they empty their products directly into the blood stream.

Glandular, pertaining to a gland.

Glandule, small gland.

Glans, cone-shaped body that forms the tip of the penis or clitoris.

Glasses, lenses to aid vision.

Glaucoma, disease of the eyes in which the pressure of the fluid in the eye increases.

Gleet, discharge from the urethra found in chronic gonorrhea.

Glioma, tumor of the nerve cells.

Globular, spherical.

Globule, small droplet.

Globulicidal, destroying red corpuscles.

Globulin, the name of a group of proteins.

Globus, ball, sphere.

Globus Hystericus, imaginary lump in the throat.

Glomerulonephritis, Kidney disease.

Glomerulus, small, round mass; important element of the kidney.

Glossa, tongue.

Glossalgia, tongue pain.

Glossitis, inflammation of the tongue.

Glottis, the space between the vocal cords.

Glucohemia, sugar in the blood.

Glucose, liquid which is sweet and important to body chemistry; sugar.

Gluteal, pertaining to the buttocks.

Gluten, protein, found in cereals.

Glutinous, sticky.

Glycemia, sugar in the blood.

Glycerin, clear, syrupy liquid used for medicinal purposes.

Glycolysis, digestion of sugar.

Glycosuria, sugar in the urine.

Glycyrrhyza, licorice.

Gnathic, pertaining to the jaw.

Gnosia, faculty of perception and recognition.

Goiter, an enlargement of the thyroid gland.

Goitrogenic, causing goiter.

Gomphiasis, looseness of teeth.

Gonad, ovary or testes.

Gonadotrophin, hormone which stimulates the ovary or testes.

Gonagra, gout in the knee.

Gonalgia, pain in the knee.

Gonococcus, germ which causes gonorrhea.

Gonorrhea, veneral disease.

Gouge, instrument for cutting bone.

Gout, disease in which there is an upset in the metabolism of uric acid, causing symptoms of joint pain.

Gouty, pertaining to gout.

G.P., general practitioner.

Gracile, slender.

Gradatim, gradually.   [tation.

Graft, piece of tissue for transplan-

Grand Mal, epileptic attack.

Granulation, process of wound healing.

Granulocytopenia, disease which reduces the defensive cells in the blood, the white blood cells.

Granum, grain.

Grave's Disease, increased activity of thyroid gland with bulging of the eyes.

Gravid, pregnant.

Gravida, pregnant woman.

Gravity, weight.

Grip, influenza; grasp.

Groin, depression between the thigh and abdomen.

Grumous, lumpy; clotted.

G. U., genitourinary.

Gumboil, a swelling in the mouth due to an abscess at the root of a tooth.

Guilt, feeling of having committed an offense.

Gullet, passage to the stomach.

Gustation, sense of taste.

Gustatory, pertaining to the sense of taste.

Gut, bowel; intestine.

Gutta, a drop.

Guttate, like a drop.

Guttur, throat.

Guttural, pertaining to the throat.

Gymnastics, physical exercise.

Gymnophobia, extreme fear of the naked body.

Gymandromorphism, condition in which one has male and female characteristics.

Gynatrisia, condition in which there is no passageway in the vagina.

Gynecic, pertaining to women.

Gynecoid, like a woman.

Gynecologist, specialist in female diseases.

Gynecology, study of the diseases of women.

Gynecomastia, enlargement of male breasts.

Gynoplasty, plastic surgery of the female genitals.

— H —

Habit, automatic action; bodily temperament.

Habituation, becoming accustomed to a thing.

Hachement, hacking.

Hacking, chopping stroke in massage.

Hair, threadlike outgrowth from the skin.

Halazone, white powder used as drinking water disinfectant.

Halitosis, offensive breath.

Halitous, covered with moisture.

Hallucination, mistaken sense impression.

Hallucinosis, condition of persistent hallucinations.

Hallux, big toe.

Ham, back part of the thigh above the knee and below the buttock; hip, thigh; buttock.

Hamarthritis, arthritis in all the joints.

Hammer, instrument for striking blows; middle ear bone.

Hammer Toe, claw-like deformity of the toe.

Hamster, rodent frequently used in laboratory tests.

Hamular, hook-shaped.

Hand, terminal part of an arm.

Handedness, tendency to use a particular hand.

Hangnail, partly detached piece of skin at the root of a fingernail.

Haphiphobia, extreme fear of contact.

Haptics, science of the sense of touch.

Hare Lip, cleft lip.

Haunch, hips and buttocks.

Haut-Mal, epileptic attack at its peak.

Hay Fever, an allergic disease caused by abnormal sensitivity to certain air borne pollens.

HB., hemoglobin.

Head, uppermost part of the body; top of anything.

Headache, pain in the head.

Heal, cure.

Healing, process of making well.

Health, state of having a normally active body and mind.

Hearing, perceiving sound.

Hearing Aid, device used by one who is deaf to amplify sound waves.

Heart, the powerful, muscular, contractile organ, the center of the circulatory system.

Heart Block, disease of the heart in which the impulse of contraction is unable to pass from the auricles to the ventricles, with the result that both beat independently of each other.

Heartburn, burning sensation, either in the back of the throat or in the left side of the chest, usually occurs after eating.

Heart Failure, inability of the heart to maintain adequate body circulation.

Heart Murmur, abnormal heart sound.

Heart Rate, number of heart beats per minute.

Heat, warmth; high temperature; form of energy; sexual excitement in certain animals; to make hot.

Heatstroke, state of dizziness, nausea and spots before the eyes due to direct exposure to high temperatures.

Hebetic, pertaining to puberty.

Hebetude, mental slowness.

Hectic, habitual; constitutional.

Hedonism, devotion to pleasure.

Heel, hind extremity of the foot.

Helcoid, resembling an ulcer.

Helcosis, formation of an ulcer.

Helicine, spiral.

Heliophobia, extreme fear of sunlight.

Heliosis, sunstroke.

Heliotherapy, treatment of disease by the rays of the sun or by the use of an ultra violet-lamp.

Heliotropism, tendency of an organism to turn toward sunlight.

Helix, margin of the external ear.

Helminthiasis, presence of parasitic worms in the body.

Helminthology, study of parasitic worms.

Heloma, callosity, corn.

Helotomy, surgical removal of a corn.

Hemafacient, blood producing agent.

Hemagogue, agent which promotes the flow of blood.

Hemal, pertaining to blood or blood vessels.

Hemangiectasis, enlargement of blood vessels.

Hemarthrosis, accumulation of blood in a joint.

Hemase, blood enzyme.

Hematemesis, vomiting of blood.

Hemathermous, warm-blooded.

Hematic, pertaining to blood.

Hematischesis, stopping of bleeding.

Hematocolpos, collection of blood in the vagina.

Hematocryal, cold-blooded.

Hematoid, resembling blood.

Hematologist, one who specializes in the study of blood and its diseases.

Hematology, science of the blood.

Hematoma, swelling containing clotted blood, usually caused by direct violence, e.g., a black eye.

Hematometachysis, blood transfusion.

Hematonosis, blood disease.

Hematuria, the passing of blood in the urine.

Hemeralopia, day blindness.

Hemi- (prefix), half.

Hemianopsia, blindness in half of the visual field of each eye.

Hemic, pertaining to blood.

Hemicrania, headache on one side of the head only; migraine.

Hemifacial, affecting one side of the face.

Hemiplezia, paralysis of one side of the body.

Hemocidal, destructive of blood cells.

Hemocyte, blood corpuscle.

Hemofuscin, brown coloring matter of blood.

Hemoglobin, red pigment in the blood.

Hemoid, resembling blood.

Hemolysis, destruction of elements of the blood.

Hemopathy, blood disease.

Hemopericardium, blood in the heart sac.   [zyme.

Hemopexin, blood coagulating enzyme.

Hemopexis, coagulation of blood.

Hemophilia, blood disease characterized by defective coagulation of the blood and a strong tendency to bleed.

Hemophiliac, one afflicted with hemophilia.

Hemophobia, aversion to blood.

Hemophoris, conveying blood.

Hemoptysis, spitting up of blood.

Hemorrhage, bleeding.

Hemorrhagenic, causing hemorrhage.

Hemorrhoids, varicose vein condition of the lower rectum and anus.

Hemopasia, withdrawal of blood.

Hemostasis, stopping of hemmorrhage.

Hemostat, instrument which stops bleeding, clamp.

Hemotherapy, using blood to treat disease.

Hemothorax, accumulation of blood between the lungs and chest wall.

Hepar, liver.

Heparin, substance which prevents clotting of blood.

Hepatic, concerning the liver.

Hepatitis, inflammation of the liver.

Hepatogenic, produced in the liver.

Hepatoma, tumor with its origin in the liver.   [liver.

Hepatomegaly, enlargement of the

Hepatopathy, liver disease.

Hereditary, transmitted from one's forefathers.

Heredity, traits and characteristics transmitted from parents and other ancestors to offspring.

Heredosyphilis, congenital syphilis.

Hermaphodite, one having both male and female sex characteristics.

Hermetic, Hermetical, airtight.

Hernia, rupture; the bulging out of a part of any of the internal organs through a weak area in the muscular wall.

Herpes, skin disease characterized by clusters of small blisters.

Heroin, narcotic.

Heroinism, addiction to the use of heroin.

Herpes Simplex, fever blisters, mouth blisters.

Herpes Zoster, acute, infectious, inflammatory skin disease; shingles.

Herpetiform, resembling herpes.

Heterogeneous, of unlike natures.

Heterosexuality, sexual desire for one of the opposite sex.

Hexavaccine, vaccine having six different organisms.

Hiatus, fissure, gap.

Hiccups, sharp, inspiratory sound caused by contractions of the diaphragm.

Hidrosis, sweating.

Hip, upper part of the thigh where it joins with the pelvis.

Hipprocrates, Greek physician, the Father of Medicine.

Hippocratic Oath, oath taken by the graduating physician on which he bases his medical ethics.

Hirsute, hairy.

Histamine, bodily substance found in most tissues, released when tissue is damaged.

Histoblast, tissue cell.

Histology, science of the microscopic structure of tissues.

Histoma, any tissue tumor.

History, patient's record of past illness, present illness and symptoms.

Hitch, knot.

Hives, skin rash characterized by large wheals.

Hoarseness, difficulty in speaking.

Hodegetics, medical etiquette.

Hodgkin's Disease, disease in which the lymph glands and spleen become enlarged.

Holarthritis, inflammation of all joints.

Homicide, murder.

Homogeneous, of uniform structure.

Homosexuality, psychological disorder which causes one to be attracted to people of same sex.

Hook, curved instrument used for traction or holding.

Hooping Cough, acute, infectious disease marked by a paroxysmal cough ending in a crowing or whooping inspiration.

Hordeolum, sty.

Hormone, a chemical that originates in the glands and is carried to all parts of the body by the blood.

Horror, fear, dread.

Hosp., hospital.

Hospital, institution for the care of those in need of medical attention.

Hospitalization, placing of a person in a hospital for treatment.

Host, organism on which a parasite lives.

Hot, having a high temperature.

Hottentotism, abnormal form of stuttering.

House Physician, doctor who lives in the hospital and is available for help at all times.

House Staff, residents, interns and certain doctors of a hospital.

Humerus, arm bone.

Humidifier, device used to increase moisture in the air of a room.

Humidity, amount of moisture in the air.

Humor, body fluid.

Humpback, curvature of the spine.

Hunger, desire, especially for food.

Hyaline, glassy.

Hybrid, product of parents of different species.

Hydatid, cyst formed in the tissues.

Hydragogue, strong laxative.

Hydrarthrosis, accumulation of fluid in a joint.

Hydraulics, science of liquids in motion.

Hydroa, skin disease with blister-like patches.

Hydrocarbon, compound of hydrogen and carbon.

Hydrocephalus, abnormal enlargement of the head due to interference with the drainage of cerebral fluid. [tents.

Hydrocyst, cyst with watery con-

Hydrogenate, combine with water.

Hydrophilia, absorbing water.

Hydrophobia, rabies.

Hydrops, dropsy.

Hydrotherapy, treatment of disease by means of water.

Hygiene, science of health and observance of its rules.

Hygienic, pertaining to health.

Hygiene, Mental, development and preservation of mental health.

Hygiene, Oral, proper care of the mouth and teeth.

Hygienist, specialist in hygiene.

Hymen, membrane fold located at the entrance to the female sex organs.

Hymenectomy, surgical removal of the hymen.

Hymenotomy, surgical opening of the hymen.

Hypacusia, faulty hearing.

Hypalgesia, reduced sensitivity to pain. [acid.

Hyperacidity, excess of stomach

Hyperacuity, sharp vision.

Hyperacusia, acute hearing.

Hyperbulia, excessive willfulness.

Hyperemesis, abnormal amount of vomiting.

Hyperglycemia, excess blood sugar.

Hyperhydrosis, excessive sweating.

Hypermastia, unusually large breasts; having more than two breasts.

Hypermotility, increased activity.

Hyperpresia, unusually high blood pressure.

Hyperpnea, hard breathing with an increase in the depth of inhalation.

Hyperrhinolalia, marked nasal quality of the voice.

Hypersensitivity, allergy.

Hypersthenia, unusual strength or tone of body.

Hypertension, high blood pressure.

Hyperthermia, abnormally high temperature.

Hyperthymia, excessive emotionalism.

Hyperthyroidism, condition caused by excessive secretion of the thyroid gland.

Hypertrichosis, excessive hairiness.

Hypnagogic, causing sleep.

Hypnagia, pain while asleep.

Hypnogenetic, causing sleep.

Hypnosis, trance induced through verbal suggestion or concentration upon an object.

Hypnotherapy, treatment by hypnotism.

Hypnotize, to put in a state of hypnosis.

Hypobaropathy, decompression sickness.

Hypocalcia, calcium deficiency.

Hypochrondria, undue concern about one's health; suffering with imaginary illnesses.

Hypochondriac, one who suffers from imaginary illness.

Hypodermic, beneath the skin; injection under the skin; needle used for injections.

Hypogastrium, lowest middle abdominal region.

Hypoglobulia, decrease of red blood cells.

Hypoglossal, under the tongue.

Hypogonadism, deficient activity of testis or ovary.

Hypomastia, unusual smallness of the breast.

Hypomenorrhea, deficient menstruation.

Hyponoia, mental sluggishness.

Hypophrenia, feeblemindedness.

Hypopraxia, deficient activity.

Hypophysis, pituitary gland.

Hypoplasia, incomplete tissue development.

Hyposensitization, treatment of allergy by giving small doses of the material to which the person is allergic and gradually increasing the doses until the allergic reaction is reduced.

Hypotension, low blood pressure.

Hypothesis, supposition.

Hypotonia, abnormally low strength or tension.

Hysterectomy, surgical removal of whole or part of the womb.

Hysteria, psychological state or neurosis resulting from failure to face reality.

Hysterosalpingectomy, surgical removal of the womb and fallopian tubes.

— I —

Iateria, therapeutics.

Iatric, medical.

Iatrogenic Disease, condition caused by a doctor's statements or procedure.

Iatrology, medical science.

Ice, frozen water.

Ichnogram, footprint.

Ichor, watery discharge from a sore.

Iconologny, sexual desire aroused by pictures or statues.

Ichthyol, coal tar product used in the treatment of skin diseases.

Icthyophobia, extreme fear of fish.

Ichthyosis, condition in which babies have dry and scaly skin.

Icterpatitis, jaundice.

Icteric, relating to or characterized by jaundice.

Icterus, jaundice.

Ictus, beat; stroke; attack.

Id, psychological term for the unconscious.

Idea, concept.

Idea, Flight of, rapid, disconnected speech characteristic of certain mental diseases.

Ideal, concept of perfection.

Ideation, thinking.

Idée Fixe, obsession.

Identical, exactly the same.

Identical Twins, twins developed from one fertilized cell.

Idiosyncrasy, peculiar characteristics whereby one person differs from another.

Idiocrasy, peculiarity.

Idiocy, mental deficiency with an I.Q. under 25.

Idiogamist, man capable of having sexual relations only with his wife, or only with a few women.

Idiot, person suffering from congenital feeblemindedness.

Idiotic, like an idiot.

Idiotypic, relating to heredity.

Idrosis, excessive sweating.

Ignis, cautery.

Ileitis, inflammation of the lower small intestine.

Ileocolitis, inflammation of the lower small intestine and the large intestine.

Ileum, lower part of the small intestine.

Ileus, intestinal obstruction.

Ilium, flank, upper wide part of the hipbone.

Ill, not healthy; diseased.

Illegal, not lawful.

Illegitimate, not according to law; born out of wedlock.

Illness, ailment.

Illusion, misinterpretation of a real sensation.

Imagery, imagination.

Imago, memory of a loved person formed in childhood.

Imbalance, lack of balance.

Imbecility, mental deficiency with the mental age between three and seven years and an I.Q. between 25 and 49.

Imbibation, absorption of a liquid.

Imbrication, surgical procedure for closing wounds.

Immature, not fully developed.

Immedicable, incurable.

Immersion, placing a body under a liquid.

Immiscible, not able to be mixed.

Immobilization, making immovable.

Immune, protected against disease.

Immunity, ability to resist infectious disease.

Immunologist, one who specializes in the science of immunity.

Immunology, science dealing with the study of the processes by which the body fights infection.

Impaction, firmly wedged in.

Impalpable, too weak or fine to be felt.

Impar, unequal.

Imperative, obligatory, involuntary.

Impermeable, not allowing to pass through.   [trated.

Impervious, unable to be penetrated.

Impetigo, infectious disease of the skin characterized by isolated pustules.

Implant, graft, insert.

Impotence, sexual weakness in the male.   [ile.

Impotent, unable to copulate; sterile.

Impregnation, fertilization; saturation.

Impulse, instinctual urge.

Inanimate, lifeless.

Inanition, starvation.

Inarticulate, without joints; not given to clear expression.

Inborn, innate; inherent.

Inbreeding, mating between close relatives.

Incest, sexual relations between those of close relationship.

Incipient, beginning; about to appear.

Incision, cut.

Incisor, any one of the four front teeth of either jaw.

Inclination, tendency.

Incompetent, not functioning properly.

Incontinency, inability to control evacuation.

Increment, increase.

Incretion, internal secretion.

Incrustation, scab.

Incubate, to provide favorable conditions for growth and development.

Incubation, stage of an infectious disease from the time the germ enters the body until the appearance of the first symptoms.

Incubus, nightmare.

Incurable, not able to be cured.

Index, forefinger.

Indication, any aspect of a disease that points out its treatment.

Indigenous, native to a particular place.

Indigestion, failure of digestive function.

Indolent, inactive.

Induced, brought about by indirect stimulation.

Indurated, hardened.

Inebriation, intoxication.

Inert, inactive.

Inertia, inactivity.

In Extremis, at the point of death.

Infant, baby.

Infanticide, killing of an infant.

Infantile, pertaining to infancy; possessing characteristics of early childhood.

Infantile Paralysis, infection of central nervous system; poliomyelitis.

Infantilism, failure of development.

Infarction, blockage of a vessel.

Infection, implantation of a germ; spread of a disease.

Infectious, liable to be transmitted by infection.   [ation.

Inferior, of a lower position or situation.

Infertility, sterility.

Infiltration, process by which substances pass into cells or into the spaces around cells.

Infirm, weak, feeble.

Infirmary, place for the care of the sick.

Infirmity, weakness, sickness.

Inflammation, changes that occur in living tissues when they are invaded by germs, e.g. redness, swelling, pain and heat.

Inflation, distention.

Inflection, bending inward.

Influenza, virus infection characterized by fever, inflammation of the nose, larynx and bronchi, neuralgic and muscular pains and gastrointestinal disorder.

Infracostal, below a rib.

Infracture, incomplete bone fracture.

Inframaxillary, below the jaw.

Infrared, beyond the red portion of the visible spectrum.

Ingestion, taking by mouth; eating; drinking.

Ingravescent, gradually becoming worse.

Inguinal, referring to the groin.

Inhalant, that which is inhaled.

Inhalation, taking of air into the lungs.

Inherent, intrinsic, innate.

Inherited, received from one's ancestors.

Inhibition, restraint.

Initial, beginning; first; commencing.

Initis, inflammation of muscular substance.

Injection, forcing a liquid into body tissue or a cavity.

Injury, hurt; damage.

Inlay, filling for a dental cavity.

Inlet, means of entrance.

Innate, hereditary; congenital.

Innervation, distribution of nerves to a part; amount of nervous stimulation received by a part.

Innocent, harmless; benign.

Innocuous, harmless.

Innominate, nameless.

Inoculation, immunization against disease by introducing one form of the germ or its products into the body.

Inoculum, material used in inoculation.

Inoperable, not surgically curable.

Inorganic, without organs; not of organic origin.

Inquest, medical examination of a corpse to determine cause of death.

Insanity, mental disorder.

Insatiable, not able to be satisfied.

Inscription, part of a prescription which states the names and amounts of ingredients.

Insecticide, agent which kills insects.

Insemination, fertilization of the female by introduction of male sperm.

Insensible, not perceived by the senses; unconscious.

Insheathed, enclosed.

Insidious, stealthy; applied to a disease that does not show early symptoms of its advent.

Insipid, without taste; without animation.

In Situ, in the normal place.

Insoluble, not capable of being dissolved.

Insomnia, sleeplessness.

Inspection, visual examination.

Inspersion, sprinkle with powder or fluid.

Inspiration, breathing in.

Inspissated, thickened.

Instillation, pouring a liquid by drops.   [tern.

Instinct, inherent behaviour pattern.

Insulin, internal secretion of the pancreas concerned with metabolism of glucose in the body.

Integration, assimilation.

Integument, skin.

Intellect, mind.

Intelligence, ability to see the relationship between things.

Intercellular, between the cells.

Intercostal, between two ribs.

Intercourse, communication between persons.

Intercourse, Sexual, coitus.

Intermittent Claudication, pain in legs after brief exercise caused by a defect in blood circulation.

Intern, an assistant physician of a hospital staff who is in training prior to receiving a license to practice medicine.

Internist, doctor who specializes in diseases of the internal organs.

Internship, term of service of an intern.

Internus, internal.

Interstice, space or gap in a tissue or structure.

Intervascular, between blood vessels.

Intestinal, pertaining to the intestines.

Intestine, the digestive tract beginning at the mouth and ending at the anus.

Intima, innermost covering of a blood vessel.

Intolerance, not able to endure.

Intoxication, drunkenness.

Intra-Abdominal, within the abdomen.

Intracapsular, within a capsule.
Intrad, inwardly.
Intramuscular; within the muscular substance.
Intravenous, within a vein.
Intravital, during life.
Intrinsic, innate.
Introvert, one whose thoughts and interests are turned inward upon himself.
Intuition, instinctual knowledge.
Inunction, massaging the skin with an ointment.
Invagination, becoming insheathed.
Invalid, one who is sickly.
Inversion, turning inside out.
Inversion, Sexual, homosexuality.
Invertebrate, having no backbone.
Invest, enclose.
Inveterate, hard to cure.
In Vitro, process or reaction that is carried out in laboratory test tube.
In Vivo, within the living organism.
Involution, return to normal that certain organs undergo after fulfilling their function, e.g., the breast after breast feeding; period of decline after middle age.
Iodine, chemical element used as an antiseptic and therapeutic agent in medicine.
Iophobia, extreme fear of poisons.
Ipecac, died plant root used against dysentery and as an emetic; expectorant and diaphoretic.
Ipsilateral, situated on the same side.
I.Q., intelligence quotient.
Iridial, pertaining to the iris.
Iridectomy, surgical removal of the iris, the colored portion of the eye.
Iris, colored portion of the eye.
Iritis, inflammation of the iris.
Iron, chemical element found mainly in the hemoglobin of the red blood cell.
Iron Lung, respirator; apparatus to aid breathing.
Irritable, capable of reacting to a stimulus; sensitive to stimuli.
Ischium, bone upon which body rests when sitting.
Ischuria, retention of urine.
ism (suffix), condition; theory; method.
Isocellular, composed of identical cells.
Isolation, separation of persons having a contagious disease.
Issue, offspring; suppurating sore kept open by a foreign body in the tissue.
Isthmus, neck or narrow part of an organ.
Itching, annoying skin sensation relieved by scatching.
Iter, tubular passage.
-itis (suffix), inflammation.
I. V., intravenously.
Ixodic, pertaining to or caused by ticks.

— J —

Jacket, covering for the thorax; plaster of Paris or leather bandage used to immobilize spine or correct deformities.
Jactitation, convulsive movements; restless tossing.
Jail Fever, typhus fever.
Jargon, incoherent speech.
Jaundice, increase in bile pigment in blood causing yellow tinge to skin, membranes and eyes; can be caused by disease of liver, gallbladder, bile system or blood.
Jaw, applied to one of two bones that form the skeleton of the mouth.
Jecur, the liver. [junium.
Jejunitis, inflammation of the je-
Jejunum, middle section of the small intestine.
Jelly, thick, homogeneous mass.
Jerk, abrupt muscular movement.
Jockey Strap, suspensory, scrotum support.
Joint, area where two different bones meet.
Jugal, pertaining to the cheek or bone.
Jugular Vein, large vein at front of throat.
Juice, body secretions.
Junction, point of meeting or coming together.
June Cold, rose fever.
Jungle Rot, tropical fungus infection.
Justo Major, larger than normal.
Justo Minor, smaller than normal.
Juvenile, pertaining to youth; young; immature.
Juxtaposition, placed side by side; close together.
Juxtaspinal, near the spinal column.

— K —

Kaif, tranquid state caused by drugs.
Kainophobia, extreme fear of new things.
Kakosmia, foul odor.
Kakotrophy, malnutrition.
Kala-Azar, disease which occurs in tropical countries and shows itself in fever, anemia, dropsy and swelling of the liver and spleen.
Kali, potash.
Kaolin, powdered aluminum silicate used for ulcerations, wounds that discharge freely or internally for inflammation of the intestines.
Karezza, prolonged sexual intercourse without ejaculation.
Karyogenesis, formation and development of a cell nucleus.
Karyomorphism, the form of a cell nucleus.
Karyon, cell nucleus.
Kata- (prefix), down.
Katabolism, breaking down process in metabolism.
Keloid, large scar formation.
Kelotomy, relief of hernia strangulation by incision.
Kenophobia, extreme fear of empty spaces.
Kephalin, commercial remedy for headache.
Kephyr, type of fermented milk.
Keratalgia, pain in the cornea.
Keratectomy, surgical removal of part of the cornea. [nea.
Keratitis, inflammation of the cor-
Keratoiritis, inflammation of both the cornea and iris.
Keratolytic, agent that causes skin to shed.
Keratoma, horny growth.
Keratosis, any skin disease that causes an overgrowth of a horny material, e.g., multiple warts.
Kelosteroid, group of chemical substances produced by the body of primary importance to normal development, body functioning and life.
Kidney, organ which secretes urine and aids in maintaing the body's chemical equilibrium.

Kidney, Floating, one loosely attached and displaced.
Kilo, one thousand.
Kilogram, one thousand grams.
Kinemia, blood output of the heart.
Kinematics, science of motion.
Kinesia, motion sickness.
Kinesis, motion.
Kinesthesia, the muscle sense.
Kinetic, pertaining to motion.
Kink, bend; twist.
K. J., knee jerk.
Kleptomania, obsessive stealing.
Kleptophobia, fear of stealing.
Kneading, type of massage.
Knee, the point of juncture of the femur and tibia.
Knife, surgical instrument.
Kneecap, patella.
Knife, surgical instrument.
Knock Knee, condition when legs are turned in at knees.
Knot, knoblike structure; small nodule.
Kolp- (prefix), vagina.
Kolpitis, inflammation of the vagina.
Kopiopia, eyestrain.
Kraurosis, dryness and hardening of skin.
Kreotoxism, meat poisoning.
Kresol, germicide.
Kyllosis, clubfoot.
Kymoscope, apparatus for measuring blood pressure variations.
Kyogenic, causing pregnancy.
Kyphosis, curvature of the spine.

— L —

Labial, pertaining to a lip.
Labialism, speech defect with the use of labial sounds.
Labile, changeable; unsteady.
Lability, instability.
Labiology, study of lip movements.
Labiomancy, lipreading.
Labium, lip.
Labor, period of giving birth to a child.
Labor, Artificial, induced labor.
Labor, Induced, labor brought on by extraneous means.
Labor Pains, pains produced by the contractions of the womb during labor.
Laboratory, place for testing and experimental work.
Labrum, edge; lip.
Labyrinth, internal ear.
Lac, milk.
Lacerate, to tear.
Laceration, tear; wound. [arm.
Lacertus, muscular portion of the
Lacrimal, pertaining to tears.
Lacrimation, secretion of tears from the eye.
Lactation, secretion of milk by the breasts.
Lacteal, relating to milk.
Lactescence, resembling milk.
Lactic Acid, an acid normal to the blood and connected with muscle fatigue.
Lactiferous, conveying milk.
Lactifuge, agent which stops milk secretion.
Lactigenous, producing milk.
Lactin, lactose; a sugar.
Lactinated, containing milk sugar.
Lactoglobulin, protein found in milk.
Lactolin, condensed milk.
Lactose, milk sugar.
Lactotherapy, treatment by milk diet.
Lacuna, small space; pit.
Lag, time between application of a stimulus and the response.

La Grippe, influenza.
Laity, non professional public.
Lake, small fluid cavity.
Labiatry, study of speech disorders.
Laliatry, babbling.
Lalopathy, any speech disorder.
Lambdacism, inability to pronounce the l sound.
Lameness, limping or abnormal walk.
Lamina, thin layer or membrane.
Laminated, in layers.
Lancet, short, double-edged, puncturing knife.
Languor, weariness; exhaustion.
Lanolin, wool fat used in ointments and cosmetics.
Lanugo, fine hair which covers a baby before birth.
Lapactic, purgative.
Laparotomy, surgical incision into the abdominal cavity.
Lapis, stone.
Larva, first stage of an insect from the egg.
Larvate, hidden.
Larvicide, agent which kills larvae.
Laryngectomy, surgical removal of part or all the voice box.
Laryngismus, muscular spasm of the voice box.
Laryngitic, due to laryngitis.
Laryngitis, inflammation of the vocal cords. [box.
Laryngology, study of the voice
Larynx, voice box.
Latent, hidden.
Lateral, pertaining to the side.
Latrine, public toilet.
Lattissimus, widest.
Lattissimus Dorsi, back muscle.
Latus, Lata, Latum, broad.
Laudable, healthy, normal.
Laughing Gas, nitrous oxide.
Laudanum, tincture of opium.
Lavage, cleansing out an organ.
Lax, without tension.
Laxative, substance when taken helps to evacuate the bowels.
Lazaretto, quarantine station, place for treatment of contagious diseases.
Lean, emaciated; thin.
Lechery, lewdness.
Lechopyra, puerperal fever; child birth fever.
Leech, blood sucking water worm.
Left-Handedness, tendency to use the left hand.
Leg, lower extremity; part of the body from the knee to the ankle.
Leiphemia, thinness of the blood.
Leitrichous, having smooth straight hair.
Lemic, pertaining to any epidemic disease. [eases.
Lemology, study of epidemic dis-
Lemostenosis, stricture of the esophagus.
Lens, magnifying glass; transparent, egg-shaped body behind the pupil of the eye.
Lenticular, lens-shaped.
Lenti-form, lens-shaped.
Lentigo, freckle. [lens.
Lentitis, inflammation of the eye
Leper, one afflicted with leprosy.
Lepra, leprosy.
Leprology, study of leprosy.
Leprosarium, place for the care of lepers.
Leprosy, chronic disease affecting the skin and nerves, caused by a germ similar to that of tuberculosis.
Leprous, afflicted with leprosy.
Leptodermic, having a thin skin.
Leptophonia, having a feeble voice.

Leresis, talkativeness in old age.
Lesbianism, homosexuality between women.
Lesion, wound; injury; tumor.
Lethal, fatal; morbid.
Lethargy, marked lack of energy; stupor.
Leucotomy, brain operation used in treatment of some mental disorders.
Leukemia, fatal disease characterized by excessive production of white blood cells.
Leukoblast, immature white blood cell.
Leukocytes, white blood cells.
Leukocythemia, leukemia.
Leukocytolysis, destruction of white blood cells.
Leukocytosis, increase in the number of white blood cells.
Leukopenia, decreased number of white blood cells.
Leukoplakia, white, thickened patches which appear on the skin following chronic irritation.
Leukorrhea, whitish discharge from the womb.
Leukosis, abnormal pallor.
Leukous, white.
Levoduction, movement of an eye toward the left.
Levorotation, turning to the left.
Libidinous, characterized by lewdness.
Libido, the instinctual energy of life, usually sexual energy.
Lichen, any form of skin disease.
Lichenification, thickening and hardening of the skin.
Licorice, dried root used in medication.
Lid, eyelid.
Lien, spleen.
Lienal, pertaining to the spleen.
Lienectomy, surgical removal of the spleen.
Lienitis, inflammation of the spleen.
Lientery, diarrhea with evacuation of undigested food.
Life, state of being alive.
Ligaments, fibrous bands that hold bones together in the region of a joint. [ment.
Ligamentous, pertaining to a liga-
Ligature, thread for tying off vessels; binding or tying.
lightening, dropping of the head of the developing infant into the mother's pelvis in the first stage of labor.
Limb, arm or leg.
Limbus, rim; border.
Liminal, barely noticeable.
Limitans, limiting.
Lingism, treatment by exercise.
Limp, impediment in walking.
Linctus, thick syrupy medicine.
Lingua, tongue.
Lingual, pertaining to the tongue.
Liniment, an oily substance rubbed into the skin to relieve pain and muscle cramps.
Lip, external soft structure around the mouth.
Liparous, fat
Lipemia, fat in the blood.
Lipocyte, fat cell
Lipogenic, producing fat.
Lipoma, fatty tumor, usually benign.
Liposarcoma, cancerous tumor composed of undeveloped fat cells.
Lip-Reading, understanding speech by watching the movements of the lips.

Listerism, principles and practice of antiseptic and aseptic surgical procedures.
Liquefacient, converting into a liquid.
Liquescent, becoming liquid.
Lisping, substitution of sounds due to a speech defect, e.g., th for s.
Lithiasis, formation of stone in the body, e.g., gallstones.
Litter, stretcher.
Livedo, discolored patch of skin.
Liver, important organ of body vitally concerned with metabolism, blood clotting and protein manufacture.
Livid, pale, ashen.
Lividity, discoloration.
Lobar, pertaining to a lobe.
Lobe, globular portion of an organ separated by boundaries.
Lobectomy, surgical removal of a lobe of an organ.
Lobites, inflammation of a lobe.
Lobatomy, cutting across of brain tissue.
Lobule, small lobe; part of a lobe.
Lobus, lobe.
Localization, limited to a definite area; determination of the place of infection.
Lochia, postnatal vaginal discharge.
Lochiopyra, puerperal fever.
Lock Jaw, tetanus.
Locomotion, movement from place to place.
Loculpus, small space; cavity.
Locus, place; site.
Logamnesia, inability to recall words.
Logokophosis, word deafness.
Logopathy, any speech disorder of central origin.
Logopedia, study and treatment of speech defects.
Loin, portion of back between thorax and pelvis.
Longevity, long life.
Longsightedness, farsightedness.
Lordosis, an abnormal curvature of the spine with the convexity towards the front.
Lotio, lotion.
Lotion, liquid substance for washing a part.
Loupe, convex lens. [eases.
Louse, parasite that transmits dis-
Loxia, wry neck.
Loxotic, slanting.
Loxotomy, oblique amputation.
Lozenge, soothing, medicated solid to be held in the mouth until it it dissolves.
Lubb-Dupp, vocal interpretation of heart sounds.
Lubricant, an agent which makes smooth.
Lucid, clear.
Lucipetal, attracted by bright light.
Lues, syphilis.
Lumbago, backache in the loin region.
Lumbar, pertaining to the loin.
Lumbodynia, lumbago.
Lumen, space within a tube.
Luminal, sedative; phenobarbital.
Lunacy, mental illness.
Lunatic, insane person.
Lungs, organs of breathing.
Lunula, pale crescent at root of nail.
Lupiform, resembling lupus.
Lupous, pertaining to lupus.
Lupus, disease of unknown origin affecting skin and vital organs.
Lusus Natural, freak of nature.
Luxation, dislocation.

Luxus, excess.

Lying-in, puerperal state; child-bed.

Lymph, special functioning fluid that flows through specific vessels, passing through the filter of the lymph glands before entering the blood stream.

Lymphadentis, inflammation of a lymph gland.

Lymphatic, relating to lymph or a vessel through which it flows.

Lysemia, disintegration of the blood.

Lysis, gradual disappearance of a disease.

Lyssa, rabies.

Lyssoid, resembling rabies.

— M —

Maceration, soften in a fluid.

Machonnement, chewing motion.

Macies, wasting.

Macrobiosis, longevity.

Macrocephalus, having an unusually large head.

Macrocyte, large red blood cell.

Macrodont, having large teeth.

Macropodia, unusually large feet.

Macroscopic, visible to the naked eye.

Macrosonia, gigantism.

Macula, pigmented spot on the skin, spot in the retina.

Maculate, spotted.

Mad, insane; angry.

Madarosis, lose of eyelashes or eyebrows.

Madescent, damp.

Madura Foot, disease of the foot caused by a fungus infection.

Maggot, worm.

Maidenhead, hymen.

Maidism, pellagra.

Maieutics, obstetrics.

Maim, injure, disable.

Main, hand.   [hands.

Main Succulente, edema of the

Mal, sickness; pain; disease.

Mala, cheek; cheekbone.

Malacosarcosis, softness of muscle tissue.

Malacosteon, softening of the bones.

Malacostic, soft.

Malady, illness.

Malaise, uneasiness, indisposition.

Malar, pertaining to the cheek or cheek bone.

Malaria, acute, febrile, infectious disease caused by the presence of parasitic organisms in the red blood cells.

Malariologist, specialist in malaria.

Malassimilation, defective assimilation.

Malaxation, kneading motion in massage.

Male, masculine; fertilizing member of the sex.

Malformation, deformity, an abnormal development.   [life.

Malignant, poisonous, threatening

Malingerer, one who fakes illness and pretends to be suffering.

Malleolus, an extension of bone having the shape of a hammerhead on either side of the ankle joint.

Malnutrition, improper nutrition.

Malposition, abnormal position of any organ or part.

Malpractice, improper medical care due to carelessness or ignorance of the doctor.

Malpresentation, faulty fetal presentation.

Malum, disease.

Mamma, breast, mammary gland.

Mammalgia, breast pain.

Mammary Glands, the breasts.

Mamma Virilis, male breast.

Mammilla, nipple.

Mammillary, resembling a nipple.

Mammose, having unusually large breasts.

Man, male of the species.

Mancinism, left-handedness.

Mandible, lower jawbone.

Mandibular, pertaining to the mandible or lower jaw bone.

Manducation, chewing.

Maneuver, skillful procedure.

Mania, violent passion or desire; extreme excitement.

Maniac, one obsessed by a violent passion or desire.

Manic-Depressive, characterized by alternate excitement and depression.

Manipulation, skillful use of the hands.

Mantle, brain cortex.

Manual, pertaining to the hands.

Manubrium, handle; top part of the breastbone.

Manus, hand.

Marantic, marasmic.

Marasmic, pertaining to marasmus.

Marasmus, progressive wasting in infants without an obvious cause.

Mareo, seasickness.

Margo, pl., **Margines,** border, margin.

Mark, spot; blemish.

Marrow, soft tissue in center of bone.

Marsh Fever, malarial fever.

Marsupium, pouch.

Masculation, having male characteristics.

Masculine, pertaining to the male.

Masculinization, acquisition of male secondary sex characteristics by the female.

Masochism, sexual pleasure derived from pain.

Masochist, one who derives pleasure from pain.

Massage, treatment of disease of the tissues.

Masseur, man who massages.

Masseuse, woman who massages.

Mastadenitis, mammary gland inflammation.

Mastadenoma, breast tumor.

Mastalgia, pain in the breast.

Mastauxe, breast enlargement.

Mastectomy, surgical removal of the breast.

Mastication, chewing.

Mastitis, inflammation of the breasts.

Mastodynia, pain in the breast.

Mastoid, bone situated behind the ear; nipple-shaped.

Mastoidectomy, surgical destruction of the cells in the mastoid.

Mastology, study of the breasts.

Mastoncus, breast tumor, swelling.

Mastoncus, breast tumor, swelling.

Masturbation, self-stimulation of the sex organs.

Materia, material; substance.

Materia Medica, pharmacology.

Maternal, pertaining to the mother.

Matrix, pl., **Matrices,** uterus, generative structure.

Maturation, achieving maturity.

Mature, fully developed.

Maxilla, bone of the upper jaw.

Maxillofacial, pertaining to the lower half of the face.

M. B., Bachelor of Medicine.

M.D., Doctor of Medicine.

Mean, average.

Measles, an infectious viral disease marked by fever, a rash of pink spots, redness of the eyes and mild bronchitis.

Measles-German, an acute viral fever which is like a mild attack of measles, running a shorter course.

Meatus, opening; passage.

Meconium, opium; first feces of the newborn.

Medi- (prefix), middle.

Medial, pertaining to the middle.

Median, located in the middle.

Medicable, receptive to cure.

Medical, pertaining to medicine.

Medical Examiner, an official whose duty it is to determine cause of death in questionable cases.

Medical Jurisprudence, medicine and its relation to law.

Medicament, medicinal substance.

Medication, giving of remedies; medicinal agent.

Medicinal, of a curative nature.

Medicine, art and science of healing.

Medicolegal, pertaining to medical jurisprudence.

Medicus, doctor.

Medulla, marrow.

Medulla Oblongata, cone-shaped part of the nervous system which is at the junction between the spinal cord and the brain.

Medullary, pertaining to a medulla.

Medullispinal, pertaining to the spinal cord.   [row.

Medullitis, inflammation of mar-

Megacephalic, having an usually large head.

Megalgia, acute pain.

Megalocornea, bulging of the cornea.

Megalogastria, enlargement of the stomach.

Megalohepatia, enlargement of the liver.

Megalomania, delusions of personal grandeur.

Megalomelia, unusual largeness of the limbs.

Megarectum, enlargement of the rectum.

Megrim, migraine.

Mel, honey.

Melaena, black vomit.

Melalgia, pain in the extremities.

Melancholia, depression and self pity.

Melanin, black or dark-brown pigment.

Melanoglossia, black tongue.

Melanoma, tumor arising from a pigmented mole.

Melanopathy, excessive skin pigmentation.

Melanosis, deposits of black pigment found in various parts of the body.

Melasma, dark pigmentation.

Melitemia, excess blood sugar.

Melitis, inflammation of cheek.

Mellite, honey preparation.

Membrana, membrane.

Membrane, thin layer of tissue covering or dividing an organ.

Membranoid, resembling a membrane.

Membrum, body; part; organ.

Memory, recall of past experience.

Menacme, years of menstrual activity in a woman's life.

Menarche, onset of the menstrual period.

Meniere's Disease, a disease of the organs of balance in the inner ear in which there is deafness

MEDICAL DICT

and sudden attacks of extreme giddiness, vomiting and loss of balance.

Meninges, thin covering of the brain and spinal cord.

Meningioma, tumor arising from membranes covering the brain.

Meningitides, inflammation of the lining membrane of the brain or spinal cord.

Meningitis, inflammation of the lining of the brain and spinal cord with both mental and motor systems usually involved.

Meningomalacia, softening of a membrane.

Meningopathy, any disease of the meninges.

Meninx, see meninges.

Meniscus, crescent-shaped piece of gristle usually found in the knee joint.

Menolipsis, temporary absence of menstruation.

Menopause, age at which normal cessation of the monthly period occurs, usually between 45 and 50.

Menorrhagia, excessive bleeding during the monthly period.

Menorrhea, normal menstruation; profuse menstruation.

Menoschesis, suppression of menstruation.

Menostaxis, prolonged menstruation.

Menses, menstruation.

Menstruation, monthly bleeding of the womb occurring between puberty and menopause.

Mensuration, measuring.

Mental, pertaining to the mind; pertaining to the chin.

Mentum, chin.

Mephitic, noxious; foul.

Meralgia, thigh pain.

Meropia, partial blindness.

Merotomy, cutting into sections.

Mesiad, toward the center.

Mesial, located in the middle.

Mesmerism, hypnotism.

Metabolism, the building-up and breaking-down processes of the body as a whole.

Metabolism, Basal, minimum amount of energy necessary to maintain life when the body is at complete rest.

Metacarpus, five bones in the palm of the hand.

Metachrosis, change of color.

Metachysis, blood transfusion.

Metacyesis, extrauterine pregnancy

Metallophobia, extreme fear of metallic objects.

Metamorphosis, change of shape or structure.

Metastasis, movement of bacteria or a disease from one part of the body to another.

Metatarsus, part of the foot between the ankle and the beginning of the toes.

Metopagus, twins joined at the forehead.

Metopic, pertaining to the forehead.

Metra, the uterus.

Metralgia, pain in the uterus.

Metrectasia, dilatation of the uterus

Metritis, inflammation of the uterus

Metrocarcinoma, cancer of the uterus.

Metrocyte, mother cell.

Metrodynia, pain in the uterus.

Metrology, science of measurements.

Metropathy, any uterine disorder.

Metrorrhagia, vaginal bleeding unrelated to monthly bleeding.

M.F.D., minimum fatal dose.

Miasm, Miasma, foul odor.

Mication, involuntary, rapid winking; fast motion.

Microbe, small, living organism discernible only through a microscope.

Microbicidal, destroying microbes.

Microbiologist, specialist in microbiology.

Microbiology, science dealing with microscopic organisms.

Microcardia, abnormal smallness of the heart.

Microcoria, smallness of the pupil.

Microcyst, tiny cyst.

Microcyte, small red blood corpuscle.

Microglossia, abnormal smallness of the tongue.

Microlesion, very small lesion.

Micromastia, unusual smallness of the breast.

Micronize, reduce to very small particles.   [ism.

Microorganism, microscopic organ-

Microphallus, abnormal smallness of the penis.

Micropsia, defective vision; seeing things smaller than they are.

Microscope, instrument which enlarges objects for visual examination.

Microscopic, able to be seen only under a microscope.

Microscopy, observation with the microscope.

Micturition, urination.

Midget, one who does not attain full growth; very small person.

Midriff, diaphragm.

Midwife, woman who helps at childbirth.

Midwifery, obstetrics.

Midriasis, enlargement of the pupil of the eye.

Migraine, severe, periodic, one-sided headache, usually accompanied by abdominal distress.

Miliaria, heat rash.

Milieu, environment.

Milphosis, loss of eyebrows or eyelashes.

Miocardia, heart contraction.

Miscarriage, loss of product of conception before age of viability; abortion.

Miscegenation, people of two different races that are married.

Miscible, able to be mixed.

Misogamy, hatred of marriage.

Misopedia, hatred of children.

Mite, tiny insect.

Mitral valve, the heart valve on left side of heart between upper and lower chambers.

Mittelschmerz, pain at time of ovulation.

M.M., mucous membrane.

Mnemonics, improvement of the memory.

Mobile, movable.

Moccasin, poisonous snake.

Modus, method.

Modus Operandi, method of performing an act.

Mogigraphia, writers' cramp.

Mogilalia, speech defect.

Mogitocia, difficult birth.

Moist, damp.

Molar, grinder tooth.

Mold, fungus.

Molding, shaping of the fetal head at birth.

Mole, skin growth usually colored and sprouting hair.

Molecule, tiny mass of matter.

Molimen, effort to establish the monthly period.

Mollities, abnormal softening.

Molluscum, chronic skin disease with pulpy bumps.

Monarticular, pertaining to a single joint.

Mongolism, arrest of physical and mental development, with features similar to the Asiatic race.

Moniliasis, fungus infection of various areas of the body, especially mouth, throat, vagina.

Moniliform, beaded.

Monocular, pertaining to or affecting one eye; having a single lens.

Monocyesis, pregnancy with one fetus.

Monocyte, type of white blood cell.

Monodiplopia, double vision in one eye.

Monogenesis, nonsexual reproduction.

Monogenous, a sexual reproduction.

Monohemerous, lasting only one day.

Monomania, obsession with one subject or idea.

Monomelic, affecting one limb.

Mononucleosis, glandular fever; virus disease in which monocytes are increased beyond normal number, lymph nodes enlarged, sore throat.

Monopathy, disease affecting a single part.

Monoplegia, paralysis of a single group of muscles or one limb.

Monosexual, having characteristics of only one sex.

Mood, attitude; state of mind.

Mons, elevated area.

Mons Pubis, Mons Veneris, area over the symphysis pubis in the female.

Monster, abnormally formed fetus.

Monstrosity, state of being a monster.

Monthlies, menses.

Monticulus, probuterance.

Morbid, pertaining to disease; the disease itself.   [ease.

Morbid Condition, condition of dis-

Morbific, causing disease.

Morbilli, measles.

Morbilliform, like measles.

Morbus, disease.

Morbus Caducus, epilepsy.

Mores, customs.

Morgue, public mortuary.

Moria, foolishness.

Moribund, dying.

Morning Sickness, nausea and vomiting during the early stages of pregnancy.

Moron, one whose mental age is from seven to twelve years.

Morosis, feeblemindedness.

Morphine, drug used as an analgesic and sedative.

Morphinism, addiction to morphine.

Mors, death.

Morsus, bite.

Morsus Humanus, human bite

Mortal, deadly.

Mortise Joint, ankle joint.

Mosquito, blood sucking insect.

Mosquitocide, agent which kills mosquitoes.

Mother, female parent.

Mother's Mark, birthmark.

Motile, able to move.

Mottling, discoloration in various areas.

Mounding, lumping.

Mountain Sickness, condition caused by low air pressure.

Mouth, oral cavity.

M.S., Master of Surgery.

M.T., Medical Technologist.

Muciferous, secreting mucus.

Mucilage, paste.

Mucilaginous, adhesive.

Mucin, main substance of mucus.

Mucopus, mucus mixed with pus.

Mucosa, mucous membrane; lining tissue that produces mucus

Mucous, pertaining to mucus.

Mucus, a thick, white liquid secreted by mucous glands.

Mulatto, anyone of both Negro and White blood.

Muliebria, female genitalia.

Muliebrity, femininity.

Multi- (prefix), many; much.

Multigravida, pregnant woman who had more than two past pregnancies.

Multipara, woman who has had more than two live children.

Mumps, infectious disease marked by swelling of the large salivary glands in front of the ears.

Murmur, abnormal heart sound with a blowing or rasping quality.

Musca, fly.

Muscae Volitantes, spots before the eyes.

Muscle, bundle of contractile fibers which produce movement.

Muscle Cramp, involuntary contraction of muscles.

Muscular, pertaining to muscle.

Musculus, muscle.

Musophobia, extreme fear of mice.

Mussitation, delirious muttering.

Mustard Plaster, home remedy no longer commonly used.

Mutation, change.

Mute, unable to speak; one who cannot speak.

Mutism, speechlessness; dumbness.

Myalgia, muscle pain.

Myasthenia, muscle weakness.

Myatonia, muscle limpness.

Mycetismus, mushroom poisoning.

Mycology, science of fungi.

Mycosis, infection caused by fungi.

Mydriasis, abnormal pupil dilation.

Myectomy, surgical removal of a piece of muscle.

Myectopia, muscle displacement.

Myelauxe, bone marrow increase.

Myelin, nerve covering.

Myelon, spinal cord.

Myelopathy, disease of the spinal cord.

Myeloplegia, spinal paralysis.

Myelitis, spinal cord inflammation.

Myeloma, bone marrow tumor that may be cancerous.

Myenteron, muscular layer of the intestine.

Myiasia, condition when larvae of flies enter eyes, ears or intestines.

Myitis, muscle inflammation.

Myocarditis, inflammation of the heart muscle.

Myocardium, muscle that makes up the heart.

Myoclonus, muscle spasm.

Myocyte, cell of muscular tissue.

Myoid, resembling muscle.

Myology, study of muscles.

Myoma, tumor from muscle tissue.

Myomectomy, surgical removal of a myoma.

Myopathy, any muscle disease.

Myope, one who is nearsighted.

Myopia, nearsightedness.

Myosis, construction of the eye pupil.

Myositis, muscle inflammation, usually a voluntary muscle.

Myospasm, muscle spasm.

Myotasis, stretching of muscle.

Myotonia, continuous muscle spasm not relieved by relaxation.

Myringitis, inflammation of the eardrum. [drum.

Myringotomy, incision into the ear-

Mythomania, habitual lying or exaggeration.

Myxedema, a disease due to failure of the thyroid gland.

Myxoma, tumor of mucous tissue.

Myxorrhea, flow of mucus.

Myzesis, sucking.

— N —

Nail, horny structure covering the ends of the fingers and toes.

Nail Bed, part of a finger or toe covered by a nail.

Nail Biting, nervous tendency to bite or or chew the fingernails.

Naked, exposed to view.

Nanism, dwarfishness.

Nanus, dwarf; stunted.

Nap, short sleep.

Nape, back of the neck.

Narcissism, self love.

Narcolepsy, disease of unknown origin in which there are periodic episodes of sleep any time of day or night.

Narcomania, morbid desire for narcotics.

Narcosis, state of unconsciousness.

Narcotic, producing a state of unconsciousness; any sleep inducing drug; one addicted to the use of narcotics.

Narcotize, to make unconscious.

Naris, nostril.

Nasal, pertaining to the nose; bone forming the bridge of the nose.

Nasus, nose.

Natal, pertaining to birth; pertain-to the buttocks.

Natality, birth rate.

Natant, floating.

Natis, buttocks.

Native, inherent; indigenous.

Natural, not artificial.

Natural Childbirth, childbirth without anesthesia.

Naturopathy, curing without drugs.

Nature Cure, any system of treatment which is based upon the belief that disease may best be cured and health maintained by the use of "natural remedies", as opposed to artificial and man-made drugs.

Naupathia, seasickness.

Nausea, stomach discomfort with the feeling of a need to vomit.

Nauseant, causing nausea.

Navel, remnant on outside of body where umbilical cord was attached at birth.

Near Point, point closest to the eye at which an object can be seen distinctly.

Nearsighted, able to see clearly only a short distance.

Nebula, haziness; cloudy urine.

Necator, hookworm.

Neck, part of the body connecting the head and trunk; narrow part near the extremity of any organ.

Necromania, obsession with death.

Necrophilism, intercourse with a corpse.

Necropneumonia, gangrene of lung.

Necropsy, autopsy.

Necrosis, death of a part of the body due to absence of blood supply.

Needle, pointed instrument for sewing or puncturing.

Negativism, a symptom in mental diseases in which the patient resists or is against everything.

Neogala, first milk after childbirth.

Neogenesis, new formation.

Neonatal, concerning the newborn.

Neonatorum, pertaining to the newborn.

Neonatus, a newborn infant.

Neopathy, new disease or complication.

Negativism, a symptom in mental diseases in which the patient resists or is against everything.

Neogala, first milk after childbirth.

Neogenesis, new formation.

Neonatal, concerning the newborn.

Neonatorum, pertaining to the new born.

Neonatus, a newborn infant.

Neopathy, new disease or complication.

Neophilism, excessive love of new things. [things.

Neophobia, extreme fear of new

Neoplasm, an abnormal growth.

Nephralgia, pain in a kidney.

Nephrectomy, surgical removal of a kidney.

Nephrelcus, renal ulcer.

Nephric, pertaining to the kidney.

Nephritis, inflammation of the kidneys.

Nephrolithiases, formation of kidney stones.

Nephrology, study of the kidney.

Nephroma, tumor of the outer portion of the kidney.

Nephropexy, sewing a floating kidney into place.

Nephros, the kidney.

Nephrosis, disintegration of the kidney without signs of inflammation.

Nepiology, study of newborn.

Nerve, bundle of nerve fibers existing outside the central nervous system.

Nervous, highly excitable.

Nervous, a condition of being easily disturbed or distressed.

Nervous System, entire nervous structure of the body.

Nervus, pl., **Nervi,** nerve.

Network, structure composed of interlacing fibers.

Neural, pertaining to nerves or nervous tissue.

Neuralgia, pain along course of nerve.

Neurasthenia, exhaustion of the nerves.

Neure, neuron.

Neurectasia, stretching of a nerve to relieve pain.

Neuritis, inflammation of a nerve.

Neurocranium, portion of the cranium enclosing the brain.

Neurocyte, any nerve cell.

Neurodynamic, pertaining to nervous energy.

Neuroid, resembling a nerve.

Neuro-induction, mental suggestion.

Neurologist, specialist in disorders of the nervous system.

Neuroma, tumor composed of nerve substance.

Neuromuscular, pertaining to the nerves and muscles.

Neuron, nerve cell.

Neuronitis, inflammation of a neuron.

Neuropathy, any disease of the nervous system.

Neurophthisis, degeneration or wasting of nerve tissue.

Neuroplasm, protoplasm of a nerve cell.

Neuropsychiatry, branch of medicine dealing with nervous and mental disorders.

Neurosis, minor mental disorder.

Neurospasm, muscular twitching.

Neurosurgeon, specialist in surgery of the brain and nervous system.

Neurosyphilis, syphilis of the nervous system.

Neurothlipsis, nerve pressure.

Neurotrauma, nerve lesion.

Nevus, birthmark; mole.

Nexus, a binding together.

Niche, depression; recess.

Nicotine, poisonous alkaloid of tobacco.

Nictitation, excessive winking.

Nidus, cluster, focus of infection; nerve nucleus.

Night Cry, cry of a child during sleep.

Nightmare, bad dream.

Nightwalking, sleepwalking.

Nigra, black.

Negrities Linguae, black tongue.

N.I.H., National Institutes of Health.

Niphablepsia, snow blindenss.

Nipple, protuberance in each breast from which the female secretes milk.

Nit, egg of a louse. [ing.

N.L.N., National League for Nurs-

Noctophobia, extreme fear of night.

Nocturia, bed wetting; frequent urination at night.

Nocuity, harmfulness.

Node, small rounded protuberance; point of constriction.

Nodule, small node; small group of cells.

Nodus, node.

Noma, form of gangrene of the mouth found in ill-nourished or weak children.

Non compos mentis, not of sound mind.

Non Repetat, do not repeat.

Nonsexual, without sex, asexual.

Nontoxic, not poisonous.

Nonunion, failure of bone fragments to knit together.

Nonviable, incapable.

Noopsyche, intellectual processes.

Norm, standard.

Normal, usual. [cell.

Normocyte, normal sized red blood

Normoptopic, normally located.

Nose, organ of the sense of smell.

Nosebleed, hemorrhage from the nose.

Nosema, sickness; disease.

Nosology, science of disease classification.

Nosophilia, extreme desire to be sick.

Nosophobia, extreme fear of illness.

Nosopoietic, causing disease.

Nostalgia, homesickness; feeling for past experiences and things.

Nostomania, extreme homesickness.

Nostril, nasal aperture.

Nostrum, patent medicine.

Notal, dorsal.

Notalgia, back pain.

Notifiable, pertaining to any disease which must be reported to health authorities.

Noxious, harmful; deadly; poisonous.

Nubile, of childbearing age.

Nucha, nape of the neck.

Nucleus, pl., Neuclei, center of a cell.

Nudomania, extreme desire to be nude.

Nudophobia, extreme fear of being nude.

Nullipara, woman who has not given birth to a child.

Numb, insensible.

Numbness, lack of sensation.

Nurse, one who is trained to care for the sick; to care for the sick; to breast feed.

Nutation, nodding.

Nutrient, nourishing.

Nutrition, food; nourishment of its assimilation.

Nutritious, giving nourishment.

Nux, nut.

Nyctalgia, pain during the night.

Nycterine, occurring at night.

Nyctalopia, night blindness due to lack of vitamin A.

Nyctophobia, extreme fear of darkness.

Nyctotyphlosis, night blindness.

Nygma, puncture wound.

Nymphectomy, surgical removal of the small lips of the vagina.

Nymphomania, excessive sexual desire in the female.

Nystagmus, jerking movement of the eyes which may be inborn or a sign of disease of the nervous system.

Nyxis, puncture; pricking.

— O —

Oaric, concerning the ovary.

Oaritis, ovarian inflammation.

Ordormition, numbness and tingling in an arm or leg.

Obduction, autopsy.

Obesity, excessive stoutness.

Obfuscation, confusion.

Oblique, diagonal.

Obliteration, complete surgical removal of a part; total memory loss.

Obmutescence, loss of power to speak.

Obnubilation, confused state.

Obsession, all consuming emotion or idea.

Obstetrical, pertaining to obstetrics.

Obstetrician, physician who specializes in pregnant women.

Obstetrics, branch of medicine dealing with pregnancy and delivery of infants.

Obstipation, constipation due to obstruction.

Obstruction, blockage of structure; usually intestine.

Obtund, to dull sensation.

Obturation, closing of an opening.

Occipital, pertaining to the bone that constitutes the back part of the skull.

Occiput, back part of skull.

Occlude, to block or obstruct.

Occlusion, shutting; the full meeting of the chewing surfaces of the upper and lower teeth.

Occult, hidden; obscure.

Occupational Disease, disease caused by one's work.

Occupational Therapy, use of an activity as treatment. [ing.

Ochlesis, disease due to overcrowding.

Ochlophobia, extreme fear of crowds. [skin.

Ochrodermia, yellowness of the

Octoroon, one who is 1/8 Negro and 7/8 Caucasian.

Ocular, pertaining to the eye or vision.

Oculist, specialist in eye diseases.

Oculus, eye.

Odaxesmus, biting of tongue or skin of mouth during a fit.

Odaxitic, stinging or itching.

Odontalgia, toothache.

Odontexesis, cleaning of teeth.

Odontiasis, teething.

Odontic, pertaining to the teeth.

Odonitis, tooth inflammation

Odontogeny, development of teeth.

Odontology, study of the teeth.

Odontechtomy, tooth extraction.

Odonterism, chattering of teeth.

Odonitoclasis, breaking a tooth.

Odontodynia, toothache.

Odontoma, tumor arising from the same tissue from which teeth are formed.

Odontoprisis, grinding teeth.

Odontotomy, incision of a tooth.

Odontotrypy, drilling of a tooth.

Odynophagia, pain with swallowing.

Odynophobia, extreme fear of pain.

Oedipus Complex, abnormal love of a child for a parent of the opposite sex, usually a boy for his mother.

Oikophobia, extreme hatred of the home.

Ointment, soft fat substance spread on skin as therapy.

Oleaginous, oily.

Olecranon, bony inner portion of elbow.

Oleum, oil.

Olfaction, smelling; sense of smell.

Olfactory, pertaining to the sense of smell.

Oligemia, deficiency of blood.

Oligocholia, bile deficiency.

Oligogalactia, deficient milk secretion.

Oligoposy, insufficient liquid intake.

Oligotrichia, lack of hair.

Oligotrophy, insufficient nutrition.

Oliguria, decreased amount of urine production.

Omagra, shoulder gout.

Omalgia, neuralgia of the shoulder.

Omentum, large fatty membrane which acts as a cover for the bowels.

Omitis, shoulder, inflammation.

Omnivorous, eating all types of food.

Omodynia, shoulder pain.

Omphalic, pertaining to the umbilicus.

Omphalitis, inflammation of the navel.

Omphalocele, hernia around navel.

Omphalos, navel.

Onanism, complete sexual intercourse with ejaculation outside, the vagina; masturbation.

Oncosis, multiple tumors.

Onocyte, tumor cell.

Oncogenous, causing tumors.

Oncoma, tumor.

Oncosis, multiple tumors.

Oncotic, pertaining to swelling.

Oneiric, pertaining to dreams.

Oniomania, excessive desire to buy things.

Onomatomania, compulsion to repeat words.

Onychia, infection and inflammation around fingernails.

Onychophagia, nail biting.

Onychosis, disease of the nails.

Onyx, fingernail; toenail.

Onyxis, ingrown nails.

Oncyesis, pregnancy in the ovary.

Oophoralgia, ovarian pain.

Oophorectomy, surgical removal of an ovary.

Oophoritis, inflammation of an ovary.   [mor.
Oophoroma, malignant ovarian tu-
Oophoron, ovary.
Oosperm, fertilized ovum.
Ootheca, ovary.
Opaque, dark; not transparent; mentally dull.
Operable, capable of being relieved by an operation.
Operation, surgical procedure.
Operation Major, one in which there is considerable risk to life.
Operation, Minor, one in which there is little or no danger to life.
Ophidism, snake poisoning.
Ophthalmia, inflammation of the eye.
Ophthalic, pertaining to the eyes.
Ophthalmologist, specialist in the eye and its diseases.
Ophthalmology, study of eye and its diseases.
Ophthalmoplegia, paralysis of the eye muscles.
Ophthalmoscope, instrument for examining the eyes.
Opiate, any opium derivative.
Opisthotonis, arched-back position with head and heel on the horizontal.
Opsialgia, pain in region of face.
Opsomania, extreme craving for a particular food.
Optic, concerning sight or eye.
Optical, pertaining to vision.
Optician, one who makes lenses or optical instruments.
O.R., operating room.
Ora, border; margin.
Orad, toward the mouth.
Oral, pertaining to the mouth.
Oralogy, oral hygiene; study of mouth diseases.
Orbicular, circular.
Orbit, eyesocket.
Orchic, pertaining to the testes.
Orchiectomy, surgical removal of a testes.
Orchiodynia, testicle pain.
Orchioncus, tumor of a testes.
Orchis, testicle.   [ticle.
Orchitis, inflammation of the tes-
Orderly, male hospital attendant.
Orexigenic, appetite stimulant.
Oreximania, abnormal desire for food.
Organ, group of tissue with specific function.
Organism, individual animal or plant.
Orgasm, sexual climax.
Orifice, opening, entrance.
Oropharynx, first part of throat starting at mouth.
Orotherapy, treatment with serums.
Orrhorrhea, watery discharge; flow of serum.
Orrhology, study of blood serum.
Orthogenics, eugenics.
Orthopedics, branch of medicine dealing with the surgery of bones and joints.   [dics.
Orthopedist, specialist in orthope-
Orthosis, correction of a deformity.
Orthostatic, concerning standing position.
Orthopnea, condition in which difficult breathing is aided by propping up head and shoulders.
Orthopschiatry, branch of psychiatry dealing mainly with adolescents.
Orthuria, normal frequency of urination.
Os, pl., **Ora,** mouth, opening.
Os, pl., **Ossa,** bone.

Oscedo, yawning; white spots in the mouth.   [tum.
Oscheitis, inflammation of the scro-
Oscitation, yawning.
Osculum, aperature.
Osculation, kissing; joining of two structures by their mouths.
Osmatic, having an acute sense of smell.
Osmesis, smelling.
Osmics, science of odors.
Osmosis, passage of fluid from lower to higher area of concentration.
Osphresis, sense of smell.
Osphus, loin.
Ossa, bones.
Osseous, bonelike.
Ossicle, small bone of ear.
Ossiferous, producing bone
Ossofication, bone formation; change of tissue to bone.
Ossify, to turn into bone.
Ostectomy, surgical removal of a bone.
Osteitis, bone inflammation.
Osteocarcinoma, bone cancer.
Osteochrondritis, inflammation of both bone and cartilage from which bone is formed.
Osteochrondroma, tumor arising from bone cartilage.
Osteology, study of bones.
Osteoma, tumor composed of various parts of bone.
Osteomalacia, softening of bone.
Osteomyelitis, an inflammatory disease of bone caused usually by infection with streptococcus or staphylococcus.
Osteopathy, system of treatment based on the idea that diseases are caused by minor dislocations of the spine, and, therefore, curable by bone manipulation.
Osteosis, formation of bony tissue.
Ostum, vaginal, outer opening of the vagina.
Ostium, small opening.
O.T., occupational therapy.
Otalgia, earache.
Otic, pertaining to the ear.
Otitis, inflammation of the ear.
Otolaryngology, medical specialty concerned with ear, nose and throat.
Otologist, ear specialist.
Otology, branch of medicine dealing with the ear.
Otopathy, any ear disease.
Otosclerosis, type of deafness caused by hardening of the tissues and bones in the inner ear.
Otoscope, instrument used to examine ear.
Oula, the gums.
Ouloid, scar-like.
Outlay, graft.
Outpatient, one who received treatment at a hospital without being admitted.
Oval, egg-shaped.
Ovarian, pertaining to the ovaries.
Ovariectomy, surgical removal of an ovary.
Ovary, the sex glands in women.
Ovate, oval.
Overgrowth, excessive growth.
Overweight, exceeding desired weight by more than 10%.
Oviduct, tube from ovary to uterus.
Ovulation, process of discharge of egg from ovary.
Ovum, pl., **Ova,** egg cell.
Oxyblepsia, very acute vision.
Oxycinesia, pain on motion.
Oxygen, an element needed for life

which is brought into the body by the process of breathing.
Oxygeusia, acute sense of taste.
Oxylalia, rapid speech.
Oxyopia, acute sight.
Oxytocic, agent used to stimulate uterus to contract.
Ozostomia, offensive breath.
Ozena, disease of nasal passage leading to the production of a foul-smelling discharge.

— **P** —

Pabulum, food, nourishment.
Pacemaker, area of heart where rhythm of heart beat starts.
Pachyblepharon, thickening of the eyelid.
Pachycephalous, thick wall.
Pachychilla, thick lips.
Pachyderma, thick skin.
Pachyglossia, thick tongue.
Pachyhemia, thickening of the blood.
Pachymeningitis, inflammation of the outer covering of the brain and spinal cord.
Pachymeter, instrument for measuring thickness.
Pachynsis, thickening.
Pachyonychia, thickening of the nails.
Pachypodous, big feet.
Pack, a dry or wet, hot or cold blanket wrapped around the patient.
Packing, material used to fill wound or cavity.
Pad, soft cushion.
Paget's Disease; Osteitis Deformans, thickening of bones, mainly skull and shin; rash of nipple connected with breast tumor.
Pain, distress; agony, suffering.
Pain, False, false labor pains.
Palate, roof of the mouth divided into hard and soft portions.
Palantine, pertaining to the palate.
Palatitis, inflammation of the palate.
Paleontology, study of early man.
Palliate, to reduce or allay discomfort.   [ing.
Palliative, relieving pain or suffer-
Pallid, lacking.
Pallor, paleness of skin.
Palm, inside portion of hand.
Palma, palm.
Palmar, pertaining to the palm.
Palpable, able to be touched.
Palpate, to examine by feeling.
Palpebra, eyelid.
Palpebra Inferior, lower eyelid.
Palpebra Superior, upper eyelid.
Palpitation, rapid pulsation in an organ, usually refers to the heart.   [sis.
Palsy, impaired function or paraly-
Paludism, malaria.
Panacea, cure for all ills.
Panarthritis, inflammation of the entire joint.
Pancarditis, infection of all parts of heart.
Panchrest, panacea.
Pancreas, gland lying behind and below the stomach which produces ferments which are passed into the intestinal tract to help in digestion; site of insulin production.
Pancreatitis, inflammation of the pancreas.
Pancreectomy, removal of pancreas in part or whole.
Pandemic, widely-spread epidemic.
Pandiculation, stretching and yawning.

Panesthesia, all of the sensations experienced.

Pang, spontaneous, sudden emotion or pain.

Panhidrosis, perspiration over entire body.

Panhysterectomy, complete removal of the womb.

Panic, extreme anxiety, with temporary loss of reason.

Panniculitis, inflammation of abdominal wall fat. [layer.

Panniculus, layer of tissue, fatty

Pannus, abnormal membrane on the cornea.

Panophobia, extreme fear of everything in general.

Pansinusitis, inflammation of all the sinuses.

Pant, breathe fast and hard.

Pap, nipple; soft food.

Pappilla, nipple-like protuberance.

Papilla, Mammary, breast nipple.

Papilledema, swelling of optic nerve where nerve enters eye.

Papilloma, benign tumor of skin or inner membranes.

Papule, small red raised area on skin.

Par, pair.

Para- (prefix), beside.

Paracentesis, puncture.

Paracusia, any hearing defect.

Parachroma, skin discoloration.

Paracyesis, pregnancy outside uterus.

Paralalia, speech disorder.

Paralgesia, painful sensation.

Paralysis, loss of the power of movement or sensation in one or more parts of the body.

Paralytic, pertaining to paralysis.

Paralyze, to cause loss of muscle control and/or feeling.

Paramenia, irregular or abnormal menstrual period.

Parametrium, tissue surrounding and supporting the womb.

Paranoia, chronic psychosis characterized by fears, suspicion and well organized imaginery thoughts.

Paraphemia, distorted speech.

Paraphobia, mild phobia.

Paraplegia, paralysis of the legs or lower part of the body.

Parapoplexy, slight apoplexy.

Parasite, any animal or plant which lives inside or on the body of of another animal or plant.

Parateresiomania, compulsion to see new sights.

Parathymia, disordered emotion.

Parathyroid Glands, group of six small glands situated around the thyroid gland concerned with calcium and phosporus in body.

Paregoric, derivative of opium used to help relieve pain or diarrhea.

Parenchyma, productive part of an organ.

Parent, one who begets offspring.

Parenchyma, functional tissue of an organ.

Parenteral, outside of digestive tract.

Paresis, paralysis due to disease of brain, usually syphilis.

Paries, wall of a cavity.

Pareunia, sexual intercourse.

Parity, capable of bearing children.

Parkinson's Disease, nervous system disorder causing tremor and odd gait.

Paronychia, infection of the tissues at the base of a nail.

Paroniria, frightful dreams.

Paropsis, disorder of vision.

Parorexia, craving for special foods.

Parosmia, smelling imaginary odors.

Parotid, located near the ear.

Parotid gland, large salivary gland located over the jaw in front of the ear.

Parotitis, inflammation of the parotid gland, a large salivary gland.

Parous, having given birth to one or more children.

Parovarian, beside the ovary.

Paroxysm, sudden attack or recurrency of symptoms.

Pars, pl., **Partes,** a part.

Particulate, composed of minute particles.

Parturient, giving birth; labor.

Parturifacient, medicine which speeds up birth.

Parturition, childbirth.

Paruria, any abnormality in excretion of urine.

Passion, strong emotion.

Pasteurization, method of sterilizing foods.

Patch Test, test carried out to determine sensitivity.

Patella, knee-cap.

Patency, state of being open, e.g., ducts, hollow tubes.

Patent Medicine, remedy for public use obtained without prescription.

Patent, open.

Pathetic, pertaining to the feelings.

Pathic, pertaining to disease.

Pathogens, anything capable of producing disease.

Pathogenic, pertaining to the ability to produce disease.

Pathology, study of diseases for their own interest, rather than directly with an immediate view to curing them.

Pathomania, abnormal wish to commit crime. [ease.

Pathophobia, extreme fear of dis-

Pathophoresis, communication of disease.

Patient, one under medical care.

Patulous, open; exposed.

Paunch, protruding abdomen.

Pavor, fear; fright.

Peccant, unhealthy.

Pectinate, like teeth of comb.

Pectoral, pertaining to the chest.

Pectus, chest; breast.

Pectus Carination, "Chicken breast"

Pedal, pertaining to the foot.

Pederasty, sexual intercourse through the anus.

Pediatrician, specialist in diseases of children.

Pediatrics, branch of medicine dealing with the diseases of children and their cure.

Pediatrist, pediatrician.

Pedicular, infested with lice.

Pediculicide, agent which kills lice.

Pediculosis, infestation with lice.

Pediculosis Capitis, head lice.

Pediophobia, extreme fear of children or dolls.

Pedodontics, branch of dentistry dealing with children.

Pedophila, abnormal fondness for children.

Peduncle, stalk or stem.

Pelada, patchy baldness.

Pelage, hair covering the body.

Pelagism, seasickness.

Pellagra, disease due to lack of vitamin B.

Pellet, small pill.

Pellicle, thin tissue; scum on a liquid.

Pellucid, translucent.

Pelvis, bony part of the body lying between the thighs and the abdomen.

Pemphigus, skin disease characterized by large blisters and pigmented spots. [ing.

Pendulous, heavy and loosely hang-

Penicillin, an antibiotic discovered in 1928 by Sir Alexander Fleming.

Penis, male sex organ.

Penitis, inflammation of the penis.

Pepo, pumpkin seed used in removal of tapeworm.

Pepsic, peptic.

Pepsin, ferment found in the gastric juice which helps in the breakdown of protein.

Peptic, pertaining to the digestive tract.

Peracidity, excessive acidity.

Per Anum, by anus.

Perception, awareness.

Percussion, striking body as an aid to physical examination and diagnosis.

Percutaneous, through the skin.

Perforating, piercing.

Perforation, opening or hole in any area of body.

Peri- (prefix), around; near.

Periorticular, surrounding a joint.

Perianal, situated around the anus.

Pericardiac, around the heart.

Pericarditis, inflammation of sac surrounding the heart.

Pericardium, sac surrounding the heart.

Pericolic, around the colon.

Pericytial, around a cell.

Perimetrium, covering tissue of the womb.

Perinephric, situated around the kidneys.

Perineum, area between the sex organs and the anus.

Periodicity, occurring at regular intervals.

Period of Gestation, period from conception to childbirth.

Periodontal, around a tooth.

Perionchyia, inflammation of area around a fingernail or toenail.

Periosteum, tissue around bone through which bone is nourished.

Periostitis, inflammation of the membrane surrounding a bone.

Periotic, located around the ear.

Peripatetic, changing from place to place.

Periphery, away from center or midline of body.

Perirenal, around the kidney.

Perirhinal, around the nose.

Perish, die; disintegrate.

Peristalsis, the normal movements of the intestines which move the food along the digestive tract.

Peritonitis, inflammation of the lining tissue of the abdominal cavity.

Peritonsillar, around the tonsil.

Perivascular, around a vessel.

Pernicious, severe; fatal.

Pernicious Anemia, disease of unknown origin affecting many systems of body.

Pernio, chillblain.

Per Os, by mouth.

Per Rectum, by rectum.

Perseveration, repetitive statements or answers to questions.

Perspiration, fluid produced by body at surface of the skin which helps to control body temperature.

Pertussis, whopping cough.
Pervert, one who practices abnormal behavior.
Pervigilium, abnormal wakefulness.
Pes, foot or footlike structure.
Pes Contortis, clubfoot.
Pes Planus, flatfoot.
Pessary, device used to hold uterus in proper position.
Pestiferous, causing pestilence.
Pestilence, epidemic of contagious disease.
Pestle, device used to break up drugs in pharmacy.
Petit Mal, type of epilepsy in which the attacks are relatively slight.
pH, concentration of hydrogen ion or acidity; Neutral = pH 7.
Phactis, inflammation of the eye lens.
Phacomatacia, soft cataract.
Phagocyte, absorbing cell.
Phalanges, bones of fingers.
Phalanx, one of the bones of the fingers or toes.
Phallectomy, amputation of the penis.
Phallic, concerning male sex organ.
Phallus, male sex organ.
Phanic, visible.
Pharm., pharmaceutical; pharmacy.
Pharmaceutical, pertaining to drugs.
Pharmacist, druggist.
Pharmacy, drug store.
Pharyngitis, inflammation of the pharynx.
Pharyngoscope, instrument for examining the throat.
Pharynx, membraneous tube extending from oral cavity to level of first part of esophagus.
Phatne, tooth socket.
Phenobarbital, barbiturate used to sedate or produce sleep.
Phenolphthalein, purgative.
Phimosis, excessive tightness of the foreskin of the penis.
Phlebitis, inflammation of a vein.
Phlebosclerosis, hardening of a vein.
Phlebothrombosis, formation of a clot in a vein.
Phlebotomy, opening of a vein.
Phlegm, thick mucus from respiratory tract.
Phlegmatic, sluggish.
Phlogistic, inducing inflammation.
Phobia, an extreme fear.
Phonal, pertaining to the voice.
Phonetics, science of vocal sounds.
Photodynia, pain in the eyes due to intense light.
Photophobia, extreme fear of light.
Photosensitive, sensitive to light.
Phrenetic, maniacal.
Phrenic, pertaining to the diaphragm or mind.
Phrenitis, delirium.
Phrenologfy, study of the mind through the shape of the skull.
Phrenoplegia, paralysis of the diaphragm.
Phthisology, study of tuberculosis.
Phthisis, tuberculosis.
Phylctenuls, small blister, usually occurring with an eye inflammation.   [fection.
Phylaxis, bodily defense against in-
Phyma, skin tumor.
Physic, cathartic; art of medicine.
Physician, licensed medical doctor.
Physics, study of natural forces and phenomena.
Physiogonomy, face.
Physiology, science which deals with the functions of the body.

Physique, body build.
Phytin, material from plants used as stimulants.
Phytotoxin, plant poison.
Pia, one of membranous coverings of brain and spinal cord.
Pica, an abnormal craving to eat odd things.
Piedra, hair disease.
Pigment, coloring substance.
Pilary, pertaining to the hair.
Pileous, hairy.
Piles, enlarged, painful veins in the rectum or around the anus.
Pill. capsule containing medication.
Pillion. temporary artificial leg.
Pilonidal, cyst containing hairs, frequently found at the base of the spine.
Pilose, hairy.
Pilus, hair.
Pimple, small pointed area on skin, at times filled with infectious material.
Pineal Gland, small gland about the size of a pea in the lower part of the brain.
Pinquecula, thickened area on edge of cornea of eye.
Pinkeye, contagious eye inflammation; conjunctivitis.   [ear.
Pinna, projecting part of external
Pinworm, parasite found in intestine and around anus.
Pit, depression.
Pithecoid, apelike.
Pituita, phlegm.
Pituitarism, disorder of pituitary function.
Pituitary Gland. small gland at the base of the brain which affects all the other glands of the body.
Pityriasis, group of diseases in which the main symptom is a scaly skin.
Placebo, inactive substance.
Placenta, organ by which the unborn infant is attached to the inside of the womb and through which infants' body needs are supplied.
Plague, epidemic disease transmitted by fleas of rats.
Planocyte, wandering cell.
Planta, sole of the foot.
Plantar, pertaining to the sole of the foot.
Plantar Wart, painful wart occcurring on the bottom of the foot.
Plasma, colorless fluid part of the blood as distinct from blood cells.
Plastic, pertaining to plastic surgery; moldable; any material that can be molded.
Platelet, small disc in blood stream used for blood coagulation.
Platycrania, flattening of the skull.
Platypodia, flat foot.
Pledget, small piece of gauze soaked in antiseptic.
Pleonemia, increased amount of blood in a part.
Pleonexia, extreme greediness.
Plethora, abnormal amount of blood.
Pleonexia, a psychic condition characterized by selfishness.
Pleura, thin tissue covering the lungs and lining the interior walls of the chest cavity.
Pleurisy, inflammation of the Pleura.
Pleurodynia, pain in the muscles between the ribs.
Plexor, percussion hammer.
Plexus, groups of nerves, lymphatic

glands or blood vessels in the body.
Plica, fold.
Plombage, filling a cavity with paraffin.
Plug, obstruction.
Plumbism, lead poisoning.
Pneoscope, the instrument that records breathing.
Pneumatic, pertaining to respiration.
Pneumococcus, germ which can attack the body, usually the lungs.
Pneumonectomy, surgical removal of a lung.
Pneumonia, inflammation of the lungs.
Pneumonopathy, any lung disease.
Pneumorrhagia, lung hemorrhage.
Pneumothorax, abnormal entrance of air or gas into lung sacs, causing an imbalance of pressures and difficult respiration.
Pock, pustule.
Podagra, gout affecting foot.
Podalgia, pain in the feet.
Podiatrist, specialist in foot ailments.
Pogoniasis, excessive beard growth.
Point, tiny spot or area.
Pointillage, massage with the finger tips.
Poisoning, ingestion of substance toxic to body.
Poison Ivy, vine causing severe skin irritation.
Poitrinaire, one having a chronic chest disease.
Poliomyelitis (Infantile Paralysis), inflammation of the grey matter of the spinal cord.
Poliosis, absence of hair coloring.
Pollen, male sex cells of plants.
Pollinosis, hay fever
Pollex, thumb or big toe.
Pollution, making impure; discharge of semen without sexual intercourse.
Polyarthritis, inflammation of several joints.
Polycholia, excessive bile secretion.
Polyclinic, medical center treating many diseases.
Polycyesis, pregnancy with more than one fetus.
Polycythemia, condition in which there is an excess of red blood cells.
Polycytosis, excess of blood cells.
Polydactylism, having more than five fingers or five toes.
Polydipsia, excessive desire to drink.
Polyemia, excessive blood in the body.
Polyglandular, affecting many glands.
Polygny, marriage to more than one woman at one time.
Polyhedral, many sides.
Polymenorrhea, unusual frequency of menstruation.
Polymyositis, inflammation of many muscles.
Polyneural, pertaining to many nerves.
Polyneuritis, inflammation of more than one group of nerves.
Polyp, outgrowths in the nose, intestines or bladder.
Polypathia, having more than one disease at a time.
Polyphagia, excessive eating.
Polyplegia, paralysis of several muscles.
Polypus, polyp.
Polyuria, excessive urination.

MEDICAL DICT

Ponophobia, extreme fear of pain or fatigue.

Pons, a part of the brain which bridges several other sections of the nervous system.

Pontic, false tooth.

Popliteal, pertaining to the back of the leg and the bend of the knee.

Pore, small opening in skin or tissue.

Pornerastic, excessive fondness for prostitutes.

Porous, having many pores.

Porrigo, ringworm.

Portio, part.

Portio Dura, facial nerve.

Porus, pore.

Position, placement of the body.

Positive, affirmative; indicating the presence of a disorder.

Posology, system of dosage.

Postcibal, after eating.

Postcoital, after sexual intercourse.

Postepileptic, after an epileptic attack.

Posterior, behind; at the back part.

Posthetomy, circumcision.

Posthumous, after death.

Postmortem, autopsy; after death.

Postnasal, situated behind the nose.

Postnatal, immediately after birth.

Postoperative, happening after an operation.

Postoral, in the back of the mouth.

Postpartum, after childbirth.

Postprandial, after a meal.

Postpubescent, after puberty.

Posture, body position.

Postuterine, behind the uterus.

Potable, adequate for drinking.

Potamophobia, extreme fear of large bodies of water.

Potency, strength; ability to perform coitus.

Potion, dose of liquid medicine.

Pouch, pocket-like cavity.

Poultice, hot, moist mass to be placed on the skin.

Pox, blisters and scars on the skin caused by certain diseases.

Practice, professional diagnosis and treatment of disease.

Practitioner, physician.

Pragmatagnosia, inability to recognize objects.

Prandial, pertaining to a meal.

Precordia, area overlying heart.

Pregnancy, state of being with child.

Pregravidic, preceeding pregnancy.

Prehensile, able to grasp.

Prehension, grasping.   [tack.

Preictal, preceeding a stroke or attack.

Premature, born before maturity.

Premature Infant, one weighing less than 5.5 pounds at birth.

Premenstrual, preceeding menstruation.

Premonitory, warning.

Premunition, immunization by vaccination.

Prenatal, before birth.

Preoral, in front of the mouth.

Prepuce, foreskin of penis.

Presbyatry, treatment of diseases of the aged.

Presbyacusia, partial loss of hearing in old age.

Presbyopia, loss of elasticity in eyes which occurs in old age.

Prescription, written order for drug authorized by a physician.

Pressure, stress; strain.

Preventive, prophylactic.

Priapism, continued erection of the penis without sexual desire.

Primary, principal.

Prickly Heat, irritations of the skin in which blisters form due to increased temperature.

Primigravida, woman in her first pregnancy.

Primipara, woman who has given birth once.

Primitive, original.

Primordial, Primitive.

Princeps, primary artery.

Principal, most important.

Probe, instrument for exploring the interior of the body.

Proconceptive, aiding conception.

Procreate, to beget children.

Proctalgia, pain in the rectum.

Proctitis, inflamation of the rectum or anus.

Proctology, branch of medicine concerned with the rectum.

Proctoscopy, examination of the rectum.

Procumbent, prone.

Prodrome, early symptoms of impending illness.

Progeny, offspring.

Progeria, condition causing early aging.   [jaws.

Prognathism, having projecting

Prognosis, medical name for the outlook of a disease.

Proiota, sexual precocity.

Prolapse, abnormal position of internal organ.

Proliferation, muplication of cells.

Prominence, projection; elevation.

Prone, lying face downward.

Prootic, in front of the ear.

Propagation, reproduction.

Prophylactic, preventing disease.

Prophylaxis, prevention of disease.

Pro Re Nata, according to circumstances.

Prorrhaphy, advancement.

Prosodemic, spread from one person to another.

Prosopospasm, facial spasm.

Prostate, small gland in the male situated at the base of the bladder, concerned with preparation of the semen.

Prostatitis, inflamation of the prostate gland.   [part.

Prosthesis, substitute for missing

Prosthetics, branch of surgery dealing with artifical parts.

Prostitution, having sexual relations for profit or gain.

Prostration, exhaustion.

Prothrombin, chemical substance important in blood coagulation.

Protistology, microbiology.

Protoplasm, prime material in living organism.

Protozoa, microscopic, one-celled organisms.

Protuberance, projection.

Provisional, of temporary use.

Proximate, nearest.

Pruritus, itching.

Prussiate, cyanide.

Psellism, stuttering.

Pseudocrisis, false crisis.

Pseudocyesis, imaginary pregnancy with some physical findings of the condition.

Psittacosis, disease spread by parrots, love-birds, canaries and other birds kept as pets.

Psoriasis, chronic skin disease in which red scaly patches develop.

Psychanalysis, psychoanalysis.

Psyche, mind.

Psychectampsia, acute mania.

Psychiatrist, one who specializes in psychiatry.

Psychiatry, study and treatment of mental disorders.

Psychic, pertaining to the mind.

Psychics, psychology.

Psychoanalysis, method of obtaining a patient's past emotional history.

Psychocoma, mental stupor.

Psychogenesis, mental development.

Psychognosis, study of mental and emotional activity.

Psychology, science dealing with mental functions.

Psychopath, one who has no sense of moral obligation.

Psychopathy, any mental disorder.

Psychophylaxis, mental hygiene.

Psychosis, type of insanity in which one loses almost complete touch with reality.

Psychosomatic Disease, physical ailments due to emotional causes.

Psychotherapy, treatment of mental and emotional disorders.

Ptarmic, causing sneezing.

Ptarmus, sneezing.

Ptomaine, specific poisoning caused by putrified food.   [lid.

Ptosis, drooping of the upper eye-

Ptyalism, excess secretion of saliva.

Ptyalorrhea, excessive secretion of saliva.

Ptysis, spitting.

Puberal, pertaining to puberty.

Puberty, period of rapid growth and development between childhood and adult life.   [tals.

Pubes, hairy area above the geni-

Pubis, bone at front of pelvis.

Pudenda, the external sex organ.

Pudic, pudendal.

Puerile, pertaining to a child.

Puerilism, childishness.

Puerpera, woman who has had a child.

Puerperium, period immediately following childbirth.

Pulmonary, pertaining to the lungs.

Pulmonic, pulmonary.

Pulpalgia, pain in the pulp of a tooth.

Pulpy, soft.

Pulsation, rhythmic throb.

Pulso, pressure variation in arteries due to action of heart; can be felt where arteries are close to skin.

Pulsus, pulse.

Pulverulent, powdery.

Punctum, point.

Punctum Caecum, blind spot.

Puncture, pierce.

Pupil, part of eye which opens or closes to adjust to light or object.

Pupillary, pertaining to the pupil.

Purgative, drug to relieve constipation.

Purge, to evacuate the bowels by medicine.

Purpura, purple areas or bruises on body due to abnormal blood clotting.

Purulent, forming or containing pus.

Pus, product of infection containing dead cell and cell debris.

Pustule, pimple.

Pyarthrosis, pus in a joint cavity.

Pyelitis, inflammation of the pelvis of the kidney, that is, the area where the kidney is connected to the ureter, the tube leading down to the bladder.

Pyemia, form of blood poisoning in which the germs are carried in the blood and produce abscesses.

Pygal, pertaining to the buttocks.

Pyknemia, thickening of the blood.

Pylorus, valve which lies at one end of the stomach and controls the entry of food into the small intestine.

Pyocele, pus around the testis.

Pyocolpos, pus in the vagina.

Pyocyst, sac of pus in body.

Pyoderma, any skin inflammation that produces pus.

Pyogenesis, formation of pus.

Pyorrhea, infection of the gums which causes the edges of the tooth sockets to bleed easily when teeth are being brushed.

Pyretic, pertaining to fever.

Pyretolysis, lowering of fever.

Pyrexia, increased body temperature, high fever.

Pyrogenic, causing fever.

Pyromania, obsessive compulsion to start fires.

Pyrophobia, extreme fear of fire.

Pyrosis, burning pain in stomach; acid taste in mouth.

Pyrotic, burning.

Pyuria, pus in urine.

— Q —

Quack, a faker in medical science.

Quadripara, woman giving birth to her fourth child. [legs.

Quadriplegia, paralysis of arms and

Quarantine, enforced isolation of people suffering from an infectious disease.

Quassation, shattering.

Quickening, the feeling of life of a baby by a pregnant woman.

Quinsy, formation of an abscess around one of the tonsils.

Quinine, drug used in the treatment of malaria.

Quintan, every fifth day.

Quintipara, woman giving birth to her fifth child.

— R —

Rabbeting, interlocking of the splintered edges of a fractured bone.

Rabbit Fever, virus disease transmitted by eating or handling infected animals; tularemia.

Rabiate, one who has rabies.

Rabic, pertaining to rabies

Rabid, pertaining to rabies.

Rabies, a fatal disease of man affecting the brain and spinal cord if untreated.

Race, class of people of similar inheritance and ethnic qualities.

Rachialgia, pain in spine.

Rachianalgesia, spinal anesthesia.

Rachicentesis, puncture into spinal canal.

Rachidian, pertaining to the spine.

Rachiocampsis, curvature of the spine.

Rachiodynia, painful condition of spinal column.

Rachis, spinal column.

Rachisschisis, spinal column fissure; congenital opening.

Rachitec, pertaining to rickets.

Radiation, rays that in proper dosage can be used to treat certain diseases.

Radicular, pertaining to a root.

Radiculitis, inflammation of a nerve root.

Radiectomy, removal of the root of a tooth.

Radioactivity, emitting of penetrating rays or small particles.

Radiograph, an x-ray film.

Radiography, taking of x-rays.

Radiologist, medical specialist who uses radiation for diagnosis and treatment.

Radiology, branch of medicine

using radiant energy in diagnosis and treatment of disease.

Radiolus, sound; probe.

Radiotherapeutic, use of x-ray or radium for treatment.

Radius, short arm bone extending from elbow to wrist.

Radix, root.

Rale, abnormal sound coming from air passages of lungs.

Rami, branch.

Ramify, to branch. [root.

Ramitis, inflammation of a nerve

Ramollissement, morbid softening of some organ or tissue.

Ramus, branch of an artery, vein or nerve; branchlike part.

Rancid, offensive; sour.

Range of Accommodation, difference between the least and greatest distance of clear vision.

Ranula, swelling under the tongue due to the blocking of a salivary gland.

Rape, sexual intercourse without consent of female.

Rash, skin eruption.

Raspatory, surgical file.

Rasura, Rasure, scraping; shaving.

Rat, rodent frequently used in experiments.

Rat Bite Fever, an infectious disease passed to human beings by bite of an infected animal.

Ratio, proportion.

Ration, fixed portion of food and drink for a certain period.

Rational, according to reason.

Rationalization, making an irrational thing appear reasonable.

Rattle, rale.

Rattle, Death, gurgling sound heard in the trachea of the dying.

Rave, talk irrationally.

Ravish, rape.

Raynaud's Disease, circulatory disturbance affecting extremities.

R.C.P., Royal College of Physicians.

R.C.S., Royal College of Surgeons.

Rauwolfia, drug which lowers blood pressure and causes relaxation in mind and body.

Re- (prefix), back; again.

Reaction, response.

Recall, memory.

Receptaculum, vessel or cavity which contains fluid.

Recessus, small hollow or recess.

Recidivation, recurrence of a disease.

Recipe, prescription; formula.

Recipient, one who receives a thing.

Recline, lie down.

Reconstituent, an agent which strengthens a part of the body by replacing lost material.

Recrement, secretion which is reabsorbed into the body after performing its function.

Recrudescence, reappearance of symptoms of a disease.

Rectal, pertaining to the rectum.

Rectal Reflex, normal desire to evacuate feces.

Rectalgia, rectal pain.

Rectectomy, surgical removal of the rectum or anus.

Rectified, made pure or straight.

Rectitis, inflammation of the rectum.

Rectoclysis, gradual introduction of fluid into rectum.

Rectocolitis, inflammation of the rectum and colon. [tum.

Rectostenosis, stricture of the rec-

Rectostomy, making an artificial opening into the rectum to relieve stricture.

Rectum, lowest six inches of the intestinal tract adjoining the anus.

Rectus, straight; any straight muscle.

Recumbent, lying down.

Recuperation, restoration to health.

Recurrent, reappearing.

Recurve, bend backward.

Red Blood Cell, blood corpuscle containing hemoglobin.

Red Softening, hemorrhagic softening of brain and spinal cord.

Redressment, correction of a deformity; dressing a wound a second time or more.

Reduce, decrease.

Reduction, restoration to normal position.

Reduction Diet, diet which eliminates fat producing foods.

Reduplicated, folded back on itself.

Referred Pain, pain felt in part of the body other than its source.

Refine, purify.

Reflex, an involuntary action caused by a stimulus to the nerves.

Reflexogenic, causing a reflex action.

Reflux, backward flow.

Refracta Dosi, in divided doses.

Refraction, eye testing to determine amount of vision.

Refractory, not easily treated.

Refracture, break again.

Refrangible, capable of refraction.

Refresh, renew, revive.

Refrigerant, medicine which relieves thirst and reduces fever.

Refusion, return flow of blood to the vessels.

Regeneration, regrowth or repair of part of body.

Regimen, course of therapy to improve health.

Region, particular body area.

Registry, placement bureau for nurses.

Regression, process of going back to a prior status in physical or mental illness.

Regressive, subsiding, reverting.

Regular, normal.

Regurgitant, backward flow.

Regurgitate, to vomit.

Rehabilitation, restoration to activity of a handicapped person.

Rehalation, rebreathing.

Reichman's Disease, constant excessive gastric secretion.

Reinfection, return of infection.

Reimplantation, replacement of a part to its original location.

Rejuvenation, return to a youthful or normal state.

Relapse, recurrence of an illness.

Relapsing Fever, an infectious disease in which periods of fever alternate with periods of normal temperature.

Relaxant, agent which lessens tension or loosens bowels.

Relaxation, reduction of tension.

Remak's Axis Cylinder, conducting part of a nerve.

Remedial, curative.

Remedy, substance that is used in treatment of disease.

Remission, abatement.

Ren, the kidney.

Renal, pertaining to the kidney.

Renifleur, one who is sexually stimulated by certain odors, especially that of urine.

Reniform, kidney-shaped.

Repair, replace; heal.

Repellent, reducing swelling; that which repels insects.

MEDICAL DICT

Repletion, full; satisfied; fullness of blood; plethora.

Reportable Diseases, diseases which must be reported to public health authorities.

Reposition, act of replacing a part.

Repositor, instrument for replacing a part.

Repression, suppression into unconsciousness of unacceptable ideas and emotion. [spring.

Reproduction, begetting of off-

Resection, excision of part of body tissue.

Reserpine, drug used to lower blood pressure.

Residue, that which remains after removal of a part.

Residuum, residue.

Resilience, elasticity.

Resilient, elastic

Resistance, ability to protect self from disease.

Resolution, subsiding of an inflammation.

Respirable, suitable for respiration.

Respiration, breathing.

Respirator, mechanical device used to aid breathing. [tion.

Respiratory, pertaining to respira-

Rest, period of inactivity.

Restiform, ropelike; rope-shaped.

Restitution, restoring.

Restorative, promoting health; remedy.

Restraint, forcible control.

Resuscitation, artificial respiration which is used to restore breathing after drowning, electric shock or other conditions interfering with breathing.

Resuscitator, mechanical device used for artificial respiration.

Retardation, delay.

Retarded Depression, depressed state of manic depressive psychosis.

Retching, unsatisfactory attempt to vomit.

Rete, network.

Retention, holding back.

Retention Cyst, cyst caused by retention of a secretion in a gland.

Retention of Urine, failure to urinate.

Reticular, netlike.

Reticulation, formation of a network mass.

Reticulum, network in cells.

Retina, part of the eye that receives the image and which is connected to the brain by the optic nerve.

Retinal, pertaining to the retina.

Retinitis, inflammation of the retina, the innermost coat of the eye.

Retinosis, degeneration of the retina.

Retractile, able to be drawn back.

Retraction, drawing back.

Retractor, surgical instrument used to hold back the edges of an incision.

Retro- (prefix), behind or in back of.

Retrocedent, going backward.

Retrocolic, behind the colon.

Retrocollic, pertaining to the back of the neck.

Retrograde, going backward.

Retroinfection, infection transmitted by the fetus to the mother.

Retrolingual, behind the tongue.

Retronasal, behind the nose.

Retropharynx, back wall of the throat.

Retroposed, displaced backward.

Retroversion, state of turning back.

Revivification, attempt to restore to life.

Revulsant, causing transfer of disease or blood from one part of body to another; agent which draws blood to inflamed site.

Rhabdophobia, extreme fear of being corrected.

Rhachis, spinal column.

Rhagades, skin cracks.

-rhagia, (suffix), bleeding.

Rhaphe, seam, ridge.

Rhegma, rupture, fracture, tear.

Rheum, watery discharge.

Rheumatalgia, rheumatic pain.

Rheumatic Fever, disease affecting joints, skin and sometimes the heart; believed due to an allergic reaction to specific bacteria.

Rheumatism, pain, swelling and deformity of joints of unknown cause.

Rheumatoid, of the nature of rheumatism.

Rhexis, rupture of a blood vessel or organ.

Rh. Factor, a substance found in the red blood cells; about 15% of people do not have this factor and are therefore called RH negative.

Rhinal, pertaining to the nose.

Rhinalgia, nasal pain.

Rhinesthesia, sense of smell.

Rhinitis, inflammation of the lining of the nose.

Rhinobyon, nasal plug.

Rhinocleisis, nasal obstruction.

Rhinodynia, nasal pain.

Rhinolalia, nasal voice quality.

Rhinologist, nose specialist.

Rhinology, branch of medicine dealing with the nose.

Rhinopathy, any nasal disease.

Rhinophonia, nasal speaking tone.

Rhinophyma, disease of the nose in which it becomes greatly enlarged.

Rhinorrhagia, nosebleed.

Rhinotomy, surgical incision of the nose.

Rhodocyte, red blood cell.

Rhoncus, rale; rattling sound in chest.

Rhypophagy, eating of filth.

Rhypophobia, extreme fear of filth.

Rhythm, measured time or movement; noting the periods of fertility and sterility in the female during the menstrual cycle.

Rhytidosis, wrinkling of skin or cornea.

Rib, bone and cartilage that form the chest cavity and protects its contents.

Ribs, False, five ribs on each side not directly attached to sternum.

Ribs, Floating, two lower ribs not attached to sternum.

Rickets, this is a disease caused by lack of vitamin D.

Ridge, narrow, elevated border.

Rigidity, stiffness. [idity

Rigor, chill preceding a fever; rig-

Rigor Mortis, stiffening of muscles after death.

Rima, crack.

Rimula, minute crack.

Rind, skin or cortex of an organ or person.

Ringworm, fungus infection.

Risus, laugh; grin.

Ritter's Disease, severe skin inflammation seen in infants.

R.N., registered nurse.

Roborant, tonic; strengthening.

Rock Mountain Spotted Fever, in-

fectious disease characterized by fever, pains in bone and muscle and reddish eruptions.

Rodent Ulcer, small, hard skin ulcer on the face in region of the inner corner of the eye or around the nose.

Roentgen, measure of radiation.

Roentgenogram, x-ray.

Rongeur, gouge forceps used to remove bone fragments.

Root, proximal end of a nerve; portion of an organ implanted in tissues.

Root Canal, pulp cavity of tooth root.

Rosacea, skin disease of the face in which there is permanent redness over the nose and cheeks.

Rose Fever, hay fever.

Roseola, red rash from various causes. [tion.

Rose Rash, any red colored erup-

Rossbach's Disease, excessive secretion of gastric juice.

Rot, decay.

Rotate, twist; revolve.

Rotular, pertaining to the kneecap.

Roughage, coarse material.

Rotula, kneecap or patella.

Roust, delivery room nurse who carries out unsterile tasks.

Rubedo, temporary redness of skin.

Rubella, German measles.

Rubeola, measles.

Rubor, redness of skin due to infection.

Rubrum, red.

Ructus, belching.

Rudimentary, elementary; undeveloped.

Ruga, fold or crease.

Rugose, wrinkled.

Rumination, regurgitation.

Rump, buttocks.

Run, to exude pus or mucus.

Runaround, infection extending around a finger or toenail.

Rupophobia, extreme dislike for dirt or filth.

Rupture, tearing apart; hernia.

Rutilizm, red-headedness.

Rx, symbol for "take" or "recipe"

— S —

Saburra, foulness of stomach or mouth.

Sac, pouch. [ener.

Saccharin, sugar substitute; sweet-

Saccharum, sugar.

Sacculation, grouping of sacs.

Saccule, small sac.

Sacrificial Operation, removal of an organ for the patient's good.

Sacroiliac, relating to the juncture of the hipbone and lower part of the spine.

Sacroiliac Strain, type of backache.

Sacrum, part of vertebral column or spine.

Sadism, perversion in which sexual pleasure is obtained by inflicting pain on someone.

Sadist, one who enjoys inflicting pain on others.

St. Vitus' Dance, involuntary muscular action.

Sal, salt.

Salacious, lustful.

Salicylate, main component of aspirin.

Saline, pertaining to salt.

Saline Solution, salt water.

Saliva, fluid secreted by the glands of the mouth.

Salivant, stimulating secretion of saliva.

Salivary, pertaining to saliva.

Salivation, excess secretion of saliva.

Sallow, having a pale, yellowish complexion.

Sal Mirabile, purgative salt.

Salmonella, bacteria causing intestinal disorder.

Salmonellosis, infestation with Salmonella bacteria.

Salpingectomy, surgical removal of Fallopian tube.

Salpingitis, inflammation of the Fallopian tubes.

Salpinx, uterine tube; eustachian tube.

Salt, sodium chloride.

Saltation, dancing.

Saltatory, characterized by leaping or dancing.

Salt Free Diet, diet which allows no more than two grams of salt.

Saltpeter, postassium nitrate.

Salubrious, promoting good health.

Salutary, healthful; curative.

Salve, ointment.

Sanative, healing.

Sanatorium, place for preserving health or caring for a long term illness.

Sanatory, promoting health.

Sane, of sound mind.

Sanger's Operation, type of Cesarean section.

Sangucolous, inhabiting the blood.

Sanguifacient, forming blood.

Sanguiferous, conducting blood.

Sanguine, bloody.

Sanguineous, bloody; having a plethora of blood.

Sanguis, blood.

Sanitarium, place for the care and cure of those suffering from mental or physical illness.

Sanitary, pertaining to health.

Sanity, soundness of mind.

Saphena, large vein of leg.

Sapid, possessing flavor.

Sapo, soap.

Saponatus, mixed with soap.

Sapphism, Lesbianism.

Saphemia, blood poisoning.

Saprodontis, tooth decay.

Sacritis, inflammation of muscle tissue.

Sarcocele, tumor of testicle.

Sarcode, protoplasm.

Sarcogenic, forming flesh.

Sarcology, study of soft body tissues.

Sarcolytic, decomposing flesh.

Sarcoma, one of the two main types of cancer, the other being carcinoma.

Sarcophagy, practice of eating flesh.

Sarcopoietic, forming flesh or muscle. [cle.

Sarcous, pertaining to flesh or muscle.

Sartorius, muscle of thigh.

Satiety, satisfying fullness.

Saturnine, pertaining to lead.

Saturnism, lead poisoning.

Satyriasis, abnormal sex drive associated with mental excitement in male.

Satyromania, excessive sexual desire in the male.

Savory, appetizing.

Saw, cutting instrument.

Scab, crust formation over wound.

Scabies, disease of the skin caused by a mite which burrows under the skin surface and causes extreme discomfort and itching.

Scald, burn of skin.

Scale, small, thin, dry particle.

Scalenus, three muscles located in the vertebrae of the neck and attached to the first two ribs.

Scall, scalp disease.

Scalp, hairy component of head.

Scalpel, surgical knife.

Scanty, insufficient.

Scapula, shoulder blade.

Scapular, pertaining to the shoulder blade.

Scapulectomy, surgical removal of scapula.

Scar, end product of healed wound.

Scarfskin, epidermis.

Scarlatina, scarlet fever.

Scarlet Fever, contagious disease causing chills, high fever, sore throat, skin rash, discolored tongue.

Scatacratia, fecal incontinence.

Scatemia, intestinal toxemia.

Scatology, study and analysis of waste product of body.

Scelalgia, pain in leg.

Schick Test, test for susceptibility to diphtheria

Schistasis, any congenital fissure.

Schizophrenia, psychiatric disorder of many and varied manifestations in which person loses contact or misinterprets reality.

Schizotrichia, splitting of hair.

Schwelle, threshold.

Sciage, sawing massage movement.

Sciatic Nerve, largest nerve in body located in back of leg.

Sciatica, inflammation of or injury to the sciatic nerve in back of thigh.

Scirrhoma, scirrhus.

Scirrhus, hard cancer.

Schlera, white of eye.

Schlerectomy, surgical removal of part of the sclera.

Schleritis, inflammation of the white of the eye.

Schleroderma, skin disease of unknown origin in which patches of skin become thickened, hard and white or yellowish.

Scleroma, sclerosis.

Sclerose, to become hardened.

Sclerosis, hardening of a tissue.

Schlerothrix, abnormal hardness and dryness of hair.

Scoliosis, curvature of the spine to one side or the other.

Scopophobia, extreme fear of being seen.

Scorbutus, scurvy. [ing.

Scordinemia, yawning and stretch-

Scotoma, blind spot.

Scotophobia, extreme fear of darkness.

Scoptopia, adjustment of eyes to darkness.

Scours, diarrhea.

Scratch, superficial injury.

Scrobiculate, pitted.

Scrobiculus, pit. [ach.

Scrobiculus Cordis, pit of the stom-

Scrofula, condition of tuberculous gland of the neck.

Scrotal, pertaining to the scrotum.

Scrotum, pouch of male containing testicles.

Scrub Nurse, operating room nurse.

Scurf, dandruff.

Scurvy, disease due to lack of vitamin C, causing bleeding, weakness and swelling of skin.

Scutum, thyroid cartilage.

Scytitis, dermatitis.

Sea Sickness, nausea, vomiting and unsteadiness due to unusual motion.

Sebaceous, pertaining to sebum.

Sebaceous Cyst, a wen; a swelling caused by the blocking of a duct of a sebaceous gland.

Sebastomania, religious insanity.

Seborrhagia, excessive secretion of sebaceous glands.

Seborrhea, condition of excessive oiliness of the skin caused by glandular upset.

Sebum, oily secretion of the oil glands of the skin.

Secondary, not of primary importance.

Secreta, waste material expelled by a gland or organ.

Secretion, fluid discharged from gland or organ.

Secretomotory, stimulating secretion.

Section, divide by cutting.

Sectorial, cutting.

Secundigravida, woman in her second pregnancy.

Secundines, afterbirth material.

Sedative, agent used to quiet patient.

Sediment, material which settles at the bottom of a fluid.

Seed, semen.

Segment, part of a whole.

Seizure, sudden attack.

Sella, saddle-shaped depression; area within skull.

Semantic, pertaining to the meaning of words.

Semeiosis, approach to disease according to symptoms.

Semel, once.

Semen, male secretion containing sperm.

Semenuria, presence of semen in urine.

Semi- (prefix), half.

Semilunar, wrist bone.

Semination, introduction of semen into the vagina.

Seminiferous, producing or carrying semen.

Seminology, study of semen.

Semis, half.

Senescence, process of growing old.

Senile, old.

Senilism, premature old age.

Sensation, awareness of stimulus to nervous system.

Sense, perceive through nervous system; perceiving faculty.

Sensibility, sensitivity.

Sensitive, responsive; unusually receptive to stimuli.

Sensorium, any sensory nerve center.

Sensory, pertaining to sensation.

Sentient, sensitive.

Sepsis, poisoning of body by products of bacteria.

Septicemia, blood poisoning.

Septum, tissue dividing cavities.

Sequela, after affects of a disease.

Sequestrum, piece of dead bone.

Serial, arranged in sequence.

Seriate, saw-toothed.

Serology, study of serum.

Serosa, layer of tissue.

Serous, thin and watery.

Serrate, notched.

Serrulate, minutely notched.

Serum, clear fluid which separates from blood when it clots.

Sex, distinctive feature between male and female; Freud-pleasure.

Sexual, pertaining to sex.

Shakes, shivering due to chill.

Shank, leg from knee to ankle.

Sheath, tubular case.

Shift, change. [tery.

Shigella, organism causing dysen-

MEDICAL DICT

Shin, front part of lower leg.

Shingles, herpes zoster, viral infection of nerve path.

Ship-Fever, typhus fever.

Shiver, chill.

Shock, decreased effective circulating fluid volume.

Shortsighted, not able to see very far.

Shoulder, joint between arm and body.

Show, vaginal discharge prior to start of labor.

Shunumitism, belief that proximity to young person rejuvenates elders.

Sialaden, salivary gland.

Sialadenitis, inflammation of a salivary gland.

Silagogue, causing the secretion of saliva.

Sialaporia, deficiency in saliva secretion.

Sialine, pertaining to saliva.

Sialism, increased production of saliva. [tion.

Sialoporia, deficient saliva secretion.

Sialorrhea, flowing of saliva.

Sibilant, whistling; hissing.

Sibling, brother or sister.

Siccative, drying.

Sick, not in normal health.

Sickness, illness.

Siderodromophobia, extreme fear of train travel.

Sigh, involuntary inspiration of emotional origin.

Sight, act of seeing.

Sigmatism, faulty pronunciation of s sound.

Sign, symptom, evidence.

Signature, directions for taking medicine on a prescription.

Silicosis, condition of the lungs found in those who work among stone dust.

Sinapism, mustard plaster.

Sinciput, upper part of head.

Sinew, tendon or fibrous tissue.

Singultus, hiccough.

Sinister, left.

Sinistrad, toward the left.

Sinistral, pertaining to the left side.

Sinuous, winding.

Sinus, hollow area of a bone.

Sinusitis, inflammation of the nasal sinuses.

Sinusotomy, incision of a sinus.

Sippy Diet, diets used to decrease acid or stomach juice.

Siriasis, sunstroke.

Sitology, study of food and its use.

Sitophobia, extreme dislike of food.

Situs, position.

Sitz-Bath, a therapeutic bath in sitting position.

Skelalgia, leg pain.

Skeleton, bones of body.

Skin, outer covering of body.

Skull, bones of head, 22 in all.

Sleep, normal loss of consciousness.

Sleeping Sickness, an infection of brain causing increased drowsiness; encephalitis.

Sling, support of arm or leg.

Slough, dead tissue which separates from living tissue.

Smallpox, serious infectious disease with fever, pain, vomiting and an eruption of red spots which later become blisters and afterwards are filled with pus.

Smear, preparation of body secretions spread on a glass slide for microscopic study.

Smegma, thick, odorous secretion of certain glands.

Smog, mixture of smoke and fog.

Smell, odor; to stimulate olfactory cells.

Sneezing, a nose irritation which causes sudden expulsion of air from mouth and nose.

Snoring, a nose or throat obstruction causing a noise when breathing during sleep.

Snowblindness, temporary loss of sight due to glare on snow.

Snuffles, yellow discharges from nose of infants.

Soak, immerse in a solution.

Sociology, study of social relationships.

Socket, hollow into which another part fits.

Sodokosis, rat-bite fever.

Sodomy, unusual sexual relations, bestiality.

Soft, not hard or firm.

Soft Palate, posterior part of palate.

Solar, pertaining to the sun.

Solar Fever, infectious febrile disease.

Solar Plexus, anatomical area in upper part of abdomen.

Sole, bottom of foot.

Soleus, soft, broad muscle of calf or leg.

Solid, not hollow, gaseous or liquid.

Soluble, able to be dissolved.

Solute, substance which is dissolved in a solution.

Solution, homogeneous mixture of a solid in a liquid.

Solvent, solution used to dissolve material.

Soma, the body.

Somal, pertaining to the body.

Somatalgia, bodily pain.

Somatesthesia, bodily sensation.

Somatic, pertaining to the body.

Somnambulism, sleepwalking.

Somnifacient, causing sleep.

Somniferous, causing sleep.

Somniloquism, talking while asleep.

Somnolent, sleepy.

Soor, thrush.

Sophistication, adulteration of a product.

Sopor, coma.

Soporific, producing sleep.

Sore, an ulcer or wound.

Sore Throat, inflammation of pharynx, tonsils or larynx.

Sororiation, growth of breasts at puberty.

Soterocyte, blood platelet.

Sound, noise; auditory sensations caused by vibrations.

Space, area; region, segment.

Span, distance from fingertip to fingertip with arms outstretched.

Spanogyny, decrease in female births.

Spargosis, swelling of female breasts with milk; thickening of skin.

Spasm, contraction of any muscle that is sudden and involuntary.

Spasmodic, occuring in spasms.

Spasmophemia, stuttering.

Spasmophilia, tendency to spasms.

Spasmus, spasm.

Spastic, rigid; flexed; pertaining to spasms.

Spasticity, sustained increased muscle tension.

Spay, to remove femile sex gland.

Specialists, one skilled in a particular field.

Species, category; classification.

Specimen, part of tissue or material used for analysis.

Spectacles, eye glasses.

Speculum, instrument which widens the opening of body cavities for examination.

Speech, thought expressed in words.

Sperm, male fertilizing cell.

Spermatocidal, killing sperm.

Sphacelate, to become gangrenous.

Sphacelation, gangrene.

Spheroma, spherelike tumor.

Sphincter, muscle that surrounds and closes an opening.

Sphincterismus, spasm of sphincter.

Sphygmic, pertaining to the pulse.

Sphygmomonometer, blood pressure gauge.

Spica, figure-of-8 bandage.

Spina, sharp protuberance; spine.

Spina Bifida, condition in which there is a defect in the development of the spinal column.

Spinal, pertaining to a spine.

Spinal Cord, part of nervous system enclosed within the backbone; part of the nervous system which transmits impulses to and from the brain.

Spinal Curvature, condition where spine is abnormally bent forward or backward.

Spinal Fracture, broken back.

Spine, sharp piece of bone; backbone.

Spinthecism, seeing sparks before the eyes. [guid.

Spirit, volatile liquid; alcoholic li-

Splanchnic, concerning abdominal organs.

Spleen, organ situated in the left upper part of the abdomen which manufactures, stores and destroys blood cells.

Splenalgia, pain in the spleen.

Splenauxe, enlargement of the spleen.

Splenectomy, surgical removal of spleen.

Splenic, pertaining to the spleen.

Splenitis, inflammation of the spleen.

Splenoma, splenic tumor. [spleen.

Splenomegaly, enlargement of the

Splint, appliance to protect or stabilize injured part.

Spondyle, vertebra.

Spondylitis, inflammation of spine.

Sporadic, intermittent; occurring at different times and places.

Spot, blemish.

Sprain, injury of a joint caused by over-stretching of the ligaments.

Sprue, disease in which the patient is unable to absorb necessary nutrients.

Spur, pointed outgrowth. [of mouth

Sputum, material that is spat out

Squama, scale.

Squatting, sitting on the heels.

Stab, puncture with sharp object.

Stabilization, making firm and steady.

Stable, immobile. [drops.

Stactometer, device for measuring

Staff, hospital personnel.

Stalagmometer, instrument for measuring drops.

Stamina, endurance.

Stammering, hesitant speech.

Stanch, to stop a flow of blood.

Stapes, small bone of middle ear.

Staphylococcus, bacteria causing body infection.

Staphyloma, budging of the white of the eye. [of food.

Starvation, continued deprivation

Stasis, stoppage of flow of blood or urine. [ing up.

Stasophobia, extreme fear of standing up.

Stat., at once.

State, condition.
Statim, at once.
Status, condition; state. [tissue.
Steatitis, inflammation of fatty
Steatopygia, having large buttocks.
Stillate, star-like shape.
Stenochoria, stenosis.
Stenosed, narrowed; constricted.
Stenosis, constricted; decrease in diameter.
Stercus, excrement. [idea.
Stereotypy, persistence of a single
Sterile, barren; aseptic.
Sterility, inability to have children.
Sterilize, to make bacteria free; remove ability to reproduce.
Sterilizer, device for eliminating bacteria on instruments.
Sternal, pertaining to the sternum.
Sternalgia, pain in the sternum.
Sternodynia, pain in breastbone
Sternum, breastbone.
Sternutation, sneezing.
Stertor, snoring.
Stethalgia, chest pain.
Stethoscope, instrument used to listen to sounds of body.
Sthenia, force; strength.
Stigma, mark or spot on tissue.
Stigmatosis, skin disease characterized by ulcerated spots.
Stillbirth, birth of a dead baby.
Stillborn, born dead. [activity.
Stimulant, anything that increases
Stimulus, exciting agent. [loop.
Stitch, localized sharp pain; sewing
Stoma, mouth. [digestion begins.
Stomach, large pouch where food
Stomach Ulcers, sores or ulcer in stomach wall usually due to increased secretion of acid.
Stomachalgia, pain in the stomach.
Stomachic, gastric stimulant.
Stomatalgia, pain in mouth.

Stomatitis, inflammation of the mouth.
Stomatodynia, pain in mouth.
Stomatopathy, any mouth disorder.
Stool, feces.
Strabismus, squint, cross-eye. [ing.
Strain, overexertion; overstretch-
Strait, narrow passage.
Strangulation, choking; stopping of blood supply.
Strangury, painful urination.
Strap, bind with bandages.
Stratified, layered.
Stratum, layer of tissue nearly uniform in thickness.
Streak, line; stripe.
Streptococcus, any organism infecting man. [sick.
Stretcher, device for carrying the
Stria, linear mark or line on body.
Striate, having streaks.
Stricture, narrowing of any tube in in the body. [sound.
Stridor, harsh, rasping breath
Stroke, apoplexy; seizure; fit.
Stroma, framework of an organ.
Struma, goiter.
Strumitis, thyroiditis.
Strumectomy, thryoidectomy.
Strychnism, strychnine poisoning.
Stump, remaining part of limb after amputation. [ness.
Stun, momentary loss of conscious-
Stupefacient, narcotic.
Stupemania, manic stupor.
Stupor, state of decreased feeling.
Stuprum, rape.
Stuttering, speech impediment characterized by repeating syllables.
Sty, infection of gland of eyelid.
Styloid, long and pointed.
Stype, tampon.
Sub- (prefix), under.

Subacute, mildly acute. [ishment.
Subalimentation, inadequate nour-
Subaural, below the ear.
Subclavian, below collar bone.
Subconscious, out of awareness.
Subcostal, below a rib.
Subcutaneous, under the skin.
Subdelirium, mild delirium.
Sublatio, detachment of a part.
Sublimation, process of passing from solid to vapor state without liquifying. [ness.
Subliminal, below conscious aware-
Sublingual Gland, salivary gland beneath tongue.
Subluxation, minor dislocation.
Submaxilla, mandible. [along jaw.
Submixillary Gland, salivary gland
Submental, beneath the chin.
Subphrenic, beneath the diaphragm.
Subscription, part of a prescription giving directions for compounding the ingredients.
Substance, material of which a thing is composed.
Substantia, substance.
Subtotal, incomplete.
Sububeres, unweaned infants.
Subungual, beneath a nail.
Subvirile, lacking in virility.
Succorrhea, excessive secretion.
Succus, fluid secretion.
Sudation, perspiring.
Sudatorium, sweat bath.
Sudor, sweat.
Sudoresis, excessive sweating.
Suffocation, blockage of air ways.
Suffusion, spreading; diffusion.
Sugar, carbohydrate.
Suicide, self-destruction.
Sulcus, groove or furrow.
Sulfa Drugs, name referring to the group of drugs used in the treat-

ment of various bacterial diseases [sun's rays.
Sunburn, skin inflammation from
Sunstroke, stroke due to excessive exposure to the sun. [ing.
Superalimentation, excessive feed-
Superciliary, concerning eyebrow.
Supercilium, eyebrow.
Superego, conscience.
Superficial, near the surface. [milk.
Superlactation, oversecretion of
Supernumeray, more than usual.
Superscription, Rx before a prescription
Supinate, turn hand upward
Supine, lying flat on back.
Suppository, solid medication for insertion into a cavity other than the mouth.
Suppurate, form infection.
Sura, calf of the leg.
Sural, pertaining to the calf.
Suralimentation, overfeeding.
Surditas, deafness.
Surdomute, deaf and dumb.
Surgeon, medical specialist performing surgery.
Surgery, specialty of medicine that deals with disease and trauma by operative means.
Surgical, pertaining to surgery.
Surrogate, a substitute.
Susceptible, having little resistance, easily influenced.
Suspiration, sigh.
Suspirious, breathing heavily.
Susurration, murmur.
Suture, to stitch together.
Swab, gauze wrapped around a stick for application of medicine.
Swallow, voluntary act of passing food from mouth to stomach.
Sweat, perspiration. [licles.
Sycosis, inflammation of hair fol-

Syllepsis, pregnancy. [ite sides.
Symmetry, similar parts on oppos-
Symphysis, immovable joint.
Symphysis Pubis, pubic bones above the midline of the external genital.
Symptom, perceptible change from normal function.
Synalgia, referred pain.
Synchronous, occurring simultaneously. [cranium.
Synciput, anterior upper half of the
Syncope, fainting. [fingers.
Syndactylus, one having webbed
Syndrome, any group of symptoms commonly occurring together.
Synechia, abnormal joining of parts.
Synergy, cooperation.
Syngamy, sexual reproduction.
Synizesis, contraction of the eye pupil.
Synovitis, inflammation of the lining of a joint.
Syntaxis, junction of two bones.
Syphilid, skin eruption due to syphilis.
Syphilis, serious venereal disease.
Syringe, instrument used to inject fluids into body.
Syrinx, cavity or tube. [ing organs.
System, group of similar function-
Systole, period during which contraction of heart takes place.

— T —

Tobacosis, tobacco poisoning.
Tobagism, tobacco poisoning.
Tabefacation, emaciation.
Tabes, gradual deterioration in a chronic illness.
Tabes Dorsalis, a disease of the nervous system leading to paralysis and caused by syphilis.

Tablet, pill.
Tabule, pill.
Tache, spot; blemish.
Tachycardia, rapid beating of the heart coming on in sudden attacks.
Tachylalia, rapid speech.
Tachyphagia, rapid eating.
Tachyphasia, rapid speech.
Tachypnea, unusually fast rate of breathing.
Tachyrhythmia, rapid heart action.
Tactile, pertaining to sense of touch.
Tactual, pertaining to touch.
Tactus, touch. [tapeworm.
Taenia, band-like muscle or tissue;
Tagma, protoplasm.
Talalgia, pain in the heel.
Talc, a powder.
Talipes, club foot.
Talipes Planus, flatfoot.
Tallus, ankle.
Tampon, round cotton plug used to close wound or cavity.
Tamponade, act of plugging.
Tap, puncture of body cavity.
Tapeworm, type of intestinal worm.
Taphephobia, extreme fear of live burial. [the instep.
Tarsal, pertaining to the eyelid or
Tarsus, arch of foot.
Tartar, dental calculus. [tongue.
Taste, sensation through nerves on
T.A.T., toxin-antoxin.
Taxonomy, science of classification of plants and animals.
Tear, saline fluid secreted by lacrimal glands.
Teat, nipple.
Technic, technique.
Technique, method; procedure.
Tectonic, pertaining to plastic surgery.

Tectum, roof-like structure.

Teeth, bony growths in jaw used for chewing.

Teeth, Milk, first set of teeth.

Teething, appearance of teeth.

Tegmen, covering.

Tegument, skin.

Teinodynia, pain in the tendons.

Tela, weblike structure.

Telalgia, referred pain.   [laries.

Telangitis, inflammation of capil-

Telangiosis, disease of capillary vessels.

Teleorganic, vital.

Telepathist, mind reader.

Telepathy, communication of two minds at a distance through means undetectable by science.

Telergy, automatism.   [tion.

Telesthesia, extrasensory percep-

Temperament, physical and mental characteristics of an individual.

Temperature, degree of heat and cold; body temperature is normally 98.6.

Temple, area in front of ear.

Temporal, pertaining to the temple or time.

Temulence, drunkenness.

Tenacious, adhesive.

Tenalgia, pain in a tendon.

Tenderness, soreness.   [don.

Tendinitis, inflammation of a ten-

Tendinous, pertaining to or composed of tendons.

Tendo, tendon.

Tendon, fibrous tissue that connects muscles to other structures.

Tenectomy, surgical removal of a tendon.   [der.

Tenesmus, spasm of anus or blad-

Tenia, tapeworm; band.

Teniacide, medication which destroys tapeworms.

Tennis Elbow, pain in the arm, particularly on twisting inwards, caused by excessive strain.

Tenodynia, pain in a tendon.

Tenonitis, inflammation of tendon.

Tenoplasty, surgical repair of a tendon.

Tenorrhaphy, suture of a tendon.

Tenosynovitis, inflammation of a tendon and its sheath.

Tension, condition of being strained or stretched.

Tentative, subject to change.

Tentigo, unusual sex desires.

Tephrosis, cremation.

Tepid, warm.

Tepidorium, warm bath.

Teras, fetal monster.

Teratism, fetal monster.

Teratoid, monster.

Teratology, science dealing with monstrosities and malformations.

Tere, to rub.

Terebration, boring.

Teres, round; smooth.   [time.

Term, boundary; definite period of

Terminal, end.

Terracing, suturing in several rows.

Terror, extreme fear.   [glands.

Testicles, the male reproductive

Testis, male reproductive gland.

Tetanus, infectious disease characterized by painful spasms of voluntary muscles.

Tetany, disease characterized by painful muscle spasms with convulsive movements, usually due to inability to utilize calcium.

Tetraplegia, paralysis of all four extremities.

Tetter, blister; pimple.

Textural, pertaining to the constitution of tissues.

Thalamus, area in the brain concerned with many bodily functions, often called the seat of the emotions.   [sea.

Thalassophobia, extreme fear of

Thanatobiologic, pertaining to life and death.

Thanatoid, resembling death.

Thanatomania, suicidal obsession.

Thebaism, opium poisoning.

Theca, case; sheath.   [of tea.

Theism, poisoning from overdose

Thelalgia, pain in nipples.

Thelerethism, erection of the nipple.

Thelitis, inflammation of nipple.

Thelium, nipple.

Thenal, pertaining to the palm.

Thenar, area beneath thumb; palm.

Theomania, delusion that one is a deity.

Theory, hypothesis.

Therapeutic, pertaining to healing.

Therapeutics, scientific treatment of disease.

Therapy, treatment of disease.

Thermal, pertaining to heat.

Thermalgesia, inability to react to heat.   [or cold.

Thermesthesia, perception of heat

Thermic, pertaining to heat.

Thermofuge, reducing fever.

Thermometer, instrument to measure heat.

Thermoplegia, heatstroke; sunstroke   [heat.

Thermostat, device for controlling

Thigh, part of leg above knee.

Thirst, desire for liquid.

Thoracalgia, chest pain.

Thoracic, pertaining to the chest.

Thoracectomy, surgical removal of a rib.

Thoracodynia, pain in thorax.

Thoracomyodynia, pain in chest muscles.

Thoracoschisis, fissure of chest wall.

Thoracotomy, surgical opening of chest.

Thorax, chest.

Threadworm, parasitic worm.

Threpsology, study of nutrition.

Threshold, point at which an effect is produced.

Thrill, heart murmur or abnormal blood vessel tremor that can be felt.

Thrix, hair.   [esophagus.

Throat, area between mouth and

Throb, pulsation.

Throe, sharp pain.

Thrombin, substance in blood which aids clotting.   [ting.

Thrombopathy, defective blood clot-

Thrombophlebitis, inflammation of a vein.

Thrombosin, thrombin.

Thrombosis, formation of a clot within a blood vessel.

Thrombus, blood clot.

Thrush, disease of the mouth and throat caused by a fungus.

Thumb, first digit of hand. [thymus.

Thymectomy, surgical removal of

Thymona, tumor of thyroid.

Thymion, wart.   [gland.

Thymitis, inflammation of thyryoid

Thymona, tumor of thymus.

Thymus, glandular structure in the chest having an unknown function.   [thyroid.

Thyroadenitis, inflammation of

Thyrocele, goiter.

Thyrogenic, originating in thyroid.

Thyroid, glandular structure in the

neck secreting thyroxin, a substance vital to life.

Thyroidectomy, surgical removal of all or part of the thyroid gland.

Thyroiditis, inflammation of the thyroid gland.   [thyroid gland.

Thyroxin, hormone secreted by the

Tibia, shin bone.

Tibial, pertaining to the tibia.

Tic, muscular twitch, usually of the face.

Tick, blood sucking parasite.

Tigroid, striped.

Tilmus, pulling out of hair.

Tinea, ringworm.

Tinnitus, noises in the ear which may take the form of buzzing, clicking or thudding.

Tiqueur, one afflicted with a tic.

Tire, exhaust, fatigue.

Tissue, structure of body made up of similar cells.

Tocalogy, obstetrical science. [birth.

Tocophobia, extreme fear of child-

Tocus, childbirth.

Toe, digit of the foot.

Tolerance, endurance.

Tongue, organ of speech and taste.

Tongue-Tie, congenital shortening of frenuum below tongue.

Tonic, muscular tightness.   [sue.

Tonsil, mass of special lymph tis-

Tonsilla, tonsil.

Tonsillectomy, removal of tonsils.

Tonsillitis, infection of the tonsils.

Tooth, hard structure in the jaws used for chewing.

Tophaceous, gritty, sandy.   [spot.

Topical, pertaining to a particular

Topoalgia, localized pain.

Toponarcosis, local anesthesia.

Torpidity, sluggishness.

Torpor, inactivity; apathy.

Torsion, twisting.

Torso, trunk of body.

Torticollis, wryneck; abnormal twisting of the neck caused by injury or infection to the muscle or nerve.

Torulus, small elevation.

Touch, tactile sense.   [bleeding.

Tourniquet, band used to control

Toxemia, any illness due to poisons absorbed from organisms in the system.

Toxenzyme, any poisonous enzyme.

Toxic, poisonous.

Toxicant, poisonous; a poison.

Toxicity, poisonous.

Toxicohemia, toxemia.

Toxicology, science dealing with poisons.   [sons.

Toxicophobia, extreme fear of poi-

Toxipathy, disease caused by poisoning.   [tion.

T.P.R., temperature, pulse, respira-

Trachea, the windpipe.

Tracheal, pertaining to trachea.

Tracheitis, inflammation of the windpipe.

Trachelagra, gout in the neck.

Trachelismus, spasm of neck muscles.

Tracheofissure, incision of trachea.

Tracheotomy, cutting into windpipe to relieve obstruction.

Trachitis, inflammation of trachea.

Trachoma, infectious disease of the eyes.

Trachyphonia, roughness of voice.

Traction, pulling or drawing.

Tragopodia, knock-knee.

Trait, distinguishing characteristic.

Trance, sleeplike state.

Tranquilizer, calming agent.

Transcalent, able to be penetrated by heat rays.

Transfix, pierce.

Transforation, perforation of the skull of a fetus. [to another.
Transfusion, giving of one's blood
Transmissable, communicable.
Transmission, communication of a disease from one person to another. [perspiration.
Transpirable, allowing passage of
Transplant, remove tissue from one part of the body to another. [side.
Transverse, extending from side to
Transvestitism, uncontrollable urge to dress in the clothing of the opposite sex.
Trapizius, muscle of back.
Trauma, injury; wound.
Trauma, Psychic, injury to subconscious due to emotional shock.
Treatment, medical care of a patient.
Tremor, shake or quiver.
Tremulous, quivering.
Trench Mouth, mouth infection caused by organism; also called Vincent's angina.
Trend, course.
Trepan, to make a hole in skull to relieve pressure on brain.
Tresis, perforation. [laries.
Trichangiectasis, dilation of capil-
Trichauxe, excessive hair growth.
Trichinosis, disease caused by the trichina organism found in raw pork.
Trichitis, inflammation of the hair roots. [testinal tract.
Trichobezar, hair-ball found in in-
Trichocardia, hairy heart.
Trichoclasia, brittleness of hair.
Trichocryptosis, brittleness of hair.
Trichology, science of hair care.
Trichoptilosis, hair splitting.
Trichosis, any hair disease.
Trifid, divided into three parts.
Trigonid, first three cusps of a lower molar tooth.
Trilobate, having three lobes.
Triorchid, having three testes.
Triphasic, having three phases.
Triplegia, paralysis of three extremities.
Triquetrum, wrist bone.
Trismus, spasm of jaw muscles.
Tristimania, melancholia.
Troche, lozenge. [on its axis.
Trochocardia, rotation of the heart
Trochoides, pivot joint.
Trophic, pertaining to nutrition.
Trophology, science of body nutrition. [ease.
Trophonosis, any nutritional dis-
Truncal, pertaining to the trunk.
Truncate, cut off limbs or branches.
Truncus, trunk.
Trunk, torso.
Truss, device to hold hernia in place. [ture.
Tube, long, hollow cylindrical struc-
Tuber, enlargement; swelling.
Tubercle, small swelling; rounded elevation on a bone; change in tissue caused by the tuberculosis germ. [cles.
Tuberculated, covered with tuber-
Tuberculophobia, extreme fear of tuberculosis.
Tuberculosis, infectious disease of man and animals caused by tubercle bacilli having many and varied manifestations in lungs, brain, bone, etc. [tuberculosis.
Tuberculous, caused by or having
Tuberosity, bone projection.
Tubule, small tube.
Tuborrhea, discharge from eustachian tube.
Tularemia, an infectious disease transmitted by insects or small

animals caused by the pasteurella organism.
Tumefaction, swelling.
Tumesence, swelling.
Tumor, a swelling or growth.
Tunic, lining membrane.
Tunnel, enclosed passage.
Turbidity, cloudiness.
Turgesence, distention; swelling.
Turgescent, becoming swollen.
Turgid, congested and swollen.
Turgor, swelling.
Tussis, cough.
Tutamen, a protection.
Twin, one of two persons of the same birth. [tion.
Twitch, slight muscular contrac-
Tyloma, callus.
Tylosis, formation of callosities.
Tympanal, pertaining to the tympanum. [due to gas or air.
Tympanites, abdominal distention
Tympanous, distended with gas.
Tympanum, ear drum.
Typhlosis, blindness.
Typhoid Fever, an infectious fever caused by the typhoid bacillus, characterized by diarrhea and other symptoms. [typhoid fever.
Typhomania, delirium found with
Typhous, pertaining to typhus.

— U —

Uberous, prolific.
Uberty, fertility.
Ulalgia, pain in the gums.
Ulatrophia, shrinkage of gums.
Ulcer, sores on skin or internal parts of body caused by various things.
Ulceration, formation of an ulcer.
Ulcus, ulcer.
Ulectomy, surgical removal of part of gums; removal of scar tissue.
Ulemorrhagia, bleeding from the gums.
Uletic, pertaining to the gums.
Ulitis, gum inflammation.
Ulna, bone of forearm.
Ulnar, pertaining to the ulna.
Ulocace, ulcer and infection of gums.
Uloid, scarlike
Ulorrhagia, bleeding from gums.
Ulosis, scar formation.
Ultimate, final; highest.
Ululation, hysterical crying.
Umbilicus, site on abdomen of attachment of umbilical cord.
Umbo, funnel-shaped area of ear drum.
Uncia, ounce; inch. [wrist.
Unciform, hook-shaped; bone of
Unconscious, state in which person is unaware of both his external and internal environment as in a faint.
Unction, ointment.
Unctuus, oily.
Undulant Fever, an infectious disease caused by the Brucella organism; found in animals and transmitted to man.
Undulation, wave.
Ungual, pertaining to the nails.
Unguent, ointment.
Unguis, fingernail or toenail.
Unilateral, pertaining to one side.
Unigravida, woman in her first pregnancy. [one live child.
Union, juncture.
Unipara, woman who has borne
Uracratia, inability to retain urine.
Uraniscus, palate.
Uranium, radioactive element. [skin.
Uredo, sensation of burning on
Uremia, poisoning from urinary substances in the blood.

Ureter, the tube leading from the kidneys to the bladder.
Ureterolith, stone in the ureter.
Uretha, tube which carries the urine from the bladder to the outside. [thra.
Urethritis, inflammation of the ure-
Uretic, promoting urination.
Urinary, pertaining to urine.
Urinate, discharge urine. [activity.
Urine, fluid end product of kidney
Urologist, medical specialist who deals with organs producing and transporting urine. [tem.
Urology, study of the urinary sys-
Uroschesis, to retain urine.
Urous, urine-like.
Urticaria, hives.
Ustion, incinerate, burn.
Ustus, burned.
Uterine, pertaining to the womb.
Uterus, womb.
Uvea, tissue layer of eye.
Uvula, small tissue projecting in the middle of palate in throat.

— V —

Vaccin, substance used for inoculation.
Vaccination, injection with a germ or germ product to produce immunity and protect against disease.
Vaccinia, contagious disease as a result of inoculation with cowpox virus.
Vagina, the passage connecting the outer and inner female sex organs. [vagina.
Vaginismus, painful spasm of the
Vaginitis, inflammation of vagina.
Vagus, tenth cranial nerve.
Valence, ability of a chemical agent to combine in a reaction.

Valetudinarian, person afflicted with frequent illness.
Valgus, bowlegged; knock-kneed.
Valve, structure which prevents backward flow in a passage.
Valvulitis, inflammation of a valve.
Valvulotomy, incision of a heart valve.
Varicella, chickenpox.
Varices, enlarged, tortuoris vein.
Varicocle, varicose veins in the area of scrotum.
Varicose Veins, swollen veins caused by improper valve function.
Variola, smallpox.
Vas, vessel, passageway.
Vascular, pertaining to blood vessels.
Vas Deferens, duct in testis which transports semen.
Vasectomy, excision of vas deferens; operation to sterilize male.
Vasoconstrictor, causing a narrowing of blood vessels.
Vasodepressor, agent which relaxes the blood vessels, thus increasing diameter and lowering blood pressure. [ber of blood vessel.
Vasospasm, sudden decrease in cali-
Vein, blood vessels carrying blood to heart. [tercourse.
Venereal, pertaining to sexual in-
Venery, sexual intercourse.
Venesection, puncture of a vein to remove blood. [a vein.
Venipuncture, surgical puncture of
Venom, poison from an animal.
Ventricle, small cavity; pouch.
Vermis, worm.
Verruca, wart.
Version, turning; changing the position of the fetus in the womb to facilitate birth.
Vertebra, bone of the spinal column.

Vertex, crown of the head.
Vertical, pertaining to the vertex.
Vertigo, dizziness.
Vesica, bladder.
Vesicant, blistering.
Vesicle, blister; small bladder.
Vessel, tube; passageway
Vestigial, non-functioning part in body more highly developed in embryo or lower animal.

Viable, alive.   [to hemorrhage.
Vibex, linear spots beneath skin due
Vibrissal, stiff hairs in nose.
Vicious, faulty.
Vigil, wakefullness.
Vincent's Angina, mouth infection; also called trench mouth.
Vinum, wine.
Virgin, one who has not experienced sexual relations.
Virile, masculine, mature.
Virilism, maleness.   [diseases.
Virology, study of virus and viral
Virose, poisonous.
Virulence, poisonousness; infectiousness; endangering life.
Viruses, minute organisms which cause certain diseases among which are the common cold, measles, mumps, poliomyelitis, chickenpox, smallpox.
Vis, energy, power.
Viscera, organs within body.
Viscid, thick; adherent.
Vision, sight; seeing.
Vitals, important body organs.
Vitamins, chemical substances found in foods that are necessary for proper bodily function.
Vitiligo, lack of pigment in certain areas of the skin.
Vitium, a defect.

Vitiation, injury; decrease in function of a part.   [animal.
Vivisect, to cut or dissect living
Vocal Cords, tissue bands whose vibration causes speech.
Voice, sounds produced by the vibration of the vocal cords.
Void, to empty bladder or rectum.
Volce, palm or sole of foot.
Volition, act of selecting.
Volvulus, twisting of the bowel causing obstruction.
Vomer, bone of nose.
Vomicose, containing ulcers.

Vomiting, dislodging the food in stomach through mouth.
Vomitus, vomited material.
Vox, voice.
Voyeur, person receiving sexual pleasure from watching activities of others.   [ing to maturity.
Vril, inborn energy from birth lead-
Vulva, female genital.
Vulvitis, inflammation of the female external genitalia.
Vulnus, wound.

— W —

Waist, area between chest and hip encircling body.
Wart, growth on the skin that may be caused by viruses.
Wash, lotion.
Wasserman Test, test of the blood to determine if syphilis is present.
Weak, lacking strength.
Wean, substitution of other substances for breast milk.   [brane.
Webbed, connected by a thin mem-
Weeping, crying; seeping of a fluid.
Wen, a sebaceous cyst.   [skin.
Wheal, a red, round elevation on
Wheeze, sound in chest due to abnormalities in lungs.
White Leg, swelling and blanching of the leg produced by thrombosis of the veins.
Whitlow, infected finger.
Whooping Cough, infectious disease characterized by episodes of coughing punctuated by whooping noises between episodes during periods of gasping for breath, pertussis.
Wisdom Tooth, the most posterior teeth or molar on each side of jaw.
Woman, mature female.
Womb, uterus; organ in which developing fetus resides.
Wound, an injury or break in the skin.
Wrist, joint between forearm and hand.

Wryneck, torticollis.

— X —

Xanthic, yellow.
Xanthoma, yellow tumor or growth.

Xanthopsia, yellow vision.
Xanthosis, jaundice.
Xenogenous, disease caused by foreign body or toxin.
Xenomenia, bleeding from other than normal site at time of menstrual period.   [ers.
Xenophobia, extreme fear of strang-
Xenopthalmia, inflammation of eye due to foreign body.
Xerocheilia, dry lips.
Xeroderma, a skin disease characterized by dryness.
Xeransis, condition of dryness.
Xerasia, dryness of hair leading to baldness.
Xerophthalmia, eye condition in which the lining membrane of the lid and eyeball is dry and thickened.
Xerosis, condition of dryness.
Xiphoid, sword-shaped cartilage at lowest part of breast bone.
X-Ray, device used to photograph interior parts of body; also used as therapeutic tool.
Xysma, membranous like material in some diarrhea stools.
Xyster, surgical instrument used to scrape bone.

— Y —

Yawn, involuntary opening mouth when fatigued.
Yaws, tropical disease.
Yeast, a rich source of vitamin B.
Yellow Fever, infectious fever found in tropical lands.
Youth, period of adolescence between childhood and adult life.

— Z —

Zein, protein from corn.
Zestocausis, to burn with steam.
Zinc, a metal used in medicines.
Zoanthropy, belief that one is an animal.
Zoetic, pertaining to life.
Zondal-Aschheim Test, test to determine pregnancy.
Zonesthesia, sensation of tightness around the waist.
Zooerastea, coitus with an animal.
Zooid, animal-like.
Zoopsia, hallucinations involving animals.   [animals.
Zoosis, disease in man carried by
Zygoma, a part of the cheek bone.
Zyme, fermenting substance.

BIBLE
DICTIONARY

BIBLE DICTIONARY

BY
JAMES P. BOYD, A.M.

KEY TO PRONUNCIATION

The hyphen (-) separates unaccented syllables. The double hyphen (=) separates compound words. (') marks the primary accent and ('') the secondary accent.

ā as in fāte; ă in courăge; ä in hät; â in câre; à in fär; a̤ in làst; ạ in fạll; ạ obscure as in liạr.

ē as in mēte; ĕ in rēdeem; ĕ in mĕt; ĕ obtuse as in tĕrm; ẹ obscure as in fuẹl.

ī as in pīne; ĭ in cĭtation; Ĭ in pĭn; ī obtuse in fĭrm; ị in familịar; ị obscure in ruịn.

ō as in nōte; ŏ in annŏtate; ŏ in nŏt; ô in fôr; ọ obscure in valọr.

ū as in mūte; ū in tūb; û obtuse as in hûrl; ụ in rụde; ụ in push.

ȳ as in stȳle; y̆ in ny̆mph.

ç soft as in çent; c hard not marked; g̵ soft as in g̵ender; g̵ hard before e, i̯ and y, as g̵et, G̵ideon; g hard otherwise not marked; ṣ as z in muṣe; x as gs in example.

A

Ā. See ALPHA.

Aâr'on (*mountaineer or enlightener*). Son of Amram and Jochebed, and elder brother of Moses and Miriam, Num. xxvi. 59. Direct descendant of Levi by both parents. Called "the Levite," Ex. iv. 14, when chosen as the "spokesman" of Moses. Married Elisheba, daughter of the prince of Judah, and had four sons, Nadab, Abihu, Eleazar, and Ithamar, Ex. vi. 23. Eighty-three years old when introduced in the Bible. Mouthpiece and encourager of Moses before the Lord and the people of Israel, and in the Court of the Pharaoh, Ex. iv. 30; vii. 2. Miracle worker of the Exodus, Ex. vii. 19. Helped Hur to stay the weary hands of Moses in the battle with Amalek, Ex. xvii. 9-12. In a weak moment yielded to idolatry among his people and incurred the wrath of Moses, Ex. xxxii. Consecrated to the priesthood by Moses, Ex. xxix. Anointed and sanctified, with his sons, to minister in the priest's office, Ex. xl. Murmured against Moses at the instance of Miriam, but repented and joined Moses in prayer for Miriam's recovery, Num. xii. His authority in Israel vindicated by the miracle of the rod, Num. xvii. Died on Mt. Hor, at age of one hundred and twenty-three years, and was succeeded in the priesthood by his son Eleazar, Num. xx. 22-29. Office continued in his line till time of Eli. Restored to house of Eleazar by Solomon, 1 Kgs. ii. 27.

Aâr'on-ītes. Priests of the line of Aaron, 1 Chr. xii. 27, of whom Jehoiada was "chief," or "leader," in the time of King Saul, 1 Chr. xxvii. 5.

Ăb (*father*). (1) A syllable of frequent occurrence in the composition of Hebrew proper names, and signifies possession or endowment. Appears in Chaldaic form of Abba in N. T., Mark xiv. 36; Rom. viii. 15; Gal. iv. 6. (2) Eleventh month of the Jewish civil, and fifth of the sacred, year; corresponding to parts of July and August. [MONTH.]

Ăb'ă-cŭc, 2 Esdr. i. 40. [HABAKKUK.]

Ȧ-bădʹdon (*destroyer*). King of the locusts, and angel of the bottomless pit. The Greek equivalent is Apollyon, Rev. ix. 11.

Ăb''ă-dīʹas, 1 Esdr. viii. 35. [OBADIAH.]

Ȧ-băgʹthȧ (*God-given*). One of the seven chamberlains in the court of King Ahasuerus, Esth. i. 10.

Ăb'ă-nȧ (*stony*). A river of Damascus, preferred by Naaman to the Jordan for healing purposes, 2 Kgs. v. 12. Believed to be identical with the present Barada, which rises in the Anti-Libanus range, twenty-three miles N. W. of Damascus, runs by several streams through the city, and thence across a plain into the "Meadow Lakes," where it is comparatively lost.

Ăb'ă-rīm (*mountains beyond*). A range of mountains or highlands of Moab, east of and facing Jordan opposite Jericho, Num. xxvii. 12; xxxiii. 47; Deut. xxxii. 49. Ije-abarim, in Num. xxi. 11, heaps or ruins of Abarim. Nebo, Peor, and Pisgah belong to this range. "Passages," in Jer. xxii. 20.

Ăb'bȧ (*father*). Chaldaic form of Hebrew Ab. Applied to God in Mark xiv. 36; Rom. viii. 15; Gal. iv. 6.

Ăb'dȧ (*servant*). (1) Father of Adoniram, 1 Kgs. iv. 6. (2) Son of Shammua, Neh. xi. 17. Called Obadiah in 1 Chr. ix. 16.

Ăb'dẹ-el (*servant of God*). Father of Shelemiah, Jer. xxxvi. 26.

Ăb'dĭ (*my servant*). (1) A Merarite, grandfather of Ethan the Singer, and father of Kishi, 1 Chr. vi. 44. (2) Father of Kish, of Levitical descent, 2 Chr. xxix. 12. (3) Son of Elam, who had married a foreign wife, in time of Ezra, Ez. x. 26.

Ăb'dĭ-as, 2 Esdr. i. 39. [OBADIAH.]

Ăb'dĭ-ĕl (*servant of God*). Father of Ahi and son of Guni. A Gadite chief of Bashan in the time of King Jotham of Judah, 1 Chr. v. 15. Milton uses the name as that of a fallen angel.

Ăb'dŏn (*servile*). (1) An Ephraimite judge of Israel for eight years, Judg. xii. 13-15. Supposed to be same as Bedan in 1 Sam. xii. 11. (2) Son of Shashak, 1 Chr. viii. 23. (3) A Benjamite, son of Jehiel, of Gibeon, 1 Chr. viii. 30; ix. 36. (4) Son of Micah in Josiah's time, 2 Chr. xxxiv. 20; supposably Achbor in 2 Kgs. xxii. 12. (5) A city in tribe of Asher, assigned to the Levites, Josh. xxi. 30; 1 Chr. vi. 74; associated with modern Abdeh, 10 miles N. E. of Accho, or Acre, the Ptolemais of N. T.

Ȧ-bĕd'=nĕ-gō (*servant of Nego, or Nebo, name of planet Mercury worshipped as scribe and interpreter*). Name given by the prince of Chaldean eunuchs to Azariah, one of the three friends and fellow-captives at Babylon of Daniel, Dan. i. 7. He refused to bow to the golden image of Nebuchadnezzar, and was condemned to the fiery furnace, from which he miraculously escaped, Dan. iii.

Ā'bĕl (*breath, vapor*). Second son of Adam and Eve. A keeper of sheep, and murdered by his brother Cain through jealousy, Gen. iv. 2-8. See also Heb. xi. 4; 1 John iii. 12; Matt. xxiii. 35.

Ā'bĕl (*meadow*). A prefix for several names of towns and places. (1) The "plain of the vineyards" in Judg. xi. 33; see marg. (2) A city in the north of Palestine, attacked by Joab, 2 Sam. xx. 14, 15. Probably same as Abel-Beth-Maachah. "Plain of the vineyard," Judg. xi. 33, marg. note. "Great stone of," 1 Sam. vi. 18.

Ā'bĕl=bĕth=mā'ȧ-chah (*meadow of house of oppression*). A town in N. Palestine, near Damascus, doubtless the same as attacked by Joab, 2 Sam. xx. 14, 15; and attacked by Benhadad, 1 Kgs. xv. 20, and by Tiglath-pileser, 2 Kgs. xv. 29.

Ā'bĕl=mā'ĭm (*meadow of waters*). Another name for Abel-beth-maachah, 2 Chr. xvi. 4.

Ā'bĕl=mẹ-hō'lah (*meadow of the dance*). A place in the Jordan valley, 1 Kgs. iv. 12, whither fled the enemy routed by Gideon, Judg. vii. 22. Home of Elisha, 1 Kgs. xix. 16.

Ā'bĕl=mĭz'rȧ-im (*meadow, or mourning, of Egypt*). A name given by the Canaanites to the threshing floor of Atad, where Joseph and his brethren mourned for Jacob, Gen. l. 11. Probably near Hebron.

Ā'bĕl=shĭt'tim (*meadow of the acacias*). A spot near Jordan, in Moabite plain, and last halting place of the wandering Israelites, Num. xxxiii. 49. Called Shittim in Num. xxv. 1; Josh. ii. 1.

Ā'bĕl, Stone of. Place in the field of Joshua, the Bethshemite, where the ark of the Lord was set down, 1 Sam. vi. 18.

Ā′bĕz (*lofty*). A town in the section allotted to the tribe of Issachar, Josh. xix. 20.

Ā′bī (*progenitor*). Mother of King Hezekiah and daughter of Zachariah, 2 Kgs. xviii. 2 ; Isa. viii. 2. Abijah in 2 Chr. xxix. 1.

Ā-bī′à, Ā-bī′ah, and **Ā-bī′jah** (*the Lord is my father*), are variants of the same word. Abia in 1 Chr. iii. 10, and Matt. i. 7, is the son of Rehoboam ; and in Luke i. 5, is the eighth of the twenty-four courses of priests. For division of priests *see* 1 Chr. xxiv. and particularly vs. 10.

Ā-bī′ah. (1) A son of Becher, 1 Chr. vii. 8. (2) Wife of Hezron, 1 Chr. ii. 24. (3) Second son of Samuel and associate judge with Joel in Beersheba, 1 Sam. viii. 2 ; 1 Chr. vi. 28.

Ā″bī=ăl′bŏn (*father of strength*). One of David's warriors, 2 Sam. xxiii. 31. Spelled Abiel in other places.

Ā-bī′à-săph (*father of gathering*). A Levite, one of the sons of Korah, and head of a Korhite family, Ex. vi. 24. Written Ebiasaph in 1 Chr. vi. 23, 37.

Ā-bī′a-thär (*father of abundance*). Son of Ahimelech, and fourth high priest in descent from Eli, of the line of Ithamar, younger son of Aaron, 1 Sam. xxiii. 9, only one of Ahimelech's sons who escaped the vengeance of Saul in the slaughter at Nob, 1 Sam. xxii. 19, 20. Fled to David at Keilah, and became a high priest. Deprived of the high priesthood by Solomon. For fuller history read 1 Sam. xxii. to 1 Kgs. iii.

Ā′bīb (*green fruits*), called also Nisan. Seventh month of Jewish civil, and first of the sacred year, Ex. xii. 2. [MONTH.]

Ā-bī′dà and **Ā-bī′dah** (*father of knowledge*). One of the sons of Midian, 1 Chr. i. 33 ; Gen. xxv. 4.

Ăb′i-dăn (*father of judgment*). Chief of the tribe of Benjamin at exode, Num. i. 11 ; ii. 22 ; vii. 60 ; x. 24.

Ā-bī′el (*father of strength*). (1) Father of Kish and grandfather of Saul and Abner, 1 Sam. ix. 1. (2) One of David's generals, 1 Chr. xi. 32, called Abialbon in 2 Sam. xxiii. 31.

Ā″bī-ē′zer (*father of help*). (1) Eldest son of Gilead and head of a family in tribe of Manasseh, Josh. xvii. 2 ; 1 Chr. vii. 18. (2) One of David's mighty men, 2 Sam. xxiii. 27 ; 1 Chr. xi. 28 ; xxvii. 12.

Ā″bī-ĕz′rīte (*father of help*). A family descended from Abiezer, Judg. vi. 11 ; viii. 32.

Ăb′ī-gāil (*father of joy*). (1) Wife of Nabal of Carmel, and afterwards of David. Noted for her beauty and wisdom, 1 Sam. xxv. 3, 14–44. (2) A sister of David, married to Jether the Ishmaelite, and mother of Amasa, 2 Sam. xvii. 25 ; 1 Chr. ii. 17.

Ăb″i-hā′il (*father of strength*). (1) Father of Zuriel, chief of the house of the families of Marari, Num. iii. 35. (2) Wife of Abishur, 1 Chr. ii. 29. (3) Son of Huri of the tribe of Gad, 1 Chr. v. 14. (4) Wife of Rehoboam, 2 Chr. xi. 18. (5) Father of Esther and uncle of Mordecai, Esth. ii. 15 ; ix. 29.

Ā-bī′hū (*God is father*). Second son of Aaron and Elisheba, Num. iii. 2 ; Ex. vi. 23. Ascended Sinai with Moses and the elders, Ex. xxviii. 1. Set apart with his brothers for the priesthood. Consumed, with his brother Nadab, for offering strange fire before the Lord, Lev. x. 1, 2.

Ā-bī′hŭd (*father of praise*). Son of Bela and grandson of Benjamin, 1 Chr. viii. 3.

Ā-bī′jah and **Ā-bī′jam** (*whose father is Jehovah*). (1) A son of King Jeroboam I. ; died in early life, 1 Kgs. xiv. (2) Son of Rehoboam, and his successor to the throne. A wicked king. Reign, 959–956 B. C., 2 Chr. xii. 16 ; xiii. Written Abijam in 1 Kgs. xv. 1. (3) A descendant of the high priest Eleazar, 1 Chr. xxiv. 10 ; Neh. xii. 17. The priestly course Abia, Luke i. 5, belonged to Zacharias, father of John the Baptist. (4) A priest who entered the covenant with Nehemiah, Neh. x. 7.

Ā-bī′jam. *See* ABIJAH (2).

Ăb-ĭ-le′nē (from Abila, *land of meadows*). A Syrian tetrarchy whose capital was Abila, situated on the eastern slopes of the Anti-Libanus range. The district was watered by the Abana River. Governed by Lysanias in the time of John the Baptist, Luke iii. 1.

Ā-bĭm′ă-el (*father of Mael*). A descendant of Joktan, and supposable father of the Arabic tribe of Mali, Gen. x. 28.

Ā-bĭm′ĕ-lech (*father of a king*). (1) A line of Philistine kings, like the Pharaohs and Cæsars. Kings of Gerar, Gen. xx., xxi., xxvi. 1. (2) Son of Gideon by his concubine of Shechem, Judg. viii. 31 ; 2 Sam. xi. 21. (3) Son of Abiathar, in David's time, 1 Chr. xviii. 16. (4) Written for the Achish of 1 Sam. xxi. 10, in title to Ps. 34.

Ā-bĭn′ă-dăb (*father of nobility*). (1) A Levite of Kirjath-jearim to whose house the ark was brought, and where it stayed for twenty years, 1 Sam. vii. 1, 2 ; 1 Chr. xiii. 7. (2) Second son of Jesse, and one of the three who followed Saul to battle, 1 Sam. xvi. 8 ; xvii. 13. (3) Son of Saul slain at Gilboa, 1 Sam. xxxi. 2. (4) Father of one of the twelve chief officers of Solomon, 1 Kgs. iv. 11.

Ăb′ĭ-nẽr, Hebrew form of Abner, 1 Sam. xiv. 50, marg.

Ā-bĭn′ŏ-ăm (*gracious father*). Father of Barak, Judg. iv. 6, 12 ; v. 1, 12.

Ā-bī′răm (*high father*). (1) A Reubenite conspirator with Korah, Num. xvi. (2) Eldest son of Hiel, 1 Kgs. xvi. 34 ; written Abiron in Ecclus. xlv. 18.

Ăb-ĭ-sē′ī, or **Ăb′ī-shū,** son of Phinehas, 2 Esdr. i. 2. Abisum in 1 Esdr. viii. 2.

Ăb′ī-shag (*ignorance of the father*). The fair Shunamite, of tribe of Issachar, whom David, in his old age, introduced into his harem, 1 Kgs. i. 1–4. After David's death, Adonijah desired to marry her, but Solomon put him to death, 1 Kgs. ii. 13, etc.

Ā-bĭsh′ă-ī (*father of gift*). (1) Eldest son of David's sister Zeruiah and brother of Joab, 1 Chr. ii. 16 ; one of the chiefs of David's mighty men, 2 Sam. ii. 18. Counselled David to take Saul's life, 1 Sam. xxvi. 5–12. Associated with Joab in assassination of Abner, 2 Sam. iii. 30. A co-general of David's army, 2 Sam. x. 14 ; xviii. 2. Rescued David from the giant Ishbi-benob, 2 Sam. xxi. 16, 17.

Ā-bĭsh′a-lŏm (*father of peace*). Father-in-law of King Jeroboam, 1 Kgs. xv. 2, 10. Called Absalom in 2 Chr. xi. 20, 21.

Ā-bĭsh′ū-à (*father of deliverance*). (1) Son of Bela, 1 Chr. viii. 4. (2) Son of Phinehas, 1 Chr. vi. 4, 5, 50 ; Ez. vii. 5.

Ăb′ī-shur (*father of the wall*). Son of Shammai, 1 Chr. ii. 28, 29.

Ăb′ī-tal (*father of dew*). One of David's wives, 2 Sam. iii. 4 ; 1 Chr. iii. 3.

Ăb′ī-tŭb (*father of goodness*). A Benjamite, 1 Chr. viii. 11.

Ā-bī′ud (*father of praise*). An ancestor of Christ, Matt. i. 13.

Ăb-lū′tion. [PURIFICATION.]

Ăb′nẽr (*father of light*). (1) Son of Ner, and commander-in-chief of Saul's armies, 1 Sam. xiv. 50, 51 ; xvii. 57 ; xxvi. 5–14. Proclaimed Ishbosheth King of Israel, and went to war with David, by whom he was defeated, 2 Sam. ii. Quarrelled with Ishbosheth and espoused the cause of David, 2 Sam. iii. 7, etc. Murdered by Joab, 2 Sam. iii. 27–39. (2) Father of a Benjamite chief, 1 Chr. xxvii. 21.

Ā-bŏm-i-nā′tion (*bad omen*). A hateful or detestable thing, Gen. xlvi. 34. Used as to animals and acts in Lev. xi. 13 ; Deut. xxiii. 18. As to idolatry in 2 Kgs. xxiii. 13 ; Jer. xliv. 4. As to sins in general, Isa. lxvi. 3. The "abomination of desolation" in Dan. ix. 27 ; xii. 11 ; Matt. xxiv. 15, doubtless refers to the standards and banners of the conquering Roman armies with their idolatrous images and legends.

Ā'brạ-hăm and **Ā'brăm** (*father of a multitude*). Son of Terah, a dweller in Ur of the Chaldees, Gen. xi. 25-31. Founder of the Jewish nation. Migrated from Chaldea to Haran. Moved thence to Canaan, to Egypt and back to Canaan, where he settled amid the oak-groves of Mamre. There confirmed in the thrice repeated promise that his seed should become a mighty nation, and his name changed from Abram to Abraham. Died, aged 175 years, and was buried in the tomb of Machpelah, Gen. xii.-xxvi.

Ăb'sạ-lŏm (*father of peace*). (1) A son of David, 2 Sam. iii. 3. Killed his brother Amnon, 2 Sam. xiii. Fled to Geshur, 2 Sam. xiii. 37, 38. Returned and conspired to usurp his father's throne, 2 Sam. xiv.-xvii. Defeated at Gilead and slain by Joab, 2 Sam. xviii. (2) Father of Mattathias, 1 Macc. xi. 70.

Ăb'sạ-lŏm's Pil'lar, built by Absalom in the " King's dale," or valley of Kedron, 2 Sam. xviii. 18.

Ăb'sạ-lŏn. An ambassador of John to Lysias, 2 Macc. xi. 17.

Ā-bū'bŭs. Son-in-law of Simon, 1 Macc. xvi. 11-15.

Ā-cā'çĭ-ạ (*point*). The *Acacia seyal* of Arabia, a large tree, highly prized for its wood, is supposed to be the Shittim wood of the Bible. A smaller species (*Acacia Arabica*) yielded an aromatic gum.

Ăc'ạ-tăn. 1 Esdr. viii. 38. [HAKKATAN.]

Ăc'căd (*fortress*). A city built by Nimrod in Shinar, Gen. x. 10.

Ăc'cạ-rŏn. [EKRON.]

Ăc'chō (*heated sand*). The Ptolemais of N. T.; now Acre, on Mediterranean coast, Judg. i. 31; Acts xxi. 7.

Ăc'cŏs. Grandfather of Eupolemus, 1 Macc. viii. 17.

Ā-çĕl'dạ-mạ (*field of blood*). A field near Jerusalem purchased with Judas' betrayal money, and in which he violently died, Acts i. 19. But bought by the priests as a potters' field in Matt. xxvii. 7.

Ā-chā'ĭạ (*trouble*). Originally a narrow strip of country on north coast of Peloponnesus, but Achaia and Macedonia came to designate all Greece, Acts xviii. 12, 27; xix. 21; Rom. xv. 26; 2 Cor. i. 1; ix. 2; xi. 10; 1 Thess. i. 7, 8.

Ā-chā'ĭ-cus (*of Achaia*). An Achaian friend of Paul, 1 Cor. xvi. 17.

Ā'chăn and **Ā'char** (*troubler*). The Judahite who was stoned to death for concealing the spoils of Jericho, Josh. vii. 16-26. Written ACHAR in 1 Chr. ii. 7.

Ā'chăz (*one that takes*). In Matt. i. 9 for AHAZ, King of Judah.

Ăch'bôr (*mouse*). (1) Father of Baal-hanan king of Edom, Gen. xxxvi. 38, 39. (2) A contemporary of Josiah, 2 Kgs. xxii. 12-14; Jer. xxvi. 22; xxxvi. 12. Written ABDON in 2 Chr. xxxiv. 20.

Ā''chĭ-ăch'ạ-rŭs. Chief minister of Esarhaddon in Nineveh, Tobit i. 21.

Ā-chĭ'ăs. A progenitor of Esdras, 2 Esdr. i. 2.

Ā'chĭm. Son of Sadoc, in Christ's genealogy, Matt. i. 14.

Ā'chĭ-ôr. A general in army of Holofernes, Judith v., vii., xiii., xiv.

Ā'chĭsh (ā'kĭsh) (*serpent-charmer*). A Philistine king of Gath to whom David twice fled for safety, 1 Sam. xxi. 10-13; xxvii.-xxix.; 1 Kgs. ii. 39, 40. Called Abimelech in title to Ps. xxxiv.

Ăch'ĭ-tôb and **Ăch'ĭ-tŭb.** A priest in genealogy of Esdras, 1 Esdr. viii. 2.

Ăch'me-thå. The Median city of Ecbatana, Ez. vi. 2.

Ā'chôr, valley of. [ACHAN.]

Ăch'sạ and **Ăch'sah** (*anklet*). Daughter of Caleb. Given in marriage to her uncle Othniel. Josh. xv. 15-18; Judg. i. 12-15. Achsa in 1 Chr. ii. 49.

Ăch'shăph (*fascination*). A city of Asher, Josh.

xi. 1; xii. 20; xix. 25.

Ăch'zĭb (*false*). (1) A town of Judah, Josh. xv. 44. (2) A town of Asher, Josh. xix. 29.

Ăc'ĭ-phă. [HAKUPHA.] 1 Esdr. v. 31.

Ăc'ĭ-thō. A progenitor of Judith, Judith viii. 1.

Ā-crăb'bim. [MAALEH-ACRABBIM.] Josh. xv. 3.

Acts of the Apostles. Fifth Book of N. T. Supposably compiled by Luke, shortly after A. D. 63. It carries on the Christian narrative from the ascension of Christ to first imprisonment of Paul, a period of about thirty-three years.

Ā-cū'ạ. [AKKUB.] 1 Esdr. v. 30.

Ā'cŭb. [BAKBUK.] 1 Esdr. v. 31.

Ăd'ạ-dah (*boundary*). A town in southern Judah, Josh. xv. 22.

Ā'dah (*beauty*). (1) One of Lamech's wives, Gen. iv. 19. (2) One of Esau's wives, Gen. xxxvi. 2, 4. Called Bashemath in Gen. xxvi. 34.

Ăd''ạ-ī'ah (*adorned by Jehovah*). (1) Maternal grandfather of King Josiah, 2 Kgs. xxii. 1. (2) A Levite, 1 Chr. vi. 41; called Iddo in vs. 21. (3) A Benjamite, 1 Chr. viii. 21. (4) A son of Jehoram, 1 Chr. ix. 12; Neh. xi. 12. (5) Ancestor of Maaseiah, 2 Chr. xxiii. 1. (6) A descendant of Bani, Ez. x. 29, 39. (7) A Judahite, Neh. xi. 5.

Ăd''ạ-lī'ạ (*fire-god*). Fifth son of Haman, Esth. ix. 8.

Ăd'ăm (*red earth*). A city of Reuben, on Jordan, Josh. iii. 16.

Ăd'ăm (*red earth*). Used generically for man and woman, and translated *man* in Gen. i. 26, 27; v. 1; Job xx. 29; xxi. 33; Ps. lxviii. 18; lxxvi. 10.

Ăd'ăm (*red earth*). The first man. Creative work of the sixth day. Placed in the " Garden of Eden." Tempted to eat of the forbidden fruit, fell under God's disfavor, and driven out of the Garden subject to the curse of sorrow and toil. Died at age of 930 years. Gen. i. 26, etc.; ii.-v.

Ăd'ạ-mah (*earth*). A fenced city of Naphtali, Josh. xix. 36.

Ăd'ạ-mănt (*diamond*). The original is translated " adamant " in Ezek. iii. 9; Zech. vii. 12; and " diamond " in Jer. xvii. 1. Used metaphorically. [DIAMOND.]

Ăd'ạ-mī (*earth*). A place on the border of Naphtali, Josh. xix. 33.

Ā'där (*height*). A boundary town of Edom and Judah, Josh. xv. 3.

Ā'där. Sixth month of Jewish civil, and twelfth of sacred, year; corresponding to parts of February and March, Esth. iii. 7.

Ăd'ạ-să. A place in Judea, 1 Macc. vii. 40, 45.

Ăd'bĕ-ĕl (*breath of God*). A son of Ishmael, Gen. xxv. 13; 1 Chr. i. 29.

Ăd'dăn (*stony*). One of the places from which Jewish captives returned, Ez. ii. 59. Addon in Neh. vii. 61.

Ăd'där (*mighty*). Son of Bela, 1 Chron. viii. 3.

Ăd'dēr (*viper*). Used in the Bible for any poisonous snake known to the Jews, of which there were several species in Palestine. In Gen. xlix. 17, the cerastes, or horned snake, is, from its habits, supposed to be alluded to. The cockatrice of Isa. xi. 8; xiv. 29; lix. 5; Jer. viii. 17, is adder and asp in Prov. xxiii. 32; Ps. lviii. 4. In Ps. cxl. 3 and Prov. xxiii. 32, a species of viper is thought to be meant.

Ăd'dī (*adorned*). Son of Cosam in Christ's genealogy, Luke iii. 28.

Ăd'dŏn. [ADDAN.]

Ăd'dŭs. (1) Son of the servant of Solomon, 1 Esdr. v. 34. (2) A priest in time of Ezra, 1 Esdr. v. 38.

Ā'der (*flock*). A Benjamite, 1 Chr. viii. 15. Properly EDER.

Ăd'ĭ-dá. A town of lower Judah, 1 Macc. xii. 38.

Ă-dī'el (*ornament of God*). (1) A prince of Simeon, 1 Chr. iv. 36. (2) A priest, 1 Chr. ix. 12. (3) An ancestor of David's treasurer, Azmaveth, 1 Chr. xxvii. 25.

Ă-dĭn (*dainty*). Head of a returned family, Ez. ii. 15; viii. 6; Neh. vii. 20; x. 16.

Ăd'ī-nå (*slender*). One of David's captains, 1 Chr. xi. 42.

Ăd'ī-nō. One of David's mighty men, 2 Sam. xxiii. 8. [JASHOBEAM.]

Ăd'ĭ-nŭs, 1 Esdr. ix. 48. [JAMIN.]

Ăd''ĭ-thā'ĭm (*double ornament*). A town of Judah, Josh. xv. 36.

Ăd-jūre'. To bind under a curse, Josh. vi. 26; 1 Sam. xiv. 24. To require a declaration of truth at the peril of God's displeasure, Matt. xxvi. 63.

Ăd'la-ī (*Jehovah's justice*). Ancestor of Shaphat, 1 Chr. xxvii. 29.

Ăd'mah (*fort*). One of the cities of the plain of Siddim, Gen. x. 19; xiv. 2. Destroyed with Sodom, Deut. xxix. 23; Hos. xi. 8.

Ăd'mă-thå (*earthy*). One of the seven Persian princes, in Esth. i. 14.

Ăd'nå (*pleasure*). (1) Father of a returned family, Ez. x. 30. (2) A priest in days of Joiakim, Neh. xii. 15.

Ăd'nah (*pleasure*). (1) One of Saul's captains who deserted to David, 1 Chr. xii. 20. (2) A captain in Jehoshaphat's army, 2 Chr. xvii. 14.

Ăd''ō-nā'ī (*Lord*). The Hebrews spoke this word where the word Jehovah occurred.

Ă-dŏn'ī=bē'zek (*lord of Bezek*). King of Bezek, vanquished by Judah, Judg. i. 3–7.

Ăd''ŏ-nī'jah (*the Lord is Jehovah*). (1) Fourth son of David, by Haggith, and rival of Solomon for the throne. Afterwards put to death by Solomon, 2 Sam. iii. 4; 1 Kgs. i., ii. (2) A Levite, 2 Chr. xvii. 8. (3) Same as Adonikam, Neh. x. 16.

Ă-dŏn'ī-kăm (*the Lord is raised*). He returned from captivity with Zerubbabel, Ezr. ii. 13; Neh. vii. 18; 1 Esdr. v. 14. Called Adonijah in Neh. x. 16.

Ăd''ŏ-nī'ram (*lord of heights*). Chief receiver of tribute under David, Solomon, and Rehoboam, 1 Kgs. iv. 6. Written Adoram in 2 Sam. xx. 24; 1 Kgs. xii. 18; and Hadoram in 2 Chr. x. 18.

Ă-dŏn'ī=zē'dec (*lord of justice*). The Amorite king of Jerusalem who formed a league against Joshua, and was slain, Josh. x. 1–27.

Ă-dŏp'tion (*a choosing to*). Receiving a stranger into one's family as an own child thereof, Ex. ii. 10; Esth. ii. 7. Figuratively, reception into the family of God, Rom. viii. 15–17; Gal. iv. 5; Eph. i. 5.

Ă-dō'rå, or Ā'dŏr, 1 Macc. xiii. 20. [ADORAIM.]

Ăd''ŏ-rā'ĭm (*double mound*). A city of Judah, 2 Chr. xi. 9.

Ă-dō'răm. [ADONIRAM and HADORAM.]

Ăd''ŏ-rā'tion (*address*). The act of paying homage to God; as in bending the knee, raising hands, inclining head, prostrating the body, etc., Gen. xvii. 3; Ps. xcv. 6; Matt. xxviii. 9.

Ă-drăm'mē-lech (*fire king*). (1) An idol introduced into Samaria and worshipped with the cruel rites of Molech, 2 Kgs. xvii. 31. (2) Son and murderer of Sennacherib, king of Assyria, 2 Kgs. xix. 37; 2 Chr. xxxii. 21; Isa. xxxvii. 38.

Ăd''ra-mỹt'tĭ-ûm (*from Adramys, brother of Cræsus*). A seaport town of Mysia in Asia, Acts xvi. 7; xxvii. 2. Now Adramyti.

Ā'drĭ-å. The Adriatic Sea, Acts xxvii. 27.

Ā'drĭ-el (*flock of God*). Son-in-law of Saul, 1 Sam. xviii. 19; 2 Sam. xxi. 8.

Ă-dū'el. An ancestor of Tobit, Tob. i. 1.

Ă-dŭl'lăm (*justice of the people*). (1) A city of Canaan allotted to Judah, Gen. xxxviii. 1; Josh. xii. 15; xv. 35; 2 Chr. xi. 7. Repeopled after the captivity, Neh. xi. 30; Mich. i. 15. (2) The cave Adullam was David's hiding-place, where his friends gathered, 1 Sam. xxii. 1; 2 Sam. xxiii. 13; 1 Chr. xi. 15.

Ă-dŭl'lăm-īte. A native of Adullam.

Ă-dŭl'ter-y (*ad=*to and *alter*, other). Under Hebrew law the crime of unchastity, wherein a man, married or single, had illicit intercourse with a married or betrothed woman, not his wife. Punished with fire, Gen. xxxviii. 24; by stoning, Deut. xxii. 22–24. In a spiritual sense, apostasy.

Ă-dŭm'mĭm (*a going up*). A steep pass on the road from Jericho to Jerusalem, Josh. xv. 7; xviii. 17; Luke x. 30–37.

Ăd'vō-cāte (*calling to*). In N. T., helper, intercessor, or comforter. Jews did not have advocates, or attorneys, till after the Roman conquest, John xiv. 16; xv. 26; xvi. 17; Acts xxiv. 1.

Æ-dī'as, Probably Eliah, 1 Esdr. ix. 27.

Æ'ne-ăs, or Æ-nē'ăs (*laudable*). The paralytic at Lydda, healed by Peter, Acts ix. 33, 34.

Æ'nŏn (*springs*). A place, west of Jordan, where John baptized, John iii. 23.

Ăf-fĭn'ī-ty. Relation by marriage and not by blood or birth, 1 Kgs. iii. 1. For preventive degrees *see* Lev. xviii. 6–17, and MARRIAGE.

Ăg'ă-bå, 1 Esdr. v. 30. [HAGAB.]

Ăg'ă-bŭs (*locust*). A prophet of Antioch, Acts xi. 28; xxi. 10.

Ā'găg (*flame*). General title of the kings of Amelek, Ex. xvii. 14; Num. xxiv. 7; Deut. xxv. 17; 1 Sam. xv. 8–32.

Ă-găg'īte. Subject of Agag, Esth. iii. 1–10.

Ă-găr. [HAGAR, HAGARENES, HAGARITES.]

Ag'ate (from *river Achates*). A species of precious quartz. Second stone in third row of high-priest's breastplate, Ex. xxviii. 19; xxxix. 12; Isa. liv. 12; Ezek. xxvii. 16. Original sometimes translated amethyst.

Ăğ'ĕ-ē (*fugitive*). Father of one of David's mighty men, 2 Sam. xxiii. 11.

Ăğ'rĭ-cul''ture (*field culture*). Patriarchal life was pastoral. After the conquest of Canaan, lands were meted and bounded, and landmarks held sacred, Deut. xix. 14. The valley soils of Palestine were fertile; natural waters abundant, Deut. viii. 7; rain plentiful, Deut. xi. 14; Jer. v. 24; James v. 7. The grains grown were wheat, barley, rye, and millet. Orchards produced the vine, olive, and fig. Gardens grew beans, fitches, pease, lettuce, endive, leeks, garlic, onions, melons, cucumbers, cabbage, etc. The implements were the plough, harrow, and hoe, but these were crude. Grains were cut with the sickle, and the sheaves were threshed by treading with oxen, usually drawing sleds; while winnowing was done in sheets before the wind. Lands rested once in seven years, Lev. xxv. 1–7. The poor were allowed to glean, Lev. xix. 9, 10; Deut. xxiv. 19.

Ă-grĭp'på. [HEROD.]

Ā'gûr (*gatherer of wisdom*). An unknown sage who compiled Prov. xxx.

Ā'hăb (*uncle*). (1) Seventh king of Israel. Reigned B. C. 919–896, 1 Kgs. xvi. 29. Married Jezebel of Tyre, who introduced the worship of Baal and Astarte. One of the most notorious of O. T. characters. Slain by a chance arrow, and the "dogs licked his blood" according to prophecy, 1 Kgs. xviii.–xxii.; 2 Chr. xviii. (2) A false prophet at Babylon, Jer. xxix. 22.

Ă-hăr'ah (*after the brother*). Third son of Benjamin, 1 Chr. viii. 1. [AHER and AHIRAM.]

Ă-hăr'hĕl (*behind the fort*). A name in the genealogy of Judah, 1 Chr. iv. 8.

Ă-hăs'ă-ī (*whom Jehovah upholds*). A priest, Neh. xi. 13. Called Jahzerah in 1 Chr. ix. 12.

Ă-hăs'ba-ī (*trusting*). Father of one of David's thirty-seven captains, 2 Sam. xxiii. 34.

Ă-hăs″ū-ē′rus (*prince*). (1) King of Media, supposably Cyaxares, whose son Astyages was Darius, Dan. ix. 1. (2) A Persian king, supposed to be Cambyses, Ez. iv. 6. (3) Another Persian king, probably Xerxes. History in Esther.

Ă-hā′vă (*water*). The place on the Euphrates whence the captives started, on their second return, Ez. viii. 15-21.

A′hăz (*who takes*). (1) Son of Jotham, whom he succeeded, and eleventh king of Israel. Reign 742-726 B. C. Weak-minded and idolatrous, 2 Kgs. xvi.; 2 Chr. xxviii. Literally sold out his kingdom. Died dishonored, 2 Kgs. xxiii. 12; 2 Chr. xxviii. 16-27. (2) A son of Micah, 1 Chr. viii. 35, 36; ix. 42.

Ă″hạ-zī′ah (*Jehovah sustains*). Son of Ahab, and his successor on the throne of Israel, as the eighth king. Reign 896-895 B. C. A weak and foolish idolater, 1 Kgs. xxii. 49-53. (2) Fifth king of Judah. Reign, B. C. 884, 2 Kgs. viii. 25-29. Killed in the rebellion of Jehu, 2 Kgs. ix. Called Azariah in 2 Chr. xxii. 6; and Jehoahaz in 2 Chr. xxi. 17.

Ah′băn (*discreet*). Son of Abishur, 1 Chr. ii. 29.

A′hĕr (*follower*). A title in genealogy of Benjamin, 1 Chr. vii. 12.

A′hī (*my brother*). (1) A Gadite chief, 1 Chr. v. 15. (2) An Asherite, 1 Chr. vii. 34.

Ă-hī′ah and Ă-hī′jah (*Jehovah's friend*). (1) A priest in Shiloh, 1 Sam. xiv. 3-18. (2) One of Solomon's princes, 1 Kgs. iv. 3. (3) A prophet of Shiloh, 1 Kgs. xiv. 2. His prophecies are in 1 Kgs. xi. 30-39 and 1 Kgs. xiv. 6-16. (4) Father of Baasha, 1 Kgs. xv. 27-34. (5) Name of several other Bible characters, 1 Chr. ii. 25; viii. 7; xi. 36; xxvi. 20; Neh. x. 26.

Ă-hī′am (*uncle*). One of David's thirty captains, 2 Sam. xxiii. 33; 1 Chr. xi. 35.

Ă-hī′an (*brotherly*). A Manassite, 1 Chr. vii. 19.

A″hi-ē′zĕr (*brother of help*). (1) A chieftain of Dan, Num. i. 12. (2) A chief of archers under David, 1 Chr. xii. 3.

Ă-hī′hud (*renown*). (1) A prince of Asher, Num. xxxiv. 27. (2) A chieftain of Benjamin, 1 Chr. viii. 7.

Ă-hī′jah. [AHIAH.]

Ă-hī′kam (*brother who raises*). An important court officer in reigns of Josiah and Jehoiakim, 2 Kgs. xxii. 12-14; Jer. xxvi. 24.

Ă-hī′lud (*brother born*). (1) Father of Jehoshaphat, the recorder of David's and Solomon's reigns, 2 Sam. viii. 16. (2) Father of Baana, 1 Kgs. iv. 12.

Ă-hĭm′a-ăz (*brother of wrath*). (1) Father-in-law of Saul, 1 Sam. xiv. 50. (2) Son of Zadok the high priest. Played a conspicuous part in the rebellion of Absalom, 2 Sam. xv. 24-37; xvii. 15-22; xviii. 19-33. (3) Solomon's son-in-law, 1 Kgs. iv. 15.

Ă-hī′măn (*brother of the right hand*). (1) One of the giant Anakim of Hebron, Num. xiii. 22, 23; Josh. xi. 21; Judg. i. 10. (2) A gate-keeper of Levi, 1 Chr. ix. 17.

Ă-hĭm′e-lech (*my brother is king*). (1) High priest at Nob, 1 Sam. xxi. 1. Priests of Nob slain by order of Saul, 1 Sam. xxii. 11-20. (2) A Hittite friend of David, 1 Sam. xxvi. 6.

Ă-hī′mŏth (*brother of death*). A Levite, 1 Chr. vi. 25. Mahath in vs. 35, and Maath in Luke iii. 26.

A′hĭn-a-dăb (*noble brother*). Royal purveyor to Solomon, 1 Kgs. iv. 14.

Ă-hĭn′o-am (*gracious*). (1) Wife of Saul, 1 Sam. xiv. 50. (2) A wife of David, 1 Sam. xxv. 43; xxvii. 3; xxx. 5, 18.

Ă-hī′o (*brotherly*). (1) He accompanied the Ark when taken from his father's house, 2 Sam. vi. 3, 4. (2) A Benjamite, 1 Chr. viii. 14. (3) Son of Jehiel, 1

Chr. viii. 31; ix. 37.

Ă-hī′rȧ (*unlucky*). A chief of Naphtali, Num. i. 15.

Ă-hī′ram (*lofty*). Founder of the Ahiramites, Num. xxvi. 38.

Ă-hĭs′a-mach (*helper*). One of the Tabernacle architects, Ex. xxxi. 6; xxxv. 34; xxxviii. 23.

Ă-hĭsh′ạ-här (*brother of dawn*). A grandson of Benjamin, 1 Chr. vii. 10.

Ă-hī′shär (*singer's brother*). A controller of Solomon's household, 1 Kgs. iv. 6.

Ă-hĭth′ọ-phel (*brother of folly*). A privy councillor of David, 2 Sam. xv. 12; xvi. 23; xxiii. 34. Joined Absalom's conspiracy, 2 Sam. xvii. Hanged himself in despair, 2 Sam. xvii. 23.

Ă-hī′tub (*brother of goodness*). (1) Grandson of Eli, 1 Sam. xiv. 3; xxii. 9-11. (2) Father of Zadok the high priest, 1 Chr. vi. 7, 8, 11, 12; 2 Sam. viii. 17.

Ah′lăb (*fertile*). A city of Canaan, Judg. i. 31.

Ah′lāi (*ornamental*). Daughter of Sheshan, and wife of his slave, Jarha, 1 Chr. ii. 31-35.

Ă-hō′ah (*brotherly*). Grandson of Benjamin, 1 Chr. viii. 4. Called Ahiah in 1 Chr. viii. 7.

Ă-hō′hite. From Ahoah, a patronymic of some of David's mighty men, 2 Sam. xxiii. 9, 28; 1 Chr. xi. 12; xxvii. 4.

Ă-hō′lah (*her tent*). The harlot used by Ezekiel to type Samaria, Ezek. xxiii. 4, 5, 36, 44.

Ă-hō′lĭ-ab (*tent of the father*). One of the Tabernacle architects, Ex. xxxv. 31-35.

Ă-hŏl′ĭ-bah (*my tent*). The harlot used by Ezekiel to type Jerusalem, Ezek. xxiii. 4, 11, 22, 36, 44.

Ă″hō-lĭb′ạ-mah (*tent of the height*). (1) Wife of Esau, Gen. xxxvi. 2, 25. Called Judith in Gen. xxvi. 34. (2) A title or district in Arabia Petrea, Gen. xxxvi. 41; 1 Chr. i. 52.

Ă-hū′mă-ī (*cowardly*). A descendant of Judah, 1 Chr. iv. 2.

Ă-hū′zam or Ă-hŭz′zam (*possession*). A son of Asher, 1 Chr. iv. 6.

Ă-hŭz′zath (*possessions*). A friend of King Abimelech, Gen. xxvi. 26.

A′ī (*heap of ruins*). (1) An ancient city of Canaan, Gen. xii. 8, where it is spelled HA′I. Captured and destroyed by Joshua, Josh. vii. 3-5; ix. 3; x. 1; xii. 9. Written Aiath in Isa. x. 28; and Aija in Neh. xi. 31; Ez. ii. 28. (2) A city of Heshbon, Jer. xlix. 3.

Ă-ī′ah (*vulture*). (1) Father of Saul's concubine, 2 Sam. iii. 7; xxi. 8-11. (2) Father of one of Esau's wives, 1 Chr. i. 40. Written Ajah in Gen. xxxvi. 24.

Ă-ī′ath. [AI.]

Ă-ī′jȧ. [AI.]

Ăij′ạ-lŏn. [AJALON.]

Ăij′e-lĕth Shā′här (*hind of the dawn*). In title to Ps. xxii. May mean a musical instrument, the argument of the Psalm, the melody, or tune name.

A′in (*eye*). (1) A landmark on eastern boundary of Canaan, Num. xxxiv. 11. (2) A Levitical city in south Judah and then in Simeon, Josh. xv. 32; xix. 7; xxi. 16. Ashan in 1 Chr. vi. 59.

Ă-ī′rus. A temple servant, 1 Esdr. v. 31.

A′jah. [AIAH.]

Aj′ạ-lŏn (*place of gazelles*). (1) A Levitical city of Dan, Josh. xix. 42. Became a city of refuge, Josh. xxi. 24, where it is written Aijalon; also in 1 Sam. xiv. 31. Prominent in Philistine wars, 2 Chr. xxviii. 18. Fortified as Aijalon by Rehoboam, 2 Chr. xi. 10. Now Yalo, 14 miles west of Jerusalem. (2) The valley in which Joshua commanded the moon to stand still, Josh. x. 12. (3) Burial place of the Judge, Elon, Judg. xii. 12.

A′kan (*keen of vision*). A Horite chieftain, Gen. xxxvi. 27. Jakan in 1 Chr. i. 42.

BIBLE
DICT

Ȧ-kĕl′da-mȧ. Spelling of Aceldama in Revised Version, Acts i. 19.

Ăk′kŭb (*insidious*). (1) A descendant of Zerubbabel, 1 Chr. iii. 24. (2) A gate-keeper of the temple, 1 Chr. ix. 17. (3) A Levite who assisted Ezra, Neh. viii. 7.

Ȧ-krăb′bim (*scorpion*). A range forming a south boundary of Judah, Num. xxxiv. 4. Maaleh-acrabbim in Josh. xv. 3. An Amorite boundary in Judg. i. 36.

Ăl′a-bàs″tĕr (*white stone*). A whitish mineral susceptible of easy carving and fine polish, much used by ancients for vases, ointment boxes, sculptures, etc., Matt. xxvi. 7; Mark xiv. 3; Luke vii. 37.

Ȧ-lăm′ĕ-lech (*king's oak*). A border place of Asher, Josh. xix. 26.

Ăl′a-mĕth (*covering*). A grandson of Benjamin, 1 Chr. vii. 8.

Ăl′a-mŏth. Perhaps a musical instrument or melody, 1 Chr. xv. 20; Ps. xlvi. title.

Ăl′çi-mŭs (*valiant*). A high priest, 1 Macc. vii. 9-25.

Ăl′e-mȧ. A city of Gilead, 1 Macc. v. 26.

Ăl′e-mĕth (*covering*). (1) A city of the priests in Benjamin, 1 Chr. vi. 60. Written Almon in Josh. xxi. 18. (2) A descendant of Jonathan, 1 Chr. viii. 36; ix. 42.

Ăl″ĕx-ăn′dĕr (*defender of men*). (1) King of Macedon; surnamed "The Great." Born B. C. 356. Succeeded his father Philip, B. C. 336. Subjugated Asia Minor, Syria, and Palestine. Overthrew the Persian Empire, B. C. 333. Conquered Egypt, B. C. 332. Founded Alexandria, B. C. 332. Consolidated his Persian conquests, with Babylon as capital, B. C. 324. Died, perhaps in Babylon, B. C. 323. Prefigured in Dan. ii. 39; vii. 6; viii. 5-7; xi. 3. (2) Alexander Balas, son of Antiochus IV. Usurped Syrian throne, B. C. 152. His coins are still preserved, 1 Macc. x., xi. (3) Son of Simon, Mark xv. 21. (4) A kinsman of Annas the high priest, Acts iv. 6. (5) A Jewish convert at Ephesus, Acts xix. 33. (6) An Ephesian Christian reprobated by Paul, 1 Tim. i. 20, and perhaps the coppersmith in 2 Tim. iv. 14.

Ăl″ĕx-ăn′drĭ-ȧ (*from Alexander*). The Grecian, Roman, and Christian capital of Egypt. Founded by Alexander the Great, B. C. 332. Situated on the Mediterranean Sea, 12 miles W. of Canopic mouth of the Nile. Noted for its libraries, architecture, and commerce. Conspicuous in early church history as a Christian centre, Acts xviii. 24; xxvii. 6; xxviii. 11.

Ăl″ĕx-ăn′drĭ-ans. Inhabitants of Alexandria; but in Acts vi. 9, Jewish colonists from Alexandria, admitted to the privilege of citizenship and worship at Jerusalem.

Ăl′gŭm or **Ăl′mŭg.** Former in 2 Chr. ii. 8; ix. 10, 11; latter in 1 Kgs. x. 11, 12. Supposed to be the red sandal-wood of India. Used in temple furniture.

Ȧ-lī′ah. [ALVAH.]

Ȧ-lī′an. [ALVAN.]

Ăl′lĕ-gō″ry (*other speech*). That figure of speech by which a subject is set forth under the guise of some other subject, Gal. iv. 24.

Ăl″le-lū′ja (*Praise ye Jehovah*). Written thus in Rev. xix. 1; but HALLELUJAH, in margin of Ps. cvi., cxi., cxii., cxiii., cxvii., cxviii., cxxxv., etc. A common exclamation of joy and praise in Jewish worship.

Ăl-lī′ance (*ans*) (*binding to*). Hebrews forbidden to make alliances with surrounding nations but finally driven to them. Alliances solemnized by presents, oaths, feasts, monuments, offerings, and other pious ceremonies, Gen. xv. 10; xxvi. 30; xxxi. 51-53; Josh. ix. 15; 1 Kgs. xv. 18; v. 2-12; ix. 27. Breach of covenant severely punished, 2 Sam. xxi. 1; Ezek. xvii. 16.

Ăl′lŏm, 1 Esdr. v. 34. [AMI and AMON.]

Ăl′lŏn (*oak*). (1) Ancestor of Ziza, 1 Chr. iv.

37. (2) A boundary place of Naphtali, Josh. xix. 33.

Ăl′lŏn=băch′uth (*oak of weeping*). The tree under which Deborah was buried, Gen. xxxv. 8.

Ăl-mō′dăd (*immeasurable*). Progenitor of an Arab tribe, Gen. x. 26; 1 Chr. i. 20.

Ăl′mŏn, Josh. xxi. 18. [ALEMETH.]

Ălm′ond (*hasten*). Tree resembles the peach in form, height, blossom, and fruit. Covering of fruit downy and succulent. Chiefly valuable for its nut. Gen. xliii. 11; Ex. xxv. 33, 34; xxxvii. 19, 20; Num. xvii. 8; Eccles. xii. 5; Jer. i. 11.

Ăl′mŏn=dīb″la-thā′ĭm (*hiding of two fig takes*). One of the last stopping places of the wandering Israelites, Num. xxxiii. 46.

Ălms (*pity*). Almsgiving enjoined by Mosaic law, Lev. xix. 9; Ruth ii. 2. Every third year the tithes of increase were shared with the Levite, the stranger, the fatherless and widow, Deut. xiv. 28. Receptacles for taking of alms placed in the Temple, Mark xii. 41. Almsgiving exhorted, Acts xi. 30; Rom. xv. 25-27; 1 Cor. xvi. 1-4.

Ăl′mŭg. [ALGUM.]

Ăl′oes (*ōz*). Written "Lign (*wood*) Aloes" in Num. xxiv. 6. A costly and sweet smelling wood of India, much prized in the East. Ps. xlv. 8; Prov. vii. 17; S. of Sol. iv. 14; John xix. 39.

Ā′lŏth. Solomon's ninth commissary district, 1 Kgs. iv. 16.

Ăl′phȧ. First letter of the Greek alphabet. Used with omega, the last letter, to express beginning and end, Isa. xli. 4; xliv. 6; Rev. i. 8, 11; xxi. 6; xxii. 13.

Ăl′pha-bĕt. *Alpha* and *beta*, first and second letters of Greek alphabet. Hebrew alphabet comprised twenty-two letters.

Ăl-phæ′us (*changing*). (1) Father of the apostle James the Less, Matt. x. 3; Mark iii. 18; Luke vi. 15; Acts i. 13. Called Clopas or Cleophas, in John xix. 25. (2) Father of Levi or Matthew, Mark ii. 14.

Ăl″ta-nē′us, 1 Esdr. ix. 33. [MATTENAI.]

Ăl′tar (*high*). First altars were simple memorial piles, Gen. viii. 20; xii. 7; xxvi. 25; xxxv. 1. Afterwards to lay sacrifices upon, Ex. xvii. 15, 16, xxvii. 1-8. Usually built of earth or stone, Ex. xx. 24-26; but sacrificial altars quite elaborate, Ex. xl. 26-33. Still more elaborate in Solomon's Temple, 1 Kgs. viii. 64; 2 Chr. vii. 7. Altar fires to burn perpetually, Lev. vi. 12, 13. *Altar of Incense*, called "golden" to distinguish it from *Altar of Sacrifice*, called "brazen," Ex. xxx. 1-10; xl. 5, 1 Kgs. vii. 48; 1 Chr. xxviii. 18.

Ăl-tăs′chith (*destroy not*). In title to Ps. lvii., lviii., lix., and lxxv. Probably the tune is meant.

Ā′lush (*crowd*). Last halting-place of Israelite before Rephidim, Num. xxxiii. 13, 14.

Ăl′vah (*wickedness*). A duke of Edom, Gen. xxxvi. 40. Called Aliah in 1 Chr. i. 51.

Ăl′văn (*tall*). A Horite, Gen. xxxvi. 23. Alian in 1 Chr. i. 40.

Ā′măd (*enduring*). An unknown place in Asher, Josh. xix. 26.

Ȧ-măd′a-thȧ, Esth. xvi. 10, and Amadathus, Esth. xii. 7; Apoch. [HAMMEDATHA.]

Ā′măl (*labor*). An Asherite, 1 Chr. vii. 35.

Ăm′a-lĕk (*valley dweller*). An Edomite chieftain, Gen. xxxvi. 12; 1 Chr. i. 36.

Ăm′a-lĕk-ītes″. A nomad tribe of the Sinai wilderness, Gen. xiv. 7. Called the first of all nations in Num. xxiv. 20. Dwelt to the South, Num. xiii. 29. Smitten by Gideon, Judg. vii. 12-23; by Saul, 1 Sam. xv. 3-9; and David, 1 Sam. xxx. 18; 1 Chr. iv. 43. "Mount of Amalekites" was in Ephraim, Judg. xii. 15.

Ā′măm (*gathering place*). A city in south Judah, Josh. xv. 26.

Ā′măn (*mother*), Esther x. 7; Apoch. [HAMAN.]

Ăm′a-nȧ (*covenant*). Probably a mount of Anti-

Libanus range, S. of Sol. iv. 8.

Ăm''a-rī'ah (*the Lord says*). (1) Father of Ahitub, 1 Chr. vi. 7. (2) A high priest, 2 Chr. xix. 11. (3) Head of a Kohathite family, 1 Chron. xxiii. 19; xxiv. 23. (4) Head of one of the twenty-four courses of priests, 2 Chr. xxxi. 15; Neh. x. 3. (5) A priest in Ezra's time, Ez. x. 42. (6) A priest who returned with Zerubbabel, Neh. x. 3; xii. 2, 13. (1) An ancestor of Zephaniah the prophet, Zeph. i. 1.

Ăm'-a-sȧ (*burden*). (1) Nephew of David, 2 Sam. xvii. 25. Rebelled with Absalom, and defeated by Joab, 2 Sam. xviii. 6. Reconciled to David, 2 Sam. xix. 13, and killed by Joab, 2 Sam. xx. 10. (2) A prince of Ephraim, 2 Chr. xxviii. 12.

Ȧ-măs'a-ī (*burdensome*). (1) A Levite, 1 Chr. vi. 25, 35. (2) A chief of captains who deserted to David, 1 Chr. xii. 18. (3) A priest who blew the trumpet before the Ark, 1 Chr. xv. 24. (4) A Kohathite, 2 Chr. xxix. 12.

Ȧ-măsh'a-ī (*burdensome*). A priest, Neh. xi. 13.

Ăm-a-sī' äh (*whom Jehovah bears*). Captain of 200,000 men in Judah, 2 Chr. xvii. 16.

Ăm''a-thē'īs, 1 Esdr. ix. 29. [ATHLAI.]

Ăm'a-this. A country north of Palestine, 1 Macc. xii. 25.

Ăm''a-zī'ah (*strength of Jehovah*). (1) Eighth king of Judah. Reign B. C. 837–809, 2 Kgs. xiv. 1–20. Rebuked by God for idolatry, 2 Chr. xxv. 1–16. Defeated by Joash and murdered at Lachish, 2 Chr. xxv. 17–28. (2) A descendant of Simeon, 1 Chr. iv. 34. (3) A Levite, 1 Chr. vi. 45. (4) An idolatrous priest of Bethel, Amos vii. 10–17.

Ăm-băs'sa-dŏr (*servant*). A person chosen by one government to represent it at the seat of another. Earliest mention in Num. xx. 14; Josh. ix. 4; Judg. xi. 17–19. Injury to them an insult to their king, 2 Sam. x. 3–6. The term includes both messenger and message, Luke xiv. 32. Ministers called ambassadors of Christ, 2 Cor. v. 20.

Ăm'bĕr. Hardly the fossil vegetable gum of commerce, Ezek. i. 4, 27; viii. 2; but rather the yellow composition of gold and silver known as *electrum*.

Ȧ-mĕn' (*true*). A final word used to fix the stamp of truth upon an assertion, Num. v. 22; Deut. xxvii. 15; Matt. vi. 13; 1 Cor. xiv. 16. Promises of God are amen, 2 Cor. i. 20. A title of Christ, Rev. iii. 14.

Ăm'ê-thyst (*not wine*). A purplish quartz, ranking among the precious stones, and forming the third stone in the third row of the high priest's breastplate, Ex. xxviii. 19; xxxix. 12. A stone in the foundations of the New Jerusalem, Rev. xxi. 20.

Ȧ'mī (*builder*). A returned captive, Ez. ii. 57. Amon in Neh. vii. 59.

Ȧ-mĭn'a-dab, Matt. i. 4; Luke iii. 33; for AMMINADAB.

Ȧ-mĭt'ta-ī (*true*). The father of Jonah, 2 Kgs. xiv. 25; Jon. i. 1.

Ăm'mah (*head*). A hill near Gibeon to which Joab pursued Abner, 2 Sam. ii. 24.

Ăm'mī (*my people*). Applied figuratively to the Israelites, Hos. ii. i. marg.

Ăm-mĭd'ī-oi. A family of returned captives, 1 Esdr. v. 20.

Ăm'mī-el (*people of God*). (1) The spy of Dan who perished for his evil report, Num. xiii. 12. (2) Father of Machir, 2 Sam. ix. 4, 5. (3) Father of Bathsheba, 1 Chr. iii. 5; called Eliam in 2 Sam. xi. 3. (4) A door-keeper of the Temple, 1 Chr. xxvi. 5.

Ăm-mī'hŭd (*people of praise*). (1) Father of the chief of Ephraim at time of Exode, Num. i. 10; ii. 18; vii. 48, 53; x. 22; 1 Chr. vii. 26. (2) A Simeonite, Num. xxxiv. 20. (3) A Naphtalite, Num. xxxiv. 28. (4) Father of Talmai, king of Geshur, 2 Sam. xiii. 37. (5) A descendant of Pharez, 1 Chr. ix. 4.

Ăm-mĭn'a-dăb (*one of the prince's people*). (1) A prince of Judah, Num. i. 7; ii. 3; Ruth iv. 19, 20; 1 Chr. ii. 10. (2) Chief of the sons of Uzziel, 1

Chr. xv. 10–12. (3) Written Amminadib in S. of Sol. vi. 12.

Ăm''mī=shăd'da-ī'' (*people of the Almighty*). Father of the prince of Dan at time of the Exode, Num. i. 12; ii. 25; vii. 66; x. 25.

Ăm-mĭz'a-băd (*people of the giver*). Commander in David's army, 1 Chr. xxvii. 6.

Ăm'mŏn, Ăm'mŏn-ītes'', Chĭl'drĕn of Ăm'mŏn. Land of the Ammonites was east of the Dead Sea between the Arnon on the south to the Jabbok on the north, Num. xxi. 24; Deut. ii. 19, 20. People called Ammonites from their ancestor Ben-Ammi; Gen. xix. 38. Nomadic, idolatrous, incursive and cruel, 1 Sam. xi. 1–3; Amos i. 13; Judg. x. 6. Reduced to servitude by David, 2 Sam. xii. 26–31. Denounced by Jeremiah and Ezekiel, Jer. xlix. 1–6; Ezek. xxv. 2–10.

Ăm''mŏn-īt'ess. A woman of Ammon.

Ăm'mŏn=nō'. [No.]

Ăm'nŏn (*faithful*). (1) Eldest son of David, killed by his brother Absalom, 2 Sam. xiii. 1–29. (2) Son of Shimon, 1 Chr. iv. 20.

Ȧ'mok (*deep*). A returned priest, Neh. xii. 7, 20.

Ȧ'mon or **Ȧ'mĕn** (*mystery*). An Egyptian god worshipped at Thebes as "Amen the Sun." Written No, in Nah. iii. 8.

Ȧ'mon (*builder*). (1) A governor of Samaria under Ahab, 1 Kgs. xxii. 26; 2 Chr. xviii. 25. (2) Fourteenth king of Judah, B. C. 642–640. A shameless idolater, and killed in a conspiracy, 2 Kgs. xxi. 19–26. Reign pictured in Zeph. i. 4; iii. 3, 4, 11.

Ăm'ŏr-ītes (*highlanders*). One of the nations of Canaan before the Hebrew conquest, Gen. x. 16; xiv. 7; Num. xiii. 29; Deut. i. 20; Josh. v. 1; x. 6; xi. 3; 1 Sam. xxiii. 29. Occupied both sides of the Jordan, Josh. xiii. 15–27; Num. xxi. 21.

Ȧ'mos (*weighty*). One of the lesser prophets. Lived during reigns of Uzziah and Jeroboam II., Amos i. 1–7; vii. 14–15. His book is 30th of O. T. It rebukes the sins of Israel and closes with God's promise. Book abounds in rural allusions.

Ȧ'moz (*strong*). Father of Isaiah, Isa. i. 1; 2 Kgs. xix. 2.

Ăm-phĭp'o-lis (*surrounded city*). A city of Macedonia, 33 miles S. W. of Philippi, Acts xvii. 1.

Ăm'plī-as (*large*). A Roman friend of Paul, Rom. xvi. 8.

Ăm'răm (*exalted*). (1) Father of Moses and Aaron, Ex. vi. 18–20. (2) A descendant of Seir, 1 Chr. i. 41; Hemdan in Gen. xxxvi. 26. (3) A son of Bani, Ez. x. 34.

Ăm'răm-ītes. Descendants of Amram, Num. iii. 27; 1 Chr. xxvi. 23.

Ăm'ra-phel (*keeper of gods*). A Hamite king who joined the expedition against Sodom, Gen. xiv.

Ăm'ū-lĕts (*charms*). Belts, rings, necklaces, ornaments, mystically inscribed or not, worn for protection against evil enchantment. Referred to in Gen. xxxv. 4; Judg. viii. 24; Isa. iii. 20; Hos. ii. 13.

Ăm'zī (*strong*). (1) A Levite, 1 Chr. vi. 46. (2) A priest, Neh. xi. 12.

Ȧ'nab (*grape*). Place in south Judah, Josh. xi. 21.

Ăn'a-ĕl. Tobit's brother, Tob. i. 21.

Ȧ'nah (*answering*). Father-in-law of Esau, Gen. xxxvi. 2–25.

Ăn''a-hā'rath (*gorge*). A border place of Issachar and Manasseh, Josh. xix. 19.

Ăn''a-ī'ah (*whom God answers*). (1) A priest who assisted Ezra, Neh. viii. 4. (2) A co-covenanter with Nehemiah, Neh. x. 22.

Ȧ'năk (*collar*), Children of, Num. xiii. 22. [ANAKIM.]

Ăn'a-kĭm or **-kĭms.** A race of giants in southern Canaan, Deut. i. 28. Defeated by Joshua, and land given to Caleb, Josh. xi. 21–22; xiv. 12–15.

Ăn'a-mĭm. A Mizraite people, not located, Gen.

x. 13.

Ā-năm′mē-lech (*kingly image*). Companion god of Adrammelech, worshipped in Samaria, and representing the female power of the sun, 2 Kgs. xvii. 31.

Ā′nan (*cloud*). A co-covenanter with Nehemiah, Neh. x. 26.

Ăn-ā′nī (*covered by Jehovah*). A descendant of Judah, 1 Chr. iii. 24.

Ăn-a-nī′ah (*covered by Jehovah*). (1) A priestly assistant of Nehemiah, Neh. iii. 23. (2) A city of Benjamin, Neh. xi. 32.

Ăn″a-nī′as (*whom Jehovah has given*). (1) Five persons mentioned in 1 Esdr. ix. (2) The doubtful convert, whose tragic ending is narrated in Acts v. 1–11. (3) A Jewish disciple at Damascus, Acts ix. 10–27 ; xxii. 12. (4) A high priest, A. D. 48, Acts xxiii. 2–5 ; xxiv. 1.

Ā-năn′ĭ-ĕl. A progenitor of Tobit, Tob. i. 1.

Ā′năth (*answer*). Father of Shamgar, Judg. iii. 31.

Ăn-ăth′e-mȧ (*devoted*). The devoted thing, if inanimate, fell to the priests, Num. xviii. 18 ; if animate, it was to be slain, Lev. xxvii. 28, 29. In N. T. a curse, Rom. ix. 3 ; 1 Cor. xii. 3 ; xvi. 22. In the latter instance Maranatha is added, the meaning being " Let him be accursed."

Ăn′a-thŏth (*answers*). (1) A descendant of Benjamin, 1 Chr. vii. 8. (2) A co-covenanter with Nehemiah, Neh. x. 19. (3) A Levitical city of Benjamin, Josh. xxi. 18 ; 1 Chr. vi. 60 ; Isa. x. 30.

Ăn′chŏr (*hook*). Anchors for holding ships to one spot were formerly cast from the stern. Acts xxvii. 29.

Ăn′drew (*manly*). An Apostle of Christ, John i. 35–40 ; Matt. iv. 18. Brother of Simon Peter, native of Bethsaida, and fisherman. Original disciple of John the Baptist, Mark xiii. 3 ; John vi. 6–13 ; xii. 22.

Ăn″drŏ-nī′cus (*man conqueror*). (1) A viceroy of Antiochus at Antioch, 2 Macc. iv. 31–38. (2) Another officer of Antiochus at Garizim, 2 Macc. v. 23. (3) A Christian friend of Paul's at Rome, Rom. xvi. 7.

Ā′nem (*two springs*). A Levitical city of Issachar, 1 Chr. vi. 73.

Ā′nĕr (*boy*). (1) A Levitical city in Manasseh, 1 Chr. vi. 70. (2) An Amorite chief of Hebron, Gen. xiv. 13–24.

Ăn′ĕ-thŏth-īte″, 2 Sam. xxiii. 27 ; **Ăn′tŏth-īte**, 1 Chr. xi. 28 ; xii. 3 ; **Ăn″ĕ-tŏth′īte**, 1 Chr. xxvii. 12. An inhabitant of Anathoth.

Ān′gĕl (*messenger*). A messenger, 2 Sam. ii. 5 ; Luke vii. 24. In a spiritual sense, a messenger of God, Gen. xxiv. 7 ; Heb. i. 14. Nature, Matt. xviii. 10. Number, 1 Kgs. xxii. 19 ; Matt. xxvi. 53 ; Heb. xii. 22. Strength, Ps. ciii. 20 ; Rev. v. 2. Activity, Isa. vi. 2–6. Appearance, Matt. xxviii. 2–4 ; Rev. x. 1, 2. Office, Isa. vi. 1–3 ; Rev. vi. 11 ; Matt. xiii. 49 ; xvi. 27 ; xxiv. 31.

Ā′nĭ-am (*sighing of the people*). A Manassite, 1 Chr. vii. 19.

Ā′nĭm (*fountains*). A city in mountains of Judah, Josh. xv. 50.

Ăn′īse. A plant of the parsley family, producing aromatic seeds used in medicine and cookery, and with which tithes were paid, Matt. xxiii. 23.

Ănk′lĕt. Much worn in the East as ornaments for the ankles, sometimes with bells, Isa. iii. 16–20. [BELLS.]

Ăn′nȧ (*gracious*). (1) Wife of Tobit, Tob. i. 9. (2) A prophetess at Jerusalem, Luke ii. 36.

Ăn′nȧ-as, 1 Esdr. v. 23. [SENAAH.]

Ăn′nas (*humble*). (1) 1 Esdr. ix. 32. Same as Harim in Ez. x. 31. (2) A Jewish high priest, A. D. 7–23. Succeeded by his son-in-law, Caiaphas, A. D. 25, John xviii. 13 ; Luke iii. 2.

Ā-noint′ (*to smear on*). Anointing with oil or

ointment, a common practice in East, Gen. xxviii. 18 ; xxxi. 13 ; Deut. xxviii. 40 ; Ruth iii. 3. A mark of respect, Luke vii. 46, Ps. xxiii. 5 ; or of induction to priestly office, Ex. xl. 15 ; Num. iii. 3 ; or to kingly office, 1 Sam. ix. 16 ; x. 1 ; or as an act of consecration, Ex. xxviii. 41 ; or as an act of healing, Mark vi. 13. Christ was anointed with the Holy Ghost, Luke iv. 18 ; Acts iv. 27 ; x. 38 ; Isa. lxi. 1 ; Ps. xlv. 7.

Ănt (*emmet*). Twice referred to in O. T. ; first as to its diligence, and second as to its wisdom. Prov. vi. 6 ; xxx. 25.

Ăn′te-lōpe (*animal*). The word translated " fallow deer " in Deut. xiv. 5, as well as " pygarg," implies a species of antelope.

Ăn′tĭ-chrīst (*against Christ*). In 1 John ii. 18, 22 ; iv. 3 ; 2 John 7, applied to those who hold heretical opinions of the incarnation.

Ăn′tĭ-ŏch (*after Antiochus*). (1) Capital of the Greek kings of Syria, on the Orontes. First Gentile church founded there, and disciples first called Christians there ; Acts xi. 19–21, 26. (2) A city of Pisidia, Acts xiii. 14. Starting point of the persecutions which followed Paul all through Asia Minor, Acts xiv.

Ăn-tī′o-chŭs (*opponent*). (1) A messenger of Jonathan to the Romans, 1 Macc. xii. 16. (2) King of Syria, B. C. 261. Prefigured as " King of the North " in Dan. xi. 6, etc. (3) Antiochus III., called " The Great," B. c. 223, Dan. xi. 14–19. (4) Antiochus IV., called Epiphanes, 1 Macc. i. (5) Antiochus V., Eupator, B. c. 164 ; 1 Macc. vi. 10. (6) Antiochus VI. and VII., 1 Macc. xii.–xvi.

Ăn′tĭ-păs (*like the father*). A martyr of Pergamos, Rev. ii. 13.

Ăn-tĭp′a-tĕr (*for the father*). An ambassador to Lacedemon, 1 Macc. xii. 16.

Ăn-tĭp′a-trĭs (*for his father*). Ancient Capharsaba, rebuilt and renamed by Herod ; 34 miles N. W. of Jerusalem, Acts xxiii. 31.

Ăn-tō′nĭ-ȧ. A fortress on N. W. side of Temple at Jerusalem, Acts xxi. 31–40.

Ăn″to-thī′jah (*answers of Jehovah*). A son of Jehoram, 1 Chr. viii. 24.

Ăn′tŏth-īte. A native of Anathoth, 1 Chr. xi. 28 ; xii. 3.

Ā′nub (*confederate*). A descendant of Judah, 1 Chr. iv. 8.

Ā′nus, 1 Esdr. ix. 48. [BANI.]

Ăp-ā′me. Daughter of Bartacus, 1 Esdr. iv. 29.

Ā-pĕl′lĕs (*called*). Friend of Paul, Rom. xvi. 10.

Āpes. Were brought from the same countries which supplied ivory and peacocks, 1 Kgs. x. 22 ; 2 Chr. ix. 21.

Ā-phär′săch-ītes,   Ā-phär′săth-chītes, Ā-phär′sītes (*rending*). Assyrian nomads settled in Samaria, Ez. iv. 9 ; v. 6.

Ā′phĕk (*strength*). (1) A royal city of the Canaanites, near Hebron, Josh. xii. 18. Probably Aphekah, Josh. xv. 53. (2) A city in the extreme north of Asher, Josh. xix. 30. Probably Aphik, Judg. i. 31. (3) A place N. W. of Jerusalem, 1 Sam. iv. 1. (4) A Philistine encampment near Jezreel, 1 Sam. xxix. 1. (5) A walled city of Syria, 1 Kgs. xx. 26.

Ā-phē′kah, Josh. xv. 53. [APHEK.]

Ā-phĕr′e-ma. Governor of Judea, 1 Macc. xi. 34.

Ā-phĕr′ra. Son of one of Solomon's servants, 1 Esdr. v. 34.

Ā-phī′ah (*refreshed*). A progenitor of Saul. 1 Sam. ix. i.

Ā′phĭk, Judg. i. 31. [APHEK.]

Ăph′rah (*dust.*) An uncertain place, Micah i. 10.

Ăph′sēs (*dispersion*). Chief of the 18th course of the temple service, 1 Chr. xxiv. 15.

Ā-pŏc′ȧ-lypse (*uncovered*). The Greek name for Revelation.

Ā-pŏc′rў-pha (*hidden*). That collection of 14

O. T. books not regarded as canonical. Also the rejected N. T. books.

Ăp''ŏl-lō'nĭ-à (*belonging to Apollo*). A city of Macedonia, Acts xvii. 1.

Ăp''ŏl-lō'nĭ-us. (1) A governor of Celo-Syria, 2 Macc. iv. 4. (2) A general under Antiochus, 1 Macc. iii. 10–12. (2) Several other Syrian generals of same name, 1 and 2 Macc.

Ăp''ŏl-lŏph'a̤-nēs. A Syrian general, 2 Macc. x. 37.

Ȧ-pŏl'lŏs (*belonging to Apollo*). A learned Jew and Christian convert of Alexandria, who became a preacher and friend of Paul, Acts xviii. 24–28; 1 Cor. iii. 6–9; Tit. iii. 13.

Ȧ-pŏll'yon (*destroyer*). Greek name of Abaddon, "angel of the bottomless pit," Rev. ix. 11. [ABADDON.]

Ăp'pa̤-im (*nostrils*). Son of Nadab. 1 Chr. ii. 30, 31.

Ȧ-pŏth'ē-ca̤''ry (*to place away*). The apothecary's art was called for in the mixing of perfume. Ex. xxx. 35.

Ȧ-pŏs'tle (*one sent forth*). Official name of the twelve disciples. As to power and names *see* Matt. x. 1–42; John xvi. 13; Mark xvi. 20. In a broad sense, any one commissioned to preach the gospel, 2 Cor. viii. 23; Phil. ii. 25. Term applied to Christ, Heb. iii. 1.

Ăp-păr'ĕl. [CLOTHES.]

Ăp-peal' (*drive to*). This right acknowledged by Jewish law, Deut. xvii. 8, 9. It lay to the judges, Judg. iv. 5; then to the kings; later to a special tribunal, 2 Chr. xix. 8–10; Ez. vii. 25; finally to the Sanhedrim. Paul appealed to the Roman Emperor, Acts xxv. 11.

Ăp'phĭ-a̤ (*productive*). A Christian woman addressed by Paul, Phile. 2.

Ăp'phŭs (*wary*). Surname of Jonathan Maccabeus, 1 Macc. ii. 5.

Ăp''pĭ-ī fō'rŭm (*market-place of Appius*). A town, 43 miles S. E. of Rome, on the Appian Way, Acts xxviii. 15.

Ăp'ple, Ăp'ple=tree (*bursting forth, in Hebrew*). The fruit is alluded to in Prov. xxv. 11; S. of Sol. ii. 5; vii. 8. Tree mentioned in S. of Sol. ii. 3; viii. 5; Joel i. 12. For figurative use *see* Prov. vii. 2; Zech. ii. 8; Ps. xvii. 8; Lam. ii. 18.

Aq'uĭ-là (*eagle*). A Jewish convert of Pontus, and valuable assistant of Paul, Acts xviii. 2; 1 Cor. xvi. 19; Rom. xvi. 3, etc.

Är, Är of Mō'ab (*city*). A chief place of Moab, Num. xxi. 28; Isa. xv. 1. Aroer in Deut. ii. 36. Used to type the Moabite people or land, Deut. ii. 9, 18, 29.

Ā'rà (*lion*). Head of a family of Asher, 1 Chr. vii. 38.

Ā'rab (*ambush*). A city of Hebron, Josh. xv. 52.

Är'a̤-bah (*burnt up*). A Hebrew word, Josh. xviii. 18, designating the valley of Jordan and the Dead Sea, and the depression through Arabia to the Gulf of Akabah.

Ȧ-rā'bĭ-à (*desert*). Known in O. T. as "East Country," Gen. x. 30; xxv. 6; and "Land of the Sons of the East," Gen. xxix.; Judg. vi. 3; vii. 12. Arabia, from *Arab* the people, in 2 Chr. ix. 14; Isa. xxi. 13; Jer. xxv. 24; Ezek. xxvii. 21. That extensive peninsula lying south of Palestine and between the Red Sea, Indian Ocean, and Persian Gulf. Home of many nomadic races, and in close commerce and even kinship, through Ishmael, with the Hebrews, 1 Kgs. x. 15; 2 Chr. ix. 14. Paul visited it, Gal. i. 17. Often referred to by prophets, Isa. xlii. 11; Jer. xxv. 24.

Ā'răd (*wild ass*). (1) A valorous Benjamite, 1 Chr. viii. 15. (2) A royal city of the Canaanites, Num. xxi. 1; Josh. xii. 14.

Ār'a̤-dus, 1 Macc. xv. 23. [ARVAD.]

Ā'rah (*wandering*). (1) An Asherite, 1 Chr. vii. 39. (2) Head of a returned family, Ez. ii. 5; Neh. vii. 10.

Ā'ram (*high*). (1) Translated Mesopotamia in Gen. xxiv. 10. The high part of Syria to the N. E. of Palestine. Absorbed by Syria, with capital at Damascus, 1 Kgs. xx. 1; Isa. vii. 8; 1 Kgs. xi. 24. (2) A descendant of Nahor, Gen. xxii. 21. (3) An Asherite, 1 Chr. vii. 34. (4) An ancestor of Christ, Matt. i. 4; Luke iii. 33.

Ā'ram=nā-ha̤-rā'im (*highlands of two rivers*), Ps. lx. title.

Ā'ram=zō'bah [Ā'ram]. Ps. xl. title.

Ā'ra̤m-ĭt''ess. A female inhabitant of Aram, 1 Chr. vii. 14.

Ā'răn (*wild goat*). A Horite, Gen. xxxvi. 28.

Âr'a̤-rat (*high land*). A high mountain of Armenia, and resting place of Noah's ark, Gen. viii. 4.

Ȧ-ra̤u'nah (*ark*). A Jebusite prince who sold his threshing-floor to David, 2 Sam. xxiv. 18–24; 1 Chr. xxi. 25.

Är'bà (*one of four*). A forefather of Anak, Josh. xiv. 15; xv. 13; xxi. 11.

Är'bah. Hebron, or Kirjath-arba, Gen. xxxv. 27.

Är'băth-īte. An inhabitant of the Arabah, 2 Sam. xxiii. 31; 1 Chr. xi. 32.

Är-băt'tĭs. A district in Palestine, 1 Macc. v. 23.

Är'bel. Hos. x. 14. [BETH-ARBEL.]

Är-bē'la. A town in Galilee, 1 Macc. ix. 2.

Är'bīte. A native of Arab, 2 Sam. xxiii. 35.

Ärch-an'gel (ärk-ān'jel) (*chief angel*). 1 Thess. iv. 16; Jude 9.

Är''chĕ-lā'us (*prince of the people*). A son of Herod the Great, and ethnarch (B. C. 4–A. D. 9) of Idumea, Judea, and Samaria, Matt. ii. 22.

Ärch'e-ry (*use of the arcus, or bow*). Use of the bow and arrow, an important art in Biblical times, Gen. xxvii. 3; Isa. xxii. 6; xlix.; 2 Ps. cxxvii. 4, 5. Benjamites noted archers, Judg. xix.–xxi.

Är'chĕ-vītes. Probably inhabitants of Erech, Ez. iv. 9.

Är'chī. A place or clan in Joseph, Josh. xvi. 2. [ARCHITE.]

Är'chĭp'pus (*chief of stables*). A Christian teacher at Colossæ, Col. iv. 17; Phil. 2.

Är'chīte. Supposed to refer to a clan of Erech, 2 Sam. xv. 32; xvi. 16; xvii. 5–14. 1 Chr. xxvii. 33.

Är'chĭ-tec''ture (*builder's art*). Descendants of Shem were city builders, Gen. iv. 17; x. 11, 12. Hebrew ideas of architecture ripened in Egypt, and by contact with Tyre. David enlarged Jerusalem. Solomon built a palace and temple, 2 Sam. v. 11; 1 Kgs. vii. The returned captives were great builders, Ez. iii. 8–10; Neh. iii.; vi. 15.

Ärc-tū'rus (*the bear*). The constellation Ursa Major, commonly called the "Great Bear" or "Charles's Wain," Job ix. 9; xxxviii. 32.

Ärd (*fugitive*). A grandson of Benjamin, Gen. xlvi. 21; Num. xxvi. 40.

Är'dăth. A field, 2 Esdr. ix. 26.

Ärd'ītes. Descendants of Ard or Addar, Num. xxvi. 40.

Är'dŏn (*fugitive*). A son of Caleb, 1 Chr. ii. 18.

Ȧ-rē'lī (*heroic*). A son of Gad. Children called Arelites, Num. xxvi. 17; Gen. xlvi. 16.

Är''ĕ-op'a̤-ḡīte. A member of the court of Areopagus, Acts xvii. 34.

Är''ĕ-op'a̤-gus (*hill of Mars*). A rocky hill near the centre of Athens, where the court of justice sat, Acts xvii. 19–34.

Ā'rēs, 1 Esdr. v. 10. [ARAH 2.]

Ăr'e-tas (*excellence*). (1) An Arab chief, 2 Macc. v. 8. (2) Father-in-law of Herod Antipas, 2 Cor.

xi. 32.

Ā-rē'us. A Lacedæmonian king, 1 Macc. xii. 20–23.

Ăr'gŏb (*stony*). A country of Bashan, and one of Solomon's commissary districts, Deut. iii. 4 ; 1 Kgs. iv. 13.

Ā''rĭ-ȧ-rā'thes. Mithridates IV., king of Cappadocia, B. C. 163–130, 1 Macc. xv. 22.

Ā-rĭd'ạ-ī (*strong*). Ninth son of Haman, Esth. ix. 9.

Ā-rĭd'ạ-thȧ. Sixth son of Haman, Esth. ix. 8.

Ā-rī'eh (*lion*). A prince of Israel, killed by Pekah, 2 Kgs. xv. 25.

Ā'rĭ-el (*lion of God*). (1) A leader of returning captives, Ez. viii. 16. (2) The city of Jebus-Salem, Jerusalem, Isa. xxix. 1, 2.

Ăr''ĭ-mȧ-thæ'ȧ (*heights*). Home of Joseph in Judea, Matt. xxvii. 57 ; Mark xv. 43 ; Luke xxiii. 51 ; John xix. 38.

Ā'rĭ-ŏch (*venerable*). (1) A King of Elassar, Gen. xiv. 1–9. (2) Captain under Nebuchadnezzar, Dan. ii. 14, etc. (3) A king of the Elymeans, Judith i. 6.

Ā-rĭs'ạ-ī (*lion like*). Eighth son of Haman, Esth. ix. 9.

Ăr''ĭs-tär'chus (*best ruler*). A Thessalonian companion of Paul on his third missionary tour, Acts xix. 29 ; xx. 4 ; xxvii. 2 ; Col. iv. 10 ; Phil. 24.

Ăr-ĭs''tō-bū'lus (*best counselor*). (1) A Christian and resident at Rome, Rom. xvi. 10. (2) A priest of the Egyptian Jews, 2 Macc. i. 10.

Ärk (*chest*). The vessel in which Noah and his family were saved, Gen. vi., vii., viii. Also a little boat of rushes, Ex. ii. 3.

Ärk of the Cŏv'ĕ-nänt. Built by direction, Ex. xxv. A chest of Shittim wood for tabernacle use, 3 ft. 9 in. long, by 2 ft. 3 in. wide and high, lined and covered with gold, whose lid was the mercy-seat, on either end of which were cherubs. Golden rings were on the sides, through which poles passed for carrying. Captured by Philistines, 1 Sam. iv. 10, 11 ; returned to Kirjath-Jearim ; brought thence by David to Jerusalem, 2 Sam. vi. 1 ; 1 Chr. xv. 25, 28, etc. ; placed in temple by Solomon, 2 Chr. v. 2–10.

Ärk'īte. A descendant of Arka, Gen. x. 17 ; 1 Chr. i. 15.

Ăr-ma-gĕd'don (*hill of Megiddo*). A typical battlefield between the hosts of good and evil, Rev. xvi. 16.

Ăr-mē'nĭ-ȧ (*Land of Aram*). The plateau of Western Asia, whence flow its great rivers Euphrates, Tigris, Araxes, etc., 2 Kgs. xix. 37 ; Isa. xxxvii. 38.

Ärm'-let (*for the arms*). An arm ornament in general use in the East. "Bracelet," 2 Sam. i. 10.

Ăr-mō'nī. A son of Saul, 2 Sam. xxi. 8.

Ärmṣ, Är'mor. Hebrew offensive weapons were the sword, 1 Sam. xvii. 51 ; xxv. 13 ; 2 Sam. xx. 8 ; Judg. iii. 16 ; spear, 1 Sam. xvii. 7 ; 2 Sam. ii. 23 ; xxiii. 8 ; bow and arrow [ARCHERY] ; sling, 2 Kgs. iii. 25 ; battle-axe, Jer. li. 20. Among defensive armor were breastplates, cuirasses, coats of mail, helmets, greaves, habergeons, shields, bucklers, 1 Sam. xvii. 5–7 ; 2 Chr. xxvi. 14.

Ăr'my. Hebrew males twenty years old and upward subject to military duty, Num. i. 2, 3. Tribes formed army divisions. Numerated by hundreds and thousands, each with captains, Num. xxxi. 14. Kings had body-guards, 1 Sam. xiii. 2 ; xxv. 13. Later, a standing army formed, 2 Chr. xxv. 6. No cavalry till Solomon's time. War declared and exempts used as in Deut. xx. 1–14 ; xxiv. 5. In N. T. Roman army composed of legions, with chief captains, Acts xxi. 31 ; tents of legions, or cohorts, and bands, Acts x. 1 ; mæniples, or thirds of legions ; centuries, 100 men each and two to a maniple. Captain of a 100 called a Centurion, Matt. viii. 5 ; xxvii.

54.

Är'na. A forefather of Ezra, 2 Esdr. i. 2.

Är'nan. Head of a returned family, 1 Chr. iii. 21.

Är'nŏn (*noisy*). A stream emptying into Dead Sea from the East, and boundary between the Amorites and Moabites, Num. xxi. 13 ; Judg. xi. 18. Afterwards between Moab and Israel, Deut. ii. 24 ; Josh. xii. 1 ; xiii. 9 ; Judg. xi. 13.

Ā'rŏd (*wild ass*). Gadite founder of the **Ā'rŏd-ītes**, Num. xxvi. 17. Called **Ăr'ŏ-dī** in Gen. xlvi. 16.

Ā'rŏd-ītes. [AROD.]

Ăr'ŏ-ër (*ruins*). (1) A Reubenite city on the Arnon, Deut. ii. 36 ; Josh. xii. 1, 2 ; Judg. xi. 26. Later fell back to Moab, Jer. xlviii. 19, 20. (2) A town of Gad, Num. xxxii. 34 ; Josh. xiii. 25 ; 2 Sam. xxiv. 5. (3) An unidentified place, Isa. xvii. 2. (4) A town in South Judah, 1 Sam. xxx. 28.

Ăr'ŏ-ër-īte''. Designation of Hothan, 1 Chr. xi. 44.

A'rom. A returned family, 1 Esdr. v. 16.

Ăr'pad or **Ăr'phad** (*strong*). A city, or district, in Syria, dependent on Damascus, Isa. xxxvi. 19 ; xxxvii. 13 ; Jer. xlix. 23 ; 2 Kgs. xviii. 34 ; xix. 13.

Ăr-phax'ăd (*Chaldean fortress*). (1) A son of Shem, Gen. x. 22, 24 ; xi. 10–13 ; 1 Chr. i. 17, 18, 24. (2) A king of the Medes, Judith i. 1–4.

Ăr'rows. [ARMS.]

Ăr''tăx-ĕrx'eṣ (*brave warrior*). (1) A Persian king who stopped the rebuilding of the temple at Jerusalem, Ez. iv. 7, 23, 24. (2) Another Persian king, friendly to Nehemiah, Neh. ii. 1.

Ăr'tẹ-mȧs (*gift of Artemis*). A friend of Paul, Tit. iii. 12.

Är-tĭl'lĕ-ry. The missile equipment of a Jewish soldier, lance, arrows, etc., 1 Sam. xx. 40. [ARMS.]

Ärts. The tricks of magic and astrology, Acts xix. 19. [ASTROLOGERS.]

Ăr'ụ-bŏth (*windows*). The third commissary district of King Solomon, 1 Kgs. iv. 10.

Ā-rụ'-mah (*height*). Residence of Abimelech, near Shechem, Judg. ix. 41.

Ăr'văd (*wandering*). An island, now Ruad, lying three miles off Tyre, Ezek. xxvii. 8–11.

Ăr'vad-īte. A native of Arvad, Gen. x. 18 ; 1 Chr. i. 16.

Ăr'zȧ. Keeper of King Elah's palace at Tirzah, 1 Kgs. xvi. 9.

Ā'sȧ (*physician*). (1) Third king of Judah, 1 Kgs. xv. 8–34 ; reigned B. C. 955–914 ; abolished idolatry ; battled victoriously with Ethiopia, 2 Chr. xiv. ; involved with Israel ; buried with pomp, 2 Chr. xvi. (2) A Levite, 1 Chr. ix. 16.

Ăs''ā-dī'as. An ancestor of Baruch, Bar. i. 1.

Ăs'ā-el. An ancestor of Tobit, Tob. i. 1.

Ā'sȧ-hĕl (*creature of God*). (1) The fleet-footed nephew of David, killed by Abner, 2 Sam. ii. 18–23. (2) A Levitical legal instructor, 2 Chr. xvii. 8. (3) A Levite and tithing-man, 2 Chr. xxxi. 13. (4) A priest, Ez. x. 15.

Ā''sa-hī'ah (*the Lord made*). A learned servant of King Josiah, 2 Kgs. xxii. 12–14. Asaiah in 2 Chr. xxxiv. 20.

Ā''sa-ī'ah (*whom the Lord made*). (1) Prince of a Simeonite family, 1 Chr. iv. 36. (2) A Levite chief, 1 Chr. vi. 30 ; xv. 6–11. (3) A Shilonite, 1 Chr. ix. 5. Maaseiah in Neh. xi. 5. (4) Asaiah, 2 Chr. xxxiv. 20.

Ăs'ạ-nȧ, 1 Esdr. v. 31. [ASNAH.]

Ā'saph (*gatherer*). (1) Levitical leader of David's choir, 1 Chr. vi. 39 ; 2 Chr. xxix. 30 ; Neh. xii. 46. Twelve of the Psalms are attributed to him, to wit, Ps. l. and lxxiii. to lxxxiii. (2) Ancestor of Joah the chronicler, 2 Kgs. xviii. 18 ; Isa. xxxvi. 3, 22. (3

Keeper of royal forests under Artaxerxes, Neh. ii. 8. (4) Another conductor of the Temple choir, 1 Chr. ix. 15; Neh. xi. 17.

Ā'saph, Sons of. A school of poets and musicians founded by Asaph.

Ă-sā'rĕ-el (*oath bound*). A descendant of Judah, 1 Chr. iv. 16.

Ăs''ă-rē'lah (*upright*). A minstrel prophet under David, 1 Chr. xxv. 2. Jesharelah in vs. 14.

Ăs'ca-lŏn. [ASHKELON.]

Ăs-çen'sion, see CHRIST.

Ăs'ē-năth (*devotee of Neith*, the Egyptian Minerva), Egyptian wife of Joseph, Gen. xli. 45-50; xlvi. 20.

Ă'sēr, Luke ii. 36; Rev. vii. 6. [ASHER.]

Ăsh. Ash was not indigenous to Palestine; perhaps pine or cedar is meant, Isa. xliv. 14.

Ă'shan (*smoke*). A city in Judah, Josh. xv. 42; and Simeon, Josh. xix. 7; 1 Chr. iv. 32.

Ăsh-bē'à (*I adjure*). A doubtful genealogical name, 1 Chr. iv. 21.

Ăsh'bel (*reproof*). Second son of Benjamin, Gen. xlvi. 21; Num. xxvi. 38; 1 Chr. viii. 1.

Ăsh'chĕ-naz. 1 Chr. i. 6; Jer. li. 27. [ASHKENAZ.]

Ăsh'dŏd or **Ăz-ō'tus** (*stronghold*). A Philistine city between Gaza and Joppa; assigned to Judah, Josh. xv. 47; 1 Sam. v. 1. Azotus, Acts viii. 40.

Ăsh'dŏd-ītes''. Dwellers in Ashdod, Neh. iv. 7.

Ăsh'dŏth-ītes. Dwellers in Ashdod, Josh. xiii. 3.

Ăsh'dŏth=pĭṣ'gah (*Springs of Pisgah*). Probably the "slopes of Pisgah," to the east, Deut. iii. 17; iv. 49; Josh. xii. 3; xiii. 20.

Ăsh'ēr (*happiness*). (1) Eighth son of Jacob, Gen. xxx. 13. Aser in Apochrypha and N. T. For boundaries of his allotment *see* Josh. xix. 24-31; xvii. 10, 11; Judg. i. 31, 32. (2) A boundary town of Manasseh, Josh. xvii. 7.

Ăsh'ĕ-rah (*straight*). [ASHTAROTH.]

Ăsh'ĕr-ītes. Members of the tribe of Asher. Judg. i. 32.

Ăsh'es. To sprinkle with or sit in ashes, marked humiliation, grief, and penitence, Gen. xviii. 27; 2 Sam. xiii. 19; Esth. iv. 3; Job ii. 8; Jer. vi. 26; Lam. iii. 16; Matt. xi. 21. The altar ashes, when a red heifer was sacrificed, were watered and used for purifying the unclean, Num. xix. 17-22.

Ăsh'ĭ-mà (*offence*). A Syrian god worshipped in Samaria, 2 Kgs. xvii. 30.

Ăsh'kĕ-lŏn, Ăs'kĕ-lŏn (*migration*). A Philistine city and seaport on the Mediterranean, 10 miles N. of Gaza, Josh. (Eshkalon) xiii. 3; Judg. (Askelon) i. 18; Judg. (Ashkelon) xiv. 19; 1 Sam. vi. 17. Its destruction predicted in Jer. xlvii. 5-7; Am. i. 8; Zech. ix. 5; Zeph. ii. 7.

Ăsh'kĕ-năz (*fire that spreads*). A grandson of Japhet, Gen. x. 3. Ashchenaz in 1 Chr. i. 6; Jer. li. 27.

Ăsh'nah (*change*). Two towns of Judah, one N. W. the other S. W. of Jerusalem, 16 miles distant, Josh. xv. 33, 43.

Ăsh'pĕ-naz (*horse-nose*). Master of eunuchs under Nebuchadnezzar, Dan. i. 3.

Ăsh'rĭ-el, 1 Chr. vii. 14. [ASRIEL.]

Ăsh'ta-rŏth and **Ăs'ta-rŏth** (*star*). A city of Bashan, noted for its worship of Ashtoreth, Deut. i. 4; Josh. ix. 10; xii. 4; xiii. 12.

Ăsh'tĕ-răth-īte''. An inhabitant of Ashtaroth, 1 Chr. xi. 44.

Ăsh'tĕ-rŏth Kär-nā'im (*Ashteroth of two peaks*). A city of the giant Rephaim in Bashan, Gen. xiv. 5.

Ăsh'tŏ-rĕth (*star*). The principal female deity of the Phœnicians; the Ishtar of the Assyrians, and

Astarte of the Greeks and Romans. Solomon introduced her worship into his kingdom, Judg. ii. 13; 1 Kgs. xi. 5, 33; 2 Kgs. xxiii. 13.

Ăsh'ŭr (*black*). Founder of Tekoa, 1 Chr. ii. 24; iv. 5.

Ăsh'ŭr-ītes. Asherites, 2 Sam. ii. 9.

Ăsh'vath. A son of Japhlet, 1 Chr. vii. 33.

Ā'ṣĭà (*eastern*). Only in N. T., and then with reference to Asia Minor, or even to western Asia Minor, with the capital at Ephesus, Acts ii. 9; vi. 9; xvi. 6; 1 Cor. xvi. 19.

Ā'ṣĭà-arch (*-ark*). Chief of the religious rites and public games of the Roman province of Asia, Acts xix. 31.

Ăs''ĭ-bī'as, 1 Esdr. ix. 26. [MALCHIJAH.]

Ā-sĭ-el (*made by God*). (1) A progenitor of Jehu, 1 Chr. iv. 35. (2) A scribe under Esdras, 2 Esdr. xiv. 24.

Ăs'kĕ-lŏn. [ASHKELON.]

Ăs''mō-dē'us. An evil spirit, classed with Abaddon and Apollyon, Tob. iii. 8-17.

Ăs'nah (*thorn-bush*). Father of a returned family, Ez. ii. 50.

Ăs-năp'pēr (*swift*). Leader of Cuthæan colonists into Samaria, Ez. iv. 10.

Ăsp (*viper*). The hooded venomous serpent known as the African cobra. Adder in Ps. lviii. 4; xci. 13, answers the description of asp, Deut. xxxii. 33; Job xx. 14-16; Isa. xi. 8; Rom. iii. 13.

Ăs-pal'ā-thus. A perfume, or ointment, product of Rhodian wood, Ecclus. xxiv. 15.

Ăs'pă-thà. Third son of Haman, Esth. ix. 7.

Ăs'phar. A pool in the wilderness of Thecoe, 1 Macc. ix. 33.

Ăs'rĭ-el (*help of God*). Founder of the Asrielites, Num. xxvi. 31; Josh. xvii. 2; Ashriel, 1 Chr. vii. 14.

Ăss. Five different Hebrew words give it name in the Bible. A patient beast of burden, and palfrey for even kings, Gen. xxii. 3; xii. 16; xxxvi. 24; 1 Chr. xxvii. 30; Job i. 3; Zech. ix. 9, which last is the prophecy of Christ's entry into Jerusalem, Matt. xxi. 1-9.

Ăs'shur. Second son of Shem, Gen. x. 22. Also Hebrew form for Assyria, Ezek. xxvii. 23.

Ăs-shu'rim (*steps*). A tribe descended from Abraham, Gen. xxv. 3.

Ăs''ṣĭ-dē'ans (*pious*). A sect of orthodox Jews, bound to the external observance of the law, 1 Macc. ii. 42.

Ăs'sĭr (*prisoner*). (1) A Levite, Ex. vi. 24; 1 Chr. vi. 22. (2) A forefather of Samuel, 1 Chr. vi. 23, 37. (3) Son of Jeconiah, 1 Chr. iii. 17.

Ăs'sŏs or **Ăs'sus** (*approaching*). A Roman seaport on northern shore of Gulf of Adramyttium, Acts xx. 13, 14.

Ăs'sur, Ez. iv. 2; Ps. lxxxiii. 8. [ASSHUR; ASSYRIA.]

Ăs-ṣy̆r'ĭ-à (*country of Asshur*). That ancient empire on the Tigris whose capital was Nineveh, Gen. ii. 14; x. 11-22. In its splendor it embraced Susiana, Chaldea, Babylon, Media, Armenia, Assyria proper, Mesopotamia, Syria, Phœnicia, Palestine, and Idumea. Assyrian kings frequently invaded Israel, 2 Kgs. xv. 19; xvi. 7-9; xv. 29; 2 Chr. xxviii. 20. Shalmaneser destroyed Samaria, B. C. 721, and carried the people captive. Assyria was overthrown by the Medes and Babylonians, 625 B. C., after an existence of 1200 years.

Ăs'ta-rŏth, Deut. i. 4. [ASHTAROTH.]

Ăs-tär'te. [ASHTORETH.]

Ā-sty̆'ă-gēs. Last king of the Medes, B. C. 500. Bel and Drag. 1.

Ā-sŭp'pim, House of (*gatherings*). Probably store-rooms in the Temple, 1 Chr. xxvi. 15, 17. "Thresholds" in Neh. xii. 25.

Ā-sy̆n'crĭ-tus (*incomparable*). A Christian

friend of Paul, at Rome, Rom. xvi. 14.

Ā'tad, THRESHING FLOOR OF. Name changed to Abel-mizraim, which see, Gen. l. 10, 11.

Ăt'ạ-rah (crown). Mother of Onam, 1 Chr. ii. 26.

Ā-tăr'gạ-tis (opening). A Syrian goddess with a woman's body and fish's tail, 2 Macc. xii. 26.

Ăt'ạ-rŏth (crowns). (1) A town of Gilead, Num. xxxii. 3, 34. (2) A place on the southern boundary of Ephraim, Josh. xvi. 2, 7. (3) Perhaps same as above, 1 Chr. ii. 54.

Ā'tĕr (shut up). Heads of two different returned families, Ez. ii. 42; Neh. vii. 21.

Ā'thăch (stopping place). A town in southern Judah, 1 Sam. xxx. 30.

Ăth''ạ-ī'ah (whom God made). A descendant of Pharez, Neh. xi. 4. Uthai in 1 Chr. ix. 4.

Ăth''ạ-lī'ah (afflicted by God). (1) Wicked wife of Jehoram, king of Judah, who introduced the worship of Baal and was slain by her own guards, 2 Kgs. xi.; 2 Chr. xxii.–xxiv. (2) A Benjamite, 1 Chr. viii. 26. (3) Head of a returned Jewish family, Ez. viii. 7.

Ā-thē'nĭ-ạns. Inhabitants of Athens, Acts xvii. 21.

Ath''ĕ-nō'bĭ-us. An envoy of King Antiochus, 1 Macc. xv. 28.

Ăth'ĕns (city of Athena, or Minerva). Capital of Attica and chief seat of Grecian learning and civilization. Situate in S. E. part of the Grecian Peninsula, five miles from its seaport, the Piræus. Paul preached on its Areopagus or Mars' Hill, Acts xvii. 19–22, and founded a church there.

Ăth'lāī (whom God afflicts). A son of Bebai, Ez. x. 28.

Ā-tōne'mĕnt (reconciliation). The expiation of sin and propitiation of God by the incarnation, life, suffering, and death of Christ. Day of Atonement, an annual day of Hebrew fasting and humiliation, Ex. xxx. 16; Lev. xvi.; xxiii. 27–32.

Ăt'rŏth (crowns). A city of Gad, Num. xxxii. 35.

Ăt'tāi (ready). (1) A grandson of Sheshan, 1 Chr. ii. 35, 36. (2) A lion-faced warrior of Gad, 1 Chr. xii. 11. (3) A son of King Rehoboam, 2 Chr. xi. 20.

Ăt-tā'lĭ-à. A coast town of Pamphylia, Acts xiv. 25.

Ăt'tạ-lus (increased). Names of three kings of Pergamos, 1 Macc. xv. 22.

Ạu-gŭs'tus (venerable). Caius Julius Cæsar Octavianus, grand-nephew of, and heir to, Julius Cæsar. Made first emperor of Rome B. C. 27, with title of Augustus. During his reign Christ was born, Luke ii. 1. Died A. D. 14, aged 76 years.

Ạu-gŭs'tus' Band, Acts xxvii. 1. [ARMY.]

Ạu-rā'nus. A riotous fellow at Jerusalem, 2 Macc. iv. 40.

Ā'vạ (ruin). A place in Assyria, 2 Kgs. xvii. 24.

Ăv'ạ-răn. Surname of Eleazer, 1 Macc. ii. 5.

Ā'ven (nothingness). (1) An unidentified plain, Amos i. 5. (2) Beth-aven, or Bethel, Hosea x. 8. (3) Heliopolis or city of On, Ezek. xxx. 17.

Ā-vĕnge', **Ā-vĕn'ger.** Exaction of just satisfaction, Luke xviii. 8; 1 Thess. iv. 6. "Avenger of Blood" was the pursuer of a slayer to avenge the blood of the slain. He must be a relative of the dead one, Deut. xix. 6.

Ā'vĭm, Ā'vĭms, Ā'vĭtes (ruins). (1) A primitive people who pushed into Palestine from the desert of Arabia, Deut. ii. 23. (2) Colonists from Ava sent to people Israel, 2 Kgs. xvii. 31.

Ā'vĭth (ruins). The king's city of Edom, Gen. xxxvi. 35; 1 Chr. i. 46.

Ạwl. Shape not known, but use expressed in Ex. xxi. 6; Deut. xv. 17.

Ăxe. Seven Hebrew words so translated. It

was of stone or iron, crudely fastened to a handle of wood, Deut. xix. 5; 2 Kgs. vi. 5–7.

Ā'zăl. Probably a common noun, Zech. xiv. 5.

Ăz''ạ-lī'ah (near Jehovah). Father of Shaphan the scribe, 2 Kgs. xxii. 3.

Ăz''ạ-nī'ah (whom God hears). Father of Jeshua, Neh. x. 9.

Ā-zā'phĭ-on. Probably Sophereth, 1 Esdr. v. 33.

Ăz'ạ-rà. A servant of the temple, 1 Esdr. v. 35.

Ā-zăr'ạ-el (whom God helps). A Levite musician, Neh. xii. 36.

Ā-zăr'ę-el (whom God helps). (1) A companion of David at Ziklag, 1 Chr. xii. 6. (2) A Levite musician, 1 Chr. xxv. 18. (3) A prince of Dan, 1 Chr. xxvii. 22. (4) Son of Bani, Ezra x. 41. (5) A priest, Neh. xi. 13.

Ăz''ạ-rī'ah (whom God helps). (1) Grandson of Zadok, 1 Kgs. iv. 2; 1 Chr. vi. 9. (2) A chief officer under Solomon, 1 Kgs. iv. 5. (3) Tenth king of Judah, commonly called Uzziah, 2 Kgs. xiv. 21; xv. 1–27; 1 Chr. iii. 12. (4) A son of Ethan, 1 Chr. ii. 8. (5) A son of Jehu, 1 Chr. ii. 38, 39. (6) A high priest under Abijah and Asa, 1 Chr. vi. 10. (7) A wrongly inserted name, 1 Chr. vi. 13. (8) An ancestor of Samuel, vi. 36. (9) A prophet in Asa's reign, 2 Chr. xv. 1. (10) Son of King Jehoshaphat, 2 Chr. xxi. 2. (11) Another son of Jehoshaphat, 2 Chr. xxi. 2. (12) For Ahaziah, 2 Chr. xxii. 6. (13) A captain of Judah, 2 Chr. xxiii. 1. (14) High priest in reign of Uzziah, 2 Chr. xxvi. 17–20. (15) A captain of Ephraim in reign of Ahaz, 2 Chr. xxviii. 12. (16) A Levite, 2 Chr. xxix. 12. (17) Another Levite, 2 Chr. xxix. 12. (18) High priest in time of Hezekiah, 2 Chr. xxxi. 10–13. (19) One who helped to rebuild the walls of Jerusalem, Neh. iii. 23, 24. (20) Leader of a returned family, Neh. vii. 7. (21) A Levite who helped Ezra, Neh. viii. 7. (22) A co-covenanter with Nehemiah, Neh. x. 2. (23) Jer. xliii. 2, for Jezaniah. (24) Hebrew name of Abed-nego, Dan. i. 6.

Ăz''ạ-rī'as. A frequent name in Esdras.

Ā'zaz (strong). A Reubenite, 1 Chr. v. 8.

Ăz''ạ-zī'ah (whom God strengthens). (1) A Levite musician, 1 Chr. xv. 21. (2) A chief of Ephraim, 1 Chr. xxvii. 20. (3) Custodian of tithes and offerings under Hezekiah, 2 Chr. xxxi. 13.

Ăz-băz'ạ-rĕth. Probably Esarhaddon, 1 Esdr. v. 69.

Ăz'bŭk (devastation). Father of Nehemiah, Neh. iii. 16.

Ā-zē'kah (dug over). A town of Judah, Josh. x. 10, 11.

Ā'zel (noble). A descendant of Saul, 1 Chr. viii. 37, 38; ix. 43, 44.

Ā'zem (bone) A city of Judah and Simeon, Josh. xv. 29; xix. 3. EZEM, elsewhere.

Ā-zē'tas. A returned Hebrew family, 1 Esdr. v. 15.

Ăz'gad (strength of fortune). (1) Head of a large returned family, Ez. ii. 12; viii. 12; Neh. vii. 17. (2) A co-covenanter with Nehemiah, Neh. x. 15.

Ā'zĭ-el (whom God comforts). A Levite, 1 Chr. xv. 20; Jaaziel in vs. 18.

Ā-zī'zạ (strong). A returned captive, Ez. x. 27.

Ăz'mạ-vĕth (strong unto death). (1) One of David's mighty men, 2 Sam. xxiii. 31; 1 Chr. xi. 33. (2) A descendant of Mephibosheth, 1 Chr. viii. 36; ix. 42. (3) A Benjamite, 1 Chr. xii. 3. (4) David's treasurer, 1 Chr. xxvii. 25. (5) A place in Benjamin, Ez. ii. 24; Neh. xii. 29. The Beth-azmaveth of Neh. vii. 28.

Ăz'mŏn (strong). A place in southern Palestine, Num. xxxiv. 4, 5; Josh. xv. 4.

Ăz'nŏth=tā'bŏr (summits of Tabor). A boundary of Naphtali, Josh. xix. 34.

Ā'zŏr (helper). One of Christ's ancestors, Matt. i. 13, 14.

Ȧ-zō'tus. Greek form of Ashdod in Acts viii. 40. [ASHDOD.]

Ăz'rĭ-el (*help of God*). (1) Head of Manassite family, 1 Chr. v. 24. (2) A Naphtalite, 1 Chr. xxvii. 19. (3) Father of Seraiah, Jer. xxxvi. 26.

Ăz'rĭ-kam (*avenging help*). (1) A descendant of Zerubbabel, 1 Chr. iii. 23. (2) A descendant of Saul, 1 Chr. viii. 38; ix. 44. (3) A Levite, 1 Chr. ix. 14; Neh. xi. 15. (4) Prefect of King Ahaz's palace, 2 Chr. xxviii. 7.

Ȧ-zū'bah (*forsaken*). (1) Wife of Caleb, 1 Chr. ii. 18, 19. (2) Mother of Jehoshaphat, 1 Kgs. xxii. 42; 2 Chr. xx. 31.

Ā'zur (*helper*). (1) Father of the false prophet Hananiah, Jer. xxviii. 1. (2) Father of one of the princes against whom Ezekiel prophesied, Ezek. xi. 1.

Ăz'zah (*strong*). In Deut. ii. 23; 1 Kgs. iv. 24; Jer. xxv. 20, for GAZA.

Ăz'zan (*very strong*). A chief of Issachar, Num. xxxiv. 26.

Ăz'zur (*helper*). A co-covenanter with Nehemiah, Neh. x. 17. Azur, elsewhere.

B

Bā'al (*lord*). (1) Baal, Bel, or Belus, supreme male god of Phœnicians and Canaanites, worshipped with self-torture and human offerings, Jer. xix. 5. Even house-tops were temples, 2 Kgs. xxiii. 12, Jer. xxxii. 29. Hebrews infected with the worship, Num. xxii. 41; xxv. 3-18; Deut. iv. 16. Became the court religion, 1 Kgs. xvi. 31-33. xviii. 19-28; 2 Kgs. x. 22; xvii. 16. Bel in Isa. xlvi. 1. Baalim, plural form, in Judg. ii. 11; x. 10, and elsewhere. (2) A Reubenite, 1 Chr. v. 5. (3) Grandson of Saul, 1 Chr. viii. 30; ix. 36. (4) A town of Simeon; Bealoth and Baalath-beer, 1 Chr. iv. 33.

Bā'al-ah (*mistress*). (1) For Kirjath-jearim in Josh. xv. 9, 10; Baale, 2 Sam. vi. 2; Kirjath-baal, Josh. xv. 60; xviii. 14. (2) A town in south Judah, Josh. xv. 29. Balah in Josh. xix. 3; and Bilhah in 1 Chr. iv. 29.

Bā'al-ath (*mistress*). A town in Dan, Josh. xix. 44; 1 Kgs. ix. 18; 2 Chr. viii. 6.

Bā'al-ath=bē'ẽr (*lord of the well*). [BAAL.] (4) [BEALOTH.]

Bā'al=bē'rith (*Baal of the covenant*). Form of Baal worshipped by the Shechemites, Judg. viii. 33; ix. 4.

Bā'ă-lē of Jū'dah. Name for Kirjath-jearim. [BAALAH.]

Bā'al=gad (*troop of Baal*). Northern limit of Joshua's conquest, Josh. xi. 17; xii. 7; xiii. 5.

Bā'al=hā'mŏn (*lord of a multitude*). Solomon had a vineyard there, S. of Sol. viii. 11.

Bā'al=hā'nan (*lord of Hanan*). (1) A king of Edom, Gen. xxxvi. 38, 39; 1 Chr. i. 49, 50. (2) Superintendent of David's groves, 1 Chr. xxvii. 28.

Bā'al=hā'zôr (*village of Baal*). The shearing-place where Absalom killed Amnon, 2 Sam. xiii. 23.

Bā'al=hẽr'mŏn (*lord of Hermon*). A peak of Hermon, Judg. iii. 3; 1 Chr. v. 23.

Bā'al-ī (*my lord*). My idol! A repudiated word of endearment, Hos. ii. 16.

Bā'al-ĭm. [BAAL.]

Bā'ă-līs (*son of exultation*). A king of the Ammonites, Jer. xl. 14.

Bā'al=mē'on (*lord of the house*). A Reubenite town, Num. xxxii. 38; 1 Chr. v. 8; Ezek. xxv. 9.

Bā'al=pē'or (*lord of the opening*). The form of Baal worship in Peor, Num. xxv. 3-5, 18. Israelites shared in it, Deut. iv. 3; Josh. xxii. 17; Ps. cvi. 28; Hos. ix. 10.

Bā'al=pẽr'ă-zĭm (*lord of divisions*). Scene of David's victory over the Philistines, 2 Sam. v. 20;

1 Chr. xiv. 11. Mount Perazim in Isa. xxviii. 21.

Bā'al=shal'ĭ-shȧ. An unknown place, 2 Kgs. iv. 42.

Bā'al=tā'mär (*lord of palms*). A place in Benjamin, Judg. xx. 33.

Bā'al=zē'bŭb (*god of the fly*). The form of Baal worshipped at Ekron, 2 Kgs. i. 16.

Bā'al=zē'phon (*lord of the north*). A place on western coast of Red Sea near where the Israelites crossed, Ex. xiv. 2; Num. xxxiii. 7.

Bā'ȧ-nȧ (*son of affliction*). (1) Son of Solomon's commissary in Jezreel, 1 Kgs. iv. 12. (2) Father of Zadok, Neh. iii. 4.

Bā'ȧ-nah (*son of affliction*). (1) Co-murderer of Ish-bosheth, killed by David, 2 Sam. iv. 2-9. (2) Father of one of David's mighty men, 2 Sam. xxiii. 29; 1 Chr. xi. 30. (3) 1 Kgs. iv. 16; Baana in vs. 12. (4) One of the returned, Ez. ii. 2; Neh. vii. 7.

Bā'ȧ-räh (*brutish*). Wife of Shaharaim, 1 Chr. viii. 8.

Bā''ȧ-sē'ĭah (*work of Jehovah*). A Levite, 1 Chr. vi. 40.

Bā'ȧ-shȧ (*bravery*). Third king of Israel, 1 Kgs. xv. 27-34; xvi. Warred continually with King Asa, 1 Kgs. xv. 33, and ruled wickedly for 24 years, B. C. 953 to 931. Family cut off according to prophecy, 1 Kgs. xvi. 3-11.

Bā'bel (*confusion*). One of Nimrod's cities in the plain of Shinar, Gen. x. 10. [BABYLON.]

Bā'bel, Tower of. That brick structure, built in the plain of Shinar, and intended to prevent the very confusion and dispersion it brought about, Gen. xi. 4-9.

Băb''ў-lon (*Greek form of Babel*). Capital city Babylonian empires. Situate on both sides of the Euphrates, 200 miles above its junction with the Tigris, Gen. x. 10; xi. 4-9; Jer. li. 58; Isa. xlv. 1-3. Once the capital of Assyria, 2 Chr. xxxiii. 11. Reached height of its splendor and strength under Nebuchadnezzar, Isa. xiii. 19; xiv. 4; xlvii. 5; Jer. li. 41. Chief home of the captive Jews. Captured by Cyrus the Persian, through his leader Darius, B. C. 539, as prophesied in Jer. li. 31, 39, and narrated in Dan. v. Its decay dates from that date. The Babylon of 1 Pet. v. 13 is conjectural. In Rev. xiv. 8; xvii. 18, Babylon types the power of Rome.

Băb''ў-lō'nĭ-ans. Inhabitants of Babylon, Ez. iv. 9.

Băb''ў-lō'nish Gär'mĕnt (*robe of Shinar*). A richly embroidered robe worn in Babylon and prized by other peoples, Josh. vii. 21.

Bā'cȧ (*weeping*). Perhaps a figurative "valley;" but if real, probably Gehenna, Ps. lxxxiv. 6.

Băc'chĭ-dēs. A noted Syrian general, 1 Macc. vii. 8.

Băc-chū'rus. One of the "holy singers," 1 Esdr. ix. 24.

Băc'chus. [DIONYSUS.]

Bā-çē'nor. A Jewish captain, 2 Macc. xii. 35.

Băch'rites. Becherites, Num. xxvi. 35.

Bădg'ers' Skins (*striped skins*). The badger not found in Palestine. Seal, porpoise, or sheep skins may be meant, Ex. xxv. 5; xxxv. 7.

Băg (*swelling*). The bag of 2 Kgs. v. 23; xii. 10, was for holding money; that of Deut. xxv. 13-15 for carrying weights. Sack was the Hebrew grain-bag, Gen. xlii. 25. The shepherd's bag was for carrying feeble lambs, Zech. xi. 15-17. The bag of Judas was probably a small chest, John xii. 6; xiii. 29.

Bā-gō'as (*eunuch*). An attendant of Holofernes, Judith xii. 1-3.

Bā-hū'rim (*low grounds*). A village between the Jordan and Jerusalem, 2 Sam. iii. 16; xvi. 5; xvii. 18; 1 Kgs. ii. 8.

Bā'jith (*house*). Temple of the gods of Moab,

Isa. xv. 2.

Băk-băk′kar (*pleasing*). A descendant of Asaph, 1 Chr. ix. 15.

Băk′bŭk (*bottle*). His children returned, Ez. ii. 51.

Băk″bŭk-ī′ah (*destruction by Jehovah*). A Levite porter, Neh. xi. 17; xii. 9, 25.

Bāke. Baking done at home and by the women, Lev. xxvi. 26; 1 Sam. viii. 13; 2 Sam. xiii. 8; Jer. vii. 18. Perhaps public bakeries in Hos. vii. 4–7.

Bā′laam (*glutton*). Son of Beor, or Bosor, Deut. xxiii. 4. A man of note and given to prophecy. Slain in battle by the Hebrews, Num. xxii.–xxiv., xxxi.; Rev. ii. 14.

Bā′lăc, Rev. ii. 14. [BALAK.]

Băl′a-dăn. [MERODACH-BALADAN.]

Bā′lah, Josh. xix. 3. Short form of Baalah.

Bā′lăk (*destroyer*). The king of Moab who hired Balaam to curse Israel, Num. xxii.–xxiv.; Josh. xxiv. 9; Judg. xi. 25. Balac in Rev. ii. 14.

Băl′ăn-çes (*two scales*). Were in general use among the ancients for weighing gold and silver, and in traffic, Lev. xix. 36; Mic. vi. 11; Hos. xii. 7.

Băld′ness (*ball-like*). Priests forbidden to make themselves bald, Lev. xxi. 5; Deut. xiv. 1; Ezek. xliv. 20. " Bald-head " a cry of contempt, 2 Kgs. ii. 23; as indicating leprosy, Lev. xiii. 40–43. Voluntary baldness a sign of misery, Isa. iii. 24; Ezek. vii. 18; or else the conclusion of the Nazarite vow, Num. vi. 9.

Bălm (*balsam*). The Balm of Gilead, or Mecca balsam, exudes an agreeable balsamic resin, highly prized in the East as an unguent and cosmetic, as the crushed leaves were for their odor, Gen. xxxvii. 25; xliii. 11; Jer. viii. 22; xlvi. 11; Ezek. xxvii. 17.

Băl-thā′sar, Bar. i. 11, 12. [BELSHAZZAR.]

Bā′mah (*high place*). Applied to places of idolatrous worship, Ezek. xx. 29.

Bā′mŏth, Num. xxi. 19. [BAMOTH-BAAL.]

Bā′mŏth=bā′al (*heights of Baal*). A sanctuary of Baal in Moab, Josh. xiii. 17. Bamoth in Num. xxi. 19.

Band. Tenth part of a Roman legion; called also " cohort," Matt. xxvii. 27; Acts xxi. 31.

Bā′nī (*built*). (1) One of David's captains, 2 Sam. xxiii. 36. (2) A forefather of Ethan, 1 Chr. vi. 46. (3) A Judahite, 1 Chr. ix. 4. (4) " Children of Bani " returned, Ez. ii. 10; x. 29–34; Neh. x. 14. (5) A son of Bani, Ez. x. 38. (6) Three others, Levites, Neh. iii. 17; viii. 7; xi. 22.

Băn′ner. [ENSIGN.]

Băn′quet (*sitting*). A favorite part of social enjoyment and religious festivity among Hebrews. The posture was usually sitting, Gen. xxi. 8; xl. 20. Morning banquets a mark of excess, Eccles. x. 16; Isa. v. 11. Banquet incidents were foods, wines, flowers, fine robes, music vocal and instrumental, dancing, jests, riddles and merriment, Prov. ix. 2; 2 Sam. xix. 35; Neh. viii. 10; Eccl. x. 19; Isa. v. 12; xxv. 6; Matt. xxii. 11; Luke xv. 25. [FEASTS.]

Băp′tism (*dipping, bathing*). The sacrament ordinance or rite commanded by Christ, Matt. xxviii. 19, in which water is used to initiate the recipient into the Christian Church. Christ did not baptize, John iv. 2. John's baptism with water, Christ's " with the Holy Ghost and with fire," Matt. iii. 1–12; Luke iii. 16. Jesus baptized by John, Matt. iii. 13–17. Outpouring of the Holy Spirit, Acts ii. John's baptized persons re-baptized, Acts xix. 1–6; xviii. 25, 26.

Bă-răb′bas (*son of Abba*). The prisoner at Jerusalem when Christ was condemned, Matt. xxvii. 16–28; Mark xv. 7; Luke xxiii. 18; John xviii. 40.

Băr′a-chel (*blessed of God*). Father of Elihu, Job xxxii. 2–6.

Băr″a-chī′as, Matt. xxiii. 35. [ZECHARIAS.]

Bā′rak (*lightning*). A Hebrew chieftain, Judg. iv.

Bär-bā′rĭ-an (*bearded*). In N. T. sense one not a Greek, Acts xxviii. 2; Rom. i. 14; 1 Cor. xiv. 11.

Bär-hū′mīte, 2 Sam. xxiii. 31; of BAHURIM.

Bā-rī′ah (*fugitive*). Son of Shemaiah, 1 Chr. iii. 22.

Bär″=jē′ṣus (*son of Jesus*), Acts xiii. 6. [ELYMAS.]

Bär″=jō′nà (*son of Jonah*), Matt. xvi. 17. [PETER.]

Bär′kŏs (*painter*). " Children of Barkos " returned, Ez. ii. 53; Neh. vii. 55.

Bär′lêy. Much cultivated by the Hebrews, Ex. ix. 31; Lev. xxvii. 16; Deut. viii. 8; Ruth ii. 7. Used for bread chiefly among the poor, Judg. vii. 13; 2 Kgs. iv. 42; John vi. 9–13; and for fodder, 1 Kgs. iv. 28. Barley harvest preceded wheat harvest, Ruth i. 22; ii. 23; 2 Sam xxi. 9, 10

Bär′na-băs (*son of comfort*). Joseph or Joses, a convert of Cyprus, and companion of Paul, Acts iv. 36; ix. 27; xi. 25, 26; xv. 22–39.

Bā-rō′dis. Servant of Solomon, 1 Esdr. v. 34.

Bär′sa-băs. [JOSEPH, JUDAS.]

Bär′ta-cŭs. Soldier of Darius, 1 Esdr. iv. 29.

Bär-thŏl′ŏ-mew (*son of Tolmai*). One of the twelve apostles, Matt. x. 3; Mark iii. 18; Luke vi. 14; Acts i. 13; perhaps Nathanael in John i. 45.

Bär″tĭ-mæ′us (*son of Timæus*). A blind beggar of Jericho, Mark x. 46–52.

Bā′ruch (*blessed*). (1) Jeremiah's friend, amanuensis and fellow prisoner, Jer. xxxvi. 4–32; xxxii. 12; xliii. 3–7. (2) Nehemiah's assistant, Neh. iii. 20. (3) A co-covenanter, Neh. x. 6. (4) A Judahite, Neh. xi. 5. (5) Eighth Apocryphal book.

Bär-zĭl′la-ī (*strong*). (1) A Gileadite, 2 Sam. xvii. 27; xix. 32–39. (2) Father-in-law of Michal, 2 Sam. xxi. 8. (3) Son-in-law of Barzillai, Ez. ii. 61; Neh. vii. 63.

Băs′cà-mà. A place in Gilead, 1 Macc. xiii. 23.

Bā′shăn (*thin soil*). A country east of Jordan between Gilead on the south and Hermon on the north, Deut. iii. 10–13; Josh. xii. 4, 5; xiii. 12–30. Conquered by the Israelites, Num. xxi. 33, and allotted to the half tribe of Manasseh, Josh. xiii. 29, 30.

Bā′shăn=hā′voth=jā′ĭr (*Bashan of the villages of Jair*). Name given to Argob in Bashan, Deut. iii. 14. Havoth-Jair, Num. xxxii. 41.

Băsh′ĕ-măth (*pleasing*). Wife of Esau, Gen. xxvi. 34; xxxvi. 3, 4, 13. Mahalath, Gen. xxviii. 9.

Bā′sin. One of the smaller vessels of the tabernacle, for holding the blood of the sacrificial victims. A larger vessel in John xiii. 5.

Băs′ket. Mostly of wicker, and variously used for bread, Gen. xl. 16–19; Ex. xxix. 2, 3, 23; Lev. viii. 2; Matt. xiv. 20; xv. 37; first fruits, Deut. xxvi. 2–4; fruits, Jer. xxiv. 1, 2; bulky articles, 2 Kgs. x. 7; Ps. lxxxi. 6.

Băs′măth (*pleasing*). Daughter of Solomon, 1 Kgs. iv. 15.

Băs′tărd. Not applied to one born out of wedlock, but to issue within the prohibited degrees, Deut. xxiii. 2.

Băt. An unclean beast. Same as our bat, Lev. xi. 19; Deut. xiv. 18; Isa. ii. 20.

Băth. A Jewish liquid measure, varying from 4¾ to 6½ gallons.

Băth, Bā′thing. Part of the Jewish ritual of purification, Lev. xiv. 8; xv. 5, 16; xvii. 15; xxii. 6; Num. xix. 7; 2 Sam. xi. 2–4; 2 Kgs. v. 10. Customary after mourning, Ruth iii. 3; 2 Sam. xii. 20. Public bathing pools usually sheltered by porticos, 2 Kgs. xx. 20; Neh. iii. 15; Isa. xxii. 11; John v. 2; ix. 7.

Băth=răb′bim (*daughter of many*). A gate of ancient Heshbon, S. of Sol. vii. 4.

Băth′=shĕ-bà″ (*daughter of the oath*). Wife of David, and mother of Solomon, 2 Sam. xi; 1 Kgs. i.

15; ii. 13–22. Bathshua in 1 Chr. iii. 5.

Băth′=shu̧-â″ [BATHSHEBA.]

Băt′tēr-ing=ram. A heavy beam of hard wood, with the end sometimes shaped like a ram, used for battering down the gates and walls of a city, Ezek. iv. 2; xxi. 22.

Băt′tle=axe. [ARMS.]

Băt′tle-ment. The barrier around the flat-roofed houses of the East, Deut. xxii. 8; Jer. v. 10.

Băv′ă-ī. A builder, Neh. iii. 18.

Bāy=tree, Ps. xxxvii. 35. The laurel, or sweet-bay (*Laurus nobilis*).

Băz′lith (*stripping*). His descendants returned, Neh. vii. 54; Ez. ii. 52.

Băz′lŭth. [BAZLITH.]

Bdĕl′li-um (*del′i-um*) (*a plant and its gum*). A fragrant gum resin. But in Gen. ii. 12 and Num. xi. 7, a precious stone.

Bea′con (*signal*). A lighted signal for warning, Isa. xxx. 17.

Bē″a-lī′ah (*Jehovah is Baal*). A friend of David, 1 Chr. xii. 5.

Bē′ă-lŏth (*mistresses*). A town of south Judah, Josh. xv. 24.

Bē′an. A Bedouin tribe, 1 Macc. v. 4.

Beans, Much cultivated in Palestine, as food for man and beast, 2 Sam. xvii. 28; Ezek. iv. 9.

Bear, Found in Syria and the mountains of Lebanon, 2 Sam. xvii. 8; 2 Kgs. ii. 24; Prov. xvii. 12.

Beard (*barbed*). Badge of manhood. Tearing, cutting, or neglecting, a sign of mourning, Ez. ix. 3, Isa. xv. 2; l. 6; Jer. xli. 5; xlviii. 37. To insult it a gross outrage, 2 Sam. x. 4. Taken hold of in salutation, 2 Sam. xx. 9. Removed in leprosy, Lev. xiv. 9.

Bĕb′ă-ī (*fatherly*). (1) Head of a returned family, Ez. ii. 11; Neh. vii. 16; x. 15. (2) Father of Zechariah, Ez. viii. 11.

Bē′chĕr (*first born*). (1) Second son of Benjamin, Gen. xlvi. 21; 1 Chr. vii. 6. (2) An Ephraimite, Num. xxvi. 35. Bered in 1 Chr. vii. 20.

Bĕ-chō′răth (*first fruits*). An ancestor of Saul, 1 Sam. ix. 1.

Bĕc′tĭ-leth. A plain, Judith ii. 21.

Bed. The Jewish bed consisted of a mattress and coverings, Gen. xlvii. 31; 1 Sam. xix. 13; Matt. ix. 6. Placed on the floor, or on a bench, 2 Kgs. i. 4; xx. 2; Ps. cxxxii. 3; Am. iii. 12; and later became ornamental and canopied, Am. vi. 4; Esth. i. 6. For bed-chamber furnishings *see* 2 Kgs. iv. 10.

Bē′dăd (*alone*). Father of Hadad, king of Edom, Gen. xxxvi. 35; 1 Chr. i. 46.

Bē′dăn (*according to judgment*). (1) A judge of Israel, 1 Sam. xii. 11. (2) A son of Gilead, 1 Chr. vii. 17.

Bĕ-dē′ĭah. A son of Bani, Ez. x. 35.

Bee. Honey bees and honey abounded in Palestine, Deut. i. 44; 1 Kgs. xiv. 3; Ps. lxxxi. 16; Isa. vii. 15, 18.

Bē″ĕl-ī′a-dă (*Baal knows*). A son of David, 1 Chr. xiv. 7; Eliada in 2 Sam. v. 16 and 1 Chr. iii. 8.

Bē-ĕl-tĕth′mus. An officer of Artaxerxes, 1 Esdr. ii. 16.

Bē-ĕl′ze-bŭb, properly **Bē-ĕl′ze-bŭl** (*lord of the house*). N. T. form of Baalzebub, "lord of the fly." It personified Satan, and the general sovereignty of evil spirits, Matt. x. 25; xii. 24; Mark iii. 22; Luke xi. 15.

Bē′er (*a well*). (1) A halting place of the Israelites, Num. xxi. 16–18. (2) Place to which Jotham fled, Judg. ix. 21.

Bĕ-ē′ră (*a well*). Son of Zophar, 1 Chr. vii. 37.

Bĕ-ē′rah (*well*). A Reubenite, 1 Chr. v. 6.

Bĕ-er=ē′lim (*well of Elim*), Isa. xv. 8. [BEER.]

Bĕ-ē′rī (*my well*). (1) Father-in-law of Esau, Gen. xxvi. 34. (2) Father of Hosea, Hos. i. 1.

Bĕ′er=Lā-hāī′=roi (*well of the living*). Hagar's well, Gen. xvi. 6–14; xxiv. 62; xxv. 11.

Bĕ-ē′rŏth (*wells*). (1) A Hivite city, Josh. ix. 17. (2) A halting place of the Israelites, Deut. x. 6. Benejaakan in Num. xxxiii. 31.

Bĕ′er=shē′bă (*well of the oath*). An old place in southern Palestine; so named by Abraham, Gen. xxi. 31–33; or Isaac, Gen. xxvi. 32, 33.

Bĕ-ĕsh′=te-rah″ (*house of Ashterah*). A city of Manasseh, Josh. xxi. 27.

Bee′tle (*biting animal*). A species of locust is evidently meant in Lev. xi. 21, 22.

Beeves. Same as cattle, when limited to the bovine species, Lev. xxii. 19.

Bĕg′gar (*asker*). Pauperism was discouraged, Lev. xix. 10; xxv. 5, 6; Deut. xxiv. 19. Poor invited to feasts, Deut. xiv. 29; xxvi. 12. Beggars abhorred, Ps. cix. 10. In N. T. times beggars had a fixed place to beg, Mark x. 46; Acts iii. 2; Luke xvi. 20.

Bĕ-hē′mŏth (*water-ox*). From the poet's description a hippopotamus is meant, Job xl. 15–24.

Bĕ′kah. A half shekel, valued at about thirty-three cents.

Bĕl. [BAAL.]

Bē′là (*destroying*). (1) A city of the plain; afterwards called Zoar, Gen. xiv. 2; xix. 22. (2) A king of Edom, Gen. xxxvi. 31–33; 1 Chr. i. 43. (3) Eldest son of Benjamin, Gen. xlvi. 21; and founder of the Belaites, Num. xxvi. 38; 1 Chr. vii. 6; viii. 1. (4) Son of Azaz, 1 Chr. v. 8.

Bē′lah. [BELA, 3.]

Bē′la-ītes, Num. xxvi. 38. [BELA, 3.]

Bē′lĭ-al (*lawlessness*). A vile, worthless person, reckless of God and man, Deut. xiii. 13; Judg. xix. 22; 1 Sam. ii. 12. Hence, Satan, 2 Cor. vi. 15.

Bĕl′lows (*bag, blow-skin*), though crude, did not differ in principle and use from ours, Jer. vi. 29.

Bĕlls (*bellowers*). Bells of gold were appended to priestly robes, Ex. xxviii. 33–35. Attached to anklets, Isa. iii. 16–18. Horses ornamented with bells, Zech. xiv. 20.

Bĕl-mā′im, Bĕl′men. A town of Samaria, Judith iv. 5.

Bĕl-shăz′zar (*prince of Bel*). Last king of Babylon; ruling at time of the great feast and handwriting on the wall, B. C. 539, Dan. v.

Bĕl″te=shăz′zar (*protected by Bel*). Name given to Daniel by Nebuchadnezzar, Dan. i. 7.

Bĕn (*son*). A Levite, and porter, appointed to carry the ark, 1 Chr. xv. 18.

Bĕ-nā′ĭah (*son of the Lord*). (1) Son of Jehoiada, 1 Chr. xxvii. 5; captain in David's body-guard, 2 Sam. viii. 18; and commander-in-chief of Solomon's army, 1 Kgs. i. 36; ii. 34–46. (2) One of David's mighty men, 2 Sam. xxiii. 30; 1 Chr. xi. 31; and chief of eleventh monthly course, 1 Chr. xxvii. 14. (3) A priest and trumpeter, 1 Chr. xv. 18, 20; xvi. 5. (4) A priest, 1 Chr. xv. 24; xvi. 6. (5) A Levite, 2 Chr. xx. 14. (6) A Levite, 2 Chr. xxxi. 13. (7) Prince of a family of Simeon, 1 Chr. iv. 36. (8) Four of the returned, Ez. x. 25, 30, 35, 43. (9) Father of Pelatiah, Ezek. xi. 1, 13.

Bĕn″=am′mī (*son of my people*). Grandson of Lot, and progenitor of the Ammonites, Gen. xix. 38.

Bĕn′e=bē′răk (*sons of lightning*). A city of Dan, Josh. xix. 45.

Bĕn′e=jā′a-kăn (*sons of Jaakan*). A desert tribe, Num. xxxiii. 31, 32. [BEEROTH.] Akan in Gen. xxxvi. 27.

Bĕn′e=kē′dem. "People of the East," Gen. xxix. 1; Judg. vi. 3, 33; vii. 12; viii. 10; Job i. 3.

Bĕn=hā′dăd (*son of Hadad*). (1) King of Syria, B. C. 950, called Benhadad I. Conqueror of northern Israel, 1 Kgs. xv. 18. (2) Benhadad II., son and successor of former, 1 Kgs. xx. 1. Defeated by Jehoram, 2 Kgs. vi. 8–33. Murdered by his servants, 2

Kgs. viii. 1–15 ; B. C. 890. (3) Benhadad III., son and successor of Hazael on Syrian throne, about B. C. 840. Defeated by King Joash, 2 Kgs. xiii. 3–24.

Běn=hā'íl (*son of strength*). A prince in Judah, 2 Chr. xvii. 7.

Běn=hā'năn (*son of grace*). Son of Shimon, 1 Chr. iv. 20.

Běn'ĭ-nū (*our son*). A co-covenanter, Neh. x. 13.

Běn'ja-mĭn (*son of the right hand*). (1) Youngest of Jacob's children. First named Benoni, afterwards Benjamin, Gen. xxxv. 16–18. Beloved by Jacob, Gen. xlii. ; visited Egypt, Gen. xliii. ; tribe distinguished as Jacob prophesied, Gen. xlix. 27 ; 1 Sam. xx. 20, 36 ; 2 Sam. i. 22 ; Judg. xx. 16 ; 1 Chr. viii. 40. Their allotment described in Josh. xviii. 11–28. Tribe awfully visited, Judg. xx., xxi. (2) Head of a Benjamite family, 1 Chr. vii. 10. (3) A returned captive, Ez. x. 32.

Bě'nō (*his son*). A Levite, 1 Chr. xxiv. 26, 27.

Běn=ō'nĭ (*son of my sorrow*), Gen. xxxv. 18. [BENJAMIN.]

Běn=zō'heth (*son of Zoheth*). A descendant of Judah, 1 Chr. iv. 20.

Bě'ŏn, Num. xxxii. 3. [BAAL-MEON.]

Bě'or (*burning*). (1) Father of Bela, an early king of Edom, Gen. xxxvi. 32. (2) Father of Balaam, Num. xxii. 5 ; xxiv. 3, 15 ; xxxi. 8 ; Deut. xxiii. 4 ; Josh. xiii. 22 ; xxiv. 9 ; Micah vi. 5. Bosor in N. T.

Bě'rà (*son of evil*). A king of Sodom, Gen. xiv. 2–22.

Běr'ă-chah (*blessing*). (1) A Benjamite, 1 Chr. xii. 3. (2) The valley in which Jehoshaphat celebrated his victory, 2 Chr. xx. 26.

Běr''a-chī'ah (*God has blessed*). Father of Asaph, 1 Chr. vi. 39.

Běr''a-ī'ah (*created by God*). A Benjamite, 1 Chr. viii. 21.

Bě-rē'à (*watered*). (1) A city of Macedonia, Acts xvii. 1–15. (2) A Syrian city, now Aleppo, 2 Macc. xiii. 4. (3) A place in Judea, 1 Macc. ix. 4.

Běr'e-chī'ah (*blessed of Jehovah*). (1) A descendant of David, 1 Chr. iii. 20. (2) A Levite, 1 Chr. ix. 16. (3) Father of Asaph, 1 Chr. xv. 17. (4) A door-keeper for the Ark, 1 Chr. xv. 23. (5) An Ephraimite, 2 Chr. xxviii. 12. (6) Father of a builder, Neh. iii. 4, 30 ; vi. 18. (7) Father of Zechariah. Zech. i. 1–7.

Bě'red (*hail*). (1) A place in south Palestine, Gen. xvi. 14. (2) An Ephraimite, 1 Chr. vii. 20.

Běr''ĕ-nī'çe. [BERNICE.]

Bě'rī (*well*). An Asherite, 1 Chr. vii. 36.

Bě-rī'ah (*evil*). (1) A descendant of Asher, Gen. xlvi. 17 ; Num. xxvi. 44, 45 ; 1 Chr. vii. 30, 31. (2) An Ephraimite, 1 Chr. vii. 23. (3) A chief of Benjamin, 1 Chr. viii. 13, 16. (4) A Levite, 1 Chr. xxiii. 10, 11.

Bě-rī'ītes, Num. xxvi. 44. Descendants of Beriah (1).

Bě'rītes. A people in north Palestine, 2 Sam. xx. 14.

Bě'rith (*covenant*), Judg. ix. 46. [BAAL-BERITH.]

Běr-nī'çe (*bringing victory*). Eldest daughter of Herod Agrippa, Acts xii. 1, and sister of the younger Agrippi, Acts xxv. 13–23 ; xxvi. 30.

Bě-rō'dăch=băl'a-dăn, 2 Kgs. xx. 12. [MERODACH-BALADAN.]

Bě-rō'thah (*of a well*). A boundary town of north Palestine, Ezek. xlvii. 16.

Běr'ō-thāi (*my wells*). A city of north Palestine, 2 Sam. viii. 8.

Bě'rŏth-ite, 1 Chr. xi. 39, of Beeroth.

Běr'yl (*beril*) (*jewel*). The first stone in fourth row of a high priest's breastplate, Ex. xxviii. 20.

Bě'sāi (*sword*). His children returned, Ez. ii. 49 ; Neh. vii. 52.

Běs''ŏ-dē'jah (*in the Lord's secret*). Father of an architect, Neh. iii. 6.

Bě'sŏm (*broom*). Twig broom for sweeping, Isa. xiv. 23.

Bě'sôr (*cool*). A brook in south Judah, 1 Sam. xxx. 9–21.

Bě'tah (*confidence*). A city of Zoba, 2 Sam. viii. 8. Tibhath in 1 Chr. xviii. 8.

Bět'a-nà. A place close to oak of Abraham, Judith i. 9.

Bě'ten (*raised*). Border city of Asher, Josh. xix. 25.

Běth (*house*). Used in combinations.

Beth''=ab'ă-rà (*house at the ford*). A place beyond, or at, Jordan where John baptized Christ, John i. 28.

Běth''=ā'năth (*house of reply*). City of Naphtali, Judg. i. 33.

Běth''=ā'nŏth (*house of reply*). A mountain town of Judah, Josh. xv. 59.

Běth'ă-nў (*house of affliction*). A village on the slope of Olivet close to Bethphage, Matt. xxi. 17 ; Mark xi. ; Luke xix. 29 ; John xi. 18. Now *Lazarieh*.

Běth''=ăr'ă-bah (*house of the desert*). A city of Judah and Benjamin, Josh. xv. 61 ; xviii. 22.

Běth''=ā'răm, properly BETHHARAN (*house of height*). A town of Gad, Josh. xiii. 27.

Běth''=ăr'bel (*house of ambush*). Scene of the massacre by Shalman, Hos x. 14.

Běth''=ā'ven (*house of idols*). A place in Benjamin, Josh. vii. 2 ; xviii. 12 ; 1 Sam. xiii. 5 ; xiv. 23. Stands for Bethel in Hos. iv. 15 ; v. 8 ; x. 5.

Běth''=ăz'ma-veth (*house of Azmaveth*). A town of Benjamin, Neh. vii. 28 ; Azmaveth and Beth-samos, elsewhere.

Běth''=bā'al-mē'on (*house of Baal-meon*). A place in Reuben, Josh. xiii. 17. Beon in Num. xxxii. 3 ; Baal-meon in xxxii. 38.

Běth''=bā'rah (*house of the ford*), Judg. vii. 24. [BETH-ABARA.]

Běth''=bā'sī. A town near Jericho, 1 Macc. ix. 62–64.

Běth''=bĭr'e-ī (*house of my creation*). A town in south Simeon, 1 Chr. iv. 31. Beth-lebaoth in Josh. xix. 6.

Běth'=căr (*house of the lamb*). A place where the Israelites' pursuit ended, 1 Sam. vii. 11.

Běth''=dā'gon (*house of Dagon*). (1) Town in Judah, Josh. xv. 41. (2) Town in Asher, Josh. xix. 27.

Běth''=dĭb''la-thā'im (*house of dried figs*). A town of Moab, Jer. xlviii. 22. [ALMON-DIBLATHAIM.]

Běth'=el (*house of God*). (1) City of Palestine, 12 mls. N. of Jerusalem, Gen. xii. 8 ; xiii. 3, 4 ; scene of Jacob's vision, then called Luz, Gen. xxviii. 11–19 ; xxxi. 13 ; xxxv. 1–8 ; Judg. i. 23 ; residence of "sons of the prophets" and priests, 2 Kgs. ii. 2, 3 ; xvii. 27, 28. Now *Beitin.* (2) A town in south Judah, Josh. xii. 16 ; 1 Sam. xxx. 27 ; Chesil in Josh. xv. 30 ; Bethul in xix. 4 ; and Bethuel in 1 Chr. iv. 30. (3) Mount Bethel, near Bethel, Josh. xvi. 1 ; 1 Sam. xiii. 2.

Běth''=ē'měk (*house of the valley*). A boundary of Asher, Josh. xix. 27.

Bě'thér. Figurative mountains, S. of Sol. ii. 17.

Bě-thěs'dà (*house of mercy*). A pool near the sheep-gate, Jerusalem, John v. 2.

Běth''=ē'zěl (*neighbor's house*). A place in Philistia, Mic. i. 11.

Běth''=gā'der (*house of a wall*). A doubtful place or person, 1 Chr. ii. 51.

Běth''=gā'mŭl (*camel-house*). A town of Moab, Jer. xlviii. 23.

Běth''=gil'gal, Neh. xii. 29. [GILGAL.]

Běth''=hăc'çě-rěm (*house of the vine*). A beacon station near Tekoa, Neh. iii. 14 ; Jer. vi. 1.

Běth''=hā'ran, Num. xxxii. 36. [BETH-ARAM.]

Běth''=hŏg'la, and **Hŏg'lah** (*partridge-house*).

A place in boundary of Judah and Benjamin, Josh. xv. 6 ; xviii. 19-21.

Bĕth″=hō′rŏn (*cave-house*). A town of Benjamin, Josh. xvi. 3, 5 ; 1 Kgs. ix. 17 ; 1 Chr. vii. 24.

Bĕth′=jĕsh′ĭ-mŏth and **Jĕs′ĭ-mŏth** (*house of deserts*). A town of Moab, allotted to Reuben, Num. xxxiii. 49 ; Josh. xii. 3 ; xiii. 20.

Bĕth″=lĕb′a̤-ŏth (*house of lionesses*), Josh. xix. 6. [BETH-BIREI.]

Bĕth′=lĕ-hĕm, Bĕth′lĕ-hĕm (*house of bread*). (1) A town of Palestine, six miles S. of Jerusalem. First called Ephrath or Ephratah, Gen. xxxv. 16-19 ; xlviii. 7. Called Bethlehem-judah after the conquest, Judg. xvii. 7. Home of Ruth, Ruth i. 19. Birthplace of David, 1 Sam. xvii. 12. Here Christ was born, Matt. ii. 1, 2 ; Luke ii. 15-18. (2) A town in Zebulun, Josh. xix. 15.

Bĕth″=lō′mŏn, 1 Esdr. v. 17. [BETHLEHEM.]

Bĕth″mā′a̤-chah, 2 Sam. xx. 14, 15. Same as Abel, Abel-maim, and Abel-beth-maachah.

Bĕth″=mär′c̤a̤-bŏth (*house of chariots*). A town of Simeon, Josh. xix. 5 ; 1 Chr. iv. 31. Madmannah in Josh. xv. 31.

Bĕth″=mē′on, Jer. xlviii. 23. Contraction of Beth-baal-meon.

Bĕth″=nim′rah (*house of leopards*). A fenced city of Gad, Num. xxxii. 36. Nimrah in vs. 3.

Bĕth″=pā′let (*house of expulsion*). A town in south Judah, Josh. xv. 27. Bethphelet in Neh. xi. 26.

Bĕth″=păz′zez (*house of dispersion*). A town of Issachar, Josh. xix. 21.

Bĕth=pē′or (*house of Peor*). A spot opposite Jericho, dedicated to Baal-peor, Deut. iii. 29 ; iv. 46 ; Josh. xiii. 20.

Bĕth′pha̤-g̤e̤ (*house of figs*). A place on Olivet, close to Bethany, Matt. xxi. 1 ; Luke xix. 29 ; Mark xi. 1.

Bĕth″=phē′let, Neh. xi. 26. [BETH-PALET.]

Bĕth″=rā′phä (*house of health*). Son of Eshton, 1 Chr. iv. 12.

Bĕth″=rē′hŏb (*house of Rehob*). A province of Aram, or Syria, 2 Sam. x. 6. Rehob in vs. 8.

Bĕth-sā′ĭ-dȧ (*fishing-house*). A fishing-village on Sea of Galilee, and west of Jordan. Birthplace of Andrew, Peter and Philip, Matt. xi. 21 ; John i. 44 ; xii. 21. Bethsaida, where the five thousand were fed, Mark vi. 31-53 ; Luke ix. 10-17, appears to have been on eastward side of Jordan.

Bĕth″=sā′mos, 1 Esdr. v. 18. [BETH-AZMAVETH.]

Bĕth=shăn′, 1 Macc. v. 52. [BETH-SHEAN.]

Bĕth″=shē′ăn, Bĕth′=săn, Bĕth′=shăn (*house of rest*). A city of Manasseh, Josh. xvii. 11 ; Judg. i. 27 ; 1 Chr. vii. 29 ; Bethshan in 1 Sam. xxxi. 10-12. A commissary district of Solomon, 1 Kgs. iv. 12. Now Beisan.

Bĕth″=shē′mĕsh (*house of the sun*). (1) A Levitical town of N. Judah, Josh. xv. 10 ; xxi. 16. Now Ainshems. (2) A border city of Issachar, Josh. xix. 22. (3) A fenced city of Naphtali, Josh. xix. 38 ; Judg. i. 33. (4) Probably Heliopolis, Egypt, Jer. xliii. 13.

Bĕth″=shĭt′tah (*house of the acacia*). The place where Gideon's pursuit ended, Judg. vii. 22.

Bĕth″=sū′rȧ, 1 Macc. iv. 29. [BETH-ZUR.]

Bĕth″=tăp′pṳ-ah (*house of apples*). A town of Judah, near Hebron. Now Teffuh, Josh. xv. 53.

Bĕth-ṳ′el (*filiation of God*). (1) Father of Laban and Rebekah, Gen. xxii. 22, 23 ; xxiv. 15, 24, 47 ; xxviii. 2-5. (2) [BETHUL.]

Bĕ′thŭl (*dweller in God*). A town of Simeon, Josh. xix. 4 ; Chesil in Josh. xv. 30 ; Bethuel in 1 Chr. iv. 30.

Bĕ-thṳ′lĭ-ȧ. Scene of Judith's exploits, Judith iv. 6 ; vi. 11-14.

Bĕth′=zûr (*house of rock*). Now Beit Sûr, 4 mls. N. of Hebron, Josh. xv. 58 ; 2 Chr. xi. 7.

Bĕ-tō′lĭ-us, 1 Esdr. v. 21. [BETHEL.]

Bĕt″ŏ-mĕs′them. A town near Esdraelon, Judith iv. 6.

Bĕt′ŏ-nim (*bellies*). A town of Gad, Josh. xiii. 26.

Bĕ-trōth′ (*in promise*). To pledge troth, *i. e.*, engage to marry. A betrothed woman was regarded as the lawful wife of her spouse, and he could not break off the match without a divorce, while she, if unfaithful, would be considered an adulteress.

Beṳ′lah (*married*). The land of Israel when the Jewish Church is again in its true relation to God, Isa. lxii. 4.

Bē′zāi (*conqueror*). His children returned, Ez. ii. 17 ; Neh. vii. 23.

Bĕ-zăl′ĕ-el (*in the shadow of God*). (1) A Tabernacle architect, Ex. xxxi. 1-6. (2) A returned Jew, Ez. x. 30.

Bē′zek (*lightning*). (1) A place in Judah, Judg. i. 1-5. (2) Where Saul numbered Israel, 1 Sam. xi. 8.

Bē′zĕr (*ore*). (1) A city of refuge east of Jordan, Deut. iv. 43 ; Josh. xx. 8. (2) An Asherite, 1 Chr. vii. 37.

Bē′zeth. Encampment of Bacchides, 1 Macc. vii. 19.

Bī′ble (*the book*). The term applied, not further back than the fifth century, to that collection of *biblia*, or holy books, which comprises the Old and New Testaments.

Bĭch′rĭ (*first-born*). A Benjamite, 2 Sam. xx. 1.

Bĭd′kär (*stabber*). One of Jehu's captains, 2 Kgs. ix. 25.

Bier (*that bears*). The frame on which a dead body was carried to the grave, Luke vii. 14 ; 2 Chr. xvi. 14.

Bĭg′thȧ, Bĭg′thăn, Bĭg′than-ȧ (*gift of God*). A chamberlain of King Ahasuerus, Esth. i 10. Bigthan in ii. 21 ; Bigthana in vi. 2.

Bĭg′va̤-ī (*happy*). (1) His children returned, Ez. ii. 14 ; viii. 14 ; Neh. vii. 19. (2) A chief under Zerubbabel, Ezra ii. 2 ; Neh. vii. 7 ; x. 16.

Bĭl′dăd (*son of strife*). The Shuhite friend of Job ii. 11 ; viii., xviii., xxv.

Bĭl′ĕ-ăm (*foreigners*). A town of Manasseh, 1 Chr vi. 70.

Bĭl′gah (*first-born*). (1) Head of the fifteenth temple course, 1 Chr. xxiv. 14. (2) A returned priest, Neh. xii. 5, 18. Bilgai in x. 8.

Bĭl′ga̤-ī, Neh. x. 8. [BILGAH.]

Bĭl′hah (*timid*). (1) Mother of Dan and Naphtali, Gen. xxix. 29 ; xxx. 3-8 ; xxxv. 25 ; xlvi. 25 ; 1 Chr. vii. 13. (2) A town of Simeon, 1 Chr. iv. 29.

Bĭl′hăn (*modest*). (1) A Horite chief, Gen. xxxvi. 27. (2) A Benjamite, 1 Chr. vii. 10.

Bĭl′shăn (*eloquent*). A returned captive, Ez. ii. 2 ; Neh. vii. 7.

Bĭm′häl (*circumcised*). A son of Japhlet, 1 Chr. vii. 33.

Bĭn′e̤-ȧ (*fountain*). A descendant of Saul, 1 Chr. viii. 37.

Bĭn′nṳ-ī (*building*). Name of five returned captives, Ez. viii. 33 ; x. 30, 38 ; Neh. vii. 15 ; x. 9.

Bīrds. Many birds of Palestine similar to our own. The "speckled bird" of Jer. xii. 9 means a vulture. Birds were snared, Ps. cxxiv. 7 ; Prov. vii. 23 ; Am. iii. 5. Used for curing leprosy, Lev. xiv. 2-7. List of birds not to be eaten, Lev. xi. 13-19 ; Deut. xiv. 11-19.

Bĭr′shȧ (*son of godliness*). A king of Gomorrah, Gen. xiv. 2.

Birth′days. Observed among ancients by feasts, Gen. xl. 20 ; Job i. 4 ; Hos. vii. 5 ; Matt. xiv. 6-10.

Birth′right. Among Jews the first-born son enjoyed the right of consecration, Ex. xxii. 29 ; great dignity, Gen. xlix. 3 ; a double portion of the paternal estate, Deut. xxi. 17 ; right to royal succession, 2

BIBLE DICT

Chr. xxi. 3.

Bĭr′za-vĭth. An Asherite, 1 Chr. vii. 31.

Bĭsh′ŏp (*looking upon, or over*). Greek *episkopos*, overseer. An officer of the Apostolic church, identical with presbyter, or elder, Acts xx. 17, 18 ; 1 Tim. iii. 1–13 ; v. 17 ; Tit. i. 5–8 ; 1 Pet. v ; 1 Thess. v. 12 ; James v. 14.

Bĭsh′ŏp-ric″. The jurisdiction and charge of a bishop, Acts i. 20 ; 1 Tim. iii. 1.

Bĭth′ī-ah (*daughter of the Lord*) Daughter of a Pharaoh, 1 Chr. iv. 18.

Bĭth′rŏn (*ravine*). A place east of Jordan, 2 Sam. ii. 29.

Bĭ-thȳn′ĭ-à. A province of Asia Minor, bordering on the Euxine (Black) sea and west of Pontus, Acts xvi. 7 ; 1 Pet. i. 1. Capital, Nice or Nicæa.

Bĭt′ter Herbs. A part of the passover feast, Ex. xii. 8.

Bĭt′tern. A bird of the heron family, solitary in its habits, and noted for its melancholy night booming, Isa. xiv. 23 ; xxxiv. 11 ; Zeph. ii. 14.

Bĭz-jŏth′jah (*contempt*). A town of south Judah, Josh. xv. 28.

Bĭz′thà (*eunuch*). A eunuch, Esth. i. 10.

Blains (*boils*). The ulcerous inflammations which constituted the sixth Egyptian plague, Ex. ix. 9–11 ; Deut. xxviii. 27, 35.

Blăs′phē-mȳ (*injurious speaking*). Speaking evil of God, Lev. xxiv. 11 ; Ps. lxxiv. 18 ; Isa. lii. 5 ; Matt. xii. 32 ; Acts xviii. 6 ; Rom. ii. 24 ; Col. iii. 8. Royalty could be blasphemed, 1 Kgs. xxi. 10. Punished by stoning, Lev. xxiv. 11–14.

Blăs′tus (*that buds*). Chamberlain of Herod Agrippa, Acts xii. 20.

Blĕm′ish (*wound, stain*). For ceremonial blemishes *see* Lev. xxi. 18–20 ; xxii. 20–24.

Blind′ness. Blind treated with compassion, Lev. xix. 14 ; Deut xxvii. 18. A punishment, Judg. xvi. 21 ; 1 Sam. xi. 2 ; 2 Kgs. xxv. 7.

Blood. The vital fluid, Gen. ix. 4. Forbidden as food, Ex. xxix. 12 ; Lev. vii. 26 ; xvii. 11–13. For N. T. atoning blood *see* Heb. ix, x. ; Acts xx. 28 ; Rom. v. 9 ; Eph. i. 7 ; Col. i. 14 ; Heb. vii. 27 ; 1 John i. 7.

Bō′″ăn-êr′ges (*sons of thunder*). A name given by Christ to James and John, sons of Zebedee, Mark iii. 17.

Boar. Found wild in the thickets of Jordan and on the Lebanon ranges, Ps. lxxx. 13.

Bō′ăz (*lovely*). (1) The Bethlehemite who married Ruth. *See* Book of Ruth ; Matt i. 5. (2) A brazen pillar in the porch of Solomon's temple, 1 Kgs. vii. 21 ; 2 Chr. iii. 17 , Jer. lii. 21.

Bŏch′e-ru (*young*). Son of Azel, 1 Chr. viii. 38.

Bō′chim (*weepers*). A place near Gilgal, Judg. ii. 1–5.

Booth (*hut*). Temporary structures, usually of boughs, Gen. xxxiii. 17 ; Lev. xxiii. 42.

Boot′y (*dealt out*). Spoils of war, regulated as in Num. xxxi. 26–47 ; 1 Sam. xxx. 24, 25.

Bō′oz, Matt. i. 5 ; Luke iii. 32. [Boaz.]

Bŏs′căth, 2 Kgs. xxii. 1. [Bozkath.]

Bos′om (*buz′um*). To lean on, implied great intimacy, John xiii. 23. Figuratively, Paradise, Luke xvi. 23 ; xxiii. 43.

Bō′sŏr. Greek form of Beor, 2 Pet. ii. 15.

Bŏs′ŏ-rà. Bozrah, 1 Macc. v. 26, 28.

Bŏs′ses (*humps*). Knobs on shields and bucklers, Job xv. 26.

Bŏtch. [Blain.]

Bŏt′tle (*little boot*). Primitive bottles, either of skin or earthenware, Gen. xxi. 14 ; Jer. xix. 1 ; Matt. ix. 17 ; of different sizes and shapes. Tear bottles used, Ps. lvi. 8.

Bō′han (*thumb*). A Reubenite, Josh. xv. 6 ; xviii. 17.

Boil. Burning inflammation, Lev. xiii. 23.

Bŏnd′age. [Slave.]

Bŏll′ed (*budded*). Podded, as flax, Ex. ix. 31.

Book (*beech*). Letters were at first engraved on stone, brick, or metal, Deut. xxvii. 2, 3 , Job xix. 24 ; later, on papyrus, bark of trees, tablets of wax, cloth of linen or cotton , the latter in long rolls, or "scrolls," which were the books of the Hebrews.

Bōw. Besides the bow and arrow the bow-gun was used by the ancients as an offensive weapon, 1 Macc. vi. 20. [Archery.] [Arms.]

Bŏw. The Eastern mode of salutation by kneeling on one knee and bending the head forward, Gen. xxxvii. 10 ; 1 Kgs. i. 53 ; ii. 19.

Bŏw′els. Used figuratively for the emotions, Col. iii. 12 ; 1 John iii. 17.

Box=tree. The evergreen, whose wood is so prized by engravers, Isa. xli. 19 ; lx. 13.

Bō′zĕz (*height*). Sharp rocks mentioned in 1 Sam. xiv. 4, 5.

Bŏz′kăth (*craggy*). A lowland city of Judah, Josh. xv. 39 ; 2 Kgs. xxii. 1.

Bŏz′rah (*strong-hold*). (1) Ancient capital of Edom, Gen. xxxvi. 33 ; Isa. xxxiv. 6 ; lxiii. 1 ; Jer. xlix. 13, 22. (2) A city of Moab, Jer. xlviii. 24.

Brāce′let. A wrist and arm ornament worn by both sexes, Gen. xxiv. 30 ; Ezek. xvi. 11. A badge of royalty, and worn above elbow, 2 Sam. i. 10.

Brăm′ble (*blackberry*). [Thorns.]

Brass. An alloy of copper and zinc, not known to the Jews. The brass of Scripture was probably copper, or a copper alloy, Gen. iv. 22 ; Deut. viii. 9 ; Judg. xvi. 21 ; 2 Kgs. xxv 7 ; 1 Sam. xvii. 5 ; Job xxviii. 2 ; 1 Cor. xiii. 1.

Brā′zen Serpent. [Serpent.]

Breach′es (*broken*). Creeks, bays, and river-mouths ; havens in case of storm, Judg. v. 17 ; Josh. xix. 29.

Bread (*brewed, baked*). Early used, Gen. xviii. 5, 6 ; Ex. xii. 34 ; Jer. vii. 18. Made of wheat, barley, rye, fitches, and spelt, in loaves or rolls, leavened or unleavened ; the kneading being in troughs, bowls, or on flat plates, and the baking in portable ovens of earthenware, or upon heated stones, or on the coals.

Breast′plate. The breastplate of the high priest, Ex. xxviii. 15, was of embroidered stuff, some 10 inches square ; its upper corners fastened with gold or lace to the ephod, its lower to the girdle, Ex. xxviii. 28. Adorned with 12 precious stones, Ex. xxviii. 12–29.

Breech′es (*broken, i. e. crotched*). Drawers or light trousers worn by priests, reaching from loins to thighs, Ex. xxviii. 42.

Brick (*fragment*). Bricks were made of clay, mixed with straw, usually larger than our bricks, and burned in a kiln or dried in the sun, Gen. xi. 3 ; Ex. i. 14 ; v. 7 , 2 Sam. xii. 31 ; Jer. xliii. 9.

Bride, Bridegroom. [Marriage.]

Brĭg′an-dine (*brawl*), Jer. xlvi. 4 ; elsewhere as habergeon.

Brĭm′stone (*burn-stone*). Sulphur, Gen. xix. 24 ; of frequent figurative use, Job xviii. 15 ; Ps. xi. 6 ; Isa. xxxiv 9 ; Rev. xxi. 8.

Bŭck′ler (*cheek*). The small round shield used to catch blows. [Armor.]

Bŭk′kī (*void*). (1) A prince of Dan, Num. xxxiv. 22. (2) Fifth from Aaron in line of high priests, 1 Chr. vi. 5, 51.

Bŭk-kī′ah (*wasting*). A Temple musician, 1 Chr. xxv. 4, 13.

Bŭl (*rain*). Marchesvan or Bul, the second month of the Hebrew civil and eighth of the sacred year, corresponding to parts of October and November, 1 Kgs. vi. 38.

Bŭl′bŭl. The Persian nightingale, common in the Jordan valley; also the titmouse, in the Latin version.

Bull, Bullock (*bellow*). A term used generically for ox, cattle, etc., Ps. xxii. 12. Bullock in Isa. lxv. 25; cow in Ezek. iv. 15; oxen in Gen. xii. 16. The "wild bull" of Isa. li. 20, and the "wild ox" of Deut. xiv. 5, mean probably the oryx.

Bul′rush (*large rush*). The bulrush of Ex. ii. 3–5 is supposed to be the papyrus, from which paper was made, Job viii. 11.

Bū′nah (*discretion*). A descendant of Judah, 1 Chr. ii. 25.

Bŭn′ni (*built*). (1) A Levite, Neh. ix. 4. (2) A co-covenanter with Nehemiah, Neh. x. 15. (3) A Levite, Neh. xi. 15.

Bŭr′ĭ-al, Bŭr-ў̄ (*mounding*). Place, a cave or hewn rock, Gen. xxiii. 4; xxv. 9; l. 5–13; Matt. xxvii. 60. Body washed, Acts ix. 37; swathed and spiced, Matt. xxvii. 59; Mark xv. 46; xvi. 1. Head covered separately, 2 Chr. xvi. 14; John xix. 40; pall-bearers and mourners, relatives and friends, 2 Sam. iii. 31; Luke vii. 12; sometimes hired mourners, Jer. ix. 17; Ezek. xxiv. 17; Matt. ix. 23.

Burnt offering. The offering which was wholly consumed by fire. For ceremonies *see* Lev. viii., ix., xiv., xxix.

Bush. Supposably the dwarf acacia, Ex. iii. 2–6. In Deut. xxxiii. 16, Mark xii. 26, Luke xx. 37, the reference is to the locality.

Bush′el (*little box*). Hebrew *seah*, twenty pints.

Bŭt′ler (*bottler*). Officer of a royal household in charge of the wines and drinking vessels, Gen. xl. 1–13; xli. 9; "cup-bearer," Neh. i. 11; 1 Kgs. x. 5.

Bŭt′ter (*cow-cheese*). A curd, or curded milk, evidently meant, Gen. xviii. 8; Job xxix. 6; Judg. v. 25.

Bŭt′ter-fly. Nine Hebrew words confusedly translated locust and associated insects. Butterfly a natural incident to caterpillar life.

Bŭz (*despised*). (1) Progenitor of Elihu, Gen. xxii. 21. (2) A Gadite, 1 Chr. v. 14. (3) Land of Buz, Jer. xxv. 23.

Bŭz′ite. Elihu so called, Job xxxii. 2, 6. [ELIHU, 1.]

Bū′zī (*despised*). Father of Ezekiel, Ezek. i. 3.

C

Căb. A Jewish dry measure, about a quart, 2 Kgs. vi. 25.

Căb′bon (*understanding*). A town in lowlands of Judah, Josh. xv. 40.

Căb′ins. Cells in a dungeon, Jer. xxxvii. 16.

Cā′bŭl (*displeasing*). (1) A boundary of Asher, Josh. xix. 27. (2) The district given to Hiram by Solomon, 1 Kgs. ix. 10–14.

Căd′dis. Joannan, 1 Macc. ii. 2.

Cā′des, 1 Macc. xi. 63. [KEDESH.]

Căd′mĭ-el, 1 Esdr. v. 26. [KADMIEL.]

Çæ′sar (*hairy, or elephant*). With Julius Cæsar and Augustus Cæsar a surname, but with the latter it became official and remained so till the death of Nero. In Luke ii. 1, Augustus Cæsar is meant; in Luke iii. 1, Tiberius Cæsar; in Acts xi. 28, Claudius Cæsar; in Acts xxv. 8, Phil. iv. 22, Nero.

Çæs′′a-rē′ȧ (*for Cæsar*). Political capital of Palestine, on Mediterranean, and official residence of Herodian kings and Roman procurators; home of Philip and Cornelius, Acts viii. 40; x., xi. 1–18.

Çæs′′a-rē′ȧ Phĭ-lĭp′pī. A city of Galilee marking the northern limit of Christ's pilgrimage, and probable scene of the configuration, Matt. xvi. 13–20; xvii. 1–10; Mark viii. 27.

Cāge (*hollow*). Bird-trap in Jer. v. 27; prison in Rev. xviii. 2.

Cā′ia-phăs (*depression*). Appointed high priest by Valerius, and reappointed by Pontius Pilate; A. D. 27–36. Deposed by Vitellius, Matt. xxvi. 3–57; John xi. 49–51; xviii. 13–28; Acts iv. 6.

Cāin (*possession*). (1) Eldest son of Adam, Gen. iv. (2) A city in lowlands of Judah, Josh. xv. 57.

Cā-ī′nan (*possessor*). (1) Son of Enos, Gen. v. 9; Luke iii. 36. Kenan in 1 Chr. i. 2. (2) Son of Arphaxad, Luke iii. 36.

Cāke. [BREAD.]

Cā′lah (*old age*). City of Assyria, Gen. x. 11.

Căl′′ȧ-mŏl′ȧ-lus. A compound of Elam, Lor?, and Hadidad, 1 Esdr. v. 22.

Căl′a-mus (*reed*). Ex. xxx. 23, S. of Sol. iv. 14, Ezek. xxvii. 19, identified with the lemon-grass, or sweet-flag. "Sweet cane" in Isa. xliii. 24, Jer. vi. 20.

Căl′cŏl (*nourishment*). A Judahite, 1 Chr. ii. 6.

Căl′drŏn (*hot*). A vessel for boiling meats, 1 Sam. ii. 14; 2 Chr. xxxv. 13; Job xli. 20; Micah iii. 3.

Cā′leb (*capable*). (1) Son of Hezron, 1 Chr. ii. 18, 19, 42, 50. Chelubai in ii. 9. (2) The spy of Judah, Num. xiii. 6; Josh. xiv., xv.; 1 Sam. xxx. 14. (3) Son of Hur, 1 Chr. ii. 50. (4) Caleb's district, 1 Sam. xxx. 14.

Călf. Fatted calf a luxury, Gen. xviii. 7; 1 Sam. xxviii. 24; Am. vi. 4; Luke xv. 23. Molten calf, Ex. xxxii. 4; 1 Kgs. xii. 28, gilded structures. Calf worship denounced, Hos. viii., x., xiii. 2. "Calves of our lips," Hos. xiv. 2, fruits of our lips.

Căl-lis′thĕ-nēs. Friend of Nicanor, 2 Macc. viii. 33.

Căl′neh, Căl′nō (*fortress*). A city of Nimrod, Gen. x. 10; Am. vi. 2; Isa. x. 9. Canneh in Ezek. xxvii. 23.

Căl′phī. A general, 1 Macc. xi. 70.

Căl′vȧ-rў (*skull*). Latin for Greek *Kranion*, "skull" (referring to shape), and Hebrew "Golgotha." Spot of crucifixion. Calvary, only in Luke xxiii. 33.

Căm′el (*carrier*). The Arabian, or one-humped camel, generally meant. Used for carriage, and source of wealth, Gen. xii. 16; Judg. vii. 12; 2 Chr. xiv. 15; Job ′. 3; xlii. 12; Isa. xxx. 6. An unclean beast, Lev. xi. 4. Hair used for clothing, 2 Kgs. i. 8; Zech. xiii. 4; Matt. iii. 4. Figuratively for something beyond human power, Matt. xix. 24; xxiii. 24.

Cā′mŏn (*straw*). Burial place of Jair, Judg. x. 5.

Cămp. [ENCAMPMENT.]

Căm′phire. The gum of the camphor-tree. But in S. of Sol. i. 14; iv. 13; the cyprus flower or henna.

Cā′nȧ (*reedy*). A town of Galilee, 7 mls. N. of Nazareth, John ii. 1–11; iv. 46; xxi. 2.

Cā′năan (*low*). (1) Fourth son of Ham, Gen. x. 6–19; 1 Chr. i. 8–13. (2) The country between the Mediterranean and Jordan, given by God to the Israelites, Ex. vi. 4; Lev. xxv. 38. "Holy Land," after the captivity, Zech. ii. 13. Palestine, from Philistia.

Cā′năan-īte. Dwellers in Canaan, and all tribes known to the Israelites at time of conquest, Gen. x. 18–20; xiii. 7; xiv. 7; xv. 20; Num. xiii. 29; Josh. xi. 3; xxiv. 11.

Căn′dȧ-çē (*queen of servants*). The Ethiopian queen whose servant was converted, Acts viii. 27.

Căn′dle-stĭck. The golden candlestick rather a lamp, Ex. xxv. 31–37; xxxvii. 17–24. Ten candelabra used instead, in Solomon's temple, 1 Kgs. vii. 49.

Cāne. [CALAMUS.]

Cănk′er-worm (*cancer-worm*). A variety of caterpillar. But in Joel i. 4; ii. 25; Nah. iii. 15, 16, probably an undeveloped locust.

Căn′neh. Ezek. xxvii. 23. [CALNEH.]

Căn′on (*cane, rule*). Word first applied to the Scriptures by Amphilochius about A. D. 380, Gal. vi. 16; Phil. iii. 16. O. T. canon fixed by the Jews, and accepted by Christ and his times. N. T. canon ratified by third council of Carthage, A. D. 397.

Căn′ō-pў (*bed with mosquito curtains*). Judith x. 21; xiii. 9; xvi. 19.

Căn′tĭ-cles (*song of songs*). The Latinized title of "The Song of Solomon."

Că-pĕr′na-ŭm (*hamlet of Nahum*). A city on N. W. shore of Sea of Galilee. Chief residence of Christ and his apostles, Matt. iv. 12–16; viii. 5; ix. 1; xvii. 24; Mark ii. 1; Luke vii. 1–5; John vi. 17.

Căph′ar (*hamlet*). Common Hebrew prefix.

Căph″ăr-săl′a-ma. A battlefield, 1 Macc. vii. 31.

Că-phĕn′a-tha. A suburb of Jerusalem, 1 Macc. xii. 37.

Căph′tôr, Căph′tŏ-rĭm. Either Philistines or Copts of Egypt, Gen. x. 14; Deut. ii. 23; Jer. xlvii. 4; Am. ix. 7.

Căp″pa-dō′çĭ-à (*fine horses*). Largest Roman province in Asia Minor, with Cæsarea as metropolis, Acts ii. 9; 1 Pet. i. 1.

Căp′tain (*head*). Title for a leader of a band of ten, fifty, hundred or thousand, Deut. i. 15; Josh. x. 24; Judg. xi. 6, 11. Also a civic meaning, Isa. i. 10; iii. 3. "Captain of the Guard," Acts xxviii. 16, was commander of the Prætorian troop of Rome. "Captain of the Temple," Acts iv. 1, was chief of the Temple watchmen.

Căp′tĭve (*taken*). Captives in war treated with great cruelty in early times, Gen. xiv. 14; Judg. i. 7; 1 Sam. xi. 2; 2 Sam. viii. 2; 2 Kgs. xxv. 7. Later, treated as servants and slaves, 1 Kgs. xx. 31–34.

Căp-tĭv′ĭ-ty. Six partial captivities mentioned in Judges. Israel had several, 2 Kgs. xv. 29; 1 Chr. v. 26, the final one being that by Shalmaneser, B. C. 721, 2 Kgs. xvii. 6. Judah was captive to Assyria B. C. 713, and finally to Nebuchadnezzar B. C. 606–562. This captivity broken, Ez. i. 11. Last captivity was to Rome, A. D. 71.

Căr′bŭn-cle (*little coal*). A gem of deep red color, Isa. liv. 12. A stone in the high-priest's breastplate, Ex. xxviii. 17; xxxix. 10.

Căr′cas. A eunuch, Esth. i. 10.

Căr′chĕ-mĭsh (*fortress of Chemosh*). A city on the Euphrates, Isa. x. 5–9; 2 Chr. xxxv. 20–23; Jer. xlvi. 2.

Că-rē′ah (*bald*). Father of Johannan, 2 Kgs. xxv. 23. Kareah, elsewhere.

Cā′rĭ-à. Southwest province of Asia Minor. Cnidus and Miletus were in it, Acts xx. 15; xxvii. 7.

Căr′mel (*fruitful*). (1) The promontory which forms the bay of Acre, 1 Kgs. xviii.; 2 Kgs. ii. 25; iv. 25; Isa. xxxiii. 9; xxxv. 2. (2) A city of Judah, 1 Sam. xv. 12; xxv. 2–44; 2 Chr. xxvi. 10.

Căr′mĭ (*vine dresser*). (1) Progenitor of the Carmites, Gen. xlvi. 9; Ex. vi. 14; Num. xxvi. 6; 1 Chr. v. 3. (2) Father of Achan, Josh. vii. 1, 18; 1 Chr. ii. 7.

Căr′nă-im. City in Manasseh, 1 Macc. v. 26–44.

Căr′pĕn-tĕr (*cart-wright*). Carpentry an early art, Gen. vi. 14–16; Ex. xxv. 23; xxvii. 1–15. David and Solomon employed foreign wood-workers, 2 Sam. v. 11; 1 Kgs. v. 6. Joseph a carpenter, Matt. xiii. 55; and Christ, Mark vi. 3.

Căr′pus (*fruit*). Paul's friend, 2 Tim. iv. 13.

Căr′rĭage (*car*). Baggage, Judg. xviii. 21; Isa. x. 28; xlvi. 1; Acts xxi. 15.

Căr-shē′nà (*distinguished*). A Persian, Esth. i. 14.

Cărt (*carry*). A two-wheeled vehicle usually drawn by oxen, 1 Sam. vi. 7–15; Amos ii. 13.

Căr′ving (*cutting*). Carving and engraving in much request, Ex. xxxi. 5; xxxv. 33; 1 Kgs. vi. 18; 2 Chr. ii. 7–14; Ps. lxxiv. 6; Zech. iii. 3.

Cāse′ment (*house-frame*). The latticed opening of the Kiosk, or summer house, of the East, Prov. vii. 6; S. of Sol. ii. 9; Judg. v. 28.

Că-sĭph′ĭ-à (*white*). An unknown place, Ez. viii. 17.

Căs′leu, 1 Macc. i. 54. [CHISLEU.]

Căs-lu′hĭm (*fortified*). A Mizraite people, Gen. x. 14; 1 Chr. i. 12.

Căs′phor. City of Gilead, 1 Macc. v. 26.

Căs′pis, 2 Macc. xii. 13. [CASPHOR.]

Căs′sĭa (*that peels*). The cinnamon cassia in Ex. xxx. 24; Ezek. xxvii. 19. In Ps. xlv. 8, the shrub is unidentified.

Căs′tle (*fort*). The "Tower of Antonia," N. W. corner of the Temple at Jerusalem, Acts xxi. 34, 37; xxii. 24; xxiii. 10, 16, 32.

Căs′tŏr and Pŏl′lux. Two mythologic heroes; figurehead and name of Paul's ship, Acts xxviii. 11.

Căt′ĕr-pĭl″lar (*hairy consumer*). The larva of the butterfly, 1 Kgs. viii. 37; 2 Chr. vi. 28; Ps. lxxviii. 46; Isa. xxxiii. 4; Joel i. 4.

Căts. Only in Baruch vi. 22.

Căt′tle (*capital*). Domestic bovine animals, as oxen, cows, bulls, and calves; also any live-stock, Gen. xiii. 2; Ex. xii. 29; xxxiv. 19; Num. xx. 19; xxxii. 16; Ps. l. 10; Job. i. 3. [BULL.]

Cau′dà, Clauda in R. V.

Caul (*kŏl*) (*cap*). A net for a woman's hair, Isa. iii. 18. In Hos. xiii. 8, the membrane around the heart.

Cāve (*hollow*). Used for storage houses, dwellings, hiding and burial places, Gen. xix. 30; Josh. x. 16; Judg. vi. 2; 1 Sam. xiii. 6; xxii. 1; xxiv. 3; 2 Sam. xxiii. 13; 1 Kgs. xviii. 4; Heb. xi. 38.

Çē′dăr (*resinous*). A cone-bearing tree whose reddish fragrant wood was much prized, 1 Kgs. vii. 2; Ps. xcii. 12; S. of Sol. v. 15; Isa. ii. 13; Ezek. xxxi. 6.

Çē′drŏn (*turbid*). (1) A brook, Kedron or Kidron, below the eastern wall of Jerusalem, John xviii. 1.

Çeī′lăn. His sons returned, 1 Esdr. v. 15.

Çeil′ing (*heavens*). Hebrew temple ceilings were generally of cedar, richly carved, 1 Kgs. vi. 9–15; vii. 3; 2 Chr. iii. 5–9.

Çĕn′chrĕ-à (*millet*). The eastern harbor of Corinth, Acts xviii. 18. Seat of a Christian church, Rom. xvi. 1.

Çĕn″dē-bē′us. A Syrian general, 1 Macc. xv. 38.

Çĕn′sĕr (*set on fire*). A small portable vessel of copper, Num. xvi. 39; Lev. xvi. 12, or gold, 1 Kgs. vii. 50; Heb. ix. 4, for carrying the coals on which incense was burned.

Çĕn′sus (*assess*). Twelve different censuses noted in the O. T., Ex. xxxviii. 26; Num. i. 2; xxvi.; 2 Sam. xxiv. 9; 2 Chr. ii. 17, 18; 1 Kgs. xii. 21; 2 Chr. xiii. 3; xiv. 8; xvii. 14; xxv. 5, 6; xxvi. 13; Ez. ii. 64; viii. 1–14. The census in Luke ii. 1–3, was for taxation.

Çĕn-tū′rĭ-ŏn (*hundred*). A Roman officer who had command of a hundred soldiers, Matt. viii. 5; Mark xv. 39; Luke vii. 1–10; Acts x. 1.

Çē′phas (*stone*). Name given to Peter, John i. 42.

Çē′ras, 1 Esdr. v. 29. [KEROS.]

Çē′tab. A doubtful name, 1 Esdr. v. 30.

Chā′bris. Ruler of Bethulia, Judith vi. 15.

Chā′dĭ-as. Her citizens returned, 1 Esdr. v. 20.

Chaff. Was separated from the grain by throwing all into the air from sheets, or forks, the wind carrying away the chaff, Ps. i. 4; Isa. xvii. 13; Hos. xiii. 3; Zeph. ii. 2.

Chains (*links*). Used for ornament on man and beast, and for fetters, Gen. xli. 42; Judg. viii. 21; xvi. 21; 2 Sam. iii. 34; 2 Kgs. xxv. 7; Isa. iii. 19; Acts xii. 6; xxi. 33; xxviii. 20.

Chăl″çe-dō′nў (*from Chalcedon*). A many-colored precious stone of the agate variety, Rev. xxi. 19.

Chăl′cŏl, 1 Kgs. iv. 31. [CALCOL.]

Chăl-dē′à, Chăl-dæ′à (*as demons*). The country lying along the Euphrates on both sides, and between it and the Tigris, for three or four hundred miles back from their mouths, Gen. x. 10; xi. 31; Job i. 17.

Chăl-dē′ănş, Chăl′deeş. The people of that country having Babylon for its capital, Dan. i. 4, v. 15; ix. 1.

Chălk=stōnes. Possibly burnt lime, Isa. xxvii. 9.

Chăm′bĕr (*vault, arched*). Sleeping apartment, Gen. xliii. 30; 2 Sam. xviii. 33; Ps. xix. 5; Dan. vi. 10; Acts ix. 37. Dining room, Mark xiv. 14; Luke xxii. 12.

Chăm′bĕr-ing. Amorous intrigue, Rom. xiii. 13.

Chăm′bĕr-lain (*man of the chamber*). Officer in charge of the king's chamber, 2 Kgs. xxiii. 11; Esth. i. 10, 12, 15; Dan. i. 8–11. A more dignified office, in Acts xii. 20; Rom. xvi. 23.

Chȧ-mē′lĕ-ŏn (*ground lion*). A species of lizard, arboreal in habit. But the word thus translated implies a frog, Lev. xi. 30.

Chăm′ois (*sham-my*) (*buck*). The chamois not known in Palestine. A wild sheep, or goat, may be meant, Deut. xiv. 5.

Chā′năan. Greek spelling of Canaan, Acts vii. 11; xiii. 19; Judith v. 3.

Chăn′çel-lŏr (*usher of a law-court*). A keeper of the king's seal, Ez. iv. 8.

Chăp′ĭ-ter (*head*). The ornamental head of a pillar, Ex. xxxvi. 38; xxxviii. 17; 1 Kgs. vii. 31, 38.

Chăp′man (*cheap-man*). A trader, 1 Kgs. x. 15; 2 Chr. ix. 14.

Chär″a-ăth′ā-lar, 1 Esdr. v. 36. [CHERUB.]

Chär′a-cȧ. An obscure place, 2 Macc. xii. 17.

Chär′a-shĭm, Valley of (*ravine of craftsmen*). Where Joab's ancestors lived, 1 Chr. iv. 14.

Chär′chĕ-mĭsh, 2 Chr. xxxv. 20; **Chär′chä-mĭs,** 1 Esdr. i. 25. [CARCHEMISH.]

Chär′cus, 1 Esdr. v. 32. [BARKOS.]

Chär′ger (*car*). A dish for receiving water and blood, and for presenting offerings of flour and oil, Num. vii. 13, 79; later, a large service plate, Matt. xiv. 8.

Chär′ĭ-ot (*car*). A two-wheeled vehicle, used for travel and war, Gen. xli. 43; xlvi. 29; 1 Kgs. xviii. 44; 2 Kgs. v. 9. In use by enemies of Israel, Josh. xi. 4; Judg. iv. 3; 1 Sam. xiii. 5. Adopted for war by David and Solomon, 2 Sam. viii. 4; 1 Kgs. ix. 19; x. 26; xxii. 34; 2 Kgs. ix. 16; Isa. xxxi. 1.

Chär′mis. Ruler of Bethulia, Judith vi. 15.

Chär′ran, Acts vii. 2–4. [HARAN.]

Chăs′ĕ-ba, 1 Esdr. v. 31. [GAZERA.]

Chē′bär (*strength*). A river of Chaldea; seat of Ezekiel's visions, Ezek. i. 3; iii. 15, 23.

Chĕd″ŏr-lā′o-mĕr (*handful of sheaves*). King of Elam, Gen. xiv. 1–24.

Chēese. The Hebrew words imply curds, or curdled milk, 1 Sam. xvii. 18; Job x. 10; 2 Sam. xvii. 29.

Chē′lăl (*perfect*). A returned captive, Ez. x. 30.

Chĕl′çi-as. Hilkiah, Bar. i. 7.

Chĕl′lŭh (*perfection*). A returned captive, Ez. x. 35.

Chĕl′lus. A place west of Jordan, Judith i. 9.

Chē′lŭb (*basket*). (1) A Judahite, 1 Chr. iv. 11. (2) Father of one of David's overseers, 1 Chr. xxvii. 26.

Chȧ-lū′bāi (*capable*). Caleb, 1 Chr. ii. 9.

Chĕm′a-rims (*black ones*). Sun-worshippers, Zeph. i. 4.

Chē′mosh (*subduer*). National god of Moab, and Ammon, Num. xxi. 29; Judg. xi. 23, 24; 1 Kgs. xi. 7; 2 Kgs. xxiii. 13.

Chĕ-nā′a-nah (*merchant*). (1) Father of Zedekiah, 1 Kgs. xxii. 11. (2) A Benjamite, 1 Chr. vii. 10.

Chĕn′a-nī (*contraction of Chenaniah*). A Levite, Neh. ix. 4.

Chĕn″a-nī′ah (*made by God*). A Levite, 1 Chr. xv. 22.

Chĕ′phär=hȧ-ăm′mo-nāi. "Hamlet of the Ammonites," in Benjamin, 2 Chr. xviii. 24.

Chĕ-phī′rah (*hamlet*). A Gibeonite city, Josh. ix. 17; Ez. ii. 25; Neh. vii. 29.

Chē′ran (*lyre*). A Horite, Gen. xxxvi. 26; 1 Chr. i. 41.

Chē′rĕ-as. A general, 2 Macc. x. 32–37.

Chĕr′ĕth-īms, Ezek. xxv. 16. [CHERETHITES.]

Chĕr′ĕth-ītes (*executioners*). A portion of David's body guard, 2 Sam. viii. 18; xv. 18; xx. 7, 23; 1 Kgs. i. 38, 44; 1 Chr. xviii. 17.

Chē′rĭth (*cutting*). The place where Elijah was fed by ravens, 1 Kgs. xvii. 3–5.

Chē′rub. A place in Babylonia, Ez. ii. 59; Neh. vii. 61.

Chĕr′ub, Chĕr′u-bĭm (*terrible*). Guards of Paradise, Gen. iii. 24; and the mercy seat, Ex. xxv. 18. Wrought in gold or wood, Ex. xxxvi. 35; xxxvii. 7–9. Of immense size in Solomon's Temple, 1 Kgs. vi. 27. Four-winged and four-faced, Ezek. i. 6; x. 14; Rev. iv. 8.

Chĕs′ȧ-lon (*hopes*). A landmark of Judah, Josh. xv. 10.

Chē′sed (*gain*). Fourth son of Nahor, Gen. xxii. 22.

Chē′sĭl (*fool*). A place in south Judah, Josh. xv. 30.

Chĕst (*box*). A coffin, Gen. l. 26. Treasure chest, 2 Kgs. xii. 9; 2 Chr. xxiv. 8–11. Trunk or packing-case, Ezek. xxvii. 24. In all other places, "Ark."

Chĕst′nut=tree, Gen. xxx. 37; Ezek. xxxi. 8; the plane-tree is meant.

Chĕ-sŭl′lŏth (*loins*). Town of Issachar, Josh. xix. 18.

Chĕt-tī′īm, 1 Macc. i. 1. [CHITTIM.]

Chē′zĭb (*lying*), Gen. xxxviii. 5. Probably Achzib.

Chī′don (*dart*). Spot where the accident befel the Ark, 1 Chr. xiii. 9–13. Nachon, 2 Sam. vi. 6.

Chief of Asia, Acts xix. 31. [ASIAARCH.]

Chief Priest. [HIGH PRIEST.]

Chĭl′dren. Children an honor, childlessness a misfortune, Gen. xvi. 2; Deut. vii. 14; 1 Sam. i. 6; 2 Sam. vi. 23; 2 Kgs. iv. 14; Ps. cxxvii. 3; Isa. xlvii. 9, Jer. xx. 15. Males circumcised on eighth day, Lev. xii. 3. Weaning an occasion of rejoicing, Gen. xxi. 8.

Chĭl′ę-ăb (*like the father*). Son of David, 2 Sam. iii. 3.

Chil′i-on (*sickly*). Husband of Orpah, Ruth 1:2–4.

Chĭl′măd (*closed*). A country on the Euphrates, Ezek. xxvii. 23.

Chĭm′ham (*longing*). A friend of David, 2 Sam. xix. 37, 38; Jer. xli. 17.

Chĭn′nę-rĕth, Chĭn′nę-rŏth. (1) A city on or near coast of Sea of Galilee, Josh. xi. 2. (2) Old name for the inland sea known as Lake Gennesareth, or Sea of Galilee, Num. xxxiv. 11; Deut. iii. 17; Josh. xiii. 27.

Chī′os (*open*). The island of Scio, Acts xx. 15.

Chĭs′lĕū. Ninth month of the Jewish sacred, and third of the civil, year, corresponding to parts of Nov. and Dec., Neh. i. 1.

Chĭs′lon (*hope*). A Benjamite, Num. xxxiv. 21.

Chĭs′lŏth=tā′bôr, Josh. xix. 12. [CHESULLOTH.]

Chĭt′tim, Kĭt′tim (*bruisers*). Descendants of Javan, and their country, supposably Cyprus, Gen. x. 4; Num. xxiv. 24; 1 Chr. i. 7; Isa. xxiii. 1–12.

Chī′ŭn. An Israelite idol, Am. v. 26. [REMPHAN.]

Chlō′ĕ (*green herb*). A Christian woman of Corinth, 1 Cor. i. 11.

Chō′bȧ, Chō′bāi. A place in Bethulia, Judith vi. 4; xv. 4.

Chôr-ā′shan. A haunt of David, 1 Sam. xxx. 30.

BIBLE DICT

Chŏ-rā′zin (*secret*). A city on the coast of the Sea of Galilee, Matt. xi. 21 ; Luke x. 13.

Chō′ze-bȧ. Descendants of Judah, 1 Chr. iv. 22.

Christ. The Anointed ; the Messiah. A title of Jesus, the Saviour : at first with the article, "The Christ ; " later, as part of a proper name, "Jesus Christ." [JESUS.]

Chrĭs′tian. Follower of Christ. First so called at Antioch, Syria, A. D. 43, Acts xi. 26 ; xxvi. 28.

Chrŏn′i̯-cles ("*words of days*," *annals*). Thirteenth and fourteenth of O. T. Books. Originally one book called Paraleipomena, "things omitted." A supplement to Kings, compiled, no doubt, by Ezra. The history covers a period of 3500 years.

Chrȳs′ō-līte (*gold stone*). Evidently the yellow topaz, Rev. xxi. 20.

Chrȳs′′ō-prā′sus (*golden leek*). An apple-green variety of chalcedony, Rev. xxi. 20.

Chŭb. Allies of Egypt, Ezek. xxx. 5.

Chŭn (*ready*). A city that supplied brass to Solomon, 2 Sam. viii. 8.

Chŭrch (*assembly*). A congregation of religious worshippers, Acts vii. 38 ; Matt. xvi. 18. Visible, Acts ii. ; Col. i. 24. Invisible, Heb. xii. 23.

Chŭrn-ing, Prov. xxx. 33. The milk was enclosed in skin bags, which were shaken or trodden.

Chū′shan=rĭsh′′a-thā′im (*great conqueror*). A king of Mesopotamia, Judg. iii. 8–10.

Chū′si. A place, Judith vii. 18.

Chū′zȧ (*seer*). Steward of Herod, Luke viii. 3 ; xxiv. 10.

Çi̯-lĭ′çi̯a (*rolling*). A province of Asia Minor. Chief city, Tarsus, birthplace of Paul, Acts ix. 11, 30 ; xv. 41.

Çĭn′nȧ-mŏn (*dried*). Inner bark of the cinnamon-tree, Ex. xxx. 23 ; Rev. xviii. 13. A perfume, Prov. vii. 17.

Çĭn′ne-rŏth. A district of Naphtali, 1 Kgs. xv. 20. [CHINNERETH.]

Çĭr′a-mȧ. Returned Jews, 1 Esdr. v. 20.

Çĭr′′cŭm-çĭ′şion (*cutting around*). Cutting off the foreskin. A rite, performed on males on eighth day after birth, Gen. xvii. ; Lev. xii. 3 ; Ex. xii. 44 ; John vii. 22. Antagonized by Christianity, Acts xv. ; 1 Cor. vii. 18 ; Gal. v. 2.

Çĭs, Acts xiii. 21. [KISH.]

Çī′sai, Esther xi. 12. [KISH.]

Çĭs′tern (*chest*). Common and necessary in the East. Sometimes synonymous with "wells," Num. xxi. 22, and "pits," Gen. xxxvii. 22 ; 2 Sam. xvii. 18 ; Eccl. xii. 6 ; Jer. xxxviii. 6.

Çĭt′ims, 1 Macc. viii. 5. [CHITTIM.]

Çĭt′i̯-zĕn-ship. Roman citizenship exempted from imprisonment or scourging without trial, and gave the right of appeal to the Emperor, Acts xvi. 37 ; xxii. 28, 29 ; xxv. 11.

Çĭt′ȳ (*place for citizens*). Cain and Nimrod city-builders, Gen. iv. 17 ; x. 9–11. "Fenced cities," fortified cities, 2 Kgs. x. 2 ; Isa. xxvi. 1. "City of David," Jerusalem, Bethlehem, 1 Chr. xi. 5 ; Luke ii. 11. "City of God," Jerusalem, Ps. xlvi. 4 ; Neh. xi. 1. "Cities of Refuge," six in number, Deut. xix. 7–9 ; Num. xxxv. 6–15.

Clȧu′dȧ (*lamentable*). A small island near Crete, Acts xxvii. 16.

Clȧu′di̯-ȧ (*lame*). A female friend of Paul and Timothy, 2 Tim. iv. 21.

Clȧu′di̯-us (*lame*). Claudius Cæsar. Fifth Roman Emperor. Reign, A. D. 41–54. Banished the Jews from Rome, Acts xviii. 2.

Clȧu′di̯-us Lȳs′i̯-as. [LYSIAS.]

Clāy. Used variously, Ps. xviii. 42 ; Isa. lvii. 20 ; Jer. xxxviii. 6 ; John ix. 6 ; for making pottery, Isa. xli. 25 ; for brick-making, 2 Sam. xii. 31 ; for sealing, Job xxxviii. 14 ; for writing tablets.

Clēan and Un′clean. Words applied to personal and ceremonial conditions, and to edibility of animals. Gen. vii. 2 ; Lev. xi.–xv. ; Num. xix. ; Ex. xxii. 31 ; xxxiv. 15–26.

Clĕm′ent (*mild*). A co-worker with Paul, Phil. iv. 3.

Clē′o-pas (*renowned father*). One of the two disciples to whom Christ appeared, Luke xxiv. 18.

Clē′o-phas (*renowned*). Husband of Mary, John xix. 25. Called also Alphæus.

Clŏth. Skins first supplied the place of cloth. Art of weaving cloth early known, Ex. xxxv. 25. Judg. v. 30.

Clō′thing. [DRESS.]

Clŏud (*round mass*). A prominent feature in Oriental imagery, Prov. xvi. 15 ; Isa. xxv. 5 ; Job xxx. 15. A token of Divine presence and protection, Ex. xvi. 10 ; Num. xii. 5.

Clout′ed. Worn out and patched, Josh. ix. 5.

Cnī′dus (*ni′dus*) (*age*). The peninsula of Caria, and the city upon it, Acts xxvii. 7 ; 1 Macc. xv. 23.

Cōal (*glow*). The coal of scripture is charcoal, or embers, Prov. xxvi. 21 ; John xviii. 18 ; xxi. 9 ; heated stones, 1 Kgs. xix. 6 ; Isa. vi. 6 ; metaphorical, 2 Sam. xxii. 9–13 ; Ps. xviii. 8, 12, 13 ; Rom. xii. 20.

Cōast (*rib*). Often used as border or boundary, Judg. xi. 20 ; 1 Sam. v. 6 ; Matt. viii. 34.

Cōat (*coarse mantle*). [DRESS.]

Cŏck. The crowing of the cock in Matt. xxvi. 34 ; Mark xiv. 30 ; Luke xxii. 34, indicated the third watch of the night, from midnight to daylight.

Cŏck′a-trīce (*crocodile like.*) The basilisk, Jer. viii. 17 ; Isa. xi. 8 ; xiv. 29 ; lix. 5 ; in all which some species of hissing, venomous serpent is meant.

Cŏck′le (*stinking*). A weed that grows among grain ; doubtless the tare, identified as darnel, Job xxxi. 40.

Çœl′e=Sȳr′i̯-ȧ and Çēl′o=Sȳr′i̯-ȧ (*hollow Syria*). That part of Syria lying between the Libanus and Anti-Libanus ranges, 1 Macc. x. 69.

Cŏf′fer (*basket*). A movable box hanging from the side of a cart, 1 Sam. vi. 8, 11, 15.

Cŏf′fin (*basket*). [BURIAL.]

Cō′hŏrt (*company*). [ARMY.]

Cŏl-hō′zeh (*all-seeing*). A man of Judah, Neh. iii. 15 ; xi. 5.

Cō′li̯-us, 1 Esdr. ix. 23. [KELAIAH.]

Cŏl′lar. "Collars" in Judg. viii. 26, and "chains" in Isa. iii. 19, should be "ear-drops."

Cŏl′lĕge (*collected*). That part of Jerusalem north of the old city, 2 Kgs. xxii. 14.

Cŏl′lops (*tender meat*). Slices of meat, Job xv. 27.

Cŏl′ō-ny (*cultivated*). Philippi, colonized by Rome, Acts xvi. 12.

Cŏl′ors (*tints*). Royal colors, purple, Judg. viii. 26 ; Esth. viii. 15 ; Luke xvi. 19 ; Rev. xvii. 4 ; blue, Ex. xxv. 4 ; Esth. i. 6. Vermilion used for beams, walls and ceilings, Jer. xxii. 14 ; Ezek. xxiii. 14.

Cō-lŏs′sē (*punishment*). A city of Phrygia. Paul wrote to the church there, Col. i. 2 ; iv. 13.

Cō-lŏs′si̯-ans, Epistle to. Written by Paul from Rome, A. D. 61 or 62, and delivered by Tychicus, Acts xxviii. 16 ; Col. iv. 7, 8.

Cōlt (*young camel or ass*). The young of camels and asses, Gen. xxxii. 15 ; xlix. 11 ; Judg. x. 4 ; Job xi. 12 ; Matt. xxi. 2–7.

Cŏm′fŏrt-er (*brave together*). Defender and helper. Applied to the Holy Ghost, and Christ, John xiv. 16.

Cŏm′merce (*buying together.*) Limited among Hebrews, Gen. xiii. 2 ; xxiv. 22, 53. Outside enterprises a failure, 1 Kgs. xxii. 48–9. Used some foreign articles, Ez. iii. 7 ; Neh. xiii. 16 ; supplied some, 1 Kgs. v. 11 ; Acts xii. 20. Temple commerce led to Christ's rebuke, Matt. xxi. 12 ; John ii. 14.

Cŏm-mū′nion (*bound together*). Mutual love, confidence and fellowship, 1 Cor. x. 16 ; 2 Cor. xiii. 14 ; 1 John i. 3. The Lord's supper called the "holy communion."

Cŏm′pass (*encircle*). To make a circuit, 2 Sam. v. 23 ; Acts xxviii. 13.

Cŏn-a̤-nī′ah (*made by Jehovah*). A Levite, 2 Chr. xxxv. 9.

Cŏn-çī′şion (*cutting off*). A sarcastic use by Paul of the word circumcision, Phil. iii. 2.

Cŏn′cū-bine (*lying with*). In the Jewish economy, a secondary wife, betrothed according to custom, Gen. xxi. 14 ; xxv. 6 ; Ex. xxi. 7 ; Deut. xxi. 10–14. Concubinage repudiated in N. T., Matt. xix. 4–9 ; 1 Cor. vii. 2–4.

Cŏn′duit (*wit*) (*conductor*). A water pipe or aqueduct, 2 Kgs. xviii. 17 ; xx. 20 ; Isa. vii. 3 ; xxxvi. 2 ; ditch, Job xxxviii. 25.

Cō′nĕy, Cō′nў (*rabbit*). The small rabbit-like animal known as the *Hyrax Syriacus*, Lev. xi. 5 ; Deut. xiv. 7 ; Prov. xxx. 26.

Cŏn″grē-gā′tion (*collected together*). Biblically, the Hebrew nationality, Num. xv. 15. Generally, collected Jewry, Ex. xii. 19. A popular assembly, Acts xix. 32, 39, 41. A religious assembly, or church, Acts vii. 38.

Cō-nī′ah. [JECONIAH.]

Cŏn″o̤-nī′ah (*the Lord's appointed*). Treasurer of tithes, 2 Chr. xxxi. 12, 13.

Cŏn′sĕ-crāte (*together sacred*). The tribe of Levi consecrated to the priesthood, Ex. xxxii. 28, 29 ; Lev. vii. 37. Consecrate vessels, Josh. vi. 19 ; profits, Mic. iv. 13 ; fields, Lev. xxvii. 28 ; cattle, 2 Chr. xxix. 33 persons, Num. vi. 9–13 ; nations, Ex. xix. 6.

Cŏn″vō-cā′tion (*called together*). The "congregation," when called in a purely religious capacity, Ex. xii. 16 ; Lev. xxiii. 2 ; Num. xxviii. 18.

Cook′ing. Done by both sexes, Gen. xviii. 6–8 ; later by servantage, 1 Sam. viii. 13. Kids, lambs and calves furnished meat for guests, Gen. xviii. 7 ; Luke xv. 23.

Cō′ŏs (*summit*), Acts xxi. 1. [Cos.]

Cō′ping. The top and projecting layer of a wall, 1 Kgs. vii. 9.

Cŏp′per (*from Cyprus*). The "brass" of the Bible. Known to antediluvians, Gen. iv. 22. Used largely in the temple, 1 Chr. xxii. 3–14 ; and for vessels, ornaments and mirrors, Ex. xxxviii. 8 ; helmets and spears, 1 Sam. xvii. 5, 6 ; 2 Sam. xxi. 16.

Cŏr. [HOMER.]

Cŏr′al. Used by Hebrews for beads and ornaments. Ranked among precious stones, Job xxviii. 18 ; Ezek. xxvii. 16.

Cŏr′ban (*offering*). The offering in fulfilment of a vow, Lev. xxvii. ; Num. xxx. The plea of corban reprehended by Christ, Matt. xv. 3–9.

Cŏr′be, 1 Esdr. v. 22. [ZACCAI.]

Cŏrd (*string*). Variously made and used, Isa. xix. 9 ; scourge, John ii. 15 ; ship-ropes, Acts xxvii. 32.

Cō′rĕ, Ecclus. xlv. 18 ; Jude 11. [KORAH.]

Cō″rḭ-ăn′der (*smelling like a bed-bug*). A plant of the parsley family producing aromatic seeds. Ex. xvi. 31 ; Num. xi. 7.

Cŏr′inth (*ornament*). Anciently Ephyra ; capital of Achaia. Destroyed by Rome, B. C. 146. Rebuilt by Julius Cæsar, B. C. 46, as a Roman colony. Paul founded a church there, Acts xviii. 1 ; xx. 2, 3.

Cŏr-ĭn′thḭ-ans, Epistles to. I. written by Paul at Ephesus, 1 Cor. xvi. 8 ; treats of church organization, social practices, holy observances, and doctrinal affairs. II. written a few months afterwards, at suggestion of Titus ; largely refers to Paul's right to preach and teach, 2 Cor. vii. 5 ; ix. 2.

Cŏr′mō-rant (*sea raven*). A large, greedy water-bird, pronounced "unclean." Lev. xi. 17 ; Deut. xiv. 17. Doubtless "pelican" in Isa. xxxiv. 11 ; Zeph.

ii. 14.

Cŏrn (*kernel*). In a Bible sense, grain of all kinds except our maize, or Indian corn. Used largely in figurative speech, Gen. xli. 22 ; Ex. ix. 32 ; Deut. xi. 14 ; xviii. 4 ; xxviii. 51 ; 2 Chr. ii. 15 ; Isa. xxviii. 25 ; Ezek. xxvii. 17 ; Matt. xii. 1.

Cŏr-nē′lḭus (*of a horn*). A Roman centurion and first Gentile convert, Acts x. 1–33.

Cŏr′ner (*horned*). Grain-field corners not allowed to be wholly reaped, Lev. xix. 9 ; xxiii. 22. "Legal corner," one sixtieth of the field. "Length and breadth" of a country, Num. xxiv. 17 ; Jer. xlviii. 45. "Cornerstone," chief stone in a foundation, Job xxxviii. 6. Figuratively in Isa. xxviii. 16 ; Matt. xxi. 42.

Cŏr′net (*horn*). The curved signal horn of the Jews, usually made of the horn of a ram, ox, chamois, or wild goat, Lev. xxv. 9 ; Ezek. xxxiii. 4, 5 ; 1 Chr. xv. 28.

Cŏs, Cō′ŏs (*summit*). A small island of the Grecian archipelago, Acts xxi. 1.

Cō′sam (*diviner*). One of Christ's ancestors, Luke iii. 28.

Cōte (*cot, den*). A sheepfold, 2 Chr. xxxii. 28.

Cŏt′t̤age (*cot*). A rustic tent or shelter, Isa. xxiv. 20.

Cŏt′ton (*wool-plant*). Not known to Hebrews. Cotton garments mentioned on the Rosetta stone.

Cŏuch (*placed*). [BED.]

Cŏun′çĭl (*called together*). In N. T., (1) The Sanhedrim, Matt. xxvi. 49. (2) Lesser courts, Matt. x. 17 ; Mark xiii. 9. (3) A jury of councillors, Acts xxv. 12. [SANHEDRIM.]

Cŏur′ses (*running*). Priests divided into twenty-four classes, courses, or orders, 1 Chr. xxiv. [ABIA.]

Cŏurt (*enclosure*). The enclosed space within the limits of Oriental houses. The outer area of the tabernacle and temple, Ex. xxvii. 9 ; Lev. vi. 16 ; 2 Sam. xvii. 18 ; 1 Kgs. vi. 36 ; 2 Kgs. xxiii. 12 ; 2 Chr. xxxiii. 5.

Cŏu′tha. One of the returned, 1 Esdr. v. 32.

Cŏv′ē-nant (*coming together*). Ratified by eating together, oaths, witnesses, gifts, pillars, Gen. ix. 15 ; xxi. 30, 31 ; xxxi. 50–52. Covenant of the law through Moses, Ex. xx. 24 ; of the gospel through Christ, Gal. iii. ; Heb. viii.

Cŏv′et (*desire*). Rightful desire, 1 Cor. xii. 31, good. Wrongful desire, sinful, Ex. xx. 17 ; xviii. 21 ; Prov. xxviii. 16 ; Luke xii. 15–34 ; 1 Tim. vi. 9, 10.

Cow. Cow and calf not to be killed on same day, Lev. xxii. 28. Symbol of plenty, Isa. vii. 21.

Cŏz (*thorn*). A Judahite, 1 Chr. iv. 8.

Cŏz′bī (*liar*). Daughter of Zur, Num. xxv. 15–18.

Crăck′nels (*that cracks*). Hard brittle cakes, 1 Kgs. xiv. 3.

Crāne. A large, long-necked, heron-like bird, of gray plumage, noisy on the wing, Isa. xxxviii. 14 ; Jer. viii. 7.

Crā′tes. Governor of Cyprus, 2 Macc. iv. 29.

Crē-āte′, Crē-ā′tion (*make, made*). To produce out of nothing by Almighty fiat, Gen. i. ii. The universe.

Crĕs′çens (*increasing*). Assistant of Paul, 2 Tim. iv. 10.

Crēte (*carnal*). Now Candia. One of the largest islands in the Grecian archipelago. Paul founded a church there in charge of Titus, Acts ii. 11 ; xxvii. 1–12 ; Tit. i. 5–13.

Crētes. Inhabitants of Crete, Acts ii. 11.

Crĭb. A stall for cattle, and the manger or rack for hay or straw, Job xxxix. 9 ; Prov. xiv. 4 ; Isa. i. 3.

Crĭm′son (*carmine*). A deep-red color ; or a red tinged with blue, Jer. iv. 30.

Crĭsp′ing=pins (*curling pins*). Crimping pins, Isa. iii. 22.

Crĭs′pus (*curled*). Chief ruler of the synagogue at Corinth, Acts xviii. 8. Baptized by Paul, 1 Cor. i. 14.

Crŏss (*across*). A gibbet of wood of various forms, Deut. xxi. 23; John xix. 17; Gal. iii. 13. Now a sacred emblem.

Crown (*curved*). A head-dress, Ezek. xvi. 12· Head-dress of priests, kings, and queens, Ex. xxviii. 36–38; 2 Chr. xxiii. 11; Esth. ii. 17. Symbol of power, honor, and eternal life, Prov. xii. 4; Lam. v. 16; 1 Pet. v. 4.

Crū″cĭ-fīx′ĭon (*fixing to the cross*). A method of death punishment by fixing to a cross, Gen. xl. 19; Esth. vii. 10. Limbs sometimes broken to hasten death, John xix. 31. Sepulture denied, Deut. xxi. 22, 23, but an exception allowed in Christ's case, Matt. xxvii. 58.

Crū′cĭ-fy. [CRUCIFIXION.]

Crūse (*pot*). A bottle, flask, or jug for holding liquids, 1 Sam. xxvi. 11; 1 Kgs. xvii. 12; xix. 6.

Crȳs′tal (*frost*). A disputed original, variously translated crystal, Job xxviii. 17; frost, Gen. xxxi. 40; ice, Job xxxviii. 29.

Cū′bit (*elbow*). Distance from the elbow to end of the middle finger, or about 21.8 inches, Gen. vi. 15; 1 Sam. xvii. 4.

Cuck′oo (*crower*). A mistranslation; and perhaps the storm-petrel is meant, Lev. xi. 16; Deut. xiv. 15.

Cū′cŭm-ber (*cumberer*). Much used for food in the East, Num. xi. 5; Isa. i. 8.

Cŭm′min. An annual of the parsley family, producing aromatic seeds, Isa. xxviii. 25; Matt. xxiii. 23.

Cŭn′ning (*test*). Skilful, Gen. xxv. 27; 1 Sam. xvi. 16.

Cŭp (*coop, tub*). A drinking vessel of various designs, made of horn, clay, or metal, Gen. xliv. 2; 1 Sam. xvi. 13; 1 Kgs. vii. 26. Used figuratively in Ps. xxiii. 5; Isa. li. 17; Rev. xiv. 10; Matt. xx. 22; xxvi. 39.

Cŭp′beăr″er. [BUTLER.]

Cŭsh (*black*). (1) Oldest son of Ham, Gen. x. 6, 8; 1 Chr. i. 8–10. (2) That indefinite country translated Ethiopia in Gen. ii. 13. (3) The country settled by Ham's descendants, Gen. x. 6–8; Isa. xviii. 1; Jer. xiii. 23; Dan. xi. 43. (4) A Benjamite, Ps. vii. title.

Cu′shan (*blackness*), Hab. iii. 7. Some refer it to Cush.

Cu′shi (*Ethiopian*). (1) A foreigner in David's army, 2 Sam. xviii. 21–32. (2) An ancestor of Jehudi, Jer. xxxvi. 14. (3) Father of Zephaniah, Zeph. i. 1.

Cŭth (*burning*). The land in Persia whence colonists came into Samaria, 2 Kgs. xvii. 30. Cuthah in vs. 24.

Cū′thah, Cŭth-ītes, 2 Kgs. xvii. 24. [CUTH.]

Cŭt′tings, Of the flesh, forbidden by Levitical law, Lev. xix. 28; xxi. 5; Deut. xiv. 1.

Çȳ′ă-mon. A place near Carmel, Judith vii. 3.

Çym′bal (*hollow of a vessel*). Metallic plates, slightly concave, used as musical instruments, by striking them together, 1 Chr. xiii. 8; xvi. 5; Ps. cl. 5; 1 Cor. xiii. 1.

Çȳ′press (*from Cyprus*). Not indigenous to Palestine. Juniper may be meant, Isa. xliv. 14.

Çȳp′rĭ-an. Dweller in Cyprus, 2 Macc. iv. 29.

Çȳ′prus (*fairness*). A large island in N. E. angle of the Mediterranean. Christianity introduced quite early, Acts xi. 19. Birthplace of Barnabas, Acts iv. 36. Paul visited it, Acts xiii. 4–13.

Çȳ-rē′nē (*wall*). Capital of Cyrenaica, in northern Africa, and corresponding to Tripoli. Simon was of Cyrene, Matt. xxvii. 32; Mark xv. 21. Cyreneans present at Pentecost, Acts ii. 10; vi. 9.

Çȳ-rē′nĭ-us (*of Cyrene*). Roman governor of Syria, B. C. 4–1, and A. D. 6–11; Luke ii. 2; Acts v. 37.

Çȳ′rus (*sun*). Founder of the Persian empire, Dan. vi. 28; xi. 13; 2 Chr. xxxvi. 22. United Media to Persia. Conquered Babylon, B. C. 538, and reigned over the consolidated empire till B. C. 529. A guardian and liberator of captive Jews, Isa. xliv. 28; xlv. 1–7. Daniel was his favorite minister. *See* Dan., also Ez. i. 1–4; iii. 7; iv. 3; v. 13–17; vi. 3.

D

Dăb′a-reh, Josh. xxi. 28. [DABERATH.]

Dăb′ba-shĕth (*hump*). A boundary of Zebulun, Josh. xix. 11.

Dăb′e-răth (*pasture*). A Levitical city, Josh. xix. 12.

Dăb′rĭ-ă. A swift scribe, 2 Esdr. xiv. 24.

Dă-cō′bī, 1 Esdr. v. 28. [AKKUB.]

Dăd-dē′us, or **Săd-dē′us,** 1 Esdr. viii. 45, 46. [IDDO.]

Dā′gŏn (*fish*). National male idol of the Philistines, 1 Chr. x. 10. Noted temples at Ashdod, 1 Sam. v. 1–7; Gaza, Judg. xvi. 23; Beth-dagon, Josh. xv. 41; and in Asher, Josh. xix. 27. Represented with human hands and face and a fish's body.

Daī′san, 1 Esdr. v. 31. [REZIN.]

Dăl″a-ī′ah (*freed by God*). A Judahite, 1 Chr. iii. 24.

Dāle, the King′s. A valley near Jerusalem, Gen. xiv. 17; 2 Sam. xviii. 18.

Dăl″ma-nū′thă. A town on Sea of Galilee, Mark viii. 10.

Dăl-mā′tĭ-ă (*-she-a*) (*deceitful*). A province of Illyricum, 2 Tim. iv. 10; Rom. xv. 19.

Dăl′phon (*swift*). Son of Haman, Esth. ix. 7.

Dăm′a-rĭs (*heifer*). An Athenian woman converted by Paul, Acts xvii. 34.

Dă-măs′cus. A city of Asia, 133 miles N. E. of Jerusalem, Gen. xiv. 15; xv. 2. Adjacent region called "Syria of Damascus," 2 Sam. viii. 5. Taken by David, 2 Sam. viii. 6; and by Jeroboam, 2 Kgs. xiv. 28. Scene of Paul's conversion, Acts ix. 1–27; xxii. 1–16.

Dăm-nā′tion (*condemnation*). Consignment to everlasting perdition, Matt. xxiii. 33; Mark iii. 29; John v. 29; 2 Pet. ii. 3.

Dăn (*judge*). (1) Fifth son of Jacob, Gen. xxx. 6; xlix. 16. Allotment, Josh. xix. 40–46. Portion of the tribe moved north, Josh. xix. 47, 48; Judg. xviii. (2) Changed name of Laish, or Leshem, Josh. xix. 47; Judg. xviii. 29. (3) A place in Arabia, Ezek. xxvii. 19.

Dăn′ītes. Members of the tribe of Dan, Judg. xiii. 2; 1 Chr. xii. 35.

Dăn=jā′an (*Danite*). Probably the northern Danites, 2 Sam. xxiv. 6.

Dănce (*drag along*). (1) In Hebrew, "leaping for joy." Not a measured step, Ps. xxx. 11. Common on festal occasions, Ex. xv. 20, 21; Judg. xi. 34; 1 Sam. xviii. 6, 7; 2 Sam. vi. 14; Jer. xxxi. 4; Luke vi. 23; xv. 25; Acts iii. 8. (2) A musical instrument, Ps. cl. 3–5. "Pipe," in margin.

Dăn′iel (*judgment of God*). (1) Fourth of the greater prophets. Carried captive to Babylon, B. C. 604; and named Belteshazzar, Dan. i., ii. Made a governor under Darius, Dan. vi. 2. Last vision on the Tigris in third year of Cyrus, B. C. 534, x. 1–4. (2) Second son of David, 1 Chr. iii. 1. (3) Son of Ithamar, Ez. viii. 2. (4) A co-covenanter, Neh. x. 6.

Dăn′iel, Book of. First six chapters historic. Chapters vii.–xii. contain the earliest model of apocalyptic literature. Largely acknowledged in N. T., Matt. xxiv. 15; Luke i. 19, 26; Heb. xi. 33, 34.

"The Song of the Three Holy Children," "History of Susanna," and "History of Bel and the Dragon," are apocryphal additions to Daniel's writings.

Dăn′nah (*judging*). A city of Judah, Josh. xv. 49.

Dăph′ne (*bay-tree*). Sanctuary of Apollo, near Antioch, 2 Macc. iv. 33.

Dā′rà, 1 Chr. ii. 6. [DARDA.]

Där′dà (*pearl of wisdom*). One of four famed for wisdom, 1 Kgs. iv. 31.

Där′ic (*kingly*). A Persian coin of gold and silver; former worth about five dollars; latter fifty cents. "Dram," in 1 Chr. xxix. 7; Ez. ii. 69; Neh. vii. 70–72.

Dā-rī′us (*Persian "dara," king*). (1) Darius the Mede, Dan. v. 31; vi.; ix. 1; xi. 1. Captured Babylon from Belshazzar, B. C. 538. (2) Darius Hystaspes, King of Persia, B. C. 521–486. He restored the captive Jews, Ez. iv. 5, 24; vi. 14, 15; Hag. i. 1, 15; Zech. i. 1, 7; vii. 1. (3) Darius the Persian, Neh. xii. 22. Darius Codomanus, B. C. 336–330, last king of Persia.

Därk′ness (*blackness*). Absence of light, Gen. i. 2; 9th plague, Ex. x. 20–23; State of misery, Job xviii. 6; God's dwelling, Ex. xx. 21; 1 Kgs. viii. 12; typical of national convulsion, Acts ii. 19, 20; state of the fallen, Matt. viii. 12; ignorance, John i. 5; sympathetic, Luke xxiii. 44.

Där′kon (*scatterer*). His children returned, Ez. ii. 56; Neh. vii. 58.

Dāte (*like a finger*). Fruit of the date-palm, 2 Chr. xxxi. 5, marg. [PALM.]

Dā′than (*of a spring*). A Reubenite chief and conspirator, Num. xvi.; xxvi. 9; Deut. xi. 6.

Dăth′e-ma. Ramoth-gilead, 1 Macc. v. 9.

Daugh′ter (*milk*). Daughter or any female descendant, Gen. xxiv. 48; female inhabitant, Gen. vi. 2; Isa. x. 32; xxiii. 12; Luke xxiii. 28; singing birds, Eccl. xii. 4.

Dā′vid (*well-beloved*). Youngest son of Jesse, 1 Sam. xvi. 8–12, born at Bethlehem. Anointed king by Samuel, 1 Sam. xvi. 13. Re-anointed at Hebron, 2 Sam. ii. 4. United his kingdom and raised it to great strength and splendor. Died at the age of 70, B. C. 1015, after a reign of seven and a half years over Judah and thirty-three years over the entire kingdom of Israel. History told in 1 Sam. xvi. to 1 Kgs. ii.

Dā′vid, City of. [JERUSALEM.]

Dāy (*shining*). Natural Hebrew day from sunset to sunset, Gen. i. 5; Ex. xii. 18. Sabbath the only day named; others numbered, Lev. xxiii. 32. Morning, noon, and evening divisions, Ps. lv. 17. Hours introduced, Dan. iii. 6; John xi. 9. Indefinite time, Gen. ii. 4; of birth, Job iii. 1; of ruin, Hos. i. 11; of judgment, Joel i. 15; of Christ's kingdom, John viii. 56.

Dāys′man. Umpire or moderator, Job ix. 33.

Dāy′spring. Dawn, Job xxxviii. 12; Luke i. 78.

Dāy′star. Morning star, 2 Pet. i. 19.

Dēa′con (*servant*). A subordinate minister or officer in early Christian Church, Acts vi. 1–6. Qualifications in 1 Tim. iii. 8–12.

Dēa′con-ess. A female officer in early Church, Rom. xvi. 1; 1 Tim. v. 10.

Dĕad Sea. Not so called until the second century. In O. T. "Salt Sea" and "Sea of the Plain." [SALT SEA.]

Dēarth. [FAMINE.]

Dē′bĭr (*oracle*). (1) A Levitical city of Judah, Josh. xxi. 15; Kirjath-sepher, Josh. xv. 15; Kirjath-sannah, xv. 49. (2) A northern boundary of Judah, Josh. xv. 7. (3) A boundary of Gad, Josh. xiii. 26. (4) A king of Eglon, Josh. x. 3–26.

Dĕb′o-rah (*bee*). (1) Nurse of Rebekah, Gen. xxxv. 8; xxiv. 59. (2) Prophetess and Judge, Judg.

iv. 5–14; v. (3) Grandmother of Tobit, Tob. i. 8.

Dĕbt′ŏr (*ower*). Lands or the person might be taken for debt, and held till the year of jubilee, Ex. xxi. 2; Lev. xxv. 29–34; 2 Kgs. iv. 1; Neh. v. 3–5.

Dĕ-căp′ŏ-lis (*ten cities*). A Roman province embracing parts of Syria and Palestine, Matt. iv. 25; Mark v. 20; vii. 31.

De-cĭ′şion, Valley of. Joel iii. 14. "Valley of Jehoshaphat," "or judgment," as in verses 2 and 12.

Dē′dan (*low*). (1) Grandson of Cush, Gen. x. 7. (2) Son of Jokshan, Gen. xxv. 3. Both founders of Arabian or Idumean tribes, Isa. xxi. 13; Ezek. xxxviii. 13.

Dĕd′a-nīm. Descendants of Dedan, Isa. xxi. 13.

Dĕd′′i-cā′tion (*declaration*). Devoting person, place or thing to holy use, Ex. xl.; Num. vii.; 2 Sam. viii. 11; 1 Kgs. viii.; Ez. vi.; Neh. xii. 27; "Feast of Dedication" commemorated the purging of the temple, John x. 22; 1 Macc. iv. 52–59.

Dēep. Abyss, or abode, of lost spirits, Luke viii. 31; Rom. x. 7. "Bottomless pit," Rev. ix. 1, 2, 11; xi. 7.

Dēer (*wild*), Deut. xiv. 5; 1 Kgs. iv. 23. [FALLOW-DEER.]

Dĕ-grēe′ (*step or grade down*). Rank or station, Ps. lxii. 9; 1 Tim. iii. 13. "Song of Degrees," title to Pss. cxx.–cxxxiv.

Dĕ-hā′vītes. Colonists planted in Samaria, Ez. iv. 9.

Dē′kär (*lancer*). Father of one of Solomon's commissaries, 1 Kgs. iv. 9.

Del′′a-ī′ah (*freed by God*). (1) Leader of the 23d priestly course, 1 Chr. xxiv. 18. (2) Returned Jews, Ez. ii. 60; Neh. vii. 62. (3) Father of Shemaiah, Neh. vi. 10. (4) A courtier, Jer. xxxvi. 12.

Dĕ-lī′lah (*longing*). A woman of Sorek, employed to discover the secret of Samson's strength, Judg. xvi. 4–20.

Dĕl′ūge (*washing away*). The usual modern word for Noah's flood, Gen. vi.–viii.

Dē′lus (*suddenly visible*). Smallest of the Cyclades islands, 1 Macc. xv. 23.

Dē′mas (*popular*). A friend of Paul at Rome, Col. iv. 14; 2 Tim. iv. 10.

Dĕ-mē′trī-us (*belonging to Ceres*). (1) A silversmith at Ephesus, Acts xix. 24–30. (2) A disciple, 3 John, 12. (3) Demetrius (I.) Soter, of Syria, 1 Macc. x. 48–50. (4) Demetrius (II.) Nicator, 1 Macc. x.

Dĕ-nā′rī-us (*ten asses*). A Roman silver coin worth about 15 cents. The "penny" of N. T., Matt. xx. 2.

Dĕp′ū-tỹ (*selected*). In N. T., a proconsul, or governor, Acts xiii. 7, 8, 12.

Dĕr′bē (*sting*). A city of Lycaonia in Asia Minor, Acts xiv. 20; xx. 4.

Dĕs′ert (*deserted*). An arid sandy plain, or wild mountainous waste, Ex. xxiii. 31; Deut. xi. 24; Ps. lxv. 12.

Dĕs′sä-ŭ. A village, 2 Macc. xiv. 16.

Deū′el (*knowledge of God*). Father of Eliasaph, Num. i. 14. Reuel in ii. 14.

Deū′′te-rŏn′o-mỹ. So called because it "repeats the law." Fifth book of O. T. and last of the Pentateuch. Authorship ascribed to Moses, except last chapter. Chapters i.–iv. 40, rehearse the wanderings; v.–xxvi. recapitulate the law; the others deliver the law into keeping of the Levites, and describe the death of Moses.

Dĕv′il (*slanderer*). The Hebrew Satan, "adversary," Matt. xvi. 23; Mark viii. 33; Luke xxii. 3; Rev. xx. 2. The devil of bodily possession was rather the polluting power of disease — dumbness, Matt. ix. 32; blindness, xii. 22; epilepsy, Mark ix. 17–27; insanity, Matt. viii. 28; murderous antipathy, John vii. 20.

Dẹw. Source of fertility, Gen. xxvii. 28; Judg. vi

BIBLE DICT

37–40; object of rich imagery, Deut. xxxii. 2; Job xxix. 19; Ps. cxxxiii. 3.

Dī′al (*daily*). An instrument for telling the time of day, 2 Kgs. xx. 11; Isa. xxxviii. 8.

Dī′a-mŏnd (*adamant*). Pure crystallized carbon. Third stone in second row of high-priest's breast-plate, Ex. xxviii. 18; Ezek. xxviii. 13.

Dī-ăn′à (*safety*). A Roman goddess. Artemis of the Greeks. Her temple at Ephesus regarded as one of the seven wonders of the world, Acts xix. 24–28.

Dĭb′la-ĭm (*two cakes*). Mother-in-law of Hosea, Hos. i. 3.

Dĭb′lăth. Unidentified place, Ezek. vi. 14.

Dī′bŏn (*wasting*). (1) A town of Gad, Num. xxxii. 3, 34. Dibon-gad, Num. xxxiii, 45, 46. Accounted to Reuben, Josh. xiii. 9, 17. Now Dhiban, within the gateway of which the famous Moabite stone was found in 1868. (2) A town in south Judah, Neh. xi. 25.

Dī′bon=găd. [DIBON, 1.]

Dĭb′rī (*orator*). A Danite, Lev. xxiv. 11.

Dĭd′y̆-mus (*twin*). Surname of Thomas, John xi. 16; xx. 24; xxi. 2.

Dĭk′lah (*palm*). A son of Joktan, Gen. x. 27; 1 Chr. i. 21.

Dĭl′ĕ-an (*cucumber*). A lowland city of Judah, Josh. xv. 38.

Dĭm′nah (*dung*). A Levitical city, Josh. xxi. 35.

Dī′mon (*reddish*). A stream of Moab, Isa. xv. 9.

Dī-mō′nah (*dunghill*) A city in south Judah, Josh. xv. 22.

Dī′nah (*judged*). First daughter of Jacob and Leah, Gen. xxx. 21; xxxiv.

Dī′na-ītes. Cuthean colonists in Samaria, Ez. iv. 9.

Dĭn′hă-bah. A capital of Edom, Gen. xxxvi. 32; 1 Chr. i. 43.

Dī″ŏ-ny̆s′ĭus (*devotee of Dionysos, or Bacchus*). A member of the court of Areopagus at Athens, Acts xvii. 34.

Dī″ŏ-ny̆s′us (*Bacchus*). Bacchus, 2 Macc. xiv. 33.

Dī′os=cŏr-ĭn′thĭ-us (*Corinthian Jove*). A month in the Cretan calendar, 2 Macc. xi. 21.

Dĭ-ot′rĕ-phēs (*nourished by Jupiter*). A Christian, 3 John 9.

Dĭs-çĭ′ple (*learner*). Follower of Christ, Matt. x. 24; of John, Matt. ix. 14. Applied specially to the twelve, Matt. x. 1; xi. 1; xx. 17.

Dĭs′cus (*round plate*). The quoit, 2 Macc. iv. 14.

Dĭs-cŏv′er (*uncover*). Uncovering, making bare, Ps. xxix. 9; Isa. xxii. 8; Mic. i. 6.

Dĭs-ēas′es (*uneasy*). Visitations of plagues and pestilences frequent in Bible lands, Gen. vii. viii.; Ex. xii. 21–29; 2 Kgs. xix. 35; 1 Chr. xxi. 12; Acts xii. 23. Principal bodily diseases were, ophthalmia, leprosy, brain and malarial fevers, lung disorders.

Dī′shan (*antelope*). Youngest son of Seir, Gen. xxxvi. 21.

Dī′shon (*antelope*). Sons of Seir, Gen. xxxvi. 21–30.

Dĭs″pĕn-sā′tion (*weighing out*), 1 Cor. ix. 17; Eph. i. 10; iii. 2; Col. i. 25. In these instances, authority to preach and teach.

Dĭs-pĕr′sion (*scattering*). The breaking up of the Jewish kingdoms and scattering of the tribes by conquest, James i. 1; 1 Pet. i. 1.

Dĭs′taff (*flax-staff*). The staff around which flax was wound for spinning, Prov. xxxi. 19.

Dī′vęs (*rich*). A popular name for the rich man in Luke xvi. 19–31.

Dĭv″ĭ-nā′tion (*belonging to a god*). In Scripture, the false use of means to discover the divine will; by rods, Hos. iv. 12; arrows, Ezek. xxi. 21; cups, Gen. xliv. 5; the liver, Ezek. xxi. 21; dreams,

Deut. xiii. 3; Zech. x. 2; consulting oracles, Isa. xli. 21–24; xliv. 7. Faith in divination forbidden, Lev. xix. 26.

Di-vôrçe′ (*turning asunder*). Allowed by Mosaic law, Deut. xxiv. 1–4, yet forbidden in certain cases, xxii. 19, 29. Christ regarded adultery as an only cause for divorce, Matt. v. 31, 32; xix. 9; Mark x. 11; Luke xvi. 18.

Dĭz′a-hăb (*gold region*). Scene of one of Moses' addresses, Deut. i. 1.

Dŏc′tor (*teacher*). A teacher of the Law of Moses, Luke ii. 46; v. 17. Teacher of the Christian faith, 1 Cor. xii. 28.

Dō′cus. Springs near Jericho, 1 Macc. xvi. 15.

Dŏd′a-ī (*loving*). Leader of David's second military course, 1 Chr. xxvii. 4.

Dŏd′a-nĭm (*leaders*). Descendants of Javan, Gen. x. 4; 1 Chr. i. 7.

Dŏd′a-vah. Father of Eliezer, 2 Chr. xx. 37.

Dō′dō (*loving*). (1) Father of one of David's captains, 2 Sam. xxiii. 24. (2) Father of Eleazar, 2 Sam. xxiii. 9; 1 Chr. xi. 12. (3) Grandfather of Tola, Judg. x. 1.

Dō′eg (*fearful*). An overseer of Saul's herds, 1 Sam. xxi. 7; xxii. 9–22.

Dŏg. An unclean animal, Ex. xi. 7; xxii. 31; Deut. xxiii. 18; regarded with contempt, 1 Sam. xvii. 43; xxiv. 14; 2 Sam. ix. 8; 2 Kgs. viii. 13; Matt. vii. 6; Rev. xxii. 15; guards, Isa. lvi. 10; Job xxx. 1; scavengers, 1 Kgs. xiv. 11; xxi. 19–23; xxii. 38; enemies, Ps. xxii. 16–20.

Dōor (*through*). [GATE.]

Dŏph′kah (*drover*). A desert station of the Israelites, Num. xxxiii. 12.

Dôr (*dwelling*). A city on the coast north of Cæsarea, Josh. xi. 2; xii. 23; xvii. 11; Judg. i. 27; 1 Kgs. iv. 11.

Dō′rà, 1 Macc. xv. 11. [DOR.]

Dŏr′cas (*gazelle*). The woman of Joppa whom Peter raised from the dead, Acts ix. 36–42. [TABITHA.]

Dō-ry̆m′ĕ-nēs. Father of Ptolemy Macron, 1 Macc. iii. 38.

Dō-sĭth′ĕ-us. (1) A Jewish captain, 2 Macc. xii. 19–35. (2) A priest, Esth. xi. 1, 2.

Dō′tha-ĭm, Judith iv. 6. [DOTHAN.]

Dō′than (*two wells*). The place where Joseph was sold, Gen. xxxvii. 17; 2 Kgs. vi. 13.

Do You To Wit. To make known, 2 Cor. viii. 1.

Dove (*diver*). Clean by the law and offered as a sacrifice by the poor, Gen. xv. 9; Lev. v. 7; xii. 6–8; Luke ii. 24; symbol of innocence, Matt. x. 16; harbinger of God, Gen. viii.; emblem of Holy Spirit, Matt. iii. 16.

Dove's Dŭng. Eaten as a last resort, in time of famine, 2 Kgs. vi. 25.

Dow′ry̆ (*gift*). The consideration paid the father of the bride by the bridegroom, Gen. xxix. 18; xxxiv. 12; 1 Sam. xviii. 25; Hos. iii. 2.

Drăch′mà, Drăchm (*handful*). A silver coin of Greece, corresponding to the Roman denarius, and worth about fifteen and a half cents. A piece of silver, Luke xv. 8, 9.

Drăg′on (*serpent*). An animal of the lizard species. Evidently a wild beast, as a jackal, in Job xxx. 29; Isa. xxxiv. 13; Ps. xliv. 19; Jer. ix. 11; Mic. i. 8; sea-serpent, Gen. i. 21; land-serpent, Ex. vii. 9–12; Deut. xxxii. 33; devil, Rev. xii. 3–17.

Drăg′on Well. Possibly Gihon, Neh. ii. 13.

Drăm (*handful*), 1 Chr. xxix. 7; Ez. ii. 69; Neh. vii. 70–72. [DARIC.]

Drăught House. Cesspool, 2 Kgs. x. 27; Matt. xv. 17.

Dream (*phantom*). Seriously regarded by ancients, Gen. xl. Divine method of approach, Gen.

xx. 3–7 ; 1 Sam. xxviii. 6 ; Acts xxvii. 22–25. Interpretation of an exceptional gift, Gen. xl. 5–23 ; xli. 14–45 ; Dan. iv. 19–27.

Dress (*keeping straight*). Of leaves, Gen. iii. 7; skins, iii. 21 ; woolens, xxxviii. 12 ; Ex. xxv. 4; Lev. xiii. 47 ; linen, 1 Chr. iv. 21 ; silk, Rev. xviii. 12 ; mixed materials forbidden, Lev. xix. 19 ; colors rich, Ex. xxxv. 25 ; Luke xvi. 19 ; no sexual interchanges, Deut. xxii. 5 ; common inner dresses, armless shirt, second tunic, linen wrapper, Mark xiv. 51 ; outer, for men, woolen wrap, 2 Sam. xv. 30 ; Esth. vi. 12 ; for women, a long shawl, Ruth iii. 15 ; Isa. iii. 22–24 ; Jer. xiii. 22 ; girdled, Matt. xxiv. 18 ; Acts xii. 8 ; 1 Kgs. xviii. 46 ; poor man's bedclothes, Ex. xxii. 26, 27.

Drink offering. The pouring of a small quantity of wine on the daily morning and evening sacrificial lamb, Ex. xxix. 40 ; Lev. xxiii. 18.

Drink, Strong. Use of, not uncommon among Hebrews, Gen. ix. 21 ; xix. 34, 35 ; Ps. cvii. 27 ; Isa. xxiv. 20 ; xlix. 26 ; li. 17–22 ; John ii. 1–11 ; but under prohibitions, Prov. xx. 1 ; Isa. v. 11.

Drom'ę-dā-ry (*running*). Post camel of the East, usually the one-humped species, as distinguished from the two-humped, or Bactrian, camel, 1 Kgs. iv. 28 ; Isa. lx. 6 ; Jer. ii. 23 ; Mic. i. 13.

Dru-sĭl'là (*watered by dew*). Daughter of Herod Agrippa I., Acts xii. 1–4, 20–23 ; xxiv. 24.

Duke (*leader*). Hereditary chief or sheikh of Edom, Gen. xxxvi. 15–43.

Dŭl'çi-mer (*sweet song*). The bagpipe and not the stringed dulcimer is meant, Dan. iii. 5–15.

Du'mah (*silence*). (1) A son of Ishmael, Gen. xxv. 14 ; 1 Chr. i. 30. (2) A town in Judah, Josh. xv. 52. (3) A region, Isa. xxi. 11.

Dŭng (*excrement*). Dung of cattle used for fuel, Ezek. iv. 12. Manure made from straw, Isa. xxv. 10. A fertilizer, Luke xiii. 8.

Dŭn'geon (*tower, keep*). [PRISON.]

Du'rà (*circle*). A plain of Babylon, Dan. iii. 1.

Dŭst (*storm breath*). Symbol of mourning, Josh. vii. 6 ; Isa. xlvii. 1 ; feebleness, Gen. xviii. 27 ; Job xxx. 19 ; countless numbers, Gen. xiii. 16 ; low condition, 1 Sam. ii. 8 ; rage, 2 Sam. xvi. 13 ; Acts xxii. 23 ; renunciation, Matt. x. 14 ; Mark vi. 11 ; Acts xiii. 51. A sand storm, Deut. xxviii. 24.

Dwĕll'ings. [HOUSES.]

E

Ea'gle (*dark-colored*). The eagle of Scripture is probably the griffon vulture, Mic. i. 16 ; Matt. xxiv. 28 ; Luke xvii. 37 ; unclean, Lev. xi. 13 ; Deut. xiv. 12; noted for height and rapidity of flight, Prov. xxiii. 5 ; 2 Sam. i. 23 ; Job ix. 26 ; Deut. xxviii. 49 ; Jer. iv. 13 ; great age, Ps. ciii. 5 ; care of young, Ex. xix. 4 ; Deut. xxxii. 11, 12 ; Isa. xl. 31.

E'ạ-nēs. A returned captive, 1 Esdr. ix. 21.

Ear'ing (*plowing*). Earing time was plowing time, Gen. xlv. 6 ; Ex. xxxiv. 21 ; Deut. xxi. 4 ; 1 Sam. viii. 12.

Earn'est (*pledge*). Pledge, Gen. xxxviii. 17 ; surety, Prov. xvii. 18 ; hostage, 2 Kgs. xiv. 14 ; deposit or advance, 2 Cor. i. 22 ; Eph. i. 14.

Ear'rings. Included "nose-rings ; " worn by both sexes ; Gen. xxxv. 4 ; Ex. xxxii. 2 ; Judg. viii. 24 ; Job xlii. 11 ; offerings, Num. xxxi. 50.

Earth (*producer*). The world, Gen. i. 1 ; dry land, i. 10 ; the soil, ii. 7.

Earth'en-wǎre. [POTTERY.]

Earth'quāke (*earth-shaking*). A natural and historic phenomenon, in Am. i. 1 ; Zech. xiv. 5 ; 1 Kgs. xix. 11, 12 ; Matt. xxvii. 51. Token of God's wrath, Judg. v. 4 ; 2 Sam. xxii. 8 ; Ps. lxxvii. 18 ; xcvii. 4 ; civ. 32 ; Am. viii. 8 ; Hab. iii. 10.

East (*dawn*). The Hebrew idea was "before" "in front of," "to the East," Gen. xxix. 1 ; Num.

xiii. 7 ; Job i. 3 ; Ezek. xlvii. 8 ; Matt. ii. 1.

East'er (*Eastre, Saxon goddess*). The day commemorative of Christ's resurrection. Wrongly associated with the Saxon Eastre festival, and the Jewish Passover feast, but corrected in R. V., Acts xii. 4.

East Sea. Ezek. xlvii. 18 ; Joel ii. 20. The Dead Sea.

Eat. Offensive to eat or drink outside of certain limits, Gen. xliii. 32 ; Matt. ix. 11 ; John iv. 9.

E'bal (*stone*). (1) Son of Shobal, Gen. xxxvi. 23. (2) Son of Joktan, 1 Chr. i. 22. Obal, Gen. x. 28.

E'bal, Mount. The mount of curses in Samaria, Deut. xi. 29 ; Josh. viii. 30–35.

E'bed (*servant*). (1) Father of Gaal, Judg. ix. 26–35. (2) One of the returned, Ez. viii. 6.

E'bĕd=mē'lĕch (*king's servant*). An Ethiopian, Jer. xxxviii. 12 ; xxxix. 15–18.

Ĕb''en=ē'zĕr (*stone of help*). A memorial stone, 1 Sam. iv. 1–5 ; vii. 12.

E'bĕr (*beyond*). (1) Great-grandson of Shem, Gen. x. 24 ; 1 Chr. i. 19. (2) A Benjamite, 1 Chr. viii. 12. (3) A priest, Neh. xii. 20.

E-bī'ạ-săph (*father that adds*). A Levite, 1 Chr. vi. 23, 37.

Ĕb'ŏ-nў (*stone-like*). A hard, heavy, dark wood, used for ornamental work and musical instruments, Ezek. xxvii. 15.

E-brō'nah (*gateway*). A desert encampment, Num. xxxiii. 34.

E-cā'nus. A swift scribe, 2 Esdr. xiv. 24.

Ec-băt'ạ-nà (*egress*). Greek for Achmetha, Ez. vi. 2, marg.

Ec-clē''sĭ-ăs'tēs (*preacher*). Twenty-first book of O. T. Authorship ascribed to Solomon. An old man's confession of the vanities of life.

Ec-clē''sĭ-ăs'tĭ-cus (*of the assembly*). The Latin name of the "Wisdom of Jesus, Son of Sirach," seventh of the Apocryphal books.

Ĕd (*witness*). A word, Josh. xxii. 34.

E'där (*flock*). A tower, Gen. xxxv. 21.

Ĕd-dī'as, 1 Esdr. ix. 26. [JEZIAH.]

E'dĕn (*pleasure*). (1) First residence of man, Gen. ii. 15. Paradise. Site not fixed. (2) A mart of Mesopotamia, 2 Kgs. xix. 12 ; Isa. xxxvii. 12. (3) Beth-eden, Am. i. 5. (4) A Levite, 2 Chr. xxix. 12. (5) Another Levite, 2 Chr. xxxi. 15.

E'dĕr (*flock*). (1) A town of Judah, Josh. xv. 21. (2) A Levite, 1 Chr. xxiii. 23 ; xxiv. 30.

E'dēs, 1 Esdr. ix. 35. [JADDUA.]

Ĕd'nà. Wife of Raguel, Tob. vii. 2–16.

E'dom (*red*). Called also Idumea and Mount Seir. Name given to Esau, his country and people, Gen. xxxii. 3–19 ; xxxiii. 1–16. It lay to the south of Palestine and Moab.

Ĕd're-ī (*fortress*). (1) A capital of Bashan, Num. xxi. 33 ; Deut. iii. 10 ; Josh. xii. 4. (2) Town of northern Palestine, Josh. xix. 37.

Ĕg'lah (*heifer*). A wife of David, 2 Sam. iii. 5 ; 1 Chr. iii. 3.

Ĕg'la-ĭm (*ponds*). A place in Moab, Isa. xv. 8.

Ĕg'lŏn (*calf-like*). (1) A King of Moab, Judg. iii. 12–23. (2) A lowland town of Judah, Josh. x. 3–5 ; xv. 39.

E'gўpt (*Coptic land*). Northeastern country of Africa ; the Hebrew "Mizraim," Gen. x. 6, and "Land of Ham," Ps. cv. 23, 27. Bondage place of Israelites, Ex. i.–xiv. Noted for Nile river, rich soil and gigantic ruins. Ancient religion monotheistic, with sun as central object ; and attributes of nature in form of trinities. Vast temples and numerous priests. Kings called Pharaohs, who perpetuated their reigns in obelisks, temples, sculptures, sphinxes, pyramids, etc. In intimate commerce with Hebrews, 1 Kgs. iii. 1. Conquered Judea, 1 Kgs. xiv. 25, 26. Frequently mentioned in Scripture.

E′hī, Gen. xlvi. 21. [AHIRAM.]

E′hŭd (*united*). (1) Son of Bilhan, 1 Chr. vii. 10. (2) A judge of Israel, Judg. iii. 15–21.

E′kĕr (*tearing up*). A Judahite, 1 Chr. ii. 27.

Ĕk′rĕ-bel. A place in Esdraelon, Judith vii. 18.

Ĕk′rŏn (*migration*). One of the five Philistine cities, Josh. xiii. 3 ; xv. 45 ; xix. 43 ; 1 Sam. v. 10.

Ĕk′rŏn-ītes. Inhabitants of Ekron, Josh. xiii. 3.

E′là, 1 Esdr. ix. 27. [ELAM.]

Ĕl′ă-dah (*eternity of God*). An Ephraimite, 1 Chr. vii. 20.

E′lah (*oak*). (1) Son and successor of Baasha on the throne of Israel, B. C. 928–27, 1 Kgs. xvi. 8–10. (2) Father of Hosea, 2 Kgs. xv. 30 ; xvii. 1. (3) A duke of Edom, Gen. xxxvi. 41. (4) Father of Solomon's commissary, 1 Kgs. iv. 18. (5) Son of Caleb, 1 Chr. iv. 15. (6) A chief of Benjamin, 1 Chr. ix. 8. (7) The valley in which David slew Goliath, 1 Sam. xvii. 2–19.

E′lăm (*age*). (1) Son of Shem, Gen. x. 22, and his country, xiv. 1–9 ; Dan. viii. 2, in Mesopotamia. (2) A chief of Benjamin, 1 Chr. viii. 24. (3) A Korhite Levite, 1 Chr. xxvi. 3. (4) Persons whose children returned, Ez. ii. 7, 31 ; Neh. vii. 12, 34. (5) A priest, Neh. x. 14.

E′lăm-ītes. Inhabitants of Elam, Ez. iv. 9.

Ĕl′a-sah (*whom God made*). (1) A priest, Ez. x. 22. (2) Son of Shaphan, Jer. xxix. 3.

E′lăth, E′lŏth (*oaks*). A city of Edom, Deut. ii. 8 ; Seat of Solomon's navy, 1 Kgs. ix. 26 ; 2 Chr. viii. 17.

Ĕl=bĕth′=el (*God of Bethel*). Place where God appeared to Jacob, Gen. xxxv. 7.

Ĕl′çī-à. Progenitor of Judith, Judith viii. 1.

Ĕl′da-ah (*called of God*). Last son of Midian, Gen. xxv. 4 ; 1 Chr. i. 33.

Ĕl′dăd (*loved of God*). One of the seventy assistants of Moses, Num. xi. 16, 26–29.

Ĕl′dĕr (*old man*). Highest in tribal authority, Gen. xxiv. 2 ; l. 7 ; Ex. iii. 16 ; iv. 29 ; Num. xxii. 7. One of the 70 justiciars, Num. xi. 25, or Sanhedrim, Judg. ii. 7 ; 2 Sam. xvii. 4 ; Jer. xxix. 1. An official in early Christian church, like presbyter or bishop, Acts xx. 17, 28.

E′le-ăd (*praised of God*). An Ephraimite, 1 Chr. vii. 21.

E″le-ā′leh (*ascent of God*). A Moabite town, assigned to Reuben, Num. xxxii. 3, 37 ; Isa. xv. 4 ; Jer. xlviii. 34.

Ĕ-lē′a-sà. A place near Ashdod, 1 Macc. ix. 5–18.

Ĕ-lē′a-sah (*made by God*). (1) A Judahite, 1 Chr. ii. 39. (2) A descendant of Saul, 1 Chr. viii. 37 ; ix. 43.

E″le-ā′zar (*help of God*). (1) Third son of Aaron, Ex. vi. 23. Chief of the Levites, Num. iii. 32 ; and high priest, Num. xx. 28. (2) Son of Abinadab, 1 Sam. vii. 1. (3) One of David's mighty men, 2 Sam. xxiii. 9 ; 1 Chr. xi. 12. (4) A Levite, 1 Chr. xxiii. 21. (5) A priest, Neh. xii. 42. (6) Son of Phinehas, Ez. viii. 33. (7) Son of Parosh, Ez. x. 25. (8) Surnamed Avaran, 1 Macc. vi. 43. (9) A scribe, 2 Macc. vi. 18. (10) Father of Jason, 1 Macc. viii. 17. (11) Son of Eliud, Matt. i. 15.

E″le-à-zū′rus, 1 Esdr. ix. 24. [ELIASHIB.]

Ĕ-lĕct′ (*chosen out*). One called to everlasting life ; the saved collectively, Matt. xxiv. 22 ; Mark xiii. 27 ; Luke xviii. 7 ; Rom. viii. 33 ; Tit. i. 1. The "elect lady," 2 John i. 1, probably refers to the Christian church.

Ĕl=e-lō′hĕ=Ĭs′ra-el (*strength of the God of Israel*). Name of Jacob's altar, Gen. xxxiii. 19, 20.

E′leph (*ox*). A town of Benjamin, Josh. xviii. 28.

Ĕl′e-phănt (*ox*). The Hebrew *eleph* means an ox, 1 Kgs. x. 22 ; 2 Chr. ix. 21 ; Job xl. 15, margins.

Ĕ-leu′thĕ-rus. A Syrian river, 1 Macc. xi. 7.

Ĕl-hā′nan (*grace of God*). (1) A noted Hebrew warrior, 2 Sam. xxi. 19 ; 1 Chr. xx. 5. (2) One of David's body-guard, 2 Sam. xxiii. 24.

E′lī (*going up*). A descendant of Aaron, Lev. x. 12. First of a line of high priests, 1 Sam. i. 9–17 ; ii. 22–36 ; iii. 1–14 ; and Judge of Israel for 40 years, iv. 14–18. Line extinguished, 1 Kgs. ii. 26, 27.

E′lī, E′lī, lā′mà sā-bäch-thā′nī. The Lord's cry upon the cross, Matt. xxvii. 46 ; Mark xv. 34, " My God, my God, why hast thou forsaken me ? " Ps. xxii. 1.

Ĕ-li′ab (*God is father*). (1) A Chief of Zebulun, Num. i. 9. (2) A Reubenite, Num. xxvi. 8, 9. (3) A Levite musician, 1 Chr. xv. 18–20. (4) Eldest brother of David, 1 Chr. ii. 13. (5) A Gadite leader, 1 Chr. xii. 9. (6) An ancestor of Samuel, 1 Chr. vi. 27. (7) Son of Nathaniel, Judith viii. 1.

Ĕ-li′a-dà (*known of God*). (1) A younger son of David, 2 Sam. v. 16 ; 1 Chr. iii. 8. (2) A Benjamite general, 2 Chr. xvii. 17.

Ĕ-li′a-dah. Father of Rezon, 1 Kgs. xi. 23–25.

Ĕ-li′ah (*God the Lord*). (1) A Benjamite chief, 1 Chr. viii. 27. (2) One of the returned, Ez. x. 26.

Ĕ-li′ah-bà (*hidden by God*). One of David's guard, 2 Sam. xxiii. 32 ; 1 Chr. xi. 33.

Ĕ-li′a-kīm (*raised of God*). (1) Master of Hezekiah's household, 2 Kgs. xviii. 18–37 ; Isa. xxxvi. 3. (2) Original name of King Jehoiakim, 2 Kgs. xxiii. 34 ; 2 Chr. xxxvi. 4. (3) A priest, Neh. xii. 41. (4) Forefather of Joseph, Matt. i. 13. (5) Father of Jonan, Luke iii. 30, 31.

Ĕ-li′a-lī, 1 Esdr. ix. 34. [BINNUI.]

Ĕ-li′ăm (*God's people*). (1) Father of Bathsheba, 2 Sam. xi. 3. (2) One of David's warriors, 2 Sam. xxiii. 34.

Ĕ-li′as. N. T. form of Elijah. [ELIJAH.]

Ĕ-li′a-săph (*God increaseth*). (1) Chief of Dan, Num. i. 14 ; ii. 14 ; vii. 42 ; x. 20. (2) A Levite chief, Num. iii. 24.

Ĕ-li′a-shib (*restored of God*). (1) Eleventh priest of "order of governors," 1 Chr. xxiv. 12. (2) A Judahite, 1 Chr. iii. 24. (3) High priest, Neh. iii. 1–21. (4) Three of the returned, Ez. x. 24, 27, 36.

Ĕ-li′a-thah (*to whom God comes*). Leader of the twentieth temple course, 1 Chr. xxv. 4, 27.

Ĕ-li′dad (*beloved of God*). A Benjamite, Num. xxxiv. 21.

Ĕ-li′el (*God, my God*). (1) A chief of Manasseh, 1 Chr. v. 24. (2) A forefather of Samuel, 1 Chr. vi. 34. (3, 4) Two chiefs of Benjamin, 1 Chr. viii. 20, 22. (5, 6) Two heroes of David's guard, 1 Chr. xi. 46, 47. (7) A Gadite, 1 Chr. xii. 11. (8) A Levite, 1 Chr. xv. 9–11. (9) Overseer of Temple offerings, 2 Chr. xxxi. 13.

Ĕ″lī-ē′na-ī (*eyes toward God*). A chief of Benjamin, 1 Chr. viii. 20.

Ĕ″lī-ē′zĕr (*help of God*). Servant of Abraham, Gen. xv. 2, 3. (2) Second son of Moses, Ex. xviii. 4 ; 1 Chr. xxiii. 15–17 ; xxvi. 25. (3) A chief of Benjamin, 1 Chr. vii. 8. (4) A priest, 1 Chr. xv. 24. (5) A Reubenite chief, 1 Chr. xxvii. 16. (6) A prophet, 2 Chr. xx. 37. (7) Messenger of Ezra, Ez. viii. 16. (8, 9, 10) Returned Jews, Ez. x. 18, 23, 31. (11) Ancestor of Christ, Luke iii. 29.

Ĕl″i-hō-ē′nă-ī (*eyes toward God*). A returned leader, Ez. viii. 4.

Ĕl″i-hō′reph (*God his reward*). A scribe, 1 Kgs. iv. 3.

Ĕ-li′hū (*God is his*). (1) A forefather of Samuel, 1 Sam. i. 1. (2) Eldest brother of David, 1 Chr. xxvii. 18. (3) A captain of Manasseh, 1 Chr. xii. 20. (4) A Levite door-keeper, 1 Chr. xxvi. 7. (5) One of Job's friends, Job xxxii. 2.

Ĕ-li′jah (*God is God*). (1) The prophet ; Elias in N. T., Matt. xvii. 3. A Tishbite of Gilead ; appears suddenly ; is fed by ravens ; restores the widow's son, 1 Kgs. xvii. 1–24 ; invokes fire on the prophets of Baal, xviii. 17–40 ; anoints Hazael, Jehu, and Elisha, xix. ;

denounces Ahab and Jezebel, xxi. 17–24; is translated in a chariot of fire, 2 Kgs. ii.; reappears on the mount of Transfiguration, Luke ix. 28–35. (2) A son of Harim, Ez. x. 21.

Ĕl′i-kà (*rejected of God*). One of David's guard, 2 Sam. xxiii. 25.

Ē′lĭm (*oaks*). Second encampment of the Israelites after crossing the Red Sea, Ex. xv. 27; Num. xxxiii. 9.

Ĕ-lĭm′ĕ-lech (*my God is king*). Husband of Naomi, Ruth i. 1–3.

Ĕl′′i-ō-ē′nă-ī (*eyes toward God*). (1) A descendant of David, 1 Chr. iii. 23, 24. (2) A Simeonite, 1 Chr. iv. 36. (3) A Levite doorkeeper, 1 Chr. xxvi. 3. (4) A Benjamite, 1 Chr. vii. 8. (5) Two priests, Ez. x. 22, 27.

Ĕl-i-ō′nas, 1 Esdr. ix. 22–32. [ELIOENAI.]

Ĕl′ĭ-phal (*judged of God*). Son of Ur, 1 Chr. xi. 35. Eliphelet, 2 Sam. xxiii. 34.

Ĕ-lĭph′ạ-lĕt (*God of deliverance*). A son of David, 2 Sam. v. 16; 1 Chr. xiv. 7.

Ĕl′ĭ-phăz (*God his strength*). (1) A son of Esau, Gen. xxxvi. 4; 1 Chr. i. 35, 36. (2) One of Job's friends, Job iv., v., xv., xxii.

Ĕ′lĭph′ĕ-leh (*who exalts God*). A harper, 1 Chr. xv. 18–21.

Ĕ-lĭph′ĕ-lĕt (*God of deliverance*). (1) One of David's warriors, 2 Sam. xxiii. 34. (2) Name of two sons of David, 1 Chr. iii. 6, 8. (3) A descendant of Saul, 1 Chr. viii. 39. (4) Two of the returned, Ez. viii. 13; x. 33.

Ĕ-lĭṣ′a-bĕth (*oath of God*). Wife of Zecharias, Luke i. 36–80.

Ĕl′′i-sē′us. Greek form of Elisha, Luke iv. 27.

Ĕ-lī′shà (*God his salvation*). Anointed prophet by Elijah, 1 Kgs. xix. 16–21. Prophesied in reigns of Jehoram, Jehu, Jehoahaz and Joash, a period of sixty years. Life and works in 2 Kgs. ii.–ix.; xiii. 14–21.

Ĕ-lī′shah (*God saves*). Eldest son of Javan, Gen. x. 4; Ezek. xxvii. 7.

Ĕ-lĭsh′a-mà (*whom God hears*). (1) Grandfather of Joshua, Num. i. 10. (2) Two sons of David, 2 Sam. v. 16; 1 Chr. iii. 6, 8. (3) A priest, 2 Chr. xvii. 8. (4) A Judahite, 1 Chr. ii. 41. (5) Grandfather of Ishmael, 2 Kgs. xxv. 25. (6) A scribe, Jer. xxxvi. 12, 20–21. (7) A priest, 2 Chr. xvii. 8.

Ĕ-lĭsh′a-phăt (*whom God judges*). Captain of a hundred, 2 Chr. xxiii. 1.

Ĕ-lish′ĕ-bà (*God her oath*). Wife of Aaron, Ex. vi. 23.

Ĕl′′i-shụ′à. A son of David, 2 Sam. v. 15; 1 Chr. xiv. 5. Elishama, 1 Chr. iii. 6–8.

Ĕ-lĭs′ĭ-mus, 1 Esdr. ix. 28. [ELIASHIB.]

Ĕ-lī′ū. A forefather of Judith, Judith viii. 1.

Ĕ-lī′ŭd (*God my praise*). Ancestor of Joseph, Matt. i. 15.

Ĕ-lĭz′a-phan (*protected of God*). (1) A Levite chief, Num. iii. 30; 1 Chr. xv. 8. Elzaphan, Ex. vi. 22; Lev. x. 4. (2) A chief of Zebulun, Num. xxxiv. 25.

Ĕ-lī′zŭr (*God his rock*). A prince of Reuben, Num. i. 5; ii. 10.

Ĕl′kă-nah, Ĕl′kŏ-nah (*provided of God*). (1) Grandson of Korah, Ex. vi. 24; 1 Chr. vi. 23. (2) Another descendant of Korah, 1 Chr. vi. 26, 35. (3) Another Levite, 1 Chr. vi. 27, 34; 1 Sam. i. 1–23; ii. 11, 20. (4) A Levite, 1 Chr. ix. 16. (5) A Korhite, 1 Chr. xii. 6. (6) An officer under Ahaz, 2 Chr. xxviii. 7.

Ĕl′kosh (*my bow is of God*). Modern Alkush on the Tigris, Nahum i. 1.

Ĕl′lạ-sär (*oak*). City of King Arioch, Gen. xiv. 1–9.

Ĕlm, Hosea iv. 13; elsewhere translated "oak."

Ĕl-mō′dăm (*measure*). Son of Er. Elmadam in R. V., Luke iii. 28.

Ĕl′na-ạm (*God his delight*). Father of two of David's guard, 1 Chr. xi. 46.

Ĕl′nạ-than (*gift of God*). (1) Grandfather of Jehoiachin, 2 Kgs. xxiv. 8; Jer. xxvi. 22. (2) Names of three Levites, Ez. viii. 16.

Ē-lō′ī, Ē-lō′hī, Ĕl′ō-him. God. Eloi is also Aramaic form of Elias, or Elijah, Mark xv. 34.

Ē′lon (*oak*). (1) A Hittite, Gen. xxvi. 34; xxxvi. 2. (2) A son of Zebulun, Gen. xlvi. 14; Num. xxvi. 26. (3) A Zebulunite, Judg. xii. 11, 12. (4) A town of Dan, Josh. xix. 43.

Ē′lon=bĕth=hā′′nạn (*oak of house of grace*). Part of one of Solomon's commissary districts, 1 Kgs. iv. 9.

Ē′lŏn-ītes, Num. xxvi. 26. [ELON, 2.]

Ē′lŏth, 1 Kgs. ix. 26; 2 Chr. viii. 17; xxvi. 2. [ELATH.]

Ĕl′pă-al (*wages of God*). A Benjamite, 1 Chr. viii. 11, 12.

Ĕl′pa-let, 1 Chr. xiv. 5. [ELIPHELET, 2.]

Ĕl-pā′ran. Oak of Paran, Gen. xiv. 6. [PARAN.]

Ĕl′tẹ-keh (*fear of God*). A city of Dan, Josh. xix. 44; xxi. 23.

Ĕl′tẹ-kon (*founded by God*). A town in Judah, Josh. xv. 59.

Ĕl′to-lăd (*kindred of God*). A city of Judah, and Simeon, Josh. xv. 30; xix. 4; Tolad, 1 Chr. iv. 29.

Ē′lŭl (*vine*). Twelfth month of Hebrew civil, and sixth of sacred, year, corresponding to parts of September and October, Neh. vi. 15.

Ē-lū′za-ī (*God my praise*). A Benjamite warrior, 1 Chr. xii. 5.

Ĕl′′ŷ-mæ′ans, Judith i. 6. [ELAMITES.]

Ĕl′ŷ-măs (*wise*). Arabic name of Bar-jesus, Acts xiii. 6–12.

Ĕl′za-băd (*gift of God*). (1) A Gadite, 1 Chr. xii. 12. (2) A Korhite Levite, 1 Chr. xxvi. 7.

Ĕl′zạ-phăn (*protected by God*). Second son of Uzziel, Ex. vi. 22; Lev. x. 4; 2 Chr. xxix. 13. Elizaphan in Num. iii. 30; 1 Chr. xv. 8.

Ĕm-bälm′ (*to put in balsam*). Embalming carried to great perfection by the Egyptians, whom the Jews feebly imitated, Gen. l. 2–26.

Ĕm-brôi′der (*to work a border*). Ex. xxviii. 39; xxxv. 35; xxxviii. 23. Possibly nothing beyond the common weaver's art is meant. "Cunning work," Ex. xxvi. 1, implies embroidery.

Ĕm′ĕr-ăld. A bright green variety of beryl. The emerald of Ex. xxviii. 18; xxxix. 11; Ezek. xxvii. 16; xxviii. 13; Rev. iv. 3; xxi. 19, is supposably the carbuncle, a fiery garnet.

Ĕm′ĕ-rŏds (*flowing with blood*). Hemorrhoids or piles, Deut. xxviii. 27; 1 Sam. v. 6–12; vi. 4–11.

Ē′mĭms (*terrors*). A race of Anakim east of Dead Sea, Gen. xiv. 5; Deut. ii. 10, 11.

Ĕm-măn′ū-el, Matt. i. 23. [IMMANUEL.]

Ĕm′mạ-us (*warm springs*). A village of Palestine, 7½ mls. from Jerusalem, Luke xxiv. 13–33.

Ĕm′mer, 1 Esdr. ix. 21. [IMMER.]

Ĕm′môr (*ass*), Acts vii. 16. [HAMOR.]

Ĕn. A fountain. Used in compounds.

Ĕn-ā′bled. Qualified, 1 Tim. i. 12.

Ē′nam (*two fountains*). A city of Judah, Josh. xv. 34.

Ē′nan (*eyes*). A prince of Naphtali, Num. i. 15; ii. 29; vii. 78, 83; x. 27.

Ē-năs′ĭ-bus, 1 Esdr. ix. 34. [ELIASHIB.]

Ĕn-câmp′ment (*field*). Halting place of army or caravan, Ex. xiv. 19; xvi. 13; Num. ii., iii.; Josh. x. 5.

Ĕn-chânt′ment (*song-spell*). Enchantments unlawful, Lev. xix. 26; Deut. xviii. 10–12; as Egyptian trickery, Ex. vii. 11–22; viii. 7; Balaam's omens, Num. xxiv. 1; muttered spells, 2 Kgs. ix. 22; Mic. v. 12; Nah. iii. 4; serpent charming, Eccl. x. 11; magical spells, Isa. xlvii. 9–12; auguries, Jer. xxvii. 9. [DIVINATION.]

Ĕn'=dôr (*fountain of Dor*). A village of Manasseh, Josh. xvii. 11; Ps. lxxxiii. 9, 10; 1 Sam. xxviii.

Ĕn=eg'la-ĭm (*fountain of two calves*). An unknown place, Ezek. xlvii. 10.

Ĕn''ĕ-mĕs'sär. Shalmaneser, Tob. i. 2, 15.

Ē-nē'nĭ-us. A returned leader, 1 Esdr. v. 8.

Ĕn-găd'dī, Ecclus. xxiv. 14. [ENGEDI.]

Ĕn=găn'nĭm (*fount of the garden*). (1) A city of Judah, Josh. xv. 34. (2) A Levitical city, Josh. xix. 21; xxi. 29.

Ĕn=gē'dī (*fount of the kid*). A town on west shore of Dead Sea, Josh. xv. 62; Ezek. xlvii. 10; 1 Sam. xxiv. 1–7; S. of Sol. i. 14. Hazezon-tamar, Gen. xiv. 7; 2 Chr. xx. 2.

Ĕn'gīne (*skilled product*). The ballista for throwing spears, arrows, stones, 2 Chr. xxvi. 15; the catapult, Ezek. xxvi. 9; battering ram, Ezek. iv. 2; xxi. 22.

Ĕn-gra'vẽr (*digger in*). The commandments were engraved, Ex. xxxii. 16; also stones and signets, Ex. xxviii. 11, 21, 36; Job xix. 24; Acts xvii. 29. Graven images were objects of idolatry, Ex. xx. 4; xxxii. 4.

Ĕn-hăd'dah (*fountain*). A city of Issachar, Josh. xix. 21.

Ĕn=hak'kŏ-rē (*fount of the caller*). Samson's fountain, Judg. xv. 19.

Ĕn=hā'zôr (*fount of Hazor*). A fenced city in Naphtali, Josh. xix. 37.

Ĕn=mish'pat (*fount of judgment*). Gen. xiv. 7. [KADESH.]

Ē'nŏch (*dedicated*). (1) A son of Cain, Gen. iv. 17. (2) Father of Methuselah, Gen. v. 18–24; Heb. xi. 5–13; Jude 14. (3) "Behemoth," 2 Esdr. vi. 49–51.

Ē'non (*springs*). John i. 28; iii. 23. [ÆNON.]

Ē'nos (*mortal*). Son of Seth, Gen. iv. 26; v. 6–11; Luke iii. 38. Enosh, 1 Chr. i. 1.

Ē'nosh, 1 Chr. i. 1. [ENOS.]

Ĕn=rĭm'mon (*fount of the pomegranate*). A settlement of returned Jews, Neh. xi. 29.

Ĕn=rō'gel (*fuller's fount*). A celebrated spring, Josh. xv. 7; xviii. 16; 2 Sam. xvii. 17; 1 Kgs. i. 9.

Ĕn=shē'mesh (*fount of the sun*). A spring, Josh. xv. 7; xviii. 17.

Ĕn'sīgn (*mark upon*). A simple device, elevated on a pole, bearing some emblem to distinguish the tribes and army divisions, Num. i. 52; S. of Sol. ii. 4; Isa. xiii. 2; xviii. 3.

Ĕn-sūe'. Pursue, 1 Pet. iii. 11.

Ĕn=tăp'pu-ah (*fount of the apple*). Tappuah in Manasseh, Josh. xvii. 7.

Ĕp'a-phrăs (*lovely*). A Roman friend of Paul, Col. i. 7; iv. 12.

Ē-pæn'ĕ-tus (*praised*). A Christian at Rome, Rom. xvi. 5.

Ē-păph''ro-dī'tus (*lovely*). Probably Epaphras, Phil. ii. 25; iv. 18

Ē'phah (*gloomy*). (1) First son of Midian, Gen. xxv. 4; 1 Chr. i. 33; Isa. lx. 6. (2) Caleb's concubine, 1 Chr. ii. 46. (3) A Judahite, 1 Chr. ii. 47. (4) A Hebrew dry measure, estimated at 2¼ to 3¼ pecks, Ruth ii. 17; Num. v. 15. (5) A Hebrew liquid measure equal to 7½ gallons.

Ē'phāi (*gloomy*). His sons were captains left behind in Judah, Jer. xl. 8.

Ē'pher (*calf*). (1) A son of Midian, Gen. xxv. 4; 1 Kgs. iv. 10. (2) A son of Ezra, 1 Chr. iv. 17. A chief of Manasseh, 1 Chr. v. 24.

Ē'pheş=dam'mim (*border of blood*). A Philis-

tine encampment, 1 Sam. xvii. 1. Pasdammim, 1 Chr. xi. 13. [ELAH.]

Ē-phē'şianş. (1) Inhabitants of Ephesus, Acts xix. 28. (2) Epistle to, written by Paul to the Christians at Ephesus, about A. D 61 or 62, and while he was a prisoner at Rome. Forwarded by Tychicus, Eph. vi. 21. Of general import.

Ĕph'ĕ-sŭs (*desirable*). Capital of Ionia, on the Ægean Sea. Noted for its commerce, learning, and architecture. Paul visited it, Acts xviii. 1–20, and founded a church there, to which he addressed one of his best epistles, Acts xix. 1–10; xx. 17–38.

Ĕph'lăl (*judgment*). A Judahite, 1 Chr. ii. 37.

Ĕph'ŏd (*clothe*). (1) A sleeveless linen garment for priests, covering breast and back, Ex. xxviii. 4–35; 1 Sam. xxii. 18, with onyx clasp at shoulder, and breastplate at breast, crossing. Worn later by other than priests, 1 Chr. xv. 27. [BREASTPLATE.] (2) A Manassite, Num. xxxiv. 23.

Ĕph'phă-thả (*be opened*). Christ's utterance in Mark vii. 34.

Ē'phră-ĭm (*doubly fruitful*). (1) Second son of Joseph, Gen. xli. 52. Obtained Jacob's blessing, Gen. xlviii. 8–20. Tribe numerous, Num. i. 33; xxvi. 37. Allotment as in Josh. xvi. 1–10. (2) Site of Absalom's sheep-farm, 2 Sam. xiii. 23. (3) Place to which Christ retired, John xi. 54. (4) A gate of Jerusalem, 2 Kgs. xiv. 13; 2 Chr. xxv. 23; Neh. viii. 16; xii. 39. (5) "Mount of," in Ephraim, 1 Sam. i. 1. (6) "The wood of," east of Jordan, 2 Sam. xviii. 6.

Ē'phră-ĭm-ītes''. Members of the tribe of Ephraim, Judg. xii. 5. Sometimes Ephrathites.

Ē'phră-ĭn (*doubly fruitful*). A city of Israel, 2 Chr. xiii. 19.

Ĕph'ra-tah, Ĕph'rath (*fruitful*). (1) Second wife of Caleb, 1 Chr. ii. 19, 50. (2) Ancient name of Bethlehem-judah, Gen. xxxv. 16, 19; xlviii. 7.

Ĕph'rath-ītes. (1) Inhabitants of Bethlehem, or Ephrath, Ruth i. 2. (2) Ephraimites, Judg. xii. 5; 1 Sam. i. 1; 1 Kgs. xi. 26.

Ĕph'ron (*fawn-like*). (1) A Hittite who sold Machpelah to Abraham, Gen. xxiii. 8–20; xlix. 29; l. 13. (2) Landmarks of Judah, Josh. xv. 9. (3) A city east of Jordan, 1 Macc. v. 46–52.

Ĕp''ĭ-cū-rē'anş (*followers of Epicurus*). A sect of pleasure-loving philosophers at Athens, Acts xvii. 18.

Ē-pĭph'a-nēş, 1 Macc. i. 10. [ANTIOCHUS, 4.]

Ē-pĭs'tle (*sending to*). In O. T. a letter, 2 Sam. xi. 14; 2 Kgs. v. 5, 6; 2 Chr. xxi. 12; Ez. iv. 6–11. In N. T., a formal tract containing Christian doctrine and salutary advice.

Ēr (*watchman*). (1) First-born of Judah, Gen. xxxviii. 3–7; Num. xxvi. 19. (2) A descendant of Shelah, 1 Chr. iv. 21. (3) Son of Jose, Luke iii. 28.

Ē'răn (*watchful*). Founder of the Eranites, Num. xxvi. 36.

Ē-răs'tŭs (*beloved*). (1) A friend of Paul at Ephesus, Acts xix. 22; 2 Tim. iv. 20. (2) A Corinthian convert, Rom. xvi. 23.

Ē'rĕch (*healthy*). A city of Shinar, Gen. x. 10.

Ē'rī (*watching*). A son of Gad, Gen. xlvi. 16, and founder of the Erites, Num. xxvi. 16.

Ē-şā'ĭas. N. T. name of Isaiah, Matt. iii. 3.

Ē''sar-hăd'don (*conqueror*). A king of Assyria, 2 Kgs. xix. 37; 2 Chr. xxxiii. 11. He united Babylon to Assyria and reigned over both B. C. 680–667.

Ē'sau (*hairy*). Eldest son of Isaac and twin brother of Jacob, Gen. xxv. 25. Called also Edom. Sold his birthright to Jacob, Gen. xxv. 26–34; xxxvi. 1–10. Gave his name, Edom, to a country and to his descendants, Gen. xxvi., xxxvi. [EDOM.]

Ē'say, Ecclus. xlviii. 20–22. [ISAIAH.]

Ĕṣ″dra̤-ē′lon. Greek for Jezreel, Judith iii. 9; iv. 6.

Ĕṣ′dras. (1) A scribe in 1 and 2 Esdras. (2) First and second books of the Apocrypha. First a supplement to Ezra; second a series of visions.

Ē′sĕk (*strife*). A well in Gerar, Gen. xxvi. 20.

Ĕsh=bā′al (*Baal's man*). Ishbosheth, Saul's fourth son, 1 Chr. viii. 33; ix. 39.

Ĕsh′băn (*wise man*). Son of Dishon, Gen. xxxvi. 26; 1 Chr. i. 41.

Ĕsh′cŏl (*bunch of grapes*). (1) Brother of Mamre, Gen. xiv. 13-24. (2) A valley or brook near Hebron, Num. xiii. 22-27; xxxii. 9; Deut. i. 24.

Ē′shĕ-an (*slope*). A city of Judah, Josh. xv. 52.

Ē′shĕk (*oppression*). A descendant of Saul, 1 Chr. viii. 39.

Ĕsh′ka̤-lŏn-ītes″, Josh. xiii. 3. [ASHKELON.]

Ĕsh′ta̤-ŏl (*a way*). Town in Judah and Dan, Josh. xv. 33; xix. 41; burial place of Samson, Judg. xiii. 25; xvi. 31; xviii. 2-11.

Ĕsh′ta̤-ul-ītes″. Families of Kirjath-jearim, 1 Chr. ii. 53.

Ĕsh″te-mō′a̤, Ĕsh′te-mŏh (*bosom of a woman*). A Levitical town of Judah, Josh. xv. 50; xxi. 14; 1 Sam. xxx. 28.

Ĕsh′ton (*weak*). A Judahite, 1 Chr. iv. 11, 12.

Ĕs′lī (*reserved*). Ancestor of Joseph, Luke iii. 25.

Ē-sō′ra̤. Hazor or Zorah, Judith iv. 4.

Ĕs-pouse′ (*promise*). [BETROTH.]

Ĕs′rom, Matt. i. 3; Luke iii. 33. [HEZRON.]

Ĕs-sēne′ (*priest*). Member of a Jewish ascetic sect, the Essenes.

Ĕs-tāte′ (*standing*). In Mark vi. 21, a class or order representing the government. The "estate of the elders," Acts xxii. 5, was a body of advisers co-operating with the Sanhedrim.

Ĕs′thêr (*star*). Persian name of Hadassah, Mordecai's cousin, who married King Ahasuerus, and saved the lives of her countrymen. Her book, seventeenth of O. T., tells her story.

Ē′tam (*lair*). (1) A village in Simeon, 1 Chr. iv. 32. (2) Favorite resort of Solomon, 2 Chr. xi. 6; Judg. xv. 8-19. (3) A doubtful name, 1 Chr. iv. 3.

Ē′tham (*sea bound*). An Israelite encampment, Ex. xiii. 20; Num. xxxiii. 6-8.

Ē′than (*strong*). (1) One noted for wisdom, 1 Kgs. iv. 31; 1 Chr. ii. 6; title to Ps. lxxxix. (2) A Levite singer, 1 Chr. vi. 44; xv. 17-19. (3) An ancestor of Asaph, 1 Chr. vi. 42.

Ĕth′a̤-nĭm (*flowing*). Seventh month (Tisri) of Jewish sacred, and first of civil, year; corresponding to parts of Sept. and Oct., 1 Kgs. viii. 2.

Ĕth′bā-al (*favored of Baal*). King of Sidon, 1 Kgs. xvi. 31.

Ē′thêr (*plenty*). Town in Judah and Simeon, Josh. xv. 42; xix. 7.

Ē″thĭ-ō′pĭ-à (*burnt faces*). Greek and Roman for Hebrew "Cush." The unbounded country south of Egypt, Ezek. xxix. 10; settled by Hamites, Gen. x. 6; merchants, Isa. xlv. 14; Jer. xiii. 23; Job xxviii. 19; wealthy, Acts viii. 27-37; strongly military, 2 Chr. xii. 3; xiv. 9-12; 2 Kgs. xvii. 4.

Ē″thĭ-ō′pĭ-anṣ. Dwellers in Ethiopia; Cushites, Num. xii. 1; 2 Chr. xiv. 9; Jer. xxxviii. 7; xxxix. 16; Acts viii. 27-37.

Ĕth′nan (*hire*). A Judahite, 1 Chr. iv. 5-7.

Ĕth′nī (*liberal*). A Levite, 1 Chr. vi. 41.

Eū-bū′lus (*prudent*). A Roman Christian, 2 Tim. iv. 21.

Eū-êr′gĕ-tēṣ (*benefactor*). A common Grecian surname, and title of honor; applied especially to the Ptolemies.

Eū′na̤-tan, 1 Esdr. viii. 44. [ELNATHAN.]

Eū′nĭçe (*good victory*). Mother of Timothy, Acts xvi. 1; 2 Tim. i. 5.

Eū′nŭch (*couch guardian*). A castrated male. Eunuchs became court officials, 2 Kgs. ix. 32; Esth. ii. 3; Acts viii. 27; could not enter the congregation, Deut. xxiii. 1. A celibate, Matt. xix. 12.

Eū-ō′dĭ-as (*fragrant*). Euodia in R. V.; a Christian woman of Philippi, Phil. iv. 2.

Eū-phrā′tēṣ (*fructifying*). A great river of western Asia, rising in Armenia and emptying into the Persian Gulf. Boundary of Eden, Gen. ii. 14; "great river," Gen. xv. 18; Deut. i. 7; eastern boundary of the promised land, Deut. xi. 24; Josh. i. 4; 1 Chr. v. 9; and of David's conquests, 2 Sam. viii. 3; 1 Chr. xviii. 3. *See also*, Jer. xiii. 4-7; xlvi. 2-10; li. 63; Ps. cxxxvii. 1; Rev. ix. 14; xvi. 12.

Eū-pŏl′e-mus. An envoy, 1 Macc. viii. 17.

Eū-rŏc′lȳ-don. A stormy northeast wind of the Levant, Acts xxvii. 14.

Eū′tȳ-chus (*fortunate*). A sleepy youth of Troas, Acts xx. 6-12.

Ē-văn′gĕl-ĭst (*publisher of glad tidings*). One of the four writers of the gospels Matthew, Mark, Luke and John. A preacher of the gospel inferior in authority to the Apostles, Acts viii. 14-19, and apparently to the prophets, Eph. iv. 11, yet superior to the pastor and teacher, Acts xxi. 8; Eph. iv. 11; 2 Tim. iv. 5. A travelling and corresponding missionary, Acts xx. 4, 5.

Ēve (*life*). The first woman; made *of* man and *for* him, Gen. ii. 18-25; iii.-iv.

Ēve′nĭng (*decline of day*). Two evenings recognized, one before, the other after, sunset, Gen. xxiv. 63; Ex. xii. 6; Num. ix. 3; xxviii. 4.

Ē′vī (*desire*). A King of Midian, Num. xxxi. 8; Josh. xiii. 21.

Ē′vĭl=mĕ-rō′dach (*fool of Merodach*). King of Babylon, B. C. 561-559, 2 Kgs. xxv. 27; Jer. lii. 31-34.

Ĕx″cŏm-mū″nĭ-cā′tion (*putting out of the community*). Threefold in Jewry. (1) Temporary suspension. (2) Further temporary suspension. (3) Final cutting off. Now rests on Matt. xvi. 19; xviii. 17; 1 Cor. v. 11; 2 Cor. ii. 5-11; 1 Cor. i. 20; Tit. iii. 10.

Ĕx″ē-cū′tion-êr (*a follower out*). In O. T. a position of dignity, Gen. xxxvii. 36, marg.; 1 Kgs. ii. 25, 34. Even in Mark vi. 27, the executioner belonged to the king's body-guard.

Ĕx′ō-dus (*going out*). Second Book of the Bible and Pentateuch. Written by Moses. Historic from i. to xviii. 27; legislative from xix. to end. Its history covers the period (about 142 years) of Jewish preparation to leave Egypt, the departure, the desert wanderings and the arrival at Sinai. Its legislation comprises the giving of the law at Sinai, directions for the priesthood, the establishment of the tabernacle and its service.

Ĕx′ŏr-çĭsts (*swearers out*). Those who pretended to drive out evil spirits by prayers and conjurations, Matt. xii. 27; Mark ix. 38; Acts xix. 13.

Ĕx″pĭ-ā′tion, Feast of. [ATONEMENT.]

Ēye. Putting out the eye a warfare custom, especially with dangerous prisoners. Judg. xvi. 21; 1 Sam. xi. 2; 2 Kgs. xxv. 7. Painting the eyelids a fashion, 2 Kgs. ix. 30; Jer. iv. 30; Ezek. xxiii. 40. "Eyeservice," reluctant service, Col. iii. 22; Eph. vi. 6.

Ē′zär, 1 Chr. i. 38. [EZER, 1.]

Ĕz′ba̤-ī (*shining*). Father of one of David's mighty men, 1 Chr. xi. 37.

Ĕz′bŏn (*bright*). (1) A son of Gad, Gen. xlvi. 16; Ozni in Num. xxvi. 16. (2) A Benjamite, 1 Chr. vii. 7.

Ēz-ē-chī′as, 2 Esdr. vii. 40. [HEZEKIAH.]

Ēz-ē-çī′as, 1 Esdr. ix. 43. [HILKIAH.]

Ēz-ē-kī′as, 2 Macc. xv. 22; Matt. i. 9, 10. [HEZEKIAH.]

Ē-zē'kĭ-ĕl (*strength of God*). One of the four greater prophets; carried captive to Babylon B. C. 598; entered the prophetic calling in fifth year of his captivity, Ezek. i. 1-3. Chapters i.-xxiv. of his book contain predictions before the fall of Jerusalem, and xxv.-xlviii. predictions after that event. The visions of the Temple, xl.-xlviii., are a unique feature of the book.

Ē'zĕl (*going away*). Scene of the parting of David and Jonathan, 1 Sam. xx. 19.

Ē'zĕm (*bone*). A town of Simeon, 1 Chr. iv. 29; Azem in Josh. xix. 3.

Ē'zĕr (*help*). (1) A Horite duke, Gen. xxxvi. 21, 27, 30; 1 Chr. iv. 4. (2) An Ephraimite, 1 Chr. vii. 21. (3) A Gadite, 1 Chr. xii. 9. (4) A Levite, Neh. iii. 19. (5) A priest, Neh. xii. 42.

Ez''ĕ-rī'as, Ē-zī'as, 1 Esdr viii 1, 2. [AZARIAH.]

Ē'zĭ-on=gā'bĕr, or gē'bĕr (*backbone of a giant*). An Israelite encampment, Num. xxxiii. 35, 36; Deut. ii. 8. Compare 1 Kgs. ix. 26; 2 Chr. viii. 17; 1 Kgs. xxii. 48.

Ĕz'nīte, 2 Sam. xxiii. 8, for Tachmonite in same verse and Hachmonite in 1 Chr. xi. 11.

Ĕz'rȧ (*help*). The famous scribe and priest, resident at Babylon, who returned to Jerusalem with his countrymen, B. C. 458, where he began instant reforms. He collected and revised the previous O. T. writings and largely settled the O. T. canon. His book, 15th of O. T., tells the story of the return and the establishment of a new order of things at Jerusalem and in Judea.

Ĕz'ra-hite''. A title applied to Ethan and Heman, 1 Kgs. iv. 31; Ps. lxxxviii. title; lxxxix. title.

Ĕz'rī (*my help*). A superintendent of David's farm laborers, 1 Chr. xxvii. 26.

F

Fā'ble (*spoken*). A narrative in which inanimate things are personalized, Judg. ix. 8-15; 2 Kgs. xiv. 9.

Fair Hā'vens. A harbor of Crete, Acts xxvii. 8-13.

Fairs (*holidays*). Wares, Ezek. xxvii. 12-33.

Făl'low=deer (*yellowish brown*). The bubalis or African deer, Deut. xiv. 5; 1 Kgs. iv. 23. Some say the Arabian wild ox.

Făl'low (*yellow*). Plowed land left to mellow. Tillage, Prov. xiii. 23. Figurative, Jer. iv. 3; Hos. x. 12. The Sabbatical, or fallow year; year of land-rest, Lev. xxv. 1-7; Deut. xxxi. 9-14.

Făm'ĭne (*hunger*). Generally foretold and regarded as a judgment, Gen. xii. 10; xxvi. 1; xli. 54-56; 2 Kgs. vii.

Făn (*winnower*). Winnowing shovel or fork used to throw chaff up into the wind, to separate it from the kernels, Isa. xxx. 24; Matt. iii. 12.

Fạr'thïng. Two Roman bronze coins. One, Matt. v. 26; Mark xii. 42; worth ¼ of a cent; the other, Matt. x. 29; Luke xii. 6, worth 1½ cents.

Făsts (*keep*). One legal fast, the Atonement, kept by Jews, Lev. xvi. 29-34; Deut. ix. 9; Jonah iii. 5; Zech. vii. 1-7. Special fasts observed, 1 Sam. vii. 6; Jer. xxxvi. 6-10; Esth. iv. 16; Matt. ix. 14; Mark ii. 18; Luke v. 33; Acts x. 30; xiii. 3.

Făt (*fed*). Forbidden food, as belonging to God, Lev. iii. 3-17; vii. 3, 23; Neh. viii. 10; yet fatted cattle enjoyed, 1 Kgs. iv. 23; Luke xv. 23. Vat is meant in Joel ii. 24; iii. 13; Hag. ii. 16.

Fä'ther (*sire*). Source of authority, Gen. iii. 16; 1 Cor. xi. 3. Disrespect of, condemned, Ex. xxi. 15-17; xxii. 17; Lev. xx. 9; 1 Tim. i. 9. Parental obedience bears a promise, Ex. xx. 12. Father also a priest, Gen. viii. 20. Any ancestor, Deut. i. 11; Matt. xxiii. 30. A title, Judg. xvii. 10; 1 Sam. x. 12; Acts vii. 2. Protector, Ps. lxviii. 5. Author and founder, Gen. iv. 21; Rom. iv. 12. Divine appellation, Deut. xxxii. 6; Matt. vi. 4; Rom. i. 7.

Făth'om (*embrace*). Space to which a man can extend his arms; about 6 feet, Acts xxvii. 28.

Fēasts (*joyful*). Observed for joyous events, Gen. xxi. 8; xxix. 22; xl. 20; Mark vi. 21, 22. Numerous religious feasts, Ex. xii. 16; Lev. xxiii. 21-24; Jude 12.

Fēet. To wash, a sign of hospitality, Gen. xviii. 4; 1 Sam. xxv. 41; John xiii. 5, 6. To remove shoes, a reverence, Ex. iii. 5; sign of mourning, Ezek. xxiv. 17.

Fē'lix (*happy*). A procurator of Judea, Acts xxiii. 26.

Fĕnced Cĭties (*defenced*). Walled or palisaded cities. [CITY.]

Fĕr'ret (*thief*). A domesticated animal of the weasel family used for catching rats, Lev. xi. 30.

Fĕs'tŭs. Procurator, Acts xxiv. 27.

Fĕt'ters (*shackles*). Instruments of brass or iron for fastening feet of prisoners, Ps. cv. 18; cxlix. 8.

Fĭeld. Open area beyond the enclosed gardens or vineyards, Gen. iv. 8; xxiv. 63; Deut. xxii. 25. Landmarks, sacred, Deut. xix. 14; Job xxiv. 2; Prov. xxii. 28.

Fĭg, Fĭg=tree. Common in Palestine, Deut. viii. 8; Isa. xxxiv. 4; 1 Kgs. iv. 25. Pressed figs, 1 Sam. xxv. 18. Fruit appears before leaves, Matt. xxi. 19.

Fĭr. A tree of the pine family, 2 Sam. vi. 5; 1 Kgs. v. 8; S. of Sol. i. 17.

Fĭre. Symbol of God's presence, Gen. iv. 4, 5; xv. 17; Ex. iii. 2; Judg. xiii. 19, 20. Worshipped, 2 Kgs. xvii. 17; punishment, Lev. xx. 14; xxi. 9. Christ comes in, 2 Thess. i. 8. World destroyed by, 2 Pet. iii. 7.

Fĭre=pan. The censer and snuff-dish of the temple, Ex. xxv. 38; xxvii. 3; xxxvii. 23; xxxviii. 3; 2 Kgs. xxv. 15.

Fĭr'kin (*fourth*). A Greek measure equal to Hebrew bath, 4 to 6 gals., John ii. 6.

Fĭrm'a-ment (*made firm*). Overhead expanse, Gen. i. 17; solid, Ex. xxiv. 10; with windows and doors, Gen. vii. 11; Isa. xxiv. 18; Ps. lxxviii. 23.

Fĭrst=born. Consecrated to God, Ex. xiii. 2; received a double portion, Deut. xxi. 17. Paid redemption money after the priesthood started, Num. iii. 12, 13; xviii. 15, 16.

Fĭrst=fruits were offerings and priest's perquisites, Ex. xxii. 29; xxiii. 19; xxxiv. 26; Lev. ii. 12; xxiii. 10-12; Num. xviii. 12; Deut. xviii. 3, 4.

Fĭsh, Fĭsh-ing. Grand division of animal kingdom, Gen. i. 21, 22. Without scales, unclean, Lev. xi. 9-12. Plenty in waters of Palestine, Luke v. 5. Worship of, prohibited, Deut. iv. 18. Caught with nets, hooks, and spears, Hab. i. 15; Luke v. 5-7; Job xli. 7.

Fĭsh=gate. A Jerusalem gate, 2 Chr. xxxiii. 14.

Fĭsh=hooks. [FISH.]

Fĭsh=pools. Should read "pools," S. of Sol. vii. 4.

Fĭtch'es (*vetches*). "Spelt," Ezek. iv. 9. "Fennel," or black cummin, Isa. xxviii. 25-27.

Flăg (*fluttering*). Embraces many water plants, Ex. ii. 3-5; Isa. xix. 6.

Flăg'on (*flask*). Small vessel for liquids, Isa. xxii. 24; 2 Sam. vi. 19; 1 Chr. xvi. 3; S. of Sol. ii. 5.

Flăx (*flexible*). Grown and used largely in East, Ex. ix. 31; Josh. ii. 6; Isa. xix. 9. For lamp wicks, Isa. xlii. 3; Matt. xii. 20. Spinning honorable, Prov. xxxi. 13, 19, 24.

Flēa. Pests throughout the East, 1 Sam. xxiv. 14; xxvi. 20.

Flĕsh. Everything living, Gen. vi. 13-19; mankind, vi. 12; the body, Col. ii. 5; 1 Pet. iv. 6; seat of appetites, Rom. viii. 1, 5, 9; Gal. v. 17-19; Eph. ii. 3. Used much figuratively.

Flĕsh=hooks. Three-tined hooks for taking meat from a boiling vessel, Ex. xxxviii. 3; 1 Sam. ii. 13, 14.

Flĭnt. Quartz; abounds in Palestine, Ps. cxiv. 8. Types abundance, Deut. xxxii. 13; firmness, Isa. l. 7; Ezek. iii. 9.

Flōats. Rafts for floating timber, 1 Kgs. v. 9; 2 Chr. ii. 16.

Flŏck. [SHEEP.]

Flŏod (*flow*). The Noachian deluge; "the flood," Gen. vi.–viii; Matt. xxiv. 37; 2 Pet. ii. 5; iii. 6. [NOAH.]

Flōor. [AGRICULTURE.]

Flŏur. [BREAD.]

Flūte (*blow, flow*). Flute or "pipe," made of reeds or copper, and similar to those of to-day, Dan. iii. 5–15; 1 Kgs. i. 40.

Flŭx (*flow*). Violent dysentery, Acts xxviii. 8.

Fly. Of many varieties in East, and very noisome, Ex. viii. 21–31; Ps. lxxviii. 45; Eccl. x. 1; Isa. vii. 18.

Food (*feed*). Vegetable foods, soups, eggs, curds, honey, bread, etc., preferred by Hebrews to animal food, Lev. xxvi. 26; Ps. cv. 16; Ezek. iv. 16. Animal food a feature of entertainments, Gen. xviii. 7; 1 Sam. xvi. 20; Luke xv. 23. Fish used, Num. xi. 5; Matt. xiii. 47, 48; xv. 34.

Foot. Used in pumping water from Nile, Deut. xi. 10.

Foot'men. Swift runners, couriers, 1 Sam. xxii. 17; 1 Kgs. xiv. 28; 2 Kgs. xi. 4.

Foot'stool. Kings used them, 2 Chr. ix. 18. God's footstool, 1 Chr. xxviii. 2; Ps. xcix. 5.

Fŏre'hĕad. Unveiled women "hard of forehead," Gen. xxiv. 65; Ezek. iii. 7–9; Jer. iii. 3. Mark of beast on forehead, Rev. xiii. 16; God's name there, Rev. xxii. 4.

Fŏr'eĭgn-er (*out of doors*). One not of Hebrew stock, Ex. xii. 45; Eph. ii. 12.

Fŏre=knowl'edge. God's knowledge of the future, Acts ii. 23; xv. 18; 1 Pet. i. 2.

Fŏre=rŭn'ner. Preparer of the way "within the veil," Heb. vi. 19, 20.

Fŏr'est. Woodland and waste land, 1 Sam. xxii. 5. "House of the Forest" was built of cedars thereof, 1 Kgs. vii. 2.

Fŏrks, 1 Sam. xiii. 21. [FLESH-HOOKS.]

Fŏr''ni-cā'tion (*crime under the arch*). Crime of impurity between unmarried persons. Figuratively, infidelity to God, Ezek. xvi. 2; Jer. ii. 20; Matt. v. 32.

Fŏr''tū'nā'tus (*fortunate*). A Corinthian friend of Paul, 1 Cor. xvi. 17, and postscript.

Fŏun'tain (*font*). Springs of Palestine many but uncertain, Deut. viii. 7. They furnish many figures of speech, Ps. xxxvi. 8, 9; Isa. xlix. 10; Jer. ii. 13; John iv. 10; Rev. vii. 17.

Fowl (*flying*). The Hebrew original embraces birds in general, Gen. i. 20; 1 Kgs. iv. 23. The Greek provides the domestic limitation, Luke xii. 24.

Fŏx (*hairy*). The jackal meant, as it is gregarious and feeds on carcasses, Judg. xv. 4; Ps. lxiii. 10; S. of Sol. ii. 15; Ezek. xiii. 4; Luke ix. 58.

Frănk'ĭn-çĕnse (*free burning*). The yellowish gum used in sacrificial fumigation, Ex. xxx. 7–9; Lev. xvi. 12, 13; Rev. viii. 3. A mixture of gums and spices in Ex. xxx. 34–38.

Frĭn'gĕs (*fibres*). The ornamental hem of the outer garment. Wearing enjoined, Num. xv. 37–40; Deut. xxii. 12; Matt. ix. 20; xiv. 36.

Frŏg. The Egyptian species akin to our own. Source of one of the plagues, Ex. viii. 2–14. Elsewhere only in Ps. lxxviii. 45; cv. 30; Rev. xvi. 13.

Frŏnt'lets (*little foreheads*). Phylacteries in Greek. Parchment strips inscribed with texts, Ex. xiii. 2–17; Deut. vi. 4–22; enclosed in calf-skin case, worn at prayers on forehead or left arm, Matt. xxiii. 5; Mark vii. 3, 4; Luke v. 33.

Ful'ler (*tramper on*). Fuller's art used for cleaning clothes. They were placed in vessels of water impregnated with natron or soap and trodden with the feet, Prov. xxv. 20; Jer. ii. 22; Mal. iii. 2. Chalk and fuller's earth used for bleaching, 2 Kgs. xviii. 17; Isa. vii. 3; xxxvi. 2.

Fū'nẽr-al. [BURIAL.]

Fŭr'long (*furrow long*). In N. T. for Greek stadium, 600 feet long, Luke xxiv. 13.

Fŭr'nace (*oven*). Oven in Gen. xv. 17; Neh. iii. 11. Smelting furnace or lime-kiln in Gen. xix. 28; Ex. ix. 8; Isa. xxxiii. 12. Refining furnace in Prov. xvii. 3. Furnace like a brick-kiln in Dan. iii. 15–27.

Fŭr'ni-ture (*provided*). Oriental furniture scanty, 2 Kgs. iv. 10–13. Camel's trappings in Gen. xxxi. 34. [BED.]

Fŭr'row (*ridge*). Usual meaning, except in Hos. x. 10, where it means transgressions.

G

Gā'al (*contempt*). Son of Ebed, Judg. ix. 26–41.

Gā'ăsh (*earthquake*). The hill on which Joshua was buried, Josh. xxiv. 30; 2 Sam. xxiii. 30.

Gā'bà, Josh. xviii. 24; Ez. ii. 26. [GEBA.]

Găb'ā-el. Ancestor of Tobit, Tob. i. 1, 14.

Găb'bạ-ī (*gatherer*). A Benjamite family, Neh. xi. 8.

Găb'bạ-thà (*elevated*). The pavement on which Christ was sentenced, John xix. 13.

Găb'dēs, 1 Esdr. v. 20. [GEBA.]

Gā'brĭ-as. Brother of Tobit, Tob. i. 14; iv. 20.

Gā'brĭ-el (*man of God*). The announcing angel, Luke i. 11, 19, 26, 38; Dan. viii. 16; ix. 21.

Găd (*troop*). (1) Jacob's seventh son, Gen. xxx. 11–13; xlix. 19; Num. i. 24, 25. Tribe settled east of Jordan, and became a fierce, warlike people. Carried captive by Tiglath-pileser, 1 Chr. v. 26. (2) A prophet and David's seer, 1 Sam. xxii. 5; 1 Chr. xxi. 9–19; xxix. 29; 2 Chr. xxix. 25.

Găd'ạ-rà (*walled*). A city six miles S. E. of Sea of Galilee. Now Um-keis.

Găd'ạ-rēnes, Gĕr'gĕ-sēnes, Gĕr'ạ-sēnes. A people east of the Sea of Galilee, Matt. viii. 28–34; Mark v. 1–20; Luke viii. 26–40.

Găd'dī (*fortunate*). One of the spies, Num. xiii. 11.

Găd'dĭel (*fortune of God*). Another of the spies, Num. xiii. 10.

Gā'dī (*of Gad*). Father of King Menahem, 2 Kgs. xv. 15, 17.

Gā'hăm (*browned*). Son of Nahor, Gen. xxii. 24.

Gā'hăr (*hiding place*). His sons returned, Ez. ii. 47.

Gā'ĭus, Cā'ĭus (*lord*). (1) Of Macedonia, a friend of Paul, Acts xix. 29. (2) Of Derbe, co-worker with Paul, Acts xx. 4. (3) Of Corinth, baptized by Paul, Rom. xvi. 23; 1 Cor. i. 14. (4) John's third epistle addressed to Gaius.

Găl'ạ-ad. Greek form of Gilead.

Gā'lăl (*prominence*). Three Levites, 1 Chr. ix. 15, 16; Neh. xi. 17.

Gà-lā'tĭà (*land of the Galli, Gauls*). A central province of Asia Minor, and part of Paul's missionary field, Acts xvi. 6; xviii. 23; 2 Tim. iv. 10.

Gà-lā'tĭans, Epistle to. Written by Paul to people of Galatia, A. D. 56 or 57, to strengthen their faith in the divinity of his mission, unfold his doctrine of justification by faith, and urge persistency in Christian work.

Găl-bā′num (*fat*). A gum-resin of yellowish color, and pungent, disagreeable odor when burning, Ex. xxx. 34.

Găl′ĕ-ed (*heap of witness*). Memorial heap of Jacob, Gen. xxxi. 47, 48.

Găl′gă-là, 1 Macc. ix. 1. [GILGAL.]

Găl′ĭ-lee (*circle*). Originally the circuit containing the 20 towns given by Solomon to Hiram, Josh. xx. 7; 1 Kgs. ix. 11; 2 Kgs. xv. 29. In time of Christ, one of the largest provinces of Palestine, in which he spent the greater part of his life and ministry. Luke xiii. 1; xxiii. 6; John i. 43–47; Acts i. 11.

Găl′ĭ-lee, Sea of. [GENNESARET.]

Găll (*yellow, bitter*). The fluid secreted by the liver. Bitter, Job xvi. 13; poison, xx. 14, 25; Deut. xxxii. 33; "hemlock" in Hos. x. 4; probably myrrh, in Matt. xxvii. 34; as in Mark xv. 23; great troubles, Jer. viii. 14; Acts viii. 23.

Găl′lĕr-ȳ (*show*). An eastern veranda or portico; but panel work in S. of Sol. i. 17; or pillared walk, Ezek. xli. 15.

Găl′ley, Isa. xxxiii. 21. [SHIP.]

Găl′lĭm (*heaps*). A village of Benjamin, 1 Sam. xxv. 44; Isa. x. 30.

Găl′lĭ-ō (*who lives on milk*). Roman proconsul of Achaia, A. D. 53, Acts xviii. 12–17.

Găl′lōws. [PUNISHMENT.]

Găm′ă-el, 1 Esdr. viii. 29. [DANIEL.]

Gâ-mā′lĭ-el (*recompense of God*). (1) A prince of Manasseh, Num. i. 10; ii. 20; vii. 54; x. 23. (2) A learned president of the Sanhedrim, and Paul's legal preceptor, Acts v. 34; xxii. 3.

Gāmes (*sports*). Simple among Hebrews. Falconry, Job xli. 5; foot-racing, Ps. xix. 5; Eccl. ix. 11; bow and sling contests, 1 Sam. xx. 20; Judg. xx. 16; 1 Chr. xii. 2; dancing, Matt. xi. 16, 17; joking, Prov. xxvi. 19; Jer. xv. 17.

Găm′ma-dĭms (*dwarfs*). Perhaps watchmen, Ezek. xxvii. 11.

Gā′mŭl (*weaned*). Leader of the 22d priestly course, 1 Chr. xxiv. 17.

Gär. Sons of, in 1 Esdr. v. 34.

Gär′den (*yard*). In Hebrew sense, enclosures for fruits, etc., well watered, Gen. ii. 10; xiii. 10; xxi. 33; Num. xxiv. 12; Job viii. 16; hedged, Isa. v. 5; walled, Prov. xxiv. 31; protected, Isa. i. 8; Job xxvii. 18; Mark xii. i.

Gā′rĕb (*scab*). (1) One of David's warriors, 2 Sam. xxiii. 38; 1 Chr. xi. 40. (2) A hill near Jerusalem, Jer. xxxi. 39.

Găr′ĭ-zĭm, 2 Macc. v. 23. [GERIZIM.]

Gär′lic (*spear leek*). A bulbous plant similar to an onion and leek, Num. xi. 5.

Gär′ment. [DRESS.]

Gär′mīte. A Judahite, 1 Chr. iv. 19.

Găr′rĭ-sŏn (*warning*). In Hebrew sense, a place manned, provisioned, and fortified, 1 Sam. xiii. 23; 2 Sam. xxiii. 14; 1 Chr. xi. 16; guards in 2 Chr. xvii. 2; 1 Chr. xviii. 13.

Găsh′mū, Neh. vi. 6. [GESHEM.]

Gā′tam (*burnt valley*). A duke of Edom, Gen. xxxvi. 11, 16.

Gāte (*opening*). Those of walled cities made of wood, iron, or brass, Judg. xvi. 3; Deut. iii. 5; Ps. cvii. 16; Acts xii. 10; flanked by towers, 2 Sam. xviii. 24, 33; market and judgment places near, 2 Sam. xv. 2; 2 Kgs. vii. 1; Job xxix. 7; Deut. xvii. 5; xxv. 7; Am. v. 10; Ruth iv. 1–12; symbol of power, Gen. xxii. 17; Isa. xxiv. 12; Matt. xvi. 18; the city itself, Deut. xii. 12.

Găth (*wine press*). A city of Philistia, Josh. xiii. 3; 1 Sam. vi. 17; home of Goliath, 1 Sam. xvii. 4; refuge of David, 1 Sam. xxi. 10.

Găth=hē′phĕr, Gĭt′tah=hē′phĕr (*wine press of Hepher*). A town in Zebulun, now el Meshed, Josh. xix. 13; 2 Kgs. xiv. 25.

Găth=rĭm′mon (*high wine press*). (1) A Levitical city of Dan, Josh. xxi. 24; 1 Chr. vi. 69. (2) A Levite town of Manasseh, Josh. xxi. 25. Bileam, 1 Chr. vi. 70.

Gā′zà (*strong*). Hebrew Azzah, now Ghuzzeh. A city of Philistia, Gen. x. 19; assigned to Judah, Josh. x. 41; xv. 47; Judg. i. 18; scene of Samson's exploits, Judg. xvi.; 1 Kgs. iv. 24; Acts viii. 26.

Găz-a-rà, 1 Macc. ix. 52. [GEZER.]

Gā′zăth-ītes. Inhabitants of Gaza, Josh. xiii. 3.

Gā′zĕr, 2 Sam. v. 25; 1 Chr. xiv. 16. [GEZER.]

Găz′ĕ-rà. (1) 1 Macc. iv. 15. [GEZER.] (2) His sons returned, 1 Esdr. v. 31.

Gā′zĕz (*shearer*). Son of Caleb, 1 Chr. ii. 46.

Gā′zītes. Inhabitants of Gaza, Judg. xvi. 2.

Găz′zam (*consuming*). His descendants returned, Ez. ii. 48; Neh. vii. 51.

Gē′bà (*hill*). Gaba in Josh. xviii. 24; now Jeba, 6 miles N. of Jerusalem. A Levitical city of Benjamin, Josh. xxi. 17; 1 Chr. vi. 60; 1 Sam. xiii. 3; 1 Kgs. xv. 22; 2 Kgs. xxiii. 8; Isa. x. 29.

Gē′bal (*mountain*). A maritime town of Phœnicia, near Tyre, Ezek. xxvii. 9. Inhabitants called Giblites, Josh. xiii. 5.

Gē′bĕr (*man*). Two of Solomon's commissaries, 1 Kgs. iv. 13, 19.

Gē′bim (*ditches*). A place near Jerusalem, Isa. x. 31.

Gĕc′ko. The fan-footed lizard of Palestine. "Ferret," in A. V., Lev. xi. 30; "Gecko" in R. V.

Gĕd′′a-lī′ah (*God my greatness*). (1) A governor of Judea, 2 Kgs. xxv. 22; and friend of Jeremiah, Jer. xl. 5, 6; xli. 2. (2) A Levite harpist, 1 Chr. xxv. 3. (3) A priest, Ez. x. 18. (4) A persecutor of Jeremiah, Jer. xxxviii. 1. (5) Grandfather of Zephaniah, Zeph. i. 1.

Gĕd′dur, 1 Esdr. v. 30. [GAHAR.]

Gĕd′e-on. Greek form of Gideon, Heb. xi. 32.

Gē′dĕr (*wall*). Its king was conquered by Joshua, Josh. xii. 13.

Gē-dē′rah (*sheepfold*). A town in lowlands of Judah, Josh. xv. 36.

Gĕd′e-răth-īte′′. Inhabitant of Gederah, 1 Chr. xii. 4.

Gĕd′e-rīte. Inhabitant of Geder, 1 Chr. xxvii. 28.

Gĕ-dē′rŏth (*sheepfolds*). A city in lowlands of Judah, Josh. xv. 41; 2 Chr. xxviii. 18.

Gĕd′′e-rŏth-ā′im (*two sheepfolds*). A town in lowlands of Judah, Josh. xv. 36.

Gē′dôr (*wall*). (1) A hill town of Judah, Josh. xv. 58. (2) A town of Benjamin, 1 Chr. xii. 7. (3) 1 Chr. iv. 39, probably Gerar. (4) An ancestor of Saul, 1 Chr. viii. 31.

Gē-hā′zī (*valley of vision*). Messenger of Elisha, 2 Kgs. iv. 12–37; v. 20–27; viii. 4.

Gē-hĕn′nà. [HINNOM.]

Gĕl′ĭ-lŏth (*circuit*). A landmark of Benjamin, Josh. xviii. 17.

Gĕ-măl′lī (*camel driver*). Father of Ammiel, Num. xiii. 12.

Gĕm′′a-rī′ah (*perfected by God*). (1) Son of Shaphan, Jer. xxxvi. 10–27. (2) Messenger of King Hezekiah, Jer. xxix. 3, 4.

Gĕms. [STONES, PRECIOUS.]

Gĕn′′e-ăl′o-gy (*birth record*). In Hebrew, "book of generations," Gen. v.; x.; 1 Chr. i.-viii.; ix. 1; Matt. i. 1–17; Luke iii. 23–38.

Gĕn′′ĕr-ā′tion (*begotten*). In plural, the genealogical register, Gen. ii. 4; v. 1; Matt. i. 1; family history, Gen. vi. 9; xxv. 12; men of the existing age, Lev. iii. 17; Isa. liii. 8; Matt. xxiv. 34; Acts ii. 40.

Gĕn'ĕ-sĭs (*beginning*). First book of the Bible and Pentateuch. Chapters i.-xi. give history of Creation, Adam, Deluge, Noah, first inhabitants, Babel. Balance devoted to history of the patriarchs Abraham, Isaac, Jacob and Joseph. Covers a period of nearly 2500 years. Authorship attributed to Moses.

Gĕn-nĕs'a̱-rĕt (*garden of the prince*). (1) Land of, the small crescent country N. W. of Sea of Galilee, Matt. xiv. 34; Mark vi. 53. (2) Lake of, "Sea of Chinnereth," in O. T., Num. xxxiv. 11; Josh. xii. 3; and "Sea of Galilee," in N. T.; enlargement of Jordan river; 13 miles long, 6 wide, 700 below bed of ocean. "Lake of Gennesaret," Luke v. 1; "Sea of Tiberias," John vi. 1; "the sea," Matt. iv. 15.

Gĕn-nĕs'a̱-rĕth. [GENNESARET.]

Gĕn-nē'us. Father of Apollonius, 2 Macc. xii. 2.

Gĕn'tīles (*nations*). In O. T. sense, all peoples not Jewish, Gen. x. 5; xiv. 1; Neh. v. 8. In N. T., Greeks and Romans seem to type Gentiles, Luke ii. 32; Acts xxvi. 17-20; Rom. i. 14-16; ix. 24. "Isles of the Gentiles," Gen. x. 5, supposed to embrace Asia Minor and Europe.

Gĕ̇-nū'bă̱th (*theft*). An Edomite, 1 Kgs. xi. 20.

Gē'on, Ecclus. xxiv. 27. [GIHON.]

Gē'ra̱ (*grain*). (1) A Benjamite, Gen. xlvi. 21; 1 Chr. viii. 3-7. (2) Father of Ehud, Judg. iii. 15. (3) Father of Shimei, 2 Sam. xvi. 5; xix. 16; 1 Kgs. ii. 8.

Gē'rah. One twentieth of a shekel; about 3 cents, Ex. xxx. 13.

Gē'rär (*halting place*). A town of Philistia, Gen. x. 19; xx. 1; xxvi. 26; 2 Chr. xiv. 13, 14.

Gĕr''a̱-sēnes'. For Gadarenes in Luke viii. 26, R. V.

Gĕr'gĕ-sēnes, Matt. viii. 28. [GADARENES, GERASENES.]

Gĕr'ĭ-zĭm (*cutters*). The mountain of blessings in Ephraim, Deut. xi. 29; xxvii. 12-26; xxviii.

Gĕr-rhē'nĭ-a̱ns. Of Gerar, 2 Macc. xiii. 24.

Gĕr'shŏm (*exile*). (1) Son of Moses, Ex. ii. 22; xviii. 3. (2) A priest, Ez. viii. 2.

Gĕr'shŏn (*exile*). Eldest son of Levi, Gen. xlvi. 11; Ex. vi. 16: 1 Chr. vi. 1. Founder of the Gershonites. Given thirteen cities in Canaan, Josh. xxi. 6. Gershom in 1 Chr. vi. 62-71.

Gĕr'zītes. Dwellers south of Palestine, 1 Sam. xxvii. 8 marg.

Gē'sem, Judith i. 9. [GOSHEN.]

Gĕ'shăm (*filthy*). A descendant of Caleb, 1 Chr. ii. 47.

Gē'shem, Găsh'mū (*rain*). A scoffing Arabian, Neh. ii. 19; vi. 1, 2.

Gē'shŭr (*bridge*). A province of Syria peopled by Geshuri or Geshurites, Deut. iii. 14; Josh. xiii. 11; 2 Sam. iii. 3; xv. 8; 1 Chr. ii. 23.

Gĕsh'u-rī, Deut. iii. 14; Josh. xiii. 2. [GESHUR.]

Gĕsh'u-rītes. Besides above, a people of Arabia and Philistia, Josh. xiii. 11; 1 Sam. xxvii. 8.

Gē'thĕr (*fear*). Son of Aram, Gen. x. 23; 1 Chr. i. 17.

Gĕth-sĕm'a̱-nē (*oil press*). Scene of Christ's agony and betrayal, at the foot of Olivet, near Jerusalem, Matt. xxvi. 36-56; Mark xiv. 26-52; Luke xxii. 39-49; John xviii. 1-13.

Gĕ̇-ū'el (*majesty of God*). The Gadite spy, Num. xiii. 15.

Gē'zĕr (*steep*). Gazer, Gazara, Gazera, and Gad. A Levitical city, Josh. x. 33; xii. 12; xvi. 3; xxi. 21; whose native people remained, Judg. i. 29.

Gĕz'rītes. [GERZITES.]

Ghōst (*that terrifies*). The spirit, Matt. xxvii. 50.

Gī'ah (*waterfall*). A hill near Ammah, 2 Sam. ii. 24.

Gī'ants (*sons of Gaea*). Huge men — Nephilim, Gibborim, Gen. vi. 4; Rephaim, xiv. 5; Emim, Ana-

kim, Zuzim, etc., Num. xiii. 28-33; Deut. iii. 11; 1 Sam. xvii. 4.

Gĭb'bar (*huge*). His children returned, Ez. ii. 20.

Gĭb'be-thon (*high*). A Levitical town of Dan, Josh. xix. 44; xxi. 23; 1 Kgs. xv. 27; xvi. 17.

Gĭb'e-a̱ (*hill*). A Judahite, 1 Chr. ii. 49.

Gĭb'e-ah (*hill*). (1) A town of Judah, Josh. xv. 57. (2) Place where the ark was left, 2 Sam. vi. 3, 4. (3) A place in Benjamin, Judg. xix. 12-15; xx. 19-25; 1 Sam. xiii. 2. (4) Saul's birthplace, 1 Sam. x. 26; xi. 4; xv. 34; xxii. 6; xxiii. 19; Isa. x. 29. (5) Probably Geba, Judg. xx. 31.

Gĭb'e-ath, Josh. xviii. 28. [GIBEAH, 3.]

Gĭb'e-on (*lofty hill*). A Hivite city of Canaan, given to Levites, Josh. ix. 3-15; x. 12, 13; xxi. 17; 2 Sam. ii. 12-24; xx. 8-10. Tabernacle set up there, 1 Chr. xvi. 39; 1 Kgs. iii. 4, 5; ix. 2; 2 Chr. i. 3, 13; Jer. xli. 12-16.

Gĭb'e-on-ītes''. Inhabitants of Gibeon, 2 Sam. xxi. 1-9.

Gĭb'lītes, Josh. xiii. 5. [GEBAL.]

Gĭd-dăl'tī (*trained up*). Son of Heman, and leader of 22d musical course, 1 Chr. xxv. 4.

Gĭd'del (*great*). His children returned, Ez. ii. 47, 56.

Gĭd'e-on (*destroyer*). The powerful warrior of Manasseh, and judge of Israel for 40 years, Judges vi.-viii.

Gĭd''e-ō'nī (*destroyer*). A Benjamite, Num. i. 11.

Gī'dom (*desolation*). A place near Rimmon, Judg. xx. 45.

Gĭer (*jer*) **Ēagle** (*sacred eagle*). An unclean bird of prey; probably the Egyptian vulture, Lev. xi. 18; Deut. xiv. 17.

Gĭft (*given*). A common way of showing esteem and confidence and securing favors, Gen. xxxii. 13-15; xlv. 22, 23. Kings were donees, 1 Kgs. iv. 21; 2 Chr. xvii. 5. Not to give, a mark of contempt, 1 Sam. x. 27. Cattle given, Gen. xxxii. 13; garments, 2 Kgs. v. 23; money, 2 Sam. xviii. 11; perfumes, Matt. ii. 11.

Gī'hon (*stream*). (1) Second river of Paradise, Gen. ii. 13. (2) A spot, or pool, near Jerusalem, 1 Kgs. i. 33-38; 2 Chr. xxxii. 30; xxxiii. 14.

Gĭl'a̱-lāi (*weighty*). A musician, Neh. xii. 36.

Gĭl-bō'a̱ (*fountain*). The mountain range east of Esdraelon and overlooking Jezreel, 1 Sam. xxviii. 4; xxxi. 1; 2 Sam. i. 6.

Gĭl'e-ăd (*rocky*). (1) Mount and Land of Gilead, east of Jordan, Gen. xxxi. 21-25; Num. xxxii. 1; Josh. xvii. 1. (2) A mountain near Jezreel, Judg. vii. 3. (3) Grandson of Manasseh, Num. xxvi. 29, 30. (4) Father of Jephthah, Judg. xi. 1, 2.

Gĭl'e-ăd-ītes''. Manassites of Gilead, Num. xxvi. 29.

Gĭl'găl (*rolling*). (1) First encampment of Israelites west of Jordan, Josh. iv. 19, 20; v. 9, 10. Became a city and headquarters, Josh. ix. 6; xv. 7. Saul crowned there, 1 Sam. vii. 16; x. 8; xi. 14, 15. (2) Another Gilgal in Sharon plain, Josh. xii. 23. (3) Another near Bethel, 2 Kgs. iv. 38.

Gī'loh (*exile*). A town of Judah, Josh. xv. 51; 2 Sam. xv. 12.

Gī'lo-nīte. Inhabitant of Giloh, 2 Sam. xv. 12; xxiii. 34.

Gĭm'zō (*producing sycamores*). Now Jimzu, a village 2½ miles from Lydda, 2 Chr. xxviii. 18.

Gĭn (*engine*). A bird-trap, Isa. viii. 14; Am. iii. 5.

Gī'nath (*protection*). Father of Tibni, 1 Kgs. xvi. 21, 22.

Gĭn'nĕ-thō (*gardener*). A priest, Neh. xii. 4.

Gĭn'nĕ-thon (*gardener*). A priest, Neh. x. 6; xii. 16.

Gĭr'dle (*gird*). Worn by men and women to hold the looser garments. Made of leather, 2 Kgs. i. 8;

Matt. iii. 4 ; of linen, Jer. xiii. 1 ; Ezek. xvi. 10 ; embroidered, Dan. x. 5 ; Rev. i. 13 ; used for carrying swords and daggers, Judg. iii. 16 ; 2 Sam. xx. 8.

Gĭr′ga-sīte, Gĭr′ga-shītes. An original tribe of Canaan, Gen. x. 16 ; xv. 21 ; Deut. vii. 1.

Gĭs′pȧ (*fondle*). An overseer, Neh. xi. 21.

Gĭt′tah=hē′phêr, Josh. xix. 13. [GATH-HEPHER.]

Gĭt′ta-ĭm (*two wine presses*). An unknown place, 2 Sam. iv. 3.

Gĭt′tītes. Gathite followers of David, 2 Sam. xv. 18, 19. [GATH.]

Gĭt′tĭth. A musical instrument or melody, Ps. viii., lxxxi., lxxxiv., titles.

Gī′zȯ-nīte. Hashem, 1 Chr. xi. 34.

Glȧss. Only once in O. T. as "crystal," Job xxviii. 17 ; N. T. "glass" mirrors were metal, 1 Cor. xiii. 12 ; 2 Cor. iii. 18 ; James i. 23 ; Rev. iv. 6.

Glēan′ing (*handful*). Field-gleanings were reserved for the poor, Lev. xix. 9, 10 ; Ruth ii. 2. [CORNER.]

Glēde (*glide*). An unclean bird of prey, Deut. xiv. 13. The European kite ; but vulture in Lev. xi. 14.

Gnȧt. A small insect ; figuratively mentioned in Matt. xxiii. 24.

Gōad (*gad, strike*). A rod spiked at the end for driving oxen, Judg. iii. 31 ; and iron-shod at the other end for cleaning plows, or even for plowing, 1 Sam. xiii. 21.

Gōat. Several varieties in Palestine, both wild and tame. An important source of food, clothing, and wealth, Gen. xxvii. 9 ; 1 Sam. xxiv. 2 ; xxv. 2 ; Job xxxix. 1. "Scape-goat," one of the two offered on Day of Atonement, over which the priest confessed the sins of Israel, and then let it escape to the wilderness, Lev. xvi. 7–26.

Gō′ath (*lowing*). An unknown place, Jer. xxxi. 39.

Gŏb (*cistern*). A battlefield, 2 Sam. xxi. 18, 19. Gezer in 1 Chr. xx. 4.

Gŏb′let (*little cask*). A wine cup.

God (*good*). In Hebrew, Jehovah, "the self-existent and eternal," and especially the covenant God. Generally rendered Lord. The ineffable name, not pronounced by the Jews, who substituted for it Adonai, "my Lord ;" or Elohim — God, the creator and moral governor — when Adonai was written with Jehovah.

God′head. The Supreme Being in all his nature and attributes, Acts xvii. 29 ; Rom. i. 20 ; Col. ii. 9.

Gŏg (*roof*). (1) A Reubenite, 1 Chr. v. 4. (2) [MAGOG.]

Gō′lan (*circuit*). A refuge city in Bashan, Deut. iv. 43 ; Josh. xx. 8 ; xxi. 27.

Gōld (*yellow*). Known early to Hebrews, Gen. ii. 11 ; used for ornaments, Gen. xxiv. 22 ; money, temple furniture and utensils, Ex. xxxvi. 34–38 ; 1 Kgs. vii. 48–50 ; emblem of purity and nobility, Job xxiii. 10 ; Lam. iv. 1. Obtained chiefly from Ophir, Job xxviii. 16 ; Parvaim, 2 Chr. iii. 6 ; Sheba and Raamah, Ezek. xxvii. 22.

Gŏl′gȯ-thȧ (*skull*). Hebrew name of the spot where Christ was crucified, Matt. xxvii. 33 ; Mark xv. 22 ; John xix. 17. [CALVARY.]

Gō-lī′ath (*splendor*). The Philistine giant who defied the army of Israel, 1 Sam. xvii. 4–54. Another Goliath in 2 Sam. xxi. 19–22.

Gō′mer (*complete*). (1) Eldest son of Japheth, Gen. x. 2, 3 ; 1 Chr. i. 5, 6. (2) Wife of Hosea, Hos. i. 3.

Gȯ-mŏr′rah (*submersion*). Gomorrha in N. T. A city of the plain destroyed by fire, Gen. xiv. 1–11 ; xviii. 20 ; xix. 24–28 ; Deut. xxix. 23 ; xxxii. 32 ; Matt. x. 15 ; Mark vi. 11.

Gō′pher. The unknown wood of Noah's ark, Gen. vi. 14.

Gŏr′gĭ-as (*frightful*). A Syrian general, 1 Macc. iii. 38.

Gŏr-tȳ′na. Capital of Crete, 1 Macc. xv. 23.

Gō′shen (*drawing near*). (1) The extreme province of Egypt, northward toward Palestine ; assigned to the Jews, Gen. xlv. 5–10 ; xlvi. 28–34 ; xlvii. 1–6 ; l. 8. (2) An undefined part of southern Palestine, Josh. x. 41 ; xi. 16. (3) A city of Judah, Josh. xv. 51.

Gŏs′pels (*good tidings*). The four initial books of N. T., containing the biographies of Christ.

Gŏth′′ō-lī′as. One who returned, 1 Esdr. viii. 33.

Gō-thŏn′ī-el. Father of Chabris, Judith vi. 15.

Gōurd (*encumberer*). A large plant family, covering the melon, pumpkin, squash, calabash, etc., Jonah iv. 6–10. A poisonous apple or cucumber, 2 Kgs. iv. 39–41.

Gŏv′êr-nôr (*director*). Often captain, chief, or civic official ; but generally the political officer in charge of a province, Gen. xlii. 6 ; 1 Kgs. x. 15 ; Ez. viii. 36 ; Neh. ii. 9 ; Matt. xxvii. 2.

Gō′zan. Place or river in Mesopotamia, 2 Kgs. xvii. 6 ; xviii. 11 ; 1 Chr. v. 26.

Grā′bȧ, 1 Esdr. v. 29. [HAGABA.]

Grāpe (*hook, grab*). Grapes of Palestine noted for size and flavor, Gen. xlix. 11 ; Num. xiii. 24. Used for wine and food, 1 Sam. xxv. 18 ; xxx. 12 ; 2 Sam. xvi. 1 ; 1 Chr. xii. 40.

Grȧss (*for gnawing*). Large figurative use, Ps. xc. 5, 6 ; Isa. xl. 6, 8 ; James i. 10, 11 ; 1 Pet. i. 24 ; sometimes herbage in general, Isa. xv. 6 ; a fuel, Matt. vi. 30 ; Luke xii. 28.

Grȧss′hop-per. An insect of the locust species, often translated locust, 2 Chr. vii. 13. A clean animal, Lev. xi. 22 ; timid, Job xxxix. 20 ; gregarious and destructive, Judg. vi. 5 ; vii. 12 ; Eccl. xii. 5 ; Jer. xlvi. 23 ; type of insignificance, Num. xiii. 33 ; Isa. xl. 22.

Grāve. [BURIAL.] [ENGRAVER.]

Grēaves (*shins*). Armor, metallic or leathern, to protect the shins from foot to knee, 1 Sam. xvii. 6.

Grēeçe, Grēeks, Grē′çians. The well known country in S. E. of Europe, called also Hellas. Javan in O. T., Gen. x. 2–5 ; Isa. lxvi. 19 ; Ezek. xxvii. 13, 19 ; but direct in Dan. viii. 21 ; x. 20 ; xi. 2 ; Joel iii. 6 ; Acts xx. 2. Greek the original N. T. language.

Grey′hound, Prov. xxx. 31. The original implies a "wrestler," not a quadruped.

Grīnd′ing. [MILL.]

Grōve. Except in Gen. xxi. 33, the Hebrew original means an idol ; primitively set up and worshipped in groves, 1 Kgs. xviii. 19 ; 2 Kgs. xiii. 6.

Gŭd′go-dah, Deut. x. 7. [HOR-HAGIDGAD.]

Guĕst. [HOSPITALITY.]

Gū′nī (*painted*). (1) Son of Naphtali and founder of the Gunites, Gen. xlvi. 24 ; Num. xxvi. 48 ; 1 Chr. vii. 13. (2) A son of Gad, 1 Chr. v. 15.

Gûr (*whelp*). Spot where King Ahaziah was slain, 2 Kgs. ix. 27.

Gûr=bā′al (*abode of Baal*). A district south of Palestine, 2 Chr. xxvi. 7.

H

Hā′′a-hȧsh′ta-rī (*runner*). Son of Ashur, 1 Chr. iv. 6.

Hȧ-bā′ịah (*God hides*). His children returned, Ez. ii. 61.

Hȧ-bȧk′kŭk (*embrace*). A minor prophet during reigns of Jehoiakim and Josiah. His book, thirteenth of the prophetic, denounces Chaldea, and concludes with a striking poem and prayer.

Hȧb′′a-zī-nī′ah (*God's light*). A Rechabite, Jer. xxxv. 3.

Hăb'ba-cuc, B. and D. 33–39. [HABAKKUK.]

Hăb'ēr-ġeon (*neck protector*). Coat of mail for neck and breast, Ex. xxviii. 32.

Hā'bôr (*fertile*). A tributary of the Euphrates, 2 Kgs. xvii. 6; 1 Chr. v. 26.

Hăch''a-lī'ah (*who waits*). Father of Nehemiah, Neh. i. 1.

Hăch'ī-lah (*dark hill*). A hill in Ziph, 1 Sam. xxiii. 19.

Hăch'mŏ-nī (*wise*). A Hachmonite, 1 Chr. xi. 11; xxvii. 32.

Hā'dăd (*brave*). (1) An Ishmaelite, 1 Chr. i. 30; Hadar, Gen. xxv. 15. (2) A king of Edom, Gen. xxxvi. 35; 1 Chr. i. 46. (3) Another king of Edom, 1 Chr. i. 50; Hadar, Gen. xxxvi. 39. (4) An Edomite, 1 Kgs. xi. 14–25.

Hăd''ăd-ē'zĕr, 2 Sam. viii. 3–12. [HADAREZER.]

Hā'dăd=rĭm'mon. From two Syrian idols. Spot of mourning for Josiah, Zech. xii. 11.

Hā'dar, Gen. xxv. 15; xxxvi. 39. [HADAD.]

Hăd''ăr-ē'zĕr (*Hadad's help*). A king of Zoba, 2 Sam. viii. 3; x. 16; 1 Chr. xviii. 7; xix. 16–19.

Hăd'a-shah (*new*). Town of Judah, Josh. xv. 37.

Hă-dăs'sah (*myrtle*). Hebrew name of Esther, Esth. ii. 7.

Hă-dăt'tah (*new*). Town of Judah, Josh. xv. 25.

Hā'deş. Place of departed spirits. Greek equivalent of Hebrew "sheol," unseen world. Hell in A. V.; Hades in R. V., Matt. xi. 23; xvi. 18; Acts ii. 31; Rev. i. 18.

Hā'dĭd (*sharp*). Place named in Ez. ii. 33; Neh. vii. 37.

Hăd'la-ī (*restful*). An Ephraimite, 2 Chr. xxviii. 12.

Hă-dō'ram (*power*). (1) Son of Joktan, Gen. x. 27. (2) An ambassador to David, 1 Chr. xviii. 10. (3) 2 Chr. x. 18. [ADONIRAM.]

Hā'drăch (*dwelling*). A Syrian country, Zech. ix. 1.

Hā'găb (*locust*). His sons returned, Ez. ii. 46.

Hăg'a-bà, Neh. vii. 48. Hagabah, Ez. ii. 45. [HAGAB.]

Hā'gar (*flight*). Abraham's concubine, Gen. xvi. 3; mother of Ishmael, xxi. 9–21. Type of law and bondage, Gal. iv. 24, 25.

Hā'gar-ītes, Hā'gar-ēneş. Ishmaelites, 1 Chr. v. 10–20; xxvii. 31; Ps. lxxxiii. 6.

Hăg'ga-ī (*festive*). A minor prophet. His book, fifteenth of the prophetic, exhorts the Jews to crown the work of Zerubbabel.

Hăg-gē'rī (*wanderer*), 1 Chr. xi. 38. [BANI.]

Hăg'gī (*festive*). Son of Gad, Gen. xlvi. 16.

Hăg-gī'ah (*Lord's feast*). A Levite, 1 Chr. vi. 30.

Hăg'gītes. Of Haggi, Num. xxvi. 15.

Hăg'gĭth (*dancer*). A wife of David, 2 Sam. iii. 4; 1 Kgs. i. 5.

Hā'ġi-à, 1 Esdr. v. 34. [HATTIL.]

Hā'ī. Ancient form of Ai, Gen. xii. 8; xiii. 3.

Hāil. The seventh plague, Ex. ix. 18–29. God's weapon, Josh. x. 11; Rev. xvi. 21.

Hâir. Worn short with elderly men, long with young men, vowed men and women, Num. vi. 5–9; 2 Sam. xiv. 26; Luke vii. 38. Lepers shorn, Lev. xiv. 8, 9.

Hăk'ka-tăn (*little*). Father of Johanan, Ez. viii. 12.

Hăk'kŏz (*thorn*). Priest of 7th course, 1 Chr. xxiv. 10.

Hă-kū'phà (*bent*). His children returned, Ez. ii. 51.

Hā'lah. Probably Habor, 2 Kgs. xvii. 6.

Hā'lăk (*smooth*). An unlocated mountain, Josh. xi. 17; xii. 7.

Hāle. Haul, Luke xii. 58; Acts viii. 3.

Hăl'hŭl (*trembling*). Town of Judah, Josh. xv. 58.

Hā'lī (*necklace*). Border of Asher, Josh. xix. 25.

Hăl''ĭ-căr-năs'sus. City of Caria, 1 Macc. xv. 23.

Hăll. Court of a high priest's house, Luke xxii. 55; Matt. xxvii. 27.

Hăl''le-lū'jăh (*ya*). [ALLELUIA.]

Hăl-lō'hesh (*enchanter*). Co-covenanter with Nehemiah, Neh. x. 24.

Hă-lō'hesh (*enchanter*). A builder of the wall, Neh. iii. 12.

Hăm (*hot*). Third son of Noah, Gen. v. 32; ix. 22. Father of the Hamitic races, x. 6, etc.

Hā'man (*famed*). Prime minister of Ahasuerus, Esth.

Hā'math (*fortress*). Chief city of upper Syria, Gen. x. 18; Num. xxxiv. 8. Became part of Solomon's kingdom, 1 Kgs. viii. 65; 2 Chr. viii. 3, 4. Now Hamah.

Hăm'măth (*hot springs*). A town near Tiberias, Josh. xix. 35. Hammoth-Dor, Josh. xxi. 32. Hammon, 1 Chr. vi. 76.

Hăm-mēd'a-thà (*double*). Father of Haman, Esth. iii. 1.

Hăm'me-lĕch (*king*). Hardly a proper name, Jer. xxxvi. 26; xxxviii. 6.

Hăm'mĕr. Same as now, Judg. iv. 21; Isa. xliv. 12. Mighty force, Jer. xxiii. 29; l. 23.

Hăm-mŏl'e-kĕth (*queen*). Sister of Gilead, 1 Chr. vii. 17, 18.

Hăm'mŏn (*warm springs*). (1) City in Asher, Josh. xix. 28. (2) Levitical city in Naphtali, 1 Chr. vi. 76.

Hăm'moth=dôr, Josh. xxi. 32. [HAMMATH].

Hă-mō'nah (*multitude*). Unknown city, Ezek. xxxix. 16.

Hā'mon-gŏg (*multitude of Gog*). Unlocated valley, Ezek. xxxix. 11–15.

Hā'mor (*ass*). Father of Shechem, Gen. xxxiii. 19; xxxiv. 26. Emmor, Acts vii. 16.

Hă-mū'el (*wrath*). A Simeonite, 1 Chr. iv. 26.

Hā'mŭl (*pity*). Son of Pharez, and founder of Hamulites, Gen. xlvi. 12.

Hā'mŭl-ītes, Num. xxvi. 21. [HAMUL.]

Hă-mū'tal (*like dew*). A wife of Josiah, 2 Kgs. xxiii. 31; Jer. lii. 1.

Hă-năm'e-el (*given of God*). Jeremiah's cousin, Jer. xxxii. 6–12.

Hā'nan (*merciful*). (1) A Benjamite, 1 Chr. viii. 23. (2) Descendant of Saul, 1 Chr. viii. 38. (3) One of David's guard, 1 Chr. xi. 43. (4) His sons returned, Ez. ii. 46. (5, 6, 7) Co-covenanters with Nehemiah, Neh. x. 10, 22, 26. (8) A tithe-keeper, Neh. xiii. 13. (9) One who had temple rooms, Jer. xxxv. 4.

Hă-năn'e-el (*given of God*). A tower on wall of Jerusalem, Neh. iii. 1; xii. 39; Jer. xxxi. 38.

Hă-nā'nī (*gracious*). (1) Head of the 18th temple course, 1 Chr. xxv. 4, 25. (2) A seer, 2 Chr. xvi. 7–10. (3) A priest, Ez. x. 20. (4) Brother of Nehemiah, Neh. i. 2; vii. 2.

Hăn''a-nī'ah (*given of God*). (1) Leader of 16th temple course, 1 Chr. xxv. 4, 5, 23. (2) A general, 2 Chr. xxvi. 11. (3) Father of Zedekiah, Jer. xxxvi. 12. (4) A false prophet, Jer. xxviii. (5) Grandfather of Irijah, Jer. xxxvii. 13. (6) Hebrew name of Shadrach, Dan. i. 3–19. (7) Son of Zerubbabel, 1 Chr. iii. 19. Joanna in Luke. (8) A Benjamite, 1 Chr. viii. 24. (9) One of the returned, Ez. x. 28. (10) Others, Neh. iii. 8; vii. 2, 3; x. 23; xii. 12.

Hănd. Conspicuous in Hebrew ceremonial and other customs, Gen. xiv. 22; Deut. xxi. 6, 7; Matt. xxvii. 24; Job xxxi. 27; Isa. lxv. 2.

Hănd′breadth. Palm width; about four inches, Ex. xxv. 25.

Hănd′ī-craft. Though not noted for artisanship, Hebrew boys were taught trades, and reference is made to smiths, Gen. iv. 22; carpenters, Isa. xliv. 14; Matt. xiii. 55; masons, 1 Kgs. v. 18; ship-building, 1 Kgs. ix. 26; apothecaries, Ex. xxx. 25, 35; weavers, Ex. xxxv. 25, 26; dyers, Josh. ii. 18; barbers, Num. vi. 5–19; tent-makers, Acts xviii. 3; potters, Jer. xviii. 2–6; bakers, xxxvii. 21; engravers, Ex. xxviii. 9–11; tanners, Acts ix. 43.

Hănd′kĕr-chiefs. These, and napkins and aprons, signify about same as to-day, Luke xix. 20; John xi. 44; Acts xix. 12.

Hănd′stāves. Javelins, Ezek. xxxix. 9.

Hā′nēs. A city in Egypt, Isa. xxx. iv.

Hăng′ing, Hăng′ings. In strict law, culprits were strangled first, then hung, Num. xxv. 4; Deut. xxi. 22, 23. Hangings for doors and tabernacle use, quite the same as modern tapestries, Ex. xxvi. 9, 36; Num. iii. 26.

Hăn′ī-el (*grace of God*). An Asherite, 1 Chr. vii. 39.

Hăn′nah (*grace*). Mother of Samuel, 1 Sam. i., ii.

Hăn′na-thon (*gracious*). A city of Zebulun, Josh. xix. 14.

Hăn′nĭ-el (*grace of God*). A prince of Manasseh, Num. xxxiv. 23.

Hā′noch (*dedicated*). (1) Son of Midian, Gen. xxv. 4; Henoch, 1 Chr. i. 33. (2) A son of Reuben, and founder of Hanochites, Gen. xlvi. 9; Num. xxvi. 5.

Hā′nŭn (*gracious*). (1) A king of Ammon, 2 Sam. x. 1–6. (2) Two architects, Neh. iii. 13, 30.

Hăph-rā′im (*pits*). A city of Issachar, Josh. xix. 19.

Hā′rà (*hill*). No doubt Haran, 1 Chr. v. 26.

Hăr′a-dah (*fear*). An Israelite encampment, Num. xxxiii. 24, 25.

Hā′ran (*mountainous*). (1) Brother of Abraham, Gen. xi. 26–31. (2) A Levite, 1 Chr. xxiii. 9. (3) Son of Caleb, 1 Chr. ii. 46. (4) The spot in Mesopotamia where Abraham located after leaving Ur, Gen. xi. 31, 32; xxiv. 10; xxvii. 43. Charran, Acts vii. 2–4.

Hā′ra-rīte. Three of David's guard so called, 2 Sam. xxiii. 11, 33.

Hăr-bō′nà (*ass driver*). A chamberlain, Esth. i. 10. Harbonah in vii. 9.

Hâre (*leaper*). A species of rabbit, wrongly thought to chew the cud, Lev. xi. 6; Deut. xiv. 7.

Hā′reph (*plucking*). Son of Caleb, 1 Chr. ii. 51.

Hā′reth (*thicket*). A forest of Judah, 1 Sam. xxii. 5.

Hăr′hà-ī′ah (*God's anger*). Father of Uzziel, Neh. iii. 8.

Hăr′has (*poor*). Ancestor of Shallum, 2 Kgs. xxii. 14.

Hăr′hûr (*inflamed*). His children returned, Neh. vii. 53.

Hā′rim (*flat-nosed*). (1) Priestly head of third course, 1 Chr. xxiv. 8. (2) Name of several who returned, Ez. ii. 32, 39; x. 21; Neh. iii. 11; vii. 35, 42; x. 27; xii. 15.

Hā′riph (*plucking*). His children returned, Neh. vii. 24; x. 19.

Hăr′lot (*vagabond*). An abandoned woman, Gen. xxxviii. 15. Harlotry forbidden, Lev. xix. 29. Type of idolatry, Isa. i. 21; Ezek. xvi. Classed with publicans, Matt. xxi. 32.

Hăr′ma-gĕd′don. R. V. for Armageddon.

Hăr′ne-phĕr (*panting*). An Asherite, 1 Chr.

vii. 36.

Hā′rod (*fear*). A spring near Jezreel, Judg. vii. 1.

Hā′rod-īte. Two of David's guard, so called, 2 Sam. xxiii. 25.

Hăr′ŏ-eh (*seer*). Son of Shobal, 1 Chr. ii. 52.

Hă-rō′sheth (*handicraft*). A city of Naphtali, Judg. iv. 2–16.

Hărp (*sickle shaped*). Prominent Jewish musical instrument, invented by Jubal, Gen. iv. 21; of various shapes and sizes; different number of strings; played with fingers or plectrum (quill).

Hăr′row (*rake*). "Threshing-machine," 2 Sam. xii. 31; 1 Chr. xx. 3. Pulverizer of ground, Isa. xxviii. 24; Job xxxix. 10, and elsewhere.

Hăr′shà (*deaf*). His children returned, Ez. ii. 52; Neh. vii. 54.

Hărt. Male of the red deer, Deut. xii. 15; xiv. 5; 1 Kgs. iv. 23; S. of Sol. ii. 9.

Hā′rum (*high*). A Judahite, 1 Chr. iv. 8.

Hă-ru′maph (*slit-nosed*). Father of Jedaiah, Neh. iii. 10.

Hăr′u-phīte, The. A friend of David, 1 Chr. xii. 5.

Hā′ruz (*careful*). Amon's grandfather Kgs. xxi. 19.

Hăr′vest. [AGRICULTURE.]

Hăs′′a-dī′ah (*loved of God*). One of David's line, 1 Chr. iii. 20.

Hăs′′e-nū′ah (*hated*). A Benjamite, 1 Chr. ix. 7.

Hăsh′′a-bī′ah (*regarded*). (1) Two Levites, 1 Chr. vi. 45; ix. 14. (2) Leader of twelfth course, 1 Chr. xxv. 3, 19. (3) A Hebronite, 1 Chr. xxvi. 30. (4) Other Levites, 1 Chr. xxvii. 17; 2 Chr. xxxv. 9; Ez. viii. 19, 24; Neh. iii. 17; x. 11; xi. 15, 22; xii. 24.

Hă-shăb′nah (*regarded*). A co-covenanter with Nehemiah, Neh. x. 25.

Hăsh′′ăb-nī′ah (*regarded*). (1) His son repaired the wall, Neh. iii. 10. (2) A Levite, Neh. ix. 5.

Hăsh-băd′a-nà (*judge*). Assistant to Ezra, Neh. viii. 4.

Hā′shem (*fat*). His sons were of David's guard, 1 Chr. xi. 34.

Hăsh-mō′nah (*fatness*). A desert station, Num. xxxiii. 29.

Hā′shub (*informed*). (1) Hasshub, a Levite, 1 Chr. ix. 14. (2) Other Levites and builders, Neh. iii. 11, 23; x. 23.

Hă-shu′bah (*informed*). One of David's line, 1 Chr. iii. 20.

Hā′shum (*rich*). (1) His children returned, Ez. ii. 19. (2) Assistant to Ezra, Neh. viii. 4.

Hă-shū′phà (*stripped*). His children returned, Ez. ii. 43; Neh. vii. 46.

Hăs′rah, 2 Chr. xxxiv. 22. [HARHAS.]

Hăs′′se-nā′ah (*thorny*). His sons built the fish-gate, Neh. iii. 3.

Hăs′shub. [HASHUB.]

Hă-sū′phà. [HASHUPHA.]

Hā′tăch. Chamberlain of Ahasuerus, Esth. iv. 5–10.

Hā′thăth (*fear*). Son of Othniel, 1 Chr. iv. 13.

Hăt′ī-phà (*captive*). His sons returned, Ez. ii. 54.

Hăt′ī-tà (*searching*). Returned porters, Ez. ii. 42.

Hăt′til (*doubtful*). His sons returned, Ez. ii. 57.

Hăt′tŭsh (*gathered*). (1) A Judahite, 1 Chr. iii. 22; Ez. viii. 2. (2) Others of the returned, Neh. iii. 10; x. 4; xii. 2.

Hau′ran (*caves*). Present Hauran, S. of Syria in Bashan, Ezek. xlvii. 16–18.

Hăv′ī-lah (*circle*). (1) Son of Cush, Gen. x. 7. (2) Son of Joktan, x. 29. (3) An unlocated region,

Gen. ii. 11 ; xxv. 18 ; 1 Sam. xv. 7.

Hā′voth=jā′ir (*villages of Jair*). Villages in Gilead or Bashan, Num. xxxii. 41 ; Deut. iii. 14.

Hăwk (*havoc*). An unclean bird ; species of falcon, Lev. xi. 16 ; Deut. xiv. 15 ; Job xxxix. 26.

Hāy (*cut*). Grass ; but hardly cut and dried grass, Prov. xxvii. 25 ; Ps. lxxii. 6 ; Isa. xv. 6.

Hăz′a-el (*God sees*). A Syrian king, 1 Kgs. xix. 15 ; 2 Kgs. viii. 7–16 ; x. 32 ; xiii. 24.

Hȧ-zā′ḷah (*whom God sees*). A Judahite, Neh. xi. 5.

Hā′zar. [HAZER.]

Hā′zar=ăd′dar. [HAZER.]

Hā′zar=mā′veth. Son of Joktan, Gen. x. 26.

Hā′zel. The almond doubtless meant, Gen. xxx. 37.

Hăz′′e-lĕl-pō′nī (*coming shadows*). Sister of Judahites, 1 Chr. iv. 3.

Hā′zer (*village*). In composition. (1) Hazar-addar, a landmark of Israel, Num. xxxiv. 4 ; Adar, Josh. xv. 3. (2) Hazar-enan, a boundary of Israel, Num. xxxiv. 9, 10. (3) Hazar-gaddah, a town of Judah, Josh. xv. 27. (4) Hazar-shual, in southern Judah, Josh. xv. 28. (5) Hazar-susah, in Judah, Josh. xix. 5 ; Hazar-susim, 1 Chr. iv. 31. (6) Hazar-hatticon, Ezek. xlvii. 16.

Hȧ-zē′rĭm, Deut. ii. 23. Villagers. [HAZER.]

Hȧ-zē′roth (*villages*). An Israelite encampment, Num. xi. 35 ; Deut. i. 1.

Hăz′e-zon=tā′mar (*felling of palms*). Old name of Engedi, Gen. xiv. 7. Hazazon-tamar, 2 Chr. xx. 2.

Hā′zĭ-el (*vision*). A Levite, 1 Chr. xxiii. 9.

Hā′zō (*vision*). Son of Nahor, Gen. xxii. 22.

Hā′zôr (*court*). (1) City of Naphtali, Josh. xi. 10 ; 1 Kgs. ix. 15 ; 2 Kgs. xv. 29. (2) Town of Judah, Josh. xv. 23–25. (3) Place in Benjamin, Neh. xi. 33.

Hĕad′dress. Sacerdotal and ornamental, Ex. xxviii. 40. Mantle or veil the usual head-dress.

Heärth (*ground*). Hot stones, Gen. xviii. 6. Pan or brazier, Jer. xxxvi. 23.

Heath (*country*). No heath in Palestine. Evidently a desert scrub, Jer. xvii. 6 ; xlviii. 6.

Hea′then (*dwellers on the heath*). All except Jews, Ps. ii. 1. Non-believer, Matt. xviii. 17.

Hĕav′en (*heaved*). Firmament, Gen. i. 1 ; Matt. v. 18. Abode of God, 1 Kgs. viii. 30 ; Dan. ii. 28 ; Matt. v. 45. Paradise, Luke xxiii. 43.

Hē′bĕr (*alliance*). Eber, Luke iii. 35. Others in Gen. xlvi. 17 ; Num. xxvi. 45 ; Judg. iv. 17 ; 1 Chr. iv. 18 ; v. 13 ; vii. 31 ; viii. 17, 22.

Hē′brews. "Abram the Hebrew," Gen. xiv. 13, that is, *eber*, the one who had "passed over" the Euphrates, westward. Hence, "seed" or descendants of Abraham. Among themselves, preferably, Israelites, from Gen. xxxii. 28. Jews, *i. e.* Judahites, Judeans, after the captivity.

Hē′brews, Epistle to. Written probably by Paul, from Rome, A. D. 62 or 63, to overcome Hebrew favoritism for the old law.

Hē′bron (*friendship*). (1) Son bf Kohath, Ex. vi. 18 ; Num. iii. 19, 27. (2) Person or place, 1 Chr. ii. 42. (3) Ancient city of Judah, 20 mls. S. of Jerusalem, Gen. xiii. 18 ; Num. xiii. 22 Arba in Josh. xxi. 11 ; Judg. i. 10.

Hē′bron-ītes. Kohathite Levites, Num. iii. 27 ; xxvi. 58.

Hĕdge (*haw*). In Hebrew sense, anything that encloses — wall, fence, or thorn bushes, Num. xxii. 24 ; Prov. xxiv. 31 ; Hos. ii. 6.

Hĕg′a-ī, Hē′gē. Chamberlain of Ahasuerus, Esth. ii. 3, 8, 15.

Hĕif′er (*high-bullock*). Red heifers sacrificial, Num. xix. 10. Frequent source of metaphor, Judg. xiv. 18 ; Isa. xv. 5 ; Jer. xlvi. 20 ; Hos. iv. 16.

Heir (*inheritor*). Eldest son became head of tribe or family with largest share of paternal estate ; sons of concubines given presents ; daughters, a marriage portion, Gen. xxi. 10, 14 ; xxiv. 36 ; xxv. 6 ; xxxi. 14 ; Judg. xi. 2, etc. Real estate apportioned as in Deut. xxi. 17 ; Num. xxvii. 4–11.

Hē′lah (*rust*). Wife of Ashur, 1 Chr. iv. 5.

Hē′lam (*fort*). A battlefield, 2 Sam. x. 16, 17.

Hĕl′bah (*fertile*). Town of Asher, Judg. i. 31.

Hĕl′bon (*fertile*). A Syrian city, Ezek. xxvii. 18.

Hĕl-chī′ah, 1 Esdr. viii. 1. [HILKIAH.]

Hĕl′da-ī (*worldly*). (1) Captain of 12th course, 1 Chr. xxvii. 15. (2) One who returned, Zech. vi. 10. Helem in vs. 14.

Hē′lĕb, Hē′lĕd (*passing*). One of David's guard, 2 Sam. xxiii. 29 ; 1 Chr. xi. 30.

Hē′lek (*portion*). Founder of Helekites, Num. xxvi. 30.

Hē′lem (*strength*). (1) An Asherite, 1 Chr. vii. 35. (2) Probably Heldai, Zech. vi. 14.

Hē′leph (*exchange*). Starting point of Naphtali's boundary, Josh. xix. 33.

Hē′lez (*strong*). (1) Captain of 7th course and one of David's guard, 2 Sam. xxiii. 26 ; 1 Chr. xi. 27. (2) A Judahite, 1 Chr. ii. 39.

Hē′lī (*climbing*). Eli, father of Joseph, Luke iii. 23.

Hē′′lī-ō-dō′rus. A Syrian treasurer, 2 Macc. iii.

Hĕl′ka-ī (*portion*). A priest, Neh. xii. 15.

Hĕl′kăth (*part*). (1) Starting point of Asher's boundary, Josh. xix. 25. (2) Hĕl′kăth-hăz′zu-rĭm, a battlefield ; 2 Sam. ii. 16.

Hĕl-kī′as, 1 Esdr. i. 8. [HILKIAH.]

Hĕll (*conceal*). Hebrew "sheol ;" translated "grave," 1 Sam. ii. 6 ; "pit," Num. xvi. 30 ; "hell," Job xi. 8, in O. T. In N. T., Hades and Gehenna are translated hell, Acts ii. 27 ; Matt. v. 29. Gehenna, or Valley of Hinnom, alone implies a place of burning or torture.

Hĕl′lĕn-ist. A Grecian ; but limited to Greek-speaking Jews in Acts vi. 1 ; ix. 29 ; xi. 20.

Hĕl′met (*hide*). Armor, generally metal, for head, 1 Sam. xvii. 5 ; 2 Chr. xxvi. 14. [ARMOR.]

Hē′lon (*strong*). Father of Eliab, Num. i. 9 ; ii. 7.

Hĕm (*field*). Edge, or fringe, of a garment, Num. xv. 38, 39 ; Matt. xxiii. 5.

Hē′mam (*driving out*). Grandson of Seir, Gen. xxxvi. 22.

Hē′man (*trusty*). (1) Son of Zerah, 1 Chr. ii. 6. (2) Grandson of Samuel, 1 Chr. vi. 33 ; xv. 16–22 ; xxv. 5.

Hē′măth (*heat*). Person or place, 1 Chr. ii. 55. Hamath, 1 Chr. xiii. 5 ; Am. vi. 14.

Hĕm′dan (*pleasant*). Son of Dishon, Gen. xxxvi. 26. Amram, 1 Chr. i. 41.

Hĕm′lock. Not the bitter, poisonous hemlock as in Hos. x. 4 ; Am. vi. 12, but "gall," as elsewhere.

Hĕn (*rest*). (1) Son of Zephaniah, Zech. vi. 14. (2) The domestic fowl, common in Palestine, but mentioned only in Matt. xxiii. 37 ; Luke xiii. 34.

Hē′nà (*troubling*). A city of Mesopotamia, 2 Kgs. xviii. 34 ; xix. 13 ; Isa. xxxvii. 13.

Hĕn′a-dăd (*favor of Hadad*). His sons returned, Ez. iii. 9 ; Neh. x. 9.

Hē′noch. (1) 1 Chr. i. 3. [ENOCH, 6.] (2) 1 Chr. i. 33. [HANOCH, 1.]

Hē′phĕr (*pit*). (1) Founder of Hepherites, Num. xxvi. 32 ; Josh. xii. 17. (2) Son of Ashur, 1 Chr. iv. 6. (3) One of David's guard, 1 Chr. xi. 36. (4) A place W. of Jordan, Josh. xii. 17.

Hĕph′zĭ-bah (*my delight in her*). (1) Name of restored Jerusalem, Isa. lxii. 4. (2) Wife of Hezekiah, 2 Kgs. xxi. 1.

Hĕr′ăld (*army ruler*). Crier, Dan. iii. 4; preacher, as in 1 Tim. ii. 7; 2 Pet. ii. 5.

Hĕr′cū-leş. The god "Melkart," 2 Macc. iv. 19.

Hĕrd. A collection of cattle. Herdsmen despised by Egyptians, Gen. xlvi. 34, but honored by Hebrews, 1 Sam. xi. 5; xxi. 7.

Hē′rēş (*sun*). A place in Dan, Judg. i. 35.

Hē′resh (*carpenter*). A Levite, 1 Chr. ix. 15.

Hĕr′mas, Hĕr′mĕş (*Mercury*). Two friends of Paul, Rom. xvi. 14.

Hĕr-mŏg′e-nēş (*born of Mercury*). One who deserted Paul, 2 Tim. i. 15.

Hĕr′mŏn (*lofty*). Highest peak of Anti-Libanus range and northern landmark of Palestine, 10,000 ft. high, Deut. iii. 8; Josh. xi. 17.

Hĕr′mon-ītes. The three peaks of Hermon, Ps. xlii. 6.

Hĕr′od (*heroic*). (1) Herod the Great, tetrarch of Judea, B. C. 41; King of Judea, B. C. 41–4; liberal, yet tyrannical and cruel. Issued murderous edict against children of Bethlehem, Matt. ii. 16. (2) Herod Antipas, son of former; tetrarch of Galilee and Perea, B. C. 4–A. D. 39; murderer of John the Baptist, Matt. xiv. 1; Luke iii. 19; xxiii. 7–15; Acts xiii. 1. (3) Herod Philip, son of Herod the Great. Married Herodias, Matt. xiv. 3; Mark vi. 17; Luke iii. 19. Lived and died in private life. (4) Herod Philip II., son of Herod the Great, and tetrarch of Batanea, Ituræa, etc., B. C. 4–A. D. 34, Luke iii. 1. (5) Herod Agrippa I., grandson of Herod the Great; tetrarch of Galilee; king of his grandfather's realm, A. D., 37–44, Acts xii. 1–19. (6) Herod Agrippa II., son of former, and king of consolidated tetrarchies, A. D. 50–100, Acts xxv. 13–27; xxvi. 1–28.

Hē-rō′dī-anş. A Jewish political party who favored the Herods and Roman dependence, Matt. xxii. 16; Mark iii. 6; viii. 15.

Hē-rō′dī-as. Granddaughter of Herod the Great. Wife of her uncle Herod Philip and her step-uncle. She requested the head of John the Baptist, Matt. xiv. 3–6; Mark vi. 17; Luke iii. 19.

Hē-rō′dī-on. Kinsman of Paul, Rom. xvi. 11.

Hĕr′on. A large aquatic bird, pronounced unclean, Lev. xi. 19; Deut. xiv. 18.

Hē′sed (*kindness*). Father of one of Solomon's commissaries, 1 Kgs. iv. 10.

Hĕsh′bŏn (*device*). An Amorite capital, N. E. of Dead Sea, Num. xxi. 26; Josh. xiii. 17; Isa. xv. 4.

Hĕsh′mŏn (*fertile*). Place in south Judah, Josh. xv. 27.

Hĕs′rŏn. [HEZRON.]

Hĕth (*fear*). Progenitor of the Hittites, Gen. x. 15; xxiii. 3–20; xxv. 10; xxvii. 46.

Hĕth′lŏn (*hiding place*). A mountain pass, probably Hamath, Ezek. xlvii. 15; xlviii. 1.

Hĕz′e-ki (*strong*). A Benjamite, 1 Chr. viii. 17.

Hĕz-e-ki′ah (*strength of God*). (1) Twelfth king of Judah, B. C. 726–698. Noted for abolition of idolatry and powerful resistance to neighboring nations, 2 Kgs. xviii.–xx.; 2 Chr. xxix.–xxxii. (2) Son of Neariah, 1 Chr. iii. 23. (3) [ATER.]

Hē′zī-on (*sight*). A king of Syria; probably Rezon, 1 Kgs. xv. 18; xi. 23.

Hē′zīr (*swine*). (1) Leader of 17th course, 1 Chr. xxiv. 15. (2) A co-covenanter, Neh. x. 20.

Hĕz′ra-ī (*enclosure*). One of David's guard, 2 Sam. xxiii. 35. Hezro, 1 Chr. xi. 37.

Hĕz′ron (*surrounded*). (1) A Reubenite, Gen. xlvi. 9. (2) Son of Pharez, Gen. xlvi. 12; Ruth iv. 18.

Hĕz′ron-ītes. Reubenite and Judahite families, Num. xxvi. 6, 21.

Hĭd′dạ-ī (*joyful*). One of David's guard, 2 Sam. xxiii. 30.

Hĭd′de-kel (*rapid*). Third river of Eden, no doubt Tigris, Gen. ii. 14; Dan. x. 4.

Hī′el (*God lives*). A Bethelite who rebuilt Jericho, 1 Kgs. xvi. 34.

Hī″e-răp′o-lĭs (*holy city*). City of Phrygia, on the Meander near Colossæ, Col. iv. 13.

Hī-er′e-el, 1 Esdr. ix. 21. [JEHIEL.]

Hī-er′e-moth. Jeremoth, Ramoth, in Esdr.

Hī″e-rŏn′y̆-mus (*sacred name*). A Syrian general, 2 Macc. xii. 2.

Hĭg-gā′ion (*meditation*). Musical pause for meditation, Ps. ix. 16; xix. 14, xcii. 3, marg.

High Plā′ces. Altars, temples, and dedicated places originally on high ground, Gen. xii. 8; Judg. vi. 25; Isa. lxv. 7; Jer. iii. 6. When the groves and mounts of idolatry overshadowed true worship, "high places" became a reproach.

High Priēst. Chief priest, Aaron being the first. Originally a life office, limited to a line or family, Ex. xxviii. 1; Lev. xxi. 10; Num. iii. 32; xx. 8; Deut. x. 6.

Hī′len (*caves*). A Levitical city in Judah, 1 Chr. vi. 58.

Hĭl-kī′ah (*God my portion*). (1) Father of Eliakim, 2 Kgs. xviii. 37. (2) A high priest, 2 Kgs. xxii. 8. (3) Four Levites, 1 Chr. vi. 45; xxvi. 11; Neh. viii. 4; xii. 7, 21. (4) Father of Jeremiah, Jer. i. 1. (5) Father of an ambassador, Jer. xxix. 3.

Hĭl′lel (*praise*). Father of Abdon, Judg. xii. 13, 15.

Hĭn. A Hebrew liquid measure, about 1¼ gallons, Ex. xxx. 24.

Hīnd. Female of the red deer, Gen. xlix. 21; Ps. xxix. 9; Prov. v. 19.

Hĭnge (*hanged*). A pivot and socket for swinging doors, 1 Kgs. vii. 50; Prov. xxvi. 14.

Hĭn′nom (*wailing*). A narrow valley south and west of Jerusalem, Josh. xv. 8; xviii. 16, where Molech was worshipped, 1 Kgs. xi. 7; 2 Kgs. xvi. 3; hence called Tophet, "drum," noise, Isa. xxx. 33; defiled, 2 Kgs. xxiii. 10, and called ge-Hinnom, gehenna, "place of Hinnom," to type a place of eternal torment. "Hell" in N. T., Matt. v. 22, 29; x. 28; xxiii. 15; Mark ix. 43; Luke xii. 5.

Hī′rah (*noble*). An Adullamite, Gen. xxxviii. 1, 12, 20.

Hī′ram, Hū′ram (*noble*). (1) King of Tyre who furnished men and material to David and Solomon, 2 Sam. v. 11; 1 Kgs. v.; 1 Chr. xiv. 1. (2) Hiram's chief architect, 1 Kgs. vii. 13, 40.

Hĭr-cā′nus. Son of Tobias, 2 Macc. iii. 11.

Hĭt′tītes. Descendants of Heth, Gen. x. 15; xxv. 9; Josh. iii. 10; 2 Sam. xi. 3.

Hī′vītes (*villagers*). Descendants of Canaan, Gen. x. 17; located at Shechem, xxxiv. 2; noted for craft, Josh. ix.

Hĭz-kī′ah (*strength*). Ancestor of Zephaniah, Zeph. i. 1.

Hĭz-kī′jah (*strength*). A co-covenanter, Neh. x. 17.

Hō′băb (*live*). Brother-in-law of Moses, Num. x. 29–32.

Hō′bah (*hiding*). A place beyond Damascus, Gen. xiv. 15.

Hŏd (*splendor*). Son of Zophah, 1 Chr. vii. 37.

Hŏd-ạ-ī′ah (*praise ye*). A Judahite, 1 Chr. iii. 24.

Hŏd-a-vī′ah (*praise ye*). (1) A Manassite, 1 Chr v. 24. (2) A Benjamite, 1 Chr. ix. 7 (3) A Levite, Ez. ii. 40.

Hō′desh (*new moon*). A Benjamite woman, 1 Chr. viii. 9.

Hō-dē′vah, Neh. vii. 43. [HODAVIAH, 3.]

Hŏ-dī′ah (*splendor*). Wife of Ezra, 1 Chr. iv. 19.

Jehudijah in vs. 18.

Hō′dī-jah (*splendor*). Three Levites, Neh. viii. 7; x. 13, 18.

Hŏg′lah (*quail*). Daughter of Zelophehad, Num. xxvi. 33.

Hō′ham (*driven*). A king of Hebron, Josh. x. 3.

Hōlm=tree. Holm-oak, Sus. 58.

Hŏl-ō-fẽr′nĕs. The general slain by Judith, Judith ii. 4, etc.

Hō′lŏn (*sandy*). (1) A town of Judah, Josh. xv. 51. (2) A city of Moab, Jer. xlviii. 21.

Hō′mam, 1 Chr. i. 39. [HEMAM.]

Hō′mẽr. A Hebrew liquid and dry measure, from 47 to 64 gals., according to time, and 6 to 8 bush., Ezek. xlv. 14.

Hŏn′ey. Bees numerous and honey plentiful in Palestine. Much used, Lev. xx. 24; Deut. xxxii. 13; Matt. iii. 4.

Hooks. Various kinds. Fishing, Job xli. 2; leading, 2 Kgs. xix. 28; pruning, Isa. ii. 4; hanging meats, Ezek. xl. 43; curtains, Ex. xxvi. 32–37; lifting boiled food, 1 Sam. ii. 13.

Hŏph′nī (*fighter*). Impious son of Eli, 1 Sam. i. 3; ii. 12–17; iii. 11–14; iv. 11.

Hōr (*hill*). (1) Mount in Edom on which Aaron died, Num. xx. 22–29; xxxiii. 37. (2) A peak of Lebanon range, Num. xxxiv. 7, 8.

Hō′ram (*hill*). King of Gezer, Josh. x. 33.

Hō′reb (*desert*). [SINAI.]

Hō′rem (*offered*). A place in Naphtali, Josh. xix. 38.

Hōr=ha̅-gĭd′gad (*cleft mountain*). A desert station of the Israelites, Num. xxxiii. 32.

Hō′rī (*cave-dweller*). (1) Grandson of Seir, Gen. xxxvi. 22. (2) A Simeonite, Num. xiii. 5.

Hō′rītes, Hōrims. Original people of Mt. Seir, Gen. xiv. 6.

Hŏr′mah (*laid waste*). A Canaanite town in southern Judah, Josh. xv. 30; 1 Sam. xxx. 30.

Hōrn. Made of horn or metal, and of various shapes, sizes, and uses. Used much figuratively, Deut. xxxiii. 17; 1 Sam. xvi. 1; Job xvi. 15; Jer. xlviii. 25.

Hŏr′net (*horner*). Plenty in Palestine, Ex. xxiii. 28; Deut. vii. 20; Josh. xxiv. 12.

Hŏr′′o-nā′im (*two caves*). City of Moab, Isa. xv. 5; Jer. xlviii. 3.

Hŏrse (*neigher*). Used chiefly for war, Ex. xiv. 9–23; 2 Chr. i. 14–17; ix. 25; Esth. vi. 8; for threshing, Isa. xxviii. 28.

Hŏrse′leech (*adherer*). Found in stagnant waters of East, and fastens to nostrils of animals when drinking, Prov. xxx. 15.

Hō′sah (*refuge*). (1) City of Asher, Josh. xix. 29. (2) A Levite, 1 Chr. xxvi. 10.

Hō-ṣăn′na. "Save, we pray," Ps. cxviii. 25, 26. The cry when Christ entered Jerusalem, Matt. xxi. 9–15; Mark xi. 9, 10.

Hō-ṣē′a (*help*). First of minor prophets. Prophetic career, B. C. 784–725, in Israel. Denounces the idolatries of Israel and Samaria. Style obscure.

Hŏsh′′a-ī′ah (*helped by God*). (1) Nehemiah's assistant, Neh. xii. 32. (2) Jezaniah's father, Jer. xlii. 1.

Hŏsh-a′ma (*whom God hears*). Son of Jeconiah, 1 Chr. iii. 18.

Hō-shē′a (*salvation*). (1) Nineteenth and last king of Israel, B. C. 730–721. Conquered and imprisoned by Shalmaneser, 2 Kgs. xv. 30; xvii. 1–6; Hos. xiii. 16. (2) Son of Nun, Deut. xxxii. 44. (3) An Ephraimite, 1 Chr. xxvii. 20. (4) A co-covenanter, Neh. x. 23.

Hŏs′′pĭ-tăl′ĭ-ty (*guest treatment*). Regulated in Lev. xix. 33, 34; xxv. 14–17; Deut. xv. 7–11.

Hō′tham (*seal*). An Asherite, 1 Chr. vii. 32.

Hō′than (*seal*). Father of Shama, 1 Chr. xi. 44.

Hō′thir (*fulness*). Son of Heman, 1 Chr. xxv. 4, 28, and leader of 21st course

Hough (*hok*) (*hock*). Cutting the sinews of the hind. leg, hamstringing, Josh. xi. 6, 9; 2 Sam. viii. 4.

Hour (*time*). First division of Jewish day, morning, noon, evening, Ps. lv. 17. Night had three watches, Ex. xiv. 24; Judg. vii. 19; Lam. ii. 19. Later, day was, morning, heat, midday, evening. Hours introduced from Babylon, after captivity, Matt. xx. 1–10. An indefinite time, Dan. iii. 6; Matt. ix. 22.

House (*cover*). Prevailing Oriental style, low, flat roofed, with court in centre. A tent, palace, citadel, tomb, family, Gen. xii. 17; property, 1 Kgs. xiii. 8; lineage, Luke ii. 4; place of worship, Judg. xx. 18.

Hŭk′kŏk (*cut*). A border of Naphtali, Josh. xix 34.

Hū′kŏk, 1 Chr. vi. 75. [HELKATH.]

Hŭl (*circle*). Grandson of Shem, Gen. x. 23.

Hŭl′dah (*weasel*). A prophetess, 2 Kgs. xxii. 14–20; 2 Chr. xxxiv. 22.

Hŭm′tah (*place of lizards*). A city of Judah, Josh. xv. 54.

Hŭnt′ing. Hebrews not a hunting people, yet various devices mentioned for capturing wild animals, 2 Sam. xxiii. 20; Job xviii. 9, 10; Prov. xxii. 5; Isa. li. 20; Am. iii. 5.

Hū′pham (*coast-man*). Founder of Huphamites, Num. xxvi. 39.

Hŭp′pah (*covered*). Leader of 13th priestly course, 1 Chr. xxiv. 13.

Hŭp′pĭm (*covered*). A Benjamite, 1 Chr. vii. 12.

Hûr (*hole*). (1) The man who helped stay the hands of Moses, Ex. xvii. 10; xxiv. 14. (2) A Judahite, Ex. xxxi. 2. (3) A king of Midian, Num. xxxi. 8. (4) Father of one of Solomon's commissaries, 1 Kgs. iv. 8. (5) Father of a wall-builder, Neh. iii. 9.

Hū′rāi (*weaver*). One of David's guard, 1 Chr. xi. 32.

Hū′ram (*noble*). (1) A Benjamite, 1 Chr. viii. 5. (2) Hiram, 2 Chr. ii. 3–13; iv. 11–16.

Hū′rī (*weaver*). A Gadite, 1 Chr. v. 14.

Hū′shah (*haste*). A Judahite, 1 Chr. iv. 4.

Hū′shāi (*haste*). A friend of David, 2 Sam. xv. 32; 1 Kgs. iv. 16.

Hū′sham (*haste*). A king of Edom, Gen. xxxvi. 34, 35.

Hū′shath-īte. Two of David's guard so called, 2 Sam. xxi. 18; xxiii. 27.

Hū′shim (*haste*). (1) Son of Dan, Gen. xlvi. 23. Shuham, Num. xxvi. 42. (2) A Benjamite, 1 Chr. vii. 12. (3) Wife of Shaharaim, 1 Chr. viii. 8, 11.

Hŭsks (*hulls*). The original means the carob, or locust bean, Luke xv. 16.

Hŭz (*strong*). Son of Nahor, Gen. xxii. 21.

Hŭz′zăb (*fixed*). A possible queen of Nineveh, Nah. ii. 7.

Hȳ-ē′na (*hog*). A bristled, fierce, carnivorous animal. "Zeboim," in 1 Sam. xiii. 18; Neh. xi. 34, means hyenas. So, it is thought, the original of "speckled bird," Jer. xii. 9, should be rendered.

Hȳ-dàs′pēs (*watery*). A river in India, Judith i. 6.

Hȳ′′mĕ-næ′us (*hymeneal*). A convert and pervert, 1 Tim. i. 20; 2 Tim. ii. 17.

Hȳmn (*praise-song*). Spiritual song, Matt. xxvi. 30; Acts xvi. 25; Eph. v. 19; Col. iii. 16.

Hȳs′sop (*aromatic plant*). A bushy herb, of the mint family, Ex. xii. 22; Lev. xiv. 4, 6, 51; 1 Kgs. iv. 33; John xix. 29.

Hȳp′ō-crīte (*stage-player*). Who feigns what he

is not, Job viii. 13; Luke xii. 1.

I

Ĭb′här (*God's choice*). Son of David, 2 Sam. v. 15.

Ĭb′lḗ-ăm (*destroying*). City of Manasseh, Josh. xvii. 11; Judg. i. 27.

Ĭb-nē′ĭah (*God builds*). A Benjamite, 1 Chr. ix. 8.

Ĭb-nī′jah (*God builds*). A Benjamite, 1 Chr. ix. 8.

Ĭb′rī (*Hebrew*). A Levite, 1 Chr. xxiv. 27.

Ĭb′zăn (*famous*). A judge of Israel, Judg. xii. 8–10.

Ĭ′=chạ-bŏd (*inglorious*). Son of Phinehas, 1 Sam. iv. 19-22; xiv. 3.

Ĭ-cō′nĭ-um (*image*). City of Lycaonia, visited twice by Paul, Acts xiii. 51; xiv. 1-22; xvi. 2; 2 Tim. iii. 11.

Ĭ-dā′lah (*memorial*). City of Zebulun, Josh. xix. 15.

Ĭd′băsh (*stout*). A Judahite, 1 Chr. iv. 3.

Ĭd′dō (*timely*). (1) Father of Ahinadab, 1 Kgs. iv. 14. (2) A Levite, 1 Chr. vi. 21. (3) A Manassite chief, 1 Chr. xxvii. 21. (4) A seer and chronicler, 2 Chr. ix. 29; xiii. 22. (5) Grandfather of Zechariah, Zech. i. 1, 7. (6) One of the returned, Ez. viii. 17.

Ĭ′dol, Ĭ-dŏl′ạ-try (*apparent*). An object of worship, other than God, Gen. xxxi. 19; idolatry forbidden, Ex. xx. 3, 4; xxxiv. 13; Deut. iv. 16-19; vii. 25, 26; yet existed largely, especially under the judges and later kings, Ex. xxxii.; Judg. ii. 10-23; 1 Kgs. xi. 33; xii. 27-33; xiv. 22-24; Isa. lvii. 5-8.

Ĭ″dụ-mē′ả (*red*), Isa. xxxiv. 5. Idumæa, Mark iii. 8. Greek name of Edom.

Ĭ′găl (*redeemed*). (1) The spy of Issachar, Num. xiii. 7. (2) One of David's guard, 2 Sam. xxiii. 36.

Ĭg″dạ-lī′ah (*great*). "A man of God," Jer. xxxv. 4.

Ĭg′ẹ-ăl (*redeemed*). A Judahite, 1 Chr. iii. 22.

Ĭ′ĭm (*heaps*). (1) Num. xxxiii. 45, Ije-abarim. (2) Town of southern Judah, Josh. xv. 29.

Ĭj′ẹ=ăb′ạ-rĭm (*ruins of Abarim*). An Israelite encampment near Moab, Num. xxi. 11.

Ĭ′jon (*ruin*). Town of Naphtali, 1 Kgs. xv. 20; 2 Kgs. xv. 29.

Ĭk′kĕsh (*wicked*). Father of Ira, 2 Sam. xxiii. 26; 1 Chr. xi. 28; xxvii. 9.

Ĭ′lāi (*exalted*). One of David's guard, 1 Chr. xi. 29.

Ĭl-lȳr′ĭ-cŭm (*joy*). A country on E. shore of Adriatic, N. of Macedonia. Reached by Paul, Rom. xv. 19.

Ĭm′ạge (*likeness*). As in Gen. i. 26, 27; Col. i. 15. Also Idol.

Ĭm′lả (*full*). Father of Micaiah, 2 Chr. xviii. 7, 8. Imlah, 1 Kgs. xxii. 8, 9.

Ĭm-măn′ū-el (*God with us*). Name of the prophetic child, Isa. vii. 14. The Messiah, Matt. i. 23.

Ĭm′mẽr (*loquacious*). (1) A priestly family in charge of 16th course, 1 Chr. ix. 12; xxiv. 14. (2) Place in Babylonia, Ez. ii. 59; Neh. vii. 61.

Ĭm′nả (*lagging*). An Asherite, 1 Chr. vii. 35.

Ĭm′nah (*lagging*). (1) An Asherite, 1 Chr. vii. 30. (2) A Levite, 2 Chr. xxxi. 14.

Ĭm′rah (*stubborn*). An Asherite, 1 Chr. vii. 36.

Ĭm′rī (*talkative*). (1) A Judahite, 1 Chr. ix. 4. (2) Father of Zaccur, Neh. iii. 2.

Ĭn′çense (*set on fire*). A mixture of gums, spices, etc., Ex. xxx. 34-38, constituted the official incense. Burned morning and evening on the altar of incense, xxx. 1-10. Used also in idolatrous worship, 2 Chr. xxxiv. 25; Jer. xi. 12-17, and by angels, Rev. viii. 3.

Ĭnd′ĭa (*Indus*). The indefinite country which bounded the Persian empire on the east, Esth. i. 1; viii. 9.

Ĭn-hĕr′ĭ-tance (*heirship*). [HEIR.]

Ĭnk, Ĭnk′hôrn (*burnt in*). Ancient ink heavy and thick and carried in an ink-horn, Jer. xxxvi. 18; Ezek. ix. 2.

Ĭnn (*in*). In O. T. a halting place for caravans, Gen. xlii. 27; Ex. iv. 24. In N. T. a caravansary afforded food and shelter for man and beast, Luke x. 34, 35.

Ĭn′stant (*stand in*). Urgent, Luke vii. 4; xxiii. 23: fervent, Acts xxvi. 7; Rom. xii. 12.

Ĭ-ō′nĭạ. India in 1 Macc. viii. 8.

Ĭph″ẹ-dē′ĭah (*free*). A Benjamite, 1 Chr. viii. 25.

Ĭr (*city*). A Benjamite, 1 Chr. vii. 12. Iri, vs. 7.

Ĭ′rả (*watchful*). (1) "Chief ruler about David," 2 Sam. xx. 26. (2) Two of David's warriors, 2 Sam. xxiii. 38; 1 Chr. xi. 28.

Ĭ′răd (*fleet*). Son of Enoch, Gen. iv. 18.

Ĭ′ram (*citizen*). A duke of Edom, Gen. xxxvi. 43: 1 Chr. i. 54.

Ĭ′rī (*watchful*). A Benjamite, 1 Chr. vii. 7.

Ĭ-rī′jah (*seen of God*). A ward-keeper, Jer. xxxvii. 13, 14.

Ĭr-nā′hăsh (*serpent city*). Unknown person or place, 1 Chr. iv. 12.

Ĭ′ron (*pious*). (1) City of Naphtali, Josh. xix. 38. (2) Iron, the metal, and copper early known, Gen. iv. 22. Prepared in furnaces, 1 Kgs. viii. 51; used for tools, Deut. xxvii. 5; weapons, 1 Sam. xvii. 7; implements, 2 Sam. xii. 31; war-chariots, Josh. xvii. 16, etc.

Ĭr′pẹ-el (*healed*). City of Benjamin, Josh. xviii. 27.

Ĭr-shḗ′mĕsh (*sun city*). A Danite cĭty, Josh. xix. 41.

Ĭ′rụ (*watch*). Son of Caleb, 1 Chr. iv. 15.

Ĭ′şaac (*laughter*). Son of Abraham, Gen. xvii. 17-22. Second of the patriarchs, and father of Jacob and Esau, Gen. xxi.–xxxv.

Ĭ-şā′ĭah (*salvation of Jehovah*). Son of Amoz, Isa. i. 1, and first of greater prophets. His book, 23d of O. T., covers sixty years of prophecy, Isa. i. 1, at Jerusalem. It reproves the sins of the Jews and other nations, and foreshadows the coming of Christ. Called "prince of prophets." Poetically for Israel, Am. vii. 9, 16.

Ĭs′cah (*who looks*). Sister of Lot, Gen. xi. 29.

Ĭs-căr′ĭ-ot. [JUDAS ISCARIOT.]

Ĭs′dà-el, 1 Esdr. v. 33. [GIDDEL.]

Ĭsh′bah (*praising*). A Judahite, 1 Chr. iv. 17.

Ĭsh′băk (*leaving*). Son of Abraham, and father of northern Arabians, Gen. xxv. 2; 1 Chr. i. 32.

Ĭsh-bĭ=bē′nŏb (*dweller at Nob*). A Philistine giant, 2 Sam. xxi. 16, 17.

Ĭsh=bō′sheth (*man of shame*). Son and successor of Saul. Original name, Esh-baal. Reigned two years, then defeated by David, and assassinated, 2 Sam. ii. 8-11; iii.; iv. 5-12.

Ĭsh′ī (*saving*). (1) Two Judahites, 1 Chr. ii. 31; iv. 20. (2) A Simeonite, iv. 42. (3) A Manassite, v. 24.

Ĭsh-ī′ah (*loaned*). Chief of Issachar, 1 Chr. vii. 3.

Ĭsh-ī′jah (*loaned*). A lay Israelite, Ez. x. 31.

Ĭsh′mả (*ruin*). A Judahite, 1 Chr. iv. 3.

Ĭsh′ma-el (*whom God hears*). (1) Son of Abraham and Hagar, Gen. xvi. 15, 16. Banished to wilderness; became progenitor of Arabian tribes, Gen. xxi.; xxv. 9; xxxvii. 25-28. (2) Descendant of Saul, 1 Chr. viii. 38. (3) A Judahite, 2 Chr. xix. 11. (4) A Judahite captain, 2 Chr. xxiii. 1. (5) A priest, Ez. x. 22. (6) Crafty son of Nethaniah, 2 Kgs. xxv. 23-25; Jer. xli.

Ĭsh′ma-el-ītes″. Descendants of Ishmael, Judg. viii. 24. Ishmeelites, Gen. xxxvii. 25; 1 Chr. ii. 17.

Ĭsh″ma-ī′ah (*God hears*). Ruler of Zebulun, 1 Chr. xxvii. 19.

Ĭsh′mĕ-rāi (*God keeps*). A Benjamite, 1 Chr. viii. 18.

Ĭ′shod (*famed*). A Manassite, 1 Chr. vii. 18.

Ĭsh′păn (*bald*). A Benjamite, 1 Chr. viii. 22.

Ĭsh′=tŏb (*men of Tob*). Part of Aram, 2 Sam. x. 6-8. [Tob.]

Ĭsh′u-ah (*quiet*). An Asherite, Gen. xlvi. 17; 1 Chr. vii. 30.

Ĭsh′u-āi (*quiet*). Son of Asher, 1 Chr. vii. 30.

Ĭsh′u-ī (*quiet*). Son of Saul, 1 Sam. xiv. 49.

Ĭsle (*island*). Habitable place, Isa. xlii. 15; island, Gen. x. 5; Isa. xi. 11; coast lands, Isa. xx. 6; xxiii. 2, 6; Ezek. xxvii. 7.

Ĭs″mạ-chī′ah (*supported*). Overseer of offerings, 2 Chr. xxxi. 13.

Ĭs′mă-el, 1 Esdr. ix. 22. [Ishmael.]

Ĭs″ma-ī′ah (*God hears*). A chief of Gibeon, 1 Chr. xii. 4.

Ĭs′pah (*bald*). A Benjamite, 1 Chr. viii. 16.

Ĭṣ′rạ-el (*who prevails with God*). Name given to Jacob, Gen. xxxii. 28; xxxv. 10; became national, Ex. iii. 16; narrowed to northern kingdom after the revolt of the ten tribes from Judah, 1 Sam. xi. 8; 2 Sam. xx. 1; 1 Kgs. xii. 16, with Shechem as capital, 1 Kgs. xii. 25, and Tirzah as royal residence, xiv. 17; afterwards, capital at Samaria, xvi. 24. Kingdom lasted 254 years, with 19 kings, b. c. 975-721, when it fell a prey to the Assyrians. The returned of Israel blended with those of Judah.

Ĭṣ′rạ-el-ītes″. "Children of Israel." [Israel.]

Ĭs′sạ-char (*rewarded*). (1) Fifth son of Jacob by Leah, Gen. xxx. 17, 18. Tribe characteristics foretold, Gen. xlix. 14, 15. Place during march at east of Tabernacle, Num. ii. 5. Allotment N. of Manasseh, from Carmel to Jordan, Josh. xix. 17-23. (2) A temple porter, 1 Chr. xxvi. 5.

Ĭs′shĭ-ah (*loaned*). Descendant of Levi, 1 Chr. xxiv. 21. (2) A Levite, 1 Chr. xxiv. 25.

Ĭs″tăl-cū′rus, 1 Esdr. viii. 40. [Zabbud.]

Ĭs′u-ah, 1 Chr. vii. 30. [Jesui.]

Ĭs′ui, Gen. xlvi. 17. [Jesui.]

Ĭt′a-lȳ (*kingdom of Italus*). In N. T. the whole of Italy between the Alps and sea, Acts xviii. 2; xxvii. 1; Heb. xiii. 24.

Ĭth′ạ-ī (*with God*). A Benjamite, 1 Chr. xi. 31.

Ĭth′ạ-mär (*land of palms*). Son of Aaron, Ex. vi. 23; xxviii. 1-43; Num. iii. 2-4. Eli was high priest of his line, 1 Chr. xxiv. 6.

Ĭth′ī-el (*God with me*). (1) Friend of Agur, Prov. xxx. 1. (2) A Benjamite, Neh. xi. 7.

Ĭth′mah (*orphan*). One of David's guard, 1 Chr. xi. 46.

Ĭth′nan (*given*). Town in south Judah, Josh. xv. 23.

Ĭth′rȧ (*plenty*). David's brother-in-law, 2 Sam. xvii. 25.

Ĭth′ran (*plenty*). (1) A Horite, Gen. xxxvi. 26. (2) An Asherite, 1 Chr. vii. 37.

Ĭth′rẹ-ăm (*populous*). Son of David, 2 Sam. iii. 5.

Ĭth′rīte. Two of David's warriors so called, 2 Sam. xxiii. 38; 1 Chr. xi. 40.

Ĭt′tah=kā′zin (*hour of a prince*). A landmark of Zebulun, Josh. xix. 13.

Ĭt′tạ-ī (*timely*). (1) One of David's generals, 2 Sam. xv. 19; xviii. 2-12. (2) One of David's guard, 2 Sam. xxiii. 29.

Ĭ′tụ-ræ′ȧ. From Jetur, Gen. xxv. 15; 1 Chr. i. 31. A small province N. W. of Palestine, now Jedur, Luke iii. 1.

Ĭ′vah, Ā′va. An Assyrian city, possibly Hit, 2 Kgs. xviii. 34; xix. 13.

Ĭ′vŏ-rȳ (*elephant tooth*), Much used by Hebrews, 1 Kgs. x. 22; 2 Chr. ix. 17-21; Ezek. xxvii. 15.

Ĭz′ẹ-här, Num. iii. 19. [Izhar.]

Ĭz′här (*oil*). Uncle of Moses, Ex. vi. 18-21; Num. iii. 19. Founder of Izharites, 1 Chr. xxiv. 22.

Ĭz″ra-hī′ah (*sparkling*). Descendant of Issachar, 1 Chr. vii. 3.

Ĭz′ra-hīte. A captain of David, so called, 1 Chr. xxvii. 8.

Ĭz′rī (*created*). Leader of the 4th musical course 1 Chr. xxv. 11.

J

Jā′a-kăn, Deut. x. 6. [Jakan.]

Jặ-ăk′ŏ-bah (*supplanter*). Prince of Simeon, 1 Chr. iv. 36.

Jặ-ā′lah (*wild goat*). His children returned, Ez. ii. 56. Jaala, Neh. vii. 58.

Jặ-ā′lam (*hidden*). Duke of Edom, Gen. xxxvi. 5, 18.

Jặ-ā′nāi (*answered*). A Gadite, 1 Chr. v. 12.

Jặ-är′ĕ=ŏr′e-gĭm (*weaver's forests*). Father of Elhanan, slayer of Goliath's brother, 2 Sam. xxi. 19.

Jặ′a-sạu (*created*). Son of Bani, Ez. x. 37.

Jặ-ā′sĭ-el (*created*). Son of Abner, 1 Chr. xxvii. 21.

Jặ-ăz″ạ-nī′ah (*heard of God*). (1) A Hebrew captain, 2 Kgs. xxv. 23. (2) A denounced prince, Ezek. xi. 1. (3) Son of Jeremiah, Jer. xxxv. 3. (4) Son of Shaphan, Ezek. viii. 11.

Jặ-ā′zĕr, Jā′zĕr (*helped*). City and province of Gilead, Num. xxi. 32; xxxii. 1; Josh. xxi. 39; 1 Chr. xxvi. 31.

Jặ′ạ-zī′ah (*comforted*). A Levite, 1 Chr. xxiv. 26, 27.

Jặ-ā′zī-el (*comforted*). A temple musician, 1 Chr. xv. 18.

Jặ′băl (*stream*). Son of Lamech, Gen. iv. 20.

Jăb′bok (*flowing*). A tributary of Jordan, on east side; and northern boundary of Ammon, Gen. xxxii. 22; Num. xxi. 24; Deut. ii. 37.

Jā′besh (*dry*). (1) King Shallum's father, 2 Kgs. xv. 10, 13. (2) Jabesh-gilead, a city of Gilead, Judg. xxi. 8-14; 1 Sam. xi. 1-11; xxxi. 11-13.

Jā′bĕz (*sorrow*). Persons or places, 1 Chr. ii. 55; iv. 9, 10.

Jā′bin (*observed*). (1) King of Hazor, Josh. xi. 1-14. (2) Another king of Hazor, defeated by Barak, Judg. iv. 2-24.

Jăb′nĕ-el (*building of God*). (1) Stronghold in Judah, Josh. xv. 11; Jabneh, 2 Chr. xxvi. 6. (2) Place in Naphtali, Josh. xix. 33.

Jăb′neh. [Jabneel.]

Jā′chan (*affliction*). A Gadite, 1 Chr. v. 13.

Jā′chin (*established*). (1) A temple pillar, 1 Kgs. vii. 21; 2 Chr. iii. 17. (2) Fourth son of Simeon, Gen. xlvi. 10. (3) Head of 21st priestly course, 1 Chr. ix. 10; xxiv. 17.

Jā′chin-ītes. Descendants of Jachin, Num. xxvi. 12.

Jā′cinth (*hyacinth*). Zircon, a vari-colored gem, Rev. ix. 17; xxi. 20.

Jā′cŏb (*supplanter*). Son of Isaac and second born twin with Esau, Gen. xxv. 24-34. Bought Esau's birthright, fled to Padan-aram, married Rachel and Leah, wandered to Hebron, name changed to Israel, drifted to Egypt, where he died, aged 147 years, Gen. xxv.-l.

Jā-cū′bus, 1 Esdr. ix. 48. [Akkub, 4.]

Jā′dȧ (*knowing*). A Judahite, 1 Chr. ii. 28, 32.

Jặ-dā′u (*loving*). Son of Nebo, Ez. x. 43.

Jad-dū′ȧ (*known*). (1) A co-covenanter, Neh. x. 21. (2) High priest, and last mentioned in O. T., Neh. xii. 11, 22.

Jā′don (*judge*). Assistant wall builder, Neh.

BIBLE DICT

iii. 7.

Jā′el (*goat*). Heber's wife; murderess of Sisera, Judg. iv. 17–23; v.

Jā′gur (*lodging*). Southern town of Judah, Josh. xv. 21.

Jāh. Jehovah, in poetry, Ps. lxviii. 4.

Jā′hăth (*united*). (1) A Judahite, 1 Chr. iv. 2. (2) Four Levites, 1 Chr. vi. 20; xxiii. 10, 11; xxiv. 22; 2 Chr. xxxiv. 12.

Jā′hăz (*trodden*). Place in Moab where Moses conquered the Ammonites, Num. xxi. 23, 24; Deut. ii. 32.

Jā-hā′zȧ, Josh. xiii. 18. [JAHAZ.]

Jā-hā′zah, Josh. xxi. 36. [JAHAZ.]

Jā″hȧ-zī′ah (*seen of God*). A priest, Ez. x. 15.

Jā-hā′zǐ-el (*seen of God*). (1) A Benjamite, 1 Chr. xii. 4. (2) A trumpeter, 1 Chr. xvi. 6. (3) A Levite, 1 Chr. xxiii. 19; xxiv. 23. (4) A Levite, 2 Chr. xx. 14. (5) His sons returned, Ez. viii. 5.

Jäh′da-ī (*directed*). A Judahite, 1 Chr. ii. 47.

Jäh′dǐ-el (*joyful*). A Manassite, 1 Chr. v. 24.

Jäh′dō (*united*). A Gadite, 1 Chr. v. 14.

Jäh′lĕ-el (*hoping*). Founder of Jahleelites, Gen. xlvi. 14; Num. xxvi. 26.

Jäh′ma-ī (*guarded*). Son of Tola, 1 Chr. vii. 2.

Jäh′zah, 1 Chr. vi. 78. [JAHAZ.]

Jäh′zĕ-el (*allotted*). Founder of the Jahzeelites, Gen. xlvi. 24; Num. xxvi. 48.

Jäh′zĕ-rah (*led back*). A priest, 1 Chr. ix. 12.

Jäh′zǐ-el, 1 Chr. vii. 13. [JAHZEEL.]

Jā′ir (*enlightened*). (1) Conqueror of Argob and part of Gilead, Num. xxxii. 41; Deut. iii. 14. (2) A judge of Israel, Judg. x. 3–5. (3) A Benjamite, Esth. ii. 5. (4) Father of Elhanan, 1 Chr. xx. 5.

Jā′ir-īte. Ira so called, 2 Sam. xx. 26.

Jā-ī′rus (*enlightened*). Ruler of a synagogue, Luke viii. 41.

Jā′kan (*thoughtful*). A Horite, 1 Chr. i. 42. [JAAKAN, AKAN.]

Jā′keh (*pious*). Father of Agur, Prov. xxx. 1.

Jā′kim (*confirmed*). (1) Head of 12th course, 1 Chr. xxiv. 12. (2) A Benjamite, 1 Chr. viii. 19.

Jā′lon (*tarrying*). A Judahite, 1 Chr. iv. 17.

Jăm′brĕṣ. An Egyptian magician, Ex. vii. 9–13, 2 Tim. iii. 8, 9.

Jăm′brī. Supposably Ammonites, 1 Macc. ix. 36–41.

Jāmes (*Jacob*). (1) "The Greater" or "Elder," son of Zebedee and brother of John, Matt. iv. 21, 22. A fisherman of Galilee, called to the Apostolate about A. D. 28, and styled Boanerges, Matt. x. 2, 3; Mark iii. 14–18; Luke vi. 12–16; Acts i. 13. Labored at Jerusalem. Beheaded by Herod, A. D. 44. (2) "The Less," another Apostle, son of Alphæus, Matt. x. 3; Mark iii. 18; Luke vi. 15. (3) Christ's brother, or more likely cousin, and identical with James the Less, Gal. i. 19. Compare Matt. xiii. 55; Mark vi. 3; Acts xii. 17. Resident at Jerusalem and author of The Epistle of James, written before A. D. 62 to the scattered Jews, urging good works as the ground-work and evidence of faith.

Jā′min (*right hand*). (1) Founder of Jaminites, Gen. xlvi. 10; Ex. vi. 15; Num. xxvi. 12. A Judahite, 1 Chr. ii. 27. (3) Ezra's assistant, Neh. viii. 7.

Jăm′lech (*reigning*). A Simeonite chief, 1 Chr. iv. 34.

Jăm′nǐ-ȧ, 1 Macc. iv. 15. [JABNEEL.]

Jăn′nȧ (*God-given*). Ancestor of Christ, Luke iii. 24.

Jăn′nĕṣ. An Egyptian magician, 2 Tim. iii. 8, 9; Ex. vii. 9–13.

Jā-nō′ah (*rest*). Town of Naphtali, 2 Kgs. xv. 29.

Jā-nō′hah (*rest*). Border town of Ephraim, Josh. xvi. 6, 7.

Jā′num (*sleeping*). Town of Judah, Josh. xv. 53.

Jā′pheth (*enlarged*). Son of Noah, Gen. v. 32; vi. 10; ix. 27; x. 21. His generations peopled the "isles of the Gentiles," and type the Indo-European and Caucasian races, Gen. x. 1–5.

Jā-phī′ȧ (*splendor*). (1) A border of Zebulun, Josh. xix. 12. (2) King of Lachish, Josh. x. 3. (3) A son of David, 2 Sam. v. 15; 1 Chr. iii. 7.

Jăph′let (*delivered*). An Asherite, 1 Chr. vii. 32, 33.

Jăph-lē′tī. Landmark of Ephraim, Josh. xvi. 3.

Jā′phō, Josh. xix. 46. [JOPPA.]

Jā′rah (*honey*). Son of Micah, 1 Chr. ix. 42.

Jā′reb (*enemy*). Unknown person or place, Hos. v. 13; x. 6.

Jā′red (*descent*). Father of Enoch, Gen. v. 15–20; Luke iii. 37.

Jăr-ĕ-sī′ah (*nourished*). A Benjamite, 1 Chr. viii. 27.

Jär′hȧ. An Egyptian servant, 1 Chr. ii. 34, 35.

Jā′rib (*enemy*). (1) A Simeonite, 1 Chr. iv. 24. (2) One who returned, Ez. viii. 16. (3) A priest, Ez. x. 18.

Jär′ǐ-moth, 1 Esdr. ix. 28. [JEREMOTH.]

Jär′mŭth (*high*). (1) Town of lower Judah, Josh. x. 3; xv. 35. (2) A Levitical city of Issachar, Josh. xxi. 29.

Jā-rō′ah (*moon*). A Gadite, 1 Chr. v. 14.

Jā′shen (*sleeping*). His sons were in David's guard, 2 Sam. xxiii. 32.

Jā′sher (*upright*). Book of, wholly lost, Josh. x. 13; 2 Sam. i. 18.

Jā-shō′bĕ-ăm (*turned to*). A chief of David's captains, 1 Chr. xi. 11; xii. 6; xxvii. 2. Adino, 2 Sam. xxiii. 8.

Jăsh′ŭb (*he turns*). (1) Founder of Jashubites, Num. xxvi. 24; 1 Chr. vii. 1; Job, Gen. xlvi. 13. (2) Son of Bani, Ez. x. 29.

Jăsh′u-bī=lē′hĕm (*turning back for food*). Person or place of Judah, 1 Chr. iv. 22.

Jā′sǐ-el (*created*). One of David's heroes, 1 Chr. xi. 47.

Jā′son (*healer*). (1) Son of Eleazar, 1 Macc. viii. 17. (2) Father of Antipater, xii. 16. (3) An historian, 2 Macc. ii. 23. (4) High priest, 2 Macc. iv. 7–26. (5) A friend of Paul, Acts xvii. 5–9.

Jăs′pĕr. A colored quartz. Last stone in high priest's breastplate, and first in New Jerusalem foundation, Ex. xxviii. 20; Rev. xxi. 19.

Jăth′nǐ-el (*God-given*). A Levite, 1 Chr. xxvi. 2.

Jăt′tir (*prominent*). Town of south Judah, Josh. xv. 48; xxi. 14; 1 Sam. xxx. 27.

Jā′văn (*clay*). (1) Fourth son of Japheth, and type of Ionians and Grecians, Gen. x. 2–5; 1 Chr. i. 5–7. (2) An Arabian trading post, Ezek. xxvii. 13, 19.

Jăve′lǐn. A short, light spear. [ARMS.]

Jā′zär, 1 Macc. v. 8. [JAAZER.]

Jā′zĕr, Num. xxxii. 1–3; Josh. xxi. 39. [JAAZER.]

Jā′zǐz (*moved*). Herdsman of David, 1 Chr. xxvii. 31.

Jē′a-rīm (*woods*). Border mountain of Judah, Josh. xv. 10.

Jē-ăt′e-rāi (*led*). A Levite, 1 Chr. vi. 21.

Jĕ″bĕr-e-chī′ah (*blessed*). Father of Zechariah, Isa. viii. 2.

Jē″bus (*threshing floor*). Original name of Jerusalem; the "threshing floor" of the Jebushi or Jebusites, Josh. xv. 8; xviii. 16, 28; Judg. xix. 10, 11; 1 Chr. xi. 4, 5.

Jĕb′u-sīte, Jĕ-bū′si. Original people of Jebus, Deut. vii. 1; Josh. xi. 3; 2 Sam. v. 6–10; xxiv, 16–25.

Jĕc″ȧ-mī′ah (*gathered*). One of David's line, 1

Chr. iii. 18.

Jĕch″o̤-lī′ah (*enabled*). Mother of King Azariah, 2 Kgs. xv. 2. Jecoliah, 2 Chr. xxvi. 3.

Jĕch″o̤-nī′as, Matt. i. 11, 12; Esth. xi. 4. Greek form of Jeconiah and Jehoiachin.

Jĕc′o̤-lī′ah, 2 Chr. xxvi. 3. [JECHOLIAH.]

Jĕc′o̤-nī′ah, 1 Chr. iii. 16; Jer. xxiv. 1. [JEHOIACHIN.]

Jĕ-dā′iah (*praise God*). (1) Head of 2d temple course, 1 Chr. xxiv. 7. (2) A priest, Zech. vi. 10-14. (3) A Simeonite, 1 Chr. iv. 37. (4) A wall-repairer, Neh. iii. 10.

Jĕ-dī′a-el (*known of God*). (1) A Benjamite, 1 Chr. vii. 6-11. (2) One of David's guard, 1 Chr. xi. 45. (3) A Manassite chief, 1 Chr. xii. 20. (4) A Levite, 1 Chr. xxvi. 1, 2.

Jĕ-dī′dah (*beloved*). Mother of King Josiah, 2 Kgs. xxii. 1.

Jĕd″ĭ-dī′ah (*beloved of God*). Name given to Solomon by Nathan, 2 Sam. xii. 25.

Jĕd′u-thŭn (*praising*). A leader of the temple choir, 1 Chr. xxv. 6; Ps. xxxix., lxii., lxxvii., title.

Jĕ-ē′zẽr (*father of help*). A Manassite, Num. xxvi. 30. Abiezer, elsewhere.

Jĕ-ē′zẽr-ītes. Descendants of above.

Je′gar=sā-hȧ-dū′thȧ (*testimonial heap*). Heap of compact between Jacob and Laban, Gen. xxxi. 47.

Jĕ″hȧ-lē′le̤-el (*who praises*). A Judahite, 1 Chr. iv. 16.

Jĕ-hăl′e̤-lĕl (*who praises*). A Levite, 2 Chr. xxix. 12.

Jĕh-dē′iah (*made joyful*). (1) A Levite, 1 Chr. xxiv. 20. (2) David's herdsman, 1 Chr. xxvii. 30.

Jĕ-hĕz′e̤-kĕl (*made strong*). Head of the 20th priestly course, 1 Chr. xxiv. 16.

Jĕ-hī′ah (*God lives*). A doorkeeper of the ark, 1 Chr. xv. 24.

Jĕ-hī′el (*God lives*). (1) A Levite, 1 Chr. xv. 18, 20. (2) A treasurer, 1 Chr. xxiii. 8. (3) Son of Jehoshaphat, 2 Chr. xxi. 2. (4) An officer of David, 1 Chr. xxvii. 32. (5) A Levite, 2 Chr. xxix. 14. (6) Ruler of God's house, 2 Chr. xxxv. 8. (7) An overseer, 2 Chr. xxxi. 13. (8) Returned captives, Ez. viii. 9; x. 2, 21, 26.

Jĕ-hī′el (*treasured*). (1) Father of Gibeon, 1 Chr. ix. 35. (2) One of David's guard, 1 Chr. xi. 44.

Jĕ-hī′e-lī. A Levite family, 1 Chr. xxvi. 21, 22.

Jĕ″hĭz-kī′ah (*strengthened*). An Ephraimite, 2 Chr. xxviii. 12.

Jĕ-hō′a-dah (*adorned*). A descendant of Saul, 1 Chr. viii. 36.

Jĕ″hŏ-ăd′dan (*adorned*). Mother of King Amaziah, 2 Kgs. xiv. 2; 2 Chr. xxv. 1

Jĕ-hō′a-hăz (*possession*). (1) Son and successor of Jehu on throne of Israel, B. c. 856-840, 2 Kgs. xiii. 1-9. Reign disastrous. (2) Son and successor of Josiah on throne of Judah. Reigned 3 months, B. c. 610. Called Shallum. Deposed and died in Egypt, Jer. xxii. 11, 12. (3) Ahaziah, Azariah, 2 Chr. xxi. 17; xxii. 1, 6.

Jĕ-hō′ash. [JOASH.]

Jĕ″hŏ-hā′nan (*God-given*). (1) A temple porter, 1 Chr. xxvi. 3. (2) A general of Judah, 2 Chr. xvii. 15; xxiii. 1. (3) Returned Levites, Ez. x. 28; Neh. xii. 13, 42.

Jĕ-hoi′a-chin (*God-appointed*). Jeconiah, 1 Chr. iii. 17; Coniah, Jer. xxii. 24; Jechonias, Matt. i. 12. Son and successor of Jehoiakim on throne of Judah. Reigned 100 days, B. c. 597; carried prisoner to Babylon; released after 36 years' captivity, 2 Kgs. xxiv. 6-16; Jer. xxix. 2; Ezek. xvii. 12.

Jĕ-hoi′a-dȧ (*known of God*). (1) Father of Benaiah, 2 Sam. viii. 18; 1 Kgs. i., ii. (2) An Aaronite leader, 1 Chr. xii. 27. (3) No doubt same as (1), 1 Chr.

xxvii. 34. (4) High priest and religious reformer under Athaliah and Joash, 2 Kgs. xi. 4-21; xii. 1-16. (5) Second priest, or sagan, Jer. xxix. 25-29. (6) A wall-repairer, Neh. iii. 6.

Jĕ-hoi′a-kim (*God-established*). Eliakim, son of Josiah; name changed to Jehoiakim; successor to Jehoahaz, and 19th king of Judah, B. c. 609-598. Nearly entire reign one of vassalage to Egypt or Babylon, 2 Kgs. xxiii. 34-37; xxiv. 1-6; Jer. xxii. 18, 19; xxxvi. 30-32.

Jĕ-hoi′a-rĭb (*God-defended*). Head of 1st temple course, 1 Chr. xxiv. 7.

Jĕ-hŏn′a̤-dăb, Jŏn′a-dăb (*God-impelled*). Son of Rechab, and adherent of Jehu, 2 Kgs. x. 15-23; Jer. xxxv. 6.

Jĕ-hŏn′a̤-than (*God-given*). (1) David's storehouse keeper, 1 Chr. xxvii. 25. (2) A Levite teacher, 2 Chr. xvii. 8. (3) A priest, Neh. xii. 18.

Jĕ-hō′ram, Jō′ram (*God-exalted*). (1) Son of Ahab and successor to Ahaziah on throne of Israel, B. c. 896-884. Victoriously allied with Judah, but defeated and slain in Jehu's revolt. Last of Ahab's line, 1 Kgs. xxi. 21-29; xxii. 50; 2 Kgs. i. 17, 18; ii.-ix. (2) Son and successor of Jehoshaphat on throne of Judah, B. c. 893-885. Murderer and Baal worshipper. Reign calamitous. Died a terrible death, 2 Chr. xxi.

Jĕ″hŏ-shăb′e-ăth, 2 Chr. xxii. 11. [JEHOSHEBA.]

Jĕ-hŏsh′a̤-phăt (*judged of God*). (1) Recorder under David and Solomon, 2 Sam. viii. 16; 1 Kgs. iv. 3. (2) A trumpeter, 1 Chr. xv. 24. (3) Solomon's purveyor, 1 Kgs. iv. 17. (4) Father of Jehu, 2 Kgs. ix. 2-14. (5) Valley of Cedron, or else a visionary spot, Joel iii. 2-12. (6) Son and successor of Asa on throne of Judah, B. c. 914-890. A God-fearing king, in close alliance with Israel, 1 Kgs. xv. 24; 2 Kgs. viii. 16; 2 Chr. xvii.-xxi. 1.

Jĕ-hŏsh′e-bȧ (*oath of God*). Daughter of king Joram and wife of Jehoiada, the high priest, 2 Kgs. xi. 2; 2 Chr. xxii. 11.

Jĕ-hŏsh′u-ȧ. Full form of Joshua, Num. xiii. 16; Jehoshuah, 1 Chr. vii. 27.

Jĕ-hō′vah. "He that is." "I am," Ex. iii. 14. The self-existent and eternal one. Hebrew word for God, generally rendered "Lord." Not pronounced; but Adonai, "Lord," or Elohim, "God," substituted, Ex. vi. 3. [GOD.]

Jĕ-hō′vah=jī′reh (*God will provide*). Abraham's name for spot where Isaac was offered, Gen. xxii. 14.

Jĕ-hō′vah=nĭs′sī (*God my banner*). The altar built in honor of Joshua's victory, Ex. xvii. 15.

Jĕ-hō′vah=shā′lom (*God is peace*). Gideon's altar in Ophrah, Judg. vi. 24.

Jĕ-hŏz′a-băd (*God-given*). (1) A storekeeper and porter, 1 Chr. xxvi. 4. (2) Co-murderer of King Joash, 2 Kgs. xii. 21. (3) A Benjamite captain, 2 Chr. xvii. 18.

Jĕ-hŏz′a-dăk (*God justifies*). Captive father of Jeshua, the high priest, 1 Chr. vi. 14, 15; Ez. iii. 2.

Jĕ′hū (*who exists*). (1) Prophet of Judah, 1 Kgs. xvi. 1-7. (2) Tenth king of Israel, B. c. 884-856. He extirpated Ahab's line according to the prophecies, 1 Kgs. xix. 16, 17; 2 Kgs. ix., x. (3) A Judahite, 1 Chr. ii. 38. (4) A Simeonite, 1 Chr. iv. 35. (5) A Benjamite, 1 Chr. xii. 3.

Jĕ-hŭb′bah (*hidden*). An Asherite, 1 Chr. vii. 34.

Jĕ′hū-cal (*mighty*). Messenger to Jeremiah, Jer. xxxvii. 3.

Jĕ′hŭd (*famed*). Town of Dan, Josh. xix. 45.

Jĕ-hū′dī (*Jew*). A messenger, Jer. xxxvi. 14-23.

Jĕ″hū-dī′jah (*Jewess*). Mother of Jered, 1 Chr. iv. 18.

Jĕ′hŭsh (*collector*). Son of Eshek, 1 Chr. viii. 39.

Jĕ-ī′el (*God's treasure*). (1) Reubenite chief, 1

Chr. v. 7. (2) Levites, 1 Chr. xv. 18 ; 2 Chr. xx. 14 ; xxvi. 11 ; xxix. 13 ; xxxv. 9 ; Ez. viii. 13 ; x. 43.

Jĕ-kăb′ze-el (*gathered*). Kabzeel, in south Judah, Neh. xi. 25 ; Josh. xv. 21 ; 2 Sam. xxiii. 20.

Jĕk″a-mē′am (*who gathers*). A Levite, 1 Chr. xxiii. 19 ; xxiv. 23.

Jĕk″a-mī′ah (*gathered*). A Judahite, 1 Chr. ii. 41.

Jĕ-kū′thĭ-el (*piety*). A Judahite, 1 Chr. iv. 18

Jĕ-mī′ma (*dove*). Job's daughter, Job xlii. 14.

Jĕm′nă-an, Judith ii. 28. [JABNEEL.]

Jĕ-mū′el (*God's day*). A Simeonite, Gen. xlvi. 10 ; Ex. vi. 15.

Jĕph′thă-ĕ, Heb. xi. 32. Greek form of Jephthah.

Jĕph′thah (*set free*). A judge of Israel, B. C. 1143–1137, Judg. xi., xii.

Jĕ-phŭn′neh (*favorably regarded*). (1) Father of Caleb the spy, Num. xiii. 6. (2) An Asherite, 1 Chr. vii. 38.

Jē′räh (*moon*). Son of Joktan, Gen. x. 26 ; 1 Chr. i. 20.

Jĕ-räh′me-el (*God's mercy*). (1) Son of Hezron, 1 Chr. ii. 9, 42. (2) A Levite, 1 Chr. xxiv. 29. (3) An official of Jehoiakim, Jer. xxxvi. 26.

Jĕ-räh′me-el-ītes″. Descendants of above (1), 1 Sam. xxvii. 10.

Jĕr′ĕ-cus, 1 Esdr. v. 22. [JERICHO.]

Jē′rĕd (*descent*). (1) Father of Enoch, 1 Chr. i. 2. (2) A Judahite, 1 Chr. iv. 18.

Jĕr′e-māi (*mountaineer*). A layman, Ez. x. 33.

Jĕr″e-mī′ah (*exalted*). (1) Second of greater prophets. His prophecies cover reigns of Josiah, Jehoiakim, and Zedekiah, B. C. 628–586, and constitute the 24th O. T. book. Life one of vicissitude. Prophecies noted for boldness and beauty, and chiefly denunciative of Judah and her policy. Withdrew to Egypt, where he probably died. (2) Seven others in O. T., 2 Kgs. xxiii. 31 ; 1 Chr. xii. 4–13 ; v. 24 ; Neh. x. 2 ; xii. 1, 12, 34 ; Jer. xxxv. 3.

Jĕr″e-mī′as, **Jĕr′e-mў.** Greek form of Jeremiah, Matt. ii. 17 ; xvi. 14 ; xxvii. 9.

Jĕr′e-mŏth (*heights*). Persons in 1 Chr. viii. 14 ; xxiii. 23 ; xxv. 22 ; Ez. x. 26, 27.

Jĕ-rī′ah (*founded*). A chief of the house of Hebron, 1 Chr. xxiii. 19 ; xxiv. 23.

Jĕr′ĭ-bāi (*defended*). One of David's guard, 1 Chr. xi. 46.

Jĕr′ĭ-chō (*fragrance*). Ancient city of Canaan, 5 miles W. of Jordan and 18 from Jerusalem. Strongly fortified, and conquered by Joshua. Fell to Benjamin, Deut. xxxiv. 3 ; Num. xxii. 1 ; Josh. vi.; xvi. 7 ; xviii. 21 ; 1 Kgs. xvi. 34 ; Matt. xx. 29 ; Mark x. 46.

Jē′rĭ-el (*founded*). An Issacharite, 1 Chr. vii. 2.

Jĕ-rī′jah, 1 Chr. xxvi. 31. [JERIAH.]

Jĕr′ĭ-mŏth (*heights*). Persons in 1 Chr. vii. 8; xii. 5 ; xxiv. 30 ; xxv. 4, 22 ; xxvii. 19 ; 2 Chr. xi. 18 ; xxxi. 13.

Jē′rĭ-ŏth (*curtains*). Caleb's wife, 1 Chr. ii. 18.

Jĕr″o-bō′am (*many-peopled*). (1) First king of Israel after the division, B. C. 975–954. Plotter for Solomon's throne, 1 Kgs. xi. 26–40 ; fled to Egypt ; returned on death of Solomon ; set up kingdom of ten tribes ; established idolatry ; warred with Judah ; defeated by Abijah ; soon after died, 1 Kgs. xii.–xiv. ; 2 Chr. x.–xiii. (2) Jeroboam II., 13th king of Israel. Successor to Joash. Reigned B. C. 825–784. Idolatrous, but mighty and illustrious. Raised Israel to greatest splendor, 2 Kgs. xiv. 23–29 ; xv. 8, 9 ; Am. ⸺ ; ii. 6–16.

Jĕr′o-hăm (*cherished*). (1) Father of Elkanah, 1 Sam. i. 1 ; 1 Chr. vi. 27. (2) A Benjamite, 1 Chr. viii. 27 ; ix. 8. (3) Father of Adaiah, 1 Chr. ix. 12. (4) Others in 1 Chr. xii. 7 ; xxvii. 22 ; 2 Chr. xxiii. 1.

Jĕ-rŭb′ba-ăl (*contender with Baal*). Surname of Gideon, Judg. vi. 32.

Jĕ-rŭb′be-shĕth (*strife with the idol*). Another surname of Gideon, 2 Sam. xi. 21.

Jĕr′u-el (*founded*). Unknown battlefield, 2 Chr. xx. 16.

Jĕ-rụ′sa-lĕm (*place of peace*). Capital of Hebrew monarchy and of kingdom of Judah, 24 miles west of Jordan and 37 east of the Mediterranean. "Salem," Ps. lxxvi. 2, and perhaps, Gen. xiv. 18. "Jebus," Judg. xix. 10, 11. "Jebus-salem," Jerusalem, Josh. x. 1. "City of David," Zion, 1 Kgs. viii. 1 ; 2 Kgs. xiv. 20. "City of Judah," 2 Chr. xxv. 28. "City of God," Ps. xlvi. 4. "City of the great King," Ps. xlviii. 2. "The holy city," Neh. xi. 1. Captured and rebuilt by David, and made his capital, 2 Sam. v. 6–13 ; 1 Chr. xi. 4–9. Destroyed by Nebuchadnezzar, B. C. 588. Rebuilt by returned captives. Captured by Alexander the Great, B. C. 332 ; by Antiochus, B. C. 203 ; by Rome, B. C. 63.

Jĕ-rụ′sa-lĕm, New. Metaphorically, the spiritual church, Rev. iii. 12 ; xxi. ; compare Gal. iv. 26 ; Heb. xii. 22.

Jĕ-rụ′sha (*possessed*). Daughter of Zadok, 2 Kgs. xv. 33. Jerushah, 2 Chr. xxvii. 1.

Jĕ-sā′iah (*saved*). (1) Grandson of Zerubbabel, 1 Chr. iii. 21. (2) A Benjamite, Neh. xi. 7.

Jĕ-shā′iah (*God's help*). (1) Head of 8th singing course, 1 Chr. xxv. 3, 15. (2) A Levite, 1 Chr. xxvi. 25. Isshiah, xxiv. 21. (3) Two who returned, Ez. viii. 7, 19.

Jĕsh′a-nah (*old*). Unidentified town, 2 Chr. xiii. 19.

Jĕ-shär′e-lah (*right*). Head of 7th singing course, 1 Chr. xxv. 14. Asarelah, vs. 2.

Jĕ-shĕb′e-ăb (*father's seat*). Head of 14th priestly course, 1 Chr. xxiv. 13.

Jĕ′sher (*right*). Son of Caleb, 1 Chr. ii. 18.

Jĕsh′ĭ-mŏn (*waste*). Perhaps desert or plain, Num. xxi. 20 ; xxiii. 28.

Jĕ-shĭsh′a-ī (*ancient*). A Gadite, 1 Chr. v. 14.

Jĕsh″o-ha-ī′ah (*bowed*). A Simeonite, 1 Chr. iv. 36.

Jĕsh′u-å (*saviour*). (1) Joshua, Neh. viii. 17. (2) Priest of 9th course, Ez. ii. 36 ; Neh. vii. 39. Jeshuah, 1 Chr. xxiv. 11. (3) A Levite, 2 Chr. xxxi. 15. (4) High priest and returned captive, called also Joshua and Jesus, Zech. iii. ; vi. 9–15. (5) Other Levites and returned captives, Ez. ii. 6, 40 ; viii. 33 ; Neh. iii. 19 ; viii. 7. (6) A town peopled by returned captives, Neh. xi. 26.

Jĕsh′u-rŭn (*blessed*). Symbolically, Israel, Deut. xxxii. 15 ; xxxiii. 5, 26. Jesurun, Isa. xliv. 2.

Jĕ-sī′ah (*loaned*). (1) One of David's warriors, 1 Chr. xii. 6. (2) Jeshaiah, 1 Chr. xxiii. 20.

Jĕ-sĭm′i-el (*set up*). A Simeonite, 1 Chr. iv. 36.

Jĕs′se (*strong*). Father of David, 1 Sam. xvi. 1–18.

Jĕs′su-e, 1 Esdr. v. 26. [JESHUA.] Jesu, viii. 63.

Jes′u-ī (*level*). Founder of Jesuites, Num. xxvi. 44. Isui, Gen. xlvi. 17. Ishuai, 1 Chr. vii. 30.

Jē′ṣus (*saviour*). (1) Greek form of Joshua, Jeshua, contraction of Jehoshua, Num. xiii. 16 ; Acts vii. 45. (2) Compiler of the Apocryphal book, Ecclesiasticus. (3) Justus, Paul's friend, Col. iv. 11.

Jē′ṣus Chrīst. Jesus the Saviour ; Christ, or Messiah, the anointed. Jesus the Christ. Name given to the long promised prophet and king, Matt. xi. 3 ; Acts xix. 4. Only begotten of God. Born of Mary at Bethlehem, B. C. 5 ; reared at Nazareth, baptized at age of 30, Luke iii. 23. Ministerial career, extending over Galilee, Judea, and Perea, began A. D. 27 and ended with the crucifixion, April 7, A. D. 30. Matthew, Mark, and Luke record his Galilean ministry ; John his Judean ministry. The four gospels embrace Christ's biography.

Jē′thĕr (*who excels*). (1) Son of Gideon, Judg. viii. 20. (2) Father of Amasa, 1 Chr. ii. 17. (3) Others in 1 Chr. ii. 32; iv. 17; vii. 38.

Jĕ′thĕth (*nail*). A duke of Edom, Gen. xxxvi. 40.

Jĕth′lah (*high*). City of Dan, Josh. xix. 42.

Je′thrŏ (*his excellence*). Honorary title, Ex. iii. 1, of Reuel, Ex. ii. 18, or Raguel, Num. x. 29, the father-in-law of Moses, Ex. xviii.

Jē′tŭr, Gen. xxv. 15; 1 Chr. i. 31. [ITURÆA.]

Jĕ-ū′el (*treasured*). A Judahite, 1 Chr. ix. 6.

Jē′ŭsh (*assembler*). (1) Son of Esau, Gen. xxxvi. 5, 14, 18. (2) A Benjamite, 1 Chr. vii. 10. (3) A Levite, 1 Chr. xxiii. 10, 11. (4) Son of Rehoboam, 2 Chr. xi. 18, 19.

Jē′ŭz (*assembler*). A Benjamite, 1 Chr. viii. 10.

Jew. Contraction of Judah. Man of Judea, 2 Kgs. xvi. 6; xxv. 25. After captivity, Hebrews in general, Ez. iv. 12; Dan. iii. 8–12. Antithesis of Christian in N. T., John; Rom. i. 16.

Jew′ĕl (*joy*). Ornament, Gen. xxiv. 22; Num. xxxi. 50.

Jew′ĕss. Hebrew woman, Acts xvi. 1.

Jew′rў. Judah, Judea, Jewish dynasty, Dan. v. 13.

Jĕz″a-nī′ah (*heard*). A Jewish captive, Jer. xl. 7–12. Jaazaniah, 2 Kgs. xxv. 23.

Jĕz′e-bĕl (*chaste*). Idolatrous wife of Ahab, 1 Kgs. xvi. 29–33; xvii.–xxi.; 2 Kgs. ix. 30–37.

Jĕ-zē′lus, 1 Esdr. viii. 32–35. [JAHAZIEL.]

Jē′zĕr (*help*). A Naphtalite, Gen. xlvi. 24; founder of Jezerites, Num. xxvi. 49.

Jĕ-zī′ah (*sprinkled*). One with a foreign wife, Ez. x. 25.

Jē′zĭ-el (*sprinkled*). A Benjamite, 1 Chr. xii. 3.

Jĕz-lī′ah (*preserved*). A Benjamite, 1 Chr. viii. 18.

Jĕz′o-ar (*white*). A Judahite, 1 Chr. iv. 7.

Jĕz″ra-hī′ah (*brought forth*). A Levite singer, Neh. xii. 42.

Jĕz′re-el (*seed of God*). (1) A Judahite, 1 Chr. iv. 3. (2) A city in plain of Jezreel. Ahab's royal residence, Josh. xix. 18; 1 Kgs. xxi. 1; 2 Kgs. ix. 30. (3) Valley of, stretches from Jezreel to Jordan. Greek form, Esdraelon. (4) Town of Judah, Josh. xv. 56; 1 Sam. xxvii. 3. (5) Son of Hosea, Hos. i. 4.

Jĭb′sam (*pleasant*). An Issacharite, 1 Chr. vii. 2.

Jĭd′laph (*weeping*). Son of Nahor, Gen. xxii. 22.

Jĭm′na̤ (*prosperity*). Son of Asher and founder of Jimnites, Num. xxvi. 44. Jimnah, Gen. xlvi. 17. Imnah, 1 Chr. vii. 30.

Jĭph′tah. Lowland city of Judah, Josh. xv. 43.

Jĭph′thah=el (*God opens*). Valley between Zebulun and Asher, Josh. xix. 14, 27.

Jō′ăb (*God his father*). (1) General-in-chief of David's army, 2 Sam. ii. 18–32; iii., xviii., xx., xxiv.; 1 Kgs. ii. (2) Son of Seraiah, 1 Chr. iv. 14. (3) One who returned, Ez. ii. 6.

Jō′a-chaz, 1 Esdr. i. 34. [JEHOAHAZ.]

Jō′a-chĭm, Bar. i. 3. [JEHOIAKIM.]

Jō″a-dā′nus. Son of Jeshua, 1 Esdr. ix. 19.

Jō′ah (*God's brother*). (1) Hezekiah's recorder, 2 Kgs. xviii. 18. (2) Josiah's recorder, 2 Chr. xxxiv. 8. (3) Levites, 1 Chr. vi. 21; xxvi. 4; 2 Chr. xxix. 12.

Jō′a-hăz (*held of God*). Father of Joah, 2 Chr. xxxiv. 8.

Jō-ăn′na̤ (*God-given*). (1) An ancestor of Christ, Luke iii. 27. (2) Wife of Chusa, Luke viii. 3; xxiv. 10.

Jō′ash (*God-given*), 2 Kgs. xiii. 1. Jehoash, 2 Kgs. xii. 1. (1) Son of Ahaziah and his successor on throne of Judah, B. C. 878–839. Cruel and idolatrous. Murdered by his servants, 2 Kgs. xi., xii.; 2 Chr. xxiv. (2) Son and successor of Jehoahaz on

throne of Israel, B. C. 840–825. Successful warrior, 2 Kgs. xiii. 9–25; xiv. 1–16; 2 Chr. xxv. 17–25. (3) Father of Gideon, Judg. vi. 11–31. (4) Son of Ahab, 2 Chr. xviii. 25. (5) A Judahite, 1 Chr. iv. 22. (6) One of David's heroes, 1 Chr. xii. 3. (7) Son of Becher, 1 Chr. vii. 8. (8) Officer of David, 1 Chr. xxvii. 28.

Jō′a-thăm, Matt. i. 9. [JOTHAM.]

Jōb (*persecuted*). (1) The pious and wealthy patriarch of Uz, whose poem constitutes the 18th O. T. book, and first of the poetical. It is a dramatic narrative of his life of vicissitude, the gist being, whether goodness can exist irrespective of reward. Poetry noted for its sublimity, pathos, and beauty. Authorship disputed. Oldest of sacred writings. (2) Son of Issachar, Gen. xlvi. 13. Jashub, 1 Chr. vii. 1.

Jō′băb (*desert*). (1) Son of Joktan, Gen. x. 29. (2) King of Edom, Gen. xxxvi. 33. (3) King of Madon, Josh. xi. 1. (4) Two Benjamites, 1 Chr. viii. 9, 18.

Jŏch′e-bed (*glorified*). Mother of Moses, Ex. vi. 20; Num. xxvi. 59.

Jō′da̤, 1 Esdr. v. 58. [JUDAH.]

Jō′ed (*witnessed*). A Benjamite, Neh. xi. 7.

Jō′el (*Jehovah his God*). (1) Son of Pethuel and second of minor prophets. Probably of Judah and contemporary with Uzziah, B. c. 810–758. His book, 29th of O. T., depicts calamities, rises into exhortation, and foreshadows the Messiah. (2) Son of Samuel, 1 Sam. viii. 2. (3) Others in 1 Chr. iv. 35; v. 4, 8, 12; vi. 36; vii. 3; xi. 38; xv. 7; xxiii. 8; xxvii. 20; 2 Chr. xxix. 12; Ez. x. 43; Neh. xi. 9.

Jō-ē′lah (*helped*). A Benjamite chief, 1 Chr. xii. 7.

Jō-ē′zer (*aided*). A Benjamite, 1 Chr. xii. 6.

Jŏg′be-hah (*high*). City of Gad, E. of Jordan, Num. xxxii. 35.

Jŏg′lī (*exiled*). A prince of Dan, Num. xxxiv. 22.

Jō′ha̤ (*given life*). (1) A Benjamite, 1 Chr. viii. 16. (2) One of David's guard, 1 Chr. xi. 45.

Jō-hā′nan (*God's mercy*). (1) A Judahite captain who escaped captivity, 2 Kgs. xxv. 23, and carried Jeremiah and other Jews into Egypt, Jer. xl.–xliii. (2) Others in 1 Chr. iii. 15, 24; vi. 9, 10; xii. 4, 12; 2 Chr. xxviii. 12; Ez. viii. 12; x. 6; Neh. vi. 18.

Jŏhn (*God's gift*). Johanan, contraction of Jehohanan. (1) Kinsman of the high priest, Acts iv. 6. (2) Hebrew name of Mark, Acts xii. 25; xiii. 5; xv. 37. (3) John the Baptist, son of Zacharias. Birth foretold, Luke i. Born about six months before Christ. Retired to wilderness. Emerged to preach and baptize. Baptized Jesus, Matt. iii. Imprisoned by Herod, Luke iii. 1–22. Beheaded, Matt. xiv. 1–12. (4) John, Apostle and Evangelist; son of Zebedee, Matt. iv. 21; a fisherman of Galilee, Luke v. 1–10; a favorite apostle, noted for zeal and firmness, John xiii. 23; xix. 26; xx. 2; xxi. 7. He remained at Jerusalem till about A. D. 65, when he went to Ephesus. Banished to Patmos, and released A. D. 96. His writings, doubtless done at Ephesus, are the fourth Gospel, giving Christ's ministry in Judea; his three epistles, and Revelation. (5) A frequent name among the Maccabees, 1 Macc.

Joi′a-da̤ (*favored*). A high priest, Neh. xii. 10, 11, 22; xiii. 28.

Joi′a-kĭm (*exalted*). A high priest, Neh. xii. 10.

Joi′a-rĭb (*defended*). Two who returned, Ez. viii. 16; Neh. xii. 6, 19.

Jŏk′de-ăm (*peopled*). City of Judah, Josh. xv. 56.

Jō′kim (*exalted*) A Judahite, 1 Chr. iv 22.

Jŏk′me-ăm (*gathered*). Levitical city in Ephraim, 1 Chr. vi. 68.

Jŏk′ne-ăm (*gathered*). Levitical city in Zebulun, Josh. xxi. 34.

Jŏk'shan (*fowler*). Son of Abraham, Gen. xxv. 2, 3; 1 Chr. i. 32.

Jŏk'tan (*small*). Son of Eber and progenitor of Joktanite Arabs, Gen. x. 25; 1 Chr. i. 19.

Jŏk'the-el (*subdued*). (1) City in Judah, Josh. xv. 38. (2) An Edomite stronghold, 2 Kgs. xiv. 7.

Jō'nà (*dove*). Father of Apostle Peter, Matt. xvi. 17; John i. 42.

Jŏn'a-dăb (*God-impelled*). (1) David's subtle nephew, 2 Sam. xiii. 3, 32–35. (2) Jer. xxxv. 6–19, Jehonadab.

Jō'nah (*dove*). Son of Amittai. Commissioned to denounce Nineveh. His book, 32d of O. T. and 5th of minor prophets, narrates his refusal, escape from drowning, final acceptance and successful ministry. This lesson is God's providence over all nations.

Jō'nan (*grace*). Ancestor of Christ, Luke iii. 30.

Jō'nas. Greek form of Jonah, Matt. xii. 39–41; Luke xi. 30–32.

Jŏn'a-than (*God-given*). (1) A Levite, Judg. xvii. 7–13; xviii. (2) Eldest son of Saul, and friend of David, 1 Sam. xiii. 2, 3; xviii. 1–4; xix. 1–7; xx. Fell in battle of Gilboa. David's lament, 2 Sam. i. 17–27. (3) Others in 2 Sam. xv. 27, 36; xxi. 20, 21; xxiii. 32; 1 Chr. ii. 32, 33; xxvii. 32; Ez. viii. 6; x. 15; Neh. xii. 11, 14, 35; Jer. xxxvii. 15, 20; xl. 8.

Jŏn'a-thas, Tob. v. 13. [JONATHAN.]

Jō'nath=ē''lem=re-chō'kim (*a dumb dove of distant places*). Title to, and probably melody of, Ps. lvi.

Jŏp'pà (*beauty*). Mediterranean seaport of Jerusalem; now Jaffa, 1 Kgs. v. 9; 2 Chr. ii. 16; Ez. iii. 7.

Jŏp'pē. For Joppa in Apoc.

Jō'rah (*rain*). His family returned, Ez. ii. 18.

Jō'ra-ī (*taught of God*). A Gadite chief, 1 Chr. v. 13.

Jō'ram (*exalted*). (1) Short form of Jehoram, king of Israel, 2 Kgs. viii. 16, etc.; and of Jehoram, king of Judah, 2 Kgs. viii. 21, etc.; Matt. i. 8. (2) Son of Toi, 2 Sam. viii. 10. (3) A Levite, 1 Chr. xxvi. 25.

Jŏr'dan (*descender*). Chief river of Palestine, rising in the Anti-Libanus range, flowing southward, enlarging into Sea of Galilee, emptying into Dead Sea. A swift, narrow, yet fordable stream, with an entire course of about 200 miles, Gen. xiii. 10; Josh. ii. 7; Judg. iii. 28; 2 Sam. x. 17; Matt. iii. 13.

Jō'rim (*exalted*). An ancestor of Christ, Luke iii. 29.

Jŏr'ko-ăm. A person or place, 1 Chr. ii. 44.

Jŏs'a-băd (*dowered*). (1) One of David's warriors, 1 Chr. xii. 4. (2) Persons in 1 Esdr.

Jŏs'a-phăt, Matt. i. 8. [JEHOSHAPHAT.]

Jō'se. An ancestor of Christ, Luke iii. 29.

Jŏs'e-dĕch, Hag. i. 1. [JEHOZADAK.]

Jō'seph (*increase*). (1) Son of Jacob and Rachel, Gen. xxxvii. 3; sold into Egypt; promoted to high office by the Pharoah; rescued his family from famine; settled them in Goshen; died at advanced age; bones carried back to Shechem, Gen. xxxvii.–l. (2) An Issacharite, Num. xiii. 7. (3) Two who returned, Ez. x. 42; Neh. xii. 14. (4) Three of Christ's ancestors, Luke iii. 24, 26, 30. (5) Husband of Mary, and a carpenter at Nazareth, Matt. i. 19; xiii. 55; Luke iii. 23; John i. 45. (6) Of Arimathea, a member of the Sanhedrim, who acknowledged Christ, Matt. xxvii. 57–59; Mark xv. 43; Luke xxiii. 51. (7) The apostle Barsabas, substituted for Judas, Acts i. 23. (8) Frequent name in Apoc.

Jō'ses (*helped*). (1) One of Christ's brethren, Matt. xiii. 55; xxvii. 56; Mark vi. 3; xv. 40, 47. (2) Barnabas, Acts iv. 36.

Jō'shah (*dwelling*). A Simeonite chief, 1 Chr. iv. 34.

Jŏsh'a-phăt (*judged*). One of David's guard, 1 Chr. xi. 43.

Jŏsh''a-vī'ah (*dwelling*). One of David's guard, 1 Chr. xi. 46.

Jŏsh-bĕk'a-shah (*hard seat*). Head of 17th musical course, 1 Chr. xxv. 4, 24.

Jŏsh'u-à (*saviour*). (1) Jehoshuah, 1 Chr. vii. 27. Oshea, Num. xiii. 8. Jesus, Acts vii. 45; Heb. iv. 8. Son of Nun, of tribe of Ephraim. The great warrior of the Israelites during the desert wanderings and conquest and apportionment of Canaan, Ex. xvii. 9–14; 1 Chr. vii. 27; Num. xiii. 8, 16; xxvii. 18–23. His book, 6th of O. T., contains the history of his conquests and governorship, B. C. 1451–1426. (2) A Bethshemite, 1 Sam. vi. 14. (3) A governor of Jerusalem, 2 Kgs. xxiii. 8. (4) A high priest, Hag. i. 1, 14.

Jō-sī'ah (*God-healed*). (1) Son and successor of Amon on throne of Judah, B. C. 641–610. He abolished idolatry, propagated the newly discovered law, aided Assyria against Egypt, and fell in the celebrated battle of Esdraelon, 2 Kgs. xxii.–xxiii. 1–30; 2 Chr. xxxiv.–xxxv. (2) Son of Zephaniah, Zech. vi. 10.

Jō-sī'as. (1) Greek form of Josiah, 1 Esdr. i. 1; Matt. i. 10, 11. (2) 1 Esdr. viii. 33. [JESHAIAH.]

Jŏs''ĭ-bī'ah (*dwelling*). A chief of Simeon, 1 Chr. iv. 35.

Jŏs''ĭ-phī'ah (*increase*). His family returned, Ez. viii. 10.

Jŏt. The Greek i, iota. A little thing, Matt. v. 18.

Jŏt'bah (*goodness*). Residence of Haruz, 2 Kgs. xxi. 19.

Jŏt'băth (*goodness*). Jotbathah, Num. xxxiii. 33. An Israelite encampment, Deut. x. 7.

Jō'tham (*God is upright*). (1) Youngest son of Gideon and author of the bramble fable, Judg. ix. 5–21. (2) Son and successor of Uzziah, or Azariah, on throne of Judah, B. C. 758–741. Reign prosperous, 2 Kgs. xv. 5, 6, 32–36; 2 Chr. xxvii. (3) A Judahite, 1 Chr. ii. 47.

Joûr'ney (*daily*). A day's journey, indefinite. Sabbath day's journey, 2000 paces, or ¾ of a mile from the walls of a city, Deut. i. 2; Acts i. 12.

Jŏz'a-băd (*God-given*). (1) Two Manassite chiefs, 1 Chr. xii. 20. (2) Five Levites, 2 Chr. xxxi. 13; xxxv. 9; Ez. viii. 33; x. 22; Neh. viii. 7; xi. 16.

Jŏz'a-chär (*remembered*). Zabad, 2 Chr. xxiv. 26. One of Joash's murderers, 2 Kgs. xii. 21.

Jŏz'a-dăk, Ez. iii. 2, 8, etc.; Neh. xii. 26. [JEHOZADAK.]

Jū'băl (*music*). Son of Lamech, and inventor of harp and organ, Gen. iv. 19–21.

Jū'bi-lee (*blast of trumpets*). Year of, celebrated every fiftieth year; ushered in by blowing of trumpets; land rested; alienated lands reverted; slaves freed; outer circle of seventh or sabbatical system, year, month, and day, Lev. xxv. 8–55.

Jū'cal, Jer. xxxviii. 1. [JEHUCAL.]

Jū'dà (*praised*). (1) Ancestors of Christ, Luke iii. 26, 30. (2) One of Christ's brethren, Mark vi. 3. (3) The patriarch Judah, Luke iii. 33. (4) The tribe of Judah, Heb. vii. 14; Rev. v. 5.

Jū-dæ'à, Jū-dē'à (*from Judah*). Vaguely, Joshua's conquest, Matt. xix. 1; Mark x. 1, or Canaanite land. Limitedly, the part occupied by returned captives; the "Jewry" of Dan. v. 13; the "province" of Ez. v. 8; Neh. xi. 3. "Land of Judea" in Apoc. A Roman province jointly with Syria, with a procurator, after A. D. 6.

Jū'dah (*praise*). (1) Fourth son of Jacob, Gen. xxix. 35; xxxvii. 26–28; xliii. 3–10; xliv. 14–34. His tribe the largest, Num. i. 26, 27. Allotted the southern section of Canaan, Josh. xv. 1–63. (2) Kingdom of, formed on disruption of Solomon's empire, out of Judah, Benjamin, Simeon, and part of Dan, with Jerusalem as capital, B. C. 975. Had 19 kings, and lasted for 389 years, till reduced by Nebuchadnezzar, B. C. 586. Outlived its rival, Israel, some 135 years. (3) City of Jerusalem, 2 Chr. xxv. 28. (4) A town in Naphtali, Josh. xix. 34. (5) Persons in Ez. iii. 9; x. 23; Neh. xi. 9.

Ju'das. Greek form of Judah. (1) Judah, Matt. i. 2, 3. (2) Iscariot, or of Kerioth. Betrayer of Christ, Matt. x. 4; Mark iii. 19; Luke vi. 16; John vi. 71; xii. 6; xiii. 29. (3) Man of Damascus, Acts ix. 11. (4) Barsabas, chief among the brethren, and prophet, Acts xv. 22, 32. (5) A Galilean apostate, Acts v. 37. (6) Frequent name in Apoc.

Jude, Jude i. 1. Judas, brother of James the Less, Luke vi. 16; John xiv. 22; Acts i. 13; Matt. xiii. 55. Thaddæus, Lebbæus, Matt. x. 3; Mark iii. 18. An Apostle and author of the epistle which bears his name, 26th N. T. book. Written about A. D. 65. Place not known.

Judg'es. Governors of Israel between Joshua and the kings. They were called of God, elective or usurpative. Qualification, martial or moral prowess. Rule arbitrary. Fifteen are recorded. Period, B. C. 1400–1091, about 310 years. Book of Judges, 7th of O. T., probably compiled by Samuel. Its history is that of a tumultuous period, completing Joshua's conquests and leading to legitimate kingly rule.

Judg'ment Hall. Pilate's residence in Jerusalem, John xviii. 28, 33; xix. 9. Prætorium or court, Acts xxiii. 35.

Ju'dith (*praised, Jewess*). (1) Wife of Esau, Gen. xxvi. 34. (2) Heroine of the 4th Apocryphal book.

Ju'el, Apoc. [JOEL.]

Ju'li̇a (*feminine of Julius*). A Christian woman at Rome, Rom. xvi. 15.

Ju'lius (*soft-haired*). A Roman centurion, Acts xxvii. 1–3, 43.

Ju'ni̇a (*youth*). Roman friend of Paul, Rom. xvi. 7.

Ju'ni̇-pẽr (*young producer*). Not the evergreen, but the desert broom-shrub, 1 Kgs. xix. 4, 5; Job xxx. 4; Ps. cxx. 4.

Ju'pĭ-tẽr (*father Jove*). Supreme god of Greeks and Romans, Acts xiv. 12; xix. 35.

Ju'shăb=hē'sĕd (*requited love*). Son of Zerubbabel, 1 Chr. iii. 20.

Jŭs"tĭ-fĭ-cā'tion. Pardon and acceptance of the just through faith, Rom. iii. 20–31; iv. 25.

Jŭs'tus (*just*). (1) Surname of Joseph, or Barsabas, Acts i. 23. (2) A Corinthian convert, Acts xviii. 7. (3) Surname of Jesus, a friend of Paul, Col. iv. 11.

Jŭt'tah (*extended*). A Levitical city in mountains of Judah; now Yutta, Josh. xv. 55; xxi. 16.

K

Kăb'ze-el (*gathered*). A city of Judah, Josh. xv. 21. Jekabzeel, Neh. xi. 25.

Kā'desh (*holy*). Halting place of Israelites near borders of Canaan, and scene of Miriam's death, Num. xiii. 26; xx. 1. Kadesh-barnea, Deut. ii. 14; Josh. xv. 3. Enmishpat, Gen. xiv. 7.

Kăd'mi-el (*before God*). One who returned, Ez. iii. 9; Neh. ix. 4.

Kăd'mŏn-ītes (*eastern*). Ancient Canaanites, Gen. xv. 19.

Kăl'la-ī (*runner*). A priest, Neh. xii. 20.

Kā'nah (*reedy*). (1) A boundary of Asher, Josh. xix. 28. (2) Boundary stream between Ephraim and Manasseh, Josh. xvi. 8; xvii. 9.

Kā-rē'ah (*bald*). Father of Johanan, Jer. xl. 8–16.

Kär'ka-à (*floor*). A southern boundary of Judah, Josh. xv. 3.

Kär'kôr (*foundation*). Scene of Gideon's victory, Judg. viii. 10.

Kär'tah (*city*). Levitical city in Zebulun, Josh. xxi. 34.

Kär'tan, Josh. xxi. 32. [KIRJATHAIM.]

Kăt'tath (*small*). Town of Zebulun, Josh. xix. 15.

Kē'där (*dark*). Son of Ishmael and founder of Arabic tribe, Gen. xxv. 13; Isa. xxi. 13–17; Ezek. xxvii. 21.

Kĕd'e̤-mah (*eastward*). Son of Ishmael, Gen. xxv. 15; 1 Chr. i. 31.

Kĕd'e̤-mŏth (*eastern*). Levitical town of Reuben, Josh. xiii. 18; xxi. 37; 1 Chr. vi. 79.

Kē'desh (*sacred*). (1) Josh. xv. 23. [KADESH.] (2) Levitical city in Issachar, Josh. xii. 22; 1 Chr. vi. 72. (3) City of refuge in Naphtali, Josh. xix. 37; Judg. iv. 6; 2 Kgs. xv. 29. Now Kades.

Kē'dron. [KIDRON.]

Kē-hĕl'a̤-thah (*assembly*). A desert encampment, Num. xxxiii. 22, 23.

Kēi'lah (*fortress*). (1) Lowland town of Judah, Josh. xv. 44; 1 Sam. xxiii. 1–13; Neh. iii. 17, 18. (2) Person or place, 1 Chr. iv. 19.

Kĕ-lā'i̤ah, Ez. x. 23. [KELITA.]

Kĕl'ĭ-ta (*dwarf*). Assistant of Ezra, Neh. viii. 7.

Kĕ-mu'el (*helper*). (1) Son of Nahor, Gen. xxii. 21. (2) A prince of Ephraim, Num. xxxiv. 24. (3) A Levite, 1 Chr. xxvii. 17.

Kē'nan, 1 Chr. i. 2. [CAINAN.]

Kē'nath (*possession*). A city or section of Gilead, Num. xxxii. 42.

Kē'năz (*hunting*). (1) A duke of Edom, Gen. xxxvi. 15, and founder of Kenezites, Josh. xiv. 14. (2) Father of Othniel, Josh. xv. 17. (3) Grandson of Caleb, 1 Chr. iv. 15.

Kĕn'ez-īte (*hunter*). Kenizzite, Gen. xv. 19. An ancient Edomite tribe, Num. xxxii. 12; Josh. xiv. 6, 14.

Kĕn'ītes (*smiths*). A Midianite tribe allied to Israelites, Gen. xv. 19; Num. xxiv. 21, 22; Judg. iv. 11.

Kĕr'en=hăp'puch (*horn of beauty*). Third daughter of Job, Job xlii. 14.

Kē'rĭ-ŏth (*cities*). (1) A town of Judah, Josh. xv. 25. (2) A city of Moab, Jer. xlviii. 24.

Kē'ros (*crooked*). His children returned, Ez. ii. 44.

Kĕt'tle (*deep vessel*). Used for cooking and sacrifices, 1 Sam. ii. 14. Basket, Jer. xxiv. 2; caldron, 2 Chr. xxxv. 13; pot, Job xli. 20.

Kĕ-tu'rah (*incense*). A wife of Abraham, Gen. xxv. 1; 1 Chr. i. 32.

Kĕ-zī'a̤ (*cassia*). Job's second daughter, Job xlii. 14.

Kē'ziz (*end*). A town of Benjamin, Josh. xviii. 21.

Kĭb'roth=hăt-tā'a̤-vah (*graves of lust*). A desert encampment of the Israelites, Num. xi. 31–35.

Kĭb'za̤-im (*heaps*). Levitical city in Ephraim, Josh. xxi. 22. Jokmeam, 1 Chr. vi 68.

Kĭd. Young goat. An offering, Num. vii. 12–82. A favorite meat, Gen. xxxviii. 17; 1 Sam. xvi. 20.

Kĭd'ron (*turbid*). The brook or ravine between Jerusalem and Olivet, 2 Sam. xv. 23; 2 Kgs. xxiii. 6. Cedron, John xviii. 1.

Kī'nah (*dirge*). City of south Judah, Josh. xv. 22.

Kine. Plural of cow, Gen. xli. 17–21.

King (*tribe*). Title of Hebrew rulers from Saul to Zedekiah, B. C. 1095–588. Other rulers, Gen. xxxvi. 31; Ex. iii. 19; Num. xxxi. 8. Supreme ruler, 1 Tim. i. 17; vi. 15.

Kings. Eleventh and twelfth O. T. books. Originally one. Compilation credited to Ezra or Jeremiah. 1 Kings gives history of Hebrew kingdoms from Solomon, B. C. 1015, to Jehoshaphat, B. C. 890. 2 Kings completes the history, B. C. 890–588.

Kĭr (*fortress*). An unlocated eastern country, 2 Kgs. xvi. 9; Am. ix. 7.

Kĭr=hăr′ạ-sĕth (*brick fortress*). A stronghold of Moab, 2 Kgs. iii. 25. Kirhareseth, Isa. xvi. 7. Kirharesh, Isa. xvi. 11. Kirheres, Jer. xlviii. 31, 36. Kir of Moab, Isa. xv. 1.

Kĭr″ĭ-a-thā′ĭm, Jer. xlviii. 1, 23; Ezek. xxv. 9. [KIRJATHAIM.]

Kĭr″ĭ-ạth-ĭ-ā′rĭ-us, 1 Esdr. v. 19. [KIRJATH-JEARIM.]

Kĭr′ĭ-ŏth, Am. ii. 2. [KERIOTH.]

Kĭr′jath (*city*). City in Benjamin, Josh. xviii. 28.

Kĭr″jath-ā′im (*double city*). (1) A Moabite town, Num. xxxii. 37. (2) Levitical town in Naphtali, Josh. xiii. 19; 1 Chr. vi. 76.

Kĭr′jath=är′bȧ (*city of Arba*). Old name of Hebron, Gen. xxiii. 2; Josh. xiv. 15.

Kĭr′jath=ā′rim, Ez. ii. 25. [KIRJATH-JEARIM.]

Kĭr′jath=bā′al, Josh. xv. 60; xviii. 14. [KIRJATH-JEARIM.]

Kĭr′jath=hū′zoth (*city of streets*). City in Moab, Num. xxii. 39.

Kĭr′jath=jē′ạ-rĭm (*city of woods*). A Gibeonite city which fell to Judah, Josh. ix. 17; Judg. xviii. 12. Baalah, Josh. xv. 9. Kirjath-baal, xviii. 14.

Kĭr′jath=san′nah (*palm city*). [DEBIR.]

Kĭr′jath=se′phĕr (*city of books*). [DEBIR.]

Kĭr of Mō′ab. [KIR-HARASETH.]

Kĭsh (*bow*). (1) Father of Saul, 1 Sam. x. 21. (2) A Benjamite, 1 Chr. viii. 30. (3) A Levite, 1 Chr. xxiii. 21. (4) A Levite, 2 Chr. xxix. 12. (5) Ancestor of Mordecai, Esth. ii. 5.

Kĭsh′ĭ (*bow*). A Levite, 1 Chr. vi. 44.

Kĭsh′ĭ-ŏn (*hardness*). Levitical city in Issachar, Josh. xix. 20.

Kĭ′shŏn (*crooked*). (1) Josh. xxi. 28. [KISHION.] (2) The brook or wady which drains the valley of Esdraelon, Judg. iv. 7–13; v. 21; 1 Kgs. xviii. 40. Kison, Ps. lxxxiii. 9.

Kĭ′son, Ps. lxxxiii. 9. [KISHON.]

Kĭss. Form of salutation, Gen. xxix. 13; token of allegiance, 1 Sam. x. 1; pledge of Christian brotherhood, Rom. xvi. 16; 1 Pet. v. 14.

Kĭte (*quick of wing*). An unclean bird of the hawk species, Lev. xi. 14; Deut. xiv. 13. Vulture, Job xxviii. 7.

Kĭth′lish (*wall*). Lowland town in Judah, Josh. xv. 40.

Kĭt′rŏn (*knotty*). Town in Zebulun, Judg. i. 30.

Kĭt′tim, Gen. x. 4; 1 Chr. i. 7. [CHITTIM.]

Knēad′ing=troughs. Were bowls, or leather surfaces, Gen. xviii. 6; Ex. xii. 34.

Knīfe (*waster*). Primitively of stone or bone; later of metal. Little used at meals. For killing and cutting, Lev. viii. 20; sharpening pens, Jer. xxxvi. 23; pruning, Isa. xviii. 5; lancing, 1 Kgs. xviii. 28.

Knŏp (*knob*). Ornamental knobs, or reliefs, Ex. xxv. 31–36; 1 Kgs. vi. 18.

Kō′ȧ (*male camel*). An eastern prince, Ezek. xxiii. 23.

Kō′hath (*assembly*). Second son of Levi, and head of the house of Kohathite Levites, Gen. xlvi. 11; Ex. vi. 16, 18; Num. iii. 27; xxvi. 57; Josh. xxi. 4–42.

Kŏl″ạ-ī′ah (*God's voice*). (1) A Benjamite, Neh. xi. 7. (2) Father of the false prophet Ahab, Jer. xxix. 21.

Kō′rah (*baldness*). (1) Dukes of Edom, Gen. xxxvi. 5–18. (2) Son of Hebron, 1 Chr. ii. 43. (3) Leader of the rebellion against Moses, Num. xvi.; xxvi. 9–11.

Kō′rah-ītes. Descendants of Korah, 1 Chr. ix. 19. Korhites, 2 Chr. xx. 19. Korathites, Num. xxvi. 58.

Kō′rḗ (*quail*). (1) A Korahite, 1 Chr. ix. 19. (2) Korhites, 1 Chr. xxvi. 1–19. (3) A Levite, 2 Chr. xxxi. 14.

Kŏz (*thorn*). (1) A Judahite, 1 Chr. iv. 8. [COZ.] (2) A priest, 1 Chr. xxiv. 10. [HAKKOZ.] (3) Returned captives, Ez. ii. 61; Neh. iii. 4, 21.

Kŭsh-ā′ịah, 1 Chr. xv. 17. [KISHI.]

L

Lā′ạ-dah (*order*). A Judahite, 1 Chr. iv. 21.

Lā′ạ-dặn (*ordered*). (1) An Ephraimite, 1 Chr. vii. 26. (2) Son of Gershon, 1 Chr. xxiii. 7–9; xxvi. 21. Libni, elsewhere.

Lā′ban (*white*). (1) Father-in-law of Jacob, Gen. xxiv.-xxx. (2) A landmark, Deut. i. 1.

Lăb′ạ-nȧ, 1 Esdr. v. 29. [LEBANA.]

Lăç″e-dē-mō′nĭ-ans. Inhabitants of Lacedemon. Spartans, 1 Macc. xii. 2–21.

Lā′chish (*impregnable*). An Amorite city in southern Judah, Josh. x.; 2 Kgs. xviii. 17; xix. 8; 2 Chr. xi. 9; Neh. xi. 30.

Lā-cū′nus. A returned captive, 1 Esdr. ix. 31.

Lā′dan, 1 Esdr. v. 37. [DELAIAH.]

Lā′el (*of God*). A Gershonite, Num. iii. 24.

Lā′hăd (*oppression*). A Judahite, 1 Chr. iv. 2.

Lā-hāi′=roi (*well of the living God*). Well of Hagar's relief, Gen. xxiv. 62; xxv. 11.

Lăh′mam (*bread*). Lowland town of Judah, Josh. xv. 40.

Lăh′mĭ (*warrior*). Brother of Goliath, 1 Chr. xx. 5.

Lā′ish (*lion*). (1) A northern Danite city, Judg. xviii. 7–29; Isa. x. 30. (2) Father of Phaltiel, 1 Sam. xxv. 44; 2 Sam. iii. 15. Leshem, Josh. xix. 47.

Lā′kŭm (*fortress*). A border of Naphtali, Josh. xix. 33.

Lămb. Young of sheep or goat. Favorite sacrifices, Ex. xxix. 38–41; Num. xxviii. 9–29.

Lā′mech (*strong*). (1) Father of Noah, Gen. v. 28–32. (2) Father of Jubal, inventor of the harp and organ, Gen. iv. 18–26.

Lăm″ĕn-tā′tions (*weepings*). Twenty-fifth O. T. book. An elegiac poem by Jeremiah, on the destruction of Jerusalem.

Lămp (*shine*). The temple candlestick, Ex. xxv. 31–40; 1 Kgs. vii. 49. Torches, Judg. vii. 16. Oriental lamps of many shapes and ornamental. Fed with oil, tallow, wax, etc., Matt. xxv. 1.

Lăn′çet (*little lance*). Light spear, 1 Kgs. xviii. 28.

Lănd′märks. Were trees, stones, towns, mountains, streams, etc. Removal forbidden, Deut. xix. 14; Prov. xxii. 28.

Lăn′guȧge (*tongue*). Originally one, Gen. xi. 1. Diversified at Babel, Gen. xi. 7–9.

Lăn′tĕrn (*shining*). Covered candle or lamp, John xviii. 3.

Lā-ŏd″ĭ-çē′ȧ (*just people*). Ancient Diospolis; modern Eski-hissar. A city of Phrygia, and seat of an early Christian church, Col. ii. 1; iv. 15; Rev. i. 11; iii. 14–22.

Lăp′ĭ-dŏth (*lamps*). Husband of Deborah, Judg. iv. 4.

Lăp′wĭng. An unclean bird, thought to be the beautiful migratory hoopoe, Lev. xi. 19.

Lā-sē′ȧ. City in Crete, Acts xxvii. 8.

Lā′shȧ (*cleft*). A Canaanite border, Gen. x. 19.

Lā-shȧr′on (*plain*). A Canaanite town, Josh. xii. 18.

Lăs′thĕ-nēṣ. A Cretan, 1 Macc. xi. 31.

Lătch′et (*lace*). Sandal lacings, or fastenings, Gen. xiv. 23; Mark i. 7.

Lăt′in. Language of Latium, *i. e.* the Romans,

Luke xxiii. 38 ; John xix. 20.

Lăt'tĭçe (*lath*). Open work of wood or metal ; also window, blind, or screen, Judg. v. 28 ; 2 Kgs. i. 2 ; Prov. vii. 6.

Lā'ver (*wash*). Brazen vessel holding water for priestly washings — hands, feet, and the sacrifices, Ex. xxx. 18-21 ; xxxviii. 8 ; 1 Kgs. vii. 38-40 ; 2 Chr. iv. 6.

Law (*rule*). In Scripture, reference is nearly always to the Hebrew civil, moral, and ceremonial law, Matt. v. 17 ; John i. 17 ; Acts xxv. 8.

Law'yĕr. Scribe or divine who expounded the Mosaic law in school or synagogue, Matt. xxii. 35 ; Luke x. 25.

Lăz'a-rus (*whom God helps*). Abbreviation of Eleazar. (1) Brother of Mary and Martha, John xi. 1 ; xii. 1-11. (2) Type of poverty and distress in the parable, Luke xvi. 19-31.

Lĕad. Early known, imported and used by Hebrews, Ex. xv. 10 ; Num. xxxi. 22 ; Job xix. 24 ; Ezek. xxvii. 12.

Lĕaf. Of trees, Gen. viii. 11 ; Matt. xxi. 19 ; double doors, 1 Kgs. vi. 34 ; of books, Jer. xxxvi. 23 ; prosperity, Jer. xvii. 8 ; decay, Job xiii. 25.

Lē'ah (*weary*). Jacob's wife through deceit of her father, Laban, Gen. xxix., xxx., xlix. 31.

Lēas'ing (*lying*). Falsehood, Ps. iv. 2 ; v. 6.

Lĕath'er. Used by Hebrews, 2 Kgs. i. 8 ; Matt. iii. 4.

Lĕav'en (*raise*). Old fermented dough used to lighten new dough, Matt. xiii. 33. Passover bread unleavened, Ex. xii. 15-17. Corrupt doctrines, Matt. xvi. 6 ; evil passions, 1 Cor. v. 7, 8.

Lĕb'a-nà (*white*). His children returned, Neh. vii. 48. Lebanah, Ez. ii. 45.

Lĕb'a-non (*white*). Two mountain ranges running N. E., between which was Cœlo-Syria. The western is Libanus, or Lebanon proper. The eastern is Anti-Libanus, and skirted Palestine on the north, Deut. i. 7 ; Josh. i. 4. Many scripture allusions, Isa. x. 34 ; Jer. xxii. 23.

Lĕb'a-ŏth (*lionesses*). Boundary town of southern Judah, Josh. xv. 32.

Lĕb-bæ'us (*brave*). Thaddæus, the apostle Jude, Matt. x. 3, Mark iii. 18.

Lĕ-bō'nah (*incense*). Place north of Bethel, Judg. xxi. 19.

Lĕ'cah (*walking*). Person or place, 1 Chr. iv. 21.

Lēech. [Horse-leech.]

Lēek. Closely allied to the onion, Num. xi. 5.

Lēes (*dregs*). Sediment of liquor. Settled, pure wine, Isa. xxv. 6 ; sloth, Jer. xlviii. 11 ; extreme suffering, Ps. lxxv. 8.

Lē'gion (*gathered*). Division of Roman army ; when full, 6200 men and 730 horse. N. T. use indefinite, Matt. xxvi. 53 ; Mark v. 9.

Lē'hă-bĭm (*flame*). A Mizraite tribe ; Libyans, Gen. x. 13. Lubim, 2 Chr. xii. 3.

Lē'hĭ (*jawbone*). Where Samson slew the Philistines, Judg. xv. 9, 19.

Lĕm'u-el (*dedicated*). The unknown king in Prov. xxxi. 1-9.

Lĕn'tĭl (*little lens*). A podded food plant, like the pea or bean, Gen. xxv. 34 ; 2 Sam. xvii. 28.

Lĕop'ard (*lion-panther*). This fierce, spotted beast of the cat species once found in Jordan jungles, Jer. xiii. 23 ; Dan. vii. 6 ; S. of Sol. iv. 8.

Lĕp'er (*peeled*). Who has leprosy ; a loathsome, incurable skin disease, common in East, Ex. iv. 6 ; treatment of, Lev. xiv. 3-32 ; Luke xvii. 12-19.

Lē'shem, Josh. xix. 47. [Laish.]

Lĕt'tus, 1 Esdr. viii. 29. [Hattush.]

Lĕ-tū'shim (*hammered*). Son of Dedan, and his Arabian tribe, Gen. xxv. 3.

Lĕ-ŭm'mim (*nations*). Son of Dedan, and his Arabian tribe, Gen. xxv. 3.

Lē'vī (*joined*). (1) Third son of Jacob, Gen. xxix. 34 ; avenged Dinah's wrong, xxxiv. 25-31 ; cursed, xlix. 5-7 ; went to Egypt, Ex. vi. 16 ; blessed, Ex. xxxii. 25-28. (2) Two of Christ's ancestors, Luke iii. 24, 29. (3) Original name of Matthew, Mark ii. 14 ; Luke v. 27, 29 ; compare Matt. ix. 9.

Lĕ-vī'a-than (*aquatic monster*). The crocodile is described in Job xli. ; and probably meant in Ps. lxxiv. 14 ; civ. 26.

Lē'vītes. Descendants of Levi, Ex. vi. 16-25 ; Lev. xxv. 32, etc. ; Num. xxxv. 2-8 ; Josh. xxi. 3. In above, the tribe is meant. But Levites came to mean the priestly branch, *i. e.*, descendants of Aaron, Josh. iii. 3 ; 1 Kgs. viii. 4 ; Ez. ii. 70 ; John i. 19. Three Levitical lines, Kohathite, Gershonite, Merarite, Num. iii. 17. Assigned 48 cities among the other tribes, Num. xxxv.

Lĕ-vīt'ĭ-cus (*for Levites*). Third book of Bible and Pentateuch, containing the ceremonial law for guidance of Levites. Authorship ascribed to Moses and Aaron.

Lĭb'a-nus. Greek form of Lebanon, 1 Esdr. iv. 48.

Lĭb'er-tīneş (*free*). Emancipated Jewish slaves ; freedmen, Acts vi. 9.

Lĭb'nah (*white*). (1) An Israelite encampment, Num. xxxiii. 20, 21. (2) Levitical city in Judah, Josh. x. 29-31 ; 2 Kgs. xix. 8-35 ; 1 Chr. vi. 57.

Lĭb'nī (*whiteness*). (1) A Levite, founder of Libnites, Ex. vi. 17 ; Num. iii. 18-21. (2) Probably the above, 1 Chr. vi. 29.

Lĭb'ў-à, Ezek. xxx. 5 ; Acts ii. 10. The African continent west of Egypt and contiguous to Mediterranean. *See* Lubim and Lehabim.

Līçe (*destroyers*). Constituted the third Egyptian plague, Ex. viii. 16-18 ; Ps. cv. 31.

Lĭeu-tĕn'ants (*place-holders*). Satraps or viceroys, Ez. viii. 36. Princes, Dan. iii. 2 ; vi. 1.

Līfe. Natural, Gen. iii. 17 ; spiritual, Rom. viii. 6 ; eternal, John iii. 36 ; Rom. vi. 23.

Līght. First gush of creation, Gen. i. 3. Frequent source of imagery, Matt. iv. 16 ; Luke ii. 32 ; John i. 7-9.

Līgn=aloes (*wood-aloes*). [Aloes.]

Lĭg'ūre (*lynx urine*). Possibly amber. First stone in third row of high priest's breastplate, Ex. xxviii. 19 ; xxxix. 12.

Lĭk'hī (*learned*). A Manassite, 1 Chr. vii. 19.

Lĭl'y (*pale*). Source of rich imagery, 1 Kgs. vii. 19 ; S. of Sol. ii. 1, 2 ; v. 13 ; Matt. vi. 28 ; Luke xii. 27.

Līme (*glue*). Was known and used for plaster and cement work, Deut. xxvii. 2 ; Isa. xxxiii. 12 ; Am. ii. 1.

Lĭn'en (*flax*). Used for stately robes, Gen. xli. 42 ; priestly vestments, Ex. xxviii. 42 ; Lev. vi. 10 ; temple veil, 2 Chr. iii. 14 ; choral gowns, 2 Chr. v. 12, and ordinary dress. Symbol of purity, Rev. xv. 6 ; of luxury, Luke xvi. 19.

Lĭn'tel (*boundary*). Support over window or door, Ex. xii. 22 ; 1 Kgs. vi. 31.

Lī'nus (*net*). Roman friend of Paul, 2 Tim. iv. 21.

Lī'on (*seeing*). Once found in Palestine, Judg. xiv. 5, 6 ; 1 Sam. xvii. 34-36 ; 2 Sam. xxiii. 20. Symbol of strength, Gen. xlix. 9.

Lĭt'ter (*bed*). Covered couch or chair, carried by men or animals, Isa. lxvi. 20. "Wagons," Num. vii. 3.

Lĭz'ärd (*muscular*). Abundant in Palestine. Unclean, Lev. xi. 30.

Lō=ăm'mī (*not my people*). Figurative name of Hosea's son, Hos. i. 9.

Lōans. Allowed by Hebrews, but all debts cancelled in Sabbatical year, Deut. xv. 1-11. Usury not allowed, Ex. xxii. 25 ; Lev. xxv. 36 ; Deut. xv. 3-10.

Lŏck (*bar*). A bar of wood or metal for outer.

and bolt for inner, doors, 1 Kgs. iv. 13 ; Judg. iii. 24.

Lŏ′cust (*leaping*). Confused original, supposably embracing the destructive insects, — locust, grasshopper, caterpillar, palmer-worm, etc. They constituted the eighth Egyptian plague, Ex. x. 1-15 ; Joel ii. 3-10.

Lŏd, 1 Chr. viii. 12 ; Ez. ii. 33. [LYDDA.]

Lō=dē′bär (*barren*). A place east of Jordan, 2 Sam. ix. 4 ; xvii. 27.

Lŏg. Hebrew liquid measure ; about five sixths of a pint, Lev. xiv. 10-24.

Lō′ĭs (*pleasing*). Timothy's grandmother, 2 Tim. i. 5.

Looking = glass. Polished metal plate, Ex. xxxviii. 8 ; Job xxxvii. 18.

Lôrd (*loaf-guardian*). Jehovah, LORD, Gen. xv. 4 ; Ps. vii., c. Adonai, Lord, Christ, The Lord, Our Lord. Supreme ruler, and not the Saxon dignitary.

Lôrd's Dāy. First day of the week ; resurrection day of Christ, Rev. i. 10. Sunday, after A. D. 321.

Lôrd's Sŭp′per. Substitute for the O. T. Paschal feast. Instituted by Christ the night before the crucifixion, as a reminder of his covenant with mankind, Matt. xxvi. 19 ; Mark xiv. 16 ; Luke xxii. 13. "Breaking of bread," Acts ii. 42 ; xx. 7. "Communion," 1 Cor. x. 16. "Lord's Supper," only in 1 Cor. xi. 20.

Lō̇=ru̇′ha̤-mah (*unpitied*). Hosea's daughter, Hos. i. 6.

Lŏt (*veil*). Abraham's nephew, Gen. xi. 27-31. Settled in Jordan valley, Gen. xiii. 1-13. Escaped to mountains, Gen. xix. Progenitor of Moabites and Ammonites.

Lō′tan (*hidden*). A Horite duke, Gen. xxxvi. 20-29.

Lŏth′′a̤-sū′bus, 1 Esdr. ix. 44. [HASHUM.]

Lŏts, Feast of. [PURIM.]

Lŏts. Casting or drawing of, a usual way of settling questions. Possibly marked pebbles were used, in a bag or box. Canaan was allotted to the tribes of Israel, Num. xxvi. 55 ; Josh. xv., xix. Scapegoat so chosen, Lev. xvi. 8 ; priest's courses, 1 Chr. xxiv., xxv. ; property divided, Matt. xxvii. 35.

Love Fēasts. Feasts of offerings, after the community of goods ceased, Jude 12 ; 2 Peter ii. 13. Forbidden by Council of Laodicea, A. D. 320.

Lu̇-bĭm, 2 Chr. xii. 3 ; xvi. 8. [LIBYA.]

Lu̇′cas. Luke the evangelist, Phile. 24.

Lu̇′çĭ-fẽr (*light-giver*). Types the king of Babylon, Isa. xiv. 12. Popularly, Satan.

Lu̇′çĭus (*morning born*). (1) Paul's kinsman, Rom. xvi. 21. (2) A Cyrenean convert and teacher, Acts xiii. 1.

Lŭd (*strife*). Son of Shem, Gen. x. 22.

Lu̇′dĭm (*strife*). A Mizraite tribe, Gen. x. 13 ; Isa. lxvi. 19 ; Ezek. xxvii. 10.

Lu̇′hĭth (*board-made*). Place in Moab, Isa. xv. 5 ; Jer. xlviii. 5.

Lu̇ke (*luminous*). Evangelist and physician, Col. iv. 14 ; 2 Tim. iv. 11. Author of third gospel and of Acts of the Apostles.

Lu̇′nä-tĭcs (*moon-struck*). Epileptics are probably meant, Matt. iv. 24 ; xvii. 15.

Lŭz (*almond*). Site of Bethel, Gen. xxviii. 19 ; Josh. xvi. 2 ; Judg. i. 23.

Lȳc′′a̤-ō′nĭ-à (*wolf-land*). Wild district of Asia Minor, containing towns of Derbe, Lystra, and Iconium, Acts xiv. 6-11. Twice visited by Paul.

Lȳ′çĭà. A southwestern district of Asia Minor, with Myra and Patara as cities, Acts xxi. 2 ; xxvii. 5.

Lȳd′dà (*strife*). Hebrew Lud or Lod. Now Lidd or Ludd. In Sharon plain, 9 miles east of Joppa, Acts ix. 32.

Lȳd′ĭ-à (*Lydus land*). (1) A province of Asia Minor, on Mediterranean. Cities, Sardis, Thyatira,

Philadelphia, 1 Macc. viii. 8. (2) Woman convert of Thyatira, Acts xvi. 14.

Lȳ-sā′nĭ-as (*that drives away sorrow*). Tetrarch of Abilene, Luke iii. 1.

Lȳs′ĭa̤s (*dissolving*). Claudius Lysias, captain of the band that rescued Paul, Acts xxi.–xxiv. 1-9. (2) Governor of southern Syria, 1 Macc. iii. 32.

Lȳ-sĭm′a̤-chus. (1) Translator of Esther, Esth. xi. 1. (2) Brother of Menelaus, 2 Macc. iv. 29-42.

Lȳs′trà (*dissolving*). City of Lycaonia, where Paul was honored, Acts xiv. 6-18 ; and stoned, 19-21.

M

Mā′a̤-cah (*oppression*). (1) A wife of David, 2 Sam. iii. 3. Maachah, 1 Chr. iii. 2. (2) A petty kingdom, N. E. of Palestine, 2 Sam. x. 6-8. Syria-maachah, 1 Chr. xix. 6, 7.

Mā′a̤-chah (*oppression*). (1) Daughter of Nahor, Gen. xxii. 24. (2) A Gathite, 1 Kgs. ii. 39. (3) Wife of Rehoboam, 1 Kgs. xv. 2. (4) Concubine of Caleb, 1 Chr. ii. 48. (5) A Benjamitess, 1 Chr. vii. 15, 16. (6) Wife of Jehiel, 1 Chr. viii. 29. (7) Father of Hanan, 1 Chr. xi. 43. (8) A Simeonite, 1 Chr. xxvii. 16.

Ma̤-ăch′a̤-thī. Maachathites. People of Maacah, Deut. iii. 14 ; Josh. xii. 5.

Ma̤-ăd′āi (*ornament*). Son of Bani, Ez. x. 34.

Mā′′a̤-dī′ah. A returned priest, Neh. xii. 5. Moadiah, vs. 17.

Ma̤-ā′ī (*merciful*). A Levite, Neh. xii. 36.

Ma̤-ăl′eh=a̤-crăb′bim, Josh. xv. 3. Scorpion pass. [AKRABBIM.]

Ma̤-ā′nī, 1 Esdr. ix. 34. [BAANA.]

Mā′a̤-răth (*open*). Town in Judah, Josh. xv. 59.

Mā′′a̤-sē′ĭah (*work of God*). (1) Returned Levites and captive families, Ez. x. 18, 21, 22, 30 ; Neh. iii. 23 ; viii. 4, 7 ; x. 25 ; xi. 5, 7 ; xii. 41, 42. (2) Father of Zephaniah, Jer. xxi. 1. (3) Father of Zedekiah, Jer. xxix. 21. (4) A porter, 1 Chr. xv. 18-20. (5) Son of Adaiah, 2 Chr. xxiii. 1. (6) Others in 2 Chr. xxvi. 11 ; xxviii. 7 ; xxxiv. 8 ; Jer. xxxv. 4.

Mā′ath (*small*). An ancestor of Christ, Luke iii. 26.

Mā′ăz (*wrath*). Son of Ram, 1 Chr. ii. 27.

Mā′′a̤-zī′ah (*consolation*). Two priests, 1 Chr. xxiv. 18 ; Neh. x. 8.

Măb′dā-ī, 1 Esdr. ix. 34. [BENAIAH.]

Măc′a̤-lon, 1 Esdr. v. 21. [MICHMASH.]

Măc′ca̤-bēeṣ (*hammer*). The Asmonean princes who upheld the cause of Jewish independence, B. C. 166-40. The two Apocryphal books of Maccabees contain their history.

Măç′′e-dō′nĭ-à (*extended*). The ancient empire north of Greece proper, whose greatest kings were Philip and Alexander the Great. Often visited by Paul, who made here his first European converts, Acts xvi. 9-12 ; xvii. 1-15 ; xx. 1-6.

Măch′ba̤-nāi (*stout*). A Gadite chief, 1 Chr. xii. 13.

Măch′be̤-nah (*cloak*). Person or place, 1 Chr. ii. 49.

Mā′chī (*decrease*). Father of the Gadite spy, Num. xiii. 15.

Mā′chĭr (*sold*). (1) Eldest son of Manasseh, Num. xxxii. 39 ; Josh. xvii. 1. (2) Son of Ammiel, 2 Sam. ix. 4 ; xvii. 27.

Mā′chĭr-ītes. Descendants of Machir, Num. xxvi. 29.

Măch′mas, 1 Macc. ix. 73. [MICHMASH.]

Măch′′nä-dē′bāi (*liberal*). Son of Bani, Ez. x. 40.

Măch-pē′lah (*double*). Abraham's burial cave at Hebron, Gen. xxiii. 17-19 ; xxv. 9 ; xlix. 29-32 ; l. 13.

Măd′a-ī (*middle*). Son of Japheth, and progenitor of the Medes, Gen. x. 2.

Mā′dĭ-an, Acts vii. 29. [MIDIAN.]

Măd-măn′nah (*dunghill*). Town in southern Judah, near Gaza, Josh. xv. 31.

Măd′men (*dunghill*). A place in Moab, Jer. xlviii. 2.

Măd-mē′nah (*dunghill*). Town in Benjamin, Isa. x. 31.

Măd′ness. Lunacy and passionate outburst, John x. 20.

Mā′dŏn (*strife*). Ancient city of Canaan, Josh. xi. 1; xii. 19.

Măg′bĭsh (*gathering*). Person or place, Ez. ii. 30.

Măg′da-lȧ (*tower*). Village on W. shore of Sea of Galilee, Matt. xv. 39. Magadan in R. V.

Măg′dĭ-el (*praise*). A duke of Edom, Gen. xxxvi. 43.

Mā′gĕd, 1 Macc. v. 36. [MAKED.]

Mā′gī (*priests*). Oriental priests and learned men. A Median and Persian caste of royal advisers, Jer. xxxix. 3; Matt. ii. 1–11.

Măg′ĭc (*of Magi*). The magician's art. Acting through occult agencies. Potent in Oriental religions, Ex. vii., viii. Forbidden, Lev. xix. 31; xx. 6.

Mā′gŏg (*Gog's region*). (1) Second son of Japheth, and his people, Gen. x. 2. (2) Gog's land; probably Scythia, Ezek. xxxviii. 2; xxxix. 2–6. (3) Symbolical enemies, Rev. xx. 7–9.

Mā′gôr=mĭs′sa-bĭb (*fear everywhere*). Pashur, who imprisoned Jeremiah, Jer. xx. 1–3.

Măg′pĭ-ăsh (*moth killer*). A co-covenanter, Neh. x. 20.

Mā-hā′lah (*sickness*). A Manassite, 1 Chr. vii. 18.

Mā-hā′la-lē′′el (*God's praise*). (1) Son of Cainan, Gen. v. 12–17. Maleleel, Luke iii. 37. (2) A Judahite, Neh. xi. 4.

Mā′ha-lath (*harp*). (1) Wife of Esau, Gen. xxviii. 9. (2) Wife of Rehoboam, 2 Chr. xi. 18. (3) The tune or the instrument, Ps. liii., lxxxviii. titles.

Mā′ha-lī (*sick*), Ex. vi. 19. [MAHLI.]

Mā′′hȧ-nā′im (*two camps*). Place where Jacob met the angels, Gen. xxxii. 2. Afterwards a Levitical town in Gad, Josh. xxi. 38; 2 Sam. ii. 8–12.

Mā′hȧ-neh=dăn (*camp of Dan*). Located as in Judg. xiii. 25; xviii. 12.

Mȧ-hăr′a-ī (*swift*). One of David's captains, 2 Sam. xxiii. 28; 1 Chr. xi. 30; xxvii. 13.

Mā′hath (*grasping*). Two Kohathite Levites, 1 Chr. vi. 35; 2 Chr. xxix. 12.

Mā′hȧ-vīte. Designation of one of David's captains, 1 Chr. xi. 46.

Mȧ-hā′zĭ-ŏth (*visions*). Son of Heman, 1 Chr. xxv. 4, 30.

Mā′hĕr=shăl′′al-hăsh′=băz (*speeding to the prey*). Name of Isaiah's son, symbolizing the Assyrian conquest of Damascus and Samaria, Isa. viii. 1–4.

Măh′lah (*disease*). Daughter of Zelophehad, Num. xxvii. 1–11.

Măh′lī (*sickly*). (1) A Levite, Num. iii. 20. Mahali, Ex. vi. 19. (2) Another Levite, 1 Chr. vi. 47.

Măh′lītes. Descendants of Mahli, Num. iii. 33.

Măh′lon (*sickly*). Ruth's first husband, Ruth i. 2–5; iv. 9, 10.

Mā′hol (*dancing*). Father of the four wise men, 1 Kgs. iv. 31.

Mā′kăz (*end*). Unidentified place, 1 Kgs. iv. 9.

Mā′kĕd. City of Gilead, 1 Macc. v. 26–36.

Măk-hē′loth (*meeting place*). A desert encampment, Num. xxxiii. 25.

Măk-kē′dah (*shepherd place*). An ancient Canaanite city, Josh. x. 10–30; xii. 16; xv. 41.

Măk′tesh (*mortar*). Denounced quarter of Jerusalem, Zeph. i. 11.

Măl′a-chī (*God's messenger*). Last of minor prophets. Nothing known of nativity or lineage. Contemporary with Nehemiah, B. C. 445–433. His book foretells the coming of Christ and John the Baptist.

Măl′cham (*their king*). (1) A Benjamite, 1 Chr. viii. 9. (2) The idol Molech, Zeph. i. 5.

Măl-chī′ah (*king*). (1) A Levite, 1 Chr. vi. 40. (2) Jeremiah's prison-keeper, Jer. xxxviii. 6. (3) Returned captives, Ez. x. 25, 31; Neh. iii. 14; viii. 4; xi. 12.

Măl′chĭ-el (*God's king*). An Asherite and founder of Malchielites, or Birzavith, Gen. xlvi. 17; Num. xxvi. 45; 1 Chr. vii. 31.

Măl-chī′jah (*king*). Priests and returned captives, 1 Chr. xxiv. 9; Ez. x. 25, 31; Neh. iii. 11; xii. 42.

Măl-chī′ram (*king of height*). Son of Jehoiachin, 1 Chr. iii. 18.

Măl′chĭ=shū′ȧ (*king of help*). Son of Saul, 1 Chr. ix. 39. Melchishua, 1 Sam. xiv. 49.

Măl′chus (*ruling*). The one whose ear Peter cut off, Matt. xxvi. 51; Luke xxii. 50.

Mȧ-lē′le-el, Luke iii. 37. [MAHALALEEL.]

Măl′lŏs. City in Cilicia, 2 Macc. iv. 30.

Măl′lŏ-thī (*fulness*). Chief of the 19th musical course, 1 Chr. xxv. 4, 26.

Măl′lōws (*soft*). Jews'-mallows of the East, used for pot-herbs, Job xxx. 4.

Măl′luch (*ruling*). Levites, 1 Chr. vi. 44; Ez. x. 29. 32; Neh. x. 4; xii. 2.

Măm′mon (*riches*). A Chaldee word used by Christ, Matt. vi. 24; Luke xvi. 9.

Măm′′nĭ-tȧ-naī′mus. 1 Esdr. ix. 34. [MATTANIAH.]

Măm′rē (*strength*). The Amorite chief who gave his name to the plain where Abraham dwelt, Gen. xiv. 13–24. Hebron, Gen. xiii. 19.

Mȧ-mū′chus, 1 Esdr. ix. 30. [MALLUCH.]

Măn. Adam, *ruddy*, Gen. i. 26. The human race, Gen. v. 2; viii. 21. As distinguished from woman, Deut. xxii. 5; 1 Sam. xvii. 33. Mortal, Isa. xiii. 14.

Măn′a-ĕn (*comforter*). A Christian teacher at Antioch, Acts xiii. 1.

Măn′a-hăth (*rest*). (1) A Horite progenitor of the Manahethites, Gen. xxxvi. 23; 1 Chr. ii. 52. (2) Place or person, 1 Chr. viii. 6.

Mȧ-năs′seh (*forgetting*). (1) First son of Joseph, Gen. xli. 51. The tribe divided and occupied both sides of Jordan, Josh. xvi., xvii. (2) Son and successor of Hezekiah on the throne of Judah, B. C. 698–643. Idolatrous, 2 Kgs. xxi. 1–18. Captive in Babylon; repented; restored, 2 Chr. xxxiii. 1–20. (3) Returned captives, Ez. x. 30, 33.

Mȧ-năs′sēs. (1) King Manasseh, Matt. i. 10. (2) Manasseh, Joseph's son, Rev. vii. 6.

Mȧ-năs′sītes. Descendants of Manasseh (1), Deut. iv. 43; Judg. xii. 4.

Măn′drāke (*field speaker*). A narcotic plant, resembling rhubarb, bearing a yellow, aromatic fruit, Gen. xxx. 14–16; S. of Sol. vii. 13.

Mā′nĕh. The mina; a variable Hebrew weight, Ezek. xlv. 12.

Măn′ger (*eating place*). Feeding crib or trough for cattle. The stall, and even the cattleyard, Luke ii. 7–16; xiii. 15.

Mā′nī, 1 Esdr. ix. 30. [BANI.]

Măn′na (*what is this?*). The bread substitute sent to the wandering Israelites, Ex. xvi. 14–36; Num. xi. 7–9; Deut. viii. 3; Josh. v. 12.

Mȧ-nō′ah (*rest*). Father of Samson, Judg. xiii. 1–23.

Măn′slāy-er. The involuntary manslayer found escape in a city of refuge, Num. xxxv. 22, 23; Deut. xix. 5.

BIBLE DICT

Măn'tle (*hand-woven*). Blanket, Judg. iv. 18. Garment, 1 Sam. xv. 27. Sleeved wrapper, Isa. iii. 22. Chief outer garment, 1 Kgs. xix. 13–19.

Mā'och (*breast-bound*). A Gathite, 1 Sam. xxvii. 2.

Mā'on (*dwelling*). Town in Judah, Josh. xv. 55; 1 Sam. xxiii. 24, 25.

Mā'on-ītes. Mehunims, Judg. x. 12.

Mā'rå (*bitter*). Naomi so called herself, Ruth i. 20.

Mā'rah (*bitter*). The desert spring whose waters were sweetened, Ex. xv. 22–25; Num. xxxiii. 8, 9.

Măr'a-lah (*trembling*). A border of Zebulun, Josh. xix. 11.

Măr'an=ā'thå. "Our Lord cometh," 1 Cor. xvi. 22.

Măr'ble (*shining*). Any white or shining stone is meant, 1 Kgs. vii. 9–12; Esth. i. 6; Rev. xviii. 12.

Măr-chĕs'van. [BUL.]

Măr'cus, Col. iv. 10; Phile. 24; 1 Pet. v. 13. [MARK.]

Măr''dŏ-chē'us. Mordecai in Apoc.

Mā-rē'shah (*hill-top*). (1) A Hebronite, 1 Chr. ii. 42. (2) Lowland city of Judah, Josh. xv. 44; 2 Chr. xi. 8; xiv. 9–12.

Măr'ĭ-mŏth, 2 Esdr. i. 2. [MERAIOTH.]

Mărk (*polite, shining*). John Mark, Acts xii. 12, 25; xv. 37. John, Acts xiii. 5, 13. Mark, Acts xv. 39. Convert of Peter, 1 Pet. v. 13. Companion of Paul, Col. iv. 10. Author of second Gospel, which was probably written in Rome.

Mā'roth (*bitter*). Town in Judah, Micah i. 12.

Măr'riåge (*husbanding*). Monogamous, Gen. ii. 18–24; vii. 13. Polygamous, Gen. iv. 19; vi. 2. Forbidden within certain degrees, Lev. xviii.; Deut. xxvii.; and with foreigners, Ex. xxxiv. 16. Monogamy re-instituted, Matt. xix. 5, 6; Mark x. 5–10.

Mărs' Hill, Acts xvii. 22. [AREOPAGUS.]

Măr'se-nå (*worthy*). A Persian prince, Esth. i. 14.

Măr'thå (*lady*). Sister of Mary and Lazarus, Luke x. 38–42; John xi. 5–28.

Măr'tyr (*witness*). Matt. xviii. 16; Luke xxiv. 48. Who seals his faith with his blood, Acts xxii. 20; Rev. ii. 13; xvii. 6.

Mā'rȳ (*rebellion*). Greek form of Miriam. (1) The betrothed of Joseph and mother of Christ, Matt. i. 18–25; xii. 46; Mark vi. 3; Luke viii. 19; John ii. 1–5; xix. 26; Acts i. 14. (2) Wife of Cleophas, Matt. xxvii. 56, 61; xxviii. 1–9; Mark xvi. 1–8; Luke xxiv. 1–10. (3) Mother of John Mark, Acts xii. 12; Col. iv. 10. (4) Sister of Martha and Lazarus, Luke x. 41, 42; John xi., xii. (5) Mary Magdalene; *i. e.*, of Magdala, Matt. xxviii. 1–10; Mark xvi. 1–10; Luke xxiv. 10; John xx. 1–18. (6) A Roman convert, Rom. xvi. 6.

Măs'å-lŏth. Place in Arbela, 1 Macc. ix. 2.

Măs'chĭl. "Didactic," or "melody." Title of thirteen Psalms.

Măsh (*drawn out*). Son of Aram, Gen. x. 23. Meshech, 1 Chr. i. 17.

Mā'shal (*entreaty*). A Levitical city in Asher, 1 Chr. vi. 74. Misheal, Josh. xix. 26. Mishal, Josh. xxi. 30.

Măs'phå, 1 Macc. iii. 46. [MIZPEH.]

Măs're-kah (*vineyard*). City in Edom, Gen. xxxvi. 36; 1 Chr. i. 47.

Măs'så (*gift*). Son of Ishmael, Gen. xxv. 14; 1 Chr. i. 30.

Măs'sah (*temptation*). Meribah; spot of temptation, Ex. xvii. 7; Ps. xcv. 8, 9; Heb. iii. 8.

Mā-thụ'sa-lå, Luke iii. 37. [METHUSELAH.]

Mā'tred (*shoving*). Mother of Mehetabel, Gen. xxxvi. 39.

Mā'trī (*rain*). A Benjamite family, 1 Sam. x. 21.

Mā'trĭx (*mother*). The womb, Ex. xiii. 12–15.

Măt'tan (*gift*). (1) A priest of Baal, 2 Kgs. xi. 18. (2) Father of Shephatiah, Jer. xxxviii. 1.

Măt'tạ-nah (*gift*). A desert encampment, Num. xxi. 18, 19.

Măt''tạ-nī'ah (*God's gift*). (1) Original name of Zedekiah, 2 Kgs. xxiv. 17. (2) Levites, 1 Chr. ix. 15; xxv. 4, 16; 2 Chr. xx. 14; xxix. 13; Ez. x. 26, 27, 30, 37; Neh. xi. 17; xiii. 13.

Măt'tạ-thả (*God's gift*). Grandson of David, Luke iii. 31.

Măt'tạ-thah. One who returned, Ez. x. 33.

Măt''tạ-thī'as (*God's gift*). (1) Two of Christ's progenitors, Luke iii. 25, 26. (2) Father of the Maccabees, 1 Macc. ii.

Măt''te-nā'ī. Levites, Ez. x. 33, 37; Neh. xii. 19.

Măt'than. Grandfather of Joseph, Matt. i. 15.

Măt''thạ-nī'as, 1 Esdr. ix. 37. [MATTANIAH.]

Măt'that, Luke iii. 24, 29. [MATTHAN.]

Măt'thew (*gift of God*). Contraction of Mattathias. The Apostle and Evangelist. Levi in Luke, v. 27–29. Son of Alphæus, Mark ii. 14. Tax-collector at Capernaum when called, Matt. ix. 9. His gospel is first of N. T. Its original claimed to be the Hebrew, or Syro-Chaldaic, of Palestine. Time of writing placed at A. D. 60–66. Gist, to establish Jesus as O. T. Messiah.

Măt-thī'as (*God's gift*). Apostle allotted to fill the place of Judas, Acts i. 26.

Măt''tĭ-thī'ah (*God's gift*). Levites, 1 Chr. ix. 31; xv. 18; xvi. 5; Ez. x. 43; Neh. viii. 4.

Măt'tŏck (*hoe*). A crude hoe, Isa. vii. 25.

Maul (*hammer*). Heavy wooden hammer, Prov. xxv. 18. Battle axe, Jer. li. 20.

Măz''ị-tī'as, 1 Esdr. ix. 35. [MATTITHIAH.]

Măz'za-rŏth. The twelve signs of the zodiac, Job xxxviii. 32.

Mĕad'ōw (*mead*). Water-plant, flag, Gen. xli. 2. Cave, Judg. xx. 33.

Mē'ah (*hundred*). Tower in Jerusalem, Neh. iii. 1; xii. 39.

Mĕ-ā'rah (*cave*). Unknown place, Josh. xiii. 4.

Mĕas'ures. Hebrew standard weights and measures provided for, Lev. xix. 35, 36; Deut. xxv. 13–15. Money passed by weight till era of coinage. For various weights and measures, *see* respective titles.

Mĕat. In Bible sense, food of any kind, Gen. i. 29; Lev. ii.; vi. 14–23; Matt. xv. 37; Luke xxiv. 41.

Mĕat=ŏf'fĕr-ing. Conditions in Lev. ii.; vi. 14–23.

Mĕ-bŭn'nāi (*building*). One of David's warriors, 2 Sam. xxiii. 27. Sibbechai, 2 Sam. xxi. 18. Sibbecai. 1 Chr. xi. 29.

Mĕch''e-rath-īte'', 1 Chr. xi. 36. Maacathite. [MAACAH.]

Mē'dăd (*love*). A camp prophet, Num. xi. 26, 27.

Mē'dan (*strife*). A son of Abraham, Gen. xxv. 2; 1 Chr. i. 32.

Mĕd'e-bå (*quiet waters*). Town in Reuben, east of Dead Sea, Num. xxi. 30; Josh. xiii. 9; 1 Macc. ix. 36.

Mēdes. Medians, 2 Kgs. xvii. 6.

Mē'dĭ-å (*middle land*). Madai, Gen. x. 2; Media, Esth. i. 3. The country northwest of Persia and south of Caspian Sea. Held early sway in Babylon. Tributary to Assyria, B. C. 880. Independent, and conquered Babylon; next, Assyria. Empire at its height, B. C. 625. Overthrown by Persian Cyrus, B. C. 558. Medo-Persian empire overthrown by Alexander the Great, B. C. 330, Isa. xiii. 17, 18; Esth. i. 19; Dan. vi. 8–12; 1 Chr. v. 26.

Mĕd'ĭ-çine (*of a physician*). The science, as known in Egypt, was copied by Hebrews, Lev. xiii.–

xv. ; 2 Kgs. viii. 29 ; Prov. iii. 8 ; vi. 15.

Mĕ-ḡĭd′dô (*crowded*). A city in plain of Esdrae-lon, Josh. xii. 21 ; xvii. 11 ; 2 Kgs. xxiii. 29. Also the plain, or valley, itself and scene of Barak's victory over Sisera, and of Josiah's death, Judg. iv. 6–17 ; 2 Chr. xxxv. 20–24.

Mĕ-ḡĭd′don, Zech. xii. 11. [MEGIDDO.]

Mĕ-hĕt′a-beel. Ancestor of Shemaiah, Neh. vi. 10.

Mĕ-hĕt′a-bel (*God-favored*). Wife of Hadar, king of Edom, Gen. xxxvi. 39.

Mĕ-hī′dȧ (*famed*). His family returned, Ez. ii. 52 ; Neh. vii. 54.

Mĕ′hĭr (*price*). A Judahite, 1 Chr. iv. 11.

Mĕ-hŏl′ath-īte. Meholaite, 1 Sam. xviii. 19.

Mĕ-hū′ja-el (*smitten*). Son of Irad, Gen. iv. 18.

Mĕ′hū-man (*true*). Chamberlain of Ahasuerus, Esth. i. 10.

Mĕ-hū′nĭmṣ (*dwellings*). Maonites, 2 Chr. xxvi. 7 ; Ez. ii. 50.

Mĕ-jär′kŏn (*yellow waters*). Town in Dan, Josh. xix. 46.

Mĕk′o-nah (*pedestal*). Town in Judah, Neh. xi. 28.

Mĕl″a-tī′ah (*saved*). Assistant wall-builder, Neh. iii. 7.

Mĕl′chī (*king*). Two ancestors of Christ, Luke iii. 24, 28.

Mĕl-chī′ah (*royal*). A priest, Jer. xxi. 1.

Mĕl-chī′el. Governor of Bethulia, Judith vi. 15.

Mĕl-chĭṣ′e-dĕc. N. T. form of Melchizedek, Heb. v.–vii.

Mĕl″chī-shu̧′ȧ, 1 Sam. xiv. 49. [MALCHISHUA.]

Mĕl-chĭz′e-dek (*king of justice*). King of Salem, and priest, Gen. xiv. 18–20. Prototype of Christ, Ps. cx. 4 ; Heb. v.–vii.

Mĕ′le-ȧ (*full*). Ancestor of Joseph, Luke iii. 31.

Mĕ′lech (*king*). Son of Micah, 1 Chr. ix. 41.

Mĕl′i-cū, Neh. xii. 14. [MALLUCH.]

Mĕl′i-tȧ (*honey*). The island of Malta, in Medi-terranean, south of Sicily, Acts xxvii., xxviii.

Mĕl′on (*mellow apple*). Melons of Egypt prized as food, Num. xi. 5.

Mĕl′zar. Common noun — steward or tutor, Dan. i. 11, 16.

Mĕm′phis (*abode of the good*). Ancient Egyp-tian city, Hos. ix. 6, on west bank of Nile, near pyra-mids and sphinx, and 10 miles south of Cairo. Noph, Isa. xix. 13 ; Jer. ii. 16 ; Ezek. xxx. 13–16.

Mĕ-mū′can. A Persian prince, Esth. i. 14–21.

Mĕn′a-hĕm (*comforter*). Usurper of Israel's throne. Idolatrous and cruel. Reigned B. C. 772–761, 2 Kgs. xv. 14–22.

Mĕ′nan. Ancestor of Joseph, Luke iii. 31.

Mĕ′nĕ. First word of Belshazzar's warning. Entire, "Mene," he is numbered ; "Tekel," he is weighed ; "Upharsin," they are divided, Dan. v. 25–28.

Mĕn″e-lā′us. High priest, 2 Macc. iv. 23.

Mĕ-nĕs′the-us. Father of Apollonius, 2 Macc. iv. 21.

Mĕ-ŏn′e-nĭm (*enchanter*). Unlocated plain, Judg. ix. 37.

Mĕ-ŏn′o-thāi. A Judahite, 1 Chr. iv. 14.

Mĕph′a-ăth (*height*). Levitical town in Reuben, Josh. xiii. 18.

Mĕ-phĭb′o-shĕth (*idol breaker*). (1) A son of Saul, 2 Sam. xxi. 8. (2) Son of Jonathan, 2 Sam. iv. 4 ; ix. 6–13 ; xvi. ; xix. 24–30.

Mĕ′rab (*increase*). Daughter of Saul, 1 Sam. xiv. 49 ; xviii. 17.

Mĕr″a-ī′ah (*rebellion*). A priest, Neh. xii. 12.

Mĕ-rā′ioth (*rebellious*). Three priests, 1 Chr. vi. 6 ; Ez. vii. 3 ; Neh. xii. 15.

Mĕ′ran, Bar. iii. 23. [MEDAN.]

Mĕ-rā′rī (*bitter*). (1) Third son of Levi, and head of family of Merarites, Gen. xlvi. 11 ; Ex. vi. 16 ; Num. iii. 17 ; iv. 29–33 ; Josh. xxi. 7–30. (2) Father of Judith, Judith viii. 1.

Mĕr″a-thā′im (*double rebellion*). Symbol of Chaldea, Jer. l. 21.

Mĕr-cū′rĭ-us (*Mercury*). Name applied to Paul in Lystra, Acts xiv. 12.

Mĕr′cy̆ Seat. Lid of the ark, Ex. xxv. 17–22 ; hence, covering, or atonement for sin, Heb. ix. 5.

Mĕ′rĕd (*rebellion*). Son of Ezra, 1 Chr. iv. 17.

Mĕr′e-mŏth (*heights*). Three priests, Ez. viii. 33 ; x. 36 ; Neh. x. 5.

Mĕ′rēṣ (*lofty*). One of Ahasuerus' wise men, Esth. i. 14.

Mĕr′ī-bah (*strife*). A desert encampment, where the rock was smitten, Ex. xvii. 7. Kadesh, Num. xx. 13–24.

Mĕr′ib=bā′al, 1 Chr. viii. 34 ; ix. 40. [MEPHIB-OSHETH, 2.]

Mĕ-rō′dăch (*death*). A Babylonian god, and royal surname, Jer. l. 2.

Mĕ-rō′dăch = băl′a-dăn (*Baal - worshipper*). King of Babylon, B. C. 721, Isa. xxxix. 1. Berodach-baladan, 2 Kgs. xx. 12.

Mĕ′rom (*heights*). The lake on Jordan above Sea of Galilee, Josh. xi. 5–7.

Mĕ-rŏn′o-thīte. Designations in 1 Chr. xxvii. 30 ; Neh. iii. 7.

Mĕ′rŏz (*refuge*). Unknown place, Judg. v. 23.

Mĕ′sech, Mĕ′shech (*drawn out*). (1) Son of Ja-pheth, Gen. x. 2 ; Ezek. xxvii. 13 ; xxxii. 26 ; Ps. cxx. 5. (2) 1 Chr. i. 17. [MASH.]

Mĕ′shȧ (*freed*). (1) A Joktanite border, Gen. x. 30. (2) A king of Moab, 2 Kgs. iii. 4. (3) Son of Ca-leb, 1 Chr. ii. 42. (4) A Benjamite, 1 Chr. viii. 9.

Mĕ′shach (*guest*). Chaldean name of Mishael, Daniel's companion, Dan i. 6, 7 ; iii.

Mĕ-shĕl″e-mī′ah (*rewarded*). A Levite gate-keeper, 1 Chr. ix. 21 ; xxvi. 1–9.

Mĕ-shĕz′a-be-el (*delivered*). Returned captives, Neh. iii. 4 ; x. 21 ; xi. 24.

Mĕ-shĭl′le-mĭth (*repaid*). A priest, 1 Chr. ix. 12.

Mĕ-shĭl′le-mŏth (*repaid*). (1) A chief of Ephraim, 2 Chr. xxviii. 12. (2) Meshillemith, Neh. xi. 13.

Mĕ-shŭl′lam (*friend*). (1) Ancestor of Shaphan, 2 Kgs. xxii. 3. (2) Son of Zerubbabel, 1 Chr. iii. 19. (3) A Gadite, 1 Chr. v. 13. (4) Three Benjamites, 1 Chr. viii. 17 ; ix. 7, 8. (5) Eleven Levites, in Ez. and Neh.

Mĕ-shŭl′le-mĕth (*friend*). Mother of King Amon, 2 Kgs. xxi. 19.

Mĕs′o-bā-īte″. Designation of Jasiel, 1 Chr. xi. 47.

Mĕs″o-po-tā′mĭ-ȧ (*between rivers*). The coun-try between the rivers Tigris and Euphrates, Gen. xxiv. 10 ; Deut. xxiii. 4 ; Judg. iii. 8–10 ; Acts ii. 9 ; vii. 2.

Mĕs-sī′ah (*anointed*). Applied to regularly anointed priests or kings, Lev. iv. 3, 5, 16 ; 1 Sam. ii. 10, 35 ; xii. 3–5. The Greek *kristos*, "anointed," takes its place in N. T., except in John i. 41 ; iv. 25.

Mĕs-sī′as. Greek form of Messiah, John i. 41 ; iv. 25.

Mĕt′als (*mined*). Precious and useful metals, such as gold, silver, tin, lead, copper, and iron, known to Hebrews and much used, Gen. ii. 11, 12 ; Num. xxxi. 22.

Mĕ-tē′rus. His family returned, 1 Esdr. v. 17.

Mĕ′theg=ăm′mah (*curb of the city*). A Philistine stronghold, 2 Sam. viii. 1.

Mĕ-thŭ'ṣạ-el (*man of God*). Father of Lamech, Gen. iv. 18.

Mĕ-thŭ'ṣẹ-lah (*dart - man*). Grandfather of Noah ; oldest of antediluvians. Lived 969 years, Gen. v. 21–27.

Mĕ-ū'nim, Neh. vii. 52. [MEHUNIMS.]

Mĕz'a-hăb (*gilded*). An Edomite, Gen. xxxvi. 39.

Mī'a-mĭn (*right hand*). Two who returned, Ez. x. 25 ; Neh. xii. 5.

Mĭb'har (*chosen*). One of David's heroes, 1 Chr. xi. 38.

Mĭb'sam (*odorous*). (1) An Ishmaelite, Gen. xxv. 13. (2) A Simeonite, 1 Chr. iv. 25.

Mĭb'zar (*fort*). A duke of Edom, Gen. xxxvi. 42.

Mī'cah (*God-like*). (1) The erratic Ephraimite whose story is told in Judg. xvii., xviii. (2) Sixth of the minor prophets. Prophesied B. C. 750–698. He foretells the destruction of Samaria and Jerusalem, and prefigures the Messiah. (3) A Reubenite, 1 Chr. v. 5. (4) Grandson of Jonathan, 1 Chr. viii. 34, 35. (5) A Levite, 1 Chr. xxiii. 20. (6) Father of Abdon, 2 Chr. xxxiv. 20.

Mī-cā'ịah (*God-like*). A Samarian prophet, 1 Kgs. xxii. 8–38 ; 2 Chr. xviii. 7–27.

Mī'chå. Persons in 2 Sam. ix. 12 ; Neh. x. 11 ; xi. 17, 22.

Mī'chaël (*God-like*). (1) Prince of angels, Dan. x. 13 ; xii. 1 ; Rev. xii. 7. (2) Characters in Num. xiii. 13 ; 1 Chr. v. 13, 14 ; vi. 40 ; vii. 3 ; viii. 16 ; xii. 20 ; xxvii. 18 ; 2 Chr. xxi. 2 ; Ez. viii. 8.

Mī'chah, 1 Chr. xxiv. 24, 25. [MICAH, 5.]

Mī-chā'ịah (*God-like*). (1) Full form of Micah in 2 Chr. xxxiv. 20. (2) Same as Micha, 1 Chr. ix. 15 ; Neh. xii. 35. (3) A priest, Neh. xii. 41. (4) Wife of Rehoboam and mother of Abijah, king of Judah, 2 Chr. xiii. 2. (5) A prince and teacher of the law, 2 Chr. xvii. 7. (6) Son of Gemariah, Jer. xxxvi. 11–14.

Mī'chal. Daughter of Saul and wife of David, 1 Sam. xiv. 49 ; xxv. 44 ; 2 Sam. iii. 14 ; vi. 23.

Mī-chē'as, 2 Esdr. i. 39. [MICAH.]

Mĭch'mash (*hidden*). Noted town in Benjamin, 1 Sam. xiii. 11 ; Isa. x. 28. Michmas, Ez. ii. 27.

Mĭch'mĕ-thah (*stony*). Border mark of Manasseh, Josh. xvii. 7.

Mĭch'rī (*precious*). A Benjamite, 1 Chr. ix. 8.

Mĭch'tam. Musical term for six Psalms.

Mĭd'din (*measures*). City in Judah, Josh. xv. 61.

Mĭd'ĭ-an (*strife*). Son of Abraham, and founder of Midianites, Gen. xxv. 2 ; Ex. iii. 1 ; Num. xxii. 4 ; Judg. vii. 13.

Mĭg'dal=ĕl (*tower of God*). Fenced city of Naphtali, Josh. xix. 38.

Mĭg'dal=găd (*tower of Gad*). Town in Judah, Josh. xv. 37.

Mĭg'dol (*tower*). Place in Egypt, Ex. xiv. 2 ; Num. xxxiii. 7, 8. Perhaps same in Jer. xliv. 1 ; xlvi. 14.

Mĭg'rŏn (*pinnacle*). Town near Gibeah, 1 Sam. xiv. 2 ; Isa. x. 28.

Mĭj'a-mĭn (*right hand*). (1) Chief of the 6th priestly course, 1 Chr. xxiv. 9. (2) Co-covenanters, Neh. x. 7.

Mĭk'loth (*staves*). (1) A Benjamite, 1 Chr. viii. 32 ; ix. 37, 38. (2) One of David's generals, 1 Chr. xxvii. 4.

Mĭk-ne'ịah (*God-possessed*). A temple musician, 1 Chr. xv. 18–21.

Mĭl''ạ-lā'ī (*eloquent*). A priest, Neh. xii. 36.

Mĭl'cah (*queen*). (1) Wife of Nahor, Gen. xi. 29 ; xxiv. 15–47. (2) Daughter of Zelophehad, Num. xxvi. 33 ; Josh. xvii. 3.

Mĭl'com. [MOLECH.]

Mīle. Roman mile in Matt. v. 41 ; 1618 yards.

Mī-lē'tus, Mī-lē'tum (*red*). City in Ionia, Acts xx. 15–38 ; 2 Tim. iv. 20.

Mĭlk, Of cows, goats, camels, and sheep a favorite Oriental food, Gen. xxxii. 15 ; Deut. xxxii. 14. Symbol of fertility, Josh. v. 6 ; Heb. v. 12.

Mĭll (*grind*). A mortar and pestle ; or, two stones, upper and nether, the former turned by hand, Job xli. 24 ; Isa. xlvii. 1, 2 ; Matt. xxiv. 41. Millstones not pawnable, Deut. xxiv. 6.

Mĭl'let. Here a grass ; abroad a cereal, like broom-corn, Ezek. iv. 9.

Mĭl'lō (*mound*). (1) A rampart of Jerusalem, 2 Sam. v. 9 ; 1 Kgs. ix. 15. (2) Where Joash was murdered, 2 Kgs. xii. 20. (3) A Shechem family, Judg. ix. 6–20.

Mī'na. [MANEH.]

Mī-nī'a-mĭn. Levites, 2 Chr. xxxi. 15 ; Neh. xii. 17, 41.

Mĭn'ĭs-tẽr (*assistant*). Attendant, Ex. xxiv. 13 ; Josh. i. 1 ; 1 Kgs. xix. 21 ; Ez. viii. 17. Magistrate, Rom. xiii. 6. Preacher and teacher, 1 Cor. iv. 1 ; 2 Cor. iii. 6. Celestial high priest, Heb. viii. 1–3.

Mĭn'nī. Part of Armenia, Jer. li. 27.

Mĭn'nith (*division*). An Ammonite section east of Jordan, Judg. xi. 33 ; Ezek. xxvii. 17.

Mĭn'strel (*minister*). A musician employed, or strolling, 1 Sam. x. 5 ; xvi. 16 ; 2 Kgs. iii. 15. Professional mourners, Matt. ix. 23.

Mĭnt. An aromatic herb, varieties numerous, Matt. xxiii. 23 ; Luke xi. 42.

Mĭph'kăd. A Jerusalem gate, Neh. iii. 31.

Mĭr'ạ-cle (*wonderful*). In scripture, a supernatural event, Num. xxii. 28 ; 1 Kgs. xvii. 6 ; Matt. ix. 18–33 ; xiv. 25.

Mĭr'ĭ-am (*rebellion*). (1) Sister of Moses and Aaron. Musician and prophetess, Ex. ii. 4–10 ; xv. 20, 21 ; Num. xii. 1–15 ; xx. 1 ; 1 Chr. vi. 3. (2) A Judahite, 1 Chr. iv. 17.

Mĭr'må (*fraud*). A Benjamite, 1 Chr. viii. 10.

Mĭr'rôr (*wonder at*). Egyptian mirrors, which the Hebrew women affected, were highly polished metal plates, chiefly of copper, Ex. xxxviii. 8 ; Job xxxvii. 18 ; 1 Cor. xiii. 12.

Mĭs'gab (*high*). Place in Moab, Jer. xlviii. 1.

Mĭsh'ạ-el (*what God is*). (1) Uncle of Moses, Ex. vi. 22 ; Lev. x. 4. (2) Ezra's assistant, Neh. viii. 4. (3) Daniel's captive companion, Dan. i. 6–19 ; ii. 17.

Mī'shal, Mī'shẹ-al (*entreaty*). Levitical town in Asher, Josh. xix. 26 ; xxi. 30.

Mī'sham (*fleet*). A Benjamite, 1 Chr. viii. 12.

Mĭsh'må (*hearing*). (1) An Ishmaelite, Gen. xxv. 14. (2) A Simeonite, 1 Chr. iv. 25.

Mĭsh-măn'nah (*fatness*). A Gadite, 1 Chr. xii. 10.

Mĭsh'ra-ītes. Colonists from Kirjath-jearim, 1 Chr. ii. 53.

Mĭs'pẹ-rĕth. A returned captive, Neh. vii. 7.

Mĭs're-photh=mā'im (*burning waters*). Place in northern Palestine, Josh. xi. 8 ; xiii. 6.

Mīte (*little*). Half a farthing, or fifth of a cent, Mark xii. 41–44 ; Luke xxi. 1–4.

Mĭth'cah (*sweetness*). A desert encampment, Num. xxxiii. 28.

Mĭth'nīte. A designation, 1 Chr. xi. 43.

Mĭth're-dăth (*Mithra-given*). (1) Cyrus' treasurer, Ez. i. 8. (2) Persian governor of Samaria, Ez. iv. 7.

Mĭth''rĭ-dā'tēs, 1 Esdr. ii. 11. [MITHREDATH.]

Mī'tre (*turban*). The priestly head-dress of linen, wrapped round the head, and bearing a frontal inscription, "Holiness to the Lord," Ex. xxviii. 4, 36–39 ; xxix. 6 ; xxxix. 28–30 ; Lev. viii. 9 ; xvi. 4.

Mĭt''y̆-lē'nĕ (*curtailed*). Chief town of the island of Lesbos, Acts xx. 14, 15.

Mīxed Multitude. Camp followers, Ex. xii. 38; Num. xi. 4; Neh. xiii. 3.

Mī′zar (*little*). Unlocated hill, Ps. xlii. 6.

Mĭz′pah, Mĭz′peh (*watch tower*). (1) Jacob's covenant heap, Gen. xxxi. 47–49. (2) Mizpeh-moab, 1 Sam. xxii. 3. (3) Hivite section in northern Palestine, Josh. xi. 3–8. (4) A city in Judah, Josh. xv. 38. (5) A city of Benjamin, Josh. xviii. 26; 1 Sam. x. 17–21; 1 Kgs. xv. 22.

Mĭz′par, Ez. ii. 2. [MISPERETH.]

Mĭz′ra-ĭm (*red soil*). Son of Ham, Gen. x. 6. The O. T. word translated Egypt, Gen. xlv. 20; Isa. xi. 11.

Mĭz′zah (*fear*). Grandson of Esau, Gen. xxxvi. 13.

Mnā′son (*remembering*). A Cyprian convert, Acts xxi. 16.

Mō′ab (*of his father*). Son of Lot by his daughter, and progenitor of the Moabites. The country lay east of the Dead Sea and south of the Arnon, Num. xxi. 13–15; xxii.; Judg. xi. 18. Though idolatrous, worshipping Chemosh, they were a strong, progressive people, holding Israel subject, Judg. iii. 12–14; but finally subdued, 15–30; 2 Sam. viii. 2; Isa. xv., xvi.; Jer. xlviii.; Ruth i., ii.

Mō′ab-īte Stōne. The celebrated stone found at Dhiban (Dibon) in Moab, in A. D. 1868, on which is engraved, in Hebrew-Phœnician, the record of Mesha, king of Moab's, rebellion against Israel, 2 Kgs. iii. 4–27.

Mō″a-dī′ah, Neh. xii. 17. [MAADIAH.]

Mŏch′mur. Brook or wady, Judith vii. 18.

Mō′din. Burial ground of the Maccabees, near Lydda, 1 Macc. xiii. 25.

Mō′eth, 1 Esdr. viii. 63. [NOADIAH.]

Mŏl′a-dah (*birth*). City in south Judah, Josh. xv. 26; xix. 2; Neh. xi. 26.

Mōle (*dirt thrower*). No ground-moles in Palestine. Chameleon or lizard in Lev. xi. 30; and rat or weasel in Isa. ii. 20.

Mō′lech (*king*). Moloch, Acts vii. 43. Milcom, 1 Kgs. xi. 5. Malcham, Zeph. i. 5. Tutelary divinity (fire-god) of the Ammonites, Lev. xviii. 21; 2 Kgs. xxiii. 10.

Mō′lī, 1 Esdr. viii. 47. [MAHLI.]

Mō′lid (*begetter*). A Judahite, 1 Chr. ii. 29.

Mō′lŏch, Acts vii. 43. [MOLECH.]

Mŏm′dis, 1 Esdr. ix. 34. [MAADAI.]

Mon′ĕy (*warning*). Gold and silver passed by weight among Hebrews, Gen. xvii. 13; xxiii. 16; though the ring tokens of Egypt may have been current, Gen. xx. 16; xxxvii. 28. Persian coined money (daric or dram) came into use after the captivity, Ez. ii. 69; Neh. vii. 70–72. The Maccabees first coined Jewish money, B. C. 140, — shekels and half shekels of gold and silver, with minor copper coins. The N. T. coins, Matt. xvii. 27; xxii. 19; x. 29; v. 26; Mark xii. 42, were Roman or Grecian.

Mon′ĕy Chān′gers. Those who made a business of supplying the annual half-shekel offering at a premium, Ex. xxx. 13–15; Matt. xxi. 12; Mark xi. 15.

Month (*moon*). Hebrew month lunar, from new moon to new moon, Num. x. 10; xxviii. 11–14. Intercalary month every three years. Months named, but usually went by number, Gen. vii. 11; 2 Kgs. xxv. 3. *See* month names in place.

Moon (*measurer*). Conjointly with the sun, appointed for signs, seasons, days, months and years. Regulator of religious festivals, Gen. i. 14–18. Worship of, forbidden, Deut. iv. 19. Used largely figuratively, Isa. xiii. 10; Matt. xxiv. 29; Mark xiii. 24.

Mō′ras-thīte. Of Moresheth, Jer. xxvi. 18; Mic. i. 1.

Môr′de-cāi (*little*). A Benjamite captive at court of Ahasuerus, and deliverer of Jews from plot of Haman, Esth.

Mō′reh (*teacher*). (1) First halting place of Abram in Canaan, Gen. xii. 6. (2) Hill in valley of Jezreel, Judg. vii. 1.

Mŏr′esh-eth=găth (*possession of Gath*). Place named in Mic. i. 14.

Mō″-rī′ah (*chosen*). (1) The land in which Abraham offered up Isaac, Gen. xxii. 2. (2) Site of Solomon's temple in Jerusalem, 2 Sam. xxiv. 24; 1 Chr. xxi. 24–27; 2 Chr. iii. 1, 2.

Môr′tar. (1) Hollow vessel of wood or stone, in which corn was ground with a pestle, Num. xi. 8; Prov. xxvii. 22. (2) Various cementing substances used in building, as bitumen, clay, and ordinary mixture of sand and lime, Gen. xi. 3; Ex. i. 14; Lev. xiv. 42; Isa. xli. 25.

Mō″-sē′ra (*bonds*). A desert encampment, Deut. x. 6.

Mō″-sē′roth, Num. xxxiii. 30. [MOSERA.]

Mō′ses (*drawn out*). The great leader and lawgiver of the Hebrews. Son of Amram, a Levite. Born in Egypt, about B. C. 1571. Adopted by Pharaoh's daughter, liberally educated, fled to Midian, Ex. ii. Called to lead the Exode, Ex. iii.–xix. Promulgated the law, Ex. xx.–xl.; Lev.; Num.; Deut. Died on Nebo, aged 120 years. Reputed author of Pentateuch and Job.

Mō″-sŏl′lam, 1 Esdr. viii. 44. [MESHULLAM.]

Mŏth. Frequent scripture references to the destructiveness of this insect, Job xiii. 28; Ps. xxxix. 11; Isa. l. 9; Matt. vi. 19.

Moth′er. Held in high respect by Hebrews, Ex. xx. 12. Often used for grandmother, or remote ancestor, Gen. iii. 20; 1 Kgs. xv. 10.

Môurn′ing. Very public and demonstrative, Gen. xxiii. 2; xxxvii. 29–35. Period, seven to seventy days, Gen. l. 3; 1 Sam. xxxi. 13. Hired mourners, Eccl. xii. 5; Matt. ix. 23. Methods, weeping, tearing clothes, wearing sackcloth, sprinkling with ashes or dust, shaving head, plucking beard, fasting, laceration, etc.

Mouse (*pilferer*). Many species in Palestine, but Bible word generic, Lev. xi. 29; 1 Sam. vi. 4; Isa. lxvi. 17.

Mōw′ing. Reaping with sickle, Ps. cxxix. 7 "King's mowings," perhaps a royal right of pasturage, Am. vii. 1.

Mō′za (*departing*). (1) A son of Caleb, 1 Chr. ii. 46. (2) Descendant of Saul, 1 Chr. viii. 36, 37.

Mō′zah (*departing*). City in Benjamin, Josh. xviii. 26.

Mŭl′bĕr-rў (*dark berry*). Translation disputed, 2 Sam. v. 23, 24; 1 Chr. xiv. 14. The bacah or balsam tree is probably meant.

Mūle. Mules not bred in Palestine, but imported, 2 Sam. xiii. 29; 1 Kgs. i. 33; 2 Chr. ix. 24. Warm springs meant in Gen. xxxvi. 24.

Mŭp′pim (*serpent*). A Benjamite, Gen. xlvi. 21. Shupham, Num. xxvi. 39.

Mûr′der (*death*). Punished with death, Ex. xxi. 12; Num. xxxv. 30, 31; but cities of refuge provided for the escape of the involuntary slayer, Ex. xxi. 13; Num. xxxv. 32; Deut. xix. 1–13.

Mûr′rain (*die*). The malignant cattle disease which constituted the fifth Egyptian plague, Ex. ix. 1–7.

Mū′shī (*deserted*). A son of Merari, Ex. vi. 19; Num. iii. 20.

Mū′shītes. Descendants of Mushi, Num. iii. 33; xxvi. 58.

Mū′sĭc (*muse*). Anciently known, Gen. iv. 21; xxxi. 27; Job xxi. 12. Vocal and instrumental, reached highest perfection in temple choirs, 2 Sam. vi. 5; 1 Chr. xxv. Usual instruments, harp, timbrel, psalter, trumpet, flute, pipe, etc.

Mŭs′tard (*must*). The black mustard of the East grows quite large and strong, Matt. xiii. 31, 32; xvii. 20; Mark iv. 31, 32; Luke xvii. 6.

BIBLE DICT

Mŭth=lăb′ben. Enigmatical title to Ps. ix.

Mўn′dus. Town in Caria, 1 Macc. xv. 23.

My′rȧ (*weeping*). Ancient seaport of Lycia, in Asia Minor, Acts xxvii. 5.

Mўrrh (*bitter*). A gum resin much prized and variously used, Ex. xxx. 23; Esth. ii. 12; Ps. xlv. 8; Prov. vii. 17; Mark xv. 23; John xix. 39.

Mўr′tle. A bushy evergreen, whose flowers, leaves, and berries were much used by Hebrews for perfume, ornament, and spicery, Isa. xli. 19; lv. 13; Zech. i. 8–11.

Mўs′ĭȧ (*beech land*). Northwestern district of Asia Minor, Acts xvi. 7, 8.

N

Nā′am (*pleasant*). Son of Caleb, 1 Chr. iv. 15.

Nā′ạ-mah (*pleasing*). (1) Sister of Tubal-cain, Gen. iv. 22. (2) A wife of Solomon and mother of King Rehoboam, 1 Kgs. xiv. 21; 2 Chr. xii. 13. (3) Town in Judah, Josh. xv. 41.

Nā′ạ-man (*pleasantness*). (1) The leprous Syrian, cured by Elisha's orders, 2 Kgs. v. (2) Founder of the Naamites, Gen. xlvi. 21; Num. xxvi. 40.

Nā′ạ-math-īte″. Designation of Job's friend, Zophar, Job ii. 11.

Nā′ạ-mītes, Num. xxvi. 40. [NAAMAN, 2.]

Nā′ạ-rah (*youth*). Wife of Ashur, 1 Chr. iv. 5, 6.

Nā′ạ-rāi (*youthful*). One of David's warriors, 1 Chr. xi. 37. Paarai, 2 Sam. xxiii. 35.

Nā′ạ-răn, 1 Chr. vii. 28. [NAARATH.]

Nā′ạ-răth (*youthful*). A border of Ephraim, Josh. xvi. 7.

Nȧ-ăsh′on, Ex. vi. 23. [NAHSHON.]

Nȧ-ăs′son. Greek form of Nahshon, Matt. i. 4; Luke iii. 32.

Nā′ạ-thus. Son of Addi, 1 Esdr. ix. 31.

Nā′băl (*fool*). The Carmelite shepherd who refused food to David, 1 Sam. xxv.

Năb″ạ-rī′as, 1 Esdr. ix. 44. [ZECHARIAS.]

Nā′băth-ītes, 1 Macc. v. 25. [NEBAIOTH.]

Nā′bŏth (*fruits*). The vineyardist of Jezreel whom Jezebel caused to be murdered, 1 Kgs. xxi. 1–16; 2 Kgs. ix. 26.

Năb″ū-chȯ-dŏn′ȯ-sȯr. Apocryphal form of Nebuchadnezzar.

Nā′chŏn (*ready*). Owner of the threshing-floor where the over-zealous Uzzah died, 2 Sam. vi. 6, 7.

Nā′chŏr, Josh. xxiv. 2; Luke iii. 34. [NAHOR.]

Nā′dăb (*liberal*). (1) Son of Aaron, Ex. vi. 23; xxiv. 1. Struck dead for offering strange fire, Lev. x. 1–3. (2) Son and successor of Jeroboam on throne of Israel, B. C. 954–953. Slain by Baasha, his successor, 1 Kgs. xv. 25–31. (3) A Judahite, 1 Chr. ii. 28. (4) Uncle of Saul, 1 Chr. viii. 30.

Nȧ-dăb′ạ-thȧ. Place east of Jordan, 1 Macc. ix. 37.

Năg′gē (*shining*). Ancestor of Joseph, Luke iii. 25.

Nā′ha-lăl (*pasture*). Levitical city in Zebulun, Josh. xxi. 35.

Nȧ-hā′lĭ-el (*God's valley*). Israelite encampment in Ammon, Num. xxi. 19.

Nȧ-hăl′lăl, Josh. xix. 15. [NAHALAL.]

Nā′hạ-lŏl, Judg. i. 30. [NAHALAL.]

Nā′ham (*comforter*). Brother of Hodiah, 1 Chr. iv. 19.

Nā-hăm′ạ-nī (*compassionate*). One who returned, Neh. vii. 7.

Nȧ-hăr′ạ-ī (*snorer*). Joab's armor-bearer, 1 Chr. xi. 39.

Nā′ha-rī, 2 Sam. xxiii. 37. [NAHARAI.]

Nā′hăsh (*serpent*). (1) A king of Ammon, 1 Sam. xi. 1–11; 2 Sam. x. 2. (2) Father of Abigail, 2 Sam. xvii. 25.

Nā′hăth (*rest*). (1) A duke of Edom, Gen. xxxvi. 13, 17. (2) Two Levites, 1 Chr. vi. 26; 2 Chr. xxxi. 13.

Năh′bī (*secret*). The spy of Naphtali, Num. xiii. 14.

Nā′hôr (*snoring*). (1) Abraham's grandfather, Gen. xi. 22–25. (2) Abraham's brother, Gen. xi. 27–29.

Năh′shon (*enchanter*). A prince of Judah, Num. i. 7.

Nā′hum (*comforter*). Seventh of minor prophets. Probably an exile in Assyria. Approximate time of prophecy, B. C. 726–698. It relates to the fall of Nineveh. Noted for vigor and beauty.

Nā′ĭ-dus, 1 Esdr. ix. 31. [BENAIAH.]

Năil (*hold, claw*). Nails of captives to be pared, Deut. xxi. 12. Ordinary metal nail, 1 Chr. xxii. 3; stylus, Jer. xvii. 1; stake, Isa. xxxiii. 20; tent-peg wood or metal, Ex. xxvii. 19; Judg. iv. 21, 22.

Nā′in (*beauty*). A village in Galilee, now Nein, Luke vii. 11.

Nā′ioth (*dwellings*). Samuel's dwelling place and school in Ramah, 1 Sam. xix. 18–23; xx. 1.

Nȧ-nē′ȧ. A Persian goddess, 1 Macc. vi. 1–4.

Nȧ-ō′mī (*my delight*). Mother-in-law of Ruth, Ruth i. 2, etc.

Nā′phish (*pleasure*). Son of Ishmael, Gen. xxv. 15; 1 Chr. i. 31.

Năph′ĭ-sī, 1 Esdr. v. 31. [NEPHUSIM.]

Năph′tạ-lī (*wrestling*). Fifth son of Jacob, Gen. xxx. 8. Large tribe at Sinai and Jordan, Num. i. 43; xxvi. 50. Allotment in northern Canaan, Josh. xix. 32–39. Tribe carried captive in reign of Pekah, 2 Kgs. xv. 29. For "mount Naphtali," Josh. xx. 7, read, mountains of Naphtali.

Năph′thȧr (*cleansing*). Naphtha, 2 Macc. i. 36.

Năph′tu-hĭm. A Mizraite (Egyptian) tribe, Gen. x. 13.

Năr-çĭs′sus (*narcotic*). Roman friend of Paul, Rom. xvi. 11.

Närd (*smell*). [SPIKENARD.]

Năs′băs. Nephew of Tobit, Tob. xi. 18.

Nā′sith, 1 Esdr. v. 32. [NEZIAH.]

Nā′sôr, 1 Macc. xi. 67. [HAZOR.]

Nā′than (*given*). (1) Distinguished prophet, and royal adviser and biographer of David and Solomon, 2 Sam. vii. 2–17; xii. 1–22; 1 Kgs. i. 8–45; 1 Chr. xxix. 29; 2 Chr. ix. 29. (2) A son of David, 1 Chr. iii. 5; Luke iii. 31. (3) Father of one of David's warriors, 2 Sam. xxiii. 36. (4) A returned captive, Ez. viii. 16.

Nȧ-thăn′ạ-el (*gift of God*). (1) A disciple of Christ, and native of Cana in Galilee, John i. 47–51; xxi. 2. (2) Ancestor of Judith, Judith viii. 1.

Năth″ạ-nī′as, 1 Esdr. ix. 34. [NATHAN.]

Nā′than=mē′lech. Chamberlain under King Josiah, 2 Kgs. xxiii. 11.

Nā′um (*comfort*). Father of Amos, Luke iii. 25.

Nāve. Hub of a wheel, 1 Kgs. vii. 33.

Nā′vē, Ecclus. xlvi. 1. [NUN.]

Năz′ạ-rēne. Inhabitant of Nazareth; Jesus so-called, Matt. ii. 23. Nazarenes, followers of Jesus, Acts xxiv. 5.

Năz′ạ-rĕth (*separated*). A town of Galilee, now En-nazirah. Home of Jesus, Matt. iv. 13; Mark i. 9; Luke i. 26; iv. 16, 29; John i. 45, 46.

Năz′a-rīte (*separated*). One bound by a temporary or life vow, Num. vi. 1–21; Am. ii. 11, 12; Acts xxi. 20–26.

Nē′ah (*shaking*). A Zebulun boundary mark, Josh. xix. 13.

Nē-ăp′ȯ-lis (*new city*). Seaport in northern Greece; now Kavalla, Acts xvi. 11; xx. 1, 6.

Nē″a-rī′ah (*child of God*). (1) A Judahite, 1 Chr. iii. 22. (2) A chief of Simeon, 1 Chr. iv. 42.

Nĕb′a̤-ī (*budding*). A co-covenanter, Neh. x. 19.

Nĕ-bā′ḷoth, Nĕ-bā′joth (*heights*). Son of Ishmael, Gen. xxv. 13; 1 Chr. i. 29; Isa. lx. 7.

Nĕ-băl′lat (*secret folly*). Re-peopled town of Benjamin, Neh. xi. 34.

Nĕ′băt (*view*). Father of King Jeroboam, 1 Kgs. xi. 26; xii. 2-15.

Nĕ′bŏ (*prophet*). (1) A mountain of Moab, whence Moses viewed the promised land, Deut. xxxii. 49; xxxiv. 1. (2) A Reubenite city, Num. xxxii. 3, 38; xxxiii. 47. (3) Father of returned captives, Ez. ii. 29. (4) A Chaldean god, presiding over learning. Counterpart of the Greek Hermes, Isa. xlvi. 1; Jer. xlviii. 1.

Nĕb′′u-chăd-nĕz′zar (*may Nebo protect*). King of Babylonish Empire, B. C. 605-561. Brought empire to greatest height of prosperity. Defeated Pharaoh-necho at Carchemish, Jer. xlvi. 2-26. Captured Jerusalem three different times, 2 Kgs. xxiv., xxv.; Dan. i.-iv.

Nĕb′′u-chăd-rĕz′zar. Jeremiah so writes Nebuchadnezzar.

Nĕb′′u-shăs′ban (*Nebo saves*). A chief of eunuchs under Nebuchadnezzar, Jer. xxxix. 13.

Nĕb′′u-zär′a̤-dan (*whom Nebo favors*). Chief of Nebuchadnezzar's body-guard, 2 Kgs. xxv. 8-21; Jer. xxxix. 11; xl. 1-5.

Nĕ′chŏ, 2 Chr. xxxv. 20. [PHARAOH-NECHO.]

Nĕ-cō′dan, 1 Esdr. v. 37. [NEKODA.]

Nĕd′′a̤-bī′ah (*driven*). A Judahite, 1 Chr. iii. 18.

Nĕg′ĭ-nah. Singular of Neginoth, Ps. lxi. title.

Nĕg′ĭ-nŏth. Stringed musical instruments. Title to Ps. iv., vi., liv., lv., lxvii., lxxvi.; Hab. iii. 19.

Nĕ-hĕl′a̤-mīte (*dreamer*). Designation of Shemaiah, Jer. xxix. 24-32.

Nĕ-he̤-mī′ah (*consolation*). (1) The Hebrew captive who returned, as leader of his people, to rebuild Jerusalem and administer its affairs. His book, 16th of O. T., B. C. 445-433, tells of his work. (2) Leader of returning captives, Ez. ii. 2; Neh. vii. 7. (3) An assistant wall-builder, Neh. iii. 16.

Nĕ′′he̤-mī′as, 1 Esdr. v. 8, 40. [NEHEMIAH.]

Nĕ′hĭ-lŏth (*perforated*). The flute and similar wind instruments, Ps. v. title.

Nĕ′hum (*comfort*). A returned captive, Neh. vii. 7.

Nĕ-hŭsh′ta̤ (*brazen*). Mother of King Jehoiachin, 2 Kgs. xxiv. 8.

Nĕ′hŭsh-tan (*little brazen thing*). Name of the preserved brazen serpent destroyed by King Hezekiah, 2 Kgs. xviii. 4.

Nē′ĭ-el (*God-moved*). An Asherite boundary, Josh. xix. 27.

Nē′keb (*cave*). A boundary town of Naphtali, Josh. xix. 33.

Nĕ-kō′da̤ (*famous*). Two fathers of returned captive families, Ez. ii. 48, 60.

Nĕ-mū′el (*God's day*). (1) A Reubenite, Num. xxvi. 9. (2) A Simeonite, Num. xxvi. 12; Jemuel, Gen. xlvi. 10.

Nĕ-mū′el-ītes′′. Descendants of Nemuel (2), Num. xxvi. 12.

Nĕ′pheg (*sprout*). (1) Korah's brother, Ex. vi. 21. (2) Son of David, 2 Sam. v. 15.

Nĕph′ew (*grandson*). Grandchild or descendant, Job xviii. 19; Isa. xiv. 22.

Nĕ′phish, 1 Chr. v. 19. [NAPHISH.]

Nĕ-phĭsh′e̤-sĭm. His children returned, Neh. vii. 52.

Nĕph′ta̤-lī, Tob. i. 2-5. [NAPHTALI.]

Nĕph′tha-līm, Matt. iv. 13. [NAPHTALI.]

Nĕp′tha-līm, Rev. vii. 6. [NAPHTALI.]

Nĕph′to-ah (*opening*). A spring on boundary of Judah and Benjamin, Josh. xv. 9.

Nĕ-phū′sim, Ez. ii. 50. [NEPHISHESIM.]

Nĕr (*lamp*). Grandfather of Saul, 1 Chr. viii. 33; ix. 39. Appears as an uncle of Saul in 1 Chr. ix. 36.

Nē′re-us. A Roman Christian, Rom. xvi. 15.

Nĕr′gal (*hero*). A man-lion god of Assyria, corresponding to Mars, 2 Kgs. xvii. 30.

Nĕr′gal=shă-rē′zer (*fire prince*). A prince of Babylon who released Jeremiah, Jer. xxxix. 3, 13.

Nĕ′rī (*lamp*). Son of Melchi, Luke iii. 27.

Nĕ-rī′ah (*light*). Father of Baruch, Jer. xxxii. 12.

Nĕ-rī′as, Bar. i. 1. [NERIAH.]

Nĕt. Used for hunting and fishing, Isa. xix. 8; Matt. xiii. 47. Style, manufacture, and method borrowed from Egyptians.

Nĕ-thăn′e̤-el (*gift of God*). Persons of this name in Num. i. 8; 1 Chr. ii. 14; xv. 24; xxiv. 6; xxvi. 4; 2 Chr. xvii. 7; xxxv. 9; Ez. x. 22; Neh. xii. 21, 36.

Nĕth′′a̤-nī′ah (*God-given*). Persons in 2 Kgs. xxv. 23; 1 Chr. xxv. 2, 12; 2 Chr. xvii. 8; Jer. xxxvi. 14; xl. 8.

Nĕth′ĭ-nĭm (*dedicated*). Assistant priests. A class, or order, associated with the temple service and wardship, 1 Chr. ix. 2; Ez. vii. 24; viii. 17-20.

Nĕ-tō′phah (*dropping*). Town near Bethlehem, Ez. ii. 22; Neh. vii. 26.

Nĕ-tŏph′a̤-thī. Netophathites. Dwellers in Netophah, 1 Chr. ii. 54; Neh. xii. 28.

Nĕt′tle (*sting*). The stinging nettle in Isa. xxxiv. 13; Hos. ix. 6. Supposably the prickly acanthus in Job xxx. 7; Prov. xxiv. 31; Zeph. ii. 9.

New Moon, 1 Sam. xx. 5. [MOON.]

New Tĕs′ta̤-ment. [BIBLE.]

New Year. [TRUMPETS, FEAST OF.]

Nĕ-zī′ah (*famed*). Returned Nethinim, Ez. ii. 54; Neh. vii. 56.

Nē′zib (*pedestal*). Lowland city of Judah, Josh. xv. 43.

Nĭb′hăz (*barker*). The Avite god, in form of a dog-headed man, introduced into Samaria, 2 Kgs. xvii. 31.

Nĭb′shăn (*sandy*). Town in wilderness portion of Judah, Josh. xv. 62.

Nĭ-cā′nor (*conqueror*). (1) A governor of Judea. 1 Macc. iii. 38. (2) One of the first seven deacons of the early church, Acts vi. 1-6.

Nĭc′′o̤-dē′mus (*people's victor*). The Pharisee ruler and timid convert who assisted at Christ's sepulture, John iii. 1-10; vii. 50; xix. 39.

Nĭc-o-lā′ĭ-tanes. An heretical sect condemned in Rev. ii. 6, 15.

Nĭc′o̤-lăs (*people's victor*). Native of Antioch. First a Jewish and then a Christian convert. One of the first seven deacons, Acts vi. 5.

Nĭ-cŏp′o̤-lĭs (*city of victory*). Many ancient cities of this name. Probably the one in Epirus is meant, Tit. iii. 12.

Nī′ġer (*black*). Surname of Simeon, Acts xiii. 1.

Nīght. The Hebrew day, from sunset to sunset, embraced the entire night, Gen. i. 5. Death, John ix. 4; sin, 1 Thess. v. 5; sorrow, sin, and death, Rev. xxi. 25; xxii. 5.

Nīght=ha̤wk. An unclean bird, Lev. xi. 16; supposably the owl or night-jar.

Nīle (*dark blue*). The great river of Egypt, worshipped as a god, famous for its annual and fertilizing overflows and its many mouths. Name not mentioned in scripture, but alluded to as "the river," Gen. xli. 1; Ex. ii. 3; vii. 21; "the river of Egypt," Gen. xv. 18; "flood of Egypt," Am. viii. 8; Sihor, "black," Josh. xiii. 3; Shihor, "dark blue," 1 Chr. xiii. 5; "Nachal of Egypt," "river of Cush," etc.

Nĭm′rah (*clear*). City in Gad, east of Jordan, Num. xxxii. 3.

Nĭm′rim (*clear*). A stream in Moab, S. E. of

Dead Sea, Isa. xv. 6 ; Jer. xlviii. 34.

Nĭm′rŏd (*brave*). Son of Cush. A renowned hunter, city builder, empire founder in Shinar (Babylonia), Gen. x. 8-12 ; 1 Chr. i. 10.

Nĭm′shī (*rescued*). Father of Jehu, 1 Kgs. xix. 16 ; 2 Kgs. ix. 2, 14.

Nĭn′e-veh (*dwelling of Ninus*). Capital of Assyria, on river Tigris. Founded by Asshur, Gen. x. 11. At height of its wealth and splendor during time of Jonah and Nahum, and burden of their prophecies. Taken by Medes about B. C. 750, and destroyed by combined Medes and Babylonians, B. C. 606. Jonah ; Nah. i.-iii ; Zeph. ii. 13. Among the ruins of Nineveh, which was supposed to embrace Nimrud and other suburbs, have been discovered many palaces and temples, and a richly sculptured obelisk whose references are to Syria and Israel.

Nĭn′e-vītes. Dwellers in Nineveh, Luke xi. 30.

Nī′san (*standard*). Abib, Ex. xiii. 4. First month of Hebrew sacred and seventh of civil year, corresponding to parts of March and April, Ex. xii. 2.

Nĭs′rŏch (*great eagle*). The eagle headed and winged Assyrian god, 2 Kgs. xix. 37 ; Isa. xxxvii. 38.

Nī′tre. The saltpetre of commerce. Evidently natron or washing soda is meant in Prov. xxv. 20 ; Jer. ii. 22.

Nō (*place*). Ancient Thebes and capital of Upper Egypt. The Diospolis of the Greeks. Situate on both banks of the Nile. Populous and splendid from B. C. 1600 to B. C. 800. Site of many imposing ruins. No-amon, "place of Amon," in marg. notes, Ezek. xxx. 14-16 ; Jer. xlvi. 25 ; Nah. iii. 8.

Nō′a-dī′ah (*met by God*). (1) A Levite, Ez. viii. 33. (2) A hostile prophetess, Neh. vi. 14.

Nō′ah (*rest*). (1) Ninth in descent from Adam, Gen. v. 28-32. Chosen to build the ark, Gen. vi. 8-22. Saved from the flood, with his three sons, Shem, Ham, and Japheth, Gen. vii., viii. Re-peopled the earth, Gen. ix., x. Died at age of 950 years. (2) A daughter of Zelophehad, Num. xxvi. 33.

Nō=ā′mon (*place of Amon*). [No.]

Nŏb (*height*). Levitical city in Benjamin, noted as scene of the massacre of the priests, 1 Sam. xxi. 1 ; xxii. 19-23 ; Neh. xi. 32.

Nō′bah (*barking*). Name given by Nobah to Kenath, Num. xxxii. 42 ; Judg. viii. 11.

Nŏd (*fleeing*). The land to which Cain the murderer fled, Gen. iv. 16.

Nō′dăb (*noble*). An Arab tribe, 1 Chr. v. 19.

Nō′e, N. T. and Apoc. form of Noah, Matt. xxiv. 37 ; Luke iii. 36.

Nō-ē′bá, 1 Esdr. v. 31. [NEKODA.]

Nō′gah (*bright*). A son of David, 1 Chr. iii. 7.

Nō′hah (*rest*). A Benjamite, 1 Chr. viii. 2.

Nŏn. Form of Nun, 1 Chr. vii. 27.

Nŏph, Isa. xix. 13 ; Jer. ii. 16 ; Ezek. xxx. 13. [MEMPHIS.]

Nō′phah (*blast*). Town in Moab, Num. xxi. 30.

Nōṣe=jew′elṣ. Rings worn in the nose. Still affected in the East, Isa. iii. 21.

Nŏv′īçe. "Newly planted." A recent convert, 1 Tim. iii. 6.

Nŭm′bêrṣ (*distribute*). (1) Hebrews used alphabetic letters for notation. They also had preferential numbers, as "three," "seven," "ten," "seventy," etc., Gen. iv. 24 ; Ex. xx. 5-17 ; Num. vii. 13 ; Rev. xv. 1. (2) Fourth book of Bible and Pentateuch. Authorship ascribed to Moses. Chapters i.-x. 10 describe the departure from Sinai ; x. 11-xiv. the marches to borders of Caanan ; xv.-xvi. contain laws ; xx.-xxxvi. describe events leading to the passage of Jordan and the conquest.

Nū-mē′nĭ-us. Jonathan's ambassador to Greece and Rome, 1 Macc. xii. 16.

Nŭn (*fish*). Father of Joshua, Ex. xxxiii. 11 ; 1

Chr. vii. 27.

Nûrse (*nourish*). Position of importance and honor among Hebrews, Gen. xxiv. 59 ; xxxv. 8 ; 2 Sam. iv. 4.

Nŷm′phas (*bridegroom*). A Laodicean Christian, Col. iv. 15.

O

Ōak (*strong*). Three varieties in Palestine, usually of great girth and expanse, but not noted for height, Gen. xxxv. 8 ; Judg. vi. 11, 19 ; 2 Sam. xviii. 9-14.

Ōath. Appeals to God to attest the truth of an assertion in early use, Gen. xxi. 23 ; xxvi. 3 ; Heb. vi. 16. Regulated in Ex. xx. 7 ; Lev. xix. 12. Forms: lifting hands, Gen. xiv. 22 ; placing hand under thigh, Gen. xxiv. 2 ; before the altar, 1 Kgs. viii. 31 ; laying hand on the law.

Ō′′ba-dī′ah (*servant of God*). (1) A Judahite, 1 Chr. iii. 21. (2) A chief of Issachar, 1 Chr. vii. 3. (3) Son of Azel, 1 Chr. viii. 38. (4) A Levite, 1 Chr. ix. 16. (5) A Gadite, 1 Chr. xii. 9. (6) A court officer under Ahab, 1 Kgs. xviii. 3-16. (7) A teacher of the law, 2 Chr. xvii. 7. (8) Others, in 1 Chr. xxvii. 19 ; 2 Chr. xxxiv. 12 ; Ez. viii. 9 ; Neh. x. 5 ; xii. 25. (9) Fourth of minor prophets. Prophesied after capture of Jerusalem. His book, 31st of O. T., is a denunciation of Edom. Nothing known of his history.

Ō′bal (*naked*). Son of Joktan, Gen. x. 28. Ebal in 1 Chr. i. 22.

Ŏb′dĭ-à, 1 Esdr. v. 38. [HABAIAH.]

Ō′bed (*servant*). (1) Son of Boaz and Ruth, Ruth iv. 17 ; Luke iii. 32. (2) Descendant of Sheshan, 1 Chr. ii. 37, 38. (3) One of David's warriors, 1 Chr. xi. 47. (4) A temple porter, 1 Chr. xxvi. 7. (5) Father of Azariah, 2 Chr. xxiii. 1.

Ō′bed=ē′dom (*servant of Edom*). (1) He kept the ark for three months, 2 Sam. vi. 10-12 ; 1 Chr. xiii. 13, 14. (2) A temple treasurer, 2 Chr. xxv. 24.

Ō′beth, 1 Esdr. viii. 32. [EBED.]

Ō′bil (*camel-keeper*). David's camel-keeper, 1 Chr. xxvii. 30.

Ŏb-lā′tion (*spread out*). Act of offering. The offering itself, Lev. ii. 4.

Ō′both (*bottles*). An Israelite encampment, east of Moab, Num. xxi. 10 ; xxxiii. 43.

Ō′chĭ-el, 1 Esdr. i. 9. [JEIEL.]

Ŏc′ran (*disturber*). An Asherite, Num. i. 13 ; ii. 27.

Ŏd′′a-när′keṣ. Chief of a nomad tribe, 1 Macc. ix. 66.

Ō′ded (*restoring*). (1) Father of Azariah, 2 Chr. xv. 1. (2) A Samaritan prophet, 2 Chr. xxviii. 9-11.

Ō-dŏl′lam. Greek form of Adullam, 2 Macc. xii. 38.

Ŏf′fẽr-ĭng (*bearing towards*). Either bloody, as of animals, or bloodless, as of vegetables. They embraced the burnt, sin, trespass, peace, and meat offerings, Lev. i.-ix.

Ŏg (*giant*). King of Bashan, last of the giant Rephaim, Num. xxi. 33 ; Deut. i. 4 ; iii. 3-13 ; Josh. ii. 10.

Ō′hăd (*strength*). Son of Simeon, Gen. xlvi. 10.

Ō′hel (*tent*). Son of Zerubbabel, 1 Chr. iii. 20.

Oil (*olive*). Used for preparing food, Ex. xxix. 2 ; anointing, 2 Sam. xiv. 2 ; illuminating, Matt. xxv. 1-13 ; in worship, Num. xviii. 12 ; in consecration, 1 Sam. x. 1 ; in medicine, Mark vi. 13 ; in burial, Matt. xxvi. 12. Types gladness, Ps. xcii. 10.

Oint′ment (*smear*). Highly prized, and made of perfumes in oil. For uses, *see* Oil.

Ŏl′īve. A tree resembling the apple in size and shape, bearing a plum-like fruit, prized for its oil, Gen. viii. 11 ; Deut. vi. 11 ; Job xxiv. 11. Olive wood used in the temple, 1 Kgs. vi. 23, 31-33.

Ŏl′īveṣ, Ŏl′ĭ-vĕt. The mount of Olives, or Olivet,

is the ridge east of Jerusalem, beyond the brook Kidron. So named from its olive-trees. On its slopes were Gethsemane, Bethphage and Bethany, 2 Sam. xv. 30; Zech. xiv. 4; Matt. xxi. 1; Mark xi. 1; Luke xxii. 39; John viii. 1; Acts i. 12.

Ŏ-lŷm'pas (*heavenly*). A Roman Christian, Rom. xvi. 15.

Ŏ-lŷm'pĭ-us. The Grecian Zeus, or Jupiter, dwelling on Olympus, 2 Macc. vi. 2.

Ŏm″a̯-ē'rus, 1 Esdr. ix. 34. [AMRAM.]

Ō'mar (*speaker*). A duke of Edom, Gen. xxxvi. 11, 15.

Ŏ-mĕg'å or **Ŏ-mē'gå** (*great or long O*). Last letter of Greek alphabet, Rev. i. 8.

Ō'mĕr. A Hebrew dry measure, equal to tenth part of an ephah, Ex. xvi. 36.

Ŏm'rĭ (*pupil*). (1) A general under Elah, king of Israel, and eventually king, B. C. 929-918. He built Samaria and made it the capital, 1 Kgs. xvi. 16-28. (2) A Benjamite, 1 Chr. vii. 8. (3) A Judahite, 1 Chr. ix. 4. (4) A chief of Issachar, 1 Chr. xxvii. 18.

Ŏn (*strength*). (1) Grandson of Reuben, Num. xvi. 1. (2) City of Lower Egypt, Gen. xli. 45, 50. Bethshemesh or "house of the sun," Jer. xliii. 13. In Greek, Heliopolis, "city of the sun," Ezek. xxx. 17 marg. Noted for its learning, opulence, temples, shrines, monuments, sphinxes, and religious schools.

Ō'nam (*strong*). (1) Grandson of Seir, Gen. xxxvi. 23. (2) Son of Jerahmeel, 1 Chr. ii. 26.

Ō'nan (*strong*). Second son of Judah, slain for wickedness, Gen. xxxviii. 4-10; Num. xxvi. 19.

Ŏ-nĕs'ĭ-mus (*useful*). Slave of Philemon, at Colosse, in whose behalf Paul wrote the epistle to Philemon, Col. iv. 9; Phile. 10, 15.

Ŏn″e̯-sĭph'o̯-rus (*profit-bearing*). Friend of Paul at Ephesus and Rome, 2 Tim. i. 16-18; iv. 19.

Ŏ-nī'a̯-rĕs. Onias and Areus, 1 Macc. xii. 19.

Ŏ-nī'as. Name of five high priests during time of Maccabees.

Ŏn'ĭon (*one*). The single-bulbed plant growing to perfection in the Nile valley, Num. xi. 5.

Ō'no̊ (*strong*). Town in Benjamin, 1 Chr. viii. 12.

Ō'nus, 1 Esdr. v. 22. [ONO.]

Ŏn'ŷ-chå (*nail*). Incense ingredient; probably burnt seashell, Ex. xxx. 34.

Ō'nŷx (*nail*). A cryptocrystalline quartz, veined and shelled, Ex. xxviii. 9-12; 1 Chr. xxix. 2.

Ō'phel (*hill*). A fortified hill in Jerusalem, 2 Chr. xxvii. 3; Neh. iii. 26; xi. 21.

Ō'phĭr (*fruitful*). (1) Son of Joktan, and his country in Arabia, Gen. x. 29. (2) Place whence the Hebrews drew gold, ivory, peacocks, and woods. Variously located, 1 Kgs. ix. 28; x. 11-22; xxii. 48; 1 Chr. xxix. 4; Job xxviii. 16; Ps. xlv. 9.

Ŏph'nī (*mouldy*). Town in Benjamin, Josh. xviii. 24.

Ŏph'rah (*fawn*). (1) Town in Benjamin, Josh. xviii. 23; 1 Sam. xiii. 17. (2) Native place of Gideon, Judg. vi. 11, 24. (3) Son of Meonothai, 1 Chr. iv. 14.

Ŏr'a̯-cle (*speaking*). In O. T. sense, the holy place whence God declared his will, 1 Kgs. vi. 5; viii. 6. Divine revelation, Acts vii. 38; Rom. iii. 2.

Ō'reb (*raven*). (1) A Midianite chief, Judg. vii. 25. (2) The rock, "raven's crag," east of Jordan, where Oreb fell, Judg. vii. 25; Isa. x. 26.

Ō'ren (*pine*). Son of Jerahmeel, 1 Chr. ii. 25.

Ŏr'gan (*instrument*). The "pipe," or any perforated wind instrument, Gen. iv. 21; Job xxi. 12; Ps. cl. 4.

Ŏ-rī'on (*hunter, Orion*). The constellation, Job ix. 9; xxxviii. 31; Am. v. 8.

Ŏr'na̯-ments (*adornments*). Of infinite variety among Oriental peoples, Gen. xxiv. 22; Isa. iii. 16-25; Jer. ii. 32; Ezek. xvi. 11-19.

Ŏr'nan (*active*). The Jebusite prince from whom David bought the threshing-floor on which he built the altar, 1 Chr. xxi. 15-25. [ARAUNAH.]

Ŏr'pah (*fawn*). Daughter-in-law of Naomi, Ruth i. 4-14.

Ŏr-thō'ṣĭ-as. City of northern Phœnicia, 1 Macc. xv. 37.

Ō-sē'å, 2 Esdr. xiii. 40. [HOSEA.]

Ō'ṣee. Greek form of Hosea, Rom. ix. 25.

Ō-shē'å. Original name of Joshua, Num. xiii. 8.

Ŏs'prāy (*ossifrage, bone-breaker*). An unclean bird; probably the osprey or sea-eagle, Lev. xi. 13; Deut. xiv. 12.

Ŏs'sĭ-frȧge (*bone-breaker*). An unclean bird; the lammergeir, or bearded vulture, Lev. xi. 13; Deut. xiv. 12.

Ŏs'trĭch (*bird*). In Hebrew, "daughter of greediness." In Arabic and Greek "camel-bird." Largest of the bird species, Job xxxix. 13-18.

Ŏth'nī (*lion*). Son of Shemaiah, 1 Chr. xxvi. 7.

Ŏth'nĭ-el (*lion*). A judge of Israel, Josh. xv. 17; Judg. i. 13; iii. 9-11.

Oū'ches (*brooches*). Jewel settings, Ex. xxxix. 6.

Ŏv'en (*arch*). Fixed ovens, Hos. vii. 4. Portable, consisting of a large clay jar, Ex. viii. 3; Lev. xxvi. 26.

Qwl (*howl*). An unclean bird and type of desolation. Five species found in Palestine, Lev. xi. 17; Deut. xiv. 16; Ps. cii. 6; Isa. xxxiv. 11-15.

Ŏx (*sprinkle*). (1) Ancestor of Judith, Judith viii. 1. (2) The male of the cow kind, and in scripture synonymous with bull. Used for plowing, Deut. xxii. 10; threshing, without muzzle, xxv. 4; draught, Num. vii. 3; burden, 1 Chr. xii. 40; beef, Deut. xiv. 4; sacrifices, 1 Kgs. i. 9.

Ō'zem (*strength*). (1) A brother of David, 1 Chr. ii. 15. (2) Son of Jerahmeel, 1 Chr. ii. 25.

Ŏ-zī'as. (1) Governor of Bethulia, Judith vi. 15. (2) Ancestor of Ezra, 2 Esdr. i. 2. (3) N. T. form of Uzziah, Matt. i. 8, 9.

Ō-zī'el. Ancestor of Judith, Judith viii. 1.

Ŏz'nī (*hearing*). Son of Gad, Num. xxvi. 16; Ezbon, Gen. xlvi. 16.

Ŏz'nītes. Descendants of Ozni, Num. xxvi. 16.

Ŏ-zō'rå, 1 Esdr. ix. 24. [SHELAMIAH.]

P

Pā'a̯-rāi (*opening*). One of David's warriors, 2 Sam. xxiii. 35; Naarai, 1 Chr. xi. 37.

Pā'dan (*table-land*), Gen. xlviii. 7. [PADAN-ARAM.]

Pā'dan=ā'ram (*table-land of Aram*). The plain region of Mesopotamia, Gen. xxiv. 10; xxv. 20; xxviii. 2-7; xxxi. 18; xxxiii. 18; xxxv. 9-26; xlvi. 15.

Pā'don (*escape*). His children returned, Ez. ii. 44.

Pā'gĭ-el (*God-allotted*). A chief of Asher, Num. i. 13; ii. 27; vii. 72, 77; x. 26.

Pā'hath=mō'ab (*ruler of Moab*). His children returned, Ez. ii. 6; viii. 4; Neh. iii. 11.

Pā'ī, 1 Chr. i. 50. [PAU.]

Pāint. Much used in East as cosmetic and beautifier, 2 Kgs. ix. 30; Jer. iv. 30. Houses, walls, beams, idols, painted, Jer. xxii. 14; Ezek. xxiii. 14. Painting as a fine art not encouraged by Hebrews.

Păl'açe. Royal residence, 1 Kgs. vii. 1-12; citadel, 1 Kgs. xvi. 18; fortress, 2 Kgs. xv. 25; entire royal court, Dan. i. 4; capital city, Esth. ix. 12. In N. T. any stately residence, Matt. xxvi. 3; Luke xi. 21.

Pā′lal (*judge*). An assistant wall-builder, Neh. iii. 25.

Păl″es-tī′nȧ, Păl′es-ţīne (*land of sojourners*). Philistia, land of the Philistines, Ps. lx. 8; lxxxiii. 7. Palestina, Ex. xv. 14; Isa. xiv. 29, 31. Palestine, Joel iii. 4. Canaan, Gen. xii. 5; Ex. xv. 15; Holy Land, Zech. ii. 12. The indefinitely bounded region promised to Abraham, lying between the Mediterranean Sea and Jordan River and Dead Sea. It also embraced the Hebrew settlements beyond Jordan, Gen. xv. 18; xvii. 8; Num. xxiv. 2–12; Deut. i. 7.

Păl′lu (*famous*). Son of Reuben, Ex. vi. 14.

Păl′lu-ītes. Descendants of Pallu, Num. xxvi. 5.

Pălm′er=worm (*pilgrim-worm*). Cankerworm, or caterpillar, Joel i. 4; ii. 25; Amos iv. 9.

Pălm=tree (*hand-leaved*). The date-palm. Once grew luxuriantly in Palestine. Evergreen and stately, often rising to 100 feet, Ex. xv. 27; Deut. xxxiv. 3; Judg. i. 16; 1 Kgs. vi. 32; S. of Sol. vii. 7.

Pạl′sȳ (*paralysis*). Partial or total death of muscle and nerve, 1 Kgs. xiii. 4–6; Matt. iv. 24; Luke vi. 6.

Păl′tī (*deliverance*). The Benjamite spy, Num. xiii. 9.

Păl′tĭ-el (*deliverance*). A prince of Issachar, Num. xxxiv. 26.

Pặl′tīte. Designation of one of David's guardsmen, 2 Sam. xxiii. 26.

Păm-phȳl′ĭ-ȧ (*mixture of nations*). A seacoast province of Asia Minor. Its chief town was Perga, where Paul preached, Acts xiii. 13; xiv. 24; xxvii. 5.

Păn (*open*). A flat plate for baking, and a deeper vessel for holding liquids, Lev. ii. 5; vi. 21.

Păn′năg. Disputed word. Probably a place, Ezek. xxvii. 17.

Pā′per. [PAPYRUS.]

Pā′phos (*hot*). Town on island of Cyprus, visited by Paul, Acts xiii. 6–13.

Pȧ-pȳ′rus. The writing-paper of the Egyptians, Greeks, and Romans, made from the papyrus plant, a rush or flag growing in Egypt, Job xl. 21.

Păr′ȧ-ble (*comparison*). Allegorical representation of something real in nature or human affairs, whence a moral is drawn. A favorite method of Oriental teaching, 2 Sam. xii. 1–4; Isa. v. 1–7. Christ spoke over 30 parables, Matt. xiii. 3–8; 24–30, 31, 32, and elsewhere in Gospels.

Păr′ȧ-dīse (*pleasure ground*). "Garden of Eden;" and, figuratively, abode of happy souls — heaven, Luke xxiii. 43; 2 Cor. xii. 4; Rev. ii. 7.

Pā′rah (*place of heifers*). City in Benjamin, Josh. xviii. 23.

Pā′ran, El=pā′ran (*places of caves*). The "desert of wandering," with Canaan on the north, desert of Sinai on the south, Etham on the west, and Arabah on the east, Gen. xxi. 14–21; Num. x. 12, 33; xii. 16; xiii. 3, 26; xxxiii. 17–36.

Pā′ran, Mount of. A mount of the Sinaitic range, Deut. xxxiii. 2; Hab. iii. 3.

Pär′bar (*suburb*). A spot between the west wall of temple at Jerusalem and the city beyond, 1 Chr. xxvi. 18.

Pärched Corn. Roasted grain, Ruth ii. 14.

Pärched Ground. Supposably the mirage frequently seen on desert tracts, Isa. xxxv. 7.

Pärch′ment (*from Pergamum*). Skin of sheep or goats prepared for writing on, 2 Tim. iv. 13.

Pär′lor (*speaking chamber*). King's audience-chamber, Judg. iii. 20–25.

Pär-măsh′tȧ (*stronger*). A son of Haman, Esth. ix. 9.

Pär′me-năs (*steadfast*). One of the first seven deacons, Acts vi. 5.

Pär′nach (*swift*). A Zebulunite, Num. xxxiv. 25.

Pā′rŏsh (*flea*). His children returned, Ez. ii. 3; Neh. vii. 8.

Pär-shăn′da-thȧ (*prayer-given*). Eldest son of Haman, Esth. ix. 7.

Pär′thĭ-anş. Jews settled in Parthia, that undefined country north of Media and Persia, Acts ii. 9.

Pär′trĭdge (*squatting*). Three varieties found in Palestine. Their flesh and eggs esteemed as food, 1 Sam. xxvi. 20; Jer. xvii. 11.

Pȧr′ụ-ah (*blooming*). Father of Solomon's commissary in Issachar, 1 Kgs. iv. 17.

Pär-vā′im (*eastern*). Unknown place whence Solomon shipped gold, 2 Chr. iii. 6.

Pā′sach (*cut off*). An Asherite, 1 Chr. vii. 33.

Păs-dăm′mim (*blood-border*). Spot of battles between Israel and Philistia, 1 Chr. xi. 13. Ephesdammim, 1 Sam. xvii. 1.

Pā-sē′ah (*lame*). (1) A Judahite, 1 Chr. iv. 12. (2) His sons returned, Ez. ii. 49.

Păsh′ụr (*freedom*). (1) Head of a priestly family, 1 Chr. ix. 12; Neh. xi. 12; Jer. xxi. 1. (2) Priestly governor of the house of the Lord, 1 Chr. xxiv. 14; Jer. xx. i.

Păs′sion (*suffering*). Last sufferings of Christ, Acts i. 3. Kindred feelings, Acts xiv. 15; Jas. v. 17.

Păss′ō-ver (*passing over*). First of three great Jewish feasts, instituted in honor of the "passing over" of the Hebrew households by the destroying angel, Ex. xii., xiii. 3–10; xxiii. 14–19; Lev. xxiii. 4–14. Called the "feast of unleavened bread." The Christian Passover is "The Lord's Supper," eucharist, Matt. xxvii. 62; Luke xxii. 1–20; John xix. 42.

Păs′tor (*shepherd*). Figuratively, one who keeps Christ's flocks, Eph. iv. 11.

Păt′ạ-rȧ (*trodden*). City on southwest coast of Lycia, Acts xxi. 1, 2.

Pāte (*flat*). Top of the head, Ps. vii. 16.

Pȧ-thē′us, 1 Esdr. ix. 23. [PETHAHIAH.]

Păth′ros (*southern*). An ancient division of Upper Egypt occupied by the Pathrusim, Isa. xi. 11; Jer. xliv. 1–15; Ezek. xxix. 14.

Păth-rụ′sīm, Gen. x. 14. [PATHROS.]

Păt′mos. The rocky island in the Ægean Sea, to which John was banished, Rev. i. 9.

Pā′trĭ-arch (*father*). Father of the family and chief of its descendants. The Hebrew form of government till Moses established the theocracy, Acts ii. 29; vii. 8, 9; Heb. vii. 4.

Păt′rȯ-băs (*paternal*). A Roman Christian, Rom. xvi. 14.

Pȧ-trō′clus. Father of Nicanor, 2 Macc. viii. 9.

Pā′u (*bleating*). Capital of Hadar, king of Edom, Gen. xxxvi. 39. Pai, 1 Chr. i. 50.

Paụl (*small*). In Hebrew, Saul. Born at Tarsus in Cilicia, of Benjamite parents, about the beginning of 1st century; a Pharisee in faith; a tent-maker by trade, Phil. iii. 5; Acts xviii. 3; xxi. 39; xxii. 6. Studied law with Gamaliel at Jerusalem; persecuted early Christians; converted near Damascus, Acts v. 34; vii. 58; ix. 1–22. Commissioned an apostle to the Gentiles, Acts xxvi. 13–20. Carried the gospel to Asia Minor, Greece, and Rome. Author of fourteen epistles, amplifying the Christian faith. Supposably a martyr at Rome, A. D. 68.

Pāve′ment (*beaten floor*). [GABBATHA.]

Pȧ-vĭl′ion (*butterfly tent*). Movable tent or dwelling. Applied to tabernacle, booth, den, etc., 1 Kgs. xx. 12; Ps. xviii. 11; xxvii. 5; Jer. xliii. 10.

Pēa′cock (*eye-feathered cock*). An import from Tarshish, 1 Kgs. x. 22; 2 Chr. ix. 21. The peacock of Job xxxix. 13 should be ostrich.

Pĕarls (*little pears*). Stony secretions of the pearl-oyster. Reckoned as gems and highly prized as ornaments. Source of frequent metaphor, Matt. xiii. 45; 1 Tim. ii. 9; Rev. xvii. 4; xxi. 21. Pearl, in Job xxviii. 18, should be crystal.

Pĕd′a-hĕl (*saved*). A chief of Naphtali, Num. xxxiv. 28.

Pĕ-däh′zur (*rock-saved*). Father of Gamaliel, Num. i. 10.

Pĕ′dā′iah (*God-saved*). (1) Grandfather of King Jehoiakim, 2 Kgs. xxiii. 36. (2) Father of Zerubbabel, 1 Chr. iii. 18, 19. (3) A Manassite, 1 Chr. xxvii. 20. (4) Returned captives, Neh. iii. 25; viii. 4; xi. 7; xiii. 13.

Pĕ′kah (*open-eyed*). Murderer and successor of Pekahiah, king of Israel, B. C. 758–738. Conspired with Damascus against Judah, and perished in a conspiracy, 2 Kgs. xv. 25–31; xvi. ; 2 Chr. xxviii.

Pĕk″a-hī′ah (*God opens*). Son and successor of Menahem on the throne of Israel, B. C. 760–758. Murdered and succeeded by his general, Pekah, 2 Kgs. xv. 22–26.

Pĕ′kŏd. The Chaldeans are so called in Jer. l. 21; Ezek. xxiii. 23.

Pĕl″a-ī′ah (*distinguished*). (1) A Judahite, 1 Chr. iii. 24. (2) A co-covenanter, Neh. viii. 7; x. 10.

Pĕl″a-lī′ah (*judged*). A returned priest, Neh. xi. 12.

Pĕl″a-tī′ah (*saved*). (1) Grandson of Zerubbabel, 1 Chr. iii. 21. (2) A Simeonite warrior, 1 Chr. iv. 42. (3) A co-covenanter, Neh. x. 22. (4) One struck dead for defying Ezekiel, Ezek. xi. 1–13.

Pĕ′leg (*division*). Son of Eber. His family remained in Mesopotamia, Gen. x. 25; xi. 16–19.

Pĕ′let (*freedom*). (1) A Judahite, 1 Chr. ii. 47. (2) An adherent of David, 1 Chr. xii. 3.

Pĕ′leth (*freedom*). (1) Father of the rebellious On, Num. xvi. 1. (2) Son of Jonathan, 1 Chr. ii. 33.

Pĕ′leth-ītes (*runners*). Retainers and messengers of David, 2 Sam. viii. 18; xv. 18; xx. 7.

Pĕ-lī′as, 1 Esdr. ix. 34. [BEDEIAH.]

Pĕl′ī-can (*axe-bill*). A voracious water-bird, large and strong-billed. The female is supplied with a pouch for supplying itself and young with water and food. Symbol of desolation. Original sometimes translated "cormorant," Lev. xi. 18; Deut. xiv. 17; Ps. cii. 6; Isa. xxxiv. 11.

Pĕl′o-nīte. Designation of two of David's warriors, 1 Chr. xi. 27, 36.

Pĕn (*feather*). Anciently, a metal graver for tracing on hard substances; the stylus, of pointed metal or bone, for writing in wax; the reed pen and hair pencil for writing on parchment and linen, Judg. v. 14; Job xix. 24; Jer. xvii. 1.

Pĕ-nī′el (*face of God*). Place beyond Jordan where Jacob wrestled with the angel, Gen. xxxii. 30. Penuel in Judg. viii. 17; 1 Kgs. xii. 25.

Pĕ-nĭn′nah (*pearl*). A wife of Elkanah, 1 Sam. . 1–4.

Pĕn′nȳ (*cattle*). The Roman silver denarius, worth 15 to 17 cents. The Greek silver drachma was a corresponding coin, Matt. xx. 2; xxii. 19–21; Mark vi. 37; Luke xx. 24; Rev. vi. 6.

Pĕn′tȧ-teuch (*five-fold book*). Greek name for the first five O. T. books, or books of Moses. Called Torah, "the law," by Hebrews.

Pĕn′tė-cŏst (*fiftieth day*). The Hebrew harvest-home festival, celebrated on fiftieth day from the Passover, or on the date of the giving of the law at Sinai, Ex. xxiii. 16; xxxiv. 22; Lev. xxiii. 15–22; Num. xxviii. In the Christian Church, Pentecost is celebrated seven weeks after Easter, to commemorate the day in Acts ii. 1–14.

Pĕ-nū′el. (1) [PENIEL.] (2) A Judahite, 1 Chr. iv. 4. (3) A Benjamite, 1 Chr. viii. 25.

Pĕ′or (*cleft*). (1) The mountain in Moab to which Balak brought Balaam, Num. xxiii. 28; xxv.

18; xxxi. 16. (2) [BAAL-PEOR.]

Pĕr′a-zĭm (*breach*). A figurative mountain, Isa. xxviii. 21.

Pĕ′resh (*dung*). Son of Machir, 1 Chr. vii. 16.

Pĕ′rez (*rent*). An important Judahite family, 1 Chr. xxvii. 3; Neh. xi. 4–6.

Pĕ′rez=ŭz′zah (*breaking of Uzzah*). Where Uzzah died, 2 Sam. vi. 6–8. Perez-uzza, 1 Chr. xiii. 9–11.

Pĕr′fūme (*thorough-fume*). Perfumes largely used by Hebrews in religious rites and for toilet purposes, Ex. xxx. 35; Prov. xxvii. 9.

Pĕr′gȧ (*earthy*). A city of Pamphylia, Acts xiii. 13.

Pĕr′ga-mŏs (*heights*). Pergamum in R. V. A city of Mysia, in Asia Minor, celebrated for its library, which was transferred to Alexandria. Seat of one of the "seven churches," Rev. i. 11; ii. 12–17.

Pĕ-rī′dȧ (*kernels*). His children returned, Neh. vii. 57.

Pĕr′ĭz-zītes (*villagers*). Original village-dwellers in Canaan, Gen. xiii. 7; Josh. xvii. 15.

Pĕr-sĕp′o-lis (*city of Persia*). Capital of Persia. Ruins very extensive, 2 Macc. ix. 2.

Pĕr′seus (*destroyer*). Last king of Macedonia; defeated by Rome, 1 Macc. viii. 5.

Pĕr′sia (*land of Perses*). Originally the country around the head of the Persian Gulf; afterwards the great empire, including all western Asia, and parts of Europe and Africa. Reached its height under Cyrus, B. C. 486–485. Conquered by Alexander, B. C. 330, Ezek. xxxviii. 5; 2 Chr. xxxvi. 20–23; Ez. i. 8.

Pĕr′sis (*Persian*). A Christian woman at Rome, Rom. xvi. 12.

Pĕ-ru′dȧ, Ez. ii. 55. [PERIDA.]

Pĕs′tĭ-lence (*the plague*). In Hebrew, all distempers and calamities, Ex. ix. 14; xi. 1; 1 Kgs. viii. 37.

Pĕ′ter (*stone, rock*). Simon, or Simeon; son of Jonas, Matt. xvi. 17; Acts xv. 14. A fisherman, resident at Capernaum, Matt. viii. 14; called, Matt. iv. 18–20; name changed to Peter, John i. 42. Founder of Christian Church among the Jews, Acts ii. ; spokesman of the apostles, Acts x. ; author of two epistles; a probable martyr at Rome. His first epistle is dated from Babylon; his second is his valedictory. Both are advisory and exhortatory.

Pĕth″a-hī′ah (*freed*). (1) Head of the 19th priestly course, 1 Chr. xxiv. 16. (2) Returned captives, Ez. x. 23; Neh. ix. 5; xi. 24.

Pĕ′thôr (*prophet*). Balaam's residence in Mesopotamia, Num. xxii. 5, Deut. xxiii. 4.

Pĕ-thu′el (*vision*). Father of Joel, Joel i. 1.

Pĕ′trȧ (*rock*). Edom. Modernly, Arabia Petræa.

Pĕ-ŭl′thāi (*wages*). Eighth son of Obed-edom, 1 Chr. xxvi. 5.

Phāi′sur, 1 Esdr. ix. 22. [PASHUR.]

Phā′lec, Luke iii. 35. [PELEG.]

Phăl′lū, Gen. xlvi. 9. [PALLU.]

Phăl′ti (*deliverance*). The man to whom Saul gave Michal, his daughter and David's wife, 1 Sam. xxv. 44. Phaltiel, 2 Sam. iii. 15, 16.

Phăl′tĭ-el, 2 Sam. iii. 15. [PHALTI.]

Phăn-u′el (*face of God*). Father of Anna the prophetess, Luke ii. 36.

Phăr′a-cim. His sons returned, 1 Esdr. v. 31.

Phā′raōh (*sun-king*). General name of Egyptian kings. Only a few are definitely named in the Bible. Different ones alluded to are, Gen. xii. 15; xli. ; Ex. i. 8; v. 1; 1 Chr. iv. 18; 1 Kgs. xi. 18–22; ix. 16; 2 Kgs. xviii. 21; Pharaoh-nechoh, 2 Kgs. xxiii. 29; Pharaoh-hophra, Jer. xxxvii. 5–8.

BIBLE DICT

Phā′raōh's Dạugh′ter. (1) Guardian of Moses, Ex. ii. 5–10. (2) Wife of Mered, 1 Chr. iv. 18. (3) Wife of Solomon, 1 Kgs. iii. 1.

Phā′rĕṣ, Matt. i. 3; Luke iii. 33. [PHAREZ.]

Phā′rĕz (*breach*). A Judahite, Gen. xxxviii. 29; xlvi. 12. Father of Pharzites, Num. xxvi. 20. Perez, Neh. xi. 4, 6. Phares, Matt. i. 3; Luke iii. 33.

Phär′ī-see (*set apart*). A Jewish sect, strictly orthodox in religion, and politically opposed to foreign supremacy, Matt. xxiii. 23–33; Luke xviii. 9–14.

Phā′rōsh, Ez. viii. 3. [PAROSH.]

Phär′par (*swift*). A river of Damascus, 2 Kgs. v 12.

Phär′zītes. Descendants of Pharez, Num. xxvi. 20.

Phȧ-sē′ah, Neh. vii. 51. [PASEAH.]

Phȧ-sē′lis. A town on border of Lycia and Pamphylia, 1 Macc. xv. 23.

Phăs′ī-ron. An Arab chief, 1 Macc. ix. 66.

Phăs′sȧ-ron, 1 Esdr. v. 25. [PASHUR.]

Phē′bĕ (*shining*). A servant of the church at Cenchrea, Rom. xvi. 1, 2.

Phĕ-nī′çē. (1) Acts xi. 19; xv. 3. [PHŒNICIA.] (2) Phœnix in R. V. A seaport of Crete, Acts xxvii. 12.

Phī′col (*strong*). Chief of Abimelech's army, Gen. xxi. 22; xxvi. 26.

Phĭl″ȧ-dĕl′phī-ȧ (*brotherly love*). A city of Lydia in Asia Minor, and seat of one of the seven churches of Asia, Rev. i. 11; iii. 7–13.

Phĭ-lär′chus. A cavalry leader, 2 Macc. viii. 32.

Phī-lē′mon (*friendship*). A Christian convert at Colosse in Phrygia, to whom Paul wrote an epistle during his captivity at Rome, in favor of Onesimus, Philemon's servant. Eighteenth N. T. book.

Phī-lē′tus (*amiable*). The convert whom Paul denounced for error, 2 Tim. ii. 17.

Phĭl′ĭp (*lover of horses*). (1) The apostle of Bethsaida, of whom little is known, Matt. x. 3; Mark iii. 18; Luke vi. 14; John vi. 5–9; Acts i. 13. (2) The evangelist and deacon, resident at Cæsarea, and preacher throughout Samaria, Acts vi. 5; viii. 5–13; xxi. 8–10. (3) The tetrarch. [HEROD.] (4) Husband of Herodias, Matt. xiv. 3. [HEROD.] (5) Governor of Jerusalem under Antiochus, and regent of Syria, 2 Macc. v. 22. (6) Philip V., king of Macedonia, 1 Macc. viii. 5. (7) King of Macedonia, B. C. 360–336, and father of Alexander the Great, 1 Macc. i. 1.

Phĭ-lĭp′pī (*city of Philip*). City in Macedonia, founded by Philip II., 12 miles from the port of Neapolis. Paul founded a vigorous church there, Acts xvi.; xx. 1–6.

Phĭ-lĭp′pĭ-anṣ. Dwellers in Philippi. Paul's epistle to the Christians there was written from Rome, A. D. 62 or 63. In it he sends thanks for gifts, praises their Christian walk and firmness, warns against Judaizing tendencies, and exhorts to steadfast faith.

Phĭ-lĭs′tĭȧ (*land of sojourners*). The plain and coast country on the southwest of Palestine, which imparted its name to Palestine, Ps. lx. 8; lxxxvii. 4; cviii. 9. [PALESTINE.]

Phĭ-lĭs′tīneṣ (*villagers*). Dwellers in Philistia. Origin disputed, but associated with Cretans; also with the Caphtorim of Egypt, Jer. xlvii. 4; Am. ix. 7. Permanent settlers in time of Abraham, Gen. xxi. 32. Wealthy, energetic, and warlike, with many strong cities. Land not conquered by Joshua. Gaza, Ashkelon, Ashdod, Gath, and Ekron, their chief strongholds. Subdued by David, 2 Sam. v. 17–25; but became practically independent under the kings. Disappeared as a distinct people after the time of the Maccabees.

Phĭ-lŏl′o-gus (*learned*). A Roman Christian saluted by Paul, Rom. xvi. 15.

Phĭ-lŏs′o-phȳ (*loving wisdom*). The prominent Grecian schools of philosophy in N. T. times were the Stoic and Epicurean, Acts xvii. 18. But the most formidable enemy of early Christian thought was the tendency of the learned to engraft the speculations of Eastern Gnosticism and Greek philosophy upon the evolving doctrines of Christianity, 1 Cor. i. 18–27; 1 Tim. vi. 20; Col. ii. 8, etc.

Phĭn′e-es. Apocryphal form of Phinehas.

Phĭn′e-has (*brazen mouth*). (1) Chief of the Korhite Levites, and high priest, Ex. vi. 25; Num. xxv. 6–15; Josh. xxii. 30–32. (2) Wicked son of Eli, 1 Sam. i. 3; ii. 34; iv. 4–19; xiv. 3. (3) A Levite, Ez. viii. 33.

Phī′son. Greek form of Pison, Ecclus. xxiv. 25.

Phlē′gon (*burning*). A Roman Christian saluted by Paul, Rom. xvi. 14.

Phœ′be. [PHEBE.]

Phœ-nī′çĭȧ (*land of palm-trees*). Phenicia in Acts xxi. 2. Phenice in Acts xi. 19; xv. 3. In O. T. referred to as Tyre and Sidon, or coasts of Tyre and Sidon. The small coast country north of Palestine, noted for its commercial enterprise, learning, and skill in arts. Included in the Land of Promise but never conquered, Josh. xiii. 4–6. David and Solomon employed its sailors and artisans, 2 Sam. v. 11; 1 Kgs. v.

Phœ-nī′çĭanṣ. Dwellers in Phœnicia. In intimate commercial, political, and even religious relations with Hebrews, 1 Kgs. xvi. 31–33; xviii. 40; 1 Chr. xiv. 1; Isa. xxiii.; Ezek. xxvii. 2–8.

Phrȳ̆ǵ′-ĭ-ȧ (*barren*). An undefined section of Asia Minor, out of which several Roman provinces were formed, Acts ii. 10; xvi. 6; xviii. 23.

Phŭd. Judith ii. 23. [PHUT.]

Phū′rah (*bough*). Armor - bearer of Gideon, Judg. vii. 10, 11.

Phū′rim, Esth. xi. 1. [PURIM.]

Phŭt, Pŭt (*bow*). Son of Ham, Gen. x. 6; 1 Chr. i. 8. Name is rendered Libya and Libyans, people of north Africa, in Jer. xlvi. 9; Ezek. xxx. 5; xxxviii. 5.

Phū′vah (*mouth*). Son of Issachar, Gen. xlvi. 13. Pua, Num. xxvi. 23. Puah, 1 Chr. vii. 1.

Phȳ-ġĕl′lus (*fugitive*). A Christian pervert of Asia, 2 Tim. i. 15.

Phȳ-lăc′te-rȳ (*safeguard*). [FRONTLET.]

Pī=bē′seth (*house of Bast*). City of Lower Egypt, on Pelusiac branch of the Nile. Bubastis of the Greeks, noted for its temple of Bast, goddess of fire, Ezek. xxx. 17.

Pĭc′tūre (*painting*), Ezek. xxiii. 14; Prov. xxv. 11. Sculptures, reliefs, or cornices, meant. Movable or hanging pictures not favored by Hebrews.

Pīēce (*part*). In O. T., "pieces of gold," "pieces of silver," may well be read shekels' weight, or shekels, of gold or silver, Gen. xx. 16; 2 Kgs. v. 5. In N. T., "pieces," Matt. xxvi. 15; xxvii. 3–9, are unknown. In Luke xv. 8, for "pieces" read drachmas.

Pĭġ′eŏn (*chirping bird*). [DOVE.]

Pī=ha-hī′roth (*place of sedges*). Last Israelite encampment before crossing the Red Sea, Ex. xiv. 2, 9; Num. xxxiii. 7, 8.

Pī′lạte (*spear-armed*). Pontius Pilate in Matt. xxvii. 2. Sixth Roman procurator of Judea, A. D. 26–36. Official residence at Cæsarea, with judicial visits to other places. Christ was brought before him at Jerusalem for judgment. He found no guilt, but lost his moral courage in the presence of the mob. Eventually banished to Gaul, Luke xxiii. 1–7; John xviii. 27–40; xix.

Pĭl′dăsh (*flame*). Son of Nahor, Gen. xxii. 22.

Pĭl′e-hȧ (*worship*). A co-covenanter, Neh. x. 24.

Pĭl′lar (*pile*). Prominent in Oriental architecture, monumental evidences, and scripture metaphor, Gen.

xxviii. 18; xxxv. 20; Ex. xiii. 21; Josh. xxiv. 26; Judg. xvi. 25-30; 1 Tim. iii. 15; Rev. iii. 12.

Pĭlled (*peeled*). Peeled, stripped, plundered, Gen. xxx. 37, 38; Isa. xviii. 2.

Pĭl′tāi (*saved*). A priest, Neh. xii. 17.

Pīne (*pitch*). Disputed rendering. Probably plane-tree is meant, Isa. xli. 19; lx. 13.

Pĭn′na-cle (*feather, edge*). Not a pinnacle, or summit, but the pinnacle, or wing, of the temple, Matt. iv. 5; Luke iv. 9.

Pī′non (*darkness*). A duke of Edom, Gen. xxxvi. 41.

Pīpe. Flute. Type of perforated wind instruments, as the harp was of stringed instruments, 1 Sam. x. 5; 1 Kgs. i. 40; Isa. v. 12.

Pī′ram (*fleet*). An Amorite king, Josh. x. 3.

Pĭr′a-thon (*princely*). Now Ferata, six miles southwest of Shechem, Judg. xii. 15.

Pĭr′a-thon-īte″. Dweller in Pirathon, Judg. xii. 13, 15; 1 Chr. xxvii. 14.

Pĭs′gah (*hill*). The elevation, in Moab, whence Moses viewed the Promised Land, Num. xxi. 20; Deut. iii. 27; iv. 49; xxxiv. 1.

Pĭ-sĭd′ĭ-à (*pitchy*). A province of Asia Minor, with Antioch as its capital. Twice visited by Paul, Acts xiii. 14; xiv. 21-24.

Pī′son (*flowing*). One of the four rivers of Eden. Unlocated, Gen. ii. 11.

Pĭs′pah (*swelling*). An Asherite, 1 Chr. vii. 38.

Pĭt (*well*). Cistern or well, Gen. xxxvii. 20; grave, Ps. xxviii. 1; game-trap, Ezek. xix. 8; device, Ps. cxix. 85; Prov. xxvi. 27.

Pĭtch (*pine-resin*). The pitch of scripture was asphalt or bitumen, found in Dead Sea regions. Used for mortar, cement, calk, etc., Gen. vi. 14; xi. 3; Ex. ii. 3; Isa. xxxiv. 9.

Pĭtch′er (*goblet, wine-vessel*). A large earthen water-jar with one or two handles, Gen. xxiv. 15-20; Mark xiv. 13; Luke xxii. 10.

Pī′thom (*house of Tum*). A store-city of Egypt, built by the Israelites, Ex. i. 11.

Pī′thon (*harmless*). A son of Micah, 1 Chr. viii. 35.

Plāgue (*blow*). Pestilential disease, Lev. xiii. 2-8; xxvi. 25. Any calamitous visitation, Mark v. 29; Luke vii. 21. The judgments of God on Egypt are called plagues. They were (1) Nile changed to blood, Ex. vii. 14-25. (2) Visitation of frogs, Ex. viii. 1-15. (3) Lice, Ex. viii. 16-19. (4) Flies, Ex. viii. 20-32. (5) Murrain, Ex. ix. 1-7. (6) Boils, Ex. ix. 8-12. (7) Hail, Ex. ix. 13-35. (8) Locusts, Ex. x. 1-20. (9) Darkness, Ex. x. 21-28. (10) Smiting of the firstborn, Ex. xii. 29, 30.

Plāin (*flat*). Hebrew words so rendered have various significations. Plain, Gen. xi. 2; meadow, Judg. xi. 33; oak-grove, Gen. xiii. 18.

Plāit′ing (*folding*). Folding or pleating, as of the hair, 1 Pet. iii. 3.

Plăn′et (*wanderer*). The reference is evidently to the signs of the zodiac, as in marg. 2 Kgs. xxiii. 5.

Plăs′ter (*forming on*). Used by Hebrews as wall and stone coating, Lev. xiv. 42; Deut. xxvii. 2, 4; Dan. v. 5.

Plĕdge (*holding before*). [EARNEST.] [LOAN.]

Plē′ĭa-dēṣ or **Pleī′a-dēṣ** (*daughters of Pleione*). The "seven stars." A group of stars in the constellation Taurus, Job ix. 9; xxxviii. 31; Am. v. 8.

Plọw (*plowland*). In early times, a crude implement made of a forked stick, one branch of which was shod, or shared, with iron. Drawn by oxen, camels, and asses, Gen. xlv. 6; Deut. xxii. 10; Job i. 14.

Pŏch′e-rĕth (*beguiling*). His children returned, Ez. ii. 57; Neh. vii. 59.

Pō′ĕt-rẙ (*made up*). Hebrew literature largely poetical, and of lyrical style. Job, Psalms, Proverbs, Ecclesiastes, and Song of Solomon are distinctively poetical.

Pōll (*head*). The head, Num. iii. 47. To cut the hair, 2 Sam. xiv. 26.

Pŏl′lux. [CASTOR and POLLUX.]

Pọme′grăn-āte (*many - seeded fruit*). A low, straight - stemmed tree, native of Persia, Syria, and Arabia, bearing an orange-like fruit, Num. xiii. 23; Deut. viii. 8; S. of Sol. iv. 3; vi. 7; viii. 2.

Pŏm′mels (*knobs*). Globular ornaments on the capitals of pillars, 2 Chr. iv. 12, 13. Called "bowls" in 1 Kgs. vii. 41.

Pŏnds (*confined*). Egyptian ponds were pools left by subsidence of the Nile waters, Ex. vii. 19. Fish-ponds in Isa. xix. 10.

Pŏn′tĭ-us Pī′late. [PILATE.]

Pŏn′tus (*the sea*). Northeastern province of Asia Minor, bordering on the Pontus Euxinus, Euxine Sea. Empire of Mithridates, defeated by Pompey, B. C. 66. Many Jews settled there, Acts ii. 9; xviii. 2; 1 Pet. i. 1.

Pool (*hole*). Artificial reservoir for water. Very necessary in the East and sometimes built very elaborately and expensively, Eccl. ii. 6; Isa. xlii. 15.

Poor (*bare*). Poor especially cared for under Jewish dispensation, Ex. xxiii. 6; Lev. xix. 9, 10; Deut. xv. 7. Spirit continued, Luke iii. 11; xiv. 13; Acts vi. 1.

Pŏp′lär (*butterfly-leaf*). The white poplar supposed to be meant, Gen. xxx. 37; Hos. iv. 13.

Pŏr′a-thà (*favored*). A son of Haman, Esth. ix. 8.

Pōrch (*door*). In oriental architecture, veranda, colonnade, vestibule, Judg. iii. 23; 1 Chr. xxviii. 11; John x. 23. Any passage from street to inner hall, Matt. xxvi. 71.

Pŏr′çĭ-us Fĕs′tus, Acts xxiv. 27. [FESTUS.]

Pōr′terṣ (*gate-keepers*). Keepers of city, temple, palace, and private gates and doors. The temple had 4000 of them, in classified service, 2 Sam. xviii. 26; 2 Kgs. vii. 10; 1 Chr. xxiii. 5; xxvi. 1-19; 2 Chr. xxxi. 14.

Pŏs″ĭ-dō′nĭ-as. Nicanor's envoy to Judas, 2 Macc. xiv. 19.

Pōsts (*placed*). Runners, messengers, on foot, on horses, or on dromedaries, Esth. viii. 10-14; Job ix. 25; Jer. li. 31.

Pŏt (*drinking-vessel*). Pots of various designs, sizes, and uses. Made of clay or metal, Lev. vi. 28; 1 Sam. ii. 14; 2 Kgs. iv. 2; Jer. xxxv. 5; Ezek. iv. 9.

Pŏt′ĭ-phar (*belonging to the sun*). Captain of Pharaoh's guard, Gen. xxxvii. 36; xxxix.

Pọ-tī′=phe-rah (*belonging to the sun*). A priest of On, in Egypt, and father-in-law of Joseph, Gen. xli. 45.

Pŏt′sherd (*pot-fragment*). A piece of broken pottery, Prov. xxvi. 23.

Pŏt′tage (*pot-cooked*). A thick stew of meat or vegetables, or both, Gen. xxv. 29; 2 Kgs. iv. 39.

Pŏt′ter's Field. The burial-ground for strangers, outside of Jerusalem, bought with the betrayal money, Matt. xxvii. 7. [ACELDAMA.]

Pŏt′ter-y (*pot-ware*). A very ancient art and carried to great perfection. Vessels variously moulded, and often elaborately decorated. The ceramic art furnishes many valuable contributions to ancient history, Gen. xxiv. 14; 1 Chr. iv. 23; Isa. xli. 25; Jer. xviii. 3.

Pound (*weight*). A weight; the maneh, 1 Kgs. x. 17; Ez. ii. 69; Neh. vii. 71. One sixtieth of a Grecian talent, Luke xix. 13-27.

Præ-tō′rĭ-um (*governor's headquarters*). The court, hearing-hall, and judgment-hall of a Roman governor, wherever he might be, Matt. xxvii. 27; Mark xv. 16; John xviii. 28; Acts xxiii. 35; Phil. i. 13.

Prāy′er (*seeking favor*). Reverent petition to a divinity a universal custom. The Jews had three daily periods of prayer: 9 A. M., 12 M., 3 P. M., Ps. lv. 17 ; Dan. vi. 10.

Prĕş′ent. [GIFT.]

Prĭcks. [GOADS.]

Prĭēst (*presbyter, elder*). Representative of man in things appertaining to God. Assistants of Moses as mediator, Ex. xxiv. 5. Function of priesthood conferred on Levites, Ex. xxviii. Priests divided into regular courses, 1 Chr. xxiv. 1–19 ; 2 Chr. xxiii. 8 ; Luke i. 5.

Prĭnce (*first*). In Bible sense, patriarch, head of a family or chief of a tribe ; governor or magistrate, 1 Kgs. xx. 14 ; satrap or ruler, Dan. vi. 1.

Prĭn″çĭ-păl′ĭ-ty. Territory of a prince. Seemingly an order of angels in Eph. i. 21 ; vi. 12 ; Col. i. 16 ; ii. 10.

Prĭs′cả (*ancient*), 2 Tim. iv. 19. [PRISCILLA.]

Prĭs-çĭl′lả (*little Prisca*). Wife of Aquila, Acts xviii. 2, 18, 26 ; Rom. xvi. 3.

Prĭş′on (*seizing*). Ward or lock-up, Lev. xxiv. 12 ; Num. xv. 34 ; well or pit, Gen. xxxvii. 24 ; Jer. xxxviii. 6–11 ; part of a palace, 2 Chr. xvi. 10 ; Jer. xxxii. 2 ; Acts xxiii. 10, 35.

Prŏch′o-rus (*choir leader*). One of the first seven deacons, Acts vi. 5.

Prō-cŏn′sul (*for a consul*). A Roman official, beneath a consul, who exercised authority in a province. Appointed by the senate, Acts xiii. 7 ; xix. 38.

Prŏc′ū-rȧ″tor (*caring for*). A Roman provincial officer, governor, or viceroy, appointed by the emperor, Matt. xxvii. ; Acts xxiii. 24 ; xxvi. 30.

Prŏg-nŏs′tĭ-cȧ″tor (*knowing before*). Conjurer and fortune-teller, aided by the heavenly bodies, Isa. xlvii. 13.

Prŏph′et (*speaking beforehand*). Who tells the future under God's inspiration. The prophetic order embraced political, as well as spiritual, advisers and warners. The books of seventeen — four greater and thirteen lesser prophets — are comprised in the O. T. Christ is the prëeminent and eternal prophet, Luke xxiv. 27, 44.

Prŏs′e-lȳte (*come to*). A convert to the Jewish faith. "Stranger" in O. T., Deut. x. 18, 19 ; Matt. xxiii. 15 ; Acts xiii. 43.

Prŏv′ĕrb (*for a word*). Wise utterance ; enigma, Num. xxi. 27. The proverbs, collected and poetically arranged by Solomon, or by his authority, constitute the twentieth O. T. book.

Psȧlms (*play a stringed instrument*). In Hebrew, "Praises." The collection of one hundred and fifty lyrics which compose the nineteenth O. T. book. The liturgical hymnbook of the Hebrews, and accepted by early Christians. Authorship of seventy of them ascribed to David. The most perfect specimens of Hebrew poetry extant.

Psȧl′tĕr-y̆ (*play on a stringed instrument*). A stringed instrument to accompany the voice, and supposed to resemble a guitar, 2 Sam. vi. 5 ; 2 Chr. ix. 11. The original frequently translated "viol," Isa. v. 12 ; xiv. 11.

Ptŏl″e̱-mæ′us, Ptŏl′e̱-my. (1) The Ptolemies were a race of Egyptian kings sprung from Ptolemy Soter, who inherited that portion of the conquests of Alexander the Great. They are supposed to be alluded to in the visions of Daniel. Ptolemy I., Soter, B. C. 323–285, Dan. xi. 5. Ptolemy II., Philadelphus, B. C. 285–247, Dan. xi. 6. Ptolemy III., Euergetes, B. C. 247–222, Dan. xi. 7–9. Ptolemy IV., Philopator, B. C. 222–205, Dan. xi. 10–12. Ptolemy V., Epiphanes, B. C. 205–181, Dan. xi. 13–17. Ptolemy VI., Philometor, B. C. 181–146, Dan. xi. 25–30. Their kingdom fell under Rome. (2) Father of Lysimachus, Greek translator of Esther, Esth. xi. 1.

Ptŏl″le-mā′ĭs, Acts xxi. 7. [ACCHO.]

Pū′ȧ, Num. xxvi. 23. [PHUVAH.]

Pū′ah (*mouth*). (1) Father of Tola, a judge of Israel, Judg. x. 1. (2) An Egyptian midwife, Ex. i. 15.

Pŭb′lĭ-can (*people's servant*). Gatherer of public revenue ; tax-collector, abhorred by Jews, Matt. xviii. 17 ; Luke iii. 12, 13 ; xix. 2.

Pŭb′lĭ-us (*common*). Governor of the island of Melita, Acts xxviii. 7, 8.

Pū′denş (*modest*). A Roman Christian who saluted Timothy, 2 Tim. iv. 21.

Pū′hītes. A Judahite family, 1 Chr. ii. 53.

Pŭl (*lord*). (1) A possible African region, Isa. lxvi. 19. (2) A king of Assyria, 2 Kgs. xv. 19, 20.

Pŭlse (*pottage*). Peas, beans, lentils, etc., and, in a Hebrew sense, perhaps the cereals, Dan. i. 12–16.

Pŭn′ĭsh-ment (*pain*). Capital punishment was by hanging, 2 Sam. xxi. 6 ; stoning, Ex. xvii. 4 ; John x. 31 ; burning, Gen. xxxviii. 24 ; shooting, Ex. xix. 13 ; the sword, 1 Kgs. ii. 25 ; drowning, Matt. xviii. 6 ; sawing, 2 Sam. xii. 31 ; crucifixion. The death penalty was inflicted for parental reviling, blasphemy, adultery, rape, idolatry, perjury. Secondary punishments were generally those of retaliation, an "eye for an eye," etc., Ex. xxi. 23–25 ; Deut. xix. 18–21.

Pū′nītes. Descendants of Phuvah, or Pua, Num. xxvi. 23.

Pū′non (*darkness*). A desert encampment, Num. xxxiii. 42.

Pū″rĭ-fĭ-cā′tion (*cleansing*). A ritualistic form and sanitary precaution among Hebrews, Lev. xiv. 4–32 ; Mark vii. 3, 4 ; John xi. 55.

Pū′rim (*lots*). The Jewish festival commemorative of the preservation of the Jews in Persia. Celebrated yearly on 14th and 15th of the month Adar, Esth. iii. 7 ; ix. 20–32.

Pŭt, 1 Chr. i. 8. [PHUT.]

Pū-tē′o-lī (*sulphurous wells*). Now Pozzuoli, seaport of Campania, on Bay of Naples, Acts xxviii. 13.

Pŭ′tĭ-el (*afflicted*). Father-in-law of Eleazar, Ex. vi. 25.

Py̆′garg (*white-rumped*). A species of antelope, Deut. xiv. 5.

Py̆r′rhus. Father of Sopater, in R. V., Acts xx. 4.

Py̆′thon (*serpent*). Pythian Apollo, Acts xvi. 16 marg.

Q

Quāils (*quackers*). Quails of the Old World species, *Coturnix coturnix*, abound in the Arabian desert, and migrate northward, in spring, in enormous flocks, Ex. xvi. 13 ; Num. xi. 31, 32 ; Ps. cv. 40.

Quär′tus (*fourth*). A Christian at Corinth, Rom. xvi. 23.

Quȧ-tĕr′nĭ-on (*file of four*). A Roman guard of four soldiers, two of whom watched prisoners within the door, and two watched the door outside, Acts xii. 4–10.

Quēen (*woman*). The three Hebrew words so rendered imply a queen-regnant, queen-consort, and queen-mother, with a dignity very like that of the present day, 1 Kgs. ii. 19 ; x. 1 ; xv. 13 ; Esth. i. 9 ; ii. 17 ; Jer. xiii. 18 ; xxix. 2.

Quēen of Heaven. The moon, worshipped as Astoreth or Astarte by idolatrous Hebrews, Jer. vii. 18 ; xliv. 17–25.

Quĭck′sȧnds. The Syrtis, greater and lesser. Two dangerous sandbanks or shoals off the north coast of Africa between Carthage and Cyrene, Acts xxvii. 17.

Quĭv′er (*cover*). Case or cover for arrows, Gen. xxvii. 3 ; Job xxxix. 23.

R

Rā′a̱-mah (*shaking*). Son of Cush, and father of a trading tribe on the Persian Gulf, Gen. x. 7 ;

Ezek. xxvii. 22.

Rā″a-mī′ah (*God's thunder*). A chief who returned, Neh. vii. 7. Reelaiah, Ez. ii. 2.

Rȧ-ăm′seş, Ex. i. 11. [RAMESES.]

Răb′bah (*great*). (1) A strong Ammonite city east of Jordan; rebuilt by Ptolemy Philadelphus, B. C. 285–247, and called Philadelphia, Josh. xiii. 25; 2 Sam. xi. 1; xii. 27–29; 1 Chr. xx. 1. Rabbath-ammon, *i. e.*, Rabbath of the Ammonites, or of the children of Ammon, in Deut. iii. 11; 2 Sam. xii. 26; xvii. 27; Jer. xlix. 2; Ezek. xxi. 20. (2) Town in Judah, Josh. xv. 60.

Răb′bath=am′mŏn. [RABBAH.]

Răb′bath=mō′ab. [AR.]

Răb′bī (*my master*). A title of respect applied to Hebrew doctors and teachers. Applied also to priests, and to Christ, Matt. xxiii. 7; Mark ix. 5; John i. 38. Rabboni in John xx. 16.

Răb′bĭth (*many*). Town in Issachar, Josh. xix. 20.

Răb-bō′nī, John xx. 16. [RABBI.]

Răb′=măg (*chief of magi*). An important office at the court of Babylonia, Jer. xxxix. 3, 13.

Răb′sa-rĭs (*chief of eunuchs*). (1) An Assyrian general, 2 Kgs. xviii. 17. (2) A Babylonian prince, Jer. xxxix. 3, 13.

Răb′sha-keh (*cup bearer*). An Assyrian general, 2 Kgs. xviii. 17–37; xix.; Isa. xxxvi.

Rā′cȧ (*worthless*). A Hebrew term of contempt and reproach, Matt. v. 22.

Race (*rush*). As a public game, not patronized by Hebrews. A favorite game with Greeks and Romans, 1 Cor. ix. 24; Heb. xii. 1.

Rā′chăb. Greek form of Rahab, Matt. i. 5.

Rā′chăl (*trade*). A town in southern Judah, 1 Sam. xxx. 29.

Rā′chel (*ewe*). Daughter of Laban, wife of Jacob, and mother of Joseph and Benjamin, Gen. xxix.–xxxv.

Răd′da-ī (*trampling*). Brother of David, 1 Chr. ii. 14.

Rā′gau. (1) Judith i. 5. [RAGES.] (2) Luke iii. 35. [REU.]

Rā′geş. City in Media, Tob. i. 14.

Rȧ-gū′el (*friend of God*). (1) A priest, or prince, of Midian, Num. x. 29. Reuel in Ex. ii. 18. (2) Father-in-law of Tobias, Tob. iii. 7.

Rā′hăb (*large*). (1) The harlot of Jericho who received the spies, and married Salmon, Josh. ii. 1–21; vi. 17–25; Ruth iv. 21; Matt. i. 5. (2) Symbolical term for Egypt, implying insolence and violence, Ps. lxxxix. 10; Isa. li. 9.

Rā′hăm (*belly*). A descendant of Caleb, 1 Chr. ii. 44.

Rā′hel, Jer. xxxi. 15. [RACHEL.]

Rāin. The early rains of Palestine fall in October, in time for seeding; the later, in April, in time for fruits. May to October is the dry season, Deut. xi. 14; Hos. vi. 3; Joel ii. 23.

Rāin′bōw. A sign of the covenant that the earth should not again be destroyed by water, Gen. ix. 12–17.

Rā′kem (*flower culture*). Descendant of Manasseh, 1 Chr. vii. 16.

Răk′kăth (*coast*). A fenced city in Naphtali, Josh. xix. 35.

Răk′kŏn (*void*). Town in Dan, near Joppa, Josh. xix. 46.

Răm (*high*). (1) A Judahite, 1 Chr. ii. 9. Aram, Matt. i. 3, 4; Luke iii. 33. (2) Son of Jerahmeel, 1 Chr. ii. 25. (3) Kinsman of Elihu, Job xxxii. 2.

Răm (*strong*). (1) Male of the sheep, or any ovine species, Gen. xxii. 13. (2) Battering-ram for breaking down gates and walls, Ezek. iv. 2; xxi. 22.

Rā′mȧ, Matt. ii. 18. [RAMAH.]

Rā′mah (*height*). (1) City in Benjamin, near

Jerusalem, Josh. xviii. 25; 1 Kgs. xv. 17–22. Point of departure for Jewish captives, Jer. xxxix. 8–12; xl. 1. (2) Birthplace of Samuel, 1 Sam. i. 19; vii. 17. (3) A border place of Asher, Josh. xix. 29. (4) Town in Naphtali, Josh. xix. 36. (5) Ramoth-gilead, 2 Kgs. viii. 28, 29. (6) A place repeopled by returned captives, Neh. xi. 33.

Rā″math-ā′im=zō′phim (*two watch-towers*). Full form of the town in which Samuel was born, 1 Sam. i. 1. [RAMAH, 2.]

Răm′ȧ-them. A part of Samaria added to Judea, 1 Macc. xi. 34.

Rā′math-īte. Dweller in Ramah, 1 Chr. xxvii. 27.

Rā′math=lē′hī (*hill of the jaw bone*). Where Samson slew the Philistines, Judg. xv. 17.

Rā′math=mĭz′peh (*watch-tower hill*). A border town of Gad, Josh. xiii. 26.

Rā′math of the South. A border place of Simeon, Josh. xix. 8; 1 Sam. xxx. 27.

Rȧ-mē′seş, Rȧ-ăm′seş (*sun-born*). Country and city in lower Egypt, associated with Goshen; the city being the capital, and one of the Pharaohs' store-cities, located on the Pelusiac mouth of the Nile, Gen. xlvii. 11; Ex. i. 11; xii. 37; Num. xxxiii. 3, 5.

Rȧ-mī′ah (*exaltion*). One who had taken a foreign wife, Ez. x. 25.

Rā′moth (*high*). A son of Bani, Ez. x. 29.

Rā′moth=gĭl′e-ăd (*heights of Gilead*). An ancient Amorite stronghold east of Jordan, and chief city of Gad. Both a Levitical city and city of refuge. Centre of one of Solomon's commissary districts, Deut. iv. 43; Josh. xx. 8; xxi. 38; 1 Kgs. iv. 13.

Răm′s Hôrns, Josh. vi. 4–20. [CORNET.]

Rā′phȧ (*tall*). (1) A Benjamite, 1 Chr. viii. 2. (2) A descendant of Saul, 1 Chr. viii. 37.

Rā′phȧ-el (*God's healer*). One of the seven holy angels, Tob. xii. 15.

Răph′ȧ-im. An ancestor of Judith, Judith viii. 1.

Rā′phŏn. A city in Gilead, 1 Macc. v. 37.

Rā′phu (*healed*). Father of the Benjamite spy, Num. xiii. 9.

Răs′seş. A land ravaged by Holofernes, Judith ii. 23.

Rȧ-thū′mus, 1 Esdr. ii. 16. [REHUM.]

Rā′ven (*seizer*). An unclean bird of the crow (*corvus*) family. Translation much disputed, Lev. xi. 15; 1 Kgs. xvii. 6; S. of Sol. v. 11.

Rā′zis. An elder at Jerusalem, 2 Macc. xiv. 37–46.

Rā′zor (*scraper*). Known to and much used by Hebrews. Levites shaved the entire body, Lev. xiv. 8; Num. vi. 9, 18; viii. 7; Judg. xiii. 5; Acts xviii. 18.

Rē″a-i′ȧ (*seen of God*). A Reubenite prince, 1 Chr. v. 5.

Rē″a-i′ah (*seen of God*). (1) A Judahite, 1 Chr. iv. 2. (2) His children returned, Ez. ii. 47; Neh. vii. 50.

Rē′bȧ (*fourth*). A Midianite king slain by Israel, Num. xxxi. 8; Josh. xiii. 21.

Rĕ-bĕc′cȧ. Greek form of Rebekah, Rom. ix. 10.

Rĕ-bĕk′ah (*snare*). Wife of Isaac and mother of Jacob and Esau, Gen. xxii. 23; xxiv.–xxviii.; xlix. 31.

Rē′chăb (*horseman*). (1) Father of Jehonadab, 2 Kgs. x. 15, 23; 1 Chr. ii. 55. (2) A traitorous captain under Ishbosheth, 2 Sam. iv. 2, 5–9. (3) Father of Malchiah, an assistant wall-builder, Neh. iii. 14.

Rē′chab-ītes. Kenite or Midianite descendants of Rechab, 1 Chr. ii. 55, who became an order or sect — said to still exist near Mecca — whose tenets were abstinence from wine, tent habitations only, freedom from agricultural labor, Jer. xxxv. 2–19.

Rē′chah (*uttermost*). Place unknown, 1 Chr. iv.

12.

Rĕ-cŏr′der (*record keeper*). The high and responsible office of annalist and royal counselor in the Hebrew state, 2 Sam. viii. 16; xx. 24; 1 Kgs. iv. 3; 1 Chr. xviii. 15.

Rĕ-dēem′ (*buying back*). In O. T., buying back a forfeited estate. Metaphorically, freeing from bondage, Ex. vi. 6; Isa. xliii. 1. In N. T., rescuing or ransoming from sin and its consequences, Matt. xx. 28; Gal. iii. 13; 1 Pet. i. 18.

Rĕd Sēa. The arm of Gulf of Aden which separates Egypt from Arabia. "The sea," Ex. xiv. 2, 9, 16, 21, 28; xv. 1–19; Josh. xxiv. 6, 7. "Egyptian sea," Isa. xi. 15. "Sea of *Suph*," *weedy* or *reedy sea*, translated "Red Sea," Ex. x. 19; xiii. 18; xv. 4; xxiii. 31; Num. xxi. 4. In N. T., the Greek "Erythrean," or Red Sea, Acts vii. 36. At its head it separates into gulfs of Akaba and Suez, the latter of which the Israelites crossed.

Rēed (*rod*). Used generically for the tall grasses, sedges, flags, or rushes which grow in marshy soils. Applied to various uses by Hebrews, and source of frequent metaphor, 2 Kgs. xviii. 21; Job xl. 21; Isa. xix. 6; Ezek. xxix. 6; Matt. xi. 7; xii. 20; xxvii. 29.

Rē″el-ā′iah, Ez. ii. 2. [RAAMIAH.]

Rĕ-fī′ner (*who makes fine*). A worker in precious metals, Isa. i. 25; Jer. vi. 29; Mal. iii. 3.

Rĕf′uge, Cities of. The six Levitical cities set apart for the temporary escape of involuntary manslayers, Num. xxxv. 6, 11–32; Deut. xix. 7–9; Josh. xx. 2–8. [CITY.]

Rē′gem (*friend*). A descendant of Caleb, 1 Chr. ii. 47.

Rē′gem=mē′lech (*royal friend*). A messenger sent by captive Jews to inquire about the ritual, Zech. vii. 2.

Rĕ-gĕn″ĕr-ā′tion (*begetting again*). The renovation of the world at and after the second coming of Christ, Matt. xix. 28. The new birth from the Holy Spirit, Tit. iii. 5.

Rē″ha-bī′ah (*enlarged*). Only son of Eliezer, 1 Chr. xxiii. 17.

Rē′hŏb (*breadth*). (1) Father of Hadadezer, king of Zobah, 2 Sam. viii. 3, 12. (2) A co-covenanter, Neh. x. 11. (3) Spot where the journey of the spies ended, Num. xiii. 21; 2 Sam. x. 8. Beth-rehob in 2 Sam. x. 6. (4) Place in Asher, Josh. xix. 28. (5) A Levitical town in Asher, Josh. xix. 30.

Rē″ho-bō′am (*emancipator*). Son of Solomon, 1 Kgs. xi. 43; xiv. 21, and successor to his father's throne, B. C. 975–958. During his reign the ten tribes, under Jeroboam, revolted and set up the kingdom of Israel. Shishak, of Egypt, captured Jerusalem from him, 1 Kgs. xiv. 21–31.

Rĕ-hō′both (*places*). (1) A city of Assyria founded by Asher or Nimrod, Gen. x. 11, 12. (2) A city on the Euphrates, home of Shaul or Saul, an early Edomite king, Gen. xxxvi. 37; 1 Chr. i. 48. (3) The third well dug by Isaac. It is located south of Beersheba, Gen. xxvi. 22.

Rē′hŭm (*merciful*). Levites and returned captives, Ez. ii. 2; iv. 8, 9, 17, 23; Neh. iii. 17; x. 25; xii. 3. Nehum in Neh. vii. 7, and Harim in xii. 15.

Rē′ī (*friendly*). A friend of David, 1 Kgs. i. 8.

Reins (*kidneys*). Once believed to be the seat of emotions; hence coupled with the heart, Ps. vii. 9; xvi. 7; Jer. xvii. 10; xx. 12.

Rē′kem (*flowered*). (1) A Midianite king slain by the Israelites, Num. xxxi. 8; Josh. xiii. 21. (2) Son of Hebron, 1 Chr. ii. 43, 44. (3) Town in Benjamin, Josh. xviii. 27.

Rĕm″a-lī′ah (*God-exalted*). Father of Pekah, king of Israel, 2 Kgs. xv. 25–37.

Rē′meth (*height*). Town in Issachar, Josh. xix. 21.

Rĕm′mon (*pomegranate*). Town in Simeon. Properly Rimmon, Josh. xix. 7.

Rĕm′mon=meth′o-är (*Remmon to Neah*). A landmark of Zebulun, Josh. xix. 13.

Rĕm′phan. An idol worshipped secretly by the Israelites in the wilderness, Acts vii. 43. Rephan in R. V. Chiun, Amos v. 26.

Rē′pha-el (*God-healed*). A Levite porter, 1 Chr. xxvi. 7.

Rē′phah (*wealth*). An Ephraimite, 1 Chr. vii. 25.

Rĕph″a-ī′ah (*God-healed*). (1) Descendant of David, 1 Chr. iii. 21. (2) A Simeonite chief, 1 Chr. iv. 42. (3) Descendant of Issachar, 1 Chr. vii. 2. (4) Descendant of Saul, 1 Chr. ix. 43. Rapha in viii. 37. (5) A wall-repairer and ruler of half of Jerusalem, Neh. iii. 9.

Rĕph′a-īm (*giants*). (1) A giant race east of Jordan, and probably driven to the west side, Gen. xiv. 5; xv. 20. (2) "Valley of Rephaim" was a landmark of Judah, and supposably the valley stretching from Jerusalem to Bethlehem, Josh. xv. 8; 2 Sam. v. 18; Isa. xvii. 5.

Rĕph′ī-dim (*rests*). Last Israelite encampment before Sinai, Ex. xvii. 1, 8–16; xix. 2.

Rē′sen (*bridle*). An Assyrian city built by Asher or Nimrod, Gen. x. 12.

Rē′sheph (*fire*). A descendant of Ephraim, 1 Chr. vii. 25.

Rĕṣ″ŭr-rĕc′tion (*rising again*). The rising again from the dead, Ps. xvi. 10, 11; Matt. xvi. 21; xx. 19; Acts ii. 31.

Rē′u (*friend*). Son of Peleg, Gen. xi. 18–21.

Reu′ben (*behold a son!*). Eldest son of Jacob and Leah, Gen. xxix. 32. Lost his birthright through crime, Gen. xxxv. 22; xlix. 3, 4. Tribe numerous and pastoral, and settled east of Jordan, Num. i. 20, 21; Josh. xiii. 15–23. Idolatrous, averse to war, carried captive by Assyria, Judg. v. 15, 16; 1 Chr. v. 26.

Reu′ben-ītes. Descendants of Reuben, Num. xxvi. 7; Josh. i. 12; 1 Chr. v. 26.

Reu′el (*God's friend*). (1) A son of Esau, Gen. xxxvi. 4, 10, 13, 17. (2) Ex. ii. 18. [RAGUEL.] (3) Father of Eliasaph the Gadite leader, Num. ii. 14. (4) A Benjamite, 1 Chr. ix. 8.

Reu′mah (*lofty*). Nahor's concubine, Gen. xxii. 24.

Rĕv″ĕ-lā′tion (*veil drawn back*). (1) Scripturally, revealing truth through divine agency or by supernatural means, 2 Cor. xii. 1–7. (2) Book of Revelation, or Apocalypse; last of N. T. books; written by the Apostle John, about A. D. 95–97, probably at Ephesus. It is a record of his inspired visions while a prisoner on the island of Patmos. Its aim is much disputed, but it is seemingly a prophetic panorama of church history to the end of time.

Rē′zeph (*heated stone*). An unknown place, 2 Kgs. xix. 12; Isa. xxxvii. 12.

Rĕ-zī′à (*delight*). An Asherite, 1 Chr. vii. 39.

Rē′zin (*firm*). (1) A king of Syria or Damascus, 2 Kgs. xv. 37; xvi. 5–9; Isa. vii. 1–8; viii. 6; ix. 11. (2) His descendants returned, Ez. ii. 48; Neh. vii. 50.

Rē′zon (*prince*). A Syrian who set up a petty kingdom at Damascus, 1 Kgs. xi. 23–25.

Rhē′gǐ-um (*breach*). Now Rheggio, port and capital of Calabria, southern Italy, Acts xxviii. 13.

Rhē′sà (*head*). One mentioned in Christ's genealogy, Luke iii. 27.

Rhō′dà (*rose*). A maid in the house of Mary, mother of John Mark, Acts xii. 12–15.

Rhōdes (*roses*). An Ægean island, just off the coast of Asia Minor. Noted for the splendor of its capital city, Rhodes. Paul touched there, Acts xxi. 1.

Rhŏd′o-cus. A traitorous Jew, 2 Macc. xiii. 21.

Rhō′dus, 1 Macc. xv. 23. [RHODES.]

Rī′bāi (*pleader*). Father of Ittai, one of David's

guard, 2 Sam. xxiii. 29 ; 1 Chr. xi. 31.

Rĭb′lah (*fertile*). An ancient strategic city on N. E. frontier of Canaan, and on military route from Palestine to Babylonia, Num. xxxiv. 11 ; 2 Kgs. xxiii. 33 ; xxv. 6–21 ; Jer. xxxix. 5–7.

Rĭd′dle (*counsel*). Oriental peoples fond of rid- d′es. Hebrew riddles embraced proverbs, Prov. i. 6 ; oracles, Num. xii. 8 ; songs, Ps. xlix. 4 ; parables, Ezek. xvii. 2 ; intricate sentences, questions, and problems, Judg. xiv. 12–14 ; 1 Kgs. x. 1 ; 2 Chr. ix. 1 ; Dan. viii. 23.

Rĭm′mŏn (*pomegranate*). (1) Father of Ishbo- sheth′s murderers, 2 Sam. iv. 2–9. (2) A Syrian deity worshipped at Damascus, 2 Kgs. v. 18. (3) Levitical city in Zebulun, 1 Chr. vi. 77. Remmon-methoar, Josh. xix. 13. (4) Town in Judah and Simeon, Josh. xv. 32. (5) A rock or fastness, now Rummon, 10 miles north of Jerusalem, to which the defeated Ben- jamites retreated, Judg. xx. 45, 47 ; xxi. 13.

Rĭm′mon=pā′rez (*pomegranates of the wrath*). A desert encampment, Num. xxxiii. 19.

Rĭng (*around*). Rings were indispensable articles of Jewish ornament. Worn on fingers, wrists, ankles, in ears and nostrils, Isa. iii. 20, 21 ; Luke xv. 22 ; Jas. ii. 2. Symbols of authority, Gen. xli. 42 ; Esth. iii. 10. Used as seals, Esth. iii. 12 ; Dan. vi. 17.

Rĭn′nah (*song*). A Judahite, 1 Chr. iv. 20.

Rī′phăth (*spoken*). Son of Gomer, and founder of a northern nation, Gen. x. 3 ; 1 Chr. i. 6.

Rĭs′sah (*ruin*). A desert encampment of the Israelites, Num. xxxiii. 21, 22.

Rĭth′mah (*bush*). A desert encampment of the Israelites, Num. xxxiii. 18, 19.

Rĭv′ĕr (*banked*). In Hebrew sense, a large flow- ing stream, rivulet, ravine, valley, or wady. "River of Egypt" is the Nile, Gen. xv. 18 ; Num. xxxiv. 5 ; Josh. xv. 4, 47 ; 1 Kgs. viii. 65 ; 2 Kgs. xxiv. 7. "The river" is the Euphrates, Gen. xxxi. 21 ; Ex. xxiii. 31.

Rĭz′pah. Concubine of Saul, and the mother who watched over the remains of her slain sons, 2 Sam. iii. 7 ; xxi. 8–11.

Rōad (*ride*). In Bible sense, a path or way. For "road" in 1 Sam. xxvii. 10, read "raid" or "inroad."

Rŏb′bĕr-ȳ (*breaking, riving*). Oppression, pil- lage, and thievery formed almost an employment among nomad tribes, Gen. xvi. 12 ; Judg. ii. 14 ; Luke x. 30 ; John xviii. 40.

Rŏ-bō′am. Greek form of Rehoboam, Matt. i. 7.

Rŏd. Shoot or branch. Figuratively, Christ, Isa. xi. 1 ; root, Ps. lxxiv. 2 ; Jer. x. 16 ; support, Ps. xxiii. 4 ; authority, Ps. ii. 9 ; affliction, Job ix. 34 ; tithing-rod, Ezek. xx. 37.

Rōe, Rōe′bŭck (*animal*). A beautiful fleet animal, probably the roe-deer of Western Asia ; but associated with antelope and gazelle, 2 Sam. ii. 18 ; 1 Chr. xii. 8 ; S. of Sol. ii. 17 ; viii. 14.

Rŏ-ḡē′lĭm (*fullers*). Home of Barzillai, in Gilead, 2 Sam. xvii. 27.

Rōh′gah (*clamor*). A chief of Asher, 1 Chr. vii. 34.

Rōll (*little wheel*). The book of ancient times, consisting of long strips of linen, papyrus, or parch- ment written upon and wrapped on a stick, Isa. viii. 1 ; Ezek. ii. 9, 10.

Rŏ-măm′tĭ=ē′zĕr. One of Heman′s fourteen sons, 1 Chr. xxv. 4, 31.

Rōme, Rō′mans. First mentioned in Bible in 1 Macc. i. 10, when Rome was pushing her conquests in Palestine and Syria. The capital, Rome, is on the Tiber, about 15 miles from the sea. Founded B. C. 752. Governed by kings till B. C. 509 ; then by consuls till Augustus Cæsar became emperor, B. C. 30. At the Christian era Rome was virtual mistress of the civilized world. Empire declined rapidly after re- moval of capital to Constantinople by Constantine, A. D. 328. Gospel early introduced among Romans, but

Christians persecuted till time of Constantine. Pal- estine was ruled from Rome by kings, procurators, governors, or proconsuls. Paul wrote his celebrated epistle to the Romans from Corinth, about A. D. 58, to show that Jew and Gentile were alike subject to sin and in equal need of justification and sanctification.

Roof. [HOUSE.]

Room (*wide*). Frequently used in N. T. for spot, seat, place, as at table, Matt. xxiii. 6 ; Mark xii. 39 ; Luke xiv. 7 ; xx. 46.

Rōṣe (*ruddy*). Disputed translation. Some say narcissus is meant ; others would simply read "flower" for "rose," S. of Sol. ii. 1 ; Isa. xxxv. 1.

Rŏsh (*head*). A Benjamite, Gen. xlvi. 21.

Rŏṣ′in (*resin*). The resin left after turpentine is distilled. But in Bible naphtha is meant, Ezek. xxvii. 17 marg. ; Song of Three Children, 23.

Ru′bȳ (*red*). A ruddy, valuable gem ; but the original word is thought to mean coral or pearl, Job xxviii. 18 ; Prov. iii. 15.

Rue (*thick-leaved*). A shrubby, medicinal plant, cultivated in the gardens of the east. Tithable, Luke xi. 42.

Ru′fus (*red*). Son of Simon of Cyrene, Mark xv. 21. Probably the same in Rom. xvi. 13.

Ru′ha-mah (*having received mercy*). A symbol- ical name used in Hos. ii. 1.

Ru′mah (*high*). A place, 2 Kgs. xxiii. 36, asso- ciated with Arumah and Dumah.

Rŭsh (*reed*). [REED.]

Ruth (*beauty*). The Moabite wife of Mahlon and Boaz. The beautiful pastoral of Ruth, 8th of O. T. books, contains her life. It supplements Judges and prefaces Samuel, and traces the lineage of David. Time of writing and authorship are unknown.

Rȳe. Not an Egyptian cereal. "Spelt" is doubt- less meant, it being a common Egyptian food, Ex. ix. 32 ; Isa. xxviii. 25. Same Hebrew word is rendered "fitches" in Ezek. iv. 9.

S

Sā′′băch-thā′nī (*hast thou forsaken me?*). An Aramaic, or Syro-Chaldaic, word, part of Christ′s ex- clamation on the cross, Matt. xxvii. 46 ; Mark xv. 34. [ELI.]

Săb′a-ŏth (*hosts*). Used usually with Jehovah, — "Lord of hosts ;" — hosts being comprehensive, and signifying the powers of earth and heaven, Isa. i. 9 ; Rom. ix. 29 ; Jas. v. 4.

Sā′bat (*around*). (1) His sons were returned captives, 1 Esdr. v. 34. (2) 1 Macc. xvi. 14. [SEBAT.]

Săb′băth (*rest*). Rest day, or seventh of the week, Gen. ii. 2, 3. Became a Mosaic institution for rest and festal occasions, Ex. xvi. 23–30 ; xx. 8–11 ; Lev. xix. 3, 30 ; xxiii. 3 ; xxv. 4–9 ; Deut. v. 12–15. Day for consulting prophets, 2 Kgs. iv. 23. A day of teaching and joy, Neh. viii. 1–12 ; Hos. ii. 11. A whole week of time is implied in Matt. xxviii. 1 ; Mark xvi. 1 ; Luke xxiv. 1 ; John xx. 1 ; Acts xx. 7 ; 1 Cor. xvi. 2. Among Christians, the day after the Hebrew Sabbath, or seventh-day, gradually and till fully established, became the Sabbath, or first-day, in commemoration of the resurrection of Christ. Hence, "The Lord′s Day," John xx. 26 ; Acts xx. 6–11 ; 1 Cor. xvi. 2 ; Rev. i. 10.

Săb′băth Day′s Journey. Travel on the Sab- bath was limited, Ex. xvi. 29. Custom seemed to sanction 2000 paces from the walls of a city as suffi- cient for all needs on the day of rest, Acts i. 12.

Săb′′ba-thē′us, 1 Esdr. ix. 14. [SHABBETHAI.]

Săb-băt′ĭ-cal Year. By the Mosaic code, each seventh year was sacred. The land rested, the poor were entitled to what grew, and debtors were re- leased, Ex. xxiii. 10, 11 ; Lev. xxv. 2–7 ; Deut. xv. 1–18.

Săb-bē′us, 1 Esdr. ix. 32. [SHEMAIAH.]

Să-bē′ans. (1) Descendants of Sheba, son of Joktan, Joel iii. 8. (2) Evidently the descendants of Seba, son of Cush, Isa. xlv. 14. (3) Perhaps a third tribe, though it may be one of the two just mentioned. (4) A wrong translation in Ezek. xxiii. 42, "drunkards," in margin.

Sā′bī, 1 Esdr. v. 34. [ZEBAIM.]

Săb′tà, Săb′tàh (*striking*). Third son of Cush, Gen. x. 7 ; 1 Chr. i. 9.

Săb′te-chà, Săb′te-chàh (*striking*). Fifth son of Cush, Gen. x. 7 ; 1 Chr. i. 9.

Sā′car (*hire*). (1) Father of one of David's warriors, 1 Chr. xi. 35. Sharar in 2 Sam. xxiii. 33. (2) A Levite porter, 1 Chr. xxvi. 4.

Săck′bŭt (*pull and push*). A wind instrument, trombone. But in Dan. iii. 5–15, a stringed instrument of triangular shape with from four to twenty strings.

Săck′cloth (*coarse cloth*). A coarse, goat-hair cloth used for making sacks and rough garments. The latter were worn next the skin by mourners and repentants, Gen. xxxvii. 34 ; xlii. 25 ; 2 Sam. iii. 31 ; 1 Kgs. xxi. 27 ; 2 Kgs. vi. 30 ; Esth. iv. 1, 2 ; Job xvi. 15 ; Rev. vi. 12.

Săc′rĭ-fīçe (*making sacred*). Propitiatory, atoning or thanksgiving offering to God. An ordained rite, Lev. xvii. 4–9 ; Deut. xvi. 5–19. Sacrificial offerings numerous ; but chiefly, the "burnt-offering," Lev. i. 1–17 ; "sin-offering," and "trespass-offering," Lev. vii. 1–10 ; "peace-offering," Lev. vii. 11–34 ; the latter also a "free-will" offering. Among Christians all sacrificial offerings merged in the universal offering of Christ's body, Heb. ix., x.

Săd′′a-mī′as, 2 Esdr. i. 1. [SHALLUM.]

Sā′das, 1 Esdr. v. 13. [IDDO.]

Săd′du-çees (*disciples of Zadok*). A Jewish sect, supposably Zadokites, 1 Kgs. i. 32–45, whose chief tenets were (1) rejection of the divinity of the Mosaic oral law and traditions ; (2) rejection of the later O. T. books, but acceptance of the Mosaic teachings ; (3) denial of angel and spiritual existence, and consequent immortality of the soul ; (4) belief in the absolute moral freedom of man. Their hatred of Christianity was as bitter as that of the Pharisees, Matt. iii. 7 ; Mark xii. 18 ; Luke xx. 27 ; Acts iv. 1 ; v. 17 ; xxiii. 6–10. Though composed of men of position, the sect was never very numerous nor influential, and it disappeared from history after the first century of the Christian era.

Sā′dŏc (*just*). (1) 2 Esdr. i. 1. [ZADOK.] (2) One in the genealogy of Christ, Matt. i. 14.

Săf′fron (*yellow*). The fall crocus, much cultivated in the Orient for its perfume and medicinal properties, S. of Sol. iv. 14.

Săint (*sanctified*). In O. T., a pious Jew, Ps. xvi. 3. In N. T., a Christian believer, Rom. i. 7 ; viii. 27 ; Heb. vi. 10.

Sā′là, Sā′lah (*sprout*). A descendant of Shem, Gen. x. 24 ; xi. 12–15 ; Luke iii. 35. Shelah in 1 Chr. i. 18, 24.

Săl′a-mis (*shaken*). A city of the island of Cyprus, visited by Paul. It was afterwards called Constantia, Acts xiii. 5. The old city was once the capital of the island and carried on a large trade in fruit, wine, flax, and copper with adjacent continents. The Jewish population was large. Its site is now traced by masses of ruins.

Sā-lā′thĭ-el (*asked of God*). Son of Jechonias, 1 Chr. iii. 17 ; Matt. i. 12 ; Luke iii. 27. Shealtiel elsewhere.

Săl′cah, Săl′chah (*moving*). A city in Bashan which fell to Manasseh. Now Sulkhad, Deut. iii. 10 ; Josh. xii. 5 ; xiii. 11 ; 1 Chr. v. 11.

Sā′lem (*peace*). The place over which Melchizedek was king, supposably Jerusalem, Gen. xiv. 18 ;

Ps. lxxvi. 2 ; Heb. vii. 1, 2.

Sā′lim (*peace*). The place near Ænon, where John baptized, John iii. 23.

Săl′la-ī (*basket-maker*). (1) A returned Benjamite, Neh. xi. 8. (2) A returned priest, Neh. xii. 20.

Săl′lu (*measured*). (1) A Benjamite, 1 Chr. ix. 7. (2) A priest, Neh. xi. 7 ; xii. 7.

Săl-lū′mus, 1 Esdr. ix. 25. [SHALLUM.]

Săl′mà, Săl′mŏn (*clothed*). (1) Father of Boaz and husband of Rahab, Ruth iv. 20, 21 ; 1 Chr. ii. 11 ; Matt. i. 5 ; Luke iii. 32. (2) One of the high hills surrounding Shechem, which afforded pasturage for Jacob's flocks, Ps. lxviii. 14. Zalmon in Judg. ix. 48.

Săl-mō′ne (*clothed*). Eastern promontory of Crete, Acts xxvii. 7.

Sā′lŏm. (1) Bar. i. 7. [SHALLUM.] (2) 1 Macc. ii. 26. [SALLU.]

Să-lō′me (*clothed*). (1) Wife of Zebedee, Mark xv. 40 ; xvi. 1. Mentioned indirectly in Matt. xx. 20–22 ; xxvii. 56. (2) The daughter of Herodias, who danced before Herod, Matt. xiv. 6 ; Mark vi. 22.

Sąlt (*sea product*). Abundant in Palestine. Used with food and sacrificial offerings, Job vi. 6 ; Lev. ii. 13 ; Num. xviii. 19 ; Mark ix. 49. Monument of divine displeasure, Gen. xix. 26 ; token of indissoluble alliance, Lev. ii. 13 ; Num. xviii. 19 ; 2 Chr. xiii. 5 ; used to rub new-born children, Ezek. xvi. 4 ; type of maintenance, Ez. iv. 14 marg. ; emblem of sterility, Judg. ix. 45 ; Jer. xvii. 6 ; a manure, Luke xiv. 35 ; emblem of holy life and conversation, Matt. v. 13 ; Mark ix. 50 ; Col. iv. 6.

Sąlt, City of. Fifth of the six cities of Judah, situate in the wilderness of Judah, Josh. xv. 62.

Sąlt Sēa. The Dead Sea. "Sea of the plain," Deut. iv. 49 ; 2 Kgs. xiv. 25. "Salt sea," Deut. iii. 17 ; Josh. iii. 16 ; xii. 3. "East sea," Ezek. xlvii. 18 ; Joel ii. 20 ; Zech. xiv. 8. "The sea," Ezek. xlvii. 8. "Vale of Siddim," Gen. xiv. 3. "Sodomitish sea," 1 Esdr. v. 7. Title "Dead Sea" not found among Hebrew writers, but introduced by Greek authors. Situate 16 miles E. of Jerusalem ; 46 miles long by 10 wide ; 1300 feet below the level of the Mediterranean ; waters intensely salt ; receives waters of Jordan from the north ; no outlet.

Sąlt, Văl′ley of. Supposably the valley, or depression, of Akabah, extending from Dead Sea to Gulf of Akabah, 2 Sam. viii. 13 ; 2 Kgs. xiv. 7 ; 1 Chr. xviii. 12 ; 2 Chr. xxv. 11 ; Ps. lx. title. But many excellent authorities limit it to a section of Edom near Petra.

Sā′lu (*weighed*). Father of Zimri, a chief of Simeon, Num. xxv. 14.

Sā′lum, 1 Esdr. v. 28. [SHALLUM.]

Săl′′ū-tā′tion (*good health, greeting*). Personal salutation very formal in East. The "peace be with thee," or similar expression, was accompanied by a profound bow, kiss, embrace, or other courtesy, Gen. xix. 1 ; 1 Sam. xxv. 23 ; Matt. x. 12 ; Luke i. 41. Epistolary salutation took the form found in the opening and closing of the epistles, Rom. i. 7 ; 1 Cor. i. 3 ; etc.

Săl-vā′tion (*deliverance*). Temporal deliverance, Ex. xiv. 13. Spiritual deliverance, 2 Cor. vii. 10 ; Eph. i. 13 ; Heb. ii. 3.

Săm′′a-rā′is. Son of Ozora, 1 Esdr. ix. 34.

Sà-mā′rĭ-à (*watch mountain*). (1) The kingdom of Samaria, synonymous with the kingdom of Israel, lay to the north of Judah. It varied in size at different times, but in general embraced the territory of the ten revolting tribes on either side of the Jordan, 1 Kgs. xiii. 32. Named from its capital, Samaria. In N. T. times, Samaria was one of the three subdivisions of Palestine, lying between Judea on the south and Galilee on the north. (2) Capital of the kingdom of Samaria or Israel, and located 30 miles north of Jerusalem. Founded by Omri, king of Israel, about B. C. 925, and called Samaria, after

Shemer, from whom he bought the ground, 1 Kgs. xvi. 23, 24. It became a beautiful and strong city and remained the capital till Shalmaneser, the Assyrian, destroyed it and the empire, B. C. 721, 2 Kgs. xviii. 9-12. Herod rebuilt it and restored much of its ancient splendor, naming it Sebaste in honor of Augustus, who gave it to him. Philip preached the gospel there, Acts viii. 5-9. It is now a modest village called Sebastiyeh, which perpetuates the name Sebaste, and is noted for its many ruins, chief of which is the famous colonnade, 3000 feet in length, 100 columns of which are still standing. Respecting the city the prophecy, Mic. i. 6, has been literally fulfilled.

Să-măr′ĭ-tanṣ. Inhabitants of Samaria, 2 Kgs. xvii. 29. The planting of Assyrian colonists in Samaria, 2 Kgs. xvii. 24-34, led to a strange admixture of people, language, laws, religions, and customs, and brought the name Samaritan into reproach with Jews, Matt. x. 5; John iv. 9-26; viii. 48; Acts viii. 1; ix. 31.

Săm′găr=nē′bŏ (*sword of Nebo*). A general of Nebuchadnezzar at the taking of Jerusalem, Jer. xxxix. 3.

Săm′mus, 1 Esdr. ix. 43. [SHEMA.]

Săm′lah (*raiment*). A king of Edom, Gen. xxxvi. 36, 37; 1 Chr. i. 47, 48.

Să′mos (*height*). An island of the Grecian archipelago, off the coast of Lydia. Visited by Paul on his third tour, Acts xx. 15.

Săm″o-thrā′çĭā (*Thracian Samos*). An island in the northern Ægean belonging to Thrace. Visited by Paul on his first tour, Acts xvi. 11.

Sămp′să-mēṣ. Probably Samsun, on Black Sea coast, 1 Macc. xv. 23.

Săm′son (*sunlike*). Son of Manoah, of Dan, and judge of Israel for 20 years, Judg. xiii. 3-25. Noted for his great strength, marvellous exploits, and moral weakness. Contrary to the wishes of his parents, and to the law as laid down in Ex. xxxiv. 16, Deut. vii. 3, he married a Philistine woman of Timnath, whom he deserted on account of her treachery, Judg. xiv. Wishing to return to her, and finding her given to another, he wreaked his vengeance on the Philistines by burning their crops and slaughtering great numbers of them, Judg. xv. 1-8. He was surrounded by 3000 of his enemies, while he dwelt on the rock Etam, and surrendered to them, but burst his bands, and routed them with great slaughter, Judg. xv. 9-19. Again he was surrounded by enemies in Gaza, but escaped by carrying away the gates of the city. The secret of his strength was finally detected by Delilah, and he was imprisoned and made blind. He finally killed himself and numerous enemies by pulling down the pillars of the house in which they were feasting, Judg. xvi.

Săm′u-el (*God hath heard*). Son of Elkanah and Hannah, celebrated Hebrew prophet and last of the judges, 1 Sam. i. 19-28. Educated under Eli, 1 Sam. iii. 4-14, and became his successor in the prophetic office. His sons proved so recreant that the people demanded a king, and Samuel anointed Saul, and resigned his authority to him, 1 Sam. xii. He also anointed David, Saul's successor, 1 Sam. xvi. 13. He died at Ramah, 1 Sam. xxv. 1. The two books which bear his name, the 9th and 10th of O. T., are called also First and Second Books of Kings. They were originally one book and contain the lives of Samuel, Saul, and David. The authorship is ascribed to a period subsequent to the secession of the ten tribes, and it is clearly an authorship different from Kings, for in Kings there are many references to the law, while in Samuel there are none. In Kings the Exile is alluded to; it is not so in Samuel. The plans of the two works vary; Samuel is biographical, Kings annalistic.

Săn-băl′lat (*strong*). A Persian officer in Samaria who opposed Ezra and Nehemiah and persistently misrepresented them at court, Neh. ii. 10; iv. 1-9; xiii. 28.

Sănc′tĭ-fȳ (*to make holy*). To prepare or set apart persons or things to holy use, Ex. xiii. 2. It was in allusion to the law that Christ spoke in John xvii. 19. To establish union with Christ by faith, John xvii. 17. To exercise the graces of knowledge, such as faith, love, repentance, humility, etc., toward God and man, 2 Thess. ii. 13; 1 Pet. i. 2.

Sănc′tụ-ar″ȳ (*made holy*). A holy or sanctified place, Ps. xx. 2. The secret part of the temple in which the ark of the covenant was kept, and which none but the high priest might enter, and he only once a year, on the day of solemn expiation, Lev. iv. 6. Also applied to the furniture of the holy place, Num. x. 21; to the apartment where the altar of incense, table of shewbread and holy candlestick, etc., stood, 2 Chr. xxvi. 18; to the whole tabernacle or temple, Josh. xxiv. 26; 2 Chr. xx. 8. "Sanctuary of strength," because belonging to God, Dan. xi. 31. Any place of public worship of God, Ps. lxxiii. 17. Heaven, Ps. cii. 19. Place of refuge, Isa. viii. 14; Ezek. xi. 16. Land of Israel called God's sanctuary, Ex. xv. 17. "Worldly sanctuary," one of an earthly type, Heb. ix. 1.

Sănd (*whirling*). Abundant in the wastes of Palestine, Arabia, and Egypt. Used much figuratively. Innumerable multitudes, Gen. xxxii. 12; abundance, Gen. xli. 49; weight, Job vi. 3; Prov. xxvii. 3; sea boundary, Jer. v. 22; hiding place, Ex. ii. 12; Deut. xxxiii. 19.

Săn′dal (*board*). A sole of wood, leather, or plaited material, bound to the foot with straps. The shoe of the Bible. Not worn in the house nor in holy places, Ex. iii. 5; Deut. xxv. 9; Josh. v. 15.

Săn′he-drim, Săn′he-drin (*seated together*). The supreme council of the Jewish nation, whose germ was in the seventy elders, Num. xi. 16, 17, and further development in Jehoshaphat's tribunal, 2 Chr. xix. 8-11. In full power after the captivity, and lasted till A. D. 425. The "great Sanhedrim" was composed of 71 priests, scribes, and elders, and presided over by the high priest. The "lesser Sanhedrims" were provincial courts in the towns, and composed of 23 members appointed by the "great Sanhedrim." The word usually appears as "council" in N. T., Matt. v. 22; Mark xiv. 55; John xi. 47; Acts iv. 5-7. The members of the Sanhedrim embraced the three classes, priests, elders, and scribes. After the Roman conquest it had no control of the death power, but the confirmation and execution of capital sentences rested with the Roman procurator. Thus it was that while the Sanhedrim condemned Christ for blasphemy, he was not brought under the Roman judgment of death till accused by the Jews of treason, Matt. xxvi. 65, 66; John xviii. 31; xix. 12. The stoning of Stephen, Acts vii. 57-59, was either due to mob excitement, or else illegal.

Săn-săn′nah (*branch*). A town in southern Judah, Josh. xv. 31.

Săph (*giant*). A Philistine giant, 2 Sam. xxi. 18. Sippai, 1 Chr. xx. 4.

Sā′phat, 1 Esdr. v. 9. [SHEPHATIAH.]

Săph′ĭr (*fair*). A village addressed by Micah, Mic. i. 11.

Săp-phī′rå (*handsome*). Wife of Ananias, and participator in his crime and punishment, Acts v. 1-10.

Săp′phīre. A light blue gem, next to the diamond in hardness, Ex. xxiv. 10. Second stone in second row of high priest's breastplate, Ex. xxviii. 18. A foundation stone of the holy Jerusalem, Rev. xxi. 19.

Sā′rå. (1) Daughter of Raguel, Tob. iii. 7. (2) Heb. xi. 11; 1 Pet. iii. 6. [SARAH.]

Sā′rah (*princess*). (1) Wife of Abraham and mother of Isaac, Gen. xi. 29; xxi. 2, 3. Name changed from Sarai to Sarah, Gen. xvii. 15, 16.

At Abraham's request she passed herself off as his sister during their sojourn in Egypt, Gen. xii. 10–20, which angered the Pharaoh and led to their banishment. Relentless toward Hagar (whom she had given to Abraham as a concubine) when she bore Ishmael, and caused her to be banished to the desert, Gen. xvi. 5–16; deceitful when Isaac was promised, Gen. xviii. 15; cruel again toward Hagar on the occasion of Isaac's weaning, causing her to be banished finally from the household, Gen. xxi. 9–21. Commended for her faith, Heb. xi. 11; and obedience, 1 Pet. iii. 6. Died at age of 127 years and buried at Machpelah, Gen. xxiii. (2) Daughter of Asher, Num. xxvi. 46.

Sā′rāi, Gen. xi. 29. [SARAH.]

Sär′a-mel (*court*). Meeting place where Simon Maccabeus was made high priest, 1 Macc. xiv. 28.

Sā′räph (*burning*). A Judahite, 1 Chr. iv. 22.

Sär-chĕd′ō-nus, Tob. i. 21. [ESARHADDON.]

Sär′dīne, Sär′dĭ-us (*stone of Sardis*). The sard or carnelian, a blood-red or flesh-colored stone, first in first row of high priest's breastplate, Ex. xxviii. 17; Rev. iv. 3.

Sär′dis. Capital of Lydia in Asia Minor. Once noted for beauty and wealth; now the miserable village of Sert-Kalessi, Rev. iii. 1–6. It was the residence of Crœsus, renowned for riches, and Cyrus, when he conquered it, B. C. 548, is said to have captured fabulous treasure there. Alexander captured it from the Persians, and it was again sacked and captured by Antiochus, B. C. 214. It was destroyed by an earthquake. A. D. 17, but was speedily rebuilt. The art of wool-dyeing was discovered there. Seat of one of the seven churches of Asia, Rev. iii. 1.

Sär′dītes. Descendants of Sered, Num. xxvi. 26.

Sär′dō-nyx. A precious stone combining the sard and onyx varieties, whence its name, Rev. xxi. 20.

Sā′rĕ-à. A swift scribe, 2 Esdr. xiv. 24.

Sä-rĕp′tà. Greek form of Zarephath, Luke iv. 26.

Sär′gon (*sun-prince*). An Assyrian king whom recently discovered inscriptions make the successor of Shalmaneser and father of Sennacherib, B. C. 722–705, 2 Kgs. xvii. 6; Isa. xx. 1.

Sā′rid (*survivor*). A landmark of Zebulun, Josh. xix. 10–12.

Sā′ron, Acts ix. 35. [SHARON.]

Sä-rō′thie. His sons returned, 1 Esdr. v. 34.

Sär-sē′chim (*master of wardrobes*). A prince of Babylon at taking of Jerusalem, Jer. xxxix. 3.

Sā′ruch, Luke iii. 35. [SERUG.]

Sā′tăn (*adversary*). In O. T. a common noun, meaning enemy or adversary in general, 1 Sam. xxix. 4; 2 Sam. xix. 22; except in Job i. 6, 12; ii. 1; Zech. iii. 1, where the word becomes a proper noun, and spiritual representative of evil. In N. T. sense, chief of the evil spirits; great adversary of man; the devil, Matt. iv. 10; xxv. 41; Rev. xx., and elsewhere. Called also "the prince of this world;" "the wicked one;" "the tempter;" and in Rev. xii. 9, the old serpent, the devil, and Satan.

Săt′ўr. A mythical creature, half man, half goat, inhabiting woods and waste places, Isa. xiii. 21; xxxiv. 14.

Saul (*wished*). (1) An early king of Edom, Gen. xxxvi. 37, 38. Shaul in 1 Chr. i. 48, 49. (2) A Benjamite, son of Kish, and first king of Israel. Anointed by Samuel; reigned B. C. 1095–1055; slain with his sons at Gilboa. His versatile career is described in 1 Sam. ix.–xxxi. He stands in Bible history for the stature, strength, and ruggedness of character so essential to judges in times of danger or necessary reform, and for the bravery, generalship and self-confidence of one called on to institute a new empire. Of boundless ambition and erratic judgment, he usurped the priestly function, and drew the reproaches of the aged prophet Samuel, who had surrendered his line

in anointing him. The announcement that royalty could not be perpetuated in his family drove him to inexcusable follies, yet with the courage of youth he fought his last despairing battle with the Philistines, and finished his course on his own sword. (3) Hebrew name of Paul, Acts xiii. 9.

Săv′a-ran, 1 Macc. vi. 43. [AVARAN.]

Sā′vĭ-as, 1 Esdr. viii. 2. [UZZI.]

Saw (*cutter*). Hebrew saws doubtless patterned after those of Egypt, being single-handled, with teeth inclined toward the handle, so that cutting was done by pulling. Used for sawing wood, Isa. x. 15; stone, 1 Kgs. vii. 9; torture, 2 Sam. xii. 31; 1 Chr. xx. 3; Heb. xi. 37.

Scāpe′gōat, Lev. xvi. 7–26. [GOAT.]

Scär′let (*orange-red*). A Tyrian color much prized by ancients, Ex. xxv. 4; Prov. xxxi. 21.

Scĕp′tre (*prop*). Any rod or staff. A shepherd's crook or tithing rod, Lev. xxvii. 32; Mic. vii. 14. A symbol of royal power, Gen. xlix. 10; Num. xxiv. 17; overlaid with gold, Esth. iv. 11.

Scĕ′va (*fitted*). An Ephesian priest, Acts xix. 14–16.

Scôr′pĭ-on (*crawler*). A venomous creature allied to the spider, but resembling the lobster. Its sting is painful and often fatal, Deut. viii. 15; 1 Kgs. xii. 11; Rev. ix. 3–10. A dangerous gift, Luke xi. 12.

Scoûrg′ing (*thonging*). A common Hebrew punishment. The scourge was made of three lashes of leather or cord. Not more than forty stripes could be administered, Deut. xxv. 1–3; Matt. x. 17; xxiii. 34. Rods or twigs were also used, 2 Cor. xi. 25.

Scrībe (*writer*). The Hebrew scribe or writer appears to have been at first a court or military official, Ex. v. 6; Judg. v. 14; then secretary or recorder, for kings, priests, and prophets, 2 Sam. viii. 17; xx. 25; finally a secretary of state, doctor, or teacher, Ez. vii. 6. Scribes became a class or guild, copyists and expounders of the law, and through their innovations fell under the same denunciations as priests and Pharisees, Matt. xxiii. 1–33; Mark vii. 5–13; Luke v. 30.

Scrĭp (*bag*). A shepherd's bag, 1 Sam. xvii. 40. A wallet for carrying food and traveller's conveniences, Matt. x. 10; Luke x. 4.

Scrĭp′ture (*written*). By way of prëeminence, the sacred writings contained in the Old and New Testaments. [BIBLE.]

Scўth′ĭ-an (*fierce-looking*). Name applied to the fierce, nomadic nations north of the Black and Caspian seas, Col. iii. 11.

Scўth-ŏp′ŏ-lis (*Scythian city*). The city of Bethshean in Palestine was for a time so called because captured and held by Scythian nomads, 2 Macc. xii. 29.

Sēa. The Hebrews so designated any large body of water, whether lake, river, sea, or ocean, Gen. i. 10; Deut. xxx. 13; Job xiv. 11; Isa. xix. 5; Jer. li. 36; Ezek. xxxii. 2. (1) "Molten sea" was the immense brass laver of Solomon's temple, 1 Kgs. vii. 23–26. (2) "Sea of the Plain," Deut. iv. 49. [SALT SEA.] (3) "Great Sea," Josh. xv. 47, "uttermost sea," Deut. xi. 24, the Mediterranean, between Europe and Africa. (4) "Sea of Tiberias" [GENNESARET.] (5) "Sea of Merom." [MEROM.]

Sēal (*little mark*). Much used by ancients to authenticate documents and secure packages and doors, the impression being made in clay or wax. Seals were frequently engraved stones set in rings; Gen. xli. 42; Job xxxviii. 14; Jer. xxxii. 10; Matt. xxvii. 66.

Sē′bà. A son of Cush, Gen. x. 7. Mentioned as a nation or country in Ps. lxxii. 10; Isa. xliii. 3; xlv. 14, and associated with Meroe on the upper Nile.

Sē′băt, Shē′băt (*rod*). Fifth month of Jewish civil and eleventh of sacred year, corresponding to parts of February and March, Zech. i. 7.

Sĕc′a-cah (*thicket*). A city in Judah, Josh. xv. 61.

Sē′chu (*tower*). A place between Gibeah and Ramah, noted for its well, 1 Sam. xix. 22.

Sĕct (*way, school*). A party adhering to a doctrine, as the sect of Sadducees, Acts v. 17, or Pharisees, Acts xv. 5; xxvi. 5. Christians in general were for a long time called by the Jews, in a spirit of contempt, "the sect of the Nazarenes," Acts xxiv. 5. The word is also applied to a certain set of doctrines or mode of life, Acts xxiv. 14; 2 Pet. ii. 1; and to heresies proper, or perversions of Christian truth, Gal. v. 20.

Sĕ-cŭn′dus (*second*). A Thessalonian friend of Paul. Acts xx. 4.

Sĕd″ē-çī′as (1) Ancestor of Baruch, Bar. i. 1. (2) Son of King Josiah, Bar. i. 8.

Sēed (*sowed*). Seed for sowing must not be mingled, Lev. xix. 19. Children, descendants, Gen. xvii. 12; Gal. iii. 16. Pedigree, Ez. ii. 59. The male fertilizing element, Gen. xxxviii. 9.

Sēer (*who sees*). 1 Sam. ix. 9. [PROPHET.]

Sēethe (*boil*). To boil, Ex. xvi. 23.

Sē′gub (*lifted up*). (1) A son of Hiel who rebuilt Jericho, 1 Kgs. xvi. 34. (2) A Judahite, 1 Chr. ii. 21, 22.

Sē′īr (*hairy*). (1) A Horite chief, Gen. xxxvi. 21; Deut. ii. 12. (2) Land or country corresponding with valley and mountains of Arabah, stretching from the Dead Sea to the Gulf of Akaba, Gen. xiv. 6; xxxii. 3; xxxiii. 14–16. The region was first occupied by the Horites, and fell into possession of Esau and his posterity, Gen. xxxvi. 8–9. Hence Seir and Edom are sometimes spoken of as identical. The Israelites, when refused permission to march through Edom to Moab, marched round the granite ranges of Seir and entered Moab by the east and north. (3) A boundary mark of Judah, Josh. xv. 10.

Sē′ī-răth (*hairy*). Place to which the murderer Ehud fled, Judg. iii. 26.

Sē′là, Sē′lah (*rock*). A rock-founded city of Edom, the Petra of the Greeks, half way between the Dead Sea and Gulf of Akaba. Subdued by King Amaziah and called Joktheel, "subdued of God." Remarkable now for its ruins, among which are a rock-hewn temple and amphitheatre, 2 Kgs. xiv. 7; Isa. xvi. 1. The complete destruction and desolation of the place fulfils the prophecy of Jeremiah, Jer. xlix. 16, 17.

Sē′lah. A word of frequent occurrence in Psalms, and supposed to mean an interlude in vocal music, or a pianissimo of all parts, Ps. ix. 16; Hab. iii. 3, 9, 13.

Sē′là=hăm″mah-lē′koth (*rock of escapes*). Rocky stronghold in wilderness of Maon, where David escaped from Saul, 1 Sam. xxiii. 28.

Sē′led (*lifted up*). A Judahite, 1 Chr. ii. 30.

Sĕl″ē-mī′ah. A swift scribe, 2 Esdr. xiv. 24.

Sē-leū′çī-à (*city of Seleucus*). The seaport of Antioch in Syria, Acts xiii. 4. It was the port whence Paul and Barnabas started on their first missionary journey, and lay sixteen miles to the west of Antioch. The city was founded by Seleucus Nicator about B. C. 300, and to distinguish it from other cities of the same name was frequently called "Seleucia by the sea." The harbor is now choked with sand, and the once beautiful city is but the insignificant village of Elkalusi.

Sē-leū′cus. The Seleuci, or Seleucidæ, sprung from Seleucus I., a general of Alexander the Great, were a line of Syrian kings, B. C. 312–65, 2 Macc. iii. 3.

Sĕm. Greek form of Shem, Luke iii. 36.

Sĕm″a-chī′ah (*God-sustained*). A Levite porter, 1 Chr. xxvi. 7.

Sĕm′e-ī (*distinguished*). (1) 1 Esdr. ix. 33. [SHIMEI.] (2) Father of Mattathias, Luke iii. 26. Semein in R. V.

Sē′mel, Esth. xi. 2. [SHIMEI.]

Sē-mĕl′lī-us, 1 Esdr. ii. 16. [SHIMSHAI.]

Sē-nā′ah (*brambly*). His sons were returned captives, Ez. ii. 35.

Sĕn′āte (*elders*). First body, or class, of Hebrew Sanhedrim; the other two being priests and scribes, Acts v. 21.

Sē′neh (*bramble*). One of two rocks in the pass of Michmash, 1 Sam. xiv. 4, 5.

Sē′nĭr (*glistening*). Amorite name for Mount Hermon, 1 Chr. v. 23; Ezek. xxvii. 5.

Sĕn-năch′e-rĭb (*not the first-born*). Son and successor of Sargon, king of Assyria, B. C. 702–680. He extended his conquests to the Mediterranean and to Egypt, 2 Kgs. xviii. 13–37; xix. Most powerful and magnificent of eastern sovereigns, Isa. xxxvi., xxxvii. He made Nineveh his capital and adorned it with many palaces and public structures. His monuments have been found in many places, and a record of his arrival in Egypt has been unearthed close by an inscription of Rameses the Great.

Sĕ-nū′ah (*bristling*). A Benjamite, second in rule over Jerusalem after the captivity, Neh. xi. 9. Hasenuah, 1 Chr. ix. 7.

Sĕ-ō′rim (*bearded*). Head of fourth priestly course, 1 Chr. xxiv. 8.

Sē′phar (*number*). A Joktanite border in Arabia, Gen. x. 30.

Sĕph′a-răd (*severed*). Unlocated place whence captive Jews would return to possess the cities of the south, Obad. 20.

Sĕph″ar-vā′im (*two Sipperas*). One of the two cities of Sippera in Syria, whence colonists were sent to Samaria, 2 Kgs. xvii. 24–34; xix. 13; Isa. xxxvii. 13.

Sĕph′ar-vītes. Inhabitants of Sepharvaim, 2 Kgs. xvii. 31.

Sĕp-tū′a-gint (*seventy*). The traditional 70 or 72 translators of the Hebrew Scriptures into Greek; but especially, the Greek version of the O. T. made by 72 learned Jews at Alexandria, at command of Ptolemy Philadelphus, about B. C. 270. The beginning of active work on this, the best known of ancient Bible translations, is fixed for the years B. C. 280–285, and it covered a long period of time, the translation of the Apocryphal books having been gradually added. It was made from Egyptian Hebrew manuscripts, and in its completed form is designated by the Roman numerals LXX. It was the version used by Hebrews in Christ's time and by the Greek Fathers and early N. T. writers, and the Latin version was made from it.

Sĕp′ul-chre (*ker*) (*bury*), 2 Kgs. xxiii. 16; Isa. xxii. 16; Matt. xxvii. 60; Mark xvi. 2; Luke xxiii. 53. Though the Egyptians and nearly all peoples adjacent to the Hebrews have made the name of sarcophagus familiar as a stone coffin, a chest-like tomb, often ornamented and inscribed, there seems to have been nothing akin to it in all the mention of funeral customs and burial rites in the Scriptures, if we except certain titles and inscriptions over tombs such as are mentioned in 2 Kgs. xxiii. 17. [BURIAL.] [TOMB.]

Sē′rah (*lady*). A daughter of Asher, Gen. xlvi. 17; 1 Chr. vii. 30. Sarah, Num. xxvi. 46.

Sĕr″a-ī′ah (*warrior of God*). (1) David's scribe, 2 Sam. viii. 17. Sheva, 2 Sam. xx. 25. Shisha, 1 Kgs. iv. 3. Shavsha, 1 Chr. xviii. 16. (2) A high priest, slain at Riblah, 2 Kgs. xxv. 18–21. (3) One who submitted to Gedaliah, 2 Kgs. xxv. 23. (4) A Judahite, 1 Chr. iv. 13, 14. (5) A Simeonite, 1 Chr. iv. 35. (6) A returned priest, Ez. ii. 2; Neh. x. 2. (7) Ancestor of Ezra, Ez. vii. 1. (8) One of the officers who arrested Jeremiah, Jer. xxxvi. 26. (9) Jeremiah's messenger to Babylon, Jer. li. 59–64.

Sĕr′a-phĭm (*burning*). An order of celestial beings, pictured in Isaiah's vision as around the throne of God, Isa. vi. 2–7.

Sĕr′ed (*fear*). First-born of Zebulun, Gen. xlvi. 14; Num. xxvi. 26.

Sĕr′gĭ-us Pₐu′lus (*little net*). Proconsul of Cyprus at time of Paul's visit, Acts xiii. 7, 12.

Sē′ron. A Syrian general, 1 Macc. iii. 13, 23.

Sẽr′pent (*creeper*). The Hebrew original embraces the entire serpent genus. Serpents numerous and venomous in Bible lands. The word appears in Scripture under various names; adder, supposably the cerastes, Gen. xlix. 17; asp, or cobra, Deut. xxxii. 33; cockatrice, Jer. viii. 17; viper, Job xx. 16. Subtile, Gen. iii. 1; wise, Matt. x. 16; poisonous, Prov. xxiii. 32; sharp-tongued, Ps. cxl. 3; charmed, Ps. lviii. 5; emblem of wickedness, Matt. xxiii. 33; cruelty, Ps. lviii. 4; treachery, Gen. xlix. 17; the devil, Rev. xii. 9–15; fiery serpents sent as a punishment, Num. xxi. 6; sight of "brazen serpent," an antidote for poison of bite, Num. xxi. 8, 9; "fiery flying serpent," a probable allusion to dragon, Isa. xiv. 29.

Sē′rug (*branch*). Son of Reu and great-grandfather of Abraham, Gen. xi. 20–23. Saruch, Luke iii. 35.

Sẽr′vant (*server*). In a broad Bible sense, subject, assistant, person under tribute; in special sense, bondman or slave, by right of purchase, pledge for indebtedness, or indenture; which relationship was carefully guarded by Mosaic law, Lev. xxv. 39–55; Deut. xv. 12–18. [SLAVE.]

Sẽrv′ị-tôr (*server*). A servant, 2 Kgs. iv. 43.

Sĕth (*pay*). Third son of Adam, Gen. iv. 25; v. 3–8.

Sē′thur (*hidden*). An Asherite spy, Num. xiii. 13.

Sĕv′en. A favorite, and often symbolic, number among Hebrews, Gen. ii. 2; vii. 2; xli. 2, 3. Used as a round number, 1 Sam. ii. 5; Matt. xii. 45. Type of abundance and completeness, Gen. iv. 15, 24; Matt. xviii. 21, 22. These references, and other places, show a seventh day and seventh year sabbath and a seven times seventh year of Jubilee; also sacrificial animals limited to seven, and the golden candlesticks. Seven priests with seven trumpets surrounded Jericho for seven days, and seven times on the seventh day. In the Apocalypse we find seven churches, seven candlesticks, seven stars, seven seals, seven trumpets, seven vials, seven plagues, seven angels.

Shā′′al-ăb′bin (*place of foxes*). A boundary place of Dan, Josh. xix. 42. Shaalbim, Judg. i. 35; 1 Kgs. iv. 9.

Shā-ăl′bim. [SHAALABBIN.]

Shā-ăl′bo-nīte. One of David's heroes, so called. Place unknown, 2 Sam. xxiii. 32; 1 Chr. xi. 33.

Shā′aph (*division*). (1) A Judahite, 1 Chr. ii. 47. (2) Son of Caleb, 1 Chr. ii. 49.

Shā′′a-rā′im (*two gates*). (1) Town in Judah, 1 Sam. xvii. 52. Sharaim, Josh. xv. 36. (2) Town in Simeon, 1 Chr. iv. 31.

Shā-ăsh′găz (*lover of beauty*). Keeper of concubines in palace of Xerxes, Esth. ii. 14.

Shăb-bĕth′a-ī (*my rest*). An assistant to Ezra, Ez. x. 15; Neh. viii. 7; xi. 16.

Shăch-ī′ă (*God-protected*). A Benjamite, 1 Chr. viii. 10.

Shăd′da-ī (*mighty*). *El-Shaddai,* "God Almighty." The name used by Hebrews for God, before "Jehovah" acquired its full significance, Gen. xvii. 1; Ex. vi. 3.

Shā′drach (*royal*). Chaldean name given to Hananiah, Dan. i. 7–21; ii.; iii.

Shā′ḡē (*erring*). Father of one of David's guard, 1 Chr. xi. 34.

Shā′′ha-rā′im (*double morning*). A Benjamite, 1 Chr. viii. 8.

Shā-hăz′ị-mah (*heights*). Town in Issachar. Josh. xix. 22.

Shā′lem (*peaceful*). For "to Shalem," Gen. xxxiii. 18, read "in peace to."

Shā′lim, Land of (*land of foxes*). The wild place through which Saul passed when searching for his father's asses, 1 Sam. ix. 4.

Shăl′ị-shă, Land of (*triangular*). A wild district near Mt. Ephraim through which Saul passed, in search of his father's asses, 1 Sam. ix. 4.

Shăl′le-chĕth (*thrown down*). A westward gate of the temple at Jerusalem, 1 Chr. xxvi. 16.

Shăl′lum (*revenge*). (1) Fifteenth king of Israel, B. C. 771; slew King Zachariah, and usurped his throne; reigned one month; slain and succeeded by Menahem, 2 Kgs. xv. 10–15. (2) Husband of Huldah the prophetess, 2 Kgs. xxii. 14; 2 Chr. xxxiv. 22. (3) A descendant of Sheshan, 1 Chr. ii. 40, 41. (4) Fourth son of Josiah king of Judah, who became King Jehoahaz, B. C. 610, and reigned for three months, 1 Chr. iii. 15; Jer. xxii. 11, 12; 2 Kgs. xxiii. 30, 31; 2 Chr. xxxvi. 1–4. (5) A Simeonite, 1 Chr. iv. 25. (6) A high priest, 1 Chr. vi. 12; Ez. vii. 2. (7) Shillem, a Naphtalite, 1 Chr. vii. 13. (8) A chief of porters, 1 Chr. ix. 17; Ez. ii. 42. (9) A porter, 1 Chr. ix. 19, 31. (10) An Ephraimite, 2 Chr. xxviii. 12. (11) Uncle of Jeremiah, Jer. xxxii. 7. (12) Four Levites, Ez. x. 24, 42; Neh. iii. 12; Jer. xxxv. 4.

Shăl′lun (*revenge*). A wall-repairer and governor of part of Mizpah, Neh. iii. 15.

Shăl′ma-ī (*thanks*). His children were returned captives, Ez. ii. 46.

Shăl′man, Hos. x. 14. [SHALMANESER.]

Shăl′′man-ē′ṣer (*Shalman is lenient*). An Assyrian king, B. C. 727–722, who twice conquered Hoshea, king of Israel, the last time capturing his capital, Samaria, 2 Kgs. xvii. 3–6; xviii. 9–12.

Shā′mă (*dutiful*). One of David's guard, 1 Chr. xi. 44.

Shăm′′a-rī′ah (*God-kept*). Son of King Rehoboam, 2 Chr. xi. 19.

Shăm′bles (*little benches*). In general, slaughter-houses, but meat-market in 1 Cor. x. 25.

Shā′med (*destroyer*). A Benjamite, 1 Chr. viii. 12.

Shāme′fāçed-ness. Wrong writing of shamefastness, modesty. Corrected in R. V., 1 Tim. ii. 9.

Shā′mer (*keeper*). (1) A Levite, 1 Chr. vi. 46. (2) An Asherite, 1 Chr. vii. 34. Shomer in vs. 32.

Shăm′găr (*sword*). A judge of Israel who slew 600 Philistines with an ox-goad, Judg. iii. 31; v. 6.

Shăm′huth (*destruction*). One of David's captains, 1 Chr. xxvii. 8.

Shā′mir (*thorn*). (1) A town in the mountains of Judah, Josh. xv. 48. (2) Residence of Tola, the judge, in Mount Ephraim, Judg. x. 1, 2. (3) Son of Michah, 1 Chr. xxiv. 24.

Shăm′mă (*desolation*). A chief of Asher, 1 Chr. vii. 37.

Shăm′mah (*desolation*). (1) A duke of Edom, Gen. xxxvi. 13, 17; 1 Chr. i. 37. (2) Third son of Jesse, 1 Sam. xvi. 9; xvii. 13. Called also, Shimea, Shimeah, and Shimma. (3) One of the three greatest of David's mighty men, 2 Sam. xxiii. 11–17, 33. (4) Another of David's mighty men, 2 Sam. xxiii. 25. Shammoth, 1 Chr. xi. 27. Shamhuth, 1 Chr. xxvii. 8.

Shăm′ma-ī (*desolated*). Three Judahites, 1 Chr. ii. 28, 32, 44, 45; iv. 17.

Shăm′moth, 1 Chr. xi. 27. [SHAMMAH, 4.]

Shăm-mū′ă, Shăm′mū-ah (*heard*). (1) The Reubenite spy, Num. xiii. 4. (2) A son of David, born in Jerusalem, 2 Sam. v. 14; 1 Chr. xiv. 4. Shimea, 1 Chr. iii. 5. (3) A Levite, Neh. xi. 17. (4) A priest representing the family of Bilgah, Neh. xii. 18.

Shăm′′she-rā′ī (*hero*). A Benjamite, 1 Chr. viii. 26.

Shā′pham (*bare*). A Gadite, 1 Chr. v. 12.

Shā′phan (*rabbit*). Scribe or secretary of King Josiah, 2 Kgs. xxii. 3–14; 2 Chr. xxxiv. 8–20.

Shā′phat (*judge*). (1) The Simeonite spy, Num. xiii. 5. (2) Father of the prophet Elisha, 1 Kgs. xix. 16, 19; 2 Kgs. iii. 11; vi. 31. (3) One in the royal line of Judah, 1 Chr. iii. 22. (4) A Gadite chief, 1 Chr. v. 12. (5) A herdsman of David, 1 Chr. xxvii. 29.

Shā'pher (*bright*). A desert encampment of the Israelites, Num. xxxiii. 23.

Shăr'a-ī (*set free*). A descendant of Bani, who had married a foreign wife, Ez. x. 40.

Shăr-ā'īm, Josh. xv. 36. [SHAARAIM.]

Shā'rär (*navel*). Father of one of David's warriors, 2 Sam. xxiii. 33. Sacar, 1 Chr. xi. 35.

Shā-rē'zer (*prince*). Son of Sennacherib, who helped to murder his father, 2 Kgs. xix. 37.

Shăr'on (*plain*). (1) The plain skirting the Mediterranean coast from Judah to Cæsarea. It is an extension of the "shefelah" or lowlands of Judah, and was renowned for its fertility. Called Saron in Acts ix. 35. First mentioned as Lasharon, Josh. xii. 18. David's flocks fed there, 1 Chr. xxvii. 29. Celebrated in S. of Sol. ii. 1; Isa. xxxv. 2; lxv. 10. (2) A town or district east of Jordan, and perhaps in Gilead, 1 Chr. v. 16.

Shăr'on-īte. Designation of Shitrai, one of David's herdsmen, 1 Chr. xxvii. 29.

Shā-ru'hen (*gracious house*). A town first allotted to Judah and then to Simeon, Josh. xix. 6.

Shăsh'a-ī (*noble*). A son of Bani, who had taken a foreign wife, Ez. x. 40.

Shā'shak (*eager*). A Benjamite, 1 Chr. viii. 14, 25.

Shā'ul (*asked*). (1) A son of Simeon and founder of the Shaulites, Gen. xlvi. 10; Num. xxvi. 13. (2) A king of Edom, 1 Chr. i. 48, 49. Saul in Gen. xxxvi. 37.

Shā'ul-ītes. Descendants of Shaul, Num. xxvi. 13.

Shā'veh (*plain*). The unidentified place in Palestine mentioned as the "king's dale," Gen. xiv. 17; 2 Sam. xviii. 18.

Shā'veh Kĭr''ĭ-a-thā'im (*plain of Kiriathaim*). Spot where the Emims dwelt when smitten by Chedorlaomer, Gen. xiv. 5. It is supposably the place that afterwards belonged to Reuben, under the name of Kirjathaim, Num. xxxii. 37; Josh. xiii. 19.

Shăv'sha (*God's warrior*). Royal secretary or scribe in time of King David, 1 Chr. xviii. 16. Seraiah, 2 Sam. viii. 17. Sheva, 2 Sam. xx. 25. Shisha, 1 Kgs. iv. 3.

Shā'ving. [RAZOR.]

Shăwm (*pipe*). A cornet or clarionet. Only in Prayer-book version of Ps. xcviii. 6.

Shē'al (*asking*). One who had a foreign wife, Ez. x. 29.

Shē-ăl'tĭ-el (*asked of God*). Father of Zerubbabel, Ez. iii. 2, 8; v. 2; Neh. xii. 1; Hag. i. 1, 12, 14; ii. 2, 23.

Shē''a-rī'ah (*prized of God*). A descendant of Saul, 1 Chr. viii. 38; ix. 44.

Shear'ing=house. A spot between Jezreel and Samaria where Jehu slaughtered the royal family of Judah, 2 Kgs. x. 12–14.

Shē'är=jā'shŭb (*a remnant shall return*). Symbolical name given by Isaiah to his son, Isa. vii. 3.

Shē'bȧ (*oath*). (1) Son of Bichri, a Benjamite, who revolted from David and was beheaded, 2 Sam. xx. 1–22. (2) A Gadite chief, 1 Chr. v. 13. (3) A descendant of Ham, Gen. x. 7; 1 Chr. i. 9. (4) Son of Joktan, Gen. x. 28. (5) Son of Jokshan, Gen. xxv. 3; 1 Chr. i. 32. (6) The kingdom of Sheba, whose queen visited Solomon, 1 Kgs. x. 1–13; 2 Chr. ix. 1–12. This country has been variously located in Africa, in Arabia, on the Persian Gulf, and in Arabia, on the Red Sea. The burden of authority identifies it with Yemen or Arabia Felix, on the Red Sea, and peopled by descendants of Sheba, son of Joktan. (7) A town in Simeon, Josh. xix. 2. Probably the Shema of Josh. xv. 26.

Shē'bah (*oath*). The famous well, or series of wells, dug by the servants of Isaac, in accordance with his compact with the Philistines. It gave name to Beersheba, Gen. xxvi. 31–33.

Shē'bam (*odor*). A town east of Jordan, given to Reuben and Gad, Num. xxxii. 3. [SIBMAH.]

Shĕb''a-nī'ah (*grown by God*). (1) A priestly trumpeter at the bringing up of the ark, 1 Chr. xv. 24. (2) Three co-covenanters with Nehemiah, Neh. ix. 5; x. 4, 10, 12; xii. 14.

Shĕb'a-rīm (*ruins*). Place near Ai to which the defeated Israelites were pursued, Josh. vii. 5.

Shē'bȧt. [SEBAT.]

Shē'ber (*breaking*). A son of Caleb, 1 Chr. ii. 48.

Shĕb'nȧ (*strength*). (1) Prefect of the palace under King Hezekiah, Isa. xxii. 15–25. (2) Scribe under King Hezekiah, 2 Kgs. xviii. 18, 37; xix. 2; Isa. xxxvi. 3.

Shĕb'u-el (*captive of God*). (1) A descendant of Moses, 1 Chr. xxiii. 16; xxvi. 24. Shubael, 1 Chr. xxiv. 20. (2) A Levite minstrel, son of Heman, 1 Chr. xxv. 4. Shubael, 1 Chr. xxv. 20.

Shĕc''a-nī'ah (*dweller with God*). (1) A priest in time of David, 1 Chr. xxiv. 11. (2) A Levite, 2 Chr. xxxi. 15.

Shĕch''a-nī'ah (*dweller with God*). (1) A descendant of the royal line, 1 Chr. iii. 21, 22. (2) Levites and returned captives, in Ez. viii. 3, 5; x. 2; Neh. iii. 29; vi. 18; xii. 3.

Shē'chem (*shoulder*). (1) The Canaanite who abducted Dinah and was slain by Simeon and Levi, Gen. xxxiv. (2) An ancient and highly historic city, between mounts Ebal and Gerizim, 34 miles N. of Jerusalem. Called also Sichem, Sychem, Sychar, later Neapolis, now Nablus. Halting place of Abraham, Gen. xii. 6. A Hivite city in time of Jacob, Gen. xxxiii. 18–20; Josh. xxiv. 32. Captured by Simeon and Levi, Gen. xxxiv. Joseph buried there, Josh. xxiv. 32. Destroyed by Abimelech, Judg. ix. Rebuilt by Rehoboam, and fortified and made capital of Israel by Jeroboam, 1 Kgs. xii. 1–19, 25; 2 Chr. x. A centre of Samaritan worship after the captivity, John iv. 5, 39–42. (3) A Manassite, of Gilead, Num. xxvi. 31. (4) A Gileadite, nephew of former, 1 Chr. vii. 19.

Shē'chem-ītes. The family of Shechem of Gilead, Num. xxvi. 31.

Shē-chī'nah (*dwelling-place*). The visible majesty of God, as in the "pillar of cloud" and the "glory" which covered the tabernacle and filled Solomon's temple. A word found only in the targums, Chaldaic version of Bible, and among early Christian writers. Alluded to in Luke ii. 9; John i. 14; Rom. ix. 4.

Shĕd'ē-ur (*light-sender*). Father of Elizur, chief of Reuben at time of exode, Num. i. 5; ii. 10; vii. 30, 35; x. 18.

Sheep. An important animal among Hebrews, and a main source of wealth. Shepherd's occupation highly respectable, Gen. iv. 2; Ex. iii. 1; 1 Sam. xvi. 11; Job xlii. 12, though odious to Egyptians. Used for sacrifices, Ex. xx. 24; xxix. 38; Lev. ix. 3; for food, 1 Sam. xxv. 18. Wool used for clothing, Lev. xiii. 47. Skins used for tabernacle coverings, Ex. xxv. 5. Paid as tribute, 2 Kgs. iii. 4. Sheep and shepherd employed much figuratively, 2 Chr. xviii. 16; Ps. cxix. 176; Matt. ix. 36; John x. 11; Heb. xiii. 20. The common sheep of Syria and Palestine was the broad-tailed variety.

Sheep'fold. Place for herding sheep, especially at night. Usually built strong to keep out wild animals, Num. xxxii. 16; 2 Sam. vii. 8; John x. 16. The fold, cote, or enclosure was also the place where the sheep were collected at shearing time, Jer. xxiii. 3; Zeph. ii. 6, which was a season of festivity, 1 Sam. xxv. 7–11; 2 Sam. xiii. 23. Hence "shearing-house," 2 Kgs. x. 12–14.

Sheep=gate. One of the gates of Jerusalem as rebuilt by Nehemiah, Neh. iii. 1, 32; xii. 39.

Sheep=mär'ket. Should read "sheep-gate" as

above, John v. 2.

She′′ha-rī′ah (*Jehovah dawns*). Son of Jeroham of Benjamin, 1 Chr. viii. 26.

Shĕk′el (*weight*). A weight for weighing uncoined money, of Assyrian and Babylonian origin. There seem to have been two standards, that of the sanctuary and the king, Ex. xxx. 13; 2 Sam. xiv. 26. Both approximated half an ounce, valued in silver at about 64 cents. Later, a Hebrew silver coin, with bronze half and quarter shekels. Probably the "pieces of silver" in Matt. xxvi. 15, though the "pieces of silver" in Luke xv. 8 are clearly the Greek drachmas. The first Jewish coins were struck by Simon Maccabeus, who obtained permission to coin money from Antiochus, King of Syria. His shekel showed a vase on one side, representing a pot of manna, and on the other an almond branch with flowers, representative supposably of Aaron's rod.

She′lah (*prayer*). (1) Youngest son of Judah and founder of Shelanites, Gen. xxxviii. 5–26; Num. xxvi. 20. (2) 1 Chr. i. 18, 24. [SALAH.]

She′lan-ītes. Descendants of Shelah, Num. xxvi. 20.

Shĕl′′e-mī′ah (*God repays*). (1) 1 Chr. xxvi. 14. [MESHELEMIAH.] (2) Two who married foreign wives, Ez. x. 39, 41. (3) Father of Hananiah, Neh. iii. 30. (4) A priest appointed treasurer, Neh. xiii. 13. (5) Father of Jehucal, Jer. xxxvii. 3. (6) Father of one of Jeremiah's accusers, Jer. xxxviii. 1. (7) Father of the officer who arrested Jeremiah, Jer. xxxvii. 13.

She′leph (*drawn out*). Son of Joktan, Gen. x. 26.

She′lesh (*strength*). An Asherite chief, 1 Chr. vii. 35.

Shĕl′o-mī (*my peace*). An Asherite, Num. xxxiv. 27.

Shĕl′o-mĭth (*my peace*). (1) Daughter of Dibri, of Dan, Lev. xxiv. 11. (2) Daughter of Zerubbabel, 1 Chr. iii. 19. (3) Two Levites, 1 Chr. xxiii. 9, 18. (4) A descendant of Eliezer, 1 Chr. xxvi. 25–28. (5) A returned captive, Ez. viii. 10.

Shĕl′o-mŏth, 1 Chr. xxiv. 22. [SHELOMITH, 3.]

She-lū′mĭ-el (*God's peace*). A prince of Simeon, Num. i. 6; ii. 12; vii. 36, 41; x. 19.

Shĕm (*name*). Oldest son of Noah, preserved with his father in the ark, Gen. v. 32. Blessed by Noah for his conduct, Gen. ix. 18–27. His descendants are the Hebrews, Arameans, Persians, Assyrians, and Arabians, whose languages are called Shemitic.

She′mȧ (*hearing*). (1) A Judahite, 1 Chr. ii. 43, 44. (2) A Reubenite, 1 Chr. v. 8. (3) A Benjamite chief, 1 Chr. viii. 13. (4) An assistant of Ezra, Neh. viii. 4. (5) Josh. xv. 26. [SHEBA, 7.]

She-mā′ah (*God hears*). A Benjamite whose sons joined David at Ziklag, 1 Chr. xii. 3.

Shĕm′′a-ī′ah (*God hears*). (1) Prophet and chronicler in reign of Rehoboam, 1 Kgs. xii. 22; 2 Chr. xi. 2. (2) Twenty-four others, mostly priests, Levites, and returned captives, 1 Chr. iii. 22; iv. 37; v. 4; ix. 14; ix. 16; xv. 8, 11; xxiv. 6; xxvi. 4–7; 2 Chr. xxix. 14; xvii. 8; xxxi. 15; xxxv. 9; Ez. viii. 13, 16; x. 21, 31; Neh. vi. 10; x. 8; xii. 6, 18, 34, 36, 42; Jer. xxvi. 20; xxix. 24–32; xxxvi. 12.

Shĕm′′a-rī′ah (*God keeps*). (1) An adherent of David at Ziklag, 1 Chr. xii. 5. (2) Two who took foreign wives, Ez. x. 32, 41.

Shĕm′e-ber (*high flight*). King of Zeboiim, Gen. xiv. 2.

She′mer (*guarded*). Owner of the hill which King Omri bought, and on which he built Samaria, giving it the former owner's name, 1 Kgs. xvi. 24.

She-mī′dȧ (*wise*). A son of Gilead and founder of the Shemidaites, Num. xxvi. 32; Josh. xvii. 2. Shemidah, 1 Chr. vii. 19.

She-mī′dah, 1 Chr. vii. 19. [SHEMIDA.]

She-mī′dȧ-ītes. Descendants of Shemida, Num. xxvi. 32.

Shĕm′i-nĭth (*eighth*). A musical term, variously surmised to mean the instrument, one of eight strings, the octave, the time of the piece, the part, air, pitch, or key, 1 Chr. xv. 21; Ps. vi; xii. titles.

She-mīr′a-mŏth′′ (*heights of heaven*). (1) A musical Levite in time of David, 1 Chr. xv. 18, 20; xvi. 5. (2) A Levite in reign of Jehoshaphat, 2 Chr. xvii. 8.

She-mĭt′ic. The family of languages spoken by the descendants of Shem. [SHEM.]

She-mū′el (*heard of God*). (1) Representative of Simeon during the apportionment of Canaan, Num. xxxiv. 20. (2) Samuel the prophet, 1 Chr. vi. 33. (3) A chief of Issachar, 1 Chr. vii. 2.

Shĕn (*tooth*). An unknown place, 1 Sam. vii. 12.

She-nā′zar (*ivory keeper*). A descendant of David, 1 Chr. iii. 18.

She′nir, Deut. iii. 9; S. of Sol. iv. 8. [SENIR.]

She′pham (*wild*). A landmark on eastern boundary of Promised Land, Num. xxxiv. 10.

Shĕph′′a-thī′ah (*God judges*). A Benjamite, 1 Chr. ix. 8.

Shĕph′′a-tī′ah (*God judges*). (1) Fifth son of David, 2 Sam. iii. 4; 1 Chr. iii. 3. (2) A Benjamite warrior, 1 Chr. xii. 5. (3) A chief of Simeon, 1 Chr. xxvii. 16. (4) Son of Jehoshaphat, 2 Chr. xxi. 2. (5) Four others in Ez. ii. 4, 57; Neh. vii. 9, 59; xi. 4: Jer. xxxviii. 1–4.

Shĕp′hĕrd (*herder of sheep*). A highly honorable occupation among pastoral Hebrews, engaged in by both sexes, Gen. xxix. 6; xxx. 29–35; Ex. ii. 16–22. Often arduous and dangerous employment, Gen. xxxi. 40; 1 Sam. xvii. 34. Equipment consisted of a sheepskin mantle, a scrip or wallet, a sling and crook. He led the flock to pasture in the morning, tended them by day and folded and watched them at night, Job xxx. 1; Luke ii. 8; John x. 4. The office of sheep-master or chief shepherd was one of great trust as well as honor, 2 Kgs. iii. 4; Heb. xiii. 20; 1 Pet. v. 4. It was the shepherd's duty to count the sheep daily and to tithe them, and he was held responsible for lost ones, Gen. xxxi. 38, 39; Ex. xxii. 12, 13; Lev. xxvii. 32; Jer. xxxiii. 13. Shepherd is used figuratively for Jehovah in Ps. lxxx. 1; Jer. xxxi. 10; for kings, Ezek. xxxiv. 10; in N. T. for Christ, John x. 11; Heb. xiii. 20; 1 Pet. v. 4. It is applied also to teachers in the synagogue and to those who preside over it. Hence pastor and minister of the gospel.

She′phī (*barren*). A descendant of Seir, 1 Chr. i. 40. Shepho, Gen. xxxvi. 23.

She′phŏ, Gen. xxxvi. 23. [SHEPHI.]

She-phū′phan (*serpent*). A grandson of Benjamin, 1 Chr. viii. 5. Shupham, Num. xxvi. 39. Shuppim, 1 Chr. vii. 12, 15. Muppim, Gen. xlvi. 21.

She′rah (*relation*). A daughter of Ephraim, 1 Chr. vii. 24.

Shĕr′′e-bī′ah (*heat of God*). A co-covenanter with Nehemiah, and assistant to Ezra, Ez. viii. 18, 24; Neh. viii. 7; ix. 4; x. 12.

She′resh (*root*). Son of Machir, of Manasseh, 1 Chr. vii. 16.

She-rē′zer (*fire prince*). A messenger of the people, Zech. vii. 2.

Shĕr′iff (*shire officer*). A Babylonian official, Dan. iii. 2.

She′shȧch (*from the goddess Shach*). Symbolical name for Babylon, Jer. xxv. 26.

She′shāi (*princely*). A son of Anak, slain by Caleb, Num. xiii. 22; Josh. xv. 14; Judg. i. 10.

She′shan (*princely*). A Judahite, 1 Chr. ii. 31–35.

Shĕsh-băz′zar (*fire-worshipper*). Zerubbabel's name at the Persian court, Ez. i. 8–11.

Shĕth (*tumult*). (1) 1 Chr. i. 1. [SETH.] (2) For Sheth in Num. xxiv. 17, read "tumult," as in Jer. xlviii. 45.

Shē′thär (*star*). A Persian prince, Esth. i. 14.

Shē′thär=bŏz′na-ī (*star of splendor*). A Persian officer in Syria, Ez. v. 3, 6 ; vi. 6, 13.

Shē′vä. Corruption of Seraiah. (1) A son of Caleb, 1 Chr. ii. 49. (2) The scribe of David, 2 Sam. xx. 25. Shavsha, 1 Chr. xviii. 16. Shisha, 1 Kgs. iv. 3. Seraiah, 2 Sam. viii. 17.

Shew′brĕad (*showbread*). Unleavened bread baked in twelve loaves corresponding to the twelve tribes, and placed fresh every Sabbath on the golden table of the sanctuary. Eaten only by the priests, Ex. xxv. 30 ; Lev. xxiv. 8 ; 1 Sam. xxi. 1-6 ; Matt. xii. 3, 4. The arrangement of loaves on the table was in two rows of six loaves each. Salt and frankincense were put on each row. It was called "shewbread," "bread of the face," or "bread of the setting before," because it stood continually before the Lord. In later times it was called the "bread of ordering," 1 Chr. ix. 32 marg. ; Neh. x. 33.

Shĭb′bo-lĕth (*ear of corn, stream*). Pronounced *sib′bo-leth* by Ephraimites, and *shib′bo-leth* by Gileadites. When the latter conquered the former, and held the fords of Jordan, they exacted the pronunciation of this word in order to distinguish friend from foe. Any other word beginning with *sh* would have answered the same purpose, Judg. xii. 6.

Shĭb′mah (*fragrant*). A town in Reuben, east of Jordan, Num. xxxii. 38. Shebam, Num. xxxii. 3. Sibmah, Josh. xiii. 19.

Shĭ′crŏn (*drunkenness*). A boundary mark of northern Judah, Josh. xv. 11.

Shĭēld (*cover*). A defensive piece of armor, varying in size and shape, and made of skin or metal. Worn on left arm. Metaphorically, divine protection, Judg. v. 8 ; 1 Kgs. x. 17 ; Ps. iii. 3.

Shĭg-gā′ĭon (*mournful*). A word which probably designates the character of the ode, Ps. vii. title.

Shĭ-gī′o-noth. Plural of Shiggaion, Hab. iii. 1.

Shĭ′hŏn (*ruin*). A town in Issachar, Josh. xix. 19.

Shĭ′hôr (*blackness*). (1) Southern boundary of David's empire, 1 Chr. xiii. 5. [SIHOR.] (2) Shihor-libnath, a boundary of Asher, and probably identical with the stream called " Blue River," which empties into the Mediterranean eight miles south of Dor, Josh. xix. 26.

Shĭl′hī (*armed*). Grandfather of King Jehoshaphat, 1 Kgs. xxii. 42 ; 2 Chr. xx. 31.

Shĭl′him (*armed*). A city in southern Judah, Josh. xv. 32.

Shĭl′lem (*retribution*). Son of Naphtali and founder of Shillemites, Gen. xlvi. 24 ; Num. xxvi. 49.

Shĭl′lem-ītes. Descendants of Shillem, Num. xxvi. 49.

Shĭ-lō′ah. The softly flowing waters of Siloam, Isa. viii. 6.

Shĭ′lōh (*peace*). (1) A disputed rendering ; referred to a town and to the Messiah, Gen. xlix. 10 ; Isa. ix. 6. (2) A city in Ephraim, midway between Bethel and Shechem. Now Seilun. Joshua's capital and site where he apportioned his conquests. The ark remained there for three hundred years, till captured by the Philistines, Josh. xviii. 1, 8-10 ; Judg. xxi. 19-23. Residence of Eli and Samuel, 1 Sam. iii., and it was there that Eli received word of the capture of the ark, and died, 1 Sam. iv. The ark was not returned to Shiloh after its capture, and the tabernacle was removed to Nob and thence to Jerusalem, but the odor of sanctity clung about the venerable city for generations, and it was long a place for annual pilgrimages and religious festivals. The prophet Ahijah dwelt at Shiloh, 1 Kgs. xiv. 1-18. Jeremiah pictures Shiloh as desolate in his day, Jer. vii. 12-14 ; xxvi. 6-9.

Shĭ-lō′nī. A descendant of Shelah, Neh. xi. 5.

Shĭ′lo-nīte. Dweller in Shiloh, 1 Kgs. xi. 29.

Shĭ′lo-nītes. Members of the family of Shelah, 1 Chr. ix. 5.

Shĭl′shah (*third*). An Asherite chief, 1 Chr. vii. 37.

Shĭm′e-à (*hearing*). (1) A son of David born in Jerusalem, 1 Chr. iii. 5. (2) A Levite, 1 Chr. vi. 30. (3) Another Levite, 1 Chr. vi. 39. (4) A brother of David, called also Shammah, Shimeah, and Shimma, 1 Chr. xx. 7.

Shĭm′e-ah (*hearing*). (1) Brother of David, called also Shammah, Shimma and Shimea, 2 Sam. xxi. 21. (2) A descendant of Jehiel, founder of Gibeon, 1 Chr. viii. 32.

Shĭm′e-ăm (*hearing*), 1 Chr. ix. 38. [SHIMEAH, 2.]

Shĭm′e-ăth (*hearing*). Mother of one of the murderers of King Joash, 2 Kgs. xii. 21 ; 2 Chr. xxiv. 26.

Shĭm′e-ath-ītes″. A family of scribes, 1 Chr. ii. 55.

Shĭm′e-ī (*famed*). (1) A son of Gershon, Num. iii. 18. Shimi, Ex. vi. 17. (2) A Benjamite who cursed David, 2 Sam. xvi. 5-13 ; 1 Kgs. ii. 44-46. (3) One of David's warriors, 1 Kgs. i. 8. (4) A commissary of Solomon, 1 Kgs. iv. 18. (5) Brother of Zerubbabel, 1 Chr. iii. 19. (6) A Simeonite, 1 Chr. iv. 26, 27. (7) A Reubenite, 1 Chr. v. 4. (8) A Levite, 1 Chr. vi. 42. (9) Leader of 10th musical course, 1 Chr. xxv. 17. (10) David's vineyardist, 1 Chr. xxvii. 27. (11) Ancestor of Mordecai, Esth. ii. 5. (12) Levites in 2 Chr. xxix. 14 ; xxxi. 12, 13 ; Ez. x. 23, 33, 38.

Shĭm′e-on (*hearing*). One who married a foreign wife, Ez. x. 31.

Shĭm′hī (*famed*). A Benjamite, 1 Chr. viii. 21.

Shī′mī, Ex. vi. 17. [SHIMEI, 1.]

Shĭm′ītes. Descendants of Shimei (1), Num. iii. 21.

Shĭm′mà (*hearing*). Third son of Jesse, 1 Chr. ii. 13.

Shī′mon (*waste*). A Judahite, 1 Chr. iv. 20.

Shĭm′rath (*watcher*). A Benjamite, 1 Chr. viii. 21.

Shĭm′rī (*vigilant*). (1) A Simeonite, 1 Chr. iv. 37. (2) Father of one of David's guard, 1 Chr. xi. 45. (3) A Levite, 2 Chr. xxix. 13.

Shĭm′rith (*vigilant*). A Moabitess, mother of Jehozabad, one of the murderers of King Joash, 2 Chr. xxiv. 26. Called Shomer in 2 Kgs. xii. 21.

Shĭm′rŏm, 1 Chr. vii. 1. [SHIMRON, 2.]

Shĭm′rŏn (*watch-place*). (1) An ancient Canaanite city allotted to Zebulun, Josh. xi. 1 ; xix. 15. (2) Fourth son of Issachar and founder of Shimronites, Gen. xlvi. 13 ; Num. xxvi. 24.

Shĭm′ron-ītes. Descendants of Shimron (2), Num. xxvi. 24.

Shĭm′ron=mē′ron, Josh. xii. 20. Probably complete name of Shimron (1).

Shĭm′shāi (*bright*). A scribe and Persian satrap in Judea. He, together with the chancellor, Rehum, wrote a letter to King Artaxerxes in opposition to the rebuilding of the temple by Zerubbabel, Ez. iv. 8, 9, 17, 23.

Shī′năb (*splendor*). A king of Admah in time of Abraham, Gen. xiv. 2.

Shī′năr (*two rivers*). The alluvial plain through which the Tigris and Euphrates pass, and probably inclusive of Babylon and Mesopotamia, Gen. x. 10 ; xi. 1-9 ; Isa. xi. 11 ; Dan. i. 2. It was the seat of the kingdom founded by Nimrod, and which reckoned among its cities, as beginnings, Babel, Erech, Accad, and Calneh, Gen. x. 9, 10. Asshur went forth from Shinar to found Nineveh, Gen. x. 11. It was in the plain in the land of Shinar that the migrating nations undertook to build the tower of Babel, and where the confusion of tongues occurred, Gen. xi. 1-9.

Ship. Ships of Scripture dependent on oars and sails for propulsion. Hebrews not sailors. The ships of Acts, xxi. 1-6; xxvii. 6-44; xxviii. 11-13, were capable of carrying many people and much freight. Primitive ships were generally coasters. They were mounted with figure-heads and had figures painted on the sides of the bow. These composed the ship's "sign," Acts xxviii. 11. Among their furnishings were under-girders, anchors shaped like those of modern times, but without flukes, sounding-lines, rudder-bands, Acts xxvii. 40. Ancient ships, being wholly or in part propelled by oars, were properly called galleys.

Shi'phi (*many*). A prince of Simeon, in time of Hezekiah, 1 Chr. iv. 37.

Shiph'mite. Probably a native of Shepham, and a designation of Zabdi, David's overseer of vineyard increase and wine cellars, 1 Chr. xxvii. 27.

Shiph'rah (*handsome*). A Hebrew midwife in Egypt, Ex. i. 15.

Shiph'tan (*judging*). Father of a prince of Ephraim, Num. xxxiv. 24.

Shi'sha (*God's strife*). Father of Solomon's scribes, 1 Kgs. iv. 3.

Shi'shak. The king of Egypt to whom Jeroboam fled, 1 Kgs. xi. 40. He invaded Judea, B. C. 969, defeated Rehoboam, and spoiled the temple, 1 Kgs. xiv 25, 26; 2 Chr. xii. 2-9. Inscriptions, reliefs, and statuary at Karnak, on the Nile, record his invasion of Palestine.

Shit'ra-i (*scribe*). Keeper of David's herds in Sharon, 1 Chr. xxvii. 29.

Shit'tah, Shit'tim (*thorny*). (1) An Asiatic tree, a species of acacia, producing a close-grained, yellowish wood used in making the sacred furniture of the tabernacle, Ex. xxv. 10-13; xxvi. 15, 26; xxvii. 1; Isa. xli. 19. (2) Last encampment of the Israelites before crossing the Jordan. Scene of the completion of the law and farewell of Moses, Num. xxv.; xxxi. 1-12; Josh. ii. 1; iii. 1. The spies were sent out from Shittim to Jericho, and there the final preparations were made for crossing the Jordan. It was also called Abel-shittim, "meadow of acacias," and was the well-watered, fertile plain stretching from the foot of the mountains of Moab to the banks of the Jordan. (3) "Valley of Shittim," Joel iii. 18, is doubtless same as Shittim (2), which was also known as Abel-shittim.

Shi'za (*loving*). Father of a Reubenite captain, 1 Chr. xi. 42.

Sho'a (*fruitful*). An undetermined name or place, Ezek. xxiii. 23.

Sho'bab (*hostile*). (1) A son of David, 2 Sam. v. 14; 1 Chr. iii. 5; xiv. 4. (2) A son of Caleb, 1 Chr. ii. 18.

Sho'bach (*enlarging*). A Syrian general whom David defeated, 2 Sam. x. 15-18. Shophach, 1 Chr. xix. 16-18.

Sho'ba-i (*captive*). A family of temple doorkeepers who returned from captivity, Ez. ii. 42; Neh. vii. 45.

Sho'bal (*current*). (1) Second son of Seir, and a Horite duke, Gen. xxxvi. 20; 1 Chr. i. 38. (2) A son of Caleb, 1 Chr. ii. 50, 52. (3) 1 Chr. iv. 1, 2, probably same as above.

Sho'bek (*forsaken*). A co-covenanter with Nehemiah, Neh. x. 24.

Sho'bi (*captive*). An Ammonite who succored David during Absalom's rebellion, 2 Sam. xvii. 27-29.

Sho'co, Sho'cho, Sho'choh, 2 Chr. xi. 7 xxviii. 18; 1 Sam. xvii. 1. [SOCOH.]

Shoe. [SANDAL.]

Sho'ham (*onyx*). A Levite, 1 Chr. xxiv. 27.

Sho'mer (*keeper*). (1) An Asherite, 1 Chr. vii. 32. Shamer in vs. 34. (2) Mother of Jehozabad, a co-murderer of King Joash, 2 Kgs. xii. 21. Called Shimrith in 2 Chr. xxiv. 26.

Sho'phach, 1 Chr. xix. 16-18. [SHOBACH.]

Sho'phan (*burrow*). A fenced city east of Jordan, which fell to Gad, Num. xxxii. 35.

Sho-shan'nim (*lilies*). Variously construed as a melody, bridal-song, and musical instrument, Ps. xlv., lxix., lxxx., titles. In the latter, *eduth*, "testimony," is added.

Shoul'der. Baring of, signified servitude, Gen. xlix. 15; withdrawing of, denoted rebellion, Neh. ix. 29; bearing upon, meant to sustain, Isa. ix. 6; xxii. 22.

Shov'el (*shove*). [FAN.] [WINNOW.]

Shu'a (*wealth*). Father-in-law of Judah, 1 Chr. ii. 3. Shuah in Gen. xxxviii. 2, 12.

Shu'ah (*pit*). (1) A son of Abraham, Gen. xxv. 2; 1 Chr. i. 32. (2) Brother of Chelub, 1 Chr. iv. 11. (3) Gen. xxxviii. 2, 12. [SHUA.]

Shu'al (*fox*). (1) An Asherite, 1 Chr. vii. 36. (2) An unlocated land, 1 Sam. xiii. 17.

Shu'ba-el (*God's captive*). (1) Shebuel, son of Gershon, 1 Chr. xxiv. 20. (2) Shebuel, son of Heman the singer, and leader of the thirteenth musical course, 1 Chr. xxv. 20.

Shu'ham (*well-digger*). A son of Dan, Num. xxvi. 42. Hushim, Gen. xlvi. 23.

Shu'ham-ites. Descendants of Shuham, Num. xxvi. 42.

Shu'hite. Designation of Bildad, one of Job's friends; associated with *Tsukhi*, an Arabic tribe, Job ii. 11.

Shu'lam-ite. One belonging to Shulem or Shunem, S. of Sol. vi. 13.

Shu'math-ites. One of the four families of Kirjath-jearim, 1 Chr. ii. 53.

Shu'nam-ite. A native of Shunem. The nurse of David and hostess of Elisha were so called, 1 Kgs. i. 3; 2 Kgs. iv. 12.

Shu'nem (*double sleeping-place*). A city of Issachar, near Jezreel. Place where the Philistines encamped before the great battle of Gilboa; home of David's nurse and wife, Abishag; residence of the woman who entertained Elisha. Now Solam, Josh. xix. 18; 1 Sam. xxviii. 4; 2 Kgs. iv. 8.

Shu'ni (*resting*). A son of Gad, Gen. xlvi. 16.

Shu'nites. Descendants of Shuni, Num. xxvi. 15.

Shu'pham, Num. xxvi. 39. [SHUPPIM.]

Shu'pham-ites. Descendants of Shupham, Num. xxvi. 39.

Shup'pim (*serpents*). (1) Great-grandson of Benjamin, 1 Chr. vii. 12. Shupham, Num. xxvi. 39. (2) A Levite gate-keeper, 1 Chr. xxvi. 16.

Shur (*wall*). A desert region of Arabia, and its town, bordering on Egypt, Gen. xvi. 7; xxv. 18. "Wilderness of Etham," Num. xxxiii. 8. Inhabited by Amalekites, 1 Sam. xv. 7; xxvii. 8.

Shu'shan (*lily*). The Greek Susa, ancient capital of Elam, a province in Mesopotamia. A seat of wealth and power after the Persian conquest of Babylon. The events of Esther's history occurred there. Spot of Daniel's visions. Nehemiah commissioned there, Gen. x. 22; xiv. 1; Neh. i. 1; Esth.; Isa. xxi. 2; Jer. xlix. 34; Dan. viii. 2. The decline of this ancient city dates from its capture by Alexander the Great, or from its later conquest by Antigonus, B. C. 315. The site, nearly due east from Babylon and north of the Persian Gulf, is marked by ruins, some three miles in circumference, in the midst of which have been found the remains of the great palace of Darius, scene of the events narrated in the book of Esther.

Shu'shan=e'duth. Abbreviated form of Shoshannim-eduth, which *see*, Ps. lx. title.

Shu'thal-ites. Descendants of Shuthelah, Num. xxvi. 35.

Shu'the-lah (*discord*). Head of the Ephraimite

family of Shuthalhites, Num. xxvi. 35 ; 1 Chr. vii. 20, 21.

Shŭt′tle (*shooter*). This weaver's device for throwing the filling thread between the warp threads is figurative of fleeting time in Job vii. 6.

Sī′à (*assembly*). His children returned from captivity, Neh. vii. 47. Siaha, Ez. ii. 44.

Sī′a-hà, Ez. ii. 44. [SIA.]

Sĭb′be̯-cāi, 1 Chr. xi. 29 ; xxvii. 11. [SIBBECHAI.]

Sĭb′be̯-chāi (*weaver*). One of David's guard, and eighth captain of eighth month, 2 Sam. xxi. 18 ; 1 Chr. xx. 4. Sibbecai, 1 Chr. xi. 29 ; xxvii. 11. Mebunnai, 2 Sam. xxiii. 27.

Sĭb′bo̯-lĕth, Judg. xii. 6. [SHIBBOLETH.]

Sĭb′mah (*fragrant*). A fortified city of Reuben, east of Jordan, Josh. xiii. 19. Shebam, Num. xxxii. 3. Shibmah, Num. xxxii. 38. Noted for its grapes. Isa. xvi. 8, 9 ; Jer. xlviii. 32.

Sĭb′ra̯-īm (*twice hopeful*). A boundary mark of northern Palestine, Ezek. xlvii. 16.

Sī′chem, Gen. xii. 6. [SHECHEM.]

Sĭck′le (*cutter*). The reaping and mowing implement of the ancients. In its size and curvature, as represented on Egyptian monuments, it resembled the implement as known to us, Deut. xvi. 9.

Sĭç′y̆-ŏn. A city of the Peloponnesus near the Isthmus, 1 Macc. xv. 23.

Sĭd′dim (*pitted vale*). A vale, full of slime-pits, supposably near the Dead Sea, in which the kings of the plain cities met their invaders, Gen. xiv. 1–10.

Sī′de (*trading*). A trading city in Pamphylia, 1 Macc. xv. 23.

Sī′dŏn, Gen. x. 15, 19. [ZIDON.]

Sı̆-dō′nĭ-ans̟. Zidonians, Deut. iii. 9 ; Josh. xiii. 4, 6 ; Judg. iii. 3 ; 1 Kgs. v. 6.

Sie̱ge (*sit*), Deut. xx. 19. [WAR.]

Sieve. Ancient sieves, or sifters, were crudely made of rushes, though the Gauls are credited with their manufacture from horsehair. They were used for separating the flour from the bran, or broken kernels, and what was left in the sieve was thrown back into the mill to be reground, Isa. xxx. 28.

Sī′hŏn (*rooting out*). An Amorite king, defeated by the Israelites, who occupied his country between the Arnon and Jabbok, Num. xxi. 21–31 ; Deut. i. 4 ; ii. 24–37 ; Josh. xiii. 15–28.

Sī′hŏr (*blackness*). The Sihor, or Shihor, of Egypt, 1 Chr. xiii. 5 ; Isa. xxiii. 3 ; Jer. ii. 18, has ever been construed as " the Nile." But when unqualified, some Arabian ravine or wady may be meant.

Sī′las (*Silvanus, woody*). An eminent member of the early Christian church. Written Silvanus in Paul's epistles. Resided at Jerusalem as teacher, but accompanied Paul on his tours, and was his fellow-prisoner at Philippi. Said to have been bishop of Corinth, Acts xv. 22, 32–34, 40 ; xvii. 14 ; xviii. 5 ; 2 Cor. i. 19 ; 1 Thess. i. 1.

Sĭlk (*Seric stuff*). Silk hardly known to ancient Hebrews. In Prov. xxxi. 22 ; Ezek. xvi. 10, 13, some fine linen fabric is supposed to be meant. Undoubtedly known in N. T. times, Rev. xviii. 12.

Sĭl′là (*branch*). The place near which King Joash was slain, 2 Kgs. xii. 20.

Sĭ-lō′ah, Neh. iii. 15. [SILOAM.]

Sĭ-lō′am (*sent*). (1) The celebrated pool, or tank, at Jerusalem, on the south side, near the opening of the Tyrophean valley into the Kidron valley. Originally a part of the water supply of the city, Neh. iii. 15 ; Isa. viii. 6 ; John ix. 7–11. (2) An unlocated tower whose fall killed eighteen men, Luke xiii. 4. Siloam still retains its ancient name under the form of the Arabic *Silwân*. It is partly hewn from rock and partly built with masonry. A flight of steps leads down to it. It is no longer a natural spring of fresh, limpid water, but is fed from the Foun-

tain of the Virgin through a rock tunnel over 1700 feet in length. The waters are brackish and colored, and the walls and steps in ruins.

Sĭl-vā′nus (*woody*). [SILAS.]

Sĭl′ver (*white*). Used by Hebrews from earliest times for money, vessels, and ornaments, but not in form of coins till after the captivity, Gen. xiii. 2 ; xxiv. 53 ; xliv. 2 ; Job xxviii. 1 ; Matt. xxvi. 15 ; Acts xix. 24. Silver supplied to Jerusalem from Arabia and Tarshish, 2 Chr. ix. 14, 21.

Sĭl′ver-lings (*little silvers*). Evidently bits of silver money, but whether by weight or coinage is not known, Isa. vii. 23.

Sī′mal-cū′e. An Arabian chief, guardian of Antiochus, son of Balas, 1 Macc. xi. 39.

Sĭm′e̯-on (*who hears*). (1) Son of Jacob and Leah, Gen. xxix. 33. For the crime in Gen. xxxiv. 25–30 his father denounced him, Gen. xlix. 5–7. His tribe was small, Num. i. 22, 23 ; xxvi. 14, and their inheritance a scattered portion of Canaan, Josh. xix. 1–9. (2) Son of Judah in genealogy of Christ, Luke iii. 30. (3) Simon Peter, Acts xv. 14. (4) A venerable and pious Jew who blessed the child Jesus in the temple, Luke ii. 25–35. (5) Simeon Niger, Acts xiii. 1. [NIGER.]

Sī′mon (*Simeon*). (1) Several distinguished Jews bore this name during the Maccabean period. (2) A native of Samaria and famous sorcerer, who professed Christ for mercenary purposes, Acts viii. 9–24. (3) Simon Peter, Matt. iv. 18. [PETER.] (4) Simon the Canaanite, or Simon Zelotes, was a member of the party of Zealots who advocated the Jewish ritual, and an apostle, Matt. x. 4. (5) Simon the brother of Jesus, Matt. xiii. 55 ; Mark vi. 3. (6) Simon the Pharisee, in whose house a woman anointed the feet of Jesus, Luke vii. 36–50. (7) Simon, the leper of Bethany, Matt. xxvi. 6. (8) Simon of Cyrene, who was compelled to bear Christ's cross, Matt. xxvii. 32 ; Mark xv. 21 ; Luke xxiii. 26. (9) The tanner of Joppa with whom Peter lodged, Acts ix. 43. (10) Simon the father of Judas Iscariot, John vi. 71 ; xiii. 2, 26.

Sĭm′rī (*alert*). A Merarite Levite in David's time, 1 Chr. xxvi. 10.

Sĭn (*clay*). (1) A city of Egypt identified with Pelusium, " town of clay or mud," on eastern mouth of Nile near the sea, Ezek. xxx. 15, 16. (2) A desert portion of Arabia between Gulf of Suez and Sinai, Ex. xvi. 1 ; xvii. 1 ; Num. xxxiii. 11, 12. It was in this wilderness that the Israelites were first fed with manna and quails. It skirts the eastern coast of the gulf for a distance of 25 miles.

Sĭn=mŏn′ey. Money sent from a distance to buy offerings. The surplus, if any, became a perquisite of the priest, and was called sin-money, 2 Kgs. xii. 16.

Sĭn=ŏf′fĕr-ing. Like the trespass-offering, the sin-offering was expiatory, but seemingly of general sins. It was presented on the great day of atonement, when one confessed the sins of the nation with his hand on the head of the scapegoat, Lev. xvi. 1–34 ; Num. xviii. 9.

Sī′nà. Greek form of Sinai, Acts vii. 30, 38.

Sī′nāi (*bushy*). The peninsula of Sinai lies between the two great arms of the Red Sea, Gulf of Akaba on the east, and Gulf of Suez on the west. This region contains the mountain system of Horeb or Sinai, on one of whose mounts, or peaks, God appeared to Moses in the burning bush, Ex. iii. 1–5, amid whose surrounding wilderness the wandering Israelites encamped, Ex. xix. 1, 2, and from whose cloud-obscured heights the law was delivered to Moses, Ex. xix. 3–25 ; xx.–xl. ; Lev. The numbering also took place there, Num. i.–x. 1–12. The peninsula is a triangle whose base extends from the head of Suez to Akaba. This base is pierced by the plateau of Tih, the " desert of wandering," south of which are those tumultuous mountain clusters above mentioned, central among which is Mount Sinai. The coast ranges along Akaba and Suez are systematic and elevated. The region was a dependency of Egypt from earliest times, but became subject to Rome.

Sī′nim. An unidentified land mentioned in Isa. xlix. 12. Referred by some to China.

Sīn′īte. A tribe descended from Canaan, Gen. x. 17; 1 Chr. i. 15.

Sī′ŏn (*lofty*). (1) An ancient name of Mount Hermon, Deut. iv. 48. (2) Greek form of Zion, Matt. xxi. 5; John xii. 15; Heb. xii. 22; Rev. xiv. 1.

Sĭph′moth (*fertile*). A haunt of David, while an outlaw, in South Judah, 1 Sam. xxx. 28.

Sĭp′pāi (*threshold*). Saph, the Philistine giant slain at Gezer, 1 Chr. xx. 4.

Sī′rach. Father of Jesus, writer of the Apocryphal book of Ecclesiasticus.

Sī′rah (*retreat*). The well, now *Ain Sarah*, from which Abner was called by Joab. It was near Hebron, 2 Sam. iii. 26.

Sĭr′i̇-ŏn. Zidonian name of Mount Hermon, Deut. iii. 9; Ps. xxix. 6.

Sĭ-săm′a̤-ī (*famed*). A descendant of Sheshan, of Judah, 1 Chr. ii. 40.

Sĭs′e̤-ra̤ (*ready for war*). (1) Captain of King Jabin's forces when defeated by Barak. Slain by Jael, Judg. iv.; v. (2) His children returned, Ez. ii. 53; Neh. vii. 55.

Sĭ-sĭn′nē̤ṣ. Governor of Syria and Phœnicia under Darius, 1 Esdr. vi. 3.

Sĭt′nah̤ (*strife*). Second of the two wells dug by Isaac in valley of Gerar, over which the herdsmen disputed, Gen. xxvi. 21.

Sĭ′van. Third month of Jewish sacred and ninth of civil year, beginning with the new moon of June, Esth. viii. 9.

Slāve (*Sclavonian*). Slavery came about under Hebrew institutions. (1) By poverty, when a man sold himself to cancel debt, Lev. xxv. 39; (2) by theft, when restitution could not be made, Ex. xxii. 3; (3) by parents selling their daughters as concubines, Ex. xxi. 7–11. It ended (1) when the debt was paid; (2) on the year of Jubilee, Lev. xxv. 40; (3) at the end of six years of service, Ex. xxi. 2; Deut. xv. 12. This as to Hebrews. As to non-Hebrew slaves, by far the most numerous class, they were purchased, Lev. xxv. 45; or captured in war, Num. xxxi. 26, 40. They were freed if ill treated, Ex. xxi. 26, 27; to slay one was murder, Lev. xxiv. 17, 22; they were circumcised and had religious privileges, Gen. xvii. 12, 13.

Slīme. The slime of Babel, and that of the pits of Siddim, and the ark of Moses, was mineral pitch or bitumen, Gen. xi. 3; xiv. 10; Ex. ii. 3.

Slĭng. The weapons of shepherds and light troops. It consisted of leather or sinew strings with a pouch at the end for the missile, Judg. xx. 16; 1 Sam. xvii. 40.

Smĭth (*smiter*). An artificer in iron, brass, or other metals, Gen. iv. 22; 1 Sam. xiii. 19–22.

Smy̆r′na̤ (*myrrh*). A coast city of Ionia, Asia Minor, 40 miles north of Ephesus. Mentioned in Rev. ii. 8–11 as site of one of the seven churches of Asia. The old city of Smyrna dates back to Theseus, 1300 years B. C. Alexander the Great built the new city B. C. 320. It became subject to Rome and was noted for its beauty. Christianity got an early foothold there and the city sent a bishop to the council of Nice, A. D. 325. It is still a large city of mixed nationalities and creeds, and of considerable commercial importance.

Snāil (*snake*). In Lev. xi. 30 a lizard is meant. In Ps. lviii. 8, the common snail, slug, or slime-snake is meant. Snails abound in the Orient and are not eschewed as a food.

Snōw. Only mentioned once as actually falling, 2 Sam. xxiii. 20; but of frequent poetic and meta-

phoric use, Ex. iv. 6; Num. xii. 10; 2 Kgs. v. 27; Ps. li. 7; Isa. i. 18.

Snŭff=dĭsh′es̤. Small dishes, made of gold, for receiving the snuff from the tabernacle lamps, Ex. xxv. 38.

Snŭf′fer̤ṣ. Scissor-like instruments, made of gold, for snuffing the wicks of the tabernacle lamps, Ex. xxxvii. 23.

Sō. A king of Egypt with whom Hoshea formed an alliance against Assyria. The discovery of this led to the imprisonment of Hoshea, the siege and capture of Samaria, and the captivity of the ten tribes of Israel, 2 Kgs. xvii. 4, 6.

Sōap (*sap, resin*). The Hebrew word for soap implies any alkaline substance used for cleansing, Jer. ii. 22; Mal. iii. 2.

Sō′chō, 1 Chr. iv. 18. [Socoh.]

Sō′choh, 1 Kgs. iv. 10. [Socoh.]

Sō′coh (*brambly*). (1) A town in lowlands of Judah, Josh. xv. 35. Shocho, 2 Chr. xxviii. 18. Shoco, 2 Chr. xi. 7. Shochoh, 1 Sam. xvii. 1. (2) A town in the mountains of Judah, Josh. xv. 48.

Sō′dī (*secret*). Father of the spy from Zebulun, Num. xiii. 10.

Sŏd′om (*consuming*). Most prominent of the cities in the plain of Siddim. Destroyed by fire from heaven, Gen. x. 19; xiii. 10–13; xix. 1–29. Site of "the cities of the plain" is not known, but variously referred to the southern end, the northern end, and bottom of the Dead Sea. Sodom is often referred to in Scripture as a symbol of wickedness and warning to sinners, Deut. xxix. 23; Isa. i. 9, 10; xiii. 19; Jer. xxiii. 14; xlix. 18; Ezek. xvi. 49, 50; Matt. x. 15; xi. 23; Rev. xi. 8.

Sŏd′om-a̤. Greek and Vulgate form of Sodom, Rom. ix. 29.

Sŏd′om-ītes̤. Dwellers in Sodom, or, by figure, those who practise the abominations of Sodom, Deut. xxiii. 17; 1 Kgs. xiv. 24; xv. 12.

Sŏl′o-mon (*peaceful*). Last of David's sons by Bathsheba. Named Jedidiah, "beloved of God," by Nathan, 1 Chr. iii. 5; 2 Sam. xii. 25. Placed in Nathan's care. Secured the throne according to David's pledge, 1 Kgs. i. 13–53, and much to the consternation of Adonijah, the legal successor. Reigned forty years, B. C. 1015–975. Confirmed his father's conquests, built the palace and temple, extended commerce, contracted favorable alliances, grew famous for wisdom, raised his kingdom to great wealth, splendor, and power, mingled justice with cruelty, endorsed true and false worship, encouraged literature, and wrote largely himself, fell a prey to the sensualities of his time and position, died leaving his kingdom under the eclipse of faction and on the edge of decay, 1 Kgs. ii.–xi.; 2 Chr. i.–ix.

Sŏl′o-mon's Pools. Reservoirs erected by Solomon near Bethlehem, whence water was conveyed to the distributing pools at Jerusalem. They are still in partial use, Eccl. ii. 6.

Sŏl′o-mon's Porch. The colonnade on east side of the temple, John x. 23; Acts iii. 11; v. 12.

Sŏl′o-mon's Sĕr′vants. Returned captives, and probable descendants of a class of servants favored by Solomon, Ez. ii. 55, 58; Neh. vii. 57, 60.

Sŏl′o-mon's Sŏng. [Song of Solomon.]

Son. In Hebrew sense, any descendant however remote, Gen. xxix. 5; 2 Sam. xix. 24. Applied also to pupils, adopted persons, those of kindred faith, etc., Gen. xlviii. 5; 1 Sam. iii. 6; Acts xiii. 6.

Son of God. A term applied to the angels, Job xxxviii. 7; to Adam, Luke iii. 38; to believers, Rom. viii. 14; 2 Cor. vi. 18; but preëminently to Christ, signifying his divine origin and nature, Dan. iii. 25; Matt. xi. 27; xvi. 16; John i. 18; v. 19–26; ix. 35.

Son of Man. In a limited sense, "man," Num. xxiii. 19; Job xxv. 6; Ps. viii. 4. In a broader, higher, and perhaps more generally received Hebrew sense, "the Messiah." In the N. T. sense, where the term is used some eighty times, it means Christ in incarnate form and relation, Dan. vii. 13 ; Matt. ix. 6 ; xii. 8 ; xviii. 11 ; Mark ii. 10 ; John i. 51 ; iii. 13 ; vi. 53.

Sŏng of Sŏl'o-mon. "Song of Songs," or "Canticles," in Latin. Twenty-second O. T. book and last of poetic. Authorship and meaning much disputed. Some make it type conjugal love ; others regard it as purely allegorical ; still others as literal and descriptive of Solomon's marriage to some beautiful woman.

Sooth'say-er (*truth-sayer*). One who pretends to foretell future events, Dan. ii. 27. [DIVINATION.]

Sŏp (*sip*). Bread dipped in soup, milk, wine, sauce, or other liquid, Ruth ii. 14 ; John xiii. 26.

Sŏp'a-tēr (*father saved*). A Berean companion of Paul, Acts xx. 4.

Sŏph'e-rĕth (*scribe*). His children were returned captives, Ez. ii. 55.

Sŏph''ō-nī'as. The prophet Zephaniah, 2 Esdr. i. 40.

Sŏr'çer-er (*fate-worker*). [DIVINATION.]

Sō'rek (*vine*). A valley of Philistia, where Delilah lived, Judg. xvi. 4.

Sō-sĭp'a-tēr (*Sopater*). (1) A general of Judas Maccabeus, 2 Macc. xii. 19-24. (2) A friend of Paul ; probably Sopater, Rom. xvi. 21.

Sŏs'the-nĕs (*saviour*). (1) A ruler of the synagogue at Corinth, who was beaten by the Greeks, Acts xviii. 17. (2) Perhaps the former, after conversion, 1 Cor. i. 1.

Sŏs'tra-tus. A Syrian general commanding in Jerusalem, 2 Macc. iv. 27.

Sō'ta-ī (*fickle*). His children were returned captives, Ez. ii. 55 ; Neh. vii. 57.

Sōul. The Hebrew ideal of man was threefold : (1) The body, or material part. (2) The vital part, seat of sensations, passions, etc. (3) The sentient, thinking, or spiritual part, Gen. i. 20 ; ii. 7 ; Num. xvi. 22 ; 1 Thess. v. 23 ; Heb. iv. 12.

South Rā'moth. A place in southern Judah, bordering on the desert, and one of the resorts of David during the period of his outlawry by Saul, 1 Sam. xxx. 27.

Sow. [SWINE.]

Sōw'er, Sōw'ing. Cereal seeds were sown by hand, Ps. cxxvi. 6 ; Am. ix. 13 ; Mark iv. 3–29. In moist ground seeds were tramped in by cattle, Isa. xxxii. 20. Mixed seeds prohibited, Lev. xix. 19 ; Deut. xxii. 9.

Spāin. Anciently the whole peninsula of southwestern Europe, embracing Spain and Portugal ; known to Greeks as Iberia and to Romans as Hispania. If identical with Tarshish, then known to Hebrews in Solomon's time ; certainly to Phœnicians. Known to Paul, who contemplated a visit to it, Rom. xv. 24–28. Christianity early introduced there.

Spăn (*bind*). Distance from tip of thumb to that of little finger, when stretched apart ; about nine inches. Also any small interval of space or time, 1 Sam. xvii. 4 ; Isa. xl. 12 ; Lam. ii. 20.

Spăr'row (*spurrer*). The Hebrew word signifies "twitterer" and is mostly rendered " bird " or " fowl." Though tree-sparrows abounded in Palestine, any small bird meets the sense in Ps. lxxxiv. 3 ; cii. 7. In N. T. the reference is directly to the sparrow species, used as a cheap food, Matt. x. 29 ; Luke xii. 6, 7.

Spēar (*spar*). In general, a wooden staff with a sharp metallic head. Some were light for throwing, others long and heavy for attack either by footmen or horsemen, 1 Sam. xiii. 22 ; xvii. 7 ; xxvi. 7 ; 2 Sam. ii. 23.

Spēar'men. Light-armed troops are evidently meant, Acts xxiii. 23.

Spĕck'led Bird, Jer. xii. 9. [HYENA.]

Spīce, Spī'çes (*species*). Hardly, as with us, the entire list of aromatic vegetable substances, but rather the fragrant gums, barks, etc., of ceremonial, medicinal, and toilet value, and for embalming, Gen. xxxvii. 25 ; xliii. 11 ; S. of Sol. iv. 14 ; Mark xvi. 1 ; John xix. 39, 40.

Spī'der (*spinner*). The common spider is meant in Job viii. 14 ; Isa. lix. 5 ; but the gecko, or lizard, is probably intended in Prov. xxx. 28. The lightness and frailty of the spider's web are made emblematic of visionary hopes and wicked schemes.

Spīke'närd (*pointed leaf yielding perfume*). An ancient fragrant and costly ointment made from the spikenard plant of India, S. of Sol. i. 12 ; iv. 13, 14 ; Mark xiv. 3 ; John xii. 3.

Spĭn'ning (*spanning, drawing*). A well-known and necessary female occupation among Hebrews. The instrument — distaff and spindle — permitted of much the same drawing and twisting process as is now employed in the East, in the absence of the more modern spinning-wheel, Ex. xxxv. 25 ; Prov. xxxi. 19 ; Matt. vi. 28.

Spĭr'it (*breath*). The breath, 2 Thess. ii. 8. The vital principle, Eccl. viii. 8. Elsewhere, the soul. [SOUL.] Holy Spirit, or Ghost, is the third person in the Trinity, 2 Cor. xiii. 14 ; Acts xv. 28. Though Holy Spirit and Holy Ghost are synonymous in meaning, preference is given to the latter form in the Scriptures, Matt. i. 18 ; John i. 33 ; Acts ii. 4 ; Rom. v. 5, and elsewhere, the former being used only four times.

Spŏil. Plunder seized by violence, as the spoils of an army or of bandits, 1 Sam. xxx. 19-22 ; but in Ex. iii. 22, the sense is that of recovery without violence of unjustly taken property. David instituted very strict regulations for the division of spoils of war among his soldiers, 1 Sam. xxx. 20-25.

Sponge. Only mentioned in N. T., though probably known to ancient Hebrews, Matt. xxvii. 48 ; Mark xv. 36 ; John xix. 29.

Spouse. [MARRIAGE.]

Sprĭn'kling (*springing*). The blood of the sin-offering was sprinkled with the finger of the priest upon the mercy-seat of the inner sanctuary as an atonement for the holy place because of national uncleanness, Lev. xvi. 14–16. The " blood of sprinkling " or mediatorial blood of the new covenant, Heb. xii. 24, is made antithetical with the blood of vengeance, Gen. iv. 10.

Stā'chỹs (*ear of corn*). A Roman Christian saluted by Paul, Rom. xvi. 9.

Stăc'tĕ (*drop*). An oriental gum or spice, one of the components of the holy incense, Ex. xxx. 34.

Stănd'ard. [ENSIGN.]

Stär (*strew*). All the heavenly bodies, except sun and moon, called stars by Hebrews, Gen. xv. 5 ; Ps. cxlvii. 4. The " star in the east," seen and followed by the " wise men," and designed to announce the birth of the Messiah, was, according to some, wholly phenomenal, and to others, natural. Stars symbolize rulers and princes, Dan. viii. 10 ; angels, Job xxxviii. 7 ; ministers, Rev. i. 16–20. Christ is " the bright and morning star," Rev. xxii. 16.

Stā'ter (*standard*). The standard gold coin of ancient Greece, worth about $4.00. Later, the silver stater, containing four drachmæ, or about sixty cents. This is thought to be the " piece of money " of Matt. xvii. 27.

Stēel. Hebrews were not acquainted with carbonized iron, or steel. Wherever the word is found in Scripture, copper is meant, Ps. xviii. 34.

Stĕph'a-năs (*crown*). One of Paul's earliest converts at Corinth, 1 Cor. i. 16 ; xvi. 15.

Stē'phen (*crown*). Chief of the first seven deacons, and first Christian martyr. A Greek convert of strong faith and great eloquence. Arrested and tried before the Sanhedrim, but stoned to death by an angry mob, before he had time to finish his defence. The date of his martyrdom is fixed at about A. D. 37. It was followed by the conversion of Saul, who was present at the stoning, and a bitter persecutor of early Christians at the time, Acts vi. 5–15, vii., viii. 1–3.

Stŏcks (*sticks*). Tree-trunks, Job xiv. 8; idols, Jer. ii. 27; instruments of punishment made of beams of wood which closed over the arms or ankles, Job xiii. 27; xxxiii. 11; Jer. xx. 2; Acts xvi. 24.

Stō′ïcs (*porch scholars*). Members of a Grecian philosophical school, or sect, founded by Zeno, 308 B. C., who taught in the *stoa*, or porch, of the Agora at Athens. They held to a high morality, proud independence of spirit, fateful, in place of providential, superintendence, wisdom as the source of happiness, Acts xvii. 18. Paul encountered both Stoics and Epicureans at Athens, and, on being taken into Areopagus by them, delivered to them the oration in Acts xvii. 22–31.

Stom′ach-er. An article of dress worn over breast and stomach. Much affected in the 17th century; but whether that of Isa. iii. 24 was similar is not known.

Stōneṣ. Used for building, 1 Kgs. v. 17; Am. v. 11; memorial marks, Gen. xxviii. 18; xxxv. 14; knives, Ex. iv. 25; ballots, Rev. ii. 17. Symbols of hardness, 1 Sam. xxv. 37; of firmness, Gen. xlix. 24; Christian aggregation, 1 Pet. ii. 4–6. Precious stones highly prized by Hebrews and much used on priestly vestments and as ornaments. Twenty gems are mentioned in the Bible, Gen. ii. 12; Ex. xxviii. 9–21. India, Arabia, and Syria were the sources of gems used by Hebrews, Ezek. xxvii. 16–22.

Stō′ning. [PUNISHMENT.]

Stŏrk (*vulture*). A large wading bird, plentiful in Palestine, gregarious, migratory, nesting in trees and noted for tenderness to its young. Unclean under the law, Lev. xi. 19; Deut. xiv. 18; Ps. civ. 17; Jer. viii. 7.

Strāin at a, Matt. xxiii. 24. "Strain out the," in R. V.

Strān′ger (*without*). One away from his country, Gen. xxiii. 4. One not a Jew, Ex. xx. 10. One not of Aaron's family, Num. iii. 10. One not of royal blood, Matt. xvii. 25, 26. One alienated or neglected, Ps. lxix. 8. But, in general, any naturalized foreigner in the Jewish State, Deut. xvii. 15. Strangers, in Hebrew acceptation, were numerous in Israel, owing to the mixed multitudes which were permitted to follow the wanderers in the wilderness, to the fact that very many Canaanites remained in the land, and to the liberal regulations respecting captives taken in war.

Strąw. Straw used for cattle fodder and litter, Gen. xxiv. 25; 1 Kgs. iv. 28; Isa. xi. 7; lxv. 25; in making bricks, Ex. v. 7, 16.

Sū′ah (*sweeping*). An Asherite, 1 Chr. vii. 36.

Sū′bå. His sons returned, 1 Esdr. v. 34.

Sŭc′coth (*tents*). (1) The place east of Jordan where Jacob built a house and booths, Gen. xxxiii. 17; Josh. xiii. 27; Judg. viii. 5–16. Between Succoth and Zarthan, in the plain of Jordan, lay the clay ground in which were cast the brazen utensils for the temple, 1 Kgs. vii. 46; 2 Chr. iv. 17. (2) First station of the Israelites after starting from Egypt, a day's journey from Rameses, Ex. xii. 37; xiii. 20; Num. xxxiii. 5, 6.

Sŭc′coth=bē′noth (*tents of daughters*). Some refer it to a Babylonian idol set up by colonists in Samaria, others to booths or tents in which the daughters of Babylon prostituted themselves in honor of their goddess, 2 Kgs. xvii. 30.

Sū′chath-ītes. A family of scribes at Jabez, 1 Chr. ii. 55.

Sŭd. River of Sura, probably Euphrates, Bar. i. 4.

Sŭk′kĭ-ĭmṣ. An African people who supported Shishak when he invaded Judah, 2 Chr. xii. 3.

Sŭn. The greater light, Gen. i. 15–18. Worshipped by idolatrous Hebrews, 2 Kgs. xxi. 3, 5; xxiii. 5; and by other nations, Job xxxi. 26, 27; Gen. xli. 45; furnishes many metaphors, Ps. lxxxiv. 11; John i. 9; Rev. i. 16.

Sûr. A place on sea-coast of Palestine, Judith ii. 28.

Sụre′tỹ (*security*). Suretyship in the older sense of pledge was regulated by the Mosaic law, Gen. xliv. 32; Ex. xxii. 25, 26; Deut. xxiv. 6–17. When Solomon opened Palestine to commerce, suretyship took the forms of general law and trade, Prov. vi. 1; xi. 15; xvii. 18; xx. 16; xxii. 26. [LOANS.] [PLEDGE.]

Sụ′så, Esth. xi. 3. [SHUSHAN.]

Sụ′san-chītes. Dwellers in Shushan or Susa, Ez. iv. 9.

Sụ′ṣăn′nå (*lily*). (1) Heroine of the story of the Judgment of Daniel, as found in "The History of Susanna," one of the Apocryphal books. (2) One of the women who ministered to Christ, Luke viii. 3.

Sū′sī (*horseman*). Father of the Manassite spy, Num. xiii. 11.

Swąl′low (*throat sweller*). The common swift or swallow abounds in Palestine, and its habits, according to Bible mention, are such as we observe : building under the eaves of houses, beneath temple cornices and porticos, and in the sides of cliffs, and rapidly circling above their homes in search of their aerial food, Ps. lxxxiv. 3; Prov. xxvi. 2; Isa. xxxviii. 14; Jer. viii. 7.

Swąn. Swans rare in Palestine. Unclean, Lev. xi. 18; Deut. xiv. 16. The original seems to imply some other bird, as the ibis or water-hen.

Sweâr′ing. [OATH.]

Swĕat. The bloody sweat of the agony is known to medical science, and ascribed to violent mental emotion, Luke xxii. 44.

Swīne. The hog was pronounced unclean, Lev. xi. 7; Deut. xiv. 8. Priests and Arabians abstained from the meat for dietetic reasons. Swine-keeping a degrading business, Luke xv. 15; yet swine were kept, Matt. viii. 32. To cast "pearls before swine" was to waste truth on those who despised it, Matt. vii. 6.

Swôrd. A short, two-edged, dagger-like weapon, carried in a sheath or scabbard, and suspended to the girdle or belt, Gen. xxvii. 40; Judg. iii. 16; 2 Sam. xx. 8; Jer. xlvii. 6; Ezek. xxi. 9, 30.

Sўc′ą-mine, Luke xvii. 6. [SYCAMORE.]

Sўc′ą-mōre (*fig-mulberry*). Not our sycamore or plane-tree, but a tree of the fig species growing in Egypt and Palestine and valued for its fruit and light, soft, durable wood, 1 Kgs. x. 27; 1 Chr. xxvii. 28; Ps. lxxviii. 47; Luke xix. 4. Sycamine in Luke xvii. 6. Sycamore fruit grows singly or in clusters and in almost direct contact with the branches. It resembles the fig in shape, and though of acrid taste when first pulled soon becomes sweetish. Egyptian mummy-cases were made of the wood of the sycamore tree.

Sȳ′char, John iv. 5. [SHECHEM.]

Sȳ′chem, Acts vii. 16. [SHECHEM.]

Sȳ-ē′ne (*key*). A city of Egypt bordering on Ethiopia. Situated on the Nile below the first cataract, and noted for its quarries of syenite stone, Ezek. xxix. 10; xxx. 6. Syene was an important city during the reigns of the Hyksos, or Shepherd Kings, in Egypt. It is now represented by the Arab village of Aswan.

Sўn′ą-gŏgue (*led together*). The Jewish assembly for social and religious purposes seems to have had its origin during the captivity, or to have been an outgrowth of it, Ez. viii. 15; Neh. viii. 2; ix. 1. The casual, or house, assemblages soon ran into regular congregations, with suitable buildings and stated meetings, at requisite points. These were the synagogues, often elaborate and costly, presided over by a chief, or rabbi, assisted by a council of elders, Mark v. 22, 35; Luke iv. 20; John xvi. 2; Acts xviii. 8.

Sўn'tў-chē (*fate*). A woman of the church at Philippi, Phil. iv. 2.

Sўr'a-cūse. A noted city on eastern coast of Sicily, where Paul spent three days on his voyage to Rome, Acts xxviii. 12.

Sўr'ĭ-à. The Hebrew Aram. So indefinitely bounded at different times as to have been associated with Assyria (whence its name) and Babylon. More definitely the country to the north of Canaan, extending from the Tigris to the Mediterranean, and northward to the Taurus ranges. Damascus was the capital, and centre of wealth, learning, and power. Joshua subdued its petty kings, Josh. xi. 2–18; David reduced it to submission, 2 Sam. viii., x. During Solomon's reign it became independent, 1 Kgs. xi. 23–25. The earliest recorded settlers in Syria were Hittites and other Hamitic races. The Shemitic element entered it from the southeast under Abraham and Chedorlaomer. After Syria became independent it was a persistent enemy of the Jews, 1 Kgs. xv. 18–20; xx., xxii.; 2 Kgs. vi. 8–33; vii., ix. 14, 15; x. 32, 33; xiii. 3, 14–25. The attempt of the Syrian king to ally Israel with him for the overthrow of Judah led Ahaz to call in the help of Assyria, and Syria was soon merged into the great Assyrian empire. It was conquered by Alexander the Great, B. C. 333, and finally fell to the lot of Seleucus Nicator, who made it the central province of his empire, with the capital at Antioch. The Syriac language was closely allied to the Hebrew.

Sўr'ĭ-ac. The ancient language of Syria, an Aramean dialect. In Dan. ii. 4, the word "Syriac" should read "Aramaic," the court language of Babylon at the time.

Sўr'ĭ-à=mā'a-chah, 1 Chr. xix. 6. [SYRIA and MAACHAH.]

Sўr'ĭ-an. Inhabitant of Syria, Gen. xxv. 20, and elsewhere.

Sў'rŏ=phē-nĭ'çĭan. A Phœnician at the time Phœnicia was part of the Roman province of Syria; or it may mean one of half Syrian and half Phœnician blood, Mark vii. 26.

Syr'tis, in Acts xxvii. 17, R. V. The dangerous quicksands or shallows on the African coast, southwest of Crete.

T

Tā'a-nāch (*sandy*). A Canaanite city conquered by Joshua and assigned to Levites, Josh. xii. 21; xvii. 11–18; Judg. i. 27; 1 Kgs. iv. 12. Now Taanak, 4 miles from Megiddo. Tanach, Josh. xxi. 25.

Tā'a-nāth=shī'lŏh (*pass to Shiloh*). A border mark of Ephraim, Josh. xvi. 6.

Tăb'ba-ŏth (*rings*). Father of returned Nethinim, Ez. ii. 43; Neh. vii. 46.

Tăb'bath (*famous*). Where the fleeing Midianites stopped after Gideon's night attack, Judg. vii. 22.

Tā'be-al (*good God*). Father of a general under Pekah, or in Rezin's Syrian army, whom it was proposed to make king of Judah, Isa. vii. 6.

Tā'be-el (*good God*). A Persian officer in Samaria under King Artaxerxes, Ez. iv. 7.

Tā-bĕl'lĭ-us, 1 Esdr. ii. 15. [TABEEL.]

Tăb'e-rah (*burning*). A place in the wilderness of Paran, where the Israelites encamped. It was so called because God there consumed the murmurers. The encampment remained there for a month, and the excessive eating of quail led to a pestilence, for which reason the place was called Kibroth-hattavah, or "graves of lust," Num. xi. 3, 34; Deut. ix. 22.

Tā'bēr-ing. Beating upon the taber, tabret, or small drum. Word now obsolete, Nah. ii. 7.

Tăb'ēr-nā-cle (*little shed or tent*). Tent of Jehovah, or movable sanctuary, which Moses was directed to erect in the wilderness, Ex. xxv. 8. Its plan, materials, and furnishings are described in Ex. xxv. 9–40; xxvi., xxvii. It could be readily taken down and set up and accompanied the Israelites during their wanderings, Ex. xl. 38. During the conquest it was stationed at Gilgal, Josh. iv. 19; ix. 6; x. 15; and at Ebal, Josh. viii. 30–35. After the conquest it was set up at Shiloh, Josh. xviii. 1, where it remained during the time of the Judges and where the ark was captured by the Philistines, 1 Sam. iv. 17, 22. Sometime after the return of the ark it was taken to Jerusalem and placed in a new tabernacle, and finally in the temple, 2 Sam. vi. 17; 1 Chr. xv. 1, but the old structure was still venerated, as long as it remained at Shiloh. It was afterwards removed to Nob, 1 Sam. xxi. 1–9, and in the reign of David to Gibeon, 1 Chr. xvi. 39; xxi. 29, where it was at the beginning of Solomon's reign. Some suppose that the tabernacle and its furniture were moved into Solomon's temple when it was completed.

Tăb'ēr-nā-cle of Tĕs'tĭ-mŏ-nў. As the stone tables of the Ten Commandments were called the "tables of testimony," Ex. xxxi. 18; xxxii. 15; xxxiv. 29; and the ark which contained them was called the "ark of testimony," Ex. xxv. 22, so the tabernacle in which the ark was placed was called the "tabernacle of testimony," Ex. xxxviii. 21; Num. i. 50. Called also "the tabernacle of witness," in Num. xvii. 7, 8.

Tăb'ēr-nā-cles, Feast of. Third of the three great Hebrew feasts, celebrated from the 15th to 22d of Tisri. It commemorated the long tent life of the Israelites, and during its celebration the people dwelt in booths. Called also "feast of ingathering," Ex. xxiii. 16, because it came at end of harvest. It was closed with a holy convocation, Lev. xxiii. 36; and on Sabbatical years was similarly opened and closed, when the law was read anew, Deut. xxxi. 11–13. For law as to solemnization *see* Lev. xxiii. 34–43; Num. xxix. 12–40. Its observance is referred to in Neh. viii. 13–18; Hos. xii. 9; Zech. xiv. 16–19; John vii. 2, 37, 38.

Tăb'ĭ-thà (*gazelle*). The Christian woman of Joppa whom Peter raised from the dead, Acts ix. 36–42. [DORCAS.]

Tā'ble (*board*). Primitive tables were merely leather or skins spread on the floor. After the captivity they were slightly raised. Beds or couches are meant in Mark vii. 4; writing tablet of wax in Luke i. 63. The "tables" of Matt. xxi. 12; John ii. 15, were doubtless sufficiently raised to answer the purposes of a counter for money-changing purposes. The meaning of "serve tables" in Acts vi. 2, is that duty which fell to the early Christian ministry of attending to the gathering and distributing of food to the poor, or of collecting and distributing the church funds. This duty was transferred to the deacons, Acts vi. 5, 6.

Tā'bôr (*mound*). (1) A high mountain on north side of plain of Esdraelon; landmark between Issachar and Zebulun, Josh. xix. 22; gathering place of Barak's forces, Judg. iv. 6–14; scene of murder of Gideon's brothers, Judg. viii. 18–21. (2) Levitical town in Zebulun, 1 Chr. vi. 77. (3) "Plain of Tabor," 1 Sam. x. 3, should read "oak of Tabor."

Tăb'ret (*little tabor*). A small drum or tambourine, without jingles; used to accompany pipes, 1 Sam. xviii. 6. [TIMBREL.]

Tăb'rĭ-mŏn (*Rimmon is good*). Father of Benhadad I., King of Syria in time of Asa, 1 Kgs. xv. 18.

Tāche (*tack*). Taches were hooks or clasps of gold or copper for connecting the tabernacle curtains, Ex. xxvi. 6, 11.

Tăch'mo-nīte, 2 Sam. xxiii. 8. Hachmonite, or "son of Hachmoni."

Tăd'môr (*Tamar, palms*). The Palmyra of the Greeks and Romans. A city built by Solomon in Syria, toward the Euphrates, for the purpose of facilitating trade with the east. Its ruins are numerous and suggestive, 1 Kgs. ix. 18; 2 Chr. viii. 4. Tadmor, or Palmyra, reached the height of its splendor, wealth, and power under the celebrated Zenobia, "Queen of the East," who made it the capital of her empire. It fell a prey to the victorious Romans. Among its notable ruins are the Temple of the Sun, dedicated to Baal, a Street of Columns, of which 150 are still standing, and a series of magnificent tombs intended for both burial places and places of worship. The old name still exists in the form of Thadmor.

Tā′hăn (*camp*). An Ephraimite, Num. xxvi. 35; 1 Chr. vii. 25.

Tā′hăn-ītes. Descendants of Tahan, Num. xxvi. 35.

Tȧ-hăp′a-nēs, Jer. ii. 16. [TAHPANHES.]

Tā′hăth (*station*). (1) A desert station of the Israelites, Num. xxxiii. 26, 27. (2) A Levite, 1 Chr. vi. 24, 37. (3) Two Ephraimites, 1 Chr. vii. 20.

Tăh′pan-hēs. An ancient city of Egypt on the Tanitic mouth of the Nile. Identical with the Daphne of the Greeks. A favorite resort of exiled Jews, Jer. xliii. 7–9; xliv. 1; xlvi. 14. Jeremiah was taken thither, after the murder of Gedaliah, and the Pharaoh erected a brick palace there. The children of Noph and Tahpanhes are made to type the entire population of Egypt, Jer. ii. 16.

Tăh′pen-ēs. An Egyptian queen, wife of the Pharaoh who received Hadad, king of Edom, 1 Kgs. xi. 18–20.

Tăh-rē′a (*cunning*). A descendant of Saul, 1 Chr. ix. 41. Tarea, 1 Chr. viii. 35.

Tăh′tim=hŏd′shī. An unknown land visited by Joab during his census tour, 2 Sam. xxiv. 6.

Tāle (*number*). A reckoning by number and not by weight, Ex. v. 8.

Tăl′ent (*weight*). A Hebrew weight and denomination for money, equal to 3,000 shekels, or 93¾ pounds of silver, and varying in value from $1,550 to $2,000, Ex. xxxviii. 25; Matt. xviii. 24. The Attic, or Greek talent, was worth about $1,200; the Roman great talent, $500; the Roman small talent, $375.

Tăl′ĭ-thȧ cū′mī. Two Syro-Chaldaic words spoken by Christ, and meaning "Damsel, arise," Mark v. 41.

Tăl′māi (*brave*). (1) A son of Anak, Num. xiii. 22; Josh. xv. 14; Judg. i. 10. (2) King of Geshur and father-in-law of David, 2 Sam. iii. 3.

Tăl′mon (*captive*). A temple porter, 1 Chr. ix. 17, and father of a family of returned captives, Ez. ii. 42; Neh. vii. 45; xi. 19; xii. 25.

Tăl′mŭd (*instruction*). The body of Jewish civil and canonical law not comprised in the Pentateuch, and commonly including the *Mishna* (traditions and decisions) and *Gemara* (expositions).

Tā′mah (*mirth*). Ancestor of returned Nethinim, Neh. vii. 55. Thamah, Ez. ii. 53.

Tā′mar (*palm-tree*). (1) Widow of Er and Onan, of Judah, and mother of Pharez and Zarah, by Shelah, Gen. xxxviii. (2) Daughter of David and sister of Absalom, 2 Sam. xiii. 1–32. (3) Daughter of Absalom, wife of Uriel and mother of Maachah, queen of Abijah, 2 Sam. xiv. 27; 2 Chr. xiii. 2. (4) A frontier place in south Judah, a day's journey from Hebron, Ezek. xlvii. 19; xlviii. 28.

Tăm′mŭz (*sprout*). A Syrian idol corresponding to the Greek Adonis, Ezek. viii. 14.

Tā′năch, Josh. xxi. 25. [TAANACH.]

Tăn′hu-mĕth (*comfort*). Father of one of Gedaliah's captains, 2 Kgs. xxv. 23; Jer. xl. 8.

Tā′nis, Ezek. xxx. 14 marg. [ZOAN.]

Tăn′nĕr (*oaker*). Tanning not a reputable occupation among Hebrews. It was carried on outside of cities and towns. Peter stopped with Simon, a tanner of Joppa, Acts ix. 43.

Tā′phath (*drop*). A daughter of Solomon, 1 Kgs. iv. 11.

Tā′phŏn, 1 Macc. ix. 50. [BETH-TAPPUAH.]

Tăp′pu-ah (*apple*). (1) A descendant of Judah,

1 Chr. ii. 43. (2) A city in the plain-country of Judah, four miles N. W. of Hebron, Josh. xv. 34. (3) A border place between Ephraim and Manasseh, Josh. xvi. 8; xvii. 8.

Tā′rah (*station*). A desert encampment of the Israelites, Num. xxxiii. 27.

Tăr′a-lah (*winding*). A town in Benjamin, Josh. xviii. 27.

Tā′re-a, 1 Chr. viii. 35. [TAHREA.]

Târes (*tears*). The darnel is supposed to be meant. It grows somewhat like wheat till near ripening time, and chokes the growth of cereals, Matt. xiii. 25–30.

Tăr′gĕt (*shield*). A small shield is meant, and not a target or mark in a modern sense, 1 Sam. xvii. 6. In the margin it is called "gorget," which was a defensive piece of armor, in the days of chivalry, used to protect the joint or opening between the helmet and cuirass.

Tăr′pel-ītes. Assyrian colonists in Samaria after the captivity, Ez. iv. 9.

Tăr′shish, Thär′shish (*solid, rocky*). (1) Second son of Javan, Gen. x. 4. (2) The city with which the Phœnicians traded. Associated with Tartessus in Spain, Jer. x. 9; Ezek. xxxviii. 13. (3) Another Tarshish is inferable from the statement that Solomon's ships at Ezion-geber on the Red Sea traded with Tarshish or Tharshish, 1 Kgs. ix. 26; xxii. 48; 2 Chr. ix. 21; 2 Chr. xx. 36. But many suppose that a class of ships — "ships of Tarshish," like "East India merchantmen" — is referred to rather than a port.

Tăr′sus (*wing*). Chief city of Cilicia, Asia Minor, on river Cydnus, six miles from the Mediterranean. Birthplace of Paul and rival of Athens and Alexandria in literature and fine arts, Acts ix. 11, 30; xi. 25; xxi. 39; xxii. 3. At the mouth of the Cydnus were fine docks, and Tarsus had, at one time, considerable commercial importance. Some would identify it with Tarshish. It was founded by the Assyrian, Sardanapalus, and was captured by the Romans and made a free city. It is now represented by Tersons, a mean Turkish city with a fluctuating population.

Tăr′tăk (*prince of darkness*). An idol introduced into Samaria by Avite colonists, and worshipped under the form of an ass, symbolizing darkness, 2 Kgs. xvii. 31.

Tăr′tan. Not a proper name, but an army official, like general or commander-in-chief, 2 Kgs. xviii. 17; Isa. xx. 1.

Tăt′na-ī (*gift*). A Persian governor in Palestine, Ez. v. 3, 6; vi. 6, 13.

Tăv′ĕrns (*huts*). "Three Taverns" was a place on the Appian Way, 33 miles south of Rome, where Paul met some of his Roman brethren, Acts xxviii. 15.

Tăx′es (*touches*). First Hebrew taxes were tithes, first-fruits, redemption money, for use of the priests. Taxes amplified under the kings and became burdensome, 1 Kgs. x. 28, 29; xii. 4. Jews under heavy tribute while subject to foreign rulers, Neh. v. The tithe-tax became a poll-tax, Neh. x. 32, 33; and continued, Matt. xvii. 24. The enrollment, or census, of Luke ii. 2, and Acts v. 37, was for the purpose of Roman taxation, which was onerous, being on the head, the field-hand, the ground and the products thereof, the harbors, city-gates, and city houses.

Tears. In Ps. lvi. 8, allusion is supposed, by some, to be made to a custom of preserving the tears of mourners in a bottle and placing it in the sepulchre. Others regard the words as a bold metaphor, expressive of David's wish that God would keep in memory his many penitential tears, as the traveller stores his water, milk, or wine in leather bottles for a journey.

Tē′bah (*slaughter*). A son of Nahor, Gen. xxii. 24.

Tĕb′′a-lī′ah (*purged*). Third son of Hosah the Merarite, 1 Chr. xxvi. 11.

Tĕ′beth (*goodness*). Tenth month of Hebrew sacred, and fourth of civil, year; commencing with new moon in January, Esth. ii. 16.

Tĕ-hăph′nĕ-hes, Ezek. xxx. 18. [TAHPANHES.]

Tĕ-hĭn′nah (*entreaty*). Son of Eshton and founder of Ir-nahash, city of Nahash, 1 Chr. iv. 12.

Tĕil=trēē (*lime-tree*). Terebinth, or oak of Palestine, Isa. vi. 13.

Tĕ-kō′à, Tĕ-kō′ah (*fort*). A town of Judah on the Hebron ridge, six miles from Bethlehem, and on the border of the wilderness, 2 Chr. xx. 20; Jer. vi. 1. Colonized by Ashur, 1 Chr. ii. 24; iv. 5; fortified by Rehoboam, 2 Chr. xi. 6. Home of the " wise woman " who interceded for Absalom, 2 Sam. xiv. 2-9. Birthplace and residence of the prophet Amos, Am. i. 1. Now Tekua.

Tĕ-kō′īte. Dweller in Tekoa, 2 Sam. xxiii. 26; 1 Chr. xi. 28; xxvii. 9; Neh. iii. 5, 27.

Tĕl=ā′bĭb (*grain-heap*). A city in Chaldea or Babylonia where captive Jews resided, Ezek. iii. 15.

Tĕ′lah (*strength*). An Ephraimite ancestor of Joshua, 1 Chr. vii. 25.

Tĕl′ạ-im (*lambs*). Place where Saul collected his forces before attacking the Amalekites, 1 Sam. xv. 4.

Te-lăs′sar, Thĕ-lā′sar (*Assyrian hill*). Place in western Mesopotamia, near Haran and Orfa, 2 Kgs. xix. 12; Isa. xxxvii. 12.

Tĕ′lem (*oppression*). (1) A city in extreme southern Judah, Josh. xv. 24. (2) A temple doorkeeper in time of Ezra, Ez. x. 24.

Tĕl=här′sà, Tĕl=hạ-rē′shà (*uncultivated hill*). A place in Babylonia whence captive Jews returned, Ez. ii. 59; Neh. vii. 61.

Tĕl=mē′lah (*salt hill*). A city mentioned with the above. Identified by some with the Thelme of Ptolemy, near the Persian Gulf, Ez. ii. 59; Neh. vii. 61.

Tē′mà (*desert*). Ninth son of Ishmael, and name of his tribe and country. Referred to Teyma in Syria, on the caravan route from Damascus to Mecca, Gen. xxv. 15; 1 Chr. i. 30; Job vi. 19; Isa. xxi. 14; Jer. xxv. 23.

Tē′man (*desert*). Oldest son of Eliphaz, and grandson of Esau, Gen. xxxvi. 11. Also the tribe and country of Temani or Temanites, in Edom, Jer. xlix. 7; Ezek. xxv. 13; Am. i. 12; Obadiah 9; Hab. iii. 3.

Tĕm′ạ-nī, Tē′man-īte, Gen. xxxvi. 34; Job ii. 11. [TEMAN.]

Tĕm′ẹ-nī. A son of Ashur, father of Tekoa, 1 Chr. iv. 6.

Tĕm′ple. (1) Solomon's temple erected at Jerusalem on Mount Moriah. David proposed to transform the tabernacle into a permanent temple at Jerusalem, and collected much material, but its construction was forbidden by the prophet Nathan, 1 Chr. xvii.; 2 Sam. vii. 7-29. Solomon completed the work after David's plans and with the assistance of Hiram, king of Tyre. He began to build in the fourth year of his reign, B. C. 1012, and finished and dedicated it B. C. 1005, 1 Chr. xxi., xxii., xxviii., 11-19; xxix. 4-7; 1 Kgs. vi.-viii.; 2 Chr. iii.-vii. This costly and imposing structure, for the age, was pillaged several times during the Eastern invasions, and was finally destroyed during the last siege of Jerusalem by Nebuchadnezzar, B. C. 588. (2) The temple of Zerubbabel was begun in B. C. 534, by the returned captives under the lead of Zerubbabel and the patronage of King Cyrus of Persia. Owing to discords and direct opposition it was not completed till B. C. 515. It was much inferior to the first in cost and beauty, though one third larger in dimensions. It was partially destroyed by Antiochus Epiphanes, B. C. 163, and restored by Judas Maccabeus, Ez. iii.-vi.; 2 Macc. x. 1-9. (3) Herod the Great removed the decayed temple of Zerubbabel and began the erection of a new one B. C. 17. This gorgeous and costly structure was not completed till the time of Herod Agrippa II., A. D. 64. It was of marble, after Græco-Roman designs, and was destroyed by the Romans under Titus, A. D. 70, thus verifying Mark xiii. 2.

Tĕmpt (*hold*). Ordinarily, the offering of an inducement to do wrong, Matt. iv. 1-11; Luke iv. 13; but in Gen. xxii. 1; James i. 2, 3, a trial of one's faith; trial of God's patience, Ex. xvii. 2; 1 Cor. x. 9; an effort to ensnare, Matt. xvi. 1; xix. 3; xxii. 18; Mark x. 2; Luke x. 25.

Tĕnt (*stretched*). The house of nomad and pastoral peoples. It was made of strong cloth, chiefly of goat's hair, stretched on poles, and firmly pegged to the ground, Gen. iv. 20; xviii. 1; Judg. iv. 21; Isa. xxxviii. 12.

Tē′rah (*laggard*). Father of Abraham. He was of Ur in Chaldea, started west with his family, stopped in Haran, and died there, aged 205 years. Through his sons, Abraham, Nahor, and Haran, he was the ancestor of the Israelites, Ishmaelites, Midianites, Moabites, and Ammonites, Gen. xi. 27-32.

Tĕr′ạ-phim (*images*). Little images kept in Eastern households for private consultation and worship. This species of idolatry or superstition was in favor with Hebrews, though often denounced, Gen. xxxi. 19, 34, 35; Judg. xviii. 17; 1 Sam. xv. 23; xix. 13, 16; 2 Kgs. xxiii. 24; Hos. iii. 4; Zech. x. 2.

Tĕr′ẹ-bĭnth. [TEIL-TREE.]

Tē′resh (*strict*). A eunuch of Ahasuerus, whose plot to murder his master was discovered by Mordecai, Esth. ii. 21-23.

Tĕr′tĭus (*third*). Paul's scribe in writing his Epistle to the Romans, Rom. xvi. 22.

Tĕr-tŭl′lus (*little third*). A Roman lawyer or orator hired by the high priest and Sanhedrim to prosecute Paul before the procurator Felix, Acts xxiv. 1-9.

Tĕs′tạ-ment (*witness*). One of the two volumes of the Sacred Scriptures, which treat of the old and new dispensations; distinguished as the Old Testament, treating of revelation before the Advent of Christ, and the New Testament, containing that made after the Advent, 2 Cor. iii. 6; Heb. ix. 15.

Tĕs′tĭ-mŏ-nȳ (*witness*). The entire revelation of God, Ps. cxix. 88, 99; the tables of stone, Ex. xxv. 16; the ark in which the tables were deposited, Ex. xxv. 22; the gospel of Christ, 1 Cor. i. 6; Rev. i. 2.

Tĕt′rärch (*fourth ruler*). Originally, one governing the fourth part of a country. Under Roman rule, any ruler or petty prince of the republic and empire, especially in Syria, Matt. xiv. 1; Luke iii. 1; ix. 7; Acts xiii. 1. Sometimes called king, Matt. xiv. 9; Mark vi. 14, 22.

Thăd-dæ′us (*wise*). Surname of the apostle Jude, and another form of Lebbæus, Matt. x. 3; Mark iii. 18. [JUDE.]

Thā′häsh (*badger*). Son of Nahor, Gen. xxii. 24.

Thā′mah, Ez. ii. 53. [TAMAH.]

Thā′mar, Matt. i. 3. [TAMAR, 1.]

Thăm′mŭz. [TAMMUZ.]

Thăm′nạ-thà, 1 Macc. ix. 50. [TIMNATH.]

Thănk Ŏf′fĕr-ing. The peace offering of Lev. iii., as offered with thanksgiving in Lev. vii. 11-15.

Thā′rà, Luke iii. 34. [TERAH.]

Thär′rà, Esth. xii. 1. [TERESH.]

Thär′shish (*rocky*). (1) 1 Kgs. x. 22; xxii. 48. [TARSHISH.] (2) A Benjamite, 1 Chr. vii. 10.

Thăs′sī. Surname of Simon, son of Mattathias, 1 Macc. ii. 3.

Thē′ạ-trē (*sight*). A place where dramatic performances are exhibited, as in Acts xix. 29; but the spectacle or performance itself in 1 Cor. iv. 9. The introduction of the theatre by Herod the Great greatly offended the Jews.

Thēbes (*life of the god*). Classical name of No or No-amon, Jer. xlvi. 25; Nah. iii. 8; Ezek. xxx. 14, 16. [No.]

Thē′bez (*prominent*). Now Tubas, a village near Shechem, and scene of Abimelech's tragic death, Judg. ix. 50–55 ; 2 Sam. xi. 21.

Thḗ-cō′e, 1 Macc. ix. 33. [TEKOA.]

Thĕft, Thĭef. Punishment of theft was severe under the Mosaic law, as in all pastoral countries where the property was chiefly in flocks, more or less exposed to persons of felonious intent. The thief was compelled to make restitution, five-fold for a stolen ox and four-fold for a sheep. To kill a thief, caught in the act, was not a capital offence. If restitution was impossible a thief could be sold, Ex. xxii. 1–4.

Thḗ-lā′sar, 2 Kgs. xix. 12. [TELASSAR.]

Thḗ-lĕr′sas, 1 Esdr. v. 36. [TELHARSA.]

Thē′man, Bar. iii. 22. [TEMAN.]

Thḗ-ŏd′ō-tŭs (*God-given*). Envoy of Nicanor to Judas Maccabeus, 2 Macc. xiv. 19.

Thḗ-ŏph′ĭ-lŭs (*lover of God*). The unknown person, probably an official, to whom Luke addressed his Gospel and his history of the Acts of the Apostles, Luke i. 3 ; Acts i. 1.

Thē′ras, 1 Esdr. viii. 41. [AHAVA.]

Thĕs′′sa-lō′nĭ-ans. People of Thessalonica, to whom Paul addressed two epistles, 13th and 14th N. T. books. The first was written at Corinth, A. D. 52 or 53, soon after the author had founded a church at Thessalonica, and upon the strength of favorable reports from Timothy. Its design was to confirm the new converts in the faith, strengthen them against persecution, correct their errors of doctrine and work, and inculcate purity of life. The second was also written from Corinth, soon after the first, and designed to correct false impressions concerning Christ's advent, and especially to place the author right before the world as an authorized apostle and teacher.

Thĕs′′sa-lō-nī′cà. Ancient Thermæ, " hot springs ; " now Salonika. Enlarged by Cassander and called Thessalonica after his wife, daughter of Alexander the Great. An important city of Macedonia, at the head of the Gulf of Thessalonica, or Thermæ. Paul visited it during his second tour and founded a strong church there, to whose members he wrote two epistles, Acts xvii. 1–9.

Theū′das (*God's gift*). An insurgent Jew mentioned in Gamaliel's speech before the council, Acts v. 34–39.

Thĭgh. Placing the hand under the thigh was a form of adjuration mentioned in Gen. xxiv. 2 ; xlvii. 29, and supposedly prevalent in patriarchal times, but only taken by inferiors, as by servants or sons, and as significant of subjection and the purpose of obedience.

Thĭm′na-thah, Josh. xix. 43. [TIMNAH.]

Thĭs′bḗ. A city in Bœotia, Tob. i. 2.

Thĭs′tle, Thôrn. No less than eighteen Hebrew words embrace the thistle, thorn, brier, and bramble species, which is prolific in Palestine, Gen. iii. 18. Figurative for desolation, Prov. xxiv. 31 ; Isa. v. 6 ; Hos. ii. 6 ; providential visitation, Num. xxxiii. 55 ; Judg. ii. 3 ; 2 Cor. xii. 7 ; hindrance, Prov. xv. 19 ; troubles, Prov. xxii. 5. " Crown of thorns," both punishment and derision, Matt. xxvii. 29.

Thŏm′as (*twin*). The cautious, susceptible, even doubtful, apostle, whose name, in Greek, was Didymus, " twin," Matt. x. 3 ; Mark iii. 18 ; Luke vi. 15 ; John xi. 16 ; xiv. 5, 6 ; xx. 24–29 ; Acts i. 13.

Thôrn. [THISTLE.]

Thrā′çĭà. Classic name for the country now embraced in the northern part of Turkey in Europe, 2 Macc. xii. 35.

Thrȧ-sē′us. Father of Apollonius, 2 Macc. iii. 5.

Thrēe Tăv′ẽrns. [TAVERNS.]

Thrĕsh′ing (*thrashing*). Done anciently by treading with oxen or horses, or by drawn sleds, sometimes spiked, on earthen floors, usually on high spots of ground, Deut. xxv. 4 ; 1 Chr. xxi. 15–28 ; Isa.

xxviii. 27, 28 ; xli. 15, 16. The flail or stick is mentioned in Ruth ii. 17.

Thrōne (*seat*). The seat of one in authority, as high priest, 1 Sam. i. 9 ; military chief, Jer. i. 15 ; but especially of a king, 2 Sam. iii. 10 ; 1 Kgs. ii. 12 ; vii. 7 ; x. 18–20 ; xxii. 10 ; Acts xii. 21.

Thŭm′mĭm, Ex. xxviii. 30. [URIM.]

Thŭn′der (*sound*). Rare in Palestine, hence regarded as God's displeasure, 1 Sam. xii. 17 ; Jehovah's voice, Job xxxvii. 2 ; Ps. xviii. 13 ; Isa. xxx. 30, 31 ; John xii. 29 ; symbol of divine power, Ex. xix. 16 ; 1 Sam. ii. 10 ; 2 Sam. xxii. 14 ; Isa. xxix. 6 ; Rev. viii. 5.

Thȳ′′a-tī′rà (*burning incense*). A city of northern Lydia in Asia Minor, founded by Seleucus Nicator, much inhabited by Jews, seat of one of the seven churches of Asia, Acts xvi. 14 ; Rev. ii. 18–29.

Thȳ′ine=wood. Wood of the thyia, sandarac, or pine variety, yielding a choice gum and hard, dark colored, fragrant wood. Indigenous to northern Africa, Rev. xviii. 12.

Tĭ-bē′rĭ-as. (1) Sea of, John vi. 1 ; xxi. 1. [GENNESARET.] (2) A town of Galilee on the west shore of Lake Gennesaret or Sea of Galilee, founded by Herod Antipas, A. D. 16–22, and named in honor of the emperor Tiberius. It seems to have imparted its name to the lake or sea. Once noted for its learning and architectural beauty, but now the miserable village of Tabariyeh, John vi. 1, 23 ; xxi. 1.

Tĭ-bē′rĭ-us. Tiberius Claudius Nero, second emperor of Rome, A. D. 14–37. Stepson of Augustus, a vigorous warrior, eloquent orator, and able statesman, but an indolent, despotic ruler. He is the Cæsar of Luke iii. 1 ; xx. 22–25 ; xxiii. 2 ; John xix. 12.

Tĭb′hath (*killing*). Capital of Hadadezer, king of Zobah, 1 Chr. xviii. 8. Betah, 2 Sam. viii. 8.

Tĭb′ni (*knowing*). Competitor of Omri for the throne of Israel, 1 Kgs. xvi. 21, 22.

Tĭ′dal (*great chief*). A chief of nomadic tribes, who joined Chedorlaomer in his attack on the cities of the plain, Gen. xiv. 1–16.

Tĭg′lath=pĭ-lē′ṣer (*Adar's son my help*). Second of the Assyrian kings in contact with Israel. He invaded Samaria, 2 Kgs. xv. 29, and a few years afterwards returned, taking many captives, 1 Chr. v. 26. King Ahaz, of Judah, became his vassal, 2 Kgs. xvi. 7–10. He reigned B. C. 747–739.

Tĭ′gris (*arrow*). Great eastern tributary of the Euphrates, rising in the Armenian mountains and flowing southeastwardly 1146 miles. Between it and the Euphrates lay Mesopotamia. In the Septuagint version it stands for Hiddekel, one of the rivers of Eden, Gen. ii. 14 ; Tob. vi. 1 ; Judith i. 6 ; Ecclus. xxiv. 25.

Tĭk′vah, Tĭk′vath (*hope*). (1) Father-in-law of Huldah the prophetess, 2 Kgs. xxii. 14 ; 2 Chr. xxxiv. 22. (2) Father of Jahaziah, Ez. x. 15.

Tĭle (*cover*). A broad, thin slab of burnt clay, used as a shingle on Oriental houses, Ezek. iv. 1.

Tĭl′gàth=pĭl-nē′ṣer, 1 Chr. v. 6 ; 2 Chr. xxviii. 20. [TIGLATH-PILESER.]

Tĭ′lon (*gift*). A Judahite, 1 Chr. iv. 20.

Tĭ-mæ′us (*honored*). Father of the blind Bartimæus, Mark x. 46.

Tĭm′brel (*bell, drum*). A Hebrew musical instrument somewhat resembling the tambourine, Ex. xv. 20 ; Judg. xi. 34 ; Ps. lxviii. 25. [TABRET.]

Tĭm′nȧ, Tĭm′nah (*portion*). (1) Mother of Amalek, Gen. xxxvi. 12. (2) A duke of Edom, Gen. xxxvi. 40, who gave his name to a boundary of Judah, Josh. xv. 10. (3) A mountain town of Judah, Josh. xv. 57. Thimnathah, Josh. xix. 43.

Tĭm′nȧth. (1) Gen. xxxviii. 14. [TIMNA, 2.] (2) Home of Samson's wife, Judg. xiv. 1–5.

Tĭm′nȧth=hē′reṣ, Judg. ii. 9. [TIMNATH-SERAH].

Tĭm′năth=sē′rah (*fruitful portion*). A city in Ephraim given to Joshua, and his home and burial place, Josh. xix. 50; xxiv. 30. Written Timnath-heres in Judg. ii. 9.

Tĭm′nĭte. Designation of Samson's father-in-law, the Timnathite, Judg. xv. 6.

Tī′mon (*honorable*). One of the first seven deacons, Acts vi. 1–6.

Tĭ-mō′the-ŭs (*honoring God*). (1) An Ammonite leader defeated by Judas Maccabeus, 1 Macc. v. 6–44. (2) Acts xvi. 1; xvii. 14, etc. [TIMOTHY.]

Tĭm′o-thў (*honoring God*). Son of Eunice, a Jewess, by a Gentile father. Born in Derbe or Lystra, Lycaonia, Acts xvi. 1; 2 Tim. i. 5. Converted by Paul and became a close friend and valuable assistant, Rom. xvi. 21; Heb. xiii. 23. Recipient of two of Paul's epistles, 15th and 16th N. T. books. The first was written to him while at Ephesus, probably from Macedonia, and about A. D. 65. The second seems to have been written from Rome some three years later. They are called pastoral epistles, because devoted to description of church work and earnest exhortation to faithfulness.

Tĭn. A metal well known to ancients, Num. xxxi. 22; evidently dross in Isa. i. 25. Imported from Tarshish, Ezek. xxvii. 12.

Tĭph′sah (*ford*). The Greek and Roman Thapsacus, a crossing point of the Euphrates, and eastern limit of Solomon's empire, 1 Kgs. iv. 24. Smitten by Menahem, 2 Kgs. xv. 16.

Tī′ras (*longing*). Youngest son of Japheth, and supposable progenitor of the Thracians, Gen. x. 2.

Tī′rath-ītes. Designation of a family of scribes at Jabez, 1 Chr. ii. 55.

Tīre (*attire*). A head-dress, Isa. iii. 18; Ezek. xxiv. 17, 23; but the original implies any round ornament, as a necklace, worn by persons or animals, Judg. viii. 21, 26.

Tĭr′ha-kah (*exalted*). A king of Ethiopia and Upper Egypt who became King Hezekiah's ally against Sennacherib, about B. C. 695, 2 Kgs. xix.; Isa. xxxvii. 9.

Tĭr′ha-nah (*favor*). A son of Caleb, son of Hezron, 1 Chr. ii. 48.

Tĭr′ĭ-à (*dread*). A Judahite, 1 Chr. iv. 16.

Tĭr′sha-thà (*governor*). Title of the governors of Judea under Persian rule, Ez. ii. 63; Neh. vii. 65, 70; viii. 9; Neh. x. 1.

Tĭr′zah (*pleasing*). (1) Youngest of the five daughters of Zelophehad, Num. xxvi. 33. (2) An ancient Canaanite city captured by Joshua, and which afterwards became the capital of the kingdom of Samaria, till Samaria, the new capital, was founded by King Omri. It was some 30 miles north of Jerusalem, and 5 miles east of Samaria, Josh. xii. 24; 1 Kgs. xiv. 17; xv. 21, 33; xvi. 6; 2 Kgs. xv. 14, 16; S. of Sol. vi. 4.

Tĭsh′bĭte. Elijah is so designated, 1 Kgs. xvii. 1; xxi. 17, 28; 2 Kgs. i. 3, 8; ix. 36. The place is generally referred to Thisbe in Naphtali, where Tobit lived, Tob. i. 2.

Tĭs′rĭ. Seventh month of the Jewish sacred, and first of the civil, year, corresponding to parts of September and October. Called also Ethanim, 1 Kgs. viii. 2; 2 Chr. v. 3.

Tīthe (*tenth*). One tenth of all produce of lands and herds was set apart, under the Levitical law, for the support of the Levites, and a tenth of their tenth went to the priests. There were tithe regulations among other nations, Gen. xiv. 20; xxviii. 22; Lev. xxvii. 30–33; Num. xviii. 21–32; Deut. xii. 17, 18; xiv. 22–27. The Pharisees tithed their mint, anise, cummin, and rue, Matt. xxiii. 23.

Tĭt′tle (*title*). Jot; iota; any minute quantity, Matt. v. 18; Luke xvi. 17.

Tī′tus (*pleasant*). A distinguished Grecian who became a Christian convert and a companion of Paul in his trials and on his missionary tours, Tit. i. 4; Gal. ii. 3–5; 2 Cor. viii. 6, 16, 23. Entrusted with many important commissions, 2 Cor. xii. 18; 2 Tim. iv. 10; Tit. i. 5. Paul wrote an epistle to Titus, the 17th N. T. book, about A. D. 65, designed to instruct him in his ministerial duties in Crete, which were arduous, on account of the immorality of the people.

Tī′zīte. Designation of Joha, one of David's guardsmen. Place unknown, 1 Chr. xi. 45.

Tō′ah (*bent*). A Levite ancestor of Samuel, 1 Chr. vi. 34. Tohu, 1 Sam. i. 1.

Tŏb (*good*). A place or district beyond Jordan and between Gilead and the desert, to which Jephthah fled when banished from Gilead, Judg. xi. 3–5. Ish-tob, 2 Sam. x. 6, 8.

Tŏb=ăd″o-nī′jah (*my good God*). A Levite sent out by King Jehoshaphat to teach the law, 2 Chr. xvii. 8.

Tŏ-bī′ah (*God's goodness*). (1) His children returned with Zerubbabel, Ez. ii. 60; Neh. vii. 62. (2) An Ammonite servant of Sanballat who joined his master in opposing Nehemiah, Neh. ii. 10–20.

Tŏ-bī′as. Greek form of Tobiah and Tobijah. (1) Son of Tobit, and hero in his book, Tob. (2) Father of Hyrcanus, and a man of great prominence at Jerusalem, B. C. 187.

Tŏ′bĭē, 1 Macc. v. 13. [TOB.]

Tŏ-bī′jah (*God's goodness*). (1) A Levite sent out by King Jehoshaphat to teach the law, 2 Chr. xvii. 8. (2) One of the captivity in whose presence Joshua was crowned high priest, Zech. vi. 10–14.

Tō′bĭt (*goodness*). Father of Tobias, and author of Tobit, the fifth Apocryphal book. It was written in Greek, with the scene in Assyria, and is a didactic narrative of Jewish social life after the captivity.

Tō′chen (*task*). An unidentified place in Simeon, 1 Chr. iv. 32.

Tŏ-gär′mah (*bony*). Son of Gomer, of the family of Japheth, Gen. x. 3. His descendants became horse and mule merchants, and have been associated with the ancient Armenians, Ezek. xxvii. 14.

Tō′hu, 1 Sam. i. 1. [TOAH.]

Tō′ĭ (*wandering*). A king of Hamath, who sent his son to congratulate David on his victory over Hadadezer, 2 Sam. viii. 9, 10. Tou, 1 Chr. xviii. 9, 10.

Tō′là (*worm*). (1) First-born of Issachar, and progenitor of the Tolaites, Gen. xlvi. 13; Num. xxvi. 23; 1 Chr. vii. 1, 2. (2) Successor of Abimelech as judge of Israel for twenty-three years, Judg. x. 1, 2.

Tō′lăd (*generation*). A city in South Judah, called also El-tolad, 1 Chr. iv. 29.

Tō′là-ītes. Descendants of Tola, Num. xxvi. 23.

Tŏl′ba-nēs, 1 Esdr. ix. 25. [TELEM.]

Tōll (*tell*). The Persian taxation of conquered Judea consisted of " tribute " levied on each province and collected by the authorities thereof; " custom," which could be paid in kind; " toll," which was a cash exaction for the use of bridges, fords, and highways, Ez. iv. 13; vii. 24.

Tomb. Burial places among Hebrews were caves, recesses in rocks, natural or artificial, and walled sepulchres. [SEPULCHRE.]

Tongues. " And the whole earth was of one language, and of one speech," Gen. xi. 1. Confusion of tongues and dispersion of peoples coincident, Gen. xi. 7–9. " New tongues," Mark xvi. 17, is the first notice of a gift specially characteristic of the first outpouring of the Spirit. Ten days afterward the promise was fulfilled in the Pentecostal phenomenon, Acts ii. 1–13.

Tooth. The Jewish law of retaliation permitted the deprivation of " eye for eye, tooth for tooth,"– Ex. xxi. 24. The principle of this law was condemned by Christ, Matt. v. 38–42. Teeth used figuratively for the inheritable quality of sin, Ezek. xviii. 2;

"cleanness of teeth" a figure for famine, Am. iv. 6; "gnashing of teeth" indicative of rage and despair, Matt. viii. 12.

Tō′păz. A variously hued gem, corresponding to the modern chrysolite, which the Hebrews obtained from Ethiopia, Job xxviii. 19, and which constituted the second stone in first row of the high priest's breastplate, Ex. xxviii. 17, and a foundation stone of the New Jerusalem, Rev. xxi. 20.

Tō′phel (*mortar*). A place east of the Dead Sea near Bozrah, Deut. i. 1.

Tō′phet, Tō′pheth (*drum, noise, place of burning*). Part of the valley of Hinnom east or south of Jerusalem. Perhaps once a pleasure garden, but afterward polluted by the abominations incident to the worship of Baal and Molech, 2 Kgs. xxiii. 10; Jer. vii. 31; xix. 13, and then turned into a dumping and burning place of the city's refuse. Hence a place of judgment, Jer. xix. 6–14. [HINNOM.]

Tôr′mah, Judg. ix. 31 marg. [ARUMAH.]

Tôr′toïse (*twisted - foot*). A faulty rendering. The Septuagint has "land-crocodile," and doubtless one of the large lizard species is meant, Lev. xi. 29.

Tō′u, 1 Chr. xviii. i. 10. [TOI.]

Tōw. The coarser part of flax, Judg. xvi. 9.

Tow′er (*shot up*). Watch-towers, or fortified posts, were frequent on frontiers and exposed places, Gen. xxxv. 21; 2 Chr. xxvi. 10; around vineyards, Isa. xxi. 5, 8, 11; Matt. xxi. 33, and for the use of shepherds, Mic. iv. 8. "Tower of Shechem," Judg. ix. 47, evidently a citadel or stronghold. Tower of Babel [BABEL]. "Tower of Siloam," possibly an observatory, Luke xiii. 4.

Town Clĕrk. An official in Ephesus, who recorded the laws and decisions and read them in public, Acts xix. 35–41.

Trăch″o-nī′tis (*stony*). One of the Roman provinces into which the country north of the Jordan was divided, and generally associated with Argob, south of Damascus, Luke iii. 1.

Trănce (*going over*). The word in Num. xxiv. 4, 16, is an interjection, without a Hebrew equivalent. In Acts x. 10, xi. 5, xxii. 17, an ecstasy is implied, which carried the subject beyond the usual limits of consciousness and volition.

Trăns-fĭg″u-rā′tion (*formed over*). The supernatural change in the appearance of Christ upon the mount — Hermon or Tabor. It served as an attestation of his Messiahship and an emblem of glorified humanity, Matt. xvii. 1–13; Mark ix. 2–13; Luke ix. 28–36.

Trĕaş′ûre Cĭ′tĭeş. The kings of Judah, and of other nations, kept their treasures in designated cities, called treasure-cities, and in special buildings called treasure-houses, Ex. i. 11; 1 Chr. xxvii. 25; Ez. v. 17.

Trĕas′ûr-ȳ (*place*). The place in the temple where gifts were received, 1 Chr. ix. 26; Mark xii. 41; Luke xxi. 1; John viii. 20.

Trĕnch (*cut*). In military usage, a ditch for protection, but in 1 Sam. xxvi. 5, the place where the wagons were grouped or packed.

Trĕs′păss (*passing over*). To violate the personal or property rights of another, Lev. v. 6. To violate a positive law of God, Matt. vi. 15.

Trĕs′păss Ŏf′fer-ing. This offering was closely allied to the sin offering, and in some cases offered with it as a distinct part of the same sacrifice, Lev. v. 15; xiv. 13–32.

Trībe (*division*). In a Roman sense, the third part of the empire, but with Hebrews any division of the people, especially that division which sprung from the twelve sons of Jacob, and was perpetuated in their descendants, Gen. xlviii. 5; Num. xxvi. 5–51; Josh. xiii. 7–33; xv.–xix. Of these tribes two, Ephraim and Manasseh, sprang from Joseph. Still there were only twelve partitions of conquered Canaan, for the tribe of Levi received no allotment of lands, but was diffused in cities among the other tribes and supported by them. Each tribe was headed by a prince, and each possessed considerable independence even under the monarchy. They waged war separately and among themselves, Judg. i. 2–4; 1 Chr. v. 18–22; 2 Sam. ii. 4–9; and finally ten of the tribes revolted and set up the separate kingdom of Israel, xix. 41–43; 1 Kgs. xii. For history of each tribe *see* its title.

Trĭb′ūte (*gift*). A payment made as a token of submission, or for sake of peace, or in pursuance of treaty, Gen. xlix. 15. The head-tax of half a shekel paid annually by Jews for the support of the temple service, Ex. xxx. 13.

Trĭp′o-lis (*three cities*). The commercially linked cities of Aradus, Sidon, and Tyre, in Phœnicia, 2 Macc. xiv. 1.

Trō′ăs (*Troad*). Alexandria Troas, or in the Troad, was an important city in Mysia, Asia Minor, 6 miles south of the entrance to the Hellespont and 4 from the site of Ancient Troy. It was founded by Alexander the Great and was for many centuries the key of commerce between Europe and Asia. Paul visited it more than once, Acts xvi. 8–11; xx. 5–10; 2 Tim. iv. 13.

Trŏ-ġȳl′lĭ-um (*fruit-port*). Town and promontory on the western coast of Asia Minor, opposite Samos. Paul visited it on his third missionary tour, Acts xx. 15.

Troop, Band. These words imply small bodies of marauders in Gen. xlix. 19; 2 Sam. xxii. 30; Jer. xviii. 22; Mic. v. 1.

Trŏph′ĭ-mŭs (*fostered*). A Christian convert residing at Ephesus, and co-worker with Paul, Acts xx. 4; xxi. 29; 2 Tim. iv. 20.

Trōw (*trust*). Signifies to think or believe in, Luke xvii. 9.

Trŭm′pet (*pipe*). A wind instrument with a flaring mouth, made of horn or metal and differing but little in form and use from the cornet, Ex. xix. 16. [CORNET.]

Trŭm′pets, Feast of. The feast of the new moon which fell on the first of Tisri, Num. xxix. 1–6; Lev. xxiii. 24, 25. It was the New Year's day of the Jewish civil year, and was ushered in by the blowing of trumpets and observed by offerings.

Trȳ-phē′nà (*shining*). A Christian woman of Rome, saluted by Paul, Rom. xvi. 12.

Trȳ′phŏn (*effeminate*). Surname of Diodotus, who usurped the Syrian throne, 1 Macc. xii. 39.

Trȳ-phō′sà (*shining*). A Christian woman of Rome, saluted by Paul, Rom. xvi. 12.

Tu′bal (*tumult*). Fifth son of Japheth, Gen. x. 2; 1 Chr. i. 5. His descendants supposably inhabited the country between the Caspian and Euxine seas, Isa. lxvi. 19; Ezek. xxvii. 13, xxxii. 26.

Tu′bal=cāin. Son of Lamech the Cainite, by Zillah. He was instructor of artificers in brass and iron, Gen. iv. 22.

Tu″bĭ-ē′nī. Inhabitants of Tubion, the O. T. Tob, 2 Macc. xii. 17.

Tûr′pĕn-tīne=trēe. The terebinth, or teil-tree, Ecclus. xxiv. 16.

Tûr′tle, Tûr′tle-dọve (*cooer*). The turtle embraces several species of plaintive-noted doves. Gen. xv. 9; Ps. lxxiv. 19; Isa. lix. 11. Those who could not afford the costlier sacrifices could offer two doves or pigeons, Lev. xii. 6–8; Luke ii. 24. They were migratory, S. of Sol. ii. 12; Jer. viii. 7.

Tȳch′ĭ-cŭs (*fate*). A disciple of Paul, Acts xx. 4, and his messenger and spokesman, Eph. vi. 21, 22; Col. iv. 7, 8.

Tȳ-răn′nus (*tyrant*). A Greek rhetorician at Ephesus in whose school Paul taught for two years, Acts xix. 9.

Tȳre (*rock*). The celebrated commercial city of Phœnicia on the Mediterranean coast. It fell to the lot of Asher, but was never conquered, Josh. xix. 29. In intimate commercial relation with Hebrews, and King Hiram furnished the artificers and material for the temple and royal houses at Jerusalem, 2 Sam. v. 11; 1 Kgs. v. 1; vii. 13; ix. 11–14; 1 Chr. xiv. 1; 2 Chr. ii. 2–18. The city was denounced by the prophets, Isa. xxiii. 1–17; Jer. xxvii. 3; Ezek. xxvi. 3–21. It resisted the five-year siege of Shalmaneser and the thirteen-year siege of Nebuchadnezzar, but fell before that of Alexander. Referred to in N.T., Matt. xi. 21, 22; xv. 21; Mark vii. 24. Paul visited it, Acts xxi. 3, 4.

Tȳ′rus. Name for Tyre in O. T. prophecies and in Apocrypha.

U

Ū′cal (*power*). The prophecy of Agur is addressed to Ithiel and Ucal, Prov. xxx. 1. Some regard the names as symbolical, while others treat them as real.

Ū′el (*God's will*). One of the sons of Bani, Ez. x. 34. Juel in 1 Esdr. ix. 34.

Ŭk′năz. The name is made to stand for Kenaz in margin of 1 Chr. iv. 15.

Ū′la͡-ī (*pure water*). A river in the province of Elam, where the palace of Shushan stood, on whose banks Daniel saw the vision of the ram and the he-goat, Dan. viii. 2–16.

Ū′lam (*porch*). (1) A descendant of Manasseh, 1 Chr. vii. 16, 17. (2) Son of Eshek, a Benjamite, of the line of Saul, 1 Chr. viii. 39, 40.

Ŭl′là (*yoke*). Head of an Asherite family, 1 Chr. vii. 39.

Ŭm′mah (*community*). A city in Asher, associated with modern Alma, five miles from the Mediterranean coast, Josh. xix. 30.

Ŭn″çĭr-cŭm-çi′ṣion (*not cut around*). In a Scriptural sense, Gentiles, Rom. ii. 25–29.

Ŭn-clēan′. A word which, with clean, was applied to personal and ceremonial conditions, as well as to the edibility of animals. The division of animals into clean and unclean existed before the Flood, Gen. vii. 2. Uncleanness and the processes of purification are particularly described in Lev. xi.–xv.; Num. xix. Unclean animals are specially mentioned in Lev. xi. 9–31; Deut. xiv. 3–20.

Ŭn″dĕr-gĭrd′ing. A primitive way of keeping the hull of a ship from opening by passing a cable tightly around it. The ship in which Paul sailed from Crete to Italy was undergirded, Acts xxvii. 17.

Ŭn″dĕr-sĕt′tĕrṣ. The molten projections which ornamented and supported the brazen laver in Solomon's temple, 1 Kgs. vii. 30.

Ū′nĭ-côrn (*one-horned*). A fabulous animal pictured as having one horn on its forehead and the body of a horse. The Hebrew word *re'em*, which is translated "unicorn," Num. xxiii. 22; xxiv. 8; Deut. xxxiii. 17; Job xxxix. 9; Ps. xxii. 21; xxix. 6; Isa. xxxiv. 7, does not refer to the one-horned creature of fable, but evidently to a two-horned animal, Deut. xxxiii. 17, possibly the now nearly extinct wild ox, auroch or urus of naturalists.

Ŭn′nī (*afflicted*). (1) A Levite appointed to play upon the psaltery, in the time of David, 1 Chr. xv. 18, 20. (2) Another Levite, who acted as watchman after the return from captivity, Neh. xii. 9.

U-phär′sin, Dan. v. 25–28. [MENE.]

Ū′phăz. Only in Jer. x. 9; Dan. x. 5, where it has been generally treated as an error for Ophir.

Ûr (*light, region*). (1) Place where Abraham lived with his father Terah and his wife Sarah, before they started for the land of Canaan, Gen. xi. 28, 31. Mentioned in Gen. xv. 7, as of the Chaldees, and Acts vii. 2, as in Mesopotamia. (2) Father of Eliphal, one

of David's guard, 1 Chr. xi. 35. Called Ahasbai in 2 Sam. xxiii. 34.

Ûr′bane (*of a city, polite*). Greek form of the Latin Urbanus, a Christian disciple of Paul at Rome whom he salutes in Rom. xvi. 9. Urbanus in R. V.

Ū′rī (*fire*). (1) Father of Bezaleel, one of the architects of the tabernacle, Ex. xxxi. 2; xxxv. 30; xxxviii. 22; 1 Chr. ii. 20; 2 Chr. i. 5. (2) Father of Geber, Solomon's commissary officer in the land of Gilead, 1 Kgs. iv. 19. (3) A gate-keeper of the temple in the time of Ezra, Ez. x. 24.

U-rī′ah (*light*). (1) A Hittite, 2 Sam. xi. 3, and commander of one of the thirty divisions of David's army, 2 Sam. xxiii. 39; 1 Chr. xi. 41. He was husband of the beautiful Bathsheba whom David coveted, and with whom he had committed the crime of adultery, 2 Sam. xi. 4, 5. In order to conceal his crime and procure her for a wife, he ordered Joab, commander-in-chief, to place Uriah and his forces in the hottest part of the battle with Ammon, and then to desert him, leaving him to be overwhelmed and slain by superior numbers, 2 Sam. xi. 15–17. (2) A high priest in the reign of Ahaz, Isa. viii. 2, and probably the same as Urijah in 2 Kgs. xvi. 10–16. (3) A priest of the family of Hakkoz, in time of Ezra, and head of the seventh priestly course, Ez. viii. 33; written Urijah in Neh. iii. 4, 21.

U-rī′as. (1) Matt. i. 6. [URIAH, 1.] (2) 1 Esdr. ix. 43. [URIJAH, 3.]

Ū′rĭ-el (*fire of God*). (1) One of the angels, 2 Esdr. iv. 1, 36. (2) A chief of the Kohathite Levites in the time of David, 1 Chr. xv. 5, 11. (3) A Kohathite Levite, son of Tahath, 1 Chr. vi. 24. (4) Father of Michaiah, or Maacha, wife of Rehoboam and mother of Abijah, 2 Chr. xiii. 2.

U-rī′jah (*light of God*). (1) A priest in the reign of Ahaz, and probably the same as Uriah (2), 2 Kgs. xvi. 10–16. (2) A priest of the family of Hakkoz or Koz, and probably same as Uriah (3), Neh. iii. 4, 21; viii. 4. (4) A prophet of Kirjath-jearim, and son of Shemaiah, who prophesied in the days of King Jehoiakim against Jerusalem and Judah according to the words of Jeremiah, and whom Jehoiakim sought to put to death. He fled to Egypt, but was pursued, caught, brought back and slain, Jer. xxvi. 20–23.

Ū′rim and Thŭm′mim (*light and perfection*). From the way these mysterious words are spoken of in Ex. xxviii. 30, and in Lev. viii. 8, compared with Ex. xxviii. 15–21, they appear to denote some material things, separate from the high priest's breastplate and its gems, and previously well known. Their purpose seems to be indicated in Num. xxvii. 21; 1 Sam. xxviii. 6, and, since they were connected with the ephod, in 1 Sam. xxii. 14, 15; xxiii. 9–12; xxx. 7, 8, it may be inferred they were consulted to ascertain the will of Jehovah, and that they were preserved in the bag of the high priest's breastplate to be borne "upon his heart before the Lord continually," Ex. xxviii. 30. Not in use after the captivity, Ez. ii. 63; Neh. vii. 65; Hos. iii. 4.

Ū′ṣu-rȳ (*use*). Exorbitant or unlawful interest for money loaned; but in a Bible sense the taking of any interest at all. The law of Moses prohibited Hebrews from exacting interest of one another on loans, though not of foreigners, Lev. xxv. 36, 37; Deut. xxiii. 19, 20. Usury is severely denounced, Neh. v. 7, 10; Ps. xv. 5; Prov. xxviii. 8; Ezek. xxii. 12.

Ū′tà, 1 Esdr. v. 30. [AKKUB.]

Ū′thạ-ī (*helpful*). (1) The son of Ammihud, of Judah, 1 Chr. ix. 4. Athaiah in Neh. xi. 4. (2) Son of Bigvai, who returned from captivity, Ez. viii. 14.

Ū′thī, 1 Esdr. viii. 40. [UTHAI, 2.]

Ŭz (*fertile*). (1) The land of Uz was Job's country, Job i. 1. It was located east or southeast of Palestine, Job i. 3; adjacent to the Sabeans or Chaldeans, Job i. 15, and to the Edomites, who once occupied it as conquerors, Lam. iv. 21. It is grouped with Egypt, Philistia, and Moab, Jer. xxv. 19–21. (2) The first son of Aram, son of Shem, Gen. x. 23 ; 1 Chr. i. 17. (3) Son of Nahor by Milcah, Gen. xxii. 21. Huz in A. V. and probably correct name for Uz. (4) Son of Dishan and grandson of Seir, Gen. xxxvi. 28.

Ŭ′za-ī (*strong*). Father of Palal, who assisted in rebuilding the walls of Jerusalem, Neh. iii. 25.

Ŭ′zal (*wanderer*). Sixth son of Joktan, Gen. x. 27 ; 1 Chr. i. 21. His descendants occupied the district of Yemen in Arabia and built the city of Uzal, since changed to Sana, and still the capital.

Ŭz′zȧ (*strength*). (1) The garden attached to the house of Manasseh, king of Judah. It evidently contained the family sepulchre, 2 Kgs. xxi. 18, 26. (2) A Benjamite descendant of Ehud, 1 Chr. viii. 7. (3) One of the drivers of the cart which bore the ark from Kirjath-jearim to Jerusalem, and who was slain by the Lord for putting his hand to the cart when the oxen stumbled, 1 Chr. xiii. 7–11. Uzzah elsewhere. (4) A Merarite Levite, 1 Chr. vi. 29.

Ŭz′zah (*strength*). 2 Sam. vi. 3–8. [UZZA, 3.]

Ŭz′zen=shē′rah (*ear of Sherah*). A town built by Sherah, a daughter of Ephraim, 1 Chr. vii. 24.

Ŭz′zī (*mighty*). (1) A son of Bukki and father of Zerahiah, in the line of high priests, but never a high priest, 1 Chr. vi. 5, 6 ; Ez. vii. 4. (2) A son of Tola and grandson of Issachar, 1 Chr. vii. 2, 3. (3) A son of Bela, of the tribe of Benjamin, 1 Chr. vii. 7. (4) A Benjamite progenitor of several families settled in Jerusalem after the captivity, 1 Chr. ix. 8, 9. (5) A Levite, son of Bani, and overseer of the Levites at Jerusalem after the captivity, Neh. xi. 22. (6) A priest, and chief of the house of Jedaiah, in the time of the high priest Joiakim, Neh. xii. 19. (7) A priest who assisted Ezra at the dedication of the walls of Jerusalem, Neh. xii. 42.

Ŭz-zī′ȧ (*God's strength*). Designated as the Ashterathite, one of David's guard, 1 Chr. xi. 44.

Ŭz-zī′ah (*God's strength*). (1) Son and successor of Amaziah on the throne of Judah, B. c. 810–758, 2 Chr. xxvi. 1–3. He is called Azariah in 2 Kgs. xiv. 21 and elsewhere. He was a godly king, an excellent general, and renowned city builder. But for daring to enter the temple and burn incense in violation of the law, Num. xvi. 40, xviii. 7, he was stricken with leprosy and forced to live in a separate house till he died, 2 Kgs. xv. 1–7 ; 2 Chr. xxvi. (2) A Kohathite Levite, son of Uriel and ancestor of Samuel, 1 Chr. vi. 24. (3) Father of Jehonathan, superintendent of David's storehouses in fields, cities, villages and castles, 1 Chr. xxvii. 25. (4) A priest of the sons of Harim, Ez. x. 21. (5) A Judahite, Neh. xi. 4.

Ŭz′zĭ-el (*God's might*). (1) Fourth son of Kohath, son of Levi, Ex. vi. 18, 22 ; ancestor of the Uzzielites, Lev. x. 4 ; and also, through Elizaphan, of the Kohathites, Num. iii. 19, 27, 30 ; 1 Chr. xv. 10. (2) A captain of the sons of Simeon, 1 Chr. iv. 42, 43. (3) A son of Bela and grandson of Benjamin, 1 Chr. vii. 7 ; (4) A son of Heman and one of the temple musicians in time of David, 1 Chr. xxv. 4. Azareel in 1 Chr. xxv. 18. (5) A descendant of Heman, 2 Chr. xxix. 14–19. (6) An assistant wall-builder, Neh. iii. 8.

Ŭz′zĭ-ĕl-ītes″. Descendants of Uzziel (1), Num. iii. 27 ; 1 Chr. xxvi. 23.

V

Văg′ȧ-bŏnd (*wanderer*). In the Bible vagabond has the original meaning of fugitive or wanderer, Gen. iv. 12 ; Ps. cix. 10 ; Acts xix. 13.

Vȧ-jĕz′ȧ-thȧ (*strong as the wind*). One of the ten sons of Haman, Esth. ix. 9.

Vāle, Văl′ley. Five Hebrew words are rendered vale or valley in the Bible, only one of which seems to imply that broad sweep of land between mountains or hills generally understood by valley. The others imply (1) a narrow ravine, gorge, or glen, Deut.

xxxiv. 3, 6 ; (2) a wady, dry in summer but a torrent in rainy weather ; (3) a plain, Josh. xi. 8, 17 ; xiii. 17 ; 2 Chr. xxxv. 22 ; Zech. xii 11 ; (4) a stretch of sloping ground, Deut. i. 7 ; Josh. x. 40 ; 1 Kgs. x. 27 ; 2 Chr. i. 15 ; Jer. xxxiii. 13.

Vȧ-nī′ah (*praise of God*). A son of Bani, who had married a foreign wife, Ez. x. 36.

Văsh′nī (*second*). Name of Samuel's oldest son, 1 Chr. vi. 28. In 1 Sam. viii. 2, Joel appears as his firstborn son.

Văsh′tī (*beautiful*). Wife of King Ahasuerus and queen of Persia, Esth. i. 9–22.

Văt. A large vessel for holding liquids. "Fat" in Joel ii. 24 ; iii. 13. [WINE-FAT.]

Veil (*carry*). The veil of Gen. xxiv. 65 ; xxxviii. 14 ; Ruth iii. 15 ; S. of Sol. v. 7 ; Isa. iii. 23, was a shawl or mantle. The veil proper was worn by Hebrew women only on special occasions, as in marriage, Gen. xxiv. 65 ; for ornament, S. of Sol. iv. 1, 3 ; for concealment as in harlotry, Gen. xxxviii. 14.

Vĕr-mĭl′ļon (*little worm*). A bright red color much affected by Hebrews in the painting of beams, ceilings, and conspicuous objects, Jer. xxii. 14 ; Ezek. xxiii. 14.

Vĕtch′eş. A plant of the bean family. [FITCHES.]

Vī′al (*shallow cup*). In a general sense any bottle or vessel, 1 Sam. x. 1.

Vĭl′laġe. In addition to the ordinary meaning, the unwalled suburbs of a walled town, Lev. xxv. 31.

Vīne (*wine*). A favorite Oriental plant of many varieties and cultivated from the earliest times, Gen. ix. 20 ; Num. xiii. 23. Subject of frequent metaphor, Deut. xxxii. 32 ; emblem of felicity and contentment, 1 Kgs. iv. 25 ; Ps. cxxviii. 3 ; Mic. iv. 4 ; rebellious Israel compared to "wild grapes," Isa. v. 2, "strange vine," Jer. ii. 21, "empty vine," Hos. x. 1 ; symbol of spiritual union, John xv. 1–5.

Vĭn′ę-gär (*sharp wine*). A thin wine, Num. vi. 3 ; Ruth ii. 14 ; acid, Prov. x. 26 ; unpalatable, Ps. lxix. 21. The thin sour wine of the Roman soldiers was the beverage in Matt. xxvii. 48 ; Mark xv. 36 ; John xix. 29, 30.

Vīne′yärd. Vineyards were generally on hills, Isa. v. 1 ; Jer. xxxi. 5 ; Am. ix. 13 ; surrounded by walls or hedges to keep out boars, Ps. lxxx. 13 ; jackals and foxes, Num. xxii. 24 ; Neh. iv. 3 ; S. of Sol. ii. 15 ; Ezek. xiii. 4 ; Matt. xxi. 33. Towers were erected within the vineyard for watch-houses and dwellings for the vine-keeper, Isa. i. 8 ; v. 2 ; Matt. xxi. 33.

Vĭnt′aġe (*taking wine away*). The vintage season a time of joy. Town people went out and lived among the vineyards in lodges and tents, Judg. ix. 27 ; Isa. xvi. 10 ; Jer. xxv. 30. Grapes were gathered in baskets, Jer. vi. 9. [WINE-PRESS.]

Vīne of Sŏd′om, Deut. xxxii. 32. A phrase used to describe the character of Israel.

Vīne′yärdş, Plain of. A place east of Jordan, beyond Aroer, Judg. xi. 33. [ABEL.]

Vī′ol (*keep holiday, sacrifice*). A stringed instrument like the psaltery, Am. vi. 5. [PSALTERY.]

Vī′per (*bringing forth its young alive*). The Hebrew word implies a hissing and venomous serpent, as the common European viper or adder, the horned vipers of the *cerastes* genus, and the Indian vipers, Job xx. 16 ; Isa. xxx. 6 ; Acts xxviii. 1–6. A symbol of deceit and destruction, Matt. iii. 7 ; xii. 34 ; xxiii. 33 ; Luke iii. 7.

Vĭs′ļon (*seeing*). An inspired dream, phantasy, or apparition, Num. xxiv. 4 ; Isa. vi. ; Ezek. i. viii.-x. ; Dan. vii., viii. ; Acts xxvi. 13–19.

Vŏph′sī (*gain*). Father of Nahbi, the spy selected to represent the tribe of Naphtali, Num. xiii. 14.

Vow (*wish*). Vows were threefold, vows of devotion, abstinence, and destruction, and respecting them certain laws were laid down, Deut. xxiii. 21–23. The law in Lev. xxvii. regulated the vow of Corban, and that in Num. vi. 1–21 the Nazarite vow.

Vŭl'ture (*tearer*). A large falconoid bird, with naked head and neck, feeding mostly on carrion. The bird is pronounced unclean in Lev. xi. 14; Deut. xiv. 13; but the original implies the kite, as also in Isa. xxxiv. 15.

W

Wā'fer (*waffle*). Among Hebrews a thin cake of fine flour used in offerings. The flour was wheaten and the wafers were unleavened and anointed with oil, Ex. xvi. 31; xxix. 2, 23; Lev. ii. 4; vii. 12; viii. 26; Num. vi. 15, 19.

Wā'ġĕṣ (*pledges*). The earliest O. T. mention of wages shows that they were paid in kind and not in money, Gen. xxix. 15, 20; xxx. 28; xxxi. 7, 8, 41. Wages paid in money are mentioned in N. T., Matt. xx. 2. The Mosaic law was very strict in requiring daily payment of wages, Lev. xix. 13; Deut. xxiv. 14, 15.

Wăg'on (*mover*). Wagons of the Hebrews, like those of the ancient Egyptians, were carts, consisting of planks or at most of crude box-like bodies, supported upon axles which connected two solid wooden wheels. They were mostly drawn by oxen or kine, Num. vii. 3, 8; 1 Sam. vi. 3–14.

Wălk (*move*). Walk has figurative use in the Bible to denote the behavior and spiritual character of a person, Ezek. xi. 20; Rom. viii. 1.

Wăll of Pär-tī'tịon. The allusion in Eph. ii. 14 is to the " wall of partition " which separated the holy of holies from the holy place in Solomon's temple, 1 Kgs. vi. 31, 35.

Wăllṣ (*palisades*). Solid walls limitedly used in Oriental countries for ordinary dwellings, but at times solidly laid and strongly built for palaces and temples, and as a protection to cities. They were of various materials, palisades, clay, cemented pebbles, brick, and stone. Houses were frequently erected on the walls of cities, and towers for archers and slingers, Josh. ii. 15; Ps. lxii. 3; Isa. xxx. 13; Luke vi. 48.

Wăn'dĕr-ĭngṣ (*windings*). The wilderness wanderings of the Israelites began at Rameses, the place of rendezvous, west of the Red Sea. The time as fixed by modern Egyptologists was during the reign of the Pharaoh Menephthah, B. C. 1317, though another date, B. C. 1491, was for a long time received. After crossing into Arabia, the line of march was southerly to the wilderness of Sinai, where a long halt was made, the law given, the tabernacle built, and the people were numbered, Ex. xv. 23, 27; xvi.–xl.; Lev.; Num. i.-x. 12. From Sinai the route was northward to Kadesh near the southern border of Canaan, the time thus far consumed being two years, Num. xiii. 26. Here they were condemned to further wilderness wanderings for a period of thirty-eight years. This period was seemingly one devoted to nomadic existence like that of other Arabian tribes. When the time came for another move on Canaan, the route lay around the head of the Gulf of Akaba and thence eastward and northward to Moab and the Jordan crossing, Num. xxxiii. 48, 49.

Wăr (*embroil*). Primitive Hebrew weapons were clubs, arrows, slings, swords, and spears. No army divisions except those indicated by the tribes. The contests of this period often hand-to-hand and brutal, 2 Sam. i. 23; ii. 18; 1 Chr. xii. 8; 2 Chr. xiii. 17. Many of the modern stratagems employed, as the double attack, Gen. xiv. 15; ambush, Josh. viii. 12; false retreat, Judg. xx. 37; night attack, 2 Kgs. vii. 12. Sometimes battles were settled by single-handed combats, 1 Sam. xvii.; 2 Sam. ii. 15, 16; 1 Chr. xi. 6. King David's army was divided into regularly disciplined and officered bands under a general-in-chief, 2 Sam. xviii. 1, 2; xxiii. 8–39; 1 Chr. xi. 25–47; xii., xxvii. He introduced the heavier weapons, such as catapults and battering-rams for siege-work and chariots for field-work, 2 Sam. viii. 4. Soldiers killed in action were plundered, 1 Sam. xxxi. 8; survivors were mutilated or killed, Judg. i. 6; ix. 45; 2 Sam. xii. 31; 2 Chr. xxv. 12; or carried into captivity, Num. xxxi. 26.

Wặrd (*watch*). A guard-room or lock-up, Gen. xl. 3; Acts xii. 10. A garrison or military post, Neh. xii. 25. A detachment of persons, guard, for any purpose, 1 Chr. ix. 23; Neh. xiii. 30.

Wặrd'rōbe (*watch-robe*). Place where the royal robes and priest's vestments were kept under watch or care, 2 Kgs. xxii. 14.

Wāreṣ. [COMMERCE.]

Wặsh'ĭng. The custom of washing hands before meals or of feet after a journey or on entering a stranger's house was not only a polite ceremony but a religious observance, Matt. xv. 2; Mark vii. 3; Luke xi. 38. After the salutation the first act of hospitality was to proffer a basin of water to the guest for washing the feet, Gen. xviii. 4; Ex. xxx. 19, 21; Judg. xix. 21; 1 Sam. xxv. 41; Luke vii. 37, 38, 44; John xiii. 5–14.

Wặtch (*wake*). The Hebrew night was divided into three watches, instead of hours. The first was called " the beginning of watches," beginning at sunset and lasting till ten o'clock, Lam. ii. 19: the second, the " middle watch," from ten P. M till two A. M., Judg. vii. 19; the " morning watch," from two A. M. till sunrise, Ex. xiv. 24; 1 Sam xi. 11. After the captivity the Jews gradually adopted the Greek and Roman division of the night into twelve hours of four watches; " evening," 6 to 9; " midnight," 9 to 12; " cock-crowing," 12 to 3; " morning," 3 to 6, Matt. xiv. 25; Mark xiii. 35; Luke xii. 38.

Wặ'ter of Jĕal'oŭs-ў. The jealous husband brought his suspected wife before the priest, with her offering of barley meal, without oil or frankincense, in her hand. The priest took holy water in an earthen vessel in his hand and sprinkled it with the dust of the floor. Then the priest administered the oath to her. If she confessed to guilt she was compelled to drink the water, and stood accursed. If otherwise, she was allowed to go free, Num. v. 12–31.

Wặ'ter of Sĕp''ặ-rā'tion. The preparation and use of the water of separation are described in Num. xix.

Wặ'ter-spouts. The word translated " water-spouts " in Ps. xlii. 7 is rendered " gutter " in 2 Sam. v. 8.

Wāve=ŏf'fĕr-ĭng. The wave-offering, together with the heave-offering, was a part of the peace-offering. The right shoulder of the victim, which was considered the choicest part, was " heaved " or held up in the sight of the Lord, and was, therefore, to be eaten only by the priests. The breast portion was " waved " before the Lord and eaten by the worshippers. On the second day of the passover feast, a sheaf of wheat and an unblemished lamb of the first year were waved, Ex. xxix. 24–27; Lev. vii. 30–34: viii. 27; ix. 21; x. 14, 15; xxiii. 10–20; Num. vi. 20; xviii. 11–18, 26–29.

Wăx. Wax in its original sense, an animal product as of bees, is frequently used in Scripture as a means of illustration, Ps. lxviii. 2; xcvii. 5; Mic. i. 4.

Wēan (*accustom*). Weaning-time a festal occasion, and probably late, Gen. xxi. 8; 2 Chr. xxxi. 16.

Wĕap'onṣ. [ARMS.] [WAR.]

Wēa'ṣel. It is thought that " mole " would be a better translation, Lev. xi. 29.

Wēave. Most ancient nations knew the art of weaving. The Egyptians were skilled weavers, Gen. xli. 42. That the Hebrews brought the art along with them from bondage is clear from the fabrics manufactured in the wilderness: goat-hair covers, linen curtains, Ex. xxvi. 1–13; embroidered raiment, Ex. xxviii. 4, 39; woolen garments, Lev. xiii. 47. Though the loom is not mentioned, its various parts are, as the shuttle, beam, etc., 1 Sam. xvii. 7; 2 Kgs. xxiii.

7; 1 Chr. iv. 21; Job vii. 6; Prov. xxxi. 13, 24; Isa. xxxviii. 12.

Wĕd'ding. [MARRIAGE.]

Wĕd'ding=gär'ment. A special garment, required to be worn at marriage-suppers, seems to have been furnished by the host, Matt. xxii. 11.

Wēek. The division of time into weeks of seven days each dates from the earliest historic times among many and wide-apart nations. The Hebrew week began on our Sunday, their Sabbath being the seventh day or Saturday. The only day of their week they named was the Sabbath. The rest ran by numbers, as first, second, third, etc. Besides their week of days, Hebrews had their week of years, every seven years, and their week of seven times seven years, or year of jubilee, every fiftieth year, Gen. viii. 10; xxix. 27. The "feast of weeks" corresponded with Pentecost, Ex. xxiii. 15; xxxiv. 22; Lev. xxiii. 15–22; Num. xxviii.

Weights and Meas'ures. The standard of Hebrew weights and measures was kept in the sanctuary, Lev. xix. 35, 36. A copy of said standard was kept in the household, Deut. xxv. 13–15. The destruction of the ancient standard with the tabernacle led to the adoption of the various weights and measures of such countries as the Hebrews happened to be subject to or in commercial intercourse with. Hence the subject of Hebrew weights and measures is full of perplexity and uncertainty. *See* various weights and measures under their respective headings.

Wĕll (*boil*). Wells were of great importance in Palestine, Gen. xxiv. 11; Num. xx. 17–19; Judg. vii. 1. They were sometimes deep, John iv. 11; frequently owned in common, Gen. xxix. 2, 3; covered at times with a stone and surrounded by a low wall to protect them from drifting sand, Gen. xxix. 2–8; to stop them up an act of hostility, Gen. xxvi. 15, 16; to invade them a cause for contention, Gen. xxi. 25; water sometimes drawn by sweeps or windlasses, but generally by a bucket attached to a rope, and in some cases steps led down to them, Gen. xxi. 25–31; Judg. i. 13–15; 1 Sam. xxix. 1; emblem of blessings, Jer. ii. 13; xvii. 13.

Whāle. The Hebrew original translated "great whales" in Gen. i. 21 is used of "serpents" in Ex. vii. 9; Deut. xxxii. 33, and of the "crocodile" in Ezek. xxix. 3; xxxii. 2. In Job vii. 12; Isa. xxvii. 1, the name belongs to sea monsters. It is thought that the shark of the Mediterranean is meant in Jonah i. 17; Matt. xii. 40.

Whēat. This well-known cereal was cultivated in the East from the earliest times, Gen. xxx. 14, and grew luxuriantly and of many varieties in Egypt, Gen. xli. 22. Syria and Palestine were both fine wheat-growing countries, Ps. lxxxi. 16; cxlvii. 14; Matt. xiii. 8. Wheat-harvest denoted a well-known season, Gen. xxx. 14.

Whĭrl'wĭnd. Whirlwinds of great violence and frequency were well-known desert visitations and gave rise to many Scripture metaphors, Job xxxvii. 9; Isa. xvii. 13.

Whĭt'ed Sĕp'ŭl-chres. Inasmuch as contact with the burial place was a cause of ceremonial defilement, Num. xix. 16, sepulchres were whitewashed that they might be seen and avoided, Matt. xxiii. 27.

Wĭd'ŏw (*lack*). When a married man died without children, his brother, if still living with the family, had a right under the law to marry the widow in order to preserve the family name and inheritance, Deut. xxv. 5, 6; Matt. xxii. 23–30. Other provisions of the Mosaic law show great consideration for widows, Ex. xxii. 22; Deut. xiv. 29; xvi. 11, 14; xxiv. 19–21; xxvi. 12; xxvii. 19.

Wĭfe. [MARRIAGE.]

Wĭl'dĕr-ness (*place of wild beasts*). Like the word desert, wilderness does not necessarily imply an absolutely arid, sandy, and uninhabitable place, but an uncultivated waste, which it was possible for pastoral tribes to occupy, and with stretches of pas-

turage, Josh. xv. 61; Isa. xlii. 11. The wilderness of wandering in which the Israelites spent forty years, Deut. i. 1; Josh. v. 6; Neh. ix. 19, 21; Ps. lxxviii. 40–52; cvii. 4; Jer. ii. 2, was practically the great peninsula of Sinai lying between Seir, Edom, and Gulf of Akaba on the east, and Gulf of Suez and Egypt on the west. It embraced many minor divisions or wildernesses, as those of Sin or Zin, Paran, Shur, Etham, and Sinai. [WANDERINGS.]

Wĭll. The laws respecting realty rendered wills useless, but nuncupative disposition of personalty seems to be implied in 2 Sam. xvii. 23; 2 Kgs. xx. 1; Isa. xxxviii. 1.

Wĭl'lŏw. Before the captivity the willow was an emblem of joy, Lev. xxiii. 40; Job xl. 22; Isa. xliv. 4; but in allusion to the captivity, the weeping willow of Babylonia became the poetical type of sorrow, Ps. cxxxvii. 2. The "brook of willows," Isa. xv. 7, was in the land of Moab, and is called "valley of Arabians" in margin.

Wĭm'ple. In a Bible sense, a hood or veil as in Isa. iii. 22, or a mantle or shawl as in Ruth iii. 15.

Wĭnd (*blow*). Hebrews recognized the cardinal winds in their "four winds," north, south, east, west, Ezek. xxxvii. 9; Dan. viii. 8; Zech. ii. 6; Matt. xxiv. 31. The east wind injured vegetation, Gen. xli. 6; Job i. 19; Isa. xxvii. 8. The south wind brought heat, Luke xii. 55. The southwest and north winds brought clear cool weather, Job xxxvii. 9, 22; Prov. xxv. 23. The west wind, coming from the Mediterranean, brought rain.

Wĭn'dŏw (*wind-eye*). In primitive Oriental houses the windows were simply openings upon the inner or court side of houses. But on the street or public side there were frequently latticed projections both for ventilation and sitting purposes, 2 Kgs. ix. 30; Judg. v. 28; probably the casements of Prov. vii. 6; S. of Sol. ii. 9.

Wīne (*drink*). The Hebrews manufactured and used wine from earliest times, Gen. ix. 20, 21; xix. 32; xxvii. 25; xlix. 12; Job i. 18; Prov. xxiii. 30, 31; Isa. v. 11. A usual drink-offering at the daily sacrifices, Ex. xxix. 40; at the presentation of first fruits, Lev. xxiii. 13; and at other offerings, Num. xv. 5. It was tithable, Deut. xviii. 4. Nazarites could not drink it during their vow, Num. vi. 3, nor priests before service, Lev. x. 9.

Wīne=făt, Wīne=prĕss. The Hebrew winefat, vat, or press, consisted of an upper and lower receptacle, the former for treading the grapes, the latter for catching the juice, Isa. lxiii. 3; Joel iii. 13; Hag. ii. 16.

Wĭn'nŏw (*wind*). The process of winnowing or winding grain was that of tossing the mixed chaff and kernels into the air, on a high, windy spot, with a fork or shovel, so that the wind could carry the chaff away. The floor on which the kernels fell was usually clean and solid, and when not so, a sheet was used to catch the grains, Isa. xxx. 24; xli. 16; Matt. iii. 12. Evening was the favorite winnowing time because the breezes were then steadiest, Ruth iii. 2.

Wĭn'ter. Winters in Palestine are short, lasting from December till February, S. of Sol. ii. 11.

Wĭs'dom of Jē'sŭs. [ECCLESIASTICUS.]

Wĭs'dom of Sŏl'o-mon. Fifth of the Apocryphal books, devoted to an exposition of wisdom in its moral, philosophic, and historic aspects.

Wīse Mĕn, Matt. ii. 1. [MAGI.]

Wĭst. Same as "knew," Ex. xvi. 15; Acts xii. 9; xxiii. 5.

Wĭt (*know*). To become aware, learn, know, Gen. xxiv. 21; Ex. ii. 4.

Wĭtch (*wizard*). One who pretends to deal with evil spirits in order to work a spell on persons or their belongings; conjurer, fortune-teller, exorcist, supernatural curer of diseases, Deut. xviii. 10; 1 Sam. xxviii. 3–25. The word formerly embraced both sexes, but is now applied to women. Witches were not allowed to live, Ex. xxii. 18.

Witch′craft. The occult practices of witches and wizards, 1 Sam. xv. 23. The art, the pretender, and the person deceived were alike denounced, Lev. xx. 6; Nah. iii. 4; Gal. v. 20.

Wit′ness (*see*). Under the Mosaic law at least two witnesses were required to establish a capital charge, Num. xxxv. 30; Deut. xvii. 6, 7. False swearing forbidden, Ex. xx. 16; Lev. vi. 1–7.

Wiz′ard (*cunning*). A male witch, Lev. xx. 27.

Wolf. Wolves of Palestine were numerous and the dread of shepherds, as they were a terrible enemy to sheep, Matt. vii. 15; x. 16; John x. 12; Acts xx. 29. A wolf typed the rapacity of Benjamin, Gen. xlix. 27; and the cruelty of Israel's oppression, Ezek. xxii. 27; and the destruction of the wicked, Jer. v. 6.

Wom′an (*wife-man*). Hebrew women cared for the household, Gen. xviii. 6; carried water, Gen. xxiv. 15; tended flocks, Gen. xxix. 6; spun, Ex. xxxv. 26; made clothes, 1 Sam. ii. 19; acted as hostess and guest on social occasions, Job i. 4; John ii. 3; xii. 2; prophesied, composed, sang, and danced, Ex. xv. 20, 21; Judg. xi. 34; xxi. 21; fêted, 1 Sam. xviii. 6, 7; held public positions, Judg. iv., v.; 2 Kgs. xxii. 14; Neh. vi. 14; Luke ii. 36; acted as workers and officials in the early Christian church, Acts xviii. 18, 26; Rom. xvi. 1.

Wool. A highly prized material for clothing among Hebrews, Lev. xiii. 47; Job xxxi. 20; Prov. xxxi. 13; Ezek. xxvii. 18; xxxiv. 3. Mixed woolen and linen fabrics forbidden, Lev. xix. 19; Deut. xxii. 11.

Word. The *logos*, or Word, in John i. 1–14; 1 John i. 1; Rev. xix. 13, stands for the Son of God, the Word incarnate.

Worm. Many Hebrew words are translated worm, all indicative of something loathsome, destructive, helpless, or insignificant, as the moth, Isa. li. 8; maggot, Job xix. 26; possibly the serpent, Mic. vii. 17. The allusion in Isa. lxvi. 24; Mark ix. 44–48, is thought to be to the valley near Jerusalem where the refuse of the city constantly bred worms and where fires were kept burning to consume the collections. The helplessness of the worm affords the figures in Job xxv. 6; Ps. xxii. 6; Isa. xli. 14.

Worm′wood. A bitter plant found in Palestine, and often mentioned in Scripture in connection with gall to denote what is offensive and nauseous, Deut. xxix. 18; Prov. v. 4; Jer. ix. 15; xxiii. 15; Lam. iii. 15, 19; Am. v. 7.

Wor′ship-per, Acts xix. 35. The word should be temple-keeper as in marg. and in R. V.

Wot. "Wotteth not," Gen. xxxix. 8, means "knows not."

Wri′ting. The first mention of writing in the Bible is in Ex. xvii. 14. The art among Hebrews was limited to persons of learning and position and to the class of scribes, Isa. xxix. 11, 12. [SCRIBE.] The oldest Semitic writings are the bricks and tablets of Nineveh and Babylon. The Hebrew alphabet was a development of the Phœnician, and it underwent many changes in the course of time. The record of Sinai was written on stone with the finger of God, Ex. xxxi. 18; xxxii. 15–19; xxxiv. 1–29. Later materials were wax, wood, metal, or plaster, Deut. xxvii. 2; Josh. viii. 32; Luke i. 63; and perhaps vellum, or fine parchment from skins, and linen were in early use for other than monumental writings, as they surely were at a later day, 2 Tim. iv. 13. Pliable substances, when written upon, were rolled on sticks, sealed and preserved as books, Ps. xl. 7; Isa. xxix. 11; Dan. xii. 4; Rev. v. 1. Hebrews doubtless knew the use of papyrus, 2 John 12. Rolls were generally written upon one side only, except in Ezek. ii. 9, 10; Rev. v. 1. Hebrew instruments of writing were the stylus and graver for hard materials, Ex. xxxii. 4; Job xix. 24; Ps. xlv. 1; Isa. viii. 1; Jer. viii. 8; xvii. 1; and for pliable materials, a reed

pen, 2 Cor. iii. 3; 2 John 12; 3 John 13. Paul used an amanuensis, but authenticated his letters in a few lines with his own pen, 1 Cor. xvi. 21; Col. iv. 18; 2 Thess. iii. 17. Ancient ink was made of pulverized charcoal or burnt ivory in water to which gum had been added. It was carried in an ink-horn suspended to the girdle, Ezek. ix. 3, 4.

Y

Yarn. Though the art of spinning was well known to Hebrews, Ex. xxxv. 25; Prov. xxxi. 19; Matt. vi. 28, the spun product is only mentioned in 1 Kgs. x. 28; 2 Chr. i. 16, and in both these instances the word is rather significant of "band" as applied to a troop or drove of horses than to yarn.

Year. The Hebrew year was sacred and civil, with two beginnings. The sacred year began with the month Abib, April, the civil with the month Tisri, October. The months were lunar, twelve in number, with, of course, the necessary intercalary month *ve-adar* at the proper time, about every three years. As divided by seasons, the year was solar. There were two seasons, summer and winter, Ps. lxxiv. 17; Jer. xxxvi. 22; Am. iii. 15; Zech. xiv. 8.

Year of Ju′bi-lee. [JUBILEE.]

Year, Sab-bat′i-cal. [SABBATICAL.]

Yoke (*join*). This well-known means of coupling oxen for agricultural purposes was primitively laid upon the necks of the cattle, and held there by thongs which passed around their necks. A thong served also as an attachment to the cart-tongue or plow-beam. A pair of oxen yoked together were called a yoke, as to-day, 1 Sam. xi. 7; 1 Kgs. xix. 21. It would seem as if asses and mules went by pairs like oxen, Judg. xix. 10; 2 Kgs. v. 17, and even horses, camels, and chariots, Isa. xxi. 7. The word, like the Latin *jugum*, gave rise to a measurement of land, 1 Sam. xiv. 14, the amount a yoke of oxen could plow in a day. Yoke is used metaphorically for subjection, 1 Kgs xii. 4, 9–11; Isa. ix. 4; Jer. v. 5. An unusually heavy bondage was typed by "iron yoke," Deut. xxviii. 48; Jer. xxviii. 13. Removal of the yoke implied deliverance, Gen. xxvii. 40; Jer. ii. 20; Matt. xi. 29, 30. Breaking of the yoke meant repudiation of authority, Nah. i. 13.

Z

Za′′a-na′im (*changing*). The plain, or rather the oak, where Heber the Kenite was encamped when Sisera sought refuge in his tent, Judg. iv. 11, 17–22. It is mentioned as near Kedesh.

Za′a-nan (*flocking-place*). A place in the lowlands of Judah, Mic. i. 11.

Za′′a-nan′nim. A border place of Naphtali, near Kedesh, and supposed to be same as Zaanaim, Josh. xix. 33.

Za′a-van (*disturbed*). Son of Ezer and descendant of Seir the Horite, Gen. xxxvi. 27. Zavan in 1 Chr. i. 42.

Za′bad (*gift*). (1) A son of Nathan, 1 Chr. ii. 36, 37, and one of David's mighty men, 1 Chr. xi. 41. (2) An Ephraimite whom the Gathites slew while on a thieving expedition, 1 Chr. vii. 21. (3) Son of Shimeath, an Ammonitess, and one of the murderers of King Joash, 2 Chr. xxiv. 25, 26. Jozachar in 2 Kgs. xii. 21. (4) Three returned captives, Ez. x. 27, 33, 43.

Zab′′a-da′ias, 1 Esdr. ix. 35. [ZABAD, 4.]

Zab′′a-de′ans. An Arab tribe smitten by Jonathan Maccabeus, 1 Macc. xii. 31.

Zab′bai (*limpid*). (1) One who had taken a foreign wife, Ez. x. 28. (2) Father of Baruch, one of the repairers of the walls of Jerusalem, Neh. iii. 20.

Zăb′bud (*given*). One who returned from captivity with Ezra, Ez. viii. 14.

Zăb′dĭ (*gift*). (1) Son of Zerah of the tribe of Judah, and ancestor of Achan, who concealed the spoils of Jericho, Josh. vii. 1, 17, 18. (2) One of the sons of Shimhi, a Benjamite, 1 Chr. viii. 19. (3) An officer who had the care of King David's wine cellars, 1 Chr. xxvii. 27. (4) Son of Asaph the minstrel, and leader of thanksgiving in prayer, Neh. xi. 17. Zaccur, Neh. xii. 35. Zichri, 1 Chr. ix. 15.

Zăb′dĭ-el (*gift of God*). (1) Father of Jashobeam, captain of first course for the first month of David's guard, 1 Chr. xxvii. 2. (2) Overseer of a returned troop of captives, Neh. xi. 14. (3) An Arabian chieftain who put Alexander Balas to death, 1 Macc. xi. 17.

Zā′bud (*given*). A friend of Solomon and his principal officer, 1 Kgs. iv. 5.

Zăb′u-lon. Greek form of Zebulun, Matt. iv. 13; Rev. vii. 8.

Zăc′ca-ī (*pure*). His descendants, 760 in number, returned with Zerubbabel, Ez. ii. 9; Neh. vii. 14.

Zăc-chæ′us (*just*). The rich chief among publicans, resident at Jericho, who climbed a tree to see Jesus pass, was invited down, became the host of Jesus, and was converted, Luke xix. 1–10.

Zăc-chē′us. An officer under Judas Maccabeus, 2 Macc. x. 19.

Zăc′chur (*mindful*). A Simeonite of the family of Mishma, 1 Chr. iv. 26.

Zăc′cur (*mindful*). (1) Father of Shammua, the spy sent out by the tribe of Reuben, Num. xiii. 4. (2) A Merarite Levite, 1 Chr. xxiv. 27. (3) A son of Asaph the minstrel, and leader of the third musical course, 1 Chr. xxv. 2, 10; Neh. xii. 35. (4) One who assisted in rebuilding the walls of Jerusalem, Neh. iii. 2. (5) One who signed the covenant with Nehemiah, Neh. x. 12. (6) Father of Hanan, whom Nehemiah made one of his treasurers, Neh. xiii. 13.

Zăch′′a-rī′ah (*remembered by Jehovah*). In better Hebrew, Zechariah. (1) Son of Jeroboam II., and his successor on the throne of Israel, 2 Kgs. xiv. 29; B. C. 773–72. He reigned only six months, 2 Kgs. xv. 8–11. (2) Father of Abi, mother of Hezekiah king of Judah, 2 Kgs. xviii. 2. Written Zechariah in 2 Chr. xxix. 1.

Zăch′′a-rī′as (*remembered by Jehovah*). Greek form of Zachariah. (1) The name is borne by many priests and laymen in the books of Esdras. (2) Father of John the Baptist and husband of Elizabeth. He was a priest of the course of Abia, or Abijah, 1 Chr. xxiv. 10, and probably lived at Hebron, Luke i. 5–25, 57–80. (3) Son of Barachias, who was slain between the temple and the altar, Matt. xxiii. 35; Luke xi. 51.

Zăch′a-rў. 2 Esdr. i. 40. [ZECHARIAH, THE PROPHET.]

Zā′cher (*testimony*). A Benjamite, one of the sons of Jehiel by Maachah, 1 Chr. viii. 29, 31.

Zā′dŏk (*just*). (1) Son of Ahitub, of the line of Eleazar. He was one of the high priests in the time of David, the other being Abiathar, 2 Sam. viii. 17. He joined David at Hebron, as a chieftain of his father's house, 1 Chr. xii. 28, remained faithful to him and subsequently anointed Solomon, 1 Kgs. i. 39. (2) A priest in the reign of King Ahaziah, 1 Chr. vi. 12. (3) Father of Jerusha, wife of Uzziah and mother of Jotham king of Judah, 2 Kgs. xv. 33. (4) Son of Baana, who helped Nehemiah to repair the walls of Jerusalem, Neh. iii. 4. (5) Another assistant wall-builder, Neh. iii. 29. (6) A co-covenanter with Nehemiah, Neh. x. 21. (7) A scribe and treasurer under Nehemiah, Neh. xiii. 13.

Zā′ham (*hateful*). A son of King Rehoboam by his wife Abihail, 2 Chr. xi. 19.

Zā′ir (*little*). A vague spot or place, where King Joram overcame the Edomites, 2 Kgs. viii. 21.

Zā′laph (*hurt*). Father of Hanun who helped to repair the walls of Jerusalem, Neh. iii. 30.

Zăl′mŏn (*shade*). (1) The Ahohite who was one of David's guard, 2 Sam. xxiii. 28. Ilai in 1 Chr. xi. 29. (2) A wooded eminence near Shechem, Judg. ix. 47–49.

Zal-mō′nah (*shady*). A desert encampment of the wandering Israelites, Num. xxxiii. 41, 42.

Zal-mŭn′nă (*shadow*). One of two kings of Midian captured and slain by Gideon, Judg. viii. 5–21; Ps. lxxxiii. 11.

Zăm′bĭs, 1 Esdr. ix. 34. [AMARIAH.]

Zăm′brī, 1 Macc. ii. 26. [ZIMRI.]

Zā′moth, 1 Esdr. ix. 28. [ZATTU.]

Zăm-zŭm′mims. An Ammonite name for a race of Rephaim or giants, Deut. ii. 20.

Ză-nō′ah (*swamp*). (1) A town in the lowlands of Judah, ten miles southwest of Jerusalem, Josh. xv. 34; 1 Chr. iv. 18. Its inhabitants helped Nehemiah to repair the walls of Jerusalem, Neh. iii. 13; xi. 30. (2) Another town of Judah in the mountains, about ten miles southwest of Hebron, Josh. xv. 56.

Zăph′nath=pā′′a-nē′ah (*revealer of secrets*). A name given by the Pharaoh to Joseph upon his promotion to a high place in the royal service, Gen. xli. 45.

Zā′phŏn (*north*). An unidentified place in Gad, Josh. xiii. 27.

Zā′ră (*dawn*). Zarah, a son of Judah, in genealogy of Christ, Matt. i. 3.

Zăr′a-çēs. A brother of Jehoiakim, King of Judah, 1 Esdr. i. 38.

Zā′rah (*dawn*). A son of Judah by Tamar, Gen. xxxviii. 30; xlvi. 12. Called Zerah in Num. xxvi. 20, and founder of the family of Zarhites; also Zerah in Josh. vii. 1, 18; xxii. 20; 1 Chr. ii. 4, 6; ix. 6; Neh. xi. 24. Zara in Matt. i. 3.

Zăr′′a-ī′as. The name stands for Zerahiah and Zebadiah in the Apocrypha, 1 Esdr. viii.

Zā′re-ah (*hornet*). Neh. xi. 29. [ZORAH, ZOREAH.]

Zā′re-ath-ītes′′. Dwellers in Zareah or Zorah, 1 Chr. ii. 53.

Zā′red, Num. xxi. 12. [ZERED.]

Zăr′e-phăth (*smelting-place*). The Sarepta of Luke iv. 26. A town in Phœnicia on the Mediterranean coast between Tyre and Sidon, and about seven miles from the latter. Residence of the prophet Elijah during the great drought, 1 Kgs. xvii. 8–24.

Zăr′e-tăn, Josh. iii. 16. [ZARTHAN, 2.]

Zā′reth=shā′har (*beauty of dawn*). A town in Reuben, Josh. xiii. 19.

Zăr′hītes. A branch of the tribe of Judah descended from Zerah the son of Judah, Num. xxvi. 13, 20; Josh. vii. 17; 1 Chr. xxvii. 11, 13.

Zăr′ta-nah (*cooling*). A place usually identified with Zarthan, 1 Kgs. iv. 12.

Zăr′than (*cooling*). (1) A town in the Jordan valley. Between it and Succoth was the clay-ground in which Solomon cast the utensils for the temple service. Now the mound called *Tell-sa-rem*, 1 Kgs. vii. 46. (2) The same place is doubtless meant by Zaretan, Josh. iii. 16, and by Zererath in Judg. vii. 22. (3) Supposably another name for the Zartanah of 1 Kgs. iv. 12. (4) Doubtless Zarthan (1) is meant by the Zeredathah of 2 Chr. iv. 17.

Zăth′o-ē̆, 1 Esdr. viii. 32. [ZATTU.]

Zăt′thu (*branch*). One who sealed the covenant with Nehemiah, Neh. x. 14.

Zăt′tu (*branch*). The children of Zattu returned from the captivity, Ez. ii. 8; x. 27; Neh. vii. 13.

Zā′van, 1 Chr. i. 42. [ZAAVAN.]

Zā′ză (*for all*). A son of Jonathan, and descendant of Judah, 1 Chr. ii. 33.

Zĕal′ŏts (*zealous*). Name of a fanatical Jewish

party, strongest from A. D. 6 to 70. It was political, having for its aim the overthrow of Roman authority; and religious, seeking a Jewish theocracy over the whole earth. In Acts v. 37 it seems to have been headed by one Judas of Galilee.

Zĕb″a-dī′ah (*portion of God*). (1) A son of Beriah, of Benjamin, 1 Chr. viii. 15. (2) A son of Elpaal of Benjamin, 1 Chr. viii. 17. (3) A son of Jeroham of Gedor, a Benjamite, 1 Chr. xii. 7. (4) A Korhite Levite, son of Meshelemiah, and one of the temple porters, 1 Chr. xxvi. 2. (5) A son of Asahel, brother of Joab, who succeeded his father as captain of the military course of the fourth month, 1 Chr. xxvii. 7. (6) A Levite sent out by King Jehoshaphat to teach the law to the people, 2 Chr. xvii. 8. (7) A son of Ishmael and ruler of the house of Judah in reign of King Jehoshaphat, 2 Chr. xix. 11. (8) One who returned with Ezra from the captivity, Ez. viii. 8. (9) A priest who had married a foreign wife, Ez. x. 20.

Zā′bah (*sacrifice*). One of the two Midianite kings slain by Gideon, Judg. viii. 5-21; Ps. lxxxiii. 11.

Zĕ-bā′im (*gazelles*). A disputed word, regarded as identical with Zeboim, Ez. ii. 57; Neh. vii. 59

Zĕb′e-dee (*God's portion*). A fisherman of Galilee, husband of Salome, and father of the apostles James the Great and John, Matt. iv. 21; xxvii. 56; Mark i. 19, 20; xv. 40. His home is located at or near Bethsaida, and he appears to have been able to employ help in his occupation, Mark i. 20.

Zĕ-bī′na (*buying*). A son of Nebo who had taken a foreign wife after the captivity, Ez. x. 43.

Zĕ-bō′im (*deer*). (1) One of the five cities of the plain, or circle, of Jordan, Gen. x. 19; Deut. xxix. 23; Hos. xi. 8. It is called Zeboiim in Gen. xiv. 2, 8. (2) A valley, or mountain gorge, contiguous to Michmash, 1 Sam. xiii. 18. (3) A place inhabited by Benjamites after the return from captivity, Neh. xi. 34.

Zĕ-bŏi′ĭm, Gen. xiv. 2, 8. [ZEBOIM, 1.]

Zĕ-bū′dah (*given*). Wife of King Josiah and mother of King Jehoiakim, 2 Kgs. xxiii. 36.

Zĕ′bul (*habitation*). Ruler of the city of Shechem at the time of the contest between Abimelech and the native Canaanites, Judg. ix. 28-41.

Zĕb′u-lon-īte″, Judg. xii. 11. [ZEBULUNITES.]

Zĕb′u-lun (*dwelling*). (1) Tenth son of Jacob, and sixth and last by Leah, Gen. xxx. 20; xxxv. 23. Three sons are ascribed to him at the time of the migration to Egypt, Gen. xlvi. 14. Zebulun was one of the six tribes stationed on Ebal to pronounce the curse, Deut. xxvii. 13. The allotment of the tribe was bounded as in Josh. xix. 10-16, and in general stretched from Acre to Jordan, taking in the plain of Esdraelon. The tribe did not expel the natives in its allotment, but associated with them and fell into easy commercial intercourse with Phœnicia on the west, Judg. i. 30. It became an idolatrous tribe, 2 Chr. xxx. 10-18, and its territory was depopulated in the captivity of Israel by Tiglath-pileser, 2 Kgs. xv. 29. (2) A boundary place of Asher, Josh. xix. 27.

Zĕb′u-lun-ites″. Descendants of Zebulun, Num. xxvi. 27.

Zĕch″a-rī′ah (*memory of God*). Son of Berechiah, Zech. i. 1; of Iddo, Ez. v. 1. Eleventh of the minor prophets and contemporary of Haggai, born in Babylon during the captivity, returned with Zerubbabel, Ez. v. 1; vi. 14. The time of his prophecies is reckoned as between B. C. 520 and 518, during the period of building the second temple, whose completion was largely due to his energies as priest and prophet. His book, 38th of O. T., is divided into two parts. Chapters i.-viii. contain hopeful visions of the restored Hebrew state, exhortations to turn to Jehovah, warnings against God's enemies. Chapters ix.-xiv. are prophetic of the future fortunes of the

theocracy, the conversion of Israel, the glorification of God's kingdom and of the coming of the Messiah. The style of the book is obscure. Many critics attribute the authorship of the second division of the book to Jeremiah. (2) A Reubenite chief, at time of the captivity by Tiglath-pileser, 1 Chr. v. 7. (3) A Korhite Levite, keeper of one of the doors of the tabernacle, 1 Chr. ix. 21. (4) A son of Jehiel, 1 Chr. ix. 37. (5) A Levite of the second order, one of the temple musicians, 1 Chr. xv. 18, 20. (6) A priest who blew the trumpet before the ark on its return, 1 Chr. xv. 24. (7) A Kohathite Levite, 1 Chr. xxiv. 25. (8) A Merarite Levite, 1 Chr. xxvi. 11. (9) A Manassite, 1 Chr. xxvii. 21. (10) A prince of Judah in reign of Jehoshaphat, 2 Chr. xvii. 7. (11) Father of Jahaziel, 2 Chr. xx. 14. (12) A son of Jehoshaphat, 2 Chr. xxi. 2. (13) Son of the high priest Jehoiada, in reign of Joash king of Judah, 2 Chr. xxiv. 20, and probably same as the Zacharias of Matt. xxiii. 35. (14) A prophet and royal counsellor in reign of Uzziah, 2 Chr. xxvi 5. (15) Father of Abijah, mother of King Hezekiah, 2 Chr. xxix. 1. (16) A member of the family of Asaph in time of Hezekiah, 2 Chr. xxix. 13. (17) A Kohathite Levite in the reign of Josiah, 2 Chr. xxxiv. 12. (18) One of the temple rulers in reign of Josiah, 2 Chr. xxxv. 8. (19) Nine priests, Levites and returned captives in Ez. viii. 3, 11, 16; x. 26; Neh. viii. 4; xi. 4, 5, 12; xii. 16, 35, 41. (20) A witness for Isaiah, Isa. viii. 2.

Zē′dăd (*hillside*). A landmark on the northern border of Canaan, Num. xxxiv. 8; Ezek. xlvii. 15.

Zĕd″e-chī′as, 1 Esdr. i. 46. [ZEDEKIAH.]

Zĕd″e-kī′ah (*justice of God*). (1) Last king of Judah, son of Josiah, and brother of Jehoahaz. He reigned eleven years, B. C. 598-588, 2 Kgs. xxiv. 18; 2 Chr. xxxvi. 11. He was raised to the throne by Nebuchadnezzar, who changed his name from Mattaniah to Zedekiah, 2 Kgs. xxiv. 17. In the ninth year of his reign, he revolted against Nebuchadnezzar, who thereupon completed the captivity of Judah and ended the kingdom, 2 Kgs. xxv. 1-21; 2 Chr. xxxvi. 11-21; Jer. xxi.-xxxviii.; Ezek. xvii. 15-21. (2) Son of Chenaanah, a prophet and head of the prophetic school in reign of Jehoshaphat, 1 Kgs. xxii. ; 2 Chr. xviii. 10-24. (3) Son of Hananiah, and a court officer under Jehoiakim, Jer. xxxvi. 12. (4) A false prophet burnt to death by Nebuchadnezzar, Jer. xxix. 21. 22.

Zē′eb (*wolf*). A prince of Midian, slain by the Ephraimites, Judg. vii. 25; Ps. lxxxiii. 11.

Zē′eb, Wine=press of. The place where Zeeb was slain by the Ephraimites, Judg. vii. 25.

Zē′lah (*rib*). A city in Benjamin in which was located the family tomb of Kish, father of Saul, Josh. xviii. 28; 2 Sam. xxi. 14.

Zē′lek (*chasm*). An Ammonite and one of David's guard, 2 Sam. xxiii. 37; 1 Chr. xi. 39.

Zē-lō′phe-hăd (*firstborn*). A son of Hepher, descendant of Manasseh. The law of female inheritance was changed in favor of his daughters, Num. xxvi. 33; xxvii. 1-11; Josh. xvii. 3, 4; 1 Chr. vii. 15.

Zē-lō′tēs (*zealous*). A name added to that of the apostle Simon to distinguish him from Simon Peter, and to emphasize his membership of the party of Zealots, Luke vi. 15. [SIMON, 4.]

Zĕl′zah (*shade*). A place in the border of Benjamin, near which was Rachel's tomb, 1 Sam. x. 2.

Zĕm″a-rā′im (*two fleeces*). (1) A town in Benjamin, four miles north of Jericho, Josh. xviii. 22. (2) Mount Zemaraim in the mountains of Ephraim, 2 Chr. xiii. 4.

Zĕm′a-rīte. An Hamitic tribe or family descended from Canaan, Gen. x. 18; 1 Chr. i. 16.

Zĕ-mī′ra (*song*). Son of Becher, a descendant of Benjamin, 1 Chr. vii. 8.

Zē′nan (*target*). A town in the lowlands of Judah, Josh. xv. 37.

Zē′nas. A Christian lawyer whom Paul wished Titus to bring along with him, Tit. iii. 13.

Zĕph″a-nī′ah (*God's secret*). (1) Ninth in order of the twelve minor prophets. Son of Cushi and a descendant of Hezekiah. He flourished during the reign of King Josiah, B. C. 641–610. His prophecy constitutes the 36th O. T. book, and denounces Judah, Nineveh, and surrounding nations, and records many cheerful promises of gospel blessings. The style is characterized by grace, strength, and dignity. (2) Son of Maaseiah and priest in the reign of Zedekiah; Jer. xxi. 1 ; xxix. 25–29 ; xxxvii. 3 ; lii. 24–27. (3) A Kohathite Levite, 1 Chr. vi. 36. (4) Father of Josiah and Hen, Zech. vi. 10, 14.

Zē′phath (*watchtower*). An Amorite town in the mountains near Kadesh. Called Hormah after it was conquered by the Israelites, Judg. i. 17. [HORMAH.]

Zĕph′a-thah (*watchtower*). The valley near Mareshah in which King Asa marshalled his forces for battle against Zerah, 2 Chr. xiv. 9, 10.

Zē′phī, 1 Chr. i. 36. [ZEPHO.]

Zē′phŏ (*watchtower*). Zephi, 1 Chr. i. 36. One of the dukes of Edom, Gen. xxxvi. 11, 15.

Zē′phon (*watchman*). A son of Gad, Num. xxvi. 15. Called Ziphion in Gen. xlvi. 16.

Zē′phon-ītes. Descendants of Zephon, Num. xxvi. 15.

Zĕr (*flint*). A city in Naphtali, Josh. xix. 35.

Zē′rah (*eastern*). (1) A grandson of Esau and one of the dukes of Edom, Gen. xxxvi. 13, 17, 33 ; 1 Chr. i. 37, 44. (2) Num. xxvi. 20 ; Josh. vii. 1, 18 ; xxii. 20 ; 1 Chr. ii. 4, 6 ; ix. 6 ; Neh. xi. 24. [ZARAH.] (3) A son of Simeon and ancestor of a family of Zarhites, Num. xxvi. 13 ; 1 Chr. iv. 24. Called Zohar in Gen. xlvi. 10. (4) A Gershonite Levite, 1 Chr. vi. 21, 41. (5) An Ethiopian king whom Asa, king of Judah, defeated, 2 Chr. xiv. 9.

Zĕr″a-hī′ah (*rising of God*). (1) Son of Uzzi and priest of the line of Eleazar, 1 Chr. vi. 6, 51 ; Ez. vii. 4. (2) One whose descendants returned from captivity with Ezra, Ez. viii. 4.

Zē′red (*growth of reeds*). A brook or wady separating Moab from Edom, Deut. ii. 13, 14. Called Zared in Num. xxi. 12.

Zĕr′e-dà (*ambush*). Native place of Jeroboam, in the mountains of Ephraim, 1 Kgs. xi. 26.

Zĕ-rĕd′a-thah, 2 Chr. iv. 17. [ZARTHAN.]

Zĕr′e-răth, Judg. vii. 22. [ZARTHAN.]

Zē′resh. Wife of Haman, and his adviser in the conspiracy against Mordecai, Esth. v. 10–14.

Zē′reth (*bright*). A son of Ashur, founder of Tekoa, 1 Chr. iv. 7.

Zē′rī (*built*). A son of Jeduthun, a musician in the time of David, 1 Chr. xxv. 3.

Zē′rôr (*tied*). An ancestor of Kish, the father of Saul, 1 Sam. ix. 1.

Zĕ-ru′ah (*leprous*). Mother of King Jeroboam I., 1 Kgs. xi. 26.

Zĕ-rŭb′ba-bĕl (*born in Babylon*). He was of the family of David, and son of Shealtiel, Hag. i. 1, or Salathiel, Matt. i. 12, or Pedaiah, 1 Chr. iii. 19. Born at Babylon, commissioned governor of Judea by the Persian king, Cyrus, Neh. xii. 47 ; leader of the first colony of captives back to Jerusalem, B. C. 536, Ez. ii. 2 ; Neh. vii. 7 ; laid the foundation of the new temple, Zech. iv. 6–10 ; began the work of reconstruction, in which he was greatly hindered by Samaritan opposition, and petty Persian intrigue ; finally succeeded in completing the structure, restored the order of priests according to the institution of David, Ez. vi. 14–22 ; Hag. i. 12, 15 ; ii. 2–4. Zorobabel in N. T., Matt. i. 12.

Zĕr″u-ī′ah (*bruised*). Sister of David and mother of the three leading heroes of David's army, 1 Sam. xxvi. 6 ; 1 Chr. ii. 16.

Zē′tham (*olive*). A Levite, son of Laadan, 1 Chr. xxiii. 8 ; xxvi. 22.

Zē′than (*olive*). A son of Bilhan, of Benjamin, 1 Chr. vii. 10.

Zē′thär (*star*). One of the seven chamberlains of King Ahasuerus, Esth. i. 10.

Zī′à (*moving*). A Gadite, Chr. v. 13.

Zī′bà (*statue*). A steward of Saul, and tiller of the lands of Saul which David restored to Mephibosheth, 2 Sam. ix. 2–13 ; xvi. 1–4 ; xix. 17–29.

Zĭb′e-on (*robber*). A Horite and son of Seir, Gen. xxxvi. 2, 24, 29 ; 1 Chr. i. 38, 40.

Zĭb′ī-à (*deer*). A Benjamite, 1 Chr. viii. 9.

Zĭb′ī-ah (*deer*). Mother of King Jehoash or Joash, 2 Kgs. xii. 1 ; 2 Chr. xxiv. 1.

Zĭch′rī (*remembered*). (1) A son of Izhar, son of Kohath, Ex. vi. 21. (2) A Benjamite of the sons of Shimhi, 1 Chr. viii. 19. (3) A Benjamite of the sons of Shashak, 1 Chr. viii. 23. (4) A Benjamite of the sons of Jeroham, 1 Chr. viii. 27. (5) A son of Asaph the musician, 1 Chr. ix. 15. Zabdi, Neh. xi. 17 ; Zaccur, Neh. xii. 35. (6) Son of Eliezer, a descendant of Moses, 1 Chr. xxvi. 25. (7) Father of Eliezer, a ruler of Reuben in reign of David, 1 Chr. xxvii. 16. (8) Father of Amasiah, a captain of 200,000 men of valor under King Jehoshaphat, 2 Chr. xvii. 16. (9) Father of Elishaphat, a captain of hundreds under Jehoiada, 2 Chr. xxiii. 1. (10) A mighty man of Ephraim in the army of Pekah, 2 Chr. xxviii. 7. (11) A Benjamite, father of Joel, overseer of Jerusalem after the captivity, Neh. xi. 9. (12) Priest of the family of Abijah, Neh. xii. 17.

Zĭd′dim (*steeps*). A fenced city of Naphtali, Josh. xix. 35.

Zī′dŏn (*fishing*). The Sidon of Gen. x. 15, 19, the N. T., and Apocrypha. An ancient and wealthy commercial city of Phœnicia on the Mediterranean coast, twenty miles north of Tyre. It was a limit of the allotment of Asher, but was never conquered, Judg. i. 31 ; x. 12 ; xviii. 7, 28. The Zidonians assisted in building the temple, 1 Kgs. v. 6 ; 1 Chr. xxii. 4 ; Ezek. xxvii. 8. Israel imported her idolatries, 1 Kgs. xi. 5, 33 ; 2 Kgs. xxiii. 13. Paul's ship touched at Sidon, Acts xxvii. 3.

Zī-dō′nī-anṣ. Dwellers in Zidon, Judg. x. 12.

Zĭf (*bloom*). Second month of Hebrew sacred and eighth of the civil year, corresponding to parts of April and May, 1 Kgs. vi. 1.

Zī′hà (*dried*). (1) His children returned from captivity, Ez. ii. 43 ; Neh. vii. 46. (2) A ruler of the Nethinims in Ophel, Neh. xi. 21.

Zĭk′lăg (*flowing, winding*). A city in southern Judah, Josh. xv. 31, afterwards assigned to Simeon, Josh. xix. 5. It became of great historic importance as the rendezvous of David when outlawed by Saul, and was then, or had just been, in the hands of the Philistines, 1 Sam. xxx. 1, 14, 26 ; 2 Sam. i. 1 ; iv. 10 ; 1 Chr. iv. 30 ; xii. 1–20.

Zĭl′lah (*shadow*). One of the wives of Lamech and mother of Tubal-cain, Gen. iv. 19, 22, 23.

Zĭl′pah (*dropping*). A Syrian woman who became Jacob's concubine and the mother of Gad and Asher, Gen. xxix. 24 ; xxx. 9–13 ; xxxv. 26 ; xxxvii. 2 ; xlvi. 18.

Zĭl′thāi (*shadow*). (1) A Benjamite of the sons of Shimhi, 1 Chr. viii. 20. (2) A Manassite captain who deserted to David at Ziklag, 1 Chr. xii. 20.

Zĭm′mah (*wickedness*). (1) A Gershonite Levite, son of Jahath, 1 Chr. vi. 20. (2) Another Gershonite Levite, 1 Chr. vi. 42. (3) A Levite and father of Joah, 2 Chr. xxix. 12.

Zĭm′răn (*sung*). A son of Abraham by Keturah, Gen. xxv. 2 ; 1 Chr. i. 32.

Zĭm′rī (*sung*). (1) Son of Salu, a prince of Simeon slain by Phinehas, Num. xxv. 6–15. (2) Captain of half the chariots under Elah king of Israel. He smote his master in Tirsah, and reigned in his stead for a period of seven days, B. C. 929, 1 Kgs. xvi.

8-18. (3) A son of Zerah, of Judah, 1 Chr. ii. 6. Zabdi in Josh. vii. 1, 17, 18. (4) Son of Jehoadah and a descendant of Saul, 1 Chr. viii. 36; ix. 42. (5) An obscure name mentioned in Jer. xxv. 25.

Zĭn (*shrub*). That part of the Arabian wilderness or desert lying south of Palestine, adjacent to Judah, and bounded on the east by the Dead Sea and valley of Arabah; Num. xiii. 21, 26; xx. 1; xxvii. 14; xxxiii. 36; xxxiv. 3; Josh. xv. 1-3.

Zĭ′na (*fruitful*). The second son of Shimei the Gershonite, 1 Chr. xxiii. 10. Zizah in vs. 11.

Zĭ′ŏn (*mount, sunny*). Zion or Sion in its literal and restricted sense was the celebrated mount in Jerusalem, the highest and southernmost or southwesternmost of the city. It was the original hill of the Jebusites, Josh. xv. 63. After David became king, he captured it, "the stronghold of Zion," from the Jebusites, dwelt in the fort there, and greatly enlarged and strengthened its fortifications, calling it "the city of David," 2 Sam. v. 6-9; 1 Chr. xi. 5-8. Despite David's prestige the name of Zion still clung to it, 1 Kgs. viii. 1; 2 Kgs. xix. 21, 31; 2 Chr. v. 2. The O. T. poets and prophets exalted the word Zion by frequent use and gave it a sacred turn, so that in time it came to type a sacred capital, Ps. ii. 6; holy place, Ps. lxxxvii. 2; cxlix. 2; Isa. xxx. 19; God's chosen people, Ps. li. 18; lxxxvii. 5; the Christian church, Heb. xii. 22; the heavenly city, Rev. xiv. 1.

Zĭ′or (*little*). A town in the mountains of Judah, Josh. xv. 54.

Zĭph (*that flows*). (1) An unidentified place in South Judah, Josh. xv. 24. (2) A town in the mountains of Judah, Josh. xv. 55. It was in the wilderness, or wastes, of Ziph that David hid himself when pursued by Saul, 1 Sam. xxiii. 14, 15, 24; xxvi. 2. (3) Son of Jehaleleel, of Judah, 1 Chr. iv. 16.

Zĭ′phah. A brother of the above, 1 Chr. iv. 16.

Zĭph′ĭms. Dwellers in Ziph, Ps. liv. title.

Zĭph′ītes. Dwellers in Ziph, 1 Sam. xxiii. 19.

Zĭph′ĭ-on, Gen. xlvi. 16. [ZEPHON.]

Zĭph′rŏn (*perfume*). A northern boundary of the promised land, Num. xxxiv. 9.

Zĭp′por (*little bird*). Father of Balak, king of Moab, Num. xxii. 2, 4, 10, 16; xxiii. 18.

Zĭp-pō′rah. A daughter of Reuel or Jethro, whom Moses married, Ex. ii. 16-22; iv. 25; xviii. 2-4.

Zĭth′rī (*protected*). A Kohathite Levite, son of Uzziel, Ex. vi. 22.

Zĭz (*cliff*). The cliff or pass of Ziz was that by which the Moabites and Ammonites came up from the shores of the Dead Sea to give battle to King Jehoshaphat's forces, 2 Chr. xx. 16.

Zĭ′za (*plenty*). (1) A son of Shiphi and a prince of Simeon in the reign of Hezekiah, 1 Chr. iv. 37. (2) A son of King Rehoboam, 2 Chr. xi. 20.

Zĭ′zah (*plenty*), 1 Chr. xxiii. 11. [ZINA.]

Zō′an (*departure*). An ancient city of Lower Egypt, the Tanis of the Greeks and the San of modern times. It occupied a highly strategic position on the east side of the Tanitic branch of the Nile, and was built seven years before the very ancient city of Hebron, Num. xiii. 22. Isaiah mentions the "princes of Zoan," Isa. xix. 11-13; xxx. 4, and Ezekiel foretells its fate by fire, Ezek. xxx. 14.

Zō′ar (*little*). One of the most ancient cities of Canaan, mentioned as in the "plain of Jordan" and in connection with Sodom and Gomorrah, Gen. xiii. 10. It was originally called Bela, Gen. xiv. 2, 8. It was spared from the fiery destruction which came upon Sodom and the other cities of the plain, Gen. xix. 20-23. Isaiah and Jeremiah speak of Zoar as in the land of Moab, Isa. xv. 5; Jer. xlviii. 34.

Zō′ba, Zō′bah (*encampment*). That portion of Syria which formed a separate empire in the time of Saul, David, and Solomon. It lay to the northeast of Palestine and probably extended to the Euphrates. Though ruled by petty kings at first, it became united and strong and engaged in frequent wars with Israel, 1 Sam. xiv. 47; 2 Sam. viii. 3-8; x. 6-19; 1 Chr. xviii. 3-8; xix. 6. Hamath became the capital of Zobah, and it was captured by Solomon, 2 Chr. viii. 3.

Zō-bē′bah (*slothful*). A Judahite, 1 Chr. iv. 8.

Zō′har (*white*). (1) Father of Ephron, from whom Abraham bought the field of Machpelah, Gen. xxiii. 8; xxv. 9. (2) A son of Simeon, Gen. xlvi. 10; Ex. vi. 15. Zerah in 1 Chr. iv. 24.

Zō′he-lĕth (*serpent*). A stone or rock by En-rogel, where Adonijah slew "sheep, oxen, and fat cattle," 1 Kgs. i. 9.

Zō′heth. A Judahite, 1 Chr. iv. 20.

Zō′phah (*viol*). An Asherite, 1 Chr. vii. 35, 36.

Zō′phāi (*honeycomb*). A Kohathite Levite, 1 Chr. vi. 26. Written Zuph in vs. 35.

Zō′phar (*little bird*). A Naamathite, and one of the three friends of Job, Job ii. 11.

Zō′phim (*watchmen*). The field on the top of Pisgah to which Balak conducted Balaam for sacrifices, Num. xxiii. 14.

Zō′rah (*hornet*). A town in the lowlands of Judah, afterwards assigned to Dan, Josh. xix. 41. Written Zoreah in Josh. xv. 33, and Zareah in Neh. xi. 29. Residence of Manoah and burial place of his son Samson, Judg. xiii. 2, 24, 25; xvi. 31.

Zō′rath-ites. Inhabitants of Zorah; but the designation seems to be limited to the family of Judah descended from Shobal, 1 Chr. iv. 2.

Zō′re-ah, Josh. xv. 33. [ZORAH.]

Zō′rites. Descendants of Salma of Judah, and probably dwellers in Zorah, 1 Chr. ii. 54.

Zŏ-rŏb′a-bĕl. Greek form of Zerubbabel, which *see*, Matt. i. 12, 13; Luke iii. 27.

Zū′ar (*little*). Father of Nethaneel, chief of Issachar, Num. i. 8; ii. 5; vii. 18, 23; x. 15.

Zŭph (*honeycomb*). (1) The land reached by Saul while in search of his father's asses, 1 Sam. ix. 5. It was there he met Samuel the prophet, 1 Sam. ix. 6-15. (2) A Kohathite Levite, and ancestor of Elkanah and Samuel, 1 Sam. i. 1; 1 Chr. vi. 35. Called Zophai in 1 Chr. vi. 26.

Zûr (*rock*). (1) A Midianite king slain by the Israelites, Num. xxv. 15; xxxi. 8. (2) Son of Jehiel, founder of Gibeon, 1 Chr. viii. 30; ix. 36.

Zū′rĭ-el. (*God my rock*). Son of Abihail, and a chief of the Merarite Levites, Num. iii. 35.

Zū′rĭ-shăd′da-ī (*the Almighty my rock*). Father of Shelumiel, chief of the tribe of Simeon at the exodus, Num. i. 6; ii. 12; vii. 36; x. 19.

Zū′zims. An Ammonite name for one of the races of giants, Gen. xiv. 5.

RHYMING
DICTIONARY

RHYMING DICTIONARY

OF ONE AND TWO SYLLABLE RHYMES

PRONUNCIATION GUIDE

a *as in* at		ēe *as in* sēen	o *as in* rod ·	ōō *as in* tōō	ū *as in* ūnit
ā *as in* gāte	ay *as in* bay	ew *as in* new	ō *as in* ōld	ou *as in* out	û *as in* ûrn
à *as in* àkin	e *as in* end		ö *as in* wön	ow *as in* owl	
â *as in* fâre	ē *as in* hē	i *as in* ill	ô *as in* fôr	oy *as in* boy	
ä *as in* cär	è *as in* dèfy ·	ī *as in* īce	oi *as in* oil		y *as in* try
ă *as in* ăll	ê *as in* hêr	î *as in* sîr	oo *as in* good		ẏ *as in* mẏth
				u *as in* pup	

-ä, -äh: ah, baa, bah, blah, bra, fa, ha, la, ma, pa, shah, spa; faux pas, hurrah, mama, papa; algebra, cha cha cha, cinema, fistula. (And many other false rhymes ending in "à" such as "America".)

-ab: bab, blab, cab, crab, dab, drab, gab, grab, jab, Mab, nab, scab, slab, stab, tab; bedab, confab, Punjab; taxicab. (For rhymes to "swab," see -ob.)

-ābe: Abe, babe, wabe; outgrabe (Lewis Carroll); astrolabe.

-ac, -ack: bac, back, black, cack, clack, claque, crack, hack, jack, Jack, knack, lac, lack, "mack", Mac, pack, plaque, quack, rack, sac, sack, sacque, shack, slack, smack, snack, stack, tack, thwack, track, whack, wrack, yak; aback, alack, attack, bivouac, bootblack, cognac, drawback, gimcrack, haystack, horseback, knapsack, ransack, shellac; almanac, Appotomac, bric-a-brac, cardiac, haversack, maniac, Sarawak, stickleback, zodiac; demoniac; hypochondriac, sacroiliac.

-āce, -āse: ace, base, bass, brace, case, chase, dace, face, grace, Grace, lace, mace, pace, place, plaice, race, space, Thrace, trace, vase; abase, apace, bullace, debase, deface, disgrace, displace, efface, embrace, encase, grimace, horse-race, misplace, outface, replace, retrace, staircase, transplace, uncase, unlace; commonplace, interlace, interspace, market-place, populace, steeplechase.

-ach, -atch: batch, catch, hatch, latch, match, patch, ratch, scratch, slatch, snatch, thatch; attach, detach, dispatch, unlatch; unattach. (For rhymes to "watch", see -otch.)

-act: act, bract, fact, pact, tact, tract; abstract, attract, co-act, compact, contact, contract, detract, distract, enact, epact, exact, extract, impact, infract, intact, protract, react, redact, refract, retract, subtract, transact; cataract, counteract, overact, re-enact, retroact; matter-of-fact. (Extend -ack for "blacked" and other preterites.)

-ad: ad, add, bad, brad, cad, chad, clad, dad, fad, gad, glad, had, lad, mad, pad, plaid, sad, scad, shad, tad; Bagdad, bedad, begad, footpad, monad, nomad; ironclad, olympiad, Stalingrad. (For rhymes to "wad," see -od.)

-āde, -āid: aid, bade, blade, braid, cade, fade, glade, grade, jade, lade, laid, maid, neighed, paid, plaid, raid, shade, skaid, Slade, sleighed, spade, stade, staid, suède, they'd, trade, wade, weighed; abrade, afraid, arcade, Belgrade, blockade, brigade, brocade, cascade, charade, cockade, crusade, decade, degrade, dissuade, evade, grenade, home-made, housemaid, invade, limeade, mermaid, nightshade, okayed, orangeade, parade, persuade, pervade, prepaid, stockade, unlade, unlaid, unmade, unpaid, upbraid, waylaid; accolade, ambuscade, balustrade, barricade, cannonade, cavalcade, citigrade, colonnade, custom-made, enfilade, escalade, esplanade, gasconade, lemonade, marmalade, masquerade, orangeade, overlade, overlaid, palisade, pasquinade, plantigrade, promenade, renegade, retrograde, serenade, underlaid, underpaid. (Also see "flayed", "grayed", and many other preterites of verbs ending in **-ay** and **-ey**.)

-āfe: chafe, Rafe, safe, strafe, waif; unsafe.

-adge: badge, cadge, fadge, Madge.

-adze: adze. (See plurals of words in **-ad**.)

-aff: calf, chaff, gaff, graph, half, quaff, staff, Taff; behalf, carafe, distaff, giraffe, Llandaff, riff-raff, seraph; autograph, cenotaph, epitaph, paragraph, phonograph, photograph, telegraph; cinematograph.

-aft: aft, chaffed, craft, daft, draft, draught, graft, haft, Kraft, laughed, quaffed, raft, shaft, staffed, "straffed", Taft, waft; abaft, aircraft; handicraft. (Also preterites of **-aff** words.)

-ag: bag, brag, crag, dag, drag, fag, flag, gag, hag, jag, knag, lag, nag, quag, rag, sag, scrag, shag, slag, snag, stag, swag, tag, wag; dishrag, grabbag, sandbag, zigzag.

-āge: age, cage, Drage, gage, gauge, page, rage, sage, stage, swage, wage; assuage, engage, enrage, greengage, outrage, presage; disengage, overage. (And nearly 100 false rhymes in words ending in **-àge** in which the final syllable is not accentuated, such as "sausage", "advantage".)

-àge: see **-idge**.

-āgue: Hague, plague, Prague, vague.

-āid: See **-āde**.

-āil, -āle: ail, ale, bail, bale, brail, Braille, dale, fail, flail, frail, gale, Gail, Grail, hail, hale, jail, kail, kale, mail, male, nail, pail, pale, quail, rail, sail, sale, scale, shale, snail, stale, swale, tail, tale, they'll, trail, vale, veil, wale, whale, wail, Yale; assail, avail, bewail, blackmail, bobtail, cocktail, curtail, detail, dovetail, entail, exhale, female, hobnail, impale, inhale, prevail, regale, retail, travail, unveil, wagtail, wassail, wholesale; Abigail, countervail, farthingale, nightingale.

-āim, -āme: aim, blame, came, claim, dame, fame, flame, frame, game, lame, maim, name, same, shame, tame; acclaim, aflame, became, declaim, defame, disclaim, exclaim, inflame, misname, nickname, proclaim, reclaim, surname; overcame.

-āin, -āne: ain (Scotch), bane, blain, brain, Cain, cane, chain, crane, Dane, deign, drain, fain, fane, feign, gain, grain, Jane, lain, lane, main, Maine, mane, pain, pane, plain, plane, rain, reign, sane, Seine, skein, slain, Spain, sprain, stain, strain, swain, thane, thegn, train, twain, vain. vane, vein, wain, wane, zane; abstain, again, airplane, amain, arraign, attain, biplane, campaign, Champagne, chicane, chilblain, chow mein, cocaine, complain, constrain, contain, detain, disdain, distrain, domain, Duquesne, Elaine, enchain, engrain, entrain, explain, germane, henbane, humane, inane, insane, Louvain, maintain, membrane, misfeign, moraine, murrain, obtain, ordain, pearmain, pertain, plantain, profane, ptomaine, refrain, regain, remain, restrain, retain, sustain, terrain, urbane; appertain, Chamberlain, entertain, hurricane, monoplane, porcelain, scatterbrain, windowpane; legerdemain.

-āint: ain't, faint, feint, mayn't, paint, plaint, quaint, saint, taint; acquaint, attaint, complaint, constraint, depaint, distraint, restraint.

-āir, -āre: air, ayr, bare, bear, blare, care, chair, Claire, Clare, dare, e'er, ere, fair, fare, flair, flare, gare, glare, hair, hare, heir, Herr, lair, mare, mayor, pair, pare, pear, prayer, rare, snare, spare, square, stair, stare, swear, tare, tear, their, there, they're, ware, wear, where; affair, armchair, aware, beware, co-heir, compare, corsair, declare, despair, eclair, elsewhere, ensnare, fanfare, forbear, forswear, howe'er, impair, mohair, nightmare, Mayfair, outstare, prepare, repair, unfair, welfare, whate'er, whene'er, where'er; anywhere, commissionaire, concessionaire, debonair, Delaware, doctrinaire, everywhere, millionaire, solitaire, unaware.

-āise, -āys, -āise, -āze: baize, blaze, braise, braze, chaise, craze, daze, faze, gaze, glaze, graze, haze, laze, maize, maze, naze, phase, phrase, praise, raise, raze, traits, yeas; ablaze, adaze, amaze, appraise, dispraise; chrysoprase, Marseillaise, mayonnaise, nowadays, outgaze, paraphrase, polonaise, selfpraise, upgaze, upraise. (Plurals of **-ay**, **-ey**.)

-āit, -āte, -eight: ait, ate, bait, bate, crate, date, eight, fate, fete, frate, freight, gait, gate, grate, great, hate, Kate, late, mate, Nate, pate, plait, plate, prate, rate, sate, skate, slate, spate, state, straight, strait, Tait, trait, wait, weight; abate, aerate, agnate, alate, await, baccate, berate, bookplate, bromate, casemate, castrate, caudate, cerate, checkmate, chelate, collate, cordate, costate, create, cremate, curate, curvate, debate, dilate, donate, elate, equate, estate, falcate, filtrate, frustrate, furcate, gemmate, globate, gradate, gyrate, helpmate, hydrate, inflate, ingrate, inmate, innate, irate, ligate, locate, mandate, migrate, narrate, oblate, orate, ornate, placate, prostrate, sedate, translate, vacate; abdicate, abrogate, acerbate, advocate (verb), aggravate, aggregate, agitate, allocate, amputate, animate, annotate, antedate, antiquate, appellate, arbitrate, arrogate, aspirate, bifurcate, cachinate, calculate, cancellate, candidate, captivate, carbonate, castigate, catenate, celebrate, circulate, cogitate, colligate, compensate, complicate, concentrate, confiscate, conformate, congregate, conjugate, consecrate, constipate, consulate, contemplate, correlate, corrugate, coruscate, crenellate, cultivate, cumulate, cyanate, decimate, decollate, decorate, dedicate, dehydrate, delegate, delicate, demarcate, demonstrate, derogate, desperate, detonate, devastate, dislocate, dissipate, dominate, duplicate, educate, elevate, elongate, emanate, emigrate, emulate, enervate, estimate, excavate, exculpate, extricate, fabricate, fascinate, federate, floriate, formulate, fornicate, generate, germinate, glaciate, gladiate, glomerate, graduate, granulate, gravitate, hesitate, hibernate, imprecate, impregnate, incubate, indicate, indurate, infiltrate, innovate, inoculate, insolate, instigate, insufflate, insulate, integrate, intimate, intonate, intricate, inundate, irrigate, irritate, isolate, iterate, jubilate, lacerate, laminate, laureate, legislate, liquidate, litigate, lubricate, macerate, machinate, magistrate, mediate, medicate, meditate, militate, mitigate, moderate, modulate, mutilate, nauseate, navigate, nominate, nucleate, oscillate, oscitate, osculate, overrate, overstate, penetrate, percolate, perforate, permeate, personate, pollinate, postulate, potentate, predicate, principate, profligate, promulgate, propagate, radiate, radicate, recreate, regulate, relegate, remonstrate, renovate, reprobate, resonate, ruminate, rusticate, satiate, saturate, scintillate, segregate, selenate, separate, simulate, spiflicate, stipulate, subjugate, sublimate, suffocate, sulfurate, syndicate, tabulate, terminate, tete-a-tete, titivate, tolerate, triplicate, triturate, ultimate, umbellate, underrate, understate, underweight, vaccinate, validate, venerate, ventilate, vindicate; abominate, accelerate, accentuate, accommodate, accumulate, acidulate, adulterate, affiliate, agglutinate, alleviate, anticipate, articulate, assassinate, capacitate, coagulate, commemorate, commensurate, commiserate, communicate, compassionate, conciliate, congratulate, consolidate, contaminate, co-operate, coordinate, corroborate, debilitate, deliberate, denominate, depopulate, depreciate, dilapidate, discriminate, ejaculate, elaborate, electorate, eliminate, elucidate, emaciate, equivocate, eradicate, evacuate, expectorate, expostulate, exterminate, facilitate, felicitate, gesticulate, illuminate, immaculate, initiate, inoculate, intimidate, intoxicate, invalidate, investigate, manipulate, matriculate, necessitate, negotiate, participate, precipitate precogitate, preconsulate, predistinate, predominate, premeditate, prevaricate, procrastinate, prognosticate, proliferate, reciprocate, recriminate, recuperate, redecorate, reduplicate, reiterate, reverberate, subordinate, substantiate, syllabicate, transliterate, triumverate, variegate, differentiate, misappropriate, proletariate, rehabilitate, reinvigorate, transsubstantiate. (And many other false rhymes in words ending in **-ăte** such as "adequate".)

-āith: faith, Snaith, wraith; misfaith.

-âird: Baird, braird, Caird, laird. (Also preterites of **-âir, -āre** words.)

-āke: ache, bake, Blake, brake, break, cake, crake, drake, fake, flake, hake, Jake, lake, make, quake, rake, sake, shake, slake, snake, spake, stake, steak, strake, take, wake; awake, backache, bespake, betake, corn crake, forsake, earache, earthquake, heartache, keepsake, mandrake, mistake, namesake, opaque, outbreak, partake, snowflake, sweepstake, toothache, upbreak, uptake; bellyache, johnnycake, overtake, pattycake, rattlesnake, undertake.

-al: Al, chal (Romany), Hal, mal, pal, Sal, shall; banal, cabal, canal, corral, locale, morale, Natal, timbale; musicale; Guadalcanal. (And more than 100 false rhymes in words ending in **-àl** in which the final syllable is not accented, such as "animal".)

-äl: Transvaal. (See **-ärl.**)

-alc: talc; catafalque.

-ăld: bald, scald; Archibald, piebald, so-called. (See preterites of verbs ending in **-ăll, -ăul,** and **-ăwl.**)

-āle: See **-āil.**

-alf: See **-aff.**

-ălk, -ăuk, ăwk: auk, balk, calk, caulk, chalk, gawk, hawk, squawk, stalk, talk, walk; catwalk, Dundalk, Mohawk, tomahawk. (See **-ôrk.**)

-älm: alm, balm, calm, Guam, palm, psalm, qualm, becalm, embalm, madame, salaam.

-ăll, -ăul, -ăwl: all, awl, ball, brawl, call, caul, crawl, drawl, fall, gall, Gaul, hall, haul, mall, maul, pall, Paul, pawl, Saul, scrawl, shawl, small, sprawl, squall, stall, tall, thrall, trawl, wall, yawl; appall, befall, Bengal, baseball, catcall, enthrall, football, footfall, install, Nepal, rainfall, snowfall, Whitehall, windfall; basketball, overhaul, waterfall; wherewithal.

-alp: alp, Alp, palp, scalp.

-ält, -ăult: fault, halt, malt, salt, smalt, vault; asphalt, assault, basalt, cobalt, default, exalt; somersault.

-alve (silent L): calve, halve, have, salve. (See **-ärve.**)

-alve (L sounded): salve, valve; bivalve.

-am: am, Cam, Cham, clam, cram, dam, damn, drachm, dram, flam, gam, gram, ham, jam, jamb, lam, lamb, mam, pam, pram, ram, Sam, scram, sham, slam, swam, tram, wham, yam; Assam, flimflam, madame, Siam. (And many false rhymes including bantam, bedlam, cryptogram.)

-āme: See **-āim.**

-amp: amp, camp, champ, clamp, cramp, damp, gamp, lamp, ramp, samp, scamp, stamp, tamp, tramp, vamp; decamp, encamp, enstamp, firedamp, revamp; safety-lamp, signal lamp. (For rhymes to "swamp", see **-omp.**)

-an: an, Ann, Anne, ban, bran, can, clan, Dan, fan, flan, Fran, Jan, khan, man, Nan, pan, Pan, plan, ran, scan, span, tan, than, van; Afghan, began, corban, divan, fireman, foreran, inspan, Iran, Koran, merman, Milan, outran, outspan, pavan, pecan, rattan, redan, Sedan, trepan, unman; artisan, barbican, barracan, caravan, Castellan, charlatan, clergyman, countryman, courtesan, fisherman, fugleman, Indian, juryman, Mexican, Michigan, midshipman, nobleman, Ottoman, overran, pelican, puritan, superman, Thespian, talisman. (And about 100 false rhymes in words in which the final syllable is not accentuated, such as "African".) For rhymes to "swan," see **-on.**

-ance, -anse: chance, dance, France, glance, lance, manse, prance, stance, trance; advance, askance, bechance, enhance, entrance, expanse, finance, mischance, perchance, puissance, romance, seance; circumstance; extravagance. (And about 30 false rhymes in words ending in **-ance** in which the final syllable is not accentuated, such as "ambulance", "vigilance", etc.)

-anch: blanch, Blanche, branch, flanch, ganch, ranch, scranch, stanch; carteblanche; avalanche.

-anct: sacrosanct. (Extend **-ank + ed** as in spanked, cranked.)

-and: and, band, bland, brand, gland, grand, hand, land, manned, rand, Rand, sand, stand, Strand, strand; command, demand, disband, expand, imband, remand, unhand, unland, withstand; contraband, countermand, fairy-land, fatherland, firebrand, hinterland, Holy Land, overland, reprimand, Rio Grande, saraband, Sunderland, understand, upper-hand, wonderland. (And preterites of verbs ending in **-an.** For rhymes to "wand", see **-ond.**)

-āne: See **-āin.**

-ang: bang, bhang, clang, fang, gang, gangue, hang, Lang, pang, rang, sang, slang, spang, sprang, stang, swang, tang, twang, whang, yang; harangue, meringue, mustang, orang-outang, Penang, serang, shebang, trepang, uphang; boomerang, overhang.

-ānge: change, grange, mange, range, strange; arrange, derange, enrange, estrange, exchange; disarrange, interchange, rearrange.

-ank: bank, blank, brank, chank, clank, crank, dank, drank, flank, franc, frank, Frank, hank, lank, plank, prank, rank, sank, shank, shrank, slank, spank, stank, swank, tank, thank, twank, yank, Yank; embank, enrank, disrank, mountebank, outflank, outrank, point-blank; savings-bank.

-ant: ant, aunt, bant, brant, can't, cant, chant, grant, Grant, Kant, pant, plant, rant, scant, shan't, slant; aslant, decant, descant, displant, enchant, extant, gallant, implant, Levant, recant, supplant, transplant; adamant, commandant, disenchant, gallivant, heirophant. (And about 50 false rhymes by wrongly accentuating the final syllable of such words as "arrogant", etc. For rhymes to "want", see ônt.)

-anx: francs, Lancs, Manx. (And pluralize words ending in **-ank**.)

-ap: cap, chap, clap, dap, flap, frap, gap, hap, Jap, knap, lap, map, nap, pap, rap, sap, scrap, slap, snap, strap, tap, trap, wrap, yap; bestrap, claptrap, entrap, enwrap, kidnap, madcap, mayhap, mishap, nightcap, unwrap; afterclap, handicap, overlap, rattletrap, thunderclap.

-āpe: ape, cape, Cape, chape, crape, dape, drape, gape, grape, jape, nape, rape, scrape, shape, tape, trape; agape, escape, landscape, red-tape, seascape, ship-shape, transshape, uncape, unshape.

-āpes: traipse, jackanapes. (And add "s" to the above.)

-aph: See **-aff.**

-apse: apse, craps, lapse, schnapps; collapse, elapse, illapse, perhaps, relapse; interlapse, after-claps. (And add "s" to words under **-ap**.)

-aque: See **-ack.**

-är: Aar, are, bar, car, char, czar, dar, far, jar, knar, Loire, mar, par, parr, Saar, scar, spar, star, tar, tsar; afar, ajar, bazaar, bizarre, catarrh, cigar, cymar,

daystar, debar, disbar, embar, feldspar, guitar, horsecar, hussar, instar, jaguar, Lascar, Navarre, pourboire, unbar, upbar; Calabar, calendar, cinnabar, circular, consular, globular, insular, Malabar, modular, ocular, registrar, regular, scapular, secular, seminar, similar, tabular, vinegar, Zanzibar.

-ärb: barb, garb, yarb; rhubarb.

-ärce, -ärse: carse, farce, parse, sparse. (For rhymes to "parse", pluralize some words in **-är**.)

-ärch: arch, larch, march, March, parch, starch; outmarch; countermarch, overarch, overmarch.

-ärd: bard, card, chard, guard, hard, lard, nard, pard, sard, shard, yard; Bernard, bombard, canard, closebarred, discard, enguard, foulard, Girard, life-guard, petard, placard, regard, retard, unguard, unmarred; afterguard, avant-garde, bodyguard, boulevard, disregard, interlard, leotard, poultry-yard. (Extend **-är** for "barred" and other preterites. For rhymes to "ward", see **-ôard.**)

-āre (as in "rare"): See **-air.**

-ärf: corf, dwarf, wharf; endomorph, mesomorph.

-ärge: barge, charge, Farge, large, marge, sparge, targe; discharge, enlarge, litharge, surcharge, uncharge; overcharge, supercharge, undercharge.

-ärk: arc, ark, bark, barque, cark, clerk, dark, hark, knark, lark, marc, mark, Mark, marque, nark, park, Sark, shark, "Snark", spark, stark, Starke; aardvark, bedark, debark, dispark, embark, hierarch, landmark, remark, tanbark; disembark, hierarch, matriarch, oligarch, patriarch.

-ärl, -äal: Basle, carl, Carl, gnarl, marl, snarl; ensnarl, imparl; Albemarle.

-ärm: arm, barm, charm, farm, harm, marm, smarm; alarm, disarm, forearm, gendarme, schoolmarm, unarm. (For rhymes to "warm", see ôrm.)

-ärn: barn, darn, "garn", Larne, Marne, tarn, yarn; incarn. (For rhymes to "warn", see -ôrn.)

-ärp: carp, harp, scarp, sharp, Zarp; counterscarp, epicarp, monocarp, pericarp.

-ärse: farce, parse, sparse. (And add "s" to

words in **-är**.)

-ärsh: harsh, marsh.

-ärt: art, bart, cart, chart, dart, hart, heart, mart, part, smart, start, tart; apart, depart, dispart, impart, rampart, sweetheart, upstart; counterpart.

-art: See **-ort**.

-ärve: carve, larve, starve. (See **-alve**.)

-as, -azz: as, has, jazz, "razz"; LaPaz.

-āse: See **-āce**.

-ash: ash, bash, brash, cache, cash, clash, crash, dash, fash (Scotch), flash, gash, gnash, hash, lache, lash, mash, Nash, pash, plash, rash, sash, slash, smash, splash, tache, thrash, trash; abash, calash, moustache, panache, Wabash; balderdash, calabash, sabretache, succotash.

-äsh: quash, squash, wash; goulash, musquash; mackintosh, mishmash. (And slang words as follows: Boche, bosh, cosh, gosh, josh, posh, slosh, splosh, tosh.)

-ask: ask, bask, Basque, cask, casque, flask, mask, task; bemask, unmask, overtask, water-cask.

-asm: chasm, plasm, spasm; miasm, orgasm, phantasm, sarcasm; cataplasm, pleonasm, protoplasm; enthusiasm, iconoclasm.

-asp: asp, clasp, gasp, grasp, hasp, rasp; enclasp, engrasp, unclasp.

-ass: ass, bass, brass, class, crass, gas, glass, grass, lass, mass, pass; alas, amass, crevasse, cuirasse, culrass, harass, impass, Madras, morass, paillasse, repass, surpass; unclass; coup-de-grace, demitasse, hippocras, looking glass, sassafras, underpass.

-ast: bast, blast, cast, caste, fast, gassed, hast, last, massed, mast, past, vast; aghast, avast, bombast, contrast, cuitassed, downcast, forecast, handfast, outcast, peltast, repast, steadfast, unfast; elegiast, metaplast, paraphrast; ecclesiast, enthusiast, flabbergast, iconoclast. (And preterites of **-ass** words.)

-āste: baste, chaste, haste, paste, taste, waist, waste; distaste, foretaste, impaste, lambaste, unchaste; aftertaste. (And preterites of many **-āce** and **-āse** words.)

-at: at, bat, brat, cat, chat, drat, fat, flat, "gat", gnat, hat, Jat, mat, Matt, Nat, pat, Pat, plait, plat, Platte, rat, sat, scat, slat, spat, sprat, tat, that, vat; combat, cravat, hellcat, Herat, loquat, polecat, whereat, wombat; acrobat, autocrat, automat, democrat, diplomat, habitat, hemostat, photostat, plutocrat, thermostat, tit for tat; aristocrat, Montserrat.

-āte: See **-āit**.

-atch: See **-ach**.
-ath: bath, Bath, Gath, hath, lath, math, path, "rath" (Carroll), scath, wrath; bypath; aftermath, allopath, philomath, psychopath; homeopath, osteopath, physiopath.

-āthe: bathe, lathe, scathe, snathe, spathe, swathe; unswathe.

-ăub, -ôrb: daub, orb, Taube; adsorb.

-ăud: bawd, broad, Claude, fraud, gaud, laud, Maud; abroad, applaud, belaud, defraud, maraud. (And many preterites of verbs on **-aw**, as "clawed". See **-ôard** and **-ôrde**.)

-augh: See **-aff**.

-ăught, -ôught: aught, bought, brought, caught, fought, fraught, naught, nought, ought, sought, taught, taut, thought, wrought; besought, bethought, Connaught, distraught, dreadnought, forethought, methought, onslaught; aeronaut, afterthought, Argonaut, astronaut, juggernaut, overwrought. (See **-ôrt**.)

-ăuk, ăulk, -awk: See **-alk**.

-ăun: See **-ăwn**.

-ăunch: craunch, haunch, launch, paunch, staunch.

-ăunt: aunt, chaunt, daunt, flaunt, gaunt, haunt, jaunt, taunt, vaunt, want; avaunt, romaunt.

-ăuse, -ăuze: awes, cause, clause, gauze, hawse, pause, tawse, yaws; applause, because, turquoise. (And add "s" to certain words in **-aw**.)

-ăv: have, Slav, sauve (compare **-alve**.)

-āve: brave, cave, crave, Dave, drave, frave, gave, Glaive, grave, knave, lave, nave, pave, rave, save, shave, slave, stave, suave, they've, trave, waive, wave; behave, concave, conclave, deprave, engrave, enslave, exclave, forgave, impave, margrave, misgave, outbrave, ungrave; misbehave.

-ăw: awe, caw, chaw, claw, craw, daw, draw,

faugh, flaw, gnaw, haw, jaw, law, maw, paw, pshaw, raw, saw, Shaw, squaw, straw, taw, thaw, yaw; cat's-paw, Choctaw, coleslaw, foresaw, guffaw, jackdaw, jigsaw, macaw, papaw, seesaw, southpaw, Warsaw, withdraw ; Arkansas, overawe, usquebaugh.

-ăwk: See **-ălk.**

-ăwl: See **-ăll.**

-ăwn: awn, bawn, brawn, dawn, drawn, faun, fawn, gone, lawn, pawn, prawn, sawn, Sean, spawn, yawn; indrawn. (See **-orn.**)

-ax: ax, claques, flax, lax, Max, pax, plaques, sax (for saxophone), tax, wax, zax; addax, Ajax, anthrax, borax, climax, relax, syntax, thorax; Analax, battle-ax, Halifax, parallax. (See **-ac** and **-ack** and add "s".)

-az: as, has, jazz, razz; whereas. (See **-as.**)

-āze: See **-āise.**

-āste: baste, chaste, haste, paste, taste, waist, waste; distaste, foretaste, impaste, lambaste, unchaste; aftertaste. (Also preterites of **-ace** and **-ase** words.)

-āy, -ey, -eigh: a, aye, bay, bey, brae, bray, Bray, clay, day, dray, drey, eh, fay, Fay, fey, flay, fray, gay, gray, greige, grey, hay, jay, Kay, lay, lah, Mae, may, May, nay, née, neigh, pay, play, pray, prey, ray, Ray, say, shay, slay, sleigh, spay, spray, stay, stray, sway, Tay, they, tray, trey, way, weigh, whey, yea; abbé, affray, agley, allay, array, assay, astray, away, belay, beret, betray, bewray, Bombay, bouquet, cabaret, café, Calais, Cathay, causeway, chambray, convey, coupé, croquet, curé, decay, defray, delay, dismay, display, doomsday, dragée, embay, endplay, essay, filet, foray, foyer, Friday, gainsay, gangway, hearsay, Herne Bay, heyday, hooray, horseplay, inlay, inveigh, Malay, Manet, melee, mid-day, mislay, Moray, Monday, Monet, nosegay, obey, okay, ole!, passé, per se, portray, prepay, purée, purvey, relay, repay, replay, risqué, Roget, roué, sachet, sashay, soirée, soufflé, subway, Sunday, survey, throughway, Thursday, today, tokay, touché, toupée, Tuesday, waylay, Wednesday ; appliqué, cabaret, canapé, castaway, Chevrolet, consommé, disarray, disobey, émigré, exposé, holiday, matinée, Monterey, negligée, popinjay, protégé, résumé, runaway, Santa Fe, Saturday,

sobriquet, stowaway, yesterday; Appian Way, cabriolet, communiqué, habitué. (And more than 30 false rhymes, such as "highway", "Monday", "popinlay", etc.)

-ē, -ēa, -ēe: be, bee, Cree, Dee, dree, fee, flea, flee, free, gee, ghee, glee, he, key, knee, lea, lee, Lee, Leigh, ley, li, me, "oui", pea, plea, quay, rhe, scree, sea, see, she, si, ski, snee, spree, Spree, tea, tee, thee, three, tree, we, wee, ye; agree, alee, bailee, banshee, bargee, bohea, bootie, coo-ee, debris, decree, degree, donee, drawee, Dundee, esprit, fäerie, fusee, grandee, grantee, jinnee, kildee, lessee, levee, M.D., McGee, mustee, "on dit", Parsee, payee, pledgee, pongee, pontee, raki, rani, rupee, settee, squeegee, suttee, tehee, Torquay, trustee, vendee, vouchee; absentee, addressee, advowee, allottee, alshantee, assignee, avowee, baloney, botany, bourgeoisie, bumblebee, calorie, cap-a-pie, Cherokee, chickadee, chimpanzee, consignee, coterie, debauchee, devotee, disagree, divorcee, dungaree, fricasee, Galilee, garnishee, guarantee, harmony, honey-bee, hyperbole, irony, jamboree, Japanee, jeu d'esprit, jubilee, legatee, licensee, Lombardy, manatee, mortgagee, nominee, Normandy, oversea, patentee, pedigree, Pharisee, pugaree, recipe, referee, refugee, releasee, remittee, repartee, Sadducee, scarabee, selvagee, simile, symphony, systole, third degree, tyranny, unforesee, vertebrae, warrantee, whiffletree; abalone, anemone, apostrophe, Antigone, Ariadne, calliope, catastrophe, facsimile, hyperbole, macarone, Penelope, synonymy.

-ēace, -ēase: cease, crease, creese, fleece, geese, grease, Greece, lease, Nice, niece, peace, piece; apiece, caprice, cerise, Clarice, decease, decrease, Felice, increase, Lucrece, Maurice, obese, police, release, surcease, Therese, valise; afterpiece, ambergris, battlepiece, cantatrice, frontispiece, mantelpiece, masterpiece.

-ēach: beach, beech, bleach, breach, breech, each, leech, peach, preach, reach, screech, speech, teach; beseech, impeach, outreach, unbreech, unpreach; overreach.

-ead: See **-ed.**

-ēad, -ēde, -ēed: bead, Bede, bleed, breed, cede, creed, deed, feed, freed, glebe, greed, heed, keyed, knead, lead, mead, Mede, meed, need, plead, read, reed, screed, seed, speed, steed, swede, Swede, teed, tweed, Tweed, weed; accede, agreed, concede, decreed, exceed, impede, indeed, knock-kneed, linseed, misdeed, mislead, precede, proceed, recede, refereed, secede, stampede, succeed; antecede, centipede, filigreed, Ganymede, guaranteed, intercede, millipede, overfeed, supersede; velocipede.

-eaf, -ef: chef, clef, deaf, Jeff; Khrushchev.

-ēaf: See -ēef.

-ēague, -igue: Greig, league, teague; colleague, enleague, fatigue, intrigue.

-ēak, -ēek, -ique: beak, bleak, cheek, chic, cleek, clique, creak, creek, eke, freak, Greek, leak, leek, meek, peak, peek, pique, reek, seek, sheik, shriek, Sikh, sleek, sneak, speak, squeak, streak, teak, tweak, weak, week, wreak; aleak, antique, apeak, bespeak, bezique, critique, forespeak, oblique, physique, relique, unique, unspeak, upseek; Chesapeake, Frederique, Martinique, Mozambique, Pathétique.

-ēal, -ēel: ceil, creel, deal, Deal, eel, feel, heal, heel, he'll, keel, Kiel, kneel, leal, meal, Neal, Neil, peal, peel, real, reel, seal, she'll, skeel, spiel, squeal, steal, steel, streel, sweal, teal, veal, weal, we'll, wheel, zeal; anele, anneal, appeal, Bastille, cartwheel, Castille, chenille, conceal, congeal, genteel, ideal, Lucille, misdeal, mobile, pastille, repeal, reveal, unreal; cochineal, commonweal, deshabille, mercantile; automobile.

-ēald, -iēld: field, shield, weald, wield, yield; afield, enshield; battlefield, Chesterfield. (And preterites of verbs in previous list.)

-ealm: elm, heim, realm, whelm; overwhelm,

-ealth: health, stealth, wealth; commonwealth.

-ēam, -ēem: beam, bream, Cheam, cream, deem, dream, fleam, gleam, ream, scheme, scream, seam, seem, steam, stream, team, teem, theme; abeam, beseem, blaspheme, centime, daydream, esteem, extreme, ice cream, moonbeam, redeem, regime, supreme, unseam, unteam; disesteem, self-esteem.

-eamt, -empt: dreamt, kempt, tempt; attempt, contempt, exempt, pre-empt, unkempt.

-ēan, -ēen: bean, been, clean, dean, Deane, e'en, Gene, glean, green, Jean, jean, keen, lean, lien, mean, mesne, mien, quean,

queen, scene, screen, seen, sheen, spleen, teen, wean, ween, yean; advene, atween, baleen, beguine, between, canteen, careen, chlorine, Christine, codeine, convene, cuisine, demean, demesne, Doreen, eighteen, Eileen, Eugene, fifteen, foreseen, fourteen, Kathleen, machine, MacLean, marine, nineteen, obscene, Pauline, poteen, praline, protein, quinine, ravine, routine, sardine, serene, shagreen, sixteen, sordine, spalpeen, subvene, terrene, tontine, tureen, umpteen, unclean, unseen, zebrine; Aberdeen, Abilene, aniline, Argentine, atabrine, bombazine, brigantine, contravene, crinoline, damascene, evergreen, Florentine, gabardine, Geraldine, gelatine, go-between, guillotine, indigene, intervene, Jacqueline, kerosene, magazine, mezzanine, Nazarene, nectarine, nicotine, overseen, quarantine, saccharine, seccotine, serpentine, seventeen, submarine, tambourine, tangerine, unforeseen, vaseline, velvetine, wolverine; aquamarine, elephantine, ultramarine.

-ēand, -iēnd: fiend. (And preterites of some verbs in previous list.)

-eant: See -ent.

-ēap, -ēep: cheap, cheep, chepe, clepe, creep, deep, heap, jeep, keep, leap, neap, peep, reap, seep, sheep, sleep, steep, sweep, threap, weep; asleep, beweep, overleap.

-ēar, -ēer, -ēir, -ēre, -iēr: beer, bier, blear, cere, cheer, clear, dear, deer, drear, ear, fear, fleer, gear, hear, Heer, here, jeer, lear, leer, meer, mere, mir, near, peer, pier, queer, rear, sear, seer, sere, shear, sheer, "skeer", smear, sneer, spear, sphere, steer, tear, tier, vere, veer, weir, year; adhere, appear, arrear, austere, besmear, career, cashier, Cashmere, cohere, compeer, emir, endear, fakir, frontier, inhere, insphere, madrier, rehear, reindeer, revere, severe, sincere, Tangier, uprear, veneer; atmosphere, auctioneer, bandoleer, bombardier, brigadier, buccaneer, carabineer, cannoneer, cavalier, chandelier, chanticleer, chevalier, chiffonier, commandeer, disappear, domineer, engineer, fusilier, gazetteer, gondolier, grenadier, halberdier, hemisphere, insincere, interfere, mountaineer, muleteer, musketeer, mutineer, overhear, overseer, pamphleteer, persevere, pioneer, privateer, profiteer, scrutineer, sonneteer, volunteer, Windemere.

-êarch, -êrch, -îrch, ûrch: birch, church, Kertch, lurch, perch, search, smirch; besmirch, research.

-eard (short), **-erd, -ird, -urd:** bird, curd, gird, heard, herd, Kurd, shirred, surd, third, word; absurd, blackbird, lovebird, songbird, ungird, unheard; hummingbird, ladybird, mockingbird, overheard; unsepulchred. (And preterites of many verbs in **-êr, îr,** and **ûr** words.)

-ēard (long), **-ēird:** beard, tiered, weird; afeard. (And more than 40 preterites of **-ear, -eer, -ere.**)

-êarl, îrl, -ûrl: Beryl, burl, churl, curl, earl, furl, girl, hurl, jurl, knurl, pearl, purl, skirl, swirl, twirl, whirl, whorl; uncurl, unfurl.

-êarled, îrled, -orld: world. (And preterites of verbs in previous list.)

-êarn, -êrn, -ûrn: Berne, burn, churn, earn, erne, fern, hern, kern, learn, querne, spurn, stern, tern, turn, urn, yearn; adjourn, astern, concern, discern, eterne, intern, Lucerne, return, sojourn, unlearn; overturn, taciturn, unconcern.

-êarse: See **-êrce.**

-eärt: See **-art.**

-êarth, -êrth, îrth: berth, birth, dearth, earth, firth, girth, mirth, Perth, worth; stillbirth, unearth.

-ēase (as in "lease"): See **-ēace.**

-ēase, -ēz, -ēeze, -ise: bise, breeze, cheese, ease, freeze, frieze, Guise, grease (verb), he's, lees, mise, pease, please, seize, she's, skis, sneeze, squeeze, tease, these, wheeze; appease, Bernice, Burmese, cerise, chemise, Chinese, disease, displease, Louise, Maltese, Thales, trapeze, valise; ABC's, Achilles, Androcles, antifreeze, Antilles, Balinese, Cantonese, Hercules, Japanese, Javanese, journalese, obsequies, overseas, Pekingese, Portuguese, Siamese, Tyrolese, Viennese. (And plurals of **-ē, -ēa, -ēe.**)

-ēast, -iēst: beast, east, feast, least, priest, yeast; artiste. (And preterites of **-ēace** and **-ēace** and **-ēase** (**-ēz**).)

-ēat, -ēet, -ēit, -ite: beat, beet, bleat, cheat, cleat, Crete, eat, feat, feet, fleet, greet, heat, meat, meet, mete, neat, peat, Pete, pleat, seat, sheet, skeet, sleet, street, suite, sweet, teat, treat, wheat; accrete, aesthete, afreet, athlete, compete, complete, conceit, concrete, deceit, defeat, delete, deplete, discreet, discrete, effete, elite, entreat, escheat, petite, receipt, repeat, replete, retreat, secrete; bittersweet, Easy Street, incomplete, indiscreet, obsolete, overeat, parakeet, sunny-sweet, winding-sheet. (For rhymes to "great", see **-āit.**)

-eath (eth): Beth, breath, death, saith, Seth; Macbeth; Elizabeth, twentieth.

-ēath: heath, Keith, Meath, 'neath, Neath, sheath, teeth, wreath; beneath, bequeath, Blackheath, Dalkeith, unsheathe; underneath.

-ēathe: breathe, seethe, sheathe, sneathe, teethe, wreathe; bequeathe, ensheath, enwreathe, inbreathe, unsheathe, upbreathe.

-ēave, -ēive, -ēve, -iēve: beeve, breve, cleave, deev, eave, eve, Eve, greave, grieve, heave, keeve, leave, lieve, peeve, reave, reeve, screeve, seave, sheave, sleave, sleeve, Steeve, Steve, thieve, vive, weave, we've; achieve, aggrieve, believe, bereave, conceive, deceive, perceive, receive, relieve, reprieve, retrieve, unreave, unreeve, unweave, upheave; Christmas-eve, disbelieve, interweave, misconceive.

-eaw: See **-ōw.**

-eb, -ebb: bleb, deb, ebb, Feb., neb, reb, web; sub-deb.

-eck: beck, check, cheque, Czech, deck, fleck, "heck", neck, peck, reck, sec, speck, tech, trek, wreck; bedeck, bewreck, henpeck, Quebec, zebec; Kennebec, leatherneck, neck-and-neck, quarter-deck.

-ect: sect; abject, adject, affect, bisect, collect, conflect, connect, correct, defect, deflect, deject, detect, direct, dissect, effect, eject, elect, erect, expect, infect, inject, insect, inspect, neglect, object, pandect, perfect, prefect, project, prospect, protect, reflect, reject, respect, select, subject, suspect, traject; architect, circumspect, dialect, disaffect, disconnect, disinfect, disrespect, incorrect, intellect, interject, intersect, introspect, misdirect, non-elect, recollect, retrospect, self-respect, unsuspect. (And preterites of **-eck** words.)

-ed, -ead (short): bed, bled, bread, bred, dead, dread, Ed, fed, fled, Fred, head, lead, led, Ned, pled, read, red, said, shed, shred, sled, sped, spread, stead, Ted, thread, tread, wed, zed; abed, ahead, behead, bestead, biped, blockhead, bulkhead, coed, hogshead, inbred, instead, misled, outspread, unread, unsaid; aforesaid, gingerbread, loggerhead, quadruped, thoroughbred, thunder-head, timber-head, trucklebed, underfed, watershed, Winifred. (And endings in **-ed** when accentuated, as in "visited.")

-ēde: See **-ēad.**

-edge: dredge, edge, fledge, hedge, kedge, ledge, pledge, Reg (for Reginald), sedge, sledge, veg. (for vegetables), wedge; allege, enhedge, impledge, unedge; interpledge, privilege, sacrilege.

-ēe: See **ē.**

-ēece: See **-ēace.**

-ēech: See **-ēach.**

-ēed: See **-ēad.**

-ēef, -iēf: beef, brief, chief, fief, feoff, grief, leaf, lief, reef, sheaf, thief; belief, fig leaf, relief, shereef, bas relief, disbelief, enfeoff, handkerchief, interleaf, neckerchief, unbelief; aperitif.

-ēek: See **-ēak.**

-ēel: See **-ēal.**

-ēem: See **-ēam.**

-ēer: See **-ēar.**

-ēese: See **-ēase.**

-ēet: See **-ēat.**

-eft: cleft, deft, eft, heft, left, reft, theft, weft; aleft, bereft; enfeoffed, unbereft.

-eg: beg, clegg, dreg, egg, keg, leg, Meg, peg, Peg, seg, skeg, teg, yegg; nutmeg, pegleg, unpeg; beglerbeg, philabeg, Winnipeg.

-egm: See **-em.**

-eigh: See **-āy**

-eign, -ein: See **-āin.**

-el, -elle: bel, bell, belle, cell, dell, dwell, El, ell, fell, hell, jell, knell, Nell, pell, quell, sell, shell, smell, snell, spell, swell, tell, well, yell, Zel, Zell; befell, compel, Cornell, debel, dispel, Estelle, excel, expel, farewell, foretell, gazelle, harebell, hotel, impel, inshell, lapel, pell-mell, propell, Purnell, rebel, repel, rondelle, sea-shell, sentinel, unshell, unspell; asphodel, Astrophel, A.W.O.L., bagatelle, bechamel, calomel, caramel, citadel, cockerel, demoiselle, div-

ing-bell, doggerel, immortelle, infidel, Lionel, mackerel, muscatel, nonpareil, parallel, personnel, pimpernel, philomel, sentinel, undersell, vesper-bell, villanelle; mademoiselle.

-elch: belch, squelch, Welch, Welsh.

-eld: eld, geld, held, meld, weld; beheld, unknelled, upheld, unquelled, withheld; unbeheld; unparalleled. (And preterites of **-el** words.)

-elf: delf, delph, elf, Guelph, pelf, self, shelf; herself, himself, itself, myself, ourself, thyself, yourself.

-elk: elk, whelk, yelk.

-elm: See **-ealm.**

-elp: help, kelp, skelp, swelp, whelp, yelp; self-help.

-elt: belt, Celt, dealt, dwelt, felt, gelt, Kelt, knelt, melt, pelt, smelt, spelt, svelte, veldt, welt; heart-felt, misspelt, unbelt, unfelt.

-elve: delve, helve, shelve, twelve.

-em: em, femme, gem, hem, Jem, phlegm, Shem, stem, them; ahem, begem, condemn, contemn, pro tem; apothegm, Bethlehem, diadem, requiem, stratagem, theorem; ad hominem.

-ēme: See **-ēam.**

-emp: hemp, kemp.

-empt: See **-eampt.**

-en: Ben, den, fen, glen, Gwen, hen, ken, men, pen, sen, ten, then, wen, when, wren, yen, zen; again, amen, cayenne, Cheyenne, Darien, sen-sen, unpen; aldermen, brevipen, cyclamen, denizen, halogen, hydrogen, nitrogen, oxygen, regimen, specimen, waterhen; comedienne, equestrienne, Parisienne, tragedienne.

-ence, -ense: cense, dense, fence, hence, pence, sense, tense, thence, whence; commence, condense, defense, dispense, expense, Hortense, immense, incense, intense, offense, prepense, pretense, suspense, abstinence, accidence, affluence, ambience, audience, commonsense, competence, conference, confidence, consequence, continence, difference, diffidence, diligence, eloquence, eminence, evidence, excellence, frankincense, immanence, imminence, impotence, impudence, incidence, indigence, inference, influence, innocence, insolence, negligence, opulence, penitence, permanence, pertinence, pestilence, preference, prevalence, prominence, recompense, redolence, reference, residence, resilience, sapience, succulence, truculence, turbulence, vehemence, violence, virulence; beneficence, benevolence, circumference, grandiloquence, inconsequence, intelligence, intransigence, magnificence, munificence, obedience, omnipotence, preeminence, subservience. (Also **ent + s** as in "tents.")

-ench: bench, blench, clench, drench, flench, French, quench, stench, tench, trench, wench, wrench; intrench, retrench, unclench; monkey-wrench.

-end: bend, blend, end, fend, friend, kenned, lend, mend, penned, rend, send, spend, tend, trend, vend, wend; amend, append, ascend, attend, befriend, commend, contend, defend, depend, descend, distend, expend, extend, forfend, impend, intend, misspend, offend, Ostend, perpend, portend, pretend, South End, subtend, suspend, transcend, unbend, unfriend, unkened, unpenned, upend, upsend; apprehend, comprehend, condescend, dividend, minuend, recommend, reprehend, subtrahend; overextend, superintend.

-ength: length, strength; full-length.

-ens: cleanse, ens, lens. (Also **-en + s** as in "pens" and **-end + s** as in "trends".)

-ense: See **-ence.**

-ent, -ent: bent, blent, cent, dent, fent, gent, Ghent, Kent, leant, lent, Lent, meant, pent, rent, scent, sent, spent, tent, Trent, vent, went; absent (verb), accent (verb), anent, ascent, assent, augment, cement, comment, consent, content, descent, dissent, event, extent, ferment, forment, frequent, indent, intent, invent, lament, lenient, misspent, ostent, portent, present (verb), prevent, relent, repent, resent, torment, unbent, unspent; abstinent, accident, ailment, argument, armament, banishment, battlement, betterment, blandishment, blazonment, blemishment, botherment, chastisement, competent, complement, compliment, condiment, confident, confluent, consequent, continent, corpulent, dazzlement, decrement, deferent, detriment, different, diffident, diligent, discontent, dissident, document, element, eloquent, eminent, emollient,

esculent, evident, excellent, exigent, filament, firmament, fosterment, fraudulent, government, gradient, immanent, imminent, implement, impotent, impudent, incident, increment, indigent, indolent, innocent, insolent, instrument, languishment, lavishment, liniment, malcontent, management, measurement, merriment, miscontent, monument, negligent, nourishment, nutriment, occident, opulent, orient, ornament, parliament, pediment, penitent, permanent, pertinent, precedent, president, prevalent, prisonment, provident, punishment, ravishment, redolent, regiment, represent, resident, reticent, reverent, rudiment, sacrament, sediment, sentiment, settlement, subsequent, succulent, supplement, tenement, testament, truculent, turbulent, underwent, vehement, violent, virulent, wonderment; accomplishment, acknowledgment, advertisement, astonishment, belligerent, benevolent, development, disarmament, embarrassment, embodiment, enlightenment, environment, establishment, experiment, impenitent, impertinent, imprisonment, improvident, intelligent, irreverent, magnificent, magniloquent, predicament, presentiment, replenishment, subservient, temperament; accompaniment. (Also see **-ant.**)

-epp: hep, nep, pep, "prep", rep, repp, skep, step, steppe, yep; Dieppe, footstep, demirep; Amenhotep. (Pluralize to rhyme with "Schweppes" and "steppes".)

-ept: crept, drept, kept, lept, leapt, pepped, Sept, slept, stepped, swept, wept; accept, adept, concept, except, inept, precept, unkept, unwept, y-clept; intercept, overslept, overstepped.

-êr, ûr, îr: blur, bur, burr, cur, err, fir, fur, her, knur, myrrh, per, purr, shirr, sir, slur, spur, stir, were, whir; astir, aver, Ben Hur, bestir, Big Sur, chasseur, chauffeur, coiffeur, concur, confer, defer, demur, deter, douceur, hauteur, incur, infer, inter, occur, prefer, recur, refer, transfer; amateur, arbiter, barrister, calendar, chronicler, chorister, colander, comforter, connoisseur, cylinder, de rigueur, disinter, doughtier, dowager, drowsier, earlier, gossamer, harbinger, huskier, Jennifer, Jupiter, lavender, Lucifer, mariner, massacre, messenger, minister, officer, passenger, prisoner, register, scimitar, sepulcher, traveler, voyageur ; administer, astrologer, astronomer, barometer, Excalibur, idolater, practitioner, relinquisher, thermometer, topographer, upholsterer, worshipper.

-êrb, ûrb: blurb, curb, herb, kerb, Serb, verb; ascerb, adverb, disturb, perturb, suburb, superb.

-êrce, -êrse, -ûrse: curse, Erse, hearse, herse, nurse, purse, terse, verse, worse; accurse, adverse, amerce, asperse, averse, coerce, commerce, converse, disburse, disperse, diverse, imburse, immerse, inverse, obverse, preverse, precurse, rehearse, reverse, sesterce, subcerse, traverse, transverse, intersperse, reimburse, universe.

-êrd: See -êard.

-ēre: See -ēar.

-êrf, ûrf: scurf, serf, turf.

-êrge, -îrge, -ûrge, -oûrge: dirge, gurge, merge, purge, scourge, serge, splurge, Spurge, surge, urge, verge ; converge, deterge, diverge, emerge, immerge, submerge; demuirge, dramaturge, thaumaturge.

-êrk, -îrk, -ûrk: Burke, Chirk, cirque, clerk, dirk, irk, jerk, kirk, lurk, merk, murk, perk, quirk, shirk, smirk, stirk, Turk, work, yerk; frostwork, rework; Albuquerque, handiwork, masterwork, overwork, underwork.

-êrls: see -êarl.

-êrm, îrm: berm, derm, firm, germ, Herm, perm, sperm, squirm, term, therm, worm; affirm, confirm, glowworm, infirm, mistherm; disaffirm, isotherm. pachyderm.

-êrn: See -êarn.

-êrse: See -êrce.

-êrt, -îrt, ûrt: Bert, blurt, Burt, cert, chert, curt, dirt, flirt, Gert, girt, gurt, hurt, pert, "quirt", shirt, skirt, spirt, spurt, squirt, syrt, vert, wert, Wirt, wort ; advert, alert, assert, avert, begirt, concert, convert, desert, dessert, divert, engirt, exert, expert, exsert, filbert, Gilbert, inert, insert, invert, obvert, overt, pervert, revert, subvert, transvert, ungirt, unhurt; Adelbert, controvert, disconcert, Englebert, extrovert, indesert, inexpert, intersert, introvert; animadvert.

-êrth: See -êarth.

-êrve -ûrve: curve, nerve, serve, swerve, verve; conserve, deserve, incurve, observe, outcurve, preserve, reserve, subserve, unnerve.

-es, -esce, -ess: Bess, bless, cess, chess, cress, dress, fess, guess, jess, Jess, Kress, less, mess, ness, press, stress, Tess, tress, yes; abscess, access, actress, address, aggress, assess, caress, compress, confess, depress, digress, distress, duress, egress, empress, excess, express, finesse, impress, ingress, largesse, Loch Ness, mattress, noblesse, obsess, oneness, oppress, possess, princess, profess, progress, recess, redress, regress, repress, sheerness, success, suppress, transgress, undress, unless; acquiesce, archeress, baroness, bottomless, coalesce, convalesce, dispossess, effervesce, hardiness, Inverness, obsolesce, opalesce, overdress, poetess, politesse, prophetess, repossess, shepherdess, sorceress, votaress, wilderness; nevertheless, proprietress. (Also many words with the suffix **-ness** as in "ugliness".)

-esh: flesh, fresh, mesh, nesh, thresh; afresh, enmesh, refresh, secesh.

-esk, -esque: desk, Esk; burlesque, Dantesque, grotesque, moresque; arabesque, barbaresque, chivalresque, gigantesque, picaresque, picturesque, Romanesque, sculpturesque, statuesque.

-est: best, blest, breast, Brest, cest, chest, crest, Gest, guest, hest, jest, lest, nest, pest, quest, rest, test, vest, west, wrest, zest ; abreast, arrest, attest, behest, bequest, congest, contest, depressed, detest, devest, digest, distressed, divest, imprest, increst, ingest, inquest, invest, molest, obtest, protest, recessed, request, suggest, unblest, unguessed, unpressed; Alkahest, anapest, Bucharest, Budapest, Everest, interest, manifest, predigest, Trieste; disinterest. (See the preterites of many verbs in **-ess,** such as "stressed". Also a number of false rhymes in which the accent is not on the final syllable such as "conquest".)

-et, -ette: bet, Brett, Cette, debt, flet, fret, frett, get, jet, ket, let, Lett, met, net, pet, ret, set, sett, stet, sweat, threat, tret, vet, wet, yet; abet, aigrette, ailette, alette, backset, baguette, barbette, Barnett, beget, benet, beset, bewet, brevet, brunette, cadet, corvette, coquette, croquette, curvet, duet, forget, fossette, fourchette, fumette, gazette, genet, Gillette, inset, prisette, lunette, Nannette, offset, omelette, parquet, pipette, piquet, piquette, pirouette, quartette, quintet, regret, rosette, sestet, sextet, sunset, Thibet, Tibet, upset, vignette, wellmet; alphabet, amulet, anchoret, Antoinette, bassinet, bayonet, cabinet, calumet, castanet, cellaret, chansonette, cigarette, coverlet, epaulet, epithet, etiquette, falconet, farmerette, flannelette, floweret, globulet, Juliet, laudaulet, lazarette, leaderette, luncheonette, maisonette, marmoset, martinet, mignonette, minaret, minuet, novelette, overset, parapet, parroket, pierette, pirouette, quadruplet, sarcenet, serviette, silhouette, somerset, statuette, suffragette, tabaret, tourniquet, underset, wagonette.

-etch: etch, fetch, ketch, fletch, retch, sketch, stretch, vetch, wretch; outstretch.

-ēte: See -ēat.

-eūd: See -ōōd.

-ēve: See -ēave.

-ew, -ieū, -ūe: blew, blue, boo, brew, chew, crew, cue, dew, do, drew, due, ewe, few, flew, flu, flue, glue, gnu, goo, grew, hew, hue, Hugh, Jew, jue, knew, Lew, lieu, loo, Lou, mew, moo, mu, new, nu, pew, queue, rue, screw, shoe, shrew, skew, thew, threw, through, to, too, true, two, view, who, woo, yew, you, zoo; accrue, adieu, ado, ague, anew, Anjou, askew, Baku, bamboo, bedew, bellevue, beshrew, cachou, canoe, cashew, cuckoo, curfew, curlew, debut, emu, endue, ensue, eschew, Hindu, imbue, issue, juju, menu, mildew, Peru, pooh-pooh, pursue, purview, ragout, renew, review, shampoo, subdue, taboo, tattoo, tissue, undo, venue, voodoo, withdrew, yahoo, Zulu; avenue, barbecue, billet-doux, catechu, cockatoo, curlicue, interview, kangaroo, misconstrue, parvenu, rendezvous, residue, retinue, revenue, toodle-oo, Timbuktu, Kalamazoo, merci beaucoup. (Also see -ōō.)

-ex: cheques, Ex, flex, hex, lex, rex, Rex, sex, "specs", treks, vex; annex, apex, codex, complex, convex, index, perplex, reflex; circumflex. (The present tense of verbs and the plurals of nouns in **-eck,** as in "decks" and "wrecks".)

-ext: next, text; pretext. (Also **-ex** + ed as "vexed".)

-ey (ā): See -āy.

-ez: Fez, fez, sez, Les (for Leslie); Juarez, Suez; Marseillaise.

-ī: See -y.

-īar: (As in "liar", see two-syllable rhymes.)

-ib: bib, Bibb, crib, dib, drib, fib, gib, Gibb, glib, jib, nib, quib, rib, sib, squib; ad lib, Carib.

-ībe: bribe, gibe, jibe, kibe, scribe, tribe; ascribe, describe, imbibe, inscribe, prescribe, proscribe, subscribe, transcribe; circumscribe, diatribe, interscribe, superscribe.

-ic, -ick: brick, chic, chick, click, crick, dick, Dick, flick, hick, kick, lick, mick, Mick, nick, Nick, pick, prick, quick, rick, sic, sick, slick, snick, spick, stick, thick, tic, tick, trick, Vic, wick, Wick; beatnik, bestick, caustic, heartsick, lovesick, sputnik, toothpick, triptych, yardstick; acoustic, arsenic, artistic, bailiwick, Benedick, bishopric, Bolshevik, candlestick, candlewick, Catholic, chivalric, choleric, double-quick, heretic, limerick, lunatic, maverick, politic, rhetoric, single-stick, turmeric; arithmetic, impolitic.

-ice, -ise (short): bice, Brice, dice, ice, gneiss, lice, mice, nice, price, rice, slice, spice, splice, thrice, trice, twice, vice, vise; advice, allspice, concise, device, entice, precise, suffice; paradise, sacrifice.

-ich: See -itch.

-ick: See -ic.

-ict: Pict, strict; addict, afflict, astrict, conflict, constrict, convict, delict, depict, edict, evict, inflict, predict, relict, restrict; benedict, Benedict, contradict, derelict. (See preterites of **-ick**.)

-id: bid, chid, Cid, did, fid, Gid, grid, hid, kid, lid, mid, quid, rid, skid, slid, squid, thrid, yid; amid, eyelid, forbid, Madrid, outbid, outdid, unbid, undid; invalid, katydid, overbid, pyramid, underbid, unforbid.

-īde, -īed: bide, bride, chide, Clyde, glide, gride, guide, hide, Hyde, pied, pride, ride, Ryde, side, slide, snide, stride, tide, wide; abide, aside, astride, backside, backslide, beside, bedside, bestride, betide, broadside, bromide, Carbide, cockeyed, collide, confide, cowhide, cross-eyed, decide, deride, divide, elide, excide, hillside, inside, landslide, meek-eyed, misguide, noontide, outride, outside, outstride, pie-eyed, preside, provide, reside, seaside, subside, sulfide, wall-eyed, wayside, Yuletide; alongside, bonafide, coincide, countrified, dignified, eventide, fortified, fratricide, goggle-eyed, homicide, justified, matricide, misallied, override, parricide, patricide, peroxide, purified, qualified, regicide, riverside, satisfied, subdivide, suicide, unapplied, undertide, vitrified; formaldehyde, infanticide, insecticide, tyrannicide, vulpicide. (And "cried", "died", "signified", and about 70 other preterites of verbs in **-y, -ie** and **-ye.**)

-īdes: ides; besides. (And add "s" to words in previous list.)

-idge: bridge, midge, ridge; abridge, cartridge, partridge; acreage, beverage, brokerage, cartilage, factorage, foliage, fuselage, hemorrhage, heritage, lineage, parentage, patronage, pilgrimage, privilege, sacrilege, tutelage, vicarage.

-idst: bidst, chidst, didst, hidst, midst, ridst, slidst; amidst, forbidst.

-īe: See **-y.**

-īef: See **-ēef.**

-iēge: liege, siege; besiege, prestige.

-iēnd: See **-ēand.**

-iēr: See **-ēar.**

-iēld: See **-ēald.**

-iērce: Bierce, fierce, Pearce, pierce, tierce; transpierce.

-iēve: See **-ēave.**

-if, -iff, -ўph: biff, cliff, diff, glyph, griff, if, Jiff, miff, niff, quif, "Riff", skiff, sniff, stiff, tiff, whiff, wiff; handkerchief, hieroglyph, neckerchief, Teneriffe.

-īfe: fife, Fife, knife, life, naif, rife, strife, wife; fishwife, goodwife, housewife, jackknife, midwife; afterlife.

-ift: clift, drift, gift, lift, rift, shift, shrift, sift, swift, thrift; adrift, snowdrift, spendthrift, spindrift, uplift. (Also preterites of verbs in **-if.**)

-ig: big, brig, dig, fig, gig, grig, jig, pig, prig, rig, shig, sprig, swig, trig, twig, Whig, wig; renege; guinea-pig, periwig, thimblerig, whirligig; thingumajig.

-īgh: See **-y.**

-īght: See **-īte.**

-īgn: See **-īne.**

-igue: See **-ēague.**

-īke: bike, dyke, hike, Ike, like, Mike, pike, psych, shrike, spike, strike, type, Wyke; alike, dislike, Klondyke, manlike, midlike, mislike, turnpike, unlike, Vandyke; maidenlike, womanlike, workmanlike.

-il, -ill: bill, Bill, brill, chill, dill, drill, fill, frill, gill, grill, grille, hill, ill, jill, Jill, kill, mill, nil, pill, prill, quill, rill, shrill, skill, spill, squill, still, swill, thill, thrill, till, trill, twill, 'twill (it will), vill, will, Will; befrill, bestill, Brazil, distil, downhill, freewill, fulfil, instil, quadrille, Seville, until, unwill, uphill; chlorophyll, codicil, daffodil, domicile, imbecile, Louisville, versatile, volatile, whippoorwill.

-ilch: filch, milch, pilch, Zilch.

-ild: build, gild, guild; rebuild, unskilled; unfulfilled. (And preterites of **-il** words.)

-īld: aisled, child, Childe, mild, wild; beguiled, enfiled. (And preterites of verbs in **-ile,** as in "filed", "exiled".)

-īle, īsle, -yle: aisle, bile, chyle, file, guile, I'll, isle, Lyle, mile, Nile, pile, rile, smile, spile, stile, style, tile, vile, while, wile; Argyle, beguile, Carlyle, compile, defile, exile, gentile, meanwhile, puerile, revile, servile, somewhile, tensile; Anglophile, crocodile, diastyle, domicile (verb), Francophile, infantile, juvenile, mercantile, peristyle, puerile, reconcile; bibliophile.

-ile (-ēl): See **-ēal.**

-ilk: bilk, ilk, milk, silk; spun silk.

-iln: biln, kiln, Milne.

-ilt: built, gilt, guilt, hilt, jilt, kilt, lilt, milt, quilt, silt, spilt, stilt, tilt, wilt; atilt, begilt, rebuilt, unbuilt, ungilt; Vanderbilt.

-ilth: filth, spilth, tilth.

-im: brim, dim, glim, grim, Grimm, gym, him, hymn, Jim, Kim, limb, limn, Lympne, prim, rim, shim, skim, slim, swim, Tim, trim, vim, whim; bedim, betrim, enlimn, pilgrim, prelim; antonym, cherubim, eponym, homonym, interim, pseudonym, Sanhedrim, seraphim, synonym.

-īme: chime, chyme, climb, clime, crime, cyme, dime, grime, I'm, lime, Lyme, mime, prime, rhyme, rime, slime, thyme, time;

bedtime, begrime, belime, berhyme, birdlime, daytime, lifetime, meantime, sublime, upclimb, Guggenheim, maritime, overtime, pantomime, paradigm, summertime, wintertime.

-īmes: betimes, sometimes. (Also -īme + s as in "chimes" and -yme + s as in "rhymes".)

-imp: blimp, "chimp", crimp, gimp, guimpe, imp, jimp, limp, pimp, primp, scimp, scrimp, shrimp, simp, skimp, tymp.

-impse: glimpse. (And pluralize words in above list.)

-in, -inn, -ine: been, bin, chin, din, djinn, fin, Finn, gin, Glynne, grin, in, inn, jinn, kin, lyn, Lynn, pin, quin, shin, sin, skin, spin, thin, tin, twin, whin, win; agrin, akin, bearskin, begin, Berlin, buckskin, chagrin, Corinne, herein, sidespin, tailspin, therein, unpin, wherein, within; alkaline, almandine, Argentine, aspirin, bulletin, Byzantine, cannikin, crinoline, crystalline, culverin, discipline, feminine, finickin, gelatin, genuine, glycerine, harlequin, heroine, Jacobin, javelin, jessamine, kilderkin, libertine, mandarin, mandolin, manikin, masculine, minikin, moccasin, origin, paladin, pavonine, peregrine, Philistine, ravelin, saccharine, sibylline, violin, zeppelin.

-inc: See **-ink.**

-ince: blintz, chintz, mince, prince, quince, rinse, since, Vince, wince; convince, evince, unprince. (Also, -int + s as in "hints".)

-inch: cinch, chinch, clinch, finch, flinch, inch, linch, lynch, pinch, winch; bepinch, Goldfinch, unclinch.

-inct, -inked: tinct; distinct, extinct, instinct, precinct, succinct; indistinct. (And preterites of verbs in **-ink,** as in "blinked".)

-īnd and -īned: bind, blind, find, grind, hind, kind, mind, rind, wind; behind, inbind, mankind, purblind, remind, snow-blind, unbind, unkind, unwind; color-blind, disinclined, gavelkind, humankind, mastermind, undersigned, undesigned, unrefined, womankind. (And preterites of **-īgn** and **-īne** words.)

-ind, -inned: ind, Scinde, wind; abscind, rescind; Rosalind, tamarind. (And preterites of verbs in **-in** and **-ine,** as in "pinned", and "disciplined".)

-īne: abine, brine, chine, dine, eyne, fine,

kine, Klein, line, mine, nine, pine, Rhine, shine, shrine, sign, sine, spine, spline, Stein, swine, syne, thine, tine, trine, twine, tyne, vine, whine, wine; airline, align, assign, benign, beshine, calcine, canine, carbine, carmine, coastline, combine, condign, confine, consign, decline, define, design, divine, enshrine, entwine, feline, Holstein, incline, indign, lifeline, malign, moonshine, opine, outline, outshine, recline, refine, reline, repine, resign, saline, sunshine, supine, untwine, vulpine, woodbine; alkaline, anodyne, aquiline, Argentine, asinine, brigantine, Byzantine, celandine, Clementine, columbine, concubine, countermine, crystalline, disincline, eglantine, incardine, interline, intertwine, iodine, leonine, palatine, porcupine, saturnine, serpentine, superfine, turpentine, underline, undermine, valentine, verperine.

-ine (ēne): See **-ēan.**

-ing: bing, bring, cling, ding, fling, king, ling, Ming, ping, ring, sing, sling, spring, sting, string, swing, synge, thing, thring, wing, wring, ying; evening, hireling, lifespring, mainspring, something, starveling, unsling, unstring; anything, chitterling, easterling, everything, underling, wedding-ring. (And more than 1,000 false rhymes in present participles, as in "happening", "issuing", etc.)

-inge: binge, cringe, fringe, hinge, Inge, singe, springe, stinge, tinge, twinge; astringe, befringe, impinge, infringe, syringe, unhinge.

-ink: blink, brink, chink, cinque, clink, drink, fink, gink, inc., jink, kink, link, mink, pink, prink, rink, shrink, sink, skink, slink, stink, swink, think, tink, trink, twink, wink, zinc; bethink; hoodwink, methink; bobolink, counter-sink, Humperdinck, interlink, tiddlywink.

-inks: See **-inx.**

-inse: See **-ince.**

-int: dint, flint, Flint, glint, hint, lint, mint, print, quint, splint, sprint, squint, stint, tint, vint; asquint, footprint, imprint, misprint, reprint, spearmint; peppermint.

-īnt: pint; ahint, behint.

-inth: plinth; absinthe, Corinth; hyacinth, labyrinth, terebinth.

-inx, -inks: jinx, lynx, minx, sphinx; larynx, methinks, salpinx, tiddlywinks. (And add "s" to nouns and verbs in **-ink.**)

-ip: blip, chip, clip, dip, drip, flip, grip, grippe, gyp, hip, kip, lip, nip, pip, quip, rip, scrip, ship, sip, skip, slip, snip, strip, tip, trip, whip, yip, zip, atrip, cowslip, equip, horse-whip, landslip, outstrip, transship, unship, unzip, warship. And false rhymes as follows: apprenticeship, battleship, censorship, championship, citizenship, chaplainship, deaconship, dictatorship, fellowship, guardianship, horsemanship, ladyship, partnership, penmanship, scholarship, sizarship, stewardship, workmanship and, etc.

-īpe: gripe, pipe, ripe, snipe, stipe, stripe, swipe, tripe, type, wipe; bagpipe, blowpipe, hornpipe, pitchpipe, sideswipe, tintype, unripe, windpipe; antitype, archetype, autotype, guttersnipe, linotype, monotype, over-ripe, prototype; daguerreotype, electrotype, stereotype.

-ipt: script; manuscript. (And preterites of verb s in **-ip,** as in "snipped".)

-ipse, -ips: eclipse, ellipse; apocalypse. (And add "s" to nouns and verbs in **-ip,** as in "snips".)

-ique: See **-ēak** and **-īc.**

-īr: See **-êr.**

-īrch: See **-êarch.**

-īrd: See **-êard.**

-īre, -yre: byre, choir, dire, fire, gyre, hire, ire, lyre, mire, pyre, quire, shire, sire, spire, squire, tire, tyre, Tyre, vire, wire; acquire, admire, afire, aspire, attire, bonfire, con-spire, desire, empire, enquire, entire, es-quire, expire, grandsire, inquire, inspire, perspire, quagmire, require, respire, retire, sapphire, satire, spitfire, suspire, transpire, wildfire. (See **iā** in list of two syllable rhymes.)

-īrge: See **-êrge.**

-īrk: See **-êrk.**

-īrl: See **-êarl.**

-īrm: See **-êrm.**

-īrn: See **-êarn.**

-īrp, -ûrp: burp, chirp, twerp; extirp, usurp, (Past tense to rhyme with "excerpt".)

-īrst, -êrst, -ûrst: burst, curst, durst, erst, first, Hearst, Hurst, thirst, verst, worst; accurst, athirst, becurst, outburst, uncursed, unversed. (And preterites of verbs in **-êrce, -êrse,** and **-ûrse,** as in "coerced", "versed" and "cursed".)

-îrt: See **-êrt.**

-îrth: See **-êarth.**

-is, -iss, -ice: bis, bliss, Chris, Diss, hiss, kiss, Liss, mis, Swiss, this, wys; abyss, amiss, dismiss, jaundice, remiss; armistice, arti-fice, avarice, Beatrice, benefice, chrysalis, cicatrice, coclatrice, cowardice, dentifrice, edifice, emphasis, genesis, nemesis, orifice, precipice, prejudice, prolapsis, synthesis, verdigris; analysis, antithesis, diaeresis, di-athesis, hypostasis, hypothesis, liquorice, metatasis, metropolis, necropolis, paralysis, parenthesis; metamorphosis.

-is (iz), -iz: biz, fizz, friz, his, is, Liz, phiz, quiz, 'tis, viz, whiz, wiz; Cadiz.

-īse, -īze: guise, prise, prize, rise, size, wise; advise, apprise, arise, assize, baptize, cap-size, chastise, cognize, comprise, demise, despise, devise, disguise, emprize, excise, incise, Judaize, misprize, moonrise, realize, remise, reprise, revise, sunrise, surmise, sur-prise, unwise, uprise; adonize, advertise, aggrandize, agonize, alkalize, analyze, ap-petize, atomize, authorize, barbarize, botan-ize, brutalize, canonize, cauteriize, central-ize, christianize, circumcise, civilize, clima-tize, colonize, compromise, criticize, crystal-lize, dogmatize, dramatize, ecstasize, emphasize, energize, enterprise, equalize, eulogize, exercise, exorcise, fertilize, feudal-ize, focalize, formalize, fossilize, fraternize, galvanize, gentilize, gormandize, Hellenize, humanize, hypnotize, idealize, idolize, im-provise, jeopardize, journalize, legalize, lionize, localize, magnetize, martyrize, mechanize, memorize, mercerize, methodize, minimize, mobilize, modernize, moralize, nasalize, neutralize, organize, ostracize, otherwise, oxidize, paralyze, patronize, pau-perize, penalize, pilgrimize, plagiarize, pluralize, polarize, pulverize, rapturize, rec-cognize, rhapsodize, royalize, ruralize, sac-rifice, satirize, scandalize, scrutinize, ser-monize, socialize, specialize, subsidize, sum-marize, supervise, syllogize, sympathize, symphonize, synchronize, synthetize, tan-talize, terrorize, tranquillize, tyrannize, vocalize, vulcanize, vulgarize; acclimatize, actualize, allegorize, alphabetize, amalga-mize, anatomize, antagonize, apologize, apostatize, apostrophize, astrologize, astron-omize, authorize, capitalize, catholicize, characterize, circularize, commercialize, congenialize, contrariwise, decentralize, dehumanize, demobilize, democratize, demonetize, demoralize, deodorize, devitalize, dichotomize, disorganize, economize, epilogize, epitomize, extemporize, externalize, familiarize, fanaticize, federalize, hypothesize, imperialize, italicize, legitimize, liberalize, macadamize, materialize, mediatize, militarize, mineralize, monopolize, nationalize, naturalize, philosophize, phlebotomise, popularize, puritanize, regularize, reorganize, ritualize, secularize, sensualize, soliloquize, systematize, theologize, theosophize, ventriloquize, visualize; Americanize, anathematize, departmentalize, etheralize, etymologize, familiarize, materialize, particularize, professionalize, proverbialize, revolutionize, spiritualize, universalize; institutionalize, internationalize. (Also add "s" to words ending in **-y**.)

-ish: dish, fish, Gish, knish, Nish, pish, squish, tish, wish; anguish, bluefish, goldfish; gibberish, babyish, betterish, cleverish, devilish, feverish, gibberish, heathenish, kittenish, lickerish, quakerish, vaporish, waterish, willowish, womanish, yellowish; impoverish.

-isk: bisk, bisque, brisk, disc, disk, frisk, risk, whisk; asterisk, basilisk, obelisk, odalisque, tamarisk.

-ism: chrism, ism, prism, schism; abysm, Baalism, Babism, baptism, Buddahism, deism, Fascism, monism, purism, realism, snobbism, sophism, technism, theism, truism; actinism, agonism, altruism, anarchism, aneurism, anglicism, animism, aphorism, archaism, asteism, atheism, atomism, babysim, barbarism, biblicism, bloomerism, bogeyism, Bolshevism, braggardism, brutalism, cabalism, Calvanism, cataclysm, catechism, centralism, Chauvinism, classicism, communism, cretinism, Darwinism, despotism, devilism, dualism, egotism, embolism, etherism, euphuism, exorcism, fairyism, fatalism, fetishism, feudalism, fossilism, frivolism, Gallicism, galvanism, heathenism, hedonism, heroism, hibernism, Hinduism, Hitlerism, humanism, hypnotism, idealism, Islamism, jockeyism, journalism, Judaism, laconism, Latinism, localism, loyalism, lyricism, magnetism, mannerism, mechanism, mesmerism, methodism, modernism, monkeyism, moralism, mysticism, nativism, nepotism, nihilism, occultism, optimism, organism, ostracism, pacifism, paganism, pantheism, paroxysm, pauperism, pedantism, pelmanism, pessimism, plagiarism, pugilism, pythonism, quietism, rabbinism, rheumatism, rigorism, royalism, ruralism, satanism, savagism, Saxonism, scepticism, socialism, solescism, stoicism, subtilism, syllogism, symbolism, synchronism, terrorism, tigerism, tribalism, vandalism, vocalism, verbalism, vulgarism, witticism, yankeeism, Zionism; absolutism, academism; achromatism, aestheticism, agnosticism, alcoholism, alienism, anachronism, anatomism, Anglicanism, animalism, antagonism, asceticism, capitalism, characterism, classicalism, clericalism, conservatism, democratism, determinism, diabolism, diplomatism, eclecticism, empiricism, evangelism, exoticism, expressionism, externalism, fanaticism, favoritism, federalism, generalism, histrionism, hyperbolism, idiotism, imperialism, impressionism, Italicism, Jesuitism, laconicism, liberalism, literalism, monasticism, naturalism, nominalism, parallelism, parasitism, paternalism, patriotism, pedagogism, philosophism, secularism, sensualism, separatism, subjectivism, sychophantism, universalism, ventriloquism; abolitionism, agrarianism, Americanism, colloquialism, colonialism, conventionalism, equestrianism, evolutionism, existentialism, histrionicism, imperialism, indeterminism, indifferentism, industrialism, materialism, medievalism, Orientalism, phalansterism, phenomenalism, professionalism, proverbalism, Republicanism, Utopianism, vernacularism, antiquarianism, bacchanalianism, Congregationalism, constitutionalism, cosmopolitanism, experimentalism, internationalism, presbyterianism, proletarianism, supernaturalism, Unitarianism, vegetarianism; humanitarianism, utilitarianism.

-iss: See **-is**.

-ist, -issed, -ÿst: cist, cyst, fist, gist, grist, hist, list, mist, schist, tryst, twist, whist, wist, wrist; artist, assist, Babist, baptist, blacklist, Buddhist, chartist, chemist, consist, Cubist, cyclist, deist, dentist, desist, dismissed, druggist, dualist, duellist, enlist, entwist, faddist, Fascist, florist, flutist, harpist, hymnist, insist, jurist, linguist, palmist, persist, psalmist, purist, realist, resist, simplist, sophist, statist, stylist, subsist, theist; alchemist, amethyst, amorist, atheist, beneficed, bicyclist, bigamist, bolshevist, Calvinist, casuist, catechist, co-exist, colonist, colorist, columnist, communist, conformist, copyist, cymbalist, Darwinist, diarist, dogmatist, dramatist, dualist, egoist, eucharist, eulogist, extremist, fabulist, fatalist, fetishist, feudalist, fictionist, guitarist, Hebraist, hedonist, hellenist, herbralist, hobbyist, humanist, humorist, hypnotist, idealist, idolist, journalist, lapidist, latinist, loyalist, medallist, Methodist, modernist, moralist, motorist, novelist, oculist, optimist, organist, pacifist, passionist, pessimist, physicist, pianist, pietist, plagiarist, platonist, pluralist, pragmatist, publicist, pugilist, quietist, rapturist, rigorist, royalist, ruralist, satanist, satirist, scientist, scripturist, socialist, soloist, specialist, strategist, suffrag.st, symbolist, sympathist, synthesist, technicist, terrorist, theorist, unionist, verbalist, visionist, vitalist, vocalist, votarist; absolutist, academist, allegorist, analogist, anatomist, annualist, antagonist, apologist, athetist, biblicist, biologist, capitalist, chiropodist, classicalist, contortionist, corruptionist, cremationist, destructionist, devotionist, diplomatist, empiricist, enamelist, epitomist, eternalist, evangelist, externalist, federalist, fossilogist, illusionist, immortalist, liberalist, misogamist, monogamist, monopolist, mythologist, nationalist, naturalist, nominalist, obstructionist, opinionist, pathologist, perfectionist, philanthropist, philologist, progressionist, protagonist, protectionist, psychologist, rationalist, religionist, revivalist, ritualist, secularist, sensualist, sexualist, spiritualist, subjectivist, synonymist, technologist, telegraphist, telephonist, textualist, topographist, traditionist, ventriloquist, vocabulist, zoologist, anthropologist, archaeologist, bibliophilist, conversationist, educationalist, entomologist, epigrammatist, evolutionist, genealogist, horticulturist, instrumentalist, materialist, memorialist, mineralogist, occidentalist, oppositionist, Orientalist, ornithologist, pharmacologist, physiognomist, physiologist, preferentialist, prohibitionist, revolutionist, sensationalist, sentimentalist, transcendentalist, universalist; constitutionalist, contraversialist, conversationalist, educationalist, experimentalist, individualist, institutionalist, intellectualist, meteorologist, ministerialist, supernaturalist. (And preterites of verbs in -iss, as in "kissed".)

-it, -ite: bit, bitt, chit, cit, fit, flit. frit, grit, it, it, kit, knit, lit, mitt, nit, pit, Pitt, quit, sit, skit, slit, smit, spit, split, sprit, tit, twit, whit, wit, Witt, writ; acquit, admit, befit, beknit, bowsprit, commit, demit, DeWitt, emit, immit, misfit, moon-lit, omit, outfit, outsit, outwit, permit, pewit, refit, remit, respite, starlit, submit, sunlit, titbit, tomtit, transmit, unfit, unknit; apposite, benefit, counterfeit, definite, exquisite, favorite, hypocrite, infinite, interknit, opposite, pretermit, preterite, recommit, requisite.

-itch: bitch, ditch, fitch, flitch, hitch, itch, lych, niche, pitch, rich, snitch, stitch, switch, twitch, which, witch; bewitch, distich, enrich, hemstitch, sandwich, unhitch.

-īte, -ight, -eīght: bight, bite, blight, bright, cite, dight, Dwight, fight, flight, fright, height, hight, kite, knight, light, might, mite, night, pight, plight, quite, right, rite, sight, site, sleight, slight, smite, spite, sprite, tight, trite, white, wight, wright, write; accite, affright, alight, aright, Baalite, bedight, benight, contrite, daylight, delight, despite, disunite, downright, eremite, excite, foresight, forthright, goodnight, ignite, incite, indite, insight, invite, midnight, moonlight, outright, polite, recite, requite, starlight, sunlight, tonight, twilight, unite, unsight, unwrite, zincite, zoolite; acolyte, aconite, anchorite, appetite, bedlamite, belemnite, bipartite, Canaanite, candlelight, Carmelite, chrysolite, composite, copyright, crystallite, disunite, dynamite, ebonite, erudite, expedite, Fahrenheit, grapholite, impolite, Israelite, Jacobite, midshipmite, Muscovite, neophyte, overnight, oversight, parasite, plebiscite, proselite, recondite, reunite, satellite, stalactite, stalagmite, Sybarite, troglodyte, underwrite, vulcanite, watertight, weathertight; cosmopolite, electrolyte, entomolite, meteorite, theodolite.

-ite: See -it.

-ith, -yth: fifth, frith, kith, myth, pith, sith, smith, with, withe; forthwith, herewith, Penrith, therewith, wherewith, zenith; acrolith, Arrowsmith, monolith; paleolith.

-īthe: blithe, hithe, Hythe, lithe, scythe, tithe, withe, writhe.

-its, -itz: Blitz, Fritz, quits, Ritz, Schlitz. (And plurals of words in **-it**.)

-īve: chive, Clive, dive, drive, five, gyve, hive, I've, live, rive, shive, shrive, skive, stive, strive, thrive, wive; alive, arrive, beehive, connive, contrive, deprive, derive, revive, survive, unhive; power drive.

-ive: give, live, sieve, spiv; active, captive, costive, cursive, forgive, furtive, massive, missive, motive, native, outlive, passive, pensive, relive, restive, sportive, votive; ablative, abductive, acquisive, amative, causative, combative, curative, curvative, expletive, formative, fugitive, genitive, lambative, laudative, laxative, lenitive, lucrative, narrative, negative, nutritive, primitive, pulsative, punitive, putative, quantitive, sanative, sedative, semblative, sensitive, siccative, substantive, talkative, tentative, transitive, vibrative, vocative; abdicative, accusative, affirmative, alternative, appelative, applicative, cogitative, comparative, consecutive, conservative, contemplative, contributive, copulative, correlative, declarative, decorative, definitive, demonstrative, derivative, derogative, desiccative, diminutive, distributive, emanative, executive, explicative, figurative, generative, illustrative, imperative, imputative, incarnative, indicative, infinitive, informative, inquisitive, insensitive, intuitive, justifactive, meditative, operative, palliative, performative, preparative, prerogative, preservative, prohibitive, precreative, provocative, recitative, reformative, reparative, restorative, retributive, speculative, superlative; accumulative, administrative, alliterative, appreciative, argumentative, authoritative, commemorative, communicative, co-operative, corroborative, defenerative, deliberative, depreciative, determinative, discriminative, eradicative, illuminative, imaginative, insinuative, interrogative, opinionative, prejuducative, recriminative, refrigerative, regenerative, remunerative, representative, reverberative, significative.

-ix: fix, mix, pyx, six, Styx; admix, affix, commix, infix, matrix, onyx, prefix, prolix, suffix, transfix, unfix; cicatrix, crucifix, fiddlesticks, intermix, politics, sardonyx, executrix. (And plurals of nouns in **-ick**, as in "kicks".)

-ō, -ōw, -eau, -ōe: beau, blow, bo, bow, co. (company), crow, do (music), doe, dough, eau, Flo, floe, flow, foe, fro, glow, go, grow, ho, hoe, Joe, know, lo, low, mot, mow, no, O, oh, owe, Po, pro, rho, roe, row, sew, show, sloe, slow, snow, so, sow, stow, strow, though, throe, throw, toe, tow, trow, whoa, woe, zoe; aglow, ago, although, banjo, below, bestow, Bordeaux, bravo, bureau, chapeau, chateau, cocoa, dado, de trop, depot, dido, duo, forego, foreknow, foreshow, heigh-ho, hello, how-so, inflow, jabot, long-bow, morceau, oboe, outflow, outgrow, pierrot, plateau, rainbow, rondeau, rouleau, Soho, tableau, trousseau, unknow, upgrow, upthrow, allegro, apropos, buffalo, bungalow, calico, cameo, comme-il faut, Diderot, domino, embryo, entrepot, Eskimo, gigolo, haricot, Idaho, indigo, momento, mistletoe, mulatto, nuncio, oleo, overflow, overgrow, overthrow, Pimlico, portico, proximo, stiletto, studio, tobacco, torpedo, tremolo, ultimo, undergo, under-tow, vertigo, volcano, Westward-ho; adagio, bravissimo, embroglio, fortissimo, incognito, intaglio, Ontario, pistachio; braggadacio, oratorio.

-ōach: broach, brooch, coach, loach, poach, roach; abroach, approach, cockroach, encroach, reproach.

-ōad, -ōde, -ōwed: bode, clode, code, goad, load, lode, mode, node, ode, road, rode, spode, strode, toad, woad; abode, bestrode, commode, corrode, erode, explode, forebode, unload; antipode, discommode, episode, incommode, lycopode, overload, pigeon-toed, unbestowed. (And preterites of verbs in **-ōe, -ōw** and **-ōwe**.)

-ōaf: goaf, loaf, oaf.

-ōak, -ōke: bloke, broke, choke, cloak, coak, coke, croak, folk, joke, loke, moke, oak, poke, sloke, smoke, soak, spoke, stoke, stroke, toke, toque, woke, yoke, yolk; asoak, awoke, baroque, bespoke, convoke, evoke, forspoke, invoke, outbroke, provoke, revoke, uncloak, unyoke; artichocke, counterstroke, equiwoke, gentlefolk, masterstroke, understroke.

-ōal, -ōle, -ōl, -ōll, -ōul, -ōwl: bole, boll, bowl, coal, cole, dhole, dole, droll, foal, goal, hole, jole, jowl, knoll, kohl, mole, pole, poll, role, roll, scroll, shoal, shole, sole, soul, stole, stroll, thole, toll, troll, vole, whole; cajole, comptrol, condole, console, control, Creole, enroll, extoll, inscroll, loophole, maypole, parole, patrol, pistole, porthole, segol, tadpole, tophole, unroll, unsoul, uproll, virole; aureole, banderole, barcarolle, buttonhole camisole, capriole, caracole, casserole, curtainpole, girasole, pigeon-hole, rigmarole, self-control, Seminole, vacuole.

-ōam, -ōme: chrome, clomb, comb, dome, foam, Frome, gnome, holm, home, loam, "mome" (Carroll), Nome, ohm, pome, roam, Rome, sloam, tome; afoam, befoam, endome, Jerome, sea-foam; aerodrome, catacomb, chromosome, currycomb, gastronome, hippodrome, metronome, microsome, monochrome, palindrome, polychrome.

-ōan, ōne, -ōwn: blown, bone, cone, crone, drone, flown, groan, grown, hone, Joan, known, loan, lone, moan, mown, own, phone, pone, prone, Rhone, roan, scone, sewn, shown, Sloane, sown, stone, strown, tone, throne, thrown, zone: alone, atone, begroan, bemoan, bestrown, brimstone, Cologne, condone, depone, dethrone, disown, dispone, enthrone, engone, flagstone, foreknown, foreshown, full-blown, grindstone, hailstone, intone, keystone, limestone, milestone, moonstone, ozone, postpone, propone, trombone, unblown, ungrown, unknown, unsewn, unsown; chaperone, cornerstone, dictaphone, gramaphone, interpone, knucklebone, megaphone, microphone, monotone, overgrown, overthrown, saxophone, semitone, telephone, unbeknown, undertone, vitaphone, xylophone.

-ôar, -ôre: boar, Boer, bore, chore, core, corps, door, floor, fore, frore, four, gore, hoar, lore, more, nore, Nore, oar, o'er, pore, pour, roar, score, shore, snore, soar, sore, store, swore, tore, war, whore, wore, yore; adore, afore, ashore, before, Cawnpore, claymore, deplore, encore, explore, folklore, footsore, forbore, foreshore, forswore, galore, heartsore, ignore, implore, restore; albacore, battledore, Baltimore, commodore, evermore, furthermore, heretofore, matador, nevermore, pinafore, sagamore, semaphore, Singapore, sophomore, stevedore, sycamore, underscore. (See ôr and ôor.)

-ôarse: See ôrse.

-ōast, -ōst: boast, coast, ghost, grossed, host, most, oast, post, roast, toast; almost, engrossed, foremost, hindmost, riposte, sea-

coast, signpost; aftermost, bettermost, furthermost, hindermost, hithermost, innermost, lowermost, nethermost, outermost, undermost, uppermost, uttermost, westernmost.

-ōat, -ōte: bloat, boat, bote, Chote, coat, cote, Croate, dote, float, gloat, goat, groat, moat, mote, note, oat, quote, rote, shoat, smote, stoat, throat, tote, vote, wrote; afloat, capote, connote, demote, denote, devote, emote, footnote, lifeboat, misquote, outvote, promote, remote, steamboat, topcoat, unquote; anecdote, antidote, assymptote, billygoat, creosote, nanny goat, overcoat, petticoat, redingote,, table d'hôte, underwrote; Witenagemot.

-ōath, -ōth: both, growth, loath, oath, quoth, sloth, troth, wroth; Arbroath, betroth; aftergrowth, overgrowth, undergrowth.

-ōathe: clothe, loathe; betrothe.

-ōax: coax, hoax. (And pluralize -ōak, -ōke, as in "oaks", "jokes".)

-ob, -äb: blob, bob, Bob, cob, Cobb, dod, fob, glob, gob, hob, job, knob, lob, mob, nob, quab, rob, slob, snob, sob, squab, swab, throb; athrob, cabob, corncob, demob, hobnob, nabob; thingumbob.

-ōbe: globe, Job, lobe, Loeb, probe, robe; conglobe, disrobe, enrobe, unrobe; Anglophobe, Francophobe, Gallophobe, Slavophobe.

-ock: Bach, Bloch, block, bock, brock, chock, clock, cock, crock, doc, dock, flock, frock, hock, jock, Jock, knock, Knoche, loch, lock, Mach, mock, pock, roc, rock, shock, smock, sock, stock; acock, amok, Bangkok, bedrock, belock, bemock, deadlock, fetlock, Hancock, hemlock, padlock, peacock, petcock, shamrock, Sherlock, Shylock, tick-tock, unfrock, unlock, woodcock; alpenstock, Antioch, billycock, havelock, hollyhock, interlock, Little Rock, shuttlecock, weathercock.

-oct: concoct, decoct, shell-shocked. (And preterites of -ock, as in "locked".)

-od: clod, cod, God, hod, nod, odd, plod, pod, prod, quad, quod, rod, scrod, shod, sod, squad, tod, trod, wad; ballade, façade, roughshod, roulade, slipshod, unshod, untrod; demi-god, golden-rod, lycopod, platypod, promenade.

-odge: bodge, dodge, hodge, lodge, podge, splodge, stodge; dislodge, hodge-podge.

-ōe: See -ō.

-ôff: cough, doff, koff, off, prof, scoff, shroff, "soph", toff, trough; takeoff; philosophe.

-ôft: croft, loft, oft, soft, toft; aloft; undercroft. (And preterites of verbs in -off.)

-og, ogue: bog, clog, cog, flog, gog, grog, jog, nog, Prague, slog, shog, stog; agog, eggnogg, incog, unclog, demogogue, epilogue, monologue, pedagogue, synagogue.

-ôg, -ôgue: dog, fog, frog, hog, log, bulldog, analogue, apologue, catalogue, decalogue, dialogue, duologue, pettifog, travelogue.

-ōgue: brogue, rogue, vogue; prorogue; disembogue.

-oice: Boyce, choic, Joyce, voice; invoice, rejoice, Rolls-Royce.

-oid: Boyd, Floyd, Freud, Lloyd, void; avoid, devoid, Negroid, ovoid, rhomboid, tabloid; alkaloid, aneroid, anthropoid, asteroid, celluloid, Mongoloid, trapezoid; paraboloid, pyramidoid. (And preterites of verbs in -oy, as "destroyed".)

-oil: boil, Boyle, broil, coil, Doyle, foil, Hoyle, moil, oil, roil, soil, spoil, toil; despoil, embroil, entoil, gumboil, Lough Foyle, parboil, recoil, tinfoil, trefoil, turmoil, uncoil; counterfoil, disembroil, quatrefoil. (See -oyàl.)

-ōin, -ōyne: Boyne, coign, coin, foin, groin, groyne, join, loin, quoin; adjoin, benzoin, Burgoyne, conjoin, Des Moines, disjoin, enjoin, purloin, rejoin, sejoin, sirloin, subjoin; tenderloin.

-oint: joint, oint, point; adjoint, anoint, appoint, aroint, conjoint, disjoint, repoint, West Point; counterpoint, coverpoint, disappoint, reappoint.

-oise, -oys: froise, noise, poise, Troyes; counterpoise, equipoise, Illinois, Iroquois; avoirdupois. (And add "s" to -oy.)

-oist: foist, hoist, joist, moist, voiced; invoiced, rejoiced. (And add "s" to -oice.)

-oit: coit, doit, quoit; adroit, Beloit, dacoit, Detroit, exploit, introit; maladroit.

-ōke: See -ōak.

-ol, -oll: doll, loll, Moll, poll, Sol; atoll, extol; alcohol, capitol, folderol, parasol, vitriol.

-ōl, -ōll, -ōle: See -ōal.

-ōld: bold, cold, fold, gold, hold, mold, mould, old, scold, sold, told, wold; behold, blindfold, cuckold, enfold, foothold, foretold, freehold, household, retold, stronghold, threshold, toehold, twofold, unfold, untold, uphold, withhold; manifold, marigold, overbold. (And preterites of -ōal, -ōle, -ōll and -ōwl.)

-ōlk: See -ōak.

-ōlt: bolt, colt, dolt, holt, jolt, molt, poult, volt; revolt, unbolt; thunderbolt.

-olve: solve; absolve, convolve, devolve, dissolve, evolve, involve, resolve, revolve.

-om: bomb, dom, from, pom, "Prom", rhomb, Somme, Tom; aplomb, pogrom, pom-pom, therefrom, tom-tom, wherefrom.

-ōme: See -ōam.

-omp: comp, pomp, romp, stomp, swamp.

-ompt: prompt, romped, swamped.

-on: Bonn, con, don, John, non, swan, wan, yon; anon, Argonne, Aswan, bonbon, Canton, Ceylon, chiffon, cretonne, icon, neutron, proton, upon, Yvonne; amazon, autophon, Babylon, benison, celadon, dies non, gonfalon, hereupon, lexicon, marathon, narbonne, octagon, Oregon, paragon, Parthenon, pentagon, polygon, Rubicon, silicon, tarragon, thereupon, phenomenon. (See -un for some words of three syllables ending in -on as in "champion".)

-ôn: on, "scone" (Scotch), begon, bygone, hereon, undergone. (Also see -ăwn.)

-once, -onse: nonce, ponce, sconce, wants; ensconce, response, séance, liederkranz. (For rhymes to "once", see -unce.)

-ond, -onned: blond, blonde, bond, fond, frond, pond, wand, yond; abscond, beyond, despond, diamond, respond; correspond, co-respond, demimonde, vagabond. (And preterites of verbs in -on, as in "conned".)

-öne: See -un.

-ōne: See -ōan.

-ong: gong, prong, thong, throng, tong, dingdong, diphthong, Hongkong, mahjongg, ping-pong.

-ong: long, song, strong, Tong, wrong, along, belong, dugong, headlong, headstrong, lifelong, oblong, prolong; evensong, overlong.

-onk: bonk, conch, conk, honk, plonk. (For "Bronx", add "s" to above.)

-ont: font, want; Vermont; Hellespont.

-ōnt: don't, wont, won't.

-önt: front. See -unt.

-onze: bonze, bronze, "onze" (French.) (And add "s" to words in -on, as in "cons".)

-ōō: See -ew.

-öod: See -ud.

-ood: could, good, hood, should, stood, wood, would; childhood, Goodwood, manhood, unhood, wildwood, withstood; babyhood, brotherhood, fatherhood, hardihood, Hollywood, likelihood, livelihood, maidenhood, motherhood, neighborhood, Robin Hood, sandalwood, sisterhood, understood, widowhood; misunderstood.

-ōōd (as in "food"), -ēud, -ewed, ūde: brood, Bude, crude, dude, feud, food, Jude, lewd, mood, nude, prude, rood, rude, shrewd, snood, you'd, who'd; allude, collude, conclude, delude, denude, detrude, elude, étude, exclude, extrude, exude, illude, include, intrude, obtrued, occlude, preclude, prelude, protrude, secude; altitude, amplitude, assuetude, attitude, beatitude, certitude, consuetude, crassitude, desuetude, finitude, fortitude, gratitude, habitude, interlude, lassitude, latitude, longitude, magnitude, mansuetude, multitude, parvitude, platitude, plenitude, promptitude, pulchritude, quietude, restitude, sanctitude, servitude, solitude; disquietude, exactitude, inaptitude, incertitude, ineptitude, infinitude, ingratitude, necessitude, serenitude, similitude, solicitude. (See under -ew for preterites of verbs in -ew, -ō, -ūe.)

-ōōf: goof, hoof, oof, pouf, proof, roof, spoof, woof; aloof, behoof, disproof, fireproof, rainproof, reproof, Tartuffe; waterproof, weatherproof.

-ook: book, brook, cook, crook, hook, look, nook, rook, shook, spook, took; betook, Chinook, forsook, mistook, nainsook, outlook, partook; overlook, overtook, pocketbook, undertook.

-ōōl, -ūle: buhl, cool, drool, fool, ghoul, Goole, pool, Poole, rule, school, spool, stool, tool, tulle, who'll, Yule; ampoule, befool, footstool, home rule, misrule, toadstool, sporrule, Stamboul, whirlpool; Istanbul, Liverpool, molecule, overrule, ridicule, vestibule. (See -ūle, with diphthong, as in "mule". See also, -ūēl in two-syllable rhymes as in "fuel".)

-ool: wool. See -ul.

-ōōm, -ūme: bloom, boom, broom, brougham, brume, coomb, coombe, doom, flume, fume, gloom, groom, loom, plume, rheum, room, spoom, spume, tomb, whom, womb, zoom; abloom, assume, Batoum, beplume, bridegroom, consume, costume, entomb, exhume, Ezroum, Fiume, heirloom, Khartoum, legume, perfume, presume, relume, resume, simoon, subsume, unplume, untomb; anteroom, diningroom, disentomb, drawingroom, dressingroom, hecatomb, reassume. (See -ūme with diphthong, as in "fume".)

-ōōn, ūne: boon, Boone, coon, croon, Doon, dune, goon, hewn, June, loon, lune, Lune, moon, noon, prune, rune, screwn, shoon, soon, spoon, strewn, swoon, Troon, tune; attune, baboon, balloon, bassoon, bestrewn, buffoon, cartoon, cocoon, commune, doubloon, dragoon, Dunoon, eftsoon, eschewn, festoon, forenoon, galloon, harpoon, high noon, immune, impugn, jejune, lagoon, lampoon, maroon, midnoon, monsoon, oppugn, platoon, poltroon, pontoon, quadroon, raccoon, Rangoon, shalloon, simoon, spittoon, tycoon, typhoon, walloon; afternoon, brigadoon, honeymoon, importune, macaroon, musketoon, octoroon, opportune, pantaloon, picaroon, picayune, rigadoon. (See -ūne with diphthong, as in "tune".)

-ōōp, -oūp: coop, croup, droop, drupe, dupe, goop, group, hoop, jupe, Krupp, loop, poop, scoop, sloop, snoop, soup, stoop, stoup, stupe, swoop, troop, troupe, whoop; recoup, unhoop; Guadeloupe, nincompoop. (See -ūpe.)

-ôor: boor, floor, moor, more, poor, Ruhr, spoor, tour, you're; amour, contour, detour; blackamoor, paramour. (See -ūre, -ewer in two-syllable rhymes, and -ōar.)

-ōōse, -ūce, -ūice (when pronounced -ōōse, short): Bruce, deuce, goose, juice, loose, moose, noose, puce, sluice, spruce, truce, use, zeus; abduce, abstruse, abuse, adduce, burnoose, caboose, conduce, deduce, diffuse, disuse, excuse, induce, misuse, obtuse, papoose, produce, profuse, recluse, reduce, seduce, Toulouse, traduce, vamoose; introduce, reproduce; hypotenuse. (Also see -uce.)

-ōōse (long), -ōōze, -ūes: blues, booze, bruise, choose, cruise, lose, Ouse, ooze, ruse, shoes, snooze, trews, whose, who's; enthuse, peruse. (Compare -ūse, as in "fuse", and see -ew,

-ieū, -ūe and -ōō for plurals of nouns and third person singular of verbs, as in "pews", adieus, "hues", etc.)

-ōōst, -ūced, -ūsed (sharp); coost, juiced, loosed, noosed, roost, suiced, spruced, used; adduced, conduced, deduced, educed, induced, produced, reduced, seduced, subduced; superinduced.

-oot (short): foot, put, soot; afoot, forefoot; pussyfoot, underfoot.

-ōōt, -ūte: boot, bruit, brute, chute, coot, flute, fruit, hoot, jute, loot, moot, root, route, shoot, skoot, toot; adjute, Beirut, cahoot, Canute, cheroot, galloot, recruit, uproot; arrowroot, attribute, overshoot, parachute, waterchute. (See **-ūte** with diphthong, as in "cute", "newt", etc.)

-ōōth (short th) **-ūth:** booth, couth, ruth, Ruth, sleuth, sooth, "strewth", tooth, truth, youth; Duluth, forsooth, uncouth, untruth, vermouth.

-ōōth (length): smooth, soothe.

-ōōve: groove, hoove, move, prove, who've, you've; amove, approve, behoove, disprove, improve, remove, reprove; disapprove.

-ōōze: See **-ōōse.**

-op: bop, chop, cop, crop, drop, flop, fop, hop, lop, mop, plop, pop, prop, shop, slop, sop, stop, strop, swap, top, whop, wop; Aesop, atop, bedrop, co-op, eavesdrop, estop, flipflop, foretop, galop, snowdrop, tiptop, unstop; ginger-pop, lollipop, overtop, soda pop, underprop.

-öp: develop. See **-up.**

-ōpe, -ōap: cope, dope, grope, hope, lope, mope, nope, ope, pope, rope, scope, slope, soap, taupe, tope, trope; elope, Good Hope; antelope, antipope, bioscope, cantaloupe, envelope, gyroscope, horoscope, interlope, isotope, microscope, misanthrope, periscope, polyscope, stethoscope, telescope; helioscope, heliotrope, kaleidoscope.

-opse, -ops: copse. (And extend **-op.**)

-opt: copped, copt, dropped; adopt, outcropped, uncropped, unstopped. (And preterites of verbs in **-op.**)

-ôr: for, lor, nor, or, Thor, tor, war; abhor, lessor, señor, therefore, ancestor, corridor, councillor, counsellor, cuspidor, dinosaur, Ecuador, escritoire, Labrador, legator, matador, metaphor, meteor, minotaur, monitor, mortgagor, orator; picador, Salvador, servitor, troubador, visitor, warrior; ambassador, apparitor, conspirator, contributor, depositor, executor, expositor, inheritor, inquisitor, progenitor, proprietor, solicitor, superior, toreador, ulterior; primogenitor.

-ör: donor, furor, junior, senior, vendor; auditor, bachelor, chancellor, conqueror, creditor, editor, emperor, janitor, senator, warrior; ambassador, anterior, competitor, excelsior, exterior, inferior, interior, posterior.

-ôrce, -ôrse, -ôarse, -ôurce: coarse, corse, course, force, gorse, hoarse, horse, Morse, Norse, source, torse; concourse, discourse, divorce, endorse, enforce, perforce, recourse, remorse, resource, sea horse, unhorse; hobbyhorse, intercourse, reinforce, watercourse.

-ôrch: Borsch, porch, scorch, torch.

-ôrd (as in "cord"): See **-ōard.**

-örd (as in "word"): See **-êard.**

-ôrge: forge, George, gorge; disgorge, engorge, regorge; overgorge.

-ôrk: cork, Cork, fork, pork, stork, torque, York; New York, pitchfork, uncork.

-örld: world. See **-earled.**

-ôrm: form, norm, storm, swarm, warm; bestorm, conform, deform, Great Orme, inform, misform, perform, reform, transform, unwarm, upswarm; aeriform, chloroform, cruciform, cuneiform, misinform, multiform, thunderstorm, uniform, vermiform; iodoform.

-ôrn, ôrne: born, borne, bourn, corn, horn, lorn, morn, mourn, scorn, shorn, sorn, shorn, sworn, thorn, torn, warn, worn; acorn, adorn, blackthorn, buckthorn, Cape Horn, first-born, foghorn, forborne, forewarn, forlorn, forsworn, greenhorn, Leghorn, lovelorn, outworn, popcorn, suborn, toilworn, unborn; barley-corn, Capricorn, disadorn, longicorn, peppercorn, readorn, unicorn. (See **-ôurn** and **-ăwn.**)

-ôrp: dorp, thorp, warp.

-ôrse: See **-ôrce.**

-ôrt: bort, court, fort, forte, mort, ort, port, porte, quart, short, snort, sort, sport, swart, thwart, tort, wart; abort, assort, athwart, cavort, cohort, comport, consort, contort, deport, disport, distort, escort, exhort, export, extort, import, passport, purport, rapport, report, resort, retort, seaport, support, transport; misreport.

-ôrth: forth, fourth, north, Porth, swarth; henceforth, thenceforth.

-ōse (short "s"): close, cose, dose, gross; engross, floccose, gibbose, globose, glucose, jocose, morose, nodose, verbose; cellulose, comatose, diagnose, foliose, grandiose, overdose, underdose; Barbados.

-ōse (-ōze): chose, close, clothes, does (plural of "doe"), doze, froze, gloze, hose, nose, pose, prose, "pros", rose, Rose, those; Ambrose, arose, banjos, compose, depose, depots, disclose, dispose, enclose, expose, foreclose, impose, inclose, Montrose, oppose, repose, suppose, transpose, unclose, unfroze; decompose, discompose, indispose, interpose, predispose, presuppose, recompose, superpose, tuberose. (For more than 60 other good rhymes, see plurals of nouns and third person singulars of verbs in -ō, -ōw and -ōe.)

-ösh: See -äsh.

-ôss: boss, Cos, cross, doss, dross, floss, fosse, gloss, "Goss", hoss, joss, loss, moss, os, poss, Ross, sauce, toss; across, cerebos, enboss, lacrosse, reredos; albatross, applesauce.

-ôst: cost, frost, lost, wast; accost, exhaust; holocaust, pentecost. (And preterities of -ôss, as in "bossed".)

-ōst: See -ōast.

-ot, -otte: blot, clot, cot, dot, Dot, got, grot, hot, jot, knot, lot, mot, not, plot, pot, rot, scot, Scot, shot, slot, snot, sot, spot, squat, swat, swot, tot, trot, watt, what, wot, yacht; allot, boycott, calotte, capot, cocotte, culotte, dogtrot, ergot, forgot, foxtrot, garotte, gavotte, kumquat, loquat, somewhat, unknot; Aldershot, aliquot, apricot, bergamot, camelot, chariot, counterplot, eschalot, gallipot, Hottentot, Huguenot, idiot, Lancelot, misbegot, patriot, polygot, unbegot, undershot; forget-me-not.

-otch: blotch, botch, crotch, notch, potch, scotch, Scotch, splotch, swatch, watch; hopscotch, hotchpotch, topnotch.

-ōte: See -ōat.

-ōth: See -ōath.

-ôth: broth, cloth, froth, Goth, moth, troth, wroth; betroth, broadcloth, sackcloth; Ashtaroth, behemoth, Ostrogoth, Visigoth.

-ouch: couch, crouch, grouch, ouch, pouch, slouch, vouch; avouch; scaramouch. (For "touch," see -uch.)

-ouch (soft **ch**): mouch; bedouch.

-oud, -owd: cloud, crowd, dowd, loud, proud, shroud, Stroud; aloud, becloud, beshroud, encloud, enshroud, unbowed, uncloud, unshroud; disendowed, overcloud, overcrowd, thundercloud. (And preterites of -ow, as in "bowed".)

-ough: See -ō, -ock, -off, -ōw, -uf.

-ôught: See -äught.

-ōul: See -ōal.

-ōuld: See -ōld.

-ounce: bounce, flounce, frounce, ounce, pounce, trounce; announce, denounce, enounce, pronounce, renounce. (Also, the plurals of -ount, as in "counts".)

-ound, -owned: bound, found, ground, hound, mound, pound, round, sound, wound; abound, aground, around, astound, background, bloodhound, compound, confound, dumbfound, expound, hidebound, homebound, icebound, inbound, outbound, profound, propound, rebound, redound, renowned, resound, spellbound, surround, unbound, unfound, unsound; underground, merry-go-round. (And preterites and adjectives of words in -own, as in "clowned" and "renowned".)

-ōund: See preterites of verbs in **ōōn,** as in "crooned".

-ounge: lounge, scrounge.

-ount: count, fount, mount; account, amount, discount, dismount, miscount, recount, remount, surmount; catamount, paramount, tantamount.

-ōup: See -ōōp.

-our: dour, flour, hour, our, scour, sour; bescour, besour, deflour, devour. See -owėr in two-syllable rhymes.)

-ôurd: gourd, Lourdes, moored. (And preterites of -ôr, -ōre, -ôar words.)

-ôurn: bourn, mourn. (See -ôrn.)

-ôurse: See -ôrce.

-ous: See -us.

-ouse (short): blouse, douse, grouse, house, louse, mouse, nous, souse, spouse, Strauss; backhouse, doghouse, madhouse, outhouse, penthouse, poorhouse, storehouse, warehouse, workhouse; Fledermaus, flindermouse.

-ouse (**-ouze**): drowse, blouse, blowze, browse, house (verb), rouse, touse; carouse (verb), expouse, unhouse, uprouse. (And plurals of nouns and third person singulars of verbs in **-ow** and **-ough,** as in "brows", "bows", "boughs" and "ploughs".)

-out: bout, clout, doubt, drought, flout, gout, grout, knout, kraut, lout, nowt, out, owt, pout, rout, scout, snout, spout, sprout, stout, tout, trout; about, beshout, bespout, devout, knockout, mahout, redoubt, thereout, throughout, without; gadabout, hereabout, knockabout, roundabout, sauerkraut, stirabout, thereabout, whereabout.

-outh: drouth, Louth, mouth, south. (For rhymes to "youth", see **-ōōth.**)

-ŏve: dove, glove, love, of, shove; above, below, foxglove, hereof, thereof, unglove, whereof; ladylove, turtledove.

-ōve: clove, cove, dove, drove, grove, hove, Hove, Jove, mauve, rove, shrove, stove, strove, throve, trove, wove; alcove, behove; interwove, treasure-trove. (**-ove,** as in "proove", **-ōōve.**)

-ow, -ough: bough, bow, brow, chow, cow, dhow, frau, how, now, plough, plow, prow, row, scow, slough, Slough, sow, tau, thou, trow, wow, vow; allow, avow, bowwow, endow, enow, Foochow, highbrow, kowtow, landau, lowbrow, Mau Mau, meow, Moldau, Moscow, powwow, snowplow, somehow; anyhow, disallow, disavow, disendow, middlebrow.

-ōw: See **-ō.**

-ōwed: See **-ōde.**

-owl, -oul: cowl, foul, fowl, growl, howl, jowl, owl, prowl, scowl, yowl; befoul, waterfowl. (Compare **-owĕl** in two syllable rhymes.)

-own: brown, clown, crown, down, drown, frown, gown, noun, town; adown, decrown, discrown, downtown, embrown, pronoun, renown, uptown; eiderdown, hand-me-down, tumble-down, upside down.

-ōwn: See **-ōan.**

-owned: See **-ound.**

-ōws: See **-ōse.**

-ox, -ocks: box, "chocs.", cox, fox, lox, ox, phlox, pox, sox, vox; approx, bandbox, hatbox, icebox, mailbox, postbox, smallpox; chickenpox, equinox, orthodox, paradox; heterodox. (And plurals of nouns and third person singulars of verbs in **-ock.**)

-oy: boy, buoy, cloy, coy, gloy, goy, hoy, joy, oy, ploy, poi, soy, toy, troy, Troy; ahoy, alloy, Amoy, annoy, convoy, decoy, deploy, destroy, employ, enjoy, envoy, hoi polloi, Leroy, Savoy, sepoy, yoi-yoi!, corduroy, Illinois, Iroquois, overjoy, pomeroy, saveloy.

-oys: See **-oise.**

-ōze: See **-ōse.**

-ub: bub, blub, chub, club, cub, drub, dub, grub, hub, nub, pub, rub, scrub, shrub, snub, stub, sub, tub; hubbub; sillabub, Beelzebub.

-ūbe: boob, cube, "rube", Rube, tube; jujube.

-ūce, -ūse: Bruce, duce, juice, puce, use, (noun); abstruse, abuse (noun), conduce, deduce, diffuse, educe, excuse (noun), obtuse, produce, reduce, refuse (noun), seduce; traduce, introduce. (See **-ōōse,** (hards), and under same heading.)

-uch, -utch: clutch, crutch, Dutch, hutch, much, smutch, such, touch; retouch; inasmuch, insomuch, overmuch.

-uck: buck, chuck, cluck, duck, luck, muck, pluck, puck, Puck, ruck, shuck, struck, stuck, suck, truck, tuck; amok, amuck, awestruck, Canuck, ill-luck, misluck, pot-luck, roebuck, woodchuck, horrorstruck, terrorstruck, thunder-struck, wonderstruck.

-ucked: See **-uct.**

-ucks: See **-ux.**

-uct, -ucked: duct; abduct, conduct (verb), construct, deduct, induct, instruct, obstruct; aqueduct, misconduct, oviduct, usufruct, viaduct. (And preterites of verbs in **-uck,** as in "mucked".)

-ud: blood, bud, cud, dud, flood, mud, rudd, scud, spud, stud, sud, thud; bestud, lifeblood, rosebud.

-ūde: See **-ōōd.**

-udge: budge, drudge, fudge, grudge, judge, nudge, Rudge, sludge, smudge, snudge, trudge; adjudge, begrudge, forejudge, misjudge, prejudge, rejudge.

-ūe: See **-ew.**

-uff: bluff, buff, chough, chuff, clough, cuff, duff, fluff, Gough, gruff, guff, huff, luff, muff, puff, rough, ruff, scruff, scuff, slough, snuff, sough, stuff, tough, tuff; bepuff, besnuff, breadstuff, enough, rebuff; blindman's-buff, counterbuff, powder-puff.

-uft: cruft, tuft; candytuft. (And past participles of verbs in **-uff.**)

-ūise: See **-ōōse.**

-ūit: See **-ōōt.**

-uīse: See **-īze.**

-ug: bug, chug, drug, dug, hug, jug, lug, mug, plug, pug, rug, shrug, slug, smug, snug, thug, tug, ugh; humbug; bunnyhug, doodlebug, jitterbug.

-ūke: duke, fluke, Juke, Luke, puke, snook, spook, uke; archduke, caoutchouc, peruke, rebuke; Heptateuch, Hexateuch, mameluke, Marmaduke, Pentateuch.

-ul, -ull (as in "bull"): bull, full, pull, wool; abull, annul, cupful, graceful, lambswool; beautiful, bountiful, dutiful, fanciful, masterful, merciful, pitiful, plentiful, powerful, sorrowful, teaspoonful, wonderful, worshipful; tablespoonful.

-ul, -ull (as in "dull"): cull, dull, gull, hull, Hull, lull, mull, null, scull, skull, trull; annul, bulbul, mogul, numskull, seagull; disannul.

-ūle: fuel, mewl, mule, pule, tuhl, you'll, Yule; ampule; molecule, reticule, ridicule, vestibule. (See **-ōōl**, and under same heading, **-ule,** without "u" sound, as in "rule". Also **-ūėl** in two-syllable rhymes.)

-ulge: bulge; divulge, effulge, indulge, promulge.

-ulk: bulk, hulk, pulque, skulk, sulk.

-ulp: gulp, pulp, sculp.

-ulse: mulse, pulse; appulse, convulse, expulse, impulse, insulse, repulse.

-ult: cult, ult; adult, consult, exult, insult, occult, result, tumult; catapult, difficult.

-um: Brum, bum, chum, come, crumb, drum, dumb, from, glum, gum, hum, mum, numb, plum, plumb, rum, scum, scrum, slum, some, strum, stum, sum, swum, thrum, thumb; become, benumb, humdrum, spec-

trum, succumb; burdensome, cardamom, Christendom, cranium, cumbersome, drearisome, flunkeydom, frolicsome, heathendom, humorsome, laudanum, martyrdom, maximum, meddlesome, minimum, misbecome, nettlesome, odium, opium, overcome, pabulum, pendulum, platinum, premium, quarrelsome, quietsome, radium, rebeldom, speculum, tedium, troublesome, tweedledum, tympanum, vacuum, venturesome, wearisome, worrisome, wranglesome; adventuresome, chrysanthemum, compendium, delirium, empirium, encomium, exordium, fee-fifo-fum, geranium, gymnasium, harmonium, magnesium, millenium, opprobrium, palladium, petroleum, residuum, sensorium, solatium, symposium; auditorium, crematorium, equilibrium, pandemonium, sanitarium.

-ūme: fume, plume, spume; assume, consume, exhume, Fiume, illume, perfume, presume, relume, resume; reassume. (Compare **-ōōm.**)

-ump: bump, chump, clump, crump, dump, frump, grump, gump, hump, jump, lump, mump, plump, pump, rump, slump, stump, sump, thump, trump, tump, ump; bethump, mugwump.

-un: bun, done, dun, fun, gun, Hun, none, nun, one, pun, run, shun, son, spun, stun, sun, ton, tun, won; begun, foredone, forerun, homespun, outdone, outrun, rerun, someone, undone, unrun; Albion, amazon, benison, cinnamon, colophon, Chesterton, galleon, ganglion, garrison, gonfalon, jettison, octagon, orison, overdone, paragon, pentagon, polygon, simpleton, singleton, skeleton, unison, venison; accordion, companion, oblivion, phenomenon.

-unce: bunce, dunce, once. (Also, see **-unt +** s, as in "hunts".)

-unch: brunch, bunch, Clunch, crunch, hunch, lunch, munch, punch, scrunch.

-unct, -unked: bunked, flunked; adjunct, defunct, debunked.

-und: bund, fund; fecund, jocund, obtund, refund, rotund; cummerbund, moribund, obrotund, rubicund, verecund. (And preterites of verbs in **-un,** as in "punned".)

-ūne: dune, hewn, June, tune, viewn; commune, immune, impugn, jejune, pursuen, subduen, triune; importune, opportune; inopportune. (Compare **-ōōn,** and, under same heading, **-ūne.**)

-ung: bung, clung, dung, flung, hung, lung, rung, slung, sprung, strung, stung, sung, swung, tongue, wrung, young; among, high-strung, Shantung, unhung, unstrung, unsung; overhung, underslung.

-unge(j): lunge, plunge, sponge; expunge.

-unk: bunk, chunk, drunk, dunk, flunk, funk, hunk, junk, monk, plunk, punk, shrunk, skunk, slunk, spunk, stunk, sunk, trunk; kerplunk, quidnunc.

-unt: blunt, brunt, bunt, front, grunt, hunt, lunt, punt, runt, shunt, stunt; affront, confront, forefront.

-up: crup, cup, pup, sup, tup, up; hiccup, makeup, setup, teacup, tossup; buttercup, develop, lovingcup.

-ūpe: drupe, dupe. (See **-ōōp**.)

-upt: abrupt, corrupt, disrupt, erupt; incorrupt, interrupt. (And preterites of words in **-up,** as in "cupped".)

-ûr: See **êr**.

-ûrb: See **-êrb**.

-ûrd: See **-êard**.

-ūre: cure, dure, lure, Muir, pure, sure, your, you're; abjure, adjure, allure, brochure, cocksure, coiffure, demure, endure, ensure, impure, inure, manure, mature, obscure, perdure, procure, secure, unmoor, unsure; amateur, aperture, armature, calenture, comfiture, conoisseur, coverture, curvature, cynosure, forfeiture, furniture, immature, insecure, manicure, overture, paramour, pedicure, premature, quadrature, reassure, reinsure, signature, sinecure, tablature, troubador, vestiture; caricature, discomfiture, divestiture, entablature, expenditure, investiture, literature, miniature, temperature; primogeniture. (See **-ôor,** also **-ewêr** in two-syllable rhymes.)

-ûrf: See **êrf**.
-ûrge: See **-êrge**.

-ûrk: See **-êrk**.

-ûrl: See **-êarl**.

-ûrn: See **-êarn**.

-ûrp: See **îrp**.

-ûrse: See **-êrce**.

-ûrst: See **-îrst**.

-urt: See **-êrt**.

-ûrve: See **-êrve**.

-ûrze: furze, thyrse. (And add "s" to words in **-êr, -îr** and **-ûr**.)

-us, -uss: bus, buss, cuss, fuss, Gus, Hus, muss, plus, pus, Russ, thus, truss, us; cirrus, discuss, nimbus, nonplus, percus, Remus, stratus, abacus, Angelum, animus, blunderbuss, emulus. (And nearly 300 false, rhymes in words of two syllables and over, which end in **-us** and **-ous**. Thus "sarcopgagus", "bulbous", and "impetuous".)

-ūse: See **-ūce**.

-ūse (ūze): blues, fuse, fuze, mews, muse, news, use (verb); abuse, accuse, amuse, bemuse, confuse, contuse, diffuse, disuse, enthuse, excuse, infuse, misuse, peruse, refuse, suffuse, transfuse; disabuse, Syracuse. (See **-ew, -ieu, -ūe** and **-ōō** for plurals of nouns and third person singulars of verbs as in "pews", "adieus", and "blues".)

-ush: bush, "cush" (billiards), push, shush, swoosh; ambush; bramblebush, Hindu Kush.

-ush (as in "blush"): blush, brush, crush, flush, frush, gush, hush, lush, mush, plush, rush, slush, thrush, tush; outblush, outrush, uprush.

-usk: brusque, busk, dusk, fusc, husk, lusk, musk, rusk, tusk, Usk; adusk, dehusk, subfusk.

-ust: bust, crust, dost, dust, gust, just, lust, must, rust, thrust, trust; adjust, adust, august, August, combust, disgust, distrust, encrust, entrust, incrust, mistrust, piecrust, robust, stardust, unjust, untrussed. (And preterites in **-uss,** as in "fussed".)

-ut, -utt: but, butt, crut, cut, glut, gut, hut, jut, Kut, mutt, nut, phut, putt, rut, scut, shut, slut, smut, strut, tut; abut, astrut, besmut, catgut, clear-cut, englut, gamut, outshut, peanut, rebut, woodcut; betel-nut, cocoanut, halibut, Lilliput, occiput, surrebut, waterbutt. (For rhymes to "put", see **-ōot**.)

-ūte: beaut, boot, brute, Butte, chute, coot, cute, flute, fruit, hoot, jute, loot, lute, moot, mute, newt, root, route, scoot, scute, shoot, snoot, soot, suit, toot. Ute; acute, argute, astute, cahoot, cheroot, commute, compute, confute, depute, dilute, dispute, emeute, enroot, en route, galoot, hirsute, imbrute, impute, minute, outshoot, permute, pollute, pursuit, recruit, refute, repute, salute, solute, unboot, unroot, uproot, volute; absolute, arrowroot, attribute, baldicoot, constitute, destitute, disrepute, dissolute, institute, involute, overshoot, prosecute, prostitute, resolute, substitute. (See **-ōōt** and, under same heading, **-ūte**.)

-ūth: See **-ōōth**.

-ux, -ucks: Bucks, crux, dux, flux, lux, shucks, tux; conflux, efflux, influx, reflux. (And plurals of nouns and third person singulars of verbs in **-uck**, as in "ducks", "mucks".)

-uz: buzz, coz, does, doz., fuzz, Luz, muzz, Uz; abuzz.

-y(ī): ay, aye, buy, by, bye, cry, die, dry, eye, fie, fly, fry, guy, Guy, hi!, hie, high, I, lie, lye, my, nigh, phi, pi, pie, ply, pry, psi, rye, Rye, shy, sigh, sky, Skye, sly, spry, spy, sty, Thai, thigh, thy, tie, try, vie, why, wry, Wye; ally, apply, awry, belie, comply, decry, defy, descry, espy, go-by, good-bye, hereby, imply, July, magpie, mudpie, outcry, outvie, popeye, rely, reply, Shanghai, shoofly, standby, supply, thereby, untie, whereby; alibi, alkali, amplify, beatify, beautify, brutify, butterfly, candify, certify, clarify, classify, codify, crucify, damnify, dandify, dignify, edify, falsify, firefly, fortify, fructify, gasify, genii, glorify, gratify, horrify, hushaby, justify, lignify, liquefy, lullaby,

magnify, modify, mollify, mortify, multiply, mystify, notify, nullify, occupy, ossify, petrify, purify, qualify, ramify, rarefy, ratify, rectify, sanctify, satisfy, scarify, signify, simplify, specify, stupefy, terrify, testify, torpify, typify, underlie, unify, verbify, verify, versify, vilify, vivify; angelify, disqualify, dissatisfy, exemplify, fossilify, identify, indemnify, intensify, personify, preoccupy, revivify, solidify.

-yle: See **-īle**.

-yme: See **-īme**.

-ẏmph: lymph, nymph.

-yne: See **-īne**.

-ẏnx: See **-inx**.

-ẏp: See **-ip**.

-yre: See **-īre**.

-ẏst: See **-ist**.

-ẏpse: See **-ipse**.

-yre: See **-īre**.

-yrrh: See **-êr**.

-ẏsm: See **-ism**.

-ẏst: See **-ist**.

-ẏth: See **-ith**.

-ythe: See **-īthe**.

-yve: See **-īve**.

-ẏx: See **-ix**.

TWO OR MORE SYLLABLE RHYMES

-abȧrd: jabbered, scabbard, slabbered, tabard.

-abble: babble, cabble, dabble, drabble, gabble, rabble, scrabble; bedabble, bedrabble. (For rhymes to "squabble", see **-obble**.)

-abböt: abbot, Cabot, jabot, sabot.

-abbey, -abby: abbey, cabby, crabby, flabby, scabby, shabby, tabby. (And extend **-ab** for such rhymes as "cabby".)

-ābėl: See **-āble**.

-abid: rabid, tabid.

-ābiȧn, -ābiön: fabian, gabion, Sabian, Arabian.

-ābiēs: babies, gabies, Jabez, rabies, scabies.

-abit: habit, rabbet, rabbit; cohabit, inhabit.

-āble, -ābėl: Abel, able, Babel, babel, cable, fable, gable, label, Mabel, sable, stable, table; disable, enable, unable, unstable.

-ābör, -ābêr: caber (Scotch), labor, neighbor, saber, tabor; belabor.

-äbrȧ: candelabra.

-āby: baby, gaby, maybe.

-acȧ: "bacca", dacca, paca, alpaca, malacca, polacca. (Compare **-ackêr**.)

-ācėnt, -āscėnt: jacent, naissant, nascent; adjacent, complacent, complaisant, renaissant, renascent, subjacent; interjacent, superjacent.

-acėt: See **-assėt**.

-ācial: facial, glacial, racial, spatial; abbatial, palatial.

-ācious, -ātious: gracious, spacious; audacious, bibacious, bulbaceous, capacious, cetaceous, cretaceous, disgracious, edacious, fallacious, feracious, flirtatious, fugacious, herbaceous, Horatius, Ignatius, linguacious, loquacious, mendacious, minacious, misgracious, mordacious, predaceous, procacious, pugnacious, rampacious, rapacious, sagacious, salacious, sebaceous, sequacious, setaceous, tenacious, ungracious, veracious, vexatious, vivacious, voracious; carbonaceous, contumacious, disputatious, efficacious, execratious, farinaceous, incapacious, ostentatious, perspicacious, pertinacious, resinaceous, violaceous.

-ācis, -āsis: basis, crasis, glacis, phasis; oasis. (Compare plurals in **-ēce**.)

-ackáge: package, stackage, trackage.

-ackén: blacken, bracken, slacken.

-ackêr, -acquêr: backer, blacker, cracker, hacker, lacquer, packer, hijacker, quacker, slacker, stacker.

-ackét: bracket, jacket, packet, placket, racket, tacket.

-ackey, -acky: baccy, blackie, Jacky, knacky, Lackey, quacky, tacky, wacky.

-ackle: cackle, crackle, grackle, hackle, macle, quackle, shackle, tackle; ramshackle.

-actêr, -actör: actor, factor, tractor; abstractor, attracter, character, compacter, contractor, detractor, distracter, enacter, exacter, extracter, infractor, olfactor, protractor, refractor, retractor, subtracter, transactor; benefactor.

-actic: lactic, tactic; didactic, emphractic, galactic, syntactic; prophylactic.

-actice: cactus, practice.

-actile: dactyle (or dactyl), tactile, tractile; contractile, protractile, retractile.

-action: action, faction, fraction, paction, taction, traction; abstraction, attraction, coaction, compaction, contaction, contraction, detraction, distraction, exaction, extraction, impaction, inaction, infraction, protraction, reaction, refraction, retraction, stupefaction, subaction, subtraction, transaction; arefaction, benefaction, calefaction, counteraction, interaction, labefaction, liquefaction, malefaction, petrifaction, putrefaction, rarefaction, retroaction, satisfaction; dissatisfaction.

-active: active, tractive; abstractive, attractive, coactive, distractive, enactive, inactive, protractive, reactive, refractive, retractive; calefactive, counteractive, purifactive, putrefactive, retroactive, stupefactive.

-actly: compactly, exactly; matter-of-factly.

-actréss: actress, factress; benefactress, detractress, malefactress.

-acture: facture, fracture; compacture, manufacture.

-ācy: Casey, Gracie, lacy, Macy, racy, Tracy.

-ädà: Dada; armada, haggada, Nevada.

-adám: Adam, madam; macadam.

-addén: bad'un, gladden, madden, sadden; engladden.

-addêr: adder, bladder, gadder, gladder, ladder, madder, padder, sadder; stepladder. (See **-attêr**.)

-addést, -addist: fadist, gladdest, maddest, saddest; invadest. (See **-attést**.)

-addle: addle, faddle, paddle, raddle, saddle, spraddle, straddle; skedaddle, unsaddle. (See **-attle**.)

-addöck: Braddock, haddock, Maddock, paddock, shaddock.

-addy: caddy, daddy, faddy, laddie, paddy; sugar daddy.

-ādén, -āidén: Aden, Haydn, laden, maiden; mermaiden, overladen, unladen.

-ādêr: aider, trader; crusader, evader. (See **-āter**.)

-adgêr: badger, cadger.

-ādiênt: gradient, radiant.

-adish, -addish: baddish, caddish, faddish, gaddish, maddish, radish, saddish.

-ādium: radium, stadium, palladium.

-ādle: cradle, ladle; encradle.

-ādō: bravado, Mikado, passado; avocado, desperado, Colorado.

-ādō: dado; crusado, grenado, stoccado, tornado; bastinado, renegado.

-ädre: cadre, padre.

-ādy, ādi: Brady, braidy, cadi, glady, lady, maidie, O'Brady, Sadie, shady; landlady.

-āfêr: safer, wafer.

-àffêr, -àffīr, -aughêr: chaffer, gaffer, Kaffir, laugher, quaffer; cinematographer, photographer.

-affic: graphic, "maffick", traffic; autographic, lithographic, paragraphic, phonographic, photographic, pornographic, seismographic, telegraphic; autobiographic, cinematographic.

-affle: baffle, gaffle, raffle, snaffle.

-affled, -afföld: baffled, raffled, scaffold, snaffled.

-affy: baffy, chaffy, daffy, draffy, taffy.

-aftêr: after, dafter, grafter, laughter, rafter, shafter, wafter; hereafter, thereafter; thereinafter.

-ägà, -ägêr (hard): lager, saga.

-ägêr, -äjôr: cager, gauger, major, pager, sager, stager; assuager, presager, wager.

-aggàrd: blackguard, baggard, haggard, laggard, staggered, swaggered.

-aggêr: bagger, bragger, dagger, flagger, gagger, jagger, nagger, ragger, tagger, wagger; carpet-bagger.

-aggish: haggish, naggish, waggish.

-aggle: draggle, gaggle, haggle, raggle, straggle, waggle; bedraggle.

-aggöt, -agàte: agate, Baggot, faggot, maggot.

-aggy, -aggie: Aggie, baggy, craggy, jaggy, knaggy, laggy, Maggie, quaggy, raggy, scraggy, shaggy, snaggy, swaggy, waggy.

-agic: magic, tragic; ellagic, pelagic.

-agile: agile, fragile.

-ägō: dago, sago; farrago, lumbago, Tobago, virago.

-ägō: farrago, Chicago.

-agön: dragon, flagon, wagon; snap-dragon.

-ägrànt: flagrant, fragrant, vagrant; infragrant.

-agship: flagship, hagship.

-äic: algebraic, archaic, Hebraic, Judaic, mosaic, prosaic, sodaic, trochaic; paradisaic.

-äidèn: See -ädèn:

-äiety, äity: gaiety, laity.

-äiler: gaoler. (And extend -ail for "jailer", "sailor", etc.)

-äiliff: bailiff, Caliph.

-äiling: ailing, grayling, paling. (And extend -äil for "prevailing", etc.)

-äilmènt, -älemènt: (Extend -äil, -äle for "ailment", "regalement", etc.)

-äily, -äly: bailey, bailie, daily, Daly, gaily, mailly, palely, scaly, shaly, snaily, stalely, vale; shillelagh, ukelele.

-äimènt, -äymènt: claimant, clamant, payment, raiment; defrayment, displayment, repayment.

-äindêr: attainder, remainder.

-äinful, -äneful: baneful, gainful, painful; disdainful.

-äinly: gainly, mainly, plainly, sanely, vainly; humanely, inanely, insanely, mundanely, profanely, ungainly, urbanely.

-äintêr: fainter, painter, tainter.

-äintly: faintly, quaintly, saintly.
-äinty: dainty, fainty.

-äiny: brainy, drainy, grainy, rainy, veiny, zany; "champagney", Delaney.

-äiry, -äry: airy, chary, dairy, eyrie, fairy, Gary, hairy, Mary, merry, nary, prairie, scary, snary, vary, wary; canary, contrary, vagary; Tipperary, voluntary; confectionary. (False rhymes, such as "bury", etc.)

-äisêr: See -azör.
-äisy: See -äzy.

-äitèn, -àtàn: Dayton, Leyton, Satan, straighten, straiten.

-äitêr: See -ätêr.

-äithful: faithful, scatheful.

-äitréss: creatress, traitress, waitress.

-äjör: See -ägêr.

-äkèn, -äcön: bacon, shaken, waken; mistaken; undertaken.

-äkèr, -äcre: acher, acre, baker, breaker, faker, fakir, maker, Quaker, raker, shaker, taker, waker; bookmaker, peacemaker, wiseacre.

-akō, -accō: Jacko, shako; tobacco.

-äky: achey, Blaikie, braky, flaky, quaky, shaky, snaky.

-alà: Bala, gala, Scala, cicala. (See -arlêr.)

-alàce, -allous: callous, chalice, Dallas, palace, Pallas, phallus. (Compare -alice.)

-alàd, -allàd: ballad, salad.

-alànce: balance, valance.

-àlder: alder, balder, Calder, scalder.

-àlding: balding, scalding, Spalding.

-alàte, -allèt, -allöt: ballot, mallet, palate, pallet, shallot, valet.

-älià: dahlia, Thalia; Australia, interalia, regalia, Westphalia.

-alice: Alice, chalice, malice. (See -alàce.)

-alid, -allied: calid, dallied, pallid, rallied, sallied, tallied, valid; invalid (adj.).

-āliph: See -ailiff.

-ălker, -ăwker, -ôrker: (Extend -ălk, -ăwk, -ôrk.)

-allànt: gallant, talent.

-ăller, -ăwler: (Extend -ăll, -ăwl.)

-allèt: See -alàte.

-allic: Alec, Gallic, phallic; medallic, metallic, vandallic.

-ăllmènt: appallment, installment.

-alliön: galleon, scallion, stallion; battalion, medallion, rapscallion.

-ăllish: Dawlish, Gaulish, smallish, tallish.

-allön: Alan, Allen, gallon, Stalin, talon.

-allöp: gallop, jalap, scallop, shallop.

-ăllöp, -ollöp: dollop, gollop, scallop, trollop, wallop.

-al!ör: pallor, valor.

-allow: aloe, callow, fallow, hallow, mallow, Mallow, sallow, shallow, tallow; marshmallow. (Add "s" to the above for "gallows".)

-ally: alley, bally, challis, dally, galley, pally, rally, sally, Sally, tally, valley; O'Malley, reveille, shilly-shally. (A number of false rhymes by wrongly accentuating last two syllables of certain adverbs, such as "principally".)

-ämà: Brahma, drama, lama, llama, mamma, pajama, Rama; Alabama, melodrama, panorama, Yokahama. (See -ălmêr and -ärmêr.)

-ălmêr: calmer, palmer; embalmer, salaamer. (See -ämà and -ärmêr.)

-ălmèst, -ălmist: calmest, palmist, psalmist; embalmist.

-almön: See -ammön.

-ălmy: See -ärmy.

-ăltàr, -ăltêr, -ăultêr: altar, alter, falter, halter, Malta, palter, psalter, salter, vaulter, Walter; assaulter, defaulter, drysalter, exalter, Gibraltar, unalter.

-ăltry: paltry, psaltery, drysaltery.

-ălty, -ăulty: faulty, malty, salty, vaulty, walty.

-ambeau, -ambō: ambo, crambo, flambeau, Sambo, zambo.

-ambêr: amber, camber, clamber, tambour, timbre. (See -ammêr.)

-ambit: ambit, gambit.

-amble: amble, bramble, Campbell, gamble, gambol, ramble, scamble, scramble, shamble, wamble; preamble.

-ambō: See -ambeau.

-āmeful: blameful, flameful, shameful.

-amèl: camel, mammal, trammel; enamel.

-āmely: gamely, namely, lamely, tamely.

-amine: famine, gamin, stamin; examine, cross-examine.

-amlèt: camlet, hamlet, Hamlet, samlet.

-ammàr, -ammêr, -amör: clamor, dammer, gammer, glamor, grammar, hammer, stammer, yammer; enamor, windjammer. (And extend -am for "crammer". See -ambêr.)

-ammön, -almön: gammon, mammon, salmon, backgammon.

-ammy: clammy, damme, drammie, gammy, hammy, jammy, mammy, Sammy, tammy, whammy.

-āmous, -āmus: famous, hamous, squamous; mandamus, ignoramus.

-ampèr: camper, champer, clamper, cramper, damper, hamper, pamper, ramper, scamper, stamper, tamper, tramper, vamper; decamper.

-ample: ample, sample, trample; example.

-ampus: campus, grampus, pampas, wampus.

-anà: Anna; banana, bandanna, Diana, Havana, iguana, Montana, Nirvana; Indiana, Juliana; Americana, Louisiana.

-anàte: See -anèt.

-ancèr, -answèr: answer, cancer, chancer, dancer, lancer, prancer; advancer, enhancer, romancer; geomancer, necromancer.

-ancèt, -ansit: lancet, transit; Narragansett.

-anchor, -ancour: See -anker.

-ancid: fancied, rancid.

-ancy: chancy, fancy, Nancy; aeromancy, arithimancy, chiromancy, geomancy, hesitancy, lithomancy, mendicancy, necromancy, occupancy, onomancy, pyromancy, romancy, sycophancy, termagancy, vagrancy.

-anda: panda, propaganda, Uganda. (Compare -andêr.)

-andàl: See -andle.

-andàm, -andèm, -andöm: granddam, random, tandem; desperandum, memorandum.

-ander, -andor: blander, brander, candour, dander, gander, glander, grander, hander, pander, slander, stander; Alexander, commander, coriander, demander, expander, gerrymander, Leander, Lysander, meander, oleander, philander, pomander, reprimander, salamander. (Compare **-antêr**.)

-andid, -anded: candid, uncandid. (Extend **-and**. Compare **-andied**.)

-andiēd: bandied, brandied, candied, dandied.

-andier, -andeur: bandier, candier, grandeur, handier, sandier. (Extend **-andy**.)

-andish: blandish, brandish, grandish, standish; outlandish.

-andit: bandit, pandit.

-andle, -andàl: candle, dandle, Handel, handle, Randall, sandal, scandal, vandal; mishandle.

-andlêr: candler, chandler, dandler, handler; tallow-chandler.

-andöm: See **-andàm**.

-andör: See **-andêr**.

-andrél, -andril: band-drill, hand-drill, mandrel, mandrill.

-andy: Andy, bandy, brandy, candy, dandy, Gandhi, handy, Kandy, Mandy, pandy, randy, sandy, Sandy, shandy, organdie, unhandy.

-anél, -anil, -annél: anil, cannel, channel, flannel, panel, scrannel; empanel.

-ānêr, āinêr: Extend **-āne, -āin**.

-āney, -āiney: Extend **-āin, -āne**.

-anét, -annét, -anite: gannet, granite, Janet, planet, Thanet: pomegranate.

-angêr (hard "g"): anger, angor, banger, Bangor, clangor, ganger, hangar, hanger, languor; haranguer.

-angêr (soft "g"): changer, danger, Grainger, granger, manger, ranger, stranger; arranger, endanger; disarranger, interchanger.

-angle: angle, bangle, dangle, jangle, mangle, rangle, spangle, strangle, tangle, twangle, wangle, wrangle; entangle, triangle, untangle; disentangle.

-angled, -anglêr, -angling. (Adapt above.)

-angō: mango, tango; contango, fandango; Pago Pago.

-anguish: anguish, languish.

-anic, -annic: Alnwick, panic, stannic, tannic: botanic. Britannic, galvanic, Germanic,

mechanic, organic, Romanic, Satanic, titanic, tyrannic, volcanic, vulcanic; charlatanic, diaphanic, oceanic.

-aniél, -annuàl: annual, Daniel, granule, manual, spaniel; Emmanuel, Nathaniel.

-anish, -annish: banish, clannish, Danish, mannish, planish, Spanish, vanish; evanish.

-ankàrd, -ankered, -anchöred: anchored, bankered, cankered, hankered, tankard.

-ankêr, -anchör, -ancör: anchor, blanker, canker, hanker, rancor. (And extend **-ank** for "banker", etc.)

-ankle: ankle, rankle.

-ankly: Extend **-ank**.

-anky: Frankie, hanky, thankee, Yankee. (Extend **-ank** for "swanky", etc.)

-anly: Cranleigh, Hanley, manly, Stanley; unmanly.

-annà, -annàh:. anna, Anna, Hannah, manna; Havana, hosannah, Savannah, Susannah. (Compare **-anà** and **-annêr**.)

-annêr, -anör: banner, canner, manner, manor, spanner, tanner. (And extend **-an** for "fanner", etc.)

-annéx: annex, panics; galvanics, mechanics.

-anön: anon, canon, cannon, Shannon.

-anny: Annie, branny, canny, cranny, Fanny, granny, mannie, nanny; uncanny.

-ansack: Anzac, ransack.

-ansion: mansion, panchion, scansion, stanchion; expansion.

-ansöm, -andsöme: handsome, hansom, ransom; transom; unhandsome.

-answêr: See **-ancêr**.

-antàm, -antöm: bantam, phantom.

-ante, -anti, -anty; ante, anti, auntie, chanty,* Dante, pantie, scanty, shanty; Bacchante, Chianti; dilettante.

-antél: See **-antle**.

-antêr: banter, canter, cantor, chanter, granter, grantor, panter, planter, ranter, scanter; decanter, displanter, enchanter, implanter, recanter, supplanter, transplanter.

-anthêr: anther, panther.

-antic: antic, frantic; Atlantic, corybantic, gigantic, pedantic, romantic; geomantic, sycophantic, transatlantic.

-antīle: infantile. (Compare -ile.)

-antle: cantle, mantel, mantle, scantle; dismantle.

-antlêr: antler, mantler, pantler; dismantler.

-antling: bantling, mantling, scantling; dismantling.

-antō, -anteau: canto, coranto, panto; Esperanto, Lepanto, portmanteau.

-antöm: See -antam.

-anty: See -antė.

-antry: Bantry, chantry, gantry, pantry.

-annual: See -aniėl.

-any: See -enny.

-āny: brainy, chaney, grainy, Janie, rainy, zany.

-anyàrd: lanyard, Spaniard, tan-yard.

-anzà: stanza; bonanza; Sancho Panza; extravaganza. ("Kansas" for plurals.)

-āpàl: See -āple.

-apėl: See -apple.

-āpėn, -āpön: capon; misshapen, unshapen.

-āpêr, -āpîr, -āpör: caper, draper, paper, taper, tapir, vapor; newspaper, sandpaper. (Extend -ape.)

-aphic: See -affic.

-apid: rapid, sapid, vapid.

-āpist: papist, rapist; escapist, landscapist, redtapist.

-āple, -āpàl: capel, maple, papal, staple.

-aplėss: capless, chapless, hapless, napless, sapless, strapless, tapless, wrapless.

-apling, -appling: dappling, grappling, knappling, sapling.

-apnėl: grapnel, shrapnel.

-āpör: See -āpêr.

-appėr: dapper. Extend -ap.

-appėt: lappet, tappet.

-apple, -apėl: apple, chapel, dapple, grapple, knapple, rappel, scapple, scrapple, thrapple; pineapple.

-appy: chappie, flappy, gappy, happy, knappy, nappy, sappy, scrappy, snappy; serape, slap-happy, unhappy.

-aptêr, -aptör: apter, captor, chapter; adapter,

adoptor, recaptor.

-aption: caption; adaption, collapsion, contraption, recaption.

-aptist, aptėst: aptest, Baptist, raptest; adaptest, inaptest; anabaptist.

-apture: capture, rapture; enrapture, recapture.

-aràb: arab, Arab, scarab.

-aräge: barrage, garage.

-ärbêr, -ärbör: arbor, barber, harbor; unharbor.

-ärbêred, -ärböard: barbered, harbored, larboard, starboard.

-ärble, -ärbėl: barbel, garble, marble, warble.

-ärcėl: parcel, sarcel, tarsal, varsal; metatarsal.

-ärchêr: archer, marcher, parcher, starcher; departure.

-ärchy: See -arky.

-ärchy (soft "ch"): Archy, larchy, starchy, Karachi.

-ärdén, -ärdön: Arden, garden, harden, pardon; beergarden, bombardon, caseharden, enharden, roularden.

-ärdêr: ardor, carder, harder, larder; bombarder, Cunarder.

-ärdy: hardy, lardy, mardy, tardy; foolhardy, Lombardy, Picardy. (Compare -ärty.)

-âreà: area; Bavaria, Bulgaria, wistaria; Berengaria.

-arėl, -arrėl, -aröl: barrel, carol, Carroll, Darrell, apparel. ("Harold" for past tense.)

-ârely: barely, fairly, rarely, squarely, yarely; unfairly, debonairly.

-ârėm, -ârum: Aram, harem, Sarum; harum-scarum.

-arénce: Clarence, transparence. (Also -ant, -ent + "s".)

-arét, -aràt, -arrėt -arröt: arret, Baratt, carat, caret, carrot, claret, garret, karat, parrot.

-ärgent: argent, sergeant.

-ärgêr: charger, larger; enlarger.

-ärging: barging, charging; discharging, enlarging; overcharging.

-ärgō, -ärgōt: Argo, argot, cargo, Dargo, largo, Margot; botargo, embargo, Wells

Fargo; supercargo.

-âriês: charier, hairier, warier.

-âriȧn, -âryȧn: Arian, aryan; agrarian, Bavarian, barbarian, Bulgarian, caesarean, grammarian, librarian, Rotarian, vulgarian; centenarian, proletarian; abecedarian, disciplinarian, predestinarian; valetudianarian. (Compare -ariön.)

-ariȧt, -ariöt: chariot, Harriet, lariat, Marriott, Marryatt; Iscariot.

-âric: baric, carrick, Garrick; Amharic, barbaric, Bulgaric, Megaric, pimaric, Pindaric, polaric, saccharic, stearic, tartaric; Balearic, cinnabaric.

-arice, -arris: Clarice, Farris, Harris, Paris; phalaris, polaris.

-arid, -arried: arid, carried, harried, married, parried, tarried, varied; miscarried, remarried, unmarried, unvaried; intermarried.

-âring, -âiring, -eāring: bearing, glaring. (Extend -âre, -âir, -eār.)

-ariön, -arriön: carrion, clarion, Marion; Hilarion. (Compare -ariȧn.)

-arious: Darius, Marius, various; Aquarius, bifarious, contrarious, gregarious, hilarious, nefarious, ovarious, precarious, vicarious; multifarious, Sagittarius, temerarious.

-ârish, -eārish: barish, bearish, fairish, garish, perish, rarish, sparish, squarish; debonarish.

-arity: charity, clarity, parity, rarity; vulgarity; angularity, jocularity, popularity, regularity, secularity, similarity, singularity; dissimilarity, irregularity, particularity; perpendicularity.

-ärkėn: darken hearken.

-ärkêr: (Extend -ärk. Compare "parka".)

-ärkėt: market; Newmarket.

-ärkish: darkish, larkish, sparkish.

-ärkle: darkle, sparkle; monarchal; matriarchal, patriarchal.

-ärkling: darkling, sparkling.

-ärkly: darkly, sparkly, starkly.

-ärky: barky, darkie, heark'ee, larky, marquee, parky, sparky, Starkey; malarkey; heterarchy, hierarchy, matriarchy, oligarchy, patriarchy.

-ärlêr, -ärlör: gnarler, marler, parlor, snarler; Transvaaler.

-ärlėt: carlet, harlot, scarlet, starlit, varlet.

-ärley, -ärly: barley, Charlie, gnarly, Marley, parley, snarly. (Extend -är for "particularly", etc.)

-ärlic: garlic, Harlech, sarlyk; pilgarlick.

-ärling: darling, marling, snarling, sparling, starling. (Extend -ärl.)

-ärlōw: Barlow, Carlow, Harlow, Marlow.

-ärly: See -ärley.

-ärmêr, -ärmör: armor, charmer, farmer, harmer; alarmer, disarmer, plate-armor.

-ärmêst, -ärmist: alarmist. (Extend -ärm. Compare -älmist.)

-ärmy, -älmy: army, balmy, barmy, psalmy, smarmy.

-ärnȧl, -arnėl: carnal, charnel, darnel, Farnol.

-ärnêr: darner, garner, yarner.

-ärnėss: farness, harness.

-ärnėt: Barnet, garnet; incarnate.

-ärnēy: barney, blarney, Carney; Killarney.

-ärnish: barnish, garnish, tarnish, varnish.

-arön: Arran, baron, barren, Charon, marron, Sharon; fanfaron, McLaren.

-ärpêr: carper, harper, scarper, sharper.

-arräck: arrack, barrack, carrack. (See -aric.)

-arränt: arrant, parent; apparent, transparent.

-ärrȧnt, -orrėnt: torrent, warrant; abhorrent.

-arräs: arras, Arras, harass; embarrass. (See -aris.)

-arrėl: See -arėl.

-ärrėl: See -orȧl.

-arrėn: See -arön.

-ärrėn: florin, foreign, sporran; warren.

-arriȧge, -arȧge: carriage, marriage; disparage, miscarriage, mismarriage; intermarriage.

-arriêr: barrier, carrier, charier, farrier, harrier, marrier, parrier, tarrier.

-arried: See -arid. (Extend -arry.)

-ärriêr, -ōrriör: quarrier, sorrier, warrior.

-arriön: See -ariön.

-arrōw: arrow, barrow, Barrow, faro, farrow, harrow, Harrow, Jarrow, marrow, narrow, Pharoah, sparrow, taro, yarrow, Yarrow; bolero, dinero, pierrot, primero, sombrero, torero, vaquero; caballero, banderillero, Embarcadero.

-arry: Barry, Carrie, carry, charry, harry, Harry, Larry, marry, parry, sàri, scarry, sparry, starry, tarry; miscarry; hari-kari, intermarry.

-ärry: barry, charry, scarry, sparry, starry, tarry (from "tar"); Araçari, Carbonari.

-ärshàl, -ärtial: marshal, Marshall, martial, partial; immartial, impartial.

-ärsley: parsley, sparsely.

-ärsön: arson, Carson, parson, squarson.

-ärtàn, -ärtèn: barton, Barton, carton, hearten, marten, martin, Martin, smarten, Spartan, tartan; dishearten, enhearten; kindergarten.

-ärtàr, -ärtêr: barter, carter, charter, darter, garter, martyr, parter, smarter, starter, tartar, tarter; bemartyr, imparter, self-starter, upstarter.

-ärtel: cartel.

-ärtful: artful, cartful, heartful.

-ärtial: See **-ärchàl.**

-ärtist, -ärtèst: artist, chartist, smartest. (Extend **-ärt.**)
-ärtle: dartle, startle.

-ärtlèt: Bartlett, chartlet, heartlet, martlet, partlet, tartlet.

-ärtly: partly, smartly, tartly.

-ärtnêr: heartener, partner, smartener; disheartener.
-ärtridge: cartridge, cart-ridge, partridge.

-ärty: arty, hearty, party, smarty; Astarte, ecarte, ex parte; Cancarty.

-ärture: See **-ärchêr.**

-ärvèl: carvel, Darvel, larvel, marvel.

-ärvèst: carvest, harvest, starvest.

-âry: See **-āiry.**

-āsàl, -āzèl: basal, basil, hazel, nasal, phrasal; appraisal, witch hazel.

-ascàl, -aschàl: paschal, rascal.

-ascàr: See **-askêr.**

-āscènce: nascence; complacence, obeisance, renascence.

-āscènt: nascent, renascent. (See **-ācent.**)

-ascot: Ascot, mascot.

-āsemènt: basement, casement, placement; abasement, begracement, belacement, debasement, defacement, displacement, efface-ment, embracement, emplacement, enlacement, erasement; misplacement, replacement; interlacement.

-ashèn, -ashion, -assion, -ation: ashen, fashion, passion, ration; compassion, dispassion.

-ashêr: Dasher, rasher; haberdasher. (And extend **-ash** for "masher", etc.)

-ashy: ashy, flashy, mashy, plashy, slashy, splashy, trashy.

-āsià: Asia, Dacia, fascia; acacia, Alsatia, Dalmatia, fantasia.

-āsian: Asian, abrasion, Caucasian, Eurasian, occasion, persuasion. (Compare **-ātion.**)

-āsin, -āsön, -āstèn: basin, caisson, chasten, hasten, Jason, mason.

-āsis: See **-ācis.**

-askêr, -ascà, -ascār: asker, basker, lascar, masker, tasker; Alaska, Nebraska, Madagascar.

-askèt: basket, casket, flasket, gasket.

-aspêr: aspen, Caspar, clasper, gasper, grasper, jasper, Jasper, rasper. (Extend **-asp.**)
-assèl: castle, hassle, passel, tassel, vassal, wassail; entassel, envassal.

-asses: molasses. (Extend **-ass.**)

-assèt, -acèt, -acit: asset, basset, facet, fascet, placet, tacit. (Compare **-acid.**)
-assic: classic, boracic, Jurassic, potassic, sebacic, thoracic, Triassic.

-assion: See **-ashèn.**

-assive: massive, passive; impassive.

-assle: See **-assèl.**

-assock: bassock, cassock, hassock.

-assy: brassie, brassy, chassis, classy, gassy, glace, glassy, grassy, Jassy, lassie, massy, passe, sassy; Coomassie, Malagasy, morassy, Tallahassee; Haile Selassie.

-astà: pasta. (Compare **-astêr.**)

-astàrd, -astêred: bastard, castored, dastard, mastered, plastered.

-āstèn: See **-āsin.**

-astèn: fasten.

-astêr: aster, Astor, blaster, caster, castor, faster, master, pastor, plaster, vaster; bandmaster, beplaster, cadaster, disaster, schoolmaster, taskmaster; alabaster, burgomaster, criticaster, medicaster, oleaster, quartermaster.

-āstêr: baster, chaster, haster, paster, taster, waster; poetaster.

-astic: clastic, drastic, mastic, plastic, spastic; bombastic, dichastic, dynastic, elastic, emplastic, fantastic, gymnastic, monastic, proplastic, sarcastic, scholastic; amphiblastic, anaclastic, antiphrastic, bioplastic, ceroplastic, deutoplastic, docimastic, Hudibrastic, metaphrastic, neoplastic, onomastic, paraphrastic, periphrastic, phelloplastic, pleonastic, protoplastic, scholiastic; antonomastic, ecclesiastic, encomiastic, enthusiastic, iconoclastic, paronomastic.

-astle: See -assèl.

-astlý: ghastly, lastly, vastly; steadfastly.

-āsty: hasty, pasty, tasty.

-asty: blasty, nasty, vasty.

-ātà: beta, data, eta, strata, theta, zeta; albata, dentata, errata, pro rata, postulata, ultimata, vertebrata; invertebrata.

-atà: data, strata; pro rata; matamata, serenata.

-ätà: cantata, errata, regatta, sonata.

-ātàl: datal, fatal, natal, Statal; prenatal, postnatal, antenatal.

-ātàn: See -āitén

-ātànt, -ātènt: blatant, latent, natant.

-atchèt: Datchet, hatchet, latchet, ratchet.

-ätchmàn: Scotchman, watchman.

-atchy: batchy, patchy, scratchy; Apache.

-atènt: patent. (Compare -atin.)

-āter, -ātör: cater, crater, freighter, gaiter, greater, Hayter, later, mater, pater, straighter, traitor, waiter; creator, cunctator, curator, dictator, equator, scrutator, spectator, testator; alligator, carburetor, commentator, conservator, valuator. (Extend -āte for about 200 other good rhymes. Thus "bater", "navigator", etc.)

-athêr: blather, gather, lather, rather; foregather.

-äther: farther, father.

-āthing: See -āything.

-āthos: Athos, bathos, pathos.

-ātial: See -ācial.

-aki: khaki, saki.

-attic: attic, static; agnatic, aquatic, astatic, asthmatic, chromatic, climatic, commatic, dalmatic, dogmatic, dramatic, ecstatic, emphatic, erratic, fanatic, hepatic, hieratic, lavatic, mathematic, phlegmatic, piratic, pragmatic, prismatic, prostatic, quadratic, rheumatic, sabbatic, schematic, schismatic, sciatic, spermatic, stigmatic, thematic, traumatic; acrobatic, Adriatic, aerostatic, aromatic, Asiatic, autocratic, automatic, bureaucratic, diplomatic, emblematic, Hanseatic, hydrostatic, kinematic, operatic, pancreatic, plutocratic, problematic, symptomatic, thermostatic; anagrammatic, aristocratic, axiomatic, epigrammatic, idiocratic, idiomatic, melodramatic; idiosyncratic. (Compare -adic.)

-atin, -attèn: Latin, matin, patin, platen, satin; batten, fatten, flatten; Prestatyn.

-ātion, ātian: nation, ration, station; ablation, aëration, agnation, aration, Asian, carnation, cassation, castration, causation, cessation, citation, collation, creation, cremation, crustacean, crustation, curvation, Dalmatian, delation, dentation, dictation, dilation, donation, duration, efflation, elation, equation, filtration, fixation, flirtation, flotation, formation, frustration, furcation, gestation, gradation, gunation, gustation, gyration, hortation, hydration, illation, inflation, lactation, laudation, laxation, legation, libation, location, lunation, migration, mutation, narration, negation, nervation, notation, novation, oblation, oration, ovation, palpation, pausation, phonation, placation, plantation, predation, privation, probation, prostration, pulsation, purgation, quotation, relation, rogation, rotation, saltation, salvation, sensation, serration, signation, stagnation, stellation, striation, sublation, tarnation, taxation, temptation, testacean, testation, titration, translation, vacation, venation, vexation, vibration, vocation; abdication, aberration, abjuration, abnegation, abrogation, acclamation, acclimation, accubation, accusation, activation, actuation, adaptation, adjudication, adjuration, admiration, adoration, adornation, adulation, advocation, affectation, affirmation, aggeration, aggravation, aggregation, agitation, allegation, alligation, allocation, alteration, altercation, alternation, ambulation, ampliation, amputation, angulation, animation, annexation, annotation, annulation, appellation, application, approbation, arbitration, argentation, arrogation, aspiration, assentation, assignation, attestation, auguration, aviation, avocation, bifurcation, blusteration, calcination, calculation, cameration, cancellation, capitation, captivation, castellation, castigation, celebration, cementation, cerebration, circulation, cogitation, coloration, combination, commendation, compensation, compilation, complication, compurgation, computation, concentration, condemnation, condensation, condonation, confirmation, confiscation, conflagration, conformation, confrontation, confutation, congelation, congregation, conjugation, conjuration, connotation, consecration, conservation, consolation, constellation, consternation, consultation, conversation, convocation, copulation, coronation, corporation, correlation, corrugation, crepitation, crimination, culmination, cultivation, cumulation, decimation, declamation, declaration, declination, decoration, decrustation, decussation, dedication, defalcation, defamation, defecation, defloration, degradation, degustation, delectation, delegation, demarcation, dementation, demonstration, denudation, deportation, depredation, deprivation, deputation, derivation, derogation, desecration, dessication, designation, desolation, destination, detestation, detonation, detruncation, devastation, deviation, digitation, disclamation, dislocation, dispensation, disputation, dissertation, dissipation, distillation, divagation, divination, domination, edentation, education, elevation, elongation, emanation, embarkation, embrocation, emendation, emulation, enervation, epuration, equitation, estimation, estivation, evagation, evocation, exaltation, exclamation, exculpation, execration, exhalation, exhortation, exhumation, expectation, expiation, expiration, expiscation, explanation, explication, exploitation, exploration, exportation, expugnation, expurgation, extirpation, extrication, exudation, exultation, exundation, fabrication, falcation, fascination, fecundation, federation, fenestration, fermentation, festimation, figuration, flagellation, flagitation, fluctuation, foliation, fomentation,

forcipation, formication, fornication, fraternation, frumentation, fulmination, fumigation, furfuration, generation, germination, glaciation, glomeration, graduation, granulation, gratulation, gravitation, gubernation, habitation, hesitation, hibernation, humectation, ideation, illustration, imitation, immanation, immigration, immolation, impanation, implication, importation, imprecation, impregnation, imputation, incantation, incarnation, incertation, inchoation, incitation, inclination, incremation, incrustation, incubation, inculcation, inculpation, incurvation, indication, indignation, induration, inequation, infestation, infeudation, inflammation, information, inhalation, inhumation, innervation, innovation, insolation, intimation, intonation, inundation, incitation, inclination, incrassation, incremation, incrustation, incubation, inculcation, inculpation, incurvation, indentation, indication, indignation, induration, inequation, infestation, infeudation, infiltration, inflammation, information, inhalation, innervation, innovation, inspiration, installation, instigation, instillation, insufflation, insulation, integration, intensation, intonation, intrication, inundation, invitation, invocation, irrigation, irritation, isolation, jaculation, jubilation, laceration, lachrymation, lamentation, lamination, lapidation, laureation, legislation, levigation, levitation, liberation, limitation, lineation, liquidation, lubrication, lucubration, maceration, machination, maculation, malleation, mediation, medication, meditation, mensuration, ministration, moderation, modulation, molestation, mutilation, natation, navigation, nictitation, nidulation, nomination, numeration, obduration, obligation, occulation, occupation, operation, ordination, oscillation, oscitation, osculation, ostentation, oxidation, ozonation, pabulation, pagination, palliation, palpitation, peculation, penetration, percolation, perfectation, perforation, permeation, permutation, pernoctation, peroration, perscrutation, personation, perspiration, perturbation, polliation, postillation, postulation, predication, preparation, preservation, proclamation, procreation, procuration, profanation, prolongation, promulgation, propagation, propogation, provocation, publication, punctuation, racemation, radiation, realization, recantation, recitation, reclamation, recreation, recubation, reformation, refutation, regelation, registration, regulation, relaxation, relocation, remonstration, renovation, reparation, replication, reprobation, reservation, resignation, respiration, restoration, retardation, revelation, revocation, reogation, rumination, rustication, salication, salutation, satiation, saturation, scintillation, separation, sequestration, siccation, signation, simulation, situation, speculation, spoliation, sternutation, stimulation, stipulation, stridulation, stylobation, subjugation, sublevation, subligation, sublination, subluxation, subornation, subrogation, succusation, suffocation, sulphuration, suppuration, suspiration, sustenation, termination, titillation, titurbation, toleration, transformation, transmigration, transmutation, tribulation, trepidation, triplication, turbination, ulceration, ululation, undulation, usurpation, vacillation, validation, valuation, vegetation, veneration, ventilation, vesication, vindication, violation, visitation, vitiation, vulneration; abbreviation, abomination, accentuation, accumulation, administration, adulteration, agglomeration, alienation, alimentation, alleviation, alliteration, amalgamation, amplification, annihilation, annunciation, anticipation, appropriation, approximation, argumentation, articulation, asphyxiation, assassination, asseveration, assimilation, association, attenuation, authorization, brutalization, calumniation, canonization, capitulation, carbonization, carnifivation, civilization, clarification, classification, coagulation, codification, cognomination, cohabitation, colonization, columniation, commemoration, commensuration, commiseration, communication, concatenation, conciliation, confabulation, confederation, configuration, conglomeration, congratulation, consideration, consolidation, contamination, continuation, cooperation, co-ordination, corroboration, crystallization, debilitation, degeneration, delineation, denomination, denunciation, depopulation, depreciation, despoliation, determination, dignification, dilapidation, disapprobation, discoloration, disfiguration, disinclination, disintegration, disobligation,

dissemination, dissimulation, dissociation, divarication, documentation, domestication, dulcification, ebonkfication, edification, edulcoration, effectuation, effemination, ejaculation, elaboration, elicitation, elimination, elucidation, elutriation, emaciation, emancipation, emasculation, enumeration, enunciation, equalization, equilibration, equivocation, eradication, etiolation, evacuation, evagination, evaporation, exacerbation, exaggeration, examination, exasperation, excoriation, excrusiation, exhilaration, exoneration, expatiation, expectoration, expostulation, expropriation, extenuation, extermination, facilitation, falsification, felicitation, ferrumination, fertilization, florification, fortification, fossilization, fructification, galvanization, gelatination, gesticulation, glorification, gratification, habilitation, habituation, hallucination, harmonization, Hellenization, horrification, humanization, humiliation, hypothecation, idealization, illiteration, illumination, imagination, immaculation, immoderation, impersonation, imperturbation, impropriation, improvisation, inaffectation, inanimation, inapplication, inauguration, incarceration, incineration, incorporation, incrimination, inebriation, infatuation, ingemination, initiation, inoculation, inosculation, insanitation, insemination, insinuation, interpolation, interpretation, interrogation, intoxication, investigation, irradiation, jollification, Judaization, justification, legalization, legitimation, licentiation, liquidation, manifestation, manipulation, masticulation, matriculation, melioration, mellification, misinformation, modernization, modification, mollification, moralization, mortification, multiplication, mystification, nasalization, negotiation, notification, nullification, obliteration, origination, organization, ossification, pacification, participation, perambulation, peregrination, perpetuation, petrification, polarization, precipitation, predestination, predomination, prefiguration, prejudication, premeditation, preoccupation, preponderation, prevarication, procrastination, prognostication, prolification, pronunciation, propitiation, protuberation, purification, qualification, ramification, ratification, recalcitration, reciprocation, reclimination, recommendation, recrimination, rectification, recuperation, refrigeration, regeneration, regurgitation, reiteration, re-integration, rejuvenation, remuneration, renunciation, representation, repudiation, resuscitation, retaliation, revivication, reverberation, sanctification, sanguification, scarification, signification, solemnization, solicitation, sophistication, specialization, specification, stabilization, stratification, stultification, sublineation, subordination, symbolization, tartarization, temporization, tergiversation, testamentation, thurification, tranquillization, triangulation, vaporization, variegation, vaticination, verbalization, vermiculation, versification, vigesimation, vilification, vitriolation, vituperation, vivification, vociferation; alcoholization, amelioration, beatification, circumnavigation, contra-indication, cross-examination, demonetization, deterioration, differentiation, discontinuation, disqualification, diversification, electrification, excommunication, exemplification, experimentation, extemporization, identification, inconsideration, indemnification, individuation, misrepresentation, naturalization, personification, predetermination, ratiocination, recapitulation, reconciliation, spiritualization, syllabification, tintinabulation, transubstantiation. (Also see **-asion**.)

-àtist: See **-attèst**.

-ātive: dative, native, sative, stative; collative, creative, dilative, translative; abrogative, aggregative, alterative, animative, approbative, cogitative, copulative, criminative, cumulative, decorative, deprecative, designative, dominative, duplicative, emanative, emulative, execrative, explicative, glutinative, gravitative, hesitative, imitative, implicative, incubative, innovative, irritative, iterative, lacerative, legislative, meditative, mitigative, operative, procreative, radiative, recreative, replicative, separative, stimulative, vegetative, violative; appreciative, associative, communicative, degenerative, deliberative, denunciative, discriminative, enumerative, enunciative, exonerative, imaginative, incogitative, incriminative, interpretative, manipulative, opinionative, participative, pronunciative, recuperative, retaliative, verificative, vituperative.

-atlèss: Atlas, fatless, hatless; cravatless.

-atling, -attling: battling, catling, fatling,

gatling, ptattling, rattling, spratling, tattling; tittle-tattling.

-atly: fatly, flatly, patly, rattly.

-ātō: Cato, Plato; potato, tomato.

-äto: chateau; legato, mulatto, tomato, staccato; obbligato, pizzicato; enamorato.

-ātör: See **-ātêr**.

-atrap: bat-trap, cat-trap, rat-trap, satrap.

-ātress: traitress, waitress; creatress, dictatress, spectatress, imitatress.

-ātrix: matrix; cicatrix, testatrix, spectatrix, testatrix; aviatrix, generatrix, imitatrix, mediatrix; administratrix, inpropriatrix.

-ātron: matron, natron, patron.

-atten: See **-atin**.

-attêr: attar, batter, blatter, chatter, clatter, fatter, flatter, hatter, latter, matter, patter, platter, ratter, satyr, scatter, shatter, smatter, spatter, splatter, tatter; bescatter, bespatter, Mad Hatter. (See **-addêr, -atà**.)

-attern, -aturn: pattern, Saturn, slattern.

-attèst, -atist, -atticed: bratticed, fattest, latticed, statist. (And extend **-at** for "flattest".)

-attle: battle, cattle, chattel, prattle, rattle, tattle; death-rattle, embattle, Seattle; tittle-tattle. (See **-addle**.)

-attlêr, -atlêr: battler, prattler, rattler, Statler, tattler. (Extend **-attle, -addle**.)

-attling: See **-atling**.

-attō, -atteau: chateau, gateau, plateau, mulatto.

-atty: batty, catty, chatty, fatty, gnatty, Hattie, matty, natty, Patti, patty, ratty, scatty; Cincinnati. (Compare **-addy**.)

-ātum: datum, stratum; eratum, pomatum, substratum; postulatum, ultimatum; desideratum, superstratum.

-āture: nature; good-nature, ill-nature, plicature, legislature, nomenclature.

-ature, -atchêr: stature. (There is no good rhyme to this but extensions of **-ach** and **-atch** may be permitted, as in "catcher".)

-ātus: status, stratus; afflatus, hiatus, senatus; apparatus, literatus, saleratus.

-atus: gratis, lattice, status; apparatus.

-āty̆, -eighty̆, -atey̆: eighty, Haiti, Katie, matey, platy, praty, slaty, weighty.

-ăucêr: Chaucer, saucer. (Compare **-ôarsêr**.)

-ăucus: caucus, Dorcas, raucous.

-ăuction: auction; concoction, decoction.

-ăudàl: caudal, caudle, dawdle.

-ăudit: audit, plaudit.

-ăudy, -ăwdy: bawdy, dawdy, gaudy, Maudie. (See **-ăughty**.)

-aufféur: chauffeur, gopher, loafer, sofa.

-aughtêr (as in "laughter") : See **-aftêr**.

-ăughtêr: daughter, slaughter, tauter, man-slaughter. (Compare **-ōrtêr, -ôrdêr**.)

-ăughty: haughty, naughty. (See **-ăudy**.)

-ăulic: aulic; hydraulic; interaulic. (Compare **-olic**.)

-ăultêr: See **-ăltàr**.

-ăulty: faulty, malty, salty, vaulty, walty.

-ăundêr: launder, maunder.

-ăuntêr: chaunter, flaunter, gaunter, haunter, jaunter, saunter, taunter, vaunter.

-auntie: See **-antè**.

-ăupêr: pauper. (Compare **-ôrpör**.)

-ăuseous, ăutious: cautious, nauseous; precautious.

-ăusêr, -ăwsêr: causer, hawser, pauser, Mauser.

-ăustràl: austral, claustral.

-ăution: caution; precaution. (See **-ōrtion**.)

-ävà: Ava, guava, Java, lava, larva; cassava, palaver. (Compare extensions of **ärve**.)

-avàge: lavage, ravage, savage, scavage.

-àvàl: naval, navel, cave-ale, Wavell.

-avél: cavil, gavel, gravel, ravel, Savile, travel; unravel.

-avélin: javelin, ravelin.

-àvelỳ: bravely, gravely, knavely.

-àvemént: lavement, pavement; depravement, engravement, enslavement.

-àvén: craven, graven, haven, mavin, raven, shaven; engraven, New Haven.

-avêr: cadaver, palaver.

-àvêr: See **-ävör**.

-avêrn: cavern, tavern.

-àviour: clavier, pavior, saviour, Xavier; Batavia, behavior, Belgravia, Moravia.

-avid: avid, gravid, pavid; impavid.

-āvis: avis, Davis, mavis, Mavis; rara avis.

-avish: lavish, ravish; enravish, McTavish.

-āvish: bravish, knavish, slavish.

-ävör, -āvêr: favor, flavor, quaver, savor; disfavor; demiquaver, hemiquaver, semiquaver. (Extend **-āve** for "braver", etc.)

-āvy: cavy, Davy, gravy, navy, slavey, wavy.

-avvy: navvy, savvy.

-ăwdry: Audrey, bawdry, tawdry.

-ăwdỳ: See **-ăudy**.

-ăwkêr: See **-ălkêr**.

-ăwful: awful, lawful; unlawful.

-ăwky, -ălky: gawky, pawky, "talkie"; Milwaukee. (Extend **-ălk** for "stalky".)

-ăwning: awning, dawning, fawning, spawning, yawning. (Extend **-āwn**. Compare **-ôrning**.)

-ăwny: brawny, fawny, lawny, Pawnee, sawney, scrawny, Shawnee, tawny, yawny; mulligatawny. (Compare **-ôrny**.)

-ăwyêr: foyer, lawyer, sawyer; topsawyer.

-axén, -axön: flaxen, Jackson, Saxon, waxen.

-axy: flaxy, Laxey, staxy, taxi, waxy; galaxy; ataraxy.

-āydāy, -eydāy: heyday, Mayday, payday, playday.

-āyêr, -eyôr: Mayor. (Extend **-āy** and **-ey** for "gayer", "surveyor". Compare **-āre, -āir**.)

-āymàn: Bremen, cayman, Damon, drayman, flamen, Haman, layman, Lehman, Ramon, stamen; highwayman.

-āymént: claimant, payment, raiment; allayment, betrayment, defrayment, prepayment, repayment.

-āything: bathing, plaything, scathing, swathing.

-äzà: Gaza, plaza, Zaza; piazza.

-azàrd: brassard, hazard, mazard; haphazard.

-āzél: See **-āsàl**.

-āzén, -āzön, -āisin: blazon, brazen, glazen, raisin, scazon; emblazon; diapason.

-āzör, -āisêr: blazer, Fraser, gazer, lazar, phraser, praiser, raiser, razer, razor; appraiser, dispraiser, self-praiser, star-gazer, upgazer, upraiser; paraphraser.

-āzier: brazier, crazier, glazier, hazier, lazier.

-āzön: See **-āsin**.

-āzy, āisy: crazy, daisy, Daisy, hazy, jasey, lazy, mazy, Maisie, quasi; lackadaisy.

-azzle: Basil, dazzle, drazil, frazzle, razzle; bedazzle, razzle-dazzle.

-ēà: Leah, Rhea, Zea; Althea, Crimea, Hygeia, idea, Korea, Judea, Maria, Medea, obeah, spirea; dahabeah, Dorothea, gonorrhea, Latakia, panacea, ratafia ; Cassiopea.

-ēachêr, -ēature, -ēechêr: creature, feature. (And extend ēach and -ēech.)

-ēabōard: keyboard, seaboard.

-ēachmènt: preachment; beseechment, impeachment.

-ēachy: beachy, beechy, bleachy, Nietzsche, peachy, preachy, reachy, queachy, reechy, screechy, speechy.

-ēacön: beacon, deacon, weaken; archdeacon.

-ēadèd: Extend -ēad, -ēat.

-ēadèn: deaden, Heddon, leaden, redden, Sedden, threaden; Armageddon.

-ēadèr, -ēdàr, -ēdèr, -ēedèr: cedar. (And extend -ēad, -ēde and -ēed.)

-ēadle, -ēedle: beadle, Cheadle, daedal, needle, tweedle, wheedle; bipedal; centipedal, semipedal. (Compare -ēetle.)

-ēadlock: deadlock, headlock, wedlock.

-ēadwāy: dead-way, headway, Medway.

-eady: See **-eddy.**

-ēady: See **-ēedy.**

-eafêr: deafer, feoffor, heifer, zephyr; Strathpeffer, "whateffer".

-eafèst (ef): deafest, prefaced.

-eafy, -ēefy: beefy, feoffee, Fifi, leafy, reefy, sheafy.

-ēagêr, -ēagre, -ēaguêr, -iguêr: eager, leaguer, meager, beleaguer, intriguer; overeager.

-ēagle, -ēgal: beagle, eagle, gragal, legal, regal, sea-gull; illegal, inveigle, vice-regal.

-ēakèn: See **-ēacön.**

-ēakêr, -ēekêr: beaker, speaker. (And extend -ēak, -ēek.)

-ēakling: meekling, treacling, weakling.

-ēakly: bleakly, meekly, sleekly, treacly, weakly, weekly; biweekly, obliquely, uniquely; semi-weekly.

-ēaky, -ēeky: beaky, bleaky, cheeky, cliquey, creaky, leaky, peeky, reeky, sheiky, sleeky, sneaky, squeaky, streaky.

-ēal: real; ideal, unreal; hymeneal. (Compare -ēal and -ēel in one-syllable rhymes.)

-ēalêr, -ēelêr: Extend -ēal and -ēel.

-ealöt: See **-elàte.**

-ealöus: jealous, trellis, zealous; apellous, entellus, procellous, vitellus; overzealous.

-ealthy: healthy, stealthy, wealthy.

-ēalty: fealty, realty.

-ēaly: eely, freely, Healy, mealy, peely, really, seely, squealy, steely, wheely; genteely.

-ēamàn, -ēemàn, -ēmàn, -ēmön: beeman, demon, freeman, gleeman, G-man, he-man, leman, seaman, semen, tea-man.

-ēamêr, -ēmêr, -ēmûr: beamer, dreamer, femur, lemur, reamer, schemer, screamer, seamer, seemer, steamer, streamer, teemer; blasphemer, redeemer. (And extned -ēam.)

-ēamish: beamish, dreamish, squeamish.

-ēamstêr: See **-ēemstêr.**

-ēamy: beamy, creamy, dreamy, gleamy, screamy, seamy, steamy, streamy, teemy.

-ēàn, -iàn: Ian, paean; Achean, Aegean, Argean, Cadmean, Chaldean, Crimean, Judean, Korean, lethean, lyncean, nymphean, pampean, perigean, plebeian, protean ; amoebean, amphigean, apogean, Caribbean, empyrean, European, Galilean, gigantean, hymenean, Jacobean, Maccabean, perigean, phalangean, Tennessean; adamantean, antipodean, Archimedean, epicurean, Pythagorean.

-ēanêr, -ēanör: cleaner, demeanour, gleaner, greener, meaner, wiener; machiner; misdemeanor.

-ēanèst, -ēenist, -ēnist: plenist, machinist. (Extend words under -ean in one-syllable rhymes for "cleanist", "obscenist", etc.)

-ēaning: gleaning, meaning. (Extend -ēan, -ēen, -ēne, -ine.)

-ēanō: beano, keno, Reno; Albino, bambino, casino, festino, merino, Sereno, tondino; andantino, baldachino, maraschino, peacherino, vetturino.

-ēanly: cleanly, keenly, leanly, meanly, queenly; obscenely, serenely. (And extend -ēan.)

-ēapêr: See **-ēap** and extend.

-ēaràncē, -ērèncē: clearance; adherence, appearance, arrearance, coherence, inherence; disappearance, interference, perseverance, reappearance.

-ēarêr: mirror. (Extend **-ēar, -ēre;** compare **-erȧ.**)

-ēarful: cheerful, earful, fearful, sneerful, tearful; uncheerful, unfearful.

-ēarest, -ērist: merest, querist, theorist. (And extend **-ēar, -ēer** and **-ēre.**)

-ēareth, -ērith: Erith. (Extend **-ēar.**)

-ēariêr, -ēeriêr, -ēriör: eerier; anterior, exterior, inferior, interior, Liberia, posterior, Siberia, superior. (And extend **-ēarẏ, -ēerẏ** for "wearier", "beerier", etc.)

-ēaring, -ēering: earring. (And extend **-ēar, -ēer** for "hearing", "leering", etc.)

-êarly, -îrly, -ûrly: burly, churly, curly, early, girlie, girly, pearly, Purley, Shirley, surly, swirly, twirly, whirly; hurly-burly.

-ēarly, -ēerly, -ērely: cheerly, clearly, dearly, merely, nearly, queerly, yearly; austerely, severely, sincerely; cavalierly. (Extend **-ēar.**)

-ēarment: cerement; endearment.

-ēarnèss, -ēernèss: sheerness. (And extend **-ēar** and **-ēer** for "clearness", "queerness", etc.)

-êarnèst, -êrnèst, -ûrnèst: earnest, Ernest, furnaced, sternest, internist. (And extend words under **-êarn** for "sternest".)

-êarnêr, -êrner, -ûrner: burner, earner, learner, sojouner. (Extend **-êarn.**)

-êarning, -êrning, -ûrning: burning, earning, learning, spurning, turning, yearning; concerning, discerning, returning.

-ēary, -ēery, -ēry: aerie, beery, bleary, cheery, deary, dreary, eerie, Erie, jeery, leary, peri, query, smeary, sneery, sphery, teary, veery, weary; aweary, miserere, uncheery.

-ēasȧnd, -ēasönd: reasoned, seasoned, treasoned, weasand, wizened; unseasoned.

-easȧnt, -escènt: crescent, peasant, pheasant, pleasant, present; decrescent, excrescent, incessant, putrescent, quiescent; convalescent, deliquescent, delitescent, effervescent, efflorescent, obsolescent, phosphorescent.

-ēasèl: Diesel, easel, measle, teasel, weasel.

--ēasȧr, -ēasèr: beezer, Caesar, easer, freezer, friezer, geezer, greaser, leaser, pleaser,

sneezer, squeezer, teaser, tweezer, wheezer; Ebenezer.

-ēasön: reason, season, treason, wizen; unreason, unseason.

-ēastêr: Easter, feaster; northeaster, southeaster.

-ēasting: bee-sting, easting, feasting.

-ēastlẏ: beastly, priestly.

-easure, -eisure: leisure, measure, pleasure, treasure; admeasure, displeasure, entreasure, outmeasure.

-ēasy, -ēezy: breezy, cheesy, easy, freezy, greasy, queasy, sleazy, sneezy, wheezy; Brindisi, speakeasy, uneasy, Zambesi.

-ēatèn, -ēetèn: Beaton, Cretan, Eaton, Eton, Keaton, Keyton. (And extend **-ēat** and **-ēet.**)

-ēatêr, -ēetêr, -ētêr, -ētre: beater, bleater, cheater, eater, fleeter, greeter, heater, liter, meeter, meter, metre, neater, Peter, praetor, seater, skeeter, sweeter, teeter, treater; beefeater, cake-eater, competer, completer, defeater, depleter, entreater, escheator, goldbeater, receipter, repeater, retreater, saltpeter, smoke-eater, unseater; centimeter, decaliter, kilometer, overeater, superheater. (Compare **-ēadêr.**)

-eathê, -ethêr: blether, feather, heather, Heather, leather, nether, tether, weather, wether, whether; aweather, pinfeather, together; altogether.

-ēathêr: breather, either, neither, seether, sheather, wreather.

-ēathing, -ēething: breathing, seething, sheathing, tea-thing, teething, wreathing; bequeathing.

-ēature: creature, feature. (See **-ēachêr.**)

-ēaty, -ēety: Beattie, meaty, peaty, sleety, sweetie, sweety, treaty; entreaty, Tahiti.

-eaty: See **-etty.**

-eavèn, -evèn: Bevan, Devon, Evan, heaven, leaven, Leven, seven; eleven.

-ēavèn: even, Stephen, Steven; uneven.

-ēavêr: beaver, cleaver, Eva, fever, griever, keever, leaver, lever, livre, reaver, riever, stiver, weaver, weever; achiever, believer, conceiver, deceiver, enfever, Geneva, receiver, cantilever; unbeliever. (Extend **-ēve, -iēve.**)

-eavy, -evy: bevy, Chevy, heavy, levee, levy, "nevvy"; top-heavy.

-ēbē: Bebe, Hebe, Phoebe, T.B.

-ebėl, -ebble: pebble, rebel, treble ; arch-rebel.

-ēeble: feeble, Keble; enfeeble.

-eccā: Mecca; Rebecca. (Compare -eckėr.)

-ēcėnt: decent, puissant, recent; indecent.

-echêr, -etchêr: etcher, fetcher, fletcher, lecher, retcher, sketcher, stretcher.

-echō: "dekko", echo, gecko, secco; El Greco, re-echo.

-ēcian, -ētion: Grecian, accretion, completion, concretion, deletion, depletion, excretion, impletion, Phoenician, repletion, secretion, Venetian; incompletion, internecion.

-ēciės: Decies, species. (Add "s" to -ēace; thus "fleeces", "ceases", "mantelpieces", etc.)

-ēcious: specious; facetious.

-eckêr, -equêr: "brekker", checker, chequer, decker, flecker, pecker, trekker, wrecker; bedecker, exchequer, henpecker, woodpecker. (And extend -eck and -eque. Compare -eccȧ.)

-eckle, -ekėl: deckle, freckle, heckle, keckle, Seckel, shekel, speckle; bespeckle; Dr. Jekyll.

-ecklėss, -ecklȧce: feckless, fleckless, necklace, reckless, speckless.

-eckön: beckon, reckon. (Preterites of same rhyme with "second" and "fecund".)

-ectȧnt: expectant, reflectent; disinfectant.

-ectful: neglectful, respectful; disrespectful.

-ectic: hectic, pectic; eclectic, electric; analectic, apoplectic, catalectic, dialectic.

-ection, -exion: flection, lection, section; affection, bisection, collection, complexion, confection, connection, convection, correction, defection, deflection, dejection, detection, direction, dissection, ejection, election, erection, infection, inflection, injection, inspection, objection, perfection, projection, protection, reflection, rejection, selection, subjection, subsection; circumspection, disaffection, disinfection, imperfection, indirection, insurrection, interjection, introspection, misdirection, recollection, resurrection, vivisection.

-ective: sective; affective, collective, connective, corrective, defective, deflective, detective, directive, effective, elective, erective, infective, inflective, injective, inspective, invective, neglective, objective, perfective, perspective, prospective, protective, refective, reflective, rejective, respective, selective, subjective; circumspective, ineffective, introspective, irrespective, recollective, retrospective.

-ectör, -ectre: flector, hector, Hector, lector, nectar, rector, sector, specter, vector; collector, deflector, detector, director, ejecter, elector, injecter, inspector, objector, prospector, protector, reflector, selector.

-ecture: lecture; confecture, conjecture, prefecture, projecture; architecture.

-edȧl, -eddle, -edule: heddle, medal, meddle, pedal, peddle, reddle, schedule, treadle; intermeddle. (Compare -ettle.)

-ēdȧr: cedar. (And extend -ēad.)

-eddar: Cheddar. (See -ettêr.)

-eddy, -eady: eddy, Freddy, heady, Neddy, ready, shreddy, steady, Teddy; already, unready, unsteady.

-ēdėd: Extend -ēad. (Compare -ēatėd.)

-ēdėn: Eden, Sweden. (Compare -ēatėn.)

-ēdėd: Extend -ead. (Compare -ēated.)

-ēdėnce: credence, precedence; antecedence, intercedence.

-ēdėnt: credent, needn't, sedent; decedent, precedent; antecedent, intercedent, retrocedent.

-ēdêr: See -ēadêr.

-edgêr: edger, dredger, hedger, ledger, pledger, sledger, spedger, wedger.

-edgewȧre: Edgeware, sledge-wear.

-edit: credit, edit; accredit, discredit, miscredit, sub-edit.

-ēdium: medium, tedium.

-edlȧr: medlar, meddler, peddler, pedlar, treadler. (Extend -edȧl. Compare -ettle.)

-ēedlėss: Extend -ēad; compare -ēat.

-edlėy, eadly: deadly, medley, redly, Sedley.

-ēdō: credo, Lido; libido, stampedo, teredo, toledo, Toledo, torpedo, tuxedo.

-ēechy, -ēachy: Extend -ēach and -ēech.

-ēecy: fleecy, greasy.

-ēedle: See -ēadle.

-ēedy: beady, creedy, deedy, greedy, heedy, Leedy, needy, reedy, seedy, speedy, weedy; indeedy, unheedy.

-ēely: See -ēaly.

-ēefy: beefy, leafy, reefy, sheafy.

-ēemstêr: deemster, seamster, teamster.

-ēenish, -ēanish: Extend -ēan and -ēen in one-syllable rhymes.

-ēeny, -ēnē: Cheney, Sheyney, genie, greeny, meanie, meany, Selene, sheeny, spleeny, Sweeney, teeny, visne, weeny; Athene, bi-kini, Cellini, Houdini, martini, Puccini; Mussolini.

-ēepėn: cheapen, deepen, steepen.

-ēeper: cheaper, creeper, deeper, keeper, leaper, peeper, reaper, sleeper, steeper, sweeper. (Extend -ēap.)

-ēepiêr: creepier, sleepier.

-ēeple, -ēople: people, steeple; unpeople.

-ēeply: cheaply, deeply. (Extend -ēep.)

-ēeráge: beerage, clearage, peerage, pierage, steerage; arrearage.

-ēerful: See -ēarful.

-ēery: See -ēary.

-ēestōne: freestone, keystone; sea-stone.

-ēesy: See -ēasy.

-ēetėn: See -ēatėn.

-ēetêr: See -ēatêr.

-ēetle: beetle, betel, fetal; decretal.

-ēety: See -ēaty.

-ēevish, -iēvish: peevish, thievish.

-ēezêr: See -ēasár.

-efty: hefty, lefty, wefty.

-ēgål: See -ēagle.

-eggår, -eggêr: beggar, dregger, egger, keg-ger, pegger; bootlegger.

-eggy: dreggy, eggy, leggy, Meggie, Peggy.

-ēgian, -ēgion: Fijian, kegion, legion, region; collegian, Glaswegian, Norwegian.

-egnånt: pregnant, regnant; impregnant.

-ēgrėss: egress, Negress, regress.

-ēgret: egret, regret.

-eifêr: See **eaf-êr.**

-eighbör: See -ābör.

-eighty: See -āty.

-ēiling: ceiling. (Extend -ēel, -ēal.)

-eirėss (āir): heiress; mayoress.

-ēist: deist, beest, fleest, freest, seest, theist.

-ēithêr: See -ēathêr.

-eīthêr: See -īthêr.

-ēivêr: See -ēavêr.

-elåte, -elöt: helot, pellet, prelate, stellate, zealot; appellate, constellate; interpellate.

-eldåm, -eldöm: beldam, seldom.

-eldêr: elder, gelder, melder, welder.

-elding: gelding, welding.

-elfish: elfish, selfish, shell-fish.

-elic: bellic, melic, relic, telic; angelic, nick-elic, parhelic, Pentelic, pimelic; archangelic, evangelic.

-ēlīne: beeline, feline, sea-line.

-elish, -ellish: hellish, relish; embellish.

-ellå: Bella, Ella, Lella, Stella; capella, Lou-ella, patella, prunella, umbrella; Arabella, Cinderella, Isabella, tarantella. (Compare -ellêr.)

-ellêr: cellar, dweller, feller, heller, seller, smeller, speller, stellar, teller; impeller, pro-peller, saltcellar; fortune teller.

-ellis: trellis. (See **-ealous.**)

-ellist, -ellised: trellised, 'cellist. (And extend -ell for "dwellest", etc.)

-ellō, -ellōe, -ellōw: bellow, 'cello, felloe, fel-low, hello, Jello, mellow, yellow; duello, good-fellow, Martello, morello, niello, pru-nello; Portobello, Punchinello; violoncello.

-elly: belly, Delhi, felly, helly, jelly, Kelly, Nelly, Shelley, shelly, smelly; cancelli; Dona-telli, vermicelli.

-elön: felon, melon.

-elpêr: Belper, helper, yelper.

-elsiē: Elsie, Chelsea, Selsey.

-eltêr: belter, felter, helter, kelter, melter, pelter, shelter, skelter, smelter, spelter, svelter, swelter, welter.

-embêr: ember, member; December, dismem-ber, November, remember, September; dis-remember.

-emble: Kemble, semble, tremble; assemble, dissemble, resemble; reassemble.

-embly: trembly, Wembley; assembly.

-emi, -emmy: clemmy, demi, hemi, Jemmy.

-ēmiêr, -ēamiêr: creamier, dreamier, steamier.

-emisēs: nemesis, premises.

-emic: chemic; alchemic, endemic, pandemic, polemic, systemic, totemic; academic, epidemic, theoremic; stratagemic.

-emish: blemish, Flemish; unblemish.

-emist: chemist, hemmest, premised, stemmest.

-ēmist: extremest. (Extend **-ēam, -ēme.**)

-emlin: gremlin, Kremlin.

-emmà: Emma, gemma; dilemma.

-emör: hemmer, tremor; condemner, contemner.

-emplár: templar; exemplar.

-emptêr: tempter; attempter, exempter, preemptor, unkempter.

-emption: emption; ademption, co-emption, diremption, exemption, pre-emption, redemption.

-ēmū: emu, seamew.

-ēmûr: See **-ēamêr.**

-ēmūse: bemuse, emus, seamews.

-ēnà: Ena, Gena, Lena, Nina, scena, Tina, Zena; arena, Athena, catena, farina, Galena, hyena, Medina, Modena, patina, Serena, Tsarina; Argentina, concertina, Pasadena, scarlatina, semolina, signorina, Wilhelmina. (Compare **-ēanêr, -ēanör.**)

-enàce, -ennis, -ennous: Dennis, menace, pennous, tenace, tennis, Venice; impennous, vaginopennous.

-ēnàl: penal, renal, venal; adrenal, machinal; duodenal.

-enànt: pennant, tenant; lieutenant.

-enàte: See **-ennèt.**

-encêr: See **-ensêr.**

-encefôrth: henceforth, thenceforth.

-encêr: See **-ensêr.**

-enchêr, -ensure, -entûre: bencher, blencher, clencher, drencher, quencher, trencher, wrencher; adventure, bedrencher, debenture, indenture; misadventure, preadventure. (Extend **-ench.**)

-encil, -ensàl: mensal, pencil, pensil, pensile, stencil, tensile; extensile, prehensile, utensil.

-endà: Brenda, Zenda; agenda, delenda; corrigenda, hacienda. (Compare **-endêr.**)

-endànt, -endènt: pendant, pendent; appendant, ascendant, attendant, contendant, defendant, dependant, dependent, descendant, descendent, impendent, intendant, resplendent, transcendent, transplendent; equipendent, interdependent, superintendent.

-endêr, -endör: bender, blender, ender, fender, gender, lender, mender, render, sender, slender, spender, splendor, tender, vendor, wender; amender, ascender, attender, commender, contender, defender, depender, descender, emender, engender, expender, extender, intender, offender, pretender, surrender, suspender; apprehender, comprehender, money-lender, recommender, reprehender.

-endön: Hendon, tendon.

-endous: horrendous, stupendous, tremendous.

-endum: addendum, agendum, credendum; corrigendum, referendum.

-ènglish: English, jinglish, tinglish.

-engthèn: lengthen, strengthen.

-ēniàl: genial, menial, venial; congenial.

-enic: phrenic, scenic, splenic; arsenic (adj.), eugenic, Hellenic, irenic, lichenic, parthenic, selenic; callisthenic, diplogenic, neurasthenic, oxygenic, paragenic, pathogenic, photogenic, protogenic, pyrogenic, telegenic.

-enin: Benin, Lenin, Menin.

-ēniôr: senior, senor, signor; teenier, weenier.

-enish: plenish, rhenish, tenish, wennish; replenish.

-ēnist: See **-ēanèst.**

-ennà: henna, senna; antenna, duenna, Gehenna, Ravenna, Siena, sienna, Vienna.

-ennèl: fennel, kennel, phenyl; antennal.

-ennêr, -enör: penner, tenor. (And extend **-en.**)

-ennèt, -enàte: Bennett, jennet, kennet, rennet, senate, tenet.

-ennis: See **-enàce.**

-ennön, -enön: pennon, tenon.

-enny, -any: any, Benny, Denny, fenny, jenny, Jenny, Kenny, Lenny, many, penny, tenny, wenny; Kilkenny, Albergavenny.

-ensêr, -ensör, -encêr: censer, censor, Spencer. (Extend **-ence, -ense.**)

-ensive: pensive, tensive; **ascensive, defensive,** descensive, distensive, expensive, extensive, offensive, ostensive, protensive, suspensive; **apprehensive, comprehensive, inexpensive,** recompensive, reprehensive, self-defensive.

-ension: See **-entian.**

-entàl, -entil, -entle: cental, dental, dentil, dentile, gentle, Lental, mental, rental, trental; fragmental, parental, placental, segmental, tridental, ungentle; accidental, argumental, complemental, continental, departmental, detrimental, documental, elemental, fundamental, governmental, incidental, instrumental, monumental, occidental, oriental, ornamental, parliamental, regimental, rudimental, sacramental, sentimental, supplemental, testamental, transcendental.

-entànce, -entènce: sentence, repentance.

-entêr, -entôr: centaur, center, enter, lentor, mentor, renter, tenter; dissenter, frequenter, inventor, lamenter, off-center, precentor, re-enter, repenter, tormentor; ornamenter; experimenter.

-entian, -ention, -ension: gentian, mention, pension, tension; abstention, ascension, ascention, attention, contention, convention, declension, detension, dimension, dissension, distension, extension, intension, intention, invention, prehension, pretension, prevention, propension, subvention, suspension; apprehension, circumvention, comprehension, condescension, intervention, reprehension, supervention.

-entice, -entis: pentice, prentice, apprentice; compos mentis.

-entīle: Gentile, pentile; percentile.

-entist, -entèst, -enticed: dentist; Adventist, apprenticed, preventist. (And extend **-ent.**)

-entle, -entil: See **-entàl.**

-entràl: central, ventral.

-entrỳ: entry, gentry, sentry, comment'ry, invent'ry; element'ry, parliament'ry.

-enture: See **-enchêr.**

-enty: plenty, scenty, twenty; festina lente, dolce far niente.

-enū: menu, venue.

-ēnus: genus, Venus.

-ēō: Cleo, Leo, Rio, trio, yeo.

-ēōle: creole, key-hole.

-ēon: aeon, Creon, Fijian, Leon, neon, peon, pheon, pantheon, plebeian; Anacreon.

-eopàrd, -ephêrd, -eppêred: jeopard, leopard, peppered, shepherd.

-epid: tepid, trepid; intrepid.

-ephỳr: deafer, heifer, zephyr. (See **-eafêr.**)

-ēpōt (pō): Beppo, depot: Aleppo.

-eppêr, -epêr: leper, pepper, stepper; highstepper.

-epping: Epping, stepping.

-eppy: peppy, Sheppey.

-eptic: peptic, sceptic, septic, skeptic; **aseptic,** dispeptic, enpeptic, eupeptic; **antiseptic,** cataleptic, epileptic.

-eptör: sceptre; accepter, adepter, excepter, inceptor, preceptor, susceptor; **intercepter.**

-ēquàl, -ēquèl: equal, sequel; co-equal, unequal.

-ēquènce: frequence, sequence.

-erà: era, Hera, lira, Vera; chimera, Madeira. (Compare **-ēarêr, -errör.**)

-eràld: Gerald, ferruled, herald; imperilled.

-êrbàl, -ûrble: burble, herbal, verbal.

-êrcêr, -êrsêr, -ûrsàr: bursar, cursor, mercer, nurser, purser; disburser, precursor. (And extend **-êrse** for "terser", etc.)

-êrcy, -ûrsy: Circe, mercy, nursey, Percy, pursy; grammercy; controversy.

-êrdêr: Extend **-êrd;** compare **-êrtêr, -îrdêr.**

-ērēàl, -ēriàl: cereal, ferial, serial, arterial, ethereal, funereal, imperial, material, venereal; immaterial, ministerial.

-ērèst: severest. (See **-ēarèst.**)

-êrgency: emergency, urgency.

-êrgent: convergent, detergent, divergent, emergent, resurgent, urgent.

-êrgêr, -êrdure, -ûrger: merger, perjure, purger, scourger, urger, verdure, verger; deterger, converger, diverger, emerger; submerger.

-êrgènce: convergence, divergence, emergence, resurgence, submergence.

-erèt: See **-erit.**

-êrgy, -îrgy, -ûrgy: clergy, dirgy, sergy, surgy; liturgy; dramaturgy, metallurgy.

-eric, -errick: Berwick, cleric, Derek, derrick, Eric, ferric, Herrick, Lerwick, spheric; chimeric, enteric, generic, Homeric, hysteric, mesmeric, numeric, suberic, valeric; atmospheric, Chromospheric, esoteric, exoteric, hemispheric, peripheric.

-eril, -errule, -erýl: beryl, Beryl, Errol, ferrule, imperil, peril, spherule, sterile.

-erish: cherish, perish.

-erit. -errét: ferret, merit; demerit, inherit; disinherit.

-êrjûre: See **-êrgêr.**

-êrkin: firkin, gherkin, jerkin, merkin, Perkin.

-êrky, -ûrky: jerky, murky, perky, smirky, turkey, Turkey.

-êrling: See **-îrling.**

-ermál: dermal, thermal.

-êrmán, -êrmön: Burman, Firman, German, Herman, merman, sermon; Omdurman.

-êrment: ferment; affirmant, averment, bestirment, deferment, determent, interment, preferment, referment; disinterment.

-êrmin, -êrmine: ermine, vermin; determine, predetermine. (See **-êrmán.**)

-êrmit: hermit, Kermit, permit (noun).

-êrmý: fermi, squirmy, wormy; diathermy, taxidermy.

-êrnál, -êrnél, -olonél, -oûrnál, -ûrnál: colonel, journal, kernel, sternal, urnal, vernal; cavernal, diurnal, eternal, external, fraternal, hibernal, infernal, internal, lucernal, maternal, nocturnal, paternal, supernal; coeternal, hodiernal, sempiternal.

-êrnárd: Bernard, gurnard.

-ērō: hero, Nero, pierrot, zero.
-errànd: errand, gerund.

-erriêr: burier, ferrier, merrier, terrier.

-êring: derring, erring, herring.

-errör: error, parer, terror. (Extend **-âir, āre;** compare **-erà.**)

-errule: See **-eril.**

-erry: berry, bury, Bury, cherry, Derry, ferry, Jerry, Kerry, merry, Perry, sherry, skerry, Terry, very, wherry; Bambury, blackberry,

blueberry, cranberry, gooseberry, mulberry, raspberry, strawberry; beriberi, cemetery, lamasery, millinery, monastery, presbytery, stationary, stationery. (Compare **-àrý.**)

-êrseý, -ûrzý: furzy, jersey, Jersey, kersey, Mersey; New Jersey.

-êrsion, -êrtian, -êrtion, -ûrsion: mersion, Persian, tertian, version; abstersion, aspersion, assertion, aversion, coercion, conversion, demersion, desertion, detersion, discursion, dispersion, diversion, emersion, excursion, exertion, immersion, incursion, insertion, inversion, perversion, recursion, reversion, submersion, subversion; extroversion, introversion; animadversion.

-êrsön, -ôrsén: person, worsen; McPherson.

-êrsus: thyrsus, versus.

-êrtain, -ûrtain: Burton, certain, curtain, Gerton, Merton; uncertain.

-êrtêr: blurter, curter, flirter, hurter, squirter; asserter, averter, converter, deserter, diverter, exerter, inserter, inverter, perverter, subverter. (Extend **-êrt, -îrt, -ûrt.** See **-êrdêr, -îrtêr.**)

-êrtést: Extend **-êrt, -îrt, -ûrt.**

-êrtile: See **-îrtle.** (Compare **-îrdle.**)

-êrtion: See **-îrsion.**

-êrtly: curtly, pertly; alertly, expertly, inertly, invertly, overtly; inexpertly.

-êrtive: furtive; assertive, divertive, exertive.

-êrvànt, -êrvènt: curvant, fervent, servant; conservant, observant, recurvant; unobservant.

-êrvêr, -êrvör: fervor, nerver, server, swerver; conserver, observer, preserver, reserver, timeserver.

-êrvid: fervid, perfervid, scurvied. (And accentuate "-ed" on **-êrve, -ûrve.**)

-êrvish: curvish, dervish, nervish, swervish.

-êrvy, -ûrvy: curvy, nervy, scurvy; topsyturvy.

-ēry: See **-ēary.**

-esàge, -essàge: dressage, message, presage; expressage.

-escénce, -essénce: essence; excrescence, florescence, pubescence, putrescence, quiescence, quintessence, senescence, turgescence, vitrescence; adolescence, coalescence, convalescence, deliquescence, delitescence, effervescence, efflorescence, evanescence, inflorescence, incalescence, incandescence, iridescence, obsolescence, phosphorescence, recrudescence, revalescence, revirescence, virilescence.

-escience: nescience, prescience.

-escènt: cessant, crescent, jessant; accrescent, depressant, excrescent, fluorescent, incessant, increscent, liquescent, putrescent, quiescent, rubescent, senescent, virescent, vitrescent; adolescent, coalescent, convalescent, deliquescent, effervescent, incandescent, obsolescent, opalescent, phosphorescent, recrudescent, superscrescent. (See **-aasènt.**)

-escō: fresco, Tresco; alfresco.

-escū: fescue, rescue; Montesquieu.

-esènce, -easànce: pleasance, presence; omnipresence. (Extend **-easànt** as in "pheasants".)

-eshêr: fresher, pressure, thresher; refresher.

-eshly: fleshly, freshly; unfleshly.

-esion: session, concession, discretion, secession. (And extend **-ess** for "profession", etc.)

-ēsion: lesion; adhesion, artesian, cohesion, Ephesioan, inhesion, magnesion, Parisian, Silesian; Indonesian, Polynesian.

-ēsis: thesis; anthesis, deesis, diesis, mimesis; catachresis, exegesis, synteresis; hyperesthesis. (And extend certain words under **-ēace** for "ceases", etc.)

-essàge: See **-esàge.**

-essàl: See **-estle.**

-essènce: See **-escènce.**

-essêr, -essôr: dresser, guesser, lesser, lessor, messer, presser; addresser, aggressor, assessor, compressor, confessor, depressor, oppressor, possessor, professor, successor, suppressor, transgressor; antecessor, intercessor, predecessor, second-guesser.

-essure: pressure. (And extend **-esh** for "flesher", "refresher", etc.)

-essy: Bessie, Crecy, dressy, Jessie, messy, Tessie, tressy.

-estàl, -estle: festal, pestle, vestal.

-estèd: rested, vested. (Extend **-est.**)

-estêr: Chester, Ester, Esther, fester, Hester, jester, Leicester, Lester, Nestor, pester,

tester, vester, wrester; digester, investor, Manchester, molester, protester, semester, sequester, Sylvester, trimester, Westchester; midsemester. (Extend **-est.**)

-estial: bestial; celestial.

-estic: gestic; **agrestic, asbestic, majestic,** telestic; anapestic, catachrestic.

-estige: prestige, vestige.

-estine: destine; clandestine, intestine, predestine.

-estive: estive, festive, restive; attestive, congestive, digestive, infestive, investive, suggestive, tempestive.

-estle (silent "t"): Cecil, Chessel, nestle, pestle, trestle, vessel, wrestle; redressal, unnestle.

-esto: presto; manifesto.

-estral, estrel: kestrel, ancestral, fenestral, orchestral, trimestral.

-estûre: gesture, vesture; divesture, investure.

-esty: chesty, cresty, pesty, resty, testy.

-ētāil: detail, retail.

-etàl: See **-ettle.**

-etchêr: See **-echêr.**

-etchy: fetchy, sketchy, stretchy, tetchy.

-ētely: fleetly, meetly, neatly, sweetly; completely, concretely, discreetly, unmeetly; incompletely, indiscreetly, obsoletely.

-etful: fretful, forgetful, regretful.

-ethèl: Bethel, Ethel, ethyl, methyl.

-ethêr: See **-eathêr.**

-etic: aesthetic, ascetic, athletic, bathetic, colletic, cosmetic, docetic, emetic, frenetic, genetic, hermetic, kinetic, magnetic, paretic, pathetic, phonetic, phrenetic, poetic, prophetic, splenetic, syncretic, synthetic, theoretic; **alphabetic, amuletic, anesthetic, anchoretic, antithetic, apathetic, arithmetic, catechetic, dietetic, energetic, epithetic, eugenetic, hypothetic, pangenetic, parathetic, parenthetic, strategetic, sympathetic,** theoretic; **antipathetic, apologetic, biomagnetic, diamagnetic, diaphoretic, homogenetic, logarithmetic, pathogenetic, peripatetic;** abiogenetic, idiopathetic; onomatopoetic.

-ētion: See **-ēcian.**

-ētör, -ētêr: See **-ēatêr.**

-ettêr, -ettör: better, bettor, debtor, fetter, getter, letter, setter, wetter, whetter; abettor, begetter, forgetter, go-getter, typesetter, unfetter.

-ettish, -etish: fetish, Lettish, pettish, wettish; coquettish.

-ettle, -etàl: fettle, Gretel, kettle, metal, mettle, nettle, petal, settle; abettal, unsettle. (Compare **-edàl, -eddle**.)

-ettō: ghetto, petto; falsetto, libretto, palmetto, stiletto, terzetto, zucchetto; allegretto, amoretto, lazaretto, Rigoletto.

-etty, -eti, -etti: betty, Betty, fretty, Hettie, Hetty, jetty, Letty, netty, petti, petty, sweaty; confetti, libretti, Rosetti, spaghetti; spermacetti, Vanizetti. (See **-eddy**.)

-ētus: Cletus, fetus; acetous, quietus.

-eūdàl: See **-ōōdle**.

-eūtêr: See **-ōōtêr**.

-evèl: bevel, devil, Greville, level, Neville, revel; bedevil, dishevel.

-evèn: See **-eavèn**.

-ēvèn: See **-ēavèn**.

-evêr: clever, ever, lever, never, sever, Trevor; assever, dissever, endeavor, however, whatever, whenever, wherever, whichever, whomever, whoever; howsoever, whatsoever, whensoever, wheresoever, whomsoever, whosoever.

-ēvêr: See **-ēavêr**.

-evêrèst: Everest, cleverest.

-ēvil: evil, weevil; coeval, primeval, retrieval, upheaval; medieval.

-evil: See **-evèl**.

-ēvious: devious, previous.

-evy: See **-eavy**.

-ewàge: brewage, "New Age", sewage; escuage.

-ewàrd, -ewêred: leeward, Seward, sewered, secured, skewered, steward.

-ewèl, -ūèl: crewel, cruel, dual, duel, Ewell, fuel, gruel, jewel, newel, ruelle; bejewel, eschewal, pursual, renewal, reviewal, subdual. (Compare **-ōōl** and **-ūle**.)

-ewêr: bluer, booer, grewer, chewer, Clewer, cooer, doer, fewer, hewer, newer, screwer, sewer, skewer, strewer, truer, twoer, viewer, wooer; construer, pursuer, renewer, re-

viewer; interviewer.

-ewèss: Jewess, Lewis, Louis, U.S., St. Louis.

-ewish: blueish, Jewish, newish, shrewish, truish, twoish.

-ewtêr, -eūtêr, -ūtêr, -ūtör: cuter, hooter, looter, mooter, muter, neuter, pewter, rooter, scooter, suitor, tutor; commuter, computer, disputer, freebooter, polluter, refuter.

-ewy, -ouè, -ūey: bluey, chewy, coo-ee, Coue, dewy, fluey, gluey, gooey, hooey, Louie, Louis, pfui, roue, screwy, thewy; viewy; chop suey.

-exīle: exile, flexile.

-exôr, -exêr: flexor, vexer; annexer, perplexer.

-exion: See **-ection**.

-extànt: extant, sextant.

-extīle: sextile, textile.

-exus: nexus, plexus; Texas; Alexis.

-exy: prexy, sexy; apoplexy.

-eyànce: seance; abeyance, conveyance, purveyance.

-eyör: See **-āyêr**.

-īad: dryad, dyad, naiad, triad; hamadryad, jeremiad.

-īàl, -īöl: dial, Dyall, phial, Lyell, trial, vial, viol; decrial, denial, espial, retrial, sundial, supplial. (Compare **-īle** in one-syllable list.)

-iàn: See **-ēön**.

-īànce, -īènce: clients, giants, science; affiance, alliance, appliance, compliance, defiance, reliance, suppliance; misalliance.

-īànt, -īènt: Bryant, client, giant, pliant, scient; affiant, compliant, defiant, reliant; self-reliant.

-īär: briar, brier, buyer, drier, Dwyer, dyer, flier, friar, fryer, higher, liar, mire, nigher, plier, prior, pryer, shyer, sigher, slyer, spryer, spyer, tire, trier, Tyre, vier. (Extend **-y**. Compare **-īre**.)

-īàs: bias, pious; Elias, Tobias; Ananias, nisi-prius.

-īàt, -īèt, -īöt: diet, fiat, quiet, riot, ryot, striate, Wyatt; disquiet.

-ibàld: ribald. (Extend **-ibble** for "quibbled", etc.)

-ibbêr: bibber, cribber, dibber, fibber, gibber, glibber, jibber, nibber, quibber, squibber; wine-bibber.

-ibbèt, -ibit: gibbet, Tibbett; cohibit, exhibit, inhibit, prohibit.

-ibble: cribble, dibble, dribble, fribble, gribble, kibble, nibble, quibble, Ribble, scribble, Sybil, thribble; ish ka bibble.

-ibbling: Extend **-ibble.**

-ibbly: dribbly, fribbly, glibly, nibbly, quibbly, scribbly, tribbly.

-ibbon: gibbon, ribbon.

-ībêr: briber, fiber, giber, Khyber, Tiber; ascriber, imbiber, inscriber, prescriber, subscriber, transcriber.

-īble, -ībàl: Bible, liable, libel, tribal.

-iblèt: driblet, giblet, triblet.

-icàr, -ickêr: bicker, clicker, dicker, flicker, kicker, knicker, licker, liquor, nicker, picker, pricker, quicker, sicker, slicker, snicker, sticker, thicker, ticker, tricker, vicar, wicker.

-ichès, -itchès: breeches, riches. (And extend **-itch.**)

-ician, -icion, -ition, -ission: fission, mission; addition, admisson, ambition, attrition, audition, cognition, coition, commission, condition, contrition, edition, emission, fruition, Galician, ignition, insition, logician, magician, nutrition, omission, optician, partition, patrician, perdition, permission, petition, physician, position, prodition, reddition, remission, rendition, sedition, submission, suspicion, transition, transmission, tuition, volition; ammunition, apparition, apposition, circuition, circumcision, coalition, competition, composition, definition, demolition, deposition, disparition, disquisition, ebullition, electrician, emolition, erudition, exhibition, expedition, exposition, imposition, inanition, inhibition, inquisition, intermission, intromission, intuition, opposition, parturition, politician, precognition, premonition, preposition, preterition, prohibition, proposition, readmission, recognition, recommission, repetition, reposition, requisition, rhetorician, superstition, supposition, transposition; arithmetician, contraposition, decomposition, geometrician, indisposition, interposition, juxtaposition, mathematician, metaphysician, predisposition, presupposition, recomposition.

-icious, -itious: vicious; ambitious, auspicious, capricious, cilicious, delicious, factitious, fictitious, flagitious, ignitious, judicious, malicious, Mauritius, nutritious, officious, pernicious, propitious, seditious, suspicious; adventitious, avaricious, expeditious, inauspicious, injudicious, meretricious, superstitious, supposititious, surrepititious.

-ickèn: chicken, quicken, sicken, stricken, thicken, wicken.

-ickêr: See **-icàr.**

-ickèt: clicket, cricket, picket, piquet,, pricket, snicket, spicate, thicket, ticket, wicket; intricate.

-ickle, -ickèl: chicle, fickle, mickle, nickel, pickle, prickle, sickle, stickle, strickle, tickle, trickle. (See **-ẏcle.**)

-ickly: prickley, quickly, sickly, slickly, thickly, trickly.

-ickshăw: kickshaw, rickshaw.

-icky: bricky, dickey, Dickey, Ficke, Mickey, Nickey, quickie, rickey, sticky, thicky, tricky, Vicki; doohickey, Kon-tiki.

-ictêr, -ictör: lictor, stricter, victor, Victor; afflicter, conflicter, constrictor, inflicter, predicter; contradicter; boa constrictor.

-iction, -ixion: diction, fiction, friction; addiction, adstriction, affliction, affixion, affriction, astriction, confliction, constriction, conviction, depiction, eviction, indiction, infliction, abstriction, prediction, prefixion, reliction, restriction, reviction, transfixion; benediction, contradiction, dereliction, interdiction, jurisdiction, malediction, valediction.

-ictive: fictive; addictive, afflictive, conflictive, constrictive, convictive, depictive, indictive, inflictive, predictive, restrictive, vindictive; benedictive, contradictive, interdictive, jurisdictive.

-icture: picture, stricture; depicture.

-ictus: ictus; Benedictus, acronyctous.

-īcy: icy, spicy.

-īdàl, -īdle, -idöl: bridal, bridle, idle, idol, idyll, sidle, tidal; fratricidal, homicidal, matricidal, parricidal, regicidal, suicidal; infanticidal, tyrannicidal.

-idàẏ: See **-idy.**

-iddèn: bidden, chidden, hidden, midden, ridden, slidden, stridden; forbidden, unbidden.

-idder: bidder, kidder. (Compare **-itter.**)

-iddish: kiddish, Yiddish.

-iddle: diddle, fiddle, griddle, middle, piddle, quiddle, riddle, tiddle, twiddle. (See **-ittle.**)

-iddling: Extend **-iddle.** See **-ittle.**

-iddy: Biddy, giddy, kiddie, middy, skiddy, stiddy.

-īdė: See **-īdy.**

-īdėn, -īdön: guidon, Haydn, Leyden, Sidon, widen.

-īdėnt: bident, guidant, rident, strident, trident; dividant.

-īdėous: hideous; fastidious, insidious, invidious, lapidious, perfidious.

-īdėr: cider, eider, glider, guider, hider, rider, spider, wider; backslider, confider, divider, insider, outrider, provider.

-idgėt, -igit: Bridget, digit, fidget, midget.

-idgy: midgy, ridgy.

-īdle: See **-īdàl.**

-īdly, -īdely: idly, widely.

-idnēy: kidney, Sidney.

-īdy: Friday, sidy, tidy; untidy; bona fide.

-iēflỹ: briefly, chiefly.

-iėnce: See **-iànce.**

-iėnt: See **-iànt.**

-iėr: See **-iär.**

-iėst, -ighėst: Extend **-y, -igh;** also "biassed."

-iėstly: See **-ēastly.**

-iėt: See **-iàt.**

-iēvėr: See **-ēavėr.**

-ifėr, -iphėr: cipher, fifer, knifer, lifer, rifer; decipher.

-iffėr: biffer, differ, sniffer.

-iffin: Biffen, biffin, griffin, griffon, stiffen, tiffin.

-iffle: piffle, riffle, sniffle, whiffle.

-iffy: jiffy, Liffy, niffy, sniffy, spiffy, squiffy, whiffy.

-ific: glyphic; deific, grandific, horrific, magnific, pacific, pontific, prolific, pulsific, rubific, sacrific, sensific, somnific, specific, tabific, terrific, vivific; beatific, anaglyphic, calorific, colorific, dolorific, hieroglyphic, honorific, humorific, lapidific, photoglyphic, saporific, scientific, sonorific, soporific.

-ifle: Eiffel, eyeful, rifle, stifle, trifle.

-ifling: rifling, stifling, trifling.

-iftėr: drifter, grifter, lifter, shifter, sifter, snifter, swifter, shop-lifter, uplifter.

-iftlėss: driftless, shiftless, thriftless.

-ifty: clifty, drifty, fifty, "giftie", nifty, rifty, shifty, thrifty.

-igàte: See **-igöt.**

-igeön, -idgeön: pigeon, Phrygian, Stygian, widgeon; religion; irreligion.

-īgėr: Niger, tiger.

-īgest: digest (noun); obligest.

-iggėr, -igör: bigger, chigger, digger, figger, jigger, nigger, rigger, rigor, snigger, swigger, trigger, twigger, vigor; configure, disfigure, gold digger, grave digger, outrigger, transfigure.

-iggêred: figgered, jiggered, niggard.

-iggin: biggin, piggin.

-iggish: riggish. (And extended **-ig.**)

-iggle: giggle, higgle, jiggle, niggle, sniggle, squiggle, wiggle, wriggle.

-igly, iggly: bigly, giggly, sniggly, wriggly; piggly-wiggly.

-iggy: iggy, piggy, twiggy.

-ighėr: See **-iär.**

-ighlànd: highland, island.

-ighly: See **-īly.**

-ightėn, -itėn: brighten, Brighton, Crichtin, frighten, heighten, lighten, tighten, Titan, whiten; enlighten. (And extend **-ite** and **ight.**)

-ightėr, -itėr: biter, blighter, brighter, citer, fighter, flighter, lighter, miter, niter, plighter, righter, sighter, slighter, smiter, tighter, triter, whiter, writer; alighter, exciter, igniter, inciter, indicter, inviter, moonlighter, politer, typewriter, uniter; copywriter, dynamiter, underwriter.

-ightful: frightful, mightful, rightful, spiteful, sprightful; delightful.

-ightly: brightly, knightly, lightly, nightly, rightly, sightly, slightly, sprightly, tightly, tritely, whiteley, whitely; politely, unknightly, unsightly, uprightly.

-ightning: brightening, frightening, lightning, tightening, whitening.

-ighty: Blighty, Clytie, flighty, mighty,

nightie, whitey, almighty, Aphrodite.

-igil: sigil, strigil, vigil.

-igmà: sigma, stigma, enigma.

-igmènt: figment, pigment.

-igöt, -igàte: bigot, frigate, gigot, spigot.

-igûr: See **-iggêr.**

-īgress: digress, tigress.

-īkèn, -īcön: Dicon, icon, lichen, liken.

-īking: biking, dyking, piking, spiking, striking, viking; well-liking.

-īky: Ikey, crikey, Psyche, spiky.

-īlacs, īlax: lilacs, smilax.

-ilbêrt: filbert, Gilbert, Wilbert.

-ildêr: builder, gilder, guilder, Hilda; bewilder, Matilda, St. Kilda.

-īldêr: milder, wilder.

-īldish: childish, mildish, wildish.

-īldly: childly, mildly, wildly.

-ilè: See **-illy.**

-ilful: skillful, wilful; unskillful.

-īlīght: dry-light, highlight, skylight, twilight, Xylite.

-īling: filing, piling, riling, smiling, styling, tiling, whiling, wiling; beguiling, compiling, defiling, reviling, up-piling.

-īlkèn: milken, silken.

-ilky: milky, silky, Willkie.

-illà: Scylla, villa; anilla, armilla, barilla, cedilla, chinchilla, codilla, gorilla, guerrilla, Manila, mantilla, maxilla, Priscilla, Sybilla, vanilla; camarilla, cassarilla, granadilla, sabadilla, sapodilla, seguidilla.

-illàge: billage, grillage, pillage, spillage, tillage, village.

-illèr, -illàr: chiller, driller, filler, griller, killer, miller, pillar, Schiller, spiller, swiller, thriller, tiller; distiller, Joe Miller, maxillar; caterpillar, killer-diller, ladykiller.

-illèt: billet, fillet, millet, quillet, rillet, skillet, Willett.

-illiant: brilliant; resilient.

-illiàrds: billiards, milliards, mill-yards.

-illing: billing, shilling, willing; unwilling. (And extend **-ill** for "drilling", etc.)

-illiön, -illiàn: billion, Gillian, Lillian, million, pillon, trillion; carillon, Castilian, civilian, cotillion, pavilian, postilion, quadrillion,

Quintilian, reptilian, vermilion; Marillian.

-illious: bilious, punctilious; antrabilious, supercilious.

-illōw: billow, kilo, pillow, willow; negrillo, armadillo, peccadillo.

-illy: billy, Billy, Chile, chili, chilly, filly, frilly, gillie, grilly, hilly, killi, lily, Lillie, Millie, Philly, Scilly, silly, shrilly, skilly, stilly, Tillie, Willie, Willy; Piccadilly, tiger lily, water lily, willy-nilly.

-īlöm: whilom, asylum.

-iltêr: filter, gilter, jilter, kilter, lilter, milter, philter, quilter, tilter, wilter.

-iltön: Chilton, Hilton, Milton, Stilton, Tilton.

-īly, -īghly: drily, Filey, highly, Reilly, Rilely, shyly, slily, smiley, wily, wryly.

-imàge: image; scrimmage.

-īmàte: climate, primate; acclimate.

-imbêr: limber, timber, timbre; unlimber.

-imble, -ymbàl: cymbal, fimble, gimbal, gimble (Lewis Carroll), nimble, symbol, thimble, tymbal, wimble.

-imbō: kimbo, limbo; akimbo.

-īmêr: chimer, climber, primer, rhymer, timer; begrimer, old-timer, sublimer.

-imic: chymic, mimic; alchimic, etymic; cherubimic, eponymic, metronymic, pantomimic, patronymic, synonymic.

-immy: gimmie, jimmy, Jimmy, shimmy.

-īmön, -ymàn: flyman, Hymen, limen, pieman, Simon, Timon, Wyman.

-impêr: crimper, limper, scrimper, shrimper, simper, whimper.

-imple: crimple, dimple, pimple, rimple, simple, wimple.

-imply: crimply, dimply, limply, pimply, simply.

-impy: crimpy, impi, impy, skimpy.

-imsy: flimsy, "mimsy" (Lewis Carroll), slimsy, whimsy.

-īmus: High Mass, primus, thymus, timous.

-īmy: blimey, grimy, limey, limy, rimy, slimy, stymie, thymy; "gorblimey".

-īnà: china, China, Dinah, Heine, Ina, myna; regina; Carolina. (Compare **-īnêr.**)

-īnàl: binal, crinal, final, rhinal, spinal, trinal, Vinal, vinyl; acclinal, caninal, declinal, equinal, piscinal; anticlinal, endo-crinal, officinal, periclinal.

-incêrs: mincers, pincers, rinsers.

-inchêr: clincher, flincher, lyncher, pincher,

-incture: cincture, tincture, vincture.

-indêr: cinder, flinder, hinder, tinder; re-scinder.

-īndêr: Extend **-ine** for "blinder", etc.

-indle: brindle, dwindle, Hindle, kindle, spindle, swindle, windle, enkindle, rekindle.

-īndnèss: blindness, kindness, color-blindness, loving-kindness.

-indy: Hindi, Lindy, shindy, windy.

-inēàr, -inniêr: finnier, linear, skinnier, whinnier.

-īnely: finely; benignly, caninely, divinely, supinely; saturninely.

-inêr, -inōr: diner, finer, liner, miner, minor, shiner, signer, winer, airliner, assigner, consignor, definer, designer, refiner.

-inèt: ginnet, linnet, minute, spinet.

-inew, -inūe: sinew; continue, retinue; discontinue.

-inful: sinful, skinful. (Extend **-in.**)

-ingènt: stringent; astringent, constringent, contingent, restringent.

-ingêr: bringer, clinger, dinger, finger, flinger, linger, malinger, ringer, singer, slinger, springer, stinger, stringer, swinger, whing-er, wringer, unslinger, unstringer.

-ingêr (soft "g"): ginger, injure. (And extend **-inge** for "cringer", etc.)

-ingle: cingle, cringle, dingle, ingle, jingle, mingle, shingle, single, springall, swingle, tingle, tringle; commingle, surcingle; intermingle.

-inglèt: kinglet, ringlet, singlet.

-ingly: jingly, mingly, shingly, singly, tingly.

-ingō: bingo, dingo, gringo, jingo, lingo, stingo; Domingo, flamingo.

-ingy: cringy, dingy, fringy, stingy, twingy.

-ingy (with hard "g"): clingy, dinghy, springy, stringy, swingy.

-inic: clinic, cynic, finic, pinic, quinic, vinic; aclinic, actinic, delphinic, fulminic, platinic, rabbinic; Jacobinic, monoclinic, narcotinic, nicotinic, polygynic.

-iniön, -iniàn: Binyon, minion, Ninian,

pinion; Darwinian, dominion, opinion, Virginian; Carolinian, Carthaginian, Palestinian.

-inis: finis, Guinness.

-inish: finish, Finnish, thinnish, tinnish, diminish.

-īnish: brinish, nineish, swinish.

-inkêr: blinker, clinker, drinker, inker, shrinker, sinker, slinker, stinker, thinker, tinker, winker. (Extend **-ink.**)

-inkle: crinkle, inkle, sprinkle, tinkle, twinkle, winkle, wrinkle; besprinkle; periwinkle.

-inkling: inkling, sprinkling, tinkling, twinkling, wrinkling.

-inky: blinky, dinky, inky, kinky, pinky; Helsinki.

-inly: inly, thinly; McKinley.

-innêr: dinner, finner, grinner, inner, pinner, sinner, skinner, spinner, tinner, winner; beginner.

-innōw: minnow, winnow.

-inny: finny, guinea, Guinea, hinny, Minnie, ninny, pinny, Pliny, skinny, spinney, tinny, vinny, whinny, Winnie; Verginny, New Guinea; ignominy.

-īnō: lino, rhino; albino.

-instêr: Leinster, minster, Minster, spinster; Westminster.

-intèl: lintel, pintle, quintal.

-intêr: dinter, hinter, minter, printer, splinter, sprinter, squinter, stinter, tinter, winter.

-intō: pinto, Shinto.

-intry: splintery, vintry, wintry.

-inty: Dinty, flinty, glinty, linty, minty, squinty; pepperminty.

-īnus: binous, dryness, highness, linous, Linus, minus, Pinus, sinus, spinous, vinous; echinus, salinous.

-īny: briny, liny, miny, piney, shiny, spiny, tiny, twiny, viny, whiney, winy; sunshiny.

-iön: Brian, ion, lion, Lyon, scion, Zion; anion, O'Brien, orion; dandelion.

-īpèd: biped, striped, typed, wiped.

-īpènd: ripened, stipend.

-īpêr, -ypêr: diaper, griper, piper, riper, sniper, striper, swiper, typer, wiper; bagpiper.

-īphön, -yphèn: siphon, hyphen.

-īpist, -īpĕst: typist. (And extend **-īpe**.)

-ippêr: chipper, clipper, dipper, dripper, flipper, gripper, kipper, nipper, ripper, shipper, sipper, skipper, slipper, snipper, stripper, tipper, tripper, whipper.

-ippĕt: sippet, skippet, snippet, tippet, whippet.

-ipple: cripple, nipple, ripple, stipple, tipple, triple.

-ippling, -ipling: crippling, Kipling, strippling, stippling, tippling.

-ippō: hippo, Lippo.

-ippy: chippy, dippy, drippy, grippy, hippy, lippy, nippy, snippy, zippy ; Mississippi.

-ipstêr: tipster, whipster.

-ipsy: gipsy, "ipse", tipsy.

-iptic: cryptic, diptych, glyptic, styptic, triptych; ecliptic, eliptic; apocalyptic.

-iquant: piquant, secant; cosecant; intersecant.

-īrȧ: Ira, Lyra, Myra, Thyra; Palmyra.

-īrȧnt: gyrant, spirant, tyrant, virant; aspirant, conspirant, expirant.

-īrate: gyrate, irate.

-îrchĕn, -ûrchin: birchen, urchin.

-îrdȧr, -îrdêr, -êrdêr, -ûrdêr: girder, herder, murder, sirdar; absurder, engirder, sheepherder. (Compare **-îrter**.)

-îrdle, -ûrdle: curdle, girdle, hurdle; engirdle. (Compare **-îrtle**.)

-îrdlẏ: birdly, curdly, thirdly; absurdly.

-īreling: hireling, squireling.

-īrĕn: Byron, siren, syren; environ.

-îrkin: See **-êrkin**.

-îrling, -êrling, -êarling, -ûrling: sterling, Stirling, yearling, whirling. (Extend **-êarl**.)

-îrlish, -ûrlish: churlish, girlish.

-îrloin: purloin, sirloin.

-îrmêr, -êrmêr, -ûrmûr: firmer, murmur, squirmer, termer; affirmer, confirmer, infirmer.

-îrmish: firmish, skirmish, squirmish, wormish.

-īrō: Cairo, giro, gyro, tyro; autogiro.

-irrȧh: mirror, sirrah.

-irrĕl: Birrel, Cyril, squirrel, Tyrell, Tyrol, virile.

-irrup: chirrup, stirrup, syrup.

-îrtle, -ûrtle: fertile, hurtle, kirtle, myrtle, Myrtle, spirtle, turtle, whirtle. (See **-îrdle**.)

-îrty, -ûrty: Bertie, cherty, dirty, flirty, Gertie, shirty, skirty, spurty, squirty, thirty.

-īrus: Cyrus, virus; desirous, papyrus.

-īry, -īary, -īĕry: briery, diary, fiery, friary, miry, priory, spiry, squiry, wiry; enquiry.

-īsal: reprisal; paradisal.

-iscȧl: discal, fiscal.

-iscȧrd: discard, Liscard.

-iscount: discount, miscount.

-iscuit: See **-iskĕt**.

-iscus: discous, discus, viscous; hibiscus, lentiscus, meniscus.

-īsect: bisect, trisect.

--īsêr, -īsōr: geyser, Kaiser, miser, sizar, visor; advisor, divisor, incisor; supervisor.

-ishêr, -issure: disher, fisher, fissure, swisher, wisher; kingfisher, well-wisher.

-ishöp: bishop; fish-shop.

-isic: Chiswick, phthisic, physic; metaphysic.

-ision, -ission: scission, vision; abscission, allision, collision, concision, decision, derision, division, elision, envision, excision, misprision, precison, prevision, provision, recision, rescission, revision; circumcision, stratovision, subdivision, supervision, television. (See **-ician**.)

-īsis: crisis, Isis, phthisis. (And compare plurals of **-īce**.)

-isit: visit; exquisite.

-īsive: decisive, derisive, divisive, incisive; indecisive.

-iskêr: brisker, frisker, risker, whisker.

-iskĕt: biscuit, brisket, tisket, trisket, wisket.

-isky: frisky, risky, whisky.

-isly, izzly: Bisley, drizzly, frizzly, grisly, grizzly, sizzly.

-ismȧl: dismal; abysmal, baptismal; cataclysmal, catechismal, paroxysmal.

-isön: See **-izzen**.

-īsön: bison, Meissen, Tyson.

-ispêr: crisper, lisper, whisper.

-issȧl: See **-istle**.

-ission: See **-ician**.

-issūe: issue, fichu, tissue; atishoo, reissue.

-issure: See **-ishêr.**

-istánce: distance; assistance, consistence, desistance, existence, insistence, resistance, subsistence; co-existence, equidistance, inconsistence, inexistence, nonexistence, nonresistance. (Also **-istant, -istént** + "s".)

-istánt: distant; assistant, consistent, existent, persistent, resistant, subsistent; coexistent, equidistant, inconsistent, inexistent, nonexistent, nonresistant, pre-existent.

-istén: christen, glisten, listen.

-istêr: bister, blister, glister, mister, sister, twister; assister, enlister, insister, persister, resister, subsister.

-isthmus: See **-istmás.**

-istic: cystic, fistic, mystic; artistic, ballistic, baptistic, Buddhistic, deistic, juristic, logistic, monistic, papistic, patristic, phlogistic, puristic, realistic, simplistic, sophistic, statistic, stylistic, theistic, touristic; agonistic, altruistic, animistic, annalistic, anarchistic, aphoristic, atheistic, cabalistic, canonistic, catechistic, Chauvinistic, communistic, dualistic, Eucharistic, eulogistic, euphemistic, euphuistic, familistic, fatalistic, humoristic, idealistic, intermistic, journalistic, Judaistic, methodistic, nihilistic, optimistic, pantheistic, pessimistic, polaristic, pugilistic, socialistic, syllogistic, talmudistic, unionistic; anachronistic, antagonistic, cameralistic, communalistic, dialogistic, formularistic, liberalistic, naturalistic, philosophistic, polytheistic, rationalistic, ritualistic, sensualistic; materialistic, spirtualistic; individualistic.

-istine (ēn): Christine, pristine, Sistine; Phillistine; amethystine.

-istle, -issál: bristle, fissile, gristle, istle, missal, missel, missile, scissel, sissile, thistle, whistle; abyssal, dismissal, epistle.

-istmás: Christmas, isthmus.

-istöl: Bristol, crystal, pistol.

-ītál: title, vital; entitle, recital, requital, subtitle.

-ītêr: miter, niter. (And extend **-ite** and **-ight.**)

-īthêr: blither, either, lither, neither, tither, writher.

-ithêr: blither, dither, hither, slither, thither, whither, wither, zither.

-itian: titian. (See **-ician.** Compare **-ision.**)

-itic: critic; arthritic, mephitic, pleuritic, Semitic; aerolitic, analytic, biolytic, catalytic, diacritic, dialytic, eremitic, hypercritic, hypocritic, Jesuitic, paralytic, parasitic, stalactitic, tonsilitic, uranitic.

-ition: See **-ician.** (Compare **-ision.**)

-ītish: lightish, whitish. (Extend **-īte.**)

-itish, -ittish: British, fittish, kittish, skittish.

-itlêr: brittler, Hitler, littler, whittler.

-itnéss: fitness, witness.

-ittánce: pittance, quittance; acquittance, admittance, omittance, permittance, remittance, transmittance.

-ittén: bitten, Britain, Briton, kitten, mitten, smitten, Witan, written; Thames Ditton.

-ittêr: bitter, "crittur", fitter, flitter, fritter, glitter, hitter, jitter, knitter, litter, pitter, quitter, sitter, slitter, spitter, splitter, titter, twitter; acquitter, committer, embitter, omitter, permitter, remitter, submitter, transmitter. (Compare **-iddêr.**)

-ittle, -ittál, -ictual: brittle, knittle, little, quittal, skittle, spittle, tittle, victual, whittle, wittol; acquittal, belittle, committal, remittal, transmittal. (Compare **-iddle.**)

-itty: chitty, city, ditty, flitty, gritty, kitty, Kitty, nitty, pity, pretty, witty; banditti, committee.

-itūál: ritual; habitual.

-īvál: rival; archival, arrival, estival, outrival, revival, salival, survival; adjectival, conjunctival; nominatival.

-ivél, -ivil: civil, drivel, rivel, shrivel, snivel, swivel; uncivil.

-ivén: driven, given, riven, scriven, shriven, shiver, sliver; deliver, forgiver.

-ivét, -ivit: civet, pivot, divot, privet, rivet, shiver, sliver; deliver, forgiver; Guadalquivir.

-īvêr: diver, driver, fiver, hiver, Ivor, liver, shriver, skiver, sliver, stiver, striver, thriver; conniver, contriver, depriver, reviver, surviver.

-ivét, -ivit: civet, pivot, divot, privet, rivet, trivet; Glenlivet.

-ivid: livid, vivid.

-ivöt: See **-ivét.**

-ivý: civvy, dhivy, Livy, privy, skivvy, skivy,

tivy; tantivy.

-ixêr, -ixîr: fixer, mixer; elixir.

-ixie: dixie, Dixie, nixie, pixy, tricksy, Trixie.

-ixture: fixture, mixture; admixture, commixture, immixture; intermixture.

-izàrd, -izzàrd, -issöred: bizard, blizzard, gizzard, izzard, lizard, scissored, vizard, wizard.

-izèn, -izzèn, -isön: dizen, mizzen, prison, wizen; arisen, bedizen, imprison.

-īzön: horizon. (False rhymes as "arisin' ".)

-izzier: busier, dizzier, fizzier, frizzier, vizier.

-izzêr: quizzer, scissor, whizzer.

-izzle: chisel, drizzle, fizzle, grizzle, mizzle, sizzle, swizzle.

-izzling: quisling. (And extend **-izzle.**)

-izzy, -usy: busy, dizzy, fizzy, frizzy, Lizzie, mizzy, tizzy.

-istic: cystic, fistic, mystic; deistic, fascistic, theistic; anarchistic, atheistic, bolshevistic, cabalistic, characteristic, communistic, pantheistic, polytheistic, socialistic, syllogistic, tritheistic.

-ōà: boa, Goa, moa, Noah, poa, proa; aloha, Genoa, Iowa, jerboa, Samoa; protozoa.

-ōadêr, -ōdör: goader, loader, odor; corroder, exploder, foreboder, malodor, unloader.

-ōafy: feofee, loafy, oafy, Sophie, strophe, trophy.

-ōakêr, -ōkêr, -ōchre: broker, choker, cloaker, croaker, joker, ocher, poker, smoker, soaker, stoker, stroker, yoker; convoker, provoker, revoker, uncloaker.

-ōakum, -ōcum: hocum, locum, oakum, Slocum.

-ōaly, -ōly, -ōley, -ōlly, -ōwly: coaly, drolly, goalie, holey, holy, lowly, molly, Rowley, shoaly, slowly, solely, wholly; roly-poly.

-ōamêr: comber, Cromer, foamer, Homer, omer, roamer; beachcomber, misnomer. (Compare **-ōmà.**)

-ōanêr, -ōnêr, -ōnör, -ōwnêr: boner, donor, droner, groaner, loaner, loner, moaner, Mona, owner, phoner, stoner; atoner, Corona, condoner, deponer, intoner, postponer; telephoner, Arizona. (Compare **-ōnà.**)

-ōapy: dopey, Hopi, mopey, ropey, soapy, topee.

-ōarish: boarish, whorish.

-ōarsêr: coarser, courser, forcer, hawser, hoarser.

-ōary, -ōry: dory, flory, glory, gory, hoary, lorry, more (Latin), storey, story, Tory; Old Glory, vain-glory; allegory, amatory, aratory, auditory, bibitory, category, crematory, damnatory, desultory, dictatory, dilatory,, dormitory, gradatory, grallatory gustatory, hunky-dory, inventory, mandadory, migratory, monitory, negatory, offertory, oratory, piscatory, predatory, prefatory, probatory, punitory, purgatory, repertory, rotatory, signatory, sudatory, territory, transitory, vibratory; abjuratory, adulatory, ambulatory, calculatory, circulatory, commendatory, compensatory, conciliatory, confirmatory, conservatory, declaratory, delineatory, depilatory, depository, derogatory, dispensatory, exclamatory, explanatory, execratory, expiratory, incantatory, incubatory, inspiratory, judicatory, laboratory, liberatory, obligatory, observatory, oscillatory, prohibitory, reformatory, repository, respiratory, salutatory, speculatory, transpiratory, undulatory.

-ōastàl, -ōstàl: coastal, postal.

-ōastêr, -ōstêr: boaster, coaster, poster, roaster, throwster, toaster; four-poster.

-ōatêr, -ōtêr, ōtôr: bloater, boater, doter, floater, gloater, motor, noter, quoter, rotor, scoter, toter, voter; demoter, denoter, devoter, promoter; locomotor, rotomotor.

-ōaty: bloaty, coyote, Doty, Doughty, floaty, goaty, throaty.

-obbêr: blobber, clobber, cobber, jobber, knobber, lobber, robber, slobber, snobber, sobber, slobber, swabber, throbber; beslobber.

-obbin: bobbin, Dobbin, robbin, robin, Robin.

-obble: cobble, gobble, hobble, nobble, squabble, wobble.

-obby: bobby, Bobby, cobby, hobby, lobby, mobby, nobby, Robbie, snobby.

-ōbelèss, -ōblesse: noblesse, robelesse.

-ōbêr: prober, rober, sober; disrober, October.

-ōbōe: hobo, lobo, oboe, zobo; Launcelot Gobbo.

-obstêr: lobster, mobster.

-ōcàl: bocal, focal, local, phocal, vocal; yokel; bifocal.

-ōcean: See **-ōtion.**

-ōcêr, -ōsêr, ōssêr: closer, doser, grocer,

grosser; engrosser, jocoser, moroser.

-ōchre: See -ōakêr.

-ockāde: blockade, brocade, cockade, dock-aid, okayed, stockade.

-ockêr: blocker, cocker, docker, knocker, locker, mocker, rocker, shocker, soccer, socker, stocker; knickerbocker.

-ockèt: brocket, brockett, docket, locket, pocket, rocket, socket, sprocket; pickpocket, vest-pocket.

-ockney: cockney, knock-knee.

-ocky: cocky, crocky, flocky, hockey, jocky, locky, rocky, Saki, stocky; sukiyaki.

-ōcōa, -ōcō, -ōkō: boko, coco, cocoa, loco, toko; baroco, rococo; Orinoco.

-oction: concoction, decoction.

-octör: doctor, proctor; concocter, decocter.

-ōcum: See -ōakum.

-ōcus: crocus, focus, hocus, locus, trochus; hocus-pocus.

-ōcust: focused, hocused, locust.

-ōdà: coda, Rhoda, soda; Baroda, pagoda, Fashoda.

-ōdàl: modal, nodal, yodel; trinodal; internodal.

-oddèn: Flooden, hodden, sodden, trodden; downtrodden, untrodden.

-oddêr: codder, dodder, fodder, nodder, odder, plodder, prodder, solder. (Compare -otter.)

-oddèss, -odice: bodice, goddess.

-oddèst, -odèst: modest, oddest; immodest.

-oddle, -odèl: coddle, model, noddle, swaddle, toddle, twaddle, waddle; remodel. (Compare -ottle.)

-oddy, -ody: body, cloddy, Mahdi, noddy, shoddy, soddy, toddy, wadi; embody, nobody, somebody; anybody, busybody, everybody, Tom Noddy.

-odgêr: dodger, codger, lodger, stodger.

-odgy: podgy, splodgy, stodgy.

-odic: odic; anodic, exodic, iodic, melodic, methodic, parodic, rhapsodic, sarcodic, spasmodic, synodic; episodic, kinesodic, periodic.

-ōdium: odium, podium, sodium; allodium.

-odling: coddling, codling, godling, swaddling, toddling, twaddling, waddling; remodelling.

-odly: godly, oddly, twaddly; waddly; ungodly.

-ōdôr: See -ōadêr.

-ōdus: modus, nodus.

-ody: See -oddy. Compare -otty.

-ōèm: poem, proem.

-ōey: blowy, Bowie, Chloe, doughy, goey, Joey, snowy, showy.

-ōfêr: chauffeur, gopher, loafer, Ophir, sofa.

-ôffēe: coffee, toffee.

-offêr: coffer, cougher, doffer, golfer, offer, proffer, scoffer.

-ôftèn: coffin, often, soften.

-ofty: lofty, softy.

-ōgà: snoga, toga, yoga; Saratoga; Ticonderoga.

-ōgàn: brogan, Hogan, slogan.

-ōgey: bogey, bogie, fogey, stogie; Yogi.

-ôggish: doggish, froggish, hoggish.

-oggle: boggle, coggle, goggle, joggle, toggle; boondoggle.

-oggy: boggy, cloggy, doggy, foggy, froggy, groggy, joggy, moggie, soggy.

-ōgle: bogle, fogle, ogle.

-ogrèss: ogress, progress.

-ōic: stoic; azoic, heroic; diapnoic, protozoic.

-oidêr: moider; avoider, embroider.

-oily: coyly, coily, doily, oily, roily. (Compare "loyally" and "royally".)

-oinêr: coiner, joiner; enjoiner, purloiner.

-ointmènt: ointment; anointment, appointment, disjointment; disappointment.

-oistêr, -oystêr: cloister, foister, hoister, moister, oyster, roister; Roister-Doister.

-oitêr: goiter, loiter, Ruyter; adroiter, exploiter; reconnoiter. (Compare -oidêr.)

-ōkay: bouquet, okay, Tokay, Touquet.

-ōkèn, -ōakèn: broken, oaken, token; bespoken, betoken, forespoken, foretoken, freespoken, outspoken, soft-spoken, unbroken, unspoken.

-ōkêr: See -ōakêr.

-ōkey: choky, cokey, croaky, hokey, joky, Loki, moky, oaky, poky, roky, smoky, yoky; okey-dokey, slow-pokey.

-ōlàr, -ōllêr, -ōwlêr: bowler, coaler, doler, droller, molar, polar, roller, solar, stroller, toller, troller; cajoler, comptroller, condoler, consoler, controller, enroller, extoller; patroller, unroller; circumpolar.

-ōldén: golden, olden; beholden, embolden.

-ōldêr, -ōuldêr: bolder, boulder, colder, folder, holder, molder, older, polder, scolder, shoulder, smolder; beholder, enfolder, freeholder, householder, landholder, upholder.

-ōldly: boldly, coldly; manifoldly.

-ōleful: bowlful, doleful, soulful.

-olémn, -olumn: column, solemn.

-ōlén, -ōlön: colon, Nolan, solen, solon, stolen, swollen; semi-colon.

-olic, -ollöck: colic, frolic, rollick; bucolic, carbolic, embolic, symbolic, systolic; alcoholic, apostolic, epistolic, metabolic, parabolic, vitriolic.

-olid, -ollied: dollied, jollied, dolid, squalid, stolid, volleyed.

-olish, -ollish: dollish, polish; abolish, demolish.

-ōlish: Polish. (Extend -ōle, -ōal.)

-ōlium: scholium; linoleum, petroleum.

-ollár, -olár, -olêr: choler, collar, dollar, dolor, loller, scholar, squalor, Waller.

-ollárd, -olláred: bollard, collared, dollared, Lollard, pollard, "scholard".

-ollége, -owlédge: college, knowledge; acknowledge, foreknowledge.

-ōllér: See -ōlêr.

-ollét: collet, wallet.

-olliér: collier, jollier.

-ollöp: collop, dollop, gollop, lollop, scallop, trollop, wallop.

-ollōw: follow, hollo, hollow, Rollo, swallow, wallow; Apollo.

-olly, -olley: Bali, collie, Dollie, dolly, Dolly, folly, golly, holly, jolly, Molly, polly, Solly, trolley, volley; finale, tamale; melancholy.

-ōlō: bolo, polo, solo.

--ōlon: See -ōlén.

-ölöred: colored, dullard.

-ōlstêr: bolster, holster, oldster; upholster.

-ōltêr, -ōultêr: bolter, colter, jolter, molter, poulter; revolter.

-ōltish: coltish, doltish.

-olumn: See -olémn.

-ōly: See -ōaly.

-ōmá: coma, Roma, soma; aboma, aroma, diploma, Natoma, sarcoma, Tacoma; la paloma. (Compare -ōamêr.)

-ōmách, -ummöck: hummock, stomach. (Add "s" to rhyme with "flummox".)

-ōmāin: domain, ptomaine, romaine.

-ōmán, -ōwmán: bowman, foeman, gnomon, omen, Roman, showman, snow-man, yeoman; abdomen.

-ombat: combat, wombat.

-ombêr: bomber, omber, somber.

-ōmént: foment (noun), loment, moment; bestowment.

-omét, -omit: comet, vomit; Mahomet.

-omic: comic, gnomic; atomic; agronomic, anatomic, astronomic, autonomic, economic, gastronomic, metronomic, taxonomic.

-ōming, -umbing, -umming: coming, plumbing. (And extend -um.)

-ommá: comma, momma, rama; pajama.

-ommy: Tommy, mommy; bonhomie, salami.

-ōmō: chromo, Como, homo; major-domo.

ömpáss: compass, rumpus; encompass.

-omptêr: compter, prompter; accompter.

-ōná: Jonah, Mona; Arizona, Catriona, corona, Cremona, Iona, Verona; belladonna. (Compare -ōanên, -ōwnêr.)

-onáge: nonage, Swanage.

-ondánt, -ondént: fondant, frondent; despondent, respondent; correspondent.

-ondél, -ondle: Blondel, fondle, rondle, Wandle.

-ondêr: blonder, bonder, condor, fonder, ponder, squander, wander, yonder; absconder, desponder, responder; corresponder.

-ōnely: lonely, only.

-ōnêr: See -ōanêr.

-onést: connest, donnest, honest, wannest.

-öney: honey, money. (See -unny.)

-ôngêr: conger, longer, stronger, Tonga, wronger; prolonger.

-ônging: longing, thronging, wronging; belonging, prolonging.

-ôngly: longly, wrongly.

-ongō: bongo, Congo, pongo.

-onic: chronic, conic, phonic, sonic, tonic; adonic, agonic, bubonic, Byronic, canonic, carbonic, crotonic, cyclonic, demonic, draconic, euphonic, harmonic, hedonic, ionic, ironic, laconic, masonic, parsonic, platonic, sardonic, sermonic, Slavonic, symphonic, tectonic, Teutonic; Alcyonic, diaphonic, diatonic, embryonic, gramophonic, histrionic, macaronic, monophonic, philharmonic, polyphonic, telephonic, theogonic.

-öniön: See **-union.**

-onish, -onnish: donnish, wannish; admonish, astonish, premonish.

-onky, -onkey: conkey, donkey; honky-tonky.

-önkey: As in "monkey"; see **-unkẏ.**

-ōnlẏ: lonely, only.

-önnàge, -unnàge: dunnage, Dunwich, tonnage.

-onnét: bonnet, sonnet.

-onny: Bonnie, bonny, Connie, Johnny, Lonny, Ronnie.

-onör, -onêr: goner, honor, wanner; dishonor.

-onsil, -onsul: consul, sponsal, tonsil; proconsul, responsal.

-öntàl: See **-untle.**

-ontract: contract, entr'acte.

-ōnus: bonus, onus, tonous.

-ōny, -ōney: bony, cony, coney, crony, drony, phony, pony, stony, tony, Tony; boloney, Marconi, polony, spumoni; alimony, antimony, macaroni, matrimony, parsimony, sanctimony, testimony.

-onẏx: onyx, phonics.

-ōōby: booby, looby, ruby, Ruby.

-ōōdle: boodle, doodle, feudal, noodle, poodle, strudel; caboodle, canoodle, flapdoodle; Yankee-Doodle. (Compare **-ōōtle.**)

-oody: goody, woody.

-ōōdy: broody, Judy, moody, Rudy.

-ookish: bookish, rookish, spookish.

-ooky: bookie, cookie, hookey, rookie.

-ōōky: fluky, spooky, Sukie.

-ōōlish, -ūlish: coolish, foolish, mulish.

-ōōnêr: See **-ūnár.**

-ōōnful: See **-ūneful.**

-ōōny, -ūny: loony, moony, pruny, puny, spoony, tuny. (And extend **-ōōn, -une.**)

-ōōpêr, -ūpêr, -ūpör: cooper, Cupar, drooper, duper, grouper, hooper, looper, scooper, snooper, stooper, stupor, super, swooper, trooper, whooper; recouper.

-ōōpy, -oūpy: croupy, droopy, loopy, rupee, soupy, whoopee, whoopy.

-ōōrish: boorish, Moorish, poorish.

-ōōsêr: boozer, bruiser, chooser, cruiser, loser.

-ōōstêr: booster, rooster.

-ōōtêr: booter, chuter, cuter, fluter, hooter, looter, luter, mooter, muter, neuter, pewter, rooter, shooter, suitor, tooter, tutor; astuter, commuter, computer, disputer, freebooter, imputer, polluter, recruiter, refuter, saluter, uprooter; substitutor.

-ōōtle: brutal, futile, tootle; refutal. (Compare **-ōōdle.**)

-ōōty: beauty, booty, cootie, cutie, duty, fluty, fruity, rooty, snooty, sooty.

-ōōvêr: grover, prover; maneuver, Vancouver. (And extend **-ōōve** and **-ove** (ōōv) for "hoover", "remover", etc.)

-ōōzle, -oūsél, -ūsil: boozle, fusel, ousel; bamboozle, perusal, refusal.

-ōōzẏ: boozy, floosie, newsy, oozy, woosy.

-ōpàl: Bhopal, copal, opal; Constantinople.

-ōpêr, -ōapêr: coper, doper, groper, moper, roper, sloper, soaper, toper; eloper; interloper. (Extend **-ōpe.**)

-ophét: profit, prophet, Tophet.

-ophist: officed, sophist. (And extend **-off** for "doffest", etc.)

-opic: topic, tropic; myopic; horoscopic, microscopic, misanthropic, periscopic, stethoscopic, telescopic, theanthropic; heliotropic, kaleidoscopic, stereoscopic.

-ōpish: mopish, Popish.

-oplàr: poplar, toppler.

-oppêr: chopper, copper, cropper, dropper, hopper, lopper, mopper, plopper, popper, proper, propper, shopper, sopper, stopper, swapper, topper, whopper; grasshopper, improper, tiptopper; overtopper.

-opping: chopping, hopping. (Extend **-op.**)

-opple: hopple, popple, stopple, topple.

-oppy: choppy, copy, croppy, droppy, floppy,

hoppy, loppy, moppy, poppy, shoppy, sloppy, soppy.

-opsy: copsy, dropsy, topsy, Topsy; autopsy.

-optêr: copter; adopter; helicopter.

-optic: Coptic, optic; synoptic.

-option: option; adoption.

-ōpy, -ōapy: dopey, mopy, ropy, slopy, soapy, topee.

-ôrà: aura, Cora, Dora, flora, Flora, hora, Laura, mora, Norah, Torah; Andorra, angora, aurora, Endora, Pandora, signora; Floradora, Theodora. (And compare extensions of -ôre.)

-ôràge: borage, forage, porridge, storage.

-oràl: coral, laurel, moral, quarrel, sorrel; Balmoral, immoral, unmoral.

-ôral: aural, choral, floral, horal, oral, thoral; binaural, femoral.

-örale: chorale, morale.

-ôran: Koran, Oran.

-ôrax: borax, corax, storax, thorax.

-ôrbél: bauble, corbel, warble.

-ôrchàrd, -ôrchêr: orchard, tortured, Slorcha, scorcher, torture.

-ôrdêr, -ôardêr: boarder, border, corder, forder, hoarder, Lauder, order, warder; accorder, awarder, disorder, recorder, rewarder.

-ôrdial: cordial; primordial.

-ôrdön: Bordon, cordon, Gordon, Jordan, warden.

-ôrdship: lordship, wardship.

-ôrēàl, -ôriàl: voreal, oriel; armorial, memorial, pictorial; equatorial, immemorial; ambassadorial, conspiratorial, dictatorial, sinatorial; inquisitorial.

-orèign, -orin: florin, foreign, sporran, warren.

-ôrelock: forelock, Porlock, warlock.

-orénce: Florence, Lawrence, torrents; abhorrence. (Also -àrrent + "s".)

-ôrêr: borer, corer, floorer, gorer, porer, pourer, roarer, scorer, snorer, soarer, sorer, storer; adorer, deplorer, encorer, explorer, ignorer, implorer, restorer.

-ôrést, -ôrist: forest, florist, sorest.

-ôrgàn: gorgon, Morgan, organ; Glamorgan.

-ôrgêr: Borgia, forger, gorger, ordure; dis-gorger.

-ôrgi, -ôrgy: Corgi, Georgie, orgy.

-ôric: chloric, choric, doric, Warwick, Yorkrick; caloric, historic, phosphoric; allegoric, categoric, metaphoric, paregoric, prehistoric, sophomoric.

-orid, -orrid: florid, forehead, horrid, torrid.

-oris: Boris, Doris, Horace, loris, Morris, Norris; deoch-an-doras.

-ôrky: corky, door-key, porky. (Compare -ăwky.)

-ôrmàl: formal, normal; abnormal, informal.

-ôrmàn: doorman, floorman, foreman, Mormon, Norman, storeman; longshoreman.

-ôrmànt: dormant, torment; conformant, informant.

-ôrmêr: dormer, former, stormer, warmer; barn-stormer, conformer, deformer, informer, performer, reformer, transformer.

-ôrnêr: corner, Lorna, mourner, scorner, warner, yawner; adorner, suborner.

-ôrnét: cornet, hornet.

-ôrning: horning, morning, scorning, adorning, suborning. (Extend -ôrn. Compare -ăwning.)

-ôrny: corny, horny, thorny.

-öröugh: borough, burro, burrow, furrow, thorough. (Compare -ûrrōw.)

-ôrus: chorus, Horus, porous, torous, torus; canorous, decorous, imporous, pylorus, sonorous; indecorous.

-ôrpör: torpor, warper.

-ôrpus: corpus, porpoise; habeas corpus.

-orràl, -orrél: See -oràl.

-orrént: torrent, warrant; abhorrent.

-orrid: See -orid.

-orrör: horror; abhorror.

-orrōw: borrow, morrow, Morro, sorrow; tomorrow.

-orrÿ: Florrie, Laurie, lorry, quarry, soiree, sorry. (For rhymes to "worry", see -ûrry.)

-ôrsàl, -ôrsél: dorsal, foresail, morsel, torsal.

-ôrsét: corset, Dorset.

-ôrtàge: cortege, portage.

-ôrtàl, -ôrtle: chortle, mortal, portal, tortile; aortal, immortal.

-ôrtár, -ôrtêr: mortar, porter, quarter, shorter, snorter, sorter, sporter; assorter, consorter, contorter, distorter, escorter, exporter, importer, reporter, supporter, transporter. (Compare **-ôrder.**)

-ôrtèn: Horton, Morton, Norton, quartan, shorten, Wharton.

-ôrtex: cortex, vortex.

-ôrtion: portion, torsion, abortion, apportion, consortion, contortion, distortion, extortion, proportion. (Extend **-ôrt** for "contortion", etc. Compare **-äution.**)

-ôrtive: sportive, tortive; abortive, transportive.

-ôrtly, -ôurtly: courtly, portly.

-ôrtréss: court-dress, fortress, portress.

-ôrtune: fortune; importune, misfortune.

-ôrture: See **-ôrchêr.**

-ôrty: forty, porty, rorty, snorty, sortie, sporty, warty. (Compare **-aughty.**)

-ôrum: forum, jorum, quorum, Shoreham; decorum; ad valorem, cockalorem, indecorum, pons asinorum.

-ôrus, -äurus: aurous, chorus, chlorous, porous, taurus, torus; canorous, decorous, imporous, sonorous.

-ôrway: doorway, Norway.

-ôry: dory, flory, glory, gory, hoary, lory, oary, shory, snory, story, tory, whory; vainglory; allegory, a priori, auditory, category, crematory, dictatory, dormitory, gradatory, hunky-dory, laudatory, mandatory, migratory, monitory, narratory, piscatory, predatory, purgatory, sanitory, territory, transitory, vibratory; ambulatory, aspiratory, circulatory, conciliatory, conservatory, declaratory, depilatory, derogatory, exclamatory, expiratory, explanatory, gladiatory, inflammatory, judicatory, obligatory, osculatory, premonitory, preparatory, prohibitory, reformatory, repository, respiratory, retributory, revocatory, salutatory, speculatory, supplicatory, transpiratory, vindicatory; retaliatory.

-ōsely: closely; jocosely, morosely, verbosely.

-ōsä: Formosa, mimosa; amorosa.

-ōsèn: chosen, frozen, squozen; boatswain.

-osèt, -osit: closet, posit, posset; deposit.

-oshêr: cosher, Kasher, posher, swasher, washer.

-ōsiêr: cosier, crozier, dozier, hosier, osier, mosier, rosier. (Extend **-ōse.** Compare **-osure.**)

-ōsion: corrosion, erosion, explosion. (Compare **-ōtion.**)

-ōsive: corrosive, erosive, explosive; inexplosive.

-osky: bosky, drosky.

-osmic: cosmic, osmic.

-ossacks: Cossacks, Trossachs.

-ôssäge: Osage, bossage, sausage.

-ôssêr, bosser, crosser, dosser, josser, prosser, tosser; emboser. (Extend **-ôss.**)

-ossum: blossom, possum; oppossum.

-ôssy: bossy, drossy, Flossie, flossy, glossy, mossy, posse, tossy.

-ostál, -ostèl: costal, hostel, hostile, postil; pentecostal.

-ōstál: coastal, postal.

-ostêr: coster, foster, Gloucester, roster; accoster, imposter; paternoster, Pentecoster.

-ōstêr: See **-ōastêr.**

-ōstèss: ghostess, hostess.

-ostic: caustic, gnostic, joss-stick; accostic, acrostic, agnostic, prognostic; anacrostic, diagnostic, pentacostic.

-ostle, -ossil: docile, dossil, fossil, jostle, throstle, wassail; apostle, colossal.

-ostlêr: hostler, jostler, ostler, wassailer.

-ōstly: ghostly, mostly.

-ostrèl, -ostril: costrel, nostril.

-ostrum: nostrum, rostrum.

-ōsure: closure; composure, disclosure, enclosure, exposure, foreclosure. (Compare **-osiêr.**)

-ōsy, -ōzy: cozy, dozy, Josie, mosey, nosy, posy, prosy, Rosie, rosy.

-ōtá: quota, rota; Bogota, Dakota, iota, Minnesota. (Compare **-ōater.**)

-ōtál: dotal, notal, rotal, total; teetotal; anecdotal, antidotal, extradotal, sacerdotal, teetotal.

-ōtárd: dotard, motored.

-otchêr: blotcher, botcher, notcher, splotcher, watcher; top-notcher.

-ōtêr, -ōtör: See **-ōatêr.**

-othêr: bother, father, pother.

-öthêr: brother, mother, other, smother; another, Anstruther.

-ōthing: clothing, loathing.

-otic: azotic, chaotic, despotic, erotic, exotic, hypnotic, neurotic, narcotic, quixotic; idiotic, patriotic.

-ōtion, -ōceàn: lotion, motion, notion, ocean, potion; commotion, devotion, emotion, promotion, remotion; locomotion. (Compare -ōsion.)

-ōtive: motive, votive; emotive, promotive; locomotive.

-otly: hotly, motley, Otley, squatly.

-otnèss: hotness, squatness.

-ottàge: cottage, pottage, wattage.

-ottèn, -ottön: cotton, gotten, rotten; begotten, forgotten, misgotten.

-ottêr: blotter, clotter, cotter, dotter, jotter, knotter, ottar, otter, plotter, potter, rotter, spotter, squatter, totter, trotter, yachter; globe-trotter. (Compare -oddêr.)

-ottish: schottische, Scottish, sottish.

-ottle: bottle, dottel, glottal, mottle, pottle, throttle, tottle, twattle, wattle. (Compare -oodle.)

-ottō: blotto, grotto, lotto, motto, Otto, Watteau; ridoto, what ho!

-otty: blotty, clotty, dotty, knotty, Lottie, spotty, totty.

-ōtum, -ōtèm: pro tem, quotum, totem.

-öuble, ubble: bubble, double, rubble, stubble, trouble.

-öublèt: doublet, sub-let.

-ouchêr: coucher, Goucher, poucher, sloucher, voucher.

-oudêr: See -owdêr.

-oudly: loudly, proudly.

-oughboy: cowboy, ploughboy.

-ōughboy: doughboy, hautboy.

-oughen: roughen, toughen.

-ôughty: See -ăughty.

-ōuldêr: See -ōldêr.

-ōulticed: poulticed. (And extend -ōlt.)

-oundêr: bounder, flounder, founder, pounder, rounder, sounder; compounder, confounder, dumfounder, expounder, impounder, profounder, resounder, surrounder.

-oundly: roundly, soundly; profoundly, unsoundly.

-ounsèl: council, counsel, groundsel.

-ountain: fountain, mountain.

-ountêr: counter, mounter; accounter, discounter, encounter, recounter, remounter, surmounter; reencounter.

-ounty: bounty, county, "mounty".

-oūpêr: See -ōōpêr.

-öuple: See -upple.

-oūpẏ: See -ōōpẏ.

-oûràge: borage, courage; demurrage, discourage, encourage.

-oûrish: currish, flourish, nourish.

-ourly: dourly, hourly, sourly.

-oûrney, -êrny: Burney, Czerny, Ernie, ferny, journey, tourney; attorney.

-ousàl: housel, spousal, tousel; arousal, carousal, espousal.

-ousêr: See -owsêr.

-öusin: See -özèn.

-ousy, -owsy: blowsy, drowsy, frowsy, lousy, mousy.

-outêr: clouter, douter, flouter, jowter, pouter, router, scouter, shouter, spouter, sprouter, touter.

-oūthful: See -ūthful.

-outy, -oughty: doughty, droughty, flouty, gouty, grouty, pouty, snouty, sprouty.

-ōvà: nova; Casanova, Jehovah; Villanova. (Compare -ōvêr.)

-ovàl: approval, disproval, removal, reproval; disapproval.

-ovèl: grovel, hovel, novel.

-övèl: hovel, Lovel, shovel.

-ovemènt: movement; approvement, improvement.

-övèn: covin, oven, sloven.

-ōvèn: cloven, woven; interwoven.

-övêr: cover, glover, lover, plover, shover; discover, recover, uncover.

-ōvêr: clover, Dover, drover, over, plover, rover, stover, trover; moreover, pushover; helf-seas-over. (Compare -ōvà.)

-övetāil: dovetail, love-tale.

-ōwàge: stowage, towage.

-owàrd: See -owêred.

-owdêr, -oudêr: chowder, crowder, louder, powder, prouder.

-owdẏ: cloudy, dowdy, howdy, rowdy; pandowdy.

-owėl: bowel, dowel, Powell, rowel, towel, trowel, vowel; avowal; disembowel. (Compare **-owl.**)

-ōwêr: blower, goer, grower, knower, lower, mower, ower, rower, sewer, slower, sower, thrower; bestower; overthrower.

-owêr: bower, cower, dower, flower, Giaour, power, shower, tower; endower, overpower. (Compare **-our.**)

-owêred: coward, Howard. (Extend **-owêr, -our.**)

-owêry: bowery, cowry, dowry, flowery, houri, showery, towery.

-ōwing: blowing, crowing, flowing, glowing, going, growing, knowing, mowing, owing, rowing, sewing, showing, snowing, sowing, towing, throwing. (Extend **-ōw** + "ing".)

-owlėdge: See **-ollėge.**

-ōwlêr: See **-ōlàr.**

-ōwmàn: See **-ōmàn.**

-ōwnêr: See **-ōanêr.**

-ownsmàn: gownsman, roundsman, townsman.

-owny, -ownie: brownie, browny, downy, frowny, Rowney, towny.

-owsêr: Browser, browser, dowser, grouser, Mauser, mouser, rouser, towser, trouser; carouser, espouser.

-ōwy: blowy, Bowie, Chloe, doughy, glowy, goey, Joey, showy, snowy.

-oxėn: cockswain, oxen, Oxon.

-oxy: Coxey, doxy, foxy, poxy, proxy; Biloxi; orthodoxy, paradoxy; heterodoxy.

-oyal: loyal, royal; disloyal. (Compare **-oil.**)

-oyàlty: loyalty, royalty.

-oyànt: bouyant, clairvoyant, flamboyant.

-oyêr: annoyer, destroyer, employer, enjoyer.

-oyly: See **-oily.**

-oymėnt: deployment, employment, enjoyment; unemployment.

-ōzėn, -ōusin: cousin, cozen, dozen.

-ōzėn: See **-ōsėn.**

-ozzle, -osel: losel, nozzle, sozzle, schnozzle;

schlemmozzle.

-ūàl: See **-ūėl.**

-ūànt: fluent, truant; diluent, pursuant.

-uäve: suave, Zouave.

-ūbà: Cuba, tuba.

-ubbêr: blubber, clubber, drubber, dubber, grubber, lubber, rubber, scrubber, slubber, snubber, stubber, tubber; landlubber; india-rubber.

-ubbêred: blubbered, cupboard, Hubbard, rubbered.

-ubbish: cubbish, clubbish, grubbish, rubbish, tubbish.

-ubble: See **-ōuble.**

-ubbly bubbly, doubly, knubbly, rubbly, stubbly.

-ubby: chubby, cubby, grubby, hubby, nubby, scrubby, shrubby, stubby, tubby.

-ūbic: cubic, pubic; cherubic.

-ublish: bubblish, publish.

-ūby: See **-ōōby.**

-uccör: See **-uckêr.**

-ūcėnt: lucent; abducent, adducent, recusant, reducent, traducent, translucent.

-ūcial: crucial; fiducial.

-ūcid: deuced, loosed, lucid, mucid; pellucid.

-uckêr: bucker, chucker, clucker, ducker, mucker, pucker, shucker, succor, sucker, trucker, tucker; seersucker.

-uckėt: bucket, tucket; Nantucket.

-uckle: buckle, chuckle, huckle, knuckle, muckle, stuckle, suckle, truckle; unbuckle; honeysuckle.

-uckled: cuckold. (And extend **-uckle.**)

-ucklêr: buckler, chuckler, knuckler, truckler; swashbuckler.

-uckling: buckling, duckling, suckling.

-ucky: ducky, lucky, mucky, plucky; unlucky, Kentucky.

-ūcre: euchre, fluker, lucre, puker; rebuker.

-uction, -uxion: fluxion, ruction, suction; abduction, adduction, affluxion, construction, deduction, defluxion, destruction, effluxion, induction, influxion, instruction, obduction, obstruction, production, reduction, seduction, traduction; introduction, misconstruction, reproduction, superstruction; over-production, superinduction.

-uctive: adductive, conductive, constructive, deductive, destructive, inductive, instructive, obstructive, productive, reductive, seductive, traductive; introductive, reconstructive, reproductive, superstructive.

-uddêr: "brudder", dudder, flooder, mudder, rudder, scudder, shudder, udder. (Compare **-uttêr.**)

-udding: hooding, pudding, wooding.

-uddle: cuddle, fuddle, huddle, muddle, puddle, ruddle. (Compare **-uttle.**)

-uddlêr: cuddler, huddler, muddler.

-uddy: bloody, buddy, cruddy, muddy, ruddy, studdy, study. (Compare **-utty.**)

-ūdėnt: prudent, student; concludent, imprudent; jurisprudent.

-ūdêr, -ūdôr: Tudor. (And extend **-ūde** for "ruder", etc.)

-udgeon: bludgeon, dudgeon, gudgeon; curmudgeon.

-ūdish: blue-dish, crudish, dudish, lewdish, nudish, prudish, rudish, shrewdish.

-ūdist: Buddhist, crudist, feudist, lewdest, nudest, nudist, rudest, shrewdest.

-ūdō: judo, pseudo; escudo.

-ūėl: crewel, cruel, dual, duel, Ewell, fuel, gruel, jewel, newel; bejewel, eschewal, pursual, renewal. (Compare **-ōōl** and **-ūle.**)

-ūėnt: See **-ūànt.**

-ūėt: chuet, cruet, Hewett, suet.

-ūeẏ: See **-ewẏ.**

-uffêr: bluffer, buffer, cuffer, duffer, gruffer, huffer, luffer, puffer, rougher, snuffer, stuffer, suffer, tougher. (And extend **-uff** and **-ough.**)

-uffin: muffin, puffin; raggamuffin, roughen.

-uffing: bluffing, cuffing, huffing, puffing, roughing, ruffing, stuffing.

-uffle: buffle, duffel, muffle, ruffle, scuffle, shuffle, snuffle, truffle.

-uffling: muffling, ruffling, scuffling, shuffling, snuffling; unruffling.

-uffly: bluffly, gruffly, muffly, roughly, ruffly, scuffly, sluffly, toughly, truffly.

-uffẏ: bluffy, buffy, chuffy, fluffy, huffy, pluffy, puffy, sloughy, snuffy, stuffy.

-ufty, -ufti: mufti, tuftly.

-ūgàl, -ūgle: bugle, frugal, fugal; McDougall; centrifugal.

-uggêr: bugger, drugger, hugger, lugger, mugger, plugger, rugger, shrugger, slugger, snugger, tugger; hugger-mugger.

-uggle: guggle, juggle, smuggle, snuggle, struggle.

-uggy: buggy, muggy, puggy, sluggy.

-ūgle: See **-ūgàl.**

-ugly: smugly, smuggly, snugly, ugly.

-ūicy: goosey, juicy, Lucy, sluicy; Debussy, retroussee.

-ūid: druid, fluid.

-uildêr: See **-ildêr.**

-ūin: bruin, ruin, Trewin.

-ūisànce: nuisance, usance.

-ūish: blueish, Jewish, newish, shrewish.

-ūitêr: See **-ōōtêr.**

-ūkẏ: See **ōōky.**

-ūlà: Beulah, Eula, hula; Ashtabula, Boola-Boola, hula-hula. (Compare **-ōōlêr.**)

-ulgàr: Bulgar, vulgar.

-ulgénce: effulgenge, indulgence, refulgence; self-indulgence.

-ulgént, fulgent; effulgent, emulgent, indulgent, refulgent; self-indulgent.

-ulky: bulky, hulky, sulky.

-ūllàh: mullah, nullah; Abdullah. (Compare **-ullêr.**)

-ullàrd: dullard, colored.

-ullêr, -ōlôr: color, cruller, culler, duller, guller, luller, sculler; annuller, discolor, medullar, tricolor; multicolor, technicolor, water color. (Compare **-ullàh.**)

-ullét (-ool): bullet, pullet.

-ullét: cullet, gullet, mullet.

-ullion: cullion, mullion, scullion; rapscallion.

-ully (-ool): bully, fully, pulley, woolly. (And many false rhymes in adverbs ending in **-ully,** thus "beautifully", etc.)

-ully: cully, dully, gully, hully, sully, Tully.

-ulpit: bull-pit, pulpit.

-ulsion: pulsion; compulsion, convulsion, divulsion, emulsion, expulsion, impulsion, propulsion, repulsion, revulsion.

-ulsive: compulsive, convulsive, divulsive, emulsive, expulsive, impulsive, propulsive, repulsive, revulsive.

-ultry: sultry; adult'ry.

-ulture: culture, multure, vulture; agriculture, horticulture, pisciculture, sylviculture, viticulture.

-ūlū: Lulu, pulu, Zulu; Honolulu.

-ūly, -ūely, -ewly, -ōōlie, -ōōly: bluely, coolie, coolly, cruelly, Dooley, duly, Julie, newly, ruly, truly, viewly; unduly, unruly, untruly.

-ūmà: Duma, puma, Yuma; Montezuma.

-ūmàge: fumage, plumage, roomage.

-ūmàn: cueman, Crewe-man, crewman, human, Kew-man, Krooman, lumen, Newman, pew-man, Truman; acumen, albumen, bitumen, legumen; superhuman.

-umbàr, -umbêr: cumber, Humber, lumbar, lumber, number, Rumba, slumber, umber; cucumber, encumber, outnumber; disencumber.

-umbêr: See **-ummêr.**

-umble: bumble, crumble, dumb-bell, fumble, grumble, humble, jumble, mumble, rumble, scumble, stumble, tumble, umble.

-umbly, -omely: comely, crumbly, dumbly, grumbly, humbly, numbly.

-umbril: tumbril, umbril.

-umbō: Dumbo, gumbo; mumbo-jumbo.

-ūmèn: See **-umàn.**

-ūmêr: See **-ūmòr.**

-ūmid: fumid, humid, tumid.

-ummêr, -umbêr: comer, crumber, drummer, dumber, glummer, grummer, gummer, hummer, mummer, number, plumber, dummer, scummer, strummer, summer; midsummer.

-ummit: plummet, summit.

-ummy; chummy, crumby, crummy, drummy, dummy, gummy, lummy, mummy, plummy, rummy, scrummy, scummy, thrummy, tummy, yummy.

-umnàl: autumnal, columnal.

-ūmòr, -ūmêr, -ōōmêr: bloomer, boomer, doomer, fumer, humor, roomer, rumor, tumor; consumer, entomber; ill-humor, presumer.

-ūmous: fumous, glumous, grumous, humous, humus, plumous, spumous, strumous.

-umpêr: bumper, dumper, jumper, lumper, mumper, plumper, pumper, stumper.

-umpét: crumpet, strumpet, trumpet.

-umpish: bumpish, dumpish, grumpish, humpish, jumpish, lumpish, mumpish, plumpish, slumpish.

-umpkin: bumpkin, lumpkin, pumpkin.

-umple: crumple, rumple.

-umption: gumption, sumption; assumption, consumption, presumption, resumption.

-umptious: bumptious, gumptious, scrumptious; assumptious.

-umpus, -ömpàss: compass, rumpus; encompass.

-ūnà: luna, una; fortuna, lacuna, vicuna.

-ūnàr, -ūnêr, -ōōnêr: crooner, lunar, pruner, schooner, sooner, spooner, swooner, tuner; attuner, ballooner, communer, harpooner, lacunar, lampooner, sublunar, translunar.

-uncheön: luncheon, muncheon, puncheon, truncheon.

-uncle: Funchal, truncal, uncle; carbuncle, siphuncle.

-unction: function, junction, unction; compunction, conjunction, defunction, disjunction, expunction, injunction, subjunction.

-unctive: adjunctive, conjunctive, disjunctive, subjunctive.

-uncture: juncture, puncture; conjuncture, compuncture.

-undànce: abundance, redundance; superabundance.

-undànt; abundant, redundant; superabundant.

-unday: See **-undy.**

-undêr: blunder, dunder, plunder, sunder, thunder, wonder; asunder, fecunder, jocunder, refunder, rotunder, thereunder; thereinunder.

-undle: bundle, Blundell, rundle, trundle.

-undy, -unday: Grundy, Lundy, Monday, sundae, Sunday, undie.

-ūneful: spoonful, tuneful.

-ūnêr: See **-ūnàr.**

-ungêr (soft "g"): blunger, lunger, plunger, sponger, spunger; expunger.

-ungêr (hard "g"): hunger, monger, younger;

fishmonger, newsmonger; costermonger, ironmonger.

-ungle: bungle, jungle.

-ūnic: Munich, punic, runic, tunic.

-uniön: bunion, Bunyan, onion, ronion, Runyon, trunnion.

-unkård, unkêred: bunkered, drunkard.

-unkén: drunken, Duncan, shrunken, sunken.

-unkêr: bunker, drunker, dunker, flunker, junker, plunker, punker.

-unkėt: junket, plunket.

-unkẏ: chunky, donkey, flunkey, funky, hunky, monkey, spunky, trunky.

-unlit: sunlit, unlit.

-unnåge: dunnage, gunnage, monage, tonnage.

-unnėl: funnel, gunwale, runnel, tunnel.

-unny, -öny, -oney: bunny, funny, gunny, honey, money, sonny, sunny, tunny.

-unstêr: Dunster, funster, gunster, Munster, punster.

-untêr: blunter, bunter, grunter, hunter, punter, shunter, stunter; affronter, confronter.

-untle: frontal, gruntle; disgruntle, contrapuntal.

-upbōard: See **-ubbêred.**

-ūpid: Cupid, stupid.

-ūpil, ūple: pupil, scruple; octuple, quintuple, septuple, sextuple.

-uplėt: octuplet, quituplet, septuplet, sextuplet.

-ūplėt: drupelet; quadruplet.

-uppêr: crupper, scupper, supper, upper.

-upple: couple, supple.

-uppẏ: guppy, puppy.

-ūrå: pleura, sura; bravura, caesura, datura; Angostura, Cuticura; coloratura; appoggiatura.

-ūrål: crural, jural, mural, neural, pleural, plural, rural, Ural; intermural, intramural, sinecural.

-ūrånce: durance; assurance, endurance, insurance; reassurance.

-ûrbån: bourbon, Durban, turban, urban; suburban.

-ûrbêr, -ûrbår: curber, Durbar; disturber, per-

turber, superber.

-ûrbish: furbish, Serbish; refurbish, superbish.

-ûrchåsed, -ûrchėst: purchased. (And extend **-êarch, -êrch, -îrch, -ûrch** for "birchest", etc.)

-ûrdén: burden, guerdon, Purdon; disburden; overburden.

-ûrdêr: See **-îrdår.**

-ûrdẏ, -îrdie: birdie, curdy, Ferdie, sturdy, Verdi, wordy; hurdy-gurdy.

-ûreau: bureau, Douro, Truro, futuro.

-ūrelẏ: purely; demurely, maturely, obscurely, securely.

-uremėnt: abjurement, allurement, conjurement, immurement, obscurement, procurement.

-ūrêr: curer, führer, juror, lurer, moorer, poorer, purer, surer, tourer; abjurer, adjurer, allurer, assurer, conjurer, demurer, endurer, ensurer, maturer, procurer, securer.

-ûrfẏ: Murphy, scurfy, surfy, turfy.

-ûrgent: purgent, surgent, turgent, urgent; convergent, detergent, divergent, emergent, insurgent, resurgent.

-ûrgeön: bourgeon, Sir John, Spurgeon, sturgeon, surgeon, virgin.

-ûrgẏ: See **-êrgẏ.**

-ūrist, -ūrést: jurist, poorest, purist, tourist; caricaturist. (And extend **-ūre** for "purest", etc.)

-ūrious: curious, furious, spurious; Asturias, incurious, injurious, juxurious, penurious, usurious.

-ûrky: See **-êrky.**

-ûrlêr: burler, curler, furler, hurler, pearler, purler, skirler, twirler, whirler.

-ûrlew: curlew, purlieu.

-ûrling: See **-îrling.**

-ûrlish: See **-îrlish.**

-ûrlẏ: See **-earlẏ.**

-ûrmå: Burma, derma, Irma, syrma.

-ûrmûr: See **-îrmêr.**

-ûrnêr: See **-êarnêr.**

-ûrnėt: burnet, gurnet, ternate; alternate.

-ûrnish: burnish, furnish, sternish.

-ûrör: furor, juror. (And extend **-ôor** and **-ure**

for "poorer", "surer", etc.)

-ûrrièr: currier, furrier, hurrier, skurrier, spurrier, worrier.

-ûrrōw: burrow, furrow. (Compare **-örōugh.**)

-ûrrẏ: burry, curry, flurry, furry, hurry, Murray, scurry, slurry, Surrey, worry.

-ûrsàr, -ûrsêr: See **-êrcêr.**

-ûrtàin: See **-êrtàin.**

-ûrtle: See **-îrtle.**

-ûrvànt: See **-êrvànt.**

-ûrvey: purvey, survey.

-ûruy: See **-êrvy.**

-ūry, -ewry, ōōry: brewery, Drury, ewry, fury, houri, Jewry, jury, moory; Missouri.

-ūsà: Sousa, Susa; Medusa; Tuscaloosa.

-uscàn: dusken, Tuscan; Etruscan, molluscan.

-uscle, -ussèl, -ustle: bustle, hustle, justle, muscle, mussel, Russell, rustle, tussle; corpuscle.

-ūsêr: See **-ōōsêr.**

-ushêr: blusher, brusher, crusher, flusher, gusher, husher, plusher, rusher, usher.

-ushy: brushy, cushy, gushy, lushy, mushy, plushy, rushy, slushy.

-ushy (-ooshy): Bushey, bushy, wushy, pushy.

-ūsion: fusion; allusion, collusion, conclusion, confusion, contusion, delusion, diffusion, effusion, elusion, exclusion, extrusion, illusion, inclusion, infusion, intrusion, Malthusian, obtrusion, obtusion, occlusion, pertusion, profusion, protusion, reclusion, seclusion, suffusion, transfusion; circumfusion, disillusion. (Compare **-ūtion.**)

-ūsive: abusive, allusive, collusive, conclusive, conducive, delusive, diffusive, effusive, exclusive, illusive, inclusive, infusive, intrusive, obtrusive, reclusive, seclusive; inconclusive.

-uskin: buskin, Ruskin.

-usky: dusky, husky, musky, tusky.

-ūsō: Crusoe, trousseau; Caruso.

-ussèt: gusset, russet.

-ussià: Prussia, Russia.

-ussiàn: Prussian, Russian; concussion, discussion, percussion, repercussion.

-ussive: concussive, discussive, percussive; repercussive.

-ussy: fussy, Gussie, hussy, mussy.

-ustàrd: blustered, bustard, clustered, custard, flustered, mustard, mustered.

-ustêr: bluster, cluster, Custer, duster, fluster, juster, luster, lustre, muster, thruster, truster; adjuster, distruster, robuster; coadjuster, filibuster.

-ustful: lustful, trustful; disgustful, distrustful, mistrustful.

-ustian: fustian, combustion.

-ustic: fustic, rustic.

-ustice: custis, justice; Augustus.

-ûrvẏ: See **-êrvẏ.**

-ustle: See **-uscle.**

-ustlêr: bustler, hustler, rustler, tussler.

-ustly: justly; augustly, robustly, unjustly.

-ustöm: custom, frustum; accustom.

-usty: busty, dusty, gusty, lusty, musty, rusty, trusty.

-usy: busy, dizzy. (See **-izzy.**)

-ūtàl: See **-ōōtle.**

-ūthful: ruthful, toothful, truthful, youthful; untruthful.

-ūthlèss: ruthless, toothless, truthless.

-ūtile: futile, utile; inutile.

-ūtion: ablution, dilution, locution, pollution, solution, volution; absolution, allocution, attribution, collocution, condecution, constitution, contribution, convolution, distitution, devolution, diminution, dissolution, distrubution, elocution, evolution, execution, institution, envolution, Lilliputian, persecution, prosecution, prostitution, resolution, restitution, retribution, revolution, substitution; circumlocution, circumvolution, electrocution, interlocution, irresolution. (Compare **-ūsion.**)

-ūtist: cutest, flutist, lutist, mutest, pharmaceutist, therapeutist. (Compare **-ūdist.**)

-ūtive: indutive; coadjutive, constitutive, persecutive, resolutive.

-utlêr: butler, cutler, scuttler, subtler, sutler,

-utney: chutney, Putney, gluttony, muttony.

-ūtön: Luton, Newton, Teuton.

-uttêr: butter, clutter, cutter, flutter, gutter, mutter, putter, shutter, splutter, sputter, stutter, utter; abutter, Calcutta, rebutter. (Compare **-uddêr.**)

-utish: ruttish, sluttish.

-uttle: buttle, cuttle, scuttle, shuttle, subtle; rebuttal.

-uttöck: buttock, futtock, puttock.

-uttön: button, Dutton, glutton, mutton, Sutton; unbutton; bachelor button.

-utty: butty, nutty, puttee, putty, rutty, smutty, tutty. (Compare -uddy.)

-ūty: See -ōōty.

-ūture: future, moocher, puture, suture.

-ūvial: pluvial; alluvial.

-uxiön: See -uction.

-uyêr: See -īár.

-uzzle: guzzle, muzzle, nuzzle, puzzle.

-uzzlêr: guzzler, muzzler, nuzzler, puzzler.

-uzzy: buzzy, fuzzy, huzzy, muzzy; Fuzzy-Wuzzy.

-yán: See -īön.

-ycle: cycle, Michael; Lake Baikal.

-ýcle: sickle, bicycle, tricycle. (See -ickle.)

-yer: See -iêr.

-ylon: nylon, pylon, trylon.

-ẏmbál: See -imble.

-ẏmbol: See -imble.

-ymén: hymen, flymen (stage), piemen, Simon.

-ẏmic: See -imic.

-ẏnchêr: See -inchêr.

-ẏnic: See -inic.

-ẏntax: syntax, tin-tacks.

-ypist: typist. (And extend īpe.)

-ẏptic: cryptic, diptych, glyptic, styptic, triptych; ecliptic, elliptic; apocalyptic.

-yrāte: gyrate, irate, lyrate; circumgyrate, dextrogyrate.

-ẏric: lyric; butyric, empiric, satiric, satyric; panegyric.

-yrön: See -īren.

-yrtle: See -ûrtle.

-ẏsmál: See -ismal.

-ẏthám: lytham, rhythm, Withem.

-ẏstic: See -istic.

GLOSSARY OF POETIC TERMS

accent: stress indicated by a (′) mark placed above certain emphasized syllables in a line of verse.
Ex.: The night is white.

alexandrine: a verse consisting of six iambic feet.

alliteration: close repetition of a consonant

sound at the beginning of a word.
Ex.: She sells sea shells by the seashore.

amphibrach: a metrical foot of three syllables consisting of the following pattern.
Ex.: I sprang to | the stirrup.

anacrusis: an additional unaccented syllable at the begining of a line.

analogy: likeness between two different things.
Ex.: T's with our judgment as our watches, none.

anapest: a metrical foot consisting of two unaccented syllables followed by one accented syllable.
Ex.: Oh, he flies | through the air.

anaphora: repeated use of a word or group of words throughout a verse.

Ex.: I gave her cakes and I gave her ale
I gave her Sack and Sherry.

antepenult: the third syllable from the end of a word.
Ex.: antepenult.

anthology: collection of poetry.

apostrophe: An inanimate object is addressed directly as if it were actually a listening person.

assonance: the repeated sound of similar vowels in accented syllables.
Ex.: Like a diamond in the sky.

ballad: a verse consisting of three stanzas and a conclusion. It is usually written in iambic or anapestic tetrameter. The rhyme scheme is ab-ab-bc-bc bc-bc.

ballad stanza: a verse consisting of four lines in which the first and third lines are in iambic tetrameter and the second and fourth lines are in iambic trimeter. The rhyme scheme is abcb.

blank verse: unrhymed iambic pentameter verse which was the standard form of the

Elizabethan time.

Ex.: Tomorrow, and tomorrow, and tomorrow,

    Creeps in this petty pace from day to day. "Macbeth"—Shakespeare.

Broadside Ballad: a poem written on a large sheet of paper and sung by the street singers in the sixteenth century.

cacophony: harsh sounds which are used in poetry for effect.

Ex.: a quick sharp scratch.

cadence: the pattern arrangements of rhythm in verse.

caesura: a pause usually in the middle of a line.

Ex.: A little learning | is a dangerous thing.

catalexis: omission of one or more final unstressed syllables.

Ex.: Irish poets learn your trade.

complaint: a Rennaissance lyrical poem in which the speaker moans for his absent or unresponsive lover.

consonance: the repeated use of the same consonant sounds before and after different vowels. Ex.: tip-top trip-trap.

couplet: two successive rhyming lines of poetry.

dactyl: poetic foot consisting of an accented syllable followed by two unaccented syllables.

Ex.: possible, wonderful.

didactic: poetry that teaches a moral lesson such as Pope's "Essay on Man".

dimeter: a line of poetry consisting of two feet.

doggerel: irregular rhyming lines that are made regular by accenting normally unaccented syllables.

Elegy: personal poem of mourning.

envoy: a concluding stanza that is shorter than the ones it follows.

epic: a long narrative poem describing a hero and his brave deeds and following a set form.

Ex.: Beowulf.

epic simile: an elaborately written comparison.

epigram: a short witty poem or a short pithy statement.

fable: a short moral tale in verse having animals as its main characters.

Ex.: Uncle Remus Stories.

feminine ending: an extra unaccented syllable at the end of a verse.

Ex.: ev*er*.

foot: basic unit of measurement in poetry consisting of two or more syllables, one of which is accented.

heptameter: a line of verse consisting of seven feet.

heroic couplet: a rhyming couplet of iambic pentameter used in the heroic poems of the eighteenth century.

hexameter: a line of verse consisting of six feet.

hyberbole: exaggeration or overstatement.

hypermeter: the additon of one or more unaccented syllables at the beginning and end of a line of poetry.

iamb: one unaccented syllable followed by one accented syllable. This pattern is the most common one used in verse.

Ex.: The world is still deceived with ornament.

incremental repetition: the repetition of a line or lines with some slight variation to further the rhyme.

internal rhyme: a rhyme that is located within a line.

Ex.: The night is white.

invocation: the addressing of a God whose help is sought.

lampoon: a personal attack in poetry.

Ex.: Pope's "The Rape of the Lock".

lyric: songlike poem expressing the writer's emotions.

macaronic verse: verse containing a mixture of languages.

masculine ending: a word ending with an accented syllable.

Ex.: remark, resound, confer.

meter: the pattern of accented and unaccented syllables in a line of poetry.

monometer: a line of poetry consisting of one foot.

octave: the first eight lines of an Italian sonnet.

octometer: a line of poetry consisting of eight

feet.

ode: a long lyrical poem characterized by lofty feelings.

onomatopoeia: sound of a word that suggests its meaning. Ex.: buzz, hiss, clang, bang.

ottava rima: right-line stanza of iambic pentameter using ab ab ab c c as its rhyme pattern.

paradox: a statement that is usually self-contradictory.
Ex.: That I may rise and stand.

pastoral: any poem concerning the country.

pentameter: a line of poetry consisting of 5 feet.

personification: the transfering of human qualities to inanimate objects.
Ex.: Time's hand.

poetic license: liberty for an author to use figures of speech and archaic words and to change form.

Poet Laureate: chief poet of England who writes all of the official poetry for the government.

pyrrhic foot: two unstressed syllables.

quatrain: four-line stanza.

refrain: a line or lines repeated during a poem.

rhyme: repetition of similar sounds at regular intervals.

rhyme royal: a seven-line stanza of iambic pentameter using ababbcc as its rhyme pattern.

rondeau: a French verse form which consists of 15 lines in 3 stanzas with only two rhymes used. The first line of the first stanza is used as a refrain in the second and third verse.

run-on verse: a line of poetry which continues into the next line without a grammatical break.

sapphics: classical verse form of four lines named after the Greek poetess, Sappho.

scansion: the study of a line to determine the meter used and number of feet in a line.

septet: a stanza of six lines.

sestet: last six lines of an Italian sonnet.

Shakespearian sonnet: fourteen lines of iambic pentameter having three quatrains and a concluding couplet using abab cdcd efef gg as its rhyme pattern.

simile: the comparison of two or more objects using like or as.
Ex.: She walks in beauty, like the night.
(Byron)

sonnet: a fourteen-line poem of iambic pentameter following a set rhyme scheme.

Spenserian stanza: a nine-line stanza named after its originator Edmund Spenser.

spondee: two stressed syllables used as a substitute for an iamb.
Ex.: watch out.

stanza: a group of lines of poetry used as a division of poetry.

stress: accent.

tercet: a group of three lines that rhyme.

terza rima: a three-line stanza that is joined by rhyme to the next stanza.
Ex.: aba bcb.

tetrameter: a line of poetry consisting of four feet.

trimeter: a line of poetry consisting of three feet.

triplet: a three-line stanza usually with one rhyme.

trochee: poetic foot consisting of a long syllable followed by a short one.
Ex.: legal, hateful.

Vers de société: playful lyrical verse that is sophisticated and deals with social customs.

verse: a. a single line of poetry. b. particular form of poetry such as blank verse. c. a stanza.

villanelle: short poem consisting of several tercets and a conclusion using only two rhymes throughout.

MUSIC
DICTIONARY

MUSIC DICTIONARY

COMPILED BY
M. H. GUANDOLA

ABBREVIATIONS*

Abb—Abbreviation	Hung—Hungarian
E—English	I—Italian
F—French	L—Latin
G—German	R.C.—Roman Catholic
Gr—Greek	S—Spanish

—A—

A—Sixth step in the typical diatonic scale of C.
Ab (G)—Off.
A ballata (I)—Ballad style.
Abandonné (F)—Unrestrained.
A battuta (I)—Strictly in time.
Abbassamento di mano (I)—To lower the hand for a downbeat.
Abbassamento di voce (I)—To lower the voice.
Abbellimenti (I)—Embellishments.
A-b-c-dieren (G)—Use of pitch letters in place of do, re, me.
Abdampfen (G)—To mute.
Abendlied (G)—Evening song.
Abendmusik (G)—Serenade.
Abendständchen (G)—Serenade.
A bene placito (I)—Freedom in performance.
Aber (G)—But.
Abgemessen (G)—Measured.
Abgestossen (G)—Staccatto.
Abkürzung (G)—Abridgment.
Abnehmend (G)—Diminishing.
Abrege (G)—Abridged.
Absatz (G)—Pause.
Abschwellend (G)—Decreasing.
Absolute music—Music which appeals through its material, form and structure in contra-distinction to program music.
Absolute pitch—Ability to identify a musical sound accurately upon hearing it.
Abstand (G)—Interval.
Abwechselnd (G)—Alternating.
Abstract music—Absolute music.
Abstrich (G)—Down-bow.
A Capp. (Abb)—A cappella.
A cappella (I)—Choral music without instrumental accompaniment.
A capriccio (I)—According to the performer.
Acathistus (Gr)—Byzantine hymn in honor of Virgin Mary.
Accarezzevole (I)—Caressing.
Accel. (Abb)—Accelerando.
Accelerando (I)—Becoming faster.
Accent (I)—Emphasis on a certain tone, chord or beat.
Accentuare (I), accentuer (F), accentuieren (G)—To accentuate.

Acciaccato (I)—Notes of a chord sounded not quite simultaneously.
Acciaccatura (I)—Single grace note placed before the principal note.
Accidentals—Sharps, flats, naturals introduced apart from the key signature.
Accidental chords—Chords containing notes foreign to their proper harmony.
Acclamation—Byzantine music saluting the emperor (9th-10th c.).
Accomodare (I)—To tune.
Accomp. (Abb)—Accompaniment.
Accompagnato (I), accompagné (F), beglietet (G) — Accompanied.
Accompaniment—Musical background for the principal part.
Accoppiato (I)—Tied notes (♪♪).
Accord (F)—Accord, chord, string, manner of tuning.
Accord à l'ouvert (F)—String not pressed down.
Accordamento (I)—Consonance.
Accordare (I), accorder (F), stimen (G)—To tune.
Accordatura (I)—Notes to which stringed instruments are tuned.
Accordion — Portable free-reed wind instrument producing tone by bellows, altering pitch by keys.
Accordo (I)—Chord.
Accresc. (Abb)—Accrescendo.
Accrescendo (I)—Increasing in tone and volume.
Accusé (F)—With emphasis.
A cembalo (I)—For the harpsichord or piano.
Achromatic—Diatonic.
Achtel (G)—Eighth.
Acoustics (E)—Science of sound.
Action—Mechanical connection between keyboard and strings or pipes.
Acuta (I)—Sharp.
Acute (E)—High pitch.
Adagietto (I)—Faster than adagio.
Adagio (I)—Slower than andante; faster than largo.
Adagio assai (I)—Very slow.

Adagissimo (I)—Extremely slow.
Addolorato (I)—Sadly.
À demi jeu (F)—Half volume.
Adeste fideles (L) — Christmas Hymn.
À deux (F)—For two.
À deux cordes (F), a due corde (I), auf zwei saiten (G)—On 2 strings.
À deux mains (F)—For two hands.
Adirato (I)—Angrily.
Adjunct notes—Unaccented auxiliary notes.
Ad lib. (Abb)—Ad libitum.
Ad libitum (L)—Passage played as performer wishes.
Adoucir (F)—To soften.
A due (I), a deux (F)—For two.
A due corde (I)—On 2 strings.
A dur (G)—A major.
Aengstlich (G)—Anxiously.
Aeolian harp—Stringed instrument sounded by air currents.
Aevia (Abb)—For Alleluia found in Gregorian Chant.
Affabile (I)—In a pleasing manner.
Affannato (I)—Distressed.
Affet. (Abb)—Affettuoso.
Affettivo (I)—Pathetic.
Affettuoso (I)—Tender expression.
Affinity—Close relationship of keys, etc.
Afflitto (I)—Sorrowfully.
Affrett. (Abb)—Affrettando.
Affrettando (I)—Hurrying.
After-note—Small, unaccented note named from the preceding note.
Agevole (I)—Lightly.
Aggiustatamente (I)—In strict time.
Aggradevole (I)—Agreeably.
Agilmente (I)—Lightness, rapidity.
Agitato (I)—Hurried.
Agnus Dei (L)—Last division in the Ordinary of the R. C. Mass.
Agogic—An accent effected by longer duration of the note.
À grand choeur (F)—For full chorus.
Agréments (F)—Grace notes.
Ahnlich (G)—Similar.
Aigrement (F)—Sharply.
Aigue (F), acuta (I), acute (E)—

MUSIC DICT

Shrill.

Air—Short, tuneful melody.

Air à boire (F)—Drinking song.

Air varié (F)—Theme with variations.

Ais (G)—A sharp (A#).

Aisément (F)—Easily.

Aisis (G)—A double sharp (A⤬·).

Akkord (G)—Chord.

À la, aux (F)—To the, in the manner of.

Alala—Gallican folk song of passion.

À la mesure (F)—In strict time.

Alberti bass—An accompaniment consisting of a bass in broken chords.

Alborada (S)—Morning song.

Albumblatt (G), **feuille d'album** (F)—Album leaf; short simple piece.

Alcuna licenza (I)—A little license.

Alcuno (I)—Some.

Al fine (I)—Repeat to the end.

Aliquot tones—Partial overtones.

A livre ouvert (F)—At sight.

All 'antico (I)—In ancient style.

Alla breve (I)—Tempo mark (¢) indicating quick duple time.

Alla caccia (I)—Like hunting music.

Alla camera (I)—In the style of chamber music.

Alla cappella, a cappella (I)—Sung without accompaniment.

Allarg. (Abb)—Allargando.

Allargando (I)—Growing louder and slower.

Alla zoppa (I)—Accent on the second beat.

Alle (G)—All.

Allegramente (I)—Quickly.

Allegrettino (I)—Slower than allegretto.

Allegretto (I)—Tempo between allegro and andante.

Allegrissimo (I) — Extremely quick.

Allegro (F)—Quick tempo.

Allegro assai (F)—Very fast.

Allein (G)—Alone.

Alleluia (Heb)—Hallelujah.

Allemande (F)—Lively German dance in four-in-a-measure time.

Allentando (I)—Slowing.

Alle saiten (G)—All strings.

Allmählich (G)—Gradually

Al loco (I)—Back to position after a shift.

Allonger (F)—To prolong.

Allontandosi (I)—Dying away.

Allora (I), **alors** (F)—Then.

All'ott. (Abb.)—All 'ottava.

All 'ottava (I)—To be played an octave higher than written.

All 'ottava bassa (I)—To be played an octave lower than written.

All 'unisono (I)—In unison; in octaves.

Alphorn, alpine horn—Primitive wind instrument used by Alp herdsmen.

Al rigore di tempo (I)—In vigorous and strict time.

Al riverso (I)—Theme which may be sung backward or forward.

Al segno (I)—Play "to the sign".

Al solito (I)—As usual.

Alt (G)—High.

Alterato (I), **alteré** (F)—Chords changed by half steps.

Alternativo (I)—Contrasting section between a theme and its repetition.

Altgeige (G)—Viola.

Altieramente (I)—With grandeur.

Altissimo (I)—Highest.

Altisono (I)—Sonorous.

Altistin (G)—Contralto singer.

Alto (I)—High; low female voice.

Alto clef—C clef on third line of the staff.

Alt 'ottava (I)—An octave higher.

Altra volta (I)—Encore.

Alzamento di mano (I)—upbeat.

Alzati (I)—Remove the mutes.

Amabile (I)—Lovable.

Amarevole (I)—Sadly.

Amaro (I)—Grief.

Ambitus (L)—Melodic range of Gregorian chant.

Ambrosian Chant—Diatonic, religious chant developed by St. Ambrose (374 A.D.)

Âme (F), **anima** (I)—Soundpost of the violin.

A mezza di voce (I)—At half voice.

A moll (G)—A minor.

Amorévole (I)—Tenderly.

Amorosamente (I)—Tender and affectionate style.

Amphibrach (G)—Musical foot comprised of short, long, short (‿—‿).

Anacrusis (Gr)—Upbeat.

Anapest (Gr)—A musical foot composed of short, short, long (‿‿—).

Anche (F)—Reed.

Ancora (I)—Once more.

Ancora piu forte (I)—Louder.

Andacht (G)—Devotion.

Andamento (I)—Unusually long fugue episode.

Andante (I)—Moderate in time, but flowing easily.

Andantino (I)—Faster than andante.

Anfang (G)—Beginning.

Angenehm (G)—Pleasing.

Anglaise (F)—English country folk dance.

Angosciosamente (I)—Anguished.

Anhaltend (G)—Continuous.

Anhang (G)—Coda.

Anhemitonic (Gr)—Scale with no semitones.

Anima (L)—Animation.

Animoso (I)—Spirited.

Anklang (G)—Harmony.

Anlage (G)—Outline of composition.

Anlaufen (G)—To increase sound.

Anleitung (G)—Introduction.

Anmutig (G)—Gracefully.

Ansatz (G)—Proper adjustment of the lips to a wind instrument.

Anschlag (G)—Percussion of a chord.

Anschwellend (G)—Increasing sound.

Ansioso (I)—Anxiously.

Anstimmen (G)—To give a keynote.

Anstimmung (G)—Intonation.

Answer—Response to the subject of a fugue in a second voice.

Antecedent—First theme of a fugue or first phrase of a musical period.

Anthem—Sacred Choral composition.

Anticipation (E), **anticipazione** (I)—Pre-sounding of a tone or tones in a coming chord.

Antiphon (Gr)—Response of one choir to another.

Antithesis—Answer in a fugue.

Antwort (G)—Answer.

Anwachsend (G)—Crescendo.

À peine (F)—Barely.

Aperto (I)—Press down the damper pedal.

A piacere (I)—According to the performer.

A poco (I)—Gradually.

Apollo—Mythological god of music.

Apostrophe—Pause mark in music.

Appassionata (I)—Impassioned.

Appena (I), **à peine** (F)—Barely.

Appenato (I)—Distressed.

Application (F), **applicatura** (I), **applikatur** (G)—Fingering.

Appoggiatura (I), **vorschlag** (G)—Grace note.

Apprestare (I)—To prepare to be played.

Âpre (F)—Harsh.

A punta d'arco (I)—With the point of the bow.

Arabesque (F), **arabeske** (G)—Highly ornamented composition.

Aragonesa (S), **aragonaise** (F)—Spanish dance.

Arbitrio (I)—According to the performer.

Arc. (Abb)—Arcato.

Arcato (I)—Bowed.

Archet (F), **arco** (I)—Violin bow.

Arco in giù (I)—Down-bow. (⅃ or ⌐).

Arco in su (I)—Up-bow (⅃).

Ardemment (F), **ardentemente** (I)—Ardently.

Ardito (I)—Boldly.

Aretinian syllables—Syllables of the scale (ut, re, mi, etc.).

Aria (I)—Elaborate solo in an opera or oratorio.

Aria buffa (I)—Comic air.

Aria cantabile (I)—Smooth, slow, lyrical solo.

Aria concertata (I)—Vocal solo with elaborate instrumental accompaniment.

Aria di bravura (I)—Ornamented vocal solo.

Aria d'entrata, di sortita (I)—Vocal solo in opera to mark singer's first entrance.

Aria fugata (I)—Vocal solo accompanied in fugue style.

Aria parlante (I)—Spoken or recitative *a tempo*.

Arietta (I)—Short, simple aria.

A rigore del tempo (I)—In strict time.

Arioso (I)—Style between an aria and a recitativo.

Armonica (I)—Earliest form of the accordian.

Armonizzare (I)—To harmonize.

Armure (F)—Key signature.

Arp. (Abb)—Arpeggio.

Arpa (I)—Harp.

Arpeggiando (I)—Music played arpeggio.

Arpeggiare (I)—To play the harp.

Arpeggio (I)—A chord the notes of which are played successively instead of together.

Arpicordo (I)—16th c. name for a harpsichord.

Arrache (F)—Forceful pizzicato.

Arrangement—Adaptation of a composition for instruments other than those for which it was originally written.

Ars antiqua (L)—School of F. composers of the 12th and 13th c.

Arsis (Gr)—Up-beat; light accent of the measure.

Ars nova (L)—Florentine music of 14th c. reaching its height in the madrigal.

Articolato (I), **articulé** (F), **artikuliert** (G), **articulation** (E)—Distinctly enunciated.

Artificial harmonics — Flute-like tones produced by pressing down the string of an instrument and touching the same string lightly with another finger at intervals of a third, a fourth or a fifth.

Art songs—Music composed to fit already written words.

As (G)—A flat (A♭).

Asas, ases (G)—A double flat (A♭♭).

As dur (G)—A flat major.

As moll (G)—A flat minor.

Aspiratamente (I)—Aspiringly.

Aspramente (I)—Harshly.

Asprezza (I)—Roughness.

Assai (I)—Very quick.

Assai piu (I)—Much more.

Assez (F)—Enough.

Assez vite (F)—Fairly fast.

Assieme (I)—Together.

Assoluto (I)—Absolute, free, one voice.

Assonant (E-F), **assonante** (I), **assonanza** (G)—Similarity of tone.

Assottigliando (I)—Softening.

Assourdir (F)—To muffle.

A suo arbitrio (I)—According to the performer.

A table sec (F)—Without accompaniment.

A tanto possibile (I)—As much as possible.

A tem. (Abb)—A tempo.

A tempo (I)—Return to normal tempo after deviations.

Atemlos, athemlos (Gr)—Breathlessly.

Atonality—Composition outside the classic frame of tonality and of the traditional concept of harmony founded on the major triad.

A tre (I), **à trois** (F)—For 3 parts or people.

Attacca (I)—Begin the next.

Attacca subito (I)—Begin the next movement immediately.

Attacco (I)—Short theme used as subject matter for fugue or imitation.

Attack (E), **attaca** (I), **attaque** (F)—Method or clearness of beginning a phrase.

Attendent keys—Tonalities having tones in common, used in modulation.

Atto (I)—Act of a drama.

Aubade (F)—Morning song.

Audace (I)—Bold, spirited.

Auf dem oberwerk (G)—On the highest row of the keys of the organ.

Auf führung (G)—Performance.

Aufgeregt (G)—Excitedly.

Aufgeweckt (G)—Lively, wide awake.

Aufhalten (G)—Retard.

Auflösung (G)—Resolution.

Aufsatz (G)—Tube of an organ reed pipe.

Aufschlag (G)—Up-beat.

Aufschnitt (G)—Mouth of an organ pipe.

Aufstrich (G)—Up-bow.

Auftakt (G)—Up-beat.

Auftritt (G)—Scene of an opera.

Augmentation—Restatement of a theme or thematic pattern in notes of longer time value.

Augmented intervals—Those which are larger by a half step than major or perfect intervals.

Au même temps (F)—In the original tempo.

A una corda (I)—The soft pedal of piano; one string.

Aurrescu (S)—Ancient ceremonial dance.

Ausdehnung (G)—Expansion.

Ausdruck (G)—Expression.

Ausdrucksvoll (G)—Expressively.

Ausgabe (G)—Edition.

Ausgehalten (G)—Restrain.

Ausgelassen (G)—Exuberant.

Aushatten (G)—To sustain a note.

Ausweichung (G)—Modulation.

Auszug (G)—Arrangement.

Authentic—Part of scale between the first note (tonic) and the fifth (dominant) above.

Authentic cadence—A cadence in which the harmony passes from the dominant to the tonic.

Authentic mode—A church mode or scale in which the final or key-note was the lowest tone.

Auxiliary notes—Notes not essential to the harmony.

Auxiliary scales—Those which belong to related keys.

Ave Maria (L)—Hymn to the Virgin Mary.

Ave Maris Stella (L)—R. C. hymn to Mary.

Ave Regina (L)—Vesper hymn to the Virgin Mary.

A vista (I)—At sight.

— B —

B—Seventh step in the typical diatonic scale of C.

Babillage (F)—Playful chatter.

Baborak—A Bohemian national dance.

Bacchanale—Drinking song.

Bachelor of Music—First musical degree taken at the universities.

Bach trumpet—Clarin trumpet.

Backfall—17th c. name for the appoggiatura.

Badinage (F)—Playful composition.

Bagatelle (F)—Short, light piece.

Bagpipe—Several reed pipes attached to a windbag from which the air is blown into the pipes.

Baguette (F)—Drumstick.

Baisser (F)—To lower

Baisser le ton (F)—To lower the pitch.

Balalaika—Russian instrument of the guitar family.

Balancement (F), **bebung** (G)—A wavering of tone (vibrato).

Baldamente (I)—Boldly.

Ballabile (I)—Dance-like.

Ballad (E), **ballade** (F-G), **ballata** (I)—A short, simple song of natural construction, usually in the narrative or descriptive form.

Ballade (F)—Poem-song usually of three stanzas, each of 7 or 8 lines, the last two of which are identical in all the stanzas, i.e., the refrain.

Ballet (F), **balletto** (I)—Dance spectacle set to music.

Ballo (I)—Ball or dance.

Band—An orchestral group composed principally of wind instruments.

Bandola (S)—An instrument resembling a lute.

Bandurria (S)—Species of Spanish guitar.

Banjo—An instrument composed of 5 to 6 strings, a drum-like body, and a long neck; a jazz instrument of the American Negro.

Bar—Vertical line on a staff, separating one measure from another; the measure itself.

Barcarola (I), **barcarolle** (F)—A boat song associated with Venetian gondoliers.

Bar, double—Heavy lines drawn across the staff separating different parts of the movement or

showing the end of a piece.

Bards—Celtic minstrals.

Bariolage (F)—Medley.

Bariton (F), **baritono** (I)—A male voice between bass and tenor.

Barocco (I), **baroque** (F)—Music from 1600-1750 in which harmony is confused and modulations are unnatural and excessive.

Barré (F)—In guitar playing the stopping of several or all strings with the forefinger.

Barrel Organ—Street organ with a barrel-like cylinder.

Bartered Bride—19th c. comic opera by Bedric Smetana.

Baryton (F)—Baritone.

Bas-dessus (F)—Mezzo soprano.

Base, bass—Deepest male voice; lowest part in a musical composition.

Bassa (I)—Ottava Bassa (8va bassa), lower octave of the written notes.

Bass Bar—Strip of wood inside a violin designed to strengthen the belly and equalize vibrations.

Bass chiffreé—(F) Figured bass; a bass part with numbers instead of notes indicating the harmonies to be played.

Bass clarinet—A clarinet an octave lower in pitch than an ordinary clarinet in B flat or A.

Bass clef—F clef placed upon the fourth line.

Bass double—Double bass viol; contra bass.

Bass drum—Largest and deepest sounding drum in the orchestra.

Basset horn (E), **corno di bassetto** (I)—Alto clarinet.

Bass, fundamental—Bass which contains the roots of the chords only.

Bass, given—Bass to which harmony is added above.

Bass, ground—Bass consisting of a few notes or measures containing a subject of its own repeated throughout the movement and each time accompanied by a new or varied melody.

Bassist (G), **bassista** (I)—Bass singer.

Basso (I)—Deepest male voice; lowest part in a musical composition.

Basso buffo (I)—Comic bass singer.

Basso cantante (I)—Bass voice of normal register.

Basso concertante (I)—Principal bass.

Basso continuo (I)—Figured bass.

Bassoon—Double reed woodwind; the bass of the oboes.

Basso ostinato (I)—Ground bass.

Basso profondo (I)—Heavy male voice of unusually low register.

Bassoposaune (G)—Bass trombone.

Bass-Saite (G)—Lowest string on any stringed instrument.

Basschulüssel (G)—F clef.

Bass trombone—Trombone with a compass from C below the bass staff to E above.

Bass tuba—Brass wind instrument, the lowest in pitch of the saxhorn family.

Bass viol—Largest and lowest pitched instrument in viol family.

Basta (I)—Enough.

Baton (F)—Conductor's stick.

Battaglia (I) — Programmatic

MUSIC DICT

pieces in which fanfares, drum rolls, cries and battle noises are imitated.

Battement (F), **battimento** (I)— 17th c. F. term for ornament.

Batterie (F), **battery** (E)—Roll of a drum; percussion instruments.

Battre à deux temps (F)—To beat two in a measure.

Battuta (I)—Beat, measure, bar.

Bauernleier (G)—Hurdy-gurdy.

Bauernlied (G)—Peasant song.

B. C. (Abb)—Basso continuo.

B dur (G)—B flat major.

Bearbeitet (G)—Arrangement.

Beat—Temporal unit of a composition indicated by the movements of a conductor's hand.

Bebung (G)—Wavering of tone.

Bec (F), **becco** (I)—Mouthpiece.

Becarre (F), **bequadro** (I)—Sign for natural (♮).

Becken (G)—Cymbals.

Bedächtig (G)—With moderation.

Bedeckte stimme (G)—Husky voice.

Bedeutend (G)—With importance.

Bedeutend schneller (G)—Faster.

Bedeutungsvoll (G)—Full of meaning.

Be (G)—B flat (B♭).

Begleiten, begleitung (G)—Accompaniment.

Behaglich (G)—Comfortably.

Behend (G)—Nimbly.

Beherzt (G)—With heart.

Beide (G)—Both.

Beide Hände (G)—Both hands.

Beinahe (G)—Almost.

Beispiel (G)—Example.

Beizeichen (G)—Accidentals, sharps, flats, naturals.

Bel canto (I)—18th c. I. vocal technique emphasizing beauty of sound and brilliancy of performance.

Belebt (G)—Lively.

Belegt (G)—Veiled.

Belieben (G)—At pleasure.

Bell—Percussion instrument of metal sounded by a clapper placed inside the bell.

Bell diapason—Organ stop with bell-mouthed pipes.

Bellezza (I)—Beauty of tone and expression.

Bell gamba—Organ stop with conical pipes, producing a delicate tone.

Bellicosamente, bellicoso (I)— Warlike.

Bellows—A pneumatic apparatus for supplying organ pipes with air.

Belly—Sound board of an instrument; that part over which the strings are distended.

Bémol (F), **Bémolle** (I)—Flat sign (♭).

Ben, bene (I), **bien** (F)—Well.

Benedicamus Domino (L)—Salutation of the Roman liturgy.

Benedictus (L)—Movement in the R. C. Mass.

Benedictus qui vent (L)—Section of the R. C. Mass following the Sanctus.

Bene placito (I)—At pleasure.

Ben marcato (I)—Well marked rhythm.

Ben sostenuto (I)—well sustained.

Bequem (G)—Convenient.

Berceuse (F)—Lullaby.

Bergamasca (I), **bergomask** (E)— Rustic dance.

Bergerette (F)—Pastoral song or dance.

Bes (G)—D double flat (B♭♭).

Beschleunigend (G)—Accelerating.

Bestimmt (G)—With decision.

Betonend, betont (G)—Accented.

Bertrübt (G)—Saddened.

Bewegt (G)—Rather fast.

Beziffert (G)—Figured.

Bianca (I), **blanche** (F)—Half note (♩).

Bicinum (G)—16th c. G. name for vocal compositions in two parts.

Binary Form—Musical form of two main sections; founded on two principal themes.

Binary measure—Two beats to a measure.

Bind, tie—Curved line above two notes indicating that they are to be played as one note with the combined duration of both (♪♪).

Bis (L)—Encore.

Biscroma (I), **double croche** (F)— Sixteenth note (♪).

Bisdiapason (L)—Interval or range of two octaves.

Bitonality—Use of two tonalities at the same time.

Biwa—Japanese lute.

Bizzarramenti, bizzaro (I) — Whimsical.

Blanche (F)—Cf. Bianca.

Blasinstrument (G)—Wind instrument.

Blasmusik (G)—Music for wind instruments.

Blatt (G)—Reed.

Blattspiel (G)—Sightreading.

Blechinstrumente (G)—Brass instruments.

Blockflöte (G)—End blown flute; organ stop with pyramid shaped pipes, producing a full, broad tone.

Blues, Blue notes—American Negro song using a flatted third or seventh note.

Bluette (F)—Short brilliant piece.

Blumen (G)—Name for coloraturas of the Meistersinger.

B moll (G)—B Flat minor.

B. Mus. (Abb)—Bachelor of Music.

Bob—Term in bell ringing applied to the changes that can be rung on six bells.

Bocel (F)—Mouthpiece of a brass instrument.

Bocca (I)—Mouth or Mouthpiece.

Bocca chiusa (I), **bouche fermée** (F), **mit brummstimme** (G)— Humming.

Bocca ridente (I)—Singing with lips in a smiling position.

Body—Resonance of tone; main structure of a musical instrument.

Boehm flute—Flute with perfect system of sound holes, closed by pads (1834).

Boehm system—System of keying a woodwind instrument which allows the holes to be cut in the proper acoustical position and size.

Bogen (G)—Bow of a stringed instrument; tie.

Bogenstrich (G)—Stroke of the bow.

Boèhme, La—Grand opera by Giacomo Puccini composed in 1896.

Bois (F)—Woodwind

Bolero (S)—Lively Spanish dance in 3/4 time performed solo or by couples.

Bombard (E)—Early oboe.

Bombarde (F), **bombardo** (I)— Powerful reed stop in an organ of 16 ft. scale.

Bombardon (E-G)—Brass saxhorn, trumpet; organ stop.

Bones—Strips of bones or hard wood clicked like castanets in Negro minstrel music.

Bon temps de la mesure (F)—Accented portion of a measure.

Boot—Foot of a reed pipe.

Bordone (I), **bourdon** (F)—Organ stop.

Boris Godunov—Opera by Modest Moussorgsky.

Borre, borry, borea (I)—Cf. Bourée.

Boston, valse Boston—American ballroom dance popular in 1915.

Bouche (F)—Muted; stopped.

Bouche fermée (F)—Humming.

Bouffe (F)—Comic.

Bourdon (F)—Low tone of long duration

Bourrée (F)—17th c. F. dance in quick duple meter with a single upbeat.

Boutade (F)—Impromptu ballet or composition.

Bow—An instrument of wood and horsehair used to vibrate the string of the violin.

Bow hand—Right hand; hand which holds the bow.

Bowing—Technique of using the bow on stringed instruments; marks indicating how a piece should be played (⊓ downstroke; V upstroke).

Br. (Abbr)—Bratsche.

Braccio (I)—Arm; instruments held at arm level.

Brace—Perpendicular line combined with a bracket joining the different staves in piano music or scores.

Bradenberg Concertos—Six concertos written by Bach in 1721 dedicated to Christian Ludwig.

Branle (F)—Lively dance in 4/4 time, the motions of the leading couple being imitated.

Brass band—Band consisting chiefly of brasses, woodwinds, and percussion instruments.

Brasses—Horns, trumpets, trombones and tubas of an orchestra.

Bratsche (F)—Vioila.

Brautlied (G)—Bridal song.

Bravo, Bravissimo (I)—Exclamation of approval.

Bravoure (F), **bravura** (I)—Spirit and skill.

Brawl—Cf. Branle.

Break—Point of change in the quality of tenor, soprano and alto voices; a pause in jazz music.

Breit (G)—Broad.

Breve (I)—Formerly the shortest, now the longest note, equal to two whole notes, eight quarter beats.

Bridge—Part of a stringed instrument which supports the strings.

Bridge passage—Subordinate passage of a composition serving as a connection between two themes.

Brill (Abb)—Brillante.

Brillante (I)—Brilliant.

Brindisi (I)—Drinking song.

Brio (I)—Vigor and brilliance.

Brioso (I)—Lively.

Brise (G)—Split; broken into arpéggio.

Broadcast—Distribution of sound by radio.

Broadsides—Single sheets on which words of ballads were printed for distribution (16th-18th c.).

Broderies (F)—Ornaments.

Broken chords—Chords whose notes are played successively instead of together.

Broken octaves—Octaves whose notes are played separately.

Bruit (F)—Noise.

Brumeux (F)—Veiled.

Brummeisen (G)—Jew's harp.

Brummstimmen (G)—Humming voices.

Brunette (F)—Popular F. song on idyllic, pastoral or amorous subjects (17th & 18th c.).

Bruscamente (I)—Brusquely.

Bruststimme (G)—Chest voice.

Buffet (F)—Organ case.

Buffo, buffa (I)—Comic, grotesque.

Bugle—Small trumpet with cupped mouthpiece usually for military signals.

Bühne (G)—Stage.

Buona nota (I)—Accented note.

Burden—Refrain.

Burla, burlesca, burletta (I)—Composition in a jesting mood.

Burletta (I)—Musical farce.

Burrasca (I)—Composition that describes a storm.

— C —

C—First step in the typical diatonic scale of C.

C. A. (Abb)—Coll'arco.

Cabaletta (I)—Simple melody with accompaniment in triplets, like hoofbeats; operatic air like the rondo in form.

Cabinet organ—Portable reed organ.

Caccia (I), **chasse** (F), **jagd** (G)—Music connected with hunting and fishing scenes.

Cachucha (S)—Popular S. dance in triple time similar to the bolero.

Cacophony (Gr)—Discordant noise.

Cad. (Abb)—Cadenza.

Cadence (F)—Shake or trill; close harmony.

Cadence—Two or more chords which bring a line or melody to a point of rest.

Cadence, amen, church, plagal—Cadence in which harmony passes from the subdominant (4th) to the tonic (1st).

Cadence, authentic, perfect, complete—Cadence in which harmony passes from the dominant (5th) to the tonic (1st).

Cadence, avoided, broken, false, interrupted—Cadence in which the final tone or chord is not the tonic.

Cadence, church—Cf. Cadence, amen.

Cadence, complete—Full cadence; cadence in which the final sound of a verse in a chant is on the keynote.

Cadence, deceptive—Cf. Cadence, avoided.

Cadence, half or imperfect—Cadence in which the dominant harmony is preceded by the common chord of the tonic, a half cadence.

Cadence, mixed—Cadence which contains in the last three or four chords, dominant, subdominant and tonic hormonies.

Cadence, plagal — Cf. Cadence, amen.

Cadenza (I), **kadenz** (G),—Ornamental passage near the close of a song or solo.

Cadenzato (I)—With determination.

Caesura, cesura—Rhythmic pause within a musical period; point

where two phrases in a period are divided.

Caisse (F)—Drum.

Caisse claire (F)—Snare drum.

Caisse grosse (F)—Bass drum.

Caisse roulante (F)—Side drum.

Cal. (Abb)—Calando.

Calando (I)—Diminuendo, growing softer.

Calata (I)—Lute dance of the early 16th c.

Calcando (I)—Accelerando, gradually quickening.

Calliope—Greek muse of heroic verse; organ possessing a strong, harsh tone, produced by forcing steam through the pipes.

Calm. (Abb)—Calmato, Calmandosi.

Calmato (I)—Calm.

Calore (I)—Warmly.

Cambiare (I)—To change.

Camera (I)—Music composed for private performance or small concerts.

Camminando (I)—Andante, gentle progression.

Campagnuolo (I)—Pastoral.

Campana, campanella (I)—Bell, little bell.

Campanology—Art of making and playing bells.

Campestre (I), **champêtre** (F)—Pastoral.

Canaries—F. dance of 17th c. designed in imitation of the natives of the Canary Islands.

Cancan—Popular F. dance of 19th c. developed from the quadrille, becoming famous for its vulgarity.

Cancel—Natural sign (♮) employed to remove the effect of a previous accidental.

Canción (S)—Song.

Cancionero (S)—Collection of folk songs.

Cancrizans (L), **cancrizzante** (I)—Retrograde movement.

Canon—Strict form of contrapuntal writing in which the subject or antecedent announced by one voice, is exactly imitated by the answer or consequent in the same or harmonizing key.

Canon, infinite, perpetual—Canon which has no definite ending.

Canonic imitation—Strict imitation of one voice by another.

Cantab. (Abb)—Cantabile

Cantabile (I)—Singable

Cantando (I)—Singing.

Cantare (I)—To sing.

Cantante (I)—Singer.

Cantata (I), **cantate** (F-G)—Poem set to music; vocal composition of several movements, comprising airs, recitatives and choruses.

Cantatore, cantatrice (I)—Singer.

Canticae (I), **cantici, canticum** (L)—Ancient sacred songs of the R. C. Church.

Canticle—Non-metrical hymns of praise in the bible.

Cantiga—Spanish monophonic songs of the 13th c., mostly honoring the Virgin Mary.

Cantilena (I)—Vocal melody or song-like instrumental piece; smooth, connected style of performance.

Cantillation—Chanting in plainsong style, especially of Jewish character.

Cantino (I), **chanterelle** (F)—Highest string of an instrument; Violin E string.

Cantio sacra—L. for motet.

Canto (I)—Song; soprano; highest part.

Canto fermo (I), **cantus firmus** (L) — Unaccompanied choral singing in unison; in contrapuntal writing, a given melody around which melodic and harmonic figures are woven.

Canto primo (I)—First soprano.

Cantor (I)—Singer, chanter.

Cantoris (L)—Passages sung by those singers on the cantor's (north) side of the church.

Canto secondo (I)—Second soprano.

Cantus (L)—Song; treble or soprano part.

Cantus firmus (L)—Cf. Canto fermo.

Cantus Gregorianus (L)—Gregorian chant; plainsong—unmeasured, unison, unaccompanied chant based on the eight modes introduced into R. C. ritual by Pope Gregory.

Cantus mensurabilis (L)—Music divided into measures.

Cantus planus (L)—Plainsong.

Cantus prius factus (L)—Cf. Cantus firmus, canto fermo.

Canzo, canso (F)—Troubadour music and poetry.

Canzona, canzone (I)—Song, ballad; song-like instrumental piece; an air in two or three parts with passages of fugue and imitation, somewhat similar to the madrigal.

Canzone sacra (I)—Sacred song.

Canzonet, canzonetta (I)—Little song.

Caoine (Keen)—Irish dirge of ancient tradition.

Capelle, Kapelle (G), **capella** (I), **chapelle** (F)—Chapel; band, orchestra.

Capellmeister (G)—Choirmaster, orchestra conductor.

Capo (I)—Begining.

Capolavoro (I)—Masterpiece.

Capotasto (I)—Mechanical device for guitars, lutes, etc. to shorten the vibrating length of all the strings simultaneously.

Cappella (I)—Band of musicians who perform in a church or privately; orchestra.

Cappriccietto (I)—Short capriccio.

Capriccio (I), **caprice** (F)—Composition in a free fanciful style.

Capricciososamente (I), **capricieusement** (F)—Fancifully.

Carcelera (S)—Composition describing prison scenes.

Caressant (F), **carezzandro, carezzevole** (I)—Tenderly.

Caricato, caricatura (I)—Exaggerated representation.

Carillon (F)—Chime.

Carita (I)—Tenderness.

Carmagnole—Dance song of the F. revolution.

Carmen—Opera in four acts by Georges Bizet (1875).

Carnaval—Piano composition by Robert Schumann consisting of twenty short pieces describing scenes of a masquerade.

Carnival of Venice—19th c. I. popular melody used by many composers as a theme for variations.

Carol—Song of devotion.

Carole—Medieval F. name for round dances in a closed circle.

Carrée (F)—Double whole note (breve).

Cassa (I), **caisse** (F)—Large drum.

Cassa grande (I)—Bass drum.

Cassa rullante (I)—Tenor drum.

Cassation (E-F), **cassazione** (I)—18th c. instrumental piece for outdoor performance.

Casse-Noisette (F)—Original title of Tschaikovski's ballet *The Nutcracker.*

Castanets (E), **castagnette** (I-F)—Clappers used in S. music to accompany dancing.

Castrato, evirato (I)—Eunuch singer whose adult voice retains the range of a boy's.

Catch—Humorous composition for three or four voices.

Catgut—Strings for violins, etc. made of sheep's or horses' intestines.

Catholica—Name given by Glareanus to contrapuntal pieces designed so that they may be sung in various church modes.

Cavalleria Rusticana—Opera in one act by Pietro Mascagni (1890).

Cavelletto (I)—Break between registers of the voice; simple melody with hoof-beat accompaniment.

Cavata—Inscription in which an important thought is concisely expressed.

Cavatina (I), **cavatine** (F)—Short aria in one section.

C. B. (Abb)—Contra bass.

C clef—Gives the name and pitch of middle C to the notes on the same line with it.

C. d. (Abb)—Colla destra.

C dur (G)—C major.

Cebell—Old E. name for the gavotte.

Cedendo (I), **cédant** (F)—Gradually giving way.

Cédez (F)—Direction to retard speed.

Celere (I)—Quick

Celesta (I)—Small keyboard instrument that produces a pure, bell-like sound.

Celeste (F)—Organ stop.

Cello (Abb)—Violoncello.

Cemb. (Abb)—Cembalo.

Cembalo (I)—Harpsichord.

Cento (L), **centone** (I)—Musical works formed by selections from other works.

Ces (G)—C flat (C♭).

Ceses (G) C double flat (C♭♭).

Ces dur (G)—C flat major.

Cetera, cetra (I)—Zither; cittern.

C. f. (Abb)—Cantus firmus.

Ch. (Abb)—Choir organ.

Chaconne (F), **ciacona** (I)—Graceful, slow S. movement in 3/4 time composed on a ground bass.

Chaleureux (F)—With warmth.

Chalumeau (F)—Lowest register of the clarinet family.

Chamade (F)—Beat of a drum declaring surrender or parley.

Chamber music—Instrumental ensemble music performed one player to the part, as opposed to orchestral music which has several players to the part.

Chamber opera—An opera of small dimensions, of an intimate character and for small orchestra.

Chamber orchestra—Small orchestra of about 25 players.

Champêtre (F)—Rustic.

Changes—Various alterations and different passages produced by a peal of bells.

Changing note (E), **nota cambiata** (I), **wechselnote** (G)—Passing notes or discords which occur on the accented parts of a measure.

Chanson (F)—Song.

Chanson d'amour (F)—Love song.

Chanson bachique (F)—Drinking song.

Chanson de geste (F)—F. epic poems of the Middle Ages which were probably sung.

Chanson de la rue—(F)—Street song.

Chanson de toile (F)—Similar to chanson de geste but with the chief character a woman.

Chanson de travail (F)—Work song.

Chanson sans paroles (F)—Songs without words.

Chant—General denomination for liturgical music of plainsong and is monophonic, unaccompanied and in free rhythm.

Chantant (F)—Adapted to singing.

Chant, double—Chant extending through two verses of a psalm.

Chanter—Melody pipe in a bagpipe.

Chanterelle (F)—Treble string; highest string of a stringed instrument.

Chanting—The ecclesiastical singing of the psalms and canticles.

Chant, plain—Single chant seldom higher than an octave or longer than once verse of a psalm.

Chant, single—Simple harmonized melody extending only through one verse of a psalm.

Chanteur (Masc.), **chanteuse** (Fem.) (F)—Singer.

Chanty, shanty (E)—Rhythmical work song, usually of the sea or mountains.

Chapelle (F)—Cf. Cappella.

Characteristic piece—Short piece expressing mood or sentiment and emphasizing character rather than form.

Charivari (F)—Deliberately distorted and noisy performance.

Chasse (F)—In the hunting style.

Che (I)—Than, that, which.

Check—A part of the action of the pianoforte.

Chef d'oeuvre (F)—Masterpiece.

Chef d'orchestre (F)—Orchestra conductor.

Cheng—Chinese string instrument.

Chest of viols—Set of six viols (2 basses, 2 tenors, 2 trebles) fitted in a case.

Chest tone, chest voice—Lowest register of the voice.

Chest wind—A reservoir in an organ for holding the air supplied by the bellows.

Chevalet (F), **ponticello** (I), **steg** (G)—Bridge of a stringed instrument.

Cheville (F)—Peg of a stringed strument.

Chevrotement (F)—Unsteadiness in singing.

Chiamare (I)—To chime.

Chiaramente, chiaro (I)—Clearly.

Chiaroscuro (I)—Loud and soft in music.

Chiave (I)—Clef.

Chiesa (I)—In Baroque music, pieces designed for Church use.

Chime—Set of bells tuned to the scale.

Ch'in—Traditional instrument of the Chinese and Japanese, also called the koto or Chinese lute.

Chitarra (I)—Guitar.

Chiudendo, chiuso (I)—Closed.

Choir (E)—Body of Church sing-ers; instrumental group of the orchestra, e.g. brass choir.

Choir, grand—In organ playing, the union of all the reed stops.

Choir organ—Lowest row of keys containing the softer and more delicate stops.

Choral—Pertaining to a choir or chorus.

Choral, chorale (G)—Hymn tunes of the early G. protestant church.

Choral cantata—Canta which employs a chorus as opposed to a soloist.

Chord—Simultaneous occurrence of several tones.

Chordal style—Style in which chords play a predominant part.

Chord, accidental—Chord produced either by anticipation or suspension.

Chord, altered, chromatic—Chord containing tones other than those of the diatonic scale to which it belongs.

Chord, common—Chord consisting of a fundamental note together with its third and fifth.

Chord, dominant—Chord built on the fifth of a key.

Chord, inverted—Chord, the notes of which are so dispersed that the root does not appear at the lowest note.

Chord of the dominant seventh—Chord built upon the fifth as its root, adding the third, fifth and seventh above.

Choreography—Generally applied to the pattern or design of a dance composition.

Chorister—Choir singer or leader.

Chorlied (G)—Choral song.

Chorogel (G)—Choir organ.

Chorus—Group of singers; music composed for a singing group; a refrain.

Christe Eleison (Gr)—Part of the Kyrie of the R. C. Mass.

Chromatic (E), **chromatique** (F), **chromatisch** (G)—Proceeding by half-steps; any music or chord containing notes not belonging to the diatonic scale.

Chromatic alteration—Process of modifying an interval, passage or chord by a chromatic sign.

Chromatic instrument—One that plays semitones.

Chromatic keys—Black keys of a pianoforte; every key in the scale of which one or more chromatic tones occur.

Chromatic modulation—Transition from one tonality to another by altering a note in a chord a half-step.

Chromatic scale—A scale composed entirely of half-steps.

Chromatic signs — Sharp (#), flat (♭), natural (♮).

Chronos (Gr)—Temporal or rhythmic unit of ancient Gr. music (smallest unit).

Church cadence—Cf. Plagal cadence.

Church modes—Tonal basis for the Gregorian chant; fourteen scales used in Medieval Church music.

Ciacona (I)—Cf. Chaconne.

Ciaramella (I)—Bagpipe.

Cimbalom (Hung.)—Dulcimer.

Cinelli (I)—Cymbals.

Cinfonie—Hurdy Gurdy.

Cinque-pas (F)—Elizabethan term for the galliard.

Ciphering—Irregular sounding of the organ pipes when not touched due to a mechanical defect.

Circle of fifths—Method of modulation from dominant to dominant, passing through all the keys back to the starting point.

Gis (G)—C sharp (C#).

Cis cis (G)—C double sharp (C✗).

C dur (G)—C sharp major.

Cis moll (G)—C sharp minor.

Cither, cithern, cittern, cithara—Ancient wire stringed instrument similar to the lute.

Civetteria (I)—Coquettish.

Cl., clar. (Abb)—Clarinet.

Clairon (F)—Bugle; organ stop.

Claque (F)—Group paid to applaud.

Claquebois (F)—Xylophone.

Clarabella (L)—Organ stop with a soft tone.

Clarinet (E), **clarinette,** (F), **clarinetto** (I)—Single reed woodwind with a cylindrical tube, played vertically, with a range of several octaves.

Clarinet, alto—Clarinet pitched in E flat or F.

Clarinet, bass—Clarinet whose tones are an octave deeper than those of the C or B flat clarinet.

Clarinet, large soprano—Clarinet in C, B flat or A; the normal treble instrument.

Clarinet, small soprano—Clarinet pitched in D, E, F, or A flat.

Clarino—High register of trumpet.

Clarion—Ancient E. trumpet in round form.

Clarone (I)—Bass clarinet.

Clarsech—Irish harp.

Classical music—Music of certain composers from 16th-18th c. noted for perfection of form, purity of style and content.

Clausula (L)—Cadential formulae of 16th c. polyphonic music.

Clave (L)—Clef.

Clavecin (F), **clavicembalo** (I)—Harpsichord.

Clavichord—Early keyed instrument played by striking a metal tangent which determined pitch.

Clavicymbal—Harpsichord.

Clavicytherium—Harpsichord with a vertical body.

Clavier (G-F)—Any stringed, keyboard instrument.

Clavierauszug (G)—Full score arrangement for piano players.

Clavier de récit (F)—Keyboard of the swell organ.

Clavierübung (G)—Piano exercise.

Cle, clef (F)—A key; character used to denote the name and pitch of the notes on the staff to which it is prefixed.

Cloche (F)—Bell.

Clock Symphony—Haydn's symphony no. 101 in D major (1794).

Clog box—Jazz percussion instrument consisting of a 7″ block of wood with slots to be struck with a drum stick.

Close—Cadence.

Close harmony—Harmony in which the notes or parts are kept as close together as possible.

C moll (G)—C minor.

Coda—Section added to the form proper of a composition as a conclusion.

Codetta (I)—Short coda.

Cogli, col, colla, coll', colle (I)—With the.

Cogli stromenti (I)—With the instruments.

Coll'arco (I)—With the bow.

Colla destra (I)—With the right hand.

Colla parte (I)—With the soloist.

Colla punta del arco (I)—With the point of the bow.

Colla voce (I)—With the voice, the accompaniment taking the time from the singer.

Collect—R. C. prayer of the day originally "collected" from the prayers of the people.

Col'legno (I)—With the bow stick.

Coll'ott, c 8va (Abb)—Coll'ottava.

Coll'ottava (I)—Directive to sound an octave higher or lower with the tones indicated.

Colophane (F)—Resin.

Color—Tone quality (timbre) determined by the combination of overtones.

Coloratura (I)—Florid vocal music.

Coloratura soprano — Extremely flexible high voice able to perform florid music.

Colpo d'arco (I)—Stroke of the bow.

Combination pedal—Cf. Composition pedals.

Combination tone—Tone of different pitch heard when two loud tones are sounded simultaneously.

Come (I)—Same as, like.

Come da lontano (I)—As if from a distance.

Come prima (I)—As at first.

Come retro (I)—As farther back.

Comes (L)—Answer to fugue subject.

Come sopra (I)—As before, as above.

Come sta (I)—Perform exactly as written.

Comma—Breathing mark; scientific term for the slight differences which exist between the pitches of the same tone in different systems of tuning or calculation.

Commodo (I)—Convenient.

Common Chord—Triad.

Common hallelujah metre—Six line stanza of iambic measure, the syllables arranged in number and order as: 8, 6, 8, 6, 8, 8.

Common measure—One which has an even number of parts in a measure.

Common metre—Four line stanza in iambic measure, the syllables arranged in number and order as: 8, 6, 8, 6.

Common time—4/4 meter.

Comodante (I)—With composure.

Compass—Range of notes obtainable from an instrument or a voice.

Compiacevole, compiacevolmenti (I)—Pleasing.

Complement—Difference between the octave and any interval.

Complementary Part—That part which is added to the subject and countersubject of a fugue.

Compline (L)—Latest evening service of the Catholic Church.

Composition—Any musical production; the art of writing music.

Composition pedal—Pedals connected with a system of mechanism for arranging the stops of an organ.

Compound binary form—Name for sonata form.

Compound harmony—Simple harmony with an octave added.

Compound intervals — Intervals greater than an octave.

Compound measure—One that has more than one principal accent.

Compound stop—Organ stop which controls more than one rank of pipes.

Compound times—Those which include or exceed six parts in a measure and contain two or more principal accents.

Con (I)—With.

Concentus—(L)—That part of the Gregorian service sung by the choir.

Concert—Public musical performance.

Concertante (F), **concertato** (I)—Composition for several solo instruments with orchestral accompaniment in the style of a concerto.

Concerted music—Music in which several voices or instruments are heard at the same time.

Concert grand—Largest size pianoforte for concert performance.

Concertina—Small instrument similar to the accordian with sound boxes hexagonal instead of oblong.

Concertino (I)—Small concerto; solo group rather than the orchestra in early music.

Concertmaster (E), **konzertmeister** (G)—Chief violinist of the orchestra.

Concerto (I)—Sonata for solo instrument or instruments with orchestra, usually in three movements.

Concerto da camera (I)—19th c. vocal concerto which developed into chamber music for small groups of instruments.

Concerto doppio (I)—Concerto for two instruments with orchestral accompaniment.

Concerto grosso—Concerto for several soloists with full orchestra.

Concert pitch—Pitch which fixes A at 440 vibrations per second at a temperature of 68°F.

Concertstück (G)—Short, one-movement concerto.

Concitato (I)—Disturbed.

Concord—Harmonious combination of sounds.

Conductor—Leader of an orchestra, chorus or band.

Conductus (L)—Monophonic or polyphonic L. songs of the 12th and 13th c.

Conga—Modern dance which originated in Cuba characterized by brief melodic phrases and normal rhythmic accents in alternating syncopation.

Conjoint tetrachords—Two tetrachords or fourths of which the highest note of one is the lowest of the other.

Conjunct degrees—Adjoining steps in the scale.

Conjunct succession—A succession of tones which proceed regularly up or down several degrees.

Connecting note—Note held in common by two successive chords.

Consecutive fifths—Two or more perfect fifths immediately following one another in similar motion.

Consecutive intervals—Intervals of the same kind which follow immediately upon one another.

Consecutive octaves—Two parts moving in octaves with each other.

Consequent (L)—Answer to the antecedent or subject in a fugue or canon.

Conservatoire (F) — Conservatory music school.

Consolante (I)—Consoling.

Console—The case which encloses the keyboard stops, etc. of an organ.

Consonance (E), **consonanza** (I)—Agreeable sounds.

Consonance, imperfect—Major and minor thirds and sixths.

Consonance, perfect—Unison, octave, fourths and fifths.

Consonare (I)—To tune in unison with another.

Con sordini (I)—with mutes in violin playing; with dampers in piano with the damper pedal not to be used.

Consort—Old English for concert.

Cont. (Abb)—Contano

Contano (I)—One part to rest while the others play.

Conte (F), **märchen** (G)—Fairytale.

Continuato (I)—Sustained.

Continued harmony — Harmony that does not change though the bass varies.

Continued rest—Long rest for a certain part while others proceed.

Continuo (I)—Without cessation.

Contra (I)—An octave lower.

Contrabass (E-G) **contrabasso** (I), **contrebasse** (F)—Lowest pitched of the viol family.

Contrabassoon (E), **contrebasson** (F), **contrafagotto** (I)—Double bassoon.

Contraction — Part of a composition in which two parts of a fugue compress the subject, counter-subject or an intervening subject.

Contradanza (I), **contredanse** (F), **country dance** (E)—E. dance in which pairs dance opposite one another.

Contrafactum (L)—Vocal composition in which the original text is replaced by a new one, particularly a secular one by a sacred one.

Contra-fagatto (I) — Contrabassoon.

Contralto (I)—Deepest of the female voice parts.

Contra-posaune (G)—16 or 32 ft. organ reed-stop.

Contrappunto (I)—Counterpoint.

Contrappunto doppio (I)—Double counterpoint.

Contrapuntal—Relating to counterpoint.

Contrapunto a la mente (I)—Improvised counterpoint.

Contrary motion—Motion in which one part rises and the other falls.

Contrasoggito (I), **contre-sujet** (F.), **countersubject** — Special contrapuntal theme which is heard against the subject or its answer in a fugue.

Contrattempo (I), **contretemps** (F)—Syncopated.

Contrepoint (F), **contrapunctus** (L)—Cf. Counterpoint.

Coperto (I)—Covered, muffled.

Copla (S)—Couplet or stanza of refrain song.

Coptic Church music—Liturgical music of the Christians living in Egypt.

Copula (I), **copule** (F)— Organ coupler; connecting phrases in a fugue.

Copyright — Legal protection against reproduction of the work of a composer.

Cor. (Abb)—Cornet, corno.

Cor (F), **corno** (I)—French horn.

Corale (I)—Plain chant.

Cor Anglais (F), **corno inglese** (I)—Alto oboe turned a fifth lower than the treble oboe.

Coranto, corrente (I), **courante** (F)—Dance in 1/4 or 3/2 time.

Cor à pistons—F. horn.

Corda (I)—String.

Cordatura (I)—Series of notes to which the strings of an instrument are tuned.

Corda vuota (I) **corde à vide** (F) a string not pressed down by the finger.

Corista—Orchestral pitch; tuning fork.

Cornamusa (I), **cornemuse** (F)—Bagpipe.

Cornet (E), **cornett** (G), **cornet à pistons** (F)—Small brass wind instrument with three valves, similar to the trumpet but of slightly different model.

Cornet stop—Organ stop from three to five pipes to each note.

Corno (I), **cor** (F)—Horn.

Corno di bassetto (I)—Basset horn; organ sto p of 8 ft. scale.

Corno inglese (I)—English horn.

Cornopean—Early coronet.

Coro (I)—Choir; choir music.

Corona (I), **couronne** (F)—Pause; hold.

Cornach—Celtic dirge.

Corps—Body of musical instruments; troupe of musicians.

Corps de ballet (F)—Ballet performers.

Corrente (I), **courante** (F)—Dance in 1/4 or 3/2 time.

Corrido—Mexican folk ballad.

Cortège (F)—Procession.

Corto (I)—Short.

Coryphée (F)—Lead ballet dancer.

Cosaque (F)—Cossack dance.

Cotillion (E), **cotillon** (F)—Lively, quadrille-like dance of the 19th c.

Couac (F)—Sound of a clarinet when the reed is out of order.

Coulé (F)—Two notes slurred.

Coulisse (F)—Trombone or trumpet slide.

Count—Beat, method of measuring beats.

Counter exposition—Second exposition of a fugue.

Counter fugue—Fugue in which the answer is the inverted form of the subject.

Counterpoint—A combination of two or more independent and significant melodies with a musical texture.

Counterpoint, double—A counterpart with an inversion of two parts.

Counterpoint, invertible—Counterpoint in which upper and lower voices may change places without harming the effect.

Counterpoint, single—Counterpoint in which the parts are not invertible.

Counterpoint, triple—Three part invertible counterpoint.

Countersubject—Second division in a fugue coming against the answer in the second voice.

Counter theme—Cf. countersubject.

Country Dance—E. dance in which pairs dance opposite one another.

Coup d'archet—Stroke of the bow.

Coupler—Organ coupler; connecting phrases in a fugue.

Courante (F), **corrente** (I)—Old danec in triple time.

Couronne (F)—Pause; hold.

C. P. (Abb)—Colla Parte.

Cracovienne (F)—Polish dance in 2/4 time.

Credo (L)—Principal movement of the R. C. mass.

Cremona—Organ stop; superior make violin.

Cresc. (Abb)—Crescendo.

Crescendo (I)—Increasing in volume ($<$).

Crescendo-zug (G)—Swell box in the organ.

Crescent — Turkish instrument made of small bells hung on an inverted crescent.

Croissant les mains (F)—Crossing the hands.

Croma (I)—Eighth note (♪).

Crook—Small movable curved tube inserted in a brass instrument which regulates the pitch.

Cross-flute—Horizontal flute.

Crotales (F)—Castanets.

Crotalum (L)—Rattle used in ancient Greece and Rome.

Crotchet—Quarter note (♩).

Crotchet rest—Quarter rest.

Crucifixus (L)—Section of Credo in the R. C. Mass.

Cruth, crwth, crowth, croud—Ancient Celtic bowed, string instrument.

C. S. (Abb)—Colla sinistra.

Csardas—Hungarian dance with alternating fast and slow parts.

Cto. (Abb)—Concerto.

Cue—Short passage taken from another leading instrument and printed in small characters to indicate to a player his entrance.

Cueca—Most popular dance of Chile.

Cuivre—Forced, harsh notes in the playing of a brass instrument.

Cuivres—Brasses.

Cum Sancto Spiritu (L)—Part of the Gloria in the R. C. Mass.

Cupo (I)—Obscure, dark.

Curtain tune—Act tune.

Cycle of fifths—Sequence of 12 perfect fifths, starting from C and returning to C.

Cycle of songs—A set of songs on texts with related subjects.

Cyclic, cyclical form—Any musical form composed of several movements, e.g., sonata; compositions in which the same thematic material is used in all or some of the movements.

Cymbals—Circular brass plate percussion instruments struck together to produce various effects.

— D —

D—Second step in the typical diatonic scale of C.

Da (I)—By, from, for.

Da ballo (I)—In dance style.

Da camera (I)—For a room.

Da capo (I)—From the beginning.

Da capo al fine, da capo sin'al fine (I)—Return to the beginning and end with the word Fine.

Da capo, e poi la coda (I)—Return to the beginning and play to the coda.

Da capo senza replica (I)—Play from the beginning without repeats.

Da capo sin'al segno (I)—Return to the beginning and play to the sign ⊕, and then play to the coda.

D'accord (F), **d'accordo** (I)—In tune, in harmony.

Dach (G)—Sounding board.

Da chiesa (I)—In church style.

Dal, dall', dalla, dalle, dallo, dagla (I)—By the, from the, for the, of the, etc.

Da lontano (I)—From a distance.

Dal S. (Abb)—Dal segno.

Dal segno (I)—Return to the sign ⊕ and repeat to the word Fine or a double bar with a pause sign.

Damp—To muffle tone.

Damper pedal—Pedal in a piano which raises all the dampers from the strings at once.

Dampers—Felted blocks which prevent undue vibration by resting on the piano strings after a note is struck.

Dämpfen (G)—To muffle.

Danse (F), **danza** (I), **tanz** (G)—Dance tune.

Danseuse (F)—Female dancer.

Danse de matelot (F)—Hornpipe.

Danse macabre (F)—Dance of death.

Da prima (I)—From the beginning.

Dar la voce (I)—To give the key note.

Darstellung (G)—Performance.

Dash—Staccato mark over or under a note.

Dasselbe (G)—Same.

Dauer (G)—Duration.

Dauernd (G)—Enduring.

Daum, daumen (G)—Thumb.

D. C. (Abb)—Da capo.

D dur (G)—D major.

De, du, de la, des (F)—Of the, from the.

Dead interval—Interval occurring between the last note of a melodic phrase and the first note of the next.

Deagan marimbaphone, nabimba—Xylophone-like instruments.

Death and The Maiden Quartet—Schubert's String Quartet in D minor (1826).

Debile, debole (I)—Weak, faint.

Début (F)—First professional appearance.

Debutant, debutante (F)—A performer who is making his (her) initial appearance before the public.

Decastich—Poem consisting of 10 lines.

Deceptive cadence—A cadence, the last chord of which is not the keynote.

Décidé (F)—Decisively.

Decima (L) — Interval of 10 degrees in a scale.

Decimole, decuplet—Group of 10 notes of artificial value equal to 8 notes of the same denomination.

Deciso (I)—Decisively.

Decke (G)—Violin soundboard; cover of a stopped organ pipe.

Declamando (I), **declamation** (F)—Declamatory singing or expression.

Déclaver (F)—To change the key.

Decr., decresc. (Abb)—Decrescendo.

Decrescendo (I)—Gradually diminishing in tone (⟍).

Degli, dei, del, della, delle, dello (I)—Than the, of the

Degree (E), **degré** (F)—Step between 2 consecutive notes of the scale; a line or space on the staff.

Dehnen (G)—To extend or prolong.

Dehors, en dehors (F)—With emphasis.

Deliberatamente (I)—Deliberately.

Delicatamente, delicato (I)—Delicately.

Delirante, delirio (I)—Frenzy.

Delivery—Controlling the respiration and using the vocal organs so as to produce a good tone.

Deliziosamente (I), **délicieusement** (F)—Deliciously.

Dem (G)—To the.

Démancher (F)—Shifting of the left hand from one position to another on stringed instruments.

Demi (F)—Half.

Demi-cadence—Half cadence, cadence on the dominant.

Demiquaver, semi-quaver—Sixteenth note or rest.

Demisemiquaver — Thirty-second note or rest.

Demi-soupir (F) — Eighth rest (ɣ).

Demi-ton (F)—Semitone.

Demi-voix (F), **mezza voce** (I)—With half the vocal power possible.

Demuthsvoll (G)—Humble, devotional.

Demütig (G)—Meekly.

Dependent chord—Chord which requires resolution.

De Profundis (L) — Penitential Psalm No. 129.

Derivative chord—Chord gotten from others by inversion.

Dernière fois (F)—Last time.

Des (G)—D flat (D♭).

Descant, discant—Treble or soprano voice; addition of a part or parts to a tenor or subject.

Deses—D double flat (D♭♭).

Des dur (G)—D flat major.

Des moll (G)—D flat minor.

Dessous (F)—Lower part; alto.

Dessus (F)—Treble or soprano.

Desterita (I)—Dexterity.

Desto (I)—Brisk.

Destra mano (I)—Right hand.

Détaché (F)—Staccato.

Determinato (I)—Determined.

Detonieren (G)—To sing in the wrong pitch.

Deutlich (G)—Clearly.

Deux (F)—Two.

Deuxième (F)—Second.

Development (E), **durchführung** (G)—Elaboration of a theme by rhythmic, melodic, harmonic or contrapuntal variation.

Devisen-arie (G)—Modern term for da capo aria with preliminary announcement of the initial subject.

Devoto (I)—Religious.

Dextra (L)—Right, right hand.

Di (L)—Of, with, for, from to.

Dia (Gr)—Throughout.

Diap. (Abb)—Diapason.

Diapason (Gr)—Medieval theory of the interval which includes all tones; range of voice; chief foundation stops of the organ.

Diapason, normal—Standard pitch.

Diapente—Gr. name for the fifth.

Diaphonia, diaphony—In Gr. theory, dissonance.

Diatessaron — Gr. name for the interval of the fourth.

Diatonic (E) **diatonico** (I), **diatonique** (F), **diatonisch** (G) Scale built of tetrachords, including major and minor scales.

Diatonic modulation—Change of key effected by using related diatonic intervals.

Diatonic scale—Different gradations of tone of the scale arranged in proper order in conformity to some particular key.

Diatonic scale, major—Scale in which the semitones occur between the third and fourth, seventh and eighth degrees.

Diatonic scale, minor—Scale in which the semitones occur between the second and third, fifth and sixth, seventh and eighth degrees.

Dichtung (G)—Poem.

Di colpo (I)—Suddenly.

Dieci (I)—Ten.

Dies Irae (L)—Second part of the Requiem Mass.

Diesis (I), **dièse** (F)—Sharp (♯).

Dietro (I)—After, following.

Diferencia—16th c. S. name for variations.

Differentiae, differences—Various endings of a psalm tone.

Difficile (I)—Difficult.

Digital—Finger lever on a keyboard.

Dignita (I)—Dignity, grandeur.

Di grado (I)—By degrees of the scale.

Dilettante (I)—Amateur.

Diluendo (I)—Dying away.

Dim. (Abb)—Diminuendo.

Diminished — Applied to intervals which are less than minor or perfect intervals.

Diminished chords—Chords which have a diminished interval between their highest and lowest notes.

Diminished seventh—An interval a semitone less than a minor seventh.

Diminished triad—Chord composed of a root tone, the minor third and diminished fifth above.

Diminuendo (I)—Growing softer.

Diminution — Restatement of a theme or thematic pattern in notes of shorter time value.

Di molto (I)—Very much.

Di nuovo (I)—Once more.

Direct—A mark (∨) at the end of a line indicating the notes to follow.

Direct motion—Parts rising or falling in the same motion.

Dirge—Funeral music.

Diriger (F), **dirigieren** (G), **dirigere** (I)—To conduct.

Diritta (I), **droit** (F)—Right hand.

Diritto (I)—Straight on in ascending or descending intervals.

Dis (G)—D sharp (D♯).

Di salto (I)—By a "jump".

Discant—Cf. Descant.

Disciolto (I)—Skilful, dexterous.

Discord (E), **discorde** (F), **discordanza** (I)—Dissonance, disagreeable combination of sounds.

Discord, prepared—Instance where the discordant note has been held over from a previous concord.

Discreto (I)—Discreetly.

Disis (G)—D double sharp (D𝄪).

Disinvolto (I)—Assured, easy.

Disjunct succession — Progressing by skips.

Dis moll (G)—D sharp minor.

Di sopra (I)—Above.

Disperato (I)—Desperate.

Dispersed Harmony — Harmony which has wide intervals between the notes of the chcords.

Disposition — Arrangement of stops, pedals, manuals, couplers, etc. of an organ.

Dissonance—Discord.

Disque (F)—Record.

Distinto (I)—Clear, distinct.

Dithyramb—Hilarious composition in honor of Bacchus, god of wine.

Dito (I)—Finger.

Ditonus (L)—Medieval name for the major third, equal to 2 whole tones.

Div. (Abb)—Divisi.

Diva (I)—Prima Donna.

Divertimento (I), **divertissement** (F)—Short, light composition; instrumental composition of several short movements.

Divided accompaniment—Accompaniment in which intervals are taken by both hands in pianoforte playing.
more notes written as a chord be played separately by a group of stringed instruments, divided for that purpose.

Dix (F)—Ten.

Dixième (F)—Tenth.

D. M. (Abb)—Destra mano.

D moll (G)—D minor.

Do (I), **ut** (F)—Syllable used in singing the first note of the diatonic scale.

Doch (G)—Still, nevertheless.

Doctor of Music—Highest musical degree conferred by universities.

Dodecuplet—Group of 12 notes occupying the time of 8 of the same value.

Doigt (F)—Finger.

Dol. (Abb)—Dolce.

Dolcan—Organ stop of 8 ft. scale; the dulciana.

Dolce (I)—Sweetly.

Dolcezza (I)—Sweetness, softness.

Dolciano—Soft-voiced organ stop.

Dolciss. (Abb)—Dolcissimo.

Dolent (F), **dolente** (I)—Sorrowfully.

Doloroso (I)—Sorrowful.

Dominant—Fifth tone of the ascending diatonic scale.

Dominant chord—Chord founded on the fifth note of the ascending diatonic scale.

Dominant harmony—Harmony on the fifth of the key.

Dominant seventh—The fifth with the third, fifth and seventh above.

Dominant triad—A triad built on the fifth tone of the ascending diatonic scale.

Domra—Russian long-necked lute of the 16th and 17th. c.

Dona nobis pacem (L)—Concluding movement of the R. C. Church.

Don Giovanni—Opera in 2 acts by Mozart (1787).

Dopo (I)—After.

Dop Ped. (Abb)—Doppio pedale.

Doppel (G), **doppio** (I)—Double.

Doppel-B (G) — B double flat (B♭♭).

Doppelgriff (G), **double corde** (F) —Double stop of violin, etc.

Doppelkreuz (G), **double-dièse** (F) —Double sharp (✕).

Doppelschlag (G)—A turn.

Doppelt so schnell (G)—Twice as fast.

Doppio (I)—Double.

Doppio movimento (I)—Twice as fast.

Doppio pedale (I)—Playing 2 notes on the pedals of an organ at the same time, generally in octaves.

Dot—Musical notation after a note indicating augmentation of its value by one-half.

Double—Series of variations; tone played with its octave.

Double bar—Two vertical strokes on the staff, indicating the end of a section, movement or piece.

Double bass, contrabass, bass viol —Largest and lowest pitched of the viol family.

Double bassoon-Woodwind pitched an octave lower than the bassoon.

Double chorus—Two choruses used in alternation.

Double concerto—A concerto for two solo instruments and orchestra.

Double corde (F)—Double stop.

Double counterpoint—Counterpoint with parts inverted.

Double croche (F)—Sixteenth note (♪).

Double diapason—Organ stop an octave below the diapasons.

Double dot—Two dots placed after a note, augmenting its time value 3/4 of original value.

Double flat—Sign (♭♭) indicating a note is to be played two half steps lower than written.

Double fugue—Fugue with two subjects.

Double note—Note twice the length of a whole note.

Double octave—Interval of two octaves.

Double pedal — In organ playing, the use of both feet simultaneously for the rendering of intervals or two parts.

Double quartet—Composition for 8 voices or instruments.

Double reed—Mouthpiece of the hautboy, etc., formed of two pieces of cane joined together.

Double sharp—Cf. Doppelkreuz.

Double stop—Executiion of 2 or more simultaneous tones on the violin and similar instruments.

Double stopped diapason—Organ stop of 16 ft. tone on the manuals.

Doublet—Irregular note groups in which 2 notes are performed in the time ordinarily allowed for 3 of the same value.

Double tierce—An organ stop tuned a tenth above the diapasons.

Double tonguing—Method of playing on a wind instrument done by applying the tongue alternately to the upper front teeth and the palate in rapid passages.

Double trill—Simultaneous trill on two different notes. usually in the distance of a third.

Doucement (F)—Sweetly.

Douloureux (F)—Sorrowfully.

Douze (F)—Twelve.

Douzième (F)—Twelfth.

Downbeat—First or accented beat in a measure.

Down-bow—Downward stroke of the bow from nut to point.

Down-bow sign—Sign which indicates the down-bow (⊓).

Doxology—Hymn of praise.

Dramatic soprano—Soprano voice with dramatic power.

Dramatic tenor—Tenor voice with dramatic power.

Dramma lirica, dramma per musica (I)—Opera.

Drammatico (I)—Dramatic.

Drängend (G)—Urging forward.

Dreher (G)—Austrian dance similar to the Landler.

Drehleier (G)—Hurdy gurdy.

Drehorgel (G)—Street organ.

Drei (G)—Three.

Dreifach (G)—Three-fold.

Dreiklang (G)—Triad.

Dreist (G)—Confidant.

Dreistimmig (G)—Three parts or voices.

Dreitaktig (G)—In phrases of three measures.

Dringend (G)—Urging.

Dritte (G)—Third.

Drittel (G)—A third.

Drohend (G)—Menacing.

Droite (F)—Right.

Drone—Low pipes of the bagpipe; long, sustained notes, usually in the lowest parts.

Drone-bass—Persistent accompaniment, in the bass, of one or two tones—tonic and dominant.

Drum—Percussion instrument consisting of a wood or metal cylinder over whose two ends, vellum heads are stretched. It is played by striking with sticks.

Drum, kettle (E), **timpani** (I)—A drum with a cup-shaped shell of copper, over which a parchment head is stretched.

Drum, side or snare—Small drum which has catgut or metal cords beneath the head.

Drum, tenor — Military or field drum without snares.

Drum, trap—Bass drum with cymbals attached and a foot pedal for playing both drum and cymbals.

D. S. (Abb)—Dal segno.

Dudelsack (G)—Bagpipe.

Due corde (I)—Two strings.

Due cori (I)—Two choirs or choruses.

Due pedali (I)—Use both pedals.

Duet (E), **duo** (I), **duett** (G)— Two voices or performers.

Due volte (I)—Twice.

Dulciana—Soft voiced organ stop.

Dulcimer (E), **hackbrett** (G), **cimbalom** (Hung), **tympano** (F)— Shallow box with wire strings over a soundboard which are struck by a hammer.

Dumka (Bohem.) Elegy or dirge with a change from melancholy to exuberance.

Dump, domp—An old dance with peculiar rhythm usually in 4/4 time.

Duo (I)—Duet.

Duo concertante (I)—Duet in which 2 instruments and the orchestra take turns at the principal part.

Duodecimo (I), **douzième** (F)— Twelfth note from the tonic.

Duodecuple scale—Chromatic scale, a series of 12 tones of equal rights.

Duodrama—Spoken dialogue with musical accompaniment.

Duolo (I)—Sorrow.

Duple—double.

Duplet—A group of 2 notes to be played in the time of 3.

Duple time—Two or a multiple of two beats to the measure.

Duplex longa—13th c. name for the maxima.

Dur (F)—Hard, harsh.
Dur (G)—Major.
Duramente (I)—Harshly.
Duration—Length of time a tone, rest or composition continues.
Durchbrochene arbeit (G)—Technique of writing in which fragments of a melody are given to different instruments to play in turn.
Durchdringend (G)—Piercing.
Durchführung (G), développement (F)—Development or working out of thematic material.
Durchimitieren (G)—A style in which imitation is applied equally to all parts.
Durchkomponiert (G)—Song in which the music is composed to fit the already written words, each stanza being different.
Durchspielen (G)—To play to the end.
Durement (F)—Harshly.
Durezza (I)—To play with harshness and determination.
Duro (I)—Rude, harsh.
Düster (G)—Gloomy.
Dux (L)—Subject of a fugue.
Dynamics—Gradations in volume of sound.

— E —

E—Third step in the typical diatonic scale of C.
E, ed (I), et (F)—And.
Ebollimente (I)—Sudden expression of passion.
Eccheggiare (I)—To resound.
Ecclesia (I)—Church.
Ecclesiastical modes—Scales used in Medieval Ch. music.
Echappement (F)—Escapement.
Echelette (F)—Xylophone.
Echelle (F)—Scales.
Echo (E), eco (I)—Repetition or imitation with less intensity than the previous passage.
Echo attachment—A special valve attached to brass instruments by which a bell of smaller opening is brought into operation, producing a distant sound.
Echo cornet—An organ stop with small scale pipes which produce a light, delicate tone.
Echos—Ancient Syrian and Byzantine system of tonal classification which corresponds to the system of modes of the R. chant.
Éclat (F)—Brilliant, piercing.
Eclogue—Short pastoral piece of music.
École (F)—Method or course of instruction; style originated by some eminent artist.
École de chant (F) — Singing school.
Écossais, écossaise (F)—A contradance of lively tempo in 2/4 rhythm.
Edel (G)—Distinguished.
E dur (G)—E major.
Effetto (I)—Effect of music upon an audience.
Également (F), egualmente (I)—Equally.
Eguale (I)—A composition for several voices or instruments of one kind.
Eifrig (G)—Zealous.
Eighth—An octave; 1/8 of whole note (♪).
Eighth rest—1/8 of whole rest (𝄾).
Eilend, eilig (G)—Hurrying.
Ein (G)—One.

Einfach (G)—Simple.
Eingang (G)—Preface.
Eingestrichen (G)—One Line.
Einhalt (G)—Pause.
Einheit (G)—Unity.
Einigkeit (G)—Harmony.
Einklang (G)—Unison.
Einlage (G)—Interpolation.
Einleitung (G)—Introduction.
Einlenken (G)—To lead back.
Einmal (G)—Once.
Einsatz (G)—Entrance of an orchestra part.
Einschlafen (G)—To slacken in time and to diminish in tone.
Einschmeichelnd (G)—Flattering, insinuating.
Einstimmig (G)—Monophonic.
Eintönig (G)—Monotonous.
Eintracht (G)—Monotonous.
Eintretend (G)—Beginning.
Eintritt (G)—Entrance.
Eis (G)—E sharp, (♯).
Eisis (G)—E double sharp, (E.𝄪).
Eisteddfod (Welsh) — Annual Welsh bardic congress.
Elargissant (F)—Broadening.
Electric action organ—Organ in which electricity takes the place of direct mechanical action.
Electronic, electrotonic — Production of tone purely by electricity.
Elégamment (F), Elegantemente (I)—Gracefully.
Elegante (I)—Elegant, graceful.
Elegia (I)—Mournful.
Élégie (F)—Monody.
Elegiac (E), elegiaco (I), élégiaque (F)—Mournfully.
Elementary music — Exercises especially adapted to beginners in the study of music.
Elevation—Motet played at the Elevation of the R. C. Mass.
Elevato (I)—Exulted.
Elevazione (I)—Grandeur.
Eleventh—An Interval of 11 diatonic degrees.
Embellishments—Ornaments such as trills, grace notes, etc.
Embouchure (F), ansatz (G)—Mouthpiece of instruments; proper disposition of the lips and tongue in playing wind and brass instruments.
E moll (G)—E minor.
Emozione (I)—Emotion, agitation.
Emperor Concerto—Colloquial name for Beethoven's Piano Concerto in E flat, op. 72 (1809).
Emperor Quartet—Colloquial name for Haydn's String Quartet in C, op. 76, no. 4.
Empfindungsvoll (G)—With sensitivity.
Emphase (F-G), emphasis (E), (I)—Stress, accent.
Emphatique (F), emphatisch (G) Emphatical.
Emporté (F)—Carried away.
Empressé (F)—Eager.
Emu (F)—With emotion.
En (F)—In.
En accélérant (F)—In speeding the pace.
En augmentant (F)—Getting louder.
En badinant (F)—Scherzando.
Enchaînement (F)—Voice-leading; proper connection of chords.
Enchiriadis, enchiridion (Gr.)—Medieval term for handbook, manual.
Enclume (F)—Anvil.
Encore (F), ancora (I)—Audience demand for repetition of a piece.
Encore une fois (F)—Once again.

Ende (G)—Conclusion.
Energ. (Abb)—Energico.
Energico (I)—Energetically.
Énergiquement (F), energisch (G) —Energetically.
Enfatico (I)—Emphatically.
Enfler (F)—To increase in tone.
Engführung (G), stretto (I)—The overlapping of subject with answer in a fugue.
English fingering, American fingering—The use of the sign X to designate the thumb on the piano as opposed to the number I used in Continental fingering.
English flute — 18th c. name for the end-blown flutes.
English horn (E), cor anglais (F) —Alto oboe pitched lower than the treble oboe.
Enharmonic (E), enarmonica (I)—Writing the same sound in 2 different ways when changing from one key to another.
Enharmonic change—A passage in which the notation is changed but the same keys of the instrument are employed.
Enharmonic instruments—Instruments capable of realizing the distinction between enharmonic tones such as G♯ and A♭.
Ensemble (F)—Combination of voices or instruments; music written for such a group.
Entendu (F)—Heard, understood.
Entfernt (G), da lontano (I)—From a distance.
Entführung aus dem Serail—Comic opera in three acts by W. A. Mozart (1782).
Entr'acte (F)—Between-the-acts music.
Entrata (I), entrée (F)—Prelude or introduction.
Entrechat (F)—Ballet term referring to the rapid crossing of the dancer's feet several times while in a jump.
Entremes (S)—A variety of the operatic intermezzo.
Entremet (F)—A short entertainment period between banquet courses in 14th and 15th c. F. and Burgundian courts.
Entschieden (G)—Determined.
Entschlossen (G)—Determined.
Entusiasmo (I)—Enthusiasm.
Entwicklung (G)—Development.
Entwurf (G)—Outline of a composition; exposition of a fugue.
Enunciare (I)—To declare.
Enunciation — Correct pronunciation; synonym for exposition in sonata form.
Epilogue—Concluding piece, coda.
Epinette (F)—Spinet, harpsichord.
Episode—Secondary sections of a fugue or rondo in which the principal subjects are missing but replaced by subordinate subjects or motifs derived from the principal subjects.
Epistle—A passage for the R. C. liturgy which is monotone or chanted.
Epistle sonata—17th and 18th c. instrumental piece designed to be played in the church before the reading of the epistle.
Epithalamium (Gr) — Wedding song.
Epode—Conclusion of a chorus.
E poi (I)—And then.
Equabile (I)—Smoothly.
Equale — Composition for equal voices—all male, all female or equal instruments.

Equal counterpoint — Composition written in 2 to 4 or more parts composed of notes of equal time value.

Equal temperament—A system of tuning which divides the octave into 12 equal semitones.

Equal voices—Cf. Equale.

Ergriffen (G)—Deeply moved.

Erhaben (G)—Exulted.

Erhöhungszeichen (G) — Sharp, flat.

Erklingen (G)—To ring or resound.

Erleichterung (G) — Simplified version.

Erlöschend (G)—Dying away.

Ermattend (G)—Wearied.

Ermunterung (G)—Animation, excitement.

Erniedrigungszeichen (G)—Signs which lower the pitch; flats and naturals following sharps.

Ernsthaft (G)—Earnest.

Erntelied (G)—Harvest song.

Eroica (I)—Heroic; Beethoven's Third Symphony.

Erotic (Gr)—Love song.

Erschüttert (G)—Shaken.

Erst (G)—First.

Erstickt (G)—Suffocated.

Erweckung (G)—Animation.

Erzähler (G)—Narrator.

Es (G)—E flat (E♭).

Esaltato (I)—With exaltation.

Esatto (I)—Exact.

Escapement — The action of the piano causing the hammer to recoil immediately after striking the string.

Es dur (G)—E flat major.

Esempio (I)—Example.

Es es (G)—E double flat (E♭♭).

Escercizio (I), **exercice** (F)—Exercise.

Esitamento (I)—Hesitation.

Es moll (G)—E flat minor.

Espagnol (F), **Spagnuolo** (I)—Spanish.

Espirando (I)—Fading away.

Espr. (Abb.)—Espressivo.

Espressione (I)—Expression.

Espressivo (I)—To be played or sung with expression.

Esquisse (F)—Sketch.

Essential harmonies—Tonic, dominant and subdominant triads.

Esterbend (G)—Dying away.

Estinto (I)—Dying away in time and strength of tone.

Estompé (F)—Toned down.

Estravagante (I)—Fanciful and extravagant work.

Estremamente (I)—Extremely.

Esultazione (I)—Exultation.

Et (L-F)—And.

Étendue (F)—Compass or range.

Et incarnatus est (L)—Part of the Credo in the R. C. Mass.

Et in Spiritum Sanctum (L)—Part of the Credo in the R. C. Mass.

Étouffé—Smothered, muffled.

Et resurrexit (L)—Part of the Credo in the R. C. Mass.

Etta, etto—Italian diminutive.

Étude (F)—A study or exercise.

Étude de concert (F)—An etude for concert performance.

Et vitam (L)—Part of the credo in the R. C. Mass.

Etwas (G)—Somewhat, a little.

Etwas stärker (G)—A little louder.

Euphonium—Baritone tuba.

Euphony—Concord.

Eurhythmics — Technique which correlates bodily movement with music.

Euterpe—Gr. muse of music and lyric poetry.

Éveillé (F)—Awakened.

Evensong—Anglican evening prayer; R. C. vespers.

Evirato, castrato (I) — Eunuch singer whose voice retains that of a boy's range.

Exaltation (F)—Exalted, dignified manner.

Execution—Technique of performance.

Exposition—First statement of a theme; first section in sonata form; first statement of a fugue theme in all voices.

Expression—Conveyance of the aesthetic and emotional content of music through its performance.

Expressionism—19th c. style of music which was supposed to indicate inner experience.

Expression marks—Signs indicating the interpretation of music.

Extemporaneous (E), **extempore** (L)—Improvised.

Extended phrase—Phrase which by modification is extended to include one or several measures more than in its original form.

Extraneous—Outside, foreign.

Extravaganza (I)—Musical burlesque.

Extreme interval—Augmented interval.

Extreme keys—Keys not closely related.

Extreme parts—Highest and lowest parts in music.

— F —

F—Fourth step in the typical diatonic scale of C.

Fa—Fourth syllable in any typical diatonic scale as sung in syllables.

Fa bémol (F)—F flat (F♭).

Fabliau (F)—Fable.

Facile (I), **facilement** (F)—With ease.

Fackeltanz (G)—19th c. Prussian torch dance.

Fa Dièse (F)—F sharp (F♯).

Fag. (Abb.)—Fagotti.

Fagott (G), **fagotto** (I)—Bassoon.

Fagotto-contra (I)—Contra-bassoon.

Faible (F)—Weak.

Faire (F)—To make or do.

Faire des fredons (F)—To trill.

Fa-la—16th c. part song with the refrain fa-la.

Fall—Cadence.

False (E), **falsa** (I), **falsch** (G), **faux** (F)—Inaccurate in pitch.

False accent—Removal of the accent from the first beat of a measure to the second or fourth.

False cadence — Interrupted cadence.

False relation—Note which occurs in one chord and found chromatically altered in the following chord but in a different part.

Falsetto (I-E), **falsett** (G), **fausett** (F)—Adult male voice forced to an upper register.

Falstaff—Opera in three acts by Giuseppe Verdi (1893).

Fa majeur (F)—F major.

Fa mineur (F)—F minor.

Fancy—Fantasia.

Fandango—S. dance in 3/4 or 3/8 time accompanied by castanets with strong emphasis upon the second beat of each measure.

Fanfare (E-F), **fanfara** (I), **tusch** (G)—Flourish of trumpets or hunting horns.

Fantaisie (F), **fantasia** (I), **fantasie** (G)—Imaginative composition which does not adhere to strict form.

Fantasia section—Same as development section in sonata form.

Fantasiren (G)—To improvise.

Fantastico (I)—Free play of fancy.

Farandole (F)—Lively, Provençal dance in 6/8 or 4/4 time in which a group holds hands and follows the leader.

Farsa (I)—Farce.

Farewell Symphony (G)—Haydn's symphony in F sharp minor (1772).

Fassung, mit (G)—Calm.

Fast (G)—Almost.

Fastosamente (I)—Pompously.

Fauxbourdon (F), **falso bordone** (I)—A form of medieval music having three part harmonization of melody in parallel thirds and sixths above.

F clef—Bass clef (𝄢).

F dur (G)—F major.

Feier (G)—Celebration.

Feierlich (G)—Festive.

Feis Ceoil—Annual Irish music festival.

Ferial—Liturgy for a weekday, not a feast day.

Ferma (I)—Firm.

Fermamente (I)—Firmly.

Fermare il tuono (I)—To sustain the tone in the central part of the "messa di voce" before diminishing.

Fermata (I), **fermate** (G)—Pause or hold, marked (⌢ ⌣).

Fermo (I), **fermament** (F)—Firmly.

Fern (G)—Distant.

Fernwerk (G)—Echo organ.

Feroce (I)—Fiercely.

Ferocita (I)—Fierceness.

Fertig (G)—Quick.

Fervente (I), **fervent, fervido** (I)—Fervent, vehement.

Fes (G)—F flat (F♭).

Feses (G)—F double flat (F♭♭).

Fest (G)—Festival.

Festal—Liturgy for a feast day.

Festiglich (G)—Firmly.

Festivo (I)—Gaily.

Festlich (G)—Festive.

Festoso (I)—Gay.

Festouvertüre (G)—Festival overture.

Festspiel (G)—Festival play.

Feuer (G)—Fire, ardor, passion.

Feuerig (G)—Ardently.

Feuille d'album (F), **albumblatt** (F)—Short lyric piece usually for piano.

Ff. (Abb.)—Fortissimo.

F-holes—F shaped sound holes of the violin family.

Fiacco (I)—Feeble, weak.

Fiasco (I)—Failure.

Fiato (I)—The breath, the voice.

Fiddle (E), **fiedel** (G)—Any instrument of the violin family.

Fidelio—Opera by Beethoven (1805).

Fidicen—16th c. humanistic name for string player.

Fiducia (I)—Confidence.

Field music—Martial music.

Fier (F), **fiero** (I)—Proudly.

Fife—Small, shrill-toned flute without keys used mostly in military bands.

Fifteenth—Interval of two octaves; an organ stop.

Fifth—Fifth degree of the diatonic scale or the interval formed by a tone and the fifth tone above.

Figuration—Ornamental treatment of a passage.

Figurato (I), figuré (F), figuriet (G)—Figured, florid.

Figure—Smallest element into which a musical phrase can be divided.

Figured—Free and florid.

Figured bass, thoroughbass (E), basse chiffrée (F), basso continuo (I), bezifferter bass (G)—A bass with figures over or under the notes to indicate the harmony.

Filare il tuono (I), filer la voix (F)—Prolongatior of a tone, gradually augmenting or diminishing the sound.

Filo (I)—The "line" of a piece.

Filo di voce (I)—Thread of tone.

Fin (F), fine (I)—End.

Fin al (I)—End at; play as far as.

Final—Keynote in ecclesiastical modes.

Finale (I)—Conclusion of a composition.

Fin 'al segno (I)—Indication to repeat from the beginning of a sign.

Fine (I)—End.

Finement (F)—Finely, acutely.

Fingerboard (E), clavier (F), tastiera (I), griffbrett (G)—Flat piece of wood over which the strings are stretched on stringed instruments; keyboard.

Fingerfertigkeit (G)—Virtuosity.

Fingering—Method of finger application to an instrument; figures written to indicate which fingers are to be used.

Fingering, American—Sign (X) which indicates the use of the thumb.

Fingering, foreign or German—Thumb is designated as the first finger.

Finger-satz (G)—Fingering.

Finire il tuono (I)—Diminishing of a sustained note in singing at the end of the "messa di voce".

Finite—Canon which comes to a definite end.

Fino (I)—As far as.

Fioritura (I)—Embellishment of a melody.

Fipple flute—Recorder.

First—Unison or prime; highest part.

First inversion—Triad rearranged so that the third of the triad becomes the bass.

Fis (G)—F sharp (F♯).

Fis dur (G)—F sharp major.

Fisis (G)—F double sharp (F𝄪).

Fis moll (G)—F sharp minor.

Fistelstimme (G)—Falsetto.

Fistula (L)—Medieval name for flute.

Five, The—Refers to the late 19th c. Russian composers: Cesar Cui, Alexander Borodin, Mily Balakirev, Modest Moussorgsky, Nicholas Rimsky-Korsakov.

Fixed-do—A system in which do in any typical diatonic scale is always C.

Fixed pitch—Pitch of such instruments such as piano, organ, etc.

in which the pitch of the individual notes cannot be changed by the performer.

Fixed syllables—Vocal syllables which do not change with the change of the key.

Fl. (Abb)—Flauto, flute.

Flag. (Abb)—Flageolet.

Flageolet (E-F), flageolett (G), flagioletta (I)—Six-hole wooden flute, blown from the end, a form of recorder.

Flageolet tones—Flute-like tones produced on a stringed instrument by touching a string lightly.

Flamenco—The gypsy style of S. dance and dance music.

Flat—Sign (♭) indicating a pitch a half-step lower than the original; too low in intonation.

Flat, double—Two flats which lower a note two semi-tones (♭♭).

Flatterzunge (G)—Flutter tonguing.

Flautando (I)—Producing flute-like tones on instruments of the violin family by drawing the bow lightly across the strings at a greater distance from the bridge than usual.

Flauto (I), flöte (G), flûte (F)—Flute; organ stop.

Flautone (I)—16 ft. pedal-stop in an organ characterized by a soft tone.

Flauto piccolo (I)—Small flute of very shrill tone.

Flauto tedesco, flauto traverso (I), querflöte (G)—A flute blown from the side.

Flaviol—Small S. one-handed flute used for dance music.

Flebile (I)—Mournful.

Flehend (G)—Imploring.

Flessibile (I)—Pliant.

Fliegende Holländer, Der (The Flying Dutchman)—Opera by Richard Wagner (1843).

Fliessend (G)—Flowing.

Fling—Scottish dance of the highlands.

Florid—Ornamental, figured.

Florid counterpoint—Free counterpoint.

Flos—13th c. term for embellishments.

Flöte (G)—Flute.

Flott (G)—Quick, without hesitation.

Flottant (F)—Floating.

Flourish—Trumpet or brass instrument fanfare; embellishment.

Flüchtig (G)—Nimbly.

Flue pipes—Labial pipes; organ pipes with lips.

Flügel—Grand piano.

Flügelhorn (G)—Bugle.

Fluit (Dutch), fluta (L)—Flute.

Flute—Wooden or metal wind instrument, made in six sizes; part of the woodwind choir.

Flute—An organ stop of the diapason species with a flute-like tone.

Flûte à bec (F)—Old E. flute with a lip or beak.

Flute-work—In the organ this includes all flue stops not belonging to the principal-work and gedackt-work and modifications of these two groups.

Flutez (F)—Direction to play harmonics.

F moll (G)—F minor.

F. O. (Abb)—Full organ.

Focoso (I)—Fiery.

Foglietto (I)—Conductor's small

score.

Fois (F)—Time.

Folgend (G)—Following.

Folia (S), follia (I)—Old Portuguese dance similar to a fandango.

Folio—Music printed on pages which are the result of folding a large sheet into two leaves.

Folk-music—Traditional music of a people expressed in song and dance.

Fonds d'orgue (F)—Foundation stops of the organ.

Foot—Rhythmic unit of two or more syllables or a unit of measure to designate the pitch of organ pipes.

Forefall—E. 17th c. term for appoggiatura.

Forlana (I), forlane (F)—Venetian dance in 6/8 time.

Form—the architecture of music; sound arranged in an orderly manner according to numerous obvious principles as well as subtle and hidden relationships.

Formare il tuono (I)—To attack and sell in singing.

Forte (I)—Loud, strong.

Forte piano (I)—A strong attack instantly diminished.

Forte possibile (I)—As loud as possible.

Fortezza (I)—Force, power.

Fortfahren (G)—Continue.

Fortissimo (I)—Very loud.

Fortsetzung (G)—Continuation or development.

Fortspinnung (G)—Process of continuation, development or working out of material rather than a symmetrical arrangement.

Forty-Eight, The—Popular name for Bach's 48 preludes and fugues.

Forza (I)—Force, strength.

Forzando (I)—Stress upon one note or chord (or).

Fougeux (F)—Impetuous.

Foundation stops—8 ft. stops of the organ.

Fourniture (F)—Mixture stops of the organ.

Fourth—The fourth note of the diatonic scale or the interval formed by a tone and the fourth tone above.

Fp. (Abb)—Forte piano.

Frais (F)—Fresh.

Francaise (F)—Country dance in 3/4 time.

Francese (I), französisch (G)—French.

Franchezza I)—Freedom, boldness.

Frapper (F)—To strike.

Frase larga (I)—Broad phrasing.

Frauenchor (G)—Women's choir.

Freddo (I)—Without animation.

Fredon (F)—Trill.

Fredonner (F)—To hum.

Free canon, free fugue—One written not according to established rules.

Free composition—A composition not in strict accordance with the rules of musical form.

Free part—A voice which is added, in strict contrapuntal writing, to fill in the harmony.

Free pitch—Applicable to instruments in which the pitch is not fixed, but altered by the performer.

Free reed—One which vibrates within an aperture without striking the edges, e.g. reed organ.

Frei (G)—Free, unrestrained.

Freischütz, Der ("The Free-shooter")—Opera in three acts by Carl Maria von Weber (1821).

French harp—Older name for mouth organ.

French horn—Brass i nstrument with circular coiled tubing, a flaring bell at one end and a cupped mouthpiece at the other, the pitch being controlled by valves and by the adjustment of player's lips.

Frenetico (I)—Frenzied.

Fresco (I)—Fresh.

Frets—Ridges of wood, metal or ivory across the fingerboard of banjo, guitar, etc. to indicate where the strings should be pressed down.

Fretta (I)—Increasing the time.

Frettevole (I)—Hurried.

Freudig (G)—Joyfully.

Frisch (G)—Fresh.

Frog (E)—Lower part of the bow.

Frog Quaret—Popular name for Haydn's Quartet in D.

Fröhlich (G)—Happy.

Froid (F)—Cold.

Frosch (G)—Cf. Frog.

Frottola (I)—Ancient I. Ballad, usually amorous.

Frühlingslied (G)—Spring song.

F-schlüssel (G)—F or bass clef.

Fuga (I)—Fugue.

Fugara (L)—An organ stop of the gamba species.

Fugato (I)—A passage or movement in sound like a fugue, but not developed as a fugue.

Fughetta (I)—Short fugue.

Fugitive pieces—Ephemeral compositions.

Fugue—A composition strict in style, in which a subject is announced and followed by an answer in another voice or voices, this being imitated by one or more other voices in the manner of a flight.

Fugue, double—A fugue on two subjects.

Fugue, free—A fugue that does not follow the rules of strict fugue form.

Fugue, manifold—A fugue of more than one subject.

Fugue, perpetual—A canon.

Fugue, simple—A fugue contain-only one subject.

Fugue, strict—A fugue constructed according to rule.

Führer (G)—Fugue subject.

Full—Complete as applied to chords, cadences, etc.

Full anthem—An anthem in four or more parts without verses or solo passages, to be sung by full choir in chorus.

Full orchestra—One in which all string and bras instruments are employed.

Full organ—Organ with all its register and stops in use.

Full score—A complete score of all the parts of a composition, vocal or instrumental or both combined, written on separate staffs placed under each other.

Fundamental—Basic tone producing a series of harmonics or a root of a tread or chord.

Fundamental chord—A chord based on the key-note.

Fundamental key—Original key.

Fundamental note—Root of a chord.

Fundamental position—The posi-tion of a chord in which the root is at the bottom.

Fundamental tones—The tonic, dominant and subdominant of any scale or key.

Funèbre (F), funerale (I)—Mournful.

Funf (G)—Five.

Fuoco (I)—Fiery.

Für (G)—For.

Furia (I)—Fury, rage.

Furiant—Fast and fiery Bohemian dance in 3/4 time.

Furioso (I)—Mad.

Furniture stop—Mixture stop.

Furore (I)—A success.

Fz. (Abb)—Forzando, forzato.

— G —

G—Fifth step in the typical diatonic scale of C.

G. (F) (Abb)—Gauche.

Gabelgriff (G)—Cross fingering.

Gagliarda (I), guillarde (F), galliard (E)—Spirited F. dance in triple time.

Gagliardamente (I)—Briskly.

Gai (F), gaio (I)—Gay.

Galant (F), galante (I)—Gallantly.

Galanterien (G)—18th c. name for short, entertaining pieces in non-fugal style, e.g. dances.

Gallant style (F)—18th c. light and elegant style of Rococo as opposed to elaborate Baroque.

Galliard—Cf. Gagliarda.

Gallican chant—F. branch of the plainsong tradition of the medieval Western Church.

Galop (E), galopp (G), galoppo (I)—A hopping round-dance in 2/4 time.

Gamba, Viola da (I)—Viola held between the knees.

Gamba-bass—16 ft. organ stop, on the pedals.

Gamelan—Javanese orchestra.

Gamme (F)—Gamut or scale.

Gamut—Range or compass; staff; scale.

Gang (G)—Pace; rate of movement.

Ganz (G)—Entire.

Ganzton (G)—Whole tone.

Ganzschluss (G)—Full cadence.

Garbatamente (I)—Gracefully.

Garbato (I)—Graceful.

Garbo (I)—Simplicity.

Gassenhauer, gassenlieder (G)—Street songs.

Gathering note—Pitch note of hymn to be sung by Church congregation.

Gauche (F)—Left.

Gaudioso (I)—Merry.

Gavot (E), gavotte (F)—Graceful 16th—18th c. F. Court dance in 2/4 time.

G clef—Treble clef ( ).

G dur (G)—G major.

Gebet (G)—Prayer.

Gebrauchsmusik (G)—Utility music or that which employs everyday subjects or idioms.

Gebrochen (G)—Broken.

Gebrochene akkord (G)—Broken chord.

Gebunden (G)—Connected in regard to style of playing or writing; legato.

Ged. (Abb)—Gedämpft.

Gedackt (G)—Stopped.

Gedämpft (G)—Muted.

Gedehnt (G)—Sustained.

Gefährte (G)—Answer in a fugue.

Gefällig (G)—Agreeable.

Gefühl, gefühlvoll (G)—Feeling.

Gegen (G)—Contrary.

Gegenbewegung (G) — Contrary motion.

Gegenfuge (G)—Counter-fugue.

Gegengesang (G)—Antiphony.

Gegensatz (G)—Contrast.

Gegenstimme (G)—Countersubject or voice.

Gegenthema (G)—Countersubject, second voice.

Gehalten (G)—Sustained.

Gehaucht (G)—Whispered.

Geheimnisvoll (G)—Mysteriously.

Gehend (G)—Andante, walking.

Geige (G)—Violin.

Geisslerlieder (G)—14th c. songs of the Flagellants.

Geistertrio (G)—Beethoven's Pianoforte Trio in D, op. 70.

Geistlich (G)—Spiritual.

Geistvoll (G)—Spirited.

Gekkin—Japanese guitar.

Gekoppelt (G)—Coupled.

Gelassen (G)—Calm.

Geläufig (G)—Rapid.

Gelinde (G)—Gently.

Gemächlich (G)—Comfortable.

Gemählig (G)—Gradually.

Gemässigt (G)—Moderate tempo.

Gemeindelied (G)—Congregational hymn.

Gemendo (I)—Moaning.

Gemessen (G)—Precise time.

Gemisch (G)—Compound stops in an organ.

Gemischte stimmen (G)—Mixed voices.

Gemshorn (G)—Organ stop with a horn-like tone.

Gemüth (G)—Mind, soul.

Gemüthlich (G)—Genial.

Genau (G)—Exact.

Generalbass (G)—Figured bass.

Generalpause (G)—Rest for the entire orchestra.

Generalprobe (G)—Dress rehearsal of symphonic concerts.

Generoso (I)—Dignified.

Genouillère (F)—Knee lever.

Genre (F)—Style, manner.

Gentil (F), gentile (I)—Kindly.

Gentilezza (I)—Elegance.

Gequält (G)—Painful.

German—Dance resembling the cotillion.

German fingering—Piano fingering using the thumb as the first finger.

German flute—Modern transverse flute.

German scale—Scale of natural notes—A, H, C, D, E, E, G. B reserved to denote B flat.

German sixth—Chord composed of a major third, perfect fifth and augmented sixth.

Gerührt (G)—Moved.

Ges (G)—G flat (G♭).

Gesamtausgabe (G) — Complete edition.

Gesang (G)—Song.

Gesangbuch (G)—Hymnbook.

Gesangvoll (G)—Cantabile.

Geschick (G)—Skill.

Geschlagen (G)—Struck.

Geschleift (G)—Slurred.

Geschwind (G)—Rapid.

Ges dur (G)—G flat major.

Gesellschaft (G)—Club.

Geses (G)—G double flat (G♭♭).

Ges moll (G)—G flat minor.

Gesprochen (G)—Spoken.

Gesteigert (G)—Becoming louder.

Gestopft (G)—Stopped notes of the horn.

Gestossen (G)—Separated, staccato.

Geteilt (G), divisi (I)—Divided.
Getragen (G)—Well sustained.
Gewichtig (G)—With importance.
Gewidmet (G)—Dedicated.
Gewiss (G)—Resolute.
Gewöhnlich (G)—Usual.
Gezogen (G)—Drawn out.
Ghironda (I)—Hurdy-gurdy.
Giga (I), gigue (F), gige (G)—Jig.
Gigelira (I)—Xylophone.
Gigue-fugue—Bach's Organ Fugue in G Major.
Giochévole (I)—Merry.
Giocondo (I)—Mirthful.
Giocoso (I)—Playful.
Gioioso (I)—Humorously.
Gioja (I)—Joy.
Giojoso (I)—Blitheful.
Giovale (I)—Jovial.
Giraffe—Early upright piano; harpsichord.
Giro (I)—Turn.
Gis (G)—G sharp (G♯).
Gis dur (G)—G sharp major.
Gisis (G)—G double sharp (G✕).
Gis moll (G)—G sharp minor.
Gitana (I), gitano—S. dance.
Giù (I)—Down.
Giubiloso (I)—Jubilantly.
Giuocoso (I)—Playfully.
Giusto (I)—Precise time.
Giustezza (I)—Precision.
Given bass—Figured bass.
Glänzend (G)—Brilliant.
Glatt (G)—Even.
Glee—Part-song for a group of solo, unaccompanied voices.
Gleich (G)—Equal; alike.
Gleiten (G)—To slide the fingers; glissando.
Gli (I) (Pl)—The.
Glide—Portamento.
Gliding—Sliding movement of the fingers in flute playing to blend tones.
Glissando (I), gleitend (G), glissant (F)—Slurred, sliding the finger.
Glocke, glocken (G)—Bells.
Glockenspiel (G), jeu de clochettes (F)—Graduated steel bars played by striking with hammers.
Gloria (L)—Movement in R. C. Mass following the Kyrie.
Glottis (Gr)—Narrow opening in the larynx forming the mouth of the windpipe which modulates the voice by its dilation and contraction.
Glühend (G)—Glowing.
G moll (G)—G minor.
Gnàcchere (I)—Castanets.
G. O. (Abb)—Great organ.
G. O. (Abb) (F)—Grand orgue.
Gola (I)—Throat.
Golden sequence—Veni Sancti Spiritus.
Gondellied (G), gondoliera (I)—Gondolier song.
Gong—Chinese instrument consisting of a large circular metal plate.
Goose (E), couac (F)—Harsh break in the tone of a woodwind.
G. P. (Abb)—Generalpause.
Grace notes—Notes played as ornaments, usually written very small.
Graces—Decorative additions (16th-18th c.).
Gracieux (F)—Graceful.
Grad (G), grado (I)—Step, degree.
Gradatamente (I)—Gradually.
Gradevole (I)—Pleasing.
Gradual (E), graduale (L)—Antiphonal response sung between

the Epistle and Gospel in the R. C. Mass.
Gramophone—British word for phonograph.
Gran (I)—Great, grand.
Gran cassa (I)—Bass drum.
Grand-barré (F)—Laying the first finger on all six strings of the guitar at once.
Grand bourdon—Organ stop of 32 foot plus one in the pedal.
Grand choeur (F) grand choir (E)—Union of all the stops of the choir organ.
Grand détaché (F)—A style of bowing on stringed instruments.
Grandezza (I)—Grandeur.
Grandioso (I)—Grand, noble.
Grand'messe (F)—High Mass.
Grand Opera—Opera without spoken dialogue, usually tragic.
Grand orgue (F)—Great organ.
Gran tamburo (I)—Bass drum.
Gratias agamus (L)—Part of the Gloria in R. C. Mass.
Grave (E-I)—Slow and silent movement with a deep pitch.
Gravicembalo (I)—Harpsichord.
Gravita (I)—Majesty.
Graz. (Abb)—Grazioso.
Grazioso (I)—Gracefully.
Great octave—Tablature; octave which begins two octaves below middle C.
Great staff—Staff of 11 lines, consisting of bass and treble clef with middle C between.
Greek modes—Ancient Gr. scales.
Gregorian Chant—Plainsong of the R. C. Church adopted under Pope Gregory I in the 6th c.
Gregorian modes or tones—Fourteen systems of octave scales adopted by the medieval Church.
Griffbrett (G)—Fingerboard.
Griffloch (G)—Fingerhole.
Grimmig (G)—Grim, furious.
Grob-gedackt (G)—Large stop diapason of full tone.
Gross (G), gros (F), grosso (I)—Big, great, major.
Grossartig (G)—Grand.
Grosses orchester (G)—Full orchestra.
Grosso (I)—Full, great.
Grosse caisse (F)—Bass drum.
Gross gedackt (G)—Double stopped diapason of 16 ft. tone in an organ.
Grottesco (I)—Grotesque.
Ground bass, ground (E), basso ostinato (I)—Bass phrase which is repeated over and over again with varied upper parts.
Group—Several short notes tied together.
Gruppetto (I)—A turn; embellishment of several short, rapid notes.
G—schlüssel (G)—G clef.
Gsp. (Abb)—Glockenspiel.
Guaracha (S)—A S. dance.
Guerriero (I)—Warlike.
Guida (I), guide (E), guidon (F)—A mark called the "direct" which indicates the note following the subject of a fugue.
Guidon (F)—Direct.
Guidonian syllables—Ut, re, me, fa, sol, la.
Guimbarde (F)—Jew's harp.
Guitar (E), guitare (F)—Stringed instrument with a fretted keyboard played by plucking the strings.
Gusla, gusle—Chief instrument of Bulgarian folk music.
Gusto (I)—Taste or expression.

Gymel (L)—Eng. two—voice discant of the 12th c.

— H —

H (G)—B natural.
H (Abb)—Hand; heel; horn.
Habanera (S)—Cuban dance in 3/4 or 6/8 time.
Hackbrett (G)—Dulcimer.
Haffner Collection—Important collection of early pianoforte sonatas published by Haffner (1760-1770).
Haffner Serenade—Mozart's Serenade in D composed in 1776.
Halb (G)—Half.
Half-cadence—Tonic chord followed by the do minant chord giving the sense of temporary close.
Half-close—Cf. Half-cadence.
Half-note—A minim; half of a whole note held for two quarter beats (♩).
Half-rest—A pause equal in duration to a half-note.
Half-step—Semitone.
Hallelujah (Heb)—"Praise ye the Lord", a hymn of thanksgiving.
Halling—Norwegian folk dance.
Halten (G)—To hold.
Hammer—Felt covered part of piano mechanism which strikes strings and causes vibrations.
Hammerklavier (G)—Early name for the piano.
Hanacca—Rapid Moravian dance.
Handstück (G)—Late 18th c. name for instructive piano pieces.
Handtrommel (G)—Tambourine.
Hardiment (F)—Boldly.
Harfe (G)—Harp.
Harmonic—Referring to harmony; partial or overtone.
Harmonica—Mouth organ; musical glasses.
Harmonic figuration — Arpeggios or broken chords.
Harmonic flute—An open metal organ stop of 8 or 4 ft. pitch, the pipes being of double length.
Harmonic mark—Sign indicating that certain passages are to be played upon the open strings which will produce the harmonic sounds, marked O.
Harmonic minor scale—A minor scale: A BC D EF G♯ A.
1 23 4 56 7 8.
Harmonic modulation—Change in harmony from one key to another.
Harmonic, natural—Flute-like tone sounded by placing the finger lightly on an untouched open string (♪ or ♬).
Harmonic series—When a tone is produced it is accompanied by overtones which occur in a definite order — the "harmonic series."
Harmonic triad—Three tone chord composed of a root tone, the third and fifth above.
Harmonious Blacksmith—Air with variations from Handel's Harpsichord Suite No. 5 in E (1720).
Harmonium—Small reed organ.
Harmonize—To add chords as accompaniment to a melody.
Harmony—Agreement or consonance of 2 or more united sounds; the art of chordal combination and treating such chords according to certain rules.
Harmony, close—One in which the tones are compact, the upper 3 voices lying within the compass

MUSIC DICT

of an octave.

Harmony, dispersed—Harmony in the notes composing the different chords are separated by wide intervals.

Harp—Triangular stringed instrument played by plucking the strings.

Harp lute—Early 19th c. instrument with features of the guitar combined with those of the harp.

Harp Quartet—Popular name for Beethoven's Quartet, op. 74, in E flat.

Harpsichord (E), clavecin (F), clavicembalo (I) — Keyboard stringed instrument which preceded the piano, the strings being plucked by quills or tips of leather fastened to pieces of wood manipulated from the keyboard.

Hastig (G)—Hasty.

Haupt (G)—Principal.

Haupt-satz (G)—Principal theme.

Hauptstimme (G)—Principal voice.

Haupt-werk (G)—Chief work.

Hausmusik (G)—Music for domestic use.

Haut (F), hoch (G)—Shrill.

Hautb. (Abb)—Hautboy.

Hautbois (F), hautboy (E)—Oboe.

Haye, hay, hey—Dance of the Elizabethan period.

H dur (G)—B major.

Head—Membrane stretched over drum; scroll and peg box of violin.

Head voice—Upper register; men's falsetto.

Hebrides, The or Fingal's Cave—Mendelssohn's Concert Overture in B minor, op. 26 (1830).

Heckelphone—Baritone oboe.

Heftig (G)—Violent.

Heftigkeit (G)—Impetuosity.

Heiss (G)—Ardent.

Heiter (G)—Serenely.

Heldentenor (G)—Tenor voice of great brilliancy and volume.

Helicon (E)—Tuba designed to encircle the body and rest on the shoulder, used for marching.

Hell (G)—Clear, bright.

Hemidemisemiquaver — Sixty-fourth note.

Hemitonium (Gr)—Semitone.

Heptachord (Gr)—Interval of a seventh; instrument with 7 strings.

Herabstimmen (G)—To tune a string down.

Herabstrich, herunterstrich (G)—Downbow.

Heraufstimmen (G)—To tune a string up.

Heraufstrich, hinaufstrich (G)—Upbow.

Herbstlied (G)—Harvest song.

Hervortretend (G)—Prominently.

Herz (G)—Heart.

Herzhaft (G)—Courageous.

Herzlich (G)—Heartfelt.

Hes (G)—B flat (B♭).

Hexachord (Gr)—Interval of a sixth; instrument with 6 strings.

Hichiriki—A Japanese oboe.

Hidden notes, hidden intervals—Notes or intervals implicit in the music, but not actually sounded.

Hieratic—Sacred.

Highland Fling—Scotch dance.

High Mass (E), hochamt (G), grand'messe (F), messa grande (I)—R. C. Mass which is sung.

Hilfs (G)—Auxiliary note.

Hilfslinie (G)—Ledger line.

Hindu music—The music of India.

Hinsterbend (G)—Dying away.

Hirtenflöte (G)—Shepherd's pipe.

Hirtlich (G)—Pastoral.

His (G)—B Sharp (B♯).

Hisis (G)—B double sharp (B𝄪).

H moll (G)—B minor.

Hoboe (G)—Oboe.

Hochamt (G)—High Mass.

Hochzeitslied (G)—Wedding song.

Hochzeitsmarsch (G)—Wedding march.

Höflich, mit höflichkeit (G)—Politely.

Ho-hoane (Irish)—Lament.

Hohflöte (G)—Organ stop producing thick and powerful hollow tones.

Hold (E), fermata (I)—A character (𝄐) indicating that a note or a rest is to be prolonged.

Holding-note—A note that is sustained while the others are in motion.

Holzbläser (G)—Woodwind players.

Holzblasinstrumente (G) — Woodwinds.

Holz-flöte (G)—Organ stop.

Homophonic, homophony, monophonic—Unison; in modern music, a prevailing melody with the accompaniment of chords.

Hook—A stroke attached to notes indicating their value (♪ 𝅘𝅥𝅮).

Hopak, gopak—Russian dance in 2/4 time.

Horn (E-G), cor (F), corno (I)—Metal wind instrument with a long tube ending in a large bell.

Hornpipe—Old E. dance popular with sailors.

Hornquinten, hornsatz (G)—Horn fifths.

Hosanna (Heb)—Part of the Sanctus in the R. C. Mass.

Hr., hrn. (Abb)—Horns.

Huitième (F)—Eighth.

Hummel, hummelchen—Primitive G. bagpipe.

Humoreske (G), humoresque (F)—Short instrumental caprice, not necessarily humorous.

Hurdy gurdy—An old instrument consisting of 4 strings, sounded by a wheel rubbed in resin powder, which serves as a bow.

Hurtig (G)—Quick.

Hydraulic organ—Ancient organ which used water to create wind pressure.

Hymn—Song of praise or adoration to the Deity.

Hymn, vesper—Hymn sung in the vesper service of the R. C. Church.

Hymnal—Collection of hymns.

Hyper (Gr)—Above.

Hyper ditonos (Gr)—The third above.

Hypo (Gr)—Below.

Hzbl. (Abb)—Holzbläser.

— I —

I (I) (m. pl.)—The.

Iambic, iambus—Musical foot consisting of one short unaccented and one long accented note or syllable (⏑ —).

Idea—A structural unit in music also called theme, subject, strain, figure, motive.

Idée fixe—Berlioz's name for the principal subject of his Symphonie Phantastique.

Idiomatic style—A style proper to the instrument for which the music is written.

Idyl—Pastoral composition.

Ilarita (I)—Hilarity.

Il faut (F), bisogna (I)—It is necessary; there are needed.

Il più (I)—The most.

Il più forte possibile (I) — The loudest possible.

Il più piano possibile (I) — The softest possible.

Im (G)—In the.

Imbroglio (I)—A passage meant to sound confused.

Imitando (I)—Imitating.

Imitation—Repetition of a theme or subject by another voice.

Imitative counterpoint — Contrapuntal music which uses the same thematic material in all parts.

Immer (G)–Always.

Immer langsam (G) — Always slowly.

Impaziente (I)—Impatiently.

Imperfect cadence—A cadence in which a tonic chord is followed by a dominant chord.

Imperfect consonance—Major and minor thirds and sixths.

Imperfect time—Two or four-in-a-measure time.

Imperioso (I)—Pompous.

Impeto, impetuoso (I), impeteux (F)—Impetuous.

Imponente (I)—Imposingly.

Imponierend (G)—Imposing, grand style.

Impresario (I)—Manager or conductor of operas or concerts.

Impressionism—Music initiated by Claude Debussy, which suggests in tone, elusive, emotional or mental impressions.

Impromptu (F)—Extemporaneous production.

Improperia (L)—Chants proper to Good Friday morning in the R. C. liturgy.

Improvisation—The act of extemporaneous performance.

In (I-L)—In, into, in the.

In alt (I)—First octave above the treble staff.

In altissimo (I)—Notes more than an octave above the treble staff.

Incalcando (I)—Becoming faster and louder.

Incalzando (I)—Pressing.

Incantation—A song designed to to spell magic.

Incarnatus (L)—Part of the Credo in the R. C. Mass.

Incidental music—Music incidental to plays.

Inconsolato (I)—Mournful style.

Inconsonant—Discordant.

Incordamento (I)—Tension of the strings of an instrument.

Incordare (I)—To string an instrument.

Indeciso (I)—Undecided.

Independent chord—A consonant chord that needs no resolution.

Indicato (I)—Assured, prominent.

Indifferente, (I)—Indifferently.

Infinite canon—A canon with no definite ending.

Inflection—Change or modification in pitch or tone of the voice.

Inganno (I)—Deceptive cadence.

In modo di (I)—In the manner of.

Initium—Opening notes of a psalm tone.

Inner parts, inner voices — Parts that lie between the highest and the lowest.

Innig (G)—Sincere.

Innocentemente (I)—Innocently; artless, simple style.
Ino (I)—Italian final diminutive.
Inquiet (F), **inquieto** (I), **unruhig** (G)—Restless.
Insensibile (I)—Imperceptibly.
Insieme (I), **ensemble** (F), **zusamen** (G)—Together.
Inständig (G)—Imploring.
Instante (I)—Vehement.
Instrument à cordes (F)—Stringed instrument.
Instrument à l'archet (F)—Bowed instrument.
Instrumental music—Music performed on instrument rather than sung.
Instrumentation (E-F), **instrumentazione** (I), **instrumentierung** (G)—Writing for an instrumental ensemble, providing for the characteristics of each instrument.
Instrument à vent (F), **instrumento da fiato** (I)—Wind instrument.
Instruments—
  I. Strings
    a. violin
    b. viola
    c. violoncello
    d. double bass
    e. harp
    f. piano
    g. guitar
  II. Woodwinds
    a. piccolo
    b. flute
    c. fife
    d. oboe
    e. clarinet
    f. bassoon
    g. contrabassoon
    h. English horn
  III. Brasses
    a. trumpet
    b. French horn
    c. trombone
    d. tuba
    e. saxaphone
    f. cornet
    g. bugle
  IV. Percussion
    a. kettle drum
    b. cymbal
    c. triangle
    d. gong
    e. xylophone
    f. glockenspiel
    g. celesta
    h. tambourine
    i. castanets
Inszenierung (G)—Get-up.
In tempo, a tempo (I)—In time.
Intabulierung (G)—16th c. arrangement of vocal music for the keyboard or lute.
Interlude—Short musical representation between the acts of a play or opera.
Intermezzo (I)—Interlude.
International pitch (E), **Diapason normal** (F)—Pitch which fixes A at 435 vibrations per second at a temperature of 68 degrees Farenheit.
Interval—Distance between two tones, inclusive of them both.
Intervals, compound—Intervals of more than octave.
Intervals, perfect—The unison, fourth, fifth and octave remain perfect when inverted.
Intime (F), **intimo** (L)—Intimate.
Intonation—Emission of the tone according to an exact standard.
Intrada (I)—Prelude.
Intrepidamente, intrepidezza, in-

trepido (I)—Boldly.
Introd. (Abb)—Introduction.
Introduction (E-F), **introduzioni** (I), **vorspiel** (G)—Preparatory section to the principal part of a composition.
Introit (L)—Entrance; hymn sung at the beginning of the R. C. Mass.
Invention (F), **invenzione** (I)—Term by Bach for short contrapuntal compositions.
Inverted chord—A chord which has as its bass a tone of the chord other than the root.
Inverted intervals — Change of position of intervals and chords, the lower notes being placed above, and the upper notes below.
Inverted melody—A melody with its intervals reversed.
Inverted turn—A turn beginning with the lowest note instead of the highest.
Invertible counterpoint—Counterpoint in which two or more voices may change places effectively.
Invocazione (I)—Prayer, invocation.
Ionian mode—A Greek mode; ecclesiastical mode, but not derived from the Greek.
Ira, irato, (I)—Irate.
Irlandais (F)—A dance tune in the Irish style.
Ironciamente (I)—Ironically.
Irresoluto, (I)—Irresolutely.
Isometric—Compositions in which all the voices proceed approximately in the same rhythmic pattern.
Issimo—Italian final superlative.
Istesso (I)—Same.
Istesso tempo (I)—The same time.
Italiano (I), **Italienisch** (G), **Italienne** (F)—Italian.
Italian sixth—Chord composed of a major third and an augmented sixth.
Italian symphony — Mendelssohn's Fourth Symphony in A (1831).
Ite, missa est (L)—End of the R. C. Mass.

—J—

Jack—Quill which strikes the strings of a harpsichord, or the upright lever in piano action.
Jagd-horn (G)—Hunting horn.
Jagd-stück (G)—Hunting piece.
Jaleo—S. national solo dance in triple time.
Jam session—Gathering of jazz performers at which they improvise.
Janissary, janizary band—Military band.
Jarabe—S. dance with music similar to a mazurka.
Jazz—American folk music originating with the Negro.
Jedoch (G)—Still, however.
Jeu (F)—Style of playing.
Jeu d'anche (F)—Reed stop in an organ.
Jeu de clochettes (F), **glockenspiel** (G)—Graduated steel bars played by striking with hammers.
Jew's harp (E), **guimbarde** (G), **maultrommel** (G)—Small horseshoe shaped instrument of brass or steel with a thin vibrating tongue of metal, played between the teeth and struck with forefinger.
Jig (E), **giga** (I), **gigue** (F)—

Brisk dance in three-in-a-measure or six-in-a-measure-time.
Jodeln (G)—Style of singing peculiar to the Tyrolese peasants.
Jongleur (F)—Wandering musicians of the early middle ages.
Joropo—Characteristic dance of Venezuela in 3/4 time.
Jota—S. national dance in triple time and rapid movement.
Jouer (F)—To play.
Jovialisch (G)—Jovial.
Juba—Am. Negro dance.
Jubel-lied (G)—Song of jubilation.
Jubilate (L)—100th Psalm in Anglican liturgy.
Jubilee—Season of great joy and festivity.
Jubiloso (I)—Jubilant.
Jupiter Symphony—Mozart's symphony in C major, K. V. 551 (1788).
Juste (F), **giusto** (I)—Exact in time and pitch.
Just intonation—Precise pitch.

— K —

K., K. V. (Abb)—Köchel verzeichnis
Kadenz (G)—Cadence; cadenza.
Kalevala—Finnish national epic.
Kalt (G)—Cold.
Kammer (G)—Chamber.
Kammerkonzert (G)—Chamber concert.
Kammermusik (G)—Chamber music.
Kammermusiker (G)—Player in a prince's private orchestra.
Kanon (G)—Canon.
Kantate (G)—Cantata.
Kapelle (G)—Chapel.
Kapellmeister (G)—Choir-master.
Katzenmusik (G)—Charivari.
Kaum (G)—Barely.
Kazoo (E), **mirliton** (F)—Toy musical instrument.
Keck (G)—Bold.
Keckheit (G)—Boldness.
Kehraus (G)—Last dance.
Kent Bugle—A bugle with six keys, four commanded by the right hand, two by the left.
Keraulophon (G)—8 ft. organ stop of reedy tone.
Kesselpauke, kesseltrommel (G)—Kettledrum.
Kettledrums (E), **timpani** (I)—Percussion instruments composed of metal half-spheres covered with sheepskin over open end.
Key (Mechanical)—Lever which sounds the pitch in many instruments.
Key (Tonal)—Scale.
Keyboard—Rows of keys upon organ, piano, etc.
Keynote—Tonic (first) note of every scale.
Keys, pedal—Keys belonging to an organ acted upon by the feet.
Key signature—Signs written on the staff at the beginning of a composition.
Kielflügel (G)—Harpsichord.
Kindermusik (G)—Children's music.
Kindlich (G)—Childlike.
Kirche (G)—Church.
Kirchen musik (G)—Church music
Kit (E), **pochette** (F)—Small pocket violin formerly used by dancing masters.
Kithara—Foremost instrument of ancient Greece.
Kl. (Abb)—Klarinette.

Klagend (G)—Plaintive.
Klang (G)—Sound.
Klangfarbe (G)—Tone color.
Klappe (G)—Key of a wind instrument.
Klar (G)—Clear, bright.
Klarinette (G)—Clarinet.
Klausel (G)—Cadence.
Klaviatur (G)—Keyboard.
Klavier (G)—Any keyboard instrument.
Klaviermässig—Suitable for the piano.
Klein (G)—Minor intervals; small.
Kleine oktave (G)—Octave from c - b.
Klein-gedackt (G)—Small covered organ stop; stopped flute.
Klingbar, klingen, klingend (G)—Resonant.
Knabenstimme (G)—Counter-tenor.
Knarre (G)—Rattle.
Knee-stop—Knee-lever beneath the manual of the reed organ.
Köchel catalog—Chronological list of Mozart's works.
Komponieren (G)—To compose.
Kontrapunkt (G)—Counterpoint.
Kontretanz (G)—Contredanse.
Konzert (G)—Concert.
Konzertmeister (G)—Concert master.
Konzertstück (G)—One-movement concerto.
Kopfstimme (G)—Head voice.
Koppel (G)—Coupler.
Kräftig (G)—Powerful.
Krakoviak, crakovienne—Polish dance in 2/4 time.
Kreisleriana—8 "Fantasien" composed by Schumann (1838).
Kreuz (G)—Sharp (#).
Kreuz-doppeltes (G)—Double sharp (𝄪).
Kriegerisch (G)—Martial.
Kriegslied, kriegsgesang (G)—War song.
Krummhorn (G), **cromorne** (F)—Double reed woodwind; organ stop.
Kujawiak—Polish dance variety of the mazurka.
Kunstlied (G)—Art song with words following the music specially composed for them.
Kurz (G)—Short.
K. V. (Abb)—Köchel Verzeichnis.
Kyrie eleison (Gr)—First section of the R. C. Mass.

— L —

L (Abb)—Left hand.
La—Sixth step in the typical diatonic scale of C.
La bémol (F)—A flat (A♭).
Labial—Organ pipes with lips.
Lacrimosa (L)—Division of the Requiem Mass.
La dièse (F)—A sharp (A♯).
Lage (G)—Chord or hand position.
Lagenwechsel (G) — Change of position.
Lagnoso (I)—Doleful.
Lagrimoso (I)—Weeping.
Lament—Scotch and Irish music for bagpipes.
Lamentando, lamentoso (I)—Mournfully.
Lamentations—Funeral music of the ancient Jews.
Lamentevole (I)—Lamentable.
Lancers (E), **lanciers** (F)—Quadrilles.
Ländler (G)—Austrian folk dance similar to a slow waltz.
Landlich (G)—Rural.

Landlied (G)—Rural song.
Lang (G)—Long.
Langsam (G)—Slow.
Langsamer (G)—Slower.
Languendo, languente, longuido (I)—Languishingly.
La Poule (F)—Haydn's Symphony in G Minor, no. 83 (1786).
La Reine (F)—Haydn's Symphony in B Flat, no. 86 (1786).
Largamente, largamento (I)—Broadly, fully.
Largando (I)—Growing broader and slower.
Large (E), **maxima** (L)—In ancient measured music, 8 whole notes.
Larghetto (I)—Faster than largo, but still slow and broad.
Larghissimo (I)—Slower than largo.
Largo (I)—Very slow tempo.
Largo assai (I)—Prior to 19th c., slow enough; after 19th c., very slow.
Largo di molto (I)—Very slow and broad.
Largo ma non troppo (I)—Slow and broad, but not too much.
Larigot (F)—Shepherd's pipe.
Larynx—Upper part of the trachea, across which are stretched the vocal chords, the vibrations of which produce sound.
Laryngoscope—Instrument for examining the larynx.
Lauda (I)—Praise.
Laudamus Te (L)—Part of the Gloria of the R. C. Mass.
Laudes—Part of matins, one of the canonical hours of the R. C. Church.
Laudi—Devotional songs of early Italy.
Lauds—Cf. Laudes.
Lauf, läufer (G)—Rapid passage.
Launedda—Sardinian triple clarinet.
Launig (G)—Capricious.
Laut (G)—Loud.
Laute (G)—Lute.
Lautenclavicymbel—Harpsichord with gut strings.
Le (F)—The.
Lead—Leading part; announcement of subject or theme.
Leader—First violin in an orchestra; conductor.
Leading chord—One that leads toward the tonic.
Leading note—Major seventh; the semitone below the keynote.
Leaning note—Appoggiatura.
Leap—Skip.
Leben (G)—Life, vivacity.
Lebendig, lebhaft (G)—Lively.
Leçon (F)—Lesson or exercises.
Ledger lines—Short lines through the stem of notes too high or low to be represented on the staff.
Leere Saite (G)—Open string.
Leg. (Abb)—Legato.
Legatissimo (I)—Exceedingly smooth.
Legato (I)—Notes played without interruption between them, indicated by a slur (⌢).
Legatura (I)—Bind.
Légende (F)—Legend.
Léger, légère (F)—Lightly.
Legg. (Abb)—Leggiero.
Leggiadra (I)—Graceful.
Leggiero (I)—Delicately.
Legni (I)—Woodwinds.
Legno (I)—Wood.
Legno, col (I)—Direction to tap the strings with the bow stick.
Leichenmusik (G)—Funeral music.

Leicht (G)—Light.
Leicht bewegt (G)—Emotionally.
Leichtfertig (G)—Carelessly.
Leid (G)—Sorrow.
Leidenschaftlich (G)—Passionate.
Leidvoll (G)—Mournfully.
Leier (G)—Lyre.
Leierkasten (G)—Street organ.
Leise (G)—Soft.
Leiter (G)—Leader.
Leitmotif(v) (G) — A musical theme or phrase associated with a character, thought or action in the modern music-drama.
Leitton (G)—Leading tone.
Lent, lentement (F), **lento, lentament** (I)—Slowly.
Lentando (I)—Slowly.
Lentissimo (I)—Extremely slow.
Lento (I)—Slow.
Lento assai (I)—Cf. Largo assai.
Lento di molto (I)—Very slow.
Leonora Overtures—Three overtures which Beethoven wrote before his final overture for Fidelio.
Lesser—Minor.
Lesson—Exercise.
Lestezza (I)—Quickness.
Lesto (I)—Lively.
Letzter, letzte (G)—Last.
Leva il sordino (I)—Lift the mute.
Levare (I)—To lift.
L. H. (Abb)—Left hand.
Liaison (F)—Tie.
Libero (I)—Unrestrained.
Libitum (L)—At the performer's pleasure.
Librement (F)—Freely.
Libretto (I)—Text of an opera or extended piece of music.
Licenza (I)—Freedom.
Liceo (I)—Conservatory.
Lié (F)—Tied.
Liebesfuss (G)—Pear shaped bell of the E. horn.
Liebesleid (G)—Love song.
Lieblich (G)—Charming.
Lieblich-gedackt (G)—Stopped diapason organ register.
Lied (G)—Song.
Liedchen, liedlein (G)—Little song.
Liederbuch (G)—Song book.
Liedercyclus, liederkreis (G)—Song cycle.
Liederkranz (G)—Choral society.
Liederkreis (G)—Song cycle.
Lieder ohne worte (G)—Songs without words.
Liedform (G)—Song form.
Lieto (I)—Happy.
Lievemente (I)—Lightly.
Ligature—Slur, tie, bind.
Line (E), **linea** (I), **ligne** (F), **linie** (G)—Continuity of a musical piece.
Lingua (I)—Tongue.
Linke hand (G)—Left hand.
Linz Symphony—Mozart's Symphony in C, no. 36, K. V. 425, (1783).
Lip (E), **ansatz** (G), **embouchure** (F)—Mouthpiece of an instrument; adjustment of the lips to the mouthpiece.
Lippenpfeife (G)—Labial pipe.
Lira (I)—Early bowed instrument similar to the violin.
Lira da braccio (I)—A lyre played while resting on the arm.
Lida da gamba (I)—Lyre played between the knees.
Lirico (I)—Songlike.
Liscio (I)—Simple, unadorned.
Lispelnd (G)—Lisping.
L'istesso, lo stesso (I)—The same.
L'istesso tempo (I)—Same pace.
Litany—Form of supplication in

public worship.

Liturgy—Prescribed form of worship.

Liuto (I)—Lute.

Livre (F)—Book.

Livret (F)—Libretto.

Lo (I)—The.

Lob-gesang (G)—Song of praise.

Loco, luogo (I)—Return to the original place after playing in another register.

Lohengrin—Opera by Wagner (1846-1848).

Loin, lointain (F), lontano (I)—Remote.

London Symphonies—Last 12 symphonies of Haydn.

Long (E), longa (L)—Formerly four whole notes.

Long meter—Four lines in iambic measure, each line containing 8 syllables.

Lontano (I), loin, lointain (F)—Remote.

Lo stesso tempo (I)—Same pace.

Lösung (G)—Solution.

Lourd (F)—Heavy.

Loure (F)—An old slow, dignified dance in 3 or 6 quarter notes to the measure.

Luftpause (G)—Breathing space.

Lugubre (I)—Lugubrious.

Lullaby—Cradle song.

Lunga (I)—Long.

Lunga pausa—Long pause or rest.

Lusing. (Abb)—Lusingando.

Lusingando, lusinghevole, lusinghiero (I)—Coaxing.

Lustig (G)—Happily.

Lute—Ancient stringed instrument played by plucking the strings.

Lutherie (F) — Art of making stringed instruments.

Luthier (F)—Maker of stringed instruments.

Luttuoso (I)—Sorrowful.

Lydian mode—Gr. octave scale.

Lyre—Ancient stringed instrument.

Lyric, lyrical—Melodius.

Lyric drama—Opera.

Lyric opera—Ballad opera.

Lyric soprano (E), soprano leggiero (I)—Light, female voice.

Lyric tenor (E), tenor leggiero (I)—Light, male tenor.

— M —

M (Abb) — Mezzo, metronome, mano, main, manual.

Ma (I), mais (F), aber (G)—But.

Mächtig (G)—Mighty.

Madrigal—Polyphonic vocal composition in 2 or more voices without accompaniment.

Madrigal Comedy—16th c. play set to music in the form of madrigals.

Maelzel Metronome — Instrument which can be set to tick beats at various speeds.

Maestevole (I)—Majestic.

Maestoso (I)—Dignified.

Maestro (I)—Director.

Maestro del coro (I)—Choral conductor.

Maestro di canto (I)—Singing teacher.

Maestro di cappella (I), kapellmeister (G), maître de chapelle (F)—Choirmaster.

Magadis—Ancient Gr. harp with 20 strings.

Magg. (Abb)—Maggiore.

Maggiolata (I)—May songs.

Maggiore (I)—Major key.

Magnificat (L)—Part of vespers

of the R. C. Church.

Main (F), mano (I)—Hand.

Main droite (F)—Right hand.

Main gauche (F)—Left hand.

Maître (F)—Teacher.

Maître de chapelle (F)—Conductor.

Maître de musique (F)—Music teacher.

Maîtrise (F)—School of Church Music.

Majeur (F), maggiore (I), dur (G)—Major key.

Major—Greater in reference to intervals, scales and chords.

Major cadence—Cadence ending on a major triad.

Major scale—Diatonic scale with half steps between the third and fourth, seventh and eighth tones.

Major triad—A three-tone chord composed of a root, the major and perfect fifth above.

Mal (F)—Bad.

Mal (G)—Time.

Malagueña—Popular S. dance.

Malincolico, malinconia (I)—Melancholy.

Malinconico (I)—Melancholic.

Man. (Abb)—Manual.

Manc. (Abb)—Mancando.

Mancando (I)—Decreasing.

Mancante (I)—Dying away.

Manche (F), manico (I)—Neck of a stringed instrument.

Mandola (I)—Large size mandolin.

Mandolin(e) (E)—Pear shaped instrument with 8 strings tuned in pairs, fingered the same as the violin but having a fretted keyboard. It is played with a plectrum.

Manica (I)—Shift of position in violin playing.

Manico (I)—Fingerboard of the violin.

Manier (G)—Ornaments.

Maniera (I), manière (F)—Style.

Manifold fugue—Fugue with more than one subject.

Männerchor (G)—Men's chorus.

Männergesangverein (G) — Male choral society.

Mano (I)—Hand.

Mano destra (I), main droite (F), rechte hand (G)—Right hand.

Mano sinistra (I), main gauche (F), linke hand (G)—Left hand.

Manual—Keyboard.

Manualiter (G)—Organ piece to be played without the pedals.

Manualkoppel (G)—Manual coupler.

Manubrio—Knobs and handles of organ stops.

Marc. (Abb)—Marcato.

Marcando, marcato (I)—Marked, accented.

March (E), marche (F), marcia (I), marsch (G)—Military air adapted to martial instruments, usually with 4 beats to the measure.

Marche funèbre (F), marcia funebre (I)—Funeral march.

Marche militare (F) — Military march.

Märchen (G)—Fairytale.

Marimba—Percussion instrument having graduated wooden blocks which are struck by mallets.

Markieren (G), marquer (F)—To emphasize.

Markig (G)—Vigorous.

Marseillaise (F)—Song of the F. Revolution.

Martellato (I), martelé (F)—Strongly marked.

Marziale (I)—Martial.

Mask, maske (G), masque (F)—16th-18th c. musical drama or operetta combining poetry, singing, dancing performed in masks.

Mass—Vocal composition performed during the celebration of High Mass in the R. C. Church, the principal divisions being Kyrie, Gloria, Credo, Sanctus, Benedictus, Agnus Dei.

Mässig (G)—Moderate.

Massima (I), maxima (L)—Largest.

Matinée (F), mattinata (I)—Morning song.

Matins—First of the R. C. canonical hours.

Maultrommel (G)—Jew's harp.

Maxixe—Brazilian dance in duple meter with syncopated rhythms.

Mazeppa—Opera by Tschaikovsky (1883).

Mazurka—Polish national dance in 3/4 time.

M. D. (Abb)—Mano destra.

Me (E), mi (F-I)—Third step in the typical diatonic scale of C.

Measure—Division of time in music by which movements are regulated; space between 2 bar lines.

Measure, compound—A measure having more than one accent, the main accent being on the first beat.

Measure, simple—A measure having one accent, that being on the first beat.

Medesimo (I), meme (F)—Same.

Mediant (L)—Third note of the typical diatonic scale of C.

Medley (E), mélange (F), mescolanza (I)—Mixture of tunes.

Mehr (G)—More.

Mehrere (G)—Several.

Mehstimmig (G)—Polyphonic.

Meistersinger (G)—Guilds of poets and singers in Germany from the 14th-16th c.

Melisma (Gr)—Vocal ornamentation; vocal cadenza.

Melodeon, melodium, cabinet organ—American reed organ, the air being blown in, the reeds smaller and the tone softer.

Melodia (I)—Melody.

Melodic—Pertaining to melody.

Melodic minor scale—Minor scale with ascending half steps between the second and third, seventh and eighth degree and having a raised sixth. Descending the half steps lie between the sixth and fifth, third and second degrees.

with musical accompaniment.

Melodrama—Dramatic presentation with musical accompaniment.

Melody—Musical sounds arranged to produce a pattern having a pleasing effect upon the hearer.

Melos (Gr)—Song.

Même (F), medesimo (I)—Same.

Men, meno (I)—Less.

Ménestrandise—Early F. professional musicians guilds.

Meno mosso (I)—Slower.

Mensural music—Music written in mensural notes (13th c.).

Mensural notes (13th c.)—All notes and rests are given a definite time value, these being maxima, longa, brevis, semibrevis, minima and semiminima.

Mente, alla (I)—Improvised.

Menuetto (I), menuett (G), menuet (F)—Stately F. court dance in 3/4 time.

Mescolanza (I)—Medley.

Messa (I), messe (F-G)—Mass; R. C. service.

Messa di voce (I), mise de voix (F)—Gradual increase and decrease of the vocal tone. (< >).

Mesto (I)—Sadly.

Mesure (F)—Measure, meter, strict time.

Meta (I) Half.

Meter, metre—Rhythm of phrase; symmetrical arrangement of rhythmic units.

Meter, common—4 line stanza in iambic pentameter, the syllable order being 8,6,8,6.

Meter, eights and sevens—4 lines in trochaic measure, the syllable order being 8,7,8,7.

Meter, hallelujah—6 line stanza in iambic measure, the syllable order being 6,6,6,6,8,8.

Meter, long—4 lines in iambic measure, each line having 8 syllables.

Meter, sevens—4 lines in trochaic measure, each line having 7 syllables.

Meter, sevens and sixes—4 iambic lines, the syllable order being 7,6,7,6.

Meter, short—Four lines in iambic measure, the syllable order being 6,6,8,6.

Metronom, metronome — Instrument for measuring the duration of notes by means of a graduated scale and pendulum.

Metronome marks—Directions for setting the metronome.

Mette (G)—Matins.

Mettre d'accord (F)—To tune.

Mettre en musique (F)—To put to music.

Mettre en répétition (F)—To put in rehearsal.

Mettre la sourdine (F)—To use the mute.

Mez. (Abb)—Mezzo.

Mezza, mezzo (I)—Half.

Mezza voce (I), demi voix (F)—Half volume.

Mezzo forte (I)—Half as loud.

Mezzo piano (I)—Half as soft.

Mezzo soprano (I), bas-dessus (F)—Female voice between soprano and alto.

Mezzo tenore (I)—Low tenor.

mf. (Abb)—Mezzo forte.

M. G. (Abb)—Main gauche.

Mi (I-F)—Third note of the major scale.

Mi bémol (F)—E flat (E♭).

Mi bémol mineur (F)—E flat minor.

Middle C—C between the bass and treble staffs.

Mi Dièse (F)—E sharp (E♯).

Militare (I)—Martial style.

Military band—Group of players on wind, brass and percussion instruments.

Military music—Music for military bands (marches, quicksteps, etc.).

Milonga—Argentinian dance.

Mimodrame—Pantomime.

Minacciando, minaccievole, minaccioso (I)—Menacing.

Mineur (F)—Minor.

Minim (L)—Half note (♩).

Minim rest—Half rest.

Minnesinger (G)—12th-13th c. G. troubadours who specialized in love songs.

Minor (E), mineur (F), minore (I), moll (G)—Smaller.

Minor interval—Interval a half step smaller than a major interval.

Minor scale, Harmonic—Scale with half steps between the second and third, fifth and sixth, seventh and eighth degrees, ascending and descending.

Minor scale, Melodic—Scale with half steps between the second and third, seventh and eighth degrees ascending and between the sixth and fifth, third and second descending.

Minor triad — Three-tone chord composed of a root tone, the minor third and perfect fifth above.

Minstrels — Troubadours of the Middle Ages; modern black-face comedy.

Minuet (E), menuet (F), minuetto (I)—Stately F. court dance in 3/4 time.

Mirliton (F)—Kazoo.

Mise-en-scène (F)—Stage setting.

Miserere (L)—Psalm of supplication, principally used in Holy Week.

Missa (L)—Mass.

Missal—Book containing the text of the R. C. Mass.

Misterioso (I)—Mysteriously.

Misura (I)—Measure.

Misurato, alla misura (I)—Strict time.

Mit (G)—With, by.

Mit verschiebung (G), una corda (I), petite pédale (F)—Direction to use the una corda pedal of the the piano.

Mixed cadence — Cadence having the last 3 or 4 chords dominant, subdominant and tonic harmonies.

Mixed chorus—Both male and female voices used together.

Mixed voices—Cf. Mixed chorus.

Mixolydian mode—Gr. octave scale, ecclesiastical mode named from the Gr.

Mixture stop—Organ stop having 3 or more ranks of pipes voiced to sound the harmonies of any note played.

M. M. (Abb)—Maelzel's Metronome.

Mobile (I)—Changeable.

Mod. (Abb)—Moderato.

Modal—Pertaining to modes.

Modaltheorie (G)—Modal interpretation.

Mode—System of sounds by which the octave is divided into certain intervals, according to genus.

Mode, major—Mode in which the third degree from the key note forms a major interval.

Mode, minor—Mode in which the third degree from the keynote forms a minor interval.

Moderato (I), modéré (F)—Moderately.

Modes, Church—Ancient modes: Dorian, Phrygian, Lydian, Mixolydian, Aeolian, Ionian, Iastian.

Modes, ecclesiastical—Ancient Ch. modes.

Modulation—Transition of key.

Modulation, abrupt—Sudden transition into keys not closely related to the original key.

Modulation, chromatic—Transition effected by means of chromatic intervals.

Modulation, deceptive—Modulation by which the ear is deceived and led to an unexpected harmony.

Modulation diatonic — Transition effected by means of related diatonic intervals.

Modulation, enharmonic — Transition effected by altering the notation of one or more intervals of some characteristic chord.

Möglich (G)—Possible.

Moins (F)—Less.

Moins vite (F)—Slower.

Moitié (F)—Half.

Moll (G)—Minor.

Molto (I)—Very.

Molto adagio (I)—Very slow.

Molto allegro (I)—Very fast.

Molto espressivo (I)—Very expressively.

Monacordo (I)—16th c. term for clavichord.

Mondscheinsonate (G)—Moonlight Sonata.

Monochord—Ancient single-stringed instrument; one stringed zither.

Monody (E)—Composition for one voice.

Monotone—Unvarying tone.

Monter (F)—To ascend; to string; to tune.

Moonlight Sonata — Beethoven's Sonata Quasi Una Fantasia, op. 27, no. 2.

Mor. (Abb)—Morendo.

Morbido (I)—Gentle.

Morceau (F)—Musical piece.

Mordent (I)—Group of 2 or more grace notes played rapidly before a principal note, indicated by ∿ over the principal note calling for the upper auxiliary or ∿ for the lower auxiliary.

Morendo (I)—Dying.

Moresca, morisco (I) — Moorish dance.

Mormorando, mormoroso (I)—Murmuringly.

Morris dance—E. country dance in duple time.

Mosso (I)—Moved.

Mosso, meno (I)—Slower.

Mosso, più (I)—Quicker.

Motet (E), motetto (I)—Sacred composition, generally contrapuntal.

Motif (F), motiv (G), motive (E), motivo (I)—Short melodic pattern.

Motion—Progression of a melody or part.

Motion, conjunct—Stepwise motion of a voice.

Motion, contrary—Motion in which one of two voices ascends, the other descending.

Motion, oblique—Motion in which one voice moves, the other remaining stationary.

Motion, parallel—Motion in which two voices move in the same direction at the same interval.

Motion, similar—Motion in which two voices move in the same direction.

Motive—Theme or subject of a composition.

Moto (I)—Motion.

Moto, con—Quick.

Moto perpetuo (I), perpetuum mobile (L), mouvement perpétuel (F)—Rapidity in execution.

Mouth harmonica—Graduated metal reeds in a narrow frame blown by the mouth to produce different tones.

Mouth-piece—Part of a wind instrument applied to the lips.

Mouvement (F), movimento (I)—Motion.

Mouvementé (F)—Animated.

Mouvement modéré (F)—Moderately fast.

Movable do—System having do as the first note of every typical diatonic scale.

Movement—Any portion of a composition comprehended under the same general measure or time.

Movente (I)—Moving.

mp. (Abb)—Mezzo piano.

M. S. (Abb)—Mano sinistra.

Müde (G)—Tired, languid.

Mühelos (G)—Effortless.

Mundharmonika (G)—Mouth organ.

Munter (G)—Lively.

Murmelnd (G), **mormorando** (I)—Murmuring.

Mus. B., Mus. Bac. (Abb)—Bachelor of Music.

Mus. D., Mus. Doc. (Abb)—Doctor of Music.

Musetta (I), **musette** (F-E)—Small bagpipe; organ stop; primitive oboe; alternate composition for a gavotte in classical suites.

Music (E), **musica** (I), **musik** (G), **musique** (F)—Art and science of expression in sound.

Musica di camera (I)—Chamber music.

Music drama—Music based on text and dramatic action.

Musicology—Science of musical research.

Muta (I)—Directive to change key.

Mutation—Change of voice at adolescence.

Mutation stops—Stops which give no corresponding tone to the key pressed down.

Mute (E), **sordino** (I), **sourdine** (F), **dämpfer** (G)—A clamp for muffling instrumental tone.

Muthig (G)—Bold.

M. V.—Mezza voce.

Mystic chord—Chord with fourths instead of thirds.

— N —

Nacaire (F), **nacara** (I)—Brass drum with a loud metallic tone.

Nacchere (I)—Castanets.

Nach (G)—After.

Nachahmung (G)—Imitation.

Nach belieben (G)—According to the performer.

Nachdruck, nachdrücklich, nachdrucksvoll (G)—Emphatic.

Nachfolge (G)—Imitation.

Nachlassend (G)—Slackening.

Nachlässig (G)—Carelessly.

Nachschlag (G)—After note.

Nachspiel (G)—Postlude.

Nachthorn (G)—Organ stop of 8 ft. tone.

Nachtmusik (G)—Serenade.

Nach und nach (G)—Little by little.

Nänien (G)—Dirges.

Narrator—One who recites the story in a composition.

National Anthem—Song adopted by a nation to be played at official functions.

National music—Music which is peculiarly characteristic of its own country as opposed to that of other countries.

Natural—A sign (♮) used to cancel a sharp or a flat; a note neither sharpened nor flatted.

Natural horn—Old F. horn without valves or keys.

Naturalmente (I)—Naturally.

Natural keys—Those having no sharp or flat at the signature (E major; A minor).

Naturhorn (G)—Natural horn.

Neopolitan sixth—Chord composed of the minor third and sixth above, occurring on the fourth degree of the scale.

Neck—That part of an instrument in the violin family holding the the fingerboard.

Negli, nei, nel, nella, nelle, nello, nell' (I)—In the, at the.

Negligente (I)—Indifferent.

Negligenza (I)—Negligence.

Negro spirituals—Religious songs of the slaves, now a part of America folksong.

Neighbor-tone—Appoggiatura.

Neo-classicism—Modern imitation of 18th c. classic music.

Nero (I), **noire** (F)—Quarter note (♩).

Nettement (F)—Clearly.

Netto. (I)—Quick.

Neu (G)—New.

Neuf (F)—Nine.

Neuvième (F) **neunte** (G), **nona** (I)—Ninth.

Nexus (L)—Tie.

Nicht (G)—Not.

Nicht schleppen (G)—Do not drag.

Niederschlag (G)—Accented part of a measure.

Niederstrich (G)—Downbow (⊓ ⊔).

Niente (I)—Nothing.

Nineteenth—An organ stop tuned two octaves plus a fifth from the diapason.

Ninth (E), **none** (G), **neuvième** (F) **nona** (I)—Interval of an octave and a second.

Nobile (I)—Noble, grand.

Noch (G)—Still.

Nocturn nocturne (F), **notturno** (I)—Evening music.

Nodal points, nodes—The points of rest or of minimum amplitude in a vibrating string.

Noel (F)—Christmas carol.

Noire (F), **nero** (I)—Quarter note (♩).

Noise—Sound made by irregular vibrations.

Non (I-F)—Not, no.

Nones (L)—Canonical hour of the R. C. Church.

Nonet (E), **nonetto** (I)—Composition for 9 performers.

Non troppo (I)—Not too much.

Normal pitch, normal tone—Standard reference in acoustics, having a fixed number of vibrations per second.

Nota cambiata (I), **wechselnote** (G)—A note not in immediate harmony.

Notation—Music expressed in writing.

Notehead—The principal part of the notes as opposed to the stem and hook.

Notes de passage (F)—Grace notes.

Notturno (I)—Nocturne.

Nourrir le son (F)—To hold a note.

Novellette—Designation introduced by Schumann for free, romantic, instrumental pieces.

Nozze di Figaro, Le (F)—The Marriage of Figaro, a comic opera in 4 acts by Mozart (1786).

Nuance (F)—Variety in tempo, intensity or tone color.

Nunc dimittis (L)—Canticle of the R. C. Church.

Nuovo (I)—New.

Nuptial song—Wedding song.

Nut—A bridge at the upper end of the fingerboard of a violin over which the strings pass.

Nutcracker Suite—Suite by Tschaikovsky, op. 71a, (1891).

— O —

O (Abb)—Indication of an open string; sign for harmonic tone; directive to use the thumb on cello; medieval notation for triple time.

O, od (I)—Or.

Ob. (Abb)—Oboes.

Obb. (Abb)—Obbligato.

Obbligato (I), **obligé** (F), **obligat** (G)—Formerly, parts which could not be omitted; now, accompanying parts which may be omitted.

Ober (G)—Upper.

Oberstimme (G)—Upper part.

Ober-manual (G)—Upper manual.

Oberton—Upper harmonic.

Oberwerk (G)—Swell-organ.

Oblique motion—A piece in which one part moves while the other remains stationary.

Oboe (E-I-G), **hautboy** (E), **hautbois** (F)—Double reed wind instrument with a conical tube.

Oboe, alto—E. horn.

Oboe, bass—Bassoon.

Oboe d'amore (I)—Transposing woodwind with a range between the treble oboe and the E. horn.

Oboe da caccia (I)—A large oboe with music written in the alto clef.

Obw., oberw. (Abb)—Oberwerk.

Ocarina (I)—A wind instrument in the shape of a sweet potato with a mouthpiece and fingerholes.

Octave—Eighth tone of the diatonic scale.

Octave coupler—A device used on organs to add the upper or lower octave as needed to the notes actually played.

Octave, fifteenth—Organ stop of sharp tone, an octave above the fifteenth.

Octave flute (E), **piccolo** (I)—A small flute having a range an octave higher than the flute.

Octave hautboy—4 ft. organ reed stop.

Octavo music—Music printed on one large sheet folded into 8 leaves.

Octet, octett—Composition for 8 parts or voices.

Octuplet—Group of 8 equal notes having the time of 6 of the same value.

Ode—Heroic lyric poem.

Oder (G)—Or, or else.

Ode Symphonie—Beethoven's Symphony No. 9.

Oeuvre (F)—Opus, work.

Off—Directive to push in an organ stop.

Off-beat—Unaccented beat.

Offertory (E), **offertorium** (L)—Prayer sung or played during the collection of the offering.

Office, officium—The service of the hours of the R. C. Church.

Ohne (G)—Without.

Oiseau de Feu, L'—The Firebird Suite by Stravinsky.

Oktave (G)—Octave.

Oliphant—Medieval instrument for signaling, usually made of elephant tusks.

Ombra scene (I)—Operatic scene depicting Hades or similar sur-

MUSIC DICT

Omnes, omnia (L), **tutti** (I)—All.

Omnitonic—Instrument producing all tones, chromatic and diatonic.

Ondeggiando (I), **ondulé** (F)—Swaying.

Ongarese All' (I) — Hungarian style.

Onzième (F)—Eleventh interval.

Op. (Abb)—Opus.

Open—Not stopped (string) or closed (pipe).

Open diapason—Most important organ stop, commanding the whole scale.

Open fifth, open triad—Triad without the third.

Open notes—Notes produced without stopping the strings of an instrument, or without valves, crooks or keys.

Open pedal—Pedal which raises dampers and allows string vibration to continue.

Open string—String not pressed down by the finger.

Open unison stop—Open diapason stop.

Oper (G), **opera** (E-I)—Drama set to music.

Opera, ballad—18th & 19th c. E. musical comprised of folk songs with new words and much dialogue.

Opéra bouffe (F)—Light comic opera.

Opera buffa (I)—Classical I. comic opera.

Opera chamber (E), **kammeroper** (G)—Opera with smal chorus and orchestra.

Opera comique (F)—Drama, not necessarily comic, set to music and having spoken words.

Operetta—Little opera in a light vein.

Ophicleide—Large brass wind instrument.

Ophicleide stop — Most powerful manual reed stop.

Op. (Abb)—Opus.

Opp. (Abb)—Oppure.

Oppure (I)—Or, or else.

Opus (L-G)—Work, composition.

Orageux (F)—Stormy.

Oratorio—Religious composition performed in a concert hall or church by solo voices, chorus and orchestra.

Orchester (G), **orchestra** (I), **orchestre** (F)—Body of performers on string instruments, or string instruments in conjunction with other instruments.

Orchestration—Arranging of music for an orchestra.

Orchestrion—Large mechanical instrument having various organ pipes, reeds, bells, etc.

Ordinaire (F), **ordinario** (I)—Ordinary.

Ordres (F)—Suites.

Orrechiante (I)—Playing by ear.

Org. (Abb)—Organ.

Organ, pipe—Keyboard instrument having a series of pipes on a wind chest supplied with valves operated by the keys through a purely mechanical apparatus.

Organpoint, pedal point—A sustained note upon which is formed a series of chords or harmonic progressions.

Organum (L)—First attempts at harmony in which two parts progressed in parallel fourths and fifths.

Orgel (G), **orgue** (F), **organo** (I)—Organ.

Orgelpunkt (G)—Organ point.

Orgue (F)—Organ.

Ornamental notes, ornaments—Embellishments.

Osservanza (I)—Observation.

Ossia (I)—Alternative version.

Ostinato (I)—Recurring.

Otello—Opera in 4 acts by Giuseppi Verdi (1887).

Otez (F)—Remove.

Otez la sourdine (F)—Remove the mute.

Ott. (Abb)—Ottava.

Ottava (I)—Octave; eighth.

Ottava alta—Octave above.

Ottava bassa (I)—Octave below.

Ottavino (I)—Piccolo.

Ottetto (I)—Octet.

Otto (I)—Eight.

Ottoni (I)—Brass instruments.

Ou (F)—Or.

Outer voices—Highest and lowest voices.

Ouvert (F)—Open.

Over blowing—Forcing wind so strongly into a wind instrument that a tone higher than the natural one is sounded.

Overture (E), **ouverture** (F), **preludio** (I), **vorspiel** (G)—Introduction to an opera, oratorio, drama, suite, etc.

Oxford Symphony—Haydn's Symphony No. 92 (1788).

Oxyrynchos Hymn—Earliest Christian hymn for which the music exists (300 A.D.).

— P —

P. (Abb)—Pedal, piano.

Pacato (I)—Peaceful.

Padovano pavan (I), **pavane** (F)—Stately I. dance named from the peacock.

Paean—Song of victory.

Pandean Pipes, Pan's pipes—Ancient instrument made of graduated reeds fastened together, stopped at the bottom and blown by mouth at the top.

Papillons (F)—12 short piano pieces by Robert Schumann.

Parallel intervals—Consecutive intervals.

Parallel keys—Major and minor founded on the same key notes.

Parallel motion—2 parts continuing their course at the same interval and in the same direction.

Paralleltonart (G)—Relative keys.

Paraphrase—Rearrangement of a composition intended for another musical medium.

Parlando, parlante (I)—Recitative; speaking style.

Paroles (F)—Words.

Parsifal—Opera in 3 acts by Richard Wagner (1882).

Part—Division of a composition; music for a separate voice or instrument.

Parte cantante (I)—Vocal part.

Partials—Tones that vibrate in ratio to tone, deriving its quality and timbre.

Parti di ripieno (I), **parties de remplissage** (F)—Fill in parts.

Partita (I)—Earliest form of instrumental suite.

Partition (F), **partitur** (G)—partitura (I)—Score.

Part-song—Song for 2 or more voices in harmony.

Pas (F)—Not; ballet step.

Pasacalle (S)—Gay Latin American dance.

Passacaglia (I), **passecaille** (F)—Slow dance with divisions on a ground bass in triple rhythm.

Pas de deux (F)—Dance for 2 performers.

Passage (E), **passaggio** (I)—Any division of a composition.

Passagio (I)—Transition.

Passamezzo (I)—Old slow dance in 2/4 rhythm.

Passecaille (F)—Cf. Passacaglia.

Passepied (F), **paspy** (E)—Lively jig in 3/8 or 6/8 time found in suites.

Pas seul (F)—Dance for one performer.

Passing notes—Notes foreign to the immediate harmony, but which connect those which are essential.

Passionato (I)—Impassioned.

Passion music—Music picturing the suffering and death of Christ.

Pasticcio (I), **pastiche** (F)—Medley of songs by various composers with poetry written to the music.

Pastoral, pastorale—Music depicting rural scenes.

Pastoral Symphony — Beethoven's Symphony No. 6, Opus 68 in F (1809).

Pastoso (I)—With pomp.

Pastourelle (F), **pastorela**—Songs of troubadours dealing with rural love scenes.

Patetica (I), **pathetique** (F), **pathetisch** (G)—Pathetic.

Pathetique — Beethoven's Pianoforte Sonata, Opus 13 (1799); Tschaikovsky's Symphony No. 6, Opus 74 (1893).

Patimento—Grief.

Patouille (F)—Xylophone.

Patter-song—Rapid comic song.

Pauken (G), **Timpani** (I)—Kettledrums.

Pauroso (I)—Timidly.

Pausa (I), **pause** (G-E) — Pause, rest.

Pavan (E), **pavana, padovano** (I)—Stately I. dance named from the peacock.

Paventato, paventoso (I)—Timorous.

Pavillon (F)—Bell of a wind instrument.

Pavillon chinois (F)—Instrument with many little bells.

Peal—Changes rung on a set of bells.

Ped. (Abb)—Pedal.

Pedal—Mechanism moved by the foot.
brass and percussion instruments.

Pedal clarinet—Double bass clarinet.

Pedal, damper—Right pedal of the piano which raises the dampers.

Pedal harp—Chromatic harp.

Pedalier (F)—Pedal board of the organ.

Pedalpauke (G) — Kettledrums tuned by pedals.

Pedal-point, organ-point—Sustained bass held while the other voices move above it.

Pedal, soft—Left pedal of the piano which lowers the tone.

Peg—Tuning pin.

Pelléas et Mélisande—Opera in 5 acts by Claude Debussy (1902).

Pentatonic scale—Five note scale, the fourth and seventh degrees being omitted.

Per (I)—For, by, from.

Percussion (E), percussione (I)—Instruments which are struck, e.g., cymbals, gongs.

Perd. (Abb)—Perdendosi.

Perdendosi—Dying away.

Perfect—Term applied to certain intervals and chords.

Perfect cadence—Cf. Cadence, perfect.

Perfect intervals—Unison, octave, fifth and fourth.

Perfect time—Triple measure in medieval music.

Period—Musical sentence having at least two phrases and a cadence.

Perpetual canon—Canon with no definite ending.

Perpetuum mobile (L), moto perpetuo (I)—Rapid piece having no pauses.

Pes. (Abb)—Pesante.

Pesante (I)—Heavy.

Petit (F)—Small.

Petite flûte (F)—Piccolo.

Petite pedale (F), una corda (I), mit verschiebung (G)—Directive to use the left pedal of the piano.

Petto (I), poitrine (F)—Chest.

Peu (F)—Little.

Pezzo (I), pièce (F), stück (G)—Piece.

PF (Abb)—Pianoforte; piano followed by forte.

Pfeife (G)—Fife; organ pipe.

Pfte. (Abb)—Pianoforte.

Phantasie (G)—Short romantic piece.

Phonetics—Science of representing sounds.

Phonofilm—Film on which sound is photographed for movies.

Phonograph—Instrument invented by Thomas A. Edison in 1897 which reproduces sound.

Phorminx—Kithara lyra.

Phrase—Dependent division of a musical sentence.

Phrasing—Division of musical sentences into rhythmical sections.

Phrygian mode—Gr. octave scale; ecclesiastical mode.

Piaceu (I)—Pleasure.

Piacevole (I)—Agreeable.

Pianamente (I)—Softly.

Piagnevole (I)—Mournful.

Piang. (Abb)—Piangendo.

Piangevole, piangendo (I)—Plaintive.

Pianino (G)—Upright piano.

Pianissimo (I)—Extremely soft.

Pianoforte—Keyboard, stringed instrument with tone produced by keyboard-controlled felt hammers striking the strings.

Pianola—Player piano.

Piano score—Orchestral score reduced for piano use.

Piano trio—Composition for piano, violin and trio.

Piatti (I)—Cymbals.

Pibroch—Music for the bagpipe.

Picchiettato (I), piqué (F), piquirt (G)—Violin stacatto.

Piccolo (I)—Little; small flute; organ stop.

Pick—Plectrum of bone, wood, ivory or metal used to pluck the strings of an instrument.

Pied (F)—Foot.

Piena, pieno (I)—Full.

Pieta (I)—Pity.

Pietoso (I)—Sympathetic.

Pincé (F), pizzicato (I)—Directive to pluck the strings of a bowed instrument with the fingers.

P'ip'a—Chinese short lute in the shape of a bottle.

Pipe—Any tube which being blown at one end produces sound.

Pitch—Acuteness or gravity of a tone in relation to others, or in the absolute measurement of the number and rate of its vibrations.

Pitch, concert—Pitch at 440 vibrations per second for A.

Pitch, international (E), diapason normal (F)—Pitch of 435 vibrations per second for A.

Pitch pipe—Small pipe used as an aid for tuning instruments.

Più (I)—More.

Più allegro (I)—Quicker.

Più forte (I)—Louder.

Più mosso (I)—Quicker.

Più stretto (I)—More hurried.

Più tosto (I)—Rather.

Pizz. (Abb)—Pizzicato.

Pizzicato—Directive to pluck the string of an instrument with the fingers.

Placido (I)—Placid.

Plagal cadence—Cf. Cadence, amen.

Plagal mode—Church mode in which the fourth tone upward is the final or keynote.

Plain chant, plain song—Unison, unaccompanied, unmeasured singing found in R. C. ritual.

Plaqué (F)—Played simultaneously and deliberately.

Plaudernd (G)—Babbling.

Plectrum—Small piece of bone, wood, ivory or metal used to pluck the strings of an instrument.

Plein-jeu—(F)—Full organ.

Plica—13th c. notation for an ornamental tone to be inserted between written notes.

Plötzlich (G)—Suddenly.

Plus (F)—More.

Pneumatic organ—Organ in which air pressure replaced direct mechanical action.

Pochette (F), kit (E)—Small pocket violin of 17th-19th c.

Pochettino, pochetto (I)—Very little.

Poco (I)—Little.

Poco a poco (I)—Little by little.

Poi (I)—Then, after.

Poi a poi (I)—By degrees.

Poi a poi tutte le corde (I)—Lift soft pedal gradually.

Point (F)—Upper end of the violin bow; dot; note.

Point d'orgue (F)—Pause and its sign (⌒); pedal point; cadenza.

Pointe (F)—Toe in organ playing.

Pointe d'archet (F)—Point of the bow.

Poitrine (F), petto (I), brust (G)—Chest.

Polacca (I), polonaise (F)—Polish national dance in 3/4 time.

Polka—Lively Bohemian folk dance in 2/4 time.

Polka mazurka—Slow dance in triple time accented on the last part of the measure.

Pollice (I), pouce (F)—Thumb.

Polonaise—Polish national dance in 3/4 time.

Polyphonic, polyphony—Music having two or more melodies carried on separately.

Polytonality—Simultaneous use of two or more tonalities.

Pomposo (I)—Pompous.

Ponderoso (I)—Ponderously.

Ponticello (I), chevalet (F), steg (G)—Bridge of a stringed instrument.

Portamento (I)—Gliding from one note to the next through all intermediate pitches.

Portar la battuta (I)—To follow the beat.

Portar la voce (I), porter la voix (F)—Vocal portamento.

Portata (I), portée (F)—Staff.

Portato (I)—Between legato and staccato.

Portunal-flaut (G)—An organ stop with pipes larger at top than at the bottom.

Pos. (Abb)—Posaune.

Posaune—Trombone; organ stop.

Posé (F)—Steady.

Positif (F), positiv (G) — Choir organ.

Position—Place taken by the left hand on fingerboard of any stringed instrument; place taken by the slide in trombone playing, a chord and its inversions.

Possibile (I)—Possible.

Posthumous work—Work published after the composer's death.

Postlude, postludium (L)—After piece.

Potpourri—Medley.

Pouce (F)—Thumb.

Pour (F)—For.

Pousé (F)—Upbow.

Poussez (F)—Speed up.

pp., ppp., (Abb)—Pianissimo.

Prachtvoll (G)—Grand, pompous.

Prague Symphony—Mozart's Symphony in D, K. V. 504 (1786).

Pralltriller (G)—Inverted mordent.

Precentor—Choirmaster.

Precipitato (I)—Hastily.

Preciso, precisione (I)—Precision.

Preghiera (I), pierè (F), gebet (G)—Prayer.

Prelude (E), prélude (F), vorspiel (G), preludio (I), praeludium (L)—Short introductory composition.

Première (F)—First performance.

Preparation—A dissonant note is prepared by sounding it in the preceding chord, and in the same part as a consonance.

Près (F)—Near.

Presque (F)—Almost.

Presser (F)—Accelerate.

Prestissimo (I)—Very quickly.

Presto (I)—Quickly.

Prick song—Early E. name for written or printed music.

Prière (F)—Prayer.

Prima (I)—First, principal.

Prima donna (I)—Principal female singer.

Primary accent—Accent at the beginning of a measure.

Primary chord—First chord; common chord.

Prima vista (I)—Sight reading.

Prima volta (I)—First time.

Prime—First note of a scale; a unison; canonical hours.

Primgeiger (G) — First violinist; concertmaster.

Primo (I)—Principal.

Principal (octave)—Organ stop an octave above the diapasons.

Principal bass—Organ stop of open diapason on the pedals.

Principio (I), anfang (G), commencement (F)—Beginning.

Prix de Rome—Annual prize awarded by the Institute de France to a Paris Conservatoire student.

Prix de Rome, American—Annual award given by the American

Academy in Rome.

Probe (G), **prova** (I), **répétition** (F)—Rehearsal.

Program music—Instrumental music describing a character or event or telling a story.

Progression, harmonic — Advance from one chord to another.

Progression, melodic — Advance from one tone to another.

Prologue—Introduction

Prolongement (F)—Sostenuto pedal of the pianoforte.

Prometheus — Beethoven's Ballet, Opus 43 (1801).

Pronto (I)—At once.

Pronunziato (I)—Pronounced.

Prooemium (L)—Humanistic.

Proposta (I)—Subject of a fugue.

Proslambanomenos (G) — Lowest tone A of the Gr. Scale.

Prova (I), **prope** (G), **repetition** (F)—Rehearsal.

Provencales—11th-13th c. troubadours.

Psalm (E), **psaume** (F)—Sacred song or hymn.

Psalmody—Psalm singing.

Psaltery—Ancient stringed instrument similar to the lyre; book of psalms.

Pult (G), **pupitre** (F) — Music stand.

Punctus (L), **punkt** (G), **punto** (I) —Dot.

Punta (I)—Point; top.

Punta d'arco (I)—Point of the bow.

Puntato (I)—Staccato.

Punto d'organo (I)—Organ-point.

Pyramidon—Organ stop invented by the Rev. F. A. G. Ously with its top four times wider than the mouth.

—Q—

Quadrat (G), **quadratum** (L), **quadro** (I), **becarre** (F) — Natural (♮).

Quadrille (F)—Square dance of 5 movements in 6/8 or 2/4 rhythm.

Quadruple counterpoint—Counterpoint in 4 voices.

Quadruple fugue—Fugue with 4 different subjects.

Quadruplet—Group of 4 notes to be played in the time of 3.

Quality—Timbre.

Quantity—Duration.

Quanto (I)—As much.

Quart (F), **quarta** (I), **quarte** (G) —Interval of the fourth.

Quart de mesure (F)—Quarter rest.

Quart de soupir (F)—Eighth rest.

Quarter note—One fourth duration of a whole note.

Quarter tone—Interval of half a semitone.

Quartet (E), **quartett** (G), **quartetto** (I)—Composition for four voices or instruments; group of four players or singers.

Quarto—Fourth.

Quartsextakkord (G)—Second inversion of the triad.

Quasi (I)—In the style of.

Quasi niente (I)—Very soft.

Quasi sonata (I)—In the style of a sonata.

Quatre (F), **quattro** (I)—Four.

Quatrième (F)—Fourth.

Quatuor (F)—Quartet.

Quaver (E), **croma** (I), **croche** (F), **achtel** (G)—Eighth note or rest.

Quelque (F)—Some.

Querflote (G)—Horizontal flute.

Queue (F)—Stem of a note.

Quickstep—Lively march in 6/8 time.

Quieto (I)—Quiet.

Quill—Plectra for harpsichord.

Quindezime (G)—Interval of the fifteenth.

Quint (L), **quinta** (I)—A fifth; organ stop sounding a fifth above its normal pitch.

Quintadena—Organ stop.

Quintaton (G) — Manual organ stop of 8 ft. tone.

Quinte—Fifth; tenor viol of 5 strings, a fifth lower than the violin.

Quintet (E), **quintett** (G), **quintetto** (I), **quintuor** (F)—Music for 5 voices or instruments.

Quinton (F)—18th c. F. violin.

Quintoyer (F)—Overblowing a wind instrument, causing a tone a fifth above the octave.

Quintsaite (G)—E string of the violin.

Quintuor (F)—Quintet.

Quintuple time—5 beats to a measure.

Qui tollis (L)—Part of the Gloria in the R. C. Mass.

Quitter (F)—To leave.

Quoniam tu solus (F)—Part of the Gloria of the R. C. Mass.

Qtte. (Abb)—Quartet.

Quodlibet—Several humorous tunes played successively.

— R —

R (Abb)—responsorium; clavier de récit.

Rabbia (I)—Rage.

Raccontando (I)—Recounting.

Raddolcendo (I)—Becoming dolce.

Raddoppiare (I)—To double.

Radical—Root of a chord.

Radleyer (G)—Hurdy-gurdy.

Raffrenando (I)—Slowing the speed.

Ragtime—Popular American music of the 1890's.

Rakoczy March—Hung. national anthem by Janos Bihari (1809).

Rall. (Abb)—Rallentando.

Rallentando (I)—Gradually slowing.

Range—Compass of a voice or instrument.

Rank—Row of organ pipes which belong to one stop.

Rant—17th c. dance found in fantasies.

Ranz des vaches (F)—Tune played on horns by Alpine herdsmen.

Rapido (I)—Rapid.

Rasch (G)—Fast.

Ratsche (G)—Rattle.

Rattenuto (I)—Heed back.

Rattle—Percussion instrument.

Rauco (I), **rauh** (G), **rauque** (F)— Harsh.

Rauschend (G)—Exuberant.

Ravvivano (I)—Quickening.

Razor Quartet — Haydn's string Quartet No. 61, (op. 55, no. 2) in F minor.

Re—Second note in any typical diatonic scale.

Real fugue—Fugue having the answer match the subject, interval by interval.

Rebec, rebecca—Moorish instrument similar to the mandolin, having 2 strings played by a bow.

Re beémol (F)—D flat (D♭).

Re bémol majeur (F)—D flat major.

Re bémol mineur (F)—D flat min-

or.

Rebute—Jew's harp.

Recapitulation—Final section of the sonata-form; restating of a passage or a theme.

Recessional—Hymn sung at the close of Church services as the choir and clergy retire.

Recht (G)—Right.

Récit (F)—Recitative; leading part.

Recital—Performance by one or two artists or one devoted to works of one or two composers.

Recitative (E), **recitatif** (F), **recitativo** (I)—Musical declamation.

Recitativo secco (I)—Free, quick moving recitative.

Recitativo stromentato (I)—Measured recitative with interesting instrumental accompaniment.

Recoeuilli (F)—Collected, reserved.

Recorder—End blown flute.

Recte et retro (L)—Canon able to be played forward or backward.

Re dièse (F)—D sharp (D♯).

Redoubled interval—Compound interval.

Redoute (F-G), **ridotto** (I)—Masquerade.

Redowa—Bohemian polka in 2/4 and 3/4 time alternately.

Reduction (E), **riduzione** (I)—A condensation or rearrangement of a composition for fewer instruments.

Reed—Thin strip of reed wood or metal which produces musical tones when set in vibration by a current of air.

Reed, beating—Reed in an enclosed column which strikes the edge of an aperture.

Reed, double—Two flat pieces of cane tied together at the narrow end, which are placed in the mouthpiece of a double reed instrument so as to vibrate freely and produce tones.

Reed, fifth—A stopped-quint register in an organ, the stopper having a hole or tube in it.

Reed, free — Reed which vibrates without striking the edges of the column enclosing it.

Reed nasat—Cf. Reed, fifth.

Reed-organ—Keyboard instrument producing tones through reeds.

Reed stops—Stops in an organ with tones produced by wind passing against a reed at the bottom of the pipe and putting the tongue in vibration.

Reel—Lively Scotch and Irish dance in 4/4 or 6/8 time.

Réexposition (F)—Recapitulation.

Refrain—Repeated chorus; burden.

Regal—Portable reed-organ.

Régisseur (F)—Director.

Register—Compass of a voice or instrument; rows of pipes in an organ.

Registering, registration—Proper use of organ stops.

Reigen, reihen (G)—Round dance.

Reimsequenz (G)—12th c. rhymed sequences.

Rejouissance (F)—18th c. light and playful pieces.

Related keys, attendant keys— Keys, which becouse of tones possessed in common, make an easy transition from one to the other.

Relative keys—Keys having a close relation and the same signature.

Relative major—Major scale beginning on the third step of a minor scale and having the same signature.

Relative minor—Minor scale beginning on the sixth step of the major scale and having the same signature.

Religieux (F), **religioso** (I)—Religious.

Remote keys—Keys with scales having few tones in common (C, D♭).

Remplissage (F)—Padding.

Renforcer (F)—To increase.

Renversement (F)—Inversion.

Repeat (E)—Character indicating a measure or passage to be played twice.

Repercussion—Frequent repetition of the same sound.

Répertoire (F), **repertory** (E)—Works which a performer or musical group is prepared to perform.

Répétiteur (F), **repetitore** (I), **repetitor** (G) Director of an opera chorus.

Répétition (F), **ripetizione** (I), **probe** (G)—Rehearsal.

Replica (I), **réplique** (F)—A repeat or reply.

Replicato (I)—Repeated.

Replicazione (I)—Repetition.

Reprendere (I)—To take up again.

Reprise (F), **reprise** (I)—Burden of a song.

Resotument (F), **risolutamente** (I)—Resolutely.

Requiem (L)—R.C. Mass for the dead.

Resolution—Progression from a dissonant into a consonant according to the rules of harmony.

Resonance—Transmission of vibrations from one body to another.

Resonater—Acoustical device which reinforces sounds by resonance.

Response—Answer of a choir or a fugue.

Restatement—Recapitulation.

Restez (F)—Remain on the same string or in the same position.

Rest—Sign indicating a rhythmic pause of fixed duration (▬ ; whole rest; ▬, half rest; 𝄽, quarter rest; 𝄾 , eighth rest; 𝄿, sixteenth rest; 𝅀, thirty-second rest; 𝅁 , sixty-fourth rest).

Retardation—Slackening in time.

Retenant—Holding back.

Réunis (F)—Unison; coupled.

Reveille (F)—Military morning signal to awaken.

Reverberation—Effect due to the reflection of sound waves.

Reverie—Dream-like composition.

Reverse motion—Contrary motion.

Revidiert (G)—Revised.

rf., rfz., rinf. (Abb)—Rinforzando.

r.h. (Abb)—Right hand.

Rhapsodie (F-G), **rhapsody** (E)—Free, exuberant composition.

Rhythm—That which pertains to the duration of musical sound; temporal quality.

Ribs—Sides of instruments of the violin family.

Ricercare (I)—16th-18th c. contrapuntal composition.

Richtig (G)—Right.

Rideau (F)—Curtain.

Ridevolmente (I)—Laughingly.

Ridotto (I), **redoute** (F)—18th c. public masquerade ball.

Riduzione (I)—Arrangement.

Rigaudon (F), **rigadoon** (E)—17th c. dance in 2/4 or 4/4 time.

Rigo (I)—Staff.

Rigoletto (I)—Opera in 3 acts by Giuseppi Verdi (1812-1901).

Rigore, rigoroso (I)—Strictness.

Rilasciando (I)—Becoming slower.

Rimmettendo (I)—Resuming the former tempo.

rinf., rfz. (Abb)—Rinforzando.

Rinforzando, rinforzare, rinforzato, rinforzo (I)—Reinforcement of tone for several notes.

Rip. (Abb)—Ripieno.

Ripetizione (I)—Repetition.

Ripieni (pl.), **ripieno** (I)—Tutti or full parts which augment the chorus and instruments.

Riposato (I)—With repose.

Ripresa (I), **reprise** (F)—Refrain.

Riscaldano (I)—Become livelier.

Risoluto (I)—Resolved.

Risonare (I)—To resound.

Risposta (I)—Answer to the subject in a fugue.

Ristringendo (I)—Quickening.

Risvegliato (I)—Animated.

Rit., ritard. (Abb)—Ritardando.

Ritardando (I)—Gradually slowing.

Riten. (Abb)—Ritenuto.

Ritenuto (I)—Slower.

Ritmo (I)—Rhythm.

Ritornando (I)—Returning.

Ritornello (I), **ritournelle** (F)—Burden or refrain.

Riverso (I)—Reverse.

Rivolto (I)—Inversion.

Rococo music, baroque—Highly embellished music of the 18th c.

Rogue's March—English tune played when a soldier was dismissed in disgrace.

Rohrblatt (G)—Reed of a wind instrument.

Rohr-flöte (G)—Stopped diapason in an organ.

Rohr-Quinr (G)—Organ stop a fifth above the diapasons.

Roll—Trill.

Rollschweller (G)—Crescendo pedal of the organ.

Romance (E-F), **romanza** (I), **romanze** (G)—Informal delicate composition; long lyric tales sung by minstrels.

Romantic music—19th c. subjective music emphasizing imagination, emotion and freedom of expression.

Rondo (I-E)—Musical form with a recurring theme in alternation with contrasted themes (ABA, ABACA).

Root—Fundamental tone of a chord.

Rotando (I)—Full quality.

Roulade (F)—Florid vocal passage.

Round—Vocal canon for several voices.

Roundel, roundelay—14th c. ballad with a refrain.

Rovescio (I)—Inversion.

Rubato (I)—Giving one note a portion of the duration of another.

Rhelos (G)—Restless.

Ruhepunkt, ruhezeichen (G)—Rest.

Ruhig (G)—Quiet.

Ruhrtrommel (G)—Tenor drum.

Rührung (G)—Emotion.

Run—Rapid flight of notes.

Russian Quartets—Beethoven's String Quartets, op. 59, nos. 1-3 (1807).

Rustico (I)—Rural.

— S —

S (Abb)—Segno, senza, sinistra, subito, solo, soprano, sordino.

Saccadé (F)—Accented.

Sackbut—14th c. trombone.

Sackpfeife (G)—Bagpipe.

Saite (G)—String.

Saitenspiel (G)—Stringed instrument.

Salcional, salicit, salicional (F)—Organ stop of small scale and delicate tone.

Salon music—19th c. term for superficial drawing room music.

Saltando (I), **sautille** (F)—Short stroke in rapid tempo in middle of bow in such a manner that bow bounces slightly from strings.

Salterella (I)—Skipping I. dance in 2/4 or 6/8 time.

Salve Regina (L)—Hymn to Virgin Mary.

Sammlung (G)—Collection.

Sämtlich (G)—Complete.

Sanctus (L)—Part of the Canon in R. C. Mass before the Consecration.

Sanft (G)—Soft.

Sängerbund, sängerverein (G)—Singing society.

Sanglot (F)—Sob.

Sans (F)—Without.

Saraband (E), **sarabanda** (I), **sarabande** (F)—Slow, majestic S. dance in 3/4 or 3/2 time.

Sarrusphone—Double reed brass instrument invented by Sarrus.

Satz (G)—Theme, movement, composition.

Sautille (F), **saltando** (I)—Cf. Saltando.

Sax horns—Family of brass wind instruments consisting of a gradually widening tube ending in a flaring bell and having a system of 3 to 5 piston valves which control pitch.

Saxophone—Group of 12 single reed, keyed brass wind instruments.

Scala (I), **scale** (E), **gamme** (F), **tonleiter** (G)—Succession of tones belonging to any one key.

Scale, chromatic—Scale composed of half-steps.

Scale, diatonic—Succession of 8 tones proceeding from one tonic to the next.

Scale, major—A diatonic scale composed of half steps between the third and fourth, seventh and eighth, the others being whole steps.

Scale, minor (harmonic)—Diatonic scale composed of half steps between the second and third, fifth and sixth, seventh and eighth degrees with an augmented second between the sixth and seventh degrees.

Scale, minor (melodic, ascending)—Diatonic scale composed of halfsteps between the second and third, seventh and eighth degrees with a raised sixth.

Scale, minor (melodic, descending)—Diatonic scale composed of half steps between the sixth and fifth, third and second degrees only.

Scale, pentatonic—Primitive 5 whole tone scale corresponding to the black keys of the piano.

Scale, whole tone—Scale completely composed of whole steps.

Scemando (I)—Diminishing.

Scena (I), scène (F), scene (E)—Most brilliant vocal solo from either part of an opera or an independent composition.

Scenario—Skeleton libretto of an opera or play.

Schablone (G)—Conventionalism.

Schäferlied (G)—Shepherd's song.

Schalkhaft (G)—Roguish.

Schallbecken (G)—Cymbals.

Scharf (G)—Sharply.

Schaurig (G)—Ghastly.

Schauspiel (G)—Drama.

Schellen (G)—Tambourine.

Schelmisch (G)—Roguish.

Scherz. (Abb)—Scherzando.

Scherzando (I), scherzhaft (G)—Playful.

Scherzetto (I)—Little scherzo.

Scherzo (I)—Rapid, sportive piece with animated rhythm; third movement of the sonata or symphony.

Schietto (I)—Sincere, simple.

Schag (G)—Beat.

Schlaginstrumente (G)—Percussion instruments.

Schlagzither (G)—Modern zither.

Schlegel (G)—Drumstick.

Schleifen (G)—To slide.

Schleifer (G)—Ornament.

Schleppend (G)—Dragging.

Schlummerlied (G)—Lullaby.

Schluss (G)—End.

Schlüssel (G)—Clef.

Schlusszeichen (G)—Double bar indicating the end.

Schmaetend (G)—Languishing.

Schmalz (G)—Sentimentality.

Schmeichelnd (G), lusingando (I)—Coaxing.

Schmelzend (G)—Lyrical.

Schmerzhaft (G)—Dolorous.

Schmetternd (G)—Blared.

Schnabel (G)—Mouthpiece.

Schnabelflöte (G)—Old name for recorder.

Schnadahupfl—Bavarian-Austrian folk song with improvised humorous texts.

Schnarre (G)—Rattle.

Schnarrtrommel (G)—Snare drum.

Schneidend (G)—With precision.

Schnell (G)—Fast.

Schöpfing, Die (G)—Haydn's oratorio, The Creation.

Schopfungsmesse (G)—Haydn's Mass in B flat.

Schottisch (G)—Mid-19th c. dance in 2/4 time.

Schreiend (G)—Shrill.

Schrittmässig (G)—As if walking.

Schüchtern (G)—Sky.

Schuhplattler (G)—Bavarian dance characterized by clapping of the knees and shoe soles with the hands.

Schwach (G)—Soft, weak.

Schwankend (G)—Staggering.

Schwebung (G)—Tremolo.

Schweigen (G)—A rest, to be silent.

Schweig (G) Direction to be silent.

Schweller (G)—Swell.

Schwellkasten—Swell box.

Schwellwerk (G)—Swell organ.

Schwer (G)—Heavy.

Schwermütig (G)—Melancholic.

Schwindend (G)—Diminishing.

Schwingung (G)—Vibration.

Schwung (G)—Swing.

Scintillante (I)—Sparkling.

Scioltezza (I)—Freedom.

Sciolto (I)—Free, light.

Scivolando (I)—Sliding.

Scoop—In singing, slurring up to a tone.

Scordato (I)—Out of tune.

Scordatura (I)—Special tuning of a stringed instrument to obtain unusual chords, facilitate difficult passages or change tone color.

Score (E), partiteur (G), partitura (I), partition (F)—Complete draft of a composition showing each part on a separate staff.

Score, full—Complete score of all the parts of a composition.

Score, instrumental—Score giving the complete instrumental parts.

Score, orchestral—Complete score of an orchestral work.

Score, piano—Arrangement of music for the piano.

Score, short—An abbreviated score.

Score, vocal—Notes of all voice parts placed in proper order, with orchestra reduced to piano.

Scoring—The process of orchestration.

Scorrendo, scorrevole (I)—Flowing.

Scotch scale—Scale which omits the fourth and seventh degrees.

Scotch snap—The rhythmic motive of Scotch music where a quarter note is divided into a sixteenth and a dotted eighth note.

Scozzese (I)—Scottish.

Scrittura (I)—Commission by an opera company to write an opera.

Scroll—The end of the head of an instrument of the violin family.

Scucito (I)—Disconnected.

Sdegno (I)—Anger.

Sdrucciolando (I)—Glissando.

Se (I)—If.

Sec (F), secco (I)—Dry.

Sechs (G), sei (I), six (E)—Six.

Sechzehntel (G)—Sixteenth.

Second (E-F), seconda (I)—An interval of 2 diatonic degrees.

Seconda votta (I)—Second time.

Secondo (I)—Second.

Section—Complete but dependent musical idea.

Secular music—Worldly as opposed to sacred music.

Seele (G)—Soul.

Seelenvoll (G)—Soulful.

Seg. (Abb)—Segue.

Segno (I)—Sign; al segno, repeat to the sign.

Segue (I)—As follows.

Seque la finale (I)—The finale follows.

Seguidilla (S)—Dance in 3/4 time similar to the bolero.

Sehnsucht, sehsuchtig (G)—Yearning.

Sehr (G)—Very.

Sei (I), six (E-F), sechs (G)—Six.

Seikilos Song—Ancient Gr. lyrical song dating to 2nd c. B. C.

Seite (G)—Page.

Seizième (F), sedecima (I), sechzehntel (G)—Sixteenth.

Sekunde (G)—Second.

Semi (I-L)—Half.

Semibreve (E-I), ronde (F), ganze taktnote (G)—Whole note.

Semiminima (I), crotchet (E), noire (F), viertel (G)—Quarter note.

Semiquaver (E), semicroma (I), double croche (F), sechzehntel (G)—Sixteenth note.

Semiseria (I)—18th c. opera seria containing numerous comic scenes.

Semitone—Half step.

Semplice (I)—Simple.

Sempre (I)—Always.

Sensibile (I)—Sensitive.

Sensible (F)—Leading tone.

Sentito (I)—With expression.

Senza (I)—Without.

Senza accompagnamento (I)—Without accompaniment.

Senza sordino (I), sans sourdine (F)—Without mute or dampers.

Séparé (F)—Separated.

Sept (F)—Seven.

Septet (E), septetto (I), septuo. (F)—Composition for 7 voices or instruments.

Septième (F)—Seventh.

Septimenakkord (G)—Seventh chord.

Septimole, septole (G)—A group of 7 notes to be played in the time of 4 or 6.

Sepulchrum play (I)—Medieval play depicting the burial of Christ.

Sequela—Term for pre-existing melodies of sequences.

Sequence—Repetition of a passage at a higher or lower level.

Serenade (E), ständchen (G)—Evening song.

Serenata (I)—18th c. short operatic works called dramatic cantatas.

Sereno (I)—Serene.

Serinette (F)—Miniature barrel organ.

Serio, serioso (I), serieusement (F)—Serious.

Serpent—Ancient brass wind instrument replaced by the modern tuba.

Serrando (I), serre (F)—Pressing.

Sesquialtera (L)—Organ stop of 2 or more ranks of pipes, with acute pitch.

Sestetto (I), sextet (E), sextett (G), sextuor (F)—Composition for 7 voices or instruments.

Sesto (I), sexte (G), sixième (F)—Sixth.

Sette (I), sept (F), sieben (G)—Seven.

Settimo (I), septieme (F), siebente (G)—Seventh.

Setzart (G)—Style of composition.

Seufzend (G)—Sighing.

Seul (F)—Alone.

Seventeenth—Organ stop.

Seventh—Interval of 7 diatonic degrees.

Seventh chord—A chord built on the third, fifth and seventh above.

Severamente (I)—Strictly.

Severita (I)—Severity.

Sext (G)—Interval of the sixth.

Sextet (E), sestetto (I), sextett (G), sextuor (F)—Chamber music for an ensemble of 6.

Sextolet (G)—Six notes played in the time of 4.

Sfogato (I)—Light.

Sfoggiando (I)—Ostentatious.

Sforzando, sforzato (I)—Emphasis on a particular chord or note.

Sforzando piano (I)—An accented tone followed by a soft tone.

sfp. (Abb).—Sforzando piano.

Sfuggito (I)—Avoided.

sfz. (Abb)—Sforzando, sforzato.

Sfumato (I)—Very lightly.

Shading—Variation in tone and color.

Shake—Trill.

Shanty, chanty, chantey—Work songs of E. and American sailors.

Sharp (E), dièse (F), diesis (I), kreuz (G)—A sign before a note which indicates its pitch is to be raised by a semitone, (#).

Shawm (E), **chálumeau** (F), **chalmei** (G), **cialamello** (I)—Ancient instrument similar to the oboe and clarinet.

Sheng—Chinese wind instrument.

Shivaree—Cf. Charivari.

Shofar—Ancient Jewish instrument made from a ram's horn.

Si—Seventh step in the typical diatonic scale of C.

Si bémol (F)—B flat (B♭).

Si dièse (F)—B sharp. (B♯).

Si majeur—B major.

Si mineur (F)—B minor.

Siciliano (I)—17th-18th c. Sicilian dance in 6/8 or 12/8 meter.

Side drum—Snare drum.

Sieben (G)—Seven.

Siebente (G)—Seventh.

Sight reading—Adeptness at reading and performing music at first sight.

Signature—Sharps and flats at the beginning of a composition indicating its key.

Signature, time—Fractional figures at the begining of a composition indicating the kind and number of beats to a measure.

Silence (F)—Rest.

Sillet (F)—Nut of the violin.

Similar motion—Two or more parts moving in the same direction at the same time.

Simile (I)—In the same manner.

Simple—Intervals of less than an octave.

Simple measure—Measure with one accent.

Sin, sino (I)—As far as.

Sin 'al fine (I)—To the end.

Sincopa (I)—Syncopation.

Sinf. (Abb)—Sinfonia.

Sinfonia (I), **sinfonie** (F)—Symphony; three voice inventions by Bach.

Sinfonie da camera (I)—Chamber symphony.

Sinfonietta (I)—Small symphony.

Sinfonische dichtung (G)—Symphonic poem.

Singend (G)—Singing.

Singhiozzando (I)—Sobbing.

Singspiel (G)—Opera.

Sinistra (I)—Left.

Sink-a-pace—Cinque pas.

Sino, sin (I)—As far as.

Si replica (I)—Repeat.

Sirventes—Troubadour poetry of heroic, political or moral content.

Si scriva (I)—As written.

Si seque (I)—It follows.

Sistine choir—Papal choir.

Si tace (I)—To be silent.

Si volta (I)—Turn the page.

Sixteenth note—Semiquaver.

Sixteenth rest—A pause equal in time to a sixteenth note.

Sixth—Interval of 6 diatonic degrees.

Sixtylfourth note—Hemidemisemiquaver.

Sixty-fourth rest—A pause equal in time to a sixty-fourth note.

Skala (G)—Scale.

Skip—Any transition exceeding a whole step.

Skizzen (G)—Sketches.

Slancio, con (I)—Impetuously.

Slargando (I)—Becoming slower and larger.

Slentando (I)—Gradually slowing.

Slide—Movable portion of the trombone which alters the pitch; a method of passing quickly from one note to another.

Slur—Curved line above or below

a group of notes indicating they are to be played legato.

Smanioso (I)—Frenzied.

Smarfioso (I)—Affected.

Sminuendo (I)—Diminishing.

Smorz. (Abb)—Smorzando.

Smorzando (I)—Dying away.

Snare drum—Small drum with strings of rawhide or catgut drawn over its lower head.

Snello (I)—Nimble.

Soave (I)—Suave.

Soggetto (I)—Theme.

Sognando (I)—Dreaming.

Sol—Fifth note of the typical diatonic scale of C.

Solea—Andalusian folk song.

Sol bémol (F)—G flat (G♭).

Sol dièse (F)—G sharp (G♯).

Solenne (I), **solennel** (F)—Solemn.

Sol-fa (E), **solfège** (F), **solfeggio** (I)—System of vocal exercise employing the syllables do, re, etc.

Solito (I)—Usual.

Sollicitando (I)—Hastening.

Sol majeur—G major.

Sol mineur (F)—G minor.

Solmisation—Designation of degrees of the scale by use of the syllables do, re, mi, fa, sol, la, si(ti).

Solo (I-F-G)—For one performer.

Solo pitch—A pitch slightly higher than normal.

Sollanto (I)—Solely.

Sommesso (I)—Subdued.

Son (F)—Sound.

Sonabile (I)—Resonant.

Sonante (I)—Resonant.

Sonare (I)—To sound.

Sonare alla mente (I)—To improvise.

Sonata (I), **sonate** (F-G.)—An instrumental composition of 3 or 4 movements usually beginning with an allegro followed by andante, adagio or largo, then the minuet, trio or scherzo.

Sonata form—Exposition, development, recapitulation.

Sonatina (I), **sonatine** (F)—Short sonata usually composed of only an exposition followed by a recapitulation.

Song—Vocal composition.

Song cycle—Group of songs related in thought and style forming a musical entity.

Song form—Generally considered the ternary form—ABA.

Sonneries (F)—Signals given by trumpets or church bells.

Sono (I)—Sound.

Sonore (F), **sonoro** (I)—Sonorous.

Sans bouchés (F)—Stopped notes in horn playing.

Sopra (I)—Above.

Soprano—Highest female voice.

Soprano clef—The C clef placing middle C on the first line of the staff.

Sordamente (I)—Subdued.

Sordini alzati (I)—Take off the mutes.

Sordino (I), **sourdine** (F)—Mute.

Sordo (I), **sourd** (F)—Muffled.

Sorgfältig (G)—Carefully.

Sortita (I)—Postlude.

Sospirando (I)—Plaintive.

Sost., sosten. (Abb)—Sostenuto.

Sostenuto (I) — Sustaining the note.

Sotto (I)—Under.

Sotto voce (I)—Softly.

Souffleur (F)—Prompter.

Sound board—A board beneath the strings of an instrument serving

as a resonater and intensifying sound.

Sound holes—Holes in the belly of stringed instruments.

Sound post—Small pillar of wood inside the body of stringed instruments which carries vibrations from front to back.

Soupir (F)—Quarter rest ( ).

Soupirant (F)—Sighing.

Sourd (F), **sordo** (I)—Muffled.

Sourdine (F), **sordino** (I)—Mute.

Sous (F)—Under.

Soutenir (F)—To sustain.

Souvenir (F)—Recollection.

Sp. (Abb)—Spitze.

Space—Interval between the lines of the staff.

Spandendo (I) — Expanding in power.

Spasshaft (G)—Jocular.

Spatium (L)—Space between two lines of a staff.

Sperdendosi (I)—Fading away.

Spianato (I)—Legato.

Spiccato (I)—Separated; playing the violin with the point of the bow.

Spiegando (I)—Becoming louder.

Spieldose (G)—Music box.

Spielen (G)—To play.

Spieloper—G. 19th c. comic opera.

Spinet (E)—Stringed instrument similar to the harpsichord.

Spirito (I)—Spirit, life.

Spiritoso (I)—Spirited.

Spirituals—Religious songs of the American Negro.

Spitze (G)—Point of the violin bow.

Spitz-flöte (G), **spitz-flute** (E)—Pointed flute.

Spitzig (G)—Pointed.

Spöttisch (G)—Mocking.

Sprechend (G)—Recitative.

Springing bow (E), **spiccato, saltato** (I), **sautillé** (F)—A type of bowing. Cf. Saltando.

Squillante (I)—Clear.

Sta (I)—As it stands.

Stabat Mater (L)—R. C. hymn on the crucifixion.

Stabile (I)—Firm.

Stabreim (G)—Alliteration.

Stacc. (Abb)—Staccato.

Staccato (I), **detaché** (F)—Detached, distinct notes.

Staff, stave—The five horizontal lines upon and between which musical notes are written.

Stanchezza (I)—Weariness.

Ständchen (G)—Serenade.

Stark (G)—Strong.

Star Spangled Banner, The—National anthem of the U. S. A.

Statement—Exposition.

St. Diap. (Abb)—Stopped diapason.

Steam organ—Calliope.

Steg (G)—Bridge of violin.

Stegrief (G)—Improvisation.

Stellung (G)—Position.

Stentando (I)—Retarding.

Step—An interval.

Sterbend (G)—Dying away.

Stesso (I)—Same.

Stets (G)—Continuously.

Stil (G), **stile** (I)—Style.

Stimme (G)—Voice.

Stimmen (G)—To tune.

Stimmenkreuzung (G) — Crossing of voice parts.

Stimmung (G)—Mood.

Stinguendo (I)—Fading out.

Stirando (I)—Retarding.

Stop—Register in an organ; pressure on a violin string.

Str. (Abb)—Strings.

Stracciacalando (I)—Prattling.

Stradivari—Superior make of violin.

Straff (G)—Tense.

Strain—Melody.

Strascinando (I)—Dragging.

Strathspey—Scotch dance in 4/4 time with many dotted notes.

Stravagante (I)—Extravagant.

Straziante (I)—Piercing.

Streichinstrumente (G) — Stringed instrument.

Streng (G)—Strict.

Strepitoso (I)—Noisy .

Stretta (I)—Concluding passage in quick time.

Stretto (I)—Part in a fugue in which the subject overlaps the answer.

Strich (G)—Bow stroke.

Strict—According to rule.

Stridente (I)—Shrill.

String. (Abb)—Stringendo.

Stringed instruments—Instruments whose sound is produced by a stretched string.

Stringendo (I)—Accelerating.

String Quartet—Chamber music for 2 violins, one viola, one cello.

String trio—Chamber music for 3 stringed instruments.

Strisciando (I)—Slurred.

Stromento (I)—Instrument.

Stromentato (I)—Instrumental.

Stromenti a corde (I)—Stringed instruments.

Stromenti d'arco (I)—Bowed instruments.

Stromenti da tasto (I)—Keyboard instruments.

Strophic—Song in which all stanzas are sung to the same tune.

Stück—(G)—Piece.

Stufe (G)—Step.

Stürmisch (G)—Stormy.

Stutzflügel (G)—Baby grand piano.

Style—Characteristic mode of musical presentation.

Styrienne (F)—Melody in 2/4 time, often minor with a yodel after each verse.

Su (I), sur (F)—On, upon.

Suave (I)—Sweet.

Sub (L), sous (F), sotto (I)—Under.

Subdominant — Fourth degree of the scale.

Subito (I)—Suddenly.

Subject (E), soggetto (I), sujet (F)—Theme.

Submediant—Sixth tone of the scale.

Subtonic—Leading tone, a semitone below the tonic.

Suite (F-E), partita (I-G) — Instrumental piece composed of several movements, each of dancelike character.

Suivez (F)—Accommodation of the accompaniment to the performer.

Sujet (F), soggetto (I)—Subject.

Sul (I)—On, upon.

Sul P. (Abb)—Sul ponticello.

Sul ponticello (I), sur le chevalet (F)—Bowing near the bridge.

Summen (G)—To hum.

Suono (I)—Sound.

Super (L), sopra (I)—Su dessus de (F)—Above.

Superbo (L)—Proud.

Superdominant—Second tone above the tonic.

Surprise Symphony—Haydn's symphony in G major (1791).

Surtout (F)—Especially.

Suspension—Creation of dissonance by holding one or more tones in a chord while the others progress.

Süss (G)—Sweetly.

Sussurando (I)—Whispering.

Sustain—To hold a note.

Svegliato (I)—Brisk.

Svelto (I)—Quick.

Sw. (Abb)—Swell organ.

Swell—Gradual increase of sound.

— T —

T. (Abb)—Talon, tasto, toe, tonic, trill, tutti.

Tablature—Former method of notation for the lute, viol and organ.

Tabor—Tambourine without jingles.

Tac. (Abb)—Tacet.

Tacet (L) taci, tacissi (I) — Be silent.

Taille (F)—Viola; tenor.

Takt (G)—Time, measure, beat.

Taktmesser (G)—Metronome.

Talon (F)—Nut of the violin bow.

Tambour (F)—Drum.

Tambourin (F)—Provencal dance accompanied by the tambourine.

Tambourine (F)—Small, shallow drum with a single head of parchment, surrounded by jingles.

Tamburo (I)—Drum.

Tampon (F)—Two headed drumstick used for producing a roll on the bass drum.

Tamtam—Gong.

Tanbur—Type of lute found in Near Eastern countries.

Tändelnd (G)—Bantering.

Tango — Spanish-American dance with syncopation as its characteristic trait.

Tant (F), tanto (I)—Much, so much.

Tantum ergo (L) — Benediction hymn of the R. C. Church.

Tarbouka—North African drum.

Tardo (I)—Slow.

Tanz (G)—Dance.

Tarantella—Swift I. dance in 6/8 meter.

Tastatur (G), tastiera (I), clavier (F)—Keyboard.

Taste (G)—Key.

Tastiera (I)—Cf. Tastatur.

Tasto (I)—touche (F)—Key of a keyboard instrument.

Tattoo (F)—Drum roll or bugle call recalling soldiers for the eveing.

T. C. (Abb)—Tre corde.

Technic, technique — Mechanical skill in musical performance.

Tecla (S)—16th-17th c. S. name for key and keyboard.

Tedesco (I)—German.

Te deum laudamus (L)—Hymn of praise.

Teil (G)—Part.

Teiltöne (G)—Partials, overtones.

Telyn—Welsh harp.

Tem. 1° (Abb)—Tempo prima.

Tema (I)—Theme, subject.

Temperament, equal—Tuning system dividing the scale into 12 equal semitones.

Temperament—Systems of tuning which differ from those using acoustically correct intervals.

Tempestoso (I)—Stormy.

Tempo—Rate of speed of a composition.

Tempo giusto (I)—Normal speed.

Tempo ordinario (I) — Moderate time.

Tempo primo (I)—Original time.

Tempo rubato (I)—Irregular time in which one note is retarded and another quickened without losing the basic rhythm.

Temps (F)—Beat.

Temps faible (F)—Weak beat.

Temps fort (F)—Strong beat.

Ten. (Abb)—Tenuto; tenor.

Tenendo (I)—Sustaining.

Tenendo il canto (I)—Sustaining the melody.

Teneramente (I)—Tenderly.

Tenete (I)—Hold out.

Tenor (E), tenore (I)—Highest natural adult male voice.

Tenor C—Lowest C in the tenor voice; lowest string of the tenor violin.

Tenor clef—C clef placing middle C on the fourth line.

Tenorhorn—Baritone.

Tenore di grazia, tenore leggiero (I)—Light.

Tenore robusto (I)—Heavy tenor.

Tenorschlüssel (G)—Tenor clef.

Tenso—Troubadours whose songs dealt with debatable topics.

Tenor trombone—B flat trombone.

Tenth (E), decima (L)—Interval of 10 diatonic degrees.

Tenue (F), tenuto (I)—Sustained.

Tepido (I)—Unimpassioned.

Ternary—That which is made up of 3.

Ternary form—Rondo form.

Ternary measure—3-beat measure.

Terpsichore—Gr. muse of song and dance.

Tertian harmony—Harmonic system based on the triad.

Terz (G)—Third.

Terzen (G), tierces (F)—Thirds.

Terzetto (I)—Trio.

Terzina (I)—Triplet.

Tessitura (I)—Position, as to pitch, of the tones in a song.

Testa (I)—Head.

Testo (I)—Narrator.

Tetrachord (Gr)—Perfect fourth.

Theme—Subject.

Themenaufstellung (G)—Exposition.

Theory of music—Science of composition.

Thesis (Gr)—Accented beat of a measure.

Third—Interval of 3 diatonic degrees.

Thirteenth—Interval of 13 diatonic degrees.

Thirty-second note — Demisemiquaver.

Thorough bass — Figured bass using numerals instead of notes to indicate harmony.

Threnody—Dirge.

Tibia (L)—Old flute made from an animal's shin bone.

Tie or bind—Curved line connecting 2 notes of the same pitch, the second being merely a continuation of the first.

Tief (G)—Deep.

Tierce (F)—Third.

Timbale (F), timballo (I)—Kettledrum.

Timbre (F)—Quality of tone.

Timbrel—Hebrew tambourine.

Time—Meter, tempo, duration.

Time signature—Fraction at the beginning of a staff which indicates the kind and number of beats to a measure, the numerator indicating the number of units per measure and the denominator indicating the units of measurement (whole note, half note, etc.).

Timoroso (I)—With fear.

Timp., tymp. (Abb)—Timpani.

Timpani—Kettledrums.

Timpani coperti (I) — Muffled drums.

Tintat (F), **tintinnando** (I)—Tinkling.

Tintinnabulum (L)—Bell.

Tiple (S)—Soprano.

Tirare (I)—To draw.

Tirer, tirez, tiré (F)—Downbow.

Tocsin—An alarm bell.

Todesgesang, todeslied (G)—Dirge.

Todtenglöckchen (G) — Funeral bell.

Tombeau (F)—Musical elegies.

Tom-tom — American Indian or Oriental drum.

Ton (F)—Pitch, key, sound.

Tonabstend (G)—Interval.

Tonada (S)—Song.

Tonadilla—Short S. comic opera.

Tonal—Pertaining to tones or key.

Tonart' (G)—Key.

Tonausweichung, tonveränderung (G)—Modulation.

Tonbuchstaben (G)—Tone letters.

Tondichtung (G)—Tone poem.

Tone—Sound of definite pitch or duration.

Tone color—Timbre.

Tone deafness—Inability to distinguish different pitches.

Tone poem (E), **tondichtung** (G)—Symphonic poem.

Tonfall (G)—Cadence.

Tonfarbe (G)—Timbre.

Tonführung (G)—Modulation.

Tongang (G)—Melody.

Tongeschlecht (G)—Distinction of a chord or key as to major or minor.

Tongue—Reed or clapper.

Tonguing—In playing wind instruments, a mode of articulating quick notes by the use of the tongue.

Tonhöne (G)—Pitch.

Tonic—First and main note of a key; keynote.

Tonic sol-fa—Method of teaching vocal music using a movable-do system and using syllables do, re, etc.

Tonic triad—Triad built on a keynote.

Tonika (G)—Tonic.

Tonkunst (G)—Music.

Tonleiter (G)—Scale.

Tonlos (G)—Toneless.

Ton majeur (F)—Major key.

Tonmalerei (G)—Descriptive music.

Tonmass (G)—Time, measure, meter.

Ton mineur (F)—Minor key.

Tono (I)—Tone.

Tonsatz (G)—Composition.

Tonschluss (G)—Cadence.

Tonschlüssel (G)—Clef.

Tonschrift (G)—Notation.

Tonstufe (G)—Step.

Tonus (L)—Whole tone.

Tornada (S)—Refrain.

Tornando (I)—Returning.

Tosto (I)—Quick.

Tost Quartets—12 Quartets by Haydn (1789-90).

Touch—Method of striking or pressing the keys of an instrument.

Touche (F), **tasto** (I)—Keyboard or fingerboard.

Toujours (F)—Always.

Tour de force (F)—Difficult passage.

Tous ensemble (F)—Direction for all to play together.

Tout (F), **tous, toutes** (pl.)—All.

Tr. (Abb)—Trill.

Trackers—Rods which constitute action in a tracker-action organ.

Tradolce (I)—Very sweet.

Traduction (F). **traduzione** (I)—Arrangement; translation.

Traîné (F)—Lingering.

Trait (F)—Tract.

Tranquillo (I)—Tranquillity.

Transcription—Arrangement.

Transition—Passing from one key to another.

Transposing instruments — Instruments for which the music is written in another key then that of their natural sound.

Transposition — Changing of key or pitch of a piece.

Transverse flute—Modern flute.

Traps—Noise - producing attachments on a drum.

Trascinando (I)—Dragging.

Tratt. (Abb)—Trattenuto.

Trattenuto (I)—Sustained.

Trauermusik (G)—Funeral music.

Traumerisch (G)—Dreamy.

Traümerei (G)—Reverie.

Trauerig (G)—Sad.

Traviata, La—Opera in 3 acts by Giuseppi Verdi (1853).

Tre (I)—Three.

Treble—Soprano.

Treble clef—G Clef.

Tre corde (I)—3 strings.

Tredecime (G) — Interval of the thirteenth.

Treibend (G)—Hurrying.

Trem. (Abb)—Tremolo.

Tremando (I)—Trembling.

Tremblement (F)—Shake, trill.

Tremolo (I)—Rapid reiteration of the same tone, produced by a swift up and down movement of the bow.

Trenchmore—16th c. E. country dance in triple meter.

Trepak—R. Cossack dance in 2/4 time.

Très (F)—Very.

Triad—Any chord having a root with its third and fifth above.

Triangle—Percussion instrument of steel bent in triangular form.

Trias (L)—Triad.

Tricinium (L)—16th c. term for vocal compositions in 3 parts.

Trill—2 adjacent notes alternating in rapid succession.

Triller (G), **trillo** (I)—Trill.

Trinklied (G)—Drinking song.

Trio—Composition for 3 voices or instruments; the voices or instruments themselves.

Triole (G), **triolit** (F)—Triplet.

Triomphale (F), **trionfale** (I)—Triumphant.

Trio sonata—Type of Baroque Chamber music.

Triple concerto — Concerto for 3 solo instruments.

Triple conuterpoint—Counterpoint in 3 voices which can be interchanged.

Triple croche (F)—Thirty-second note or rest.

Triple time (E), **mesure à trois temps** (F), **tripeltakt** (G)—3 beats to the measure.

Triplet—Group of 3 notes played in the time of 2 similar ones.

Tristan und Isolde — Opera in 3 acts by Richard Wagner (1865).

Triste (I), **trüb** (G)—Sad.

Triste—Melancholic Argentine type of love song.

Tritone—Augmented fourth, i.e., an interval of 3 whole tones.

Trochee (L)—Musical foot having one long and one short syllable (— ◡).

Trois (F), **tre** (I), **dei** (G)—Three.

Troisieme (F), **terzo** (I), **dritte** (G)—Third.

Tromb. (Abb)—Trombones.

Tromba (I)—Trumpet; 8 ft. reed organ-stop.

Tromba sorda (I)—Muted trumpet.

Trombetta (I)—Formerly a small trumpet.

Trombone (E), **posaune** (G)—Brass wind instrument having a cylindrical metal bore which terminates in a flaring bell, pitch being controlled by a U-shaped slide.

Trommel (G)—Drum.

Trommelbass (G)—Derogatory reference to stereotyped bass figures.

Trompete (G), **trompette** (F), **tromba** (I)—Trumpet.

Tronco (I) — Indication to cut sounds short.

Troppo (I)—Too much.

Troubadour (E), **trouvères** (F), **trovatori** (I), **minnesinger** (G)—Traveling poet-musicians of the Middle Ages who wandered through France, Spain, Germany and Italy.

Trüb (G)—Sad.

Trugschluss (G)—Deceptive cadence.

Trumpet—Brass wind instrument having a cylindrical narrow tube terminating in a moderate sized bell, pitch being controlled by valves, keys or a crook.

T. s. (Abb)—Tasto solo.

Tuba—Deepest saxhorn of the brass choir with a range of 4 octaves.

Tucket—Elizabethan term for a trumpet flourish.

Tumultuoso (I)—Tumultuously.

Tune—Air; melody.

Tuning—Regulation of the pitch of stringed instruments by propper adjustment of the strings.

Tuning fork—U-shaped pair of steel prongs used to indicate absolute pitch.

Tuning hammer—A metal instrument used by piano tuners.

Tuning slide—A crook used to adjust the pitch of all brass instruments.

Tuning wire—A wire used to adjust the pitch of organ reed pipes.

Tuono (I), **ton** (G-F)—Tone.

Tuono mezzo (I)—Semitone.

Turba—Term for choral movements representing Jewish or heathen population.

Turca (I), **turque** (F)—Turkish.

Turn (E), **groupe** (F), **gruppetto** (I), **doppelschlag** (G)—An embellishment of a group of 4 or 5 notes connecting one principal note with another indicated by (∽).

Tusch (G)—Fanfare on brass inments.

Tutti (I)—Parts for the whole orchestra.

Tuyau (F)—Tube, pipe.

Twelfth—Interval of 12 diatonic degrees.

Tymbalon, tymbal—Early kettledrum.

Tympani (I)—Kettledrums.

Tyrolienne—Song or dance of the Tyrolese.

Tzigane (F)—Gypsy.

— U —

Üben (G)—To practice.
Über (G)—Above, over.
Übergang (G)—Transition.
Übermässig (G)—Augmented.
Übersetzung (G)—Translation.
Übung (G), étude (F)—Exercise, study.
U. C. (Abb)—Una corda.
Uguale (I)—Equal.
Uilleann pipes—Irish bagpipe.
Ukulele—Hawaiian instrument of the guitar family.
Umano (I)—Human.
Umfang (G)—Compass.
Umkehrung (G)—Inversion.
Umore (I)—Humor.
Umstimmen (G)—A change in tuning.
Un. (Abb)—Unison.
Una, uno (I)—A, an, one.
Una corda (I), petite pédale (F), mit verschiebung (G)—Direction to use the left or soft pedal of the piano thereby striking one string instead of the usual three.
Unda maris (L)—Organ stop with a wavy sound.
Undezime (G)—Eleventh.
Unequal voices — Mixed male and female voices.
Unfinished Symphony — Schubert's Symphony no. 8 in B minor.
Ungar (G)—Hungarian.
Ungebunden (G)—Free.
Ungeduldig (G)—Impatient.
Ungezwungen (G)—Natural.
Ungrader takt (G)—Triple meter.
Unheimlich (G)—Uncanny.
Unison (E), unisono (I)—Two or more voices or instruments sounding precisely the same tone or tones.
Unmerklich (G)—Imperceptibly.
Uno a uno (I)—One by one.
Un peu (F), un poco (I)—A little.
Un pochettino (I)—Very little.
Unruhig (G)—Restless.
Unschuldig (G)—Innocently.
Unter (G)—Under.
Unterdominante (G) — Subdominant.
Unterhaltungs-stück (G) — Light, entertaining piece of music.
Unterwerk (G)—Choir organ.
Up-beat—Unaccented beat of a measure.
Up-bow—Stroke beginning at the point (V).
Ut (L)—Do, C.
Ut bémol (F)—C flat (C♭).
Ut dièse (F)—C sharp (C♯).
Ut supra (L)—As above.

— V —

V. (Abb)—Vide, violino, volti, volte, voce.
Va! (I)—Go on.
Va. (Abb)—Viola.
Vacillando (I)—Wavering.
Vaghezza, con (I)—With charm.
Vago (I)—Vague.
Valse (F)—Waltz.
Value (E), valeur (F), valore (I), wert (G)—Length of a note.
Valve—Device designed to regulate the sound of brass instruments.
Vamp — Improvised accompaniment.
Vaporeux (F)—Hazy.
Var. (Abb)—Variations.
Variants—Various versions of the same piece.

Variations—A musical form in which a musical idea is stated and then repeated with various modifications, yet retaining its identity.
Varsoviana (I), varsovienne (F)—Polish dance in slow mazurka rhythm.
Vc. (Abb)—Violoncello.
Veemenza (I)—Vehemence.
Velato (I), voilé (F)—Veiled.
Vellutato (I)—Velvety.
Veloce (I)—Quick.
Vene Sancte Spiritus (L)—Pentecostal sequence in the R. C. Church.
Vent (F)—Wind.
Ventil (G), ventile (I)—Valve.
Veränderungen (G)—Variations.
Verdoppeln (G)—To double.
Vergleichende Musikwissenschaft (G)—Comparative musicology.
Vergnügt (G)—Happily.
Vergrösserung (G) — Augmentation.
Verhallend (G)—Dying away.
Verism (E), verismo (I)—20th c. school of musical realism.
Verklärt (G)—Transfigured.
Verkleinerung, verkürzung (G)—Diminution.
Verlierend (G)—Fading away.
Verlöschend (G)—Extinguishing.
Vermindert (G) — Diminished interval.
Verschiebung (G)—Soft pedal.
Verschieden (G)—Various.
Verschwindend (G)—Dying away.
Verse (E), verso (I)—Stanza; solo portion of an anthem.
Versetzung (G)—Transposition.
Versetzungzeichen (G)—Accidental.
Versicle—Verse chanted by the priest.
Versmaas (G)—Poetic meter.
Verstärken (G)—To reinforce.
Verstimmt (G)—Out of tune.
Verwandt (G)—Related.
Verweilend, Zögernd (G)—Retarding.
Verzierung (G)—Ornamentation.
Verzweiflungsvoll (G) — Despairingly.
Vespers—Evening canonical hour of the R. C. Church.
Vezzoso (I)—Tender.
Via (I)—Away.
Vibra. (Abb)—Vibrato.
Vibration—Undulation of a sonorous body thereby producing sounds.
Vicendevole (I)—Alternately.
Vide (F), vuoto (I), leer (G)—Empty.
Viel (G)—Much.
Viella, vielle—Stringed instrument of the 12th-13th c.
Vielstimmig (G)—Polyphonic.
Vier (G)—Four.
Vierhändig (G)—For 4 hands.
Vierte (G)—Fourth.
Viertel (G)—Quarter.
Vif (F)—Lively.
Vihuela—Early S. name for the viola.
Vigoroso (I), vigoureux (F)—Vigorous.
Villanella (I), villanelle (F)—16th c. Neopolitan madrigal.
Vingt-Quatre Violons—Group of 24 violinists in the employ of the F. Kings Louis XIII, Louis XIV, Louis XV.
Viol—Instrument similar to the violin but having 6 strings and a fretted keyboard.

Viola (I), bratsche (G), taille (F)—Tenor violin.
Viol, bass—Violoncello.
Viola da spalla—18th c. cello-like instrument held against the shoulder.
Viola pomposo—18th c. instrument of the violin family invented by J. S. Bach.
Violento (I)—Violently.
Violin (E), violine (G), violino (I), violon (F)—Bowed instrument having 4 strings (GDAE). The soprano of the string choir, it is the most important stringed instrument of the orchestra.
Violinbogen (G)—Violin bow.
Violinsaite (G)—Violin string.
Violinschlüssel (G)—Treble clef.
Violoncello (I)—Large 4 stringed (CGDA), bowed instrument held between the knees. It is the bass baritone of the string choir.
Violone (I)—Double bass.
Virginal—16th c. type of harpsichord.
Virtuoso (I)—Skillful performer.
Vista (I), vue (F)—Sight.
Vite (F)—Quickly.
Vivace (I)—Animated.
Vl. (Abb)—Violin.
Vla. (Abb)—Viola.
Vlc. (Abb)—Violoncello.
Vll. (Abb)—Violins.
Vocal—Pertaining to the human voice.
Vocalise (F)—Voice exercise using vowel sounds.
Vocal music—Music written for voices.
Voce (I), voix (F), stimme (G)—Voice.
Voce umana (I)—An organ stop imitating human quality.
Voice—Sound produced by vocal organs in singing or speaking.
Voicing—Adjustment of the timbre and pitch of organ pipes.
Voilé (F)—Subdued.
Voix (F)—Voice.
Voix céleste (F), vox angelica (L)—Organ stop; soft stop on the harmonium.
Vokal (G)—Vowel.
Volante (I)—Swift.
Volkslied (G)—Folksong.
Voll (G)—Full.
Volles Werk (G)—Full organ.
Vollstimmig (G)—Full voiced.
Volltönend (G)—Sonorous.
Volta (I)—Time.
Volta prima (I)—First time.
Voltare (I)—To turn.
Volteggiando (I) — Crossing the hands in piano playing.
Volti (I)—Turn over.
Volti subito (I)—Turn quickly.
Volubile (I)—Flowing.
Volume—Quantity of tone.
Voluntary—Introductory performance on the organ.
Voluttuoso (I)—Voluptuously.
Vom, von (G)—From.
Vom anfang (V)—From the beginning
Vom blattspiel (G)—Sight reading.
Vorausnahme (G)—Anticipation.
Vorbereitung (G)—Preparation.
Vordersatz (G)—First subject.
Vorhalt (G)—Suspension.
Vorher (G)—Before.
Vornehm (G)—Dignified.
Vorschlag (G)—Appoggiatura.
Vorspiel (G)—Prelude, overture.
Vortrag (G)—Execution.
Vortragzeichen (G) — Expression

marks.

Vorwärts (G)—Faster.

Vorzeichnung (G)—Signature.

Vox (L)—Voice.

Vox angelica (L) — Cf. Voix céleste.

Vox humana (L) — Cf. Voix céleste.

V. s. (Abb)—Volti subito.

Vuoto (I), **vide** (F)—Empty.

Vv. (Abb)—Violins.

— W —

Wachsend (G)—Crescendo.

Wachtel (G)—Toy pipe which mimicks the quail.

Wahnsinnig (G)—Frenzied.

Wald-flöte (G)—Shepherd's flute; organ stop.

Waldhorn (G)—French horn.

Waldstein Sonata — Beethoven's Piano Sonata in C, op. 53.

Waltz (E), **walzer** (G), **valse** (F) —A dance in moderate triple time.

Walze (G)—Crescendo pedal of the organ.

Wankend (G)—Wavering.

Wärme (G)—Warmth.

Water Music—Orchestral Suite by Handel (1715).

Wechselnote (G), **nota cambiata** (I)—Changing note.

Wehmütig (G)—Sad.

Weich (G)—Soft.

Weihnachtslied (G) — Christmas music.

Well-tempered—Satisfactory pitch relationship.

Weltlich (G)—Secular.

Wenig (G)—Little.

Werdend (G)—Becoming.

Werk (G)—Work.

Wert (G)—Value.

Whole note—Four quarter beats; semibreve (◯).

Whole rest—A pause equal in time to a whole note.

Whole step—Major second.

Wiederholung (G)—Repetition.

Wiegend (G)—Swaying.

Wiegenlied (G)—Lullaby.

Wie oben (G)—As above.

Wie vorher (G)—As before.

Wie zuvor (G)—As previously.

Wind-chest — An air-tight box which receives the wind from the bellows of the organ.

Wind-gauge—A device on the organ indicating the amount of air in the bellows.

Wind instruments — All instruments sounded by air.

Wirbel (G)—Violin peg; drum roll.

Wohlklang (G)—Harmony.

Wohltemperiert (G) — Well-tempered.

Wolf—Disagreeable effect due to improper tuning.

Woodwinds—Orchestral wind instruments made of wood.

Wuchtig (G)—Ponderous.

Würdig (G)—Dignified.

Wütend (G)—Furious.

— X —

Xylophone—A percussion instrument made of graduated wooden bars which are struck with a hammer to produce tones.

— Y —

Yobel, yodel, jodel—Special type of singing among the Swiss and Tyrolean mountaineers characterized by falsetto tones interspersed with chest tones.

Yüeh ch'in—Chinese guitar.

— Z —

Zähle (G), **si conta** (I), **comptez** (F)—Direction to count.

Zahlzeit (G)—Beat.

Zampogna (I)—Bagpipe.

Zanfonia (S)—Hurdy gurdy.

Zarge (G)—Ribs of the violin.

Zart (G)—Tender.

Zarzuela—Type of S. opera having music interspersed with dialogue.

Zauber (G)—Magic.

Z. B. (Abb)—Zum beispiel.

Zeffroso (I)—Like a zephyr.

Zehn (G)—Ten.

Zeit (G)—Time.

Zeitmass (G)—Tempo.

Zeitmesser (G)—Metronome.

Zeloso (I)—Zealous.

Zerstreut (G)—Scattered.

Ziemlich (G)—Moderately.

Zierlich (G)—Graceful.

Zigeunermusik (G)—Gypsy music.

Zimbalon—Hungarian dulcimer.

Zirkelkanon (G)—Circular canon.

Zither—Instrument consisting of a flat wooden soundbox over which are stretched about 30 strings, these being plucked by plectrum and fingers.

Zitternd (G)—Trembling.

Zögernd (G)—Hesitating.

Zornig (G)—With anger.

Zortziko — Basque folk dance in 5/8 time and dotted rhythm.

Zu (G)—To, at, by.

Zuffolo (I) — Shepherd's pipes, shawms.

Zug (G)—Slide.

Zugeeignet (G)—Dedicated.

Zugposaune (G)—Slide trombone.

Zugtrompete (G)—Slide trumpet.

Zum beispiel (G)—For example.

Zunehmend (G)—Increasing.

Zunge (G)—Reed, tongue.

Zurückhaltend (G)—Retarding.

Zusammenklang (G)—Consonance, harmony.

Zutraulich (G)—Confiding.

Zwei (G)—Two.

Zweite (G)—Second.

Zweimal (G)—Twice.

Zwischensatz (G)—Episode.

Zwischenspiel (G)—Interlude.

Zwolf (G)—Twelve.

Zymbel (G)—Cymbal.

FAMILIAR
QUOTATIONS

Ability.

Ability wins us the esteem of the true men; luck that of the people.
La Rochefoucauld.

Consider well what your strength is equal to, and what exceeds your ability.
Horace.

An able man shows his spirit by gentle words and resolute actions; he is neither hot nor timid. *Chesterfield.*

Absence.

In my Lucia's absence
Life hangs upon me, and becomes a burden;
I am ten times undone, while hope, and fear,
And grief, and rage and love rise up at once,
And with variety of pain distract me.
Addison.

O thou who dost inhabit in my breast,
Leave not the mansion, so long tenantless;
Lest growing ruinous the building fall,
And leave no memory of what it was.
Shakespeare.

Abstinence.

To set the mind above the appetites is the end of abstinence, which one of the Fathers observes to be, not a *virtue*, but the *groundwork of a virtue*. *Johnson.*

Abuse.

The bitter clamour of two eager tongues.
Shakespeare.

Account.

No reckoning made, but sent to my account
With all my imperfections on my head.
Shakespeare.

Acquaintance.

There is a wide difference between general acquaintance and companionship. You may salute a man and exchange compliments with him daily, yet know nothing of his character, his inmost tastes and feelings. *Wm. Matthews.*

Acquaintances.

If a man does not make new acquaintances, as he advances through life, he will soon find himself left alone. A man should keep his friendship in constant repair.
Johnson.

Make the most of the day, by determining to spend it on *two* sorts of acquaintances only—those by whom something may be got, and those from whom something may be learned.
Colton.

Acquirements.

That which we acquire with the most difficulty we retain the longest; as those who have earned a fortune are usually more careful of it than those who have inherited one.
Colton.

Acting.

All the world's a stage.
Shakespeare.

Action.

We should often be ashamed of our very best actions, if the world only saw the motives which caused them.
La Rochefoucauld.

When we cannot act as we wish, we must act as we can. *Terrence.*

The end of man is an action, and not a thought, though it were the noblest.
Carlyle.

Think that day lost whose low descending sun
Views from thy hand no noble action done.
Jacob Bobart.

Advise well before you begin, and when you have maturely considered, then act with promptitude. *Sallust.*

Strong reasons make strong actions.
Shakespeare.

Actions.

Our actions are our own; their consequences belong to Heaven. *Francis.*

The evil that men do lives after them;
The good is oft interr'd with their bones.
Shakespeare.

All our actions take
Their hues from the complexion of the heart,
As landscapes their variety from light.
W. T. Bacon.

Actions of the last age are like almanacs of the last year. *Sir Thomas Denham.*

Act well at the moment, and you have performed a good action to all eternity.

Lavater.

Acts.

The best portion of a good man's life,
His little, nameless, unremembered acts of
kindness and of love.   *Wordsworth.*

Our acts our angels are, or good or ill,
Our fatal shadows that walk by us still.

John Fletcher.

Activity.

Run, if you like, but try to keep your
breath ;
Work like a man, but don't be worked to
death.   *Holmes.*

Acuteness.

The keen spirit
Seizes the prompt occasion—makes the
thought
Start into instant action, and at once
Plans and performs, resolves and executes.

Hannah Moore.

A man who knows the world will not
only make the most of everything he does
know, but of many things that he does not
know ; and will gain more credit by his
adroit mode of hiding his ignorance than
the pedant by his awkward attempt to exhibit his erudition.   *Colton.*

Adversity.

Adversity borrows its sharpest sting
from our impatience.   *Bishop Horne.*

Adversity has the effect of eliciting talents. which in prosperous circumstances
would have lain dormant.   *Horace.*

The good are better made by ill,
As odors crush'd are sweeter still.

Rogers.

The firmest friendships have been
formed in mutual adversity, as iron is
most strongly welded by the fiercest fire.

Such a house broke !
So noble a master fallen ! All gone and not
One friend to take his fortune by the arm
And go along with him.   *Shakespeare.*

Adversity's sweet milk, Philosophy.

Shakespeare.

He is the most wretched of men who
has never felt adversity.

Sweet are the uses of adversity,
Which like the toad, ugly and venomous,
Wears yet a precious jewel in his head ;
And this our life, exempt from public
haunt.
Find tongues in trees, books in the run-
ning brooks.
And good in everything.   *Shakespeare.*

We ask advice, but we mean approbation.   *Colton.*

Let no man presume to give advice to
others that has not first given good counsel to himself.   *Seneca.*

Love all, trust a few.
Do wrong to none ; be able for thine enemy
Rather in power than use ; and keep thy
friend
Under thine own life's key ; be checked
for silence.
But never taxed for speech.   *Shakespeare.*

The worst men often give the best advice.   *Bailey.*

We give advice, but we cannot give the
wisdom to profit by it.   *La Rochefoucauld.*

Give thy thoughts no tongue,
Nor any unproportioned thought his act.
Be thou familiar, but by no means vulgar.
The friends thou hast, and their adoption
tried,
Grapple them to thy soul with hooks of
steel ;
But do not dull thy palm with entertain-
ment
Of each new-hatched, unfledged comrade.
Beware
Of entrance to a quarrel ; but, being in,
Bear it that the opposer may beware of
thee.
Give every man thine ear, but few thy
voice.
Take each man's censure, but reserve thy
judgment.
Costly thy habit as thy purse can buy,
But not expressed in fancy ; rich, not
gaudy ;
For the apparel oft proclaims the man.
Neither a borrower nor a lender be,
For loan oft loses both itself and friend ;
And borrowing dulls the edge of hus-
bandry.
This above all : To thine own self be true ;
And it must follow, as the night the day,
Thou cans't not then be false to any man.

Shakespeare.

He who can take advice is sometimes
superior to him who can give it.

Von Knebel.

Let no man value at a little price
A virtuous woman's counsel ; her winged
spirit
Is feathered often times with heavenly
words,
And, like her beauty, ravishing and pure.

Chapman.

Affection.

Fathers alone a father's heart can know
What secret tides of still enjoyment flow

When brothers love, but if their hate succeeds,
They wage the war, but 'tis the father bleeds. *Young.*

Affections.

Of all the tyrants the world affords,
Our own affections are the fiercest lords.
Earl of Sterling.

O you much partial gods!
Why gave ye men affections, and not power
To govern them? *Ludovick Barry.*

Nothing can occur beyond the strength of faith to sustain, or, transcending the resources of religion, to relieve. *Binney.*

Man is born to trouble, as the sparks fly upward. *Job v. 7*

Age.

Age sits with decent grace upon his visage,
And worthily becomes his silver locks;
He bears the marks of many years well spent,
Of virtue truth well tried, and wise experience. *Rowe.*

As you are old and reverend, you should be wise. *Shakespeare.*

These are the effects of doting age,
Vain doubts, and idle cares, and over caution. *Dryden.*

But an old age serene and bright,
And lovely as a Lapland night,
Shall lead thee to thy grave.
Wordsworth.

How blest is he who crowns, in shades like these,
A youth of labor with an age of ease.
Goldsmith.

Eternal sunshine settles on its head.
Goldsmith.

Care keeps his watch in every old man's eye. *Shakespeare.*

When men grow virtuous in their old age, they are merely making a sacrifice to God of the Devil's leavings. *Swift.*

Last scene of all
That ends this strange, eventful history,
Is second childishness, and mere oblivion;
Sans teeth, sans eyes, sans taste, sans everything. *Shakespeare.*

These old fellows have
Their ingratitude in them hereditary;
Their blood is caked, 'tis cold, it seldom flows;
'Tis lack of kindly warmth, they are not kind,
And nature, as it grows toward earth,
Is fashion'd for the journey—dull and heavy. *Shakespeare.*

Every man desires to live long; but no man would be old. *Swift.*

Age is a tyrant, who forbids, at the penalty of life, all the pleasures of youth.
La Rochefoucauld.

Ambition.

Ambition is an idol, on whose wings
Great minds are carried only to extreme;
To be sublimely great or to be nothing.
Southey.

O cursed ambition, thou devouring bird,
How dost thou from the field of honesty
Pick every grain of profit or delight,
And mock the reaper's toil! *Havard.*

What is ambition? 'Tis a glorious cheat.
Angels of light walk not so dazzlingly
The sapphire walls of heaven. *Willis.*

Dream after dream ensues,
And still they dream that they shall still succeed,
And still are disappointed. *Cowper.*

Ambition's like a circle on the water,
Which never ceases to enlarge itself,
'Till by broad spreading it disperse to nought. *Shakespeare.*

Accurst ambition,
How dearly I have bought you.
Dryden.

Airy ambition, soaring high. *Sheffield.*

Why dost thou court that baneful pest, ambition? *Potter.*

—— brave thirst of fame his bosom warms.
Churchill.

Ah! curst ambition! to thy lures we owe,
All the great ills that mortals bear below.
Teckell.

The dropsy'd thirst of empire, wealth or fame. *Nugent.*

The glorious frailty of the noble mind.
Hoole.

No bounds his headlong, vast ambition knows. *Rowe.*

Ambition is like love, impatient
Both of delays and rivals.
Denham.

———— ambition, idly vain;
Revenge and malice swell her train.
Penrose.

Vaulting ambition which o'erleaps itself.
Shakespeare.

What's all the gaudy glitter of a crown?
What but the glaring meteor of ambition,
That leads the wretch benighted in his errors,
Points to the gulf and shines upon destruction? *Brooke.*

Who soars too near the sun, with golden

wings,
Melts them; to ruin his own fortune brings.
Shakespeare.

Farewell, a long farewell, to all my greatness!
This is the state of man. To-day he puts forth
The tender leaves of hope; to-morrow blossoms,
And bears his blushing honors thick upon him;
The third day comes a frost, a killing frost. *Shakespeare.*

'Tis a common proof,
That lowliness is young ambition's ladder,
Wherto the climber upwards turns his face;
But when he once attains the utmost round,
He then unto the ladder turns his back,
Looks in the clouds, scorning the base degrees
By which he did ascend. *Shakespeare.*

Ambition is a lust that's never quenched,
Grows more inflamed, and madder by enjoyment. *Otway.*

A slave has but one master; the ambitious man has as many masters as there are persons whose aid may contribute to the advancement of his fortune.
La Bruyere.

Our natures are like oil; compound us with anything,
Yet will we strive to swim at the top.
Beaumont and Fletcher.

Dreams, indeed, are ambition; for the very substance of the ambitious is merely the shadow of a dream. And I hold ambition of so airy and light a quality, that it is but a shadow's shadow. *Shakespeare.*

Oh, sons of earth! attempt ye still to rise,
By mountains pil'd on mountains to the skies?
Heaven still with laughter the vain toil surveys,
And buries madmen in the heaps they raise. *Pope.*

Amusements.

The mind ought sometimes to be amused, that it may the better return to thought, and to itself. *Phaedrus.*

Ancestry.

.I am one
Who finds within me a nobility
That spurns the idle pratings of the great,
And their mean boast of what their fathers were,
While they themselves are fools effeminate,

The scorn of all who know the worth of mind
And virtue. *Percival.*

The man who has not anything to boast of but his illustrious ancestors, is like a potato—the only thing belonging to him is under ground. *Sir T. Overbury.*

Angels.

So dear to heaven is saintly chastity,
That when a soul is found sincerely so
A thousand liveried angels lackey her.
Milton.

Man hath two attendant angels
Ever waiting by his side,
With him wheresoe'r he wanders,
Wheresoe'r his feet abide;
One to warn him when he darkleth,
And rebuke him if he stray;
One to leave him to his nature,
And so let him go his way. *Prince.*

A guardian angel o'er his life presides,
Doubling his pleasures and his cares dividing. *Rogers.*

We are ne'er like angels 'till our passion dies. *Dekker.*

Fools rush in where angels fear to tread.
Pope.

Anger.

Be ye angry and sin not; let not the sun go down upon your wrath. *Eph. iv, 26.*

Anger
Is blood, pour'd and perplexed into a froth.
Davenant.

My rage is not malicious; like a spark
Of fire by steel inforced out of a flint
It is no sooner kindled, but extinct.
Goffe.

There is not in nature
A thing that makes a man so deform'd, so beastly,
As doth intemperate anger.
Webster's Duchess of Malp.

To be angry, is to revenge the fault of others upon ourselves. *Pope.*

The intoxication of anger, like that of the grape, shows us to others, but hides us from ourselves, and we injure our own cause, in the opinion of the world, when we too passionately and eagerly defend it.
Colton.

When a man is wrong and won't admit it, he always gets angry. *Haliburton.*

My indignation, like th' imprisoned fire,
Pent in the troubled breast of glowing Ætna,
Burnt deep and silent. *Thomson.*

If anger is not restrained, it is frequently more hurtful to us, than the injury that provokes it. *Seneca.*

O that my tongue were in the thunder's mouth!
Then with a passion would I shake the world. *Shakespeare.*

Angling.

In genial spring, beneath the quiv'ring shade,
Where cooling vapors breathe along the mead,
The patient fisher takes his silent stand,
Intent, his angle trembling in his hand;
With looks unmoved, he hopes the scaly breed,
And eyes the dancing cork and bending reed. *Pope.*

I in these flowery meads would be;
These crystal streams would solace me;
To whose harmonious, bubbling noise
I with my angle would rejoice.
Isaac Walton.

Animals.

Let cavillers deny
That brutes have reason; sure tis something more,
'Tis heaven directs, and stratagems inspires
Beyond the short extent of human thought.
Somerville.

Answering.

Any man that can write, may answer a letter. *Shakespeare.*

Anticipation.

By the pricking of my thumbs
Something wicked this way comes.
Shakespeare.

Antipathy.

Some men there are love not a gaping pig;
Some that are mad, if they behold a cat.
Masterless passion sways it to the mood,
Of what it likes or loathes *Shakespeare*

Antiquary.

They say he sits
All day in contemplation of a statue,
With ne'er a nose, and dotes on the decays
With greater love than the self-lov'd Narcissus
Did on his beauty. *Shakerly Marmyon.*

Antiquity.

Time's gradual touch
Has moulder'd into beauty many a tower
Which when it frown'd with all its battlements,

Was only terrible. *Mason.*

All those things which are now held to be of the greatest antiquity, were at one time new; and what we to-day hold up by example, will rank hereafter as a precedent. *Tacitus.*

Anxiety.

It is not work that kills men; it is worry. Work is healthy; you can hardly put more upon a man than he can bear. Worry is rust upon the blade. It is not the revolution that destroys the machinery, but the friction. Fear secretes acids; but love and trust are sweet juices.
Beecher.

Apology.

What! shall this speech be spoke for our excuse?
Or shall we on without apology?
Shakespeare.

Appeal.

And here I stand; judge, my masters.
Shakespeare.

Appearance.

He has, I know not what
Of greatness in his looks, and of high fate
That almost awes me. *Dryden.*

Within the oyster's shell uncouth
The purest pearl may hide,
Trust me you'll find a heart of truth
Within that rough inside.
Mrs. Osgood.

'Tis not the fairest form that holds
The mildest, purest soul within;
'Tis not the richest plant that holds
The sweetest fragrance in. *Dawes.*

Appearances.

Appearances deceive
And this one maxim is a standing rule:
Men are not what they seem. *Havard.*

The ass is still an ass, e'en though he wears a lion's hide.

The chameleon may change its color, but it is the chameleon still.

The world is still deceived by ornament.
In law, what plea so tainted and corrupt,
But being seasoned with a gracious voice,
Obscures the show of error? In religion,
What damn'd error, but some sober brow
Will bless it and approve it with a text,
Hiding the grossness with fair ornament?
There is no vice so simple, but assumes
Some mark of virtue on its outward parts.
How many cowards, whose hearts are all as false
As stairs of sand, wear yet upon their chins
The beards of Hercules, and frowning

Mars;
Who inward search'd have livers white as
    milk?
And these assume but valor's excrement,
To render them redoubted. Look on beauty,
And you shall see 'tis purchas'd by the
    weight;
Which therein works a miracle in nature,
Making them lightest that wear most of it.
So are those crisped, snaky, golden locks,
Which make such wanton gambols with the
    wind,
Upon supposed fairness, often known
To be the dowry of a second head,
The skull that bred them, in the sepulchre.
Thus ornament is but the guilded shore
To the most dangerous sea; the beauteous
    scarf
Veiling an Indian beauty; in a word,
The seeming truth which cunning times
    put on
To entrap the wisest.   *Shakespeare.*

Appetite.

Now good digestion wait on appetite,
And health on both.   *Shakespeare.*

Applause.

Applause is the spur of noble minds, the
end and aim of weak ones.   *Colton.*

Apple.

He kept him as the apple of his eye.
                        Deut. xxxii, 10.

Appreciation.

A primrose on the river's brim,
    Or by the cottage door,
A yellow primrose was to him,
    And it was nothing more.
                        Wordsworth.

Apprehensions.

Better to be despised for too anxious ap-
prehensions, than ruined by too confident a
security.   *Burke.*

Appropriation.

It is a special trick of low cunning to
squeeze out knowledge from a modest man,
who is eminent in any science, and then to
use it as legally acquired, and pass the
source in total silence.   *Horace Walpole.*

Aptitude.

I cannot draw a cart, nor eat dried oats;
If it be man's work I will do it.
                        Shakespeare.

Architect.

Every man is the architect of his own
fortune.   *Appius Claudius.*

Architecture.

Architecture is the printing press of all

ages, and gives a history of the state of
the society in which it was erected.
                        Lady Morgan.

Argument.

Who shall decide when doctors disagree,
And sound casuists doubt like you and me?
                        Pope.
The Devil can quote scripture for his pur-
    pose.   *Shakespeare.*
Be calm in arguing; for fierceness makes
Error a fault, and truth discourtesy.
Why should I feel another man's mistakes
More than his sickness or poverty?
In love I should; but anger is not love,
Nor wisdom neither; therefore gently
    move.
Calmness is great advantage; he that lets
Another chafe may warm him at his fire,
Mark all his wand'rings and enjoy his
    frets,
As cunning fencers suffer heat to tire.
                        Herbert.
    A man convinced against his will
    Is of the same opinion still.   *Butler.*
No argument can be drawn from the
abuse of a thing against its use.   *Latin.*
In arguing, too, the parson owned his skill,
For even tho' vanquish'd he could argue
    still.   *Goldsmith.*
He'd undertake to prove, by force
    O' argument, a man's no horse.
He'd prove a buzzard is no fowl,
And that a lord may be an owl,
A calf an alderman, a goose a justice,
And rooks committeemen and trustees.
                        Butler.

Arguments.

Examples I could cite you more:
But be contented with these four;
For when one's proofs are aptly chosen
Four are as valid as four dozen.   *Prior.*

Army.

All in a moment through the gloom were
    seen
Ten thousand banners rise into the air,
With orient colors waving: With them
    rose
A forest huge of spears, and thronging
    helms
Appear'd, and serried shields and thick
    array
Of depth immeasurable.   *Milton.*

Artifice.

It is sometimes necessary to play the
fool to avoid being deceived by cunning
men.   *La Rochefoucauld.*

Artist.

A flattering painter, who made it his care
To draw men as they ought to be, not as

they are. *Goldsmith.*

Ascendency.

Whatever natural right men have to freedom and independency, it is manifest that some men have a natural ascendency over others. *Greville.*

Aspect.

The tartness of his face sours ripe grapes. *Shakespeare.*

Assertions.

There is nothing as cheap and weak in debate as assertion that is not backed by fact.

Assignation.

An assignation sweetly made,
With gentle whispers in the dark.
Francis.

Associates.

Choose the company of your superiors, whenever you can have it; that is the right and true pride. *Lord Chesterfield.*

He who comes from the kitchen, smells of its smoke; and he who adheres to a sect, has something of its cant; the college air pursues the student; and dry inhumanity him who herds with literary pedants. *Lavater.*

Associations.

There's not a wind but whispers of thy
    name;
And not a flow'r that grows beneath the
    moon,
But in its hues and fragrance tells a tale
Of thee, my love. *Barry Cornwall.*

Astonishment.

I could a tale unfold, whose lightest word
Would harrow up thy soul; freeze thy
    young blood;
Make thy two eyes, like stars, start from
    their spheres;
Thy knotted and combined locks to part,
And each particular hair to stand on end,
Like quills upon the fretful porcupine.
Shakespeare.

Astronomy.

The contemplation of celestial things will make a man both speak and think more sublimely and magnificently when he descends to human affairs. *Cicero.*

Atheism.

Atheism is the result of ignorance and pride; of strong sense and feeble reasons; of good eating and ill-living. It is the plague of society, the corrupter of manners, and the underminer of property.
Jeremy Collier.

There is no being eloquent for atheism. In that exhausted receiver the mind cannot use its wings—the clearest proof that it is out of its element. *Hare.*

Atheism is rather in the life than in the heart of man. *Bacon.*

Atheist.

No atheist, as such, can be a true friend, an affectionate relation, or a loyal subject. *Dr. Bentley.*

By night an atheist half believes a God.
Young.

Atmosphere.

When you find that flowers and shrubs will not endure a certain atmosphere, it is a very significant hint to the human creature to remove out of that neighborhood.
Mayhew.

Attention.

Lend thy serious hearing to what I shall unfold. *Shakespeare.*

Author.

Never write on a subject without having first read yourself full on it; and never read on a subject 'till you have thought yourself hungry on it. *Richter.*

If an author write better than his contemporaries, they will term him a plagiarist; if as well, a pretender; but if worse, he may stand some chance of commendation as a genius of some promise, from whom much may be expected by a due attention to their good counsel and advice.
Colton.

Authority.

Man, proud man!
Drest in a little brief authority,
Most ignorant of what he's most assur'd,
His glassy essence, like an angry ape,
Plays such fantastic tricks before high
    heaven
As make the angels weep. *Shakespeare.*

Authority intoxicates,
And makes mere sots of magistrates.
The fumes of it invade the brain,
And make men giddy, proud and vain;
By this the fool commands the wise
The noble with the base complies.
The sot assumes the rule of wit,
And cowards make the base submit.
Butler.

Authorship.

The two most engaging powers of an author are to make *new* things *familiar,* and *familiar* things *new.* *Johnson.*

None but an author knows an author's
    cares,

Or fancy's fondness for the child she bears.
Cowper.

'Tis pleasant, sure, to see one's name in print;
A book's a book, although there's nothing in't.
Byron.

Autumn.

Then came the autumne, all in yellow clad,
As though he joy'd in his plenteous store,
Laden with fruits that made him laugh, full glad
That he had banished hunger, which tofore
Had by the belly oft him pinched sore;
Upon his head a wreath that was enrol'd
With ears of corne of every sort, he bore,
And in his hand a sickle did he holde,
To reape the ripened fruit the which the earth had yold.
Spenser.

Thrice happy time,
Best portion of the various year, in which
Nature rejoiceth, smiling on her works
Lovely, to full perfection wrought.
Phillips.

Avarice.

It may be remarked for the comfort of honest poverty, that avarice reigns most in those who have but few good qualities to recommend them. This is a weed that will grow in a barren soil.
Hughes.

Because men believe not in Providence, therefore they do so greedily scrape and hoard. They do not believe in any reward for charity, therefore they will part with nothing.
Barrow.

O, cursed love of gold; when for thy sake,
The fool throws up his interest in both worlds,
First starved in this, then damn'd in that to come.
Blair.

Extreme avarice is nearly always mistaken; there is no passion which is oftener further away from its mark, nor upon which the present has so much power to the prejudice of the future. *La Rochefoucauld.*

Avarice is always poor, but poor by her own fault.
Johnson.

'Tis strange the miser should his cares employ
To gain those riches he can ne'er enjoy.
Pope.

Aversion.

I do not love thee, Doctor Fell.
The reason why, I cannot tell;
But this alone I know full well
I do not love thee, Doctor Fell.
Tom Brown.

Awkwardness.

Not all the pumice of the polish'd town
Can smooth the roughness of the barnyard clown;
Rich, honor'd, titled, he betrays his race
By this one mark—he's awkward in his face.
Holmes.

Axe.

When I see a merchant over-polite to his customer, begging them to take a little brandy, and throwing his goods on the counter, thinks I, that man has an axe to grind.
Franklin, (Poor Richard.)

Babbler.

Fie! what a spendthrift he is of his tongue!
Shakespeare.

Badness.

Damnable, both sides rogue.
Shakespeare.

Bag.

It is hard for an empty bag to stand upright.
Franklin (Poor Richard.)

Ball.

A thousand hearts beat happily; and when
Music arose with its voluptuous swell
Soft eyes looked love to eyes that spake again,
And all went merry as a marriage bell.
Byron.

I saw her at a country ball.
There, when the sound of flute and fiddle,
Gave signal sweet in that old hall.
Of hands across and down the middle.
Her's was the subtlest spell by far
Of all that sets young hearts romancing;
She was our queen, our rose, our star;
And when she danced—oh, heaven, her dancing!
Praed.

Ballads.

I knew a very wise man that believed that, if a man were permitted to make all the ballads, he need not care who should make the laws of a nation.
Fletcher of Saltoun.

Ballot.

As lightly falls
As snow flakes fall upon the sod.
But executes a freeman's will.
As lightning does the will of God.
Halleck.

Banishment.

All places that the eye of heaven visits,
Are, to a wise man, ports and happy havens.
Teach thy necessity to reason thus:
There is no virtue like necessity.
Shakespeare.

Banquet.

A table richly spread in regal mode,
With dishes piled, and meats of noblest
    sort,
And savor; beasts of chase, or fowl of
    game,
In pastry built, or from the spit, or boil'd
Gris-amber-steam'd; all fish from sea or
    shore,
Freshet or purling brook, for which was
    drain'd
Pontus, and Lucrine bay, and Afric coast
                 Milton.

Bashfulness.

So sweet the blush of bashfulness
Even pity scarce can wish it less.
                 Byron.

There are two distinct sorts of what we
call bashfulness; *this*, the awkwardness of
a booby, which a few steps into the world
will convert into the pertness of a cox
comb; *that*, a consciousness, which the
most delicate feelings produce, and the
most extensive knowledge cannot always
remove.   *Mackenzie.*

Battle.

His back against a rock he bore,
And firmly placed his foot before;
"Come one, come all! this rock shall fly
From its firm base as soon as I." *Scott.*
Now night her course began, and over
    heaven
Inducing darkness, grateful truce, impos'd
Her silence on the odious din of war;
Under her cloudy covert hath retired
Victor and vanquish'd.   *Milton.*
Hark! the death - denouncing trumpet
    sounds
The fatal charge, and shouts proclaim the
    onset;
Destruction rushes dreadful to the field,
And bathes itself in blood; havoc let loose
Now undistinguish'd rages all around,
While ruin, seated on her dreary throne,
Sees the plain strewed with subjects truly
    hers,
Breathless and cold.   *Harvard.*
That awful pause, dividing life from death,
Struck for an instant on the hearts of men,
Thousands of whom were drawing their
    last breath!
A moment all will be life again.
*   *   *   *   *   *   one moment more,
The death-cry drowning in the battle's
    roar.   *Byron.*
         This day hath made
Much work for tears in many an English
    mother,
Whose sons lie scatter'd on the bleeding
    ground;

Many a widow's husband groveling lies,
Coldly embracing the discolor'd earth.
              Shakespeare.
When Greeks join'd Greeks, then was the
    tug of war;
The labour'd battle sweat, and conquest
    bled.   *Lee.*

Beard.

It has no bush below;
Marry a little wool, as much as an unripe
    Peach doth wear;
Just enough to speak him drawing towards
    a man.   *Suckling.*
He that hath a beard is more than a youth;
And he that hath none is less than a man.
              Shakespeare.

Beautiful.

The beautiful are never desolate,
But some one always loves them.
               Bailey.

Beauty.

       O she is all perfection,
All that the blooming earth can send forth
    fair,
All that the gaudy heavens could drop
    down glorious.   *Lee.*
         When I approach
Her loveliness, so absolute she seems,
And in herself complete, so well to know
Her own, that what she wills to do or say,
Seems wisest, virtuousest, discretest, best;
All higher knowledge in her presence falls
Degraded. Wisdom in discourse with her
Loses, discount'nanc'd, and like folly
    shows.   *Milton.*
Nature was here so lavish of her store,
That she bestow'd until she had no more.
              Brown.
    Oh! she has a beauty might ensnare
A conqueror's soul, and make him leave his
    crown
At random, to be scuffled for by slaves.
              Otway.
Grace was in all her steps, heav'n in her
    eye,
In every gesture dignity and love. *Milton.*
        Beauty is a witch,
Against whose charms faith melteth into
    blood.   *Shakespeare.*
Her eyes, her lips, her cheeks, her shapes,
    her features,
Seem to be drawn by love's own hand; by
    love
Himself in love.   *Dryden.*

The criterion of true beauty is, that it
increases on examination; of false, that it
lessens. There is something, therefore, in

FAM QUOTES

true beauty that corresponds with the right reason, and it is not merely the creature of fancy. *Greville.*

Beauty, like ice, our footing does betray:
Who can tread sure on the smooth, slippery way?
Pleased with the surface, we glide swiftly on,
And see the dangers that we cannot shun. *Dryden.*

I long not for the cherries on the tree,
So much as those which on a lip I see;
And more affection bear I to the rose
That in a cheek than in a garden grows. *Randolph.*

A thing of beauty is a joy forever,
Its loveliness increases; it will never
Pass into nothingness. *Keats.*

O fatal beauty! why art thou bestow'd
On hapless woman still to make her wretched!
Betray'd by thee, how many are undone! *Patterson.*

For her own person,
It beggar'd all description; she did lie
In her pavilion,
O'er-picturing that Venus, where we see
The fancy outwork nature. *Shakespeare.*

That is the best part of beauty which a picture cannot express. *Bacon.*

Beauty is worse than wine; it intoxicates both the holder and the beholder. *Zimmerman.*

Beauty is truth, truth beauty—that is all
Ye know on earth, and all ye need to know. *Keats.*

When I forget that the stars shine in air,
When I forget that beauty is in stars—
Shall I forget thy beauty. *Thomson.*

But then her face
So lovely, yet so arch, so full of mirth,
The overflowings of an innocent heart. *Rogers.*

All orators are dumb when beauty pleadeth. *Shakespeare.*

Socrates called beauty, a short lived tyranny; Plato, a privilege of nature; Theophrastes, a silent cheat; Theocritus, a delightful prejudice; Carneades, a solitary kingdom; Domitian said that nothing was more grateful; Aristotle affirmed that beauty was better than all the letters of recommendation in the world; Homer, that 'twas a glorious gift of nature; and Ovid alluding to him, calls it a favor bestowed by the Gods.

Remember if you marry for beauty, thou bindest thyself all thy life for that which

perchance, will neither last nor please thee one year; and when thou hast it, it will be to thee of no price at all. *Raleigh.*

Without the smile from partial beauty won,
O, what were man! a world without a sun! *Campbell.*

Beauty,
That transitory flower; even while it lasts
Palls on the roving sense, when held too near,
Or dwelling there too long; by fits it pleases,
And smells at distance best; its sweets familiar
By frequent converse, soon grow dull and cloy you. *Jeffry.*

The mate for beauty should be a man and not a money chest. *Bulwer.*

Ye tradeful merchants! that with weary toil,
Do seek most precious things to make you gaine,
And both the Indies of their treasures spoil:
What needeth you to seek so far in vain?
For lo! my love doth in herself contain
All this world's riches that may far be found;
If saphyrs, lo! her eyes be saphyrs plain;
If rubies, lo! her lips be rubies sound;
If pearls, her teeth be pearls, both pure and round;
If ivory, her forehead's ivory I ween;
If gold, her locks are finest gold on ground;
If silver, her fair hands are silver sheen:
But that which fairest is, but few behold,
Her mind, adorn'd with virtues manifold. *Spenser.*

Every trait of beauty may be traced to some virtue, as to innocence, candour, generosity, modesty, and heroism. *St. Pierre.*

Beauty is but a vain and doubtful good,
A shining gloss, that fadeth suddenly,
A flower that dies when first it 'gins to bud,
A brittle glass, that's broken presently:
A doubtful good, a gloss a glass, a flower,
Lost, faded, broken, dead within an hour. *Shakespeare.*

Beauty is as summer fruits, which are easy to corrupt and cannot last; and for the most part it makes a dissolute youth, and an age a little out of countenance; but if it light well, it makes virtue shine and vice blush. *Bacon.*

Honesty coupled to beauty, is to have honey sauce to sugar. *Shakespeare.*

What is beauty? Not the show
Of shapely limbs and features. No;

These are but flowers
That have their dated hours,
To breathe their momentary sweets and go.
'Tis the stainless soul within
That outshines the fairest skin.

Sir A. Hunt.

Beauty. without virtue. is like a flower without perfume. *From the French.*

Bed.

Bed is a bundle of paradoxes; we go to it with reluctance, yet we quit it with regret; and we make up our minds every night to leave it early, but we make up our bodies every morning to keep it late.

Colton.

Bed-Chamber.

Sweet pillows, sweetest bed;
A chamber deaf to noise, and blind to light;
A rosy garland, and a weary head.

Sir Philip Sydney.

Bee.

How doth the little busy bee
  Improve each shining hour,
And gather honey all the day
  From every opening flower. *Watts.*

Many colored, sunshine loving, spring-betokening bee!
Yellow bee, so mad for love of early blooming flowers!
Till thy waxen cells be full, fair fall thy work and thee,
Buzzing round the sweetly-smelling garden plots and flowers.

Professor Wilson.

Bees.

Even bees, the little alms-men of spring bowers,
Know there is richest juice in poison-flowers. *Keats.*

    So work the honey-bees;
Creatures, that by a rule in nature teach
The art of order to a peopled kingdom.
They have a king and officers of sorts;
Where some, like magistrates, correct at home;
Others, like merchants, venture trade abroad;
Others, like soldiers, armed in their stings,
Make boot upon the summer's velvet buds;
Which pillage they, with merry march, bring home,
To the tent royal of their emperor;
Who, busied in his majesty, surveys
The singing masons building roofs of gold;
The civil citizens kneading up the honey;
The poor mechanic porters crowding in
Their heavy burdens at his narrow gate;

The sad-ey'd justice, with his surly hum,
Delivering o'er to executors pale
The lazy yawning drone. *Shakespeare.*

Beggar.

The beggar, as he stretch'd his shrivel'd hand,
Rais'd not his eyes and those who dropp'd the mite
Pass'd on unnoticed. *Bailey.*

The adage must be verified—
That beggars mounted, run heir horse to death. *Shakespeare.*

Well, while I am a beggar, I will rail,
And say,—there is no sin but to be rich;
And being rich my virtue then shall be,
To say,—there is no vice but beggary.

Shakespeare.

Behavior.

Levity of behavior is the bane of all that is good and virtuous. *Seneca.*

What is becoming is honorable, and what is honorable is becoming. *Tully.*

Never put off till to-morrow what you can do to-day.

Never trouble another for what you can do yourself.

Never spend your money before you have it.

Never buy what you do not want because it is cheap.

Pride costs us more than hunger, thirst, and cold.

We seldom repent having eaten too little.

Nothing is troublesome that we do willingly.

How much pain the evils have cost us that have never happened!

Take things always by the smooth handle.

When angry, count ten before you speak: if very angry, a hundred. *Jefferson.*

Belief.

'Tis with our judgments as our watches; none
Are just alike, yet each believes his own.

Pope.

You believe that easily which you hope for earnestly. *Terence.*

Bells.

How soft the music of those village bells,
Falling at intervals upon the ear
In cadence sweet! now dying all away,
Now pealing loud again and louder still,
Clear and sonorous as the gale comes on,
With easy force it opens all the cells
Where memory slept. *Cowper.*

Benefactor.

And he gave it for his opinion, that whoever could make two ears of corn, or two blades of grass to grow upon a spot of ground, where only one grew before, would deserve better of mankind, and do more essential service to his country, than the whole race of politicians put together.
Swift.

Beneficence.

Men resemble the gods in nothing so much as in doing good to their fellow creatures. *Cicero.*

Benevolence.

The conqueror is regarded with awe, the wise man commands our esteem, but it is the benevolent man who wins our affection.
From the French.

A poor man served by thee, shall make thee rich. *Mrs. Browning.*

Think not the good,
The gentle deeds of mercy thou hast done,
Shall die forgotten all; the poor, the pris'ner,
The fatherless, the friendless, and the widow,
Who daily own the bounty of thy hand,
Shall cry to heav'n and pull a blessing on thee. *Rowe.*

The truly generous is the truly wise;
And he who loves not others lives unblest.
Home.

Bible.

This Book, this Holy Book, on every line,
Mark'd with the seal of high divinity,
On every leaf bedew'd with drops of love
Divine, and with the eternal heraldry
And signature of God Almighty stamp'd
From first to last; this ray of sacred light,
This lamp, from off the everlasting throne,
Mercy took down, and in the night of time
Stood, casting on the dark her gracious bow;
And evermore beseeching men with tears
And earnest sighs, to read, believe and live.
Pollok.

It has God for its author, salvation for its end, and truth, without any mixture of error, for its matter;—it is all pure, all sincere; nothing too much, nothing wanting. *Locke.*

The Scriptures teach us the best way of living, the noblest way of suffering, and the most comfortable way of dying.
Flavel.

A glory gilds the sacred page,
Majestic like the sun,
It gives a light to every age;
It gives, but borrows none.
Cowper.

Within that awful volume lies
The mystery of mysteries. *Scott.*

Bigotry.

She has no head, and cannot think; no heart, and cannot feel. When she moves, it is in wrath; when she pauses, it is amid ruin; her prayers are curses—her God is a demon—her communion is death—her vengeance is eternity—her decalogue written in the blood of her victims; and if she stops for a moment in her infernal flight, it is upon a kindred rock, to whet her vulture fang for a more sanguinary desolation. *Daniel O'Connell.*

To follow foolish precedents, and wink
With both our eyes is easier than to think.
Cowper.

Bird.

A light broke in upon my soul—
It was the carol of a bird;
It ceased—and then it came again
The sweetest song ear ever heard.
Byron.

Birth.

When real nobleness accompanies that imaginary one of birth, the imaginary seems to mix with real, and becomes real too. *Greville.*

Birthday.

Yet all I've learnt from hours rife,
With painful brooding here,
Is, that amid this mortal strife,
The lapse of every year
But takes away a hope from life,
And adds to death a fear.
Hoffman.

Blessings.

The dews of heaven fall thick in blessings on her. *Shakespeare.*
How blessings brighten as they take their flight! *Young*

Blindness.

He whom nature thus bereaves,
Is ever fancy's favorite child;
For thee enchanted dreams she weaves
Of changeful beauty, bright and wild.
Mrs. Osgood.

Blockhead.

A bee is not a busier animal than a blockhead. *Pope.*

Bluntness.

This is some fellow,
Who having been prais'd for bluntness, doth affect
A saucy roughness, and constrains the

garb,
Quite from his nature: he can't flatter, he!
An honest mind and plain,—he must speak
    truth!
And they will take it so; if not he's plain.
These kind of knaves I know, which in
    this plainness
Harbor more craft, and far corrupter ends,
Than twenty silly, duckling observants,
That stretch their duty nicely.
                        Shakespeare.

I have neither wit, nor words, nor worth,
Nor actions, nor utterance, nor the power
    of speech,
To stir men's blood: I only speak right on.
                        Shakespeare.

Blushes.

The heart's meteors tilting in the face.
                        Shakespeare.

Give me the eloquent cheek,
    When blushes burn and die
Like thine its changes speak,
    The spirit's purity.   *Mrs. Osgood.*
————the blush is formed—and flies—
Nor owns reflection's calm control;
It comes, it deepens—fades and dies,
    A gush of feeling from the soul.
                        Mrs. Dinnies.

The blush is Nature's alarm at the approach of sin and her testimony to the
dignity of virtue.   *Fuller.*

Confusion thrill'd me then, and secret joy
Fast throbbing, stole its treasure from
    my heart,
And mantling upward, turn'd my face to
    crimson.   *Brooke.*

Boasting.

When you begin with so much pomp and
    show,
Why is the end so little and so low?
                        Roscommon.

The empty vessel makes the greatest
sound.   *Shakespeare.*

For men (it is reported) dash and vapor
Less on the field of battle than on paper.
Thus in the hist'ry of dire campaign
More carnage loads the newspaper than
    plain.   *Dr. Wolcott.*

Body.

What! know ye not that your body is
the temple of the Holy Ghost which is in
you, which ye have of God: and ye are not
your own?   *Cor.* vi, 19.
For of the soul the body form doth take,
For soul is form, and doth the body make.
                        Spenser.

Books.

Books are a guide in youth, and an entertainment for age. They support us
under solitude, and keep us from becoming
a burden to ourselves. They help us to
forget the crossness of men and things,
compose our cares and our passions, and
lay our disappointments asleep. When we
are weary of the living, we may repair to
the dead, who have nothing of peevishness, pride or design in their conversation.
                        Collier.

Books should to one of these four ends
    conduce,
For wisdom, piety, delight or use.
                        Denham.

————The place that does
Contain my books, the best companions, is
To me a glorious court, where hourly I
Converse with the old sages and philoso-
    phers;

And sometimes for variety, I confer
With kings and emperors, and weigh their
    counsels;
Calling their victories, if unjustly got,
Unto a strict account; and in my fancy,
Deface their ill-plac'd statutes. *Fletcher.*

Books are men of higher stature,
And the only men that speak aloud for
future times to hear! *Mrs. Browning.*

Books, as Dryden aptly termed them, are
spectacles to read nature. * * They
teach us to understand and feel what we
see, to decipher and syllable the hiero-
glyphics of the sense.   *Hare.*

Books cannot always please, however good,
Minds are not ever craving for their food.
                        Crabbe.

He that will have no books but those
that are scarce, evinces about as correct a
taste in literature as he would do in friendship, who would have no friends but those
whom all the rest of the world have sent
to Coventry.   *Colton.*

As good almost kill a man, as kill a good
book; who kills a man, kills a reasonable
creature, God's image; but he who destroys a good book, kills reason itself.
                        Milton.

Reading maketh a full man, conference
a ready man, and writing an exact man.
                        Bacon.

History makes men wise; poets, witty:
the mathematics, subtile; natural philosophy, deep; moral, grave; logic and rhetoric
able to contend.   *Bacon.*

A good book is the precious life-blood of
a master spirit, embalmed and treasured
up on purpose to a life beyond life.
                        Milton.

FAM QUOTES

'Tis in books the chief
Of all perfections to be plain and brief.
Butler.

Some books are to be tasted, others to be swallowed, and some few to be chewed and digested. *Bacon.*

Many books require no thought from those who read them, for a very simple reason;—they made no such demand upon those who wrote them. Those works, therefore, are the most valuable that set our thinking faculties in the fullest operation. *Colton.*

I have somewhere seen it observed, that we should make the same use of a book that the bee does of a flower: she steals sweets from it, but does not injure it. *Colton.*

Borrowing.

Go to friends for advice;
To women for pity;
To strangers for charity;
To relatives for nothing.
Spanish Proverb.

I can get no remedy against this consumption of the purse; borrowing only lingers and lingers it out, but the disease is incurable. *Spanish Proverb.*

Bottle.

In the bottle, discontent seeks for comfort, cowardice for courage, and bashfulness for confidence. *Johnson.*

Bounty.

Such moderation with thy bounty join,
That thou may'st nothing give that is not thine.
That liberality is but cast away,
Which makes us borrow what we cannot pay. *Denham.*

Boxes.

The four boxes that rule the world—Cartridge-box, Ballot-box, Jury-box and Band-box.

Boyhood.

O! enviable, early days,
When dancing thoughtless pleasure's mazes.
To care, to guilt unknown!
How ill exchang'd for riper times,
To feel the follies, or the crimes
Of others, or my own!
Ye tiny elves, that guiltless sport,

Like linnets in the bush,
Ye little know the ill ye court,
When manhood is your wish!
The losses, the crosses,
That active men engage;
The fears all, the tears all,

Of dim declining age. *Burns.*

Ah! happy years! once more who would not be a boy. *Byron.*

Brains.

Not Hercules
Could have knock'd out his brains, for he had none. *Shakespeare.*

Bravery.

A spirit yet unquell'd and high,
That claims and seeks ascendency.
Byron.

A brave man may fall, but cannot yield.
A brave man may yield to a braver man.
None but the brave deserve the fair.
Dryden.

That's a valiant flea that dares eat his breakfast on the lip of a lion.
Shakespeare.

He is not worthy of the honeycomb
That shuns the hive because the bees have stings. *Shakespeare.*

The best hearts, Trim, are ever the bravest, replied my uncle Toby. *Sterne.*

Nature often enshrines gallant and noble hearts in weak bosoms—oftenest, God bless her! in female breasts. *Dickens.*

Breeding.

A well-bred dog generally bows to strangers.

Brevity.

Brevity is the soul of wit
And tediousness the outward limbs, and flourishes. *Shakespeare.*

If you would be pungent, be brief; for it is with words as with sunbeams—the more they are condensed the deeper they burn. *Southey.*

Bribery.

Who thinketh to buy villainy with gold,
Shall ever find such faith so bought—so sold. *Shakespeare.*

Silver, though white,
Yet it draws black lines; it shall not rule my palm
There to mark forth its base corruption,
Middleton and Rowley.

Broken-Heart.

The heart will break, yet brokenly live on.
Byron.

Brook.

Oh for a seat in some poetic nook
Just hid with trees and sparkling with a brook. *Leigh Hunt.*

Building.

Never build after you are five and forty: have five years' income in hand before you lay a brick; and always calculate the expense at double the estimate. *Kett.*

Bully.

A brave man is sometimes a desperado; a bully is always a coward. *Haliburton.*

Business.

A man who cannot mind his own business, is not to be trusted with the king's. *Saville.*

There are in business three things necessary—knowledge, temper and time. *Feltham.*

Never shrink from doing anything which your business calls you to do. The man who is above his business, may one day find his business above him. *Drew.*

But.

Oh, now comes that bitter word—but
Which makes all nothing that was said before,
That smooths and wounds, that strikes and dashes more
Than flat denial, or a plain disgrace. *Daniel.*

But yet
I do not like "but yet;" it does allay
The good precedence; fie upon "but yet;"
"But yet" is as a jailer to bring forth
Some monstrous malefactor. *Shakespeare.*

Cake.

My cake is dough. *Shakespeare.*

Calamity.

How wisely fate ordain'd for human kind
Calamity! which is the perfect glass,
Wherein we truly see and know ourselves. *Davenant.*

The willow which bends to the tempest, often escapes better than the oak which resists it; and so in great calamities, it sometimes happens that light and frivolous spirits recover their elasticity and presence of mind sooner than those of a loftier character. *Sir Walter Scott.*

Calamity is man's true touchstone. *Beaumont and Fletcher.*

Thus sometimes hath the brightest day a cloud;
And, after summer, ever more succeeds
Barren winter with his wrathful nipping cold,
So cares and joys abound, as seasons fleet. *Shakespeare.*

Calm.

How calm,—how beautiful comes on
The stilly hour, when storms have gone,
When warring winds have died away
And clouds, beneath the dancing ray
Melt off and leave the land and sea,
Sleeping in bright tranquillity. *Moore.*

The tempest is o'er-blown, the skies are clear,
And the sea charm'd into a calm so still
That not a wrinkle ruffles her smooth face. *Dryden.*

Calumny.

False praise can please, and calumny affright
None but the vicious, and the hypocrite. *Horace.*

Be thou as chaste as ice, as pure as snow, thou
Shalt not escape calumny. *Shakespeare.*

Candor.

I hold it cowardice
To rest mistrustful where a noble heart
Hath pawn'd an open hand in sign of love. *Shakespeare.*

The brave do never shun the light;
Just are their thoughts, and open are their tempers;
Truly without disguise they love and hate;
Still are they found in the fair face of day
And heav'n and men are judges of their actions. *Rowe.*

In simple and pure soul I come to you. *Shakespeare.*

Cant.

'Tis too much prov'd—that, with devotion's visage
And pious action, we do sugar o'er
The devil himself. *Shakespeare.*

Care.

Care keeps his watch in every old man's eye
And where care lodgeth, sleep will never lie. *Shakespeare.*

Care is no cure, but rather a corrosive
For things that are not to be remedied. *Shakespeare.*

Care seeks out wrinkled brows and hollow eyes,
And builds himself caves to abide in them. *Beaumont and Fletcher.*

Still though the headlong cavalier,
O'er rough and smooth, in wild career,
Seems racing with the wind;
His sad companion, ghastly pale,
And darksome as a widow's veil,
Care keeps her seat behind. *Horace.*

FAM QUOTES

God tempers the wind to the shorn lamb.
Sterne.

Care that is once enter'd into the breast
Will have the whole possession ere it rest.
Johnson.

Man is a child of sorrow, and this world,
In which we breathe, has cares enough to
plague us,
But it hath means withal to soothe these
cares,
And he who meditates on others' woe,
Shall in that meditation lose his own.
Cumberland.

Cares.

Providence has given us *hope* and *sleep*,
as a compensation for the many cares of
life. *Voltaire.*

But human bodies are sic fools,
For a' their colleges and schools,
That when nae real ills perplex them,
They make enow themselves to vex them.
Burns.

Although my cares do hang upon my soul
Like mines of lead, the greatness of my
spirit
Shall shake the sullen weight off.
Clapthorne.

Quick is the succession of human events:
the cares of to-day are seldom the cares of
to-morrow; and when we lie down at
night, we may safely say to most of our
troubles, "Ye have done your worst, and
we shall meet no more." *Cowper.*

Cause.

A good cause makes a strong arm.

God befriend us, as our cause is just.
Shakespeare.

A noble cause doth ease much a grievous case. *Sir Philip Sidney.*

A rotten cause abides no handling.
Shakespeare.

Causes.

Small causes are sufficient to make a man
uneasy, when great ones are not in the
way; for want of a block he will stumble
at a straw. *Swift.*

Caution.

It is a good thing to learn caution by the
misfortunes of others. *Publius Syrus.*

All's to be fear'd where all is to be lost.
Byron.

More firm and sure the hand of courage
strikes,
When it obeys the watchful eye of caution.
Thomson.

Trust-none.
For oaths are straws, men's faiths are
wafer cakes,
And hold-fast is the only dog.
Shakespeare

Beware equally of a sudden friend, and
a slow enemy. *Home.*

Cautious Man.

He knows the compass, sail, and oar
Or never launches from the shore;
Before he builds computes the cost,
And in no proud pursuit is lost. *Gay.*

Celibacy.

But earlier is the rose distill'd
Than that which withering on the virgin
thorn
Grows, lives and dies in single blessedness.
Shakespeare.

Censure.

Horace appears in good humor while
he censures, and therefore his censure has
the more weight as supposed to proceed
from judgment, not from passion. *Young.*

The censure of those that are opposed
to us, is the nicest commendation that can
be given us. *St. Evremond.*

Few persons have sufficient wisdom to
prefer censure which is useful to them, to
praise which deceives them.
La Rochefoucauld.

Ceremony.

Ceremony was but devis'd at first
To set a gloss on faint deeds—hollow wel-
comes,
Recanting goodness, sorry e'er 'tis shown;
But where there is true friendship, there
needs none. *Shakespeare.*

All ceremonies are, in themselves, very
silly things; but yet a man of the world
should know them. They are the out-
works of manners and decency, which
would be too often broken in upon, if it
were not for that defence, which keeps
the enemy at a proper distance. It is for
this reason that I always treat fools and
coxcombs with great ceremony: true
good breeding not being a sufficient barrier
against them. *Chesterfield.*

As ceremony is the invention of wise
men to keep fools at a distance, so good
breeding is an expedient to make fools and
wise men equal. *Steele.*

Chance.

A lucky chance that oft decides the fate
Of mighty monarchs. *Thomson.*

Although men flatter themselves with their great actions, they are not so often the result of a great design as of chance.
La Rochefoucauld.

As the ancients wisely say
Have a care o' th' main chance,
And look before you ere you leap;
For as you sow y'ere like to reap.
Butler.

Be careful still of the main chance.
Dryden.

Change.

Ships, wealth, general confidence,—
All were his;
He counted them at break of day,
And when the sun set! where were they?
Byron.

Gather ye rosebuds while ye may,
Old Time is still a flying;
And that same flower that blooms to-day,
To-morrow shall be dying. *Herrick.*

Character.

Those who see thee in thy full blown pride,
Know little of affections crushed within
And wrongs which frenzy thee.
Talfourd.

Thou wilt quarrel with a man that hath a hair more or a hair less in his beard than thou hast. Thou wilt quarrel with a man for cracking nuts, having no other reason but because thou hast hazel eyes; what eye but such an eye, would spy out such a quarrel? Thy head is as full of quarrels, as an egg is full of meat.
Shakespeare.

Those who quit their proper character to assume what does not belong to them, are for the greater part ignorant of both the character they leave and of the character they assume. *Burke.*

He who when called upon to speak a disagreeable truth, tells it boldly and has done, is both bolder and milder than he who nibbles in a low voice and never ceases nibbling. *Lavater.*

Decision of character is one of the most important of human qualities, philosophically considered. Speculation, knowledge, is not the chief end of man; it is action. * * * "Give us the man," shout the multitude, "who will step forward and take the responsibility." He is instantly the idol, the lord, and the king among men. He, then, who would command among his fellows, must excel them more in energy of will than in power of intellect. *Burnap.*

Character is a perfectly educated will.

Novalis.

Spare in diet;
Free from gross passion, or of mirth, or anger;
Constant in spirit, not swerving with the blood;
Garnish'd and deck'd with modest compliment;
Not working with the eye, without the ear,
And, but purged in judgment, trusting neither. *Shakespeare.*

The best rules to form a young man are, to talk little, to hear much, to reflect alone upon what has passed in company, to distrust one's own opinions, and value others that deserve it. *Sir Wm. Temple.*

Best men are often moulded out of faults.
Shakespeare.

Every man has in himself a continent of undiscovered character. Happy is he who acts the Columbus to his own soul.
Sir J. Stevens.

The most trifling actions that affect a man's credit are to be regarded. The sound of your hammer at five in the morning, or nine at night, heard by a creditor, makes him easy six months longer; but if he sees you at a Billiard table, or hears your voice at a Tavern, when you should be at work, he sends for his money the next day. *Franklin.*

Characters.

Nature hath fram'd strange bed-fellows in her time;
Some, that will evermore peep through their eyes,
And laugh like parrots, at a bag-piper;
And other of such vinegar aspect,
That they'll not show their teeth in way of smile
Though Nestor swear the jest be laughable.
Shakespeare.

Charity.

Charity suffereth long, and is kind; charity envieth not; charity vaunteth not itself, is not puffed up, doth not behave itself unseemly, seeketh not her own, is not easily provoked, thinketh no evil; rejoiceth not in iniquity but rejoiceth in the truth; beareth all things, believeth all things, hopeth all things, endureth all things.
I Cor. xiii. I.

And now abideth faith, hope and charity, these three; but the greatest of these is charity. *I Cor. xiii, 13.*

Gently to hear, kindly to judge.
Shakespeare.

Give to him that asketh thee; and from him that would borrow of thee turn not

FAM QUOTES

thou away.   *Matthew.*

Charity shall cover a multitude of sins.
     1 Peter iv, 8.

He who receives a good turn should never forget it; he who does one should never remember it.   *Charron.*

The drying up a single tear has more
Of honest fame than shedding seas of gore.
     Byron.

     Charity ever
Finds in the act reward, and needs no trumpet
In the receiver.   *Beaumont and Fletcher.*

     For true charity
Though ne'er so secret finds its just reward.   *May.*

A woman who wants a charitable heart, wants a pure mind.   *Haliburton.*

A physician is not angry at the intemperance of a mad patient, nor does he take it ill to be railed at by a man in a fever. Just so should a wise man treat all mankind, as a physician treats a patient, and look upon them only as sick and extravagant.   *Seneca.*

Chastity.

O, she is colder than the mountain's snow,
To such a subtile purity she's wrought.
     Crown.

     Chaste as the icicle
That's curdled by the frost of purest snow,
And hangs on Dian's temple.
     Shakespeare.

Cheerfulness.

Give us, O give us, the man who sings at his work! Be his occupation what it may, he is equal to any of those who follow the same pursuit in silent sullenness. He will do more in the same time—he will do it better—he will persevere longer.
     Carlyle.

A merry heart goes all the day,
A sad tires in a mile.   *Shakespeare.*
Cheerfulness is health; the opposite, melancholy, is disease.   *Haliburton.*

Child.

The child is father of the man.
     Wordsworth.

How sharper than a serpent's tooth it is
To have a thankless child.
     Shakespeare.

Train up a child in the way he should go; and when he is old he will not depart from it.   *Proverbs xxii, 6.*

Childhood.

Sweet childish days that were as long

As twenty days are now.   *Wordsworth.*
     A simple child,
That lightly draws its breath,
And feels its life in every limb,
What should it know of death?
     Wordsworth.

Children.

Fragile beginnings of a mighty end.
     Mrs. Norton.

Delightful task! to rear the tender thought,
To teach the young idea how to shoot,
To pour the fresh instruction o er the mind,
To breathe the enlivening spirit and to fix
The generous purpose in the glowing breast!   *Thomson.*

Call not that man wretched, who whatever ills he suffers, has a child to love.
     Southey.

Choice.

When better cherries are not to be had,
We needs must take the seeming best of bad.   *Daniel.*

The measure of choosing well, is whether a man likes what he has chosen.
     Lamb.

Jesus Christ the same yesterday, to-day, and forever.   *Hebrews xiii, 8.*

     The best of men
That e'er wore earth about Him was a sufferer,
A soft, meek, patient, humble, tranquil spirit,
The first true gentleman that ever breathed.   *Decker.*

There's a small choice in rotten apples.
     Shakespeare.

Christian.

A christian in this world is but gold in the ore; at death the pure gold is melted out and separated and the dross cast away and consumed.   *Flavel.*

A christian is the highest style of man.
     Young.

A christian is God Almighty's gentleman.   *J. C. Hare.*

Christianity.

Ours is a religion jealous in its demands, but how infinitely prodigal in its gifts! It troubles you for an hour, it repays you by immortality.   *Bulwer.*

Church.

What is a church? Our honest sexton

tells,
'Tis a tall building, with a tower and bells.
Crabbe.

Look on this edifice of marble made—
How fair it swells, too beautiful to fade.
See what fine people in its portals crowd,
Smiling and greeting, talking, laughing
    loud!
What is it? Surely not a gay exchange,
Where wit and beauty social joys arrange,
Not a grand shop, where late Parisian
    styles
Attract rich buyers from a thousand
    miles?
But step within; no need of further
    search.
Behold, admire a fashionable church!
Look how its oriel window glints and
    gleams,
What tinted light magnificently streams
On the proud pulpit, carved with quaint
    device,
Where velvet cushions, exquisitely nice,
Presse'd by the polish'd preacher's dainty
    hands,
Hold a large volume clasp'd by golden
    bands. *Park Benjamin.*

Ciphers.

There are foure great cyphers in the
world; hee that is lame among dancers,
dumbe among lawyers, dull among schol-
lars, and rude amongst courtiers.
Bishop Earle.

Civility.

Whilst thou livest keep a good tongue in
thy head. *Shakespeare.*

A good word is an easy obligation, but
not to speak ill, requires only our silence,
which costs us nothing. *Tillotson.*

The insolent civility of a proud man is,
if possible, more shocking than his rudeness could be; because he shows you, by
his manner, that he thinks it mere condescension in him; and that his goodness
alone bestows upon you what you have no
pretense to claim. *Chesterfield.*

Cleanliness.

Even from the body's purity, the mind
Receives a secret, sympathetic aid.
Thomson.

Let thy mind's sweetness have its operation upon thy body, clothes, and habitation. *Herbert.*

Clock.

A clock! with its ponderous embowel-
ments of lead and brass, its pert or solemn
dullness of communication. *Lamb.*

Cloud.

Was I deceived, or did a sable cloud
Turn forth her silver lining on the night?
Milton.

That look'd
As though an angel, in his upward flight,
Had left his mantle floating in mid-air.
Joanna Baillie.

Clouds.

Those playful fancies of the mighty sky.
Smith.

Cock.

I have heard
The cock, that is the trumpet to the morn,
Doth, with his lofty and shrill-sounding
    throat,
Awake the god of day. *Shakespeare.*

Coffee.

Coffee, which makes the politician wise,
And see through all things with his half
    shut eyes. *Pope.*

Comfort.

Sweet as refreshing dews or summer
    showers,
To the long parching thirst of drooping
    flowers;
Grateful as fanning gales to fainting
    swains
And soft as trickling balm to bleeding
    pains.
Such are thy words. *Gay.*
I would bring balm and pour it into your
    wound,
Cure your distemper'd mind and heal your
    fortunes. *Dryden.*
Thy words have darted hope into my soul
And comfort dawns upon me. *Southern.*

Commander.

It is better to have a lion at the head of
an army of sheep, than a sheep at the head
of an army of lions. *De Foe.*

Commendation.

Commend a fool for his wit, or a knave
for his honesty, and they will receive you
into their bosom. *Fielding.*

Commerce.

A well regulated commerce is not, like
law, physic, or divinity, to be overstocked
with hands; but, on the contrary, flourishes by multitudes, and gives employment
to all its professors. *Addison*

FAM
QUOTES

Companions.

The most agreeable of all companions is a simple, frank man, without any high pretensions to an oppressive greatness; one who loves life, and understands the use of it; obliging, alike at all hours; above all, of a golden temper, and steadfast as an anchor. For such an one we gladly exchange the great genius, the most brilliant wit, the profoundest thinker. *Lessing.*

Company.

No company is far preferable to bad, because we are more apt to catch the vices of others than virtues, as disease is far more courageous than health. *Colton.*

Bad company is like a nail driven into a post, which, after the first or second blow, may be drawn out with little difficulty; but being once driven up to the head, the pincers cannot take hold to draw it out, but which can only be done by the destruction of the wood. *Augustine.*

Take rather than give the tone to the company you are in. If you have parts you will show them more or less upon every subject; and if you have not, you had better talk sillily upon a subject of other people's than of your own choosing. *Chesterfield.*

No man can possibly improve in any company for which he has not respect enough to be under some degree of restraint. *Chesterfield.*

Compensation.

When articles rise the consumer is the first that suffers, and when they fall, he is the last that gains. *Colton.*

Competence.

O grant me, heav'n, a middle state
Neither too humble or too great;
More than enough for nature's ends,
With something left to treat my friends. *Mallet.*

Complaining.

I will not be as those who spend the day in complaining of the head-ache, and the night in drinking the wine that gives the head-ache. *Goethe.*

Compliments.

Compliments of congratulation are always kindly taken, and cost nothing but pen, ink and paper. I consider them as draughts upon good breeding, where the exchange is always greatly in favor of the drawer. *Chesterfield.*

Concealment.

We shall find that it is less difficult to hide a thousand guineas than one hole in your coat. *Colton.*

To conceal anything from those to whom I am attached, is not in my nature. I can never close my lips where I have opened my heart. *Dickens.*

Conceit.

Conceit is to nature what paint is to beauty; it is not only needless, but impairs what it would improve. *Pope.*

A strong conceit is rich; so most men deem;
If not to be, 'tis comfort yet to seem. *Marston.*

The more any one speaks of himself, the less he likes to hear another talked of. *Lavater.*

Conceit in weakest bodies strongest works. *Shakespeare.*

Conceit and Confidence.

Success seems to be that which forms the distinction between confidence and conceit. Nelson, when young, was piqued at not being noticed in a certain paragraph of the newspapers, which detailed an action wherein he had assisted "But never mind," said he, "I will one day have a gazette of my own." *Colton.*

Conciliation.

Agree with thine adversary quickly while thou art in the way with him. *Matt. v, 25.*

Conclusion.

O most lame and impotent conclusion. *Shakespeare.*

Conduct.

Have more than thou showest,
Speak less than thou knowest,
Lend less than thou owest,
Learn more than thou trowest,
Set less than thou throwest. *Shakespeare.*

Confession.

A man should never be ashamed to own he has been in the wrong, which is but saying, in other words, that he is wiser today than he was yesterday. *Pope.*

Confidence.

There is a kind of greatness which does not depend upon fortune; it is a certain manner that distinguishes us, and which seems to destine us for great things; it is the value we insensibly set upon ourselves; it is by this quality, that we gain the deference of other men, and it is this which commonly raises us more above them, than birth, rank, or even merit itself.

La Rochefoucauld.

Confusion.

Confusion now hath made his masterpiece!
Shakespeare.

With ruin upon ruin, rout on rout,
Confusion worse confounded.   *Milton.*

Conscience.

Suspicion haunts the guilty mind
The thief doth fear each bush an officer.
Shakespeare.

I feel within me
A peace above all earthly dignities,
A still and quiet conscience.
Shakespeare.

The torture of a bad conscience is the hell of a living soul.   *Calvin.*

What stronger breast-plate than a heart untainted?
Thrice is he arm'd, who hath his quarrel just;
And he but naked, though lock'd up in steel,
Whose conscience with injustice is corrupted.   *Shakespeare.*

My conscience hath a thousand several tongues,
And every tongue brings in a several tale;
And every tale condemns me for a villain.
Shakespeare.

Man's conscience is the oracle of God!
Byron.

Conscience has no more to do with gallantry than it has with politics. *Sheridan.*

Thus conscience doth make cowards of us all.   *Shakespeare.*

A still, small voice.   *1 Kings xix, 12.*

Consequences.

As the dimensions of the tree are not always regulated by the size of the seed, so the consequences of things are not always proportionate to the apparent magnitude of those events that have produced them.
Colton.

Consistency.

Either take Christ in your lives, or cast him out of your lips; either be that thou seemest, or else be what thou art. *Dyer.*

Conspiracies.

Conspiracies no sooner should be form'd
Than executed.   *Addison.*

Constancy.

There are two kinds of constancy in love. one arising from incessantly finding in the loved one fresh objects to love. the other from regarding it as a point of honor to be constant.
La Rochefoucauld.

I am constant as the northern star;
Of whose true fix'd and resting quality
There is no fellow in the firmament.
Shakespeare.

Contemplation.

There is no lasting pleasure but contemplation; all others grow flat and insipid upon frequent use; and when a man hath run through a set of vanities, in the declension of his age, he knows not what to do with himself, if he cannot think; he saunters about from one dull business to another, to wear out time; and hath no reason to value Life but because he is afraid of death.   *Burnet.*

Contempt.

Those only are despicable who fear to be despised.   *La Rochefoucauld.*

Despise not any man, and do not spurn any thing. For there is no man that hath not his hour, nor is there any thing that hath not its place.   *Rabbi Ben Azai.*

Content.

There is a jewel which no Indian mine can buy,
No chemic art can counterfeit;
It makes men rich in greatest poverty,
Makes water wine, turns wooden cups to gold,
The homely whistle to sweet music's strain;
Seldom it comes to few from Heaven sent,
That much in little—all in naught—*content.*
Wilbye.

Poor and content is rich and rich enough;
But riches. fineless, is as poor as winter,
To him that ever fears he shall be poor.
Shakespeare.

Contentment.

Contentment, rosy, dimpled maid,
Thou brightest daughter of the sky.
Lady Manners.

Contentment, parent of delight. *Green.*

Contentment produces in some measure, all those effects which the alchymist usually ascribes to what he calls the philosopher's stone; and if it does not bring riches. it does the same thing, by banishing the desire of them. If it cannot remove the disquietudes arising from a man's mind, body, or fortune, it makes him easy under them. *Addison.*

Happy the man who void of care and strife,
In silken or in leather purse retains
A good old shilling. *Goldsmith.*

As for a little more money and a little more time, why it's ten to one, if either one or the other would make you one whit happier. If you had more time, it would be sure to hang heavily. It is the working man who is the happy man. Man was made to be active, and he is never so happy as when he is so. It is the idle man who is the miserable man. What comes of holidays, and far too often of sight-seeing, but evil? Half the harm that happens is on these days. And, as for money—Don't you remember the old saying, "Enough is as good as a feast"? Money never made a man happy yet, nor will it. There is nothing in its nature to produce happiness. The more a man has, the more he wants. Instead of its filling a vacuum, it makes one. If it satisfies one want, it doubles and trebles that want another way. That was a true proverb of the wise man, rely upon it: "Better is little with the fear of the Lord, than great treasure, and trouble therewith." *Franklin.*

Contiguity.

Speaking generally, no man appears great to his contemporaries, for the same reason that no man is great to his servants—both know too much of him. *Colton.*

Conversation.

Speak little and well, if you wish to be considered as possessing merit. *From the French.*

It is a secret known to but few, yet no small use in the conduct of life, that when you fall into a man's conversation, the first thing you should consider is, whether he has a greater inclination to hear you, or that you should hear him. *Steele.*

The fullest instruction, and the fullest enjoyment are never derived from books, till we have ventilated the ideas thus obtained, in free and easy chat with others. *Wm. Matthews.*

Talking is a digestive process which is absolutely essential to the mental constitution of the man who devours many books. A full mind must have talk, or it will grow dyspeptic.

Wm. Matthews.

The first ingredient in conversation is truth, the next, good sense, the third, good humor, and the fourth, wit. *Sir Wm. Temple.*

He who sedulously attends, pointedly asks, calmly speaks, coolly answers, and ceases when he has no more to say, is in possession of some of the best requisites of man. *Lavater.*

Converser.

He is so full of pleasant anecdote;
So rich, so gay, so poignant in his wit,
Time vanishes before him as he speaks,
And ruddy morning through the lattice peeps
Ere night seems well begun. *Joanna Baillie.*

Coquette.

There affectation, with a sickly mein,
Shows in her cheeks the roses of eighteen,
Practis'd to lisp and hang the head aside,
Faints into airs and languishes with pride;
On the rich quilt sinks with becoming woe,
Wrapt in a gown for sickness and for show. *Pope.*

See how the world its veterans rewards!
A youth of frolics, an old age of cards;
Fair to no purpose, artful to no end,
Young without lovers, old without a friend;
A fop their passion but their prize a sot,
Alive ridiculous, and dead forgot! *Pope.*

The vain coquette each suit disdains,
And glories in her lover's pains:
With age she fades—each lover flies,
Contemn'd, forlorn, she pines and dies. *Gay.*

Corpulence.

Let me have men about me that are fat;
Sleek-headed men and such as sleep o'nights.
Yond' Cassius has a lean and hungry look;
He thinks too much; such men are dangerous. *Shakespeare.*

Still she strains the aching clasp
That binds her virgin zone:
I know it hurts her, though she looks
As cheerful as she can.
Her waist is larger than her life
For life is but a span. *Holmes.*

Corruption.

E'en grave divines submit to glittering gold,
The best of consciences are bought and sold. *Dr. Wolcot.*

Countenance.

The countenance may be rightly defined as the title page which heralds the contents of the human volume, but like other title pages, it sometimes puzzles, often misleads, and often says nothing to the purpose. *Wm. Matthews.*

Physically, they exhibited no indication of their past lives and characters. The greatest scamp had a Raphael face, with a profusion of blonde hair; Oakhurst, a gambler, had the melancholy character and intellectual abstraction of a Hamlet; the coolest and most courageous man was scarcely over five feet in height, with a soft voice, and an embarrassed manner. *Bret Harte.*

The cheek
Is apter than the tongue to tell an errand. *Shakespeare.*

A countenance more
In sorrow than in anger. *Shakespeare.*

Country.

Scenes must be beautiful which daily view'd
Please daily, and whose novelty survives
Long knowledge and the scrutiny of years. *Cowper.*

God made the country and man made the town;
What wonder then, that health and virtue, gifts
That can alone make sweet the bitter draught
That life holds out to all, should most abound,
And least be threaten'd in the fields and groves? *Cowper.*

And see the country, far diffused around,
One boundless blush, one white impurpled shower
Of mingled blossoms; where the raptured eye
Hurries from joy to joy. *Thomson.*

He who loves not his country can love nothing. *Johnson.*

And lives there a man, with soul so dead
Who never to himself hath said—
This is my own, my native land! *Scott.*

Had I a dozen sons, each in my love alike, I had rather have eleven die nobly for their country, than one voluptuously surfeit out of action. *Shakespeare.*

Country Life.

Here too dwells simple truth; plain innocence:

Unsullied beauty; sound unbroken youth,
Patient of labor, with a little pleas'd;
Health ever blooming; unambitious toil,
Calm contemplation; and poetic ease. *Thomson.*

How various his employments, whom the world
Calls idle, and who justly in return
Esteems that busy world an idler too!
Friends, books, a garden, and perhaps his pen,
Delightful industry enjoyed at home,
And nature in her cultivated trim,
Dressed to his taste, inviting him abroad. *Cowper.*

Courage.

Courage consists not in blindly overlooking danger, but in seeing it, and conquering it. *Richter.*

The intent and not the deed
Is in our power; and, therefore, who dares greatly,
Does greatly. *Brown.*

Most men have more courage than even they themselves think they have. *Greville.*

The smallest worm will turn, being trodden on;
And doves will peck, in safeguard of their brood. *Shakespeare.*

I do not think a braver gentleman,
More active-valiant, or more valiant young,
More daring, or more bold, is now alive,
To grace this latter age with noble deeds. *Shakespeare.*

True courage scorns
To vent her prowess in a storm of words,
And to the valiant action speaks alone. *Smollett.*

Prithee peace:
I dare do all that may become a man,
Who dares do more is none. *Shakespeare.*

Rocks have been shaken from their solid base,
But what shall move a firm and dauntless mind? *Joanna Baillie.*

Courtesy.

Ill seemes (say'd he) if he so valiant be,
That he should be so sterne to stranger wight;
For seldom yet did living creature see
That courtesie and manhood ever disagree *Spenser.*

As the sword of the best-tempered metal is the most flexible; so the truly generous are most pliant and courteous in their behavior to their inferiors.
Fuller.

Courtiers.

A toad-eater's an imp I don't admire.
Dr. Wolcot.

I am no courtier, no fawning dog of state,
To lick and kiss the hand that buffets me;
Nor can I smile upon my guest and praise
His stomach, when I know he feeds on poison,
And death disguised sits grinning at my table.
Sewell.

A mere court butterfly,
That flutters in the pageant of a monarch.
Byron.

Courtship.

There is, sir, a critical minute in
Ev'ry man's wooing, when his mistress may
Be won, which if he carelessly neglect
To prosecute, he may wait long enough
Before he gain the like opportunity.
Marmion's Antiquary.

Men are April when they woo, December when they wed, and maids are May when they are maids, but the sky changes when they are wives.
Shakespeare.

Women are angels wooing;
Things won are done, joy's soul lies in the doing;
That she belov'd knows nought, that knows not this,—
Men prize the thing ungain'd more than it is.
Shakespeare.

Courtship consists in a number of quiet attentions, not so pointed as to alarm, nor so vague as not to be understood.
Sterne.

Say that she rail; why then I'll tell her plain,
She sings as sweetly as a nightingale;
Say that she frown; I'll say she looks as clear
As morning roses, newly wash'd with dew;
Say she be mute and will not speak a word,
Then I'll commend her volubility
And say she uttereth piercing eloquence.
Shakespeare.

Trust me—with women worth the being won,
The softest lover ever best succeeds.
Hill.

That man that hath a tongue I say is no man,
Win her with gifts if she respect not words;
Dumb jewels often in their silent kind,
More quick than words do move a woman's mind.
Shakespeare.

If with his tongue he cannot win a woman.
Shakespeare.

She is a woman, therefore may be woo'd,
She is a woman, therefore may be won.
Shakespeare.

Covetousness.

We never desire earnestly what we desire in reason.
La Rochefoucauld.

He deservedly loses his own property, who covets that of another.
Phoedrus.

The things which belong to others please us more, and that which is ours, is more pleasing to others.
Syrus.

Coward.

Bold at the council board
But cautious in the field.
Dryden.

A coward; a most devout; religious in it.
Shakespeare.

I know him a notorious liar,
Think him a great way fool, solely a coward.
Shakespeare.

Go—let thy less than woman's hand
Assume the distaff—not the brand.
Byron.

Cowards fear to die; but courage stout,
Rather than live in snuff, will be put out.
Sir Walter Raleigh.

Cowards die many times before their deaths;
The valiant never taste of death but once.
Shakespeare.

Cowardice.

Those that fly may fight again,
Which he can never do that's slain,
Hence timely running's no mean part
Of conduct in the martial art.
Butler.

Creation.

The heavens declare the glory of God, and the firmament showeth his handiwork. Day unto day uttereth speech, and night unto night showeth knowledge. There is no speech nor language where their voice is not heard.
Psalms xix, 1.

The spacious firmament on high,
With all the blue ethereal sky,
And spangled heavens, a shining frame
Their great Original proclaim.

* * * * * *

Forever singing as they shine
The hand that made us is divine.
Addison.

Creditor.

The creditor whose appearance gladdens the heart of a debtor, may hold his head in sunbeams and his foot on storms.
Lavater.

Creditors.

Creditors have better memories than debtors; and Creditors are a superstitious sect, great observers of set days and times.
Franklin.

Crime.

One crime is concealed by the commission of another. *Seneca.*

Where have you ever found that man who stopped short after the perpetration of a single crime? *Juvenal.*

For he that but conceives a crime in thought,
Contracts the danger of an actual fault.
Creech.

Every crime
Has, in the moment of its perpetration,
Its own avenging angel—dark misgiving,
An ominous sinking at the inmost heart.
Coleridge.

Criticism.

Criticism is like champagne, nothing more execrable if bad, nothing more excellent if good; if meagre, muddy, vapid, and sour, both are fit only to engender colic and wind; but if rich, generous and sparkling, they communicate a glow to the spirits, improve the taste, expand the heart, and are worthy of being introduced at the symposium of the gods. *Colton.*

Damn with faint praise, assent with civil leer,
And without sneering, teach the rest to sneer;
Willing to wound, and yet afraid to strike,
Just hint a fault, and hesitate dislike.
Pope.

Get your enemies to read your works in order to mend them, for your friend is so much your second selve that he will judge too like you. *Pope.*

Critics.

Critics are a kind of freebooters in the republic of letters,—who like deer, goats and divers other gramniverous animals, gain subsistence by gorging upon buds and leaves of the young shrubs of the forest, thereby robbing them of their verdure, and retarding their progress to maturity. *Washington Irving.*

A poet that fails in writing, becomes often a morose critic. The weak and in-

sipid white wine makes at length excellent vinegar. *Shenstone.*

Crown.

Uneasy lies the head that wears a crown.
Shakespeare.

Cruelty.

I would not enter in my list of friends,
(Though grac'd with polish'd manners and fine sense,
Yet wanting sensibility), the man
Who needlessly sets foot upon a worm.
An inadvertent step may crush the snail
That crawls at evening in the public path,
But he that has humanity, forwarn'd,
Will tread aside, and let the reptile live.
Cowper.

Cunning.

Cunning and treachery are the offspring of incapacity. *La Rochefoucauld.*

It is sometimes necessary to play the fool to avoid being deceived by cunning men. *La Rochefoucauld.*

Cunning and Wisdom.

We take cunning for a sinister and crooked wisdom, and certainly there is a great difference between a cunning man and a wise man, not only in point of honesty but in point of ability. *Bacon.*

Curiosity.

Inquisitive people are the funnels of conversation; they do not take in anything for their own use, but merely to pass it to another. *Steele.*

I loathe that low vice curiosity.
Byron.

Cursing.

This nor hurts him, nor profits you a jot:
Forbear it, therefore; give your cause to heaven. *Shakespeare.*

Custom.

Custom is the law of fools. *Vanburgh.*

Custom does often reason overrule
And only serves for reason to the fool.
Rochester.

Custom, 'tis true, a venerable tyrant
O'er servile man extends her blind dominion. *Thomson.*

Dancing.

Dear creature! you'd swear
When her delicate feet in the dance twinkle round,
That her steps are of light, that her home is the air,
And she only "par complaisance" touches the ground. *Moore.*

Her feet beneath her petticoat.
Like little mice, stole in and out,
  As if they feared the light.
And oh! she dances such a way,
No sun upon an Easter day
  Is half so fine a sight.   *Suckling.*

  Come, trip it as you go,
  On the light fantastic toe.   *Milton.*

Danger.

For danger levels man and brute
And all are fellows in their need.
             Dryden.

Darkness.

How sweetly did they float upon the wings
Of silence, through the empty-vaulted
  night,
At every fall smoothing the raven-down
Of darkness till it smiled.   *Milton.*

Dark night that from the eye his functio
  takes,
The ear more quick of apprehensio
  makes.
Wherein it doth impair the seeing sense,
It pays the hearing double recompense.
             Shakespeare

Day.

One of the heavenly days that cannot die.
             Wordsworth.

"I've lost a day"—the prince who nobly
  cried
Had been an emperor, without his crown.
             Young.

Daybreak.

At last the golden oriental gate
Of greatest heaven 'gan to open fair;
And Phœbus, fresh as bridegroom to his
  mate,
Came dancing forth shaking his dewy hair,

And hurl'd his glist'ning beams through
  gloomy air.   *Spenser.*

It was a lark, the herald of the morn,
No nightingale; look love, what envious
  streaks
Do lace the severing clouds in yonder
  east;
Night's candles are burnt out, and jocund
  day
Stands tip-toe on the misty mountain tops.
             Shakespeare.

Dead.

Weep not for him that dieth,
  For he hath ceased from tears,
And a voice to his replieth
  Which he hath not heard for years.
             Mrs. Norton.

    All that tread
The globe are but a handful to the tribes
That slumber in its bosom.   Take the
  wings

Of morning, and the Barcan desert pierce,
Or lose thyself in the continuous woods
Where rolls the Oregon, and hears no
  sound
Save his own dashings,—yet the dead are
  there;
And millions in those solitudes, since first
The flight of years began, have laid them
  down
In their last sleep; the dead reign there
  alone.   *Bryant.*

    Duncan is in his grave;
After life's fitful fever he sleeps well;
Treason has done his worst; nor steel, nor
  poison,
Malice domestic, foreign levy, nothing
Can touch him further.   *Shakespeare.*

Death.

O death! the poor man's dearest friend,
  The kindest and the best!
Welcome the hour, my aged limbs
  Are laid with thee at rest!   *Burns.*

Let no man fear to die, we love to sleep
  all,
And death is but the sounder sleep.
             Beaumont.

To what base uses may we return!
Why may not imagination trace the noble
dust of Alexander, till it find it stopping
a bunghole? As thus: Alexander died,
Alexander was buried, Alexander return-
eth to dust; the dust is earth: of earth
we make loam. And why of that loam,
whereto he was converted, might they
not stop a beer barrel?
             Shakespeare.

But yesterday the word of Cæsar might
Have stood against the world; now lies he
  there,
And none so poor to do him reverence.
             Shakespeare.

Death opens the gate of fame, and shuts
the gate of envy after it; it unlooses the
chain of the captive, and puts the bondsman's task into another man's hand.
             Sterne.

  O grave! where is thy victory?
  O death! where is thy sting?   *Pope.*
Whom the Gods love die young.
             Byron.

Why, what is pomp, rule, reign, but earth
  and dust?
And live we how we can, yet die we must.
             Shakespeare.

And thou art terrible—the tear,
The groan, the knell, the pall, the bier;
And all we know, or dream, or fear
Of agony, are thine.   *Halleck.*

    Nothing in his life
Became him like the leaving it; he died

As one who had been studied in his death,
To throw away the dearest thing he owed,
As 'twere a careless trifle.   *Shakespeare.*

Weep not for those
Who sink within the arms of death
Ere yet the chilling wintry breath
    Of sorrow o'er them blows;
But weep for them who here remain,
The mournful heritors of pain,
Condemn'd to see each bright joy fade,
And mark grief's melancholy shade
    Flung o'er Hope's fairest rose.
        Mrs. Embury.

If I must die
I will encounter darkness as a bride
  And hug it in my arms.   *Shakespeare.*

It is hard
To feel the hand of death arrest one's
  steps,
Throw a chill blight o'er all one's budding
  hopes,
And hurl one's soul untimely to the
  shades
Lost in the gaping gulf of blank oblivion.
        Kirk White.

Death is but what the haughty brave,
The weak must bear, the wretch must
  crave.   *Byron.*

O death all eloquent, you only prove
What dust we dote on, when 'tis man we
  love.   *Pope.*

Neither the sun nor death can be looked
at steadily.   *La Rochefoucauld.*

To die—to sleep—
No more;—and, by a sleep, to say we
  end
The heart-ache, and the thousand natural
  shocks,
That flesh is heir to,—'Tis a consumma-
  tion
Devoutly to be wish'd.   *Shakespeare.*

Leaves have their time to fall,
  And flowers to wither at the north
    wind's breath,
And stars to set; but all—
  Thou hast all seasons for thine own, O,
    death!   *Mrs. Hemans.*

Lay her i' the earth;
And from her fair and unpolluted flesh
May violets spring!   *Shakespeare.*
Oh my love, my wife!
Death, that hath suckt the honey of thy
  breath,
Hath had no power yet upon thy beauty,
Thou art not conquer'd; beauty's ensign
  yet
Is crimson in thy lips, and in thy cheeks,
And death's pale flag is not advanced
  there.
Why art thou yet so fair?   *Shakespeare.*

Pale death approaches with an equal
step, and knocks indiscriminately at the
door of the cottage, and the portals of the
palace.   *Horace.*

Death's but a path that *must* be trod,
If man would ever pass to God.
        Parnell.

It is impossible that anything so natural,
so necessary, and so universal as death,
should ever have been designed by Providence as an evil to mankind.   *Swift.*

For good men but *see* death, the wicked
taste it.   *Johnson.*

Death is a commingling of eternity
with time; in the death of a good man,
eternity is seen looking through time.
        Goethe.

Thou know'st 'tis common; all that live
  must die,
Passing through nature to eternity.
        Shakespeare.

Early, bright, transient
Chaste as morning dew
She parkled, was exhaled,
And went to heaven.   *Young.*

So live, that when thy summons comes to
  join
That innumerable caravan that moves
To that mysterious realm, where each
  shall take
His chamber in the silent halls of death,
Thou go not like the quarry-slave at night,
Scourged to his dungeon; but sustain'd
  and sooth'd
By an unfaltering trust, approach thy
  grave,
Like one that draws the drapery of his
  couch
Around him, and lies down to pleasant
  dreams.   *Bryant.*

All was ended now, the hope, the fear and
  the sorrow,
All the aching of heart, the restless, unsatisfied longing,
All the dull, deep pain, and constant anguish of patience!   *Longfellow.*

A sleep without dreams, after a rough day
Of toil, is what we covet most; and yet
How clay shrinks back from mere quies-
  cent clay.   *Byron.*

It is not strange that that early love of
the heart should come back, as it so often
does when the dim eye is brightening with
its last light. It is not strange that the
freshest fountains the heart has ever
known in its wastes should bubble up anew
when the life-blood is growing stagnant.
It is not strange that a bright memory
should come to a dying old man, as the

sunshine breaks across the hills at the close of a stormy day; nor that in the light of that ray, the very clouds that made the day dark should grow gloriously beautiful.   *Hawthorne.*

How wonderful is death!
Death and his brother sleep.
    Shelley.

Debt.

Run not into debt, either for wares sold, or money borrowed; be content to want things that are not of absolute necessity, rather than run up the score.
    Sir M. Hale.

A public debt is a kind of anchor in the storm; but if the anchor be too heavy for the vessel, she will be sunk by that very weight which was intended for her preservation.   *Colton.*

Debtor.

The ghost of many a veteran bill
Shall hover around his slumbers.
    Holmes.

The ghostly dun shall worry his sleep,
  And constables cluster around him,
And he shall creep from the wood-hole deep.
  Where their spectre eyes have found him.   *Holmes.*

Decay.

    My way of life
Is fall'n into the sear and yellow leaf.
    Shakespeare.

Deceit.

Smooth runs the water, where the brook is deep;
And in his simple show he harbors treason.
The fox barks not when he would steal the lamb.   *Shakespeare.*

Decency.

Immodest words admit of no defence
For want of decency is want of sense.
    Earl of Roscommon.

Deception.

Of all the agonies of life, that which is most poignant and harrowing—that which for the time annihilates reason and leaves our whole organization one lacerated, mangled heart—is the conviction that we have been deceived where we placed all the trust of love.   *Bulwer.*

No man was ever so much deceived by another as by himself.   *Greville.*

The first and worst of all frauds is to cheat oneself. All sin is easy after that.
    Baily.

Defects.

If we had no defects ourselves, we should not take so much pleasure in noting those of others.
    La Rochefoucauld.

In the intercourse of life we please, often, more by our defects than by our good qualities.   *La Rochefoucauld.*

Deformity.

Deformity of the heart I call
The worst deformity of all;
For what is form, or what is face,
But the soul's index, or its case?
    Colton.

Degeneracy.

What a falling off was there.
    Shakespeare.

Dejection.

Ah, there are moments for us here, when seeing
Life's inequalities, and woe, and care,
The burdens laid upon our mortal being
  Seem heavier than the human heart can bear.   *Phoebe Carey.*

Delays.

Be wise to-day, 'tis madness to defer
Next day, the fatal precedent will plead
Thus on, till wisdom is push'd out of life.
    Young.

Delicacy.

If you destroy delicacy and a sense of shame in a young girl, you deprave her very fast.   *Mrs. Stowe.*

Dependence.

There is none made so great, but he may both need the help and service, and stand in fear of the power and unkindness, even of the meanest of mortals.   *Seneca.*

Depend on no man, on no friend, but him who can depend on himself. He only who acts conscientiously towards himself will act so towards others, and vice versa.
    Lavater.

Desire.

O, fierce desire, the spring of sighs and tears,
  Reliev'd with want, impoverish'd with store,
Nurst with vain hopes, and fed with doubtful fears,
  Whose force withstood, increaseth more and more!   *Brandon.*

The desire of the moth for the star—

Of the night for the morrow—
The devotion to something afar
From the sphere of our sorrow.
Shelley.

The passions and desires, like the two twists of a rope, mutually mix one with the other, and twine inextricably round the heart; producing good if moderately indulged; but certain destruction, if suffered to become inordinate. *Burton.*

Desolation.

Such a house broke!
So noble a master fallen? all gone! and not
One friend to take his fortune by the arm,
And go along with him.
Shakespeare.

What is the worst of woes that wait on age?
What stamps the wrinkle deeper on the brow?
To view each lov'd one blotted from life's page,
And be alone on earth as I am now.
Byron.

Despair.

To doubt
Is worse than to have lost; And to despair
Is but to antedate those miseries
That must fall on us. *Massinger.*

He that despairs, degrades the Deity, and seems to intimate, that He is insufficient, or not just to his word; and in vain hath read the Scriptures, the world, and man.
Feltham.

Spirits of peace, where are ye? Are ye all gone?
And leave me here in wretchedness behind ye? *Shakespeare.*

Beware of desperate steps!—the darkest day
Live till to-morrow, will have passed away.
Cowper.

'Tis late before
The brave despair. *Thomson.*

Talk not of comfort, 'tis for lighter ills;
I will indulge my sorrows, and give way
To all the pangs and fury of despair.
Addison.

Despondency.

My heart is very tired—my strength is low—
My hands are full of blossoms pluck'd before
Held dead within them till myself shall die.
Mrs. Browning.

Despots.

Despots govern by terror. They know that he who fears God fears nothing else; and, therefore, they eradicate from the mind, through their Voltaire, the Helœtius, and the rest of that infamous gang, that only sort of fear which generates true courage. *Burke.*

Destiny.

The wheels of nature are not made to roll backward; everything presses on toward Eternity; from the birth of Time an impetuous current has set in, which bears all the sons of men toward that interminable ocean. Meanwhile Heaven is attracting to itself whatever is congenial to its nature, is enriching itself by the spoils of earth, and collecting within its capacious bosom, whatever is pure, permanent and divine.
Robert Hall.

Destruction.

The gates of hell are open night and day;
Smooth the descent, and easy is the way;
But to return, and view the cheerful skies,
In this the task and mighty labor lies.
Dryden.

Determination.

I'll speak to it though hell itself should gape,
And bid me hold my peace. *Shakespeare.*

Devotion.

Private devotions and secret offices of religion are like the refreshing of a garden with the distilling and petty drops of a water-pot; but, addressed from the temple, are like rain from heaven.
Jeremy Taylor.

Dew.

As fresh as morning dew distill'd on flowers. *Shakespeare.*

I must go seek some dew-drops here,
And hang a pearl in every cowslip's ear.
Shakespeare.

The starlight dews
All silently their tears of love instil
Weeping themselves away, till they infuse
Deep into nature's breast, the spirit of her hues.
Byron.

Diet.

All courageous animals are carnivorous, and greater courage is to be expected in a people, such as the English, whose food is strong and hearty, than in the half starved commonalty of other countries.

FAM QUOTES

Sir W. Temple.

Simple diet is best;—for many dishes bring many diseases; and rich sauces are worse than even heaping several meats upon each other. *Pliny.*

Differences.

In differing breasts what differing passions glow!
Ours kindle quick, but yours extinguish slow. *Garth.*

Difficulty.

Difficulty is a severe instructor, set over us by the supreme ordinance of a parental guardian and legislator, who knows us better than we know ourselves; and He loves us better too. He that wrestles with us strengthens our nerves, and sharpens our skill. Our antagonist is our helper. This amicable conflict with difficulty obliges us to an intimate acquaintance with our object, and compels us to consider it in all its relations. It will not suffer us to be superficial. *Burke.*

Digestion.

A light supper, a good night's sleep and a fine morning have often made a hero of the same man, who, by indigestion, a restless night and a rainy morning would have proved a coward. *Chesterfield.*

Things sweet to taste, prove in digestion sour. *Shakespeare.*

Dignity.

True dignity is never gained by place,
And never lost when honors are withdrawn. *Massinger.*

A fit of anger is as fatal to dignity as a dose of arsenic to life. *Dr. Holland.*

Diligence.

Who makes quick use of the moment is a genius of prudence. *Lavater.*

Dinner.

A good dinner sharpens wit, while it softens the heart. *Doran.*

Disappointment.

Out of the same substances one stomach will extract nourishment, another poison; and so the same disappointments in life will chasten and refine one man's spirit, and embitter another's. *Wm. Matthews.*

Discipline.

Train up a child in the way he should go; and when he is old he will not depart from it. *Prov.* xxii, 6.

Discipline, like the bridle in the hand of a good rider, should exercise its influence without appearing to do so; should be ever active, both as a support and as a restraint, yet seem to lie easily in hand. It must always be ready to check or to pull up, as occasion may require; and only when the horse is a runaway should the action of the curb be perceptible.

Discontent.

Sour discontent that quarrels with our fate
May give fresh smart, but not the old abate;
The uneasy passion's disingenuous wit,
The ill reveals but hides the benefit. *Sir Richard Blackmore.*

What's more miserable than discontent? *Shakespeare.*

Discretion.

Open your purse and your mouth cautiously; and your stock of wealth and reputation shall, at least in repute, be great *Zimmerman.*

There are many shining qualities in the mind of man, but there is none so useful as discretion; it is this, indeed, that gives a value to all the rest, which sets them to work in their proper times and places, and turns them to the advantage of the person who is possessed of them. Without it, learning is pedantry, and wit impertinence; virtue itself looks like weakness; the best parts only qualify a man to be more sprightly in errors, and active to his own principle. *Addison.*

It show'd discretion, the best part of valor. *Beaumont and Fletcher.*

Discretion in speech is more than eloquence. *Bacon.*

Discussion.

Men are never so likely to settle a question rightly as when they discuss it freely. *Macaulay.*

Free and fair discussion will ever be found the firmest friend to truth. *George Campbell.*

Disease.

It is not the disease but neglect of the remedy which generally destroys life. *From the Latin.*

Dishonesty.

That which is won ill, will never wear well, for there is a curse attends it, which will waste it; and the same corrupt dispositions which incline men to the sinful ways of getting, will incline them to the like sinful ways of spending. *Matthew Henry.*

Who purposely cheats his friend. would cheat his God. *Lavater.*

Distance.

'Tis distance lends enchantment to the view,
And robes the mountain in its azure hue. *Campbell.*

Divinity.

It is a good divine that follows his own instructions. *Shakespeare.*

There's a divinity that shapes our ends,
Rough-hew them how we will. *Shakespeare.*

Dog.

Every dog must have his day. *Swift.*

Doubt.

When you doubt, abstain. *Zoroaster.*
To believe with certainty we must begin to doubt. *Stanislaus.*
Our doubts are traitors
And make us lose the good we oft might win
By fearing to attempt. *Shakespeare.*

Dreams.

Dreams are but interludes that fancy makes
When monarch reason sleeps, this mimic wakes;
Compounds a medley of disjointed things.
     *   *   *   *   *
That neither were nor are not e'er can be.
Sometimes forgotten things, long cast behind
Rush forward in the brain, and come to mind. *Dryden.*

I talk of dreams;
Which are the children of an idle brain,
Begot of nothing but vain phantasy
Which is as thin of substance as the air;
And more inconstant than the wind, which woos
Even now the frozen bosom of the north,
And, being anger'd, puffs away from thence,
Turning his face to the dew dropping south. *Shakespeare.*

Dress.

The person whose clothes are extremely fine I am too apt to consider as not being possessed of any superiority of fortune, but resembling those Indians who are found to wear all the gold they have in the world in a bob at the nose. *Goldsmith.*

Drinking.

The first draught a man drinks ought to be for thirst, the second for nourishment, the third for pleasure, the fourth for madness.

Drunkard.

When he is best, he is little worse than a man; and when he is worst he is little better than a beast. *Shakespeare.*

Drunkenness.

Drunkenness is the vice of a good constitution, or of a bad memory! of a constitution so treacherously good, that it never bends until it breaks; or of a memory that recollects the pleasures of getting drunk, but forgets the pains of getting sober. *Colton.*

Duties.

Happy the man, and happy he alone,
He, who can call to-day his own;
He who, secure within, can say
To-morrow do thy worst, for I have lived to-day. *Dryden.*

Be not diverted from your duty by any idle reflections the silly world may make upon you, for their censures are not in your power, and consequently should not be any part of your concern. *Epictetus.*
Stern duty, daughter of the voice of God!
O, duty! if that name thou love,
Who art a light to guide, a rod
To check the erring and reprove;
Thou who art victory and law,
When empty terrors overawe,
Give unto me, made lowly wise,
The spirit of self-sacrifice. *Wordsworth.*

Ear.

One ear heard it, and at the other out it went. *Chaucer.*

Early Rising.

The early morning has gold in its mouth. *Franklin.*

Early to bed and early to rise,
Makes a man healthy, wealthy and wise.

Few ever lived to a great age, and fewer still ever became distinguished, who were not in the habit of early rising. *Todd.*

Earnestness.

Earnestness alone makes life eternity. *Carlyle.*

There is no substitute for thorough going, ardent, and sincere earnestness. *Dickens.*

Earth.

The earth, that's nature's mother, is her tomb. *Shakespeare.*

The earth is bright,
And I am earthly, so I love it well;
Though heaven is holier, and full of
    light
Yet I am frail, and with frail things
    would dwell.   *Mrs. Judson.*

And fast by, hanging in a golden chain
This pendant world, in bigness as a star.
    Milton.

Ease.

Ease leads to habit, as success to ease.
He lives by rule who lives himself to
    please.   *Crabbe.*

Eating.

The chief pleasure (in eating) does not
consist in costly seasoning, or exquisite
flavor, but in yourself. Do *you* seek
sauce by sweating.   *Horace.*

The turnpike road to people's hearts I find
Lies through their mouths, or I mistake
    mankind.   *Dr. Wolcot.*

The difference between a rich man and a
poor man is this—the former eats when he
pleases, and the latter when he can get it.
    Sir Walter Raleigh.

Eccentricity.

He that will keep a monkey should pay
for the glasses he breaks.   *Selden.*

Echo.

The babbling gossip of the air.
    Shakespeare.

Economy.

Beware of little expenses; a small leak
will sink a great ship.   *Franklin.*

Economy is of itself a great revenue.
    Cicero.

Education.

A college education shows a man how
little other people know.   *Haliburton.*

'Tis education forms the common mind.
Just as the twig is bent, the tree's inclin'd.
    Pope.

All of us who are worth anything, spend
our manhood in unlearning the follies, or
expiating the mistakes of our youth.
    Shelley.

They who provide much wealth for their
children, but neglect to improve them in
virtue, do like those who feed their horses
high, but never train them to the manage.
    Socrates.

Effort.

The rider likes best the horse which
needs most breaking in.
    Edward Garrett.

The general prizes most the fortress
which took the longest siege.
    Edward Garrett.

The vain beauty cares most for the conquest which employed the whole artillery
of her charms.   *Edward Garrett.*

Egotism.

We often boast that we are never bored,
but yet we are so conceited that we do not
perceive how often we bore others.
    La Rochefoucauld.

Eloquence.

The clear conception, outrunning the deductions of logic, the high purpose, the
dauntless spirit, speaking on the tongue,
beaming from the eye, informing every
feature, and urging the whole man onward,
right onward, to his object,—this is eloquence, or rather it is something greater
and higher than all eloquence—it is action,
noble, sublime, godlike action.   *Webster.*

God gave you that gifted tongue of
yours, and set it between your teeth, to
make known your true meaning to us, not
    be rattled like a muffin man's bell.
    Carlyle.

Pour the full tide of eloquence along,
Serenely pure, and yet divinely strong.
    Pope.

        His tongue
Dropp'd manna, and could make the worse
    appear
The better reason to perplex and dash
Maturest counsels.   *Milton.*

It is but poor eloquence which only
shows that the orator can talk.
    Sir Joshua Reynolds.

Her tears her only eloquence.   *Rogers.*
Whene'er he speaks, Heaven, how the
    list'ning throng
Dwell on the melting music of his tongue!
His arguments are emblems of his mien,
Mild but not faint, and forcing, though
    serene:
And when the power of eloquence he'd try,
Here lightning strikes you, there soft
    breezes sigh.   *Garth.*
When he spoke, what tender words he
    us'd!
So softly, that like flakes of feather'd snow,
They melted as they fell.   *Dryden.*
Your words are like the notes of dying
    swans;
Too sweet to last.   *Dryden.*
True eloquence consists in saying all
that should be, not all that could be said.
    La Rochefoucauld.

Empire.

Nations and empires flourish and decay,
By turns command, and in their turns
   obey. *Ovid.*

Westward the course of empire take its
   way,
The four first acts already past.
A fifth shall close the drama with the day;
Time's noblest offspring is the last.
   Bishop Berkeley.

Emulation.

Keeps mankind sweet by action: without
   that
The world would be a filthy settled mud.
   Crown.

End.

The end crowns all;
And that old common arbitrator, time,
Will one day end it. *Shakespeare.*

All's well that ends well, still the finis is
the crown. *Shakespeare.*

Endurance.

He conquers who endures. *Persius.*

Enemies.

If you want enemies excel others; if
you want friends let others excel you.
   Colton.

The fine and noble way to kill a foe
Is not to kill him: you with kindness may
So change him, that he shall cease to be
   so;
Then he's slain. *Aleyn.*

There's not so much danger
In a known foe as a suspected friend.
   Nabb.

Ennui.

Give me to drink, Mandragora,
That I may sleep away this gap of time.
   Shakespeare.

Enthusiasm.

Nothing is so contagious as enthusiasm; it is the real allegory of the tale of
Orpheus; it moves stones, it charms
brutes. Enthusiasm is the genius of sincerity, and truth accomplishes no victories
without it. *Bulwer.*

Enthusiast.

No wild enthusiast ever yet could rest
'Till half mankind were like himself possess'd. *Cowper.*

Entreaty.

Once more into the breach, dear friends,
once more! *Shakespeare.*

Envy.

The most certain sign of being born with
great qualities is to be born without envy.
La Rochefoucauld.

As rust corrupts iron, so envy corrupts
man. *Anisthenes.*

Envy is but the smoke of low estate,
Ascending still against the fortunate.
   Lord Brooke.

Envy is a weed that grows in all soils
and climates, and is no less luxuriant in
the country than in the court; is not confined to any rank of men or extent of fortune, but rages in the breasts of all degrees. *Lord Clarendon.*

He who envies another admits his own
inferiority. *From the Latin.*

Our envy always lasts longer than the
happiness of those we envy.
   La Rochefoucauld.

Equality.

In the gates of Eternity, the black hand
and the white hand hold each other with
an equal clasp. *Mrs. Stowe.*

Equity.

All things whatsoever ye would that
men should do unto you, do ye even so to
them. *Matt.* vii, 12.

Error.

O, hateful error—Melancholy's child!
Why dost thou show to the apt thoughts of
   men
The things that are not? O, Error, soon
   conceived!
Thou never coms't unto a happy birth,
But kill'st the mother that engendered
   thee. *Shakespeare.*

From the errors of others, a wise man
corrects his own. *Syrus.*

I will not quarrel with a slight mistake,
Such as our nature's frailty may excuse.
   Roscommon.

A man's errors are what make him amiable. *Goethe.*

The best may slip, and the most cautious
   fall;
He's more than mortal that ne'er err'd at
   all. *Pomfret.*

Great errors seldom originate but with
men of great minds. *Petrarch.*

Errors like straws upon the surface flow:
He who would search for pearls must dive
   below. *Dryden.*

Estrangement.

There is not so agonizing a feeling in the
whole catalogue of human suffering, as the
first conviction that the heart of the being
whom we most tenderly love is estranged
from us. *Bulwer.*

Eternity.

Eternity stands always fronting God;
A stern colossal image with blind eyes,
And grand dim lips, that murmur ever-
　　more,
"God, God, God!"　　　*Mrs. Browning.*

　　None can comprehend eternity but the
eternal God. Eternity is an ocean, whereof we shall never see the shore; it is a
deep, where we can find no bottom; a
labyrinth from whence we cannot extricate
ourselves and where we shall ever lose the
door.　　　　　　　　*Boston.*

　　　　Why shrinks the soul
Back on herself, and startles at destruc-
　　tion?
'Tis the divinity that stirs within us;
'Tis heaven itself that points out an here-
　　after,
And intimates eternity to man.
Eternity, thou pleasing dreadful thought!
Thro' what variety of untry'd being
Thro' what new scenes and changes must
　　we pass?
The wide, the unbounded prospect lies be-
　　fore me;
But shadows, clouds, and darkness rest
　　upon it.　　　　　　*Addison.*

Etiquette.

There was a general whisper, toss, and
　　wriggle,
But etiquette forbade them all to giggle.
　　　　　　　　　　　Byron.

Evening.

The curfew tolls the knell of parting day,
　　The lowing herd winds slowly o'er the
　　lea;
The ploughman homeward plods his weary
　　way,
And leaves the world to darkness and to
　　me.
Now fades the glimm'ring landscape on
　　the sight,
　　And all the air a solemn stillness holds,
Save where the beetle wheels his drony
　　flight
　　And drowsy tinklings lull the distant
　　folds.
Save that from yonder ivy-mantled tower,
　　The moping owl does to the moon com-
　　plain
Of such as wand'ring near her secret
　　bower
　　Molest her ancient, solitary reign.
　　　　　　　　　　　Gray.

The summer day has clos'd—the sun is
　　set;
Well have they done their office, those
　　bright hours,
The latest of whose train goes softly out
In the red west.　　　　*Bryant.*

Sweet is the hour of rest,
　　Pleasant the wind's low sigh,
And the gleaming of the west,
　　And the turf whereon we lie.
　　　　　　　　Mrs. Hemans.

Now stir the fire, and close the shutters
　　fast,
Let fall the curtains, wheel the sofa
　　round,
And while the bubbling and loud hissing
　　urn
Throws up a steamy column, and the cups,
That cheer but not inebriate, wait on each,
So let us welcome peaceful evening in.
　　　　　　　　　　　Cowper.

　　　　How still the evening is
As hush'd on purpose to grace harmony!
　　　　　　　　　　Shakespeare.

An eve intensely beautiful; an eve
Calm as the slumber of a lovely girl
Dreaming of hope. The rich autumnal
　　woods,
With their innumerable shades and color-
　　ings,
Are like a silent instrument at rest:
A silent instrument—whereon the wind
Hath long forgot to play.　　*Houseman.*

Evidence.

　　Hear one side, and you will be in the
dark; hear both sides, and all will be
clear.　　　　　　　　*Haliburton.*

Evil.

　　He who will fight the devil with his own
weapons, must not wonder if he finds him
an over-match.　　　　　　*South.*

　　The doing evil to avoid an evil cannot
be good.　　　　　　　*Coleridge.*

　　An evil at its birth, is easily crushed, but
it grows and strengthens by endurance.
　　　　　　　　　　　Cicero.

This is the curse of every evil deed
That, propagating still, it brings forth evil.
　　　　　　　　　　　Southey.

　　Timely advis'd, the coming evil shun!
　　　　　　　　　　　Prior.

Examinations.

Examinations are formidable even to the
best prepared, for the greatest fool may
ask more than the wisest man can answer.

Example is a living law, whose sway
Men more than all the written laws obey.
　　　　　　　　　　　Sedley.

　　People seldom improve, when they have
no other model but themselves to copy.
　　　　　　　　　　　Goldsmith.

Excellence.

Excellence is never granted to man, but as the reward of labor. It argues, indeed, no small strength of mind to persevere in the habits of industry, without the pleasure of perceiving those advantages which, like the hands of a clock, whilst they make hourly approaches to their point, yet proceed so slowly as to escape observation.

Sir Joshua Reynolds.

Excess.

To gild refined gold, to paint the lily,
To throw a perfume on the violet,
To smoothe the ice, or add another hue
Unto the rainbow, or, with taper-light,
To seek the beauteous eye of heaven to
　　garnish,
Is wasteful and ridiculous excess.

Shakespeare.

The desire of power in excess caused angels to fall; the desire of knowledge in excess caused man to fall; but in charity is no excess, neither can man or angels come into danger by it. *Bacon.*

Excesses.

The excesses of our youth are drafts upon our old age, payable with interest, about thirty years after date. *Colton.*

Excuse.

An excuse is worse and more terrible than a lie; for an excuse is a lie guarded.

Pope.

And, oftentimes, excusing of a fault,
Doth make a fault the worse by the excuse:
As patches set upon a little breach,
Discredit more in hiding of the fault,
Than did the fault before it was so patch'd.

Shakespeare.

Exertion.

With every exertion, the best of men can do but a moderate amount of good: but it seems in the power of the most contemptible individual to do incalculable mischief. *Washington Irving.*

Expectation.

How slow
This old moon wanes! she lingers my desires,
Like to a stepdame, or a dowager,
Long withering out a young man's revenue. *Shakespeare.*

Experience.

Experience keeps a dear school, but fools will learn in no other, and scarcely in that; for it is true, we may give *advice*, but we cannot give *conduct*. Remember this; they that will not be counseled cannot be helped. If you do not hear reason she will rap you over your knuckles.

Franklin.

I had rather have a fool to make me merry, than experience to make me sad.

Shakespeare.

Ah! the youngest heart has the same waves within it as the oldest; but without the plummet which can measure the depths. *Richter.*

All is but lip wisdom which wants experience. *Sir Philip Sydney.*

Extravagance.

The man who builds and wants wherewith
　　to pay
Provides a home from which to run away.

Young.

Dreading the climax of all human ills,
The inflammation of his weekly bills.

Byron.

Eye.

An eye like Mars, to threaten and command. *Shakespeare.*

A beautiful eye makes silence eloquent, a kind eye makes contradiction an assent, an enraged eye makes beauty deformed. This little member gives life to every part about us; and I believe the story of Argus implies no more, than that the eye is in every part; that is to say, every other part would be mutilated, were not its force represented more by the eye than even by itself. *Addison.*

The eye sees not itself
But by reflection, by some other things.

Shakespeare.

Eyes with the same blue witchery as those
Of Psyche, which caught Love in his own
　　wiles. *From the Italian.*

The soft blue eye,
That looks as it had open'd first in heaven,
And caught its brightness from the seraph's gaze
As flowers are fairest where the sunbeams
　　fall. *Mrs. Hale.*

His eye was blue and calm, as is the sky
In the serenest noon. *Willis.*

A gray eye is still and sly;
A roguish eye is the brown;
The eye of blue is ever true;
But in the black eye's sparkling spell
Mystery and mischief dwell.

A pair of bright eyes with a dozen glances suffice to subdue a man; to enslave him, and inflame; to make him even forget; they dazzle him so, that the past becomes straightway dim to him; and he so prizes them, that he would give all his

life to possess them. What is the fond love of dearest friends compared to his treasure? Is memory as strong as expectancy. fruition as hunger, gratitude as desire?
Thackeray.

Men with grey eyes are generally keen, energetic, and at first cold : but you may depend upon their sympathy with real sorrow. Search the ranks of our benevolent men and you will agree with me.
Dr. Leask.

His eyes have all the seeming of a demon's that is dreaming.   *Poe.*
From women's eyes this doctrine I derive ;
They sparkle still the right Promethean fire ;
They are the books, the arts, the academies,
That show, contain, and nourish all the world,
Else, none at all in aught proves excellent.
Shakespeare.

Face.

But then her face,
So lovely, yet so arch, so full of mirth,
The overflowings of an innocent heart.
Rogers.

Her face was like an April morn,
  Clad in a wint'ry cloud ;
And clay-cold was her lily hand,
  That held her sable shroud.   *Mallet.*
His face was of the doubtful kind ;
That wins the eye and not the mind.
Scott.

Facts.

One fact is better than one hundred analogies.

The Right Honorable Gentleman is indebted to his memory for his jests and to his imagination for his facts.   *Sheridan.*

Facts are to the mind the same thing as food to the body. On the due digestion of facts depends the strength and wisdom of the one, just as vigor and health depend on the other. The wisest in council, the ablest in debate, and the most agreeable in the commerce of life, is that man who has assimilated to his understanding the greatest number of facts.   *Burke.*

Fail.

Macbeth.—If we should fail—
Lady M.—We fail ?
But screw your courage to the sticking place
And we'll not fail.   *Shakespeare.*
In the lexicon of youth, which fate reserves

For a bright manhood, there is no such word
As *fail.*   *Bulwer.*
There is not a fiercer hell than failure in a great object.   *Keats.*

Fairies.

Did you ever hear
Of the frolic fairies dear?
They're a blessed little race,
Peeping up in fancy's face,
In the valley, on the hill.
By the fountain and the rill ;
Laughing out between the leaves
That the loving summer weaves.
Mrs. Osgood.

Oft fairy elves,
Whose midnight revels by a forest side,
Or fountain, some belated peasant sees,
Or dreams he sees, while o'erhead the moon
Sits arbitress, and nearer to the earth
Wheels her pale course, they on their mirth and dance
Intent, with jocund music charm his ear ;
At once with joy and fear his heart rebounds.   *Milton.*

Fairy Land.

Wherever is love and loyalty, great purposes and lofty souls, even though in a hovel or a mine, there is fairy-land.
Kingsley.

Faith.

Faith builds a bridge across the gulf of death,
To break the shock blind nature cannot shun,
And lands thought smoothly on the further shore.   *Young.*
Nought shall prevail against us, or disturb
Our cheerful faith, that all which we behold
Is full of blessings.   *Wordsworth.*

Faith is the substance of things hoped for, the evidence of things not seen.
Hebrews xi, 1.

Faith is the soul going out of itself for all its wants.   *Boston.*
Faith lights us through the dark to Deity.   *Davenant.*
For modes of faith let graceless zealots fight,
His can't be wrong whose life is in the right.   *Pope.*
Faith is not reason's labor, but repose.
Young.

Works without *faith* are like a fish without water, it wants the element it should live in. A building without a basis can-

not stand; faith is the foundation, and every good action is as a stone laid.
Feltham.

We should act with as much energy as those who expect everything from themselves; and we should pray with as much earnestness as those who expect everything from God. *Colton.*

Fall.

I've touch'd the highest point of all my
    greatness:
And from that full meridian of my glory
I haste now to my setting. I shall fall,
Like a bright exhalation in the evening
And no man see me more. *Shakespeare.*

Falsehood.

A goodly apple rotten at the heart;
O, what a goodly outside falsehood hath!
    Shakespeare.

The seal of truth is on thy gallant form,
For none but cowards lie. *Murphy.*

A lie should be trampled on and extinguished wherever found. I am for fumigating the atmosphere, when I suspect that falsehood, like pestilence, breathes around me. *Carlyle.*

Fame.

Fame is an ill you may with ease obtain,
A sad oppression to be borne with pain;
And when you would the noisy clamour
    drown,
You'll find it hard to lay the burden down.
    Cooke.

And what is fame, that flutt'ring noisy
    sound,
But the cold lie of universal vogue?
    H. Smith.

In Fame's temple there is always a niche to be found for rich dunces, importunate scoundrels or successful butchers of the human race. *Zimmerman.*

Vain empty words
Of honor, glory, and immortal fame,
Can these recall the spirit from its place,
Or re-inspire the breathless clay with life?
What tho' your fame with all its thousand
    trumpets,
Sound o'er the sepulchres, will that awake
The sleeping dead? *Sewell.*

I courted fame but as a spur to brave
And honest deeds; and who despises
    fame
Will soon renounce the virtues that deserve it. *Mallet.*

If a man do not erect in this age his own tomb ere he dies, he shall live no longer in monument than the bell rings, and the widow weeps. *Shakespeare.*

Fame may be compared to a scold; the best way to silence her is to let her alone, and she will at last be out of breath in blowing her own trumpet. *Fuller.*

Fame is the spur that the clear spirit doth
    raise
(That last infirmity of noble minds)
To scorn delights and live laborious days;
But the fair guerdon when we hope to
    find,
And think to burst out into sudden blaze,
Comes the blind Fury with the abhorr'd
    shears,
And slits the thin-spun life. *Milton.*

Famine.

This famine has a sharp and meagre face;
'Tis death in an undress of skin and bone,
Where age and youth, their landmark
    ta'en away,
Look all one common sorrow. *Dryden.*

Fanatacism.

The Puritans hated bearbaiting not because it gave pain to the bear, but because it gave pleasure to the spectators.
    Macaulay.

Fancy.

Tell me where is fancy bred,
Or in the heart, or in the head?
How begot, how nourished?
It is engendered in the eyes,
With gazing fed; and fancy dies
In the cradle where it lies.
    Shakespeare.

Farewell.

Twere vain to speak, to weep, to sigh,
Oh, more than tears of blood can tell
When wrung from guilt's expiring eye,
Are in the word farewell—farewell.
    Byron.

Farewell a word that must be, and hath
    been,
A sound which makes us linger;—yet—
    farewell. *Byron.*

Fashion.

Fashion, leader of a chatt'ring train,
Whom man for his own hurt permits to
    reign,
Who shifts and changes all things but his
    shape,
And would degrade her vot'ry to an ape,
The fruitful parent of abuse and wrong,
Hold a usurp'd dominion o'er his tongue,
There sits and prompts him to his own disgrace,
Prescribes the theme, the tone, and the

grimace,
And when accomplish'd in her wayward
    school,
Calls gentleman whom she has made a
    fool.   *Cowper.*

I see that fashion wears out more apparel than the man.   *Shakespeare.*

We laugh heartily to see a whole flock
of sheep jump because one did so; might
not one imagine that superior beings do
the same by us, and for exactly the same
reason?   *Greville.*

Be neither too early in the fashion, nor
too long out of it; nor at any time in the
extremities of it.   *Lavater.*

Fate.

Heaven from all creatures hides the
book of Fate.   *Pope.*

What must be, shall be; and that which
is a necessity to him that struggles is little
more than choice to him that is willing.
                                      Seneca.

With equal pace, impartial fate,
Knocks at the palace and the cottage gate.
                                      Horace.

Fate steals along with silent tread,
Found oftenest in what least we dread;
Frowns in the storm with angry brow,
But in the sunshine strikes the blow.
                                      Cowper.

Faults.

O wad some pow'r the giftie gie us
To see oursels as others see us!
It wad frae mony a blunder free us,
    And foolish notion.   *Burns.*

Men have many faults;
    Poor women have but two;
There's nothing good they say,
    And nothing right they do.
                                      Anon.

Fear.

In politics, what begins in fear usually
ends in folly.   *Coleridge.*

In morals, what begins in fear usually
ends in wickedness; in religion, what begins in fear usually ends in fanatacism.
Fear, either as a principle or a motive, is
the beginning of all evil.   *Mrs. Jameson.*
Fear is the tax that conscience pays to
guilt.   *Sewell.*

The thing in the world I am most afraid
of is fear, and with good reason, that
passion alone in the trouble of it exceeding other accidents.   *Montaigne.*

What are fears but voices airy?

Whispering harm where harm is not,
And deluding the unwary
    Till the fatal bolt is shot! *Wordsworth.*

Feasting.

It is not the quantity of the meat, but
the cheerfulness of the guests, which
makes the feast.   *Lord Clarendon.*

        Mingles with the friendly bowl
The feast of reason and the flow of soul.
                                      Pope.

Feeling.

The last, best fruit which comes to perfection, even in the kindliest soul, is, tenderness toward the hard, forbearance toward the unforbearing, warmth of heart
toward the cold, philanthropy toward the
misanthropic.   *Richter.*

A fellow-feeling makes one wondrous
kind.   *Garrick.*

Fidelity.

            Faithful found
Among the faithless, faithful only he;
Among innumerable false, unmov'd,
Unshaked, unseduced, unterrified;
His loyalty he kept, his love, his zeal
Nor number, nor example with him
    wrought
To swerve from truth, or change his constant mind
Though single.   *Milton.*

She is as constant as the stars
That never vary, and more chaste than
    they.   *Proctor.*

Finis.

My pen is at the bottom of a page,
Which being finished, here the story ends;
'Tis to be wished it had been sooner done,
But stories somehow lengthen when begun.
                                      Byron.

Finery.

All that glisters is not gold,
Gilded tombs do worms enfold.
                                      Shakespeare.

Fire.

Behold how great a matter a little fire
kindleth.   *James iii. 5*

And where two raging fires meet together,
They do consume the thing that feeds
    their fury.   *Shakespeare*

Fire that's closest kept burns most of all.
                                   Shakespeare.

Fireside.

The cat's Eden.   *Southey.*

Firmness.

I said to Sorrow's awful storm,
 That beat against my breast,
Rage on—thou may'st destroy this form,
 And lay it low at rest;
But still the spirit that now brooks
 Thy tempest raging high,
Undaunted on its fury looks
 With steadfast eye. *Mrs. Stoddard.*

First and Last.

First must give place to last, because
last must have his time to come; but last
gives place to nothing, for there is not
another to succeed. *Bunyan.*

Flatterers.

Of all wild beasts preserve me from a
 tyrant;
Of all tame—a flatterer. *Johnson*
 Hold!
No adulation!—'tis the death of virtue!
Who flatters, is of all mankind the lowest
Save him who courts the flattery.
 Hannah More.

When flatterers meet the devil goes to
dinner. *De Foe.*

Flattery.

Flattery is a sort of bad money, to
which our vanity gives currency.
 La Rochefoucauld.

Nothing is so great an instance of ill-
manners as flattery. If you flatter all the
company you please none; if you flatter
only one or two, you affront all the rest.
 Swift.

Sirs, adulation is a fatal thing—
Rank poison for a subject, or a king.
 Dr. Wolcot.

Folly.

Sick of herself is folly's character,
As wisdom's is a modest self applause.
 Young.

None but a fool is always right. *Hare.*

Fool.

For every inch that is not fool is rogue.
 Dryden.

This fellow is wise enough to play the
 fool;
And, to do that well, craves a kind of wit.
 Shakespeare.

The greatest of fools is he who imposes
on himself, and in his greatest concern
thinks certainly he knows that which he
has least studied, and of which he is most
profoundly ignorant. *Shaftesbury.*

Though thou shouldst bray a fool in a
mortar among wheat with a pestle, yet will
not his foolishness depart from him.
 Prov. xxvii, 22.

Fop.

Knows what he knows as if he knew it
 not,
What he remembers, seems to have forgot.
 Cowper.

So gentle, yet so brisk, so wondrous sweet.
So fit to prattle at a lady's feet.
 Churchill.

The soul of this man is in his clothes.
 Shakespeare.

Forbearance.

Whosoever shall smite thee on thy right
cheek, turn to him the other also. And
if any man will sue thee at the law, and
take away thy coat, let him have thy cloak
also. *Matt.* v, 39.

Use every man after his deserts, and
who shall 'scape whipping. *Shakespeare.*

Everything has two handles; the one
soft and manageable, the other such as will
not endure to be touched. If then your
brother do you an injury, do not take it
by the hot hard handle, by representing to
yourself all the aggravating circumstances
of the fact; but look rather on the soft
side, and extenuate it as much as is possible, by considering the nearness of the
relation, and the long friendship and familiarity between you—obligations to kindness which a single provocation ought not
to dissolve. And thus you will take the
accident by its manageable handle.
 Epictetus.

Forgetfulness.

Of all affliction taught a lover yet
'Tis sure the hardest science to forget.
 Pope.

Forgiveness.

'Tis easier for the generous to forgive,
Than for offence to ask it. *Thomson.*

Forms.

Of what use are forms, seeing at times
they are empty?—Of the same use as barrels, which are at times empty too. *Hare.*

Fortitude.

Brave spirits are a balsam to themselves;
There is a nobleness of mind that heals
Wounds beyond salves. *Cartwright.*
———Gird your hearts with silent forti-
 tude
Suffering yet hoping all things.
 Mrs. Hemans.

Fortune.

To catch dame fortune's golden smile,
 Assiduous wait upon her;
And gather gear by every wile
 That's justified by honor.

Not for to hide it in a hedge,
  Nor for a train attendant;
But for the glorious privilege
  Of being *independent*.   *Burns.*

Fortune brings in some boats that are not steered.

Fortune is like the market, where, many times, if you can stay a little, the price will fall.   *Bacon.*

To be thrown on one's own resources is to be cast in the very lap of fortune; for our faculties undergo a development, and display an energy, of which they were previously unsusceptible.   *Franklin.*

When fortune means to men most good
She looks upon them with a threat'ning
    eye.   *Shakespeare.*

        Fortune is merry,
And in this mood will give us anything.
    Shakespeare.

When fortune sends a stormy wind,
Then show a brave and present mind;
And when with too indulgent gales
She swells too much, then furl thy sails.
    Creech.

The wheel of fortune turns incessantly round, and who can say within himself, I shall to-day be uppermost.   *Confucius.*

Free.

Who then is free? The wise man who can command himself.   *Horace.*

—— Freedom hath a thousand charms to
    show,
That slaves howe'er contented never know.
    Cowper.

Friend.

Give me the avow'd, the erect, the manly
    foe,
Bold I can meet,—perhaps may turn his
    blow;
But of all plagues, good heaven, thy wrath
    can send,
Save, save, oh! save me from the candid
    friend.   *Canning.*

Chide a friend in private and praise him in public.   *Solon.*

To lose a friend is the greatest of all losses.   *Syrus.*

A friend to everybody is a friend to nobody.   *Spanish Proverb.*

Friends.

Friend after friend departs;
  Who hath not lost a friend?
There is no union here of hearts
  That hath not here its end.
    Montgomery.

It is better to decide between our ene-
mies than our friends; for one of our friends will most likely become our enemy; but on the other hand, one of your enemies will probably become your friend.
    Bias.

He who hath many friends, hath none.
    Aristotle.

Old friends are best. King James used to call for his old shoes; they were easiest to his feet.   *John Selden.*

Purchase not friends with gifts; when thou ceasest to give, such will cease to love.   *Fuller.*

    A friend in need
    Is a friend indeed.

Friendship.

    So we grew together,
Like to a double cherry, seeming parted
But yet a union in partition,
Two lovely berries moulded on one stem:
So, with two seeming bodies, but one
    heart.   *Shakespeare.*

Friendship's the wine of life.   *Young.*

We still have slept together
Rose at an instant, learn'd, play'd, eat to-
    gether;
And wheresoe'er we went, like Juno's
    swans,
Still we went coupled, and inseparable.
    Shakespeare.

Friendship is no plant of hasty growth;
Tho' planted in esteem's deep fixed soil,
The gradual culture of kind intercourse
Must bring it to perfection.
    Joanna Baillie.

Great souls by instinct to each other turn,
Demand alliance, and in friendship burn.
    Addison.

      Friendship's the privilege
Of private men, for wretched greatness
    knows
No blessing so substantial.   *Tate.*

—— O friendship! of all things the
Most rare, and therefore most rare, be-
    cause most
Excellent; whose comforts in misery
Are always sweet, whose counsels in
Prosperity are ever fortunate.   *Lilly.*

Friendship is composed of a single soul inhabiting two bodies.   *Aristotle.*

Friendship is the only thing in the world concerning the usefulness of which all mankind are agreed.   *Cicero.*

Frugality.

Frugality may be termed the daughter of prudence, the sister of temperance, and the parent of liberty. He that is extravagant will quickly become poor, and poverty will

enforce dependence and invite corruption. *Johnson.*

Fury.

I understand a fury in your words,
But not your words. *Shakespeare.*

Future.

Heaven from all creatures hides the book
 of fate,
All but the page prescribed, their present
 fate. *Pope.*

God will not suffer man to have the
knowledge of things to come: for if he
had prescience of his prosperity he would
be careless: and understanding of his adversity he would be senseless. *Augustine.*
There is no hope—the future will but turn
The old sand in the falling glass of time.
    R. H. Stoddard.

Trust no future howe'er pleasant!
Let the dead past bury its dead!
Act—act in the living present!
Heart within and God o'erhead!
    Longfellow.

The veil which covers the face of futurity is woven by the hand of mercy.
    Bulwer.

Gallantry.

Conscience has no more to do with gallantry than it has with politics. *Sheridan.*
Gallantry consists in saying the most
empty things in an agreeable manner.
    La Rochefoucauld.

Gambler.

The gamester, if he die a martyr to his
profession, is doubly ruined. He adds his
soul to every other loss, and by the act of
suicide, renounces earth to forfeit heaven.
    Colton.

Look round the wrecks of play behold,
Estates dismember'd, mortgaged, sold;
Their owners now to jail confin'd,
Show equal poverty of mind. *Gay.*
Bets at the first were fool-traps where
 the wise
Like spiders lay in ambush for the flies.
    Dryden.
Some play for gain; to pass time others
 play
For nothing; both play the fool, I say:
Nor time nor coin I'll lose, or idly spend;
Who gets by play, proves loser in the end.
    Heath.

Gaming is the son of avarice, but the
father of despair.

General.

A gen'ral sets his army in array

In vain, unless he fight and win the day.
    Denham.

Generosity.

God blesses still the generous thought
 And still the fitting word He speeds,
And truth, at His requiring taught,
 He quickens into deeds. *Whittier.*
The truly generous is the truly wise;
And he who loves not others, lives unblest.
    Horace.

Genius.

The three indispensables of genius are
understanding, feeling, and perseverance.
The three things that enrich genius, are
contentment of mind, the cherishing of
good thoughts, and exercising the memory.
    Southey.

No enemy is so terrible as a man of
genius. *Disraeli.*

Men of genius are often dull and inert
in society, as a blazing meteor when it descends to earth, is only a stone.
    Longfellow.

Talent, lying in the understanding, is
often inherent; genius, being the action of
reason and imagination, rarely or never.
    Coleridge

There is no great genius free from some
tincture of madness. *Seneca.*

The greatest genius is never so great as
when it is chastised and subdued by the
highest reason. *Colton.*

When a true genius appears in the
world you may know him by this sign, that
the dunces are all in confederacy against
him. *Swift.*

Genius and Talent.

Genius is the highest type of reason—
talent the highest type of the understanding. *Hickok.*

Gentleman.

A gentleman has ease without familiarity, is respectful without meanness; genteel
without affectation, insinuating without
seeming art. *Chesterfield.*
His years are young, but his experience
 old;
His head unmellow'd, but his judgment
 ripe;
And in a word (for far behind his worth
Come all the praises that I now bestow)
He is complete in feature and in mind,
With all good grace to grace a gentleman.
    Shakespeare.

The grand old name of gentleman
Defam'd by every charlatan
And soil'd with all ignoble use.
    Tennyson.

Education begins the gentleman, but reading, good company and reflection must finish him. *Locke.*

I am a gentleman,
   I'll be sworn thou art!
Thy tongue, thy face, thy limbs, action and spirit,
Do give the five-fold blazon.
Shakespeare.

When Adam dolve and Eve span
Who was then the gentleman? *Pegge.*

Gentleness.

Sweet speaking oft a currish heart reclaims. *Sidney.*

Ghosts.

Glendower.—I can call spirits from the vasty deep.
Hotspur.—Why so can I, or so can any man;
   But will they come when you do call for them? *Shakespeare.*

Gift.

The manner of giving, shews the character of the giver, more than the gift itself.
Lavater.

Gifts.

Those gifts are ever the most acceptable which the giver has made precious.
Ovid.

There is no grace in a benefit that sticks to the fingers. *Seneca.*

Your gift is princely, but it comes too late,
And falls like sunbeams on a blasted blossom. *Suckling.*

Win her with gifts, if she respect not words;
Dumb jewels often, in their silent kind.
More quick than words do move a woman's mind. *Shakespeare.*

And with them, words of so sweet breath compos'd
As make the things more rich; their perfume lost.
Take these again; for to the noble mind
Rich gifts wax poor, when givers prove unkind. *Shakespeare.*

Never look a gift horse in the mouth.

Glory.

Real glory
Springs from the silent conquest of ourselves;
And without that the conqueror is nought,
But the first slave. *Thomson.*

Glory is the fair child of peril. *Smollett.*

Glory, the casual gift of thoughtless crowds!

Glory, the bribe of avaricious virtue!
Johnson.

**Who pants for glory finds a short repose,
A breath revives him, and a breath o'erthrows.** *Pope.*

Our greatest glory consists not in never falling, but in rising every time we fall.
Goldsmith.

The paths of glory lead but to the grave.
Gray.

Glutton.

Honor's a thing too subtle for his wisdom;
If honor lie in eating, he's right honorable. *Beaumont and Fletcher.*

Gluttony.

Fat paunches have lean pates, and dainty bits
Make rich the ribs, but bankrupt quite the wits. *Shakespeare.*

God.

God of my Fathers! holy, just and good!
My God! my Father, my unfailing Hope!
Jehovah! let the incense of thy praise,
Accepted, burn before thy mercy seat,
And let thy presence burn both day and night. *Pollok.*

A God alone can comprehend a God.
Young.

There is an Eye that never sleeps
   Beneath the wing of night:
There is an Ear that never shuts
   When sink the beams of light.

There is an Arm that never tires
   When human strength gives way;
There is a Love that never fails
   When earthly loves decay.

That Eye is fix'd on seraph throngs:
That Ear is fill'd with angel's songs:
That Arm upholds the worlds on high;
That Love is thron'd beyond the sky.
Heber.

God moves in a mysterious way
   His wonders to perform:
He plants His footsteps in the sea,
   And rides upon the storm. *Cowper.*

**All things that are on earth shall wholly pass away.
Except the love of God, which shall live and last for aye.** *Bryant.*

How calmly may we commit ourselves to the hands of Him who bears up the world—of Him who has created, and who provides for the joy even of insects, as carefully as if He were their Father!
Richter.

'Tis hard to find God, but to comprehend
Him, as He is, is labor without end.
Herrick.

At whose sight all the stars
Hide their diminish'd heads.
Milton.

Gold.

—— The picklock,
That never fails. *Massinger.*

O cursed lust of gold! when for thy sake
The fool throws up his interest in both
worlds
First starved in this, then damn'd in that
to come. *Blair.*

O, what a world of vile ill-favor'd faults
Look handsome in three hundred pounds a
year. *Shakespeare.*

'Tis gold so pure
It cannot bear the stamp without alloy.
Dryden.

Good.

That which is good to be done, cannot
be done too soon; and if it is neglected to
be done early, it will frequently happen
that it will not be done at all.
Bishop Mant.

Hard was their lodging, homely was their
food
For all their luxury was doing good.
Garth.

Good, the more
Communicated, more abundant grows.
Milton.

Good Breeding.

Virtue itself often offends when coupled
with bad manners. *Middleton.*

Good breeding shows itself most where,
to an ordinary eye, it appears the least.
Addison.

One principal object of good-breeding
is to suit our behavior to the three several degrees of men —our superiors, our
equals, and those below us. *Swift.*

A man's good-breeding is the best security against another's bad manners.
Chesterfield.

The scholar without good-breeding is a
pedant, the philosopher a cynic, the soldier
a brute, and every man disagreeable.
Chesterfield.

Good-Humor.

Good humor is the health of the soul,
sadness its poison. *Stanislaus.*

Good-Nature.

That inexhaustible good nature, which is
itself the most precious gift of Heaven,

spreading itself like oil over the troubled
sea of thought, and keeping the mind
smooth and equable in the roughest
weather. *Irving.*

Goodness.

Goodness is beauty in its best estate.
Marlowe.

Kind hearts are more than coronets,
And simple faith than Norman blood.
Tennyson.

He has more goodness in his little finger
Than you have in your whole body.
Swift.

Good-night.

To all, to each, a fair good night,
And pleasing dreams, and slumbers light.
Scott.

Gossip.

For my part I can compare her to nothing but the sun; for, like him, she takes
no rest, nor ever sets in one place but to
rise in another. *Dryden.*

Governing.

A man must first govern himself ere he
be fit to govern a family, and his family
ere he fit to bear the government in the
commonwealth. *Sir Walter Raleigh.*

Government.

It is better for a city to be governed by
a good man than by good laws. *Aristotle.*
They that govern most make the least
noise. You see, when they row in a barge,
they that do drudgery work, slash and
puff, and sweat, but he that governs sits
quietly at the stern, and is scarce seen to
stir. *Selden.*

For forms of government let fools contest:
Whate'er is best administer'd is best.
Pope.

We are more heavily taxed by our idleness, pride and folly than we are taxed by
government. *Franklin.*

Grace.

Some hae meat that canna eat,
And some would eat that want it;
But we hae meat, and we can eat.
Sae let the Lord be thankit. *Burns.*

Gratitude.

To the generous mind
The heaviest debt is that of gratitude,
When 'tis not in our power to repay it.
Dr. Thomas Franklin.

The debt immense of endless gratitude.

Milton.

What is grandeur, what is power?
Heavier toil, superior pain!
What the bright reward we gain?
The grateful mem'ry of the good.
Sweet is the breath of vernal shower,
The bee's collected treasure sweet.
Sweet music's melting fall, but sweeter yet
The still small voice of gratitude. *Gray.*

He who receives a good turn should
never forget it; he who does one should
never remember it. *Charron.*

Grave.

The reconciling grave
Swallows distinction first, that made us
foes:
There all lie down in peace together.
Southern.

There the wicked cease from troubling;
and the weary be at rest. There the prisoners rest together; they hear not the
voice of the oppressor. The small and
great are there; and the servant is free
from his master. *Job* iii, 17, 18.

A grave, wherever found, preaches a
short and pithy sermon to the soul.
Hawthorne.

Grave-digger.

The houses that he makes, last till
doomsday. *Shakespeare.*

Gravity.

Gravity is a mystery of the body, invented to conceal the defects of the mind.
La Rochefoucauld.

Too much gravity argues a shallow
mind. *Lavater.*

Greatness.

He doth bestride the narrow world,
Like a Colossus; and we petty men
Walk under his huge legs, and peep about
To find ourselves dishonorable graves.
Shakespeare.

In my stars I am above thee, but be not
afraid of greatness; some are born great,
some achieve greatness, and some have
greatness thrust upon them. *Shakespeare.*

Oh! greatness! thou art a flattering dream,
A wat'ry bubble, lighter than the air.
Tracy.

Lives of great men all remind us
We can make our lives sublime.
And departing leave behind us
Footsteps on the sands of time;
Footsteps that perhaps another,
Sailing o'er life's solemn main,
A forlorn and shipwreck'd brother,
Seeing, shall take heart again.
Longfellow

What millions died that Cæsar might be
great! *Campbell.*

The greatest truths are the simplest: so
are the greatest men.

Grief.

And but he's something stain'd
With grief, that's beauty's canker, thou
might'st call him
A goodly person. *Shakespeare.*

What a rich feast the canker grief has
made;
How has it suck'd the roses of thy cheeks!
And drunk the liquid crystal of thy eyes.
Sewell.

Oh! grief hath chang'd me since you saw
me last;
And careful hours, with time's deform'd
hand,
Have written strange defeatures in my
face. *Shakespeare.*

Excess of grief for the deceased is madness; for it is an injury to the living, and
the dead know it not. *Xenophon.*

What's gone, and what's past help
Should be past grief. *Shakespeare*

'Tis impotent to grieve for what is past,
And unavailing to exclaim. *Havard*

A malady
Preys on my heart, that medicine cannot
reach
Invisible and cureless. *Maturin.*

Grief, madam! 'Tis the pensiveness of joy,
Too deep for language—too serene for
mirth. *Talfourd.*

Grief knits two hearts in closer bonds
than happiness ever can; and common sufferings are far stronger links than common
joys. *Lamartine.*

The storm of grief bears hard upon his
youth,
And bends him like a drooping flower to
earth. *Rowe.*

Thine is a grief that wastes the heart,
Like mildew on a tulip's dyes—
When hope, deferr'd but to depart,
Loses its smiles but keeps its sighs.
L. E. Landon

Grudge.

If I can catch him once upon the hip
I will feed fat the ancient grudge I bear
him. *Shakespeare.*

Grumbling.

Everyone must see daily, instances of
people who complain from a mere habit of
complaining.

Guard.

It is better to be always upon your
guard, than to suffer once. *Latin Proverb.*

Guest.

A pretty woman is a welcome guest.
Byron.

Unbidden guests
Are often welcomest when they are gone.
Shakespeare.

Guilt.

He swears, but he is sick at heart;
He laughs, but he turns deadly pale;
His restless eye and sudden start—
These tell the dreadful tale
That will be told: it needs no words from
thee
Thou self-sold slave to guilt and misery
Dana.

From the body of one guilty deed
A thousand ghostly fears and haunting
thoughts proceed. *Wordsworth.*

So full of artless jealousy is guilt
It spills itself in fearing to be split
Shakespeare

And oh! that pang where more than mad
ness lies,
The worm that will not sleep, and never
dies. *Byron.*

God hath yok'd to guilt
Her pale tormentor—misery. *Bryant.*

Habit.

Habit gives endurance, and fatigue is
the best nightcap. *Kincaid*

The chain of habit coils itself around the
heart like a serpent, to gnaw and stifle it
Hazlitt

A new cask will long preserve the tincture of the liquor with which it was first
impregnated. *Horace.*

Habits.

All habits gather by unseen degrees
As brooks make rivers, rivers run to seas.
Dryden.

The diminutive chains of habit are seldom heavy enough to be felt until they are
too strong to be broken. *Johnson.*

Small habits well pursued, betimes,
May reach the dignity of crimes.
Hannah More.

Happiness.

The sweetest bird builds near the ground,
The loveliest flower springs low;
And we must stoop for happiness
If we its worth would know. *Swain.*

That something still . . . .
For which we bear to live or dare to die.
Pope.

How cheap
Is genuine happiness, and yet how dearly

Do we all pay for its base counterfeit!
We fancy wants, which to supply, we dare
Danger and death, enduring the privation
Of all free nature offers in her bounty,
To attain that which, in its full fruition,
Brings but satiety. The poorest man
May taste of nature in her element:
Pure, wholesome, never cloying; while the
richest,
From the same stores, does but elaborate
A pungent dish of well-concocted poison.
J. N. Barker.

I earn what I eat, get what I wear, owe
no man hate, envy no man's happiness,
glad of other men's good, content with my
harm. *Shakespeare.*

Know then this truth, enough for man to
know
Virtue alone is happiness below. *Pope.*

Our happiness in this world depends on
the affections we are enabled to inspire.
Duchesse de Praslin.

What nothing earthly gives, or can destroy
The soul's calm sunshine and the heartfelt joy. *Pope.*

Perfect happiness, I believe, was never
intended by the Deity to be the lot of one
of His creatures in this world; but that
He has very much put in our power the
nearness of our approaches to it, is what
I have steadfastly believed. *Jefferson.*

Happiness is in the taste, and not in the
things themselves; we are happy from possessing what we like, not from possessing
what others like. *La Rochefoucauld.*

Surely happiness is reflective like the
light of heaven; and every countenance,
bright with smiles and glowing with innocent enjoyment, is a mirror, transmitting
to others the rays of a supreme and ever-
shining benevolence. *Washington Irving.*

After long storms and tempests overblown,
The sun at length his joyous face doth
cleare;
So when fortune all her spight hath
showne,
Some blissful houres at last must needs
appeare,
Else should afflicted wights oft-times de-
speare. *Spenser.*

If solid happiness we prize,
Within our breast this jewel lies,
And they are fools who roam;
The world has nothing to bestow:
From our own selves our joys must flow
And that dear hut—our home. *Cotton.*

All who joy would win
Must share it—happiness was born a twin.
Byron.

Happiness and Wisdom.

There is this difference between happiness and wisdom; he that thinks himself the happiest man really is so; but he that thinks himself the wisest, is generally the greatest fool.
Colton.

Harlot.

She weaves the winding-sheets of souls,
and lays
Them in the urn of everlasting death.
Pollok.

'Tis the strumpet's plague
To beguile many, and be beguiled by one.
Shaftesbury.

Harvest.

Glowing scene!
Nature's long holiday! luxuriant—rich
In her proud progeny, she smiling marks
Their graces, now mature, and wonder
fraught!
Hail! season exquisite!—and hail ye sons
Of rural toil!—ye blooming daughters! ye
Who, in the lap of hardy labor rear'd,
Enjoy the mind unspotted.
Mary Robinson.

Haste.

Running together all about,
The servants put each other out,
Till the grave master had decreed,
The more haste, ever the worst speed.
Churchill.

Hatred.

A man should not allow himself to hate even his enemies, because if you indulge this passion on some occasions, it will rise of itself in others: if you hate your enemies, you will contract such a vicious habit of mind, as by degrees will break out upon those who are your friends, or those who are indifferent to you.
Plutarch.

Thou mayst hold a serpent by the tongue,
A chafed lion by the mortal paw,
A fasting tiger safer by the tooth,
Than keep in peace that hand which thou
dost hold.
Shakespeare.

It is the nature of the human disposition to hate him whom you have injured.
Tacitus.

Now hatred is by far the longest pleasure;
Men love in haste, but they detest at
leisure.
Byron.

Health.

He who has health has hope, and he who has hope has everything.
Arabian Proverb.

People who are always taking care of their health are like misers, who are hoarding a treasure which they have never spirit enough to enjoy.
Sterne.

The only way for a rich man to be healthy is, by exercise and abstinence, to live as if he were poor.
Sir W. Temple.

The common ingredients of health and
long life are:
Great temp'rance, open air,
Easy labor, little care.
Sir P. Sidney.

For life is not to live, but to be well.
Martial.

Be sober and temperate, and you will be healthy.
B. Franklin.

The surest road to health, say what they
will,
Is never to suppose we shall be ill.
Churchill.

Heart.

Heaven's Sovereign spares all beings but
himself,
That hideous sight—a naked human heart.
Young.

The honest heart that's free frae a
Intended fraud or guile,
However fortune kick the ba'
Has aye some cause to smile. *Burns.*

A young maiden's heart
Is a rich soil, wherein lie many germs
Hid by the cunning hand of nature there
To put forth blossoms in their fittest season;
And though the love of home first breaks
the soil,
With its embracing tendrils clasping it,
Other affections, strong and warm will
grow
While that one fades, as summer's flush of
bloom
Succeed the gentle budding of the spring.
Mrs. F. Kemble Butler.

The heart aye's the part aye
That makes us right or wrang.
Burns.

I have ease and I have health,
And I have spirits light as air;
And more than wisdom, more than
wealth—
A merry heart that laughs at care.
H. H. Milman.

The human heart is often the victim of the sensations of the moment; success intoxicates it to presumption, and disappointment dejects and terrifies it. *Volney.*

A recent moralist has affirmed that the human heart is like a jug. No mortal can look into its recesses, and you can only judge of its purity by what comes out of it. *Anon.*

Heaven.

Heaven is above all yet: there sits a judge
That no king can corrupt. *Shakespeare.*

Heaven's gates are not so highly arch'd
As princes' palaces: they that enter there
Must go upon their knees. *Webster.*

By heaven we understand a state of happiness infinite in degree, and endless in duration. *Franklin.*

Eye hath not seen it, my gentle boy;
Ear hath not heard its deep song of joy;
Dreams cannot picture a world so fair;
Sorrow and death may not enter there;
Time doth not breathe on its fadeless
  bloom
For beyond the clouds, and beyond the
  tomb,
  It is there, it is there, my child.
    Mrs. Hemans.

A Persian's heaven is easily made.
'Tis but black eyes and lemonade.
    Moore.

Heaven and Earth.

Heaven—it is God's throne. The earth
—it is his footstool. *Matthew v, 34.*

Hell.

Hell is truth seen too late. *H. G. Adams.*
Divines and dying men may talk of Hell
But in my heart her several torments
  dwell. *Shakespeare.*
Hell has no limits, nor is circumscribed
In one self place; but where we are is hell
And where hell is, there must we ever be
And to be short, when all the world dissolves,
And every creature shall be purified,
All places shall be hell that are not heaven.
    Marlowe.

Hero.

Whoever, with an earnest soul,
  Strives for some end from this low
    world afar,
Still upward travels though he miss the
  goal,
And strays—but towards a star. *Bulwer.*

All may be heroes:—
"The man who rules his spirit," saith the
  voice
Which cannot err,—"is greater than the
  man
Who takes a city." Hence it surely follows,
If each man would govern wisely, and
  thus show
Truth, courage, knowledge, power, benevolence
All, all the princely soul of private virtues,
Then each would be a prince, a hero—
  greater—
He will be a man in likeness of his maker!
    Mrs. Hale.

Heroism.

Heroism—the divine relation which in all times unites a great man to other men.
    Carlyle.

Highwayman.

Gentlemen of the shade, minions of the moon. *Shakespeare.*

History.

Her ample page
Rich with the spoils of time. *Gray.*

Some are to be read, some to be studied, and some may be neglected entirely, not only without detriment, but with advantage. *Bolingbroke.*

Some write a narrative of wars and feats,
Of heroes little known, and call the rant
A history; describe the man of whom
His own coevals took but little note,
And paint his person, character, and
  views,
As they had known him from his mother's
  womb. *Cowper.*

What are most of the histories of the world, but lies? Lies immortalized and consigned over as a perpetual abuse and a flaw upon prosperity. *South.*

Holiness.

Blessed is the memory of those who have kept themselves unspotted *from* the world! Yet more blessed and more dear the memory of those who have kept themselves unspotted in the world.
    Mrs. Jameson.

Home.

Bare walls make a gadding housewife.
    Fielding.

The paternal hearth, that rallying place of the affections. *Washington Irving.*

His warm but simple home where he en-
    joys
With her who shares his pleasures and his
    heart
Sweet converse.   *Cowper.*

Mid pleasures and palaces though we may
    roam,
Be it ever so humble there's no place like
    home.   *J. Howard Payne.*

Home is the sacred refuge of our life,
Secured from all approaches but a wife;
If thence we fly, the cause admits no
    doubt,
None but an inmate foe could force us out.
                  Dryden.

Honesty.

Honesty coupled to beauty, is to have
honey a sauce to sugar.   *Shakespeare.*

What is becoming is honest, and what
ever is honest must always be becoming.
                  Cicero.

Who is the honest man?
He that doth still and strongly good pur-
    sue,
To God, his neighbor, and himself most
    true:
Whom neither force nor fawning can
Unpin, or wrench from giving all their
    due.   *Herbert.*

Let honesty be as the breath of thy soul,
and never forget to have a penny, when all
thy expenses are enumerated and paid:
then shall thou reach the point of happiness, and independence shall be thy
shield and buckler, thy helmet and crown;
then shall thy soul walk upright, nor stoop
to the silken wretch because he hath
riches, nor pocket an abuse, because the
hand which offers it wears a ring set with
diamonds.   *Franklin.*

Lands mortgag'd may return, and more
    esteem'd,
But honesty once pawn'd, is ne'er re-
    deem'd.   *Middleton.*

The maxim that "Honesty is the best
policy" is one which, perhaps, no one is
ever habitually guided by in practice. An
honest man is always before it, and a
knave is generally behind it.   *Whately.*

A wit's a feather, and a chief's a rod;
An honest man's the noblest work of God.
                  Pope.

Heav'n that made me honest, made me
    more
Than ever king did when he made a lord.
                  Rowe.

To be honest, as this world goes,
Is to be one pick'd out of ten thousand.
              Shakespeare.

The more honesty a man has, the less he
affects the air of a saint.   *Lavater*

Honor.

Honor's a good brooch to wear in a
man's hat at all times.   *Jonson.*

Honor is like that glassy bubble,
That finds philosophers such trouble,
Whose least part crack'd, the whole does
    fly
And wits are crack'd to find out why.
                  Butler.

Honor and shame from no condition rise;
Act well your part; there all the honor
    lies.   *Pope.*

Honor's a fine imaginary notion.
That draws in raw and unexperienced men
To real mischiefs, while they hunt a
    shadow.   *Addison.*

No man of honor, as that word is usually understood, did ever pretend that his
honor obliged him to be chaste and temperate, to pay his creditors, to be useful to
his country, or to do good to mankind, to
endeavor to be wise or learned, to regard
his word, his promise, or his oath. *Swift.*
The noblest spur unto the sons of fame,
Is thirst for honor.   *John Hall.*

Our own heart, and not other men's
opinions forms our true honor. *Coleridge.*

Better to die ten thousand deaths
    Than wound my honor.   *Addison.*

Woman's honor
Is nice as ermine,—'twill not bear a soil.
                  Dryden.

Hope.

It is best to hope only for things possible and probable; he that hopes too
much shall deceive himself at last; especially if his industry does not go along
with his hopes; for hope without action is
a barren undoer.   *Feltham.*

Hope
Is such a bait, it covers any hook. *Jonson.*
Come then, oh care! oh grief! oh woe!
    Oh troubles! mighty in your kind,
I have a balm ye ne'er can know,
    A hopeful mind.   *F. Vane.*

Auspicious hope! in thy sweet garden grow
Wreaths for each toil, a charm for every
    woe.   *Campbell.*
All, all forsook the friendless guilty mind,
But hope, the charmer, linger'd still be-
    hind.   *Campbell.*

Hope deferred maketh the heart sick.
Prov. xiii, 12.

Hope is the pillar that holds up the world.

Hope is the dream of a waking man.
Pliny.

—Hopes that beckon with delusive gleams.
Till the eye dances in the void of dreams.
Holmes.

Hope springs eternal in the human breast.
Man never is, but always to be blest.
Pope.

Hope is a flatterer, but the most upright of parasites; for she frequents the poor man's hut, as well as the palace of his superior. *Shenstone.*

Hope, of all passions, most befriends us here. *Young.*

Our greatest good, and what we least can spare,
Is hope; the last of all our evils, fear.
Armstrong.

Hope is like the cork to the net, which keeps the soul from sinking in despair: and fear is like the lead to the net, which keeps it from floating in presumption.
Watson.

The setting of a great hope is like the setting of the sun. The brightness of our life is gone, shadows of the evening fall around us, and the world seems but a dim reflection itself—a broader shadow. We look forward into the coming lonely night; the soul withdraws itself. Then stars arise, and the night is wholly.
Longfellow.

He that loses hope may part with anything. *Congreve.*

Where no hope is left, is left no fear.
Milton.

Hope! fortune's cheating lottery
Where for one prize a thousand blanks there are. *Cowley.*

The mighty hopes that make us men.
Tennyson.

However deceitful hope may be, yet she carries us on pleasantly to the end of life.
La Rochefoucauld.

A propensity to hope and joy is real riches; one to fear and sorrow real poverty. *Hume.*

True hope is swift and flies with swallow's wings;
Kings it makes gods, and meaner creatures kings. *Shakespeare.*

Hope is the fawning traitor of the mind,
Which, while it cozens with a color'd friendship

Robs us of our best virtue—resolution.
Lee.

Hospitality.

Hospitality to the better sort, and charity to the poor; two virtues that are never exercised so well as when they accompany each other. *Atterbury.*

Hours are golden links;—God's tokens reaching heaven. *Dickens.*
Catch, then, oh! catch the transient hour,
Improve each moment as it flies;
Life's a short summer—man a flower;
He dies—alas! how soon he dies.
Johnson.

House.

A house is never perfectly furnished for enjoyment, unless there is a child in it rising three years old, and a kitten rising six weeks. *Southey.*

My precept to all who build is, that the owner should be an ornament to the house, and not the house to the owner. *Cicero.*
Nothing lovelier can be found
In woman, than to study household good,
And good works in her husband to promote. *Milton.*

Human Nature.

If we did not take great pains, and were not at great expense to corrupt our nature, our nature would never corrupt us.
Lord Clarendon.

Our humanity were a poor thing were it not for the divinity which stirs within us.
Bacon.

Humility.

Highest when it stoops
Lowest before the holy throne; throws down
Its crown abased; forgets itself, admires,
And breathes ador'ing praise. *Pollok.*
Humility, that low sweet root,
From which all heavenly virtues shoot.
Moore.

The sufficiency of my merit is to know that my merit is not sufficient.
Augustine.

Humility is a virtue all preach, none practice, and yet everybody is content to hear. The master thinks it good doctrine for his servant, the laity for the clergy, and the clergy for the laity. *Selden.*

Be wise,
Soar not too high to fall, but stoop to rise.
Massinger.

My endeavors
Have ever come too short of my desire
Shakespeare.

Humor.

Let your humor always be good humor in both senses. If it comes of a bad humor, it is pretty sure not to belie its parentage.

Some things are of that nature as to make One's fancy chuckle while his heart doth ache. *Bunyan.*

Hunger.

Famish'd people must be slowly nursed, And fed by spoonfuls, else they always burst. *Byron.*

Hunger is the best seasoning for meat, and thirst for drink. *Cicero.*

Hypocrisy.

O serpent heart, hid with a flow'ring face! Did ever dragon keep so fair a cave? *Shakespeare.*

Obey me, features, for one supple moment: You shall not long be tortured. Here in courts
We must not wear the soldier's honest face. *H. Thompson.*

Trust not those cunning waters of his eyes, For villainy is not without much rheum; And he long-traded in it, makes it seem Like rivers of remorse and innocence. *Shakespeare.*

Thy very looks are lies; eternal falsehood Smiles in thy lips, and flatters in thine eyes. *Smith.*

The devil can cite Scripture for his purpose.
An evil soul, producing holy witness, Is like a villain with a smiling cheek; A goodly apple rotten at the heart; Oh, what a goodly outside falsehood hath! *Shakespeare.*

Hypocrisy is the homage which vice pays to virtue. *La Rochefoucauld.*

Hypocrite.

The fawning, sneaking, and flattering hypocrite, that will do, or be anything, for his own advantage. *Stillingfleet.*

Hypocrites do the devil's drudgery in Christ's livery. *Matthew Henry.*

Idea.

An idea, like a ghost, (according to the common notion of ghost,) must be spoken to a little before it will explain itself. *Dickens.*

He doth nothing but talk of his horse; and he makes it a great appropriation to his own good parts, that he can shoe him himself. *Shakespeare.*

Idleness.

Absence of occupation is not rest.
A mind quite vacant is a mind distress'd. *Cowper.*

Evil thoughts intrude in an unemployed mind, as naturally as worms are generated in a stagnant pool. *From the Latin.*

Sluggish idleness—the nurse of sin. *Spenser*

Idleness travels very slowly, and poverty soon overtakes her. *Hunter.*

Idolatry.

'Tis mad idolatry, To make the service greater than the god. *Shakespeare.*

If.

Your If is the only peace-maker,— Much virtue in If. *Shakespeare.*

Ignorance.

Where ignorance is bliss 'Tis folly to be wise. *Gray.*

I hardly know so true a mark of a little mind as the servile imitation of another. *Greville.*

It is impossible to make people understand their ignorance, for it requires knowledge to perceive it: and, therefore, he that can perceive it hath it not. *Jeremy Taylor.*

Ills.

Common and vulgar people ascribe all ill that they feel, to others; people of little wisdom ascribe to themselves; people of much wisdom, to no one. *Epictetus.*

Keep what you've got; the ills that we know are the best. *Plautus.*

Illusion.

Some there be that shadows kiss; Some have but a shadow's bliss. *Shakespeare.*

Imagination.

The beings of the mind are not of clay; Essentially immortal, they create And multiply in us a brighter ray And more beloved existence. *Byron.*

Imitation.

A good imitation is the most perfect originality. *Voltaire.*

Men are so constituted that everybody undertakes what he sees another successful in, whether he has aptitude for it or not. *Goethe.*

Immodesty.

Immodest words admit of no defence
For want of decency is want of sense.
Pope.

Immortality.

Immortality o'ersweeps
All pains, all tears, all time, all fears—and peals,
Like the eternal thunders of the deep,
Into my ears this truth—Thou liv'st for ever. *Anon.*

Love, which proclaims thee human bids thee know
A truth more lofty in thy lowliest hour
Than shallow glory taught to human power,
"What's human is immortal!" *Bulwer.*

Impatience.

Impatience dries the blood sooner than age or sorrow. *Creon.*

Implacability.

There's no more mercy in him than there is milk in a male tiger. *Shakespeare.*

Impossible.

Impossible is a word only to be found in the dictionary of fools. *Napoleon I.*

Impressions.

The mind unlearns with difficulty what it has long learned. *Seneca.*

Impudence.

The way to avoid the imputation of impudence is not to be ashamed of what we do, but never to do what we ought to be ashamed of. *Tully.*

What! canst thou say all this and never blush? *Shakespeare.*

Impulse.

Act upon your impulses, but pray that they may be directed by God.
Emerson Tennent.

Since the generality of persons act from impulse much more than from principle, men are neither so good nor so bad as we are apt to think them. *Hare.*

Inaction.

Or doing nothing with a deal of skill.
Cowper.

It is better to have nothing to do, than to be doing nothing. *Attilus.*

Incivility.

A man has no more right to say an uncivil thing, than to act one; no more right to say a rude thing to another, than to knock him down. *Johnson.*

Inconstancy.

The dream on the pillow,
That flits with the day,
The leaf of the willow
A breath bears away;
The dust on the blossom,
The spray of the sea;
Ay,—ask thine own bosom—
Are emblems of thee.
L. E. Landon.

O heaven! Were man
But constant, he were perfect: that one error
Fills him with faults; make him run through sins:
Inconstancy falls off ere it begins.
Shakespeare.

Independence.

Bow to no patron's insolence; rely
On no frail hopes, in freedom live and die.
Seneca.

Slave to no sect, who takes no private road
But looks through nature up to nature's God. *Pope.*

Industry.

Sloth makes all things difficult, but industry all easy; and he that riseth late, must trot all day, and shall scarce overtake his business at night; while laziness travels so slowly, that poverty soon overtakes him. *Franklin.*

It sweeteneth our enjoyments, and seasoneth our attainments with a delightful relish. *Barrow.*

At the working-man's house hunger looks in, but dares not enter! nor will the bailiff or the constable enter; for industry pays debts, but despair increaseth them.
Franklin.

Inexperience.

He jests at scars who never felt a wound.
Shakespeare.

Infancy.

Heaven lies about us in our infancy.
Wordsworth.

Infant.

Or as the plumage of an angel's wing
Where every tint of rainbow beauty blends. *Mrs. Welby.*

Ere sin could blight, or sorrow fade,
Death came with friendly care;
The opening bud to heav'n convey'd,
And bade it blossom there. *Coleridge.*

He smiles and sleeps! sleep on
And smile, thou little young inheritor
Of a world scarce less young; sleep on and smile!
Thine are the hours and days when both

are cheering
And innocent. *Byron.*

Infidelity.

When once infidelity can persuade men that they shall *die like beasts*, they will soon be brought to *live like beasts* also. *South.*

Influence.

Not one false man but does unaccountable mischief. *Carlyle.*

As a little silvery circular ripple, set in motion by the falling pebble, expands from its inch of radius to the whole compass of a pool, so there is not a child—not an infant Moses—placed, however softly, in his bulrush ark upon the sea of time, whose existence does not stir a ripple, gyrating outward and on, until it shall have moved across and spanned the whole ocean of God's eternity, stirring even the river of life, and the fountains at which the angels drink. *Elihu Burritt.*

Ingratitude.

I hate ingratitude more in a man,
Than lying, vainness, babbling, drunkenness
Or any taint of vice, whose strong corruption
Inhabits our frail blood. *Shakespeare.*

Blow, blow thou winter wind,
Thou art not so unkind
As man's ingratitude;
Thy tooth is not so keen,
Because thou art not seen,
Although thy breath is rude. *Shakespeare.*

Injuries.

A man should be careful never to tell tales of himself to his own disadvantage; people may be amused, and laugh at the time, but they will be remembered, and brought up against him upon some subsequent occasion. *Johnson.*

Innocence.

O innocence, the sacred amulet,
'Gainst all the poisons of infirmity,
Of all misfortunes, injury and death! *Chapman.*

Against the head which innocence secures,
Insidious malice aims her dart in vain;
Turn'd backwards by the powerful breath
of heav'n. *Johnson.*

There is no courage, but in innocence,
No constancy, but in an honest cause. *Southern.*

O that I had my innocence again!
My untouch'd honor! But I wish in vain.
The fleece that has been by the dyer stain'd

Never again its native whiteness gain'd. *Waller.*

They that know no evil will suspect none. *Ben Jonson.*

Innocence is always unsuspicious. *Haliburton.*

Instinct.

In the nice bee what sense so subtly true
From pois'nous herbs extract the healing dew? *Pope.*

By a divine instinct, men's minds distrust
Ensuing danger; as by proof we see
The waters swell before a boisterous storm. *Shakespeare.*

Insult.

Of all the griefs that harass the distress'd,
Sure the most bitter is a scornful jest;
Fate never wounds more deep the generous heart,
Than when a blockhead's insult points the dart. *Dr. Johnson.*

Intellect.

The intellect of the wise is like glass: it admits the light of heaven and reflects it. *Hare.*

Intentions.

A man who is always forgetting his best intentions, may be said to be a thorough fare of good resolutions. *Mrs. Jameson.*

Intrusiveness.

The great secret of life is never to be in the way of others. *Haliburton.*

Irresolution.

I hope when you know the worst you will at once leap into the river and swim through handsomely, and not weatherbeaten by the divers blasts of irresolution, stand shivering upon the brink. *Suckling.*

Ivy.

As creeping ivy clings to wood or stone
And hides the ruin that it feeds upon. *Cowper.*

Jealousy.

Trifles light as air
Are to the jealous, confirmations strong
As proofs of holy writ. *Shakespeare.*

Beware of jealousy.
It is the green-eyed monster which doth mock
The meat it feeds on. *Shakespeare.*

Yet there is one more cursed than them all,
That canker-worm, that monster, jealousy,
Which eats the heart and feeds upon the gall,
Turning all love's delight to misery,
Through fear of losing his felicity.

Ah, gods! that ever ye that monster placed
In gentle love, that all his joys defaced!
Spenser.

The venom clamors of a jealous woman
Poison more deadly than a mad dog's
tooth. *Shakespeare.*

Jest.

A jest's prosperity lies in the ear
Of him that hears it, never in the tongue
Of him who makes it. *Shakespeare.*

Jests.

Laughter should dimple the cheek, not
furrow the brow. A jest should be such,
that all shall be able to join in the laugh
which it occasions; but if it bear hard
upon one of the company, like the crack of
a string, it makes a stop in the music.
Feltham.

Jollity.

Give me health and a day, and I will
make ridiculous the pomp of emperors.
Emerson.

Journalism.

A journalist is a grumbler, a censurer, a
giver of advice, a regent of sovereigns, a
tutor of nations. Four hostile newspapers
are more to be feared than a thousand bay-
onets. *Napoleon I.*

Joy.

Joy descends gently upon us like the
evening dew, and does not patter down
like a hail-storm. *Richter.*

We show our present joking, giggling race,
True joy consists in gravity and grace.
Garrick.

How much better it is to weep at joy
than joy a weeping.
Shakespeare.

Joys.

Little joys refresh us constantly, like
house-bread, and never bring disgust; and
great ones, like sugar-bread, briefly, and
then bring it. *Richter.*

Judge.

He softens the hard rigor of the laws,
Blunts their keen edge, and grinds their
harpy claws. *Garth.*

Four things belong to a judge: to hear
courteously, to answer wisely, to consider
soberly, and to decide impartially.
Socrates.

Judging.

Forbear to judge, for we are sinners all.
Shakespeare.

'Tis better that a man's own works,
than that another man's words should
praise him. *L'Estrange.*

Every one complains of the badness of
his memory, but nobody of his judgment.
La Rochefoucauld.

You think it is a want of judgment that
he changes his opinion. Do you think it
a proof that your scales are bad because
they vibrate with every additional weight
that is added to either side? *Edgeworth.*

Justice.

Justice like lightning, ever should appear
To few men's ruin, but to all men's fear.
Swetnam.

1. Do you know me, Mr. Justice?
2. Justice is blind; he knows nobody.
Dryden.

Justice is lame as well as blind among
us. *Otway.*

Be just and fear not:
Let all the ends thou aim'st at be thy coun-
try's,
Thy God's, and truth's. *Shakespeare.*

Kick.

A kick, that scarce would move a horse
May kill a sound divine. *Cowper.*

Kin.

One touch of nature makes the whole
world kin. *Shakespeare.*

Kindness.

That best portion of a good man's life
His little nameless, unremembered acts of
kindness and of love. *Wordsworth.*

The drying up a single tear has more
Of honest fame, than shedding seas of
gore. *Byron.*

King.

A crown
Golden in show, is but a wreath of thorns;
Brings danger, troubles, cares, and sleep-
less nights
To him who wears a regal diadem.
Milton.

Then happy low, lie down!
Uneasy lies the head that wears a crown.
Shakespeare.

A king that would not feel his crown too
heavy for him, must wear it every day;
but if he think it too light, he knoweth not
of what metal it is made. *Bacon.*

Kiss.

Soft child of love—thou balmy bliss,
Inform me, O delicious kiss!

FAM
QUOTES

Why thou so suddenly art gone
Lost in the moment thou art won.
                                        Dr. Wolcot.

I came to feel how far above
All fancy, pride, and fickle maidenhood
All earthly pleasure, all imagined good
Was the warm tremble of a devout kiss.
                                        Keats.

My lips pressed themselves involuntarily
to hers—a long, long kiss, burning intense
—concentrating emotion, heart, soul, all
the rays of life's light, into a single focus.
                                        Bulwer.

Sweet were his kisses on my balmy lips,
As are the breezes breath'd amidst the
    groves
Of ripening spices on the height of day.
                                        Behn.

**Kiss the tear from her lip, you'll find the
    rose
The sweeter for the dew.**   *Webster.*

Kissing.

Then kiss'd me hard;
As if he pluck'd up kisses by the roots,
That grew upon my lips.   *Shakespeare.*

A pleasing trembling thrills through all
    my blood
Whene'er you touch me with your melting
    hand;
But when you kiss, oh! 'tis not to be spoke.
                                        Gildon.

Knave.

What a pestilent knave is this same!
                                        Shakespeare.

A beetle-headed, flat-ear'd knave.
                                        Shakespeare.

A slippery and subtle knave; a finder out
of occasions; that has an eye can stamp
and counterfeit advantages, though true
advantage never presents itself; a devilish
knave.   *Shakespeare.*

Knowledge.

The first step to knowledge is to know
that we are ignorant.   *Cecil.*

Knowledge is power.   *Bacon.*

The desire of knowledge, like the thirst
of riches, increases ever with the acquisition of it.   *Sterne.*

The profoundly wise do not declaim
against superficial knowledge in others, as
much as the profoundly ignorant.   *Colton.*

He that sips of many arts, drinks of none.
                                        Fuller.

The shortest and surest way of arriving
at real knowledge is to unlearn the lessons
we have been taught, to remount first
principles, and to take nobody's word
about them.   *Bolingbroke.*

Knowledge of Self.

The most difficult thing in life is to
know yourself.   *Thales.*

Man know thyself! All wisdom centers there.   *Young.*

Labor.

It is only by labor that thought can be
made healthy, and only by thought that labor can be made happy; and the two cannot be separated with impunity.   *Ruskin.*

Where love is there is no labor; and if
there be labor, that labor is loved.
                                        Austin.

Numbering sands and drinking oceans
dry.   *Shakespeare.*

You may as well go about to turn the
sun to ice, by fanning in his face with a
peacock's feather.   *Shakespeare.*

Letting down buckets into empty wells,
And growing old with drawing nothing
    up.   *Cowper.*

Language.

Languages are the pedigrees of nations.
                                        Johnson.

Language is fossil poetry.   *Anon.*

When nature's end of language is declined,
And men talk only to conceal the mind.
                                        Young.

Speak the language of the company you
are in: speak it purely, and unlarded with
any other.   *Chesterfield.*

Lark.

Hark! how with lone and fluttering start
    The sky-lark soars above,
And with her full, melodious heart,
    She pours her strains of love.
                                        Mrs. Welby.

Laughter.

Madness, we fancy, gave an ill-timed birth
To grinning laughter and to frantic mirth.
                                        Prior.

Man is the only creature endowed with
the power of laughter; is he not the only
one that deserves to be laughted at?
                                        Greville.

How much lies in laughter; the cipher-
key wherewith we decipher the whole
man! some men wear an everlasting barren simper; in the smile of others lies
the cold glitter, as of ice; the fewest are
able to laugh what can be called laughing, but only sniff and titter and sniggle
from the throat outwards, or at least
produce some whiffling, husky cachinnation, as if they were laughing through

wool; of none such comes good. The man who cannot laugh is only fit for treasons, stratagems and spoils; but his own whole life is already a treason and a stratagem. *Carlyle.*

The most utterly lost of all days, is that in which you have not once laughed. *Chamfort.*

Law.

The good needs fear no law,
It is his safety, and the bad man's awe. *Massinger, Middleton and Rowley.*

The English laws punish vice; the Chinese laws do more, they reward virtue. *Goldsmith.*

To go to law, is for two persons to kindle a fire at their own cost, to warm others, and singe themselves to cinders; and because they cannot agree, to what is truth and equity, they will both agree to unplume themselves, that others may be decorated with their feathers. *Feltham.*

Laws.

When the state is most corrupt, then the laws are most multiplied. *Tacitus.*
Laws can discover sin, but not remove. *Milton.*

Lawyers and Physicians.

Commonly, physicians, like beer, are best when they are old, and lawyers, like bread, when they are young and new. *Fuller.*

Learning.

A little learning is a dangerous thing! *Pope.*
Learning maketh young men temperate, is the comfort of old age, standing for wealth with poverty, and serving as an ornament to riches. *Cicero.*

Lecture.

And every married man is certain
T' attend the lecture called the curtain. *Lloyd.*

Leisure.

I am never less at leisure than when at leisure, nor less alone than when I am alone. *Scipio Africanus.*

Lending.

If you lend a person any money, it becomes lost for any purposes of your own. When you ask for it back again, you find a friend made an enemy by your own kindness. If you begin to press still further—either you must part with that which you have intrusted, or else you must lose that friend. *Plautus.*

Letters.

Kind messages that pass from land to land,
Kind letters that betray the heart's deep history,
In which we feel the pressure of a hand
One touch of fire, and all the rest is mystery. *Longfellow.*
Letters which are warmly sealed are often but coldly opened. *Richter.*

Liars.

Past all shame—so past all truth. *Shakespeare.*

They begin with making falsehood appear like truth, and end with making truth itself appear like falsehood. *Shensione.*

Liberty.

Oh! liberty, thou goddess, heavenly bright,
Profuse of bliss, and pregnant with delight! *Addison.*

Liberty! Liberty! how many crimes are committed in thy name. *Madame Roland.*

Oh! give me liberty,
For were ev'n Paradise my prison,
Still I should long to leap the crystal walls. *Dryden.*
Liberty consists in the power of doing that which is permitted by law. *Cicero.*

Libraries.

Libraries are the shrines where all the relics of the ancient saints, full of true virtue, and that without delusion or imposture, are preserved and reposed. *Bacon.*

Lie.

Sin has many tools, but a lie is the handle which fits them all. *Holmes.*

He who tells a lie is not sensible how great a task he undertakes; for he must be forced to invent twenty more to maintain that one. *Pope.*

Life.

Life is but a day at most. *Burns.*
O life! thou art a galling load
Along a rough, a weary road. *Burns.*
My life is but a wind
Which passeth by, and leaves no print behind. *Sandys.*
Life is as tedious as a twice told tale
Vexing the dull ear of a drowsy man. *Shakespeare.*

At twenty years of age the will reigns; at thirty, the wit; and at forty, the judgment. *Grattan.*

FAM QUOTES

Our care should not be so much to live long, as to live well. *Seneca.*

Life is real, life is earnest,
And the grave is not its goal;
Dust thou art, to dust returnest,
Was not spoken of the soul.
Longfellow.

Like some fair hum'rists, life is most enjoy'd
When courted least; most worth, when disesteemed. *Young.*

Life's but a walking shadow—a poor player,
That struts and frets his hour upon the stage,
And then is heard no more. It is a tale
Told by idiot, full of sound and fury
Signifying nothing. *Shakespeare.*

Nor love thy life, nor hate; but whilst thou liv'st
Live well: how long, how short, permit to Heaven. *Milton.*

That life is long which answers life's great end. *Young.*

Live while you live the epicure would say
And seize the pleasures of the present day:
Live while you live the sacred preacher cries,
And give to God each moment as it flies.
Lord in my views let both united be:
I live in pleasure when I live in thee.
Philip Doddridge.

To live long, it is necessary to live slowly. *Cicero.*

Our life so fast away doth slide
As doth an hungry eagle through the wind;
Or as a ship transported with the tide,
Which in their passage leave no print behind. *Sir J. Davies.*

The youngest in the morning are not sure
That till the night their life they can secure. *Sir J. Denham.*

The vanity of human life is like a river, constantly passing away, and yet constantly coming on. *Pope*

Light.

The first creation of God in the works of the days was the light of the sense, the last was the light of the reason; and his Sabbath work ever since is the illumination of the spirit. *Bacon.*

Ethereal, first of things, quintessence, pure. *Milton.*

Is not light grander than fire? It is the same element in a state of purity. *Carlyle.*

And storied windows richly dight,
Casting a dim religious light. *Milton.*

Light-footedness.

Pray you tread softly, that the blind mole may not
Hear a footfall. *Shakespeare.*

Light-heartedness.

They pass best over the world who trip over it quickly; for it is but a bog—if we stop we sink. *Queen Elizabeth.*

A light heart lives long. *Shakespeare.*

Lion.

A lion among ladies is a most fearful thing; for there is not a more fearful wild-fowl than your lion living. *Shakespeare.*

Lips.

Her lips are roses over-washed with dew. *Greene.*

Listening.

Were we as eloquent as angels, yet should we please some men and some women much more by listening than by talking. *Colton.*

Literature.

Literature is the grindstone, to sharpen the coulters, and to whet their natural faculties. *Hammond.*

Living.

The man who will live above his present circumstances is in great danger of living in a little time much beneath them. *Addison.*

From the time we first begin to know,
We live and learn, but not the wiser grow. *Pomfret.*

He that spends all his life in sport is like one who wears nothing but fringes and eats nothing but sauces. *Fuller.*

Logic.

It was a saying of the ancients, "Truth lies in a well;" and to carry on this metaphor, we may justly say that logic does supply us with steps, whereby we may go down to reach the water. *Dr. I. Watts.*

Logician.

He was in logic a great critic,

Profoundly skilled in analytic;
He could distinguish and divide
A hair 'twixt south and southwest side;
On either which he would dispute,
Confute, change hands, and still confute.
                    Butler.

Loquacity.

Learn to hold thy tongue. Five words
cost Zacharias forty weeks' silence.
                    Fuller.

Gratiano speaks an infinite deal of nothing, more than any man in Venice; but
his reasons are as two grains of wheat
hid in two bushels of chaff; you seek all
day ere you find them; and when you
have them, they are not worth the search.
                    Shakespeare.

Love.

Love is the salt of life; a higher taste
It gives to pleasure, and then makes it
  last.   *Buckingham.*

The sweetest joy, the wildest woe is love;
The taint of earth, the odor of the skies
                    is in it.   *Bailey.*

Love is not altogether a delirium, yet it
has many points in common therewith.
I call it rather a discerning of the infinite
in the finite—of the ideal made real.
                    Carlyle.

It is better to have loved and lost,
Than never to have loved at all.
                    Tennyson

Love is life's end! an end, but never ending;
All joys, all sweets, all happiness, awarding;
Love is life's wealth, (ne'er spent, but
  ever spending,)
More rich by giving, taking by discarding;
Love's life's reward, rewarding in rewarding;
Then from thy wretched heart fond care
  remove;
Ah! shouldst thou live but once love's
  sweets to prove,
Thou wilt not love to live, unless thou
  live to love.   *Spenser.*

Let none think to fly the danger
For soon or late love is his own avenger.
                    Byron.

Love that has nothing but beauty to
keep it in good health is short lived, and
apt to have ague fits.   *Erasmus.*

But love is blind, and lovers cannot see
The pretty follies that themselves commit.
                    Shakespeare.

Love's a capricious power; I've known it
  hold
  Out through a fever caused by its own
    heat;
But be much puzzled by a cough or cold.
  And find a quinsy very hard to treat.
                    Byron.

Love not! love not! the thing you love
  may change,
  The rosy lip may cease to smile on you,
The kindly beaming eye grow cold and
    strange,
  The heart still warmly beat, and not for
    you.   *Mrs. Norton.*

The more we love the nearer we are to
hate.   *La Rochefoucauld.*

I know a passion still more deeply charming
That fever'd youth e'er felt; and that is
  love,
By long experience mellow'd into friend
  ship.   *Thomson*

                    She never told her love,
But let concealment, like a worm in the
  bud
Feed on her damask cheek; she pined in
    thought;
And, with a green and yellow melancholy
She sat like patience on a monument,
Smiling at grief.   *Shakespeare.*

Love me little, love me long.   *Marlowe.*
                    Love will find its way
Through paths where wolves would fear
  to prey,
And if it dares enough 'twere hard
If passion met not some reward.   *Byron.*

For the memory of love is sweet,
  Though the love itself were vain
And what I have lost of pleasure,
  Assuage what I find of pain.   *Lyster.*

                    Love is a god
Strong, free, unabounded, and as some de-
  fine
Fears nothing, pitieth none.   *Milton.*

  O! love is like the rose,
  And a month it may not see,
  Ere it withers where it grows.
                    Bailey.

For oh! so wildly do I love him
That paradise itself were dim
And joyless, if not shared with him.
                    Moore.

Love is not in our choice, but in our
fate.   *Dryden.*
Who loves, raves—'tis youth's phrenzy;
  but the cure
Is bitterer still.
                    Byron.

Love is a passion
Which kindles honor into noble acts.
Dryden.

Nuptial love maketh mankind, friendly love perfecteth it; but wanton love corrupteth and embaseth it. *Bacon.*

It warms me, it charms me,
 To mention but her name;
It heats me, it beats me,
 And set me a' on flame. *Burns.*

All the passions make us commit faults; love makes us commit the most ridiculous ones. *La Rochefoucauld*

Men have died from time to time, and worms have eaten them, but not for love.
Shakespeare.

To write a good love-letter you ought to begin without knowing what you mean to say, and to finish without knowing what you have written. *Rousseau.*

Love's like the measles—all the worse when it comes late in life. *Jerrola.*

Love is merely madness; and I tell you, deserves as well a dark house and a whip, as madmen do; and the reason why they are not so punished and cured, is that the lunacy is so ordinary, that the whippers are in love too. *Shakespeare.*

If you cannot inspire a woman with love of you, fill her above the brim with love of herself;—all that runs over will be yours. *Colton.*

A mother's love!
If there be one thing pure,
Where all beside is sullied,
That can endure,
When all else passes away;
If there be aught
Surpassing human deed or word, or
  thought,
  It is a mother's love.
  Marchioness de Spadara.

What *is* a mother's love?
A noble, pure, and tender flame
Enkindled from above.
  James Montgomery.

Love moderately; long love doth so;
Too swift arrives as tardy as too slow.
  Shakespeare.

When love's well-timed, 'tis not a fault to
 love;
The strong, the brave, the virtuous, and
 the wise,
Sink in the soft captivity together.
  Addison.

Love did his reason blind,
And love's the noblest frailty of the mind.
  Dryden.

Love is a pearl of purest hue,
 But stormy waves are round it;
And dearly may a woman rue,
 The hour that first she found it.
  L. E. Landon.

When poverty comes in at the door, love flies out at the window.

No cord or cable can draw so forcible, or bind so fast, as love can do with only a single thread. *Burton.*

Man while he loves, is never quite depraved,
And woman's triumph is a lover saved.
  Lamb.

Is there no way to bring home a wandering sheep, but by worrying him to death? *Fuller.*

To love and to be wise is scarcely granted to the highest. *Laberius.*

Love, the sole disease thou canst not cure. *Pope.*

Who ever loved that loved not at first sight? *Marlowe.*

Love is strong as death. Many waters cannot quench love, neither can the floods drown it; if a man would give all the substance of his house for love, it would utterly be contemned.
  Solomon's Song viii, 6. 7.

To her love was like the air of heaven. —invisible, intangible; it yet encircled her soul, and she knew it; for in it was her life. *Miss M'Intosh.*

All thoughts, all passions, all delights,
Whatever stirs this mortal frame,
All are but ministers of love,
And feed his sacred frame. *Coleridge*

The first symptom of love in a young man is timidity, in a girl it is boldness. The two sexes have a tendency to approach, and each assumes the qualities of the other. *Victor Hugo.*

That you may be loved be amiable.
  Ovid.

All love at first, like gen'rous wine,
Ferments and frets until 'tis fine,
But when 'tis settled on the lee,
And from the impurer matter free,
Becomes the richer still the older,
And proves the pleasanter the colder.
  Butler.

The proverb holds, that to be wise and
 love,
Is hardly granted to the gods above.
  Dryden.

Alas! the love of women! it is known
To be a lovely and a fearful thing;
For all of theirs upon that die is thrown,
And if 'tis lost, life has no more to bring
To them but mockeries of the past alone.

Byron.

The wound's invisible
That love's keen arrows make.

Shakespeare.

Love and Friendship.

Friendship often ends in love; but love
in friendship never.   *Colton.*

Lover.

If I freely may discover
What should please me in my lover,
I would have her fair and witty,
Savouring more of court than city;
A little proud, but full of pity;
Light and humorous in her toying,
Oft building hopes, and soon destroying,
Long, but sweet in the enjoying;
Neither too easy nor too hard;
All extremes I would have bar'd.

Ben. Jonson.

A lover's like a hunter—if the game be
got with too much ease he cares not for't.

Mead.

In lover's quarrels, the party that loves
most is always most willing to acknowledge the greater fault.   *Scott.*

Doubt thou the stars are fire!
Doubt that the sun doth move;
Doubt truth to be a liar;
But never doubt I love.

Shakespeare.

A reserved lover, it is said, always
makes a suspicious husband.   *Goldsmith.*

Yet, if thou swear'st,
Thou may'st prove false; at lover's vows,
They say, Jove laughs.   *Shakespeare.*

O, men's vows are women's traitors.

Shakespeare.

Lust.

Capricious, wanton, bold, and brutal lust
Is meanly selfish; when resisted, cruel:
And, like the blast of pestilential winds,
Taints the sweet bloom of nature's fairest
     forms.   *Milton.*

Luxury.

War destroys men, but luxury mankind
At once corrupts the body and the mind.

Crown.

Lying.

And he that does one fault at first,
And lies to hide it, makes it two.

Isaac Watts.

He who has not a good memory, should
never take upon him the trade of lying.

Montaigne.

Madness.

How pregnant, sometimes, his replies are!
A happiness that often madness hits on,
Which sanity and reason could not be
So prosp'rously deliver'd of.

Shakespeare.

I am not mad; I would to heaven I
    were!
For then, 'tis like I should forget my-
    self;
O, if I could, what grief should I forget!

Shakespeare.

There is a pleasure in being mad,
Which none but madmen know.

Dryden.

Great wits are sure to madness near al-
    lied,
And thin partitions do their bounds di-
    vide.

Dryden.

Maiden.

Maidens, like moths, are ever caught by
    glare,
And mammon wins his way where seraphs
    might despair.   *Byron.*

A child no more! a maiden now—
A graceful maiden, with a gentle brow;
A cheek tinged lightly and a dove-like
    eye;
And all hearts bless her as she passes by.

Mary Howitt.

Main Chance.

As the ancients say wisely
Have a care o' th' main chance;
And look before you ere you leap;
For as you sow, y' are like to reap.

Butler.

Man.

God made him, and therefore let him
pass for a man.   *Shakespeare.*

Like a man made after supper of a
cheese-paring; when he was naked, he
was, for all the world, like a forked radish, with a head fantastically carved upon
it with a knife.   *Shakespeare.*

Know thou this:—that men
Are as the time is.   *Shakespeare.*

What a piece of work is man! How
noble in reason; how infinite in faculties;
in form and moving, how express and
admirable! In action, how like an angel;
in apprehension, how like a god; the
beauty of the world—the paragon of ani-

mals! And yet to me what is this quintessence of dust?   *Shakespeare.*

Every man is a volume, if you know
how to read him.   *Channing.*

Men are but children of a larger
growth.   *Dryden.*

He is the whole encyclopedia of facts.
The creation of a thousands forests is in
one acorn; and Egypt, Greece, Rome,
Gaul, Britain, America, lie folded already
in the first man.   *Emerson.*

Men are machines, with all their boasted
     freedom,
Their movements turn upon some favor-
     ite passion;
Let art but find the foible. out,
We touch the spring and wind them at
     our pleasure.   *Brooke.*

The way to conquer men is by their pas-
     sions;
Catch but the ruling foibles of their
     hearts,
And all their boasted virtues shrink be-
     fore you.   *Tolson.*

A man he seems of cheerful yesterdays
and confident to-morrows.
     Wordsworth.

Men are born with *two* eyes, but with
one tongue, in order that they should see
twice as much as they say.   *Colton.*

The mind of man is vastly like a hive;
His thoughts are busy ever—all alive;
     But here the simile will go no further;
For bees are making honey, one and all;
Man's thoughts are busy in producing
     gall,
     Committing, as it were, self-murther.
     Dr. Wolcot.

O man! while in thy early years,
     How prodigal of times,
Misspending all thy precious hours,
     Thy glorious youthful prime!
Alternate follies take the sway;
     Licentious passions burn;
Which tenfold force give nature's law,
     That man was made to mourn.
     Burns.

Beware the fury of a patient man.
     Dryden.

Know then thyself; presume not God to
     scan;
The proper study of mankind is man.
     Pope.

Manners.

Of manners gentle, of affections mild;
In wit a man, simplicity a child. *Pope.*

Evil habits soil a fine dress more than
mud; good manners, by their deeds, easily
set off a lowly garb.   *Plautus.*

Nothing so much prevents our being
natural as the desire of appearing so.
     La Rochefoucauld.

Those that are good manners at the
court are as ridiculous in the country, as
the behavior of the country is most mock-
able at the court.   *Shakespeare.*

Marriage.

Hail, wedded love, mysterious law, true
     source
Of human offspring, sole propriety
In paradise of all things common else!
     Milton.

The best time for marriage will be towards thirty, for as the younger times are
unfit, either to choose or to govern a wife
and family, so, if thou stay long, thou
shalt hardly see the education of thy
children, who, being left to strangers, are
in effect lost; and better were it to be
unborn than ill-bred; for thereby thy posterity shall either perish or remain a
shame to thy name.   *Sir Walter Raleigh.*

Domestic happiness, thou only bliss
Of paradise that has survived the fall.
     Cowper.

Marriage is a feast where the grace is
sometimes better than the feast.   *Colton.*

The moment a woman marries, some
terrible revolution happens in her system;
all her good qualities vanish, presto, like
eggs out of a conjuror's box. 'Tis true
that they appear on the other side of the
box, but for the husband they are gone
forever.   *Bulwer.*

First get an absolute conquest over thyself, and then thou wilt easily govern thy
wife.   *Fuller.*

Masters and Servants.

If thou art a master, be sometimes
blind; if a servant, sometimes deaf.
     Fuller.

Maxims.

Maxims are the condensed good sense
of nations.   *Sir J. Mackintosh.*

Medicines.

Joy, temperance, and repose,
Slam the door on the doctor's nose.
     Longfellow.

Mediocrity.

Persevering mediocrity is much more
respectable, and unspeakably more use-

ful than talented inconstancy.
Dr. James Hamilton.

Meditation.

Though reading and conversation may furnish us with many ideas of men and things, yet it is our own meditation must form our judgment. *Dr. I. Watts.*

Melancholy.

Melancholy is the nurse of frenzy.
Shakespeare.

Go, you may call it madness, folly,—
  You shall not chase my gloom away;
There's such a charm in melancholy,
  I would not, if I could, be gay!
Rogers.

    Melancholy
Sits on me, as a cloud along the sky,
Which will not let the sunbeams through, nor yet
Descend in rain, and end, but spreads itself
Twixt heaven and earth, like envy between man
And man—an everlasting mist. *Byron.*

Memory.

Lull'd in the countless chambers of the brain,
Our thoughts are link'd by many a hidden chain;
Awake but one, and lo, what myriads rise!
Each stamps its image as the other flies.
Pope.

Tears, idle tears, I know not what they mean,
Tears from the depth of some divine despair,
Rise in the heart and gather in the eyes,
In looking on the happy autumn fields
And thinking of the days that are no more. *Tennyson.*

A strong memory is generally coupled with an infirm judgment. *Montaigne.*

Men.

Men are the sport of circumstances, when the circumstances seem the sport of men. *Byron.*

There are but three classes of men: *the retrograde, the stationary* and *the progressive.* *Lavater.*

It is far easier to know men than to know man. *La Rochefoucauld.*

Never have anything to do with an unlucky place, or an unlucky man. I have seen many clever men, very clever men, who had not shoes to their feet. I never act with them. Their advice sounds very well, but they cannot get on themselves; and if they cannot do good to themselves, how can they do good to me?
Rothschild.

Men, Great.

Lives of great men all remind us,
  We can make our lives sublime,
And departing, leave behind us
  Footprints in the sands of time.

Footprints, that perhaps another,
  Sailing o'er life's solemn main,
A forlorn and shipwreck'd brother,
  Seeing, shall take heart again.
Longfellow.

Mercy.

The quality of mercy is not strain'd:
It droppeth, as the gentle rain from heaven
Upon the place beneath; it is twice bless'd,
It blesseth him that gives, and him that takes:
'Tis mightiest in the mightiest: it becomes
The throned monarch better than his crown:
His sceptre shows the force of temporal power,
The attribute to awe and majesty,
Wherein doth sit the dread and fear of kings;
But mercy is above this scepter'd sway,
It is an attribute to God himself;
And earthly power doth then show likest God's,
When mercy seasons justice.
          Consider this,—
That, in the course of justice, none of us
Should see salvation: we do pray for mercy;
And that same prayer doth teach us all to render
The deeds of mercy. *Shakespeare.*

Merit.

Modesty is to merit as shades to figures in a picture: giving it strength and beauty. *La Bruyere.*

Good actions crown themselves with lasting bays
Who deserves well, needs not another's praise. *Heath.*

Metaphysics.

He knew what's what, and that's as high
As metaphysics wit can fly. *Meta.*

Midnight.

Midnight.—strange mystic hour,—when

the veil between the frail present and the eternal future grows thin. *Mrs. Stowe.*

Mind.

My mind to me an empire is.
Southwell.

In my mind's eye, Horatio.
Shakespeare.

A mind content both crown and kingdom is. *Greene.*

Cultivation to the mind is as necessary as food to the body. *Cicero.*

Canst thou not minister to a mind diseased;
Pluck from the memory a rooted sorrow;
Raze out the written troubles of the brain;
And, with some sweet oblivious antidote,
Cleanse the foul bosom of that perilous stuff
Which weighs upon the heart?
Shakespeare.

'Tis the mind that makes the body rich.
Shakespeare.

It is the mind that maketh good or ill,
That maketh wretch or happy, rich or poor. *Spenser.*

A narrow mind begets obstinacy, and we do not easily believe what we cannot see. *Dryden.*

The mind ought sometimes to be diverted, that it may return the better to thinking. *Phoedrus.*

A weak mind is like a microscope, which magnifies trifling things, but cannot receive great ones. *Chesterfield.*

Ah! noblest minds
Sink soonest into ruin; like a tree,
That with the weight of its own golden fruitage
Is bent down to the dust. *H. Neele.*

Minister.

Of right and wrong he taught
Truths as refined as ever Athens heard;
And (strange to tell!) he practised what he preach'd. *Armstrong.*

The life of a pious minister is visible rhetoric. *Hooker.*

It would be well, if some who have taken upon themselves the ministry of the Gospel, that they would first preach to themselves, then afterwards to others.
Cardinal Pole.

Mirth.

O spirits gay, and kindly heart!
Precious the blessings ye impart!
Joanna Baillie.

From the crown of his head to the sole of his foot he is all mirth; he has twice or thrice cut Cupid's bowstring, and the little hangman dare not shoot at him: he hath a heart as sound as a bell, and his tongue is the clapper; for what his heart thinks his tongue speaks.
Shakespeare.

Jest and youthful jollity,
Quips, and cranks, and wanton wiles,
Nods and becks, and wreathed smiles.
Milton.

Care to our coffin adds a nail, no doubt;
And ev'ry grin so merry, draws one out.
Dr. Wolcot.

Misanthrope.

I am *misanthropos*, and hate mankind.
For thy part, I do wish thou wert a dog,
That I might love thee something.
Shakespeare.

As prone to mischief, as able to perform it. *Shakespeare.*

Miser.

Some o'er-enamour'd of their bags, run mad;
Groan under gold, yet weep for want of bread. *Young.*

I can compare our rich misers to nothing so fitly as to a whale; that plays and tumbles, driving the poor fry before him, and at last devours them all at a mouthful. *Shakespeare.*

Misery.

This iron world
Brings down the stoutest hearts to lowest state:
For misery doth bravest minds abate.
Spenser.

Misfortune.

Misfortune, like a creditor severe,
But rises in demand for her delay;
She makes a scourge of past prosperity
To sting thee more and double thy distress. *Young.*

Mistrust.

I hold it cowardice,
To rest mistrustful, where a noble heart
Hath pawn'd an open hand in sign of love.
Shakespeare.

It is more disgraceful to distrust than to be deceived by our friends.
La Rochefoucauld.

The world is an old woman, that mistakes any gilt farthing for a gold coin;

whereby being often cheated, she will henceforth trust nothing but the common copper. *Carlyle.*

Modesty.

The crimson glow of modesty o'erspread
Her cheek, and gave new lustre to her
   charms. *Dr. Thomas Franklin.*

The violet droops its soft and bashful
   brow,
   But from its heart sweet incense fills
      the air;—
So rich within—so pure without—art
   thou,
   With modest mien and soul of virtue
      rare. *Mrs. Osgood.*

They oft-times take more pains
Who look for pins, than those who find
   out stars. *John Fountain.*

Moments.

Think nought a trifle, though it small appear;
Small sands the mountain, moments make
   the year,
And trifles life. *Young.*

Money.

If you make money your god, it will
plague you like the devil. *Fielding.*
   Mammon has enriched his thousands,
and has damned his ten thousands.
   South.

The love of money is the root of all
evil; which while some coveted after they
have erred from the faith, and pierced
themselves through with many sorrows.
   I Tim. vi, 10.

For they say, if money go before, all
ways do lie open. *Shakespeare.*

Money is a good servant, but a dangerous master. *Bonhours.*

Put not your trust in money, but put
your money in trust. *Holmes.*

He that wants money, means and content, is without three good friends.
   Shakespeare.

Moon.

The cold chaste Moon, the Queen of
   Heaven's bright isles,
Who makes all beautiful on which she
   smiles!
That wandering shrine of soft, yet icy
   flame,
Which ever is transform'd yet still the
   same,
And warms, but not illumines. *Shelley.*
      The queen of night
Shines fair with all her virgin stars about
   her. *Otway.*

Now through the passing clouds she seems
   to stoop,

Now up the pure cerulean rides sublime.
Wide the pale deluge floats, and streaming mild
O'er the sky'd mountain to the shadowy
   vale,
While rocks and floods reflect the quivering gleam,
The whole air whitens with a boundless
   tide
Of silver radiance, trembling round the
   world. *Thomson.*

Moral Law.

The moral law is written on the tablets
of eternity. For every false word or unrighteous deed, for cruelty and oppression, for lust or vanity, the price has to
be paid at last. *J. A. Froude.*

Morning.

But, look, the morn in russet mantle clad
Walks o'er the dew of yon high eastern
   hill. *Shakespeare.*

Now from night's womb the glorious day
   breaks forth,
And seems to kindle from the setting
   stars. *Lee.*

Morn, in the white wake of the morning
   star,
Came furrowing all the orient into gold.
   Tennyson.

Now morn her rosy steps in th' eastern
   clime
Advancing, sow'd the earth with orient
   pearl. *Milton.*

Mother.

She was my friend—I had but her—no
   more,
No other upon earth—and as for heaven,
I am as they that seek a sign, to whom
No sign is given. My mother! Oh, my
   mother! *Taylor.*

   A mother is a mother still,
   The holiest thing alive. *Coleridge.*

Mourning.

None acted mourning forced to show,
Or squeeze his eyes to make the torrent
   flow. *Dryden.*

Excess of grief for the deceased is madness; for it is an injury to the living, and
the dead know it not. *Xenophon.*

Murmuring.

Murmur at nothing: if our ills are reparable, it is ungrateful; if remediless, it
is vain. *Shakespeare.*

FAM QUOTES

Music.

The man that hath no music in himself,
Nor is not moved with concord of sweet
    sounds,
Is fit for treasons, stratagems and spoils;
The motions of his spirit are dull as
    night,
And his affections dark as Erebus;
Let no such man be trusted.
                     Shakespeare.

Music hath charms to soothe a savage
    breast,
To soften rocks, or bend a knotted oak.
I've read that things inanimate have
    moved,
And as with living souls have been in-
    form'd
By magic numbers and persuasive sound.
                     Congreve.

There's music in the sighing of a reed;
There's music in the gushing of a rill;
There's music in all things, if men had
    ears
Their earth is but an echo of the spheres.
                     Byron.

Name.

He left a name, at which the world grew
    pale.
To point a moral, or adorn a tale.
                     Johnson.

Nature.

The sea is like a silvery lake,
    And o'er its calm the vessel glides
Gently as if it fear'd to wake
    The slumbers of the silent tides.
                     Moore.

Man's rich with little, were his judgment
    true;
Nature is frugal, and her wants are few;
These few wants, answer'd bring sincere
    delights;
But fools create themselves new appetites.
                     Young.

All things are artificial, for
    Nature is the art of God.
                Sir Thos. Browne.

Surely there is something in the unruffled calm of nature that overawes our little anxieties and doubts: the sight of the
deep-blue sky, and the clustering stars
above, seems to impart a quiet to the
mind.
                     Edwards.

To him who in the love of nature holds
Communion with her visible forms, she
    speaks
A various language.
                     Bryant.

Nature the vicar of the Almighty Lord.
                     Chaucer.

One impulse from a vernal wood
    May teach you more of man,
Of moral evil and of good,
    Than all the sages can.
                     Wordsworth.

Nature and Art.

Nature is mighty. Art is mighty. Artifice is weak. For nature is the work of a
mightier power than man. Art is the
work of man under the guidance and inspiration of a mightier power. Artifice is
the work of mere man in the imbecility of
his mimic understanding.   *Anon.*

Nature is the chart of God, mapping
out all His attributes: art is the shadow
of His wisdom, and copieth His resources.
                     Tupper.

Necessity.

The tyrant's plea.   *Milton.*

When fear admits no hope of safety,
Necessity makes dastards valiant men.
                     Herrick.

Necessity is the mother of invention.

Neck.

A lover forsaken
    A new love may get;
But a neck that's once broken
    Can never be set.   *Walsh.*

Negligence.

A little fire is quickly trodden out;
Which being suffer'd, rivers cannot
    quench.   *Shakespeare.*

Omittance is no quittance.
                     Shakespeare.

Negotiation.

It is better to sound a person with
whom one deals afar off, than to fall upon
the point at first.   *Bacon.*

Nervousness.

He experienced that nervous agitation
to which brave men as well as cowards
are subject; with this difference, that the
one sinks under it, like the vine under the
hailstorm, and the other collects his energies to shake it off, as the cedar of Lebanon is said to elevate its boughs to disperse the snow which accumulates upon
them.   *Sir Walter Scott.*

New.

Nothing is new; we walk where others
    went;
There's no vice now but has its precedent.
                     Herrick.

News.

For evil news rides post, while good news baits.   *Milton.*

Newspapers.

An abstract and brief chronicle of the times.

Every editor of newspapers pays tribute to the Devil.   *La Fontaine.*

Nickname.

A nickname is the heaviest stone the devil can throw at a man.   *Anon.*

A good name will wear out; a bad one may be turned; a nickname lasts forever.   *Zimmerman.*

Night.

Night whose sable hand
Hangs on the purple skirts of flying day.   *Dyer.*

Why does the evening, does the night, put warmer love in our hearts? Is it the nightly pressure of helplessness? or is it the exalting separation from the turmoils of life, that veiling of the world in which for the soul nothing there remains but souls? Is it therefore that the letters in which the loved name stands written in our spirit appears like phosphorous writing by night, *in fire*, while by day, in their cloudy traces, they but smoke?   *Richter.*

How like a widow in her weeds, the night,
Amid her glimmering tapers, silent sits!
How sorrowful, how desolate, she weeps
Perpetual dews, and saddens nature's scene.   *Young.*

In her starry shade
Of dim and solitary loveliness,
I learn the language of another world.   *Byron.*

Nobility.

Better not be at all,
Than not be noble.   *Tennyson.*

Would'st thou clearly learn what true nobility is? inquire of noble-minded women.   *German Saying*

He is noble only who in word, thought and deed, proves himself a man.   *Anon.*

Nonsense.

A little nonsense now and then,
Is relish'd by the best of men.   *Anon.*

Nonsense and noise will oft prevail,
When honor and affection fail.   *Lloyd.*

Novels.

Writers of novels and romances in general bring a double loss on their readers, they rob them both of their time and money; representing men, manners, and things, that never have been, nor are likely to be; either confounding or perverting history or truth, inflating the mind, or committing violence upon the understanding.   *Lady Montague.*

Novelty.

Of all the passions that possess mankind,
The love of novelty rules most the mind;
In search of this, from realm to realm we roam;
Our fleets come fraught with ev'ry folly home.   *Foote.*

Now.

Now! it is gone.—Our brief hours travel post,
Each with its thought or deed, its why or how;
But know, each parting hour gives up a ghost
To dwell within thee—an eternal now!   *Coleridge.*

Oak.

The monarch oak, the patriarch of the trees,
Shoots rising up, and spreads by slow degrees:
Three centuries he grows, and three he stays
Supreme in state; and in three more decays.   *Dryden.*

Oaths.

An oath is a recognizance to heaven,
Binding us over in the courts above,
To plead to the indictment of our crimes,
That those who 'scape this world should suffer there.   *Southern.*

I'll take thy word for faith, not ask thine oath;
Who shuns not to break one, will sure crack both.   *Shakespeare.*

Obedience.

I hourly learn a doctrine of obedience.   *Shakespeare.*

Wicked men obey for fear, but the good for love.   *Aristotle.*

Let them obey that know not how to rule.   *Shakespeare.*

Obligation.

An extraordinary haste to discharge an obligation is a sort of ingratitude.   *La Rochefoucauld.*

Observation.

He alone is an acute observer who can observe minutely without being observed.   *Lavater.*

FAM
QUOTES

Obstinacy.

Narrowness of mind is often the cause of obstinacy: we do not easily believe beyond what we see. *La Rochefoucauld.*

An obstinate man does not hold opinions, but they hold him. *Pope.*

Stiff opinion, always in the wrong. *Dryden.*

Occasion.

Let me not let pass
Occasion, which now smiles. *Milton.*

Ocean.

Whosoever commands the sea commands the trade; whosoever commands the trade of the world commands the riches of the world, and, consequently, the world itself. *Sir Walter Raleigh.*

Offence.

Who fears t' offend takes the first step to please. *Cibber.*

Offences ought to be pardoned, for few offend willingly, but as they are compelled by some affection. *Hegesippus.*

At every trifle scorn to take offence,
That always shews great pride or little sense. *Pope.*

Omissions.

Omissions, no less than commissions, are often times branches of injustice. *Antoninus.*

Opiniators.

There are a sort of men, whose visages
Do cream and mantle, like a standing pond;
And do a wilful stillness entertain,
With purpose to be dress'd in an opinion
Of wisdom, gravity, profound conceit;
As who should say, *I am Sir Oracle,
And, when I ope my lips, let no dog bark?*
. . . I do know of these
That therefore only are reputed wise.
For saying nothing. *Shakespeare.*

Opinion.

Opinion, the blind goddess of fools, foe
To the virtuous, and only friend to
Undeserving persons. *Chapman.*

If a man would register all his opinions upon love, politics, religion, and learning, what a bundle of inconsistencies and contradictions would appear at last! *Swift.*

Opinion, that great fool, makes fools of all. *Field.*

There's nothing good or bad, but thinking makes it so. *Shakespeare.*

Opinion is that high and mighty dame
Which rules the world; and in the mind doth frame
Distaste or liking: for in human race,
She makes the fancy various as the face. *Howel.*

Opinions.

He that never changed any of his opinions never corrected any of his mistakes; and he who was never wise enough to find out any mistakes in himself will not be charitable enough to excuse what he reckons mistakes in others.

Opportunity.

There is a tide in the affairs of men,
Which, taken at the flood, leads on to fortune;
Omitted, all the voyage of their life
Is bound in shallows and in miseries:
On such a full sea are we now afloat,
And we must take the current when it serves,
Or lose our ventures. *Shakespeare.*

Opportunity has hair in front, behind she is bald; if you seize her by the forelock, you may hold her, but, it suffered to escape, not Jupiter himself can catch her again. *From the Latin.*

There sometimes wants only a stroke of fortune to discover numberless latent good or bad qualities, which would otherwise have been eternally concealed: as words written with a certain liquor appear only when applied to the fire. *Greville.*

Opposed.

Equally to God and truth opposed:
Opposed as darkness to the light of heaven. *Pollok.*

Orator.

What the orators want in depth, they give you in length. *Montesquieu.*

Fire in each eye, and papers in each hand,
They rave, recite, and madden round the land. *Pope.*

Order.

Order is the sanity of the mind, the health of the body, the peace of the city, the security of the state. As the beams to a house, as the bones to the microcosm of man, so is order to all things. *Southey.*

Order is heaven's first law; and this confest,
Some are, and must be, greater than the rest,
More rich, more wise; but who infers

from hence
That such are happier, shocks all common
sense.   *Pope.*

Originality.

The little mind who loves itself, will
write and think with the vulgar; but the
great mind will be bravely eccentric, and
scorn the beaten road, from universal benevolence.   *Goldsmith.*

Orphan.

An orphan's curse would drag to hell
A spirit from on high.   *Coleridge.*

Pain.

Long pains, with use of bearing, are
half eased.   *Dryden.*

Parasite.

Your friend, your pimp, your hanger-on,
      what not?
Your lacquey, but without the shoulder-
      knot.   *Horace.*

Pardon.

Pardon, I beseech Thee, the iniquity of
this people, according unto the greatness
of Thy mercy! And the Lord said I have
pardoned, according to thy word.
      Numbers xiv, 19.

Thou art a God ready to pardon, gracious and merciful, slow to anger, and of
great kindness.   *Nehemiah* ix, 17.

Parents.

A suspicious parent makes an artful
child.   *Haliburton.*

Parting.

Abruptness is an eloquence in parting,
when spinning out the time is but the
weaving of new sorrow.
      Sir John Suckling.
      To die and part
Is a less evil; but to part and live,
There—there's the torment.   *Lansdowne.*
Farewell; God knows, when we shall
      meet again,
I have a faint cold, fear thrills through
      my veins,
That almost freezes up the heat of life.
      Shakespeare.

My heart is heavy at the remembrance
of all the miles that lie between us; and
I can scarcely believe that you are so
distant from me. We are parted; and
every parting is a form of death, as every
re-union is a type of heaven.   *Edwards.*
Good night, good night! parting is such
      sweet sorrow
That I shall say—good night till it be
      morrow.   *Shakespeare.*

Passion.

How terrible is passion! how our reason
Falls down before it! whilst the tortur'd
      frame,
Like a ship dash'd by fierce encount'ring
      tides,
And of her pilot spoil'd, drives round and
      round,
The sport of wind and wave.   *Barford.*
The ruling passion, be it what it will,
The ruling passion conquers reason still.
      Pope.

Passions.

Passion often makes a madman of the
cleverest man, and renders the greatest
fools clever.
The passions are the only orators that
always persuade.
The passions often engender their con-
traries.   *La Rochefoucauld.*
Passions, like seas, will have their ebbs
and flows.   *Lee.*

The wither'd frame, the ruin'd mind,
The wreck by passion left behind:
A shrivell'd scroll, a scatter'd leaf,
Sear'd by the autumn-blast of grief.
      Byron.
Our passions are like convulsion fits,
which, though they make us stronger for
a time, leave us the weaker ever after.
      Pope.
The passions, like heavy bodies down
steep hills, once in motion, move them-
selves, and know no ground but the bot-
tom.   *Fuller.*
Oh! she has passions which outstrip the
      wind,
And tear her virtue up, as tempests root
      the sea.   *Congreve.*

Patience.

If the wicked flourish, and thou suffer,
be not discouraged. They are fatted for
destruction: thou art dieted for health.
      Fuller.
Patience is sorrow's salve.   *Churchill.*
There is a limit at which forbearance
ceases to be a virtue.   *Burke.*
He that would have a cake out of the
wheat must tarry the grinding.
      Shakespeare.

Patriot.

Who, firmly good in a corrupted state,
Against the rage of tyrants singly stood,
Invincible.   *Thomson.*
'Tis home-felt pleasure prompts the patri-
      ot's sigh

This makes him wish to live, and dare to
die. *Campbell.*

Peace.

Down the dark future, through long gen-
erations,
The echoing sounds grow fainter and then
cease;
And like a bell, with solemn, sweet vi-
brations,
I hear once more the voice of Christ say
"Peace!" *Longfellow.*

Peace hath her victories,
No less renown'd than war. *Milton.*

Peacemakers.

Blessed are the peacemakers, for they
shall be called the children of God.
St. Matthew v, 9.

Pedantry.

Brimful of learning, see that pedant
stride,
Bristling with horrid Greek, and puff'd
with pride!
A thousand authors he in vain has read,
And with their maxims stuff'd his empty
head;
And thinks that without Aristotle's rule,
Reason is blind, and common sense a
fool! *Boileau.*

Pedantry crams our heads with learned
lumber, and takes out our brains to make
room for it. *Colton.*

Pen.

Oh! nature's noblest gift—my grey goose
quill:
Slave of my thoughts, obedient to my
will,
Torn from thy parent bird to form a pen,
That mighty instrument of little men!
Byron.

Penetration.

The balls of sight are so formed, that
one man's eyes are spectacles to another,
to read his heart within. *Johnson.*

Penury.

Chill penury weighs down the heart, itself; and though it sometimes be endured
with calmness, it is but the calmness of
despair. *Mrs. Jameson.*

People.

The world may be divided into people
that read, people that write, people that
think, and fox hunters. *Shenstone.*

Perfection.

To arrive at perfection, a man should
have very sincere friends or inveterate
enemies; because he would be made sensible of his good or ill conduct, either by
the censures of the one, or the admoni-
tions of the other. *Diogenes.*

Perseverance.

Yet I argue not
Against heaven's hand or will, nor bate a
jot
Of heart or hope, but still bear up and
steer
Right onward. *Milton.*

When I take the humor of a thing
once, I am like your tailor's needle—I go
through. *Ben Jonson.*

By gnawing through a dyke even a rat
may drown a nation. *Edward Burke.*

Let us only suffer any person to tell us
his story morning and evening, but for
one twelve-month, and he will become our
master. *Burke.*

Perseverance and Obstinacy.

The difference between perseverance
and obstinancy is that one often comes
from a strong will, and the other from a
strong won't.

Perversity.

Some men put me in mind of half-bred
horses, which often grow worse in proportion as you feed and exercise them for improvement. *Greville.*

Philosophy.

Philosophy, when superficially studied,
excites doubt; when thoroughly explored,
it dispels it. *Bacon.*

A little philosophy inclineth man's
mind to atheism, but depth of philosophy
bringeth a man's mind about to religion.
Bacon.

Do not all charms fly,
At the mere touch of cold philosophy?
Keats.

Physicians.

If you need a physician, employ these
three—a cheerful mind, rest, and a temperate diet.

The patient can oftener do without the
doctor, than the doctor without the patient. *Zimmerman.*

Physiognomy.

As the language of the face is universal, so 'tis very comprehensive; no laconism can reach it: 'tis the short hand of

the mind, and crowds a great deal in a little room. *Jeremy Collier.*

Picture.

A picture is a poem without words. *Horace.*

Pity.

The truly brave are soft of heart and eyes,
And feel for what their duty bids them do. *Byron.*

No radiant pearl which crested fortune wears,
No gem that, twinkling, hangs from beauty's ears,
Not the bright stars which night's blue arch adorn,
Nor rising suns that gild the vernal morn,
Shine with such lustre as the tear that breaks
For other's woe, down virtue's manly cheeks. *Darwin.*

Villain, thou know'st no law of God or man:
No beast so fierce, but knows some touch of pity. *Shakespeare.*

Plagiarism.

It is one thing to purloin finely-tempered steel, and another to take a pound of literary old iron, and convert it in the furnace of one's mind into a hundred watchsprings, worth each a thousand times as much as the iron. When genius borrows, it borrows grandly, giving to the borrowed matter, a life and beauty it lacked before. *Anon.*

Pleasure.

The seeds of repentance are sown in youth by pleasure, but the harvest is reaped in age by pain. *Colton.*

Enjoy your present pleasures so as not to injure those that are to follow. *Seneca.*

Flowers are like the pleasures of the world. *Shakespeare.*

Pleasure soon exhausts us and itself also; but endeavor never does. *Richter.*

Pleasure, or wrong or rightly understood,
Our greatest evil, or our greatest good. *Pope.*

Pleasure that comes unlooked for is thrice welcome. *Rogers.*

Why, all delights are vain; but that most vain,
Which, with pain purchas'd, doth inherit pain. *Shakespeare.*

Pleasures.

Choose such pleasures as recreate much, and cost little. *Fuller.*

Put only the restriction on your pleasures—be cautious that they hurt no creature that has life. *Zimmerman.*

Venture not to the utmost bounds of even lawful pleasure; the limits of good and evil join. *Fuller.*

It is sad
To think how few our pleasures really are:
And for the which we risk eternal good. *Bailey.*

Poet.

Just writes to make his barrenness appear,
And strain from hard-bound brains, eight lines a year. *Pope.*

Poet! esteem thy noble part,
Still listen, still record,
Sacred historian of the heart,
And moral nature's lord. *Richard M. Milnes.*

Poetry.

Poetry is the eloquence of truth. *Campbell.*

Poetry has been to me "its own exceeding great reward;" it has soothed my afflictions; it has multiplied and refined my enjoyments; it has endeared solitude; and it has given me the habit of wishing to discover the good and the beautiful in all that meets and surrounds me. *Coleridge.*

Poets.

Poets are all who love—who feel great truths—
And tell them. *Bailey.*

Policy.

The devil knew not what he did, when he made man politic. *Shakespeare.*

Politeness.

As charity covers a multitude of sins before God, so does politeness before men. *Chesterfield.*

When two goats met on a bridge which was too narrow to allow either to pass or return, the goat which lay down that the other might walk over it, was a finer gentleman than Lord Chesterfield. *Cecil.*

Politician.

A politician, Proteus-like must alter
His face, and habit; and, like water, seem
Of the same color that the vessel is

That doth contain it; varying his form
With the chameleon at each object's
change. *Mason.*

Politics.

Who's in or out, who moves the grand
  machine,
Nor stirs my curiosity, or spleen;
Secrets of state no more I wish to know
Than secret movements of a puppet-show;
Let but the puppets move, I've my desire,
Unseen the hand which guides the master
  wire. *Churchill.*

Popularity.

He who can listen pleas'd to such applause,
Buys at a dearer rate than I dare purchase,
And pays for idle air with sense and virtue. *Mallett.*

Oh, popular applause, what heart of man
Is proof against thy sweet seducing
  charms?
The wisest and the best feel urgent need
Of all their caution in thy gentlest gales;
But swelled into a dust—who then, alas!
With all his canvas set, and inexpert,
And therefore heedless, can withstand thy
  power. *Cowper.*

Please not thyself the flattering crowd to
  hear;
'Tis fulsome stuff, to please thy itching
  ear.
Survey thy soul, not what thou dost appear,
But what thou art. *Persius.*

Possibilities.

To him nothing is impossible, who is always dreaming of his past possibilities.
Carlyle.

Poverty.

It is not poverty so much as pretence
that harasses a ruined man—the struggle
between a proud mind and an empty
purse—the keeping up a hollow show that
must soon come to an end. Have the
courage to appear poor, and you disarm
poverty of its sharpest sting.
Mrs. Jameson.

O blissful poverty!
Nature, too partial to thy lot, assigns
Health, freedom, innocence, and downy
  peace,
Her real goods; and only mocks the great
With empty pageantries. *Fenton.*

This mournful truth is everywhere con-
  fessed,
Slow rises worth by poverty depressed.
Johnson.

He is poor whose expenses exceed his income. *La Bruyere.*

To mortal men great loads allotted be;
But of all packs no pack like poverty.
Herrick.

Poverty makes people satirical,—soberly, sadly, bitterly satirical. *Friswell.*

Power.

Nothing, indeed, but the possession of
some power can with any certainty discover what at the bottom is the true character of any man. *Burke.*

Even in war, moral power is to physical
as three parts out of four. *Napoleon I.*

Praise.

Let another man praise thee, and not
thine own mouth; a stranger, and not
thine own lips. *Proverbs xxvii, 2.*

Allow no man to be so free with you
as to praise you to your face. Your vanity by this means will want its food. At
the same time your passion for esteem
will be more fully gratified; men will
praise you in their actions: where you
now receive one compliment, you will
then receive twenty civilities. *Steele.*

Praise was originally a pension, paid
by the world. *Swift.*

Those men who are commended by
everybody, must be very extraordinary
men; or, which is more probable, very
inconsiderable men. *Greville.*

It gives me pleasure to be praised by
you whom all men praise. *Tully.*

The more you speak of yourself, the
more you are likely to lie. *Zimmerman.*

There's not one wise man among twenty will praise himself. *Shakespeare.*

Prayer.

If any of you lack wisdom, let him ask
of God, that giveth to all men liberally
and upbraideth not; and it shall be given
him. But let him ask in faith, nothing
wavering. *James i, 5, 6.*

God is a spirit: and they that worship
Him, must worship Him in spirit and in
truth. *St. John iv, 24.*

Ye ask, and receive not, because ye ask
amiss. *James iv, 3.*

He that cometh to God, must believe
that He is, and that He is a rewarder of
them that diligently seek Him.
Heb. xi, 6.

Fountain of mercy! whose pervading eye
Can look within and read what passes
  there,

Accept my thoughts for thanks; I have no
words.
My soul o'erfraught with gratitude, rejects
The aid of language—Lord!—behold my
heart. *Hannah More.*

Prayer purifies; it is a self-preached
sermon. *Richter.*

Any heart turned Godward, feels more
joy
In one short hour of prayer, than e'er was
rais'd
By all the feasts on earth since their
foundation. *Bailey.*

More things are wrought by prayer
Than this world dreams of.
Tennyson.

In prayer it is better to have a heart
without words, than words without a
heart. *Bunyan.*

Is not prayer a study of truth—a sally
of the soul into the unfound infinite? No
man ever prayed heartily without learning
something; but when a faithful thinker
resolute to detach every object from personal relations, and see it in the light of
thought, shall, at the same time, kindle
science with the fire of the holiest affections, then will God go forth anew into
the creation. *Emerson.*

Let prayer be the key of the morning
and the bolt of the evening.
Matthew Henry.

Prejudice.

To divest one's self of some prejudices,
would be like taking off the skin to feel
the better. *Greville.*

Press.

"The Press!" all lands shall sing;
The press, the press we bring
All lands to bless.
O pallid Want! O Labor stark!
Behold, we bring the second ark!
The press! the press! the press!
Ebenezer Elliott.

Presumption.

Fools rush in where angels fear to
tread. *Pope.*

Pretension.

Where there is much pretension, much
has been borrowed; nature never pretends. *Lavater.*

It is no disgrace not to be able to do
everything; but to undertake, or pretend
to do, what you are not made for, is not
only shameful, but extremely troublesome
and vexatious. *Plutarch.*

Pride.

The lofty pine is oftenest agitated by
the winds—high towers rush to the earth
with a heavier fall—and the lightning
most frequently strikes the highest mountains. *Horace.*

What is pride? a whizzing rocket
That would emulate a star.
Wordsworth.

Pride that dines on vanity, sups on
contempt. *B. Franklin.*

He whose pride oppresses the humble
may, perhaps, be humbled, but will never
be humble. *Lavater.*

Defeated, but not dismayed,—crushed
to the earth, but not humiliated,—he
seemed to grow more haughty beneath
disaster, and to experience a fierce satisfaction in draining the last dregs of bitterness. *Washington Irving.*

When pride begins, love ceases.
Lavater.

The vile are only vain; the great are
proud. *Byron.*

Principles.

Let us cling to our principles as the
mariner clings to his last plank when
night and tempest close around him.
And oftener changed their principles
than their shirts. *Dr. Young.*

Prison.

A felon's cell—
The fittest earthly type of hell!
Whittier.

Emblem of hell, nursery of vice.
Tom Brown.

Procrastination.

Procrastination is the thief of time.
Dr. Young.

Defer not till to-morrow to be wise,
To-morrow's sun to thee may never rise.
Congreve.

Progress.

Living movement. *Carlyle.*
The goal of yesterday will be the starting point of to-morrow. *Carlyle.*

Promises.

He who is most slow in making a promise, is the most faithful in the performance
of it. *Rousseau.*

Prosperity.

Take care to be an economist in prosperity; there is no fear of your not being
one in adversity. *Zimmerman.*

Knaves will thrive,
When honest plainness knows not how to
live. *Shirley.*

FAM
QUOTES

Whilst you are prosperous you can number many friends; but when the storm comes you are left alone. *Ovid.*

Proverbs.

The wisdom of many, and the wit of one. *Lord John Russell.*

Jewels five-words long,
That on the stretch'd forefinger of all time
Sparkle forever. *Tennyson.*

Providence.

The ways of heaven are dark and intricate,
Puzzled in mazes, and perplex'd with errors;
Our understanding traces them in vain,
Lost and bewilder'd in the fruitless search;
Nor sees with how much art the windings run,
Nor where the regular confusion ends.
Addison.

How just is Providence in all its works.
How swift to overtake us in our crimes!
Lansdowne.

Prudence.

Men are born with two eyes, but with one tongue, in order that they should see twice as much as they say. *Colton.*

Want of prudence is too frequently the want of virtue; nor is there on earth a more powerful advocate for vice than poverty? *Goldsmith.*

Punishment.

Let rules be fix'd that may our rage contain,
And punish faults with a proportion'd pain;
And do not flay him, who deserves alone
A whipping for the fault that he has done. *Horace.*

The seeds of our punishment are sown at the same time we commit sin. *Hesiod.*

Purity.

An angel might have stoop'd to see,
And bless'd her for her purity.
Dr. Mackay.

Purity is the feminine, truth the masculine, of honor. *Hare.*

Purse.

Their love
Lies in their purses; and whoso empties them,
By so much fills their hearts with deadly hate. *Shakespeare.*

Quarrels.

Those who in quarrels interpose,
Must often wipe a bloody nose. *Gay.*

If he had two ideas in his head, they would fall out with each other.
Johnson.

I consider your very testy and quarrelsome people in the same light as I do a loaded gun, which may, by accident, go off and kill one. *Shenstone.*

Quotations.

Some for renown on scraps of learning dote
And think they grow immortal as they quote.
To patchwork learn'd quotations are allied,
But strive to make our poverty our pride.
Young.

I am but a gatherer, and a disposer of other men's stuff. *Watton.*

If the world like it not, so much the worse for them. *Cowper.*

Rabble.

They condemn what they do not understand. *Cicero.*

A hundred mouths, a hundred tongues,
And throats of brass, inspired with iron lungs. *Virgil.*

Rage.

They could neither of 'em speak for rage and so fell a sputtering at one another like two roasting apples.
Congreve.

My rage is not malicious; like a spark
Of fire by steel inforced out of a flint.
It is no sooner kindled, but extinct.
Goffe.

Rain.

How beautiful is the rain!
After the dust and heat,
In the broad and fiery street,
In the narrow lane;
How beautiful is the rain!
How it clatters along the roofs,
Like the tramp of hoofs;
How it gushes and struggles out
From the throat of the overflowing spout. *Longfellow.*

Dashing in big drops on the narrow pane,
And making mournful music for the mind,
While plays his interlude the wizard wind,
I hear the singing of the frequent rain.
Wm. H. Burleigh.

Rainbow.

How glorious is thy girdle cast.

O'er mountain, tower, and town ;
Or mirror'd in the ocean vast,
A thousand fathoms down.   *Campbell.*

That gracious thing, made up of tears
and light.   *Coleridge.*

What skillful limner e'er would choose
To paint the rainbow's various hues,
Unless to mortal it were given
To dip his brush in dyes of heaven ?
   Scott.

Rank.

The rank is but the guinea's stamp,
The man's the gowd for a' that.   *Burns.*

Rant.

Nay, an' thou 'lt mouth,
I'll rant as well as thou.   *Shakespeare.*

Rapture.

Not the poet in the moment
Fancy lightens on his e'e,
Kens the pleasure, feels the rapture
That thy presence gi'es to me.   *Burns.*

Rascals.

Make yourself an honest man, and then
you may be sure that there is one rascal
less in the world.   *Carlyle.*

Rashness.

That's a valiant flea that dare eat his
breakfast on the lip of a lion.
   Shakespeare.

Reading.

As a man may be eating all day, and
for want of digestion is never nourished,
so these endless readers may cram themselves in vain with intellectual food.
   Dr. I. Watts.

Read not to contradict and confute, nor
to believe and take for granted, nor to
find talk and discourse,—but to weigh and
consider.   *Bacon.*

To read without reflecting, is like eating without digesting.   *Burke.*

Reason.

He who will not reason, is a bigot ; he
who cannot, is a fool ; and he who dares
not, is a slave.   *Byron.*

When a man has not a good reason
for doing a thing, he has one good reason
for letting it alone.   *Sir Walter Scott.*

One can never repeat too often, that
reason, as it exists in man, is only our intellectual eye, and that, like the eye, to
see, it needs light,—to see clearly and far,
it needs the light of heaven.   *Anon.*

Reason is the test of ridicule—not ridicule the test of truth.   *Warburton.*

Neither great poverty, nor great riches,
will hear reason.   *Fielding.*

Reckoning.

I am ill at reckoning ; it fits the spirit
of a tapster.   *Shakespeare.*

So comes a reck'ning when the banquet's
   o'er,
The dreadful reck'ning and men smile no
   more.   *Gay.*

Recreation.

Amusements to virtue are like breezes
of air to the flame—gentle ones will fan
it, but strong ones will put it out.
   David Thomas.

Refinement.

That only can with propriety be styled
refinement which, by strengthening the intellect, purifies the manners.   *Coleridge.*

Reflection.

There is one art of which man should
be master,—the art of reflection.
   Coleridge.

Reform.

Reform, like charity, must begin at
home. Once well at home, how will it radiate outwards, irrepressible, into all that
we touch and handle, speak and work ;
kindling every new light by incalculable
contagion, spreading, in geometric ratio,
far and wide, doing good only wherever it
spreads, and not evil.   *Carlyle.*

He who reforms himself, has done more
towards reforming the public, than a crowd
of noisy, impotent patriots.   *Lavater.*

Regularity.

Regularity is unity, unity is godlike,
only the devil is changeable.   *Richter.*

Religion.

Religion is the best armor that a man
can have, but it is the worst cloak.
   Bunyan.

True religion
Is always mild, propitious, and humble,
Plays not the tyrant, plants no faith in
   blood ;
Nor bears destruction on her chariot-
   wheels ;
But stoops to polish, succor, and redress,
And builds her grandeur on the public
   good.   *Miller.*

Genuine religion is not so much a matter
of feeling as of principle.

An atheist is but a mad ridiculous de-
rider of piety ; but a hypocrite makes a
sober jest of God and religion ; he finds it
easier to be upon his knees than to rise
to a good action.   *Pope.*

Men will wrangle for religion; write for it; fight for it; die for it; anything but—
live for it.   *Colton.*

Measure not men by Sundays, without regarding what they do all the week after.
                                            Fuller.

I have lived long enough to know what I did not at one time believe—that no society can be upheld in happiness and honor without the sentiment of religion.
                                            La Place.

Pure religion and undefiled before God and the Father is this: To visit the fatherless and widows in their affliction, and to keep himself unspotted from the world.
                                    James i, 27.

For in religion as in friendship, they who profess most are ever the least sincere.
                                            Sheridan.

A man devoid of religion, is like a horse without a bridle.   *From the Latin.*

Remembrance.

Let never day nor night unhallow'd pass, But still remember what the Lord has done.   *Shakespeare.*

Remorse.

Remorse is the echo of a lost virtue.
                                    Bulwer Lytton.

One of those terrible moments when the wheel of passion stands suddenly still.
                                    Bulwer Lytton.

Repentance.

Repentance,
A salve, a comfort, and a cordial;
He that hath her, the keys of heaven hath:
This is the guide, this is the post, the path.
                                            Drayton.

Repose.

Our foster-nurse of nature is repose.
                                            Shakespeare.

When a man finds not repose in himself it is in vain for him to seek it elsewhere.
                                    From the French.

Reproof.

Forbear sharp speeches to her; she's a lady,
So tender of rebukes that words are strokes,
And strokes death to her.   *Shakespeare.*

Reputation.

O reputation! dearer far than life,
Thou precious balsam, lovely, sweet of smell,
Whose cordial drops once split by some rash hand,

Not all the owner's care, nor the repenting toil
Of the rude spiller, ever can collect
To its first purity and native sweetness.
                                    Sir W. Raleigh.

How many people live on the reputation of the reputation they might have made!
                                            Holmes.

How difficult it is to save the bark of reputation from the rocks of ignorance.
                                            Petrarch.

Thy credit wary keep, 'tis quickly gone:
Being got by many actions, lost by one.
                                            Randolph.

The reputation of a man is like his shadow: It sometimes follows and sometimes precedes him, it is sometimes longer and sometimes shorter than his natural size.   *French Proverb.*

Resignation.

Whate'er my doom;
It cannot be unhappy: God hath given me
The boon of resignation.   *Wilson.*

It is the Lord: let Him do what seemeth Him good.   *Samuel iii, 18.*

The Lord gave, and the Lord hath taken away; blessed be the name of the Lord.
                                        Job i, 21.

Rest.

Rest is the sweet sauce of labor.
                                            Plutarch.

Alternate rest and labor long endure.
                                            Ovid.

Retreat.

In all the trade of war, no feat
Is nobler than a brave retreat.
                                            Butler

Retribution.

Man never fastened one end of a chain around the neck of his brother, that God's own hand did not fasten the other end round the neck of the oppressor.
                                            Lamartine.

And thus the whirligig of time brings in his revenges.   *Shakespeare.*

Revenge.

How rash, how inconsiderate is rage!
How wretched, oh! how fatal is our error,
When to revenge precipitate we run;
Revenge, that still with double force recoils
Back on itself, and is its own revenge,
While to the short liv'd, momentary joy,
Succeeds a train of woes, an age of torments.   *Frowde.*

The best sort of revenge is not to be like him who did the injury.   *Antoninus.*

Rhetoric.

The heart's still rhetoric, disclosed with eyes.
Shakespeare.

Rhyme and Reason.

I was promised on a time,
To have reason for my rhyme;
From that time until this season,
I received no rhyme nor reason.
Spenser.

Riches.

And his best riches, ignorance of wealth.
Goldsmith.

As riches and favor forsake a man, we discover him to be a fool, but nobody could find it out in his prosperity.
La Bruyere.

He hath riches sufficient, who hath enough to be charitable.
Sir Thomas Browne.

A great fortune is a great slavery.
Seneca.

Believe not much them that seem to despise riches; for they despise them that despair of them; and none are worse when they come to them. Be not penny-wise: riches have wings, and sometimes they fly away of themselves, sometimes they must be set flying to bring in more. *Bacon.*

Rich, be not exalted; poor, be not dejected.
Cleobulus.

Ridicule.

If ridicule were employed to laugh men out of vice and folly, it might be of some use; but it is made use of to laugh men out of virtue and good sense, by attacking everything solemn and serious *Addison.*

Ring.

Oh! how many torments lie in the small circle of a wedding ring. *Colley Cibber.*

Rivalry.

Two stars keep not motion in one sphere.
Shakespeare.

Roaring.

I will roar, that it will do any man's heart good to hear me.

I will aggravate my voice so, that I will roar you as gently as any suckling dove; I will roar you an 'twere any nightingale.
Shakespeare.

Rod.

Take thy correction mildly. Kiss the rod.
Shakespeare.

He that spareth his rod hateth his son.
Proverbs xiii, 24.

Rudeness.

A man has no more right to say an uncivil thing, than to act one; no more right to say a rude thing to another, than to knock him down.
Johnson.

Rumor.

The flying rumors gather'd as they roll'd
Scarce any tale was sooner heard than told
And all who told it added something new,
And all who heard it made enlargement, too,
In every ear it spread, on every tongue it grew.
Pope.

Sabbath.

The poor man's day.
Grahame.

The Sabbath was made for man, and not man for the Sabbath. *St. Mark* ii, 27.

Sailor.

I love the sailor; his eventful life—
His generous spirit—his contempt of danger—
His firmness in the gale, the wreck, the strife;
And though a wild and reckless ocean-ranger,
God grant he make the port, when life is o'er,
Where storms are hush'd, and billows break no more
Walter Colton.

Satan.

Th' infernal serpent; he it was, whose guile,
Stirr'd up with envy and revenge, deceiv'd
The mother of mankind.
Milton.

Here we may reign secure; and in my choice
To reign is worth ambition, though in hell.
Better to reign in hell than serve in heaven.
Milton.

Satiety.

A surfeit of the sweetest things,
The deepest loathing to the stomach brings.
Shakespeare.

Satire.

Wit larded with malice.
Shakespeare.

A bitter jest. when the satire comes too near the truth, leaves a sharp sting behind.
Tacitus

Scandal.

Nor do they trust their tongues alone,
But speak a language of their own;
Can read a nod, a shrug, a look,

Far better than a printed book ;
Convey a libel in a frown,
And wink a reputation down ;
Or, by the tossing of a fan,
Describe the lady and the man. *Swift.*

Scar.

A scar nobly got is a good livery of honor. *Shakespeare.*

Scepticism.

I would rather dwell in the dim fog of superstition than in air rarified to nothing by the air pump of unbelief ; in which the panting breast expires, vainly and convulsively gasping for breath. *Richter.*

Schemes.

The best laid schemes o' mice an' men,
    Gang aft agley,
And lea'e us nought but grief and pain,
    For promised joy. *Burns.*

Scorn.

Oh ! what a thing, ye gods, is scorn or
    pity !
Heap on me, Heaven, the heat of all mankind,
Load me with envy, malice, detestation ;
Let me be horrid to all apprehension ;
Let the world shun me, so I 'scape but
    scorn. *Lee.*

Sculpture.

A statue lies hid in a block of marble ; and the art of the statuary only clears away the superfluous matter, and removes the rubbish. *Addison.*

Sea.

Praise the sea, but keep on land. *Geo. Herbert.*

Secret.

    'Tis in my memory lock'd,
And you yourself shall keep the key of it. *Shakespeare.*

    A secret in his mouth,
Is like a wild bird put into a cage ;
Whose door no sooner opens, but 'tis out. *Jonson.*

Generally he perceived in men of devout simplicity this opinion ; that the secrets of nature were the secrets of God, part of that glory into which man is not to press too boldly. *Bacon.*

Self.

And though all cry down self, none means
His ownself in a literal sense. *Butler.*

Be always displeased with what thou art, if thou desirest to attain to what thou art not ; for where thou hast pleased thyself, there thou abidest. But if thou sayest I have enough, thou perishest. Always add, always walk, always proceed. Neither stand still, nor go back, nor deviate. *Augustine.*

Self-Confidence.

For they can conquer who believe they can. *Virgil.*

Self-Control.

He who reigns within himself, and rules passions, desires and fears, is more than a king. *Milton.*

Self-Deception.

No man was ever so much deceived by another as by himself. *Greville.*

Self-Defense.

Self-defense is nature's eldest law. *Dryden.*

Self-Help.

Help yourself, and Heaven will help you. *La Fontaine.*

I have ever held it as a maxim, never to do that through another, which it was possible for me to execute myself. *Montesquieu*

Self-Love.

Self-love is more cunning than the most cunning man in the world. *La Rochefoucauld.*

Self-love is the greatest of flatterers. *La Rochefoucauld.*

Of all mankind, each loves himself the best. *Terence.*

Self-Respect.

The reverence of a man's self is, next religion, the chiefest bridle of all vices. *Lord Bacon.*

Sense.

Something there is more needful than expense,
And something previous e'en to taste—'tis sense :
Good sense which only is the gift of heaven,
And though no science, fairly worth the seven. *Pope.*

Sensibility.

The heart that is soonest awake to the flowers,
Is always the first to be touch'd by the thorns. *Moore.*

Servant.

Master, go on, and I will follow thee
To the last gasp, with truth and loyalty. *Shakespeare.*

If thou hast a loitering servant, send him of thy errand just before his dinner.
Fuller.

Services.

The daisy, by the shadow that it casts,
Protects the ling'ring dewdrop from the sun. *Wordsworth.*

Shame.

It is the guilt, not the scaffold, which constitutes the shame. *Cornville.*

Shaving.

Men for their sins
Have shaving, too, entail'd upon their chins. *Byron.*

Ship.

She comes majestic with her swelling sails,
The gallant bark; along her watery way
Homeward she drives before the favoring gales;
Now flirting at their length the streamers play,
And now they ripple with the ruffling breeze. *Southey.*

Silence.

The temple of our purest thoughts is—silence! *Mrs. Hale.*

Fellows who have no tongues are often all eyes and ears. *Haliburton.*

Let us be silent, that we may hear the whispers of the gods. *Emerson.*

Simplicity.

Whose nature is so far from doing harm,
That he suspects none. *Shakespeare.*

Sin.

He that falls into sin is a man; that grieves at it may be a saint; that boasteth of it is a devil. *Fuller.*

Few love to hear the sins they love to act. *Shakespeare.*

Sincerity.

The more honesty a man has, the less he affects the air of a saint. The affectation of sanctity is a blotch on the face of piety. *Lavater.*

Sincerity is like traveling in a plain beaten road, which commonly brings a man sooner to his journey's end than by-ways, in which men often lose themselves. *Tillotson.*

Skull.

Where be your gibes now? your gambols? your songs? your flashes of merriment that were wont to set the table on a roar? *Shakespeare.*

Slander.

Slander—
Whose edge is sharper than the sword.
Shakespeare.

Slander meets no regard from noble minds;
Only the base believe, what the base only utter. *Beller.*

Slanderers.

Long-breath'd talkers, minion lispers,
Cutting honest throats by whispers. *Scott.*

Sleep.

Sleep, that knits up the ravell'd sleeve of care;
The death of each day's life, sore labor's bath,
Balm of hurt minds, great Nature's second course,
Chief nourisher in life's feast.
Shakespeare.

Downy sleep, death's counterfeit.
Shakespeare.

How wonderful is death, death and his brother, sleep! *Shelley.*

O magic sleep! O comfortable bird,
That broodest o'er the troubled sea of the mind
Till it is hush'd and smooth! O unconfin'd
Restraint! imprison'd liberty! great key
To golden palaces—ay, all the world
Of silvery enchantment! *Keats.*

Sneer.

There was a laughing devil in his sneer,
That raised emotions both of rage and fear,
And where his frown of hatred darkly fell,
Hope, withering, fled, and mercy sighed farewell. *Byron.*

A habit of sneering, marks the egotist, or the fool, or the knave, or all three.
Lavater.

Society.

Society is like a lawn, where every roughness is smoothed, every bramble eradicated, and where the eye is delighted by the smiling verdure of a velvet surface. He, however, who would study nature in its wildness and variety, must plunge into the forest, must explore the glen, must stem the torrent, and dare the precipice.
Washington Irving.

Solitude.

Alone on a wide, wide sea,
So lonely 'twas, that God himself
Scarce seemed there to be. *Coleridge.*

Oh, lost to virtue—lost to manly thought,
Lost to the noble sallies of the soul!
Who think it solitude to be alone. *Young.*

The thought,
The deadly thought of solitude. *Keats.*

FAM QUOTES

Sorrow.

When sorrows come, they come not single
 spies,
But in battalions!   *Shakespeare.*

Any mind that is capable of a *real sorrow* is capable of good.   *Mrs. Stowe.*

Sorrow seems sent for our instruction, as we darken the cages of birds when we would teach them to sing.   *Richter.*

The first sharp sorrow—ay, the breaking up
Of that deep fountain, ne'er to be seal'd
Till we with time close up the great account.   *Caroline Bowles.*

Soul.

Alas! while the body stands so broad and brawny, must the soul lie blinded, dwarfed, stupefied, almost annihilated? Alas! this was, too, a breath of God, bestowed in heaven, but on earth never to be unfolded!   *Carlyle.*

There are souls which fall from heaven like flowers, but ere they bloom are crushed under the foul tread of some brutal hoof.   *Richter.*

Speaking.

Speak but little and well, if you would be esteemed as a man of merit.   *Trench.*

Speech.

A sentence well couched takes both the sense and the understanding. I love not those cart-rope speeches that are longer than the memory of man can fathom.   *Feltham.*

Spite.

Spite is a little word, but it represents as strange a jumble of feelings and compound of discords, as any polysyllable in the language.   *Dickens.*

Spoon.

He must have a long spoon that must eat with the devil.   *Shakespeare.*

Spring.

Wide flush the fields; the softening air is
 balm;
Echo the mountains round; the forest
 smiles;
And every sense and every heart is joy.   *Thomson.*

Stars.

There they stand,
Shining in order like a living hymn
Written in light.   *Willis.*

The stars hang bright above,
Silent, as if they watch'd the sleeping
 earth.   *Coleridge.*

Those gold candles fix'd in heaven's air.   *Shakespeare.*

Stoicism.

To feel for none is the true social art
Of the world's stoics—men without a
 heart.   *Byron.*

Story-Telling.

I cannot tell how the truth may be;
I say the tale as 'twas said to me.   *Sir Walter Scott.*

Study.

Much study is a weariness of the flesh.   *Ecclesiastes* xii, 12.

Success.

'Tis not in mortals to command success;
But we'll do more, Sempronius.—We'll
 deserve it.   *Addison.*

It is success that colors all in life;
Success makes fools admir'd, makes villains honest,
All the proud virtue of this vaunting world
Fawns on success and power, howe'er acquired.   *Thomson.*

Suicide.

Child of despair, and suicide my name.   *Savage.*

Self-murder, that infernal crime,
Which all the gods level their thunder at!   *Fane.*

Sun.

The glorious lamp of heaven, the sun.   *Herrick.*

Open the casement, and up with the sun!
His gallant journey has now begun,
Over the hills his chariot is roll'd,
Banner'd with glory and burnish'd with
 gold;
Over the hills he comes sublime,
Bridegroom of earth, and brother of time!   *Martin F. Tupper.*

Sunrise.

And see—the sun himself! on wings
Of glory up the east he springs.
Angel of light! who from the time
Those heavens began their march sublime,
Hath first of all the starry choir
Trod in his Maker's steps of fire!   *Moore.*

Sunset.

See the descending sun,
Scatt'ring his beams about him as he sinks,
And gilding heaven above, and s'as beneath,
With paint no mortal pencil can express.   *Hopkins.*

Superstition.

Superstition renders a man a fool, and scepticism makes him mad.   *Fielding.*

Suspense.

It is a miserable thing to live in suspense, it is the life of the spider.   *Swift.*

Suspicion.

It is hardly possible to suspect another without having in one's self the seeds of baseness the party is accused of.
Stanislaus.

Swearing.

Swear not at all: neither by heaven; for it is God's throne: nor by the earth; for it is his footstool: neither by Jerusalem; for it is the city of the great king. Neither shalt thou swear by thy head, because thou canst not make one hair white or black. But let your communication be yea, yea; nay, nay: for whatsoever is more than these cometh of evil.   *St. Matthew.*

Tact.

Never join with your friend when he abuses his horse or his wife, unless the one is about to be sold, and the other to be buried.   *Colton.*

Talents.

It seems that nature has concealed at the bottom of our minds, talents and abilities of which we are not aware. The passions alone have the privilege of bringing them to light, and of giving us sometimes views more certain and more perfect than art could possibly produce.

La Rochefoucauld.

Talkers.

As empty vessels make the loudest sound, so they that have the least wit are the greatest babblers.   *Plato.*
Talkers are no good doers. *Shakespeare.*

Talking.

Words learned by rote a parrot may re-
     hearse,
But talking is not always to converse;
Not more distinct from harmony divine,
The constant creaking of a country sign.
Cowper.

Does a man speak foolishly?—suffer him gladly, for you are wise. Does he speak erroneously?—stop such a man's mouth with sound words that cannot be gainsaid. Does he speak truly?—rejoice in the truth.   *Oliver Cromwell.*

Taste.

May not taste be compared to that exquisite sense of the bee, which instantly discovers and extracts the quintessence of every flower, and disregards all the rest of it.   *Greville.*

Tea.

Tea! thou soft, thou sober sage, and venerable liquid;—thou female tongue-running, smile-smoothing, heart-opening, wink-tippling cordial, to whose glorious insipidity I owe the happiest moments of my life, let me fall prostrate!   *Colley Cibber.*

Tears.

Beauty's tears are lovelier than her smile.
Campbell.
The safety-valves of the heart, when too much pressure is laid on.   *Albert Smith.*
The tears of penitents are the wine of angels   *St. Bernard.*

Temper.

A sunny temper gilds the edges of life's blackest cloud.   *Guthrie.*

Temptation.

He who has no mind to trade with the devil, should be so wise as to keep from his shop.   *South.*
     'Tis one thing to be tempted,
Another thing to fall.   *Shakespeare.*

Testimony and Argument.

Testimony is like an arrow shot from a long bow; the force of it depends on the strength of the hand that draws it. Argument is like an arrow from a cross-bow, which has equal force though shot by a child.   *Bacon.*

Thinkers.

There are very few original thinkers in the world; the greatest part of those who are called philosophers have adopted the opinions of some who went before them.
Dugald Stewart.

Thought.

There's too much abstract willing, purposing,
In this poor world. *We talk by aggregates,
And think by systems,* and being used to face
Our evils in statistics, are inclined
To cap them with unreal remedies,
Drawn out in haste on the other side the slate.   *Elizabeth Barrett Browning.*

Man is a thinking being, whether he will or no: all he can do is to turn his thoughts the best way.   *Sir W. Temple.*

Thoughts are but dreams till their effects be tried.   *Shakespeare.*

Kindred objects kindred thoughts inspire,
As summer clouds flash forth electric fire.
Rogers.

Time.

Time is the chrysalis of eternity.
Richter.

I never knew the old gentleman with the scythe and hour-glass bring anything but grey hairs, thin cheeks, and loss of teeth.
Dryden.

All that time is lost which might be better employed. *Rousseau.*

The inaudible and noiseless foot of time.
Shakespeare.

Time is the old Justice, that examines all offenders. *Shakespeare.*

Who shall contend with time, unvanquished time,
The conqueror of conquerors, and lord of desolation? *Kirk White.*

Still on it creeps.
Each little moment at another's heels,
Till hours, days, years, and ages are made up
Of such small parts as these, and men look back
Worn and bewildered, wondering how it is.
Thou trav'llest like a ship in the wide ocean,
Which hath no bounding shore to mark its progress. *Joanna Baillie.*

As every thread of gold is valuable, so is every minute of time. *Mason.*

Dost thou love life? Then waste not time, for time is the stuff that life is made of. *B. Franklin.*

Time, as he passes us, has a dove's wing,
Unsoil'd and swift, and of a silken sound.
Cowper.

Title.

A fool, indeed, has great need of a title,
It teaches men to call him count and duke,
And to forget his proper name of fool.
Crowne.

To-day.

To-day is ours: why do we fear?
To-day is ours: we have it here:
Let's banish bus'ness, banish sorrow:
To the gods belongs to-morrow. *Cowley.*

To-morrow.

To-morrow cheats us all. Why dost thou stay,
And leave undone what should be done to-day?
Begin—the present minute's in thy power;
But still t' adjourn, and wait a fitter hour,
Is like the clown, who at some river's side

Expecting stands, in hopes the running tide
Will all ere long be past. Fool! not to know
It still has flow'd the same, and will forever flow. *Hughes.*

Tongue.

The tongue the ambassador of the heart.
Lyly.

Restrain thy mind, and let mildness ever attend thy tongue. *Theognis.*

To many men well-fitting doors are not set on their tongues. *Theognis.*

Toothache.

There was never yet philosopher
That could endure the toothache patiently.
Shakespeare.

Treason.

Treason doth never prosper. What's the reason?
Why, when it prospers, none dare call it treason. *Sir John Harrington.*

Trifles.

Those who bestow too much application on trifling things, become generally incapable of great ones. *La Rochefoucauld.*

Truth.

Truth is God's daughter.
Spanish Proverb.

He who conceals a useful truth is equally guilty with the propagator of an injurious falsehood. *Augustine.*

"Truth," I cried, "though the heavens crush me for following her; no falsehood, though a whole celestial Lubberland were the price of apostacy!" *Carlyle.*

Truth is a gem that is found at a great depth; whilst on the surface of this world, all things are weighed by the false scale of custom. *Byron.*

There are three parts in truth: first, the inquiry, which is the wooing of it; secondly, the knowledge of it, which is the presence of it; and thirdly, the belief, which is the enjoyment of it. *Bacon.*

Truth needs no flowers of speech. *Pope.*

Twilight.

How fine to view the sun's departing ray
Fling back a lingering lovely after-day;
The moon of summer glides serenely by,
And sheds a light enchantment o'er the sky.
These, sweetly mingling, pour upon the

sight
A pencill'd shadowing, and a dewy light—
A softened day, a half-unconscious night.
Alas! too finely pure on earth to stay,
It faintly spots the hill, and dies away.
Anon.

Tyrants.

It is worthy of observation, that the most imperious masters over their own servants, are at the same time, the most abject slaves to the servants of other masters.
Seneca.

Uncertainty.

How happy could I be with either,
Were t'other dear charmer away.
John Gay.

Unkindness.

Sharp-tooth'd unkindness. *Shakespeare.*

Unworthiness.

You are not worth the dust which the rude wind blows in your face.
Shakespeare.

Urgency.

The affair cries—haste,
And speed must answer it. *Shakespeare.*

Usurer.

A money-lender. He serves you in the present tense; he lends you in the conditional mood; keeps you in the subjunctive; and ruins you in the future!
Addison.

Utility.

Crab apples may not be the best kind of fruit; but a tree which every year bears a great crop of crab apples is better worth cultivating than a tree which bears nothing.

Valor.

The better part of valor is discretion; in the which better part I have saved my life.
Shakespeare.
The truly valiant dare everything but doing anybody an injury.
Sir Philip Sidney.

Vanity.

She neglects her heart who studies her glass.
Lavater.
In a vain man, the smallest spark may kindle into the greatest flame, because the materials are always prepared for it.
Hume
Every man has just as much vanity as he wants understanding. *Pope.*

Vanity and Pride.

Pride makes us esteem ourselves; vanity makes us desire the esteem of others. It is just to say, as Dean Swift has done, that a man is too proud to be vain. *Blair.*

Variety.

Variety's the very spice of life,
That gives it all its flavor. *Cowper.*

Verbiage.

Words, words, mere words. no matter from the heart. *Shakespeare.*

Vice.

Vice repeated like the wandering wind,
Blows dust in others' eyes. *Shakespeare.*
Ah, vice! how soft are thy voluptuous ways,
While boyish blood is mantling, who can 'scape
The fascination of thy magic gaze?
A cherub-hydra round us dost thou gape,
And mould to every taste thy dear delusive shape.
Byron.
Vice is a monster of so frightful mien,
As to be hated needs but to be seen;
Yet seen too oft, familiar with her face,
We first endure, then pity, then embrace.
Pope.
Our pleasant vices
Are made the whip to scourge us.
Shakespeare.
Vice stings us even in our pleasures, but virtue consoles us, even in our pains.
Colton.

Vicissitudes.

Thus doth the ever-changing course of things
Run a perpetual circle, ever turning;
And that same day, that highest glory brings,
Brings us unto the point of back-returning.
Daniel.

Vigilance.

The master's eye makes the horse fat.
From the Latin.

Villainy.

The evil you teach us, we will execute, and it shall go hard but we will better the instruction. *Shakespeare.*
He hath out-villained villainy so far, that the rarity redeems him. *Shakespeare.*

Virtue.

The only amaranthine flow'r on earth
Is virtue; the only lasting treasure. truth.
Cowper.
A heart unspotted is not easily daunted.
Shakespeare.
And virtue is her own reward. *Prior.*

Vituperation.

The bitter clamor of two eager tongues.
Shakespeare.

Vocation.

Why, Hal, 'tis my vocation.
'Tis no sin for a man to labor in his vocation. *Shakespeare.*

Voice.

Her voice was ever soft,
Gent'e. and low; an excellent thing in
woman. *Shakespeare.*

Vulgar.

To endeavor to work upon the vulgar
with fine sense, is like attempting to hew
blocks with a razor. *Pope.*

Wagers.

I've heard old cunning stagers
Say fools for arguments use wagers.
Butler.

Want.

His wit being snuft by want burnt clear.
Killigrew.

Wants.

The fewer our wants the nearer we resemble the gods. *Socrates.*

Where necessity ends, curiosity begins;
and no sooner are we supplied with every
thing that nature can demand, than we sit
down to contrive artificial appetites.
Johnson.

War.

O war! begot in pride and luxury,
The child of malice and revengeful hate;
Thou impious good, and good impiety!
Thou art the foul refiner of a state,
Unjust scourge of men's iniquity,
Sharp easer of corruptions desperate!
Is there no means but that a sin-sick land
Must be let blood with such a boist'rous
hand? *Daniels.*

Give me the money that has been spent
in war, and I will purchase every foot of
land upon the globe. I will clothe every
man, woman and child in an attire of
which kings and queens would be proud.
I will build a school house on every hillside, and in every valley over the whole
earth; I will build an academy in every
town, and endow it; a college in every
State, and fill it with able professors; I
will crown every hill with a place of worship, consecrated to the promulgation of
the gospel of peace; I will support in every
pulpit an able teacher of righteousness, so
that on every Sabbath morning the chime
on one hill should answer to the chime on
another round the earth's wide circumference; and the voice of prayer, and the
song of praise, should ascend like an universal holocaust to heaven. *Henry Richard.*

That mad game the world so loves to
play. *Swift.*

War, my lord,
Is of eternal use to human kind,
For ever and anon when you have pass'd
A few dull years in peace and propagation,
The world is overstock'd with fools, and
wants
A pestilence at least if not a hero.
Jeffrey.

Warriors.

If Europe should ever be ruined, it will
be by its warriors. *Montesquieu.*

Waste.

What maintains one vice, would bring
up two children. Remember, many a little makes a mickle: and farther, beware of
little expenses; a small leak will sink a
great ship. *Franklin.*

Water.

Traverse the desert, and then ye can tell
What treasures exist in the cold deep well,
Sink in despair on the red parch'd earth,
And then ye may reckon what water is
worth. *Miss Eliza Cook.*

Wealth.

It is far more easy to acquire a fortune
like a knave than to expend it like a gentleman. *Colton.*

The way to wealth is as plain as the way
to market. It depends chiefly on two
words, industry and frugality; that is,
waste neither time nor money, but make
the best use of both. Without industry
and frugality nothing will do, and with
them everything. *Franklin.*

Wickedness.

Wickedness may prosper for awhile, but
at the long run, he that sets all knaves at
work will pay them. *L'Estrange.*

Wife.

What is there in the vale of life
Half so delightful as a wife;
When friendship, love, and peace combine
To stamp the marriage-bond divine?
Cowper.

All other goods by Fortune's hand are
given,
A wife is the peculiar gift of heaven.
Pope.

She who ne'er answers till her husband
cools;
Or, if she rules him, never shows she
rules:
Charms by accepting, by submitting sways,
Yet has her humor most when she obeys.
Pope.

Will.

In idle wishes fools supinely stay,
Be there a will,—and wisdom finds a way.
George Crabb.

Wills.

What you leave at your death, let it be without controversy, else the lawyers will be your heirs. *Osborne.*

Wind.

The wind has a language, I would I could learn!
Sometimes 'tis soothing, and sometimes 'tis stern,
Sometimes it comes like a low sweet song,
And all things grow calm, as the sound floats along,
And the forest is lull'd by the dreamy strain,
And slumber sinks down on the wandering main,
And its crystal arms are folded in rest,
And the tall ship sleeps on its heaving breast. *L. E. Landon.*

Wine.

Wine is a turncoat; first a friend, and then an enemy. *Fielding.*

Wisdom.

Common sense in an uncommon degree is what the world calls wisdom. *Coleridge.*

It is far easier to be wise for others than to be so for oneself.
La Rochefoucauld.

Call him wise whose actions, words and steps are all a clear *because* to a clear *why.*
Lavater.

The wisest man is generally he who thinks himself the least so. *Boileau.*

Wishes.

What ardently we wish we soon believe.
Young.

Wit.

Wit and judgment often are at strife,
Though meant to be each other's aid like man and wife. *Pope.*

True wit is nature to advantage drest,
What oft was thought, but ne'er so well exprest,
Something whose truth, convinc'd at sight we find,
That gives us back the image of our mind.
Pope.

Woman.

'Tis beauty that doth oft make women proud;
'Tis virtue, that doth make them most admired;
'Tis modesty, that makes them seem divine. *Shakespeare.*

If the heart of a man is depress'd with cares,
The mist is dispelled when a woman appears. *Gay.*

Ould nature swears, the lovely dears
Her noblest work she classes, O;
Her 'prentice han' she tried on man,
An' then she made the lasses, O. *Burns.*

Woman is something between a flower and an angel.
First, then, a woman will or won't,—depend on't;
If she will do't, she will; and there's an end on't,
But, if she won't, since safe and sound your trust is,
Fear is affront; and jealousy injustice.
Aaron Hill.

O woman! lovely woman! nature made thee
To temper man: we had been brutes without you! *Otway.*

Women have more strength in their looks than we have in our laws, and more power by their tears than we have by our arguments. *Saville.*

O woman! in our hours of ease,
Uncertain, coy, and hard to please,
And variable as the shade
By the light quivering aspen made;
When pain and anguish wring the brow
A ministering angel thou! *Scott.*

Woman's natural mission is to love, to love but one, to love always. *Michelet.*

Woman knows that the better she obeys the surer she is to rule. *Michelet.*

Woman's happiness is in obeying. She objects to men who abdicate too much.
Michelet.

Disguise our bondage as we will,
'Tis woman, woman rules us still.
Tom Moore.

What manly eloquence could produce such an effect as woman's silence.
Michelet.

He's a fool, who thinks by force, or skill,
To turn the current of a woman's will.
Tuke.

Words.

Words are men's daughters, but God's sons are things. *Johnson.*

If you would be pungent, be brief; for it is with words as with sunbeams—the more they are condensed the deeper they burn.
Southey.

He that uses many words for the explaining any subject, doth like the cuttlefish, hide himself for the most part in his own ink. *Ray.*

Words are things; and a small drop of ink,
Falling like dew upon a thought, produces
That which makes thousands, perhaps millions, think. *Byron.*

Apt words have power to 'suage
The 'tumults of a troubled mind
And are as balm to fester'd wounds.
Milton.

Working and Talking.

By work you get money, by talk you get knowledge. *Haliburton.*

World.

O what a glory doth this world put on,
For him who with fervent heart goes forth,
Under the bright and glorious sky and looks
On duties well performed, and days well spent. *Longfellow.*

Ay beauteous is the world, and many a joy
Floats through its wide dominion. But, alas,
When we would seize the winged good, it flies,
And step by step, along the path of life,
Allures our yearning spirits to the grave.
Goethe.

The world's a wood, in which all lose their way,
Though by a different path each goes astray. *Buckingham.*

Worth.

For what is worth in anything,
But so much money as 'twill bring?
Butler.

Worth makes the man, and want of it the fellow;
The rest is all but leather or prunella.
Pope.

Writers.

Every great or original writer in proportion as he is great or original, must himself create the taste by which he must be relished. *Wordsworth.*

Writing.

The world agrees
That he writes well who writes with ease.
Prior.

You write with ease to show your breeding
But easy writing's curst hard reading.
Sheridan.

To write well is at once to think well, to feel rightly, and to render properly! it is to have, at the same time, mind, soul, taste. *Buffon.*

Years.

Winged time glides on insensibly, and deceives us; and there is nothing more fleeting than years. *Ovid.*

Youth.

What is youth?—a dancing billow,
Winds behind and rocks before. *Moore.*

Crabbed age and youth
Cannot live together;
Youth is full of pleasure,
Age is full of care;
Youth like summer morn,
Age like winter weather;
Youth like summer brave,
Age like winter bare;
Youth is full of sport,
Age's breath is short;
Youth is nimble, age is lame;
Youth is hot and bold,
Age is weak and cold;
Youth is wild and age is tame.
Age, I do abhor thee;
Youth, I do adore thee;
O, my love, my love is young.
Age, I do defy thee,
O sweet shepherd, hie thee,
For methinks thou stay'st too long.
Shakespeare.

Zeal.

No wild enthusiast ever yet could rest
'Till half mankind were like himself possessed. *Cowper.*

Famous Lines from Favorite Authors

SHAKESPEARE.

A little more than kin, and less than kind.

Seems, madam; nay, it is; I know not seems.

Frailty, thy name is woman.
Like Niobe, all tears.

O that this too, too solid flesh would melt.

Springes to catch woodcocks.

When shall we three meet again,
In thunder, lightning, or in rain?
When the hurly-burly's done,
When the battle's lost and won.

Come what come may,
Time and the hour run through the longest day.

Your face, my Thane, is as a book, where men
May read strange matters.

Letting *I dare not* wait upon *I would.*
Like the poor cat i' the adage.

I dare do all that may become a man;
Who does more, is none.

We have scotched the snake, not killed it.

Infirm of purpose!
Thou canst not say I did it; never shake
Thy gory locks at me.

Double, double, toil and trouble.

        Lay on, Macduff,
And damned be he that first cries, "Hold, enough!"

One fire burns out another's burning,
One pain is lessen'd by another's anguish.

For you and I are past our dancing days.

He jests at scars that never felt a wound.

Too early seen unknown, and known too late.

Parting is such sweet sorrow.

I am the very pink of courtesy.

Adversity's sweet milk, philosophy.

      Eyes, look your last;
Arms, take your last embrace.

We have seen better days.

Beware the Ides of March.

But, for mine own part, it was Greek to me.

Cowards die many times before their death,
The valiant never taste of death but once.

Though last, not least in love.

If you have tears prepare to shed them now.

This was the most unkindest cut of all.

A friend should bear his friend's infirmities,
But Brutus makes mine greater than they are.

This was the noblest Roman of them all.

    I am no orator as Brutus is,
   . . . I only speak right on.

One touch of nature makes the whole world kin.

So wise so young, they say, do ne'er live long.

A horse! a horse! my kingdom for a horse!

Misery acquaints a man with strange bedfellows.

He that dies pays all debts.

This is the long and short of it.

The King's English.

How use doth breed a habit in a man!

Condemn the fault, and not the actor of it.

What's mine is yours, and what is yours is mine.

Benedick the married man.

Sets the wind in that corner?

O, what men dare do! what men may do! what men daily do, not knowing what they do!

Are you good men and true?

Done to death by slanderous tongues.

My cake is dough

There's small choice in rotten apples.

In maiden meditation, fancy free.

       My heart
    Is true as steel.

      Gives to airy nothing
  A local habitation and a name.

A bright particular star.

The inaudible and noiseless foot of time.

Life is as tedious as a twice-told tale,
Vexing the dull ear of a dreaming man.

Midsummer madness.

Still you keep o' the windy side o' the law.

I like not fair terms and a villain's mind.

'Tis vile, unless it may be quaintly order'd,
And better, in my mind, not undertook.

Who chooseth me shall gain what many men desire.

Who chooseth me shall get as much as he deserves.

Who chooseth me must give or hazard all he hath.

I will assume desert.

O, these deliberate fools! when they do choose,
They have the wisdom by their wit to lose.

What, wouldst thou have a serpent sting thee twice?

A Daniel come to judgment!

     O wise and upright judge!
How much more elder art thou than thy looks!

Is it so nominated in the bond?

I cannot find it; 'tis not in the bond.

A Daniel, still say I, a second Daniel!
I thank thee, Jew, for teaching me that word.

He is well paid that is well satisfied.
Sir, you are very welcome to our house;
It must appear in other ways than words,
Therefore I scant this breathing courtesy.

Motley's the only wear.

I had rather have a fool to make me merry, than experience to make me sad.

The Retort Courteous.—The Lie Circumstantial.—The Lie Direct.

Good wine needs no bush.

Your *If* is the only peacemaker; much virtue in *If*.

The ripest fruit first falls.

He will give the devil his due.

I know a trick worth two of that.

It would be argument for a week, laughter for a month, and a good jest forever.

Brain him with a lady's fan.

A good mouth-filling oath.

Shall I not take mine ease in mine inn?

I could have better spared a better man.

He hath eaten me out of house and home.

Uneasy lies the head that wears a crown.

Thy wish was father, Harry, to that thought

How sharper than a serpent's tooth it is
To have a thankless child!

Striving to better, oft we mar what's well.

I am a man
More sinned against than sinning.

O, that way madness lies; let me shun that.

The little dogs and all,
Tray, Blanche, and Sweetheart, see, they
bark at me.

Ay, every inch a king.

But I will wear my heart upon my sleeve
For daws to peck at.

Put money in thy purse.

Framed to make women false.

For I am nothing, if not critical.

Iago.—What, are you hurt, lieutenant?

Cas.—Ay, past all surgery.

O thou invisible spirit of wine, if thou hast no name to be known by, let us call thee devil!

O that men should put an enemy in their mouths to steal away their brains!

Trifles, light as air,
Are to the jealous confirmations strong
As proofs of holy writ.

Speak of me as I am; nothing extenuate,
Nor set down aught in malice; then must
you speak
Of one that lov'd, not wisely, but too well.

My salad days,
When I was green in judgment.

It beggared all description.

Age cannot wither her, nor custom stale
Her infinite variety.

Let's do it after the high Roman fashion.

As it fell upon a day
In the merry month of May.

We are such stuff
As dreams are made on, and our little life
Is rounded with a sleep.

JONATHAN SWIFT.

Bread is the staff of life.

No wise man ever wished to be younger.

I shall be like that tree; I shall die at the top.

EDWARD YOUNG.

At thirty man suspects himself a fool;
Knows it at forty and reforms his plan.

Be wise with speed;
A fool at forty is a fool indeed.

How blessings brighten as they take their flight.

Wishing, of all employments, is the worst.

And all may do what has by man been done.

Beautiful as sweet!
And young as beautiful! and soft as young
And gay as soft! and innocent as gay!

'Tis impious in a good man to be sad.

JOHN DRYDEN.

None but the brave deserve the fair.

And like another Helen, fired another Troy.

Who think too little, and who talk too much.

Everything by starts, and nothing long.

The young men's vision, and the old men's dream.

She hugged the offender and forgave the offense.

Sex to the last.

For Art may err, but Nature cannot miss.

Errors, like straws, upon the surface flow;
He who would search for pearls must dive below.

All delays are dangerous in war.

ALEXANDER POPE.

Thou wert my guide, philosopher, and friend.

'Tis education forms the common mind:
Just as the twig is bent the tree's inclined.

Odious! in woolen! 'twould a saint provoke!

Who shall decide when doctors disagree,
And soundest causists doubt, like you and me?

Heaven from all creatures hides the book of fate.

Shoot folly as it flies.

Lo, the poor Indian! whose untutored mind
Sees God in clouds, or hears Him in the wind.

Honor and shame from no condition rise;
Act well your part, there all the honor lies.

Curst be the verse, how well soe'er it flow,
That tends to make one worthy man my foe.

There St. John mingles with my friendly bowl,
The feast of reason, and the flow of soul.

Welcome the coming, speed the departing guest.

The last and greatest art, the art to blot.

I am his Highness' dog at Kew,
Pray tell me, sir, whose dog are you?

Thou great First Cause, least understood.

Whatever is, is right.

JOHN MILTON.

Tears, such as angels weep, burst forth.

Which, if not victory, is yet revenge.

The bright consummate flower.

Deep-versed in books and shallow in himself.

When more is meant than meets the ear.

The oracles are dumb.

That old man eloquent.

License they mean when they cry liberty.

JOSEPH ADDISON.

My voice is still for war,
Gods! can a Roman senate long debate
Which of the two to choose, slavery or death?

A day, an hour, of virtuous liberty
Is worth a whole eternity in bondage.

The woman who deliberates is lost.

The spacious firmament on high,
With all the blue ethereal sky—
.   .   .   .   .
Forever singing, as they shine,
The hand that made us is divine.

EDMUND BURKE.

There is, however, a limit at which forbearance ceases to be a virtue.

But the age of chivalry is gone. That of sophisters, economists, and calculators has succeeded.

Early and provident fear is the mother of safety.

WILLIAM COWPER.

England, with all thy faults, I love thee still,
My country!

She that asks
Her dear five hundred friends.

The beggarly last doit.

A fool must now and then be right by chance.

A hat not much the worse for wear.

And Satan trembles when he sees
The weakest saint upon his knees.

Beware of desperate steps. The darkest day,
Live till to-morrow, will have passed away.

OLIVER GOLDSMITH.

And learn the luxury of doing good.

These little things are great to little man.

But winter lingering, chills the lap of May.

He cast off his friends, as a huntsman his pack,
For he knew, when he choosed, he could whistle them back.

SAMUEL TAYLOR COLERIDGE.

As idle as a painted ship
Upon a painted ocean.

Water, water, everywhere,
Nor any drop to drink.

A sadder and a wiser man
He rose the morrow morn.

He prayeth best, who loveth best
All things, both great and small.

A sight to dream of, not to tell.

Alas! they had been friends in youth;
But whispering tongues can poison truth;
And constancy lives in realms above;
And life is thorny, and youth is vain,
And to be wroth with one we love,
Doth work like madness in the brain.

Motionless torrents! silent cataracts!
Ye living flowers that skirt the eternal
frost.

Our myriad-minded Shakespeare.

A dwarf sees father than the giant
when he has the giant's shoulder to mount
on.

THOMAS CAMPBELL.

'Tis distance lends enchantment to the
view,
And robes the mountain in its azure hue.

The combat deepens. On, ye brave,
Who rush to glory or the grave!

To bear is to conquer our fate.

LORD BYRON.

'Tis pleasant, sure, to see one's name in
print;
A book's a book, although there's nothing
in't.

With just enough of learning to misquote.

Maid of Athens, ere we part,
Give, oh! give me back my heart.

Had sighed to many, though he loved
but one.

The dome of Thought, the palace of the
Soul.

Hereditary bondsmen! know ye not,
Who would be free, themselves must
strike the blow.

Music arose with its voluptuous swell—
Soft eyes looked love to eyes which spake
again,
And all went merry as a marriage bell.

On with the dance! let joy be unconfined.

And there was mounting in hot haste.

I stood in Venice, on the Bridge of Sighs;
A palace and a prison on each hand.

Man!
Thou pendulum betwixt a smile and tear.

"While stands the Coliseum Rome shall
stand;
When falls the Coliseum, Rome shall fall;
And when Rome falls—the world."

I die—but first I have possess'd,
And come what may, I have been blest.

He makes a solitude, and calls it—
peace.

Hark! to the hurried question of despair,
"Where is my child?"—an Echo answers
—"Where?"

The power of Thought—the magic of
the mind.

And both were young, and one was
beautiful.

A change came o'er the spirit of my
dream.

My boat is on the shore
And my bark is on the sea.

The precious porcelain of common clay

Society is now one polished horde.

Formed of two mighty tribes, the Bores,
and Bored.

I awoke one morning and found myself
famous.

The best of Prophets of the future is
the Past.

And what is writ, is writ—
Would it were worthier?

JOHN KEATS.

Philosophy will clip an angel's wings.

Thou foster-child of Silence and slow
Time.

TALLEYRAND.

Prudence in women should be an instinct, not a virtue.

What I have been taught I have forgotten; what I know I have guessed.

The love of glory can only create a
hero: the contempt of it creates a great
man.

If you wish to appear agreeable in society, you must consent to be taught many
things which you know already.

There are two things to which we never
grow accustomed—the ravages of time
and the injustice of our fellow-men.

He who cannot feel friendship is alike
incapable of love. Let a woman beware
of the man who owns that he loves no
one but herself.

It is sometimes quite enough for a man to feign ignorance of that which he knows, to gain the reputation of knowing that of which he is ignorant.

Human life is like a game of chess—each piece holds its place upon the chessboard—king, queen, bishop, and pawn. Death comes, the game is up, and all are thrown, without distinction, pell-mell in the same bag.

CHARLES DICKENS.

In a Pickwickian sense.

When found, make a note of.

My life is one demd horrid grind.

Barkis is willin'.

Lor! let's be comfortable.

In came Mrs. Fezziweg, one vast substantial smile.

Oh! a dainty plant is the ivy green,
  That creepeth o'er ruins old!
Of right choice food are his meals,
    ween,
  In his cell so lone and cold.
Creeping where no life is seen,
A rare old plant is the ivy green.

Miscellaneous Quotations.

Build thee more stately mansions, O my soul,
  As the swift seasons roll!
  Leave thy low vaulted past!
Let each new temple, nobler than the last,
Shut thee from heaven with a dome more vast,
  Till thou at last art free,
Leaving thine outgrown shell by life's unresting sea.   *O. W. Holmes.*

For myself alone I doubt;
All is well, I know, without;
I alone the beauty mar,
I alone the music jar.
Yet with hands by evil stained,
And an ear by discord pained,
I am groping for the keys
Of the heavenly harmonies.
        J. G. Whittier.

Into the sunshine,
  Full of the light,
Leaping and flashing
  From morn till night!
. . . .
Glorious fountain!
  Let my heart be
Fresh, changeful, constant,
  Upward, like thee!
          J. R. Lowell.

I knew a very wise man that believed that if a man were permitted to make all the ballads he need not care who should make the laws of a nation.
        Andrew Fletcher.

Then gently scan your brother man,
  Still gentler, sister woman;
Though they may gang a kennin wrang,
  To step aside is human.
. . . .
What's done we partly may compute,
  But know not what's resisted. *Burns.*

    Alas for the rarity
    Of Christian charity
      Under the sun! *Thomas Hood.*

Like the dew on the mountain,
  Like the foam on the river,
Like the bubble on the fountain,
  Thou art gone, and forever! *Scott.*
Philosophy is the romance of the aged, and Religion the only future history for us all. *Balbi, Life and Times of Dante.*

Boston State House is the hub of the Solar System. You couldn't pry that out of a Boston man if you had the tire of all creation straightened out for a crowbar.
        O. W. Holmes, Autocrat.

Say—the world is a nettle; disturb it, it stings:
Grasp it firmly, it stings not. On one of two things,
If you would not be stung, it behooves you to settle:
Avoid it, or crush it. *Owen Meredith.*

    Tender-handed grasp a nettel
      And it stings you for your pains;
    Grasp it like a man of mettle
      And it soft as silk remains.
            Aaron Hill.

Every man has in himself a continent of undiscovered character. Happy he who acts the Columbus to his own soul!
        Stephen.

Conquering, not as anger is cowed by fiercer anger, or hate by bitterer hate, but as anger is subdued by patience and hatred is conquered by love. And the conquests of patience and love are slow.
  Author of Schonberg-Cotta Family.

O noble conscience, upright and refined,
How slight a fault inflicts a bitter sting.
  Dante, Purgatorio III, Wright, Tr.

Nature fits all her children with something to do,
He who would write and can't write, can surely review. *J. R. Lowell*

Meanwhile the guilty soul cannot keep its own secret. It is false to itself; or, rather, it feels an irresistible impulse of conscience to be true to itself. . . . It must be confessed—it *will* be confessed—there is no refuge from confession but suicide, and suicide is confession.

Daniel Webster, in the Knapp Trial.

How sink the brave who sink to rest,
By all their country's wishes blest!

. . . .

By fairy hands their knell is rung;
By forms unseen their dirge is sung;
There Honor comes, a pilgrim gray,
To bless the turf that wraps their clay;
And Freedom shall awhile repair,
To dwell a weeping hermit there.

Collins.

Was it something said,
    Something done,
Vexed him? was it touch of hand,
    Turn of head?
Strange! that very way
    Love began.
I as little understand
    Love's decay. *Robert Browning.*

The mossy marbles rest
On the lips that he has prest
    In their bloom:
And the names he loved to hear
Have been carved for many a year
    On the tomb. *O. W. Holmes.*

We may live without poetry, music, and art;
We may live without conscience, and live without heart;
We may live without friends; we may live without books;
But civilized man cannot live without cooks.
He may live without books—what is knowledge but grieving?
He may live without hope—what is hope but deceiving?
He may live without love—what is passion but pining?
But where is the man that can live without dining. *Owen Meredith.*

Not a drum was heard, not a funeral note,
As his corpse to the rampart we hurried.

. . . .

But he lay like a warrior taking his rest,
With his martial cloak around him.

. . . .

We carved not a line, and we raised not a stone,
But we left him alone in his glory.
Charles Wolfe, The Burial of Sir John Moore.

The consciousness of clean linen is in and of itself a source of moral strength only second to that of a clean conscience. A well-ironed collar, or a fresh glove, has carried many a man through the emergency in which a wrinkle or a rip would have defeated him. *E. S. Phelps.*

Grant me, O sweet and loving Jesus, to rest in Thee, above all other creatures, above all health and beauty, above all glory and honour, above all power and dignity, above all knowledge and subtlety, above all riches and arts, above all joy and gladness, above all fame and praise, above all sweetness and comfort, above all hope and promise, above all desert and desire, above all gifts and benefits that Thou canst give and impart unto us, above all mirth and joy that the mind of man can receive and feel; finally, above angels and archangels, and above all the heavenly host, above all things visible and invisible, and above all that Thou art not, O my God. *Thomas à Kempis.*

Within that awful volume lies
The mystery of mysteries!

. . . .

And better had they ne'er been born,
Who read to doubt, or read to scorn.

Scott.

The paths of glory lead but to the grave.
Gray's Elegy.

A dull mind, once arriving at an inference that flatters a desire, is rarely able to retain the impression that the notion from which the inference started was purely problematic. *George Eliot.*

Sometimes, I think, the things we see
Are shadows of the things to be:
    That what we plan we build;
That every hope that hath been crossed,
And every dream we thought was lost,
    In Heaven shall be fulfilled.

Phoebe Cary.

Life! we have been long together,
Through pleasant and through cloudy weather;
'Tis hard to part when friends are dear;
Perhaps 'twill cost a sigh, a tear;
Then steal away, give little warning,
Choose thine own time:
Say not "Good night," but in some brighter clime
Bid me "Good mornin." *Mrs. Barbauld.*

The love of Ophelia, which she never once confesses, is like a secret which we have stolen from her, and which ought to die upon our hearts as upon her own.
Mrs. Jamison.

When love and skill work together, expect a masterpiece.   *Charles Reade.*

Love feels no burden, thinks nothing of trouble, attempts what is above its strength, pleads no excuse of impossibility; for it thinks all things lawful for itself, and all things possible.

It is therefore able to undertake all things, and it completes many things, and brings them to a conclusion, where he who does not love, faints and lies down.
Thomas à Kempis.

Shall I, wasting in despair,
Die because a woman's fair?
Or make pale my cheeks with care,
'Cause another's rosy are?

Be she fairer than the day,
Or the flowery meads in May,
If she be not so to me,
What care I how fair she be?
George Wither.

I could not love thee, dear, so much,
Loved I not honor more.
Richard Lovelace.

Where true love has found a home, every new year forms one more ring around the hearts of those who love each other, so that in the end they cannot live apart.   *Julius Stinde.*

Fain would I climb, yet fear I to fall.
Sir Walter Raleigh.

If thy heart fails thee, climb not at all.
Queen Elizabeth's reply.

No mistress of the hidden skill,
No wizard gaunt and grim,
Went up by night on heath or hill
To read the stars for him;
But the merriest maid in all the land
Of vine-encircled France
Bestowed upon his brow and hand
Her philosophic glance:
"I bind thee with a spell," said she,
"I sign thee with a sign;
No woman's love shall light on thee,
No woman's heart be thine!"
Mrs. Hemans, The Child's Destiny.

I remember, I remember,
How my childhood fleeted by
The mirth of its December,
And the warmth of its July.
W. M. Praed.

I love it, I love it, and who shall dare
To chide me for loving that old arm-chair?   *Eliza Cook.*

Oft in the stilly night,
Ere slumber's chain has bound me,
Fond memory brings the light
Of others days around me!
The smiles, the tears

Of boyhood's years,
The words of love then spoken;
The eyes that shone,
Now dimmed and gone,
The cheerful hearts now broken!

. . . .

I feel like one
Who treads alone
Some banquet-hall deserted,
Whose lights are fled,
Whose garlands dead,
And all but he departed!
Thomas Moore.

The old oaken bucket, the iron-bound bucket,
The moss-covered bucket, which hung in the well.   *Samuel Woodworth.*

Near the lake where drooped the willow,
Long time ago!   *George P. Morris.*
Woodman, spare that tree!
Touch not a single bough!
In youth it sheltered me,
And I'll protect it now.
George P. Morris.

When the sun sinks to rest,
And the star of the west
Sheds its soft silver light o'er the sea,
What sweet thoughts arise,
As the dim twilight dies—
For then I am thinking of thee!
O! then crowding fast
Come the joys of the past,
Through the dimness of days long gone by,
Like the stars peeping out,
Through the darkness about,
From the soft silent depth of the sky.

And thus, as the night
Grows more lovely and bright
With the clustering of planet and star,
So this darkness of mine
Wins a radiance divine
From the light that still lingers afar.
Then welcome the night,
With its soft holy light!
In its silence my heart is more free
The rude world to forget,
Where no pleasure I've met
Since the hour that I parted from thee.
Samuel Lover.

Through days of sorrow and of mirth,
Through days of death and days of birth,
Through every swift vicissitude
Of changeful time, unchanged it has stood.
And as if, like God, it all things saw,
It calmly repeats those words of awe—
"Forever—never!
Never—forever!"
Longfellow, The Old Clock.

Stone walls do not a prison make,
  Nor iron bars a cage;
Minds innocent and quiet take
  That for an hermitage.
                    Richard Lovelace.

Could we forbear dispute and practice
    love,
We should agree as angels do above.
                    Waller.

I hold every man a debtor to his profession; from the which as men of course do seek to receive countenance and profit, so ought they of duty to endeavor themselves by way of amends to be a help and ornament thereunto.   *Bacon.*

Music hath charms to soothe the savage
    breast,
To soft'n rocks, or bend a knotted oak,
By magic numbers and persuasive sound.
                    Congreve.

When Music, heavenly maid, was young,
While yet in early Greece she sung.

Filled with fury, rapt, inspired,

'Twas sad by fits, by starts 'twas wild.

In notes by distance made more sweet,
In hollow murmurs died away.

O Music! sphere-descended maid,
Friend of pleasure, wisdom's aid.
      William Collins, Ode to the Passions.

  Come forth unto the light of things,
  Let Nature be your teacher.

  . . . .

  One impulse from a vernal wood
  May teach you more of man,
  Of moral evil and of good,
    Than all the sages can. *Wordsworth.*

The melancholy days are come, the saddest of the year,
Of wailing winds, and naked woods, and
    meadows brown and sere.
Heaped in the hollows of the grove the
    withered leaves lie dead,
They rustle to the eddying gust, and to
    the rabbit's tread.   *W. C. Bryant.*

  Nature, before it has been touched by man, is almost always beautiful, strong, and cheerful in man's eyes; but nature, when he has once given it his culture and then forsakes it, has usually an air of sorrow and helplessness. He has made it live the more by laying his hand upon it, and touching it with his life. It has come to relish of his humanity, and it is so flavored with his thoughts, and ordered and permeated by his spirit, that if the stimulus of his presence is withdrawn it cannot for a long while do without him, and live for itself as fully and as well as it did before. *Jean Ingelow.*

The sea! the sea! the open sea!
The blue, the fresh, the ever free!
Without a mark, without a bound,
It runneth the earth's wide region round.

  . . . .

I never was on the dull, tame shore,
But I loved the great sea more and more,
And backward flew to her billowy breast,
Like a bird that seeketh its mother's
    nest.   *Bryan W. Procter.*

Like a spear of flame the cardinal flower
Burned out along the meadow.   *Eddy.*

  A strong nor'wester's blowing, Bill;
    Hark! don't ye hear it roar now!
  Lord help 'em, how I pities them
    Unhappy folks on shore now!
    William Pitt, The Sailor's Consolation.

Dearest, has Heaven aught to give thee
    more?
  I thought the while I watched her
    changing face,
  Heard her fine tones and marked her
    gestures' grace—
Yea, one more gift is left all gifts before.

We go our separate ways on earth, and
    pain,
  God's shaping chisel, waits us as the
    rest,
  With nobler charm thy beauty to invest,
And make thee lovelier ere we meet again.
                    Celia Thaxter

Not perfect, nay, but full of tender wants
No angel, but a dearer being, all dipt
In angel instincts, breathing Paradise.
                    Tennyson.

  Sink or swim, live or die, survive or perish, I give my heart and my hand to this vote.   *Webster.*

  The Guard dies, but never surrenders.
                    Rougemont.

  There is one certain means by which I can be sure never to see my country's ruin—*I will die in the last ditch.*
                    William of Orange.

  Cæsar had his Brutus—Charles the First, his Cromwell—and George the Third ("Treason!" cried the Speaker)—*may profit by their example.* If *this* be treason, make the most of it.
                    Patrick Henry, Speech, 1765.

Praise the Power that hath made and
    preserved us a nation!
Then conquer we must, when our cause
    it is just,
And this be our motto: "In God is our
    trust;"
And the star-spangled banner, O long may
    it wave
O'er the land of the free, and the home
    of the brave.   *Francis Scott Key.*

Forever floats that standard sheet!
  Where breathes the foe but falls before
    us,
With Freedom's soil beneath our feet,
  And Freedom's banner streaming o'er
    us.   *Joseph Rodman Drake.*

Give me liberty or give me death!
              Patrick Henry.

A song for our banner? The watchword
  recall
Which gave the Republic her station:
"United we stand—divided we fall!"
It made and preserves us a nation!
The union of lakes—the union of lands—
  The union of States none can sever—
The union of hearts, the union of hands—
  And the flag of our Union forever!
              George P. Morris.

O rally 'round the flag, boys, rally once
  again,
  Shouting the battle-cry of Freedom.
              George F. Root.

We join ourselves to no party that does
not carry the flag and keep step to the
music of the Union.   *Rufus Choate.*

  When can their glory fade?
  Oh! the wild charge they made!
    All the world wondered.
  Honour the charge they made!
  Honour the Light Brigade,
    Noble six hundred!   *Tennyson.*

And he gave it as his opinion, that
whoever could make two ears of corn, or
two blades of grass, to grow upon a spot
of ground where only one grew before,
would deserve better of mankind, and
do more essential service to his country,
than the whole race of politicians put together.   *Swift, Gulliver's Travels.*

I never could believe that Providence
had sent a few men into the world ready
booted and spurred to ride, and millions
ready saddled and bridled to be ridden.
  Richard Rumbold, on the scaffold.

Millions for defense, but not one cent
for tribute.   *C. C. Pinckney.*

To the memory of the man, first in
war, first in peace, and first in the hearts
of his country.   *General Henry Lee.*

But whether on the scaffold high,
  Or in the battle's van,
The fittest place where man can die
  Is where he dies for man.
              Michael J. Barry.

Let the soldier be abroad if he will, he
can do nothing in this age. There is another personage, a personage less imposing in the eyes of some, perhaps insignificant. The schoolmaster is abroad, and I

trust to him, armed with his primer,
against the soldier in full military array.
              Lord Brougham.

O for a seat in some poetic nook,
Just hid with trees, and sparkling with a
  brook.   *Leigh Hunt.*

In winter, when the dismal rain
  Came slanting down in lines,
And Wind, that grand old harper, smote
  His thunder-harp of pines.
              Alexander Smith.

There were two or three pretty faces
among the female singers, to which the
keen air of a frosty morning had given a
bright rosy tint; but the gentlemen choristers
had evidently been chosen, like old Cremona fiddles, more for tone than looks;
and as several had to sing from the same
book, there were clusterings of odd phys-
iognomies, not unlike those groups of
cherubs we sometimes see on country
tombstones.   *Irving.*

Seemed washing his hands with invisible
  soap
  In imperceptible water.   *Hood.*

Reason is the life of the law; nay, the
common law itself is nothing else but
reason. . . . The law which is the
perfection of reason.   *Coke.*

      Remorse—she ne'er forsakes us—
A bloodhound staunch—she tracks our
  rapid step
Through the wild labyrinth of youthful
  frenzy,
Unheard, perchance, until old age hath
  tamed us;
Then in our lair, when Time hath chilled
  our joints,
And maimed our hope of combat, or of
  flight,
We hear her deep-mouthed bay, announcing all
Of wrath, and woe, and punishment that
  bides us.   *Old Play*

Do what lieth in thy power, and God
will assist in thy good will.
              Thomas à Kempis.

Weep no more, lady, weep no more,
  Thy sorrow is in vain;
For violets plucked, the sweetest showers
  Will ne'er make grow again.
              John Fletcher.

God will not give any soldier ammunition who is not willing to go into battle.   *Anon.*

What does little baby say,
In her bed at peep of day?
Baby says, like little birdie,
Let me rise and fly away.

Baby, sleep a little longer,
Till the little limbs are stronger.
If she sleeps a little longer
Baby, too, shall fly away.
Tennyson, Cradle Song in Sea Dreams.

Sweet and low, sweet and low,
Wind of the western sea,
Low, low, breathe and blow,
Wind of the western sea!
Over the rolling waters go,
Come from the dying moon and blow,
Blow him again to me:
While my little one, while my pretty one,
sleeps.

Sleep and rest, sleep and rest,
Father will come to thee soon;
Rest, rest, on mother's breast,
Father will come to thee soon;
Father will come to his babe in the nest,
Silver sails all out of the west,
Under the silver moon:
Sleep, my little one, sleep, my pretty one,
sleep. *Tennyson, The Princess.*

Were I to adopt a pet idea as so many people do, and fondle it in my embraces to the exclusion of all others, it would be, that the great want which mankind labors under at this present period is sleep. The world should recline its vast head on the first convenient pillow and take an age-long nap. It has gone distracted through a morbid activity, and, while preternaturally wide awake, is nevertheless tormented by visions that seem real to it now, but would assume their true aspect and character were all things once set right by an interval of sound repose.
Hawthorne, Mosses from an Old Manse.

Oh! would I were dead now
Or up in my bed now,
To cover my head now,
And have a good cry!
Thomas Hood.

When death, the great Reconciler, has come, it is never our tenderness that we repent of, but our severity. *George Eliot.*

My best thoughts always come a little too late. *Hawthorne.*

Thought is deeper than all speech;
Feeling deeper than all thought;
Souls to souls can never teach
What unto themselves was taught.
Christopher P. Cranch.

Too late I stayed—forgive the crime—
Unheeded flew the hours;
How noiseless falls the foot of time,
That only treads on flowers.
Wm. Robt. Spencer.

Gather ye rosebuds while ye may,
Old Time is still a-flying,
And this same flower that smiles to-day,
To-morrow may be dying.
Robert Herrick.

O! a wonderful stream is the river Time,
As it runs through the realm of tears!
With a faultless rhythm, and a musical rhyme,
And a broader sweep and a surge sublime,
As it blends in the ocean of years!
B. F. Taylor.

By Woden, God of Saxons,
From whom comes Wensday, that is, Wednesday,
Truth is a thing that I will ever keep
Unto thylke day in which I creep into
My sepulcre. *Cartwright's Ordinary.*

O God, who art the truth, make me one with Thee in everlasting love.
Thomas à Kempis.

LEGAL
DICTIONARY

LEGAL DICTIONARY

COMPILED BY

M. H. GUANDOLA

ABBREVIATIONS

Abb.	Abbreviation.	m.	male.
Coll.	Colloquial.	pl.	plural.
E., Eng.	England.	sing.	singular.
f.	female.	U.S.	United States

A

A.A.C. (Abb.) Anno ante Christum (year before Christ).

A Aver et Tener. To have and to hold.

Ab., Abr. (Abb.). Abridgment.

A.B.A. (Abb.). American Bar Association.

A.C. (Abb.). Anno Christi (year of Christ).

A/C. Account.

Abactor. One who steals cattle in large numbers.

Ab Agendo. Unable to act.

Abandon. To relinquish rights to an object; to desert, forsake or surrender.

Abandum. That which is proscribed or abandoned.

Ab Ante, Ab Antecedented. In advance.

Ab Antiquo. From antiquity.

Abarnare. Exposure of a secret crime.

Abatare. To abate, put an end to, reduce.

Abate. Quash, beat down, destroy; to nullify, lessen or diminish.

Abatement. Reduction, decrease or diminution.

Abatement of Taxes. Reduction of a tax either before or after payment.

Abatement, Plea in. Dilatory plea in procedural law asking for abatement of the action for reasons not connected with the controversy.

Abator. One who occupies property without right of title, before the heir.

Ab Auctoritate. From authority.

Abatuda. Anything diminished.

Abbettator. One who abets.

Abbey. Monastery or convent.

Abbot. Spiritual superior of a monastery.

Abbreviate. An abstract.

Abbreviate of Adjudication. An abstract of judgment.

Abbrochment. Forestalling the market by buying up commodities wholesale for selling at retail.

Abdication. Voluntary surrender of rights to the throne by a reigning monarch.

Abdicatio Tutelae. Resignation of a guardian.

Abditorium. Hiding place for valuables.

Abduction. Taking away of wife, child or ward by fraud, persuasion or violence.

Abearance. Behavior.

Aberemurder. Intentional murder.

Abet. To aid or assist.

Abettare. To aid or abet.

Abettor. One who instigates a crime; one who incites another to commit a crime, thus becoming a principal.

Ab Extra. From without.

Abeyance. In expectation, remembrance and contemplation of law.

Abiactus, Aviactus. Grandson.

Abide. To obey, comply with, execute, conform to.

Abide by. To stand by the consequences of one's actions.

Abiding Conviction. A definite conviction of the guilt of the accused.

Abiding Faith. Belief in the guilt of the accused which remains in the minds of the jury.

Abigeat. Crime of stealing cattle.

Abigeatore. Cattle thief.

Ability. In legal terminology, usually refers to pecuniary ability.

Ab Inconvenienti. From hardship.

Ab Initio. From the beginning.

Ab Intestate. From a decedent who dies without leaving a will.

Ab Invito. Against one's will.

Ab Irato. Done in anger.

Abishering. Freedom and exemptions from forfeitures and amercements.

Abjudicate. To deprive by a judgment of the court.

Abjuration. Renunciation or abandonment by oath.

Abjuration of Allegiance. Declaration by a naturalized citizen of U.S., whereby he renounces and abjures all fidelities and allegiances which he owes to any foreign power.

Abjure. Renounce.

Able. Legally qualified.

Able-Bodied. Absence of visible defects which incapacitate a person from performing ordinary duties.

Able Buyer. One who has actual cash to meet payment.

Able Customer. One has the actual cash to make required payment and who can meet deferred payments.

Able Seaman. Grade of merchant seaman.

Ablocate. To lease.

Ablocatio. Leasing for money.

Abnegation. Renunciation; self-denial; abjuration.

Abode. Place of residence.

Ab Olim. Formerly.

Abolish. To annul.

Abolitio Legis. Repeal of a law.

Abolition. Leave to stop a prosecution; annihilation or extinguishment of anything.

Abomination. Anything wicked.

Aborage. Collision of vessels.

Aborticide. Killing of the fetus in the uterus.

Abortifacient. Any drug used to produce an abortion.

Abortion. Expulsion of a human fetus before time of viability.

Abortionist. One who practices the crime of producing abortions.

Abortive Trial. A trial in which no verdict is reached due to no fault of the parties.

Abortus. An aborted fetus.

About. Near in time, quality, quantity or degree.

Above Cited. Quoted before.

Abridge. Reduce or cut down.

Abridgment. Condensation of the work of another.

Abridgment of Damages. Reduction of damages by order of court.

Abrogate. Annul.

Abrogatio Legis. Repeal of a law.

Abrogation. Repeal of a law; an annulment.

Abscond. Clandestine withdrawal of one's self in order to avoid legal proceedings.

Absent. Being away from.

Absentee. One who is not present at his usual place of residence.

Absente Reo. In the absence of the defendant.

Absolute. Free from condition or qualification; perfect.

Absolute Assignment. Outright transfer of title.

Absolute Contraband. Munitions and primary material of war.

Absolute Control. Freedom to act without hindrance or direction by others.

Absolute Law. Immutable law of nature.

Absolute Majority. More than half of those entitled to vote on an issue.

Absolutely. Wholly; completely.

Absolution. A judgment of the court declaring a defendant innocent.

Absolutism. Principle of absolute power in the sovereign.

Absolve. To free or release from obligation, debt or responsibility.

Absolvitor. Acquittal.

Absque. Without.

Abstract. An abridgment; a complete history in abbreviated form of the case as found in the record.

Abstract Instruction. Instructions to the jury amounting to an abstract statement of the law.

Abstract of Title. An historical summary to the title of land covering all conveyances, transfers and other facts of title, together with all such facts appearing of record as may impair the title.

Abstract Question. Moot question.

Absurdity. That which is physically and morally impossible.

Abuse. To injure, misuse; excessive or improper use of a legal right.

Abut. To reach, to touch.

Abutments. Parts of a bridge which support the extremes.

Abuttals. Boundaries at which lands touch neighboring lands.

Abutting Owners. Owners whose lands touch a highway or other public place.

Accede. To attain an office or dignity.

Acceleration. Shortening of the time within which a future estate is to vest.

Accept. To agree by some overt act to the terms of a contract.

Acceptance. The actual or implied taking and receiving of that which is offered.

Acceptance of Bill of Exchange. A promise to pay the bill when due.

Acceptare. To accept.

Access. The power of approaching; (sometimes used in reference to the right of sexual intercourse between husband and wife).

Accessary. See Accessory.

Accession. The addition by natural or artificial means of new matter to one's property.

Accessorial. Pertaining to a principal thing.

Accessory. One who encourages or incites another to commit a crime.

Accessory after the Fact. One who, knowing a crime to have been committed, aids or assists the felon in any way.

Accessory before the Fact. One who contributes to the commission of a crime by will, although not present at the time of the act.

Accident. An unforseen, unplanned, unexpected event.

Accidental. Happening by chance.

Accommodation. Acceptance of an obligation without consideration.

Accommodation Paper. A loan without restriction as to its use.

Accommodation Party. One who has signed a negotiable instrument as maker, drawer, acceptor or indorser, without receiving value therefor, and for the purpose of lending his name to some other party.

Accomplice. One who knowingly and willingly participates in the planning or carrying out of a crime.

Accord. Mutual agreement.

Account. To render a detailed statement of a transaction; the statement so rendered.

Accountable. Liable; responsible.

Accountable Receipt. Acknowledgment of the receipt of money or property by a person who is under obligation to account therefor.

Accountant. One skilled in keeping books or accounts.

Account Book. Ledger in which is kept the record of commercial transactions.

Account Current. A running account.

Accounts Receivable. Amounts owing to a person on an open account.

Accouple. To unite or marry.

Accredit. To acknowledge a diplomatic agent and give him credentials and rank accord-

Accredulitare. To clear a person of an offense by oath.

Accrescere. To increase or grow.

Accretion. Addition to land by natural causes, such as deposits.

Accroach. The exercising of power without due authority.

Accrocher. To delay.

Accrual of Cause of Action. The coming into existence of the right to sue.

Accrue. To increase or augment.

Accumulated Surplus. Funds which a corporation has in excess of its capital and liabilities.

Accumulations. Requirement that profits from a fund or trust be invested for a definite period.

Accumulative. Additional; one thing added to another.

Accumulative Judgment. A judgment which is to take effect upon the expiration of a prior judgment.

Accusation. A complaint; formal charge.

Accuse. To formally charge one of being guilty of a punishable offense.

Accused. The defendant in a criminal case.

Accustomed. Habitual; used.

Acknowledge. To own, avow or admit; to confess.

Acknowledgment. Admission or confirmation.

A Consiliis. Of counsel.

Acquaintance. Familiar knowledge.

Acquest. Property acquired other than by inheritance.

Acquiesce. Consent implied by silence.

Acquit. To set free; to discharge from an accusation.

Acquittal. Verdict of not guilty; release from pecuniary liability.

Acquittance. Written confirmation of payment of money due.

Acre. 160 square rods of land.

Ac si. As if.

Act. That which is done; a statute.

Acting. Substituting; taking the place of temporarily.

Actio. An action or suit; a right or cause of action.

Act of God. An act caused solely by violence of nature.

Actionize. To use.

Acts of Congress. Statutes passed by the Congress of the U.S. as opposed to resolutions or other Congressional acts.

Actual. Real; substantial.

Actum. A deed; something done.

A.D. (Abb.). Anno Domini (from the Year of our Lord).

A Dato. From the date.

Ad Colligendum. Of an administrator or trustee, for collecting.

Ad Culpam. Until misbehavior.

Ad Damnum. To the damage.

Ad Exitum. At issue.

Addicere. To condemn.

Addict. One who is in the habit of using alcohol or narcotics to the point of losing self-control.

Addiction. Formal commission of a prisoner by judicial sentence.

Ad Diem. At the day.

Addition. That which is added to another thing; extension; increase.

Adduce. To bring forward; to present.

Adeem. To revoke.

Ademption. Revocatio of a legacy by act of the testator.

Adeo. So far.

Adeprimes. In the first place.

Adequate. Sufficient.

Aderere. In arrears.

Adesse. To be present.

Adeu. Without day, implying dismissal of a matter from court.

Adevant. Before.

Ad Exitum. At the end.

Ad Extremum. Finally.

Ad Faciendum. To make or do.

Ad Fidem. An allegiance.

Adhibere. To apply, employ or use.

Adhibere Diligentiam. To employ care.

Adhibere Vim. To use force.

Ad Hoc. To this.

Ad Hominem. To the man; personal.

Ad Idem. To the same thing (agreement).

Adieu. See Adeu.

Ad Illud. To that.

Adimere. To remove.

Ad Infinitum. Without end.

Ad Inquirendum. To inquire.

Ad Instantiam. At the instance.

Ad Interim. Meanwhile.

Adiratus. Lost.

Aditus. An approach; right of entrance.

Adjacent. Lying near but not necessarily touching.

Adjectire. To summon to court.

Adjective Law. Rules of procedure and court organization.

Adjoining. Contiguous as opposed to adjacent.

Adjourn. To postpone or defer.

Adjourned Term. A term of court continued at a later date.

Adjudge. To make a judicial decision.

Adjudicare. To deprive by judgment of a court.

Adjudication. A judgment or decree in a cause.

Adjunct. Something added to another.

Adjunction. Uniting of a thing belonging to one person to that of another.

Adjuration. Placing under oath.

Adjurnare. To adjourn.

Adjust. To settle.

Adjuster. One who ascertains the extent of a claim.

Adjustment. Arrangement or settlement, usually applied to insurance.

Adjutor. Helper or assistant.

Ad Largum. At large.

Ad Libitum. At pleasure.

Ad Litem. During the interim of an action or proceeding, e.g. appointment of a guardian for a minor.

Ad Majus. For the greater.

Ad Manum. At hand.

Admeasurement. Assignment or apportionment of one's share; a division.

Ad Melius Inquirendum. Writ of further inquiry.

Adminicular. Corroborative.

Administer. To take charge, manage or conduct.

Administration. The managing or conduct of anything.

Administation of Estates. Supervision by an executor or administrator.

Administrative Law. That branch of law which deals with the activities of executive or administrative agencies.

Administrator (m.) **Administratrix** (f.). One given the authority by court to settle the estate of a decedent.

Administrator ad Colligendum. One appointed to temporarily preserve the estate of a decedent.

Admiralty. Court having jurisdiction in civil and criminal maritime cases.

Admissable Evidence. Evidence which, in the opinion of the court, may properly be introduced.

Admission. Acknowledgment made by a party of the existence of certain facts; recognition of attorneys and counsellors as officers of the court.

Ad Modum. In such a way.

Asmonition. Cautionary statement by judge in his advice to the accused or his charge to the jury.

Admr. (Abb.). Administrator.

Adnihilare. To annul.

Adolescence. Period between childhood and maturity (f. 12–21; m. 14–25).

Adopt. To accept as one's own that which was not so originally.

Adoptivus. Adopted child or parent.

Adpromissor. A surety.

Adquieto. Payment.

Adquirere. To acquire.

Adrectare. To corrent.

Ad Respondendum. To respond.

Adrogation. Adoption of a child who has not reached the age of puberty.

Adscendentes. Ancestors.

Adscriptus. Annexed by writing.

Ad Sectam. At the suit of.

Adsecurare. To assure; to insure.

Adsessores. Judges appointed as substitutes or advisors to the regular magistrates.

Adsignare. To seal.

Ad Testari. To attest.

Adult. One who has attained the legal age, usually twenty-one years.

Adulter. One who corrupts.

Adultera. Adulteress.

Adulterated. Impure.

Adulteration. Mixing of a foreign substance with something pure, usually applied to food and beverage sold to the public.

Adulterine. Issue of adulterous intercourse.

Adultery. Voluntary sexual intercourse of a married person with one other than his or her spouse.

Ad Valorem. According to the value.

Advance. Rendering before due.

Advancement. Money or property given by a parent to child. not required by law, which represents part of the whole of the recipient's share of the donor's estate.

Advances. Payments made before they are due.

Advena. Unnaturalized alien.

Adverse. Opposed.

Adverse Possession. Open occupation of real property without title or permission of the person holding title.

Advertise. To give public notice.

Advertisement. Publication of information designed to attract public attention.

Advice. Counsel.

Advise. To give an opinion.

Advisedly. With deliberation.

Advisement. Consideration.

Advisory. By way of suggestion; not imperative.

Advisory Opinion. Opinion rendered by a court to a lower court or legislature, being neither binding nor decisive.

Advocare. To defend.

Advocate. One who pleads the cause of another in court.

Aequitas. Equity.

Aequum et Bonum. Fair and good.

Aequus. Equal.

Aeronautics. The science of flying in the air.

Aes Alienum. Debt.

Aesnecia. See Esnecy.

Aesthetic. Relating to that which is beautiful or in good taste.

Aetas. Age.

Affect. To act upon.

Affected with a Public Interest. Phrase applied to a business whose activities are deemed vital to the public and, therefore, its use in effect granted to the public.

Affectus. Intention.

Affere. To appraise.

Affiance. To engage to marry.

Affiant. One who makes an affidavit.

Affidare. To swear.

Affidavit. Voluntary oath in writing sworn to before one authorized to administer oaths or affirmations.

Affilare. To put on record.

Affile. To file.

Affiliate. The state of being close to, allied with or united.

Affines. Relatives by marriage.

Affinity. Relationship of a husband to the blood relatives of his wife and vice versa.

Affirm. To ratify; confirm; reassert.

Affirmation. A solemn and formal declaration, substituted for a sworn statement by one whose beliefs will not permit him to swear.

Affirmative. That which declares as a fact.

Affirmative Defense. One which, assuming the complaint to be true, sets up new matter constituting a defense outside the ordinary scope of denial, e.g. Act of God.

Affirmative Statute. Mandatory rather than prohibitive.

Affix. Fasten or attack physically.

Affliction. Distriss of mind or body.

Afforare. To set a price.

Afforce. To add to; to increase.

Afforer. To assess.

Afforest. To make into a forest, in a legal sense.

Affranchir, Affranchise. To free.

Affray. Fighting of two or more persons in a public place.

Affreightment. Contract for the hiring of a ship.

Affront. Insult.

Aforesaid. Already said or mentioned.

Aforethought. Premeditated.

A Fortiori. With greater reason.

After. Later; succeeding.

After-Acquired. Acquired after a certain date or event.

After-Born Child. Child born after the testator has made his will.

Against. Adverse to.

Age. Number of years which a person has lived.

Agency. Contract by which one person acts for or represents another by the latter's authority.

Agenda. Things to be done.

Agenesia. Sexual impotence.

Agens. Manager; plaintiff.

Agent. One intrusted with another's business and given the authority to act for him.

Age of Consent. Age at which a statue presumes a girl capable of agreeing to the sexual act.

Aggravated Assault. Malicious assault.

Aggrevation. Any circumstance which increases the gravity of an offense.

Aggregate. Entire number.

Aggressor. One who initiates hostile force.

Aggrieved. Injured.

Aggrieved Party. Party whose rights have been damaged by a judgement.

Agiser. To lie.

Agist. To feed or pasture another's cattle for a fee.

Agitator. One who stirs up.

Agnates, Agnation. Relationship by the father's side.

Agnise. To acknowledge, admit.

Agnomen. Nickname.

Agony. Violent physical or mental distress.

Agrarian. Pertaining to land.

A Gratia. By gratuity.

Agree. To give mutual assent.

Agricultural. Pertaining to agriculture.

Agriculture. Science of cultivating the ground.

Aid. Support; help; assist.

Aid and Abet. To assist in the commission of a crime.

Ail. Grandfather.

Ailment. Indisposition of body or mind.

Air. Atmosphere. See Easement of Light and Air.

Aisne, Eigne. Eldest or first born.

A Latere. Collaterally.

Alcholic Liquor. Beverage, which when drunk excessively, will produce intoxication.

Alcoholism. Addiction to the excessive use of intoxicating beverages.

Alderman. Judicial or administrative magistrate.

Ale. An intoxicating liquor made from an infusion of malt by fermentation.

Alea. Game of chance.

Aleator. Gambler.

Aleatory. Uncertain.

Aleager. To redress.

Alia. Other things.

Aliamenta. Freedom of passage.

Alias. Otherwise or also known as.

Alias Writ. A second writ.

Alibi. Usually a defense plea stating at the time of the crime the accused was elsewhere or in another place.

Alien. Foreigner; one who is not a citizen.

Alien. To transfer.

Alienable. Lawfully transferable.

Alien and Sedition Laws. Four acts of Federalist Congress in July, 1798 imposing penalties on conspirators against government measures.

Alienate. To transfer title to property; to cause one to lose affection for a spouse.

Alienation of Affections. Causing a spouse to lose the society, affections and assistance of his marital partner.

Alien Enemy. One owing allegiance to an enemy state.

Alieni Generis. Of another kind.

Alieni Juris. Subject to the authority of another person.

Alimenta. Necessities of Life.

Alimony. The support of a wife by her husband required by order of the court on divorce or separation.

Alimony in Gross. Alimony awarded in a gross sum rather than periodically.

Aliquid. Something; somewhat.

Aliquis. Anyone.

Aliquot. Fraction of the whole.

Aliter. Otherwise.

Aliud Examen. Another trial.

Aliunde. From another source.

All and Singular. Without exception.

Allegation. An assertion, declaration or statement of fact in a pleading.

Allege. To assert or charge; to make an allegation.

Alleged. Claimed; asserted; charged.

Allegiare. To defend one's self.

Alliance. Banding together.

Allocate. To allot.

Allocatur. It is allowed.

Allocution. The inquiry made of a defendent after a verdict of guilty as to whether he has anything to say as to why the court should not pronounce sentence against him.

Alloidal. Free.

Allot. To distribute.

Allotment. Share, portion.

Allow. To approve.

Allowance. Authorization of payments in legal proceedings; a deduction; **average** payment; portion allowed.

Alloy. In coining, a cheaper metal mixed with

gold or silver the amount being fixed by law.

Alms. Charitable donations.

Also. Besides; in addition; likewise.

Alter. To change.

Alteration. Making different.

Altercation. Angry dispute.

Alter Ego. Second self.

Alternatim. Interchangeably.

Alternative. Choice between two things or acts.

Alteruter. One of two; either.

A.M. (Abb). Ante meridem; before noon.

Amalgemation. Consolidation.

Ambassador. Diplomatic agent of a country representing that country in a foreign state.

Ambulance Chaser. Lawyer who makes a practice of following up accidents, inducing injured persons to sue for damages.

Ambiguity. Doubleness of meaning; doubtful.

Ambit. Boundary line.

Amblotic. Anything used to produce an abortion.

Ambulatory. Revocable; movable.

Ameliorations. Improvements.

Amenable. Subject to answer to the law.

Amend. To change for the better.

Amendment. Addition or change.

Amends. Satisfaction for an injury.

Amentia. Insanity.

Amercement. Pecuniary fine assessed by a court.

American. Pertaining to the Western Hemisphere.

Ami. Friend.

Amicable. Friendly.

Amicable Action. Action brought to court with the agreement of all parties to obtain a decision on doubtful questions of law.

Amicus Curiae. Friend of the court.

Amittere. To lose.

Amnesia. Loss of memory.

Amnesty. An act of government granting general pardon to certain classes of people for past, usually political, crimes.

Amortize. To provide for the paying off of a liability; to transfer lands in mortmain.

Amotion. Eviction.

Ampliare. To enlarge.

Anaesthetic. Any drug producing insensibility to pain.

Anagraph. Inventory.

Analytical Jurisprudence. A system of jurisprudence based upon analysis of existing legal theories and institutions rather than principles of right and equity.

Anarchy. Absence of government.

A Nativitate. From birth.

Anatocism. Compound interest.

Ancestor. One from whom a person is lineally descended.

Ancient Deeds. Deeds more than 30 years old.

Ancillary. Auxiliary; aiding.

Androgyne. Hermaphrodite.

Andromania. Nymphomania.

Androphonomania. Homicidal insanity.

Anew. Over again.

Anguish. Extreme pain of body or mind.

Aniens. Null; void.

Animal. Irrational, sentient being.

Animo. With intent.

Annex. To attach to.

Anni Nubiles. The age of marriage for a girl.

Anno Domini. In the year of our Lord.

Annoyance. Nuisance; vexation.

Annual. Of or pertaining to a year.

Annuity. Yearly payment of money to another in fee for life or years.

Annul. To make void.

Annus. A year.

Annuum. Yearly pension.

Anomalous. Deviating from the common rule.

Anonymous. Nameless.

Answer. A plea by which a defendent resists an allegation of facts.

Ante. Before.

Ante Bellum. Before the war.

Antecedent. Prior in point of time.

Antedate. To date an instrument prior to the date of actual execution.

Ante Litem. Before suit.

Antestari. To subpoena a witness.

Antichresis. A contract pledging real property as security for a debt.

Anticipation. The performance of an act before its proper time.

Antigraphy. A copy of a document.

Antinomy. Real or apparent inconsistency in a statute.

Antitrust Act. Statute forbidding the formation of monopolies.

Apertus. Open; unsealed.

Apex. Highest point.

Apex Juris. Legal subtlety.

Apocal, Apocha. Receipt for payment.

Apograph. Copy of a document.

Apographa, Apographia. An inventory.

A Posteriori. Reasoning from the effect to the cause.

App. (Abb.). Appellate.

App. Ct. (Abb.). Appellate Court.

Apparent. Obvious, e.g. apparent danger or obvious danger.

Apparent Authority. Authority which a principal permits his agent to exercise or which he holds the agent out as possessing.

Appeal. Complaint to a superior court of an injustice or error committed by an inferior court.

Appearance. To be before a court as a party to a suit.

Appellant. One who files an appeal.

Appellate Court. Court which reviews appeals from inferior courts.

Appellee. One against whom a cause is appealed.

Appellor. One who prosecutes an appeal.

Append. To add or attach.

Appendant. Any right or thing of a subordinate nature which is permanently connected to a more worthy right or thing.

Appertaining. Belonging to.

Applicant. Petitioner.

Application. Request; petition.

Appoint. Designate; name; assign.

Appointee. One appointed for a particular office or duties.

Apportion. To divide proportionally.

Appraise, Appraisal. Estimation of value of property.

Appreciate. To increase in value.

Apprehend. To place in legal custody.

Approbate and Reprobate. To accept one part and reject another.

Appropriate. To make a thing one's own; to set apart for a particular use.

Approval. Sanction of a thing or an act of another.

Appurtenances. That which belongs to another thing, but which has not always belonged to it, e.g. addition of a barn to a piece of land.

A Priori. Reasoning from the cause to the effect.

Apt. Fit.

Apud. With; at; among.

Aqua. Water.

Aqua Ductus. Right to run water through the land of another.

A Quo. From which.

Arable Land. Land suitable for plowing.

Arbiter. Arbitrator; one chosen to settle a controversy.

Arbitrarily, Arbitrary. Unreasonably.

Arbitration. Submission of a disputed matter to private, unofficial persons.

Arbitrator. One chosen to settle disputes.

Archetype. Original document.

Archives. Repository of public records; the records themselves.

A Retro. In arrears.

Argument. A course of reasoning intended to establish belief.

Aristocracy. A government ruled by a class of men.

Arma. Arms; weapons.

Arraign. To summon a person to court to answer charges made against him in an indictment.

Array. The whole body of persons summoned for jury duty at the same time.

Arrears. Money past due in payment.

Arrest. To detain one by legal authority.

Arret. Decree of a court.

Arson. The felony of wilfully and maliciously burning the house of another.

Article. One of a series of clauses.

Articles. System of rules; a statute; written contract containing terms of agreement.

Articles of Agreement. A written contract.

Articulately. Article by article.

Artifice. Fraud; trick.

Artificial. See Artificial Person.

Artificial Boundary. Boundary erected by man.

Artificial Person. An entity created by law and given the attributes of a natural person, e.g. a corporation.

Ascendants. Ancestors.

Ascertain. To make certain; to fix.

Asexualization. Sterilization.

Ask. To petition.

Aspersion. Defamation; criticism.

Asportation. Carrying away of personal property from one place to another.

Assailant. An aggressor.

Assassination. Murder committed for hire alone; murder committed by stealth or surprise.

Assault. An intentional, unlawful attempt to inflict immediate injury on another.

Assault and Battery. Assault is the attempt to strike; battery is the actual striking.

Assay. A test by chemical analysis of the purity of metals.

Assecurare. To give security.

Assembly. A meeting of a group of persons at the same place: persons so gathered.

Assent. Compliance.

Assess. To estimate the value of.

Assessed Value. Value of property as estimated for taxation.

Assets. Property which can be made available for the payment of debts.

Assign. To make over to another.

Assignation House. Brothel.

Assignment. The transfer of property or right from one person to another.

Assignor. Maker of an assignment.

Assist. To help or aid.

Assize. A jury or inquest; a court; a statute; a tax.

Association. A group of persons who have joined together to act for a common end.

Assume. To undertake; engage; promise.

Assumpsit. An agreement of service or payment to another, not under seal.

Assurance. Pledge, guaranty, surety; insurance.

Assurer. Insurer or underwriter.

Astipulate. To agree.

Asylum. A sanctuary.

At Arms Length. Careful to avoid being imposed upon.

At Bar. Before the court.

Atheist. One who denies the existence of a Supreme Being.

At Maturity. At the due date.

Atrocity. Conduct outrageously criminal or cruel.

Attach. To take, bind or fasten.

Attaché. One attached to a foreign legation or embassy.

Attachment. The taking of persons or property into legal custody by virtue of a writ, summons or other judicial order.

Attainder. The forfeiture of civil rights which occurs when a person is convicted of a capital offense.

Attendant Term. A mortgage or lease, the term of which has extended beyond the date of expiration.

Attest. To witness.

Attested Copy. A copy of a document which has been witnessed.

Attorn. To turn over a transfer to another.

Attorney. One authorized to act in the place of another to manage his matters of law.

Attorney General. Head of the Department of Justice.

Attorney at Large. Formerly an attorney who

LEGAL DICT

practiced in all courts.

Auction. Public sale of land or goods to the highest bidder.

Audience. A hearing.

Audit. To examine and verify figures and computations.

Auditor. Public agent who examines and verifys the accounts of those who have received and expended public money by lawful authority.

Aunt. Sister of one's father or mother.

Authentic. Properly attested.

Author. One who originates a literary work.

Authorize. To empower.

Autocracy. Self-government.

Autograph. One's handwriting.

Autopsy. The dissection of a dead body in order to ascertain cause of death.

Autre. Other.

Autrefois. Formerly.

Auxiliary. Collateral; incidental; aiding.

Avails. The proceeds or profits of a sale.

Aviation. The art of flying.

A Vinculo Matrimonii. From the bonds of matrimony.

Avoid. To annul.

Avoucher. To call upon a warrantor of lands to fulfill his undertaking.

Avow. To acknowledge and justify an act which has been committed.

Award. The decision of an arbitrator.

Award. To grant.

Axiom. Self-evident truth.

B

Baby Act. Plea of infancy as a defense.

Bachelor of Laws. Degree granted to one graduating from law school.

Back-Bond. Indemnity bond.

Backing. Indorsement.

Bad. Evil.

Bad Debt. One which is uncollectable.

Bail. Release of a person from legal custody after security has been given for his appearance to answer the charge against him at the designated time; the security thus given.

Bail Bond. Bond issued on behalf of a person who has been arrested in connection with a civil suit.

Bailiff. Keeper; protector; guardian; sheriff's deputy.

Bailiwick. District under jurisdiction of a bailiff.

Ban. Public edict or proclamation.

Bandit. Outlaw.

Bane. Malefactor.

Banishment. A penalty which consists of compelling a citizen to leave a city, place or country for a specific period of time or life.

Bank. An institution empowered to receive deposits of money, to discount negotiable paper and to lend money.

Bank Note. A promissory note issued by a bank payable to bearer on demand.

Bankruptcy. The state or condition of one who is unable to pay a debt without respect to time.

Bannitus. One who has been banished.

Banns of Marriage. Public announcement of an intended marriage.

Bar. Collective term for those persons licensed to practice law; obstruction to a suit or action.

Bar Association. Society composed of members of the bar.

Bargain. A contract or agreement between two parties, the one to sell goods or lands, the other to purchase them.

Barratry. Frequently stirring up quarrels and suits.

Barrenness. Sterility.

Barrister. An advocate learned in the law who is permitted to plead at the bar of England.

Barter. A contact whereby one commodity is exchanged for another.

Base Coin. Adulterated or alloyed coin.

Bastard. An illegitimate child.

Battery. Any unlawful touching or physical violence inflected on the person of another without his consent.

Bawd. One who procures opportunities for persons of opposite sexes to cohabit in an illicit manner.

Bawdy House. House of prostitution.

Beach. The area of land between ordinary high and low water marks.

Bearer. One in actual possession of a negotiable paper payable to bearer.

Beast. An animal.

Beat. To strike with successive blows; a subdivision of a county; a voting precinct.

Beaupleader. Fair pleading; a writ to prohibit exacting a fine for bad pleading.

Beget. To procreate.

Beggar. One who solicits alms.

Begin. To originate.

Behalf. Benefit; defense; in the name of.

Behavior. Manner of conducting one's self.

Belief. Conviction of the truth of a proposition existing in the mind and based on argument, persuasion or proof.

Belligerent. A nation, power or state engaged in war.

Belong. To be the property of.

Bench. A court; judges of the court.

Bench Warrant. Process issued by the court for the apprehension of a person either for contempt of court or a criminal offense.

Bene. Well; properly.

Beneficiary. One entitled to profit, benefit or advantage from a contract or estate; one to whom a policy of insurance is payable.

Benevolent Associations. Charitable societies.

Bequeath. To devise; to give personal property to another by last will and testament.

Bequest. Legacy.

Beseech. To implore.

Besot. To stupefy.

Best Evidence. Primary evidence.

Bestiality. Sexual relations between man and beast.

Bestow. To give or confer.

Betrayal. Wrongful disclosure of a professional

secret, e.g. a doctor violating a patient's trust.

Betroth(al). To enter into an agreement of marriage.

Betterment. Improvement to real property.

Bias. Preconceived opinion.

Bicameral. Two-house legislature.

Biennium. Period of two years.

Bigamy. The crime of wilfully and knowingly contracting a second marriage when already legally married to another.

Big with Child. Pregnant.

Bilan. Balance sheet.

Bilateral Contract. A contract in which both parties involved are bound to fill reciprocal obligations.

Bilinguis. Of two languages.

Bill. A proposed statute; first pleading in an equity case; an itemized statement.

Bill of Exchange. A draft.

Bill of Indictment. That paper which contains a criminal charge and which is submitted to the grand jury to be acted upon by them.

Bill of Lading. A document evidencing a contract for the carriage and delivery of the listed goods.

Bill of Rights. First ten amendments to the Constitution of the U.S. and that part of each state constitution which guarantees certain rights of the citizen.

Bill of Sale. A written instrument professing to pass title to personal property.

Bind. To obligate.

Binder. A memorandum of an agreement issued by an insurer to give temporary protection pending the investigation and issuance of a formal policy.

Bind Over. To hold on bail for trial.

Bipartite. In two parts; in duplicate; a document involving two parties.

B.L. (Abb). Bachelor of Laws.

Blackleg. Swindler; strike breaker.

Blacklist. A list of persons who are to be refused employment circulated among various employers.

Blackmail. Extortion of money by threat.

Blanc. White; having no marks or writing.

Blank. Having no marks or writing.

Blank Indorsement. Indorsement of a negotiable instrument by merely writing the name of the indorsee on the back.

Blasarius. An incendiary; arsonist.

Blasphemy. Malicious revilement of God or religion.

Blind Tiger. Place where intoxicants are sold contrary to the law.

Blockade. The prevention by a belligerent of access to enemy territory.

Blood. Kindred; family relationship.

Blood Money. The price paid for causing a person's death.

Blue Laws. Laws restricting Sunday sports, entertainment or trade.

Blue Sky Law. Popular name for statutes regulating investment companies.

Board. An official or representative body entrusted with executive duties and acting for and in the interest of others.

Bodily. Pertaining to or concerning the body.

Bodily Injury. Any physical or corporeal injury intentionally inflicted by another.

Body. Person; corporation; board.

Body Corporate. Corporation.

Body Snatching. Secret and unlawful disinterment of corpses.

Bogus. Spurious.

Bona. Goods; chattels.

Bona Fide. In good faith.

Bond. Long-term promissory note with stipulated interest issued by a corporation or the government; and obligation under seal.

Bondage. Slavery or serfdom.

Bondsman. A surety.

Bonus. Additional payment beyond the stipulated compensation.

Boodle. Money paid as a bribe for corrupt official action.

Bookmaker. Professional betting man.

Bookmaking. The registering of bets on any contest.

Bootlegger. One who sells liquor unlawfully.

Booty. Goods captured on land from the enemy during war.

Born. Brought forth.

Borrow. To take or receive any article of value from another with the intention of returning it or its equivalent.

Bottom. National registry of a vessel.

Bottomry. A mortgage made by the owner of a ship as security for a loan given, to make a voyage possible.

Bought and Sold Notes. Memoranda made by brokers employed to buy and sell goods.

Boundary. Markings which divide two contiguous estates.

Bounty. A gratuity given by the government to encourage the doing of a special act.

Boy. Male child from birth to the age of puberty.

Boycott. To combine against a named person or business in a policy of nonintercourse.

Brand. A mark made with a hot iron.

Breach. A break; a violation.

Breach of Close. Trespassing.

Breach of Promise of Marriage. Violation of an agreement to marry each other made between a man and woman.

Break. To separate; to violate.

Breve. A writ or brief.

Bribe. A reward or gift offered with a view to pervert the judgement of a person in a position of trust.

Brief. A written document; a written statement of the points of law made by the parties upon an appeal.

Bring Suit. Initiation of legal proceedings.

Broker. A person employed in the purchase and sale of goods or other commodities for a principal.

Brokerage. Broker's commission.

Brothel. House of prostitution.

Bruise. Temporary contusion.

Bubble. Dishonest investment scheme.

Budget. Statement of estimated receipts and expenditures.

Buggery. Carnal copulation against nature.

Bull. Papal edict.

Bulla. Seals used by the Roman emperors.

Bulletin. An official notice concerning public affairs.

Bullion. Uncoined gold or silver.

Burden of Proof. The necessity of affirmatively proving a fact in dispute by a quantum of evidence as the law demands.

Burglary. Breaking into and entering a dwelling by night with the intention of committing a felony.

Burkism. Murder committed by smothering the victim for the purpose of selling the body to be used for dissection.

Burn. To destroy by fire.

Bursar. College treasurer.

Business Month. A month of 30 days.

Buttals. End boundary lines.

By-Laws. Rules and regulations adopted by a corporation for its government.

By-Product. A secondary product of value.

Bystander. One who is present, but not taking part.

C

©. A designation accompanied by the mark of a copywrite proprietor to give notice to the public of the existence of the copyright.

Cabal. An intrigue.

Cabinet. Advisory board or council.

Cadavar. Corpse.

Cadit. Ends.

Cadit Qusestio. No further dispute.

Caesarian Operation. The delivery of a fetus by cutting above the pelvis.

Caeterus. Other.

Cahoots. Partnership.

Calaboose. A city jail.

Calcea, Calcetum. Causeway.

Calculated. Adapted by design.

Calendar. List of cases to be tried before a court during each term.

Calends. First day of the month.

Call. A notice of a meeting to be held by the board of directors or stockholders of a corporation; demand for payment.

Calling. Vocation.

Calumnia. Calumny or false charge.

Calumniatrix. Female slanderer.

Calumny. Libel.

Camarage. Rent paid for storage.

Cambio. Exchange.

Campus. A field.

Cancellaria. Chancery.

Cancellation. Abandonment of contract.

Candidate. One who seeks election to an office.

Cannot. Not able to.

Canon. A law; church officer.

Canonic. Pertaining to a canon or church law.

Canon Law. Roman ecclesiastical law.

Canvass. Examination of election returns.

Capable. Competent.

Capacity. The ability to understand the nature and effect of one's acts.

Capax. Capable.

Capita. Heads.

Capital. Assets of a corporation used to conduct corporate business and derive profits.

Capital Gains Tax. A tax on gains from the exchange or sale of capital assets.

Capital Punishment. Punishment by death.

Capital Stock. Money which a corporation regards as the basis for prosecution of business, such funds raised by subscription, divided into shares.

Capitation. Poll tax.

Capitulate. Conditional surrender.

Caption. Heading or title of a document.

Captives. Prisoners.

Capture. The seizing of property from one of two belligerents by the other.

Caput. Head; chief.

Carat. Weight of four grains.

Carcelage. Prison fee.

Care. Freedom from negligence.

Careless. Negligent.

Cargo. The load of a vessel.

Carnal Knowledge. Sexual intercourse.

Carrier. One who transports persons or merchandise.

Carte Blanche. Unrestricted authority to act.

Case. Law suit.

Case Law. Law as laid down in the decisions of the courts.

Case System. Study of law by analysis of cases and decisions.

Cash. Ready money.

Cash and Carry. Payment of goods and immediate transportation thereof by the purchaser.

Cassare. To make void.

Cast. To defeat at law.

Castigation. Chastisement.

Casting Vote. The deciding vote cast by the presiding officer of a legislative body, who ordinarily does not vote.

Casual. Occasional; incidental.

Casualty. An unavoidable accident.

Casus. Case.

Casus Major. Extraordinary casualty.

Catalla. Chattels.

Caucus. Political meeting, usually secret.

Causa. Cause; reason.

Causa Proxima. The proximate cause.

Causa Sine Qua Non. A cause without which the effect in question could not have happened.

Cause. To be the cause of; an action or suit.

Cause Celebre. Celebrated case or cause.

Cautio. Caution; care; security.

Caveat. Let him beware.

Caveat Emptor. Let the buyer beware, maxim' of common law that the buyer purchases at his own risk.

Caveat to Will. Demand that the will be produced and probated in open court.

C.C.P. (Abb.). Court of Common Pleas.

Cease. Stop.

Cede. To yield.

Celation. Concealment of pregnancy.

Celebrate. To solemnize.

Celibacy. State of being unmarried.

Censorship. Governmental restrictions over publications and public performances.

Census. The official counting of people of a state, nation or district.

Cent (Abb.). One hundred.

Centum. One hundred.

Cepi. I have taken.

Certain. Free from doubt.

Certificate. A signed statement testifying to the truth of the facts therein stated.

Certified Check. A check which is recognized and accepted by the bank drawn upon.

Certified Copy. A copy certified as authentic by the officer to whose custody the original is entrusted.

Certified Public Accountant. One who has received a certificate qualifying him to practice as a public accountant.

Cessare. To cease or stop.

Cession. A yielding or giving up.

Cessionary. Assignee.

Cessment. Assessment or tax.

Cf. (Abb.). Compare.

C.H. (Abb.). Courthouse.

Chairman. Presiding officer of a deliberative body.

Challenge. To object.

Chamberlain. Treasurer.

Chambers. Private office of a judge.

Champerty and Maintenance. The act of inducing another party to bring a civil action with or without an agreement to receive part of the resultant profits.

Chancellor. Judge of a court of chancery.

Chancellor, Lord High. Head of the judicial system of Great Britain.

Chancery. Equity.

Character. Qualities of an individual.

Charge. To impose a duty, obligation or lien; to accuse; to instruct a jury; the duty, obligation, lien, or accusation itself.

Chargé d'Affaires. Diplomatic representative of inferior rank.

Charitable Institution. An institution supported by public expense or charity.

Charitable Trust. One established for the public and intended to carry out benevolent, educational or similar purposes.

Charity. Anything done to relieve poverty, advance religion or education or any activity beneficial to the community at large.

Charlatan. Cheat.

Charta. Charter or deed.

Charter. An instrument emanating from the sovereign power which grants certain rights and privileges.

Chastity. Virtuous abstinence from sexual intercourse.

Chattels. Articles or personal property.

Chauvinism. Excessive nationalism.

Cheat. Defraud.

Check. A negotiable instrument drawn on a bank by a depositor, which is payed by the bank to the payee in the check.

Checkoff. A method of paying union dues whereby the employer deducts the dues from wages.

Cheque. Check.

Chicane. Fraud.

Chief. Head.

Chief Justice. Presiding justice of the court.

Chief Magistrate. Head of the executive department of government of a nation, state or municipal corporation.

Children. Progeny; between infancy and youth.

Chirograph. An indenture.

Chit. A promissory note.

Chose in Action. Any claim that can be pleaded in law or equity.

Chronic. Of long duration.

Cicatrix. Scar.

C.I.F. (Add.). Cost, freight and insurance.

Cipher. Secret, disguised message.

Circa. About; around.

Circuit. Division of territory where justice is usually administered by a travelling judge.

Circuit Courts. Courts presided over by a judge or judges at different places in the same district.

Circuity of Action. Indirect method of adjustment by unnecessary litigation.

Circular Notes. Letters of credit.

Circumduction. Annulment; cancellation.

Circumstantial Evidence. Indirect proof.

Circumstantibus. Bystanders in the court.

Circumvention. Fraud.

Cite. To summon to appear.

Citizen. In the U. S., one born therein or naturalized as such; a member of the political community, sharing in its rights, privileges and duties.

City. A large community, organized as a chartered municipal corporation.

Civil. Pertaining to a city or state.

Civil Action. A legal proceeding brought to enforce a civil right.

Civilian. One versed in civil law; a private citizen.

Civil Death. The state of one who loses all civil rights.

Civil Law. The system of law derived from the Roman Law as codified by Justinian.

Civil Rights. Rights which an individual possesses and which may not be impaired by the government.

Civil Service. The system providing for government employment on the basis of competitive examinations.

Civil Year. Solar year.

C.J. (Abb.). Chief Justice.

Claim. Assertion of a right to have money paid.

Claimant. One who makes a claim.

Clamor. Outcry.

Clandestine. Secret.

Classify. Group, by similar character.

Clause. Single paragraph or subdivision of a written instrument.

Clausum. Land enclosed by a boundary.

Clean. Irreproachable; innocent of fraud.

Clear. To acquit.

Clear. Obvious.

Clergy. Ministers of religion.

Clericus. Clergyman; clerk.

Clerk. Clergyman; one employed to keep accounts or records; shop or store assistant.

Client. One who engages an attorney to represent him or give legal advice.

Close. An enclosed piece of land; closed.

Closed Shop. One which employs only union members.

Closed Seasons. Periods in which certain game and fish may not be taken.

Cloth. Clergy.

Co. (Abb.). Company; county.

Coagent. Accomplice.

Coalition. Alliance.

Coast. Seaboard of a country.

C.O.D. (Abb.). Cash on delivery.

Code. System of law.

Codicil. Amendment of or addition to a will.

Coercion. Compulsion; compel by force.

Coexecutors. Persons appointed to act jointly in the administration of a testator's estate.

Cognati. Blood relations on the mother's side.

Cognizance. Recognition.

Cognomen. Family name.

Cognosce. To adjudge.

Cohabit. To live together as man and wife.

Coitus. Sexual intercourse.

Cojudices. Associate judges.

Collateral. Blood relationship other than lineal; additional security besides principal.

Collateral Attack. Attack on a prior judicial act in an independent action.

Collateral Facts. Facts not directly connected with the facts in issue.

Collateral Security. See Collateral.

Collect. To gather together.

Collection Agency. An agency which collects claims for others.

Collegium. An assembly or society; corporation.

Collide. To strike against.

Collision. A striking against.

Colloquium. Term used in an action for slander which alleges the words used were spoken of the plaintiff.

Collusion. An agreement to defraud another of his rights by forms of law or to secure an object forbidden by law.

Color. Deceptive appearance.

Combat. To fight.

Combustible. Inflammable.

Come. To appear in court.

Comfort. To give security from want.

Comitas. Courtesy.

Comitatus. County.

Comity. Courtesy; respect; recognition by states and nations of each other's laws.

Comme. As.

Commerce. Exchange of goods.

Commerce Clause. Article 1, Section 8, Clause 3 of the U.S. Constitution giving Congress power to regulate commerce with foreign powers, the states and the Indians.

Commercial Law. Law which relates to commercial enterprise.

Commercial Paper. Negotiable instruments.

Commission. Authority; writ; authorization.

Commissioner. A subordinate administrative Federal, State or Municipal official.

Commitment. The order of a court sending a person to an institution.

Committee. A group of persons appointed by a court to perform some public service or duty.

Committitur. An order naming the committed.

Commodate. Gratuitous loan.

Commodity. Any movable or tangible thing that is ordinarily used in trade.

Common. A right of incorporeal hereditament which one man may have in the land of another.

Common Assurances. Title deeds.

Common Barratry. Habitual instigation of quarrels and suits.

Common Carrier. One engaged in the transportation of freight or passengers for hire.

Common Highway. Public highway.

Common Intent. Concerted action or intention of several persons to commit a crime.

Common Law. General and ordinary law of a country or community; unwritten law founded on immemorial usage and natural justice and reason.

Common-Law Action. A civil suit.

Common-Law Marriage. Marriage by contract without religious or other ceremony.

Common Nuisance. Public danger.

Common Recovery. Fictitious suit used to break entails.

Common Seal. Corporation seal.

Commons. Public grounds.

Common Schools. Public schools.

Commonwealth. Public; state; body politic.

Commorancy. Temporary residence.

Commorant. Staying or dwelling.

Commotion. Disturbance.

Commune. Small town.

Communia. Common or ordinary.

Communism. A system of social organization in which goods are held in common.

Community. Neighborhood.

Community Property. Property owned jointly by husband and wife.

Commutation of Sentence. Reduction of a punishment of a person to a lesser one.

Compact. Agreement or contract.

Compact. Closely united.

Company. A union of two or more persons for the purpose of carrying on a business.

Compass. To plot.

Compel. To force.

Compensation. Indemnification.

Competency. Admissibility of evidence.

Competent. Legally qualified; capable.

Complainant. One who brings suit.

Complaint. Formal allegation or charge.

Complete. Full; entire.

Complete Jurisdiction. Power to hear and determine the cause, as well as to enforce judgment.

Complice. Accomplice.

Complot. To conspire.

Comply. To accomodate.

Composition. A settlement between a debtor and his creditors.

Compos Mentis. Sound of mind.

Compound. To compromise.

Compound Interest. Interest upon interest.

Compromise. To settle a controversy, usually out of court.

Compulsion. Duress.

Compulsory. Involuntary.

Compurgator. Character witness.

Conceal. To keep secret.

Conception. The beginning of pregnancy.

Concession. A grant, ordinarily that of specific privileges by a government.

Concessor. Grantor.

Concisely. Briefly.

Conclude. To make a final statement.

Conclusion. Termination.

Conclusive. Decisive.

Concord. Settlement.

Concordant. Agreement.

Concubine. A woman who cohabits with a man to whom she is not married.

Concur. To agree.

Concurrent. Running together.

Concussion. Extortion; a jolt to the brain.

Condemn. To find guilty; to appropriate private property for public use legally.

Condition. A provision in a written instrument which is to take effect upon the occurence of an uncertain contingency.

Conduct Money. Expense money paid to a witness.

Confederacy. Conspiracy.

Confederation. An agreement between two or more governments.

Confession. An admission by a person charged with a crime.

Confidence. Trust.

Confidence Game. Obtaining of money or property by means of fraud.

Confidence Man. Swindler.

Confidential Relation. Fiduciary relation.

Confirmation. Affirmation.

Confiscation. Seizure of property by the government.

Confrontation. Bringing a witness face to face with the accused in a criminal action.

Confusion. Blending, mingling; merger.

Congé. Permission to depart.

Congeable. Lawful.

Congress. The legislature of the U.S., consisting of the Senate and House of Representatives.

Conjecture. Guess.

Conjoints. Husband and wife.

Conjugal. Pertaining to the marital state.

Conjunct. Concurrent; joint.

Conjurator. Conspirator.

Connubium. Marriage.

Consanguinity. Blood relationship.

Conscience. Faculty of discriminating between right and wrong.

Conscionable. According to the principles of honesty.

Conseil. Counsel; advice.

Consent. An agreement.

Conserve. To save from loss.

Consider. To examine.

Consign. To entrust goods for care or sale.

Consignee. One to whom goods are consigned.

Consignor. One who sends goods to another by consignment.

Consolidate. To unit into one.

Consolidation. Merger of two or more corporations.

Consortium. Right of conjugal fellowship of husband and wife.

Conspiracy. An agreement between two or more persons to do an unlawful deed.

Constate. To prove.

Constituent. The principal of an agent.

Constituere. To appoint.

Constitution. Fundamental law of a state or nation.

Constitutional Law. In the U.S., the body of law created by applying and interpreting the the Constitution of the U.S. and its amendments.

Constitutional Right. Any right guaranteed under the constitution.

Constraint. Duress.

Construction. Interpretation.

Constructive. Presumed.

Construe. To put together.

Constuprate. To violate or rape.

Consuetudinary. Customary.

Consuetudo. Custom.

Consul. A government official, residing in a foreign country, who watches over the interests of his countrymen.

Consultation. A writ which returns an action from a temporal to an ecclesiastical court; conference between the counsels.

Consummate. To complete.

Consummation of Marriage. Sexual intercourse between two parties after marriage.

Contango. Broker's charge.

Contemner. One who commits a contempt.

Contempt. Disregard or disobedience of a public authority.

Contempt of Court. Disobedience of a lawful order of a court or any act which hinders the proper functioning of a court or impairs its standing in the community.

Conterminous. Adjoining.

Contested. Opposed.

Contiguous. In close proximity.

Continens. Joined together.

Contingent. Dependent upon an uncertainty.

Continuing. Enduring.

Continuous. Uninterrupted.

Contra. Against.

Contraband. Goods brought in or out of a country against its laws.

Contracausator. Criminal.

Contract. A promissory agreement by which two or more legally competent persons to do or not to do a particular thing.

Contract Clause. Article 1, Section 10, of the U.S. Constitution prohibiting a State from imparing the obligation of contracts.

Contradict. To disprove.

Contradiction in Terms. An expression which contradicts itself.

Contrafactio. Counterfeiting.

Contrary. Against.

Contrary to Law. Illegal.

Contravention. Violation of a law.

Contribute. To give assistance or aid.

Contributory. Additional.

Contrivance. Disguise.

Control. To restrain or regulate.

Controller. One who has charge of the financial affairs of a public or private corporation.

Controvert. To dispute.

Contumacy. Contemptuous disobedience of a court order.

Contumax. Outlaw.

Contusion. Bruise.

Contutor. Joint guardian.

Conus. Known.

Convenable. Suitable.

Convene. To file suit.

Conventio. Agreement.

Conventional. Based upon agreement.

Conventus. Contract.

Conveyance. The transfer of title to property from one person to another.

Convicium. An insult; slander.

Convict. To condemn after judicial investigation.

Convict. One found guilty of a crime.

Convocation. Assembly.

Copia. Copy; opportunity.

Copia Vera. True copy.

Copr. (Abb). Copyright.

Copula. Sexual intercourse.

Copulative Condition. A condition, the happening of which, depends on several events.

Copy. Transcript of an original.

Copyright. The exclusive right to print, multiply, publish and sell a literary, artistic or technical work.

Coram. Before.

Coram Judice. Within the court's jurisdiction.

Coram Nobis. Before us.

Coram Non Judice. Before one who is not a judge.

Co-Respondent. One accused in a divorce suit of having committed adultery with the defendant.

Corner. A plan to gain control of the available supply of a commodity.

Corona. The crown.

Coronor. An officer whose duty it is to make inquiry into the cause and circumstances of any death occurring within his territory caused by violence or marks of suspicion.

Corporal. Bodily.

Corporal Punishment. Physical punishment.

Corporate. Belonging to a corporation.

Corporate Franchise. Right to conduct business and exist as a corporation.

Corporation. An artifical being or institution created under the law consisting of a group of members associated in a common enterprise, and having a personality distinct from those men who compose it.

Corporator. A member of a corporation.

Corporeal. Tangible.

Corpse. Dead body of a human being.

Corpus. Body; an aggregate or mass.

Corpus Delicti. Remains of a committed crime.

Corpus Juris. Body of law.

Corpus Juris Civilis. Body of civil law.

Correi. Co-stipulators.

Corroborate. To add credibility by evidence.

Corrupt. Tainted; debased; depraved.

Cosmus. Clean.

Cost. Expense.

Cost Price. Price actually paid for goods.

Co-Stipulator. Joint promisor.

Costs. Expenses incurred in a lawsuit.

Council. Legislative department of a city or other municipal corporation.

Counsel. Attorney.

Counselor at Law. An attorney who has been admitted to the bar.

Count. Statement of a cause of action.

Countenance. Credit; credibility.

Counter. Against.

Counterfeit. To copy or imitate without authority, with the intent to deceive or to defraud by passing the imitation for the genuine.

Countermand. To revoke on order given.

Counterpart. Corresponding part of an instrument; a copy.

Countersign. To verify by an additional signature.

County. An administrative unit of the state created and organized by statute for judicial and political purposes.

County Court. A court whose jurisdiction is limited to a specific county.

Coupons. Interest and dividend certificates.

Court. Persons appointed under law and vested with the power of rendering judgments, issuing writs and hearing appeals.

Court Martial. A military court for the enforcement of military regulations.

Court of Admiralty. A court having jurisdiction in maritime cases.

Court of Appeals. A court in which appeals from a lower court are heard.

Court of Conscience. Court of equity.

Court of Convocation. Ecclesiastical Court.

Court of First Instance. Court of Primary Jurisdiction.

Court of General Jurisdiction. Court of record.

Court of Inquiry. A military court which conducts preliminary investigations of charges.

Court of Law. A duly constituted tribunal administering the laws of the state or nation.

Cousin German. First Cousin.

Coustom. Duty; toll.

Covenant. In the wide sense, a contract in general.

Covenant, Action of. Common law action for breach of contract under seal; a written agreement executed by a sealing and delivery.

Covert. Covered; protected.

Coverture. Status of a married woman.

Covin. Fraud.

Cozen. To cheat.

C.P.A. (Abb.). Certified Public Accountant.

Crassus. Gross; large.

Crave. To demand.

Crazy. Deranged.

Creance. Collateral security.

Creancer. Creditor.

Create. To bring into existence.

Credibility. Worthiness of belief.

Credible Witness. Competent witness.

Credit. Capacity of being trusted.

Creditor. One to whom a debt is owing.

Creed. Formal declaration of religious belief.

Cremation. Reduction of a corpse to ashes.

Crepusculum. Twilight.

Crime. An act in violation of penal law.

Crime Against Nature. Unnatural sexual relations.

Crimen. Crime.

Crimen Furti. Larceny.

Crimen Incendii. Arson.

Crimen Majestatis. Treason.

Criminal. Pertaining to a crime; one who commits a crime.

Criminal Homicide. Unlawful taking of another's life in such a manner that he dies within a year and one day from the time the mortal wound is inflicted.

Cross Action; Cross Bill. An action or bill against the plaintiff or codefendent, set up in the defendant's plea or answer.

Cross Examination. Examination of a witness by an adverse party.

Crude. Raw or unfinished.

Cruelty. Abusive treatment.

Ct. (Abb.). Cent; cents.

C.T.A. (Abb). Cum Testamento Annexo, with the will annexed.

Cts. (Abb.). Cents.

Cui Bono. For whose good.

Cul. Guilty.

Cul de Sac. A street open at only one end.

Culpa. Fault, guilt.

Culpable. Guilty.

Culprit. One indicted for a criminal offense.

Cum. With.

Cum Grano Salis. With a grain of salt.

Cum Testamento Annexo. With the will annexed.

Cumulative. Additional; two things which are to be added together.

Cura. Care.

Curator. Guardian.

Curatrix. Female guardian.

Curia. A court.

Curia Admiralitatis. Court of Admiralty.

Curia Comitatus. County court.

Currency. Money.

Current. Running; now in transit.

Currere. To run.

Cursing. Profane swearing.

Curtis. A yard.

Custa. Costs.

Custodes Pacis. Justices of the Peace.

Custody. Control without ownership of personal property.

Custom. A rule of conduct which has been followed for an appreciable time and which has become compulsory.

Customs. Tariffs and duties on imported and exported merchandise.

Custum. Cost.

Cut. A wound inflicted by a sharp instrument.

Cwt. (Abb.). Hundredweight.

D

Dactylography. Scientific study of fingerprints.

Daily. Every day.

Damage. Injury; loss.

Damages. Compensation from an injury.

Damn. To condemn.

Damnify. To injure.

Danger. Jeopardy; peril.

Danism. Usurious loan.

Dans. In.

Day. Time between two successive midnights.

Daysman. An arbiter.

D.C. (Abb.). District Court.

De. From; of.

Dead. Without life.

Dead body. Corpse.

Death. Cessation of life.

Death, Civil. Loss of all legal personality.

Debase. To adulterate.

Debauchery. Excessive indulgence in sensual pleasures.

De Bene Esse. Done conditionally.

Debenture. Various kinds of evidence of debt issued by a corporation.

Debit. That which is due and owing.

Debita Fundi. A debt secured by real estate.

Debt. An obligation to pay money.

Debt, National. The total sum of obligations owing by the government.

Debtor. One who owes money.

Decalogue. The Ten Commandments.

Decapitation. Beheading.

Deceased. A dead person.

Decedent. A deceased person who has left property.

Deceit. Fraud.

Decency. Propriety of action.

Decision. Judgment of a court.

Declaration. First pleading of a plaintiff in which the cause of action is set out; an admission or statement subsequently used as evidence in the trial of an action.

Darbies. Handcuffs.

Darrein. Last.

Darrein Continuance. The last continuance.

Date. The calendar designation of the date on which an instrument is issued or signed.

Dation. A giving or transfer in the fulfillment of a duty.

Daughter. An immediate female descendant.

Daughter-in-Law. The wife of one's son.

Declaration of Intention. A declaration by an alien of his intention to become a citizen.

Declaratory. Explanatory.

Declare. To make known, manifest or clear.

Decline. To object.

Decollation. Decapitation.

Decoy. To entice or lure.

Decree. The judgment of a court of equity.

Decree Absolvitor. A decree acquitting.

Decree Nisi. A provisional decree to be made absolute on motion unless cause be shown

LEGAL DICT

against it.

Decretal Order. Order of a court of chancery.

Decry. To discredit.

Dedbaba. Homicide.

Dedicate. To set private property aside for public use.

Deed. An instrument conveying real property.

Deeded. Transferred by deed.

Deed Poll. A deed made by one party only.

Deem. To judge.

De Facto. In fact, as opposed to "by right."

De Facto Government. One which maintains itself by force.

Defalcation. Misappropriation of moneys.

Defamation. Libel, slander and any wilful injury to the reputation of another.

Default. Fault; neglect.

Defeasance, Defeasible. Subject to be revoked upon the happening of a future event or a conditional limitation.

Defect. Deficiency.

Defend. To oppose a claim or action.

Defendant. One being sued in a civil action or prosecuted in a criminal action.

Defeneration. Usurious rate of interest when lending money.

Defense. Facts in answer to a complaint.

Defiance. Open contempt.

Defile. To debauch.

Definitive. Final; final determination of an issue in controversy.

Defloration. Seduction.

Deforce. To withhold wrongfully, particularly land.

Defraud. To cheat.

Degradation. A deprivation of dignity.

Degree. Grade of crime according to its gravity; one's rank in life.

Dehors. Outside of; unconnected with.

Dejeration. An oath.

De Jure. By right or lawful authority.

Delate. To accuse.

Delay. To retard.

Delegate. A representative; to transfer a power to another.

Delete. To erase.

Deleterious. Morally or physically harmful.

Deliberate. Carefully considered; willful.

Delict. Wrong; injury; tort.

Delinquency. Failure of duty.

Delinquent Taxes. Taxes which are owing.

Delivery. Transfer of movable and personal property or deed to another.

De Lunatico Inquirendo. A writ issued for an inquisition of lunacy.

De Malo. Of sickness.

Demand. To claim as on's due.

Demand Instrument or Note. Note payable on demand.

Demens. One who is demented.

Demented, Dementia. Of unsound mind.

Demesne. Domain; held in one's own right.

Demi. One-half.

Demi-Sangue. Half-blood.

Demise. To convey an estate for years or life.

Demise and Redemise. Mutual leasing of the same land, the owner paying a nominal rental.

Democracy. A form of government which is directed according to the will of the people.

Demonstration. Description or designation.

Demonstrative Legacy. A legacy which designates a particular source out of which it is to be paid.

Demurrage. Monetary allowance; a compensation for the detention of a vessel by the freighter beyond the time allowed.

Demurrer. A denial by the defendant that the allegations of the declaration, even if true, would legally constitute a cause for action.

Denial. A refusal.

Denumeration. Act of present payment.

Department. Division of public administration.

Departure. A deviation in the course of pleading, except by a formal amendment.

Depeculation. Embezzlement of public moneys.

Dependent. One who relies on another.

De Pone. A writ to remove a cause to a superior court.

Depone. To give a deposition.

Deponent. Witness.

Deport. To arrest and remove an alien.

Depose. To testify under oath.

Deposit. To commit to custody; the goods or money received by the bank.

Depositary. An person or institution receiving a deposit.

Deposition. An affidavit.

Depreciation. Reduction in value.

Depredation. Plundering.

Deprive. To take.

Deputy. The subordinate of a public officer.

Deranged. Insane.

Derelict. Abandoned.

Derivative. Subordinate; secondary.

Derogation. Substantial change.

Descend. To pass by succession.

Descent. Hereditary succession.

Description. An account of a particular subject by the narration of its characteristics.

Desert. To forsake or abandon.

De Son Tort. By his own wrong.

Desperate. Hopeless.

Despite. Contempt.

Desponsation. Betrothal.

Despot. Tyrant.

Destitute. Impoverished.

Detachiare. To seize.

Detainer. Wrongful withholding of another's property; restraint without consent.

Deter. To discourage or stop by fear.

Determinable. Liable to come to an end upon the happening of a future event.

Determinate. Ascertained.

Determine. To bring to an end.

Detinue. A common law action used to recover personal chattels wrongfully held by a person whose original holding was lawful.

Deternicari. To discover.

Deuterogamy. A valid second marriage after the death of one's former spouse.

Devest. Deprive.

Devisa. Boundary.

Devise. To leave real property by will.

Devisee. One to whom real property is willed.

Devolution. Legal transfer of property from one person to another.

Diatim. Daily.

Dictator. An absolute ruler.

Dictum. A remark or observation made by a judge in pronouncing an opinion which does not embody the resolution of the court.

Dies. Day.

Dies Datus. A continuance.

Dies Dominicus. The Lord's day.

Dies Juridicus. A court day.

Diet. A legislative assembly.

Diffacere. To multilate.

Differential Duty. A duty placed on imported goods in addition to ordinary duty.

Digamy. A valid second marraige.

Digests. Pandects of Justinian.

Dilation. A delay.

Dilatory Plea. Any plea which tends to delay.

Diligence. Prudence.

Diligiatus. An outlaw.

Dimidia. Half.

Diminution. A lessening.

Dimittere. To dismiss.

Diocese. The district subject to a bishop.

Dipsomania. An uncontrollable desire for intoxicating drinks.

Direct. To instruct, advise or request.

Direct. Immediate.

Direct Examination. The interrogation of a witness by the party who called him.

Direction. Command; court's instruction to a jury; the complainant's address to the court.

Directive. An order issued by an administrative agency.

Directly. Without deviation.

Director. A member of the governing board.

Directory. That which is advisory or instructive as opposed to obligatory.

Diriment Impediments. In canon law, absolute bars to lawful matrimony.

Disability. Legal or physical incapacity.

Disable. To render incapable of proper and effective action.

Disabling Statute. One which limits rights.

Disadvocare. To deny.

Disaffirm. To repudiate.

Disagreement. Difference of opinion.

Disallow. To overrule.

Disalt. To disable a person.

Disavow. To repudiate.

Disbar. To deprive a lawyer from practice.

Discharge. To release.

Disclaimer. Renunciation of any claim or power vested in a person.

Disclose. To make known.

Discontinuance. Termination of an action on the part of the plaintiff before a decision.

Disconvenable. Improper.

Discount. A deduction made from a gross sum on any account whatever.

Discovert. Not married.

Discovery. The ascertainment of that which was previously unknown; the right to demand examination under oath of an adverse party or to have documents produced which will aid the litigant in the presentation.

Discredit. To injure a person's credit or reputation.

Discreetly. Prudently.

Discrepancy. A variance.

Discretely. Separately.

Discretion. Individual judgment.

Discrimination. A failure to treat all equally.

Discussion. The right of a surety to demand that the creditor resort to the principal before holding the surety liable.

Disfranchise. To deprive of the right to vote.

Disgrace. Shame.

Disguise. To change the appearance of.

Dishersion. Disinheritance.

Disheritor. One who disinherits.

Dishonesty. Lack of integrity.

Dishonor. To refuse to honor a negotiable instrument when duly represented.

Disincarcerate. To free from prison.

Disinhersion. Disinheriting an heir.

Disinherit. The act by which a testator passes over a person who would be his heir.

Disinter. To take a body out of the grave.

Disinterested. Unprejudiced.

Disjunctim. Separately.

Disjunctive Allegation. An allegation which expresses a thing alternatively.

Disloyal. Unfaithful.

Dismiss. To order a discontinuance.

Disorderly. In violation of good behavior.

Disorderly Conduct. Conduct which constitutes a breach of public peace or morality.

Disorderly House. House of prostitution.

Disparage. To match unsuitably.

Dispensation. An exemption from some laws.

Dispersonare. To scandalize.

Displace. To remove.

Dispone. To grant or convey.

Dispossess. To legally exclude from realty.

Dispossession. Ouster.

Disprove. To refute.

Disputable. Refutable.

Dispute. Controversy.

Disqualify. To incapacitate.

Disrationare. To clear one's self.

Disrepute. Of bad reputation.

Disseise. To deprive of the possession of land.

Desseisin. Dispossession.

Dissent. To disagree.

Dissignare. To break a seal.

Dissolution. A breaking up; a termination.

Dissolve. To terminate.

Dissuade. To persuade one not to perform a positive legal duty.

Distinct. Clear.

Distinctively. Characteristically.

Distraited. Insane.

Distrahere. To sell.

Distrain. To seize goods and chattels as security for the payment of any obligation

Distraint. Seizure.

Distress. The act of distraining.

Distribute. To divide in proportion.

Distributee. An heir.

District. Geographical division.

District Attorney. Public prosecutor of the U.S. Government in each of the federal judicial districts; state prosecuting office.

District Courts. Courts of limited jurisdiction.

Districtio. A distress.

Disturb. To throw into confusion.

Divers. Various.

Diverse. Different.

Diversion. Alteration of the natural cause of a thing.

Diversity. The plea of a prisoner in a criminal action that he is not the man.

Divest. To deprive of a right or title.

Dividend. That share of the net profits of a corporation to be distributed to stockholders.

Dividenda. An indenture.

Divinare. To guess.

Divine Law. Law of God.

Divisional Opinion. The opinion of a divided court with regard to the matter before it.

Divorce. The legal dissolution of a marriage.

Divorcee. A women who has been divorced.

Divulge. To disclose.

Do. I give. Apt word of feoffment and gift.

Dock. The space enclosed between two wharves; the place reserved in a court-room for the prisoner.

Docket. A formal record of court proceedings.

Doctrine. A rule, principle or theory.

Document. A written instrument in which is recorded matter which may be used as evidence in court.

Doe, John. The fictitious plaintiff in the action of ejectment.

Doer. One who performs an act.

Dole. A part, share or portion; money or commodities distributed to the public in times of disaster.

Doli Capax. Capable of evil intent.

Dollar. Legal currency in the U.S.

Dolus. Malicious fraud.

Domain. The absolute ownership of land.

Dome. Sentence.

Domestic. Pertaining to the family and household; the internal affairs of a country.

Domestic Corporation. One which does business in the state it was organized.

Domestic Relations Court. One which settles controversies between members of the family.

Domicile, Domicil. A place where a person has his permanent residence.

Dominant. Principal.

Dominate. To rule.

Dominion. Ownership.

Dominium. Dominion.

Dominium Directum. Direct ownership.

Dominus. Lord or master.

Dominus Litis. The person in control of any litigation.

Domitae. Domesticated.

Domus. House.

Dona. Gifts.

Donare. To give.

Donate. To give.

Donation. Gift.

Donor. One who gives.

Dormant. Sleeping; inactive; in abeyance.

Dormant Claim. One which is in abeyance.

Dormant Partner. Silent partner.

Dos. Dowry.

Dot. Dowry.

Dotage. Mental feebleness due to old age.

Dote. To be silly, delirious or insane.

Double. Twofold.

Double Bond. Bond which carries a penalty for its non-fulfillment.

Double Damages. Twice the amount of actual damages, provided for by statute in some-cases of injuries due to negligence etc.

Double Entry. Bookkeeping system which provides a credit and debit entry.

Double Jeopardy. The defense in a criminal action that the defendant has previously been tried for the same offense as now charged.

Doubt. Uncertainty of mind.

Dowager. A widow assigned her dower.

Dower. The legal right of a widow to the real estate of her husband.

Dowry. The property which a woman brings to her husband upon marriage.

Draft. Bill of exchange.

Draftsman. One who prepares a legal document.

Drawback. Money collected by customs officials on imported merchandise and remitted if the goods are re-exported.

Drawee. One on whom a bill of exchange is drawn.

Drawer. One who issues a bill of exchange.

Droit. Right; justice.

Droit Commun. Common law.

Droit-Droit. Double right; title and possession.

Droit Écrit. Written law.

Drunkenness. The condition of one whose rational actions are affected by alcohol.

Dry. In the legal sense, formal or nominal; without profit.

Dry Law. A statute prohibiting the manufacture and sale of alcoholic beverages.

Dry Rent. A rent reserved without a clause of distress.

Duarchy. A government with two rulers.

Dubitans, Dubitante. Doubting.

Due. Just; proper; owing.

Due Bill. A written acknowledgment that a debt is owing.

Due Care. Care which a reasonably prudent man would exercise under similar conditions.

Due Process of Law. The regular procedure in the administration of the law.

Duellum. Trial by battle.

Dues. Payments to retain membership.

Duly. In due course; according to the law.

Dumb. Unable to speak.

Dumb-Bid. A previously arranged price below which no bid is accepted by an auctioneer.

Dummage. Loose material placed around a ship's cargo to prevent chafing or injury.

Dummodo. Provided.

Dummy. One who legally acts for another, while posing as acting for himself.

Duodena. Jury of twelve men.

Duplex Querela. Double complaint.

Duplicate. The copy of a document, being equal to the original.

Duplicity. The technical fault of using more than one cause of action in a declaration or more than one defense in any subsequent pleading; fraud.

Durante. During.

Durante Absentia. During absence.

Durante Vita. During life.

Duration. Limit of time.

Duress. Unlawful use of force or fear to compel another to act against his will.

During. Throughout the course of.

Duties. Customs.

Duty. Obligation.

Dwell. To inhabit.

Dwelling-House. Residence.

Dying Without Issue. Dying without a child being born to one.

Dysnomy. Bad legislation.

Dyvour. A bankrupt.

E

E, Ex. From.

Eagle. Gold coin of the U.S. worth ten dollars.

Earmark. Any mark of identification.

Earn. To obtain by labor.

Earned Income. Income as a result of labor.

Earnest. Something given by a buyer to a seller as a part of the purchase price.

Earnest Money. Money paid in anticipation of the fulfillment of some agreement.

Earnings. Compensation for services.

Ear Witness. One who testifies to what he has heard.

Ease. Comfort.

Easement. The right to use the realty of another for a specific purpose or to limit the use of someone else's realty.

Easement of Light and Air. Right to free enjoyment of unobstructed light and air.

Easterly. Due east.

Eau. Water.

Ebb. The going out of the tides of the sea.

Ebriety. Drunkenness.

Eccentricity. Personal peculiarity of mind and disposition.

Ecchymosis. Bruise.

Ecclesia. Assembly.

Ecclesiastical. Pertaining to an organized church.

Ecclesiastical Corporation. A private corporation organized for religious purposes.

Economy. Frugality.

E Contra. On the contrary.

E Converso. On the other hand.

Ecumenical. Universal.

Edict. Any proclamation or announcement promulgated by a sovereign of a country and having the force of law.

Editus. Issued.

Education. Proper moral, physical and intellectual instruction.

E.E. (Abb.). Errors excepted.

Effect. To do; to produce.

Effect. Result.

Effects. Personal property.

Effectus Sequitus Causam. The effect follows the cause.

Efficient Cause. That cause which produces results; primary cause.

Effigy. A corporeal representation of a person.

Efflux. The flow of time.

Effort. An attempt.

Effractor. Burgular.

E.G. (Abb.). For example.

Egality. Equality.

Ego. I; myself.

Egress and Regress. The right to enter and leave land without hindrance.

Eighteenth Amendment. Prohibition.

Eigne. The eldest son.

Eignesse. The share of the eldest son.

Eisna. The eldest son.

Either. Each of two.

Eject. To throw out.

Ejection. A compulsory turning out.

Ejectment. An action in which the right of corporeal hereditaments may be tried.

Ejectum. That which is tossed up by the sea.

Ejurare. To abjure or renounce.

Ejusdem Generis. Of the same kind.

Election. The selection by popular vote of a public representative.

Election, Right of. The right of a widow to choose between the will or the statute.

Elective. Subject to choice.

Elector. One who has the right to vote.

Electoral College. The body that elects the President and Vice-President of the U.S.

Electrocution. The infliction of the death penalty by passing through the body a current of electricity of high power.

Eleemosynary. Charitable.

Eleganter. Accurately.

Elements. Forces of nature.

Eligible. Qualified.

Ell. A lineal measure equal to one yard.

Eloign. To remove from jurisdiction.

Eloin. See Eloign.

Elopement. The act of a wife who abandons her husband and subsequently cohabits with another man.

Elsewhere. In another place.

Emancipate. To set free.

Emasculate. To castrate.

Embargo. A proclamation of state forbidding vessels to enter or leave without permission.

Embezzle. To misappropriate funds.

Embody. To include in a written instrument.

Embracery. The offense of attempting to bribe or corruptly influence a jury.

Emendatio. An amendment.

Emergency. A pressing situation.

Emigrant. One who departs from his native land and settles in another country.

Eminent Domain. The right of the government to take private property for public use after just compensation.

Emit. To send forth.

Emolument. Compensation of a public servant.

Emplead. To indict.

Employ. To engage; hire.

Employee. One who works for another.

Empower. To authorize.

Emption. Buying.

Emptor. Buyer.

En. In.

Enact. To establish by law.

Enacting Clause. The introductory clause of a statute declaring the authority of the body.

En Autre Droit. In the right of another.

En Bloc. In mass.

Enceinte. Pregnant.

En Coste. Collateral.

Encroachment. An unlawful extension of rights over another's.

Encumbrance. A burden; charge or lien resting on property which limits its use.

En Demeure. In default.

Endorse. See Indorse.

Endorsement. See Indorsement.

Endow. To bestow money or property for maintaining a person or institution.

Enforce. To put into execution.

Enfranchise. To make free; to grant a person the right to vote.

Engage. To employ; to take part in.

Engagement. Contract; an agreement between a man and woman to marry.

Engross. To copy a document.

Enhanced. Increased in value.

Enitia Pars. The share of the elder.

Enjoin. To issue an injunction.

Enjoyment. Dominion over or possession of.

Enlarge. To increase; to extend.

Enlargement. A conveyance from a reversioner or remainderman to the holder of the particular limited estate.

Enlist. To volunteer for military service.

Enormia. Crimes.

Enroll. To register.

Enroute. On the way.

Ensemble. Together.

Ensue. To follow after.

Entail. To settle the succession to property.

Entail. An estate in fee limited to certain heirs.

Entendment. Understanding.

Enter. To take part in; to record or make entry; to place anything before a court formally.

Enterlesse. Omitted.

Enterprise. A hazardous undertaking.

Entice. To wrongfully persuade.

Entire. Whole.

Entire Contract. An indivisible contract.

Entire Tenancy. Sole ownership.

Entirety. Joint tenancy by husband and wife whereby either is the owner of the whole.

Entitle. To give a right or title.

Entity. Being.

Entrebat. Intruder.

Entrepot. Warehouse.

Entry. The making of a record; going upon land to make claim; in burglary, the actual going into a place after breaking.

Entry, Writ of. A real action brought to recover possession of lands by one from whom the lands are wrongfully withheld.

Enumerate. To mention specifically.

Enumerators. Persons appointed to take census.

En Vie. In life.

Eo Intuitu. With that intention.

Eo Nominee. By that name.

Epistola. Letter.

E Pluribus Unum. The motto of the U.S. Government, "One out of many".

Equal. Alike; unbiased.

Equality. Possessing the same rights.

Equip. To furnish for service against a need.

Equitable. Fair; just; in accordance with the special rules enforceable in a Court of Equity.

Equity. Body of law which aids and supplements the common law; justice; fairness; a mortgagor's interest; a right of any sort.

Equity of Statute. The reason or meaning underlying a statute.

Equity of Redemption. The right of a mortgagor to redeem his land after it has been forfeited at law by paying the mortgage debt.

Equivalent. In patent law, a device by which an inventor reaches the same result as that achieved by the patent which he is charged.

Equivocal. Having more than one meaning.

Erasure. The obliteration of any words of a document.

Ergo. Therefore.

Ergot. A drug sometimes used for abortions.

Erosion. The gradual wearing away of soil.

Errant. Wandering.

Error. A mistake of law or fact.

Error Apparent. A defect on the face of the proceedings, pleadings or decree.

Error, Writ of. A writ to review a judgment of an inferior court in a higher court for errors.

Errors, Court of. Common law court of appeals.

Escape. The voluntary departure of a prisoner from lawful custody before he is released.

Escheat. The right of the state to succeed to property either real or personal where there is no heir.

Escrier. To proclaim.

Escrow. A written instrument for a transfer of property or interest in property which is deposited with a third person and is not to be delivered to the grantee until some condition is fulfilled.

Esne. One in a position of servitude.

Esnecy. The privilege of the eldest to have first choice in the division of an inheritance.

Espera. The period of time which a court has fixed for the performance of an act.

Esplees. The products and profits of the land.

Espousal. Mutual promise to marry.

Espouse. To engage to marry.

Espurio. Bastard.

Esq. (Abb.). Esquire.

Esquire. Attorney-at-law; title of respect.

Esse. To be.

Essence. The substance of a thing.

Essoin, Essoign. An excuse for non-appearance when a defendant was summoned.

Establish. To make or form; to found.

Estate. An interest in land; the assets and liabilities, real and personal property left by a decedent when taken together.

Estate in Fee Simple. An estate free of any restriction, limitation or condition.

Estate Tail. An estate wherein lands and tenements are given to the donee's issue.

Estate Tax. Inheritance tax; probate duty.

Estop. To prevent.

Estoppel. The equitable rule that when anyone executes some deed, or is connected with or does some act either of deed or record, he is precluded from stating anything to the contrary.

Estreat. To extract.

Estrepe. Waste.

Estrepement, Writ of. The common law writ to prevent waste on the part of a defendant in a writ of right pending the outcome of any real action.

Et. And; also.

Et Al. And another.

Et Alii. And others.

Et Als. And others.

Etc. (Abb.). Et cetera (and other things).

Et Non. And not.

Et Seq. (Abb.). Et sequitur (and as follows).

Et Sic. And so.

Eugenics Law. A statute requiring a medical certificate of good physical condition, as a condition for receiving a marriage license.

Every. Each.

Evict. To turn out of possession of land.

Evidence. Any species of proof that may legally be admitted to court in settlement of an issue.

Evident. Obvious.

Evidentiary. Being used as evidence.

Ewage. Toll paid for water passage.

Ewbrice. Adultery.

Ewe. Water.

Ex. From; out of.

Exaction. Unauthorized demanding of fees or taxes by an officer or one impersonating.

Ex Aequitate. According to equity.

Examen. A trial.

Examination. An investigation.

Examination in Chief. The first examination of a witness by the party who has called him.

Examiner. One authorized to examine.

Excambium. An exchange.

Ex Causa. From or with cause.

Exception. An objection; reservation.

Excerpta. Excerpts.

Excerpts. Extracts.

Excess. Extreme force.

Excessive Force. Undue or unnecessary force.

Excess Profits Tax. A tax levied in profits beyond a specified amount.

Exchange. To barter.

Exchange Broker. One who handles bargains for others in money or merchandise.

Exchequer. The English department of revenue.

Excise. A duty levied upon the manufacture, sale or consumption of commodities within a country.

Exclusion Laws. Federal statutes which exclude certain specified foreigners.

Exclusive. Undivided; sole.

Ex Concessis. From what has been conceded.

Ex Continenti. At once.

Ex Contractu. From contract.

Ex Culpa Levissima. From the least negligence.

Ex Curia. Out of court.

Excusable. That which can be forgiven.

Excusable Homicide. Justifiable homicide is accidental, or in self-defense.

Excuse. To pardon.

Excuss. To seize goods under court process.

Ex Debito Justitiae. As a debt of justice.

Ex Defectu Sanguinis. From want of issue.

Ex Delicto. From the wrongdoing.

Ex Demissione. On the demise of.

Ex Directo. Directly; immediately.

Ex Dolo Malo. From fraud.

Execute. To complete; to do; to carry out.

Executed. Completed.

Executed Consideration. A past consideration.

Executed Gift. A gift which has been delivered.

Executed Remainder. A remainder whereby a present interest passes to the tenant, although the enjoyment is postponed.

Executed Use. An equitable estate which, under the Statute of Uses, is a legal estate.

Execution. The term for the process by which judgments are enforced; the final act necessary to make legal a document effective; the enforcement of capital punishment.

Executor. One designated n a will to administer the estate of the testator.

Executory. Not yet completed.

Executory Consideration. A promise to do something in the future.

Executory Contract. A contract in which the obligation lies in a future act.

Executory Instrument. One which has not been fully executed by the parties.

Executory Trust. One in which the directions to the trustee are general and to be determined by some future deed or declaration.

Executrix. Female executor.

Exemplary Damages. Punitive damages.

Exemplification. Certified copy of a document or legal proceeding under the seal of a court or public office.

Exempli Gratia. For example; (Abb.) e.g.

Exemplum. An example; a copy.

Exempt. Free from obligation or liability.

Exemption. Freedom from taxation on certain property or a certain amount of one's income; freedom from military service; property which may not be legally levied upon or sold to satisfy a debt after judgment.

Ex Empto. From purchase.

Exequatur. Permission issued by any government authorizing some person to act within the jurisdiction of that government, as the consul of a foreign government.

Exercise. To carry out; to execute.

Ex Facie. On the face.

Exfrediare. To break the peace.

Ex Gratia. Out of grace.

Ex Gravi Querela. As a ground of complaint.

Exhaeridatio. A disinheritance.

Exhibere. To produce in a court of justice.

Exhibit. Something offered in evidence.

Exhibition. A suit to compel a person to produce writings.

Exhumation. Disinterment.

Exigence, Exigency. Urgency, need, demand.

Exigency of a Bond. The condition upon which the enforcement of the bond depends.

Exigent. A writ forming part of the process of outlawry, ordering the sheriff to bring the person summoned before court.

Exile. Banishment.

Exilium. Exile.

Ex Improviso. Without preparation.

Ex Industria. Intentionally.

Ex Intervallo. After an interval.

Exist. To be.

Existing Person. A child conceived; not born.

Existing Rights. Rights as they exist under general laws.

Exit. The process of issuance is complete.

Exitus. Issues of land and tenements; off-spring.

Ex Jurae Natural. By the law of nature.

Ex Justa Causa. From a just cause.

Exlegalitas. Outlawry.

Ex Lege. According to law.

Ex Maleficio. From wrong or tortious conduct.

Ex Malitia. Out of malice.

Ex Mero Motu. Of his own accord.

Ex Mora. Because of delay.

Ex More. By custom.

Ex Natura Rei. From the nature of the thing.

Ex Necessitate Legis. By necessity of law.

Ex Necessitate Rei. From the necessity of the case.

Ex Officio. By virtue of the office.

Exonerate. To relieve from liability; clear.

Exorbitant. Beyond the rule of established.

Exordium. Introduction to a speech.

Ex Parte. From one part or side.

Expatriation. The voluntary renouncing of one's country and becoming the citizen of another.

Expectancy. That which is hoped.

Expectant. Dependent upon a contingency.

Expeditio. Service; execution.

Expel. To eject; to put out.

Expensae. Expenses.

Expensae Litis. Costs of suit.

Expert. Term applied to a witness qualified to speak authoritatively by virtue of the special training, skill or familiarity with the subject.

Expilare. To plunder.

Expiration. Termination due to lapse of time.

Expire. To terminate; to die.

Explicatio. In civil law, the fourth pleading; equivalent to the surrejoinder.

Export. To send goods from one country to another.

Export Tax. Tax on goods shipped out of the country.

Expose. To disclose.

Exposé. A statement, account or explanation.

Expositio, Exposition. Explanation.

Ex Post Facto. After the act is done.

Exposure. Openness to danger.

Express. Explicit; definite; clear.

Express Acceptance. Complete acceptance.

Express Business. The carrying of goods for hire.

Express Consideration. A consideration which is stated in the contract.

Express Warranty. In the law of sales, a statement in regard to the nature, quality or use.

Expropriation. The taking of private property for public use under the right of eminent domain, upon payment of compensation.

Ex Proprio Motu. Of his own accord.

Ex Proprio Vigore. Of its own force.

Ex Provisione Viri. By provision of the husband.

Expulsion. A putting out; ejectment.

Expunge. To strike from the record.

Expurgation. A cleansing; a purification.

Ex Relatione. On the relation or information of.

Exscript. Copy.

Ex Tempore. Temporarily.

Extend. To prolong.

Extension. A grant of further time.

Extenuate. To lessen.

Extenuating Circumstances. Circumstances to be considered when imposing punishment.

Exterritoriality. The privilege enjoyed by diplomats of not being subject to the laws of the country in which they are residents.

Ex Testamento. By will or testament.

Extinct. Extinguished.

Extinguish. To destroy, terminate.

Extinguishment of Debt. Cancellation of debt.

Extortion. Unlawful obtaining (usually by force) of money or property from another.

Extra. Outside of.

Extradition. The surrender by one nation to another of an individual accused of committing a crime in the latter country.

Extrajudicial. That which is done outside the course of regular judicial proceedings.

Extra-Jus. Beyond the law.

Extra Legal. Outside the law.

Extra Legem. Outside the law.

Extraneus. Alien; foreigner.

Extraneus Evidence. Evidence derived not from the document in question.

Extraordinary. Exceeding the normal measure or degree of care; extreme diligence.

Extraordinary Legislative Session. A session of a legislative body held between normal sessions to consider special measures.

Extraparochial. Out of the parish.

Extraterritorial. Outside the boundaries of the state or country.

Extraterritoriality. Any place or building in a country which is treated as a part of another country; the privilege of not being subject to the laws of the country in which one is a resident; the effect of a statute or legal rule beyond the jurisdiction in which the statute or legal rule was instituted.

Extra Viam. Off the highway.

Extra Viris. In excess of power or authority.

Extreme. At the utmost point; excessive.

Extremity. The furthest point.

Extrinsic. Outside; foreign.

Extrinsic Evidence. External evidence or evidence in regard to the meaning of a document which is derived from a source other than the document itself.

Extum. Thence.

Exulare. To exile.

Ex Vi Termini. By the intrinsic meaning.

Ex Voluntate. Voluntarily.

Eye Witness. One who testifies as to what he has seen.

F

F.A.A. (Abb.). Free of all average; in marine insurance, denotes that the insurance is against total loss only.

Fabricate. To deceive a court by giving false evidence; to forge or falsify.

Fabula. Contract; agreement.

Face. The matter which appears on a written instrument.

Facere. To make or do.

Facias. That you make or cause.

Face of a Judgment. The sum for which the judgment was rendered, exclusive of interest.

Face of Record. Entire record in a case.

Face Value. Par value.

Faciendo. In doing or making.

Facilitate. To make less difficult.

Facio Ut Des. I do that you may give; an agreement to pay money in return for the performance of an act.

Facsimile. An exact copy.

Fact. A thing done; that which is real or true.

Fact. Deed or act.

Fact Enrolle. An enrolled deed.

Facta. Facts; deeds.

Facto. In fact or deed.

Factor. A commercial agent engaged in the sale and purchase of goods for a principal.

Factorage. Commission paid to a factor for his services.

Factum. Deed; a thing done.

Factum Probans. A proving fact.

Faculties of Husband. The ability of the husband to render support to his wife in the form of alimony.

Faggot Votes. Sham or illegal votes.

Faida. Malice.

Failure. Bankruptcy; insolvency.

Failure of Consideration. Absence of consideration necessary to make a valid contract; failure to perform what was agreed.

Failure of Issue. To die without lineal descendants.

Failure to Provide. Failure of a husband to provide his wife and children with the necessities of life.

Faint Pleading. A fraudulent or collusive manner of pleading with the intent of deceiving a third party.

Fair. A market.

Fair. Reasonable; equitable.

Fair Comment. In a suit of libel, the defense that the defamatory words were a fair comment on a matter of public interest.

Fair Consideration. Adequate consideration.

Fair Knowledge. Ordinary knowledge.

Fairly. Impartially.

Fair Pleader. See Beaupleader.

Fair Trial. Legal trial.

Faith. Confidence.

Fall of Land. A quantity of land equal to 160th of an acre.

Fallow. Barren or unproductive.

Fallow Land. Land ploughed but not sown in order that it may recuperate its fertility.

Falsa Demonstratio. False description.

Falsa Moneta. Counterfeit money.

Falsare. To falsify or forge.

False. Untrue.

False Appeal. An unsuccessful appeal of felony.

False Arrest. Illegal restraint by one person of the liberty of another.

False Character. Fradulent letter of recommendation used to aid a person seeking employment.

Falsedad. Deception.

Fasehood. Lie.

False Imprisonment. Illegal arrest or detention of a person.

False Instrument. Forged instrument.

False Personation. Criminal offense of pretending to be another person in order to deceive others.

False Pretense. An intentional false statement about a present or past fact.

False Representation. A representation which is untrue as to matter of fact.

False Swearing. A common law misdemeanor not amounting to perjury since the testimony need not be as to a fact material to the issue or point of inquiry and in perjury it must.

False Verdict. A verdict which is not the proper verdict of the jury, i.e. arrived at by some improper means such as drawing lots.

Falsi Crimen. Concealment of the truth for fradulent purposes.

Falsify. To fraudulently alter a record or document; to prove false.

Fama. Character; reputation.

Famacide. Slanderer.

Familia. Family.

Family. Usually refers to parents and children, but can be extended to many relationships.

Family Bible. Bible containing family records which may be used as evidence or to prove age or place of birth.

Family Settlement. An agreement between the members of a family settling the distribution of family property among them.

Famosus Libellus. A libelous writing.

Fanatic. A religious enthusiast.

Fardel. A fourth part.

Farding Deal. One-fourth of an acre of land.

Fare. Charge for transportation.

Farlingarii. Panderers.

Farm. A body of land used for agricultural purposes.

Farm Let. In a lease, formal words signifying a letting on a certain rent payable in produce.

Farthing. The fourth part of an English penny.

Farthing Damages. Nominal damages.

Fatal Injury. Injury causing death.

Father. Male parent.

Father's Natural Guardianship. Guardianship over one's children until they have reached the age of twenty-one.

Farthing of Land. A great quantity of land.

Farvand. Passage by water.

Fast Writ. Any matter which is entitled to precedence on the court calendar.

Fathom. Nautical measure of six feet in length.

Fatua Mulier. Whore.

Fatuitas. Idiocy.

Fatum. Fate.

Fatuous Person. One with no mind; an idiot.

Fatuus. Fatuous, foolish.

Fatuum Judicum. Foolish judgment or verdict.

Faubourg. In Louisiana, a suburb.

Fauces Terrae. Narrow headlands enclosing a bay.

Fault. Negligence; an error or defect in judgment or conduct.

Fautor. An abettor.

Faux. False.

Fauxer. To falsify or forge.

Favor. Bias or prejudice; an act of kindness.

Feal. Faithful.

Feasance. Performance.

Feasant. Performing; making.

Federal. Relating to the U.S.

Federal Courts. The courts of the U.S.

Federal Bureau of Investigation. An agency of the U.S. government, under the Justice Department, which has the duty of enforcing the laws of the U.S.

Federal Government. A union of independent sovereignties.

Federal Question. A question arising under the U.S. Constitution of or under Federal statute.

Fee. An estate of inheritance; compensation for professional services.

Fee Conditional. At common law, a fee limited to some particular heirs, exclusive of others.

Fee Expectant. One which is limited to a man and his wife and their direct heirs.

Fee Farm. An estate in land, subject to rent.

Fee Simple. An estate in which the owner is entitled to the entire property without limitations or qualifications.

Fee Simple Absolute. See Fee Simple.

Fee Tail. An estate in land limited to the grantee and all or certain of his descendants.

Feigned. Fictitious.

Feigned Action. An action brought to secure the decision of the court on a point of law and not founded on any actual controversy.

Feigned Issue. An issue framed to try questions of fact.

Fello-Heir. Joint heir.

Felo. Felon.

Felo de Se. A suicide.

Felon. One who commits felony.

Felonious. Done with intent to commit crime.

Felonious Homicide. An unjustifiable killing.

Felony. A capital crime or one of graver nature than those designated as misdemeanors.

Feme. Woman.

Feme Covert. Married woman.

Feme Sole. Unmarried woman.

Feme Sole Trader. A married woman who engages in business independently.

Femicide. The killing of a woman.

Femme. Woman.

Fender. A protection against danger.

Feneration. The lending of money for interest.

Feod. Fee.

Feoda. Feudal.

Feofee. The grantee of an estate in land.

Feoffor. The grantor of an estate in land.

Feoffment. The transfer of the title to an estate in freehold.

Ferriage. The fare for transportation by ferry; the transportation itself.

Ferry. A place where person or goods are carried across a body of water for a toll.

Festinum Remedium. A speedy remedy.

Festum. Feast.

Fet. Done.

Feticide. Criminal abortion.

Fetters. Chains or shackles.

Fetus. Unborn child.

Feud. A grant of land to be held by a form of feudal tenure.

Fiancer. To pledge or promise.

Fiat. Let it be done.

Fiat Justitia. Let justice be done.

Fiat Money. Currency whose value is decided by the issuing government without regard to its equivalent value in specie.

Fictio. Fiction.

Fiction. A false statement on the part of the plaintiff which the defendant is not allowed to deny, giving the court jurisdiction.

Fictitious. False; feigned.

Fidei. In civil law, a species of trust.

Fidelis. Faithful.

Fides. Trust; faith.

Fiduciary. One who is put in control of property in the interests of others.

Fieri Facias. That you cause to be made.

Fight. Hostile encounter.

Filare. To file.

File. A record of the court; to put away papers.

Filiate. To determine paternity.

Filiation Proceeding. A statutory proceeding to establish the paternity of an illegitimate child in order to impose the duty of support.

Filius. Son.

Filius Nullius. Illegitimate child.

Fille. Girl; daughter.

Fils. Son.

Filium. Thread; edge.

Fin. End.

Final. Last; the end.

Final Decree. A concluding decree.

Final Judgment. A judgment which is not subject to appeal because of a statutory determination or because the time for appeal has expired; a judgment of the highest court in any jurisdiction, a judgment which ends the legal proceeding by resolving the controversy.

Finance. Public or government funds.

Finding. The determination of an issue of fact

by judge or jury.

Fine. Financial penalty.

Fine Force. Necessity, compulsion.

Finem Facere. To impose or pay a fine.

Fines. Boundaries; limits.

Finger Prints. Patterns made by the ends of the fingers used for identification.

Finire. To finish; end; fine.

Finis. Finish; end; fine; limit; boundary.

Finitio. The end.

Fire. The effect of combustion.

Firearm. Gunpowder weapon.

Firebug. Arsonist; pyromaniac.

Fire Insurance. Insurance against fire.

Fire-Proof. Incombustible.

Firm. Partnership; agricultural lease.

Firma. Farm.

Firman. Passport; permit.

Firm Name. Name under which a firm transacts business.

First. Preceeding all others; foremost.

First Class. Of the most superior grade.

First Class Mail. Written matter and all else sealed against inspection.

First Class Misdemeanant. One found guilty of a misdemeanor but judged deserving.

First Degree Burn. Burn which causes inflammation of the outer layer of skin.

First Impression. A case without precedent.

First Instance, Court of. Trial court.

First Mortgage. One having priority as a lien over the lien of any other mortgage of the same property.

First Purchaser. The one who first acquired the state by any method other than descent.

Fisc, Fiscus. Treasury.

Fiscal. Pertaining to public revenue.

Fiscal Year. For accounting purposes, a year beginning other than the first day of January.

Fishery. Right to take fish from water.

Fish Royal. Whale, porpoise, sturgeon.

Fisticuffs. A pre-arranged fist fight.

Fistula. Water conduit or pipe.

Fit. Proper, suitable.

Fitz. Son.

Fix. Fasten a thing immovably; to adjust.

Fixed Liabilities. Those definite in obligation.

Fixed Opinion. Conviction or prejudgment which disqualifies a juror.

Fixture. Personal property attached to realty.

Flag. National standard, ensign, banner.

Flagellat. Whipped.

Flagging. Pavement of flat stones.

Flagrans. Burning; raging.

Flagrans Crimen. As the crime was committed.

Flagrant Necessity. An illegal act made lawful due to urgent necessity.

Flat. Area covered with shallow water.

Flattery. Insincere praise.

Fleece. To cheat.

Fleet. Where the tide flows; creek; ships.

Flem. Outlaw.

Flet. House.

Flight. Offense of running away.

Flim-Flam. Confidence game.

Float. Checks in process of collection; a

government certificate authorizing the holder to enter a specific amount of public lands.

Floating Capital. Funds for general expenses.

Float Policy. Insurance policy covering the interest of the insured without describing particular property.

Flodemark. Highwater mark.

Flogging. Whipping.

Flood. Inundation of water.

Flood-Tide. Rising tide of the sea.

Floor. Section of a building between horizontal boundaries.

Flotsam. Wreckage found at sea.

Flourish. Brandish; wave.

Fluctus. Flood; flood-tide.

Flume. Artificial channel; viaduct.

Fluvius. River; stream.

Fluxus. Flow of tides.

F.O.B. (Abb.) **Free on Board.** Transportation term signifying that no price is due until the seller has delivered the goods.

Fodder. Feed for cattle.

Foedus. Treaty.

Foenus. Interest on money.

Foeticide. Criminal abortion.

Foetus. Unborn child.

Fog. In navigation laws, any atmospheric condition.

Foi. Fealty, loyalty.

Fois. Time.

Folgarii. Followers; menial servants.

Folio. Page with a certain number of words.

Folk Right. Right or law of the people.

Fontana. Fountain; spring.

Food. Nourishment.

Fool Natural. An idiot.

Foot. Measurement of 12 inches; terminal part of leg.

Foot Frontage Rule. Taxation confined to actual frontage on line of improvement.

Footman. Pedestrian.

Foot of the Fine. Concluding part of the fine.

For. Because of; on account of; by reason of.

Foraneus. Foreigner.

Forbarrer. To exclude.

Forbatudus. An agressor killed.

Forbear. To suspend the enforcement of a legal right.

Force. Violence.

Force and Arms. An act of violence.

Forced Heir. One to whom the testator must leave a certain portion of his property.

Forces. Military and naval power.

Forcible Detainer. Unlawfully held chattels.

Forcible Entry. Illegal entry on real property.

Forda. A ford.

Fordanno. Agressor.

Fore. Before.

Foreclosure. Legal proceeding to enforce a lien, pledge or mortgage.

Foreclosure Sale. Sale of mortgaged property.

Foregoer. Ancestor.

Foregift. Premium for a lease.

Forehand Rent. Rent paid in advance.

Foreign. Belonging to another nation.

Foreign Bill of Exchange. A bill drawn in

one state or country and payable in another.

Foreign Corporation. One doing business in a state other than where incorporated.

Foreigner. Citizen of another country; alien.

Foreign Exchange. Drafts drawn on a foreign state or country.

Foreign Plea. One which raises an objection to the jurisdiction of the court.

Forejudge. To expel from court; deprive.

Foreman. Presiding member of jury.

Forensic. Pertaining to the courts.

Forensic Medicine. Medical jurisprudence.

Forensis. Forensic.

Foreright. Right of primogeniture.

Foresaid. Aforesaid; previously mentioned.

Foreshore. Land lying between the greatest and least high tides.

Forest. Large tract of land covered with trees.

Forestall. Lie in wait; obstruct a highway.

Forethought Felony. Premeditated felony.

Forefeit. Loss of a right by default.

Forfeiture of Bond. Failure to meet the condition of the bond and imposition of the stipulated penalty.

Forfeiture of Lease. Failure to meet conditions of a lease causing its termination.

Forgery. The making or altering of a written instrument for fraud or deceit.

Forinsic. Foreign, external.

Foris. Outside.

Forisbanitus. Banished.

Forisfacere. Forfeit.

Forisjurare. Forswear; abjure; renounce.

Form. Model instrument to be used in judicial proceedings; the legal or technical manner to be observed in legal instruments.

Forma. Form.

Forma Dat Esse. Form imparts existence.

Formaldehyde. Preservative.

Formality. Adherence to forms and customs.

Formed Design. Wilful, malicious act.

Formedon. Writ of right to recover property.

Former Jeopardy. Plea under which one cannot be tried for the same offense twice.

Forms of Action. Classes of personal action at common law.

Formula. Set form of words.

Fornication. Illicit intercourse between two unmarried persons.

Fornix. Brothel.

Forno. Oven.

Foro. In the court.

Foro Seculari. In the secular court.

Forprise. An exception.

Forsque. Only; but.

Forswear. Adjure; swear falsely.

Forsworn. Having committed perjury.

Fort. Place protected against attack.

Fortax. Tax heavily.

Forthcoming. Action whereby an arrestment is made effectual.

Forthwith. Immediately.

Fortia. Force; violence.

Fortior. Stronger, more effective.

Fortis. Strong, forcible.

Fortuitous. Accidental.

Fortuitous Event. One depending upon chance.

Forty. Quarter section of land; forty acres.

Forum. Court; tribunal.

For Value Received. Attestation of value.

Forward. Transmit.

Forwarder. One who transports merchandise.

Fossa. Ditch; grave; moat.

Fosterage. Rearing of another's child.

Fosterlean. Remuneration for rearing a foster child.

Foundation. Endowment of an institution.

Founded. Based upon.

Founder. One who initially endows an educational or charitable institution.

Founderosa. In need of repair.

Foundling. An abandoned child.

Four Corners. Contents of an instrument.

Four Seas. Water surrounding England.

Fractio. Fraction; fragment.

Fraction. Fragment; portion; part of whole.

Fraction of a Day. Portion of a day.

Fractura Navium. Shipwrecks.

Frais. Expenses.

Frame-Up. Conspiracy to falsely incriminate.

Franc. Free.

Franchilanus. Freeman.

Franchise. Special privilege conferred on an individual or corporation by the government.

Francus. Free.

Francus Tenens. Freeholder.

Frank. Free; send mail exempt from postage.

Franking Privilege. Use of public mails without payment of postage.

Frassetum. Tract of wooded land.

Frater. Brother.

Frater Consanguineus. Brother born of the same father but different mother.

Frater Nutricius. Bastard brother.

Frater Uterinus. Brother born of the same mother but different father.

Fraternity. Group of men associated for common interests.

Fratriage. Inheritance by a younger brother.

Fratricide. Killing of one who kills a brother or sister.

Fraud. Intentional deception to induce another to part with something of value or to surrender a legal right; deceit; trickery.

Fraudulent. That which is done with intent to defraud.

Fraudulent Concealment. Suppression of a material fact, duty bound to communicate.

Fraudulent Conveyance. Transfer of property to defraud or hinder creditors.

Fraus. Fraud.

Fray. An affray.

Frectare. To freight or load.

Frectum. Freight.

Free. Unconstrained; exonerated; public.

Free and Clear. Not encumbered by any liens.

Free-Bench. Widow's dower in some copyhold lands.

Free-Board. Land claimed outside a fence.

Free Course. Sailing with a favorable wind.

Freedman. One freed from bondage.

Freedom. Liberty.

Free Enterprise. Right to conduct a business

Free Entry, Egress, Regress. Right to enter

and leave another's land.

Freehold. Full ownership or title to land.

Freeholder. One having title to realty.

Free List. Articles exempted by Congress from import duty.

Free On Board. Freight term meaning that the subject of the sale is to be loaded for shipment without expense to the buyer.

Free Ships. During war, neutral ships.

Free Tenure. Tenure by free service.

Freight. Sum paid for transportation of goods; the goods transported.

French Pool. System of gambling.

Freneticus. Madman.

Frequent. To visit often.

Fresh. New; recent.

Fresh Fine. Fine levied within the past year.

Freshet. Flood; inundation.

Fresh Pursuit. Immediate pursuit of an offender after the commission of a crime.

Fret. Freight.

Frettum. Freight.

Fretum. Strait.

Friars. Members of monastic religious order.

Friendly Society. Mutual aid society.

Friendly Suit. An action brought by mutual agreement of parties involved in order to clarify a question of legal right.

Frigidity. Incapacity for sexual intercourse.

Frilinger. Freemen.

Friscus. Fresh; recent; new.

Frisk. To run hands over another's person.

Frithman. Member of a company or fraternity.

Frivolous. Lacking in legal sufficiency.

From. Starting point; out of.

Frontage. Extent of land facing a street.

Fructuarius. Lessee.

Fructus. Fruit; fruits; increase.

Fructus Civiles. Revenues; compensations.

Fructus Legis. Fruit of the law, i.e. execution.

Fructus Naturales. Products of nature.

Fructus Separati. Plucked fruit.

Fruges. Fruits; produce.

Fruit. Seed or edible pulp of plants.

Fruits of Crime. Loot, booty.

Frusca Terra. Uncultivated land.

Frustra. In vain.

Frustrum Terrae. Land lying by itself.

Frutex. Bush; shrub.

Ft. (Abb.). Foot; feet.

Fuer. Flee.

Fuer en Fait. Actual flight.

Fugacia. Chase; hunt.

Fugatio. Hunting privilege.

Fugie. Fugitive.

Fugie-Warrant. Warrant for a debtor.

Fugitate. To outlaw by sentence of court.

Fugitation. Outlawry.

Fugitive. One who flees to escape arrest.

Fugitive Slave. Slave who has fled.

Fugitivus. Fugitive.

Full. Ample; complete, perfect.

Full Age. Age of legal maturity, usually 21.

Full Court. Duly organized with judges present.

Full Faith and Credit. Article IV, Section I of the U.S. Constitution which provides that full faith and credit shall be given in each state to the public acts of other states.

Full Hearing. The right to present evidence and an opportunity to know the claims.

Full Jurisdiction. Complete jurisdiction.

Full Life. Life in fact and law.

Full Pardon. One which releases the punishment and obliterates the guilt.

Full Right. Good title with possession.

Fully. Amply, sufficiently.

Function. Office; duty.

Functionary. Public officer.

Functus. Dead; void.

Functus Officio. Having performed his duty.

Fund. Money or securities for a purpose.

Fundamental. Basic.

Fundatio. Founding or foundation.

Fundator. Founder.

Funded Debt. A debt for which a specific fund has been appropriated, usually to redeem public obligations.

Fundi. Lands.

Fundi Patrimoniales. Lands of inheritance.

Fundi Publici. Public lands.

Funditores. Pioneers.

Fundus. Land; soil; farm; estate.

Fungible. Consumable by use and returnable in kind.

Fungible Goods. Personal property divided into units in such a way that they are considered interchangeable.

Fur. Thief.

Furandi Animo. With intent to steal.

Furca. Gallows.

Fur Diurnus. Daytime thief.

Furiosity. Raving madness.

Furiosus. Madman.

Furlong. One-eighth of a mile.

Furlough. Leave of absence.

Furnish. Provide for use.

Fur Nocturnus. Nighttime thief.

Furor Brevis. Sudden anger.

Further Advance. Additional loan.

Further Assurance. Covenant in real property that the vendor will execute any other documents necessary to perfect the vendee's title.

Furtively. Stealthily.

Furtum. Theft; larceny.

Furtum Grave. Aggravated larceny.

Fustis. Staff.

Future Debt. Existing debt which is not due.

Futures. Commodities or stocks on which delivery is not made until some future time.

G

Gabel. Excise; rent.

Gag. Something forced into a person's mouth to prevent outcry.

Gage. Pledge; challenge.

Gain. Profit.

Gainage Lands. Lands reclaimed from the sea.

Gainful. Profitable.

Gallon. Liquid measure of 4 quarts.

Gallows. Scaffold.

Gamacta. Assault.

Gamalis. Legitimate child.

Gamble. Play for money or other stake.

LEGAL DICT

Game. Animals hunted for sport; sport.

Game. Laws for the preservation of game.

Gaming. To play a game of chance.

Ganancial System. Spanish system of community property.

Gang. Group united for criminal purposes.

Gaol. Jail.

Gaoler. Jailer.

Garage. Place to house motor vehicle.

Garandia. Warranty.

Garaunt. Warranty.

Garaunter. To warrant.

Garauntor. Warrantor.

Garbage. Refuse.

Garble. Sort good from bad.

Gard. Guardianship; care; custody.

Gardein. Guardian.

Garens. Private game preserve.

Garnish. Warn, notify.

Garnishes. One owing money to a debtor or on whom a garnishment is levied.

Garnishment. Statutory proceeding whereby property, money or credits of a debtor in possession of another, the garnishee, is applied to the payments of the debtor by means of process.

Garrant. Warrant; authority.

Garrantie. Warranty.

Garrote. Capital punishment by strangulation.

Gast. Waste.

Gastaldus. Bailiff; steward.

Gaster. To waste.

Gastine. Uncultivated land.

Geld. Sum of money, fine, tribute.

Gemma. Gem, jewel.

Genealogy. Family history.

Gener. Son-in-law.

General. Extensive; prevalent.

General Circulation. Circulation of a newspaper among the public.

General Credit. General reputation of a witness for veracity.

General Estate. Entire estate held by one in his individual capacity.

General Exception. An objection to a pleading or any part thereof for want of substance.

General Indorsement. An indorsement of a negotiable instrument without payee named.

Generalis. General.

General Issue. Denial by the defendant of every material allegation of fact in the plaintiff's complaint.

Generaliter. Generally.

General Law. Law that applies to the community at large.

General Legacy. One which is to be paid to the legatee from the estate's general assets.

General Lien. Lien on a chattel not only for an existing debt, but for any other debt.

General Mortgage. Blanket mortgage on all the chattels of the mortgagor.

General Ownership. Unqualified dominion.

General Power of Appointment. Right to appoint any person the donee pleases.

General Public Law. Law which binds all members of the community, always.

General Property Tax. Tax on real or personal property to obtain revenue.

General Statute. Public statute.

General Strike. Strike of all or most of the workingmen in a particular area.

Generation. Single succession of living beings in natural descent.

Generosa. Gentlewoman.

Generosus. Gentleman.

Geniculum. Degree of consanguinity.

Gens. People; race; tribe.

Gentes. People.

Gentiles. Member of a common tribe or gens.

Genuine. Real; original; not counterfeit.

Genus. Class comprising many species.

Gerens. Bearing.

Gerens Datum. Bearing date.

Gerere. To act; behave; engage in.

German. Fully related; of the same parents.

German Cousin. First Cousin.

Germane. Closely related; appropriate.

Germanus. Of the same stock.

Gerrymander. To subdivide or redistrict a political area for political purposes.

Gestation. Period of pregnancy.

Gestio. Behavior, conduct.

Gestor. Agent.

Gestum. Deed; transaction; business.

Gestura. Behavior.

Gibbet. Gallows.

Gift. Voluntary transfer of personal property without compensation therefor.

Gift Deed. Deed for a nominal sum.

Gift Note. Donor's promissory note.

Gift Tax. Tax levied on gifts of property, to supplement estate and inheritance tax.

Gild, Guild. English fraternal society of artisans or merchants.

Gilt Edge. Of best quality.

Girth. Linear measure of 36 inches.

Gisant. Resting; reclining.

Giser. To lie, rest or recline.

Gist. Main point of a question.

Give. Transfer; grant; bequeath.

Give Bail. Furnish security for one's appearance.

Given Name. First name; Christian name.

Giver. Donor.

Gladiolus. Small sword; dagger.

Gladius. Sword.

Glanders. Contagious disease of horses.

Glans. Fruits of trees.

Gleaning. Gathering together of reaped crops.

Gleba. Turf; sod; soil.

Glider. Form of aircraft.

Glos. A husband's sister.

Gloss. Translation; explanation.

Glossator. Translator; commentator.

Glyn. Glen; ravine.

Go. To be dismissed or issue from court.

God's Acre. Cemetery.

Go Hence. Depart from court.

Going Price. Current price.

Going Witness. One about to leave the jurisdiction of the court.

Golda. Coin.

Goldwit. Fine in gold.

Goliardus. Jester.

Gonorrhea. Venereal disease.

Good. Valid; effective; unobjectionable.

Good Abearing. Good behavior.

Good and Lawful Men. Those qualified to serve on juries.

Good and Valid. Reliable; adequate.

Good Behavior. Orderly conduct; conduct of a prisoner warrenting sentence reduction.

Good Cause. Substantial reason.

Good Faith. Honesty of intention and absence of information causing doubt of validity.

Good Health. Sound of body.

Good Repute. Good reputation.

Goods. Chattels.

Goods and Chattels. Personal property.

Goods Sold and Delivered. An action for goods sold and delivered is brought by the seller to recover the purchase price.

Good Time Provision. Statutory provision by which the prison term of a convict is shortened because of good behavior.

Go Quit. Exonerated.

Gouge. Cheat; defraud; deceive.

Govern. To direct and control.

Government. Political agency through which the state or community acts.

Government de Facto. Government of fact, i.e. actually exercising power in the state as opposed to the lawful government.

Government de Jure. Government of right, i.e. true and lawful government.

Governor. Chief executive officer of a state or territory of the U.S.

Grace. Indulgence; favor.

Gradation. Gradually.

Grade. Line of a street's inclination from the horizontal; quality; value; rank.

Graduate. One who has received a degree in a college or university.

Graduated Tax. Progressive tax.

Gradus. Step; grade; status.

Gradus Parentelae. Family tree.

Graf. Magistrate.

Graffer. Notary; copyist.

Graft. Dishonest transaction in relation to public or official acts.

Grafter. Swindler or dishonest person.

Gram Stain Test. Gonorrhea test.

Grammatophylacium. Place for keeping written instruments.

Grand (Coll.). One thousand dollars.

Grand-Stand Play. An act to draw applause.

Grandchild. Child of one's child.

Grand Jury. A body of citizens of a county organized for the purpose of inquiring into the commission of crimes within the county.

Grandfather. Father of either of one's parents.

Grandmother. Mother of either parents.

Grand Larceny. Larceny or theft of property worth more than the amount fixed in statute.

Grand Theft. See Grand Larceny.

Grange. Farm and all its buildings.

Grangiarius. Keeper of a grange.

Grant. Transfer of real property or of some license or authority; bestow; permit; allow.

Grantee. One to whom a grant is made.

Grantor. One who makes a grant.

Grasson, Grassum. Fine paid upon the transfer of a copyhold estate.

Gratificaion. Gratuity; recompense; reward.

Gratis. As a favor; free.

Gratuitous. Without charge, free.

Gratuity. Free gift; recompense.

Gratulance. Bribe.

Gravamen. Substance of a complaint.

Gravatio. Charge; accusation.

Grave. Excavation in the earth in which a corpse is or is to be buried.

Gravel. Mixture of small stones and sand.

Graveyard. Cemetery.

Gravis. Grave; important; serious.

Great. Important; serious.

Great Seal. Seal of state.

Gree. An agreement.

Green Bag. Symbol of the legal profession.

Green Goods. American slang for counterfeit paper money.

Gremium. Safeguard; protection.

Grievance. Injury; injustice.

Grievance Committee. A committee, usually of workingmen, which presents complaints connected with their employment.

Grieved. Aggrieved.

Grievous. Causing sorrow or pain.

Griff. Offspring of a Negro and mulatto.

Gros. Large, great.

Grocer. Merchant.

Gross. Twelve dozen.

Gross. Great; culpable; general; absolute.

Gross Average. General average.

Grossement. Greatly.

Gross, In. Phrase used to describe a right.

Gross Income. Income before deduction..

Gross Negligence. Lack of care or attention.

Gross Weight. Total weight of goods.

Ground. Soil; earth.

Ground Rent. Rent reserved by one who conveys land to another in fee simple.

Groundage. Port fee.

Ground Annual. Annual rent.

Guadia. Pledge.

Guarantee. One to whom a guaranty is made; to make a contract of guaranty.

Guarantor. One who makes a contract of guaranty.

Guaranty. Mercantile contract whereby a person undertakes to answer for the debt, default or miscarriage of another.

Guardage. Wardship.

Guardia. Ward of a guardian.

Guardian. One who has been legally intrusted with the custody and control of the person and/or property of an incompetent.

Guardian ad Litem. Guardian for the litigation.

Guarra. War.

Gubernator. Pilot; governor.

Gubernatorial. The office of governor.

Guerpi. Abandoned.

Guess. Conjecture.

Guest. One lodged for pay at an inn or hotel.

Guilde. See Gild.

Guilt. Cupability.

Guillotine. French instrument for beheading.

Gule of August. August 1st.

Gun. Firearm.

Gynarchy. Government ruled by a woman.

Gyves. Fetters.

H

Hab. Corp. (Abb.). Habeas corpus.

Habeas Corpora Juratorum. That you have the bodies of the jurors. Writ formerly used in Common Pleas to secure compulsory attendance of the jury.

Habeas Corpus. You are to bring the body. Name given to various writs having as their object to bring a party before a court.

Habeas Corpus ad Subjiciendum. Writ requiring a person detaining a prisoner to produce him and submit to the court's order.

Habendum. Part of deed beginning with, "To have and to hold".

Habendum et Tenendum. To have and to hold.

Habentia. Riches.

Habere. To have.

Habere Facias Possessionem. Old common law writ issued after a successful suit in ejectment, to put the claimant in possession.

Habere Facias Siesinam. Writ to put a claimant in possession of a freehold.

Habere Facias Visum. Writ directing the sheriff to view the premises in controversy.

Habere Licere. To allow possession.

Habilis. Suitable; fit.

Habilis ad Matrimonium. Fit for marriage.

Habit. Disposition or condition of the body acquired by frequent repetition.

Habitable. Tenantable.

Habitancy. Fixed place of abode.

Habitant. Resident tenant.

Habitatio. Right of dwelling.

Habitation. Temporary or permanent abode.

Habitual. Customary; usual; familiar.

Habitual Offender. One who consistently violates the law.

Habitus. Habit; garb; apparel.

Hackney. Let out for hire.

Hade. Grassy slope.

Haec Est Conventio. This is the agreement.

Haec Verba. These words.

Haeredes. Heirs.

Haeredes Proxime. Nearest heirs.

Haeredipeta. One seeking an inheritance.

Haereditas. An inheritance.

Haereditas Jacens. An inheritance held in abeyance pending possession by the heir.

Haereditas Paterna. Paternal inheritance.

Haeres. Heir.

Haeres Ex Asse. Sole heir.

Haeres Institutus. Testamentary heir.

Haeres Legitimus. Lawful heir.

Haeres Natus. Born heir.

Hafne. Haven; port.

Haga. House.

Hagia. Hedge.

Hagne. Small hand-gun.

Hakh. Truth; the true God; legal claim.

Half-Blood. Having one parent in common.

Half-Brother. Brother through a common mother or father.

Half-Proof. Testimony of a single witness.

Half-Sister. Sister through a common mother or father.

Half-Tongue. Jury half speaking one language, the other half another.

Half Year. In law, period of 182 days.

Hall Day. Court day.

Hallucination. Trick of the senses.

Ham. Home, house.

Hamel. Village.

Hamlet. Small village.

Hand. Length of 4 inches.

Handcuffs. Wrist shackles.

Handle. Control; direct.

Hand Sale. Shaking hands over a bargain.

Handwriting. Chirography of a person.

Handy Man. Man of all work.

Hang. Remain undetermined.

Hanging. Form of capital punishment.

Hangman. Executioner.

Hanse. German merchants and traders guild.

Hansgrave. Head of a corporation.

Hap. To catch.

Happiness. Comfort; contentment.

Harbor. Port.

Harbor. To conceal a fugitive from justice.

Hard Cider. Fermented cider.

Hard Labor. Punishment which includes useful labor as well as imprisonment.

Hard Money. Lawful coined money.

Harlot. Prostitute.

Harrow. Hue and cry.

Hat Money. Small duty paid to the captain.

Haula. Court.

Haut. High.

Haut Chemin. Highway.

Have. To possess.

Hawker. Peddler.

Hazar-Zamin. Bail; surety.

Hazard. Game of chance; danger; risk.

Hazardous. Perilous.

Head. Chief; principal.

Head Money. Poll tax; money distributed among officers and crew of a ship.

Head of a Family. One who supports and maintains a household.

Head Taxes. Taxes levied on aliens.

Headnotes. Printed synopses of court decisions which appear in most reports.

Healer. One who cures disease by prayer.

Health. Absence of disease.

Hearing. Examination of one accused of a crime and of the witnesses for and against him; session of court to conduct a trial.

Hearsay Evidence. Evidence based on something which has been told to a witness rather than on personal knowledge.

Head of Passion. Spontaneous anger aroused by some reasonable provocation which will reduce a homicide from the grade of murder.

Heat Prostration. Sunstroke.

Heat Stroke. Sunstroke.

Hebdomad. A week.

Heda. Haven; wharf.

Hedagium. Toll for landing goods at a wharf.

Hedging. Means of making sales contracts in advance at current prices to protect against loss due to fluctuations.

Hegemony. Leadership by one of a group of states or nations.

Heifer. Young cow.

Heir. One who inherits property.

Heir Apparent. One who is sure to succeed to the estate if he survives his ancestor.

Heiress. Female who inherits an estate.

Heirloom. Any personal chattels which go directly to the heir and not to the executor.

Heirship. Condition of being an heir.

Heir Testamentary. One to whom property is left by will.

Hemiplegia. Paralysis of one side of the body, usually due to a lesion in the brain.

Henchman. Attendant; servant.

Henghen. Prison.

Heptarchy. Government by seven rulers.

Herald. Messenger.

Herbage. Right or easement of pasturing cattle on another's land.

Herd. Indefinite number of cattle assembled.

Hereafter. At a future time.

Hereby Granted. Transfer of interest.

Hereditaments. Anything inherited.

Hereditament, Corporeal. Any hereditament that can be perceived by the senses.

Hereditaments, Incorporated. Any right concerning a corporeal hereditament.

Hereditary. Pertaining to inheritance.

Hereditary Succession. Title by descent.

Heredity. Biological law whereby all beings tend to repeat themselves in their descendants.

Heres. Heir.

Heresy. False belief.

Heretofore. Formerly.

Heritable. Inheritable.

Heritable Rights. Rights in real property.

Heritage. An inheritance.

Heritor. Proprietor of an inheritance.

Hermaphrodite. One having the sexual organs of both sexes.

Heroin. Narcotic drug.

Hesia. Easement.

Hidel. Sanctuary.

Hierarchy. Organization of a governing body in the order of their importance and rank.

Highbinder. Member of a Chinese society organized for murder or blackmail.

High Diligence. Great diligence.

High-Jacker. Robber.

High Justice. The right to try all crimes.

High Seas. Open and enclosed parts of ocean.

High Treason. Treason against the king or the government.

High-Water Mark. Line on shore reached at high tide.

Highway. A road open to public use and broad enough to permit the passage of vehicles.

Highwayman. Robber.

H.I.H. (Abb.:. His or Her Imperial Majesty.

Hiis Testibus. With these witnesses.

Hinc Inde. On each side.

Hind. Agricultural servant.

Hire. To receive for payment, the temporary use of a thing or to stipulate for services.

Hire. Compensation for the use of a thing.

Hireman. A subject.

Hirer. One who acquires the right to use a thing belonging to another.

Hissa. Lot or portion.

Hoc. This.

Hoc Paratus Est Verificare. This he is ready to verify.

Hoc Titulo. Under this title.

Hoc Voce. Under this word.

Hogshead. Liquid measure equal to 63 gallons.

Hold. To possess; to bind under contract; to maintain; to administer.

Holder. One who has legal possession of a negotiable instrument.

Holder in Due Course. A holder of a negotiable instrument who has paid value for it.

Holding. Tenure.

Holding Company. Corporation organized to hold the stocks of other corporations.

Hold Over. Retention of real property by a tenant after expiration of the lease.

Hold-Up. Robbery by threat and use of lethal weapons.

Holiday. A day on which public business is suspended by statute.

Holographic Will. Will written entirely in the testator's hand.

Holt. Grove.

Holy Orders. Ecclesiastical orders.

Home. House in which one lives.

Home Office. Office of the British Government which supervises the internal affairs of the empire; the office of a corporation in the state where it was created.

Homestead. The residence of the family.

Homicide. Any killing of a human being.

Homicide Infortunium. Excusable homicide.

Homicide Se Defendendo. Justifiable homicide committed in self-defense.

Homicide, Excusable. Killing of a human being by accident or in self-defense.

Homicide, Felonious. Killing of a human being without justification or excuse in law.

Homicide, Justifiable. Intentional killing of a human being without evil intent.

Homocidium. Homocide.

Hominum Causa Jus Constitutum. Law is constituted for the benefit of mankind.

Homiplagium. Mayhem.

Homme. A man.

Homo. A man.

Homo Liber. A free man.

Homologation. Ratification or confirmation.

Homonymial. Cases in which the same principles and rules of law as set down in previous cases are repeated.

Honestus. Of good character.

Honesty. Financial integrity; loyalty.

Honor. To accept a negotiable instrument at maturity and according to tenor.

Honorable. Title used when addressing certain officials, e.g. judges, congressmen.

Honorarium. Compensation for services.

Honorary Service. Service rendered gratis.

Honoris Causa. As a mark of honor.

Hony. Shame, evil.

Hooch. (Slang). Intoxicating beverage.

Hora. An hour.

Horae Judiciae. Hours of the court sessions.

Hordera. Treasurer.

Hornswoggle (Slang). Triumph over.

Hors. Out, out of; without.

Horse Power. Unit of power capable of lifting 33,000 pounds a foot a minute.

Hors Pris. Taken out; except.

Hortus. Garden.

Hospes. Guest.

Hospita. Inns.

Hostage. Person held as security.

Hostel. Inn.

Hosterler. Host; innkeeper.

Hostelry. Inn.

Hostes. Enemies.

Hosticide. Killing of or one who kills an enemy.

Hostile. Adverse; the character of an enemy.

Hostile Act. Act of war.

Hostile Witness. A witness who is subject to cross-examination by the party who called him because of obvious hostility or prejudice against that party.

Hot (Slang). Term applied to recently stolen goods.

Hotel. Inn.

Housage. Charges for storage of goods.

House. Structure intended for human dwelling; one of the bodies of a bicameral legislature; mercantile firm; reigning family.

Housebreaking. Forcible entry into a dwelling with intent to commit a felony.

Household. The family living together.

Household Furniture, Goods or Stuff. Personal chattels used for the house.

House of Commons. Lower house of English Parliament.

House of Correction. Reformatory.

House of Ill Fame. Brothel.

House of Lords. Upper house of English Parliament.

House of Refuge. Reformatory for juveniles.

House of Representatives. Lower house of U.S. Congress and some state legislatures.

House of Worship. Building for religious services; church.

Hovel. Hut; cottage.

How. Hill.

Hoy. Small sailboat.

H.R.M. (Abb.). His or Her Royal Highness.

Huckster. Peddler, particularly of garden produce.

Humagium. A humid place.

Humane. Kind; benevolent.

Humbug. Imposter.

Hung Jury. Jury which cannot agree.

Hunger. The desire to eat; hunger is not an excuse for larceny.

Hunting. Pursuing of wild animals.

Hurdle. A sledge in which criminals were formerly dragged to execution.

Hurricane. Violent storm with high winds.

Hurst. Grove; wood.

Hurt. Physical injury or mental discomfort.

Husband. Married man.

Husband and Wife. Man and woman married.

Husbandman. Farmer.

Husbandry. Agriculture.

Hush-Money (Coll.). Bribe for silence.

Hustings. Council; court.

Hybrid. Mongrel.

Hypermetropia. Farsightedness.

Hypotism. Induced somnambulism.

Hypothecation. A contract whereby specific property is pledged as security.

Hypothesis. Supposition; theory.

Hypothetical Question. A supposition creating a specific situation upon which the opinion of an expert is asked.

Hysterotomy. Caesarian operation.

I

Ibi. There; then.

Ibid. See Ibidem.

Ibidem. In the same place; indicate that a phrase appears in a passage already quoted.

Ibimus. We will go.

I.C. (Abb.). Inspected and condemned.

Icona. Image or representation of a thing.

Ictus. Blow.

Ictus Orbis. A blow causing a bruise.

Id. It; that.

Idem. The same.

Idem Sonans. Sounding the same; names pronounced the same but varied in spelling.

Identical. Exactly the same.

Identification. Proof that a person or thing is the same as he or it is represented.

Identity. Sameness; see Identification.

Ideo. Therefore; on that account.

Ides. Roman division of time.

Id Est. That is.

Idiochira. Privately executed instrument.

Idiocy. Extreme mental deficiency.

Idiot. One who has been mentally deficient from his birth.

Idiota. An unlearned man.

Idoneare. To prove one's own innocence.

Idoneus. Fit, responsible, qualified.

Idonietas. Fitness.

I.E. (Abb.). Id est; that is.

If. Word which implies a condition.

Ignis Judicium. Trial by fire.

Ignitegium. Curfew.

Ignominy. Public disgrace.

Ignoramus. We do not know. Formerly the indorsement on a bill of indictment when the Grand Jury thought the charge groundless.

Ignorance. Absence of knowledge.

Ignorantia. Ignorance.

Ignorare. To be ignorant of; to ignore.

Ignore. To be unacquainted with.

Il. He; it.

Ilet. Small island.

Illegal. Unlawful.

Illegal Interest. Usury.

Illegitimate. Begotten and born out of wedlock; contrary to law.

Illeviable. Exempt from levy.

Ill Fame. Evil repute.

Illicenciatus. Unlicensed.

Illicit. Unlawful.

Illiterate. Unlettered; unlearned.

Illocable. Not able to be hired.

Illud. That.

Illusion. That which a person believes he sees, but really does not.

Illusory. Deceiving by false appearances.

Imbargo. See Embargo.

Imbecile. One who is mentally deficient and incapable of managing his own affairs.

Immaterial. Not pertinent.

Immediate. At once.

Immediately. Without delay.

Immediate Death. Instantaneous death.

Immediate Family. Members of the same household bound by relationship.

Immemorial. Beyond human memory.

Immemorial Usage. Custom.

Immigration. Coming into a country to take up permanent residence.

Imminent. Impending; threatening; perilous.

Immiscere. To mingle.

Immittere. To put into; admit.

Immobilis. Immovable.

Immoderate. Exceeding reasonable limits.

Immoral. Contrary to accepted standards.

Immovables. Property which by its nature cannot be removed.

Immunity. Exemption from legal punishment.

Immunity of Witness. Constitutional provision protecting witnesses from giving self-incriminating testimony.

Impair. To weaken; make worse.

Impalare. To impound.

Impalement. Inclosure.

Imparcare. Impound; imprison.

Impargamentum. Right of impounding.

Imparl. To discuss a controversy with the opposing party in a suit in order to settle.

Imparlance. Discussion between parties of a suit to settle the dispute amicably.

Impartial. Disinterested.

Impeach. Accuse; censure.

Impeachment. Criminal proceeding against a public official.

Impeachment of Waste. Liability for waste.

Impechiare. To impeach.

Impede. To obstruct; hinder.

Impediens. One who impedes or hinders.

Impediments. Disabilities; bars to marriage.

Impensae. Expenses.

Imperative. Imposing an obligation.

Imperator. Emperor.

Imperfect. Defective, incomplete.

Imperfect Obligation. One which cannot be enforced but depends on an individual's will.

Imperfect Trust. One which has not been executed.

Imperite. Without skill.

Imperium. Rule, authority.

Impertinence. Irrelevancy.

Impertinent. Applied to allegations of a bill in equity which do not belong to a pleading.

Impescare. Impeach.

Impetere. Impeach.

Impierment. Impairing.

Impignorata. Pledged, mortgaged.

Implead. Sue.

Implements. Things necessary to perform the work of any trade.

Implication. That which is inferred.

Implied. Not explicit; not expressed.

Implied Authority. Actual authority possessed by an agent.

Implied in Fact. Applied to situations when the conduct of individuals is used to prove the existence of a transaction.

Implied Power. Powers exercised by a governing body which are proper and necessary.

Import. Bring goods into a country.

Importunity. Pressing solicitation.

Impose. To levy or exact.

Imposition. Impost; tax.

Impossibility. That which cannot be done.

Impotence. Inability to perform the sexual act; any physical incapacity.

Impotent. Incapable of the sexual act.

Impound. To shut up stray animals in a pound; to place disputed property in the custody of the court.

Imprescriptible Rights. Rights not capable of being lost, whether used or not.

Impression. Image fixed in the mind; a belief.

Impressment. Seizing seamen for compulsory service in the navy.

Imprest Money. Money paid on enlisting.

Impretiabilis. Invaluable.

Imprimatur. Let it be printed.

Imprimere. Impress; print.

Imprimis. First of all.

Imprison. Confine; deprive of liberty.

Impristi. Followers.

Improbable. Unlikely.

Improbare. Disallow; disprove.

Improbation. Action to have an instrument declared false and forged.

Improper. Not suitable; unfit.

Improper Influence. Undue influence.

Improve. Disprove; impeach; augment.

Improved Land. Land used to good purpose.

Improvement. Anything that enhances the value of property.

Impruiare. To improve.

Impubes. Minor not the age of puberty.

Impulse. Act of driving onward with force.

Impunity. Exemption from punishment.

Imputatio. Legal liability.

Imputation of Payment. Application of a payment made by a debtor to his creditor.

Imputed. In the legal use, attributed vicariously.

In Action. Not in possession; recoverable by action.

Inadequate. Insufficient.

Inadmissible. Not receivable as evidence.

In Adversum. Against a hostile party.

Inadvertence. Lack of care or attention.

Inaedificatio. Building on another's land with one's own materials or on one's own land with another's material.

In Aequali. In equal right.

Inalienable. That which cannot be transferred.

In Alio Loco. In another place.

In Ambiquo. In doubt.

In and About. In connection with.

In Aperta Luce. In broad daylight.

In Apicibus Juris. In the extremes of the law.

In Articulo. On the point.

In Articulo Mortis. On the point of death.

In Auditu. Within the hearing.

Inauguration. The installing into office.

In Autre Droit. In the right of another.

In Banco. On the bench.

In Being. Alive.

In Blank. Without qualification.

Inblaura. Profit or produce from the soil.

In Bonis. Among the goods.

Inc. (Abb.). Incorporated.

In Camera. In chambers.

Incapacity. Lack of legal power.

In Case. In the event.

In Casu Consimili. In a similar case.

Incarceration. Imprisonment.

Incaustum. Ink.

Incendiary. One guilty of arson.

Inception. Beginning; commencement.

Incest. Sexual intercourse between persons so closely related that marriage is prohibited.

In Chief. Primary; applied to direct examination of a witness.

Inchoate. Incomplete; imperfect.

Incident. A minor characteristic found in connection with a more important or principal quality.

Incidental. Depending upon something else.

cidere. Happen; occur.

Incipitur. It is begun; used at the beginning of a common law pleading or judgment.

Incineration. Burning to ashes.

Incite. Arouse to action.

Incivile. Unjustly; irregular; improper.

Incivism. Hostility to one's government.

Inclose. To surround.

Inclose Lands. Lands surrounded by barriers.

Include, Inclusive. Contain; embrace.

Incola. Inhabitant.

Incombustible. Incapable of being burned.

Income. Money which one receives from business, labor or capital invested.

Income Excise Tax. Tax on income.

Income Tax. A tax levied directly upon incomes of an individual or corporation.

In Commendam. In the care of; in trust.

In Common. Sharing the use of a thing.

In Communi. In common.

Incompatibility. Not able to exist together.

Incompetency. Lack of ability.

Incompetent. One not mentally capable to manage his affairs.

Inconclusive. Subject to disproof or rebuttal.

Inconsistent. Mutually contradictory.

Inconsulto. Unadvisedly; unintentionally.

Incontinency. Illicit sexual intercourse.

Incontinenti. Immediately.

Incontrovertible. Too certain to admit of dispute.

Inconvenience. Disquiet, annoyance.

Incorporamus. We incorporate.

Incorporate. To form a corporation.

Incorporation. The formal act of creating a corporation according to statute.

Incorporator. One of the persons who institutes the steps to form a corporation.

In Corpore. In body.

Incorporeal. Without body.

Incorporeal Property. Intangible property.

Incorrigible. Incapable of being corrected.

Increase. Growth; development; profit.

Increment. Increase; improvement; addition.

Incrementum. Increase.

Incriminate. To charge with a crime.

Inculpate. To accuse.

Inculpatory. Tending to establish guilt.

Incumbent. One presently holding office.

Incumber. To make land subject to a liability.

Incumbrancer. One who has a legal claim upon an estate.

Incur. To become liable for.

In Curia. In court.

Incurramentum. Liability to fine or penalty.

In Custodia Legis. In legal custody.

In Damno. Doing damage.

Inde. Thence.

Indebitatus. Indebted.

Indebitatus Nunquam. Never indebted.

Indebitum. Not due or owing.

Indebtedness. Any liability.

Indecency. That which is against good behavior.

Indecent. Unfit to be seen or heard.

Indecent Exposure. Intentional exposure of the private parts of one's body in public.

Indefeasible. That which cannot be defeated.

Indefensus. Undefended.

Indefinite. Not having fixed boundaries or distinguishing characteristics.

In Delicto. Guilty; at fault.

Indemnatus. Uncondemned.

Indemnificatus. Indemnified.

Indemnify. To save harmless against loss or damage by another; to make good.

Indemnis. Without harm or damage.

Indemnity. Contract by which one person promises to make good any loss or damage another has incurred while acting at his request.

Indemnity Mortgage. A mortgage executed to indemnify the mortgagee against future loss.

Indenture. A written agreement between two.

In Descendu. By descent.

Indeterminate. Uncertain.

Indeterminate Sentence. Criminal sentence imposing a punishment not greater than the maximum nor less than the minimum penalty.

Indicare. Show; reveal; declare.

Indication. A fact pointing to some inference.

Indicia (pl.). Signs or evidence.

Indicia of Ownership. Evidence of title.

Indicium. Mark; sign; evidence.

Indictable Offense. Felony.

Indictare. To indict.

Indicted. Charged in an indictment with a criminal offense.

Indictee. One who has been indicted.

Indictio. Indictment; declaration.

Indictment. Formal accusation made by a Grand Jury charging a person with a crime.

Indicator. One who causes indictment.

In Diem. For, on or at a day.

Indifferent. Impartial; neutral; unprejudiced.

Indigent. Destitute; poor.

Indigent Person. Pauper.

Indignity. Any act which manifests contempt or incivility toward another.

Indirect. Not an immediate relationship.

Indirect Evidence. Circumstantial evidence.

Indispensable. Vital; essential.

Indispensable Evidence. Evidence without which the proof of a given fact is impossible.

Indisputable. Undeniable; conclusive.

Indistanter. Without delay.

Individual. A single person.

Individually. Separately and personally.

Individuum. Indivisible.

Indivisible. Inseparable; whole; entire.

Indivisum. Undivided; owned in common.

Indorsat. Indorsed.

Indorse. To write one's name on the back of a paper or document.

Indorsee. One to whom a negotiable instrument is indorsed.

Indorsement. Writing on the back of an instrument.

Indorser. One who indorses a negotiable instrument.

In Dorso. On the back.

In Dubio. In doubt.

Induce. Request; entice; cause.

Inducement. Motive for an act; matter stated in a pleading by way of introduction.

Induct. Install; inaugurate.

Inductio. Cancellation; obliteration.

Indulgence. Remission of punishment due to sin, granted by the R.C. Church; grade; favor.

In Duplo, in Duplum. In double the amount.

Industry. Habitual diligence; any business conducted for profit.

Inebriate. Alcoholic; drunkard.

Inebriation. Intoxication.

In Effect. In force; in operation.

Ineligible. Not qualified to be elected to office.

In Equity. In a court of equity.

In Esse. In existence or being.

In Essentialibus. In the essentials.

In Evidence. Before the court after having been introduced and received as evidence.

Inevitable. Unavoidable.

In Excambio. In exchange.

In Extenso. Fully; verbatim.

In Extremis. In the last extremity; at the end.

In Facie Curiae. In the presence of the court.

In Faciendo. In doing or making.

In Facto. In fact or deed.

Infamia. Infamy; disgrace.

Infamis. Of ill repute; disreputable.

Infamous. Wicked; criminal.

Infamy. Any criminal or vicious conduct which implies bad character as well as violation of law and involves the guilty person in disgrace.

Infancy. One under 21 years of age.

Infans. A child under the age of 7.

Infant. A minor.

Infantia. Between birth and 7 years.

Infanticide. Killing of a new born child.

In Favorem Libertatis. In favor of liberty.

In Favorem Vitae. In favor of life.

In Fee. In fee simple.

Inference. Conclusion derived from the proof of certain facts.

Inferential. Deducible from proven facts.

Inferior Court. Any court subordinate to the chief appellate tribunal in the particular judicial system.

Inficiari. To deny.

Inficiatio. Denial; denial of a debt or liability.

Infidel. One who does not believe in God.

Infidelis. Infidel.

Infidelitas. Infidelity.

Infidelity. Unfaithfulness in marriage.

In Fieri. In the process of being done.

In Fine. At the end.

Infirm. Weak; feeble.

Infirmative. Having the tendency to weaken.

Infirmity. A defect in a document which subjects it to attack on the ground of invalidity; ailment of substantial character.

In Flagrante Delicto. In the act of the crime.

Informal. Deficient in legal form.

Informality. Want of legal form.

Information. A written accusation made by an official prosecutor, without a presentment by a Grand Jury, charging a person.

Informer. One who gives information to public officials concerning criminal offenses.

In Foro. In the court.

In Foro Conscientiae. In good faith.

In Foro Conteintioso. In a court of litigation.

In Foro Domestico. In the home.

In Foro Legis. In a court of law.

Infortunium. Misfortune.

Infra. Under; below; within; during.

Infra Aetatem. Under age.

Infra Anno Nubiles. Under marriageable age.

Infra Annum. Within a year.

Infra Civitatem. Within the state.

Infra Corpus Comitatus. With the county body.

Infraction. Violation of a law or contract.

Infra Dignitatem. Beneath the dignity.

Infra Furorem. While insane.

Infra Sex Annos. Within 6 years.

Infra Tridium. Within 3 days.

In Fraudem Legis. In fraud of the law.

Infraction. Violation.

Infringement. Encroachment upon; violation of a law, contract or right.

Infugare. To chase.

In Full Life. Alive both civilly and physically.

In Futuro. In the future.

In Genere. In class or kind.

Inge. Meadow; pasture.

Ingenium. Trick; fraud.

In Gremio Legis. In the bosom of the law; applied to that held in abeyance.

Ingress. Entry.

Ingress, Egress and Regress. Used in leases to express the right of a lessee to enter, go upon and return from the land in question.

Ingressu. Writ of entry.

Ingressus. Ingress.

In Gross. In large quantity, personal.

Ingrossing. Making a clear copy from a rough draft of a document.

Inguinal. Term referring to the groin.

Inhabit. Dwell; live.

Inhabitant. One residing in a particular place.

In Hac Parte. On this side; in this behalf.

In Haec Verba. In these words.

Inherent. Intrinsic; a part of.

Inherent Power. Authority possessed.

Inheretrix. Heiress.

Inherit. To take by descent on the death of another.

Inheritance. The right to succeed to the estate of an intestate; the estate itself.

Inheritance Tax. Tax on property transfer.

Inhibition. Prohibition.

In His Verbis. In these words.

In Hoc. In this.

Inhonestus. Dishonorable.

Inhuman Treatment. As a ground for divorce, any cruelty which endangers the life or health of the party concerned.

In Hunc Modum. In this manner.

In Iisdem Terminis. In the same terms.

In Infinitum. Without end.

In Initialibus. In the beginning.

In Initio Litis. At the beginning of the litigation.

In Invidium. With ill will.

In Invitum. Against an unwilling person.

Iniquity. A judicial error.

In Issue. Applied to a matter regularly and properly in controversy before the court.

Initiate. Begun, commenced.

Initiate Curtesy. The interest of the husband during the lifetime of his wife in her lands after a child is born who may inherit.

Initiative. The right of the people to propose bills and laws to be enacted by the legislature on which the people may vote.

In Itinere. On a journey or voyage.

Initium. Beginning.

In Judgment. In a court.

In Judicio. In a legal or judicial proceeding.

Injunction. A restraining order.

In Jure. In law, legally.

In Jure Alterius. In the right of another.

Injuria. A wrong; violation of a legal right.

Injury. Any wrong or damage done to another.

In Jus Vocare. To summon to court.

Inlagare, Inlagation. To restore to the law.

Inland. Within the limits of a state, territorty or country.

Inland Bill of Exchange. Bills drawn and payable in the state where made.

In Law. Implied by law.

Inlaw. To restore an outlaw.

Inleased. Trapped.

In Lecto. In bed.

In Lieu of. In place of.

In Limine. At the outset.

In Linea Recta. In the direct line.

In Litem. In or for a litigation.

In Loco. In the place.

In Loco Parentis. In place of a parent.

In Majorem Cautelam. Of greater caution.

In Malam Partem. In an evil sense.

Inmate. One who resides in an institution or part of another's house.

In Medias Res. In the heart of the matter.

In Misericordia. At the mercy.

In Mitiori Sensu. In a milder sense.

In Mora. In delay.

Inn. Public house where transients can receive food, lodging and other accomodations.

Innamium. Pledge.

Innings. Lands reclaimed from the sea.

Innkeeper. One who keeps a house for the lodging of travelers.

Innocence. Freedom from guilt.

Innocent. Not guilty.

Innocent Woman. One who has never had illicit sexual intercourse.

Innominate. In civil law, unclassified.

Innotescimus. We make known.

In Notis. In the notes.

Innoxiare. To exculpate.

In Nubilius. In the clouds; applied to that held in abeyance.

Innuendo. That part of a declaration or complaint in an action for libel or slander in which the alleged libelous words are explained.

In Nullo Est Erratum. No error committed.

In Octavis. In 8 days.

In Odium Spoliatoris. In hatred of one who despoils.

Inofficiosum. Contrary to natural duty.

Inofficiosum Testamentum, Inofficious Will. A will which violates the natural wish of a dying man to provide for his family.

In Omnibus. In everything.

In Open Court. Before the court while it is in public session.

Inopportune. At the wrong time.

Inops Consilii. Without legal counsel.

Inordinatus. An intestate; one who dies without leaving a valid will.

In Ore. In the mouth.

In Pacato Solo. On peaceful soil.

In Pais. In the country; outside the court or legal proceeding.

In Pari Causa. In a similar case.

In Pari Delicto. Equally in the wrong.

In Pari Materia. In the same matter.

In Pari Passu. On equal footing.

In Patiendo. In suffering or permitting.

In Pendente. In suspense.

In Perpetuum Rei Memoriam. In perpetual memory of the thing.

In Person. Appearing in court on one's own behalf without benefit of counsel.

In Personam. In the law of procedure, applied

to an action which is instituted by giving notice to the party affected, either by personal or by substituted service of process; applied to describe the fact that a court of equity usually enforces its decree by ordering persons to do or not to do certain acts.

In Plena Vita. In full life.

In Pleno Lumine. In the daytime.

In Poenam. By way of punishment.

In Posse. In possibility.

In Posterum. In the future.

In Potentia. In possibility.

In Potestate Parentis. Under the control of a parent.

In Praesenti. In the present.

In Praesentia Diversorum. In the presence of divers persons.

In Prender. That which is to be taken.

In Primis. In the first place.

In Prinicipio. In the beginning.

In Promptus. Impromptu; in readiness.

In Propria Persona. In one's own behalf.

Inquest. A general name for any judicial inquiry; an investigation held by a coronor.

In Quindena. In 15 days.

Inquirendo. Authorization to institute an inquiry on behalf of the government.

Inquisitio. Inquest; investigation.

Inquisition. Inquest; inquiry.

Inquisitor. An official investigator.

In Re. In the matter.

In Rebus. In matters; in transactions.

In Rem. Action instituted against a thing rather than a person.

In Rem Suam. In his own business.

In Render. That which is to be paid or given.

In Rerum Natura. In the nature of things.

In Rixa. In a quarrel.

Inroll. Enroll.

Insane, Insanity. Of unsound mind.

Inscribere. To charge with a crime.

Inscriptio. Written accusation of crime.

Insecure. Unsafe and dangerous.

Insensible. Unintelligible.

In Separali. In severalty.

Insidiator. One who lies in wait.

Insignia. Emblems of rank; distinctive marks.

Insilium. Bad counsel.

In Simile Materia. In a like matter.

Insimul. Together; jointly.

Insimul Computassent. They have together calculated; a common law action to recover a balance due in an account stated.

Insinuare. To deposit in the records.

Insinuatio. Suggestion, information.

Insinuation. In Civil Law, copying something into a public record.

Insinuation of a Will. In Civil Law, the production of a will of a decedent for probate.

Insolation. Sunstroke.

Insolent. Rude; abusive.

In Solido. In entirety.

In Solidum. As a whole.

In Solutum. In payment.

Insolvency. Inability to pay one's debts.

Insolvent. Status of one who is unable to pay.

In Spe. In hope.

In Specie. In kind; in U.S. currency.

Inspect. Examine.

Inspectator. Adversary.

Inspection. Careful investigation.

Inspeximus. We have seen; an official copy.

Install. Induct into office.

Installment. Partial payment of a debt.

Instance. Request; precedent; solicitation.

Instant. Present, current.

Instantaneous. Applied to a crime, one which is fully consummated in and by a single act.

Instanter. At once, immediately.

Instantly. Immediately.

Instar. Image; likeness; equal.

Instar Dentium. Like teeth.

In Statu Quo. In the situation in which.

Instaurum. Farming equipment.

Instigate. Incite to action.

Instirpare. To establish.

Institor. In Civil Law, a clerk or agent.

Institute. To begin or inaugurate an action; one named in a will as heir but directed to transfer the property.

Institutes. Elementary treatises on the law.

Institution. Inauguration of anything.

In Stricto Jure. In strict law.

Instruct. Direct; advise; to give instructions.

Instructions. Directions of a superior.

Instrument. Formal document in writing.

Instrumenta. Unsealed writings admitted as evidence.

Instrumental. Helpful.

Insubordination. Disobedience to authority.

In Subsidium. By way of subsidy.

In Substantialibus. Substantially.

Insufficiency. Failure of an answer to meet the allegations of any pleading.

Insula. Island; separated building.

Insultus. An assault.

In Summa. On the whole.

In Summo Jure. In strictest law.

Insuper. Moreover.

In Superficie. On the surface.

Insurance. A contract whereby one party, the insurer, agrees to indemnify another, the insured, against loss, damage or liability.

Insurance Agent. One authorized to negotiate policies for an insurance company.

Insurance Broker. One who negotiates insurance contracts.

Insurer. One who promises to indemnify.

Insurgent. One who participates in an insurrection.

Insurrection. Rebellion.

In Suspenso. In abeyance.

Intaker. Receiver of stolen goods.

In Tantum. In so much.

Integer. Whole; entire; untouched.

Integral. Complete.

Integration. The act of making whole or entire.

Integrity. Sound principles and character.

Intemperance. Inclination to drink to excess.

Intend. To design; resolve.

Intendant. Manager; director; superintendent.

Intended Wife. Betrothed.

Intendment. Meaning.

Intendment of Law. The meaning of the law.

Intent, Intention. The purpose with which a person acts.

Intentio. In Civil Law, intent, intention.

Intentional. Willful.

Intentional Injury. Willful, conduct.

Inter. Among or between.

Inter Alia. Among other things.

Inter Alios. Between or among others.

Inter Amicos. Among or between friends.

Inter Apices Juris. Among the subtleties of the law.

Inter Caeteros. Among others.

Intercedere. In Civil Law, intervene; to become bound for another's debt.

Intercommon. To enjoy mutual rights.

Inter Conjuges. Between husband and wife.

Intercourse. Communication.

Interdiction. In Civil Law, court order depriving a person of the exercise of his civil rights; in International Law, cessation of all trade between two countries.

Interesse. Interest.

Interesse Termini. Interest of the term; interest a lessee acquires in the lands.

Interest. Right or title of any extent in any property or estate; compensation for the use of money which is due.

Interest Bearing Stock. Preferred stock.

Interested Person. One who has some legal right or who is under some legal liability.

Interests. Any rights of property less title.

Interfere. Hinder; intervene.

Interference. Proceedings in patent law to determine priority of two inventions.

Interim. Meanwhile.

Interim Curator. Temporary guardian.

Interlineation. Writing between the lines.

Interlocking Directors. Persons who simultaneously serve as members of the boards of directors of two or more corporations.

Interlocutory. Provisional; temporary.

Interlopers. Persons operating without the license required by law.

Intermarriage. The act of marriage between two persons considered as members of different groups.

Intermeddle. To interfere officiously.

Intermediary. Broker; one who negotiates.

Intermediate. Intervening.

Inter Minora Crimina. Among the minor crimes.

Intermittent Easement. An easement used only occasionally.

Intern. To incarcerate a person as a political prisoner.

Internal Revenue. Revenue raised from any source except duties on imports.

International Copyrights. Copyrights which are recognized as such by states or countries other than that of the writer.

International Law. Law which governs the intercourse of nations.

Internuncio. Representative of the Pope.

Internuncius. Messenger, go-between.

Inter Partes. Between the parties.

Interpellation. Summons.

Interpleader. Proceeding in equity in which a person in possession of property claimed by two or more persons adversely to each other, surrenders the property to the court to settle.

Interpolate. Add words in a written document.

Interpret. Construe; discover the meaning of a statute; to translate.

Interpretation. The art of discovering the true meaning of any form of words.

Interregnum. The period between the death of one sovereign and the election of another.

Interrogatories. Written questions prepared as part of a commission to take an oral deposition; written questions propounded by one party and served on an adversary before trial of the action and answered in writing.

In Terrorem. As a threat; applied to legacies given upon condition that the legatee shall not dispute the validity of the will.

Interruptio. Interruption.

Interruption. An arrest in the running of the statute of limitations or the period of prescription by the voluntary act of the party in whose favor the period runs, by an act of the adverse party, or by the advent of some incapacity of the adverse party.

Inter Se. Among themselves.

Intersection. The space occupied by two streets at the point where they cross.

Interstate. Between two or more states.

Interstate Commerce. Transactions which involve the movement of persons or goods from one state to another.

Intervener. One who voluntarily enters a litigation in which he was not an original party.

Intervening Cause. An independent cause which breaks the chain between the original negligent act and ensuing damage or loss.

Intervention. Proceeding permitted by statute in a number of states to enable persons to protect their rights when they are in danger of being injuriously affected by attachment proceedings; procedure whereby persons may intervene in litigation though not originally a party in the suit.

Inter Virum et Uxorem. Between husband and wife.

Inter Vivos. Between living persons.

Intestabilis. One disqualified from testifying.

Intestable. One not qualified to make a will.

Intestacy. State or condition of dying without leaving a valid will.

Intestate. One who dies without a will.

Intestatus. Intestate.

In Testimonium. In testimony.

Intimacy. Proper, friendly relation between persons; sometimes improper relation.

Intimidation. Unlawful coercion.

In Totidem Verbis. In so many words.

In Toto. In all; entirely.

Intoxicated. Under the influence of alcohol.

Intoxicating Liquor. Any alcoholic beverage which will produce intoxication in such quantities as may practically be drunk.

Intoxication. Drunkenness.

Intra. Inside; within.

In Transitu. In transit.

Intrastate Commerce. Trade within a state.

Intra Vires. Applied to a person or corporation when acting within authority.

Intrinsic Evidence. Evidence derived from a document without anything to explain it.

Intrinsic value. Inherent value.

Introduction. Part of a document which sets forth preliminary matter.

Intruder. One who wrongfully enters.

Intrusion. Wrongful entry of a stranger on land after a particular estate of freehold in them is determined.

Intrust. To confer a trust upon.

Intuitu Matrimonii. Contemplation of marriage.

Intuitus. View; regard; contemplation.

In Tuto. In safety.

Inundation. Flood.

Inure. To take effect as to benefit a person.

Invade. To assault.

Invadiare. To mortgage.

Invadiatio. Mortgage.

Invadiatus. One who has had pledges given for him.

In Vadio. In pledge; by way of security.

Invalid. Without binding force; null; void.

Invasion. Encroachment upon the rights of another; entry of an army for conquest.

Inveigle. Entice.

Inveniendo. Finding.

Inventio. In Civil Law, finding of goods.

Invention. A new and original creation upon which a patent may be issued.

Inventory. An itemized, detailed list of articles of property in an estate which executors and administrators are required by law to make.

Inventus. Found.

Inveritare. To verify.

Invest. To place money where it will yield an income or revenue.

Investment. The placing of capital in a business or for the purchase of secuirities.

In Vinvulis. In chains; in bondage.

Inviolable. Not to be violated.

In Vita. In life; living.

Invitee. One who is invited onto the premises.

Invito Domino. The owner being unwilling; used in an indictment for larceny to indicate that the act done in regard to property was not permitted.

Invitus. Against the wish.

Invoice. An itemized account of merchandise shipped from merchants to their correspondents setting forth the quantity, prices and charges.

Invoice Price. Prime cost.

Involuntary. Unintentional.

Involuntary Payment. Made under coercion.

Iota. Minutest quantity possible.

I.O.U. I owe you; written acknowledgment of indebtedness.

Ipse. Himself; itself.

Ipse Dixit. He said it himself; a bare asser-

tion resting on the authority of the individual.

Ipsissimis Verbis. In the very words.

Ipso Facto. By the fact itself.

Ipso Jure. By the law itself.

Ira Motus. Excited by anger.

Ire Ad Largum. To go at large.

Iron Safe Clause. Clause in an insurance policy stipulating that books of account and inventory be kept in an iron safe.

Irrational. Unreasonable.

Irrebuttable Presumption. One which is indisputable and cannot be changed.

Irrecusable. Contractual obligation imposed without one's consent.

Irregular. Not according to rule or form.

Irregular Judgment. One contrary to the course and practice of the courts.

Irrelevant. Not pertinent.

Irreparable Injury. One which cannot be adequately compensated by damages.

Irrepleviable. Anything which is not subject to an action for replevin.

Irresistible Impulse. A mental state amounting to a disease which overpowers the will.

Irrevocable. That which cannot be revoked or withdrawn.

Irritus. Ineffectual, void.

Irrogare. To impose: levy; as a fine.

Irrotulatio. An enrollment.

Island. Body of land surrounded by water.

Issint. Thus.

Issuable. Producing or relating to an issue; plea which permits issue of fact.

Issue. Lineal descendents; send forth; point in which one pleading contradicts the allegations of another; a question arising which must be determined for one side or the other; to send forth; to promulgate.

Issues. The profits of land.

Ita. Thus.

Ita Est. It is thus.

Ita Quod. So that.

Ita Te Deus Adjuvet. So help you God.

Item. Also; formerly used to mark the beginning of a new paragraph or every addition to a list of articles or of statements.

Itemize. To list.

Iteratio. Repetition.

Itinerant. Wandering; traveling.

J

J. (Abb.). Judge.

J.A. (Abb.: Judge Advocate.

Ja. Now; yet.

Jacens. Lying in abeyance.

Jactitation. False boast.

Jactitation of Marriage. Wrongful assertion of any person that he or she is married.

Jactivus. Lost by default.

Jactura. Jettison; tossing of goods overboard.

Jail. Prison.

Jailer. Warden of a prison or jail.

Jake. Colloquialism applied to a mixture of Jamaica ginger and some other drink.

Janitor. Doorkeeper.

Jay Walking. Crossing a street intersection diagonally.

Jeopardy. Danger, particularly of conviction and punishment for a crime.

LEGAL DICT

Jetsam. Goods cast from a ship to lighten it.

Jettage. Tax on incoming ships.

Jettison. Voluntary throwing overboard of part of a vessel's cargo to lighten the ship.

Jetty. A projection devised to serve as protection against waves.

Jim Crow Car. Railway car for the exclusive accomodation of colored passengers.

Jimmy. Prying-bar used by burglars.

J.J. (Abb.). Judges.

Jobber. One who buys and sells goods.

Jocalia. Jewels.

Jocelet. Small farm.

Jocus. Game of chance.

John Doe. Fictitious name frequently used to indicate a party in an action or proceeding.

Join. Unite; act together.

Joinder. Uniting of several causes of action in one suit; uniting of different persons as parties plaintiff or defendent.

Joint. United; combined; coupled together.

Joint Account. An account in two or more names.

Joint Action. An action prosecuted or defended by two or more persons.

Joint Adventure. A community of interests among several persons.

Joint and Several. A liability in which the creditor may sue one or more of the obligors separately or together.

Joint Creditors. Creditors who can only enforce their claim by acting together.

Joint Executor. Co-executor.

Jointist. One who sells intoxicating liquors where such sales are prohibited by law.

Jointly. Unitedly; sharing in interest.

Joint Resolution. Resolution adopted concurrently by both houses of legislature.

Joint Stock Company. A company engaged in business for profit, possessing a common capital divided into shares, of which each member possesses one or more.

Joint Tenancy. A holding of property by several persons in such a way that any one of them can act as owner of the whole.

Jour. Day.

Jour in Court. Day in court.

Journal. Book in which daily entries are made.

Journée. A court day.

Journey. Travel from place to place.

Journeyman. A laborer hired by the day.

Journey-Work. Work by the day.

J.P. (Abb.). Justice of the Peace.

Jr. (Abb.). Junior.

Jubere. To order, command, direct.

Judaism. Religion of the Jews.

Judex. Judge.

Judge. One appointed or elected to preside.

Judge Advocate. An officer of a court martial whose duty it is to advise the court and to act as prosecuting attorney.

Judge Made Law. Applied to decisions made by the courts as distinct from statute laws.

Judge pro Tem. A substitute judge.

Judge's Chambers. A judge's private office.

Judge's Minutes or Notes. Memoranda jotted down by the judge in the trial of an action.

Judgement. An opinion; the court decision.

Judgment Book. An official record of court judgments.

Judgment by Default. A judgment rendered in consequence of non-appearance.

Judgment Creditor. One in whose favor a judgment is rendered.

Judgment Debtor. One against whom a judgment has been rendered.

Judgment Docket. An official record of court judgments and their satisfaction.

Judgment in Error. Judgment of the higher court rendered on a writ of error.

Judgment Lien. A lien on real property arising from the filing of a judgment.

Judgment Nihil. A judgment against a party due to his failure to plead.

Judgment Nisi. A judgment which will become final unless cause is shown.

Judgment Note. A promissory note with the provision that upon default the holder may have judgment for the principal with interest.

Judgment of His Peers. Trial by jury.

Judgment Paper. The paper on which the final judgment of the court is written.

Judicial Writ. A writ subsequent to the original writ with which the litigation began.

Judicare. To judge, decide.

Judicatio. The passing of a sentence.

Judicatories. That department of government intended to interpret and administer the laws.

Judicatory. Court of justice.

Judicature. Court of justice; jurisdiction.

Judicial. Any act done under direction of a court; involving the exercise of judgment.

Judicial Admission. Statements made by a party in a legal proceeding, such a statement being admissable in evidence.

Judicial Cognizance. Knowledge upon which a judge is bound to act without having it proved in evidence.

Judicial Confession. A confession made by a party, such a confession being admissable in evidence against the party.

Judicial Divorce. One granted by the sentence of a court of justice.

Judicial Function. An act performed by virtue of judicial powers.

Judicially. Belonging to a judge.

Judicial Mortgage. A lien on real property arising from the filing of a judgment.

Judicial Notice. The power of a court to accept as proved certain notorious facts.

Judicial Power. The power granted to a court or judicial tribunal.

Judicial Proceedings. Any proceeding before a judge or court of justice.

Judicial Review. The power of the courts to review statutes or administrative acts and to determine their constitutionality.

Judicial Separation. Separation of man and wife by court decree, without divorce.

Judiciary. That branch of government which interprets and applies the laws; a judge.

Judiciously. Directed by good judgment.

Judicium. Judicial authority; trial; verdict.

Judicium Capitale. Death sentence.

Judicium Dei. The judgment of God; name for trial by ordeal or battle.

Jugulator. Cutthroat; murderer.

Jumenta. Beasts of burden.

Jump Bail. To flee in violation of a bail bond.

Junior. Younger; of secondary standing.

Junk. Rubbish.

Junk Shop. Place where odds and ends are bought and sold.

Junty, Junto. Political faction; secret council.

Jura (sing. Jus). Rights.

Jura in Re. Rights in a thing.

Jural. Relating to law or right.

Juramentum. An oath.

Juramentum Calumniae. Oath of calumny.

Juramentum Corporalis. Corporal oath; oath taken on the Bible.

Juramentum Necessarium. Necessary oath.

Juramentum Voluntarium. Voluntary oath.

Jura Personam. Rights of persons.

Jura Praediorum. The rights of landed estates.

Jura Publica. Public rights.

Jurare. To swear or take an oath.

Jurat. Certificate stating the time and place of an affidavit and the person before whom it was sworn.

Jurata. Jury.

Juration. The administration of an oath.

Jurator. One who swears; member of a jury.

Jure. By right; by the law.

Jure Civili. By the Civil Law.

Jure Divino. By divine right.

Jure Gentium. By the law of nations.

Jure Mariti. By the right of a husband.

Jure Naturae. By the law of nature.

Jure Propinquitatis. By right of nearness.

Jure Representationes. By right of representation.

Jure Uxoris. In the right of the wife.

Juridical. Pertaining to the law and the administration of justice.

Juridical Day. Day court is in session.

Juris. Of right; of law.

Juris Consultus. Learned in the law.

Jurisdiction. The authority whereby a court can render a valid judgment.

Jurisdictional Dispute. A dispute between rival labor organizations affecting their right to control workingmen.

Juris et de Jure. Of law and from law.

Juris et Seisinae Conjunctio. The union of right and possession forming a complete title.

Juris Gentium. Of the law of nations.

Jurisperitus. Learned in the law.

Juris Positivi. Of positive law.

Juris Privati. Of private right.

Jurisprudence. The science of law.

Juris Publici. Of common right or public use.

Jurist. One learned in the law.

Juristic Act. One to have a legal effect.

Juristic Person. Any legal entity other than a natural person.

Juror. Member of a jury.

Juror's Book. List of those qualified to serve on juries.

Jury. A body of men, usually 12, selected according to law and sworn to hear and determine issues of fact in a trial at law.

Jury Box. Enclosed area in a courtroom.

Jury List. List of those eligible for jury duty.

Juryman. Member of a jury.

Jury Process. Process or writ to summon jurors.

Jury Wheel. Contrivance by means of which the names of those to serve are selected.

Jus. Right; justice; law.

Jus Abutendi. The right to abuse, i.e. the right of full ownership.

Jus Accrescendi. Right of survivorship.

Jus ad Rem. The right to a thing, which has its foundation in an obligation incurred by another person.

Jus Anglorum. The law of the Anglo-Saxons.

Jus Belli. The law of war.

Jus Bellum Dicendi. The right to declare war.

Jus Canonicum. The canon law.

Jus Civile. The Civil Law.

Jus Civitatis. The right of citizenship.

Jus Cloacae. The right of sewage or drainage.

Jus Coronae. The right of succession to the throne.

Jus Dare. To make or enact the law.

Jus Dicere. To declare or state the law.

Jus Disponendi. The right of disposing of one's property.

Jus Dividendi. The right of disposing of realty by will.

Jus Duplicatum. A double right; right of possession united with right of property.

Jus Edicere. Right to issue edicts.

Jus Est Ars Boni et Aequi. Law is the science of that which is good and just.

Jus Fiduciarium. A right in trust.

Jus Fluminum. The right of using rivers.

Jus Futurum. A future right.

Jus Gentium. Law of nations.

Jus Gladii. The right of the sword; the executory power of the law.

Jus Habendi. The right to have a thing.

Jus Haereditatis. The right of inheritance.

Jus Immunitatis. Exemption from service in public office.

Jus Incognitum. An unknown law.

Jus Individuum. An indivisible right; an individual right.

Jus In Personam. A right against a person, the right arising out of a personal obligation.

Jus In Re. A right in a thing; ownership.

Jus in Re Propria. Complete ownership.

Jusjurandum. An oath.

Jus Legitimum. A legal right.

Jus Mariti. The right of the husband.

Jus Naturae. The law of nature.

Jus Naturalis aut Divini. Natural or divine law.

Jus Navigandi. The right of navigation.

Jus Non Scriptum. The unwritten law.

Jus Pascendi. The right to pasture cattle.

Jus Personarum. Rights of persons.

Jus Possessionis. The right of possession.

Jus Postliminii. The right, after war, of the restoration to former state.

Jus Praescens. A present or existing right.

Jus Presentationis. The right of presentation.

Jus Privatum. A private right.

Jus Proprietatis. The right of property only.

Jus Publicum. Public law.

Jus Quaesitum. The right to recover a thing.

Jus Representationis. The right of representing or of being represented by another.

Jus Respicit Aequitatem. Law regards equity.

Jus Sanguinis. The principle that the nationality of a person is the same as his parents.

Jus Scriptum. The written law.

Jus Soli. The principle that nationality is determined by the place of birth.

Jus Strictum. Strict law.

Just. Conforming to what is legally right.

Just Cause. Legitimate cause.

Just Claim. A claim which can be enforced.

Just Compensation. Compensation paid to one whose property has been taken in condemnation proceedings.

Jus Tertii. The right of a third party.

Justice. Judge; a standard of action on the part of public officials in accordance with the entire body of law.

Justice of the Peace. A public official having minor judicial power.

Justices' Courts. Courts presided over by justices of the peace.

Justiceship. Rank or office of a justice.

Justice's Judgment. A judgment rendered by a justice of the peace.

Justiciable. Subject to court action.

Justiciar(y). Justice; judge.

Justiciatus. Judicature; perogative.

Justifiable. Rightful; lawful.

Justifiable Homicide. Excusable homicide.

Justification. Valid defense for the performance or non-performance of an act.

Justify. Quality as a surety or as bail.

Justinianist. Civilian; one studying civil law.

Justitia. Justice.

Justitia Piepoudrous. Speedy justice.

Justitium. Suspension of the court business.

Jus Tripertitum. The law of wills.

Jus Utendi. The right to use a thing.

Juvenile Courts. Court having special jurisdiction over delinquent or neglected children.

Juxta. Near; following; according to.

Juxta Formam Statuti. According to the form of the statute.

Juxtaposition. Being placed in nearness; side by side.

K

Kasier. Emperor.

Kalendae. First day of the Roman month.

Kalendar. Calendar.

Kalends. See Kalendae.

Kangaroo Court. Mock court held in prison whereby prisoners judge another inmate.

Karat. Weight of four grains, in weighing gems.

Kay. Quay; key.

Keelage. Duty for anchoring in a harbor.

Kadi. Turkish civil magistrate.

Kaia. Key; quay.

Kaiagium. Quayage; wharfage-due.

Keehaul. To punish a sailor by dragging him under the ship's keel with a rope.

Keels. Coal barges.

Keep. To continue; maintain; conduct.

Keep Down Interest. Payment of interest periodically as it becomes due.

Keeper. Custodian; superintendent.

Keep the Peace. Prevent a public disturbance.

Keno. Gambling game.

Kern. Vagrant.

Kerosene. Rock or earth oil.

Key. Wharf for the loading and unloading of goods from vessels.

Khedive. Governor of Egypt.

Kidnapping. Forcible abduction of anyone.

Kilderkin. Measure of 18 gallons.

Kill. To deprive of life, slay; stream.

Kin, Kindred, Kinship. Related by blood.

Kind. Class; grade; sort.

Kind, In. Payment by means of property or service and not in specie.

King. Ruler or sovereign of a kingdom.

Kingdom Dominion of a king or queen.

Kings Evidence. State's evidence.

Kinsfolk. Relations.

Kip. Brothel

Kirk. Church.

Kleptomania. An irresistible impulse to steal.

Knave. Swindler; cheat.

Knight. Lowest order of nobility.

Knight's of the Garter. The highest order of knighthood.

Knock Down. At an auction, to indicate property is going to the last bidder.

Knot. A marine mile of 6086.7 feet.

Know. To have information.

Knowingly. Intentionally.

Koran. Mohammedan book of faith.

Koshuba. Jewish marriage contract or settlement.

Kyn. Kin.

L

La. There.

Label. A slip of paper attached to a written instrument in order to hold the appending seal; identification tag.

Labor. Work; toil; name for all workmen.

Labor Agitator. One actively engaged in promoting the interest of laboring men.

Labor a Jury. To tamper with a jury.

Labor Arbitration. Arbitration of controversies arising out of the relationship between management and labor.

Labor Dispute. Controversy regarding terms or conditions of employment.

Laborer. One engaged in manual labor.

Labor Union. An organization of workmen formed to promote common interests.

Laches. Term used in equity to indicate unreasonable delay to claim a right.

Lacta. Defect in weight.

Lacuna. Blank space in a written instrument.

Lacus. Lake.

Laden in Bulk. In maritime law, loaded with a loose, unboxed cargo.

Lady Day. March 25, Feast of the Annunciation of the Blessed Virgin Mary.

Laesa Majestas. Injured majesty; high treason.

Laga. Law.

Laicus. Layman.

Lais Gents. Laymen; a jury.

Laity. Laymen, secular persons.

Lake. Large body of fresh water surrounded by land.

Laissez Faire. Non-governmental interference in business or economic affairs.

Land. Ground, soil, earth; realty, real estate.

Landed Estate. An interest in lands.

Landed Property. Real estate.

Land Gabel. Tax or rent for the use of land.

Landing. A place on navigable water for loading and unloading.

Landlord. One who leases land to a tenant.

Landmark. Boundary marker.

Land Patent. Document whereby the government title to portions of the public domain passes to private ownership.

Land Poor. To be in possession of a large amount of unproductive land.

Land Offices. Government offices in which titles to public lands and sales of such land are registered, and other business dealing with public land is transacted.

Lands, Tenements and Hereditaments. Inheritable lands or interests therein.

Land-Tax. Tax laid upon the legal or beneficial owner of land.

Land-Tenant. One in possession of land.

Language. Any way of communicating ideas.

Languidas. Sick; ill.

Lapidation. Stoning to death.

Lapidicina. Stone quarry.

Lapilli. Precious stones.

Lapse. To end, cease or fail; forfeiture.

Lapsed Policy. Policy on which there has been default in payment of premiums.

Lapsus Lingual. Slip of the tongue.

Larceny. Theft.

Larcyn. Larceny.

Laron. Thief.

Lascivious. Wanton; lustful.

Last. Latest; ultimate.

Lastage. Ballast or lading of a ship.

Last Clear Chance. Doctrine that the one who has last clear chance is liable.

Last Illness. Illness which immediately precedes and results in one's death.

Last Resort. Applied to courts from which there is no appeal to a higher court.

Last Will and Testament. An instrument whereby one makes a disposition of his property to take effect after his death.

Lata Culpa. Gross negligence.

Latching. Underground survey.

Late. Last; defunct; dead; formerly.

Latent. Hidden; concealed.

Latent Deed. A deed kept hidden for 20 years or more.

Latent Defect. Defect not apparent but which becomes evident in use.

Lateral. Proceeding from the side.

Lateral Support. Support which adjoining land or the soil beneath gives one's own land.

Laterare. To lie sideways.

Latifundium. Great or large possessions.

Latin. Language of the ancient Romans.

Latitare. To lie hidden.

Latitatio. Concealment of one's person.

Latori Praesentium. To the bearer of these presents.

Lato Sensu. Broadly speaking.

Latro. Thief; bandit.

Latrocination. Pillage.

Latrociny. Larceny.

Laudare. To name, cite or quote; advise.

Laudatio. Testimony favorable to the accused's character.

Laudator. Favorable witness; arbitrator.

Laus Deo. Praise be to God.

Law. Statute; legislative enactment.

Law Charges. Court costs.

Law Day. The day specified in a contract upon which money was to be paid.

Lawful. Legal.

Lawful Age. Legal Age; majority.

Lawful Heirs. Those designated by law to take by descent.

Lawful Interest. Lawful rate fixed by statute.

Lawful Issue. Descendents.

Lawful Money. Legal tender.

Lawless. Not subject to or controlled by law.

Lawless Man. Outlaw.

Law of a General Nature. One which relates to a subject that may exist everywhere.

Law of Nations. International law.

Law of Nature. Scientifically determined law of natural phenomena; binding all mankind.

Law of the Land. Due process of law.

Law Spiritual. Ecclesiastical law.

Lawsuit. A suit, action or proceeding in a civil court; a suit at law or in equity.

Law Worthy. Entitled to legal protection.

Lawyer. One licensed to practice law.

Lay. Pertaining to person or things not clerical.

Lay Corporation. A corporation of lay persons.

Lay Damages. Damages claimed by plaintiff.

Lay Gents. Laymen.

Laying Out. Expression for locating and establishing a new highway.

Laying the Venue. In pleading, stating the county in which the plaintiff proposes that the trial of the action shall take place.

Layman. One not of the clergy.

Lay People. Jurymen.

Layoff. Termination of work by the employer.

Lazaret. Quarantine station.

Le. The.

Leading Case. A case frequently cited.

Leading Counsel. Counsel who is in charge of the conduct of a lawsuit.

Leading Question. One which suggests answer.

League. Treaty of alliance among states.

Leakage. Loss in a vessel's cargo by leaking or breaking in transit.

Lean. To include in opinion or preference.

Leap Year. Year having 366 days and occuring every 4 years.

Learn. To gain knowledge or information of.

Lease. Grant by one person, the lessor, to another, the lessee, of the used and possession of land for a limited time.

Leasehold. Tenancy under a lease.

Leave. Give by will; to put, place, deposit.

Leave and License. A defense in an action of trespass that the plaintiff consented to the act complained of.

Leave of Court. Permission granted by court.

Leccator. Lecherous person.

Lecit. It is legal.

L. Ed. (Abb.). Lawyer's edition.

Ledger. Account book.

Lega. An alloy once used in making coins.

Legacy. Bequest; property left by will.

Legacy Tax. Inheritance tax.

Legal. Lawful.

Legal Age. The age (usually 21) at which one acquires the full capacity to enter into contracts and transact business.

Legal Aid Society. An organization for the purpose of giving legal advice and assistance to the indigent.

Legal Cause. Substantial factor that caused harm.

Legal Conclusion. Legal inference.

Legal Duty. An obligation arising from a contract or operation of the law.

Legal Entity. Legal existence.

Legal Ethics. The usages and customs among members of the legal profession involving their moral and professional duties.

Legal Evidence. All admissable evidence.

Legal Heirs. Next of kin.

Legal Holiday. A day on which juridical proceedings cannot be held.

Legal Injury. Violation of legal right.

Legal Interest. Rate of interest.

Legal Liability. Liability which the courts recognize and enforce.

Legalis Homo. A lawful man.

Legalize. To make lawful.

Legally. According to law.

Legally Determined. Determined by process of law.

Legally Proved. Established by evidence.

Legally Reside. Domicile.

Legal Malice. Constructive malice, arising from the circumstances.

Legal Name. Christian name and surname.

Legal Negligence. Negligence per se.

Legal Notice. Notice complying with the requirements of law.

Legal Obligation. An obligation to do and perform what the law requires.

Legal Rate of Interest. A rate which is not in excess of the maximum rate allowed by law.

Legal Representative. Usually applied to the executor or administrator of a decedent.

Legal Right. A claim recognizable and enforceable at law.

Legal Tender. That which may be legally offered to a creditor by his debtor in payment.

Legal Voter. One authorized by law to cast his ballot at an election.

Legal Wilfulness. Intentional negligence.

Legare. Bequeath.

Legatee. One to whom property is left by will.

Legation. An embassy; a diplomatic minister.

Legator. One who makes a will and leaves legacies.

Legatum. Legacy; bequest.

Legem. Law.

Legem Facere. To make an oath.

Legem Habere. To give evidence under oath.

Legem Pone. To lay down the law.

Leges. Law.

Leges Scriptae. Written or statute laws.

Legislate. To enact laws or pass resolutions.

Legislation. Preparation and enactment of laws.

Legislative. Pertaining to the statute-making branch of the government or legislature.

Legislative Courts. Courts created by Legislature not named by the Constitution.

Legislative Power. Lawmaking power.

Legislator. One who makes laws; member of a legislative body.

Legislature. That branch of government which makes laws for a state or nation.

Legisperitus. One learned in the law.

Legitimacy. Status of being born in wedlock.

Legitimation. Making lawful.

Legitimate. Lawful; born in wedlock.

Legitimize. To make lawful.

Legitimus. Lawful.

Lego. I bequeath.

Leguleius. One learned in the law.

Lend. Give, grant; put out for hire.

Lender. He from whom a thing is borrowed.

Leod. The people; country; nation.

Les. The.

Lésé Majesté. High treason.

Lesion. Damage; injury.

Lessa. Legacy.

Lessee. One to whom property is leased.

Lessor. One who gives a lease.

Let. To make a lease of real property; to award a contract.

Let In. To admit a party as a matter of favor.

Lethal. Deadly; mortal.

Letter. Character of the alphabet; a written message inclosed, sealed, stamped and sent.

Letter of Administration. Written authority by a court giving permission to administer.

Letter of Advice. A written notice of an act performed by the writer.

Letter of Attorney. Power of attorney.

Letter of Credit. An instrument ordering money to be paid to the bearer.

Letter of License. An agreement between creditors and their debtor extending time.

Letter of Recall. A notice sent to a foreign government by another government of the recall of its representative.

Letter of Recredentials. The reply of a foreign government to a letter of recall.

Letter of Safe Conduct. Passports issued by a government in time of war.

Letters Patent. A governmental grant of property, status, title, authority or privilege.

Letters Testamentary. Letters issued by a court empowering an executor of a will to act.

Letting Out. The award of a contract.

Lettre de Change. A bill of exchange.

Levee. An embankment constructed along the bank of a river to prevent overflow.

Leviable. That which may be levied.

Levis. Light; slight.

Levissima Deligentia. Slight diligence.

Levitical Degrees. Degrees of kindred within which marriage is prohibited.

Levy. To assess, raise, exact, collect, seize.

Lewd. Obscene.

Lewdness. Open and public indecency.

Lex. Law.

Lex Amissa. Infamous or outlawed person.

Lex Angliae. The law of England.

Lex Apparens. Apparent law.

Lex Domicilii. Law of the domicile.

Lex Est ab Aeterno. Law is from eternity.

Lex et Consuetudo Regni. The law and custom of the nation.

Lex Fori. The law of the court; the law of the jurisdiction in which the litigation occurs.

Lex Ligeantiae. The law of the country of one's allegince.

Lex Loci. The law of the place in which the circumstance arose.

Lex Loci Actus. The law of the place of the act.

Lex Loci Commissi. The law of the place where the act was committed.

Lex Loci Contractus. The law of the place of making of the contract.

Lex Loci Delictus. The law of the place of the crime.

Lex Mercatoria. The law merchant.

Lex Nil Frustra Facit. The law does nothing in vain.

Lex Non Scripta. The unwritten law.

Lex Patriae. National law.

Lex Reprobat Moram. The law disapproves of delay.

Lex Respicit Acquitatem. The law regards equity.

Lex Scripta. The written law.

Lex Spectat Naturae Ordinem. The law regards the order of nature.

Lex Succurrit Minoribus. Law aids minors.

Lex Talionis. The law of retaliation.

Lex Terrae. The law of the land.

Ley. Law; an oath.

Ley Civile. The civil law.

Le Gager. To wage one's law.

Leze Majesty. High treason.

Liability. The condition of one who is under obligation to pay; an obligation to pay money.

Liability Insurance. Indemnity against liability.

Liable. Bound in law or equity; responsible.

Libel. To defame a person's reputation.

Libellus Conventionis. A bill or complaint.

Libellus Famosus. A defamatory publication.

Libelous. Defamatory.

Liber. Book; volume; free or open.

Libera. Free; exempt.

Liberal. Generous, open-minded, not literal.

Liberam Legem Amittere. To lose one's status as a free man.

Liberare. To free.

Liberation. The extinguishment of a contract, by which he who was bound becomes free.

Liber et Legalis Homo. A free and lawful man; juryman.

Libertas. Liberty; freedom; privilege.

Libertas Inaestimabilis Res Est. Liberty is a thing of inestimable value.

Liberticide. Destroyer of liberty.

Liberties. Privileged communities or districts.

Liberty. Freedom; all the rights, privileges and immunities of the Constitution.

Liberty of the Press. Freedom from censorship.

License. A certificate which gives permission.

Licensee. One who holds a license.

Licensor. One who gives a license.

Licentia. License; leave; permission.

Licentia Concordandi. Permission to come to an agreement, a step in levying a fine.

Licentia Loquendi. Permission to speak.

Licentiate. One who has license to practice.

Licentious. Unrestrained; dissolute.

Licentiously. Freely; loosely; dissolutely.

Licentiousness. Disregard the rights of others.

Licere. To be allowed by law.

Licet. It is allowed by law.

Licitare. To bid.

Licitation. An offering for sale to the highest bidder or to the one who will give the most.

Lie. To be admissable, as an action or an appeal; to be appropriate as a remedy; an untruth deliberately told.

Liege. One bound in fealty to a superior.

Liegeman. A feudal vassal.

Lie in Franchise. Property is said to lie in franchise when it may be seized by those entitled to it without the aid of a court.

Lie In Grant. Property which can be transferred from one person to another.

Lien. A charge, security or incumbrance upon property for the payment of a debt.

Lien Creditor. One whose claim is secured by a lein on particular property.

Lienee. One whose property has a lien.

Lienor. One who has a lien.

Lien for Improvements. Lien sometimes decreed in equity to one who claims compensation for improvements made on the land of another.

Lieu. Place or stead well-known.

Lieu Conus. A well known place.

Lieutenant. Deputy, substitute, agent; lowest rank commissioned officer in the U.S. Army.

Life Annuity. An annual payment made to a person during his lifetime.

Life Estate. An estate whose duration is limited to the lifetime of the possessor.

Life Insurance. Insurance on the life of a particular individual on whose death payment of a specified amount is made.

Life Interest. An interest in property which is to terminate upon the death of the holder of the interest or some other designated person.

Life-Land. Land held on a lease for lives.

Life Policy. A written contract of life insurance.

Life-Tables. Statistical tables showing the length of expectancy of survival of persons at certain ages.

Life Tenant. One who has the right to enjoy certain property for the period of his own life or that of another certain person.

Lift. To raise or take up; as applied to a promissory note, to cause its cancellation.

Liga. League; association.

Ligan. Goods cast into the sea to lighten a ship but attached to a buoy so they may be recovered.

Ligare. Bind together, unite.

Ligealty. Allegiance.

Ligeantia. Allegiance.

Light. An easement to have natural light unobstructed by buildings, etc.

Lighter. Vessel used in assisting to load and unload other vessels.

Lignum. Firewood.

Like. Equal; exactly corresponding.

Like Effect. With like results.

Like a Shot. Quickly.

Likelihood. Probability.

Likely. Probable.

Limb. Member of the human body.

Limit. To confine, restrict; boundary.

Limitatio. Limitation.

Limitation. Restriction; settling an estate.

Limitation of Actions. See Limitations, Statute of.

Limitations, Statute of. A statute establishing fixed periods of time within which various actions or proceedings in law or equity must be brought, after a cause of action has arisen.

Limited. Restricted.

Limited Guaranty. Usually a guaranty restricted in its application to a single act.

Limited Jurisdiction. Jurisdiction which does not extend to the general administration.

Limited Owner. One whose ownership is less than full.

Limited Partnership. A partnership in which one or more of the partners are not personally liable for partnership debts, beyond the amount they have invested.

Line. Course of descent; lineal measure containing one-twelfth of an inch; a boundary between two estates.

Linea. Line of descent.

Lineage. Progeny.

Lineal. In direct line.

Lineal Consanguinity. Relationship through some common ancestor.

Linea Recta. Direct descent.

Liquere. To be clear, evident, apparent.

Liquet Satis. It is clear enough.

Liqueur. An alcoholic cordial.

Liquidate. To settle a debt or an obligation in the form of money; to reduce all the assets and liabilities of a business or estate to a precise sum in money in order to settle the business or estate.

Liquidated Damages. Damages which are agreed upon in advance between two parties should either of them breach their contract.

Liquidation. The act of settling or winding up business affairs; payment of due amount.

Liquor. Alcoholic beverage.

Lis. Law suit; dispute.

Lis Mota. A controversy which has begun.

Lis Pendens. A pending suit; jurisdiction which courts acquire over property in suit pending action and until final judgment.

List. Court docket; to enter in an official list.

Listed. Included in a list.

Lister. One who makes lists of taxables.

Listing Contract. An agreement whereby an owner of real property employs a broker to procure a purchaser without right to sell.

Lite Pendente. While the action is pending.

Liter. A liquid containing 1.056 quarts.

Litera. A letter.

Litera Acquietantia. A letter of acquittance.

Literacy Test. A test in reading and writing required by some states as a qualification to vote.

Literae. Letters, written documents, words.

Literae Mortuae. Dead letters; superflous words.

Literae Patentes. Letters patent.

Literae Procuratoriae. Power of attorney.

Literal. Closely following the exact words.

Literal Proof. Proof by writings in evidence.

Litera Scripta Manet. The written word endures.

Literatura. Education.

Litigant. A party to a lawsuit.

Litigare. To carry on a suit.

Litigate. To carry on a suit.

Litigated. Applied to questions about which there has been a legal hearing.

Litigation. A law suit.

Litigiosity. The pendency of a suit.

Litigious. Contested suit; fond of litigation.

Litis. Of a litigation, suit or action.

Litis Aestimatio. The measure of damages.

Litis Contestatis. A defense to an action.

Litis Dominum. Control or direction of a suit.

Litis Dominus. One who controls a suit.

Litis Magister. One who directs a suit.

Litispendence. Pendency of a suit or action.

Litre. See Liter.

Littoral. Relating to the shore.

Litura. Erasure; correction.

Litus Maris. Sea-shore.

Live. To reside.

Livelode. Maintenance; support.

Livery. The act of transferring physical possession of property to some person; particular dress appropriate to certain persons.

Livery Stable. Building for horses or vehicles.

Live Oil. Oil that has gas in it.

Live Stock. Domestic animals used on a farm.

Live Trust. An active or operative trust.

Live Wire. A wire charged with current.

Living. Existing; surviving.

Living Apart. To live in a separate abode.

Living Together. Cohabitation.

Lloyd's. London insurance association.

Loadman. Pilot.

Loadmanage. Pay to loadsmen.

Loaf. Loiter.

Loan. Borrowing with a promise to repay.

Loan for Consumption. Lending of goods for consumption to be repayed in kind.

Lobby. To try to influence the passage or rejection of legislative measures; group of persons engaged in this activity.

Lobbyist. Member of a lobby.

Local. Pertaining to a particular place.

Local Action. Action which must be brought in a particular place.

Local Agent. Agent of a definite district.

Local Assessment. Property charges levied.

Local Chattel. Fixture.

Local Courts. Courts whose jurisdiction is confined to particular area.

Local Government. Government of county, city, town.

Local Improvement. Public improvement conferring a benefit on a particular property.

Locality. Place; vicinity; neighborhood.

Local Law. Law directed to a particular place.

Local Nature. Pertaining to an action situated wholly within the district in which filed.

Local Option. Local choice whether or not to have prohibition of alcoholic beverages.

Local Prejudice. Prejudice or influence warranting the removal of a case from state to federal courts.

Local Statute. Local law.

Local Taxes. Taxes levied for the benefit of a district or town.

Locare. To let for hire; bestow in marriage.

Locatarius. Depositee.

Locate. Discovery by survey.

Locatio. Hiring out of property.

Locatio Custodiae. Placing in custody or safe-keeping for hire.

Location. Site; place; a mining claim.

Locatio Operis. Contract to make repairs and to supply materials.

Locatio Operis Faciendi. Hiring of work or services upon a thing.

Locatio Rei. Hire of a thing.

Locative Calls. Landmarks and physical objects whereby land can be identified.

Lockout. A cut-off from work by the employer in an effort to bring the matter to terms.

Lockup. Prison; jail.

Loco Citato. In the place cited.

Loco Parentis. In the place of the parent, e.g. the school teacher.

Locum Tenens. Holding the place, e.g. a deputy.

Locuples. Wealthy.

Locus. Place.

Locus Contractus. Place contracted.

Locus Criminis. Place where the crime was committed.

Locus Delicti. Place where the crime tort was committed.

Locus in Quo. The place in which or where.

Locus Poenitentiae. A place for repentence; an opportunity to change one's mind.

Locus Publicus. Public place.

Locus Regit Actum. Place governs the act.

Locus Rei Sitae. Place where a thing is located.

Locus Sigilli. Place of the seal, (Abb. "l.s."), indicating the document as sealed.

Locus Solutionis. Place of payment or performance.

Locus Standi. Place of standing, i.e. right to appear in court.

Lode. In mining law, a vein.

Lodeman. Pilot.

Lodge. Fraternal order; meeting place.

Lodger. One who has the use but not possession of a dwelling.

Logbook. Ship's daily journal.

Logia. Lodge.

Log Rolling. Legislative practice of combining several unrelated bills into one in order to combine various minorities into a majority.

Logic. Science of reasoning.

Loiter. To idle or linger.

Lond. Land.

Long. An order is given to a stockbroker to buy or credit the account with stocks.

Long and Short Haul. Practice of some railroad companies of charging lower rates in the face of competition, regardless of distance.

Loose Waman. An unchaste woman.

Loquella. Speech; talk; discourse.

Loss. Damage.

Losses. Tax deductible items, if incurred in trade or business or by casualty.

Lost or Not Lost. In marine insurance, coverage for past and future losses.

Lost Papers. Papers which cannot be found.

Lost Property. Property involuntarily parted with through neglect or carelessness.

Lot. Group of persons or things; a share; a portion of land.

Lottery. A gamble for a prize at a price.

Low. Lacking in dignity or character; mean.

Lower House. House of Representatives of the U.S. Congress.

Low Water Mark. Line on the shore made by receding water at low tide.

Loyal. Faithful; lawful.

Loyalty. Faithfulness.

L.S. (Abb.). Locus sigilli.

Ltd. (Abb.). Limited.

Lucid. Temporary period of sanity, any affairs conducted at this time being valid.

Lucre. Gain; profit.

Lucri Causa. In criminal law, for the sake of gain, in regard to larceny.

Lumen. Light; window; right to light.

Lump Sum Payment. Payment before due.

Lunacy. Madness.

Lunatic. One who is insane.

Lupanatrix. Prostitute.

Lustful. Lewd.

Lying by. Acquiescing.

Lying in Wait. Lying in ambush.

Lynching. Punishment by a mob without trial

Lynch Law. Mob law.

M

Mace Proof. Safe from arrest.

Machination. Artful contrivance formed with deliberation.

Machine. Mechanical device.

Mactater. Murderer.

Maculare. To wound.

Mad Point. Central idea of a monomania.

Magis. More; more fully; in a higher degree.

Magister. Master; ruler; chief; head.

Magisterial. Pertaining to a magistrate.

Magister Litis. One in charge of a suit.

Magister Navis. Captain of a ship.

Magister Rerum Usus. Use is the master.

Magister Societas. Manager of a partnership.

Magistra. Mistress; directress.

Magistralia Brevia. Magisterial writs.

Magistrate. One vested with power.

Magistrate's Certificate. Certificate of proof of loss without fraud obtained from a magistrate required by some fire insurance.

Magistratus. Magistrate.

Magna Carta (Charta). The great charter issued by King John of Eng. in 1215, considered basis of Eng. constitutional liberty.

Magna Culpa. Gross negligence.

Magna Culpa Dolus Est. Gross negligence is the equivalent of fraud.

Magnum Concilium. Eng. Parliament.

Maiden. Young, unmarried woman.

Maihematus. Maimed; wounded.

Mail. Letters; correspondence.

Mailable Matter. Matter which may legally handled through U.S. mails.

Maile. Rent money.

Maim. Cripple; mutilate; disable.

Main-a-Main. Immediately.

Mainovre. Manual labor.

Mainpernable. Bailable.

Mainpernor. One who provides bail.

Mainsworn. Perjured.

Maintain. Sustain; support.

Maintainor. One guilty of maintenance.

Maintenance. To aid someone with the means of prosecuting a suit; supporting someone.

Maintenance Curialis. Maintenance in a court of justice.

Maintenant. Now.

Mais. But; however.

Major. Greater, more important.

Major Annus. Leap year.

Majority. Full age; the greater number.

Majus Jus. Greater or better right.

Make. To execute, do or perform.

Maker. One who makes, executes or signs.

Mal. Prefix meaning bad or evil.

Mala. Bad or evil things.

Maladministration. Mismanagement.

Mala Fides. Bad faith.

Mala in Se. Evil in themselves.

Mala Mens. Bad intention.

Malandrinus. Thief.

Mala Praxis. Malpractice.

Mala Prohibita. Acts forbidden by law.

Male. Badly; improperly.

Male. Belonging to the masculine sex.

Malefaction. Crime.

Malefactor. Criminal.

Maleficium. Crime.

Malfeasance. Commission of a wrongful act.

Malformation. Deformity.

Malice. State of mind of one who deliberately commits a wrongful act.

Malice Aforethought. Intention to kill existing some time before the actual deed is done.

Malice in Fact. Express with intent to injure.

Malice in Law. Deliberate commission of a wrongful act without just cause.

Malice Prepense. Malice aforethought.

Malicious. Committed with evil intentions.

Malicious Arrest. Arrest of a person without probable cause during the proceeding.

Malicious Injury. Wrongful and wilful infliction of injury upon another.

Maliciously. Wilfully.

Malicious Mischief. Wilful injury to the personal property of another.

Malicious Prosecution. Instigation of legal proceedings without probable cause.

Malignare. To malign, defame or maim.

Malinger. To pretend sickness.

Malingerer. One who pretends sickness to avoid some duty.

Malitia. Malice.

Malitia Implicita. Implied malice.

Malitia Praecogitata. Malice aforethought.

Malo Animo. With evil intent.

Malo Grato. In spite of.

Malpractice. Professional misconduct.

Malum in Se. A wrong in itself.

Malum Prohibitum. A prohibited wrong.

Malus, Mala, Malum. Evil; bad wrong.

Malus Animus. Evil intent.

Malversation. Misconduct in office.

Man. A human being; one of the male sex.

Manacles. Hand shackles.

Manage. To control; direct; govern.

Management. Government, control.

Manager. One who directs anything.

Manas Mediae. Inferior persons.

Mancipate. To enslave.

Mandamus. We command; a writ issuing from a court of higher jurisdiction commanding the performance of a public duty.

Mandans. Commanding; entrusting.

Mandatary. An agent or bailee who receives instructions to act by another person; one to whom a charge is given.

Mandate. An order of the court; writ of mandamus; gratuitous bailment for work.

Mandator. One who employs a mandatary.

Mandatory. Imperative; peremptory.

Mandatum. In civil law, contract involving the bailment of property.

Manens. Remaining.

Mania. Type of mental disorder characterized by obsession with particular subjects.

Mania a Potu. Type of temporary insanity caused by excessive use of intoxicating drinks.

Mania Transitoria. Emotional insanity.

Manifest. Evident; declaration of ship's cargo.

Manifesto. Public declaration authorized by the government of a nation.

Manifest Theft. Open theft.

Mann Act. White Slave Traffic Act.

Manner. Method; mode of operation.

Mannire. To cite an adverse party into court.

Mannus. Horse.

Man of Straw. A non-existent bondsman.

Manor. House; dwelling; residence.

Manser. An illegitimate child.

Manslaughter. Unlawful or negligent killing of a human being, without malice.

Manstealing. Kidnapping.

Manticulate. To pick pockets.

Man Trap. Device to catch trespassers.

Manual. Pertaining to the hand or hands.

Manu Brevi. Briefly; directed.

Manu Longa. Indirectly; circuitously.

Manufacture. Process of making products.

Manumission. Act of freeing a slave.

Manus. Hand; oath; compurgator.

Manuscript. A writing; a handwritten book.

Many. Numerous.

Mar. Damage greatly; to do serious injury.

Marauder. Soldier who plunders and steals.

Mare. The sea.

Mare. Female horse.

Mare Altum. Open sea.

Mare Apertum. High sea.

Maretum. Overflowed marsh land.

Margin. Edge; border.

Margin. Money given a stockbroker by one on whose account a purchase or sale is to be made as security against loss.

Marginal Transactions. Dealing in stocks on margin.

Margin of Profit. Difference between purchase price and selling price of merchandise.

Marine. Naval; pertaining to the sea.

Marine Contract. One for chartering a vessel or shipping goods for transportation over sea.

Marine Insurance. Insurance against loss in maritime transactions.

Marine League. Distance equal to three geographical miles.

Marine Risk. Perils of the sea.

Mariner, Seaman; sailor.

Marital. Pertaining to marriage.

Marital Portion. In Louisiana, the share of the widow in her husband's estate.

Marital Rights, Duties and Obligations. Arising from the marriage contract and constituting its object.

Maritime. Pertaining to the sea.

Maritime Belt. Part of the sea under control of the riparian states.

Maritime Blockade. Blockade by sea.

Maritime Causes. All causes of action arising in connection with acts done at sea.

Maritime Contract. One relating to commerce and navigation.

Maritime Law. Law dealing with cases arising on the high seas.

Maritime Lien. Claim on a vessel for work done in relation to maritime employment.

Maritime Tort. Civil wrongs committed on navigable waters.

Maritus. Married man.

Mark. Character used by one unable to write.

Market. Place of commercial activity where wares are bought and sold; the demand there is for a particular article; collective name for a group of buyers and sellers of a commodity.

Market Overt. Open market.

Market Price. Price which a commodity would command if sold at public sale.

Market Value. Price which property or a commodity would command in the market.

Marriage. A legal contract between a man and a woman to unit for life to the exclusion of all.

Marriageable Age. Age of consent.

Marriage Articles. Written agreement between parties comtemplating marriage.

Marriage Ceremony. Form for the soleminization of a marriage.

Marriage Certificate. Document certifying a marriage and executed by person officiating.

Marriage License. License issued by public authority, often an essential prerequisite.

Marriage Portion. Property a woman brings with her upon marriage; dowry.

Marriage Promise. Betrothal, engagement.

Marriage Settlement. Written agreement by which title to certain property is settled in the event of the husband's death.

Marshal. Ministerial officer in each Federal district whose duties are similar to a sheriff.

Marshaling of Assets. In equity, the arrangements of assest in due order of administration.

Marshaling Securities. In equity, the ranking of classes of creditors, with respect to the assets of the common debtor, to provide for the satisfaction of the greatest number of claims.

Mart. Public market.

Martial Law. Law dealing with military affairs; state existing when military authorities carry on government or exercise control over civilians in domestic territory.

Masochism. Sexual perversion in which one enjoys infliction of pain by another.

Massa. Mass; raw material.

Massachusetts Trust. Business trust; trust in which property is conveyed to trustees to manage and deal with.

Master. Head of a college or school; employer in relation of master and servant; captain of a merchant ship; a subordinate judge in equity appointed to hear testimony and report his findings to the court.

Master and Servant. Relation between two people in which the former may determine what work is to be done and how to do it.

Master Builder. Contractor who employs men to build.

Mate. Officer second in command on a merchant vessel.

Mater Familias. Mother of the family.

Materia. Material; subject matter.

Material. Physical matter or substance; important; having influence or effect.

Material Allegation. One which forms a substantive part of the case presented by the pleading.

Material Alteration. One which changes the legal effect of the instrument.

Material Evidence. Evidence that might

determine a decision on the facts of a case.

Material Fact. One which influences a person to enter into a contract; an essential fact.

Material Injury. One resulting in damages of a substantial nature.

Materiality. Bearing which facts may have on a controversy; importance.

Materials. Matter of which a thing is made.

Materia Prima. Primary matter.

Maternal. Pertaining to a mother.

Maternal Property. Property which comes from the mother's side of the family.

Maternity. Motherhood.

Matima. Godmother.

Matricide. Killing of one's mother.

Matriculate. Enroll.

Matrimonial. Pertaining to matrimony.

Matrimonial Causes. Cases involving actions for divorce, annulment, and separation.

Matrimonial Cohabitation. The living together of a man and woman.

Matrimonial Domicile. Place where parties live together as husband and wife.

Matrimonial Res. Marriage state.

Matrimony. State of being married.

Matrix. An original document.

Matron. Married woman; female head of an institution, e.g. prison or nursing home.

Matter. Substantial facts constituting the basis of claim or defense.

Matter in Controversy or in Dispute. Subject of the litigation.

Matter in Pais. Matter of fact.

Matter of Fact. Issues of fact to be determined by the jury.

Matter of Form. Established mode.

Matter of Law. Issues of law to be determined by the court.

Matter of Record. Matter in the court records.

Matter of Substance. See Matter of Form.

Maturity. Time at which payment is due.

Maxim. Tradtionally and generally accepted.

Maximum. Greatest amount, quality or value.

Mayhem. Wrongful act resulting in the loss or damage of some part of the body of the person.

Mayor. Governor or chief magistrate of a city.

Mayor's Court. Municipal court presided over by the mayor.

M.D. (Abb.). Doctor of Medicine.

Mean, Mesne. Middle between two extremes.

Meander Line. Line used in surveying to indicate the end of a plot of ground that has unsurveyable real boundaries.

Meaning. Signification; sense.

Means. Intermediate agent, instrument.

Means of Support. Resources from which the necessities and comforts of life are supplied.

Measure. A definite, specific act or resolution.

Measure of Damages. Means of determining the amount of the plaintiff's damages sustained by a breach of contract or tort.

Mechanic. One skilled in the use of tools.

Mechanic's Lien. Claim created by law in order to secure a priority of payment for the price or value of work performed and materials furnished in erecting or repairing a building or structure.

Media Concludendi. Steps of an argument.

Mediae et Infirmae Manus Homines. Men of mean and lowly condition.

Media Nox. Midnight.

Mediate. Intervening; indirect; arbitrate.

Mediately. That which is derived by inference from facts known or proved.

Mediate Testimony. Secondary evidence.

Mediation. Intervention; the act of a third party attempting to reconcile a dispute between two parties.

Mediator. One who attempts to reconcile.

Medical. Pertaining to the science, practice or study of medicine.

Medical Evidence. Testimony given by medical men.

Medical Jurisprudence. Branch of the science of medicine concerned with the law.

Medicine. Science and art of dealing with the prevention, cure and relief of diseases.

Medico-Legal. Law concerning medical questions.

Medio Tempore. In the meantime.

Medium Concludendi. Means of reaching a conclusion.

Medley. Affray; sudden fight.

Meet. To come together.

Meeting. Coming together of persons.

Meeting of the Minds. Concurrence of intention between two parties to make a contract.

Melancholia. Type of mental illness characterized by depression and grief.

Melior. Better.

Meliorations. Betterments; improvements.

Member. Part or organ of the body; one of the persons constituting a family.

Member of Congress. Member of the Senate or House of Representatives of the U.S. Congress.

Membrana. Membrane; parchment.

Memoranda. Notes used by a witness.

Memorandum. Notes or record of fact.

Memorandum Decision. Decision of an appellate court usually a brief paragraph.

Memorial. Memorandum or note.

Memoriter. From memory.

Memory. Recollection of past events.

Menace. Threats of bodily violence.

Menial. Household servants.

Mens. Mind; intention.

Mensis. A month.

Mensa et Thora. From bed and board.

Mensor. Surveyor.

Mens Rea. A guilty mind.

Mensura. A measure.

Mental. Pertaining to the mind.

Mental Alienation. Descriptive of insanity.

Mental Anguish. Mental grief, suffering.

Mental Capacity or Competence. Ability to understand the nature of a transaction.

Mental Cruelty. Cruelty on the part of one spouse toward another of such a nature that it may endanger the health of the spouse.

Mental Imbecility. Childishness; dotage.

Mental Reservation. An exception in mind only to a term or terms of a promise.

Mentiri. To lie.

Mentition. A lie.

Mera Noctis. Midnight.

Mercantile. Pertaining to merchants.

Mercantile Law. Law of commercial transactions.

Mercantile Paper. Commercial paper.

Mercat. Market.

Mercative. Pertaining to trade.

Merces. Wages for labor.

Merchandise. Commodities which merchants usually buy and sell.

Merchantable. Of good and salable quality.

Merchant Seamen. Seamen employed on private vessels.

Merciament. Amerciament; penalty; fine.

Mercy, In. In criminal law, discretion of a judge within the limits prescribed by positive law to remit punishment.

Mere. Mother.

Mere Motion. A voluntary act.

Mere Right. Mere right of property without either possession or right of possession.

Meretricious. Lewd; of unlawful sexual connection.

Merger. The absorption of one thing by another.

Meritorious Consideration. Consideration consisting in moral obligations.

Merits. Strict legal rights of parties.

Merit System. System of appointing employees to office in the civil service.

Mere Motu. See Mere Motion.

Merscum. Lake.

Merx. Merchandise.

Mese. House.

Mesen. Intermediate; intervening.

Mesne Conveyance. Any conveyance or transfer of property executed prior to the last one.

Mesne Encumbrance. An intermediate charge, burden or liability.

Mesne Process. Those writs intervening between the first and the judgment.

Mesque. Unless; except.

Message. Any communication sent from one person to another.

Messenger. The bearer of messages or one who performs errands.

Messuage. House.

Mestizo. One of mixed blood.

Meter. Instrument of measurement.

Metes and Bounds. Boundary lines of land with determination of terminal points and angles.

Metropolis. A mother city.

Metus. Fear; dread.

Meum et Teum. Mine and thine.

Middleman. An agent who brings persons together to make their own contracts.

Midwife. Woman who assists at childbirth.

Mile. Distance of 1,760 yards or 5,280 feet.

Mileage. Allowance for traveling expense at a certain sum per mile.

Military. Pertaining to war or the army.

Military Courts. Courts of military jurisdiction.

Military Law. System of law for governing the armed forces.

Military Testment. Verbal or nuncupative will by which a soldier engaged in actual military operation may make his will by either word of mouth or informal writing.

Militia. Body of citizens trained to military duty, but not engaged in actual service.

Milled Money. Coined money.

Mind. Ability to will, direct, permit or assent.

Mind and Memory. Applied to the ability of a testator to make a will.

Mine. Excavation in the earth from which minerals are removed.

Mineral. Any mined inorganic substance.

Minerator. Miner.

Minimus. The least; the smallest.

Mining Claim. Portion of land containing precious metal appropriated by an individual.

Mining Partnership. Partnership created for the purpose of operating a mine but differing in many respects from ordinary partnership.

Minister. Clergyman; diplomat.

Ministerial. That which is performed by a subordinate official under the directions of a superior.

Ministerial Duty. A simple, definite duty.

Minor. One under the legal age of competence.

Minor Aetas. Under age.

Minor Fact. A relative, collateral or subordinate fact in giving evidence.

Minority. Under age; lesser of two factions.

Mint. Place where money is legally coined.

Mintage. Charge made for coining money.

Minus. Less; smaller; not.

Minute. Small portion; 1/60 of an hour.

Minute Book. Book kept by the court clerk for entering memoranda of the court.

Minutes. Notes of a transaction or proceeding.

Minutio. A reduction; subtraction.

Misadventure. An accident.

Misae. Costs of a suit; expenses.

Misallege. To state or cite falsely.

Misappropriate. To use funds or property entrusted to an agent for other purposes.

Misbehavior. Misconduct; improper or unlawful conduct.

Misbranding. False labeling.

Miscarriage. Failure of a judicial proceeding to observe the ends of justice while observing legal forms; expulsion of a human fetus before maturity.

Miscasting. An error in an account audit.

Miscegenation. Intermarriage of a person of the white race with one of a colored race.

Miscognizant. Without knowledge of.

Misconduct. A transgression of some established and definite rule of action.

Misconduct in Office. Any willful, unlawful behavior of a public official in relation to the duties of his office.

Misdemeanant. One who has committed a misdemeanor.

Misdate. A false date on a document.

Misdemeanor. Any crime punishable by fine or imprisonment other than in a penitentiary.

Misdirection. An error made by the judge.

Mise. The issue on a writ of right.

Miserecordia. Mercy; a fine.

Misfeasance. Wrongful doing of an act which might be done lawfully.

Misfortune. Ill luck; calamity.

Mishering. A freedom from amercement.

Misjoinder. Joining together of different causes of action which under rules of procedure may not be litigated together; the adding of a litigant in a pleading as a party plaintiff or defendant in an action or suit in which he is not a proper plaintiff or defendant.

Misnomer. A mistake in a name.

Mispleading. Essential errors in defense.

Misprision. Applied to a misdemeanor which does not have a specific name; misapprehension; applied to a clerical error; applied to offenses involving concealment of crime.

Misprision of Felony. Offense of concealing a felony that has been committed.

Misreading. The false reading of a written instrument to one who cannot read.

Misrecital. Misstatement of facts.

Misrepresentation. A false statement or other conduct by one person to another which amounts to a false assertion.

Missio. Discharging.

Mistake. An unintentional act, omission or error due to ignorance, surprise, imposition or misplaced confidence.

Mistake of Fact. Mistake consisting of unconscious ignorance or forgetfulness of a fact material to the transaction.

Mistake of Law. A mistake of a party who having full knowledge of the facts.

Mistery. Trade; calling.

Mistrial. Erroneous or invalid trial.

Misuser. Unlawful use of a right.

Mitigate. To reduce or lessen.

Mitigation. Reduction of damages or punishment by reason of extenuating facts.

Mitigation of Damages. Reduction of the amount of damages.

Mitior Sensus. More favorable interpretation.

Mittimus. Warrant to remove records from one place to another; a warrant to the prison official to receive or keep a prisoner.

Mixed Action. Action both real and personal.

Mixed Contract. Contract in which parties exchange things of different value.

Mixed Gift. One in which there is included both real and personal property.

Mixed Insurance Company. One which is both a mutual and a stock company.

Mixed Larceny. Larceny which is complicated by the presence of aggravating factors.

Mixed Marriage. Marriage between a white and colored person.

Mixed Personalty. Personal property which is associated with real property.

Mixed Property. Property which has the characteristics of realty and personalty.

Mixed Questions of Law and Fact. Questions which cannot be decided by the judge or jury.

Mob. An assemblage of people acting violent.

Mobilia. Movables.

Mock. To deride or ridicule.

Mode. Manner; method.

Moderata Misericordia. Writ to prevent an excessive fine.

Moderator. Presiding officer of an assembly.

Modification. Change; alteration; variance.

Modo et Forma. In the manner and form.

Modus. Mode; manner; method; form.

Modus Hiabilis. A proper manner.

Modus Injuriae. The means of injury.

Modus Operandi. The method of operation.

Modus Transferrendi. Manner of transfer.

Modus Vivendi. The mode of living.

Moiety. One half.

Molest. To annoy a person to the extent of a criminal offense.

Molliter. Gently.

Momentum. An instant.

Monarchy. Government controlled by one.

Money. Coin or that which is lawfully and actually current in buying and selling.

Money Bill. Bill for raising money.

Money Demand. Claim for a fixed and liquidated amount of money.

Moneyed Capital. Capital of a corporation used for investing and reinvesting.

Moneyed Corporation. One engaged in investing money for profit.

Money Judgment. A judgment which can be fully satisfied by a monetary payment.

Monition. In admiralty, an order to appear.

Monogamy. The state of being married to only one person at a time.

Monomachy. Single combat.

Monomania. Mental derangement on some particular subject, apparently sane on others.

Monopoly. The exclusive control of a particular business or trade, manufacture of a particular article, sale of the whole supply.

Monster. Human being abnormal at birth.

Month. In statutes and contracts, a calendar month of the ordinary year.

Monument. Something erected in memory.

Moonshine. Whiskey illicitly distilled or produced.

Moot. A subject for argument; unsettled.

Moot Case. Case which seeks to determine an abstract question.

Moot Court. Practice court for law students.

Moot Question. Undecided point of law.

Mora. Delay; hindrance.

Moral. Pertaining to character and right conduct.

Moral Certainty. Certainty beyond a reasonable doubt.

Moral Consideration. A consideration good only in conscience.

Moral Insanity. Mental disease which destroys the ability to distinguish between right and wrong as to a particular act.

Moral Law. Law of conscience.

Moral Turpitude. Applied to an act which is dishonest, and contrary to good morals.

Morari. To delay or hinder.

Moratorium. The temporary suspension by statute of the enforcement of liability for debt because of an existing emergency.

Moratory Interest. Interest by way of damages.

Moratur in Lege. Plaintiff demurs in favor of a judgement of the court.

Morbus Sonticus. An illness which prevents one from attending to business.

More Colonico. In a husbandlike manner.

More or Less. An uncertain amount.

Moreover. In addition to; furthermore.

Morgue. Place where unidentified dead are temporarily kept.

Moron. One with the mentality of a child between 7 and 12 years of age.

Morphine. A narcotic drug.

Mors. Death.

Mort. Death.

Mortal. Deadly.

Mortality Tables. Life expectancy tables.

Mort Civile. Cessation of one's legal rights.

Mortgage. A conditional conveyance of property to a creditor as security for a debt.

Mortgage, Chattel. Mortgage in the form of personalty.

Mortgage, Conventional. Contact by which a person binds the whole part of his property in favor of another to secure the execution of some engagement.

Mortgage, Equitable. Specific lien upon real property to secure the performance of an obligation by a court of equity.

Mortgage, First. The first in a series of two or more mortages covering the same property.

Mortgage, General. One which binds all property, present and future, of the debtor.

Mortgage of Goods. Mortgage of personal property.

Mortgage, Second. One which ranks immediately after a first mortgage on the same property, without any intervening liens.

Mortgage Pools. Groups of mortgages.

Mortgagee. Holder of mortgage.

Mortgagor. Debtor under a mortgage.

Mortis Causa. By reason of death; in contemplation of death.

Mortmain. Inalienable ownership; the holding of land by a corporation beyond the period of time or in violation of the law.

Mortmain Statute. One which restricts the granting of lands to corporations by will or limits the amount that any testator leaving a wife and children may donate to charity or restricts the period before death in which a charitable bequest may be made.

Mortuary. Undertaking establishment.

Mortuary Tables. See Mortality Table.

Mortuus. Dead.

Mortuus Sine Prole. Dead without issue.

Mos Pro Lege. Custom instead of law.

Mother. Woman who has given birth to a child.

Motion. An application to the court for some rule or order granting some type of relief.

Motive. That which induces one to indulge in a criminal act, admissable as evidence in order to arrive at the truth of the matter.

Mourant. Dying.

Movables. Movable objects.

Move. To make a motion.

Movent. One who makes a motion.

Mugging. Photographing of persons arrested.

Muggle. Marihuana.

Mulatto. Child of Negro and white parents.

Mulct. Fine, penalty.

Mulier. Woman; wife; legitimate child.

Mulierty. Legitimacy.

Multifariousness. The misjoinder of causes of action in a bill.

Multipartite. Having several parts.

Multiple Taxation. Taxation of the same property by several states.

Multiplicity of Actions or Suits. A large number of unnecessary attempts to litigate.

Multitude. In legal parlance, an assembly of 10 or more persons.

Multi Will. Will executed by more than one.

Municipal. Belonging to a city or town.

Municipal Affairs. Internal business activities of a city or town.

Municipal Corporation. An organized town, generally established by the legislature.

Municipal Law. Law dealing with municipalities or municipal corporations.

Municipal Securities. Bonds issued by cities and towns.

Municipality. A legally incorporated association of inhabitants of a prescribed area for local governmental or other public purposes.

Muniments. Documents which prove title.

Muniments of Title. Original title deeds.

Murder. The intentional and unlawful killing.

Murder in the First Degree. Murder committed after deliberation.

Murder in the Second Degree. Murder committed in the heat of passion.

Muster. To assemble troops.

Mustizo. Child of an Indian and Negro.

Mutato Nominis. Change of name.

Mutation. Change; transfer; conveyance.

Mutilate. To deprive of an essential part.

Mutilation. Rendering a document imperfect.

Muting. Insurrection.

Mutual. Reciprocal.

Mutual Insurance. Type of insurance in which the insured becomes a company member.

Mutuality. Reciprocation; that element of every contract making it binding.

Mutual Promises. Promises reciprocally exchanged a bilateral contract is formed.

Mutual Wills. Similar wills made by two parties giving the property to each other.

Mutuari. To borrow.

Mutuatis. A loan of money.

Mutus. Dumb; mute.

Mutus et Surdus. Dumb and deaf.

Mutuum. A loan of personal property for consumption, the loan to be returned in kind.

Myelitis. Chronic inflammation of the spine.

LEGAL DICT

Myself Note. Promissory note with the word "myself" inserted as the name of the payee.

Mystery. Trade; art; occupation.

N

Naked. Nude; lacking in power.

Naked Authority. Authority granted by a principal to an agent without obligations.

Naked Confession. One not corroborated.

Naked Contract. Promise without consideration, therefore not really a contract.

Naked Title. One which gives the holder no rights in relation to the property.

Naked Trust. One which requires no action on the part of the trustee other than turning over money or property to the beneficiary.

Name. Word used to identify.

Narrare. To allege in a declaration.

Narratio. A declaration or complaint.

Nasciturus. One conceived but not yet born.

Nastre. To be born.

Natale. The state of a man at birth.

Natio. Nation; birthplace.

Nation. A political group of persons having a government, associated with a particular territory and organized for the purpose of obtaining mutual interests.

National. Of a nation as a whole.

National Bank. Bank incorporated and doing business under the laws of the U.S.

National Corporations. Corporations organized under the authority of acts of Congress.

National Currency. Notes issued by national banks and the U.S. government.

National Emergency. State of national crisis.

Nationality. A person's natural political allegiance with all its duties and obligations.

Native. A citizen by reason of birth.

Naturae Vis Maxima. The force of nature is greatest.

Natural. Normal; in accordance with nature.

Natural Affection. Presumed affection between two close relatives.

Natural Allegiance. Allegiance by birth.

Natural Child. Illegitimate child.

Natural Consequences. Those consequences which flow from an act.

Natural Fool. Idiot.

Natural Guardian. Parent of a minor child.

Natural Infancy. Child under seven years.

Naturalization. The act of giving a foreigner the privilege of citizenship.

Natural Citizen. Person made a citizen of the U.S. by act of Congress.

Natural Law. Rules of conduct founded in nature and man, discoverable by reason, which act as a guide to civil conduct.

Naturally. In the normal course of events.

Natural Monopoly. One based on control of a natural resource.

Natural Obligation. One which rests wholly in the conscience.

Natural Person. An individual.

Natural Presumption. Presumption based upon proof of a fact from which other facts may be naturally presumed.

Natural Year. 365¼ days.

Naulage. The freight of a ship's passengers.

Naulum. Freight; fare.

Nauta. Sailor.

Ne. Not; lest.

Nearest Kin. Next of kin.

Nearest of Blood. Next of kin.

Neat Cattle. Bulls, cows or oxen.

Ne Baila Pas. Denial of defendent's suit.

Necation. The act of killing.

Necessaries. Those things which one actually needs; those things indispensable to maintain human life.

Necessary. Applied to that which is indispensable or an obsolute physical necessity.

Necessary Domicile. One established by law.

Necessitas. Necessity; need; poverty.

Necessitas Vincit Legem. Necessity supersedes the law.

Necessity. Controlling force.

Nee. Born.

Needs. Requirements.

Needy. Indigent.

Nee Vife. Born alive.

Ne Exeat. Writ forbidding a person to leave.

Nefas. Unlawful act.

Negare. To deny.

Negative. A denial.

Negative Condition. One which provides against the occurrence of some event.

Negative Evidence. Testimony that an alleged fact did not exist.

Negative Pregnant. Negative statement which contains an affirmative statement.

Negative Statute. Statute which prohibits.

Negative Testimony. See Negative Evidence.

Negatum. Denied.

Neglect. To omit or fail to do an act; lack of care or attention.

Negligence. Failure to use the amount of care a reasonable man would exercise.

Negligent Escape. Escape occurring through the negligence of the officer.

Negligently. Without due caution.

Negotiability. Transferable quality.

Negotiable. Any written security which can be negotiated, transferred or assigned.

Negotiable Bonds. Bonds of railroad, industrial and municipal corporations.

Negotiable Instrument. Any written securities which may be transferred by endorsement and/or delivery.

Negotiate. To transfer a negotiable instrument in due course of business; to bargain or trade.

Negotiorum Gestor. On who without authority to do so acts as agent for another.

Negro. One of African descent.

Neighborhood. A surrounding district.

Ne Luminibus Officiatur. An easement preventing a person from obstructing light to another's dwelling.

Nemine Contradicente. No one saying the contrary; indicates a unanimous vote.

Nemo. No man.

Nemo Debit Bis Puniri pro Uno Delicto. No one ought to be punished twice for one offense.

Nemy. Not.

Nephew. Male child of a brother or sister.

Nepos. Grandson.

Neptis. Granddaughter.

Ne Recipiatur. A warning given to a law officer, by a defendant, not to receive the next proceedings of his opponent.

Net. That which remains after all deductions.

Net Cash. As applied to a payment, payment in cash without the allowance of any discount.

Net Earnings. The gross receipts of a business less the expenses of operating.

Net Gains. Profits.

Net Income. Income remaining after the subtraction of allowable deductions and exemptions from gross income.

Net Loss. Any operational deficit, plus any reduction in value of plant investment.

Net Premium. In life insurance, that portion of the premium intended to meet the cost.

Net Price. Price after all discounts.

Net Profits. Investment gain after deductions.

Net Weight. The weight of the commodity shipped exclusive of all crating, etc.

Ne Unques Accouple. Never married.

Ne Varietur. Not to be altered; a notary's endorsement upon a negotiable instrument.

Never Indebted. General issue of debt.

New and Useful. Two qualities essential to a product to make it patentable.

New Assignment. A restatement in detail.

Newly Discovered Evidence. As a basis for a new trial, it must be likely to change the result if a new trial is granted, must have been discovered after the trial.

New Matter. Statements of facts made during the course of a litigation.

New Trial. A complete retrial of a case in the same court before another jury.

Next. Nearest; closest.

Next Friend. One who appears without official appointment or designation on behalf of an infant or other person who cannot appear.

Next of Kin. Those persons who stand in the closest degree of blood relationship.

Nickname. Short name.

Niece. Female child of a brother or sister.

Nient. Not.

Nient Comprise. Not included.

Nient Culpable. Not guilty.

Nient Dedire. To say or deny nothing.

Night. Period between sunset and sunrise.

Nightwalker. Prostitute.

Nihil, Nil. Nothing.

Nihil ad Rem. Nothing to the point.

Nihil Dicit. He says nothing; failure of the defendant to plead.

Nil. Contracted form of nihil.

Nil Debet. He owes nothing; form of the general issue in all actions of debt.

Nimmer. Thief.

Nisi. Unless.

Nisi Prius. Civil causes before a jury and judge.

No Award. Plea which denied that the award sued upon was made.

Nocent. Guilty.

Nocere. To harm or injure.

Nocumentum. Nuisance; annoyance.

Nolens Volens. Willing, unwilling.

Nolle. To be unwilling.

Nolle Proseque. To refuse to prosecute, the power to enter a nolles proseque.

Nolo Contendere. A plea in a criminal prosecution by which the defendant announces his intention not to contest the action.

Nol. Pros. (Abb.). Nolle Proseque.

Nomen. Name.

Nomen Collectivum. Collective name.

Nomen Generale. General name.

Nomen Juris. Legal term.

Nominal. Titular; not substantial.

Nominal Damages. Trifling sum awarded to a plaintiff in an action where no serious loss or damage has been sustained.

Nominal Partner. One who allows his name to be used in a business although he has no interest in it.

Nominal Plaintiff. One who appears as a plaintiff in an action, although not the real party in interest.

Nominate. To name, designate or appoint; to choose for election to office.

Nomination. By name; the act of nominating.

Nominee. One chosen as a candidate.

Nomini Poenae. Under the name of a penalty.

Non. Not; by no means.

Nonability. Legal incapacity.

Non Acceptavit. Denial of agreement.

Nonaccess. Absence of sexual intercourse between husband and wife.

Nonage. Under age.

Non Assumpsit. Plea in an action of special assumpsit which denies a promise was made.

Non Assumpsit infra Sex Anno. Plea assumsit is null if not within six year limitation.

Non Claim. Failure to assert a claim or right.

Non Compos Mentis. Not in possession of his full mental faculties; totally incompetent.

Non Constant. It is not certain.

Non Culpabilis. Not guilty.

Non Damnifactus. Not injured.

Non Demisit. Not granted, leased.

Non Est Factum. It was not made.

Non Est Inventus. He has not been found.

None Effect. Void.

Nonfeasance. Failure to perform a duty.

Non Fecit. He did not make it.

Non Infregit Conventionem. He has not broken the agreement; denial of breach of contract.

Nonissuable Plea. No issue of fact plea.

Nonjoinder. Failure of the plaintiff to include in his declaration all of the necessary parties.

Non Juridicus. Not legal.

Non Liquet. It is not clear.

Nonmailable Matter. Material which cannot legally be sent through the U.S. mails.

Non Memini. Not remembered.

Non Obstante. Notwithstanding.

Non Obstante Veredicto. Notwithstanding the verdict of the jury.

Nonpar Value Stock. Corporation stock having no face or par value.

Nonpayment. Failure of payment of a debt.

Non Pros. (Abb.). Non Prosequitur.

Non Prosequitur. He has not proceeded.

Non-Residence. Residence beyond the limits of a particular jurisdiction.

Non Sanae Mentis. Not of sound mind.

Nonsane Memory. Unsound mind.

Nonsense. Unintelligible written matter.

Non Sequitur. It does not follow.

Non Sui Juris. Not in his own right.

Nonsuit. Judgement against a plaintiff for technical failure to prove his case.

Nonsupport. Failure of a husband to provide.

Non Tenuit. He did not hold.

Non-Term. Court vacation.

Non-User. Neglect to use.

Non Vult Contendere. At common law, a plea in a criminal prosecution that the defendant will not contest.

Noon. The middle of the day.

Nota. A note; a distinguishing mark.

Nota Bene. Note well.

Notarial. Pertaining to a notary.

Notary Public. A public official authorized to attest to the authenticity.

Note. A written instrument containing a promise of signer to pay another.

Note of Hand. Promissory note.

Not Found. Indorsement by a grand jury on a bill of indictment upon failure to indict.

Not Guilty. Plea of the general issue in trespass and certain other civil actions; verdict in favor of a defendant.

Notice. Information; knowledge.

Notice, Averment of. Allegation in a pleading that required notice has been given.

Notice of Dishonor. Notice given by the holder to the drawer of a bill, that the person primarily liable has failed to honor it.

Notice of Motion. Written notice advising the defendant when and where he is to appear and states cause of complaint.

Notice of Protest. Notice given by the holder of a bill to the drawer that the bill has been protested for refusal of payment.

Notice to Plead. Written notice served upon the defendant by the plaintiff.

Notice to Produce. Written notice requiring the adverse party to produce a certain described document at the trial.

Notice to Quit. Written notice given by a landlord to a tenant according to the terms of the lease, requiring him to leave the premises.

Notify. To inform in words or writing.

Noting Protest. The notation by a notary on a bill exchange showing it was dishonored.

Notitia. Notice; knowledge.

Notoriety. State of being well-known.

Notorious. Applied to things universally known and recognized; flagrant.

Notorious Possession. Conspicious possession of real property which may lead to the acquisition of title by adverse possession.

Nova Customa. New duties or customs.

Novation. Substitution of new contract.

Novel. New; recent.

Noverint Universi per Praesentes. Know all men by these presents.

Novi Operis Nunciato. Protest a new work.

Novitas. Novelty.

Novum Opus. A new work.

Novus Homo. A new man; a man pardoned.

Now. At this time.

Noxious. Harmful; offensive.

Nubilis. Marriageable.

Nuda. Nude, naked; mere.

Nuda Pactio Obligationem Non Parit. A naked agreement does not beget an obligation.

Nuda Patientia. Mere sufferance.

Nuda Possessio. Mere possession.

Nude. Naked, unclothed; mere.

Nude Contract. One without consideration.

Nudum Pactum. Promise with no consideration.

Nuisance. Anything which interferes with the enjoyment of property or common right.

Nuisance Per Se. That which is a nuisance at all times and under all circumstances.

Nul. No; no one; none.

Nul Agard. No award.

Nul Disseisin. Name given to a plea of the general issue in a writ of entry.

Null. Void.

Null and Void. Binding on no one.

Nullity. That which has no legal effect.

Nullity of Marriage. Defect in the marriage state which renders it void.

Nullus, Nulla. No.

Nullius Juris. Without legal effect.

Nul Tiel Corporation. No such corporation.

Nul Waste. Plea in a common law action of waste denying waste has been committed.

Nunciato. Protest; declaration.

Nuncius. Messenger.

Nuncupate. To make a verbal will.

Nuncupative Will. An oral or verbal will.

Nunquam. Nowhere; never.

Nuquam Indebitatus. Never indebted.

Nuptial. Pertaining to or concerning marriage.

Nuture. To rear or educate a child.

Nutander. By right.

Nute. Night.

Nymphomania. A woman with a morbid, uncontrollable desire for sexual intercourse.

O

Oath. Statement by a witness at a trial, with God as his witness, that he will tell the truth.

Oath in Litem. An oath respecting the value of the property which is the subject.

Oath of Office. Oath by one assuming office.

Oathworthy. Credible.

Ob. On account of.

Obedient. Submissive to authority.

Obiter. On the way; in passing.

Obiter Dictum. That which is said in passing.

Obit Sine Prole. He died without issue.

Objection. Argument against a statement.

Object of Statute. Purpose of the statute.

Oblatio. An offer of payment of debt.

Obligatio. Obligation.

Obligation. A legal and/or moral duty.

Obligee. One to whom another is bound.

Obligor. One bound by some obligation.

Obliquus. Oblique; collateral; indirect.

Obliteration. Erasure of written words.

Oblivion. Forgetfulness.

Obloquy. Disgrace; reproach.

Obreption. Obtaining a thing by fraud.

Obrogation. The annulling of a law.

Obscene. Words, actions or representation which shock the public ideas of sexual purity.

Observe. To perform that which is prescribed.

Obsignare. To sign and seal an instrument.

Obsolete. Term applied to a law which is not enforced although it has not been repealed.

Obstante. Obstructing.

Obstetrics. Branch of medicine for the care of women during pregnancy and birth.

Obstriction. A bond; an obligation.

Obstruct. To hinder, prevent from progress.

Obstruction of Justice. An act or acts hindering or tending to hinder justice.

Obtain. To get possession of, procure.

Obtest. To protest.

Obventio. Rent; revenue; income.

Obvious. Easily seen or understood.

Obvious Risk. One apparent to a reasonable man.

Occasion. An incident as opposed to a cause.

Occasional. Not regularly; casual.

Occision. A killing.

Occult. Hidden; secret.

Occultatio. Concealment.

Occupancy. Mode of acquiring property, which before belonged to nobody.

Occupant. One in actual possession.

Occupare. To occupy.

Occupation. An occupation; a seizure.

Occupation. Taking possession; trade.

Occupational Disease. Disease resulting as a natural consequence of one's occupation.

Occupy. To hold in possession.

Of Course. As a matter of right.

Occur. To happen.

Odium. Hatred; dislike.

Oeconomicus. An executor of the estate.

Oeconomus. Administrator.

Oeps. Use.

Of Age. Over 21 years of age.

Of Counsel. An associate counsel in an action.

Offend. To commit a public offense.

Offender. Person implicated in a crime.

Offense. Violation of law or established rules.

Offer. Proposal by one person to another.

Office. A public position in any branch of government.

Office Copy. Transcript of legal proceedings.

Officer. One entrusted with the duties of either a public or private office.

Official. Pertaining to a public office; officer.

Officious Will. Will in which the testator leaves his property to his family.

Offset. A deduction; counterclaim.

Offspring. Issue.

Of New. Anew a second time.

O.K. (Abb.). All right.

Olographic Will. One which is hand written in entirety by the testator.

Omissio. An omission.

Omission. Failure to do that which is required.

Omme. Man; anyone.

Omnibus Bill. A statute which contains a number of bills.

Omnium. The aggregate value of the different stock in which a loan is usually funded.

On. Upon; as soon as; near to.

On Account. In partial payment.

On Account of Whom It May Concern. An insurance term used to include all persons having an insurable interest in the subject matter for whose benefit the policy is intended.

On Call. On demand.

On Demand. A promissory note payable on demand.

Onerari Non. Not chargeable with the debt.

Onerous. Burdensome; difficult.

Onerous Gift. Gift which imposes some obligation upon the donee by the donor.

Only. Solely; alone.

Onomastic. Applied to the signature of an instrument which is different than the writing.

On or About. An approximation of date.

Onus Probandi. The burden of proof.

Ope Consilio. By aid and counsel.

Open. To begin a trial; to be first to present argument during a trial.

Open and Current Account. One in which there is a series of financial transactions in which debits and credits are balanced.

Open and Notorious. Flagrant misconduct.

Open Court. Public session of court.

Opening. Beginning; first statement of counsel.

Open Policy. An insurance policy in which the value is determined after loss.

Open Season. Part of the year when the laws for the preservation of game and fish permit the unlimited killing or taking of a particular species of game or fish.

Open Shop. Business or industry in which both union and non-union labor is employed.

Open Theft. A larceny wherein the thief is caught in the act.

Operation of Law. Manner in which rights and liabilities pass to a person with no act done by the party.

Operative. Workmen.

Operative Words. Words in a deed or lease which effect the transaction intended to be consummated by the instrument.

Operis Novi Nuntiato. A protest or warning against a new work.

Opiates. Drugs, sedatives.

Opinion. Expression of a conclusion or inferences based upon observation.

Opinion Evidence. Evidence based upon what

LEGAL DICT

the witness thinks or believes.

Opium. Drug made from poppy.

Oportet. It is necessary, fitting or proper.

Oppignerare. To pledge.

Opposition. Act of resisting; antagonism.

Opposite Party. One whose interests are antagonistic to the protected party.

Oppression. An act of cruelty.

Opprobrium. Infamy; shame.

Optimacy. Nobility.

Option. Choice; contract to keep an offer open.

Optional. Left to choice.

Optionee. One who has secured by contract the right to keep an offer open.

Optioner. One bound by contract to keep an offer open.

Opus. Work.

Opus Locatum. Work let out to another.

Opus Manificium. Manual labor.

Opus Novum. New work.

Oral. Spoken.

Oral Defamation. Slander.

Orator. (m.), **Oratrix** (f.). Petitioner in an action in equity.

Ordain. To decree or enact.

Order. Command; direction; written direction.

Order of Business. Order in which legislative business is conducted.

Order of Filiation. Court order determining the paternity of a bastard child.

Order of the Coif. Legal fraternity.

Ordnance. A rule established by authority.

Ordinandi Lex. Law of procedure.

Ordinary. Common; usual.

Ordinary Care. Care exercised by a reasonable man under the particular conditions.

Ordinary Conveyances. Deed of transfer entered into without an assurance.

Ore Tenus. By word of mouth.

Organic Act. Federal statute conferring powers of government upon a territory.

Organic Law. Constitutional law.

Original. First in time or importance.

Original Bill. Bill filed at the beginning of a suit in equity.

Original Conveyance. Conveyance which creates an estate.

Original Evidence. Original document.

Original Jurisdiction. Jurisdiction of a court to hear a case at its beginning.

Orphan. A minor child who has lost one or both of his parents.

Orphans' Court. Courts of probate jurisdiction in a number of states.

Ostensible. Applied to that which claims to be what it is not.

Ostensible Partner. One who although not a member of a firm, allows the use of his name as a general partner in transactions with third persons.

Ostentum. Monster.

Osteopath. One who treats disease by manipulation.

Oust. To put out.

Ouster. A wrongful dispossession.

Outer Door. The door of each separate apartment where there are different apartments having a common outer door.

Outlaw. One violating the law.

Outlawed. As applied to debt, to have become invalid by lapse of time.

Out of Benefit. Term applied to insurance policy holders who have been suspended for nonpayment of premiums.

Out of Term. Between terms of court.

Output. Amount of material produced within a certain time.

Outrage. A grave wrong; violation of a right.

Outre. Outside; beyond.

Outroper. Licensed auctioneer.

Outstanding. Unpaid; uncollected.

Over. In conveyance, used to describe a gift or limitation that comes into existence on the termination of a previous estate.

Overcharge. A charge in excess of that permitted by law.

Overcyted. Found guilty.

Overdraft. Taking out more than deposited.

Overdraw. To write checks on a bank for a larger amount than one has deposited.

Overdue. Delayed or unpaid.

Overlive. Survive.

Overload. To burden too heavily.

Overplus. Remaining balance.

Overrule. To deny; to annul or make void.

Overseer. Superintendent; supervisor.

Overt. Open; manifest, public.

Owe. To be bound to pay a debt.

Owing. Unpaid.

Own. To have title.

Ownership. Group of rights to use and enjoy property, including the right to transmit it to others.

Owner's Risk. The risk, assumed by the owner of merchandise, in transit that the goods may be damaged.

Oyer and Terminer. Name of a court in several states with general jurisdiction.

Oyez. Hear ye.

P

Pace. 2½ feet.

Paceatur. Let him be freed or discharged.

Package. A parcel made up of smaller parcels.

Packing a Jury. Use of improper means in selecting a jury.

Pact. Agreement.

Pactio. Pact.

Pactitious. Settled by a pact or contract.

Pagus. A county.

Paid-Up Insurance. Insurance upon which no further premiums are due.

Pais. The country; the jury; outside of court.

Palam. Openly.

Palm Off. To impose by fraud.

Palpable. Obvious.

Pander. Procurer; pimp.

Panel. Persons available each month for Federal and State jury duty.

Paper. A document or pleading.

Paper Title. Title shown only by deeds.

Par. Equal.

Paragraph. An entire statement of action.

Paramount. Above; upwards.

Paramount Title. Superior title to property.

Paranoia. Type of insanity.

Paraphernalia. Property of a married woman other than that included in her dowry.

Parcel. In regard to land, a lot or tract.

Parcenary. The holding of an inheritable estate jointly by parceners.

Parcener. Joint heir.

Parchment. A document on parchment.

Par Delictum. Equal wrong or fault.

Pardon. The release from the legal consequenses of a specific crime.

Parens Patriae. Father of his country.

Parent. The natural father or mother.

Parenticide. One who kills or the killing of a parent.

Pari. With equal or in equal.

Pari Causa. With equal right.

Pari Delicto. In equal guilt.

Pari Materia, In. On the same subject.

Pari Passu. Of the same degree.

Pari Ratione. By the same reasoning.

Parish. In Louisiana, a district corresponding to a county in other states.

Parity. Equality.

Park. A public ground for recreation.

Parking. The stationing of automobiles.

Parking on the Highway. The voluntary act of leaving an automobile on the highway.

Parliament. The legislative branch of the English government.

Parliamentary Law. The body of regulations of procedure governing legislative assemblies.

Parliamentary Procedure. The procedure and rules governing the conduct of business.

Par of Exchange. The value of the money of one country in that of another.

Parol. Oral; verbal.

Parol Contract. A contract not under seal.

Parole. A conditional release from prison.

Parol Evidence. Oral testimony of a witness.

Parol Evidence, Rule of. A rule which prohibits the receipt of oral agreements to contradict or modify a written agreement.

Parricide. One who murders or the murder of one's parent.

Pars. A part; a party to a deed or action.

Pars Gravata. The party aggrieved.

Pars Rationabilis. A reasonable part or share.

Pars Rea. A party defendant.

Part. Portion, share.

Parte Inaudia. One side being unheard.

Parte Non Comparente. The party not having appeared; a party in default.

Particips Criminis. A party to the crime.

Particeps Doli. A party to the fraud.

Participate. To take part in.

Particular Averment. An allegation or pleading a particular fact.

Particular Malice. Grudge.

Particulars. The items of an account.

Parties. Those persons who take part in any act or directly interested in the action.

Partition. Any division of real or personal property by co-owners.

Partitione Facienda. Concerned with making a division.

Partner. Member of a partnership or firm.

Partnership. An association of two or more persons sharing profits and losses.

Part Owners. Owners in common property.

Part Payment. Partial payment of a debt due.

Part Performance. Partial completion.

Parturition. Giving birth to a child.

Partus. A child.

Party. One who takes part in a legal transaction; a litigant; a political group.

Party Aggrieved. One who has been directly and injuriously affected by the act or omission.

Party in Interest. One who has a beneficial interest in the result of an action or who might be injured as the result thereof.

Party To Be Charged. In the statute of frauds, the party against whom the contract is sought.

Par Value. As applied to bonds, a value equal to the face of the bonds.

Parum. Little.

Parvise. Moot.

Pas. Precedence.

Pass. To utter or pronounce; to transfer.

Passage. Voyage over water or the money paid for such a voyage; enactment.

Passagium. A voyage.

Pass Book. Bank book in which deposits made by a customer are entered.

Passenger. One who uses a public conveyance.

Passim. Scattered; indiscriminately.

Passion. Any emotion which renders the mind incapable of cool reflection.

Passive. Inactive; permissive.

Passive Bond. One which bears no interest.

Passive Trust. One in which the trustee no longer has any active duty to perform.

Passport. A document issued to a citizen by his country, certifying his status.

Past Consideration. In the law of contracts, a consideration which was furnished or rendered in the absence of any previous request.

Patent. A document by which a state or government grants public lands to an individual; the exclusive right granted to an inventor to make, use and sell his invention.

Patent Ambiguity. An apparent error on the face of an instrument.

Patentee. One to whom letters patent are granted by the government.

Patent Medicine. Medicine made by secret formula.

Patent Writ. An open or unsealed writ.

Pater. Father.

Paterfamilia. The father of a family.

Parternal. Pertaining to the father.

Paternal Power. Paternal authority of a father over his children.

Paternity. Fatherhood.

Pathology. That branch of medicine which deals with the nature, causes and symptoms.

Patiens. A patient.

Patria. A country; a jury.

Patria Potestas. Paternal power.

Patricide. One who kills or the killing of one's own father.

Patrimonial. Paternal.

Patrimony. An inherited estate; property inherited from the paternal side.

Patrinus. A godfather.

Patronymic. Surname.

Patruelis. Paternal first cousin.

Pauper. One who is destitute.

Pawn. A bailment of goods to a creditor as security for some debt.

Pawnbroker. One licensed to lend money on the security of personal property.

Pawnee. One to whom goods are pledged.

Pax. Peace.

Pay. To discharge a debt.

Payable. To be paid.

Payable on Demand. Indicates a bill is payable on its date.

Payee. One to whom a payment is made.

Payment. The discharge of a debt.

Payment into Court. The placing of money in the custody of the court by a person who is actually sued for it or is so threatened.

Peace. State of public order, tranquility.

Peace, Justice of the. A public official having minor judicial power.

Peace Offfcers. Those charged with the enforcement of the law.

Peccatum. A sin; a crime.

Peculation, Peculatus. The embezzlement of public funds.

Peculiar. Particular; special.

Pecunia. Money; property.

Pecunia Non Numerata. Money not paid.

Pecuniary. Financial.

Pecuniary Injury. One estimated financially.

Peddler. An itinerant trader.

Pederasty. Copulation between two men.

Pedestrian. Person traveling on foot.

Pedigree. Genealogy.

Peeping Tom. One who peers in windows on the sly in the hope of seeing nude women.

Peine. Punishment.

Penal. Pertaining to punishment.

Penal Action. An action to recover.

Penal Statute. Statute which forbids an act and imposes a penalty for it.

Penalty. Punishment for a crime.

Pendency. Suspense; undecided; pending.

Pendente Lite. While the suit is pending.

Pending. During; before the conclusion of.

Penses Me. In my possession.

Penetration. In a case of rape, the insertion of the male sex organ into the female sex organ.

Penitentiary. Prison.

Pensa. A weight.

Pensio. A payment; a rent.

Pension. A regular allowance paid to a public or private employee, retired from the service.

Pensioner. One who receives a pension.

Pentways. Byways; private roads.

Per. By, through, by means of.

Per and Cui. By and to whom.

Per Annum. Yearly.

Per Autre Vie. For the lifetime of another.

Per Bouche. Orally.

Per Capita. As applied to descent and distribution of estates, equally.

Perception. Taking into possession.

Per Consequences. In consequence.

Per Contra. On the other hand.

Per Curiam. By the court.

Per Defaltam. By default.

Per Diem. Daily.

Perduellio. Treason.

Perdurable. Lasting forever.

Peregrini. Foreigner; alien.

Peremptory. Imperative; positive; conclusive.

Peremptory Defense. A defense denying suit.

Peremptory Mandamus. A writ of obedience.

Per Equipollens. By an equivalent.

Perfect. Free from error; to complete.

Perfect Trust. Executed trust.

Perfidy. Treachery, faithlessness.

Perform. To execute or fulfill according to terms.

Performance. Fulfillment of a duty.

Per Fraudem. By fraud.

Periculum. Danger; hazard.

Periel. Risk; hazard.

Per Incuriam. Through inadvertence.

Per Industriam. By industry.

Per Infortunium. Accidentally.

Period. Any point, space or division of time.

Period of Gestation. Time between a child's conception and birth.

Peripharasis. Verbosity.

Perjury. Lying under oath.

Per Legem Terrae. By the law of the land.

Permanent. Lasting; fixed; stable.

Permenent Abode. Fixed residence.

Permanent Disability. One which is more than temporary and presumably permanent.

Per Minas. By threats or duress.

Permission. Leave; license; authority to do.

Permissive. Allowed.

Permissive Waste. Negligent waste.

Permit. A license.

Per Omnes. By all persons.

Perpetrator. One who commits a crime.

Perpetual. Everlasting; eternal; continuous.

Perpetual Injunction. Injunction which is final.

Perpetual Lease. One which the tenant has the option of renewing as soon as it expires.

Perpetuating Testimony. Procedure for taking and preserving testimony.

Perpetuity. An interest under which property is less than completely alienable for longer than allowed by law.

Per Plegium. By a security or pledge.

Per Procuration. By an agent.

Perquisites. Anything lawfully acquired by an officer beyond the salary or regular fees.

Perquisitio. A purchase.

Per Quod. By which.

Per Se. In itself.

Persecutio. A suit or prosecution.

Person. A human being (natural person) or a corporation (artificial person).

Persona. Person.

Persona Designata. Person pointed out as an individual.

Persona Grata. An acceptable person.

Personal. Pertaining to an individual person.

Personal Action. Action to recover damages due to breach of contract or injury.

Personal Chattels. Movable property.

Personal Contract. Contract involving personal property.

Personal Effects. Items having an intimate relation to the possessor; movable or chattel

Personal Injury. An invasion of a personal right; bodily injury.

Personality. The law dealing with persons.

Personal Knowledge. First-hand knowledge.

Personal Liberty. Freedom of movement.

Personal Representative. Executor or administrator of a deceased person.

Personality. Personal property; chattels.

Persona Non Grata. A person not acceptable.

Personate. To assume another's identity with intent to deceive and defraud.

Persona Non Compos Mentis. Persons of unsound mind.

Per Stirpes. By representation.

Persuade. Induce.

Per Testes. By witnesses.

Pertinens. Appurtenant.

Pertinent. Relevant.

Perturbation. A disturbance.

Perverse Verdict. Verdict in which the jury does not follow the directions of the judge.

Petitio. Petition; demand; claim.

Petition. In equity, an application for a court order giving the circumstances.

Petit Jury. A trial jury.

Petitor. Petitioner; plaintiff.

Petitory Action. An action in which the plaintiff seeks to establish right of property or title.

Petty. Small; trifling.

Petty Larceny. A misdemeanor; larceny or theft of property worth less than the amount fixed by statute.

Pharmacist. Druggist.

Philanthropic. Charitable.

Physical. Relating to the body.

Physical Force. Actual violence.

Physical Incapacity. Inability to copulate due to an incurable physical imperfection.

Physical Injury. Bodily harm.

Physician. A doctor of medicine.

Picaroon. Robber.

Picketing. The posting of men before a business organization to make public protest.

Pickpocket. One who secretly steals from the person of another.

Pierage. Toll charge for the use of a pier.

Pignus. Property pledged as security.

Pilfer. Steal.

Pillage. Robbery by force or violence.

Pillory. A frame erected on a pillar, made with holes through which a man's head, hands or fingers could be fixed and held.

Pimp. A procurer; a pander.

Piracy. Robbery on the high seas.

Pirate. A sea-robber.

Piscary. The right of fishing.

Pistol. A short, hand firearm.

P.J. (Abb.). Presiding judge.

Placard. Edict; declaration.

Place of Abode. Residence.

Placit, Placitum. Decree; determination.

Placitabile. Pleadable.

Placita Communia. Common pleas.

Placita Juris. Rules of law.

Placitamentum. Pleading.

Placitum. Marginal title.

Plaga. Wound; stroke.

Plagerism. Copying an author's work.

Plaint. Complaint; the introductory pleading.

Plaintiff. One who brings an action at law.

Plat. A scale map of land.

Plea. In common law pleading, the formal answer of the defendant; in criminal law, the answer of "guilty" or "not guilty"; any action.

Plead. To deliver the defendant's answer to the plaintiff's declaration.

Pleader. One who prepares a pleading.

Pleadings. The successive statements delivered alternately by the parties involved.

Plea in Bar. Plea which defeats the plaintiff's.

Plea of Guilty. Admission of guilt in court.

Plea of Nolo Contendere. Implied confession.

Plea Side. Civil department of a court.

Plebian. One of the common people.

Plebiscite. Popular vote.

Pledge. Personal property given as security.

Pledgee. One to whom goods are pledged.

Pledgery. Suretyship; an answering for.

Pledgor. One who delivers goods in pledge.

Plee. Plea; an action.

Plenary. Full; complete; entire.

Plenary Suit. A suit on formal pleadings.

Plene Administravit. Plea of an administrator when sued for a debt of his decedent.

Plenipotentiary. One fully empowered to act for another.

Plenum Dominum. Full ownership.

Plenum Rectum. Absolute right.

Plumbism. Lead poisoning

Plunder. To take by open force.

Plural. More than one.

Plurality. The largest number of votes cast.

Pluries. Often; frequently.

Plus. More.

Poach. To steal game from another man.

Poena. Punishment.

Poena Corporalis. Corporal punishment.

Point. A question of law in a particular case.

Poison. Any substance which when taken internally can destroy life.

Police. Branch of the government which enforces the law.

Police Court. Municipal court for the trial of minor criminal offenses.

Policy of Insurance. Contract between the insured and the insurer.

Political Offense. An offense against the state.

Politics. The science of government.

Poll. To examine each juror to determine whether they agree with the verdict.

Polling the Jury. See Poll.

Polls. Place where votes are cast in an election.

Polyandry. Marriage of a woman to several men at the same time.

Polygamy. Marriage to more than one person at the same time.

Ponere. To place or put.

Pool. The combined money, property or interests of a group of people.

Poor. Needy; destitute.

Poor Person. Pauper.

Populus. The people.

Port. Place where vessels load and unload.

Portatica. Port duties.

Portion. Part; share; division.

Port of Entry. Port where there is a custom-house.

Portorium. Customs duty.

Positive. Certain; absolute.

Positive Evidence. Direct proof.

Positive Juris. Of positive law.

Positive Law. Law established by members of a society to govern their actions.

Posse. Possible.

Posse Comitatus. The force of the county.

Possess. To occupy, control.

Possessed. A temporary interest in lands.

Possessio. To have full right and control.

Possessio Bonorum. The possession of goods.

Possessio Malae Fidei. Possession in bad faith.

Possession. Exclusive ownership and control.

Possession in Fact. Actual possession.

Possession in Law. Possession which the law annexes to the title.

Possession, Writ of. In an action of ejectment, a writ used to put a plaintiff in possession of real property.

Possessor. One who possesses.

Possessory. Pertaining to possession.

Post Entry. An entry of goods at a custom house to correct an original entry.

Posthumous Child. Born after father's death.

Possibilities. A possibility.

Possibility. An uncertain future event.

Possibility of Reverter. Possibility of estate.

Post. After.

Post-Act. An act done afterwards.

Postage. Charge for the delivery of mail.

Post-Date. To put a future date on.

Post Diem. After the day.

Postea. Afterwards.

Posterity. Direct descendants.

Post Facto. After the commission of a crime.

Post Litem Motam. After the start of suit.

Post Mortem. After death; autopsy.

Post Notes. Bank notes payable at a future date.

Post-Nuptial. After the marriage has taken place.

Post Obit. After death; an agreement to pay a sum of money after the death of a person from whom the promisor hopes to inherit property.

Postpone. Delay.

Post Rem. After the transaction.

Post Terminum. After the term.

Potable. Drinkable.

Potentia. Power; authority; possibility.

Potential. Existing in possibility.

Potestas. Power; authority.

Pound. Place to confine animals.

Poverty Affidavit. An affidavit filed by one of the parties in an action, that he is unable to pay court costs.

Power. The authority to do a thing; the authority to dispose of real or personal property.

Power Coupled with an Interest. Authority to do some act coupled with an interest in the thing itself.

Power of Attorney. Formal instrument by which an agent is appointed.

Powers that Be. Duly constituted authorities.

Practice. Habit, custom, usage; execution of legal proceedings in all its stages and forms; the exercise of the profession of law.

Practitioner. One engaged in the practice of his profession.

Praecipe. An original writ; an order; a command.

Praecognita. Things which must be known in order to understand that which follows.

Praedictus. Aforesaid.

Praedium. Land.

Praefatus. Aforesaid.

Praejudicialis. Prejudged.

Praejudicium. Prejudgment; prejudice.

Praemissa. The premises.

Praemium. Reward; price.

Praesens in Curia. Present in court.

Prayer. In equity, that part of the bill or complaint which asks for the relief sought by the party.

Preamble. A clause at the beginning of a constitution or statute stating the reason and purpose of the legislation.

Precarious. Descriptive of anything which may be ended at the will of the person who granted it.

Precatory. Having the character of a request.

Precatory Trust. A trust created by words of entreaty and request rather than by command.

Precaution. Foresight.

Precedence. Superiority in rank.

Precedent. Previous decision of court relied upon as authority.

Prece Partium. By the prayer of the parties.

Precept. A written order issued to an officer(s) to give him (them) the authority to perform some act.

Precinct. A police district; an election district.

Preclude. Estop.

Preconceived Malice. Malice aforethought.

Predecessor. One who goes before.

Pre-Emption. The right to buy property before some other person.

Pre-Existing Debts. Debts previously contracted.

Prefer. To bring before; to prosecute.

Preference. The transfer of property by an insolvent debtor to one or more of his creditors, to the exclusion of the rest.

Preferred. Having a priority, advantage or privilege.

Preferred Stock. Stock having a priority over other stock in the distribution of dividends.

Pregnant. The state of being with child.

Prejudice. Bias; preconceived opinion; to injure or damage.

Preliminary. Introductory; preceding.

Premeditation. The planning of a deed before the doing thereof; plotting.

Premises. Foregoing statements; in equity, the stating part of a bill; in estates, the actual property conveyed; in insurance, the subject matter insured.

Premium. Reward; compensation; money paid by the insured to the insurer under a policy of insurance.

Prenomen. First name.

Prepense. Forethought.

Preponderance of Evidence. Greater weight of or more credible evidence.

Prerogative. An exclusive privilege.

Prescribe. To make invalid or to outlaw; to claim title by virtue of long use and enjoyment.

Prescription. Mode of acquisition to title of land by long use and enjoyment.

Presence. State of being in a certain place.

Present. A gift; now existing.

Presently. Immediately; now.

Presentement. The written statement of a grand jury concerning an offense based on their own knowledge and observation without any bill of indictment being laid before them; the presentation of a negotiable instrument to the maker, drawee or acceptor at the proper time and place.

Preservation. To keep safe from harm.

Preside. To direct some proceeding.

President. One in a position of authority over others.

Presume. Assume beforehand.

Presumed Bias. Implied bias.

Presumption. That which may be taken for granted.

Presumption of Fact. Inference drawn from evidence adduced at a trial.

Presumption of Law. Legal conclusion derived from the proof of certain facts.

Presumptive. Based upon a presumption.

Presumptive Title. Titled inferred from possession and use.

Pretend. To feign, sham.

Preterition. Omission by a testator of a legally entitled heir.

Preter Legal. Not legal.

Pretermission. See Preterition.

Pretermit. To omit.

Pretext. Pretense.

Pretium. Price; cost; value.

Pretium Affectionis. The price of affection.

Pretium Periculi. The price of risk, such as an insurance policy premium.

Prevailing. Predominant; effectual.

Prevarication. Breach of confidence; lie.

Prevent. To impede; to obstruct.

Previous. Prior; former.

Price. Monetary consideration paid for a thing.

Prima Facie. At first sight; a fact presumed true unless proven otherwise.

Prima Facie Case. Case supported by sufficient evidence to justify a favorable verdict unless contradicted by other evidence.

Primary. First in importance or time.

Primary Cause. The responsible cause of a legal liability.

Primary Evidence. The best evidence to prove a fact.

Primary Legacy. A gift of money by will.

Primer Election. First choice.

Primogeniture. The state of being of the eldest of several children of the same parents.

Principal. One who grants authority to an agent to transact business for him; one primarily liable to a creditor, but jointly a third person, the surety; the one who actually commits a crime; the amount of a debt, not including interest.

Principal Fact. The main fact at issue in a cause.

Principalis. A principal.

Principium. The beginning.

Principle. A fundamental doctrine of law.

Prior. Earlier, preceding; preferable.

Priority. Precedence; preference.

Prison. Place of confinement.

Prisoner. One confined to a prison by due process of law.

Private. Pertaining to a private individual as opposed to the public.

Private Law. Law concerned with the legal relations between private individuals.

Private Person. An individual not holding public office.

Private Property. Property belonging to an individual who has the exclusive right of disposition thereof.

Private Residence. Residence for one family.

Private Trust. Trust created for purposes other than public or charitable.

Privies. Persons mutually interested in a thing due to some relation other than actual contract between them.

Previgna. Step-daughter.

Prevignus. Step-son.

LEGAL DICT

Privilege. A benefit or immunity.

Privileged Communications. A communication made in professional confidence (client to lawyer, patient to doctor) which may not be divulged.

Privilege Tax. Excise tax.

Priviligium. Privilege.

Privity. A succession of relationship to the same rights of property.

Privity of Contract. Relationship among two or more contracting parties.

Privy. One who participates in any action, matter or thing; private.

Privy in Representation. Executor of a testator; administrator of an intestate.

Privy Verdict. Verdict given privately to the judge out of court.

Prize. A reward for some feat.

Pro. For; before; by way of; in place of.

Pro and Con. For and against.

Probability. Likelihood.

Probable. Appearing to be true.

Probable Cause. Reasonable cause.

Probable Consequence. One most likely to follow its supposed cause.

Probate. The process of proving a will.

Probate Court. Court established for the administration of the estates of decedents, and the control of the adoption and guardianship of minors; Orphan's Court.

Probate Duty. Estate tax.

Probatio. Proof; trial.

Probation. Proof; trial; test; suspended sentence during good behavior, usually under supervision of a probation officer.

Probationer. One on probation.

Probation Officer. An officer who supervises those on probation or suspended sentence.

Probatio Viva. Living proof.

Probe. An inquiry or investigation.

Pro Bono et Malo. For good and evil.

Procedure. Method of proceeding by which a legal right is enforced.

Proceeding. The form and manner of conducting a legal action before a court; an inquiry before a grand jury.

Process. Method, mode or operation producing a result or effect; all the acts of the court from the beginning to the end of a proceeding.

Prochein. Next.

Prochein Ami. Next friend; the adult representative (not a guardian) of an infant plaintiff.

Proclamare. To proclaim, warn.

Proclamation. A public notice.

Pro Concilio. For advice.

Pro Confesso. As confessed; in equity, applied to the decree founded upon a bill where no answer is made to it by the defendant.

Proctor. One authorized to act for another; an attorney in a court of probate or admiralty or in an ecclesiastical court.

Procuracy. A written instrument empowering a procurator to act.

Procuration. Power or authority given in writing.

Procurator. Proctor.

Procure. To initiate a proceeding; to cause or bring about; to obtain.

Procurer. One who brings about a thing.

Pro Defectu. Because of the lack of.

Pro Defectu Exitus. For failure of issue.

Pro Defendente. In favor of the defendant.

Prodigal. Spendthrift.

Prodition. Treason.

Proditor. Treason.

Produce. To make, manufacture; to bring forward.

Producent. One who produces a person as a witness.

Pro Emptore. As a purchaser.

Pro Facti. As a fact.

Pro Falso Clamore Suo. By reason of his false claim.

Profanity. Cursing; swearing.

Profectitus. Property which can be inherited.

Profert. An offer to produce a written instrument in court.

Profert in Curia. He produces in court.

Profess. To make a public declaration.

Profession. A public declaration; vocation; occupation.

Proffer. To offer, propose.

Profit. Gain.

Profiteering. Acquisition of excessive profits.

Profits. Net gain from a business investment.

Pro Forma. As a matter of form.

Pro Hac Vice. For this occasion.

Prohibit. To forbid by law.

Prohibition. Writ issued from a superior court forbidding an inferior court to hear a case because of lack of jurisdiction; restraint on the sale of alcoholic beverages.

Pro Indiviso. As undivided.

Pro Legato. As a legacy.

Proles. Offspring; posterity.

Prolicide. The killing by a parent of his child.

Prolixity. Superfluous statement of facts in pleading.

Prolongation. Extension of time.

Promise. An agreement or declaration to perform a certain act.

Promisee. One to whom a promise is made.

Promisor. One who makes a promise.

Promissory Note. A negotiable instrument.

Promote. Encourage; advance.

Promoter. Informer; one who undertakes the organization of a corporation.

Promulgation. Publication of the enactment of a law.

Proof. Evidence.

Proper. Suitable; correct.

Proper Care. Care exercised by a prudent man under like circumstances.

Proper Name. Christian name.

Proper Party. One other than a necessary party who has an interest in the subject matter of the litigation.

Property. Means the exclusive and unrestricted right to a thing as well as the physical thing itself.

Property Insurance. A contract for the indemnification against loss or damage to certain property named in the policy.

Propinquity. Relationship.

Propinquus. Next of kin.

Propone. To propound; to offer; to make a motion.

Proponent. One who offers a will for probate or makes a motion.

Proportum. Import.

Proposal. Offer; expression of intention.

Proposition. An offer to do a thing.

Pro Posse Suo. According to his own ability.

Proprietary. Pertaining to an owner.

Proprietas. Property; ownership.

Proprietor. Owner.

Proprio Vigore. By its own force; automatically.

Propter. Because of; for.

Propter Adulterium. By reason of adultery.

Propter Affectum. Term applied to the challenge of a juryman for bias.

Propter Defectum. Because of the lack of.

Propter Delictum. On account of some defect.

Propter Saevitiam. Because of cruelty.

Pro Querente. For the plaintiff.

Pro Rata. Proportional.

Prorate. To divide or distribute proportionately.

Pro Re Nata. According to the occasion as it arises.

Proscribed. Outlawed.

Pro Se. On his own behalf.

Prosecute. To act against through law.

Prosecuting Attorney. Public officer who conducts trial on behalf of the state.

Prosecution. Legal proceedings for purpose of determining guilt or innocence.

Prosecutor. Witness or public official who instigates a criminal proceeding.

Prosequi. Pursue; prosecute.

Prospective Law. Law applicable to cases arising after its enactment.

Prospectus. Document setting forth nature and objectives of securities; an invitation to purchase stock, bonds, debentures.

Prostitution. Practice of a woman who engages in sexual intercourse for pay.

Protectim Order. Order protecting wife's property in willful direction by husband.

Protest. Expression of dissent or disapproval.

Pro Tempore. Temporarily.

Protestation. Manner of pleading involving an indirect affirmation or denial of fact that cannot be definitely alleged or denied.

Prothonotary. Office of courts having custody of court records and seals.

Protocol. A record.

Prout. As charged.

Prove. To establish; make certain.

Pro Veritate. For the truth.

Proviso. Part of legal document which provides for certain conditions of the basic instrument.

Provocation. Act of inciting to do particular act.

Provoke. Arouse; stimulate.

Proximity. Relationship; closeness.

Proxeneta. One who arranges contract between two parties.

Proxy. One who is charged with representing another.

Pseudo. False; counterfeit.

Puberty. The age of maturity at which person is capable of begetting children (Common Law).

Public. The citizens of a community, state or nation.

Publish. To make known, circulate.

Pudendum. External female sexual organ.

Pudicity. Purity; modesty.

Pierita. Age from 7 to 14 years.

Punish. To impose a penalty for an act.

Punitive Damages. Exemplary or vindictive damages.

Purchaser. Buyer.

Pure. Free of conditions or restrictions; chaste.

Purge. To cleanse.

Purloin. To steal.

Purpart. Part of an estate, after having been held in common, allotted to a single person.

Purport. Convey; imply.

Pusue. Prosecute.

Purveyor. One who purchases or procures for another.

Purview. Enacting pact of a statute.

Put. Stockbroker's privilege of delivering or not delivering the thing sold.

Putative. Assumed; supposed.

Put in Suit. To sue upon.

Pyx. Receptacle in mint for testing coins.

Pyromania. Morbid desire for house burning.

Q

Qua. Considered as; in what manner; how; in the capacity of.

Quack. An incompetent physician.

Quadrans. A fourth part.

Quadripartite. Divided into four parts; having four parties.

Quadroon. Offspring of mulatto and white.

Quaere. Query.

Quaerens. Plaintiff.

Quaeritus. It is doubted.

Quaestio Facti. A question of fact.

Quaestio Juris. A question of law.

Quaestus. An estate acquired by purchase as opposed to inheritance.

Qualification. A requisite, essential; condition which must be fulfilled in order to attain a certain status; a modification.

Qualified. Adapted; entitled; capable; competent; possessing legal power or capacity.

Qualified Acceptance. Conditional acceptance.

Qualified Elector. One legally qualified to vote.

Qualified Indorsement. Indorsement of a negotiable instrument qualifying the liability of the endorser.

Qualified Interest. An interest in property which is less than absolute.

Qualified Privilege. In the law of libel and slander, applied to all communications made in good faith upon any subject matter in which the person communicating has an interest, or in reference to which he has a duty to a person having a corresponding interest or duty, although not a legal one, but of moral or social character.

Qualified Voter. One who votes.

Qualify. To prepare to exercise a right, office or franchise; to limit; modify or restrict.

Quamdiu. As long as; until.

Quando Acciderint. When they shall come in.

Quandocumque. Whenever; as often as.

Quantes Fois. How many times.

Quantum. How much; the whole; a totality.

Quantum Indemnificatus. To what amount he should be indemnified.

Quantum Meriut. As much as deserved; in the common counts, which evaluates services rendered.

Quantum Valebant. As much as they were worth; in the common counts which evaluate for goods sold and delivered.

Quarantine. Isolation of infected persons to prevent spread of serious disease; period during which a ship with infectious disease aboard is isolated.

Quare. Wherefore; why; because.

Quarrel. Applied to real and personal actions and the causes of actions and suits; controversy; debate.

Quarry. An open excavation where marble, stone, etc. are dug.

Quart. A liquid measure of one-fourth of a gallon.

Quarter. One-fourth.

Quarter-Dollar. 25 cents.

Quarter-Eagle. U.S. coin worth $2.50.

Quarterly. Every 3 months.

Quarter of a Year. 91 days.

Quarter Section. In U.S. land law, one of the square divisions employed in the survey and designation of public lands, containing 160 acres and measuring ¼ of a mile on each side.

Quarter Year. 91 days.

Quash. To annul or make void.

Quasi. As; as if; as it were.

Quasi Affinity. Relationship of an engaged person to the relatives of the person to whom he or she is engaged.

Quasi-Contractus. An obligation arising not from an agreement of parties, but from some relationship between them.

Quasi Corporation. Name sometimes given to a county.

Quasi-Delict. A tort in which there is an absence of malice.

Quasi Ex-Contractu. As if from a contract; applied to obligations which are not really contractual but to which the actions of assumpsit have been extended.

Quasi-Fee. Estate gained wrongfully.

Quasi Judicial Act. Judicial act performed by one other than a judge.

Quay. Wharf.

Querela. An action preferred in any court.

Querens. Plaintiff.

Querulous. Fault-finding; fretful; whining.

Question. Query; inquiry; problem.

Quia. Because; inasmuch as.

Quibble. Verbal objection; unnecessary objection.

Quick. Alive.

Quickening. First motion of the fetus in the womb felt by the mother.

Quick with Child. Having conceived.

Quid Pro Quo. What for what; something for something.

Quidam. Somebody.

Quiet. To pacify; to silence; peaceful; free from disturbance.

Quietare. To acquit, discharge.

Quinquepartite. Divided into 5 parts.

Quintal. 100 pounds.

Quit. Clear; discharged; free.

Quitclaim. To relinquish a claim; a release or acquittance given to one man by another in respect of any action that he has against him.

Quitclaim Deed. Deed of conveyance operating by way of release.

Quittance. Acquittance; a release.

Quoad Hoc. As to this; with respect to this.

Quo Animo. With what intention.

Quod Computet. That he account.

Quod Recuperet. That he recover; the ordinary form of judgments for the plaintiff in actions at law.

Quod Vide. Which see.

Quorum. A majority.

Quota. A proportional part or share.

Quote. To copy or repeat a passage from; to cite.

Quousque. How long; how far.

Quovis Modo. In whatever manner.

R

Race. An ethnical stock; a contest for stakes with judges presiding.

Rachater. To redeem or buy back.

Rachetum. Redemption; ransom.

Rack. Instrument of torture.

Racketeer. One who make money in violation of the Penal Law.

Racketeering. An organized conspiracy to gain control of a business or commodity through acts of violence.

Rack-Rent. A rent amounting to the full value of the tenement or close to it.

Radiograph. X-ray.

Radius. A straight line drawn from the center of the circle to its periphery.

Raffle. Game of chance in the form of a lottery.

Railroad. To force through legislation over the objection of a minority; a road or way on which iron rails are laid for purposes of transportation.

Railroad Commission. A state board empowered to make and enforce regulations concerning railroad companies.

Railway. Railroad.

Raise. To create; to infer; to produce; to rear.

Raise an Issue. To bring pleadings to an issue.

Raise a Rate. Levy a tax.

Raising a Check. Forgery of a check in which the amount has been increased, but the signatures are genuine.

Random. Without aim, purpose or direction.

Rank. Grade; official standing.

Ransom. Money paid for the release of a person or property from captivity.

Rape. Forcible and unlawful sexual knowledge of a woman without her consent.

Rapina. Robbery.

Raptim et Sparsim. Hastily and spasmodically.

Raptor. One who commits rape.

Raptus. Rape.

Rasure. Erasure.

Rasus. Erased.

Ratable. Taxable.

Ratable Value. Appraised or assessed value of property for purposes of taxation.

Ratam Rem Habere. To consider the matter as ratified.

Rate. Tax; assessment; proportional or relative value.

Rate of Exchange. The actual value in a foreign country of a negotiable instrument drawn upon a person in that country.

Ratification. Confirmation by a principal of an act performed by his agent in his behalf; affirmation.

Ratify. To make valid; to confirm.

Ratihabito. Ratification.

Ratio. Rate; proportion.

Ratio Decidendi. The reason for deciding.

Ratio Legis. The reason underlying the law.

Rationabilis. Reasonable; rational.

Rational. Sane.

Rational Doubt. Reasonable doubt.

Ratione Contractus. By reason of the contract.

Ratione Loci. By reason of the place.

Ratione Materiae. By reason of the matter involved.

Ratione Personae. By reason of the person concerned.

Rationes. The pleadings filed in an action.

Ratione Tenurae. By reason of one's tenure.

Ravish. Forcible and unlawful sexal knowledge of a woman without her consent.

Ravishment. A rape.

Raze. Erase.

R.C.L. (Abb.). Ruling Case Law.

Re. In the matter of; in regard to.

Read. To make known the contents of a writing or document.

Ready. Prepared.

Ready and Willing. Not only the capacity, but the disposition to act.

Ready Money. Cash.

Real. Pertaining to a thing or realty.

Real Action. An action brought for the specific recovery of lands, tenements and hereditaments.

Real Estate. Right, interest or ownership existing in the land.

Real Evidence. Evidence furnished by physical objects brought into court.

Real Injury. Physical injury due to an unlawful act.

Real Law. Body of laws relating to real property; law relating to specific property, movable or immovable.

Realize. To bring into actual possession; to convert property into money; to receive returns on an investment.

Realm. State; country.

Real Party in Interest. One directly interested in a litigation.

Real Property. Lands, tenements and hereditaments and all that makes up the earth in its natural condition.

Real Security. Security upon property.

Real Statute. Statute regulating property within the state where it is in force.

Real Things. Things which are permanent, fixed and immovable.

Realty. Real property.

Real Value. Market value under normal conditions.

Reason. Intellect; sanity; motive or cause for action.

Reasonable. Just; proper.

Reasonable Care. Prudent action.

Reason and Probable Cause. Existing grounds for suspecting one of a crime.

Reasonable Creature. A human being.

Reasonable Doubt. Such a doubt as will leave the juror's mind uncertain after examination of the evidence.

Reasonable Prudence. Ordinary care.

Reasonable Time. Length of time fairly and properly allowed for the performance of a duty or obligation.

Reattachment. A second attachment of a defendant's person subsequent to his release from a previous attachment in the same action.

Rebate. Discount; refund; reduction in consideration of prompt payment.

Rebel. One who unjustly and unlawfully acts against the government or duly constituted authority.

Rebellion. Insurrection.

Rebouter. To rebut; to bar.

Rebut. To deny, contradict or avoid.

Rebuttable Presumption. A presumption which may be contradicted by evidence.

Rebuttal. Showing that a statement of a witness is not true; testimony addressed to evidence of the opposition.

Rebutter. A defendant's answer of fact to a plaintiff's surrejoinder.

Recall. To set aside; method of removal from office.

Recall of Pardon. Cancellation of a pardon before its delivery and acceptance.

Recapture. A taking back; a remedy or reprisal.

Receipt. Written acknowledgment that an obligation has been discharged.

Receive. To get by transfer; accept custody of.

Receiver. One appointed to hold in trust, property under litigation.

Receiver Pendente Lite. One appointed to take charge of the fund or property to which the receivership extends while the case is still undecided.

Receptus. Arbitrator.

Recess. A brief cessation or interruption to a meeting or proceeding.

Recession. A giving back of property by the grantee to his grantor.

Recessus. An exit.

Rechater. To ransom.

Recidivist. An habitual criminal.

Reciprocal. Mutual.

Reciprocal Contract. A bilaterial contract.

Reciprocal Wills. Wills giving the property of each testator to the other.

Reciprocity. Mutuality.

Recital. The formal statement in any deed or writing setting forth the reasons upon which the transaction is founded.

Reck. To care, mind or heed.

Reckless. Negligent.

Reckless Driving. Operating a motor vehicle in a negligent manner with disregard of consequences and indifference to the rights of others.

Recognition. Ratification; adoption.

Recognizance. An obligation of record, entered into before some court of record or a duly authorized magistrate, to do some particular act.

Recognize. To try; to examine in order to determine the facts; to ratify.

Recognizee. One to whom the promise is made in a recognizance.

Recognizor. One who binds himself by a recognizance.

Recommend. To advise or counsel.

Recommendatory. Precatory; advisory.

Recompense. Reward; compensation.

Reconcile. To harmonize.

Reconduction. Renewal of a lease.

Recontinuance. The recovery of an incorporeal hereditament of which one has been wrongfully deprived.

Reconvenire. To plead a cross-demand.

Reconvention. An action by a defendant against a plaintiff in a former action; a cross-bill or litigation.

Record. To write or transcribe for the purpose of preservation; an official memorandum of proceedings, acts, etc.

Recordare. A writ to bring up judgments of justices of the peace.

Recorder. Public officer who keeps record books required by law.

Recordum. Record.

Recount. A counting over again of election ballots.

Recoupment. A keeping back and stopping of something which is due because there is an equitable reason to withhold it.

Recourse. Resort; recur.

Recover. To collect; to regain; to acquire by litigation.

Recovery. Obtained by process and course of law; payment compelled by action in the revenue laws of the state.

Recreant. Coward.

Recrimination. Charge by an accused person against the accuser.

Recte. Rightly; correctly.

Rectifier. A person who purifies spirits in any manner or who makes a mixture of spirits with anything else and sells it under any name.

Rectify. To correct; to purify by distillation; to adjust.

Rectum. Right.

Rectum Esse. To be right in court.

Recurrent Insanity. Temporary insanity which returns from time to time.

Recusation. A challenge directed against a judge before whom the case is to be tried on the ground of prejudice or some others diqualification.

Recusatio Testis. Rejection of a witness on the ground of his incompetency.

Red. Communist; anarchist.

Reddendum. In conveyancing, rendering; yielding; a clause in which the grantor creates some new thing to himself out of that which he has granted.

Reddition. Surrender; restoration.

Redditus Assisus. A fixed rent.

Redeem. To buy back.

Redeemable Bonds. Bonds which are due and payable at a specified time, but redeemable on demand of the issuing body.

Redelivery. A yielding back of a thing.

Redemption. A buying back.

Red-Handed. While committing the crime.

Redhibition. Avoidance of a sale because of a defect in the thing sold which renders it useless or undesirable.

Redirect Examination. Re-examination of a witness by the party who called him, after the cross examination.

Reditus. Revenue; return.

Reditus Assisus. A set rent.

Red Light District. Area where houses of prostitution are located.

Redraft. The drawing of a new bill of exchange which has been protested by the holder of the original draft.

Redraw. To make a redraft.

Redress. Reparation.

Red Tape. Order or system carried to extremes.

Reduced. Improverished.

Reduce to Possession. To convert a claim in action to a tangible possession.

Redundancy. Introduction of superfluous matter into a legal document.

Re-Entry. The act of resuming possession pursuant to a right reserved when the party exercising the right quit his possession.

Refare. To bereave; to rob.

Refection. Redress; reparation.

Refer. To call in an auditor or referee in a case which requires special handling.

Referee. One appointed by the court to perform certain duties in a cause pending in court.

Reference. An agreement to arbitrate; to send a cause pending in court to a referee.

Referendum. The determination of legislation by direct vote of the people.

Reform. Correct; rectify

Reformatory. Penal institution directed toward rehabilitation.

Refunding Bond. Bond which replaces an outstanding bond which the holder surrenders in return for the new security.

Refund. To repay or return.

Refuse. To fail to comply with a demand.

Regency. Rule; government; kingship.

Regent. Temporary ruler; governor; member of governing board of some colleges.

Regicide. Murder of or one who murders a sovereign.

Régime. System of rules.

Regina. Queen.

Register. To record; to enroll; an officer who keeps such a record; the book containing a record.

Registered. Entered; recorded.

Registered Letter. A letter which is recorded and for which the sender receives a receipt.

Registered Trade-Mark. A trade-mark filed in U.S. patent office.

Registered Voter. One lawfully registered and who has the right to vote.

Register of Deeds. Officer who records instruments affecting realty.

Registry. Record book; recording of an instrument in the proper office.

Regnant. Regent.

Regress. A going back.

Regula. Rule.

Regulae Juris. Rules of law.

Regular. Conforming to law; steady; according to custom.

Regular Army. Standing army.

Regulate. To control or direct.

Regulation. Rule; precept.

Rehabilitate. To return to a former state.

Rehearing. Second consideration of a cause.

Reimburse. To refund; pay back.

Reinstate. To restore to a former state.

Reinstate A Case. To put a case in the same position as before dismissal.

Reinsurance. A contract by which an insurer insures himself with another insurer against loss in the original policy.

Reissuable Note. Bank notes, which after having been paid, may be put into circulation again.

Reject. To discard, throw away.

Rejoin. To answer a plaintiff's replication.

Rejoinder. The second pleading on the part of the defendant in answer to the plaintiff's replication.

Relate. To pertain to or refer to.

Related. Connected; akin.

Relation. Relative.

Relations by Affinity. Persons related through marriage.

Relations by Consanguinity. Persons related by blood.

Relative. Kinsman.

Relative Fact. One which has bearing on another fact.

Relative Impediment. Bar to marriage because of relationship.

Relative Powers. Powers which relate to land.

Relator. One who brings an action in which he is beneficially interested, but which under existing procedure can only be brought by some state official.

Relaxare. To free or discharge.

Relaxatio. A release.

Release. Relinquishment; liberation; to surrender a claim due at a specified time; the conveyance of the rights of one person to another who is actually in possession.

Releasee. One who is released or to whom a release is given.

Release of a Debt. Discharge of a debt by writing under seal.

Releasor. One who releases or executes a release.

Relegatio. Type of exile in which one retains his civil rights.

Relevancy. Applicability; connection between two facts.

Relevant. In relation to testimony, directly touching upon the issue.

Relict. Surviving spouse.

Relief. Assistance given to the indigent.

Religion. Body of beliefs encompassing man's relationship to the supernatural

Religious Freedom. The right to worship God according to the dictates of one's conscience as safeguarded in the First Amendment of the Constitution.

Relinquish. To abandon or give up.

Reliqua. Balance of an account.

Relocatio. Renewal of a lease without change in terms.

Remainder. An estate in expectancy, created by the act of the parties, which becomes an estate in possession upon the determination of a particular prior estate, created by the same instrument at the same time.

Remainderman. One entitled to the remainder of an estate after a particular estate out of it has expired.

Remand. To order or send back.

Remanet. A cause, the trial of which must await the next term of court.

Remedial. Able to be remedied or redressed.

Remedial Action. An action brought to obtain compensation or indemnity.

Remedy. Means by which a right is protected or enforced.

Remise. To remit or give up; to pass title of property.

Remission. Release of a debt; pardon; exoneration.

Remit. To send or transmit; to pardon.

Remittance. Money sent by one person to another.

Remittee. One to whom a remittance is sent.

Remitter. One who remits.

Remittere. To release.

Remittitur. Writ of reversal issued by an appellate court upon reversing the order or judgement appealed.

Remonstrance. Giving reasons against a proposal.

Remote. Afar; slight.

Remote Cause. In negligence, improbable cause.

Remote Damages. Result over and beyond which the negligent party has no control.

Removal of Cause. Change of venue; transfer of a cause from one court to another.

Remover. Trasfer of a suit or cause from one court to another.

Renant. Denying.

Rencounter. A sudden fight or dispute.

Render. To give up, yield.

Render an Account. To present an account.

Rendezvous. Meeting place.

Rendition of Judgment. Oral pronouncing of a judgment which determines the rights of the parties to an action.

Renegade. Deserter.

Renew. To remake, rebuild, re-establish.

Renewal. The act of renewing or reviving; an obligation on which time of payment is extended.

Renounce. To relinquish; disclaim; forsake; abandon.

Rent. Compensation paid for the use or occupation of property.

Rentage. Rent.

Rental. Amount paid periodically for the use of property.

Rental Agent. One who leases premises and collects rents thereon.

Rent Sec. Rent created by a deed without any clause for distress.

Rents of Assize. The certain and demanded rents of freeholders and copyholders of ancient manors.

Renunciation. A legal act by which a person abandons a right acquired without transferring it to another.

Repair. To mend; restore; renovate.

Reparable Injury. An injury which can be fully compensated.

Reparation. Compensation; redress.

Repatriation. Restoration of citizenship.

Repay. To return or restore money or goods.

Repeal. Recall or revoke; annulment of a law by a subsequent statute.

Repeaters. Habitual offenders or criminals.

Repetition. A demand or action for the recovery of payment made under mistake on a condition which had not been performed.

Repleader. Permission by the court to plead over again.

Repleviable. Subject to an action of replevin.

Replevin. A personal action whereby the owner recovers possession of his own goods.

Replevisor. Plaintiff in an action of replevin.

Replevy. To secure the possession of personal property by means of replevin.

Repliant. Plaintiff who pleads a replication in answer to a defendant's plea.

Replication. Reply; answer; rejoinder; a reply made by the plaintiff in an action to the defendant's plea, or a suit in chancery to the defendant's answer.

Reply. Answer of the plaintiff to the defendant' replication.

Report. Official statement of facts.

Represent. To stand in someone's place; to substitute.

Representative. One who stands in place of another.

Representative Form of Government. Government conducted by delegates elected by the people.

Reprieve. Temporary suspension of a death sentence.

Reproach. Censure; rebuke.

Republic. Commonwealth; the state.

Repudiation. Rejection; disclaimer; denial of responsibility.

Repudium. Breach of marriage contract.

Repugnancy. Inconsistency between two or more clauses in the same deed, contract or statute or in the same count or plea.

Reputable. Worthy; honorable.

Reputable Citizen. One of good character.

Repute. Esteem with which a man is held by his neighbors.

Reputed. Accepted by public opinion.

Request. Petition; asking for that which is desired.

Require. Need; command; demand; to ask by right and authority.

Requisition. Demand in writing.

Res. Thing; object; subject matter of a suit; property; transaction.

Res Accessoria. An accessory thing.

Res Aliena. The property of another.

Res Caduca. An escheat.

Recind. To terminate a contract as to future transactions; to annul a contract from the beginning.

Rescissio. Repeal; abrogation.

Rescession. Termination or annulment of a contract.

Res Communes. Common property.

Res Corpales. Corporeal property.

Rescript. Duplicate; copy; written court order to the clerk, giving directions concerning the further disposition of a case.

Rescue. Unlawfully and knowingly aiding another to escape from prison without any effort of the prisoner to free himself; unlawful setting free of a distrained animal.

Rescyt. Haboring of a felon.

Res Derelicta. Abandoned property.

Reservation. A clause in a deed or other instrument of conveyance whereby something is created or reserved out of the thing granted which was not in existence before.

Reserve. In insurance, the amount of money which insurance companies are legally required to have to mature or liquidate claims made upon them.

Reserve Fund. See Reserve.

Reset. Harboring of an outlaw.

Res Fungibles. Property consumable by use and returnable in kind.

Res Furtivae. Stolen things.

Res Gestae; Res Gesta. Things done; thing done; circumstances incidental to an act ligitated.

Resiant. Residing.

Reside. Live, dwell.

Residence. Place of abode; dwelling place.

Resident. One who lives in a place.

Resident Freeholder. One who lives in a particular place, and who owns property amounting to a freehold interest.

Residual. Pertaining to the remaining part.

Residuary. That which remains of an estate after the legacies have been paid.

Residuary Clause. Clause in a will providing for the disposition of property remaining after the legacies have been paid.

Residuary Device. The person to whom all the land is given which is not specifically disposed of in a will.

Residuary Estate. Property of a testator not disposed of by the will and which may not be legally disposed of.

Residue. Surplus.

Residum. Residue; balance.

Resignation. Formal renouncement of office.

Resignee. One in favor of whom a resignation is tendered.

Res Immobiles. Immovable corporeal things.

Res in Re. In rape, reference to the entering of the male organ into that of the female.

Resist. Oppose.

Resisting an Officer. Obstructing, opposing or endeavoring to prevent an officer from legally discharging his duty.

Res Mobiles. Corporeal movable things.

Res Nova. A new matter; something without precedent.

Res Nullius. Property of no one.

Resolution. A formal decision; determination or expression of an opinion by an official body or any assembly or meeting.

Resolutory. Determinative.

Resolutory Condition. A condition subsequent; one which, when accomplished, revokes an obligation valid until its happening.

Reson. Right; justice; reason.

Resort. To go back; to frequent; a place of frequent assembly.

Resources. Assets; means; income.

Respectable. Decent; proper.

Res Perit Domino. The thing is lost for the owner.

Respite. Temporary suspension or reprieve; delay.

Respond. Answer; to be liable or answerable.

Respondeat Ouster. A judgment against a defendant upon an issue of law raised by his dilatory plea.

Respondent. Defendant; appellee.

Responsibility. Obligation; duty; liability.

Responsible. Liable; answerable.

Responsio. Answer; reply of a witness.

Res Private. Private property.

Res Publica. Public property.

Res Quotidianae. Common, everyday matters.

Rest. Repose; to announce that no more testimony will be presented because the plaintiff or defendant considers his case completed.

Restitution. Act of restoring; to return a thing to its rightful owner; remedy for breach of contract whereby the aggrieved party occupies as good a position as he occupied before the contract.

Restitutor. Restorer.

Restore. To bring back or return.

Restrain. Prohibit; limit; confine or abridge a thing.

Restraining Order. Order similar to an injuction; court order to prevent the doing of some act.

Restraint of Marriage. A condition in a gift or will which prohibits the free choice of husband or wife of the donee or grantee.

Rest, Residue and Remainder. Phrase used in will to device and bequeath all of the property of the testator not specifically bequeathed.

Restrictive Covenant. A covenant in a lease or deed limiting the way in which the land may be used.

Restrictive Indorsement. Indorsement restricting the use of a negotiable instrument, e.g. "for deposit."

Resulting Trust. Trust which arises by implication of law or through equity, and which is established as consonant to the presumed intentions of the parties as inferred from the nature of the transaction.

Res Universitatis. Things in common.

Retail. To sell in small quantities, directly to the consumer.

Retain. To keep possession; to engage the services of an attorney.

Retainer. Fee which a client pays an attorney.

Retaining Fee. See Retainer.

Retaliation. Reprisal.

Retorna Brevum. Return of Writs with an indorsement of an officer as to what he has done in execution of the writ.

Retorsion, Retortion. Retaliation; in international law, the treatment by one State of citizens of another State in a similar way as that State treats the first State's citizens.

Retraction. Withdrawal of a renunciation.

Retraxit. He has withdrawn; the formal withdrawal of a suit by a plaintiff.

Retreat to the Wall. In self-defense, to avail oneself of all means of escape.

Retroactive. Retrospective; acting on things past.

Rette. Accusation.

Return. To bring back; an official statement by an officer in respect to a writ which he has executed; filing of a tax form or other form required by authority.

Return-Day. The day on which a writ or process must be returned.

Returns. Number of ballots cast in an election.

Reus. Defendant; one accused of a crime; party to a suit.

Reus Stipulandi. Promise.

Revendication. To reclaim or to demand the restoration of.

Revenge. To inflict malicious injury in return for harm done.

Revenue. Return; yield; income.

Revenue Law. Law authorizing taxation.

Reversal. Annulment; making void of a judgment.

Reve Se. To set aside; make void; annul.

Reversion. This residue of an estate which the grantor has not disposed of in a grant, which commences in possession after the determination of some particular estate.

Reversionary. Relating or pertaining to a reversion.

Reversionary Lease. Lease the term of which begins at a future time.

Reversioner. One entitled to a reversion.

Revert. To turn back; to return to.

Reverter. Reversion.

Revest. To come into possession again; to restore an interest in property to one who has been divested of that property.

Review. Judicial re-examination. reconsideration, revision; the power, by a bill in equity, to correct errors in a court record.

Revise. To review for correction.

Revival. Agreement to maintain as valid a rescinded contract; restoration of power to levy execution on a judgment, which while still valid, has been dormant for a specified time.

Revivor. Bill in equity to reestablish and continue proceedings which have been abated.

Revocation. Withdrawal; recall; annulment; repudiation.

Revocation of a Will. Annulment of a will by some subsequent act of the testator.

Revoke. To annul or make void by calling back.

Revolution. The overthrow of an established government.

Reward. Recompense for some service or attainment.

Rex. King.

Ribaldu. A vagrant.

Ribaud. Rogue; vagrant.

Rider. An additional clause or provision annexed to a bill while in the course of passage in order to "slip" it through.

Rien. Nothing.

Rien Culp. Not guilty.

Right. Legally enforceable claim; privilege; power of appointment or choice.

Rightful. Lawful; proper.

Right in Personam. Right against the person.

Right of Conscience. Religious freedom.

Right of Dower. Legal interest which a wife acquires by marriage in the property of her husband.

Right of Eminent Domain. Right of a community to possess itself of the property of an individual when necessary for public welfare.

Right of Entry. Right to take possession of certain land in a peaceful manner.

Right of Possession. Right to occupy and enjoy property.

Right of Privacy. Right to be let alone.

Right of Redemption. Right to redeem real property from judicial sale.

Right of Sufferage. Right of qualified citizen to vote.

Right of Way. Right to pass over the land of another.

Rights in Action. See Chose in Action.

Right to Counsel. Right of one accused of a crime to have legal assistance.

Rigor Juris. Strict Law.

Rigor Mortis. Cadaveric rigidity.

Ring Fight. Prize fight.

Riot. Tumultuous public disturbance committed by 3 or more persons.

Riotous. Violent.

Riparian. Of or belonging to the bank of a river.

Riper. Mature; ready.

Risicum. Insurance risk.

Rising Of Court. Final adjournment of court for the term.

Rite. Duly and formally; legally.

Rixa. Quarrel.

Road. Highway; place of public passage.

Road Tax. Tax for the maintenance of public roads.

Robbery. Felonious taking of something of value from the person of another by forcible means.

Rod. 16½ feet.

Rogo. I ask, expression used in wills.

Rogue. Cheat; rascal.

Rogues' Gallery. A collection of photographs of criminals kept for purposes of identification.

Roll. Record.

Roll. To rob.

Rondo. Game of chance.

Rood. ¼ acre.

Root. Stock of descent.

Roster. List of persons; register.

Rota. A court.

Rough Minutes. Unofficial memoranda made by the court clerk.

Roup. Auction sale.

Rout. Group of persons assembled with the intention to incite riot.

Royalty. Money paid to the holder of a patent or copyright for the right to manufacture, sell or use the patented or copyrighted article.

Rudely. Uncivilly; violently.

Rule. Regulation; principle set up by authority.

Rule Absolute. Court order to be immediately enforced without conditions.

Rule Nisi. A rule which shall become imperative or final unless cause be shown why it should not.

Rules. Times or seasons when motions are entertained by the court.

Rule To Show Cause. Rule summoning an adverse party to appear before court and show cause why a certain thing shall not be done.

Ruling. A settlement of a point of law arising during the course of a trial.

Rumor. Popular report; current story.

Running Account. Current or open account.

Running at Large. Applied to domestic animals wandering without restraint.

Running Policy. In insurance, a policy which anticipates that the property insured shall be added to or further defined by later additions to the policy.

Rusticum Jus. Simple justice.

Rustler. Cattle thief.

S

Sabbath. Sunday.

Sabotage. Intentional damage to the property of an employer by an employee.

Sacrilege. Stealing of things from a churco.

Sadism. Type of sexual perversion in which the man enjoys inflecting pain on the woman he desires.

Safe. Receptacle for valuables.

Safe Deposit Company. Company which rents boxes in vaults for the safe-keeping of valuables.

Safe-Pledge. Surety for a person's appearance in court.

Said. Aforesaid; mentioned before.

Salarium. Salary; wages.

Salary. Recompense for services rendered.

Sale. Transfer of property from one man to another for recompense.

Sale at Auction. Public sale of property to the highest bidder.

Sale for Payment. Judicial sale of the property of a decedent to pay his debts.

Sale in Gross. Sale by the tract without regard to quantity.

Sale Notes. Memorandum with respect to the sale of merchandise usually given to the buyer by the broker.

Sale on Approval. Conditional sale which becomes effective only in case the buyer, on trial, is satisfied with the merchandise.

Sale on Execution. Public sale conducted by a writ of execution.

Sale or Return. Sale, usually by manufacturer to a retailer, with the understanding that he may consider some or all of the goods as a consignment and return them within a certain period of time.

Sales Guaranteed. If goods purchased by the buyer cannot be sold, they may be returned to the seller.

Sales Tax. Tax upon retail merchandise, usually paid by the buyer.

Saloon. Place where alcoholic beverages are sold.

Salus. Health; safety.

Salvage. Compensation paid to persons by whose voluntary services a ship or her cargo are saved, in whole or in part in time of peril.

Salvo. Saving; excepting.

Salvor. One who conducts a salvage operation.

Salvus Plegius. A safe-pledge.

Same. Identical; of a kind or species.

Same Offense. Constitutional provision that no person shall be twice put in jeopardy for the same crime.

Sample. A part used to show the quality of the whole.

Sanae Mentis. Of sound mind.

Sanction. To consent, concur, ratify; penalty or punishment for disobedience to the law.

Sane. Of sound mind.

Sanguis. Blood-relationship; blood.

Sanipractice. Method of drugless healing.

Sanitarium. Health retreat.

Sanitary. That which pertains to health and cleanliness.

Sanity. Mental soundness.

Sans. Without.

Sans Ceo Que. Without this.

Sans Frais. With expense.

Sans Recours. Without recourse.

Sanus. Sane; whole; sound.

Satisdare. To guaranty the obligation.

Satisdatio. Security given by a party to an action.

Satisfaction. Fulfilling of a legal obligation

Satisfaction Contract. Contract whereby one party agrees to perform his obligation to the satisfaction of the other.

Satisfaction of the Jury. To prove to the jury that a thing existed.

Satisfaction Piece. A written instrument stating that satisfaction is acknowledged between the parties, plaintiff and defendant.

Satisfactory. To meet with one's approval or expectation.

Satisfactory Evidence. Evidence or proof which ordinarily satisfies an unprejudiced mind.

Satisfy. To answer or discharge a claim or obligation; to convince a jury.

Save. To except, reserve or exempt; to suspend the running or operation of.

Saving Clause. In a statute, an exception of a special thing out of general things mentioned in the statute.

Savings Bank. An institution for the deposit and safekeeping of money.

Savings Bank Check. A receipt for the money withdrawn from a savings account.

S.C. (Abb.). Same Case.

Scab. Working man who works contrary to union rules.

Scale. To cut down; to proportion.

Scale Tolerance. Nominal weight variation between different scales in weighing the same goods.

Scaling Laws. Laws which formerly regulated the relation between depreciated currency and specie.

Scalped Ticket. Ticket purchased from a ticket broker.

Scandal. Defamatory rumors; scandalous talk.

Scandalous Matter. Allegations of fact in a pleading which are immaterial and impertinent and unbecoming the court's dignity.

Schedule. List; inventory.

Schedule in Bankruptcy. An inventory filed by the bankrupt listing all his property and credits.

Scheme. Plan; plot.

School. Educational institution.

School Taxes. Taxes levied for the support and maintenance of the public schools.

School Trustees. School directors.

Sciagraph. X-ray, admissible as evidence.

Sciant Praesentes et Futuri. Know all men present and in future.

Scienter. Knowingly; in torts, an allegation that the defendant knew a fact which was essential to create liability.

Scit. (Abb.) Scilicet.

Scilicet. To wit.

Scintilla of Evidence. Spark of evidence; any material evidence, which if true, might create interest in a reasonable juror.

Scintilla Rule. Rule that if there is any evidence supporting a claim it must be submitted to jury.

Scire Facia. A judicial writ, founded upon some matter of record, requiring the person against whom it is brought to show cause why the plaintiff should not have advantage of such a record, or why the record should not be annulled.

Scire Facias ad Audiendum Errores. To hear the errors.

Scire Facias ad Disporbandum. To disprove the debts.

Scire Facias Quare Restitutionem Habere Non Debet. Make it known why he ought not to have restitution.

Scire Feci. I have made known or notified.

Scite. Site; location.

Scold. Troublesome woman.

Scolding. Personal reproof.

Scope. Design; aim; intention.

Scope of Authority. Actual and implied authorization conferred upon an agent by his principal.

Scoundral. Villian; rascal.

Scrambling Possession. Situation where two or more persons are struggling for the possession of land.

Scrawl. Scroll.

Screwball. Eccentric person.

Scribere Est Agers. Writing is the doing of an act..

Script Certificates of ownership.

Script. An original written instrument.

Scriptum. A written instrument.

Scrivener. Draftsman; copyist; clerk; conveyancer.

Scroll. A writing designed to be rolled up; a scrawl intended as a seal; an escrow.

Se. Himself; themselves; itself.

Seal. Wax impression giving authenticity to a document; a written or printed circle or scroll with the initials "l.s." (locus sigilli, place of seal).

Sealed. Under seal.

Sealed Instrument. An instrument to which the party to be bound has affixed both his name and seal.

Sealed Verdict. The verdict of the jury placed in a sealed envelope.

Seaman. Sailor.

Search. Examination by an officer of the law.

Searchers and Seizures. The power possessed by public authority to inspect private premises for the purpose of arresting a man or obtaining evidence of his guilt of a crime.

Search of Title. Examination of public records to ascertain a person's title to real estate.

Search Warrent. A written order issued by legal authority for the examination or inspection of one's premises or person in the search for stolen goods or evidence to be used in prosecution of a criminal.

Seasonable Appearance. A defendant's appearance within the time allowed by law, after receiving a summons.

Seated Land. Land used for residence or farming; productive land.

Seat of Justice. A county seat.

Seat On Exchange. Membership in a stock exchange.

Seaworthy. Applied to a ship reasonably fit to transport cargo.

Sebastomania. Religious mania.

Secession of State. An attempt of a state to withdraw from the Union.

Seck. Without the right or remedy of distraining.

Secondary. Of a subsequent or subordinate class.

Secondary Boycott. A boycott directed against relations with those against whom there is a primary boycott.

Secondary Conveyance. One which alters or modifies an interest already granted by a conveyance.

Secondary Easement. Evidence which is admissible after proof is offered of the excused absence of primary evidence.

Second Degree Murder. Statutory degree of murder usually punishable by life imprisonment.

Second-Hand Evidence. Hearsay.

Second Mortgage. Mortgage on previously mortgaged property.

Secret. Hidden; not public.

Secretary. Corporate officer in charge of records; correspondence, etc.; one who acts as the agent of a person in matters of communication; title given to several Cabinet officers of U.S. government.

Secretary of State. Member of Cabinet of U.S. government charged with the general administration of the international and diplomatic affairs of the government.

Secret Service. Agency of the Department of Treasury charged with the protection of the president and his family, and the suppression of counterfeiting.

Sect. Religious denomination.

Sectarian. Pertaining to a religious sect.

Sectarian School. Denominational school.

Section. Division; part; portion; division of land consisting of 640 acres and equal to one square mile.

Secular. Temporal; worldly.

Secundum. According to; in favor of.

Secundum Aequum et Bonum. According to justice and right.

Secundum Allegata. According to the allegations contained in the pleadings.

Secundum Allegata et Probata. According to what has been alleged and proved.

Secundum Formam Statuti. According to the form of the statutes.

Secundum Naturam. According to nature.

Secundum Regulam. According to rule.

Secure. To give security; to guaranty; safe; free from danger.

Securities. Negotiable instruments; evidences of debt or of property.

Security. Protection; assurance; indemnification; a negotiable instrument; one who becomes a guarantor for another.

Security for Costs. A bond required of a party to an action to ensure the fact that the costs of the action will be paid if he loses.

Securus. Safe; secure; sure.

Secus. Otherwise; not so.

Sed. But; however.

Sedato Animo. With settled intent.

Sed Contra. But otherwise.

Se Defendendo. In self-defense.

Sedente Curia. During a session of the court.

Sedition. Insurrection; acts which disturb the peace and imperil the government.

Se Non Allocatur. But it is not allowed.

Sed per Curiam. But by the court.

Seduce. To corrupt.

Seduction. To persuade a chaste woman to have illicit sexual intercourse.

Sed Vide. But see.

See. The area of a bishop's jurisdiction.

Seen. Used to denote acceptance of a bill of exchange.

Segration Laws. Laws authorizing separate accommodations for people of different races.

Seigneur. Lord.

Seised. State of ownership coupled with right of possession.

Seised in His Demesne as of Fee. Seised in fee simple.

Seized. See Seised.

Seizin. Possession of premises after full investiture, coupled with a claim to the right of exclusive possession.

Seizin in Fact. Seizin in deed; actual seizin; possession with intent to claim a freehold interest.

Seizin in Fee. Person's actual possession of land, with a fee-simple estate therein.

Seizin in Law. Right of immediate possession according to the nature of the estate.

Seizure. Taking possession of goods by public authority.

Select. To pick out.

Selectmen. Officers constituting a local council.

Self-Defense. Protection of one's person or property from injury by another; the right to such protection.

Self-Destruction. Suicide.

Self-Disserving Evidence. Evidence unfavorable to the person offering it.

Self-Executing Constitutional Provision. Effective immediately without additional legislation.

Self-Incrimination. Subjecting of one's self to criminal prosecution by the disclosure of certain facts during the course of a trial.

Self-Serving Evidence. Evidence favorable to the party offering it.

Sell. To dispose of for profit.

Seller. One who sells anything.

Seller's Option. Transaction wherein stock is sold to be delivered at a future time.

Semble. It seems; a dictum holds.

Semblement. Similarly.

Semi-Matrimonium. Concubinage.

Seminary. Ministerial school.

Semi-Plena Probatio. Half proof.

Semper. Always; at all times.

Semper Paratus. Always ready.

Senate. Upper house of Congress.

Senator. Member of the senate.

Senatus Consultum Ultimae Necessitatis. The act of the senate in an emergency.

Senile Dementia. Imbecility due to old age.

Senility. Mental state of an aged person.

Senior. Higher in rank; older.

Senior Mortgage. One which has priority over another incumbrance.

Sentence. Judgment passed by the court on a convicted criminal.

Sentence of Nullity. Legal annulment of a marriage.

Sententia. An opinion; decision; judgment.

Separable. Severable.

Separaliter. Separately.

Separate. Disconnected; independent; distinct.

Separate Action. An action brought by each of several complainants for himself although all are concerned in the same transaction, but cannot legally join in suit.

Separate Estate. Individual property of one of two persons who have a social or business relationship; the property of a married woman over which her husband has no right in equity.

Separate Examination. Questioning of a married woman by a notary, apart from her husband, to determine if she acts on her own will.

Separate Maintenance. Support granted to a wife and her children by the husband upon their voluntary separation; alimony.

Separate Property. Property owned by a husband or wife in his or her own right during marriage.

Separatin. Separately.

Separatim. Cessation of cohabitation by man and wife by mutual consent.

Sepulchre. Grave; tomb.

Sequela. Suit; prosecution.

Sequela Curiae. Suit of court.

Sequester. To renounce or disclaim; to seize property under a writ of sequestration.

Sequestration. The setting apart of something in controversy to await final disposition; a form of seizure of property to be held as a means of enforcing a decree from the payment of money.

Sergeant-at-Arms. An officer of a legislative body charged with keeping order.

Serial Bonds. Bonds issued in a series, different parts being redeemable at different specified dates.

Seriatim. Successively.

Serious. Important; weighty.

Serious and Wilful Misconduct. Intentionally doing something likely to have serious consequences.

Servant. One who gives domestic help.

Servato Juris Ordine. In keeping with the order of the court.

Serve. To deliver legal papers.

Service. Employment; performance of labor; the delivery of an order, a summons or a writ; the furnishing of public utilities.

Service by Publication. Publication of a summons or other process in the newspaper in order to reach an absent or nonresident defendant.

Service of Process. The delivering of writs, summonses, rules, etc. to the party to whom

Serviens ad Legem. A sergeant-at-law.

Servient Tenement. An estate in land burdened with an easement for the benefit of some other estate or tenement.

Servitium. Service.

Servitude. An easement; a right or interest which one proprietor has in the estate of another proprietor.

Servitus. Slavery; servitude.

Servitus Luminum. Easement of having unobstructed light come into one's premises.

Servitus Viae. Right of way over the land of a neighbor.

Servus. Slave; servant.

Sess. Assessment; tax.

Sessio. Session; meeting.

Session. Period of time during which a legislative body transacts business.

Session Laws. All of the enactments passed by a legislative body at a single session.

Sessions. A meeting of the justices.

Set. Lease.

Set Aside. Annulled; made void; cancelled.

Set of Exchange. A set of bills of exchange in duplicate or triplicate, the honoring of any one of them voiding the others.

Set-Off. The discharge of one demand by an opposite one; a counter-demand.

Set Out. In pleading, to state the facts; to allege; to set out a deed or contract.

Settle. To come to an agreement in a legal dispute; to pay; to compromise.

Settlement. An arrangement by which property is to be held by several persons in succession; establishment of a permanent residence in a place, entitling the settlor to the privileges of such residence; a compromise by the parties in a litigation to settle the dispute.

Settlement, Deed of. Deed settling a controversy or property.

Settling Day. Day in the month when transactions on the stock exchange are accounted for and settled.

Settlement in Paris. Settlement out of court.

Settlor. Grantor or donor in a deed of settlement; a person who creates a trust.

Sever. To separate; to divide; to disjoin; to separate one cause of action from another and plead them separately; to try persons separately who were jointly indicted.

Severable Contract. Contract in which consideration may be apportioned or divided.

Several Actions. Actions which are separate.

Several Inheritance. An inheritance in which the heirs take severally in equally parts.

Severally. Separately.

Several Ownership. Ownership by one person.

Severalty. An estate held by one person alone.

Severance. Act of separating; partition; separation.

Severance of Actions. Entering of separate pleas by several defendants, instead of joining in the same plea.

Severe Illness. An illness having a permanent, detrimental effect.

Sexual Commerce. Sexual intercourse.

Sexual Intercourse. Copulation.

Shackles. Chains used to bind a prisoner.

Shakedown. Extortion.

Sham. False; counterfeit.

Sham Pleading. A pleading which is false.

Share. To have a portion of; a part or portion; a stock certificate.

Share and Share Alike. To take in equal shares or portions.

Shareholder. Stockholder.

Share of Stock. The right which a stockholder has in the management, profits and assets of a corporation.

Share Tenant. Tenant who leases land with the provision that crops produced be shared with his landlord.

Shave. To lend money on usury; to extort; the buying of notes and securities at a discount.

Sheriff. The chief executive officer of a county, elected by the people.

Sheriff's Sale. Sale by a sheriff under a writ of execution of property of the judgment debtor.

Shifting. Changing; varying.

Shifting Use. A use limited to take effect and arise in derogation of another use.

Ship. To place on board a ship; to transport; any vessel used in navigation.

Shipmaster. Commander of a merchant vessel.

Shipment. Transport of goods on a ship or other carrier; delivery of goods to a carrier and his issuance of a bill of lading therefore; the property transported.

Shipper. One who makes a contract with a carrier for the transportation of goods.

Shipping. General term of the use of ships or vessels for any public or private purposes; collective term for ships.

Ship's Bill. Ship's bill of lading, kept by the master.

Ship's Husband. General agent of the owner of a ship who manages the concerns of the ship.

Ship's Papers. Papers which every ship must carry, showing the nationality of her registry and cargo and compliance with the navigational laws of her country.

Shire. County.

Shock. Sudden physical or mental agitation.

Shoot. To injure someone with a bullet; to kill.

Shop. Place where merchandise is retailed.

Shopbook Rule. Introduction of a party's account books of original entry as evidence in his favor, this being an exception to the hearsay rule.

Shop-Right. Right of an employer to the invention of an employee without payment of royalties.

Shore. Land lying between the lines of high water and low water, over which the tides ebb and flow; beach; shore line.

Shore of Watercourse. The spaces between high and low water marks.

Short Cause. A suit the trial of which is estimated to be brief.

Short Haul. Transportation of merchandise for a short distance.

Short Sale. Sale of stock before purchase in hope to acquire at a lower price than that of the delivery price; sales upon margin.

Show. To prove; to make clear.

Show Cause. Court order to a party in a law suit to show good reason why a certain action should not be taken.

Shut Down. To stop work.

Shyster. A dishonest and unethical attorney; a pettifogger.

Si. If; although; as if.

Sic. So; such; in this manner.

Sic Hic. So here.

Sic. Jubeo. I so order.

Sick. Ill.

Sickness. Illness.

Si Contingat. If it happens.

Sicut Alias. As on another occasion.

Sicut Me Deus Adjuvet. So help me God.

Sic Volo. I so will it.

Side Judge. An associate judge.

Sidewalk. Part of the street reserved for pedestrians.

Siens. Scions; descendants.

Sight. In regard to negotiable instruments, presentment.

Sight Draft. A bill of exchange payable on presentment.

Sigillare. To affix a seal.

Sigillum. A seal.

Sigla. Abbreviations.

Sign. To place one's signature on; to ratify by hand or seal.

Signa. Evidence addressed to the senses.

Signare. To sign or seal.

Signature. The affixing of one's name at the end of an instrument intended to authenticate the instrument; the name itself.

Signed, Sealed and Delivered. Executed.

Signum. Sign; signature; mark.

Si Ita Est. If it be so.

Silent Partner. Dormant partner.

Silver. Base metal used in coins.

Similar. Resembling; nearly corresponding.

Similiter. Likewise; a short formula in pleading expressive of the acceptance of an issue tendered by the adversary.

Simony. The buying or selling of religious favor.

Simple. Pure; unadulterated; not aggravated.

Simple Assault. Futile attempt to do bodily injury to another.

Simple Confession. Plea of guilty.

Simple Contract. Oral contract; one which is not sealed.

Simple Interest. Interest paid for the principal, at a certain rate or allowance, made by law or mutual agreement.

Simple Trust. A conveyance of property in trust without further specifications or directions.

Simplex. Simple.

Simplex Dictum. Mere allegation.

Simplex Justitiarius. Simple justice.

Simplex Loquela. A mere allegation.

Simpliciter. Simply.

Simulated. Counterfeited; pretended.

Simul cum. Together with.

Simul et Simul. Together and at the same time.

Simultaneously. At the same time.

Sine. Without.

Sine Animo Revertendi. Without intention of returning.

Sine Consideratione Curiae. Without having been considered by the court.

Sine Cura. Without care.

Sinecure. An office which yields a revenue, but imposing little responsibility.

Sine Decreto. Without a decree.

Sine Die. Without day; final adjournment; final dismissal of a cause.

Sine Hoc Quod. Without this, that.

Sine Liberis. Without children.

Sine Prole. Without issue.

Sine Qua Non. Without which not; an indispensable requisite or condition.

Sine Vi aut Dolo. Without force or fraud.

Single. One; alone; detached; unmarried.

Single Adultery. Adultry between two persons, only one of whom is married.

Single Bill. Written promise to pay a certain person a certain amount on a certain date.

Single Bond. Single Bill.

Singulariter. Singly.

Sinking Fund. A fund put aside for the extinguishment of a debt, expecially of a government or corporation, by the accumulation of interest.

Si Prius. If before.

Si Quis. If anyone.

Sit. To preside.

Sit Down Strike. Strike in which the employees occupy the property of the employer until agreement is reached.

Site. Land suitable or set apart for special use.

Sit in Bank. To hold a session of court with all judges present.

Sit in Camera. To hold a session of court in chambers or privately.

Sitting In Bank. Session of the court with all judges present.

Sitting of Court. Term of court.

Situated. Located.

Situs. Location; location of a concrete object, particularly land.

Skeleton Bill. Bill drawn, indorsed or accepted in blank.

Skill. Slip; failure of automobile tires to grip the road.

Skilled Witness. Expert witness.

Slacker. One derlict in his duty or responsibility; one who shirks military duty.

Slander. False statements made orally which bring another into disrepute.

Slander of Title. A false and malicious statement made in regard to a person's title to property.

Slave. One subject to the will of another.

Slavery. State of bondage.

Slay. To kill.

Sleep. To delay action in securing one's right.

Sleeping Partner. Dormant partner.

Sleeping Rent. Fixed rent.

LEGAL DICT

Slight. Inconsiderable; unimportant; remote.

Slot Machine. An automated gambling machine into which one deposits coins, hoping to win a prize or money.

Slum. Dirty, impoverished area.

Slush Fund. Money used for corrupt purposes, e.g. lobbying.

Slut. Careless, sloppy woman; female dog; a bitch.

Small Claims Courts. Courts with jurisdiction over very small amounts.

Smart Money. Punitive damages in addition to actual damages.

Smuggling. Unlawful bringing in of goods into the U.S., such importation being prohibited without payment of duty.

Snap Judgement. Judgement by default.

So. In this way.

Sober. Moderate in use of alcoholic beverages.

Socer. A father-in-law.

Social Security Acts. Acts designed for the economic security of the individual.

Societas. Partnership.

Societe Anonyme. Stock corporation; an association in which the liability of the members is limited.

Society. An association of people united in a common purpose; the capacity of usefulness, aid and comfort which a wife possesses in regard to her husband in her normal state.

Sodomy. Sexual relations between two men.

Soit. Let it be.

Soit Droit Fait al Partie. Let right be done to the party.

Solar Day. Period from sunrise to sunset.

Solar Month. Calendar month.

Solatium. Compensation for injury to feelings.

Sold Note. Note given by a broker to a buyer indicating the sale of certain goods.

Sole. Single; only; separate.

Sole and Unconditional Ownership. In insurance, the insured is the only one having any interest in the property as owner, that property not being limited to or affected by any condition.

Sole Corporation. A corporation consisting of a single person in which there is a succession of interest.

Solemnitas. Solemnity.

Solemn. Following certain set forms.

Solemnity. Rite or ceremony.

Solicit. To ask for something; to entreat or implore.

Solicitation. Asking; enticing; inciting another to commit a crime, particularly one which affects society.

Solicitation of Chastity. To entice a woman to give up her chastity.

Solicitor. In E. a lawyer licensed as a legal representative; in U.S., a lawyer in the Court of Bankruptcy.

Solidum. The whole.

Solitary Confinement. Complete isolation of a prisoner from human contacts.

Solum. Soil; ground.

Solutio. Payment of a debt.

Solutio Indebite. Payment of a debt which does not exist.

Solutus. Free; released from debt or mortgage.

Solvency. Ability to pay one's debts.

Solvendum in Futuro. To be paid in the future.

Solvent. Able to pay one's debts.

Solvere. To pay; to release.

Solviet ad Diem. He paid at the day; plea made that the money was paid on the day mentioned in the condition.

Somnambulism. Sleep-walking.

Son. An immediate male descendant.

Son Assault Demesne. His own assault; a plea of self-defense.

Son-in-Law. The husband of one's daugher.

Sonticus. That which delays; injurious; hindering.

Soon. Within a reasonable time.

Sortitio. Drawing of lots.

Sound Health. Good health.

Sounding in Damages. Applied to an action seeking satisfaction only in money damages.

Sound Mind. Sane.

Sound Physical Condition. Good health.

Souvent. Often.

Sovereign. Ruler; supreme power in government.

Sovereign. Right reserved to the state or its agencies.

S.P. (Abb.). Sine Prole.

Spado. Impotent person.

Sparsim. Sparsely; rarely.

Spay. To remove the ovaries of a female animal to prevent propagation.

Speak. In practice, to argue.

Speaking Demurrer. A demurrer which alleges and relies on new matter as well as the ground of the demurrer.

Special. Pertaining to a particular thing or person.

Special Acceptance. Qualified acceptance of a bill of exchange.

Special Act. Private statute.

Special Action. Statutory action.

Special Agent. An agent authorized to act in a specific transaction but not employed in continuous service.

Special Assessment. A tax on property to finance public improvements.

Special Assumpsit. An action brought on an express promise.

Special Bastard. One born before marriage of his parents.

Special Count. A statement of the facts of a particular cause of action.

Special Damages. Damages which are the actual, but not the necessary result of the injury complained of.

Special Demurrer. One which states the exact ground on which the complaint or pleading is alleged to be inadequate.

Special Deposit. Deposit of something to be returned in kind.

Special Finding. Answer of a jury to a particular question of fact submitted to them.

Special Imparlance. An imparlance reserving exceptions and objections.

Special Indorsement. Indorsement of a negotiable instrument naming the payee to whom or to whose order the instrument is to be paid.

Special Issue. A plea denying a particular material and traversable allegation of the preceding pleading.

Specialist. One skilled in a particular field.

Special Legislation. Legislation which applies to particular persons and things.

Special Letter of Credit. One addressed to a particular person.

Special Lien. Lien upon particular property.

Special Matter. Matter of a certain nature which upon notice may be raised at a hearing after a plea of the general issue.

Special Partner. Limited partner.

Special Pleading. A pleading which avoids an allegation without expressly denying it.

Special Property. Property in which a person's interest is less than that of ownership, existing only to carry out a specific legal right or interest.

Special Sessions, Court of. Court of limited jurisdiction in criminal cases.

Special Statute. One applying to particular persons and things.

Special Tail. An estate tail which is limited to the issue of named persons.

Special Tax. A tax levied for a particular public person.

Special Trust. An operative trust in which the trustee performs certain specified acts.

Specialty. An instrument or document under seal.

Special Verdict. Verdict whereby a jury finds facts only, submitting the decision of the case to the court.

Specie. Gold or silver coins.

Species. Kind; class.

Specifically. Explicitly.

Specification. In Patent Law, a particular or detailed statement of the various elements involved; detailed statement of the acts constituting a military offense charged against the defendant in a court martial.

Specific Denial. A denial of each material allegation of the declaration or complaint.

Specific Legacy. A legacy consisting of a definitely described article or thing which is not a sum of money.

Specific Performance. Accomplishment of a contract according to the precise terms agreed upon.

Speculate. To risk loss in view of possible gain.

Speculative Damages. Damages awarded in excess of the actual loss suffered by the plaintiff.

Speedy Trial. The constitutional guaranty that a trial be conducted according to fixed rules, regulations and proceedings of law, free from unreasonable delay.

Spendthrift. One who spends money foolishly; prodigal.

Spendthrift Trust. A trust created to provide for the maintenance of the beneficiary at the same time guarding against his improvidence or incapacity.

Spermatozoa. Seminal fluid.

Spes. Hope.

Spex Accrescendi. The hope of surviving.

Spes Recuperandi. Hope of recovering.

Spinster. A woman who has never married.

Spiritual. Relating to the religious or ecclesiastical.

Speritual Courts. Ecclesiastical courts.

Spirituous Liquor. Liquor produced by distillation.

Spite Fence. Fence erected solely to annoy an adjoining neighbor.

Spoliation. A material change or alteration in a written document by a stranger, this not changing the legality of such a document.

Spondeo. I promise.

Sponsalia. Mutal promises to marry.

Sponsor. A surety; one who voluntarily intervenes for another.

Sporting Woman. Prostitute.

Spot Cash. Cash on delivery.

Spotter. Paid informer.

Spouse. A husband or wife.

Spouse-Breach. Adultery.

S.P.Q.R. (Abb.). The senate and people of Rome.

Spring Gun. Device used against trespassers.

Springing Use. A use limited to arise on a future event either absolutely or contingently.

Spur. A railroad siding.

Spurius. Illegitimate child.

Squatter. One who takes possession of the land of another without authority.

SS. (Abb.). Scilicet; that is to say.

Stab. A wound inflicted with a pointed weapon.

Stabilize. To keep steady.

Stabilize Prices. To hold prices steady against increases.

Stagiarius. A resident.

Stake. Deposite made as coverage for a wager.

Stakeholder. One who holds money or property pending the outcome of a wager or claim.

Stale Claim or Demand. A claim which has not been asserted for an unreasonable period of time, whether or not barred by the statute of limitations.

Stamp. Instrument for making imprinted mark; mark imprinted; die; piece of gummed paper used as postage.

Stand. To pause or remain stationary; to submit to; to remain as is; to appear in court.

Standard. General recognition of and conformity to established practice; flag; type; model.

Stand By. In the equitable principle of estoppel, to make no effort to change a situation, when the situation will cause a false impression on some other person.

Stand Mute. To refuse to plead.

Staple. Principle commodity of a region.

Stare ad Rectum. To stand trial.

Stare Decisus. To abide by; the decisions of the court should stand as precedents for future guidance.

Stare in Judicio. To stand in judgement; the right to appear in court.

State. Politically organized community; civil powers of such.

State Aid. Support or help given by the state to institutions or individuals for a public purpose.

Stated Account. An action for money admitted to be due, after both parties have computed their claims against each other.

State-Lands. Lands belonging to the Government which may be acquired by private citizens under general land laws.

Statement. An allegation; a declaration of matters of fact.

State's Attorney. Public prosecutor; district attorney.

State's Evidence. Evidence of an accomplice who testifies for the prosecution, usually in expectancy of a lighter punishment or pardon.

State Tax. Any tax levied for general state purposes.

Statim. Immediately.

Stating Part. Part of a bill in equity in which the plaintiff states the facts of his case.

Statu Liber. A free person.

Status. Standing; state; condition.

Status Quo. Existing state of things at any given date.

Statute. Law passed by legislature.

Statute of Amendment. Statute which provides for the correction of certain omissions and imperfections in pleadings.

Statute of Limitations. A statute establishing fixed periods of time within which actions must be brought after cause for such an action has arisen.

Statutes of Repose. See Statute of Limitations.

Statutory. Created or existing by statute.

Statutory Interpretation. The sum total of methods used in aiding the court to apply law derived from statutes.

Statutory Pardon. Pardon effected by act of legislature.

Statutory Rape. Felony of sexual intercourse with a girl under the aged fixed by statute, whether with or without her consent.

Stay. Temporarily stop further proceedings; restraining order.

Stay of Execution. The stopping or arresting of an execution on a judgment for a limited period.

Stay Laws or Statutes. An act of legislature which provides a temporary suspension of the enforcement of an obligation or liability for a debt.

Steal. To commit larceny; to take property feloniously.

Stellionate. Fraud of contracting for the sale of property which the vendor has previously sold.

Step-Child. Child of one of the spouces by former marriage.

Sterility. Barrenness; inability to have children.

Sterilize. To make incapable of reproduction.

Stet Processus. An entry of the dismissal of an action voluntarily made by the plaintiff.

Stick Up. Rob at gun point.

Stiletto. Dagger.

Still. Apparatus for the distillation of alcholic beverages.

Still-Born. Born dead.

Stillicidium. The drip of water from the eves of a house.

Stipend. Salary.

Stipulate. To enter into an agreement.

Stipulated Damages. Liquidated damages; damages designated to be paid in the event of breach of contract.

Stipulation. A material article in an agreement; an agreement between the parties in a litigation, as to the proceeding or part of it.

Stirps, Stirpes. Descent; lines of descent.

Stock. Commodity which a merchant sells; the capital or principal fund of a corporation, usually divided in equal shares held by members of the corporation.

Stock, Common. Ordinary stock of a corporation.

Stock, Preferred. Stock given a preference or priority in respect to dividends, over the remainder of the stock of the corporation, the common stock.

Stockbroker. One who buys and sells stock for others.

Stock Certificate. A certificate issued by a corporation stating that a specified person owns a certain number of shares of the capital stock of the corporation.

Stock Dividend. Dividend payable to stockholders of a corporation in shares of stock of that corporation.

Stock Exchange. Place where stock is bought and sold.

Stockholder. Member of a corporation who owns one or more shares of stock in the company.

Stock in Trade. The goods or chattels which a merchant holds for sale.

Stock of Descent. An ancestor in whom a succession of inheritance begins.

Stock of Merchandise. See Stock in Trade.

Stocks. Formerly, a device used to publicly punish criminals.

Stop, Look and Listen Rule that anyone who fails to stop at a railroad crossing, look both ways and listen for an oncoming train is guilty of contributory negligence.

Stop Order. Direction to a stock broker that if a commodity touches a certain price, the broker shall close trade at the best available price.

Stoppage. Hindrance to doing a certain thing.

Stowage. Storage; payment for storage.

Stowaway. One who conceals himself on board ship.

Stramineus Homo. Man of Straw.

Stramonium. Narcotic poison.

Stranding. Causing a ship to run on the shore.

Stranger. One not a party to an instrument or legal proceeding.

Straw Bail. Nominal or worthless bail.

Straw-Bond. An undertaking sgined by irresponsible or fictitious sureties.

Straw Man. Fictitious person used in a number of transactions.

Street. An urban way or throughfare.

Street Intersection. A street or highway common to two or more streets or highways.

Streetwalker. Prostitute.

Strict. Exact; precise; undeviating.

Strict Construction. Interpretation of a statute confined to the actual language used rather than the intentions of the legislators.

Stricti Juris. According to strick law.

Strictissimi Juris. Of the strictest right or law.

Strictly. Closely; precisely; stringently.

Stricto Jure. In strict law.

Strictum Jus. The strict law; the letter of the law.

Strike. The cessation of work by a group of workmen in order to force their employer to accede to some demand.

Strikebreaker. One who takes the place of a striking workman.

Strike Out. To expunge from a court record or pleading.

Strip. The spoiling or unlawful taking away of anything from the land.

Struck Jury. A jury of 12 men selected from names remaining after each side has exercised his right of striking out a certain number of those eligible for jury duty.

Structure. Any construction; an edifice for any use.

Strumpet. Prostitute.

Stub Line. Small branch line of a railroad.

Stuffing Ballot Box. Fraudulent placing in ballot boxes of ballots which have not been voted.

Stultify. To plead one's self mentally incapacitated for the performance of an act.

Stumpage. Fee paid for permission to enter on another man's land and cut standing timber.

Stuprum. Rape of a virgin.

Style. To call, name or entitle one; a title or official name.

Strong. Cogent; powerful; forceful.

Suable. Liable to be sued.

Suapte Natura. In its own nature.

Sua Sponte. Upon his own responsibility; of his own motion.

Sub. Under.

Sub Colore Officii. Under color of right or office.

Sub Conditions. Upon condition.

Subcontractor. One who takes a portion of a contract from the principal contractor or another subcontractor.

Sub Cura Mariti. Under the care of the husband.

Sub Curia. Under law

Subdivision. Division into smaller parts of the same thing or subject matter.

Sub Disjunctione. In the alternative.

Subhastatio. Sale at public auction.

Subject. One subject to and who owes allegiance to the government of a state; matter of public or private concern for which

law is enacted.

Subject-Matter. That which is under consideration or in dispute.

Subject to. Liable; subordinate; governed by; provided; answerabe for.

Sub Judice. Before the court; in litigation.

Subalta Causa Tollitur Effectus. By removing the cause, the effect is removed.

Sublease. A lease executed by the lessee of an estate to a third person; to enter into a sublease; to sublet.

Subletting. See Sublease.

Submission. Yielding to authority; agreement to abide by a decision of an arbiter.

Submit. To commit to the discretion of another.

Sub Modo. Subject to a modification or qualification; on condition.

Subordinate. To place in a lower class, order or rank; accessory.

Subornation. Procuring another to commit a crime.

Subpoena. Under penalty; writ, process or mandate requiring a person to appear in court to testify in a certain case.

Subpoena ad Testificandum. See Subpoena.

Sub Potestate. Under the protection.

Sub Potestate Parentis. Under the protection of a parent.

Sub Potestate Viri. Under control of her husband.

Subreption. Obtaining property by concealment of the truth.

Subrogation. The substitution of one person in place of another with reference to a lawful claim, demand or right.

Subrogee. One who by subrogation acquires the rights of another, the subrogor.

Subrogor. See Subrogee.

Subscribe. To sign one's name; to agree to pay.

Subscribing Witness. One who attests the signature of a party to an instrument by signing the instrument himself.

Subscription. A written signature; an agreement to give or pay some amount to a designated purpose.

Subsequent. Coming after.

Subsidiary Corporation. A corporation controlled by a parent corporation.

Subsidy. Aid given or appropriated by the government through its proper agencies.

Sub Sigillo. Under seal.

Sub Silento. Silently.

Subsistence. Support.

Sub Spe Reconcilliationis. In the hope of reconciliation.

Substance. Essence; that which is essential.

Substantial. Of real worth and importance; valuable.

Substantial Claim. One which is real and actual.

Substantiate. To establish the existance or truth of by competent evidence.

Substantive Law. Law concerned with the determination of rights and legal powers.

Substitute. To put in the place of another person or thing; the thing or person so put.

Substitution. In the law of wills, to bequeath property to one or more persons, to be succeeded in the enjoyment thereof by others designated by the testator.

Sub Suo Periculo. At his own risk.

Subtenant. A sub-lessee; an undertenant.

Sub Voce. Under the word or title.

Succession. The taking of property by inheritance or will or by operation of law.

Succession Tax. Probate or estate tax levied on the transfer of the decedent's estate; a legacy tax levied on the right to receive such property.

Successor. One who succeeds to the place of another.

Sudden. Happening without notice; unforseen.

Sue. To bring an action in a court of law or equity.

Sue Out. To obtain by application; to petition for certain relief.

Suffer. To permit or authorize.

Sufferance. Toleration; passive consent.

Sufficent. Adequate; competent.

Sufficient Cause. Indicates the presence of facts which will justify an action, especially by a court.

Sufficient Evidence. Adequate evidence; satisfactory evidence.

Suffocate. To kill by stopping respiration, e.g. strangling.

Suffrage. The right to vote at public elections.

Suggest. To hint; to intimate.

Suggestio Falsi. A false suggestion; a misrepresentation.

Suicide. Taking of one's own life.

Sui Generis. Of its own kind.

Sui Juris. In his own right; capable of making a contract.

Suit. An action of any kind, in law or equity; prosecution of a claim or right in a court of law.

Suit Money. An allowance granted the wife in divorce cases to cover court costs and provide temporary alimony.

Suitable. Fit; appropriate.

Suitor. Party to a suit or action in court.

Sum. Money.

Summa Injuria. The greatest injury.

Summa Providentia. The greatest prudence.

Summary. Short, brief; without formal trial or proceeding.

Summary Abatement. Abatement of a nuisance by physical means.

Summary Conviction. Conviction of a person without a formal trial.

Summary Judgment. A judgment in an action which is entered without plenary trial, based upon the affidavits of the parties.

Summary Jurisdiction. Power of a court to give a judgment or make an order itself forthwith.

Summary Proceedings. Proceeding which dispenses with many formalitites.

Summary Trial. Trial on a criminal charge without jury.

Summation. Closing address to the jury.

Summing Up. See Summation.

Summon. To notify a defendant that an action has been instituted against him; to notify to appear in court.

Summonea. A summons.

Summons. A writ or process by which a defendant is notified to appear in court. See Summon.

Summum Jus. A strict insistence on a legal right.

Sunday. The first day of the week.

Suo Nomine. In his own name.

Suo Periculo. At his own risk.

Super. Above, over; on; during; concerning.

Supercargo. One employed by the owner of a vessel to take charge of the cargo.

Superficies. The surface; anything erected upon the land so as to become a part of it.

Superhuman Cause. Act of God.

Superintend. To direct; to manage; to take care of with authority.

Superintendence. Direction; guidance.

Superintendent. Manager; director; employer's representative who directs work of employees.

Superior Court. Court of general jurisdiction in the first instance.

Superior Lien. A prior lien.

Supersede. Set aside; annul.

Supersedeas. In practice, a writ that stays the proceedings at law.

Supersedere. To supersede; to stay.

Supervise. To superintend or inspect.

Supervision. Inspection.

Supervisor. One who has authority over and directs others.

Supervisor of Elections. One appointed to supervise the registration of voters.

Super Visum Corporis. On view of the body (at a coroner's inquest).

Supplemental. Additional.

Supplemental Bill. In equity practice, a new bill filed to supply a defect in the original bill or add something to it.

Supplemental Pleading. A pleading consisting of facts arising since the institution of the suit.

Supplementary Proceedings. Proceedings by which a judgment debtor, against whom execution has been returned unsatisfied, may be examined under oath about his property.

Suppletory Oath. Oath taken by a party to an action who testified in his own behalf.

Suppliant. Petitioner.

Supplicium. Death penalty.

Support. Source or means of living; maintenance; subsistence; sustenance.

Supposition. Conjecture based on probability or possibility.

Suppress. To prevent, subdue or prohibit.

Suppressio Veri. Concealment of the truth, known to be relevant to a transaction.

Supra. Above; upon; in addition to.

Supra Dictus. As stated above.

Suprema Voluntas. The last will.

Supremacy. Paramount authority; sovereignty.

Supreme Court. Highest court of U.S. government; highest court in many states; in New York, the court of general jurisdiction in the first instance.

Supreme Law of the Land. The Constitution of the U.S. and all laws and treaties enacted thereunder.

Sur. On; upon.

Surcharge. In equity, to place an item in an account to the debit of a trustee or other holder of property, which in the account has not been so debited.

Sur Disclaimer. On disclaimer.

Surety. One legally liable for another.

Surgeon. One who cures disease by manual operation.

Surname. One's name; family name.

Surplus. Remainder; residue; undistributed profits of a business.

Surplusage. Unnecessary, extraneous matter.

Surplus Earnings. Amount owned by a corporation over and above its capital and liabilities.

Surprise. Taken unawares; sudden confusion and perplexity.

Surrebutter. Plaintiff's answer to the defendant's rebutter.

Surrejoinder. Plaintiff's answer to the defendant's rejoinder.

Surrender. To give back; yield; restore; to relinquish patent rights; to yield up an estate for life or for years so that the reversioner or remainderman may enter into possession at once.

Surreptitious. Stealthily; fraudulently.

Surrogate Court. Court with jurisdiction in guardianship and probate matters.

Sursise. Negligence; default.

Surtax. Tax levied in addition to the normal tax.

Survey. To ascertain boundaries, corners, diversions, etc. of land; process by which land is measured; an examination.

Survival. Living longer than another.

Survive. To outlive another; to remain alive.

Survivor. One who outlives others.

Suspect. To have a vague idea concerning.

Suspend. To interrupt; to hold in abeyance; to delay or hinder.

Suspendatur per Collum. Let him be hanged by the neck.

Suspended Sentence. A sentence which is delayed by the trial court after the defendant has been found guilty.

Suspension. Temporary delay; temporary extinguishment of a right of an estate.

Suspension of Sentence. Postponement of the execution of a sentence for an indefinite period.

Sus. Per. Co., (Abb.). Suspendature per Collum.

Suspicion. Imagination of something wrong without proof.

Sustain. To carry on; to maintain.

Sustenance. Food; that which maintains life.

Suus. His own.

Swear. To take an oath; to use profane language.

Swear in. To administer an oath.

Swearing. Cursing.

Sweating. Abusing prisoners under interrogation.

Sweat Shop. A plant whose employees work under extremely unfavorable conditions.

Sweepstakes. In a public race, the sum of the stakes for which the subscribers agree to pay for each horse nominated.

Swindle. To cheat and defraud; to obtain property by false pretenses.

Swindler. A cheat; one who defrauds others.

Sworn. Verified.

Sworn Evidence. Testimony given under oath.

Syllabi. The headnotes which precede the decisions in the printed reports.

Syllabus. An abstract; a headnote.

Sympathetic Strike. A boycott.

Synallagmatic Contract. In civil law, a contract in which both parties are bound.

Syndic. Business agent or representative of a corporation.

Syndicate. An association of individuals formed to carry out some special financial transaction or group of transactions.

Synonymous. Expressing the same ideas.

Syphilis. A venereal disease.

T

Table. A condensed, tabulated statement; synopsis.

Tabularius. Notary.

Tacit. Silent; implied.

Tacite. Tacitly.

Tacit Law. Law deriving its authority from the common consent of the people.

Tail. An estate tail or in fee tail is an estate of inheritance limited to the heirs of the body of the grantee.

Taini. Freeholders.

Take. To acquire, obtain or procure.

Take Back. Revoke; retract.

Take by Stealth. Steal.

Take Effect. To become operative.

Take Testimony. To receive evidence.

Take Up. To pay or discharge a note.

Taking. To seize or grasp.

Tales. Talesman. Jurors called to fill vacancies in the regular panel of jurors.

Tales de Circumstantibus. Jurors from the bystanders.

Tacit Hypothecation. Type of lien or mortgage which is created by operation of the law without any express agreement of the parties.

Taking per Capita. In the distribution of estates, equally.

Tales Jurors. See Tales.

Talesmen. See Tales.

Talio. Punishment in the same kind.

Talis Qualis. As much as; such as.

Taliter. Thus; so.

Tallagium. A term including all taxes.

Tallia. Tax.

Tam. So; to such extent.

Tamen. However; nevertheless.

Tamper. To interfere with a thing for some improper purpose; to meddle.

Tam Quam. As much as; as well as.

Tangible. Capable of being touched; tactile; real; substantial; evidence.

Tangible Property. Property which may be felt or touched.

Tanquam Testamentum Inofficiosum. An improvident will; one which overlooks the nearest relatives.

Tantus. So much; so great.

Tarde. Return of an officer stating that he received the process too late to execute it.

Tare. An allowance for the weight of a container made by customs officers in computing duties on imports.

Tariff. Duty on imports; tabulated list of rates.

Tavern. Place where alcoholic beverages are sold to be drunk on the premises.

Tax. To assess, particularly money for the support of the government; to demand; to lay a burden upon; financial burden levied upon persons or property by the government for public purposes.

Taxable. Subject or liable to taxation.

Taxable Costs. Expenses of the prevailing party in an action which may be included in the judgment of a court.

Taxable Credit. Any obligation or contract which creates an enforceable indebtedness on the part of the promisor.

Taxable Property. Property liable to or subject to taxation.

Taxable Value. The bonded indebtedness together with the stock of a corporation.

Taxation. The act of levying or imposing a tax.

Taxation of Costs. The fixing of the costs which are to be paid by the party losing the suit.

Tax Avoidance. The legal attempt to minimize one's taxes.

Tax Certificate. A certificate of the scale of real estate for delinquent taxes.

Tax Collector. One authorized to collect and to enforce payment of taxes.

Tax Deed. The conveyance given upon a sale of property upon which taxes have not been paid.

Tax Ferrets. Persons who search for property omitted from taxation.

Taxi, Taxicab. Vehicle for public hire.

Taxing Power. Power of a government to levy taxes.

Tax Levy. Establishment of a rate of taxation by a duly authorized government.

Tax Lien. A lien existing in favor of state or municipality upon the property of a delinquent taxpayer on which unpaid taxes are due, or on all his property.

Tax List. Official listing of the descriptions of property and the names of those liable to assessment.

Taxpayer. One subject to and chargeable with a tax.

Tax Roll. List of persons and property subject to the payment of a particular tax, with the amounts severally due.

Tax Sale. Sale of property for unpaid delinquent taxes.

Tax Title. Title acquired by purchase of land land at a tax sale.

Teacher. One who instructs.

Teamster. One engaged in the hauling of freight for others.

Teazer. Railroad operated at a loss.

Technical. Pertaining or peculiar to an art or science; immaterial.

Technical Error. An error during the course of a trial which is not serious.

Technical Mortgage. A true and formal mortgage.

Tegula. A title.

Teller. Bank employee who takes in and pays out money; one who keeps tallies, e.g. of votes.

Temere. Rashly; accidentally.

Temperance. Moderation; restrained indulgence.

Temperate Damages. Reasonable damages.

Temporalis. Temporary.

Temporalis Actio. An action which had to be brought within a certain time.

Temporary. For a limited time.

Temporary Alimony. Allowance paid a wife pending court action.

Temporary Damages. In real estate, recovery made from time to time as damages accrue.

Temporary Disability. One which is not permanent, lasting for a limited time.

Temporary Injunction. Restraining Order; an injunction to maintain the status quo until the action is finally determined.

Temporary Loan. A loan which is to be paid with and by the taxes of a current fiscal year.

Temporary Statute. Statute limited in duration from the time of its inception.

Tempore et Loco. In time and place.

Temporis Exceptio. A plea of lapse of time, in bar of an action.

Tempus. Time.

Tempus Continuum. A continuous time.

Tempus Semestrae. The six-months period.

Tempus Utile. The period to be used; indicates how a period of time for procedure or limitations is to be reckoned.

Tenancy. The estate of a tenant; a mode of holding an estate; temporary possession of another's property.

Tenancy at Sufferance. Possession of land by lawful title but holding thereof after title has expired.

Tenancy by the Entirety. Joint tenenacy by husband and wife, each being seized and possessed of the entire estate, after the death of one, the survivor taking the whole.

Tenancy for Life. One which continues for the period of a designated life or lives.

Tenancy for Years. One which terminated after a fixed time.

Tenancy from Year to Year. Tenancy which can be terminated after a year, usually by giving six months' notice.

Tenancy in Common. Tenancy in lands by more than one person in such a way that each owns an undivided share.

Tenant. One who holds land in return for service or rent.

Tenant at Sufferance. See Tenancy at Sufferance.

Tenant by Entirety. See Tenancy by Entirety.

Tenant for Life. See Tenancy for life.

Tenant for Years. See Tenancy for Years.

Tenant from Year to Year. See Tenancy from Year to Year.

Tenant in Common. See Tenancy in Common.

Tenant in Fee Simple. One who holds land or tenements for himself and his heirs forever.

Tenant in Severalty. A sole tenant.

Tenants by the Entireties. Tenants who hold by one title, e.g. joint tenancy.

Tenants in Common. Tenants who hold in unity of possession.

Tender. Offer to perform an obligation which is due.

Tender of Issue. In pleading, an offer to submit the question to the court or jury.

Tenement. Landed property held by one person of another; a large building for the occupation of three or more persons, usually of the poorer class.

Tenements. Corporeal hereditaments, and incorporeal hereditaments issuing out of corporeal ones or which are annexed thereto.

Tenementum. A tenement; an estate held by a tenant.

Tenens. A tenant.

Tener. To hold or keep.

Tenere. To hold or keep; to understand.

Tenet. He holds.

Tenor. The actual wording of a document; an exact copy.

Tenor Praesentium. By tenor of these presents.

Tenor of Bill of Exchange. Refers to the time and manner of payment of the bill.

Tenure. The nature of the holding or tenancy of lands; term of office.

Terce. Dower.

Tercerone. Mulatto.

Term. A word; a phrase; a fixed period of time; the limit of time in a leasehold; a session of court; time for which one holds an office.

Terminare. To terminate; to decide finally.

Terminating Building and Loan Association. One in which all of the stock matures at the same time.

Terminus. Limit; term; boundary; an estate for years.

Terminus ad Quem. Limit to which.

Term of Court. Sesson of court.

Terra. Land.

Terra Affirmata. Farmed land.

Terra Debilis. Barren land.

Terra Firma. Dry land.

Terra Frisca. Uncultivated land.

Terra Lucrabilis. Reclaimed land.

Terra Testamentalis. Land transferrable by will.

Terre. Land.

Terre-Tenant. One actually in occupation or possession of land.

Terrible. Frightful; dreadful.

Territorial Waters. Waters contiguous to the coast of a country.

Territory. A part of the national domain of the U.S.

Terror. Fright; dread.

Tertia. The third part; dower.

Tertius Interveniens. A third party who intervenes in an action.

Test. Examination; trial; a criterion; standard; norm.

Testacy. The state or condition of leaving a valid will at one's death.

Testament. The disposition of personal property according to the decedent's will and desire.

Testamentary. Pertaining to a will.

Testamentary Capacity. The mental ability recognized by law as sufficient for making a will.

Testamentary Disposition. The disposition of property not to take effect until after the grantor dies.

Testamentary Guardian. The guardian of a decedent's child appointed by his will.

Testamentary Instrument. Any instrument intended as a will; an unprobated will.

Testamentary Power. Power to dispose of one's property by will.

Testamentum. Testament; will.

Testari. To testify; to attest; to make a will.

Testate. One who has made a will or dies leaving a will.

Testation. Witness; evidence.

Testator. A man who dies leaving a valid will.

Testatrix. Woman who dies leaving a valid will.

Testatum. Testified.

Testatus. Testate; a testator.

Test Case. Case seeking to answer an abstract question.

Teste. Bear witness.

Tested. Witnessed; attested.

Teste of Writ. The concluding clause, showing date of issuance.

Testify. To bear witness; to give evidence under oath.

Testimonia. Testimony; evidence.

Testimonium, Testimonium Clause. See Teste of Writ.

Testimony. Evidence given by a witness under oath.

Testis. Witness.

Test Oath. Oath required as a criterion of the fitness of a person to hold a public or political office; an oath of past and present fidelity to an established government.

Thalweg. Middle of the main channel of a river.

Theft. Larceny; the unlawful taking of the personal property of another.

Then. At that time; a specific time; also used to denote a contingency.

LEGAL DICT

Theocracy. Government which recognizes God as its ruler.

Theolonium. Toll.

Theory of a Case. Facts or basis on which a right of action is claimed.

Thearapy. Treatment of a disease.

There. In or at that place.

Thereafter. After that time; afterward.

Thereby. Because of; by reason of.

Therefor. For that thing.

Therein. In that place.

Thereupon. Without delay.

Thesaurus Inventus. Treasure-trove.

Thief. One who commits larceny.

Things. Objects of ownership or property.

Things in Action. A right to recover money or personal property by court proceedings.

Things of Value. Tangible objects recognized by the law as personal property.

Things Personal. Goods, money and all other movables which a person may move about with him.

Things Real. Permanent, fixed, immovable things which cannot be moved about, e.g. land.

Think. To believe; to conclude; to recollect.

Third Degree. Method used to force a prisoner to confess or give information.

Third House. An organized and generally unscrupulous lobby.

Third Party. One who has an interest in a legal transaction but not actually a party to it.

Third Party Beneficiary. One not a party to a contract, who receives a benefit thereunder and who may bring suit to protect his interest.

Third Possessor. One who buys mortgaged property without assuming the mortgage.

Thoroughfare. A passage through.

Thread. A middle line; center line of the main channel of a stream or river.

Threat. Declaration of an intention to harm another by the doing of some unlawful act; a menace.

Three Mile Limit. Territorial waters which mark the limit of jurisdiction of national control.

Throw Out. To ignore a bill.

Thus. In the way indicated.

Tick. (Coll.). Credit or trust.

Ticket. A certificate entitling the holder to some right or privilege; list of candidates running for office; a ballot.

Ticket Speculator. One who sells tickets at an advance over the price charged by the management.

Tide. The ebb and flow of the ocean.

Tide Lands. Lands which are covered and uncovered by the daily ebb and flow of the tides.

Tie. To bind; the failure of either of two candidates to obtain a majority.

Tiel. Such.

Tignum. Building material.

Timber. Trees which can be used for building purposes.

Time. The measure of duration.

Time Bargain. An agreement to buy or sell stock at a future time at a fixed price.

Time Immemorial. Time beyond the memory of man.

Tipstaff. A court bailiff.

Tithes. Tenths.

Title. Ownership; means whereby the owner has just possession of his property; certificate of ownership; a claim or right; a distinctive appellation; the caption describing a statute or legal proceeding.

Title Bond. Bond given to the purchaser of real property as security in the transfer of title to property.

Title by Descent. Title by hereditary succession.

Title by Prescription. Title acquired by use and time.

Title, Chain of. Record of the succession of conveyances of real property, giving the origin and history to the title of property.

Title Deeds. Deeds which give evidence of title to lands.

Title in Fee Simple. Full and unconditional ownership in fact.

Title Insurance. Insurance against loss or damage resulting from defects or failure of title or from the enforcement of liens existing at the time of the insurance.

Through. By means of; within; from one side to the other; by agency of.

Title of a Cause. Manner of designating a suit at law, e.g. Brown vs. Jones.

Title of an Act or Statute. The name of a statute, usually the first part.

Title Search. A search of public record to ascertain the state of a person's title to real estate.

Title Theory. The theory that the mortage passes legal title to the property.

Titulus. Title.

Toft. Vacant site on which a building formerly stood.

To Have and To Hold. Clause in an instrument which defines and limits the extent of the estate granted.

Token. A sign or mark; symbol of the existence of a fact.

Tolerate. To permit, although not wholly approved of.

Toll. To bar, defeat or take away; to interrupt the statute of limitations; a tax for the use of something.

Tollage. Toll; the payment of or exaction of a toll.

Toll Bridge. A bridge built and maintained under public authority, the use of which is subject to a reasonable toll.

Tollere. To raise, lift up or elevate; to take away; to defeat.

Toll Gate. Gate erected on private or public property allowing passage only upon payment of toll.

Toll Road. Turnpike.

Toll the Statute. To stop the running of the statute of limitations.

Toll-Traverse. A toll on passage over private property.

Tonnage. The capacity of a vessel for carrying

freight, etc., calculated in tons.

Tontine. Insurance whereby perpetual or life annuities and benefits are enjoyed by several persons with the agreement that on the death of any one of them, his share goes to the survivors.

Tort. An act or omission which causes injury and which creates a claim for damage in the injured party; a private or civil wrong or injury.

Tort-Feasor. One who commits a tort.

Tortious. Wrongful; injurious.

Torture. The use of instruments to inflict pain in order to extort confessions or information.

Tota Curia. The whole court.

Total. Whole; complete; full.

Total Loss. Complete loss of insured property.

Totidem Verbis. In so many words.

Toties Quoties. As often as.

Toujours et Uncore Prist. Now and always ready.

Tout. All; whole.

Towage. The towing of ships and vessels; the fee therefor.

Toward. In the direction of.

To Wit. That is to say; namely.

Town. A civil and political division of a state larger than a village, but not incorporated as a city.

Town-Clerk. An officer of a municipality who acts as a recorder and general secretary.

Town-Meeting. A legal assembly of the qualified voters of an incorporated town.

Town-Plat. A map or chart showing the arrangement of streets and the division of lots of a town.

Township. A division of land, six miles square.

Townsite. Portion of public domain set apart to be the site for a town.

Toxic. Poisonous.

Toxicant. A poison.

Toxicology. The science of poisons.

Tp (Abb.). Township.

Tracing. A mechanical copy or facsimile of an original document.

Tract (of Land). Lot; parcel.

Tradas in Bailium. To deliver for bail.

Trade. Commerce; barter; any bargain or sale; the business of buying and selling for money.

Trade Acceptance. A draft or bill of exchange drawn by the seller of goods on the buyer and accepted by him.

Trademark A distinguishing mark or charac-f teristic,. through which the products o particular manufacturers are identified.

Trade-Name. Name under which a person, firm or corporation does business.

Trader. One who deals in the purchase and sale of goods for profit.

Trade-Union. A labor organization formed to protect the rights and interests of the workingman through collective bargaining with the employer.

Tradition. Delivery of real or personal property.

Traffic. Commerce; trade; sale or exchange of merchandise; the transportation of passengers, goods and merchandise.

Trahere. To draw.

Traitor. One who betrays; one who commits treason.

Tramp. A vagrant.

Tramp Corporation. A corporation which does not intend to do business in the state of incorporation.

Transact. To conduct, manage or carry out.

Transactio. A voluntary compromise or settlement of a litigation.

Transaction. The conducting of any business; negotiation; proceeding; a compromise.

Transcript. A copy of a writing.

Transcript of Judgment. A certificate that a judgment has been entered.

Transcript of Record. Printed copy of the record of an entire case.

Transfer. To convey from one person or place to another.

Transfer by Indorsement. The indorsement and delivery of a negotiable instrument.

Transferee. One to whom a transfer is made.

Transferor. One who makes a transfer.

Transgressio. Trespass.

Transient. Passing across; not lasting or permanent.

Transient Foreigner. A foreigner who comes to a country without intending to remain.

Transient Person. One who has no fixed address in the state in which he is.

Transire. To go or pass over.

Transit. Carriage and delivery of goods in accordance with the terms of a contract.

Transitory. Passing from one place to another.

Transitus. Transit; a conveyance.

Translation. Reproduction of a document, paper, etc. in another language; a testamentary provision in the same will or in a codicil, by which a legacy previously given is transferred to another person.

Transport. To carry; to convey.

Transportation. The removal of goods or persons from one place to another.

Transhipment. Transfer of cargo from one ship to another before reaching the ultimate destination.

Trassans. Drawing; the drawer of a bill of exchange.

Trassitus. The drawee of a bill of exchange.

Trauma. A wound; bodily injury.

Traumatic Disease. Disease caused by physical injury.

Travail. Childbearing; suffering.

Travel. To go from one place to another; journey.

Traveler. One who goes from one place to another.

Travel Pay. Allowance given to military officers upon their honorable discharge to return to their place of enlistment.

Traverse. To deny an allegation in a pleading.

Traverse Jury. Trial jury.

Traverser. Party to an action who pleads by way of denial.

Treason. The attempt to overthrow by overt acts the state to which one owes allegiance.

Treasurer. Officer of the state, a corporation or organization entrusted with the custody and disbursement of money.

Treasure-Trove. Money or other precious metals hidden away by an unknown owner and accidentally found by another.

Treasury. Place where public funds are kept.

Treasury Note. Bill issued by the U.S. Treasury and circulating as legal tender.

Treaty. Formal agreement between two or more sovereign states.

Treble Damages. Three times the actual damages sustained.

Tres. Three.

Trespass. Any violation of law; unlawful and intentional injury to another's person or property.

Trespass Quare Clausum Fregit. "Trespass wherefore he broke the close;" common-law action for trespass upon the plaintiff's land.

Trespasser. One who enters upon the property of another without permission.

Tret. An allowance made for water or dust in weighing certain commodities.

Trial. Judicial examination, according to the law of the land, of issues presented in due course of procedure.

Trial by Jury. Trial by a body of 12 men duly selected, impaneled and sworn.

Trial by Court. Trial by one or more judges without a jury.

Trial de Novo. A re-trial in a superior court on an appeal of the case from an inferior court.

Trial Judge. Judge who presides at a court case.

Trial per Testes. Trial by witnesses; a trial without the intervention of a jury.

Triare. To try.

Triatio. A trial.

Tribunal. Court; the place where a judge administers justice.

Tribute. A tax levied by a sovereign on his subjects or by one nation on another.

Triens. The third part; dower.

Trigamus. One who has been lawfully married three separate times.

Trinkets. Small, decorative ornaments.

Triors. Persons appointed by the court to determine whether a juror challenged for favor is or is not qualified to serve.

Trip. Journey from one place to another.

Tripartite. Having three parts or parties.

Trithing. The third of a country.

Trivial. Trifling; of small importance.

Trove. Found.

Troy Weight. A weight of 12 oz. to the pound.

Truce. A suspension of hostilities between belligerents.

True. Correct; actual; genuine; honest.

True Bill. Indorsement on an indictment when the jury finds that the accused should be prosecuted.

Trust. Reliance upon another; confidence; credit given; that committed to another for management or safekeeping; a right of property, real or personal, held by one party for the benefit of another; a confidence reposed in one person, the trustee, for the benefit of another, the cestui que-trust, respecting arrangements of rights over property which is held by the trustee for the benefit of the cestui que trust; term used for combinations of large industrial corporations or individuals which control or tend to control an industry or groups of industries.

Trust Company. A bank organized under general statutes for the purpose of accepting, and executing trusts and managing the various financial matters of corporations organized as trusts.

Trust Deed. A species of mortgage given to a creditor to secure a loan.

Trustee. One in whom property is vested in trust for others; one appointed to execute a trust.

Trustee in Bankruptcy. An officer of the court appointed to collect and reduce to money the estate of a bankrupt.

Trustee Process. In New England States, the process of garnishment.

Trustee Estate. Either the estate of the trustee, i.e. legal title, or the estate of the beneficiary.

Trust Fund Doctrine. The doctrine that the capital stock of a corporation is held by the corporation in trust for its creditors and stockholders.

Trust in Invitum. A trust imposed by operation of law without consent of the trustee.

Trustor. One who settles or creates a trust; the grantor.

Try. To examine judicially.

Tug. Tow-boat.

Tulit. He brought.

Tumult. Noisy quarrel; brawl.

Tunc. Then; at that time.

Turn-Over. Repeated use of the same invested capital in the buying and selling of goods.

Turnpike. Toll gate; road having toll gates.

Turpis. Bad; wicked; immoral.

Turpis Contractus. Dishonorable contract.

Turpitude. Inherent baseness; depravity; everything contrary to justice, honesty or good morals.

Tuta. Safe; secure.

Tutela. Guardianship; tutelage.

Tutor. Guardian of a minor.

Twelve Mile Limit. Provision in an agreement between Britian and U.S. allowing the latter to search British ships within 12 miles of shore.

Tyrant. Despot.

U

Uberrima Fides. The most complete good faith.

Ubi Re Vera. Where, in truth.

Ulterior. Beyond what is apparent.

Ulterior Estate. An estate in remainder.

Ulterius Concilium. Further consideration or argument.

Ultimo Ratio. The last reason or resort.

Ultimate. The last in a sequence; final.

Ultimate Facts. The facts that are in issue in a

case; facts necessary and essential for decision by the court.

Ultimatum. The last proposition.

Ultima Voluntas. A last will.

Ultimum Supplicium. The extreme punishment; punishment of death.

Ultimus Haeres. Ultimate heir.

Ultra. Beyond; outside of; in excess of.

Ultra Mare. Beyond the sea.

Ultra Reprises. After deductions.

Ultra Vires Act. An act beyond the scope of the power of a corporation.

Umpirage. The decision of the umpire.

Umpire. Arbitrator.

Una cum. Together with.

Una cum Omnibus Aliis. Together with all the others.

Unalienable. Inalienable.

Unanimous. Agreeing.

Una Voce. With one voice; unanimously.

Unavoidable Accident. An inevitable, unforseeable accident.

Unavoidable Cause. Accidental cause.

Uncertain. Vague; indefinite.

Unchaste Woman. Woman who is not sexually pure.

Unchasity. Impurity in mind and conduct.

Uncle. The brother of one's father or mother.

Unclean Hands. Principle which will prevent a court of equity from giving equitable relief to a person whose conduct is unconscionable.

Unconditional. Without conditions or reservations; not limited.

Unconscionable. Morally reprehensible.

Unconstitutional. That which is contrary or irreconcilable to the constitution.

Uncontrollable. Ungovernable; irresistible.

Uncontrollable Impulse. Irresistible impulse.

Uncore. Again; now.

Unde. Whence; from what.

Undefended. Without defense; applied to one who must make his own defense when on trial.

Unde Petit Judicium. Whereof he demands judgment.

Under-Lease. Where lessee lets premises for a part only of his unexpired terms.

Under Seal. Applied to any document to which a seal has been attached.

Undertake. To take on oneself; set about; attempt; to perform or execute; to contract; to accept responsibility for.

Undertaker. One who contracts to do something, ordinarily in the public service; one who prepares the dead for burial.

Undertaking. A guaranty; a bond.

Under-Tenant. Sub-tenant.

Under the Law. In conformity with the law.

Underwriter. Insurer; investment banker who underwrites corporate bonds and stocks.

Underwriting Contract. Contract to insure the sale of bonds.

Undique. In all directions.

Undisclosed Principal. A principal in an agency relationship whose identity is not known to the persons with whom the agent transacts business.

Undisputed. Uncontested.

Undivided Profits. Profits which have not been distributed or set aside as surplus.

Undres. Minors.

Undue. More than necessary or proper; illegal.

Undue Influence. Pressure brought to bear upon a person so as to interfere with the exercise of freedom of will.

Unearned Income. Income received from property.

Unequal. Not uniform.

Unequivocal. Clear; capable of being interpreted in only one way.

Unerring. Sure; infallible.

Unethical. Not according to business or professional standards.

Unexpected. Sudden.

Unfair. In regard to labor, unfriendly to organized labor.

Unfair Competition. All dishonest or fradulent rivalry in trade and commerce; the endeavor to drive a competitor out of business by fraud, intimidation, counterfeiting, etc.

Unfit. Unsuitable; incompetent.

Unforseen. Not expected.

Unforseen Event. An uncontrollable force.

Unified. Made one.

Uniform. Unvarying; equable; as applied to statutes, one which treats alike all persons similarly situated.

Uniform Operation of Laws. In constitutional law, the requirement that laws of a general nature have uniform application to all persons within a legitimate class.

Unilateral. One-sided.

Unilateral Contract. Contract in which one party undertakes the performance of an act without receiving in return any express promise of performance from the other party, the promise becoming binding only when the act is performed.

Unilateral Mistake. A mistake on the part of only one of the parties to a contract.

Unintelligible. That which cannot be understood.

Union. League; federation; an unincorporated association of workingmen. See Trade Union.

Union Labels. Certain labels attached to goods made by union members.

Union Shop. One in which only union members may work.

Unitas Personarum. Merger of two legal persons into one.

Unite. To join in an act.

United Kingdom. Great Britain and Ireland.

United Nations. An international organization chartered in 1945 with the objective of maintaining peace and friendly relations among nations.

United States. Collective name of the states united by and under the Constitution; territory under the sovereignty of the U.S.

United States Bond. Obligations for payment of money issued by the U.S. government at various times.

LEGAL DICT

United States Commissioners. Subordinate judicial officers appointed by the Federal District Court for a term of four years.

United States Courts. Under the Constitution, the judicial power of the U.S. is vested in a supreme court and other inferior courts as established by Congress.

United States Notes. Promissory notes issued by the U.S. government intended to circulate as money and with the national bank notes to constitute the credit currency of the country.

Unity of Interest. The identity of the interest of joint tenants with respect to the property which is subject to the tenancy.

Unity of Possession. Joint possession of two rights in the same property, one dependent upon the other.

Unity of Time. That essential aspect of joint tenancy, that the estates of the joint tenants be vested at one and the same time.

Unity of Title. That essential aspect of joint tenancy, that the estates of the joint tenants be created by one and the same act.

Universal. That which pertains to all without exception.

Universal Agent. One authorized to transact all of his principal's business.

Universal Legacy. A legacy which beqneaths all of the decedent's property.

Universal Partnership. Partnership in which each partner contributes all of his property.

Universites. Corporation.

Universitas Bonorum. All of a person's goods or estate.

Universitas Juris. A quantity of things which for legal purposes may be treated as a whole.

Universum Jus. Sole ownership.

Universus. Whole; entire.

Unjust. Contrary to right and justice.

Unjust Enrichment. Principle that one should not profit inequitably at another's expense.

Unkerjay. Morphine addict.

Unlawful That which is contrary to the law; wrong.

Unlawful ab Inirio. Unlawful from the beginning.

Unlawful Act. Act contrary to law.

Unlawful Assembly. Meeting of three or more persons for an unlawful purpose by force or violence.

Unlawful Cohabitation. The living together as husband and wife of two persons not married to each other.

Unlawful Combination. Agreement with tendency to restrain trade, inhibit competition, or create a monopoly.

Unlawful Conspiracy. Two or more persons acting together in a criminal transaction.

Unlawful Contract. Agreement calling for performance of acts prohibited by law.

Unlawful Detainer. Refusal to grant possession to property being unlawfully held.

Unlawful Entry. Peaceful entry upon lands by means of fraud or willful wrong.

Unlimited. Unrestricted.

Unliquidated. Unsettled or unassessed.

Unmarried. Not having husband or wife; single; never married.

Unnatural Offense. Crime against nature, i.e. sodomy.

Uno Actu. By a single act.

Uno Flatu. In one breath.

Unprecedented. New; no prior example.

Unques. Always; ever; still.

Unques Prist. Always ready.

Unrestricted. Absolute; without limits or conditions.

Unsafe. Dangerous; applied to a bank, insolvent.

Unseated. Unsettled; uncultivated.

Unseaworthy. Vessel incapable of withstanding dangers of sea.

Unsolemn War. War without formal declaration.

Unsound Mind Person incapable of handling own affairs due to infirmity of mind.

Untenantable. Unfit for occupacy.

Unthrift. A spendthrift.

Unwritten Law. Customs, mores; principles accepted without enactment; common law.

Uplands. Lands bordering on waters.

Urban. Referring to city or town.

Ure. Practice; effect.

User. Exercise or enjoyment of a right or property.

Uso. Usage.

Usque. Until; up to.

Usufruct. Enjoying property not belonging to user as long as nature of property is not altered.

Usura. Interest on money borrowed.

Usura Manifesta. Open usury.

Usurare. To pay interest.

Usura Velata. Concealed usury.

Usurp. To unlawfully seize and hold by force.

Usurpaticn. To unlawfully assume possession of the property of another.

Usury. Illegal rate of interest.

Usus. Use.

Usus Fori. The practice of the court.

Ut. That; so that; as.

Ut Audivi. As I have heard.

Ut Credo. As I believe.

Uterine. Applied to children born of the same mother.

Utero Gestation. Pregnancy.

Utilis. Useful; profitable.

Utility. Industrial value; capable of use.

Utmost Care. Highest or greatest care.

Ut Supra. As above.

Utter. To publish or put in circulation; entrice; complete.

Uxor. Wife.

Uxorcide. Killing of one's own wife.

V

V. (Abb.). Versus.

Vacant. Empty; without inanimate objects.

Vacantia Bona. Goods without an owner or claimant and which may be held by the first occupant or finder.

Vacate. To leave empty; to annul or cancel.

Vacatio. An immunity; an exemption.

Vacation. Time between court terms.

Vacation of Judgment. Setting aside of a judgment.

Vacatur. Let it be vacated.

Vaccination. Innoculation with vaccine for purposes of immunization.

Vacuity. Vacancy.

Vacuus. Empty; void.

Vadari. To give bail.

Vades. Pledges; sureties; bail.

Vadiari. To wage; to give security.

Vadiare Legem. To wage law.

Vadium. A pledge.

Vadium Mortuum. A mortgage or "dead pledge".

Vagabond. Vagrant; tramp.

Vagrant. Person without visible means of support or of fixed residence.

Vague. Indefinite.

Vale. A promissory note.

Valentia. Value or price of a thing.

Valid. Having legal effect; operative; not void.

Validate. To make valid; to confirm.

Validating Statute. Statute which cures or makes valid past transactions.

Validity. Legal effectiveness.

Valuable. Of financial value; estimable.

Valuable Consideration. A class of consideration in which some right, interest or profit may accrue to one party, or some detriment or loss to the other party.

Valuation. Estimated worth of a thing.

Value. The utility or worth of a thing.

Valued Policy. Insurance policy which states the value of the thing insured.

Valuer. Appraiser.

Value Received. Phrase used in negotiable instruments to indicate that a lawful consideration has been given for it.

Variance. A material difference; any substantial difference between the allegations of a pleading and the evidence addressed to sustain it.

Various. Separate.

Vary. To change to something else.

Vas. A surety or pledge.

Vasectomy. Surgical operation for the purpose of sterilization.

Vastitas. Wasteland.

Vauderie. Witchcraft.

Vectura. Freight.

Vehicle. That which is used for transportation.

Vel. Whether; or.

Velle. To consent.

Vel Non. Or not.

Vend. To transfer title for a monetary consideration.

Vendee. Purchaser.

Vender. To sell; vendor.

Vendetta. Private blood feud.

Vendition. A sale.

Venditor. A seller or vendor.

Vendor. One who transfers property by sale.

Vendor's Lien. Right of the vendor to retain possession of goods until their price has been paid.

endue. Sale; auction.

Veneral. Sexual.

Venereal Disease. Disease associated with sexual intercourse.

Venire. To come; to appear in court.

Venireman. One summoned as a juror.

Venit et Dicit. Comes and says.

Venture. To take chances; a risky undertaking.

Venue. Neighborhood; area in which an injury is claimed to have occurred; geographical unit in which a trial court has jurisdiction.

Veracity. Truth; honesty.

Vera Copula. True and natural intercourse.

Veray. True.

Verba. Words.

Verbal. In words; by word of mouth.

Verbal Act. That which a person says or writes.

Verba Precaria. Precatory words.

Verba Sunt Indices Animi. Words are the indexes of the mind.

Verdict. Decision of the jury.

Verdict Against Evidence. Verdict contrary to the evidence.

Verdicto Non Obstante. Notwithstanding the verdict.

Verification. Confirmation.

Verify. To confirm by oath.

Verily. Beyond doubt; really.

Veritas. Truth; correctness.

Veritatem Dicere. To speak the truth.

Versari. To be employed; to be conversant with.

Versus. Against; vs. (Abb.).

Verus. Genuine.

Vessel. Ship..

Vest. To give immediate right of present or future enjoyment; to give possession; to give power or authority.

Vested. An unconditional right to property.

Vested Interest. A fixed, present right or title to a thing which carries an existing right of alienation.

Vested Legacy. A legacy which is given to be paid at a future time.

Vested Remainder. An interest in real property to be enjoyed at a future time, with no other condition imposed other than the determination of the precedent estate.

Vestigium. A vestage or trace.

Vestimentum. Investitute; seisin.

Vestire. To vest.

Veteran's Preference. Preference given to honorably discharged veterans by the civil service.

Vetitio Principii. A begging of the question.

Veto. I forbid; refusal of assent by an executive officer.

Veto Power. Constitutional power of the President and most Governors to prevent acts of Legislature from becoming law.

Vetustas. Antiquity.

Vexatae Quaestiones. Moot questions.

Vi. By force or violence.

Via. Way; road.

Via Alta. Highway.

Via Amicabili. In a friendly way.

Viability. Ability of the newborn to live.

Viaggio, Viagium. A voyage.

Via Publica. A public road.

Vi aut Clam. By force or fraud.

Vicarious. Through an agent or representative.

Vice. Fault; defect; imperfection; in place of; as a substitute for, e.g. vice-president.

Vice Versa. On the contrary; the other way around.

Vicinage. Vicinity; neighborhood.

Vicious. Wicked; harmful.

Vi Clam aut Precario. Forcible, secretly or by sufferance.

Victuals. Food prepared to eat.

Victus. Means of support; the vanquished.

Vicus. Village.

Vide. See; refer to.

Videlicet. That is to say; to wit; namely.

Vidimus. We have seen.

Vidua. A widow.

Viduity. Widowhood.

Vi et Armis. Force and arms.

View. The taking of the jury to the place where an event is alleged to have happened.

Vigilia. Vigil; watch.

Vigilance. Watchfulness; precaution.

Vigore Cujus. By the force of which.

Vill. Village.

Village. A community of limited area and population, smaller than a city or town.

Villein. Serf attached to the soil.

Vinculum. Chain; bond.

Vinculum Matrimonii. Bond of marriage.

Vindex. A defender.

Vindicare. To claim or challenge.

Vindictive Damages. Punitive or exemplary damages.

Vinous. Alcoholic.

Vintner. Wine seller.

Vinum. Wine.

Violate. To disobey a law; to force; to rape.

Violence. Force.

Virtue. Effect; chastity.

Virtuous. Pure.

Virilia. The testicles.

Viripotens. Capable of sexual intercourse.

Virtuate Cujus. By virtue of which.

Virtute Officii. By virtue of his office.

Vis. Force; violence.

Visa. Indorsement on a passport allowing the holder to enter a foreign state.

Vis Armata. An armed force.

Vis Divina. Divine force.

Vise. To certify that a document has been examined and found to be correct.

Vis et Metus. Force and fear.

Visible. Noticeable; apparent.

Vis Impressa. Force directly applied.

Visitation. Inspection; superintendence.

Vis Laica. A lay force.

Vis Major. An act of God.

Visores. Viewers.

Visus. A view.

Vita. Life.

Vital Statistics. Statistics relating primarily to the subject of health, usually including the registration of births, deaths and marriages.

Vitium. Vice; error.

Vitium Clerici. Clerical mistake.

Viva Voce. The living voice; by word of mouth.

Vix. Scarcely; with difficulty.

Vix. (Abb.). Videlicet; that is to say; to wit; namely.

Vocabula Artis. Technical terms.

Vocans. A voucher.

Vocare. To call or summon.

Vocation. Calling; occupation.

Vociferatio. Hue and cry.

Vociferous. Noisy; clamerous.

Void. Wholly without effect.

Voidable. Able to be nullified.

Voidance. A vacancy.

Void Tax. Tax which never had any effect.

Voir Dire. To speak the truth.

Volo. I will.

Volstead Act. National Prohibition Act of 1919.

Voluntarily. Willingly.

Voluntary. Intentional.

Voluntary Association. An organization not constituted as a legal entity.

Voluntary Bankruptcy. Bankruptcy proceeding brought by the bankrupt.

Voluntary Deed. Deed executed without consideration.

Voluntary Manslaughter. Intentional killing of a person under the influence of sudden passion, but without malice.

Voluntary Waste. Intentional and deliberate waste committed by a tenant.

Voluntas. Volition, purpose or intention.

Volunteer. One who freely gives of his services.

Vote. Suffrage; choice.

Voter. An elector; one possessing the legal qualifications to vote.

Voting Trust. A trust in which the shares of stock belonging to various stockholders are transferred to a trustee who has the power to cast votes for the stockholders in the various corporations which have issued the stock.

Votum. Vow; promise.

Vouch. To call upon; to call in to warranty; to quote as an authority; to request a warrantor to defend a grantee's title.

Vouchee. Person called or summoned; one for whom another vouches.

Voucher. A receipt or release discharging a person or giving evidence of payment of a debt.

Vouch to Warranty. To call a person, under a warranty title, to defend a suit in which the voucher's title is attacked.

Vox Dei. Voice of God.

Voyage Policy. Policy insuring a ship's voyage on a specific course.

Vs. (Abb.). Versus.

Vulgo Concepti. Bastards.

W

Wager. Bet.

Wagering Contract. Gambling contract.

Wager of Law of Nonsummons. A form of plea in real action.

Wager Policy. An insurance policy wherein the person insured has no interest in the subject matter.

Wages. Compensation for manual labor.

Waifs. Goods found, but claimed by nobody.

Waive. To abandon or throw away; to surrender a claim or privilege voluntarily.

Waiver. Intentional relinquishment of a right or privilege.

Want of Issue. Having no children.

Wanton. Wilful; reckless; unrestrained; wicked.

Wanton Act. An act performed with reckless disregard for the rights of others.

Wanton Injury. Injury inflicted by conscious and intentional wrongful act or omission of duty with flagrant disregard for consequences.

War. Mutual hostility between two nations carried on by armed forces.

Warantia. Warranty; guaranty.

Warantus. Warrantor.

Ward. A minor under care of a guardian municipal district.

Warda. A ward; guard.

Warden. Guardian; prison superintendent.

Warehouse. Place for storage of goods.

Warentare. To warrant; to guarantee.

Wares. Goods and merchandise.

Warrant. Judicial writ authorizing the arrest of a person or the seizure of property; authorization for a policeman to search the premises of a private citizen; to defend; to guarantee.

Warantee. One to whom a warranty is made.

Warrant in Deed. A written warrant under seal.

Warrant in Law. Authority of law.

Warrant Officer. Noncommissioned officer of U.S. Navy.

Warrantor. Maker of a warranty.

Warranty. A promise or guaranty that a proposition of fact is true; a collateral undertaking in the sale of real or personal property whereby one party promises another to indemnify or make good any defect in the contemplation of the parties; a provision in an insurance policy making certain statements about the person or thing insured or about the risk insured.

Warranty of Goods. Warranty that goods are of a specified quality.

Warranty of Title. A warranty that title to property sold is good.

Warren. Game preserve.

Wash Sale. The operation of simultaneously buying and selling the same stock.

Wasserman Test. Test for syphilis.

Waste. Destruction or abuse of property.

Wastors. Thieves.

Water Company. A public utility to supply water to the inhabitants of a municipality.

Watered Stock. Stock of a corporation issued as paid in full, whereas the cash or property value of the stock has not in fact been received by the corporation in exchange.

Water Right. Right to the use of water from a running stream.

Waterscape. Aqueduct.

Way. Right of passage.

Way-Bill. List of passengers or freight transported by a common carrier.

Wayfarer. Traveler.

Ways and Means Committee. Committee of a legislative body which determines how necessary revenues are to be raised.

Weapon. Combat instrument.

Wedlock. Matrimoney.

Week. Period of seven days.

Weight. Measure of heaviness.

Weight of Evidence. Valuation made of the credibility of evidence based on its quality; the preponderance of evidence.

Welfare. State or condition of well-being.

Welsh Mortgage. Mortgage whereby the rents and profits of the mortgaged property go to the creditor until the debt is paid.

Wharf. Place for the loading and unloading of ships.

Wharfage. Charge for use of a wharf.

When. At the time that; at what time.

Whereby. By or through which.

Whiteacre. Term used to distinguish one parcel of land from another, particularly in moot cases.

White Person. Caucasian.

White Slavery. The procurement and transportation of women across state lines for immoral purposes.

Whole. Hearty; strong.

Whole Blood. Relationship of children who have the same parents.

Wholesale. Selling to retailers rather than consumers.

Wholesale Price. Price paid by the retailer.

Wholly. Entirely.

Whore. Woman who practices illicit sexual intercourse; prostitute.

Wick. Town; village.

Widow. Woman who survives her husband.

Widower. Man who survives his wife.

Wife. Woman who has a living husband.

Wild Land. Land in its natural state.

Wilful. Intentional; deliberate.

Wilful Desertion. In divorce, unjustifiable refusal to maintain the family relationship.

Will. Directions for the disposal of one's property after death.

Winding Up. Dissolution of a corporation or partnership.

Wire Tapping. Unauthorized interception of telephone conversations.

Wit. To know.

Wit. (Abb.). Witness.

With Child. Pregnant.

Withdrawal. Removal of money or securities from a bank.

Withold. To keep in one's possession that which is sought or claimed by another; to conceal.

Without Day. Without naming a special day.

Without Impeachment of Waste. Without liability for the commission of waste.

Without Notice. In good faith.

With Strong Hand. With force.

LEGAL DICT

Witness. One called to give testimony under oath; one present at a transaction; one who attests the genuineness of a document by offering his signature thereto.

Wittingly. With knowledge and by design.

Wolf's Head. Outlaw.

Woman Suffrage. Right of women to vote and participate in government.

Woods. Forest; land covered by trees.

Words, Act for. An action of slander.

Words Actionable in Themselves. Language from which the law would presume damage.

Words of Art. Words having a special or technical meaning.

Words of Limitation. Words used to define the character of an interest granted.

Words of Procreation. Words necessary to create an estate-tail.

Work. To put forth effort for a particular purpose.

Workhouse. Place where prisoners convicted of minor offenses are confined and kept at labor.

Working Capital. Cash or quick assets.

Workman. One who labors.

Workmen's Compensation Acts. Statutes which protect the working man and give security against injury and death occurring during the course of employment.

Works. An establishment for performing industrial labor.

World. All those who have an interest in the subject matter.

Worship. Paying respect to the Divine Being.

Worth. The quality of a thing, giving it value.

Worthless. Having no value.

Worthy. Having merit or value.

Wound. A physical injury which breaks the skin.

Wreck. To destroy or damage; unclaimed goods cast upon the shore by the sea; ship damaged so that it cannot be navigated.

Writ. Mandatory precept issued by a court of justice; a court order directing a party to do a specific act, usually to appear in or report to court.

Writing. Expression of ideas in visible form.

Writing Obligatory. A bond.

Writ of Attachment. A writ used to enforce a court order or judgment.

Writ of Covenant. Writ to recover damages for breach of a covenant.

Writ of Debt. Writ for recovery of a debt.

Writ of Delivery. A writ of execution to enforce a judgment for the delivery of chattels.

Writ of Entry. A real property possessory action to recover possession of property of which the claimant was wrongfully dispossessed.

Writ of Error. A writ used to review the judgment of an inferior court.

Writ of Error Coram Nobis. Writ of error used to correct errors of fact.

Writ of Execution. Writ to enforce the judgment of a court.

Writ of Injunction. A restraining or preventive court order.

Writ of Mandamus. A writ to compel the performance of an act.

Writ of Mandate. See Writ of Mandamus.

Writ of Possession. Writ of execution for the recovery of possession of land.

Writ of Prevention. Writ to prohibit filing of a suit.

Writ of Review. Writ to bring up for review the record or decision of an inferior court.

Writ of Right. Writ to recover real property.

Written Contract. A contract in writing signed by the parties involved.

Written Law. Statute law.

Wrong. Violation of a legal right; a legal injury; a tort.

Wrongful. Injurious; reckless; unfair.

X

X. Symbol of the word "by"; symbol used by those who cannot write.

X-Ray Photographs. Photographs of the interior body which may be submitted as evidence.

Y

Yacht. Pleasure boat.

Yard. Measure of three feet or thirty-six inches.

Yea or Nay. Yes and No.

Year. 365 days; leap year, 366 days.

Year and a Day. Period of limitation in which the right to seize and sell land under a judgment must be exercised.

Year of Our Lord. The beginning of the Christian era.

Yeas and Nays. The affirmative and negative votes on a bill or proposal.

Yellow Dog Contract. Contract between an employer and employee whereby the employee promises not to join a labor union.

Yen Pock. Opium pill.

Yield. Proceeds or returns from an investment; to produce; to earn; to perform; to resign or surrender.

Yielding and Paying. In conveyancing, the words which create the agreement to pay rent.

Z

Zealous Witness. One who shows partiality for the side calling him.

Zetetick. Proceeding by inquiry.

Zone. An area restricted by municipal regulation to certain purposes, i.e. residental industrial or commercial.

DICTIONARY
OF
SCIENTIFIC
TERMS

DICTIONARY OF
SCIENTIFIC TERMS

A

ab'acus: A term applied to various early forms of an instrument used for mechanically performing addition and subtraction.

abamu'rus (Build.): A supporting wall or buttress built to add strength to another wall.

aba'picul (Zool.): Situated at, or pertaining to, the lower pole: remote from the apex.

abatjour, ab-a-joor' (Build.): An opening to admit light, generally deflecting it downwards as a skylight.

abatvoix, ab-a-vwa' (Acous.): A sounding board over a rostrum or pulpit, to deflect speech downwards and in the direction of the listeners.

abaxial (Bot.): The side of a leaf, petal etc. which is farthest from the axis. (Zool.): Remote from the axis.

Abbe refractometer (Chem.): An instrument for measuring directly the refractive index of oils, etc.

abbreviated (Bot.): Shortened suddenly.

A. B. C. process (Sewage): A process of sewage treatment in which charcoal, blood, clay and alum are used as precipitants.

abdo'men (Zool.): In mammals, the region of the body, lying between the diaphragm and the pelvis, which contains the urinogenital and digestive organs.

abduction (Zool.): The action of pulling a limb or part away from the main axis.

abductor (Zool.): Any muscle that draws a limb or part away from the median axis.

aber'rant (Bot., Zool.): Showing some unusual difference of structure.

aberration (Astron.): An apparent change of position of a heavenly body, due to the velocity of light having a finite ratio to the relative velocity of the source and the observer. (Bot.): Some peculiarity of an individual plant not capable of transmission to offspring, and usually due to some special environmental condition.

abjection (Bot.): The forcible projection of spores from the sporophore.

ablation (Surg.): Removal of body tissue by surgical methods.

abnormal (Psychol.): Said of a person who is maladjusted to himself and/or to the outside world.

aboma'sum (Zool.): The true or fourth stomach in ruminant mammals. Also called rennet, reed.

abo'ral (Zool.): Leading away from or distant from the mouth.

abortifa'cient (Med.): Anything which causes artificial abortion.

abortion (Med.): Expulsion of the foetus from the uterus during the first three months of pregnancy. May be induced or spontaneous. (Bot.): A state of incomplete development, or the product of such defective development. (Zool.): Cessation of development in a foetus or in an organ.

abran'chiate (Zool.): Lacking gills.

abrasion: A rubbing away.

abrasive (Chem.): A substance used for the removal of matter by grinding and scratching.

Abney level (Surv.): A particular form of reflecting level, devised for the measurement of vertical angles.

abreac'tion (Psycho-an.): A release of blocked psychic energy attached to repressed and forgotten memories and phantasies; effected by living through these in action or feeling.

abscess (Med.): Pus localised in infected tissue and separated from healthy tissue by an abscess wall.

absciss layer (Bot.): A layer of parenchymatous cells across the base of a petiole or a branch, or embedded in bark, through which the scale of bark, the branch or leaf, separates off.

absolute potential (Chem.): The true potential difference between a metal and a solution.

absolute pressure (Phys.): Pressure measured with respect to zero pressure, in units of force per unit of area.

absolute transpirations (Bot.): The rate of loss of water from a plant, as determined by experiment.

absolute weight (Chem.): The weight of a body in a vacuum.

absorber (Nucleonics): Material for capturing neutrons without generating more neutrons.

absorptiom'eter (Chem.): An apparatus for determining the solubilities of gases in liquids.

abutment (Eng.): A surface or point provided to withstand thrust; e.g. the end supports of a bridge or an arch.

abys'sal, abys'mal (Ocean.): Relating to the greatest depths of the ocean.

A. C. (Elec. Eng.): Abbreviations for alternating current.

acana'ceous (Bot.): A general term for prickly.

acan'tha (Bot.): A spine or prickle.

acantho'sis ni'gricans (Med.): A condition in which warty pigmented growths appear on the surface of the body.

acap'nia (Med.): Excessive diminution of carbon dioxide in the blood.

ac'arus (Biol.): A mite.

a'cauline, a'caulose (Bot.): Stemless or nearly so.

acceleration (Mech.): The rate of change of velocity, expressed in feet or centimetres per second.

accelerator (Nucleonics): Any device for accelerating to high kinetic energy protons, electrons, deuterons and helium ions.

accelerator (Bot.): Any substance which increases the efficient action of an enzyme. (Chem.): A substance which increases the speed of a chemical reaction. (Automobiles): A pedal connected to the carburetor throttle valve of a motor vehicle, or to the fuel injection control where oil engines are used. (Zool.): Any nerve or muscle which increases rate of action.

accelerom'eter (Aero.): An instrument carried in aircraft for measuring acceleration in a specific direction.

accentuation (Photog.) : High-lights or high contrasts in the composition of a photographic picture.

acceptor (Chem.) : (1) The reactant in an induced reaction which does not react directly with the inductor. (2) The atom which contributes no electrons to a semi-polar bond.

accesso'rius (Zool.) : A muscle which supplements the action of another muscle : in Vertebrates, the eleventh cranial nerve or spinal accessory.

acclimatisation (Chem.) : The change produced in a colloidal sol by the addition of a precipitating agent in small quantities, resulting in less complete precipitation for the addition of a given total amount of precipitant.

accommodation (Bot.) : The capacity possessed by a plant to adjust itself to new conditions of life, provided the changed conditions come gradually into operation. (Physiol.) : The ability of the eye to change its effective focal length in order to see objects distinctly at varying distances.

accouplement (Carp.) : A tie or brace of timber.

accres'cent (Bot.) : Enlarged ; usually applied to a calyx which increases in size as the fruit ripens.

accretion (Zool.) : External addition of new matter : growth by such external addition.

accuracy : Implies exactitude in measurement.

A.C.E. mixture (Med.) : A common general anaesthetic, containing 1 part of alcohol, 2 parts of chloroform and 3 parts of ether.

aceph'alous (Bot.) : Said of a style which does not terminate in a well-marked stigma.

acerose, acerous (Bot.) : Needle-shaped.

acetates (Chem.) : The salts of acetic acid ; e.g. sodium acetate.

acetic acid (Chem.) : $CH_3 \bullet COOH$, an important raw material of the chemical industry, synthesised from acetylene ; also obtained by the oxidation of alcohol and by the destructive distillation of wood.

achala'sia (Med.) : Failure to relax.

achene, akene, achae'nocarp (Bot.) : A small, dry, one-seeded fruit which ripens without bursting its thin outer sheath or pericarp.

achlorhy'dria (Med.) : Absence of hydrochloric acid from the gastric juice.

achon'drite (Geol.) : A type of stony meteorite which compares with some basic igneous rocks ; e.g. eucrite.

achon'dropla'sia (Med.) : A condition of dwarfism characterised by shortness of the legs and the arms and by a big head.

achondroplas'tic (Zool.) : Having a normal body with stunted limbs or appendages.

achro'matin (Cyt.) : That part of the nucleus which does not stain with basic dyes.

acic'ular (Bot., Zool.) : Stiff, pointed and slender, like a pine needle.

acic'ulate (Bot.) : Marked on the surface by fine scratches.

acid (Chem.) : (1) A substance which tends to lose a proton. (2) A substance containing hydrogen which may be replaced by metals with the formation of salts. (3) A substance which dissolves in water with the formation of hydrogen ions.

acid solution (Chem.) : An aqueous solution containing more hydrogen ions than hydroxye ions ; one which turns blue litmus red.

acid'ophil (Zool.) : Said of structures which stain intensely with acid dyes.

acina'ceous (Bot.) : Full of pips.

acinaciform (Bot.) : Scimitar-shaped.

ac'me (Biol.) : The period of maximum vigor of an individual, race or species.

ac'ne (Med.) : Inflammation of a sebaceous gland. Pimples in adolescents are commonly due to infection with the acne bacillus.

acoustics : The science of sounds.

acre (Surv.) : A unit of area equal to 4,840 square yards.

acrocar'pons (Bot.) : Having fruit at the end of the stem or branch.

acrodro'mous (Bot.) : Said of venation when the main

veins, after running parallel along most of the leaf, unite at the leaf apex.

ac'ron (Zool.) : In insects, the region in front of the mouth.

acti'noid (Zool.) : Star-shaped.

acti'nomere (Zool.) : A radial segment.

action (Acous.) : The mechanism for selecting notes in musical instruments.

activity (Nucleonics) : Rate of breakdown of atoms through radioactivity.

acu'leate (Bot.) : Bearing prickles, or covered with needle-like outgrowths.

acute (Bot.) : Bearing a sharp and abrupt point ; said usually of a leaf-tip. (Med.) : Said of a disease which rapidly develops to a crisis.

acy'clic (Bot.) : Having the parts of the flower arranged in spirals.

adaptation (Bot.) : Any morphological or physiological characteristic which may be supported to help in adjusting the organism to the conditions under which it lives. (Zool.) : The process by which an animal becomes fitted to its environment.

adapter (Elec. Eng.) : An accessory used in electrical installations for connecting a piece of apparatus fitted with one type of terminals to a supply-point fitted with another size.

addict (Med.) : One who is unable to resist taking harmful drugs.

adductor (Zool.) : A muscle that draws a limb or part inwards, or towards another part.

adelomor'phic (Zool.) : Of indefinite form.

adeni'tis (Med.) : Inflammation of a gland.

adhesion (Elec.) : The mutual force which tends to hold two electrified non-conducting bodies together. (Med.) : Abnormal union of two parts which have been inflamed.

a'biabat'ic (Bot.) : Not capable of translocation. (Phys.) : Without gain or loss of heat.

adit (Civ. Eng.) : An access tunnel, that is usually nearly horizontal, leading to a main tunnel.

adjustor (Zool.) : An organ or faculty determining the behavior of an organism in response to stimuli received.

adj'utage (Hyd.) : A tube or nozzle through which water is discharged.

adj'uvant (Med.) : A remedy which assists the action of other remedies.

adnexa (Anat.) : Appendages ; usually refers to Fallopian tubes and ovaries.

ado'ral (Zool.) : Adjacent to the mouth.

adpressed, appressed (Bot.) : Pressed closely together but not joined.

adre'nal (Zool.) : Adjacent to the kidney.

adsorption (Chem.) : The taking up of one substance at the surface of another.

adulares'cence (Min.) : A milky or bluish sheen in gemstones.

advection (Meteor.) : The transference of heat by horizontal motion of the air.

adven'tive (Bot.) : Denotes a plant which has not secured a permanent foothold in a given locality.

aeolotro'pic (Phys.) : Having physical properties which vary according to the position or direction in which they are measured.

aerial (Radio) : Any exposed wire capable of radiating or receiving the energy to or from an electromagnetic wave.

aer'obe, aerobi'ont (Bot.) : A plant which requires elementary oxygen for respiration.

aerodynam'ics (Aero.) : That part of the mechanics of fluids that deals with the dynamics of gases. Primarily, the study of forces acting upon bodies in motion in air.

aero-engine (Aero.) : The power unit of an aircraft.

aer'olites (Geol.) : A general name for stony as distinct from iron meteorites.

aerol'ogy (Aero.) : The study of the upper air, that part of the atmosphere removed from the effect of surface conditions.

aeronautical engineering: That branch of engineering concerned with the design, production and maintenance of aircraft structures and power units.

aeronautics: All activities concerned with aerial locomotion.

aeroph'agy (Med.): The swallowing of air, with consequent inflation of the stomach.

aeroplane (Aero.): Any power-driven heavier-than-air flying machine with fixed wings.

aer'ostat (Aero.): Any form of aircraft deriving support in the air primarily from its buoyancy.

aes'tival (Bot., Zool.): Occurring in summer.

aestivation (Bot.): The arrangement of the sepals and petals.

aetiology, etiol'ogy (Med.): The medical study of the causation of disease.

afeb'rile (Med.): Without symptoms or signs of fever.

af'fect (Psychol.): The degree of pleasantness or unpleasantness accompanying any emotional state.

affinity (Bot.): Likeness, especially in relationships.

agalac'tia, agala'cia (Med.): Failure of the breast to secrete milk.

agamic (Bot.): Said of reproduction without the co-operation of a male gamete.

agam'ogen'esis (Bot., Zool.): Asexual reproduction.

agamotro'pic (Bot.): Said of a flower which does not shut after having once opened.

agar'ic (Bot.): A mushroom or toadstool.

agene'sia, agen'esis (Med.): Imperfect development or failure to develop of any part of the body.

age'otro'pism (Bot.): The condition of not reacting to gravity.

agglomerate (Bot.): Crowded or heaped into a cluster.

agglutinate (Bot.): Cemented together by sticky material.

aggregate (Bot.): Closely packed but not confluent. (Zool.): Massed or clustered. (Geol., Min.): A mass consisting of rock or mineral fragments.

aggressiveness (Bot.): The capacity of a parasite to attack its host.

aglos'sate, aglos'sal (Zool.): Lacking a tongue.

agno'sia (Med.): Loss of the ability to recognize the nature of an object through the senses of the body.

ag'orapho'bia (Psychol.): The fear of being alone in an open space.

agraph'ia (Med.): Loss of the power to express thought in writing, as a result of a lesion in the brain.

agres'tal (Bot.): Growing in cultivated ground, but not itself cultivated; e.g. a weed.

agrostol'ogy (Bot.): The study of grasses.

air-cooling (Eng.): The cooling of hot bodies by means of a stream of cold air, as distinct from water-cooling.

air brake (Aero.): An extendable device to increase the drag of an aircraft.

air-drain (Build.): A cavity in the external walls of a building, designed to prevent damp from getting through to the interior.

aircraft (Aero.): All air-supported vehicles.

air ducts (Eng.): Pipes or channels through which air is distributed throughout buildings for heating and ventilation.

airflow meter (Aero.): An instrument for measuring the airflow in ducts.

air gate (Eng.): A passage from the interior of a mold to allow the escape of air and gases as the metal is poured in.

air log (Aero.): An instrument for registering the distance travelled by an aircraft relative to the air.

air pocket (Aero.): A colloquialism for a localized region of low air density, a rising or descending air current.

air speed (Aero.): Speed measured relative to the air in which the aircraft is moving, as distinct from speed relative to the ground.

akine'sia (Med.): A disinclination to move, as a result of a brain lesion.

a'lar (Zool.): Pertaining to wings.

al'binism (Bot.): An abnormal condition due to the absence of chlorophyll or other pigments. (Zool.): Absence of pigmentation especially marked in the skin, epidermal outgrowths and the eyes.

albu'men (Zool.): White of an egg.

alex'ia (Med.): Loss of the ability to interpret written language, due to a brain lesion.

Algae (Bot.): A large group of simple organisms, mostly aquatic. They contain chlorophyll and/or other photosynthetic pigments and have simple organized reproductive organs.

algebra (Maths.): The abstract investigation of the properties of numbers by means of symbols; e.g. x, y, etc.

algesim'eter (Med.): An instrument for measuring sensitivity to pain.

alignment (Civ. Eng.): A setting in line, usually straight.

alimentary: Pertaining to the nutritive functions or organs.

alinentary canal (Zool.): The digestive tract.

al'kali (Chem.): A substance which dissolves in water to form an alkaline solution, especially the sodium and potassium hydroxides.

alkaline solution (Chem.): An aqueous solution containing more hydroxyl ions than hydrogen ions; one which turns red litmus blue.

aller'gy (Med.): A state in which the cells of the body are supersensitive to substances.

allette (Build.): A wing of a building or a buttress.

allocar'py (Bot.): Fruiting after cross-fertilization.

allom'eric (Chem.): Having the same crystalline form but a different chemical composition.

allomor'phous (Chem.): Having the same chemical composition but a different crystalline form.

allotro'pous flower (Bot.): A flower in which the nectar is readily accessible to all kinds of visiting insects.

alloy (Chem.): Any metal other than a pure metallic element. (Met.): Metal prepared by adding other metals or non-metals to a basic metal to obtain desirable properties.

alopecia (Med.): Baldness.

alternate (Bot.): Said of leaves and branches which are placed singly on the parent axis; not opposite.

alternating current (Elec. Eng.): An electric current the direction of flow of which alternates in direction.

altri'ces (Zool.): Birds whose young are hatched in a very immature condition.

alu'minum (Met.): Light ductile metal with high electrical conductivity and good resistance to corrosion.

amal'gam (Chem.): The solution of a metal in mercury.

amaweo'sis (Med.): Blindness due to a lesion of the optic nerve, the retina, or optic tracts, or to hysteria.

ama'zia (Med.): Non-development of the female mammary glands.

am'bergris (Zool.): A grayish fatty substance obtained from the intestines of diseased sperm whales; used as a fixative in perfumery.

am'bient (Biol.): Environmental.

ambiva'lence (Psychol.): The co-existence, in one person, of opposing emotional attitudes, as love and hate, towards the same object.

ambula'tory (Zool.): Having the power of walking.

amelification (Zool.): The formation of enamel.

amenorrhoe'a (Med.): Suppression or absence of menstruation.

amenta'ceous (Bot.): Bearing catkins.

am'ntia (Med.): Mental deficiency.

amito'sis, amitot'ic division (Cyt.): Direct nuclear division.

am'meter (Elec. Eng.): An indicating instrument for measuring the current in an electric circuit.

am'modyte (Bot.): A plant living in sandy places.

amne'sia (Med.): Loss of memory.

amoe'ba (Zool.): A form of primitive Protozoon of indeterminate shape.

ampere (Elec. Eng.): The most frequently used unit of current.

amphibian (Aero.): Aeroplane capable of taking off

and landing on land or water.

amphibious (Zool.) : Adapted for life on land or in the water.

amphicar'pic (Bot.) : Having two kinds of fruits.

amphig'ony (Zool.) : Reproduction by fertilization.

amphilep'sis (Gen.) : Inheritance such that the offspring has characteristics derived from both parents.

amphitheatre (Build.) : An oval or circular building in which the spectators' seats surround the arena in which the spectacle is presented, the seats rising away from the arena.

amphoter'ic (Chem.) : Having both basic and acidic properties.

amplitude (Phys.) : The maximum value of a periodically varying quantity during a cycle.

ampoule (Med.) : A small, sealed glass capsule for holding measured quantities of serums, drugs, vaccines etc., ready for use.

amyg'dale, amyg'dule (Geol.) : An almond-shaped infilling by secondary minerals of elongated steam cavities in igneous rocks.

amyla'ceous (Bot.) : Starchy.

anabat'ic (Meteor.) : A term applied to winds caused by the upward convection of heated air.

anae'mia, ane'mia (Med.) : Diminution of the amount of hemoglobin in the blood, from lowering of the quality or the quantity of the red blood cells.

anesthe'sia (Med.) : Loss of sensibility to touch.

anesthet'ic (Med.) : A drug which produces insensibility to touch, temperature and pain, with or without loss of consciousness.

anesthetist : One skilled in the administration of an anesthetic drug.

analep'tic (Med.) : A drug or medicine that strengthens.

analge'sia (Med.) : Loss of sensibility to pain.

analogy (Bot., Zool.) : Likeness in function but not in origin.

analysis (Struct.) : The process of reducing a problem to its primary parts.

anamne'sis (Med.) : The past history of all matters relating to a patients' health.

anamor'pha (Zool.) : Larvae which do not possess the full number of segments at the time of hatching.

anas'tral (Cyt.) : Without asters.

anatomy (Bot., Zool., etc.) : The study of the form and structure of animals and plants.

anax'ial (Zool.) : Asymmetrical.

an'con (Arch.) : A console built on each side of a door-opening to carry a cornice.

anconeal (Zool.) : Pertaining to, or situated near, the elbow.

andiron (Build.) : A metal support for wood in an open fire.

an'drocyte (Bot.) : A sperm mother-cell.

androdivecious (Bot.) : Said of a species in which some of the plants bear staminate flowers, other hermaphrodite flowers.

androgen'esis (Bot., Zool.) : Development from a male cell.

androl'ogy (Med.) : That branch of medical science which deals with the functions and diseases peculiar to the male sex.

anemom'eter (Meteor.) : An instrument for measuring the velocity of the wind.

ane'mophily (Bot.) : Pollination by means of the wind.

an'emotro'pism (Biol.) : Active response to the stimulus of an air current.

anenceph'aly (Med.) : Developmental defect of the skull and absence of the brain.

anen'terous (Zool.) : Without a gut.

an'er (Zool.) : A male ant.

aneroid barometer (Meteor., Surv.) : A portable instrument for the recording of changes in atmospheric pressure and for the approximate determination of altitude.

Angiosper'mae (Bot.) : A major group of flowering plants in which the seeds develop and ripen inside a closed ovary.

angle : The inclination of one line to another, measured in degrees, of which there are 360 to one complete revolution.

angle bar, angle iron, angle steel (Eng.) : Mild steel bar rolled to the cross-section of the letter L, much used for light structural work.

angle-bead (Build.) : A small round molding placed at an external angle formed by plastered surfaces in order to preserve the corner from accidental fracture.

angle block (Carp.) : A small wooden block used in woodwork to make joints more rigid, especially right angle joints.

angle-board (Carp.) : One used as a gauge by which to plane boards to a required angle between two faces.

angle brace (Carp.) : (1) Any bar fixed across the inside of an angle in a framework in order to make the latter more rigid. (2) A special tool for drilling in corners where there is not room to use the cranked handle of an ordinary brace.

angle-closer (Build.) : A portion of a whole brick, used to close up the bond of brickwork at corners.

angle of contact (Phys.) : The angle made by the surface separating two fluids (one of them usually air) with the wall of the containing vessel or with any other solid surface cutting the fluid surface.

angle of depression (Surv.) : The vertical angle measured below the horizontal from the surveyors's instrument to the point observed.

angle of elevation (Surv.) : The vertical angle measured above the horizontal, from the surveyor's instrument to the point observed.

angle of incidence, angle of reflection (Acous.) : Respectively, the angle with which a beam of sound arrives at a surface, and the angle with which it leaves after reflection, the angle being measured with respect to the normal at the point of incidence.

angle plate (Eng.) : A bracket used to support work on a lathe faceplate or other machine-tool.

anglesite (Min.) : A common lead ore.

Angström unit (Phys.) : The unit employed for expressing wave lengths of light, X-rays, and ultraviolet radiations.

angular diameter (Astron.) : The angle which the apparent diameter of a heavenly body subtends at the observer's eye.

angular velocity (Phys.) : The rate of change of angular displacement, usually expressed in radians per second.

anhidro'sis (Med.) : Diminution of the secretion of sweat.

anhy'drides (Chem.) : Substances which either combine with water to form acids, or which may be obtained from the latter by the elimination of water.

an'ima (Analytical Psychol.) : Term used in Jungian psychology to denote the unconscious feminine component of a male personality.

animal charcoal (Chem.) : The carbon residue obtained from the carbonization of organic matter as flesh, blood, etc.

an'imus (Analytical Psychol.) : A Jungian term denoting the unconscious masculine component of a female personality.

annealing : General term denoting heating followed by slow cooling.

annoyance (Acous.) : The psychological effect arising from excessive noise.

annual (Bot.) : A plant which, in the same season that it develops from a seed, flowers, fruits, and dies.

annual equation (Astron.) : One of the four principal periodic terms in the mathematical expression of the moon's orbital motion.

annual ring (Bot.) : One of the circular bands seen when a branch or trunk is cut across ; the band is a section of the cylinder of secondary wood added in one season of growth.

annular (Bot.) : Having the form of a ring.

annular eclipse (Astron.) : A central eclipse of the sun, in which the moon's disc does not completely cover the sun's disc at the moment of greatest eclipse but leaves a ring of the solar surface visible.

an'ode (Elec.): The positive electrode of an electrolytic cell.

anodon'tia: Absence of teeth.

an'olyte (Elec. Eng.): That part of the electrolyte of an electrolytic cell which is near the anode.

anomaly: Any departure from the strict characteristics of the type.

anorex'ia (Med.): Loss of appetite.

anosmat'ic (Zool.): Lacking the sense of smell.

anox'ia, anoxe'mia (Med., Zool.): Deficiency of oxygen in the blood.

antagonist (Physiol.): A muscle which opposes the action of another muscle.

antenna (Radio): An elevated or extended system of conductors used for the transmission and/or reception of electromagnetic waves. (Zool.): One of a pair of anterior appendages, usually many jointed and of sensory function.

ante-sola'rium (Build.): A balcony which faces the sun.

anther (Bot.): The fertile part of a stamen.

an'thophore (Bot.): An elongation of the floral receptacle between the calyx and the corolla.

anthoxanthin (Bot.): Yellow pigment in flowers.

anthacite coals (Fuels): Slow burning coals, yielding little ash, moisture and volatiles.

anthraco'sis (Med.): "Coal-miners' lung," produced by inhalation of coal dust.

an'tibody (Bacteriol.): Specific substances liberated into the plasma in response to the presence of bacteria and their toxins, and antagonistic to them.

anticathode (Phys., Radiol.): The anode target of an X-ray tube on which the cathode rays are focused, and from which the X-rays are emitted.

anticline (Geol.): A type of fold, the strata dipping outwards, away from the fold-axis.

anticy'clone (Meteor.): A distribution of atmospheric pressure in which the pressure increases towards the center.

an'tigen (Med.): Any bacterium, toxin or other vegetable or animal substance which, introduced into the body, gives rise to an antibody.

an'timony (Met.): A white metallic element with a bluish tinge.

antinode (Phys.): A point of maximum amplitude in a system of stationary waves.

anti-neutron (Nucleonics): Recently discovered particle which can mutually annihilate a neutron, with the evolution of vast energy.

antisep'sis (Med.): The inhibition of growth, or the destruction, of bacteria in the field of operation by chemical agents.

antiseptic (Med.): An agent which destroys bacteria or prevents their growth.

antithrom'bin (Chem.): An anti-enzyme, produced by the liver, preventing the intravascular clotting of the blood.

antitox'ins (Path.): Substances, produced by the organism, which, by uniting with toxins, prevent their poisonous action.

antler (Zool.): In deer, the annual outgrowth of bony material from the frontal bone.

antrorse (Zool.): Directed or bent forwards.

anu'ral (Zool.): Without a tail.

anu'ria (Med.): Suppression of the secretion of urine.

a'nus (Zool.): The opening of the alimentary canal by which indigestible residues are voided, generally posterior.

anvil (Anat.): One of the three small bones which transmit mechanical vibrations between the outer ear drum and the inner ear. (Eng.): A block of iron on which work is supported during forging.

anvil cloud (Meteor.): A common feature of a thundercloud, consisting of a wedge-shaped projection of cloud suggesting the point of an anvil.

anxiety (Psychol.): A state of mental apprehension and tension.

aor'ta (Zool.): The main arterial vessel or vessels by which blood leaves the heart and passes to the body.

ap'atite (Min.): Naturally occurring phosphate of calcium, widely distributed in igneous rock.

aperiodic (Acous., Elec.): Said of any potentially vibrating system which, because of sufficient damping, does not vibrate when impulsed.

apeture (Build.): An opening provided in a wall for ventilation purposes.

apex: The top or pointed end of anything.

apha'sia (Med.): Loss of, or defect in, the faculty of expressing thought in words.

aphonia (Med.): Loss of voice in hysteria, laryngitis, or in paralysis of the vocal cords.

apho'tic (Bot.): Able to grow with little or no light.

Apjohn's formula (Phys.): A formula which may be used for determining the pressure of water vapor in the air from readings of the dry and wet bulb hygrometer.

apla'sia (Med.): Defective structural development.

apneu'sis (Physiol.): Want of oxygen.

apo'dal, apo'dous (Zool.): Without feet.

ap'ogee (Astron.): The point farthest from the earth on the apse line of a central orbit having the earth as a focus.

ap'ogeny (Bot.): Sterility.

apomecom'eter (Surv.): An instrument which may be used to measure the height of trees, buildings, etc.

apopet'alous (Bot.): Lacking petals.

ap'oplexy (Med.): Sudden loss of consciousness and paralysis as a result of thrombosis of a cerebral artery or of hemorrhage into the brain.

appendage: A general term for any external outgrowth; as fins, limbs, etc.

appendix (Zool.): An outgrowth.

applaus'eograph (Acous.): A recording noise-meter, suitable for recording applause in a theatre.

approach (Civ. Eng.): The access road leading to a tunnel or bridge.

apron (Aero.): A firm surface laid down adjacent to aerodrome buildings to facilitate the movements, loading and unloading, of airplanes.

apt'erous (Zool.): Without wings.

apty'alism (Med.): Deficiency or absence of salivary secretion.

apyrex'ia (Med.): Absence of fever.

aquamarine (Min.): A variety of beryl, of blue-green color, used as a gemstone.

aqueduct (Civ. Eng.): An artificial conduit used to convey water.

aqueous: Made of, or pertaining to, water.

arachnid'ium (Zool.): The spinnerets and silk glands in spiders.

arach'noid (Bot., Zool.): Cobweb-like.

arc: A portion of a circle. (Elec.): A luminous discharge of electricity through an ionised gas.

arch (Civ. Eng.): A form of structure having a curved shape, used to support loads or to resist pressure.

Archimedes' principle (Phys.): When a body is wholly or partly immersed in a fluid, it suffers a loss in weight equal to the weight of fluid which it displaces.

architectural acoustics (Acous.): The study of the propagation of sound-waves in interiors.

ar'chitype (Zool.): A primitive type from which others may be derived.

archoplasmic apparatus (Cyt.): In cell-division, the asters, and the spindle-shaped bundle of fibers between them.

arc'uate (Bot., Zool.): Bent like a bow.

are (Surv.): The metric unit of area. 1 are = 119.6 sq. yds.

arena'ceous (Bot.): Growing best in sandy soil.

a'reopyknom'eter (Chem.): An instrument for the measurement of the specific gravity of viscous liquids.

ar'gentite (Min.): An important silver ore.

argilla'ceous rocks (Geol.): Sedimentary rocks of the clay grade.

argument (Maths.): The angle between a vector and its reference axis.

ar'istate (Bot.): Bearing a beard or awn.

arithmetic: The science of numbers.

armature (Elec.): A moving part in a magnetic circuit to indicate the presence of electric current as the agent of actuation.

arrhi'zal (Bot.): Lacking roots.

arrhyth'mia (Med.): Abnormal rhythm of the heart beat.

arrow (Surv.): The steel pin, looped at one end and pointed at the other, used to mark in the field the end of a chain.

arrowroot: Starch derived from the roots of plants of the maranta genus.

ar'senic (Chem.): An element which occurs in a large number of minerals. Symbol As.

ar'tefact: A man-made stone implement.

arte'rioscle'rosis (Med.): Hardening or stiffening of the arteries.

artery (Zool.): One of the vessels of the vascular system, that conveys the blood from the heart to the body.

arthri'tis (Med.): Inflammation of a joint.

arthro'dia (Zool.): A joint.

article (Bot.): A joint of a stem or fruit, breaking apart at maturity.

articulation (Eng.): The connection of two parts in such a way as to permit the same relative movements. (Zool.): The movable or immovable connection between two or more bones.

artiodac'tyl (Zool.): Possessing an even number of digits.

asexual (Bot., Zool.): Without sex.

asphalt: The name given to various bituminous substances.

asphyxia (Med.): State of suspended animation as a result of deficiency of oxygen in the blood.

aspirator (Chem.): A device for draining a stream of liquids or air through an apparatus by suction.

assimilation (Zool.): The conversion of food material into protoplasm.

aster (Cyt.): A group of radiating fibrils formed of cytoplasmic granules surrounding the centrosome, seen immediately prior to and during cell-division.

asteroid (Astron.): A small planetary body.

asthe'nic type (Psychol.): One of Kretschmer's three types of individuals, characterized by tall thin men, with hands long in proportion to the trunk.

asthma (Med.): A disorder in which there occur attacks of difficult breathing due to spasm of 'the bronchial muscles.

ast'roid (Cyt.): In cell division, the star-shaped figure formed by the looped chromosomes aggregated around the equator of the nuclear spindle.

as'trolabe (Astron.): In ancient Greece, a circular instrument for stellar observation.

astrology: The pseudo science which treats of the influences of the stars upon human affairs, and of foretelling terrestrial events by their aspects and positions.

astronomy: The science of the heavens in all its branches.

astrophysics: That branch of astronomy which applies the laws of physics to the study of interstellar matter and the stars.

astyl'len (Civ. Eng.): A small dam built across an adit to restrict the flow of water.

asymmetric: Irregular in form; not divisible into halves.

at'avism (Gen.): The recurrence, in a descendant, of characters of a remote ancestor, as a great-grandparent.

ataxia (Med.): Inco-ordination of muscles.

a'telomit'ic (Cyt.): Said of a chromosome having the spindle fibre attached somewhere along the side.

athletic type (Psychol.): One of Kretschmer's three types of individual, characterized by a well-developed skeletal musculature, in which the relation of limbs to trunk is well-proportioned.

atmosphere, pressure of (Phys.): The pressure exerted by the atmosphere at the surface of the earth is due to the weight of the air.

atmospheric electricity (Meteor.): The electric charges which exist in the atmosphere.

at'olls: Coral reefs.

atom (Chem.): The smallest particle of an element which can take part in a chemical reaction.

atom'ic (Chem.): Pertaining to an atom or atoms.

atomic mass (Phys.): The mass of an atom.

atomic number (Phys.): The number of an element when arranged with others in order of increasing atomic weight.

atomic weight (Chem.): The relative weight of an atom of an element when the weight of an atom of oxygen is taken as 16.000.

atomicity (Chem.): The number of atoms contained in a molecule of an element.

at'omiser (Eng.): A nozzle through which oil fuel is sprayed into the combustion chamber of an oil engine or boiler furnace.

at'rophy (Med.): Wasting of a cell or of an organ of the body.

attenuate (Bot.): Narrowing gradually to a point.

attenuation (Bot.): A weakening by parasitic bacteria and fungi in culture.

attracted-disc electrometer (Elec. Eng.): An instrument in which potential is measured by the attraction between two oppositely charged discs.

attrition test (Civ. Eng.): A test for the determination of the wear-resisting properties of stone.

audibility (Acous.): Ability to be heard.

audiom'eter (Acous.): An electrical apparatus for measuring the minimum intensities of sounds perceivable by an ear, for specified frequencies.

auditory, aural (Zool.): Pertaining to the sense of hearing.

aug'er (Carp., Civ. Eng.): A tool used for boring holes.

aur'eole (Meteor.): (1) The clear transparent space between the sun or moon and a halo or corona. (2) The bright indefinite ring around the sun in the absence of clouds.

Auro'ra Borea'lis (Astron.): The Northern Lights, a phenomenon consisting of luminous arcs.

Australasian region (Zool.): One of the primary faunal regions into which the land surface of the globe is divided.

aut'ocarp (Bot.): A fruit resulting from self-fertilization.

autoclave (Chem.): A vessel for carrying out chemical reactions under pressure and at high temperatures.

autog'amy (Bot., Zool.): Self-fertilization.

auto-infection (Zool.): Re-infection of a host by its own parasites.

auto-intoxication (Med.): Poisoning of the body by toxins produced in it.

automatic digital computer (Maths.): Electronic calculating machine using conventional arithmetical digits.

automatic pilot (Aero.): A device for guiding and controlling an aircraft on a given path.

automation: Industrial technique in which the whole of a manufacturing process is performed automatically under electronic control.

autonomic, auton'omous (Bot., Zool.): Self-regulating, independent.

autoph'agous (Zool.): Capable of self-feeding from birth.

aut'ophyte (Bot.): A plant which builds up its food substances from simple compounds.

auxe'tic (Zool.): Stimulating cell-division.

awl (Carp.): A small pointed tool for making holes which are to receive screws or nails.

awn (Bot.): A long bristle borne on some cereals and grasses.

axil (Bot.): The solid angle between a stem and the upper surface of a leaf base growing from it.

axis (Aero.): The three axes of an aircraft are the straight lines through the center of gravity about which change of altitude occurs.

axis: A line, usually imaginary, which has a peculiar importance in relation to a particular set of circumstances.

axle (Eng.): The cross-shaft or beam which carries the wheel of a vehicle.

B

bacil'lus (Bacteriol.): A rod-shaped member of bacteria.

backlash (Eng.): The lost motion between two elements of a mechanism.

backing (Meteor.): The changing of a wind into a counter-clockwise direction.

bacteria (Bacteriol.): A large group of unicellular or filamentous microscopic organisms, lacking chlorophyll and well-defined nuclei, multiplying rapidly by simple fissure.

bacteriology: The scientific study of bacteria.

bacte'rium (Bacteriol.): A rod-shaped member of bacteria.

badger (Build.): An implement used to clear mortar from a drain after it has been laid.

baffle (Acous.): A rigid structure for regulating the distribution of sound-waves from a reproducer.

baffle plate (Eng.): A plate used to prevent the movement of a fluid in the direction in which it would normally flow, and to direct it into the desired path.

baffle tube: A pipe of sufficient length to lower the temperature of hot gases before they enter a furnace.

balance: Equilibrium of the body.

balcony (Build.): A projecting platform, either inside or outside a building.

baleen' (Zool.): In certain whales, horny plates arising from the mucous membrane of the palate, and acting as a food strainer.

ball-pane hammer (Eng.): A hammer, the head of which has a flat face at one end, and a smaller hemispherical face at the other.

ballis'tics (Mech.): The science of projectiles.

balloon (Aero.): A general term for aircraft supported by buoyancy and not driven mechanically.

balsa wood (Acous.): A highly porous wood valued for its lightness.

baluster (Build.): A small pillar supporting the handrail of a staircase.

band: A transverse marking broader than a line.

banker (Build.): A bench upon which bricklayers and stonemasons shape their material.

banking (Aero.): Angular displacement of the wings of an airplane about the longitudinal axis, to cause turning.

bar (Civ Eng.): A deposit of sand or gravel in a river or across the mouth of a river. (Eng.): Material of uniform cross-section which may be extruded or rolled.

barb (Bot.): A hooked hair-like bristle. (Zool.): One of delicate thread-like structures extending obliquely from a feather rachis, and forming the vane.

barbate (Zool.): Bearded.

barbel (Zool.): A tactile process arising from the head of various fishes.

bark (Bot.): The external group of tissues, from the cambrium outwards, of a woody stem.

bar'nacle (Zool.): A crustacean.

barometer (Meteor.): An instrument used for the measurement of atmospheric pressure.

barophore'sis (Chem.): Diffusion of suspended particles at a speed dependent on extraneous forces.

baroscope (Meteor.): An instrument giving rough indications of changes in atmospheric pressure.

barren (Bot.): Infertile.

barysphere: The solid heavy interior core of the earth inside the lithosphere.

bas relief (Arch.): Sculpture in which the figures project their true proportions from the surface on which they are carved.

basal (Bot.): At, or near the base.

basal metabolic rate (Zool.): The rate of oxygen consumption in a resting organism or organ.

bas'alt (Geol.): A fine-grained, dark colored igneous rock.

base (Bot.): That end of a plant member nearest to the point of attachment to another member. (Chem.): A substance which tends to gain a proton.

base bullion (Met.): Impure lead.

base line (Surv.): A survey line the length of which is accurately measured.

ba'seost (Zool.): One of the distal elements of a fin-ray in fish.

basichro'matin (Cyt.): A form of chromatin which stains relatively deeply.

basicity (Chem.): The number of hydrogen atoms of an acid replaceable by a metal atom.

basid'ium (Bot.): A special cell or rom of cells, of certain fungi, forming spores by abstriction.

basin (Geol.): A geological formation in which the strata dip towards the center.

bass frequencies (Acous.): Those frequencies towards the lower end of the audible scale.

bathom'eter (Ocean.): An instrument used for deep-sea soundings.

bathoph'ilous (Zool.): Adapted to an aquatic life at great depths.

bathotonic (Chem.): Tending to diminish surface tension.

bath'yal zone (Geol.): The sea-floor between 600 & 3,000 ft. below sea-level.

bath'ybic (Biol.): Relating to the deep sea.

bath'ysphere (Ocean.): A spherical diving apparatus capable of resisting tremendous pressure.

batter (Build.): Slope of the face of a structure from the vertical.

batter pile (Civ. Eng.): A pile which is driven in at an angle to the vertical.

battery (Elec.): A group of two or more primary cells electrically connected in series or in parallel.

bauxite (Min.): A residual clay formed by the chemical weathering of basic igneous rocks.

bead (Carp.): A small convex molding formed on wood or other material.

beaked (Bot.): Bearing a pointed prolongation.

bearing (Build.): The part of a girder which rests on the supports.

bearing (Surv.): The horizontal angle between any survey line and a given reference direction.

Beaufort notation (Meteor.): A code of letters used for indicating the state of the weather.

Beckmann apparatus (Chem.): Apparatus used for measuring the boiling and freezing points.

bed (Geol.): A term used for stratum.

beha'viourism (Psychol.): A school of thought that bases its doctrine on objective observation and experiment.

bell: A sound-emitting metal device, operated by striking.

belt (Eng.): An endless strip of leather used to transmit rotary motion from one shaft to another by running over pulleys.

benthos (Ecol.): The animal and plant life on the sea bottom.

benzine (Chem.): Petroleum hydrocarbons.

ber'iber'i (Med.): A disease resulting from thiamine deficiency.

berm (Civ. Eng.): A horizontal ledge on the side of an embankment to intercept earth rolling down the slopes.

berry (Bot.): A simple fleshy fruit.

beryllium (Met.): Used in nuclear reactors, as it reflects neutrons.

betatron (Phys.): An apparatus for imparting high velocities to electrons.

Bethell's process (Build.): A process for preserving timber.

bevel (Carp.): The sloping surface formed when two surfaces meet at an angle which is not a right angle.

bicar'bonates (Chem.): The acid salts of carbonic acid.

bi'ceps (Zool.): A muscle with two parts at one end.

bicon'jugate (Bot.): Said of a compound leaf when each of the two main ribs bears a pair of leaflets.

bicus'pid (Bot.): Having two short horn-like points.

bien'nial (Bot.): A plant which completes its life cycle within two years and then dies.

bifa'cial (Bot.): Flattened, and having the upper and lower faces of different structure.

bifa'rious (Bot.) : Arranged in two rows, one on each side of an axis.

bi'fid (Bot., Zool.) : Forked.

bigem'inate (Bot.) : In two pairs.

bigener'ic (Zool.) : Hybrids produced by crossing two distinct genera.

bight: A loop formed in a rope or chain.

bila'biate (Bot.) : With two lips.

bilat'eral (Med.) : Pertaining to, or having, two sides.

bilateral symmetry (Biol.) : The arrangement of body parts so that the right and left halves are mirror images of each other.

bile (Physiol.) : A viscous liquid produced by the liver.

bile ducts (Zool.) : The excretory ducts of the liver and gall bladder.

bilge: The space above the double bottom of a ship, into which waste water from the engine-room and holds is drained.

bill (Zool.) : In birds, the beak.

biloc'ular (Bot.) : Consisting of two chambers.

bilo'phodent (Zool.) : Having the two anterior and the two posterior cusps of the grinding teeth joined by ridges.

bi'manous (Zool.) : Having two hands.

biman'ual (Med.) : Performed with both hands.

bimolec'ular reaction (Chem.) : A reaction in which two molecules interact.

bi'nary (Astron.) : A double star in which the two components revolve about their common center of mass under the influence of gravitational attraction. (Chem.) : Consisting of two components.

binary fission (Biol.) : The type of asexual reproduction in which division in two parts is approximately equal.

bi'nate (Bot.) : Occurring in pairs.

binaur'al (Acous.) : Pertaining to the use of two ears.

binding energy (Nucleonics) : Total energy required to separate the protons and neutrons in a nucleus.

binding screw (Eng.) : The general name for a set-screw used for clamping two parts together.

Binet's test (Psychol.) : A method of testing a child's intelligence.

binomial nomenclature (Biol.) : The system of denoting an organism by two Latin words, the first the name of the genus and the second the specific name.

biochemistry: The chemistry of living things.

biocoenosis (Ecol.) : The association of plants and animals together, especially in relation to a feeding area.

biocoenotic (Ecol.) : Pertaining to the inter-relationship between the organisms of a community.

bi'ogen (Bot.) : A hypothetical protein molecule of instable nature which is assumed to be primarily responsible for life.

biogen'esis (Biol.) : The doctrine that life comes only from pre-existing life.

biology: The science of plant and animal life.

biolumines'cence (Biol.) : The production of light by living organisms.

biom'eter (Biol.) : An instrument for measuring the amount of life by assessing the respiration.

bi'on (Bot.) : An individual plant.

bi'ophore (Bot.) : A hypothetical particle of minute size, assumed to be capable of growth and reproduction.

bi'opsy (Med.) : Diagnostic examination of tissue removed from the living body.

bi'os (Chem.) : A group of substances which act as a growth promoter for yeast.

biot'is (Biol.) : Relating to life.

bi'otite (Min.) : A form of black mica distributed in igneous rocks as shiny black crystals.

bi'otype (Biol.) : One individual of a population composed of organisms which are alike in their inheritable characters.

bip'arous (Zool.) : Giving birth to two young at a time.

biped (Zool.) : A two-footed animal.

bipen'niform (Zool.) : Feather-shaped, with the sides of the vane of equal size.

bipolar (Zool.) : Having two poles.

bipyramid (Crystal.) : A crystal form consisting of two pyramids on a common base, the one being the mirror-image of the other.

bird's-eye grain (Bot.) : The appearance when worked timber shows large numbers of small circular areas dotted about the wood.

bi'refrin'gence (Min.) : The double bending of light by crystalline minerals.

bi'sac'cate (Bot.) : Having two sepals each with a small pouch at the base.

bise'riate (Bot.) : (1) In two rows. (2) A vascular ray two cells wide.

bisex'ual (Bot., Zool.) : Possessing both male and female sexual organs.

bismuth (Chem.) : A gray-white metallic element.

bis'toury (Med.) : A long, narrow surgical knife for cutting abscesses, etc.

bisul'cate (Bot.) : Marked by two furrows.

bisymmet'ric (Bot.) : Symmetrical in two planes at right-angles to one another.

bit (Carp.) : A boring tool.

bittern (Chem.) : The residual liquid remaining from the evaporation of sea water.

biva'lent (Cyt.) : Paired homologous chromosomes.

bi'valve (Zool.) : Having the shell in the form of two plates.

biva'riant (Chem.) : Having two degrees of freedom.

bivol'tine (Zool.) : Having two broods in each year.

bladder (Bot.) : A device which catches small aquatic animals. (Zool.) : Any membranous sac containing fluid or gas.

blade (Bot.) : The flattened part of a leaf, sepal or petal.

blast: The ignition of an explosive charge. (Met.) : Air under pressure, blown into a furnace.

blaste'ma (Bot.) : The axial part of an embryo (Zool.) : The protoplasmic part of an egg.

blasting (Civ. Eng.) : The operation of disintegrating rock, etc.

blast'ocyst (Zool.) : The germinal vesicle.

blast'oderm: The germinal disc.

blastogen'esis (Gen.) : Transmission of inherited characters by means of germ-plasm only.

blast'okine'sis (Zool.) : Migration of embryo in insect eggs.

blast'omere (Zool.) : One of the cells formed during the early stages of cleavage of the ovum.

Blavier's text (Elec. Eng.) : A method of locating a fault on an electric cable.

bleb (Med.) : A small blister containing clear fluid.

bleeder (Med.) : One afflicted with hemophilia.

bleeding (Bot.) : The exudation of sap from wounds.

blinding (Civ. Eng.) : The process of sprinkling small stone chips over a tár-dressed road surface.

blink microscope (Astron.) : An instrument in which two photographic plates of the same region are viewed simultaneously.

blister (Med.) : A subcutaneous bubble filled with fluid.

block time (Aero.) : The time elapsed from the moment an aircraft starts to leave to the moment it comes to rest.

blood (Zool.) : The fluid circulating in the vascular system of animals, distributing food material and oxygen and collecting waste products.

blood corpuscle (Physiol.) : A cell normally contained in suspension in the blood.

blood count (Med.) : The number of red or white corpuscles in the blood.

blood dust (Physiol.) : Neutral fats carried by the blood-plasma in the form of very fine globules.

blood groups: A classification of human bloods based on their mutual agglutination reactions.

blood plasma (Physiol.) : The fluid part of the blood, under normal conditions.

blood serum (Physiol.) : The fluid part of the blood remaining after the corpuscles and the fibrin have been removed.

blood-vessel (Physiol.) : An enclosed space with well-defined walls, through which blood passes.

blow-holes (Met.): Gas-filled cavities in solid metals.

blowpipe (Chem.): An apparatus using a mixture of air under pressure and coal gas in order to give a hot localized flame.

blower (Eng.): A rotary air-compressor for supplying a large volume of air at low pressure.

blub (Build.): A swelling on the surface of newly plastered work.

blubber (Zool.): In marine mammals, a thick fatty layer on the dermis.

blur (Acous.): The introduction of alien frequencies into reproduced sounds, making the sounds indistinct.

board (Build.): Timber cut to a thickness of less than 2 in., and to any width from 4 in. upwards.

board-foot (Build.): The unit of measurement in the board-measure system, being a piece of lumber of 1 in. thickness by 12 in. square.

bobbin (Elec. Eng.): A flanged structure used for the winding of a coil. Also called a spool.

body cell (Zool.): Somatic cell.

body wall (Zool.): The wall of the perivisceral cavity, comprising the skin and muscle layers.

Bohr magneton (Nucleonics): Unit for expressing magnetic moments of electrons or nuclei.

boiler (Eng.): A steam-generator consisting of tubes and water-drums, exposed to the heat of a furnace and arranged so as to promote rapid circulation.

boiling: The rapid conversion of a liquid into vapor by the violent evolution of bubbles; it occurs when the temperature reaches such a value that the saturated vapor pressure of the liquid equals the pressure of the atmosphere.

boiling point: The temperature at which a liquid boils when exposed to the atmosphere.

bole (Bot.): A tree trunk.

bo'lide (Astron.): A large meteor, generally one that explodes.

boll (Bot.): The fruit of a cotton plant.

bollard: On a vessel or quay, a short upright post round which ropes are secured for mooring purposes.

bolom'eter (Elec. Eng.): An instrument for measuring radiant energy.

bolt (Eng.): A cylindrical, screwed metal bar with a nut, it is the most common means of fastening two parts together.

bomb: A high-explosive, incendiary, smoke or gas projectile. (Geol.): A spherical or ovoid mass of lava formed by explosions in an active volcano vent.

bone (Zool.): Connective tissue in which the ground substance contains salts of lime.

bone beds (Geol.): Strata characterized by a high content of fossil remains.

boning-in (Surv.): The process of locating and driving in pegs so that they are in line.

booking (Surv.): A surveyor's term to describe the operation of recording field observations.

boom (Eng.): Any long beam.

boost control (Aero.): A capsule device regulating reciprocating-engine manifold pressure so that super-charged engines are not over-stressed at low altitude.

booster transformer (Elec. Eng.): A transformer connected in series with a circuit in order to raise or lower the voltage of that circuit.

booted (Zool.): Having the feet protected by horny scales.

bora (Meteor.): A squally winter wind blowing on the shores of the Adriatic and Aegean seas.

borax (Min.): A mineral deposited by evaporation of the waters of alkaline lakes.

boring (Civ. Eng.): The process of drilling holes into ground or rock.

bornite (Min.): A copper ore.

bo'ron (Chem.): A non-metallic element.

botany: The branch of science that deals with plant life.

botryoi'dal (Zool.): Shaped like a bunch of grapes.

bottoming (Civ. Eng.): The lowest layer of foundation material for a road.

boulder (Geol.): The unit of largest size occurring in rocks.

bow (Elec. Eng.): A sliding type of current collector, used on electric vehicles to collect the current from an overhead contact-wire.

Boyle's law (Phys.): The volume of a given mass of gas kept at a uniform temperature varies inversely as the pressure.

braccate (Zool.): Feathered legs or feet; said of birds.

brace (Carp., Eng.): A tool used to hold a bit and give it rotary motion.

bra'chial (Zool.): Pertaining to the ar of a vertebrate.

bra'chiate (Bot., Zool.): Branched; bearing arms.

brachycerous (Zool.): Having short antennae.

brach'ycla'dous (Bot.): Having very short branches.

brach'ymeio'sis (Cyt.): A simplified form of meiosis, completed in one division.

brachypterous (Zool.): With short wings that do not cover the abdomen.

bracing (Civ. Eng.): The supporting ties or rods which are used in the strengthening of a structure.

bracket (Build.): A projecting support for a shelf.

bract (Bot.): A modified leaf from the axil of which arises a flower or an inflorescence.

brad: A nail with a small head.

bradyar'thria (Med.): Abnormally slow delivery of speech.

bradycar'dia (Med.): Slowness of the heart beat.

bradykine'sia (Med.): Abnormal slowness of the movements of the body.

brad'yspore (Bot.): A plant from which the seeds are liberated slowly.

Bragg method (Min.): A method of investigating crystal structure by X-rays.

brain (Zool.): Center of nervous system; mass of nervous matter in vertebrates at the anterior end of the spinal cord, lying in the cranium; in invertebrates, the pre-oral ganglia.

brake (Eng.): A device for applying resistance to the motion of a body.

bran'chin (Zool.): Gills.

brass (Met.): Primarily an alloy of zinc and copper.

brazing (Eng.): The process of joining two pieces of metal by fusing a layer of brass between the adjoining surfaces.

break (Elec. Eng.): The shortest distance between the contacts of a switch or similar apparatus, when the contacts are in an open position.

breakwater (Civ. Eng.): A natural or artificial coastal barrier to break the force of the waves.

breast (Anat.): An accessory gland of the generative system; rudimentary in the male and secreting milk in the female.

brick: A shaped and hardened block of special clay, used for building purposes.

bridge (Civ. Eng.): A structure built over or under a road or railway, or over a body of water, to provide a continuous roadway from one side to the other for transportation.

bristle (Bot.): A very stiff, erect hair.

brittleness (Met.): The tendency to fracture without appreciable deformation and under low stress.

brochone'ma (Cyt.): In cell division, the spireme thread when it has become arranged in the form of loops.

bromides (Chem.): Salts of hydrobromic acid.

bromine (Chem.): A non-metallic element.

bronchi'tis (Med.): Inflammation of the bronchi.

bron'choscope (Med.): An instrument consisting of a hollow tube with light and mirrors arranged for inspecting the interior of the bronchi.

bronchus (Zool.): One of the two branches into which the trachea divides, and which leads to the lungs.

bronze (Met.): Primarily an alloy of copper and tin.

brood (Zool.): A set of offsprings produced at the same birth or from the same batch of eggs.

Brückner cycle (Meteor.): A recurrence of periods of cold and damp alternating with warm and dry years, the period of a cycle being about 35 years.

bruise (Med.): Rupture of blood-vessels in a tissue.

brush (Elec. Eng.): A conductor arranged to make electrical contact between a stationary and a moving surface.

Bry′ophy′ta (Bot.) : One of the main divisions of the plant kingdom ; the liverworts and masses.

bubble (Surv.) : The bubble of air and spirit vapor within a level tube ; sometimes the level tube itself.

buc′cal (Zool.) : Pertaining to the cheek or the mouth.

buckle (Eng.) : To twist or bend out of shape.

bud (Bot.) : The undeveloped stage of a branch.

budding (Bot.) : (1) The production of daughter cells in the form of rounded outgrowths, characteristic of yeasts. (2) The production of buds. (3) A means of artificial propogation.

buff (Eng.) : A revolving disc composed of layers of cloth charged with abrasive powder ; used for polishing metals.

building line (Build.) : The line beyond which a building may not be erected on any given plot.

bulb (Bot.) : A large underground bud consisting of swollen leaf bases containing reserved food material, arranged on a short conical stem. (Illum.) : The glass container holding the filament of an electric filament lamp or the electrodes of an ·electric discharge lamp.

bulbous (Bot.) : Having underground bulbs. Swollen like a bulb.

bulkhead (Civ. Eng.) : A timber or masonry partition to retain earth.

bullate (Bot.) : Having a blistered surface.

bulldozer (Civ. Eng.) : A power-operated machine provided with a blade for spreading and levelling material.

bulling (Civ. Eng.) : The operation of detaching a piece of loosened rock by exploding blasting charges inserted in the surrounding fissures.

bullion (Met.) : Gold or silver in bulk.

bulwark (Civ. Eng.) : A sea-wall built to withstand the force of the waves.

bundle (Anat.) : Fibers collected into a band in the nervous system or in the heart.

bunker (Eng.) : A storage room for coal or oil fuel for use in steam boilers.

Bunsen burner (Chem.) : A gas burner consisting of a tube with a small gas jet at the lower end, and an adjustable air inlet which controls the heat of the flame.

buoy (Hyd. Eng.) : A floating vessel moored in ship-canals to mark the position of minor shoals and to show the limits of the navigable channel.

buoyancy (Phys.) : The loss in weight of a body when immersed in a fluid.

buran (Meteor.) : A frequent winter north-easterly wind in Russia and Central Asia.

burden (Elec. Eng.) : A term used to signify the load on an instrument transformer.

burette (Chem.) : A long glass tube with a ground-glass tap at one end and open at the other end ; used in volumetric analysis.

burial (Nuclear Eng.) : Place for the safe deposition of the highly radioactive products of the operation of nuclear reactors.

bu′rin (Engraving) : A tool of tempered steel used in engraving and for retouching etched plates.

burnisher (Engraving) : A polished steel tool used to soften or remove lines on engraved plates.

burr (Acous.) : The rough edge which a victrola record has when it is removed from the press. (Eng.) : (1) A rough edge left on metal by a cutting tool. (2) A blank punched from sheet-metal. (Engraving) : A ridge raised on an engraved plate by a cutting tool.

bursa (Zool.) : Any sac-like cavity.

bush (Bot.) : A low woody plant forming a number of branches at ground level.

butt joint (Carp.) : A joint formed between the squared ends of the two jointing pieces, which come together but do not overlap.

butte (Geol.) : A steep-sided flat-topped hill.

buttress (Civ. Eng.) : A supporting pier built on the exterior of a wall to enable it to resist outward thrust.

Buys Bal′lot's law (Meteor.) : The law giving the direction of rotation of cyclones and anticyclones.

buzzer (Elec. Comm.) : A vibrating reed used to generate a note to indicate the presence of actuating current.

bys′malith (Geol.) : A form of igneous intrusion bounded by a circular fault and having a dome-shaped top.

byssa′ceous (Bot.) : Consisting of a mass of fine threads ; delicate, filamentous structure.

C

cab (Eng.) : The covered shelter for the driver of a locomotive or road-transport vehicle.

cabin altitude (Aero.) : The nominal pressure altitude maintained in the cabin of a pressurized airplane.

cable (Eng.) : A general term for rope or chain used for engineering purposes. (Elec. Comm.) : An electrical circuit suitable for laying on the bed of the ocean for carrying telegraphic signals.

cable code (Teleg.) : The modification of the Morse code in which a dash becomes a dot reserved in polarity ; used for telegraph transmission in submarine cables.

cable-length : One-tenth of a nautical mile (6080 feet).

cabling (Arch.) : A round molding used to decorate the lower parts of the flutes of a column. (Elec. Comm.) : The collection of cables required for distributing the power supplies in a telephone exchange.

caboose (Rail.) : A separate car at the end of a freight train for the guide and brakemen.

cada′ver (Anat.) : A dead human body.

cadmium (Nucleonics) : Metal element characterized by high absorption of neutrons, and hence used for controlling nuclear reactors.

cadmium (Met.) : A white metallic element.

cadu′cous (Bot.) : Lasting for a short time only.

Caesa′rean section (Med.) : Artificial delivery of a foetus through the incised abdomen and uterus.

cae′sions (Bot.) : Bearing a bluish-gray waxy bloom.

cae′spitose (Bot.) : Growing from the root in tufts.

cage (Civ. Eng.) : The platform on which goods are hoisted up or down a vertical shaft.

Cainozo′ic (Geol.) : The word signifies "recent life" and is applied to the fourth of the great geological eras.

caisson (Civ. Eng.) : A water-tight box used to surround the works involved in laying the foundations of a bridge.

calamif′erous (Bot.) : Having a hollow stem.

cal′amus (Zool.) : A quill.

calca′reous (Bot.) : Coated with or containing lime.

cal′cicole (Bot.) : Flourishing on soils or rocks rich in calcium carbonate.

calcico′sis (Med.) : Lung disease caused by the inhalation of marble dust.

calcifica′tion (Bot.) : The accumulation of calcium carbonate on or in cell walls. (Zool.) : The deposition of lime salts.

calcination (Chem.) : The process of subjecting a material to the effect of prolonged heating at fairly high temperatures.

calcium (Met.) : A silvery-white metallic element.

caldera (Geol.) : A volcanic crater of large size.

calibration (Phys.) : The process of determining experimentally the absolute values corresponding to the graduations on an arbitrary or inaccurate scale on an instrument.

caliber : The internal diameter or bore of a pipe.

caliduct (Build.) : A hot water or steam pipe used for heating purposes.

callipers : An instrument, consisting of a pair of hinged legs, used to measure external and internal dimensions.

callous (Bot., Med.) : Hardened, usually thickened.

cal′lus (Bot.) : A mass of parenchymatous cells formed by plants over a wound. (Med.) : Newly formed bony tissue between the broken end of a fractured bone.

cal'orie (Physics.): (1) Used as a unit in expressing the heat or energy producing value of food. (2) The unit quantity of heat.

calor'ifier (Heat): An apparatus for heating water in a tank.

calorim'etry (Heat): The measurement of thermal constants.

calvities (Med.): Baldness.

ca'lyx (Bot.): The outer whorl of the flower, consisting of sepals. (Zool.): A pouch of an oviduct, in which eggs may be stored.

cam (Eng.): A projection on a revolving shaft.

cambium (Bot.): A soft meristematic tissue which gives rise to new tissue (wood, bark).

campanile (Build.): A bell-tower.

canal (Bot.): An elongated intercellular space. (Hyd. Eng.): An artificial water channel used for irrigational or navigational purposes.

can'cellate (Bot.): Lattice-like.

Cancer (Astron.): Crab. Fourth sign of the Zodiac.

candle (Illum.): The unit of luminous intensity.

candle-power (Illum.): The luminous flux emitted by a source of light per unit solid angle in a given direction.

canes'cent (Bot.): Having a somewhat hoary appearance.

canine (Zool.): Pertaining to a dog. In mammals, a pointed tooth with a single cusp.

canker (Bot.): A name applied to various diseases of trees, caused by fungi.

cañon (Geol.): A deep, narrow, steep-sided valley.

canopy (Aero.): The fabric body of a parachute. (Build.): An enriched roof-like part projecting from a wall or supported on pillars.

cant: To tilt. (Build.): A molding having plane surfaces and angles instead of curves. (Surv.): The transverse slope given to the surface of the rails on a railway curve or to the road surface on a highway curve.

cantilever (Struct.): A beam or girder fixed at one extremity and free at the other.

canyon (Nuclear Eng.): Long narrow space with heavy shielding for essential processing of wastes from reactors.

capacitor (Elec. Eng.): A piece of electrical apparatus consisting of two conducting plates separated by a layer of insulating material.

capacity (Elec. Eng.): A term commonly used to denote the output of a piece of electrical apparatus.

capilla'ceous (Bot.): Hair-like.

capillarity (Phys.): A phenomenon associated with surface tension and angle of contact.

capil'lary (Bot., Zool.): Of very small diameter; slender, hair-like.

capillit'ium (Bot.): A mass of threads.

cap'itate (Bot.): (1) Resembling a pin-head in appearance. (2) Bearing a rounded swelling at the apex. (3) Having flowers grouped in a head.

cap'reolate (Bot.): Having tendrils.

capricornus (Astron.): Goat. Tenth sign of the Zodiac.

capsule (Med.): A soluble case of gelatine in which a dose of medicine may be enclosed.

carat: A standard of weight for precious stones.

carbohy'drates (Chem.): Any of a group of neutral compounds composed of carbon, hydrogen, and oxygen, and including the sugars, starches, etc.

carbon (Chem.): A non-metallic element.

carbon compounds (Chem.): Compounds containing one or more carbon atoms in the molecule.

carbon dioxide (Chem.): A colorless gas with a slight smell.

carbon disulphide (Chem.): Sulphur vapor passed over heated charcoal combines with the carbon to form carbon disulphide.

carbona'ceous (Bot.): Hard, blackened and appearing as if charred.

carbonaceous rocks (Geol.): Sedimentary deposits of which the chief constituent is carbon, derived from plant residues.

carbonated (Chem.): Said of a liquid saturated with carbon dioxide under pressure.

carbonic acid (Chem.): A weak acid formed when carbon dioxide is dissolved in water.

carburetor (Eng.): A device for mixing air and a volatile fuel in correct proportions, in order to form a combustible mixture.

carceru'lus (Bot.): A fruit which splits at maturity into several one-seeded portions.

car'cinogen'esis (Med.): The production and development of cancer.

carcinogen (Chem.): A substance which induces cancer in a living organism.

car'cinomato'sis (Med.): Cancer widely spread throughout the body.

card (Surv.): The graduated dial or face of a magnetic compass in which the card and needle are firmly connected.

cardiac: Pertaining to the heart.

car'diograph (Med.): A recording device to exhibit a wave-form determined by heart electromotive forces.

cardinal points (Astron.): The name given to the four principal points of the horizon—north, south, east, and west.

cardiol'ogy (Med.): Medical science concerned with the function and diseases of the heart.

cardiovas'cular (Med.): Pertaining to the heart and the blood vessels.

cardo (Zool.): The hinge of a bivalve shell.

car'et (Typog.): A symbol (Λ) used in proof correcting to indicate that something is to be inserted at that point.

ca'ries (Med.): (1) Pathological absorption of bone infected by the tubercle bacillus. (2) Decay of teeth.

ca'riose (Bot., Med.): Appearing as if decayed.

car'neous (Bot.): Flesh-colored.

Carniv'ora (Zool.): An order of carnivorous mammals.

carniv'orous: Flesh-eating.

car'nose (Bot.): Fleshy in texture.

car'notite (Min.): An important source of radium.

carotene (Chem.): A ruby-red crystalline hydrocarbon, found in various plants and used as a pigment.

carpel (Bot.): The ovule-bearing structure of a plant.

carpet strip (Carp.): A strip of wood secured to the floor below a door.

carpus (Zool.): The wrist.

carrar'a marble (Geol.): A well-known, pure-white, statuary marble quarried at Carrara, Italy.

carrier (Med.): One who carries pathogenic bacteria without having the disease caused by the bacteria, but does infect other people.

cartilage (Histol.): A form of connective tissue in which the cells are embedded in a stiff matrix of chondrin.

cartog'raphy (Surv.): The preparation and drawing of maps.

caruncle (Zool.): Any fleshy outgrowth.

cascade (Elec. Comm.): A number of devices connected in such a way that each operates the next one in turn.

casein (Chem.): The principal albuminous constituent of milk, in which it is present as a calcium salt.

casement (Build.): A window hinged to open about one of its vertical edges.

cast-iron (Met.): An iron-carbon alloy.

cast-steel (Met.): Steel as cast; not shaped by mechanical working.

casta'neous (Bot.): Chestnut brown.

casting (Met.): The operation of pouring molten metals into sand or metal molds in which they solidify.

catgut (Surg.): Sterilized strands of sheep's intestines used as ligatures.

catal'ysis (Chem.): The acceleration or retardation of a chemical reaction by a substance which itself undergoes no permanent chemical change.

Science
Terms

cat'alyst (Chem.): A substance which catalyses a chemical reaction.

cataract (Med.): Opacity of the lens of the eye as a result of degenerative changes in it.

catch (Carp.): A spring bolt for securing doors when shut.

catch-net (Elec. Eng.): A wire netting placed under high-voltage transmission lines.

catenation (Cyt.): The arrangement of chromosomes in chains.

caterpillar (Eng.): A device for increasing the tractive effort of a road vehicle. (Zool.): A type of larva.

cathar'sis (Psycho-an.): The purging of the effects of a pent-up emotion by bringing them to the surface of consciousness.

cathetom'eter (Phys.): An instrument for measuring vertical distances not exceeding a few centimeters.

cathode (Elec.): The electrode through which a current leaves an electrolytic cell.

cathode rays (Phys.): Streams of electrons emitted from the cathode during an electrical discharge in a rarefied gas.

cat'olyte (Elec.): The part of the electrolyte of an electrolytic cell which is near the cathode.

caud'a (Zool.): Any tail-like appendage.

caules'cent (Bot.): Having a stem.

cauline (Bot.): Growing from the stem.

caulking (Civ. Eng.): Making a joint tight to withstand pressure.

causeway (Civ. Eng.): A road carried by an embankment across water or marshy land.

caustic (Med.): Corrosive or destructive to living tissue.

cavern (Geol.): A chamber in a rock.

cavernic'olous (Ecol.): Cave-living.

cavetto (Arch.): A hollow molding, quarter round.

cavitation (Eng.): The formation of a cavity between the downstream surface of a moving body and a liquid normally in contact with it.

ceiling (Aero.): The maximum height attainable under standard conditions by an airplane.

celestial equator (Astron.): The great circle in which the plane of the earth's equator cuts the celestial sphere.

celestial poles (Astron.): The two points in which the earth's axis cuts the celestial sphere.

celestial sphere (Astron.): An imaginary sphere, of indeterminate radius of which the observor is the center.

cell (Biol.): One of the specialized units, consisting of nucleus and protoplasm, which compose the bodies of animals and plants.

cell division (Cyt.): The splitting of a cell into daughter cells.

cell inclusion (Cyt.): Any non-living material present in the cytoplasm.

cell sap (Cyt.): The fluid constituents of a cell.

cell tissue (Bot.): A group of cells formed by division of one or a few original cells, remaining associated and functioning as a whole.

cell wall (Cyt.): The membrane confining the contents of a cell.

cell (Elec.): The unit of a battery, in which chemical action takes place between two electrodes.

cellulation (Zool.): The reformation of cells in injured tissue.

cement (Build., Civ. Eng., etc.): A material for uniting other materials.

cement gun (Civ. Eng.): An apparatus for spraying cement mortar by pneumatic pressure.

Centigrade scale: The most widely used method for graduating a thermometer; the temperature interval between the freezing and boiling points of water is divided into 100 equal parts, each of which is a centigrade degree.

central heating (Build.): A system of heating a building, in which water is heated by a central boiler, and hot water or steam is circulated throughout the building through pipes and radiators.

central nervous system (Zool.): The main ganglia of the nervous system with their associated nerve cords.

center (Civ. Eng.): A timber frame built as a temporary support during the construction of a dome or an arch. (Surv.): To set up a surveying instrument vertically above a station point.

center of action (Meteor.): A position occupied by an anticyclone or a depression, which largely determines the weather conditions over a wide area.

center of buoyancy (Hyd.): The center of gravity of the liquid displaced by a floating body.

center of curvature: The point of intersection of normals drawn to a curve at two consecutive points.

center of gravity (Mech.): That point in a body at which the body may be supported in neutral equilibrium.

center square (Eng.): A device for marking the centers of bars and circular objects.

centrifugal force (Mech.): A body constrained to move along a curved path reacts against the constraint with a force directed away from the center of curvature of its path.

cen'trifuge: Apparatus rotating at very high speed, designed to separate solids from liquids, or liquids from other liquids dispersed therein.

cen'triole (Cyt.): A central granule within the centrosome.

centrip'etal force (Mech.): It is equal and opposite to the force directed towards the center of curvature which is deviating the body from a straight path.

centrodes'mose (Cyt.): A delicate thread of stainable material connecting the centrosomes at the time of nuclear division.

cen'trosome (Cyt.): A minute protoplasmic cell-inclusion associated with the nucleus and dividing with it.

cephal'ic (Zool.): Pertaining to, or situated on or in the head region.

cer'anoid (Bot.): Bearing branches shaped like horns.

cerebel'lum (Zool.): A dorsal thickening of the hindbrain in vertebrates.

cere'bral (Zool.): Pertaining to the brain.

cer'nuous (Bot.): Drooping.

cer'vix u'teri (Med.): The neck of the uterus.

chain (Chem.): A series of atoms linked together, generally in an organic molecule. (Eng.): A series of interconnected metal links forming a flexible cable. (Surv.): An instrument used for the measurement of length.

chain reaction (Chem.): A reaction in which a large number of molecules or atoms take part in succession.

chalced'ony (Min.): A cryptocrystalline variety of silica.

chalcopy'rite (or copper pyrite) (Min.): Sulphide of copper and iron.

chalk (Geol.): A fine-grained and relatively soft limestone.

character (Biol.): Any well-marked feature which helps to distinguish one species from another. (Psychol.): The quality of the whole organized self.

character trait (Psycho-an.): A distinguishing behavior pattern of an individual.

charcoal (Chem.): The residue from the destructive distillation of animal matter or wood with exclusion of air.

charge (Elec. Eng.): The quantity of electricity on a body.

charta'ceous (Bot.): Papery in texture.

chase (Build.): A trench dug to accommodate a drain pipe.

chaser (Eng.): A lathe tool the cutting edge of which is serrated to the profile of a screw thread.

chas'mogam'ous (Bot.): Having large conspicuous flowers which open and are pollinated by insects or wind.

chas'mophyte (Bot.): A plant inhabiting rocky places and rooting in a crevice containing mineral and organic debris.

chatter (Eng.): Vibration of a cutting tool or of a machine.

check-lock (Carp.): A device for locking in position the bolt of a door lock.

check valve (Eng.): A non return valve, closed automatically by fluid pressure.

cheek (Build.): One of the sides of an opening.

chemical affinity (Chem.): The force which binds atoms together in molecules.

chemical analysis (Chem.): The splitting up of a material into its component parts or constituents by chemical methods.

chemical bond (Chem.): The unit of force joining two atoms together in a molecule.

chemical change (Chem.): A change involving the formation of a new substance.

chemical compound (Chem.): A substance composed of two or more elements in definite proportion by weight, which are independent of its mode of preparation.

chemical constitution (Chem.): The number and arrangement of the atoms present in a molecule.

chemical energy (Chem.): The energy liberated in a chemical reaction.

chemical engineering: Design, construction and operation of plant and works in which matter undergoes change of state and composition.

chemical equation (Chem.): A symbolic representation of the changes occurring in a chemical reaction.

chemical kinetics (Chem.): The study of the velocities of chemical reactions.

chemical reaction (Chem.): A process in which one substance is changed into another.

chemical symbol (Chem.): A single capital letter, or a capital and small letter combined, which are used to represent either an atom or a gram-atom of a chemical element.

chemilumines'cence (Chem.): The production of light without heat in certain chemical reactions.

chemistry (Chem.): The study of the composition of substances and the changes of composition which they undergo.

chemotherapy: Treatment of disease by a chemical compound having a specific bacteriostatic effect against the micro-organism involved.

chest saw (Carp.): A small handsaw without a back; with 6 to 12 teeth to the inch.

chias'ma (Cyt.): The exchange of material between paired chromosomes during nuclear division.

chimera (Bot.): A plant in which there are at least two kinds of tissue differing in their genetic constitutions.

chili (Meteor.): A sirocco-type hot and dry southerly wind blowing in Tunis.

chimney jambs (Build.): The upright sides of a fireplace opening.

chimney lining (Build.): The tile within a chimney space.

chimney shaft (Build.): The part of a chimney projecting above a roof.

chimney stack (Build.): The unit containing a number of flues grouped together.

chim'onophi'lous (Bot.): Growing primarily during the winter.

chinook' (Meteor.): A föhn-like west wind blowing on the eastern side of the Rocky Mountains.

chipping (Met.): The removing of surface defects from semi-finished metal produces by using pneumatic chisels.

chirop'ody: The care and treatment of minor ailments of the feet.

chirop'tera (Zool.): An order of aerial mammals. Bats.

chisel (Build.): A steel tool for cutting wood, stone or metal.

chlorates (Chem.): Salts of chloric acid; powerful oxidizing agents.

chlorides (Chem.): Salts of hydrochloric acid obtained by the action of an acid on many metals.

chlorination (Chem.): The substitution or addition of chlorine in organic compounds; the sterilization of water with chlorine.

chlorine (Chem.): A greenish-yellow gas.

chlor'oform (Chem.): A colorless liquid of a peculiar odor; used as an important anesthetic.

chlor'ophyll (Bot.): The mixture of two green and two yellow pigments, present in the chloroplasts of all plants, essential for photosynthesis.

chlo'roplast: Specialized cytoplasmic body containing chlorophyll.

choke (Eng.): (1) The throat in the air passage of a carburetor. (2) A valve in a carburetor intake.

chol'era (Med.): An acute bacterial infection in Eastern countries.

chon'drin (Histol.): A firm, elastic, translucent substance of a gelatinous nature, which forms the ground substance of cartilage.

chop (Carp.): The movable wooden jaw of a carpenter's bench vice.

chord: A straight line drawn between two points on a curve.

chords (Zool.): Any string-like structure.

chre'sard (Bot.): The total amount of water in the soil which can be drawn up by plants.

chro'matin (Cyt.): The deeply staining portion of the nucleoplasm.

chro'miole (Cyt.): One of the deeply staining granules of which chromatin is composed.

chromium (Met.): A metallic element.

chromium plating (Met.): A thin layer of chromium on the surface of another metal by electrodeposition, to protect it against corrosion.

chro'momeres (Cyt.): One of the many linearly arranged bead-like structures found on a chromosome.

chro'moplast (Bot.): Specialized protoplasmic body containing orange or yellow pigments.

chro'mosome (Cyt.): Deeply staining rod-shaped bodies within the nucleus and conspicuously visible during cell division; it contains the genes.

chro'mule (Bot.): A general term for plant pigments.

chronic (Med.): Said of a disease which is long-continued.

chrys'alis (Zool.): The pupa of some insects.

cic'atrix (Bot.): A scar left on a plant where a member has been shed.

cil'lia (Zool.): Microscopic hair-like projections from certain cells which vibrate, causing fluid movement; eyelashes.

cincture (Arch.): A plain ring around a column, generally placed at the top and the bottom to separate the shaft from its capital and its base.

cip'olin (Build.): A white marble with green streaks.

circle (Geom.): A plane curve which is the locus of a point which moves so that it is at a constant distance (the radius) from a fixed point (the center).

circuit (Elec. Comm.): The whole or part of the path of transmitted electrical energy in a communication channel.

circulating pumps (Eng.): A pump used to circulate cooling water through the condenser of a steam plant.

circulation (Bot.): A rotary movement of the protoplasm inside a cell. (Physiol.): The continuous movement of the blood through the heart, arteries, capillaries and veins.

circumpolar stars (Astron.): Those stars which for a given locality on the earth revolve about the elevated celestial pole, always above the horizon.

cirrho'sis (Med.): A disease of the liver.

cirro-cumulus (Meteor.): Small white flakes of cloud without shadows, arranged in groups or in lines.

cirro-stratus (Meteor.): A thin sheet of whitish cloud.

cir'rose (Bot., Zool.): Curly.

cistern (Build.): A tank for storing up water which may later be used.

citrine, citron (Bot.): Lemon-colored.

civil engineering: The design and construction of roads, railways, bridges, aqueducts, canals, docks, ports, breakwaters, lighthouses and drainage works.

clamp (Build.): A wooden frame consisting of two parallel bars connected by two tightening screws; used to secure work.

class (Bot., Zool.): Principal sub-division of a phylum in the animal kingdom and one of the larger subdivisions in the plant kingdom.

clastic rocks (Geol.) : Rocks formed of fragments of pre-existing rocks.

claustrophobia (Med.) : Abnormal fear of being in a confined space.

clav'icle (Zool.) : The collar-bone, in vertebrates.

claw (Bot.) : The narrow, elongated, lower portion of a petal in some plants. (Carp.) : A tool with a bent and split end, used for extracting tacks. (Zool.) : A curved, sharp-pointed process at the distal extremity of a limb.

clay (Geol.) : A fine-textured, sedimentary or residual deposit.

cleavage (Bot., Zool.) : Divisions of the fertilized egg. (Chem.) : (1) The splitting of a crystal along certain planes. (2) The splitting up of a complex protein molecule into simpler molecules. (Geol.) : A property of rocks, whereby they can be split into thin sheets.

cleis'togam'y (Bot.) : The production of small flowers, which do not open and are self-pollinated.

climate (Meteor.) : The average weather conditions of a place.

climatology (Meteor.) : The study of climate and its causes in relation to a particular region.

climom'eter (Surv.) : A hand instrument for the measurement of angles of slope.

cloaca (Zool.) : A common receptacle for digestive and excretory wastes and the reproductive cells of lower vertebrates.

clone (Zool.) : A group of organisms produced by asexual reproduction from a single individual.

closed circuit (Elec. Eng.) : An electrical circuit in which there is a complete path for the current to flow.

clot (Med.) : The semi-solid state of blood or of lymph when they coagulate.

cloud (Meteor.) : A mass of water droplets remaining more or less at a constant altitude.

cloud-burst (Meteor.) : An extremely heavy downpour of rain.

club (Zool.) : The distal joints of the antenna, when they are enlarged in insects.

cluster (Bot.) : A general term for an inflorescence of small flowers closely crowded together.

clutch (Eng.) : A device by which two shafts or rotating members may be connected or disconnected, either at rest or in motion.

coagulation (Biol.) : The irreversible setting of protoplasm on exposure to heat or to poisons. (Chem.) : The process of changing a sol into gel. (Med.) : The process of clotting of blood.

coal (Geol.) : A general name for firm, brittle carbonaceous rocks.

coal-tar (Chem.) : The distillation products of the high or low temperature carbonization of coal.

coales'cent (Bot., Zool.) : Grown together, especially by union of the walls.

coating (Elec. Eng.) : The metallic sheets forming the plates of a condenser.

cob (Build.) : An unburnt brick.

cobalt (Met.) : A metallic element.

cobalt 60 : Radioactive isotope of cobalt, used in cancer treatment.

cocaine (Chem.) : Used as a local anesthetic.

coccin'eous (Bot.) : Bright red.

coccus (Bot.) : (1) A one-seeded portion formed by the break-up of a dry fruit. (2) A minute spherical bacterium.

coccyx (Zool.) : A bony structure in primates and amphibia, formed by the fusion of the caudal vertebrae.

cochleate (Bot., Zool.) : Spirally twisted, like a snail shell.

cockpit (Aero.) : The compartment in which the pilot of an aircraft is seated.

cockscomb (Min.) : Aggregate of pyrite.

coconut oil (Chem.) : Oil obtained from the fruit of a coconut palm.

cocoon (Zool.) : In insects, a special envelope constructed by the larva for protection during the pupal stage.

cod liver oil (Chem.) : Oil obtained from fresh livers of cod fish ; very rich in vitamins.

co'deine (Chem.) : An alkaloid of the morphine group.

coefficient (Phys.) : A numerical constant prefixed as a multiplier to a variable quantity, in calculating the magnitude of a physical property.

coel'iac (Zool.) : In vertebrates, pertaining to the abdomen or belly.

coe'lom (Zool.) : The body cavity lined with tissue of mesodermal origin in which the digestive and other organs lie.

co-enzyme (Chem.) : A relatively simple substance which is involved in the transfer of hydrogen atoms during oxidative reactions in protoplasm.

coercive force (Elec. Eng.) : The magnetizing force necessary to annul the residual magnetism of a substance.

coffering (Civ. Eng.) : The operation involved in the construction of dams for impounding water.

coffin (Phys.) : Heavy box of absorbing material, for the safe transportation of highly radioactive materials.

cogs (Eng.) : Separate wooden teeth.

cognition (Psychol.) : Intellectual perception ; ideas and reasons.

cohesion (Phys.) : The attraction between the molecules of a liquid which enables drops and thin films to be formed.

cohort (Bot.) : A group of related families.

coil (Elec. Comm.) : Any winding of conducting wire, with a core of air or of magnetic material for providing inductance.

coke (Min.) : The solid residue from the carbonization of coal after the volatile matter of the coal has been distilled off.

cold bend (Eng.) : A test of the ductility of a metal.

cold-blooded (Zool.) : Of animals having a body temperature which is dependent on the environmental temperature.

cold chisel (Eng.) : A chisel for chipping away surplus metal.

cold front (Meteor.) : The leading edge of an advancing mass of cold air.

cold-saw (Eng.) : A metal-cutting circular saw for cutting steel bars to length.

cold short (Met.) : Brittle at atmospheric temperature.

cold wave (Meteor.) : The fall of temperature following the passage of a depression.

Coleop'tera (Zool.) : An order of insects ; beetles.

coleop'tile (Bot.) : The first leaf to appear above the ground in a seedling of grass.

colic (Med.) : Severe spasmodic pain in the belly due to affections of abdominal organs.

collapse (Med.) : Extreme prostration and depression of vital functions.

collateral (Zool.) : Running parallel.

collimation : The process of aligning the various parts of the optical system.

colloid (Chem.) : A system in which particles larger than molecules of one substance are suspended throughout the second substance.

collum (Zool.) : Any collar-like structure.

colon (Zool.) : The wide posterior part of the hind-gut in insects. The large intestine in vertebrates.

colonnade (Arch.) : A row of columns supporting an entablature.

colony (Bot.) : A group of individuals of one species which are invading new ground. (Zool.) : A collection of individuals living together and in some degree interdependent.

column (Civ. Eng.) : A vertical shaft supporting an axial load. (Zool.) : In vertebrates, a bundle of nerve fibers running longitudinally in the spinal cord.

coma (Bot.) : A tuft of hairs attached to the testa of a seed. (Med.) : A state of complete unconsciousness.

combination (Chem.) : Formation of a compound.

combinations (Maths.) : The different groups that can be formed from a given number of items.

combustion chamber (Eng.) : In a boiler furnace, the space in which combustion of gaseous products from the fuel takes place.

co'mes (Zool.): A blood-vessel which runs parallel and close to a nerve.

comet (Astron.): A member of the solar system that revolves olliptically around the sun.

common bricks (Build.): A class of bricks used in ordinary construction.

combustion (Chem.): Chemical union of oxygen with gas, accompanied by the evolution of light and rapid production of heat.

compass (Surv.): An instrument for indicating the directions.

compass brick (Build.): A brick which tapers so as to be especially useful for curved work.

compass saw (Carp.): A handsaw with tapering blade, used for cutting curves.

compasses: An instrument for describing arcs, taking or marking distances, etc.

compatible (Bot.): Capable of self-fertilization.

competition (Biol.): The struggle between organisms for the necessities of life.

complement (Cyt.): A group of chromosomes derived from one nucleus, and consisting of one, two or more sets.

complete flower (Bot.): A flower which has both calyx and corolla.

complic'ant (Zool.): Folding one over another, as wings of some insects.

composition (Chem.): The nature of the elements present in a substance and the proportions in which they occur.

compound fruit (Bot.): A fruit formed from several closely associated flowers.

compressed (Bot.): Pressed together.

compressor (Eng.): Any kind of reciprocating rotary, or centrifugal pump for raising the pressure of gas.

computing scale (Surv.): A special scale fitted with a sliding cursor, used for the computation of area on maps, etc.

concentration (Chem.): Number of molecules or ions of a substance in a given volume.

concentric arch (Build.): An arch laid in several courses whose curves have a common center.

conception (Physiol.): The fertilization of an ovum with a spermatozoon.

concha (Arch.): The smooth concave surface of a vault. (Zool.): In vertebrates, the outer ear.

con'chate (Bot.): Shaped like a sea-shell.

concres'cence (Bot.): Growing together to form a single structure.

concrete (Bot.): Grown together to form a solid body. (Build.): A mixture of cement, sand and gravel with water.

concrete blocks (Civ. Eng., Build.): Solid or hollow pre-cast blocks of concrete used in construction.

concussion (Med.): A violent blow to the head, or the condition resulting from it.

condensation (Chem.): The linking together of two or more molecules, resulting in the formation of long chain compounds. (Meteor.): The process of forming a liquid from its vapor.

condenser (Chem.): Apparatus used for condensing vapors obtained during distillation. (Eng.): A chamber into which the exhaust steam from a steam engine or turbine is delivered to be condensed by cooling water.

conditioned reflex (Zool.): A reflex response to a stimulus which depends upon the former experience of an individual.

conductance (Elec. Eng.): The property of a material by which it allows current to flow through it when a potential difference is applied.

conductor (Elec. Eng.): (1) A material which offers a low resistance to the passage of an electrical current. (2) That part of a wiring system which actually carries the current.

conduit (Elec. Eng.): A pipe for containing electric wires in order to protect them against damage from external causes. (Hyd. Eng.): A pipe for the conveyance of water.

confluent (Bot.): Said of two or more structures which, as they enlarge, grow together and unite.

congenital (Zool.): Dating from birth.

congested (Bot.): Packed into a tight mass.

congestion (Med.): Pathological accumulation of blood in a part of the body.

conglomerate (Bot.): Clustered. (Geol.): A cemented clastic rock containing rounded small fragments.

conglu'tinate (Bot.): United onto a mass by a sticky substance.

conic section (Geom.): A curve obtained by the intersection of a right circular cone by a plane.

conif'erae (Bot.): The chief class of the Gymnospermae; primarily large evergreen trees.

conif'erous (Bot.): Cone-bearing.

conjugate (Bot.): Occurring in pairs.

conjunction (Astron.): Term signifying that two heavenly bodies have the same apparent geocentric longitude or right ascension.

connecting-rod (Eng.): In a reciprocating engine or pump, the rod connecting the piston or cross-head to the crank.

connective (Zool.): A bundle of nerve fibers uniting two nerve centers.

conni'vent (Bot.): Converging and muting at the tips.

consciousness (Psychol.): A comprehensive state of awareness of the mind to stimuli from the outside world and to emotions and thoughts from within the individual.

consen'sual (Zool.): Said of response to stimuli in which voluntary action and involuntary action are correlated.

conservatory (Build.): A glazed building in which plants may be grown under controlled atmospheric conditions.

consistom'eter (Chem.): An instrument for determining the consistency or hardness of semi-fluid and brittle materials.

constellation (Astron.): A group of stars to which have been given a pictorial configuration and a name, although of no scientific significance.

constituent (Met.): A component of a solid alloy.

constituents (Chem.): All the substances present in a system.

constricted (Bot., Zool.): Narrowed suddenly.

consumption (Med.): Wasting of the body.

contact-breaker (Elec. Eng.): A device for repeatedly breaking and making an electric circuit.

conta'gion (Med.): The communication of disease by direct contact between two persons or between an infected object and a person.

contiguous (Bot.): In contact but not in organic union.

continuous (Bot.): With a smooth surface of even uninterrupted outline.

contorted (Bot.): Twisted together.

contortion (Geol.): Of strata the deformation of rocks by directed pressure.

contour (Build.): The profile of the face of a molding. (Surv.): The imaginary intersection line between the ground surface and any given level surface.

contour gradient (Surv.): A line on the ground surface having a constant inclination to the horizontal.

contraceptive (Med.): Any agent which prevents the fertilization of the ovum with a spermatozoon.

contractility (Zool.): The power of changing shape.

control (Acous.): The regulation of the contrast between the highest and lowest power levels in a sound-reproducing system.

controller (Elec. Eng.): An assembly of equipment for controlling the operation of electric apparatus.

co'nus (Zool.): Any cone-shaped organ or structure.

convergence (Melcor.): An accumulation of air over a region caused by lack of uniformity of the winds.

converging (Bot.): Having the tips gradually approaching.

conveyor (Eng.): A device for the continuous transport of articles over a distance.

con'volute (Bot.): Coiled, folded or rolled, so that one half is covered by the other.

convulsion (Med.): Generalized involuntary spasm of the muscles normally under control of the will.

Science Terms

coping (Build., Civ. Eng.): A stone or brick covering to the top of wall exposed to the weather.

copper (Met.): A metallic element.

core (Civ. Eng.): A watertight wall built within a dam as an absolute barrier to water. (Elec. Eng.): That part of a magnetic circuit around which the winding is placed.

cork (Bot.): A layer of dead cells on the outside of a stem or root.

corm (Bot.) A rounded, swollen, underground, solid stem, resembling a bulb in appearance.

corne'a (Zool.): In vertebrates, the transparent part of the outer coat of the eyeball in front of the eye.

cornice (Build.): A projecting molding decorating the top of a window, building etc.

corol'la (Bot.) The general name for the whole of the petals of a flower.

coron'ary (Zool.): Crown shaped.

coronary thrombosis (Med.): The formation of a clot in one of the arteries of the heart.

corpus: Latin for body. Plural-corpora.

corpuscle (Zool.): A cell which lies freely in a fluid or solid matrix and is not in continuous contact with other cells.

correlation (Biol.): Mutual relationship. (Bot.): The conditions of balance existing between the various organs of a plant. (Maths.): The mathematical statements respecting the degree to which one variable is dependent on another variable.

corrosion (Chem.): The slow wearing away of solids by chemical attack.

cor'rugated (Bot.): Having a ridged surface.

cortical (Bot., Zool.): Relating to bark.

corundum (Min.): Oxide of aluminum; next to diamond in hardness.

cosmog'ony (Astron.): The science of the origins of stars, planets and satellites.

cosmog'raphy: The science of the constitution of the universe.

cosmology (Astron.): The branch of theoretical astronomy that deals with the known universe as a systematised whole.

cosmotron (Phys.): Machine for liberating nuclear energy.

Cotyle'don (Bot.): One of the leaves of the embryo in flowering plants.

counterbalancing (Eng.): The system of neutralizing the effect of a force by a counter-weight which provides an opposite effect.

coupling (Gen.): The tendency for dominant characters to remain in association. (Elec. Comm.): An arrangement for transferring electric energy from one 'circuit to another.

co-valency (Chem.): The union of two atoms by the sharing of a pair of electrons.

cramp (Carp.): A contrivance for holding parts of a frame in place during construction. (Med.): Painful spasm of muscle.

crane (Eng.): A machine for hoisting and lowering heavy weights.

cranium (Zool.): That part of the skull which encloses and protects the brain.

crater (Geol.): The orifice of a volcano through which the lavas and gases are emitted.

creep (Eng.): A slow relative movement between two parts of a structure. (Met.): Continuous deformation of metals under steady load.

cren'ate (Bot.): Having a margin bearing rounded teeth.

crevasse' (Geol.): A fissure in a glacier.

cris'pate (Bot.): Having a frizzled appearance.

cross (Gen.): An individual whose parents belong to different breeds or races.

cross-fertilization (Biol.): The fertilization of the female gametes of one individual by the male gametes of another individual.

cross pollination (Bot.): The conveyance of pollen from an anther of one flower to the stigma of another, either on the same or on a different plant of the same species.

cross section: A drawing showing the section of a body at right-angles to its length.

cross staff (Surv.): An instrument for setting out right-angles in the field.

crown (Bot.): A very short knotstock.

crown (Build., Civ. Eng.): The highest part of an arch.

croy (Civ. Eng.): A protective barrier built out into a stream to prevent erosion of the bank.

cruciate (Bot.): Having the form of a cross.

crucible (Chem., Met.): A refractory vessel in which metals are melted.

crustaceous (Bot.): Forming a crust on the surface of anything.

cryoplank'ton (Bot.): Algae which live on the surface of snow and ice in polar regions and on high mountains.

cryptocrystalline (Crystal.): Consisting of very minute crystals.

cryptozo'ic (Zool.): Living in dark places.

crystal: A body whose atoms are arranged in a definite pattern, the crystal faces being an outward expression of the regular arrangement of the atoms.

crystal nuclei (Chem.): The minute crystals whose formation is the beginning of crystallization.

crystal systems (Crystal.): A classification of crystals based on the intercepts made on the crystallographic axes by certain planes.

cryst'alline: Clear, transparent. (Bot.): Having a shining appearance.

crystalline form (Crystal.): The external geometrical shape of a crystal.

crystalline schists (Geol.): A group of rocks which have resulted from heat and pressure.

crystallization (Chem.): The preparation of a solid, especially from solution, in the form of crystals.

cryst'allites (Chem.): Very small, imperfectly formed crystals.

crystallogram (Chem.): A photograph of the X-ray diffraction pattern produced by a crystal.

crystallog'raphy: The study of the forms, properties and structures of crystals.

cubic system (Crystal.): The crystal system which has the highest degree of symmetry.

cul-de-sac (Civ. Eng.): A road which is stopped at one end.

culture (Bot., etc.): An experimental preparation containing a micro-organism growing on a medium.

cu'mulo-nimbus (Meteor.): Great masses of clouds, generally having a screen of fibrous texture at the top and a cloud mass similar to nimbus at the bottom; usually associated with thunderstorms.

cu'mulus (Meteor.): Thick cloud with a well defined, dome-shaped upper surface, while the base is generally horizontal.

cuprite (Min.): Oxide of copper.

curing (Chem.): A term applied to a fermentation process of natural products. (Civ. Eng.): A method of reducing the cracking on concrete on setting.

current: A flow.

cursorial (Zool.): Adapted for running.

curvature (Maths.): A measure of the departure of a line from the straight, or a surface from the plane. (Surv.): The difference in height at any point between the horizontal and the level lines through some other point on the earth's surface.

cu'ticle (Bot.): A deposit of waterproof, waxy material forming the external layer of the outer walls of epidermal cells. (Zool.): The epidermis.

cy'anides (Chem.): Salts of hydrocyanic acid.

cycle: A series of occurrences in which conditions at the end of the series are the same as they were at the beginning.

cyclic (Bot.): Having the parts arrayed in whorls not in spirals.

cycloid: The curved path traced out by a point on the circumference of a circle which rolls along a straight line.

cyclom'eter: A revolution counter calibrated in miles

or kilometers.

cyclone (Meteor.): A depress of small area but considerable pressure gradient, in which the winds attain hurricane force.

cyclo'sis (Biol.): The circulation of protoplasm within a cell.

cylinder: A solid of uniform cross-section which may be generated by a straight line moving round a clo ed curve and remaining parallel to a given direction.

cy'ma (Arch.): A molding showing a reverse curve in profile. Also called an ogee.

cypress knee (Bot.): A vertical upgrowth from the roots of the swamp cypress.

cyst (Zool.): A non-living membrane enclosing a cell.

cy'tode (Biol.): A mass of protoplasm without a nucleus.

cytol'ogy (Biol.): The study of the structure, functions and reproduction of cells.

cy'toplasm (Cyt.): The protoplasm of a cell, apart from that of the nucleus.

D

dactyl (Zool.): A digit.

dac'tyline, dac'tyloid (Bot.): Spreading like outstretched fingers.

da'do (Arch.): One of the faces of the solid block forming the body of a pedestal.

da'is (Build.): A raised platform at one end of a room.

dam'askeen: Inlay of ivory, metal or mother-of-pearl on metal.

damper (Acous.): A vibration-absorbing pad for reduction of the transmission of vibrational energy from a disturbing source.

damper (Aero.): Widely used term applied to devices for the suppression of unfavorable characteristics or behavior.

dasypae'des (Zool.): Birds which when hatched have a complete covering of down.

dasyphyl'lons (Bot.): Having crowded leaves or thick leaves or merely hair on leaves.

date line (Geog.): An imaginary line on the Earth's surface for the purpose of fixing the change of date; it runs approximately along the meridian of longitude 180° from Greenwich, deviating around certain islands for convenience.

da'tum (Surv.): An assumed level surface used as a reference surface for the measurement of reduced levels.

daughter (Biol.): Offspring belonging to the first generation, whether male or female.

day (Astron.): Apparent solar day-the interval, not constant due to the earth's elliptic orbit, between two successive transits of the true sun over the meridian. Mean solar day—the interval, perfectly constant, between two successive transits of the mean sun across the meridian.

deactivation (Chem.): The return of an activated atom, molecule or substance to the normal state.

dead (Elec. Eng.): Said of electric circuits which are not connected to any source of supply.

deafness (Acous.): Lack of sensitivity of hearing in one or both ears.

deammimila'tion (Bot.): The utilization of food by the plant.

death (Biol.): In a cell or an organism, complete and permanent cessation of the characteristic activities of living matter.

debacle (Meteor.): The breaking up of the surface ice of great rivers in spring.

debridement (Surg.): The removal of foreign matter and excision of infected and lacerated tissue from a wound.

decade: The time period of ten years.

decalcification (Med.): The process of absorption of lime salts from bone.

dec'androus (Bot.): Having ten stamens.

dec'aploid (Cyt.): Having ten times the haploid number of chromosomes.

dec'astyle (Arch.): A portico having ten columns.

deceleration (Mech.): The rate of diminution in the speed of a vehicle or moving part.

decid'uous (Bot.): Falling off, generally before cold or drought sets in.

decimal: The name for a system of units of which each unit is ten times the next smaller one.

decimal fraction: A fraction having a power of ten as denominator.

dec'linate (Bot.): Descending in the form of a curve.

declining (Bot.): Straight and pointing downwards.

declinom'eter (Elec Eng.): An instrument for making accurate measurements of the angle between the magn tic and geographic meridians.

decomposition (Chem.): The more or less permanent breakdown of a molecule into simpler molecules or atoms.

decomposition voltage (Elec. Eng.): The minimum voltage which will cause continuous electrolysis in an electrolytic cell.

decompound (Bot.): A term applied to a compound leaf having leaflets made up of several distinct parts.

decompression (Surg.): Any procedure for the relief of pressure.

deconjugation (Cyt.): The separation of the chromosomes before the end of the prophase of meiosis.

decor'ticated (Bot.): Having no bark.

decrepitation (Chem.): The crackling sound made when crystals are heated.

decumbent (Bot.): Lying flat, except for the tip, which ascends.

decurved (Bot.): Bent downwards.

deductive reasoning: The mental process whereby an unobserved fact is inferred from relevant observations of other facts.

deep therapy (Radiology): Treatment of diseases by deep X-rays.

deficiency (Cyt.): The loss of a portion of a chromosome.

definition (Acous.): The clarity of perception of speech sounds.

definitive (Zool.): Fully developed.

def'lagrating spoon (Chem.): A small spoon-shaped instrument used in chemical laboratories for handling materials which are liable to take fire when exposed to air.

deflagra'tion (Chem.): Sudden combustion.

deflection (Eng.): (1) The amount of bending or twisting of a structure. (2) The movement of the hand of any recording instrument.

deflection angle (Surv.): The angle between one survey line and the prolongation of another survey line which meets it.

deflectom'eter (Eng.): A device for measuring the amount of bending suffered by a beam during a transverse test.

deflexed (Bot.): Bent outwards and downwards.

degaussing (Elec. Eng.): Neutralization of the magnetization of a mass of magnetic material.

degeneration (Bot.): The loss of morphological or physiological characters by a fungus kept in culture for a long time. (Biol.): Evolutionary retrogression.

deglutit'ion (Zool.): The act of swallowing.

degradation (Chem.): The conversion of a complex alkaloid molecule into simpler fragments.

degree of a curve (Surv.): The angle subtended at the center of a curve by a standard chord length of 100 ft.

degressive (Bot.): A change towards simplification or degeneration.

dehis'cence (Bot.): The spontaneous opening at maturity of a fruit or any other reproductive body. (Zool.): The act of splitting open.

dehydration (Chem.): (1) The splitting off of H_2O from a molecule by the action of heat or by a dehydrating agent. (2) The removal of water from tars, oils, crystals etc. by heating, distillation, or by chemical action. (Med.): Excessive loss of water from the body tissues.

deionization (Au. Eng.): The process whereby an ionized gas returns to its normal neutral condition.

de-ionization (Phys.): Disappearance of ions in an

ionized gas.

dekad': The interval of ten days.

delamination (Zool.): The division of cells in a tissue, leading to the formation of layers.

delay (Elec. Comm.): The time taken for a signal to travel from one end of an electrical communication system to the other.

delayed opening (Aero.): Delaying the opening of a parachute by an automatic device.

deletion (Cyt.): The loss of a portion of a chromosome.

delinquent (Psychol.): An individual, generally a child or adolescent, who shows definite lack of moral and social sense.

deliquescence (Chem.): The change undergone by certain substances which become damp and finally liquefy when exposed to the air.

delivery (Eng.): (1) The discharge from a compressor or pump. (2) The withdrawal of a pattern from a mold. (Med.): The birth of a child.

delta (Geol.): A more or less triangular area of river-borne sediment deposited at the mouths of rivers.

deltoid (Bot., Zool.): Any triangular structure.

delusion (Psychiatry): A belief in events for which there is no objective evidence.

demagnetization (Elec. Eng.): The process whereby a magnetized body has its degree of magnetization reduced.

dementia (Psychol.): Any form of insanity characterized by the failure of mental powers.

demer'sal (Zool.): Found on the sea bottom.

demography: The study of population statistics and the estimation of their variation with time.

demul'cent (Med.): Soothing.

dena'tured alcohol (Chem.): Alcohol which according to law has been made unfit for human consumption by the admixture of poisonous substances.

dendrite (Crystal.): A tree-like crystal formation.

dendrit'ic (Bot.): Much branched.

den'drograph (Bot.): An instrument which is used to measure the periodical swelling and shrinkage of tree trunks.

dendroid (Bot.): Freely branched.

dener'vated (Med.): Deprived of nerve supply.

denig'rate (Bot.): Blackened.

denizen (Bot.): A specimen which maintains its footing as a mild plant, though probably introduced by man.

densi-tensim'eter (Chem.): An apparatus for determining the pressure and density of a vapor.

density (Phys.): The mass of unit volume of a substance.

density bottle (Chem.): A thin, glass, calibrated bottle used for the determination of the density of a liquid.

density function (Astron.): A formula expressing the total number of stars per unit volume chosen.

dental: Pertaining to the teeth.

dentate (Bot.): Having a toothed margin.

denticles (Zool.): Any small tooth-like structures.

dentine (Zool.): A hard calcareous substance of which teeth and placoid scales are mainly composed.

dentistry: The treatment of diseases and irregularities of the teeth.

denu'date (Bot.): Having a worn or stripped appearance.

deoxidation (Met.): The process of elemination of oxygen from molten metal before casting.

departure (Surv.): The projected length of a survey line upon a line at right angles to the reference meridian.

depaup'erate (Bot.): Having a starved, undeveloped appearance.

dephosphorization (Met.): Elimination of phosphorous from steel.

dep'ilate (Med.): To remove the hair from.

depil'atories (Chem.): Compounds for removing or destroying hair.

deplan'ate (Bot.): Flattened.

deposit (Elec. Eng.): The coating of metal deposited electrolytically upon any material.

deposition (Geol.): The placing into position of sheets

of sediment or of mineral veins and lodes.

depressed (Med.): Lowering functional activity.

depressed (Bot.): Flattened.

depression (Meteor.): The name for that distribution of atmospheric pressure in which the pressure decreases to a minimum at the center. (Psychol.): A state of dejection.

depth gauge (Eng.): A gauge used for measuring the depth of a hole.

derivative hybrid (Gen.): A hybrid obtained by crossing two hybrids or by crossing a hybrid with one of its parents.

dermal (Bot.): Appertaining to the epidermis. (Zool.): Pertaining to the skin.

dermati'tis (Med.): Inflamation of the skin surface.

dermatol'ogy (Med.): That branch of medical science which deals with the skin and its diseases.

derrick (Civ. Eng.): An arrangement for hoisting material.

dertrum (Zool.): In birds, the horny casing of the beak.

descending (Bot.): Growing or hanging downwards in a gradual curve.

descrt (Geol): A barren and uninhabited tract of large extent.

des'iccants (Chem.): Substances capable of absorbing moisture and used as drying agents.

dessication: The process of drying.

des'iccator (Chem.): Laboratory apparatus for drying substances.

desynap'sis (Cyt.): Abnormally early breaking up of synapsis in meiosis.

detailer (Civ. Eng.): A draughtsman who designs the details involved in steelwork construction.

detector (Elec. Eng.): A simple form of galvanometer used for detecting the presence of current in a circuit.

deter'gents (Chem.): Cleansing agents.

determinate (Bot.): With a well-marked edge.

det'onator: A substance which initiates an explosion.

detrition (Geol.): The natural process of rubbing or wearing down strata by blown wind or running water.

development (Bot., Zool.): The succession of stages in the life growth.

deviation (Matho.): The amount by which one of a set of observed values differs from the mean value.

dew (Meteor.): The deposit of moisture on exposed surfaces which accumulates during clear, calm nights.

dew claw (Zool.): The useless claw which represents the rudimentary first digit.

dew-point (Meteor., Phys.): The temperature at which a given sample of moist air will become saturated and deposit dew.

diagnosis (Med.): The identification of a diseased state.

diagonal: A straight line drawn between two non-adjacent angles of a polygon.

diagram (Geom., etc.): An outline figure to represent an object or area, to indicate the relation between parts, or to show the value of forces or quantities.

dial: The observable functional part of an indicating instrument.

diameter (Geom.): (1) A straight line passing through the center of a figure and terminated by its boundaries. (2) A straight line bisecting a system of parallel chords in a curve.

diamond (Min.): One of the crystalline form of carbon. carbon.

dian'drous (Bot.): Having two anthers or two stamens.

diaphragm (Zool.): Generally, a transverse partition subdividing a cavity.

diarrhea (Med.): The frequent evacuation of liquid faeces.

di'astase (Chem.): Enzymes capable of converting starch into sugar.

diather'manous (Phys.): Capable of transmitting radiant heat.

diather'my (Med.): The generation of heat in body tissues by the passage of electric current.

dibasic acids (Chem.): Acids containing two replaceable hydrogen atoms in the molecule.

dicar'yon (Cyt.): A pair of closely associated nuclei which divide at the same time.

dichotomy (Astron.) : The half-illuminated phase of a planet.

didac′tyl (Zool.) : Having two digits.

die (Eng.) : A metal block used in stamping operations.

diecasting (Met.) : A process by which castings of various alloys and cast-iron are produced in permanent molds.

differential calculus (Maths.) : A branch of mathematics dealing with continuously varying quantities.

differentiation (Bot.) : The organization of mature tissues or members from generalized rudiments.

dif′fluent (Bot.) : Readily becoming fluid.

difformed (Bot.) : of unusual form.

digestion (Zool.) : The process by which food material ingested by an organism is made soluble and assimilable by enzyme action.

digit (Zool.) : A finger or toe.

dilated (Bot.) : Expanded and flattened.

dilution (Chem.) : Decrease of concentration.

dimonoecious (Bot.) : Having perfect flowers as well as staminate, pistillate and neuter flowers.

dimor′phic (Bot., Zool.) : Existing in two forms.

dioecious (Bot.) : Having the male and female organs on separate plants of the same species, each plant being unisexual.

di′orite (Geol.) : A coarse-grained igneous rock.

dip (Elec. Eng.) : The angle between the earth's magnetic field at any point and the horizontal. (Geol.) : A term implying inclination of strata, measured by the horizontal.

dip stick (Eng.) : A rod inserted in a tank to measure the depth of oil or other liquids.

diphylet′ic (Biol.) : Of dual origin.

diph′yodont (Zool.) : Having two sets of teeth.

diploid (Cyt.) : Having the somatic number of chromosomes characteristic of the species.

diplo′sis (Cyt.) : The doubling of the chromosome number.

dip′lotene (Cyt.) : The fourth stage of meiotic prophase.

diplozo′ic (Zool.) : Bilaterally symmetrical.

di′pole (Chem.) : A molecule in which the effective centers of the positive and negative charges are separated.

dipping (Eng.) : The immersion of pieces of material in a liquid bath for surface treatment.

direct current (Elec. Eng.) : A current which flows in one direction only.

direct heating (Build.) : A system of heating by radiation.

direct sounds (Acous.) : The sound intensity arising from the direct radiation from a source to a listener.

disc valve (Eng.) : A form of suction and delivery valve used in pumps and compressors.

disc wheel (Eng.) : A wheel in which hub and rim are connected by a solid disc of metal instead of by separate spokes.

discharge (Elec. Eng.) : The process of taking energy from a charged accumulator.

discriminator (Elec. Eng.) : A device used in connection with the metering of an electrical supply.

disinfectant (Chem.) : Any compound for destroying germs and microbes.

disintegration (Phys.) : Radioactive breakdown in natural isotopes or radioelements.

disjunction (Cyt.) : The separation during meiosis of the two members of each pair of homologous chromosomes.

dislocation (Surg.) : The displacement of one part from another; especially two bones at a joint.

disorientation (Psychol.) : A mental state in which there is inability to judge the proper relations between events in time and space.

dispensary (Med.) : (1) A place where drugs are dispensed. (2) A clinic for the treatment of out-patients.

dispersal (Biol.) : The establishment of individuals in a new area.

dispersed phase (Chem.) : A substance in the colloidal state.

displacement (Aero.) : The mass of the air displaced by the volume of gas in any lighter-than-air craft. (Eng.) : The volume of fluid displaced by a pump

plunger per stroke or per unit time. (Psychol.) : A mechanism commonly observed in dreams, whereby a hidden element may be replaced by something more remote.

disposition (Psychol.) : The mental constitution of an individual, as formed by his reactions to environment and experience.

dissected (Bot.) : Cut deeply into many narrow leaflets or lobes.

disseminate (Bot.) : Scattered.

dissociation (Chem.) : The reversible or temporary breaking-down of a molecule into simpler molecules or atoms. (Psycho-path.) : A state of temporary loosening of control over consciousness.

dissolution (Chem.) : The taking up of a substance by a liquid, with the formation of a homogeneous solution.

distal (Biol.) : Widely spaced.

disti′chorus (Bot.) : Arranged in two opposite vertical rows.

distillation (Chem.) : A process of evaporation and recondensation used for separating liquids into various fractions according to their boiling points.

distinct (Bot.) : Said of a species which has strongly marked characters.

distortion (Elec. Comm.) : Any departure from the initial wave-form of a signal during transmission.

distributor (Elec. Eng.) : The cable forming that part of the electric distribution system to which the consumers' circuits are connected.

ditch (Civ. Eng.) : A channel cut in the surface of the ground for drainage purposes.

ditching (Aero.) : Emergency alighting of a land plane on water.

diurnal : During a day.

diva′lent (Chem.) : Capable of combining with two atoms of hydrogen or their equivalent.

dive (Aero.) : A steep descent, the nose of the aircraft being down.

divergent (Bot.) : Said of two or more organs which gradually spread so that they are farther apart at their tips than at their bases.

diving-bell (Civ. Eng.) : A water-tight working chamber, open at the bottom, which is lowered into water beneath which excavation or other works are to proceed.

doldrums (Meteor.) : Regions of calm in equatorial oceans.

dol′erite (Geol.) : The general name for basic igneous rocks of medium-grain size.

dol′omite (Min.) : An important gangue mineral.

dome (Bot.) : The growing point of the receptacle of a flower. (Geol.) : A form of igneous intrusion the roof of which has a dome-like shape.

donor (Med.) : One who gives his blood for transfusion to another.

door case (Carp.) : The frame into which a door fits to shut an opening.

door frame (Carp.) : The framework of stiles, rails and mountings into which the panels are fitted.

door strip (Carp.) : A strip attached to a door to cover the space between the bottom of the door and the floor.

dormancy (Bot.) : In seeds and other structures, a condition of inactivity.

dormer (Build.) : A small window projecting from a roof slope.

dorsal (Anat.) : Said of the back of any part.

dorsal or dorse (Arch.) : A canopy.

dorsif′erous (Zool.) : Said of animals which bear their young on their back.

dose (Med.) : The prescribed quantity of a medicine.

double-acting engine (Eng.) : Any reciprocating engine in which the working fluid acts on each side of the piston alternately.

double-acting pump (Eng.) : A reciprocating pump in which both sides of the piston act alternately.

double-beat valve (Eng.) : A hollow cylindrical valve for controlling high-pressure fluids.

double-hung window (Build.) : A window having top and bottom sashes.

double-pole (Elec. Eng.): Said of switches, circuit-breakers etc. which can make or break a circuit on two poles simultaneously.

double-wire system (Elec. Eng.): It employs separate wire for the go and return conductors.

dowel (Eng.): A pin fixed in one part which, by accurately fitting in a hole in another attached part, locates the two, thus facilitating accurate re-assembly.

down (Bot.): A fine soft coating of hairs on the surface of a plant member.

downpipe (Build.): A pipe for conveying rain water from the gutter to the drain. Also called downspout.

drag (Aero.): Resistance to motion through a fluid.

drain (Civ. Eng.): A pipe to carry away wastes and liquid sewage. (Surg.): Any piece of material used in directing away the discharges of a wound.

drain tiles (Civ. Eng.): Hollow tiles laid end to end without joints to carry off surface or excess water.

drainage (Geol.): The removal of surface meteoric waters by rivers and streams.

draught (Eng.): The flow of air through a boiler furnace.

draw-bridge (Civ. Eng.): A general name for any type of bridge of which the span is capable of being moved bodily to allow the passage of large vessels.

dredge (Civ. Eng.): Any apparatus used for excavating under water.

dresser (Eng.): (1) An iron block used in forging bent work on an anvil. (2) A mallet for flattening sheet-lead.

dressing (Surg.): The application of sterile material to a wound or infected part.

drift (Aero.): The motion of an aircraft in a horizontal plane, under the influence of an air current. (Civ. Eng.): The direction in which a tunnel is driven. (Geol.): A general name for the superficial formations of the Earth's crust.

drift currents (Meteor.): Ocean currents produced by prevailing winds.

drill (Eng.): A revolving tool used for making cylindrical holes in metal.

drizzle (Meteor.): A very fine rain.

drone (Aero.): Pilotless aircraft, electronically controlled by radio, which serves as a target for anti-aircraft weapons.

drone (Zool.): In social bees, a male.

dross (Met.): Similar to slag somewhat.

drought (Meteor.): Lack of rain.

drug: Any substance which has a physiological action on a living body.

drum (Eng.): Any hollow cylindrical barrel.

drupe (Bot.): A succulent fruit formed from a superior ovary.

dry cell (Elec. Eng.): A primary cell in which the contents are in the form of a paste.

dry dock (Civ. Eng.): A dock in which ships are repaired.

dry ice (Chem.): Solid (frozen) carbon dioxide, used in refrigeration and engineering.

dry rot (Build.): A decay of timber due to a fungus attack.

duct (Elect. Eng.): (1) A pipe for containing electric cables. (2) An air passage in the core of an electric machine along which cooling air may pass.

dust counter (meteor.): An instrument for counting dust particles in a known volume of air.

dyke (Geol.): A form of minor intrusion injected into the crust during its subjection to tension.

dy'namo (Elec. Eng.): A term used to denote any electromagnetic generator, but commonly used only for a direct-current generator.

dyspep'sia (Med.): Indigestion.

dyspha'sia (Med.): Disturbed utterance of speech, due to a lesion in the brain.

dyspho'ria (Med.): Unease.

E

ear (Zool.): The sense-organ which receives auditory impressions.

earth (Astron.): The third planet in the solar system, counting from the sun outwards.

earth pressure (Civ. Eng.): The pressure exerted on a wall by earth which is retained.

earthquake (Geol.): A shaking of the earth's crust, usually by displacement along a fault.

earthshine (Astron.): The reflected sunlight from the surface of the earth.

earth thermometer (Meteor.): A thermometer used for measuring the temperature of the earth at depths up to a few feet.

easing (Build., Civ. Eng.): The shaping of a curve so that there is no abrupt change of curvature in it.

eave (Build.): The lower part of a roof which projects beyond the face of the walls.

ecdem'ic (Zool.): Foreign.

echard (Bot.): Water present in the soil which cannot be used by plants.

echo (Acous.): A delayed sound-wave which arrives at the recipient at a later time than the directly radiated sound-wave from a source.

echo sounder (Ocean.): A sounding apparatus for determining automatically the depth of sea beneath a ship.

eclipse (Astron.): A name applicable to cases where a non-luminous body passes into the shadow of another.

eclipse seasons (Astron.): The two periods, approximately six months apart, in which solar and lunar eclipses can occur.

ecology: The study of organisms in relation to their environment.

ec'togeny (Bot.): The effect of pollen on the tissues of the female organs of the plant.

ec'tophyte (Bot.): A parasite growing on the surface of its host.

ec'toplasm (Cyt.): A layer of clear non-granular cytoplasm at the periphory of a cell.

eddy: An interruption in the steady flow of a fluid.

effervescence (Chem.): The vigorous escape of small gas bubbles from a liquid.

efficiency: The performance of a machine.

efflores'cence (Bot.): Production of flowers. (Chem.): The loss of water from a crystalline hydrate on exposure to air.

effluent (Nuclear Eng.): Radioactive waste from atomic plants.

efflux (Aero.): The mixture of combustion products and cooling air which forms the propulsive medium of any jet or rocket engine.

e'gest (Zool.): To expel.

egg albumen (Chem.): A simple protein from the white of the egg.

e'go (Psycho-an.): That part of the self formed originally from the instinctual life forces.

eidograph (Surv.): An instrument for reducing and enlarging plans.

ejector (Eng.): A device for exhausting a fluid by entraining it by a high-velocity steam or air jet.

ejection capsule (Aero.): A cockpit or cabin, in a high altitude and/or high speed military airplane which can be fired clear in emergency and which, after being slowed down, descends by parachute.

elasticity (Phys.): The tendency of a body to return to its original size or shape, after having been compressed, stretched or deformed.

elbow: A bend.

electric field (Elec. Eng.): A region in which forces are exerted on any electric charge present in the region.

electric furnace (Elec. Eng.): A furnace for industrial purposes in which the heat is produced electrically.

electric generator (Elec. Eng.): A machine for converting mechanical energy into electrical energy.

electric shock: The sudden pain or convulsion which results from the passage of an electric current through the body of a human being or animal.

electric storm (Meteor.): A condition of high electric field within a cloud.

electrical engineering: That branch of engineering chiefly concerned in the design and construction of all electrical machinery, communications, etc.

electrician: A person engaged in the construction or

maintenance of electrical apparatus or installations.

electricity: The manifestation of a form of energy believed to be due to the separation or movement of certain constituent parts of an atom known as electrons.

electrocar'diograph (Med.): An instrument used for making graphic records of the electrical changes during contraction of the muscle of the heart.

electrochemistry (Chem.): The study of the relation between electricity and chemical changes.

electrocrat'ic (Chem.): Owing its stability to an electric charge.

electro-culture (Bot.): The stimulation of the growth of plants by electrical means.

electrocution (Elec. Eng.): The causing of death by electric shock.

electrode (Elec. Eng.): A conductor whereby an electric current is led into a liquid or into a gas.

elec'trolyte (Chem.): An electrolytic conductor.

electrolytic conduction (Chem.): The conduction of electricity accompanied by the actual transfer of matter, which is shown by the occurrence of chemical changes at the electrodes.

electromagnet (Elec. Eng.): A core of iron or steel which is magnetized when a current is passed through a coil surrounding the core and behaves as a magnet.

electrom'eter (Elec. Eng.): An electrical measuring instrument for measuring potential difference.

electromotive force (Elec. Eng.): The force which tends to cause a movement of electricity around an electric circuit.

electron (Phys.): An electrically charged particle.

electronegative (Chem.): (1) Carrying a negative charge of electricity. (2) Tending to form negative ions.

electronics: The science which deals with the behavior of free electrons. Now defined as the science and technology of conduction of electricity in vacuum, in a gas, and in semi-conductors, and the utilization of devices based on these phenomena.

electro-physiology (Biol.): The science of electrical phenomena associated with living organisms.

electroplating: The production of a thin coating of one metal on another by electrodeposition.

electropositive (Chem.): (1) Carrying a positive charge of electricity. (4) Tending to form positive ions.

elec'troscope (Elec. Eng.): An apparatus which indicates the presence of a charge or a potential difference.

electrostatics (Elec. Eng.): The science which deals with the behavior of electric charges and potentials.

electro-therapy (Med.): The treatment of disease by electric currents or by electrically produced radiations.

electrova'lence (Chem.): A chemical bond in which an electron is transferred from one atom to another, the resulting ions being held together by electrostatic attraction.

element (Chem.): A substance which cannot be decomposed by chemical means into simpler substances.

elements (Meteor.): Those components, as temperature, humidity, wind, rainfall, etc., which determine the state of the weather.

elevation (Build.): The facade of a building.

elimination (Chem.): The removal of a simple molecule from different parts of the same molecule, or from two or more different molecules.

elix'ir (Med.): A strong extract or tincture.

ellipse (Geom.): A plane curve, the path of a point the sum of whose distances from two fixed points is constant; a conic section, the closed intersection of a right circular cone.

elongation (Astron.): The angular distance between the moon on planets and the sun. (Met.): The total extension produced in a tensile test.

emasculation (Med.): The removal of testes, or of testes and penis.

embankment (Civ. Eng.): A ridge of earth, stones, etc., especially constructed to carry a highway or railroad at a higher level than the surrounding ground; or as a protective bank to prevent water encroachment.

em'bolism (Med.): The blocking of a blood vessel by a mass carried, to the point of obstruction, from a remote part of the circulation.

embossed (Build.): A term applied to any form of ornamentation surface which is raised from the general surface which it is decorating.

embryo (Bot.): A young plant in a rudimentary state of development. (Zool.): An immature organism in the early stages of its development, before it emerges from the egg or the uterus.

embryol'ogy (Biol.): The study of the formation and development of embryos.

emerald (Met.): The brilliant green gemstone, a form of beryl.

emergence (Biol.): An epidermal outgrowth in insects, the appearance of the imajo from the cocoon or pupa-case.

emersed (Bot.): (1) Protruding upwards. (2) Amphibious.

emersion (Astron.): The exit of the moon, or other body, from the shadow which causes its eclipse.

emery (Min.): A finely granular admixture of corundum and magnetite or hematite; used as an abrasive.

emet'ic (Med.): Having the power to cause vomiting.

emotion (Psychol.): A mental state characterized by a strong degree of feeling.

empirical: Said of a rule or generalization which is induced solely from observation, without correlation, without scientific law.

emulsion (Chem.): A colloidal suspension of one liquid in another.

ena'tion (Bot.): A general term for an outgrowth.

encephali'tis (Med.): Inflammation of the brain substance.

enceph'alogram (Med.): An X-ray photograph of the skull and the brain.

enchyle'ma (Cyt.): The more fluid constituents of cytoplasm.

endem'ic (Med.): Prevalent in, and confined to, a particular country or area: said of disease.

endolith'ic (Bot.): Growing within the substance of rocks or stones.

endoplasm (Cyt.): The granular central portion of the cytoplasm of a cell.

en'doscope (Med.): A tubular instrument for inspecting the cavities of internal organs.

en'dosperm (Bot.): A multicellular tissue formed inside a developing seed.

en'dospore (Bot.): The innermost layer of the wall of a spore.

endurance (Aero.): The maximum time, or distance, that an aircraft can continue to fly without refueling.

energetics (Chem.): The abstract study of the energy relations to physical and chemical changes.

energy (Phys.): The capacity of a body for doing work.

engine (Eng.): Generally, a machine in which power is applied to do work.

engine speed (Aero.): In a turbine engine, the revolutions per minute of the main rotor assembly.

engineer: One engaged in the science and art of engineering practice.

enlargement (Bot.): Primary growth in thickness before secondary thickening begins.

enrich (Nuclear Eng.): To increase the proportion of fissile material in a fuel for a nuclear reactor.

entab'lature (Arch.): The whole of the parts immediately supported upon columns, consisting of an architrave, a frieze and a cornice.

entel'echy (Zool.): The vital element that controls and directs response to stimuli.

enter'ic (Med.): Pertaining to the intestines.

enthal'py (Phys.): The heat content of a substance per unit mass.

entomol'ogy: The branch of zoology which deals with the study of insects.

entomoph'agous (Zool.): Feeding on insects.

Science Terms

en'tomophi'ly (Zool.) : Pollination by insects.

entozo'ic (Bot.) : Living inside an animal.

entozo'on (Zool.) : An animal parasite living within the body of the host.

entrain (Eng.) : In a moving fluid, a suspension of bubbles or particles.

entrainment (Chem.) : Transport of small liquid particles in vapor.

entrance lock (Eng.) : A lock through which vessels must pass in entering or leaving a dock.

environment (Biol.) : The sum total of the external and internal conditions which influence existence, growth, development and activity.

en'zymes (Chem.) : Catalysts produced by living cells.

e'olith (Geol.) : A term applied to the oldest-known stone implements used by early man.

Eolith'ic (Geol.) : The time of the primitive men who manufactured and used eoliths.

ephe'bic (Zool.) : Adult ; mature.

ephemeral (Bot.) : A plant which completes its whole life-history in a very short time.

ephemeral movement (Bot.) : A movement of a plant member which cannot be repeated ; as the opening of a bud.

ephem'eris (Astron.) : A compilation, published at regular intervals, in which are tabulated the daily positions of the sun, moon, planets and certain stars with other data necessary for the astronomer and navigator.

epicenter : That point on the surface of the earth lying immediately above the focus of an earthquake.

epidem'ic (Med.) : An outbreak of an infectuous disease spreading widely among people at the same time in any region.

epide'miol'ogy (Med.) : That branch of medical science concerned with the study of epidemics.

epider'mis (Bot.) : A sheath of closely united cells forming a layer over the surface of the leaves and young stems of a plant. (Zool.) : Those layers of the integument which are ectodermal in origin.

ep'ilepsy (Med.) : A general term for a sudden disturbance of cerebral function accompanied by loss of consciousness with or without convulsion.

ep'isperm (Bot.) : The outer part of a seed coat.

equal (Bot.) : Not lop-sided.

equilibrium (Chem.) : The state reached in a reversible reaction when the reaction velocities in the two opposing directions are equal. (Mech.) : The state of a body which is at rest or is moving with uniform velocity.

equinoctial (Bot.) : Said of plants bearing flowers which open and close at definite times.

equinox (Astron.) : The instant at which the sun in its apparent annual motion crosses the celestial equator.

eq'uivalve (Zool.) : Said of bivalves which have the two halves of the shell of equal size.

erect (Bot.) : Set at right angles to the part from which it grows.

erg (Mech.) : A unit of work or energy.

eroded (Bot.) : Appearing as if gnawed or worn irregularly.

erosion (Geol.) : The lowering of the land surface by weathering.

error : Term for any small difference from the correct value.

eruption (Med.) : A rash.

escapement : A device for converting circular motion into reciprocating motion.

escarpment (Geol.) : A long cliff-like ridge. Generally consists of a short steep rise and a long gentle slope.

establishment (Bot.) : The successful germination and subsequent growth of a plant.

ester (Chem.) : Derivatives of acids.

estuary (Geol.) : An inlet of the sea at the mouth of a river.

etching (Met.) : The process of revealing the structure of metals and alloys.

ete'sian winds (Meteor.) : In the Mediterranean, winds which blow from the north-west for about 40 days in the summer.

e'theogen'esis (Zool.) : Parthenogenesis of male individuals.

e'thers (Chem.) : Compounds derived from two molecules of an alcohol by elimination of one molecule of water.

et'iola'tion (Bot.) : The condition of a green plant which has not received sufficient light.

eudiom'eter (Chem.) : An apparatus for determining the composition of gases.

eugam'ic (Zool.) : Pertaining to the period of maturity.

eumito'sis (Cyt.) : Typical normal mitosis.

eupep'tic (Med.) : Possessing a good digestion.

eupot'amous (Ecol.) : Normally living in rivers and streams.

euryha'line (Ecol.) : Normally inhabiting salt water.

euryther'mous (Ecol.) : Tolerant of a wide range of temperature.

eustatic movements (Geol.) : Changes of sea level.

eutec'tic (Chem.) : Relative to a mixture of two or more substances having a minimum melting-point.

euthana'sia (Med.) : Easy or painless death.

eu'tropy (Chem.) : The regular variation of the crystalline form of a series of compounds with the atomic number of the element.

evaporation (Phys.) : The conversion of a liquid into vapor, at temperatures below the boiling point.

evaporation, natural (Meteor.) : The evaporation that takes place at the surface of rivers, ponds, etc., which are exposed to the weather.

evaporim'eter (Meteor.) : An instrument used for measuring the rate of natural evaporation.

even (Bot.) : Having a smooth surface.

evening star (Astron.) : The name given in popular language to a planet, generally Mercury or Venus, seen in the western sky at or just after sunset.

e'volute (Biol.) : Having the margins rolled outwards.

evolution (Biol.) : The gradual development of more complex organisms from simpler forms.

evulsion (Surg.) : Plucking out by force.

exacerba'tion (Med.) : An increase in the severity of a disease.

excavation (Civ. Eng.) : The operation of digging material out from the solid mass and depositing it elsewhere.

excavator (Civ. Eng.) : A power-driven machine for excavating earth.

excision (Surg.) : The action of cutting a part out or off.

excitation (Bot.) : The action of a stimulus on a plant organ. (Zool.) : The setting of a metabolic process into activity or acceleration.

excited (Nucleonics) : Said of an atom when, by absorption of photons or by collision, its energy rises above that of the ground state.

excres'cence (Med.) : Any abnormal outgrowth of tissue.

excre'ta (Zool.) : Poisonous or waste substances eliminated from a cell, tissue or organism.

exfoliation : The process of falling away in flakes, layers or scales.

exha'lant (Zool.) : Emitting or carrying outwards a fluid or gas.

exhaust (Eng.) : The working fluid discharged from an engine cylinder after expansion.

exhaust fan (Eng.) : A fan used in artificial draught systems.

exhaust pipe (Eng.) : The pipe through which the exhaust products of an engine are discharged.

ex'oderm (Zool.) : The outer cell layer.

ex'ogan'ete (Zool.) : A gamete which unites with one from another parent.

ex'ogam'y (Bot., Zool.) : Union between gametes which are not closely related.

ex'ospore (Bot.) : The outer layer of the wall of a spore.

exotoxin (Bacteriol.) : The toxin produced by a bacterium in the medium in which it grows.

expanded: Of cellular structure and therefore light in weight.

expansion: Increase in one or more of the dimensions of a body.

expiration (Zool., etc.): The expulsion of air or water from the respiratory organs.

exploring cell (Elec. Eng.): A small coil used for measuring the flux in a magnetic field.

explosion (Chem.): A rapid increase of pressure in a confined space.

exposure (Meteor.): The method by which an instrument is exposed to the elements.

exser'ted: Stretched out.

extensom'eter (Met.): An instrument used, in the testing of metals, for measuring small values of strain.

exten'sor (Zool.): A muscle which by its contraction straightens a limb, or a part of the body.

extraction (Met.): The processes used in obtaining metals from their ores.

extravert (Psychol.): An individual well adapted to the outside world and to other people.

extrusive rocks (Geol.): Rocks formed by the consolidation of magma on the surface of the ground.

exudation (Bot.): The liberation of liquid water or sap from special pores in the plant.

eye (Eng.): A loop formed at the end of a steel wire or bolt. (Meteor.): The central calm area of a cyclone or hurricane. (Zool.): The sense organ which receives visual impressions.

eyepiece (Phys.): In an optical instrument, the lens to which the observer applies his eye in using the instrument.

F

facade (Build.): The front elevation of a building.

face: The outer, upper or more important surface of any object. (Eng.): The working surface of any part.

face lathe (Eng.): A lathe designed for work of large diameter but short length.

facette (Arch.): A projecting flat surface between adjacent flutes in a column.

facia (Arch.): A flat banded projection from the face of a member.

fa'cial (Zool.): Pertaining to or situated on the face.

facies (Bot.): The general form and appearance of a plant.

facing (Civ. Eng.): An outer covering applied to the exposed face of sea-walls, embankments, etc. (Eng.): (1) The operation of turning a flat face on a piece of work in the lathe. (2) A raised machine surface to which another part is to be attached.

fac'ulae (Astron.): The name given to large bright areas of the photosphere of the sun.

fac'ultative (Zool.): Optional; able to live under different conditions.

fadom'eter (Chem.): An instrument used to determine the resistance of a dye or pigment to fading.

faeces (Zool.): The indigestible residues remaining in the alimentary canal after digestion and absorption of food-materials.

Fahrenheit scale: The method of graduating a thermometer with the fixed points marked 32° F and 212° F.

fairing (Aero.): A secondary structure added to any part of an aircraft to reduce drag by improving the streamlining.

falcu'la (Zool.): A sharp curved claw.

fall (Civ. Eng., etc.): The inclination of rivers, streams, etc.

Fallo'pian tube (Zool.): In mammals, the oviduct.

fall-out (Nuclear Warfare): Deposition of highly radioactive particles down-wind, after being vaporized and sucked up by the heat of a nuclear explosion on or near the ground.

false ceiling (Build.): A lower dummy ceiling formed to provide covered accommodation for wires, conduits, etc.

family (Biol.): A group of individuals within an order or suborder.

fan (Eng.): A device for delivering or exhausting large volumes of air or gas.

fascia (Arch., Build.): (1) A wide flat member in an entablature. (2) A board carrying a gutter around the leaves of a building. (3) The broad flat surface below a cornice.

fas'cicle (Bot.): A tuft of leaves crowded on a short stem.

fastener (Build.): A device such as a nail, screw, dowel, etc. for securing two parts together.

fats (Chem.): An important group of naturally occurring substances consisting of the glycerides of higher fatty acids.

fathom: A unit of measurement; generally, a nautical measurement of depth = 6 ft.

fatigue (Zool.): The condition of an excitable cell or tissue which, as a result of activity, is less ready to further stimulation until it has had time to recover.

fatigue test (Eng., Met.): A test made on a material to determine the range of alternating stress.

fault: A defect in a mechanism in which normal function is impaired.

fault (Geol.): A fracture in rocks along which some displacement has taken place.

fauna (Zool.): A collective term denoting the animals occurring in a particular region or period.

fauton (Build.): A metal rod embedded in concrete.

fa'veolate (Bot., Zool.): Resembling a honeycomb in appearance.

feathers (Zool.): Epidermal outgrowths forming the body-covering of birds.

feb'rile (Med.): Pertaining to, produced by, or affected with fever.

feed (Eng.): (1) The rate at which the cutting tool of a machine is advanced. (2) Fluid pumped into a vessel. (3) Mechanism for advancing material into a machine for processing.

feeling (Psychol.): An affective experience.

feldspar (Min.): A group of rock-forming silicates.

female (Bot.): A flower having carpels and no stamens. (Zool.): An individual the gonads of which produce ova.

fen: Low marshy land.

fence (Eng.): (1) A guard or stop to limit motion. (2) A guide for material, as in a circular saw.

fenes'tra (Build.): A window or other opening in the outer walls of a building. (Zool.): An aperture in a bone or cartilage or between two or more bones.

fenestral (Build.): A window-opening covered with oiled paper or cloth.

fe'ral (Bot., Zool.): Wild.

fermentation (Chem.): A slow decomposition process of organic substances induced by micro-organisms.

ferritin (Chem.): Protein containing iron.

ferro-electric (Phys.): Said of non-magnetic material exhibiting spontaneous and substantially permanent electric polarization.

ferrous oxide (Chem.): An oxide of iron.

ferru'genous (Bot.): Reddish-brown.

ferrugenous deposits (Geol.): Sedimentary rocks containing sufficient iron to justify exploitation as iron ore.

ferrule (Eng.): A short length of tube.

fertile (Bot.): Able to produce spores or seeds.

fertile flower (Bot.): A pistillate flower.

fertilization (Biol.): The union of two sexually differentiated gametes to form a zygote.

fever (Med.): The complex reaction of the body to infection, associated with a rise in temperature.

fibre (Bot.): (1) A very narrow, elongated, thick-walled cell, tapering to a sharp point at both ends. (2) A very delicate root. (Met.): Any arrangement of the constituents of metals parallel to the direction of working.

fi'bril (Bot.): A small fibre. (Zool.): Any minute thread-like structure.

fibrin (Chem., Zool.): An insoluble protoid substance

which is precipitated in the form of a meshwork of fibres when blood coagulates.

fibrinogen (Chem., Zool.): A protein contained in the plasma of blood.

fibroid (Med.): Resembling fibrous tissue.

fibrous tissue (Zool.): Any tissue containing a large number of fibres.

fidelity (Elec. Comm.): The measure of the performance of a reproducing system.

fidu'cial (Surv.): Said of a line or point assumed as a fixed basis of reference.

field (Phys.): The region in which the forces being considered are visible. (Surv.): The term denoting the scene of operation of the surveyor.

field coil (Elec. Eng.): The coil which carries the current for producing the magnetomotive force to set up the flux in an electric machine.

filament (Bot.): (1) A chain of cells set end to end. (2) The stalk of a stamen. (Elec. Eng.): A fine wire of high resistance. (Zool.): Any fine thread-like structure.

file (Eng.): A hand metal-cutting tool.

filial generation (Gen.): The offspring of a cross-mating.

filicin'ean (Bot.): Relating to ferns.

filing block (Eng.): A wooden block which is held in the vice, and to which light flat work is secured for filing.

fillet (Arch.): A flat and narrow surface separating or strengthening curved moldings.

film (Chem.): A thin layer of a substance, generally differing in properties from other layers in contact with it.

filter (Chem.): An apparatus used for the separation of liquids from solids.

filter paper (Chem.): Paper, consisting of pure cellulose, which is used for separating solids from liquids by filtration.

filtrate (Chem.): The liquid freed from solid matter after having passed through a filter.

fin (Aero.): In an airplane, a fixed vertical surface giving lateral stability of motion.

fineness (Chem.): The state of subdivision of a substance. (Met.): The purity of a gold or silver alloy.

fin'ial (Build.): A term applied to an ornament placed at the summit of a gable, spire or pillar.

fiords or fjords (Geol.): Narrow winding inlets of the sea bounded by mountain slopes.

fire escape (Build.): A special means of exit from a building, for use in event of fire.

fire extinguishers: Generally portable with a range up to 40 ft.

fireplace (Build.): The place where a chimney opens into a room.

fire plug: A hydrant for service in extinguishing fires.

fire-stone (Geol.): A stone or rock capable of withstanding a considerable amount of heat without injury.

fire stop (Build.): An obstruction across an air passage in a building to prevent flames from spreading further.

firing (Eng.): (1) The process of adding fuel to a boiler furnace. (2) The ignition of an explosive mixture.

fissile (Bot., Zool.): Split.

fissile (Nuclear Eng.): Said of isotopes which can, in a reactor, maintain a chain reaction of neutrons.

fission (Astron.): The breaking-up of a single gaseous body into two unequal masses, to form a binary star. (Phys.): The splitting of an atomic nucleus, as the result of bombardment by neutrons, into two other atomic nuclei.

fission (Phys.): Breakdown of atomic nuclei into approximately equal parts, identifiable as isotopes of lower-number elements, yet yielding neutrons and gamma-rays with much energy.

fissure (Geol.): A cleft in rock determined in the first instance by a fracture, a joint plane or fault, subsequently widened by erosion or solution. (Med.): Any normal cleft in organs of the body.

fis'tular (Bot.): Hollow like a pipe.

fitter (Eng.): A mechanic who assembles finished parts in an engineering workshop.

fittings (Eng.): (1) Small auxiliary parts of an engine or machine. (2) Boiler accessories.

fix (Aero.): The exact geographical position of an aircraft.

fixation (Zool.): The action of certain muscles which prevent disturbance of the equilibrium of the body or limbs.

fixative (Bot., Zool.): A reagent which will permanently fix the structure of a specimen in a life-like condition.

fixture (Build.): An attachment to a building.

flaccid (Bot.): Limp and flabby.

flagstone (Civ. Eng.): A flat thin stone used as a paving material.

flagellate (Bot., Zool.): Bearing a long thread-like appendage.

flakes (Met.): Minute transverse internal fissures which appear as bright scales on fractured surfaces of steel forgings.

flame (Chem.): A region in which chemical interaction between gases occur, accompanied by the evolution of light and heat.

flame test (Chem.): The detection of the presence of an element in a substance by the coloration imparted to a Busen flame.

flame (Eng.): A projecting rim.

flap (Aero.): Any surface attached to the wing which can be adjusted in flight to alter the lift as a whole.

flare: A bright light used as a signal.

flash test (Elec. Eng.): A test applied to electrical equipment for testing its insulation strength.

flats (Eng.): Steel or iron bars of rectangular section.

flat roof (Build.): A roof surface laid nearly horizontal.

flight engineer (Aero.): A member of the flying crew of an aircraft responsible for engineering duties as management of the engineers, etc.

flocculation (Chem.): The coalescence of a finely divided precipitate into larger particles.

floccus (Zool.): A tuft.

floor plan (Build.): A separate plan drawn for each floor of a building showing dimensions of the rooms and the thicknesses of walls.

flora (Bot.): The plant population of any area under consideration.

floral envelope (Bot.): The calyx and corolla.

floret (Bot.): An individual flower in a crowded inflorescence.

flow (Eng.): A pipe by which water leaves a boiler or pressure cistern.

flow lines (Met.): Lines which appear in the surface of iron and steel when stressed to the yield points.

flower (Bot.): A group of closely crowded specialized leaves at the end of a short branch, including one or more of the following members: sepals, petals, carpels, stamens.

flower bud (Bot.): A bud enclosing one or more young flowers but no foliage leaves.

fluctuating variation (Gen.): Variation as shown by the differences between the individuals of one progeny.

fluctuation (Bot.): A change in a plant due to the effect of its environment on it. (Med.): The palpable undulation of fluid in any cavity or abnormal swelling of the body.

flue (Build.): A smoke-duct in a chimney.

fluid: A substance which flows and offers no permanent resistance to change of shape.

fluidization: The handling of solids as if they were liquids.

fluores'cence: The absorption of radiation of a particular wave length by a substance and its reemission as light of greater wave length.

fluorescope: Screen coated with fluorescent material for observing images excited by X-rays.

fluorine (Chem.): A non-metallic element. The presence of small quantities in water supplies has been found to promote strong resitsance to dental decay.

fluorophore (Chem.): A group of atoms which give a molecule fluorescent properties.

flush (Bot.): (1) A period of renewed growth in a woody plant. (2) A limited area watered by a spring, or by the run off from rainfall.

flush (Build.): In the same plane.

flute (Build.): A long vertical groove.

flying buttress (Build.): An arched buttress giving support to the foot of another arch.

foam (Chem.): A suspension, often colloidal, of a gas in a liquid.

focus (Maths.): The point of contact of the focal sphere.

foetus (Zool.): A young animal within the egg or the uterus of the mother.

fog (Meteor.): A condition of obscurity in which visibility is less than 1 kilometer; fog may consist of a cloud of water droplets, dust or smoke particles.

Fogbow (Meteor.): A bow seen opposite the sun in fog.

folding (Geol.): The bending of strata.

fo'liose (Bot.): Bearing leaving.

foliage leaf (Bot.): The ordinary green leaf of a plant.

foliation (Geol.): The arrangement of minerals normally possessing a platy habit in leaves.

fol'licle (Bot.): A fruit formed from a single carpel and containing several seeds. (Zool.): Any small sac-like structure.

foot (Zool.): A locomotor appendage.

footing (Build, Civ. Eng.): The lower part of a column or wall. (Elec. Eng.): The foundation which is set in the ground to support a tower of an overhead transmission line.

forb (Bot.): Any herb other than a grass.

force (Mech.): That which, when acting on a body which is free to move, produces an acceleration in the motion of the body.

force pump (Eng.): Any pump which delivers liquid under a pressure greater than its suction pressure.

forceps (Med.): A pincer-like instrument with two blades, for holding or extracting objects.

forcing: The process of hastening growth by artificial means.

forecast (Meteor.): A statement of the anticipated weather conditions in a given region.

forging (Eng.): The operation of shaping that metal by means of pressure or hammers.

fork lift truck: A vehicle with power operated prongs, which can be raised or lowered, for loading and unloading goods.

forked (Bot.): Dividing into two or more distinct branches which diverge as they elongate.

formal'dehyde (Chem.): A gas of pungent odor, readily soluble in water and usually used in aqueous solution.

formative stage of growth (Bot.): The stage in development when a cell is formed from a pre-existing cell.

formula: A fixed rule or set form.

fossette (Zool.): In general, a small pit.

fossil (Geol.): A relic of some former living thing—plant or animal—embedded in, or dug out of, the superficial deposits of past geological periods.

fosso'rial (Zool.): Adopted for digging.

fouling (Eng.): Coming into accidental contact with.

foundation (Build., Civ. Eng.): The formation upon which a building or construction rests.

foundry (Eng.): A workshop in which metal objects are made by casting in sand or loam molds.

fo'vea (Zool.): A small depression.

fovil'la (Bot.): The material inside a pollen grain.

fractional crystallization (Chem): The separation of substances by the repeated partial crystallization of a solution.

fractional distillation (Chem.): Distillation process for the separation of the various components of liquid mixtures.

fracture (Min.): The broken surface of a mineral as distinct from its cleavage. (Surg.): Breaking of a bone.

fragmentation (Cyt.): The separation of a portion from the main body of a chromosome.

frames (Civ. Eng.): The centring used in concrete construction.

framework: The supporting skeleton of a structure.

framed (Carp.): Said of work assembled with mortise and tenon joints.

free (Bot.): Not joined laterally to another member of the same kind.

free association (Psycho-an.): The method used for making unconscious processes conscious.

free cell formation (Bot.): The formation of daughter cells which do not remain united.

free end (Build.): The end of a cantilever which is not built in or fixed.

free nuclear division (Cyt.): Nuclear division unaccompanied by the formation of cell walls.

free pole (Elec. Eng.): A magnet pole which is imagined, for theoretical purposes, to exist separately from its corresponding opposite pole.

free radical (Chem.): A group of atoms which normally exists only in combination with other atoms, brought into independent existence by special conditions.

freezing: The conversion of a liquid into a solid form.

freezing-point: The temperature at which a liquid solidifies.

French window (Buildg.): A glazed casement, serving as both window and door.

frequency (Phys.): The number of vibrations, waves or cycles of any periodic phenomenon per second. (Ecol.): The relative number of any given species in a given place. (Elec.): The frequency at which an electric current alternates.

friction (Mech.): The resistance to motion when it is attempted to slide one surface over another.

frieze (Arch., Build.): (1) The middle part of an entablature between the architrave and the cornice. (2) The decorated upper part of a wall, below the cornice.

frigidity (Psychol.): In women, decrease or absence of the normal sexual response.

frond (Bot.): A general term for the leaf of a fern.

front (Carp.): The sole face of a plane. (Meteor.): The line of separation between masses of air at different temperatures.

frost (Meteor.): A frost is said to occur when the air temperature falls below the freezing point of water.

fructification (Bot.): A general term for the body which develops after fertilization and containing spores or seeds.

fruit (Bot.): The structure which develops from the ovary of an angiosperm after fertilization.

fuel (Nuclear Eng.): Fissile material inserted through a reactor, the source of the chain reaction of neutrons, and so of the energy released.

fuel cell (Chem.): A galvanic cell in which the oxidation of a fuel is utilized to produce electricity.

fulcrum (Mech.): The point of support or pivot of a lever.

function (Biol.): The normal vital activity of a cell, tissue or organ.

Fungi (Bot.): One of the main groups of the Thallophyta, distinguished from the algae chiefly by the absence of chlorophyll.

fun'gicide (Bot.): A substance which kills fungi.

fuse (Elec. Eng.): A device used for protecting electrical apparatus against the effect of excess current.

fu'selage (Aero.): The name generally applied to the main structural body of a heavier-than-air craft, other than the hull of a flying-boat or amphibian.

fusion (Nucleonics): Atomic condensation.

G

gabbro (Geol.): The name of a specific igneous rock type.

gable (Build.): A triangular part of an outside wall, between the sides of the roof and the line of the eaves.

gadget: A small mechanical device.

galactic plane (Astron.): The plane passing as nearly as possible through the center of the belt known as the Milky Way or Galaxy.

Gal'axy (Astron.): (1) The name given to the belt of faint stars which encircles the heavens and which is known as the Milky Way. (2) The name is also used for the entire system of dust, gases and stars within which the sun moves.

gale (Meteor.): A wind having a velocity of about 40 miles per hour or more, at a height of 32 ft. above the ground.

gale'na (Min.): Lead sulphide.

gall (Bot.): An abnormal growth formed on a plant following attack by a parasite.

gall-bladder (Zool.): A lateral diverticulum of the bile-duct in which the bile is stored.

gall-stones (Med.): Pathological concretions in the gall-bladder and bile passages.

gallery (Build.): An elevated floor projecting beyond the walls of a building so as to command a view upon the main floor.

galvanizing (Met.): The coating of steel or iron with zinc.

galvanom'eter (Elec. Eng.): An electrical instrument for measuring small electric currents.

gal'vanotro'pism (Biol., Bot.): Response of an organism to an electric stimulus.

gam'etes (Biol.): Reproductive cells which will unite in pairs to produce zygotes.

gamma rays (Phys.): Short, highly penetrating X-rays emitted by radioactive substances during their spontaneous disintegration.

gan'grene (Med.): Death of a part of the body, associated with putrefaction.

gangue (Met.): The portion of an ore which contains no metal.

gangway (Build.): Rough planks laid to provide a footway for the passage of workmen on a site.

gape (Zool.): The width of the mouth when the jaws are open.

gargoyle (Build.): A grotesquely shaped spout projecting from the upper part of a building, to carry away the rain water.

gas: A state of matter in which a substance completely fills the region in which it is contained, no matter how small its amount.

gas-turbine engine (Aero. and Eng.): The generic term of an engine deriving its energy from internal combustion gases expanded through a turbine.

gas mill (Geol.): A deep boring which yields natural gas rather than oil.

gas'oline (Chem.): Low-boiling petroleum distillates.

gas'tric (Zool.): Pertaining to the stomach.

gate (Eng.): (1) A valve controlling the supply of water in a conduit. (2) A frame in which saws are stretched to prevent buckling.

gauge: An object or instrument for the measurement of dimensions, volume, pressure, etc.

gaze'bo (Build.): A summerhouse resembling a temple in form and commanding a wide open view.

gear (Eng.): A moving part that transmits motion.

gel (Chem.): The apparently solid, often jelly-like, material formed from a colloidal solution on standing.

gel'atine (Chem.): A colorless, ordorless and tasteless glue prepared from albuminous substances.

geminate (Bot.): Paired.

Gemine (Astron.): Twins. Third sign of the Zodiac.

gem'ini (Bot.): Bivalent chromosomes.

gemma (Bot.): A small multicellular body produced by vegetative means, and able to separate from the parent plant and from a new individual. (Zool.): A bud that will give rise to a new individual.

gemmology: The science and study of gemstones.

genes (Cyt., Gem.): In the modern chromosome theory, hypothetical units supposed to be arranged in linear fashion on the chromosomes, each representing a unit character.

gene-mutation (Gen.): A heritable variation caused by spontaneous change at single points in the chromosomes.

gene string (Cyt., Gen.): A hypothetical component of a chromosome, consisting of a series of genes arranged like a string of beads.

generating plant (Elec. Eng.): The equipment necessary for the generation of electrical energy.

generation (Biol.): Origin; the individuals of a species which are separated from a common ancestor by the same number of broods in the direct line of descent.

genesis (Biol.): The origin, formation or development of a group, a species, an individual, an organ, a tissue or a cell.

genet'ics (Biol.): The study of variation and heredity.

genetic complex (Gen.): The sum-total of the hereditary factors contained in the chromosomes and in the cytoplasm.

genetic variation (Gen.): Variation due to differences in the gametes.

genial (Zool.): Pertaining to the chin.

genic'ular (Zool.): Pertaining to the region of the knee.

genita'lia (Zool.): The gonads and their ducts and all associated accessory organs.

genom (Cyt., Gen.): The total chromosome content of the nucleus of a gamete.

genotyp'ic (Gen.): Determined by the genes.

ge'nus (Biol.): A taxonomic category of closely related forms.

ge'obiot'ic (Zool.): Terrestrial.

geocen'tric (Astron.): The term applied to any system or mathematical construction which has as its point of reference the center of the earth.

ge'ochem'istry (Chem.): The study of the chemical composition of the earth's crust.

ge'odes (Geol.): Large cavities in rocks, lined with crystals that were free to grow inwards.

geodesic (Maths.): The shortest path between two points on any surface.

ge'oid (Surv.): The figure of the mean sea-level surface assumed to be continued across the land.

geological time (Geol.): The time extending from the end of the Formative Period of earth history to the beginning of the Historical Period.

geology: The science which investigates the history of the earth's crust, from the earliest times to the beginning of the Historical Period.

geophys'ics: The science concerned with the physical characteristics and properties of the earth.

geotax'y (Biol.): The response of an organism to the stimulus of gravity.

ge'otome (Bot.): An instrument used for taking soil samples without disturbing the surrounding soil.

germ (Zool.): The primitive rudiment which will develop into a complete individual.

germ cells (Zool.): Special reproductive cells which are liberated by the organism and in which the qualities of the organism are inherent.

germination (Bot.): The beginnings of growth in a seed or spore.

gerontol'ogy (Med.): The scientific study of old age and of diseases peculiar to this period of life.

gestalt (Psychol.): German, 'form," 'pattern;" an organized whole. A school of psychology based on the gestalt theory.

gestation (Zool.): Pregnancy.

geyser (Geol.): A volcano in miniature, from which hot water and steam are erupted periodically.

gibbous (Astron.): The word applied to the phase of the moon or of a planet, when it appears less than a circular disc but greater than a half disc.

gill (Zool.): A membranous respiratory outgrowth of aquatic animals.

gimlet (Carp.): A small hand tool for boring holes in wood.

gimped (Bot.): Crenate.

gin'gival (Zool.): Pertaining to the gums, in mammals.

girder (Eng.): A beam, usually steel, to bridge an open space.

glabres'cent (Bot.): Almost but not quite without hairs.

glab'rous (Bot.): Hairless.

glacial denudation (Geol.): **Disintegration of rocks consequent upon glacial conditions.**

glaciation (Geol.): The subjection of an area to glacial conditions, with the development of an ice-sheet on its surface.

glacier (Geol.): A field or body of ice.

gla'cis (Civ. Eng.): An inclined bank.

glad'iate (Bot.): Shaped like a sword blade.

gland (Bot.): A cell or group of cells, inside or on the surface of the plant, secreting an oily or resinous substance, sometimes containing digestive enzymes. (Zool.): A single epithelial cell or an aggregation of them, specialized for the elaboration of a secretion useful to the organism, or of an excretory product.

glans (Bot.): A dry, hard indehiscent fruit, containing one or a few seeds, derived from an inferior ovary and surrounded partly by a cupule; an acorn is an example.

glass: An amorphous substance, usually transparent, consisting ordinarily of a mixture of silicates.

glass-cutter (Build.): A tool for cutting glass to sizes.

glauco'ma (Med.): An eye condition causing partial or complete loss of sight.

glau'cous (Bot.): Covered with a dull greenish-gray waxy bloom.

glaze (Build.): A glass-like surface given to tiles, bricks, etc.

glazier (Build.): A workman who cuts panes of glass to size and fits them in position.

glider (Aero.): A heavier-than-air craft driven within itself.

glob'ular, glob'ose (Bot.): Almost spherical.

glob'ulites (Geol.): Minute crystallites of spherical shape occurring in natural glasses.

glom'erule (Bot.): A small ball-like cluster of spores.

glossa (Zool.): In vertebrates, the tongue.

glu'cophore (Chem.): A group of atoms which causes sweetness of taste.

glue (Carp., etc.): A substance used as an adhesive; obtained from bones, gelatine, starch, etc.

gluma'ceous (Bot.): Brownish, thin and papery in texture.

glu'tinous (Chem.): Covered by a sticky exudation.

gneiss (Geol.): A metamorphic rock.

godroon' (Arch.): An ornamentation taking the form of a bead or cable.

going (Build.): The horizontal interval between consecutive risers in a stairs.

gold (Met.): A heavy, yellow, metallic element.

gonad (Zool.): A sex gland; ovary or testis.

gones (Cyt.): The groups of four nuclei or of four cells which are the immediate results of meiosis.

goniom'eter (Min.): An instrument for measuring the angles between crystal faces.

gonorrhe'a (Med.): A contagious infection of the mucous membrane of the genital tract with the gonococcus.

gore (Aero.): One of the sector-like sections of the canopy of a parachute.

gouge (Carp.): A tool having a curved blade and a cutting edge capable of forming a rounded groove.

gout (Med.): A disorder of metabolism in which there is an excess of uric acid in the blood.

governor (Eng.): A device for controlling the fuel or steam supply to an engine in accordance with the power demand.

grade (Civ. Eng.): The degree of slope.

grade pegs (Surv.): Pegs driven into the ground as references in construction work.

grader (Civ. Eng.): A power-operated machine for shaping excavated surfaces to the desired slope or shape.

gradient (Phys.): The rate of change of a quantity with distance. (Surv.): The ratio of the difference in elevation between two given points and the horizontal distance between them, or the distance for unit rise or fall.

gradine (Arch.): A tier of seats rising above one another in an amphitheater.

grading (Build.): The proportions of the different sizes of stone used in mixing concrete. (Civ. Eng.): The operation of preparing a surface to follow a given gradient.

gradiom'eter (Surv.): An instrument for setting out long uniform gradients.

graduated circle (Surv.): A circular plate, marked off in degrees, used on surveying instruments as a basis for the measurement of horizontal or vertical angles.

graduated vessels (Chem.): Vessels which are used for measuring liquids and are adapted to measure definite volumes of liquid.

graft (Bot.): A plant consisting of a rooted part (the stock) into which another part (the scion) has been inserted so as to make organic union. (Surg.): A piece of skin, bone or tissue taken from one part of the body and grafted to another.

grain (Bot.): The pattern on the surface of wood due to variations of the cells forming the wood.

gram: The unit of mass in the metric system.

gram-atom (Chem.): The quantity of an element whose mass in grams is equal to its atomic weight.

gram-equivalent (Chem.): The quantity of a substance or radical whose mass in grams is equal to its equivalent weight.

gram-molecule (Chem.): The quantity of a substance whose mass in grams is equal to its molecular weight.

graminiv'orous (Zool.): Grass-eating.

granite (Geol.): A coarse-grained igneous rock.

granulated sugar (Chem.): A term for loose sugar crystals of grain-like appearance.

gran'ulization (Geol.): The process in regional metamorphism of reducing the components of a solid rock to grains.

graphic formula (Chem.): A formula in which every atom is represented by the appropriate symbol, valency bonds being indicated by dashes.

graphic instrument (Elec. Eng.): An electrical instrument in which the pointer consists of a pen moving over a paper chart so that a graphic record of the quantity measured is obtained.

graphical methods: The name given to those methods in which items, such as forces in structures, are determined by drawing diagrams to scale.

graphic (Min.): One of the two naturally occurring forms of crystalline carbon, the other being diamond.

grate (Build.): The cast-iron fire bars and frame of a fireplace. (Eng.): That part of a furnace which supports the fuel.

grating (Build.): A perforated cover across a drain, gulley, etc.

gravel (Build.): A natural mixture of sand, loam and flints. (Geol.): The name of an aggregate consisting of pebbles and a considerable amount of sand.

gravitation (Phys.): The name given to that force of nature which manifests itself as a mutual attraction between masses.

gravitational astronomy (Astron.): **That branch of astronomy that deals with the motions of the heavenly bodies under the forces of gravitation.**

gravity cell (Elec. Eng.): A two-fluid cell in which the electrolytes lie in separate layers because of their difference in specific gravity.

gravity water system: A system in which flow occurs under the natural pressure due to gravity.

grease gun: A device for forcing grease into bearings under high pressure.

great circle (Maths.): The intersection of a sphere by a plane passing through its center.

green (Civ. Eng.): A colloquial term for concrete in the hardening stage.

gregale (Meteor.): A north-easterly winter wind blowing in the central Mediterranean.

grega'rious (Bot.): Growing in close companies, but not matted together.

grey matter (Zool.): An area of the central nervous system, mainly composed of cell bodies.

grid (Civ. Eng.): A timber framework so built that a vessel may be floated in at high water and repairs undertaken as the tide falls. (Surv.) : A network of lines super-imposed upon a map and forming squares for referencing.

grille (Build.) : A plain or ornamental openwork of metal or wood, used as a protecting screen or grating.

grinding teeth (Zool.) : The molars and premolars of mammals.

grinding wheel (Eng.) : An abrasive wheel for cutting and finishing metal.

grit (Geol.) : Siliceous sediment, the component grains being angular.

grit cell (Bot.) : A stone cell occurring in the flesh of a fruit.

grooving (Eng.) : Cracking of the plates of steam boilers at points where stresses are set up by the differential expansion of hot and colder parts.

ground engineer (Aero.) : An individual, selected by the licensing authorities, who has power to certify the safety for flight of an aircraft.

ground loop (Aero.) : An uncontrollable and violent turn by an airplane while taxying, landing or taking-off.

ground noise (Acous.) : Extraneous noise accompanying reproduced sound.

ground plan (Build., Civ. Eng.) : A drawing showing a plan view of the foundations for a building or of the layout of rooms etc., on the ground floor.

ground-postion indicator (Aero.) : An instrument which continuously displays the dead-reckoning position of an aircraft.

ground speed (Aero.) : The speed of an aircraft relative to a point on the earth's surface.

ground state (Nucleonics) : State of a molecule when its energy is the minimum possible.

groundwork (Civ. Eng.) : The work involved in preparing a site for a foundation.

ground-zero (Nuclear Warfare) : Point on the ground directly under an air-burst of a nuclear weapon.

group (Chem.) : (1) A vertical column of the periodic system, containing elements of similar properti (2) A number of atoms which occur together several compounds.

growth (Biol.) : A change in the body of an organi and in the cells composing it, accompanied by a division and nearly always, by increase in the size and weight of the organism or of the part under consideration. (Met.) : Applied to cast-iron, the tendency to increase in volume when repeatedly heated and cooled.

growth ring (Bot.) : The cylinder of secondary wood added during one season of growth, as seen in cross-section.

gudgeon (Build.) : A metal pin used for joining adjacent stones.

guide (Civ. Eng.) : A pile driven to indicate a site.

guided weapon (Aero.) : Any missile which is guided to its target; propulsion is usually by rocket, ramjet or simplified turbojet.

gums (Zool.) : In higher vertebrates, the thick tissue masses surrounding the bases of the teeth.

gus'tatory (Zool.) : Pertaining to the sense of taste.

gut (Zool.) : The alimentary canal.

guttate (Bot.) : Containing little drops of material.

gutter (Build., Civ. Eng.) : A channel along the side of a road, or around the eaves of a building, to collect and carry away surface waters.

guy-rope (Civ. Eng.) : A rope holding a structure in a desired position.

Gym'nosperm'ae (Bot.) : One of the two main divisions of seed plants.

gynan'drous (Bot.) : Having the stamens and styles united to form a column, as in the flowers of orchids.

gyroscope : A small heavy wheel or top rotated at high speed in anti-friction bearings.

H

haar (Meteor.) : A wet set-fog advancing in summer from the North Sea upon the shores of Scotland and England.

habit (Cryst.) : A term used to cover the varying development of the crystal forms possessed by any one mineral. (Zool.) : The established normal behavior of an animal species.

habit spasm (Med.) : Tic.

habitat (Biol.) : The normal locality or place of living of an organism.

habitat form (Bot.) : A plant showing features which can be related to the place where it is growing.

habitat group (Bot.) : A set of unrelated plants which inhabit the same kind of situation.

haboob' (Meteor.) : A line-square, with dust storms, blowing in the Sudan during the rainy season.

hack-saw (Eng.) : A hand-saw for cutting metal.

hacking (Build.) : The process of making surface rough.

hade (Geol.) : The angle of inclination of a fault-plane, measured from the vertical.

had'romal (Bot.) : An enzyme present in some fungi which enables them to decompose wood.

hae'mal, haemic (Zool.) : Pertaining to the blood-vessels or to the blood.

hae'mapoi'esis (Zool.) : The formation of blood.

hae'matite (Min.) : An oxide of iron.

haematol'ogist (Med.) : One who specializes in the study of the blood and its diseases.

haemat'ozo'on (Zool.) : An animal living parasitically on the blood.

haemoglo'bin (Zool.) : The respiratory pigment in the red corpuscles of vertebrates, a compound of hematin and globin.

haemophil'ia (Med.) : A hereditary disorder in which bleeding after injury persists, owing to delayed coagulation of the blood.

haem'orrhage (Med.) : Bleeding.

haemostat'ic (Med.) : Arresting bleeding.

hail (Meteor.) : Precipitation in the form of hard pellets of ice.

hair (Anat., Zool.) : Any thread-like outgrowth of the epidermis.

half-pace (Build.) : A landing at the end of a flight of steps.

half-rip saw (Carp.) : A hand-saw designed for cutting timber along the grain.

halides (Chem.) : Fluorides, bromides, iodides and chlorides.

holite (Min.) : Common or rock salt.

halito'sis (Med.) : Offensively smelling breath.

Hall effect (Elec. Eng.) : A change in the distribution of current in a strip of metal, due to a magnetic field.

hallucination (Psychol.) : A perception of sensation for which there is no objective reality.

hallux (Zool.) : In land vertebrates, the first digit of the hind-limb.

halo (Meteor.) : A bright ring or system of rings seen surrounding the sun or moon.

ha'lobion'tic (Ecol.) : Strictly confined to salt water.

ha'logens (Chem.) : A group consisting of the non-metallic elements, fluorine, bromine, chlorine and iodine.

haloid acids (Chem.) : A group consisting of hydrogen fluoride, hydrogen bromide, hydrogen chloride and hydrogen iodide.

ha'lophile (Ecol.) : A fresh-water species capable of surviving in salt water.

ha'lophole (Bot.) : A plant which will not grow in a soil containing an appreciable amount of salt.

ha'lophyte (Bot.) : A plant which will live in a soil containing an appreciable amount of common salt or other inorganic salts.

hamiros'trate (Zool.) : Having a hooked beak, as vultures.

handle : The part of a tool by which it is grasped.

hangar (Aero.) : A special construction for the accommodation of aircraft.

hapan'thous (Bot.) : Flowering once and then dying.

hap'loid (Cyt.) : Having the basic chromosomes number half the number in somatic cells.

haplo'sis (Cyt.) : The halving in the number of the chromosomes at meiosis.

harbor (Civ. Eng.) : A sheltered area of water giving safe anchorage to ships.

hardpan (Civ. Eng.): A layer of hardened subsoil.

hard water (Chem.): Water having calcium and magnesium salts in solution and offering difficulty in making a soap lather.

hardening (Met.): The process of making steel hard.

hardness (Met.): In general, signifies resistance to deformation.

harelip (Med.): A congenital cleft in the upper lip.

harmattan' (Meteor.): A dusty, dry north-easterly wind blowing over West Africa during the dry season.

hatch (Build.): A door closing only the lower half of a door opening.

hatchet (Carp.): A small axe used for splitting timber.

hay-fever (Med.): Paroxysmal attacks of running at the nose, congestion and irritation of the nasal mucous membrane and of the eyes, due to sensitivity to grass pollens.

head: A generic term for the essential part of an apparatus. (Arch.): The capital of a column. (Bot.): A dense inflorescence of small crowded flowers.

hearing (Acous.): The subjective appreciation of externally applied sounds.

heart (Zool.): A hollow organ, with muscular walls, which by its rhythmic contractions pumps the blood through the vessels and cavities of the circulatory system.

heart wood: The dense wood which lies in the inner part of a trunk or branch.

hearth (Build.): The floor of the fireplace.

heat (Phys.): That which when given to a body raises its temperature, and when removed lowers the temperature. Heat is also a form of energy into which mechanical energy may be converted. (Zool.): The period of sexual desire.

heat index (Astron.): An indication of the proportion of heat to light received from a star.

heat insulation (Build.): The property of impeding the transmission of heat.

heater (Build.): Appliance for heating a building.

heating-element (Elec. Eng.): The heating resistor, together with its former in any device in which heat is produced by the passage of an electric current through a resistance.

height (Build., Civ. Eng.): The rise of an arch.

heliacal rising and setting (Astron.): The rising or setting of a star or planet, simultaneously with the rising or setting of the sun.

helicopter (Aero.): A rotorcraft capable of vertical take-off and landing.

helio: A prefix meaning sun.

heliom'eter (Astron.): An instrument for determining the sun's diameter and for measuring the angular distance between two celestial objects in close proximity.

he'liophyte (Bot.): A plant able to live with full exposure to the sun.

he'liostat (Astron.): An instrument used for photographic and spectroscopic study of the sun. (Surv.): An instrument used to reflect the sun's rays in a continuous beam.

heliotro'pism (Biaol.): Reaction of an organism to the stimulus of the sun's rays.

helium (Chem.): An inert element; the lightest of the rare gases.

helix (Zool.): A spirally coiled structure.

hemi: A prefix meaning half.

Hemip'tera (Zool.): An order of insects usually with the characteristic of having two pairs of wings.

hemisphere: The half of a sphere.

henry (Elec. Eng.): The practical unit of inductance.

hepat: A prefix meaning liver.

hepatic (Med.): Pertaining to the liver.

hepati'tis (Med.): Inflammation of the liver.

hept: A prefix meaning seven.

heptam'erous (Bot.): Having parts in sevens.

heptava'lent (Chem.): Capable of combining with seven hydrogen atoms or their equivalent.

herb (Bot.): A small flowering plant, of which the aerial shoots last only as long as it is necessary to develop the flowers and the fruits.

herba'ceous (Bot.): Soft and green, containing little woody tissue.

herba'rium (Bot.): A collection of dried plants; also the place where such a collection is kept.

hereditary (Biol.): Inherited.

heredity (Biol.): That factor in evolution which causes the persistence of characters in successive generations.

hermaph'rodite (Zool.): Having both male and female reproductive organs in one individual.

hernia (Med.): Protrusion of a viscus through a defective area in the cavity containing it.

heroin (Chem.): An alkaloid prepared by the acetylation of morphine.

hertz (Elec. Comm.): The unit of frequency, one cycle per second.

hesperid'ium (Bot.): A fruit like an orange; a fleshy fruit covered by a firm rind.

heter-, hetero: A prefix meaning other or different.

het'erobares (Chem.): Atoms having different atomic weights.

heteroblastic (Zool.): Showing indirect development.

heterocar'pous (Bot.): Having more than one kind of fruit.

heterochro'mosome (Cyt.): A differentiated chromosome, determining sex.

heterochro'sis (Zool.): Abnormal coloration.

heterodynam'ic (Biol.): Of unequal potentiality.

heterog'eneous (Chem.): Said of a system consisting of more than one phase.

heteromorpho'sis (Zool.): The regeneration of a part in a different form from the original part; the production of an abnormal structure.

heteromor'phous (Bot.): Existing in more than one form.

het'eroploid (Cyt.): Possessing an additional chromosome.

hetero'sis (Zool.): Cross-fertilization.

het'erospo'ry (Bot.): The formation of more than one kind of spore.

heterosynap'sis (Cyt.): Pairing of two dissimilar chromosomes.

het'erotopes (Chem.): Atoms having different atomic numbers.

heterotyp'ic (Zool.): Differing from the normal condition.

hex: A prefix meaning six.

hexam'erous (Bot.): Having parts in sixes.

hex'apod (Zool.): Having six legs.

hexap'terous (Zool.): Having six wing-like processes.

hex'astyle (Arch.): A portico formed of six columns in front.

hex'ava'lent (Chem.): Capable of combining with six hydrogen atoms or their equivalent.

hia'tus (Zool.): A large opening.

hibernation (Zool.): The condition of partial or complete torpor into which some animals relapse during the winter season.

hiccup (Med.): Sudden spasm of the diaphragm followed immediately by classure of the glottis.

hidro'sis (Zool.): Formation and excretion of sweat.

highs (Acous.): The same as top.

high-fidelity (Acous.): An inexact term generally meaning sound reproduction of a superior quality.

high-voltage (Elec. Eng.): Legally, any voltage above 650 volts.

hinge (Carp.): A means of connecting two members, such as a door to its frame, as that one may swing in relation to the other.

hipped roof (Build.): A pitched roof having sloping ends instead of gable ends.

hirsute (Bot.): Hairy.

his'tocyte (Zool.): A tissue cell as opposed to a germ cell.

his'togen (Bot.): An area within a plant where tissues undergo differentiation.

Science Terms

histogen'esis (Zool.): Formation of new tissues.

histol'ogy (Zool.): The study of the minute structure of tissues and organs.

histol'ysis (Bot.): The breakdown of a cell or tissue.

hoar-frost (Meteor.): A deposit of ice crystals formed on objects, especially during cold clear nights when the dew-point is below the freezing-point.

hoary (Bot.): Covered with short greyish-white down.

hod (Build.): A three-sided container used for carrying bricks and mortar on the site.

hoggin (Build.): A mixture of gravel and clay, used for paving garden paths, etc.

hoisting: The process of lifting materials by mechanical means.

hole (Civ. Eng.): (1) A bore hole. (2) A depression for accommodating a blasting charge.

holohe'dral (Crystal.): Crystal forms exhibiting the highest possible symmetry in their respective systems.

ho'lotype (Zool.): The original type specimen, from which the description of a new species is established.

holozo'ic (Zool.): Devouring other organisms.

homo: A prefix meaning the same.

homoblas'tic (Zool.): Showing direct development.

homoch'romy (Zool.): The resemblance of the color of the animal to the color of its surroundings.

homocy'clic (Chem.): Containing a ring composed entirely of atoms of the same kind.

homog'amy (Zool.): Inbreeding, usually due to isolation.

homoge'neous (Chem.): Said of a system consisting of only one phase.

homogen'esis (Zool.): The reproductive cycle in which the offspring resemble the parents.

homogeny (Zool.): Similarity of individuals or of parts, due to common descent.

homol'ogous (Bot., Zool.): Of the same essential nature and of common descent.

homomor'phic (Cyt.): Said of chromosome pairs which have the same form and size.

homomor'phous (Bot., Zool.): Alike in form.

homophyl'lous (Bot.): Having foliage leaves all of the same kind.

homoplas'tic (Bot.): Of the same structure and manner of development but not descended from a common source.

ho'moplas'ty (Zool.): Similarity between two different organs or organisms, due to convergent evolution.

homop'terous (Zool.): Having both pairs of wings similar.

homosexual'ity (Psycho-path.): A general term denoting sexual attraction for the same sex.

homosynap'sis (Cyt.): Pairing of two similar chromosomes.

homotyp'ic (Zool.): Conforming to the normal condition.

honey dew (Zool.): A sweet substance secreted by certain Aphididae.

honing (Eng.): The process of finishing cylinder bores etc., to a very high degree of accuracy.

hoof (Zool.): In certain mammals, a horny proliferation of the epidermis, enclosing the toes.

horizon (Astron.): That great circle of which the Zenith and the nadir are the poles, in which the plane tangent to the earth's surface, considered spherical, at the point where the observer stands, cuts the celestial sphere. (Surv.): A plane perpendicular to the direction of gravity at the point of observation.

horizontal (Bot.): Spreading at a right-angle to a support.

horizontal component (Elec. Eng.): The component of the earth's magnetic field which acts in a horizontal direction.

hormone (Physiol.): An internal secretion produced by the endocrine or ductless glands of the body and exercising a specific stimulatory physiological action on other organs to which it is carried by the blood.

horn (Zool.): One of the pointed or branched hard projections borne on the head in many mammals.

hornblende (Min.): An important rock-forming mineral of complex composition.

horological (Bot.): Said of a flower which opens and shuts at a definite time of day.

horology: The science of time-measurement, or of the construction of timepieces.

horse (Carp.): A trestle for supporting a board while it is being sawn.

horse-power (Eng.): The engineering unit of power equal to a rate of working 33,000 foot pounds per minute.

horseshoe curve (Surv.): A curve whose arc subtends an angle of more than 180' at the center, so that the intersection point lies on the same side of the curve as the center.

host (Biol.): An organism which supports another organism (parasite) at its own expense.

hot (Elec.): Charged to a dangerously high potential.

hot-air heater (Build.): One which supplies warm air through gratings in the floor or openings in the walls.

hot plate (Elec. Eng.): An electrically heated plate maintained at a moderate temperature so that dishes placed on it may be kept warm.

hot-wire (Elec. Eng.): Said of an electrical indicating instrument whose operation depends on the thermal expansion of, or change in resistance of, a wire when it carries a current.

hour angle (Astron.): The angle which the declination circle of a heavenly body makes with the observer's meridian at the celestial pole.

hour circle (Astron.): The great circle passing through the celestial poles and a heavenly body, cutting the celestial equator at 90°.

hull (Aero.): The main boat of a boat amphibian.

hum (Acous.): A single note emitted from a sound reproducer.

hu'meral (Zool.): In vertebrates, pertaining to the region of the shoulder.

humid'ifier: An apparatus for maintaining desired humidity conditions in the air supplied to a building.

humidity (Meteor.): The quantity of water vapor present per unit volume.

hu'mus (Bot.): Organic matter present in the soil, and so far decomposed that it has lost all signs of its original structure.

hurricane (Meteor.): A wind of force with a velocity of 75 miles per hour.

hy'aline (Zool.): Clear, transparent.

hy'alite (Min.): A colorless transparent variety of opal.

hy'alogen'esis (Cyt.): The secretory process in a cell.

hyalop'terous (Zool.): Having transparent wings.

hybrid (Gen.): An organism which is the offspring of a union between two different races, species or genera.

hyd, hydro: A prefix meaning water.

hy'drates (Chem.): Salts which contain water of crystallization.

hydraulics: The science relating to the flow of fluids.

hydraulic lift (Eng.): A lift or elevator operated by a ram, working in a cylinder to which water is admitted under pressure.

hydrocarbons (Chem.): A general term for organic compounds which contain only carbon and hydrogen in the molecule.

hydrochlor'ic acid (Chem.): An aqueous solution of hydrogen chloride gas.

hydro-electric generating set (Elec. Eng.): An electric generator driven by a water turbine.

hy'drogen (Chem.): The lightest element known, having both metallic and non-metallic properties.

hydrogen ion (Chem.): An atom of hydrogen carrying a positive charge.

hydrographical surveying (Surv.): A branch of surveying dealing with bodies of water at the coast-line and in harbors, estuaries and rivers.

hydrog'raphy: The study, determination and publication of the conditions of navigable water.

hydrol (Chem.): A name given to the simple water molecule H_2O.

hydrol'ysis (Chem.): (1) The formation of an acid and

a base from a salt by interaction with water. (2) The decomposition of organic compounds by interaction with water.

hydrome'teor (Meteor.): Any weather phenomenon which depends on the moisture content of the atmosphere.

hy'drophi'lous (Bot.): (1) Living in water. (2) Pollinated by water.

hydropho'bia (Med.): Rabies in man.

hy'drophyte (Bot.): A plant which lives on the surface or submerged in water

hydroplane: (1) A motor-boat which skins the surface of water. (2) A planing surface which enables a submarine to submerge.

hy'drosol (Chem.): A colloidal solution in water.

hydrosphere: The water on the surface of the earth.

hydrostatics (Phys.): The mechanics of fluids at rest.

hydrotax'is (Biol.): Response of an organism to the stimulus of moisture.

hy'etograph (Meteor.): An instrument which collects, measures and records the fall of rain.

hygro-: A prefix meaning moist or wet.

hygrom'eter (Meteor.): An instrument for measuring the amount of moisture in the atmosphere.

hy'grophile (Bot.): Living where moisture is abundant.

hy'grophobe (Bot.): Living best in dry situations.

hygroscopic (Chem.): Tending to absorb moisture.

hygrostat (Chem.): Apparatus which produces constant humidity.

hyloph'agous (Zool.): Wood-eating.

hy'lophyte (Bot.): A plant characteristic of damp woods.

hylot'omous (Zool.): Wood-cutting.

hyper: Prefix meaning above.

hyperacid'ity (Med.): Excessive acidity.

hyperchromato'sis (Cyt.): Excess of chromotin in a cell.

hypermnesia (Med.): Exceptional power of memory.

hyperon (Nucleonics): Particles whose mass is between that of neutron and deutron.

hypertension (Med.): Increase in tension; a blood pressure higher than normal.

hy'pha (Bot.): One of the branched or simple filaments of the thallus of a fungus.

hyp'nody (Zool.): The resting period in larval forms.

hypno'sis (Psychol.): A condition, induced in a person by suggestion, in which conscious control is discouraged.

hypo: A prefix meaning under.

hypochondri'asis (Med.): Morbid preoccupation with bodily sensations and functions, with the false belief that bodily diseases are indicated.

hypoder'mis (Bot.): A layer of strongly constructed cells, lying immediately beneath the epidermis and reinforcing it.

hypoder'mic (Med.): Under the skin.

hypogene (Geol.): Said of rocks formed under the earth's surface.

hypopla'sia (Zool.): Under-development.

hyposthe'nic (Med.): Having diminished strength.

hy'postyle hall (Arch.): A hall having columns to support the roof.

hypotension (Med.): Low blood pressure.

hypso: Prefix meaning height.

hypsom'eter (Phys.): An instrument used for determining the boiling point of water.

hysterec'tomy (Surg.): Removal of the uterus.

hysteria (Psycho-an.): A psychoneurosis in which repressed complexes become dissociated from the personality, forming independent units, partially or completely unrecognized by consciousness.

I

iatrochemistry (Chem.): The study of chemical phenomena in order to obtain results of medical value.

ice (Meteor.): Ice is formed when water is cooled below its freezing point.

ice action (Geol.): The work and effects of ice on the earth's surface.

ice apon, ice breaker (Civ. Eng.): A construction serving to break floating ice or to afford protection against the thrust of the ice upon the pier.

iceberg (Meteor.): A large mass of ice, floating in the sea, which has broken away from a glacier or ice barrier.

iceblink (Meteor.): A whitish glare in the sky over ice which is too distant to be visible.

Iceland spar (Min.): A very pure transparent and crystalline form of calcium carbonate, first brought from Iceland.

ichthy: A prefix meaning fish.

id (Psycho-an.): A term used to denote the sum total of the primitive instinctual forces in an individual.

idealism or mentalism: The conception of natural phenomena as arising within the mind, the external world being ultimately unknowable to the human mind.

idio: A prefix meaning distinct or peculiar.

idioblast (Min.): A crystal which developed in metamorphic rocks and is bounded by crystal contours.

idiochro'matin (Cyt.): A substance within the nucleus which controls the reproduction of the cell.

idiot (Med.): One afflicted with the severest grade of feeble-mindedness.

id'iozome (Zool.): The attraction sphere or region of char protoplasm surrounding the centrosome.

idling (Eng.): The slow rate of revolution of an automobile or aero engine, when the throttle pedal or lever is in the closed position.

ignite (Chem.): To heat a gaseous mixture to the temperature at which combustion takes place.

igni'ter (Civ. Eng.): A blasting fuse or other contrivance used to fire an explosive charge.

ignition (Elec. Eng.): The firing of an explosive mixture of gases, vapors or other substances, by means of an electric spark.

ignition laz (Eng.): Of a combustible mixture in an engine cylinder, the time interval between the passage of the spark and the resulting pressure rise due to combustion.

ileitis (Med.): Inflammation of the ileum.

i'leum (Zool.): In vertebrates, the posterior part of the small intestine.

il'ium (Zool.): In vertebrates, a dorsal cartilage bone of the pelvic girdle.

illusion (Psychol.): A false interpretation of something perceived through the special senses.

imagination (Psychol.): The faculty of forming images in the mind.

imag'o (Zool.): Final instar of an insect.

im'becile (Med.): A person whose defective mental state does not amount to idiocy, but who is incapable of managing his own affairs.

imbibition (Chem.): The absorption or adsorption of a liquid by a solid or a gel, accompanied by swelling of the latter.

im'bricate (Bot., Zool.): Said of leaves, scales, etc., which overlap.

immar'ginate (Bot.): Lacking a distinct edge.

immersed (Bot.): (1) Embedded in the tissues of the plant. (2) Arising beneath the surface of the substratum.

immersion (Astron.): The entry of the moon, or other body, into the shadow which causes its eclipse.

immiscibility (Chem.): The property of two or more liquids of not mixing and of forming more than one phase when brought together.

immune (Med.): Protected against any particular infection.

immune bodies (Bacteriol.): Antibodies.

impacted (Med.): Firmly fixed; pressed closely in.

impiller (Eng.): The rotating member of a centrifugal pump or blower, which imparts kinetic energy to the fluid.

imperforate (Med.): Not perforated; closed abnormally. (Zool.): Lacking apertures, especially of shells.

imperial (Build.): A domed roof shaped to a point at the top.

impermeable (Chem., Geol.) : Not permitting the passage of gas or liquids.

impervious (Build., etc.) : Said of materials which have the property of satisfactorily resisting the passage of water.

impeti'go (Med.) : A contagious skin disease, chiefly of the hands and face, due to infection with pus-forming bacteria.

impressed (Bot.) : Having the surface marked by slight depressions.

impulse (Elec. Comm.) : An unidirectional flow of current of non-repeated wave-form.

in vitro (Med.) : In a test-tube ; in a glass.

in vivo (Med.) : In the living body.

inactivation (Chem.) : The destruction of the activity of a serum, catalyst, etc.

inarticulate (Bot.) : Not jointed.

inbreeding (Zool.) : Breeding within the descendants of a foundation stock of related animals.

incandes'cence : The emission of light by a substance because of its high temperature.

incendiary : Tending to cause combustion.

in'cept (Bot.) : The rudiment of an organ.

incise (Arch.) : To carve.

incision (Surg.) : The act of cutting into something ; made by a surgical knife.

inci'sors (Zool.) : The front teeth of mammals.

inclinom'eter (Surv.) : An instrument for measuring ground and embankment slopes.

included (Bot.) : Not projecting beyond the surrounding members.

included angle (Surv.) : Either of the two angles between two survey lines meeting at a station.

inclusion : A particle or lump of foreign matter embedded in a solid.

incompatibility (Bot.) : Any difference in the physiological properties of the protoplasts of a host and a parasite which limits or stops the development of the latter.

incompetence (Med.) : Inability to perform proper function.

incubation (Zool.) : The process of causing eggs to hatch by the application of natural or artificial heat.

indehis'cent (Bot.) : Not opening naturally when ripe.

indeterminate (Bot.) : Indefinite.

index (Surv.) : A simple plane table alidade, having sighting vanes at the ends.

indicator (Chem.) : A substance whose color depends on the alkalinity or acidity of the solution in which it is dissolved. (Elec. Eng.) : A signalling device.

indigenous (Zool.) : Native ; not imported.

indigestion (Med.) : A condition, marked by discomfort and pain, in which the normal digestive functions are impeded.

indirect heating (Build.) : A system of heating by convection.

indium (Met.) : A metallic element.

individual (Zool.) : A single member of a species ; a single unit or specimen.

individuation (Zool.) : The formation of separation functional units which are mutually interdependent.

indolent (Med.) : Causing little or no pain.

induced charge (Elec. Eng.) : An electric charge produced as a result of a charge on a neighboring conductor.

induced reaction (Chem.) : A chemical reaction which is accelerated by the simultaneous occurrence in the same system of a second, rapid reaction.

induction (Elec. Eng.) : A term sometimes used to denote the density of an electric or magnetic field. (Zool.) : The production of a definite condition by the action of an external factor.

induction furnace (Elec. Eng.) : An electric furnace for melting metals.

induction period (Chem.) : The interval of time between the initiation of a chemical reaction and its actual occurrence.

inductor (Chem.) : A substance which accelerates a slow reaction between two or more substances by reacting rapidly with one of the reactants.

indurated : Hardened.

inequality (Astron.) : The term used to signify any departure from uniformity in orbital motion.

inequi : Prefix meaning not equal.

inert (Chem.) : Not readily changed by chemical means.

inertia (Mech., Phys.) : Reluctance of a body to change its state of rest.

infection (Med.) : The invasion of body tissue by living micro-organisms causing a diseased condition.

inferior (Zool.) : Lower, under.

inferiority complex (Psychol.) : Generally a persisting state of feelings of inferiority.

infirmary (Med.) : An institution for the surgical and/or medical treatment of disease.

inflation (Aero.) : The process of filling an airship or balloon with gas.

inflores'cence (Bot.) : In flowering plants, the part of the shoot which bears flowers.

infra : A prefix meaning below.

ingestion (Zool.) : The act of swallowing food material so that it passes into the body.

ingot (Met.) : A metal casting of a shape suitable for subsequent rolling or forging.

inhalation (Med.) : The act of breathing in into the lungs.

inhibitor (Bot.) : A substance which limits or destroys the catalytic activity of an enzyme.

initiator (Chem.) : The substance or molecule which starts a chain reaction.

injected (Bot.) : Having the intercellular spaces filled with water.

innings (Civ. Eng.) : Lands reclaimed from the sea.

inoculation (Bot.) : The conveyance of infection to a host plant by any means of transmission. (Chem.) : The introduction of a small crystal into a supersaturated solution or supercooled liquid in order to initiate crystallization.

inop'erable (Med.) : Not suitable for operation.

inorganic chemistry (Chem.) : The study of the chemical elements and their compounds.

inscribe : To draw one plane figure so that it is enclosed within another.

insecticide (Chem.) : The product used to destroy insects.

insemination (Zool.) : The approach and entry of the spermatozoon to the ovum.

insesso'rial (Zool.) : Adapted for perching.

insolation (Med.) : Sunstroke. (Meteor.) : The radiation received from the sun.

instability (Aero.) : Said of an aircraft when any disturbance of its steady motion tends to increase.

instinct (Psychol.) : An innate force in an organism attaching to certain biological ends, such as self-preservation and reproduction.

integ'ument (Bot.) : The seed coat or testa.

intelligence quotient (Psychol.) : The ratio, expressed as a percentage, of an individual's mental age to his actual age.

inter- : A prefix meaning between.

interbreeding (Gen.) : Experimental hybridization of different species.

intercel'lular (Zool.) : Between cells.

interchange (Cyt.) : The mutual transfer of portions between two chromosomes.

interference (Aero.) : The aerodynamic influence of one body upon another. (Phys.) : The effect of superposing two or more trains of waves of equal wavelength.

intern (Med.) : An assistant physician in a hospital.

interspecif'ic (Cyt.) : Said of a cross between two separate species.

inter-vari'etal (Gen.) : Said of a cross between two varieties of the same species.

intestine (Zool.) : In vertebrates, that part of the alimentary canal leading from the stomach to the anus.

intracel'lular (Biol.) : Within the cell.

intracra'nial (Anat.) : Situated within the skull.

intrader'mal (Anat.) : Situated in the skin.

intrave′nous (Anat.): Within a vein.

intra-vi′tam Staining (Biol.): The artificial staining of living cells.

intricate (Bot.): Intertwined.

intrinsic system (Chem.): The store of energy possessed by a material system.

introspection (Psychol.): The habit, which may become pathological, of "looking within" one's self.

in′trovert (Psychol.): An individual interested mainly in his own mental processes and attitudes; shy and retiring in manner.

intrusions (Geol.): Bodies of igneous rocks which, in the condition of magma, were intruded into the pre-existing rocks of the earth's crust.

in′volucre (Bot.): A crowded group of bracts around the base of a dense inflorescence.

involuntary (Zool.): Outside the control of the will.

in′volute (Bot.): Having the margins rolled inwards. (Zool.): Tightly coiled.

iodine (Chem.): A non-metallic element.

ion (Chem.): A charged atom, molecules or radical.

ionization: The production of ions from an electrically neutral substance.

i′rid,- i′rido-: Prefix meaning rainbow.

irides′cence (Phys.): The production of fine colors on a surface.

irid′ium (Met.): A brittle, steel-gray metallic element.

i′ris (Anat.): In the vertebrate eye, that part of the choroid, lying in front of the lens, which takes the form of a circular curtain with a central opening.

iron (Met.): A metallic element.

iron ores (Geol.): Rocks or deposits containing iron-rich compounds in workable amounts.

ironwork (Build.): A term applied to essentially ornamental work in iron as gates, hinges, etc.

irrigation (Civ. Eng.): The storage of flood waters by means of dams.

irritant (Biol.): Any external stimulus which produces an active response to a living organism.

i′singlass (Chem.): Fish glue.

iso: (Chem.): A prefix indicating: (1) The presence of a branched carbon chain in the molecule. (2) An isomeric compound. Also a prefix meaning equal.

i′sobar (Chem.): A curve relating quantities measured at the same pressure. (Meteor.): A line drawn on a map through places having the same atmospheric pressure at a given time.

i′sobilat′eral (Bot.): Divisible into symmetrical halves by two distinct planes.

isoch′ronism (Phys.): Regular periodicity, as the swinging of a pendulum.

isometric system (Crystal.): The cubic system.

isomorphism (Biol.): Apparent likeness between individuals belonging to different species or races.

i′soneph (Meteor.): A line drawn on a map through places having equal amounts of cloudiness.

isoster′ic (Chem.): Consisting of molecules possessing similar electronic structures.

i′sotherm (Meteor.): A line drawn on a map through places having equal temperatures.

isothermal (Chem.): Occurring at constant temperature.

i′sotopes (Phys.): Atoms of the same element having different nuclear masses but identical chemical properties and atomic numbers.

isotrop′ic (Phys.): Said of a substance which possesses the same properties in all directions.

J

jack (Eng.): A portable lifting machine for raising heavy weights through a short distance.

jacket (Eng.): An outer casing constructed around a cylinder or pipe, the space being filled with a fluid for either heating, cooling or maintaining the cylinder contents at constant temperature.

jalousies (Build.): Hanging or sliding sun-shutters giving external protection to a window, and allowing for ventilation through louvres cut in the shutters themselves.

jamb (Build.): The side of an aperture.

jaundice (Med.): Yellow coloration of the skin and and other body tissues.

jaw (Eng.): One of a pair of members between which an object is held, crushed or cut as the jaws of a vice.

jet: A fluid stream issuing from an orifice or nozzle.

jet propulsion (Eng. and Aero.): Propulsion by reaction from the expulsion of a high velocity jet of the fluid in which the machine is moving.

jet (Min.): A hard coal-block variety of lignite.

jettison, fuel (Aero.): Apparatus for the rapid emergency discharge of fuel.

jib (Eng.): The boom of a crane or derrick.

jig (Eng.): An appliance used in a machine shop for accurately guiding and locating tools during the operations involved in producing interchangeable parts.

jimmy (Build.): A small crowbar.

joggle (Eng.): A small projection on a piece of metal fitting into a corresponding recess in another piece, to prevent lateral movement.

joint: A connection made between two pieces.

joints (Geol.): Vertical, inclined or horizontal divisional planes, found in almost all rocks.

joist (Build.): A horizontal beam of steel or timber used with others as a support for a floor or a ceiling.

joystick (Aero.): Colloquialism for control column.

jug′ular (Zool.): Pertaining to the throat or neck region.

jumper-cable (Elec. Eng.): A cable for making electrical connection between two sections of conductor-rail in an electric traction system.

junket (Chem.): A product obtained from milk by the action of rennin.

Jupiter (Astron.): The largest planet in the solar system, the fifth in order of distance from the sun.

jutty (Build.): A projecting part of a building.

jet streams (Meteor.): Narrow streams of high-velocity wind occurring at altitudes between 10,000-40,000 ft.

K

karyas′ter (Cyt.): A group of chromosomes arranged like the spokes of a wheel.

karyogamy (Biol.): The union of two nuclei, especially gametic nuclei.

karyolysis (Cyt.): Dissolution of the nucleus by disintegration of the chromatin.

kar′yosome (Cyt.): A nucleus; a chromosome.

kar′yotin (Cyt.): The substance which makes up the nuclear reticulum.

katabat′ic (Meteor.): Said of a wind which is caused by the downward motion of air due to convection.

katab′olism (Biol.): The sum-total of the disruptive metabolic processes in an organism, organ or cell.

katagen′esis (Zool.): Retrogressive evolution.

katakinet′ic (Biol.): Tending to the discharge of energy.

kataklastic structures (Geol.): Structures produced in a rock by the action of severe mechanical stress, during dynamic metamorphism.

katharom′eter (Chem.): An instrument for the analysis of gases by means of measurements of thermal conductivity.

keel (Aero.): The longitudinal member along the under side of the hull of a rigid airship.

kelp (Bot.): A general name for large seaweeds.

keratogenous (Zool.): Horn-producing.

kernel (Bot.): The seed inside the stony endocarp of a drupe.

kevel (Build.): A hammer, edged at one end and pointed at the other, used for breaking and rough-hewing stone.

kham′sin (Meteor.): A hot dry wind from the south, which blows over Egypt in front of depressions moving eastward along the Mediterranean.

kilowatt (Elec. Eng.): A unit of power equal to 1000 watts.

kilowatt-hour (Elec. Eng.): The commonly used unit of electrical energy, equal to 1000 watt-hours.

kinaesthet′ic (Zool.): Pertaining to the perception of muscular effort.

kineso'dic (Zool.) : Conveying motor impulses.
kinetic body (Cyt.) : A tiny granular body lying where a chromosome is attached to the spindle.
kinetic energy (Phys.) : The energy possessed by a moving body in virtue of its motion.
kip (Eng.) : A unit of force equivalent to 1,000 lbs.
knee (Eng.) : An elbow pipe.
knot (Bot.) : A hard and often resinous inclusion in timber.

L

la'bia (Zool.) : Any structures resembling lips.
la'bile (Chem.) : Unstable.
lab'oratory : A place where specific scientific research or testing is done.
lac : A resinous substance, an excretion product of certain Coccid insects.
laccate (Bot.) : Having a shining surface.
lac'erate (Bot.) : Irregularly cut, as if torn.
lac'quer (Chem.) : A solution of film-forming substances in volatile solvents.
lac'rimal (Zool.) : Pertaining to the tear gland.
lactation (Zool.) : The formation of milk by the mammary glands.
lacte'ous (Bot.) : Milky.
lacu'na (Bot.) : (1) Any depression in a surface of a plant. (2) A large intercellular space.
lacustrine (Ecol.) : Pertaining to a lake or lakes.
lagging (Eng.) : The process of covering a vessel or pipe with a non-conducting material.
lake (Geol.) : A body of water lying on the surface of a continent, and unconnected with the ocean.
lamel'la (Bot.) : A plate of cells.
lam'ellose (Bot.) : Stratified.
lam'ina (Bot.) : The flattened blade of a leaf. (Elec. Eng.) : Thin sheet steel. (Zool.) : A flat plate-like structure.
laminated magnet (Elec. Eng.) : A permanent magnet built up of magnetized strips.
lamination (Geol.) : Stratification on a fine scale.
lan'ate (Bot., Zool.) : Covered with long and loosely tangled hairs.
lan'ceolate (Bot.) : Flattened, two or three times as long as broad, widest in the middle and tapering to a pointed apex.
landslip (Geol.) : The sudden sliding of masses of rock, soil or other superficial deposits from higher to lower levels, on steep slopes.
landing (Build.) : A flat platform at the head of a series of steps. (Civ. Eng.) : A space on a pier intended to provide access for passengers alighting.
landing beam (Aero.) : The beam of radiation from a transmitter along which an aircraft approaches a landing field during blind landing.
lan'iary (Zool.) : Adapted for tearing, as a canine tooth.
lan'thanum (Chem.) : A metallic element.
lap (Met.) : A surface defect on rolled or forged steel.
lapidic'olous (Zool.) : Living under stones.
lapil'li (Geol.) : Small rounded pieces of lava whirled from a volcanic vent during explosive eruptions.
la'pis laz'uli (Min.) : The original sapphire.
lapse (Meteor.) : The temperature gradient of the atmosphere taken vertically.
larva (Zool.) : In insects, an immature stage intervening between the egg and the adult.
lar'ynx (Anat.) : The vocal organ in all land vertebrates except birds.
la'tent (Zool.) : In a resting condition or state of arrested development, but capable of becoming active when conditions become suitable.
latent heat (Phys.) : The heat which is required to change the state of a substance from solid to liquid, or from liquid to gas, without change of temperature.
later-latero-lateri : A prefix meaning sides.
lateral : Situated on or at a side.
later'igrade (Zool.) : Moving sideways, as some crabs.
laterit'ious (Bot.) : Brick-red.
la'tex (Bot.) : A milky fluid, present in many plants.
lathe (Eng.) : A machine tool for producing cylindrical work, facing, boring and screw cutting.

latitude, terrestrial : Angular distance measured on a meridian ; now distance measured in degrees north and south from the equator.
lava (Geol.) : The molten rock material that issues from a volcanic vent or fissure.
law : A scientific law is a rule or generalization which describes specified natural phenomena within the limits of experimental observation.
lax (Bot.) : Arranged loosely.
layer (Bot.) : A stratum of vegetation, as the shrubs in a wood.
leaching (Bot.) : The removal, by percolating water, of mineral salts from the soil. (Met.) : The extraction of a soluble metallic compound from an ore.
lead (Met.) : A metallic element.
lead (Elec. Eng.) : A term often used to denote an electric wire or cable.
leader (Bot.) : One of the main shoots of a tree.
leaf (Bot.) : An outgrowth from the stem of a plant, usually green, and largely concerned with transpiration and photosynthesis.
leaf base (Bot.) : The base of the leaf stalk, where it joins the stem.
leaf bud (Bot.) : A bud containing vegetative leaves only.
leaf scar (Bot.) : The scar left on a stem at the point where a leaf has fallen off.
leaflet (Bot.) : One separate portion of the lamina of a compound leaf.
leap year (Astron.) : Those years in which an extra day, February 29, is added to the civil calendar to allow for the fractional part of a year of 365 days.
leg'ume (Bot.) : A fruit formed from a single carpel.
len'ticel (Bot.) : Structure of the bark of plants which permits passage of gas between internal tissues and atmosphere.
lenticle (Geol.) : A mass of lens-like form.
Leo (Astron.) : Lion ; the fifth sign of the Zodiac.
lep'idote (Bot.) : Said of a surface which bears scale-like hairs. (Zool.) : Having a coating of minute scales, as butterfly wings.
lesion (Med.) : Any wound or morbid change anywhere in the body.
leste (Meteor.) : A dry south wind blowing in Madeira and North Africa in front of a depression.
le'thal (Biol.) : Causing death.
leuco : A prefix meaning white.
leu'cocyte (Zool.) : A white blood-corpuscle.
level (Civ. Eng.) : To reduce a cut or fill surface to an approximately horizontal plane. (Surv.) : An instrument used by the surveyors for determining the difference in height between two points.
level line (Surv.) : A line lying wholly on a level surface, and therefore perpendicular at all points to the direction of gravity.
level man (Surv.) : The operator of a surveyor's level.
level surface (Surv.) : A surface which is everywhere perpendicular to the direction of gravity.
levelling (Surv.) : The operation of finding the difference of elevation between two points.
lever (Mech.) : One of the simplest machines ; a rigid beam pivoted at the fulcrum, with a load being applied at one point in the beam and an effort, sufficient to balance the load at another.
Leyden jar (Elec. Eng.) : A capacitor consisting of a glass jar having its inner and outer surfaces coated with a conducting material.
libido (Psycho-an.) : A term used to denote the energy attached to the sexual impulse ; subsequently used to cover vital energy in general.
Libra (Astron.) : Balance. Seventh sign of the Zodiac.
librations (Astron.) : Apparent oscillations of the moon or other body.
Liche'nes (Bot.) : A large group of composite plants, consisting of an alga and a fungus in intimate association.
life-cycle (Biol.) : The various stages through which an organism passes, from fertilized ovum to the fertilized ovum of the next generation.
lig'ament (Zool.) : A bundle of fibrous tissue joining two or more bones or cartilages.

light: Electromagnetic radiation capable of inducing visual sensation through the eye. Light is the product of the visibility and the radiant power.

light valve: Any device whereby the passage of light is controlled electrically.

light-year (Astron.): A spatial unit used to express distances in the stellar universe.

lightning (Meteor.): The very large spark which marks the discharge of an electrified thunder cloud, either to another cloud or to earth.

lig-neous (Bot.): Woody.

lig'nite (Geol.): Brown, compact, fossil wood, representing one stage in the conversion of plant remains into coal.

lig'ulate (Bot.): Strap-shaped, flattened, long and narrow.

limb (Astron.): The term applied to the rim of a heavenly body having a visible disc. (Bot.): (1) The lamina of a leaf. (2) The widened upper part of a petal. (Zool.): A jointed appendage, as a leg.

limbous (Zool.): Overlapping.

lime (Build.): A substance produced by heating limestone to 825° C or more.

limestone (Geol.): Sedimentary rock containing 50% carbonate of lime or magnesia.

limic'olous (Zool.): Living in mud.

lim'nobiot'ic (Zool.): Living in fresh water.

limnoph'ilous (Zool.): Living in marshes.

limon'iform (Bot.): Lemon-shaped.

line (Carp.): To mark a straight line on timber as a guide for erection or working. (Elec. Comm.): That part of a communication circuit which has uniformly distributed constants. (Elec. Eng.): A power transmission circuit. (Surv.): The cord to which the lead of a lead-line is secured.

line (Maths.): In a plane: the shortest distance between two points. On a sphere: a portion of a great circle.

line of action (Mech.): The line along which a force acts.

lineage (Gen.): In evolution, a time-character concept representing a racial complex of lines of descent.

lin'qua (Zool.): Any tongue-like structure.

link (Eng.): Any connecting piece in a machine. (Surv.): The one-hundredth part of a chain.

linkage (Gen.): The tendency shown by certain genetical characteristics to be inherited together.

Linnean System (Bot., Zool.): The system of classification established by the Swedish naturalist Linnaeus.

linseed oil (Chem.): An oil obtained from the seeds of flax.

lintel (Build.) A beam across the top of an aperture.

lip (Bot.): A large projecting lobe of a corolla.

lipids, lipoids (Chem.): Generic terms for fats, waxes and related products found in living tissue.

lipogenous (Zool.): Fat-producing.

lip'oplast (Bot.): A fatty globule.

liquefaction: The change of a gas or solid into a liquid state.

lithium (Min.): The lightest metallic element.

lithod'omous (Zool.): Living in rocks.

lithol'ogy (Geol.): The character of a rock expressed in terms of its structure, its mineral composition, the grain-size and arrangement of its component parts.

lithoph'agous (Zool.): Stone-eating.

lith'osphere (Geol.): The crust of the earth.

litmus (Chem.): A material of organic origin used as indicator for acids and alkalines.

litt'oral (Bot., Zool.): Pertaining to the shore; seashore.

live (Acous.): Said of an enclosure in which the reverberation is normal. (Elec. Eng.): Said of an electric circuit or conductor in which there is a difference between it and earth.

load: (1) The weight supported by a structure. (2) The power output of an engine or motor under given circumstances.

loam (Build.): A brick earth composed of clay and sand.

lobe (Bot.): One of the parts into which a flattened plant member is cut, when the parts are too large

to be called teeth, but not completely separated from one another. (Zool.): A rounded projection.

locomotive (Eng.): A vehicle driven by oil, steam or electricity for hauling on a railway.

locus (Cyt.): The position of a gene in a chromosome.

lode (Civ. Eng.): An artificial dyke.

lodestone (Min.): A form of magnetite, behaving when freely suspended, as a magnet.

loess (Geol.): An aeolian clay originating in arid regions and transported by wind.

log: The stem of a felled tree when deprived of its limbs and ready for conversion.

longi-: A prefix meaning long.

longitude, terrestrial: The portion of the equator intersected between the meridian of a given place and the prime meridian, as from Greenwich, England.

looming (Meteor.): The vague enlarged appearance of objects seen through a fog or mist, particularly at sea.

lopho: A prefix meaning crest.

loss (Elec. Comm.): The negative of gain in a transmission system.

lo'tic fauna (Ecol.): Animals living in running waters, as streams and rivers.

loudness (Acous.): The subjective measure of the intensity of a sound.

louver (Build.): A window space across which are sloping slats fixed horizontally, with spaces between for ventilation.

low (meteor.): A region of low pressure.

lubricant: A substance capable of reducing friction between bearing surfaces in relative motion; oil or graphite.

lu'bricous (Bot.): Having a slippery surface.

lucif'erin (Zool.): A protein like substance which occurs in the luminous organs of certain animals.

lucifu'gous (Ecol.): Shunning light.

luciph'ilous (Ecol.): Seeking light.

lumbago (Med.): A rheumatic affection of the muscles and ligaments in the lower part of the back.

lumines'cence (Chem.): The emission of light as a result of causes other than high temperatures.

lu'minophore (Chem.): A substance which emits light at room temperature.

luminosity (Astron.): The measure of the amount of light actually emitted by a star, irrespective of its distance.

lunar bows (Meteor.): Bows of a similar nature to rainbows but produced by moonlight.

lu'nate: Crescent-shaped.

lune (Maths.): The portion of the surface of a sphere intercepted by two great circles.

lung (Zool.): The respiratory organ in air-breathing vertebrates.

luster (Min.): This depends upon the quality and amount of light that is reflected from the surface of a mineral.

lute'cium (Chem.): A metallic element.

lutein (Chem.): A yellow unsaturated compound occurring in leaves and petals of various plants.

lymph-: A prefix meaning water.

lymph (Zool.): A colorless circulating fluid occurring in the lymphatic vessels of vertebrates and closely resembling blood plasma in composition.

ly'sin (Zool.): A substance which will cause dissolution of cells.

M

macad'amized road (Civ. Eng.): A road whose surface is formed with broken stones rolled into a 6-10 in. layer.

machine (Mech.): A device for overcoming a resistance at one point by the application of a force at some other point.

macr-, macro-: A prefix meaning large.

macrochem'istry (Chem.): The study of the composition and chemical properties of matter in bulk.

macroscop'ic: Visible to the naked eye.

macrosmat'ic (Zool.): Having a highly developed sense of smell.

Science Terms

mac'rosome (Zool.) : A large protoplasmic globule.

mac'rostructure (Met.) : The general arrangement of crystals in a solid metal as seen by the naked eye or at low magnification.

maestro (Meteor.) : A fine-weather, non-autumn north-west wind in the Adriatic.

Mae West (Aero.) : Personal lifejacket designed for airmen.

magma (Geol.) : A term given to the molten fluids and gaseous fractions which have been generated within the earth, and from which igneous rocks are considered to have been derived.

mag'nesite (Met.) : Carbonate of magnesium.

magne'sium (Chem.) : A metallic element.

magnet: A mass of iron or other material which possesses the property of attracting or repelling other masses of iron.

magnet core: The iron core within the coil of an electromagnet.

magnetic axis: A line through the effective centers of the poles of a magnet.

magnetic bearing (Surv.) : The horizontal angle between any survey line and the direction of magnetic north.

magnetic circuit (Elec. Eng.) : The closed path taken by the magnetic flux in an electric machine or other apparatus.

magnetic compass: A compass consisting of a magnetic needle which sets itself along the lines of the earth's magnetic field.

magnetic field: The region in the neighborhood of a permanent magnet or a current-carrying conductor in which magnetic forces can be detected.

Magnetic North: The direction in which the north pole of a pivoted magnet will point.

magnetic polarization (Chem.) : The production of optical activity by placing an inactive substance in a magnetic field.

Magnetic South: The direction in which the South pole of a pivoted magnet will point.

magnetizing coil (Elec. Eng.) : A current-carrying coil used to magnetize an electromagnet.

magnetism: A general term used to denote either a magnetic field or the whole science associated with the behavior of such fields.

magnetite (Min.) : An oxide of iron.

magne'to (Elec. Eng.) : A small permanent-magnet electric generator capable of producing periodic high-voltage impulses.

magnetochemistry (Chem.) : The study of the magnetic changes accompanying chemical reactions.

magnetom'eter: A pivoted magnetic needle used for measuring the strength of magnetic fields.

magnetomotive force: The force which produces a magnetic flux in a magnetic circuit.

magneto-striction: The change in dimensions produced in a magnetic material when it is magnetized.

magnitudes (Astron.) : The scale by which the brightness of stars is measured.

main (Civ. Eng.) : A principal water or gas pipe, having branch pipes leading supplies to consumers.

male (Zool.) : An individual of which the gonads produce spermatozoa or some corresponding form of gamete.

malignant (Med.) : Tending to go from bad to worse; especially, cancerous.

malleabil'ity (Met.) : The property of being able to be mechanically deformed by rolling, forging, extrusion etc., applied to metals.

mal'leate (Zool.) : Hammer-shaped.

mamil'la (Zool.) : A nipple.

Man (Zool.) : The human race, all varieties of which are included in the single species Homo sapiens, belonging to the order Primates.

manganese (Met.) : A hard, brittle, metallic element.

mania (Psychiatry) : The elated phase of manic depressive psychosis.

manic-depressive psychosis (Psychiatry) : A type of insanity characterized by disorders of affect, either of elation or of depression, with intermediate mixed states.

manom'eter (Phys.) : An instrument used to measure the pressure of a gas.

mantel (Build.) : An ornamental front and shelf to a fireplace.

marble (Geol.) : The term applies to a granular crystalline limestone.

marbled (Bot.) : Marked by irregular streaks of color.

marginate (Bot.) : Having a well-marked border.

mar'igraph (Surv.) : A guage registering the height of the tide at a given place.

maritime (Bot., Zool.) : Living by the sea.

mark (Surv.) : Any of the distinguishing tags attached at intervals to a lead-line to denote feet or fathoms.

marl (Geol.) : A general term for a very fine-grained rock, either clay or loam, with a variable admixture of calcium carbonate.

marquise (Build.) : A projecting canopy over the entrance to a building.

marrow (Zool.) : The vascular connective tissue which occupies the central cavities of the long bones in most vertebrates.

Mars (Astron.) : The fourth planet from the sun in order of distance.

marsu'pium (Zool.) : A pouch-like structure occupied by the immature young of an animal during the later stages of development.

ma'sochism (Psycho-path.) : Gratification obtained from the suffering of physical or mental pain.

mass (Phys.) : The quantity of matter in a body.

mass number (Chem.) : The atomic weight of an isotope.

mastication (Zool.) : The act of reducing solid food to a fine state of subdivision or to a pulp.

mas'ticatory (Zool.) : Pertaining to the chewing of food prior to swallowing.

ma'trix (Biol.) : An outer layer of stainable material in a chromosome. (Zool.) : The inter-cellular ground-substance of connective tissues.

matromor'phic (Biol.) : Resembling the mother.

matter (Phys.) : The substances of which the physical universe is composed.

maturation (Bot., Zool.) : The final stages in the development of the germ cells.

mean solar time (Astron.) : Time as measured by the hour angle of the mean sun.

mechanical advantage (Mech.) : The ratio of the resistance to the applied force in a machine.

mechanical engineering: That branch of engineering concerned primarily with the design and production of all purely mechanical contrivances.

mechanics: The study of the action of forces on bodies and of the motions they produce.

medi-, medio-: A prefix meaning middle.

medium (Bot., Zool.) : A nutritive substance on or in which tissues or culture of micro-organisms may be reared.

medulla (Zool.) : The central portion of an organ or tissue.

medul'lary (Bot.) : Relating to the pith.

mega-, meg-: A prefix denoting a million.

mega-, megal. megalo: A prefix meaning large.

meg'acycle (Elec. Comm.) : One million cycles.

megaloma'nia (Psychiatry) : Delusion of grandeur.

megascopic: Visible to the naked eye.

megaton (Nuclear Warfare) : Explosive force equivalent to 1,000,000 tons of T.N.T.

meg'ohm (Elec. Eng.) : A unit of resistance used for very high resistance values.

mei'ocyte (Cyt.) : Any cell in which meiosis is begun.

meiomer'ous (Bot., Zool.) : Having a small number of parts.

meio'sis (Cyt.) : The type of nuclear division by which the chromosomes are reduced from the diploid to the haploid number.

melan-, mel'ans-: A prefix meaning black.

melancho'lia (Psychiatry) : A condition seen in the depressive state of manic depressive psychosis.

mel'anin (Chem.) : A black or dark brown pigment occurring in hair and skin.

melliphagous (Zool.) : Honey-eating.

melting-point (Chem.): The temperature at which a solid begins to liquify.

member (Bot.): Any part of a plant considered from the standpoint of morphology. (Zool.): An organ of the body, especially an appendage.

membrane (Bot., Zool.): A thin sheet-like structure, usually fibrous, connecting other structures or covering or lining a part or organ.

menis'cus (Chem.): The surface of a liquid in a tube.

men'opause (Med.): The natural cessation of menstruation in women.

mensa (Zool.): The biting surface of a tooth.

menstrua'tion (Zool.): The periodical discharge from the uterus.

Mercury (Astron.): The first planet from the sun in order of distance.

mercury (Met.): A white metallic element which is liquid at atmospheric temperature.

mercury barometer (Meteor., Phys.): An instrument used for measuring the pressure of the atmosphere in terms of the height of a column of mercury which exerts an equal pressure.

mer'icarp (Bot.): A one-seeded portion of a fruit which splits up at maturity.

meridian (Astron.): That great circle passing through the poles of the celestial sphere which cuts the observer's horizon in the north and south point, and also passes through his Zenith.

meris'tic (Zool.): Segmented.

mero-: A prefix meaning part.

merog'amy (Bot.): The union of two individual gametes.

merosthen'ic (Zool.): Having the hind legs exceptionally well developed, as kangaroos.

mer'ycism (Med.): Rumination.

mes-, meso-: A prefix meaning middle.

mesons (Nucleonics): Short-lived sub-atomic particles arising in cosmic rays.

mesh (Civ. Eng.): Expanded metal used as a reinforcement for concrete.

mesomor'phous (Chem.): Existing in a state of aggregation midway between the true crystalline state and the completely irregular amorphous state.

me'sophyte (Bot.): A plant occurring in places where the water-supply is neither scanty nor excessive.

me'sostate (Zool.): An intermediate stage in metabolism.

meta-: A prefix meaning after.

metabol'ic nucleus (Cyt.): A nucleus when it is not dividing, and when the chromation is in the form of a network.

metab'olism (Biol.): The sum-total of the chemical and physical changes constantly taking place in living matter.

metab'olite (Zool.): A product of metabolism.

metab'oly (Bot.): The power possessed by some cells of altering their external form.

metachemistry: The study of atomic and sub-atomic phenomena.

metachromat'ic (Micros.): Showing other than the basic color constituent after staining.

metachro'sis (Zool.): The ability of an animal to change color by contraction and expansion of chromatophores, as a chameleon.

metal: An element which readily forms positive ions.

metallif'erous veins (Geol.): Cracks and fissures in rocks which are found to contain the ore of metals.

metallization (Chem.): The conversion of a substance into a metallic form.

metal'lochrome (Chem.): The tinting produced on a metal surface by means of metallic salts.

metallog'raphy: The branch of metallurgy which deals with the study of the structure and constitution of solid metals and alloys, and the relation of this to properties on the one hand and manufacture and treatment on the other.

met'alloid (Chem.): (1) A non-metal. (2) An element having both metallic and non-metallic properties.

metallurgy: Art and science applied to metals.

metamorphic rocks (Geol.): Rocks derived from pre-existing rocks by chemical, mineralogical and structural alterations.

metamor'phism (Geol.): The sum of the processes which can operate within the earth's crust and transform a rock into a well characterized new type.

metamorpho'sis (Zool.): Pronounced change of form and structure taking place within a short time, as an animal changing from the larval to the adult stage.

metapla'sia (Zool.): Tissue transformation.

metapla'sis (Zool.): The period of maturity in the life-cycle of an individual.

metaplasm (Biol.): Any substance within the body of a cell which is not protoplasm.

metasitism (Zool.): Cannibalism.

met'astable (Chem.): In a state which is apparently stable.

metasta'sic electron (Chem.): An electron which is transferred from one atom to another, or from one shell to another in the same atom.

metas'tasis (Med.): The transfer of deseased tissue from one part of the body to another.

me'teor (Astron.): A "shooting star".

meteorites (Astron.): Mineral aggregates of cosmic origin which reach the earth from interplanetary space.

meteorograph (Meteor.): A collection of meteorological recording instruments which are attached to small balloons and sent up to record conditions in the upper atmosphere.

meteorology: The study of the earth's atmosphere in its relation to climate and weather.

meter: A unit of length in the metric system; 1 meter equals 39.37 inches.

metric system: A system of weights and measures depending upon the meter.

metromor'phic (Bot.): Resembling the mother.

metu'liform (Bot.): Resembling a pyramid.

mez'zanine (Build.): An intermediate floor constructed between two other floors in a building.

mica (Min.): A group of minerals which crystallize in the monoclinic system.

mica-schist (Geol.): A schist composed essentially of micas and quartz.

micelle (Chem.): A particle of colloidal size.

micro-: A prefix meaning small.

microanal'ysis (Chem.): A special technique of both quantitative and qualitative analysis, by means of which very small amounts of substance may be analyzed.

mi'crobe (Bacteriol.): A bacterium which can be seen with the aid of a microscope.

microcrystalline texture (Geol.): A term applied to a rock in which the individual crystals can be seen as such only under the microscope.

mi'crolite (Geol.): A general term for minute crystals of tabular or prismatic habit found in microcrystalline rocks.

microm'eter: An instrument used primarily for measuring small angular separations visually.

mi'cron: A unit of length equal to 10^{-3} mm., used for expressing wave-lengths of light and small distances.

mi'crophone (Acous.): An acousti-electrical convertor of sound wave-forms, essential in sound-reproducing systems.

microphyl'line (Bot.): Composed of small scales or lobes.

mi'croscope: An instrument used for obtaining magnified images in small objects.

mi'crosome (Cyt.): A granular or bladder-like inclusion in the cytoplasm, of very small size.

microspe'cies (Bot.): A variety of species.

microstructure (Met.): A term referring to the size, shape and arrangement with respect to each other of the crystals of the constituents present in a metal or alloy.

mi'crotome (Bot., Zool.): An instrument for cutting thin sections of specimens.

midrib (Bot.): The largest vein of a leaf, running longitudinally through the middle of the lamella.

midwater zone (Ocean.): The depths of the ocean between the surface waters and the abyss.

migraine (Med.): Paroxysmal headache.

migration (Chem.): The steady motion of particles, ions, etc., in a given direction under the influence of a force. (Zool.): Removal from one habitat to another.

mil (Eng.): Measurement unit, 10^{-3} inch.

mile: A unit of length; 1 statute mile = 1760 yds.

mill (Eng.): (1) A machine for grinding. (2) A factory fitted with machinery for manufacturing.

mil'limeter: The thousandth part of a meter.

mil'limicron (Phys.): A unit of length, equal to 10^{-6} millimeter.

mim'icry (Zool.): The adoption by one species of the color, habits or structure of another species.

min'aret (Arch.): A lofty slender tower rising from a mosque and surrounded by galleries.

mind (Psycho-an.): According to Freud, mind consists of a relatively small conscious part and a larger unconscious part, each of which consist of the processes of feeling, thinking and wishing.

mineral (Min.): A body produced by processes of inorganic nature; usually with a definite chemical composition, a certain characteristic atomic structure, which is expressed in its crystalline form.

mineral'ogy: The scientific study of minerals.

minute: (1) A sixtieth part of an hour of time. (2) A sixtieth part of a degree. (3) A sixtieth part of the lower diameter of a column.

mio'sis (Med.): Contraction of the pupil of the eye.

mirage (Meteor.): An effect caused by total reflection of light at the upper surface of shallow layers of hot air in contact with the ground, the appearance being that of pools of water in which are seen inverted images of more distant objects.

mirror (Phys.): A high polished reflecting surface capable of reflecting light-rays without appreciable diffusion.

miscarriage (Med.): Expulsion of the foetus before the twenty-eighth week of pregnancy.

miscilibility (Chem.): The property enabling two or more liquids to mix when brought together and thus form one phase.

mist (Chem.): A suspension of a liquid in a gas. (Meteor.): A term applied to cloud in contact with the ground.

mis'tral (Meteor.): A cold, dry northerly wind occurring along the Mediterranean coast of France during fine clear weather.

mito'sis (Cyt.): The series of changes through which the nucleus passes during ordinary cell division, and by which each of the daughter cells is provided with a set of chromosomes similar to that possessed by the parent cell.

mito'tic index (Cyt.): The proportion in any tissue of dividing cells.

miter (Build.): A joint between two pieces at an angle to one another.

mixed (Zool.): Said of nerve trunks containing motor and sensory fibers.

mixer (Met.): A large furnace used as a reservoir for molten pig-iron coming from the blast-furnace.

mode (Geol.): The actual mineral composition of a rock expressed quantitatively in percentages by weight.

modification (Bot.): A change in a plant brought about by environmental conditions and lasting only as long as the operative conditions last.

modules (Arch.): The radius of the lower end of the shaft of a column.

molars (Zool.): The posterior grinding teeth of mammals.

molecular compound (Chem.): A compound formed by the combination of two or more molecules capable of independent existence.

molecular heat (Chem.): The product of the specific heat of a substance and its molecular weight.

molecular structure (Chem.): The way in which atoms are linked together in a molecule.

molecular weight (Chem.): The weight of a molecule of a substance referred to that of an atom of oxygen as 16.000.

molecule (Chem.): The smallest particle of a substance that is capable of independent existence while still retaining its chemical properties.

momentum (Mech.): The product of the mass of a body and its velocity.

mon-, mono-: A prefix meaning alone.

mongrel (Bot., Zool.): The offspring of a cross between varieties of races of a species.

monitor (Elec. Comm.): An arrangement for reproducing and checking any transmission without interfering with the regular transmission.

monkey (Civ. Eng.): The falling weighting of a pile-driver.

Monocotyle'dones (Bot.): One of the two main groups included in the Angiospermae. The embryo has one cotyledon.

monoe'cious (Bot.): Having separate staminate and pistillate flowers on the same individual plant.

monog'ony (Zool.): Asexual reproduction.

monokar'yon (Cyt.): A nucleus with only one centriole.

mon'olith (Build.): A single detached column or block of stone.

monolith'ic (Build., Civ. Eng.): A structure made of a continuous mass of material.

monomolec'ular layer (Chem.): A film of a substance one molecule thick.

monomor'phic (Zool.): Showing little change of form during the life history.

monomor'phous (Cryst.): Existing in only one crystalline form.

mononucleo'sis (Med.): Glandular fever.

monophylet'ic (Gen.): Descended from a single parent form.

mon'oplane (Aero.): A heavier-than-air aircraft, having one main supporting surface.

monova'lent (Chem.): Capable of combining with one atom of hydrogen or its equivalent.

monsoon (Meteor.): A wind which blows in opposite directions at different seasons of the year.

montic'olous (Zool.): Living in mountainous regions.

moon (Astron.): (1) The satellite which revolves about the earth in a variable orbit at a mean distance of 239,000 miles in a period of one month. (2) Any satellite of a planet.

mo'ron (Psychiatry): A feeble-minded person whose mentality is that of a child between 8 and 12 years of age.

morph-, morpho-: A prefix meaning form.

morphol'ogy (Bot., Zool.): The study of the structure and form of organisms, as opposed to the study of their functions. (Geol.): The study of the shapes and contours of objects, especially of the surface of the earth.

morpho'sis (Zool.: The development of structural characteristics; tissue formation.

mortar (Chem.): A bowl, made of porcelain, glass or agate, in which solids are ground up with a pestle.

mother cell (Bot., Zool.): A cell which divides to give daughter cells.

motor (Bot., Zool.): Pertaining to movement.

mold (Bot.): A popular name for any of numerous small fungi.

molding (Build.): An ornamental band projecting from the surface of a wall or other surface.

mound (Civ. Eng.): An undisturbed hillock left on an excavated site as an indication of the depth of the excavation.

mu'cins (Chem.): A group of glucoproteins occurring in saliva and mucus and widely distributed in nature.

mu'cus (Zool.): The viscous slimy fluid secreted by the mucous glands.

multi-: A prefix meaning many.

multicel'lular (Bot., Zool.): Consisting of a number of cells.

mul'tiform (Bot.): Diverse in shape.

multinu'cleate (Bot., Zool.): With many nuclei.

mul'tiplet (Bot.): One of several individuals derived by the segmentation of an ovum.

multiplication (Bot.): Increase by vegetative means.

muscle (Zool.): Tissue possessing the power of rapidly

and forcibly changing shape.

mus'culature (Zool.): The disposition and arrangement of the muscles in the body of an animal.

mutation (Gen.): The inception of a heritable variation.

mycol'ogy (Bot.): The study of fungi.

myol'ogy (Zool.): The study of muscles.

myo'pia (Med.): Near-sightedness.

N

na'cre (Zool.): Mother-of-pearl.

nacreous (Min.): A term applied to the luster of certain minerals.

narcot'ic (Med.): Tending to induce sleep or unconsciousness.

na'dir (Astron.): The point on the celestial sphere diametrically opposite the zenith.

nar'cissism (Psycho-path.): A state of self-love.

na'sal (Zool): Pertaining to the nose.

nas'cent (Chem.): Just formed by a chemical reaction, and therefore very reactive.

na'tal (Med., Zool.): Pertaining to birth.

nata'tory (Zool.): Adapted for swimming.

native (Min.): Said of naturally occurring metal.

natural frequency (Phys.): The frequency of free vibrations of a body.

neap tides (Astron.): High tides occurring at the moon's first or third quarter.

nebula (Astron.): Any first luminous patch seen among the stars.

nebule (Arch.): An ornamental molding characterized by a wavy lower edge.

neb'ulous (Bot.): Clouded, dark.

necro-: A prefix meaning a dead body.

necrog'enous (Biol.): Living or developing in the bodies of dead animals.

ne'cron (Bot.): Dead plant material not rotted into humus.

nec'ropsy (Med.): Autopsy.

necro'sis (Biol): Death of a cell or cells while still part of the living body.

nectar (Bot.): A sugary fluid exuded by plants.

nectary (Bot.): A glandular organ or surface from which nectar is secreted.

necto-: A prefix meaning swimming.

nectopod (Zool.): An appendage adopted for swimming.

needle (Elec. Eng.): The moving magnet of a compass or galvanometer of the moving-magnet type.

negative (Elec.): A particular point or electrode is negative with respect to another point when it is at a lower electric potential.

negative catalysis (Chem.): The retardation of a chemical reaction by a substance which itself undergoes no permanent chemical change.

negative group (Chem.): An acid radical.

nemato-: A prefix meaning thread.

neo-: A prefix meaning young.

Neo-Darwinian (Zool.): Pertaining to the modern version of the natural selection theory of Darwin.

Neolithic Period (Geol.): The later portion of the Stone Age.

ne'on (Chem.): A zero-valent element, one of the rare gases.

ne'oplasm (Med.): A new formation of tissue in the body.

nephr-, nephro-: A prefix meaning kidney.

neph'ric (Anat., Zool.): Pertaining to the kidney.

nephrite (Min.): One of the minerals grouped under the name of jade.

neph'ros (Zool.): A kidney.

Neptune (Astron.): Eighth major planet of the solar system, in order of distance from the sun.

neritic zone (Geol., Ocean.): That portion of the sea floor lying between low-water mark and the edge of the continental shelf, at a depth of about 100 fathoms.

nerve (Anat., Zool.): One of the branches of the central nervous system passing to an organ or part of the body. (Bot.): A general name for the midrib and the larger veins of a leaf.

nerve center (Zool.): An aggregation of nerve cells associated with a particular function or sense.

nerve ending (Zool.): The free distal end of a nerve or nerve fiber.

nerve fiber (Zool.): An axon.

nerve impulse (Zool.): The disturbance which passes along a nerve when it is stimulated.

nerve plexus (Zool.): A network of interlacing nerve fibers.

nerve root (Zool.): The origin of a nerve in the central nervous system.

nerve trunk (Zool.): A bundle of nerve fibers united within a connective-tissue coat.

nervous system (Zool.): The whole system of nerves, ganglia and nerve endings of the body of an animal, considered collectively.

net knot (Cyt.): A small accumulation of chromatin.

network (Elec. Comm., Elec. Eng.): A group of electrical elements connected together for the purpose of satisfying specified requirements.

net'rum (Cyt.): A minute spindle which arises within the centrosome during the division of the centriole.

neur-, neuro-: A prefix meaning nerves.

neurogen'ic (Zool.): Activity of a muscle or gland which is dependent on continued nervous stimuli.

neurogen'esis (Zool.): The development and formation or nerves.

neurol'ogy: The study of the nervous system.

neuro'sis (Med.): Any one of a group of diseases thought to be due to disordered function of the involuntary nervous system, shown by instability of the circulatory system. (Psycho-path.): A psychological disorder resulting from a conflict of repressed infantile instinctive demands with those of adult society.

neurosurgery (Surg.): That part of surgical science which deals with the nervous system.

neus'ton (Ecol.): Aquatic animals associated with the surface film.

neuter (Bot., Zool.): (1) Sexless.

neutral solution (Chem.): An aqueous solution which is neither alkaline nor acidic.

neutralization (Chem.): The interaction of an acid and a base with the formation of a salt.

neutron (Phys.): Uncharged sub-atomic particle, mass approximately equal to that of a proton, which enters into the structure of atomic nuclei.

neu'trophil (Physiol.): Stainable by neutral dyes.

new moon (Astron.): The instant when sun and moon have the same celestial longitude.

niche (Build.): A recess in a wall surface. (Ecol.): A term used to describe the status of an animal in its community.

nickel (Met.): A silver-white metallic element.

ni'dus (Zool.): A nest.

nimbus (Meteor.): A dense layer of dark shapeless cloud with ragged edges, from which steady rain or snow falls.

ni'trates (Chem.): Salts formed by the action of nitric acid on metallic oxides, hydroxides and carbonates.

nitrides (Chem.): Compounds of metals with nitrogen.

ni'trogen (Chem.): A non-metallic element.

nitrogen cycle (Bacteriol.): The sum total of the transformations undergone by nitrogen and nitrogenous compounds in nature in relation to living organisms.

noctilu'cent (Zool.): Light-producing.

nocturnal (Zool., etc.): Active at night.

nodalizer (Elec. Comm.): An arrangement for adjusting a minimum effect in an electrical circuit.

node (Bot.): The place where a leaf is attached to a stem. (Phys.): A point of minimum displacement in a system of stationary waves. (Astron.): The two points, diametrically opposite each other, in which the orbit of a heavenly body cuts some great circle.

nod'ular (Bot.): Bearing local thickenings.

noise (Acous.): Sounds which are objectionable to some people and which may or may not have significance. That class of sounds which do not exhibit clearly defined frequency components.

non-conjunction (Cyt.) : The complete failure of synopsis.

non-disjunction (Cyt.) : Failure of two chromosomes to disjoin in meiosis.

non-metal (Chem.) : An element which readily forms negative ions and are generally poor conductors of electricity.

noon (Astron.) : The instant of the sun's upper culmination at any place.

norm : The value of a quantity or of a state which is statistically most frequent.

normal (Bot., etc.) : Quite ordinary in structure and in all other respects. (Math.) : The normal to a line or surface is a line drawn perpendicular to it. (Psychol.) : Said of one who is well adjusted to himself and to the outside world.

normalizing (Met.) : A heat-treatment applied to steel.

northing (Surv.) : A north latitude.

nosol'ogy (Med.) : Systematic classification of diseases.

nostrils (Anat., Zool.) : The external nares.

notching (Carp.) : The process of joining timbers together by fitting one or both into a notch cut in the other. (Civ. Eng.) : The method of excavating cuttings for roads or railways in a series of steps marked at the same time.

nova (Astron.) : A star which makes a sudden appearance in the sky, generally decreasing rapidly in brightness.

nozzle : An outlet tube through which a discharge of fluid finally passes.

nu'clear budding (Cyt.) : Production of two daughter nuclei of unequal size by constriction of the parent nucleus.

nuclear chemistry (Chem.) : The study of reactions in which new elements are produced.

nuclear energy (Phys.) : Energy released or absorbed during reactions taking place in atomic nuclei.

nuclear isomers (Phys.) : Atomic nuclei having the same mass and charge but different radio-active properties.

nuclear membrane (Cyt.) : The delicate membrane of the nucleus.

nuclear reactor (Eng.) : Device in which chain reaction of neutrons can be sustained and regulated for the production of heat-energy, synthetic elements and radioisotopes.

nuclear spindle (Cyt.) : The fusiform structure which appears in the cytoplasm of a cell surrounding the nucleus during mitosis and meiosis.

nuclei (Met.) : Points at which crystals begin to grow during solidification.

nucleide (Nucleonics) : The atom of a specific isotope.

nucleon (Nucleonics) : Component of an atomic nucleus as the proton or neutron.

nucleonics : Science of the nucleus of the atom, its components and energies.

nu'cleoplasm (Cyt.) : The dense protoplasm composing the nucleus of a cell.

nucleus (Biol.) : The chief organ of the cell.

nut (Bot.) : A hard, dry, indehiscent fruit and usually containing one seed. (Eng). A metal collar, screwed internally, to fit a bolt.

nutation (Astron.) : An oscillation of the earth's pole about the mean position.

nutlet (Bot.) : A one-seeded portion of a fruit which fragments when it matures.

nutrient (Med.) : Providing nourishment.

nutrition (Zool.) : The process of feeding and the subsequent digestion and assimilation of food-material.

nyc'tanthous (Bot.) : Said of flowers which open at night.

nymph (Zool.) : In insects, a young stage intervening between the egg and the adult.

O

obelisk (Arch.) : A slender stone shaft and tapering towards the top, which is surmounted by a small pyramid.

oblong (Bot.) : Elliptical, blunt at each end, having almost parallel sides, and two to four times as long as broad.

o'bovate' (Bot.) : Having the general shape of the longitudinal section of an egg.

ob'ovoid' (Bot.) : Solid, egg-shaped and attached by the narrower end.

obscure (Bot.) : Said of venation which is very little developed.

obsession (Psycho-path.) : The morbid persistence of an idea in the mind, against the wish of the obsessed person.

obsid'ian (Geol.) : A volcanic glass of granitic composition.

obstetrician : A medically qualified person who practices obstetrics.

obstetrics : That branch of medical science which deals with the problems and management of pregnancy and labor.

obvol'vent (Zool.) : Folded downwards and inwards, as some insect wings.

occlusion (Zool.) : Closure of a duct or aperture. (Chem.) : The retention of a gas or a liquid in a solid mass or on the surface of solid particles.

occultation (Astron.) : The hiding of one celestial body by another interposed between it and the observer.

ocean : Any of the major expanses of salt water on the face of the globe.

ocel'lus (Bot.) : An enlarged discolored cell in a leaf.

ochlopho'bia (Med.) : Morbid fear of crowds.

o'chery (Bot.) : Yellowish-brown.

ochroleu'cous (Bot.) : Yellowish-white.

octa- (Chem.) : Containing eight atoms, groups, etc.

octant division (Bot.) : The division of an embryonic cell by walls at right-angles, giving eight cells.

octastyle (Arch.) : A building have a colonnade of eight columns in front.

octava'lent (Chem.) : Capable of combining with eight atoms of hydrogen or their equivalent.

octet (Chem.) : An extremely stable group of eight electrons.

octopod (Zool.) : Having eight feet, tentacles or arms.

octospo-rous (Bot.) : Containing eight spores.

ocul-, oculo- : A prefix meaning eye.

ocular (Zool.) : Pertaining to the eye.

o'culate (Zool.) : Possessing eyes.

oculist (Med.) : One skilled in the knowledge and treatment of diseases of the eye.

o'culomo'tor (Zool.) : Pertaining to eye movements.

oculus (Build.) : A round window.

odom'eter (Ocean.) : A recording sheave used with other machines when it is necessary to know how much warp or wire has been paid out.

odontal'gia (Med.) : Toothache.

odon'tic (Anat.) : Pertaining to the teeth.

odontogeny (Zool.) : The origin and development of teeth.

odorim'etry (Chem.) : The measurement of the intensity and permanency of odors.

Oedipus complex (Psycho-an.) : A Freudian name for a complex, present in all boys at an early age characterized by an unconscious rivalry for the mother's love, resulting in hostility to the father.

oesoph'agus (Zool.) : The section of the alimentary canal leading from the pharynx to the stomach, in vertebrates.

oestrogen (Physiol.) : The generic term for female sex hormones.

offset (Build.) : A ledge formed at a place where part of a wall is set back from the face.

o'gee arch (Arch.) : A pointed arch of which each side consists of a reverse curve.

ohm (Elec. Eng.) : The practical unit of resistance of an electrical circuit.

ohm'meter (Elec. Eng) : An indicating instrument for giving a direct reading of the resistance of an electric circuit.

oils (Chem.) : A group of neutral liquids ; fixed oils from animal, vegetable and marine sources, mineral oils from petroleum, coal, etc., and essential oils, volatile products derived from certain plants.

olfac'tory (Zool.) : Pertaining to the sense of smell.

olig-, oligo- : A prefix meaning few, small.

oligotro'phic (Ecol.) : Said of a type of lake habitat

having steep and rocky shores and scanty vegetation.

oliva'ceous, olive (Bot.): Greyish-green with a touch of orange.

ombrom'eter (Meteor.): A rain-gauge.

om'brophyte (Bot.): A plant inhabiting rainy places.

omniv'orous (Zool.): Eating both animal and vegetable tissue.

oncol'ogy (Med.): The part of medical science that deals with tumors of body-tissue.

oni'ric (Med.): Pertaining to dreams.

onyx (Min.): A cryptochrystalline variety of silica.

oö: A prefix meaning egg.

oöblas'tema (Zool.): A fertilized egg.

ooze (Geol.): A fine-grained, soft, deep-sea deposit composed of shells and fragments of other organisms.

opal (Min.): An amorphous variety of silica with a varying amount of water.

opales'cence (Chem.): The milky, iridescent appearance of a mineral or solution, due to the reflection of light from very fine, suspended particles.

opaque: Totally absorbent of rays of a specified wave-length. (Bot.): Not shining.

open circuit (Elec. Eng.): A break in an electrical circuit along which current can normally pass.

open floor (Build.): A floor which is not covered by a ceiling.

open-hearth process (Met.): A process for making steel from varying proportions of pig-iron and scrap.

oper'culate (Bot., Zool.): Possessing a lid.

ophthalmo-: A prefix meaning eye.

ophthal'mic (Zool.): Pertaining to the eye.

ophthalmol'ogy (Med.): That part of medical science which deals with the eye and its diseases.

ophthal'moscope (Med.): An instrument for inspecting the interior of the eye by means of light reflected from a mirror.

opposite (Bot.): Said of leaves inserted in pairs at each node, with one on each side of the stem.

optics: The study of light. (Zool.): Pertaining to the sense of sight.

optimism: Most favorable.

oral (Zool.): Pertaining to the mouth.

orbit (Astron.): The path of a heavenly body moving about another under gravitational attraction. (Aero.): An aircraft circling a given point is said to orbit that point.

ordinal number (Maths.): Number derived from the notion of counting and possessing the fundamental property of position in an aggregate.

ore (Min.): A term applied to any metalliferous mineral from which the metal may be profitably extracted.

organic chemistry (Chem.): The study of the compounds of carbon.

organism (Biol.): A living animal or plant.

organ'osol (Chem.): A colloidal solution in an organic liquid.

orientation (Biol.): The position or change of position, of a part or organ with relation to the whole. (Chem.): The ordering of molecule particles or crystals so that they point in a definite direction. (Met.): The position of important sets of planes in a crystal in relation to any fixed system of planes.

or'nithoph'ily (Bot.): Pollination by birds.

o'ro: Prefix meaning mouth.

ortho-: A prefix meaning straight.

orthodi'agraph (Med.): An X-ray apparatus for recording exactly the size and form of organs and structures inside the body.

orthograph: A view showing an elevation of a building or of part of a building.

orthokinet'ic (Chem.): Migrating in the same direction.

orthope'dics: That branch of surgery which deals with deformities arising from injury or disease of bones or of joints.

orthop'terous (Zool.): Having the posterior pair of wings straight folded.

or'thostyle (Arch.): A colonnade formed of columns arranged in a straight line.

os'cillograph (Elec. Eng.): An instrument for producing a curve representing the wave-form of an alternating quantity.

osmom'eter (Chem.): An apparatus for the measurement of osmotic pressures.

osmo'sis (Chem.): The diffusion of a solvent through a semi-permeable membrane into a more concentrated solution in order to equalize the concentrations on both sides of the membrane.

os'seous (Zool.): Bony.

ossifica'tion (Zool.): The formation of bone.

oste-, osteo-: Prefix meaning bone.

os'teoblast (Zool.): A bone-forming cell.

osteol'ogy (Zool.): The study of bones.

osteop'athy: A system of therapeutics based on the theory that diseases arise chiefly from displacement of bones, with resultant pressure on blood vessels and nerves, and can be remedied by manipulation of the parts.

osteot'omy (Surg.): The surgical cutting of a bone.

os'tiolate (Bot.): Having an opening.

ot-, oto-: A prefix meaning ear.

otal'gia (Med.): Earache.

o'tic (Zool.): Pertaining to the ear.

otol'ogy (Med.): That part of surgical science dealing with the organ of hearing and its diseases.

o'toscope (Med.): An instrument for inspecting the ear drum and the external canal of the ear.

outlet (Build.): An opening serving to direct the discharge of a liquid.

outrigger (Build.): A projecting beam carrying a suspended scaffold.

o'vary (Anat., Zool.): A reproductive gland producing ova.

ovate (Bot.): Flat and thin, shaped like the longitudinal section of an egg, widest below the middle.

overall efficiency (Elec. Eng.): When power is passed through a number of times of plant in succession.

overcast (Meteor.): Said of sky when more than eight-tenths of it is covered by cloud.

overfold (Geol.): A fold with both limbs dipping in the same direction, but one more steeply inclined than the other.

overhang (Aero.): In a wing structure, the distance from the outermost supporting point to the extremity of the wing tip.

overhead railway (Civ. Eng.): An elevated railway carried above ground-level on arches or viaducts.

overhead transmission line (Elec. Eng.): A transmission line in which the conductors are supported on towels or poles at a considerable height above the ground.

overlap test (Elec. Eng.): A test used for locating a fault in a cable.

overload: A load on a machine, etc., greater than that which it is designed to withstand continuously.

overshoot (Aero.): Failure to land within the intended area due to excessive speed or height.

overstrain (Eng.): The result of stressing an elastic material beyond its yield point.

ovi-: A prefix meaning egg.

o'viduct (Zool.): The tube which leads from the ovary to the exterior and by which the ova are discharged.

ovip'arous (Zool.): Egg-laying.

oviposition (Zool.): The act of depositing eggs.

ovipos'itor (Zool.): In female insects, the egg laying organ.

o'visac (Zool.): An egg receptacle.

o'void (Bot.): Solid, like an egg in form, and attached by the broader end.

o'volo (Arch.): A quarter-round convex molding.

o'vovivip'arous (Zool.): Producing eggs which hatch out within the uterus of the mother.

ovula'tion (Zool.): The formation of ova.

ov'ule (Bot.): A young seed in course of development.

o'vum (Bot., Zool.): A non-motile, female gamete.

Science Terms

oxalates (Chem.): The salts and esters of oxalic acid.

oxidase (Bot., Zool.): One of a group of enzymes occurring in plant and animal cells and promoting oxidation.

oxidation (Chem.): The addition of oxygen to a compound.

oxides (Chem.): Compounds of oxygen with another element.

oxidizing agent (Chem.): A substance which is capable of bringing about the chemical change known as oxidation.

oxy-: A prefix meaning sharp.

oxy-acetylene welding (Eng.): Welding with a flame resulting from the combustion of oxygen to acetylene.

oxycelluloses (Chem.): Products formed by the action of oxidizing agents on cellulose.

oxychro'matin (Cyt.): A form of chromatic which stains lightly and contains little nucleic acid.

oxydac'tylons (Zool.): Having narrow-pointed digits.

oxygen (Chem.): A non-metallic element.

oxy-hydrogen welding (Eng.): A method of welding in which the heat is produced by the combustion of a mixture of oxygen and hydrogen.

oxyn'tic (Zool.): Acid-secreting.

ozone (Chem.): Produced by the action of ultra-violet rays and radium emanation on oxygen; and when oxygen or air is exposed to a silent discharge of electricity.

P

pachy-: A prefix meaning thick.

pachyder'matous (Zool.): Thick-skinned.

pachyphyl'lous (Bot.): Having thick leaves.

padder (Elec. Comm.): A small adjustable condenser for fine adjustment of capacity.

pediat'ric (Med.): That branch of medical science that deals with the study of children's diseases.

pediatric'ian (Med.): A doctor who specializes in children's diseases.

palaeo-: A prefix meaning ancient.

palaeobot'any: The study of fossil plants.

Palaeolith'ic Period (Geol.): The older stone age.

palaeontol'ogy (Geol.): The study of animal life in past geological periods.

Palaeozo'ic (Geol.): A major division of geological time.

pal'ama (Zool.): The webbing of the feet in birds of aquatic habits.

palate (Zool.): The roof of the mouth in vertebrates.

paling (Build): One of the upright boards of a fence.

palisade (Build.): Fencing formed of pointed wooden poles or iron railings.

palla'dium (Met.): A metallic element.

palles'cent (Bot.): Becoming lighter in color with age.

pal'liative (Med.): A medicinal remedy affording temporary relief from pain or discomfort.

pal'mate (Bot.): Having several lobes or leaflets spreading from the same point, like the fingers from the palm.

palmat'isect (Bot.): Having the leaf blade cut nearly to the base.

palpe'bra (Anat.): An eyelid.

palpitation (Med.): Increased frequency of the heart beat.

paludic'olous (Ecol.): Living in marshes, ponds and streams.

pancaking (Aero.): The alighting of an aircraft at a steep angle with low forward speed.

pan'creas (Zool.): A large racemose gland discharging into the intestine, in vertebrates.

pandem'ic (Med.): An epidemic very widespread.

pane (Build.): (1) A panel; (2) A sheet of glass cut to fit as a window light.

panel (Elec. Eng.): A sheet of material upon which switches, instruments, etc., are mounted.

pangam'ic (Zool.): Of indiscriminate mating.

pannose (Bot.): Felted.

pantoph'agous (Zool.): Omnivorous.

pap (Build.): An outlet nozzle fitted to an eaves gutter.

papyra'ceous (Bot.): Papery in texture.

parabio'sis (Embryol.): The union of similar embryos between which a connection exists, as Siamese Twins.

parab'ola (Maths.): (1) The section of a right circular cone by a plane parallel to a generator of the cone. (2) The locus of a point equi-distant from a fixed point and a fixed line.

parabol'ic (Bot.): Having a broad base and gradually narrowing by curved sides to a blunt apex.

parachute (Aero.): An umbrella-shaped fabric device of high drag to retard the descent of a falling body.

parac'me (Zool.): The period in the history of a race or an individual when vigor is decreasing.

par'allax (Astron.): The apparent displacement of a heavenly body on the celestial sphere due to a change of position of the observer.

parallel (Elec. Eng.): When two circuits are connected so that any current flowing divides between the two.

parallel motion (Eng.): A system of links by which the reciprocating motion of one point is copied to an enlarged scale by another.

par'allelism (Bot.): Evolution along similar lines in unrelated groups of plants.

paral'ysis (Med.): The loss in any part of the body of the power of movement, or of the capacity to respond to sensory stimuli.

paraly'zer (Chem.): A catalytic poison.

param'eter (Maths.): A line or figure that serves to determine a point, figure, line or quantity in a class of such things.

parametric equations (Maths.): Equations in which coordinates of points on the surface or curve are given in terms of one or more variables of the surface or curve.

par'amorph (Min.): The name given to a mineral species which can change its molecular constitution without any change of chemical substance.

paramy'osin'ogen (Chem.): One of the chief proteins contained in living muscle.

paranoi'a (Psychiatry): A psychosis characterized by the development of a permanent delusional system and accompanied by the preservation of clear thought, action and will.

parapet (Build., Civ. Eng.): A low wall built along the edge of a quay, bridge or roof.

par'aplasm (Cyt.): The inactive vegetative portion of the cytoplasm.

paraple'gia (Med.): Paralysis of the lower part of the body and legs.

parasite (Bot., Zool.): An organism which lives in or on another organism and derives subsistence from it without rendering service in return.

parasymbio'sis (Biol.): The condition when two organisms grow together but neither assist nor harm each other.

parasynop'sis (Cyt.): Side-by-side union of the elements of a pair of chromosomes.

paraton'ic movements (Bot.): Plant movements in relation to an external stimulus.

par'esis (Med.): Incomplete paralysis.

pari'etes (Anat.): The walls of an organ or a cavity.

parity (Med.): The fact of having borne children.

parquet (Build.): A floor-covering of hardwood blocks glued to the ordinary floor boarding.

pars (Zool.): A part of an organ.

parsec (Astron.): The chief unit used in measuring stellar distances.

parted (Bot.): Cleft nearly to the base.

parthenogenet'ic (Bot., Zool.): Reproducing by the production of ova capable of development with male fertilization.

partial (Bot.): Secondary.

particulate inheritance (Gen.): Inheritance, in one individual, of distinctive characteristics of both parents.

parting (Met.): The process of removing silver from gold-silver bullion.

partition (Build.): A dividing wall between rooms.

parturition (Zool.): The act of bringing forth young.

pas'cual (Bot.): Inhabiting pastures.

passage beds (Geol.): The general name given to

strata laid down during a period of transition from one set of geographical conditions to another.

passive electrode (Elec. Eng.): The earthed electrode of an electrical precipitation apparatus.

pasteurization (Med.): Reduction of the number of micro-organisms in milk by maintaining it at a temperature of 131°-158° F. for thirty minutes.

patel'late (Bot.): Shaped like a saucer.

path'ogen (Med.): Any disease-producing micro-organism or substance.

parthogen'esis (Med.): The development or production of a disease-process.

pathological: Diseased, morbid.

pathol'ogy: Medical science that deals with the causes and nature of disease, and with the bodily changes caused by disease.

pat'ina (Chem.): The thin film of oxide formed on the surface of a metal.

patroclin'ic (Bot., Zool.): Exhibiting the characteristics of the male parent more than those of the female parent.

pat'ulous (Bot.): Spreading widely.

pavement (Civ. Eng.): The hard surfacing of a road or side-walk.

paving flags (Civ. Eng.): Thin flat stones used for surfacing pavements.

peacock ore (Min.): Bornite.

peak arch (Arch.): A pointed arch.

peak load (Elec. Eng.): The maximum load of a generating station or power distribution system.

peak value (Elec. Eng.): The maximum positive or negative value of an alternating quality.

pearl: An abnormal concretion of nacre formed inside a mollusc shell around a foreign body, as a sand particle.

pearlite (Met.): A microconstituent of steel and cast-iron.

peat (Geol.): Name given to layers of dead vegetation.

pecten (Zool.): Any comb-like structure.

pectization (Chem.): The formation of a jelly.

pec'toral fins (Zool.): The anterior pair of fins, in fish.

pedal: Pertaining to the feet.

pedestal (Build.): A base for the support of a column, a statue, etc.

ped'icel (Bot.): The stalk which bears a single flower or a single fruit.

pediculo'sis (Med.): Infestation of the body with lice.

pe'dion (Crystal.): A crystal form consisting of a single plane.

pedology: The study of soil.

pedom'eter (Surv.): An instrument recording distances travelled by foot.

ped'uncle (Bot.): The main stalk or stalks of an inflorescence.

peg'matite (Geol.): Applied to igneous rocks of coarse grain occurring in veins of larger intrusive rock bodies.

pela'gic (Geol.): A term applied to any accumulation of sediments under deep water.

pellu'cid (Bot., Zool.): Transparent.

pelvic fins (Zool.): The posterior pair of fins, in fish.

pelvis (Zool.): The pelvic girdle or posterior limb girdle of vertebrates; in mammals the funnel-shaped expansion of the upper end of the ureter.

pen'icillate (Bot.): Tufted.

penicillin (Med.): A filtrate of a broth culture of Penicillium notatum, which tends to inhibit the growth of gram-positive bacteria.

penis (Zool.): The male copulatory organ in mammals.

pennate: Winged.

pent-, penta-: A prefix meaning five.

pentad: The period of five days; used for meteorological records.

pentadac'tyl (Zool.): Having five digits.

pen'tastyle (Arch.): A row of five columns.

pentava'lent (Chem.): Capable of combining with five atoms of hydrogen or their equivalent.

pep'sin (Zool.): A protein-digesting ferment of the alimentary canal of vertebrates.

peptization (Chem.): The production of a colloidal solution of a substance; especially the formation of a sol from a gel.

peptones (Chem.): Products obtained by the action of enzymes on albuminous matter.

perambulator (Surv.): An instrument for distance measurement.

peren'nial (Bot.): A plant which lives for three or more years.

perfect (Bot., Zool.): Having all organs in a functional condition.

per'forate (Bot.): Pierced by holes. (Zool.): Having apertures.

peri-: A prefix meaning round.

per'ianth (Bot.): A general term for calyx and corolla together.

periartic'ular (Anat.): Said of the tissues around a joint.

perias'tron (Astron.): That point in an orbit about a star in which the body describing the orbit is nearest to the star.

pericar'dium (Zool.): The space surrounding the heart.

peri'carp (Bot.): The wall of a fruit, if derived from the wall of the ovary.

per'iclase (Min.): Native magnesia.

periodo'tite (Geol.): A coarse-grained igneous rock consisting primarily of olivine.

per'igee (Astron.): The point nearest to the earth on the apse line of a central orbit having the earth as a focus.

perihe'lion (Astron.): That point in the orbit of any heavenly body moving about the sun at which it is nearest to the sun.

period (Phys.): The time for one complete cycle of any periodic phenomenon.

periodic system (Chem.): A classification of the chemical elements.

periodicity (Biol.): Rhythmic activity.

per'istyle (Arch.): A colonnade encircling a building.

perlite (Geol.): An acid and glassy igneous rock which exhibits perlitic structure.

permeability (Phys.): The rate of diffusion of gas or liquid under a pressure gradient through a porous material.

person (Zool.): An individual organism.

personality (Psychol.): The integrated organization of all the psychological, emotional, physical and intellectual characteristics of an individual.

persorption (Chem.): The effective absorption of a gas by a solid.

pertus'sis (Med.): Whooping cough.

perversion (Psycho-path.): Any pathological state in which there is a deviation from the normal method of sexual gratification.

pestle (Chem.): An instrument for grinding and pounding solids in a mortar.

petal (Bot.): One of the leaves composing the corolla.

pe'tiole (Bot.): The stalk of a leaf.

petri-, petro-: A prefix meaning stone.

petrifaction (Geol.): The term applied to any organic remains which have been changed in composition by molecular replacement but whose original structure is nearly retained.

petrog'raphy (Geol.): Systematic description of rocks.

petroleum (Chem.): Crude mineral hydrocarbon oils obtained from natural oil wells.

petrology: The study of rocks.

pewter (Met.): An alloy of tin and lead.

phantasy (Psychol.): A mental state of preoccupation with thought which are associated with certain desires unobtainable in reality.

pharmacology (Med.): The scientific study of drugs.

pharynx (Zool.): In vertebrates, that portion of the alimentary canal which intervenes between the mouth cavity and the oesophagus and serves for the passage of food and also respiratory functions.

phase (Astron.): The name given to the changing shape of the visible illuminated surface of the moon. (Chem.): The sum of all those portions of a material system which are identical in chemical composition and physical state.

phenology (Biol.) : The study of organisms in relation to climate.

phe'notype (Gen.) : One of a group of individuals all of which have a similar appearance regardless of their factorial constitution.

phenotyp'ic (Biol.) : Caused or produced by environmental factors.

-philous (Bot., Zool.) : Suffix meaning preferring, inhabiting.

phleb-, phlebo- : A prefix meaning vein.

phlo'em (Bot.) : The conducting tissue present in vascular plants, concerned with the transport of food materials.

phobia (Psycho-path.) : Fear of an internal danger which has been projected on to an external object.

phon-, phono- : A prefix meaning voice.

phon (Acous.) : The unit of the objective loudness.

phonation (Zool.) : Sound production.

phonochemistry (Chem.) : The study of the effect of sound and ultrasonic waves on chemical reactions.

phoresis (Med.) : Electrical passage of ions through a membrane.

phosphates (Chem.) : Salts of phosphoric acid.

phosphores'cence (Chem.) : The greenish glow observed during the oxidation of white phosphorous in the air. (Phys.) : A glow emitted by certain substances after having been illuminated by visible or ultra-violet rays.

phos'phorous (Chem.) : A non-metallic element.

photo- : A prefix meaning light.

photo-catalysis (Chem.) : The acceleration or retardation of the rate of a chemical reaction by light.

photochemistry (Chem.) : The study of the chemical effects of radiation.

photochron'ograph (Astron.) : An instrument for recording time photographically.

photo-dissociation (Chem.) : Dissociation produced by the absorption of radiant energy.

photo-electric cell : Generally, any device in which the incidence of light causes an alteration in the electrical state.

photo-electricity : Electricity produced by the action of light.

photo-electronic : The science dealing with the interactions of electricity and light.

photo-electrons : Electrons ejected from the surface of a body by the action of incident light.

pho'togene (Zool.) : A light-producing organ.

photographic telescope (Astron.) : An astronomical telescope in which a camera replaces the eye-piece.

photol'ysis (Bot.) : The grouping of the chloroplasts in relation to the amount of light falling on the plant. (Chem.) : The decomposition of a molecule as the result of the absorption of light.

pho'ton (Phys.) : A light quantum.

photoph'ilous (Biol.) : Light-seeking.

pho'tophore (Zool.) : A luminous organ of fish.

photophy'gous (Zool.) : Shunning strong light.

photorecep'tor (Zool.) : A sensory nerve-ending receiving light stimuli.

photo-sensitive (Phys.) : The property of being sensitive to the action of visible or invisible light.

pho'tosphere (Astron.) : The name given to the visible surface of the sun on which sun-spots and other markings appear.

photosyn'thesis (Bot.) : The building up, in the green cell of a plant, of simple carbohydrates from carbon dioxide and water, with the liberation of oxygen.

phototax'is (Biol.) : Response of an organism to the stimulus of light.

photo-therapy (Med.) : Light treatment for therapeutic reasons.

phreni : A prefix meaning diaphragm.

phycol'ogy (Bot.) : The study of algae.

phylet'ic classification (Biol.) : A scheme of plant classification based on the presumed evolutionary descent of organisms.

phyllome (Bot.) : A general term for all leaves and leaf-like organs.

phy'logeny (Bot., Zool.) : The history of the development of a race.

phy'lon (Biol.) : A line of descent.

phy'lum (Zool.) : One of the major subdivisions of the animal kingdom.

physical chemistry (Chem.) : The study of the dependence of physical properties on chemical composition, and of the physical changes accompanying chemical reactions.

physiological (Bot., Zool.) : Relating to the functions of plant or animal as a living organism.

physiological anatomy (Biol.) : The study of the relation between structure and function.

physiological zero (Biol.) : The threshold temperature below which the metabolism of a cell, organ or organism ceases.

physiology (Bot., Zool.) : The study of the manner in which organisms carry on their life processes.

phy'topathology (Bot.) : The study of plant diseases.

phytoph'agous (Zool.) : Plant-feeding.

piazza (Arch.) : (1) An enclosed court in a building. (2) An arcade.

picket (Build.) : A narrow upright board in a fence. (Surv.) : A short ranging rod about 6 ft. long.

pickling (Eng.) : The process of removing a coating of scale, tarnish, oxide, etc., from metal objects by immersing in an acid bath.

pier (Civ. Eng.) : (1) A breakwater adapted for service as a landing. (2) A support for a bridge, an arch, etc.

pig (Met.) : A mass of metal cast in a simple shape for storage or transportation and subsequently remelted for casting into final shapes.

pig iron (Met.) : The crude iron produced in the blast furnace and cast into pigs.

pilas'ter (Build.) : A square tier projecting from a wall, having both a cap and a base.

pile (Civ. Eng.) : A column sunk into the ground to support vertical loading or to resist lateral pressures.

pile bridge (Civ. Eng.) : A bridge whose superstructure is carried on piles.

pile'um (Zool.) : The top of the head, in birds.

pillar (Build.) : A detached column for the support of a superstructure.

pillow structure (Geol.) : A term applied to lavas consisting of ellipsoidal and pillow-like masses which have cooled under submarine conditions.

pi'lomo'tor (Anat.) : Causing movements of hair.

pi'lose (Bot.) : Bearing a scattering of simple, fairly stiff hairs.

pilot (Aero.) : The person who operates the flying controls of an aircraft. (Elec. Eng.) : In power systems, a conductor used for auxiliary purposes, not for the transmission of energy.

pin (Carp.) : A small wooden peg.

pin'acoid (Crystal.) : An open crystal form which consists of two parallel faces.

pincers (Zool.) : Claws adapted for grasping.

pinna (Bot.) : A leaflet, when part of a pinnate compound leaf. (Zool.) : In fish, a fin; in mammals, the outer ear; in birds, a wing or feather.

pinn'iped (Zool.) : Having the digits of the feet united by a membrane or flesh.

pintle (Eng.) : (1) The pin of a hinge. (2) An iron bolt on which a chassis turns.

pi'oscope (Chem.) : An instrument in which the fat content of milk is estimated colorimetrically.

pipe : A tube for the conveyance of fluids.

pipette' (Chem.) : Laboratory apparatus consisting of a glass tube which is calibrated to deliver a measured amount of a liquid.

Pisces (Astron.) : Fishes. Twelfth sign of the Zodiac.

pisciv'orous (Zool.) : Fish-eating.

pis'tillate (Bot.) : Said of a flower which has a carpel, but the stamens are lacking or non-functional.

piston : A cylindrical metal piece which moves in a cylinder, either under fluid pressure, as in engines, or to displace or compress a fluid, as in pumps.

pit (Eng.): A small opening formed in a floor, either to accommodate the moving parts of a large engine or to facilitate inspection of the underside of a machine.

pitch: A dark-colored, fusible, more or less solid material, containing bituminous or resinous substances. (Build.): The ratio between the rise and span of a roof.

pitchblende (Min.): Uraninite.

pitching: The angular motion of a ship or aircraft in a vertical plane about a lateral axis.

pithed (Zool.): Having the central nervous system destroyed.

pitted: Having the surface marked by small excavations.

pitting (Eng.): (1) Corrosion of metal surfaces due to chemical action. (2) A form of failure of gear teeth.

placen'ta (Bot.): The portion of the carpel wall to which the ovules are attached. (Zool.): A flattened cake-like structure within the uterine wall of the mother: it serves for the respiration and nutrition of the growing young.

placers (Geol.): Superficial deposits, rich in heavy ore minerals, which have become concentrated in the course of time by long-continued disintegration and removed from the lighter associated minerals.

plane (Carp.): A wood-working tool used for smoothing surfaces.

plane of symmetry (Crystal.): When one half of a crystal is a mirror image of the other.

plane surveying (Surv.): Surveying applied to areas of small extent and the curvature of the earth's surface is negligible.

plane table (Surv.): A drawing board mounted on a tripod so that the board can be levelled and also rotated about a vertical axis and clamped in position.

plane tabling (Surv.): A method of surveying in which the fieldwork and platting are executed simultaneously.

planet (Astron.): The name given in antiquity to the seven heavenly bodies, including the sun and moon, which were thought to travel among the fixed stars.

planetarium (Astron.): A building in which an optical device displays the apparent motions of the heavenly bodies on the interior of a dome which forms the ceiling of the auditorium.

planing machine (Eng.): A machine for producing large flat surfaces.

plankton (Ecol.): Plants and animals floating in waters as distinct from those which are attached to or crawl upon, the bottom.

plan'osome (Cyt.): An odd chromosome resulting from non-disjunction of a pair during meiosis.

plant (Bot.): **An organism which has little or no power of dealing with solid food, and which takes in most or all of the material used in nutrition in solution in water.**

plan'tigrade (Zool.): Walking on the soles of the feet.

plasma-, plasmo-: A prefix meaning anything molded.

plasma (Physiol.): The watery fluid containing protein, salts and other organic compounds, in which the cells of the blood are suspended.

plasmol'ysis (Biol.): Removal of water from a cell by osmotic methods, with resultant shrinking.

plaster: A general name for plastic substances which are used for coating wall surfaces and which set hard after application.

plaster board (Build.): A building-board made of plaster with paper facings.

plaster of Paris (Chem.): Dehydrated gypsum; used for making casts.

plastics: A generic name for certain organic substances, mainly synthetic condensation products, capable of being molded.

plastic surgery (Surg.): That branch of surgery which deals with the repair and restoration of damaged or lost parts of the body.

plastid (Cyt.): Any small dense photoplasmic inclu-

sion in a cell.

plastin (Cyt.): An acidophil substance occurring in masses in the nuclei of cells.

plate (Elec. Eng.): (1) The electrode of an accumulator cell. (2) One of the conducting surfaces of a condenser.

plat'en (Eng.): The work table of a machine tool.

platform (Carp.): An area of floor raised above the general floor-level.

plat'inum (Met.): A metallic element.

platinum thermometer (Phys.): A means of measuring temperature up to 1200° C.

plat'y-: A prefix meaning broad, flat.

plat'yphyl'lons (Bot.): Having wide leaves.

plax (Zool.): A flat plate-like structure, as a scale.

pleasure (Psychol.): The feeling-tone which accompanies the emotional satisfaction of any one instinct.

plei-, pleo-, plio-: A prefix meaning more.

Pleiades (Astron.): The name given to the open cluster of 7 principal stars in the constellation Taurus.

plei'omer'ous (Bot.): Having a large number of organs or parts.

pleion (Meteor.): An area over which some weather element is above the normal average.

Pleis'tocene Period (Geol.): The Great Ice Age.

pleur-, pleuro-: A prefix meaning side.

plexus (Zool.): A mass of interwoven fibers.

pli'cate (Bot.): Folded in longitudinal plaits.

plinth (Build.): The projecting course at the base of a building.

Pli'ocene Period (Geol.): The period of geological time which followed the Miocene and preceded the Pleistocene.

plot (Build.): A ground plan.

plotting (Surv.): The operation of drawing on paper from the field notes of a surveyor.

plough (Carp.): To cut a groove.

plug (Build.): A wooden piece driven into a hole cut in surface brickwork and finished off flush, so as to provide a material to which fittings may be nailed. (Elec. Eng.): A device containing two metal contacts arranged for inserting into a socket-outlet in order

to provide a connection to portable electrical apparatus. (Geol.): A roughly cylindrical orifice through which igneous rock is injected.

plumb: (Build., Civ. Eng.): Vertical.

plumb-bob (Surv.): A small weight hanging at the end of a cord, which under the action of the weight takes up a vertical direction.

plumba'go (Chem.): Graphite.

plume (Bot.): A light feathery or hairy appendage on a fruit or seed, serving in wind dispersal. (Meteor.): Snow blown over the ridge of a mountain. (Zool.): A feather.

plu'miped (Zool.): A bird having feathered feet.

plummet (Surv.): A plumb-bob.

plu'mose (Bot., Zool.): Hairy, feathered.

plunger (Eng.): The ram or solid piston of a force pump.

plur-, pluri-: A prefix meaning several, more.

plural gel (Chem.): A gel formed from two or more sols.

pluricel'lular (Biol.): Composed of two or more cells.

Pluto (Astron.): The ninth major planet in the solar system in order of distance from the sun.

pluton'ic intrusions (Geol.): A term applied to large intrusions which have cooled at great depth beneath the surface of the earth.

pluto'nium: An element.

pneumo-, pneumat-, pneumato-: A prefix meaning breath.

pneumatic (Eng., etc.): Operated by, or relying on, air pressure.

pneumatic (Zool.): Containing air.

pneumatic brake (Eng.): A continuous braking system in which air pressure is applied simultaneously to brake cylinders throughout the train.

pneumatic drill (Eng.): A hard rock drill operated by the use of compressed air.

Science Terms

pneumatic trough (Chem.) : A vessel used for the collection of gases.

pneumaticity (Zool.) : The condition of containing air spaces, as the bones of birds.

pneumatocyst (Zool.) : Any air cavity used as a float, as the air bladder in fish.

pneumon-, pneu'mono- : A prefix meaning lung.

pneumonia (Med.) : A term generally applied to any inflammatory condition of the lung accompanied by consolidation of the lung tissue.

pocu'liform (Bot.) : Cup-shaped.

pod (Bot.) : A dry fruit formed from a single carpel, usually splitting open when mature and containing several seeds.

pod-, podo- : A prefix meaning foot.

po'dal (Zool.) : Pedal.

po'dium (Arch.) : A continuous low wall under a row of columns.

poikilother'mal (Zool.) : Cold-blooded.

point (Elec. Eng.) : In electric wiring installations a termination of the wiring for attachment to a lighting fitting socket-outlet.

Pointers (Astron.) : The name used for the two stars of the Great Bear.

pointing (Build., Civ. Eng.) : The process of raking out the exposed jointing of brickwork and refilling with cement mortar.

point of no return (Aero.) : The point in a flight which it is impossible to return to the departure base with a practical margin of fuel.

poise (Chem.) : To maintain the oxidation-reduction potential of a solution constant by the addition of a suitable compound.

poison : Any substance which, introduced into the body, is capable of destroying life.

pol (Cyt.) : The pole of a resting nucleus which lies nearest to the centrosome.

polar (Maths.) : Of a point with respect to a curve or surface.

Polaroid : Transparent plastic sheet containing oriented doubly-refracting crystals of an organic iodine compound ; transmits plane-polarized light.

polar axis (Astron.) : That diameter of a sphere which passes through the poles. (Crystal.) : A crystal to which no two- or four-fold axes are normal.

polar body (Biol.) : One of two small cells detached from the ovum during the maturation divisions.

polar caps (Astron.) : The two white regions around the poles of the planet Mars.

polar fusion nucleus (Bot.) : The nucleus formed in the embryo sac by the union of the two polar nuclei ; later it unites with a male nucleus and gives the first endosperm nucleus.

polar sequence (Astron.) : The name given to the adopted scale for determining photographic stellar magnitudes.

polarim'etry (Chem.) : The measurement of optical activity.

Polar'is (Astron.) : The name given to the star a Ursae Minoris.

polarization (Chem.) : The separation of the positive and negative charges of a molecule.

polar'ity (Elec.) : The distinction between the north and south poles of a magnet, or between the north and south poles of a circuit. (Zool.) : Existence of a definite axis.

polder (Civ. Eng.) : A piece of low-lying land reclaimed from the water.

pole : Generally, the pivot or axis on which anything turns. (Zool.) : Point, apex. (Bot.) : One end of an elongated spore. (Carp.) : A long piece of timber of circular section and small in diameter. (Elec. Eng.) : A wooden, concrete or steel column for supporting the conductors of an overhead transmission or telephone lines.

pole (Elec.) : The part of a magnet towards which the lines of magnetic flux converge or from which they diverge.

po'lioplasm (Biol.) : Granular protoplasm.

poll (Carp.) : The blunt end of an axe or hammer.

pollen (Bot.) : The sticky or dusty material produced in anthers, each grain ultimately contains two male nuclei equivalent to male gametes.

pollen sac (Bot.) : A cavity in an anther in which pollen is formed.

pollination (Bot.) : The transfer of pollen from an anther to a stigma.

polo'nium (Chem.) : A radioactive element.

poly- : A prefix meaning many.

polybasic acids (Chem.) : Acids with two or more replaceable hydrogen atoms in the molecule.

polycyclic (Chem.) : Containing more than one ring of atoms in the molecule. (Zool.) : Said of shells having numerous whorls.

polyg'amous (Bot.) : Having staminate, pistillate and hermaphrodite flowers on the same and on distinct individual plants. (Zool.) : Mating with more than one of the opposite sex during the same breeding season.

polymor'phic (Zool.) : Showing a tendency to division of labor among the members of a colony.

polyp (Zool.) : An individual of a colonial animal.

polyphylet'ic (Gen.) : Descended from diverse ancestors.

pome (Bot.) : A term for a fleshy fruit containing seeds inside a papery core formed from the inner walls of the united carpels.

pom'iform (Bot.) : Apple-shaped.

pomol'ogy (Bot.) : The study of cultivated fruits and fruit trees.

pons (Zool.) : A bridge-like or connecting structure.

pontoon (Civ. Eng.) : A floating vessel for the support of materials and men.

pore (Bot.) : The aperture of a stoma. (Zool.) : A small aperture.

porom'eter (Bot.) : An instrument for measuring the rate at which air can be drawn through a portion of a leaf.

porosity (Build.) : The percentage of pore space in a material.

por'phyry (Geol.) : A general term used for igneous rocks which contain large isolated crystals set in a fine-grained ground mass.

portico (Build.) : A colonnade at one side of a building.

positional astronomy (Astron.) : The branch that is concerned with the position of the heavenly bodies regarded as points on the observer's celestial sphere.

positive (Elec.) : A particular point or electrode is positive with respect to another point when it is at a higher electric potential than the other point.

positive rays (Phys.) : Streams of positively charged atoms or molecules which take part in the electrical discharge in a rarefied gas.

positivism : The conception which regards natural phenomena as being the only reality demonstrable by experiment, without reference to the human mind.

positron (Phys.) : A sub-atomic particle of mass and charge equal to those of the electron, but having its charge positive.

post (Build.) : (1) An upright member in a frame. (2) A column or pillar.

post- : A prefix meaning after.

posterior (Bot.) : The rear. (Zool.) : Further away from the head region.

postern (Build.) : A private door or gate.

po'table : Suitable for drinking purposes.

pot'amous (Ecol.) : Living in rivers and streams.

potas'sium (Chem.) : A very reactive alkali metal.

potential (Zool.) : Latent. (Elec.) : When a point is said to be "at a certain potential" it means there is a potential difference of that amount between the point and earth.

potential energy (Phys.) : Energy possessed by a body in virtue of its position.

potom'eter (Bot.) : An instrument for measuring the rate a plant takes in water.

pouch (Zool.) : Any sac-like structure.

pound : A unit of mass.

power (Mech.) : Rate of doing work.

pre- : A prefix meaning before.

Pre-Cambrian (Geol.) : The oldest era of geological time.

precipitation (Chem.) : The formation of an insoluble solid by a reaction which takes place in solution. (Meteor.) : Moisture falling on the earth's surface from clouds ; rain, snow or hail.

precision instrument (Elec. Eng.) : An instrument having a high degree of accuracy.

pregnancy (Med.) : Gestation.

prehensile (Zool.) : Adapted for grasping.

pressure, barometric (Meteor.) : The pressure of the atmosphere as read by a barometer.

pressure cabin (Aero.) : An airtight cabin which is maintained at greater than atmospheric pressure for the comfort and safety of the occupants.

pressure suit (Aero.) : An airtight fabric suit for very high altitude flying.

prickle (Bot.) : A hard epidermal appendage resembling a thorn but not containing woody tissue.

primary (Bot., Zool.) : Original, first-formed. (Chem.) : A substance which is obtained directly from natural raw material.

primary cell (Elec.) : A voltaic cell in which the chemical energy of the constituents is changed to electrical energy, when current flows.

Primates (Zool.) : The highest order of mammals.

primitive (Bot., Zool.) : Of early origin.

primor'dial (Bot., Zool.) : Primitive.

prism (Crystal.) : A hollow (open) crystal form consisting of three or more faces parallel to a crystal axis.

pro- : A prefix meaning before in time or place.

profile (Surv.) : A longitudinal section.

progno'sis (Med.) : The forecast of the probable course of an illness.

projection (Psycho-an.) : The process whereby we ascribe to other people and to the outside world mental factors and attributes really in ourselves.

prolapse (Med.) : The sinking of an organ or part of of the body.

proliferation (Bot.) : A renewal of growth in a mature organ after a period of inactivity. (Med.) : Growth by the multiplication of cells.

promontory (Zool.) : A projecting structure.

promotor (Chem.) : A substance which increases the activity of catalyst.

pronu'cleus (Zool.) : The nucleus of a germ cell after the maturation divisions.

propagation (Bot.) : Increase in the number of plants by vegetative means.

pro'pane (Chem.) : A colorless gas found in crude petroleum.

pro'phase (Cyt.) : The preliminary stages of mitosic or meiosis leading up to the formation of the astroid.

prophylac'tic (Med.) : Tending to prevent or protect against disease.

prophylax'is (Med.) : The preventive treatment of disease.

prosce'nium (Build.) : The stage frame in a theatre.

pros'thesis (Surg.) : The supplying of an artificial bodily part in place of one which is deficient or absent.

pro'tamines (Chem.) : The simplest proteins.

protease (Chem.) : A term for any protein-spliting enzyme.

pro'teins (Chem.) : Any of a class of naturally occurring complex combinations of amino acids which are essential constituents of all living cells and also of the diet of the animal organism.

proter-, protero- : A prefix meaning former, before.

proto- : A prefix meaning first.

protoactinium (Chem.) : A radio-active element.

pro'togam'y (Biol.) : Union of gametes without fusion of their nuclei.

protogen'ic (Chem.) : Capable of supplying a hydrogen ion.

pro'toly'sis (Bot.) : The decomposition of chlorophyll by light.

pro'ton (Phys.) : A positively charged particle of mass.

pro'tophyte (Bot.) : A simple unicellular plant.

pro'toplasm (Biol.) : The material basis of all living matter, a grayish semitransparent semi-fluid substance, of complex chemical composition.

pro'tosome (Gen.) : A hypothetical central body in a gene.

pro'totype (Zool.) : An ancestral form.

Protozo'a (Zool.) : A subkingdom of the animal kingdom.

pseud-, pseudo- : A prefix meaning false.

psych-, psycho- : A prefix meaning mind.

psyche (Psychol.) : The principle of mental and emotional life, consisting of conscious and unconscious processes.

psychiatry : That branch of medical science that deals with disorders and diseases of the mind.

psycho-analysis : The method of treatment of functional nervous disorder by bringing unconscious conflicts into consciousness, by the methods of free association, dream analysis and the use of the transference situation.

psychogen'ic (Med.) : Having a mental orgin.

psychology : The science of the mind.

psy'chopath (Psychol.) : An individual who shows a pathological degree of congenital emotional instability, but not suffering from a true organic mental disorder.

psychopathology : That brand of psychology which deals with the abnormal working of the mind.

psycho'sis (Med.) : A disorder of the mind, characterized by illusions, delusions, hallucinations, etc.

psychother'apist : An individual who practices psychotherapy.

psychother'apy : The treatment of functional psychic disorder.

psychophi'lic (Bot.) : Growing best at a low temperature.

pteropae'des (Zool.) : Young birds which are able to fly as soon as they are hatched.

pu'berty : Sexual maturity.

pubes'cense (Zool.) : A covering of fine hairs or down.

pull-out (Aero.) : The transition from a dive or spin to normal flight.

pulley (Eng.) : A wheel on a shaft having a crowned rim for carrying an endless belt, or grooved for carrying a rope or chain.

pulmo- : A prefix meaning lung.

pul'monate (Zool.) : Air-breathing.

pulp (Zool.) : A mass of soft spongy tissue situated in the interior of an organ.

pulsating current (Elec. Eng.) : An electric current which periodically changes in magnitude but not in direction.

pulse (Med.) : The periodic expansion and elongation of the arterial walls which follows each contraction of the heart.

pump : A machine driven by some prime mover, and used for raising fluids from a lower to a higher level, or for imparting energy to fluids.

pu'pa (Zool.) : An inactive stage in the life-history of an insect during which it does not feed and reorganization is taking place to transform the larval body into that of the imago.

pupil (Zool.) : The central opening of the iris of the eye.

pure culture (Bot.) : A culture containing a pure stock of one species of plant.

pure line (Zool.) : A population consisting of individuals whose descent can be traced to a single ancestor.

pure tone (Acous.) : A sound-wave of a single frequency.

purposiveness (Zool.) : Correlation of individual reactions to a definite end.

pus (Med.) : The yellowish fluid consisting of serum, pus cells bacteria, and the debris of tissue destruction.

Science Terms

pyk′nic type (Psychol.): One of Kretschmer's three types of individual, characterized by short squat stature, small feet and feet, domed abdomen, round face, the limbs being short in relation to the trunk.

pyknom′eter (Chem.): A small graduated glass vessel, of defined volume, used for determining the specific gravity of liquids.

pyramid (Crystal.): A crystal form with three or more inclined faces which cut all three axes of a crystal. (Zool.): A conical structure.

py′retother′apy (Med.): The treatment of disease by artificially increasing body temperature.

pyrhe′liom′eter (Meteor.): An instrument for measuring the rate at which heat energy is received from the sun.

pyro-, pr-: A prefix meaning fire.

pyroclas′tic rocks (Geol.): A name given to fragmental deposits of volcanic origin.

pyrocondensation (Chem.): A molecular condensation caused by heating to a high temperature.

pyrogen′ic (Chem.): Resulting from the application of a high temperature.

pyrol′ysis (Chem.): The decomposition of a substance by heat.

pyroxene group (Min.): A number of mineral species which, although falling into different systems are closely related in form, composition and structure.

Q

quadra (Arch.): A plinth at the base of a podium.

quadrant (Surv.): An angle-measuring instrument.

quadrat (Bot.): A square area of vegetation marked off for study.

quadratic system (Crystal.): The tetragonal system.

quadra′tus (Zool.): A muscle of rectangular appearance.

quad′rimolec′ular (Chem): Associated with four molecules.

quadripartition (Bot.): The division of a spore mother cell to yield four spores.

quadriplex (Gen.): Containing four dominant genes.

quadripole (Elec. Comm.): A network with two input and two output terminals.

quadrivalent (Cyt.): A nucleus having two pairs of homologous chromosomes.

quadru′manous (Zool.): Having all four podia constructed like hands, as apes.

quadruped (Zool.): Having all four podia constructed like feet, as cattle.

qualitative analysis (Chem.): The identification of the constituents of a material irrespective of their amount.

quality (Acous.): The sound reproduction, the degree to which a sample of reproduced sound resembles a sample of the original sound.

quantitative analysis (Chem.): The determination of the amounts in which the various constituents of a material are present.

quantum theory (Phys.): The conception of energy as being atomic in nature, meaning not variable continuously, but only in multiples of a minimum indivisible quantity called a quantum; a basic unit of discrete values of certain quantities.

quantum statistics (Phys.): Statistics of the distribution of particles of a specified type in relation to their energies.

quarry: An open pit for granite, slate or other rock.

quarry sap (Civ. Eng.): The moisture naturally contained in building-stone freshly cut from the quarry.

quarter (Astron.): The term applied to the phase of the moon at quadrature.

quarter (Bot.): The group of four related cells or nuclei formed as a result of meiosis. (Zool.): A set of four related cells in a segmented ovum.

quartz (Min.): Crystalline silica distributed in igneous, metamorphic and sedimentary rocks.

quartzite (Geol.): The characteristic product of the metamorphism of a siliceous sandstone.

quater′nate (Bot.): In groups of four.

quay (Civ. Eng.): A place on the seacoast for the loading and unloading of vessels.

queen (Zool.): In social insects, a sexually perfect female.

quencher (Phys.): That which is introduced into a luminescent material to reduce the duration of phosphorescence.

quenching (Met.): Generally means cooling steel or the rapid cooling of other alloys.

quicksand: Loose sand mixed with such a high proportion of water that its bearing-pressure is very low.

quicking (Elec. Eng.): Electro-deposition of mercury on a surface before regular plating.

quill (Eng.): A hollow shaft revolving on a solid spindle.

quinine (Chem.): An alkaloid of the quinoline group, present in Cinchona bark.

quinquefo′liate (Bot.): Having five leaflets.

quinquemolec′ular (Chem.): Associated with five molecules.

R

rabies (Med.): Hydrophobia.

race (Zool.): A category of variant individuals occurring within a species and differing slightly in characteristics from the typical members of the species.

raceme (Bot.): A type of simple indeterminate or centripetal inflorescence in which the elongated axis bears flowers on short pedicils in succession toward the apex.

ra′chis (Bot.): The main axis of an inflorescence. (Zool.): The shaft of a feather.

radial: Radiating out from a common center.

radian (Maths.): A unit of circular measure.

radiant (Astron.): The point on the celestial sphere from which a series of parallel tracks in space appear to originate.

radiant heat (Phys.): Heat communicated to a body by radiation.

radiation (Phys.): Energy emitted in the form of electromagnetic waves.

radiation chemistry: That which deals with chemical effects arising from the impact of high energy rays and particles on other materials.

radiation pressure (Phys.): The mechanical pressure exerted by light and other forms of radiation on surfaces on which they are incident.

radical (Bot.): Appearing as if springing from the root at soil-level. (Chem.): A group of atoms which passes unchanged through a series of reactions, but is normally incapable of separate existence.

rad′icate (Bot.): Rooted.

radicle (Bot.): The root of the embryo of a flowering plant.

radioactivity (Chem., Phys.): The emission of radiant energy; the property possessed by certain elements, of spontaneously emitting alpha, beta, or gamma rays, by the disintegration of the nuclei of atoms.

radiochemistry (Chem.): The chemistry of the radioactive elements.

radio-element (Phys.): A radioactive atom produced by an artificially induced nuclear transformation.

radiogen′ic (Chem.): Produced by radioactive disintegration.

radiology: That branch of medical science which deals with the examination of the body by means of X-rays, and with the treatment of disease by the use of radiant energy.

radium (Chem): A radioactive metallic element.

ra′dix (Zool.): The root of a structure.

ra′don (Chem.): A radioactive element.

rafter (Build., Civ. Eng.): A member in a roof framework extending from the ridge to the eaves.

rain (Meteor.): Rain is due to the condensation of excess water vapor when moist air is cooled below its dew-point.

rainbow (Meteor., Phys.): Formed by sunlight which is refracted and internally reflected by raindrops.

rain gauge (Meteor.): An instrument for measuring the amount of rainfall over a given period.

rake (Eng., etc.): An angle of inclination.

ram (Civ. Eng.): The monkey of a pile-driver.

ramification (Bot., Zool.): Branching.

ramp (Civ. Eng.): An inclined surface provided instead of steps.

ra'mus (Zool.): The barb of a feather.

range (Aero.): The distance that an aircraft can travel without refuelling. (Bot., Zool.): The area over which a species grows or feeds, and breeds in the wild state. (Surv.): To fix points to be in the same straight line.

ranging rod (Surv.): A wooden pole used to mark stations conspicuously.

rapport (Psychol.): The emotional bond existing between analyst and patient.

rapto'rial (Zool.): Adapted for snatching, as birds of prey.

rarefaction (Phys.): Diminution of air-pressure below normal.

raso'rial (Zool.): Adapted for scratching.

rate of climb (Aero.): The rate of ascent from the earth.

rating (Elec. Eng.): The maximum output or input of a piece of electrical apparatus as specified by the maker.

rationalization (Psychol.): The attempt to substitute conscious reasoning for unconscious motivations in explaining behavior.

rattle (Zool.): The series of horny rings representing the modified tail-tip scale in rattlesnakes.

rays (Phys.): A line which represents the direction in which light is travelling. (Zool.): A skeletal element supporting a fin.

raze (Build., Civ. Eng.): To demolish.

reactants (Chem.): The substances taking part in a chemical reaction.

reaction (Bot., Zool.): Any change in behavior in an organism in response to a stimulus. (Chem.): The acidity or alkalinity of a solution.

reaction chamber (Aero.): The chamber in which the combustion of a rocket's fuel and oxidant take place.

reactivation (Chem.): The restoration of an atom, molecule or substance to an activated state.

reactive (Chem.): Readily susceptible to chemical change.

reactor (Elec. Eng.): A piece of apparatus used in an electric circuit, primarily on account of its reactance.

reagent (Chem.): A substance or solution used to produce a characteristic reaction in chemical analysis.

recapitulation (Biol.): Reflection of ancestral characteristics in the developmental stages of the individual.

receiver (Elec. Comm.): The equipment which receives signals in an electrical form and converts them into the form desired.

receptor (Zool.): An element of the nervous system especially adapted for the reception of stimuli.

recess (Build.): A niche or alcove in a wall. (Zool.): A small depression or cleft.

recli'nate (Bot.): Bent back; curved downwards.

recolonization (Bot.): The reestablishment of vegetation on an area which has been stripped of plants.

recombination (Cyt., Gen.): Regroupings of linked characters caused by crossing-over.

recon'naissance (Surv.): The process of preliminary examination, by the surveyor, on the ground which he is to survey.

reconstruction (Zool.): The reconstitution of the structure of an organism or organ from a series of sections.

recorder (Acous.): A machine for registering sound.

recording (Acous.): The practice and science of registering wave-forms arising from sound sources, so that they can be re-created.

recording altimeter (Aero.): An instrument which traces height against time.

recti-: A prefix meaning straight.

rectification (Chem.): The purification of a liquid by redistillation. (Elec. Eng.): The conversion of an alternating current into a direct current by a rectifier.

rec'tinerved (Bot.): Having straight veins.

rec'trices (Zool.): In birds, the stiff tail feathers used in steering.

rectum (Zool.): The posterior terminal portion of the alimentary canal leading to the anus.

reduced (Bot.): Simplified in structure as compared with some ancestral form.

reduced level (Surv.): The elevation of a point above or below datum.

reducing flame (Chem.): The luminous tip of a small Bunsen flame.

reduc'tases (Chem.): Enzymes which bring about the reduction of organic compounds.

reduction (Chem.): Any process in which an electron is added to an atom or an ion.

re-entrant (Surv.): A term applied to an internal angle.

reflex (Zool.): Involuntary; automatic.

reflex action (Zool.): An automatic or involuntary response to a stimulus.

refrigeration: The artificial production of cold, for food preservation.

refrigerator (Eng.): A machine or plant by which mechanical or heat energy is utilized to produce and maintain a low temperature.

regeneration (Zool.): Renewal or replacement of an organ or structure which has been damaged or lost.

regional metamorphism (Geol.): All those changes in the mineral composition and texture of rocks due to compressional stresses and to the rise of temperature.

register (Build.): A metal damper to close a chimney.

reglette (Surv.): The short graduated scale attached to each end of the special measuring tape used in base-line measurement.

regression (Biol.): A tendency to return from an extreme to an average condition. (Psycho-an.): A return to an earlier stage of development.

regulating switch (Elec. Eng.): A switch used for switching the regulating cells of a battery in and out of circuit.

regurgitation (Med.): The bringing back into the mouth of undigested food.

rejuvenes'cence (Biol.): Renewal of growth from old or injured parts.

relapse (Med.): The falling back into an illness after an apparent or partial recovery.

relative density (Chem.): The ratio of the density of a gas to that of hydrogen under similar conditions of pressure and temperature.

relative humidity (Meteor.): The ratio of the amount of water vapor in the air to the amount which would saturate it at the same temperature.

relay (Elec. Comm.): Any piece of apparatus in which a small electrical power is used to control larger electrical power. (Elec. Eng.): A device which, when operated, by the current in one circuit, causes contacts to close or open to control the current in another circuit.

relict (Ecol.): A species which occurs at the present time in circumstances different from those in which it originated.

reluctance (Elec. Eng.): The ratio which the magneto-motive force acting around a magnetic circuit bears to the flux which it produces.

rem'iped (Zool.): Having the feet adapted for paddling.

remission (Med.): An abatement of the severity of a disease.

remote control (Elec. Eng.): The control of apparatus by means of a switch situated at some distance from the apparatus.

re'nal (Zool.): Pertaining to the kidneys.

rennin (Chem.): An enzyme found in the gastric juice, causing the clotting of milk.

replaceable hydrogen (Chem.): Those hydrogen atoms in the molecule of an acid which can be replaced by atoms of a metal on neutralization of a base.

repression (Psycho-an.): The unconscious mental mechanism by which complexes are kept out of consciousness.

reproduction (Biol.): The process of generation of new individuals whereby the species is perpetuated.

repulsion (Gen., Cyt.): The tendency shown by dominant characters to separate.

reservoir (Civ. Eng.): A basin for the storage of water, which is later to be used for irrigation or as a supply for cities.

residual affinity (Chem.): The chemical attractive forces which remain after saturation of the normal valencies of the atoms in a molecule.

resilience (Eng.): The stored energy of a strained material.

resin (Chem.): The product from the secretion of the sap of certain trees and plants.

resistance (Biol., Med.): The whole of the characters of an organism which enable it to resist the attacks of a disease. (Elec.): The property of a substance by virtue of which it resists the flow of an electric current through it. (Psycho-an.): An unconscious barrier in the mind against making unconscious processes conscious.

resistor (Elec. Eng.): A piece of apparatus used on account of its possessing resistance.

resolution (Chem.): The separation of an optically inactive mixture or compound into its optically active components.

resonance (Phys.): A vibration of large amplitude resulting on application of a forced vibration to a system, when the period of the force equals that of a natural vibration of the system.

respiration (Bot., Zool.): The interchange of oxygen and carbon dioxide associated with katabolic processes.

resting nucleus (Cyt.): A nucleus which is not dividing.

restorative (Med.): Capable of restoring to health.

resuscitation (Med.): Restoration to consciousness or to life one who is unconscious.

retaining wall (Civ. Eng.): A wall built to support earth at a higher level on the one side than on the other.

retardation (Med.): Arrest of mental development.

retarder (Chem.): A negative catalyst which is added to a reacting system to prevent the reaction from being too vigorous.

rete (Zool.): A net-like structure.

ret′icule (Surv.): A cell carrying cross-hairs and fitting into the diaphragm of a surveying telescope.

ret′ina (Anat., Zool.): The light-sensitive layer of the eye of all animals.

ret′inerved (Bot.): Net-veined.

retort: A vessel used in distillation.

retrac′tile (Zool.): Capable of being withdrawn.

retro-: A prefix meaning behind, backwards.

retrogression (Zool.): Degeneration.

retrorse (Bot., Zool.): Pointing backwards; retroverse.

reversible reaction (Chem.): A chemical reaction which can take place in both directions, and is therefore incomplete.

revet′ment (Civ. Eng.): A retaining wall.

rev′olute (Bot.): Rolled backwards and usually downwards.

revolution (Astron.): The term for orbital motion, as the earth about the sun. (Geol.): A period of intense change in the disposition of sea and land and of the surface configuration.

rhe′nium (Chem.): A metallic element.

rheology (Phys.): The science of flow of matter.

rhemor′phism (Geol.): Process by which a pre-existing rock is converted into magma.

rhe-ostat (Elec. Eng.): A resistor in which the value of the resistance in circuit may be varied.

rhin-, rhino-: A prefix meaning nose.

rhi′nal (Zool.): Pertaining to the nose.

rhiz-, rhizo-: A prefix meaning root.

rhi′zome (Bot.): An underground stem, having a superficial resemblance to a root, but bearing scale

leaves and one or more buds.

rhi′zophi′lous (Bot.): Growing on roots.

rhodium (Met.): A metallic element.

rhombohedron (Crystal.): A crystal form of the trigonal system.

rhomboi′dal (Bot.): Quadrangular, but not square, and attached by one acute angle.

rhynchoph′orous (Zool.): Having a beak.

ria (Geol.): A normal valley drowned by a rise of sea-level relative to the land.

rib (Bot.): One of the larger veins of a leaf. (Build., Civ. Eng.): A curved member of a center or ribbed arch. (Zool.): In vertebrates, an element of the skeleton in the form of a curved rod connected at one end with a vertebra.

ribbed arch (Civ. Eng.): An arch composed of side-by-side ribs spanning the distance between the springings.

rickets (Med.): A nutritional childhood disease characterized by defective ossification and softening of bones.

ric′tal (Zool.): In birds, of the mouth aperture.

rider (Chem.): A small piece of platinum wire used on a chemical balance as a final adjustment.

ridge (Build., Civ. Eng.): The summit-line of a roof.

riffler (Eng.): A file bent so as to be capable of operating in a shallow depression.

rigging (Aero.): The operation of adjusting and aligning the various components of an aircraft.

rigid arch (Civ. Eng.): A continuous arch without joints or hinges.

rigor (Bot.): An inert condition assumed by a plant when growing conditions are unfavorable. (Zool.): A state of rigidity when subjected to sudden shock.

rigor mortis (Med.): The stiffening of the body following death.

rim (Bot.): The overhanging part of a wall about a bordered pit.

ri′ma (Zool.): A narrow cleft.

rime (Build.): A rung of a ladder.

ri′mose (Bot.): Having the surface marked by a network of intersecting cracks.

rind (Bot.): The outer layers of the fruit body.

rip (Carp.): To saw timber along the direction of the grain.

ripcord (Aero.): A cable used for opening the pack of a parachute.

rip-saw (Carp.): A saw for cutting timber along the grain.

ripa′rean, riparious (Bot., Zool.): Living or growing on the banks of streams and rivers.

ripples (Phys.): Small waves on the surface of a liquid.

rise (Build., Civ. Eng.): (1) The vertical height from end supports to ridge of a roof. (2) The height of a step in a staircase.

riser (Build.): The vertical part of a step.

rising and setting (Astron.): The positions of a heavenly body when it is exactly on the great circle of the observer's horizon, east or west of the meridian respectively.

rising arch (Civ. Eng.): An arch whose springing line is not horizontal.

river wall (Civ. Eng.): A wall built as a side boundary to the flow of a river, thereby confining it to a definite path.

rivet (Eng.): A headed shank for making a permanent joint between two pieces.

riv′ulose (Bot.): Marked with lines, appearing as rivers on a map.

roasting (Met.): The operation of heating sulphide ores in air to convert to oxide.

roasting furnace (Met.): A furnace in which finely ground ores and concentrates are roasted to eliminate sulphur.

rock (Geol.): An aggregate of mineral particles forming part of the earth's crust.

rock drill (Civ. Eng.): A tool especially adapted to the boring of holes through rock.

rocket propulsion (Aero.): Reaction propulsion using internally stored oxygen for combustion.

rod-cell (Zool.): One of the photosensitive cells of the retina of which the percipient structure is rod-shaped.

rods and cones (Zool.): The photosensitive cells of the retina.

Roden'tia (Zool.): An order of small mammals, as squirrels, beavers, rats, rabbits, etc.

rodman (Surv.): A staffman.

rolling (Aero.): The angular motion of an aircraft tending to set up a rotation about a longitudinal axis.

Röntgen rays (Phys.): X-rays.

roof truss (Build., Civ. Eng.): The structural framework built to support the roof covering of a building.

root (Bot.): The branching lower portion of the axis of a higher plant. (Civ. Eng.): The part of a dam which runs into the natural ground surface at each end.

root tuber (Bot.): A swollen root containing reserve food material.

rosa'ceous (Bot.): Having the character of a rose.

Rose crucible (Chem.): A crucible used for igniting substances in a current of gas.

rose'ola (Med.): Any rose-colored rash.

rosin (Chem.): The residue from the distillation of turpentine.

ros'trate (Bot.): Ending in a long hard point.

rostrum (Build.): A raised platform for speakers.

rotation (Astron.): The term generally confined to the turning of a body about an axis passing through itself. (Bot.): The movement of the protoplasm in a cell in a constant direction.

rotator (Zool.): A muscle which turns a limb on its axis.

rotor (Aero.): A system of revolving aerofoils producing life. (Elec. Eng.): The rotating part of an electric machine.

rotund (Bot.): Approximately circular.

rotunda (Build.): A building or room which is circular and covered by a dome.

rough arch (Build.): An arch built of uncut bricks with wedge-shaped joints.

roughness integrator (Civ. Eng.): An instrument for measuring the roughness of a road surface.

round (Build.): A rung of a ladder.

rowlock (Build.): A term applied to a course of bricks laid on edge.

rubes'cent (Bot.): Turning red or pink.

rubid'ium (Chem.): A metallic element; one of the alkali metals.

rudiment (Bot., Zool.): The earliest recognizable stage of an organ or member.

rudimentary (Bot., Zool.): Incompletely developed.

ru'fous (Bot.): Red-brown.

ru'gose (Biol.): Having a wrinkled surface.

ru'men (Zool.): The first division of the stomach in ruminants.

rumination (Med.): The regurgitation of swallowed food and its further mastication before reswallowing.

run (Build.): A gangway. (Surv.): In a level tube, the movement of a bubble with change of inclination.

runway (Aero.): A hard path to facilitate landing and taking-off of aircraft.

rung (Build.): A bar connecting the two side posts of a ladder and serving as a step.

runner (Bot.): A prostrate shoot which roots at the end and there gives rise to a new plant.

rupic'olous (Bot., Zool.): Living or growing on or among rocks.

rupture (Med.): Forcible breaking or tearing of a bodily organ or structure.

rut (Zool.): To be sexually excited.

ruthe'nium (Chem.): A metallic element.

ru'tilant (Bot.): Brightly colored in orange, yellow or red.

S

sab'ulose (Bot.): Growing in sandy places.

sac (Bot., Zool.): Any pouch-like structure.

saccharim'eter (Chem.): A special type of polarimeter adapted for use with white light.

saccarim'etry (Chem.): The estimation of the percentage of sugar present in solutions of unknown strength.

sac'charin (Chem.): A white crystalline powder used where sugar is harmful.

saccharolyt'ic (Bacteriol.): Said of bacteria which use starches and simple carbohydrates as sources of energy.

saccharom'eter (Chem.): A hydrometer which is used to determine the concentration of sugar in solution.

sac'rum (Zool.): The vertebrae to which the pelvic girdle is attached.

saddle (Civ. Eng.): A block surmounting one of the towers of a suspension bridge. (Elec. Eng.): A U-shaped cleat for securing lighting conduits to a flat surface.

safety fuse (Elec. Eng.): A protective fuse in part of an electric circuit.

sag: To bulge downwards under load.

Sagitta'rius (Astron.): Archer. Ninth sign of the Zodiac.

salient (Surv.): (1) A jutting-out piece of land. (2) A term applied to an external angle.

salinom'eter (Phys.): A hydrometer for measuring the density of sea water.

sali'va (Zool.): The secretion, produced by the salivary glands, which facilitates the swallowing of food.

sali'vary glands (Zool.): Glands present in many land animals, the ducts of which open into or near the mouth.

salt (Chem.): A compound which results from the replacement of one or more hydrogen atoms of an acid by metal atoms or electropositive radicals.

saltant (Biol.): A changed form of a species, developed suddenly, and differing from the original in morphology or in physiological properties.

saltato'rial (Zool.): Used for jumping.

samar'a (Bot.): A single-seeded, dry, indehiscent fruit, bearing a wing-like extension of the pericarp.

sama'rium (Chem.): A metallic element.

sand (Geol.): Applied to loose, unconsolidated accumulations of detrital sediment consisting primarily of rounded grains of quartz.

sand-blasting: A method of cleaning metal surfaces by means of sand or grit directed from a nozzle at high velocity.

sand culture (Bot.): An experimental method of determining the mineral requirements of plants.

sand dunes (Geol.): Rounded mounds of loose sand piled up by wind action.

sandpaper (Carp.): Stout paper with a thin coating of fine sand glued on to one side, for use as an abrading material.

sandstones (Geol.): Compacted and cemented sedimentary rocks, which consist essentially of rounded grains of quartz.

sanding (Carp., etc.): The operation of cleaning up wood surfaces by rubbing with sandpaper.

sanguic'olous (Zool.): Living in blood.

sanguin'eous (Bot.): Blood-red.

sanguiv'orous (Zool.): Blood-feeding.

sap (Bot.): An aqueous solution of mineral salts, sugars and other organic substances, present in the xylem of plants.

saywood (Bot.): The layer of recently formed secondary wood.

sapling (Bot.): A young tree.

sapona'ceous (Bot.): Slippery.

saprobiot'ic (Biol.): Feeding on dead animals or plants.

sap'rophyte (Biol.): An organism which obtains its food from dead organic material.

sarcod'ic (Zool.): Pertaining to flesh.

sar'cody (Bot.): Conversion into something of fleshy texture.

sarco'ma (Med.): A malignant tumor.

sarcoph'agous (Zool.): Flesh-eating.

sar'cous (Zool.): Pertaining to flesh; to muscle tissue.

sash (Carp.): A framing for window panes.

sat'ellite (Astron.): The name given to a small body revolving around another, generally a planet. (Bot.): A small part of a chromosome.

saturated solution (Chem.): A solution which can exist in equilibrium with excess of the dissolved substance.

saturated vapor (Phys.): A vapor which is sufficiently concentrated to exist in equilibrium with the liquid form of the same substance.

saturation of the air (Meteor.): The air, at a given temperature, can contain water vapor up to a limit known as the saturation point.

Saturn (Astron.): The sixth planet of the solar system in order of distance from the sun.

saur'ian (Zool.): Lizard-like.

saxica'vous (Zool.): Rock-boring.

sax'icale (Bot.): Growing on rocks or stones.

scaffold (Build.): A temporary erection of timber or steelwork, used in the construction, alteration or demolition of a building.

scala (Zool.): A ladder-like structure.

scale (Bot.): A thin, flat, semi-transparent plant member. (Zool.): A small exoskeletal outgrowth of chitin, bone or some horny material, usually flat and plate-like.

scale leaf (Bot.): A leaf, usually reduced in size, membranous, of rough texture and protective in function.

scalloped (Bot.): Said of a margin bearing rounded teeth.

scandium (Chem.): A metallic element.

scanso'rial (Zool.): Adapted for climbing trees.

scape (Bot.): A peduncle arising from the middle of a rosette of leaves and bearing a flower. (Zool.): The basal joint of the antenna in insects.

sca'phoid (Bot., Zool.): Boat-shaped.

scheelite (Min.): An ore of tungsten.

schist (Geol.): The name given to a group of metamorphic rocks which have a tendency to split, as mica, talc.

schistos'ity (Geol.): The tendency in certain rocks to split easily.

schizogen'esis (Zool.): Reproduction by fission.

schizoid (Psychiatry): Showing qualities of a schizophrenic personality but without definite mental disorder.

sciat'ic (Zool.): Pertaining the the hip region.

science: The ordered arrangement of ascertained knowledge.

scintillation (Astron.): The twinkling of stars.

sci'ograph (Build.): A drawing showing a sectional view of a building.

sci'on (Bot.): (1) A portion of a plant which is inserted into a root stock in grafting. (2) A stolon.

sci'ophyte (Bot.): A plant which grows in shady situations.

scis'sile (Bot.): Capable of being split.

scler-, sclero–: A prefix meaning hard.

scleratogenous (Zool.): Skeleton-forming.

sclere (Zool.): A skeletal structure.

scler'eide (Bot.): A general term for a cell with a thick, lignified wall.

sco'pa (Zool.): The pollen brush of bees.

scop'ula (Zool.): A small tuft of hairs.

sco'ria (Geol.): A cavernous mass of volcanic rock.

scorification (Chem.): The separation of gold or silver from an ore.

Scorpio (Astron.): Scorpion. Eighth sign of the Zodiac.

screen (Build., Cirv. Eng.): A large sieve used for grading coarse or fine aggregates.

screenings (Build., Civ. Eng.): The residue from a sieving operation.

scum (Build.): A surface formation of lime crystals on new cement work.

sea: An expanse of salt water on the face of the globe.

seaplane (Aero.): An aeroplane fitted with means for taking off and alighting on water.

sealing (Build.): The operation of closing a joint by means of cement, lead, etc.

season (Astron.): One of the four divisions of the tropical year taken from the passage of the sun through the equinoctial and solstitial points.

seba'ceous (Zool.): Producing or containing fatty material.

sec'odont (Zool.): Having teeth adapted for cutting.

second: 1/60 of a minute of time.

secondary (Zool.): Arising later; of subsidiary importance.

secre'tion (Physiol.): A substance discharged by a gland or gland cell.

section (Bot.): A division of a genus. (Surv.): The representation to scale of the variations in level of the ground surface along any particular line.

sector: A plane figure enclosed by two radii of a circle and the arm cut off by them.

secto'rial (Zool.): Adapted for cutting.

sectroid (Arch.): The curved surface between adjacent groins on a vault surface.

secular changes (Geol., etc.): Changes which take many centuries to accomplish.

sedentary (Zool.): Said of animals which remain attached to a substratum.

sedimentary rocks (Geol.): All those rocks which result from the wastage of pre-existing rocks.

sedimentation (Chem.): The settling of solid particles from a liquid as a result of either gravity or centrifuging.

secd (Bot.): A multicellular structure containing the embryo of a higher plant.

seed crystal (Chem.): A crystal introduced into a supersaturated solution or a supercooled liquid in order to initiate crystallization.

seedling (Bot.): The young plant from a germinated seed.

segment (Bot.): (1) A multinucleate portion of a filament. (2) A daughter cell cut off by the division of a single apical cell. (Elec. Eng.): One of many elements, insulated from one another, which collectively form a commutator. (Geom.): A plane figure enclosed by the chord of a circle and the arc cut off by it. (Zool.): One of the joints of an articulate appendage; a cell or group of cells produced by cleavage of an ovum.

segregation (Gen.): The separation of hereditary factors from one another during spore formation. (Met.): non-uniform distribution of impurities, inclusions and alloying constituents in metals.

seis'mograph: An instrument by means of which earthquake shocks are registered.

seismology: The study of earthquake phenomena.

seistan (Meteor.): The 120 day summer north wind in East Persia.

sele'nium (Chem.): A non-metallic element.

selenog'raphy (Astron.): The description and delineation of the moon's surface.

self-pollination (Bot.): The transfer of pollen from the anthers to the stigmas of the same flower, or to the stigmas of another flower on the same plant.

semat'ic (Zool.): Warning.

semeiol'ogy (Med.): The branch of medical science dealing with the symptoms of disease.

se'men (Zool.): The fluid formed by the male reproductive organ in which the spermatozoa are suspended.

semi-: A prefix meaning half.

semi-automatic (Elec. Eng.): Said of an electric control in which the initiation of an operating sequence is manually performed and then proceeds automatically.

semicircular arch (Civ. Eng.): An arch describing half a circle.

semi-diameter (Astron.): Half the angular diameter of a celestial body.

sender (Elec. Comm.): A radio transmitting station for broadcasting.

sending end (Elec. Eng.): The end of a transmission line from which electrical energy is sent out.

senes'cent (Biol.): Said of that period in the life-history of an individual when its powers are declining prior to death.

senil'ity (Biol.): Condition of degeneration due to old age.

sensation (Psychol.): An awareness in consciousness of a physical experience.

sense organ (Bot., Zool.): A structure especially adapted for the reception of stimuli.

sensibility (Bot.): The condition of a plant of being liable to parasitic attack.

sensif'erous (Zool.): Sensitive.

sensil'la (Zool.): A small sensory structure.

sensitizer (Chem.): A substance, other than the catalyst, whose presence facilitates the start of a catalytic reaction.

sensitive (Zool.): Capable of receiving stimuli.

sensitive flame (Phys.): A gas flame which changes its shape or height when sound-waves fall on it.

sensitivity (Elec. Eng.): The change in deflection of an instrument per unit torque applied.

senso'rium (Zool.): The nervous system.

sensory (Zool.): Pertaining to the senses.

sentiment (Psycho-an.): A psychological constellation formed when instinctive emotions become attached to persons, ideas, objects, etc.

sepal (Bot.): One of the leaf-like members forming the calyx of a flower.

separation (Bot.): The liberation of a reproductive body from the parent plant.

separator (Elec. Eng.): A thin sheet of wood or perforated celluloid separating the plates of a secondary cell.

sepsis (Med.): The invasion of bodily tissue by non-specific pathogenic bacteria.

sep'tate (Bot.): Divided into cells by walls; or into two or more chambers by partitions.

sep'tenate (Bot.): Having parts in sevens.

septum (Bot.): A wall between one cell and another. (Zool.): A partition separating two cavities.

sere (Bot.): A series of plant communities making up a succession.

serein (Meteor.): The rare phenomenon of rainfall out of an apparently clear sky.

ser'eate (Bot.): Arranged in a row.

series (Elec. Eng.): A series connection of two or more electric circuits is one in which the same current traverses all the circuits.

seroti'nous (Bot.): Appearing late in the year.

serous (Zool.): Watery.

serpentine (Min.): A hydrated silicate of magnesium.

serrate (Bot.): Said of a toothed margin. (Zool.): Saw-like, notched.

se'rum (Med., Zool.): A watery secretion.

service mains (Elec. Eng.): Cables of small conductor cross-section which lead the current from a distributor to the consumer's premises.

ses'sile (Bot.): Having no stalk.

set of chromosomes (Cyt.): A group of chromosomes consisting of one each of the various kinds of chromosomes contained in the nucleus of a gamete.

se'ta (Bot.): A bristle.

setting (Build.): The name given to the hardening of lime, mortar, plaster or cement.

sex-: A prefix meaning six.

sex (Biol.): The sum-total of the characteristics which distinguish female organisms, especially with regard to the part played in reproduction.

sex chromosome (Cyt.): The chromosome which is responsible for the initial determination of sex.

sex-linked (Gen.): Said of hereditary characteristics borne by the sex chromosome.

sex ratio (Zool.): The ratio of males to females.

sexfa'rious (Bot.): In six rows.

sexpar'tite (Bot.): Divided deeply into six segments.

sextant (Surv.): A reflecting instrument in the form of a quadrant, for measuring angles up to about 120°

sexual cell (Biol.): A male or female germ-cell.

sexual organs (Zool.): Reproductive system.

sexual reproduction (Bot., Zool.): The union of gametes, preceding the formation of a new individual.

sexual selection (Zool.): A phase of natural selection, based on the struggle for mating.

shaft (Arch.): The principal portion of a column, between the base and the capital. (Civ. Eng.): A passage, usually vertical, leading from ground level into an underground excavation. (Zool.): The part of a hair distal to the root.

shaggy (Bot.): Covered with long weak hairs.

shale (Geol.): A consolidated clay-rock which possesses definite lamination.

shank (Build.): (1) The shaft of a column, pillar, etc. (2) The shaft of a tool, connecting the handle and the head.

shaping machine (Eng.): A machine tool for producing small flat surfaces, slots, etc.

sharp (Build., Civ. Eng.): Said of sand, the grains of which are angular.

sheath (Zool.): An enclosing or protective structure.

sheathing (Carp.): Close boarding nailed to the framework of a building to form the walls or the roof.

shed (Build.): A small outhouse.

sheeting (Civ. Eng.): Rough horizontal boards used to support the sides of narrow trenches during excavation in very loose soils.

shell (Chem.): A group of electrons in an atom, all of which have the same principal quantum number. (Zool.): A hard outer case of inorganic material.

shellac (Chem.): The purified product of lac.

shingle (Build.): A thin, flat rectangular piece of wood laid like a tile, as a roof covering or for the sides of a building.

shock (Eng., etc.): The sudden application of load to a member.

shoe (Build.): The short bent part at the foot of a downpipe, directing the water away from the wall.

short-circuit (Elec. Eng.): The electrical condition created when the terminals of a generator or any other conveyor or source of electrical energy are connected by a conducting path of negligible resistance.

short waves: Electromagnetic waves whose wavelength is of the order of 50 meters or less.

shrinkage (Civ. Eng.): The difference in the spaces occupied by material before excavation and after settlement in embankment.

shrub (Bot.): A woody plant in which most of the side shoots survive, so that there is no main trunk as a tree.

shutter (Build.): A removable protective covering to the outside of a window.

sid'erite (Geol.): A general term for meteoric iron.

sidereal time (Astron.): A method of reckoning intervals based on the rotation of the earth on its axis as the fundamental period.

sieve (Build.): An open container fitted with a mesh bottom.

sight: The sensation produced when light waves impinge on the photosensitive cells of the eye.

sig'moid (Bot., Zool., etc.): Curved like the letter S.

sign (Med.): Any objective evidence of disease or bodily disorder.

signal (Elec Comm.): The modification of an electrical effect having a variation wave-form or coding which represents the intelligence transmitted. (Surv.): A device used to mark a survey station, as a ranging rod, etc.

sil'ica (Met., Min.): Dioxide of silicon; used in the manufacture of glass.

sil'icates (Min.): The salts of the silicic acids, the large group among minerals.

sil'icon (Chem.): A non-metallic element.

silk (Zool.): A fluid substance secreted by various anthropoda; used for spinning cocoons, webs, etc.

sill (Geol.): A concordant minor intrusion of igneous rock injected as a tabular sheet between the bedding planes of rocks.

silt (Eng.): Material of an earthy character deposited in a finely divided form by flowing water.

silver (Met., Min.): A pure-white metallic element.

silver amalgam (Min.): A solid solution of mercury

and silver.

sim'ian (Zool.): Pertaining to the anthropoid apes.

simoom' (Meteor.): A hot dry wind of brief duration, occurring in the Arabian and African deserts.

simple (Bot.): Consisting of one piece.

simple curve (Surv.): A curve composed of a single arc connecting two straights.

simple fruit (Bot.): A fruit formed from one pistil.

simple harmonic motion (Phys.): A type of vibration represented by projecting into a diameter the uniform motion of a point around a circle.

simple tissue (Bot.): A tissue made up of cells all of the same kind.

simplex channel (Elec. Comm.): A channel of communication which transmits signals in one direction only at a time.

simplex group (Cyt.): The haploid complement of chromosomes and factors.

simulation (Zool.): Mimicry.

sine galvanometer (Elec. Eng.): A galvanometer in which the coil and scale are rotated to keep the needle at zero.

sine wave (Phys.): A wave in which the particles execute transverse vibrations of a simple harmonic type.

singlet (Chem.): A chemical bond which consists of a single shared electron.

sinking (Civ. Eng.): The operation of excavating for a shaft, well or pit.

sinter (Chem.): To coalesce into a single mass under the influence of heat, without actually liquefying.

sin'uose (Bot.): Waved from side to side.

si'nus (Bot.): A depression in a margin between two lobes. (Zool.): A cavity of irregular shape.

sipho-: A prefix meaning tube.

siphon (Civ. Eng.): A pipeline full of water connecting two reservoirs, with the flow taking place under the action of atmospheric pressure. (Zool.): A tubular organ serving for the intake and output of fluid.

sipho'neous (Bot.): Tubular.

siroc'co (Meteor.): A warm moist wind from the south or south-east, which blows before the eastward passage of a depression in Mediterranean regions.

sisal hemp (Bot.): A fibrous material used for cordage.

site (Build., Civ. Eng.): An area of ground which is to be the location of building works.

sitotro'pism (Zool.): Reaction to the stimulus of food.

skein (Cyt.): The nuclear reticulum.

skeleton (Anat., Zool.): The rigid or elastic, internal or external framework of a body.

skew: Irregular, unsymmetrical, oblique.

skin: The protective tissue layers of the body-wall of an animal. (Bot.): Epidermis. (Eng.): The hard surface layer found on iron castings.

skip (Civ. Eng.): A bucket used for the transport of materials and hung on a crane.

skirt (Elec. Comm.): The lower side portions of a resonance curve.

skull (Zool.): In vertebrates, the brain case and sense-capsules with the jaws and the bronchial arches.

skylight (Build.): A glazed opening in a roof.

skyscraper (Build.): A very tall, multistoryed building.

slab (Civ. Eng.): A thin flat piece of stone or concrete.

slag (Met.): The top layer of the two-layer melt formed during smelting and refining operations.

slaking (Build.): The process of combining quicklime with water.

slashed (Bot.): Deeply cut by tapering incisions.

slate (Geol.): A sedimentary rock of the clay or silt grade which has developed a slaty cleavage.

slaty cleavage (Geol.): The property of splitting easily with the cleavage planes lying in the directions of maximum elongation of the mass.

sledge-hammer (Eng.): A heavy hammer weighing up to 100 lb. or over, swung by both hands.

sleet (Meteor.): A mixture of rain and snow.

sleeve (Eng.): A tubular piece.

slide rule: A device for performing mechanically arithmetical processes.

slide valve (Eng.): A steam-engine inlet and exhaust valve shaped like a rectangular lid.

slimes (Met.): Particles of crushed ore which settle very slowly in water.

slip (Civ. Eng.): A sloping concrete surface for the support of a vessel in the process of being built or repaired.

slope (Civ. Eng.): The inclined side of an embankment.

slough (Med.): To form dead tissue. (Zool.): The cast-off outer skin of a snake.

sluice (Civ. Eng.): A water channel equipped with means of controlling the flow.

smell: The sensation produced by stimulation of the mucous membrane of the olfactory organs.

smelting (Met.): Fusion of an ore to produce a melt of two layers.

smoke (Chem.): A suspension of a solid in a gas.

smooth (Bot.): Said of a surface that is neither hairy nor rough.

snow (Meteor.): Precipitation in the form of small ice crystals.

soaking (Met.): A phrase of a heating operation during which metal is maintained at the requisite temperature until the temperature is uniform throughout the mass.

soaps (Chem.): The alkaline salts of palmitic, oleic or stearic acid.

social (Zool.): Living together.

socket (Elec. Eng.): The female portion of a plug-and-socket connection in an electric circuit.

sodium (Chem.): A metallic element.

softness (Met.): Tendency to deform easily.

sol (Chem.): A colloidal solution.

solar (Zool.): Having branches radially arranged.

solar plexus (Zool.): In higher mammals, a ganglionic center of the autonomic nervous system.

solar apex (Astron.): The point on the celestial sphere towards which the solar system is moving at the rate of 20 kilometers a second.

solar constant (Phys.): The quantity of energy received normally per sq. cm. per second by the earth.

Solar System (Astron.): The term designating the sun and the attendant bodies moving about it under gravitational attraction.

solation (Chem.): The liquefaction of a gel.

solder (Met.): A general term for alloys used for joining metals by soldering.

soldered (Bot.): United.

soldier (Zool.): In some social insects, a form with a large head and mandibles, adapted for defending the community.

sole (Carp.): The lower surface of the body of a plane.

solid (Chem.): A state of matter, with a definite shape, in which the constituent molecules or ions possess no translational motion, but can only vibrate about fixed mean positions.

solitary (Bot., Zool.): Occurring singly. (Zool.): Living alone.

solstices (Astron.): The two moments in the year when the sun in its apparent motion attains its maximum distance from the celestial equator.

solubility (Chem.): The weight of a dissolved substance which will saturate 100 grams of a solvent.

sol'ute (Chem.): A substance which is dissolved in another.

solution (Bot.): The abnormal separation of parts normally united. (Chem.): An extremely intimate mixture, of variable composition, of two or more substances, one of which is usually a liquid, which may be separated by simple physical processes.

solvent (Chem.): That component of a solution which is present in excess, or whose physical state is the same as that of the solution.

so'ma (Zool.): The body of an animal, as distinct from the germ-cells.

somatic cell (Zool.): One of the non-reproductive cells of the parent body.

somatic mitosis (Cyt.): Division of the metabolic nucleus.

somatic mutation (Gen.): A mutation arising in a somatic cell and not in a reproductive structure.

somatic segregation (Bot., Gen.): A change in nuclear or hereditary constitution during vegetative growth.

somatogen'ic (Zool.): Arising as the result of external stimuli. Developing from somatic cells.

so'matoids (Chem.): Small particles of definite shape and possessing a definite arrangement of matter but not homogeneous.

sonims (Met.): Solid non-metallic inclusions in metal.

sough (Civ. Eng.): A drain at the foot of a slope.

sound (Acous.): The perception of external stimuli accepted through the ear and sense of hearing.

sounder (Ocean.): Any instrument used for determining the depth of the sea.

sounding (Surv.): The depth of an under-water point below some chosen reference datum.

space: Continuous and boundless extension considered as a vacuous entity in which things may exist and move.

spa'dix (Bot.): A spike with a swollen fleshy axis, enclosed in a spathe.

span (Civ. Eng., etc.): The horizontal distance between the supports of an arch, bridge, etc. (Elec. Eng.): The distance between two transmission-line towers.

spark (Elec. Eng.): An electric discharge taking place in air or other insulating material.

spasm (Zool.): Involuntary contraction of muscle fibers.

spathe (Bot.): A large foliar organ which subtends and more or less encloses a spadix.

spawn (Zool.): To deposit eggs or discharge spermatozoa.

spay (Zool.): To remove the ovaries.

species (Bot., Zool.): A classification term used to denote a group of closely allied, mutually fertile individuals, showing differences from allied groups.

specific gravity (Phys.): The ratio of the mass of a given volume of a substance to the mass of an equal volume of water at a temperature of 4° C.

specific heat (Phys.): The quantity of heat necessary to raise the temperature of unit mass one degree.

specific volume (Phys.): The volume of unit mass.

spectrum (Phys.): An arrangement of radiated frequencies in order of their frequencies.

speed: The ratio of the distance covered by a moving body to the time taken. (Elec. Eng.): The angular velocity of an electrical machine, expressed in revolutions per minute.

speed of rotation: In a rotating body, the number of rotations about the axis of rotation divided by the time.

speleology (Zool.): The study of the flora and fauna of caves.

sperm (Zool.): A male germ-cell.

Spermatophy'ta (Bot.): Seed-bearing plants.

sphe'noid (Bot., Zool.): Wedge-shaped. (Crystal.): A wedge-shaped crystal-form consisting of four triangular faces.

sphincter (Zool.): A muscle which by its contraction narrows or closes an orifice.

sphyg'mus (Zool.): The pulse.

spi'cate (Bot.): Spike-like.

spike (Carp.): A large stout nail. (Bot.): An indefinite inflorescence with sessile flowers.

spile (Civ. Eng.): A timber pile.

spin (Aero.): The movement of an aircraft in a continuous spiral dive.

spinal (Zool.): Pertaining to the vertebral column.

spindle (Cyt., Zool.): Any spindle-shaped structure.

spine (Zool.): The vertebral column.

spinif'erous (Bot.): Thorn-bearing.

spin'neret (Zool.): One of the spinning organs in spiders.

spin'nerule (Zool.): A duct by which the fluid silk is discharged in spiders.

spi'nose (Bot.): Bearing sharp spiny teeth.

spira (Arch.): The base of a column.

spire (Build.): A slender tower tapering to a point.

spi'reme (Cyt.): A stage in which the nuclear chromatin takes the form of a long thread.

spiril'lum (Bacteriol.): A curved spiral organism.

spirit (Chem.): An aqueous solution of ethyl alcohol.

spi'rochetes (Bacteriol.): Filamentous bacteria showing 'indulations or spirals.

spirom'eter (Med.): An instrument for measuring the air inhaled and exhaled during respiration.

splint (Med.): Any appliance used for the fixation of displaced or movable parts, especially dislocated or fractured bones.

spontaneous generation (Biol.): The production of living matter or organisms from non-living matter.

spool (Elec.): The support of a coil.

sporad'ic (Bot.): Scattered over a wide area. (Med.): Of disease, occurring here and there.

spore (Bot.): A reproductive body characteristic of plants. Consists of one or a few cells, never contains an embryo, and when set free may give rise to a new plant. (Zool.): In protozoa, a minute body formed by multiple fission.

spori-, sporo-: A prefix meaning seed.

sporogen'esis (Bot., Zool.): Spore formation.

spo'rophyte (Bot.): The spore-bearing plant.

sport (Gen.): Any individual differing markedly from the normal by reason of genetical factors.

spot level (Surv.): The reduced level of a point chosen at random.

sprain (Med.): A wrenching of a joint.

spray-gun (Civ. Eng.): An apparatus for forming by pneumatic pressure a fine spray.

spread (Biol.): The establishment of a species in a new area.

sprocket (Eng.): A toothed wheel used for chain drives.

spur (Bot.): A tubular prolongation at the base of a petal. (Geol.): A hilly projection extending from the flanks of a valley.

squam'a (Bot., Zool.): A scale.

stabilizer (Chem.): (1) A negative catalyst. (2) A substance which makes a solution stable.

stability: A general property of mechanical, electrical or aerodynamical systems whereby the system returns to a state of equilibrium after disturbance.

stable (Chem., etc.): Possessing no tendency to change.

stage (Build., Civ. Eng.): A platform. (Geol.): A succession of rocks which were deposited during an age of geological time.

stainless steel (Met.): Corrosion-resistant steel with a high percentage of chromium.

stair (Build.): A series of steps.

stair-head (Build.): The top of a flight of stairs.

stake (Carp.): A piece of timber pointed at one end for driving into the ground.

stalac'tite (Geol.): A concretionary deposit of calcium carbonate which hangs icicle-like from the roofs of limestone caverns.

stalag'mite (Geol.): A concretionary deposit of calcium carbonate, precipitated from dripping solutions on the floors and walls of limestone caverns.

stalagmom'etry (Chem.): The analysis of solutions by means of surface tension measurements.

stall (Eng.): Of an engine, to stop owing to the too sudden application of a brake.

stalling speed (Aero.): The airspeed of an aeroplane at which it experiences its maximum lift.

sta'men (Bot.): One of the members of the flower which produces pollen.

stanchion (Civ. Eng.): A pillar for the support of a superstructure.

sta'sis (Bot.): Stoppage of growth.

star (Astron.): A term for any body that is self-luminous and of the same general nature as the sun though differing in size, distance, etc.

sta'sis (Bot.): Stoppage of growth.

sta'tor (Elec. Eng.): The fixed part of an electrical machine.

steam (Phys.): Water in the vapor state.

steel (Met.): Essentially an alloy of iron and carbon.

steeple (Build.): A structure surmounted with a spire.

stellate (Bot., Zool.): Radiating from a center, like a star.

stem (Bot.): The ascending axis of plant.

steno-: A prefix meaning narrow.

stenother'my (Ecol.): Tolerance of only a very narrow range of temperature.

step-down transformer (Elec. Eng.): A transformer for changing a high-voltage supply into a low-voltage supply.

stepping (Civ. Eng.): Laying foundations in horizontal steps on sloping ground.

stereo-: A prefix meaning solid, stiff.

stereochemistry (Chem.): The study of the spatial arrangement of the atoms in a molecule.

stereophon'ic (Acous.): Said of reproduced sound in which the illusion of auditory perspective is realized.

stereotax'is (Biol.): Response of an organism to the stimulus of contact with a solid body.

sterile: Unable to breed.

sterilization (Bot., Zool.): (1) Loss of sexual function. (2) The preparation, usually by heating, of a substratum free from any living organism, on which fungi or bacteria may subsequently be grown in pure culture.

steth'oscope (Med.): A tube adapted for listening to the sounds produced in the body.

stigma (Bot.): The distal end of the style on which pollen alights and germinates.

stimulus (Bot., Zool.): An agent which will provoke active reaction in a living organism.

sting (Zool.): A sharp-pointed organ by means of which a poison can be injected into a victim.

sti'pate (Bot.): Crowded.

stip'ule (Bot.): One of the two appendages, usually leaf-like, present at the base of the petiole of a leaf.

sto'a (Arch.): A covered portico or collonade.

stock (Bot.): A race. (Gen., Zool.): A direct line of descent.

stoke (Eng.): To supply fuel to a boiler furnace by mechanical means.

sto'lon (Bot.): A weak stem, growing horizontally from the main stem of the plant.

sto'ma: A small aperture.

stomach (Zool.): In vertebrates, the sac-like portion of the alimentary canal between the oesophagus and the intestines.

stone (Bot.): The hard endocarp of a drupe.

story (Build.): The part of a building included between two adjacent floors.

straight (Surv.): A straight or tangent length connecting curves in a highway or railway.

strain (Bot., Zool.): A variety of a species, with distinct physiological and/or morphological characters.

stratification (Geol.): The layering in sedimentary rocks due to changes in the rate of deposition, or in the nature of the sediment.

strat'osphere (Meteor.): A layer of the earth's atmosphere.

stratum (Geol.): A single bed of rock bounded above and below by divisional planes.

streak (Min.): The name given to the color of the powder obtained by scratching a mineral with a knife or file.

streptococ'cus (Bacteriol.): A gram-positive coccus of which the individuals tend to be grouped in chains.

stri'a: A streak, a faint ridge.

strict (Bot.): Stiff and rigid.

strike (Geol.): The horizontal direction which is at right-angles to the dip of a rock.

striped (Bot.): Bearing longitudinal stripes of color.

stripping: Removal of an electro-deposit by any means.

stud (Carp.): An upright scantling in a timber framework. (Eng.): A shank, or headless bolt.

stu'por (Med.): A state of mental and physical inertia.

style (Bot.): The portion of the carpel between the stigma and the ovary.

sty'lobate (Arch.): A continuous pedestal supporting a row of columns.

styp'tic (Med.): Astringent.

sub: A prefix meaning under.

suc'culent (Bot.): Juicy, thick and soft.

sucker (Bot.): A strongly growing shoot arising from the base of a stem or a root.

sullage (Civ. Eng.): The mud deposited by flowing waters.

sulphates (Chem.): Salts of sulphuric acid.

sulphides (Chem.): Salts of hydrosulphuric acid.

sulphur (Chem.): A non-metallic element.

summation (Physiol.): The production of an effect by repetition of causal factor which would be insufficient in a single application.

Sun (Astron.): The central body of the solar system, an incandescent gaseous sphere.

supercooled (Chem.): Cooled below the normal freezing-point without solidification.

superficial: Pertaining to the surface.

supplementary (Zool.): Additional.

supply: A source of energy.

suppression (Bot.): Failure to develop.

surveying: The art of making such measurements of the relative positions of points on the surface of the earth that will enable the features to be depicted in their true relationship by drawing them to scale on paper.

suspension (Chem.): A system in which denser particles are distributed throughout a less dense liquid or gas.

suspension bridge (Civ. Eng.): A bridge suspended from a flexible connection between the two sides.

swab (Med.): Any small mass of cotton or gauze used for mopping up blood, or discharges, or for cleansing surfaces.

swarm (Zool.): A large number of small animals in movement together.

switch (Eng.): A mechanical device for opening and closing an electric circuit.

switching-off (Elec. Eng., etc.): The opening of an electric circuit.

switching-on (Elec. Eng., etc.): The closing of an electric circuit.

sylves'tral (Bot.): Growing in woods.

symbio'sis (Biol.): An internal, mutually beneficial partnership between two organisms.

symptom (Med.): Evidence of disease as experienced by the patient.

syn-, sym-: A prefix meaning with.

synapse (Zool.): The mode of connection of one nerve-cell with another.

syn'desis (Cyt.): In meiotic nuclear division, fusion of homologous chromosomes.

syn'ecology (Bot.): The study of plant communities.

syn'gamy (Bot., Zool.): Fusion of gametes.

synodic month (Astron.): The interval between two successive passages of the moon.

synthetic: Artificial.

system (Biol.): A method or scheme of classification. (Chem.): Any portion of matter which is isolated from other matter. (Elec. Eng.): A general term covering the entire complex of apparatus involved in the transmission and distribution of electric power. (Geol.): The name given to the succession of rocks which were formed during a certain period of geological time.

systems of crystals (Crystal.): The seven large divisions into which all crystallizing substance can be placed.

systematics (Biol.): The branch of biology which deals with nomenclature and classification.

T

tabular (Bot., Geol., Min.): Horizontally flattened.

tacheom'eter (Surv.): An instrument which measures distance from any given point by telescopic observation.

tachom'eter (Eng.): An instrument for indicating the revolutions per minute of a revolving shaft.

tack (Build.): A small clout nail.

tactile (Zool.): Pertaining to the sense of touch.

tail (Aero.): The hindmost horizontal unit of an aeroplane.

talc (Min.): An acid metasilicate of magnesium.

tally (Surv.): A brass tag attached to a chain at every tenth link.

talon (Arch.): An ogee molding. (Zool.): A sharp-hooked claw.

tan'talum (Met., Min.): A metallic element.

tape (Build., Surv.): A long flexible measuring scale.

tapering (Bot.): Said of a leaf base which becomes gradually narrowed towards the petiole.

tapping (Elec. Eng.): A connection taken to an intermediate joint on a winding.

tarnish (Chem.): The discoloration produced on the surface of an exposed metal.

tars-, tarso-: A prefix meaning the sole of the foot.

tarsus (Zool.): The ankle, in vertebrates.

Taurus (Astron.): Bull. Second sign of the Zodiac.

tawny (Bot.): Dark brownish-yellow.

taxi (Aero.): Said of an aircraft that travels under its own power, while in contact with the earth.

taxis (Bot., Zool.): A movement of a whole organism towards or away from a stimulus.

taxon'omy (Biol.): The science of classification as applied to living organisms.

technology: The practice, description and terminology of the applied sciences which have commercial value.

tela (Zool.): A web-like tissue.

telecommunication (Elec. Comm.): Any communication of information by electrical means.

telegraph (Elec. Comm.): A combination of apparatus for conveying messages over a distance by means of electrical impulses.

telegraphy: The electrical communication system whereby messages are transmitted in coded signals by trained operators.

telcme'ter (Elec. Eng.): An instrument for the remote indication of electrical quantities. (Surv.): The general name for an instrument which acts as a distance measurer without the use of a chain.

teleol'ogy (Biol.): The interpretation of animal or plant structures in terms of purpose and utility.

teleph'ony: The transmission of speech-currents over wires.

telescope (Astron.): An optical instrument for making distant objects appear nearer.

television: The electrical transmission of visual scenes and images by wire or radio.

tellu'rium (Met.): A metallic element.

telo-: A prefix meaning end.

telomit'ic (Cyt.): In cell-division, having the chromosomes attached to the fibers of the spindle by their ends.

tel'ophase (Cyt.): The period of reconstruction of nuclei which follows the separation of the daughter chromosomes in mitosis.

temperament (Psychol.): The quantity and quality of the general affective nature of an individual.

temperamental (Psychol.): Displaying alternation of moods.

temperature (Phys.): The degree of heat or cold measured with respect to an arbitrary zero.

tempering (Met.): The reheating of hardened steel at any temperature below the critical range, in order to decrease the hardness.

template (Build.): A long flat stone supporting the end of a beam.

tendon (Zool.): A card or sheet of fibrous tissue by which a muscle is attached to another muscle or to a skeletal structure.

tentacle (Zool.): An elongate, slender, flexible organ having a variety of functions as grasping, feeling, holding, exploring, etc.

ter'bium (Chem.): A metallic element.

terebrate (Zool.): Possessing a sting.

terminal (Bot.): Situated at the tip of anything. (Elec. Eng.): A point of connection in an electrical circuit.

ternary (Chem.): Consisting of three components, etc.

terrestrial: Pertaining to the earth.

terrestrial poles: The two diametrically opposite points in which the earth's axis cuts the earth's surface.

Tertiary (Geol.): the era of geological time during which the strata ranging from the Eocene to the Pliocene were deposited.

test: Any routine or special procedure for ascertaining that apparatus is functioning correctly.

testa (Bot.): The seed coat.

tet'anus (Med.): Lockjaw.

tetra-: A prefix meaning four.

tet'racyte (Bot.): One of the four cells formed after a meiotic division.

tetrad (Cyt.): A bivalent chromosome which shows signs of division into four longitudinal threads.

tetrag'onal system (Crystal.): The crystallographic system in which all the forms are referred to three axes at right-angles.

tetramor'phous (Chem.): Existing in four different crystalline forms.

tet'rapod (Zool.): Having four feet.

tetrav'terous (Zool.): Having four wings.

tetrava'lent (Chem.): Capable of combining with four atoms of hydrogen or their equivalent.

thal'amus (Bot.): The receptacle of a flower.

thallium (Chem.): A metallic element.

than'atoid (Zool.): Deadly.

theod'olite (Surv.): An instrument for measuring horizontal and vertical angles.

theory: A scientific theory is a co-ordinated set of hypotheses which are found to be consistent with one another and with specially observed phenomena.

therapeu'tic (Med.): Curative.

ther'apy (Med.): The curative and preventive medical treatment of disease.

therm-, thermo-: A prefix meaning heat.

thermal (Aero., Meteor.): An ascending current due to local heating of air.

thermal analysis (Met.): The use of cooling or heating curves in the study of changes in metals and alloys.

thermal dissociation (Chem.): The dissociation of certain molecules under the influence of heat.

thermal resistance (Elec. Eng.): Resistance to the flow of heat.

thermion'ics: The science dealing with the emission of electrons from hot bodies.

thermochemistry (Chem.): The study of the heat changes accompanying chemical reactions.

thermoduric (Phys.): Resistant to heat.

thermodynam'ics (Phys.): The mathematical treatment of the relation of heat to mechanical and other forms of energy.

thermogen'esis (Zool.): Production of heat within the body.

thermo'graph (Meteor.): A continuously recording thermometer.

thermol'ysis (Chem.): The dissociation of a molecule by heat. (Zool.): Loss of body heat.

thermometer: An instrument for measuring temperature.

thermonuclear reaction (Phys.): Nuclear reaction induced by heat.

ther'mophyte (Bot.): A plant growing in warm situations.

thermoplastic (Chem.): Becoming plastic on being heated.

thermoscop'ic: Perceptive of change of temperature.

ther'mostat: A device for maintaining an inclosure at a constant temperature.

thor'ium (Chem.): A radio-active metallic element.

thorn (Bot.): A leaf or shoot which contains vascular tissue and ends in a hard sharp point.

three-point landing (Aero.): The normal perfect landing of an aeroplane.

thrombo'sis (Med.): The formation of a clot in a blood vessel. (Zool.): Coagulation.

thrust: Propulsive force developed by a jet-propelled motor.

thu'lium (Chem.): A metallic element.

thunder (Meteor.): The noise which accompanies a flash of lightning; its origin is in the violent thermal changes accompanying the discharge, which causes non-periodic wave disturbances in the air.

tide (Astron.): The effect of the gravitational attraction of the moon on the waters of the earth.

tide gauge (Surv.): An apparatus for determining the variation of sea-level with time.

tie (Eng.): A frame member sustaining a tensile load.

tile (Build): A thin slab of baked clay, cement, glass or terra-cotta used for roofing or for covering floors or walls.

timber: Felled logs or trees suitable for sawing.

time: (Astron.): In its astronomical sense of a measured quantity, essentially a measure of angle; the fundamental unit of time measurement is supplied by the earth's rotation on its axis.

tin (Met.): A metallic element.

tissue (Biol.): An aggregate of similar cells forming a definite and continuous fabric.

tissue culture (Bot., Zool.): The growth of detached pieces of tissue in nutritive fluids under conditions which exclude fungi and bacteria.

tita'nium (Met.): A metallic element.

tolerance (Bot.): The ability of a plant to endure adverse environmental conditions, and also to withstand the development of a parasite within it without showing signs of a serious disease.

ton: A unit of weight for large quantities; 1 ton = 2,000 lbs.

tone: (Acous.): Strictly, a sound-wave of one frequency. (Zool.): The condition of elasticity or tension to the living tissues of the animal body, especially muscles.

tongue (Zool.): In vertebrates, the moval muscular organ lying on, and attached to, the floor of the buccal cavity; used in connection with tasting, mastication and swallowing.

tonsils (Zool.): In vertebrates, lymphoid bodies situated at the junction of the buccal cavity and the pharynx.

tooth (Bot.): Any small irregularity on the margin of a leaf. (Zool.): A hard projecting body with a masticatory function.

topochem'istry (Chem.): The study of reactions which occur only at certain definite regions in a system.

topog'raphy (Surv.): The delineation of the natural and artificial features of an area.

torna'do (Meteor.): An intensely destructive, advancing whirlwind formed from strongly ascending currents.

torque (Mech.): The fluctuating or uniform turning moment exerted by a tangential force acting at a distance from the axis of rotation or twist.

torrent'icolis (Ecol.): Animals living in swiftly running waters.

Torrid Zone (Astron.): The region of the earth bounded by the two tropics and bisected by the equator.

torsion: The state of strain set up in a part by twisting. (Bot.): Twisting without marked displacement.

torsion balance (Phys.): A delicate device for measuring small forces such as those due to gravitation, magnetism or electric charges.

tor'ticone (Zool.): A spirally twisted shell.

tor'us (Bot.): The receptacle of a flower. (Zool.): A fold or ridge.

totipo'tent (Zool.): Capable of development into a complete embryo or organ.

toughness (Met.): A term denoting a condition intermediate between softness and brittleness.

tourniquet (Surg.): Any appliance, which by means of a constricting band, a pad to lie over the artery, and a device for tightening it, exerts pressure on the artery and controls the bleeding from it.

tower (Elec. Eng.): The lattice-type steel structure used to carry the several conductors of a transmission line at a considerable height above the ground.

toxicol'ogy (Med.): That branch of medical science which deals with the nature and effects of poisons.

trache'a (Bot.): The windpipe leading from the glottis to the lungs, in air breathing vertebrates.

tracho'ma (Med.): A highly contagious infection of the conjunctiva covering the eyelids.

tract (Zool.): The extent of an organ or system.

tractile fiber (Cyt.): A spindle fiber which begins to develop from an attachment to a chromosome and extends to the pole of the spindle.

traction: The propulsion of vehicles.

tractor: A vehicle capable of propelling itself along a track or road, or for drawing other vehicles.

trade-winds (Meteor.): A drying wind blowing almost continually in the same course toward the equator but from an easterly direction. The trade wind blows from n.e. to s.w. on the north side of the equator, and from s.e. to n.w. on the south side of the equator.

traffic lights (Elec Eng.): Red, amber and green signal-lights installed at street intersections, etc., for controlling the flow of traffic.

trails (Astron.): Long flashes of brightness seen in the wake of some large meteors in the sky.

tramontan'a (Meteor.): A northerly mountain wind blowing over Italy.

transcription (Elec. Comm.): The recording of a broadcast performance for subsequent re-broadcast.

tran'sect (Bot.): A line of vegetation marked off for study.

transference (Psycho-an.): The displacement of affect, positive or negative, from the person to whom it was originally directed, on to another.

transformer (Elec. Comm.): An electromagnetic device for separating electrical circuits while permitting the flow of electrical power from one to the other.

transforming station (Elec. Eng.): A point on an electricity supply system where a change of supply voltage occurs.

transfusion (Med.): The operation of transferring the blood of one person into the veins of another.

translocation (Bot.): The movement of material in solution inside the body of the plant. (Cyt.): The transfer of a portion of a chromosome, either to another part of the same chromosome, or to a different chromosome.

translucent (Bot., Min., etc.): More or less transparent.

transmission (Elec. Comm., Elec. Eng.): The conveying of electrical energy over a distance.

transmission line (Elec. Eng.): The overhead conductor system by which electric power is transmitted at high voltage from one place to another.

transmitter (Elec. Comm.): A generic term for the device which transmits electrical power under the control of some signal, conveyed mechanically.

transmutation (Chem.): The conversion of one element into another.

transpiration (Aero.): The flow of gas along relatively long passages. (Bot.): The loss of water vapor from a plant.

transplantation (Surg., Zool.): Grafting.

transuranic (Phys.): Pertaining to an element of atomic weight greater than that of uranium.

transverse (Bot., Zool., etc.): Broader than long.

trapez'ioid: Shaped like a triangle with one corner cut off.

trau'ma (Med.): (1) A wound or bodily injury. (2) Emotional shock.

trav'erse (Surv.): A survey consisting of a set of connected lines whose lengths and directions are measured.

tread (Build.): The horizontal part of a step.

tree (Bot.): A tall woody perennial plant having a well-marked trunk and few branches persisting from the basal parts.

trench (Civ. Eng.): A long narrow excavation for drains, pipes, etc.

tri-: A prefix meaning three.

triangular: Having three angles.

triax'on (Zool.): Having three axes.

triba'sic (Chem.): Containing three replaceable hydrogen atoms in a molecule.

tribe (Bot.): A section of a family consisting of a number of related genera.

tri'choid (Zool.): Hair-like.

triclin'ic system (Crystal.): The crystallographic system which includes all the forms referred to three unequal axes which are not at right-angles.

trigger (Chem.): The agent which causes the initial decomposition of a chain reaction.

triplet (Chem.): A chemical bond which consists of three electrons shared between two atoms. (Bot.): Individuals resulting from the division of the ovum into three parts, each then developing.

troph-, tro'pho-: A prefix meaning nourishment.

Tropics (Astron.): The name given to those two parallels of celestial latitude which pass through the solstices, and which therefore represent the limits of the sun's extreme north and south declinations.

tro'pism (Physiol.): A reflex response to an external stimulus, involving movements of the whole body rather than a part.

tro'posphere (Meteor.): The lower part of the earth's atmosphere, in which the temperature decreases with height.

trunk (Anat., Zool.): The body, apart from the limbs. (Arch.): The shaft of a column. (Bot.): The upright, massive main stem of a tree.

tuber (Bot.): A swollen underground stem.

tu'bercle (Bot.): A general name for a small swelling. (Zool.): A small rounded projection.

tufa (Geol.): A porous form of calcium carbonate, which is deposited from solution around springs.

tumor (Med.): Any swelling or enlargement.

tung'sten (Met.): A metallic element.

tu'nicate (Bot.): Having a coat or covering.

tunnel (Civ. Eng.): An underground horizontal passage through which passes a road, canal, railway, etc.

turbojet (Aero.): An internal-combustion aero-engine comprising compressors and turbines, of which the net gas energy is used for reaction propulsion through a propelling nozzle.

tur'gid (Bot.): Said of a cell which is distended and tense, well supplied with water.

tur'pentine (Chem.): An oil obtained by the steam distillation of rosin.

twin: One of a pair of two. (Biol.): (1) Individuals arising from the division into two of the fertilized egg, each part proceeding to develop. (2) In mammals, two individuals produced at the same birth.

type (Biol.): The individual specimen on which the description of a new species or genus is based.

typhoon (Meteor.): A cyclone.

U

ulcer (Med.): A localized destruction of an epithelial surface of the skin or of the gastric mucous membrane, forming an open sore.

uliginous (Bot.): Growing in wet places.

ulno-: A prefix meaning elbow.

ulot'richous (Zool.): Having wooly or curly hair.

ultra-centrifuge (Chem.): A high-speed centrifuge for the separation of submicroscope particles.

ultra-filtration (Chem.): The separation of colloidal particles by filtration, under suction or pressure, through a colloidal filter or semi-permeable membrane.

ultramicrobe (Biol.): An agent of obscure nature, able to cause disease in organisms, but too small to be visible with the microscope.

ultrasonics (Acous.): The science of mechanical vibrations and radiations in solids, gas and fluids, which have frequencies in excess of those which, in a soundwave, are normally perceivable by the ear.

ultra-violet radiation (Phys.): Invisible radiations of wave-length less than 3900 A.U.—the limit of visibility at the violet end of the spectrum.

umbel (Bot.): An inflorescence consisting of numerous small flowers in flat-topped groups, borne on stalks all arising from about the same point on the main stem.

umbil'ical cord (Anat., Zool.): In eutherian mammals, the bascular cord connecting the foetus with the placenta.

umbil'icate (Bot.): Having a small central depression.

umbra (Astron.): The dark central portion of the shadow of a large body such as the earth or moon.

umbrella (Zool.): A flat cone-shaped structure.

um'brine (Bot.): Dull darkish-brown.

unarmed (Bot.): Without prickles or thorns.

u'nary (Chem.): Consisting of one component.

un'cate, un'ciform, un'cinate (Bot., Zool.): Hook-like.

unconformity (Geol.): A geological structure involving two sets of rocks of different ages.

unconscious (Psychol.): A general term used to include all processes which cannot be made conscious by direct effort of will.

underpinning (Build., Civ. Eng.): The operation of rebuilding the lower part of a building without damaging or weakening the superstructure.

undershoot (Aero.): Failure to reach the intended landing area.

un'dulate (Bot.): Having a wavy margin.

undulated (Bot.): With gentle depressions and elevations.

unequal (Bot.): Having the two sides not symmetrical.

unguiculate (Bot., Zool.): Provided with claws.

un'gula (Zool.): A hoof.

Ungula'ta (Zool.): An order of terrestrial mammals.

uni-: A prefix meaning one.

uniaxial (Min.): A term for all the crystalline minerals in which there is only one direction of single refraction.

unicel'lular (Biol.): Consisting of one cell.

unidac'tyl (Zool.): Having one digit.

unilat'eral (Bot.): Said of members which are all inserted on one side of the axis; of a raceme with all flowers turned to one side; of a stimulus falling on the plant from one side.

unilateral conductivity (Elec. Eng.): The property of unipolarity by which current can flow in one direction only.

unilateral impedance (Elec. Comm.): Any device in which power can be transmitted in one direction only.

uniloc'ular (Bot.): Consisting of a single compartment.

uninu'cleate (Biol.): Containing one nucleus.

union (Med.): In the process of healing, the growing together of parts separated by injury.

unionized (Chem.): Not ionized.

unip'arous (Zool.): Giving birth to one offspring at a time.

unipo'lar (Zool.): Said of nerve cells having only one process.

unise'riate (Bot.): Arranged in a single series, layer or row.

unisex'ual (Bot., Zool.): Distinctly male or female.

unit cell (Crystal.): The smallest group of atoms, molecules or ions, whose repetition at regular intervals, in three dimensions, produces the lattice of a given crystal.

unit characters (Gen.): Independent characteristics, which act as units, are traceable in each generation.

univa'lent (Cyt.): One of the single chromosomes which separate in the first meiotic division. (Chem.): Monovalent.

u'nivalve (Zool.): In one piece.

universal time (Astron.): A system of time reckoning adopted by international agreement.

unsaturated (Chem.): Less concentrated than a saturated vapor or solution.

unstable (Chem.): Subject to spontaneous change.

uran'inite (Min.): When massive, known as pitchblende.

ura'nium (Chem.): A metallic, radioactive element.

U'ranus (Astron.): The seventh planet in the solar

system in order of distance from the sun.

ured-, uredo-: A prefix meaning a blight.

urine (Zool.): In vertebrates, the excretory product elaborated by the kidneys, usually of a fluid nature.

urinogen'ital (Zool.): Pertaining to the urinary and genital systems.

urn (Bot.): The capsule of a moss.

urol'ogy (Med.): That part of medical science which deals with diseases and abnormalities of the urinary tract and their treatment.

uros'copy (Med.): The scientific examination of urine for diagnostic purposes.

utero-: A prefix meaning womb.

uterus (Zool.): In female mammals, the muscular posterior part of the oviduct in which the foetus is lodged during the prenatal period.

u'va (Bot.): A berry formed from a superior ovary.

u'vea (Zool.): In vertebrates, the posterior pigment-bearing layer of the iris of the eye.

V

vacancy (Crystal.): Absence of an atom in a crystal pattern.

vaccination (Med.): (1) Inoculation into the skin of the virus of vaccinia in order to immunize the person against smallpox. (2) The therapeutic application of a vaccine made from any micro-organism.

vac'cine (Med.): A preparation of any micro-organism or virus, treated so as to lose its virulence, for introduction into the body in order to stimulate antibodies to the micro-organisms introduced, so as to confer immunity against any subsequent infection by the same type of micro-organism.

vac'uole (Biol.): A small cavity in cytoplasm, generally containing fluid.

vacuum (Phys.): A region in which the gas pressure is considerably lower than atmospheric pressure.

vagina (Zool.): Any sheath-like structure.

valency (Chem.): The combining power of an atom or group in terms of hydrogen atoms. (Zool.): The numerical arrangement of the chromosomes in a nucleus.

valley (Geol.): Any hollow tract of ground between hills or mountains.

valve (Zool.): Any structure which controls the passage of material through a tube or aperture.

vane (Build.): A weathercock. (Surv.): A disc attachment to a levelling staff.

vaporization (Chem.): The conversion of a liquid or a solid into a vapor.

vapor (Phys.): A gas which is at a temperature below its critical temperature and therefore can be liquefied by a suitable increase in pressure.

vapor pressure (Phys.): The pressure exerted by a vapor.

variable stars (Astron.): Those stars whose apparent magnitudes are not constant but vary over a range.

variance (Maths.): The square of the standard deviation.

variant (Biol.): A specimen differing slightly in its characteristics from the type.

variation (Biol.): The difference between the offspring of a single mating; the difference between the individuals of a race, species, etc.

var'icose (Bot.): Dilated.

variegated (Bot., etc.): Marked irregularly with diverse color.

variety (Biol.): A race; a breed; a stock; a subspecie.

vas (Zool.): A vessel or tube carrying fluid.

vascular (Bot., Zool.): Pertaining to vessels which convey fluids or provide for the circulation of fluids.

vascular system (Zool.): The organs responsible for the circulation of blood and lymph, collectively.

vasofor'mative (Zool.): Pertaining to the formation of blood vessels or blood.

vault (Build.): (1) An arched ceiling or roof. (2) An underground room.

vector (Maths.): A vector is one which has magnitude and which is related to a given direction in space. (Biol.): Any agent which transmits a virus disease from one host to another.

vector ratio (Elec. Comm., Elec. Eng.): The ratio between two alternating quantities.

veering (Meteor.): A change in the direction of the arrival of the wind in a clockwise direction.

vegetation (Bot.): The whole of the plants in a given area.

vegetative functions (Zool.): The autonomic or involuntary functions, as circulation, digestion.

vegetative reproduction (Zool.): Propagation by budding.

vein (Bot.): One of the smaller strands of conducting tissues in a leaf. (Geol.): An irregular minor intrusion in rocks. (Zool.): A vessel conveying blood back to the heart from the various organs of the body.

velocity (Mech.): Rate of change of position or rate of displacement, expressed in feet per second.

velum (Zool.): A veil-like structure.

velu'tinous (Bot.): Having a velvety surface.

velvet (Zool.): The tissue layers covering a growing antler.

venation (Bot., Zool.): The arrangement of the veins.

venomous (Zool.): Provided with poison-secreting glands.

vent (Aero.): The opening in a parachute canopy which stabilizes it by allowing the air to escape at a controlled rate.

ventilating fan (Elec. Eng.): An electrically driven fan whose function is to force cooling air through the ventilating ducts of an electrical machine.

ventilating tissue (Bot.): The sum total of the intercellular spaces in a plant, through which air circulates.

ventilation (Build., etc.): The process of replacement of vitiated air by fresh air.

ventilator (Build.): A device employed in order to promote and maintain ventilation.

ventral (Bot.): (1) In front. (23) Uppermost. (3) Nearest to the axis.

ven'tricle (Zool.): A chamber, especially the cavities of the vertebrate brain and the main contractile chamber of the heart.

ventro-, ventri-: A prefix meaning belly.

Venus (Astron.): The second planet in the solar system in order of distance from the sun.

veranda (Build.): A covered external balcony along the outside of a building.

veranil'lo (Meteor.): The short period of fine weather which ends the rainy season in the tropical countries of America.

veran'o (Meteor.): The dry season in the tropical countries of America.

vermic'ular (Bot.): Shaped like a worm.

vermic'ulites (Min.): A group of hydrous silicates.

ver'miform (Zool.): Worm-like.

vernal (Bot.): Of spring.

vernation (Bot.): The manner in which the leaves are packed in a bud.

vertebra (Zool.): One of the bony skeletal elements which compose the backbone.

vertex (Zool.): In higher vertebrates, the highest point in the skull.

vertigo (Med.): Dizziness.

vesic'ular (Bot., Zool.): Like a bladder.

vespoid (Zool.): Wasp-like.

vessel (Bot.): A long water-conducting tube in the xylem. (Zool.): A duct with definitive walls.

vestibule (Build.): A small antechamber just inside the entrance of a building.

vestigial (Zool.): A small or reduced structure.

ves'titure (Bot., Zool.): A covering as hairs, fur, scales, feathers.

vet'erinary: Relating to the science which treats of the diseases of domestic animals.

viable (Bot., Zool.): Capable of living and developing normally.

viaduct (Civ. Eng.): A structure which carries a road across a wide and deep valley.

vinegar (Chem.): The product of the alcoholic and acetic fermentation of fruit juices.

Virgo (Astron.) : Virgin ; the sixth sign of the Zodiac.

virology : The study of viruses.

vir'ulence (Bot.) : The capacity of a parasite to cause disease.

virus (Med., Bot.) : A particulate infective agent, smaller than accepted bacterial forms, that causes many diseases in man.

viscid (Bot.) : Said of a surface which is glutinous and covered by a sticky secretion.

viscosity (Phys.) : Internal friction due to molecular cohesion in fluids.

vis'cus (Med.) : Any one of the organs situated within the chest and the abdomen.

vise (Eng.) : A clamping device used for holding work that is to be operated on.

visibility (Meteor.) Ability to observe distant objects through suspended water-droplets in the atmosphere.

vital stain (Bot., Zool.) : A stain which can be used on living cells without killing them.

vi'tamins (Chem., Med.) : Organic substances required, in relatively small amounts, for the proper functioning of the animal organism.

vitelline (Bot., Zool.) : Pertaining to yolk ; egg-yellow.

vivip'arous (Bot.) : Producing young plants in place of flowers. (Zool.) : Giving birth to living young which have already reached an advanced stage of development.

vocal cords (Zool.) : In air-breathing vertebrates, folds of the lining membrane of the larynx which vibrate under the influence of breath and thereby the voice is produced.

voids (Civ. Eng.) : The spaces between the separate particles in a mass of granular material.

volant (Zool.) : Flying.

volcanic ash (Geol.) : The typical product of explosive volcanic eruptions, consisting of rock and lava.

volca'no (Geol.) : A center of volcanic eruption, having the form of a mountain, built of ashes and lava-flows with a central crater from which a pipe leads down to the source of magma beneath.

volt (Elec.) : The unit of electromotive force.

volt-ampere (Elec.) : Unit of apparent power.

voltage (Elec.) : The value of an electromotive force, expressed in volts.

voltaic current (Elec.) : Current produced by chemical action.

voltam'eter (Elec. Eng.) : An instrument for measuring a current.

voltmeter (Elec.) : An instrument, calibrated in volts, for measuring potential differences directly.

volume (Acous.) : The general loudness of sounds.

volumetric analysis (Chem.) : A form of chemical analysis using standard solutions for the estimation of the particular constituent present in solution.

voluntary (Zool.) : Under control of the will.

vortex (Aero.) : An eddy, or intense spiral motion in a limited region.

vulcanites (Geol.) : A general name for igneous rocks of fine grain-size.

W

wad (Min.) : Bog manganese.

waist : A narrowed-down, constricted part of an object.

wale (Civ. Eng.) : A horizontal timber used to bind together piles driven in a row.

wall plug (Elec. Eng.) : A plug-in device for connecting a flexible conductor to a circuit terminal in the form of a wall socket.

walling (Civ. Eng.) : A general term for masonry walls.

warm-blooded (Zool.) : Said of animals which have the bodily temperature constantly maintained at a point usually above the environmental temperature, of which it is independent.

warm front (Meteor.) : The leading edge of a mass of advancing warm air as it rises over colder air.

wart (Bot.) : A small blunt-topped rounded upgrowth. (Med.) : A tumor of the skin formed by overgrowth of the prickle-cell layer.

washer (Build., Eng.) : An annular piece used under a nut to distribute pressure, or between jointing surfaces to make a tight joint.

water (Chem., Phys.) : A colorless, odorless, tasteless fluid formed when hydrogen burns in oxygen.

water balance (Bot.) : The ratio between the water taken in by a plant and the water lost by it.

water culture (Bot.) : An experimental means of determining the mineral requirements of a plant.

water-gauge (Eng.) : A vertical or inclined protected glass tube connected to the steam and water spaces of a boiler, for showing the height of the water level.

water-level (Surv.) : An instrument for establishing a horizontal line of sight.

waterlogged (Civ. Eng.) : A term applied to ground when it is saturated with water.

waterproofing : The process of rendering materials impervious to water.

water-table (Geol.) : The surface below which fissures and pores in the strata are saturated with water.

watt (Elec. Eng.) : A unit of electric power.

watt-hour (Elec. Eng.) : The unit of electrical energy, being the work done by 1 watt acting for 1 hour.

wattmeter (Elec. Eng.) : An instrument that measures the circuit power in watts.

wave (Phys.) : A single pulse in a vibrational disturbance advanced through a body or an elastic medium.

wavelength (Elec. Eng.) : The distance between two similar and successive points on an alternating wave.

wax pocket (Zool.) : In bees, a ventral abdominal pouch which secretes wax.

weathering (Build.) : The deliberate slope at which an approximately horizontal surface is built or laid so that it be able to throw off the rain. (Geol.) : The processes of disintegration and decomposition effected in minerals and rocks as a consequence of exposure to the elements.

web (Zool.) : The mesh of silk threads produced by some insects and spiders. Also the membrane connecting the toes in aquatic vertebrates.

weed (Bot.) : A plant growing where it is not wanted by man.

weight : The gravitational force acting on a body.

weir (Civ. Eng.) : A dam placed across a river to raise its level in dry weather.

welding (Eng.) : The joining of two iron or steel pieces by heat.

well (Civ. Eng.) : A shaft sunk in the ground for procuring a supply of underground waters.

wet steam (Eng.) : A steam-water mixture.

wettability (Chem.) : The extent to which a solid is wetted by a liquid.

whalebone (Zool.) : Baleen.

wheel base (Eng.) : The distance between the leading and trailing axles of a vehicle.

whirlwind (Meteor.) : A small rotating wind-storm which may extend upwards to a height of many hundred feet.

white light (Phys.) : Light containing all wavelengths in the visible range at the same intensity.

whorl (Bot.) : A group of similar members arising from the same level on a stem, and forming a circular group around it. (Zool.) : A single turn of a spirally coiled shell or other spiral structure.

wilting (Bot.) : The loss of rigidity in leaves and young stems following the loss of water from the plant.

winch (Eng.) : A hand power hoisting machine attached to a crane.

wind (Meteor.) : Air in motion naturally.

wind pollination (Bot.) : The conveyance of pollen by the wind.

wind pump (Civ. Eng.) : A pump which is operated by the force of the wind rotating a multi-bladed propeller.

wind tunnel (Aero.) : Apparatus for producing a steady airstream past a model for aerodynamic investigations.

winding (Elec. Eng.) : The system of insulated conductors forming the current-carrying element of a

Science Terms

dynamo-electric machine.

window (Elec. Eng.) : The winding space of a transformer. (Geol.) : A closed outcrop of strata lying beneath a thrust plane and exposed by denudation.

wing (Bot.) : A flattened outgrowth from a seed or a fruit, serving in wind dispersal. (Build.) : A section of a building projecting from the principal part of it. (Zool.) : Any broad flat expansion; an organ used for flight.

wing nut (Eng.) : A nut with wings similar to those of a butterfly to enable it to be turned by thumb and fingers.

wire gauge (Eng.) : Any system of designating the size of wires by means of numbers.

wirephoto (Elec. Comm.) : A photograph transmitted over a wire circuit by electrical means.

wolf'ramite (Min.) : An important ore of tungsten.

woody tissues (Bot.) : Tissues which are hard because of the presence of lignin in the cell walls.

wool (Bot.) : A tangled mass of long, soft, whitish hairs on a plant. (Zool.) : A modification of hair.

work (Mech.) : Work is done when the point of application of a force moves along the line of action of the force.

working chamber (Civ. Eng.) : The compressed-air chamber at the base of a hollow caisson.

worm (Zool.) : A term loosely used to indicate any elongate invertebrate without appendages.

wow (Acous.) : Rhythmic or arrhythmic change in reproduced sound, arising from fluctuation in speed, of either recorder or reproducer.

X

x-body (Bot.) : An inclusion in a plant cell suffering from a virus disease.

x-chromosome (Cyt.) : A heterochromosome associated with sex determination.

x-generation (Bot.) : The gametes.

X-rays (Phys.) : Electromagnetic waves of short wavelength which are produced when cathode rays impinge on matter.

xanth-, xantho- : A prefix meaning yellow.

xanthoch'roism (Zool.) : A condition in which all skin pigments other than yellow and golden ones disappear, as in goldfish.

xanth'ophyll (Bot., Zool.) : One of the two yellow pigments present in the normal chlorophyll mixture of green plants.

xe'mia (Bot.) : The effect of the pollen upon the characters of the young plant resulting from pollination.

xe'nogamy (Bot.) : Pollination of a flower from a flower of the same species but on another plant.

xe'nolith (Geol.) : A fragment of rock of extraneous origin which has been incorporated in magma, and occurs as an inclusion.

xe'non (Chem.) : A zero-valent element; one of the rare gases.

xerophyt'ic (Bot.) : Able to withstand drought.

xiphoid (Zool.) : Sword-shaped.

xy'lem (Bot.) : Wood.

xylogenous, xylophilous (Bot., Zool.) : Growing on wood; living in or on wood.

xylophagous (Zool.) : Wood-eating.

xylotomous (Zool.) : Wood-cutting; wood-boring.

Y

yaw (Aero.) : The angular motion of an aircraft in a horizontal plane about its normal axis.

year (Astron.) : The calendar year consisting of 365 days in ordinary years and 366 days in leap years, and beginning with January 1.

yeast (Bot.) : Micro-organisms producing zymase, which induces the alcoholic fermentation of carbohydrates.

yield point (Met.) : The stress at which a substantial amount of plastic deformation takes place under constant or reduced load.

yoke (Civ. Eng.) : Stout timbers around the shuttering for a column to secure the part during the process of pouring and setting. (Elec. Eng.) : The field poles of an electrical machine.

yolk (Zool.) : The nutritive non-living material contained by an ovum.

yolk sac (Zool.) : The yolk-containing sac which is attached to the embryo by the yolk stalk.

yolk stalk (Zool.) : A short stalk by which the yolk sac is attached to the embryo and by which the yolk substance may pass into the alimentary canal of the embryo.

ytter'bium (Chem.) : A metallic element.

ytt'rium (Chem.) : A metallic element.

Z

zenith (Astron.) : The point on the celestial sphere vertically above the observer's head; one of the two poles of the horizon, the other being the nadir.

zenith distance (Astron.) : The angular distance from the zenith of a heavenly body.

zenith telescope (Astron.) : An instrument used to determine latitude.

ze'olites (Min.) : A group of amino-silicates.

zeph'yr (Meteor.) : A warm westerly wind blowing in the Mediterranean.

zero-potential (Elec. Eng.) : Earth potential in electric circuits.

zero-valent (Chem.) : Incapable of combining with other atoms.

zeu'gite (Bot.) : A cell in which nuclear fusion occurs.

zinc (Met.) : A white metallic element.

zircon (Min.) : A tetragonal mineral distributed in igneous and sedimentary rocks.

Zo'diac (Astron.) : A Greek name given to the belt of stars through which the ecliptic passes centrally.

zo'id (Bot.) : A zoospore.

zoid'ioph'lous (Bot.) : Pollinated by animals.

zona (Zool.) : A zone.

zonation (Bot.) : (1) The formation of bands of different colors on the surface of a plant. (2) The occurrence of vegetation in well-marked bands, each band having its characteristic dominant species.

zone (Bot.) : A band of color, or of hairs or other surface feature. (Chem.) : A region of oriented molecules. (Geol.) : A subdivision of a stratigraphical series.

zoning (Aero.) : The specification of areas in which there is a known clearance for the safe landing and taking-off of airplanes.

zo'o : A prefix meaning animal.

zo'obiot'ic (Biol.) : Parasitic on, or living in association with, an animal.

zo'ochor'ous (Bot.) : Said of seeds or spores dispersed by animals.

zo'ogam'ete (Zool.) : A motile gamete.

zoogamy (Zool.) : Sexual reproduction of animals.

zo'ogeog'raphy (Zool.) : The study of animal distribution.

zooming (Aero.) : Utilizing the kinetic energy of an aircraft in order to gain height.

zo'oplank'ton (Zool.) : Floating and drifting animal life.

zo'ospore (Bot.) : An asexual reproductive cell which can swim by means of flagella.

zyg-, zy'go- : A prefix meaning yoke.

zygobran'chiate (Zool.) : Having paired, symmetrically placed gills.

zy'gophase (Biol.) : The diploid portion of the life-history.

zy'gopleur'y (Zool.) : Bilateral symmetry.

zy'gote (Bot., Zool.) : The product of the union of two gametes.

zy'gotene (Cyt.) : The second stage of meiotic prophase, in which the chromatin threads approximate in pairs and become loops.

zy'mase (Chem.) : An enzyme inducing the alcoholic fermentation of carbohydrates.

zymot'ic (Med.) : Pertaining to or causing an infectious disease.

OUTLINE
OF
U. S.
HISTORY

OUTLINE OF
U.S. HISTORY

PART I

I. European Background to United States History
II. English Colonies in North America, 1607-1732
III. Life in the English Colonies
IV. The Colonies' Move Toward Rebellion and Unification, 1763-1789
V. The Constitution of the United States
VI. The Period of the Federalist Control, 1789-1801
VII. The Period of Jefferson's Administration, 1801-1809
VIII. James Madison, President in 1809, and the War of 1812
IX. An Era of Common National Purpose, 1815-1824
X. The Reign of the People's President, Andrew Jackson, 1829-1837
XI. Social Reform, Cultural Development and Industrial Growth Prior to the Civil War
XII. The Westward Territorial Expansion, 1840-1850
XIII. Background of the Civil War
XIV. The Civil War and Reconstruction, 1861-1877

PART II

I. The Reconstruction Period
II. American International Participation, 1865-1875
III. The New Economic Order Through the Conquest and Settlement of the West
IV. The Administrations of Grant, Hayes, Garfield and Arthur, 1869-1884
V. The First Administration of Grover Cleveland, 1885-1889
VI. The Administration of Benjamin Harrison, 1889-1893
VII. The Second Administration of Grover Cleveland, 1893-1897
VIII. The Cultural and Economic Trends, 1865-1900
IX. The Spanish American War
X. The United States in World Affairs
XI. Theodore Roosevelt's Program of Government
XII. The Progressive Movement Under President Taft
XIII. Woodrow Wilson's Liberalism
XIV. The First World War, 1914-1918
XV. The Peace Movement and Post-War Readjustment
XVI. Post-World War Readjustments in the United States
XVII. The New Deal of Franklin D. Roosevelt
XVIII. The Foreign Policy of the United States Prior to World War II
XIX. World War II
XX. The Post-War Search for Peace
XXI. The Truman Administrations, 1945 to 1953
XXII. The Republican Administration of Dwight D. Eisenhower, 1952-1960
XXIII. The New Frontier Government of John F. Kennedy, 1961-1963
XXIV. November 22, 1963, John Fitzgerald Kennedy, President of the United States, was shot and killed by an assassin
XXV. Summary of the "New Frontier" of President John Fitzgerald Kennedy, 1961-1963
XXVI. Johnson Administration, 1963-1968
XXVII. Nixon Administration, 1969-1974
XXVIII. Ford Administration, 1974-1977
XXIX. Carter Administration, 1977-

APPENDIX

Entry of States into the Union
Presidents of United States
Structure of the National Government
Index Guide to the Constitution
Constitutional Amendments

PART I

I. EUROPEAN BACKGROUND TO UNITED STATES HISTORY

A. **The darkness of the Middle Ages predominated over Europe, 500-1500.**

1. The Great Roman Empire declined.
2. Barbaric tribes overran Europe.
3. The level of civilization sank.
4. Feudalism, poverty and ignorance were indicative of the times.

B. **Bands of Norse sea rovers sailed the northern European coasts, 700-1000 A.D.**

1. These were a Nordic people, ancestors of the modern Norwegians, Swedes, and Danes.
2. They were marauders on the coasts of England, France, Germany and Russia.
3. Not only were they free-booters but also colonizers.
   a. They established a commonwealth in Ireland.
   b. They established frontier settlements in Greenland.
   c. According to Norse Sagas, Lief Ericson discovered Vineland about 1000 A.D.
      (1) This is believed to have been on the eastern shores of North America.
   d. Norse adventurers also visited the coast of Labrador, near the 56th parallel.
4. The period when the Norseman was most active was called the Viking Age.

C. **The Renaissance brought enlightenment to Europe, 1200-1500.**

1. Civilization began to rise again.
2. Learning and literature became important but limited to the wealthy and to the churchmen.
3. John Gutenberg invented the first printing press.
4. Feudalism gave way to strong monarchies.
5. National patriotism was born in England, Spain, Portugal and France.

U.S. HISTORY

D. A geographic awakening took place.

1. The Crusaders, 1096-1270, introduced new ideas and luxurious wares to Europe.

2. Marco Polo and other merchants brought back tales of the wealth in the Orient.

3. Improved methods of navigation were developed.

4. Navigation instruments, as the compass and astrolabe, were developed.

5. A demand for spices, perfumes, silks, and other articles was growing.

6. Land routes were uncertain and transportation expensive.

E. The age of exploration carried European interests into other parts of the world, 1450-1550.

1. A new route to the Indies was found by the Portuguese.
   a. Prince Henry, the Navigator, established a navigation school—1418.
   b. Bartholomew Diaz passed the Cape of Good Hope, at the southern tip of Africa—1488.
   c. Vasco da Gama reached India by sailing around Africa—1498.

2. America was discovered—1492.
   a. Christopher Columbus, an Italian sea-captain, was employed by Spain.
   b. He believed that the earth was a sphere.
   c. He planned to reach the East Indies by sailing westward.
   d. He made four voyages to America, 1492, 1493, 1497 and 1502, never realizing he discovered a new world.

3. Spain and Portugal divided the world.
   a. The papal line of demarcation in 1493 was supplemented by the Treaty of Tordesillas in 1494, and the boundaries were set.
   b. Spain had the rights to all new lands west of an imaginary line drawn between the north and south poles 370 leagues west of the Azores.
   c. Portugal had all new lands east of the line.

4. Voyages of exploration and discovery were made.
   a. John Cabot, an Italian, sponsored by England, laid the first British claim to North America in 1497.
   b. Amerigo Vespucci, after whom America was named, was an Italian, sponsored by Portugal, who sailed down the coast of Brazil and the new World in 1499.

   c. Vasco de Balboa, a Spanish, sponsored by Spain, discovered the Pacific Ocean in 1513.
   d. Ponce de Leon, a Spaniard sponsored by Spain, explored the Florida peninsula in 1513.
   e. Ferdinand Magellan, a Portuguese, sponsored by Spain, was the first to sail around the world in 1519-1522.
   f. Hernando Cortez, a Spaniard, sponsored by Spain, conquered Mexico in 1521.
   g. Francisco Pizarro, Spaniard, sponsored by Spain, conquered Peru in 1531.
   h. Jacques Cartier, a Frenchman, sponsored by France, explored the St. Lawrence River in 1534.
   i. Hernando de Soto, a Spaniard, sponsored by Spain, discovered the Mississippi River in 1539.
   j. Francis Drake, an Englishman, sponsored by England, explored the west coast of North and South America in 1577-80.
   k. Samuel de Champlain, a Frenchman, sponsored by France, founded Quebec in 1608.
   l. Henry Hudson, an Englishman, sponsored by Holland, sailed up the Hudson River in 1609.
   m. Rene de La Salle, a Frenchman, sponsored by France, explored the Mississippi River to its mouth in 1682.

F. European governments promoted colonization.

1. Spain became a great explorer and colonizer.
   a. Cortez invaded Mexico and conquered Montezuma and his followers in 1519-21.
   b. Hernando de Soto reached Florida and explored as far west as Oklahoma.
   c. The Coronado expedition, 1540-41, crossed the Rio Grande River and explored what was later to become Texas, Oklahoma and Kansas.
   d. First permanent Spanish settlement was on the island of Hispaniola, now Haiti, in 1493.
   e. Cuba was settled in 1508.
   f. Pizarro occupied Peru in 1531-33.
   g. The first permanent settlement in what is now the United States was in St. Augustine, Florida in 1565.

h. At the height of Spain's empire, she controlled most of South America, Central America, Mexico, Florida, California and most of the West Indies.

2. Spain promoted colonization for gold and for converting the natives to Catholicism.
   a. They introduced European methods of industry and agriculture.
   b. They founded churches, missions and schools.
   c. They exploited the gold and silver mines.
   d. They enslaved the natives as well as the Negro slaves imported from Africa.
   e. The form of government was autocratic.
   f. Trade was restricted to Spain only.
   g. Taxation was extremely high.

3. Holland began explorations and settlements.
   a. Henry Hudson explored the coast from Virginia to Newfoundland in 1609.
   b. Dutch fur-traders traded with the Indians.
   c. The Dutch West India Company founded New Amsterdam, now New York, on Manhattan Island in 1623.
   d. The Dutch governor, Peter Stuyvesant annexed Swedish settlements near the Delaware River.
   e. The basis of Dutch colonization was the patroon system.
   f. The chief source of wealth was fur trading.
   g. The Dutch empire was ended in 1664 by the British who took over the colony of New Amsterdam, changing its name to New York.

4. France began its empire building in the 17th century.
   a. The St. Lawrence Valley and the Great Lakes basin were secured.
   b. The explorations of Father Marquette and La Salle gave France claim to the Mississippi Valley, Louisiana territory.
   c. The French population migrated slowly.
   d. Chief occupations were fur trapping and trading.
   e. French missionaries converted Indians to Christianity.
   f. The government was a centralized despotism.

g. The French Empire was later overthrown by the British.

II. **ENGLISH COLONIES IN NORTH AMERICA, 1607-1732.**

A. **England became interested in overseas expansion.**

1. Colonies would provide raw materials in exchange for finished products from England.
2. The lure of finding gold and silver was exciting.
3. England would become more self-sufficient if the colonies would produce commodities for the mother country.
4. The unemployed and over-population could be sent to the colonies.
5. England wanted to control North American fisheries.
6. Religious dissenters would have a haven for religious freedom from the divine right rule of the Stuart monarchy.
7. England would develop prestige as a national power and weaken Spain.

B. **The English government used two methods to colonize.**

1. The chartered trading company operated under royal charters.
   a. They were composed of stockholders who shared the profits and losses of the colonial venture.
   b. The directors were more interested in profits than in the colonists.
2. The proprietorships, one or more persons, received royal grants and political power to colonize.

C. **The London Company and the Plymouth Company were organized to establish colonies in Virginia.**

1. King James granted the companies a charter with 6 provisions.
   a. The London Company could establish a settlement between 34° and 41° north latitude; the Plymouth Company between 38° and 45°.
   b. Each company would own the land 50 miles north and south of the colony and 100 miles in from the coast.
   c. Neither company could make or settle a colony in the common territory between 38° and 41°.
   d. A council of 13 men in England, appointed by the king, managed the companies.
   e. Local councils in America supervised Indian trade and preserved order.
   f. The colonists were given the same rights they had in England.
2. The Plymouth Company made an un-

successful attempt to colonize in Maine in 1607.

3. The London Company established the first permanent settlement in Virginia in 1607.
    a. At first the Virginia colony was a failure.
    b. The mistakes made benefited the colonies that were to follow.
4. England changed the form of the Virginia government.
    a. The council was replaced by a governor with a council as an advisory board.
    b. The boundary was changed to include 200 miles north and south of Point Comfort.
    c. The Virginia Company obtained the right to govern itself.
    d. The joint-stock system was ended.
    e. District representatives, called burgesses, were elected and met with the governor and council to pass legislation.
    f. The Virginia Company was dissolved in 1624 and the colony reverted to the King because of inefficiency and political opposition.
    g. The burgesses and councilors met as an upper and lower house after 1676.
        (1) The governor and council were appointed by the King.
        (2) The burgesses were elected by the colony.
        (3) The Virginia government became a model for other English colonies.

D. Other English Colonies were settled.
1. The Pilgrims arrived to settle the Plymouth Colony.
    a. Sects who did not conform with the Anglican Church had left England to seek religious freedom.
        (1) They migrated to Holland but were discontent there.
        (2) They obtained a patent from the Virginia Company to settle in Virginia.
    b. The Pilgrims reached Cape Cod in 1620 on the Mayflower.
        (1) They received a grant from the Council of New England to stay in New Plymouth.
        (2) The settlers signed the Mayflower Compact to abide by the decisions of the male majority.
        (3) The Pilgrims made their own laws and selected their own officials in their ten small towns.
2. The Massachusetts Bay Colony was started in 1628.
    a. John Endicott and others, primarily

Puritans, obtained a grant from the Council of New England.
    b. The company obtained a charter from the king, giving it governmental powers similar to the Virginia Company.
    c. A large Puritan migration began in 1630 with John Winthrop as governor of the new city of Boston.
    d. This group brought the charter with them and made Massachusetts almost independent of the crown.
    e. The main purpose was to have freedom of worship.
    f. Participation in government was limited to members of the church.
3. Massachusetts was given a new charter in 1691.
    a. Maine and Plymouth were incorporated in Massachusetts.
    b. The crown appointed the governor.
    c. The voters elected the assembly.
    d. The assembly elected the council, who was confirmed by the governor.
    e. The franchise was no longer based on religious qualification but on property ownership.
4. Connecticut was founded in 1633 by Massachusetts malcontents.
    a. The emigrants were led by Thomas Hooker.
    b. The cities of Hartford, Windsor and Wethersfield were founded.
    c. The first constitution in America was the "Fundamental Orders" adopted in 1639.
        (1) A man did not have to be a member of the church to vote.
        (2) Ministers did not control politics.
        (3) The governor and his assistants were elected at a general meeting.
        (4) The governor, his assistants and representatives from the towns formed a court with judicial and legislative powers.
5. Rhode Island was founded in 1636.
    a. Roger Williams and Anne Hutchinson were two of the original founders who fled from religious tyranny in Massachusetts.
    b. The colony was granted a patent in 1664 to form its own government.
    c. There was complete freedom of religion and franchise.
6. Mason and Gorges obtained grants for Maine and New Hampshire in 1635.
    a. Massachusetts claimed both regions and extended her control over them.
    b. New Hampshire became a crown colony in 1679.

c. Maine was considered a part of Massachusetts by the charter of 1691.

7. Maryland was first settled in 1634.
   a. A charter was issued by Charles I in 1632 making Maryland a proprietary colony under George Calvert.
   b. Calvert died before the charter was sealed and the proprietorship went to his son Cecil, also known as Lord Baltimore.
   c. Maryland was chiefly a Catholic haven.
   d. All sects were welcomed in the colony, and there was religious freedom for all who believed in Jesus as passed by the Religious Toleration Act of 1649.
   e. The proprietor was the supreme ruler, but Lord Baltimore yielded to a more liberal government of an elected assembly.

8. Charles II granted land between Virginia and Florida to 8 proprietors in 1663.
   a. North Carolina was settled by migrants from Virginia.
   b. It was governed as a separate colony from South Carolina.
   c. In 1729, the crown bought the rights of the Carolina proprietors.
   d. North and South Carolina were separate royal colonies.
   e. North Carolina was primarily a farming country with democratic principles.
   f. South Carolina consisted of wealthy aristocracy owning large plantations.

9. England seized New York from the Dutch in 1664.
   a. James, the Duke of York, brother of Charles II, was the proprietor.
   b. James became King and he made New York a royal colony in 1686.
   c. Until 1683, the governor and his council ruled when the first elected assembly convened.
   d. In 1686 the law-making powers were in the hands of the governor.
   e. In 1691, the assembly was restored by William and Mary.

10. The part of New York now New Jersey was transferred to Berkeley and Carteret by the Duke of York in 1664.
    a. New Jersey was proprietary until 1702.
    b. It became a crown colony in 1702.

11. William Penn, the proprietor, set up Pennsylvania as a haven for Quakers.

a. The Charter of Pennsylvania was issued in 1681.
b. The assembly, elected in 1682, passed a liberal code of laws.
c. Penn promoted the settlement of the colony by attractive land promotion ideas.
d. Delaware was a proprietary colony of Pennsylvania.
e. In 1701 Delaware had its separate legislature.

12. Oglethorpe obtained a charter for Georgia in 1732.
    a. Purpose of the colony was to serve as a refuge for debtors of England.
    b. Another purpose was to act as a buffer state against the Spaniards and Indians.

III. LIFE IN THE ENGLISH COLONIES.

A. Agriculture was the leading occupation.

1. In New England farming was not too productive.
   a. Except in the rich river valleys, the soil was infertile and stony.
      (1) The growing season was short.
      (2) There was diversified farming of small freeholds.
      (3) Chief crops were barley, oats, rye and corn.
   b. The people turned to other occupations.
   c. The New England system of settlement was primarily in towns.

2. In the middle colonies the farms were more fertile than in New England.
   a. Farms were usually small.
   b. Wheat was an important crop.
   c. Pasturing cattle was very important.
   d. Many tenant farmers operated the farms, with payment to the proprietors.
   e. Large surpluses of flour, wheat and livestock were exported.
   f. Crops originating in North America were beans, pumpkins, corn and squash.

3. Land was divided mainly into large estates in the southern colonies.
   a. The large estates and the use of Negro slave labor foreshadowed the plantation system.
      (1) White indentured servants were replaced by enslaved Africans.
      (2) First shipload of Africans landed in Virginia in 1619.
   b. Agriculture was the sole industry because of the large market for its products.
   c. Tobacco was the great staple crop, centering in Maryland and Virginia.

U.S. HISTORY

d. Rice was the chief staple crop of South Carolina cotton became important after the Revolution.

f. Manufactured goods were imported from the northern colonies and from England.

B. The organization of economic life was determined by land tenure, labor supply and natural resources.

1. New England was primarily a maritime region.
    a. Fishing and whaling were important in New York and in New England.
    b. Shipbuilding was centered in the same area.
    c. Intercolonial and foreign commerce played an important role in the economy of the region.
    d. The manufacturing of woolen textiles, leather goods and iron implements was important.
    e. In the 18th century, the distillation of rum was the chief manufacturing industry.
    f. Lumbering camps were numerous in New Hampshire and Maine.

2. The provision provinces were New York, New Jersey and Pennsylvania.
    a. Flour was important for export and domestic consumption.
    b. Wheat, corn, cattle, sheep, pigs, fruits and vegetables were used for export trade.

3. Other colonial industries flourished.
    a. Naval supplies as pitch, tar and turpentine were produced.
    b. Distilleries and breweries produced rum, cider and beer.
    c. Textiles were manufactured from wool and flax.
    d. Iron was mined and smelted into pig iron.
    e. Brick works and lime kilns were busy with production.
    f. Fur trade was extremely prosperous.

4. Farmers, merchants and manufacturers were confronted with labor problems.
    a. Farmers performed their own labor.
    b. Manufactured items were produced by individual craftsmen such as skilled carpenters, tailors, weavers, masons, silversmiths and others.
    c. Indentured servants paid for their passage to America by working as skilled or unskilled laborers.
        (1) Period of servitude 5 to 7 years.
        (2) They were in all the colonies.
    d. Apprentices work while they learned their particular craft.
    e. Slaves were more numerous in the South than in the North.
        (1) Harsh laws controlled the slaves.
        (2) They were used as field hands in the South.
        (3) They were used as servants and unskilled laborers in the North.

5. Money was a problem.
    a. During the early colonial period, trade was by barter.
    b. Money was a mixture of gold and silver coins from England, Spain and France.
    c. Paper currency issued by the colonies circulated with a fluctuating value.
    d. The theory of mercantilism held that the colonies serve as a source of raw products in exchange for England's finished goods, which created an adverse balance of trade.

C. The social and cultural development of the colonies were of concern to the colonists.

1. The important towns were Norfolk, Charleston, Baltimore, New York, Philadelphia and Boston.
    a. There was a class distinction between the masses and the wealthy.
    b. The towns were the centers of communication.

2. Printing and newspapers were established early.
    a. First printing press was set up in 1639 in Massachusetts.
    b. First regular newspaper, called the "Boston News-Letter" was published in 1704.
    c. First magazine was published in 1741 by Benjamin Franklin.
    d. The Zenger Trial in New York established the freedom of the press in 1793.
    e. By 1765 there were 43 newspapers published in the colonies.

3. Educational institutions were erected.
    a. Schools were more numerous in the North than in the South.
    b. The wealthy children were educated by tutors mainly; other children in town grammar schools.
    c. Colleges were primarily denominational institutions.
    d. Harvard was founded in 1636, William and Mary in 1698, Yale in 1701, and Princeton in 1746, as well as others.
    e. Most colleges were initiated by religious organizations.
    f. The first library was started by Benjamin Franklin in 1731 in Philadelphia.
    g. The legal profession was much more

advanced than the medical profession.

h. The fine arts were patterned after European types.

4. Religious intolerance receded during the late 17th century.

a. All the colonies, except Pennsylvania and Rhode Island, devoted part of the taxes to the churches.

b. Congregationalism and Anglicanism were the major denominations.

c. Puritan powers declined with the numerous non-English migrations of the 18th century.

(1) The Massachusetts Charter of 1691 abolished the Congregational church test for the right to vote.

(2) Connecticut adopted a policy of cooperation with the Presbyterians in 1708.

(3) During the early 18th century, theology overshadowed other intellectual interests.

(4) Politics, science and economics gradually replaced theology in discussions and in printed matter.

D. The British colonial system was based on the policies of mercantilism.

1. The kings all attempted to maintain the Crown's authority over the colonies.

a. James I (1603-25) imposed the royal will on the colonies.

b. Plans of Charles I (1625-49) were thwarted by the revolt against his authority in 1642.

c. Charles II (1660-1685) reasserted royal authority in America.

d. James II (1685-1688) carried out the policy of uniting the northern colonies under one royal governor.

2. Parliament maintained that the colonies were of parliamentary concern, because it was a matter of commercial regulation.

a. Mercantilism emphasized a favorable balance of trade.

(1) This meant selling more than was bought.

(2) Colonies had to furnish raw materials to the mother country for her finished products.

(3) England did not have to buy from other foreign countries thus keeping the money within her country and colonies.

b. Parliament passed a series of Trade Acts.

(1) The Navigation Laws of 1660 provided that the colonial products as sugar, tobacco, indigo and cotton could not be sold to foreign countries but had to be sent to England first.

(2) Goods imported to or exported from any British possession had to be transported in British ships or in ships built in English colonies.

(3) All European goods sent to the colonies must first be shipped to England and then reshipped to the colonies, 1663.

(4) The Molasses Act placed high duties on molasses imported from the non-British West Indies so as to protect the British West Indian planters, 1733.

(5) Other parliamentary laws prohibited the export of woolen goods and hats from the colonies.

(6) Parliament restricted excessive issuance of paper money by the colonies.

3. Regulations were poorly enforced and smuggling became widespread.

E. French colonization in America conflicted with the British.

1. A French colony was first established by the Huguenots in Florida in 1562, but it was unsuccessful.

2. French fur traders visited the areas Cartier explored.

3. Champlain founded Quebec in 1609.

4. Jesuits began their missionary activities in New France in 1615.

5. Montreal was established in 1642.

6. Marquette, a missionary, and Joliet, a fur trader, reached the Mississippi river in 1673.

7. La Salle explored in the southwestern area between the Mississippi and the Gulf of Mexico.

8. LaSalle claimed the Mississippi in 1682.

9. The French settled around the Gulf of Mexico.

10. French missions, towns and fur trading posts were set up in the St. Lawrence valley, the Great Lakes area and the Mississippi River valley from the Great Lakes to the Gulf of Mexico.

11. Fur trading and missionary settlements were the prime purposes of France.

F. France and England had a series of wars for possession of North America, 1689-1763.

1. King William's War, 1690-1697, inspired French raids on English frontier settlements.

U.S. HISTORY

a. The English won Port Royal, Acadia, 1690.

b. The Treaty of Ryswick accomplished nothing, 1697.

2. Queen Anne's War, 1702-1713, obtained Acadia for the British in 1710.

a. The Treaty of Utrecht, 1713, secured the Newfoundland, Nova Scotia and The Hudson Bay Region for England.

b. The provision called the "Assiento" gave England a monopoly of the slave trade with Spanish America.

3. King George's War, 1745-1748, contributed little towards the British and French controversy.

G. The decisive struggle was the French and Indian War, 1754-1763.

1. France had definite advantages.

a. France had effective control over New France.

b. The army in America was well disciplined.

c. France had powerful Indian allies.

d. France had forts located at strategic points from the Ohio Valley to Quebec.

2. England had disadvantages which weakened her struggle.

a. There was a lack of unified control.

b. The various colonies had conflicting plans.

c. There was disharmony between the colonial and royal troops.

3. England also had certain advantages.

a. England controlled the seas.

b. England had tremendous American resources.

c. England had an ally in the Iroquois.

d. The English population was fifteen times greater than that of New France.

4. The War went badly for England the first two years.

a. William Pitt became the leader for the English in 1757.

b. The tide turned in favor of the English.

5. The Peace of Paris in 1763 gave Great Britain the triumph over France in North America.

a. The English controlled the region from the Atlantic to the Mississippi.

b. They also controlled the land from the Arctic to the Gulf of Mexico, excluding New Orleans.

c. France was left with two islands, St. Pierre and Miquelon, off Newfoundland and the islands of Martinique and Guadeloupe in the West Indies.

d. France ceded to her ally Spain, her

possession of Louisiana.

e. The colonies now no longer needed the assistance from Great Britain against the French threat.

IV. THE COLONIES' MOVE TOWARD REBELLION AND UNIFICATION, 1763-1789.

A. There were five important acts which led to the American Revolution.

1. By the Proclamation of 1763, the English kept the colonists out of the territory between the Alleghenies and the Mississippi, which made the fur traders and land speculators resentful.

2. The Sugar Act of 1764 raised revenues by reducing the molasses duty from the West Indies, and increased the duties on refined sugar as well as other imported luxuries.

3. The Stamp Act of 1765 required that stamps be bought and placed on many items.

4. The Quartering Act of 1765 required the colonists to furnish British troops with barracks.

5. The Townshend Acts of 1767 placed duties on a great number of goods including lead, paints, glass, paper and tea, imported by the colonists.

a. The taxes were repealed, except on tea, in 1770.

b. The purpose was to let the colonists realize that Parliament had the right to tax them.

c. Colonial reactions were in the forms of an English boycott, riots, and strong anti-British literature.

d. The Boston Massacre in 1770 led the colonists to act violently against the English "Redcoats."

e. Colonists, disguised as Indians, threw tea loaded on ships in Boston Harbor overboard and created the Boston Tea Party of 1773.

6. Parliament passed the severe Intolerable Acts in 1774.

a. The Port of Boston was closed.

b. The colony was deprived of many important governmental powers.

B. The colonies united to discuss measures to help the colony of Massachusetts.

1. The First Continental Congress met in Philadelphia in 1774.

a. The Intolerable Acts were declared unconstitutional.

b. A Declaration of Rights and Grievances was issued to the crown and to the English people.

c. They agreed on a non-exportation, non-importation policy to compel

England to discontinue her objectionable policies.

2. **The Second Continental Congress met in Philadelphia in 1775.**
   a. The fighting had already begun between the colonies and England.
   b. The delegates were more rebellious and radical.
   c. Another petition was sent to the crown.
   d. A Declaration of Causes for Taking up Arms was drafted.
   e. Thomas Paine's "Common Sense," published in 1776, argued for colonial independence.
   f. An army was authorized with George Washington appointed commander-in-chief.
   g. A committee of five was appointed to draw up a Declaration of Independence.

3. **The Declaration of Independence was adopted by the Congress July 4, 1776.**
   a. Thomas Jefferson was the principal writer of the document.
   b. The preamble contained the philosophy of human rights.
   c. The second part stated a severe indictment of the British policies in America, listing 27 grievances.
   d. The concluding part stated a decisive break with England, which was a formal declaration of war.

C. **Both the Revolutionists and the English had advantages and disadvantages.**
   1. The English did not fully support the war.
   2. England had only part of its man power available in America.
   3. The English army training and discipline were superior.
   4. It was difficult to supply the English army with supplies.
   5. England was wealthy but had a large national debt.
   6. England was involved with another war with France, Spain and Holland.
   7. The Continental army was maintained with difficulty.
   8. The colonists obtained loans from friendly foreign powers as France and Holland.
   9. France furnished aid to the colonies with money, a naval fleet and army supplies.
   10. The state militias harassed invading English troops.
   11. The colonists were convinced that they were right and therefore had a deep determination to win.
   12. George Washington was a remarkable leader.

D. **The military and naval campaigns led the colonists to victory.**
   1. The Battle of Bunker Hill, 1775, caused the British to evacuate Boston and establish New York headquarters.
   2. Washington crossed the Delaware in 1776 and captured the Hessians at Trenton, New Jersey.
   3. Burgoyne was defeated near Saratoga, New York in 1777.
      a. Victory at Saratoga caused France to become an American ally.
      b. This battle became known as the turning point of the war.
   4. The winter of 1777-1778 was a bitter one for the colonial army at Valley Forge.
   5. In 1779-1781 the theatre of war shifted to the South.
      a. Sections of the Carolinas and Virginia were captured by the British.
      b. In 1781 Washington trapped Cornwallis and the British army at Yorktown with the help of the French troops and fleet.
      c. The surrender of Cornwallis brought the war to an end.

E. **The Treaty of Paris, 1783, gave America its independence.**
   1. The United States boundary was extended from the Appalachians to the Mississippi River.
   2. The United States shared in the Newfoundland fisheries.
   3. Payments of American debts were to be paid to British merchants, and Tory properties were to be returned to them.
      a. This never took place because the colonists developed social changes.
      b. The land confiscated from the Tories was sold to small farmers.
      c. Large estates held together by laws of primogeniture were broken up.

F. **The results of the Revolution created significant changes.**
   1. Democracy emphasized the belief in political equality with fairer representation.
   2. England removed her restraints on trade and industry.
   3. Penal codes were moderated.
   4. Franchises were liberalized.
   5. American manufacturers and shipping were encouraged.
   6. The spirit of nationalism and democracy were strengthened.

G. **The critical period after the Revolution was 1783-1789.**
   1. A post-war depression until 1787.

U.S. HISTORY

a. Trade with the West Indies and England deteriorated.

b. Much property was destroyed.

c. There was a great deal of unemployment.

d. Farmers could not pay their debts and Shay's Rebellion in 1786 in Massachusetts displayed the unrest of the farmers.

e. Paper money in the states circulated at unstable values.

f. High tariffs and interstate competition for revenue restricted commerce.

2. The Articles of Confederation had many weaknesses.

a. The Articles were adopted in 1781 by the thirteen states as the framework of their national government.

b. The states feared the power of a central government after revolting against the English government.

c. The Articles created a league of sovereign commonwealths which was weak.

   (1) Each state was equally represented in Congress.

   (2) All important measures had to be approved by nine of the thirteen states.

   (3) Amendments to the Articles had to be by unanimous consent.

   (4) Congress only had the power to levy its tax assessments on the states but not to collect them.

   (5) Congress had no funds to pay the national debt or provide for an army or navy.

   (6) The government was not respected by foreign powers so that treaties could not be satisfactorily negotiated.

   (7) The government did not have the power to regulate domestic or foreign commerce.

d. The government under the Articles did make some major contributions.

   (1) The Northwest Ordinance, 1787, provided for self-government in the vast Western territories, which the states transferred to the national government.

   (2) The Ordinance broke the colonial policy of England by admitting new states to share governmental powers equally with the older states.

   (3) A coinage system was developed.

   (4) Weights and measures were regulated.

V. THE CONSTITUTION OF THE UNITED STATES.

A. A general convention was held at Independence Hall in Philadelphia in 1787.

1. Prior to this, there were several smaller scale interstate conferences.

2. Alexander Hamilton suggested that delegates from all states meet in Philadelphia.

3. The purpose of the meeting was to revise the Articles of Confederation.

4. All the states were represented except Rhode Island.

5. Some of the prominent men who came to the convention were George Washton, its president, James Madison, Benjamin Franklin, Alexander Hamilton and others.

B. The delegates agreed that the national government had to be strengthened.

1. The Great Compromise gave equal representation for all states in the Senate and representation based on population in the House of Representatives.

   a. This was based on the Virginia plan which wanted representation in the two-house legislature to be based on population proportions.

   b. The New Jersey Plan wanted equal representation from all states.

2. The Three-Fifths Compromise provided that three out of five slaves would be counted for direct taxation and representation.

   a. Congress could not prohibit the importation of slaves until 1808.

3. The regulation of trade compromise assured the southern states that Congress could not tax exports from any states.

   a. The South depended on the export of agricultural crops and tobacco for the bulk of its income.

   b. Congress was given the right to tax imports and to regulate interstate and foreign commerce.

4. Congress was given the powers to negotiate and ratify treaties with foreign nations, to lay and collect taxes, to maintain an army and navy.

   a. Treaties had to be ratified by two-thirds of the Senate.

5. The government was divided into the executive, the legislative and the judicial branches with a system of checks and balances to protect the welfare of all the people.

6. The Constitution was sent to Congress with the recommendation that State conventions meet to pass upon its ratification.

a. Congress acted as it was requested.

b. Despite provisions of the Articles of Confederation that amendments must be by unanimous consent of the states, only nine states had to ratify the Constitution.

C. **The struggle to ratify the Constitution was bitter.**

1. Wealthy areas favored the ratification.
2. Some opposed the Constitution because it contained no guarantees of personal rights.
   a. Massachusetts signed provided amendments would be added.
   b. The Bill of Rights protecting individual liberties was adopted, 1791, as the first ten amendments.
3. All the states except Rhode Island and North Carolina ratified the Constitution by 1788.
4. These two states entered the Union after the new government began to operate.
5. Proponents of the new government were known as Federalists.
6. Opponents of the new government were known as anti-Federalists.

D. **The new government formally began April 20, 1789 in New York City.**

1. Washington was unanimously elected as President by electors.
2. John Adams was declared vice-president.
3. Both houses of Congress had strong Federalist majorities.
4. The capitol was moved in 1790 to Philadelphia and in 1800 to Washington.

VI. **THE PERIOD OF THE FEDERALIST CONTROL, 1789-1801.**

A. **The government started to put the Constitution to work.**

1. Washington first appointed his officials, all of whom were Federalists.
2. Thomas Jefferson was appointed as Secretary of State, Alexander Hamilton, Secretary of the Treasury, Edmund Randolph, Attorney-General and Henry Knox, Secretary of War.
3. Washington's acts set the precedents for future years.
   a. He accepted the title, "Mr. President".
   b. He established the Cabinet which is not mentioned in the Constitution.
   c. The Vice-President was not part of the Cabinet.
   d. He established the two term tradition for the Presidency which lasted until Franklin D. Roosevelt's time.
      (1) Roosevelt was elected in 1932,

1936, 1940 and 1944.
      (2) The 22nd Amendment in 1951 limited all future Presidents to two terms only.

B. **Alexander Hamilton presented a new financial program.**

1. Money was raised by the Tariff Bill of 1789 putting low duties on imports.
2. In 1792 an internal revenue tax was passed on American wine and distilled liquor.
   a. The Whiskey Rebellion in Pennsylvania in 1794 was caused by the refusal of distillers to pay the tax.
   b. The revolt was subsided by troops.
   c. The incident helped to establish the authority of the government.
3. Public land sales added to the Federal income.
4. He urged the Congress to pay off the foreign debt of $12,000,000 as well as the internal debt of $42,000,000 owed to citizens for financing the Revolutionary War.
5. The government also assumed the states' debts to individual citizens for war financing.
6. The assumption of debts was carried in 1790 by means of a bargain, whereby the Capitol would be on the Potomac banks in exchange for southern votes for assumption.
7. Hamilton recommended a central national bank to issue sound currency.
   a. Jefferson opposed the bank, because it was unconstitutional of the Federal government to charter a bank.
   b. Hamilton replied emphasizing the doctrine of implied powers which were necessary to carry into effect the specific powers.
   c. The bank was given a charter in 1791 to last for twenty years.
   d. The government owned one-fifth of the bank's stocks and four-fifths were privately owned.
8. A mint was established in 1792.

C. **Political parties were developed by opponents to the Federalist doctrines.**

1. The Federalist party was led by Hamilton and John Adams who had definite policies.
   a. The party was supported by the wealthy class.
   b. They supported Hamilton's financial program.
   c. They favored a strong central government and a broad interpretation of the Constitution.

d. They were sympathetic with England in its war against France.
 (1) England represented law and order.
 (2) French Revolution violence represented radicalism.
e. They had little confidence in the judgment of the masses.
f. They demanded maintaining an army and navy in order to obtain foreign respect.

2. Jefferson and Madison opposed the Federalist doctrines as reactionary and harsh.
 a. Jefferson organized a united body known as the Democratic-Republicans, with the word Democratic soon dropped.
 (1) This party is not to be mistaken for the Republican party of today which was founded in 1854.
 b. The party was supported by the workers in the North, the small farmers and planters of the South. They opposed the aristocratic tendencies of the Federalists wanting all men to participate in the government.
 d. They favored strong state governments with guarantees of individual liberties.
 e. They opposed the Hamiltonian financial program as an exploitation instrument of the laborers and farmers by the wealthy class.
 f. They sympathized with France in its attempt to introduce democracy and liberalism in Europe.
 g. They regarded an army and navy as a needless expense when all citizens could be called upon to be soldiers, if necessary.

3. John Adams was elected president in 1796 with Thomas Jefferson as vice president.

4. In 1800 Jefferson became president and the Republicans controlled Congress; the Federalist party never regained control and finally disappeared.

D. During the Federalist regime international problems had to be met.

1. The French Republic was at war with England and expected American aid.
 a. France sent Edmond Genet as their representative to the United States.
 b. Genet began using American ports for privateering activities.
 c. Washington issued a Proclamation of Neutrality in 1790 forbidding Americans to aid either side in the war.

d. Genet appealed to the American people over the head of Washington and attempted to promote attacks on Spanish America.
e. His activities were looked upon with disfavor even by French sympathizers.
f. France recalled Genet, but he was allowed to remain in the United States because his party had fallen from power and his enemies had gained control.

2. The disagreements between the United States and England resulted in the Jay Treaty in 1795.
 a. England was interfering with the freedom of the seas by seizing cargoes from American ships trading with the French West Indies.
 b. They were forcing American seamen to serve in the British navy.
 c. They continued to hold the fur-trading posts along the Great Lakes area.
 d. Washington sent John Jay to England to prevent a war and correct the grievances.
 e. Jay's Treaty, ratified by the Senate in 1795, was looked upon with disfavor in the United States.
 (1) The British promised to relinquish the fur-trading posts.
 (2) A commission was to settle the claims for pre-revolutionary debts.
 (3) No settlement was made of American objections to British violations of maritime rights.
 f. Washington and the Government were accused of bowing to England, but the treaty did avert a war for the new nation.

3. The United States almost went to war with France because of the XYZ Affair.
 a. The French government refused to receive C. C. Pinckney as United States Minister.
 b. In 1797 John Adams sent Gerry and Marshall to join Pinckney to establish diplomatic relations between the United States and France.
 c. Three agents of Tallyrand, called XYZ, suggested that negotiations could be made if money were paid.
 d. The American envoys refused and reported the incident to John Adams.
 e. The United States was insulted and prepared for war.
 f. Alien and Sedition Acts were passed by Congress in 1798 to stop governmental criticism and interference during a critical period.

(1) Naturalization Act lengthened time of residence from five to fourteen years; in 1801 this was changed back to five years.

(2) Alien Act gave the president power to deport or imprison undesirable aliens.

(3) Sedition Acts provided imprisonment and fines for criticism of officers of the federal government.

(a) The Acts expired by self-limitation.

g. France and the United States arranged a settlement which abrogated the Treaty of 1778 and settled their differences.

h. The Alien and Sedition Acts prompted the Kentucky and Virginia Resolutions in 1798.

(1) These Resolutions claimed that the federal government by passing the acts, had exceeded the powers delegated to the states and therefore they were null.

(2) The Resolutions were the first formal statements of the doctrine of states' rights.

4. The Pinckney Treaty of 1795 settled the differences with Spain.

a. Spain held the Louisiana Territory and controlled both banks of the Mississippi River.

b. This menaced the trade of the southwestern farmers, who needed the right of free navigation of the river for their products.

c. Spain and the United States had conflicting opinions about the southwestern boundary.

d. The Pinckney Treaty, negotiated with Spain, gave the United States her boundary claim at the thirty-first parallel, granted navigation rights on the Mississippi, and established a port of deposit for Americans at New Orleans.

e. The treaty could be renewed at the request of the United States at the end of five years.

5. United States was now accepted as a national power by Europe.

a. The disputes with England, France and Spain were settled by diplomatic negotiations by 1800.

VII. THE PERIOD OF JEFFERSON'S ADMINISTRATION, 1801-1809.

A. The Republican candidates were Jefferson and Burr, and the Federalist candidates were Adams and Pinckney.

1. Jefferson and Burr were tied in votes.

2. The election of the president was decided by Congress in accordance with the Constitution, and after some political maneuvering, Jefferson was selected.

3. The 12th Amendment, adopted in 1804, provided that the Electoral College vote separately for the president and vice-president.

B. The Federalist policies were somewhat changed.

1. Jefferson emphasized the equality of all men and their right to participate in government.

2. The change was more in a shift of attitude than in radical governmental alterations.

3. The debt continued to be paid.

4. The United States Bank charter was not renewed in 1811 but was rechartered in 1816.

5. The Army and Navy were reduced in number.

6. The excise tax was abolished.

C. Jefferson contributed much to American life.

1. He fought for free public education.

2. He regarded the small farmers as the backbone of America.

3. He fought for the abolition of slavery.

4. He fought for prison reforms.

5. He was one of the greatest fighters for democracy and freedom.

D. The Republicans were hostile to the growing power of the courts and the Federalist judges.

1. Judiciary Act of 1801, which had created new judicial posts, were repealed.

2. Impeachment proceedings were started against several Federalist Judges.

a. John Pickering, a federal judge of New Hampshire, was impeached.

b. Samuel Chase of the Supreme Court was impeached but acquitted.

E. The Tripolitan "War", 1801-1805, was caused by the Barbary States demanding increased tributes from commercial nations trading in the Mediterranean.

1. If tribute was not paid, vessels were seized and the crew sold into slavery.

2. Jefferson, provoked by the unwarranted piracy, sent an American naval force to the area.

3. The American naval vessels had a series of encounters, 1802-1804, which finally released the United States from the piracy by the Barbary States.

U.S. HISTORY

F. Jefferson doubled the area of the United States by purchasing the Louisiana Territory from France.

1. The use of the Mississippi as an outlet for trading was exceedingly important to the southwestern United States.
2. Spain retroceded Louisiana to France in 1800 by the Treaty of San Ildefonso.
   a. Spain, in preparation for the transfer, revoked the right of deposit at New Orleans.
   b. United States neglected to renew its treaty privileges.
3. Jefferson sent Monroe to join Livingston, the American minister to France, with instructions to buy New Orleans and West Florida.
   a. Napoleon decided to sell all of Louisiana to the United States.
   b. Livingston and Monroe bought Louisiana in 1803 for $15,000,000.
4. Jefferson doubted the government's constitutional power to buy territory from a foreign power.
   a. He wanted a constitutional amendment to permit it, but time required for the amending process would take too long.
   b. Jefferson was finally convinced that the purchase was an implied power in the Constitution.
   c. The treaty to purchase the land was a precedent for liberal interpretation of the Constitution.
5. Spain and the United States quarreled over the boundary of West Florida.
   a. Spain finally recognized American ownership in the Treaty of 1819.
6. The New England Federalists were dissatisfied with the center of political power shifting to the south and west.
   a. The northeast felt that they had the right to secede.
   b. They felt the federal government exceeded the powers delegated to it.
   c. The Federalists supported Burr for governor of New York in 1804 with the hopes New England and New York would unite in an eastern confederacy.
   d. Hamilton's influence on the Federalist party caused the plan to be defeated.
   e. The sequel was the fatal duel for Hamilton with Burr.
   f. Burr's conspiracy in the southwest ended with his trial for treason in 1807 in which he was acquitted.
7. The United States made efforts to prevent war with France and England.
   a. France and England were at war, 1803-1814.
   b. The United States traded with both belligerents.
   c. Both warring countries declared that any vessels trading with the opposing country would be seized.
   d. The result was the loss of numerous American vessels.
   e. The British also seized American seamen and forced them into the Royal Navy.
   f. Jefferson believed in peaceful coercion.
      (1) The Non-importation Act of 1806 stated that British articles which were produced in the United States or could be produced elsewhere were prohibited as imports.
      (2) The Embargo Act of 1807 stated that American vessels could not bring cargoes to American ports from Europe or carry cargoes to Europe from American ports.
      (3) The Embargo Act injured the United States more than France or England.
         (a) Manufacturing, agriculture and shipping were affected by the embargo.
         (b) Unemployment was prevalent.
         (c) France had her coast blockaded by England anyway.
         (d) France was pleased that United States ceased trading with England.
         (e) The Embargo Act was repealed in 1809.
      (4) Peaceful coercion was continued by the Non-intercourse Act of 1809.
         (a) Trade was resumed except with England and France.
         (b) The act was less disastrous but the shippers who obeyed it were penalized, and the illicit shippers profited.
      (5) The Non-Intercourse Act was replaced by the Macon Bill, Number 2.
         (a) Trade was restored with France and England with the provision that, if one of them should eliminate its undesirable orders, the non-intercourse would be resumed against the other.
         (b) Napoleon stated that he had repealed his decrees, but England claimed this was only a trick to create war between England and the United States.

VIII. JAMES MADISON, PRESIDENT IN 1809, AND THE WAR OF 1812.

A. **The causes of the War of 1812 came primarily from the Western frontiersmen and the Southern planters.**

1. The rise of a western group elected to Congress, known as "war hawks", promoted a war with England to realize personal ambitions.
    a. If Canada could be taken from England they could control the fur trade.
    b. They protested British support of Indian uprisings, particularly those organized by the Shawnee chieftain, Tecumseh, to unite the Northern and Southern Indian tribes.
    c. They desired to invade Spanish territory in Florida for conquest and annexation.
2. France and England were both offensive to the United States but the American attitude was more anti-British.
    a. The British ministry had an insolent diplomatic attitude.
    b. They forced American seamen into the British navy.
    c. They interfered with trade by confiscating American cargoes.
    d. Nevertheless the opposition to war came from the New England and Middle States Congressmen, even though they were most directly affected by the loss of commerce.
    e. The west favored the war because of its desire for territorial expansion.
3. The insistence of the war party in Congress, led by Clay, Calhoun, Porter and Grundy, caused the Declaration of War to be sent to Congress in June, 1812.

B. **United States was ill prepared for war.**

1. The army was small, badly equipped and handicapped by incompetent leaders.
2. The Bank of the United States was not rechartered in 1811, and financial disorder followed.
3. The government's credit collapsed.
4. New England extended little aid in manpower or finances to aid the war.

C. **The military campaigns in the war were from 1812-1814.**

1. United States made a triple movement against Canada but failed.
    a. Hull surrendered Detroit to the English in 1812.
    b. Van Rensselaer and Smythe lost at Niagara.
    c. Dearborn never attacked Montreal.
    d. In 1813, Perry won an important naval victory on Lake Erie and recovered Detroit.
    e. Andrew Jackson defeated the Creeks in the south.
    f. By 1813 it was evident that America could not conquer Canada, and the fervor for war declined.
2. Spain abstained from an alliance with England in the War of 1812 and therefore prevented any conquest of Spanish territory.
3. Napoleon's defeat in Europe paralleled the United States campaign of 1814.
    a. Washington was captured and burned by the British in retaliation for the burning of Toronto, the capital of Canada, the previous year by the Americans.
    b. The resistance of Fort McHenry prevented the British troops from entering Baltimore.
    c. Francis Scott Key wrote "The Star Spangled Banner".
    d. The Battle of New Orleans (led by Andrew Jackson in January 1815) was a decisive victory for the United States.
    e. It was fought after the signing of the peace treaty because of slow communication regarding the end of the war.
4. The British had an effective blockade of the American coast.

D. **The Hartford Convention met December, 1814-January, 1815.**

1. New England Federalists met at Hartford, Connecticut to protest the useless war.
2. The convention drafted amendments to the Constitution to protect themselves from the Republican government policies.
    a. Slaves were to be omitted from the census on which representation was based.
    b. There had to be a two-thirds vote of Congress to admit new states, declare war or impose commercial restrictions.
    c. The President was to be limited to a single term, and no two persons from the same state could be elected in succession.
3. In this way the Federalist party expressed its dislike to the southern followers of Jeffersonian doctrines.
4. The convention representatives arrived in Washington after the Treaty of Ghent.

U.S. HISTORY

a. They left Washington without taking any action.

b. After that, New England was an ardent supporter of the supremacy of the central government and stopped advocating states' rights doctrines.

E. **The Treaty of Ghent was signed December, 1814 and was ratified by the Senate February, 1815.**

1. The negotiations were greatly influenced by the course of England's struggle with Napoleon.

2. The American representatives were John Quincy Adams, Henry Clay and Albert Gallatin.

3. Claims by both countries were given up.

4. The treaty provided only for the cessation of hostilities and a return to the conditions prior to the war.

5. The United States lost the Newfoundland fishing rights.

6. Questions of other fisheries and boundaries were referred to commissions for future studies.

F. **The war did have its effect upon both countries.**

1. Little was accomplished toward the settlement of grievances against England.

2. United States was never again treated with contempt by England.

3. The war engendered a spirit of national self-sufficiency in the United States as opposed to the disruptive force of sectionalism.

IX. AN ERA OF COMMON NATIONAL PURPOSE, 1815-1824.

A. **At the end of the War of 1812, there were about 8,000,000 people in the United States.**

B. **Between 1815 and 1820, Indiana, Missippissi, Illinois and Alabama were admitted as new states to the Union.**

C. **The wave of nationalism was based on several factors.**

1. The country had the natural boundaries of the Atlantic, the Gulf of Mexico, the Great Lakes and the Rockies.

2. Everyone spoke English.

3. The growth of agriculture and industry provided prosperity.

4. All sections united because they shared a common history.

5. People in politics introduced measures to increase the power and prestige of the country.

D. **There were definite economic aspects of nationalism.**

1. A second Bank of the United States was chartered in 1816 for twenty years.

a. The bank was to curb unsound banking practices and to check currency inflation.

b. One-fifth of the capital stock was subscribed to by the federal government, and about 31,000 citizens subscribed to the other four-fifths.

c. The bank aided the government's financial operations.

d. The bank was a depository for government funds for which it offered no interest.

e. The bank was exempt from federal taxation.

f. A bonus of $1,500,000 was given to the government.

g. The bank compelled state banks to limit the volume of notes and maintain those issues at full face values.

2. Internal improvements at governmental expense were demanded to aid industry and farming.

a. Heavy western migration demanded the necessity for better canals, roads and methods of communication.

b. The National Road was completed to Wheeling on the Ohio River.

c. New settlements made it necessary to reach the markets with the products.

d. The opposition to internal improvements was that they would be of limited local benefit, and the government did not have the approved power by the Constitution to spend the money in this fashion.

e. A Bonus Bill of 1817 proposed by John C. Calhoun was passed.

(1) The purpose was to give the government a bonus of $1,500,000 for the bank charter, and the dividends from the government stock to be used for internal improvements.

(2) Madison vetoed the bill because he thought it unconstitutional.

f. New York completed the Erie Canal in 1825, which became a highway between the east and the west.

g. Other states as Virginia, Maryland, New Jersey and Pennsylvania built roads and canals.

3. American manufacturers felt they needed protection against foreign competitors.

a. Every section supported the high tariff of 1816.

b. This tariff act affected woolen and

cotton goods.

c. People in areas where there was no manufacturing felt that the protection from high tariffs would create manufacturing in all regions.

d. Manufacturing still developed slowly in the United States.

(1) Agriculture was a lesser financial risk.

(2) Eli Whitney's invention of the cotton gin in 1793 made cotton cultivation in the south profitable.

(3) The southern staple items as tobacco, rice and cotton made a profit.

(4) Money was scarce.

(5) Labor was scarce and expensive.

(6) British competition was still great.

(7) Land was cheap.

4. The Republican program had great popular appeal, and Monroe became the president in 1816.

E. The Republican administration pursued an aggressive foreign policy.

1. Madison agreed with Jefferson that West Florida was a part of the Louisiana Purchase.

a. In 1810 and 1813 executive orders were given to occupy West Florida.

2. Andrew Jackson, invading Spanish Florida in 1818, started a war against the Seminole Indians and seized Spanish forts.

a. Adams, Secretary of State, using this as an excuse, demanded that Spain control the Indians or sell the region.

b. Spain agreed to sell Florida for $5,000,000 by the Treaty of 1819.

(1) The money was to be used for American claims settlement against the Spanish government.

(2) The western boundary of Louisiana was settled.

3. Harrison's victories in the Northwest during the War of 1812 allowed treaties to be made to permit settlement in Illinois, Michigan and Indiana.

4. The Anglo-American Convention in 1818 made an agreement pertaining to the northwestern border.

a. The northern boundary of the United States was the 49th parallel to the Rockies.

b. Oregon country was to be jointly occupied with the British for ten years.

5. Central and South American colonies rebelled against Spain.

a. Monroe decided to recognize the new republics.

b. He was probably influenced by the argument that their situation was comparable to that of the new United States.

c. He also foresaw trade possibilities which were forbidden under Spain's rule.

F. The Monroe Doctrine was delivered in a presidential speech in 1823.

1. There was a possibility that the Holy Alliance of Russia, Prussia and Austria at the Verona Congress in 1822 intended to interfere in the Americas.

a. European powers wanted to reclaim the Spanish colonies.

b. The Russian-American Fur Company was extending its operations southward toward the Oregon territory.

2. President Monroe delivered his opinions in a message to Congress.

a. If any European nation would extend its control over independent American nations, it was to be considered an unfriendly act to the United States.

b. Europe could no longer colonize on the American continents.

c. The United States would practice a hands-off policy in Europe and expected Europe to do the same in the western hemisphere.

3. The effects of the Monroe Doctrine were many.

a. Europe rejected the Doctrine as having no international legal validity.

b. Latin-American republics regarded it as only a friendly gesture by the United States.

c. It was recognized as international law after World War I in the Versailles Treaty.

G. The nationalistic program of Congress was supported by the Supreme Court.

1. At first the Supreme Court was not looked upon with too much respect.

2. Leaders could not agree about the functions of the court.

a. Proponents of states' rights maintained that the power to interpret the Constitution belonged to the states.

b. Advocates of a strong national government maintained that the court had the right of judicial review of the Constitution in regard to federal and state legislation.

3. The decisions of the Court, under John Marshall as Chief Justice, upheld the supremacy of the Court and used its

U.S. HISTORY

power to strengthen the national government.

    a. Marbury vs. Madison, 1801, declared unconstitutional the Judiciary Act of 1789 passed by Congress, thereby asserting the right of the Court to pass on the Constitutionality of Congressional legislation.

    b. Fletcher vs. Peck, 1810, declared an act of the Georgia legislature unconstitutional concerning the sanctity of contracts, thereby asserting the right of the Court to pass on the constitutionality of state legislation.

    c. Martin vs. Hunter's Lessee, 1816, the Court maintained its right to review decisions over the highest state courts if the decisions were appealed on grounds of conflict with the Constitution.

    d. McCulloch vs. Maryland, 1819, the Court upheld the constitutionality of the act of chartering the Second Bank of the United States and denied the right to the states to tax the bank; both decisions reached by the doctrine of "implied powers".

      1) The "implied powers" doctrine enabled the national government to exercise powers which were in the Constitution only by implication.

    e. Dartmouth College vs. Woodward, 1819, the Court declared the pre-Revolutionary charter of Dartmouth College was a contract and therefore could not be altered by the state of New Hampshire without the consent of the college, thereby again declaring state legislation unconstitutional.

    f. Gibbons vs. Ogden, 1824, the Court denounced state interference with interstate commerce and presented an extremely broad interpretation of congressional power so that a great deal of interstate and foreign commerce could be controlled.

H. Monroe was reelected in 1820, and the Federalists died as a national party.

I. The political scene changed considerably in 1824.

1. There were four favorite candidates for president.

    a. John Quincy Adams was from the North, Andrew Jackson and Henry Clay from the West and William H. Crawford from the South.

2. Personalities were emphasized in the campaign instead of issues.

3. No one candidate received a majority of the electoral votes, so the House of Representatives had to select the president, as stated by the Constitution.

4. Adams was elected President in 1825 by the House of Representatives.

    a. He was chosen from the three leading candidates, Adams, Crawford and Jackson.

    b. Clay, having been dropped, directed his supporters to vote for Adams.

    c. Later Clay became Secretary of State in Adams' cabinet.

    d. This combination merged the New England and the northwestern sections of the country.

    e. Jackson denounced the Clay-Adams merger as a "corrupt bargain".

5. The opposing groups consolidated and caused frustration to be the keynote of the Adams' administration.

    a. Congress refused to allow his program of using federal revenues for road and canal construction, the endowment of educational institutions and the building of warships.

    b. The Senate quarreled with him for sending delegates to the Panama Congress in 1826.

    c. The Georgia legislature defied him in the harsh treatment of the Cherokee Indians.

    d. The organized politicans did a thorough job of discrediting the administration.

6. The "era of good feeling" had ended in 1824.

    a. The era of frustration ended with the Adams' administration.

    b. The reign of Andrew Jackson took over.

X. THE REIGN OF THE PEOPLE'S PRESIDENT, ANDREW JACKSON, 1829-1837.

A. The Republican party split into the National Republicans, and the Democratic Republicans.

1. The National Republicans consisted of the former followers of the Federalist party and the followers of Clay and Adams.

    a. They believed in the governmental program of internal improvements.

    b. They believed in a strong central government, high tariffs and a national bank.

2. The Democratic Republicans, who later were just called Democrats, consisted of the followers of Calhoun, Crawford, Van Buren and Jackson.

    a. They opposed internal improvements, a strong central government which would curtail the rights of states, a national bank and high tariffs.

b. The party lacked unity in its theories.

c. Jackson, their leader, primarily proclaimed the equality of mankind.

3. The campaign of 1829 was divided between democratic equality on one side and aristocracy and privilege on the other side.

4. The popularity of Jackson himself and his liberal doctrines gave him the presidency over Adams in 1828.

a. He was the first president to come from a state west of the Appalachians.

b. By contrast to the wealth of previous presidents, Jackson was born in poverty on the frontier of Carolina.

c. By the time he was elected, he was a fairly wealthy Tennessee plantation owner.

d. He was supported by city workers, small farmers and Southern plantation owners.

e. He symbolized the common man.

f. He allowed his personal relations to have direct bearing on his political policies.

(1) The Cabinet was composed of representatives who united to elect him.

(2) His only close friends in the cabinet were John H. Eaton, Secretary of War and Martin Van Buren, Secretary of State.

(3) The other officials were accepted because of political expediency, and their only common bond was an anti-Clay feeling.

(4) His true political advisors were unofficial close friends called the "Kitchen Cabinet".

(5) He used the spoils system in appointing employees who had the same political belief rather than having aptitude and experience.

B. Jackson instituted greater democracy in elections.

1. Judges, constables and public surveyors were elected rather than appointed.

2. Previously, Presidential candidates were nominated by a caucus of party leaders in congress or by state legislatures.

3. By 1832, Jackson's second nomination, the Democrats held a national nominating convention.

a. A platform was adopted at the convention.

b. The rule was adopted at the Democratic National Convention in 1832 that the nominee must be selected by two-thirds vote of the delegates.

4. The National-Republicans had their convention in 1831.

C. A major issue during his administration was the tariff which was an economic basis of sectionalism.

1. The various sections of the country could not agree on a united satisfactory program.

2. The Tariff of 1828, called "The Tariff of Abominations", provided for high rates to protect the northern factory products.

3. The South, a region exporting cotton and tobacco and importing manufactured goods, favored a low tariff.

a. This would allow the buying of manufactured goods at low prices.

b. John Calhoun of South Carolina was one of the leaders in this fight.

4. Calhoun wrote a famous paper in 1829 called "Exposition and Protest".

a. He maintained the protective tariff was unconstitutional.

b. He declared that a special state convention could declare the tariff law null and void in each state.

c. He based his arguments on the fact that the tariffs were not laws for revenue or for regulating commerce which were legally constitutional, but rather laws that were to protect the manufacturers and were not delegated to the federal government by the Constitution.

5. The controversy was brought to Congress in 1830 by the Webster-Hayne Debate.

a. Senator Hayne of South Carolina tried to encourage the West to side with the South to nullify the tariff laws.

b. Senator Daniel Webster of Massachusetts argued that states could not nullify a Congressional law, but only the Supreme Court could decide on its constitutionality.

c. The debate accomplished nothing.

6. Jackson signed the Tariff Act of 1832 which maintained Clay's protectionist doctrines, even though the rates were slightly lower than in 1828.

a. South Carolina immediately called a state convention to consider nullification, which passed.

b. The state prohibited the collection of custom duties after February 1, 1833 and threatened to secede if the government used force.

c. Jackson warned that nullification was incompatible with the maintenance of the Union and threatened the state with warships and troops held in readiness.

d. At Jackson's request Congress passed the Force Bill in 1833 granting him the authority to use force.

e. The rest of the South did not support South Carolina.

f. The Compromise Tariff in 1833 settled the crisis.

   (1) The bill systematically reduced the tariff over a period of ten years.

   (2) South Carolina accepted the compromise but had forced the government to yield to her demands.

D. There was social and political intrigue within the administration.

1. There was difficulty over the refusal of the cabinet members' wives, led by Mrs. Calhoun, to accept Mrs. Eaton, wife of the Secretary of War.

   a. The Eaton situation weakened the influence of Calhoun with the President, who resented the slander against Mrs. Eaton.

2. Jackson was informed that Calhoun had suggested that Jackson be court martialed for his invasion of Florida at the time of the Seminole War, 1818.

3. The break between Jackson and Calhoun became complete.

   a. This weakened the strength of Calhoun's followers since there was no presidential backing.

   b. In 1831, Jackson completely changed the personnel of his cabinet.

   c. Calhoun resigned the vice-presidency and became a senator from South Carolina.

   d. Van Buren resigned as Secretary of State and the Senate refused to confirm his appointment as minister to England.

   e. Jackson forced the Democrats to nominate Van Buren as Vice-President in 1832.

E. The issue of the presidential campaign of 1832 was based on Jackson's hostility to the bank.

1. The Second Bank of the United States was the most important banking institution.

   a. It acted as the government's agent in all money matters.

   b. It floated loans and accepted government deposit of funds.

   c. Its bank notes were accepted everywhere in the country and in Europe.

2. The merchants and industrialists favored the Bank.

3. Jackson disapproved of the Bank.

   a. He believed the charter was unconstitutional.

   b. He believed it was a monopoly which favored the business group.

   c. He believed the Bank used its financial power for political advantages.

4. Farmers and plantation owners opposed the Bank.

5. The re-chartering of the Bank became a major issue in 1832.

   a. Clay introduced a bill for re-chartering.

   b. Jackson vetoed the bill.

   c. Clay was the candidate of the newly formed National Republican Party which later became the Whig Party.

   d. Jackson was renominated by the Democratic Party in an overwhelming victory.

      1) He then felt the public endorsed his opposition to the Bank.

   e. He withdrew government funds and the Bank was not rechartered in 1836.

F. The Panic of 1837 followed until 1840.

1. Government funds were deposited in favored state banks called "pet banks".

   a. State banks now were able to make loans.

   b. They issued so many they became valueless.

2. Wild land speculation and internal improvement projects ran rampant so as to strain the resources of the banks.

   a. Jackson issued an order—the "Specie Circular", 1836, which required payment in gold and silver for public land.

   b. Land speculation collapsed because easy paper money loans were checked.

3. The people lost confidence in the soundness of national currency.

4. Over-extended industries closed up and created alarming unemployment, mortgage foreclosures and bankruptcies.

5. Farmers' crops also were poor in 1837.

6. Europe had an economic depression and recalled loans in the United States.

7. Many state banks failed or suspended specie payment.

G. The national government issued emergency measures to relieve the conditions.

1. The poor received relief.

2. The Van Buren administration which

followed, approved the issuing of $10,000,000 in treasury notes as an emergency act.

3. Congress passed the Independent Treasury Act in 1840, which the Whigs repealed in 1841 and re-established in 1846.
   a. The measure divorced the government from the banking system.
   b. Sub-treasuries were established in important cities as depositories for government funds, which were to be used only for government expenditures.

H. **The Whig party began to rise in 1836.**
1. The party consisted of people opposed to Jackson's doctrines.
2. The party lost the presidency to Van Buren, the Democratic nominee, in 1836.
   a. Van Buren won because of Jackson's popularity.
3. In 1840, Van Buren, an unpopular president, lost to William Henry Harrison, a Whig.
   a. The Whigs blamed Van Buren for the depression of 1837.
   b. The campaign used slogans, the most famous one being "Tippicanoe and Tyler too!"
   c. Harrison was portrayed as a simple man as against Van Buren, the aristocrat.
4. The Whig program continued under the leadership of Senator Henry Clay.
   a. Harrison died in 1841.
   b. John Tyler, the Vice-President succeeded Harrison.
      (1) Tyler was unsympathetic to Whig policies.
      (2) He was only associated with the party because he disapproved of Jackson's attitude toward the South Carolina nullification episode.
5. The Tyler administration typified his states' rights Democratic leanings.
   a. The bank charter was reissued, though Tyler vetoed the bill.
   b. The sub-treasury act was repealed.
   c. Tyler refused to approve a tariff bill protecting manufacturers.
   d. Revenue was needed so a tariff bill of 1842 restored the 1832 rates.
   e. Tyler's refusal to accept Clay's program caused his cabinet to resign, and they were replaced by political friends.
6. Daniel Webster, Secretary of State, was engaged in negotiations with England.
   a. There was a dispute concerning the boundary between Maine and New Brunswick and the unsatisfactory joint occupation of Oregon territory.
   b. There was a series of other minor irritating grievances.
   c. The Webster-Ashburton Treaty of 1842 settled the Maine-New Brunswick boundary by setting up a compromise line.
   d. There were British apologies for the grievances and Anglo-American relationship improved.

XI. **SOCIAL REFORM, CULTURAL DEVELOPMENT AND INDUSTRIAL GROWTH PRIOR TO THE CIVIL WAR.**

A. **By 1830 the Industrial Revolution was well developed.**
1. After the Revolutionary War, the factory system and production methods improved.
2. The first successful cotton factory was in Rhode Island, 1790, established by Samuel Slater.
3. A power loom for spinning and weaving was installed by Lowell in a factory in Massachusetts, 1814.
4. Elias Howe invented the sewing machine, 1846.
5. After 1825 the iron manufacturing system was improved by the hot blast furnace and the Bessemer process of molten metal and decarbonizing.
6. Eli Whitney invented the cotton gin and introduced the principle of manufacturing interchangeable parts.
7. Water power was harnessed for mills.
8. Coal replaced wood as fuel.
9. The New England, New York, New Jersey, Pennsylvania and Maryland manufacturing regions spread to Ohio, Indiana, Illinois and northern Kentucky.

B. **The improved factory system created labor problems.**
1. The labor movement's start dated from 1827, when the Mechanics Union of Trade Association began in Philadelphia.
2. By the 1830's the "closed shop", in which only union members might be employed, and the strike were used to better working conditions.
3. In 1837, a National Trades Union was organized by labor union delegates from northern cities.
4. Jackson ordered the ten-hour day on all work done for the government.
5. Labor unions worked with other groups

for more social reforms, such as; free public education, restricting child labor and demanding cheap public land.

C. **The growth of manufacturing created transportation improvements.**

1. Robert Fulton's steamboat, the Clermont, made its first successful trip between New York and Albany, 1807.
2. Other steamboats were launched on various rivers and canals.
3. Railroads became the chief means of transportation.
   a. The first steam railway was the Baltimore and Ohio which was chartered in 1827.
   b. By 1840, there were 2,818 miles of tracks and by 1860 they increased to 30,626 miles.
4. S. F. B. Morse invented the telegraph, 1837.
   a. By 1860, there were 50,000 miles of telegraph wires east of the Rocky Mountains.
5. The Adams Express Company, the first nation-wide company started in 1854.

D. **During the 1830's and 1840's there were many more tax-supported schools.**

1. By 1850, many states provided free elementary education.
2. There were few public high schools.
3. Much of the education was privately controlled.
4. Horace Mann of Massachusetts became the first Secretary of the State Board of Education.
   a. He started the establishment of normal schools to train teachers.
   b. He worked to unite local units into a state system of education.
5. Henry Barnard did the same for Connecticut and Rhode Island and became the first United States Commissioner of Education.

E. **Women began to fight vigorously for equal rights with men.**

1. More girls attended public schools.
2. Mount Holyoke Seminary, an institution of higher education for women, was founded in 1836 by Mary Lyon.
3. Oberlin College in Ohio was the first co-educational college.
4. Lucretia Mott, Susan B. Anthony and Elizabeth Stanton led the "Feminists" movement at the first women's rights convention in New York, 1848.
5. During Jackson's administration, some states passed laws allowing women to keep and manage their property after marriage.

F. **There began an active antislavery movement by the abolitionists.**

1. They demanded immediate freedom of slaves with no compensation to the owners.
2. The group was small but dedicated.
3. William Lloyd Garrison was their most outstanding spokesman.
4. Other abolitionists were Theodore Parker, Harriet Tubman, John Greenleaf Whittier, Harriet Beecher Stowe and Frederick Douglas.
5. The group had great difficulty in promoting its doctrines.

G. **A great variety of other reforms were also developing.**

1. Dorothea Dix worked to improve the treatment of the insane.
2. The treatment of criminals was improved upon.
3. The temperance movement to adopt a prohibition law began.

H. **The cultural movement in literature, music, art and science were making strides.**

1. An American literature was developing.
   a. Washington Irving wrote "Rip Van Winkle" and stories about early Dutch settlers.
   b. James Fenimore Cooper told of American boys imitating Indians and settlers in his "Leatherstocking Tales".
   c. Nathaniel Hawthorne wrote of his native New England in "The House of Seven Gables".
   d. American poets as Walt Whitman, Henry Wadsworth Longfellow, John Greenleaf Whittier, William Cullen Bryant, and Edgar Allan Poe gave us poetry concerning the new land.
   e. Ralph Waldo Emerson emphasized individualism in his essays and poems.
   f. Henry Thoreau gave us "Walden" as he rebelled against industrialism.
2. Notable scientific progress was made during Jackson's era and pre-Civil War.
   a. Asa Gray was an outstanding botanist.
   b. Joseph Henry did pioneer work in harnessing electricity.
   c. Drs. Long and Morton worked independently of each other in using ether as an anesthetic during operations.
   d. Eli Whitney, Robert Fulton and Samuel F. B. Morse created important inventions.

e. The Smithsonian Institution and National Museum was established by the federal government in 1846 with funds of James Smithson, an Englishman.

3. Professions began to improve their training and skill.
   a. The training of lawyers was emphasized by many colleges.
   b. King's College appointed a professor of law, 1773.
   c. The first law school was founded in Connecticut, 1784.
   d. Harvard Law School was opened, 1817.
   e. First medical schools were at the University of Pennsylvania, 1765 and the Harvard Medical School, 1783.
   f. By 1825, most of the important universities had medical schools.
   g. Dr. Elizabeth Blackwell was the

first woman graduate doctor, 1849.
4. Classical music was encouraged.
   a. The Philharmonic Society of Boston was founded, 1810 and that of New York, 1842.
   b. The Handel and Haydn Society of Boston started, 1815.
5. The most outstanding artists were post-Revolutionary ones, and there were no great followers until after the Civil War.
   a. Gilbert Stuart, Jonathan Trumbull, Benjamin West, Charles Wilson Peale were some of the outstanding painters.
6. The first half of the nineteenth century also saw other conveniences develop.
   a. Sewage systems and disposal of waste were established in cities.
   b. Gas illumination was used from 1816 and thereafter.
   c. Water supply systems were installed in cities.
   d. Street cars, drawn by horses, ran on the city streets.
   e. Daily newspapers were published.
      1) The New York Herald, 1835, was the first successful daily penny paper published.
7. Architecture followed various European styles.
   a. The colonial period saw Georgian types.
   b. At the end of the eighteenth century there was a classical revival of Greek and Roman architecture.
   c. The decade prior to the Civil War saw Victorian Gothic and French Romanesque architecture.

XII. THE WESTWARD TERRITORIAL EXPANSION, 1840-1850.

A. American nationalists argued it was their "manifest destiny" to reach all natural territorial limits, namely, the seas.
  1. The motives for expansion were economic, political and a search for adventure.
  2. Transportation was greatly improved, and the frontiers could be more easily reached.
  3. The West was occupied by three types of pioneers.
     a. The trappers and fur traders came first for economic reasons.
     b. The backwoodsmen followed and lived in log cabins with hunting, fishing and small scale farming as their means of subsistence.
     c. The pioneer farmers came next and improved the land and erected buildings in order to remain permanently.
     d. The establishment of churches, schools and town halls created urban communities.
  4. The frontier was plagued with problems.
     a. The Indians were an obstacle to land settlement.
        (1) The United States practiced unethical land negotiations with the Indians and thereby created violent quarrels.
        (2) By 1840, Indian titles to land east of the Mississippi were non-existent.
     b. Land title disputes created confusion and conflicts.
     c. There was insufficient currency in the West since they opposed the Bank and eastern financiers.
     d. Transportation was expensive and thereby restricted western trade.

B. Americans gained their independence in Texas.

  1. The uncertain boundaries of the Louisiana Purchase gave the United States a claim to Texas.
  2. The claim was surrendered to Spain in 1819 by the Florida treaty.
  3. Stephen Austin settled on land in Texas given to his father by the Spanish government.
     a. Soon other colonizers were recipients of large land grants.

    b. By 1830, there were almost 20,000 Americans settled in Texas.

4. Mexico overthrew the Spanish government, 1821.

    a. Mexico established a federal Republic, 1825.

    b. Joel Poinsett became minister to Mexico.

    c. No offer was encouraged by the Mexican government for the sale of Texas.

5. The Texan settlers developed anti-Mexican grievances.

    a. The Texans desired to retain their English language and American traditions.

    b. They feared the Mexican government would abolish slavery.

    c. They resented the Mexican laws imposing duties on imported goods, suspending land contracts, and prohibiting foreigners from settling there.

6. The Texans rebelled against the Mexican government, 1835.

    a. Texans won their independence at the Battle of San Jacinto, when Santa Anna's forces were routed by General Sam Houston.

    b. President Santa Anna acknowledged the independence of the province but refused to recognize the presidential signature.

7. Texas requested annexation by the United States in 1836 but was refused by Jackson and later by Van Buren.

    a. Jackson recognized Texas as an independent nation, 1837.

    b. The Senate, in 1844, refused to ratify the treaty by which Texas would gain admittance under President Tyler, 1841-45.

    c. The North feared the addition of more slave territory.

    d. Texas annexation was the presidential election issue of 1844.

      (1) James K. Polk, the Democratic candidate, favored annexation.

      (2) Henry Clay, the Whig candidate, first opposed annexation and later accepted it.

      (3) Polk was elected by a slim margin.

8. Texas was annexed by a joint resolution of the Senate and House of Representatives, 1845.

    a. Joint resolution was necessary because the Senate was unable to obtain a two-thirds ratification.

    b. Texas ratified the resolution and was admitted to the Union in December, 1845.

9. The Oregon boundary dispute was settled, 1846.

    a. Polk's campaign program for Oregon was "54-40 or fight".

    b. Oregon's value lay in the fur trade and its land fertility.

    c. Britain would not yield to the American claim.

    d. Oregon partitioned between the United States and Canada by the treaty of 1846, boundary set at the forty-ninth parallel from the Rockies to the Pacific.

C. The annexation of Texas precipitated a crisis between the United States and Mexico.

1. Americans and other foreigners arrested in Upper California were given harsh treatment and deported from Mexico, 1840.

2. Mexico was disturbed about the increasing migration of Americans into California.

3. After Texas annexation, Mexico severed relations with the United States.

4. John Slidell, an American representative who was sent to discuss amicable arrangements, was not received.

5. American troops clashed with a Mexican force in an area lying on the Texas side of the Rio Grande River.

6. Polk called a session of Congress and war was declared on Mexico, 1846.

    a. War was blamed on the invasion of American territory and the shedding of American blood by Mexican troops.

D. Military events led to America gaining control of all of California, New Mexico and Texas.

1. General Zachary Taylor led American troops to victory at the battles of Palo Alto, 1846 and Buena Vista, 1847.

2. General Kearney conquered New Mexico and led an expedition to take possession of California.

3. Commodore John Sloat seized San Francisco with the American fleet.

4. General Winfield Scott landed his troops at Vera Cruz and took Mexico City.

E. The war ended with the Treaty of Guadalupe, 1848.

1. Texas was recognized as part of the United States with the Rio Grande river as its boundary.
2. California and New Mexico were ceded to the United States for a payment of $15,000,000 and the assumption of debts owed to Americans by Mexico.
3. On today's map, the Mexican cession included California, most of New Mexico and Arizona, Utah, Nevada and parts of Wyoming and Colorado.

F. The Mexican War had two far-reaching effects in the United States.

1. Gold was discovered in the Sacramento valley, California, 1848 and created a phenomenal migration to the west.
2. Zachary Taylor, a victorious general of the Mexican War, became the elected Whig president, 1848.
   a. The defeated Democratic candidate was Lewis Cass.
   b. Taylor died in 1850 and was succeeded by the Vice-President, Millard Fillmore.

G. The Mormons settled around Salt Lake in Utah, 1847.

1. The Mormon Church was founded by Joseph Smith at Palmyra, New York in 1830.
2. The Mormons, a religious sect, migrated to Ohio, Missouri, Illinois, Iowa and finally settled permanently in Utah.
3. Their migrations were caused by the hostility shown to them by the communities in which they lived.
4. Brigham Young, their leader after Smith, became the first governor of Utah.
5. The Mormon settlements prospered because the seekers of gold passed through their territory on the way to California.
6. Utah was organized as a territory in 1850.

XIII. BACKGROUND OF THE CIVIL WAR

A. Slavery became predominantly a Southern institution.

1. During the colonial period, slaves were in all the colonies.
2. State statutes abolished slavery in the northern states after the Revolutionary War by a gradual emancipation.
3. Slaves were retained in the southern area, because they were used as laborers on the plantations.

4. The disagreement on the slave issue between the North and the South appeared at the Constitutional Convention of 1787.
5. Slavery was prohibited in the Northwest Territory by the Northwest Ordinance of 1787.
   a. Slavery was thereafter confined to the region south of the Ohio river and the Mason-Dixon line.
6. There was no slave policy set up in the territory of the Louisiana Purchase.
7. The return of runaway slaves who fled to other states was provided by the Fugitive Slave Law, 1793.
8. The most important factor for the retaining of slaves in the South was the expansion of the cotton industry.
   a. Eli Whitney's invention of the cotton gin, 1793, made the cotton industry extremely profitable.
   b. This created a great need for Negro labor on the cotton plantations.
   c. The demand was further increased by the beginning of sugar plantations.
   d. As slavery expanded, it became a gang system of enforced labor.
9. A federal law was passed in 1807 prohibiting the importation of slaves.

B. A national crisis was temporarily settled by the Missouri Compromise of 1820.

1. Missouri wanted admission to the Union in 1818 with slavery permitted.
2. Maine also sought admission in 1819 and would enter as a free state.
3. Nationalism now was replaced by sectionalism, with differences over the extension of slavery as the main antagonism.
4. Thomas of Illinois proposed the compromise of admitting Missouri as a slave state and Maine as a free state.
   a. This maintained the balance of power between slave and free states.
   b. The extension of slavery into the Louisiana Territory was limited to the section north of the 36° 30' line except in the state of Missouri.
5. The bill was passed, 1820.

C. The North organized its anti-slavery feelings as opposed to the consolidated pro-slavery Southern sentiments.

1. The South defended slavery as the basis for economic prosperity.

U.S. HISTORY

2. The North looked upon slavery as a moral evil.
   a. Abolitionists aimed to eradicate slavery.
   b. Quakers and other religious groups were actively anti-slavery.
   c. William Lloyd Garrison founded the publication "The Liberator", 1831.
   d. Abolitionist societies were formed, and the American anti-Slavery Society was organized in 1833.
   e. Even though the Abolitionists were a minority, the conscience of the North was aroused.
   f. The South used the Bible and the Constitution to back their views on slavery.
   g. The Southern postmasters refused to deliver abolitionist literature, and legislatures forbade the printing of anti-slavery literature.
   h. The Southern members of the House of Representatives passed a "gag rule", whereby all petitions pertaining to slavery were put aside without debate or action.

D. The Mexican War also complicated the slavery issue.
   1. The North opposed war with Mexico for fear newly acquired territory would become slave areas.
   2. Representative David Wilmot of Pennsylvania proposed an amendment to an appropriation bill in 1846 to bar slavery from any areas acquired from Mexico.
      a. The Wilmot Proviso was defeated in the Senate and passed in the House of Representatives.
      b. Southern leaders regarded the Proviso as a serious threat to slavery.
      c. The United States was threatened with a definite division of thought.
   3. The slavery issue split the Democratic party in New York state and thereby assured the election of Zachary Taylor, the Whig candidate for President, 1848.
   4. Threats of secession were heard when Congress convened, 1849.
   5. The vast territory gained from the Mexican War caused the controversy to start anew.
      a. California had a record population increase because of the 1849 "Gold Rush".
      b. California was ready to be admitted to the Union as a state.

   c. California would upset the balance in the Senate for its constitution banned slavery.

E. Clay, assisted by Webster, framed a compromise called the Omnibus Bill, which contained five provisions.
   1. California was admitted as a free state.
   2. Newly organized territories of New Mexico and Utah would take popular sovereignty, allowing the state to decide the slavery issue.
   3. The Fugitive Slave Act of 1793 was amended to be stronger and more effective.
   4. The slave trade, but not slavery itself, was prohibited in the District of Columbia.
   5. A payment of $10,000,000 was to be paid to Texas for yielding her claim to part of the New Mexico territory.

F. The Compromise of 1850 was passed as five separate bills.
   1. President Taylor opposed the bill, but he died in office.
   2. He was succeeded by President Fillmore who favored it.

G. The national policy of the next decade was dominated by the slavery issue.
   1. Franklin Pierce, the Democratic candidate for president, defeated Winfield Scott, the Whig candidate, 1852.
      a. The Whig party then disintegrated.
   2. The construction of a trans-continental railway between the Mississippi River and the Pacific coast was prevented by the Northern and Southern rivalry as to its location.
      a. James Gadsden, from South Carolina, was sent to Mexico in 1853 to purchase 50,000 square miles in the Gila Valley for a sum of $10,000,000 for a Southern railroad route.
      b. An era of violence followed in Kansas.
      c. President Pierce had to send troops to restore order.
      d. Kansas was finally admitted as a free state but not until 1861.
   3. The Kansas Nebraska Bill, 1854, repealing the Missouri Compromise was a fateful factor in reviving the North-South quarrel.
      a. The Bill extended the principle of popular sovereignty to Kansas and Nebraska, where formerly slavery

was banned by the Compromise of 1850.

b. The Bill was sponsored by Senator Stephen Douglas of Illinois.

c. His aims were based on the desire for the trans-continental railroad to take the central route and to curry favor with the South for his personal ambitions toward the presidency.

d. The South saw an opportunity to gain new slavery territory.

e. Douglas directed the passage of the bill through both houses of Congress.

4. The most significant result was the formation of the Republican Party in Michigan, 1854.

a. The party was composed of anti-slavery Whigs, the anti-slavery Democrats and the Free Soilers.

b. The party platform called for the repeal of the Kansas-Nebraska Act, the fugitive slave law and the restriction of slavery to its already existing boundaries.

c. The Republican party was organized nationally at Pittsburgh, 1856.

d. John C. Fremont was selected as the Republican presidential nominee to run against James Buchanan, a Democrat.

e. Buchanan was elected even though he had a minority of the popular vote.

5. The Supreme Court decision on the Dred Scott case legalized slavery in the territories, 1857.

a. Scott, a slave, sued for his freedom on the basis that temporary residency with his master on free soil emancipated him.

b. The Supreme Court of Missouri reversed a lower court decision which had given Scott his freedom.

c. Scott then sued in the Federal courts, and it became a test case backed by Northern anti-slavery men.

d. Chief Justice Taney, of the Supreme Court, speaking for the majority, ruled that since Scott was a descendant of slaves he was not a citizen and therefore could not sue in a Federal court.

e. In a supplementary opinion, the court defined the status of slaves in the United States.

(1) The Constitution guaranteed property rights, therefore Congress could not prohibit a citizen from taking slave property into any United States territory.

f. Therefore, the Missouri Compromise had always been unconstitutional.

g. The decision legalized slavery in all the territories.

6. The Lincoln-Douglas debates, 1858, in the senatorial election in Illinois brought Lincoln national prominence.

a. Douglas was the Democratic candidate, and Lincoln was the Republican.

b. Douglas was elected but his Freeport Doctrine, the indorsement of popular sovereignty, angered the southerners.

(1) The Southerners believed in the rights of owners to take slaves anywhere despite local opinion in the territories.

c. Lincoln's opposition to the extension of slavery made him a potential presidential nominee of the Republican party in 1860.

7. John Brown's Raid, 1859, increased Southern hostility.

a. John Brown, a fanatical abolitionist, hoped to free the slaves by organizing a rebellion.

b. Brown seized the Federal arsenal at Harper's Ferry, Virginia, 1859.

c. He planned to use it as a base for his revolutionary operations.

d. The arsenal was captured two days later by a detachment of marines under Colonel Robert E. Lee.

e. Brown was captured, tried, convicted and hanged.

f. The South accused the North of a slave rebellion in order to destroy slavery completely.

g. Some of the North looked upon John Brown as a martyr and others deplored his rash deed.

8. Lincoln, solidly backed by the Republicans, was elected President in 1860.

a. The Democratic party was completely split.

(1) The Northern Democrats nominated Douglas of Illinois.

(2) The Southern Democrats selected Breckinridge of Kentucky.

(3) Other Democrats from the border states, former Whigs, started the

U.S. HISTORY

Constitutional Unionist Party and nominated Bell from Tennessee.

 b. The party platform advocated a high tariff, public works, and an end to the extension of slavery.

9. The Southern states seceded from the Union, 1860.

 a. South Carolina adopted an Ordinance of Secession, Dec. 20, 1860.

 b. Five states immediately followed South Carolina.

 c. A convention was held in Alabama, January 4, 1861, where the Confederate States of America was created.

  (1) The states included South Carolina, Florida, Georgia, Alabama, Mississippi and Louisiana.

  (2) Texas joined the Confederacy, February 23, 1861.

  (3) Jefferson Davis was elected President and Alexander H. Stephens Vice-President.

10. President Buchanan remained passive during the secession of the states.

11. Schemes for reconciliation were proposed during 1860-61.

 a. The Crittenden Compromise to prohibit slavery north of 36° 31' and to guarantee federal protection south of that line was defeated by Republican members of a Senatorial committee.

 b. Lincoln, the President-elect, opposed any type of compromise.

12. Lincoln took his oath of office March 4, 1861.

 a. He pleaded with the South.

 b. He stated that he was opposed to extension of slavery not slavery itself.

XIV. THE CIVIL WAR AND RECONSTRUCTION, 1861-1877.

A. The War was basically a clash of opposing social and economic systems between the North and the South.

1. The South lived by the plantation system, employing slave labor to produce agricultural staples for export.

2. The North developed diversified agriculture and industries depending on free labor.

3. The South advanced the principle of states' rights.

 a. Calhoun believed the states possessed the right to nullify Congressional acts.

 b. Others believed that this also led to the states' rights to secession, which was an extreme interpretation.

4. The North believed in a strong central government.

5. The principle of human rights versus slavery was an obvious factor.

B. The attack on Fort Sumter by the Confederates on April 12, 1861 began the war.

1. Lincoln requested volunteers immediately, but Fort Sumter fell.

2. He declared the Southern ports blockaded.

3. During May and June, 1861, Arkansas, Virginia, North Carolina and Tennessee seceded from the Union.

C. The North was superior in materials and power.

1. Northern population was 22,000,000 as against 9,000,000 in the South of whom 3,500,000 were Negroes.

2. The North drew the armies from a manpower pool of 5,000,000 men, the South from about 1,500,000 men.

3. The quality of both troops were fairly similar.

4. The South had the advantage of better generals at the outbreak of the war.

 a. The outstanding Southern generals were Robert E. Lee, Joseph E. Johnston, "Stonewall" Jackson, P. G. Beauregard and Albert S. Johnston.

 b. General George McClellan was the only outstanding Union General with Grant, Sheridan and Sherman rising in distinction later.

 c. Jefferson Davis, the Confederate President, was a West Point graduate, a former Secretary of War and knew the art of war and leadership.

5. The material resources of the North were superior to the South.

6. The North controlled most of the naval forces.

7. The South was fighting on familiar home territory; saving their homes and land was a motivating force.

D. The Union troops were defeated at Bull Run, July 21, 1861, the first Battle.

1. The North then developed a program of offensive warfare with three major objectives.

a. Richmond, the capitol of the Confederacy had to be captured.

b. The Mississippi had to be controlled so that the Confederacy would be split in two.

c. Southern ports had to be blockaded.

2. The Southern strategy centered on defense.

3. It took four years for the North to complete its objectives.

E. The Peninsular Campaign took place from March to July, 1862.

1. General McClellan, victorious from a West Virginia campaign, took command of the Army of the Potomac to march on Richmond.

2. He decided to approach Richmond via Fortress Monroe and the Peninsula between the York and James Rivers.

3. He waited in vain for reinforcements.

4. Despite being successful against Lee's troops at Malvern Hill, he abandoned the campaign.

F. The Battle of Antietam was fought September, 1862.

1. McClellan was removed, but after Pope lost to "Stonewall" Jackson in the Second Battle of Bull Run, he was recalled to stop Lee's advancing forces.

2. The two armies met at Antietam and Lee was forced to retreat.

3. McClellan did not follow up his victory and was replaced by Burnside.

G. The Battle of Gettysburg, 1863, was a decisive battle of the war.

1. Burnside suffered a disastrous defeat at Fredericksburg, December, 1862.

2. Burnside's successor, Hooker, lost at Chancellorsville, May, 1863, but the South lost its able general, "Stonewall" Jackson.

3. Lee's advance through Maryland into Pennsylvania was stopped by General Meade at Gettysburg.

H. The Union was successful in obtaining control of the Mississippi.

1. Grant captured Fort Henry on the Tennessee River and Fort Donelson on the Cumberland River, 1862.

2. He advanced to Tennessee and withstood a Confederate attack in the Battle of Shiloh, April, 1862.

3. The Confederate troops were forced to retreat to Mississippi.

4. Farraugut's naval forces captured New Orleans, April, 1862, thus gaining control of the lower Mississippi River.

5. The Confederates now were in control of the river between Vicksburg and Port Hudson.

6. Grant captured Vicksburg, July, 1863.

7. The Union next occupied Port Hudson and thereby gained full control of the Mississippi.

8. This cut off Arkansas, Louisiana and Texas from the rest of the South.

I. Lincoln proclaimed a blockade on the Atlantic Coast from South Carolina to Florida, April, 1861.

1. By the end of 1862, the Federal Navy controlled all the major ports except Mobile, Charleston and Wilmington.

2. The Confederates reconstructed the ironclad frigate Merrimac and sent her to destroy the Federal wooden ships.

3. The Federal government sent out another ironclad, the Monitor, to meet the Merrimac.

4. The battle was indecisive but the attempt to break the blockade was unsuccessful.

5. After this, wooden ships became obsolete.

6. The effect of the blockade was successful in slowly starving the South.

J. The closing campaigns led to the collapse of the Confederacy.

1. Sheridan, Sherman, Thomas and Grant cooperated and won the battles of Chattanooga, Lookout Mountain and Missionary Ridge, in the fall of 1863.

2. Grant was made commander of the Union forces, February, 1864.

3. Sherman began his invasion of Georgia in the spring of 1864 and captured Atlanta by September 1, 1864.

4. Sherman then marched eastward to the sea laying waste the land which supplied Lee's army.

5. He then turned northward to crush the Confederacy between the two Union armies.

6. Grant advanced toward Richmond in the Wilderness campaign of 1864.

7. Grant entered Richmond, April 3, 1865; Lee's army weakened.

8. Lee surrendered April 9, 1865, at Appomattox Court House.

K. The war had imposed problems on both sides which had far reaching effects.

U.S.
HISTORY

1. Both sides depended upon taxes, paper money, and bonds to finance the war.
2. Labor saving agricultural machinery was used because of the labor shortage.
3. Northern manufacturing was stimulated.
4. Lincoln suspended the writ of habeas corpus, authorized political arrests and upheld sentences by military tribunals in order to preserve the Union.
5. Lincoln moved slowly toward the abolition of slavery.
   a. Slaves were freed in the District of Columbia with compensation to their owners, 1862.
   b. A preliminary Emancipation Proclamation was issued September 22, 1862 to become effective January 1, 1863.
      (1) It freed slaves in all states which were still in rebellion against the government on that date.
      (2) The act was a military punishment against the Confederate States.
      (3) This act pleased England in that she believed that the North had humanitarian sentiments.
      The House of Representatives received a resolution for a thirteenth amendment to the Constitution, December, 1863, to prohibit slavery within the United States or any region subject to its jurisdiction.
      (1) The necessary two-thirds majority in Congress was obtained January 31, 1865.
      (2) The amendment was then referred to the state legislatures, three-fourths of which ratified by December 12, 1865.
      (3) The abolition of slavery then became legal.

L. The Union and the Confederacy had deep concern of the European policies throughout the war.

1. The South hoped the British need for her cotton would cause her to reorganize the South as an independent nation.
   a. England did not do so because of the hostility of the working class to the Southern cause.
   b. England in general had anti-slavery sentiments.
   c. England had to rely on Northern wheat.
   d. The Lincoln administration led a successful diplomatic effort to prevent this from occurring.
2. The North almost went to war with England because of the Trent Affair.
   a. Captain Wilkes of an American war vessel removed Mason and Slidell, Confederate emissaries to Europe, from the British mailship Trent.
   b. The crisis ended when Lincoln ordered Mason and Slidell to be released.
3. The Alabama, Florida and Shenandoah, commerce raiders, were built in England for the Confederacy.
   a. The United States protested against this as a neutrality violation.
   b. England became more forceful in maintaining neutrality.
   c. The activity of the commerce-destroyers became the basis for the United States Alabama claims against England after the war.
4. Napoleon III of France paid little attention to its obligations as a neutral.
   a. He allowed ships to be built for the Confederacy.
   b. He assisted the Confederacy in making the Erlanger loan.
   c. He violated the Monroe Doctrine by placing Maximilian of Austria on the throne of a Mexican Empire he created with French troops.
   d. He refused to withdraw from Mexico until General Sheridan was sent to the Mexican border at the end of the war.

M. Lincoln was re-elected for a second term, 1864.

1. Andrew Johnson became Vice-President on the Union Republican Party ticket.
2. Lincoln won over the Democratic nominee, General McClellan.
3. McClellan had been nominated by the regular Democrats and a militant minority of Democrats, called "Copperheads".

PART II

I. THE RECONSTRUCTION PERIOD
  A. The Civil War left important aftereffects on the nation.

1. Slavery was abolished.
2. Large Southern plantations were divided.

3. The prestige and power of the national government were increased.

4. The doctrine of states' rights was discredited.

5. Northern economic policies were strengthened.

   a. The national banking system and the high protective tariff remained after the war.

   b. The trancontinental railway through Northern territory influenced the national economy.

B. **The South was left destroyed, destitute and with no social order or politica control.**

1. The financial condition was hopeless.

2. The structure of the pre-war Southern society was destroyed.

   a. Merchants, small farmers and bankers replaced the aristocratic plantation owner.

   b. The change of the Negro status from slave to paid worker created tension.

3. There was no government left when the Confederacy collapsed.

4. The status of the slave had to be determined.

   a. The Negroes were confused by their newly found freedom.

   b. Congress established a Freedman's Bureau, March 3, 1865, for one year to organize and administer the affairs of the liberated Negroes.

   c. The Bureau, headed by General Howard, worked to protect them from white exploitation.

      (1) Land was leased or purchased for them.

      (2) The Bureau attempted to establish the freed people as part of a new economic system.

C. **Lincoln's plan for reconstruction was of a moderate nature in order to avoid bitterness.**

1. On December 8, 1863, he delivered his "Proclamation of Amnesty and Reconstruction."

   a. This pardoned almost all who would swear allegiance to the Union and accept the abolition of slavery.

   b. High officers of the Confederate government, army and navy were not pardoned.

2. He set up provisional governments in areas where the Northern armies were victorious.

3. He authorized the establishment of a new civil government in any state if one tenth of its qualified voters of 1860 would take the oath of loyalty.

   a. Lincoln stated that he did not have the power to readmit Congressmen.

   b. Tennessee, Arkansas, and Louisiana were brought back.

4. Lincoln based his plan upon the theory that the South had rebelled and had not seceded, and he therefore had the power to pardon them.

D. **The Reconstruction Plan ran into strong opposition among Republican congressional leaders.**

1. Congress passed the severe Wade-Davis bill, July, 1864.

   a. The bill provided that a majority of white male citizens had to take a loyalty oath before a civil government could be established in a seceded state.

   b. Former Confederate soldiers and officials were excluded from the electorates of these states.

   c. Lincoln pocket-vetoed the bill.

2. Many thought the South should be treated as a conquered nation.

E. **Andrew Johnson became the successor to the presidency after the assassination of Lincoln, April 14, 1865.**

1. His attitude was to continue Lincoln's moderation policy.

2. His amnesty proclamation pardoned all Confederates who took the loyalty oath except leaders and large property holders.

   a. The excluded people could be pardoned individually by the President.

3. He set up provisional governments in North Carolina, Mississippi, Alabama, Georgia, Texas, Florida and South Carolina.

   a. These states had to annul secession, abolish slavery and repudiate the Confederate state debts.

F. **Congressional radicals disapproved of the President's reconstruction policy.**

1. A Joint Committee on Reconstruction with fifteen members was formed to study the conditions of the Confederate states and make new proposals for Congressional action.

   a. Sumner of the Senate and Stevens of the House were the radical leaders.

2. Freedman's Bureau Bill, July, 1866, enlarged the powers of the emergency organization and extended its existence for two years, in order to improve the Negro's welfare.

   a. The first bill introduced in January was vetoed by Johnson.

3. The Civil Rights Bill, April, 1866, was passed over Johnson's veto.

   a. The bill conferred citizenship upon the Negro and assured him equality of treatment.

   b. Johnson vetoed the bill because of its invasion of state powers.

4. The South passed "Black Codes" to ensure white supremacy.

5. The Joint Committee on Reconstruction proposed the Fourteenth Amendment, April, 1866.

   a. The provisions included citizenship to be conferred on every person born or naturalized in the United States and any state laws abridging citizenship and civil rights equality would be unconstitutional.

   b. Representation in Congress would be reduced in proportion to those who were denied the franchise by states.

   c. Ex-Confederates who had taken the loyalty oath before service were prohibited from state or federal office unless the disability was removed by a two-thirds vote in each house.

   d. The validity of the United States debt was affirmed and the Confederate debt was repudiated.

6. Congress passed the amendment with changes, June 13, 1866 and then submitted it to the states.

   a. Tennessee ratified the amendment and was readmitted to the Union.

   b. All other states rejected the amendment upon the advice of Johnson, who thought it was unconstitutional.

7. Congressional election of 1866 resulted in a majority in both houses in opposition to Johnson.

G. The radicals in Congress took control of the reconstruction policies.

1. The Tenure of Office Act, March 2, 1867, passed over Johnson's veto, subordinated the President to Congress.

   a. President was prohibited from removing any governmental official without the Senate's consent.

2. Another act required the President to issue all military orders only through the general of the army.

3. The Reconstruction Act of March 2, 1867, set up military governments in the Confederate states not readmitted to the Union.

   a. The ten states were to be divided into five military districts, each under the command of a Major General.

   b. Constitutional conventions, elected by both whites and Negroes were to frame new constitutions providing for Negro franchise.

   c. Congress had to accept the constitutions.

   d. State legislatures had to ratify the Fourteenth Amendment.

   e. Then the states could apply for representation in Congress.

4. The House voted for Johnson's impeachment February 24, 1868.

   a. Johnson had dismissed Secretary of War Stanton without the Senate's consent.

   b. Chief Justice Chase presided over the trial.

   c. The evidence against Johnson was weak, since the issue was really political opposition.

   d. His conviction would have set a precedent for the impeachment of a President when a majority of the House and two-thirds of the Senate opposed him.

   e. The Senate voted "not guilty" by 35 to 19, lacking one vote of the two-thirds needed for conviction.

5. Congress restored the Southern states to the Union, 1868.

   a. Reorganized governments with new constitutions were recognized in Georgia, Florida, Louisiana, Arkansas, and North and South Carolina.

   b. Congress declared a constitution in force for Alabama because it had been ratified by their electorate.

   c. Other states were readmitted later.

6. The Fourteenth Amendment was declared July 20, 1868, after the restored states had given the necessary three-fourths vote.

7. Ulysses S. Grant was elected President by the Republicans in 1868 over the Democratic opponent, Horatio Seymour.

8. The Fifteenth Amendment assuring the

franchise of the Negro was passed by Congress, February 27, 1869.

H. The reconstruction era of the South caused social and economic changes.

1. The Ku-Klux Klan, a terroristic organization, originated in Tennessee.
   a. They attempted to keep the Negroes in an inferior position politically and economically.
   b. They resorted to brutality and violence.
2. Other groups used peaceful coercion by intimidation in denying Negroes employment and the right to vote; "Black Codes" to ensure white supremacy.
3. The South harbored "carpetbaggers", Northerners who came South to achieve fortune and power, and "scalawags", Southerners who wanted to obtain lucrative contracts and political preferment.
4. The result was corruption, fraud and extravagance in the South.
5. By 1870, Virginia, Mississippi and Texas were readmitted to the Union by ratifying the Fifteenth Amendment.
6. Southern resistance created congressional legislation for the enforcement of its program.
   a. An act of May, 1870 imposed penalties for violations of the Fourteenth and Fifteenth Amendments.
   b. Enforcement Act of February, 1871, provided federal supervision of elections.
   c. The Ku-Klux Act of April, 1871 gave the President military power to suppress violence in the South.
7. Some of the Republican Party leaders compromised with some of the Southern Democrats and aimed for the restoration of the Conservatives.
   a. The General Amnesty Act of 1872 removed the disabilities imposed by the Fourteenth Amendment upon almost all former Confederates.
      1) In 1898 a general act restored all those who had not been pardoned.
   b. President Hayes removed all troops in 1877 from the Southern states.

I. The Reconstruction Period Had Left Predominately Negative but also Positive Effects on the South.

1. Politically, the South became solid in their adhering to the Democratic party as a result of hostility to the Republican program.
2. The South in order to insure "white supremacy" passed "Jim Crow" laws segregating Negro life from that of the white.
3. Devices were used to reduce the number of Negroes who could meet qualifications to vote.
4. The plantation system came to an end.
   a. The land was rented out in small parcels to tenants, which started the share-cropping system.
   b. Tenants paid their rent by giving the landlord a share of the crop, with the tenants usually finding themselves constantly in debt.
5. Industry and commerce were beginning to flourish.
   a. Northern capital helped in the construction of railroads.
   b. Cotton mills were built.
   c. Natural resources began to be exploited.
6. Despite improvements, the South still had many critical problems.
   a. Northern financiers controlled the Southern economy.
   b. White and Negro still lived in poverty and were uneducated.
   c. Southern politicians were more interested in sectional rather than national problems.

II. AMERICAN INTERNATIONAL PARTICIPATION, 1865-1875.

A. France occupied Mexico during the Civil War.

1. Napoleon III landed troops and set up Maximilian as emperor.
2. United States protested and demanded the withdrawal of the foreign troops and the ruler, because it violated the Monroe Doctrine.
3. France evacuated the troops in 1867 and Maximilian was shot after a court martial.

B. United States bought Alaska from Russia in 1867.

1. The Senate ratified the purchase April 9, 1867.
2. United States paid $7,200,000 in gold.
3. Little was known of the area, yet Seward favored expansion of the national domain.
4. Alaska became the 49th state, 1958.

C. United States had an anti-British reaction because of her lack of neutrality

U.S. HISTORY

during the Civil War.

1. England permitted the building of commerce destroyers, the most famous of which was the Alabama, that later flew the Confederate Flag.
2. United States claimed that England's policy cost this country two billion dollars and prolonged the war.
3. Negotiations lasted several years.
4. The Treaty of Washington was ratified in May, 1871.
   a. The "Alabama" claims were submitted to an international tribunal which met in Geneva, December, 1871.
   b. Their decision stated that England was responsible and had to pay $15,500,000 to the United States, which she did.

D. United States showed its concern over the fate of Cuba, a Spanish possession.

1. The Cubans revolted against Spanish authority.
2. Spain charged that Americans were aiding the rebels in violation of international law.
3. Spain mistreated American citizens in Cuba and executed Americans aboard a steamer, "Virginius", flying the American flag.
4. Secretary of State Fish demanded Spanish reparations.
   a. The "Virginius" and survivors were released.
   b. Spain paid a sum of money to the families of the slain Americans.
   c. War was avoided.

E. United States negotiated with the Far East.

1. Specified ports in China were opened to American trade by a treaty negotiated by Cushing in 1844.
2. The Burlingame Treaty of 1868 sanctioned reciprocal rights of residence and travel of Chinese and American citizens.
   a. Hayes negotiated a new treaty in 1880 which allowed United States to regulate, suspend or limit Chinese immigration.
   b. The Pacific Coast Americans feared limitless immigration from China, since Chinese labor was so much cheaper than American labor.
   c. The Chinese Exclusion Law of 1882 lasted ten years and afterward was

renewed until 1902 when it was extended with no time limit.
3. Commodore Perry opened trade with Japan in 1854.

III. **THE NEW ECONOMIC ORDER THROUGH CONQUEST AND SETTLEMENT OF THE WEST.**

A. **The entire country was organized into territories or states by the end of the Civil War.**

1. The Gadsden Purchase, 1853, had completed the continental boundaries.
2. For list of states and when admitted see appendix.

B. **The last frontier began to disappear because of specific factors.**

1. The land and resources of the West became available.
2. Transportation of goods and people was made possible by the building of the transcontinental railroad.
3. The industrial revolution created a manufacturing economy.
4. The government adopted a policy of encouragement.
5. The pioneers had courage and persistence.
6. There was adequate capital and labor supply was plentiful; immigration increased.
7. Natural resources were rapidly developed.

C. **The discovery of gold and other metals had hastened migration to the West.**

1. Prospectors migrated to the new mining districts and established boom towns.
2. Silver and gold were found in Nevada in 1850 and in the areas east of California.
3. Mines were worked in Idaho, Montana, Wyoming and New Mexico in the 1860's.
4. Territories were reorganized by Congress to create law and order in the mining areas.
5. Gold was discovered in the Pike's Peak area in 1858, and the town of Denver grew.

D. **Cattle towns rivaled the mining towns.**

1. Ranches as opposed to open ranges, cattle brand systems, improved breeding of stock, and round-up cattle all developed.

2. The American cowboy became an American figure.

3. Meat packing firms and slaughter houses became major industries.

4. Railroad construction aided in the accessibility of markets.

E. Settlements were facilitated by the railroads.

1. The Union Pacific Railroad Company was chartered in 1862 by Congress.

2. The Northern Pacific Railroad was chartered in 1864 by Congress.

3. The Atchison, Topeka and Santa Fe Railroad was given a liberal federal grant in 1863.

4. The government was liberal in its aid to the railroad companies through generous land grants and financial aid.

F. The Homestead act of 1862 helped to achieve Western settlement.

1. It provided that any person who lived on and improved a tract of 160 acres for five years would receive title to it.

2. Subsequent acts authorized granting additional lands.

3. Timber Act of 1873 required the planting of a specified number of trees for the receipt of 160 additional acres.

4. Grants of 640 acres were authorized by the Desert Land Act of 1877 if irrigation ditches were built.

5. Settlers also bought lands from the states or the railroads who had obtained lands for support of schools.

G. The government policy was to remove land titles from the Indians by treaties.

1. Warfare continued between 1868 and 1882 by the Indians to retain their land.

2. In 1871, Congress allowed no more treaties to be made with the Indians.

3. Indians assigned to reservations.

4. Dawes Act of 1887 granted 160 acres of land to heads of Indian families.

   a. They received full title at the end of 25 years.

   b. Citizenship was granted from the beginning of the 25 years.

5. Burke Act of 1906 granted full title of land to Indians who evidenced fitness and also conferred citizenship with it.

6. All Indians became American citizens by law in 1924.

IV. THE ADMINISTRATIONS OF GRANT, HAYES, GARFIELD AND ARTHUR, 1869-1884.

A. Many public scandals were revealed during Grant's Administrations, 1869-1877.

1. No proof was ever found connecting Grant and the scandals, but he lacked political experience and was extremely naive.

2. Jim Fiske and Jay Gould attempted to corner the gold market.

   a. The government took belated action on "Black Friday", Sept. 24, 1869 to try to save the country from economic collapse.

   b. Boutwell, Secretary of the Treasury, released $4,000,000 in gold and thus ruined the speculators.

3. There was graft and political corruption with the Credit Mobilier, a corporation formed for building the Union Pacific Railway.

4. Frauds committed against New York City were operated by the Tweed ring in Tammany Hall.

5. In 1874, a "Whiskey Ring" in St. Louis defrauded the government of large sums of money.

6. There were other lesser scandals in municipal as well as national government.

B. Grant was reelected in 1872, over Horace Greeley, the Democratic nominee.

1. The Democratic party was ineffective.

2. Greeley was a poor choice and unpopular.

3. The South was controlled by the Republican party.

C. Grant's second term continued to have governmental scandals and political corruption.

1. Fast economic expansion and political graft caused a five year depression, starting with the Panic of 1873.

2. Political reform was imminent.

D. Hayes, a Republican reform governor of Ohio, won the Election of 1876 over Tilden, a Democratic reform governor of New York in a disputed election.

1. Tilden won a majority of the popular votes, but lost in the Electoral College by one vote.

   a. The twenty electoral votes from Louisiana, Florida, Oregon and South Carolina were disputed.

   b. Law of January 29, 1877 established an Electoral Commission to pass judgment on the disputed votes.

c. The Commission awarded all disputed electoral votes to Hayes, since there were eight Republicans and seven Democrats on the Commission.

2. The election was an important test of the strength of popular government.

E. Hayes was capable, honest and yet unpopular.

1. He terminated the control of the South by federal troops.

2. His cabinet consisted of able men.

3. He made attempts to reform the civil service.

   a. He forbade the collection of political contributions from federal office holders.

   b. He removed politicians from misusing their offices for personal gain.

   c. He made Federal appointments on the basis of merit.

4. The Democratic control of Congress made the Hayes administration an unhappy one because of partisan quarreling.

F. Industrial growth affected business and labor.

1. Business organized into large units: pools, trusts, holding companies.

2. A great many labor organizations were organized.

   a. The first meeting of the National Labor Union was in 1865.

   b. Knights of Labor was organized in 1869.

   c. Serious railroad labor disturbances occurred during 1877.

G. Both Grant and Hayes backed anti-inflationist policies.

1. From the Civil War on, the country's business was carried on through depreciated greenbacks.

2. In 1873, a revision of the coinage laws omitted the silver dollar from the coins.

3. In 1875, the Resumption Act provided that $300,000,000 of greenbacks remain in circulation, but in 1879 they should be redeemable at face value in gold.

4. In 1878, Congress set the amount of greenbacks in circulation at $346,-681,016.

5. The National Greenback Party, 1875, was the extreme inflationist group but their strength declined.

6. The Bland-Allison Act, 1878, authorized the Treasury to purchase monthly $2,000,000 to $4,000,000 silver bullion

and coin it into silver dollars.

   a. It passed over Hayes' veto.

   b. The silver miners strongly advocated the use of silver in preference to the scarcer gold.

7. Businessmen feared inflation by the issuance of greenbacks or the coinage of cheap silver.

   a. They worked to base currency on actual gold reserves.

   b. In 1879, the nation began using a gold standard in maintaining the value of the currency.

8. The call for free and unlimited coinage continued.

H. Republicans nominated James A. Garfield, a former Union general, as President with Chester Arthur as Vice-President.

1. The Democrats chose General Winfield S. Hancock.

2. Garfield was elected, 1880.

3. He was assassinated in Washington, July 2, 1881 by a half-crazed office seeker.

   a. The tragedy appeared to be the result of factional quarrels over political appointments.

   b. The country became aware of the necessity to improve the merit system.

4. Vice-President Arthur became President.

   a. He refused to use the "spoils system" and urged Congress to remove the civil service from politics.

   b. He was adamant against the continuation of strife within the Republican party.

   c. He was intelligent in his approach to his duties.

   d. The Pendleton Act, 1883, intended to improve government efficiency and eliminate the abuses of the spoils system.

   (1) It created a bi-partisan civil service commission of three people to advise the President of the offices to be filled by competitive examinations.

   (2) It also prohibited the collection of funds for political purposes from federal employees.

   e. President Arthur warned against wasteful government income expenditure.

(1) He vetoed the use of $18,000,000 for harbor and river improvements that were of doubtful value.

(2) It passed over his veto.

f. Edmunds Act, 1882, attempted to suppress polygamy in Utah by fines, imprisonments and disqualification for the franchise and public office.

g. The surplus of money in the Treasury between 1870-1880 allowed Congressmen to spend freely on public works in their own districts, and

1. These were called "pork-barrel" appropriations.

I. The 1884 elections brought the first Democratic President into office since Buchanan in 1856.

1. Grover Cleveland, the highly reputable Governor of New York, won over Blaine, the Republican nominee.

2. The Democrats were successful for a variety of reasons.

a. Blaine was thought to have used his public position to further his own financial gains.

b. New York City Catholics resented Blaine's speech referring to the Democratic Party as one of "rum, Romanism and rebellion".

c. Many independent Republicans, called "Mugwumps", refused to support the party ticket.

d. Cleveland seemed to embody the hopes of political reformers despite party affiliation.

V. THE FIRST ADMINISTRATION OF GROVER CLEVELAND, 1885-1889.

A. The last remnant of reconstruction disappeared.

1. The cabinet consisted of men of ability, including Lamar of Mississippi, who had written the Secession ordinance for the state.

2. Diplomatic offices were equally divided between the North and South.

B. Cleveland continued civil service reform.

C. Tenure of Office Act was repealed in 1887.

D. Presidential Succession Act was passed, January, 1886.

1. It specified that upon the death of the president and vice-president, the presidency would pass to the members of the cabinet.

2. The order would be determined by the succession in which the offices had

been created.

3. This was changed in 1947.

E. Congress was generous in granting pensions to Civil War veterans who served in the Union Army.

1. The passage of the Arrears of Pensions Act, 1879, granted back pension from the date of the discharge from the army to the time of filing of the claim.

2. Cleveland vetoed many private pension bills.

3. Cleveland tried to keep the pension list honest.

4. He vetoed a Dependent Pension Bill passed in 1887, which provided a pension for any ex-soldier who served three months and was incapable of earning a living.

F. The Electoral Count Act, 1887, authorized the states to decide disputes over presidential electors.

G. Tariffs were revised.

1. Cleveland urged reductions.

2. Tariff policy became the issue: for revenue or protection?

H. Interstate Commerce Act, 1887, was the first attempt of the national government to regulate industry in the public interest.

1. Railroads often used objectionable fraudulent practices which impaired prosperity and created corruption.

2. Senate appointed a committee, headed by Senator Cullom of Illinois, to investigate railways.

3. The Act provided that an Interstate Commerce Commission of five members have the power to collect railroad data, hear complaints and bring about Federal Court action to force conformity with the Act.

a. Special rates, drawbacks and secret rebates were prohibited.

b. Pool agreements were illegal.

c. Rates had to be fair with no discrimination between places, persons and commodities.

d. The public had the right to inspect schedules and rates.

e. Higher costs for short hauls than for long hauls under similar conditions of traffic were forbidden.

4. The Act, a pioneer in social control,

had many weaknesses.

a. The Commission could not compel witnesses to testify.

b. The Commission had the burden of court action.

c. The Supreme Court was able to control the Commission by its interpretation.

d. The weaknesses allowed the railroads to evade the provisions.

I. The Department of Agriculture was established.

J. There were numerous labor riots and strikes.

1. Several states established labor boards but Congress did nothing despite Cleveland's recommendations.

2. Two labor parties, Greenback Labor and Union Labor parties, presented tickets in the 1888 elections.

K. Cleveland lost the presidential election, 1888.

1. Cleveland was nominated again by the Democrats.

2. The Republican nominee, Benjamin Harrison, a former Senator from Indiana, received a majority of the electoral vote but a smaller popular vote than Cleveland.

3. A major issue was the tariff, with Cleveland favoring lower tariffs.

VI. THE ADMINISTRATION OF BENJAMIN HARRISON, 1889-1893.

A. Republicans controlled the Senate and the House of Representatives.

1. The new administration's leaders were James Blaine, Secretary of State; Thomas Reed, the Speaker of the House of Representatives; and William McKinley, Chairman of the House Committee on Ways and Means.

2. The Democratic minority in the House attempted to obstruct the President's legislative program by parliamentary tactics.

a. The Reed Rules were accepted to speed up legislative processes.

(1) Actual attendance should be the basis for determining a quorum.

2) Dilatory motions should not be recognized by the Speaker.

b. In 1890, the Democrats regained control in the House.

c. In 1894, the Democrats also accepted the Reed rules.

B. The Republicans attempted to increase tariff rates.

1. The passage of the McKinley Tariff bill was delayed.

2. Western Republicans demanded the expansion of the coinage of silver.

3. As a compromise, the Sherman Silver Purchase Act was accepted.

a. It provided for the monthly purchase of 4,500,000 ounces of silver.

b. Treasury notes, redeemable in gold or silver, were to be issued against this silver bullion.

4. As a result of the compromise between Republicans and the Western party members, the McKinley Tariff bill was passed, Oct. 1, 1890.

a. The bill raised the level of duties on woolen goods, cotton goods, steel products and some farm products.

b. Raw sugar was put on the free list and the producers were to receive a two cents a pound bounty in order to compete with foreign producers.

c. The Senate included reciprocity provisions in the Act.

(1) This was intended to promote South American trade.

(2) First Pan-American Congress met in Washington, 1899, to discuss trade agreements, currency, arbitration and other measures.

(3) The President was authorized to impose duties on coffee, tea, sugar and molasses from countries which levied excessive duties on the United States products.

(4) This was to compel countries to reciprocate the United States policy.

5. The result of the McKinley Bill caused prices of protected commodities to rise.

a. Democrats foresaw disaster from the bill.

b. Foreign trade statistics did not support Democratic pessimism.

c. However, popular distaste for the bill created a Democratic landslide in the 1890 Congressional elections.

C. Sherman Anti-Trust Act, 1890, continued governmental social control.

1. Huge industrial organizations developed after the Civil War which suppressed competition and formed monopolies.

a. Examples were the Standard Oil

Trust, 1879, Sugar Refineries Company, 1887, and others.

  b. Prices would be low while suppressing competition and then rise to unfair heights.

  c. Producers exploited consumers.

2. Sherman Anti-Trust Act of July 2, 1890 declared illegal "every contract, combination in the form of trust or otherwise, or conspiracy, in restraint of trade or commerce among the several states, or with foreign nations."

  a. Violators were subject to a $5,000 fine or one year imprisonment or both; corporations were considered legal persons.

  b. During the first years, the enforcement of the law by the government was not too aggressive.

3. States also acted to hinder harmful business monopolies with little effect.

D. Several serious foreign disputes occurred during the administration of James Blaine as Secretary of State.

1. Civil War broke out in Chile between the President and the Congressional party, 1891.

  a. Egan, our Minister to Chile, antagonized the congressionalists by his support of the defeated President.

  b. Dislike for Americans provoked an attack on American sailors, as well as insults to American officials.

  c. The United States requested an apology, an indemnity to be paid for the slain and wounded sailors, and the presidential refugees at the American ministry be allowed to leave the country.

  d. War and peace hung in the balance, when Chile yielded to the demands of the ultimatum.

2. A great problem was the dispute with England over the seal fisheries in the Bering Sea.

  a. United States claimed that the Bering Sea was an interior water of Alaska and seized Canadian vessels in 1886 and 1887.

  b. The aim was to protect seal extinction and to prohibit other nations from hunting in the Bering Sea.

    (1) Congress passed such an Act in 1889.

  c. Arbitration tribunal, 1893, upheld the British position; England received $473,000 damages for seized vessels.

3. Diplomatic relations with Italy were severed in 1891 because of the lynching of eleven Italians in New Orleans, who were alleged to have killed the chief of police.

  a. Italian government demanded prosecution of the lynchers.

  b. Harrison sent a message of friendship and regret over the incident.

  c. The Italian government was mollified.

  d. A gift of money was given to the families of the dead, and diplomatic relations were restored.

4. United States, England and Germany were rivals in the Samoan Islands.

  a. The United States trading privileges and the use of Pago Pago harbor as a coaling station were obtained by a treaty in 1872 with a Samoan chief.

  b. Imperialistic disturbances among the three countries led to a possible war between United States and Germany.

  c. War was averted when a hurricane wrecked the war vessels ready for action.

  d. In 1889, the three countries established a tripartite protectorate over the islands.

  e. The arrangement was unsuccessful.

  f. In 1899, England withdrew in return for concessions in Africa, and the islands were divided between the United States and Germany.

5. A step forward was the meeting of the first Pan American Congress, 1889.

E. The Presidential election of 1892 indicated the decline of the Republican policies and popularity.

1. There was resentment over higher prices after the 1890 high tariff bill.

2. The reformers disliked Harrison's neglect of the merit system in appointments.

3. There was animosity against the compromise in the Sherman Silver Act, 1890.

4. The administration was charged with wasting the Treasury surplus.

F. The Democratic party won the 1892 election.

U.S. HISTORY

1. Farmers and laborers united to form the Populist party, with James B. Weaver as their presidential candidate.
   a. The party advocated government ownership of railroads and telegraph lines, an income tax free and unlimited silver coinage.
   b. Many of their demands were later adopted by the two major parties.
2. Benjamin Harrison was the Republican nominee, and Cleveland, the Democratic nominee.
   a. Republicans advocated a protective tariff which the Democrats denounced.
3. Cleveland won a decisive electoral and popular vote.
   a. Harrison claimed that the Homestead Strike was responsible for his defeat.
      (1) A strike occurred in the Carnegie Steel Works at Homestead, Pennsylvania.
      (2) Much violence resulted and many strikers were killed.
      (3) This seriously damaged the Republicans, who maintained that labor was secure.
      (4) The Democrats discredited the Republicans for protecting an industry which killed American workers.
4. The Democrats kept the control of the House and won a majority in the Senate.

VII. THE SECOND ADMINISTRATION OF GROVER CLEVELAND, 1893-1897.

A. Cleveland faced serious financial problems.

1. Exports fell below imports leaving a balance of $35,000,000 to be met in gold.
2. Low valued silver was accumulating in the Treasury.
3. Exchange of silver certificates for gold at the Treasury reduced the gold reserve drastically.
4. A business panic erupted in May and lasted until October.
5. Gold threatened to disappear from circulation.
6. Greenbacks could not be backed by the gold reserve on hand.

B. The Sherman Silver Purchase Act was repealed in 1893 by a special Congressional session.

1. The Western and Southern Democrats were bitterly hostile against the industrial East and the President.

C. The depleted gold reserve required replenishing.

1. $100,000,000 in bonds were sold by the Treasury in 1894.
2. Another $100,000,000 in bonds were sold by public subscription.
3. As soon as subscribers to bonds paid their gold, they withdrew them again.
4. In 1895 the reserve was down to $41,000,000.
5. J. P. Morgan and a financial syndicate agreed to deliver $65,000,000 in gold in return for 4% bonds.
   a. The public resented the profit made by Morgan, but he did supply the much needed gold.

D. Wilson-Gorman Tariff Bill, 1894, slightly reduced the tariff.

1. The original Wilson bill was revised by the Senate with 634 amendments.
2. The resulting bill resembled the McKinley Tariff with high schedules.
3. The Act became law without Cleveland's signature; he had fought for reduced tariffs.

E. The economic depression gave rise to labor disturbances.

1. Coxey's "army" of unemployed marched from Ohio to Washington, 1894.
2. The Pullman Company workers struck in Chicago, 1894, on account of wage reductions.
   a. About 4,000 of the Pullman employees belonged to the American Railway Union under the presidency of Eugene V. Debs.
   b. Mr. Pullman refused to arbitrate, and the union ordered the men not to handle trains with Pullman cars.
   c. United States mail trains carrying Pullman cars did not operate.
   d. Cleveland sent troops to Chicago to end rioting.
   e. Federal court issued an injunction forbidding the strikers to interfere with the mails.
   f. Debs and his associates were arrested for violating the Sherman Act by a conspiracy in restraint of trade and for contempt of court for violation of the injunction.
      1. Debs was sentenced to 6 months

imprisonment for contempt of court.

g. Labor organizations and others criticized the "Government by injunction" policy, claiming it violated the constitutional right of trial by jury.

F. **The Venezuela boundary dispute allowed Cleveland to defend the Monroe Doctrine as an integral part of American international policy.**

1. England claimed rich mineral country in South America.
2. The land lay within territory disputed between Venezuela and British Guiana.
3. Venezuela relied on the Monroe Doctrine to protect her against European interference.
   a. Secretary of State Olney asserted the right of the United States to intervene.
   b. England refused to recognize the Monroe Doctrine as international law.
4. Cleveland requested appropriation in 1895 for a boundary commission to investigate the situation.
5. England's offer to give the commission the necessary documents for handling the situation allowed for the dismissal of the commission.
6. A treaty in 1897 was ratified to submit the boundary controversy to an arbitration tribunal.
   a. The tribunal confirmed most of England's claims in 1899.

G. **The currency policy was the basis of the 1896 election.**

1. William Jennings Bryan was the Democratic nominee.
   a. Democrats demanded an unlimited coinage of silver at a ratio to gold of 16 to 1.
   b. They opposed the issuance of paper money by national banks.
   c. They urged that tariff schedules be imposed only for governmental revenue.
   d. They denounced "government by injunction" labor disputes.
   e. They denounced the Supreme Court's decision against the constitutionality of the income tax.
   f. They wanted the Interstate Commerce Commission to have increased powers.

2. William McKinley was the Republican nominee.
   a. Mark Hanna, a Cleveland capitalist, directed the business and financial interests of the Republican campaign.
   b. The platform advocated maintenance of a gold standard.
   c. Other platform issues favored a protective tariff, federal arbitration of labor disputes involving interstate commerce, large pensions for Union veterans, and the American control of the Hawaiian Islands.
3. The Populist party favored Bryan.
4. McKinley won a decisive victory.
   a. The farmers and industrial workers lost to the industrialists.
   b. The government was dominated by business interests.
5. The Administration passed the Dingley Tariff Act in 1897 with high tariff schedules.
6. The Gold Standard Act of 1900 placed the currency on a gold basis and increased the reserve to $150,000,000.

VIII. CULTURAL AND ECONOMIC TRENDS, 1865-1900.

A. **Big business caused population shifts from rural to urban areas, thus creating the need for social reforms.**

1. Socialist Labor party was founded in 1877, but remained unpopular.
2. The Social Democratic party was founded in 1899.
   a. It became known as the Socialist party.
   b. Eugene Debs was its presidential nominee four successive times.
3. Relief agencies, social workers and settlement houses were organized to improve slum area conditions.
4. State and municipal health boards were organized to fight disease.
5. The American Society for the Prevention of the Cruelty of Animals was started in 1866 in New York.
6. The Society for the Prevention of Cruelty to Children was founded in 1875 in New York.
7. A fight began against the sale of liquor after the Civil War.
   a. Prohibition party was organized in 1869.
   b. The Women's Christian Temperance Union was started in 1874.

8. There was agitation for the improvement of working conditions.
9. Philanthropies grew at this time.

B. **There was a marked change in immigration.**
1. Beginning about 1880, immigrants came from Southern and Central Europe, rather than Northern Europe as previously.
2. French Canadians came into New England.
3. Numerous laws were passed to prevent the immigration of "contract labor," paupers, the insane, and anarchists.

C. **Cultural progress developed fairly rapidly.**
1. Concentrated population and wealth created the openings of libraries, museums, theatres, concert halls, schools, opera houses and other fine buildings.
2. Schools and school enrollment increased with the number of students almost doubled.
3. American authors, namely, Walt Whitman, Mark Twain, Bret Harte, Henry James and others wrote of their country and of their people.
4. Newspapers became large business enterprises.
   a. The New York Sun, the New York World and the St. Louis Post-Dispatch were leading papers.
   b. William Randolph Hearst developed a chain of papers which became powerful as molders of public opinion.
   c. The invention of the Mergenthaler linotype machine enabled faster production for increased circulation.
5. Skyscrapers were built because of the high cost of land.
   a. The first skyscraper of ten floors, the Home Insurance Building, was built in Chicago in 1885.
6. Sports for amateurs and professionals became extremely popular.
   a. Baseball and football became the two most popular sports.
   b. Tennis and golf, starting after the Civil War, remained games for the wealthy.
   c. Nearly everyone rode a bicycle during the 1890's.
7. The number of women in professions and industry increased.
   a. Vassar founded in 1865 was the first college for women.
   b. Wellesley and Smith soon followed.
8. Newly formed women's suffrage organizations began fighting for the recognition of the female franchise.

D. **Invention and science made great advances.**
1. The discovery of oil and better processes for making steel had stimulated inventive genius.
1. Alexander Graham Bell invented the telephone in 1876.
3. Thomas Edison invented the electric light in 1879.
4. The electric trolly car appeared in the 1880's.
5. Water was harnessed to produce hydro-electric power by 1900.

E. **American economic supremacy began to reach great heights.**
1. Railroads swiftly opened the Western frontiers for settlement.
2. Wide use of mechanized machinery on farms and factories was encouraged.
3. Industrial and agricultural growth was encouraged by the government.
4. Individual proprietorship gave way to the growth of corporations.
5. The modern labor movement began to improve the worker's lot.
   a. Granges were organizations of farmers.
   b. Knights of Labor, 1869, was made up of both skilled and unskilled industrial workers.
   c. American Federation of Labor, 1886, was based on the crafts principle.
6. A movement began to conserve the nation's resources.
7. Production was greatly stimulated.

IX. THE SPANISH-AMERICAN WAR.

A. **Definite events led up to the War with Spain over Cuba.**
1. The harsh rule of the Spanish in Cuba created discontent and revolts starting in 1895.
2. United States demonstrated concern in Cuban affairs.
   a. The proximity of the island created interest.
   b. American capital was invested in sugar and tobacco plantations, railroads and mines.
   c. American trade with Cuba was extensive.
3. The press distorted Spanish atrocities,

and Cuban refugees in the United States reported Spanish cruelty.
   a. American anger was aroused.
   b. Cleveland, in his message to Congress in 1896, hinted at American intervention.
4. Two incidents occurred which made war imminent.
   a. A letter written by Dupuy de Lome, Spanish Minister to the United States, referred to President McKinley with insults.
      (1) The letter had been written to a friend in Cuba where it had been stolen.
      (2) The letter was then published in the New York Journal, February 9, 1898.
      (3) De Lome resigned immediately.
   b. The United States battleship "Maine" was blown up in Havana Harbor, February 15, 1898 with a loss of 260 lives.
5. McKinley sent an ultimatum to Spain, March 29, 1898.
   a. He demanded the abandonment of the "reconcentrado" policy, the retention of inhabitants in camps under horrifying conditions.
   b. He demanded an armistice between Spain and the insurrectionaries during negotiations.
   c. If negotiations failed, then United States would be appointed as arbitrator.
6. Spain agreed to the first demand but evaded the others.
7. Spain informed McKinley on April 10, 1898, she was willing to grant an armistice.
8. McKinley dismissed the concession, and urged Congress in a war message on April 11, 1898 to intervene.
9. Congress authorized war to force Spain to relinquish Cuba, April 19, 1898.
10. The Teller Amendment promised U.S. withdrawal when Cuba achieved independence.

B. **The Spanish-American War took place in 1898.**

1. The army was increased from 28,000 to 62,000 men with request for 200,000 volunteers.
2. Theodore Roosevelt, Assistant Secretary of the Navy, had the navy prepared.
   a. Admiral Dewey destroyed the Span-

ish fleet in Manila Bay, May 1, 1898.
   b. Admiral Sampon blockaded the Spanish fleet of Admiral Cervera in the harbor of Santiago, May 19, 1898.
3. An army of 16,000 troops was sent into Cuba under Major General Shafter.
   a. The most publicized division of this army was the cavalry regiment known as the "Rough Riders".
   b. They consisted of cowboys, ranchmen, hunters and Indians plus others under Colonel Wood.
      1. Theodore Roosevelt resigned as Assistant Secretary of the Navy to become their Lieutenant Colonel.
   c. The American troops captured two outposts of Santiago, El Caney and San Juan Hill on July 1st.
   d. With the capture of Cervera's fleeing fleet by Commodore Schley, Santiago surrendered.
4. Manila, in the Philippines, was captured August 13th because the news of the armistice had not reached them.

C. **War ended with the United States as victor.**

1. Armistice between Spain and the United States was signed August 12, 1898.
2. The peace treaty was signed December 10, 1898, in Paris.
   a. Spain agreed to evacuate Cuba.
   b. Spain assumed the Cuban debt.
   c. Puerto Rico and Guam were ceded to the United States.
   d. United States agreed to pay $20,-000,000 for the Philippines.
3. The treaty was ratified by the Senate February 6, 1899 after strong opposition from "anti-imperialists."
4. There were definite motives for the overseas expansion.
   a. There was a desire to increase national prestige.
   b. New business enterprises and expanding trade were important factors.
   c. The desire to thwart Germany's designs in the Pacific was a motive.
   d. There was also talk of uplifting and civilizing the population of the islands.

X. THE UNITED STATES IN WORLD AFFAIRS.

U.S. HISTORY

A. McKinley's second administration and public opinion demanded overseas expansion.
  1. McKinley was shot December 6 ,1901 by an anarchist, and he died September 14th.
  2. Theodore Roosevelt, the vice-president, succeeded to the presidency.

B. The Cuban Republic was established May 20th, 1902.
  1. Spain transferred the administration of Cuba to the United States, January 1, 1899.
  2. General Leonard Wood, following General Brooks, was its administrator until 1902.
  3. Cuba was forced by Congress in the Army Appropriation Bill of 1900 to insert a provision in her constitution called the Platt Amendment.
     a. Cuba could not make any international agreements impairing her independence without the consent of the United States.
     b. Cuba could not contract debts unless they could be paid by current revenues.
     c. Cuba would accept the intervention of the United States whenever necessary to preserve its political stability and independence.
     d. Two naval bases would be granted to the United States.
  4. The administration was transferred to the Cubans, May 20, 1902.
  5. Reciprocal tariff reductions were made between the United States and Cuba.
  6. United States intervened several times in Cuban affairs to quiet political disorders and supervise elections.
  7. Even though Cuba was politically independent, the United States was a strong economic imperialist over the island.
  8. The Platt Amendment was abrogated by a mutual treaty in 1934.

C. Puerto Ricans became American citizens in 1917.
  1. American troops occupied Puerto Rico during the Spanish-American War.
  2. Military administration lasted until 1900.
  3. Foraker Act of 1900 made Puerto Rico an unorganized territory with a governor and council appointed by the President of the United States, and an elected lower house.
  4. The inhabitants were citizens of Puerto Rico.
  5. Jones Act of 1917 conferred United States citizenship on all Puerto Ricans and replaced the council with an elected senate.
  6. Puerto Rico adopted a constitution and became a free state or commonwealth.

D. Philippine Islands received their independence in 1946.
  1. Filipinos revolted for their independence against Spain first and then against the United States.
  2. Congress made the islands an unorganized territory and its people citizens of the islands in 1902.
  3. Taft Commission prepared a framework of government.
  4. Jones Act of 1916 allowed the people to elect its two legislative house, but the governor general, appointed by the President, had veto power.
  5. Various Governor-Generals, some cooperative, others not, were appointed through the years.
  6. The Philippines were offered independence by President Roosevelt and Concongress in 1934 to become effective in 1946.

E. The Hawaiian Islands became a state in 1959.
  1. The United States' interests in Hawaii began with traders and missionaries in the 1800's.
  2. Hawaii requested annexation by the United States but was refused.
  3. Reciprocal trading agreement was ratified in 1875.
  4. Treaty of 1884 gave the United States rights to Pearl Harbor and set up conditions which would prevent annexation by any other country.
  5. By 1887, the Americans in Hawaii fully controlled the government.
  6. In 1893, the Americans in Hawaii staged a successful revolt against Queen Liliuokalani.
  7. Harrison favored annexation but left office before the treaty would be ratified.
  8. Cleveland withdrew the treaty and attempted to restore the government to the Queen if she would pardon the revolutionists.
     a. She refused and the revolutionary

government remained.

9. The United States proclaimed the Republic of Hawaii on July 4, 1894.

10. Hawaii was annexed in 1898, and made a territory in 1899.

11. The Hawaiian Islands became the fiftieth state in 1959.

F. The United States began to have direct contact with the Far East.

1. John Hay, Secretary of State in 1898, championed overseas expansion.

2. He advocated the "open door" policy which sought equal trading privileges in China along with other foreign nations.

3. The Boxer Rebellion in 1900 was an uprising against the penetration of foreigners in China.

   a. Chinese ports had been opened to American trade in 1844.

   b. Chinese immigration had been limited in 1880 and 1882.

   c. Britain, France, Germany, Russia, Japan and United States sent troops to put down the insurrection.

   d. Moderate punishment and indemnites prevailed against China in order to maintain Chinese territorial and administrative independence.

   (1) Leaders of the rebellion were punished.

   (2) Further outbreaks were to be prevented.

   (3) A monetary indemnity was paid.

4. Japanese immigrants created difficulties.

   a. Roosevelt acted as mediator in 1905 at the end of the Russo-Japanese War.

   b. California was hostile to Japanese immigrants.

   c. Root-Takahira Agreement of 1908 was a gentlemen's agreement between the United States and Japan.

   (1) Japan promised to refuse passports to laborers.

   (2) United States could refuse admittance to those without passports.

   d. Immigration Act of 1924 excluded all oriental immigrants.

G. A canal was needed between the Atlantic and the Pacific.

1. The needs were to promote trade and make naval movements easier.

2. Clayton-Bulwer Treaty, 1850, between England and the United States provided that any isthmian canal should be jointly controlled.

3. The treaty was abrogated by the Hay-Pauncefote Treaty, 1901, which provided that America might build the canal and have full control, but all nations were to use the canal on equal terms.

4. Hay-Herron Treaty was signed with Columbia in 1903.

   a. Columbia refused to ratify the treaty.

   b. Panama revolted from Columbia for fear the canal would be built in Nicaragua instead.

5. Republic of Panama was recognized by the United States on Nov. 6, 1903.

6. Hay-Bunau-Varilla Treaty was signed between Panama and the United States.

   a. The agreement leased to the United States the use of a canal zone ten miles wide for 99 years.

   b. Panama was to be paid $10,000,000 in gold and an annual rental of $250,000 beginning in 1913.

   c. New Panama Canal Company was paid $40,000,000 for its property.

7. United States paid Columbia $25,000,000 to quiet her complaints.

8. The Panama Canal construction began in 1907, and Colonel Goethals was put in charge.

   a. Dr. Gorgas eliminated yellow fever in the canal zone.

   b. The 3-lock canal was completed in 1914.

9. In 1936, the annuity was changed.

10. The Canal Zone is, in effect, a government-owned reservation subject to Congress and the President.

H. The United States reinterpreted the Monroe Doctrine to justify its intervention in Latin-American affairs.

1. President Roosevelt urged England, Germany and Italy to arbitrate the Venezuelan debt crisis in 1902.

2. The Drago Doctrine contended that no nation should be able to cause war because of financial claims of its citizens owed to another state.

3. The Roosevelt Corollary to the Monroe Doctrine in 1904 allowed the United States to exercise international police powers in the Americas.

4. Roosevelt applied the Monroe Doctrine

corollary to the Santo Domingo financial situation in 1905.

I. The Algeciras Conference in 1906, promoted by Roosevelt, led to a Franco-German agreement over the Moroccan trade crisis.

J. America participated in peace movements.

1. First Hague Conference of 1899 founded a Permanent Court of Arbitration.

2. Roosevelt called a second Hague Conference in 1907 of forty-four nations.

3. Court of Arbitration settled seventeen cases between 1902 and 1914 with the United States participating in four cases.

4. Peace movements and foundations developed rapidly prior to the outbreak of World War I.

   a. Examples were the World Peace Foundation and the Carnegie Endowment for International Peace.

XI. THEODORE ROOSEVELT'S PROGRAM OF GOVERNMENT

A. Roosevelt's policies led to far-reaching reforms.

B. He advocated greater control of corporations by the federal government.

1. Anthracite coal strike of 1902 was settled by an arbitration board, after Roosevelt threatened to use federal troops and exerted pressure in financial circles.

2. The enforcement of the Sherman Anti-Trust Act was encouraged by the court action against the Northern Securities Company in 1904.

C. Roosevelt was reelected for a second administration, 1905-1909.

1. His Democratic opponent was Alton Barker.

2. Roosevelt carried every state except the solid South.

D. He advocated greater authority for the Interstate Commerce Commission.

1. The Hepburn Act of 1906 strengthened the Commission's regulatory powers over the railroads.

   a. Membership of the Commission was increased from five to seven.

   b. Jurisdiction was extended to include express companies, terminals, ferries and pipelines.

   c. Commission had the power to inspect railway accounts.

   d. Standard bookkeeping methods were ordered.

   e. Commission had the power to fix reasonable rates upon the complaints of the shippers.

   f. The burden of proof was placed upon the carrier rather than the Commission in legal disputes.

2. The Mann-Elkins Act of 1910 again strengthened the Interstate Commerce Commission.

   a. Its authority was extended to include telegraph, telephone, cable, and wireless companies.

   b. It was empowered to institute legal proceedings against carriers who violated the law.

   c. It could suspend all new rates from four to ten months while it investigated them.

   d. A commerce court (abolished in 1913) was created to expedite the handling of railroad rate cases.

3. Pure Food and Drug Act of 1906 prevented the manufacture, sale or transportation of poisonous, adulterated or misbranded foods, drugs or liquors.

4. Meat Inspection Act also passed in 1906.

E. Roosevelt advocated greater conservation of natural resources.

1. Newlands Act of 1902 created a fund for irrigation works in arid areas.

2. Roosevelt aroused public interest in the conservation movement.

3. Roosevelt set aside 148,000,000 acres as timber reserves.

4. Roosevelt appointed an Internal Waterways Commission who worked on the utilization of the internal waterways system.

5. A national conservation commission was appointed in 1908.

F. Panic of 1907 produced the Aldrich-Vreeland Act of 1908.

1. The Treasury Department was permitted to issue emergency currency to be loaned to banks.

G. Numerous local reforms were introduced.

1. Many states began using the secret ballot.

2. Reforms were introduced in fire, police and health departments.

3. Direct primaries, though futile, were begun to remove political boss control over candidates.

4. Initiative, referendum and recall were used in many states to control unsatisfactory legislatures.

H. The civil service list was increased and the consular service improved.

XII. THE PROGRESSIVE MOVEMENT UNDER PRESIDENT TAFT.

A. William Howard Taft was elected President in 1908; William Jennings Bryan was the Democratic nominee.

B. Taft was temperamentally conservative and less aggressive for reform.

C. The tariff was revised in 1909.
1. A special congressional session was called to reduce tariff rates as promised by the Republicans.
2. Neither the Payne Bill, passed by the House, nor the Senate amended Payne-Aldrich Bill, created tariff changes of any consequence.
3. Despite protests, Taft signed the bill.

D. The Mann-Elkins Act of 1910 failed to provide for supervision of railroad security issues by the Interstate Commerce Commission.

E. Bollinger-Pinchot controversy over the conservation program alienated many Republican progressives.

F. Progressive measures of the administration included the establishment of Postal Savings Banks, 1910, the Parcel Post, 1912, an extension of Civil Service merit system, and an eight-hour maximum day for government employees.

G. The sixteenth constitutional amendment, permitting the levying of an income tax, was ratified in 1913.

H. The seventeenth constitutional amendment for direct election of senators was ratified in 1913.

I. Reforms were made in the House of Representatives.
1. Joseph Cannon, Speaker of the House, exercised great power in the legislature.
   a. He controlled the Committee on Rules which determined routine procedure.
   b. He appointed members who desired to speak from the floor and thereby could guide the course of debate.
2. Insurgent Republicans revolted against

Cannon's dictatorial power in 1910.
   a. A resolution was passed which deprived the Speaker control over the Rules Committee.
   b. In 1911, the speaker was denied the right to appoint standing committees.
   c. Speaker only retained the power of recognizing members on the floor.

J. A reciprocity agreement between United States and Canada in 1911 was rejected by Canada.

K. The 1912 presidential election of the Democratic nominee, Woodrow Wilson, was caused by a definite Republican party split.
1. The Republicans selected Taft as their nominee.
2. The Progressive Party, formed by Republican insurgents in 1911, nominated Roosevelt.
3. Wilson obtained a record electoral total of 435 votes to Roosevelt's 88 and Taft's 8, but far less than a majority of the popular vote.

XIII. WOODROW WILSON'S LIBERALISM.

A. Wilson brought to his office idealism, administrative ability, and a talent for expressing his ideas with strength and emotional impact.

B. The cabinet was composed of superior men.
1. William Jennings Bryan was Secretary of State and William McAdoo, Secretary of the Treasury.
2. Colonel Edward House of Texas was his chief advisor.

C. Wilson's inaugural address itemized his objectives for reform in tariff, and in banking and currency in the industrial and agricultural systems.

D. Domestic reforms were immediately begun.
1. Underwood-Simmons Tariff Act of 1913 substantially reduced tariff duties.
   a. An income tax was levied to compensate for any loss in revenue.
   b. World War I broke out before the effect of the measure could be determined.
2. Owen-Glass bill of 1913 created the Federal Reserve Banking system.
   a. The Federal Reserve Act had the

following provisions:

    (1) It stabilized bank reserves.

    (2) It provided for mobility of credit so funds could be shifted to any part of the country where needed.

    (3) It created a currency supply necessary to the varying needs of business.

  b. The Federal Reserve System established a Federal Reserve Bank in each of twelve districts throughout the United States.

    (1) All national banks had to become member banks or lose their charters.

    (2) Private banks and trust companies could join.

    (3) Federal Reserve Banks were not private banks.

    (4) A National Federal Reserve Board consisted of the Secretary of the Treasury, the comptroller of the currency and five members appointed by the President.

    (5) The district Federal Reserve Banks were supervised by nine directors.

3. Clayton Act of 1914 extended federal control in regulating business.

  a. It enumerated unlawful methods of business competition.

  b. It listed ways of obtaining help from illegal trade practices.

  c. It prohibited interlocking directorates in order to evade provisions of the act.

  d. It exempted labor organizations from anti-trust laws.

  e. It prohibited the use of injunctions in labor disputes except in particular instances.

  f. Strikes, boycotts and peaceful picketing were not illegal.

  g. Directors, officers and agents were responsible for violations of the Act.

4. Federal Trade Commission was established in 1914 under a bipartisan commission of five members.

  a. It could conduct investigations of unfair methods of competition in commerce.

  b. It could issue orders against unfair trade practices and apply for judicial injunctions to enforce its orders.

  c. It could require reports from corporations engaged in interstate business.

  d. Appeals from the commission's order could be made to the Circuit Court of Appeals which could be reviewed by the Supreme Court.

5. Newlands Act of 1913 created a permanent board of mediation for railway labor disputes.

6. Smith-Lever Act of 1914 granted federal funds to states for farm extension work.

7. LaFollette Seamen's Act of 1915 prescribed minimum wages, food and accommodations for seamen employed on ships under American registry.

8. Keating-Owen Act of 1915 prohibited the transit in interstate commerce of products manufactured in establishments using child labor under fourteen.

  a. The Act was declared unconstitutional by the Supreme Court in 1918.

  b. Child-labor was abolished in 1933 in codes drafted by the National Recovery Administration.

9. Adamson Act of 1916 established an eight-hour day for employees of carriers engaged in interstate commerce.

10. Hollis-Bulkley Rural Credits Act of 1916 established twelve Federal Farm Loan Banks.

  a. Farmers were able to obtain loans for farm mortgages at a reasonable rate of interest.

E. Wilson's foreign policy was dominated by perplexing international difficulties.

1. Wilson refused to befriend neighboring republics if the country had been seized and controlled by violence rather than by a democratic process.

2. A revolutionary outbreak in Haiti in 1915 was followed by the landing of the United States Marines to assume control.

  a. The Haitian government reluctantly signed a treaty allowing American control of public works, the constabulary, finances and public works.

  b. Native resistance often caused disorders.

  c. The United States continued building highways, reforming finances and improving sanitary conditions.

  d. The last troops were withdrawn in 1934.

3. Between 1912 and 1933, American-Nicaraguan relations were strained.

a. From 1912 to 1925, American marines protected the administration of Nicaraguan finances and maintained political tranquility.

b. Bryan-Chamorro Treaty of 1914 granted the United States a right to build a canal through the country, 99 year leases on Great and Little Corn Islands and a naval base in the Gulf of Fonseca.

  1) Nicaragua received $3,000,000 for these concessions.

c. New revolts caused the marines to return in 1926 until 1933.

4. The Virgin Islands were acquired for $25,000,000 from Denmark.

a. The territory was ruled by an appointed governor with limited self-government.

b. The inhabitants' became United States citizens in 1927.

5. Wilson's dealings with Mexico were well-intentioned.

a. The autocratic regime of Diaz, 1876 to 1910, was overthrown by Francisco Madero and his wealthy liberals and enslaved peons.

b. From 1910 to 1913, Madero attempted reforms which were futile.

c. General Huerta's revolt ended Madero's efforts in 1913.

d. Wilson refused to recognize the new Huerta government claiming it did not represent the will of the people.

e. Huerta retaliated by acts of reprisal on American citizens.

  (1) Arrest of American marines at Tampico in 1914 precipitated the seizure of Vera Cruz by American forces.

  (2) Huerta apologized but refused to salute the American flag.

f. Wilson accepted the offer of the "ABC" powers—Argentina, Brazil and Chili to mediate the differences between Mexico and the United States.

  (1) Huerta fled and American troops withdrew.

g. Violence continued and Carranza seized power with the promise to establish an orderly government.

h. The United States recognized the Carranza government.

i. However, Carranza failed to restrain his enemy, Pancho Villa, who led a raid against Americans in Columbus, New Mexico.

j. The United States sent a punitive expedition under General Pershing into Mexico in pursuit of Villa with Carranza's permission.

  (1) Villa was not captured but border raids ceased.

  (2) American troops withdrew in 1917.

XIV. THE FIRST WORLD WAR, 1914-1918

A. Archduke Francis Ferdinand, heir to the Austrian-Hungarian throne, and his wife, were murdered, June 28, 1914.

1. Austria-Hungary declared war on Serbia.

2. Germany declared war on Russia and France.

3. England declared war on Germany.

4. Later other nations became involved.

B. President Wilson issued a neutrality proclamation on August 4, 1914.

1. American public opinion favored England and the Allies.

2. The United States thought Germany to be an authoritarian nation and the aggressor after violating Belgian neutrality.

C. Germany began a campaign of subversive activities to prevent American shipments to the Allies.

1. England maintained a rigorous naval blockade against Germany and extended the list of contraband articles.

2. Germany attempted a similar blockade against England by the use of submarines.

a. Germany declared that the English Channel and waters around the British Isles were a war zone and all vessels could be destroyed.

b. United States protested.

3. Lusitania was torpedoed May 7, 1915 with a loss of 1,153 people including 114 Americans.

a. The act was deliberately planned.

b. Wilson demanded that Germany stop her submarine practices.

c. Germany continued sinking vessels until August, 1915, when she agreed to discontinue the practice.

d. Americans were warned not to travel on armed belligerent vessels.

e. March 24, 1916, a French vessel, Sussex, was sunk.

f. Wilson threatened a severance of diplomatic relations with Germany.

U.S. HISTORY

D. National military preparedness was actively urged in the United States despite anti-war organizations.

1. National Defense Act of June, 1916, increased the Army to 220,000 men and national guard to 425,000 men.
2. United States shipping board was created September, 1916, to build or buy ships which might be transferred to private concerns or operated by government corporations.
3. Naval Appropriations Bill authorized $500,000,000 for ship construction.

E. Wilson won the presidential election again in 1916 against Supreme Court Justice Hughes, the Republican nominee.

F. On January 31, 1917 Germany announced unrestricted submarine warfare.

1. Wilson severed diplomatic relations with Germany, February 3, 1917.
2. Publication of the Zimmermann note by the State Department revealed Germany's offer for a Mexican alliance with a promise to Mexico to recover Texas, Arizona and New Mexico.
3. Japan was also to be invited in an attack on the United States.

G. Wilson directed the arming of merchant ships in March, 1917.

H. Wilson called a special Congressional session and the war declaration was signed April 6, 1917.

I. Congressional legislation in 1917 dealt with organizing all energies on winning the war.

1. Council of National Defense began to function.
2. War Industries Board was established.
3. War Finance Corporation loaned money for war industries.
4. Herbert Hoover took charge of the Food Administration.
5. A Fuel Administration was established.
6. Railroads were nationalized.
7. War Trade Board supervised foreign trade.
8. Army camps were constructed for the American Army which totaled 3,500,000 volunteers and draftees.
9. Selective Service Act, the draft, was passed in 1917.

J. General John Pershing commanded the American Expeditionary Force, which reached Paris, June 13, 1917.

1. American, French and British troops participated in counter-offensives to the Germans at Mondidier, Cantigny, Belleau Wood and Vaux.
2. In July, 1918, American Troops fought in the Marne Valley and in the assaults at Soissons and Chateau-Thierry.
3. The first American offensive was September 12, 1918 in the reduction of the Saint Mihiel salient.
4. On September 26 began the offense against the Meuse-Argonne line.

K. During the war certain laws were passed as retaliatory measures to attacks on the war effort.

1. Espionage Act of 1917 prescribed penalties for insubordination and disloyalty in the army.
   a. Mail was censored.
2. Sedition Act of 1918 made it a criminal offense to abuse the government, the flag or the Constitution.
3. Deportation Act of 1918 deported aliens without jury trials who advocated the overthrow of the government.

L. Many civilian agencies as the Y.M.C.A., the Salvation Army, the Jewish Welfare Board and others attempted to help the troops.

M. A thriving prosperity existed caused by high prices and a large demand for products.

N. War ended at 11 A.M., November 11, 1918; the Armistice was signed.

1. Wilson's address to Congress January 8, 1918 described the fourteen points program for peace.
   a. They included abolition of secret diplomacy, freedom of the seas, disarmament, removal of international economic barriers, establishment of an association of nations, and territorial and political readjustments of Alsace-Lorraine, Italy, Belgium, Poland, Russia, Austria-Hungary, the Balkan states and sections of Turkey.
2. Chancellor von Herthing resigned and was succeeded by Prince Maximilian, a liberal.
   a. Terms of the armistice stripped Germany of her munitions and armaments.
3. Kaiser Wilhelm abdicated.

O. World War I had become a total war

necessitating the mobilizing of complete economic resources and mechanical techniques.

XV. THE PEACE MOVEMENT AND POST-WAR READJUSTMENT.

A. Peace conference was held at Paris, January 18, 1919.

1. Wilson wanted the peace terms to adhere to his fourteen points.
2. The European allies had secret treaties with their own nationalistic objectives.

B. The conference was composed of more than sixty delegates from twenty-seven nations.

1. The steering committee was the Council of Ten consisting of two representatives from England, France, Italy, Japan and the United States.
2. The "Big Four", Wilson, Lloyd George, Clemenceau and Orlando settled the most important issues.

C. Treaty of Versailles was signed June 28, 1919.

1. Germany and her allies were made to assume the responsibility of the war.
2. Germany was disarmed, lost territorial possessions, and had to pay $56,500,-000,000 in gold to the Reparations Commission.

D. The League of Nations came into being on January 10, 1920.

1. Wilson insisted that the Covenant of the League be made part of the peace treaties.
2. The League consisted of a council, an assembly and a secretariat.
3. Members originally numbered 29; by 1928 at the height of its prestige, there were 54.
3. Germany was stripped of her colonies which became League of Nations mandates; furthermore she could not join the League.

E. A hostile United States Senate refused to ratify the treaty because of the inclusion of certain articles in the League of Nations.

1. Wilson refused to make concessions, fought for the League, then suffered a paralytic stroke.
2. President Harding signed the congressional resolution ending the war with Germany on July 2, 1921.

F. New states were created in Europe by treaties and the principle of self-determination; the map of Europe was greatly changed.

XVI. POST-WORLD WAR READJUSTMENTS IN THE UNITED STATES.

A. Warren G. Harding, the Republican candidate, won the presidential election in 1920 over James M. Cox, the Democratic candidate.

B. United States began its move toward disarmament.

1. There was swift military demobilization.
2. An Army Act of 1920 set the regular peace army at 300,000 men.
3. Congress passed legislation to assist war veterans.
4. The government began a program of scrapping war machines.

C. United States began to develop its World Peace policies.

1. The government gave unofficial cooperation to the League of Nations by unofficial delegates at various conferences.
2. Since 1931, the United States had permanent representatives at Geneva to handle her interests at the League.
3. The United States, although not a member, adopted a favorable attitude towards the World Court.
   a. The court was created by the League and inaugurated at The Hague in 1922.
   b. Presidents Harding and Coolidge recommended membership, but up to 1935 there was still rejection by the Senate.
4. Fourteen nations in 1928 signed the Breand-Kellogg Peace Pact, which outlawed war.
   a. Fifty-four nations ultimately joined.
5. Washington Conference of 1921-1922 reduced naval armaments among leading naval powers.
6. London Naval Conference in 1930 produced a treaty between United States, England and Japan which Japan denounced in 1934.

D. New amendments were added to the Constitution.

1. The eighteenth amendment, prohibiting the manufacture or sale of intoxicating liquors was adopted January 16, 1920.
   a. The twenty-first amendment repealed the eighteenth in December, 1933.
2. Congress passed the nineteenth amendment in June, 1919, extending suffrage to women.

3. The twentieth amendment was proclaimed February, 1933.
   a. Terms of President and Vice-President will end on January 20.
   b. Terms of senators and representatives will end on January 3rd at noon.
   c. Congress will assemble at least once a year on January 3rd unless another date is appointed by law.
   d. A method was created in selecting a President and Vice-President in case of death before qualifying.

E. **Transportation Act of 1920 or Esch-Cummins returned the railways to the companies but extended the Interstate Commerce Commission powers.**
1. The Commission was granted control of security issues, traffic regulations and consolidation of lines.
2. The government guaranteed 5½ percent to owners for 2 years.
3. A revolving fund was created to facilitate loans for improvements.
4. Labor disputes were to be arbitrated by a Railway Labor Board.
   b. Federal Board of Mediation succeeded it in 1926.

F. **Merchant Marine Act of 1920 terminated building by the Shipping Board but continued to operate and sell ships to American buyers.**

G. **Harding died unexpectedly in 1923.**
1. His most distinguished cabinet members were Hughes, Secretary of State, Mellon, Secretary of the Treasury, and Hoover, Secretary of Commerce.
2. At the time of Harding's death the Teapot Dome scandal was disclosed.
   a. This was the secret leasing, without competitive bids, of government oil reserves, by Fall, Secretary of the Interior.

H. **Coolidge succeeded Harding and was re-elected in the presidential campaign of 1924 over John W. Davis, the Democratic nominee and La Folette, the new Progressive party candidate.**

I. **The prosperity of the Republican regime under Coolidge swept Herbert Hoover into Office in 1928 over Alfred E. Smith, the Democratic opponent.**

J. **The country flourished with great prosperity in the twenties.**
1. Labor unions had huge memberships at the end of the war.

   a. There were numerous strikes succeeding the war.
   b. During the post-war decade, trade unionism declined in activity.
2. Fear of Communists and radicals developed.
   a. Despite inconclusive evidence, Sacco and Vanzetti, two anarchists were convicted of murder.
   b. The intolerant group of the Ku Klux Klan grew rapidly in the 1920's aiming their attacks at Roman Catholics, Jews and Negroes.
   c. John Scopes was indicted for teaching the theory of evolution in high school.
     1. The case was an example of the Fundamentalist fear that the changing mood of the country would weaken traditional religious beliefs.
   d. Even the moderate reforms of the Progressive era were looked upon with suspicion during the wave of radicalism.
3. Immigration to the United States was curtailed by laws.
   a. The Act of 1921 provided that no European country could send in any year more than 3 per cent of the number of people of that nationality in the United States during 1910.
   b. Immigration Act of 1924 restricted the quota to 2 per cent of the members of that nation in the United States during 1890.
     (1) National origins provision was to go into effect in 1927, whereby immigration was restricted to 150,000 annually according to the distribution of people in the country and according to the 1890 census.
     (2) Natives of Latin America and Canada were not restricted.
     (3) Orientals were prohibited.
4. Farmers prospered because of high prices, an almost unlimited market and the mechanization of machinery during the war.
   a. Disaster followed the post-war years.
   b. Farm Bureau Federation collaborated with other farmer organizations to obtain legislative relief by having a farm bloc in Congress.
     (1) Federal Farm Loan Banks were liberal with loans to farmers.

(2) Intermediate Credits Act of 1923 allowed the farmers to borrow on crops and cattle in transit to market.

(3) Volstead Act of 1922 exempted cooperative associations from the anti-trusts acts.

(4) The McNary-Haugen bill was vetoed by Coolidge.

(5) Agricultural Marketing Act of 1929 created a Federal Farm Board to organize farm cooperatives.

5. The Republican high tariff policy was reviewed.

   a. Emergency Tariff act of 1921 placed high duties on some agricultural products and new chemicals.

   b. Fordney-McCumber Tariff Act of 1922 allowed for the most rigorous protection.

      (1) It reduced the commodities in the free list.

      (2) It increased rates on agricultural products.

      (3) It created a Tariff Commission to investigate costs abroad.

      (4) The basic principle was the equalization of costs of production between domestic and foreign producers.

   c. Hawley-Smoot Tariff Act was passed June, 1930.

      (1) It contained the highest tariff rate in American history.

      (2) As a result foreign countries increased their tariff duties.

K. Depression in 1929 succeeded the prosperous boom times.

1. A passion for speculation in 1928 and 1929 ended in disastrous results.

   a. The stock market crash of October, 1929 marked the start of a severe depression.

   b. Economic conditions grew increasingly worse.

      (1) Unemployment increased, banks and businesses failed and factories closed.

2. An elaborate system of charitable and relief agencies provided for the destitute.

   a. Reconstruction Finance Corporation in 1932 channeled government funds into private business enterprise.

   b. The Public Works Program spent large sums of money on public buildings to increase employment.

   c. The Federal Reserve Banks made loans to industry at low rates for plant improvements.

3. Income Taxes were increased in 1932 and excise taxes were imposed to pay for the huge appropriations.

L. Presidential election of 1932 was won by Franklin D. Roosevelt, a Democrat, over Hoover, the Republican.

1. Roosevelt promised "a new deal" to "the forgotten man" as against the Republican favoritism of financial and industrial interests.

2. Conditions at the beginning of 1932 were deplorable.

XVII. THE NEW DEAL OF FRANKLIN D. ROOSEVELT.

A. Roosevelt adopted emergency measures to meet the economic crisis.

1. Between 13 and 15 million people were unemployed.

2. All the banks in the country closed March 4, 1933 as a result of depositors having withdrawn their money to hoard it.

   a. Roosevelt proclaimed a bank holiday; prohibited gold to be exported.

   b. An Emergency Banking Law set up a plan to resume normal banking procedures.

      (1) Sound banks reopened in ten days.

      (2) Other banks were aided by bank conservators.

3. Under an Economy Act, government expenditures were reduced by $500 million.

B. New Deal legislation of the "hundred days" was a remarkable period of governmental cooperation.

1. Roosevelt offered an emergency relief program.

   a. Civilian Conservation Corps was established for improving the park and forest resources.

   b. Wagner Act created an employment system which later became the United States Employment Service.

   c. Federal Emergency Relief Administration provided the states with relief funds for unemployed.

   d. Works Progress Administration spent huge sums of money for relief

U.S. HISTORY

projects and for public works which gave employment to millions of people.

2. Steps were taken to aid industry and agriculture.
   a. Reconstruction Finance Corporation gave liberal loans to industry as well as railroads and banks.
   b. Home Owners Loan Corporation loaned money to mortgage holders to stimulate building construction.
   c. United States Housing Authority assisted states with slum clearance.
   d. National Industrial Recovery Act helped government representatives, employers and employees to prepare codes of agreement which regulated hours, wages, prices and production in industry.
      (1) Roosevelt was given the power to license interstate commerce.
      (2) NRA was declared unconstitutional by the Supreme Court in 1935.
      (3) Wagner-Connery Act in 1935 established a Labor Relations Board to protect the rights of labor.
   e. Agricultural Adjustment Act of 1933 tried to control production by subsidizing farmers who reduced lands farmed in specified crops.
      (1) The Act was ruled unconstitutional in 1936.
      (2) Domestic Allotment Act of 1936 provided funds by states to farmers for improved techniques, crop subsidies and soil conservation.
   f. Federal Farm Loan Act of 1933 financed farm mortgages at low rates of interest.
   g. Resettlement Administration of 1935 helped farmers in poor agricultural areas to resettle.

3. Other important reform measures were included in the New Deal.
   a. Reforms were made in banks and finance by the Glass-Steagall Act of 1933, the Truth in Securities Act of 1933, Securities Exchange Act of 1934, Securities and Exchange Commission created, 1934.
   b. The dollar was devaluated to raise prices.
   c. The gross national debt almost doubled itself between 1933-1939 despite tax raises to defray the costs

of the New Deal program.
   d. Tennessee Valley Authority Act of 1933 set up the construction of power dams where the Tennessee River flows.
      (1) The Authority sold electric power and rehabilitated the entire area.
      (2) The cheaper government rates forced private utility companies to reduce their rates.
      (3) Rural Electrification Administration in 1935 authorized the construction of electric power plants in rural areas with government funds.

4. The New Deal also included, welfare, old age and unemployment programs.
   a. The Social Security Act of 1935 provided pensions for workers at the age of sixty-five.
      (1) The pension was financed from an equal tax levied on employer and worker.
      (2) The Act also provided for unemployment compensation financed from a federal tax on payroll.
      (3) The Act also established federal aid to states for welfare assistance.

5. The New Deal evoked attacks from conservatives and radicals.

C. In 1936 the Democrats, with the renomination of Roosevelt, won the presidential election over the Republican candidate, Alfred Landon.

D. Roosevelt continued to extend his New Deal program.

1. Roosevelt attempted to reorganize the Supreme Court with appointees more favorable to his program.
   a. He attempted retirement of judges over 70.
   b. He asked to increase the number of judges to fifteen.
   c. Congress defeated his Reorganization Bill.
   d. With the retirement and death of some of the judges, Roosevelt appointed more liberal men.

2. The New Deal passed legislation to improve industrial workers and the farmers.
   a. Long-term, low-interest loans were given to sharecroppers.
   b. A new AAA replaced the one declared unconstitutional in 1933.

3. Increased membership in labor unions developed.

   a. The Congress of Industrial Organization (CIO) under John L. Lewis, organized workers on an industry-wide basis, as opposed to the American Federation of Labor (AFL) organized by crafts.

   b. The Wages and Hour Law of 1938 established a forty-hour week and a minimum hourly wage.

4. Many federal departments were reorganized.

XVIII. THE FOREIGN POLICY OF THE UNITED STATES PRIOR TO WORLD WAR II.

A. International political conditions were affecting the United States policy of isolationism.

1. Nationalism was expanding in Europe and the Far East.

2. Dictatorships were developing in Germany, Italy, Russia and Japan.

3. Japan occupied Manchuria in 1931.

4. The United States would not join the World Court.

5. Changes were made in foreign trade.

   a. London Economic Conference, 1933, failed because the United States refused to cooperate with other countries in currency stabilization.

   b. Reciprocal trade agreements were made and provisions were set for decreasing tariffs.

   c. Loans were made to countries to aid foreign trading.

   d. Trade with aggressor nations was restricted.

6. Stringent Neutrality Acts were passed in 1935-37.

B. A "Good Neighbor Policy" was adopted toward Latin America.

1. Troops withdrew from Nicaragua and Haiti.

2. A series of Pan-American conferences was held.

   a. At the Montevideo Conference, 1933, Cordell Hull, Secretary of State, stated that no nation has the right to intervene in the affairs of another state.

   b. Rio de Janeiro 1933, condemned aggression.

   c. At the Lima conference, 1938, twenty-one American republics af-

firmed their solidarity and agreed that any threat to peace in the Western Hemisphere would lead to governmental consultations.

   d. Panama Declaration, 1939, defined the neutral position of the American states in the European war and declared that the warring countries must remain out of a three hundred mile safety zone around the Western Hemisphere.

   e. Act of Havana, 1940, affirmed the position of the Latin American countries and the United States, that an act of aggression against one of

   them would be an attack on all of them and prohibited the transfer of any European colony in the area to a non-American power.

3. Money was loaned to Latin American countries to improve economic conditions.

C. The United States attempted to stay neutral.

1. Japanese aggression in China began in 1931; neither the League, Britain or the U.S. could stop the aggression which was renewed in 1937.

2. Italy conquered Ethiopia in Africa in May, 1936; League sanctions not effective.

3. In Germany, the Nazis under Hitler annexed the Saar Basin and took over the Rhineland; she had rearmed.

4. Civil war in Spain, and the recognition of Franco, 1939, added strength to Italy and Germany.

D. Foreign events caused the United States to enter World War II, December, 1941.

1. Germany made military alliances with Italy, Russia and Japan.

2. Germany occupied Austria, 1938.

3. France and England agreed to German annexation of the Czechoslovakian Sudetenland, 1938.

4. Hitler took over Czechoslovakia and then Poland, 1939.

5. England and France declared war on Germany in September, 1939.

6. Hitler overran Denmark, Norway, the Netherlands, Belgium and France with his highly mechanized army (blitzkrieg).

7. England continued to fight on alone.

U.S. HISTORY

8. The dictators established military alliances.
    a. Rome-Berlin Axis of May, 1939, was a ten year military pact between Mussolini and Hitler.
    b. Moscow-Berlin Pact of August, 1939, promised Hitler Russian support in the invasion of Poland.
    c. Rome-Berlin-Tokyo Axis of 1940 recognized the various aggressions, and the Axis leaders pledged military assistance if the United States entered the war.
9. Italy invaded Albania, 1939.
10. Russia invaded Estonia, Latvia, Lithuania and Finland.
11. Japan occupied Indo-China and British and Dutch possessions in southern Asia.
12. Relations with Japan were strained over economic restrictions.
13. On December 7, 1941, Japan attacked the United States naval base at Pearl Harbor in the Hawaiian Islands.

E. **The United States began to prepare itself for war in 1939.**

1. Selective Service Act of 1940 provided for drafting men into military service.
2. Lend-Lease Act of 1941 sent American goods to England and later to other countries.
3. The industrial resources of the country were mobilized.
4. Naval and air bases were obtained.
5. Aliens were required to register.
6. Embargo Act was modified.

F. **Roosevelt was elected President for the third time in 1940 over the Republican candidate, Wendell Willkie.**

G. **The Atlantic Charter, 1941, resulted from a meeting between President Roosevelt and England's Prime Minister, Winston Churchill, to set up their future policies and actions.**

1. Twenty-six nations, including Russia and the United States, signed the Charter, 1942.

XIX. WORLD WAR II.

A. **Congress declared war on Japan, December 8, 1941.**

1. England also declared war on Japan.
2. Germany and Italy joined Japan in the war against the United States.
3. Congress then declared war on Germany and Italy.

B. **United States became united in a tremendous effort to win the war.**

1. By 1944, the armed forces had 11 million people.
2. Food production was increased by one third between 1939 and 1944.
3. Number of airplanes increased from 17,700 to 250,000 between 1941 and 1944.
4. Warship tonnage increased from two million to five million.
5. Merchant tonnage increased from over one million to nineteen million.
6. Gigantic war appropriations were made.
    a. The national debt increased from $47 billion to $247 billion between 1941 and 1945.
    b. Taxes were increased and war savings bonds were issued to finance the war.
    c. Appropriations for national defense and war rose to approximately $220 billion between 1940 and 1943.
7. New military techniques were developed.
    a. The United States was the first to use the atomic bomb against Japan in August, 1945.
8. Price controls and rationing were established.

B. **The Japanese demonstrated their impressive military power in the beginning of the war, 1942.**

1. Netherlands East Indies, Singapore, Burma, Guam, Wake Island and Hong Kong all fell under Japanese domination.
2. General Douglas MacArthur commanded the American and Filipino troops in the Philippines.
    a. The Bataan peninsula and Corregidor fell.
    b. MacArthur retreated to Australia where he planned his return to free the Philippines.
3. Japan then held Attu and Kiska in the Aleutian Islands.

C. **United States also turned her efforts to the European front.**

1. England fought a heroic fight against the German air force.
2. Hitler invaded Russia, despite the Moscow Pact, and thereby created two battlefronts for Germany.
3. Russia joined the West.
4. Forces, under the British General Mont-

gomery and the American General Eisenhower, routed the Germans under Marshal Rommel in a 1300 mile offensive from El Alamein to Tunisia in Africa, 1943.

5. The invasion of Sicily and Mussolini's resignation caused Italy to surrender, 1943.
   a. A provisional government was created.
   b. Italy later became a cobelligerent.
6. The successful German offensive in Russia controlled Bessarabia, Moscow, Leningrad and Kiev.
   a. By 1943, Russia began to move forward breaking the German hold and entered Berlin in 1945.
7. France was invaded in 1944, and a second front was opened.
   a. The Russians were fighting on the first front.
   b. The Allies got control of air power over Western Europe.
   c. Under Generals Montgomery and Eisenhower, the German defense lines were broken.
   d. America sent unlimited amounts of food and war materials.
   e. April, 1945, the forces joined with the Russians at Torgau, Germany.
   f. European fighting ended with the complete unconditional surrender of Germany, May 7, 1945.

D. **After 1943, the United States turned its strength to the Pacific war area.**

1. The battles of Coral Sea and Midway halted the Japanese offensive, 1942.
2. Beachheads on Guadalcanal and in the Florida Islands were obtained by the United States, 1942-1943.
3. Attu and Kiska were recaptured, 1943.
4. Saipan, Guam, Iwo Jima and Okinawa were captured in order to become military air bases from which an air war could be launched against Japan.
5. The Japanese navy was reduced so that MacArthur could return and regain the Philippines.
6. After the battle of Leyte Gulf, Leyte and Luzon were occupied by the United States.
7. Assistance was given to the Chinese to push the Japanese out of the mainland.
8. American bombers dropped the first atomic bomb on Hiroshima, August 5, 1945 and the second on Nagasaki, Aug-

ust 8, almost destroying both cities.
9. Japan surrendered unconditionally September 2, 1945.
   a. The end of the European War allowed the strength to be relocated.
   b. The dropping of the atomic bombs, and Russia's declaration of war against Japan ended the Pacific war.

E. **During World War II, the United States elected Roosevelt to presidential office for a fourth term.**

1. The Republican candidate was Thomas Dewey, Governor of New York.
2. President Roosevelt died April 12, 1945, about three months after the beginning of his fourth term.
3. Vice-President Harry Truman succeeded him.

XX. THE POST-WAR SEARCH FOR PEACE.

A. **During the war, conferences were held to discuss plans for collective security and post war policy.**

1. President Roosevelt and British Prime Minister Churchill met at Washington, Quebec and Casablanca.
   a. At Casablanca, January, 1943, a decision to continue war until unconditional surrender of enemy countries was established.
   b. Chiang Kai-shek, the Nationalist Defender of China, joined them in a conference at Cairo in 1943, where a pledge was made to restore Japanese taken territory to China.
2. At Moscow, 1943, Roosevelt, Churchill and Stalin of Russia met.
3. At Teheran, 1943, they agreed to continue cooperating after the war.
4. At Yalta, 1945, they approved a plan for ending the war and for calling an international conference at San Francisco to draft a charter for world peace.
5. At Potsdam, July 1945, they dealt with reparations, etc.

B. **A conference on economic problems created the United Nations Relief and Rehabilitation Administration, 1943.**

C. **A conference at Bretton Woods, 1944, made plans for an International Bank for Reconstruction and Development.**

D. **At the Dumbarton Oaks Conference, 1945, proposals for a United Nations charter were drafted.**

E. **A United Nations Charter was adopted by forty-six nations at the San Francisco Conference, 1945.**

1. Membership was open to peace-loving countries.
2. Each nation was to have one vote in the General Assembly.
   a. The Assembly had powers of debate, recommendation, and supervision of special agencies.
   b. It handled matters on which the Security Council failed to overcome the veto.
3. The Security Council was composed of five permanent members, namely, England, Russia, China, France, the United States and six non-permanent members elected by the General Assembly for two year terms.
   a. Each of the permanent members had a right to veto any decision.
   b. The Council was to maintain international peace and was empowered to take enforcement action for this purpose.
4. An international court with fifteen members was created with its headquarters at The Hague.
5. Eighteen members from the General Assembly formed an economic and social council to alleviate war, caused by economic and social conditions.
6. A secretary-general selected by the General Assembly was to coordinate the work of the United Nations.
7. The Charter went into effect in 1945.
   a. Trygve Lie was the first secretary-general.
   b. The budget was approximately $50 million dollars.
   c. Permanent headquarters for the U.N. were to be in New York City.
8. The U.N. set up several agencies to handle non-political problems.
   a. Among these agencies were International Labor Office, Food and Agricultural Organization, United Nations Educational, Scientific and Cultural Organization and others.
   b. International Atomic Energy Commission was created in 1946 to act as an international authority controlling atomic energy uses.

F. **The United Nations was effective in settling some disputes.**

1. Under the Japanese Peace Treaty, Korea was divided at the 38th Parallel with Russia controlling the north and anti-communist forces controlling the south.
2. The U.N. sent military aid in June, 1950 to South Korea when the North Korean forces, aided by Russia, crossed the 38° parallel.
   a. This was the first time U.S. troops were used in an international police force to stop aggression.
   b. Chinese Communist soldiers intervened on the North Korean side.
   c. President Truman dismissed General MacArthur as leader of U.N. forces because of policy differences.
   d. An armistice was agreed upon in 1953, but no satisfactory conclusion for Korea was reached.
3. U.N. was also active in the Suez crisis, Arab-Israel disputes and in emerging African states.

XXI. THE TRUMAN ADMINISTRATIONS, 1945-1953.

A. **Military demobilization went ahead at a rapid pace after the war.**

1. Discharged veterans were given the G.I. Bill of Rights which provided for government loans for business and home, free education and unemployment insurance.
2. Departments of Navy and War were combined into the Department of Defense, with James Forrestal as its first Secretary in 1947.

B. **Truman continued the Roosevelt domestic policy with his "Fair Deal" program.**

1. His efforts were stymied by the 1946 Republican Congress and the Republican and Southern Democrats coalition between 1948 and 1952.
2. Industry was converted to peacetime production under the Office of War Mobilization and Reconversion.
   a. Price controls were removed, 1947.
   b. A bill to lower taxes was vetoed by Truman, 1947.
   c. Taft-Hartley Act of 1947 passed over the President's veto, replacing the Wagner-Connery Act of 1935.
      (1) Unions were placed under supervision on the same basis as management.
      (2) Unions were required to give financial reports.
      (3) Unions and management had to

give sixty days notice before strikes or lockouts.

(4) Secondary boycotts were prohibited.

(5) Closed-shop, unfair labor practices, and union contributions to federal political campaigns were prohibited.

(6) A company had the right to sue a union.

(7) Employers were guaranteed freedom of speech.

(8) Union officers were compelled to swear they were not communists.

(9) The law was to be administered by the National Labor Relations Board.

3. A twenty-second amendment to the Constitution was passed, limiting the office of the president to two full terms.

4. Truman defeated the Republican Governor Dewey in the 1948 election for presidency.

5. Truman's civil rights program was defeated.

6. Laws were enacted that expanded social security, allowed large appropriations for low-rental housing and slum clearance, and the minimum wage was raised from forty to seventy-five cents an hour.

C. Truman's foreign policy worked primarily for communist containment and for an effective United Nations.

1. Truman, Stalin and Atlee, the new British Prime Minister, had met at the Potsdam Conference in 1945 to lay the plans for dealing with a defeated Germany.

   a. Occupied Germany was divided into four military zones under United States, France, England and Russia.

   b. Berlin was controlled by a Four Power Allied Council.

2. United Nations War Crimes Commission tried the Nazi war leaders at Nuremberg under proper judicial processes.

   a. Some defendants were sentenced to death, some were given prison terms, and others were acquitted.

3. Occupied Austria was divided into four military zones under the control of the Four Powers.

4. Peace Treaties were completed in 1947 with Bulgaria, Hungary, Finland, Rumania and Italy.

   a. The countries were assessed indemnities, had their military power reduced and lost territory.

5. Four Powers failed to reach a satisfactory agreement about Germany and Austrian peace treaties.

   a. United States, England and France established a West Germany Republic.

   b. The Russian controlled section was called East Germany.

   c. Russia's attempt to gain control of Germany led to the Berlin blockade, which stopped all supplies from entering Berlin from the West by land and rail.

   d. The West retaliated with an airlift which kept the supply flow open for almost eleven months, 1948-1949.

   e. A constitution was adopted which was the basis for the Federal Republic of Western Germany, 1949.

      (1) Troops remained but the military government ceased.

6. A Japanese peace treaty was accepted in 1951.

   a. General MacArthur provided efficient leadership for the American occupation.

   b. Japanese war leaders were tried and their country demilitarized.

   c. A new constitution was adopted which led to a more democratic form of government, in limiting the emperor's power and providing Democratic elections.

   d. A new constitution was adopted which led to a more democratic form of government, in limiting the emperor's power and providing Democratic elections.

   e. The Peace Treaty removed Japan's island possessions and claims to Korea.

   f. The treaty provided for occupation troop withdrawal, but some military forces were allowed to remain.

   g. Treaty became effective April, 1952, despite the refusal of Poland, Czechoslovakia and Russia to sign.

D. The world became divided under Russian and American dominance and developed the "cold war".

1. After World War II, Russian foreign policy was based on world revolution.

2. China fell under the influence of the

Russian Communists.

3. United States allowed the Philippines to be proclaimed a Republic, July 4, 1946.

4. The Latin American ''good neighbor'' policy was continued.

 a. The Bogota Pact of 1948 provided for the Charter of the Organization of American States (OAS).

 b. This placed Pan-Americanism within the United Nations.

E. **The Truman Doctrine of 1947 declared the responsibility of the United States to approve a program of aid to people who were resisting subjugation or aggression from other countries.**

1. Congress appropriated $400 million to aid Greece and Turkey because of Russian penetration in the area.

2. The Marshall Plan, 1947, planned the Economic Cooperation Administration of 1948, which gave huge sums of money to aid European economic recovery and reconstruction.

3. Mutual Defense Assistance Pact, 1949, gave military aid to friendly countries.

4. "Point Four" program gave technical assistance to underdeveloped areas, 1950.

5. The North Atlantic Treaty Organization (NATO), 1949, was the first European alliance to be signed by the United States during peace time.

 a. Twelve nations, and later also Greece and Turkey, agreed to a defensive pact if any of them were to be attacked by a non-member nation.

6. The European Defense Community (EDC) composed of France, Italy, Belgium, Netherlands, Luxembourg, and West Germany would contribute soldiers for an army to be commanded by NATO ground headquarters, SHAPE.

F. **During this period, Russia (USSR) extended its communist control of its satellites and extended its sphere of influence.**

1. Russia controlled the governments of Bulgaria, Finland, Poland, Rumania, Estonia, Czechoslovakia, Latvia, Hungary, Lithuania, East Germany, and her area of occupied Austria.

2. In China, the Nationalists under Chiang Kai-shek fled to Formosa.

 a. The People's Republic of China, 1949, under Mao Tze-tung and Premier Chou En-lai was communist controlled.

3. Communists also gained a foothold in Viet Nam.

XXII. THE REPUBLICAN ADMINISTRATION OF DWIGHT D. EISENHOWER, 1952-1960.

A. **General Eisenhower was elected over the Democratic candidate, Adlai Stevenson.**

B. **Eisenhower's domestic policy attempted to reduce governmental control by encouraging private enterprise.**

1. Congress passed a tax act which reduced about $7,000,000 worth of taxes.

2. The end of governmental monopoly of atomic energy and the return of the tideland off-shore oil fields to the states were examples of the change of the philosophy of government.

3. Social Security pensions were increased, and they also included more people.

4. Many governmental controls started under Roosevelt and Truman were not maintained.

5. A movement was started to extend civil rights.

 a. In 1954, the Supreme Court ruled the desegregation of public schools.

 b. The Little Rock, Arkansas episode in 1957 resulted in the use of Federal troops for integration security.

 c. A bill was passed in 1957 which empowered the government to seek court orders to guarantee the individual's right to vote in any state.

6. The United States attempted a program of fighting communism within the country, which resulted in witch hunts, spy scares, McCarthy hearings and fifth amendment-pleaders.

C. **Eisenhower's foreign policy aimed for a united front of the Western countries and security through mutual protection pacts.**

1. The Korean armistice of 1953 settled nothing as far as the unity of the country was concerned.

2. Fighting in Indo-China ended in 1954 with a victory for the communists, in that the country remained divided.

3. In 1952, the United States, New Zealand and Australia signed the ANZUS treaty, pledging cooperation in mutual defense plans.

4. In 1955, the South East Asia Treaty Organization (SEATO) was formed.
   a. United States, United Kingdom, France, New Zealand, Pakistan, Thailand and the Philippine Republic agreed to cooperate for security against aggression.
5. In 1954, the United States and Nationalist China signed a treaty providing for mutual aid in defense of the Pescadores and Formosa.
   a. United States sent convoyed supply ships to the area in 1958, when Quemoy and other islands were shelled from Communist-held areas.
6. A Summit Conference was held in 1955 in Geneva where United States, England, France and the Soviet Union attempted to reach agreements for collective security.
   a. Eisenhower's proposal for mutual aerial inspections of world military installations was unaccepted by the Soviet Union, and the Conference broke up.
7. The Suez crisis brought a United Nations Emergency Force into the area for patrolling.
   a. Secretary of State Dulles promised financial aid to Egypt for building the Aswan Dam.
   b. In 1956 Nassar's request for a large loan was turned down by England and the United States.
   c. Nassar then seized and nationalized the Suez Canal.
   d. Israel, England and France successfully invaded the Canal area.
   e. United States and the Soviet Union pressed action in the U.N. for withdrawal of foreign troops from Egypt.
   f. The withdrawal took place, and U.N. forces were sent to patrol the area.
8. The Eisenhower Doctrine of 1957 was approved by Congress.
   a. He asked Congress to grant funds for economic and military assistance to nations of the Middle East to preserve their independence.
   b. He requested permission to use United States troops to resist Communist aggression in that area.
9. In 1958 Eisenhower proposed a plan for the economic and political stabilization of the Middle East under United Nations supervision.

   a. The Lebanon and Jordan crisis allowed for a compromise resolution sponsored by the Arab nations.
D. Eisenhower was reelected in 1956 over Adlai Stevenson, the Democratic candidate.
E. The Democratic control of Congress made bipartisan support necessary for Eisenhower's legislative program.
   1. The Defense Secretary was put in direct command of the armed forces.
   2. The reciprocal trade program was extended at periodic intervals.
      a. The law in 1958 authorized tariff cuts up to twenty percent below prevailing rates.
   3. The policy of granting economic, technical, and at times, military aid to countries whose defense was vital to contain Communism continued.
   4. In 1958, amendments to the Social Security Act raised the benefits and tax rates for old-age, survivors' and disability payments.
   5. Aid to farmers was continued through flexible price supports.
   6. In 1958, Congress authorized 887 million dollars to be spent over a four-year period for education purposes.
   7. During 1952 and 1958 there were serious economic recessions.
      a. To overcome these, the Federal Reserve Board reduced its discount rate and the margin requirements for stock transactions.
      b. Congress authorized large sums of money for public works.
      c. By the end of 1958 economic recovery had begun.
   8. In 1955, the AFL and the CIO merged into a powerful fifteen million member organization.
      a. During 1957 and 1958 Senate committee investigations revealed corruption among some high union officials.
      b. Steps were taken to oust some unions, and labor continued to benefit from cost-of-living wage increases.
      c. By the end of 1958, nineteen states had enacted "right-to-work" laws which stated that workers could not be barred from jobs for refusing to join a union.

U.S. HISTORY

F. Alaska was admitted as the forty-ninth state of the Union in 1958, and in 1959, Hawaii became the fiftieth.

G. The United States and the Soviet Union forged ahead with their space programs.

1. The Soviet Union successfully launched a satellite into outer space in October, 1957, "Sputnik."

2. The announcement led the United States to emphasize its space and missile programs.

    a. The first earth satellite, Explorer 1, was sent into orbit by the United States in January, 1958.

    b. The fourth Explorer sent in July, 1958, was equipped to measure radiation and to report on cosmic rays.

    c. Pioneer IV was sent around the sun in March, 1959.

3. The Soviet Union announcement that Yuri Gagarin had orbited the earth in a space capsule in April, 1961, led the United States into the race.

    a. Alan B. Shepard was the first American to soar into outer space on May 5, 1961.

4. The space race gave impetus to the competition in nuclear armaments.

    a. The United States successfully fired an Atlas missile in August, 1959.

    b. In August, 1958, the Navy Department announced that the Nautilus, the first United States atomic-powered submarine had successfully completed a transpolar trip.

H. Peace efforts continued despite the "cold war."

1. Eisenhower proposed the creation of an international stockpile of atomic materials to be used for peaceful purposes.

    a. From this proposal, the International Atomic Energy Agency was created in 1957 by the U.N.

    b. Delegates attended conferences to exchange scientific information.

2. United States representatives to the U.N. presented disarmament proposals.

    a. Nuclear tests should be suspended.

    b. A ban should be placed on the manufacturing of atomic weapons.

    c. An inspection system should be established.

    d. Some nuclear materials should be used for industrial purposes.

3. The Soviet Union was unwilling to agree with the Western powers on methods of international inspection.

4. A Summit Conference was planned in 1960.

    a. Khrushchev of the Soviet Union visited the United States in 1959.

    b. The U-2 Incident, a United States reconnaissance plane mapping military targets was brought down inside the Soviet Union.

      (1) Khrushchev demanded an apology from Eisenhower for the incident.

      (2) Eisenhower refused, and there was no Summit meeting in Paris as planned.

5. United States broke off diplomatic relations with Cuba in December, 1960.

    a. Fidel Castro had led a successful revolutionary movement against the government of President Batista.

    b. Castro's rule became dictatorial under Communist influence and turned violently anti-American.

6. East and West were drawn into the struggle for power in Congolese Africa when the Belgian colonial rule ended in 1960.

    a. The Communist bloc gave strong support to some African leaders.

    b. The U.N., under Secretary-General Dag Hammarskjold, attempted to establish order.

    c. The United States supported the U.N.

XXIII. THE "NEW FRONTIER" GOVERNMENT OF JOHN F. KENNEDY, 1960 ——.

A. The Democrats chose John F. Kennedy of Massachusetts for President, and Vice-President Richard M. Nixon was the Republican candidate.

1. The Democrats won by the closest popular vote since 1884.

2. Lyndon Johnson was Vice President; Dean Rusk became Secretary of State and Adlai Stevenson became the U.N. representative.

B. President Kennedy launched his legislative program.

1. First major controversy arose over the President's 5.6 billion dollars plan for aid to education from which he specifically barred parochial schools.

2. An executive order was issued to insure that all Americans of all colors

and religions would have equal access to government employment.

    a. President's Committee on Equal Employment Opportunity was given wide powers of investigation and enforcement.

3. Twenty-third amendment to the Constitution was approved, and thereby allowed the District of Columbia citizens to vote in presidential elections.

4. A Peace Corps was created to enlist men and women for service in world's underdeveloped countries.

    a. First project was to help local technicians plan and build roads in Tanganyika, Africa.

5. A minimum wage bill was adopted which increased the lowest legal pay for interstate commerce workers from $1 an hour to $1.25 by 1963.

6. Supreme Court decision upheld the law requiring communist members to register with the Department of Justice.

7. Social Security Act of 1961 increased old-age benefits and permitted the retirement age to be 62.

8. A United States Arms Control and Disarmament Agency was established.

9. The 87th Congress gave the country a record peacetime expenditure of over $95 billion.

10. A bill to increase permanent membership in the House of Representatives was killed.

11. Kennedy forced the steel industry to rescind a price rise.

12. The administration appealed for support for the program of medical care for the aged under Social Security, embodied in the King-Anderson bill.

13. Federal Reserve Board announced a reduction in stock margin requirements.

14. A revision of Federal tax depreciation schedules was announced.

15. Telstar, an experimental communication satellite, was developed and successfully relayed television across the Atlantic.

16. United States government forced the first Negro's admission to the University of Mississippi.

17. Thirteen men were named by Kennedy to set up and incorporate a private communications satellite corporation under direct government control.

18. Federal Aviation Act made airplane hijacking punishable by death or imprisonment.

C. The United States foreign policy continued to fight for world security.

1. United States ended diplomatic relations with Cuba after Cuban demand that the United States embassy reduce its staff to 11 people.

    a. Anti-Castro forces invaded Cuba unsuccessfully with United States taking part in the attack; known as Bay of Pigs incident.

    b. Cuba definitely became a Russian satellite with Castro's admission to being a Communist.

    c. Cuba proposed prisoners-for-tractors exchange but was rejected.

    d. United States made public reports that Cuba was a serious threat to the American republics.

        (1) She was being heavily armed by Russia.

        (2) United States placed a quarantine around Cuba.

        (3) Russia dismantled missile bases and withdrew "offensive" weapons, fall 1962.

        (4) The Cuban quarantine was lifted.

    e. Fourteen Western Hemisphere nations broke off diplomatic relations with Cuba by February, 1962.

    f. Organization of American States (OAS) completely ostracized Cuba.

    g. Kennedy warned Cuba about communist inroads in the Western Hemisphere, and the Administration was preparing a tight embargo on all shipowners transporting Soviet-bloc supplies to Cuba.

    h. A strong U.S. stand dissipated the threat of war with Russia over Cuba.

2. United States spent huge sums of money in nuclear development and research, and on space programs.

    a. Explorer IX and Discoverer XX were launched, setting records and developing scientific information.

    b. Rocket plane X-15 set 31.25 mile altitude record and later set controlled flight speed record.

    c. First United States Astronaut, Alan B. Shepard, Jr., rocketed 115 miles into space.

    d. Second Astronaut, Virgil I. Grissom, made 118 mile suborbital flight.

    e. U.S.S. Long Beach became the Navy's first nuclear surface ship.

    f. Atomic testing was resumed in Nevada.

U.S. HISTORY

g. United States orbited a chimpanzee around the earth twice.

h. The first attempt to land scientific instruments on the moon missed.

i. Five United States Polaris Subs were given to NATO.

j. United States astronauts, John H. Glenn, Jr., M. Scott Carpenter, Walter M. Schirra orbited the earth.

3. Many attempts were made to develop international cooperation for peace.

a. United States and the West Indies signed a treaty on military bases.

b. United States joined the Organization for Economic Cooperation and Development with Canada and eighteen European nations.

c. A Latin-American Aid Bill of $600 million became effective in 1962.

d. Kennedy and Khrushchev failed to reach any agreements on Germany or on nuclear testing.

    (1) East Berlin border was closed by East Germany to stop the mass exodus of refugees.

    (2) United States sent additional 1500 troops to assure the U.S. strength.

e. Japanese Premier Ikeda announced the establishment of the Joint U.S.-Japan Committee on Trade and Economic Affairs.

f. The first United States trade agreement with the Common Market of Europe was signed January, 1962, providing a partially reciprocal reduction of tariffs.

g. United States announced the creation of a new military command in Communist threatened South Vietnam.

h. Seventeen nation disarmament conference sponsored by the U.N. opened in Geneva, March, 1962, and no basis for agreement was reached.

    (1) Later Russia rejected any conference proposals.

    (2) Disarmament talks reopened in November, 1962.

i. Preliminary meetings were held between United States and Russia to join in a cooperative program of space exploration.

j. Troops were sent to Thailand to save the independence of Laos against Communist attack and to force a diplomatic solution of the Laotian Civil War; troops were removed when a coalition government was set up by three Laotian princes.

4. Economic aid to South and Central American states was formulated in the Alliance for Progress.

XXIV. NOVEMBER 22, 1963
JOHN FITZGERALD KENNEDY, PRESIDENT OF THE UNITED STATES, WAS SHOT AND KILLED BY AN ASSASSIN.

A. A shocked bewildered nation remained glued to television and radio sets for detailed reporting.

B. Lyndon Baines Johnson sworn in as President.

C. Early closing of Stock Market on the 22nd, through November 25, a Day of National Mourning, allowed the sharp stock drop following the assassination news to return confidence to investors.

D. Lee Harvey Oswald was arrested and charged on the 22nd with the murder of the president.

1. November 24, while being transferred to a county jail, Oswald was shot by Jack Ruby. Oswald died shortly after.

2. Ruby was arrested and charged with murder.

E. More than 200 world leaders came and paid their respects to the late president, his widow, family and the nation.

XXV. 1964—AN EVALUATION OF THE UNEXPECTED, UNTIMELY CLOSING OF THE "NEW FRONTIER" OF JOHN KENNEDY.

A. Legislature.

1. An unorthodox budget with a built-in deficit of over $11,000,000,000 proposed.

2. National tax reform and deduction proposed.

3. $195,000,000 fall-out shelter program.

4. Program of medical care for the aged not voted on by Congress.

5. A comprehensive civil rights bill submitted to Congress June 19 by President Kennedy.

6. A $355,000,000 mental health bill enacted October, 1963.

B. U.S. Supreme Court ruled against the required reading of the Lord's Prayer or Bible verses in public schools.

C. The Integration Movement.
1. Air Force Captain Edward J. Dwight is the first Negro to be assigned training as an astronaut.
2. Over 200,000 white and Negro citizens marched and gathered in Washington at the greatest non-violent demonstration in this country's history.
3. Demonstrations grew in frequency and size in both the North and South, receiving sympathetic religious and "celebrity" support and full news coverage.

D. Space Advancement.
1. Astronaut Gordon Cooper orbited the earth 22 times—a U.S. record.
2. Russia, a step ahead, launched Valentina Tereshkova, the first woman astronaut, into space with 48 orbits of the earth. Valery Bykovsky orbited the earth for a record 81 times.

E. The International Scene.
1. Improved relations.
   a. U.S. proposed, Russia accepted, direct line communications between White House and Kremlin (the "Hot Line").
   b. $250,000,000 U. S. wheat sales to the Soviet Union.
   c. A co-operation pact signed between France and Germany.
   d. Birth of Malaysia.
   e. Nuclear Test Ban Treaty limiting testing, signed by major powers.

2. Non-improved relations.
   a. Although unsettled Cuba tangle lost prominence in U. S. in light of uprisings in Laos and Vietnam, U. S. found no constructive resolutions.
   b. Britain vetoed from European Common Market by de Gaulle.
   c. Russian and Red Chinese relations grew progressively strained by year's end.

F. Due to unrest, scandal, death, revolution and election, many nations change heads of state.

1. In Europe, Asia and Africa—Katanga surrendered to Central Congo Government; Iraq premier ousted; revolt in Vietnam, Diem overthrown; Syrian government overthrown; Israel's Ben Gurion resigned; new Greek premier, Pipinelis; Lyng, new head of Norwegian government; Erhard succeeded Adenhauer as chancellor of West Germany; Sir Douglas Home, British Prime Mnister; the Vatican now presided over by Pope Paul VI.

2. In South America—Honduras new head, Lopez; Jijon new military head in Ecuador; Terry new president of Peru; Juan Bosch of Dominican Republic elected president, after several months in office ousted in favor of 3-man junta; Illia elected head of Argentina; and Azurdia head of new military regime in Guatemala.

3. **North America—In Canada, Diefenbaker scheduled an election after Canada turned down U. S. weapons—Lester Pierson was elected. In the U. S., Vice President Lyndon Johnson succeeded to the presidency following the assassination of President Kennedy.**

XXVI. JOHNSON ADMINISTRATION, 1963-1968.
A. The International Scene.
1. Vietnam War escalated, U.S. forces increased.
2. Unprecedented tours by Pope Paul made news: to the Holy Land, India and the U.N. in the U.S.
3. Red China tested an atomic bomb.
4. In U.S.S.R., Premier Kruschev was replaced by Kosygin as Premier and Brezhnev as party leader.
5. Mideast problems erupted into a "Six Day War" in June 1967; Israel defeated the Arab states and occupied territory including the Sinai Peninsula, the Golan Heights, all of Jerusalem and the area west of the Jordan R.
6. North Korea in 1968 seized a U.S. naval intelligence ship, the Pueblo; the men were released after 11 months.
7. President Johnson, Premier Kosygin met in Glassboro, N.J. to discuss the Mideast & Vietnam situations; no agreements were reached.
8. Preliminary meetings were held in Paris to discuss possibility of peace in Vietnam; no progress reported through early 1970.

B. The Domestic Scene.

1. The Civil Rights Act was strengthened, providing voter guarantees & prohibiting segregation in public accommodation facilities.
2. Twenty-fourth Amendment, abolishing poll taxes, was ratified.
3. Socio-economic programs received wide support by Congress; billions were allocated for the "War on Poverty"; the Office of Economic Opportunity (OEO) was created.
4. November 3, 1964, Lyndon B. Johnson won a landslide victory for a full term, defeating Ariz. Senator Barry Goldwater.
5. The Medicare program was put into effect in 1966.
6. Race riots took place in large cities in many areas of the country.
7. In 1967, Thurgood Marshall became the first Negro Supreme Court Justice.
8. The twenty-fifth Amendment was ratified, providing for continuity of office in case of Presidential disability.
9. In 1968 the nation was stunned by the assassinations of Rev. Martin Luther King, Jr. in April and of Senator Robert F. Kennedy in June.
10. The Johnson Administration asked a 10% income tax surcharge to finance the Vietnam War and to combat inflation.
11. Student unrest, demonstrations on college campuses spread across the country; the issues included the Vietnam War, the draft, national priorities.
12. The Chicago police, The National Guard and groups of demonstrators battled during the Democratic National Convention in August, 1968; Vice-pres. Hubert H. Humphrey & Sen. Edmund Muskie were the nominees.

C. Space Highlights.

1. U.S. spacecraft made soft landings on the moon, and the Apollo moon program advanced.
2. Russia sent a space vehicle to Venus, the first to reach a planet.

XXVII NIXON ADMINISTRATIONS, 1969-74

A. The Elections.

1. In November 1968, Republican Richard M. Nixon of California with Spiro T. Agnew of Maryland as his running mate won a close victory over Democrats Hubert H. Humphrey of Minnesota and Edmund S. Muskie of Maine; George C. Wallace of Alabama was the candidate of the American Independent party.
2. In November 1972, Nixon and Agnew were reelected by a vast majority over George McGovern of South Dakota and Sargent Shriver of Maryland.

B. The Vietnam Situation.

1. A negotiated peace settlement was sought through both public and private talks, but the war dragged on, causing increased discontent and demonstrations at home against continued U.S. involvement.
2. American ground forces were withdrawn by August 1972, leaving war planes in Southeast Asia and an announced policy of "Vietnamization."
3. A negotiated cease-fire was signed January 27, 1973, followed by frequent violations throughout the year.
4. Prisoners of war were returned home and the last U.S. troops left Vietnam in the spring of 1973.

C. The Domestic Scene.

1. Congress doubled the President's salary to $200,000, and provided raises for members of Congress, Supreme Court Justices, other Federal judges, the Vice President and Speaker of the House.
2. Air and water pollution became an issue locally and nationally by 1970.
3. Mounting inflation caused wage and price controls to be instituted in various phases, beginning in 1971.
4. A rash of airplane hijackings, nationally and internationally, led to passenger and baggage screening systems being put into effect in all airports.
5. Selective Service System for the draft ended in January 1973, marking the change to an all-volunteer army.
6. An uprising of militant Indians in Wounded Knee, S.D. in February 1973, demanded government discussion of grievances.
7. In October 1973, Vice President Agnew resigned after an investigation into "payoffs" from Maryland contractors and a charge of income tax invasion.
8. Michigan Congressman Gerald R. Ford named by President Nixon and approved by Congress as Vice President.
9. Energy crisis developed in U.S. as a result of Arab oil policies in fall-winter of 1973-74.

D. The Watergate Affair.

1. Five men were arrested and charged with burglary of the Washington, D.C. office of the Democratic National Committee in the Watergate Hotel-Apartment complex, June 1972; the men involved were linked to the Committee to Reelect the President.
2. After many charges and countercharges by campaign and administration personnel concerning campaign funds and other activities, a Senate Select Committee on

Presidential Campaign Activities was created to investigate "the extent, if any, to which illegal, improper or unethical activities were engaged in during the Presidential election campaign of 1972. . ." and to propose "legislation to safeguard the electoral process"; the committee to report in February 1974.

3. In May 1973 a special prosecutor was appointed to investigate, indict and bring to trial those involved in illegal activities related to the Watergate Affair; during 1974 several former members of President Nixon's cabinet and staff were indicted and sentenced.

4. In February 1974 the House of Representatives directed its Judiciary Committee to conduct an inquiry into whether grounds existed for impeachment of the President.

5. In July 1974 the Judiciary Committee voted to recommend three Articles of Impeachment and the Supreme Court ruled that tapes of White House conversations must be made available to the special prosecutor.

6. On August 9, 1974 President Nixon resigned.

E. Space Highlights

1. Unmanned spacecraft photographed Mars.

2. Manned moon orbits were followed by moon landings.

   a. In July 1968, Neil Armstrong and Edwin Aldren, Jr. became the first men to land on the moon. The command module pilot was Michael Collins.

   b. In November 1969, Charles Conrad and Alan Bean landed on the moon to gather data and samples of lunar material; Richard Gordon was pilot of the command module.

   c. In April 1970, a planned moon landing was canceled because of power failure.

   d. In February 1971, Shepard and Mitchell completed a moon mission exploring the Fra Mauro area.

   e. In July 1971, there was another successful moon landing and the first deep space walk (200,000 miles from earth) by Alfred MM. Worden.

   f. In April 1972, Charles Duke and John Young spent a record of 71 hours and 2 minutes on the moon's surface.

   g. In December 1972, Cernan, Evans and Schmitt flew the final manned space flight to the moon; it set records for the longest flight, most miles traveled, longest time spent on the moon and the most specimens brought back.

3. The most dramatic space event of 1973 was the launching of Skylab, America's first manned space station on May 14.

   a. Soon after lift-off, solar panels were damaged almost leading to cancellation of the flight; the three-man crew, Conrad, Kerwin and Weitz made the repairs in a daring series of space walks.

   b. A second three-man crew was launched in an Apollo capsule on July 28 for a 59-day flight, replacing the makeshift umbrella over Skylab erected earlier; astronauts Bran and Lousma walked in space a record 6½ hours.

   c. On November 1973, a third crew moved into the earth-orbiting 86-ton space station for another two-month stay.

4. Both the United States and the Soviet Union continued to launch spacecraft to explore Mars, Venus and Jupiter.

   a. The schedule called for flights from 1973 through 1977.

   b. A joint manned space mission was authorized for 1975.

F. International Developments

1. The United States and Russia met in Finland in 1969 to limit the arms race; an arms reduction agreement was signed in 1972.

2. The Mid-East erupted October 7, 1973 into "The Yom Kippur War", with Egyptian and Syrian attacks on Israel; Israel made inroads into Syria and crossed the Suez Canal; Secretary of State Kissinger arranged cease-fire agreements.

3. President Nixon made several European trips, making history in 1972 with visits to China and Russia.

4. Airplane hijackings and Arab terrorist activities were climaxed in Munich, Germany, September 1972 during the Olympic Games when 11 members of the Israeli team were kidnapped and shot.

XXVIII Ford Administration

A. Succession to office

1. Vice President Gerald R. Ford became 38th President August 9, 1974.

2. President Ford named Nelson A. Rockefeller as Vice President.

B. The Domestic Scene

1. Gerald Ford was the first president to serve without being chosen by the Ameri-

U.S.
HISTORY

can people in a national election.

2. On September 8, 1974, President Ford pardoned Richard Nixon for any federal crimes he might have committed as president.

3. During his first 21 months in office, Mr. Ford vetoed 48 bills believing most of them to be too costly for the economy. The Democratic controlled Congress overrode only 8 of the vetoes.

4. Three nation-wide television debates were held during 1976 between President Ford and Jimmy Carter, both major presidential candidates, prior to the November 2nd election. The results of that election were defeat for Gerald Ford.

C. International Developments

1. President Ford conferred with Chinese leaders, including Mao Tse-tung, on his visit to China December 1 through 5, 1975. The Pacific tour also included stops at Indonesia, the Philippines and Hawaii.

2. The U.S. vetoed an Arab instigated resolution at the U.N. condemning Israel for its "premeditated air attacks". This came before the U.N. on December 8, 1975.

3. Secretary of State Henry Kissinger made repeated trips abroad during the Ford administration trying to negotiate a peaceful foreign policy for the U.S. He traveled to Russia, Africa, Rhodesia, Korea, Iran, Israel and Egypt in his goal toward world peace.

D. Space Highlights

1. A U.S. Apollo and a USSR Soyuz linked together 140 miles above the Atlantic on July 17, 1975. The crews exchanged visits and meals in the 2 crafts.

2. July 20, 1976, Viking I made a successful landing on Mars, transmitting black and white photographs to earth.

3. Viking II landed on Mars on September 3, 1976. Despite a breakdown in the lander's communication system, after the landing, surface photographs and panoramic photographs were successfully transmitted.

XXIX Carter Administration

A. The Elections

1. After a long, hard political campaign, Mr. Carter won the election at the polls on November 2, 1976.

2. James Earl Carter, Jr. became 39th President on January 20, 1977. His running mate and Vice President was Walter F. Mondale of Minnesota.

B. The Domestic Scene

1. President Carter granted a pardon to almost all Vietnam draft evaders.

2. He began the reorganization of structures of various departments and agencies within the government. He proposed two new departments — energy and consumer affairs.

3. He proposed energy programs calling for reduction of the annual energy demand growth rate to 2%. Also, his programs aim at cutting oil imports from 16 million barrels per day to about 6 million barrels per day by 1985 and cutting gasoline consumption by 10%. His programs also want an increase in coal production and greater use of solar energy and effective insulation.

4. Under Carter's proposed welfare reforms, certain able welfare recipients would be required to work. These reforms also include consolidation of a number of existing federal assistance programs.

C. International Developments

1. During President Carter's administration Vietnam has been allowed to join the U.N.

2. For the first time in 16 years, a U.S. diplomat is in residence in Havana, Cuba.

3. The new American proposals on arms accord were rejected at the Strategic Arms Limitations Talks (SALT).

4. President Carter visited Egypt. He met with President Sadat and expressed his vision of a "fair settlement" of the mideast crisis.

D. Space Highlights

1. Voyager I and II are en route to Jupiter (1979) and Saturn (1980).

2. The first U.S. space shuttle orbiter, the Enterprise, had a series of approach and landing flight tests in 1977. The U.S. has plans to have operational in the 1980's.

APPENDIX

INDEX GUIDE TO THE CONSTITUTION
OF THE UNITED STATES

Preamble.

ARTICLE 1.—The Legislative Department consisting of a Senate and a House of Representatives.

Organization of Congress and terms, qualifications, apportionment and elections.

Impeachment procedures.

Privileges and compensation.

Lawmaking procedures.

Congressional powers.

Limitations on the States and Congress.

ARTICLE II.—The Executive Department.

Election of the President and the Vice-President.

Presidential duties and powers.

Ratification of treaties.

Impeachment of officers.

ARTICLE III.—The Judiciary Department.

Judicial independence.

Jurisdiction of the courts.

Trial by jury guaranteed.

Definition of treason and punishment.

ARTICLE IV.—Position of States and territories.

Full faith and credit to public acts and the judicial proceedings.

Privileges and immunities of citizens of each state.

Fugitives from justice.

Congressional control over territories.

Guarantees and protection to the States.

ARTICLE V.—Methods of amending the Constitution.

ARTICLE VI.—Supremacy of the Constitution, treaties and laws.

Oath of Office.

ARTICLE VII.—Method of ratification of the Constitution.

CONSTITUTIONAL AMENDMENTS
Original Ten—Bill of Rights

1. Freedom of religion, speech, press and assembly.
   Right to petition.
2. Right to keep and bear arms.
3. Quartering of soldiers.
4. Protection from unreasonable search and seizure.
5. Due process in criminal cases.
   Limitation on right of eminent domain.
6. Right to speedy trial, witnesses and counsel.
7. Right of trial by jury.
8. Excessive bail and cruel punishment forbidden.
9. Retention of rights of the people.
10. Undelegated powers belong to the States or to the people.
11. States exempted from suits by individuals.
12. New method of selecting the President and Vice-President.
13. Abolition of slavery.
14. Definition of citizenship.
    Guarantees of due process and protection against state action.
    Apportionment of Congressional Representatives.
    Certain public debts held valid.
15. Equal rights to vote for white and colored citizens.
16. Authorization of income tax.
17. Popular election of Senators.
18. Prohibition of intoxicating liquors.
19. Extension of suffrage to women.
20. Change in presidential and congressional terms.
21. Repeal of the Eighteenth Amendment.
22. Limitation of President's term in office to two four-year terms.
23. Extension of suffrage to District of Columbia in presidential elections.
24. Poll tax barred in Federal Elections.
25. Succession of the Vice-President to Presidency; fill the office of Vice-President.

U.S. HISTORY

STRUCTURE OF THE
NATIONAL GOVERNMENT

LEGISLATIVE BRANCH	EXECUTIVE BRANCH	JUDICIAL BRANCH
Congress	President	Supreme Court
House of Representatives	Departments	Circuit Court of Appeals
	Government Corp.	District Courts
Senate	Agencies	Special Courts
	Cabinet	

State, Treasury, Defense, Justice,
Interior, Agriculture, Commerce,
Labor, Health, Education & Welfare,
Housing and Urban Development,
Transportation

ENTRY OF STATES INTO THE UNION

State	Capital	Entered Union	State	Capital	Entered Union
1. Alabama	Montgomery	1819	26. Montana	Helena	1889
2. Alaska	Juneau	1958	27. Nebraska	Lincoln	1867
3. Arizona	Phoenix	1912	28. Nevada	Carson City	1864
4. Arkansas	Little Rock	1836	*29. New Hampshire	Concord	1788
5. California	Sacramento	1850	*30. New Jersey	Trenton	1787
6. Colorado	Denver	1876	31. New Mexico	Santa Fe	1912
*7. Connecticut	Hartford	1788	*32. New York	Albany	1788
*8. Delaware	Dover	1787	*33. North Carolina	Raleigh	1789
9. Florida	Tallahassee	1845	34. North Dakota	Bismarck	1889
*10. Georgia	Atlanta	1788	35. Ohio	Columbus	1803
11. Idaho	Boise	1890	36. Oklahoma	Oklahoma City	1907
12. Illinois	Springfield	1818	37. Oregon	Salem	1859
13. Indiana	Indianapolis	1816	*38. Pennsylvania	Harrisburg	1787
14. Iowa	Des Moines	1846	*39. Rhode Island	Providence	1790
15. Hawaii	Honolulu	1959	*40. South Carolina	Columbia	1788
16. Kansas	Topeka	1861	41. South Dakota	Pierre	1889
17. Kentucky	Frankfort	1792	42. Tennessee	Nashville	1796
18. Louisiana	Baton Rouge	1812	43. Texas	Austin	1845
19. Maine	Augusta	1820	44. Utah	Salt Lake City	1896
*20. Maryland	Annapolis	1788	45. Vermont	Montpelier	1791
*21. Massachusetts	Boston	1788	*46. Virginia	Richmond	1788
22. Michigan	Lansing	1837	47. Washington	Olympia	1889
23. Minnesota	St. Paul	1858	48. West Virginia	Charleston	1863
24. Mississippi	Jackson	1817	49. Wisconsin	Madison	1848
25. Missouri	Jefferson City	1821	50. Wyoming	Cheyenne	1890

*—Thirteen Original States to Ratify the Constitution.

PRESIDENTS	NATIVE STATE	PARTY	TERM	VICE PRESIDENTS	SECRETARIES OF STATE
1. George Washington	Virginia	Federalist	1789-1797	John Adams	Thomas Jefferson—1789 Edmund Randolph—1794 Timothy Pickering—1795
2. John Adams	Massachusetts	Federalist	1797-1801	Thomas Jefferson	Timothy Pickering John Marshall—1800
3. Thomas Jefferson	Virginia	Rep.-Dem.	1801-1809	Aaron Burr George Clinton	James Madison—1801
4. James Madison	Virginia	Rep.-Dem.	1809-1817	George Clinton Elbridge Gerry	Robert Smith—1809 James Monroe—1811
5. James Monroe	Virginia	Rep.-Dem.	1817-1825	Daniel Tompkins	John Q. Adams—1817
6. John Quincy Adams	Massachusetts	Rep.-Dem.	1825-1829	John Calhoun	Henry Clay—1825
7. Andrew Jackson	S. Carolina	Democrat	1829-1837	John Calhoun Martin Van Buren	Martin Van Buren—1829 Edward Livingston—1831 Louis McLane—1833 John Forsyth—1834
8. Martin Van Buren	New York	Democrat	1837-1841	Richard Johnson	John Forsyth
9. William Harrison	Virginia	Whig	1841	John Tyler	Daniel Webster—1841
10. John Tyler	Virginia	Democrat	1841-1845		Daniel Webster Hugh Legare—1843 Abel Upshur—1843 John Calhoun—1844
11. James K. Polk	N. Carolina	Democrat	1845-1849	George Dallas	James Buchanan—1845
12. Zachary Taylor	Virginia	Whig	1849-1850	Millard Fillmore	John Clayton—1849
13. Millard Fillmore	New York	Whig	1850-1853		Daniel Webster—1850 Edward Everett—1852
14. Franklin Pierce	New Hampshire	Democrat	1853-1857	William King	William Marcy—1853
15. James Buchanan	Pennsylvania	Democrat	1857-1861	John Breckenridge	Lewis Cass—1857 Jeremish Black—1860
16. Abraham Lincoln	Kentucky	Republican	1861-1865	Hannibal Hamlin Andrew Johnson	William Seward—1861
17. Andrew Johnson	N. Carolina	Republican	1865-1869		William Seward
18. Ulysses S. Grant	Ohio	Republican	1869-1877	Schuyler Colfax Henry Wilson	Elihu Washburne—1869 Hamilton Fish—1869
19. Rutherford B. Hayes	Ohio	Republican	1877-1881	William Wheeler	William Evarts—1877
20. James A. Garfield	Ohio	Republican	1881	Chester Arthur	James Blain—1881
21. Chester A. Arthur	Vermont	Republican	1881-1885		James Blaine F. T. Frelinghuysen—1881
22. Grover Cleveland	New Jersey	Democrat	1885-1889	Thomas Hendricks	Thomas Bayard—1885 Richard Olney—1895
23. Benjamin Harrison	Ohio	Republican	1889-1893	Levi Morton	James Blaine—1889 John Foster
24. Grover Cleveland	New Jersey	Democrat	1893-1897	Adlai Stevenson	Walter Gresham—1893 Richard Olney—1895
25. William McKinley	Ohio	Republican	1897-1901	Garret Hobart Theodore Roosevelt	John Sherman—1897 William Day—1898 John Hay—1898
26. Theodore Roosevelt	New York	Republican	1901-1909	Charles Fairbanks	John Hay Elihu Root—1905 Robert Bacon—1909
27. William Taft	Ohio	Republican	1909-1913	James Sherman	Philander Knox—1909
28. Woodrow Wilson	Virginia	Democrat	1913-1921	Thomas Marshall	William Bryan—1913 Robert Lansing—1915 Bainbridge Colby—1920
29. Warren G. Harding	Ohio	Republican	1921-1923	Calvin Coolidge	Charles Hughes—1921
30. Calvin Coolidge	Vermont	Republican	1923-1929	Charles Dawes	Charles Hughes Frank Kellogg—1925
31. Herbert Hoover	Iowa	Republican	1929-1933	Charles Curtis	Henry Stimson—1929
32. Franklin D. Roosevelt	New York	Democrat	1933-1945	John Garner Henry Wallace Harry Truman	Cordell Hull—1933 E. R. Stettinius—1944
33. Harry S. Truman	Missouri	Democrat	1945-1953	Alben Barkley	E. R. Stettinius—1945 James Byrnes—1945 Geo. Marshall—1947 Dean Acheson—1949
34. Dwight D. Eisenhower	Texas	Republican	1953-1961	Richard M. Nixon	John F. Dulles—1953 Christian Herter—1959
35. John F. Kennedy	Massachusetts	Democrat	1961-1963	Lyndon Johnson	Dean Rusk—1961
36. Lyndon B. Johnson	Texas	Democrat	1963-1968	H. Humphrey	Dean Rusk
37. Richard M. Nixon	California	Republican	1968-1974(r)	Spiro T. Agnew (r) Gerald R. Ford	William P. Rogers—1968 Henry A. Kissinger—1973
38. Gerald R. Ford	Nebraska	Republican	1974-1977	Nelson A. Rockefeller	Henry A. Kissinger
39. James Earl Carter, Jr.	Georgia	Democrat	1977-	Walter F. Mondale	Cyrus Vance

(r)—resigned

U.S. HISTORY

GAZETTEER

GAZETTEER

A dictionary of up-to-date information including geographical, historical and political facts about the major divisions and natural features of the world.

NOTE: All U.S. cities with 35,000 population or over are included.

USING THE GAZETTEER

- **Bold** type indicates an entry with pronunciation shown; commas separate alternate spellings.
- - denotes breaks between syllables.
- ′ denotes accented syllables.
- *Italic* type indicates geographical (or political) categories of the entry.

PRONUNCIATION KEY

The following are always pronounced as shown, except where noted in parentheses following the entry.

a as in at	ay as in bay	i as in ill	oi as in oil	ū as in ūse	g as in get
ā as in āte	e as′in end	ī as in īce	oo as in good	û as in ûrn	gu as in Guam
ȧ as in ȧ kin′	ē as in hē	î as in sîr	ōō as in tōō	y as in yet	j as in jet
â as in bâre	ė as in ė·vent′	o as in odd	ou as in out	ẏ as in mẏth	qu as in quit
ä as in cär	ê as in hêr	ō as in ōld	ow as in owl	ȳ as in trȳ	s as in set
ă as in ăll	ee as in sēen	ö as in wön	oy as in boy	c as in cat	
ai as in aid	ew as in new	ô as in ôr	u as in up	ch as in chat	

Abbreviations

* Capital or County seat
= same as

A

ab.	about
Ala.	Alabama
Alas.	Alaska
Amer.	American
anc.	ancient
Ariz.	Arizona
Ark.	Arkansas
A.S.S.R.	Autonomous Soviet Socialist Republic

B

(B)	Brazzaville
bel.	belongs (to)
Belg.	Belgian
bet.	between
Bib.	Biblical
Brit.	British

C

Cal., Calif.	California
cen.	center
Colo.	Colorado
Conn.	Connecticut

D

D.C.	District of Columbia
Dan.	Danish
Del.	Delaware
dept.	department
dist.	district
div.	divided
Dut.	Dutch

E

E	east, eastern
emp.	empire
Eng.	English
esp.	especially
estab.	established
Eur.	Europe

F

Fed.	Federation
Fla.	Florida
Fr.	French
ft.	feet

G

Ga.	Georgia
Ger.	German
Gk.	Greek

H

Haw.	Hawaii
hist.	historical, historically

I

I.	island
Ida.	Idaho
Ill.	Illinois
imp.	important
incl.	includes, including
Ind.	Indiana
Is.	Islands
It.	Italian

J

Jap.	Japanese

K

Kan.	Kansas
Ky.	Kentucky

L

(L)	Leopoldville
L.	Lake
La.	Louisiana
lat.	latitude
Lat.	Latin
long.	longitude

M

m.	miles
Mass.	Massachusetts
max.	maximum
Me.	Maine
Md.	Maryland
Medit.	Mediterranean
Mich.	Michigan
Minn.	Minnesota
Miss.	Mississippi
Mo.	Missouri
mod.	modern
Mont.	Montana
Mt.	mountain
Mts.	mountains

N

N	north, northern
N.C.	North Carolina
N.D.	North Dakota
N.H.	New Hampshire
N.J.	New Jersey
N.M.	New Mexico
N.Y.	New York
Neb.	Nebraska
Neth.	Netherlands
Nev.	Nevada
nr.	near

O

O.	ocean
Okla.	Oklahoma
Ore.	Oregon

P

Pa.	Pennsylvania
penin.	peninsula
Phil.	Philippine
pop.	population
Port.	Portuguese
prov.	province

R

R.	river
reg.	region
Rep.	Republic
R.I.	Rhode Island
R.S.F.S.R.	Russian Soviet Federated Socialist Republic
Russ.	Russian

S

S	south, southern
S.	sea
S.C.	South Carolina
S.D.	South Dakota
Span.	Spanish
sq.	square
S.S.R.	Soviet Socialist Republic
surr.	surrounded by

T

Tenn.	Tennessee
terr.	territory

U

U.	university
U.S.	United States (of America
U.S.S.R.	Union of Soviet Socialist Republics

V

Va.	Virginia
Vt.	Vermont

W

W	west, western
Wash.	Washington
Wisc.	Wisconsin
W.Va.	West Virginia
WW I	World War I
WW II	World War II
Wyo.	Wyoming

GAZETTE
ATLAS

A

Äa'chen (kėn) or **Aix-lä-chä-pelle'** (eks-lä-shä) *City* NW West Germany; trade, manufacturing

Äal'bôrg *County* and *City* NE Denmark

Äar'gau (gou) *Canton* N cen. Switzerland; * **Äar'au** (ou) on **Äa'rė** R.; textiles, instruments

Äar'hūs *County, City,* port on *Bay* E cen. Denmark

Ab'à-cō : Great **Ab'à-cō**, Little **Ab'à-cō** *Islands* of the Bahamas

Ä-bä-dän' *Town* on *Island* W Iran; oil refineries

Ä-be-ō'ku-tä (koo) *Town,* * of *Province* SW Nigeria; trade

Ab-êr-dēen' *Burgh* * of *County* NE Scotland; agriculture, fisheries, quarries, cattle. 2. *Lake,* Northwest Terrs., Canada

Ab-i-djän' *Town** of Ivory Coast Spart

Ab'i-lēne *City* NW cen. Texas, U.S.; pop. 89,653; dairy, food products

Ab-khä'zi-àn A.S.S.R. *Republic* NW Georgia, U.S.S.R.; agriculture, forests, minerals

Ä'brà *Province* Luzon, Phil. Is.; corn, rice, timber

Ä-brûz'zi e **Mô'li-sė** *Compartimento* cen. Italy; agriculture, livestock

À-bȳ'dös 1. *Anc. town* Asia Minor. 2. *Anc. town* anc. Egypt

Ab-ỷs-sĭn'i-à *Kingdom* E Africa, now ETHIOPIA

À-cā'di-à 1. Original name of NOVA SCOTIA. 2. *National Park,* Me. coast, U.S.

Ä-cä-pul'cō (pōōl') *Town* W Mexico; port

Ä-cä-tĕ-nän'gō *Volcano* 12,980 ft., Guatemala

Ac'crà *City* * of Ghana, SE part; pop. 491,-000; port

À-chae'à and **Ē'lis** (kē') *Department* NW Peloponnesus, Greece

Ä-ci-re-ä'le (chē-râ) *City* E Sicily; port, resort

Ac-ön-cä'guà 1. *Mountain* 23,081 ft., W Argentina; highest peak of Western Hemisphere. 2. *River, Province* cen. Chile

Ä'crė 1. *River* 330 m., W cen. South America. 2. *Territory* W Brazil; rubber. 3. *City* on *Bay* NW Israel; port

Ac'tön *Municipal borough* SE England; part of greater London

Ā'dak *Island,* Aleutian Is., SW Alas., U.S.

Ä-dä-nä' *City* S Turkey, Asia; rail, commercial cen.

Ad'dis Ab'à-bà *City* * of Ethiopia, cen. part; pop. 600,000

Ad'ė-lāide *City* * of South Australia, SE Australia; trade, educational cen.

Ä'dėn *Protectorate* Brit. crown colony and *City* its * on *Gulf,* SW Arabia; pop. ab. 600,000

Äd'di-ge (dē-jâ) *River* 220 m., NE Italy

Ad-i-ron'dack *Mountains Mountain chain* NE N.Y., U.S.; resorts

Ad'mi-ràl-tỷ Islands *Island group* W Pacific O.; part of Bismarck Arch., Territory of New Guinea

Ā-dri-at'ic Sea Arm of Mediterranean S. E of Italy

À-dỷ-gei' **Autonomous Region** (gä'i) *Region* of S R.S.F.S.R.,

U.S.S.R., Eur.; agriculture, oil

À-dzhar' A.S.S.R. (jär') *Republic* SW Georgia, U.S.S.R., Eur.

Àe-gē'àn Islands (à-jē') *Islands* of **Aegean Sea** bet. Asia Minor & Greece; incl. the Cyclades, Sporades, Dodecanese, etc.

Ae-tō'li-à and **Ac-àr-nä'ni-à** *Department* W cen. Greece

Ā'fars and Issas (E'sus) *Fr. Terr.* NE Africa; formerly **Fr. Somaliland,** 9,000 sq. mi.; pop. 125,000

Af-ghan'i-stan *Country* W Asia; 260,000 sq. m.; pop. 16,500,000; * Kabul

Af'ri-cà *Continent* world's second largest ab. 11,730,000 sq. m.

Ä-gä'nä *Town* W Guam, its * on *Bay*

Ag'in-cōurt (aj') *Village* N France; battle scene 1415

Ä'grà 1. *City* * of *Division, District* cen. India. 2. *Former province* of Brit. India, now part of United **Provinces of Agra and Oudh**

Ä-gri-gen'tō (jen') *Commune* * of *Province,* Sicily, Italy

Ä-guä-dil'lä (dē'yä) *Municipality* NW Puerto Rico; port

Ä-guäs-cä-lien'tes *City* * of *State* cen. Mexico; climate

Ä-gui-lär' *Commune* S Spain; olives, grapes

À-gul'hàs, Cape Southern point of Africa

Ä-gu'sän (goō') *Province* Mindanao, Phil. Is.; agriculture

Äh-màd-ä-bäd' *City* W cen. India

Äh-màd-nä'gàr *City* * of *District,* Bombay prov., W India

Ä-huä-chä-pän' *Town*

* of *Department* SW El Salvador; trade

Ah've-nan-mäa or **A'land Islands** (ō') *Archipelago, Department* of Finland bet. Sweden and Finland

Äh-wäz' *Town* SW Iran; oil, commerce

Ai-chi (ī-chē) *Prefecture* Honshu, Japan

Ai-gun' (ī-goon') *City* N Manchuria; port

Ain (an) *Department* E France

A-ir' (ēr') or **Az-bine'** (bēn') Mountainous area of the Sahara

Aisne (ân) *Department, River* 175 m., N France; WWI battles

Aix (āks) *City* SE France

Aix-lä-Chà-pelle' (shà) see AACHEN

Ä-jac'cio (yät'chô) *Commune* on *Gulf* * of Corsica on W coast; port, fisheries

Àj-mēr' *City* NW India; salt trade, cotton cloth

Ä-jus'cō (hōōs') *Mountain,* volcano, 13,612 ft. Mexico

Ä-kä-shi *City* Honshu, Japan; industrial

Ak-där', Je'bel (ja'bal) *Mountain range* Oman, Arabia

Ä-ki-tä *City* * of *Prefecture* Honshu, Japan; silk, lumber

À-kō'là *City* cen. India; cotton trade

Ak'rön *City* NE Ohio, U.S.; pop. 275,425; rubber goods, aircraft

Ä'kûr-ey-ri (ā) *Town* N Iceland; Iceland's 2nd city

Ak-yab' *Town* * of *District* Lower Burma; port

Al-à-bam'à *State* S U.S.; 51,610 sq. m.; pop. 3,444,165; * Montgomery; 67 counties; agriculture, mining   [Brazil

A-là-gō'às *State* E

Ä-lä-jue′lä (hwä′) *Province, Town* cen. Costa Rica; sugar, cattle, coffee

Al-à-mē′da *City* W Calif., U.S.; pop. 70,968; shipping, manufacturing, canning

Al′à-mō, The *Fort* San Antonio, Texas, U.S.

À-las′kà *State* of U.S., NW North America; 586,400 sq. m.; pop. 302,173; * Juneau; fishing, mining, furs

À-las′kà Range *Mountain range* S Alas. U.S.; highest — MT. McKINLEY

Äl-bä-ce′te (sä′tâ) *Commune,* * of *Province* SE Spain; cutlery

Al-bä′ni-à *Country* W Balkan penin.; 11,096 sq. m.; pop. 2,100-000; * Tirana; mountainous

Äl′bà-nỳ 1. *City,* * of N.Y., U.S.; pop. 114,-873; industrial cen. 2. *City* SW Ga. U.S.; pop. 72,623; pecans. 3. *River* 610 m. Ontario, Canada

Äl-bay′ (bī′) *Province* Luzon, Phil. Is.; hemp, sugar, coconuts

Al-bêr′gà *River* 350 m. N South Australia

Al′bêrt, Lake *Lake* Uganda-Congo (L)

Al-bêr′tà *Province* W Canada; 248,800 sq. m.; pop. 1,553,000; * Edmonton; wheat, cattle, fish, coal, timber

Al′bu-quer-que (kêr-kē) *City* cen. N.M., U.S.; pop. 243,751; commerce, canning, oil

Al′cà-traz *Island* San Francisco Bay, Calif., U.S.; former penitentiary site.

Äl-coy′ *Commune* SE Spain; paper manufacture

Àl-dan′ *River* 1500 m., U.S.S.R., Asia

Àl′dêr-ney (ni) *Island* of The Channel Is.; agriculture, cattle

À-len-côn (län-sôn′) *City* NW France; lace

À-lep′pō or A-lep′ *City* NW Syria

A-les′ *City* S France; raw silk trade

Ä-les-sän′dri-à *Commune,* * of *Province* NW Italy; rail, trade cen.

Ä′lè-sund (soon) *City* W Norway; port, fisheries

À-leū′tian Islands (shàn) *Island chain, District* W Alas., bet. Bering S. and N Pacific O.; fish, furs

Al-ex-an′dêr Archipelago *Island group* SE Alas., U.S.

Al-ex-an′dri-à 1. *City* N Va., U.S.; pop. 110,938; commerce, manufacturing. 2. *City* cen. La., U.S.; pop. 41,557; manufacturing. 3. *Governorate* and *City* Lower Egypt; commercial port

A-ley′ (lä′) *Town,* summer * of Lebanon

Al-gè-ci′ràs (jè-sē′) *City* SW Spain; port

Al-gē′ri-à (jē′), Rep. of *Country* NW Africa; 920,000 sq. m.; pop. 13,400,000; * Algiers; agriculture

Al-giers′ (jērz′) 1. *City* on *Bay* * of Algeria; port. 2. Former name of ALGERIA

Al-ham′brà *City* SW Calif., U.S.; pop. 62,125; residential

Ä-li-cän′te *City* * of *Province* SE Spain; port, wine, textiles

A′li-gärh *City* * of *District* N India; trade

Alk′mäar *Commune* W Netherlands; cheese, butter, grain

Al Ku-wāit′ (koo) *Town*

* of Kuwait principality; port

Al′läh-à-bad′ 1. *District* of *Division* N India. 2. *City* N cen. India; imp. trade cen.

Al-lè-ghe′nỳ (gä′) 1. *River* 325 m., W Pa., U.S. 2. *Mountain ranges* of Appalachian system, E cen. U.S.

Al′len Pärk *City* SE Mich. U.S.; pop. 40,-747

Al′len-town *City* E Pa., U.S.; pop. 109,527; commerce, industry

Al-lep′pi *Town* S India; port

Al-lier′ (yä′) *Department, River* (250 m.), cen. France

Äl′mä-Ä-tä′ *City* * of *Region,* R.S.F.S.R., U.S.S.R., Asia

Äl-mä-den′ (dän′) *Commune* S cen. Spain; quicksilver

Äl-me-ri-ä (rē′) *City* * of *Province* SE Spain; harbor

Ä′lôr *Island* of *Group* Lesser Sunda Is., Indonesia

Alpes′ - Ma-ri-times′ (alp′ma-rē-tēm′) *Department* SE France

Alps *Mountain system* S cen. Europe extending ab 660 m.; in France, Italy, Switzerland, Austria, Yugoslavia; scenery, lakes, glaciers

Al′sace (sas) *Former province* Germany and France, now in NE France

Al′sace-Lör-räine′ *Region* bet. France, Germany, Belgium and Switzerland (now French)

Al′sek *River* 260 m. SW Yukon and SE Alas., U.S.

Al′tai 1. *Mountain system* W China. 2. *Territory* R.S.F.S.R., U.S.S.R., Asia; agriculture, minerals

Ält′dôrf *Commune* cen.

Switzerland; of William Tell fame

Äl′tèn-burg (boork) *City* cen. East Germany; manufacturing; grain, livestock

Äl′ton *City* SW Ill., U.S.; pop. 39,700; shipping

Äl′tō-nä *City* N West Germany; manufacturing

Al-tōō′nà *City* S cen. Pa., U.S.; pop. 62,-900; industrial

Äl′wàr *City* * of *State* NW India

Ä-mä-gä-sä-ki *City* Honshu, Japan; chemicals, iron-steel

A′ma-gêr *Island* part of Copenhagen, Denmark

Ä-mä-kụ-sä (koo) *Island group* off W Kyushu, Japan

Ä-mäl′fi *Town* S Italy; mountain drive

Ä-mä-mi or Ō-shi-mä (shē) *Island group* S Japan [Brazil

A-mà-pá′ *Territory* N

Am-à-ril′lō *City* NW Texas, U.S.; pop. 127,010; industry, commerce

Am′à′zon *River* 4000 m., South America: worlds′ largest river

Àm-bä′lä *City* * of *Division* and *District* East Punjab, India

Am-boi′nà *Town* * of *Division* and of *Island* E Indonesia; spices, fruits

À-mer′i-cà — Name often used for U.S.; pl. The Americas incl. all lands of W Hemisphere

Āmes City *City,* Iowa, U.S.; pop. 39,505; education cen.

A-miens′ (myan′) *City* N France; textiles

Am-man′ *Town* * of Jordan, NW part; pop. 450,000; Bib. — Am′mön; Anc. —

Phil-a-del'phi-a (fil, fi)

Ä-moy' *City* on *Island* SE China; port

Am-rao'ti (rou') *Town* * of *District* cen. India; cotton cen.

Am-rit'sar *City* * of *District* N India; manufacturing

Am'ster-dam 1. *City* * of Netherlands, W part; pop. 804,000; commerce, manufacturing, bridges, canals. 2. *Island* (Fr.) S Indian O.

A-mu' Dar-yä' (mōō') *River* 1500 m., U.S.S.R., W Asia

Ä'mund-sen Gulf *Body* of water bet. N Northwest Terrs. Canada and Banks and Victoria Is.

A-mur' (mōōr') *River* 2800 m. NE Asia, Manchuria-U.S.S.R.

A-na-dyr' *River* 450 m. to *Gulf*, U.S.S.R., Asia

An'a-heim *City* SW Calif., U.S.; pop. 166,701; citrus fruits

An-a-tō'lia *Area* of Turkey from Asia Minor to Black S.

An'chor-age (ij) *City* in *District* S cen. Alas., U.S.; pop. 48,029; port

Än-co-hu'mä (ōō') *Peak* of Mt. Sorata, Bolivia; 21,490 ft; see ILLAMPU

An-cō'na *City* * of *Province* cen. Italy; Adriatic port

An-da-lu'sia (lōō'zhà) *Region* S Spain; minerals, grain, fruit

An'da-man and Nic'o-bär Islands *Island groups*, *Province*, Bay of Bengal, India

Än'der-lecht (lekt) *Commune* cen. Belgium; weaving

An'der-sön 1. *City* cen. Ind., U.S.; pop. 70,787; automobiles. 2.

City NW S.C., U.S.; shipping

An'dēs *Mountain system* W South America extending 4500 m.

Än'dhra Pra-desh' (dāsh') *State* S India on Bay of Bengal

An-di-jhan' *City*, R.S.F.S.R., U.S.S.R., Asia; cotton cen.

An-dôr'ra *Republic* and its * *City* S Eur., bet. France and Spain; 19 sq. m.; pop. 21,000; tobacco, sheep, cattle

Än-dre-ä'nöf Islands *Island group* of Aleutian Is., Alas., U.S.

Än'dri-ä *Commune* SE Italy; trade cen.

An'drös 1. *Island*, largest of the Bahamas. 2. *Island* and *Town* N Cyclades

A-ne'to, Pi'co de (pē' kō, ä-nā'tō) *Peak* 11,169 ft. NE Spain

Än-ga-ra' *River* 1100 m. U.S.S.R., Asia

Än'gel Falls (jel) *Waterfall* 3200 ft. high, SE Venezuela

Ang'êr-man (ông') *River* 279 m., cen. Sweden

Än-gers' (zhä') *City* W France; slate, liqueurs, shoes, rope

An'gle-sey (g'l-si) *Island* NW Wales; pastureland

An-glō-E-gyp'tian Su-dan' (jip'shan) see SUDAN

An-gō'la or Portuguese West Africa *Colony* (Port.) SW Africa; 481,350 sq. m.; pop. 5,362,000; * Luanda; agriculture, diamonds; wax

An-gō'ra see ANKARA

Än-gos-tu'ra (tōō') now CIUDAD BOLIVAR

Än-gou-lême (gōō-lâm') *City* W France; manufacturing, esp. paper

Angus *County* E Scotland; agriculture, livestock

Änhält *Former state* cen. Germany

Än'hwei' (hwā') *Province* E China; agriculture

An-jou' (zhōō') *Historical region* NW France

An'ka-ra *City* on *River* (115 m.), * of *Vilayet* and * of Turkey in W cen. Turkey, Asia; pop. 288,000; imp. trade cen.

Än-nam' *Region* cen. Vietnam on S China S.; rice

Än-nap'ö-lis *City* * of Md., U.S.; pop. 29,592; U.S. Naval Academy site

An-na-pûr'na *Mountain range* of Himalayas, Nepal

Ann Ar'bor *City* SE Mich., U.S.; pop. 99,797

An-ne-cy' (an-sē') *City* E France; textiles

Än'shän' *Town* S Manchuria; steel

Än-tä-kyä', anc. An'ti-och (ok) *City* S Turkey, Asia

Än-täl-yä' or Ä-dä-li-ä' *Vilayet*, *Town*, *Gulf* SW Turkey, Asia

Ant-ärc'tic *Region*, *Ocean* incl. waters of Atlantic, Pacific and Indian Oceans

Ant-ärc'ti-cä *Continent* at South Pole; ab. 5,000,000 sq. m.; mountains 10,000 to 15,000 ft.; mostly unexplored

An-tibes' (tēb') *City* SE France; port

An-tie'tam *Village* N Md., U.S.; 1862 battle site

An-ti'gua (tē'ga) *Island* Brit. West Indies, E cen. Leeward Is.; * St. Johns; harbors, sugar, cotton

Än-ti'gua (tē') *City* S cen. Guatemala, its former *

An-til'lēs *Island groups* of West In-

dies: Greater Antilles incl. Cuba, Haiti, Dominican Rep., Puerto Rica, Jamaica; Lesser Antilles incl. Virgin, Windward, Leeward Is.

An'ti-och (ok) See ANTAKYA

An-tip'o-dēs 1. *Island group* of New Zealand. 2. *Name* for Australia and New Zealand

Än-ti'que (tē'ka) *Province* Panay, Phil. Is.; fishing, sugar cane

Än-to-fä-gäs'tä *City* * of *Province* N Chile; exports minerals

Än-to-fäl'lä (fä'yä) *Volcano* 21,129 ft. NW Argentina

An'trim *County* NE Northern Ireland; basalt, oats, flax, peat

Än'tung' (doong') *Province* S Manchuria; trade

Ant'wêrp *City* * of *Province* N Belgium; harbor; trade, manufacturing

A - nu - rä'dha - pu - ra (noo, poo) *Town* Ceylon; sacred to Buddhists

A-nyui' (nyōō'i) *River* 420 m. U.S.S.R., Asia

Än-zhe'rö Sud-zhensk' *Town* R.S.F.S.R., U.S.S.R., Asia

Än-zin' (zan') *Commune* N France; coal area

An'zi-ō *City* W Italy; port; Allied landing site, WW II

A-ō-mō-ri *City* * of *Prefecture* Honshu, Japan; harbor

Ä'pä-pä *Town* SW Nigeria; port

Ä-pä-pō'ris *River* 500 m. S Colombia

A'pil-dōorn *Commune* cen. Netherlands; paper

Ap'en-nīnes *Mountain range* 800 m. long, cen. Italy; agriculture, trees, pasturage

Ä'pō, Mount *Mountain* 9690 ft., highest of Phil. Is.

À-pos'tle Islands (pos''l) *Islands* Lake Superior, U.S.

Ap-pȧ-lāch'i-ȧ *Region* SE U.S. incl. ranges of Appalachian Mts.

Ap-pȧ-lāch'i-ȧn Mountains *Mountain system* E North America: Quebec, Canada-N Ala., U.S.

Ap'pėn-zell *Canton, Commune* NW Switzerland; sheep, embroidery, agriculture

Ap'ple-tön *City* E Wisc., U.S.; pop. 57,143; manufacturing

Ap-po-mat'töx *Town* SE cen. Va., U.S.; Confederate surrender, 1865

Ä-puä'niä *Commune*, * of *Province* cen. Italy

À-pū'li-ȧ *Compartimento* SE Italy; "heel" of Italian "boot"; agriculture, livestock, salt

Ä-pu're (pōō'rå) *State* and *River* 420 m. W Venezuela

Ä-pu-ri'mäc (pōō-rē') *River* 500 m. Peru

A'qa-bȧ *anc.* **Ē'lath** *Town* at *Gulf*, SW Jordan; port

Äq'sū' *Town, Oasis* W China; trade cen.

Aq'ui-lȧ (wi) *Commune* * of *Province*, cen. Italy; linen, paper, leather

Aq-ui-tā'ni-ȧ (wi) Historical division of SW France, later **Aq'ui-tāine** (wi)

À-rā'bi-ȧ *Peninsula* SW Asia; 1,000,000 sq. m.; fertile coast areas; incl. Saudi Arabia, Qatar, Trucial Oman, Oman, Aden, Yemen

À-rā'bi-ȧn Des'êrt *Desert* E Egypt, E of Nile R. along Gulf of Suez and Red S.

À-rā'bi-ȧn Sea Part of Indian O. India-Arabia

Ar'ȧ-bẏ poetic name for ARABIA

A-rȧ-cä-ju' (zhōō') *City* E Brazil

Ä-räd' *City* W Romania; commerce, industry

Ä-rä-fu'rä Sea (fōō') *Sea* Indonesia-Australia

Ar'ȧ-gon *Region, anc. kingdom* NE Spain; manufacturing, mining, agriculture

A-rȧ-guai'ȧ (gwī') *River* 1100 m., cen. Brazil

À-raks' *River* 635 m., E U.S.S.R.

Ar'ȧl, Lake *Inland sea* U.S.S.R., Asia

Ār'ȧm *Anc. country* SW Asia, Lebanon Mts-Euphrates

Ar'ȧ-rat *Mountain* 16,916 ft., E Turkey

Är-cā'di-ȧ 1. *City* SW Calif., U.S.; pop. 42,-868. 2. *Department* cen. Peloponnesus, Greece

Ärc'tic Archipelago *Island group* in Arctic O., incl. Baffin, Victoria, Banks, Devon, etc.

Ärc'tic Red *River* 230 m. Northwest Terrs., Canada

Ärc'tic Regions incl. Arctic O. and lands in and adjacent to it

Ärc'tic Ocean *Ocean* N of Continental land masses at Arctic Circle; 5,441,000 sq. m.

Ar-dė-bĭl' (bēl') *City* NW Iran; trade

Ar-deche' (desh') *Department* SE France

Är-dennes' (den') 1. *Region* incl. parts of SE Belgium, Luxembourg, France; battles WW I, II. 2. *Department* NE France

Ä-re-ci'bō (sē') *Municipality, Town,* N Puerto Rico

Ä-re-qui'pȧ (kē') *City* * of *Department,* S Peru; industrial, educational cen.

Ä-rez'zō (rät') *Commune* * of *Province,* cen. Italy; manufacturing

Ar-gen-teuil' (zhäntu'y') *Commune* N France; grapes, chemicals

Är-gėn-ti'nȧ (jėn-tē') *Country,* S South America; 1,072,750 sq. m.; pop. 23,300,-000; * Buenos Aires; 14 provinces and 9 terrs.; livestock products, grain

Är-gŏnne' *Plateau* NE France; battles WW I and II.

Är'gös *City* NE Peloponnesus, Greece

Är'gun' (gōōn') *River* 450 m. Manchuria-U.S.S.R.

Ä-ri'cȧ (rē') *City* N Chile; port

Ar-i-zō'nȧ *State* SW US.; 113,909 sq. m.; pop. 1,772,482; * Phoenix; 14 counties; livestock, agriculture

Är'kȧn-sas (sä) 1. *River* 1450 m. Col.-Ark. U.S. 2. *State* S cen. U.S.; 53,104 sq. m.; pop. 1,923,295; * Little Rock; 75 counties; agriculture, mining, lumbering

Är-khan'gėlsk *City* * of *Region* N R.S.F.S.R., U.S.S.R., Eur.; timber port

Ärl'bêrg *Pass* Alpine valley, W Austria

Ärles (ärl) *City* SE France; medieval kingdom

Är'ling-tön 1. *Town* NE Mass., U.S.; pop. 53,524; residential. 2. *City* N Texas, U.S.; pop. 90,643. 3. *County* N Va., U.S.; Tomb of Unknown Soldier, grave of John F. Kennedy

Är'ling-tön Heights *Village* NE Ill., U.S.; pop. 64,884; residential

Är-mägh' (mä') *County* S Northern Ireland; agriculture, livestock

Är-mȧ-vir' (vyēr') *City* S R.S.F.S.R., U.S.S.R.; Eur.; agriculture

Är-mē'ni-ȧ *Anc. country* W Asia, now parts in U.S.S.R., Turkey, Iran

Är-mē'ni-ȧn S.S.R. *Republic* of U.S.S.R., S Eur.; * Yerevan; agriculture, lumbering, livestock

Är-men-tieres' (tērz') *Commune* N France; industrial cen.

Ärn'hem *Commune* E Netherlands; precision instruments

Är'nō *River* 140 m. cen. Italy; WW II crossing   [dia

Är'rȧh *Town* NE In-

Ar'rȧs *City* N France; grain market

Är'tȧ *Department* NW Greece

Ȧr-te'mövsk (tye') *City* Ukraine, U.S.S.R.; salt, coal

Är-tois' (twä') *Historical region* N cen. France

Ä-ru'bä (rōō') *Islands* (Neth.) off NW Venezuela; oil refineries

Är-va'dȧ *City* C Colo., U.S.; pop. 46,814; food processing agriculture

Ashe'ville *City* W N.C., U.S.; pop. 57,-681; resort, manufacturing

Ä-shi-kä-gä *City* Honshu, Japan; weaving

Ashkh'ȧ-bad *City* * of Turkmen S.S.R., U.S.S.R., Asia

Ā'sia (zhȧ) *Continent,* world's largest: ⅓ of world's land area ab. 16,500,000 sq. m.; over ½ world's pop.

ab. 1,164,000; Eastern hemisphere

Ā′sia Mĭ′nŏr *Peninsula* W Asia bounded by Black, Mediterranean, Aegean Seas; forms large part of Turkey

As-mä′rȧ *Town* Eritrèa, N Ethiopia

As-nieres′ (à-nyâr′) *Commune* N France; boating, dyes, perfume

Ä-sō *Volcano* Kyushu, Japan; five peaks, world's largest crater

As-sam′ *State* NE India; tea

Ȧs-sin′i-boine *River* 450 m. S Canada

Ȧs-si′si (sē′) *Commune* cen. Italy

Ȧs-syr′i-ȧ *Anc. empire* W Asia

Ä′sti *Commune* * of *Province* NW Italy; sparkling wine

As′trȧ-khan *City* * of *Region*, R.S.F.S.R., U.S.S.R., Eur.

Ä-sun-ciôn′ (sōōn-syôn′) *City*, * and chief port of Paraguay, S cen. part; pop. 360,000; commerce, industry

As-wan′ *City* * of *Province* Upper Egypt; dam

As-yut′ (yōōt′) *City* * of *Province*, Upper Egypt; pottery, ivory

Ä-tä-cä′mä *Province, Desert* N cen. Chile; borax lakes

Ät′bä-rä *River* 500 m., NE Africa

Ä - tchaf - à - lay′à (lī′) *River* 225 m. S La., U.S.

Ath-à-bas′kȧ *River* 765 m., and *Lake* 2842 sq. m. W cen. Canada

Ath′ẻns *City* * of Greece, S cen. part; pop. ab. 2,000,000; commercial, manufacturing, cultural

cen.

Ath′ẻns *City* NE Ga., U.S.; pop. 44,342; manufacturing, education cen.

Ath′ös *Mountain* 6670 ft. NE Greece; "Holy Mountain"

At′kȧ *Island* of Aleutian Is. SW Alas., U.S.

At-lan′tȧ *City*, * and largest city of Ga., U.S., NW cen part; pop. 496,973; commercial, rail, education cen.

Ȧt-lan′tic City *City* SE N.J., U.S.; pop. 47,-859; resort

Ȧt-lan′tic Ocean *Body* of water separating North and South America from Europe and Africa; ab. 31,-500,000 sq. m.

At′làs Mountains *Mountain system* 1500 m. long N Africa

Ä-trä′tō *River* 350 m. NW Colombia

Ä-trek′ *River* 300 m. NE Iran

At-tȧ-wȧ-pis′kȧt *River* 465 m. Ontario, Canada

At′ti-cȧ and Boe-ō′tia (bi-ō′shȧ) *Department* E cen. Greece

At′tu (tōō) *Island* westernmost of Aleutian Is.

Ä-tuel′ (twel′) *River* 300 m. W Argentina

Aube (ōb) *Department* NE France

Au-ber-vil-liers′ (ō-bėr-vē-lyā′) *Commune* N France; chemicals, glass, perfume, rubber

Au-bus-sôn′ (ō) *Commune* cen. France; carpets, tapestries

Ăuck′lȧnd *City* * of *District* N New Zealand; port

Aude (ōd) *Department* S France

Augs′bûrg (ouks′) *City* S West Germany;

textiles

Au-gus′tä 1. *City* E Ga., U.S.; pop. 59,-864; cotton, lumber. 2. *City* * of Me., U.S.; pop. 21,680; lumber, shoes, textiles, paper

Au - gus′tä (ou-gōōs′) *Commune* SE Sicily; salt, oil, wine, fish

Ău-rō′rȧ 1. *City* cen. Colo., U.S.; pop. 74,-974; 2. *City* NE Ill., U.S.; pop. 74,182; industry

Ausch′wits (oush′vitz) *Commune* S Poland; concentration camp WW II

Ăus′tẻr-litz *Commune* W cen. Czechoslavakia

Ăus′tin *City* * of Texas cen. part, U.S.; pop. 251,808; political, educational, commercial cen.

Ăus-trā′lia 1. *Island Continent* S Eastern Hemisphere; vast plateau, mild climate. 2. *Commonwealth*, Brit. Dominion; * Canberra; 6 states, 3 territories; 3,000,000 sq. m.; pop. 12,400,-000; wool, dairy products, flour, wheat, hides

Ăus′tri-ȧ *Republic*, former *Empire*, cen. Eur.; * Vienna; 32,-373 sq. m.; pop. 7,-349,000; 8 provinces and Vienna; agriculture, forestry

Ăus′tri - ȧ - Hun′gȧ - rẏ *Former monarchy* cen. Eur. incl. Hungary, Austria, Czechoslovakia, parts of Italy, Poland, Yugoslavia, Romania

Ȧ-vei′ro (vä′i-rōō) *City* on *Lagoon*, * of *District* NW Portugal; salt, mercury

Ä-ver′sä *Commune* S Italy; white wine

Ȧ-vi-gnôn′ (vē-nyôn′)

City SE France; commerce, manufacturing

Ä′vi-lä *City* * of *Province* cen. Spain

Ā′von *River* 96 m. cen. England; Shakespeare fame

Ä-wä-jĭ *Island* of Japan, S of Honshu

Ax′min-stêr *Town* SW England; carpets

Ay-din′ (ī) *Town* * of *Vilayet* SW Turkey, Asia; trade

Āyles′bûr-ẏ *Municipal borough* SE cen. England; lace

Āyr or Āyr′shĭre *County, Burgh* SW Scotland; port, manufacturing

Ay-sen′ (ī-sän′) *Province, Commune* S Chile

Ä-zẻr-baĭ-dzhän′ S.S.R. *Republic* of U.S.S.R., Eur.; * Baku; minerals, oil wells

Ä-zẻr-baĭ-jän′ *Province* NW Iran; fertile area

Ā′zōres *Island group* (Port.) N Atlantic O.; fruit, wine, grain

B

Bā′àl-bek, anc. **Hē-li-op′ö-lis** *Village* E Lebanon [bylon

Bā′bẻl *City*, anc. Ba-

Bȧ′bush-kin (boosh) *City* R.S.F.S.R., U.S.S.R., Eur.

Bab′ẏ-lon *Anc. city*, * of **Bab-ẏ-lō′ni-ȧ**, mod. S Iraq

Back River *River* 605 m. N Canada

Bä-cô′lôd *City*, Negros, Phil. Is.; sugar cen.

Bä-dä-jôz′ (hôth′) *City* * of *Province*, SW Spain; trade cen.

Bä-dä-lō′nä *Commune* NE Spain; port

Bä′dẻn *Former state* SW Germany, now part of **Bä′dẻn-Wûrt′tẻm-bêrg,** *State* West Germany

Bad Lands *Region* SW

S.D., U.S.; barren area

Baf'fin Bay *Inlet* of Atlantic O. Greenland-Baffin I.

Baf'fin Island *Island*, largest of Canadian Arctic Arch.

Bagh'dad *City* * of *Province* and * of Iraq, E cen. part; pop. 500,000; imp. since anc. times

Bà'ghel-khànd *Former agency* E cen. India

Bä'gō *Municipality* Negros, Phil. Is.

Bä'guiō (gyō) *City* Luzon; summer * of Phil. Is.

Bà-hä'mà Islands *Islands* (Brit.) SE of Fla., U.S.; * Nassau on New Providence I.; agriculture, fish, resort

Bà-hä'wàl-pur (poor) *Town* * of *State*, Punjab, W Pakistan

Bä-hi'ä Blänc'ä ('ē') *City* E Argentina; port

Bàh-raich' (rīk') *Town* * of *District* N India; trade cen.

Bàh-rain' Islands *Archipelago* W Persian Gulf; pearls, oil

Bahr el Ghä-zal' *River* ab 500 m., Sudan

Bà-i'ä (ē') *State* E Brazil

Baja California *State* NW Mexico

Baï-kal', Lake *Lake*, Siberia, U.S.S.R., Asia

Bä-kàr-gànj' *District* East Pakistan

Bä'kêr Island *Island* (U.S.) cen. Pacific O.

Bä'kêrs-fiēld *City* S Cal., U.S.; pop. 69,-515; oil industry

Bä-ku' (kōō') *City* * of Azerbaidzhan Rep., U.S.S.R.; oil

Bal-à-klä'và *Village* SW Crimea, U.S.S.R. Eur.; port

Bal-bō'à *District* SE

Canal Zone

Bäld'win Pärk *City* S Cal., U.S., pop. 47,-285

Bal-è-ar'ic Islands *Islands*, *Province* E Spain; incl. Majorca, Minorca, etc.

Bä'li *Island* E of Java, Indonesia

Bä-li-ke-sir' (sēr') *City* * of *Vilayet* NW Turkey, Asia

Bä-lik-pä'pän *Town* on *Bay* SE Borneo, Indonesia; oil

Bäl'kàn Peninsula *Peninsula* SE Eur., bounded by Adriatic, Ionian, Mediterranean, Aegean and Black Seas; incl. Yugoslavia, Bulgaria, Romania, Greece, Albania, Turkey in Eur. called **Bäl'kàn States**

Bäl-khäsh', Lake *Lake* Kazakh, U.S.S.R.

Bal'là-rat *City* SE Australia; gold

Bäl'tic Sea Arm of Atlantic O., N Eur.

Bäl'tic States *Republics* of U.S.S.R.: Latvia, Estonia, Lithuania

Bäl'ti-môre *City* Md., U.S.; pop. 905,759; imp. port

Bà-lū-chi-stän' *Region* W Pakistan

Ba-ma-ko' *Town* * of Mali, S part; pop. 175,000

Bam'bêrg *City* S cen. West Germany; textiles, breweries

Bä-nät' *Region* N Yugoslavia, formerly div. bet. Romania and Hungary

Bän-dä'mä *River* 370 m. Ivory Coast

Bän-djêr-mä'sin *Town* S Borneo, Indonesia; trade cen.

Bän'doeng (doong) *City* J a v a, Indonesia; manufacturing

Bän'drà *Town* W India; resort

Banff (bamf) 1. *Town*

and *National Park*, SW Alberta, Canada. 2. *County* NE Scotland

Banff'shìre *County* SE Scotland; quarries, fish, cattle

Ban'gà-lôre *City* * of *District*, Mysore, S India; trade cen.

Bang'kà *Island* off SE Sumatra, Indonesia

Bang'kok *City* * of Thailand, S part; pop. 2,800,000; port

Bang-la-desh' *Country* formerly E. Pakistan; E of India; * Dacca; pop. 78,000,000

Bän-gui' (gē') *Town* * of Central African Republic; pop. 150,-000

Bang - wē - ū'lū Lake *Lake* N Zambia

Banks Island *Island* Northwest Territories, Canada

Bän'ku-rä (koo) *Town* and *District*, NE India

Bàn'nu (noo) *Town* and *District*, N West Pakistan

Bäns-wä'rà *State* and *Town*, NW India

Bär-bä'dōs *Island*, Brit. West Indies; * Bridgetown; sugar

Bär'bà-rỳ *Region* N African Coast, Egypt to Atlantic O.; **Bär' bà-rỳ States**: Morocco, Algiers, Tunis, Tripoli

Bär-cè-lō'nà (sè) *City* * of *Province* NE Spain; chief port, manufacturing cen.

Bär-cōō' *River* 600 m., Australia

Bà-reil'lỳ (rāl') *City* * of *Division* and *District*, N India

Bar'ènts Sea *Area* of Arctic O. N of Norway and U.S.S.R.

Bä'ri *City* * of *Province* SE Italy; port, manufacturing

Bä'ri-à *State* W India

Bä-ri-sän' Mountains *Mountain system* W Sumatra

Bä-ri'tō (rē') *River* 550 m. SE Borneo

Bär'king *Urban district* SE England

Bar-lè-Dūc' *Commune* NE France; manufacturing

Bär-let'tà *City* SE Italy; port

Bar-nà-ūl' (bēr') *Town*, R.S.F.S.R., U.S.S.R., Asia; mines, factories

Bà-rō'dà *City* * of *State* and *Division*, W India; jewelry

Bà-rot'sè-land *Former Region* of Northern Rhodesia, now part of Zambia

Bär-qui-si-me'tō (kē-sē-mä') *City* NW Venezuela; export cen.

Bär-rän-quil'lä (kē'yä) *City* N Colombia; port

Bar'rōw 1. *Town* nr. *Point* N Alas., U.S. 2. *County Borough* NW England; industry. 3. *Island* off W Australia

Bär-thol'ö-mew Bay'ou mū bī'ōō) *River* 275 m. Ark.-La., U.S.

Bär'wön Upper course of Darling R., SE Australia

Bä'sil or **Bäsle** (bäl) *City* * of *Canton* NW Switzerland; manufacturing

Bash'kir A.S.S.R. *Republic*, R.S.F.S.R., U.S.S.R. Eur.; forestry, agriculture, minerals, horses

Bä-si'län (sē') *Island* of *Group*, Phil. Is.; wood, fish

B a s q u e Provinces (bask) *Region* N Spain; forests, vineyards, mines

Bäs'rà *City* * of *Province*, S Iraq; port

Bäs-Rhin' (bä-ran') *Department* NE France

Bàs-sein' (sān') *City* *

of *District*, Lower Burma; rice

Basses - Alpes' (bäs-zalp') *Department* SE France

Basses - Py - re - nees' (bäs-pē-rā-nā') *Department* SW France

Bass Islands *Islands* (3) W Lake Erie, U.S.

Bä-sti'à (stē') *City* NE Corsica; commerce

Bas-togne' (tôn'y') *Town* SE Belgium; WW II battle

Bà-su'tō-land (sōō') *Brit. Colony* now LESOTHO, republic South Africa; * Maseru; livestock

Bä'tä *Town* * of Spanish Guinea; pop. 3500; port

Bà-täan' *Province* and *Peninsula* Luzon, Phil. Is.; WW II battles

Bà-tan'gàs *Municipality* on *Bay*, * of *Province*, Luzon, Phil. Is.; sugar, lumber, coconuts

Bà-tä'vi-à *City* now DJAKARTA, on *Bay*; * of former Neth. Indîes

Bath *City* and *County borough* SW England; resort

Bath'ûrst *Town* * of Gambia; pop. 28,000; seaport

Bät'ön Rouge (rōōzh) *City* * of La., U.S.; pop. 165,963; chemicals, petroleum

Bat'tle (t'l) *River* ab. 340 m. W Canada

Bat'tle Crēēk *City* S Mich., U.S.; pop. 38,931; breakfast foods

Bà-tūm' *City* * of Adzhar A.S.S.R., U.S.S.R.; port

Baut'zèn (bou') *City* SE East Germany; manufacturing

Bà-var'i-a *State* S West Germany; * Munich; agriculture, manufacturing

Bà-var'i-àn Alps *Range*

of Alps bet. Austria and Germany

Bāy City *City* E Mich. U.S.; pop. 49,449; lumber, coal, fish

Bay'kal, Lake (bī) see BAIKAL

Bāy-ōnne' *City* NE N.J., U.S.; pop. 72,743; petroleum industry

Bay - reuth' (bī - roit') *City* SW West Germany; industrial

Bāy'town *City* SE Texas, U.S.; pop. 43,980

Bear *River* ab. 350 m. Ida. and Utah, U.S.

Bē'äs *River* ab 300 m. N India

Beau'fört Sea (bō') Part of Arctic O. N of Alaska and Canada

Beau'mont (bō') *City* SE Texas, U.S.; pop. 115,919; oil port

Bech-ū-ä'nà-land now BOTSWANA

Bed'förd *Municipal borough* SE cen. England; farm tools

Bed'förd-shîre *County* SE cen. England; agriculture, lace

Bed'lōe's Island *Island* N.Y. Bay, N.Y., U.S.; site of Statue of Liberty

Bēer-shē'bà *Town* and *Subdistrict*, S Israel

Bēes'tön and Stä'pleförd (p'l) *Urban district* N cen. England

Bei-rūt' (bā) *City* * of Lebanon, N part; pop. 700,000; port

Be'là-yà *River* ab. 700 m., U.S.S.R., Eur.

Bè-lem' *City* N Brazil; seaport

Bel'fast *County borough* * of Northern Ireland; shipbuilding, seaport, linen

Bel - fort' (fôr') *Commune* E France, manufacturing

Bel-fôrt', Ter-ri-toire' dê (twar') *Department* E France

Bel-gaum' (goum')

Town * of *District* W India; weaving

Bel'gian Con'gō (jàn) see CONGO

Bel'gium (jum), **Belgique'** (zhēk) *Country* NW Europe; 11,775 sq. m.; pop. 9,606,000; * Brussels; commercial, industrial country

Bel'grāde *City* * of Yugoslavia and of Serbia Republic; pop. 697,000; industrial and communication cen.

Bè-lize' (lēz') *City* * of *District* E Brit. Honduras; port

Bel'leau Wood (lō) *Wood* N France; WW I battle site

Bèl-lēek' *Parish* and *Village* Northern Ireland; china

Belle' Fourche' (fōōsh') *River* ab. 350 m. Wyo., U.S.

Belle'ville *City* SW Ill., U.S.; pop. 41,699; coal area

Belle'vūe *City* Va. U.S.; pop. 61,102

Bell'flow-êr *City* Calif., U.S.; pop. 51,454

Bel'ling ham *City* Va., U.S.; pop. 39,375

Bel - lu'nō (bäl - lōō') *Commune* * of *Province* NE Italy; trade

Bè-loit' *City* S Wisc., U.S.; pop. 35,729; manufacturing, dairy farms

Bel-yan'dō *River* ab. 250 m. NE Australia

Bè-nä'rès *City* * of *Division* N India; ancient holy city

Ben'è-lux = countries of Belgium, Netherlands and Luxembourg

Be-ne-ven'tō (bâ-nä) *Commune* * of *Province* S Italy

Ben'gàl *Former Province* NE Brit. India, * Calcutta; 1947 div.

into **East Ben'gàl**, Pakistan and **West Ben'gàl**, India

Ben'gàl, Bay of *Arm* of Indian O. bet. India and Burma

Ben-gä'zi *City* * of *Province*, co-* of Libya N part; port

Be'ni (bâ) *River* 1000 m. Bolivia

Be'ni Su-ef' (bâ'ni-soo-wäf') *City* * of *Province*, Upper Egypt

Bè-nō'ni *Town* NE Republic of South Africa; gold mining

Be'nue (bä'nwä) *River* ab 870 m. W Africa

Bep'pu (pōō) *City* on *Bay* Kyushu, Japan

Be-rär' (bä) *Division* of **Central Provinces and Berar**, cen. India

Bêr'bê-rà *City* N Somalia; seaport

Bêr-bice' (bĕs') *County* and *River* 300 m. E

Bêr'chèm (kèm) *Commune* N Belgium

Bêrch-tès-gä'dèn (bêrk) *Town* Bavarian Alps, West Germany

Bêr-di'chev (dyĕ'chèf) *City* Ukraine, U.S.S.R.; trade cen.

Be-re'zi-nà (bye-ryä'-zyi) *River* 350 m. White Russia, U.S.S.R.

Bè-rez'ni-ki (byi-ryôs') *City* R.S.F.S.R., U.S.S.R., Eur.; industry

Bêr'gä-mō *Commune* * of *Province* N Italy; commercial cen.

Bêr'gèn *City* NW Norway; manufacturing, seaport

Be'ring Sea *Area* of N Pacific O., bet. Alas. and Siberia

Be'ring Strait *Strait* bet. Arctic O. and Bering S.

Bêrke'ley (bêrk'li) *City* W Cal., U.S.; pop. 116,716; residential, industrial

Bêrk'shîre 1. *County* S

England; agriculture, livestock. 2. **Hills** or **Bêrk′shìres** *Mountain range* W Mass., U.S.

Bêr′lin *City* E Germany, former * of Germany; div. 1949: **West Berlin**, part of West German Federal Republic, pop. 2,200,600; **East Berlin**, * of East German Democratic Republic; pop. ab. 1,083,800

Ber-me′jō (hō) *River* 1000 m. N Argentina

Bêr - mū′dà *Islands* (Brit. Colony), ab. 360 islands, W Atlantic O., E of U.S.; * Hamilton on **Bermuda I.**

Bêrn *City* * of *Canton* and * of Switzerland; pop. 166,200; manufacturing, cultural cen.

Bêr′nēse Alps *Mountain range* S cen. Switzerland

Ber′wick (ik) *County* SE Scotland; agriculture, fish, livestock

Bêr′wyn *City* NE Ill., U.S.; pop. 52,502; residential

Bê-sän-côn′ (zän-sôn′) *City* E France; manufacturing, trade

Bes-sà-rā′bi-à 1. *Area* SE Europe from Danube R. to Black S. 2. *Former province* E Romania, now part of Moldavian S.S.R.; agriculture

Beth′el *Town* anc. Palestine, N of Jerusalem

Bê-thes′dà (thez′) *District* and *Suburb* cen. Md., U.S.; pop. 71,621

Beth′lè-hem 1. *Town* nr. Jerusalem, Jordan; City of David, birthplace of Jesus. 2. *City* E Pa., U.S.; pop. 72,686; iron,

steel, cigars, hosiery

Bet′wä (bät′) *River* 360 m. cen. India

Bev′êr-lÿ *City* NE Mass., U.S.; pop. 38,348; shoe machinery

Bex′ley (li) *Urban district* SE England; hardware

Bey-ō-glu′ (be-ē-ō-lōō′) *City*, division of Istanbul, Turkey

Be′zhi-tsà (byā) *Town* R.S.F.S.R., U.S.S.R., Eur.; locomotives

Be-ziers′ (bā-zyā′) *City* S France; commerce, industry

Bez-wä′dà (bāz) *Town* SE India; rail, trade cen.

Bhad′gaon (bud′goun) *Town* cen. Nepal

Bhä′gàl-pur (poor) *City* * of *Division* NE India; trade cen.

Bhà-mô′ *Town* * of *District* Upper Burma; trade cen.

Bhà′ràt (bu′rut) = INDIA, its anc. and official name

Bhà′ràt-pur (poor) *City* * of *State* NW India

Bhät′pä-rà *City* W Bengal India; industrial

Bhav-nà′gàr (bou-nug′) *Town* * of *State* W India; port

Bhi′mä (bē′) *River* ab. 400 m. S India

Bhō-päl′ *City* * of *State* cen. India; agriculture

Bhū - tan′, Druk - Yul *Country* NE of India; 18,000 sq. m.; pop. 750,000; * Tashi chho Dzong; foods, handicrafts

Biä-lÿ′stôk *City* NE Poland; textiles

Biar-ritz′ *Commune* SW France; resort

Biel (bēl) *Commune* nr. *Lake* NW Switzerland; manufacturing

Bie′lè-feld (bē′) *City* West Germany; manufacturing

Big Black *River* 330

m. W cen. Miss., U.S.

Big Blūe *River* 300 m. Neb. and Kan., U.S.

Big′hôrn *River* 336 m. Wyo.-Mont., U.S.

Big Sioux (sōō) *River* ab. 300 m. S.D. and Iowa, U.S.

Bi-här′ 1. *Town* in *Division* and *State* NE India; agriculture, mining. 2. **and O-ris′sà** former province of Brit. India

Bi-kä-nèr′ *City* * of *State* NW India; livestock, carpets

Bi-ki′ni (kē′) *Atoll* of Marshall Is.

Bil-bä′ō *City* N Spain; trade, manufacturing

Bi-li′rän (bē-lē′) *Island* cen. Phil. Is.

Bil′lings *City* S cen. Mont., U.S.; pop. 61,581; shipping cen.

Bil-li′ton (lē′) *Island* Java Sea, Indonesia

Bi-lox′i *City* SE Miss., U.S.; pop. 48,486; fisheries

Bin-gêr-ville′ *Town* Ivory Coast

Bing′hàm-tön (àm) *City* S N.Y., U.S.; pop. 64,123; manufacturing

Binh Dinh *Town* E South Vietnam

Bi′ō-Bi′ō (bē′) *River* 238 m. S cen. Chile

Bîr′kèn-head (hed) *County borough* NW England; shipping

Bîr′ming-ham 1. *City* N cen. Ala., U.S.; pop. 300,910; industrial cen. 2. *City* and *county borough* W cen. England; rail and metal cen.

Bi′rö-bi-dzhän′ *Town* * of *Region* (Jewish Autonomous Region) SE R.S.F.S.R., U.S.S.R., Asia

Bis′cäy or **Viz-cä′yä** *Province* N Spain

Bis′cäy, Bay of *Inlet* of Atlantic O., W France and N Spain

Bis′cäyne Bay *Inlet* of

Atlantic O., SE Fla., U.S.

Bisk (byĕsk) *Town* R.S.F.S.R., U.S.S.R., Asia

Bis′märck (biz′) 1. *City* * of N.D., U.S.; pop. 34,703; trade cen., flour. 2. **Archipelago** *Island group* (ab. 200) W Pacific O., Terr. of New Guinea; incl. New Britain, Admiralty Is., New Ireland, etc. 3. **Sea** W Pacific O.; site of WW II battle

Bis-sau′ (sou′) *Town* * of **Portuguese Guinea**; port

Bit′têr-rōōt Mountains *Range* of Rocky Mts., Idaho-Mont., U.S.

Bi′yà (bē′) *River* ab. 350 m. U.S.S.R., Asia

Bi-zêrte′ *City* N Tunisia; seaport

Black′bûrn *County borough* NW England; textiles

Black Forest *Region* S West Germany; resort area

Black Hills *Mountains* South Dakota-Wyo., U.S.; minerals

Black River 1. *River* 280 m. Mo.-Ark., U.S. 2. *River* 200 m. Wisc., U.S.

Black′pōōl *County borough* NW England; resort

Black Sea *Sea* bet. Europe and Asia; 168,000 sq. m.

Blanc′, Mont (môn blänk′) *Mountain* 15,781 ft.; highest of the Alps, SE France at Italian border

Blär′ney (ni) *Town* SW Eire

Blen′heim (im) *Village* S West Germany

Block Island *Island* Atlantic O., R.I., U.S.; fishing cen.

Bloem - fôn - tein′ (blōōm-fôn-tān′) *City* Orange Free State E Republic of South

Africa; trade cen.

Blōōm′fiēld *City* NE N.J., U.S.; pop. 52,-029; manufacturing

Blōōm′ing-tön 1. *City* cen. Ill., U.S.; pop. 39,992; commerce, manufacturing. 2. *City* SE Minn., U.S.; pop. 81,970. 3. *City* SC Ind., U.S.; pop. 42,890; education cen.

Blue′grass (blōō′) *Region* cen. Ky., U.S.

Blue Ridge Mountains *Range* of Appalachian Mts., W.Va. into Ga., U.S. [SE Asia

Bō *River* ab. 500 m.

Bö - bruisk′ (brōō′isk) *City* * of *Region* White Russia, U.S.S.R.

Bō′cà Rà-tōn′ *Town* SE Fla., U.S.

Bō′chum (koom) *City* W cen. West Germany; iron, coal, steel

Boē - ō′tià (bē - ō′shà) *Anc. republic* E cen. Greece, now part of mod. dept. of **Attica and Boeotia**

Boe′roe (bōō′rōō) *Island* Malay Arch., Indonesia

Boe′toeng (bōō′toong) *Island* off SE Celebes, Indonesia

Bō′gôr *City* Java, Indonesia

Bō-gö-tä′ *City* * of Colombia, W cen. part; pop. 2,500,000; cultural cen.

Bō-hē′mi-à *Province* W Czechoslovakia; mining, agriculture, manufacturing

Bō - hôl′ *Island* and *Province* S cen. Phil. Is.; agriculture, weaving

Boi′se (zi) *City* * of Ida., U.S., SW part; pop. 74,481; foodstuffs, quarries

Boks′bûrg *Town* NE Republic of South Africa; gold cen.

Bō′li-vär 1. *Department* N Colombia. 2.

Province W cen. Equador. 3. *State* SE Venezuela, * **Cuidad Bolivar**, port

Bō-liv′i-a, Republic of *Republic* W cen. South America; 424,-000 sq. m.; pop. 4,-800,000; legal * Sucre; administrative * La Paz; country without a coastline; minerals, rubber

Bö-lō′gnä (nyä) *Commune* * of *Province* N Italy; manufacturing

Bōl′tön *County borough* NW England; woolens

Bōl-zä′nō *Commune* * of *Province* NE Italy; trade cen.

Bom-bāy′ *City* * of *Province* on *Island* W cen. India; port, cotton cen.

Bō′mu (mōō) *River* ab. 500 m. cen. Africa

Bōne *Commune* NE Algeria; seaport, manufacturing

Bonn *City* * of West German Federal Republic, W cen. part; pop. 299,400; manufacturing, educational cen.

Bōō′thi-à, Gulf of *Gulf* SW of Baffin I. Northwest T e r r s., Canada

Bōō′tle (t′l) *County borough* NW England; seaport

Bôr-deaux′ (dō′) *City* SW France; port, industrial cen.

Bôr′gêr-hout *Commune* N Belgium

Bö-ri′slàv (ryē′) *City* Ukraine, U.S.S.R.; oil, natural gas

Bō-ri-sö-glebsk′ *City* R.S.F.S.R., U.S.S.R., Eur.; grain

Bôr′nē-ō *Island* of Malay Arch., world's 3rd largest; divided: N part = part of Malaysia (formerly Brit. colony of Sarawak); S part = unit of In-

donesia; good harbors; agriculture, minerals

Bôrn′hôlm *I s l a n d*, *County* of Denmark, Baltic S.

Bos′ni-a (boz′) *Region* cen. Yugoslavia, now part of **Bosnia and Her-zè-gö-vi′nà** (vē′) Federated Republic

Bos′pö-rus *Strait* bet. Turkey in Asia and Turkey in Eur.

Bös′siêr City *City* NW La., U.S.; pop. 41,595

Bôs′tön *City* * of Mass. U.S.; pop. 641,071; financial, commercial, industrial cen.; fish, wool

Bot′à-nỳ Bay *Inlet* of South Pacific O. SE Australia

Both′ni-à *Arm* of Baltic S. bet. Finland and Sweden

Bot-swä′na *Country* (Sept. 1966) cen. S Africa, former Brit. protectorate: Bechuanaland; 238,805 sq. m.; pop. 670,000; * Gaberones; livestock, minerals

Bôt′trôp *City* W West Germany; coal

Bouches - du - Rhône′ (bōōsh-d′rŏn′) *Department* SE France

Bou′gain-ville (bōō′gàn) *Island*, largest of Solomon Is.; fertile soil

Boul′dêr (bōl′) 1. *City* N cen. Colo., U.S.; pop. 66,870; mining area. 2. *Dam* = HOOVER DAM

Bou-logne′ (bōō-lôn′y′) *City* N France; port

Bour-bön-nais′ (boor-bön-ā′) *Hist. region* of cen. France

Bourges (boorzh) *Commune* cen. France

Bōw *River* 315 m. Alberta, Canada

Bo′wie (bōō) *Town* SC Md., U.S.; pop. 35,-028; dairy, poultry, truck farms

Bōwl′ing Grēen *City* SW Ky., U.S.; pop. 36,253; manufacturing, education cen.

Bō′zėn see BOLZANO

Brà-bant′ *Province* (former *Duchy*) cen. Belgium

Brad′förd *County borough* N England; worsted cen.

Bräh-mà-pu′trà (pōō′) *River* 1800 m. Tibet and India

Brà-i′lä (ē′) *City* E Romania; shipping

Brain′trēe *Town* E Mass., U.S.; pop. 35,-050; manufacturing, shipbuilding

Bran′cō, Ri′ō (rē′) *River* ab. 350 m. N Brazil

Bran′dėn-bûrg *City* cen. East Germany; manufacturing

Brant′förd *City* Ontario, Canada; manufacturing

Brà-sil′ià (zēl′) *City* * of Brazil, cen. part; pop. 44,000

Brä-sôv′ (shôv′), Germ. **Krōn′städt** *City* cen. Romania; manufacturing

Bra′ti-sla-va *City* E cen. Czechoslovakia; shipping

Braun′schweig (broun′shvīk) or **Bruns′wick** *City* E West Germany; trade, manufacturing

Brà-zil′, United States of *Republic* E cen. South America; 3,-286,270 sq. m.; pop. 90,000,000; * Brazilia (since 1960; formerly Rio de Janeiro); harbors, forests, agriculture, cattle, minerals

Braz′ös *River* 870 m. cen. Texas, U.S.

Braz′zà-ville *City* * of Congo Republic (B), SE part; pop. 133,-000; port

Breck′nöck-shire *County* SE Wales; farming, mining, livestock

Bre-da′ (brà) *Commune*

S Netherlands; carpets, cloth

Bre'mèn (brā') *City* * of *State* NW West Germany; commerce

Brem'êr-hä-vèn *City* NW West Germany; seaport

Brem'êr-tön *City* Va., U.S.; pop. 35,307

Bren'nêr Pass *Pass* bet. Austria and Italy, Alps

Brent'förd and Ches'wick (chez'ik) *Urban district* SE England

Bre'scia (brā'shä) *Commune* * of *Province* N Italy; manufacturing

Brest 1. *Commune* NW France; naval station, manufacturing. 2. *Region* White Russia U.S.S.R.; * **Brest Li-tôvsk'**, trade cen.

Bridge'pôrt (brij') *City* SW Conn., U.S.; pop. 156,542; industrial

Bridge'town (toun) *Town* * of Barbados on Barbados I.; port

Brigh'tön (brī) *County borough* S England; resort

Brin'di-si (zi) *Commune* * of *Province* SE Italy; trade cen.

Bris'bāne (briz') *City* * of Queensland, Australia; port

Bris'töl 1. *City* N Conn., U.S.; pop. 55,-487; manufacturing. 2. *City, county borough* SW cen. England; shipping. 3. **Bay** Arm of Bering S., SW Alas.; salmon. 4. **Channel** Arm of Atlantic O. bet. Wales and England

Brit'ain ('n) Term referring to Great Britain; Lat. **Bri-tan'ni-à**

Brit'ish Ant-ärc'ti-cà *Territories* incl. Falkland Is., South Sandwich Is., Antarctic Terr., Graham's Land

Brit'ish Cö - lum'bi - à

Province W Canada; * Victoria; harbors, forests, minerals, agriculture

Brit'ish Co m'm ö n - wealth of Nations Association of Nations under the United Kindgom of Great Britain and Northern Ireland including dominions, dependencies and colonies; mod. term for **Brit'ish Em'pīre;** * London, England

Brit'ish East Africa former terrs. now KENYA, UGANDA, TANZANIA

Brit'ish Gui-a'nà = GUYANA

Brit'ish Hon-dū'ràs *Colony* (Brit.) Central America; * Belize; forest products, fruits

Brit'ish In'di-à Parts of India under Brit. rule before 1947; * New Delhi

Brit'ish Isles (īlz) *Island group* W Europe incl. Great Britain, Ireland and nearby islands

Brit'ish South Africa *Territories* (Brit.) outside Rep. of South Africa; incl. Basutoland, Botswana, Swaziland

Brit'ish West In'diès (dēz) *Islands* (Brit.) of West Indies incl. Bahama, Leeward, and Windward Is., Barbados, Trinidad and Tobago, and Jamaica; see WEST INDIES FEDERATION (former 1958)

Brit'tà-nỳ *Hist. region* NW France

Br'nô (bûr') or **Brunn** *City* cen. Czechoslovakia; manufacturing

Broad (brôd) *River* ab. 220 m. W N.C., U.S.

Brock'tön *City* SE Mass. U.S.; pop. 89,040

Brom'ley (li) *Municipal*

borough SE England

Bronx *Borough* of N.Y. City (N) also *County* of N.Y. State, U.S.; residential, industrial

Brook'līne *Town* E Mass., U.S.; pop. 58,886; residential

Brook'lỳn *Borough* of N.Y. City (E), U.S.; same area also Kings County, N.Y.; residential

Brook'lỳn Cen'têr *City* SE Minn., U.S.; pop. 35,173; residential

Browns'ville *City* S Texas, U.S.; pop. 52,522; port

Bruges (brōōzh), **Brug'gè** *Commune* NW Belgium; commerce, canals, bridges

Bru'nei (brōō') *City* on *Bay,* formerly Brit., NW Borneo; port, oil

Bruns'wick 1. *City* SE Ga., U.S.; shrimp, shipbuilding. 2. *City* cen. Germany; see BRAUNSCHWEIG

Brus'sèls, Bru-xelles' (bruk-sel') *City* * of Belgium, cen. part; pop. 1,500,000; manufacturing

Brỳ-ansk' *City* * of *Region* SW R.S.F.S.R., U.S.S.R., Eur.; trade, manufacturing

Bu-cär-rä-män'gä (bōō) *City* N cen. Colombia; agricultural cen.

Bū'cha-rest (kà) *City* * of Romania, SE part; pop. 1,500,000; trade, industrial cen.

Bu'chen-wäld (bōō'kèn) *Village* cen. Germany; WW II concentration camp

Buck'ing - hàm - shîre *County* SE cen. England; livestock, agriculture

Bū-cö-vi'nà (vē') *Region* E cen. Europe, formerly all Romanian; N part now in Ukranian S.S.R.

Bū'dà-pest *City* * of

Hungary, cen. part; pop. 2,017,000; trade, manufacturing, political cen.

Bue'nà Pärk (bwä') *City* Cal., U.S.; pop. 63,646

Bue-nä-ven-tū'rä (bwä) *City* W Colombia; imp. port

Bue'nös Air'ēs (bwä', âr') 1. *Province* and *City* * of Argentina, E part; pop. 5,900,-000; port. 2. *Lake* SE Chile

Buf'fà-lō *City* NW N.Y. U.S.; pop. 462,768; industrial, trade cen.

Bug (boog) *River* 450 m. U.S.S.R.-Poland

Bui'tèn-zörg (boi') = BOGOR

Bu - jum - bu'rà (boo') *Town* * of Burundi; pop. 75,000

Bu'kà (bōō') *Island* of Solomon Is., Terr. of New Guinea

Bu-khä'rà (bōō) *City* Uzbek, U.S.S.R.; Islam holy place

Bu-läk' (bōō) *Port* of Cairo, Egypt

Bu-là-wä'yō (bōō) *Town* Rhodesia; trade cen.

Bul-gar'i-à *Republic* SE Eur., 42,796 sq. m.; pop. 8,400,000; * Sofia; livestock, agriculture

Bull Run (bool) *Stream* NE Va., U.S.; Civil War battle site

Bu'nà (bōō') *Village* NE New Guinea; WW II base

Bun'kêr Hill *Site* of battle 1775, Boston, Mass., U.S.

Bûr'bank *City* SW Cal., U.S.; pop. 88,871

Bûr'di-kin *River* 425 m. Queensland, Australia

Bûr-dwän' *Town* * of *Division* Bengal, NE India

Bu-re'yà (rä') *River* 480 m. U.S.S.R., Asia

Bur'gôs (bōōr') *City* * of *Province* N cen.

Spain; manufacturing

Bûr'gun-dy *Region,* former kindgom, France and Switzerland

Bur-hän'pur (b o o r , poor) *Town* cen. India; silk, brocade

Bûr'ling-tön 1. *City* NW Vt., U.S.; pop. 38,633; port. 2. *City* NC N.C., U.S.; pop. 35,930; manufacturing

Bûr'må, Union of *Republic* SE Asia; 261,-790 sq. m.; pop. 27,-000,000; * Rangoon; div.: **Lower Burma** = coast; **Upper Burma** = inland area; agriculture, minerals; formerly Brit.

Bûr'må Rōad *Highway* 2100 m. Rangoon-Chungking

Bûrn'ley (li) *County borough* NW England; textiles, iron

Bur-sä' (boor) *City* * of *Vilayet* NW Turkey, Asia; carpets, silk

Bûr'tön on Trent *County borough* W cen. England; breweries

Bu-run'di, Kingdom of (bōō-rōōn') *Country* cen. Africa; 11,000 sq. m.; pop. 3,000,-000; * Bujumburo; formerly part of Ruanda - Urundi and Germ. E Africa

Bur-yat' - Mon'göl A.S.S.R. (boor) *Republic* of R.S.F.S.R., Siberia, U.S.S.R.; forests, furs, fish

Bū-shire' (shēr') *City* SW Iran; port

Bū'stô Är-si'ziō (sē') *Commune* N Italy; cotton, wine

Būte'shire *County* SW Scotland; agriculture, fish

Būtte *City* SW Mont., U.S.; pop. 23,368; world's largest mineral deposits

Bẏd'goszcz (gôshch), **Brôm'bêrg** *City* N Poland; industrial

Bye-lö-rus'sian S.S.R. (rush'ån) = WHITE RUSSIAN S.S.R.

Bȳ'lot Island *Island* W of Baffin Bay, Canada

Bȳ'tôm *City* SW Poland; industrial

Bȳ'zån - tine Em'pīre (tin) *Empire* S and SE Eur. and W Asia, 4th-15th centuries

Bȳ-zan'ti-um *Anc. city* site of mod. Istanbul

C

Cä-bä-nä-tuän' *Municipality* Luzon, Phil. Is.; trade cen.

Cå-bin'då *Town* W Angola; seaport

Cab'öt Strait *Channel* bet. Gulf of St. Lawrence and Atlantic O.

Cä'ce-res (sâ-râs) *Commune* * of *Province* W Spain; factories

Cache (cash) *River* ab. 230 m. NE Ark., U.S.

Cå-diz' 1. *City,* * of *Province* on *Bay* (inlet of *Gulf*) SW Spain; port. 2. *Municipality,* Negros, Phil. Is.

Caen (kän) *City* NW France; commerce, manufacturing

Caer - när'vön - shire (cär) *County* NW Wales; slate, minerals

Caer-phil'lẏ (cär-fil') *Urban district* SE Wales; cheese

Cae-sa-rē'å (sē-zå) *Anc. city,* Palestine; port; now QISARYA

Cä-gä-yän' *River* 220 m. Luzon, Phil. Is.

Cä'gliä-ri (lyä) *Commune* on *Gulf* * of *Province* S Sardinia, Italy

Cä'guäs *Municipality* E cen. Puerto Rico; tobacco

Cå-ha'bå *River* 200 m. cen. Ala., U.S.

Caï'rō (kī') *Governorate*

and *City,* * of Egypt and of the United Arab Republic; pop. 4,219,800; educational, industrial cen.

Cäith'ness *County* N Scotland; fish, agriculture

Cå-jon' Pass (hōn') *Pass* S Cal., U.S.

Cä-lä'bri-ä *Compartimento* S Italy; "toe" of It. "boot"; quarries, agriculture, livestock

Cä'läh *Anc.* * of Assyria; mod. **Nimrud**

Ca'lais (lā) *City* N France; manufacturing port

Cä-lä-trä'vä *Municipality* Negros, Phil. Is.

Cal'cå-sieu (shōō) *River* ab. 200 m. La., U.S.

Cal-cut'tå *City* NE India; former seat of government; seaport, educational cen.

Cal'ė-dön *River* 230 m. SE Africa

Cal'gå-rẏ *City* S Alberta, Canada; trade

Cä'li *City* W Colombia; trade cen.

Cal'i-cut *City* S India; port, calico

Cal-i-fôr'niä *State* W U.S.; * Sacramento; 155,652 sq. m.; pop. 19,953,134; div. into 58 counties; fruit, petroleum, mining

Cäl-lä'ō (cä-yä'ō) *City* on *Bay,* * of *Province* W Peru; port

Cal-tå-nis-set'tå *Commune* * of *Province* cen. Sicily, Italy

Cal'ū-met *Industrial area* NE Ill. and NW Ind., U.S.; incl. several cities nr. Chicago

Cal-va-dôs' *Department* NW France

Cal'vå-rẏ *Site* of Jesus' crucifixion nr. anc. Jerusalem

Cä-mä-guey' (g w ā') *City* * of *Province* E cen. Cuba; trade cen.

Cä - m ä- ri'nes (rē'),

Nôr'te and Sur (sōōr) *Provinces,* Luzon, Phil. Is.

Cam-bāy' *Town* at *Gulf,* * of *State,* W cen. India

Cam'bêr-well *City* SE Australia

Cam-bō'di-å *Kingdom* SE Asia; was part of Fr. Indo-China; 69,-900 sq. m.; pop. 6,700,000; * Phom Penh; agriculture, fish, forestry

Cam-brāi' *C i t y* N France; linen, cotton, lace

Cam'bri-å = Lat. name for WALES

Cam'bridge (brij) 1. *City* NE Mass., U.S.; pop. 100,361; commercial, manufacturing, educational cen. 2. *County* and *Municipal borough* E England; university

Cam'dėn *City* SW N.J., U.S.; pop. 102,551; port

Cam'ė-lot *Legendary* site of King Arthur's court, England or Wales

Ca-mė-rōōn' *Peak* 13,-350 ft. Nigeria

Ca-me-rōōn', Federal Republic of *Republic,* W Africa; 184,000 sq. m.; pop. 5,700,000; * Yaounde; tropical products

Cam'êr-ōōns, Ca-mė-roun' (rōōn') = *Former protectorate* (variously Germ., Brit., Fr.) W Africa now CAMEROON

Cä-mi-guin' (mē-gēn') *Island* off N Mindanao, Phil. Is.

Cä-mō'tes *Island group* and *Sea,* Phil. Is.

Cäm-pä'niä *Compartimento* S Italy; fertile mountainous area

Cam-pė'chė *City* * of *State* SE Mexico; woods, hides, sisal

Cam - pi'nå *Gran'dė*

(pē') *City* E Brazil

Cam-pi'nȧs (pē') *City* SE Brazil; coffee area

Cäm-pö-bäs'sō *Commune* * of *Province* cen. Italy

Cam-pō-bel'lō *Island* New Brunswick, Canada; F.D.R. summer home

Cam'pos (pōōs) *City* SE Brazil; trade cen.

Cā'naan (nȧn) *Area* of Palestine bet. Jordan R. and Mediterranean S.

Ca'nȧ-dȧ *Country, Dominion* of Brit. Commonwealth, N North America; 3,851,800 sq. m.; pop. 21,300,000; * Ottawa; 10 provinces and 2 territories; grain, livestock, fish, fur, minerals, lumber

Cȧ-nā'di-ȧn *River* 906 m. N.M.-Texas-Okla., U.S.

Cȧ-nal' Zōne *Territory* leased to U.S. for Panama Canal, cen. America

Cȧ-nâr'ẏ Islands *Island group* (Sp.) off NW Africa; agriculture

Cȧ-nav'êr-ȧl *Peninsula* E Fla., U.S.; site of Cape KENNEDY

Can'bêr-rȧ *City* * of Australia, SE part; pop. 124,500; farm area

Can'di-ȧ *City* N Crete; island's largest city

Cȧ-nē'ȧ *City* * of *Department* and * of *Crete*, N coast; port

Cannes (kan) *Commune* SE France; resort, port

Can'nŏck *Urban district* W cen. England; coal

Cän-tal' *Department* S cen. France

Can'têr-bur-ẏ (bêr) 1. *City* SE Australia. 2. *City* and county borough SE England; ecclesiastical cen.

Can'tŏn *City* NE Ohio, U.S.; pop. 110,053;

manufacturing

Can-ton', **Kwäng'chow'** (jō') *City* SE China; imp. port

Cä-pän'nö-ri *Commune* cen. Italy = group of villages

Cāpe Bret'ön *Cape* on *Island* Nova Scotia, E Canada; coal

Cāpe Cod *Peninsula* enclosing *Bay* SE Mass., U.S.

Cāpe Fear (fēr) *River* ab. 200 m. N.C., U.S.

Cāpe Hat'têr-ȧs *Point* on island, E N.C., U.S.

Cāpe of Good Hōpe *Cape* and *Province* S Rep. of South Africa

Cāpe Town *City* SW Rep. of South Africa; seaport

Cāpe Vêrde Islands (vêrd) *Island group* (Port.) off **Cāpe Vêrde**, W Africa

Cä'piz (pēs) *Municipality* * of *Province* Panay I., Phil. Is.

Cä'pri (prē) *Island* in Bay of Naples SE Italy

Cap'u-ȧ *Commune* S Italy; WW II fighting

Cȧ-rac'ȧs *City* * of Venezuela, N part; pop. 2,175,400

Car'dä-mön Hills *Range* S India

Cär'de-näs *City* on *Bay* W cen. Cuba; seaport

Cär'diff *County borough* SE Wales; industrial port

Cär'di-gȧn-shîre *County* W Wales; livestock, lead mines

Car-ib-bē'ȧn Sea *Arm* of Atlantic O. bet. N and S America

Car'i-bōō Mountains *Range* of Rocky Mts., Brit. Columbia, Canada

Car'i-bou Mountains (bōō) *Range* W Alberta, Canada

Cär'lisle (līl) *City* and county borough NW England; rail cen.

Cär'lōw *County* SE Eire

Cärls'bad 1. *City* SE N.M., U.S.; potash mines, caverns. 2. *City*, Austria, see KARLOVY VARY

Cär - mär'thèn - shîre *County* S Wales; farming, mining, quarrying

Cär-nä'rō *Former province* Italy; now in Croatia, Yugoslavia

Car'ō-līne Islands *Archipelago* (U.S. Trust Terr.) E of Phil. Is., W Pacific O.; incl. Yap, Truk, Easter I., Palau Is.

Cä-rō-ni' (nē') *River* 550 m. E Venezuela

Cär-pä'thi-ȧn Mountains *Mountain system* bet. Czechoslovakia and Poland

Cär-pä'thi-ȧn Rū-thē'ni-ȧ *Former province* E Czechoslovakia, part of Hungary, now in Ukraine, U.S.S.R.

Cär-pèn-târ'i-ȧ, Gulf of *Gulf* NE Australia

Cär-rä'rȧ *Former commune*, now part of APUANIA, Italy

Car'röt *River* ab. 220 m. Saskatchewan, Canada

Cär-shal'tön *Urban district* S England

Cär'sön *City* Cal., U.S.; pop. 71,150

Cär'sön City *City* * of Nevada W part; pop. 15,468; farming, lumbering, mining

Cär-tȧ-gē'nȧ (jē') 1. *City* NW Colombia; seaport. 2. *City* SE Spain; port

Cär'thage (thij) *Anc. city* and *State*, N Africa nr. mod. Tunis

Cas-ȧ-blan'cȧ *City* W Morocco; seaport

Cas-cāde' Mountains *Range* NW U.S.

Cas'cō Bay *Inlet* of Atlantic O., SW Me., U.S.

Cas'pêr *City* cen. Wyo.,

U.S.; pop. 39,361; oil industry

Cas'pi-ȧn Sea *Lake* bet. Eur. and Asia; world's largest inland body of water; 169,380 sq. m.

Cäs'sèl see KASSEL

Cȧs-si'nō (sē') *Commune* cen. Italy; WW II battle site

Cä - stel' Gän - dôl'fō *Commune* cen. Italy; papal palace

Cä-stel-läm-mä're di Stä'biä *Commune* S Italy; seaport

Cäs-tel-lon' de lä Plä'nä (tâ-yôn') *City* * of *Province* E Spain

Cas-tile' (tēl') *Region* and *Anc. kingdom* cen. Spain

Cas'tle-förd (cas"l) *Urban district* N England; manufacturing

Cas'tle Här'böur *Gulf* off NE Bermuda I.

Cas'tôr 1. *Peak* 13,879 ft., E peak of ZWILLINGE (Twins). 2. *Peak* 10,800 ft. NW Wyo., U.S.

Cäs'triēs *Town* * of Saint Lucia, Brit. Windward Is.

Cä'strôp - Rau'xèl (rouk') *City* W West Germany; coal, manufacturing

Cat-ȧ-lō'ni-ȧ *Hist. region* NE Spain

Cat-ȧ-mär'cȧ *Town* * of *Province* NW Argentina; farming, mining

Cä-tän-duä'nes *Island* off SE Luzon, Phil. Is.; agriculture

Cä-tä'niä *Commune* on *Gulf*, * of *Province* E Sicily, Italy; manufacturing

Cä-tän-zä'rō *City* * of *Province* S Italy

Cȧ-tăw'bȧ *River* ab. 250 m. N.C., U.S.

Cȧ-thāy' = old name for China during Middle Ages

Cats'kill Mountains

Range of Appalachians SE N.Y., U.S.

Cau'cä (cou') *River* 600 m. W Colombia

Cău-cä'sia (zhȧ) *Region* bet. Black S. and Caspian S., U.S.S.R.; incl. **Cău'cȧ-sus Mts.**, boundary bet. Eur. and Asia

Căul'fïeld *City* SE Australia, suburb of Melbourne

Cau'rä (cou') *River* 450 m. cen. Venezuela

Cău'vê-rẏ *River* 475 m. S India

Cȧ-val'lẏ *River* 300 m. W Africa

Cav'ȧn *County* N Eire; agriculture

Cä-vi'te (vē'tâ) *City* * of *Province* Luzon, Phil. Is.; WW II battles

Căwn'pōre *City* N India; industrial cen.

Cay-enne' (kī) *City* on *Island*, * of French Guiana

Căy'mȧn Islands *Island group* of Brit. West Indies

Ce-a-ra' (sä-ȧ-ra') *State* NE Brazil

Ce-bu' (sä-bōō') *City* * of *Province* on *Island*, E cen. Phil. Is.; harbor

Cĕ'dȧr (sē') *River* 329 m. Minn.-Iowa, U.S.

Cĕ'dȧr Rapids (sē') *City* E Iowa, U.S.; pop. 110,642; rail cen., manufacturing

Ceg'led (tseg'lād) *City* cen. Hungary

Cel'ê-bĕs (sel') *Island* S of *Sea*, Malay Arch., Indonesia; forest products

Cen'tral Af'ri-cȧn Republic (sen', kȧn) *Republic* (former *Terr.*) of Fr. Community, E cen. Africa; 238,000 sq. m.; pop. 2,300,-000; * Banqui; cotton, coffee

Cen'trȧl Ȧ-mer'i-cȧ (sen') *Area* bet. Mex-

ico, N America and Colombia, S America; incl. Guatemala, Honduras, Brit. Honduras, El Salvador, Nicaragua, Costa Rica, Panama

Cen'trȧl Grēēce and Eū-boē'ȧ (sen'grēs) *Division* cen. Greece

Cen'trȧl In'di-ȧ (sen') Group of states of Brit., India; * Indore

Cen'trȧl Pro'vince (sen') *Province* S cen. Ceylon; * Kandy; tea

Cen'trȧl Pro'vin-cês and Be-rär' *Former province* cen. India; now MA'DHYA PRADESH

Ceph-ȧ-lō'ni-ȧ (sef) *Island*, Ionian Is. W Greece

Ce'räm (sä') *Island* and *Sea*, cen. Moluccas, Indonesia

Ce'ri-gō (châ') *Island*, S Ionian Is. Greece

Cer'rô dê Päl-pä-när' (ser') *Mountain* 19,830 ft. N Chile

Cer'rô dê Päs'cō (ser') *Mountain* 15,000 ft. cen. Peru

Ce-se'nä (châ-zä') *Commune* N Italy; wine, sulphur, silk

Ces'ke Bu'de-jo-vi-ce (ches'kâ boo'dye-yộ-vi-tse) *City* W Czechoslovakia; breweries, manufacturing

Ceu'tä (sä'oo) *City* NW Sp. North Africa

Cey-lon' (sē) *Island*, see SRI LANKA

Cha-blis' (shä-blē') *Commune* NE cen. France; wine

Chä-chä'ni *Peak* 20,000 ft. S Peru

Chä'cō *Region* S cen. South America incl. parts of Bolivia, Paraguay, Argentina; swamp area

Chad, Republic of *Republic* (former *Terr.*) of Fr. Community,

N cen. Africa; 495,-600 sq. m.; pop. 3,-400,000; * Fort Lamy; ivory

Chad, Lake *Lake* W Chad; 10,000 sq. m.

Chal'cê-don (kal'sê) *Anc. city*, now KADIKOY

Chal-cid'i-ce (kal-sid'i-sē) *Peninsula* and *Department*, NE Greece

Chal'cis (kal'sis) *City* cen. Greece

Chal-dē'ȧ (kal) *Anc. region* on Persian Gulf, S Babylonia

Chä-lôns'-sur-Marne' (sha) *Commune* NE France; manufacturing

Chä-mär-tin' de lä Rô'-sä (tēn') *Commune* cen. Spain

Chȧm'bȧ *State* NW India; mountainous

Chȧm'bȧl *River* 650 m. cen. India

Cham-be-ry' (shän-bā-rē') *City* E France; commerce

Cha-mô-nix' (sha-mô-nē') *Valley* E France; winter sports

Cham-pagne' (shämpan'y') *Region*, former prov., NE France; wines

Cham-paign' (shampān') *City* E Ill., U.S.; pop. 56,532; commerce, industry

Cham-pläin' **Lake** (sham) *Lake* Vt.-N.Y., U.S., into Canada

Chȧb-dêr-nȧ-gôr' *Settlement* E India, formerly French

Chȧn'di-gärh *City* N India

Chäng'än' now SIAN

Chäng'chow' (jō') now LUNGKI

Chäng'chun' (choon') or **Hsin'king** (shin'jing') *City* S Manchuria; soybean trade

Chäng'shä' *City* SE cen. China; port; brass, linen, silk

Chäng'teh' (du') *City* SE cen. China; cen. of "rice bowl".

Chäng'tse' *Peak* 24,730 ft. Mt. Everest group S Tibet

Chan'nêl Islands *Islands* (Brit.) in English Channel; incl. Alderney, Guernsey, Jersey, Sark; cattle, agriculture

Chan-til-ly' (shän-tē-yē') *Commune* N France; lace

Chao'än' (chou') *City* SE China; river trade

Chao Phrä-yä (chou p'hrä) *River* 750 m. Thailand

Chao'tung' (jou'toong') *City* S China; commerce, mining

Chȧ-pa'êvsk *Town* U.S.S.R., Eur.

Chȧ'prä *Town* NE India; commerce

Chä-pul-te-pec' (pool) *Fortress* nr. Mexico City, Mexico

Chär-dzhou' (jō'oo) *Town* U.S.S.R., Asia; cotton trade

Cha-rente' (sha-ränt') *River* 225 m., and *Department* W France

Cha-rente'-Ma-ri-time' (sha-ränt', tēm') *Department* W France

Cha-ri' (sha-re') *River* 1400 m. into Lake Chad

Char'i-tön (shar') *River* 280 m. Iowa-Mo., U.S.

Chär-khȧ'ri *State* N cen. India

Chärles'tön 1. *City* SE S.C., U.S.; pop. 66,-945; port. 2. *City* * of W.Va. W cen. part, U.S.; pop. 71,505; industrial cen.

Chär'lotte (shär') *City* S N.C., U.S.; pop. 241,178; commerce, cotton industry

Chär'lotte Ȧ-mä'lie (shär', mäl'yê) *City* * of St. Thomas I. and * of U.S. Virgin Is., West Indies; port

Chär'löttes-ville *City* C Va., U.S.; pop. 38,-880; ed. cen.

Chär'lötte-town (sh, toun) *City* * of Prince Edward I., Canada

Chär'tres (tr') *City* N cen. France; cathedral, manufacturing

Cha - teau' Thier - ry' (shä-tō' tye-rē') *Commune* N France; battles 1814, 1870, 1918

Chat'ham *Municipal borough* SE England; naval cen.

Chat-tà-hōō'chēe *River* 410 m. Ga.-Ala.-Fla., U.S.

Chat-tà-nōō'gà *City* SE Tenn., U.S.; pop. 119,082; industrial port

Chau-mont' (shō-môn') *Commune* NE France; manufacturing

Chè-chen' - In-gush' A.S.S.R. (g ō ō s h') *Former republic* of U.S.S.R., Eur.

Che'fōō' (ju') *City* NE China; commercial port

Chè'jū *Town* on *Island* S Korea

Che'ki-äng' (ju'ji) *Province* E China coast

Che-liff' (shä-lēf') *River* 430 m. Algeria

Chelms'förd *Municipal borough* SE England; trade cen.

Chel'sea (si) *Borough* of London, England

Chel'tèn-ham ('am) *Municipal borough* SW England; spas

Chè-lya'binsk *City* * of *Region* R.S.F.S.R., Asia; industrial

Chem'nitz (kem') *City* SE East Germany; manufacturing

Che-näb' *River* 590 m. W Pakistan

Cheng'tu' (chung'dōō') *City* S cen. China; anc. city, fertile area

Cher'bourg (shâr'boorg) *City* NW France; port

Cher'chen' (ju-ur'-

chung') *River* ab. 420 m. W China

Chè-rem'khö-vö *Town* U.S.S.R. Asia; coal

Cher (shâr) *Department* cen. France

Cher-i-bon' *Town* * of *Residency* Java, Indonesia; rice port

Cher-kas'sÿ *City* cen. Ukraine U.S.S.R.; refineries

Cher-kessk' *Town* * of Cher-kess', Autonomous Reg., U.S.S.R. Eur.

Chèr-ni'göv (nyē') *City* * of *Region* Ukraine, U.S.S.R.; shoes, flour

Cher-ni'kövsk (nya') *City* U.S.S.R., Eur.; manufacturing

Cher-nôv'tsÿ *City* * of *R e g i o n* Ukraine, U.S.S.R.; cultural cen.

Ches'à-pēake *City* SE Va., U.S.; pop. 89,-580; residential

Ches'à-pēake Bāy *Bay*, inlet of Atlantic O., Md.-Va., U.S.

Chesh'ire *County* NW England; dairying, mining

Ches'têr 1. *City* SE Pa., U.S.; pop. 56,331; industrial port. 2. *City* and *County borough*, NW England; port, rail cen.

Ches'têr-fièld *Municipal borough* N cen. England; coal, iron

Chev'i-öt Hills *Hills*, English-Scottish border

Chey-enne' (shī) 1. *City* * of Wyo. (W cen.), U.S.; pop. 40,-914. 2. *River* 290 m. S.D., U.S.

Chhà'tar-pur (chu', poor) *State* cen. India

Chi-äng' Maī' *City* * of *Province* NW Thailand; trade cen.

Chi-an'ti Mountains (ki) *Range* cen. Italy; wines

Chiä'päs *State* SE Mexico

Chi'bà (chē') *City* * of *Prefecture* Honshu, Japan; trade

Chi-cä'gō (shi) *City* NE Ill., U.S.; pop. 3,366,-957; port; world's leading grain and livestock market

Chi-cä'gō Heights *City* NE Ill., U.S.; pop. 40,900; manufacturing, residential

Chi-ca'pà (shi) *River* 310 m. S Africa

Chic'ö-pēe *City* SW Mass., U.S.; pop. 66,-676; rubber products

Chie'ti (kyâ') *Province* cen. Italy; textiles

Chi-huä'huä (wä'wä) *City* * of *State* N Mexico; silver mines

Chil'ē, Republic of *Republic* SW South America; 286,396 sq. m.; pop. 9,000,000; * Santiago

Chil-lan' (che-yän') *City* S cen. Chile; trade

Chi-lo-e' (chē-lō-ā') *Island, Province* SW Chile; coal

Chim-bō-rä'zō *Peak* 20,702 ft. W cen. Ecuador

Chim-kent' *Town* Kazakh U.S.S.R.

Chī'nà formerly **Cà-thāy'** *Republic* since 1912, E cen. Asia; world's most populous country, 3rd largest in area; divided: 1. **Nationalist China** (**Rep. of China**) incl. Taiwan (Formosa) and the Pescadores Is.; * Taipei; 13,885 sq. m.; pop. 14,700,-000. 2. **Communist China** (**People's Rep. of China**) the mainland, * Peiping; 3,-691,502 sq. m.; pop. 780,000,000; div. into provinces and regions; textiles, agriculture, minerals

Chī'nà Sea Part of Pacific O. bet. Japan and Malay Penin.;

div. into **East** and **South China** S.

Chin'dwin' *River* 550 m. W Upper Burma

Ching'förd *Urban district* SE England

Chin'hsien' (jin'shyen') *T o w n* Manchuria; cattle trade

Chin'kiang' (jin'ji-äng') *City* E China; port

Chin-näm-pō *City* W North Korea; port

Chin'wäng'tao' (dou') *Town* NE China; port

Chiog'gia (kyôd'jä) *City* NE Italy; fishing

Chī'os (kī') *Island, Department* and *City* of Greece, Aegean S.

Chi-ta' *City* on *River* * of *Region*, U.S.S.R., Asia; minerals, timber

Chi-träl' *River* 300 m. India-Afghanistan

Chit'ta-gông *Town* * of *Division* E Pakistan; trade cen.

Chka'löv *City* * of *Region*, U.S.S.R., Eur.; trade cen.

Choi-seul' (shwa-zûl') *Island* of Solomon Is.

Chô'lôn' *City* S Vietnam; industrial

Chô'mô Lhä'ri *Peak* 23,930 ft. bet. Tibet and Bhutan

Chöng-jin *City* NE Korea; port

Chō-pi-côl'qui (kē) *Peak* 22,000 ft. Peru

Cho'rzow (ko'zhōōf) *City* SW Poland; nitrate, iron, coal

Chō-sen 1. Jap. for KOREA. 2. *Strait* connecting S. of Japan and Yellow S.

Chō-shi *Town* Honshu, Japan; port, fishing

Chow'tsun' (jō') *Town* NE China; port, silk industry

Christ'chûrch (krīst') *City* South I. New Zealand; grain cen.

Chris-ti-ä'nà (kr) *Town* E Rep. of South Africa; diamonds

Christ'màs I s l a n d

(kris') 1. *Island* (Brit.) Indian O. 2. *Island* (Brit.) Line Is. cen. Pacific O.

Chu (chōō) *River* 600 m. U.S.S.R., Asia

Chu-but' (choo-vōōt') *Territory* S Argentina

Chu-kôt' National District (choo) *District* U.S.S.R., Asia; incl. **Chu-kôt'ski Penin.**

Chū'là Vis'tà *City* SW Calif., U.S.; pop. 67,-901; fruit

Chu-lým' (choo) *River* 700 m. S i b e r i a U.S.S.R., Asia

Chung'hsien' (joong' shyen') *City* S cen. China; river port

Chung'king' (choong') or **Päh'hsien'** (shyen') *City* S China; trade port; * of China 1937-46.

Chûrch'ill *River* 1000 m. cen. Canada

Chûrch'ill Downs *Race track* Louisville Ky., U.S.

Chū' Sän' *Archipelago* East China S.; trade

Chu-sö-va'yà (c h o o) *River* 430 m. U.S.S.R. Asia

Chu'vash A. S. S. R. (chōō') *Republic* E cen. R. S. F. S. R., U.S.S.R., Eur.; lumber

Cic'êr-ō (sis') *City* NE Ill., U.S.; pop. 67,-058; engines

Cien-fue'gōs (s y â n-fwä') *Municipality* on Bay W cen. Cuba; sugar processing

Ci-li'ci-à (si-lish'i-à) *Anc. country* SE Asia Minor

Cim'àr-rōn (sim') *River* 600 m. N.M., U.S.

Ci-nä-rū'cō (sē) *River* 280 m. Colombia-Venezuela

Cin-cin-nat'i (sin-si) *City* SW Ohio, U.S.; pop. 452,524; trade, manufacturing

Cis-cáu-cä'sia (sis, zhá) *Region* N of Caucasus

Mts. U.S.S.R.

Ci-tläl-te'petl (sē, tä') *Peak* 18,700 ft. cen. Mexico

Ciu - däd' Bō - li'vär (syōō, lē') *City* SE Venezuela; port

Ciu-däd' Juä'rez (syōō, wä') *City* N Mexico

Ciu-däd' Re-al' (syōō) *Commune* * of *Province* S cen. Spain

Ciu - däd' Tru - jil'lo (syōō, trōō - hē'yō) *City* former name of * of Dominican Rep., now SANTO DO-MINGO

Ciu - däd' Vic - tō'ri - ä (syōō) *Town* cen. Mexico; sugar cen.

Ci-vi-ta-vec'chia (chē-vē-tä-vek'kiä) *City* cen. Italy; port

Clack - man'nàn - shîre *County* cen. Scotland

Clâre *County* W Eire

Clärk Fôrk *River* 300 m. Mont.-Ida., U.S.

Clēar' wätêr *City* WC Fla., U.S.; pop. 52,-074; business, resort

Cler-mont' - Fer-rand' (môn', rän') *City* S cen. France

Cleve or **Cleves** (klâv) *City* E West Germany; manufacturing

Clēve'land *City* N Ohio, U.S.; pop. 750,903; industrial port

Clēve'land Heights (hītz) *City* N Ohio; pop. 60,767; residential

Cli-chy' (klē-shē') *Commune* N France; chemicals, rubber

Clif'tôn *City* N.J., U.S.; pop. 82,437; factories

Cluj (klōōzh), **Klau'sèn-bûrg** (klou') *City* cen. Romania; industry

Clýde *River* S Scotland into **Firth of Clýde**

Clýde'bank *Burgh* W cen. Scotland; shipbuilding

Cō-ä-hui'là (wē') *State* NE Mexico

Cōast Ranges *Moun-*

tains W North America

Cōat'bridge (brij) *Burgh* S cen. Scotland; coal, iron

Cō'blenz see **KO-BLENZ**

Cō'bûrg 1. *City* SE Australia. 2. *City* E West Germany; manufacturing

Co-cà-nä'dà *City* E India; exports

Cō-chä-bäm'bä *City* * of *Department* cen. Bolivia; trade cen.

Cō'chin *Town* in *Region*, former *State*, SW India

Cō'chin Chī'nà *Area* of S Vietnam, formerly of Fr. Indo-China

Coi or **Sông' koi'** (**Red River**) *River* 500 m. SE Asia

Coim'bà-tōre' *City* S India; mills, factories

Cō-im'bra *City* * of *District* cen. Portugal; earthenware

Cōl'ches-têr *Municipal borough* SE England; oysters, farming

Cō-li'mä (lē') *Volcano* 12,790 ft. W cen. Mexico

Cōl'mär *Commune* NE France; textiles

Cō-logne' (lōn') *City* W West Germany; imp. industrial port

Cô-lômbes' (lômb') *Commune* N France; Paris suburb

Cō-löm'bi-à, Republic of *Republic* NW South America; 455,-000 sq. m.; pop. 21,-100,000; * Bogota; 14 departments, 6 commissaries, 4 intendancies; agriculture, esp. coffee, forest products, minerals

Cō-löm'bō *City* * of Sri Lanka; pop. 551,-200; port

Cō-lōn' *City* * of *Province* N cen. Panama; port

Col-ö-rä'dō 1. *River*

1450 m. SW U.S. 2. *River* 840 m. Texas, U.S. 3. *State* W cen. U.S.; 103,658 sq. m.; pop. 2,207,259; * Denver; 63 counties; mining, livestock. 4. *Desert* SE Cal., U.S.

Col-ö-rä'dō Springs *City* E cen. Col., U.S.; pop. 135,060; site of U.S. Air Force Academy

Cö-lum'bi-à 1. *River* 1270 m. W Canada and U.S. 2. *City* * of S.C. (W cen.), U.S.; pop. 113,542; manufacturing. 3. *City* cen. Mo., U.S.; pop. 58,-804; farm area

Cö-lum'bus 1. *City* W Ga., U.S.; pop. 154,-168; cotton mills. 2. *City* * of Ohio (cen.) U.S.; pop. 539,677; trade, manufacturing

Col'ville *River* 320 m. Alas., U.S.

Cöm-man'dêr Islands = KOMANDORSKIE

Com'mū-nist P e a k *Peak* 24,590 ft. U.S.S.R., Asia; was Stalin Peak

Cō'mō *Province* and *Commune* at *Lake* N Italy; resort area

Com'ö-rō Islands *Islands* (Fr.) bet. Mozambique and Madagascar

Comp'tön *City* SW Cal. U.S.; pop. 78,611; glass, steel

Con'à-krý *Town* * of Guinea; pop. 172,500; port

Côn-cep-cion' (s e p-syôn') *City* * of *Province* cen. Chile

Côn'chôs *River* 300 m. N Mexico

Con'côrd 1. *City* * of N.H., U.S.; pop. 30,-022; manufacturing, granite. 2. *Town* NE Mass., U.S. 3. *City* W Cal., U.S.; pop. 85,-164; diversified retailing

Côn-côr'diä *City* E Argentina

Cō'ney Island (ni) *Resort* Brooklyn, N.Y., U.S.

Con'gō *River* ab. 3000 m. W Africa now **Zaire**

Con'gō, Republic of the *Republic* (formerly *Terr.*) of Fr. Community, W cen. Africa; * Brazzaville; 132,000 sq. m.; pop. 920,000; wood processing, potash, farming

Con'gō, Democratic Rep. of the *Republic* see ZAIRE

Con'nacht (ut) *Province* NW Eire

Con-nect'i-cut (net') 1. *River* 400 m. NE U.S. 2. *State* E U.S.; * Hartford; 4,820 sq. m.; pop. 3,032,217; 8 counties; insurance, manufacturing

Con'stance = KONSTANZ

Côn-stän'tä (tsä) *City* SE Romania; petroleum export

Côns-tän-tine' (tēn') *City* * of *Department* NE Algeria

Con-stan-ti-nō'ple (p'l) = ISTANBUL

Con-ti-nen'täl Di-vide' *Watershed* of North America: N.M.-Colo.-Wyo. - Ida. - Mont. - Canada; drainage to east or to west

Cooch Be-här' *State* NE India; rice, tobacco

Cook, Mount *Mountain* 13,700 ft. SE Alas., U.S.

Cook Inlet *Inlet* of Pacific O. S Alas., U.S.

Cook Islands *Island* group S Pacific O.; bel. to New Zealand

Cōō'lidge Dam (lij) *Dam* of Gila R., Ariz., U.S.

Coo'pêrs-town (toun) *Village* cen. N.Y., U.S.; site of Baseball Hall of Fame

Cōō'sä *River* 285 m. Ala., U.S.

Cō-pėn-hä'gėn *City* * of Denmark (E coast) pop. 875,000

Cop'pêr *River* 300 m. S Alas., U.S.

Cor'äl Sea *Area* of Pacific O. bet. Australia and New Hebrides

Cor'äl Gäbles *City* S Fla., U.S.; pop. 42,-494; residential, ed. center

Côr'cö-rän, Mount *Peak* 14,040 ft. SE cen. Cal., U.S.

Côr'dö-bä 1. *City* * of *Province* N cen. Argentina; industrial cen. 2. or **Côr'dö-vä** *City* * of *Province* S Spain; gold, silver

Côr-fū' *City* on *Island* within *Department* Ionian Is. off NW Greece; olives, fruits

Cor'inth *City, Gulf, Subdivision* S Greece

Côrk *City* * of *County* SW Eire; port

Côr-niche' (nēsh') *Road* (3 parallel highways) along Riviera, S Eur.

Côr'ning *City* S N.Y., U.S.; glassware

Côrn'wäll *County* SW England

Cor-ö-man'del Coast *Coast* SE India

Cō-rö-nä'dä Bay *Inlet* of Pacific O. W Costa Rica

Cō-rö-nel' *City* S cen. Chile; coal cen., port

Côr'pus Chris'ti (kris') *City* on *Bay*, S Texas, U.S.; pop. 204,525

Cör-reg'i-dôr *Island* Manila Bay, Phil. Is.; WW II battle

Côr-reze' (räz') *Department* S cen. France

Côr-rien'tes (ryän'tâs) *City* * of *Province* NE Argentina

Côrse *Department* SE France = CORSICA

Côr'si-cä *Island* (Fr.) Mediterranean S. off

SE France; wine, olives, citrus fruits

Côr-val'lis *City* W Ore., U.S.; pop. 35,153; ed. center

Cö-sen'zä *Commune* * of *Province* S Italy

Cos'tä Me'sä (mä') *City* Cal., U.S.; pop. 72,-660

Cos'tä Ri'cä, Republic of (rē') *Republic* S Cen. America; 20,240 sq. m.; pop. 1,800,-000; * San Jose; crops esp. coffee, lumber

Cō-tä-bä'tō *Province* Mindanao Phil. Is.

Côte d'A-zūr' *French coast* of Mediterranean S. [E France

Côte-d'Ôr' *Department*

Côtes-du-Nord' (kōt-du-nôr') *Department* NW France

Cō-tö-pax'i *Volcano* 19,-500 ft. cen. Ecuador

Cott'bus *City* East Germany; cloth, rail cen.

Coun'cil Bluffs (sil) *City* SW Iowa, U.S.; pop. 60,348; grain trade, nurseries

Cour'än-tȳne (cōr') *River* ab. 300 m. N South America

Cöv'ėn-trȳ *City* and *county borough* cen. England; machinery

Cöv'ing-tön *City* N Ky., U.S.; pop. 52,535

Crä-iô'vä *City* S Romania; industrial cen.

Cran'stön *City* N R.I., U.S.; pop. 73,037

Crä'têr Lake *Lake* S Ore., U.S.; National Park

Crēe *Lake* Saskatchewan, Canada

Cre-mō'nä *Commune* * of *Province* N Italy; manufacturing

Crēte or **Can'di-ä** *Island, Division* of Greece, E Mediterranean S.; fruits

Creuse (krŭz) *Department* cen. France

Crewe (krōō) *Municipal borough* NW Eng-

land; rail cen.

Crī-mē'ä *Peninsula, Former republic* S U.S.S.R., Eur.; agriculture

Cris-tō'bäl *Town* in *District*, NW Canal Zone [SE Europe

Crō-ā'tia (sha) *Region*

Crō-ā'tia, Peoples Republic of (shä) *Republic* NW Yugoslavia; * Zagreb

Crôss *River* 300 m. Nigeria-Cameroons

Croy'dön (kroi') *County borough* S England; manufacturing

Crô-zet' Islands (ze') *Islands* (Fr.) S Indian O. [cen. Angola

Cuän'zä *River* 500 m.

Cū'bä, Republic of *Island Republic* West Indies; 44,200 sq. m.; pop. 7,900,000; * Havana; sugar, tobacco, textiles

Cu'cu-tä (cōō'cōō) *City* N Colombia

Cud'dä-lōre *Town* SE India; port

Cuen'cä (cwäng') 1. *City* S Ecuador; panama hats. 2. *Commune* * of *Province* E cen. Spain

Cuer-nä-vä'cä *Town* S cen. Mexico; caverns

Cu-iä-bä' (cōō) *River* 300 m. SW Brazil

Cui'tō (cwē') *River* 400 m. Angola, SW Africa

Cū-mä-nä' *City* N Venezuela; port

Cum'bêr-länd 1. *River* 687 m. Ky.-Tenn., U.S. 2. *County* NW England; coal, iron

Cu-ne'nî (cōō-nä') *River* 700 m. Angola

Cu'ne-ō (cōō'nä) *Commune* * of *Province* NW Italy

Cu-rä-cao' (coor-ä-sou') *Island* of Netherlands Antilles

Cu-rä-ray' (cōō-rä-rī') *River* 490 m. Ecuador-Peru

Cu-ri-ti'bä (cōō-ri-tē')

City S Brazil

Cur'rent *River* 250 m. Mo.-Ark., U.S.

Cûr'zön Line *Boundary* U.S.S.R.-Poland

Cutch *State* and *Peninsula* W India; salt

Cut'tåck *City* E India; silver work

Cuy-å-hōg'å Fǎlls (cå'hōg') *City* NE Ohio, U.S.; pop. 49,678; rubber items

Cu-yū'ni (cōō) *River* 300 m. N South America

Cuz'cō (cōōs') *Peak* 17,800 ft. SW Bolivia

Cỳc'lå-dēs (sic') *Department Island group* (ab. 220) of Greece; S Aegean S.

Cy'prus (sī') *Island Republic* (former colony) of Brit. Commonwealth E Mediterranean S.; 3572 sq. m.; pop. 630,000; * Nicosia; farming, minerals

Czech - ö - slö - vä'ki - å (chek) *Socialist republic* cen. Europe; 49,375 sq. m.; pop. 14,200,000; * Prague; farming, mining, industry

Cze-stô-cho'wa (chenstô-kô'vä) *City* S cen. Poland; manufacturing

D

Dac'cå *City* * Bangladesh; muslin, jewelry

Dä'chau (kou) *Town* S West Germany; WW II concentration camp

Dag'en-håm (åm) *Urban district* SE England; automobiles

Dag-es-tan' A.S.S.R. *Republic* R.S.F.S.R., U.S.S.R., Eur.; cattle

Dä-gū'pän *Municipality* Luzon, Phil. Is.; port

Då-hō'mey, Republic of (mi) *Republic* (former Fr. terr.) W Africa; 45,000 sq. m.; pop.

2,600,000; * Porto Novo; palm oil, cotton, coffee

Daï'ren' (dī') or **Ta'lien'** (dä') *City* E China; Yellow S. port

Dä-kär' *City* * of Senegal, W part; seaport

Då-kō'tå or **Jāmes** *River* 710 m. N.D. and S.D., U.S.

Däl *River* 250 m. S cen. Sweden

Dal-hou'sie (zi) *Town* New Brunswick, Canada; resort

Dal'lås *City* NE Texas, U.S.; pop. 844,401; oil and insurance cen. cotton trade, manufacturing

Dal-mā'ti-å (shå) *Coastal area* of Yugoslavia

Dä'lỳ *River* 300 m. N Australia

Dä'lỳ City *City* W Calif. U.S.; pop. 66,922

Då-mas'cus *City* * of Syria, SW part; pop. 800,000; anc. city

Dam-ï-et'tå *City* N Egypt; port

Dä'mö-där *River* 350 m. NE India

Då Nang *U.S. base* South Vietnam

Dan'bûrỳ *City* SW Conn., U.S.; pop. 50,781; manufacturing

Dan'übe *River* 1725 m. cen. Eur.

Dan'ville 1. *City* E Ill., U.S.; pop. 42,570; trade cen. 2. *City* S Va., U.S.; pop. 46,391; tobacco market

Dan'zig, Gdänsk *City* on *Gulf* N Poland

Där-bhån'gå *City* NE India; trade cen.

Där-då-nelles' (nelz'), anc. **Hel'les-pont** *Strait* W Turkey, separates Eur.-Asia

Där-di-stän' *Region* N India and Pakistan

Där' es Så-läam' *District* and *City* E Tanganyika

Dä-rien' (ryän') 1.

Early name of PANAMA. 2. **Gulf of** *Inlet* of Caribbean S. Panama-Colombia

Där-jēe'ling *District* and *Town* NE India

Där'ling 1. *River* 1160 m. SE Australia. 2. *Range* SW Western Australia

Där'ling-tön *County borough* N England; rail cen., iron, steel

Därm'städt (shtät) *City* S cen. West Germany; manufacturing; former * of Hesse

Därt'moor *Tableland* SW England

Där'win, formerly Pôrt Där'win and **Pälm'erstön** *City* * of Northern Terr., Australia

Dasht'-i-Ka-vir' (vēr') = **Greāt Sǎlt Desert** N cen. Iran

Dāte Līne hypothetical N-S line ab. 180° from Greenwich, England; place where each day begins

Då'ti-å *State* N cen. India

Dau'gåv-pils (dou') or **Dvinsk** *City* E Latvia, U.S.S.R.; trade

Dau-phi-ne' (dō-fē-nā') *Alps* in *Hist. region* and *Former province* SE France

Dä'vao (vou) *City* on *Gulf*, * of *Province* Mindanao, Phil. Is.; volcanic soil; hemp

Dav'en-pôrt *City* E Iowa, U.S.; pop. 98,469; trade, industrial cen., cereals

Då'vis Strait *Strait* bet. Baffin I.-Greenland

Då-wa' *River* 370 m. S Ethiopia

Dǎw'sön 1. *City* Yukon Terr. N Canada; gold rush 1898. 2. *River* 380 m. E Australia

Dāy'tön *City* SW Ohio, U.S.; pop. 243,601

Dāy-tō'nå Bēach *City* E Fla., U.S.; pop. 45,327; winter resort

Dead Sea (ded) *Lake* bet. Israel and Jordan

Dēar'bôrn *City* SE Mich., U.S.; pop. 104,199; automobiles

Dēar'bôrn Heïghts *City* SE Mich., U.S.; pop. 80,069

Death Valley (deth) *Valley* Cal., U.S.; lowest point in U.S.

De'bre-cen (tsen) *City* E Hungary

De-cātûr 1. *City* cen. Ill., U.S.; pop. 90,397; corn, iron area. 2. *City* N Ala., U.S.; pop. 38,044; diversified manufacturing

Dec'cån name given to penin. of India and former states S of Narbada R.

Dēe *River* 90 m. NE Scotland; salmon

Dēep Crēek Lake *Lake*, artificial, Md., U.S.

Deh'rå Dun (dā', dōōn) *Town* N India

Del'å-wāre 1. *River* 296 m. Pa.-Del., U.S. 2. *State* E cen. U.S.; 1955 sq. m.; pop. 548,104; * Dover; 3 counties

Del'å-wāre Wǎ'ter Gap *Gorge* Pa.-N.J., U.S.

Delft *Commune* SW Netherlands; pottery

Del'hi (i) *City* now NEW DELHI

Del'men-hôrst *Commune* N cen. West Germany; manufacturing

De'los *Island*, smallest of the Cyclades S Aegean S.

Del'phï (fī), **Del-phoi'** (fē') *Town* S Greece

Dem'å-vend *Mountain* 18,550 ft. N Iran

De-mē'tri-ås *Anc. city* NE Greece

Den'bigh-shïre (bi) *County* N Wales

Den'märk 1. *Kingdom* NW Europe incl. Jutland Penin., Greenland, Faroe and Baltic S. islands; 16,619 sq. m.; pop. 4,900,-

000; * Copenhagen; 22 counties; dairying, fishing, brewing. 2. **Strait** bet. Greenland and Iceland

Den′tŏn *City* NE Texas, U.S.; pop. 39,-874; ed. center

Den′vêr *City* * of Colo., NE cen. Colo., U.S.; pop. 514,678

Der′bẏ (där′) *County borough* * of **Der′bẏ-shîre** county, N cen. England

Des-chutes′ (dȧ-shōōt′) *River* 250 m. Ore., U.S.

De-se-ä′dō (dȧ) *River* 300 m. S Argentina

De-shi-mä *Island* (artificial) Nagasaki harbor, Japan

Des Moines′ (dė moin′) 1. *City* * of Iowa S cen. part, U.S.; pop. 200,587; corn, coal area. 2. *River* 327 m. Iowa-uo., U.S.

Des-nä′ *River* 550 m. U.S.S.R., Eur.

Dės Plaines (dė) *City* NE Ill., U.S.; pop. 57,239; residential

Des′sau (sou) *City* cen. East Germany

Dė-troit′ *City* SE Mich. U.S.; pop. 1,511,482

Deur′nė (dûr′) *Commune* N Belgium

Deut′sches Reich′ (doi′, r ī k′) **Deutsch′länd** (doich′) = GERMANY

Deux-Sevres′ (du-sä′-vr′) *Department* W France

Dev′il′s Island *Island* off N Fr. Guiana

De′vėn-têr (dā′) *Commune* E Netherlands

De′vŏn Island *Island* Northwest Terrs., Canada

Dev′ŏn-shîre *County* SW England; farming, mining, livestock, textiles

De-wäs′ *Two states* cen. India

Dews′bur-ẏ (dūz′bêr)

County borough N England; iron, wool

Dhär *State* cen. India

Dhȧ′rȧm-pur (p o o r) *State* W India

Dhär-wär′ *Town* W India; cotton

Dhau′lȧ-gi′rĭ, Mount (dou′) *Peak* 26,800 ft. N India

Dhen-kä′näl (dän) *State* NE India

Dhōl′pur (poor) *State* NW India

Dhrän′gȧ-dhrä *State* W India

Dĭ-ȧ-mȧn-tĭ′nȧ (tē′) *River* 470 m. E Australia

Dĭ′ȧ-mŏnd Head *Cape* Honolulu harbor Hawaii, U.S.

Die′gō - Suä′rez (dyä′) *Town* N Madagascar; one of world's best harbors

Di-eppe′ (ep′) *City* N France; port, ivory

Di′göel (dē′gool) *River* 400 m. SE Irian

Di-jon′ (dē-zhôn′) *City* E France; trade, manufacturing

Di-näj′pur (poor) *Former district* Brit. India; now div.: Pakistan and India

Di-nar′ic Alps *Range*, Yugoslavia, parallel to Adriatic

Din′di-gul *Town* S India; tobacco cen.

Din′gle Bay (g′l) *Inlet* of Atlantic O. SW Eire

Dĭ′ŏ-mēde Islands *Islands* (2) B e r i n g Strait; one Russ.; one Amer.

Dis′kō *Island* W Greenland; coal

Dis′trict of Cö-lum′bi-ȧ *Federal district* E cen. U.S.; coextensive with U.S. *, Washington; 69 sq. m.; pop. 756,510

Dix′ie (dik′si) refers to S States of U.S.

Di-ya′la *River* 300 m. E Iraq

Di-yär-be-kir′ (kēr′) *City* SE Turkey, Asia; trade cen.

Djȧ-kär′tȧ formerly **Bȧ-tä′vi-ȧ** *City* N Java, * of Indonesia; pop. 4,774,000; imp. port

Djäm′bi *Town* Sumatra, Indonesia; oil

Djer′bȧ *Island* cen. Mediterranean S.; fruit

Dji-bou′ti (bōō′) *City* * Fr. Terr. of Afars and Issas; port

Djok - jȧ - kär′tȧ = JOGJAKARTA

Dmi′tri - ev (di - mē′) *Town* U.S.S.R., Eur.

Dne - prö-dzêr - zhinsk′ (nep-rö-dêr′) *City* Ukraine, U.S.S.R.

Dne - prö - pė - trôvsk′ (nep-rö) *City* * of *R e g i o n* Ukraine, U. S. S. R.; wheat trade, manufacturing

Dne-prö-stroi′ (nep-rö) *Dam* across Dnieper R. Ukraine; hydroelectric plant

Dnie′pêr (nē′) *River* 1400 m. R.S.F.S.R., U.S.S.R., Eur.

Dnies′têr (nēs′) *River* 850 m. U.S.S.R., Eur.

Dō′ce (sė) *River* 360 m. E Brazil

Dō-dec′ȧ-nēse *Island group* (Gk.) SE Aegean S.

Dō′hȧ *Town* * of Qatar

Dol′ö-mītes (m ī t s) *Range* of Alps NE Italy

Dö-lō′rės *River* 230 m. SW Colo., U.S.

Dōm *Peak* 14,940 ft. SW cen. Switzerland

Dom-i-ni′cȧ (nē′) *Island*, Brit. colony, Brit. West Indies; * Roseau; forests

Dö-min′i-cȧn Republic *Republic* E Hispaniola I., West Indies; 19,300 sq. m.; pop. 4,000,000; * Santo Domingo; agriculture, livestock

Dôn *River* 1200 m. U.S.S.R. Eur.

Don′bas or **Dö-nets′ Bȧ′sin** *Region* E Ukraine, U.S.S.R.

Don′cȧs-têr *County borough* N England; coal

Don Cos′sȧcks Territory *Region* of Don R., U.S.S.R.

Don′ė-gȧl *County* N Eire; fish, farming, livestock

Dö-nets′ *River* 670 m. U.S.S.R., Eur.; also see DONBAS

Don′nẏ-brook *Suburb* of Dublin, Eire

Dôr-dogne′ (dôn′y′) *Department* and *River* 300 m. SW France

Dôr′drecht (drekt) or **Dôrt** *Commune* SW Neth.; trade, shipping cen.

Dôr′set-shîre *County* S England; farming, sheep, fish, quarries

Dôrt see DORDRECHT

Dôrt′mund (moont) *City* N cen. West Germany; mining, industrial, trade cen.

Dō′thȧn *City* SE Ala., U.S.; pop. 36,733; manufacturing

Dou-ai′ (dōō-ā′) *City* N France; manufacturing, educational cen.

Dou-ä′lȧ (dōō) *Town* Cameroon; port

Doubs (dōō) *Department* and *River* 270 m. E France

Dou′ro (dō′rōō), **Due′rō** (dwä′) *River* 485 m. Spain-Portugal

Dō′vêr 1. *City* * of Del., U.S.; pop. 17,488. 2. *Municipal borough* SE England

Dō′vêr, Strait of *Channel* SE England-N France

Down *County* SE Northern Ireland; farming, livestock, granite

Down′ey (i) *City* SW Cal., U.S.; pop. 88,-445 [England

Downs, The *Hills* S

GAZETTE ATLAS

Drāke Passage *Strait* bet. Cape Horn and S Shetland Is., S America

Drä-mä *City* * of *Department* N Greece

Dräm'mėn *City* S Norway; port; mills

Drän-cy' (sē') *Commune* N France

Drä'vä, Drau (drou) *River* 450 m. Austria-Yugoslavia

Dres'dėn (drez') *City* SE East Germany; cultural, manufacturing cen.

Drö-gö-bých' *City* in *Region* Ukraine, U.S.S.R.; trade cen.

Drôme *Department* SE France

Drum'mönd Island *Island* Lake Huron, U.S.

Du-băwnt' (dōō) *River* 580 m. and *Lake*, N cen. Canada

Dub'lin *City* on *Bay*, * of *County* and * of Rep. of Ireland (Eire), E part; pop. 569,000; shipbuilding, glass, iron, breweries

Du-buque' (būk') *City* E Iowa, U.S.; pop. 62,309; Miss. R. port

Dud'ley (li) *County borough* W cen. England; coal, bricks, brass, iron

Duis'bûrg (dooz') *City* W West Germany; imp. Rhine port

Du-lä'wän (dōō) *Municipality* Mindanao Phil. Is.

Dul'ce (dōōl'sä) *River* 360 m. N Argentina

Du-luth' (lōōth') *City* NE Minn., U.S.; pop. 100,578; lake port, industrial cen.

Dum'bär-tön Oaks (ōks) *Mansion* Washington, D.C., U.S.; site of UN planning meeting 1944

Dum' Dum *Town* NE India; ammunition

Dum-fries'shire (frēs')

County S Scotland; farming, livestock

Dū-nå-gi'ri *Mountain* 23,180 ft. Himalayas N India

Dū'näv-skä *Former county* NE Yugoslavia

Dun - bär'tön - shire *County* W cen. Scotland; livestock, coal, textiles, ships

Dun'dălk Bay *Inlet* of Irish S. NE Eire

Dun-dēe' *Burgh* E Scotland; port, manufacturing

Dun-ē'din *City* South I. New Zealand; port

Dun-fêrm'ling (lin) *Burgh* E Scotland; manufacturing

Dun'gär-pur (doong', poor) *State* NW India

Dun-kêrque' (kêrk'), **Dun'kirk** *City* N France; port; WW II site

Dun Laogha'rė (lâ'), **Dun-lēa'rý** *City borough* E Eire; cattle port, fisheries

Du-ran'gō *City* * of *State* NW cen. Mexico; farm, mine, lumber cen.

Dûr'bån *City* E Natal, Rep. of South Africa; port

Dûr'håm (åm) 1. *City* NE cen. N.C., U.S.; pop. 95,438; cotton, tobacco market. 2. *County* N England; coal, iron, steel

Dus'sėl-dôrf (dōō') *City* and *District* NW West Germany; Rhine port

Dutch East Indies = INDONESIA

Dutch Gui-a'na (gi-an'å) = SURINAM

Dutch Här'bör *Village* E Aleutian Is., U.S.; port, naval base

Dutch New Gui'nea (gi'ni) = IRIAN

Dutch West Indies = NETHERLANDS ANTILLES

Dvi-nä' 1. *River* 630 m. U.S.S.R. N Eur. 2. *Gulf* N U.S.S.R., Eur.

Dvinsk = DAUGAV-PILS

Dwär'kä *City* W India; sacred city, port

Dýkh' Tau (tou) *Mountain* 17,080 ft. U.S.S.R., Eur.

Dzau-dzhi'kau (dzou-jē'kou) *City* R.S.F.S.R., U.S.S.R., Eur.; industry, trade

Dzer - zhinsk' (dyer) *City* R.S.F.S.R., U.S.S.R., Eur.

Dzham - bul' (bōō·l') *Town* * of *Region* U.S.S.R., Asia

Dzhir-gä-län-tu' (tōō') *Town* W Outer Mongolia; imp. trade cen.

E

Ēa'ling *Municipal borough* SE England

Ēast, the = Countries of Asia, the Orient

Ēast An'gli-å *Kingdom* of Anglo-Saxon England; mod. Norfolk and Suffolk

Ēast Ben'gål *Region* E Pakistan; former prov. of Brit. India

Ēast'bourne (bōrn) *County borough* S England; resort

Ēast Chi-cä'gō (shi) *City* NW Ind., U.S.; pop. 46,982; manufacturing

Ēast Clēve'lånd *City* N Ohio, U.S.; pop. 39,-600; electrical products

Ēast Dė-troit' *City* SE Mich., U.S.; pop. 45,920

Ēas'tėr Island *Island* (Chile) S Pacific O.

Ēas'têrn Hem'i-sphēre (sfēr) = E half of earth incl. Eur., Asia, Africa, Australia

Ēas'têrn Range (rānj) = KAMCHATKA MTS.

Ēas'têrn States 1. *States*

(6) of New England, NE U.S. 2. *States* of U.S. along Atlantic O. 3. *States* of India (NE) former agency

Ēast Flan'dêrs *Province* NW cen. Belgium; wheat, flax

Ēast Gêr'må-ný (jêr') = GERMAN DEMOCRATIC REP.

Ēast Ham *County borough* SE England; docks

East Härt'förd *Town* N Conn., U.S.; pop. 57,583; manufacturing, residential

Ēast In'dies refers to INDOCHINA; sometimes incl. all SE Asia

Ēast Lan'sing *City* S Mich., U.S.; pop. 47,540; educational cen.

Ēast Lön'dön *City* S Rep. of South Africa

Ēast Lō'thi-ån *County* SE Scotland

Ēast'main *River* 375 m. E Canada

Ēast Or'ange (inj) *City* NE N.J., U.S.; pop. 75,471

Ēast-phal'i-å (fäl') E part of anc. Saxony, Germany

Ēast Point *City* NW cen. Ga., U.S.; pop. 39,315

Ēast Prov'i-dence *City* R.I., U.S.; pop. 48,-151; industrial

Ēast River *Strait* Manhattan - Brooklyn - Queens, N.Y. City, U.S.

Ēast Sāint Lou'is (lōō') *City* SW Ill., U.S.; pop. 69,996; manufacturing, livestock

Eau Clâire' (ō) *City* W Wisc., U.S.; pop. 44,-987; lumber cen.

E'brō (ā') *River* 480 m. NE Spain

Ec'cles ('lz) *Municipal borough* W England

Ech'ō Can'yön (ek') *Ravine* NE Utah, U.S.

Ec'uȧ-dôr *Republic* NW South America; 116,200 sq. m.; pop. 6,100,000; * Quito; 17 provs. and 1 terr.; coffee, cacao, petroleum, minerals

Ē'dam *Commune* W Netherlands

Ē'dē (ā') 1. *Commune* E Netherlands. 2. *City* W Nigeria

E-dī'nȧ *Village* E Minn., U.S.; pop. 44,046; residential

Ed'in-burgh (bur-ö) *City* and *Burgh* * of Scotland, SE part; pop. 468,000; printing, publishing cen.

E-dir'nè *City* * of *Vilayet* NW Turkey, Eur.; trade, manufacturing

Ed'mȯn-tȯn 1. *City* * of Alberta, NW Canada; rail, air cen.; fur trade. 2. *Municipal borough* SE England

Ē'döm *Anc. country* S of Dead S.

Ed'wȧrd, Lake *Lake* E cen. Africa

E-fä'te *Island* New Hebrides Is. administrative cen.

Ē'gẏpt (jipt), now **Ū-nī'ted A'rȧb Republic** *Country*, anc. *Kingdom* NE Africa and Sinai Penin, Asia; 386,200 sq. m.; pop. 34,000,000; * Cairo; cotton, grain, vegetables

E-hi-me *Prefecture*, Shikoku, Japan

Eind'hō-vȧn (īnt') *Commune* S Netherlands; electrical equipment

Ei'rȧ (ā')=IRELAND, REPUBLIC OF

Ei'sè-näck (ī'zė-näk) *City* SW East Germany; manufacturing

Eis'le-bȧn (īs'lä) *City* W cen. East Germany

El Al-ȧ-mein' (mān') *Village* N Egypt

Ē'lath now 'AQABA

El'bȧ *Island* W cen. Italy; iron-ore

El'bė *River* 720 m. Czechoslovakia - Germany

El'bêrt, Mount *Peak* 14,431 ft. Colo., U.S.

El'blag (blông), **El'bing** *City* N Poland, formerly Germany; port

El-bö-rus' (rōōz'), **El-brus'** (brōōz') *Mountain* 18,480 ft.; Europe's highest; Caucasus Mts., U.S.S.R.

El-burz' Mts. *Range* N Iran

El Cȧ-jōn (hōn') *City* S Cal., U.S.; pop. 52,273; residential

El'che (chä') *City* SE Spain; dates, manufacturing

El'ė-phant (fȧnt) *River* 250 m. South-West Africa

El-ė-phan-tī'ne (fan) *Island* Nile R. Egypt

El Faï-yum' (yōōm') *Town* Upper Egypt

El Fer-rôl' *City* NW Spain; harbor

El'gin (jin) *City* NE Ill., U.S.; pop. 55,691; butter, watches

El'gon, Mount *Peak* 14,175 ft. E cen. Africa

E-lis'ȧ-beth-vïlle (liz') *Town* * of *Province* (now KATANGA) SE Rep. of Congo (L)

E-liz'ȧ-beth *City* NE N.J., U.S.; pop. 112,654; manufacturing

Elk'härt *City* N Ind., U.S.; pop. 43,152

Elk'tȯn *Town* NE Md., U.S.; marriage mill until 1938

Elles'mēre Island (elz') *Island* NE Northwest Terrs., Canada

El'lice Islands (lis) *Island group* (Brit.) see GILBERT and ELLICE IS.

El'lis Island *Island* N.Y. Bay, U.S.; immigration cen. til 1954

El-lōre' *City* E India

El Man-su'rȧ (soor') *City* Lower Egypt

Elm'hûrst *City* NE Ill., U.S.; pop. 50,547

El Min'yȧ *City* Upper Egypt

El-mī'rȧ *City* S N.Y., U.S.; pop. 39,945

El Mis'ti *Volcano* 19,110 ft. S Peru

El Mon'tė *City* S Cal., U.S.; pop. 69,837; manufacturing, residential

El Oued' (wed'), **El Wad'** *Town*, *Oasis*, NE Algeria

El Pas'ō *City* W Texas, U.S.; pop. 322,261; trade, manufacturing

El Sal'vȧ-dôr *Republic* Central America; 8,260 sq. m.; dense pop. 3,400,000; * San Salvador; coffee

El'si-nōre = HELSINGOR

Ē'lẏ, Isle of *County* E England

E-lẏr'i-ȧ *City* N Ohio, U.S.; pop. 53,427

Em-ba' *River* 350 m. U.S.S.R., Asia

Em'dȧn *City* N West Germany; port

Em'êr-ȧld Isle = IRELAND, the island

E-mi'liȧ (mē') *Compartimento* N Italy

E-min-ö-nū' *District* of Istanbul, Turkey

Em'mȧn *Commune* NE Netherlands

Em'press Ȧu-gus'tȧ Bay *Inlet* Bougainville NW Solomon Is.

Ems *River* 205 m. NW Germany

En'dêr-bẏ Land *Projection* (Brit.) of Antarctica

En'fïeld 1. *Urban District* SE England; rifles 2. *Town* N Conn., U.S.; pop. 46,189

Eng'ėls *Town* R.S.F.S.R., U.S.S.R., Eur.; agriculture

Eng'lȧnd (ing') *Country*

S and E Great Britain island; division of United Kingdom; 51,355 sq. m.; pop. 54,022,000; * London; 45 counties; iron, steel, coal, manufacturing

Eng'lish Channel (ing') *Strait* S England-N France

Ē'nid *City* N Okla., U.S.; pop. 44,008; grain, oil, meat industries

E-ni-wē'tok *Atoll* Marshall Is. W Pacific O.

En'nȧ *Province* Sicily, Italy

En-sche-de' (skė-dä') *Commune* E Netherlands; industry

En-teb'bė *Town* Uganda; on equator

En-ze-li' (lė') now PAHLEVI

E-per-nāy' (ā) *Commune* NE France; champagne

Eph'ė-sus (ef') *Ruins* of anc. city W Asia Minor

E-pï'rus 1. *Anc. country* NW Greece. 2. *Division* E Greece

Ep'söm and Ew'ell (ū') *Municipal borough* SE England; site of **Ep'söm Downs** racecourse

Ē-quȧ'tör = imaginary circle on earth's surface equidistant from N and S poles

E-quȧ-tōr'i-ȧl Gui'nea was Sp. Gui'nea (gi'ni) *Rep.* W Africa, * Santa Isabel, Rio Muni; coffee, cocoa, bananas

E-rä'klēi-ön = HERAKLEION

Er'ė-bus, Mt. *Peak* 13,200 ft. Ross I. Antarctica

E-rė-pe-cu-ru' (kōō-rōō') *River* 250 m. N Brazil

E-rē'tri-ȧ *City* anc. Greece, S Euboea I.

E-re-vän' = YERE-

VAN

Er′fûrt *City* * of *District* SW East Germany

Erg, El *Regions* of sand dunes, Sahara Desert

Ē′rie (ri) *City* NW Pa., U.S.; pop. 129,231

Ē′rie, Lake (ri) *Lake* NE U.S.; one of 5 Great Lakes

Ē′rie Canal (ri) *Canal* Buffalo-Albany N.Y., U.S. [poetic name

Er′in = IRELAND, a

Er′ith *Urban district* SE England; yachting

Er-i-trē′a *Area* of NE Ethiopia on Red S., former It. colony

Es′bjerg (byark) *City* SW Jutland, Denmark; meats, fish, dairy products

Es-cä-län′te *Municipality* Negros, Phil. Is.

Es-con-di′dō (dē′) *City* S Cal., U.S.; pop. 36,792; business

Ē′shêr *Urban district* S England

E′skil-stu-na (ā′shil-stŏŏ) *City* SE Sweden; steel, cutlery

Es-ki-se-hir′ (she) *City* * of *Vilayet* W Turkey, Asia; meerschaum [SPAIN

Es - pä′nä (n y ä) =

Es-pi′ri-tū Sän′tō *Island* largest of New Hebrides, SW Pacific O.

Es′sên *City* NW West Germany; Krupp works: arms, locomotives [Australia

Es′sên-dön *City* SE

Es-sê-qui′bō (kwē′) *River* 600 m. W Guyana

Es′sex *County* SE England; farming, fish, manufacturing

Ess′ling-ên *City* SW West Germany

Es-tō′ni-à or **Es-tō′ni-àn S.S.R.** *Republic* of U.S.S.R., N Eur.; * Tallin; agriculture, livestock; independent 1918-40

E-tä′wàh *Town* N India; cotton mills

Ē-thi-ō′pi-à 1. *Anc. country* NE Africa, larger than mod. Ethiopia. 2. *Kingdom* E Africa (formerly Abyssinia); * Addis Ababa; 457,266 sq. m.; pop. 24,800,000; skins, grain, coffee

Et′nà, Aet′nà *Volcano* 10,740 ft. NE Sicily

E-trur′i-à (troor′) *Anc. country* cen. Italy

Et′têr-beek (bāk) *Commune* cen. Belgium

Eu-boe′à (ū-bē′) *Island* largest of Greece, Aegean S.; with CENTRAL GREECE, a division

Eū′clid *City* N Ohio, U.S.; pop. 71,552; grapes, machinery

Eū-gēne′ (jēn′) *City* W Ore., U.S.; pop. 76,346; gold, silver

Eū-phrā′tēs (frā′) *River* 1700 m. SW Asia

Eūr-ā′sia (z h à) = world's largest land mass: Europe and Asia

Eure (ûr) 1. *Department* N France. 2. **-et-Loir′** (ā-lwar′) *Department* N cen. France

Eū′röpe *Continent*, E hemisphere; 3,800,000 sq. m.; div. into many countries

Ev′àns-tön *City* NE Ill., U.S.; pop. 79,808; education cen.

Ev′àns-ville *City* SW Ind., U.S.; pop. 138,764; machinery

E-ven′kỳ *National district* N cen. Siberia, U.S.S.R.

Ev′êr-est, Mount *Mountain*, world's highest, 29,028 ft., Nepal-Tibet, Himalayas

Ev′êr-ett 1. *City* NE Mass., U.S.; pop. 42,485; iron, paints. 2. *City* NW cen. Wash., U.S.; pop. 53,622;

port, lumber, fish

Ev′êr-glädes *Marshland* S Fla., U.S.

E′we-land (ā′wä) *Region* W African coast; former slave coast

Ex′ê-têr *City* and *county borough* SW England; rail, farming, shipping cen.

Ex-ū′mà *Island group* Bahama Is.

Eyre (âr) *Peninsula* and *Lake* S Australia

F

Fä-en′zä *Commune* N Italy; pottery

Fäer′ōes (fär′ōz) *Island group* (Dan.) N of Brit. Isles, Atlantic O.

Fair′banks *Town* cen. Alas., U.S.; pop. 14,771; port, gold, lumber

Fair′field 1. *City* SW Conn., U.S.; pop. 56,487; port 2. *City* NWC Cal., U.S.; pop. 44,146

Fāir Läwn *City* NE N.J., U.S.; pop. 37,975; cement, textiles

Fair′weath-êr, Mount (weth) *Peak* 15,315 ft. Alas., U.S.-Brit. Columbia, Canada

Faïz′à-bad 1. *Town* NE Afghanistan. 2. see FYZABAD, India

Fäl′kîrk *Burgh* cen. Scotland; flour, iron, coal, chemicals

Fälk′lànd Islands *Brit. colony* S Atlantic O.; * Stanley; whaling, sealing, sheep

Fäll Ri′vêr *City* SE Mass., U.S.; pop. 96,898.

Fal′stêr *Island* of Denmark, Baltic S.

Fä - mà - gu′stà (gōō′) *City* on *Bay*, * of *District* E Cyprus; port

Fä′nō *Commune* E cen. Italy; manufacturing

Fär East = Countries and Islands of E Asia

Fär Eas′têrn Region or **Republic** former area

of E Siberia, U.S.S.R.

Fâre′hàm *Urban district* S England

Fär′gō *City* E N.D., U.S.; pop. 53,365; manufacturing, trade

Fà-rid′kōt (rēd′) *State* NW India

Fà-rid′pur (rēd′poor) *District* E Pakistan; formerly Brit. India

Fär′ōe Islands see FAEROES

Fà-rukh′ä-bäd (rook′) *City* * of *District* N India

Fär West = area of U.S. west of Great Plains

Fä-tih′ (tē′) *District* of Istanbul, Turkey

Fät′shän′ *City* SE China; commerce, industry

Fāy′ette-ville (êt-vil) *City* S cen. N.C., U.S.; pop. 53,510; manufacturing

Fed′êr-àl District = capital area of a country

Federated Malay States, Federation of Malaya = Former states, S Malay Penin; now part of MALAYSIA

Felt′hàm *Urban district* SE England

Fen (fun) *River* 300 m. NE China

Fengh′kieh′ (fung′ji-e′) *City* S cen. China

Feng′tien′ (fung′ti-en′) now MUKDEN

Feng′tu′ (fung′dōō′) *City* S cen. China

Fen′nö-scan′di-à = Geological term for Scandinavia

Fē-ö-dō′si-yà (s h i) *Town* R.S.F.S.R., U.S.S.R., Eur.; port

Fêr-man′àgh (à) *County* Northern Ireland; farming, livestock

Fêr-nän′dō Pō′ö *Island Province* Equatorial Guinea (Sp.)

Fè-rōze′pōre *City* * of *District* NW India; grain, cotton trade

Fêr-rä′rä *Commune* * of *Province* N Italy

Fez *City* N Morocco; sacred city

Fez-zan′ *Desert, Oasis, Region,* SW Libya

Fie′sö-le (fyä′) *Commune* cen. Italy; ruins, resort

Fïfe *County* E Scotland; farming, limestone

Fi′ji Islands (fē′jē) *Island group* SW Pacific O.; 7,073 sq. m.; pop. 526,765; * Suva; agriculture, fishing

Finch′ley (li) *Urban district* SE England; residential

Find′lay (li) *City* NW Ohio, U.S.; pop. 35,-800; manufacturing

Fin′gêr Lakes *Lakes* W N.Y., U.S. (Seneca, Cayuga, Keuka, Canandaigua, Owasco, Skaneateles)

Fin-is-tere′ (târ′) *Department* NW France

Finke *River* 400 m. cen. Australia

Fin′länd *Republic* N Eur.; 130,165 sq. m.; pop. 4,700,000; * Helsinki; 10 departments.

Fin′länd, Gulf of *Arm* of Baltic S.

Fin′lay (li) *River* 250 m. Brit. Columbia, Canada

Finsch′hä-fèn *Village* SE New Guinea

Fin-stêr-äar′hôrn *Peak* 14,025 ft. Switzerland

Fïre Island *Island* N.Y., U.S.; lighthouse

Fi-ren′ze (tsä) 1. *City* = FLORENCE. 2. *Province* cen. Italy

Fitch′bûrg *City* cen. Mass., U.S.; pop. 43,343; industrial cen.

Fitz′roy *River* 300 m. W Australia

Fiü′me (mä) It. name of RIEKA

Flan′dêrs, East and **West** *Provinces* N Belgium

Flat′bush (boosh) *Dis-*

trict of Brooklyn, N.Y. City, U.S.

Flens′bûrg *City* N West Germany

Flin′dêrs *River* 500 m. NE Australia

Flint 1. *River* 265 m. W Ga., U.S. 2. *City* SE cen. Mich., U.S.; pop. 193,317

Flint′shïre *County* NE Wales

Flor′ènce, It. **Fi-ren′ze** *Commune* cen. Italy

Flô′res *Island* of Lesser Sundas, Indonesia

Flô-ri-ä-nop′ö-lis *City* S Brazil; harbor

Flor′i-dä 1. *State* SE U.S.; 58,260 sq. m.; pop. 6,789,443; * Tallahassee; 67 counties; fruit, fish, resorts. 2. *Strait* S Fla., U.S.-N Cuba. 3. *Island* SE Solomon Is.

Flor′i-dä Keys (kēz) *Islands* S Fla., U.S.

Flô′ri-nä (rē) *Department* N Greece

Flô-ris′sänt *City* E Mo., U.S.; pop. 65,-908

Flush′ing *Site* Long I. Queens, N.Y. City, U.S.; site of Worlds′ Fairs 1939, 1964

Flÿ *River* 650 m. SE New Guinea

Fond′ Du Lac *City* SEC Wisc., U.S.; pop. 35,515; manufacturing

Fog′gia (fôd′jä) *Commune* * of *Province* SE Italy

Fô-li′gnô (lē′) *Commune* cen. Italy

Fôlke′stöne (stun) *Municipal borough* SE England; port

Fon′taine - bleau (ten-blō) *Commune* N France; chateau

Fôô′chow′ see MINHOW

Foots′cräy *City* SE Australia; quarries, manufacturing

For′ä-kêr, Mount *Mountain* 17,000 ft. S cen. Alas., U.S.

For-bid′dèn City = LHASA

For′est Hills *Community* Queens, N.Y. City, U.S.; site of tennis tournaments

Fôr′fàr-shïre now ANGUS

För-li′ (lē′) *Commune* * of *Province* N Italy; manufacturing

Fôr-mö′sä or **Taï-wän** *Island* off SE China; pop. 14,700,000; * Taipei; agricultural, forest products, mining; seat of Chinese Nationalist Government since 1949

Fôr-mö′sä 1. *Territory* N Argentina. 2. *Bay* of Indian O., SE Kenya. 3. *Strait* SE China-Formosa I.

Fôrst *City* East Germany; textiles

Fôrt Ben′ning *Infantry post* W Ga., U.S.

Fôrt Col′lins *City* N Col., U.S.; pop 43,-337; ed. center

Fôrt-dè-Fränce′ *City* * of Martinique, Fr. West Indies

Fôr-tè-le′zà (lä′) *City* NE Brazil; port

Fôr′tès-cūe *River* 350 m. W Australia

Fôrt George (jôrj) *River* 520 m. Quebec, Canada

Fôrth *River* into **Fîrth of Fôrth,** arm of North S.

Fôrt Knox (nox) *Military reservation* N cen. Ky., U.S.; U.S. gold depository

Fort - La - my′ (fôr-la-mē′) *Town* * of Chad NW part; pop. 150,-000

Fôrt Läu′dêr-däle *City* SE Fla., U.S.; pop. 139,590; resort

Fôrt Leav′èn - wörth (lev′) *Military reservation* E Kan., U.S.; federal penitentiary

Fôrt Mc-Hen′rÿ *National monument* Md., U.S.; site of writing

of national anthem

Fôrt Nel′sön *River* 260 m. Brit. Columbia, Canada

Fôrt Smith *City* W Ark., U.S.; pop. 62,-802; trade, industry

Fôrt Sum′têr *Fort* Charleston S. C., U.S.; site of attack starting Civil War

Fôrt Wayne (wän) *City* SE Ind., U.S.; pop. 177,671; rail, manufacturing cen.

Fôrt Wil′liam (yàm) *City* Ontario, Canada; imp. port

Fôrt Wörth *City* N Texas, U.S.; pop. 393,476; trade, transportation cen.

Fou-geres′ (fōō-zhâr′) *City* NW France; quarries, manufacturing

Four Côr′nêrs (fôr) *Site* only place in U.S. where four states meet: Colo., N.M., Ariz., Utah

Fow′liang′ (fōō′li-äng′) *Town* SE China; porcelain

Fox Islands 1. *Islands* (2) Lake Mich., U.S. 2. *Island group* of Aleutian Is., Alas., U.S.

Frä′ming-ham *Town* NE Mass., U.S.; pop. 64,048; manufacturing

France, anc. **Gäul** *Republic* W cen. Eur.; 212,660 sq. m.; pop. 50,300,000; * Paris; div. into 90 departments; grain, wine, coal, iron, silk, fish

Frän-cô′ni-ä 1. *Former division* S cen. Germany. 2. *Mountain range* of White Mts. N.H., U.S.

Frank′fört *City* * of Ky. N cen. Ky., U.S.; pop. 21,356

Fränk′fûrt on the Main (mïn) *City* W cen. West Germany; commerce, manufacturing

Fränk′fûrt on the Ō′dêr *City* E cen. East Germany; manufacturing

Franz Jō′séf Land *Archipelago* Arctic O., U.S.S.R.

Frā′ser (zhêr) *River* 700 m. Brit. Columbia, Canada

Fred′êr-ic-tön *City* * of New Brunswick, SE Canada; lumber trade

Fred′êr-iks-bêrg *City* E Denmark; Copenhagen suburb

Frēe′pôrt *Village* SE N.Y., U.S.; pop. 40,-374; residential

Frēē′town *Town* * of Sierra Leone; pop. 110,000; fine harbor

Freī′bêrg 1. *City* S East Germany; manufacturing, silver mines. 2. *City* S West Germany

Freī′täl *City* S East Germany

Frē-man′tle *Municipality* SW Australia

Frē′mont *City* W Calif., U.S.; pop. 100,869

French Ant-ärc′ti-cå *Territory* (Fr.) incl. islands in Indian O. and area of mainland

French Cöm-mū′ni-tỷ *Federation* of France, its territories, overseas depts. and republics; replaced **French Union** 1958

French E-quá-tô′ri-ål Af′ri-cå *Former Fr. terr.* now div: CHAD, CONGO (b), GABON

French Gui-ä′nå (gi) *Department*, Fr.; NE coast of South America; * Cayenne; agriculture, woods

French Guin′ea (gin′i) *Former Fr. terr.* now GUINEA

French In′di-å *Former Fr. terr.* E India

French In′dō-chī′nå *Former Fr. colonies*, E Indochina; now

CAMBODIA, LAOS, VIETNAM

French O-ce-an′i-å (she) = Fr. islands of Pacific O.

French Pol-ỷ-nē′sia (zhà) *Territory* (Fr.) S Pacific O.; incl. Society, Marquesa, Gambier, Austral Is., Tuamotu Arch.; * Papeete on Tahiti, Society Is.

French Sö-mä′li-land *Territory* (Fr.) E Africa; * Djibouti; salt

French Sū-dan′ *Former Fr. terr.* now SUDAN

French West Africa *Former Fr. terrs.* now DAHOMEY, GUINEA, IVORY COAST, MAURITANIA, NIGER, SENEGAL, SUDAN, UPPER VOLTA

French Union now FRENCH COMMUNITY

French West In′diēs *Islands* (Fr.) of West Indies: Martinique, Guadeloupe, etc.

Fres′nō (frez′) *City* S cen. Calif., U.S.; pop. 165,972; fruit

Fri′bourg (frē′boor) *Commune* * of *Canton* W cen. Switzerland; manufacturing

′riē - drichs - hä′fen (driks) *City* S West Germany; imp. port

Friend′lỷ Islands (frend′) or TONGA ISLANDS

Friēs′land (frēz′) *Province* N Netherlands; dairying

Fri′sian Islands (frizb′-àn) *Island chain* North S.; **West** bel. to Netherlands, **East** to Germany, **North** to Germany and Denmark [Italy

Fri′ū-li *Province* NE

Frō′bish-êr Bay *Inlet* SE Baffin I., N Canada

Frön′tiēr Il-lä′qas (kàz) *Districts* NW Kashmir, N India

Frō-si-nō′ne (nä) *Province* cen. Italy

Frün′zė *City* * of Kirgiz S. S. R., U.S.S.R., Asia

Fu′ji, Fu-ji-yä′mä (fōō) *Mountain* 12,388 ft. Honshu, Japan, sacred

Fū-kä-e *Island* off Kyushu, Japan

Fū′kien′ *Province* SE China; agriculture, forestry

Fu-ku-i (foo-koo) *City* * of *Prefecture* Honshu, Japan; textiles

Fu-ku-ō-kä (foo-koo) *City* * of *Prefecture* Kyushu, Japan; manufacturing

Fu-ku-shi-mä (foo-koo) *City* * of *Prefecture* Honshu, Japan; trade

Fu-ku-yä-mä (foo-koo) *City* Honshu, Japan

Ful′då (fool′) *City* on *River* cen. W Germany; manufacturing

Ful′lêr-tön *City* SW Calif., U.S.; pop. 85,826; oil [Is.

Fū-ná-fū′ti *Atoll* Ellice

Fun-chal′ (fōōn-shäl′) *Commune* Madeira Is. Portugal; resort

Fun′dỷ, Bay of *Inlet* of Atlantic O. SE Canada

Furth (fûrt) *City* SE West Germany; manufacturing

Fu-sän (foo) or **Pu-sän** (poo) *City* S Korea

Fu′shun′ (fōō′shoon′) *Town* S Manchuria; coal

Fū-tū′nå Islands see WALLIS and FUTUNA IS.

Fu-yu′ (fōō′) *Town* cen. Manchuria

Fyn (foon) *Island* cen. Denmark

Fўz′á-bad *City* N India; rail cen., sugar refining

G

Gä-bė-rō′nes *Town* * of Bechuanaland now Botswana

Gä′bes *Town* on *Gulf* SE Tunisia; port

Ga-bôn′ Republic *Republic* of Fr. Community W cen. Africa; * Libreville; 102,300 sq. m.; pop. 500,000; forests, minerals [rail cen.

Gá′dåg *Town* W India;

Gads′dėn 1. *City* NE Ala., U.S.; pop. 53,-928; mineral, lumber area. 2. **Pûr′chàse Land** *area* SW U.S. (Ariz., N.M.); purchased from Mexico 1853

Gaines′ville *City* N Fla., U.S.; pop. 64,-510; ed. center

Gâird′nêr *Lake* S Australia

Gá-lä′på-gös Islands *Island group* of Ecuador, Pacific O.; * San Cristobal; wild life

Gå-lä′tia (shà) *Anc. country* cen. Asia Minor

Gä′lätz *City* E Romania; port

Gäles′bûrg *City* W Ill., U.S.; pop. 36,290

Gå-li′cia (shà) 1. *Region* E cen. Eur. now part of U.S.S.R. 2. *Region, Anc. Kingdom,* NW Spain

Gal′i-lēe 1. *District* N Israel; scene of Jesus' ministry. 2. **Sea of** *Lake* N Israel

Gal′lå-tin R a n g e *Mountains* S Mont., U.S. [port

Gälle *Town* Ceylon;

Gal-li′näs, Point (gä-yē′) N point of South America, Colombia

Gål-lip′ö-li 1. *Commune* SE Italy; port. 2. *Peninsula* NW Turkey, Eur.

Gal′vės-tön *City* SE Texas, U.S.; pop.

61,809; imp. port

Găl'way *County* and *Municipal borough* on Bay, W Eire

Gam'bi-à *River* 460 m. W Africa

Gam'bi-à, The *Country* of Brit. Commonwealth, former *Colony* NW Africa; 4,000 sq. m.; pop. 357,000; * Bathurst; peanuts

Gam'biêr Islands *Island group* (Fr.) S Pacific O.

Gam-tōōs' *River* 300 m. Rep. of South Africa

Găn'dàk *River* 400 m. Nepal-N India

Gan'ges (jĕz.) *River* 1550 m. NE India; sacred to Hindus

Găng'pur (poor) *Indian state* NE India

Găng'tok *Town* * of Sikkim   [S France

Gard (gar) *Department*

Gär-dē'nà *City* SW Cal., U.S.; pop. 41,021; manufacturing, residential

Gär'dĕn City *City* SE Mich., U.S.; pop. 41,864

Gär'dĕn Grōve *City* SW Calif., U.S.; pop. 122,524; residential

Gär'dĕn of the Gods *Region* ab. 500 acres, Colo., U.S.

Gär'dĕn Rēach *Suburb* of Calcutta NE India

Gär'fĭeld Heights (hīts) *City* N Ohio, U.S.; pop. 41,417; manufacturing

Gar - ian' (gur - yan') *Town* NW Libya

Gär'lànd *City* NE Texas, U.S.; pop. 81,437

Gà-ronne' *River* 355 m. SW France

Gar'rỳ, Lake *Lake* Northwest Terrs., Canada

Gâr'ỳ *City* NW Ind., U.S.; pop. 175,415

Gas-cŏn-āde' *River* 250 m. S cen. Mo., U.S.

Gas'cŏ-nỳ 1. *Hist. re-*

gion SW France. 2. *Gulf* SE part of Bay of Biscay

Gas'coyne (coin) *River* 400 m. W Australia

Gà'shêr-brum (broom) *Peak* 26,470 ft. N India

Gas'pe (pā) *Peninsula, Cape, Bay* SE Quebec Canada; hunting, fishing

Gas-tō'ni-à *City* SW N.C., U.S.; pop. 47,142; industry

Gātes'head (gāts'hed) *County borough* N England; manufacturing, mines, quarries

Gat'i-neau (nō) *River* 240 m. SW Quebec, Canada

Gà-tōō'mà *Town* Rhodesia; gold

Găul, Găulle, Gal'li-à *Anc. country* W Eur. incl. most of mod. France

Gau'ri Sàn'kàr (gou') *Peak* 23,440 ft. N Nepal

Gav'lĕ (yâv') *City* E Sweden; port

Gà-yä' *City* NE India; sacred to Buddhists

Gä'zà *City* * of *District* SW Israel; port

Gä-zi-än-tep' *Town* * of *Vilayet* S Turkey Asia; educational cen.

Gdänsk see DANZIG

Gdỳ'ni-à *City* N Poland; port

Gee-lông' (je) *Port* SE Australia; wool

Ge-hen'nà = New Testament word for "hell"; see HINNOM

Ge'lä (jâ') *Commune* S Sicily; ruins

Gel-sĕn-kir'chĕn (kĕn) *City* N cen. West Germany; industry, coal

Gĕ-nē'và (jĕ), **Ge-neve'** (zhe-nâv') *City* on *Lake,* * of *Canton* SW Switzerland; tourist, cultural cen.; manufacturing

Gen'ö-à (jen'), **Ge'nö-**

vä (jä') *City* on *Gulf* in *Province* NW Italy; imp. port

Gent see GHENT

Gen'töf-tĕ *City* E Denmark   [rea; port

Gen-zän *City* NE Ko-

George (jôrj) *River* 365 m. Quebec, Canada

George, Cape (jôrj) *Cape* Nova Scotia, Canada

George, Lake (jôrj) *Lake* E N.Y., U.S.; resort area

George'town (jôrj') 1. *Section* of Washington, D.C., U.S. 2. *City* * and chief port of Guyana

George' Town (jôrj') or **Pė-nang'** *City* Penang I. Malaysia; port

Geor'gia (jôr'jà) 1. *State* S U.S.; 58,876 sq. m.; pop. 4,589,575; * Atlanta; div. into 159 counties; agriculture esp. cotton. 2. or **Geor'gi-àn** S.S.R. (jôr'ji), anc. **I-bē'ri-à** *Republic* of U.S.S.R., Eur.; * Tiflis; mines, timber. 3. *Strait* W Canada-W U.S.

Geor-gi'nà (jôr-jē') *River* 400 m. N cen. Australia

Ge'rä (gā') *City* SW East Germany; industry

Ger'màn East Africa (jêr') *Ger. Terrs.* prior to WW I

Ger-mā'ni-à (jêr) *Anc. region* cen. Eur., larger than mod. Germany

Ger'màn Vol'gà Republic (jêr') *Former republic* U.S.S.R., Eur.

Ger'mà-nỳ (jêr'), **Deutsch'land** (doich') **Deut'sches Reich** (doi', rīk) *Country,* former empire, cen. Eur.; 1949 two governments estab.: (1) **Federal Republic of**

Germany (West Germany); 95,930 sq. m.; pop. 60,460,000; * Bonn; steel, shipping, coal, manufacturing. (2) **German Democratic Republic (East Germany);** 41,660 sq. m.; pop. 17,084,000; * East Berlin; machinery

Ger'mis-tön (jêr') *City* NE Rep. of South Africa; gold

Gers (zhâr) *Department* SW France

Get'tỳs-bûrg *Borough* S Pa., U.S.; Civil War battle site

Ghä'nà, Republic of *Republic* of Brit. Commonwealth, W Africa; formerly Gold Coast and Brit. Togoland; 91,850 sq. m.; pop. 8,600,000; * Accra; minerals, cocoa, rubber

Ghåts, Eastern and **Western** *Mountain ranges* S India

Ghent, Gent *City* NW cen. Belgium; commerce, manufacturing

Ghôr, the *Region,* valley of the Dead Sea

Gi-brăl'têr (ji) *Town* on Rock of Gibraltar, a peninsula and Brit. colony, S Spain

Gi-brăl'têr, Strait of (ji) *Passage* Spain-Africa

Gib'sön Desert *Desert* W Australia; salt lakes

Gies'sĕn (gēs') *City* cen. West Germany; manufacturing

Gi-fu (foo) *City* * of *Prefecture* Honshu, Japan; paper goods

Gi - hulng'än (h ē - hōōlng') *Municipality* Negros, Phil. Is.

Gi-jon' (hē-hôn') *City* NW Spain; port

Gi'là (hē') *River* 630 m. SW U.S.

Gil'bêrt *River* 250 m.

NE Australia

Gil′bêrt and El′lice Islands (lis) *Brit. colony* W Pacific O. incl. Gilbert Is., Ellice Is., Phoenix Is. and Line Is., Christmas I., Fanning I., Washington I.; * Tarawa; copra, phosphates

Gil′e-àd *Region* anc. Palestine, mod. NW Jordan

Gil′ling-hàm (jil′) *Municipal borough* SE England; fruit, cement

Gi-rônde′ (zhē) *Department* SW France

Giu′bä (jōō′) *River* 1000 m. Somalia

Gi′zà, El Gi′zèh (gē′) *City* * of *Province,* Upper Egypt, 5 m. from pyramids

Glâ′cier National Park (shêr) *Park* glaciers, mountains, NW Mont., U.S.

Gläd′bäch - Rheydt′ (bäk-rīt′) *City* NW West Germany; textiles

Gläd′beck *City* W West Germany; coal

Glà - môr′gàn - shìre *County* SE Wales; coal, iron, steel

Glas′gōw *Burgh* W cen. Scotland; port, manufacturing

Glei′witz (glī′vits) see GLIWICE

Glen′dāle 1. *City* SW Calif., U.S.; pop. 132,752; manufacturing 2. *City* S Ariz., U.S.; pop. 36,228

Glen-elg′ *River* 280 m. SE Australia

Glen-gar′rỳ *Valley* NW Scotland; lake

Gli-wi′ce (vē′tse) *City* SW Poland; manufacturing

Glôm′mä *River* 375 m. E Norway

Glouces′têr (glos′) *County borough* of **Glouces′têr - shìre** county, SW cen. Eng-

land; iron, textiles

Gō′à *City,* former terr. of Port. India, W India; port

Gōat Island *Island* Niagara R. N.Y., U.S.

Gō′bi, the *Desert* 500,-000 sq. m. cen. Asia

Gō-dä′và-ri *River* 900 m. cen. India

God′hāvn *Town* W Greenland; scientific station

Gôdt′haab (hôp) *Town* * of Greenland, SW coast

God′win Ăus′tèn *Peak* 28,250 ft. N Kashmir

Gog′rà *River* 570 m. N India

Gōld Cōast 1. former Brit. colony, now GHANA. 2. *Coast* of Gulf of Guinea; gold

Gōl′dèn Gāte *Strait* Pacific O.-San Francisco Bay, Calif., U.S.

Gōl′dèn Thrōne *Peak* 23,600 ft. N Kashmir

Gō′mêl *City* * of *Region* White Russia U.S.S.R., Eur.; trade

Go-me′rä (mä′) *Island* of Canary Is.

Gō-môr′ràh see SODOM

Gō′nà *Settlement* New Guinea; WW II site

Gōn′dàl *State, Town* W India

Good Hōpe, Cape of *Cape* S tip of Africa, Rep. of South Africa

Gōōse Bay = U.S.-Canada Air base Labrador, Newfoundland

Göp′ping-èn *City* S West Germany; manufacturing

Gō′ràkh-pur (poor) *City* * of *Division* N India

Gô′ri *Town* Georgia S cen. U.S.S.R.

Go-ri′ziä (rē′) *Commune* * of *Province* NE Italy; resort, manufacturing

Gôr′ki *City* * of *Region* E cen. R.S.F.S.R., U.S.S.R.; imp. industrial city

Gör′litz *City* SE East Germany; manufacturing

Gör-lôv′kà *City* Ukraine SW U.S.S.R.

Gō′rỳn *River* 485 m. E U.S.S.R.

Gôr′zow (zōōf), Ger. **Länds′bêrg** *City* W Poland; industry

Gō′sain-than′ (sīn-tän′) *Peak* 26,290 ft. S Tibet

Gos′pôrt *Municipal borough* S England; naval barracks

Go′tà (yu′) *River* and *Canal* S Sweden; 360 m., 58 locks

Go′tà-land (yu′) *S Division* of Sweden; incl. 12 provs.

Go-tė-bôrg′ (yu), **Goth′ èn-bûrg** *City* S Sweden; industrial port

Gō′tha (tä) *City* SW East Germany; manufacturing

Go′thàm = New York City, U.S.; humorous reference

Got′land *Island Province* SE Sweden; fish, agriculture, sheep

Göt′ting-èn *City* W cen. West Germany

Gôtt′wald-ôv (val-dôf), formerly Zlin (zlēn) *Town* cen. Czechoslovakia; shoes

Gou′dà *Commune* SW Netherlands; cheese

Goul′bûrn (gōl′) *River* 280 m. SE Australia

Gŏv′êr-nörs Island *Island* New York Bay, U.S.

Grā′hàms-town *Town* S Rep. of South Africa; educ. cen.

Gra-jà-u′ (ōō′) *River* 450 m. NE Brazil

Gram′pi-àn Hills *Mountains* cen. Scotland

Gram′pi-àns *Mountains* SE Australia

Grà-nä′dà 1. *City* * of *Department* SW Nicaragua; sugar, coffee, hides. 2. *City* * of

Province S Spain

Grand *Rivers* of U.S.: 1. 260 m. SW Mich. 2. 300 m. NW Mo. 3. 200 m. N S.D.

Grand Bank *Banks* E and S of Newfoundland, Atlantic O.; cod

Grand Cà-nal′ 1. *Canal,* main thoroughfare of Venice, Italy. 2. *Inland waterway* NE China

Grand Can′yön *Gorge* of Colo. R. in *National Park:* 280 m. long, mile deep; NW Ariz., U.S.

Gränd Côm-bin′ (bän′) *Peak* 14,160 ft. S Switzerland

Grand Cou′lēe *Valley* cen. Wash., U.S.; dam

Grande′, Rì′ō (rē′) see RIO GRANDE (U.S.)

Gran′dè, Rì′ō (rē′ōō) *Rivers:* 1. 250 m. W Africa. 2. 300 m. E Brazil 3. 680 m. E Brazil

Grand Fôrks *City* E N.D., U.S.; pop. 39,-008; business

Grand Prair′ie *City* N Texas, U.S.; pop. 50,904

Grand Rap′ids *City* W Mich., U.S.; pop. 197,649

Grand Tė′ton *Peak* 13,765 ft. NW Wyo., U.S.; *National Park*

Grand Tûrk *Island* dependency of Jamaica

Gran′ite City *City* SW Ill., U.S.; pop. 40,-440; steel, granite

Grän Pä-rä-di′so (dē′zō) *Peak* 13,325 ft. NW Italy

Gran′ville Lake *Lake* Manitoba Canada

Gras′, Lac de (grä′) *Lake* Northwest Terrs. Canada

Grässe *Commune* SE France; perfumes

Grätz See GRAZ

Grāves′end *Municipal*

borough SE England

Grāys Peak *Mountain* 14,275 ft. cen. Colo., U.S.

Grāz, earlier **Grätz** *City* SE Austria

G r e ā t Āu-strā′li-ȧn Bight (bĭt) *Bay* S Australia

Greāt Bar′ri-êr Rēef *Coral reef* off NE Australia, 1250 m.

Greāt Bā′sin *Elevated area* of U.S.: parts of Nev., Utah, Calif., Ida., Wyo., Ore.

Greāt Beâr Lake *Lake* 12,200 sq. m. Northwest Terrs. Canada

Greāt Brit′ain (″n) 1. *Island*, Europe's largest, W part; incl. England, Scotland, Wales. 2. *Unit* of UNITED KING-DOM OF GREAT BRITAIN AND NORTHERN IRE-LAND

Greāt Di-vīde′ = CON-TINENTAL DI-VIDE

Greāt Di-vī′ding Range or **Eastern Highlands** *Mountain ranges* E Australia

Greāt Fălls *City* cen. Mont., U.S.; pop. 60,091; copper works, mineral deposits

Greāt Lakes *Lakes,* chain of 5: Superior, Michigan, Huron, Erie and Ontario, cen. North America

Greāt Plāins *Plains,* cen. North America (U.S. and Canada)

Great Sălt Desert See DASHT-I-KAVIR

Greāt Sălt Lake *Lake* N Utah, U.S.; 2360 sq. m.

Greāt San′dy̆ Desert *Desert* W Australia

Greāt Slāve Lake *Lake* Northwest Terrs. Canada

Greāt Smŏ′ky̆ Moun-tains *Range* of Ap-palachian Mts., N.C.-Tenn., U.S.

Greāt Vĭc-tō′ri-ȧ Desert *Desert* W and S Aus-tralia

Greāt Wăll of Chī′nȧ *Wall* for defense, built 205 B.C., 2000 m. bet. Mongolia and China

Greāt Whāle *River* 365 m. Quebec, Canada

Grēece (grēs), Gk. **Hel′lȧs** *Kingdom* SE Eur., incl. Ionian Is. and Crete; 50,944 sq. m.; pop. 8,800,000; * Athens; div. into 10 divisions, 26 de-partments; grains, fruits, livestock

Grēe′ley *City* N Col., U.S.; pop. 38,902; business, ed. center

Grēen *Rivers* of U.S.: 1. 360 m. Ky.-Ohio. 2. 730 m. Wyo.-Utah-Colo.

Grēen Bay *City* on *Inlet* E Wisc., U.S.; pop. 87,809; river, lake port, factories

Grēen′lȧnd 1. *Island* 839,800 sq. m.; pop. 40,000; world's larg-est, N America, bel. to Denmark; * Godt-haab; hunting, fish-ing. 2. *Sea* part of Arctic O. NE of Greenland

G r ē e n Mountains *Range* of Appalachi-ans, Canada-Mass., U.S.

Grēen′ock *Burgh* SW Scotland; port

Grēens′bö-rö *City* N cen. N.C., U.S.; pop. 144,076

Grēen′ville 1. *City* W Miss., U.S.; pop. 39,-648; cotton. 2. *City* NW S.C., U.S.; pop. 61,208; textiles

Green′wich (gren′ij) *Borough*, London, England; Greenwich meridian is basis for standard time

Green′wich (gren′ich) 1. *Town* SW Conn., U.S.; pop. 59,755. 2. **Village** artist and student section of

N.Y. City, U.S.

Greifs′wăld *City* N East Germany

Greiz (grīts) *City* S East Germany

Grė-nā′dȧ *Island* Brit. Colony, Windward Is. Brit. West Indies; * St. George's

Gren′ȧ-dines (dēnz) *Is-lands* ab. 600 of Windward Is., Brit. West Indies

Grė-nō′ble (b′l) *City* SE France; manu-facturing, esp. gloves

Gret′nȧ Grēen *Village* S Scotland; famous as elopement site

Gri-jal′vä (häl′) *River* 350 m. SE Mexico

Grims′by̆ *County bor-ough* E England; har-bor

Gri-quȧ-land East (grē′) *Territory* S Rep. of South Africa; agri-culture, sheep

Gri′quȧ-land West (grē′) *Region* S cen. Rep. of South Africa

Griz′zly̆ *Mountain Peaks* 1. 13,800 ft. cen. Colo., U.S. 2. 14,000 W cen. Colo., U.S.

Griz′zly̆ Pēak *Peaks* 1. 13,740 ft. SW Colo., U.S. 2. 13,700 ft. SW Colo., U.S.

Grŏd′nô (or Găf-di′näs) *City* * of Region White Russia, W cen. U.S.S.R.

Grō′ning-ėn *City* * of *Province* NE Nether-lands; commerce

Grōōt-fôn-tein′ (tän′) *Town* N South-West Africa; mines

Grōs-se′tō (sā′) *Prov-ince* cen. Italy

Gro′tŏn *Town* Conn., U.S.; pop. 38,523

Grŏz′ny̆ *City* * of *Re-gion* nr. Caspian S. S U.S.S.R., Eur.; oil

Grū′dziadz (jônts), Ger. **Grau′denz** (grou′) *City* N cen. Poland; agricultural

cen.

Gru-yere′ (yâr′) *Dis-trict* W cen. Switzer-land; cheese

Guä-dä-lä-jä′rä (hä′) *City* W cen. Mexico; industrial, agricul-tural, mining cen.

Guä-dȧl-cȧ-nal′ *Island,* Brit. Solomon Is.; WW II site

Guȧl-dȧl-quiv′ir *River* 374 m. S Spain

Gua-dȧ-lupe′ (lōōp′) 1. *River* 300 m. SE Texas, U.S. 2. *Island* off NW Mexico

Guä-dȧ-lū′pe Hi-dȧl′gō, Gūs-tä′vō A Mä-de′rō (dä′) *City* cen. Mexico; pilgrimage site

Gua-dė-loupe′ (lōōp′) *Islands,* part of *De-partment* of France, E West Indies

Guä-diä′nä *River* 515 m. Spain-Portugal

Guä-ji′rä (hē′) *Penin-sula* N Columbia

Guäm = *Island* (U.S. possession) of Mari-ana Is., W Pacific O. * Agana

Guä-nä-juä′tō (hwä′) *City* * of *State* cen. Mexico

Guän-tä′nä-mō *Munici-pality* and *Town* on *Bay* E Cuba; sugar cen., U.S. naval base

Gua - po - re′ (pōō-r′) *River* 950 m. W cen. South America

Guar′di-ȧn, the (gär′) *Peak* 13,625 ft. SW Colo., U.S.

Guä-tė-mä′lȧ 1. *Re-public* Central Amer-ica; 42,000 sq. m.; pop. 5,200,000; agri-culture, esp. coffee; woods, cattle. 2. *City* * of Republic

Guä-viä′re (râ) *River* 450 m. SW cen. Co-lombia

Guä-yä-quil′ (kēl′) *City* SW Ecuador; port

Guern′sey (gêrn′zi) *Is-land* of Channel Is.;

cattle   [S Mexico

Guer-re′rō (ger) *State*

Gui-ä′nà (gi) *Region* N South America incl. Guyana, Fr. Guiana, Surinam, N Brazil, S and E Venezuela

Gui-enne′ (gē) or **Aq- ui-tā′nià** *Hist. region* SW France

Guild′förd (gīl′) *Municipal borough* S England

Guin′ea (gin′i) 1. *Region* W African coast. 2. *Republic* W Africa (was Fr. Guinea); 95,000 sq. m.; pop. 3,700,000; * Conakry

Guin′ea, Gulf of (gin′i) *Inlet* of Atlantic O. W cen. Africa

Gu-jà-rät′ (goo) *State* W India

Guj-rän-wä′là (gooj) *Town* * of *District* West Pakistan

Guj′rät (gooj′) *Town* West Pakistan; crafts

Gul′bàr-gä (gool′) *Town* S cen. India; cotton, flour, paint

Gulf′pôrt *City* S Miss., U.S.; pop. 40,791; business

Gulf States = States of U.S. bordering Gulf of Mexico

Gulf Strēam *Ocean current* (warm) from Gulf of Mexico to N Atlantic O.

Gu-mäl′ Pass *Mountain pass* W India frontier

Gum-mä (goom) *Prefecture* Honshu, Japan

Gum′ti (goom′) *River* 500 m. N India

Gun-tur′ (goon-tōōr′) *City* E India; tobacco, cotton trade

Gun-zän (goon) *Port* SW Korea; rice

Gur′là Män-dhä′tä (goor′) *Peak* 25,355 ft. SW Tibet

Gu-ru-pi′ (gōō-rōō-pē′) *River* 350 m. NE Brazil

Gu′ryèv or **Gu′rèv** (gōō) *Town* * of *Region* Kazakh, on Caspian S. U.S.S.R. SW Asia

Guy-ä′nä (gi) *Country* former Brit. colony of Brit. Guiana, N South America; * Georgetown; 83,000 sq. m.; pop. 735,000

Gwä′li-ôr *Town* and former *State* N cen. India

Gwȳ′dir *River* 450 m. SE Australia

Gyäng′tse′ *Town* SE Tibet; woolens

Györ (dyur), Ger. **Räab** *City* NW Hungary

Gy′ - Pa-rà-na′ (zhē′) *River* 500 m. W cen. Brazil

H

Häar′lem *City* W Netherlands; tulips

Habs′bûrg (haps′) *Hamlet* N cen. Switzerland

Hä-chi-nō-he *Town* Honshu, Japan

Hä-chi-ō-ji *City* Honshu, Japan; weaving

Hack′èn-sack *City* on *River* NE N.J., U.S.; pop. 35,911

Hadd, Cape *Cape* E Oman

Hà-de′ji-à (dā′) *River* 375 m. N Nigeria

Hä-dhrä-maut′ (mōōt′) *Coast region*, E Aden

Ha-fun′, Cape (fōōn′) *Cape* E point of Africa

Hä′gèn *City* cen. West Germany; industry

Hä′gèrs-town *City* N Md., U.S.; pop. 35,- 862; factories

Hague, The (hāg) *City* SW Netherlands; site of International court

Haï′fà *City* * of *District* NW Israel; imp. port

Haï′lär′ *River* 240 m. Manchuria   [China

Haï′nän′ *Island* off SE

Hai′phong′ (fông′) *Port* N Vietnam

Häi′ti, Republic of *Re-*

public W Hispaniola West Indies; 10,715 sq. m.; pop. 4,500,- 000; * Port-au- Prince; coffee, woods

Hä-kä-tä Bay *Inlet* of S. of Japan; Fukuoka harbor

Hä-ko-dä-te *City* Hokkaido, Japan; port

Häl′bêr-städt *City* W cen. East Germany; manufacturing

Hä-le-ä-kä-la′ *Mountain* and crater, Hawaii, U.S.

Ha′leb See ALEPPO

Hal′i-fax 1. **Bay** *inlet* of Pacific O., E Australia. 2. *City* * of Nova Scotia, E Canada; harbor, factories. 3. *County borough* N England

Чäl′lè *City* S cen. East Germany; trade, industry

Hal-mà-he′rà *Island*, largest of the Moluccas, Indonesia

Halm′städ *City* SW Sweden; port

Hal′sing-bôrg (hel′) *City* SW Sweden; port

Ha′ma *City* W Syria

Ha-mad′, El W part of Syrian Desert

Ham′à-dan *City* * of *Province* W Iran; commerce

Hä-mä-mä-tsu (tsoo) *City* Honshu, Japan industry

Häm-bôrn′ now part o DUISBURG - HAMBORN

Häm′bûrg *City* * of *State* NW West Germany; imp. port

Ham′dèn *Town* S Conn., U.S.; pop. 49,357

Hä′mèln, Ham′è-lin *City* cen. West Germany; factories

Häm-hung (hoong) = KANKO

Ham′il-tön 1. *City* * of Bermuda Is. on Bermuda I. 2. *City* SW Ohio, U.S.; pop.

67,865; industry. 3. *City* SE Ontario, Canada; transportation cen. 4. *River* 600 m. Labrador, Canada. 5. *Burgh* S cen. Scotland; coal, iron

Hämm *City* N cen. West Germany; machinery

Ham′mönd *City* NW Ind., U.S.; pop. 107,- 790; industry

Hamp′shîre, officially South-amp′tön *County* S England

Hamp′stead (sted) *Borough* London, England

Hamp′tön 1. *City* SE Va., U.S.; pop. 120,- 779; fisheries. 2. **Bay** *Inlet* of Atlantic O., E Long I. N.Y., U.S.

Hamp′tön Rōads *Channel,* Port Va., U.S.

Hän *River* 900 m. E cen. China

Hang′chow *City* on *Bay* E China; port, silks

Han′kow *City* E cen. China, now part of Wuhan; port

Hän-nō′vêr *City* NE West Germany; commerce, industry

Hä-noi′ *City* * of North Vietnam; pop. 1,000,- 000

Han′ō-vêr Island *Island* off SW Chile

Hän′yäng′ *City* E cen. China, now part of Wuhan

Hà′rà-muk (mook) *Peak* 16,015 ft. Kashmir   [coffee trade

Hä′ràr *City* E Ethiopia;

Här′bin or **Pin′kiang′** (bin′ji-äng′) *City* cen. Manchuria; trade

Här′bûrg - Wil′helms- bûrg (vil′) *City* NE West Germany now part of Hamburg

Här-däng′êr Fjord (fyôrd) *Inlet* SW Norway

Hàr′dwär *Town* N India; pilgrimage site

Hä′ri, was **Djäm′bi**

River 450 m. Sumatra

Hä′ri Rūd′ *River* 650 m. A f g h a n i s t a n-Turkmen S.S.R.

Här′lèm 1. *District* of Manhattan borough, N.Y. City, U.S. 2. *River channel* bet. Hudson and East Rivers, N.Y., U.S.

Här′pêrs Fer′rẏ *Town* NE W.Va., U.S.; J. Brown's raid 1859

Har-ri-can′ăw *River* 250 m. Quebec, Canada

Har′ris-bûrg *City* * of Pa., U.S.; pop. 68,-061; rail, manufacturing cen.

Har′ro-gāte *Municipal borough* N England; resort

Har′rōw *Urban district* London, England; boys' school

Härt′förd *City* * of Conn., U.S.; pop. 158,017; insurance

Här′vàrd, Mount *Peak* 14,400 ft. Colo., U.S.

Härz (härtz) *Mountains* W cen. West Germany; mines

Häs′tings *County borough* S England; battle 1066.

Hä′ti-à *Island group* in Ganges R. E Pakistan

Hat′têr-às, Cape *Cape* E N.C., U.S.

Hat′ties-bûrg *City* SE Miss., U.S.; pop. 38,277; diversified manufacturing

Haute- (ōt) *Departments,* France: **Haute-Ga-rônne′,** S; **Haute-Loire′** (lwär′), S cen.; **Haute-Marne′,** NE; **Hautes-Alpes′** (ōt-zalp′), SE; **Haute-Saône′,** E; **Haute-Sa-voie′** (vwa′), E; **Hautes - Py-re-nees′** (ōt-pē-rā-nā′) SW; **Haute-Vienne′,** W cen.; **Haut-Rhin′** (ō-ran′), NE

Hà-van′à *City* * of Cuba, NW part; pop.

ab. 1,000,000; sugar tobacco, port

Ha′vêr-hill (il) *City* NE Mass., U.S.; pop. 46,120; shoes

Hä′vrè = LE HAVRE

Hà-waï′i *Island* (*County*) largest of *Chain*

Hà-waï′i (wï′ē), **Ha-waï′iàn Islands** (earlier **Sand′wich Islands**) 1. *Island chain* (20) N cen. Pacific O. 2. *State* of U.S.; 6424 sq. m.; pop. 768,561; * Honolulu; div. into 4 counties; pineapples, sugar

Hä′wàsh *River* 500 m. E Ethiopia

Häwkes′bûr-ẏ *River* 340 m. SE Australia

Häw′thôrne *City* S Cal., U.S.; pop. 53,-304; manufacturing, residential

Hāy *River* 320 m. NW Canada

Hāyes *River* 300 m. W cen. Canada

Hāyes, Mount *Peak* 13,740 ft. E Alas., U.S.

Hāyes and Här′ling-tön *Urban District,* London, SE England

Hāy′wàrd *City* W Calif. U.S.; pop. 93,058

Ha-zär′, Kuh′i (kōō′hi) *Peak* 14,500 ft. SE Iran [Pakistan

Hà-zä′rà *Area* NW

Heard Island (hêrd) *Island* (Brit.) S Indian O.

Heart (härt) *River* 200 m. N.D., U.S.

Heb′ri-dēs 1. *Islands* (Outer and Inner) Atlantic O., W Scotland. 2. *Sea* or *Gulf* *Body* of water off NW Scotland

Hec′à-tē Strait *Channel* bet. W Canada and Queen Charlotte Is.

Heer′lèn (hār′) *Commune* SE Netherlands; industrial cen.

Heï′dèl-bêrg *City* SW

West Germany

Heï′dèn-heïm *City* S West Germany

Hei-jō (hä) see PYONG-YANG

Heil-bronn′ (hïl) *City* S West Germany

He-jaz′ *Kingdom,* W Saudi Arabia; * Mecca

Hel′é-nà *City* * of Mont., U.S.; pop. 22,730

Hel′gō-land, Hel′-i-gō-land *Island* North S. W Germany

Hē-li-op′ō-lis Anc. holy city, Lower Egypt

Hel′lès-pont see DARDANELLES

Hell Gāte *Narrow part* of East R., New York City, U.S.

Hel′mànd *River* 650 m. SW Afghanistan

Hel-sing-ör′, El′si-nōre *City* E Denmark; port; scene of Hamlet

Hel′sin-ki *City* * of Finland; pop. 534,-000

Hel-vē′tia (shà) Lat. for SWITZERLAND

Hemp′stead (sted) *Village* SE N.Y., U.S.; pop. 39,411; business, residential, ed. cen.

Hen′dön *Urban district* SE England; textiles

Heng′é-lo *Commune* E Netherlands

Hen-zà-dä′ *Town* * of *District* Lower Burma; rice, tobacco cen.

He-rät′ *City* of *Province* NW Afghanistan; palaces

Her′é-förd-shîre *County* W England

Her′fôrd *City* N cen. West Germany; manufacturing

Her′nè *City* W West Germany; coal, factories

Hert′förd-shîre *County* SE England; farms

Her′tö - gèn - bôsch, Bois-lê-Duc′ (bwä) *Commune* S Netherlands

Hêr′vey Bay (vi) *Inlet* of Pacific O., E Australia

Hêr-zè-gō-vi′nà (vē′) *Region* NW Balkan Penin.; now part of BOSNIA and HERZEGOVINA

Hesse 1. *State* SW West Germany; * Wiesbaden. 2. *State* (former) SW Germany; * Darmstadt

Hes′tön and I′sle-wörth (z′l) *Municipal borough* SE England

Hī-à-lē′àh *City* SE Fla. U.S.; pop. 102,297

Hī-bêr′ni-à Lat. = IRELAND

Hi-dal′gō *State* cen. Mexico

Hier′rô (yer′) *Island* W Canary Is.

High′lànd Pärk (hī′) *City* SE Mich., U.S.; pop. 35,444; cars

High′lànds (hī′) *Area* N of Grampians, Scotland

High Point (hī′) *City* N cen. N.C., U.S.; pop. 63,204; furniture

Hi-kō-ne (hē) *Town* Honshu, Japan

Hil′dès-heïm (hïm) *City* NE West Germany; manufacturing

Hīl′là *Town* and *Province* cen. Iraq

Hi′lō (hē′) *City* on *Bay* E Hawaii I.; harbor

Hil′vêr-sum *Commune* W Netherlands

Hi-mä′chàl Prà-desh′ (däsh′) *Territory* of India, NW India; * Simla

Hi - mà - lā′yàs, The *Mountain system* S Asia, 1500 m.; highest peak Mt. Everest

Hi-me-ji *City* Honshu, Japan; industrial cen.

Hin′dèn-bûrg *City* formerly Germ. now Polish = ZABRZE

Hin′dū Kush′ (koosh′) *Mountain range* cen. Asia

Hin-du-stan' = "place of the Hindus"-INDIA

Hin'nŏm *Valley* nr. anc. Jerusalem = GEHENNA (Gk.)

Hi-rä-tsu-kä *City* Honshu, Japan

Hi-ro-sä-kä *City* Honshu, Japan; silk, fruit, lacquer

Hi-rō-shi'mà (shē') *City* * of *Prefecture* Honshu, Japan; target of first atomic bomb used in warfare, Aug. 1945

His-pàn-iō'là *Island* cen. West Indies inc. Haiti and Dominican Rep.

Hi-tä-chi *City* Honshu, Japan; industrial cen.

Hi'và O'à (hē') *Island* Fr. Oceania; Gaugin's burial place

Hjor'ring (yûr') *City* and *County* Jutland, Denmark; shipping

Hō'bärt *City* * of Tasmania, Australia; harbor, factories

Hō-bō'kèn *City* NE N.J., U.S.; pop. 45,-380; rail cen., port, factories

Hō-dei'dà (dā') *City* Yemen; industrial port

Hŏd'me-zö-vä'sär-hely (shär-hā) *City* SE Hungary

Hŏf *City* E West Germany; factories

Hö'fei' (fā'), formerly **Lü'chow'** (jō') *City* E China

Ho-fūf' *Oasis* and *Town* S Saudi-Arabia

Hō-hèn-zŏl'lêrn *Province, Hist. region* S Germany

Hö'kiäng' (ji - äng') *Province* Manchuria NE China

Hok-kaï'dō *Island* and *Prefecture* N Japan; fish, timber, coal

Hol'länd = NETHERLANDS

Hol-lan'di-à *Division* and *Town* NE Irian, New Guinea, Indonesia

Hol'lẏ-wood 1. *City* SE Fla., U.S.; pop. 106,-873; resorts. 2. *District* Los Angeles, Calif., U.S.; movie industry

Hōl'stein *Region* N West Germany

Hŏl'yōke *City* SW Mass., U.S.; pop. 50,-112; fine papers

Hō'lẏ Rō'màn Em'pīre *Empire* cen. Eur. 800-1800

Hom'bûrg or **Bäd Hom'bûrg** *City* cen. West Germany; resort

Hôms *City* W Syria; silks

Hō'nän' *Province* E cen. China; agriculture, coal, cotton, silk

Hon-dū'ràs, Rep. of 1. *Republic* Cen. America; 44,480 sq. m.; pop. 2,535,000; * Tegucigalpa; coconuts, bananas, woods, coffee, silver. 2. **Gulf of** *Inlet* of Caribbean S. N Honduras

Hon-dū'ras, Brit. see BRIT. HONDURAS

Hong' Kong *Colony* (Brit.) SE China; 390 sq. m.; pop. 3,927,-000; * Victoria; commercial cen.

Hō-ni-ä'rà *Town* Guadalcanal, * of Brit. Solomon Is.

Hon-ö-lū'lū *City* Oahu I. Hawaii, U.S.; * of Hawaii; pop. 324,-871; imp. port

Hon'shū or **Hon'dō** *Island* largest, considered mainland of Japan

Hōōgh'lẏ *Channel*, most imp. of Ganges R. NE India

Hook'êr Island *Island* Arctic O., U.S.S.R.; meteorological station

Hōō'vêr, Bōul'dêr Dam *Dam* of Colorado R., Nev. and Ariz., U.S.

Hōpe, Point *Cape* NW Alas., U.S.; whaling

Hō'peh', Hō'pei' (pä') *Province* NE China; coal, trade

Hōpe'town *Town* S Rep. of South Africa; diamonds

Hôrn, Cape *Cape* S tip of South America on **Hôrn I.**

Hôrn'chûrch *Urban district* SE England

Hor'sèns *City* Jutland Denmark; dairy port

Hôrse'shoe Fall (shōō) see N I A G A R A FALLS

Hôs-pi-tä-lèt' *City* NE Spain; textiles

Hô-tin' (tēn') 1. *Former department* Romania. 2. *Town* = KHOTIN

Hot Springs *City* W cen. Ark., U.S.; pop. 35,631; resort

Hoūs'tön *City* SE Tex., U.S.; pop. 1,232,802 port, petroleum products

Hōve *Municipal borough* S England

Howe, Cape SE tip of Australia

How'land Island *Island* of U.S. cen. Pacific O. nr. equator

How'ràh *City* NE India; rail, industrial cen. [CHIKU

Hsin-chu = SHIN-

Hsing'än' *Region, Province* NW Manchuria

Hsin'king' (jing') = CHANGCHUN

Hual-cän' *Peak* 21,000 ft. W Hawaii I., U.S.

Huäl-lä'gä (wä-yä') *River* 700 m. N and W Peru

Huäl-lä-ti'ri (wä-yä-tē') *Peak* 19,800 ft. Bolivia-Chile

Huäs - cä - rän' (wäs) *Peak* 22,200 ft. W Peru

Hub'bàrd, Mount *Peak* 14,950 ft. Alas. U.S.-Yukon Canada

Hub'li (hoob') *Town* W India; rail cen.

Hud'dêrs-fièld *County*

borough N England; woolens, iron

Hud'sön *River* 306 m. E N.Y., U.S.

Hud'sön Bay *Inland sea* 850 m. x 600 m. E NW Terrs. Canada; joined to Atlantic O. by **Hud'sön Strait**

Hue' (hū-ä') *City* N South Vietnam; rice

Hue - hue - tè - nän'gō (wä-wä) *Town, Department* W Guatemala; mining

Huel'vä *Commune* * of *Province* SW Spain; mines, fisheries

Hues'cä (wäs') *Commune* * of *Province* NE Spain; factories

Hui'lä (wē') *Volcano* 18,700 ft. W cen. Colombia [China

Hū'kow *Town* SE

Hull 1. *City, County* SW Quebec Canada; commerce. 2. *County borough* N England; imp. port

Hum'bêr *Estuary* E England

Hum'bŏldt 1. *River* 290 m. N Nev., U.S. 2. *Bay* Pacific O. inlet NW Calif., U.S. 3. *Peak* 14,000 ft. S cen. Colo., U.S.

Hump, the *Air route* India-China, E Himalayas

Hun (hoon) 1. *River* 300 m. NE China. 2. *River* 240 m. S Manchuria

Hū'nän' *Province* SE cen. China

Hun'gà-rẏ, Mag'yàr People's Rep. *Communist Republic* cen. Europe; * Budapest; 35,900 sq. m.; pop. 10,275,000; former kingdom

Hung-nam *Town* E North Korea

Hung'shui' (shwä') *River* 700 m. S China

Hun'têr *River* 300 m. SE Australia

Hun'ting - dön - shîre

County E cen. England

Hun′ting-tön *City* W W.Va., U.S. pop. 74,-315; tobacco, apples, coal, gas

Hun′ting-tön Beach *City* SW Cal., U.S.; pop. 115,960

Hunts′ville *City* N Ala., U.S.; pop. 137,802; factories, natural gas

Hū′on Gulf *Inlet* of Solomon S. New Guinea

Hū′peh′ (pā′) *Province* E cen. China

Hū′ron, Lake *Lake* of The Great Lakes, NE cen. U.S.

Hûrst′ville *City* SE Australia

Hutch′in-sön *City* cen. Kans., U.S.; pop. 36,885; grain, salt, oil

Huy′tön with Rō′bȳ (hī′) *Urban district* NW England

Hwaī *River* 350 m. E China   [China

Hwaī′ning′ *City* E

Hwäng′ Haī′, Yellow Sea *Sea* bet. China and Korea

Hwäng′ Hō′, Yel′lōw River *River* 2700 m. N cen. and E China

Hwei (hwā) *River* 200 m. N China

Hȳ-an′nis Pôrt *Town* S Mass., U.S.; summer resort

Hȳde Pärk 1. *Village* SE N.Y., U.S.; birthplace of F. D. Roosevelt. 2. *Park* London, England

Hȳ′dėr-á-bad 1. *City* (and former state) S cen. India; factories. 2. *City* SW Pakistan; rail cen., handicrafts

Hyō-gō *Prefecture* Honshu, Japan

I

I′ao (ē′ou) *Canyon* Maui I. Haw., U.S.

Iä′si *City* NE Romania, early *   [geria

I-bä′dän *City* W Ni-

I-ba-que′ (ē-vä-gä′) *City* W cen. Colombia

I-bä-rä-ke *Prefecture* Honshu, Japan

Ī-bē′ri-á 1. *Anc. region,* now Soviet Rep. of GEORGIA. 2. *Peninsula* SW Europe incl. Spain and Portugal

I-bi-cuí′ (ē-vē-kwē′) *River* 400 m. S Brazil

I-cel′ (ē-chel′) *City* * of *Vilayet* S Turkey

Īce′lánd, Republic of *Island Republic* (formerly Danish), bet. N Atlantic O. and Arctic O.; 39,750 sq. m.; pop. 196,549; * Reykjavik; fish

I′chäng (ē′) *City* E cen. China

I-chi-nö-mi-yä *Town* Honshu, Japan

Ī′dá 1. *Mountain* NW Asia Minor, site of anc. Troy. 2. *Mountain,* highest in Crete

Ī′dá-hō *State* NW U.S.; 83,550 sq. m.; pop. 712,567; * Boise; 44 counties

I′dá-hō Fälls *City* E Ida., U.S.; pop. 35,-776; business

Ī′dle-wīld (d′l) former name of John F. Kennedy International Airport N.Y., U.S.

I′dėn-bûrg (ē′) *Peak* 15,748 ft. New Guinea

Ie′pêr (yä′) = YPRES

I-guäs-sū′ *River* 380 m. S Brazil

Ijs′sėl (ī′) *River* E Netherlands to Ijs′-sėl-meer (mär), former Zuider Zee

Ī-kar′i-á *Island* of Aegean Is.

I-ki *Island* NW Kyushu, Japan

I′län′ (ē′) *Town* E Manchuria; port, furs

Ile′-dê-Fränce (ēl′) 1. *Historical Region* N cen. France. 2. = MAURITIUS

Ile′ dê la Ci-te′ (sē-tā′) *Island* Seine R., Paris, France; Cathedral

of Notre Dame

I-lek′ (lyek′) *River* 300 m. E U.S.S.R., Eur.

Il′förd *Municipal borough* SE England; paper   [W China

I′li′ (ē′lē) *River* 800 m.

I-li-ni′zä (ē-lē-nē′) *Peak* 17,390 ft. Ecuador

Il-lam′pū (ē-yäm′) *Peak* of Mt. Sorata, W Bolivia; 21,276 ft.

Ille-et-Vi-laine′ (ēl-á-vē-len′) *Department* NW France

Il-li-mä′ni (ē-yē) *Peak* 21,180 ft. W Bolivia

Il-li-nois′ (noi′) 1. *State* N cen. U.S.; 56,400 sq. ft.; pop. 11,113,-976; * Springfield; 102 counties. 2. *River* 273 m. Ill., U.S.

Il-lȳr′i-á *Anc. country* E Adriatic coast

Il′mẻn *Lake* 300-700 sq. m. NW U.S.S.R.

I-lō′cos Nôr′te (tâ), **I-lō′cos Sūr** *Provinces* Luzon, Phil. Is.

I-lō-i′lō (ē′) *City* * of *Province* Panay I. Phil. Is.; commerce

I-lō-rin′ (rēn′) *Town* * of *Province* W Nigeria

I-mä-bä-ri *Town* Shikoku, Japan; port

I - man′drá *Lake* U.S.S.R., Eur.

Im-bä-bū′rä *Volcano* 15,028 ft. N Ecuador

Im-pe′riä (pâ′) *Province* and *Port* NW Italy

Imp′hál *City* NE India

In′cá, Pä′sö del *Pass* 15,620 ft. Argentina-Chile

In-cä-huä′si *Peak* 21,-720 ft. NW Argentina

In′chon′ or **Jin-sin** *City* Seoul's port, South Korea   [Sweden

In′däl *River* 260 m. N

In-dē-pen′dénce 1. *City* W Mo., U.S.; pop. 111,662; Harry S Truman library. 2. *Fjord* N Greenland

In-dẻ-ra-gi′ri *District* and *River* 225 m. Sumatra, Indonesia

In′di-á 1. *Peninsula* or *Subcontinent* S Asia bet. Arabian S. and Bay of Bengal; 1941 div. into PAKISTAN and 2. **Republic of India** or **Indian Union** *Rep.* of Brit. Commonwealth; confederation of states and terrs.; 1,261,600 sq. m.; pop. 537,000,000; * New Delhi; grains, textiles, rice, tea

In-di-an′á *State* N cen. U.S.; 36,291 sq. m.; pop. 5,193,669; * Indianapolis; 92 counties; agriculture, manufacturing

In-di-án-ap′ö-lis *City* * of Ind., U.S.; pop. 744,624

In′di-án or **Thär Desert** *Region* NW India; 100,000 sq. m.

In′di-án Em′pīre parts of India penin. under Brit. rule until 1947

In′di-án Ocean *Ocean* surr. by Africa, Asia, Australia, Antarctica; ab. 28,375,000 sq. m.

In′di-án River *Inlet* of Atlantic O. E Fla., U.S.

In′di-án States *Areas* ruled by natives or Brit. India, now within Rep. of INDIA

In-di-gir′ka *River* 850 m. U.S.S.R., Asia

In-dō-chī′ná *Peninsula* SE Asia, incl. Burma, Thailand, Laos, Cambodia, Vietnam, parts of Malaysia

In-dō-nē′sia, Republic of (zhá) *Republic,* formerly **Neth. East Indies,** SE Asia; incl. most of Archipelago bet. Asia and Australia; * Djakarta; 735,800 sq. m.; pop. 106,000,000

In-dōre′ *City* cen. India, * of former *State;* cotton   [m. S India

In-drä′vá-ti *River* 330

In′drė (an′) *Depart-*

ment cen. France

In′drė - et - Loire′ (an′-drä-lwar′) *Department* NW cen. France

In′dus *River* W Pakistan; 1700-1900 m.

In′gle-wood (g′l) *City* SW Calif., U.S.; pop. 89,985; chinchilla, planes

In′go-dà *River* 360 m. U.S.S.R., Asia

In′göl-städt *City* SE West Germany

In-gu-lets′ (lyets′) *River* 300 m. Ukraine U.S.S.R.

In-hàm-ba′nè *Port* on *Bay* SE Mozambique

In-ish-mōre′ *Island* Galway Bay, W Ireland

Ink′stêr *City* SE Mich., U.S.; pop. 38,595

In′lànd Sea *Waterway* Honshu-Shikoku-Kyushu, Japan

I n′l à n d Wä′têr-wäy *System* of rivers, bays and canals: 1. U.S. Atlantic coast, Mass.-Fla.; U.S. 2. Gulf coast Fla.-Tex. U.S.

Inn *River* 320 m. Switzerland, Austria, Germany

In′nes-fäil = poetic IRELAND

Inns′bruck (brook) *City* W Austria

I-nö-nu′ *Village* NW Turkey Asia

In′têr-lä-kèn *Commune* SE Switzerland

International Dāte Line see DATE LINE

In-vêr-ness′ *Burgh* * of -shire, *County* NW Scotland

Iô-än′ni-nä (yô) *City* * of *Department* NW Greece

Ī-ō′ni-à *Anc. district* W Asia Minor

Ī-ō′ni-àn Islands *Island* group in **Ī-ō′ni-àn Sea** bet. Italy and Greece; bel. to Greece

Iô′niô *Province* SE Italy

Ī′ō-wà 1. *State* N cen. U.S.; 56,290 sq. m.; pop. 2,825,041; * Des

Moines; 99 counties; agriculture, livestock, meat packing. 2. *River* 291 m. N cen. Iowa

Ī′ō-wà City *City* E Iowa, U.S.; pop. 46,-850; ed. center

I′pin′ (ē′), was Su′chow′ (jō′) *City* S cen. China; exports

I′pōh (ē′) *City* Penang, Malaysia; commerce

Ips′wich *County borough* E England; port

I-qui′que (ē-kē′kà) *City* N Chile; nitrate

I-ran′, Imperial Government of formerly **Pêr′sia** (zhà) *Kingdom* W Asia; 636,000 sq. m.; pop. 28,000,-000; * Tehran; oil, minerals, agriculture

Ī′ran 1. **Plateau of** *Highland* W Asia; 1,000,000 sq. m.; salt deserts. 2. **Mountains** Sarawak-Borneo

I-rä-puä′tō *City* cen. Mexico; farming

I-raq′, Republic of *Republic* SW Asia; 172,-000 sq. m.; pop. 8,-700,000; * Baghdad; oil, agriculture; incl. anc. Mesopotamia, Babylonia, Assyria

I-raq′, was Sul-tän-ä-bäd′ *City* cen. Iran; pottery, metals

I-rä-zū′ *Volcano* 11,200 ft. cen. Costa Rica

Īre′lànd *Island* of British Isles; div. into: 1. **Republic of Ireland** or **Ei′rė** (ā′) *Republic* S, cen. and NW Ireland; 27,135 sq. m.; pop. 2,900,000; * Dublin; agriculture, food processing. 2. **Northern Ireland** *Division* of the United Kingdom, NE Ireland; 5,450 sq. m.; pop. 1,491,000; * Belfast; agriculture, linens, ships

Ir′i-àn *Area* W half of New Guinea, part of Indonesia; formerly **Neth. New Guinea**

I-ri-ri′ *River* 570 m. N Brazil

Ī′rish Free State *Dominion* of Brit. Commonwealth 1922-37, now REP. OF IRELAND

Ī′rish Sea *Sea* bet. England and Ireland

Ir-kutsk′ *City* * of *Region* S R.S.F.S.R., U.S.S.R., Asia; furs, minerals, factories

Ir-rà-wäd′dỳ *River* 1350 m. cen. Burma

Ir-tỳsh′ *River* 2200 m. U.S.S.R., cen. Asia

Îr′ving *City* NE Tex., U.S.; pop. 97,260

Îr′ving-tön *Town* NE N.J., U.S.; pop. 59,-743; factories

I-sà-be′là 1. *Cape, Port* N Dominican Rep. 2. *Province* Luzon, Phil. Is. 3. *Municipality* Negros, Phil. Is. 4. or **Al-bè-märle** *Island*, largest of Galapagos

Is′chi-à (ki) *Town* on *Island* Tyrrhenian S., S Italy

I-sē *Old province* Honshu, Japan; shrines

I-sere′ (ē-zâr′) *Department* SE France

Is′fà-han *City* * of *Province*, former * of Persia, W cen. Iran; metalwork, brocades

I-she-kä-ri *River* 275 m. Hokkaido, Japan

I-shi-kä-wä *Prefecture* Honshu, Japan

I-shim′ *River* 1330 m. U.S.S.R., cen. Asia

I-shi-nō-mä-ki *Town* Honshu, Japan; port

Ī′sis name for upper Thames R., England

Is - ken - dė - ron′ (ēs, rōōn′), **Al-ex-an-dret′tà** *City* S Turkey, Asia; port

Is′kêr *River* 249 m. cen. Bulgaria

Isle of Man, Wīght, etc. see MAN, ISLE OF

Is-ma-i-li′à (lē′) *Town* NE Egypt

Is-pär-tä′ *Town* * of *Vilayet* SW Turkey,

Asia

Is′rà-èl (iz′) 1. *Anc. kingdom* of Palestine. 2. **State of** *Republic* SW Asia (former United K i n g d o m mandate of Palestine, bel. to Turkish Empire pre WW I); 8,-000 sq. m.; pop. 2,-850,000; * Jerusalem; agriculture, industry

Is′sỳk-Kul *Lake* Kirgiz U.S.S.R., Asia

Is-tan-bul′ (bōōl′), formerly **Con-stan-ti-nō′ple,** anc. **Bỳ-zan′-ti-um** *City* * of *Vilayet*, former * of Turkey, NW Turkey, Eur.; pop. 2,000,000

Is′tri-à *Peninsula* NE Adriatic coast, formerly It. now Yugoslavian

I-tal′iàn East Africa former It. colonies: ERITREA, ETHIOPIA, SOMALIA

It′à-lỳ, I-tä′liä *Republic* S Europe, penin. into Medit. S.; 116,375 sq. m.; pop. 53,800,-000; * Rome; 18 compartimenti incl. 94 prov.; agriculture, livestock, minerals, textiles

I-tà-pe-cu-ru′ (pä-kōō-rōō′) *River* 450 m. NE Brazil

I-tà-pi-cu-ru′ (pē) *River* 350 m. E Brazil

I-tas′cà, Lake *Lake* N Minn., U.S.; source of Miss. R.

Ith′à-cà 1. *City* S cen. N.Y., U.S.; pop. 26,-226. 2. *Island* of Ionian Is. Greece

I-và-i′ (ē′) *River* 300 m. S Brazil

I-va′nö-vö *City* * of *Region* R.S.F.S.R., U.S.S.R., Eur.; heavy industry

Ī′vö-rỳ Cōast, Republic of the *Republic*, formerly Fr., W Africa; 127,000 sq. m.; pop. 4,800,000; * Abidjan; forestry, ag-

riculture, livestock
I-wä-te *Prefecture* Honshu, Japan
I'wō (ē') *City* W Nigeria
I'wō Ji'má (ē', jē') *Island* of Volcano Is. S of Tokyo, Japan; WW II battle
Ix-elles' (ek-sel') *Commune* Brussels suburb cen. Belgium
I'zhėvsk (ē') *Town* R.S.F.S.R., U.S.S.R., Eur.; steel
Iz'má-il *City* * of *Region* Ukraine U.S.S.R.
Iz-mir', formerly **Smýr'ná** *City* * of *Vilayet*, on *Gulf* W Turkey, Asia; imp. port
Iz-täc-cî'huätl (ēs-täk-sē') *Mountain* 16,880 ft. SE Mexico

J

Já'bál-pur = JUBBULPORE
Jä'bôr *Port* Jaluit I. * of Marshall Is.
Jack'sŏn 1. *City* * of Miss., U.S.; pop. 153,968; cotton, textiles, rail cen. 2. *City* S Mich., U.S.; pop. 45,484; machinery. 3. *City* W Tenn., U.S.; pop. 39,996; manufacturing. 4. **Mount** *Peak* 13,685 ft. cen. Colo., U.S.
Jack'sŏn-ville *City* NE Fla., U.S.; pop. 528,-865; port
Já-ciu' (kwē') *River* 300 m. S Brazil
Ja-en' (hä-än') *Commune* * of *Province* S Spain
Jaf'fá, anc. **Jop'pá** *City* W cen. Israel; port; part of Tel Aviv
Jäff'ná *Town* on *Peninsula* N Ceylon; port
Jag'gėd Mountain *Peak* 13,835 ft. SW Colo., U.S.
Ja-guá-ri'bė (rē') *River* 350 m. NE Brazil
Jaï'pur (poor) *City* (and former state) NW

India; trade, industry
Jaï'sál-mer *State* NW India; mostly desert
Já-kär'tä = DJAKARTA
Já-lál'á-bad *Town* E Afghanistan
Jä-lä'pä (hä) 1. *Town* * of *Department* SE Guatemala. 2. *City* E Mexico; coffee
Jä-les'cō (hä-lēs') *State* W cen. Mexico
Jäl'ná *Town* S cen. India
Jál-paï-gu'ri (goo') 1. *Town* NE India. 2. *Former district* now div. bet. India and E Pakistan
Jal'u-it *Island* largest of Marshall Is.
Já-mäi'cá 1. *Island Republic* (former colony) Brit. Commonwealth, West Indies; 4232 sq. m.; pop. 2,-000,000; * Kingston; sugar, bananas, coffee, rum. 2. *Town* now part of Queens, N.Y. City, U.S. 3. *Bay* inlet of Atlantic O. N.Y., U.S.
Jāmes 1. *Bay* S of Hudson Bay bet. Ontario and Quebec, E Canada. 2. *River* 340 m. cen. Va., U.S. 3. *Peak* 13,260 ft. Colo., U.S.
Jāmes'town 1. *City* SW N.Y., U.S.; pop. 39,-795; manufacturing. 2. *Island* E Va., U.S.; 1st permanent Eng. settlement in America. 3. *Town* * of St. Helena I.
Jám'mū *Town* and *Region* S Kashmir
Jäm-ná'gár *City* W India
Jäm'shed-pur *City* NE India; metalwork
Jānes'ville *City* S Wisc. U.S.; pop. 46,426; industry   [W India
Jản'ji-rá *Island, State*
Jan May'ĕn Island (yän mī') *Island* (Norway) Arctic O.

Jao'rä (jou') *Town* * of *State* W cen. India
Já-pan', **Nip-pôn** *Island chain Empire* W Pacific O.; 142,690 sq. m.; pop. 102,000,000 * Tokyo; incl. 4 main islands and Ryukyu Is.; 47 prefectures; rice, tea, silk, cotton, metal products
Já-pan', **Sea of** *Sea* W of Japan
Ja-pu-ra' *River* 1750 m. NW South America
Já-ri' (rē') *River* 360 m. NE Brazil
Jär'vis Island *Island* of Line Is.; air field
Jásh'pur *State* NE India
Jath (jut) *Town* * of *State* W India
Jä'vá 1. *Island* Malay Arch., Indonesia; agriculture. 2. **Sea** *Area* of Pacific O. N of Java
Ja-vá-ri' (rē') *River* 650 m. NW cen. South America
Já-whär' *State* W India
Jef'fėr-sŏn *River* 250 m. SW Mont., U.S.
Jef'fėr-sŏn City *City* * of Mo., U.S.; pop. 32,407; agriculture, mining
Jė-hōl' *City* * of *Region, Province* NE China
Je-le'nia Go'rä (ye-le', gōō'), Ger. **Hîrsch'-bêrg** *City* SW Poland
Je'lep-lä' *Pass* 14,390 ft. Sikkim
Je'nä (yä') *City* S cen. East Germany; glass
Jė-qui-ti-nhō'nhá (kē-tē-nyō'nyá) *River* 500 m. E Brazil
Je-rez' (hâ-rāz') *City* SW Spain; trade cen.
Jer'i-chō (kō) *Village* cen. Jordan; imp. anc. city
Jêr'sey (zi) *Island* of Channel Is. * St. Helier; resort
Jêr'sey City (zi) *City* NE N.J., U.S.; pop. 260,545; port, manufactures
Jė-rū'sá-lem *City* for-

merly of S cen. Palestine; Holy city of Moslems, Christians, Jews; was div.: Old City part of Jordan; New City, (W part) = * of Israel; pop. 66,000 (in total); 1967 united under Israel
Jêr'vis Bay *Inlet* of S Pacific O. SE Australia
Jes'sėl-tŏn *Town* * of Brit. North Borneo
Jes-sōre' *District* formerly NE Brit. India, now div. bet. E Pakistan and India
Jew'ish Au-ton'ö-mous Region = BIRO-BIDZHAN
Jhä'bu-á *City* * of *State* SW cen. India
Jhä'lá-wär *State* NW India
Jhäng' - Má-ghi-ä'nä *Town* * of *Jháng* dist. N Pakistan
Jhän'si *City* * of *Division* N India
Jhe'lum (jä') 1. *River* 450 m. Kashmir. 2. *Town* * of *District* W Pakistan
Jid'dá *Port* Hejaz, W Saudi Arabia   [India
Jind *Town*, *State* NW
Jin-sen = INCHON
Joao Pės-sō'á (zhwoun) *City* E Brazil
Jodh'pur *City* * of *State* NW India; camels, wheat, metalware
Jōg-já-kär'tä *City*, *Sultanate* S Java, former * of Indonesia
Jō-han'nės-bûrg *City* NE Rep. of South Africa; gold, produce, manufactures
John Day *River* 281 m. N Ore., U.S.
Johns'town *City* SW cen. Pa., U.S.; pop. 42,476; iron, coal cen.
Jo-hōre' *State* and *Strait* Malaysia, S Malay Penin.
Jō'li-et *City* NE Ill., U.S.; pop. 8,378;

industrial cen.

Jō-lō' (hō) *Island* Sulu Arch. Phil. Is.

Jon'ko-ping (yûn'chû) *City* * of *Province* S Sweden; matches

Jop'lin *City* SW Mo., U.S.; pop. 39,256

Jôr'dȧn *River* 200 m. Syria-Israel

Jôr'dȧn, Hash'ĕm-īte Kingdom of *Kingdom* Arab state, SW Asia; formerly **Trans'jôr-dȧn**; bel. to Turkish Emp. pre WW I; 37,300 sq. m.; pop. 2,100,000; * Amman

Juä'rez (h w ä') = CIUDAD JUAREZ

Jū'bȧ *River* 1000 m. E Africa

Jū'bȧ-land *Region* S Somalia, one-time colony

Jub'bul-pōre *City* * of *Division* cen. India

Jou'cär (hōō) *River* 300 m. E Spain

Jū'dah *Kingdom*, anc. S Palestine, later **Jū-dē'ȧ**

Jū-gō-slä'vi-ȧ = YU-GOSLAVIA

Juiz' dė Fô'rȧ (zhwēzh') *City* E Brazil; manufacturing

Jūl'iȧn Alps *Mts.* NW Yugoslavia

Jū-li-an'ȧ Top *Peak* 15,420 ft. W New Guinea

Jul'lun-dur *City* * of *Division* NW India

Jum'nȧ *River* 860 m. N cen. India

Ju-nä'gȧrh *Town* * of *State* W India

Jun-cäl' (hōōn) *Peak* 19,880 ft. Chile-Argentina

Junc'tion Peak *Mt.* 13,625 ft. S cen. Calif. U.S.

Jū'neau (nō) *City* SE Alas., U.S.; * of Alas.; pop. 6,050; harbor, fisheries

Jung'frau (yoong'frou) *Peak* 13,670 ft. SW cen. Switzerland

Jū'pi-têr Peak *Mt.* 13,-835 ft. SW Colo., U.S.

Jur (joor) *River* 300 m. SW Sudan

Ju'rȧ (joor') 1. *Department* E France. 2. *Mts.* bet. France and Switzerland

Jū-rua' (rwa') *River* 1200 m. NW cen. South America

Jū-rue'nȧ (rwä') *River* 600 m. W cen. Brazil

Jū-tȧ-i' (ē') *River* 400 m. NW Brazil

Jut'lȧnd *Peninsula* N Eur. incl. Danish mainland and N West Germany

K

Kab-ȧr-di'nō - Bal-kar'-i-ȧn A.S.S.R. *Republic* SE R.S.F.S.R., U.S.S.R., Eur.

Kä'bul 1. *City* * of Afghanistan; pop. 292,000. 2. *River* 360 m. Afghanistan-India

Kä-dhi-maīn' *City* cen. Iraq; holy city

Kä-di-koy' anc. **Chal'-cė-don** (kal'sė) *City* Turkey, Asia

Kȧ-di'yĕv-kȧ (dyē') *Town* Ukraine U.S.S.R.

Kae'sông' (ka'i), **Kaī-jō** *City* W North Korea; 1951 truce site

Ka'fä *Region* SW Ethiopia; coffee said to originate here

Kä-fū'e *River* 500 m. N Rhodesia

Kä-gä-wä *Prefecture* Shikoku, Japan

Kä-ge'rä (gä') *River* 429 m. E Africa

Kä-gi *City* W cen. Taiwan

Kä-go-shi-mä *City* on *Bay*, * of *Prefecture* Kyushu, Japan

Kaī'fing' *City* E cen. China; one-time *

Kaī Islands *Island* group Malay Arch. Indonesia

Kaī-jō = KAESONG

Kaī-läs' *Mt. range* SW Tibet

Kaī-lū'ä *Village* W Hawaii I , Haw., U.S.

Kaīr-ouän', Kaīr-wän' *City* NE Tunisia; Moslem holy city

Kaī-sêrs-lau'têrn (lou') *City* SW West Ger; many; manufacturing

Kaī-shū, Hae-jū (hī) *Town* W North Korea

Kȧ-lȧ-dan' *River* 300 m. Lower Burma

Kä-lä-hȧn'di *State* NE India

Kä-lä-hä'ri Desert *Plateau* South Africa; big game

Kal-ȧ-mä'tȧ, Kä-lä'maï *City* S Greece; port

Kal-ȧ-mȧ-zōō' 1. *City* SW Mich., U.S.; pop. 85,555; factories. 2. *River* 200 m. SW Mich., U.S.

Kȧ-lät' 1. *Town* W Pakistan. 2. *Former state* Brit. India

Kä-lä-wä'ō *Village, District* Molokai I., Haw., U.S.; leper settlement [CHUAN

Käl'gän now WAN-

Kȧ-li'nin (lē') *City* * of *Region* R.S.F.S.R., U.S.S.R., Eur.

Kȧ-li'nin-grad (lē'), Ger. **Kö'nigs-bêrg** *City* * of **Kȧ-li'nin-gradsk Region** W R.S.F.S.R., U.S.S.R.

Kä'lisz (lēsh), Ger. **Kä'-lisch** *Commune* cen. Poland

Kä'lix *River* 267 m. N Sweden; many rapids

Kal'mär *City* * of *Province* SE Sweden; port

Kal'mȳk A.S.S.R. *Former republic* U.S.S.R., Eur., now div.

Kȧ-lū'gȧ *City* * of *Region* cen. R.S.F.S.R., U.S.S.R., Eur.

Kä'mä *River* 1200 m. E R.S.F.S.R., U.S.S.R., Eur.

Kä-mä-ku-rä *Town* Honshu, Japan

Kam-chat'kȧ *Peninsula* site of *River* 350 m. and *Mountains*, NE Tibet

R.S.F.S.R., U.S.S.R., Asia; fish, furs

Kȧ-mė-nets' Pö-dôl'ski *City* and *Region* Ukraine U.S.S.R.

Kȧ'met *Peak* 25,445 ft. N India

Käm-pä'lä *Town* * of Uganda; pop. 331,900

Kän *River* 350 m. SE China

Kän or **Hän** *River* 220 m. cen. Korea

Kä-nä-gä-wä *Prefecture* Honshu, Japan

Kä-nä-zä-wä *City* Honshu, Japan; imp. industrially

Kȧn-chèn-jun'gȧ *Peak* 28,145 ft. Nepal-Sikkim

Kan'dȧ-här *City* * of *Province* SE Afghanistan; trade cen.

Kan'dȳ *Town* Ceylon; Buddhist temple

Kä'nem *District* Chad

Kan'gȧ-rōō Island *Island* S Australia

Käng'e-än *Island* of *Group* Java S. Indonesia

Käng'to' *Peak* 23,260 ft. Assam-Tibet

Kan'hsien' (gän'shi-en') formerly **Kan'chow'** (gän'jō') *Town* SE China

Kan-iȧ-pis'kau (kou) *River* 445 m. N Quebec, Canada

Ka'nin Peninsula *Peninsula* into Barents S., U.S.S.R., Eur.

Kan-kȧ-kēe' *River* 225 m. Ind.-Ill., U.S.

Kän-kō or **Häm-hung** (hoong) *City* N Korea

Kä'nō *City* * of *Province* N Nigeria; trade

Kän'pur *City* N cen. India; industrial cen.

Kan'sȧs (zȧs) *State* cen. U.S.; 82,276 sq. m.; pop. 2,249,071; * Topeka; 105 counties; agriculture, livestock

Kan'sȧs City 1. *City* NE Kan., U.S.; pop. 168,213; industrial cen. 2. *City* W Mo.,

U.S.; pop. 507,087; industry, commerce

Kan′sū′ *Province* N cen. China; agriculture, cattle, minerals

Kä′poe-äs (poo) *River* 450 m. Borneo, Indonesia [Korea

Kap-san *City* N North

Kȧ-pur′thȧ-lȧ *State* NW India

Kä′rä *Strait* connecting *Sea* with Barents S., U.S.S.R., Eur.

Kȧ-rȧ-cha′ĕv *Region Former autonomous region* R.S.F.S.R., U.S.S.R., Eur.

Kȧ-rä′chi *City* W Pakistan, former *; port, trade cen.

Kä-rä′fu-tō Jap. name of SAKHALIN

Kä-rä-gän-dä′ *City* * of *Region* Kazakh, U.S.S.R., Asia; coal

Kä - rä - Käl - päk′ *A.S.S.R. Area* Uzbek U.S.S.R.

Kar-ȧ-kō′rȧm 1. *Mt. range* N Kashmir. 2. *Pass* 18,290 ft., main route Kashmir-China. 3. *Ruins* of anc. * of Mongolia

Kä′rä Kûl′ *Lake* Tadzhik U.S.S R., Asia

Kä′rä Kum′ (kōōm′) *Desert* 110,000 sq. m Turkmen, U.S.S.R., Asia

Kä-rä-tsu *City* Kyushu, Japan; port

Kȧ-rau′li (rou′) *State* N cen. India

Kär′bȧ-la *Town* and *Province* cen. Iraq; holy city

Kȧ-rē′lō - Finn′ish S.S.R. *Constituent Republic,* NW U.S.S.R., Eur.; * Petrozavodsk; forests, furs, fish

Kä-ri-käl′ *Town* and *Province* SE India; Fr. India before 1954

Kä-ri-mä′tä *Islands* and *Strait* W of Borneo, Indonesia

Kar-i-sim′bi *Peak* 14,-785 ft. E Congo (L)

Kar-kheh′ (ka′) *River* 340 m. W Iran

Kär′li *Village* W India; Buddhist caves

Kar′lô-vȳ Va′rȳ, Ger. **Kärls′bad, Cärls′bad** *Town* W Czechoslovakia; springs

Kärls-kro′na (krōō′) *City* S Sweden; harbor

Kärls′rū-hė *City* S West Germany; manufacturing

Kärl′städ *City* SW Sweden; factories

Kär′näk *Village* Upper Egypt; hist. temples

Kär′pȧ-thos *Island* of Dodecanese Is.

Kȧr-rōō′ *Tableland* Rep. of South Africa

Kä-rūn′ *River* 450 m. W Iran

Kä-saī′ 1. *River* 1200 m. SW Africa. 2. *Province* was Lusambo, Congo (L)

Kä-shän′ *City* cen. Iran; carpets, melons

Kash′gär or **Shū′fū′** *Town* W China; wool, tea, cotton

Kä′shing′, Chia′hsing′ (ji-ä′) *City* E China; eggs, poultry, rice

Kash′mir (mēr) or **Jȧm′mū** and **Kash′mir** *State* N India, in dispute bet. India and Pakistan; * Srinagar; agriculture, Cashmere goats, woods

Kas-kas′ki-ȧ *River* 300 m. SW Ill., U.S.

Käs′sėl, Cäs′sėl *City* West Germany; machinery

Kas′sė-rine (rēn) *Village* and *Pass* cen. Tunisia

Kȧ-sur′ (soor′) *Town* W Pakistan

Kȧ-täh′din *Peak* 5268 ft., highest in Me., U.S.

Kȧ-tän′gȧ *Province* S Congo (L); * Elizabethville; minerals

Kä′thi-ȧ-wär (ti) *Peninsula* W India

Kat′maī, Mount *Volcano* S Alas., U.S.

Kät-män-dū′ *City* * of Nepal

Kä-to-wi′ce (vė′tse), **Kät′to-witz** *City* S Poland; coal cen.

Kat′rine, Loch (lok) *Lake* cen. Scotland

Kä′tsi-nȧ *Town* and *anc. Kingdom* N Nigeria

Kat′tė-gat *Arm* of North S. bet Sweden and Denmark

Kȧ-tūn′ *River* 400 m. U.S.S.R., Asia

Kau′näs (kou′), **Kôv′nö** *City* * of *District* cen. Lithuania; onetime *; factories

Kȧ-val′lȧ *City* * of *Department* on *Gulf* Macedonia N E Greece

Ka-vi-eng′ *Town* NW New Ireland; port

Ka-vir′, Dasht-i- (vēr′) *Salt Desert* N cen. Iran

Kä-wä-gu-chi (goo) *City* and *Lake* Honshu, Japan

Kä-wä-sä-ki *City* Honshu, Japan; elec. equipment

Kȧ-wē′ȧh Peaks *Four Mts.* S cen. Calif., U.S.; over 13,000 ft.

Kay′ak (kī′) *Island* off SE Alas., U.S.

Kay-se-ri′ (kī, rē′) *City* * of *Vilayet* cen. Turkey Asia

Kä-zäkh′ S.S.R. *Constituent Republic* of U.S.S.R. cen. Asia; * Alma Ata; agriculture, minerals

Kȧ-zan′ 1. *River* 450 m. cen. Canada. 2. *City* * of Tatar Rep. E R.S.F.S.R., U.S.S.R., Eur.; commerce, industry

Kȧz-bek′ *Peak* 16,540 ft. U.S.S.R., Eur.

Kaz-vin′ (vēn′) *City* * of *Province* NW Iran; trade cen.

Keȧr′nȳ *Town* NE N.J.

U.S.; pop. 37,585; factories

Kecs′ke-met (kech′ke-māt) *City* cen. Hungary; market cen.

Ke′däh (kä′) *Area* S Malay Penin. Malaysia; rubber, rice

Ke-där′näth *Peak* 23,-420 ft. NE India

Ke-di′ri (dē′) *City* Java, Indonesia; sugar cen.

Ke′doe, Ke′du (kä′dōō) *Residency* Java, Indonesia; agricultural

Kēele *River* 230 m. NW Terrs. Canada

Kēe′lung′ (loong′), **Ki-run** (roon) *City* N Formosa (Taiwan); port, naval base

Keigh′ley (kē′li) *Municipal borough* N England; woolens

Kei-jo (kä) now SEOUL

Kė-lan′tan *Area* S Malay Penin., Malaysia [U.S.S.R.

Kem *River* 140 m.

Ke′mė-rō-vō *City* * of *Region* R.S.F.S.R., U.S.S.R., Asia; heavy industry

Ke′mi *Port* on *River* 300 m. N Finland

Kē′naī *Peninsula Peninsula* S Alas., U.S.

Ken′il - wörth *Urban district* cen. England; castle ruins

Ke-ni-tra′ (kä-nē) now PORT LYAUTEY

Ken′nė-bec *River* 165 m. cen. Me., U.S.

Ken′nė-dȳ, Cape *Cape* E Fla., U.S.; rocket launching cen.

Kė-nog′ȧ-mi *River* 200 m. cen. Ontario, Canada

Kė-nō′shȧ *City* SE Wisc., U.S.; pop. 78,-805; industrial

Ken′sing-tön *Borough* of London, England

Kent *County* SE England; farming, dairying, fishing, manufacturing

Ken-tuck′ȳ 1. *River* 260 m. Ky., U.S. 2. *State* E cen. U.S.; 40,395

GAZETTE· ATLAS

sq. m.; pop. 3,219,-311; * Frankfort

Ken′yȧ 1. *Republic* of Brit. Commonwealth E Africa; 225,000 sq. m.; pop. 10,900,000; * Nairobi; agriculture, mining. 2. *Mountain* 17,040 ft. cen. Kenya

Ke-ōn′jhȧr *Town* * of *State* NE India

Kė-rak (rok) *Anc emirate* now in Jordan

Ke′rä-lä (kä′) *State* SW India

Kêrch *City* on *Peninsula* E Crimea S. U.S.S.R.; metallurgy, port

Kêr′guė-lėn, Des′ö-lā-tion Island *Island* of *Arch.* of Fr. Union, S Indian O.

Kė-rin′tji (che) *Peak* 12,465 ft. Sumatra; volcanic

Kerk′ra-dė *Commune* SE Netherlands

Kêr-män′ anc. **Cär-mä′nȧ** *City* * of *Province* SE Iran; carpets

Ker-män-shäh′ *City* * of *Province* W Iran

Kêrn *River* 200 m. S cen. Calif., U.S.

Ker′rẏ *County* SW Eire

Ker′u-len *River* 650 m N Ouğer Mongolia

Ket *River* 500 m. S Siberia, U.S.S.R., Asia

Ketch′i-kȧn *Town* SE Alas., U.S.; port; salmon, pulp

Ket′têr-ing 1. *City* SW Ohio, U.S.; pop. 69,-599; manufacturing. 2. *Urban district* cen. England

Keü′kȧ, Lake *Lake* W N.Y., U.S.; one of Finger lakes

Key Lär′gō (kē) *Island* largest of Fla. Keys SE U.S.

Key West *City* on *Island* SW Fla., U.S.; pop. 27,563

Khȧ-ba′rövsk *City* * of *Territory* R.S.F.S.R., U.S.S.R., Asia; fur, mineral cen.

Khä-bur′ *River* 200 m. Turkey-Syria

Khaĭ′rä-gȧrh *Town* * of *State* NE India

Khaĭr′pur *Town* * of *State* S West Pakistan

Khȧ-kass′ Autonomous Region *Region* R.S.F.S.R., S Siberia, U.S.S.R.

Khȧ′li-fȧt *Peak* 11,440 ft. Pakistan

Khä - nȧ - qin′ (kēn′) *Town* E Iraq; oil

Khän′bä - lik′ (lēk′) *Town* (mod. PEI-PING) Mongol name of Kubla Khan's * of China   [India

Khȧnd-pä′rȧ *State* NE

Khan′kȧ, Han′kȧ *Lake* 1700 sq. m. Manchuria-U.S.S.R.

Khan′tẏ-Man′si *District* W Siberia, U.S.S.R., Asia

Khȧ′rȧg-pur *City* NE India

Khär′kôv *City* * of *Region* NE Ukraine U.S.S.R.; rail cen.

Khär′tȧ-phu (pōō) *Peak* 23,800 ft. Himalayas

Khär-ti-chäng′ri *Peak* 23,420 ft. Himalayas

Khär-toum′, Khär-tum′ (tōōm′) *City* * of *Province* and * of Sudan; pop. 160,000

Khä′si *District* NE India

Khȧ-tan′gȧ *River* 800 m. U.S.S.R., Asia

Kher-sôn′ *City* in *Region* S Ukraine U.S.S.R.; port

Khe′tȧ *River* 500 m. U.S.S.R., Asia

Khi-lôk′ *River* 350 m. U.S.S.R., Asia

Khing′än′ (shing′) *Mountain ranges* (2) E Asia

Khir-bät′ Qum-rän′ *Site* NW Jordan; Dead Sea Scrolls 1947

Khôb′dō *River* 300 m. Outer Mongolia

Khō′i (ē) *Town* NW Iran; trade cen.

Khö-per′ (pyôr′) *River*

560 m. R.S.F.S.R., U.S.S.R., Eur.

Khor-ram-shahr′ (koor) *Town* W Iran

Khō′tän′, Hō′tien′ *Town, Oasis* W China; supply cen.

Khul′nä *Town* * of *District* E Pakistan

Khȳ′bêr Pass *Pass* 33 m. long bet. Afghanistan and India

Kiä′ling′ (ji-ä′) *River* 500 m. cen. China

Kia′mu′sze′, Chia′mus′su′ (ji-ä′moo′soo′) *City* NE China

Ki′än′ (jē′), **Lü′ling′** *Town* SE China

Kiäng′ling′ (ji-äng′), **King′chow′** (jing′jō′) *City* E cen. China

Kiang′si′ (ji-äng′sē′) *Province* SE China

Kiang′sū′ (ji-äng′) *Province* E China

Kiang′tu′ (ji-äng′dōō′), **Yäng′chow′** (jō′) *City* E China

Kiao′chow′ (ji-ou′jō′) *District* and *Bay* NE China

Ki′bō (kē′) *Peak* (highest) 19,315 ft. of Mt. Kilimanjaro

Kiĕl *City* N West Germany; port

Kiĕl or **Kaĭ′sêr Wil′helm Canal** *Canal* 61 m. long, Baltic to North S.

Kiel′ce, Kel′tsẏ *City* * of *Dept.* S Poland

Ki′ev (kē′yef) *City* * of *Province* and * of Ukraine S.S.R., U.S.S.R., Eur.; commercially, industrially, historically imp.

Ki-gä′li *Town* * of Rwanda; pop. 17,000

Kil-dare′ *County* E Eire; farming, textiles, brewing

Ki-li-mȧn-jä′rō, Mount *Mountain* 19,315 ft. NE Tanzania; Africa's highest point

Kil-ken′nẏ *County* SE Eire; mining, brewing, quarrying

Kil-lär′ney (ni) *District, Lakes* (3) SW Eire

Kil-lēen′ *City* E Texas, U.S.; pop. 35,507

Kil-mär′nŏck *Burgh* SW Scotland; coal, manufactures

Kim′bêr-ley (li) *Town* Cape of Good Hope, Rep. of South Africa; world's diamond cen.

Kin (kēn) *River* 250 m. SW Korea

Kin-ȧ-bȧ-täng′än *River* 350 m. N Borneo, Malaysia

Kin-ȧ-bu-lū′ *Mountain* 13,455 ft. N Borneo, Malaysia

Kin-cär′dine-shire, formerly **The Mearns** (mûrnz) *County* E Scotland; livestock. quarrying, fishing

Ki′nėsh-mȧ (kē′) *City* R.S.F.S.R., U.S.S.R., Eur.

King′chow′ now KIANGLING

King Chris′tian IX Land (kris′) and **King Frederick VI Land** *Coastal regions* SE Greenland

King Island 1. *Island* Bering Strait W Alas. U.S.; walrus hunting. 2. *Island* Bass Strait S Australia

King′s Peak *Peak* 13,-495 ft. NE Utah, U.S.

Kings′tŏn 1. *City* SE Ontario, Canada; shipping. 2. *City* * of Jamaica; port

Kings′town 1. *City* and *Bay* St. Vincent I. West Indies. 2. now DUN LAOGHAIRE

King Wil′liam Island *Island* NW Terrs., Canada   [China

Kin′hwä (jin′) *City* E

Kin-rôss′ *County* E cen. Scotland; textiles

Kinshasa *City* * of *Province* and * of Zaire, SW part; pop. ab. 1,000,000; air cen.; formerly **Leopoldville**

Kin′tä Val′ley *Area*

Malay Penin. W Malaysia; tin

Kir-ghiz' (gēz') early name of KAZAKH S.S.R.

Kir-giz' Range (gēz') *Mountains* U.S.S.R., cen. Asia

Kir-giz' S.S.R. (gēz') *Republic* of U.S.S.R., cen. Asia; livestock, grains

Ki'rin' (kē') 1. *Province* cen. Manchuria, China. 2. or **Yung'ki'** (yoong'jē') *City* E Manchuria, China; port

Kirk-cäl'dy (cä') *Burgh* E Scotland; port

Kirk-cūd'bright (kōō'-brī) *County* and *Burgh* S Scotland

Kirk-pat'rick, Mount *Peak* 14,600 ft. S Victoria Land, Antarctica

Kir-kūk' *Town* in *Province* NE cen. Iraq; oil, sheep

Ki'röv (kē') *City* * of *Region* R.S.F.S.R., U.S.S.R., Eur.; cultural, industrial cen.

Ki-rō'vȧ-bad *City* SW U.S.S.R., Eur.; textiles, mines

Ki-rō'vō-grad *City* * of *Region* Ukraine U.S.S.R., Eur.; agriculture

Ki'rövsk (kē') *Town* R.S.F.S.R., U.S.S.R., Eur.; uranium

Ki-run (kē-roon) see KEELUNG

Kir-yū *Town* Honshu, Japan; weaving

Kish *Anc. city* now in Iraq; imp. ruins

Ki'shȧn-gärh *Former state* NW India

Ki'shi-nev *City* SW U.S.S.R., Eur.; former * of Bessarabia

Kis'kȧ *Island* W Aleutian Is., Alas., U.S.

Kis'lö-vodsk *City* R.S.F.S.R., U.S.S.R., Eur.

Kis'tnȧ, formerly **Krish'-**

nȧ *River* 800 m. S India

Kit Kär'sön Peak *Peak* 14,100 ft. S Colo., U.S.

Kitch'ė-nėr *City* SE Ontario, Canada

Kit'tẏ Hȧwk *Village* E N.C., U.S.; site of Wright brothers' first plane flight 1903

Kiu'kiang' (ji-ōō'ji-äng') *City* SE China; tea, pottery

Kiung'shän' (chi-oong') *City* Hainan I. SE China; port

Ki'vū (kē') *Lake* 1025 sq. m. cen. Africa (Congo-Rwanda)

Ki-zil' Ir-mäk' *River* 600 m. cen. Turkey, Asia

Klä'gin-furt (foort) *City* S Austria; factories

Klam'ȧth *River* 250 m. S Ore., U.S.

Klär *River* 215 m. cen. Norway-W Sweden

Klon'dīke *Region, River* Yukon, NW Canada; gold rush 1897-99

Klông or **Me-klông** *River* 300 m. W Thailand

Klū-äne' *Lake* and *River* SW Yukon, Canada

Klẏ-az'mȧ *River* 425 m. U.S.S.R., Eur.

Klyū-chev'skȧ-yȧ Sôp'-kȧ *Volcano* 15,900 ft. Siberia, U. S. S. R., Asia

Knox'ville (nox') *City* E Tenn., U.S.; pop. 174,587; commerce, industry

Kō'bē *City* Honshu, Japan; port, factories

Ko-bėn-havn' (kû-pėn-houn') = COPENHAGEN

Kō'blenz or **Cō'blenz** *City* and *District* W cen. West Germany; commerce, industry

Kō-buk' (book') *River* 275 m. NW Alas., U.S.

Kō-chi *City* * of *Prefecture* Shikoku, Japan

Kō'di-ak *Island* S

Alas., U.S.; salmon, furs

Koe'päng (kōō') = KUPANG

Koe'tä-rä'djä (kōō') = KUTARAJA

Kō'fu *City* Honshu, Japan; silk market

Kog'ȧ-rȧh *City* SE Australia

Kō-hä'lä *Village* N Hawaii I., Haw. U.S.; home of 1st king

Kō-hät' *Town* * of *District* N West Pakistan

Kō - kand' *City* S U.S.S.R., Asia; trade

Kō'kö-mō *City* N cen. Ind., U.S.; pop. 44,-042; metal goods

Kō-ku-rä (koo) *City* Kyushu, Japan; port

Kō'lä or **Kôl'ski Peninsula** *Peninsula* bet. White S. and Arctic O., NW U.S.S.R., Eur.; Murmansk area

Kō-lär' Gōld Fīelds *City* S India; gold

Kōl'hȧ-pur (poor) *City* * of *State* W India; trade cen.

Köln = COLOGNE

Kō-lō'ä *Village, District* Kauai I., Haw., U.S.; Hawaii's 1st sugar plantation

Kô-lôb'rzeg (rhek), Ger. **Kôl'bêrg** *City* NW Poland; port

Kö-lôm'nȧ *City* nr. Moscow, U.S.S.R., Eur.; factories

Kö-lẏ'mȧ 1. *River* 1110 m. U.S.S.R., Asia. 2. *Range* E U.S.S.R.

Kö-mȧn-dôr'ski-ė or **Cöm-man'dêr Islands** *Islands* Bering S., E U.S.S.R.

Kö-mä'ti *River* 500 m. S Africa

Kō'mi A.S.S.R. *Republic* NE R.S.F.S.R., U.S.S.R., Eur.; forests, minerals

Kō'mi-Pêrm'iak *National district* NW Siberia, U. S. S. R., Asia

Kom-sö-môlsk' *City*

R.S.F.S.R., SE U.S.S.R., Asia; steel, shipyards

Kö'nigs-bêrg = KALININGRAD

Kon-stȧn-ti'növ-kȧ (te') *City* Ukraine W U.S.S.R., Eur.

Kôn'stänz, Con'stȧnce *City* S West Germany; factories

Kôn-yä' *City* * of *Vilayet* SW Turkey, Asia

Koo'tė-nāi *River* 400 m. SW Canada-NW U.S.

Kö'pė-nick, Cö'pė-nik area of East Berlin

Kö-re-ä' (rä) *State* NE India

Kö-rē'ȧ, Jap. Chō-sen *Country* on *Peninsula* E coast of Asia, former Jap. dependency, divided 1948 at 38th parallel: 1. **North Korean People's Rep.**; * Pyongyang (Heijo); 48,000 sq. m.; pop. 13,000,000. 2. **South Korean Rep.** * Seoul (Keijo); 37,000 sq. m.; pop. 31,200,000

Kö-rē'ȧ Strait *Channel* Korea-Japan, site of **Korean Arch.**

Kö-ri-yä-mä *City* Honshu, Japan; silk mills

Kôrr'ce (chè), It. **Coriz'zä** (rēt') *Town* * of *Prefecture* SE Albania; textiles, flour

Kö-ryak' National District *District* E U.S.S.R. on Bering S.; fish

Kôs, Cos *Island* of Dodecanese, SW Turkey, Asia

Kos-ci-us'kō, Mount *Peak* 7330 ft., highest in Australia, SE part

Kosh'tän Tau' (tou') *Mountain* 16,875 ft. U.S.S.R., Eur.

Kō - shū, Kwäng - jū *Town* SW South Korea [Nepal-India

Kō'si *River* 305 m.

Kō'si-ce (shi-tse), Ger. **Kä'schau** *City* SE

Czechoslovakia; industrial

Kö-strö-ma′ *River* 250 m. and *City* * of *Region* N cen. R.S.F.S.R., U.S.S.R., Eur.

Kō′tåh *Town* * of *State* NW India; muslin, carpets

Kö′then (tĕn) *City* East Germany; factories

Kot′tō *River* 400 m. cen. Africa

K ö v - r ô v′ *T o w n* R.S.F.S.R., U.S.S.R., Eur.

Kow′lōōn′, Kau′lūn′ (kow′) *Town* on *Peninsula* SE China, bel. to Hong Kong; imp. commercially

Koy′u-kuk (kī′) *River* 425 m. W Alas., U.S.

Krä-kȧ-tau′ (tou′) *Island volcano* nr. Java, Indonesia

Krä′kow (kōōf), **Krä′-kau** (kou) *City* * of *Department* S Poland; educational cen.

Krȧ-mȧ-tôrsk′ *City* Ukraine, U.S.S.R.; industry

Kras′no-dȧr *City* * of *Territory* R.S.F.S.R., S U.S.S.R., Eur.; industrial, cultural cen.

Kras′no-vodsk *Town* on *Gulf* * of *Region* U.S.S.R. cen. Asia

Kras′no-yȧrsk *Town* * of *Territory* W cen. Siberia, U.S.S.R.; commerce, industry, gold

Kras′nẏ Lūch′ *City* Ukraine U.S.S.R.

Kre′feld (krä′) *City* West Germany; textiles

Kre′mĕn-chūg *City* Ukraine, U.S.S.R.

Kre-mė-nets′ *City* Ukraine, U.S.S.R.

Krem′lin = a citadel, walled part of Russ. city; site of government buildings in Moscow

Krems *City* N Austria; machinery

Krish′nȧ now KISTNA

Kri-voi′ Rôg′ *City* Ukraine, U.S.S.R.; mines

Krōn′shtadt *Town* on *Bay*, NW U.S.S.R. Eur.

Krö-pot′kin *T o w n* U.S.S.R. Eur.; grain

Krū′gêr National Park *Game reserve* NE Rep. of South Africa

Krū′gêrs-dôrp *Town* NE Rep. of South Africa; gold cen.

Krung Thep (kroong t′hāp) = BANGKOK

Kuä′lȧ Lum′pur (loom′-poor) *City* * of Malaysia, W cen. Malay Penin.; pop. 216,230

Kū-ban′ *River* 510 m. U.S.S.R. Eur.

Kū′ching *City* Borneo, Malaysia; trade cen.

Ku′fow′, Chu′fou′ (fōō′) *Town* NE China; home of Confucius

Kūh-i-Di-när′ (dē) *Peak* 14,030 ft. SW Iran

Kūi′bẏ-shev, was **Sȧ-ma′rȧ** *City* * of *Region* cen. U.S.S.R., Eur.; port

Kū′kông′ *City* SE China; coal cen.

Ku′lȧ Gulf *Gulf* Solomon Is.; WW II battles

Ku-ma′ *River* 400 m. U.S.S.R. Eur.

Ku-mä-gä-yä *Town* Honshu, Japan

Ku-mä-mō-tō *City* * of *Prefecture*, Kyushu, Japan

Kū-mä′si *City* S cen. Ghana; mod. city

Kum-bȧ-kō′nȧm *City* S India; Brahman cen.

Kun′lun′, Shän′ *Mountain ranges* cen. Asia

Kun′ming′, was **Yunnan′** *City* SW China; trade cen.

Kun-sän = GUNZAN

Kuô′piô *City* * of *Department* S Finland; lumber cen.

Kū′päng = KOEPANG

Ku-rä′ *River* 825 m. NE Turkey to Cas-

pian S.

Kûr-di-stän′ *Region* (nonpolitical) SW Asia: Turkey, Iraq, Iran

Ku-re (koo) *City* Honshu, Japan; harbor

Kur-gan′ (koor) *City* * of *Region* cen. U.S.S.R., W Asia; trade cen.

Ku-ri-hä-mä *Town* SE Honshu, Japan; Comm. Perry′s landing site, 1853

Kū′ril or **Ku′rile Islands** *Islands* (ab. 32) N of Japan; bel. to Russia

Kū′ril Strait *Strait* bet. *Islands* and U.S.S.R.

Kûr-lȧnd = K U R - ZEME

Kur′rȧm *River* 200 m. NW Pakistan

Kursk (koorsk) *City* * of *Region* E cen. R.S.F.S.R., U.S.S.R., Eur.

Ku-ru-me (koo-roo) *City* Kyushu, Japan; cotton fabric

Kur′ze-me, Kûr′lȧnd *Province* W Latvia U.S.S.R.

Ku-shi-ro *City* Hokkaido, Japan; port

Kus′ko-kwim *River* 550 m. SW Alas., U.S.

Ku-stȧ-naī′ *Town* * of *Region* Kazakh, U.S.S.R. cen. Asia

Ku-tä′i-si *City* Georgia, U.S.S.R.; trade, coal

Kūt′al I-mär′ȧ *Town* SE cen. Iraq

Kū′tä Rä′jä *Port* Sumatra, Indonesia

Ku-wāit′ *Independent Arab State* NW Persian Gulf; * **Kuwait City**; 6000 sq. m.; pop. 534,000; oil

Kuz-netsk′ (kooz) *City* R.S.F.S.R., U.S.S.R., Eur.; trade cen.

Kuz-netsk′ Basin *Basin* of Tom R., U.S.S.R., Asia; iron, coal

Kwä′jȧ-lein (lin) *Island* Marshall Is. W Pacific O. [S Africa

Kwän′dō *River* 600 m.

Kwäng′chow′ (jō′) 1.

official name for CANTON. 2. *Territory* SE China, formerly Fr.

Kwäng-jū = KOSHU

Kwäng′si′ *Province* SE China; rice, forests

Kwäng′tung′ (doong′) *Province* SE China; agriculture, harbors

Kwän′tung′ (doong′) *Territory* S Manchuria, China

Kwei′chow′ (gwā′jō′) *Province* S China; agriculture, forestry

Kwei′lin′ (gwā′) *City* SE China

Kwei′sui′ (gwā′swā′) *Town* N China; trade

Kwei′yäng′ or **Kwei′-chū′** (gwā′) *City* S China

Kyō′gȧ *Lake* 1000 sq. m. S cen. Uganda

Kyông′sông = SEOUL

Kyō′tō *City* * of *Prefecture*, anc. * of Japan; Honshu, Japan

Kȳ-rē′ni-ȧ *District* N Cyprus

Kyū′shū *Island* S Japan; fine harbors

Kẏ-zẏl′ Kum′ *Desert* 1 0 0 , 0 0 0 sq. m. U.S.S.R., cen. Asia

Kzẏl′-Ôr-dä′ *Town* * of *Region* U.S.S.R., cen. Asia

L

Lab′rȧ-dôr 1. *Peninsula* E Canada; div. bet. Quebec and Newfoundland provs. 2. *Current* flows S along W Greenland, E Newfoundland

Lȧ-bū′ȧn *Island* off NW Borneo, Malaysia

Lac′cȧ-dīve and A-min-di′vi Islands (dē′) *Islands, Terr.* of India, Arabian S.

Läch′lȧn (läk′) *River* 800 m. SE Australia

Lȧ-cō′ni-ȧ *Department* and *Anc. country* SE Greece; * Sparta

Lä Cö-rū′na (nyä) *City* * of *Province* NW Spain; port

Lä Crôsse′ *City* W Wisc., U.S.; pop. 51,-153; shipping cen., manufacturing

Là-däkh′ *District* and *Mountain range* E Kashmir

Lad′ō-gà *Lake* N U.S.S.R.; 7000 sq. m.; largest in Eur.

Lä′e *Town* SE New Guinea; WW II base

Lä-fày-ette′ 1. *City* W cen. Ind., U.S.; pop. 44,955; commerce. 2. *City* La., U.S.; pop. 68,908; market cen.

Là-gōōn′ *Islands* = ELLICE ISLANDS

Lä′gos *City* on *Island* * of Nigeria, SW part; pop. 700,000; port

Lä Guaī′rä *Town* N Venezuela

La-gū′nà *Province* Luzon, Phil. Is. [VANA

Lä Hä-bä′nä = HA-La Hä′brà *City* S Cal., U.S.; pop. 41,350

Là-hōre′ 1. *City* * of West Pakistan; trade cen. 2. *Former division* NW Brit. India, now div. Pakistan-India

Läh′ti *City* S Finland

Laī′chow′ (jō′) now YEHSIEN

Lail-lä′hue (lī-yä′wä) *Peak* 16,995 ft. Bo-livia-Peru

Läke Chärles *City* SW La., U.S.; pop. 77,998

Lake District *Region* NW England; resorts

Läke′hûrst *Borough* E N.J., U.S.; site of *Hindenburg* fire 1937

Läke′land *City* cen. Fla., U.S.; pop. 41,-550; business

Lake of the Woods *Lake* N Minn., U.S.-S Canada

Lake Plac′id (plas′) *Village* NE N.Y., U.S.

Lake Suc-cess′ (suk-ses′) *Village* SE N.Y. U.S.

Läke′wood 1. *City* N Ohio U.S.; pop. 70,-173. 2. *City* S. Cal.,

U.S.; pop. 82,973; residential. 3. *City* N Col., U.S.; pop. 92,-787

Lä Män′chä *Region* S cen. Spain

Là-märck′, Mount *Peak* 13,300 ft. S cen. Calif. U.S.

Läm-ba-re-ne′ (rä-nä′) *Town* W Gabon

La Me′sa (mä′) *City* S Cal., U.S.; pop. 39,-178

Lam′mêr-mūir or Lam′-mêr-moor **Hills** *Range* SE Scotland

Là-motte′ *Peak* *Peak* 12,720 ft. Utah, U.S.

Läm-päng *Town* * of *Province* NW Thailand

Läm′pông *Bay* and *District* S Sumatra, Indonesia

Lan′árk-shîre *County* S cen. Scotland; ships, textiles, mining

Lan′cà-shîre, Lan′càs-têr *County* NW England; mining, shipping, manufacturing

Lan′cas-têr 1. *City* SE Pa., U.S.; pop. 57,-690; tobacco, farming, livestock cen.; factories. 2. *Municipal borough* NW England; textiles

Län′chow′ (jō′) = KAOLAN

Landes (länd) *Department* SW France

Lands End *Cape* SW England

Länds′hūt *City* SE West Germany; manufacturing

Läng′chung′ (joong′) *City* S cen. China

Lang′ley, Mount (li) *Peak* 14,040 ft. S cen. Calif., U.S.

Län-gre′o (grä′) *City* NW Spain

Lang′ Son′ *Town* NE North Vietnam

Lan′sing *City* * of Mich., U.S.; pop. 131,546; automobiles

Län′tsäng′ = Chin. for MEKONG

Lä′nus *City* E Argentina

Lao′hō-kōw′ (lou′) *City* E cen. China

Laoigh′is (lä′ish), Leix (läx) *County* cen. Eire

Lao′ Kay′ (lou′ kī′) *Town* N Vietnam

Laos, Kingdom of (lous) *Kingdom* SE Asia; 91,000 sq. m.; pop. 2,900,000; * Vientiane, * Luang-prabang; formerly part of Fr. Indochina; agriculture

Lä Päl′mä *Island* of Canary Is., Spain

Lä Päm′pä *Territory* S cen. Argentina

Là Paz′ 1. *City* * of *Department* and * of Bo-livia; pop. 562,000; industry, trade. 2. *Department* S El Sal-vador. 3. *Department, Town* SW Honduras. 4. *Town* on *Bay* NW Mexico

Lap′land *Region* above Arctic Circle: parts of Norway, Sweden, Finland and Kola Penin. of U.S.S.R.; reindeer, fish

Lä Plä′tä 1. *City* E Argentina; city plan like Wash., D.C. 2. *River* 225 m. Ura-guay-Argentina. 3. *Unit* of Span. South America, 18th cent. 4. *Mountains* SW Colo., U.S. 5. *Peak* 14,340 ft. Colo., U.S.

Lap′tev Sea (tyèf) *Area* of Arctic O. U.S.S.R., Asia

La-rache′ (rash′) *City* NW Morocco; port, fisheries

Lar′à-mie *River* 200 m., *Mountain range* Colo. Wyo., U.S.

Lärch *River* 300 m. Quebec, Canada

Là-re′dō (rä′) *City* S Tex., U.S.; pop. 69,-024; industrial port

Là-ris′sà *City* * of *Department* Thessaly,

Greece

La Rô-chelle′ (shel′) *City* W France

Lärs Chris′tèn-sèn Cōast (kris′) *Coast* of Antarctica on Indian O. (Norway)

Läs Crū′cès *City* S N.M., U.S.; pop. 37,857

Lä Se-re′nä (rä′) *City* cen. Chile

Làsh′kár *City* N cen. India; trade

Läs Päl′mäs *City* * of *Province* Canary Is. Spain; port

Lä Spe′ziä (spä′) *City* on *Gulf* * of *Province* NW Italy; harbor

Las′sèn Peak *Volcano* 10,545 ft. NE Calif., U.S.

Läs Ve′gàs (vä′) *City* SE Nev., U.S.; pop. 125,787; tourists

Läs Vil′las (vē′yäs) *Province* W cen. Cuba

Lat-à-ki′à (kē′) *City* * of *Territory* (coastal region) W Syria; to-bacco

Lat′in À-mer′i-cà = *Area* incl. Span. America and Brazil

Lä-ti′nä (tē′), formerly Lit-tō′ri-à *Province* cen. Italy

Lä′ti-um (shi) *Compartimento* and *Anc. country* cen. Italy

Lä Tôr-tū′gä *Island* N cen. Venezuela

La Tri-ni-te′ (trē-nē-tä′) *Commune* E Martinique

Lat′vi-àn S.S.R. *Republic* of U.S.S.R. N Eur.; * Riga; lumber, agriculture, livestock; Balkan republic be-fore 1940

Laun′ces-tön *City* Tas-mania, Australia; trade cen.

Lä Ū-niôn′ 1. *Province* Luzon, Phil. Is.; coco-nuts, sugar. 2. *Town* * of *Department* E El Salvador

Lău-ren′tian **Mountains** (shàn) *Moun-*

tain range Quebec, Canada

Lău-sanne' *Commune* W Switzerland; manufacturing

Lau-tō'kả (lou) *Town* Fiji Is.; sugar cen.

La-val' *Commune* NW France

Lä Ven'tä (vän') *Village* SE Mexico

Läw'rénce 1. *City* NE Mass., U.S.; pop. 66,915; paper, textiles, rubber products. 2. *City* E Kan., U.S.; pop. 45,698

Lăw'tön *City* SW Okla., U.S.; pop. 74,470; cotton, factories

Lēaf 1. *River* 200 m. SE Miss., U.S. 2. *River* 295 m. Quebec, Canada

Leam'ing-tön (l e m') *Municipal borough* cen. England; resort

Leav'én-wörth (lev') *City* NE Kan., U.S.; nearby FORT LEAVENWORTH

Leb'à-nön, Republic of *Republic* E of Mediterranean S.; * Beirut; 4000 sq. m.; pop. 2,600,000; tobacco, fruits; formerly in Turkish Emp., later Fr. mandate

Le Bour-get' (boor-zhā') *Commune* N France; Lindbergh's landing 1927

Lec'ce (lāt'chä) *Commune* * of *Province* SE Italy; textiles

Lec'cō (lāk') *Commune* N Italy; manufacturing

Lè Conte' *Peak* 13,960 ft. S cen. Calif., U.S.

Lē'dō *Town* NE India; start of Stillwell (formerly **Ledo**) Road, military highway to Burma

Lēeds *City*, county borough N England; industrial cen.

Leeu'wär-dèn (lā'vär) *Commune* N Nether-

lands; commerce, industry

Leeū'win, Cape *Cape* SW tip of Australia

Lēe'wàrd Islands 1. *Island china* of Lesser Antilles E West Indies; div. bet. U.S. (Virgin Is.), France, Netherlands, Britain. 2. *Island group* of Society Is. (Fr.) S Pacific O.

Le-gäs'pi *Municipality* E Phil. Is.

Leg'hôrn, It. Li-vôr'nō *Commune* cen. Italy; straw hats

Leg-ni'ca (nē'tsä), Ger. **Līēg'nitz** *City* SW Poland; rail cen.

Lè Hä'vrè *City* N France; commercial port

Leices'têr (les') *City*, county borough of **Leices'têr-shire** *County*, cen. England; hosiery, boots, shoes, farms

Leich'härdt (līk') *River* 220 m. Queensland, Australia

Leï'dèn or **Ley'dèn** (lī') *Commune* SW Netherlands; publishing

Leigh (lē) *Municipal borough* NW England; coal, iron, glass

Lein'stèr (len') *Province* SE Eire

Leïp'zig *City* SW East Germany; publishing

Lēith *Former burgh* SE Scotland; now part of Edinburgh

Lè Mäns' (män') *City* NW France; commerce, manufacturing

Lem'bêrg = LVOV

Lem'nôs *Island* of Greece N Aegean S.

Lè Moūs-tier' (tyä') *Cave* SW France; archaeological finds

Lē'nả *River* 3000 m. E cen. Siberia, U.S.S.R.

Len'in-à-bad *Town* * of *Region* U.S.S.R.

cen. Asia

Len-in-à-kän', formerly **A - le - ksan'dro - pôl** *City* Armenia, U.S.S.R.; industrial

Len'in-grad *City* * of *Region* NW R.S.F.S.R., U.S.S.R., Eur.; * of Russia 1712-1917 as St. Pē'têrs-bûrg, and 1914-24 as Pet'ro-grad; cultural, industrial

Len'in Peak *Mountain* 23,385 ft. U.S.S.R. cen. Asia

Len'insk - Kuz-nets'kiy (kooz) *Town* S cen. U.S.S.R.; Asia

Len'nöx *Town* W Mass., U.S.; Tanglewood music festivals

Le-ôn' (lä) 1. *City* cen. Mexico; textiles. 2. *City* * of *Dept.* W Nicaragua; farming, commerce, industry. 3. *City* * of *Province* NW Spain; manufactures. 4. *Region* and *anc. kingdom* NW Spain

Lē'o-nīne City *Area* of Rome, Italy; incl. Vatican

Lē'o-pöld II, Lake *Lake* W Congo (L)

Lē'o-pöld-ville see **Kinshasa**

Le'pä-yä, Li-ba'và *City* * of *District* W Latvia; port

Le-pon'tīne Alps *Range* Italy-Switzerland

Le'ri-dä (lä') *Commune* * of *Province* NE Spain; manufactures

Lē'ros *Island* of Dodecanese Is.

Les Baux' (lä-bō') *Commune* SE France

Les'bos or **Mȳt-i-le'ne** (lē') *Island* Greek; E Aegean S.; olives

Lesotho *Kingdom* S Africa; 11,716 sq. mi.; pop. 950,000

Les'sêr An-til'lēs *Islands* one of 3 divisions of West Indies; incl. Virgin Is., Windward and Leeward

Is., and Netherlands West Indies; also Barbados, Trinidad, Tobago

Leū'kàs, It. Sän'tä Mau'rä (mou') *Island* of Ionian Is. Greece

Lê-val-lois' - Per-ret' (lwä' pe-re') *Commune* N France; port

Le-vant' *Area* E shore of Mediterranean, Greece-Egypt

Le-vant' States *Countries* of Levant area

Lè-veque', Cape *Cape* N West Australia

Le-vêr-kū'sèn (lä) *City* W West Germany; manufactures

Le-vī'à-thản Peak *Peak* 13,535 ft. Colo., U.S.

Lew'ès (lū') *River* 338 m. S cen. Yukon, Canada

Lew'is-tön (lū') *City* SW Me., U.S.; pop. 41,779; textiles

Lew'is with Har'ris *Island* of Outer Hebrides NW Scotland

Lex'ing-tön 1. *City* NE Ky., U.S.; pop. 108,-137; tobacco, horses. 2. *Town* NE Mass., U.S.; start of Am. Revolution, 1775. 3. *Town* W cen. Va., U.S.; quarries, Natural Bridge

Ley'tē (lä') 1. *Island* E Phil. Is.; agriculture, minerals, timber. 2. *Gulf* E of island; WW II battle

Ley'tön (lä') *Municipal borough* SE England

Lhä'sả *City* * of Tibet; Buddhist sacred city

Lhô'tse S *Peak* of Mt. Everest; 28,100 ft.; bauxite

Liao (li-ou') *River* 700 m. S Manchuria

Liao'ning' (li-ou'); formerly **Fèng'ti-en', Shèng'king** (jing') *Province* S Manchuria

Liao'peh' (li-ou'bā')

Province SW Manchuria

Liao'tung' (li-ou'doong') *Peninsula* and *Gulf* S Manchuria

Liao'yäng' (li-ou') *City* S Manchuria; cotton

Liao'yuän' (li-ou') *Town* SW Manchuria; market cen.

Li'ärd (lē') *River* 550 m. W Canada

Li'be-rec (rets) *City* W Czechoslovakia; cloth

Lĭ-bē'ri-å *Republic* W Africa; 43,000 sq. m.; pop. 1,200,000; * Monrovia; iron ore, rubber

Li-bre-ville' (lē-bre-vēl') *Town* * of Gabon; port

Lib'ў-å or **Libyan Arab Republic** *Rep.* N Africa; former It. colony; 679,350 sq. m.; pop. 1,900,000; * Tripoli; WW II campaigns

Li-cän-cä'bur (vōōr) *Volcano* 19,455 ft. N Chile

Lich'tën-bêrg (lik') *Village* E Berlin, Germany; WW II concentration camp

Lick'ing *River* 350 m. NE Ky., U.S.

Li'di-ce (se) *Village* W Czechoslovakia; 1942 Nazi massacre

Li'dō (lē') *Island reef* outside Venice Lagoon NE Italy; resort

Liech'tën-steīn (lik') *Principality* bet. Switzerland and Austria; 62 sq. m.; pop. 21,000; * Vaduz; agriculture, livestock

Li-ege' (äzh') *City* * of *Province* E Belgium; coal, manufacturing

Lieg'nitz (lig') = LEGNICA

Li-gü'ri-å *Compartimento* NW Italy on **Li-gūr'i-ån** S.; incl. It. Riviera; fruits, machinery, resorts

Li-gūr'i-ån Alps *Range*

NW Italy

Lille, formerly **Lisle** (lēl) *City* N France; commerce, industry

Lĭ'mà *City* NW Ohio, U.S.; pop. 53,734; heavy industry

Lĭ'mà (lē') *City* * of *Department,* * of Peru, cen. part; pop. 2,526,-000; economic, cultural, political cen.

Li-may' (mī') *River* 250 m. cen. Argentina

Lim'bûrg *Region* W Eur. div. bet.: *Province* SE Netherlands and *Province* NE Belgium; limburger cheese

Lim'êr-ick *City* * of *County* SW Eire; farming, fish, livestock

Li-moges' (mōzh') *City* W cen. France; porcelain

Li-môn' Bāy *Inlet* of Caribbean S., Canal Zone

Lim-pō'pō *River* 1000 m. SE Africa to Indian O.

Li-nä'res *Commune* S Spain; mining

Lin'coln (kön) 1. *City* * of Neb., U.S.; pop. 149,518; commerce, shipping. 2. *City,* county borough of **Lin'cöln-shîre** E England

Lin'coln, Mount (kön) *Peak* 14,285 ft. cen. Colo., U.S.

Lin'coln Pärk (kön) *City* SE Mich., U.S.; pop. 52,984

Lin'dën *City* NE N.J., U.S.; pop. 41,409; industry

Lin'di 1. *River* 400 m. NE Congo (L). 2. *Port* Tanzania

Līne Islands *Island group,* U.S. (Kingman Reef, Palmyra I.) and Brit. (Washington, Fanning, Christmas), cen. Pacific O.

Lin-gä-yen' *Gulf* and

Municipality N Luzon, Phil. Is.

Lin'ko-ping (chö) *City* SE Sweden; manufacturing

Linz *City* N Austria; river port; manufacturing

Li-pä' *Municipality* Luzon, Phil. Is.

Lip'å-ri Islands *Island group* off N Sicily

Li'petsk (lē') *Town* R.S.F.S.R., U.S.S.R., Eur.; resort

Lip'pè *Former State* NW Germany

Lis'bön *City* * of **Lis-bō'å** district and * of Portugal, W part; pop. 1,000,000; fine harbor, manufacturing

Lisle (lēl) = LILLE

Li'sū-land (lē') *Region* S China; mountains

Lith-ū-ā'ni-å, Lit-va' *Baltic republic* until 1940, now **Lith-ū-ā'-ni-ån S.S.R.** *Republic* of U.S.S.R. N Eur.; * Vilnyus; agriculture, lumber, livestock, iron

Lit'tle Å-mer'i-cå *Settlement* of Byrd Expedition, Ross S., Antarctica

Lit'tle Beâr Peak *Peak* 14,000 ft. Colo., U.S.

Lit'tle Big Hôrn *River* S Mont., U.S.; General Custer's defeat 1876

Lit'tle Col-o-rä'dō *River* 300 m. NE Ariz., U.S.

Lit'tle Mis-sou'ri (zoor') *River* 560 m. Wyo.-N.D., U.S.

Lit'tle Neck Bay *Inlet* W Long I. N.Y., U.S.

Lit'tle Rock *City* * of Ark., U.S.; pop. 132,-483; mineral, farm area; manufacturing

Lit'tle Sioux (sōō) *River* 235 m. Minn.-Iowa, U.S.

Lit-tō'ri-å now LATINA

Liu'chow' (li-ōō'jō'),

was **Mä'ping'** *City* SE China

Liv'êr-môre *City* W Cal., U.S.; pop. 37,-703

Liv'êr-pōōl *City* and county borough NW England; port, flour

Liv'ing-stöne *Town* S Zambia; former * of Northern Rhodesia

Li-vō'ni-å 1. *City* SE Mich., U.S.; pop. 110,109. 2. *Former province* of Russia, now LATVIA and ESTONIA

Li-vôr'nō *Province* cen. Italy

Liz'ård Point S point of Great Britain

Lju'blja-nä (yōō'blyä), **Laï'bach** (bäk) *City* NW Yugoslavia

Ljung'an (yung') *River* 234 m. E Sweden

Ljus'nän (yōōs') *River* 267 m. cen. Sweden

Llul-lail-la'cō (yōō-yi-yä') *Volcano* 22,055 ft. N Chile [Chile

Lō'ä *River* 275 m. N

Lo-an'gè *River* 425 m. cen. Angola

Lō'bos or **Sēal Islands** *Islands* off N Peru

Lō-cär'nō *Commune* SE cen. Switzerland

Lodz (lōōj) *City* * of *Department* cen. Poland; textile cen.

Lō'fō-tèn *Island group* NW Norway; fish

Lō'gån, Mount *Peak* 19,850 ft. SW Yukon, Canada

Lo-grō'no *Commune* * of *Province* N Spain

Loire (lwar) 1. *River* 625 m. longest in France, SE part. 2. *Departments* of France: **Loire** SE; **Loire - In-fe-rieure'** (fä-ryêr') NW; **Loi-ret'** (lwa-re') N cen.; **Loir-et-cher'** (ā-shär')

Lol'länd *Island* of Denmark, Baltic S.

Lo-mä'mi *River* 900 m. cen. Congo (L) [tina

Lō'mäs *Town* E Argentina

Löm'bärd *Village* NE Ill., U.S.; pop. 35,977

Lom'bàr-dẏ *Compartimento* N Italy

Lom-bok' *Island* and *Strait* E of Bali, Indonesia

Lô-me' (mā') *Town* * of Togo Rep.; port

Lo-me'là (mā') *River* 290 m. cen. Congo Rep. (L)

Lō'mönd, Loch (lok) *Lake* S cen. Scotland

Lön'dön 1. *City* SE Ontario, Canada; industrial. 2. *City* = Greater London: SE England incl. City of London (old city) and County of London (administrative unit); * of United Kingdom, * of Brit. Commonwealth; pop. 7,-880,760; world's largest city; commercial, industrial, cultural cen.

Lön'dön-der-rẏ 1. *County borough*, * of *County* NW Northern Ireland; harbor, trade, manufacturing. 2. *Cape* N point of W Australia

Lông Bēach *City* SW Calif., U.S.; pop. 358,633

Lông'förd *County* E cen. Eire

Lông Is'länd (ī') *Island* SE N.Y., U.S. bet. Long Island Sound and Atlantic O.

Lôngs Peak *Mountain* 14,255 ft. Colo., U.S.

Lông'view (vū) *City* NE Tex., U.S.; pop. 45,547; oil

Long'xuyen' (swē'un) *Town* S Vietnam

Look'out Peak *Peak* 13,675 ft. Colo., U.S.

Lo-pat'kà, Cape *Cape* into Kuril Strait, E U.S.S.R., Asia

Lo-pō'ri *River* 340 m. cen. Congo (L)

Lo-rāin' *City* N Ohio, U.S.; pop. 78,185;

port

Lôr'cä *Commune* SE Spain; mines

Lō'rė-leī *Rock* at Rhine R. West Germany; famous in legend

Lô-rient' (ryän') *Commune* NW France; port

Lôr-rāine' *Medieval kingdom*, later *Duchy* W Eur.; incl. in A L S A C E - L O R - RAINE

Lôs Al'à-mōs *Town* N.M., U.S.; nuclear test site

Lôs An'gė-lės (jė) *City* SW Calif., U.S.; pop. 2,816,061; resort, industrial city [China

Lō'shän' *City* S cen.

Los Ne'gros (nā') *Islands* of Admiralty Is.

Los Sän'tos *Province* cen. Panama

Lôt 1. *River* 300 m. S France. 2. *Department* S cen. France

Lôt-et-Ga-rônne' (-à-) *Department* SW France [Scotland

Lō'thi-àn *Region* S

Loū-ise', Lake (ēz') *Lake* SW Alberta, Canada

Lou-i-si-an'à (loo-i-zi) *State* S U.S.; 48,523 sq. m.; pop. 3,643,-180; * Baton Rouge; 64 parishes; agriculture, lumber, oil

Lou-i-si-an'à Pûr'chàse *Territory* of U.S.; 885,000 sq. m. from Miss. R.-Rocky Mts., Gulf of Mex.-Canada; bought from France 1803

Louis'ville (lōo'ĭ) *City* N cen. Ky., U.S.; pop. 361,472; rail, market cen.

Loup (lōop) *River* 300 m. E cen. Neb., U.S.

Lourdes (loord) *Commune* SW France; pilgrimage shrine

Lōu-ren'co Màr-ques' (rän'sū, kàsh') *City* * of Mozambique, S part

Louth *County* NE Eire

Lo-vat' *River* 320 m. U.S.S.R., Eur.

Löve'lànd *Mountain Peak* 13,625 ft. cen. Colo., U.S.

Lo-vē'ni-à, Mount *Peak* 13,225 ft. Utah, U.S.

Lōw Countries *Region* N Eur. incl. Netherlands, Belgium, Luxembourg

Lōw'ėll *City* NE Mass., U.S.; pop. 94,239; textiles, literary cen.

Lōw'êr Aus'tri-à *Province* NE Austria

Lōw'êr Bûr'mà *Coast region* of Burma

Lōw'êr Cä-li-fôr'niä *Peninsula* NW Mexico bet. Pacific O. and Gulf of Calif.; incl. a *State* and *Territory*

Lōw'êr Ē'gẏpt (jipt) *Region* Nile Delta, N Egypt

Lōw'êr Sax'ö-nẏ *State* N West Germany

Lōwes'tôft *Municipal borough* E England; china

Lōw'lànds, the *Area* S of Grampians, Scotland

Loy'àl-tẏ Islands *Island group* (Fr.) SW Pacific O.

Lō'yäng' or Hō'nan' *City* E cen. China

Lô-zere' (zär') *Department* S France

Lū-à-lä'bà *River* 400 m. cen. Africa

Lū-an'dà *City* * of *District*, * of Angola; port

Luäng'prä-bäng' *Town*, *State* N Laos; residential *

Lū-äng'wä *River* 400 m. E Zambia

Lū-à-pū'là *River* Zambia-Congo (L)

Lub'böck *City* NW Tex., U.S.; pop. 149,-101; cotton-seed oil, meats

Lū'beck *City*, * of *District* on *Bay* N East Germany; imp. port

Lū'blin (blēn) *City* * of *Department* E Poland; leather, textiles

Lū-cä'ni-ä 1. *Comparti-*

mento S Italy. 2. *Peak* 17,150 ft. Yukon, Canada

Lūc'cä *Commune* * of *Province* cen. Italy; silk

Lu-cerne' (sêrn'), Lu-zêrn' *Lake*, *Commune* * of *Canton* cen. Switzerland; tourism

Lū'chow' (jō') = HO-FEI, LUHSIEN

Luck'now (nou) *City* N India; rail cen., paper, metal

Lû'dėn-scheid (shīt) *City* W cen. Germany; resort, factories

Lu-dhi-ä'nà (loo) *Town* NW India; wool, grain cen.

Lūd'wigs-bûrg (viks) *City* SW West Germany; factories

Lūd-wigs-hä'fėn (viks) *City* W West Germany; commercial port

Lū-em'be (bä) *River* 300 m. Angola

Lū-gä'nō *Commune* on *Lake* SE cen. Switzerland; resort

Lu-gansk', Vō-ro-shi'-löv-grad (shē') *City* * of *Region*; coal, factories

Lū'go *Commune* * of *Province* NW Spain; trade cen.

Lū'hsien' (shi-en'), formerly Lū'chow' (jō') *City* S cen. China; salt trade

Luik (loik) = LIEGE

Lū-ke'nie (kā'nyâ) *River* 450 m. cen. Congo (L) [Sweden

Lū'lė *River* 280 m. N

Lū-lū'à *River* 600 m. S Congo (L)

Lund *City* SW Sweden; publishing

Lu'nė-bûrg *City* * of *District* N West Germany; factories

Lun'ga (loong') *Village*, *River* NW Guadalcanal; WW II battles

Lung'ki' (kē'), formerly Chang'chow' (jäng'-

jō′) *City* SE China; commerce

Lung′kiang′ (ji-äng′), **Tsi′tsi-här** *City* N Manchuria; port

Lū′rāy *Town* N Va., U.S.; caverns nearby

Lū-sä′kȧ *Town* E Zambia; former * of Northern Rhodesia

Lū-säm′bō = KASAI

Lū′shaï Hills *Region* NE India

Lū-si-tā′ni-ȧ = classical name of PORTUGAL

Lūt = DASHT-I-LUT

Lū′tön *Municipal borough* SE cen. England; hats

Lutsk, Luck (lōōtsk) *City* Ukraine, U.S.S.R.; textiles

Lux′ěm-bourg (bûrg, boorg) *Grand duchy* and *City* its *, W Eur.; 999 sq. m.; pop. 336,000; cattle, farming

Lux′ôr, El Uq′sor *Town* Upper Egypt; ruins

Lū-zêrn′ = LUCERNE

Lū-zon′ 1. *Island*, most imp. of Phil. Is.; agriculture. 2. **Strait** *passage* bet. *Island* and S Taiwan

Lvov, Lwow (lȧ-vôf′), **Lem′bûrg** *City* and *Region* Ukraine, U.S.S.R.; formerly Polish; factories

Lwän *River* 400 m. NE China

Lya′khöv Islands *Islands* U.S.S.R., Asia; Ice Age remains

Lȳ′ȧll-pur (poor) *Town* West Pakistan; cotton cen.

Lȳ-cē′um *Locale* anc. Athens; Aristotle's teachings

Lyd′dȧ *City* in *District* W Israel

Lȳme Bay *Inlet* SW England

Lȳnch′bûrg *City* S cen. Va., U.S.; pop. 54,-083; tobacco market

Lȳnn 1. *City* NE Mass., U.S.; pop. 90,294;

shoe cen. 2. *Canal*, fiord, SE Alas., U.S.; imp. gateway to Klondike

Lȳn′wood *City* S Cal., U.S.; pop. 43,353

Ly-ön-nais′ (lē-ö-nā′) *Hist. region* SE cen. France

Ly-ons′ (lē-ôn′) *City* E cen. France; silk manufacture

Lys′kämm (lēs′) *Peak* 14,888 ft. Italian-Swiss border

Lȳs′vȧ *City* W U.S.S.R., Asia

M

Maas (Dut.) = MEUSE

Maas-tricht′ (trikt′) *Commune* SE Netherlands; trade

Mȧ-cä′ō *Town* in *Port. Colony*, SE **Macao I.**, Pearl R., SE China

Mac′cles-field (ělz) *Municipal borough* NW England; silk cen.

Mac-e-dō′ni-ȧ (mas) 1. *Region* cen. Balkan penin. site of *Anc. country*. 2. *Division* N Greece; farming. 3. *Republic* SE Yugoslavia

Ma-cei-ô′ (sä) *City* E Brazil; sugar, cotton

Mä-ce-rä′tä (che) *Commune* * of *Province* cen. Italy

Mȧc-ken′zie *District*, *River* 1120 m. into *Bay*, Northwest Terrs., Canada

Mack′i-nac *Island* in *Straits* Lake Huron-Lake Mich., U.S.

Mä′cön *City* cen. Ga., U.S.; pop. 122,423; commerce, industry

Mȧc-quär′ie *River* 750 m. SE Australia

Mäc-tän′ *Island* off E Cebu, Phil. Is.

Mad-ȧ-gas′cȧr *Island* off E Africa, Indian O.; formerly Fr.; now MALAGASY REP.

Mä′däng *Town* * of *District* NE New Guinea; port

Mȧ-dēi′rȧ 1. *River* 2100 m. W Brazil. 2. *Island* of *Group* (Port.) E Atlantic O.; wine

Mȧ′dhyȧ Prȧ-desh′ (däsh′) *Province* cen. India; incl. former Central Provs., Berar, **Mȧ′dhyȧ Bhä′rät**

Ma-di-oen′ (yōōn′) *City* Java, Indonesia

Mad′i-sön *City* * of Wisc., U.S.; pop. 173,258

Mad′i-sön Heights *City* SE Mich., U.S.; pop. 38,599

Mȧ-doe′rȧ, Ma-du′rȧ (doo′) *Island* off Java, Indonesia

Mȧ-dras′ 1. *City* * of *State* SE India; main E coast port. 2. *States*, former agency incl. 5 states S India

Mä′dre de Diôs 1. *River* 900 m. Peru-Bolivia. 2. *Archipelago* S Pacific O. off Chile

Mȧ-drid′ *City* * of *Province*, * of Spain, cen. part; pop. 2,500,-000; commercial, manufacturing, cultural cen.

Mad′u-rȧ, Mȧ-du′raï *City* S India

Mä-e-bä-shi *City* Honshu, Japan; silk cen.

Mäel′ström *Whirlpool* Norwegian S.

Maf′ė-king *Town* former * of Bechuanaland, now Botswana; trade cen.

Mȧ-gȧ-dan′ *Port* E U.S.S.R., Asia

Mag-dȧ-lē′nȧ *Department* and *River* 1060 m. Colombia

Mag′dȧ-lėn Islands *Islands* E Quebec, Canada

Mag′dė-bûrg *City* * of *District* N East Germany; sugar cen.

Mä-ge-läng′ *City* Java, Indonesia

Mȧ-gel′lȧn, Strait of (jel′) *Strait* S South America

Mag-gio′re, Lake (maj-

ō′râ) *Lake* N Italy

Mag-ni′to-gôrsk (nē′) *City* R.S.F.S.R., U.S.S.R., Asia; imp. iron-steel cen.

Mȧ-gwe′ (gwä′) *Town*, *District*, *Division* Mandalay, Burma

Mä-hä′käm, Koe-taï′ (kōō-tī′) *River* 400 m. Borneo, Indonesia

Mȧ-hal′lȧ el Kū′brȧ *City* Lower Egypt

Mä-hä′nȧ-dȧ *River* 512 m. E India

Mä-hä′räsh′trȧ *State* W cen. India

Ma-he′ (hä′) *City* SW India; was Fr.

Mȧ′hi *River* 300 m. W India

Mä-hon′ (ôn′) *City* * of Minorca I. Spain; port

Māid′stöne *Municipal borough* SE England

Maī-kôp′ *City* S R.S.F.S.R., U.S.S.R., Eur.; mineral area

Main *River* 300 m. cen. West Germany

Māine *State* NE U.S.; 33,215 sq. m.; pop. 992,048; * Augusta; 16 counties; potatoes, lumber, granite

Māine′-et-Loire′ (ä-lwär′) *Department* W France

Maïnz *City* cen. West Germany; port, factories

Maï-pū′ *Peak* 17,355 ft. Chile-Argentina

Māit′länd *Town* SE Australia; coal, farming

Maï-zu-ru *City* Honshu, Japan; port

Mȧ-jôr′cȧ (yôr′) *Island* largest of Balearic Is. Spain; fertile, mountainous

Mȧ-jung′ȧ *Town* NW Madagascar; port

Mȧ′kȧ-lū *Peak* 27,790 ft. Himalayas, Nepal

Mä-kä-ri-kä′ri *Salt basin* Botswana

Mȧ-kas′sȧr 1. *City* Celebes I., Indonesia; port. 2. *Strait* Borneo-

Celebes

Má-ke'yėv-ká (kā') *City* Ukraine U.S.S.R.; imp. steel cen.

Mä-khäch-kä-lä', formerly **Pė-trôvsk'** *City* SE R. S. F. S. R., U.S.S.R., Eur.; fish, cotton

Mal'á-bär Coast *Region* SW India

Má-lac'cá *Municipality* on *Strait* S Malay Penin., Malaysia; rubber, port

Ma'lá-gá *City* * of *Province* S Spain; commercial port

Mal-à-gas'ý Republic, Mad-à-gas'cár *Island republic* E Africa, formerly Fr.; 230,000 sq. m.; pop. 7,000,-000; * Tananarive; agriculture

Má-lāi'tá *Island* of Brit. Solomon Is.

Má'lá-kánd *Region* West Pakistan

Mä-läng' *City* Java, Indonesia; coffee

Ma'lar-ėn *Lake* SE Sweden

Mal-à-spi'nà (spē') *Glacier* S Alas., U S

Mä-lä-tyä' *City* * of *Vilayet* E Turkey, Asia

Mä-lä'wi *Country*, formerly Brit. Protectorate of Nyasaland; E Africa; 46,000 sq m.; pop. 4,200,000; * Zomba; tea, tobacco

Má-lāy'á, Federation of Mainland area of Malaysia

Mā'lāy Archipelago *Island group* (world's largest) SE Asia, incl. East Indies, New Guinea, Phil. Is.

Mā'lāy Peninsula *Peninsula* SE Asia; incl. parts of Burma, Thailand, Malaysia; onetime **Mā'lāy States** (Brit.)

Má-lāy'sià, Federation of (zhá) *Republic* SE Asia; incl. S Malay

Penin., N Borneo; 129,000 sq. m.; pop. 10,000,000; * Kuala Lumpur

Mäl'dá *District* E Pakistan-E India

Mäl'dėn *City* NE Mass. U.S.; pop. 56,127

Mäl'dīve Islands *Kingdom, Atolls* (formerly Brit.) Indian O. SW of India; 115 sq. m.; pop. 106,969; * **Mä'le**; fish

Mä'li, Republic of *Republic* W Africa; 465,-000 sq. m.; pop. 4,-700,000; * Bamako; formerly Fr. Sudan and part of Fed. of Mali; agriculture

Mä-lin'che (lēn') *Peak* 14,635 ft.; cen. Mexico

Mal'lēe *Region* Victoria, Australia

Mal'mö *City* SW Sweden; port

Mäl'tá *Island* of **Mäl'tēse Is.**, Brit. Commonwealth nation, Mediterranean S.; 122 sq. m.; pop. 317,-000; * Valletta

Mäl'vêrn *City* SE Australia

Mäm-be-rä'mō *River* 500 m. W Irian

Mam'möth Cäve *Caverns* SW Ky., U.S.

Mä-mō-re' (rä') *River* 1200 m. Bolivia

Man, Isle of *Island* off NW England; * Douglas

Mä-nä'dō *City* Celebes I. Indonesia; coffee

Má-nä'guä *City* on *Lake* * of *Department*, * of Nicaragua

Ma-na'má *Town* * of Bahrein Is. (Brit.), Persian Gulf

Má-nas'sás *Town* NE Va., U.S.; battles of Bull Run 1861-2

Mä-nä-tä'rä *Peak* 12,-140 ft. NW Venezuela

Má-naus' (nous') *City* W Brazil; port

Mänche *Department* NW France

Man'ches-têr 1. *City* S N.H., U.S.; pop. 87,-754; factories. 2. *City* and *County borough* NW England; port, world's cotton cen. 3. *City* N Conn., U.S.; pop. 47,994; residential

Man-chu'ri-á (choo') *Territory* NE China; was **Man-chū'kuō** (kwō) 1932-45 under Jap.; agriculture

Mänd, Mund *River* 300 m. SW Iran

Man'dá-lāy' *City* * of *District* and *Division* Upper Burma

Mán'de *State* N India

Man'gá-lōre *City* S India; coffee, pepper

Man-has'set Bay *Inlet* Long I. N.Y., U.S.

Man-hat'tán *Island, Borough* of N.Y. City, N.Y., U.S.; incl. city's financial, cultural, commercial areas

Man-hat'tán Bēach *City* S Cal., U.S.; pop. 35,352

Man-i-kuä'gán *River* 310 m. Quebec, Canada

Má-nil'á *City* on *Bay* Luzon, Phil. Is.; former *; chief port

Mä'ni-pur (poor) *Territory* and *River* 210 m. NE India

Mä-ni-sä' *City* * of *Vilayet* W Turkey, Asia; manufacturing

Man-i-tō'bá *Lake* in *Province* cen. Canada; * Winnipeg; agriculture esp. wheat

Man-i-zä'les *City* W cen. Colombia; coffee

Mánj'rá *River* 320 m. S cen. India

Mán-när', Gulf of *Area* of India O. SE of India; pearl fisheries

Man'nêr-heim Line *Fortified area* (Finnish), now NW U.S.S.R.

Mann'heīm *City* cen. West Germany;

Rhine port

Mans'fïeld 1. *City* N cen. Ohio, U.S.; pop. 55,047; manufacturing. 2. *Municipal borough* N cen. England; coal area

Män'to-vä, Män'tu-á *Commune* * of *Province* N Italy; manufacturing

Mä'nus *Island*, largest of Admiralty Is.

Má-ných' *Valley* SE U S S R., Eur.

Mä'ping' =LIUCHOW

Má-pue'rá (pwä') *River* 270 m. N Brazil

Mar-à-caī'bō *Lake, City* NW Venezuela; imp. petroluem cen.

Mä-rä-cay' (kī') *City* N Venezuela

Mä - rä - non' (nyôn') *River* 800 m. Peru

Mä-räsh' *City* * of *Vilayet* S cen. Turkety, Asia

Mär'ble-head (bėl-hed) *Town* NE Mass., U.S.; yachting

Mär'chės *Compartimento* cen. Italy

Mär'cus Island *Island* (Jap.) W Pacific O.

Mär'dän *Town* N West Pakistan

Mär' del Plä'tä *City* E Argentina; resort

Mä-reb' *River* 250 m. E Africa

Māre Island *Island* W cen. Calif., U.S.; naval base

Mär-gá-ri'tá (rē') *Island* Caribbean S., Venezuela

Mär'gáte *Municipal borough* SE England

Mär-gė-län' *Town* U.S.S.R. cen. Asia

Mä'ri, A.S.S.R. *Republic* E R.S.F.S.R., U.S.S.R., Eur.

Mar - i - an'ás *Island group* (U.S.) W Pacific O.; incl. Guam, Tinian, Saipan, etc.

Mä-riä-nä'ō *Municipality* and *City* W Cuba

Má-rī'ás *River* 250 m. NW Mont., U.S.

Mä′ri-bôr, Mär′bûrg *City* NW Yugoslavia

Må-riē′ Bўrd Land *Area* of Antarctica E of Ross S.

Ma-riē′ Ga-länte′ *Island* (Fr.) E West Indies

Mä-rin-dū′que (ke) *Island, Province* cen. Phil. Is.

Må-rin′gå *River* 270 m. S cen. Africa

Mar′i-ön 1. *City* cen. Ohio U.S.; pop. 38,-079. 2. *City* NE Ind., U.S.; pop. 39,607; manufacturing

Mar′i-tīme Alps *Range* S France-Italy

Mar′i-tīme Provinces *Provinces* of Canada: New Brunswick, Prince Edward I., Nova Scotia

Mar′i-tīme Territory *Territory* SE U.S.S.R. Asia

Mä-ri′tsä (rē′) *River* 320 m. SE Eur.

Märk′håm, Mount *Peak* 15,000 ft. Antarctica

Mär′må-rå *Island* in *Sea* NW Turkey, Eur.-Asia; marble

Märne *Department, River* 325 m. NE France

Må-rō′ni *River* 420 m. N South America

Må-rōōn′ Peak *Peak* 14,125 ft. Colo., U.S.

Mär-que′sås Islands (kā′) *Islands* (Fr.) S Pacific O.

Mår-rä′kech (kesh) *City* W cen. Morocco

Mär-sä′lä *City* Sicily

Mär-seilles′ (sā′) *City* SE France; imp. port

Mär′shåll Islands *Islands* of U.S. Trust Terr. W Pacific O.

Märsh Peak *Peak* 12,-220 ft. E Utah, U.S.

Mär-ti-nique′ (nēk′) *Island* (Fr.) E West Indies; sugar

Mär′trè, Lake *Lake* Northwest Terrs. Canada

Mä-rў′, formerly **Mêrv**

Town U.S.S.R. cen. Asia

Mår′ў-lånd *State* E cen. U.S.; 10,577 sq. m.; pop. 3,922,399; * Annapolis; 23 counties; agriculture, clothing, seafood

Mä-sän, Mä-säm-pō *City* SE South Korea; port

Mäs-bä′te *Town* on *Island, Province* cen. Phil. Is.

Mas-ê-rū *Town* * of Basutoland Brit. South Africa

Mås′qat and Ō-man′ *Sultanate* SE Arabia; 82,000 sq. m.; pop. 700,000; * **Mås′qat**; agriculture, livestock, oil

Mä′sön-Dix′ön Line = S boundary of Pa., U.S.

Mas-så-chū′setts *Bay, State* NE U.S.; 8257 sq. m.; pop. 5,689,-170; * Boston; 14 counties; shoes, paper, textiles, fish

Mas-sif′ Cen-tral′ (sēf′, sän) *Plateau* SE cen. France

Mas′sive, Mount *Peak* 14,415 ft. Colo., U.S.

Må-su-li-på′tåm, Bån′-dår *City* E cen. India; port

Mat-å-mō′rōs *City* NE Mexico; hides, coffee

Må-tan′zås *Municipality* and *City* * of *Province* W cen. Cuba; harbor

Mä-te′rä (tä′) *Commune* * of *Province* S Italy

Mä′thu-rä (too) = MUTTRA

Ma′tö Grōs′sō *State, Plateau* SW Brazil

Mät′sū *Island* SE China (Nationalist)

Mä-tsu-e (tsoo) *City* Honshu, Japan

Mä-tsu-mō-tō *City,* Honshu, Japan; commerce, silkworms

Mä-tsu-shi-mä *Islands* Honshu, Japan

Phil. Is.; perfect volcanic cone, vapor halo

Ma-zär′-i-Sha-rif′ (rēf′) *City* N Afghanistan

Maz-å-rū′ni *River* 270 m. Guyana

Mä-zä-tlän′ *City* W Mexico; port

Mbä-bäne′ (bän′) *Town* * of Swaziland

McAl′lén *City* S Texas, U.S.; pop. 37,636; business

Mc-Clin′töck Channel *Passage* bet. Victoria and Prince of Wales Is. Northwest Terrs., Canada

Mc-Kēes′pôrt *City* SW Pa., U.S.; pop. 37,-977; steel, coal, gas

Mc-Kin′ley, Mount (li) *Mountain* 20,300 ft. S cen. Alas., U.S.; highest in North America

Mēad, Lake *Reservoir* Ariz.-Nev., U.S.; world's largest artificial lake

Mēath *County* E Eire

Mec′cå *City* * of Saudi Arabia; pop. 150,000; Mohammed's birthplace

Me′chè-lèn (kè), **Ma-lines′** (lēn′) *Commune* N Belgium

Mä-tsu-yä-mä *City* Skikoku, Japan

Mä-tsu-zä-kä *Town* Honshu, Japan; cotton textiles

Mat-tå-ga′mi *River* 275 m. Ontario, Canada

Mat′têr-hôrn, Mônt Cêr-van′ (sêr) *Peak* 14,780 ft., It.-Swiss border

Mat′têr-hôrn Peak *Peak* 13,585 ft. Colo., U.S.

Mau′i (mou′) *Island* of Haw., U.S. (2nd largest) S cen. part; sugar

Mau′nä Ke′å (mou′, kä′) *Volcano* 13,785 ft. Hawaii I., Haw., U.S.; world's highest island mountain

Mau′nä Lō′å (mou′)

Volcano 13,680 ft. Hawaii I., Haw., U.S.; world's largest mountain

Mău-re-tā′ni-å *Anc. country* N Africa

Mău-ri-tā′ni-å, Islamic Republic of *Republic* W Africa, (was Fr.); 419,000 sq. m.; pop. 1,200,000; * Nouakchott; agriculture, livestock

Mău-ri′ti-us (rish′i), **Ile dê Fränce′** (ēl) *Island* (Brit.) Indian O.; * Port Louis; sugar

Mä-wen′zi *Peak* 16,890 ft. Mt. Kilimanjaro

Ma′yå *River* 500 m. U.S.S.R., Asia

Mä-yä-guez′ (gwäz′) *Municipality* and *city* W Puerto Rico; port

Mä-yä-ri′ (rē′) *Municipality* E Cuba

Ma-yenne′ *Department* NW France

Măy′fāir *District* W London

Măy′myō *Town* Lower Burma, summer *

Măy′ō *County* NW Eire; fishing

Mä′yō *River* 250 m. W Mexico

Mä-yôn′, Mount *Volcano* 7943 ft. Luzon,

Meck′lén-bûrg *Former state* N Germany

Me-dän′ *City* Sumatra Indonesia

Me-dèl-lin′ (lēn′) *City* NW Colombia

Med′förd *City* NE Mass., U.S.; pop. 64,397

Med′i-cine Bōw (sin) *Peak* 12,000 ft. of *Range*, Wyo., U.S.

Me-di′nå (dē′) *City* Saudi Arabia; tomb of Mohammed

Med-i-têr-rā′nè-ån Sea *Inland sea* Eur.-Africa-Asia; 966,755 sq. m.

Mè-djêr′då *River* 230 m. N Africa

Mee′rut (mä′) *City* * of *Division* N India; Sepoy Mutiny

GAZETTE ATLAS

Mee - stêr Côr-ne'lis (mā', nā') *City*, Java Indonesia

Meiggs (megs) *Peak* 15,520 ft. cen. Peru

Meïs'sėn *City* SE East Germany; china

Mė-klông = 1. *River* KLONG. 2. *City* SA-MUT SONGKA-RAM

Mek-nes' *City* N Morocco, former *

Me-kông *River* 2600 m. SE Asia

Mel-å-nē'sia (zhå) = *Islands* of Pacific O. NE of Australia

Mel'bourne (bûrn) 1. *City* SE Australia; harbor. 2. *City* E Fla., U.S. pop. 40,236

Me-lil'la (lē'yä) *City* N Morocco

Me-li-tô'pöl *Town* Ukraine U.S.S.R., Eur.; agriculture, fish

Mė'los, Mi'lō (mē') *Island* Cyclades, Greece

Mel'ville, Lake *Lake* SE Labrador Canada

Mel'vlle, Island *Island* off N Australia

Mel'ville Sound, Vis'-count (vī') *Sound* Northwest Terrs., Canada

Me'mėl (mā'), **Klaī'pe-dä** *City* * of *Territory* W Lithuania

Mem'phis (fis) 1. *City* SW Tenn., U.S.; pop. 623,530; port, commerce, industry. 2. *Anc. city* Egypt

Men-de-res' *River* 240 m. W Turkey, Asia

Men-dō'zå *City* * of *Province* W Argentina; grape, wine cen.

Mėng' Chiang' (ji-äng') *Buffer state* (Jap.) bet. Manchukuo and Outer Mongolia 1937-45

Meng'tsz' (mung' zu') *City* S China; tin, shipping

Men'lō Pärk *Village* cen. N.J., U.S.

Men-tôn' (män) *Commune* SE France; re-

sort

Men'tôr *City* NE Ohio, U.S.; pop. 36,912

Mer-ce-dä'riō *Peak* 22,210 ft. W Argentina

Mer-ce'des (sā'dâs) 1. *Town* E Argentina. 2. *City* cen. Argentina. 3. *City* SW Uruguay; port

Mêr-gui' (gwē') *Town*, *District*, *Archipelago* Lower Burma

Me'ri-dä (mā') 1. *City* SE Mexico; sisal. 2. *Commune* SW Spain. 3. *Mountain range* W Venezuela

Mer'i-den *City* S Conn. U.S.; pop. 55,959

Me-rid'i-ån *City* E Miss., U.S.; pop. 45,-083; textiles

Mer - i - on'ėth - shîre *County* W Wales

Me-ri-ti' (mā-rē-tē') *City* SE Brazil

Mêr'thyr Tÿd'fil *County borough* SE Wales

Mêr'tön and Môr'dėn *Urban district* S England

Me'rū, Mount (mā') *Peak* 14,955 ft. N Tanzania

Me'sa (mā) *City* SC Ariz., U.S.; pop. 62,-853; business

Mė-sä'bi Range *Mountains* NE Minn., U.S.

Me'så Vêrde' (mā') *National park* SW Colo., U.S.

Mė-shed' *City* NE Iran; trade cen.

Mes-ö-pö-tä'mi-å *Region* Tigris-Euphrates rivers SW Asia; in mod. Iraq

Mesquite *City* NE Texas, U.S.; pop. 55,131

Mės-sē'ni-å *Department* Peloponnesus, Greece

Mes-si'nå (sē') *City* * of *Province* on *Strait* NE Sicily; port, silks

Me'tå (mā') *River* 685 m. Colombia

Mė-thū'en *Town* NE

Mass., U.S.; pop. 35,456

Metz *City* NE France; metal industries, coal; German before 1918

Meûrthe- et -Mō-selle' (mûr-tä-mō-zel') *Department* NE France

Meûse, Dut. Maas 1. *River* 575 m. W Eur. 2. *Department* NE France [Mexico

Mex-i-cal'ē *Town* NW

Mex'i-cō, United States of *Republic* S North America; 761,600 sq. m.; pop. 50,600,000; * Mexico City; divisions: 29 states, 2 terrs., 1 fed. distr.; minerals, esp. silver and petroleum; agriculture, esp. coffee

Mex'i-cō City *City* * of Mexico and Fed. Distr., cen. part; pop. 3,484,000

Mex'i-cō, Gulf of *Gulf* SE North America

Me'zin (mā') *River* 550 m. N U.S.S.R., Eur.

Mī-am'i *City* SE Fla., U.S.; pop. 334,859; winter resort

Mī-am'i Bēach *Island City* SE Fla., U.S.; pop. 87,072; resort

Mich'i-gån (mish') 1. *State* N cen. U.S.; 58,216 sq. m.; pop. 8,875,083; * Lansing; 83 counties; mines, lumber, agriculture. 2. *Lake* NE cen. U.S. 3rd in size of Great Lakes, 22,400 sq. m.

Mich'i-gån City *City* N Ind., U.S.; pop. 39,-369; factories, resort

Mi-chu'rinsk, formerly **Köz-lôv'** *City* W U.S.S.R., Eur.

Mī-crō-nē'sia (zhå) *Islands* of W Pacific O. E of Phil. Is., N of equator

Middle Con'gō former Fr. terr., now Rep. of Congo (B)

Middle East = indefinite area incl. countries of S, SW Asia,

NE Africa

Middle Loup (lōōp) *River* 220 m. cen. Neb., U.S.

Mid'dles-brough ('lz-bru) *County borough* N England; iron

Mid'dle-sex ('l) *County* SE England; residential

Mid'dle-town (toun) 1. *City* SW Ohio, U.S.; pop. 48,767; factories 2. *City* S Conn., U.S.; pop. 36,924; manufacturing, residential

Mid'lånd 1. *City* W Tex., U.S.; pop. 59,-463; cattle, oil. 2. *City* E Mich., U.S.; pop. 35,176; manufacturing

Mid'lånds, The = cen. counties of England

Mid-lō'thi-ån, formerly **Ed'in-burgh** (bur-ö) *County* SE Scotland; farming, factories

Mid'wāy *Islands* (Eastern I., Sand I.) cen. Pacific O.; bel. to U.S.

Mid'west City *City* Okla., U.S.; pop. 48,-114

Mi-e (mē) *Prefecture* Honshu, Japan

Mi-län' *Commune* * of **Mi-lä'nō** prov. N Italy; manufacturing, commerce, publishing

Mil'förd *City* S Conn., U.S.; pop. 50,858; oysters, hardware

Milk *River* 625 m. N Mont., U.S.

Mi'lō (mē') = MELOS

Mil-wǎu'kēe *City* SE Wisc., U.S.; pop. 717,099

Min 1. or **Min'kiang'** (ji-äng') *River* 350 m. S cen. China. 2. or **Min-kông'** *River* 250 m. SE China

Min-då-nä'ō *Island* S. of *Sea*, S Phil. Is.

Min'dėn *City* S West Germany; factories

Min-dō'rō *Island* and *Strait* cen. Phil. Is.

Min'hōw', Fōō'chow' (jō') *City* SE China;

port
Min-nē-ap'ō-lis *City* SE Minn., U.S.; pop. 434,400; St. Paul's twin city; flour mills

Min-nė-sō'tå 1. *State* N cen. U.S.; 84,068 sq. m.; pop. 3,805,069; * St. Paul; 87 counties. 2. *River* 332 m. S Minn., U.S.

Min-nė-ton'kå *City* SE Minn. U.S.; pop. 35,776

Mi-nôr'cå *Island* of Belearic Is., Spain; * Mahon

Minsk *City* * of *Region*, * of White Russia, SW U.S.S.R.

Min'tō, Lake *Lake* Quebec, Canada

Min'yå Kon'kå *Mountain* 24,900 ft. S China

Miq'ue-lon (mik'ė) *Island* (Fr.) Atlantic O. off Newfoundland

Mi-råj' *States* W India

Mi-rim' (rēm') *Lake* Uruguay-Brazil

Mir'pur Khäs' (mēr') *City* S West Pakistan

Mir'zä-pur *City* N India; pilgrimage cen.

Mi-sä'mis *Former prov.* Mindanao, Phil. Is.

Mish-å-wä'kå *City* N Ind., U.S.; pop. 35,517; manufacturing, residential

Mis'kolc (mish'kôlts) *City* NE Hungary

Mis-si-naï'bi *River* 270 m. Ontario, Canada

Mis-sis-sip'pi 1. *River* 3870 m. cen. U.S., Minn.-Gulf of Mexico. 2. *State* SE U.S.; 47,716 sq. m.; pop. 2,216,912; * Jackson; 82 counties; cotton

Mis-sou'ri (zoor') 1. *River* 2720 m. cen. U.S. 2. *State* cen. U.S.; 69,674 sq. m.; pop. 4,677,399; * Jefferson City; 114 counties

Mis-tås-si'ni (sē') *Lake* Quebec, Canada

Mi-su-rä'tå *City* * of

Province NW Libya

Mitch'åm *Municipal borough* S England

Mitch'éll *River* 300 m. NE Australia

Mi-tō (mē) *City* Honshu, Japan; industry, commerce

Mi-yä-gi (mē) *Prefecture* Honshu, Japan

Mi-yä-ji-mä (mē-yä-jē) *Island* Inland S., Japan

Mi-yä-kō-nō-jō (mē) *Town* Kyushu, Japan

Mi-yä-zä-ki (mē) *City* * of *Prefecture* Kyushu, Japan; port

Mi-zu-sä-wä *Town* Honshu, Japan; International observatory

Mjo'sä (myu') *Lake* SE Norway

Mō'ab *Anc. kingdom* Syria; now in SW Jordan

Mō-bile' (bēl') *City* on Bay SW Ala., U.S.; pop. 190,026

Mô'dė-nä *Commune* * of *Province* N Italy; leather, silk, glass

Mo-de'stō *City* C Cal., U.S.; pop. 61,712; business

Moe'si, Mu'si (mōō') *River* 325 m. Sumatra Indonesia

Mog-å-di-sci-ō (dish'-i-ō) *City* * of Somali; pop. 141,770; port

Mo'gi-lev *City* * of *Region* White Russia U.S.S.R.; industrial

Mo-ja've (hä') *Desert* S Calif., U.S.

Mō-ji *City* Kyushu, Japan; coal port

Môk'shå *River* 380 m. U.S.S.R., Eur.

Mol-dä'vi-å, Ger. Mol'dau (dou) *Former principality*; former prov. of Românía

Mol-dä'vi-ån S.S.R. *Republic* SW U.S.S.R., Eur.; * Kishenev

Mō'lèn-beek - Saint - Jean' (bäk-san-zhän') *Commune* cen. Belgium

Mol-fet'tå *City* SE Italy; port

Mō-line' (lēn') *City* NW Ill., U.S.; pop. 46,237; machinery

Mö-lô'gå *River* 340 m. W U.S.S.R., Eur.

Mo-lö-kaï' *Island* cen. Haw., U.S.

Mo-lö'pō *River bed* S Africa

Mō'lö-töv = PERM

Mō'lö-töv, Mount *Peak* ~,000 ft. U.S.S.R. cen. Asia

Mo-luc'cås or Spice Islands *Islands* E Indonesia; forests, spices

Mom-bä'så *Municipality, Island* S Kenya

Mon'å-cō *Principality* S Europe; 370 acres; pop. 23,000; * Monaco (commune); gambling, tourism

Mon'å-ghan (h a n) *County* NE Eire

Mō'nå *Island* (Sp.) in *Passage* bet. Haiti and Puerto Rico

Monch (mûnk) *Peak* 13,465 ft. W cen. Switzerland

Mon-gal'å *River* 400 m. S cen. Africa

Mon-ghyr' (gir') *Town* NE India; factories

Mon-gi-bel'lō (ji) = Mt. ETNA

Mon-gō'liå *Territory* E cen. Asia N of China, incl. Tuva Region U.S.S.R. Inner and Outer Mongolia

Mon-gō'lia, Inner *Region* SE Mongolia, Chinese

Mon-gō'liån Peoples' Republic, or Outer **Mon-gō'liå** *Republic* E cen. Asia; 626,000 sq. m.; pop. 1,290,000; * Ulan Bator; livestock

Mon'i-tör Peak *Peak* 13,700 ft. SW Colo., U.S.

Mon 'mouth - shíre (muth) *County* W England

Mön-rōe' *City* N La., U.S.; pop. 56,374; in-

dustrial

Mön-rō'vi-å *City* * of Liberia

Môns, Bêr'gėn *Commune* SW Belgium

Mon-tan'å *State* NW U.S.; 147,138 sq. m.; pop. 694,409; * Helena, 56 counties; mining, livestock

Mont-clåir' *Town* NE N.J., U.S.; pop. 44,043; residential

Mon-tė-bel'lo *City* S Cal., U.S.; pop. 42,807

Mon'tė Cär'lo *Commune* Monaco; casino

Mon-te-cris'tō *Island* (It.) off W cen. Italy

Mon-tē'gō Bay *Seaport* Jamaica I.; fruits

Mon-tė-nē'grō *Federated Republic* S Yugoslavia; former kingdom; * Titograd

Mon-tė-rey' (rā') *City* on *Bay* W Calif., U.S.; formerly * of Span. Calif.

Mon-tė-rey' Park (rā') *City* W Cal., U.S.; pop. 49,166; residential

Mon-tėr-rey' (rā') *City* NE Mexico

Mon-tė-vi-dė'ō (dā') *City* * of *Dept.*, * and chief port of Uruguay, S part

Mon-tė-zū'må *Peak* 13,130 ft., Colo., U.S.

Mont-göm'êr-ÿ 1. *City* * of Ala., U.S.; pop. 133,386; commerce. 2. *Town* * of *District* West Pakistan. 3. or -shire *County* E Wales

Mon-ti-cel'lo (sel') *Residence* of T. Jefferson, Charlottesville, Va., U.S.

Mônt-lu-côn' (sôn') *City* cen. France; steel

Mônt-mar'trė *Area* N Paris, France

Mônt-pēl'iêr *City* * of Vt., U.S.; pop. 8,609; granite, maple syrup

Mônt-pēl-lier' (yä') *City* S France

Mont-rē-ål' *City* on *Island* S Quebec, Can-

GAZETTE ATLAS

ada; Canada's largest city; port, commerce

Môn - treuil' (tru'y') *Commune* N France; factories, fruits

Môn-treux' (trû) *Villages* W Switzerland

Mont-sèr-rat' *Island* West Indies

Môn'zä *Commune* N Italy; factories

Mōōse Lake *Lake* Manitoba, Canada

Môp'pō, Môk'pō *City* S Korea; harbor

Mō-räd'à-bäd *City* N India; brasses

Mō-ran', Mount *Peak* 12,595 ft. Wyo., U.S.

Mo-rä'tu-wà *Town* Ceylon

Mo-rā'vi-à *Former Kingdom* and *Province*, cen. Czechoslovakia; now part of **Moravia** and **Silesia** prov.

Mô'rav-skä O'stra-va *City* cen. Czechoslovakia; factories, coal

Mōr'ay (i), **El'gin** *County* NE Scotland

Môr-bi-hän' (bē-än') *Department* N W France

Môr-dō'vi-àn A.S.S.R. *Republic* R.S.F.S.R., U.S.S.R., Eur.; agriculture

Mō-reau' (rō') *River* 250 m. S.D., U.S.

Mō-re'liä (rā') *City* SW Mexico; cattle farms

Mō-re'lōs (rā') *State* S cen. Mexico

Mo-rī'àh *Hill* S anc. Palestine; sacrifice of Isaac

Mō-ri-ō-kä *City* Honshu, Japan; textiles

Môr'ley (li) *Municipal borough* N England

Môr'ō *Gulf*, former *Province* Phil. Is.

Mo-roc'cō, Kingdom of *Monarchy* NW Africa; incl. Fr. Morocco (W), Span. Morocco (N), Tangier International Zone; 171,300 sq. m.; pop. 15,310,000; * Rabat; agriculture, mining

Mō-ro-cō-cä'lä *Peak* 17,000 ft. W Bolivia

Mor'ris Jes'up, Cape *Cape* N point of Greenland

Mor'ris-town *Town* N N.J., U.S.

Mos'cow (kou), **Mös-kva'** *City* on Moskva R. (315 m.); * of *Region*, * and largest city of U.S.S.R., E cen. part; pop. 6,600,000; political, cultural, economic cen.

Mō-selle' (zel') *River* 320 m., *Department* NE France

Mös-qui'tō (kē') 1. *Gulf* N Panama. 2. *Peak* 13,795 ft. Colo., U.S.

Môs-ta-ga-nem' *City* NW Algeria; port

Mo-sūl' *City* in *Province* N Iraq; trade

Mo-tä'guä *River* 340 m. Guatemala

Môth'êr-well and Wish'àw *Burgh* S cen. Scotland; coal, iron

Moū-lins' (lan') *City* cen. France

Moūl-mein' (mān') *City* Lower Burma; port

Moū-loū'yà *River* 300 m. Morocco

Moun'tàin Province *Province* Luzon, Phil. Is.

Moun'tàin View *City* W Cal., U.S.; pop. 51,092; manufacturing, residential

Mount Ath'ôs *Department* Macedonia, Greece

Mount Vêr'nòn 1. *City* SE N.Y., U.S.; pop. 72,778. 2. *Estate*, burial place of George Washington NE Va., U.S.

Mō-zam-bique' (bēk') 1. *Port. colony* SE Africa; * Lourenco Marques; agriculture, food, jute. 2. *City* on *Island* in *Channel* off coast; port

Msta ('m-sta') *River* 270 m. U.S.S.R., Eur.

Mū'äng-Thai' (tī') =

THAILAND

Muhl-hau'sèn (h o u') *City* SW East Germany; industry

Mūir, Mount *Peak* 14,025 ft. Calif., U.S.

Mūir Glacier *Glacier* SE Alas., U.S.

Mūir Woods *National monument* W Calif., U.S.; redwoods

Muk'den' (m ō ō k'), **Shèn'yäng', Fèng'-tien'** *City* S Manchuria; trade, educational cen.

Mul-ha-cen' (mōō-lä-sän') *Peak* 11,400 ft. S Spain

Mūl'heīm *City* W West Germany; commerce, industry

Mul-house' (mu-lōōz'), **Mul-hau'sèn** *Commune* NE France

Mu'ling' (mōō') *River* 260 m. E Manchuria

Mul-tän' (mool) *City* * of *Division* N West Pakistan; trade

Mun (mōōn) *River* 350 m. Thailand

Mun'chen - Gläd'bäch (kèn, bäk) *Former city* W Germany

Mun'cie (si) *City* E cen. Ind., U.S.; pop. 69,080; trade cen.

Mū'nich (nik), **Mun'chen** (kèn) *City* * of Bavaria SE West Germany; educational cen., breweries

Mun'stêr 1. *Province* S Eire. 2. *City* W cen. West Germany; manufacturing, commerce

Mū-rä'nō *Suburb* of Venice, Italy; glass

Mûr'chi-sön *River* 400 m. W Australia

Mûr'ci-à (shi) 1. *Anc. kingdom*, *Region* SE Spain. 2. *Commune* * of *Province* SE Spain; factories

Mu'res, Mu'resh (mōō') *River* 400 m. Hungary-Romania

Murgh - äb' (moorg) *River* 450 m. Afghanistan-U.S.S.R.

Mur - mansk' (moor) *City* * of *Region* NW U.S.S.R., Eur.; ice-free port

Mu-rō-rän (moo) *City* Hokkaido, Japan; port, navy base

Mûr'ray (ri) *River* 1200 m. Australia's chief river, SE part

Mûr-rum-bidg'ēe *River* 1000 m. SE Australia

Mus'cat = MASQAT

Mus-kē'gön *City* at *River* mouth, W Mich., U.S.; pop. 44,631; port, rail cen.

Mus-kō'gēe *City* E Okla., U.S.; pop. 37,331; oil, gas, factories

Mus-kō'kà *District*, *Lake* Ontario, Canada; resorts

Mus'sèl-shell *River* 300 m. Mont., U.S.

Mū'tän'kiäng' (ji-äng') *City* on **Mū'tän'** R. (300 m.) E Manchuria

Mut'trà *City* N India; cotton, paper

Mu-zàf'fàr-pur (poor) *Town* NE India; trade cen.

Muz-tagh' A-tä' (mōōs-tä') *Range, Peak* 24,390 ft. W China

Myit'nge (ngâ) *River* 250 m. Upper Burma

Mȳ'men-singh *Town* * of *District* N East Pakistan

Mȳ-sôre' *City* in *State* S India; famed palace

Mȳt-i-lē'ne 1. *Island* now LESBOS. 2. *City* Lesbos I., Greece; harbor

N

Nä'bhà *Town* * of *State* NW India

Nab'lus, anc. **Shē'chem** (kèm) *Town* NW Jordan

Nà'di-à *Town* in *District* N India [India

Nà-di-äd' *Town* W

Nä-gä-nō *City* * of *Prefecture* Honshu, Japan; silk cen.

Nä-gä-ō-kä *City* Honshu, Japan; oil cen.

Nä-gä-sä-ki *City* of *Prefecture* Kyushu, Japan; port; atomic bomb destruction WW II [of India

Nä'gêr-coil *City* S tip

Nä-gôr'nö-Kä-rä-bakh' *Autonomous region* Azerbaidzhan S.S.R., U.S.S.R.

Nä-gō-yä *City* Honshu, Japan; planes

Näg'pur (poor) *City* * of *Division* S cen. India

Nä-hä *City* Okinawa I., Ryukyu Is.; port

Nä-huel' Huä-pi', Lake *Lake* SW Argentina

Nairn'shîre *County* NE Scotland

Naī-rō'bi *Town* * of Kenya; pop. 477,600

Nä-kä-tsu *Town* Kyushu, Japan

Nä - khi - che - vän' A.S.S.R. *Republic* of Azerbaidzhan S.S.R. U.S.S.R. Asia

Nä-män-gän' *T o w n* U.S.S.R. cen. Asia; trade

Nä-mä'quä-land *Coast area* SW Africa; sandy plains, copper

Näm'chä Bär'wä *Peak* 25,445 ft. SE Tibet

Näm'hoi', Fät'chän' *City* SE China; industry, commerce

Nam'oi *River* 525 m. SE Australia

Näm' Tsô' *Salt lake* E Tiber [Thailand

Nän *River* 350 m. W

Nän'chäng' *City* SE China; commerce

Nän'cheng' (jung') *City* NE China; commerce

Nän'cÿ *City* NE France; manufacturing

Nän'dä De'vi (dä') *Peak* 25,645 ft. N India

Nan-dä-rū'ä *Peak* 12,-900 ft. cen. Kenya

Nän'gä Pär'bät *Peak* 26,660 ft. NW Kashmir

Nan'king' *City* E China; former * of Chi-

na; cloth, paper, pottery [China

Nän'kōw' *Town* NE

Nän'ning' = YUNG-NING

Nän'sei (sä) = RYU-KYU IS.

Nän' Shän' *Mountain range* cen. China

Nän-terre' (tär') *Commune* N France

Nantes (nänt) *City* NW France; commerce

Nan-tuck'ėt *Island* at *Sound* SE Mass., U.S.; resort

Nän'tung' (toong') *City* E China; port

Nap'ä *City* W Cal., U.S.; pop. 35,978; residential

Nä'ples (pulz), Nä'pö-li *Commune* (in Napoli prov.) on *Bay* SW Italy; imp. port

Nä'po *River* 550 m. NW South America

Nä-rä *City* * of *Prefecture* Honshu, Japan

Nä'rä *Channel* 250 m. East Pakistan

Nä-rä'yän-gänj *Town* East Pakistan

När-bä'dä *River* 800 m. cen. India

Nä'rew (ref) *River* 285 m. NE Poland

Nar-rä-gan'sett *Town* on *Bay* S R.I., U.S.

När'vä *City* NE Estonia; industrial cen.

Nash'u-ä *City* S N.H., U.S.; pop. 55,820

Nash'ville *City* * of Tenn., U.S.; pop. 447,877; industrial port

Nas'säu *City* New Providence I., * of Bahamas; harbor

Nä-tal' 1. *City* NE Brazil; port. 2. *Province* E Rep. of South Africa

Nä-tash'kwän *River* 250 m. Quebec, Canada

National City *City* S Cal., U.S.; pop. 43,-184; residential, Armed Forces

Nat'u-räl Bridge *Village* W cen. Va., U.S.

Nä-ū'rū *Is. country* SW Pacific 82,000 sq. mi; pop. 750,000

Nav'ä-jō Peak (hō) *Peak* 13,400 ft. Colo., U.S.

Naum'bêrg (n o u m') *City* S cen. East Germany; manufactures

Nä-vä-nä'gär *State* W India [dom N Spain

Nä-värre' *Anc. king-*

Nax'ös *Island* largest of Cyclades, Greece

Nä-yä-rit' (rēt') *State* W Mexico

Naz'ä-rėth *Town* NE Israel; site of Jesus's childhood

Ndō'lä *Town* N Zambia; copper cen.

Neagh, Lough (lok nā') *Lake* Northern Ireland, largest in Brit. Isles, 153 sq. m.

Nēar East = Countries of SW Asia and Balkan States

Nēar Islands *Islands* W Aleutians SW Alas., U.S.

Nė-bras'kä *State* cen. U.S.; 76,808 sq. m.; pop. 1,483,791; * Lincoln; 93 counties

Ne-chak'ō *River* 255 m. Brit. Columbia, Canada

Neck'är *River* 245 m. SW Germany

Nēe'dle Mountain *Peak* 12,130 ft. Wyo., U.S.

Ne-fud' (fōōd') *Desert* N Saudi Arabia

Neg-ä-pä'täm *Town* S India; port [Israel

Neg'ev *Desert area* S

Ne'grō, Ri'ō (nē', nä') 1. *River* 1400 m. Colombia - Venezuela - Brazil. 2. *River* 630 m. S cen. Argentina. 3. *River* 290 m. cen. Uruguay

Ne'grôs (nä') *Island* cen. Phil. Is.

Nei'vä (nā') *Peak* 12,-100 ft. Colombia

Nejd *Kingdom* and *Tableland* cen. Arabia

Nel-lōre' *Town* S India; imp. port

Nel'sön *River* 390 m. Manitoba, Canada

Ne'män, Nie'män (nē') *River* 500 m. U.S.S.R. E cen. Eur.

Nė-nets' National District *District* NE U.S.S.R., Eur.; reindeer

Ne-ō'shö *River* 460 m. Kans.-Okla., U.S.

Nė-pal' *Monarchy* bet. China and India; 54,-360 sq. m.; pop. 11,-100,000; * Katmandu; site of Mt. Everest; agriculture, forestry

Ner'chinsk *Town* E U.S.S.R., Asia; export trade

Ness, Loch (lok) *Lake* NW Scotland

Neth'êr-länds, Ne'dêr-länd, Hol'länd *Kingdom* NW Eur.; 13,000 sq. m.; pop. 13,119,-367; * Amsterdam; famous dikes and canals, agriculture, dairying, horticulture

Neth'êr-länds An-til'lēs (before 1949 Cū-rä-cao' (sō) or Dut. West Indies *Territory* in West Indies; * Willemstad on Curacao; oil refining

Neth'êr-länds Indies now INDONESIA

Neth'êr-länds New Gui'nêa = IRIAN

Neû - cha - tel' (shä) *Lake, Commune, Canton* W Switzerland

Neuil - ly' - sur - Seine' (nû - yē' - sur - sän') *Commune* N France; automotive cen.

Neu-köln' (noi) *Suburb* of Berlin; industrial

Neu-mun'stêr (noi) *City* N West Germany; manufactures

Ne-u-quen' (nä-ōō-kän') *River* 375 m. W cen. Argentina

Neūse (nūs) *River* 260 m. N.C., U.S.

Neuss (nois) *City* W West Germany; industry

Ne-vä'dà 1. *State* W U.S.; 110,540 sq. m.; pop. 488,738; * Carson City; 17 counties; mining, sheep. 2. *Mountain* 21,000 ft. NW Argentina. 3. *Mountain range* S Spain, **Si-er'rà Ne-vä'dà**

Ne'vis *Island* of Leeward Is. (Brit.) West Indies

New (nū) *River* 255 m. Va.-W.Va., U.S.

New Ăl'bà-ny *City* S Ind., U.S.; pop. 38,-402; residential

New Am'ster-dam *City* on Manhattan I., N.Y., U.S.; became New York City

New'ark (nū') 1. *City* NE N.J., U.S.; pop. 382,417; transportation, insurance cen.; manufacturing. 2. *City* cen. Ohio., U.S.; pop. 41,836; glass, tires, stoves

New Bed'förd *City* SE Mass., U.S.; pop. 101,777; manufacturing, fish

New Brit'ain ('n) 1. *City* N Conn., U.S.; pop. 83,441; manufacturing. 2. *Island* largest of Bismarck Arch.; cocoa, coconuts. 3. *District*, incl. *Island*, Terr. of New Guinea; * Rabaul

New Bruns'wick 1. *City* cen. N.J., U.S.; pop. 41,885; rail, manufacturing, market cen. 2. *Province* SE Canada; 28,354 sq. m.; pop. 626,000; * Fredericton; agriculture, forestry, fish

New Cal-e-do'nià *Island* of *Fr. Territory* SW Pacific O.; * Noumea; agriculture

New Cas-tle (cas"l) *City* W Pa., U.S.; pop. 38,559; industrial cen.

New'cas-tle ('l) 1. *City* SE Australia. 2. *Municipal borough* W cen. England; manufactures. 3. **Newcastle upon Tyne** *City, county borough* N England; shipbuilding, chemicals, coal, iron

New'chwäng' *City* S Manchuria

New Del'hi (del'i) *City* * of Rep. of India, N part; pop. 2,344,051

New Eng'länd *Section* NE U.S.; incl. Me., N.H., Vt., Mass., R.I., Conn.

New-found-land' (nū-fun) 1. *Island* off E Canada. 2. *Province* E Canada· includes Labrador; * St. John's; 154,734 sq. m.; pop. 513,000; fish

New Geor'gia (jôr'jà) *Island* of *Island group* Brit. Solomon Is.

New Guin'ea (gin'i) *Island* (world's 2nd largest) E Malay Arch.; div.: W = Irian, Indonesia; NE = part of Terr. of New Guinea, SE = Papua, both administered by Australia

New Hamp'shire *State* NE U.S.; 9304 sq. m.; pop. 737,681; * Concord; 10 counties; manufactures, granite

New Hā'ven *City* S Conn., U.S.; pop. 137,707; manufacturing, port

New Heb'ri-dēs *Island group* SW Pacific O.; a *Condominium* administered by Fr., Brit. and Australians; coconuts, coffee, cocoa, cotton

New Ire'länd *Island* in *District* of Terr. of New Guinea, Bismarck Arch.; coconuts

New Jer'sey (si) *State* E U.S.; 7836 sq. m.; pop. 7,168,164; * Trenton; 21 counties; factories, shipbuilding

New Lön'dön *City* SE Conn., U.S.; port

New Mex'i-co *State* SW U.S.; 122,503 sq. m.; pop. 1,016,000; * Santa Fe; 32 counties; mining, agriculture

New Or'le-àns *City* SE La., U.S.; pop. 593,-471; port

New Ply'mouth (muth) *Borough* New Zealand; port, dairy cen.

New'pôrt 1. *City* SE R.I., U.S.; pop. 34,-562; port, resort, naval base. 2. *County borough* W England; port, manufactures

New'pôrt Beach *City* S Cal., U.S.; pop. 49,-422; manufacturing, residential

New'pôrt News *City* SE Va., U.S.; pop. 138,-177; tobacco, coal

New Prov'i-dénce *Island* of Bahama Is.; site of Nassau, * of Bahamas

New Rō-chelle' (shel') *City* SE N.Y., U.S.; pop. 75,385; manufacturing

New Sī-bē'ri-àn Islands *Island group* Arctic O., U.S.S.R., Asia

New'tön *City* NE Mass. U.S.; pop. 91,066, incl. 14 Villages

New Wörld = term for Western Hemisphere

New Yôrk 1. *State* E cen. U.S.; 49,576 sq. m.; pop. 18,190,740; * Albany; 62 counties; factories, farms, shipping, finance. 2. *City* of 5 boroughs SE N.Y., U.S.; pop. 7,-867,760; largest city of U.S.; shipping, financial, commercial, industrial, cultural

New Yôrk State Barge Canal *Canal system* 525 m. connecting Hudson R. with Lake Erie N.Y., U.S.

New Zēa'länd *Dominion* of Brit. Commonwealth, S Pacific O.; incl. North I., South I. and others; 104,000 sq. m.; pop. 2,755,-092; * Wellington; harbors, meats, wool

Ne'zhin (nyä') *Town* Ukraine, U.S.S.R.

Nez' Pêrce' *Peak* 11,-900 ft. Wyo., U.S.

Nī-ag'à-rà Fălls 1. *Falls* of *River*, U.S.-Canada border, incl. Canadian Falls (Horseshoe) 158 ft. high and Amer. Falls 167 ft. 2. *City* W N.Y., U.S.; pop. 85,615; resort, hydroelectric power, manufacturing. 3. *City* Ontario, Canada; hydroelectric power, manufactures

Nia-mey' (mä') *Town* * of Rep. of Niger; pop. 43,000

Ni'äs (nē') *Island* off Sumatra, Indonesia

Nic-à-rä'guà *Lake* 2972 m. S Nicaragua

Nic-à-rä'guà, Rep. of *Republic* central America; 57,145 sq. m.; pop. 1,734,000; * Managua; bananas, coffee, forest products, gold

Nice (nēs) *City* SE France; port, resort

Nic'o-bär Islands *Island group* Bay of Bengal, with Andaman Is. forms prov. of India

Nic-ö-si'à (sē') *Town* * of *District*, * of Cyprus, cen. part; weaving, tanning

Nī'ger (jêr) *River* 2600 m. W Africa

Nī'ger, Rep. of (jêr) *Republic*, former Fr. terr., W Africa; 489,-000 sq. m.; pop. 3,700,-000; * Niamey; cattle, agriculture

Nī-gē'ri-à, Federal Rep. of (jē') *Republic* of Brit. Commonwealth W Africa; former Brit. colony; 357,000 sq. m.; pop. 55,000,-

000; * Lagos; iron, coal, fish, sugar

Ni-i-gä-tä *City* * of Prefecture Honshu, Japan; port

Ni-i-tä-kä *Peak* 13,600 ft. cen. Formosa

Nij'me-gèn (nĭ'mä) *Commune* E Netherlands; WW II battles

Nik-kō *Village* Honshu Japan; resort, shrines

Ni-kö-la'ev (yef) *City* * of *Region* Ukraine, U.S.S.R., Eur.

Ni-kô'pöl *T o w n* Ukraine, U.S.S.R., Eur.; trade

Nĭle *River*, world's longest 4100 m. E-NE Africa; incl. **Victoria Nile, White Nile, Blue Nile**

Nîmes (nēm) *City* S France; commerce

Nin'è-veh *Anc. city* * of Assyria, site now Kuyunjik, Iraq

Ning'hsien' (shi-en'), **Ning'pō'** *City* E China; port

Ning'sia' (shi-à) *Town* * of *Province* Inner Mongolia, N China

Ni-ō-brâr'à *River* 431 m. Wyo., U.S.

Nip'ĭ-gon *Lake* 1730 sq. m. Ontario, Canada

Nip'is-sing *Lake* 330 sq. m. Ontario, Canada

Nip-pon' = official name of JAPAN

Nish *City* Serbia, E Yugoslavia; industry, commerce

Ni-shä-pur' (poōr') *Town* NE Iran; turquoise mines

Ni-shi-nō-mi-yä *City* Honshu, Japan; sake

Ni-tè-roi' (nē) *City* SE Brazil

Nizh'ni Nov'gö-rod = GORKIY

Nizh'ni Tä-gil' *City* R.S.F.S.R., Asia; mineral products

Niz-wa', **Kûh-iū** *Peak* 13,500 ft. N Iran

Nmai (nà-mī') *River* 320 m. Upper Burma

Nō-ä'täk *River* 320 m.

NW Alas., U S

Nō-be-ō'kà *City* Kyushu, Japan

Nob Hill *Hill* SW San Francisco, Calif., U.S.

N o - g i n s k' *C i t y* U.S.S.R., Eur.

Nōme *City* W Alas., U.S.; pop. 2,488; commercial cen.; mining

Nön'ni *River* 660 m. N Manchuria

Nord (nôr) *Department* N France

Nōrd'kÿn *Cape* NE Norway, N point of Mainland of Eur.

Nôrd'vik *Bay, Town* N cen. U.S.S.R., Asia

Nôr'folk (fuk) 1. *City* SE Va., U.S.; pop. 307,951; port, commerce, industry. 2. *County* E England

Nôr'màn *City* Ohio, U.S.; pop. 52,117

Nôr'màn-dÿ *Hist. region* and *Former Province* NW France

Nor'ris-town *Borough* SE Pa., U.S.; pop. 38,169; manufactures

Norr'kö-ping (chö) *City* SE Sweden; port

Nôrr'land *Division* N Sweden

Nôrth A-mer'ĭ-cà *Continent* (3rd in size) W Hemisphere; 9,385,-000 sq. m.; incl. Greenland, Canada, U.S., Mexico, Cen. America, West Indies

Nôrth-amp'tön *County* borough, **Nôrth'amp-tön-shire** *county* cen. England; shoes

Nôrth Bôr'nē-ō *Area* of Malaysia, N Borneo I.; former Brit. colony

Nôrth Cà-nā'di-àn *River* 760 m. Okla., U.S.

Nôrth Cape *Cape* off N Norway; N point of Eur.

Nôrth Car-ō-lī'nà *State* SE U.S.; 52,712 sq. m.; pop. 5,082,059; * Raleigh; 100 counties

Nôrth Cău'cà-sus *Former region* R.S.F.S.R. U.S.S.R., Eur.

Nôrth Chan'nèl *Strait* of Atlantic O. Ireland-Scotland

Nôrth Chi-cä'gō *City* NE Ill., U.S.; pop. 47,275

Nôrth'côte *City* SE Australia

Nôrth Dà-kō'tà *State* NW U.S.; 70,665 sq. m.; pop. 617,761; * Bismarck; 53 counties; wheat, cattle

Nôrth-Êast New Gui'nēa *Area* NE New Guinea, *Division* of Terr. of New Guinea, Australia

Nôrth'êrn Dvi-nä' *River* 1100 m. N U.S.S.R., Eur.

Nôrth'êrn High'lànds (hī') *Region* N Scotland

North'êrn Īre'lànd *Division* of United Kingdom, NE Ireland; * Belfast

Nôrth'êrn Rhō-dē'sia (zhà) = ZAMBIA

Nôrth'êrn Terr'i-tôr-ÿ *Territory* N Australia; * Darwin

Nôrth Island *N Island* of New Zealand

Nôrth Las Ve'gàs (vā') *City* SE Nev., U.S.; pop. 36,216

Nôrth Lit'tle Rock *City* cen. Ark., U.S.; pop. 60,040; industrial

Nôrth Mà-rōōn' *Peak* *Mountain* 14.000 ft. Colo., U.S.

Nôrth Minch *Strait* Scotland-Outer Hebrides

N ô r t h Os-sē'tian A.S.S.R. (shàn) *Republic* SE R.S.F.S.R., U.S.S.R., Eur.

Nôrth Platte *River* 618 m. Colo.-Neb., U.S.

Nôrth Pōle = earth's N axis, Arctic O.

Nôrth Rhine-West-phā'lià *State* of West Germany

Nôrth Sea *Sea* arm of

Atlantic O. bet. N Eur. continent and Great Britain

Nôrth Ton-à-wän'dà *City* W N.Y., U.S.; pop. 36,012

Nôrth-um'bêr-lànd 1. *County* N England; coal, shipping. 2. *Strait* Prince Edward I. - SE Canada. 3. *Cape* SE Australia

Nôrth-um'bri-à *Early kingdom* of Britain, NE England

Nôrth-West Frön'tiêr Province *Former province* NW Brit. India, now part of Pakistan

Nôrth'west Pas'sàge (ij) *Passage* Atlantic O.-Pacific O. N of North America

Nôrth'west Territories *Division* N Canada incl. Hudson Bay and Arctic islands, mainland N of 60° lat.

Nôrth'west Territory *Region* NW of Ohio R., U.S.; incl. Ohio, Ind., Ill., Wisc., Mich., part of Minn.; first U.S. national terr. estab. 1787

Nôr'wälk 1. *City* SW Calif., U.S.; pop. 91,-827. 2. *Town* SW Conn., U.S.; pop. 79,-113; manufacturing

Nôr'wäy *Kingdom* NW Europe; 125,060 sq. m.; pop. 3,800,000; * Oslo; 20 counties

Nôr-wē'gian Sea (jàn) *Arm* of Arctic O., Greenland-Norway

Nôr'wich 1. *Town* SE Conn., U.S.; pop. 41,-433; textiles, cutlery, machinery. 2. *County borough* E England

Nō-shi-rō *Town* Honshu, Japan; timber

Nō'sop *River* 450 m. SW Africa

Nôs'si-Be (bā) *Island* (Fr.) off NW Madagasgar

Nô'tec (tets-y'), **Net'zè** *River* 275 m. W Poland

GAZETTE ATLAS

Not'tȧ-wāy *River* 400 m. Quebec, Canada

Not'ting-hȧm *City,* *County borough,* **Not'-ting-hȧm-shire** *County* N cen. England

Nou-me'ȧ (nōō-mä') *Town* * of New Caledonia colony, SW coast; fine harbor

Nō'vȧ Gō'ȧ = PANGIM

No-vä'rä *Commune* * of *Province* NW Italy

Nō'vȧ Scō'tiȧ (shȧ) *Province* SE Canada; 21,425 sq. m.; pop. 764,000; * Halifax; agriculture, fish, coal

Nô'vȧ-yȧ Zĕm-lya' 2 *Islands* (Arctic O.) off NE U.S.S.R., Eur.

Nov'go-rod *City* * of *Region* NW U.S.S.R., Eur.; meats, mills, metallurgy

No'vi Sȧd' *City* NE Yugoslavia; commerce, industry, port

Nô-vö-cher-kassk' *City* S cen. U.S.S.R., Eur.

Nô-vö-rös-sisk' *City* on Black S. U.S.S.R., Eur.; port

Nô-vo-si-birsk' *City* * of *Region* S R.S.F.S.R., cen. U.S.S.R.; Asia; imp. industrial cen.

Nü'bi-ȧn Desert *Desert area* NE Sudan

Nü'do Au-sän-gä'tĕ (ou), **Ausangate Knot** *Mountain* 20,000 ft.; SE Peru

Nü-e'ces (ā'sĕs) *River* 338 m. Tex., U.S.

Nue'vō Lä-re'dō (nwä', rä') *City* E Mexico

Nue'vō Le-ôn' (nwä', lä) *State* NE Mexico

Nü-ku-ȧ-lô'fȧ *City* * of Tonga Is.; port

Nü'ku Hi'vȧ (hē') *Island,* largest of Marquesas (Fr.) Is.

Null-ȧr'bör *Plain* SW Australia; rocket cen.

Nu-mä-zu (noo, zoo) *Town* Honshu, Japan; resort

Nun-ēa'tön *Municipal borough* cen. England

Nü'ni-vak *Island* off W Alas., U.S.

Nun'kiang' (noon'ji-äng') *Province* N cen. Manchuria

Nuô'rô *Province* Sardinia, Italy

Nûrn'bĕrg, Nü'rĕm-bĕrg *City* SE West Germany

Nȳ-as'ȧ *Lake* 11,000 sq. m. SE Africa

Nȳ-as'ȧ-land now MALAWI

Nyi'regy-hä-zä (nyē'-red-y') *City* NE Hungary; manufactures

Ny'kö-ping (nû'chû) *Town* SE Sweden

Nyông *River* 280 m. Cameroun

O

Ō-ä'hu (hōō) *Island* of Hawaiian Is., Haw., U.S.; most imp., 3rd in size

Ōak'lȧnd *City* W Calif., U.S.; pop. 361,561; industrial port

Ōak Lȧwn *Village* NE Ill., U.S.; pop. 60,305

Ōak Park 1. *Village* NE Ill., U.S.; pop. 62,511; residential. 2. *City* SE Mich., U.S.; pop. 36,762

Ōak Ridge (rij) *City* E Tenn., U.S.; pop. 28,-319; atomic research

Oä-xä'cä (wä-hä'cä) *City* * of *State* SE Mexico; wool, coffee

Ob *River* 2500 m. into *Gulf* at Arctic O., W U.S.S.R., Asia

Ō - bêr - äm'mêr - gau (gou) *Village* Germany

Ō'bêr - Gä'bĕl-hôrn *Peak* 13,365 ft. SW cen. Switzerland

Ō'bêr-hau-sĕn (hou) *City* W West Germany; industrial

Oc'ci-dent (si) = The West; refers to Western culture

Ō-ce-an'i-ȧ (she) = islands of cen. and S Pacific O.

Ō'cean Island (shȧn)

Island of Gilbert and Ellice Is.

Oceanside *City* S Cal., U.S.; pop. 40,494; business, Armed Forces

O'chil Hills (kil) *Hills* cen. Scotland

Ōc-mul'gēe *River* 255 m. cen. Ga., U.S.

Ō-cō'nēe *River* 250 m. cen. Ga., U.S.

Ō-dä-wä-rä *Town* Honshu, Japan

Ō'dĕn-sĕ *City* * of *County* Fyn I., Denmark; manufacturing

Ō'dêr *River* 560 m. cen. Eur.

Ō-des'sȧ 1. *City* W Tex., U.S.; pop. 78,-380; oil. 2. *City* * of *Region* on *Bay,* Ukraine U.S.S.R., Eur.; imp. port

Of'fȧ-lȳ *County* cen. Eire

Of'fĕn-bach (bäk) *City* cen. West Germany

Ō-gä-ki *Town* Honshu, Japan [Nigeria

Og-bo-mō'shō *City* W

Og'dĕn *City* N Utah, U.S.; pop. 69,478

Ō-gēe'chēe *River* 250 m. E Ga., U.S.

O-gō'ki *River* 300 m. Ontario, Canada

Ō-gö-oue' (wä') *River* 700 m. Gabon

Ō-hī'ō 1. *River* 980 m. Pa. - Ohio - Ind. - Ill., U.S. 2. *State* N cen. U.S.; 41,222 sq. m.; pop. 10,652,017; * Columbus; 88 counties; farming, mining, rubber industry

Oi'röt Autonomous Region *Region* R.S.F.S.R., U.S.S.R., Asia; cattle, timber

Oise (waz) *River* 186 m., *Department* N France

Ō-i-tä *City* * of *Prefecture* Kyushu, Japan

O'jos del Sä-lä'dō (hōz) *Peak* 22,572 ft. NW Argentina

Ō'kȧ 1. *River* 530 m. S R.S.F.S.R., U.S.S.R.,

Asia. 2. *River* 950 m. cen. R.S.F.S.R., U.S.S.R., Eur.

Ō-kȧ-nä'gȧn *River* 300 m., *Lake* Brit. Columbia, Canada

Ō-kä-yä-mä *City* * of *Prefecture* Honshu, Japan; port, cottons

Ō-kä-zä-ki *Town* Honshu, Japan

Ō-kēe-chō'bēe, Lake *Lake* SE Fla., U.S.; 2nd largest in U.S.

Ō-kė-fė-nō'kēe *Swamp* SE Ga., U.S.

O-khotsk' *Town* on coast of *Sea* E U.S.S.R., Asia

Ō-ki-nä-wä *Island* of *Island group* Ryukyu Is., incl. in *Prefecture* S Japan

Ō-klȧ-hō'mȧ *State* SW U.S.; 69,919 sq. m.; pop. 2,559,253; * Oklahoma City; 77 counties; agriculture, mining, petroleum

Ō-klȧ-hō'mȧ City *City* * of Okla., U.S.; pop. 366,481; commercial, financial, industrial

Ō-kō-vang'gō *River* 1000 m. SW cen. Africa

O'land *Island* off SE Sweden; alum

Ōld Bȧld'ȳ Peak *Mountain* 14,125 ft. S Colo., U.S.

Ōld'bur-ȳ *Urban district* W cen. England; steel, iron, chemicals

Ōld Cas-tile' (tēl') *Provincial region* N Spain

Ōl'dĕn-bûrg *City* and *Former state,* NW West Germany; manufacturing

Ōld Fāith'ful *Geyser* NW Wyo., U.S.

Ōld'ham (ȧm) *County borough* NW England; cotton

O-lek'ma *River* 700 m. E U.S.S.R., Asia

O-lė-nek' (nyôk') *River* 1325 m. N U.S.S.R., Asia [SE Africa

Ol'i-fȧnts *River* 350 m.

Ō-li-vä'res (räs) *Peak*

20,510 ft. W Argentina

O'lives, Mount of *Ridge* E of Jerusalem, Israel

Ol-la'gue (o-yä'gwâ) *Peak* 19,260 ft. N Chile

O'lô-mouc (mōtz) **Ol'-mutz** *City* cen. Czechoslovakia; industrial

Olsz'tўn (ôlsh'), **Äl'lèn-steīn** *City* N Poland; manufactures

Ôlt, Ger. **Ält** *River* 308 m. S Romania

Ō-lўm'pi-ä 1. *City* * of Wash., U.S.; pop. 23,111; lumber products, canneries, oysters. 2. *Plain* S Greece; religious cen.

O-lўm'pic Mountains *Mountains* of Penin. NW Wash., U.S.

Ō-lўm'pus *Mountain* *range* Thessaly NE Greece; home of gods in Gk. mythology

Ôm *River* 450 m. W Siberia, U.S.S.R.

Ō'má-hǎ *City* E Neb., U.S.; pop. 347,328; stockyards, grain, manufacturing

O'má-hǎ Beach *Coast* *area* NW France; WW II landing site June 6, 1944

Ō-man' 1. popular name of MASQAT AND OMAN. 2. *Gulf* Arm of Arabian S., Oman-Iran

Ôm-bi'lin (bē') *Village* Sumatra, Indonesia; coal cen.

Om-dûr-man' *City* NE cen. Sudan

Ō'mō *River* 400 m. SW Ethiopia

O-mö-loi' *River* 380 m. N U.S.S.R., Asia

Ö-mö-lôn' *River* 600 m. NE U.S.S.R., Asia

Ômsk *City* * of *Region* cen. U.S.S.R., W Asia; trade, industrial cen.

Ō-mu-rä (moo) *City* Kyushu, Japan; aircraft

Ō-mu-tä (moo) *City* Kyushu, Japan; coal

Ō-ne'gà *Lake* 3764 sq. m., Eur.'s 2nd largest; *River* 250 m. into *Bay* NW U.S.S.R., Eur.

O-nit'shà *Town* * of *Province* S cen. Nigeria

O-no-mi-chi *City* Honshu, Japan; industrial

Ō'non *River* 610 m. ber, fish, agriculture. 2. *Trail* Mo.-Ore. U.S. 1804-1860

O-re'khō-vō - Zū'gè-vö *City* W R.S.F.S.R., U.S.S.R., W Eur.

O-rel' *City* * of *Region* U.S.S.R., cen. Eur.; market cen.

Ō'rèn - bûrg now CHKALOV

Ō-ren'se (rän'sā) *Commune* * of *Province* NW Spain; wine, lumber

O'ri-ènt = the East; countries of E Asia, the Far East

Ō-ri-hue'lä (wä') *City* SE Spain; manufacturing, agriculture

Ō-ri-nō'cō *River* 1500 m. Venezuela

O-ris'sà *State* E India; agriculture

Ō-ri-zä'bä *City* E Mexico; agriculture

Ôr'khon *River* 450 m. N Outer Mongolia, China

Ôrk'ney Islands (ni) *Archipelago* constitutes *County* off NE Scotland; fish, agriculture, livestock

Ôr-land'ō *City* cen. Fla., U.S.; pop. 99,-006; citrus fruits

Ôr-le-ans' (lā-än') *Commune* N cen. France; manufactures; site of Joan of Arc victory

Ôr'ly (li) *Commune* N France; Paris airport

Ôr-môc' *Municipality* on *Bay* Leyte, Phil. Is.; port [France

Ôrne *Department* NW

Ôr'ping-tön *Urban district* SE England

Ôr-rè-fôrs *Town* SE Sweden; crystal

Outer Mongolia-U.S.S.R.

On-tä-ke *Peak* 10,050 ft. Honshu, Japan

On-târ'i-ō 1. *Province* S, cen. Canada; 412,580 sq. m.; pop. 7,425,-000; * Toronto; agriculture, minerals. 2. *Lake* 7540 sq. m. NE cen. U.S.; smallest of Great Lakes. 3. *City* SE Cal., U.S.; pop. 64,118; residential

Ōost-en'dè = OSTEND

O'pa-va *City* cen. Czechoslovakia

Ō-pin'á-kǎ *River* 280 m. Quebec, Canada

Ô-pô'le, Ôp'pèln *City* SW Poland

Ō-pōr'tō, Pōr'to (tōō) *City* NW Portugal

Ô-rä'deä (dyä) *City* NW Romania; industrial, cultural, commercial cen.

O-ran' *City* * of *Department* NW Algeria

Or'ange (inj) 1. *City* NE N.J., U.S.; pop. 32,566; pharmaceuticals, machinery. 2. *River* 1300 m. South Africa. 3. *City* S Cal., U.S.; pop. 77,374; residential

Or'ange Free State (inj) *Province* E cen. Rep. of South Africa

Ôrch'hä *State* cen. India [Australia

Ôrd *River* 300 m. N

Ö-rè-bro' (brōō') *City* * of *Province* S cen. Sweden; shoes

Or'e-gön 1. *State* NW U.S.; 96,981 sq. m.; pop. 2,091,385; * Salem; 36 counties; lumber

Ôrsk *Town* U.S.S.R., Eur.; oil refining

Ôr'tôn *River* 340 m. Peru-Bolivia

O-rū'ro *City* * of *Department* W Bolivia; trade cen.

O-sage' (sāj') *River* 500 m. Kans.-Mo., U.S.

Ō'sä-kä *City* on *Bay* *

of *Prefecture*, Honshu, Japan; port, chemicals, manufactures

Osh'á-wa *City* SE Ontario, Canada; port

Ō-shi-mä Islands *Island* largest of *Group*, N Japan

Osh'kosh *City* E Wisc., U.S.; pop. 53,221; trading cen., manufacturing [geria

O-shog'bō *City* W Ni-

Ō'si-jek (yek) *City* N Yugoslavia; shipping

O-si-pen'kō *Town* Ukraine W U.S.S.R., Eur.; export trade

Os'lō, formerly **Kris-ti-än'i-ä** *City* * of Norway, SE part; pop. 484,000; commerce, shipping, industry

Ôs-nä-bruck' *City* * of *District* N cen. West Germany; manufacturing

Ō'sō, Mount *Peak* 13,-700 ft. Colo., U.S.

Os-sē'ti-à (shà) *Region* U.S.S.R., SE Eur.; div. into NORTH OSSETIAN A.S.S.R. and SOUTH OSSE-TIAN AUTONO-MOUS REGION

Os'si-ning *Village* SE N.Y., U.S.; Sing Sing state prison

Os'tend *Commune* NW Belgium; port, fish

Os'ti-à *Village* nr. Rome, Italy; ruins

O'stra-va, Mô'rav-skä *City* cen. Czechoslavakia

Ö-styak'-Vö-gūl' **Na-tional District** now KHANTY-MANSI

O-tä-ru (roo) *City* on *Bay*, Hokkaido, Japan; harbor

Ō-tsu (tsoo) *City* Honshu, Japan

Ot'tá-wa 1. *City* SE Ontario, * of Canada; pop. 290,741; cultural, industrial cen. 2. *River* 685 m. Ontario-Quebec, Canada

Ot'to-mán or **Tûr'kish**

Empire *Former empire* Eur.-Africa-Asia; * Constantinople; 13th century-1923

Ouach'i-tă (wäsh') *River* 600 m. La.-Ark., U.S.

Oua-ga-doū'goū (wä) *Town* * of Upper Volta; imp. trade cen.

Oudh *Former prov.* of Brit. India

Oudj'da (ōōj'dà) *City* NE Morocco

Ou'lu, U'le-bôrg (ōō') *City* * of *Department* N cen. Finland; port

Oum êr Rė-bi'à (oom, bē') *River* 250 m. cen. Morocco

Oū-rāy' Peak *Peak* 14,000 ft. Colo., U.S.

Ou'trė-mônt (ōō') *City* Montreal I. Quebec, Canada

Ō'vêr-land Park *City* Kan., U.S.; pop. 76,623

Ō-vie'dō (vyā') *City* * of *Province* NW Spain; manufactures

Ōw'ėn, Mount *Peak* 12,920 ft. Wyo., U.S.

Ōw'ėns-bör-o *City* NW Ky., U.S.; pop. 50,329; tobacco market

Ōw'ėn Stan'ley Range (li) *Mountains* E New Guinea

Ō-wȳ'hēe *River* 250 m. Ore., U.S.

Ox'förd *County borough* * of *Ox'förd - shire county*, cen. England; university

Ox'närd *City* SW Cal., U.S.; pop. 71,225; business

O-yä'hue (wâ) *Peak* 19,225 ft. SW Bolivia; volcano

Ô-ya-pôck' *River* 300 m. N South America

Ō'yō *City* * of *Province* W Nigeria

Oys'têr Bay *Inlet* and *Village* SE N.Y., U.S.; home of Theo. Roosevelt

Ō'zärk Mountains *Tableland* Mo.-Ark.-Okla., U.S.

P

Pä-biä-ni'ce (nē'tse) *Commune* cen. Poland; linen

Pä-chū'cä *City* cen. Mexico; silver

Pà-cif'i-cà *City* W Cal., U.S.; pop. 36,020

Pà-cif'ic Islands Trust Territory (sif') *Islands* of Pacific O. assigned to U.S. 1947: Caroline, Marshall, Mariana Is. (except Guam)

Pà-cif'ic Ocean (sif') *Ocean* Arctic Circle-Antarctic R e g i o n, bet. N and S America and Australia and E Asia; 70,000,000 sq. m.

Pä'däng *City* Sumatra, Indonesia; exports

Pad'ding-tön *Borough* of London, England

Pä-dêr-bôrn' *City* cen. West Germany; manufacturing

Pad'ū-à, It. Pä'dö-vä *Commune* * of *Province* NE Italy; manufacturing, trade

Pä-gä-di'än (dē') *Municipality* Mindanao, Phil. Is.

Pà-gō'dà *Mountain Peak* 13,490 ft. Colo., U.S.

Pä'gō Pä'gō (or päng'ō) *Town* Tutuila I., Samoa; excellent harbor, * of American Samoa [E Malaysia

Pà-hang' *River* 285 m.

Pah-le-vi' (vē') *City* NW Iran; port

Päint'ėd Desert *Region* N cen. Ariz., U.S.; colored rock

Päis'ley (li) *Burgh* SW Scotland; textiles, shawls, threads

Paï'tä *Town* NW Peru; port

Pak-i-stan', Is-läm'ic Rep. of *Republic* of Brit. Commonwealth (formerly part of Brit. India), S Asia; 364,800 sq. m.; pop. 130,-

000,000; * Rawalpindi; rice, tea, jute, cotton industries

Pak-se' (sā') *Town* S Laos [SE India

Pä-lär' *River* 230 m.

Pà-lat'i-nāte *Former terr.* S Germany, ruled by counts and emperors

Pal'à-tine (tin) *Hill*, one of Rome's 7

Pä-lau' (lou'), **Pėl-lew'** (lōō') *Island group* of Caroline Is. (U.S.)

Pä-lä'wän *Island* SW Phil. Is.; fish, agriculture, forests

Pä-lem-bäng' *City* Sumatra, Indonesia; port, trade cen.

Pà-len'ci-à *City* * of *Province* N Spain; manufacturing

Pä-ler'mō *City* on *Bay*, * of *Province*, * of Sicily, S Italy; port, trade, fisheries

Pal'ės-tīne *Area* and *Anc. country* of SW Asia; * Jerusalem; now div. bet. Israel and Jordan

Päl'ghät *Town* S India

Pal - i - säde', Middle *Peak* 14,050 ft. S cen. Calif., U.S.

Pal-i-säde', North *Peak* 14,250 ft. S cen. Calif. U.S. [Ceylon-India

Pälk Strait *Channel*

Päl'mä *Commune* on *Bay* * of Majorca I. and of Baleares prov. E Spain; imp. port

Päl'mäs, Cape *Cape* S Liberia

Päl'mäs, Läs see LAS PALMAS

Pälm Beach *Town* SE Fla., U.S.; resorts

Pälm'êr Archipelago *Island group* South America-Antarctica

Pälm'êr-stön n o w DARWIN, Australia

Pälm'êr-stön, North *City* North I. New Zealand

Pal'ō Al'tō *City* W Calif., U.S.; pop. 55,966; industrial

Pä-lo-mä'ni *Peak* 18,925 ft. W Bolivia

Pal'ö-mär, Mount *Peak* 6126 ft. SW Calif., U.S.; giant telescope

Pà-louse' (lōōs') *River* 220 m. Ida.-Wash., U.S. [ft. N Chile

Päl-pä'nä *Peak* 19,815

Pà-mir' *Region* of high altitude cen. Asia

Pam'li-cō Sound *Sound* E N.C., U.S.

Päm'päs *Plains* 1000 m. cen. Argentina

Päm-plō'nä *City* N Spain; manufactures

Pan'à-mä Canal *Canal* across *Isthmus*, links North-South America, Atlantic-Pacific Oceans; canal and 10 m. strip = CANAL ZONE

Pan'à-mä, Rep. of *Republic* S Central America; 28,575 sq. m.; pop. 1,400,000; * **Pan'à-mä** *City* (pop. 306,000) on *Bay* and *Gulf* agriculture

Pä-nay' (nī') *Island* on *Gulf* cen. Phil. Is.

Pän de A-zu'cär (dâ-ä-sōō') *Peak* 15,975 ft. Venezuela

Pän-gä'ni *River* 330 m. Tanzania

Pän-gä-si-nän' *Province* Luzon, Phil. Is.

Pan-gim' (shēn') now GOA

Pan'han-dle handlelike projection of land

Pä-ni'zo (nē') *Peak* 18,025 ft. SW Bolivia

Pan-mun-jön (moon) *Village* cen. Korea, site of 1953 armistice

Pan-tà-näl' *Swamp region* SW Brazil

Pän-tel-le-ri'à (tâ-lâ-rē') *Island* (It.) Mediterranean S.

Pä'nū-cō *River* 240 m. cen. Mexico

Pä'pàl States = Temporal lands of popes 750-1870, cen. Italy

Pao'ting' (bou') now TSINGYUAN

Pä-pe-e'te (pâ-ā'tâ)

Town NW Tahiti, * of Society Is. and * of Fr. Oceania; port

Pap'u-à 1. Name for New Guinea I. 2. *Gulf* S coast of New Guinea

Pa'pu-à, Terr. of was Brit. New Guinea *Territory* of Australia, incl. SE New Guinea and adjacent islands; * Port Moresby

Pà-ra' 1. *State* NE Brazil; * **Pà-ra'** or BELEM. 2. E mouth of Amazon R., Brazil

Pä-rä'guä 1. *River* 435 m. E Venezuela. 2. *River* 230 m. E Bolivia

Pa-rà-guàs-su' (sōō') *River* 320 m. E Brazil

Par'à-guay, Rep. of (gwī or guä) 1. *Republic* cen. South America; 157,000 sq. m.; pop. 2,200,000; * Asuncion; 16 departments; cattle, agriculture, forestry. 2. *River* 1500 m. S cen. South America

Pa-rà-i'ba (ē'vä) 1. *Two rivers* = **Pa-rà-i'bà dō Nôr'tė** 240 m. E Brazil, **Pa-rà-i'bà dō Sūl** 660 m. S Brazil. 2. *State* E Brazil

Par-à-mar'i-bō *City,* * of Surinam (Dut. Guiana); port

Pä-rä-mu-shi-rō *Island* N of Kuril Is. (U.S.S.R.)

Pä-rä-nä' 1. *City* E Argentina; river port. 2. *River* 2040 m. SE cen. South America. 3. *River* 300 m. cen. Brazil. 4. *State* S Brazil

Pa-rà-nà-i'bà (ē'vä) *Headstream* of Parana R. SE Brazil

Pa - rà - na - pà - ne'mà (nä') *River* 470 m. SE Brazil

Pär'bà-ti *River* 220 m. cen. India

Par'do (dōō) 1. *River* 310 m. E Brazil. 2.

River 290 m. S Brazil. 3. *River* 230 m. SW Brazil

Par'du-bi-ce (tse) *Town* NW Czechoslovakia

Pä'riä, Gulf of *Inlet* Trinidad-Venezuela

Pä-ri'cu-tin (rē'kōō-tēn) *Volcano* (modern) 200 m. W of Mexico City, Mexico

Par'is *City* * of France, N cen. part; pop. 2,-607,600; commercial, cultural, fashion cen.

Pär'kėrs-bûrg *City* NW W. Va., U.S.; pop. 44,208; business

Pärk Ridge *City* NE Ill., U.S.; pop. 42,-466; residential

Pär'mà 1. *City* N Ohio, U.S.; pop. 100,216..2. *Commune* * of *Province* N Italy; textiles

Par-nà-i'bà (ē'vä) *River* 800 m. NE Brazil

Pär'nū *City* on *Bay* SW Estonia; imp. port

Pâr'os *Island* of Cyclades Is.; marble

Par-rà-mat'tà *Town* SE Australia

Par'ris Island *Island* S S.C., U.S.

Par'rý Islands *Islands* Northwest Terrs., Canada incl. Melville, Bathurst, Borden, Cornwallis, Prince Patrick

Pär'sōns Peak *Mountain* 12,120 ft. cen. Calif., U.S. [Brazil

Pà-rū' *River* 350 m. N

Pas-à-dē'nà 1. *City* SW Calif., U.S.; pop. 113,327; resort. 2. *City* SE Texas, U.S.; pop. 89,277; residential

Pä'say (sī) now RIZAL

Päs-dė-Ca-lais' (le') *Department* N France

Pàs-sā'ic *City* NE N.J., U.S.; pop. 55,124

Pas-sà-mà-quod'dý Bay *Inlet* bet. New Brunswick, Canada-SE Me., U.S.

Päs-tä'zä *River* 400 m. cen. Ecuador

Päs'to *Volcano* 13,990 ft., and *City* SW Colombia; gold

Pat-à-gō'nià *Barren region* Chile and Argentina, Andes Mts.-Atlantic O.

Pä-täm-bän', Cer'rô de (ser') *Peak* 12,299 SW Mexico

Pä'tän 1. *Town* W Indies; pottery, knives. 2. *Town* E cen. Nepal

Pat'êr-sön *City* N N.J., U.S.; pop. 144,824

Pà-ti-à'là *City, District,* former *State* NW India [Dodecanese

Pat'mös *Island* of

Pàt'nà 1. *City* * of *Division* NE India; was opium cen. 2. *State* NE India [Brazil

Pa'tos (tōōs) *Lake* S

Pà-tras' *City* on *Gulf* Peloponnesus, Greece; port

Pä-tū'cä *River* 300 m. Honduras

Pau (pō) *Commune* SW France

Pä-vi'à (vē') *Commune* * of *Province* N Italy

Pà-vil'iön Dōme *Peak* 11,355 ft. S Calif., U.S.

Pàw-tuck'ėt *City* N R.I., U.S.; pop. 76,-984; industrial

Pä-yà-chä'tä *Peak* 20,-765 ft. N Chile

Pāyne Lake *Lake* Quebec, Canada

Pay-sän-dū' (pī) *City* * of *Department* W Uruguay

Pä-yūn' *Peak* 12,070 ft. W Argentina

Pēa'bod-y *City* NE Mass., U.S.; pop. 48,080; residential, manufacturing

Peace (pēs) *River* 1065 m. W Canada

Pēale, Mount *Peak* 13,090 ft. Utah, U.S.

Pêarl (pûrl) 1. *River* 290 m. Miss., U.S. 2. *River* SE China

Pêarl Här'bör *Inlet* Honolulu's port,

Oahu I. Haw., U.S.; site of Jap. attack Dec. 7, 1941

Pēa'rý-land *Region* N Greenland

Pė-chen'gà *Village, Territory* NW U.S.S.R., Eur.

Pė-chō'rà *River* 1125 m. into *Bay* U.S.S.R., NE Eur.

Pe'cös (pā') *River* 735 m. N.M.-Tex., U.S.

Pecs (pāch) *Municipality* S Hungary; coal

Pe'drō Mi-guel' (pā', gel') *Town, Locks* Panama Canal

Pēe'bles-shire *County* SE Scotland

Pēe' Dēe *River* 235 m. N.C.-S.C., U.S.

Pēel 1. *River* 365 m. NW Canada. 2. *Sound* bet. Prince of Wales and Somerset Is., Canada

Pe-gu' (gōō') *Mountain range* Lower Burma

Peh, Pei (bā) *River* 220 m. SE China

Peī-hō *River* 350 m. NE China

Pei'ping' (bā'), **Pē-king** *City* * of People's Rep. of China, NE part; pop. 7,000,000; literary cen.

Peī'pus (poos) *Lake* Estonia U.S.S.R.

Pė-kä-lông'än *City* Java, Indonesia

Pē'king = PEIPING

Pel'ė-liū *Island* of Palau Is.

Pel-lew'Islands (lōō') *Islands* off N Australia

Pel'là *Department* and *Anc. city* * of Macedonia, cen. Greece

Pel'lý 1. *River* 330 m. Yukon, Canada. 2. *Lake* Northwest Terrs., Canada

Pel-o-pön-nē'sus *Division* on *Peninsula* S mainland of Greece

Pė-lō'tàs *City* S Brazil

Pel-vou' (vōō') *Mountain* 12,970 ft., of group SE France

Pem'bȧ *Island* off Tanzania

P e m ' b r o k e - s h î r e (brook) *County* SW Wales; mines, farms, quarries

Pe-nang' *City* (George Town) on *Island* off W Malay Penin., NW Malaysia

Pe'nas (pā'nyäs) *Cape, Gulf* SW Chile

Pėng'pu' (pōō') *Town* E China

Pėn'ki' (chē') *Town* S Manchuria; coal

Pėn-nell', Mount *Peak* 11,320 ft. S Utah, U.S.

Pen'nêr *Two rivers* cen. India: **Northern** 350 m., **Southern** 245 m.

Pen'nȋne Alps *Range* of Alps, Switzerland-Italy

Pen'nȋne Chāin *Range* N cen. England

Penn-sȳl-vā'niȧ *State* E cen. U.S.; 45,333 sq. m.; pop. 11,793,-909; * Harrisburg; 67 counties; mines, factories, farms

Pė-nob'scŏt *Bay* S Me., U.S.

Pen-sȧ-cō'lȧ *City* on *Bay* NW Fla., U.S.; pop. 59,507; harbor, air base, fish, lumber

Pent'lȧnd Fȋrth *Channel* Orkney Is.-Scotland

Pen'zȧ *City* * of *Region* U.S.S.R., E Eur.; agriculture, manufacturing

Pen'zhi-nȧ *Town* on *River* into *Bay* NE U.S.S.R., Asia

Pė-ō'ri-ȧ *City* NW cen. Ill., U.S.; pop. 126,-963; trade, industry

Pe'räk (pā') *State* W Malay Penin., Malaysia; tin, agriculture

Per-di'dō, Mount (dē'), **Mônt Per-dû'** *Peak* 11,000 ft. Sp.-Fr. border

Per-i-bon'kȧ *River* 280 m. Quebec, Canada

Pe-ri-gueux' (pā-rē-gû') *Commune* SW cen. France; manufacturing

Pêr'kins, Mount *Peak* 12,555 ft. S Calif., U.S.

Pêr'lis *State* S Malay Penin, Malaysia; rice

Pêrm was **Mô'lö-töv** *C i t y* R.S.F.S.R., U.S.S.R., Asia; commerce, manufactures

Pêr-nȧm-bū'cŏ 1. *State* E Brazil. 2. *City* now RECIFE

Per-pi-gnan' (pē-nyän') *City* S France; manufacturing

Pêr'sia (zhȧ) *Kingdom* anc. and mod. (now IRAN), SW Asia; anc. * **Pêr-sep'ŏ-lis**

Pêr'sian Gulf (zhȧn) *Arm* of Arabian S., Arabia-Iran

Pêr'sian Gulf States (zhȧn) *States* along Persian Gulf: incl. Bahrian, Qatar, Trucial Oman, etc.; shiekdoms. Brit. management; oil, date palms

Pêrth 1. *City* * of Western Australia, SW Australia; trade cen. 2. *Burgh* * of **Pêrth'-shȋre** *County* cen. Scotland; textiles

Pêrth Am'boy *City* cen. N.J., U.S.; pop. 38,-798; port, smelting and refining, manufacturing

Pė-ru', Rep. of (rōō') *Republic* W South America; 500,060 sq. m.; pop. 13,200,000; * Lima; 23 departments; agriculture, minerals

Pe-ru'gia (rōō'jȧ) *Commune* * of *Province* cen. Italy; velvet, silk, brandy

Pe'sä-rō (pā') *City* * of **Pe'sä-rō e Ur-bi'nō** (â oor-bē') *prov.* E cen. Italy; manufacturing

Pes-cȧ-dō'res *Island group* (Chinese) For-mosa Strait

Pe-scä'rä *City* * of *Province* cen. Italy; resort

Pė-shä'wȧr *City* * of *District* NW Pakistan; trade

Pest (pesht) = part of BUDAPEST since 1872

Pest'er-zse-bet (pesh,-ter-zhā-bet) *City* suburb of Budapest, Hungary

Pė'têr-bör-ough (bör-ŏ) 1. *City* SE Ontario, Canada; agricultural area. 2. *Municipal borough* cen. England; trade cen.

Pe-te-rō'ä (pā-tä) *Peak* 13,420 ft. cen. Chile; volcanic

Pė'têrs-bûrg *City* SE Va., U.S.; pop. 36,-103; shipping, tobacco industry

Pet'ri-fȋed Forest *National park* E Ariz., U.S.

Pet'rō-grad see LENINGRAD

Pet-rō-pav'lôvsk *City* U.S.S.R., cen. Asia; trade cen.

Pė-trop'ŏ-lis *City* SE Brazil

Pet-ro-zȧ-vodsk', Kȧ-li'ninsk (lē') *City* NW U.S.S.R., Eur.; guns

Pet'sȧ-mō *Territory* NW U.S.S.R., Eur.; formerly Finnish

Pfôrz'heim *City* SW West Germany; manufacturing

Phal'tȧn (p'hȧl') *State* W India

Phä-nöm Dông Räk (p'hä) *Mountain range* Thailand-Cambodia

Phän-räng (p'hän) *Town* on *Bay* S Vietnam; agricultural cen.

Phil-ȧ-del'phi-ȧ (fil-a-del'fi-ȧ) 1. *City* SE Pa., U.S.; pop. 1,-948,609; commercial, cultural, financial, industrial cen.; site of 1st and 2nd Conti-nental Congresses, signing of Declaration of Independence; * of U.S. 1790-1800. 2. *Anc. city* W Turkey, Asia

Phi'lippe-ville (fil') *City* NE Algeria; port

Phi'lip-pi (fil') *Anc. town* N cen. Macedonia, Greece

Phil'ip-pine I s l a n d s (fil'i - pēn) *I s l a n d group* N Malay Arch. former dependency of U.S., now **Republic of the Philippines**: 116,000 sq. m.; pop. 37,000,000, * Quezon City on Luzon; 49 provinces

Phil'lip-pine Sea (fil'i-pēn) *Area* of W Pacific O. E of Phil. Is.

Phoe-ni'ci-a (fe-nish'ȧ) *Anc. country* W Syria

Phoe'nix (fē') 1. *City* * of Ariz., U.S., SW cen. part; pop. 581,-562. 2. *Islands* of Gilbert and Ellice group

Phryg'e-a (frij') *Anc. country* W cen. Asia Minor

Phu-ket (p'hōō) *Town* on *Island* SW Thailand; tin mines, port

Piä-cen'zä (chen') *Commune* * of *Province* N Italy; manufacturing

Pic'ȧr-dȳ *Hist. region* N France

Pi-chin'chä (pē-chēn') *Volcano* 15,710 ft. Ecuador

Pi'cō Ri-ve'rȧ (pē', vä') *City* S Cal., U.S.; pop. 54,170

Pi-chu'-Pi-chu' (chōō') *Peak* 18,600 ft. S Peru

Pic'tou (tōō) *Town* N Nova Scotia, Canada; port

Piĕd'mont, Pie-môn'te (pyâ-môn'tä) *Compartimento* NW Italy

Pierre (pyâr) *City* * of S.D., U.S.; cen. part; pop. 9,699; shipping, saddles

Pit'câirn Island *Island,* Brit. colony, cen. Pacific O.

Pitts'bûrgh *City* SW Pa., U.S.; pop. 520,-117; river port; iron, steel, educational cen.

Pitts'fïeld *C i t y* W Mass., U.S.; pop. 57,-020; cultural, industrial cen.

Plå-cen'tia Bay (sen'-shà) *Bay* SE Newfoundland, Canada; site of Atlantic Charter 1941

Pla'cid, Lake (sīd) *Lake* NE N.Y., U.S.

Plāin'fïeld *City* NE N.J., U.S.; pop. 46,-862; machinery

Plä'tä-nō *River* 325 m. S Mexico

Platte 1. *River* 300 m. Iowa-Mo., U.S. 2. *River* 310 m. cen. Neb., U.S.

Platts'bûrgh *City* NE N.Y., U.S.; naval battles, 1776, 1814

Plau'ên (plou') *City* S cen. East Germany; cotton textiles

Ple'ven *City* * of *Department* N Bulgaria; cattle, wine cen.

Plô-es'ti (yesh') *City* SE cen. Romania; oil

Piē - têr - mar'it - bûrg *Town* former * of Nepal; tanneries, furniture

Pi'geon Peak (jun) *Peak* 13,970 ft. SW Colo., U.S.

Pïkes Peak *Mountain* 14,110 ft. E cen. Colo., U.S.

Pil-co-mä'yō (pēl) *River* 1000 m. S cen. South America

Pi'li (pē'lē) *Peak* 19,850 ft. N Chile

Pil'lår, Cape *Cape* SE Tasmania

Pi'löt Knob (nob) *Peak* 13,750 ft. SW Colo., U.S.

Pi'löt Peak *Peak* 11,740 ft. NW Wyo., U.S.

Pil'sèn = PLZEN

Pin'chot, Mount (shō) *Peak* 13,470 ft. S cen. Calif., U.S.

Pin'dus *Mountain chain* NW Greece

Pīne Bluff *City* SE Ark. U.S.; pop. 57,389; industrial, trade cen.

Pi-ne'gå *River* 500 m. U.S.S.R., Eur.

Ping, Me-ping *River* 360 m. W Thailand

Pin'kiang' (ji-äng') see HARBIN

Pinsk *City* * of *Region,* White Russia, U.S.S.R., Eur.; manufacturing

Piô'tr-kow (kōōf), **Pe-trö-kôv'** *Commune* cen. Poland; textiles

Pi-rà-ci-ca'bà (pē, ce) *City* SE Brazil; trade

Pī-raē'us *City* E cen. Greece; seaport for Athens

Pi-ra'nhàs (nyàs) *River* 250 m. NE Brazil

Pir'mä-sens *City* SW W e s t Germany; leather items

Pi'sà (pē'zà) *Commune* * of *Province* cen. Italy; resort, tower

Pi-stō'ià *Commune* * of *Province* cen. Italy; manufacturing

Pit *River* 280 m. N Calif., U.S.

Plõ'mō *Mountain* 22,-300 ft. S cen. Chile

Plôv'div *City* * of *Department* S Bulgaria; trade cen.

Plým'outh (u t h) 1. *Town* on *Bay* SE Mass., U.S.; site of early colony. 2. *City,* on *Sound,* SW England; port, naval base

Pl'zen (pul'), **Pil'sèn** *City* SW Czechoslovakia; breweries, industry

Pnôm'penh' *City* * of Cambodia, SE part; pop. 394,000; trade

Pō *River* 415 m. N Italy

Pō-cà-tel'lo *City* SE Ida., U.S.; pop. 40,-036

Pō'co-nō Mountains *Heights* E Pa., U.S.

Po - dolsk' *T o w n* R.S.F.S.R., U.S.S.R., Eur.; factories

Pō'dôr *Town* N Senegal

Pō Hai, Gulf of NW *Arm* of Yellow S.

Pō'hsien' (shi-en') *City* E China; commerce

Pointe-a-Pi'tre (pwan-ta-pē') *Town* E Guadeloupe

Poi-tiers' (pwa-tyä') *City* W cen. France

Pō'lånd, Pôl'skä *Communist republic* cen. Eur.; 120,360 sq. m.; pop. 32,400,000; * Warsaw

Pō'lår Regions *Areas* around N and S Poles

Pōle Crèek Mountain *Peak* 13,735 ft. SW Colo., U.S.

Pō'lish Cor'ri-dör *Land strip,* various ownership; now N Poland

Pol'lux 1. *Peak* 13,430 ft. W peak of ZWILLINGE (Twins). 2. *Peak* 11,080 ft. NW Wyo., U.S.

Pō'lotsk *City* * of *Region* White Russia, U.S.S.R.

Pöl-ta'vå *City* * of *Region* Ukraine, U.S.-S.R.; grain, leather

Pol-ÿ-nē'sia (zhà) 1. *Islands* of cen. Pacific O. 2. FRENCH POLYNESIA

Pom-êr-ā'nià 1. *Bay* NE Germany - NW Poland. 2. *Hist. region* on Baltic S. now bel. to Poland

Po-mō'nà 1. *City* SW Calif., U.S.; pop. 87,-384; shipping. 2. *Island,* largest of Orkney Is.

Pom'på-nō Beach *City* S Fla., U.S.; pop. 37,724

Pom-pe'ii (pâ'ê) *Anc. city* S Italy; excavations; mod. **Pom-pe'i**

Pō'nà-pe (pä) *Island* E Caroline Is.

Pôn'ce (sâ) *City* and

Municipality S Puerto Rico; shipping

Pon-di-cher'rÿ *Town* SE India, former * of Fr. India; textiles

Pon'do-land *Area* S Rep. of South Africa

Pōn'tà Grôs'sà *City* S Brazil

Pont'chår-trāin' *Lake* SE La., U.S.

Pôn-te-ve'drä (v ä ') *Commune* * of *Province* NW Spain

Pon'ti-àc *City* SE Mich. U.S.; pop. 85,279; automobile equipment

Pon-ti-ä'näk *City* Borneo, Indonesia; port

Pon'tine (tēn), **Pon'zä** *Islands* of *Group* W of Naples, Italy

Pon-tÿ-pōōl' *Urban district* W England; coal, factory area

Pōōle *Municipal borough* S England; fish, pottery

Pōō'nà *City* * of *District* W India; mills

Pō-pä-yän' *City* SW Colombia; cultural cen.

Po-pō-cä-tė-petl' (pet'l) *Volcano* 17,885 ft. SE cen. Mexico

Pō'quis (kēs) *Peak* 18,-830 ft. N Chile

Pôr-ban'dår *Town* * of *State* W India; port

Pôr'cū-pīne 1. *River* 400 m. Yukon, Canada-NE Alas., U.S. 2. *Range* NW Mich., U.S.

Pô'ri, Björ'nė-bôrg (byûr') *City* SW Finland; port, factories

Pôrs'äng-êr Fjord *Inlet* N Norway

Pôrt Ad'ė-lāide *City* SE Australia; seaport

Pôrt Är'thûr 1. *City* SE Tex., U.S.; pop. 57,371; shipping. 2. *City* SW Ontario, Canada; p o r t. 3. *Town* S Manchuria. E cen. China; port

Pôrt-au-Prince' *City* * and main seaport of

Haiti; pop. 300,000

Pôrt Blâir *Town* Andaman Is., Bay of Bengal, India; harbor

Pôrt E-liz′à-beth *Town* S Rep. of South Africa; imp. port, factories

Pôrt Här′côurt *City* S Nigeria; port

Pôrt Hū′ron *City* SE Mich., U.S.; pop. 35,-794; lake port

Pôrt Jack′sön *Inlet* SE Australia; harbor

Pôrt′lånd 1. *City* SW Me., U.S.; pop. 65,-116; port. 2. *City* NW Ore., U.S.; pop. 382,-619; manufacturing, industrial, shipping

Pôrt Lou′is (lōō′i) *City* * of Maurituis I.; port

Pôrt Lyau-tey′ (lyō-tā′), **Ke-ni-tra′** *Port* NW Morocco; WW II landing, 1942

Pôrt Mōres′bỳ *City* S Terr. of Papua, New Guinea; port

Pôr′to A-le′grè (tōō, lā′) *City* S Brazil; port, commercial cen.

Pôrt of Spāin *Town* NW Trinidad, * of Trinidad and Tobago; pop. 125,000; port

Pôr′tô Nō′vō *Town* * of Dahomey, SE part; pop. 80,000; port

Pôrt Phil′lip Bay (fil′) *Harbor* of Melbourne, Australia

Pôrt Saīd′ *City* NE Egypt; port

Pôrts′mouth (muth) 1. *City* SE Va., U.S.; pop. 110,963; industrial port. 2. *County borough* S England; port

Pôrt Stan′ley (li) *Town* * of Falkland Is.; port

Pôrt Su-dan′ (sōō) *Town* NE Sudan; port

Pôrt Tal′böt *Urban district* SE Wales; coal

Pôr′tū-gàl *Republic,*

former kingdom, SW Eur.; 35,500 sq. m.; pop. 9,496,000; * Lisbon; 11 provs., 18 districts; agriculture, cork, fish

Pôr′tū-guese E Africa (gēz) now MOZAMBIQUE; **W Africa** = ANGOLA

Pôr′tū-guese Guin′ea (gēz, gin′i) *Colony* W Africa, * Bissau; peanuts, oils, ivory, hides

Pôr′tū-guese India (gēz) see GOA

Pôr′tū-guese (gēs) **Ti-môr′** *Colony* E part of Timor I. Malay Arch. * Dili; agriculture

Po′sèn = POZNAN

Pô′shän′ *Town* NE China; industry

Po-ten′zä *Commune* * of *Province* S Italy

Po-tō′màc *River* 500 m. W.Va.-Va.-Md., U.S.

Pō-to-si′ (sē′) 1. *City* * of *Department* SW Bolivia; silver. 2. *Peak* 13,765 ft. SW Colo., U.S.

Pō′trô *Peak* 19,125 ft. NW Argentina

Pots′dam *City* cen. East Germany; factories; WW II conference 1945

Pour-ri′, Mônt (pōō-rē′) *Peak* 12,425 ft. E France

Pow′dêr *River* 375 m. Wyo.-Mont., U.S.

Pow′èll, Mount *Peak* 13,535 ft. Colo , U.S.

Pō′yäng′ Hū *Lake* SE China

Pôz′nän, Ger. Pō′sèn *City* * of *Department* W cen. Poland; manufacturing, cultural cen.

Prague (präg), **Pra′ha** *City* * of Czechoslovakia, W part; pop. 1,103,200; industrial, commercial cen.

Präh-ran′ *City* SE Australia

Prä′tō *Commune* cen.

Italy; textiles

Pres′cött *City* cen. Ariz., U.S.; mining

Pres-i-den′tial Range (shàl) *Range* of White Mts., N.H., U.S. [SLAVA

Press′bûrg = BRATI-

Pres′tön *County borough* NW England; port, factories

Pre-tō′ri-à *City,* administrative * of Rep. of South Africa, NE part; pop. 448,000

Prib′i-lôf Islands *Island group* SE Bering S. Alas., U.S.; fur seals

Prich′ård *City* SW Ala., U.S.; pop. 41,-578

Prince Al′bêrt *Peninsula, Sound*, Victoria I. Northwest Terrs., Canada

Prince Ed′wàrd Island *Island Province* SE Canada; pop. 110,-000; * Charlottetown; fish, forests, agriculture

Prince Ed′wàrd Islands *Islands* (2) S Indian O., South Africa

Prince of Wāles Island 1. *Island*, largest of Alexander Arch. SE Alas., U.S. 2. *Island* NW Terrs., Canada

Prince Pat′rick Island *Island* of Parry Is. NW Terrs., Canada

Prince Rū′pêrt *City* W Brit. Columbia, Canada; port, fisheries

Prince′tön, Mount *Peak* 14,175 ft. Colo., U.S.

Prin′ci-pe (si) *Island* (Port.) off W Africa; agriculture

Pri′pyàt (prē′) *River* 500 m. through Marshes White Russia-Ukraine, U.S.S.R.

Prö-kô′pèvsk *City* S cen. U.S.S.R., Asia; mines

Prōme *Town* * of *District* Lower Burma; port

Prom′ön-tō-rỳ Point *Point* NW Utah,

U.S.; Golden Spike Monument

Pros′pec-törs Mountain *Peak* 11,230 ft. Wyo., U.S.

Prô-vence′ (väns′) *Hist. region* SE France

Prov′i-dénce *City* * of R.I., U.S.; pop. 179,-213; manufacturing, port

Prov′ince-town *Town* SE Mass., U.S.; 1620 landing of Pilgrims

Prō′vō *Peak* 11,055 ft.; *City* N cen. Utah, U.S.; pop. 53,131; commerce, industry

Prus′sia (prush′à) *Former state* N and cen. Germany; div. 1945-7 Poland-U.S.S.R.

Prūt *River* 500 m. E Romania

Psel *River* 420 m. Ukraine U.S.S.R.

Pskôv *City* * of *Region* W cen. U.S.S.R., Eur.; port; rail, commercial cen.

Ptär′mi-gàn Peak (tär′) *Peak* 13,735 ft. cen. Colo., U.S.

Pue′blä (pwäb′) *City* * of *State*, SE cen. Mexico; old city; textiles, pottery

Pû-eb′lō *City* SE cen. Colo., U.S.; pop. 97,-453; commerce, industry, minerals

Puer′to Plä′tä *Commune* and *City* N Dominican Rep.; port

Puer′tö Ri′cō (rē′) *Island* of West Indies (U.S.); * San Juan; agriculture

Pū′get Sound (jèt) *Arm* of Pacific O., W Wash., U.S.

Pulj (pōōl′y′), **Pō′là** *Town* NW Yugoslavia; port

Pu′nà-khà (poo′) *Town* winter * of Bhutan

Pun′jäb 1. *Former province* NW Brit. India; 1947 div.: **East Pun′jäb** (*state*) NW India, **West Pun′jäb** part of West Pakistan

Pun′tä A-re′näs (pōōn′, rä′) *City* S Chile; port; world's southernmost city

Pu-pä-yäx′ (yäk′) *Peak* 19,080 ft. W Bolivia

Pu-rä-ce′ (sä′) *Volcano* 15,420 ft. SW Colombia

Pu-rä′li *River* 310 m. West Pakistan

Pu-rä′ri *River* 280 m. E cen. New Guinea

Pûr′gà-tô′rẏ Peak *Peak* 13,720 ft. S Colo., U.S.

Pu′ri (poo′), **Jà′gàn-näth** *Town* E India; Hindu pilgrimage site

Pu-rūs′ (pōō) *River* 2000 m. Peru-Brazil

Pu-sän, Fu-sän (oo) *City* S Korea; port

Push′kàr (poosh′) *Lake* NW cen. India; sacred water

Push′kin (poosh′) *Town* NW U.S.S.R., Eur.; resort

Put′-in-Bay (poot′) *Bay* of Lake Erie, Ohio, U.S.; Comm. Perry victory, 1813

Pu′tô′ Shän (pōō′) *Island* E China; sacred to Buddhists

Pu-tu-mä′yo (pōō-tōō) *River* 980 m. Colombia-Peru-Brazil

Puy-de-Dōme′ (pû-ĕd-dôm′) *Department* S cen. France

Pyä′si-nà *River* 350 m. N U.S.S.R., W Asia

Pya-ti-gôrsk′ *Town* S U.S.S.R., Eur.; resort

Pẏ′los, It. Nä-vä-ri′nō (rē′) SW Peloponnesus, Greece; harbor

Pyöng-yäng or Hei-jō (hä) *City* * of North Korea; pop. 653,000

Pẏr′à-mid Peak *Mountain:* 1. 14,000 ft. Colo., U.S. 2. 10,300 ft. NW Wyo., U.S.

Pẏr′à-mids *Anc monuments* (3) nr. Cairo, Egypt

Pẏr′ė-nēes, Pi-rė-ne′ōs (nä′) *Mountains* Span.-Fr. border

Pẏ-re-nees′ (rä-nä′) *Department* France

Pẏ-re-nees′ - O-rien-tale′ (rä-nä′ zô-ryän-tal′) *Department* S France

Q

Qä′tär *Arab shiekdom* on *Peninsula*, Persian Gulf; 8,000 sq. m.; pop. 80,000; * Doha; oil

Qät-tä′rä Depression *Low area* N Egypt

Qė′nà *City* * of *Province* Upper Egypt; glass jars

Qi′zel U-zun′ (oo-zoon′) *River* 450 m. NW Iran

Quän′dà-rẏ Peak *Peak* 14,256 ft. Colo., U.S.

Quän′ti-cô *Town* NE Va., U.S.; Marine Corps base

Qu'Ap-pelle′ (ka) *River* 270 m. cen. Canada

Que-bec′ 1. *Province* E Canada; 594,860 sq. m.; pop. 5,976,000; * Quebec; agriculture, fish, mining, forestry. 2. *City* its *; pop. 166,984; port, manufacturing

Quēen Al-ex-an′drà Range *Mountains*, Victoria Land, Antarctica

Quēen Chär′lötte (shär′) *Islands* and *Sound* W Brit. Columbia, Canada

Quēen Mâr′ẏ Coast *Area* at Antarctic Circle, Brit.

Quēen Mǎud Gulf *Gulf* NW Terrs., Canada

Quēen Mǎud Land (Norwegian) Antarctica

Quēens *Borough* (largest of 5) of N.Y. City, U.S.; manufacturing

Quēens′land *State* NE Australia; * Brisbane; exports sugar, animal products

Que-moy′ (kē) *Island* off SE China (Nationalist)

Que-nä-mä′ri (k ä) *Mountain* 19,190 ft. SE Peru

Que-re′tä-rō (kâ-rä′) *City* * of *State* cen. Mexico

Quet′tä (kwet′) *Town* * of *District* W cen. West Pakistan; trade

Que-zäl-te-nän′gō (kâ-säl-tä) *City* * of *Department* SW Guatemala; grain area

Que′zôn City (kä′) *City* Luzon, Phil. Is.; * of Republic of the Philippines; pop. 500,000

Quil′mes (kēl′mâs) *City* E Argentina; industry, resort

Quim-sä-chä′tä (kēm) *Peak* 19,880 ft. N Chile

Quim-sä-crūz′ (kēm) *Peak* 19,355 ft. W Bolivia

Quin′cẏ 1. *City* W Ill., U.S.; pop. 45,288; commerce, industry. 2. *City* E Mass., U.S.; pop. 87,966; shipyards; home of John, John Q. Adams

Quin′tô (kēn′) *River* 250 m. N cen. Argentina

Quir′i-nàl *Hill* one of of 7 of Rome, Italy

Qui′tô (kē′) *City* * of Ecuador, N part; pop. 530,000; cultural cen.

Qum (koom) *City* NW cen. Iran; grain, cotton region

R

Rà-bät′ *City* * of Morocco, NW part; pop. 250,000; port

Rà-baul′ (boul′, bōōl′) *Town* New Brit. I., Terr. of New Guinea

Rä-ci′borz (tsē′boosh), **Ra′ti-bôr** *City* SW Poland, formerly German

Rà-cine′ (sēn′) *City* SE Wisc., U.S.; pop. 95,162; industry, port

Rä′dhàn-pur (poor) *Town* * of *State* W India

[E Wales

Rad′nör-shìre *County*

Rä′dôm *Commune* E cen. Poland; industrial

Rä-gu′sä (gōō′) 1. *Commune* * of *Province* SE Sicily, Italy. 2. or **Dū′brov-nik** Yugoslavia port

Rä′had *River* 270 m. Ethiopia-Sudan

Raï′chur *Town* S cen. India

Raï′gärh *Town* * of *State* NE India; silk

Rai-niēr′, Mount (rà) *Peak* in *National Park* 14,400 ft. W cen. Wash., U.S.

Rāin′ẏ Lake *Lake* Canada-Minn., U.S.

Raï′pur (poor) *Town* E cen. India

Rä - jàh - mun′drẏ (moon′) *City* E India; timber

Rä′jäng *River* 300 m. Sarawak, Borneo

Rä′jà-sthän *State* NW India within *Region* (also **Räj-pu-tä′nà**)

Räj′kōt *Town* * of former *State* W India

Räj-pi′plà (pē′) *Town* * of *State* W India

Räj-shä′hi *Town* * of *District* E Pakistan

Rä-kà-häng′à *Atoll* (U.S.) cen. Pacific O.

Rà-kà-pô′shi *Peak* 25,560 ft. N Kashmir

Rä′kos-pa-lo-ta (kosh) *City* cen. Hungary

Rä-ku-tō *River* 270 m. S Korea

Rä′leigh (li) *City* * of N.C., U.S.; pop. 121,577; cotton, tobacco, educational cen.

Rà-ma′di *Town* cen. Iraq

Räm-gàn′gä *River* 370 m. N India

Räm′lèh *City*, resort of Alexandria, Egypt

Räm′pur (poor) *City* * of *State* N India; sugar, damask, pottery

Ram′sēs *Anc. city* E Egypt

Rams′gāte *Municipal*

borough SE England; yachting, fishing

Rä'mu (moō) *River* 300 m. NE New Guinea

Rän'chi *Town* NE India; health cen.

Rän'dêrs *City* Jutland, Denmark; port

Ränd-fôn-tein' (tän') *City* NE Rep. of South Africa; gold

Rand'wick *City* SE Australia

Ränge'ley (r ā n j'l i) *Lakes* W Me., U.S.

Ran-goōn' *City* on *River*, * of Burma, S part; pop. 740,000; imp. port

Rång'pur (poor) *Town* * of *District* E Pakistan

Rän-te-mä'ri-ō *Peak* 11,285 ft. Celebes I., Indonesia

Rä-päl'lō *Commune* NW Italy; port

Rap'id City *City* SW S.D., U.S.; pop. 43,-836; trade

Rä'pi-dō (pē) *River* cen. Italy; WW II site

Räp'ti *River* 400 m. Nepal [Cook Is.

Rar-o-ton'gà *Island* of

Räs' Dä-shän' *Peak* 15,160 ft. N Ethiopia

Rä-shin *Port* NE North Korea

Rat Islands *Group* W Aleutians, Alas., U.S.

Råt-läm' *Town* cen. India

Rå-ven'nà *Commune* * of *Province* N Italy

Rä'vi *River* 450 m. N India

Rä-wal-pin'di *City* * of *Division* and former.* of Pakistan, N West Pakistan; pop. 340,-200; industrial

Read'ing (red') 1. *City* SE Pa., U.S.; pop. 87,643; industrial. 2. *County borough* S England

Rēar'guärd (gärd) *Peak* 12,350 ft. S Mont., U.S.

Rè-ci'fè (sē') *City* (was Pernambuco) E Bra-

zil; imp. port

Reck'ling - hau - sèn (hou) *City* W West Germany; commerce

Red'cloud Peak *Peak* 14,050 ft. SW Colo., U.S.

Red Dēer *River* 385 m. Alberta, Canada

Red'lands *City* SE Cal., U.S.; pop. 36,355; residential

Red Mountain 1. *Peak* 11,930 ft. S cen. Calif. U.S. 2. *Peak* 13,500 ft. W cen. Colo., U.S.

Re-don'dō Beach *City* S Cal., U.S.; pop. 56,075; manufacturing, residential

Red Peak 1. *Mountain* 11,700 ft. cen. Calif., Calif., U.S. 2. *Mountain* 13,600 ft. S Colo., U.S.

Red River 1. *River* 1018 m. N.M.-Tex.-Okla -Ark.-La., U.S. 2. **of the Nôrth** *River* 310 m. cen. U.S.-cen. Canada

Red Sea *Inland sea* bet. Arabia-Africa

Red'wood City W Cal., U.S.; pop. 55,686; residential, manufacturing

Re'gèns-bûrg (rä') *City* SE West Germany

Reg'gio (räd'jō) 1. **di Cä-lä'bri-ä** *Commune* * of *Province* S Italy. 2. **nell' E-mi'lià** (nâl-lâ-mē') *Commune* * of *Province* N Italy; commerce, manufacturing

Rè-gī'nà (jī') *City* * of Saskatchewan prov. (S part) Canada; pop. 131,127; trade cen.

Reich (rīk) = Empire: 1st Reich = Holy Roman Emp.; 2nd Reich = Bismarck Emp.; 3rd Reich = Nazi Emp.

Reï'chèn-bêrg (rī'kèn) see LIBEREC

Reï'gäte *Municipal borough* S England

Rēims, Rhēims *City*

NE France; cathedral, champagne, textiles; site of German surrender 1945

Rein'dēer Lake (rän') *Lake* cen. Canada

Reïn'stein, Mount *Peak* 12,600 ft. S cen. Calif., U.S.

Re'mä-gèn (rä') *Town* W cen. West Germany; WW II battle

Rem'scheïd (shīt) *City* W cen. West Germany; cutlery, tools

Ren-frew' (froō') *Burgh*, **Ren-frew'shire** *county*, SW Scotland

Rennes (ren) *City* NW France; manufacturing

Rē'nō *City* NW Nev., U.S.; pop. 72,863; commercial cen., legal gambling

Re-pub'li-càn *River* 445 m. Neb.-Kans., U.S.

Resht *City* NW Iran

Re-sis-ten'cià (tän'sià) *City* N Argentina

Res-o-lu'tion Island (loō'shàn) *Island* off SE Baffin I., Canada

Re-ū-niôn' (rä) *Island* (Fr. *Dept.*) off Madagascar, W Indian O.

Reut'ling-èn (roit') *City* SW West Germany; manufacturing

Rè-vēre' *City* E Mass., U.S.; pop. 43,159; beach resort

Rè-vil'là-gi-gē-dō *Island* SE Alas., U.S.; site of Ketchikan

Rē'wà *Town* * of *State* E cen. India

Rey'kja-vik (rä'kyà) *Town* * of Iceland, SW coast; pop. 81,-500; port

Rhēims = REIMS

Rheïn'hau-sèn (hou) *Commune* W West Germany; port, coal

Rheïn'wäld-hôrn (vält) *Peak* 11,144 ft. SE Switzerland

Rhine, Rheïn, Rijn (rīn), **Rhin** (ran) *River* 820 m. W Eur.

Rhine'land *Area* of

West Germany W of Rhine R.

Rhīne'land - Pá-la't-i-nate *State* of W Germany, W of Rhine R.

Rhōde Is'länd (ī') *State* NE U.S.; 1,067 sq. m.; pop. 949,723; * Providence; 5 counties; textiles, jewelry

Rhōdes *City* on *Island*, * of Greek Aegean Is.; 2 harbors; fruit

Rhō-dē'sia (shà) 1. *Region* cen. S Africa: 1953-63 Fed. of Rhodesia and Nyasaland; now N Rhodesia = ZAMBIA; S Rhodesia = RHODESIA; Nyasaland = MALAWI. 2. *Country* S Africa; 150,333 sq. m.; pop. 4,670,000; * Salisbury

Rhon'ddà *Urban district* SE Wales; coal

Rhōne 1. *River* 500 m. Switzerland - France. 2. *Department* S France

Ri-äd' = RIYADH

Ri-bei-rao' Pre'to (vä-rou' pra'tōō) *City* SE Brazil; coffee area

Rich'ärd-sön *City* NE Texas, U.S.; pop. 48,582

Rich'e-lieū (rish') *River* 210 m. Quebec, Canada

Rich'fiēld *City* SE cen. Minn., U.S.; pop. 47,231

Rich'mönd 1. *City* W Calif., U.S.; pop. 79,-043; industrial port. 2. *City* E Ind., U.S.; pop. 43,999; manufacturing. 3. *County* of N.Y. and *Borough* of N.Y. City, U.S. 4. *City* * of Va., U.S.; pop. 249,621; trade cen., tobacco market, manufacturing. 5. *City* SE Australia; manufacturing. 6. *Municipal borough* S England

Rie'kä, Ri-je'kä (r'ye'), It. **Fiü'me** (mä) *City*

NW Yugoslavia; port

Rie'ti (ryā') *Commune* * of *Province* cen. Italy; livestock, agriculture

Ri'gả (rē') *City* on *Gulf* * of Latvia; port

Ri'mi-ni *City* N Italy; port, resort

Rimp'fisch-hôrn *Peak* 13,791 ft. SW Switzerland [ft. N Chile

Rin-côn' *Peak* 18,350

Ri'ō Al'tō Peak (rē') *Peak* 13,570 ft. S cen. Colo., U.S.

Ri'ō Cuär'tō *Town* N cen. Argentina; agricultural cen.

Ri'ō dė Jả-nei'rō (rē', nā') 1. *City*, former * of Brazil, SE part; one of world's finest harbors; cultural cen. 2. *State* SE Brazil

Ri'o Gran'dė (rē'ōō) *City* S Brazil; port

Ri'ō Grande or **Ri'ō Brä'vō** (rē') *River* 1800 m. Colo.-N.M.-Tex., U.S.-Mexico

Ri'o Gran'dė (rē'ōō) 1. *River* 250 m. W Africa (also **Co-rū-bäl'**, **Kom'bả**). 2. *River* 680 m. E Brazil. 3. *River* 300 m. E Brazil

Ri'ō Mu'ni (rē', mōō') *Province*, mainland of Equatorial Guinea, site of *

Ri'ō Ne'grō (rē', nā') see NEGRO, RIO

Ri'ō Pie'dräs (rē', pyä') *Municipality* NE Puerto Rico; industrial

Ri'tō Al'tō Peak (rē') *Mountain* 13,570 ft. Colo., U.S.

Rit'têr, Mount *Peak* 13,155 ft. cen. Calif., U.S.

Riv'êr-sīde *City* SE Calif., U.S.; pop. 140,089; commerce, resort; fruit area

Ri-vie'rä (vyả') *Region* on Mediterranean S., SE France-NW Italy (Fr. = Côte d'A-zūr')

Ri-yädh' *City* * of Saudi Arabia, E cen. part; pop. ab. 185,000

Ri-zäl' *Province* Luzon, Phil. Is.

Rōad' Town *Town* * of Brit. Virgin Is. on Tortola I.; pop. 1500

Rō-anne' *Commune* SE cen. France; mills

Rō'ả-nōke 1. *City* W cen. Va., U.S.; pop. 92,115; rail, manufacturing cen. 2. *Island* E N.C., U.S.; 1st English settlement in N America 3. *River* 380 m. Va.-N.C., U.S.

Rob'sön, Mount *Peak* 12,970 ft. E Brit. Colombia, Canada

Rô'cả *Cape* SW point of Portugal

Roch'dāle *County borough* NW England

Roch'es-têr 1. *City* SE Minn., U.S.; pop. 53,766; Mayo Clinic. 2. *City* W N.Y., U.S.; pop. 296,233; port; manufacturing, educational cen. 3. *City* SE England

Rock *River* 300 m. Wisc.-Ill., U.S.

Rock'dāle *City* SE Australia

Rock'förd *City* N Ill., U.S.; pop. 147,370; manufacturing

Rock-hamp'tön *City* E Australia; shipping

Rock Is'lånd (ī') *City* NW Ill., U.S.; pop. 50,166; port

Rock'ville *City* C Md., U.S.; pop. 41,564; residential

Rock'ẏ Mountains, **Rock'ies** *Mountain system* W North America; Mexico-U.S.-Canada-Arctic

Rodg'êrs Peak (roj') *Peak* 13,055 ft. Calif., U.S.

Rōes Wel'cöme *Strait* Southampton I.-mainland, Northwest Terrs., Canada

Rōgue (rōg) *River* 220 m. Ore., U.S.

Rō'kän *River* 225 m.

Sumatra, Indonesia

Ro-kel' *River* 300 m. Sierra Leone

Roll'ing Mountain *Peak* 13,695 ft. Colo., U.S.

Rō'mä = ROME, Italy

Rō-mäine' *River* 225 m. Quebec, Canada

Rō'mản Em'pīre *Anc. Empire* 264 B.C.-180 A.D., incl. S Eur., Britain, N Africa, Asia Minor, Egypt, Armenia, Mesopotamia, Syria, Palestine, NW Arabia

Ro-mā'niả, or **Rū-mā'niả, People's Republic of** *Country*, Balkan State, E cen. Europe; 91,700 sq. m.; pop. 20,300,000; * Bucharest

Rōme 1. *City* cen. N.Y., U.S.; pop. 50,148; industry. 2. *City* * of Italy, cen. part; pop. 2,731,000; cultural cen., famous ruins, site of Vatican City

Röm'förd *Urban district* SE England; iron foundries

Roo'sė-velt (rō') 1. *Dam, Lake* S cen. Ariz., U.S. 1. *Island* Ross Dependency, Antarctica. 3. *Island* (**Thē'ö-dōre**) D.C., U.S. 4. *Lake* (**Frank'lin D.**) N cen. Wash., U.S.

Rō'pêr *River* 325 m. N cen. Australia

Rō'sä, Môn'ta *Mountain* 15,215 ft. Swiss-Italian border

Rō'sả-liė Peak *Mountain* 13,575 ft. cen. Colo., U.S.

Rô-sä'rio *City* E cen. Argentina; imp. port

Rose'mėad *City* S Cal., U.S.; pop. 40,972

Rō-set'tả, Rả-shid' *City* Lower Egypt; Rosetta Stone found nearby

Rōse'ville *City* SE Mich., U.S.; pop. 60,529 [Denmark

Rös'kil-dė *City* E

Rôss and Crom'ảr-tẏ *County* N Scotland; sheep, fish

Rôss Bar'riêr or **Rôss Shelf Ice** *Ice wall* and *shelf* along S Ross S., Antarctica

Rôss Dependency *Section* of Antarctica (Brit., administered by New Zealand) bet. 160° E and 150° W long. incl. **Rôss I.** and shores of **Rôss S.**

Ros'tock *City* East Germany; port, fisheries, manufactures

Rös-tôv' *City* * of *Region* U.S.S.R., SE Eur.; cultural, industrial cen.

Roth'êr-hảm *County borough* N England; iron, coal area

Rô'ti *Island* nr. Timor, Indonesia

Rot'têr-dam *City* W Netherlands; manufacturing, commercial port

Rou-baix' (rōō-be') *City* N France; textiles, leather

Rou-en' (rōō-än') *City* N France; manufacturing, commerce

Rou-mā'niả (rōō) = ROMANIA *Republic* SE Europe; iron-steel, machinery, oil, timber, textiles, footwear, food processing

Rô-vi'gō (vē') *Commune* * of *Province* NE Italy

Rôv'nö *Commune* W Ukraine U.S.S.R.; industrial

Row'ley Rē'gis (rou'li-rē'jis) *Urban district* W cen. England; iron, coal, pottery

Row'têr, Mount (rou') *Peak* 13,750 ft. W cen. Colo., U.S.

Rox'burgh (bûr-ö) *County* SE Scotland

Roy'al, Mount *Height* Montreal City, Canada

Roy'ảl Gôrge (gôrje)

GAZETTE ATLAS

Gorge Grand Canyon, Colo., U.S.

Roy′ål Ōak *City* SE Mich., U.S.; pop. 85,499

Rū-ä′hä *River* 300 m. cen. Tanzania

Rū-än′dä-U-run′di (ōō-rōōn′) *Territory,* formerly Germ. East Africa, later Belg. Trust Terr.; div. 1962 RWANDA and BURUNDI

Rub′ al Khä′li (roob′), **Great San′dẏ Desert** *Desert* 3000 sq. m. S Arabia [Kenya

Rū′dolf, Lake *Lake* N

Rū-fi′ji (fē′) *River* 250 m. Tanzania

Ṛug′bẏ *Urban district* cen. England

Rü′gėn *Island* Baltic S.; Germany's largest island; fishing

Rūhr *Valley* of *River* 144 m. West Germany; mining area, incl. great industrial centers; imp. WW I, WW II.

Ruis′lip **Nôrth′wood** *Urban district* SE England

Ruiz (rwēz) *Peak* 17,-390 ft. W cen. Colombia

Rū′ki *River* 250 m. NW Congo (L)

Rū-mā′niä = ROMANIA

Run′nẏ-mēde *Meadow* S England; Magna Charta signing

Rū′pêrt *River* 380 m. Quebec, Canada

Rū′pêrt's Land *Territory* N Canada, now part of NW Terrs.

Rū-pu-nū′ni *River* 250 m. Guyana

Ru′se (roo′) *City* NE Bulgaria; industry, commerce

Rush′môre, Mount *Peak* 6040 ft. W S.D., U.S.; president's faces

Rus′sėll, Mount *Peak* 14,190 ft. E Calif., U.S.

Rus′sia (rush′à) 1. *Popular name* for U.S.S.R. 2. *Former empire* E Eur., N and NW Asia; * St. Petersburg

Rus′sian Sō′vi-et Fed-erated Sō′cial-ist Rep. (rush′àn, sō′-shàl) = R.S.F.S.R. *Republic,* largest of U.S.S.R., E Eur.-N and W Asia; * Moscow; incl. many autonomous reps., terrs., regions

Rü′string-ėn *City* NW West Germany; resort, manufacturing

Ru-thē′ni-à (rōō) *Region* formerly in NE Hungary, then Czechoslovakia, now incl. in Ukraine as ZAKARPATSKAYA

Rut′länd-shîre *County* E cen. England

Ru-vu′mà (rōō - vōō′) *River* 400 m. Tanzania

Ru-wėn-zō′ri (r ō ō) *Mountains* Uganda-Congo (L)

Rȳ′àn Peak *Mountain* 11,900 ft. Ida., U.S.

Ryà-zan′ *City* * of *Region* cen. R.S.F.S.R., U.S.S.R., Eur.

Rhȳ′binsk 1. **Reservoir** or **Sea** *Lake* NW U.S.S.R., Eur. 2. *City* = SHCHERBAKOV

Rwän′dä, Rep. of *Republic* E cen. Africa; 10,170 sq. m.; pop. 3,500,000; * Kigali; coffee, tin, yams

Rȳde *City* SE Australia

Ryū′kyū Islands *Island chain* W Pacific O. bet. Taiwan-Japan; bel. to U.S except for Amami group (Jap.)

R z h e v *C i t y* N W U.S.S.R., Eur.; commerce, industry

S

Säa′lė *River* 225 m. cen. Germany

Säar′länd *Region* of **Säar R.;** *State* of

West Germany, * **Säar′brûck-ėn;** coal, iron, steel

Sä-bä-dell′ *Commune* NE Spain; agriculture, manufacturing

Sä′bäh *Division* of Malaysia, N Borneo; formerly Brit. North Borneo

Sȧ-bē′tà Peak *Peak* 13,600 ft. cen. Colo., U.S.

Sȧ-bine′ (bēn′) *River* 380 m. Tex.-La., U.S.

Sä′ble *Island, Cape* SW Nova Scotia, Canada; sand bar

Sac-rȧ-men′tō 1. *City* * of Calif., U.S., N cen. part; pop. 254,413; industrial cen. 2. *River* 382 m. NW Calif., U.S.

Sad′dle Mountain *Peak* 10,680 ft. NW Wyo., U.S.

Sȧ-di-yä *Town* NE India; WW II base

Sä-dō *Island* off NW Honshu, Japan; silver, gold

Säfe′tẏ Islands *Islands* off N Fr. Guinea, incl. Devil's I.

Sa′fi *City* NW Morocco; port

Sä-gä *City* * of *Prefecture* Kyushu, Japan; fish, coal

Sȧ-gaing′ (gīng′) *Town* * of *Division* and *District,* Upper Burma; port

Sä-gay′ (gī′) *Municipality* Negros, Phil. Is.

Sag′ĭ-năw *City* cen. Mich., U.S.; pop. 91,-849; port, rail cen., machinery

Sag-uė-nāy′ *River* 400 m. (with Peribonka R.) Quebec, Canada; hydroelectricity, resorts

Sa-hand′, Kuh′i (kōō′) *Mountain* 12,100 ft. NW Iran

Sȧ-har′à *Desert area* N Africa, div.: France, Great Britain, Italy,

Spain

Sȧ-hä′rȧn-pur (poor) *City* N India

Saï′dȧ-pet *Town* S India

Saï-gon′ *City* on *River,* * of South Vietnam, SE part; pop. 2,200,-000; port

St. Äl′bȧns *City, Municipal borough* SE England; shipping

St. Äu′gus-tine (tēn) *City* NE Fla., U.S.; pop. 12,352

St. Bri-euc′ (san brē-û′) *City* NW France

St. Cath′ȧ-rines (rinz) *City* SE Ontario, Canada; manufacturing,

St. Chris′tö-phêr (kris′-tö-fêr) = ST. KITTS

St. Clâir, Lake *Lake* Mich., U.S.-Ontario, Canada

St. Clâir′ Shores *City* SE Mich., U.S.; pop. 88,093; residential

St. Cloud′ (san klōō′) *Commune* N France

St. Cloud′ *City* C Minn., U.S.; pop. 39,691; business

St. Croix′ (sânt kroi′), **San′tȧ Crŭz′** *Island* largest of U.S. Virgin Is.; sugar cane

St.-Den′is (or sand-nē′) 1. *City* * of Reunion I. (Fr.). 2. *Commune* N France

Ste. Anne′ dê Beau-pre′ (bō-prä′) *Village* S Quebec, Canada

St. E-li′ȧs *Peak* 18,000 ft. of *Range* SW Yukon Terr., Canada-E Alas., U.S.

Ste. Mȧ-rié′ *Cape* S tip Madagascar I.

Saint E-tienne′ (san-tā) *City* SE cen. France

St. Fran′cis (sĭs) *River* 425 m. Mo.-Ark., U.S.

St. Gäl′lėn *Commune* * of *Canton* NE Switzerland; trade cen.

St. Geor′ge's (jôr′jiz) 1. *Town* Grenada I., * of Windward Is., Brit. West Indies. 2.

Channel bet. Wales-Ireland

Saînt Gilles' (san-zhēl') *Commune* cen. Belgium

St. Hė-lē'nȧ *Island* (Brit.) S Atlantic O. off W Africa; Napoleon's exile 1815-21

St. Hel'ėns *County borough* NW England

St. Hel'ier (yêr) *Town* Jersey I., * of Channel Is.

St. John' 1. *City* New Brunswick, Canada; shipping, manufacturing. 2. *Lake* Quebec, Canada. 3. *Peak* 11,410 ft. Wyo., U.S. 4. *River* 450 m. NE U.S.-SE Canada

St. Johns' 1. *River* 276 m. Fla., U.S. 2. *Town* Antigua I., * of Leeward Is., Brit. West Indies

St. John's' *City* * of Newfoundland, Canada; pop. 79,884

St. Jō'seph (zef) 1. *City* NW Mo., U.S.; pop. 72,691; industrial, livestock cen. 2. *Lake* SW Ontario, Canada. 3. *River* 210 m. Mich.-Ind., U.S.

St. Kil'dȧ *City* SE Australia; residential

St. Kitts, St. Chris'tö-pher (fêr) *Island* of Brit. Leeward Is., E West Indies

St. Lȧw'rence (rėns) 1. *River* 760 m. Quebec-Ontario, Canada, into **Gulf of St. Lȧw'rence** off E Canada. 2. *Island* W Alas., U.S.; excavations. 3. **Sēa'wȧy** *Waterway* Canada-U.S., Atlantic O.-Great Lakes

Saint Lō' (san) *Commune* NW France

Saint Lou-is' (san-lwē') *City* on Island, was * of Senegal

St. Lou'is (lōō'is) 1. *City* E Mo., U.S.; pop. 622,236; fur market, manufactur-

ing. 2. *River* 220 m. Minn., U.S.

St. Lou'is Park (lōō') *City* SE Minn., U.S.; pop. 48,883; residential

St. Lū'cia (shȧ) *Island* (Brit.) of Windward Is., E West Indies

Saint-Ma-lō' (san) *Gulf* NW France

St. Mar'y's *Island* site of * of Gambia

Saint - Maur' - des - Fos-ses' (san-môr' dȧ-fô-sā') *Commune* N France; manufacturing

St. Mau'rice (mä'ris) *River* 325 m. Quebec, Canada

St. Mö-ritz' *Commune* E Switzerland; resort

St. Na-zaire' *Commune* NW France; manufacturing port

St. Ni-co-las' (nē-kô-lä'), **Sint-Ni'klass** (nē') *Commune* NW cen. Belgium; manufacturing

St. Ou-en' (san-twan') *Commune* N France; manufacturing

St. Pȧul 1. *City* * of Minn., E part, U.S.; pop. 309,980; twin city with Minneapolis; commercial, manufacturing cen. 2. *River* 280 m. Liberia

St. Pē'tėrs-bûrg 1. *City* W cen. Fla., U.S.; pop. 216,232; port, resort. 2. *City* former * of U.S.S.R., now LENINGRAD

St. Pierre' and Miq'ue-lon' (-pyâr', mē-klon') *Territory* (Fr.); 2 islands S of Newfoundland; fish

St. Quen'tin *Commune* N France; textiles

St. Thom'ȧs (tom') 1. *Island* of U.S. Virgin Is.; commercial cen. resort. 2. see SAO TOME

St. Vin'cent (sėnt) 1. *Island* of Windward Is., Brit. West Indies;

cotton, agriculture. 2. *Cape* SW Portugal

Saī-pan' *Island* of U.S. Trust Terr., W Pacific O.

Saī-shū *Town* on *Island* off S Korea

Saī-tä-mä *Prefecture* Japan

Sä-jä'mä (hä') *Peak* 21,390 ft. W Bolivia

Sä-kaī *City* Honshu, Japan; textiles

Sä-kär'yȧ *River* 300 m. Turkey, Asia

Sä-kä-tä *City* Honshu, Japan; rice cen.

Sa'khȧ-lin, Jap. Kä-rä-fū-tō *District* N part of *Island* in S. of Okhotsk; fish, oil, coal

Sä-ki-shi-mä *Islands* Island group of Ryukyu Is., Japan

Sä-lä'do *River* 250 m. NE Mexico

Sä-lä'do, Ri'ō (rē') *Rivers* (3), Argentina: 1. 1120 m., N part. 2. 850 m. W part. 3. 415 m. E part

Sä-lä'jär (yär) *Island* off SW Celebes I., Indonesia

Sal-ȧ-man'cȧ *Commune* * of *Province* W Spain; manufacturing

Sal'ȧ-mis 1. *City* imp. in anc. Cyprus, E part. 2. *Island* SE Greece

Säl-cän-tay' (tī') *Peak* 20,550 ft. Peru

Sāle (sāl) *Urban district* NW England

Sa-le' (lā'), **Sla** *City* NW Morocco; port

Sä'lėm 1. *City* NE Mass., U.S.; pop. 40,556; port, textiles, shoes. 2. *City* * of Ore., NW part, U.S.; pop. 68,296; industrial, trade cen. 3. *City* S India; trade

Sal'ėn-tīne Peninsula = "heel" of Italy

Sä-ler'nō *City* on *Gulf* * of *Province* S Italy

Säl'förd *County borough* NW England

Sȧ-lī'nȧ *City* cen. Kan., U.S.; pop. 37,714

Sȧ-li'nȧs (lē') *City* W Cal., U.S.; pop. 58,-896; business

Sȧ-line' (lēn') *River* 200 m. Kan., U.S.

Sȧlis'bur-ẏ (salz') *Town* * of Rhodesia, NE part; pop. 390,000; gold, agricultural area

Salm'ön (sam') *River* 420 m. Ida., U.S.

Sȧ-lon'i-kȧ, Thes-sä-lô-ni'ke (nyē') *City* on **Gulf of Salonika** NE Greece; port

Sal-sette' *Island* off W cen. India

Sȧlt 1. *River* 200 m. Ariz., U.S. 2. *River* 200 m. Mo., U.S.

Säl'tä *City* * of *Province* N Argentina

Säl-til'lo (tē'yō) *City* NE Mexico; mines, agriculture

Sȧlt Lake 1. see GREAT SALT LAKE. 2. *Region* SW cen. Australia; lakes, gold

Sȧlt Lake City *City* * of Utah, N part, U.S.; pop. 175,885; Mormon cen.; commerce, industry

Säl'tō *City* * of *Department* NW Uruguay; port, meat industry

Sȧ-lū'dȧ *River* 200 m. S.C., U.S.

Sal'vȧ-dôr, Bȧ-hi'ȧ (ē') *City* E Brazil; commercial port

Sal'wēen, Sal'win (wēn) *River* 1750 m. SE Asia, E Tibet-Lower Burma

Sälz'bûrg *City* * of *Province* W Austria; resort, manufacturing

Sä'mär *Island, Sea* E Phil. Is.

Sȧ-ma'rȧ *River* 360 m. U.S.S.R., Eur.

Sȧ-mâr'i-ȧ *District* of anc. Palestine, cen.

part; part in mod. Israel

Sam'ar-kand *City, Region,* Uzbek S.S.R., U.S.S.R.; industrial

Sa-mar'ra *Town* N cen. Iraq   [India

Sa-mō'a *Island group* SW cen. Pacific O., div. into: 1. **American Samoa,** * Pago Pago on Tutuila I., fish, copra; 2. **WESTERN SAMOA** (New Zealand)

Sä'môs *Island, Department,* Aegean Is., Greece

Sam'ō-thrāce *Island* (Gk.) Aegean S.

Säm-sun' (sōōn') *City* on *Bay* * of *Vilayet,* N Turkey, Asia; port

Sä-mut Söng-khräm, formerly **Me-klông** *City* W Thailand; port   [Poland

Sän *River* 280 m. SE

Sän'-a' *City* * of Yemen; trade cen.

Sä'na-ga *River* 430 m. Cameroun

San An'gė-lō (jė) *City* W cen. Texas, U.S.; pop. 63,884; commerce, manufacturing

San An-tō'ni-ō *City* on *River* (200 m.) S cen. Tex., U.S.; pop. 654,-153; commerce, industry

San Ber-nar-di'nō (dē') 1. *City* S Calif., U.S.; pop. 104,251; resort. 2. *Mountains* S Calif., U.S. 3. *Strait* Luzon-Samar Is., Phil. Is.

San Blas' *Gulf, Isthmus, Mountains* N Panama

San Brū'nō *City* W Cal., U.S.; pop. 36,254

San Cär'lôs 1. *Municipality* Luzon, Phil. Is. 2. *Municipality* Negros, Phil. Is.

Sän Cle-men'te (män'tä) *Peak* 13,315 ft. S Argentina

San Cris-tō'bal 1. *City*

W Venezuela. 2. *Commune* S Dominican Rep. 3. *Town* on *Island,* Galapagos Is.

Sän-dä'kän *Town* former * of North Borneo

San Di-e'gō (ā') 1. *City* on *Bay,* SW Calif., U.S.; pop. 696,769; port, resort, fruit cen. 2. *Cape* S Argentina

San Dō-min'gō now **DOMINICAN REP.**

San'dring-ham *Village* E England; royal residence

Sand'wich Islands now **HAWAIIAN IS.**

San'dwip (dwēp) *Island* East Pakistan

San Fêr-nan'dô 1. *City* E Argentina; port. 2. *City* SW Spain; port. 3. *Municipality* cen. Luzon, Phil. Is.; sugar cen., rice

San'förd, Mount *Peak* 16,200 ft. S Alas., U.S.

San Fran-cis'cō (sis') *City* on *Bay* W Calif., U.S.; pop. 715,674; shipping, financial, commercial, industrial cen.

San'ga *River* 400 m. Congo (L)

San'ga-mön *River* 225 m. Ill., U.S.

San-gän', Kōh'-i- *Peak* 12,870 ft. Afghanistan

Sän-gay' (gī') *Volcano* 17,750 ft. Ecuador

Säng'i Islands *Island group* Indonesia, NE of Celebes I.

Sän'gli *Town* * of *State* W India

Sän I-si'drō (sē') 1. *Town* E Argentina. 2. *Municipality* on *Bay* Leyte, Phil. Is.

San Ja-cin'tō (sin') *River* 100 m. SE Tex., U.S.; Mexican War battle

San Joa-quin' (wä-kēn')

1. *River* 350 m. Calif., U.S. 2. *Mountain* 13,-500 ft. Colo., U.S.

Sän Jor'ge (hôr'hâ) *River* 250 m. N Colombia

San Jo-se' (hō-zā') 1. *City* W Calif., U.S.; pop. 445,779; manufacturing, fruit cen. 2. *City* * of *Province* and * of Costa Rica, cen. part; pop. 580,-000; coffee trade

San Juan' (won') 1. *River* 360 m. Colo.-N.M.-Utah, U.S. 2. *Mountains* Colo., U.S.

Sän Juan' (hwän') 1. *City* and *Municipality* * of Puerto Rico, NE part; pop. 432,377; port. 2. *Hill* E Cuba; battle, Span. Am. War, 1898

Sän'kiang' (ji-äng') *Former Province* E Manchukuo

Sän-ku'ru (kōō'rōō) *River* 340 m. Congo (L)

San Lē-an'drō *City* W Calif., U.S.; pop. 68,698; dairy area

Sän Luis' Pō-tō-si' (lwēs', sē') *City* * of *State* cen. Mexico

Sän Mär'cō *Island* of Venice, Italy

Sän Mä-ri'nō (rē') *Republic* and *City* its *, S Europe surr. by Italy; 38 sq. m.; pop. 18,000; wine, cattle, stone

San Ma-te'ō (tā') *City* W Calif., U.S.; pop. 78,991; residential

Sän Mi-guel' (gel') *River* 475 m. E Bolivia

San Nic'o-las *Island Island* off SW Calif., U.S.

Sän Pä'blō, City of *City* Luzon Phil. Is.

San Ra-fael' (fel') *City* W Cal., U.S.; pop. 38,977; residential

San Sal'va-dôr 1. *City* * of *Department* and

* of El Salvador, pop. 472,000; commercial, cultural cen. 2. *Island* of Bahama Is.

San Sa-bas'tian (chan) 1. *City* N Spain; commercial port. 2. *Municipality* NW Puerto Rico

Sän Se-ve'rō (vâ') *Commune* SE Italy

Sänt *State* W India

San'ta An'a *City* SW Calif., U.S.; pop. 156,601; manufacturing

Sän'ta Ä'nä *City* * of *Department* NW El Salvador

San'ta Bär'ba-ra 1. *City* on *Channel* SW Calif., U.S.; pop. 70,215; resort. 2. *Island* of *Chain* off SW Calif., U.S.

San'ta Cat-a-li'na (lē') *Island* of Santa Barbara group SW Calif., U.S.; resort

San'ta Clar'a 1. *City* W Calif., U.S.; pop. 87,717. 2. *Municipality* and *City* W cen. Cuba; sugar, tobacco

San'ta Cruz' (krōōz') 1. *City* on *River* 250 m. in *Territory* S Argentina. 2. *City* * of *Department* E Bolivia. 3. de Te-ne-ri'fe (dâ tâ-nâ-rē'fâ) *City* * of *Province* Canary Is. Spain. 4. *Island* off SW Calif., U.S. 5. *Islands* (Brit.) SW Pacific O.

San'ta Fe' (fā') 1. *City* * of N.M., U.S.; pop. 41,167; tourist, art cen. 2. *Peak* 13,145 ft. Colo., U.S. 3. *Trail* W Mo.-Santa Fe-West

Sän'ta Fe' (fā') *City* * of *Province* E Argentina; port

San'ta Is'a-bel (iz') *Town* Equatorial Guinea; former * of Span. Guinea

San'ta Ma-ri'a (rē') 1.

City S Brazil; manufacturing. 2. *Volcano* 12,300 ft. Guatemala

San'tä Mär'tä *City* N Colombia; port

San'tä Mon'i-cà *City* on *Bay* SW Calif., U.S.; pop. 88,289; resort, residential

Sän-tän-dêr' *City* * of *Province* N Spain; commercial port

San'tä Rō'sà *City* NW Cal., U.S.; pop. 50,-006; business

Sän-ti-ä'gō 1. *City* * of *Province* and * of Chile, cen. part; pop. 2,314,000. 2. *Commune* and *City* N cen. Dominican Rep. 3. *Commune* NW Spain. 4. *Bay* E Cuba

Sän-tiä'gō de Cū'bä *Seaport* S Cuba

Sän-tiä'gō del Es-te'rō (tä') *City* * of *Province* N Argentina

Sän'tō An-dre' (drä') *City* SE Brazil

San'tō Do-min'gō *City* * of Dominican Rep.; pop. 462,000

San'tös *City* SE Brazil; coffee export

Sän Vä-len-tin' (tēn') *Peak* 13,310 ft. S Chile

Sao Fran-cis'co (sou fran-sēsh'kōō) *River* 1800 m. E Brazil

Sao Lou-ren'co (sou lō-rān'sōō) *River* 340 m. SW Brazil

Sao Luiz' (sou lwēs') *City* NE Brazil; port

Sao Mà-nuel' (sou, nwâl') *River* 600 m. cen. Brazil

Sao Mi-guel' (sou mē-gâl') *Island* largest of Azores

Saone (sōn) 1. *River* 300 m. E France. 2. -et-Loire' (lwär') *Department* E cen. France

Sao Pau'lo (sou pou'lōō) *City* * of *State* SE Brazil; imp. city, manufacturing, commerce

Sao To-me' (sou tōō-mä') *Island* and *Town* its * off W Africa; part of Port. colony: **Sao To-me' e Prin'ci-pe** (ē prēn'sē)

Sä-poe'di (pōō') *Island* Malay Arch., Indonesia

Säp-pō-rō *City* Hokkaido, Japan; breweries, manufacturing

Sar-à-gos'sä *City* * of *Province* NE Spain; trade, manufacturing

Sà-raï'ke-lä *State* NE India

Sä'rä-je-vō (ye) *City* * of Bosnia and Herzegovina Rep., cen. Yugoslavia; carpets, tobacco; site of assassination precipitating WW I

Sar'à-nac Lakes *Lakes* (3) NE N.J., U.S.

Sä'rän-gärh *State* NE India

Sà-ransk' *Town* * of Mordovian Rep. R.S.F.S.R., U.S.S.R.

Sä-rä-sä'rä *Peak* 19,-500 ft. Peru

Sar-à-sō'tà *City* SW Fla., U.S.; pop. 40,-237; business, resort

Sar-à-tō'gà *Village* now Schuylerville, E N.Y. U.S.; Revolutionary war battles

Sar-à-tō'gà Springs *City* E N.Y., U.S.; resort

Sà-ra'töv *City* * of *Region* SE R.S.F.S.R., U.S.S.R., Eur.

Sa-rä'wäk *Division* of Malaysia, N Borneo

Sär'dà *River* 220 m. N India

Sär-din'i-à *Island* of *Compartimento*, SW Italy

Sär-gō'dhà *Town* W Pakistan [Is.

Särk *Island* of Channel

Sär'ni-à *City* SE Ontario, Canada; port

Särre = SAAR

Sarthe (sart) *Department* NW France

Sä-rẏ Sū' *River* 520 m. U.S.S.R., Asia

Sä-se-bō *City* Kyushu, Japan; port

Sas-katch'i-wàn 1. *Province* W Canada; 250,000 sq. m.; pop. 961,000; * Regina; agriculture, esp. wheat. 2. *River* SW and S cen. Canada, 2 branches: **North** and **South** 1205 m. total

Sas-kà-tōōn' *City* S Saskatchewan, Canada; trade cen.

Sàs-san'drà *River* 300 m. W Ivory Coast

Säs'sä-ri *Commune* * of *Province* S India; trade, manufacturing

Sà-til'là *River* 220 m. Ga., U.S.

Sät'pu-rà Range (poo) *Hills* W cen. India

Sä-tsu-mä (tsoo) *Old province* Kyushu, Japan; pottery

Sàt-ti'mà (tē') *Peak* 13,215 ft. cen. Kenya

Sä'tū-Mà're *City* NW Romania; commerce

Sau'di A-rä'bi-à (sou') *Kingdom* SW Asia, most of Arabian penin.; 869,000 sq. m.; pop. 7,740,000; * Riyadh (Riad); oil

Sàu'gör *Town* N India

Sault' Sâinte Mà-rie' (sōō', rē') *City* S Ontario, Canada; industrial

Sä'vä, Save (sav), **Sau** (zou) *River* 450 m. N Yugoslavia

Sä-vaï'i *Island*, largest of Samoa

Sa-va-län', Kūh'-i- *Peak* 15,785 ft. NW Iran

Sà-van'nàh 1. *City* SE Ga., U.S.; pop. 118,-349; cotton port. 2. *River* 315 m. E Ga., U.S.

Sä'vànt-vä'di *Town* * of *State* W India

Sa'vè, Sä'bi *River* 400 m. SE Africa

Sa-voie' (vwa') 1. *Department* E France. 2. or SAVOY

Sä-vō'nä *City* * of

Province NW Italy; port, industry

Sà-voy' (voi') *Hist. region* SE France-NW Italy, now in France; incl. **Sa-voy' Alps**

Säv'skä *Former county* N Yugoslavia, now in Croatia

Säw'tōōth Mts. *Ranges* S cen. Ida., U.S.

Saxe = Fr. for Saxony, used in names of former duchies: **Saxe-Cō'bûrg**

Sax'ö-nẏ *Former duchy, Kingdom, State* cen. Germany; now W East Germany; minerals, manufacturing

Sä-yän' Mts. *Range* U.S.S.R., Asia

Scan-di-nä'vi-à = countries of Sweden, Denmark, Norway, Iceland

Scàr'bör-ough (bûr-ö) *Municipal borough* N England; port

Schaer'beek (skar'bāk) *Commune* cen. Belgium

Schel'dè (skel'), **Scheldt** (skelt) *River* 270 m. France-Belgium

Schè-nec'tà-dẏ (skè) *City* E N.Y., U.S.; pop. 77,859; industrial, electric plants

Sche'vè-ning-én (skā') *Resort* SW Netherlands

Schie-däm' (ske) *Commune* SW Netherlands

Schles'wig 1. *City* NW West Germany; manufacturing. 2. *Hist. region* NW Germany, former duchy; now incl. in **Schles'wig-Hōl'stein**, *State*, N West Germany

Schön-brunn' (broon') *Palace* Vienna, Austria

Schö'nè-beck *City* cen. East Germany; manufactures

Schö'nè-bêrg *Section* E Berlin, East Germany

Schreck'hôrn, Grôss

Peak 13,385 ft. SW Switzerland

Schwarz'wald (shvärts'-vält) = BLACK FOREST

Schwein'furt (shvīn') *City* S West Germany; manufacturing, port

S c h w e n ' n i n g - ė n (shven') *City* S West Germany; clocks

Schwe-rin' (shvā-rēn') *City* NW East Germany; manufacturing

Sci-ō'tō (sī) *River* 238 m. Ohio., U.S.

Scot'land *Division* of United Kingdom of Great Britain and Northern Ireland, N Great Britain; 30,400 sq. m.; pop. 5,188,-000; * Edinburgh; 33 counties

Scots'dāle *City* cen. Ariz., U.S.; pop. 67,-823

Scran'tön *City* NE Pa., U.S.; pop. 103,564

Scun'thôrpe *Urban district* E England

Scū'tȧ-ri *Lake* Yugoslavia-Albania

Sēal *River* 240 m. Manitoba, Canada

Sēa'sīde *City* W Cal., U.S.; pop. 35,935

Sē-at'tle (t'l) *City* W cen. Wash., U.S.; pop. 530,831; commercial, industrial port [VASTOPOL

Sė-bas'tö-pôl = SE-

Se-cun'dėr-ä-bäd *Town* S cen. India

Se-gō'viȧ *River* 450 m. N Nicaragua

Sei'bo (sā'vō) *Commune* * of *Province* E Dominican Rep.; coffee, cacoa, sugar

Seim (sām) *River* 435 m. U.S.S.R., Eur.

Seine (sān) 1. *River* 480 m. N France. 2. *Departments* (4) N France: **Seine'et-Marne'** (ā märn'), **-et-Oise'** (ā waz'), **-In-fe-rieure'** (an-fā-

ryûr')

Sei-shin (sâ), **Chöng-jin** *City* NE Korea; port

Sei-shū (sâ) *City* S Korea

Sė-lang'ör *State* SW Malay Penin., Malaysia; tin, rubber

Se-len-gä' *River* 750 m. N cen. Asia

Sel'kîrk 1. *County* SE Scotland; sheep. 2. *Mountains* Brit. Columbia, Canada

Sė-mä'räng *City* Java, Indonesia; port

Sė-me'növ (myô') *Peak* 15,350 ft. Kirgiz, U.S.S.R.

Sė-me'roe (rōō) *Volcano* 12,000 ft. Java, Indonesia

Se-mi-pȧ-la'tinsk *City* * of *Region* U.S.S.R., W Asia; livestock products

Sen-daī *City* Honshu, Japan; cultural cen.

Sen'ė-cȧ Lake *Lake* (of Finger Lakes) W N.Y., U.S.

Sen-ė-gal', Rep. of 1. *Republic* W Africa (formerly Fr.); 75,750 sq. m.; pop. 3,400,-000; * Dakar; agriculture, peanuts. 2. *River* 1050 m. W Africa

Seoul (sōl), was **Kei-jō** (kā) *City* * of South Korea, N part; pop. 5,000,000

Se'pik (sā') *River* 600 m. North-East New Guinea

Sė-quoi'ȧ *National Park* S cen. Calif., U.S.; trees, Mt. Whitney

Se-raing' (ran') *Commune* E Belgium; manufacturing, mining [India

Ser'ȧm-pōre *Town* NE

Sêr'bi-ȧ *Republic*, one of 6 federated republics of Yugoslavia, NW part; * Belgrade; former Balkan kingdom

Ser'gö = now KADI-YEVKA

Ser'ôv *City* R.S.F.S.R., U.S.S.R., Asia

Se-rōw'e *Town* E Botswana

Sêr-pū'khôv (pōō') *City* R.S.F.S.R., U.S.S.R., Eur.; textiles, grain, timber cen.

Ser'rȧ dos Aī-mo-res' (sâr', dōōz ī-mōō-rȧs') *Area* E Brazil

Ser'rai (sâ'rä) *City* * of *Dept.* N cen. Greece; agricultural cen.

Sete, Cette *City* S France; commercial port

Se-tif' (sā-tēf') *Commune* NE Algeria

Sė-tit', Bahr (tēt') *River* 350 m. E Africa

Sė-tu'bȧl (tōō') *City* on *Bay* SW Portugal; port

Seûl, Lake *Lake* W Ontario, Canada

Se-vän', Gök'chä *Lake* Armenian S. S. R., U.S.S.R.

Sė-vas'to-pôl *City*, *Peninsula* on *Bay* of Black S., S U.S.S.R., Eur.; port, naval base

Seven Hills *Hills* of Rome, Italy: Palatine, Capitoline, Quirinal, Aventine, Caelian, Esquiline, Viminal

Sev'êrn 1. *River* 420 m. Ontario, Canada. 2. *River* 210 m. W England

Se'vėr-nȧ-yȧ Zėm-la' (syâ') *Islands* Arctic O., U.S.S.R., Asia

Sė-vier' (vēr') *River* 279 m. Utah, U.S.

Sė-ville' *City* * of **Se-vil'la** (vē'yä) prov. SW Spain; buildings

Se'vres (sâ'vr') *Commune* N France; porcelain

Sew'ȧrd (sū') *Peninsula* W Alas., U.S.; gold

Sey-chelles' (sâ-shelz') *Islands* (Brit.) Indian O. E of Tanzania; * Port Victoria; coconuts, spices

Sey-hän' (sā) 1. *River* 780 m. S cen. Turkey, Asia. 2. *City* = ADANA

Sfax *City* E Tunisia; port, olives

's Gra-vėn-ha'gė (kė) = HAGUE, THE

Shäh Fu-lä-di' (dē') *Mountain* 16,872 ft. E cen. Afghanistan

Shäh-jȧ-hän'pur (poor) *City* N India

Shäk'êr Heights (hīts) *City* N Ohio; pop. 36,306; residential

Shakh'tẏ *City* SW U.S.S.R., Eur.

Sha'lȧ-mär Gardens *Gardens* E of Lahore West Pakistan

Shä'mō' = Chinese name of GOBI Desert

Shang'haī' *City* E China; industrial cen. and commercial port of China

Shan'nön *River* 240 m. N cen. - SW Eire; longest of Brit. Isles

Shän'si' *Province* NE China; coal, cereals, wool, opium [Burma

Shan States *States* E

Shan'tung' *Province* NE China; silk industry

Shao'hing' (shou'shing') *City* E China; trade

Shärk Bay *Bay* of Indian O. W Australia; pearls

Shärps'bûrg *Village* N Md., U.S.; Antietam battle site

Shä'si' (sē') *City* E cen. China; port

Shas'tȧ, Mt. *Peak* 14,-160 ft. N Calif., U.S.

Shȧ-vä'nō Peak *Peak* 14,180 ft. Colo., U.S.

Shȧ-win'i-gȧn Falls *City* and *Falls* S Quebec, Canada; light and power plants

Shchėr-bȧ-kôv', was **Rẏ'binsk** *City* W U.S.S.R., Eur.; port

Shē'bȧ *Anc. country* S Arabia

She-boy'gȧn *City* E Wisc., U.S.; pop. 48,-

484; cheese, plumbing fixtures

Shef′field *City, County borough* N England; cutlery cen., plating

Shek-sna′ *River* 280 m. W U.S.S.R., Eur.

Shen-an-dō′ah *Valley, River, National Park* N Va., U.S.

Shen′si′ *Province* NE cen. China; cereals, coal

Sher′brô *Island* SW Sierra Leone

Sher′brooke *City* S Quebec, Canada; manufacturing

Sher′i-dan, Mount *Peak* 13,700 ft. Colo., U.S.

Sher′man, Mount *Peak* 14,035 ft. Colo., U.S.

's Her′tō - gen - bôsch (′ser′, bôs) *Commune* S Netherlands

Sher′wood Forest *Anc. forest* cen. England

Shet′land Islands *Archipelago* off N Scotland; fishing, sheep, ponies

Shey - enne′ (shī - en′) *River* 325 m. N.D., U.S.

Shi-be′li, Web′be (bā′) *River* 700 m. E Africa

Shi-gä (shē) *Prefecture* Honshu, Japan

Shi-gä′tse *Town* SE Tibet; trade

Shi-kär′pur (poor) *City* W Pakistan; silks, precious stones

Shi-kō′ku *Island* of Japan, 4th in size; agriculture, minerals

Shil′ka *River* 300 m. U.S.S.R., Asia

Shil′la *Peak* 23,000 ft. Kashmir

Shi-mä-ne *Prefecture* Honshu, Japan

Shi-mi-zu (zoo) *City* Honshu, Japan; tea port

Shi-mōn-nō-se′ki *City* on *Strait* Honshu, Japan; port

Shi-nä-no *River* 225 m. Honshu, Japan

Shin-chi-ku (koo) *City*

NW Taiwan

Shin-gi-shu (shōō) *City* NW Korea; lumber trade, manufacturing

Shin-shu = CHINJU

Shi-räz′ *City* SW cen. Iran; industry, commerce

Shi′re (shē′) *River* 370 m. SE Africa

Shi-zu-ō-kä *City* * of *Prefecture* Honshu, Japan; industrial

Shkä′rä Tau (tou) *Mountain* 17,000 ft. U.S.S.R., Eur.

Shkō′der, Scu′ta-ri (skōō′) *Town* * of *Prefecture* NW Albania; trade cen.

Shō-kä *City* W Taiwan

Shō′lä-pur (poor) *City* W India; trade, manufacturing

Shôrt′land Islands *Island group* Brit. Solomon Is.

Shrēve′pôrt *City* NW La., U.S.; pop. 182,064; commercial, industrial cen.

Shrews′bur-y (shrōōz′) *Municipal borough* W England; brewing, tanning

Shrop′shire *County* W England; agriculture, coal, china

Shun-sen (shoon) *Town* E South Korea

Shū′shan *Anc. city,* now ruins, SW Iran

Shū′ya *Town* cen. U.S.S.R., Eur.; textiles

Shwe′li (shwā′) *River* 350 m. Upper Burma

Si (shē), **Si′kiang′** (shē′-ji-äng′) *River* over 1000 m. SE China into China S.

Si (sē) *River* 300 m. E Thailand

Si-äl′kōt *City* * of *District* W Pakistan

Si-am′ 1. *Kingdom,* since 1949 THAILAND. 2. *Gulf Inlet* of South China S., S of Thailand

Si′än′ (shē′), **Chäng′än′**

City NE cen. China; trade cen., imp. hist.

Siang, Hsiang (shi-äng′) 1. *River* 350 m. SE cen. China. 2. formerly Yü *River* 400 m. S China

Siang′tän′ (shi-äng′) *City* SE cen. China; trade cen.

Si-bē′ri-a *Area:* N Asia Ural Mts.-Pacific O., R.S.F.S.R. in Asia, U.S.S.R.; natural resources, furs

Si-biu′ *City* W cen. Romania

Sic′i-ly (sis′) *Island, Compartimento,* SW Italy; * Palermo; fruit, olives, wine, sulfur

Si′di-bel-Ab-bes′ (sē′) *Commune* NW Algeria

Sid′ley, Mount (li) *Peak* 12,000 ft. Antarctica

Si′dön *City* SW Lebanon

Sid′ra, Gulf of *Inlet* of Mediterranean S. N Libya

Sie′nä (syâ′) *Commune* * of *Province* cen. Italy; manufacturing, fine buildings

Si-er′rä Le-ōne′ *Country* of Brit. Commonwealth (former Brit. colony) W Africa; 27,700 sq. m.; pop. 2,500,000; * Freetown; farming, mining

Si-er′rä Mad′re *Mountain ranges:* 1. S Wyo., U.S.; part of Continental Divide. 2. SE Mexico. 3. Luzon, Phil. Is.

Si - er′rä Ne - vad′a *Mountain range* E Calif., U.S.

Si′käng′ (shē′) *Province* S China

Si - ka - ram′, Mount *Peak* 15,620 ft. E Afghanistan

Si′khō-te A-lin′ (sē′kō-tä ä-lēn′) *Mountain range* E U.S.S.R.

Sik′kim *Monarchy, Protectorate* of India; 2745 sq. m.; pop. 187,000; * Gangtok; agriculture

Si-lē′sia (zhä) 1. *Region* E Eur., variously bel. to Poland, Germany, Czechoslovakia. 2. *Peak* 13,600 ft. Colo., U.S.

Si′lex, Mount *Peak* 13,635 ft. Colo., U.S.

Sill, Mount *Peak* 14,255 ft. S Calif., U.S.

Sil-laj-huay′ (sē-yäk-wī′) *Peak* 19,670 ft. W Bolivia

Sil′li-man, Mount *Peak* 11,190 ft. Calif., U.S.

Sil′vêr-heels, Mount *Peak* 13,835 ft. Colo., U.S.

Sil′vêr Plūme *Mountain Peak* 13,500 ft. Colo., U.S.

Sil′vêr Run *Peak Mountain* 12,610 ft. Mont., U.S.

Sim-birsk′ now ULYANOVSK

Sim′cōe, Lake *Lake* Ontario, Canada

Sim-fêr-ô′pöl *City* S R.S.F.S.R., U.S.S.R., Eur.; industry

Simi Valley *City* SW Cal., U.S.; pop. 56,464

Sim′la *Town* NW India; former Brit. summer *

Si′nai *Mountain* (Bib. Mt. Horeb) on *Peninsula* NE Egypt

Si-nä-lō′ä *State* W Mexico

Sind 1. *Province,* formerly NW India, now W Pakistan. 2. *River* 240 m. cen. India

Sin′ga-pōre 1. *City* * and imp. port of 2. *Island State* off S Malay Penin., former Brit. Colony, later part of Malaysia, independent 1965; 225 sq. m.; pop. 2,000,000; tin, rubber

Si′ning′, Hsi′ning′ (shē′) *City* W cen. China

Sin′kiang′ (shin′ji-äng′) *Province* W China

Sint-Ni′klaas (nē′), **St.-Ni-co-las′** (san-nē-kô-lä′) *Commune* NW cen. Belgium

Sioux City (sōō) *City* W Iowa, U.S.; pop. 85,925; trade, industrial cen.

Sioux Falls (sōō) *City* SE S.D., U.S.; pop. 72,488; commerce, industry

Si′ple, Mount (p′l) *Peak* 15,000 ft. Antarctica

Si-rä-cu′sä (kōō′zä) 1. *Province* SE Sicily, Italy. 2. *City* see SYRACUSE (2.)

Sir-mur′ (moor′) *State* NW India

Si-rō′hi *State* NW India

Sit′ka *Town* Baranof I. SE Alas., U.S.; trade

Sit′täng *River* 350 m. E cen. Burma

Si-väs′ *City* * of *Vilayet* E cen. Turkey, Asia; trade

Sjael′land (shel′) *Island* of *Island group* E Denmark; site of Copenhagen [DEN

Sjen′yang′ = MUK-

Skag′êr-rak *Arm* of North S. bet. Norway and Denmark

Skag′wāy *City* SE Alas., U.S.; gold rush

Ska′nē (skō′) *Section* S Sweden

Skan-e-at′e-lês *Lake* of Finger Lakes cen. N.Y., U.S.

Skēe′nå *River* 335 m. Brit. Columbia, Canada

Skel-lef′tė (shel) *River* 325 m. N Sweden

Sker′ries (riz) *Islands* S Irish S.

Skō′kie *City* NE Ill., U.S.; pop. 68,627

Skōp′lje (lye) *City* S Yugoslavia; industry, commerce

Skunk *River* 265 m. Iowa, U.S.

Skȳe *Island* off NW Scotland; sheep, cattle, fish [S.

Skȳ′rös *Island* Aegean

Slä′met *Peak* 11,250 ft. Java, Indonesia

Slask (shlônsk) = Polish SILESIA

Slāve *River* 265 m. W cen. Canada

Slå-vō′ni-å *Region* SE Eur., now part of Croatia, Yugoslavia

Slå-vyansk′ *Town* E Ukraine U.S.S.R.; industry

Slīde Mountain *Peak* 11,095 ft. Calif., U.S.

Sli′gō *Municipal borough* and *City*, * of *County* N Eire; port

Slough (slou) *Municipal borough* SE England; motors

Slo-vä′ki-å, Slô′ven-skô *Province* E cen. Czechoslovakia; livestock, mining, farms

Slo-vē′ni-å *Federated Republic* NW Yugoslavia; * Ljubljana

Slu-bi′ce (slōō-bē′tse), **Frank′fûrt** *City* W Poland, formerly part of Frankfurt on Oder

Slupsk (slōōpsk), Ger. **Stôlp** *City* N Poland

Smeth′wick *County borough* W cen. England; factories

Smi′chov (smē′kôf) *City* W cen. Czechoslovakia

Smī′ley Mountain (li) *Peak* 11,500 ft. Ida., U.S.

Smōk′ȳ *River* 245 m. Alberta, Canada

Smō′kȳ Hill *River* 540 m. Colo.-Kans., U.S.

Smo-lensk′ *City* * of *Region* R.S.F.S.R., U.S.S.R., Eur.; trade, manufacturing, cultural cen.

Smȳr′nå now IZMIR

Snāke *River* 1038 m. NW U.S.; Wyo.-Ida.-Ore.-Wash.

Snef′fėls, Mount *Peak* 14,145 ft. Colo., U.S.

Snōw′mass Mountain *Peak* 14,080 ft. Colo.,

U.S.

Snōw Mountains *Range* New Guinea

So-ci′ė-tȳ (sī′) **Islands** *Island group* (Fr.) S Pacific O., incl. Windward and Leeward Is.; * Papeete on Tahiti [ft. N Chile

So-côm′pä *Peak* 19,785

Sod′öm *Bib .City*, with GOMORRAH; known for wickedness

Soe- see SU-

Soem-bä′wå (sōōm) = SUMBAWA

Sō-fi′å (fē′) *City*, * of *Department*, * of Bulgaria in W part; pop. 868,200; manufacturing, transportation

Sô-hag′ (haj′) *City* Upper Egypt

Sō-hō′ *District* London, England; restaurants

Sō′kō-tō *Town* * of *Province* NW Nigeria

Sō-li-mä′nä *Peak* 20,-735 ft. S Peru

Sō′ling-ėn (zō′) *City* W West Germany; industrial

Sō′lō *River* 335 m. Java, Indonesia

Sô-logne′ (lôn′y′) *Area* cen. France; reclaimed for farming

Sol′ö-mön Islands *Island group* (Brit.) W Pacific O., largest Guadalcanal; * Honiara; timber, copra

So-lö-vets′ki Islands *Island group* White S., U.S.S.R., Eur.

So-mä′lia, Sö-mä′li Republic *Republic* E Africa; 246,200 sq. m.; pop. 2,745,000; * Mogadiscio; livestock, agriculture; former Brit. and It. terrs.: So-mä′li-land

Söm′êr-set Island *Island* Northwest Terrs., Canada

Söm′êr-set-shîre *County* SW England; fruit, cattle

Söm′êr-ville *City* NE Mass., U.S.; pop. 88,779; industry

Sômme *Department* N France

Sōn *River* 487 m. NE cen. India [Italy

Sôn′dri-ō *Province* N

Sō-ne-que′rä (kä′) *Peak* 18,650 ft. SW Bolivia

Sō-nō′rä 1. *River* 300 m. NW Mexico. 2. *Peak* 11,430 ft. E Calif., U.S.

Sôn′pur (poor) *State* NE India

Sōō′chow′ (jō′) now WUHSIEN

Sōp′rōn, Ō′dėn-bûrg *City* W Hungary

Sō-rä′tä *Mountain*, Bolivia; peaks ANCO-HUMA, ILLAMPU

Sō-ro-ca′bå *City* SE Brazil; trade

Sōr-ren′tō *City* on *Peninsula* S Italy; fruits

Sôr-so-gôn′ *Municipality* on *Bay*, * of *Province* Luzon, Phil. Is.

Sôs-nô′wiec (v y e t s) *City* SW Poland; coal

Sôs′vå *River* 350 m. U.S.S.R., Asia

So-tä′rä *Peak* 14,550 ft. SW Colombia

Sou′ris (sōō′) *River* 500 m. S Canada

South Af′ri-cå, Rep. of *Republic* S tip of Africa; 471,820 sq. m.; pop. 21,314,000; legislative * Cape Town; administrative * Pretoria; minerals, manufacturing

South A-mer′i-cå *Continent* W hemisphere; ab. 7,000,000 sq. m.; pop. 190,038,000; 4th in size; Brazil, largest country; incl. 13 countries

South-amp′tön *County borough* S England

South A-rā′biå, Fed. of see YEMEN, PEOPLES DEM. REP. OF

South Är′gen-tine Peak (jėn-tēn) *Mountain* 13,600 ft. Colo., U.S.

South Äus-trāl′iå *State* cen. Australia; * Adelaide

South Bend *City* N Ind., U.S.; pop. 125,-580; manufacturing

South Bûr'rō Mountain *Peak* 12,745 ft. Utah, U.S.

South Car-o-lī'nà *State* SE U.S.; 31,055 sq. m.; pop. 2,590,516; * Columbia; 46 counties; lumber, agriculture, textiles

South Chī'nà Sea *Area* of Pacific O. surr. by China, Indonesia, Malay Penin., Phil. Is.

South Dà-kō'tà *State* NW U.S.; 77,047 sq. m.; pop. 665,507; * Pierre; 67 counties; farming, mining, flour, cattle

South'end' on Sēa *County borough* SE England; resort

Sou'thêrn Alps (su') *Mountain range* South I. New Zealand

Southern and Antarctic Terrs. *Territories* of France, S Indian O.: incl.: Karguelan Arch., New Amsterdam, Adelie Coast

Southern Ye'mèn *Rep.* S Arabian Penn.; 112,000 sq. mi.; pop. 1,300,000.

South'field *City* SE Mich., U.S.; pop. 69,285

South'gàte *Urban district* SE England

South' Gāte *City* SW Calif., U.S.; pop. 56,-909; manufacturing

South Island *Island* largest of New Zealand, cen. part

South Look'out Peak *Peak* 13,500 ft. Colo., U.S.

South Nà-han'ni *River* 250 m. Northwest Terrs., Canada

South Ork'ney Islands (ni) *Islands* (Brit.) S Atlantic O.

South Os-sē'tia (shà) *Autonomous region* Georgia, U.S.S.R.

South Platte *River* 424 m. Colo.-Neb., U.S.

South Pōle S end of earth's axis; surr. area = **South Pō'làr Regions**

South'pôrt *County borough* NW England

South San Fran-cis'cō (sis') *City* W calif., U.S.; pop. 46,646; industrial

South Seas *Area* incl. islands of Pacific O.

South Shiēlds *County borough* N England

South Tē'tön *Peak* 12,-500 ft. Wyo., U.S.

South - West Af'ri-cà *Territory* of Rep. of South Africa, NW; * Windhoek; grazing, fish, minerals

Sō'vetsk, Til'sit *City* R.S.F.S.R., U.S.S.R., Eur.; factories

Sō'vi-et Central Asia *Region* W Asia, incl. several reps.

Sō'vi-et Rus'sia (rush'à), **Sō'vi-et Un'ion** (yōōn'yön) refers to U.S.S.R.

Spāin, State of *Country* SW Eur. incl. Balearic and Canary Is.; 194,880 sq. m.; pop. 34,000,000; * Madrid; 50 provinces; agriculture, minerals, manufacturing

Spä'lä-tō see SPLIT

Spän'dau (dou) *Commune* cen. East Germany

Span'ish Guin'ea (gin'i) = EQUATORIAL GUINEA

Span'ish Nôrth Af'ri-cà *Territory* of Spain N Morocco, 2 cities: Ceuta and Melilla

Span'ish Peaks *Mountains* (2): E 12,710 ft.; W 13,625 ft.; Colo., U.S.

Span'ish Sà-har'à *Colony* (Sp.) NW Africa

Spär'tà *Anc. city* Peloponnesus S Greece

Spär'tàn-bûrg *City* NW

S.C., U.S.; pop. 44,-546; farming, factories, marble

Spe'ziä (spâ') = LA SPEZIA [LUCCAS

Spīce Islands = MO-

Spits'bêr-gèn *Archipelago* (Norway) Arctic O.; coal

Split, Ital. **Spä'lä-tō** *City* Croatia, Yugoslavia; shipping

Split Mountain *Peak* 14,050 ft. Calif., U.S.

Spō-kane' (kan') *City* E Wash., U.S.; pop. 170,516; commercial, financial, industrial

Spôr'à-dēs *Island groups* (**Northern, Southern**) Aegean S., Greece

Spree (shprā) *River* 220 m. E cen. Germany

Spring'fiēld 1. *City* * of Ill., U.S., cen. part; pop. 91,753; manufacturing, home of A. Lincoln. 2. *City* SW Mass., U.S.; pop. 163,905; manufacturing. 3. *City* SW Mo., U.S.; pop. 120,096; industrial cen. 4. *City* W Ohio, U.S.; pop. 81,926; trade, manufacturing

Springs *City* NE Rep. of South Africa; trade

Squàw Valley *Valley* E Calif., U.S.; skiing

Sri Lanka *Island Country* formerly Ceylon, Indian O.; 25,300 sq. m.; pop. 12,500,000; * Colombo; pearls, tea, rubber, minerals

Sri-nàg'àr *City* * of Kashmir, SW part

Staf'förd-shire *County* W cen. England; * **Staf'förd**; coal, factories, pottery

Stāines *Urban district* SE England

Stä'lin see BRASON, Romania; GARMO PEAK, U.S.S.R.; VARNA, Bulgaria

Stä - lin - à - bäd' since 1961 DYUSHAMBE

Stä'lin-grad now VOLGOGRAD

Stä-li-nir' (nyēr') since 1961 TSKHINVALI

Stal'i-nö now DO-NETSK

Stä-li'nö-gôrsk (lē') now BOBRIKI

Sta'linsk since 1961 NOVOKUZNETSK

Stam-boul' (bōōl') *Area* of Istanbul, Turkey; site of anc. Byzantium

Stam'förd *City* SW Conn., U.S.; pop. 108,798; manufacturing

Stan'is-laus Peak (lôs) *Peak* 11,200 ft. Calif., U.S.

Stà-ni-slav' *City* * of *Region* (incl. **Stà-ni-slä'wow** (vōōf) former Polish dept.) W Ukraine, U.S.S.R.

Stan'ley (li) *Town* * of Falkland Is.; port

Stan'ley Falls (li) *Falls* Upper Congo R., Congo (L)

Stan'ley-ville (li) *Town, Province* Congo (L)

Stan'tön Peak *Peak* 11,665 ft. Calif., U.S.

Stär Peak *Peak* 13,560 ft. Colo., U.S.

Stat'ên Island *Island* N.Y. Bay; forms Richmond, borough of N.Y. City, U.S.

Stä-väng'êr *City* SW Norway; port

Stav'rö-pôl *City* * of *Territory* SE R.S.F.S.R., U.S.S.R., Eur.

Stēele, Mount *Peak* 16,645 ft. Yukon, Canada

Sten'däl (shten') *City* W cen. East Germany

Steppes (steps) *Region* W cen. Asia; wide, treeless tracts

Stêr'ling Heights *City* Mich., U.S.; pop. 61,365

Stet-tin' (tēn'), Polish **Szcze-cin'** (che-tsēn') *City* NW Poland (for-

GAZETTE ATLAS

merly Ger.); commerce, industry, port

Stew'àrt (stū') 1. *River* 320 m. Yukon, Canada. 2. *Island, County* South I. New Zealand

Stew'àrt Peak (stū') *Peak* 14,030 ft. Colo., U.S.

Sti-kēne' (kēn') 1. *Mountains* Brit. Columbia, Canada. 2. *River* 335 m. Canada-S Alas., U.S.

Stîr'ling-shîre *County* cen. Scotland; coal, textiles

Stock'hōlm *City* * of *Province,* * of Sweden SE part; pop. 800,-000; industrial, commercial, manufacturing port

Stock'pôrt *County borough* NW England; manufacturing

Stock'tön *City* cen. Calif., U.S.; pop. 107,644; commercial, manufacturing, port

Stock'tön on Tēes *Municipal borough* N England; shipbuilding

Stōke on Trent *City, County borough* W cen. England; pottery, coal

Stôrm Bay *Inlet* of Pacific O. Tasmania, Australia

Stôrm King Peak *Peak* 13,750 ft. Colo., U.S.

Strähl'hôrn *Peak* 13,-750 ft. Switzerland

Strāits, the *Straits* bet. Mediterranean S. and Black S.; incl. Bosporus, Dardanelles

Strāits Settlements *Former Brit. colony,* Malay Penin.; incl. Singapore and areas now in Malaysia

Stras'boûrg *City* NE France; trade, manufacturing, coal

Strat'förd 1. *Town* SW Conn., U.S.; pop. 49,-775; manufacturing.

2. *Town* Ontario, Canada

Strat'förd on A'vön *Municipal borough* cen. England; Shakespeare's home

Strath-mōre' *Valley* cen. Scotland

Stret'förd *Urban district* NW England; industry

Strick'lànd *River* 225 m. cen. New Guinea

Strīp'ed Mountain *Peak* 13,160 ft. Calif., U.S.

Strom'bo-li *Volcano* on *Island* off N Sicily

Stū'àrt *Lake, River* 220 m. Brit. Columbia, Canada

Stûr'bridge (brij) *Town* cen. Mass., U.S.; colonial restoration

Stutt'gärt *City* S cen. West Germany; publishing cen., manufacturing

Stŷr *River* 300 m. Ukraine, U.S.S.R.

Sū'bo-ti-ca (tsä) *City* NE Yugoslavia; industry, commerce

Su'chow' (sōō'jō') see TUNGSHAN

Su'cre (sōō') *City,* constitutional * of Bolivia; pop. 58,400

Sū'dan *Region* N cen. Africa; deserts, plains

Sūdan', Republic of the *Republic* (formerly **Anglo-Egyptian Sudan**) NE Africa; 967,-500 sq. m.; pop. 15,-600,000; * Khartoum; livestock, cotton

Sū-dà-nēse' *Republic,* formerly **French Sūdan,** now MALI

Sud'bûr-ÿ *City* SE Ontario, Canada; nickel

Sū-de'tèn (dā') *Mountain ranges* N and NW Czechoslovakia; region seized by Germans 1938

Su-ez' (sōō) 1. *City* and *Governorate* at *Gulf,* Lower Egypt. 2. *Canal* across *Isthmus* NE Africa; 100 m.

long; Suez-Port Said; completed 1869

Suf'folk (uk) *County* E England; fish, livestock

Sug'àr-lōaf (shug') = PAO DE ACUCAR

Suisse (su-ēs') Fr. for SWITZERLAND

Sui'yuan' (swā'yu-än') *Province* N China

Su'ket (sōō'kāt) *State* NW India

Su-khô'nà (soo) *River* 350 m. N cen. U.S.S.R., Eur.

Su'khu-mi (sōō') *Town* Georgia U.S.S.R.

Suk'kur (s o o'k o o r) *Town* West Pakistan; irrigation cen.

Sū'là *River* 240 m. Ukraine, U.S.S.R.

Su - laī - män' (soo-lī) *Mountain range* NW India

Su-lāi-ma-ni'yà (nē') *Town* NE Iraq

Sul-tän-ä-bäd' n o w IRAQ *City*

Su'lu (sōō'lōō) *Archipelago, Province, Sea* SW Phil. Is.

Su-mä'trà *Island* W Indonesia; agriculture, esp. rubber, tobacco

Sum'bà (sōōm') *Island* S Indonesia; sandalwood; agriculture

Sum-bä'wà (sōōm) *Island* S Indonesia; livestock

Su'mÿ (sōō') *Town* Ukraine, U.S.S.R.; mills, factories

Sun'dà (sōōn') *Islands:* **Greater** and **Lesser,** Malay Arch., Indonesia

Sun'dêr-lànd *County borough* N England; shipping, manufacturing

Sun'gä'ri' (soon') *River* 800 m. SE Manchuria

Sung'kiang' (soong'ji-äng') 1. *Province* cen. Manchuria. 2. *Town* E China

Sun'light Peak (līt) *Peak* 14,060 ft. Colo.,

U.S.

Sun'nÿ-vāle *City* W Calif., U.S.; pop. 95,408

Sun'shīne Peak *Peak* 14,020 ft. Colo., U.S.

Sun Valley *Resort area* cen. Ida., U.S.

Su-pē'ri-ör, Lake *Lake* 31,820 sq. m. N U.S.; largest of 5 Great Lakes, world's largest fresh water lake

Sur-à-bä'jà (soor) *City* on *Strait* NE Java, Indonesia; imp. port, trade cen.

Sur-à-kär'tà (soor) *City* S cen. Java, Indonesia

Su-rat' *City* W India; brocades, carpets

Sûr'bi-tön *Municipal borough* S England; factories [NE India

Sur-gu'jà (gōō') *State*

Su-ri-bä'chi, Mount *Volcano* S Iwo Jima I., Volcano Is.; WW II fame

Su'ri-nam (soo') or **Dutch Gui-ä'na** (gi) *Territory* of Neth., N South America; * Paramaribo; bauxite, agriculture

Su-ri-na'mè *River* 400 m. N Surinam

Surkh-äb' (soor-käb') *River* 400 m. U.S.S.R. cen. Asia

Sur'mä (soor') *River* 560 m. NE India-Pakistan

Sûr'rey (ri) *County* S England; farming, sheep

Su-sit'nà (sōō) *River* 280 m. S Alas., U.S.

Sus-que-han'nà (kwe) *River* 444 m. N.Y.-Pa.-Md., U.S.

Sus'sèx *County* S England; fish, sheep, farming

Suth'êr-lànd 1. *County* N Scotland; fish, deer 2. *Falls* South I. New Zealand

Sut'lej *River* 900 m. Tibet-West Pakistan

Sut'tērs Mill *Site* nr. village of Coloma, Calif., U.S.; gold discovered 1848

Sut'tön and Chēam *Urban district* S England

Sut'tön in Ash'fiēld *Urban district* N cen. England; hosiery, coal, lime

Su'và (sōō') *Town* * of Fiji Is. Terr.; harbor

Su-wan'nēe (soo) *River* 240 m. Ga.-Fla., U.S.

Svàl'bärd *Territories* of Norway in Arctic O.

Sve'a-land (svā') = *Cen. Division* of Sweden

Svend'bôrg *City* Fyn I. Denmark; port

Svêrd-lôvsk' *City* * of *Region* S R.S.F.S.R., U.S.S.R., Asia; cultural, industrial, mining cen.

Sve'ri-ge (svar'yè) = SWEDEN

Svi-yä'gà *River* 250 m. U.S.S.R., E Eur.

Swän Islands *Islands* (2) W Caribbean S., U.S.

Swän'sēa *County borough* SE Wales; port

Swät *River* 400 m. West Pakistan

Swä'tow' (tou') *Town* SE China; harbor

Swä'zi-land *Brit. dependency* SE Africa; * Mbabane; agriculture, mining

Swē'dèn, **Sve'ri-ge** (svar'yè) *Monarchy* NW Europe; 173,665 sq. m.; pop. 8,000,000; * Stockholm; 24 provinces and *; forestry, iron, fish

Swin'dön *Municipal borough* S England; locomotives

Swit'zèr - lànd, F r. Suisse (su-ēs'), Ital. Sviz'ze-rä (svēt'tsä) *Republic* cen. Eur.; 15,940 sq. m.; pop. 6,280,000; * Bern; 22 cantons; finance,

manufacturing (watches, jewelry, textiles)

Sy̆d'ney (ni) *City* SE Australia; imp. port

Sy̆r'à-cūse 1. *City* cen. N.Y., U.S.; pop. 197,208; trade, manufacturing cen. 2. or It. **Si-rä-cu'sa** (cōō'zä) *City* * of *Province* SE Sicily, Italy; port

Sy̆r' Dar-yä' *River* 1500 m. U.S.S.R., Asia

Sy̆r'i-à 1. *Anc. country* Asia, incl. Lebanon, Palestine, Transjordan, mod. Syria. 2. *Fr. Mandate* with Lebanon, called the LEVANT STATES. 3. *Republic* = Sy̆r'i-àn **Arab Rep.**, SW Asia; 71,200 sq. m.; pop. 6,300,000; * Damascus; agriculture, textiles

Sy̆r'i-àn Desert *Desert* Arabia - Syria - Iraq - Transjordan

Sy̆z'ràn *City* U.S.S.R., Eur.; grain trade

Szcze'cin (che'tsēn) see STETTIN

Sze'chwän' (se') *Province* S cen. China

Sze'ged *City* S Hungary; industrial, commercial port

Sze'kes-fe-her-vär (sä'-kesh-fe-här-vär) *City* W cen. Hungary; trade

Sze'ping'kaī' (soo') *Town* S Manchuria

T

Tà-bas'cō *State* SE Mexico

Tä'blàs *Island, Strait* cen. Phil. Is.

Tä'ble Mountain (b'l) *Peak* 11,100 ft. Wyo., U.S.

Tà-briz' (brēz'), **Tău'ris** *City* NW Iran; imp. commercially

Tä-cä-nä' *Volcano* 13,335 ft. SW Guatemala

Tà-cō'mà *City* W cen. Wash., U.S.; pop. 154,581; port, fishing, manufacturing, lumber cen.

Tà-cō'rà *Peak* 19,520 ft. S Peru

Tà-cū-bä'yà *City* cen. Mexico, Fed. distr.

Tà-dzhik' S.S.R. *Republic* of U.S.S.R. cen. Asia; * Dyushambe

Tae-gū (ta), **Taī-kyū** *City* SE South Korea

Tae-jôn (ta), **Taī-den** *City* W South Korea

Taf-tän', Kūh-i- *Volcano* 13,260 ft. SE Iran

Ta'gàn-rog *City* on *Gulf* S R.S.F.S.R., Eur.; metal items

Tä'gus *River* 565 m. Spain-Portugal

Ta-hi'ti (hē') *Island* of Society Is. (Fr.), S Pacific O.

Tä'hōe, Lake *Lake* Nev.-Calif., U.S.; resorts

Tä'hua (wä) *Peak* 17,455 ft. W Bolivia

Taī-än *Town* NE China; nr. Mt. Taī sacred mountain

Taī-chū, was **Taī-wän** *City* W cen. Taiwan

Taī-my̆r' *National district* on *Peninsula* crossed by *River* (400 m.) through *Lake* to *Bay*, N cen. Siberia, U.S.S.R., Asia

Taī-nän *City* SW Taiwan; commercial cen.

Taī-peh (bä) *City* * of Rep. of China, Taiwan; pop. 964,000

Taī'ping' *City* NW Malaysia

Taī-wän *Island*, formerly **Fôr-mō'sà**, off SE China; site of Rep. of China; 13,885 sq. m.; pop. 14,700,000; * Taipei; agriculture, camphor

Tä - ju - mul'cō (hōō-mōōl') *Volcano* 13,815 ft. W Guatemala

Tä-kä-mä-tsu *City* Shikoku, Japan; port

Tä-kä-ō *City* SW Taiwan; port

Tä-kä-ō-kä *City* Honshu, Japan; bronze, rice cen.

Tä-kä-sä-ki *City* Honshu, Japan; silk trade

Tä'klä Mä-kän' *Desert* W China; fertile soil

Tä-ku-tu' (kōō - tōō') *River* 220 m. Brazil-Guyana

Täl'cä *City* * of *Province* cen. Chile; trade, manufacturing

Täl-cä-hua'nō (wä') *Port* S cen. Chile

Tal'dy̆-Kur-gan' (koor) *Town* * of *Region* Kazakh, U.S.S.R., cen. Asia

Tä'li', was **Tung'chow'** (toong'jō') *Town* NE cen. China

Tä-li'say (lē'sī) *Municipality* Negros, Phil. Is.

Tal'là-has'sēe *City* * of Fla. N part, U.S.; pop. 71,897; tobacco, lumber industries

Tal-là-hatch'ie *River* 300 m. Miss., U.S.

Tal-là-pōō'sà *River* 270 m. Ala., U.S.

Tal'lin *City* * of Estonian S.S.R. NW U.S.S.R., Eur.; port, manufacturing

Tä'mä *Peak* 13,125 ft. N Colombia

Tä-mau-li'päs (mou-lē') *State* E Mexico

Tàm-bôv' *City* * of *Region* cen. R.S.F.S.R., U.S.S.R., Eur.; grain

Tam'pà *City* on *Bay* W cen. Fla., U.S.; pop. 277,767; resort, fishing, cigars

Tam'pe-re, Tam-mêr-fôrs' *City* SW Finland; power plants, factories

Tam-pi'cō (pē') *City* E Mexico; commercial cen., port [Africa

Tä'nà *River* 500 m. E

Tä'nä, Te'nô *River* 200

m. NE Norway

Tä′nä, Tsä′nä *Lake* N Ethiopia

Tan′å-nå *River* 475 m. cen. Alas., U.S.

Ta-na-na-rive′ (rēv′) *City* * of Malagasy Rep., E cen. part; pop. 321,654

Tän-ci-tä′rō (se) *Mountain* 12,665 ft. SW Mexico

Tä-ne-gä-shi-mä *Island* off Kyushu, Japan

Tan-gån-yi′kå (yē′) 1. *Lake* SE Africa. 2. *Former Terr.* (Germ., then Brit.) and *Republic* E Africa; now part of TANZANIA

Tan-gier′ (jēr′) *City* on *Bay* N Morocco; former international zone (England, France, Spain)

Täng′shän′ *City* NE China; coal cen.

Tan-jōre′ *City* * of *District* S India; carpets, jewelry [Egypt

Tän′tä *City* Lower

Tan - zan′i - å, United Rep. of *Republic* E Africa, incl. former reps.: Tanganyika, Zanzibar; 362,720 sq. m.; pop. 13,300,000; * Dar es Salaam; agriculture, livestock, fish

Tao′nän′ (tou′) *Town* S Manchuria

Ta-på-joz′ (zhôs′) *River* 500 m. N Brazil

Täp′ti *River* 435 m. India; unnavigable

Ta-quå-ri′ (kwå-rē′) *River* 450 m. S cen. Brazil

Tä′rän-tō *City* * of former *Province* (now *Iionio*) SE Italy; port

Tä′rä-wä *Island* atoll, * of Gilbert and Ellice Is. (Brit.)

Tarbes (tarb) *City* SW France; trade, manufacturing

Ta′rim′ (dä′rēm′) *River* 1250 m. W China

Tarn *River* 233 m., *Department* S France

Tarn-et-Ga-ronne′ (nä-ga-rôn′) *Department* S France

Tär′now (nōōf) *City* SE Poland; industry, commerce

Tar-rå-gō′nå *Commune* * of *Province* NE Spain; manufacturing, wine industry

Tär-rä′sä *Commune* NE Spain; manufacturing

Tär′tū *City* * of *Province* E Estonia, U.S.S.R.; manufacturing

Tåsch′hôrn *Peak* 14,-760 ft. SW Switzerland

Tä′shi Dhhō Dzông′ *Town* * of Bhutan, W part

Tash-kent′ *City* * of Uzbek S.S.R., R.S.F.S.R., U.S.S.R., cen. Asia; agriculture, manufacturing

Tas′mån, Mount *Peak* 11,465 ft. South I. New Zealand

Tas-mā′ni-å (taz) *Island* S Pacific O., *State* of Australia; * Hobart

Tas′mån Sea Area of South Pacific O., W New Zealand - SE Australia

Tä′tår A.S.S.R. *Republic* E R.S.F.S.R., U.S.S.R., Eur.; * Kazan; agriculture, livestock

Tä′tå-rẏ, Gulf of *Strait* N end of Sea of Japan

Tä′trå Mountains *Mountain group* of Carpathians, Czechoslovakia

Tä′tung′ (dä′toong′) *City* NE China; trade

Täunt′ön *City* SE Mass., U.S.; pop. 43,-756; manufacturing

Täu′rus Mountains *Mountain chain* S Turkey, Asia

Tåv-da′ *River* 650 m. W Siberia, U.S.S.R.

Tāy *River* 120 m., largest in Scotland, E part

Tä-yä′bäs *Province* Luzon, Phil. Is.

Tay′lör *City* SE Mich., U.S.; pop. 70,020

Tāy′lör, Mount *Peak* 11,380 ft. N.M., U.S.

Tāy′lör Mountain *Peak* 13,600 ft. Colo., U.S.

Taz *River* 600 m. NW Siberia, U.S.S.R.

Tbi′li-si see TIFLIS

Tēa′neck *Township* NE N.J., U.S.; pop. 42,355

Tēe′wi - not, Mount *Peak* 12,315 ft. NW Wyo., U.S.

Tef-fe′ (tâ-fâ′) *River* 500 m. W Brazil

Te-gäl′ *Town* Java, Indonesia; port

Tė-gū-ci-gal′på (gōō-si) *City* * of Honduras; silver, gold mines

Teh-rän′, Te-hė-ran′ *City* * of *Province* and * of Iran N part

Teh′ri (tä′rē) *State* N India

Tė-huän′tė-pec, Gulf of *Inlet* of Pacific O. SE Mexico

Tel′ A-viv′ (vēv′) *City* W Israel; modern commercial city

Tel′ė-scōpe Peak *Peak* 11,050 ft. Calif., U.S.

Tem′ple, Mount (p′l) *Peak* 11,635 ft. Alberta, Canada

Te-mu′cō (mōō′) *City* S cen. Chile; trade

Ten′êr-ife (ēf) *Island* largest of Canary Is.

Teng′ri Khän′ *Peak* 23,620 ft. cen. Asia

Ten-nės-sēe′ 1. *River* 650 m. SE U.S. 2. *State* SE cen. U.S.; 41,687 sq. m.; pop. 3,924,164; * Nashville; 95 counties; agriculture, mining

Ten′sas (så) *River* 250 m. La., U.S.

Te′rä-mō (tâ′) *Commune* * of *Province* cen. Italy

Têr-cei′rå (sā′) *Island* cen. Azores

Te′rek (tā′) *River* 380 m. U.S.S.R., Eur.

Te-rė-si′nå (tä-rė-zē′) *City* NE Brazil

Têr-nä′te *Island* of Moluccas, Indonesia; spices

Ter′ni *Commune* * of *Province* cen. Italy; factories

Têr-nō′pöl *City* W Ukraine, U.S.S.R.

Ter′rė Haute′ (hōt′) *City* W Ind., U.S.; pop. 70,286; manufacturing, mining

Ter′rėl, Mount *Peak* 11,560 ft. Utah, U.S.

Tes′lin (tez′) *Lake* NW Canada

Tē′tön Range *Mountain range* NW Wyo., U.S.; site of **Grand Tē′tön** peak 13,766 ft. in **Grand Tē′tön** *National Park*

Te-tuän′ (twän′) *City* Spanish North Africa

Teu′co (tā′oo) *River* 350 m. N Argentina

Tex-är-kan′å *Twin cities* Tex.-Ark., U.S.

Tex′ås *State* SW U.S.; 262,800 sq. m.; pop. 11,196,730; * Austin; 254 counties

Tex′ås City *City* SE Texas, U.S.; pop. 38,908; manufacturing

Tey′de or **Te-ne-ri′fe, Pi′co de** (pē′cō dâ tē′dâ, tä-nâ-rē′fe) *Volcano* 12,190 ft. Tenerife I.

Thai′land (tī′), formerly **Si′am** *Kingdom* SE Asia; 198,450 sq. m.; pop. 35,000,000; * Bangkok

Thames (temz) *River* 210 m. S England

Thar (tär) or **In′di-ån Desert** *Region* W Pakistan-NW India; 100,000 sq. m.

Thēbes *Anc. city*, cen. of Egyptian civilization, Upper Egypt

Thêr-mop′ẏ-laē *Moun-*

tain pass E Greece

Thes-sa-lô-ni′ke (nyē′) 1. *Department* Macedonia, Greece. 2. *City* = SALONIKA

Thes′sa-ly *Division* of anc. and mod Greece, E penin.

Thomp′son *River* 270 m. Brit. Columbia, Canada

Thom′son *River* 300 m. Queensland, Australia

Thou′sand Islands *Islands* (ab. 1500) St. Laurence R. U.S.-Canada

Thou′sand Lake Mountain *Peak* 11,250 ft. Utah, U.S.

Thou′sand Ōaks *City* SW Cal., U.S.; pop. 36,334

Thrāce (thrās) *Region* E Balkan Penin., SE Eur.; div: **Wes′têrn** NE Greece, **Eas′têrn** Turkey, Eur.

Thrēe Rivers *City* S Quebec, Canada; industrial port

Thu′le (tōō′) *Settlement* NW Greenland, U.S. air base

Thumb, the (thum) *Peak* 13,880 ft. Calif., U.S.

Thun′dêr Mountain *Peak* 13,575 ft. Calif., U.S.

Thû-rin′gi-a (ji) *Former state* cen. Germany; agriculture, forests

Thûrs′day Island *Island* Queensland, Australia; pearl cen.

Ti′a Jua′na (tē′, wä′) = TIJUANA

Tī′bêr *River* 244 m. cen. Italy

Tī-bē′ri-as *Anc. town* NE Palestine; cen. of learning

Ti-bet′ *Country*, presently *Dependency* of Communist China; 470,000 sq. m.; pop. 1,300,000; * Lhasa; agriculture

Tieh′ling′ (ti-e′) *Town*

S Manchuria

Tien′ Shän′ (ti-en′) *Mountain chain* U.S.S.R.-China

Tien′shui′ (shwä′) *City* N. cen. China; trade

Tien′tsin′ *City* NE China; educational, commercial cen., port

Ti-er′ra del Fu-e′gō (fōō-ā′) *Island* of *Archipelago* off S South America; div. bet. Argentina (E)-Chile (W)

Tiė-te′ (tā′) *River* 500 m. SE Brazil

Tif′lis, Tbi′li-si *City* * of Georgian S.S.R., U.S.S.R.; trade, manufacturing

Ti′gre (tē′grä) *River* 350 m. Ecuador-Peru

Tī′gris *River* 1150 m. Iraq-Turkey

Ti-jua′nä (wä′) *Town* NW Mexico

Til′bûrg *Commune* S Netherlands; industrial cen.

Til′sit = SOVETSK

Ti-mi-soa′rä (tē-mi-shwä′) *City* nr. **Tī′-mis R.** (tē′) 270 m. SW Romania; commerce, industry

Ti-môr′ 1. *Island* Lesser Sunda Is., S Malay Arch., div. bet. Portugal (E) and Indonesia (W); agriculture, forests 2. *Sea* bet. Timor-NW Australia

Tim-pa-nō′gos, Mount *Peak* 12,000 ft. Utah, U.S.

Ti-ni-an′ . *Island* W Pacifc O.; WW II site [India

Tin-nė-vel′ly *Town* S

Tip-pė-ca-noe′ (nōō′) *River* 200 m. Ind., U.S.

Tip-pė-rar′y *County* S Eire; mining, livestock, agriculture

Tip′tön *Urban district* W cen. England; coal

Ti-rä′nė *Town* * of *Prefecture* and * of Albania, cen. part;

pop. 170,000

Ti′rich Mir′ (tē′, mēr′) *Peak* 25,260 ft. NW Pakistan

Ti-rōl′, Tȳ′rōl *Region* Austria-Italy [India

Tis′tä *River* 300 m. NE

Ti′sza, Theiss (tīs) *River* 800 m. U.S.S.R.-Hungary-Yugoslavia

Ti-tä′gärh *Town* W India

Ti-tä′nō, Mount *Mountain* 2435 ft.; site of San Marino

Ti-ti-cä′cä, Lake *Lake* Peru-Bolivia; world's highest navigable lake 12,500 ft.

Ti′tō-gräd (tē′) or **Pŏd′-gō-ri-ca** (rē-tsä) *Town* * of Montenegro Rep. S Yugoslavia

Ti′vö-li *Commune* cen. Italy; anc. ruins, fountains

Ti′zi-n-Tam-jurt′ *Peak* 14,760 ft. Morocco

Tläx-cä′lä *Town* * of *State* cen. Mexico

Tlem-cen′ (sen′) *City* NW Algeria; commerce

To-bä′gō *Island* West Indies; part of TRINIDAD and TOBAGO

To-bä-tä *Town* Kyushu, Japan; coal port

To-bôl′ *River* 800 m. Ural Mts. U.S.S.R.

Tō′bruk (brook) *Port* Libya; WW II fame

Tō - can - tins′ (tēns′) *River* 1700 m. E Brazil

Tō-chi-gi *Town* in *Province* Honshu, Japan; silk weaving

Tō-côr-pū′ri, Cer′rōs de (ser′ōz dâ) *Mountain* 22,160 ft. Bolivia

Tō′gō, Republic of *Republic* within Fr. Community, W Africa; 21,850 sq. m.; pop. 1,800,000; * Lomé; coffee, cocoa; formerly Ger. terr., later Trust Terr.

Tō-kė-wän′na *Mountain* 13,175 ft. Utah, U.S.

Tō-ku-shi-mä *City* * of *Prefecture* Shikoku, Japan; port

Tō-ku-yä-mä *Town* Honshu, Japan; port

Tō′ky̆-ō *City* on *Bay*, * of *Prefecture*, * of Japan, Honshu I.; pop. 10,863,000; manufacturing, cultural cen.

Tō-lē′dō 1. *City* NW Ohio, U.S.; pop. 383,-818; port, factories. 2. *Commune* * of *Province* cen. Spain; textiles, arms

Tō-li′mä (lē′) *Volcano* 18,435 ft. Colombia

Tol′ly̆-gunge (g u n j) *Town* E India

Tō-lu′ca (lōō′) 1. *City* * of Mexico state, cen. Mexico. 2. *Volcano* (**Ne-vä′dō de**) 15,025 ft. Mexico

Tom *River* 450 m. U.S.S.R., Asia

Tom-a-säk′i *Peak* 12,-270 ft. Utah, U.S.

Tô-mä′szow (shōōf or shō) *Commune* cen. Poland; manufactures

Tom-big′bēe *River* 410 m. Alas., U.S.

Tom′bō *Island* off Fr. Guinea; site of *

Tomb′stōne (t ō ō m′) *Town* SE Ariz., U.S.; former mining cen.

Tō′mō *River* 260 m. Colombia

Tômsk *City* * of *Region* U.S.S.R., Asia; educational cen.

Tôn′gä or **Friend′ly̆ Islands** *Archipelago* (Brit.) S Pacific O.; pop. 90,000; * Nukualofa on **Tongatapu**; copra, bananas

Ton′gä-land *Region* SE Africa, Rep. of South Africa

Tongue (tung) *River* 245 m. Mont., U.S.

Tônk *Town* * of *State* NW India

Ton′kin′ 1. *Region* of North Vietnam, former Fr. protectorate.

2. *Gulf* arm of South China S.

Ton'le Sap' (lä), **Great Lake** *Lake* W Cambodia

Töns'berg (bar) *City* NE Norway; port, Norway's oldest city

To-pē'kå *City* * of Kans., U.S.; pop. 125,011; flour, meat packing, metal works

To-ri'nō (rē') *City* (see TURIN) * of *Province* NW Italy

Tör'nė *River* 250 m. N Sweden [cen Chile

Tö'rō *Peak* 20,930 ft.

Tö-ron'tō *City* * of Ontario (SE part), Canada; pop. 664,584; commercial, industrial pórt

Tôr-quay' (kē') *Municipal borough* SW England; pottery, resort

Tôr'rä *Peak* 11,661 ft. W Colombia

Tor'rance *City* SW Calif., U.S.; pop. 134,584; industrial

Tor're An - nun - ziä'tä (rä, nōōn) *Commune* S Italy; resort

Tor're del Gre'cō (rä däl grä'kō) *Commune* S Italy; resort

Tôr-re-ôn' *City* NE Mexico; textiles, flour

Tor'rėys Peak (riz) *Peak* 14,265 ft. Colo. U.S.

Tôr'toise Islands (tis) = GALAPAGOS IS.

Tôr-tö'lå *Island* largest of Brit. Virgin Is.

Tôr-tö'så *City* NE Spain; manufacturing

Tôr-tu'gä, Lä (tōō') *Island* off N Venezuela

Tö'run (rōōn), **Thorn** (tôrn) *City* N Poland; commerce, industry

Tot'tėn-håm *Urban district* Greater London, England

Tot-to-ri *City* * of *Prefecture* Honshu, Ja-

pan; textiles, port

Toub'kal (tōōb') *Peak* 13,660 ft. Morocco

Toug-gourt' (too-goort') *Territory, Town, Oasis* NE Algeria

Tou-lôn' (tōō) *City* SE France; port

Tou-louse' (tōō-lōōz') *City* S France; educ. cen., manufacturing

Tou-rāine' (tōō) *Hist. region* NW France

Tour - coing' (t ō ō r - k w a n') *C i t y* N France; manufacturing

Tour-nāi' (tōōr), **Dōor'-nik** *Commune* SW Belgium; commerce, manufacturing

Tours (tōōr) *City* NW cen. France; manufacturing, commerce

Towns'ville *City* NE Australia; port

To-yä-mä *City* * of *Prefecture* Honshu, Japan; port

To-yo-hä-shi *City* Honshu, Japan

Träb-zôn' *City* * of *Vilayet* NE Turkey; port

Trå-fal'går *Cape* SW Spain; Nelson's victory 1805

Trå-lēe' *Bay, Port, Urban district* SW Eire [cen. Asia

Trans A-laï' *Mt. range*

Trans-cău-cā'sia (shå) *Region* S of Caucasus Mts.

Trans-jôr'dån n o w JORDAN

Trans - väal' (briefly **South African Rep.**) *Province* NE Rep. of South Africa; minerals

Tran-sȳl-vā'niä *Region* NW cen. Romania; nr. **Transylvanian Alps** South Carpathians)

Trä'pä-ni *City* * of *Province* Sicily, Italy; port

Tra'vån-cōre *Region,* former state, S India; rice, minerals

Treas'ûre Island (trezh') *Island* (manmade) San Francisco, Calif., U.S.

Treng-gä'nu (nōō) *State* Malaysia

Trent, Tren'tō *Commune* * of *Province* NE Italy; manufacturing

Tren'tön *City* * of N.J., U.S.; pop. 104,638; manufacturing

Tres Ar-rô'yōs (trâs) *City* E Argentina; cattle, farming

Tres Crû'ces (trâs, sâs) *Peak* 20,850 ft. N Chile

Tre-vi'sō (vē') *Commune* * of *Province* NE Italy

Trich-i-nop'ö-lỳ *City* S India; manufacturing, commerce

Tri-chur' (choor') *Town* S India; temple

Trier (trēr), **Treves** (trevz) *City* W cen. West Germany; manufacturing, mining

Tri-e'ste 1. *Area* **Free Terr. of Trieste** 1947-53; S part to Yugoslavia; N part: 2. *City* on *Gulf* NE Italy; port

Trik'kå-lå *City* * of *Department* c e n . Greece

Trin'i-dad *Island* West Indies; part of **Trin'-i-dad and To-bä'gō** *Dominion* former colony of Brit. Commonwealth; pop. 1,-070,000; site of * Port of Spain; petroleum, trade

Trin'i-tỳ 1. *River* 360 m. E Tex., U.S. 2. *Peak* 13,810 ft. SW Colo., U.S.

Trip'ö-li 1. *Region,* **Trip-o-li-tan'iä,** N African coast. 2. *City* * of *Province,* * of Libya; pop. 379,900; port. 3. *Town* NW Lebanon; port

Trip'o-lis *City* S Greece; manufacturing

Tri'pu-rä *Territory* NE India; former state

Tri-sul' (sōōl') *Peak* 23,380 ft. N India

Tri-van'drum *City* SW India; port

Tr'no-vo (tûr') *City* cen. Bulgaria

Trô'itsk *City* Ural area U.S.S.R., Asia

Trōm-be'tås (bä') *River* 350 m. N Brazil

Trō'men *Volcano* 12,-795 ft. W Argentina

Trōms'ö *City* N Norway; port

Trônd'heim (hām) 1. *City* cen. Norway; commercial port. 2. *Fjord* W cen. Norway

Troy 1. *City* E N.Y., U.S.; pop. 62,918. 2. *Anc. city* NW Asia Minor. 3. *City* SE Mich., U.S.; pop. 39,419

Troyes (trwä) *City* NE France

Trū'chås Peak *Peak* 13,110 ft. N.M., U.S.

Trū'cial O-man', Trū'-cial Coast, Trū'cial States (shål) *Region* and *Shiekdoms* of Persian Gulf States, SE Arabia; oil

Trū-jil'lo (hē'yō) 1. *City* now SANTO DOMINGO * of Dominican Rep. 2. *City* NW Peru; commercial cen. 3. *Town* * of *State* W cen. Venezuela

Truk *Island group* Caroline Is. (U.S. Trust Terr.)

Tsäng'wū', was **Wū'-chow'** (jō') *City* SE China; port

Tshuä'pä (chwä') *River* 420 m. S cen. Africa

Tsi'nän' (jē') *City* NE China; trade

Tsing'haï', Ching'haï' *Lake* in *Province* W cen. China

Tsing'tao' (dou') *City* NE China; port

Tsing'yuän' *City* NE China

Tsi'ning' (jē') *City* NE

China; manufacturing

Tsin′kiảng′ (jin′ji-äng′) *City* SE China; port

Tsū *City* Honshu, Japan; port

Tsū-gi-tä-kä *Peak* 12,-900 ft. Formosa

Tsun′yi′ (ē′) *Town* S China

Tsū-rū-mi *Town* Honshu, Japan; industrial

Tsū-rū-ō-kä *City* Honshu, Japan; textiles

Tsū-shi-mä *Island* of Japan on *Strait* NW of Kyushu

Tsū-yä-mä *Town* Honshu, Japan

Tū-ä-mō-tū *Archipelago Island group* of Fr. Polynesia, S Pacific O.

Tū-bū′rän *Municipality* Cebu I. Phil. Is.; port

Tu-cu-män′ (tōō-cōō′) *City* * of *Province* N Argentina; sugar

Tu-ge′lả (tōō-gä′) *River* 300 m. E Rep. of South Africa

Tuk-uh-nik′i-vätz, Mt. *Peak* 12,000 ft. Utah, U.S.

Tū′lả *City* * of *Region* cen. R.S.F.S.R., U.S.S.R., Eur.

Tū-lä′gi *Town* on *Island* of Solomon Is., W Pacific O.

Tul′sả *City* NE Okla., U.S.; pop. 331,638; financial, commercial cen., oil industry

Tū′mẻn′ *River* 220 m. NE Korea-SE Manchuria

Tū-nä′ri *Peak* 17,000 ft. cen. Bolivia

Tung (doong) *River* 280 m. SE China

Tun-gä-bhả′drä *River* 400 m. S India

Tung′chow′ (jō) now NANTUNG

Tung′hsien′ (shi-en′) *City* NE China

Tung′hwä′ *City* S Manchuria; lumber

Tung′kiang′ (ji-äng′) *Town* E Manchuria

Tung′kwän′ *Town* NE

China   [SE China

Tung′ting′ Hū′ *Lake*

Tūn-gū-rä′guä *Volcano* 16,685 ft. Ecuador

Tun-gū′skả *Rivers* (3) cen. Siberia, U.S.S.R.:
(1) **Lower** 2000 m.
(2) **Stony** 1000 m.
(3) **Upper** = lower Angara R.

Tū′nis 1. *Former Barbary State* and Fr. *Protectorate*, N Africa; now TUNISIA. 2. *City* on *Gulf* * of Tunisia; pop. 800,000

Tū-ni′sia, Republic of (shả) *Republic* N Africa; 38,330 sq. m.; pop. 5,140,000; * Tunis; agriculture, mining

Tū-pūn-gä′tō *Peak* 22,-300 ft. Argentina-Chile

Tu-ra′ *River* 400 m. U.S.S.R., Asia

Tū′rin, It. To-ri′nō (rē′) *Commune* * of Torino prov. NW Italy; manufacturing, commerce

Tûr-kẻ-stan′ *Town* R.S.F.S.R., U.S.S.R., cen. Asia

Tûr′key, Republic of (ki) *Republic* SE Eur. and SW Asia; 301,380 sq. m.; pop. 35,230,000; * Ankara; 58 vilayets; agriculture, livestock

Tûr′kish Empire = OTTOMAN EMPIRE

Tûr-ki-stan′ *Region* cen. Asia: U.S.S.R.-China-Afghanistan

Tûrk′men S.S.R. *Republic* of U.S.S.R., cen. Asia; * Ashkhabad; livestock, oil

Tûrks and Cāi′cös Islands *Islands* dependency of Jamaica

Tur′ku (toor′koo) *City* SW Finland; port

Tûr′ret Peak *Peak* 13,-825 ft. Colo., U.S.

Tus-cả-lōō′sả *City* W cen. Ala., U.S.; pop. 65,773; manufacturing

Tus′cản Archipelago *Is-*

land group bet. Corsica and Italy

Tus′cả-ny *Compartimento* cen. Italy; mining, farming, manufacturing

Tus′con (tōō′son) *City* S Ariz., U.S.; pop. 262,933; trade cen., resort

Tū-ti-cô-rin′ · *Town* S India; port

Tū-tu-i′lä (ē′) *Island* SW Pacific O.; site of Pago Pago, * of Amer. Samoa

Tū-tū-pä′cä *Volcano* 18,960 ft. S Peru

Tū′vả Autonomous Region, was Tan′nū T ū ′ v ả R e g i o n R.S.F.S.R., U.S.S.R., Asia; livestock

Twick′ẻn-hảm *Municipal borough* London, SE England

Tỷ′lêr *City* NE Tex., U.S.; pop. 57,770; commerce, industry

Tỷn′dảll, Mount *Peak* 14,025 ft. Calif., U.S.

Tỹne′mouth (m u t h) *County borough* on **Tỹne R.** N England; port

Tỹre *Town* S Lebanon; anc. * of Phoenicia

Tỷ-rōl′ = TIROL

Tỹ-rōne′ *County* W cen. Northern Ireland

Tỷr-rhẽ′ni-ản Sea *Area* of Mediterranean S. SW of Italy

Tyū-men′ *City* * of *Region* R.S.F.S.R., U.S.S.R., Asia

Tzẻ′liū′tsing′ (jing′) *City* S cen. China

Tzu, Tzẻ *River* 375 m. SE China

U

Ua-tū-ma′ (wa) *River* 350 m. N Brazil

Uau - pes′ (wow - pās′) *River* 700 m. Colombia-Brazil

Ū-ban′gi *River* 700 m. cen. Africa

Ū-ban′gi-Shä′ri *Former*

terr. Fr. Equatorial Africa, now CENTRAL AFRICAN REP.

U′bē (ōō′) *City* Honshu, Japan; port

U-bi′nä (ōō-vē′) *Peak* 16,830 ft. Bolivia

U-bi′näs (ōō-bē′) *Peak* 17,390 ft. Peru

Ub′su Nur′ (sōō-nōōr′) *Lake* Outer Mongolia

U-cä-yä′li (ōō) *River* 1200 m. Peru

U-da′ *River* 470 m. U.S.S.R., Asia

U-daï′pur (ōō-dī′poor) *City* * of *State* (also **Me-wär′**) NW India

U′di-ne (ōō′dē-nâ) *Commune* NE Italy; manufacturing

Ud′murt A.S.S.R. (ood′-moort) *Republic* R.S.F.S.R., U.S.S.R., Eur.; lumber, livestock, grain

U-e-dä (oo) *Town* Honshu, Japan

Ue′le (we′) *River* 700 m. cen. Africa

U-fa′ (oo) 1. *City* Ural area, U.S.S.R. Eur.; industrial, cultural cen. 2. *River* 430 m. U.S.S.R., Eur.

Ū-gan′dả *Republic* E Africa, former Brit. protectorate; 93,980 sq. m.; pop. 9,760,-000; * Kampala; coffee, cotton, fish

U-ji-yä-mä-dä *City* Honshu, Japan; Japan′s sacred city

Uj′jain (ōō′jin) *City* W cen. India; holy city

Uj′pest (ōō′y′pesht) *City* cen. Hungary

Uk′kẻl *Commune* cen. Belgium

Ū-krāi′ni-ản S.S.R. *Constituent republic* of U.S.S.R., SW part; * Kiẻv; agriculture, livestock

U′län Bä′tôr (ōō′) *City* * of Mongolian Rep. N cen. part; pop. 195,300; commercial, sacred city

U′län U-de′ (ōō′, ōō)

City R.S.F.S.R., U.S.S.R., Asia; industrial

Ulm (oolm) *City* West Germany; commerce, manufacturing

Ul'stêr *Former province* N Ireland, now div. into NORTHERN IRELAND and Ul'stêr prov. N Eire

U'lugh Muz-tagh' (ōō'-lōō mooz-tä') *Peak* 25,340 ft. W China

Ul-ya'nŏvsk *City* * of *Region* R.S.F.S.R., U.S.S.R., Eur.; industrial

U-man' (ōō) *City* Ukraine U.S.S.R.

Um'bri-à *Compartimento* cen. Italy; farming

U'mė (ōō') *River* 290 m. N Sweden

Ūn-à-las'kà *B..y, Island* of Aleutians SW Alas., U.S.

Un-cöm-päh'gre *Peak* 14,305 ft. Colo., U.S.

Un-gā'và *Region* E Canada, Hudson Bay-Labrador; minerals

Ū'ni-mak *Island* largest of Aleutians SW Alas. U.S.

Ūn'iön City *City* NE N.J., U.S.; pop. 58,-537; industrial

Ūn'iön of South Africa = SOUTH AFRICA, REP. of

Ūn'iön of Sō'vi-et Socialist Republics (U.S.S.R.) also Sō'vi-et Ūn'iön or Rus'sià (r u s h') *Country* world's largest: E Eur.-N and W Asia; 8,649,490 sq. m.; pop. 239,000,000; * Moscow; incl. 16 constituent reps.; heavy industry, fish, timber, minerals

Ū-nī'ted A'ràb Republic = 1. Official name of EGYPT. 2. *Union* of Egypt and Syria 1958-61

Ū-nī'ted King'döm of

Greāt Bri'tain and Nôr'thêrn Īre'lànd (U.K.) = *Kingdom* incl. Great Britain (England, Scotland, Wales) and Northern Ireland; 94,220 sq. m.; pop. 56,100,000; * London, England; varied industries, farming, shipping

Ū-nī'ted Nā-tions (shuns) *International terr.* N.Y. City, U.S.; U.N. headquarters

Ū-nī'ted Provinces now UTTAR PRADESH

Ū-nī'ted Stātes of À-mer'i-cà (U. S., U.S.A.) *Federal republic* North America, incl. 50 states and federal district; 3,-688,882 sq. m.; pop. 203,184,772; * Washington; industrialized, rich in natural resources

Ū-ni-vêr'si-ty City *City* E Mo., U.S.; pop. 46,309

U-ni-vêr'si-ty Peak *Peak* 13,585 ft. Calif., U.S.

Un'ley (li) *City* South Australia

Un'zhà (ōōn') *River* 365 m. U.S.S.R., Eur.

U-pō'lu (ōō-pō'lōō) *Island* of Western Samoa

Up'pêr Är'ling-tön *City* Ohio, U.S.; pop. 38,-630

Up'pêr Vŏl'tà, Republic of *Republic* W Africa (former Fr. terr.); 95,444 sq. m.; pop. 5,300,000; * Ouagadougou; livestock

Upp'sä-la *City* * of *Province* E Sweden; machinery, publishing

Ū'ràl 1. *Mountains:* range div. Eur.-Asia, U.S.S.R.; minerals, forests, heavy industry. 2. *River* (unnavigable) 1400 m. U.S.S.R. Eur.-Asia

Ū-ralsk' *City* Kazakh U.S.S.R. cen. Asia

U-ra-ri-coe'rà (ōō, cwà') *River* 360 m. N Brazil

U-rä'wä (ōō) *Town* Honshu, Japan

Ur-fä' *City* * of *Vilayet* SE Turkey

Ur'gä (oor') now ULAN BATOR [NW Iran

Ur'mi-à (oor') *Lake*

U-rū-bäm'bä (ōō) *River* 450 m. cen. Peru

U'ru-guay (gwĭ or gwä), **Re-pu'bli-cä Ō-rien-täl' del** 1 *Republic* SE cen. South America; 72,170 sq. m.; pop. 2,900,000; * Montevideo; div. 19 departments; animal products, agriculture. 2. *River* 980 m. SE South America

U-rum'chi (ōō-rōōm') *City* W China; commercial cen.

U-run'di (ōō-rōōn') *Former terr.* (Ger.) and Mandate (Belg.) E Africa, now BURUNDI

U-sa' *River* 350 m. U.S.S.R., Eur.

U.S. Grant Peak *Peak* 13,690 ft. SW Colo., U.S.

Ush'bä *Peak* 15,400 ft. Georgia U.S.S.R.

Us-kub' = SKOPLJE

Us-ku-där', was Scū'tà-ri *Town* Turkey, Asia; manufacturing, commerce

Us-su'ri (ōō-soor') *River* 450 m. U.S.S.R. Asia

U'sti (ōō') *City* W Czechoslovakia; manufacturing

Ust Urt (ōōst oort) *Plateau* U.S.S.R. cen. Asia

U-sū-mä-cin'tà (sēn') *River* 330 m. Guatemala-Mexico

U-sum-bu'rà (ōō-soomboor') now BUJUMBURA

Ū'täh *State* W U.S.; 84,196 sq. m.; pop. 1,059,273; * Salt Lake

City; 29 counties; mines, sheep, farms

Ūte Peak *Peak* 12,300 ft. Colo., U.S.

Ū'ti-cà *City* cen. N.Y., U.S.; pop. 91,611; port, manufacturing

Ū'trecht (trekt) *City* * of *Province* cen. Netherlands; commercial

U-tsu-mo-mi-ya *City* Honshu, Japan

Ut'tàr Prä-desh' (däsh') *State* N India incl. Ganges plains; grains

U-tuä'dō (ōō) *Municipality* W cen. Puerto Rico

U-wä-ji-mä *Town* Shikoku, Japan

Ux'bridge *Urban district* SE England (Greater London)

Uz'bek S.S.R. (ooz') *Constituent Republic* of U.S.S.R., cen. Asia; * Tashkent; agriculture, mining

Ūzh'go-rod *City* Ukraine, U.S.S.R.; trade cen.

V

Väal *River* 700 m. Rep. of South Africa

Vä-dūz' *Commune* * of Liechtenstein

Vaī'gàch *Island* N U.S.S.R., Eur.

Väkh *River* 550 m. U.S.S.R. Asia

Väksh *River* 400 m. U.S.S.R. cen. Asia

Vàl-daī' Hills *Plateaus, hills* W U.S.S.R., Eur.; Volga R. source

Väl'dez (däz) *Peninsula* S Argentina

Va-lence' (läns') *Commune* SE France; manufacturing

Và-len'ci-à (shi) 1. *Anc. kingdom* E Spain. 2. *Commune* * of *Province* E Spain; manufacturing. 3. *City* N Venezuela; manufacturing, commerce

Va-len-ciennes' (sien') *City* N France; manufacturing, coal area

Val-lả-do-lid' *Commune* * of *Province* N cen. Spain; manufacturing

Väl-le'cäs (bä-yā') *Commune* cen. Spain

Vàl-le'jo (lā'ō) *City* cen. Calif., U.S.; pop. 66,733; port, trade

Vȧl-let'tà *City* * of Malta; pop. 16,135; port, naval base

Val'ley Fôrge (li fôrj) Site of Washington's headquarters 1777-78, SE Pa., U.S.

Val'ley Strēam (li) *City* SE N.Y., U.S.; pop. 40,413

Va-lois' (lwa') *Hist. duchy* N France

Val-pȧ-rai'sō (rā' or rī') *City* on *Bay* * of *Province* cen. Chile; commercial port

Van *Salt lake, Vilayet* E Turkey

Van-cou'vȇr (cōō') 1. *City* SW Wash., U.S.; pop. 42,493; imp. shipping, lumber cen. 2. *City* Brit. Columbia, Canada; imp. port, manufacturing cen. 3. *Mountain* 15,-700 ft. Yukon, Canada. 4. *Island* off Brit. Columbia, W Canada; minerals, fish, forests

Var *Department* SE France

Vär'där *River* 200 m. Yugoslavia-Greece

Vä-re'se (rā'sâ) *Commune* * of *Province* N Italy; silk industry

Vär'nä, was Stä'lin *City* NE Bulgaria; port

Vas'quez Peak (kez) *Peak* 12,800 ft. Colo., U.S.

Vȧs-tȇr-as' (ōs') *City* E Sweden; factories

Vat'ĭ-cȧn City *State* within Rome, Italy; 109 acres; papal palaces, museums, St. Peter's Basilica

Vȧt'tȇrn *Lake* S Sweden

Vau-cluse' (vō-clōōz') *Department*   S E France

Ve-lä-de'rō (dā') *Peak* 20,735 ft. NW Argentina

Ve-län' (vâ) *Peak* 12,-350 ft. It.-Swiss border

Ve-le'tä, Pi-cä'cho de (vȧ-lä') *Peak* 11,380 ft. S Spain

Vȇ-li'kie Lu'ki (lē', lōō') *Town* * of *Region* R.S.F.S.R., U.S.S.R., Eur.

Vȇl-lōre' *City* S India

Vel'sȇn *Commune* W Netherlands; port

Ven-dee' (vän-dā') *Department* W France

Vend'sys-sȇl-Thy' (sus, tu') *Island* N Jutland, Denmark

Ve-nē'ti-ȧ (shi), **Ve-ne'ziä** (nä') *Anc.* and *mod. region* NE Italy; fertile, mineral-rich area; div. into 3 compartimenti: 1. **Vene-zia Eu-gä'ne-ȧ** (a-oo-gä'). 2. **Venezia Giu'-liä** (jōō'). 3. **Venezia Tri-den-ti'nä** (dȧn-tē')

Ven-ė-zu-e'lȧ, Republic of (wē' or wā') *Republic* N South America; 352,140 sq. m.; pop. 10,400,000; * Caracas; div. 20 states, 2 terrs., fed. distr.

Ven'ice (is), It. **Ve-ne'-ziä** (nä') 1. *City* on 118 islands in *Lagoon* NE Italy; canals, buildings, glass, lace. 2. *Gulf of* N area of Adriatic S.

Ven-tuä'ri *River* 350 m. S Venezuela

Ven-tūr'ȧ (San Buenaventura) *City* SW Cal., U.S.; pop. 55,-797; business

Ve'rȧ-crūz' *City* in *State* E Mexico; port

Ver-cel'li (vâr-chel') *Commune* * of *Province* NW Italy; trade

Vȇrde, Cape = VERT

Vȇr'di-gris (grēs) *River* 280 m. Kans.-Okla., U.S.

Vȇr-dun' 1. *City* Quebec, Canada; manufacturing. 2. *City* NE France; battles WW I, WW II

Vȇr-kho-yansk' Moun-tains U.S.S.R. Asia

Vȇr-mil'iȯn Peak *Peak* 13,870 ft. Colo., U.S.

Vȇr-mont' *State* NE U.S.; 9609 sq. m.; pop. 444,330; * Montpelier; 14 counties; quarries, agriculture

Ve-rō'nȧ *Commune* * of *Province* NE Italy; textiles

Vė-ro'ni-cȧ *Peak* 19,-340 ft. Peru

Vȇr-sailles' (sī') *City* N France; imp. treaties signed at palace

Vȇrt or Vȇrde *Cape* W point of Africa

Ver-viers' (vyā') *Commune* E Belgium

Ves'tȧl Peak *Peak* 13,-850 ft. Colo., U.S.

Ves'tȇr-ȧ-lȇn *Islands* NW Norway

Ve-sū'vi-us *Volcano* SW Italy nr. Naples

Vet-lu'gȧ (lōō') *River* 500 m. U.S.S.R. Eur.

Vi'bȯrg (vē') 1. *City* Jutland, Denmark. 2. *City* U.S.S.R. = VYBORG

Vi-cen'zä (vē-chen') *Commune* * of *Province* NE Italy

Vi-chä'dȧ *River* 335 m. Colombia

Vi'chy (vē') *Commune* cen. France; resort; Fr. seat of government 1940-42

Vicks'bûrg *City* W Miss., U.S.; Civil War battle site

Vic-tō'ri-ȧ 1. *City* * of Brit. Colombia, Canada; pop. 57,453; port, commerce, manufacturing. 2. *City* * of Hong Kong; port, trade cen. 3. *River* 400 m. N cen. Australia. 4. *State* SE Australia

Vic-tō'ri-ä 1. *Island*

and *Strait* Arctic Arch. Northwest Terrs. Canada. 2. *Lake* 26,830 sq. m. E cen. Africa. 3. *Peak* 13,240 ft. Papua, New Guinea. 4. *Point* S Burma. 5. *City* SE Texas, U.S.; pop. 41,349; business

Vic-tō'ri-à Falls 1. *Falls* Zambezi R. S Africa. 2. now IGU-ASSU

Vic-tō'ri-à Land *Area* of Antarctica, Ross Dependency

Vi-en'nȧ, Ger. **Wien** (vēn) *City* * of *District* and * of Austria E part; pop. 1,644,-900

Vienne (vyen) 1. *Department* W cen. France. 2. *River* 215 m. SW cen. France

Vien-tiane' *Town* administrative * of Laos; pop. 132,000

Vi-et'nam' *Country*, former Fr. terr., SE Asia; 1954 div. at 17th parallel: 1. **Vi-et'näm', Democratic Rep. of** (North); 61,-290 sq. m.; pop. 21,-150,000; * Hanoi; rice, fish. 2. **Vi-et'näm', Rep. of** (South); 65,-900 sq. m.; pop. 18,-330,000; * Saigon

Vi'gō (vē') *City* NW Spain; port, manufacturing

Vil-kits'ki Strait *Channel* N U.S.S.R., Asia

Ville-ûr-banne' (vēl) *Commune* E cen. France; industry

Vil'nẏ-us, Vil'nȧ, Vil'nō, Ger. **Wil'nä** (vil') *City* * of Lithuania; trade, cultural cen.

Vi-lyui' (lū'i) *River* 1500 m. U.S.S.R., Asia

Vi'nä del Mär' (vē') *City* cen. Chile; resort

Vin - cennes' (senz') *Commune* N France

Vin'dȇl *River* 225 m. N

Sweden

Vīne′lånd 1. *City* SW N.J., U.S.; pop. 47,-685; business cen. 2. *Coast area* N North America; visited by Norse 1000 B.C.

Vin′ni-tså *City* * of *Region* Ukraine U.S.S.R.; factories

Vîr-gin′iå (jin′) *State* E U.S.; 40,815 sq. m.; pop. 4,648,494; * Richmond; 98 counties; tobacco, lumber, corn

Vîr-gin′iå Beach *City* SE Va., U.S.; pop. 172,106; Armed Forces, residential, resort

Vîr-gin′iå City *Village,* now ghost town W Nev., U.S.; gold, silver mines 1850

Vir′gin Islands (jin) *Islands* NE West Indies div.: 1. **Amer. Virgin Is.** * Charlotte Amalie on St. Thomas. 2. **Brit. Virgin Is.** * Road Town

Vis (vēs), **Lis′så** *Island* off Yugoslavia

Vi-sä′yån Islands *Islands* cen. Phil. Is.; incl. Cebu, Leyte, Negros, Panay, etc.

Vis′count Mel′ville Sound (vī′) *Sound* Northwest Terrs. Canada

Vi′sō, Mount (vē′) *Peak* 12,600 ft. NW Italy

Vis′tū-lå *River* 625 m. N Poland

Vi′tebsk (vē′) *City* * of *Region* White Russia, U.S.S.R.; industrial cen.

Vi-ter′bō *Commune* * of *Province* cen. Italy; manufacturing

Vi′ti Le′vu (vē′, vōō) *Island* largest of Fiji Is.

Vi-tim′ (tēm′) *River* 1100 m. Siberia, U.S.S.R., Asia

Vi-tō′ri-å 1. *City* N Spain; manufacturing. 2. *City* E Brazil;

port

Vi-try′-sur-Seine′ (trē′, sân′) *Commune* N France; manufacturing

Vi-zä′gå-på′tàm *City* E India; port, textiles

Vi-zi-å-någ′råm *Town* E India

Vlad′i-mir *City* of *Region* R.S.F.S.R., U.S.S.R., Eur.

Vla-di-vos-tok′ *City* R.S.F.S.R., U.S.S.R., Asia; imp. port

Vlō′nä *Town* on *Bay* in *Prefecture* SW Albania; port

Vōl-cän′ *Peak* 18,075 ft. cen. Chile

Vol′gå *River* 2325 m., U.S.S.R.; Eur.'s longest

Vol′go-grad, was **Stä′-lin-grad** *City* * of *Region* U.S.S.R., Eur.; imp. industrially

Vô′lög-då *City* * of *Region* R.S.F.S.R. U.S.S.R. Eur.; trade, factories

Vō′los *City* on *Gulf* NE Greece; port

Volsk *Town* R.S.F.S.R., U.S.S.R., Eur.; port

Vol′tå 1. *River* 250 m. W Africa; formed by **Black Vol′tå** (headstream) and **White Vol′tå** 450 m. 2. *Republic* see UPPER VOLTA

Vö-lȳn′ *Region* Ukraine U.S.S.R.

Vö-rô′nezh *City* * of *Region* on *River* (290 m.) R. S. F. S. R., U.S.S.R. Eur.; imp. industrial cen.

Vō-ro-shi′lov (shē′) *City* R.S.F.S.R., U.S.S.R., Asia; industrial, agricultural cen.

Vō - ro - shi′löv - grad (shē′) *City* * of *Region* Ukraine, U.S.S.R.; coal area; factories

Vō-ro-shi′lovsk (shē) *City* Ukraine U.S.S.R.; industrial

Vôr′sklå *River* 270 m. Ukraine, U.S.S.R.

Vosges (vōzh) *Department, Mountains* NE France

Vul′cån Crest *Peak* 13,-720 ft. S Colo., U.S.

Vyat′kå 1. *River* 800 m. U.S.S.R., Eur. 2. *City* now KIROV

Vy′bôrg (vē′) *City* on *Bay* R.S.F.S.R., U.S.S.R., Eur.

Vy′chėg-då *River* 700 m. U.S.S.R., Eur.

Vȳsh′ni Vö-lô′chek *City* R.S.F.S.R., U.S.S.R., Eur.; factories

W

Wäas, Mount *Peak* 12,585 ft. Wash., U.S.

Wä′bash *River* 475 m. Ind.-Ill., U.S.

Wä′cō *City* cen. Tex., U.S.; pop. 95,326; commerce, shipping

Wä-daī′, Ouä-daī′ *Former sultanate* now in E Chad

Wad′ding-tön, Mount *Peak* 13,260 ft. Brit. Colombia, Canada

Waī-ki-kī′ (kē′) *Beach* Oahu, Haw., U.S.

Waīn-gån′gä *River* 360 m. cen. India

Wä-kä-mä-tsu 1. *City* Kyushu, Japan; coal port. 2. *City* Honshu, Japan; pottery, fabrics

Wä-kä-yä-mä *City* * of *Prefecture* Honshu, Japan; port

Wäke′fiėld *City,* county borough, N England; coal, manufacturing

Wäke Island *Island* (U.S.) N cen. Pacific O.

Wäl′brzych (bzhik), **Wäl′dėn-bûrg** *City* SW Poland

Wäl′chė-rėn (väl′kė) *Island* off SW Netherlands

Wäl′deck *Former state* W Germany

Wäles *Principality* W

Great Britain, *Division* of United Kingdom; 8000 sq. m.; pop. 2,720,000; * Cardiff; 12 counties

Wäl′grēen Coast *Region* coast of Antarctica

Wäl′lå-sey (si) *County borough* NW England; docks

Wal′ling-förd *Town* S Conn., U.S.; pop. 35,714

Wal′lis and Fu-tu′nå (fōō-tōō′) *Island groups* (Fr.) cen. Pacific O.; * Matu-Utu

Wäl-lō′ni-å = name for Fr. speaking area of Belgium

Wälls′end *Municipal borough* N England; coal area

Wäl′nut Creek *City* W Cal., U.S.; pop. 39,-844; residential

Wäl′såll *County borough* W cen. England

Wäl′tham *City* NE Mass., U.S.; pop. 61,-582; watches

Wäl′thåm-stōw *Municipal borough* SE England; industry

Wän′chuän′, was **Käl′-gän′** *City* N China

Wän′hsien′ (shi-en′) *City* S cen. China; port .

Wän′nė-Eīck′il (vän′, ĭk′) *City* W West Germany; coal, beer

Wän′stead and Wood′-förd (sted) *Municipal borough* SE England

Wäp-si-pin′i-cön *River* 255 m. E Iowa, U.S.

Wå′rån-gål *City* S cen. India

Wär′bûr-tön *River* 275 m. S cen. Australia

Wår′dhä *River* 290 m. cen. India

Wärm Springs *Village* W Ga., U.S.; site of health foundation estab. by F. D. Roosevelt

Wär′re-gō *River* 400 m. E cen. Australia

Wär′ren 1. *City* NE

Ohio, U.S.; pop. 63,-494; steel. 2. *City* SE Mich., U.S.; pop. 179,260

Wär′ring-tön *County borough* NW England; manufacturing

Wär′säw, Wär-szä′wä (vär, vä) *City* * of *Department* and * of Poland, cen. part; pop. 1,273,600; commerce, manufacturing

Wär′tå, Wär′the (vär′-tȧ) *River* 445 m. W Poland

Wär′wick (ik) *City* R.I. U.S.; pop. 83,694

Wär′wick-shire *County* cen. England

Wä′såtch Mountain *Peak* 13,550 ft. Colo., U.S.

Wäsh′ing-tön 1. *City* * of U.S., E part; co-extensive with fed. distr.: Dist. of Columbia; 69 sq. m.; pop. 756,510; political, cultural, educational cen. 2. *State* NW U.S.; 68,192 sq. m.; pop. 3,409,169; * Olympia; 39 counties; lumber, fruit, fish, quarries. 3. *Lake* W cen. Wash., U.S.

Wäsh′i-tä *River* 500 m. Okla., U.S. [Kenya

Wa′sö Nyi′rö *River* cen.

Wä′tẽr-bur-ẏ (ber) *City* S Conn., U.S.; pop. 108,033; brass. cen.

Wä′tẽr-förd *County* S Eire

Wä′tẽr-loō 1. *City* NE Iowa, U.S.; pop. 75,-533; commerce, manufacturing. 2. *Commune* cen. Belgium; Napoleon's defeat 1815

Wä′tẽr-tön - Glä′cier (shẽr) *International Park* Alberta, Canada-Mont., U.S.

Wä′tẽr-town *Town* NE Mass., U.S.; pop. 39,-307; textiles

Wät′förd *Municipal borough* SE England

Wät′lings Island was **San Sal′vå-dôr** *Island* of Bahamas

Wät′sön, Mount *Peak* 11,470 ft. Utah, U.S.

Wät′tẽn-scheid (shīt) *City* W West Germany; factories, coal

Wäu-kē′gȧn *City* NE Ill., U.S.; pop. 65,-269; wire, iron

Wäu′kė-shä *City* SE Wisc., U.S.; pop. 40,258; manufacturing

Wäu-wå-tō′sȧ *City* SE Wisc., U.S.; pop. 58,676

Wä′vẽr-ley (li) *Municipality* SE Australia

Wȧ-zir-i-stän′ *Mountain area* W Pakistan

We, Weh (wä) *Island* off Sumatra, Indonesia; imp. port

Webbe *River* 280 m. SE Ethiopia

Wed′dėll Sea *Arm* of Atlantic O., Antarctica [N cen. China

Wei (wä) *River* 400 m.

Wei′hai′wei (wä′hī′-wä′) *City* NE China; port

Wei′hsien′ (wä′shi-en′) *City* NE China; trade

Wei′mär (vī′) *City* SW East Germany; Ger. Rep., called **Wei′mär, Rep.** formed here 1919

Weiss′hôrn (vīs′) *Peak* 14,800 ft. Switzerland

Weiss′kū-gėl (v ī s′) *Peak* 12,290 ft. Austria-Italy

Weiss′miės (vīs′) *Peak* 13,225 ft. Switzerland

Wel′lånd Ship Cȧ-nal′ *Canal* L. Erie-L. Ontario, Canada

Wel′ling-tön *City* * of New Zealand, North I.; pop. 288,000; port

Wel′tė-vre-dėn (vel′, vrä) *Section* of Batavia, Indonesia

Wem′bley (bli) *Municipal borough* SE England

Wer′rä (ver′) *River* 280

m. cen. West Germany

We′sẽr (vä′) *River* 280 m. N cen. West Germany

We-sẽr-mun′dė (vä) now **BREMER-HAVEN**

Wes′sėx *Anc. kingdom* S Great Britain

West Al′lis *City* SE Wisc., U.S.; pop. 71,-723; manufacturing

West Ben′gȧl *State* NE India incl. Calcutta

West Brom′wich (ich) *County borough* W cen. England

West Co-vi′nȧ (vē′) *City* SW Calif., U.S.; pop. 68,034; fruit

Wes′tẽrn Åus-trāl′iȧ *State* W third of Australia; * Perth

Wes′tẽrn Sȧ-mō′ȧ *Republic* within Brit. Commonwealth, SW cen. Pacific O.: Upolu and Savai'u Is.; 1100 sq. m.; pop. 134,000; * Apia; agriculture

West-Ham *County borough* SE England

West Hart′förd *Town* S Conn., U.S.; pop. 68,031; residential

West Här′tle-poōl *Municipal borough* N England

West Hā′ven *City* S Conn., U.S.; pop. 52,851

West In′diēs *Islands* bet. N and S America; Greater Antilles (Cuba, Hispaniola, Jamaica, Puerto Rico), Lesser Antilles (Virgin, Leeward, Windward Is.), Bahamas

West I′ri-än (ē′) *Division* of Indonesia, W half of New Guinea

West′land *City* SE Mich., U.S.; pop. 86,749

West Lō′thi-ȧn *County* SE Scotland

West′mēath *County* N cen. Eire

West′min-stẽr 1. *City* and *Borough* cen. London England. 2. *City* S Cal., U.S.; pop. 59,865

West′môr-land *County* NW England

West New Gui′nea = WEST IRIAN

West New York *City* NE N.J., U.S.; pop. 40,627

Wes′tön Peak *Peak* 13,500 ft. Colo., U.S.

West Or′ange (ȧnj) *City* NE N.J., U.S.; pop. 43,715

West Pälm Bēach *City* SE Fla., U.S.; pop. 57,375; resort

West-phä′liȧ (fä′) *Area* (prov. of former Ger. state of Prussia) West Germany; mines

West Point U.S. Military Academy SE N.Y., U.S.

Western Sȧ-mō′ȧ, Terr. of *Islands, Terr.* of New Zealand, W Samoa Is.; copra

West Span′ish Peak *Peak* 13,620 ft. Colo., U.S.

West Vîr-gin′iȧ (jin′) *State* E cen. U.S.; 24,181 sq. m.; pop. 1,744,237; * Charleston; 55 counties; minerals

Wet′tẽr-hôrn (v e t′) *Peak* 12,150 ft. cen. Switzerland

Wet′tẽr-hôrn *Peak* 14,020 ft. Colo., U.S.

Wex′förd *County* SE Eire

Wey′mouth (wä′muth) *City* E Mass., U.S.; pop. 54,610; shoes, granite

Whēa′tön *City* Md., U.S.; pop. 66,247

Whēe′lẽr Peak 1. *Peak* 13,060 ft. E Nev., U.S. 2. *Peak* 13,150 ft. N N.M·, U.S.

Whēe′ling *City* N W.Va., U.S.; pop. 48,188; manufacturing, commerce

Whīte 1. *River* 690 m. Ark., U.S. 2. *River* 325 m. S.D., U.S. 3. *River* 280 m. NW Tex., U.S.

Whīte'crôss Mountain *Peak* 13,550 ft. Colo., U.S.

Whīte Dōme *Peak* 13,-615 ft. Colo., U.S.

Whīte'hôrse *Town* * of Yukon Terr., Canada; S part

Whīte'house Mountain *Peak* 13,490 ft. Colo., U.S.

Whīte Mountain *Peak* 14,240 ft. E cen. Calif., U.S.

Whīte Mountains 1. *Mountains* Calif.-Nev., U.S. 2. *Mountains* N.H., U.S.

Whīte Nīle see NILE R.

Whīte Peak *Peak* 13,-600 ft. Colo., U.S.

Whīte Pīne Peak *Peak* 11,490 ft. Nev., U.S.

Whīte Plāins *City* SE N.Y., U.S.; pop. 50,-220; residential

Whīte Rock Mountain *Peak* 13,530 ft. Colo., U.S.

Whīte Rus'sian or **Bye-lö-rus'sian S. S. R.** (rush'ăn) *Constituent republic* of U.S.S.R., W part; * Minsk; livestock, agriculture

Whīte Sea *Gulf* of Barents S. N U.S.S.R. Eur. [TA R.

White Vōl'tà see VOL-

Whit'ney, Mount (ni) *Peak* 14,495 ft. SE cen. Calif., highest in continental U.S.

Whit'tiêr *City* S Cal., U.S.; pop. 72,863; residential

Wich'i-tă 1. *City* S cen. Kans., U.S.; pop. 276,554; industry, commerce. 2. *River* 230 m. N Tex., U.S.

Wich'i-tă Fălls *City* N Tex., U.S.; pop. 97,-564; oil cen.

Wick'lōw *County* E Eire

Wid'nes *Municipal borough* NW England; manufacturing

Wien (vēn) = VIENNA

Wies'bä-dẽn (vēs') *City* W cen. West Germany

Wig'àn *County borough* NW England

Wight, Isle of (wīt) *Island County* of England, English Channel; resorts

Wig'tön *County* SW Scotland

Wild'spit-zẽ (vilt') *Peak* 12,380 ft. Austria

Wil-hel-mi'nà (m ē') *Peak* 15,585 ft. W cen. New Guinea

Wil-helms-hä'vẽn (vil) *City* NW West Germany; North S. port

Wilkes'-Bar-rẽ *City* E Pa., U.S.; pop. 58,-856; industry

Wilkes Land *Region* Indian O. coast, Antarctica

Wil'lẽm-städ (vil') *City* * of Netherlands Antilles on Curacao I.; port

Willes'dẽn *Municipal borough* SE England

Wil'liåms-bûrg *City* SE Va., U.S.; colonial restoration

Wil'liăm-sön, Mount *Peak* 14,385 ft. cen. Calif., U.S.

Wil'liåms-pôrt *City* N cen. Pa., U.S.; pop. 37,918; manufacturing

Wil'lough-bÿ (lô) *City* SE Australia

Wil'ming-tön 1. *City* N Del., U.S.; pop. 80,-386; port, commerce, industry. 2. *City* SE N.C., U.S.; pop. 46,-169; commercial port

Wil'nō (vil') = VIL-NYUS

Wil'sön, Mount *Peak* 14,240 ft. Colo., U.S.

Wil'sön Peak 1. *Peak* 14,025 ft. Colo., U.S. 2. *Peak* 11,095 ft. Utah, U.S.

Wilt'shîre *County* S England

Wim'ble-dön (b'l) *Municipal borough* S England; tennis events

Wim'mêr-à *River* 230 m. SE Australia

Win'chèll, Mount *Peak* 13,750 ft. Calif., U.S.

Wind'hoek (vint'hook) *Town* * of South-West Africa; minerals, educational cen.

Win'döm Peak *Peak* 14,090 ft. Colo., U.S.

Wind'sör 1. *City* SE Ontario, Canada; industrial cen. esp. cars *Municipal borough* 2. or **New Wind'sör** S England; Windsor castle

Wind'ward Islands 1. *Islands* (Brit.) S chain of Lesser Antilles, West Indies; * St. George's on Grenada I. 2. *Islands* of Society Is., Fr. Polynesia, incl. Tahiti

Wind'ward Passage *Channel* E Cuba-NW Hispaniola

Win'isk *River* 400 m. Ontario, Canada

Win'ni-peg 1. *City* * of Manitoba, Canada, S part; pop. 257,005; cattle, grain market. 2. *Lake* S cen. Manitoba, Canada

Win-ni-peg-ō'sis *Lake* W Manitoba, Canada

Win'stön-Sā'lèm *City* N cen. N.C., U.S.; pop. 132,913

Win'têr-thur' (tōōr) *Commune* NE cen. Switzerland

Wis-con'sin 1. *River* 430 m. cen. - NW Wisc., U.S. 2. *State* N U.S.; 56,154 sq. m.; pop. 4,417,933; * Madison; 71 counties; livestock, grain, lumber, minerals

Wis'têr, Mount *Peak* 11,480 ft. NW Wyo., U.S.

Wis'mär (vis') *City* on *Bay* NW East Germany; port

Wit'tẽn (vit') *City* W cen. West Germany

Wit'tẽn-bêrg (vit') *City* N East Germany; manufacturing

Wit-tẽn-bêr'gẽ (v i t) *City* S East Germany; port

Wō'bûrn *City* NE Mass., U.S.; pop. 37,406; residential

Wlo-cla'wek (vlô-tslä'-vek) *Commune* N Poland; manufacturing

Wō'king *Urban district* S England; resort

Wol'làs-tön *Lake* Saskatchewan, Canada

Wol'vêr - hamp - tön (wool') *County borough* W cen. England; iron, coal àrea

Wood, Mount *Peak* 15,880 ft. Yukon, Canada

Wood'bridge *Town* cen. N.J., U.S.; pop. 78,-846; brick, tile

Wood Grēen *Urban district* SE England; residential

Wood Mountain *Peak* 13,640 ft. Colo., U.S.

Wōōn-sock'ĕt *City* N R.I., U.S.; pop. 46,-820; manufacturing

Worces'têr (woos') 1. *City* cen. Mass., U.S.; pop. 176,572; industrial cen. 2. *County borough*, * of **Worces'-têr - shîre** (woos') county W cen. England; manufacturing

Wörms *City* SW cen. West Germany; river port

Wör'thing *Municipal borough* S England; resort

Wran'gèl Island *Island* off N U.S.S.R. Asia, Arctic O.

Wran'gèll, Mount *Peak* 14,000 ft. of **Wran'-gèll Mts.** S Alas., U.S.

Wro'claw (vrô'tsläf), Ger. **Bres'lau** (lou) *City* * of Department SW Poland; commerce, manufacturing

Wu (wōō) *River* 500 m. cen. China

Wu'chäng' (wōō') *City* E cen. China; * of Hupeh prov.

Wu'chow' (wōō'jō') now TSANGWU

Wu'hän' (wōō') = The HAN CITIES

Wu'hing' (wōō') was **Hu'chow'** (hōō'jō') *City* E China

Wu'hsien' (wōō'shi-en') was **Sōō'chow'** (jō') *City* E China; port, anc. city

Wu'hu' (wōō'hōō') *City* E China; trade cen.

Wul'stèn Peak (wool') *Peak* 13,666 ft. Colo., U.S.

Wup'pêr-täl (voop') *City* on **Wupper R.** W cen. West Germany industrial

Wûrt'têm-bêrg *Former state* S Germany; now BADEN-WURTTEMBERG

Wûrz'bûrg *City* S cen. West Germany; manufacturing

Wu'sih' (wōō'shē') *City* E China; trade

Wu' Taï' Shän' (wōō') *Mountain* 10,000 ft. NE China; sacred to Buddhists

Wu'tsin' (wōō'jin') was **Chäng'chow'** (jō') *City* E China; trade

Wu'wei' (wōō'wä') was **Liäng'chow'** (jō') *City* N cen. China

Wỹ'àn-dotte *City* SE Mich., U.S.; pop. 41,061; chemicals

Wỹn'bêrg *Town* S Rep. of South Africa

Wỹ-o'ming 1. *State* W U.S.; 97,914 sq. m.; pop. 332,416; * Cheyenne; 23 counties and Yellowstone National Park; livestock, mines, lumber. 2. *Peak* 11,360 ft. W Wyo., U.S. 3. *City* W Mich., U.S.; pop. 56,560

X

Xan'the (zan') *City* NE Greece

Xin-gu' (shēng-gōō') *River* 1300 m. cen. Brazil

Y

Yä'än', Yä'chow' (jō') *Town* S China

Yak'ï-mä *City* S Wash., U.S.; pop. 45,588; business

Yà-kutsk' A.S.S.R. (kōōtsk') *Republic* R.S.F.S.R., U.S.S.R., Asia; * Yà-kutsk'

Yäl'tà *Town* R.S.F.S.R. U.S.S.R., Eur.; WW II conference site

Yä'lu' (lōō') *River* 300 m. Manchuria-Korea

Yä'lung' (loong') *River* 725 m. S China

Yä-mä-gä-tä *City* * of *Prefecture* Honshu, Japan; silk cen.

Yä-mä-gu-chi (goo) *City* * of *Prefecture* Honshu, Japan

Yà-ma'lö-Ne-nets' *National district* R.S.F.S.R., U.S.S.R., Asia

Yä-mä-nä-shi *Prefecture* Honshu, Japan

Yä-mä-tō *Former province* Honshu, Japan; now NARA

Ya'nà *River* 750 m. U.S.S.R., Asia

Yäng'ku' (chu') *City* NE China

Yang'tzē' *River* 3200 m. China's chief river, S part

Ya-oun-de' (ōōn-da') *Town* * of Cameroun; pop. 130,000

Yap *Island* of *Group* W Caroline Is., U.S. Trust Terr.

Yä-qui' (kē') *River* 420 m. N.M., U.S.

Yär-kand' *River* 500 m. *Town, Oasis* W China

Yär'mouth, Great Yär'mouth (muth) *County borough* E England; port, herring

Yä-rö-slavl' *City* * of *Region* R.S.F.S.R., U.S.S.R., Eur.

Yär-vi-cō'yä *Peak* 17,390 ft. N Chile

Yä-wä-tä *City* Kyushu, Japan; iron works; port

Yè-gôr'èvsk *City* W cen. R.S.F.S.R., U.S.S.R., Eur.

Ye'hsien' (shi-en'), was **Lu'chow'** (jō') *City* NE China

Yeisk (yä'esk) *Town* R.S.F.S.R., U.S.S.R., Eur.; port

Yè-lets' *City* R.S.F.S.R. U.S.S.R., Eur.; trade

Yel'lōw 1. *River* China, see HWANG HO. 2. *Sea* China-Korea

Yel'lōw-stōne 1. *River* 670 m. Wyo.-Mont., U.S. 2. *Lake* in *National Park* NW Wyo., U.S.

Yem'ên Arab Republic *Republic* (former kingdom) SW Arabian penin., SW Asia; 75,390 sq. m.; pop. 5,000,000; * Sana

Yemen, Peoples Dem Rep. of *Country* SW Arabian penin.; SW Asia; 112,000 sq. mi.; pop. 1,280,000

Yè-nà-ki'yè-vö (kē') *City* Ukraine U.S.S.R., Eur.

Yen'än' or **Fu'shih'** (fōō') *Town* NE cen. China

Yen'bō, Yan'bu *City* W Arabia; Red S. port

Ye-ni-sei' (sā') *River* 2800 m. W Siberia U.S.S.R. Asia

Yer'bà Bue'nà Island (bwā'), was **Gōat I.** *Island* San Francisco Bay, Calif., U.S.

Ye-re-vän', E-re-vän' *City* * of Armenian S.S.R. SW U.S.S.R., Eur.

Yezd *City* * of *Province* cen. Iran; industrial

Ying'kōw', New' chwäng' (nū') *City* Manchuria, China; port

Yok-kaï-chi *City* S Honshu, Japan; port

Yō-ko-hä-mä *City* SE Honshu, Japan; imp. silk port, industry, commerce

Yō-ko-su-kä *City* SE Honshu, Japan; port

Yom *River* 300 m. NW Thailand

Yo-nä-go *Town* W Honshu, Japan; harbor

Yo-ne-zä-wä *City* N Honshu, Japan; weaving

Yon'kêrs *City* SE N.Y., U.S.; pop. 204,370; factories

Yônne *Department* NE cen. France

Yôrk 1. *City* S Pa., U.S.; pop. 50,335; industry. 2. *City, county borough* of **Yôrk'shïre** county N England; manufacturing

Yôrk'town (toun) *Town* SE Va., U.S.; site of surrender ending Amer. Revolution 1781

Yôr'u-bà-land *Area,* former kingdom, N Nigeria

Yō-sem'i-tē *National Park* cen. Calif., U.S.; falls, cliffs

Youngs'town (yungs'toun) *City* NE Ohio, U.S.; pop. 139,788; industrial cen.

Yp'si-lon *Peak* 13,505 ft. Colo., U.S.

Yu now SIYANG R., 400 m. S China

Yuän' *River* 500 m. SE cen. China

Yū-cä-mä'ni *Peak* 17,860 ft. S Peru

Yū-cà-tan' *Peninsula* cen. and South America; incl. *State* SE Mexico, Brit. Honduras, N Guatemala

Yug (yōōk) *River* 330

m. U.S.S.R., Eur.

Yū-go-slä'viä, Socialist Federal Rep. of *Federal rep.* SE Eur.; 98,765 sq. m.; pop. 19,392,000; * Belgrade; div. into reps. and provs.; industry, agriculture

Yū'kon 1. *Territory* NW Canada; 205,346 sq. m.; pop. 15,000; * Whitehorse; forests, minerals. 2. *River* SW Yukon terr.

Yung'ki' (yoong'ji'), **Ki'rin'** (kē') *City* E Manchuria, China; imp. trade cen.

Yung'kia' (yoong'jiä'), was **Wėn'chow'** (jō') *City* E China; port

Yung'ning' (yoong'), was **Nän'ning'** *Town* SE China; port

Yung'ting' (yoong'), or **Hun** (hoon) *River* 300 m. NE China

Yun'nän' 1. *Province* S China. 2. *City* its * now KUNMING

Z

Zaan-däm' *Commune* W Netherlands; lumber

Zab, Great *River* 260 m. SE Turkey, Asia

Zab, Little *River* 230 m. Iran-Iraq

Zäb'rze (zhe), Ger. **Hin'dėn-bêrg** *City* SW Poland; industrial

Zä-cä-te'cäs (tā') *City*

* of *State* cen. Mexico; mines

Zä'där, It. **Zä'rä** *City* W Yugoslavia; port

Zag'ä-zig *City* Lower Egypt; trade cen.

Zä-gôrsk' *Town* R.S.F.S.R., U.S.S.R., Eur.; pilgrimage spot

Zä'greb *City* * of Croatia Rep., NW Yugoslavia; industry, commerce

Zaire *Country* formerly **Democratic Rep. of the Congo,** S. cen. Africa; * Kinshasa; 905,500 sq. mi.; pop. ab. 18,400,000; cotton, forest products, uranium

Zaire *River* ab. 3000 m. W. Africa; formerly **Congo**

Za - kär - pat'skä - yä Russ. for RUTHENIA

Zä-ko-pä'ne *Commune* S Poland; resort

Zäm-bä'les (läs) *Mountain range, Province* Luzon, Phil. Is.

Zam-bē'zi *River* 1650 m. S Africa

Zam'bi-ä *Republic* (was Northern Rhodesia) E Africa; 288,130 sq. m.; pop. 4,300,000; * Lusaka; copper

Zäm-bo-än'gä *City* * of *Province* Mindanao, Phil. Is.; trade cen.

Zänes'ville *City* SE cen. Ohio, U.S.; pop.

33,045; manufacturing

Zan'te, Zä-kyn'thös *Island Department* Ionian Is., Greece

Zan'zi-bär *City* on *Island* off E Africa, former Brit. prot. and Rep., now part of Tanzania

Zä-pä'tä *Peninsula* and *Swamp* W cen. Cuba

Zä-pö-rô'zhė *City* * of *Region* Ukraine, U.S.S.R., Eur.; industrial cen.

Zä-ṛä-gō'zä Span. for SARAGOSSA

Zär'dėh Kuh (kōō) *Peak* 14,920 ft. W Iran

Zēe'länd *Province* SW Netherlands

Zem - pō - äl - te - pec' (zäm) *Peak* 11,135 ft. SE Mexico

Zen-shu *Town* SW Korea

Ze-rav-shän' *River* 400 m. U.S.S.R. cen. Asia

Zet'land = SHETLAND *County* and *Islands*

Ze'yä (zyä') *River* 765 m. U.S.S.R., Asia

Zhda'növ *City* Ukraine, U.S.S.R.; port

Zhi-tô'mir, Ji-tô'mir *City* * of *Region* Ukraine, U.S.S.R.; industrial

Zi-näl' Rôt'hôrn *Peak* 13,855 ft. SW Switzerland

Zi'ön *Hill* NE Jerusa-

lem, Israel; site of anc. Temple

Zi'ön *National park* SW Utah, U.S.; cliffs

Ziz'kôv (zhish') *Former city,* now incl. in Prague, Czechoslovakia

Zlä-tö-ust' (ōōst') *City* R.S.F.S.R., U.S.S.R., Asia; machinery, iron

Zom'bä *City* * of Malawi; pop. 11,000

Zôn-gul-däk' *City* * of *Vilayet* NW Turkey, Asia; port

Zuĭ'dėr Zēe *Former inlet* and *Lake,* now reclaimed land, N Netherlands

Zu'lu - land (zōō'lōō) *Area* of Natal prov. E South Africa

Zū'pō, Piz (pēts) *Peak* 13,120 ft. It.-Swiss border

Zu'rich (zoor'ik) *City* on *Lake* * of *Canton* NE cen. Switzerland; largest Swiss city; imp. industrial cen.; resort

Zwick'au (ou) *City* S cen. East Germany; factories, mines

Zwol'le *Commune* E Netherlands; industry

Zy-rär'dow (zhi, dōōf) *Commune* cen. Poland; textiles

Zẏr'i-än Autonomous Area now KOMI A.S.S.R.

ATLAS

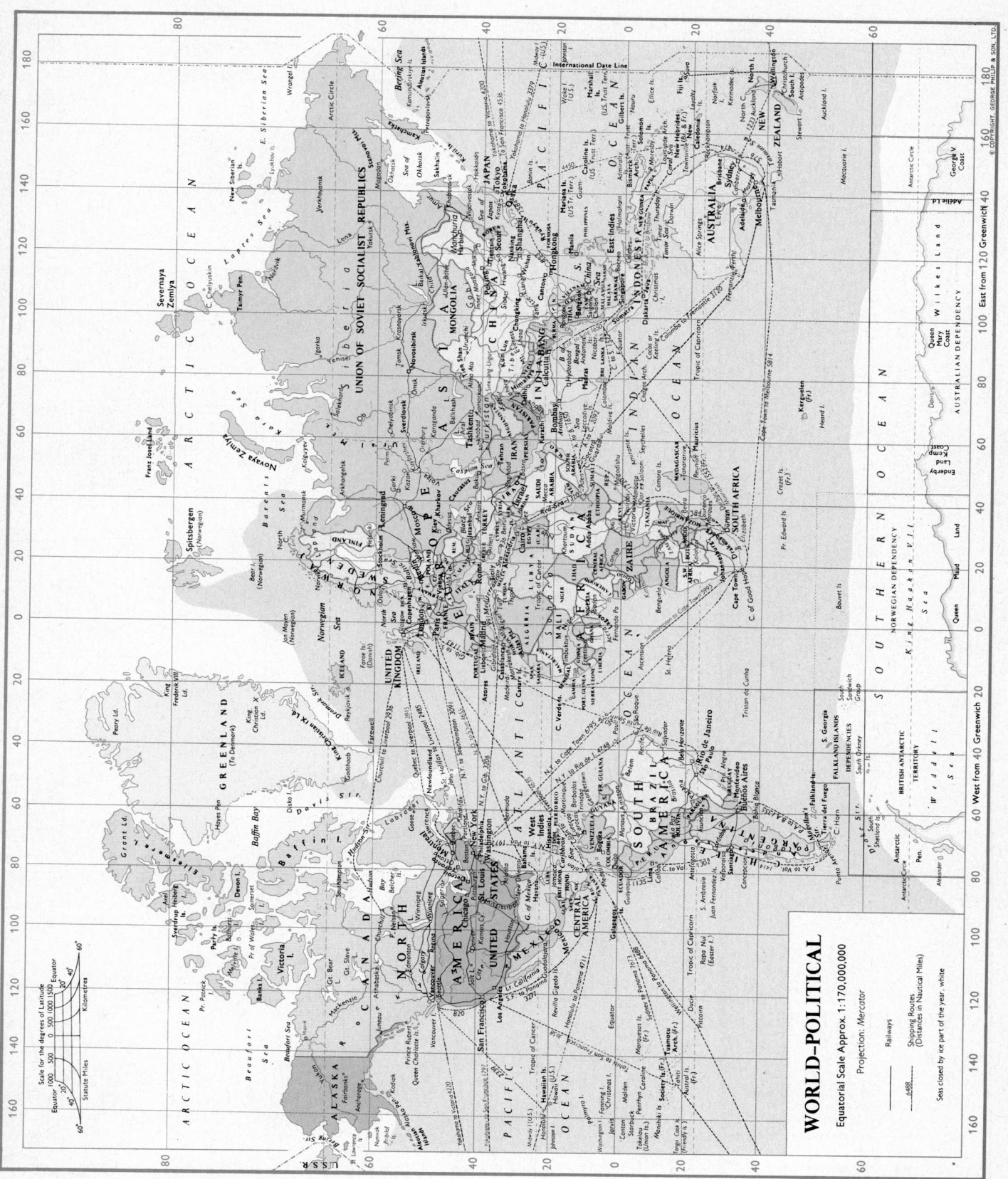

WORLD-POLITICAL

Equatorial Scale Approx. 1:170,000,000

Projection: Mercator

Railways
Shipping Routes
(Distances in Nautical Miles)

Seas closed by ice part of the year, white

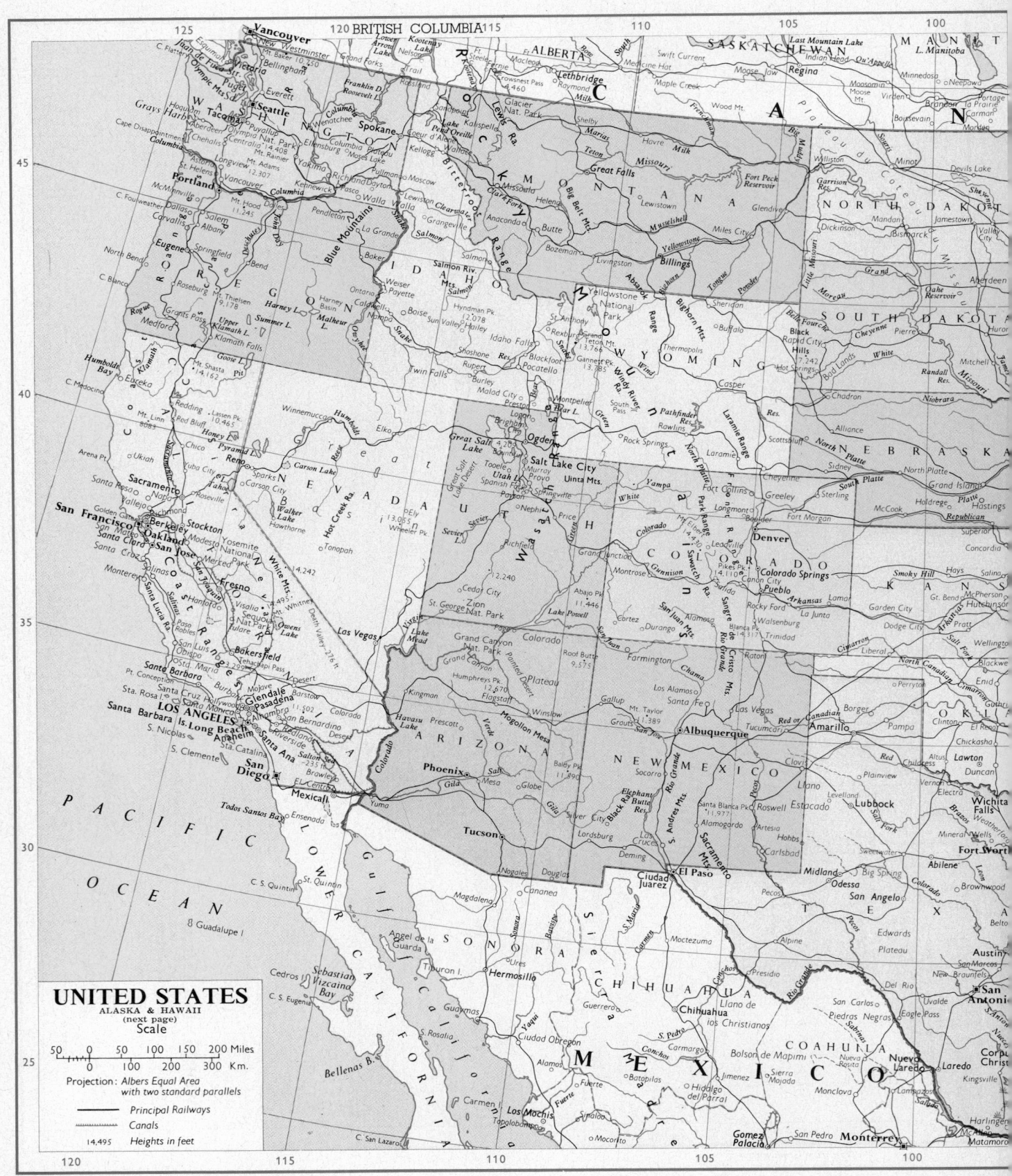

UNITED STATES

ALASKA & HAWAII
(next page)

Scale

50   0   50   100   150   200 Miles

0   100   200   300 Km.

Projection: Albers Equal Area
with two standard parallels

———— Principal Railways

··········· Canals

14,495   Heights in feet

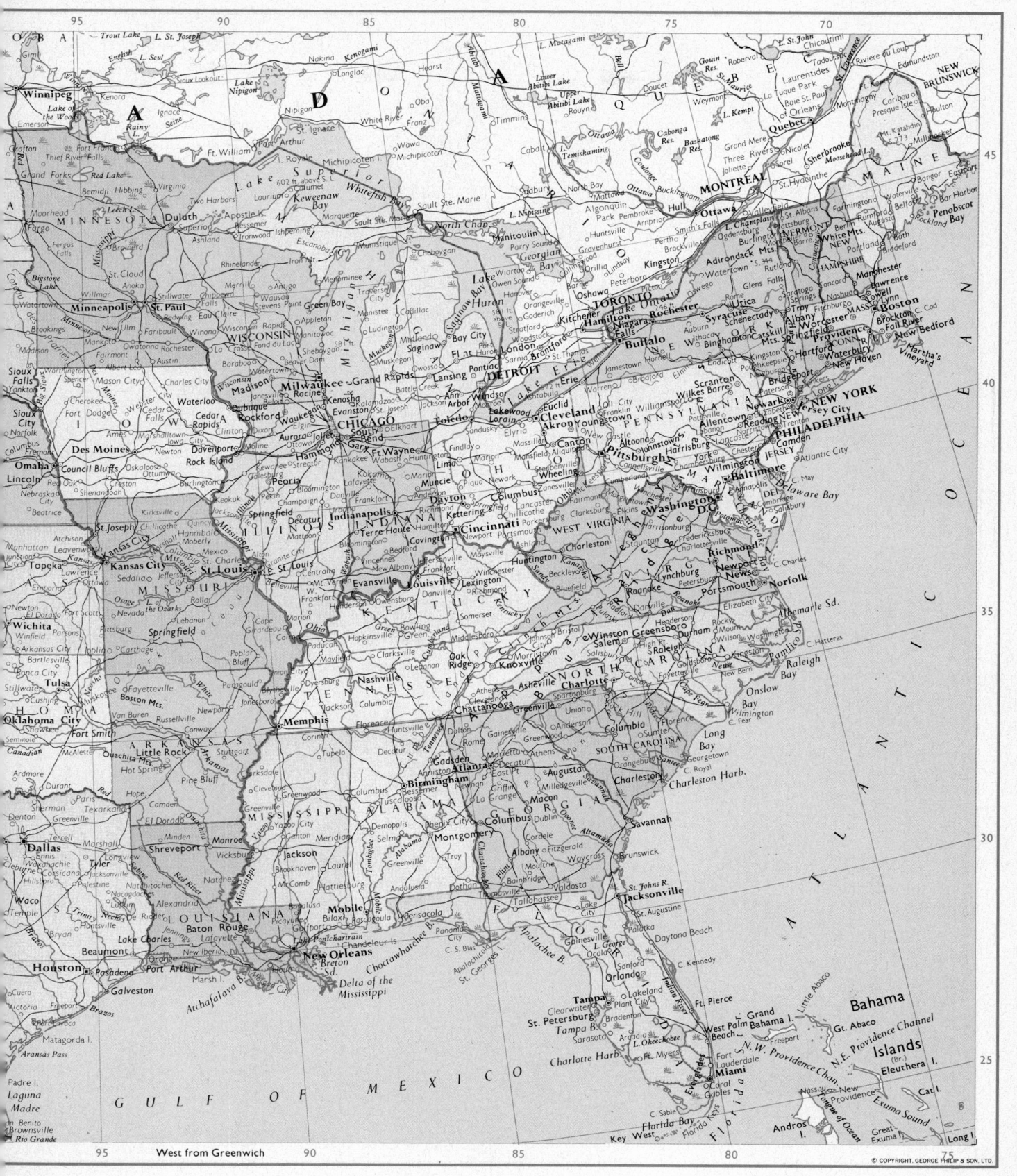

West from Greenwich

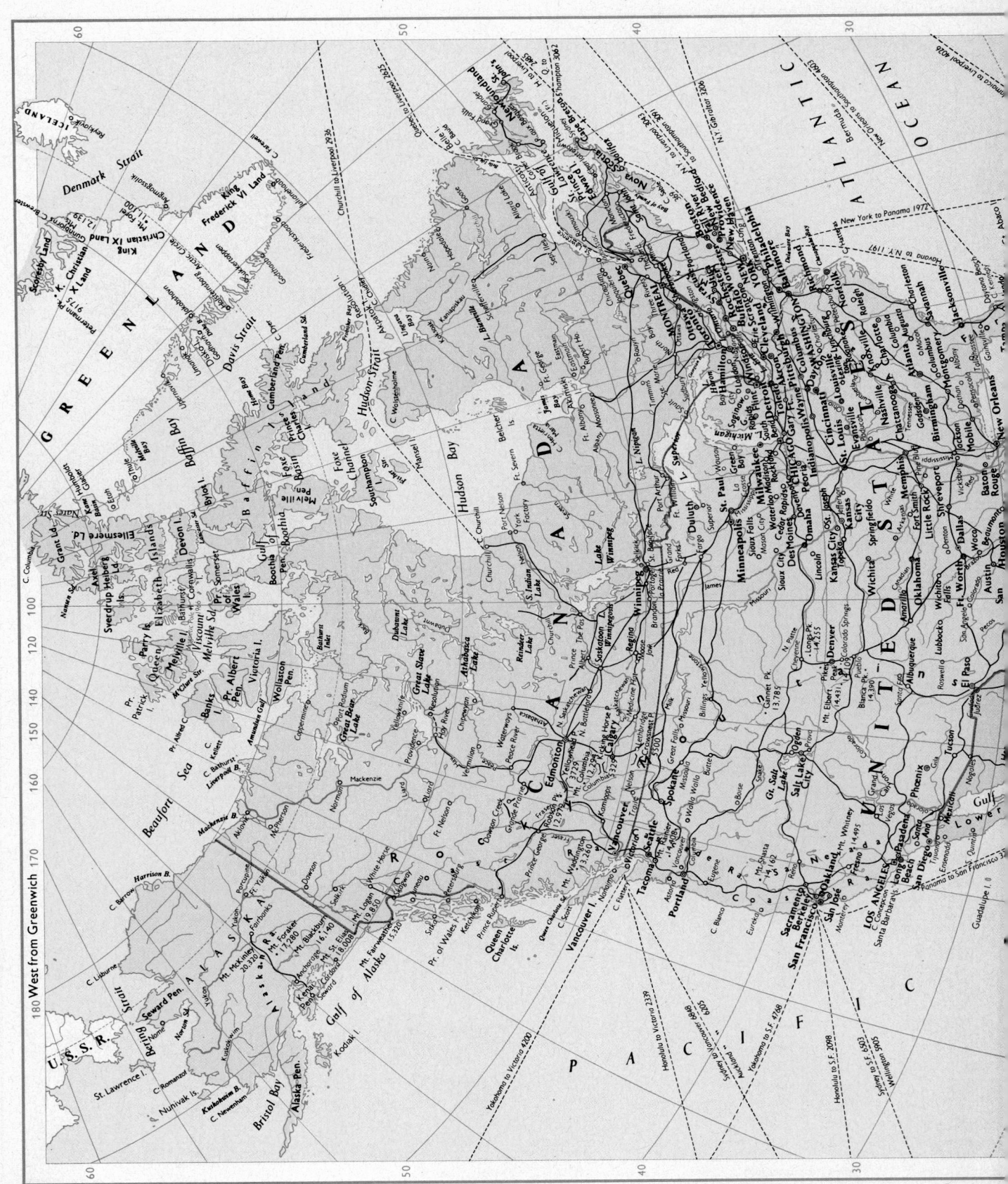

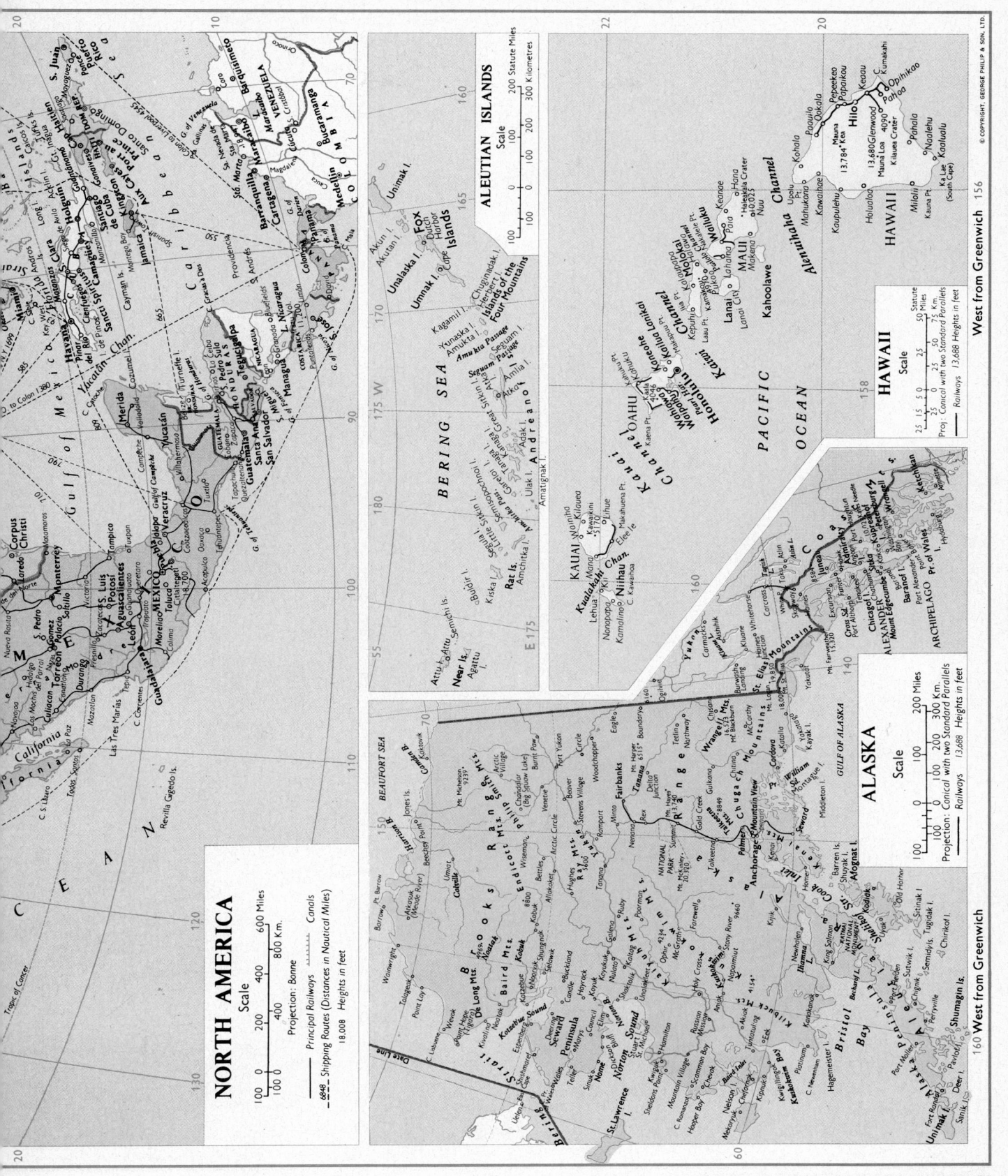

NORTH AMERICA

Scale

600 Miles
400   600 Km.
800 Km.

Projection: Bonne

—— Principal Railways   ——— Canals
—— 6848 Shipping Routes (Distances in Nautical Miles)
18,008 Heights in feet

ALEUTIAN ISLANDS

Scale
200 Statute Miles
300 Kilometres

HAWAII

Scale
Statute Miles
Proj.: Conical with two Standard Parallels
—— Railways   13,688 Heights in feet

ALASKA

Scale
200 Miles
300 Km.
Projection: Conical with two Standard Parallels
—— Railways   13,688 Heights in feet

West from Greenwich 156

BERING SEA

PACIFIC OCEAN

GULF OF ALASKA

BEAUFORT SEA

Date Line

160 West from Greenwich

PREPARED FOR DENNISON MFG. CO., FRAMINGHAM, MASS.

© COPYRIGHT, GEORGE PHILIP & SON, LTD.

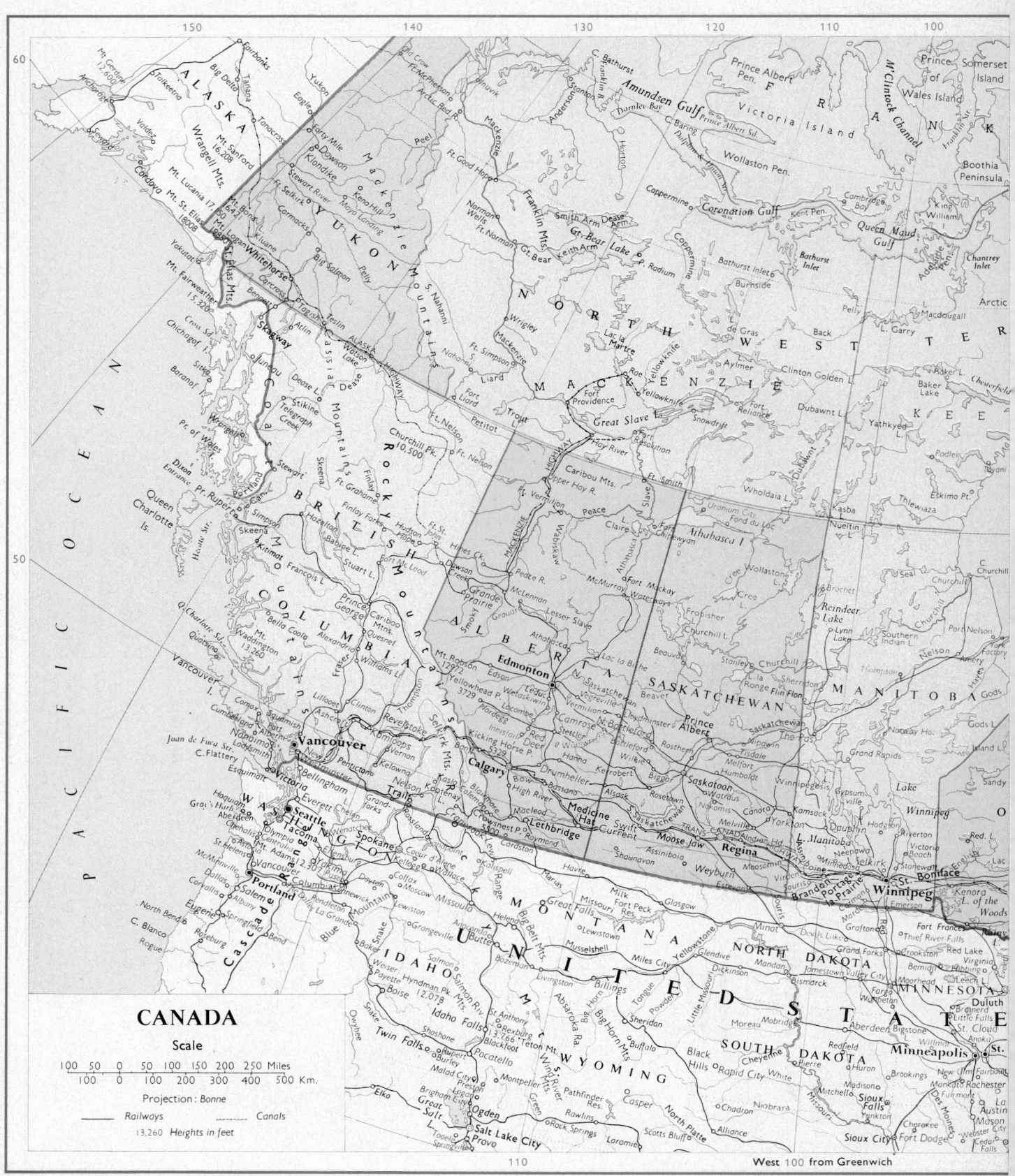

CANADA

Scale

100 50 0 50 100 150 200 250 Miles
100 0 100 200 300 400 500 Km.

Projection : Bonne

—— Railways .... Canals
13,260 Heights in feet

West 100 from Greenwich

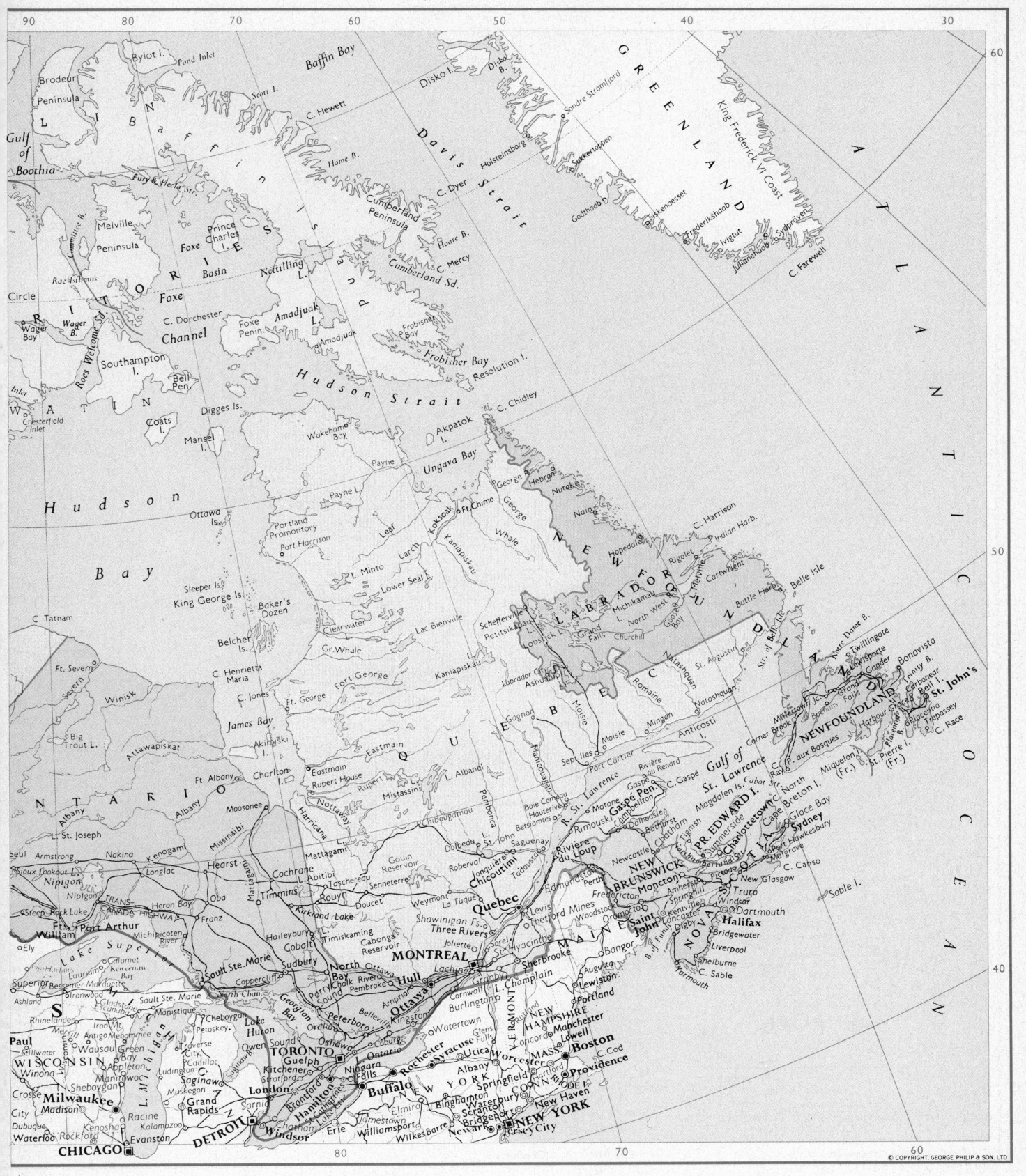

EUROPE

Scale

100 0 100 200 300 400 Miles

100 0 200 400 600 Km.

Projection: *Bonne*

——— Principal Railways   ········· Canals

_508_ Shipping Routes (Distances in Nautical Miles)

·5377 Heights in feet

West 5 from Greenwich 0 5 East from 10 Greenwich 15 20 25 30

PREPARED FOR DENNISON MFG. CO., FRAMINGHAM, MASS.

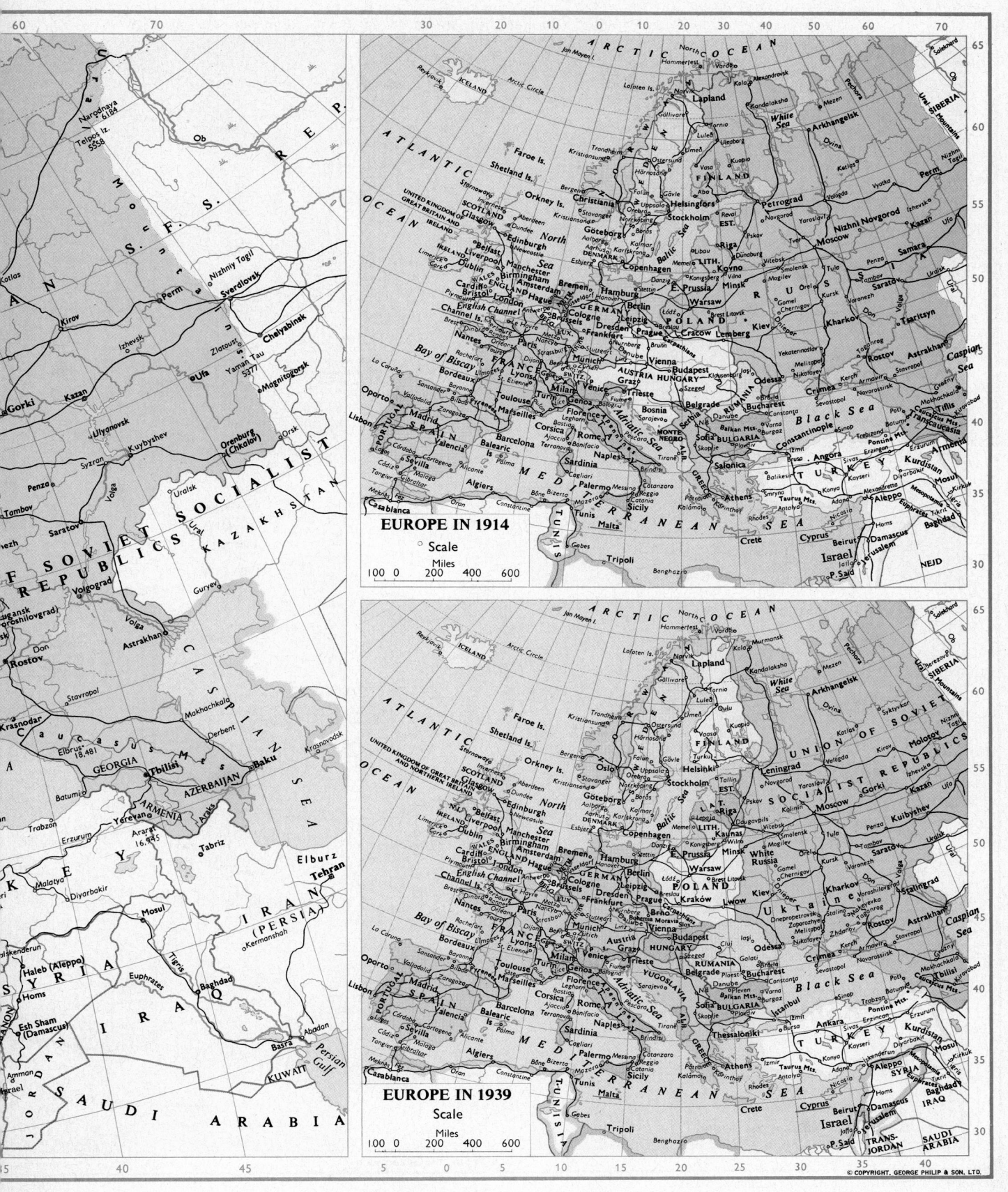

EUROPE IN 1914

Scale

Miles
100 0 200 400 600

EUROPE IN 1939

Scale

Miles
100 0 200 400 600

© COPYRIGHT, GEORGE PHILIP & SON, LTD.

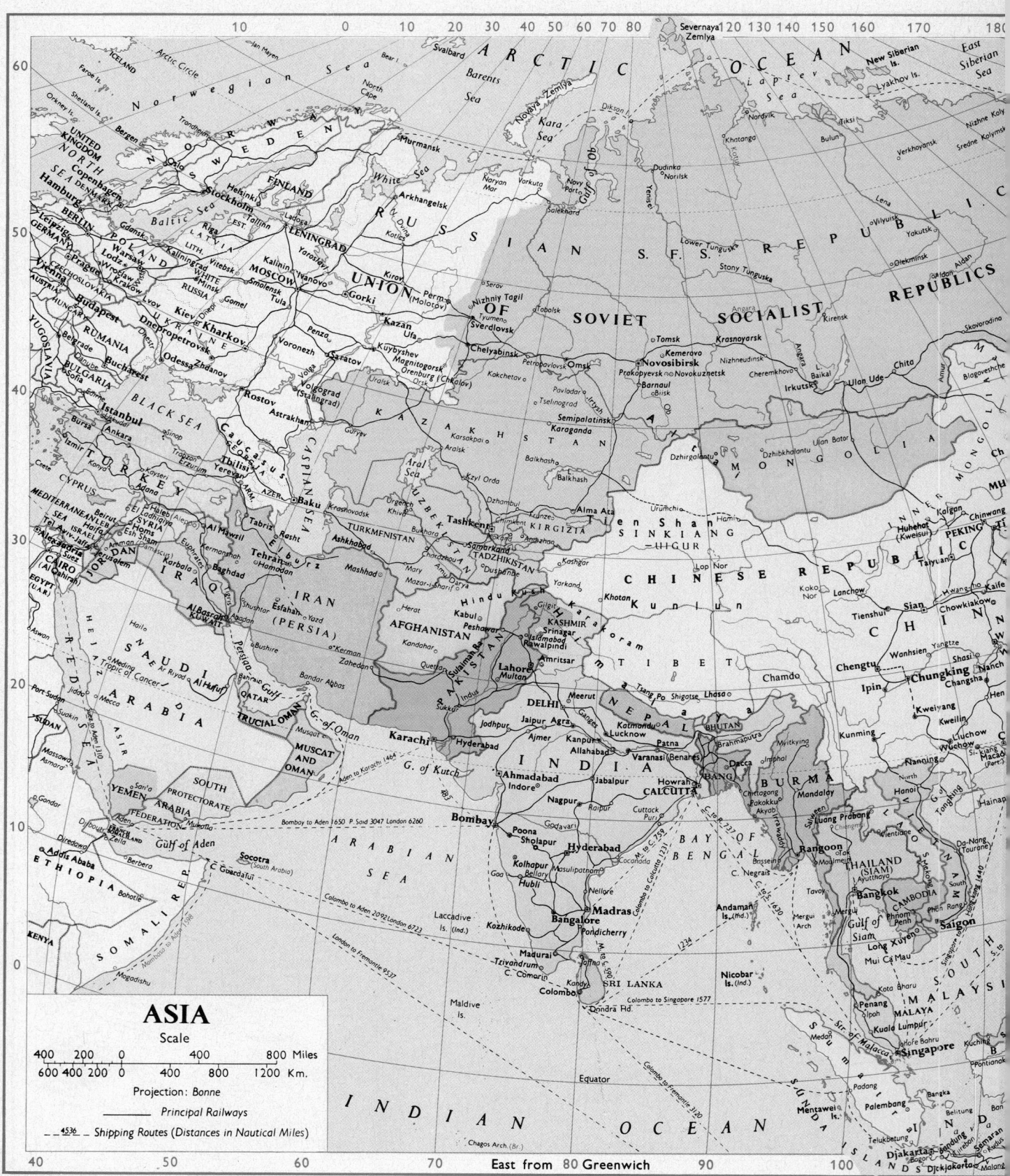

ASIA

Scale

400 200 0 400 800 Miles

600 400 200 0 400 800 1200 Km.

Projection: Bonne

——— Principal Railways

- - -1536- - - Shipping Routes (Distances in Nautical Miles)

East from 80 Greenwich

PREPARED FOR DENNISON MFG. CO., FRAMINGHAM, MASS.

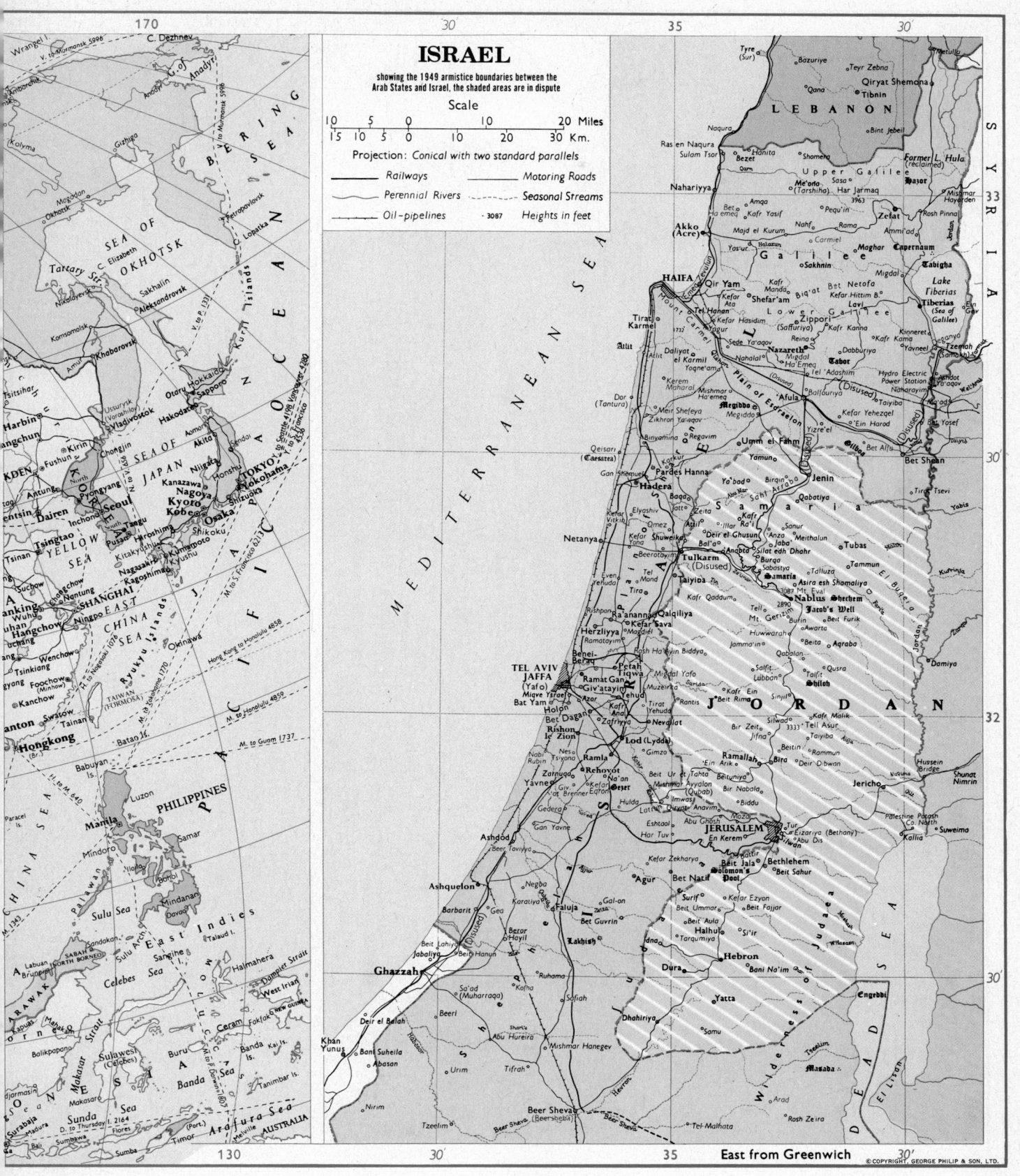

ISRAEL

showing the 1949 armistice boundaries between the
Arab States and Israel, the shaded areas are in dispute

Scale

10   5   0   10   20 Miles
15 10 5 0   10   20   30 Km.

Projection: Conical with two standard parallels

——— Railways   ——— Motoring Roads
⌁⌁⌁ Perennial Rivers   - - - Seasonal Streams
∿∿∿ Oil-pipelines   · 3087 Heights in feet

East from Greenwich

© COPYRIGHT, GEORGE PHILIP & SON, LTD.

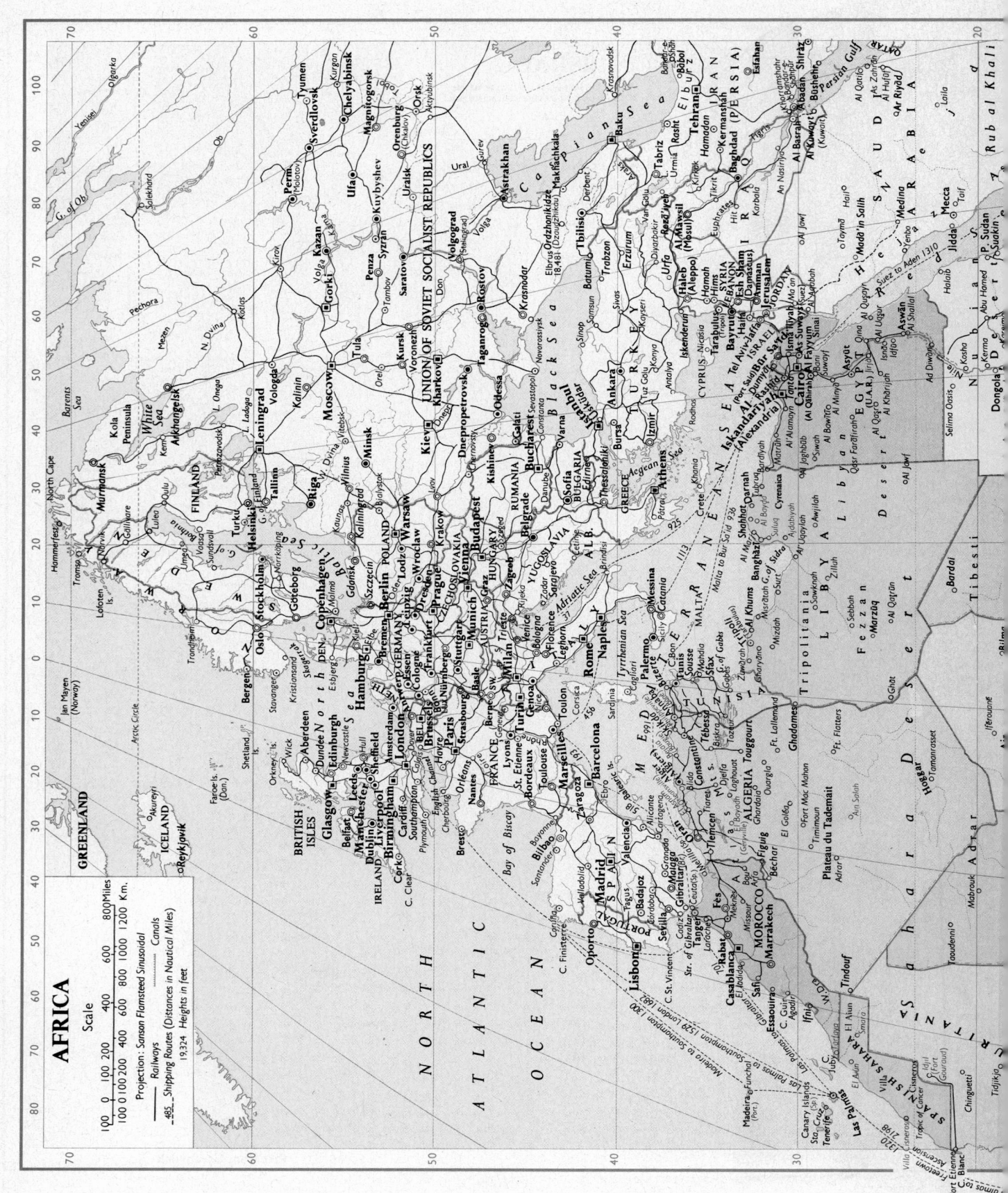

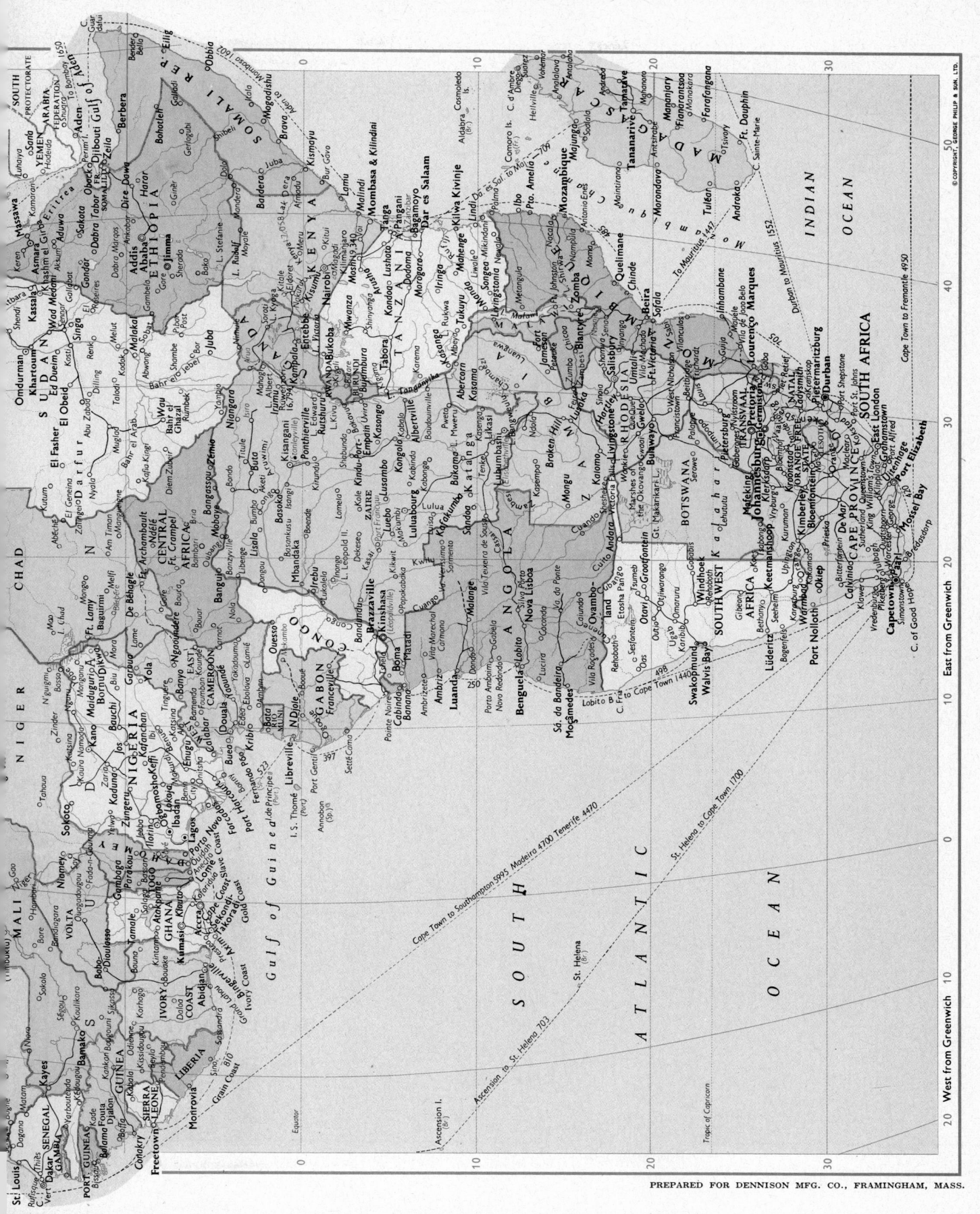

PREPARED FOR DENNISON MFG. CO., FRAMINGHAM, MASS.

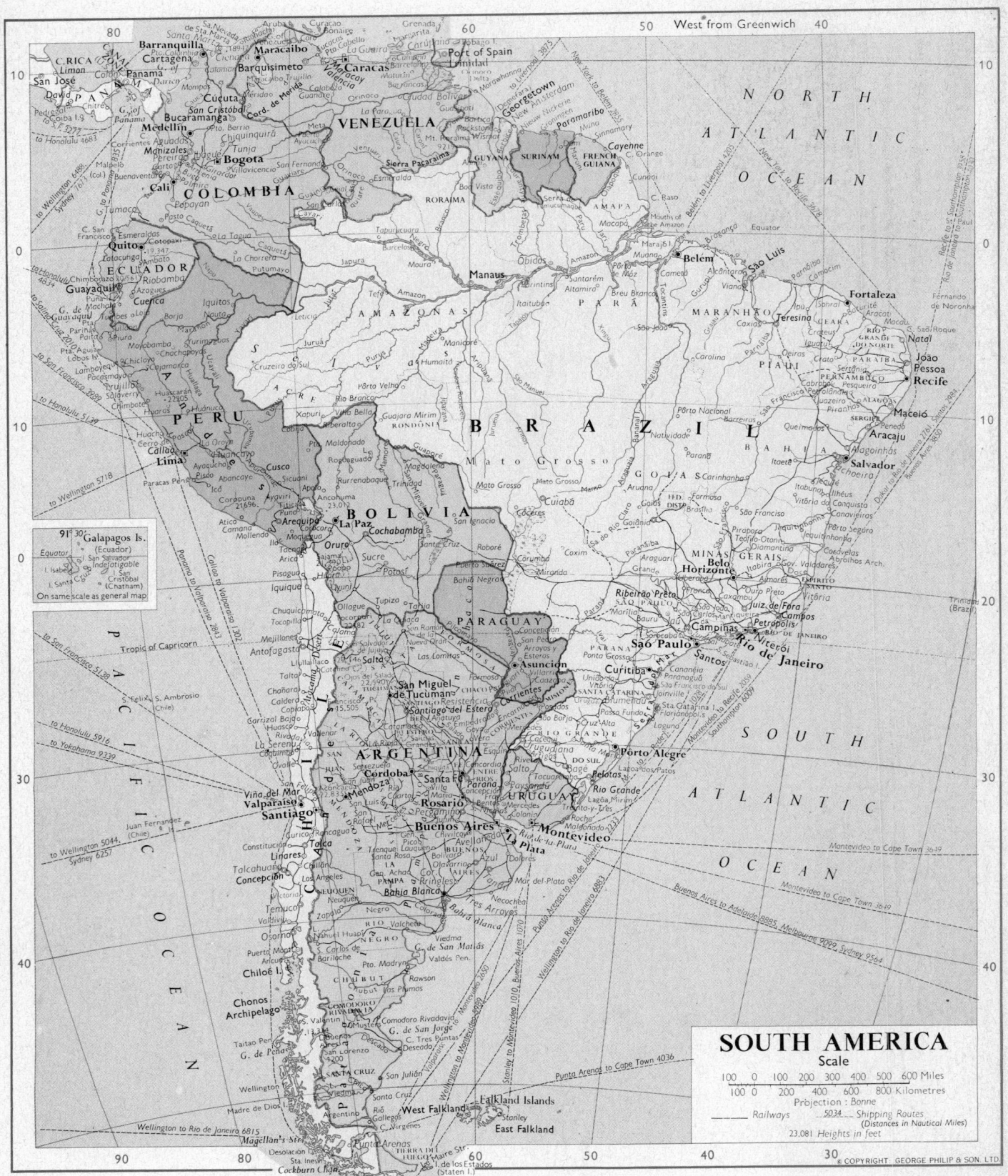

SOUTH AMERICA

Scale

100 0 100 200 300 400 500 600 Miles
100 0   200 400 600   800 Kilometres
Projection : Bonne

——— Railways   5034 Shipping Routes
(Distances in Nautical Miles)
23,081 Heights in feet

West from Greenwich

NORTH ATLANTIC OCEAN

SOUTH ATLANTIC OCEAN

PACIFIC OCEAN

VENEZUELA
COLOMBIA
ECUADOR
PERU
BOLIVIA
BRAZIL
PARAGUAY
CHILE
ARGENTINA
URUGUAY
GUYANA
SURINAM
FRENCH GUIANA

Galapagos Is.
(Ecuador)
On same scale as general map

Falkland Islands
West Falkland
East Falkland

PREPARED FOR DENNISON MFG. CO., FRAMINGHAM, MASS.

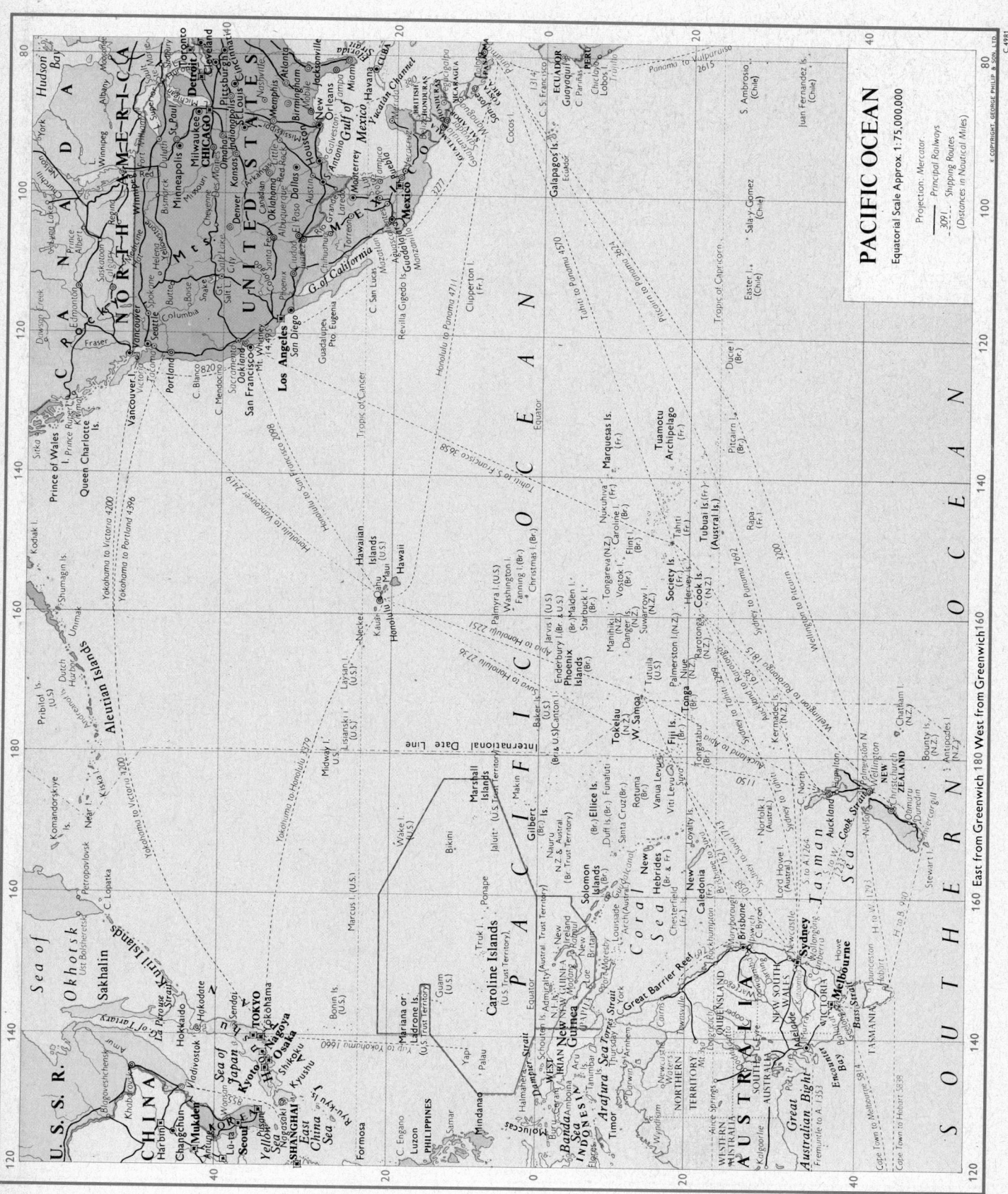

PACIFIC OCEAN

Equatorial Scale Approx. 1:75,000,000

Projection: Mercator.

Principal Railways
309 l. ——— Shipping Routes
(Distances in Nautical Miles)

© COPYRIGHT. GEORGE PHILIP & SON, LTD.

C.498 l

PREPARED FOR DENNISON MFG. CO., FRAMINGHAM, MASS.

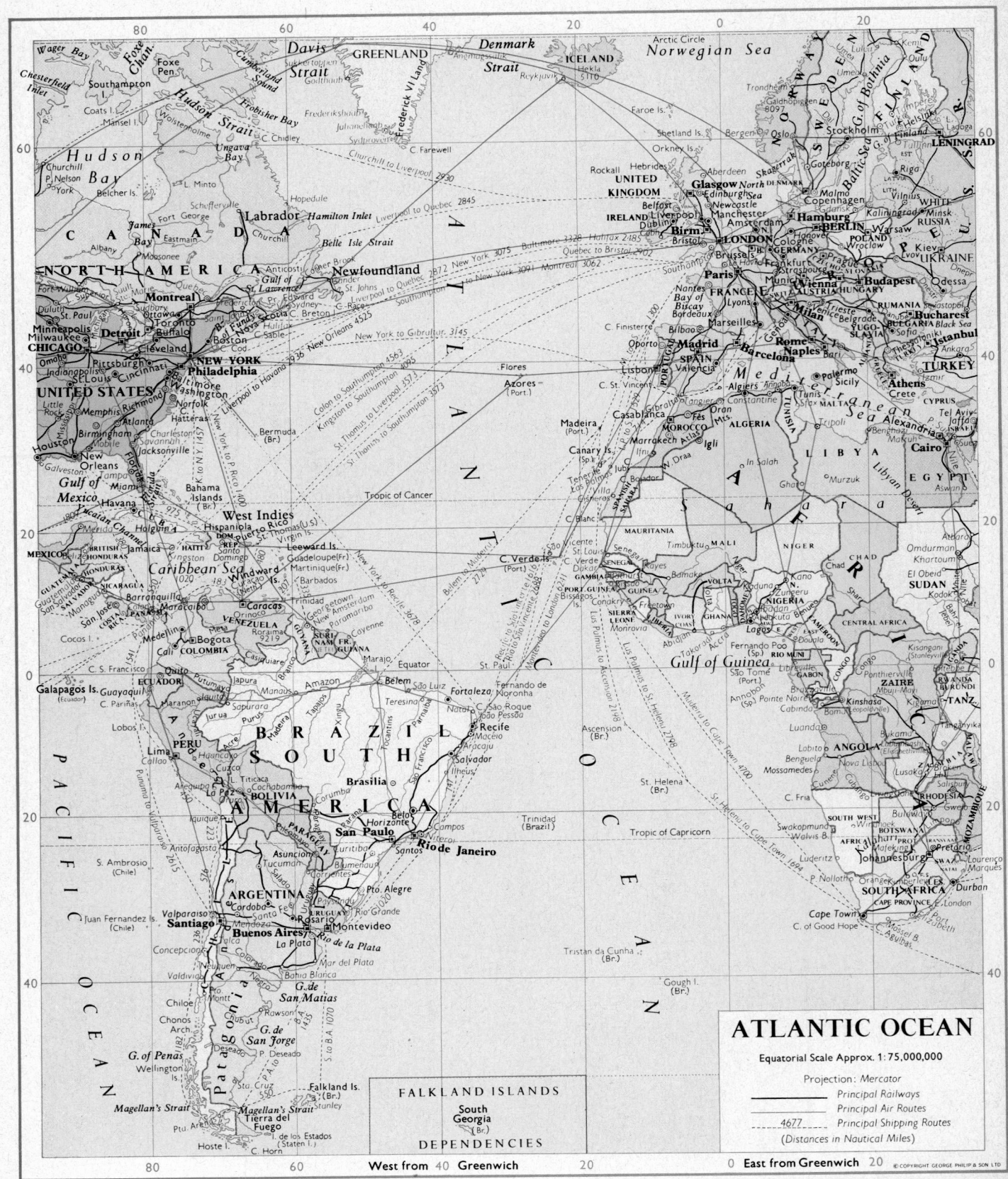

ATLANTIC OCEAN

Equatorial Scale Approx. 1:75,000,000

Projection: *Mercator*

———————— Principal Railways

———————— Principal Air Routes

– – 4677 – – Principal Shipping Routes

(Distances in Nautical Miles)

FALKLAND ISLANDS

South
Georgia
(Br.)

DEPENDENCIES

West from 40 Greenwich 20   0 East from Greenwich 20   © COPYRIGHT GEORGE PHILIP & SON LTD

STATE FLAGS AND FLOWERS III

OHIO
Buckeye State

Scarlet Carnation

OKLAHOMA
Sooner State

Mistletoe

OREGON
Beaver State

Oregon Grape

PENNSYLVANIA
Keystone State

Mountain Laurel

RHODE ISLAND
Little Rhody

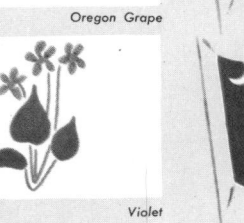

Violet

SOUTH CAROLINA
Palmetto State

Yellow Jessamine

SOUTH DAKOTA
Coyote State

Pasque Flower

TENNESSEE
Volunteer State

Iris

TEXAS
Lone Star State

Bluebonnet

UTAH
Beehive State

Sego Lily

VERMONT
Green Mountain State

Red Clover

VIRGINIA
Old Dominion State

Dogwood

WASHINGTON
Evergreen State

Western Rhododendron

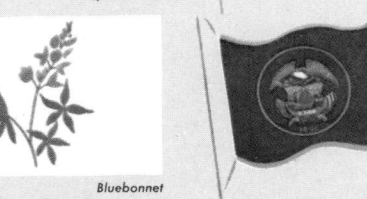

WEST VIRGINIA
Mountain or Panhandle State

Big Rhododendron

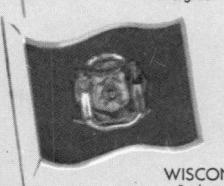

WISCONSIN
Badger State

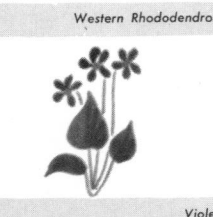

Violet

WYOMING
Equality State

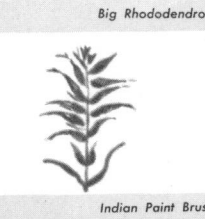

Indian Paint Brush